THE COLUMBIA
GRANGER'S®

INDEX TO POETRY

IN COLLECTED AND
SELECTED WORKS

THE COLUMBIA
GRANGER'S®
INDEX TO POETRY
IN COLLECTED AND SELECTED WORKS

EDITED BY

NICHOLAS FRANKOVICH

COLUMBIA UNIVERSITY PRESS

NEW YORK

LIBRARY OF CONGRESS CATALOGING-IN-PUBLICATION DATA

Frankovich, Nicholas
    The Columbia Granger's index to poetry in collected
and selected works / edited by Nicholas Frankovich.
    p. cm.
    ISBN 0-231-10762-5
    1. Poetry—Indexes.   2. English poetry—Indexes.
I. Granger, Edith. Index to poetry.   II. Title.
    1996
                                    96-21122
                                    CIP

CASEBOUND EDITIONS OF COLUMBIA UNIVERSITY PRESS BOOKS ARE
PRINTED ON PERMANENT AND DURABLE ACID-FREE PAPER.

PRINTED IN THE UNITED STATES OF AMERICA

c 10 9 8 7 6 5 4 3 2 1

PREFACE

Books of collected and selected poems by major poets constitute a substantial portion of the poetry in most libraries, but for decades *The Columbia Granger's® Index to Poetry* has been devoted exclusively to anthologies. With this new reference work, the range of poetry books covered by Granger indexing is greatly expanded.

Subject Indexing

In the subject index of this new work—which is what the poetry books themselves do not provide—the poems are listed alphabetically by author, so users can quickly identify poems by Robert Lowell on the subject of conscientious objectors, for example—or poems about slavery that were written by authors such as Emerson and Whittier, for whom it was a contemporary issue.

"Who Wrote It?"

Among the illustrious poets whose poems we index here are some who, by virtue of similar subject matter or style, are commonly confused with each other. Famous passages of English poetry that even a knowledgeable reader attributes to Shakespeare may turn out to be from Milton, or perhaps the King James Version of the Bible. In the poem that begins "My doctor, the comedian," an American woman in the middle decades of the twentieth century addresses her psychiatrist. Sylvia Plath or Anne Sexton? See the Title and First Line Index.

Multiple Access Points

The Columbia Granger's® Index to Poetry in Collected and Selected Works provides more access points to poetry than do the books in which the poetry was published, even those books that have first-line and title indexes. Our index turns up many famous, frequently anthologized passages from long poems whose origin is hidden from users who know the passage but not the longer poem.

For example, a hymn familiar to many as "Jerusalem" is part of Blake's "Milton." But "Jerusalem" in the title index at the back of Blake's collected works refers to a different poem, the only one to which Blake himself ever gave that title. As is proper, the Blake book strives to be faithful to what Blake actually wrote or intended, not necessarily to what readers expect to find. Users looking up "Jerusalem" in our index are directed to both poems by Blake. A note indicates that the one is a selection from "Milton," and suggests that it may be found by going to "M" in the title index of Blake's *Complete Poems*.

Our Selection of Authors

More than 50,000 poems by 251 authors, in 275 volumes, are indexed in *The Columbia*

Granger's® Index to Poetry in Collected and Selected Works. The final list of authors and books covered by this work reflect many considerations—the prominence of the author, the number of libraries that own the book, and a commonsense assessment of what authors or books are likely to be sought by those who consult it.

James Shapiro, professor of English at Columbia, joined editorial staff of the Press in drawing up a preliminary list of poets to be represented in this index. We then looked at the books themselves. The first question we asked about each volume of collected or selected works is the same as the first question we ask about every anthology we consider for standard editions of Granger's: Is it likely to be found on library shelves?

In some cases where the answer was no, the author was indisputably popular. Either no collected or selected version of the great poet had been published or, more often, it had been published as long as a hundred or more years ago. Faced with the fame of the poet and the staggering old age of the book, we tended to decide in favor of including the book.

Where authors are represented by both collected and selected versions of their works, we generally favored collected versions. In most instances where selected versions have been substituted for collected, they are of classic poets whose collected works stretch over several volumes, and who are well represented by editions of selected works that contain the poems for which they are most famous. A few poets are represented by both their collected and selected works, as some libraries have one but not the other.

Exceptional cases that need to be acknowledged here include two translated poets, Catullus and Pablo Neruda. Catullus was drawn into this index by way of a contemporary poet whose own collected works include translations of all 116 Carmina; in indexing the complete poems of Louis Zukofsky, we also indexed the complete poems of Catullus, one of the ancient poets most often translated into English. Already that far along in our coverage of Catullus, we took the next logical step, which was to index the complete poems as translated by Peter Whigham, a standard source for those who wish to read the Latin poet in English.

The release of the movie *Il Postino* has been accompanied by a surge in Neruda's popularity in the United States.

For similar reasons an exception was made for Shel Silverstein. No volume of his collected or selected works has been published. The corner we found for him, for the 128 poems that appear in what is widely regarded as his premier book, is testimony to his own stature as well as to the growing audience for contemporary children's poetry.

While the focus of this work is on individual authors and their collected and selected works, some citations also refer to anthologies. This happens where an anthology has excerpted a poem that appears in toto in a collected or selected work.

ACKNOWLEDGMENTS

In addition to the contributors who read for subjects and indexed the poetry generally, often arriving at elegant solutions to problems posed by works that seemed to defy neat indexing rules and categories, there are others whose efforts on this project have been crucial. Keith Frome helped plan the index in its earliest stages and laid much of the groundwork for it. Among those at Auto-Graphics, our compositor, who have been helpful in the design as well as in the production of the index, Susan Chriss and Kathryn Pittman deserve special mention, as does Patrick LaFollette, whose insight into the complex Granger database has been a godsend. Back at the Press, the contributions of Edith Hazen were indispensable. A heroic degree of patience and discipline went into her painstaking work on the author and subject indexes. Her advice on any number of points was informed by her detailed knowledge of English literature. We like to think that her long experience as a school librarian and as an editor sets the tone for *The Columbia Granger's® Index to Poetry in Collected and Selected Works*.

The Columbia Granger's® Index to Poetry
in Collected and Selected Works

PUBLISHER
JOHN D. MOORE

EDITORIAL DIRECTOR, REFERENCE DIVISION
JAMES RAIMES

DIRECTOR OF DESIGN AND PRODUCTION
AUDREY SMITH

EDITORIAL MANAGER
ADAM TIBBS

EDITOR
NICHOLAS FRANKOVICH

STAFF

DAVID LARZELERE   BRIAN M. LENNON   ALEXANDRE NAMOUR

ANNE LILLIAN ARRÁZOLA
BRUCE P. ALEXANDER
ALISSA BADER
ARLE BORDAS
GENEVA CHAO
DEEPA CHATTERJEE
SUSAN CIATTO
VERONICA COLEMAN
OLYMPIA FIEDLER
JENNIFER FIORE
ALISON FORNER
DIANA M. GRANT

RACHEL M. KAHN
YUNG KIM
THOMAS LEE
MICHELE LUC
DANN S. MCDORMAN
EDWARD H. MORRIS
KELCEY NICHOLS
JOHN C. NEWTON
RYAN SCHETELICK
CHRISTOPHER THOMAS
JACQUELINE WATERS
JOHN ZAVIEH

HOW TO USE THE INDEXES

This volume is divided into three sections:

— Title and First Line Index
— Author Index
— Subject Index

Each section is arranged alphabetically.

Every poem covered here is cited at least once in each of the three sections (except for those that are too abstract to be assigned to any heading in the Subject Index). Every poem cited here appears in at least one volume of the collected and selected works listed on pages XV–XXII, or in an anthology listed on pages XXIII–XXXVIII.

See also the explanatory notes at the beginning of each of the three sections, pages 1, 1143, and 1387.

Title and First Line Index

The clearest way to explain the Title and First Line Index is to begin by showing how it answers specific questions brought to it.

Where can I find a poem called "Southeast Arkanasia"? Go to the Title and First Line Index. The citation for "Southeast Arkanasia" is followed by the name of the poem's author, Maya Angelou, and by the letter code SP-AngeM. Letter codes beginning "CP-" and "SP-" refer to the List of Collected and Selected Works; all other letter codes refer to the List of Anthologies. So look up SP-AngeM in the List of Collected and Selected Works, where the codes are arranged alphabetically by author's name. There you learn that you can read "Southeast Arkanasia" in *Maya Angelou; Poems*, published by Bantam Books / Random House in 1986.

What is the title of the poem that begins "Glory be to God for dappled things"? The first-line citation is followed by the title, "Pied Beauty," and then by the author, Gerard Manley Hopkins. CP-HopkG is the letter code for the collected poems of Hopkins; the List of Collected and Selected Works indicates that the title of the book is *Gerard Manley Hopkins* and that it was published by Oxford University Press in 1986.

Titles. Initial capitals in the important words usually indicate that the citation is the title of the poem. "Song Sparrow Singing in the Fall, A," for example, by Wendell Berry, is a title.

First Lines. First-line citations are followed by the title (except where the poem has no title).

You know, for example, that "Poet, be seated at the piano" is not a title because the initial letters of all the words (except the first one) are lower-case.

"To the Richest Treasury" looks like a title, but you know it is not because it is followed by "Dedication to Anne Lovelace, The"; the initial caps in the first line reflect the antiquated spelling in *The Poems of Richard Lovelace*.

When the first line of a poem is the same as or slightly longer than the title, only the title is listed. The poem listed under the title "Up and Down," for example, has no listing for first line because the first line is "Up and down the streets they go."

Brackets.   Brackets usually show variant spellings. For example, see the first-line citation "Whan that Aprille [or April or Aprill] with his[e] shoures [or showres] sote [or soote]." In the several books in which that first line appears, the spelling may vary as indicated in brackets.

Capitalization.   The first letter of the first word in every citation is capitalized, even when in its published form it appears as lower-case.

Initial Articles.   An article—"a," "an," or "the"—that begins a title or a first line is transposed to the end of the citation. "The Jacob's Ladder" by Denise Levertov, for example, is listed as "Jacob's Ladder, The."

Parentheses.   When an entire citation is enclosed by parentheses, it usually means that it is a variant title or variant first line. Parentheses are used instead of brackets when it is necessary to indicate a version that varies widely from the standard version, with the result that, in this alphabetized index, it can also be found in a place far from where the standard version is listed.

   Look again at "Whan that Aprille...," the example used above. In the anthology indicated by the code NAWM-1, the first line is modernized to read "As soon as April pierces to the root." It is a variant first line and appears inside parentheses beneath "Whan that Aprille...," the standard version. It is also listed toward the beginning of the Index, under the "A" 's ("As soon as . . .").

Indentation.   Indentation of a citation indicates that it is a selection. See, for example, "Canterbury Tales, The."

> Canterbury Tales, The. Geoffrey Chaucer.
>> Clerk's Tale, The.
>>> Patient Griselda.

"Clerk's Tale, The" is indented because it is a selection from The Canterbury Tales. "Patient Griselda" is further indented because it in turn is a selection from The Clerk's Tale.

   The letter code PoRA after "Patient Griselda" refers to the List of Anthologies, where the letter codes, not the titles of the anthologies, are listed alphabetically. There you learn that "Patient Griselda" appears in *Poems to Read Aloud*, published by W. W. Norton in 1967.

   When you look up "Patient Griselda" under "P," you find additional information that may help you decide whether the poem is what you are looking for. A note indicates that the poem is a modernized version by Edward Hodnett. A further note indicates that it is a selection of The Clerk's Tale, which in turn is a selection of The Canterbury Tales. The letter code CP-ChauG after "Canterbury Tales, The" refers to *The Riverside Chaucer*, the volume of collected works in which the whole of The Canterbury Tales can be found. Be alert to the possibility that, while the passage of poetry on which Edward Hodnett based his modernized version can be found in *The Riverside Chaucer*, the modernized version itself cannot; as it happens, "Patient Griselda," the title given to the modernized version in *Poems to Read Aloud*, does not appear in *The Riverside Chaucer* either.

Author Index

   Under each author's name, poems are listed alphabetically by title or, where the poem has no title, by first line.

What poems can I find by Hilda Doolittle? The Author Index lists 187 poems in *The Columbia Granger's Index to Poetry in Collected and Selected Works.*

Did she write under a pseudonym? The Author Index indicates that she used the pen name H.D. and that she lived from 1886 to 1961.

Subject Index

Under each subject heading, poems are listed alphabetically by author's name.

What poems can I find about marriage? The subject index shows that there are more than 500 poems about marriage, by 154 different poets, including "Marriage of Psyche and Cupid" by Elizabeth Barrett Browning and "Marriages" by Philip Larkin. Citations for all these poems can be found in the Title and First Line Index, where the letter codes, which refer to the List of Collected and Selected Works and the List of Anthologies, indicate in which books the poems are published.

Has Rita Dove written poems about religion? Go to the heading for "Religion" and locate "Dove" in the list of poems alphabetized by author.

ABBREVIATIONS

abr.	abridged		*mod.*	modernized *or* modern
ad.	adapted		*N.T.*	New Testament
add.	additional		*O.T.*	Old Testament
arr.	arranged		*orig.*	original
at.	attributed		*par.*	paraphrase *or* paraphrased
Bk.	book		*pr.*	prose
br.	brief		*Pt.*	part
ch.	chapter		*rev.*	revised
comp.	compiled *or* compiler		*sc.*	scene
comps.	compilers		*Sec.*	section
cond.	condensed		*sel.*	selection
diff.	different		*sels.*	selections
fr.	from		*sl.*	slightly
frag.	fragment		*st.*	stanza
incl.	included *or* including		*sts.*	stanzas
introd.	introduction *or* introductory		*tr.*	translator, translation, *or* translated
ll.	lines		*trs.*	translators *or* translations
LL.	last line		*var.*	various
med.	medieval		*vers.*	version *or* versions
misc.	miscellaneous		*wr.*	wrong *or* wrongly

CONTENTS

PREFACE   V

ACKNOWLEDGMENTS   VII

HOW TO USE THE INDEXES   IX

ABBREVIATIONS   XXII

LIST OF COLLECTED AND SELECTED WORKS   XV

LIST OF ANTHOLOGIES   XXIII

TITLE AND FIRST LINE INDEX   1

AUTHOR INDEX   1143

SUBJECT INDEX   1387

LIST OF COLLECTED AND SELECTED WORKS

Ø CP-AudeW   Collected Poems [W. H. Auden] *Edward Mendelson, ed.* (1991) Vintage. 926p., pap.

Ø CP-AudWJ   Juvenilia; Poems, 1922–1928 [W. H. Auden] *Katherine Bucknell, ed.* (1994) Princeton University Press. 263p.

CP-Beatl Dynix+   The Beatles; Complete Scores (1993) Hal Leonard Publishing. 1,136p.

Ø CP-BeckS   Collected Poems 1930–1978 [Samuel Beckett] (1984) John Calder. 179p.

CP-BerrJ 811.54   Collected Poems, 1937–1971 [John Berryman] (1989) Farrar, Straus and Giroux. 348p., pap.

CP-BerrW Dynix   Collected Poems, 1957–1982 [Wendell Berry] (1984) Farrar, Straus and Giroux. 268p., pap.

Ø CP-BetjJ   The Collected Poems of John Betjeman *Earl of Birkenhead, ed.* (4th ed., 1979; reissued 1990) John Murray. 351p.

CP-BishE Dynix+   The Complete Poems, 1927–1979 [Elizabeth Bishop] (1983) Farrar, Straus and Giroux. 287p., pap.

Ø CP-BlakW   The Complete Poems [William Blake] *Alicia Ostriker, ed.* (1977) Penguin Books. 1,071p., pap.

CP-BogaL Dynix+   The Blue Estuaries; Poems 1923–1968 [Louise Bogan] (1968; repr. 1988) Ecco Press. 136p., pap.

Ø CP-BoylK   Collected Poems of Kay Boyle (1991) Copper Canyon Press. 172p., pap.

Ø CP-BradA   The Poems of Mrs. Anne Bradstreet (1897) The De Vinne Press. 347p.

CP-BroEB Dynix+   The Complete Poetical Works of Mrs. Browning [Elizabeth Barrett Browning] *Harriet Waters Preston, ed.* (1900) Houghton Mifflin. 548p.

Ø CP-BronE   The Complete Poems of Emily Jane Brontë *C. W. Hatfield, ed.* (1941) Columbia University Press. 262p.

CP-BroR1 Dynix   The Poems; Vol. 1 [Robert Browning] *John Pettigrew, ed.* (1981) Penguin. 1,191p., pap.

CP-BroR2 ?   The Poems; Vol. 2 [Robert Browning] *John Pettigrew, ed.* (1981) Penguin. 1,167p., pap.

Ø CP-BuntB   The Complete Poems [Basil Bunting] *Richard Caddel, ed.* (1994) Oxford University Press. 226p., pap.

Ø CP-BurnR   Burns; Complete Poems and Songs [Robert Burns] *James Kinsley, ed.* (1969) Oxford University Press. 786p., pap.

Ø CP-Byron   The Poems of Byron *Paul E. More, ed.* (1933) Houghton Mifflin. 1,055p.

CP-CampT Dynix 1967ed   The Works of Thomas Campion *Walter R. Davis, ed.* (1969) W. W. Norton. 521p., pap.

Ø CP-CareT   Poems of Thomas Carew *Arthur Vincent, ed.* (1899; reprinted 1972) Books for Libraries Press. 264p.

CP-CarHL Dynix+   Collected Longer Poems [Hayden Carruth] (1994) Copper Canyon Press. 205p., pap.

Ø CP-CarHS   Collected Shorter Poems, 1946–1991 [Hayden Carruth] (1992) Copper Canyon Press. 417p., pap.

CP-CarrL 821   The Humorous Verse of Lewis Carroll (1960) Dover. 446p.

Ø CP-Catul   The Poems of Catullus *Peter Whigham, tr.* (1966) Penguin Books. 246p., pap.

CP-ChauG 821.1   The Riverside Chaucer *F. N. Robinson, ed.* (3d ed., 1987) Houghton Mifflin. 1,327p.

CP-CoheL 811.54   Stranger Music; Selected Poems and Songs [Leonard Cohen] (1993) Pantheon Books. 415p.

Ø CP-ColeS   Poems [Samuel Taylor Coleridge] *John Beer, ed.* (1993) Everyman. 535p., pap.

Ø CP-CowpW   The Poetical Works of William Cowper *H. S. Milford, ed.* (1926, 3d ed.) Oxford University Press. 677p.

Ø CP-CranH   Complete Poems of Hart Crane (1986) Liveright. 269p., pap.

Ø CP-CrasR   The Complete Poetry of Richard Crashaw *George Walton Williams, ed.* (1972) New York University Press. 707p.

Ø CP-CreeR   The Collected Poems of Robert Creeley, 1945–1975 (1982) University of California Press. 671p., pap.

CP-CullC Dynix+   My Soul's High Song; the Collected Writings of Countee Cullen, Voice of the Harlem Renaissance *Gerald Early, ed.* (1991) Doubleday. 618p., pap.

CP-CummE Complete Poems, 1904–1962 [E. E. Cummings] *George J. Firmage, ed.* (1991) Liveright. 1,102p.

CP-DavDo Collected Poems [Donald Davie] (1990) University of Chicago Press. 475p., pap.

CP-DeLaW Collected Poems [Walter De La Mare] (1941) Henry Holt. 327p.

CP-DickE The Complete Poems of Emily Dickinson *Thomas H. Johnson, ed.* (1960) Little, Brown. 770p., pap.

CP-DickJ The Whole Motion; Collected Poems, 1945–1992 [James Dickey] (1992) Wesleyan University Press / University Press of New England. 475p., pap.

CP-DonnJ The Complete English Poems [John Donne] *A. J. Smith, ed.* (1971) Penguin Books. 677p., pap.

CP-DoolH Collected Poems, 1912–1944 [H.D. (Hilda Doolittle)] *Louis L. Martz, ed.* (1983) New Directions. 629p., pap.

CP-DunbP The Collected Poetry of Paul Laurence Dunbar *Joanne M. Braxton, ed.* (1993) University Press of Virginia. 396p., pap.

CP-DylaB Lyrics, 1962–1985 [Bob Dylan] (1988) Alfred A. Knopf. 524p.

CP-EberR Collected Poems, 1930–1986 [Richard Eberhart] (1988) Oxford University Press. 444p.

CP-ElioT Collected Poems 1909–1962 [T. S. Eliot] (1963; repr. 1991) Harcourt Brace. 221p.

CP-EmerR Ralph Waldo Emerson; Collected Poems and Translations *Harold Bloom and Paul Kane, eds.* (1994) The Library of America. 637p.

CP-FrosR The Poetry of Robert Frost *Edward Connery Lathem, ed.* (1979) Henry Holt. 607p., pap.

CP-GardI Isabella Gardner; the Collected Poems (1990) BOA Editions. 162p., pap.

CP-GinsA Collected Poems 1947–1980 [Allen Ginsberg] (1984) Harper & Row. 837p., pap.

CP-GravR Collected Poems, 1975 [Robert Graves] (1988) Oxford University Press. 592p.

CP-GrayT Gray's English Poems; Original and Translated from the Norse and the Welsh [Thomas Gray] *D. C. Tovey, ed.* (1922; repr. by Reprint Services) Cambridge University Press. 293p.

CP-GunnT Collected Poems [Thom Gunn] (1994) Faber and Faber. 495p.

CP-HallD Old and New Poems [Donald Hall] (1990) Ticknor & Fields. 244p.

CP-HardT The Complete Poems of Thomas Hardy *James Gibson, ed.* (1978) Macmillan. 1,002p.

CP-HartM The Collected Poems of Marsden Hartley, 1904–1943 *Gail R. Scott, ed.* (1987) Black Sparrow Press. 360p., pap.

CP-HaydR Collected Poems [Robert Hayden] *Frederick Glaysher, ed.* (1985) Liveright. 205p., pap.

CP-HemiE Complete Poems [Ernest Hemingway] *Nicholas Gerogiannis, ed.* (1992) University of Nebraska Press. 171p., pap.

CP-HerbG The Complete English Poems [George Herbert] *John Tobin, ed.* (1991) Penguin Books. 460p. pap.

CP-HerrR The Poems of Robert Herrick *L. C. Martin, ed.* (1965) Oxford University Press. 478p.

CP-HewiJ The Collected Poems of John Hewitt *Frank Ormsby, ed.* (1992) Blackstaff Press. 708p., pap.

CP-HillG New & Collected Poems, 1952–1992 [Geoffrey Hill] (1994) Houghton Mifflin. 228p.

CP-HopkG Gerard Manley Hopkins *Catherine Phillips, ed.* (1986) Oxford University Press. 429p., pap.

CP-HousA The Collected Poems of A. E. Housman (1965) Henry Holt. 254p., pap.

CP-HugoR Making Certain It Goes On; the Collected Poems of Richard Hugo (1984) W. W. Norton. 456p., pap.

CP-JarrR The Complete Poems [Randall Jarrell] (1969; repr. 1989) Farrar, Straus and Giroux. 507p., pap.

CP-JefR1 The Collected Poetry of Robinson Jeffers; Vol. 1 *Tim Hunt, ed.* (1988) Stanford University Press.

CP-JefR2 The Collected Poetry of Robinson Jeffers; Vol. 2 *Tim Hunt, ed.* (1989) Stanford University Press. 610p.

CP-JefR3 The Collected Poetry of Robinson Jeffers; Vol. 3 *Tim Hunt, ed.* (1991) Stanford University Press. 485p.

CP-JohnS The Complete English Poems [Samuel Johnson] *J. D. Fleeman, ed.* (1971) Penguin Books. 260p., pap.

CP-JonsB The Complete Poems [Ben Jonson] *George Parfitt, ed.* (1988) Penguin. 634p., pap.

CP-KeatJ The Complete Poems [John Keats] *John Barnard, ed.* (3d ed., 1988) Penguin. 754p., pap.

CP-KiplR Rudyard Kipling; Complete Verse; Definitive Edition (1989) Doubleday. 850p., pap.

CP-KuniS The Poems of Stanley Kunitz, 1928–1978 (1979) Little, Brown. 249p.

CP-LarkP   Collected Poems of Philip Larkin *Anthony Thwaite, ed.* (1988) Farrar, Straus and Giroux. 330p.
CP-LawrD   The Complete Poems [D. H. Lawrence] *Vivian de Sola Pinto and Warren Roberts, eds.* (1993) Penguin Books. 1,079p., pap.
CP-LeveD   Poems 1960–1967 [Denise Levertov] (1983) New Directions. 247., pap.
CP-LewiA   Collected Poems [Alun Lewis] *Cary Archard, ed.* (1994) Poetry Wales Press. 206p.
CP-LiddJ   Collected Poems [James Liddy] (1994) Creighton University Press. 359p., pap.
CP-LindV   Collected Poems of Vachel Lindsay (1925) Macmillan. 464p.
CP-LoveR   The Poems of Richard Lovelace *C. H. Wilkinson, ed.* (1930, repr. 1953) Oxford University Press. 367p.
CP-LowrM   The Collected Poetry of Malcolm Lowry *Kathleen Scherf, ed.; with annotation by Christopher Ackerley* (1992) University of British Columbia Press. 418p.
CP-MacLA   New & Collected Poems, 1917–1976 [Archibald MacLeish] (1976) Houghton Mifflin. 493p.
CP-MacNL   The Collected Poems of Louis MacNeice *E. R. Dodds, ed.* (1966) Faber and Faber. 575p.
CP-MarkD   Collected Poems [David Markson] (1993) Dalkey Archive Press. 94p., pap.
CP-MarlC   The Complete Poems and Translations [Christopher Marlowe] *Stephen Orgel, ed.* (1971) Penguin Books. 282p., pap.
CP-MarvA   The Complete Poems [Andrew Marvell] *Elizabeth Story Donno, ed.* (1972, repr. 1985) Penguin. 314p., pap.
CP-MerG1   The Poems of George Meredith. Vol. 1 *Phyllis B. Bartlett* (1978) Yale University Press. 707p.
CP-MerG2   The Poems of George Meredith. Vol. 2 *Phyllis B. Bartlett, ed.* (1978) Yale University Press. 542p.
CP-MertT   The Collected Poems of Thomas Merton (1977) New Directions. 1,048p., pap.
CP-MillE   Collected Poems [Edna St. Vincent Millay] *Norma Millay, ed.* (1956) Harper and Row. 738p., pap.
CP-MiltJ   The Complete Poetry of John Milton *John T. Shawcross, ed.* (1963, rev. ed. 1971) Doubleday. 654p., pap.
CP-MoorM   The Complete Poems of Marianne Moore (1981) Penguin Books. 305p.
CP-NashO   Verses from 1929 On [Ogden Nash] (1959) Random House. 522p.
CP-NemeH   The Collected Poems of Howard Nemerov (1981) University of Chicago Press. 516p., pap.
CP-OlsoC   The Collected Poems of Charles Olson *George F. Butterick, ed.* (1987) University of California Press. 675p.
CP-OppeG   The Collected Poems of George Oppen (1975) New Directions. 263p., pap.
CP-OwenW   The Collected Poems of Wilfred Owen *C. Day Lewis, ed.* (1963) New Directions. 191p., pap.
CP-PaleG   New and Collected Poems [Grace Paley] (1992) Tilbury House. 126p., pap.
CP-PatcK   Collected Poems [Kenneth Patchen] (1982) New Directions. 504p., pap.
CP-PlatS   The Collected Poems [Sylvia Plath] *Ted Hughes, ed.* (1981) HarperCollins. 351p., pap.
CP-PoCan   The Cantos of Ezra Pound (1970; repr. 1991) New Directions. 818p.
CP-PoeEd   Complete Poems and Selected Essays [Edgar Allan Poe] *Richard Gray, ed.* (1993) Everyman. 306p., pap.
CP-PopeA   Poetical Works [Alexander Pope] *Herbert Davis, ed.* (1978; repr. 1990) Oxford University Press. 754p., pap.
CP-PrinF   Collected Poems, 1935–1992 [F. T. Prince] (1993) The Sheep Meadow Press. 319p., pap.
CP-Psal   The Book of Psalms–(1991) Walker and Company. 226p., pap.
CP-RaleW   The Poems of Sir Walter Ralegh *Agnes M. C. Latham, ed.* (1929) Constable. 200p.
CP-RexKL   The Collected Longer Poems of Kenneth Rexroth (1968) New Directions. 307p., pap.
CP-RicAE   Collected Early Poems 1950–1970 [Adrienne Rich] (1993) W. W. Norton. 435p.
CP-RobiE   Collected Poems [Edward Arlington Robinson] (1922) Macmillan. 591p.
CP-RoetT   The Collected Poems of Theodore Roethke (1975) Doubleday / Anchor Books. 272p., pap.
CP-RolfE   Collected Poems [Edwin Rolfe] *Cary Nelson and Jefferson Hendricks, eds.* (1993) University of Illinois Press. 337p.
CP-RosC1   The Complete Poems of Christina Rossetti. Vol. 1 *R. W. Crump, ed.* (1979) Louisiana State University Press. 332p.
CP-RosC2   The Complete Poems of Christina Rossetti. Vol. 2 *R. W. Crump, ed.* (1986) Louisiana State University Press. 525p.

CP-RosC3 The Complete Poems of Christina Rossetti. Vol. 3 *R. W. Crump, ed.* (1990) Louisiana State University Press. 601p.

CP-RukeM The Collected Poems of Muriel Rukeyser (1978) McGraw-Hill. 588p.

CP-SandC The Complete Poems of Carl Sandburg (1970) Harcourt Brace Jovanovich. 707p.

CP-SchuJ Collected Poems [James Schuyler] *Tom Carey, Raymond Foye, and Darragh Park, eds.* (1993) Farrar, Straus and Giroux. 429p.

CP-SextA The Complete Poems [Anne Sexton] (1981) Houghton Mifflin. 622p., pap.

CP-ShaWS The Unabridged William Shakespeare *William George Clark and William Aldis Wright, eds.* (1989) Running Press. 1,421p., pap.

CP-ShelP The Complete Poems of Percy Bysshe Shelley *Mary Shelley, ed.* (1994) The Modern Library / Random House. 914p.

CP-SmitC The Poems of Charlotte Smith *Stuart Curran, ed.* (1993) Oxford University Press. 335p., pap.

CP-SmitS Collected Poems [Stevie Smith] *James MacGibbon, ed.* (1976) New Directions. 591p., pap.

CP-SnydG No Nature; New and Selected Poems [Gary Snyder] (1992) Pantheon Books. 390p., pap.

CP-SoutR The Complete Poems of Robert Southwell *Alexander B. Grosart, ed.* (1872; repr. by Reprint Services) 232p.

CP-SpenS Collected Poems [Stephen Spender] (1985) Faber and Faber. 204p.

CP-Spens The Complete Poetical Works of [Edmund Spenser] *R. E. Neil Dodge, ed.* (1936) Houghton Mifflin. 851p.

CP-SteiG The Yale Gertrude Stein *Richard Kostelanetz, ed.* (1980) Yale University Press. 464p., pap.

CP-StevR The Works of Robert Louis Stevenson; Vailima Edition; Vol. 8 (1922; repr. by Reprint Services) William Heinemann and Chatto Windus. 595p.

CP-StevW The Collected Poems of Wallace Stevens (1954, repr. 1990) Vintage. 534p., pap.

CP-SuckJ The Works of Sir John Suckling in Prose and Verse *A. Hamilton Thompson, ed.* (1910; repr. by Reprint Services) 424p.

CP-SwifJ The Complete Poems [Jonathan Swift] *Pat Rogers, ed.* (1983) Penguin Books. 956p., pap.

CP-TateA Collected Poems, 1919–1976 [Allen Tate] (1989) Louisiana State University Press. 218p., pap.

CP-TennA Tennyson; a Selected Edition *Christopher Ricks, ed.* (1989) University of California Press. 1,032p., pap.

CP-ThomD The Collected Poems of Dylan Thomas, 1934–1952 (1953, rev. ed. 1956) New Directions. 203p., pap.

CP-ThomJ The Poetical Works of James Thomson (n.d.) Houghton, Mifflin. 568p.

CP-TomlC Collected Poems [Charles Tomlinson] (1985) Oxford University Press. 388p., pap.

CP-UpdiJ Collected Poems, 1953–1993 [John Updike] (1993) Alfred A. Knopf. 387p.

CP-WalcD Collected Poems, 1948–1984 [Derek Walcott] (1986) Farrar, Straus and Giroux. 516p., pap.

CP-WalkA Her Blue Body Everything We Know; Earthling Poems, 1965–1990 Complete [Alice Walker] (1991) Harcourt Brace. 459p., pap.

CP-WhitJ The Complete Poetical Works of John Greenleaf Whittier (1904) Houghton, Mifflin; repr. by Reprint Services. 656p.

CP-WhitW The Complete Poems [Walt Whitman] *Francis Murphy, ed.* (1975; repr. 1986) Penguin Books. 892p., pap.

CP-WilbR New and Collected Poems [Richard Wilbur] (1988) Harcourt Brace Jovanovich. 393p.

CP-WillC Poems; 1963–1983 [C. K. Williams] (1988) Farrar, Straus and Giroux. 244p., pap.

CP-WilW1 The Collected Poems of William Carlos Williams; Vol. 1, 1909–1939 *A. Walton Litz and Christopher MacGowan, eds.* (1986) New Directions. 579p., pap.

CP-WilW2 The Collected Poems of William Carlos Williams; Vol. 2, 1939–1962 *Christopher MacGowan, ed.* (1988) New Directions. 553p., pap.

CP-WorW1 The Poems; Vol. 1 [William Wordsworth] *John O. Hayden, ed.* (1977; repr. 1990) Penguin Books. 1,066p., pap.

CP-WorW2 The Poems; Vol. 2 [William Wordsworth] *John O. Hayden, ed.* (1977; repr. 1989) Penguin Books. 1,104p., pap.

CP-WorW3 The Prelude; a Parallel Text [William Wordsworth] *J. C. Maxwell, ed.* (1971; repr. 1972, 1986) Penguin. 573p., pap.

CP-WrigJ Collected Poems [James Wright] (1972) Wesleyan University Press. 215p.

CP-WrotM   The Poems of Lady Mary Wroth *Josephine A. Roberts, ed.* (1983) Louisiana State University Press. 251p., pap.

CP-WyatT   Complete Poems [Sir Thomas Wyatt] *R. A. Rebholz, ed.* (1978) Penguin Books. 558p., pap.

CP-YeatW   The Collected Poems of W. B. Yeats *Richard J. Finneran, ed.* (1989) Macmillan. 544p., pap.

CP-YounA   Heaven; Collected Poems 1956–1990 [Al Young] (1992) Creative Arts Book Company. 348p., pap.

CP-ZukLS   Complete Short Poetry [Louis Zukofsky] (1991) The Johns Hopkins University Press. 365p.

SP-AmmoA   The Really Short Poems of A. R. Ammons (1990) W. W. Norton. 160p., pap.

SP-AngeM   Maya Angelou; Poems (1986) Bantam Books / Random House. 209p., pap.

SP-ArnoM   Selected Poems and Prose [Matthew Arnold] *Miriam Allott, ed.* (1993) J. M. Dent. 293p., pap.

SP-AshbJ   Selected Poems [John Ashbery] (1986) Penguin Books. 348p., pap.

SP-AtwM1   Selected Poems, 1965–1975 [Margaret Atwood] (1976) Houghton Mifflin. 240p., pap.

SP-AtwM2   Selected Poems II; Poems Selected and New, 1976–1986 [Margaret Atwood] (1987) Houghton Mifflin. 147p., pap.

SP-BergS   New & Selected Poems [Stephen Berg] (1992) Copper Canyon Press. 219p., pap.

SP-BerrT   Selected Poems [Ted Berrigan] *Aram Saroyan, ed.* (1994) Penguin Books. 142p., pap.

SP-BlyR   Selected Poems of Robert Bly (1986) HarperCollins. 211p., pap.

SP-BrooG   Selected Poems by Gwendolyn Brooks (1963) Harper & Row. 127p., pap.

SP-BukC1   Love Is a Dog from Hell; Poems 1974–1977 [Charles Bukowski] (1993) Black Sparrow Press. 307p., pap.

SP-BukC2   The Roominghouse Madrigals; Early Selected Poems 1946–1966 [Charles Bukowski] (1988) Black Sparrow Press. 256p., pap.

SP-BukC3   War All the Time; Poems 1981–1984 [Charles Bukowski] (1984) Black Sparrow Press. 280p.

SP-CarrJ   Fear of Dreaming; the Selected Poems of Jim Carroll (1993) Penguin Books. 273p., pap.

SP-CedeS   Letters from the Floating World; Selected and New Poems [Siv Cedering Fox] (1984) University of Pittsburgh Press. 183p., pap.

SP-CeraJ   The Green Lake Is Awake; Selected Poems by Joseph Ceravolo *Larry Fagin, Kenneth Koch, Charles North, Ron Padgett, David Shapiro, and Paul Violi, eds.* (1994) Coffee House Press. 131p., pap.

SP-CiarJ   Selected Poems [John Ciardi] (1984) University of Arkansas Press. 222p., pap.

SP-ClarJ   Selected Poems [John Clare] *Elaine Feinstein, ed.* (1968) University Tutorial Press. 152p.

SP-ClarT   Sleepwalker's Fate; New and Selected Poems, 1965–1991 [Tom Clark] (1992) Black Sparrow Press. 212p., pap.

SP-ClouA   Selected Poems [Arthur Hugh Clough] *Jim McCue, ed.* (1991) Penguin Books. 252p., pap.

SP-CoopJ   Scaffolding; Selected Poems [Jane Cooper] (1993) Tilbury House. 128p., pap.

SP-CrabG   Selections from the Poems of George Crabbe *Anthony C. Deane, ed.* (1903; repr. 1932) Methuen. 251p.

SP-CummE   100 Selected Poems by E. E. Cummings (1959; repr. 1988) Grove Press. 121p., pap.

SP-DickE   New Poems of Emily Dickinson *William H. Shurr, ed.; with Anna Dunlap and Emily Grey Shurr* (1993) University of North Carolina Press. 125p.

SP-DickW   In the Dreaming; Selected Poems [William Dickey] (1994) University of Arkansas Press. 106p.

SP-DobyS   Velocities; New and Selected Poems, 1966–1992 [Stephen Dobyns] (1994) Penguin. 297p., pap.

SP-DoveR   Selected Poems [Rita Dove] (1993) Vintage Books. 207p., pap.

SP-DrydJ   Dryden; Poems and Prose *Douglas Grant, ed.* (1955; repr. 1985) Penguin Books. 357p., pap.

SP-DuncR   Selected Poems [Robert Duncan] *Robert J. Bertholf, ed.* (1993) New Directions. 147p., pap.

SP-DunnS   New and Selected Poems 1974–1994 [Stephen Dunn] (1994) W. W. Norton. 296p.

SP-EdmuM   The High Road to Taos [Martin Edmunds] *Donald Hall, ed.* (1994) University of Illinois Press. 115p., pap.

SP-EverW   The Blood of the Poet; Selected Poems [William Everson] *Albert Gelpi, ed.* (1994) Broken Moon Press. 278p., pap.

SP-FentJ   Children in Exile; Poems, 1968–1984 [James Fenton] (1994) Farrar, Straus and Giroux. 110p., pap.

SP-FerlL   These Are My Rivers; New & Selected Poems [Lawrence Ferlinghetti] (1993) New Directions. 308p.

SP-FishR   Poems, 1955–1987 [Roy Fisher] (1988) Oxford University Press. 223p., pap.

SP-FletJ   Selected Poems of John Gould Fletcher *Lucas Carpenter and Leighton Rudolph, eds.* (1988) University of Arkansas Press. 340p., pap.

SP-FordC   Out of the Labyrinth; Selected Poems [Charles Henri Ford] (1991) City Lights. 113p., pap.

SP-GallT   Amplitude; New and Selected Poems [Tess Gallagher] (1987) Graywolf Press. 199p., pap.

SP-GalvB   Great Blue; New and Selected Poems [Brendan Galvin] (1990) University of Illinois Press. 162p., pap.

SP-GarrJ   Selected Poems [Jean Garrigue] (1992) University of Illinois Press. 194p., pap.

SP-GildG   Blue like the Heavens; New & Selected Poems [Gary Gildner] (1984) University of Pittsburgh Press. 142p., pap.

SP-GlücL   The First Four Books of Poems [Louise Glück] (1995) The Ecco Press. 216p.

SP-GrifS   Selected Poems [Steve Griffiths] (1993) Seren Books. 144p., pap.

SP-HackM   Selected Poems 1965–1990 [Marilyn Hacker] (1994) W. W. Norton. 250p.

SP-HainJ   New from the Glacier; Selected Poems 1960–1980 [John Haines] (1982) Wesleyan University Press. 157p., pap.

SP-HarMi   Selected & New Poems [Michael Hartnett] *Peter Fallon, ed.* (1994) Wake Forest University Press. 104p., pap.

SP-HeanS   Selected Poems 1966–1987 [Seamus Heaney] (1990) Farrar, Straus and Giroux. 273p., pap.

SP-HeskP   The Leave Train; New and Selected Poems [Phoebe Hesketh] (1994) Enitharmon Press. 157p., pap.

SP-HoffD   Hang-Gliding from Helicon; New and Selected Poems, 1948–1988 [Daniel Hoffman] (1988) Louisiana State University Press. 218p.

SP-HolmJ   Night Music; Selected Poems [John Clellon Holmes] (1989) University of Arkansas Press. 72p.

SP-HughL   Selected Poems of Langston Hughes (1959) Vintage Books. 297p., pap.

SP-HughT   Selected Poems 1957–1981 [Ted Hughes] (1982) Faber and Faber. 238p.

SP-JarrR   Randall Jarrell [Selected Poems] *William H. Pritchard, ed.* (1990) Farrar, Straus and Giroux. 115p.

SP-JongE   Becoming Light; Poems New and Selected [Erica Jong] (1991) HarperCollins. 378p., pap.

SP-JoseJ   Selected Poems [Jenny Joseph] (1992) Bloodaxe Books. 157p., pap.

SP-KinnG   Selected Poems [Galway Kinnell] (1982) Houghton Mifflin. 148p., pap.

SP-KnigE   The Essential Etheridge Knight (1986) University of Pittsburgh Press. 114p., pap.

SP-KnotB   Poems: 1963–1988 [Bill Knott] (1989) University of Pittsburgh Press. 50p., pap.

SP-KochK   Selected Poems, 1950–1982 [Kenneth Koch] (1985) Random House. 239p.

SP-KoerR   Life on the Edge of the Continent; Selected Poems by Ronald Koertge (1982) University of Arkansas Press. 68p., pap.

SP-KoosT   Sure Signs; New and Selected Poetry [Ted Kooser] (1980) University of Pittsburgh Press. 93p., pap.

SP-LeviP   New Selected Poems [Philip Levine] (1991) Alfred A. Knopf. 292p.

SP-LiebL   New and Selected Poems, 1962–92 [Laurence Lieberman] (1993) University of Illinois Press. 237p., pap.

SP-LongH   Selected Poems [Henry Wadsworth Longfellow] *Lawrence Buell, ed.* (1988) Penguin. 389p., pap.

SP-LordA   Undersong; Chosen Poems, Old and New [Audre Lord] (1992) W. W. Norton. 206p., pap.

SP-LoweR   Selected Poems [Robert Lowell] (Rev. ed. 1977; repr. 1993) Farrar, Straus and Giroux. 256p., pap.

SP-MacDH   Selected Poetry [Hugh MacDiarmid] *Alan Riach and Michael Grieve, eds.* (1992) New Directions. 289p.

SP-MahoD   Selected Poems [Derek Mahon] (1991) Viking (in association with Oxford University Press). 194p.

SP-MattW   Selected Poems and Translations, 1969–1991 [William Matthews] Houghton Mifflin. 200p., pap.

SP-McAuJ   Coming & Going; New and Selected Poems [James J. McAuley] (1989) University of Arkansas Press. 148p.

SP-McGrT   Selected Poems, 1938–1988 [Thomas McGrath] *Sam Hamill* (1988) Copper Canyon Press. 180p., pap.

SP-McNeL Hill Daughter; New and Selected Poems [Maggie Anderson] *Maggie Anderson, ed.* (1991) University of Pittsburgh Press. 139p., pap.

SP-MeinP Liquid Paper; New and Selected Poems [Peter Meinke] (1991) University of Pittsburgh Press. 117p., pap.

SP-MelvH Selected Poems of Herman Melville *Hennig Cohen, ed.* (1991) Fordham University Press. 259p., pap.

SP-MerrJ Selected Poems [James Merrill] (1992) Alfred A. Knopf. 340p., pap.

SP-MertT Selected Poems of Thomas Merton (1967) New Directions. 140p., pap.

SP-MillC Northern Fields; New and Selected Poems by Chuck Miller (1994) Coffee House Press. 190p., pap.

SP-MorgF Poems; New and Selected [Frederick Morgan] (1987) University of Illinois Press. 258p., pap.

SP-MorrJ The American Night; the Writings of Jim Morrison; Vol. 2 (1990) Vintage Books / Random House. 212p., pap.

SP-MuldP Selected Poems, 1968–1986 [Paul Muldoon] (1993) Farrar, Straus and Giroux. 153p., pap.

SP-NathL Carrying On; New and Selected Poems [Leonard Nathan] (1985) University of Pittsburgh Press. 160p., pap.

SP-NeruP Late and Posthumous Poems 1968–1974 [Pablo Neruda] *Ben Belitt, ed. and tr.* (1988) Grove Press. 239p., pap.

SP-NotlA Selected Poems of Alice Notley (1993) Talisman House. 138p., pap.

SP-OharF The Selected Poems of Frank O'Hara *Donald Allen, ed.* (1974) Vintage Books / Random House. 233p., pap.

SP-OlivM New and Selected Poems [Mary Oliver] (1992) Beacon Press. 255p.

SP-OlsoC Selected Poems [Charles Olson] *Robert Creeley, ed.* (1993) University of California Press. 225p.

SP-PackR Fathering the Map; New and Selected Later Poems [Robert Pack] (1993) University of Chicago Press. 302p.

SP-PierM Circles on the Water; Selected Poems of Marge Piercy (1982) Alfred A. Knopf. 299p., pap.

SP-PounE The Selected Poems of Ezra Pound (1957) New Directions. 184p., pap.

SP-RainK Selected Poems [Kathleen Raine] (1988) Lindisfarne Press. 157p., pap.

SP-RansJ Selected Poems of John Crowe Ransom (1969) Alfred A. Knopf. 159p.

SP-ReedL Between Thought and Expression; Selected Lyrics of Lou Reed (1991) Hyperion. 142p., pap.

SP-RexrK The Selected Poems of Kenneth Rexroth *Bradford Morrow, ed.* (1984) New Directions. 152p., pap.

SP-RicA1 Adrienne Rich's Poetry and Prose *Barbara Charlesworth Gelpi and Albert Gelpi, eds.* (1975, repr. 1993) W. W. Norton. 434p. pap.

SP-RicA2 The Fact of a Doorframe; Poems Selected and New 1950–1984 [Adrienne Rich] (1984) W. W. Norton. 341p., pap.

SP-SartM Selected Poems of May Sarton *Serena Sue Hilsinger and Lois Brynes, eds.* (1978) W. W. Norton. 206p., pap.

SP-SchwD Last & Lost Poems [Delmore Schwartz] *Robert Phillips, ed.* (1989) New Directions. 134p., pap.

SP-ScotW Selections from the Poems of Sir Walter Scott *A. Hamilton Thompson, ed.* (1921) Reprint Services. 196p.

SP-ShapK New & Selected Poems, 1940–1986 [Karl Shapiro] (1987) University of Chicago Press. 103p., pap.

SP-ShelR Selected Poems, 1969–1981 [Richard Shelton] (1982) University of Pittsburgh Press. 221p., pap.

SP-SidnP Selected Poems [Sir Philip Sidney] *Catherine Bates, ed.* (1994) Penguin Books. 219p., pap.

SP-SilS2 Where the Sidewalk Ends; the Poems and Drawings of Shel Silverstein (1974) HarperCollins. 166p.

SP-SimiC Selected Poems, 1963–1983—Revised and Expanded [Charles Simic] (1990) George Braziller. 229p., pap.

SP-SmarC Christopher Smart; Selected Poems *Karina Williamson and Marcus Walsh, eds.* (1990) Penguin Books. 390p., pap.

SP-SmitP Early Work, 1970–1979 [Patti Smith] (1994) W. W. Norton. 177p.

SP-SnodW   Selected Poems, 1957–1987 [W. D. Snodgrass] (1987) Soho Press. 270p., pap.

SP-SorrG   Selected Poems, 1958–1980 [Gilbert Sorrentino] (1981) Black Sparrow Press. 268p., pap.

SP-StafW   The Darkness around Us Is Deep; Selected Poems of William Stafford *Robert Bly, ed.* (1993) HarperCollins. 138p., pap.

SP-StJoD   Study for the World's Body; New and Selected Poems [David St. John] (1994) HarperCollins. 142p., pap.

SP-StuaD   Light Years; New and Selected Poems [Dabney Stuart] (1994) Louisiana State University Press. 196p.

SP-SuttB   The Book of Names; New and Selected Poems by Barton Sutter (1993) BOA Editions. 107p., pap.

SP-SwinA   A Choice of Swinburne's Verse *Robert Nye, ed.* (1973) Faber and Faber, 169p.

SP-TurcL   The Shifting Web; New and Selected Poems [Lewis Turco] (1989) University of Arkansas Press. 184p.

SP-VanDM   If It Be Not I; Poems, 1959–1982 [Mona Van Duyn] (1993) Alfred A. Knopf. 305p.

SP-WakoD   Emerald Ice; Selected Poems, 1962–1987 [Diane Wakoski] (1988) Black Sparrow Press. 343p., pap.

SP-WaldA   Helping the Dreamer; New & Selected Poems, 1966–1988 [Anne Waldman] (1989) Coffee House Press. 245p., pap.

SP-WarrR   Selected Poems 1923-1975 [Robert Penn Warren] (1976) Random House. 325p.

SP-WillC   Selected Poems [C. K. Williams] (1994) Farrar, Straus and Giroux. 289p.

SP-WillM   Living on the Surface; New and Selected Poems by Miller Williams (1989) Louisiana State University Press. 132p.

SP-WrigC   The World of the Ten Thousand Things; Poems 1980–1990 [Charles Wright] (1990) Farrar, Straus and Giroux. 231p., pap.

SP-YauJo   Radiant Silhouette; New & Selected Work, 1974–1988 [John Yau] (1989) Black Sparrow Press. 228p.

SP-ZimmP   Family Reunion; Selected and New Poems [Paul Zimmer] (1983) University of Pittsburgh Press. 85p., pap.

LIST OF ANTHOLOGIES

AA — An American Anthology, 1787–1900 *Edmund Clarence Stedman, ed.* (1900) Houghton Mifflin. 878p.

AAS *Dynix +* — The Anchor Anthology of Sixteenth Century Verse *Richard Sylvester, ed.* (1974) Doubleday/ Anchor Books; also published 1984 by W. W. Norton with title English Sixteenth-Century Verse. 623p.

ACP — An Anthology of Catholic Poets *Shane Leslie, ed.* (Rev. ed., 1952) Macmillan; later published by The Newman Press. 378p., o.p.

AH *R 783.952* — American Hymns Old and New. Vols. I–II *Albert Christ-Janer, Charles W. Hughes, and Carleton SpragueSmith, eds.* (1980) Columbia University Press.
v.1+2

AiP *811.008* — America in Poetry *Charles Sullivan, ed.* (1988) Harry N. Abrams. 207p.

AIW — Ain't I a Woman! a Book of Women's Poetry from around the World *Illona Linthwaite, ed.* (1988) Peter Bedrick Books. 195p.

AmFN — America Forever New; a Book of Poems *Sara Brewton and John E. Brewton, comps.* (1968) Thomas Y. Crowell. 270p., o.p.

AmFP *R 811.04* — American Folk Poetry; an Anthology *Duncan Emrich, ed.* (1974) Little, Brown. 831p.

AmMo — Amazing Monsters; Verses to Thrill and Chill *Robert Fisher, ed.* (1982) Faber and Faber. 95p.

AmNP — American Negro Poetry *Arna Bontemps, ed.* Rev. ed., (1974) Hill and Wang. 252p., pap., o.p.

AmPP *Dynix +* — American Poetry and Prose *Norman Foerster, Norman S. Grabo, Russel B. Nye, E. Fred Carlisle, and Robert Falk, eds.* (5th ed., 1970) Houghton Mifflin. 3 vols., pap., o.p.

AMV-81 — Anthology of Magazine Verse and Yearbook of American Poetry, 1981 Edition *Alan F. Pater, ed.* (1981) Monitor Book Company. 640p., o.p.

AnAmPo — Anthology of American Poetry *George Gesner, ed.* (1983) Avenel Books. 735p., o.p.

AnAn — The Antaeus Anthology *Daniel Halpern, ed.* (1986) Bantam Books. 615p., pap.

AnAnS-1 — The Anchor Anthology of Seventeenth-Century Verse. Vol. I *Louis L. Martz, ed.* (1969) Doubleday Anchor Books

AnAnS-2 — The Anchor Anthology of Seventeenth-Century Verse. Vol. II *Richard S. Sylvester, ed.* (1969) Doubleday Anchor Books

AngWe — Anglo-Welsh Poetry, 1480–1980 *Raymond Garlick and Roland Mathias, eds.* (1984) Poetry Wales Press. 377p.

AnIL — An Anthology of Irish Literature *David H. Greene, ed.* (1954) Modern Library. 602p., o.p.

AnIV — An Anthology of Irish Verse; the Poetry of Ireland from Mythological Times to the Present *Padraic Colum, ed.* (1948) Liveright. 425p., o.p.

AP — American Poetry *Gay Wilson Allen, Walter B. Rideout, and James K. Robinson, eds.* (1965) Harper & Row. 1,274p., pap., o.p.

APAS — Anthology of Poems on Affairs of State; Augustan Satirical Verse, 1660–1714 *George de F. Lord, ed.* (1975) Yale University Press. 800p., o.p.

APN-1 *811.308* — American Poetry: The Nineteenth Century. Vol. 1 *John Hollander, ed.* (1993) The Library of America. 1,099p.

∅ APN-2 — American Poetry: The Nineteenth Century. Vol. 2 *John Hollander, ed.* (1993) The Library of America. 1,050p.

APSN *Dynix +* — American Poetry since 1950: Innovators and Outsiders *Eliot Weinberger, ed.* (1993) Marsilio. 433p.

ArLo — Art & Love; an Illustrated Anthology of Love Poetry *Kate Farrell, ed.* (1990) The Metropolitan Museum of Art. 176p.

ArNa — Art & Nature: an Illustrated Anthology of of Nature Poetry *Kate Farrell, ed.* (1992) The Metropolitan Museum of Art. 175p.

ASP   American Sports Poems *R. R. Knudson and May Swenson, comps.* (1988) Orchard Books. 226p.

AWP   An Anthology of World Poetry *Mark Van Doren, ed.* (Rev. and Enl. ed., 1936) Reynal & Hitchcock. 1468p.

BeJo   Ben Jonson and the Cavalier Poets *Hugh MacLean, ed.* (1974) W. W. Norton & Company. 591p., pap.

BeLS   Best Loved Story Poems *Walter E. Thwing, ed.* (1941) Garden City. 754p., o.p.

⌀ BiHa   Bitter Harvest; an Anthology of Contemporary Irish Verse *John Montague, ed.* (1989) Scribner's. 211p.

BiP   Beginnings in Poetry *William J. Martz, ed.* (1965) Scott, Foresman. 494p., pap., o.p.

BIrV   The Book of Irish Verse; an Anthology of Irish Poetry from the Sixth Century to the Present *John Montague, ed.* (1974) Macmillan; also published as The Faber Book of Irish Verse. 400p., o.p.

BLPA   Best Loved Poems of the American People, The *Hazel Felleman, ed.* (1936) Doubleday. 670p., pap.

BLPL   Best-Loved Poems in Large Print *Virginia S. Reiser, ed.* (1983) G. K. Hall. 585p.

BLRP   The Best Loved Religious Poems *James Gilchrist Lawson, comp.* (1933) Fleming H. Revell. 253p., o.p.

BoAnP   A Book of Animal Poems *William Cole, ed.* (1973) Viking. 288p., pap., o.p.

⌀ BoLoP   A Book of Love Poetry *Jon Stallworthy, ed.* (1974) Oxford University Press; also published in Great Britain as The Penguin Book of Love Poetry. 393p.

BoNaP   A Book of Nature Poems *William Cole, comp.* (1969) Viking Press. 256p., o.p.

⌀ BoTP   The Book of a Thousand Poems; a Family Treasury *J. Murray Macbain, ed.* (1983) Peter Bedrick Books. 630p.

BoWoP   A Book of Women Poets from Antiquity to Now *Aliki Barnstone and Willis Barnstone, eds.* (1980) Schocken Books. 613p.

BPAW   Best Loved Poems of the American West *John J. Gregg and Barbara T. Gregg, eds.* (1980) Doubleday. 515p., o.p.

BPo   The Black Poets *Dudley Randall, ed.* (1971) Bantam Books. 355p., pap.

BrPo   British Poetry 1880–1920; Edwardian Voices *Paul L. Wiley and Harold Orel, eds.* (1969) Appleton-Century-Crofts. 681p., o.p.

BrRo   Bread and Roses; an Anthology of Nineteenth- and Twentieth-Century Poetry by Women Writers *Diana Scott, comp.* (1982) Virago Press. 282p., pap., o.p.

BSV   A Book of Scottish Verse *Maurice Lindsay and R. L. Mackie, eds.* (1983) St. Martin's Press. 476p., o.p.

BTR   Blood to Remember; American Poets on the Holocaust *Charles Fishman, ed.* (1991) Texas Tech University. 426p.

⌀ BWW   British Women Writers *Dale Spender and Janet Todd, eds.* (1989) Peter Bedrick Books. 921p., pap.

BXAP   The Brand-X Anthology of Poetry *William Zaranka, ed.* (1981) Apple-Wood Books. 358p., o.p.

CABA   The College Anthology of British and American Verse *A. Kent Hieatt and William Park, eds.* (1964) Allyn and Bacon. 631p., o.p.

CAD   City in All Directions; an Anthology of Modern Poems *Arnold Adoff, ed.* (1969) Macmillan. 128p., o.p.

CaPo   Cavalier Poets; Selected Poems *Thomas Clayton, ed.* (1978) Oxford University Press. 364p., pap., o.p.

CAPP   Contemporary American Poetry [Poulin, 4th ed.] *A. Poulin Jr., ed.* (4th ed., 1985) Houghton Mifflin. 728p.

CavP   The Cavalier Poets *Robin Skelton, ed.* (1970) Oxford University Press. 291p., o.p.

CBCK   The Chatto Book of Cabbages and Kings; Lists in Literature *Francis Spufford, ed.* (1989) Chatto and Windus. 313p.

CBCWP   The Columbia Book of Civil War Poetry *Richard Marius, ed.* (1994) Columbia University Press. 543p.

CBLP   The Chatto Book of Love Poetry *John Fuller, ed.* (1990) Chatto & Windus. 374p.

CBNP   The Chatto Book of Nonsense Poetry *Hugh Haughton, ed.* (1988) Chatto & Windus. 530p.

CH   Come Hither *Walter de la Mare, comp.* (3rd ed., 1957) Knopf. 777p., o.p.

ChER   A Choice of English Romantic Poetry *Stephen Spender, ed.* (1947) Dial Press. 384p.

ChIV-1   Chapters into Verse. Vol. I: Genesis to Malachi *Robert Atwan and Laurance Wieder, eds.* (1993) Oxford University Press. 481p.

ChIV-2   Chapters into Verse. Vol. II: Gospels to Revelation *Robert Atwan and Laurance Wieder, eds.* (1993) Oxford University Press. 391p.

ChMP   The Chatto Book of Modern Poetry, 1915-1955 *C. Day Lewis and John Lehmann, eds.* (1966) Chatto & Windus. 288p., pap.

ChTr   The Cherry-Tree *Geoffrey Grigson, comp.* (1959) Phoenix House. 518p.

CIP   Contemporary Irish Poetry; an Anthology *Anthony Bradley, ed.* (New and rev. ed., 1988) University of California Press. 526p.

ClHu   The Classic Hundred; All-Time Favorite Poems *William Harmon, ed.* (1990) Columbia University Press. 250p., pap.

CMoP   Chief Modern Poets of Britain and America *Gerald DeWitt Sanders, John Herbert Nelson, and M. L. Rosenthal, eds.* (5th ed., 1970) Macmillan. 962p.

CNA   Celebrations; a New Anthology of Black American Poetry *Arnold Adoff, ed.* (1977) Follett. 285p., o.p.

CoAP   The Contemporary American Poets; American Poetry since 1940 *Mark Strand, ed.* (1969) World. 390p., pap.

CoBMV   College Book of Modern Verse, A *James K. Robinson and Walter B. Rideout, eds.* (1958) Row, Peterson and Company

CoGr   Common Ground; an Anthology *Marghanita Laski, ed.* (1989) Carcanet Press. 295p.

ConAP   Contemporary American Poetry [Hall] *Donald Hall, ed.* (2d ed., 1972) Penguin Books. 280p.

CoPo   A Controversy of Poets *Paris Leary and Robert Kelly, eds.* (1965) Anchor Books. 567p., o.p.

CPA   California Bicentennial Poets Anthology *A. D. Winans, ed.* (1976) Second Coming Press. 217p., pap.

CrDW   Crossing the Danger Water *Deirdre Mullane, ed.* (1993) Doubleday. 769p., pap.

CrMA   The Criterion Book of Modern American Verse *W. H. Auden, ed.* (1956) Criterion Books. 336p., o.p.

CRP   Contemporary Religious Poetry *Paul Ramsey, ed.* (1987) Paulist Press. 227p., pap.

CrSp   Cries of the Spirit; a Celebration of Women's Spiritualities *Marilyn Sewell, ed.* (1991) Boston Beacon Press. 311p., pap.

CTC   Confucius to Cummings; an Anthology of Poetry *Ezra Pound and Marcella Spann, eds.* (1964) New Directions. 353p., pap.

DBV   The Devil's Book of Verse; Masters of the Poison Pen from Ancient Times to the Present Day *Richard Conniff, ed.; foreword by Willard R. Espy* (1983) Dodd, Mead. 269p., o.p.

DiL   Divided Light: Father & Son Poems; a Twentieth-Century American Anthology *Jason Shinder, ed.* (1983) Sheep Meadow Press. 293p., pap.

DIP   Dance in Poetry; an International Anthology of Poems on Dance *Alkis Raftis, ed.* (1991) Princeton Book Company. 170p., pap.

DiPo   The Direction of Poetry; an Anthology of Rhymed and Metered Verse Written in the English Language since 1975 *Robert Richman, ed.* (1988) Houghton Mifflin. 168p.

DL   Death in Literature *Robert F. Weir, ed.* (1980) Columbia University Press. 451p., o.p.

DTC   Dylan Thomas's Choice; an Anthology of Verse Spoken by Dylan Thomas *Ralph Maud and Aneirin Talfan Davies, eds.* (1963) New Directions. 182p., o.p.

EaLo   The Earth Is the Lord's; Poems of the Spirit *Helen Plotz, comp.* (1965) Thomas Y. Crowell. 224p., o.p.

EaPr   Earth Prayers from around the World; 365 Prayers, Poems, and Invocations for Honoring the Earth *Elizabeth Roberts and Elias Amidon, eds.* (1991) Harper Collins. 451p., pap.

EAS   English and American Surrealist Poetry *Edward B. Germain, ed.* (1978) Penguin Books. 348p., o.p.

EBCP   Eerdman's Book of Christian Poetry *Pat Alexander and Veronica Zundel, eds.* (1981) William B. Eerdmans. 125p., o.p.

EBEV *Dynix +*   Everyman's Book of English Verse *John Wain, ed.* (1981) J. M. Dent. 672p.

⊘ EBEvV   Everyman's Book of Evergreen Verse *David Herbert, ed.* (1984) J. M. Dent. 387p., pap., o.p.

⊘ EBNV   The Everyman Book of Narrative Verse *David Herbert, ed.* (1990) J. M. Dent & Sons. 315p.

EBVV *Dynix +*   Everyman's Book of Victorian Verse *J. R. Watson, ed.* (1982) J. M. Dent. 373p.

⊘ EBVVPR   The Everyman Book of Victorian Verse; the Post-Romantics *Donald Thomas, ed.* (1992) J. M. Dent. 284p., pap.

⊘ ECEV   Eighteenth-Century English Verse *Dennis Davison, ed.* (1988) Penguin Books. 321p., pap., o.p.

⊘ ECWP   Eighteenth Century Women Poets; an Oxford Anthology *Roger Lonsdale, ed.* (1989) Oxford University Press. 555p.

ElL   Elizabethan Lyrics *Norman Ault, ed.* (3d ed., 1949) William Sloane Associates; paperback edition published by G. P. Putnam's (1960). 560p.

ELP   English Lyric Poems, 1500–1900 *C. Day Lewis, ed.* (1961) Appleton- Century-Crofts. 249p., pap.

ELU   Eight Lines and Under; an Anthology of Short, Short Poems *William Cole, ed.* (1967) Mac-millan. 164p., o.p.

EnlH *Dynix +*   The Enlightened Heart; an Anthology of Sacred Poetry *Stephen Mitchell, ed.* (1989) Harper & Row. 171p.

⊘ EnLoPo   English Love Poems *John Betjeman and Geoffrey Taylor, comps.* (1957; paperback ed., 1964) Faber and Faber. 220p., pap., o.p.

EnRePo   English Renaissance Poetry; a Collection of Shorter Poems from Skelton to Jonson *John Williams, ed.* (2d ed, 1990) University of Arkansas. 416p.

EnRP   English Romantic Poetry and Prose *Russell Noyes, ed.* (1956) Oxford University Press. 1,324p.

⊘ EnVB   English Verse, 1300–1500; Longman Annotated Anthologies of English Verse. Vol. I. *John Burrow, ed.* (1977) Longman. 397p., pap.

⊘ EnVR   English Verse 1830-1890 *Bernard Richards, ed.* (1980) Longman. 543p., pap., o.p.

⊘ EPCY   English Poetry; a Poetic Record, from Chaucer to Yeats *David Hopkins, ed.* (1990) Routledge. 269p., pap.

ErPo   Erotic Poetry; the Lyrics, Ballads, Idyls, and Epics of Love—Classical to Contemporary *William Cole, ed.* (1963) Random House. 501p., o.p.

⊘ ESCV   English Seventeeth–Century Verse *Louis L. Martz, ed.* (1973) W. W. Norton & Company. 525pp., pap.

EtS   The Eternal Sea; an Anthology of Sea Poetry *W. M. Williamson, ed.* (1946) Coward-McCann. 565p.

EvOK   Everybody Ought to Know *Ogden Nash, ed.* (1961) J. B. Lippincott. 186p., o.p.

EyDe   Eye's Delight; Poems of Art and Architecture *Helen Plotz, comp.* (1983) Greenwillow Books. 150p., o.p.

FaBCIP   The Faber Book of Contemporary Irish Poetry *Paul Muldoon, ed.* (1986) Faber and Faber. 415p.

FaBoBe *R820.82* The Family Book of Best Loved Poems *David L. George, ed.* (1952) Doubleday. 485p., pap.

FaBoBl   The Faber Book of Blue Verse *John Whitworth, ed.* 1990 Faber and Faber. 305p.

FaBoCh *808.0681* The Faber Book of Children's Verse *Janet Adam Smith, comp.* (1953) Faber and Faber. 412p., pap.

FaBoCo   The Faber Book of Comic Verse *Michael Roberts and Janet Adam Smith, eds.* (Rev. ed., 1974; paperback ed., 1978) Faber and Faber. 400p., o.p.

FaBoDD   The Faber Book of Drink, Drinkers and Drinking *Simon Rae, ed.* (1991) Faber and Faber. 554p.

⊘ FaBoEE   The Faber Book of Epigrams and Epitaphs *Geoffrey Grigson, ed.* (1977) Faber and Faber. 291p., o.p.

FaBoEH   The Faber Book of English History in Verse *Kenneth Baker, ed.* (1988) Faber and Faber. 448p., o.p.

FaBoEn   The Faber Book of English Verse *John Hayward, ed.* (1958) Faber and Faber. 483p., o.p.

FaBoMo *811*   The Faber Book of Modern Verse   *Michael Roberts, ed.*   (4th ed., revised by Peter Porter, 1982) Faber and Faber. 416p., pap.

FaBoPa   The Faber Book of Parodies   *Simon Brett, ed.*   (1984)   Faber and Faber. 383p., pap.

FaBoPP   The Faber Book of Poems and Places   *Geoffrey Grigson, ed.*   (1980)   Faber and Faber. 387p., pap.

⊘ FaBoPV   The Faber Book of Political Verse   *Tom Paulin, ed.*   (1986)   Faber and Faber. 482p.

FaBoRV   The Faber Book of Reflective Verse   *Geoffrey Grigson, ed.*   (1984)   Faber and Faber. 238p., o.p.

FaBoTw *Dynix+*   The Faber Book of Twentieth Century Verse   *John Heath-Stubbs and David Wright, eds.*   (3d ed., 1975)   Faber and Faber. 348p.

FaBoUs   The Faber Book of Useful Verse   *Simon Brett, ed.*   (1981)   Faber and Faber. 254p., pap., o.p.

⊘ FaBoVe   The Faber Book of Vernacular Verse   *Tom Paulin, ed.*   (1990)   Faber and Faber. 407p.

⊘ FaBoWP   The Faber Book of 20th Century Women's Poetry   *Fleur Adcock, ed.*   (1987)   Faber and Faber. 330p.

FaBV   Family Book of Verse, The   *Lewis Gannett, ed.*   (1961)   Harper & Row. 351p., o.p.

FaFP   The Family Album of Favorite Poems   *P. Edward Ernest, ed.*   (1959)   Grosset & Dunlap. 538p., o.p.

FaPoB   The Family Poetry Book; 100 Favorite Poems   *Felicity Kendal, ed.*   (1990)   Michael Joseph. 208p.

FaPON   Favorite Poems Old and New   *Helen Ferris, ed.*   (1957)   Doubleday. 589p., pap.

FaPoR *821.008*   The Faber Popular Reciter   *Kingsley Amis, ed.*   (1978)   Faber and Faber. 256p.

FF   Fine Frenzy; Enduring Themes in Poetry   *Robert Baylor and Brenda Stokes, eds.*   (2d ed., 1978) McGraw-Hill. 417p., o.p.

FHYEP *Dynix+*   Five Hundred Years of English Poetry; Chaucer to Arnold   *Barbara Lloyd-Evans, ed.*   (1989) Peter Bedrick Books. 1200p., pap.

FiBHP   The Fireside Book of Humorous Poetry   *William Cole, ed.*   (1959)   Simon and Schuster. 522p., o.p.

FiP   Fifteen Poets; Chaucer to Arnold   *H. S. Bennett, gen. ed.*   (1941)   Oxford University Press. 503p., o.p.

FL   First Lines; Poems Written in Youth, from Herbert to Heaney   *Jon Stallworthy, ed.*   (1987) Carcanet. 119p., pap.

FM   Fellow Mortals; an Anthology of Animal Verse   *Roy Fuller, comp.*   (1981)   Macdonald and Evans. 274p.

FPL   Favorite Poems in Large Print   *Virginia S. Reiser, ed.*   (1981)   G. K. Hall. 462p.

FSW   Folksinger's Wordbook   *Irwin Silber and Fred Silber, eds.*   (1973)   Oak Publications. 430p.

FYAP *811.508*   Fifty Years of American Poetry; Anniversary Volume for the Academy of American Poets. *American Academy of Poets; introduction by Robert Penn Warren*   (1984)   Harry N. Abrams. 260p.

⊘ GBL   The Gambit Book of Love Poems   *Geoffrey Grigson, ed.*   (1973)   Gambit; originally published in Great Britain by Faber and Faber as The Faber Book of Love Poems. 407p.

GBP   The Gambit Book of Popular Verse   *Geoffrey Grigson, ed.*   (1971)   Gambit; also published in Great Britain as The Faber Book of Popular Verse. 376p., o.p.

GDP   Good Dog Poems   *William Cole, ed.*   (1981)   Scribner's. 142p., o.p.

GeHe *Dynix+*   George Herbert and the Seventeenth-Century Religious Poets   *Marie A. Di Ceare, ed.*   1978   W. W. Norton. 401p., pap.

⊘ GePo   German Poetry; from the Beginnings to 1750   *Ingrid Walsøe–Engel, ed.*   1992   Continuum. 338p., pap.

GeTw   The Generation of 2,000; Contemporary American Poets   *William Heyen, ed.*   (1984)   Ontario Review Press. 364p., pap.

GGP   The Gift of Great Poetry   *Lucien Stryk, ed.*   (1992)   Regnery Gateway. 271p.

GN   Golden Numbers   *Kate Douglas Wiggin and Nora Archibald Smith, eds.*   (1902)   Doubleday, Doran. 687p.

GOA   The Gift Outright; America to Her Poets   *Helen Plotz, ed.*   (1977)   Greenwillow Books. 204p., o.p.

GoBC   The Golden Book of Catholic Poetry   *Alfred Noyes, ed.*   (1946)   J. B. Lippincott. 440p., o.p.

GoJo   The Golden Journey; Poems for Young People *Louise Bogan and William Jay Smith, eds.* (1990) Contemporary Books. 294p., o.p.

GoTS   The Golden Treasury of Scottish Poetry *Hugh MacDiarmid, ed.* (1941) Macmillan. 410p., o.p.

∅ GrIP   Greece in Poetry *Simoni Zafiropoulos, ed.* (1993) Harry N. Abrams. 176p.

GTBS   Golden Treasury of the Best Songs and Lyrical Poems in the English Language *Francis Palgrave, comp.* (1991) Penguin Books; also published 1986, with a new fifth book, by Oxford University Press. 526p.

GTBS-6   Golden Treasury of the Best Songs & Lyrical Poems in the English Language *Francis Turner Palgrave, comp. With a sixth book selected by John Press.* Sixth ed., updated by John Press (1994). Oxford University Press. 701p.

GTBS-P   Golden Treasury of the Best Songs & Lyrical Poems in the English Language *Francis Turner*
YA 821.082 (1964 ed.) *Palgrave, comp. With a fifth book selected by John Press.* Updated ed., by Christopher Ricks (1991) Oxford University Press. 526p., pap.

HAP *821.008*   The Harper Anthology of Poetry *John Frederick Nims, ed.* (1981) Harper & Row. 842p.

HBMV   The Home Book of Modern Verse *Burton Egbert Stevenson, ed.* (1953) Henry Holt. 1,124p., o.p.

HBV 1-2   The Home Book of Verse *Burton Egbert Stevenson, ed.* (9th ed., 1953, 2 vols.) Henry Holt and Company. 1,950p., 2,063p.

HBVY   The Home Book of Verse for Young Folks *Burton Egbert Stevenson, ed.* (1929) Holt, Rinehart and Winston. 676p., o.p.

HCAP *811.508*   The Harvard Book of Contemporary American Poetry *Helen Vendler, ed.* (1985) Belknap Press. 440p.

HeIL   The Heath Introduction to Literature *Alice C. Landy, ed.* (4th ed., 1992) D. C. Heath and Company. 1142p., pap.

HeIP   The Heath Introduction to Poetry *Joseph DeRoche, ed.* (4th ed., 1992) D. C. Heath. 561p., pap.

HoFi   Holy Fire; New Visionary Poets and the Quest for Enlightenment *Daniel Halpern, ed.* (1994) HarperCollins. 328p.

HoPM *821.008*   How Does a Poem Mean? *John Ciardi and Miller Williams, eds.* (2d ed., 1975) Houghton Mifflin. 408p.

IDB   I Am the Darker Brother; an Anthology of Modern Poems by Negro Americans *Arnold Adoff, ed.* (1968) Macmillan. 128p.

IHNG   I Have No Gun But I Can Spit; an Anthology of Satirical and Abusive Verse *Kenneth Baker, ed.* 1980 Faber and Faber. 185p., pap.

∅ IIP   Ireland in Poetry *Charles Sullivan, ed.* (1990) Harry N. Abrams. 208p.

ILwL   In Love with Love; 100 of the Greatest Mystical Poems *Anne Fremantle and Christopher Fremantle, eds.* (1978) Paulist Press. 170p., o.p.

ImGa *Dynix+*   Imaginary Gardens; American Poetry and Art for Young People *Charles Sullivan, ed.* (1989) Harry N. Abrams. 111p.

ImOP   Imagination's Other Place; Poems of Science and Mathematics *Helen Plotz, comp.* (1955) Thomas Y. Crowell. 200p.

ImPo *Dynix+*   Immortal Poems of the English Language *Oscar Williams, ed.* (1952) Simon & Schuster. 637p., pap.

IMW   In the Midst of Winter; Selections from the Literature of Mourning *Mary Jane Moffat, ed.*
808.803 (1982 ed.) (1992) Vintage Books. 274p., pap.

InMe   Innocent Merriment; an Anthology of Light Verse *Franklin P. Adams, ed.* (1942) McGraw-Hill. 523p., o.p.

InPK   An Introduction to Poetry *X. J. Kennedy, ed.* (3d ed., 1974) Little, Brown & Company. 648p., pap.

InPS   An Introduction to Poetry *Louis Simpson, ed.* (3d ed., 1986) St. Martin's Press. 640p.

InvP   Invitation to Poetry; a Round of Poems from John Skelton to Dylan Thomas *Lloyd Frankenberg, ed.* (1956) Doubleday. 414p., o.p.

IPY   Irish Poetry after Yeats; Seven Poets *Maurice Harmon, ed.* (1979) Little, Brown. 231p., pap., o.p.

ISi   I Sing of a Maiden; the Mary Book of Verse   *Sister M. Therese, ed.*   (1947)   Macmillan. 459p., o.p.

Jaz   The Jazz Poetry Anthology   *Sascha Feinstein and Yusef Komunyakaa, eds.*   (1991)   Indiana University Press. 293p.

JCP   Jacobean and Caroline Poetry; an Anthology   *T. G. S. Cain, ed.*   (1981)   Methuen. 334p.

⌀ KTR   Kissing the Rod; an Anthology of Seventeenth-Century Women's Verse   *Germaine Greer, Susan Hastings, Jeslyn Medoff, and Melinda Sansone, eds.*   (1988)   Farrar Straus Giroux. 477p., pap.

LAuP   Late Augustan Poetry   *Patricia Meyer Spacks, ed.*   (1973)   Prentice-Hall. 678p., o.p.

LCAP   The Longman Anthology of Contemporary American Poetry   *Stuart Friebert and David Young, eds.*   (2d ed., 1989)   Longman. 629p., pap.

LiSp   A Literature of Sports   *Tom Dodge, ed.*   (1980)   D. C. Heath and Company

LiTA   The Little Treasury of American Poetry   *Oscar Williams, ed.*   (1948)   Scribner's. 860p., o.p.

LiTB   A Little Treasury of British Poetry   *Oscar Williams, ed.*   (1951)   Scribner's. 874p., o.p.

⌀ LiTM   A Little Treasury of Modern Poetry; English and American   *Oscar Williams, ed.*   (3d ed., 1970)   Scribner's. 937p., o.p.

LLLT   Love Is like the Lion's Tooth; an Anthology of Love Poems   *Frances McCullough, ed.*   (1984)   Harper & Row. 80p., o.p.

LO   Love   *Walter de la Mare, ed.*   1946   William Morrow. 822p., o.p.

LoBV   The London Book of English Verse   *Herbert Read and Bonamy Dobrée, eds.*   (1952)   MacMillan. 874p., o.p.

LPA   Loving: Poetry and Art   *Charles Sullivan, ed.*   (1992)   Harry N. Abrams. 160p.

MasP   Master Poems of the English Language   *Oscar Williams, ed.*   (1966)   Trident Press. 1072p., o.p.

MAT   Messages; a Thematic Anthology of Poetry   *X. J. Kennedy, ed.*   (1973)   Little, Brown. 386p., o.p.

MAYP   The Morrow Anthology of Younger American Poets   *Dave Smith and David Bottoms, eds.*   (1985)   Quill. 784p.

⌀ MDDM   Mother to Daughter, Daughter to Mother; Mothers on Mothering   *Tillie Olsen, ed.*   (1984)   The Feminist Press. 296p., pap.

MeEL   Medieval English Lyrics; a Critical Anthology   *R. T. Davies, ed.*   (1964)   Northwestern University Press. 384p., o.p.

⌀ MeLP   Metaphysical Lyrics & Poems of the Seventeenth Century; Donne to Butler   *Herbert J. Grierson, ed.*   (1921)   Oxford University Press. 302p., o.p.

MeMAP ~Dynixt~   The Mentor Book of Major American Poets   *Oscar Williams and Edwin Honig, eds.*   (1962)   New American Library. 535p.

MeMBP   The Mentor Book of Major British Poets   *Oscar Williams, ed.*   (1963)   New American Library. 576p., pap.

MePo   The Metaphysical Poets   *Helen Gardner, ed.*   (1957)   Penguin Books; reprinted by Oxford University Press, 1961. 310p.

Mes   Messages; a Book of Poems   *Naomi Lewis, comp.*   (1985)   Faber and Faber. 255p.

MiAP   Mid-Century American Poets   *John Ciardi, ed.*   (1950)   Twayne Publishers. 300p., o.p.

⌀ MLL   More Latin Lyrics; from Virgil to Milton   *Dame Felicitas Corrigan, ed.; Helen Waddell, tr.*   (1977)   W. W. Norton. 392p.

MMA   Men Who March Away; Poems of the First World War   *I. M. Parsons, ed.*   (1965)   Viking Press. 192p., o.p.

MoAB   Modern American & British Poetry   *Louis Untermeyer, ed., in consultation with Karl Shapiro and Richard Wilbur.*   (Rev., shorter ed., 1955)   Harcourt, Brace. 697p., o.p.

MoAmPo   Modern American Poetry   *Louis Untermeyer, ed.*   (8th rev. ed., 1962)   Harcourt, Brace. 701p., ~811.08 (1969 ed.)~ o.p.

MoBrPo ~YA821.08~   Modern British Poetry   *Louis Untermeyer, ed.*   (7th rev. ed., 1962)   Harcourt, Brace. 500p., o.p.

⌀ MoLi   More Light: Father & Daughter Poems: A Twentieth-Century American Selection   *Jason Shinder, ed.*   (1993)   Harcourt Brace & Company. 172p., pap.

Moon   Moonstruck; an Anthology of Lunar Poetry   *Robert Phillips, ed.*   (1974)   The Vanguard Press. 181p., o.p.

⌀ MoP   Modern Poems; an Introduction to Poetry   *Richard Ellmann and Robert O'Clair, eds.*   (1976)   W. W. Norton. 526p., pap.

MoPo	Modern Poetry; American and British. *Kimon Friar and John Malcolm Brinnin, eds.* (1951) Appleton-Century-Crofts. 580p., o.p.
MOS	Moods of the Sea; Masterworks of Sea Poetry *George C. Solley and Eric Steinbaugh, comps.* (1981) Naval Institute Press. 300p.
MoShBr	The Moon Is Shining Bright as Day: an Anthology of Goodhumored Verse *Ogden Nash, ed.* (1953) J. B. Lippincott. 178p.
MoVE	Modern Verse in English, 1900–1950 *David Cecil and Allen Tate, eds.* (1967) Macmillan. 688p., o.p.
MP	The Modern Poets; an American-British Anthology *John Malcolm Brinnin and Bill Read, eds.* (1963) McGraw-Hill; revised edition of 1970 has title Twentieth-Century Poetry; American and British (1900–1970). 427p., o.p.
MT	The Made Thing; an Anthology of Contemporary Southern Poetry *Leon Stokesbury, ed.* (1987) University of Arkansas Press. 326p.
NAAL-1	The Norton Anthology of American Literature. Vol. 1 *Nina Baym and others, eds.* (2d ed., 1985) W. W. Norton. 2,535p., pap.
NAAL-2	The Norton Anthology of American Literature. Vol. 2 *Nina Baym and others, eds.* (2d ed., 1985) W. W. Norton. 2,652p., pap.
NAAL-3	The Norton Anthology of American Literature *Nina Baym et al., eds.* (3d ed., 1989) W. W. Norton. 2459p., pap.
NAEL-1	The Norton Anthology of English Literature. Vol. I *M. H. Abrams, general ed.* (5th ed., 1986) W. W. Norton.
NAEL-2	The Norton Anthology of English Literature. Vol. II *M. H. Abrams, general ed.* (5th ed., 1986) W. W. Norton.
NALW	The Norton Anthology of Literature by Women; the Tradition in English *Sandra M. Gilbert and Susan Guber, eds.* (1985) W. W. Norton. 2457p. W. W. Norton. 2457p.
NaP	Naked Poetry; Recent American Poetry in Open Forms *Stephen Berg & Robert Mesey, eds.* (1969) Bobbs-Merrill. 392p., pap.
NAs	The Naked Astronaut; Poems on Birth and Birthdays *René Graziani, ed.* (1983) Faber and Faber. 380p., o.p.
NAWM 1-2	The Norton Anthology of World Masterpieces, Vols. I–II *Maynard Mack, general ed.* (4th Continental ed., 1980) W. W. Norton & Company
NAWM-1	The Norton Anthology of World Masterpieces. Vol. I *Maynard Mack, general ed.* (5th ed., 1985) W. W. Norton.
NAWM-2	The Norton Anthology of World Masterpieces. Vol. II *Maynard Mack, general ed.* (5th ed., 1985) W. W. Norton.
NBLV	The Norton Book of Light Verse *Russell Baker, ed.* (1986) W. W. Norton. 447p.
NBM	19th Century British Minor Poets *W. H. Auden, ed.* (1966) Delacorte Press. 383p., o.p.
NCEP	A New Canon of English Poetry *James Reeves and Martin Seymour-Smith, eds.* (1967) Barnes & Noble. 326p., o.p.
NCSH	New Coasts & Strange Harbors; Discovering Poems *Helen Hill and Agnes Perkins, eds.* (1974) Thomas Y. Crowell Co., 283p., o.p.
NeAP	The New American Poetry, 1945–1960 *Donald M. Allen, ed.* (1960) Grove Press. 454p., o.p.
NeBP	The New British Poets; an Anthology *Kenneth Rexroth, ed.* (1949) New Directions. 312p., o.p.
NePA	New Pocket Anthology of American Verse; from Colonial Days to the Present *Oscar Williams, ed.* (1966) World. 670p., o.p.
NePoAm	New Poems by American Poets *Rolfe Humphries, ed.* (1953) Ballantine Books. 179p.
NePoEA	New Poets of England and America *Donald Hall, Robert Pack and Louis Simpson, eds.* (1957) Meridian Books. 351p., o.p.
NePoEA-2	New Poets of England and America *Donald Hall and Robert Pack, eds.* (Second selection, 1962) World. 384p., o.p.
NGP	A New Geography of Poets *Edward Field, Gerald Locklin, and Charles Stetler, eds.* (1992) University of Arkansas Press. 324p.
NIP	The Norton Introduction to Poetry *J. Paul Hunter, ed.* (4th ed., 1991) W. W. Norton; First edition had title The Norton Introduction to Literature: Poetry. 578p.

NMM   No More Masks! an Anthology of Poems by Women   *Florence Howe and Ellen Bass, eds.* (1973)   Doubleday Anchor Books. 396p., o.p.

NMP   The New Modern Poetry; British and American Poetry since World War II   *M. L. Rosenthal, ed.* (1967)   Macmillan. 289p., o.p.

NNaP Dynix +   The New Naked Poetry; Recent American Poetry in Open Forms   *Stephen Berg and Robert Mesey, eds.*   (1976)   Bobbs-Merrill. 478p., o.p.

NoAM 821.008 The Norton Anthology of Modern Poetry   *Richard Ellmann and Robert O'Clair, eds.*   (2d ed., 1988)   W. W. Norton. 1863p., pap.

NOBA R811.008 The New Oxford Book of American Verse   *Richard Ellmann, ed.*   (1976)   Oxford University Press. 1,076p.

NOBC Dynix +   The New Oxford Book of Canadian Verse in English   *Margaret Atwood, comp.*   (1982)   Oxford University Press. 477p., o.p.

NOBE R821.008 The New Oxford Book of English Verse, 1250–1950   *Helen Gardner, ed.*   (1972)   Oxford University Press. 974p.

NOBL 821.08 The New Oxford Book of English Light Verse   *Kingsley Amis, ed.*   (1978)   Oxford University Press. 347p.

⌀ NOBRP   The New Oxford Book of Romantic Period Verse   *Jerome J. McGann, ed.*   (1993)   Oxford University Press. 832p.

NOBVV Dynix + The New Oxford Book of Victorian Verse   *Christopher Ricks, ed.*   (1987)   Oxford University Press. 654p.

NOCV Dynix + The New Oxford Book of Christian Verse   *Donald Davie, ed.*   (1981)   Oxford University Press. 320p.

NOEC Dynix + The New Oxford Book of Eighteenth Century Verse   *Roger Lonsdale, ed.*   (1984)   Oxford University Press. 870p.

NOIV R821.08 (OxBoIV)   The New Oxford Book of Irish Verse   *Thomas Kinsella, ed. and tr.*   (1986)   Oxford University Press. 422p.

NoP   The Norton Anthology of Poetry   *Alexander W. Allison and others, eds.*   (3d ed., 1983)   W. W. Norton. 1452p., pap.

NOSC Dynix +   The New Oxford Book of Seventeenth Century Verse   *Alistair Fowler, ed.*   (1991)   Oxford University Press. 831p.

NoSic Dynix +   The New Oxford Book of Sixteenth Century Verse   *Emrys Jones, ed.*   (1991)   Oxford University Press. 769p.

⌀ NSI   Never Such Innocence; a New Anthology of Great War Verse   *Martin Stephen, ed.*   (1988)   Buchan and Enright. 358p., pap.

NTCP J811.008 A New Treasury of Children's Poetry; Old Favorites and New Discoveries   *Joanna Cole, comp.* (1984)   Doubleday. 224p., pap.

NTP Dynix +   A New Treasury of Poetry   *Neil Philip, ed.*   (1990)   Stewart, Tabori, and Chang. 256p.

NU   News of the Universe; Poems of Twofold Consciousness   *Robert Bly, comp.*   (1980)   Sierra Club Books. 305p.

NYBP 821.91 The New Yorker Book of Poems   *The New Yorker editors, comps.*   (1969)   Viking Press; paperback edition of 1974 published by William Morrow. 835p.

NYP   New York: Poems   *Howard Moss, ed.*   (1980)   Avon Books. 345p., o.p.

OAEL-1 Dynix + The Oxford Anthology of English Literature. Vol. I   *Frank Kermode and John Hollander, general eds.*   (1973)   Oxford University Press.

OAEL-2 Dynix + The Oxford Anthology of English Literature. Vol. II   *Frank Kermode and John Hollander, general eds.*   (1973)   Oxford University Press.

OAEP   An Oxford Anthology of English Poetry   *Howard Foster Lowry and Willard Thorp, eds.*   (2d ed., 1956)   Oxford University Press. 1356p., o.p.

OBAL R811.07 The Oxford Book of American Light Verse   *William Harmon, ed.*   (1979)   Oxford University 811.07 Press. 540p.

OBCA J811.008 The Oxford Book of Children's Verse in America   *Donald Hall, ed.*   (1985)   Oxford University Press. 319p.

OBCoV Dynix + The Oxford Book of Comic Verse   *John Gross, ed.*   (1994)   Oxford University Press. 512p.

OBCP J394.268The Oxford Book of Christmas Poems *Michael Harrison and Christopher Stuart-Clark, eds.* (1983) Oxford University Press. 160p.

OBD The Oxford Book of Death *D. J. Enright, ed.* (1987) Oxford University Press. 352p.

OBEC The Oxford Book of Eighteenth Century Verse *David Nichol Smith, ed.* (1926) Oxford University Press. 727p., o.p.

OBEV 821.08 The Oxford Book of English Verse, 1250–1918 *Sir Arthur Quiller-Couch, ed.* (New ed., rev. and enl., 1939) Oxford University Press. 1083p., o.p.

OBF The Oxford Book of Friendship *D. J. Enright and David Rawlinson, eds.* (1991) Oxford University Press. 364p.

OBMV 821.08 The Oxford Book of Modern Verse, 1892–1935 *William Butler Yeats, ed.* (1936) Oxford University Press. 454p., o.p.

OBNC 821.08 The Oxford Book of Nineteenth-Century English Verse *John Hayward, ed.* (1964; reprinted, with corrections, 1965) Oxford University Press. 970p., o.p.

OBNV 821.0308The Oxford Book of Narrative Verse *Iona Opie and Peter Opie, eds.* (1983) Oxford University Press. 407p.

OBRV The Oxford Book of Regency Verse 1798–1837 *H. S. Milford, ed.* (1928) Oxford University Press; edition of 1935 had title The Oxford Book of English Verse of the Romantic Period, 1798–1837. 888p., o.p.

OBS The Oxford Book of Seventeenth Century Verse *H. J. C. Grierson and G. Bullough, eds.* (1934) Oxford University Press. 974p., o.p.

OBSC The Oxford Book of Sixteenth Century Verse *E. K. Chambers, comp.* (1932) Oxford University Press. 905p.. o.p.

∅ OBSP The Oxford Book of Story Poems *Michael Harrison and Christopher Stuart-Clark, eds.* (1990) Oxford University Press. 175p.

OBSV K827.009 The Oxford Book of Satirical Verse *Geoffrey Grigson, comp.* (1980) Oxford University Press. 454p., pap., o.p.

OBTV The Oxford Book of Travel Verse *Kevin Crossley-Holland, ed.* (1986) Oxford University Press. 423p.

OBVE Dynix+ The Oxford Book of Verse in English Translation *Charles Tomlinson, ed.* (1980) Oxford University Press. 608p., pap., o.p.

OBVV The Oxford Book of Victorian Verse *Arthur Quiller-Couch, ed.* (1971) Oxford University Press. 1,023p., o.p.

OBWP Dynix+ The Oxford Book of War Poetry *Jon Stallworthy, ed.* (1984) Oxford University Press. 358p., o.p.

OBWVE Dynix+The Oxford Book of Welsh Verse in English *Gwyn Jones, ed.* (1977) Oxford University Press, 313p.

OFC 101 Favorite Cat Poems *Sara L. Whittier, ed.* (1991) Contemporary Books. 153p., o.p.

OFD O Frabjous Day: Poetry for Holidays and Special Occasions *Myra Cohn Livingston, ed.* (1977) Atheneum. 205p., o.p.

OHCV One Hundred and One Classics of Victorian Verse *Ellen J. Greenfield, ed.* (1992) Contemporary Books. 187p.

OHFP One Hundred and One Famous Poems *Ray J. Cook, comp.* (Rev. ed., 1958) Reilly & Lee; reprinted by Contemporary Books (1981). 186p., o.p.

OHIP Our Holidays in Poetry *Mildred P. Harrington and Josephine H. Thomas, comps.* (1929) H. W. Wilson. 479p.

OLR One Little Room, an Everywhere; Poems of Love *Myra Cohn Livingstone, ed.* (1975) Atheneum

OnMSP 100 More Story Poems *Elinor Parker, comp.* (1960) Thomas Y. Crowell. 374p., o.p.

OnUR Once upon a Rhyme; 101 Poems for Young Children *Sara Corrin and Stephen Corrin, eds.* (1982) Faber and Faber. 157p., o.p.

OnYI 1000 Years of Irish Poetry; the Gaelic and Anglo-Irish Poets from Pagan Times to the Present *Kathleen Hoagland, ed.* (1975) Devin-Adair. 833p.

OPOP 100 Poems by 100 Poets; an Anthology *Harold Pinter, Geoffrey Godbert, and Anthony Astbury, comps.* (1986) Grove Press. 176p.

Ø OPOU   100 Poems on the Underground *Gerald Benson, Judith Chernaik, and Cicely Herbert, eds.*
                  (1991) Cassell Publishers. 144p., pap.
Ø OTCP   The Oxford Treasury of Children's Poems *Michael Harrison and Christopher Stuart-Clark, eds.*
                  (1988) Oxford University Press. 174p.
OtMeF   Other Men's Flowers *A. P. Wavell, ed.* (1990) Jonathan Cape. 448p.
OxAEP-1 Dynix+   The Oxford Anthology of English Poetry. Vol. I: Spenser to Crabbe *John Wain, ed.* (1990)
                  Oxford University Press. 659p., pap.
OxAEP-2 Dynix+   The Oxford Anthology of English Poetry. Vol. II: Blake to Heaney *John Wain, ed.* (1990)
                  Oxford University Press. 770p., pap.
OxBA 811.08   The Oxford Book of American Verse *F. O. Matthiessen, ed.* (1950) Oxford University Press.
      R 811.08   1,130p.
Ø OxBC   The Oxford Book of Contemporary Verse, 1945–1980 *D. J. Enright, comp.* (1980) Oxford
        J821.008 University Press. 299p., o.p.
OxBChV R821.008   The Oxford Book of Children's Verse *Iona Opie and Peter Opie, eds.* (1973) Oxford Uni-
                  versity Press. 407p.
OxBI   The Oxford Book of Irish Verse; XVIIth Century–XXth Century *Donagh MacDonagh and Len-
                  nox Robinson, eds.* (1958) Oxford University Press. 343p., o.p.
Ø OxBM   The Oxford Book of Marriage *Helge Rubinstein, ed.* (1990) Oxford University Press. 383p.
OxBM   The Oxford Book of Medieval English Verse *Celia Sisam and Kenneth Sisam, eds.* (1970)
                  Oxford University Press. 617p., o.p.
OxBoCh   The Oxford Book of Christian Verse *Lord David Cecil, ed.* (1940) Oxford University Press.
                  560p., o.p.
OxBoLi 821.08   The Oxford Book of Light Verse *W. H. Auden, ed.* (1938) Oxford University Press. 552p., pap.,
                  o.p.
Ø OxBoS   The Oxford Book of the Sea *Jonathan Raban, ed.* (1992) Oxford University Press. 522p.
OxBS 821.08   The Oxford Book of Scottish Verse *John MacQueen and Tom Scott, comps.* (1966) Oxford
                  University Press. 633p.
OxBSP Dynix+   The Oxford Book of Short Poems *P. J. Kavanagh and James Michie, eds.* (1985) Oxford
                  University Press. 307p., pap.
OxBTC R821.91   The Oxford Book of Twentieth-Century English Verse *Philip Larkin, ed.* (1973) Oxford Uni-
                  versity Press. 641p.
PAH   Poems of American History *Burton Egbert Stevenson, ed.* (Rev. ed., 1922) Houghton Mifflin.
                  704p.
PAI   Poetry; an Introduction *Ruth Miller and Robert A. Greenberg, eds.* (1981) St. Martin's Press.
                  589p.
PAL   Patriotic Poems America Loves *Jean Anne Vincent, ed.* (1968) Doubleday. 240p., o.p.
Par   Parodies; an Anthology from Chaucer to Beerbohm—and After *Dwight Macdonald, ed.* (1960)
                  Modern Library. 575p., pap.
PAW   Peace and War; a Collection of Poems *Michael Harrison and Christopher Stuart-Clark, eds.*
                  (1989) Oxford University Press. 208p.
PB   The Poetry of Birds *Samuel Carr, ed.* (1976) Taplinger. 88p., o.p.
PBBP   The Penguin Book of Bird Poetry *Peggy Munsterberg, ed.* (1984) Penguin Books; first pub-
                  lished by Allen Lane (1980). 361p., o.p.
Ø PBCIP   The Penguin Book of Contemporary Irish Poetry *Peter Fallon and Derek Mahon, eds.* (1990)
                  Penguin Books. 462p., pap.
Ø PBCV   The Penguin Book of Caribbean Verse in English *Paula Burnett, ed.* (1986) Penguin Books.
                  446p., pap.
Ø PBMP   The Premier Book of Major Poets *Anita Dore, ed.* (1970) Fawcett Publications. 336p., pap.
PBWP R808.81   The Penguin Book of Women Poets *Carol Cosman, Joan Keefe, and Kathleen Weaver, eds.*
                  (1978) Penguin Books. 399p., pap.
PCat   The Poetry of Cats *Samuel Carr, ed.* (1974) Viking Press. 96p., o.p.
PChr J808.81   Poems of Christmas *Myra Cohn Livingston, ed.* (1980) Atheneum. 172p.
PCP   Postcard Poems; a Collection of Poetry for Sharing *Paul B. Janeczko, ed.* (1979) Bradbury
                  Press. 106p., o.p.

PDV	Piping Down the Valley Wild; Poetry for the Young of All Ages *Nancy Larrick, ed.* (1968) Delacorte Press. 248p.
PeECV	The Penguin Book of English Christian Verse *Peter Levi, ed.* (1984) Penguin Books. 379p.
PeFWW	The Penguin Book of First World War Poetry *Jon Silkin, ed.* (1979) Penguin Books. 258p., pap.
PeHV	The Penguin Book of Homosexual Verse *Stephen Coote, ed.* (1983) Penguin Books. 410p., pap.
PeIV	The Penguin Book of Irish Verse *Brendan Kennelly, ed.* (1981) Penguin Books. 470p., pap.
PeLi 821.07	The Penguin Book of Limericks *E. O. Parrott, ed.* (1983) Penguin Books. 304p., pap.
PeLV	The Penguin Book of Light Verse *Gavin Ewart, ed.* (1980) Penguin Books. 639p., pap., o.p.
PeSAV	The Penguin Book of Southern African Verse *Stephen Gray, ed.* (1989) Penguin Books. 402p., o.p.
PeVV 821.808 (1969ed)	Victorian Verse *George MacBeth, ed.* (1986) Penguin Books; first published 1969 as The Penguin Book of Victorian Verse. 440p., pap.
PF	The Poorhouse Fugitives; Self-Taught Poets and Poetry in Victorian Britain *Brian Maidment, ed.* (1987) Carcanet. 374p.
PFL	Poets for Life; Seventy-Six Poets Respond to AIDS *Michael Klein, ed.* (1989) Persea Books. 244p., pap.
PFP	Poems by Favorite Poets in Large Print *Leslie Lewis, ed.* (1992) G. K. Hall. 449p.
PGD	Poems for the Great Days *Thomas Curtis Clark and Robert Earle Clark, eds.* (1948) Abingdon-Cokesbury Press. 245p.
PlP	The Pleasure of Poetry; from His Daily Mirror Column *Kingsley Amis, ed.* (1990) Cassell Publishers. 245p.
PmAP Dynix +	Postmodern American Poetry; a Norton Anthology *Paul Hoover* (1994) W. W. Norton & Company. 701p., pap.
PNI	Poets from the North of Ireland *Frank Ormsby, ed.* (New ed., 1990) The Blackstaff Press. 336p., pap.
PoA 811.52	The Poetry Anthology, 1912–1977 *Daryl Hine and Joseph Parisi, eds.* (1978) Houghton Mifflin. 555p.
PoBA R 811.54	The Poetry of Black America; Anthology of the 20th Century *Arnold Adoff, ed.* (1973) Harper & Row. 552p.
PoCh	Poet's Choice *Paul Engle and Joseph Langland, eds.* (1962) Dial Press. 303p., o.p.
PoE	Poetry in English; an Anthology *M. L. Rosenthal, general ed.* (1987) Oxford University Press. 1196p., pap.
PoEL-1 Dynix+	Poets of the English Language. Vol. I *W. H. Auden and Norman Holmes Pearson, eds.* (1950) Viking Press. 619p., o.p.
PoEL-2 Dynix +	Poets of the English Language. Vol. II *W. H. Auden and Norman Holmes Pearson, eds.* (1950) Viking Press. 556p., o.p.
PoEL-3 Dynix +	Poets of the English Language. Vol. III *W. H. Auden and Norman Holmes Pearson, eds.* (1950) Viking Press. 622p., o.p.
PoEL-4 Dynix +	Poets of the English Language. Vol. IV *W. H. Auden and Norman Holmes Pearson, eds.* (1950) 535p., o.p. (also published separately as "Romantic Poets," pap.)
PoEL-5 Dynix +	Poets of the English Language. Vol. V *W. H. Auden and Norman Holmes Pearson, eds.* (1950) Viking Press. 624p., o.p.
Poetr	Poetry *Jill P. Baumgaertner, ed.* (1990) Harcourt, Brace, Jovanovich. 703p., pap.
POL	Poems One Line & Longer *William Cole, ed.* (1973) Grossman. 182p., o.p.
PoLF 821.08	Poems That Live Forever *Hazel Felleman, ed.* (1965) Doubleday. 454p., pap.
PoNe	The Poetry of the Negro, 1746–1970 *Langston Hughes and Arna Bontemps, eds.* (Rev. ed., 1970) Doubleday. 645p., o.p.
PoPl	Poetry for Pleasure; the Hallmark Book of Poetry *Selected and arranged by the editors of Hallmark Cards* (1960) Doubleday. 470p., o.p.
PoPle	Poetry for Pleasure; a Choice of Poetry and Verse on a Variety of Themes *Ian Parsons, ed.* (1977) W. W. Norton. 352p., o.p.
PoPo	Portraits of Poets *Sebastian Barker, ed.* (1986) Carcanet. 124p., pap.

PoRA *821.008* Poems to Read Aloud   *Edward Hodnett, ed.*   (Rev. ed., 1967)   W. W. Norton. 390p., o.p.

PoSC   Poems for Seasons and Celebrations   *William Cole, ed.*   (1961)   World. 191p., o.p.

PoSH   Poems of the Scottish Hills; an Anthology   *Hamish Brown, comp.*   (1982)   Aberdeen University Press. 202p.

PoToHe *Dynix+* Poems that Touch the Heart   *A. L. Alexander, ed.*   (1956)   Doubleday. 403p.

PoWW *Dynix+* Poetry of the World Wars   *Michael Foss, ed.*   (1990)   Peter Bedrick Books. 192p.

PP   Poems on Poetry; the Mirror's Garland   *Robert Wallace and James G. Taaffe, eds.*   (1965)   E. P. Dutton. 328p., o.p.

PPoe   The Pleasures of Poetry   *Donald Hall, ed.*   (1971)   Harper and Row. 338p., o.p.

PPON   Poems of Protest Old and New   *Arnold Kenseth, ed.*   (1968)   MacMillan. 140p., o.p.

PPP   Poetry: Past and Present   *Frank Brady and Martin Price, eds.*   (1974)   Harcourt Brace Jovanovich. 527p., pap.

PPR   The Ploughshares Poetry Reader   *Joyce Peseroff, ed.*   (1986)   Ploughshares Books. 335p.

PRA   The Paris Review Anthology   *George Plimpton, ed.*   (1990)   W. W. Norton. 686p.

Prf   Preferences; 51 American Poets Choose Poems from Their Own Work and from the Past   *Richard Howard, ed.*   (1974)   Viking Press. 323p., o.p.

PrIm   The Practical Imagination; an Introduction to Poetry   *Northrop Frye, Sheridan Baker, and George Perkins.*   (1983)   Harper & Row. 500p., pap.

PV   Pith and Vinegar; an Anthology of Short Humorous Poetry   *William Cole, ed.*   (1969)   Simon & Schuster. 158p., o.p.

PWE   Poetry with an Edge   *Neil Astley, ed.*   (1988)   Bloodaxe Books. 320p.

Ø PWR   Poetry Worth Remembering; an Anthology of Poetry   *Roy W. Watson, comp.*   (1986)   Brunswick. 274p., o.p.

QFR   Quest for Reality; an Anthology of Short Poems in English   *Yvor Winters and Kenneth Fields, eds.*   (1969)   Swallow Press. 200p.

RaBo *Dynix+* The Rag and Bone Shop of the Heart: Poems for Men   *Robert Bly, James Hillman, and Michael Meade, eds.*   (1992)   Harper Collins. 536p.

Ø RB   The Rattle Bag; an Anthology of Poetry   *Seamus Heaney and Ted Hughes, comps.*   (1982)   Faber and Faber. 498p., pap.

RFM   Room for Me and a Mountain Lion; Poetry of Open Space   *Nancy Larrick, comp.*   (1974)   M. Evans. 191p.

RHPC   The Random House Book of Poetry for Children   *Jack Prelutsky, ed.*   (1983)   Random House. 248p.

RHTwFP   The Random House Book of Twentieth-Century French Poetry   *Paul Auster, ed.*   (1982)   Random House. 638p., pap.

RoGo   Roofs of Gold; Poems to Read Aloud   *Padraic Colum, ed.*   (1964)   Macmillan. 179p., o.p.

RR   Rhythm Road; Poems to Move To   *Lillian Morrison, comp.*   (1988)   Lothrop, Lee & Shepard. 148p.

SaC   Saturday's Children; Poems of Work   *Helen Plotz, comp.*   (1982)   Greenwillow Books. 174p. o.p.

SAmP *811.008* Six American Poets; an Anthology   *Joel Conarroe, ed.*   (1991)   Random House. 281p.

SBG   Salt and Bitter and Good; Three Centuries of English and American Women Poets   *Cora Kaplan, ed.*   (1975)   Paddington Press. 304p., o.p.

SBVL   Shivering Babe, Victorious Lord; the Nativity in Poetry and Art   *Linda Ching Sledge, ed.*   (1981)   Eerdmans. 188p.

SCAP *811.108* Seventeenth-Century American Poetry   *Harrison T. Meserole, ed.*   (1968)   Doubleday. 540p., o.p.

SCBI   Some Contemporary Poets of Britain and Ireland; an Anthology   *Michael Schmidt, ed.*   (1983)   Carcanet Press. 184p.

ScCV   The Scottish Collection of Verse to 1800   *Eileen Dunlop and Antony Kamm, eds.*   (1985)   Richard Drew. 256p., pap., o.p.

SCGP *Dynix+* Six Centuries of Great Poetry   *Robert Penn Warren and Albert Erskine, eds.*   (1955)   Dell. 544p., pap., o.p.

Ø SCV   Six Centuries of Verse   *Anthony Thwaite, ed.*   (1984)   Thames Methuen. 290p., pap.

SD   Sprints and Distances; Sports in Poetry and the Poetry in Sport *Lillian Morrison, comp.* (1965) Thomas Y. Crowell. 212p., o.p.

SeCePo   Seven Centuries of Poetry; Chaucer to Dylan Thomas *A. N. Jeffares, ed.* (1955) Longmans, Green. 463p.

SeCeV   Seven Centuries of Verse, English & American, from the Early English Lyrics to the Present Day *A. J. M. Smith, ed.* (1957) Scribner's. 778p., o.p.

Ø SeCP   Seventeenth Century Poetry; the Schools of Donne and Jonson *Hugh Kenner, ed.* (1964) Holt, Rinehart and Winston. 460p., o.p.

SeCV-1   Seventeenth-Century Verse and Prose. Vol. I: 1600–1660 *Helen C. White, Ruth C. Wallerstein, and Ricardo Quintana, eds.* (1951, 1952) Macmillan. 498p., o..p.

SeCV-2   Seventeenth-Century Verse and Prose. Vol. I: 1660–1700 *Helen C. White, Ruth C. Wallerstein, and Ricardo Quintana, eds.* (1951, 1952) Macmillan. 472p., o.p.

SiPS 821.3   Silver Poets of the Sixteenth Century *Gerald Bullett, ed.* (1947) J. M. Dent. 428p.

SiPSBD   Silver Poets of the Sixteenth Century—*Douglas Brooks-Davies, ed.* (2d ed., 1992) J. M. Dent. p.484, pap.

SiSoPo   Sing a Song of Popcorn; Every Child's Book of Poems *Beatrice Schenck de Regniers, Eva Moore, Mary Michaels White, and Jan Corr, eds.* (1988) Scholastic. 142p.

SiSoSe   Sing a Song of Seasons; Poems about Holidays, Vacation Days, and Days to Go to School *Sara Brewton and John E. Brewton, eds.* (1955) Macmillan. 200p., o.p.

SM   Strong Measures; Contemporary American Poetry in Traditional Forms *Philip Dacey and David Jauss, eds.* (1986) Harper & Row. 492p.

SoCa   The Sophisticated Cat; a Gathering of Stories, Poems, and Miscellaneous Writings about Cats *Joyce Carol Oates and Daniel Halpern, eds.* (1992) Penguin Books. 396p.

Ø Son   The Sonnet; an Anthology *Robert M. Bender and Charles L. Squier, eds.* (1987) Washington Square Press. 428p., pap.

SoPo   The Sound of Poetry *Mary C. Austin and Queenie B. Mills, eds.* (1963) Allyn and Bacon

SoSe   Sound and Sense; an Introduction to Poetry *Laurence Perrine and Thomas R. Arp, eds.* (8th ed., 1992) Harcourt Brace Jovanovich. 342p., pap., o.p.

SOTW   Sleeping on the Wing; an Anthology of Modern Poetry with Essays on Reading and Writing *Kenneth Koch and Kate Farrell, eds.* (1981) Random House. 313p.

Ø Spl   Splinters; a Book of Very Short Poems *Michael Harrison, ed.* (1989) Oxford University Press. 121 p.

SpRo   Speak Roughly to Your Little Boy *Myra Cohn Livingston, ed.* (1971) Harcourt Brace Jovanovich. 180p., o.p.

SRLS   She Rises like the Sun; Invocations of the Goddess by Contemporary American Women Poets *Janine Canan, ed.* (1989) The Crossing Press. 226p., pap.

STV Dynix+   Sappho to Valéry; Poems in Translation *John Frederick Nims, ed.* (Rev. and enl., 1990) University of Arkansas Press. 415p., pap.

SUS   Sung under the Silver Umbrella *Association for Childhood Education International, ed.* (1935) Macmillan. 211p., o.p.

SWP   Songs of Work and Protest *Edith Fowke and Joe Glazer, eds.* (1973) Dover Publications. 209p., pap.

SyP   The Symbolist Poem; the Development of the English Tradition *Edward Engelberg, ed.* (1967) E. P. Dutton. 350p., o.p.

TAP Dynix+   The Treasury of American Poetry *Nancy Sullivan, ed.* (1978) Doubleday. 838p.

TEP   The Treasury of English Poetry *Mark Caldwell and Walter Kendrick, eds.* (1984) Doubleday. 734p., o.p.

TFi R821.08   The Top 500 Poems *William Harmon, ed.* (1992) Columbia University Press. 1132p.

TiPo   Time for Poetry *May Hill Arbuthnot, ed.* (1959) Scott, Foresman. 512p., o.p.

Ø TIRV   Treasury of Irish Religious Verse *Patrick Murray, ed.* (1986) Crossroad. 295p., o.p.

TLR J 821.008   Talking like the Rain; a First Book of Poems *X. J. Kennedy and Dorothy M. Kennedy, eds.* (1992) Little Brown and Company. 96p.

Ø TOF   Tongues of Fire; an Anthology of Religious and Poetic Experience *Karen Armstrong, ed.* (1987) Penguin Books. 352p., pap., o.p.

TrCP *Dynix+* The Treasury of Christian Poetry *Lorraine Eitel, comp., with others.* (1982) Fleming H. Revell. 182p., o.p.

TreF A Treasury of the Familiar *Ralph L. Woods, ed.* (1942) Macmillan. 751p.

TreFS A Second Treasury of the Familiar *Ralph L. Woods, ed.* (1950) Macmillan. 722p., o.p.

TreFT A Third Treasury of the Familiar *Ralph L. Woods, ed.* (1970) Macmillan. 682p., o.p.

TrGrPo A Treasury of Great Poems, English and American *Louis Untermeyer, ed.* (Rev. and enl. ed., 1955) Simon and Schuster. 1,286p., o.p.

TrJP *YA 808.1* A Treasury of Jewish Poetry *Nathan Ausubel and Maryann Ausubel, eds.* (1957) Crown. 471p., o.p.

Ø TRP To Read a Poem *Donald Hall, ed.* (2d ed, 1992) Harcourt, Brace, Jovanovich. 411p., pap.

TrPWD A Treasury of Poems for Worship and Devotion *Charles L. Wallis, ed.* (1959) Harper. 378p., o.p.

TRV The Treasury of Religious Verse *Donald T. Kauffman, ed.* (1962) Fleming H. Revell. 371p., o.p.

TSF 365 Love Poems *John Gabriel Hunt, comp.* (1993) Gramercy Books. 320p.

TSS These Small Stones *Norma Farber and Myra Cohn Livingston, comps.* (1987) Harper & Row. 84p.

TTTS *J808.81* Talking to the Sun; an Illustrated Anthology of Poems for Young People *Kenneth Koch and Kate Farrell, eds.* (1985) Metropolitan Museum of Art/Henry Holt. 112p.

TV Tangled Vines; a Collection of Mother and Daughter Poems *Lyn Lifshin, ed.* (1978) Beacon Press, 95p., pap., o.p.

TW Tygers of Wrath; Poems of Hate, Anger, and Invective *X. J. Kennedy, ed.* (1981) University of Georgia Press. 282p.

TwAmPo Twentieth Century American Poetry *Conrad Aiken, ed.* (1963) Random House. 552p., o.p.

TwCP *821.91* Twentieth-Century Poetry; American and British (1900–1970) *John Malcolm Brinnin and Bill Read, eds.* (Rev. ed., 1970) McGraw Hill (Text edition entitled The Modern Poets). 515p., o.p.

UnAS Under All Silences; Shades of Love *Ruth Gordon, comp.* (1987) Harper & Row. 78p.

UnPo *821.008* Understanding Poetry *Cleanth Brooks and Robert Penn Warren, eds.* (4th ed., 1976) Holt, Rinehart and Winston. 602p., o.p.

UnS Untune the Sky; Poems of Music and Dance *Helen Plotz, comp.* (1957) Thomas Y. Crowell. 162p., o.p.

UnTE An Uninhibited Treasury of Erotic Poetry *Louis Untermeyer, ed.* (1963) Dial Press. 580p., o.p.

Ø UV Unauthorized Versions; Poems and Their Parodies *Kenneth Baker, ed.* (1990) Faber and Faber. 446p.

VBLP The Virago Book of Love Poetry *Wendy Mulford, ed.* (1990) Virago Press. 288p., o.p.

VCAP *Dynix+* The Vintage Book of Contemporary American Poetry *J. D. McClatchy, ed.* (1990) Vintage Books. 560p.

VGW *Dynix+* The Voice That Is Great Within Us; American Poetry of the Twentieth Century *Hayden Carruth, ed.* (1970) Bantam Books. 722p., pap.

ViBoPo The Viking Book of Poetry of the English-Speaking World. Vols. I–II *Richard Aldington, ed.* Rev., Mid-Century ed., (1958) Viking Press. 1,297p., o.p.

VLP Victorian Literature: Poetry *Donald Gray and G. B. Tennyson, eds.* (1976) Macmillan. 1060p.

VoGa Voices in the Gallery *Dannie Abse and Joan Abse, eds.* (1986) Tate Gallery. 212p., pap.

VPP Victorian Parlour Poetry; an Annotated Anthology *Michael R. Turner, ed.* (1992) Dover Publications; originally published by The Viking Press as Parlour Poetry; a Casquet of Gems. 325p., pap.

VVA The Vampire in Verse; an Anthology *Steven Moore, ed.* (1985) Dracula Press. 196p., pap. $7.95

WaaP War and the Poet; an Anthology of Poetry Expressing Man's Attitudes to War from Ancient Times to the Present *Richard Eberhart and Selden Rodman, eds.* (1945) Devin-Adair. 240p.

WaP The War Poets; an Anthology of the War Poetry of the 20th Century *Oscar Williams, ed.* (1945) John Day. 485p., o.p.

WBLP   The World's Best Loved Poems *James Gilchrist Lawson, comp.* (1927) Harper & Row. 455p.,
            o.p.
WeW   Western Wind; an Introduction to Poetry *John Frederick Nims, ed.* 3d ed., (1992) Random
            House. 639p., pap.
WGRP   The World's Great Religious Poetry *Caroline Miles Hill, ed.* (1954) Macmillan. 836p., o.p.
WHA   The Winged Horse Anthology *Joseph Auslander and Frank Ernest Hill, eds.* (1929) Double-
            day. 669p., o.p.
WhC   What Cheer; an Anthology of American and British Humorous and Witty Verse *David McCord,*
            ed. (1945) Coward-McCann. 515p., o.p.
WiR   The Wind and the Rain; an Anthology of Poems for Young People *John Hollander and Harold*
            Bloom, eds. (1961) Doubleday. 264p.
WoWa   Women on War; Essential Voices for the Nuclear Age *Daniela Gioseffi, ed.* (1988) Simon and
            Schuster. 391p., pap.
WPE 821.008 The Women Poets in English; an Anthology *Ann Stanford, ed.* (1972) McGraw-Hill. 374p., o.p.
Ø WPOW   Women Poets of the World *Joanna Bankier and Deirdre Lashgari, eds.* (1983) Macmillan.
            442p., o.p.
WSC   Why Am I Grown So Cold? Poems of the Unknowable *Myra Cohn Livingston, ed.* (1982)
            Atheneum. 269p.
YaD   Yankee Doodles; a Book of American Verse *Ted Malone, ed.* (1943) McGraw-Hill; edition of
            1948, published by Garden City Publishing Company, had title The All-American Book of
            Verse. 246p., o.p.
YeAr   The Year Round; Poems for Children *Alice I. Hazeltine and Elva S. Smith, eds.* (1956) Ab-
            ingdon Press. 192p., o.p.
ZA   A Zooful of Animals *William Cole, ed.* (1992) Houghton Mifflin. 88p.

TITLE AND FIRST LINE INDEX

Titles and first lines are arranged in one alphabetical listing in the Title And First Line Index. Titles are distinguished by initial capital letters on the important words. All first line entries are followed by the title of the poem, if there is a title. When the title and first line of a poem are identical, or nearly so, only the title is listed, although occasionally, for purposes of clarity, the first line has been added in quotation marks and in parentheses to the title entry.

Letter codes for volumes of collected and selected works are listed after titles and first lines; in some cases, letter codes for anthologies are listed as well.

Indented listings below an entry have the following significance: a single indentation indicates a selection *from the above work; double indentation, within parentheses, signifies a* variant title *or* variant first line *as used in the collected or selected works or in anthologies.*

Generic title entries, such as Ode, Song, Sonnet, are followed by the first line in quotation marks for easy identification. Such entries, of course, may also be located by first line listing.

Titles and first lines beginning with "O" and "Oh" are filed separately.

A

$$$$$$. Charles Bukowski. **SP-BukC1**

A- / float on some. Edward Estlin Cummings. **CP-CummE**

A / Ask horror for a helping hand. ABC's. Charles Henri Ford. **SP-FordC**

A. Robert Creeley. **CP-CreeR**

A / mong crum / bling people(a). Edward Estlin Cummings. **CP-CummE**

A, B & C of It, The. William Carlos Williams. **CP-WilW2**

A B C D F I J. Days and Nights. Kenneth Koch. *Fr.* Days and Nights. **SP-KochK**

A B Cs. Charles Olson. **CP-OlsoC**

A B Cs (3—for Rimbaud). Charles Olson. **CP-OlsoC**

A B Cs (2). Charles Olson. **CP-OlsoC**

A Bas Ben Adhem. Ogden Nash. **CP-NashO**

A Calais / Trop de frais. French Distichs. Samuel Johnson. **CP-JohnS**

À Constance, This Day. Charles Olson. **CP-OlsoC**

A. E. F. Carl Sandburg. **CP-SandC**

A. E. Housman. Wystan Hugh Auden. **CP-AudeW**

À elle l'acte calme. Samuel Beckett. **CP-BeckS**

A. H. Ralph Waldo Emerson. *Fr.* Quatrains. **CP-EmerR**

A. "I was a Have." B. "I was a 'Have-not.'" Equality of Sacrifice. Rudyard Kipling. **FaBoTw; OAEP** *Fr.* Epitaphs of the War [1914–1918]. **CP-KiplR**

A is for [Acland], who'd physic the Masses. Examination Statute. "Lewis Carroll." **CP-CarrL**

A is for Atom, the source. A Darkling Alphabet. William DeWitt Snodgrass. **SP-SnodW**

A is the Alphabet, A at its head. An Alphabet. Christina Georgina Rossetti. **CP-RosC3**

A. J. J. Alfred Edward Housman. **CP-HousA**

A La Bourbon. Richard Lovelace. **CP-LoveR**

A La Lune. William Carlos Williams. **CP-WilW1**

À La Maniere De D. H. Lawrence. David Herbert Lawrence. **CP-LawrD**

À l'École Berlitz. John Updike. **CP-UpdiJ**

A. Lincoln—Odd, or Even. Marsden Hartley. **CP-HartM**

À l'instant de s'entendre dire. Samuel Beckett. **CP-BeckS**

A. Love's very fleas are mine. Enter. The A, B & C of It. William Carlos Williams. **CP-WilW2**

À mi-hauteur. Rue de Vaugirard. Samuel Beckett. **CP-BeckS**

A-morwe, whan that day bigan to springe. Geoffrey Chaucer. **FiP** *Fr.* The General Prologue. **FHYEP; NAWM-1; OAEL-1; PoE** *Fr.* The Canterbury Tales. **CP-ChauG**

A peels an apple, while B kneels to God. A Primer of the Daily Round. Howard Nemerov. **CP-NemeH**

À peine à bien mené. Samuel Beckett. **CP-BeckS**

A quoy servent tant d'artifices. *see also* Desdain ("To what end serve the promises"). Sir John Suckling. **CP-SuckJ**

A Solis Ortus Cardine. Sedulius, *tr. fr. Latin by* Thomas Merton. **CP-MertT**

A' the lads o' Thornie-bank. Lady Onlie. Robert Burns. **CP-BurnR**

A Tirsi. Christina Georgina Rossetti. **CP-RosC3**

À travers la mince cloison. Ascension. Samuel Beckett. **CP-BeckS**

A-Wishing Well. Robert Frost. **CP-FrosR**

A' ye wha live by sowps o' drink. On a Scotch Bard Gone to the West Indies. Robert Burns. **CP-BurnR**

A.A.A. Emily Brontë. *See* Sleep not, dream not; this bright day.

Aardvark. Kenneth Rexroth. **SP-RexrK** *Fr.* A Bestiary. **SP-RexrK**

Aaron. George Herbert. **CP-HerbG**

Aaron Stark. Edwin Arlington Robinson. **CP-RobiE**

Ab lo dolchor qu'al cor mi vai. Canto 91. Ezra Pound. *Fr.* Cantos. **CP-PoCan**

Abacus, The. Malcolm Lowry. **CP-LowrM**

Aban Kavost and Ivar Oakeson. Robert Bly. **SP-BlyR**

Abandon for a moment, friends. Electra Becomes Morbid. Ogden Nash. **CP-NashO**

Abandon your body and soul into the abundance of light sent from above. Thomas Merton. *Fr.* Cables to the Ace. **CP-MertT**

Abandoned by their parents. The Nazi Amphitheatre. Erica Jong. **SP-JongE**

Abandoned Church, An. Walter de la Mare. **CP-DeLaW**

Abandoned Farmhouse. Ted Kooser. **SP-KoosT**

Abandoned Love. "Bob Dylan." **CP-DylaB**

Abandoned Ranch, Big Bend. Hayden Carruth. **CP-CarHS**

Abbé Voltaire, alias Arouet, The. The Caraway Seed. Ogden Nash. **CP-NashO**

Abbey Mason, The. Thomas Hardy. **CP-HardT**

Abbeyforde. Donald Davie. **CP-DavDo**

Abbot is painting me so true. On His Portrait. William Cowper. **CP-CowpW**

Abt Vogler. Robert Browning. **CP-BroR1**

Abbott previsioning the pestilent swarm. L'etat C'est Moi. John Crowe Ransom. *Fr.* Two Gentlemen in Bonds. **SP-RansJ**

ABC, An. Geoffrey Chaucer. **CP-ChauG**

ABC of Aerobics, The. Peter Meinke. **SP-MeinP**

ABC's. Charles Henri Ford. **SP-FordC**

Abdhur Rahman, the Durani Chief, of him is the story told. The Ballad of the King's Mercy. Rudyard Kipling. **CP-KiplR**

Abduction, The. Rita Dove. **SP-DoveR**

Abduction of Saints, The. Alice Walker. **CP-WalkA**

Abels Bloud. Robert Herrick. **CP-HerrR**

Abel's Bride. Denise Levertov. **CP-LeveD**

Abenaki Poem. Frederick Morgan. **SP-MorgF**

Aberdeen. Thomas Hardy. **CP-HardT**

Abiquiu. Charles Tomlinson. **CP-TomlC**

Abishag. Louise Glück. **SP-GlücL**

Ablaze / with candles sconced. Dawnbreaker. Robert Earl Hayden. **CP-HaydR**

Abnegation. Adrienne Rich. **CP-RicAE; SP-RicA2**

Aboard at a Ship's Helm. Walt Whitman. **CP-WhitW**

Abode of the nightingale is bare, The. Alone. Walter de la Mare. **CP-DeLaW**

Abominable Lake, The. Stevie Smith. **CP-SmitS**

Abominable Snowman, The. Ogden Nash. Fr. Nature-Walks, or, Not to Mention a Dopping of Sheldrakes. **CP-NashO**

Abortion, The. Anne Sexton. **CP-SextA**

Abortions will not let you forget. The Mother. Gwendolyn Brooks. **CrDW; CrSp; MDDM; NALW** Fr. A Street in Bronzeville. **SP-BrooG**

About an hour before dawn the women squeeze themselves into. The Pleasures of Exile. John Yau. **SP-YauJo**

About blood, he said, be. Concerning Exaggeration, or How, Properly, to Heap Up. Charles Olson. **CP-OlsoC**

About Cranes. Charles Bukowski. **SP-BukC1**

About Eyes. Edwin Rolfe. **CP-RolfE**

About five A.M. he hears dimly. Dressing. Dabney Stuart. **SP-StuaD**

About four, a few flakes. Robert Bly. Fr. Six Winter Privacy Poems. **SP-BlyR**

About growing up / the midget did. The Midget. Dabney Stuart. **SP-StuaD**

About Ice. Malcolm Lowry. **CP-LowrM**

About Marriage. Denise Levertov. **CP-LeveD**

About my fields, in the broad sun. Robert Louis Stevenson. Fr. The Family. **CP-StevR**

About my temples go, triumphant bays! 2.12. Ovid. **CP-MarlC**, tr. by Christopher Marlowe; Fr. Elegies.

About My Very Tortured Friend, Peter. Charles Bukowski. **SP-BukC2**

About Pain. Charles Bukowski. **SP-BukC3**

About suffering, about adoration, the old masters. The Old and the New Masters. Randall Jarrell. **CP-JarrR; SP-JarrR**

About suffering they were never wrong. Musée des Beaux Arts. Wystan Hugh Auden. **CP-AudeW**

About ten days or so. The Reassurance. Thom Gunn. **CP-GunnT**

. . . about the cool water. When We with Sappho. Kenneth Rexroth. **SP-RexrK**

About the Elk and the Coyotes That Killed Her Calf. Stephen Dunn. **SP-DunnS**

About the hour the December moon. John Haines. Fr. The Dream of the Police. **SP-HainJ**

About the Phoenix. James Merrill. **SP-MerrJ**

About the Shark, phlegmatical one. The Maldive Shark. Herman Melville. **SP-MelvH**

About the sheltered garden ground. Robert Louis Stevenson. **CP-StevR**

About the size of an old-style dollar bill. Poem. Elizabeth Bishop. **CP-BishE**

About the skull of the beloved, filled. Presentation Piece. Marilyn Hacker. **SP-HackM**

About the sweet bag of a bee. The Bag of the Bee. Robert Herrick. **CP-HerrR**

About the time that taverns shut. The Ballad of Minepit Shaw. Rudyard Kipling. **CP-KiplR**

About twenty years ago. Wild Oats. Philip Larkin. **CP-LarkP**

About Ulysses, the learned have reached two. Howard Nemerov. Fr. Runes. **CP-NemeH**

About us lies the summer night. Summer Night. Robert Louis Stevenson. **CP-StevR**

About what sort of thing. Arthur Hugh Clough. **SP-ClouA**

Above. Howard Nemerov. **CP-NemeH**

Above / the darkness of a river upon. A Marriage Ritual. William Carlos Williams. **CP-WilW1**

Above a between-the-acts prattling of. Edward Estlin Cummings. **CP-CummE**

Above a stretch of still unravaged weald. The Garden Party. Donald Davie. **CP-DavDo**

Above all, absent yourself from that affair. Malcolm Lowry. Fr. The Cantinas. **CP-LowrM**

Above all, I curse and strive to combat. My Songs Are Kandym in the Waste Land. "Hugh MacDiarmid." **SP-MacDH**

Above all, not by violence—. The Bacterial War. Howard Nemerov. **CP-NemeH**

Above, below, in sky and sod. The Over-Heart. John Greenleaf Whittier. **CP-WhitJ**

Above Carrara. Charles Tomlinson. **CP-TomlC**

Above Manhattan. Charles Tomlinson. **CP-TomlC**

Above mimosa and the flowering palm. The Cloud, Florida, 1985. Peter Meinke. **SP-MeinP**

Above my desk / the Rabbi of Auschwitz. On a Drawing by Flavio. Philip Levine. **SP-LeviP**

Above my desk, whirring and self-important. Angel. James Merrill. **SP-MerrJ**

Above my door the rushy cross. Rite, Lubitavish, Glenaan. John Hewitt. **CP-HewiJ**

Above Oblivion's Tide there is a Pier. Emily Dickinson. **CP-DickE**

Above Pate Valley. Gary Snyder. **CP-SnydG**

Above Taos now / I peer through the crack. The Man Who Rode Away. Lawrence Ferlinghetti. **SP-FerlL**

Above the Battle's Front. Nicholas Vachel Lindsay. **CP-LindV**

Above the beach, the vineyard. The Flower. Robert Penn Warren. Fr. To a Little Girl, One Year Old, in a Ruined Fortress. **SP-WarrR**

Above the Cave. Denise Levertov. **CP-LeveD**

Above the Edge of Doom. Robert Ranke Graves. **CP-GravR**

Above the forest of the parakeets. The Bird with the Coppery, Keen Claws. Wallace Stevens. **CP-StevW**

Above the fresh ruffles of the surf. Hart Crane. **AmPP; CABA; MOS; MoP; NAAL-2; OxBA; PoE; VGW** Fr. Voyages. **CP-CranH**

Above the Oxbow. Sylvia Plath. **CP-PlatS**

Above the waters in their toil. Randall Jarrell. **CP-JarrR**

Above the whispering sea. Air Raid across the Bay at Plymouth. Stephen Spender. **CP-SpenS**

Above These Cares. Edna St. Vincent Millay. **CP-MillE**

Above these Lithuanian cliffs. Bulldog on the Roof—Avenue C. Marsden Hartley. **CP-HartM**

Above trees and rooftops. Below. Wendell Berry. **CP-BerrW**

Above whorled, spindling gorse. Two Views of Withens. Sylvia Plath. **CP-PlatS**

Abracadabra Boys, The. Carl Sandburg. **CP-SandC**

Abracadabra boys—have they been in the stacks and cloisters? Have, The. The Abracadabra Boys. Carl Sandburg. **CP-SandC**

Abraham and Isaac. Isabella Gardner. **CP-GardI**

Abraham Davenport. John Greenleaf Whittier. **CP-WhitJ**

Abraham Lincoln. Robert Lowell. **SP-LoweR**

Abraham Lincoln, Born Feb. 12, 1809. Walt Whitman. **CP-WhitW**

Abraham Lincoln Walks at Midnight. Nicholas Vachel Lindsay. **CP-LindV**

Abraham Lincoln was giggling uncontrollably. Every few minutes he. The Presidentiad. Donald Hall. **CP-HallD**

Abraham to kill him. Emily Dickinson. **CP-DickE**

Abrahamic River, The. The Muster. Herman Melville. **SP-MelvH**

Abram Morrison. John Greenleaf Whittier. **CP-WhitJ**

Abroad Thoughts from Home. Donald Hall. **CP-HallD**

Abrupt tempter; close enough to survive. Little Apocalypse; Hölderlin: 1770–1843. Geoffrey Hill. **CP-HillG**

Abrupt the supernatural Cross. The Apparition. Herman Melville. **SP-MelvH**

Abruptly paused the strife;—the field throughout. The Germans on the Heights of Hochheim. William Wordsworth. **CP-WorW2**

Absalom. Walter de la Mare. **CP-DeLaW**

Absalom. Muriel Rukeyser. **CP-RukeM**

Absalom and Achitophel, Pt. I. John Dryden. **SP-DrydJ**

    Achitophel: The Earl of Shaftsbury. **NOBE**

    "From hence began that Plot, the nation's curse." **FaBoEH**

    "In pious times ere [or e'r] priest-craft did begin." **EBEvV; FHYEP; FaBoPV; HAP; NOSC; NoP; OAEL-1; PoE; SeCV-2**

    "In the first rank of these did Zimri stand." **HAP; SeCePo**

      (Zimri: "In the first rank of These did Zimri stand.") **SeCePo**

    Malcontents, The. **OBS**

    "Of these the false Achitophel was first." **AWP; FaBoEH; FiP; HAP; InPS; NOBE; NOSC; OBS; PoEL-3; SeCePo; WHA**

      (Achitophel.) **AWP; SeCePo**

      (Achitophel: The Earl of Shaftsbury.) **NOBE**

      (False Achitophel, The.) **FiP**

      (Shaft[e]sbury.) **NOSC; OBS**

    Popish Plot, The. **ACP**

"Some by their friends, more by themselves thought wise." **ChIV-1; OBSV**

"Some of their chiefs were princes of the land." **AWP; EBEV; IHNG; SCV**

(On the Duke of Buckingham.) **IHNG**

(Zimri: "Some of their chiefs were princes of the land.") **AWP**

"Sunk were his eyes, his voice was harsh and loud." **FaBoEH**

"With all these loads of injuries opprest." **EBEV**

Zimri: The Duke of Buckingham. **NOBE; OBSV**

(Zimri: "Numerous host of dreaming saints succeed.") **AWP; SeCePo**

Absalom and Achitophel, Pt. II. John Dryden *and* Nahum Tate.

"Doeg, though without knowing how or why." **SP-DrydJ**

Absence. Samuel Taylor Coleridge. **CP-ColeS**

Absence. Stephen Dobyns. **SP-DobyS**

Absence. Paul Laurence Dunbar. **CP-DunbP**

Absence. William Shakespeare. *See* Sonnet 57: "Being your slave, what should I do[e] but tend."

Absence. Stephen Spender. **CP-SpenS**

Absence! Absenting causeth me to complain. Sir Thomas Wyatt. **CP-WyatT**

Absence, alas, / Causeth me pass. Sir Thomas Wyatt. **CP-WyatT**

Absence disembodies—so does Death. Emily Dickinson. **CP-DickE**

Absence Makes the Heart Grow Heart Trouble. Ogden Nash. **CP-NashO**

Absence of a Noble Presence, The. John Ashbery. **SP-AshbJ**

Absence of heart—as in public buildings. The Chimaeras. Wystan Hugh Auden. **CP-AudeW**

Absences. Philip Larkin. **CP-LarkP**

Absent Crusader. Robert Ranke Graves. **CP-GravR**

Absent from the United States. Al Young. **CP-YounA**

Absent-Minded Are Always to Blame, The. Adrienne Rich. **CP-RicAE**

Absent-Minded Beggar, The. Rudyard Kipling. **CP-KiplR**

Absent-Minded Professor. Howard Nemerov. **ELU** *Fr.* Epigrams: "Wasp, climbing the window pane." **CP-NemeH**

Absent or present, still to thee. Lines Written on a Blank Leaf of the "Pleasures of Memory." Byron. **CP-Byron**

Absent Place—an April Day. Emily Dickinson. **CP-DickE**

Absent, this morning. Aube Provençale. Marilyn Hacker. **SP-HackM**

Absent with Official Leave. Randall Jarrell. **CP-JarrR; SP-JarrR**

Absentees, The. Ogden Nash. **CP-NashO**

Absentees, The. Ogden Nash. *Fr.* Posies from a Second Childhood, or, Hark How Gaffer Do Chaffer. **CP-NashO**

Absolute / Pity / Advancing. Roy Fisher. **SP-FishR** *Fr.* Three Ceremonial Poems.

Absolute, An / patience. The Breathing. Denise Levertov. **CP-LeveD**

Absolute Explains, The. Thomas Hardy. **CP-HardT**

Absolute Reverence. David Herbert Lawrence. **CP-LawrD**

Absolutely Sweet Marie. "Bob Dylan." **CP-DylaB**

Absolutely Vernal. Charles Olson. **CP-OlsoC**

Abstinence. Robert Herrick. **CP-HerrR**

Abstinence from Melody. Emily Dickinson. **SP-DickE**

Abstinence sows sand all over. William Blake. **EBEV; FF; FaBoEE; GBL; MeMBP; OxBM; TrGrPo** *Fr.* Gnomic Verses. **CP-BlakW**

Abstract Greek absurdity has crazed the man, An. Ribh Denounces Patrick. William Butler Yeats. **CP-YeatW**

Abstract #1, Yucatan. Charles Olson. **CP-OlsoC**

Abstract Study—Circles. Jenny Joseph. **SP-JoseJ**

Abstraction, The. Gilbert Sorrentino. **SP-SorrG**

Abstracts hover like dull angels, The. Magi. Sylvia Plath. **CP-PlatS**

Absurd in his tight black coat like a sleazy beetle. The Vanity of the Bright Boys. John Crowe Ransom. *Fr.* Sixteen Poems in Eight Pairings. **SP-RansJ**

Abt the dead he sd. Charles Olson. **CP-OlsoC**

Abundant plagues I late have had. Patience, or Comforts in Crosses. Robert Herrick. **CP-HerrR**

Abuse of Monastic Power. William Wordsworth. *Fr.* Ecclesiastical Sonnets. **CP-WorW2**

Abuse of the Gospel. William Cowper. *Fr.* Olney Hymns. **CP-CowpW**

Abysmal Immortality. David Herbert Lawrence. **CP-LawrD**

Abyss, The. Theodore Roethke. **CP-RoetT**

Acacia Tree. Kathleen Jessie Raine. **SP-RainK**

Academic. Phoebe Hesketh. **SP-HeskP**

Academic. Theodore Roethke. **CP-RoetT**

Academic Discourse at Havana. Wallace Stevens. **CP-StevW**

Academic Graffiti. Wystan Hugh Auden. **CP-AudeW**

"Henry Adams / Was mortally afraid of Madams." **OBAL**

"James Watt / Was the hard-boiled kind of Scot." **InPK**

"Sir Rider Haggard / Was completely staggered." **FaBoCo**

Academy. John Updike. **CP-UpdiJ**

Academy of the future is opening its doors, The. Ted Berrigan. **SP-BerrT** *Fr.* The Sonnets.

Accept, loved Nymph, this tribute due. To the Same. James Thomson. **CP-ThomJ**

Accept my timid happiness. Emily Dickinson. **SP-DickE**

Accept these records of pure love. Records. Robert Ranke Graves. **CP-GravR**

Acceptance. Robert Frost. **CP-FrosR**

Acceptances. Jane Cooper. **SP-CoopJ**

Graveyard, The. **NePoEA-2**

Racetrack, The.

Sundial, The.

Accepted. David Markson. **CP-MarkD**

Acceptum pro me perhibes te, Castrice, ludis. *acc. by English translation.* Thomas Campion. **CP-CampT**

Accession of King George III, The. Christopher Smart. *Fr.* Hymns and Spiritual Songs for the Fasts and Festivals of the Church of England. **SP-SmarC**

Accident. Maya Angelou. **SP-AngeM**

Accidentally on Purpose. Robert Frost. **CP-FrosR**

Accompanist, The. William Matthews. **SP-MattW**

Accomplice, The. Robert Ranke Graves. **CP-GravR**

Accomplices, The. Isabella Gardner. **CP-GardI**

Accomplished Facts. Carl Sandburg. **CP-SandC**

Accomplishment. Tess Gallagher. **SP-GallT**

According to Brueghel. Landscape with the Fall of Icarus. William Carlos Williams. **LCAP; NAAL-2; NoAM; PPP** *Fr.* Pictures from Brueghel. **CP-WilW2**

According to His Seasons. Howard Nemerov. **CP-NemeH**

According to my mother. Their Shadows. John Yau. **SP-YauJo**

According to the helicopter pilot. The Survivor. Miller Williams. **SP-WillM**

According to the Mighty Working. Thomas Hardy. **CP-HardT**

According to their need. The Host. William Carlos Williams. **CP-WilW2**

According to Thy will: That this day only. A Usual Prayer. John Berryman. **CP-BerrJ**

According to Webster's, "the condition." Neotony. John Updike. **CP-UpdiJ**

Accordingly, on weighty business bound. Robert Browning. **EBVVPR** *Fr.* Red Cotton Night-Cap Country. **CP-BroR2**

Accordingly, they commenced by an insidious. Carl Sandburg. *Fr.* The People, Yes. **CP-SandC**

Account of your what critics call Prose Style. On the Platform. Howard Nemerov. **CP-NemeH**

Accountability. Gerrit Achterberg, *tr. fr. Dutch by* Adrienne Rich. **CP-RicAE**

Accountability. Paul Laurence Dunbar. **CP-DunbP**

Accumulation. John Updike. **CP-UpdiJ**

Accumulation of reefs, The. The Distances. Jim Carroll. **SP-CarrJ**

Accusation. Robert Herrick. **CP-HerrR**

Accusation, The. James Wright. **CP-WrigJ**

Accuse me not, beseech thee, that I wear. Sonnet. Elizabeth Barrett Browning. *Fr.* Sonnets from the Portuguese. **CP-BroEB**

Accuse me thus; that I have scanted all. Sonnet 117. William Shakespeare. *Fr.* Sonnets. **CP-ShaWS**

Accused though I be without desert. Sir Thomas Wyatt. **CP-WyatT**

Ace of Destiny. Tom Clark. **SP-ClarT**

Ach, mein Kurt, when we were young we sang. Tanck's Song About Youth and Age. Hayden Carruth. **CP-CarHS** *Fr.* Songs About What Comes Down: The Complete Works of Mr. Septic Tank.

Ach, Mutter, / This old, black dress. Explanation. Wallace Stevens. **CP-StevW**

Ache of Marriage, The. Denise Levertov. **CP-LeveD**

Ache's End. Marge Piercy. **SP-PierM**

Achill. Derek Mahon. **SP-MahoD**

Achilles and Hector and Homer and all. On Hayley's Portrait. William Cowper. **CP-CowpW**

Achilles over the Trench. Homer, *tr. by* George Meredith. **CP-MerG2** *Fr.* The Iliad.

Achilles' Song. Robert Duncan. **SP-DuncR**

Achitophel. John Dryden. *See* Of these the false Achitophel was first.

Achitophel: The Earl of Shaftsbury. John Dryden. **NOBE** *Fr.* Absalom and Achitophel, Pt. I. **SP-DrydJ**

Achitophel: The Earl of Shaftsbury. John Dryden. *See* Of these the false Achitophel was first.

Acid. Mary Oliver. **SP-OlivM**

Acid and ignorant voice, desist. Louis MacNeice. *Fr.* Donegal Triptych. **CP-MacNL**

Acid dreams & Spanish Queens. L'America. Jim Morrison. **SP-MorrJ**

Acids. Charles Kenneth Williams. **CP-WillC**

Acknowledge last this human peace. Nocturne for the Heirs of Light. Kenneth Patchen. **CP-PatcK**

Acknowledgement. Archibald MacLeish. **CP-MacLA**

Acme. Christina Georgina Rossetti. **CP-RosC3**

Acme and Septimius. Catullus. *See* Carmen 45: "Phyllis Corydon clutched to him."

Acme, Septimius, sighs so amorous. Catullus. *See* Carmen 45: "Phyllis Corydon clutched to him."

Acolyte singeth, An. Holy Trinity, Sloane Street. Sir John Betjeman. **CP-BetjJ**

Acon. Hilda Doolittle. **CP-DoolH**

Acorns. Donald Hall. **CP-HallD**

Acquaintance; companion. The Results of Thought. William Butler Yeats. **CP-YeatW**

Acquaintance with Death, Sir. Carl Sandburg. **CP-SandC**

Acquainted with the Night. Robert Frost. **CP-FrosR**

Acquiescence of Pure Love, The. Jeanne Marie Bouvier de la Motte-Guyon, *tr. fr. French by* William Cowper. **CP-CowpW**

Acquit of evil intention. Canto 62. Ezra Pound. *Fr.* Cantos. **CP-PoCan**

Acquittal of the Bishops. William Wordsworth. *Fr.* Ecclesiastical Sonnets. **CP-WorW2**

Acre of Grass, An. William Butler Yeats. **CP-YeatW**

Acrid scents of autumn, The. Dolour of Autumn. David Herbert Lawrence. **CP-LawrD**

Acrobat, The. Siv Cedering Fox. **SP-CedeS**

Acrobats. Robert Ranke Graves. **CP-GravR**

Acrobats, The. Shel Silverstein. **SP-SilS2**

Across a city from you, I'm with you. Adrienne Rich. **PeHV** *Fr.* Twenty-one Love Poems. **SP-RicA1; SP-RicA2**

Across a world where all men grieve. Justice. Rudyard Kipling. **CP-KiplR**

Across from me the whole ride. The Chicago Train. Louise Glück. **SP-GlücL**

Across his path the spouseless Lady cast. George Meredith. *Fr.* The Sage Enamoured and the Honest Lady. **CP-MerG1**

Across Lamarck Col. Gary Snyder. **CP-SnydG**

Across Lock Laig / the yellow- billed blackbird. Gloss, on the Difficulties of Translation. John Hewitt. **CP-HewiJ**

Across lunar wastes of wind and snow. Robert Earl Hayden. **CP-HaydR** *Fr.* The Snow Lamp.

Across my dreams the bell. Sunday Morning. Wystan Hugh Auden. **CP-AudWJ**

Across Nevada and Utah. March of the Hungry Mountains. Carl Sandburg. **CP-SandC**

Across salt marshes north of. Little Songs for Gaia. Gary Snyder. **CP-SnydG**

Across seven thousand miles of sea and time. Alun Lewis. *Fr.* Letter From the Cape. **CP-LewiA**

Across Space and Time. Charles Olson. **CP-OlsoC**

Across the Bay. Donald Davie. **CP-DavDo**

Across the Board. Ernest Hemingway. **CP-HemiE**

Across the bridge across the dyke. The Fugitive's Ride. Stevie Smith. **CP-SmitS**

Across the cages of the keyless aviaries. Aubade—Harlem. Thomas Merton. **CP-MertT; SP-MertT**

Across the floor flits the mechanical toy. Cirque d'Hiver. Elizabeth Bishop. **CP-BishE**

Across the frontiers of the helpless world. Nineteen Thirty-Eight. John Berryman. **CP-BerrJ**

Across the frozen marshes. The Conquest of Finland. John Greenleaf Whittier. **CP-WhitJ**

Across the Great Schism, through our whole landscape. The Old Man's Road. Wystan Hugh Auden. **CP-AudeW**

Across the hills and down the narrow ways. A Winter's Day. Paul Laurence Dunbar. **CP-DunbP**

Across the landing strip, past planes. A Church Cemetery in St. Mary's. Peter Meinke. **SP-MeinP**

Across the lock-smoothed river you may see. Autumn Valley. John Hewitt. **CP-HewiJ**

Across the millstream below the bridge. The Blue Swallows. Howard Nemerov. **CP-NemeH**

Across the mud flats and the wide roads, over rivers and borders. Marilyn Hacker. **SP-HackM** *Fr.* The Navigators.

Across the open countryside. The Unsettled Motorcyclist's Vision of His Death. Thom Gunn. **CP-GunnT**

Across the Oregon plateau. Men Against the Sky. John Haines. **SP-HainJ**

Across the pond / reeds bow against. A Window in Cherry Valley. Jim Carroll. **SP-CarrJ**

Across the scorched stubble among the grey olives. Mycenae and Epidaurus. John Hewitt. **CP-HewiJ**

Across the sea I heard the groans. Italy. John Greenleaf Whittier. **CP-WhitJ**

Across the Stony Mountains, o'er the desert's drouth and sand. The Crisis. John Greenleaf Whittier. **CP-WhitJ**

Across the street my neighbor's colored lights. December 24, Alone. Richard Hugo. **CP-HugoR**

Across the street, the carpenter carries a golden. The Street. Stephen Dobyns. **SP-DobyS**

Across the thin / façade, the galleried. To Be Engraved on the Skull of a Cormorant. Charles Tomlinson. **CP-TomlC**

Across the tracks in Cheyenne, behind the biggest billboard. A Long Way Outside Yellowstone. Thomas McGrath. **SP-McGrT**

Across the trampled, program-littered grass. After Commencement. Howard Nemerov. **CP-NemeH**

Across the Universe. John Lennon *and* Paul McCartney. **CP-Beatl**

Across the Waste to Northward, go. Day-dreams of a Tourist. Wystan Hugh Auden. **CP-AudWJ**

Across the water sits a shore. Gilbert Sorrentino. **SP-SorrG**

Across the way hands / move nervously on curtains. The Other Side. Charles Kenneth Williams. **CP-WillC**

Across the wet November night. Verses Turned in Aid of a Public Subscription (1952) Towards the Restoration of the Church of St. Katherine Chiselhampton, Oxon. Sir John Betjeman. **CP-BetjJ**

Across the wide waters / something comes. The Swan. Mary Oliver. **SP-OlivM**

Across the world / in the high mountains of the West. Philip Levine. **SP-LeviP** *Fr.* A Poem with No Ending.

Acrostic. John Keats. **CP-KeatJ**

Acrostic: A boat, beneath a sunny sky. "Lewis Carroll." **CP-CarrL** *Fr.* Through the Looking-Glass.

Acrostic: "Are you deaf, Father William?" "Lewis Carroll." **CP-CarrL**

Acrostic: Around my lonely hearth, to-night. "Lewis Carroll." **CP-CarrL**

Acrostic: Dreams, that elude the Waker's frenzied grasp—. "Lewis Carroll." **CP-CarrL** *Fr.* Sylvie and Bruno Concluded.

Acrostic: Is all our Life, then, but a dream. "Lewis Carroll." **CP-CarrL** *Fr.* Sylvie and Bruno.

Acrostic: Little maidens, when you look. "Lewis Carroll." **CP-CarrL**

Acrostic: Love-lighted eyes, that will not start. "Lewis Carroll." **CP-CarrL**

Acrostic: "Maiden, though thy heart may quail." "Lewis Carroll." **CP-CarrL**

Acrostic: Maidens! if you love the tale. "Lewis Carroll." **CP-CarrL**

Act, The. William Carlos Williams. **CP-WilW2**

Act of Love, The. Robert Creeley. **CP-CreeR**

Act of love seemed a dead metaphor, The. The Metaphor. Robert Ranke Graves. **CP-GravR**

Act of seeing a tree is the act of pressing, The. A Spell of Conjunctivitis. Mona Van Duyn. **SP-VanDM**

Act of Union. Seamus Heaney. **SP-HeanS**

Act Sederunt of the Session—A Scots Ballad. Robert Burns. **CP-BurnR**

Actfive. Archibald MacLeish. **CP-MacLA**

Acting younger than I am and thinking older. To Hedli. Louis MacNeice. **CP-MacNL**

Action and Non-Action. Chuang Tzu, *tr. fr. Chinese by* Thomas Merton. **CP-MertT**

Action is a pain of being. Autumnal. Richard Eberhart. **CP-EberR**

Action of Therapy, The. May Sarton. **SP-SartM**

Active Life. Chuang Tzu, *tr. fr. Chinese by* Thomas Merton. **CP-MertT**

Activity without / Attachment. One link with the. Charles Henri Ford. **SP-FordC** *Fr.* Secret Haiku.

Actor: Decline and Death, The. James McAuley. **SP-McAuJ**

Actors. Rudyard Kipling. *Fr.* Epitaphs of the War [1914–1918]. **CP-KiplR**

Actors with their variety of voices. A Mexican Guitar. Frank O'Hara. **SP-OharF**

Actress, The. Stevie Smith. **CP-SmitS**

Acts 5; Sicke Implore St. Peter's Shadow, The. Richard Crashaw. *See* Under thy shadow may I lurk a while.

Acts 8; On the Baptized Æthiopian. Richard Crashaw. *See* Let it no longer be a forlorn[e] hope.

Acts 21; I Am Ready Not Onely To Be Bound but To Dye. Richard Crashaw. **CP-CrasR**

Acts of Light which beautified, The. Emily Dickinson. **SP-DickE**

Acts Passed Beyond. Stephen Spender. **CP-SpenS**

Actually, and weeping do nothing best. & do what I know best. Anne Waldman. **SP-WaldA**

Ad Amorem, *acc. by English translation*. Thomas Campion. **CP-CampT**

Ad ampliss. totius Angliae Cancellarium, Fr. Ba., *acc. by English translation.* Thomas Campion. **CP-CampT**

Ad Cambricum, *acc. by English trnaslation.* Thomas Campion. **CP-CampT**

Ad Carolum Fitz Geofridum, *acc. by English translation.* Thomas Campion. **CP-CampT**

Ad Caspiam, *acc. by English translation.* Thomas Campion. **CP-CampT**

Ad Castitatem. Louise Bogan. **CP-BogaL**

Ad Castricum, *acc. by English translation.* Thomas Campion. **CP-CampT**

Ad Chloen, *acc. by English translation.* Thomas Campion. **CP-CampT**

Ad Ed. Mychelburnum, *acc. by English translation.* Thomas Campion. **CP-CampT**

Ad Ed. Spencerum, *acc. by English translation.* Thomas Campion. **CP-CampT**

Ad Episcopum Salopiensem. Gerard Manley Hopkins. **CP-HopkG**

AD EUNDEM. Thomas Hamersley. *Fr.* Commendatory Poems. **CP-LoveR**

Ad Ge. Chapmannum, *acc. by English translation.* Thomas Campion. **CP-CampT**

Ad Graios, *acc. by English translation.* Thomas Campion. **CP-CampT**

Ad Guil. Camdenum, *acc. by English translation.* Thomas Campion. **CP-CampT**

Ad Infinitum. William Carlos Williams. **CP-WilW1**

Ad Invictissimum Serenissimumque Iacobum *Magnae Britanniae Regem, accompanied by English translation.* Thomas Campion. *Fr.* Lord Hay's Mask.

Ad Io. Davisium, *acc. by English translation.* Thomas Campion. **CP-CampT**

Ad Io. Dolundum, *?acc. by English translation.* Thomas Campion. **CP-CampT**

Ad Leam, *acc. by English translation.* Thomas Campion. **CP-CampT**

Ad Lesbiam. Catullus. *See* Carmen 7: "Curious to learn / how may kiss- / es of your lips."

Ad Librum, *?acc. by English translation.* Thomas Campion. **CP-CampT**

Ad Lucium, *acc. by English translation.* Thomas Campion. **CP-CampT**

Ad Lyram. Samuel Taylor Coleridge. **CP-ColeS**

Ad Man's Daughter, The. Jim Carroll. **SP-CarrJ**

Ad Mariam. Gerard Manley Hopkins. **CP-HopkG**

Ad Martialem. Robert Louis Stevenson. **CP-StevR**

Ad Matrem Virginem. Gerard Manley Hopkins. **CP-HopkG**

Ad Melleam, *acc. by English translation.* Thomas Campion. **CP-CampT**

Ad Nashum, *acc. by English translation.* Thomas Campion. **CP-CampT**

Ad Nepotem. Robert Louis Stevenson. **CP-StevR**

Ad nobiliss. virum Gul. Percium, *acc. by English translation.* Thomas Campion. **CP-CampT**

Ad Olum. Robert Louis Stevenson. **CP-StevR**

Ad Piscatorem. Robert Louis Stevenson. **CP-StevR**

Ad Pisonem. Lucan, *tr. fr. Latin.*
"Unlike the ribald, whose licentious jest." **CP-JohnS**

Ad Quintilianum. Robert Louis Stevenson. **CP-StevR**

Ad Regem Carolum Parodia [A Parody: To King Charles]. Andrew Marvell, *tr. fr. Latin by* William A. McQueen *and* Kiffin A. Rockwell. **CP-MarvA**

Ad Reinhardt's black, in *Abstract Painting 33.* Gradations of Black. John Updike. **CP-UpdiJ**

Ad Reverendum Patrem Fratrem Thomam Burke O.P. Collegium S. Beunonis Invisentem. Gerard Manley Hopkins. **CP-HopkG**

Ad Rob. Caraeum Equitem Auratum Nobilissimum, *acc. by English translation.* Thomas Campion. **CP-CampT**

Ad Rusticum, *acc. by English trnaslation.* Thomas Campion. **CP-CampT**

Ad sanctam catherinam, virginem et martyrem. Robert Southwell. **CP-SoutR**

Ad Se Ipsum. Robert Louis Stevenson. **CP-StevR**

Ad Thamesin, *acc. by English translation.* Thomas Campion. **CP-CampT**

Ad Tho. Munsonium, equitem Auratum et Baronetum, *acc. by English translation.* Thomas Campion. **CP-CampT**

A.D. 2029. David Markson. **CP-MarkD**

Ad Venetos venit corio Coryatus ab uno. Accompanied by English translation. Thomas Campion. **CP-CampT**

Ad Vilmum Axiologum, *with tr. of the Latin.* Samuel Taylor Coleridge. **CP-ColeS**

'ΑΔΑΚΡΥΝ ΝΕΜΟΝΤΑΙ ΑΙΩΝΑ. Ralph Waldo Emerson. *Fr.* Quatrains. **CP-EmerR**

Adam. Stephen Spender. **CP-SpenS**

Adam. Charles Tomlinson. **CP-TomlC**

Adam. William Carlos Williams. **CP-WilW1**

Adam and Eve. Arthur Hugh Clough. **SP-ClouA**

Adam and Eve. John Milton. *See* So passed they naked on, nor shunned the sight.

Adam and Eve. Karl Shapiro. **SP-ShapK**

Confession, The.

Exile. **CRP**

Kiss, The.

Recognition of Eve, The. **ChIV-1; MoAB**

Shame.

Sickness of Adam, The. **AP; CRP; CoBMV; MoAB**

Tree of Guilt, The.

Adam and Eve sat in their garden. Throwing the Apple. Richard Eberhart. **CP-EberR**

Adam A———'s Prayer. Robert Burns. **CP-BurnR**

Adam Cast Forth. Richard Eberhart. **CP-EberR**

Adam Fallen ("Descended, Adam to the bower where Eve"). John Milton. **NOCV** *Fr.* Book XII. *Fr.* Paradise Lost. **CP-MiltJ**

Adam Fallen ("He ended, and they both descend the hill"). John Milton. *See* He ended, and they both descend the hill.

Adam had fallen twice, if for an apple. Alexander Pope. *Fr.* Epigrams Occasion'd by an Invitation to Court. **CP-PopeA**

Adam had found what was not his to seek. Eden. Donald Davie. **CP-DavDo**

Adam in the Evening. Archibald MacLeish. *Fr.* Songs for Eve. **CP-MacLA**

Adam in Winter. James Dickey. **CP-DickJ**

Adam, Lilith, and Eve. Robert Browning. **CP-BroR2**

Adam, on such a morning, named the beasts. Adam. Charles Tomlinson. **CP-TomlC**

Adam scriveyn [*or* scrivain *or* scrivein], if ever it thee bifalle. Chaucer's Wordes unto Adam, his Owne Scriveyn. Geoffrey Chaucer. **CP-ChauG**

Adam Speaks. John Milton. **NU** *Fr.* Book X. **FHYEP** *Fr.* Paradise Lost. **CP-MiltJ**

Adam Unfallen. John Milton. **NOCV** *Fr.* Book V. *Fr.* Paradise Lost. **CP-MiltJ**

Adamant, The. Theodore Roethke. **CP-RoetT**

Adamo Me. Charles Olson. **CP-OlsoC**

Adam's Curse. William Butler Yeats. **CP-YeatW**

Adam's Jealousy: Eve's Answer. Archibald MacLeish. *Fr.* Songs for Eve. **CP-MacLA**

Adam's Morning Hymn. John Milton. *See* Morning Hymn of Adam.

Adam's Riddle. Archibald MacLeish. *Fr.* Songs for Eve. **CP-MacLA**

Adam's Song. Derek Walcott. **CP-WalcD**

Adamson. Frederick Morgan. *Fr.* Eight Triolets. **SP-MorgF**

Adaption of a Theme from Catullus. Catullus. *See* Carmen 101: "Journeying over many seas and through many countries."

Add This to Rhetoric. Wallace Stevens. **CP-StevW**

Add to your show, before you close it, France. Bravo, Paris Exposition! Walt Whitman. **CP-WhitW**

Added to / making a Republic. Charles Olson. **SP-OlsoC** *Fr.* The Maximus Poems.

Addenda Quaedam. Jonathan Swift. **CP-SwifJ**

Addendum for C ("Evil is Usury, *neschek,* The"). Ezra Pound. *Fr.* Cantos. **CP-PoCan**

Addendum for C ("Now sun rises in Ram sign"). Ezra Pound. *Fr.* Cantos. **CP-PoCan**

Addict, The. Anne Sexton. **CP-SextA**

Addio. John Ciardi. **SP-CiarJ**

Addio, diletto amico; / A me non lece amore. Amor Dormente? Christina Georgina Rossetti. *Fr.* Il Rosseggiar Dell'Oriente Canzoniere. **CP-RosC3**

Additional Poem, An. John Ashbery. **SP-AshbJ**

Address. Byron. **CP-Byron**

Address, An. William Carlos Williams. **CP-WilW2**

Address. William Carlos Williams. **CP-WilW2**

Address from the Spirit of Cockermouth Castle. William Wordsworth. *Fr.* Poems Composed or Suggested During a Tour, in the Summer of 1833. **CP-WorW2**

Address Intended to be Recited at the Caledonian Meeting. Byron. **CP-Byron**

Address of Beelzebub. Robert Burns. **CP-BurnR**

Address to Edinburgh. Robert Burns. **CP-BurnR**

Address to General Dumourier. Robert Burns. **CP-BurnR**

Address to Kilchurn Castle, upon Loch Awe. William Wordsworth. **CP-WorW1**

Address to My Infant Daughter, Dora on Being Reminded That She Was a Month Old That Day, September 16. William Wordsworth. **CP-WorW1**
"Hast thou then survived." **EvOK; Par**

Address to Silence. William Wordsworth. **CP-WorW1**

Address to the Beasts. Wystan Hugh Auden. **CP-AudeW**

Address to the Deil. Robert Burns. **CP-BurnR**

Address to the Migrations. Jean Garrigue. **SP-GarrJ**

Address to the Mob, An. William Cowper. **CP-CowpW**

Address to the National Council on the Arts. Gilbert Sorrentino. **SP-SorrG**

Address to the Ocean. William Wordsworth. **CP-WorW1**

Address to the Scholars of the Village School of—1798. William Wordsworth. **CP-WorW1**

Address to the Shade of Thomson. Robert Burns. **CP-ThomJ**

Address, to the Shade of Thomson, on Crowning His Bust, at *Ednam, Roxburgh-shire*, with Bays. Robert Burns. **CP-BurnR**

Address to the Tooth-Ache. Robert Burns. **CP-BurnR**

Address to the Unco Guid, or the Rigidly Righteous. Robert Burns. **CP-BurnR**

Address to the Woodlark. Robert Burns. **CP-BurnR**

Address to Venus. Edmund Spenser, *tr. fr. Latin*. **AWP** *Fr.* The Faerie Queene. **CP-Spens**

  (Prayer to Venus.) **ElI**

Address to you. Richard Eberhart. *Fr.* Suite in Prison. **CP-EberR**

Addressed to a Young Man of Fortune. Samuel Taylor Coleridge. **CP-ColeS**

Addressed to Haydon. John Keats. **CP-KeatJ**

Addressed to Haydon. John Keats. *See* Great Spirits Now on Earth.

Adela, Adela, Adela Chart. To Henry James. Robert Louis Stevenson. **CP-StevR**

Adela is such a silly woman. V. Stevie Smith. **CP-SmitS**

Adelaide Abner. Stevie Smith. **CP-SmitS**

Adelaide Crapsey. Carl Sandburg. **CP-SandC**

Adelard, Etienne. Three Loving Men. Marsden Hartley. **CP-HartM**

Adequacy. Elizabeth Barrett Browning. **CP-BroEB**

Adhuc sub Judice Lis. Edward Estlin Cummings. **CP-CummE**

Adieu, The. Byron. **CP-Byron**

Adieu. Walter de la Mare. **CP-DeLaW**

Adieu À Charlot, *see also* Ferlinghetti, "Poets, come out of your closets." Lawrence Ferlinghetti. **SP-FerlL**

Adieu! a heart-warm, fond adieu! The Farewell. To the Brethren of St. James' Lodge, Tarbolton. Robert Burns. **CP-BurnR**

Adieu, adieu, my Friar, he cried. George Meredith. **CP-MerG2**

Adieu, adieu! my native shore. Childe Harold's Farewell to England. Byron. **OHFP** *Fr.* Childe Harold's Pilgrimage. **CP-Byron**

Adieu O soldier. Adieu to a Soldier. Walt Whitman. **CP-WhitW**

Adieu Rydalian Laurels! that have grown. William Wordsworth. *Fr.* Poems Composed or Suggested During a Tour, in the Summer of 1833. **CP-WorW2**

Adieu sweet Sun. Mary Sidney, Countess of Montgomery Wroth. *Fr.* Part 1. *Fr.* Urania. **CP-WrotM**

Adieu to a Soldier. Walt Whitman. **CP-WhitW**

Adieu to Norman, Bon Jour to Joan and Jean-Paul. Frank O'Hara. **SP-OharF**

Adieu, ye joys of La Valette! Farewell to Malta. Byron. **CP-Byron**

Adirondacs, The. Ralph Waldo Emerson. **CP-EmerR**

Adjustment. John Greenleaf Whittier. **CP-WhitJ**

Admetus, from my marrow's core I do. Edna St. Vincent Millay. **CP-MillE**

Administration. John Hewitt. **CP-HewiJ**

Administration. Philip Larkin. **CP-LarkP**

Admiral Fan, The. Charles Kenneth Williams. **CP-WillC**

Admiral to His Lady, The. Donald Davie. **CP-DavDo**

Admiral's Caravan, The, *sels.* Charles Edward Carryl.

  Song of the Camel, The.

  Unicorn. **SP-RexrK**

Admirals Curse-You and No-More. The Little Daughters of America. Stevie Smith. **CP-SmitS**

Admirations—and Contempts—of time, The. Emily Dickinson. **CP-DickE**

Admire Cranmer! Stevie Smith. **CP-SmitS**

Admire the old man, admire him, admire him. Admire Cranmer! Stevie Smith. **CP-SmitS**

Admire, when you come here, the glimmering hair. Vuillard: "The Mother and Sister of the Artist." William DeWitt Snodgrass. **SP-SnodW**

Admiring Nature in her wildest grace. Written with a Pencil over the Chimney-Piece, in the Parlour of the Inn at Kenmore, Taymouth. Robert Burns. **CP-BurnR**

Admiring the rustic / garden, the fat thatch. At Shottery, Anne Hathaway's Cottage. John Hewitt. **CP-HewiJ**

Admit the fact, you might have stood your ground. Belfastman Abroad Argues with Himself. John Hewitt. **CP-HewiJ**

Admit the ruse to fix and name her chaste. The Romantic. Louise Bogan. **CP-BogaL**

Admit, thou darling of mine eyes. To His Jealous Mistress. Thomas Carew. **CP-CareT**

Admonition. William Wordsworth. **CP-WorW1**

Admonition to Science. John Hewitt. **CP-HewiJ**

Admonitions. Sylvia Plath. **CP-PlatS**

Admonitions to a Special Person. Anne Sexton. **CP-SextA**

Adolescence. Wystan Hugh Auden. **CP-AudeW**

Adolescence. Thom Gunn. **CP-GunnT**

Adolescence—I. Rita Dove. **SP-DoveR**

Adolescence—II. Rita Dove. **SP-DoveR**

Adolescence—III. Rita Dove. **SP-DoveR**

Adolf Eichmann. Hayden Carruth. **CP-CarHS**

Adolf Hitler ("Better stuffed in a bag; drowned"). William DeWitt Snodgrass. **SP-SnodW**

Adolf Hitler ("More than fifty millions. More"). William DeWitt Snodgrass. **SP-SnodW**

Adonais; An Elegy on the Death of John Keats. Percy Bysshe Shelley. **CP-ShelP**

  Cancelled Passages of the Poem.

  Go Thou to Rome. **ChTr**

  (Grave of Keats, The.) **FaBoPP**

  "He is made one with Nature; there is heard." **EPCY; WGRP**

  "Most musical of mourners, weep again!" **EPCY**

  "One remains, the many change and pass, The." **SCV**

  "Peace, peace! he is not dead, he doth not sleep." **FaBoEn; LO; NOBE; OBD; OBNC**

  (Elegy on the Death of John Keats, An.) **OBNC**

  (Mourn Not for Adonais.) **NOBE**

Adonis. Hilda Doolittle. **CP-DoolH**

Adorable images. To the Mannequins. Howard Nemerov. **CP-NemeH**

Adorable is an adjective and womankind is a noun. Allow Me, Madam, But It Won't Help. Ogden Nash. **CP-NashO**

Adoration of the Virgin, The. Robert Duncan. **SP-DuncR**

Adore the Roses; nor delay. Rosary Beads. Herman Melville. **SP-MelvH**

The Adorner of the uncomely—Those. Robert Louis Stevenson. *Fr.* The Family. **CP-StevR**

Adoro Te. The Hymn of Saint Thomas in Adoration of the Blessed Sacrament, *ad. fr. the medieval* Rhythmus ad Sacram Eucharistiam. Richard Crashaw. **CP-CrasR**

Adown the west a golden glow. At Sunset Time. Paul Laurence Dunbar. **CP-DunbP**

Adown winding Nith I did wander. Song. Robert Burns. **CP-BurnR**

Adriano in Syria. Pietro Metastasio.

  Translations from Metastasio ("Grown old in courts, thou art not surely done"). **CP-JohnS**

Adrian's Address to His Soul When Dying. Emperor Hadrian. *See* Ah! gentle, fleeting, wav'ring sprite.

Adrift! A little boat adrift! Emily Dickinson. **CP-DickE**

Adulation is inexpensive. Emily Dickinson. **SP-DickE**

Adult Bookstore. Karl Shapiro. **SP-ShapK**

Adult Entertainment. Marilyn Hacker. **SP-HackM**

Adult Epigram. Wallace Stevens. **CP-StevW**

Adult Grief. Louise Glück. **SP-GlücL**

Adult: That's a tattooed man. James Fenton. *Fr.* Exempla. **SP-FentJ**

Adulteress stoned to death, The. Adam's Song. Derek Walcott. **CP-WalcD**

Adultery. James Dickey. **CP-DickJ**

Adultery. Thom Gunn. **CP-GunnT**

Adultery At Forty. Donald Hall. **CP-HallD**

Adults Only. William Stafford. **SP-StafW**

Advance and take your place. Greeting for Old Age. William Carlos Williams. **CP-WilW2**

Advance—come forth from the Tyrolean ground. William Wordsworth. **CP-WorW1**

Advance is Life's condition. Emily Dickinson. **CP-DickE**

Advance your choral [*or* chorall] motions now. The Stars Dance. Thomas Campion. **OBSC** *Fr.* The Lords Mask[e].

Advanced out toward the external from. Celestial Evening, October 1967. Charles Olson. **SP-OlsoC** *Fr.* The Maximus Poems.

Advancing with a self-denying gaze, he. The Mechanist. Richard Wilbur. **CP-WilbR**

Advantage, The. Charles Olson. **CP-OlsoC**

Advantages of Learning, The. Martial, *tr. fr. Latin by* Kenneth Rexroth. **SP-RexrK**

Advent. Wystan Hugh Auden. *Fr.* For the Time Being; a Christmas Oratorio. **CP-AudeW**

  "If, on account of the political situation." **LiTA; WaP**

Advent. Donald Davie. **CP-DavDo**

Advent. Thomas Merton. **CP-MertT; SP-MertT**

Advent. Christina Georgina Rossetti. **CP-RosC1**

Advent. Christina Georgina Rossetti. **CP-RosC2**

Advent. Christina Georgina Rossetti. **CP-RosC3**

Advent. James Schuyler. **CP-SchuJ**

Advent of Summer. Robert Ranke Graves. **CP-GravR**

Advent of Today. William Carlos Williams. **CP-WilW1**

Advent Sunday. Christina Georgina Rossetti. **CP-RosC2**

Adventure, The. Frederick Morgan. **SP-MorgF**

Adventure of Giomar: Castilian footbsll / Minding doctrines. Thomas Merton. *Fr.* Cables to the Ace. **CP-MertT**

Adventures, Midnight. Muriel Rukeyser. *Fr.* Night-Music. **CP-RukeM**

Adverse and prosperous Fortunes both work on. All Things Run Well for the Righteous. Robert Herrick. **CP-HerrR**

Adversity ("Love is maintain'd by wealth; when all is spent"). Robert Herrick. **CP-HerrR**

Adversity ("Adversity hurts none, but onely such"). Robert Herrick. **CP-HerrR**

Advertisement, The, *parody of early English aliterative verse.* Rudyard Kipling. **CP-KiplR** *Fr.* The Muse among the Motors.

Adverts. James Schuyler. **CP-SchuJ**

Advice. Paul Laurence Dunbar. **CP-DunbP**

Advice. Langston Hughes. **SP-HughL**

Advice. Ted Kooser. **SP-KoosT**

Advice, The. Sir Walter Ralegh. **CP-RaleW**

Advice for Geraldine on Her Miscellaneous Birthday. "Bob Dylan." **CP-DylaB**

Advice from a Mother. Robert Ranke Graves. **CP-GravR**

Advice from the Holy Tomb. Howard Nemerov. **CP-NemeH**

Advice from the Muse. Richard Wilbur. **CP-WilbR**

Advice of the Popes Who Succeeded the Age of Rafael. William Blake. **CP-BlakW**

Advice outside a Church. Ogden Nash. **CP-NashO**

Advice the Best Actor. Robert Herrick. **CP-HerrR**

Advice to a Beauty. Countee Cullen. **CP-CullC**

Advice to a God. Mona Van Duyn. **SP-VanDM**

Advice to a Maid. Robert Herrick. **CP-HerrR**

Advice to a Parson. Jonathan Swift. **CP-SwifJ**

Advice to a Prophet. Richard Wilbur. **CP-WilbR**

Advice to a Son. Ernest Hemingway. **CP-HemiE**

Advice to a Young Prophet. Thomas Merton. **CP-MertT; SP-MertT**

Advice to My Best Brother, Colonel Francis Lovelace. Richard Lovelace. **CP-LoveR**

Advice to My Son. Peter Meinke. **SP-MeinP**

Advice to Pilgrims. Robinson Jeffers. **CP-JefR3**

Advice to the Grub Street Verse-Writers. Jonathan Swift. **CP-SwifJ**

Advice to the Old. Kay Boyle. **CP-BoylK**

Advice to Young Children. Stevie Smith. **CP-SmitS**

Advise me, draftsman of the drifting sands. Osip Emilevich Mandelstam. *Fr.* Octets. **CP-DavDo**

Advising the Prince. Chuang Tzu, *tr. fr. Chinese by* Thomas Merton. **CP-MertT**

Advocates. Robert Ranke Graves. **CP-GravR**

Adze, The. Wendell Berry. **CP-BerrW**

A.E. Emily Brontë. **NBM** *Fr.* The Two Children. **CP-BronE**

A.E. And R.C. Emily Brontë. *See* The Two Children.

A.E. and R.C. Emily Brontë. *See* The Two Children.

Ae day, as Death, that grusome carl. Lines Addressed to Mr. John Ranken. Robert Burns. **CP-BurnR**

Ae fond kiss, and then we sever. Robert Burns. **CP-BurnR**

(Song: "Ae fond kiss, and then we sever.") **CP-BurnR**

Ae weet forenicht i' the yow-trummle. The Watergaw. "Hugh MacDiarmid." **SP-MacDH**

Aegeus in Prison. Alfonso Cortes, *tr. fr. Spanish by* Thomas Merton. **CP-MertT**

Aegir. Frederick Morgan. **SP-MorgF**

Aegle, beauty and poet, has two little crimes. From the French. Byron. **CP-Byron**

Aeneas at New York. Allen Tate. **CP-TateA**

Aeneas at Washington. Allen Tate. **CP-TateA**

Aeneid [*or* Eneados, *Aeneis*], The. Virgil, *tr. fr. Latin.*

"All breathed in silence, and intensely gazed." **CP-WorW2**

"Amazons with Crescent-formed shield, The." **CP-RaleW**

"Arms, and the Man I sing, the first who bore." **CP-WorW2**

"Ev'n yet his voice from Hell's dread shades we hear." **CP-JohnS**

"For healthful indigence in vain they pray." **CP-JohnS**

"Heaven, the earth, and all the liquid mayne, The." **CP-RaleW**

"Hesperia the Gr[a]ecians call the place." **CP-RaleW**

"In the main[e] sea the i[s]le of Cre[e]te doth lie." **CP-RaleW**

"Now when the Gods had crushed the Asian State." **CP-WorW2**

"Of mortal Justice if thou scorn the rod." **CP-JohnS**

"Queene anone commands the waightie bowle, The." **CP-RaleW**

"She who to lift her heavy eyes had tried." **CP-WorW2**

"Some old Auruncans, I remember well." **CP-RaleW**

"There is a Land which Greekes Hesperia name." **CP-RaleW**

"This scarcely uttered they advance, and straight." **CP-WorW2**

"Thus was Italy mov'd—nor did the chief." **CP-CowpW**

Ænigma, An. Vincent Bourne, *tr. fr. Latin by* William Cowper. **CP-CowpW**

Æolian. Hayden Carruth. **CP-CarHS**

Æolian Harp, The. Herman Melville. **SP-MelvH**

Aequam Memento. Horace. *Fr.* Three Odes of Horace. **CP-MacNL**

Aer. Hayden Carruth. *Fr.* Journey to a Known Place. **CP-CarHL**

Aera perennius? Dissolving dialects. Louis MacNeice. *Fr.* Memoranda to Horace. **CP-MacNL**

Aërial Rock—Whose Solitary Brow. William Wordsworth. **CP-WorW2**

Aerialist. Sylvia Plath. **CP-PlatS**

Aerie. John Updike. **CP-UpdiJ**

Aerolite, The. Thomas Hardy. **CP-HardT**

Aeroplane engines in my head, The. Greetings. Alun Lewis. **CP-LewiA**

Aeschylus' Soliloquy. Robert Browning. **CP-BroR2**

Aesthete's Renunciation. John Hewitt. **CP-HewiJ**

Aesthetic. Charles Tomlinson. **CP-TomlC**

Aesthetic Distance. Miller Williams. **SP-WillM**

Aesthetic Point of View, The. Wystan Hugh Auden. *See* As the poets have mournfully sung.

Aesthetics after War. Richard Eberhart. **CP-EberR**

Instruments.

Propositions.

Pull of Memory, The.

Reality.

Aetatis suae fifty-two. The Progress of Marriage. Jonathan Swift. **CP-SwifJ**

Aeterna Poetae Memoria. Archibald MacLeish. **CP-MacLA**

Æternall love! what 'tis to love thee well. *ad. fr. the Latin.* Richard Crashaw. **CP-CrasR**

Aether. Allen Ginsberg. **CP-GinsA**

Ævo diversi tres et regione poetae. Milton. John Dryden, *tr. fr. English by* Gerard Manley Hopkins. **CP-HopkG**

Afar th' illustrious Exile roams. A Birth-Day Ode. December 31st 1787. Robert Burns. **CP-BurnR**

Affable, bibulous, / corpulent, dull. Capacity. John Updike. **CP-UpdiJ**

Affable Irregular, An. The Road at My Door. William Butler Yeats. **BIrV; CP-YeatW; LiTB; NOBE; PoE** *Fr.* Meditations in Time of Civil War. **CP-YeatW**

Affection is a noble quality. Reflection on Caution. Ogden Nash. **CP-NashO**

Affection is like bread. Emily Dickinson. **SP-DickE**

Affection wants you to know it is here. Emily Dickinson. **SP-DickE**

Affection would his vivid likeness give. R.P.M. John Hewitt. **CP-HewiJ**

Affections lose their object; Time brings forth. Sonnet (To an Octogenarian). William Wordsworth. **CP-WorW2**

Affirmed. Pent by power that holds it fast. Like a Bulwark. Marianne Craig Moore. **CP-MoorM**

Affliction. Robert Herrick. **CP-HerrR**

Affliction (5). George Herbert. **CP-HerbG**

Affliction (4). George Herbert. **CP-HerbG**

Affliction of Margaret—, The. William Wordsworth. **CP-WorW1**

Affliction (1). George Herbert. **CP-HerbG**

Affliction sore long time he bore. Henry Hardiman. Christina Georgina Rossetti. **CP-RosC3**

Affliction (3). George Herbert. **CP-HerbG**

Affliction (2). George Herbert. *See* Kill me not every [*or* ev'ry] day.

Afflictions bring us joy in times to come. Pain[e] Ends in Pleasure. Robert Herrick. **CP-HerrR**

Afflictions of England. William Wordsworth. *Fr.* Ecclesiastical Sonnets. **CP-WorW2**

Afflictions Sanctified by the Word. William Cowper. *Fr.* Olney Hymns. **CP-CowpW**

Afflictions they most profitable are. Persecutions Profitable. Robert Herrick. **CP-HerrR**

Afica. Charles Olson. **CP-OlsoC**

Afloat between lives and stale truths. The Guardian Angel. Stephen Dunn. **SP-DunnS**

Afoot and light-hearted I take to the open road. Song of the Open Road. Walt Whitman. **CP-WhitW**

Afoot and light-hearted I take to the open road. Walt Whitman. **RFM** *Fr.* Song of the Open Road. **CP-WhitW**

Afraid. Al Young. **CP-YounA**

Afraid of the Dark. Shel Silverstein. **SP-SilS2**

Afraid! Of whom am I afraid? Emily Dickinson. **CP-DickE**

Africa. Maya Angelou. **SP-AngeM**

Africa. Langston Hughes. **SP-HughL**

Africa. William Carlos Williams. **CP-WilW1**

Africa is bleeding / from the rape of her light. Words from Babylon. Jim Carroll. **SP-CarrJ**

African Images, Glimpses from a Tiger's Back. Alice Walker. **CP-WalkA**

African Violet. Louis Zukofsky. **CP-ZukLS**

Afro-American Fragment. Langston Hughes. **SP-HughL**

Aften hae I played at the cards and the dice. The Rantin Laddie. Robert Burns. **CP-BurnR**

After. Maya Angelou. **SP-AngeM**

After. Wystan Hugh Auden. **CP-AudWJ**

After. Robert Browning. **CP-BroR1**

After. Frederick Morgan. **SP-MorgF**

After a blatant dawn of red and gold. Skypiece. John Hewitt. **CP-HewiJ**

After a brief unconsciousness. Emily Dickinson. **SP-DickE**

After a Brubeck Concert. Miller Williams. **SP-WillM**

After a crazy winter / when garden flowers went mad. Northern Spring. John Hewitt. **CP-HewiJ**

After a creek. For Louise and Tom Gossett. Archie Randolph Ammons. **SP-AmmoA**

After a Death. Charles Tomlinson. **CP-TomlC**

After a hundred years. Emily Dickinson. **CP-DickE**

After a Journey. Thomas Hardy. **CP-HardT**

After a Killing. Seamus Heaney. *Fr.* Triptych. **SP-HeanS**

After a little I could not have told—. The Song of the Tortured Girl. John Berryman. **CP-BerrJ**

After a long / muggy. Release. Archie Randolph Ammons. **SP-AmmoA**

After a Long Illness. Robert Duncan. **SP-DuncR**

After a long, long course, hundreds of years, denials. Long, Long Hence. Walt Whitman. **CP-WhitW**

After a long walk in the woods clear cut for lumber. Fifty Males Sitting Together. Robert Bly. **SP-BlyR**

After a month and a half without rain. August Rain. Robert Bly. **SP-BlyR**

After a night when sky was lit with fire. After the Fire. John Hewitt. **CP-HewiJ**

After a Romantic Day. Thomas Hardy. **CP-HardT**

After a Sentence in "Malte Laurids Brigge." Adrienne Rich. **CP-RicAE**

After a Stoic, a Peripatetic, a Pythagorean. John Berryman. *Fr.* Eleven Addresses to the Lord. **CP-BerrJ**

After a string of failed romances and intensely remarked sexual adventures she'd finally married. Experience. Charles Kenneth Williams. **SP-WillC**

After a thousand mazes overgone. A Sleeping Youth. John Keats. **SeCePo** *Fr.* Endymion: Poetic Romance. **CP-KeatJ**

After a Train Trip, One Town Remains. Richard Hugo. **CP-HugoR**

After a Visit. Countee Cullen. **CP-CullC**

After a Visit. Paul Laurence Dunbar. **CP-DunbP**

After a week of physical anguish. An Evening Lull. Walt Whitman. **CP-WhitW**

After a while there were no bull fights. What the hell. Ernest Hemingway. **CP-HemiE** *Fr.* The Soul of Spain with McAlmon and Bird the Publishers.

After a while we took in the clothes. Clothes Line. "Bob Dylan." **CP-DylaB**

After Adam broke his rib in two. Rats Live on No Evil Star. Anne Sexton. **CP-SextA**

After All. Robert Pack. **SP-PackR**

After all Birds have been investigated and laid aside. Emily Dickinson. **CP-DickE**

After All Saints' Day. David Herbert Lawrence. **CP-LawrD**

After All the Tragedies Are Over. David Herbert Lawrence. **CP-LawrD**

After all, the vision was like but subtly sea-changed. Malcolm Lowry. *Fr.* Peter Gaunt and the Canals. **CP-LowrM**

After all, there's no need. Flirtation. Rita Dove. **SP-DoveR**

After all, we also stand on a height. Our blood and culture have. Decaying Lambskins. Robinson Jeffers. **CP-JefR2**

After All, What Else Is There to Say? Allen Ginsberg. **CP-GinsA**

After all white horses are in bed. Edward Estlin Cummings. **CP-CummE**

After all you are quite. Margaret Atwood. **SP-AtwM1**

After an Accident. Donald Davie. **CP-DavDo**

After an Interval. Walt Whitman. **CP-WhitW**

After an Old Song. Kenneth Patchen. **SP-PatcK**

After anemones, after almond. Louis MacNeice. *Fr.* Areopagus. **CP-MacNL**

After Apple-picking. Robert Frost. **CP-FrosR**

After, at sea a tall ship did appeare. Petrarch. *Fr.* The Visions of Petrarch. **CP-Spens**

After Auschwitz. Anne Sexton. **CP-SextA**

After Autumne, Winter. Robert Herrick. **CP-HerrR**

After Charles Sedley. Louis Zukofsky. **CP-ZukLS**

After Christmas. Wystan Hugh Auden. *See* Well, so that is that. Now we must dismantle the tree.

After close, uembittered meditation. Deed of Gift. Robert Ranke Graves. **CP-GravR**

After Commencement. Howard Nemerov. **CP-NemeH**

After Communion. Christina Georgina Rossetti. **CP-RosC1**

After comparing lives with you for years. Letter to a Friend about Girls. Philip Larkin. **CP-LarkP**

After Cumae. Geoffrey Hill. **CP-HillG**

After Dark. David Herbert Lawrence. **CP-LawrD**

After dark / Near the South Dakota border. Having Lost My Sons, I Confront the Wreckage of the Moon: Christmas, 1960. James Wright. **CP-WrigJ**

After Dark. Adrienne Rich. **CP-RicAE; SP-RicA1; SP-RicA2**

After Dark Vapours Have Oppressed Our Plains. John Keats. **CP-KeatJ**

After Dead Souls. Allen Ginsberg. **CP-GinsA**

After Death. Christina Georgina Rossetti. **CP-RosC1**

After Death. Algernon Charles Swinburne. **SP-SwinA**

After digging in the rubble of the ruined house. The Princess Casamassima. Daniel Gerard Hoffman. **SP-HoffD**

After Dinner. Robert Burns. *Fr.* Graces————at the Globe Tavern. **CP-BurnR**

    Grace after Dinner. **FaBoEE**

    "L—d, we [thee] thank an' thee adore."

After-Dinner Remarks. Philip Larkin. **CP-LarkP**

After Drinking All Night with a Friend, We Go Out in a Boat at Dawn to See Who Can Write the Best Poem. Robert Bly. **SP-BlyR**

After Dunkirk. Alun Lewis. **CP-LewiA**

After each rain the workers. Wehlener Sonnenuhr Auslese 1959. William Matthews. **SP-MattW**

After Ecclesiastes. Phoebe Hesketh. **SP-HeskP**

After Election. John Greenleaf Whittier. **CP-WhitJ**

After Eli Whitney's gin. Southeast Arkanasia. Maya Angelou. **SP-AngeM**

After Experience Taught Me. . . . William DeWitt Snodgrass. **SP-SnodW**

After explanations and regulations, he. A WASP Woman Visits a Black Junkie in Prison. Etheridge Knight. **SP-KnigE**

After Fever. Jane Cooper. **SP-CoopJ**

After Fifty-five Years. Kathleen Jessie Raine. **SP-RainK**

After 53 years. Some Love. Allen Ginsberg. **CP-GinsA**

After fifty years Amelia Earhart's Lockheed fretted with rust. Persistence of 1937. Donald Hall. **CP-HallD**

After fifty years, nearly, I remember. The King's Horses. John Hewitt. **CP-HewiJ**

After five / times the poem. Edward Estlin Cummings. **CP-CummE**

After Floods on the Wharfe. Andrew Marvell. **FaBoPP** *Fr.* Upon Appleton House [To My Lord Fairfax]. **CP-MarvA**

After-Glow. Edward Estlin Cummings. **CP-CummE**

After God. Daniel Gerard Hoffman. **SP-HoffD**

After great pain, a formal feeling comes. Emily Dickinson. **CP-DickE**

After great storms the calm returns. Sir Thomas Wyatt. **CP-WyatT**

After Greece. James Merrill. **SP-MerrJ**

After Hal'amová. James Liddy. **CP-LiddJ**

After hard rain the eaves repeat their beads. The Walk. Derek Walcott. **CP-WalcD**

After Heraclitus. Margaret Atwood. **SP-AtwM2**

After his long wakeful life. The Freedom of Loving. Wendell Berry. *Fr.* The Handing Down. **CP-BerrW**

After His Realms and States were moved. The King and the Sea. Rudyard Kipling. **CP-KiplR**

After hours under water, a mask. Flying below Sea Level. Laurence Lieberman. **SP-LiebL**

After I am dead, darling. What They Said. Muriel Rukeyser. **CP-RukeM**

After I forgot about the horses. Marching. Charles Simic. **SP-SimiC**

After it was over, though still gusting balefully. Eternity. Hart Crane. **CP-CranH**

After Job had been given back all his possessions. The End of Job. John Gould Fletcher. **SP-FletJ** *Fr.* The Parables of Antichrist.

After Joe Was at the Island. James Schuyler. **CP-SchuJ**

After Jonah. Hart Crane. **CP-CranH**

After Kraske. James Liddy. **CP-LiddJ**

After Labour Day. Malcolm Lowry. **CP-LowrM**

After Lake Leman. Robinson Jeffers. **CP-JefR3**

After Landing—The Valley of Dover, Nover, 1820. William Wordsworth. *Fr.* Memorials of a Tour of the Continent; 1820. **CP-WorW2**

After Leaving Italy. William Wordsworth. *Fr.* Memorials of a Tour in Italy, 1837. **CP-WorW2**

After Leaving Italy, Continued. William Wordsworth. *Fr.* Memorials of a Tour in Italy, 1837. **CP-WorW2**

After "Les Fleurs." Anne Waldman. **SP-WaldA**

After Life. James Liddy. *Fr.* Ossie Esmonde. *Fr.* His Resplendent Neighbours. **CP-LiddJ**

After Long Busyness. Robert Bly. **SP-BlyR**

After Long Silence, *fr.* Words for Music Perhaps. William Butler Yeats. **CP-YeatW**

After long trouble in a taedious way. Louis MacNeice. **KTR** *Fr.* Dark Age Glosses. **CP-MacNL**

After long trouble in a taedious way. Sonnet 31. Mary Sidney, Countess of Montgomery Wroth. **KTR** *Fr.* Pamphilia to Amphilanthus. **CP-WrotM**

After long wars when comes release. Herba Santa. Herman Melville. **SP-MelvH**

After looking at the enlarged photographs. Cultra Manor: The Ulster Folk Museum. John Hewitt. **CP-HewiJ**

After Lorca. Robert Creeley. **CP-CreeR**

After Losses. Stephen Dunn. **SP-DunnS**

After lunch take the half-destroyed bodies and put them to bed. Switzerland. Robert Penn Warren. **SP-WarrR**

After Making Love We Hear Footsteps. Galway Kinnell. **SP-KinnG**

After Mallarmé. Robert Creeley. **CP-CreeR**

After many battles / The good angel killed the bad one. Song of Purification. Carlos Drummond de Andrade, *tr. fr. Portuguese by* Thomas Merton. **CP-MertT**

After Many Days. Paul Laurence Dunbar. **CP-DunbP**

After Many Days. David Herbert Lawrence. **CP-LawrD**

After many scorns [*or* scornes] like these. What He[e] Suffered. Ben Jonson. *Fr.* A Celebration of Charis in Ten Lyric[k] Pieces [*or* Peeces]. **CP-JonsB**

After many strange thoughts, thoughts. After Working. Robert Bly. **SP-BlyR**

After Margrave died, nothing. History of a Literary Movement. Howard Nemerov. **CP-NemeH**

After Melville. Muriel Rukeyser. **CP-RukeM**

After Midnight. Brendan Galvin. **SP-GalvB**

After Midnight. Derek Mahon. *Fr.* Four Walks in the Country Near Saint-Brieuc. **SP-MahoD**

After midnight, and my sister Lizzie. Mona Van Duyn. **SP-VanDM**

After midnight, in the dark / The clock strikes one. Praying Always. Christina Georgina Rossetti. **CP-RosC2**

After Moving. John Yau. **SP-YauJo**

After my classes at the Faculté. At the Roman Wall, 1956. Daniel Gerard Hoffman. **SP-HoffD**

After My Grandmother's Funeral. Ted Kooser. **SP-KoosT**

After my marriage, I found myself in constant. 1930's. Robert Lowell. **SP-LoweR**

After New York—May Seventeenth. Kay Boyle. *Fr.* Two Poems for a Poet. **CP-BoylK**

After Night Flight Son Reaches Bedside of Already Unconscious Father, Whose Right Hand Lifts in a Spasmodic Gesture, as Though Trying to Make Contact: 1955. Robert Penn Warren. **NOBA; Prf** *Fr.* Mortmain. **SP-WarrR**

(After Night Flight.) **DiL**

After one first green step ahead. W. D. Creates a Device for Escaping. William DeWitt Snodgrass. **SP-SnodW**

After our death, when scholars try. Complaint and Reply. Robert Ranke Graves. **CP-GravR**

After our industrial civilisation has broken, and the civilisation of touch has begun. Future War. David Herbert Lawrence. **CP-LawrD**

After overwhelming filth and amazing betrayals Odd Nansen looked at. Shoes of Travel. Carl Sandburg. **CP-SandC**

After Pasternak. Derek Mahon. **SP-MahoD**

After Peire Vidal, & Myself. Ted Berrigan. **SP-BerrT**

After ranging at large in a region. Another. Pablo Neruda, *tr. fr. Spanish by* Ben Belitt. **SP-NeruP**

After reading. Louis Zukofsky. **CP-ZukLS**

After Reading a Child's Guide to Modern Physics. Wystan Hugh Auden. **CP-AudeW**

After Reading "Antony and Cleopatra." Robert Louis Stevenson. **CP-StevR**

After Reading H.D.'s *Hermetic Definitions*. Robert Duncan. **SP-DuncR**

After Reading Keats' Ode. Wystan Hugh Auden. **CP-AudWJ**

After Reading Psalms XXXIX, XL, etc. Thomas Hardy. **CP-HardT**

After Reading *Sonnets* by Rev. Charles Turner (1864) and *The New Day*, Sonnets by Dr T. Gordon Hake (1890). John Hewitt. **CP-HewiJ**

After Reading "The Country of the Pointed Firs." Jean Garrigue. **SP-GarrJ**

After Reading the Sad Story of the Fall of Babylon. Nicholas Vachel Lindsay. **CP-LindV**

After removing the anodized plate, the two electricians discover an. John Yau. **SP-YauJo** *Fr.* Predella.

After returning. Housecleaning. Richard Shelton. *Fr.* Three Poems For A Twenty-Fifth Anniversary. **SP-ShelR**

After Returning from Camden Harbor. Robert Pack. **SP-PackR**

After Rishikesh / the Ganges is still green. The Key of Water. Octavio Paz, *tr. fr. Spanish by* Elizabeth Bishop. **CP-BishE**

After St. John of the Cross. Jim Carroll. **SP-CarrJ**

After scanning its face again and again. John Muir on Mt. Ritter. Gary Snyder. **CP-SnydG** *Fr.* Burning. *Fr.* Myths and Texts.

After Schiller. Thomas Hardy. **CP-HardT**

After School. David Herbert Lawrence. **CP-LawrD**

After screamgroa / ning.ish:ly. Edward Estlin Cummings. **CP-CummE**

After Seeing French Funeral. Edward Estlin Cummings. **CP-CummE**

After seeing the magnificent blue sheep. The Snow Leopard. Stephen Dunn. **SP-DunnS**

After shaking paws with his dog. Terce. Wystan Hugh Auden. **CMoP; PoE** *Fr.* Horae Canonicae. **CP-AudeW**

After so many years, I come walking to you. Conversation with a Holy Woman Not Seen for Many Years. Robert Bly. **SP-BlyR**

After Song, An. William Carlos Williams. **CP-WilW1**

After Sunday Dinner We Uncles Snooze. John Ciardi. **SP-CiarJ**

After surmounting three-score and ten. My 71st Year. Walt Whitman. **CP-WhitW**

After swift blizzard and strong frost. The Turban. John Hewitt. **CP-HewiJ**

After That. Charles Kenneth Williams. **CP-WillC**

After that hot gospeller had levelled all but the churched sky. A City's Death by Fire. Derek Walcott. **CP-WalcD**

After that we'll meet in some Kingdom they forgot. Thomas Merton. *Fr.* Cables to the Ace. **CP-MertT**

After the abrupt collision. Song of the Hen's Head. Margaret Atwood. *Fr.* Songs of the Transformed. **SP-AtwM1**

After the agony in the guest / bedroom, you lying by the. Margaret Atwood. **SP-AtwM1**

After the Argument. Stephen Dunn. **SP-DunnS**

After the Argument. Walt Whitman. **CP-WhitW**

After the argument—argument? battle, war, harrowing; you need shrieks, moans from the pit. Toil. Charles Kenneth Williams. **CP-WillC; SP-WillC**

After the autumn storms, we chose a night. Night Fishers. Charles Tomlinson. **CP-TomlC**

After the ball. James Merrill. **SP-MerrJ**

After the baths and bowel-work, he was dead. Old Relative. Gwendolyn Brooks. *Fr.* Notes from the Childhood and the Girlhood. **SP-BrooG**

After the Blast. Louise McNeill. **SP-McNeL**

After the blast of lightning from the east. The End. Wilfred Owen. **CP-OwenW**

After the Blizzard. James McAuley.

"Air of an old song's in my head, The." **SP-McAuJ**

"Behind a brightening cloud." **SP-McAuJ**

"Not a sound. The house could be." **SP-McAuJ**

After the Bomb Tests. Jane Cooper. **SP-CoopJ**

"Atom bellies like a cauliflower, The."

"Now I have thought the very thoughts of God!"

"Where is the simple myth we used to have?"

After the bronzed, heroic traveller. The Mapmaker on His Art. Howard Nemerov. **CP-NemeH**

After the Burial. Wystan Hugh Auden. **CP-AudWJ**

After the Burial. Thomas Hardy. **CP-HardT**

After the burial-parties leave. The Hyænas [*or* Hyenas]. Rudyard Kipling. **CP-KiplR**

After the Calamitous Convoy (July 1942). Donald Davie. **CP-DavDo**

After the centers' naked files, the basic line. The Lines. Randall Jarrell. **CP-JarrR**

After the Christening. Ogden Nash. **CP-NashO**

After the Club-Dance. Thomas Hardy. *Fr.* At Casterbridge Fair. **CP-HardT**

After the college. What You Need to Be a Writer. Erica Jong. **SP-JongE**

After the Crash. Louis MacNeice. **CP-MacNL**

After the Dazzle of Day. Walt Whitman. **CP-WhitW**

After the Death of a Friend. Thomas Hardy. **CP-HardT**

After the doctor checked to see. First Practice. Gary Gildner. **SP-GildG**

After the door shuts and the footsteps die. A Hunt in the Black Forest. Randall Jarrell. **CP-JarrR**

After the door shuts, and the footsteps die. The Prince. Randall Jarrell. **CP-JarrR**

After the drama. Charles Henri Ford. **SP-FordC** *Fr.* Secret Haiku.

After the Earth Quaked. Kay Boyle. **CP-BoylK**

After the Earthquake. Erica Jong. **SP-JongE**

After the earthquake, a phenomenon of quiet. After the Earth Quaked. Kay Boyle. **CP-BoylK**

After the echo of your flight. Great Owl. Daniel Gerard Hoffman. **SP-HoffD**

After the Fair. Thomas Hardy. **CMoP; HAP; VLP** *Fr.* At Casterbridge Fair. **CP-HardT**

After the feast, my Shapcott, see. Oberon's Palace. Robert Herrick. **CP-HerrR**

After the fiesta, the beauty-contests, the drunken wrestling. Apple Dumps. Ted Hughes. **SP-HughT**

After the fifth beer. Sorry. Leonard Nathan. **SP-NathL**

After the fight at Otterburn. The English Way. Rudyard Kipling. **CP-KiplR**

After the final no there comes a yes. The Well Dressed Man with a Beard. Wallace Stevens. **CP-StevW**

After the Fire. John Hewitt. **CP-HewiJ**

After the Fire. James Merrill. **SP-MerrJ**

After the Fire—The Woman. Tom Clark. **SP-ClarT**

After the first astounding rush. After the Earthquake. Erica Jong. **SP-JongE**

After the first astronauts reached heaven. The Gardener. Stephen Dobyns. **SP-DobyS**

After the first powerful plain manifesto. The Express. Stephen Spender. **CP-SpenS**

After the first terror. Nuclear Winter. Thomas McGrath. **SP-McGrT**

After the flight, the tired body. Elegy for Henry Street. Charles Tomlinson. **CP-TomlC**

After the Flood. Robert Ranke Graves. **CP-GravR**

After the flood or fire or deadly cloud. Premonitory July. John Clellon Holmes. **SP-HolmJ**

After the Flood, We. Margaret Atwood. **SP-AtwM1**

After the Funeral. Dylan Thomas. **CP-ThomD**

After the Funeral: Cleaning Out the Medicine Cabinet. Ted Kooser. **SP-KoosT**

After the great intrusion of Death. Emily Dickinson. **SP-DickE**

After the grimaces of capitulation. Basil Bunting. **CP-BuntB**

After the history has been made. Adolescence. Thom Gunn. **CP-GunnT**

After the hour of illumination, when the tottering mind. Gold and Malachite. Robert Ranke Graves. **CP-GravR**

After the laboring birth, the clean stripped hull. My Father's Death. May Sarton. **SP-SartM**

After the last battle. Hideyoshi. Frederick Morgan. **SP-MorgF**

After the Last Breath. Thomas Hardy. **CP-HardT**

After the Last Bulletins. Richard Wilbur. **CP-WilbR**

After the last cold mountain. Outpost. Muriel Rukeyser. **CP-RukeM**

After the Last Dynasty. Stanley Jasspon Kunitz. **CP-KuniS**

After the last freeze, in easy air. Fighting for Roses. Muriel Rukeyser. **CP-RukeM**

After the last red sunset glimmer. Plowboy. Carl Sandburg. **CP-SandC**

After the lean road looping the narrow river. Up the Dark Valley. Thomas McGrath. **SP-McGrT**

After the leaves have fallen, we return. The Plain Sense of Things. Wallace Stevens. **CP-StevW**

After the legshows and the brandies. Night Club. Louis MacNeice. **FaBoDD; OxBSP** *Fr.* Entered in the Minutes. **CP-MacNL**

After the Levite had seen the robbed man lying on the ground. The Levite and the Samaritan. John Gould Fletcher. **SP-FletJ** *Fr.* The Parables of Antichrist.

After the lights and after the rumba and after the bourbon. A Charm for Cantinflas. Muriel Rukeyser. **CP-RukeM**

After the long snow. Capture. Archie Randolph Ammons. **SP-AmmoA**

After the long strike. Triumphal March. Thomas McGrath. **SP-McGrT**

After the long wake, when many were drunk. Irish Catholic. Richard Eberhart. *Fr.* Attitudes. **CP-EberR**

After the many courses, hot bowls of rice. Photographs of China. Donald Hall. **CP-HallD**

After the Match. Donald Davie. **CP-DavDo**

After the morning of amazing rain. The First Point of Aries. Howard Nemerov. **CP-NemeH**

After the murder. The Last Quatrain of the Ballad of Emmett Till. Gwendolyn Brooks. **SP-BrooG**

After the Night Office—Gethsemani Abbey. Thomas Merton. **CP-MertT; SP-MertT**

After the old gangster said. Law and Order. Leonard Nathan. **SP-NathL**

After the Opera. David Herbert Lawrence. **CP-LawrD**

After the Party. Meng Hao Jan, *tr. fr. Chinese by* William Carlos Williams *with* David Rafael Wang. **CP-WilW2**

After the picture show, the explanation is usually found in. New Year's Eve, 1979. Charles Wright. **SP-WrigC**

After the Pleasure Party. Herman Melville. **SP-MelvH**

After the Quarrel. Paul Laurence Dunbar. **CP-DunbP**

After the quarrel in the house I walked the grasses of the field. After Their Quarrel. Muriel Rukeyser. **CP-RukeM**

After the rapture comes, and everyone goes away. March Journal. Charles Wright. **SP-WrigC**

After the rare arch-poet Jonson died. Upon M. Ben Jo[h]nson: Epigram. Robert Herrick. **CP-HerrR**

After the Reading. Charles Bukowski. **SP-BukC1**

After the red leaf and the gold have gone. A Spell before Winter. Howard Nemerov. **CP-NemeH**

After the Revolution. Marilyn Hacker. **SP-HackM**

After the revolution came the Fuehrer. Traditional Tune. Muriel Rukeyser. **CP-RukeM**

After the Revolution for Jesus a Secular Man Prepares His Final Remarks. Miller Williams. *See* What the blind lost when radio.

After the sack of the City when Rome was sunk to a name. The King's Task. Rudyard Kipling. **CP-KiplR**

After the School's Broadcast. I Remember. John Hewitt. **CP-HewiJ**

After the Sea-Ship. Walt Whitman. **CP-WhitW**

After the Shrink. Alice Walker. **CP-WalkA**

After the songless rose of evening. The Unchanging. Walter de la Mare. **CP-DeLaW**

After the sponge bath. Nimble Rays of Day Bring Oxygen to Her Blood. Tom Clark. **SP-ClarT**

After the Storm. Wystan Hugh Auden. **CP-AudWJ**

After the Storm. Charles Tomlinson. **CP-TomlC**

After the stormy night: / the crack of lightning and. Cornflowers. James Schuyler. **CP-SchuJ**

After the Sun comes out. Emily Dickinson. **CP-DickE**

After the sunlight and the fiery vision. From a Chapter on Literature. Adrienne Rich. **CP-RicAE**

After the sun's eclipse. Teresa. Richard Wilbur. **CP-WilbR**

After the sunset in the mountains. Flat Waters of the West in Kansas. Carl Sandburg. **CP-SandC**

After the Supper and Talk. Walt Whitman. **CP-WhitW**

After the Surprising Conversions. Robert Lowell. **SP-LoweR**

After the sweet promise. The Operation. Anne Sexton. **CP-SextA**

After the swirling snowfall, days of whole. Homage to the North. Richard Eberhart. **CP-EberR**

After the tables and chairs. Explaining the Nature of Evidence. Stephen Dobyns. **SP-DobyS**

After the teach-in. Student Revolution. Erica Jong. **SP-JongE**

After the thaw after. Hayden Carruth. *Fr.* North Winter. **CP-CarHL**

After the third day ash began to shift. Halflives. Daniel Gerard Hoffman. **SP-HoffD**

After the thorns I came to the first page. The Sleeping Beauty: Variation of the Prince. Randall Jarrell. **CP-JarrR**

After the Titanic. Derek Mahon. **SP-MahoD**

After the train meandering through August. After. Wystan Hugh Auden. **CP-AudWJ**

After the tumult and conflagration in the city. The Tribunes. John Hewitt. **CP-HewiJ**

After the twenty thousand year. John Haines. *Fr.* News from the Glacier. **SP-HainJ**

After the vas deferens is cut, the constantly. Vasectomy. William Matthews. **SP-MattW**

After the Visit. Thomas Hardy. **CP-HardT**

After the War. Thomas Hardy. **CP-HardT**

After the War With the Eskimos. Stephen Dobyns. **SP-DobyS**

After the weeks of unrelenting heat. An Ending. Howard Nemerov. **CP-NemeH**

After the whirlwind when all things. The Action of Therapy. May Sarton. **SP-SartM**

After the wind-tempest, when. Sasquatch. Lewis Turco. **SP-TurcL**

After the winter thawed away, I rose. The Assignation. James Wright. **CP-WrigJ**

After Their Quarrel. Muriel Rukeyser. **CP-RukeM**

After thirteen years / nothing is changed except. Widowhood. Phoebe Hesketh. **SP-HeskP**

After Thirty Years. Richard Shelton. **SP-ShelR**

After this encounter the usual residue. Mother and Son. John Hewitt. **CP-HewiJ**

After this life, the wages shall. Wages. Robert Herrick. **CP-HerrR**

After this much time, it's still impossible. The SS man with his stiff hair and his uniform. Spit. Charles Kenneth Williams. **CP-WillC; SP-WillC**

After This the Judgement. Christina Georgina Rossetti. **CP-RosC1**

After those reverend papers, whose soul[e] is. To Sir Henry Wotton, at His Going Ambassador to Venice. John Donne. **CP-DonnJ**

After-Thought, The. Stevie Smith. **CP-SmitS**

After-Thought ("Oh Life! without thy chequered scene"). William Wordsworth. *Fr.* Memorials of a Tour of the Continent; 1820. **CP-WorW2**

After-Thought. William Wordsworth. *See* I thought of Thee, my partner and my guide.

After Thoughts. Allen Ginsberg. **CP-GinsA**

After thrashing in the water of the reservoir. Merlin and the Deer. Thomas Merton. **CP-MertT**

After Three Days. "Lewis Carroll." **CP-CarrL**

After three days dragging. The Cap. Phoebe Hesketh. **SP-HeskP**

After three years of constant courtship. The Gateway. Robert Ranke Graves. **CP-GravR**

After thy labour take thine ease. The Mount of the Muses. Robert Herrick. **CP-HerrR**

After Troy. Hilda Doolittle. **CP-DoolH**

After true sorrow for our sinnes, our strife. Sin and Strife. Robert Herrick. **CP-HerrR**

After Tu Fu (A.D. 713-770). Edwin Rolfe. **CP-RolfE**

After Twenty Years. Adrienne Rich. **SP-RicA2**

After two months, already. Humanly Speaking. Donald Davie. **CP-DavDo**

After two rainy days, a sunny one. Evenings in Vermont. James Schuyler. **CP-SchuJ**

After two sittings, now our Lady State. The Last Instructions to a Painter. Andrew Marvell. **CP-MarvA**

After two sittings, now our Lady State. Andrew Marvell. **APAS; OBSV** *Fr.* The Last Instructions to a Painter. **CP-MarvA**

After uncounted days of drought and flood. The Shortened Day. John Hewitt. **CP-HewiJ**

After venting all my spite. To a Lady. Jonathan Swift. **CP-SwifJ**

After Verlaine. Phoebe Hesketh. **SP-HeskP**

After Visiting Arl at the Hospital. Al Young. **CP-YounA**

After Visiting the Field of Waterloo. William Wordsworth. *Fr.* Memorials of a Tour of the Continent; 1820. **CP-WorW2**

After Wang Chi. Edwin Rolfe. **CP-RolfE**

After we / were all. Days and Days. Robert Creeley. **CP-CreeR**

After we / were all. Here Again. Robert Creeley. **CP-CreeR**

After we had crossed the long illness. Further Arrivals. Margaret Atwood. **SP-AtwM1**

After we had loved each other intently. Listening to the Köln Concert. Robert Bly. **SP-BlyR**

After we saw the wild ducks. To Gary Snyder. Wendell Berry. **CP-BerrW**

After While. Paul Laurence Dunbar. **CP-DunbP**

After Whitman & Reznikoff. Allen Ginsberg. **CP-GinsA**

After/Words. Patti Smith. **SP-SmitP**

After Work. Gary Snyder. **CP-SnydG**

After Working. Robert Bly. **CP-BlyR**

After Working. Roy Fisher. **SP-FishR**

After World War II. Gary Gildner. **SP-GildG**

After years of bickering. Spite Fence. Richard Eberhart. **CP-EberR**

After years smuggling poems. A Poem in Translation. Tess Gallagher. **SP-GallT**

After Yeats. Allen Ginsberg. **CP-GinsA**

After Yeats, After Ronsard, *Pace* Hopkins. James McAuley. **SP-McAuJ**

After Yesterday. Archie Randolph Ammons. **SP-AmmoA**

After You Die You Don't Give a Piddling Damn. Miller Williams. **SP-WillM**

After you finish your work. Ballad of Orange and Grape. Muriel Rukeyser. **CP-RukeM**

After you have spent all the money modistes and manicures and mannikins. Proud and Beautiful. Carl Sandburg. **CP-SandC**

After your pleasant morning travel. A Day's Journey. John Greenleaf Whittier. **CP-WhitJ**

After your poppied hair inaugurates. Edward Estlin Cummings. **CP-CummE**

After you've hit the bars a while. The Walls. Charles Bukowski. **SP-BukC3**

Afterflakes. Robert Frost. **CP-FrosR**

Afterhours. "Lou Reed." **SP-ReedL**

Afterimages. Audre Lorde. **SP-LordA**

Afterlife. Stephen Dunn. **SP-DunnS**

Afterlife, The. Ted Kooser. **SP-KoosT**

Afterlives. Derek Mahon. **SP-MahoD**
"I am going home by sea." **IIP**
"I wake in a dark flat."

Afterlude. Marsden Hartley. *Fr.* Un Recuerdo—Hermano—Hart Crane R.I.P. **CP-HartM**

Aftermath. Henry Wadsworth Longfellow. **SP-LongH**

Aftermath. Louis MacNeice. **CP-MacNL**

Aftermath. Howard Nemerov. **CP-NemeH**

Aftermath. Sylvia Plath. **CP-PlatS**

Aftermath, The. William Carlos Williams. **CP-WilW2**

Afternoon / hundreds of blackbirds, The. Meadow Foam. Leonard Nathan. **SP-NathL**

Afternoon. Charles Olson. **CP-OlsoC**

Afternoon / The Last Lesson, *also stands as sl. diff. separate poem,* Last Lesson of the Afternoon, *and incl. in* The Schoolmaster [B]. David Herbert Lawrence. *Fr.* The Schoolmaster [A]. **CP-LawrD**

Afternoon After, The. Al Young. **CP-YounA**

Afternoon breaks from a pale, The. The Art of a Novel. Marilyn Hacker. **SP-HackM**

Afternoon closed round us like a witch, The. Lyric Evening. Phoebe Hesketh. **SP-HeskP**

Afternoon Evening and Night in the Courtyard of the Museum of Modern Art. William Dickey. **SP-DickW**

Afternoon fills the grey wood, The. In the Wood. Frank Templeton Prince. **CP-PrinF**

Afternoon had opened like a rose, The. For a September Afternoon of Unexpected Brightness. John Hewitt. **CP-HewiJ**

Afternoon in School / The Last Lesson, *also stands as sl. diff. separate poem,* Last Lesson of the Afternoon, *and incl. in* The Schoolmaster [A]. David Herbert Lawrence. *Fr.* The Schoolmaster [B]. **CP-LawrD**

Afternoon lengthens like sunlight. A Wall. Robert Creeley. **CP-CreeR**

Afternoon lies glazed upon the wall, The. Glass Poem. Karl Shapiro. **SP-ShapK**

Afternoon Nocturne. Malcolm Lowry. **CP-LowrM**

Afternoon of a Faun. Stéphane Mallarmé, *tr. fr. French by* Hayden Carruth. **CP-CarHS**

Afternoon of a McGrath. Thomas McGrath. **SP-McGrT**

Afternoon of indecision. Frank! Frank! James Schuyler. *Fr.* Four Poems. **CP-SchuJ**

Afternoon of Summer, An. Jim Morrison. **SP-MorrJ**

Afternoon on a Hill. Edna St. Vincent Millay. **CP-MillE**

Afternoon Seattle. Allen Ginsberg. **CP-GinsA**

Afternoon Service at Mellstock. Thomas Hardy. **CP-HardT**

Afternoon sets red and cold, The. Christmas Eve. Wystan Hugh Auden. **CP-AudWJ**

Afternoon sunlight plays. Kathleen Jessie Raine. **SP-RainK**

Afternoon with André Breton, An. Charles Henri Ford. **SP-FordC**

Afternoon with heavy hours, The. The Traveller. Allen Tate. **CP-TateA**

Afternoons. Tom Clark. **SP-ClarT**

Afternoons. Philip Larkin. **CP-LarkP**

Afterthought, An. Christina Georgina Rossetti. **CP-RosC3**

Afterthoughts. Edwin Arlington Robinson. **CP-RobiE**

Afterwake, The. Adrienne Rich. **CP-RicAE; SP-RicA2**

Afterward. Adrienne Rich. **CP-RicAE; SP-RicA1; SP-RicA2**

Afterward. James Schuyler. **CP-SchuJ**

Afterward. James Schuyler. **CP-SchuJ**

Afterward He Repented, and Went. Christina Georgina Rossetti. **CP-RosC2**

Afterwards. Thomas Hardy. **CP-HardT**

Afterwards, An. Seamus Heaney. **SP-HeanS**

Afterwards, *ad. fr. the French of* Tristan Corbière. Randall Jarrell. **CP-JarrR**

Afterwards. Muriel Rukeyser. **CP-RukeM**

Afterwards. Robert Penn Warren. *Fr.* Fall Comes in Back-Country Vermont. **SP-WarrR**

Afterword. James Liddy. **CP-LiddJ**

Afterword on Rupert Brooke. Frank Templeton Prince. **CP-PrinF**
"To begin with he was undoubtedly in love."
"Two and a half years later the interpreter."
"Way in is to pause and look again, look back, The."
"We cannot disinter the girls of nineteen-eight."
"You go by bushes with dog-roses, through long grass."
"Young question of *What it is for* stays always, The."

Afterword: What the Poet Had Written. Hayden Carruth. *Fr.* North Winter. **CP-CarHL**

Afton Water. Robert Burns. *See* Flow Gently, Sweet Afton.

A.G.A. to A.E. Emily Brontë. **CP-BronE**

A.G.A. to A.S. Emily Brontë. **CP-BronE**

Again. Robert Creeley. **CP-CreeR**

Again. Robert Creeley. **CP-CreeR**

Again, *see also* Poverty and Riches. Robert Herrick. **CP-HerrR**

Again. Howard Nemerov. **CP-NemeH**

Again? Carl Sandburg. **CP-SandC**

Again / the bare brush of. Tree and Sky. William Carlos Williams. **CP-WilW1**

Again / The rivers of the South rise high and crest their green. The Flood Symphony. John Gould Fletcher. **SP-FletJ**

Again / Who am I? Al Young. **CP-YounA** *Fr.* The Song Turning Back into Itself.

Again a verse for sake of you. Ashes of Soldiers: Epigraph. Walt Whitman. **CP-WhitW**

Again, Again. Jean Garrigue. **SP-GarrJ**

Again! Again! Stanley Jasspon Kunitz. **CP-KuniS**

Again, again, I see this form repeated. In Attica. Stephen Spender. **CP-SpenS**

Again & again / I have read your books. To Pablo Neruda. Erica Jong. **SP-JongE**

Again and again. Again lips, again breast, again hand, thigh, loin and bed and bed. With Ignorance. Charles Kenneth Williams. **CP-WillC; SP-WillC**

Again and Again and Again. Anne Sexton. **CP-SextA**

Again and again I make the intolerable journey. The Repeated Journey. Thomas McGrath. **SP-McGrT**

Again at Christmas did we weave. Tennyson. **EBVV; IMW; OAEL-2; PeECV** *Fr.* In Memoriam A. H. H. **CP-TennA**

Again—but other faces bend with mine. At Chinese Checkers. John Berryman. **CP-BerrJ**

Again, great season, sing it through again. Again. Howard Nemerov. **CP-NemeH**

Again he fac'd the battle-field. The Death of Argentine. Sir Walter Scott. **SP-ScotW** *Fr.* The Lord of the Isles.

Again—his voice is at the door. Emily Dickinson. **CP-DickE**

Again I am summoned to the eternal field. First Love. Edwin Rolfe. **CP-RolfE**

Again I come to buy the image fated. The Fitting of the Mask. Stanley Jasspon Kunitz. **CP-KuniS**

Again I hear you piping, for I know the tune so well. The Piper. Robert Louis Stevenson. **CP-StevR**

Again I reply to the triple winds. January. William Carlos Williams. **CP-WilW1**

Again I see my bliss at hand. The Lake. Matthew Arnold. **SP-ArnoM** *Fr.* Switzerland.

Again in conversations. Never Stronger. Wystan Hugh Auden. **CP-AudeW**

Again in space, / elsewhere. Smoke. Robert Creeley. **CP-CreeR**

Again, Kapowsin. Richard Hugo. **CP-HugoR**

Again last night I dreamed the dream called Laundry. The Mad Scene. James Merrill. **SP-MerrJ**

Again? new Tumults in my breast? The First Ode of the Fourth Book of Horace Imitated. Alexander Pope. **CP-PopeA**

Again on dark looms. Hayden Carruth. **CP-CarHS** *Fr.* The Clay Hill Anthology.

Again rejoicing Nature sees. Song. Robert Burns. **CP-BurnR**

Again so I subside / nudged by the softening. Pre-Amphibian. Margaret Atwood. **SP-AtwM1**

Again the last ebb. *Author's own English vers. of his* Dieppe. Samuel Beckett. **CP-BeckS**

Again the native hour lets down the locks. Allen Tate. *Fr.* More Sonnets at Christmas. **CP-TateA**

Again the silent wheels of time. To Miss L———. Robert Burns. **CP-BurnR**

Again the wood, and long-withdrawing vale. To Spring. Charlotte Smith. **CP-SmitC**

Again this morning trembles on the swift stream the image of the sun. Images. Kathleen Jessie Raine. **SP-RainK**

Again to measure with the foe. The Red Coats & the Blue. George Meredith. **CP-MerG2**

Again, traveller, you have come a long way led by that star. Epitaph. Thomas McGrath. **SP-McGrT**

Again we drift back to these mountains, these. In Marin Again. Al Young. **CP-YounA**

Again you / feel the air. Fall. Robert Creeley. **CP-CreeR**

Againe, *see also* Upon Julia's Voice. Robert Herrick. **CP-HerrR**

Againe, / thou witty Cruell Wanton now againe. The Answer. Richard Lovelace. **CP-LoveR**

Against / darkness. Fund Appeal. Grace Paley. **CP-PaleG**

Against a gun-metal sky. The Sycamore. Marianne Craig Moore. **CP-MoorM**

Against a thunderhead's / Blue marble, the eagle. Violent Pastoral. James Merrill. **SP-MerrJ**

Against Absence. Sir John Suckling. **CP-SuckJ**

Against Confidences. Donald Davie. **CP-DavDo**

Against Despair. Christopher Smart. *Fr.* Hymns for the Amusement of Children. **SP-SmarC**

Against Disaster. Theodore Roethke. **CP-RoetT**

Against diseases here the strongest fence. Abstinence. Robert Herrick. **CP-HerrR**

Against Eutropius. Claudian.
   "Over the Medes and light Sabaeans reigns[*or* raignes]." **CP-RaleW, tr.** *by* Sir Walter Ralegh.

Against Extremity. Charles Tomlinson. **CP-TomlC**

Against Fruition ("Fie upon hearts that burn with mutual fire!"). Sir John Suckling. **CP-SuckJ**

Against Fruition ("Stay here, fond youth, and ask no more, be wise"). Sir John Suckling. **CP-SuckJ**

Against Hope. Richard Crashaw. *Fr.* The Mistress.
   (On Hope). **CP-CrasR**

Against Illuminations. Archibald MacLeish. **CP-MacLA**

Against Interested Love. William Cowper. **CP-CowpW**

Against Jealousy [*or* Jealousie]. Ben Jonson. **CP-JonsB**

Against Love. Robert Herrick. **CP-HerrR**

Against my love shall be, as I am now. Sonnet 63. William Shakespeare. **OBSC** *Fr.* Sonnets. **CP-ShaWS**

Against our puny sound and sight. For Helen Keller. Countee Cullen. **CP-CullC**

Against Portraits. Charles Tomlinson. **CP-TomlC**

Against Silence. Marilyn Hacker. **SP-HackM**

Against Slavery. William Cowper. *See* Oh for a lodge in some vast wilderness.

Against Still Life. Margaret Atwood. **SP-AtwM1**

Against that time, if ever that time come. Sonnet 49. William Shakespeare. **OXAEP-1** *Fr.* Sonnets. **CP-ShaWS**

Against the Bermudas we foundered, wherby. The Coiner. Rudyard Kipling. **CP-KiplR**

Against the bright / grass the white-knickered. The Baseball Players. Donald Hall. **CP-HallD**

Against the burly air I strode. Genesis. Geoffrey Hill. **CP-HillG**

Against the clapboards and the window panes. Elegy for Wesley Wells. Donald Hall. **CP-HallD**

Against the False Magicians. Thomas McGrath. **SP-McGrT**

Against the glass. Antique. George Oppen. **CP-OppeG**

Against the Head which Innocence secures. Samuel Johnson. **CP-JohnS** *Fr.* Irene.

Against the Love of Great Ones. Richard Lovelace. **CP-LoveR**

Against the meadow's transparency, / a black bell tower. The Bell Tower of Authenay. Pablo Neruda, *tr. fr. Spanish by* Ben Belitt. **SP-NeruP**

Against the outcrop boulders of a raised beach. The Last Conservative. Robinson Jeffers. **CP-JefR3**

Against the Personality Cult. Jenny Joseph. **SP-JoseJ**

Against the rock I climb, both high and hard. Sir Thomas Wyatt. **CP-WyatT**

Against the rubber tongues of cows and the hoeing hands of men. Thistles. Ted Hughes. **SP-HughT**

Against the Sky. William Carlos Williams. **CP-WilW2**

Against the stone breakwater. The Storm. Theodore Roethke. **CP-RoetT**

Against the sunset's glowing wall. The Wife of Manoah to Her Husband. John Greenleaf Whittier. **CP-WhitJ**

Against the Tricks of Time. Basil Bunting. **CP-BuntB**

Against the unlighted lids of morn. The Inspiration of the Great West Wind. George Meredith. *Fr.* Wandering Willie. **CP-MerG2**

Against the wall he / gropes like ivy, you pray, I. Hayden Carruth. **CP-CarHS** *Fr.* The Clay Hill Anthology.

Against the wall of this sky. Elegy on an Empty Skyscraper. John Gould Fletcher. **SP-FletJ**

Against the War in Vietnam. Wendell Berry. **CP-BerrW**

Against the wooded hills it stands. The Homestead. John Greenleaf Whittier. **CP-WhitJ**

Against Unworthy Praise. William Butler Yeats. **CP-YeatW**

Against Witchcraft. Robert Ranke Graves. **CP-GravR**

Against Women Unconstant [*or* A Ballade against Woman Inconstant]. Geoffrey Chaucer. **CP-ChauG**

Agamemnon in the Fight. Homer, *tr. by* George Meredith. **CP-MerG1** *Fr.* The Iliad.

Agatha Christie and Beatrix Potter. John Updike. **CP-UpdiJ**

Agatha Fry, she made a pie. Helping. Shel Silverstein. **SP-SilS2**

Agave in the West. Donald Davie. **CP-DavDo**

Age. Walter de la Mare. **CP-DeLaW**

Age. Philip Larkin. **CP-LarkP**

Age. Grace Paley. **CP-PaleG**

Age, and the deaths, and the ghosts. He Resigns. John Berryman. **CP-BerrJ**

Age and Youth. John Hewitt. **CP-HewiJ**

Age and Youth. William Shakespeare. *See* Crabbed age and youth cannot live together.

Age Demanded, The. Ernest Hemingway. **CP-HemiE**

Age Demanded, The. Ezra Pound. *Fr.* Mauberly (1920). *Fr.* Hugh Selwyn Mauberley. (Life and Contacts). **SP-PounE**

Age demanded an image, The. Ezra Pound. **HAP; MoAmPo; VGW** *Fr.* Hugh Selwyn Mauberley. (Life and Contacts). **SP-PounE**

Age Gap. Robert Ranke Graves. **CP-GravR**

Age hath been when Earth was proud, An. Ode to Lycoris; May, 1817. William Wordsworth. **CP-WorW2**

Age in Prospect. Robinson Jeffers. **CP-JefR1**

Age is a pale bird, film of ice on the sea. The Vindication of Jovan Babic. Donald Davie. **CP-DavDo**

Age is dull and mean, The. Men creep. For Righteousness' Sake. John Greenleaf Whittier. **CP-WhitJ**

Age is when to a man. Song. Samuel Beckett. **CP-BeckS** *Fr.* Words and Music.

Age of Anxiety, The. Wystan Hugh Auden. **CP-AudeW**

Age of Bronze, The. Byron. **CP-Byron**

"Alas, the country! how shall tongue or pen." **OBSV**

Age of Desire, The. Richard Shelton. *Fr.* The Seven Ages of Man. **SP-ShelR**

Age of Despair, The. Richard Shelton. *Fr.* The Seven Ages of Man. **SP-ShelR**

Age of Elegance, The. Richard Shelton. *Fr.* The Seven Ages of Man. **SP-ShelR**

Age of Miracles, The. Richard Shelton. *Fr.* The Seven Ages of Man. **SP-ShelR**

Age of Pericles, The. Kenneth Patchen. **CP-PatcK**

Age of petty tit-for-tat, An. George Meredith. **CP-MerG2**

Age of Progress, The. Richard Shelton. *Fr.* The Seven Ages of Man. **SP-ShelR**

Age of Romance, The. Richard Shelton. *Fr.* The Seven Ages of Man. **SP-ShelR**

Age of the Antonines, The. Herman Melville. **SP-MelvH**

Age of War, The. Richard Shelton. *Fr.* The Seven Ages of Man. **SP-ShelR**

Age saw two quiet children. Carpe Diem. Robert Frost. **CP-FrosR**

Age shall not daunt me, nor sorrow for youth that is gone. The Strange Spirit. Walter de la Mare. **CP-DeLaW**

Age! twine thy brows with fresh spring flowers. The Matron of Jedborough and Her Husband. William Wordsworth. **CP-WorW1**

Age Unfit for Love. Robert Herrick. **CP-HerrR**

Aged catch their breath, The. Preface. Wystan Hugh Auden. **LiTA** *Fr.* The Sea and the Mirror. **CP-AudeW**

Aged Newspaper Soliloquizes, The. Thomas Hardy. **CP-HardT**

Aged Tamba Temple Plum Tree Song. Gary Snyder. **CP-SnydG**

Aged twenty-odd, I spent. Joycentenary Ode. Derek Mahon. **SP-MahoD**

Ageing House, The. Thomas Hardy. **CP-HardT**

Ageless Reason. Robert Ranke Graves. **CP-GravR**

Agenda. John Hewitt. **CP-HewiJ**

Agent, The. Richard Wilbur. **CP-WilbR**

Agent death assails me now, The. Life and Death. Richard Eberhart. **CP-EberR**

Ages and Ages Returning at Intervals. Walt Whitman. **CP-WhitW**

Ages blaspheme, The. Breughel. Stevie Smith. **CP-SmitS**

Ages of Oath, The. Robert Ranke Graves. **CP-GravR**

Agh—man / thinks. Robert Creeley. **CP-CreeR**

Aging. Randall Jarrell. **CP-JarrJ; SP-JarrR**

Aging. Erica Jong. **SP-JongE**

Aging Actress Sees Herself a Starlet on the Late Show, The. Miller Williams. **SP-WillM**

Aging Female Poet on Laundry Day. Margaret Atwood. **SP-AtwM2**

Aging Female Poet Reads Little Magazines. Margaret Atwood. **SP-AtwM2**

Aging Female Poet Sits on the Balcony. Margaret Atwood. **SP-AtwM2**

Aging pilgrim on a, An. Kenneth Rexroth. **SP-RexrK** *Fr.* On Flower Wreath Hill.

Agitation of the air, An. End of Summer. Stanley Jasspon Kunitz. **CP-KuniS**

Agitations of April in the sky, The. Spring 1967. Hayden Carruth. **CP-CarHS**

Agitato Ma Non Troppo ("I have a grief"). John Crowe Ransom. **OxBA** *Fr.* Sixteen Poems in Eight Pairings. **SP-RansJ**

Agitato Ma Non Troppo ("This is what the man said"). John Crowe Ransom. *Fr.* Sixteen Poems in Eight Pairings. **SP-RansJ**

Agitator. John Hewitt. **CP-HewiJ**

Aglaura. Sir John Suckling. **CP-SuckJ**

Epilogue: "Our play is done; and yours doth now begin."

Epilogue for the Court.

Fifth Act of Aglaura As Presented to the Court, The.

Epilogue: "Plays are like feasts; and every act should be."

Prologue: "'Fore love, a mighty session; and (I fear)."

Prologue to the Court ("'Tis strange, perchance you'll think, that she, that died").

Prologue: "I've thought upon't; and cannot tell which way."

Prologue to the Court ("Those common passions, hopes, and fears, that still").

Song: "No, no, fair heretic[k], it needs must be." **AnAnS-2; BeJo; CABA; CaPo; LoBV; OBS; PrIm**

To the King.

"Why so pale and wan, fond lover?" **AWP; AnAnS-2; BeJo; BoLoP; CABA; CaPo; ClHu; EBEvV; ELP; EnLoPo; EvOK; FPL; FaBV; FaFP; GTBS; GTBS-6; GTBS-P; HAP; HBV; HeIP; HoPM; InPS; JCP; LoBV; MePo; NAEL-1; NBLV; NIP; NOBE; OBEV; OBS; OPOP; OtMeF; OxAEP-1; PAI; PBMP; PlP; PoE; PoEL-3; PoPl; PoRA; PrIm; SeCP; SeCV-1; SeCePo; TEP; TFi; TrGrPo; TreFS; UnPo**

(Encouragements to a Lover.) **FaFP; GTBS; GTBS-6; GTBS-P; PBMP**

(Song: "Why so pale and wan, fond lover?") **AnAnS-2; BeJo; BoLoP; CABA; CaPo; ClHu; EBEvV; EnLoPo; HBV; HeIP; InPS; JCP; LoBV; MePo; NAEL-1; NBLV; NIP; OPOP; OxAEP-1; PAI; PlP; PoEL-3; PoPl; PrIm; SeCP; SeCV-1; TFi**

Agnellina orfanellina. Christina Georgina Rossetti. **CP-RosC3**

Agnostic, The. Edna St. Vincent Millay. **CP-MillE**

Agnostic, An. Stevie Smith. **CP-SmitS**

Agnosto Theo [To an Unknown God]. Thomas Hardy. **CP-HardT**

Agonies confirm His hour. Bahá'u'lláh in the Garden of Ridwan. Robert Earl Hayden. **CP-HaydR**

Agonized Spires, The. William Carlos Williams. **CP-WilW1**

Agony [or Agonie], The. George Herbert. **CP-HerbG**

Agony Among the Crowd, The. Nicolas Calas, *tr. fr. French by* William Carlos Williams. **CP-WilW2**

Agosta the Winged Man and Rasha the Black Dove. Rita Dove. **SP-DoveR**

Agree. David Markson. **CP-MarkD**

Agree we call the place. The She-Bear (II). Charles Olson. **CP-OlsoC**

Agreed: Familiarity breeds. Adult Entertainment. Marilyn Hacker. **SP-HackM**

Agreed that all these birds. All These Birds. Richard Wilbur. **CP-WilbR**

Agricultural Caress. Sir John Betjeman. **CP-BetjJ**

Agrigento, Sicily. John Hewitt. **CP-HewiJ**

Agrigentum Road, The. Salvatore Quasimodo, *tr. fr. Italian by* Richard Wilbur. **CP-WilbR**

Agrippina. Thomas Gray. **CP-GrayT**

Ah. . . . Charles Bukowski. **SP-BukC1**

Ah. Archie Randolph Ammons. **SP-AmmoA**

Ah / Because the world is round, it turns me on. Because. John Lennon *and* Paul McCartney. **CP-Beatl**

Ah / Lovely Rita meter maid. Lovely Rita. The Beatles. **CP-Beatl**

Ah! / Our floating and inconstant life. Phoenix Undying, *sel.* Kuo Mo-jo, *tr. fr. Chinese by* William Carlos Williams *with* David Rafael Wang. **CP-WilW2**

Ah / You say you want a revolution. Revolution. The Beatles. **CP-Beatl**

A.H., 1855–1912. Thomas Hardy. **CP-HardT**

Ah Ah mm / You be good to me; you made me glad when I was blue. Thank You Girl. The Beatles. **CP-Beatl**

Ah, Are You Digging on My Grave? Thomas Hardy. **CP-HardT**

Ah bed, the field where joy's peace some do owe. Sonnet 98. Sir Philip Sidney. **EnLoPo** *Fr.* Astrophil and Stella. **SP-SidnP**

Ah Ben! / Say how, or when. An Ode for Him. Robert Herrick. **CP-HerrR**

Ah Biancha! now I see. To Biancha. Robert Herrick. **CP-HerrR**

Ah, bird, / our love is never spent. Cuckoo Song. Hilda Doolittle. **CP-DoolH**

Ah, broken garden, frost on the melons and on the beans! Thanksgiving Dinner. Edna St. Vincent Millay. **CP-MillE**

Ah, broken is the golden bowl! the spirit flown forever! Lenore. Edgar Allan Poe. **CP-PoeEd**

Ah, Brother, good-day. *Act I, Scene 4.* Molière, *tr. fr. French by* Richard Wilbur. **CP-WilbR**

Ah brother Poet! send me of your shade. William Cowper. **CP-CowpW**

Ah, but a good wife! Late Abed. Archibald MacLeish. **CP-MacLA**

Ah, but—because you were struck blind, could bless. With Gerard de Lairesse. Robert Browning. **CP-BroR2**

Ah, but how each loved each, Marquis! Cristina and Monaldeschi. Robert Browning. **CP-BroR2**

Ah, cannot the curled shoots of the larkspur that you loved so. Spring in the Garden. Edna St. Vincent Millay. **CP-MillE**

Ah cease thy Tears and Sobs, my little Life! To an Infant. Samuel Taylor Coleridge. *Fr.* Effusions. **CP-ColeS**

Ah! changed and cold, how changed and very cold! Dead before Death. Christina Georgina Rossetti. **CP-RosC1**

Ah child, no Persian—perfect art. Horace. *See* 1.38: Simplicity.

Ah, child, thou art but half thy darling mother's. To a Motherless Child. Thomas Hardy. **CP-HardT**

Ah, Chloris, since it may not be. To Chloris. Robert Burns. **CP-BurnR**

Ah, Christ, I love you rings to the wild sky. Allen Tate. PoNe; Son *Fr.* Sonnets at Christmas. **CP-TateA**

Ah, Christ, what a CREW. O, We Are the Outcasts. Charles Bukowski. **SP-BukC2**

Ah, come with me. To an Usherette. John Updike. **CP-UpdiJ**

Ah, could I hide me in my song. Hafiz, *tr. by* Ralph Waldo Emerson. **CP-EmerR** *Fr.* Odes.

Ah, could I lay me down in this long grass. Journey. Edna St. Vincent Millay. **CP-MillE**

Ah could we wake in mercy's name. Song for an Allegorical Play. John Ciardi. **SP-CiarJ**

Ah! County Guy, the hour is nigh. Serenade, A. Sir Walter Scott. **SP-ScotW** *Fr.* Quentin Durward.

Ah, cruell Love! must I endure. To Pansies. Robert Herrick. **CP-HerrR**

Ah! dainty—dainty Death! Emily Dickinson. **SP-DickE**

Ah, did you once see Shelley plain. Memorabilia. Robert Browning. **CP-BroR1**

Ah, Douglass, we have fall'n on evil days. Douglass. Paul Laurence Dunbar. **CP-DunbP**

Ah downward through the dark coulisse. Orfeo. James Merrill. **SP-MerrJ**

Ah, drink again. Lethe. Edna St. Vincent Millay. **CP-MillE**

Ah fading joy, how quickly art thou past! John Dryden. **SP-DrydJ** *Fr.* The Indian Emperor.

(Song: "Ah fading joy, how quickly art thou past!") **SP-DrydJ**

Ah! faint are her limbs, and her footstep is weary. The Drowned Lover. Percy Bysshe Shelley. *Fr.* Poems from St. Irvyne, or, The Rosicrucian. **CP-ShelP**

Ah, Fate! cannot a man. Fame. Ralph Waldo Emerson. **CP-EmerR**

Ah, Faustus,/ Now hast thou but one bare hour [*or* hower] to live. Christopher Marlowe. FaBoVe; HelP; ILwL; PeECV; PoEL-2; TrGrPo *Fr.* Doctor Faustus. **CP-JefR2**

(End of Doctor Faustus, The.) PoEL-2

(End of Faustus, The.) TrGrPo

Ah, Feare! abortive impe of drouping mind. Fear. Robert Southwell. CBCK *Fr.* Saint Peter's Complaint. **CP-SoutR**

Ah for that time when open daylight pours. George Meredith. **CP-MerG2**

Ah, friend! 'tis true—this truth you lovers know—. To Mr. Gay, Congratulating Pope on Finishing His House and Gardens. Alexander Pope. **CP-PopeA**

Ah! gentle, fleeting, wav'ring sprite. Emperor Hadrian. *Fr.* Hadrian's Address to His Soul When Dying.

(Adrian's Address to His Soul When Dying.) **CP-Byron**

Ah, George Bubb Dodington Lord Melcombe,—no. With George Bubb Dodington. Robert Browning. **CP-BroR2**

Ah, God, dear Brother, the mild and frowning rose. Kenneth Patchen. **CP-PatcK**

Ah God, life, law, so many names you keep. Martyr à la Mode. David Herbert Lawrence. **CP-LawrD**

Ah! grasp the dire dagger and couch the fell spear. Song: Translated from the German. Percy Bysshe Shelley. *Fr.* Original Poetry by Victor and Cazire. **CP-ShelP**

—Ah, green Elysia. Drama. Howard Nemerov. **CP-NemeH**

Ah! Hannah, why should'st thou despair. Hope. Christopher Smart. ChIV-1 *Fr.* Hymns for the Amusement of Children. **SP-SmarC**

Ah, happy blindness! Enion sees not the terrors of the uncertain. It Is Not So with Me. William Blake. SeCePo *Fr.* Vala; or The Four Zoas. **CP-BlakW**

Ah, happy, happy boughs! that cannot shed. John Keats. *Fr.* Ode on a Grecian Urn. **CP-KeatJ**

Ah! have you seen a bird of sweetest tone. On the Death of an Unfortunate Lady. William Wordsworth. **CP-WorW1**

Ah heaven, send. No News. David Herbert Lawrence. **CP-LawrD**

Ah, heedless girl! why thus disclose. To a Vain Lady. Byron. **CP-Byron**

Ah! hills belov'd!—where once a happy child. To the South Downs. Charlotte Smith. **CP-SmitC**

Ah, how the human mind wearies her self. John Milton. *See* Nature Does Not Suffer Decay.

Ah, how was I to know that the chink through. Open Your Mouth and Say. Gilbert Sorrentino. **SP-SorrG**

Ah, I have changed, I do not know. A Lost Dream. Paul Laurence Dunbar. **CP-DunbP**

Ah I know how you have sought me. Separated. David Herbert Lawrence. **CP-LawrD**

Ah, in the night, all music haunts me here. The Amaranth. Nicholas Vachel Lindsay. **CP-LindV**

Ah, in the past, towards rare individuals. Desire. David Herbert Lawrence. **CP-LawrD**

Ah in the thunder air. Trees in the Garden. David Herbert Lawrence. **CP-LawrD**

Ah, it's a damn pity that you were put to all the trouble. Portrait of the Artist as an Interior Decorator. Kenneth Patchen. **CP-PatcK**

Ah—it's the skeleton of a lady's sunshade. The Sunshade. Thomas Hardy. **CP-HardT**

Ah Jean Dubuffet. Naphtha. Frank O'Hara. **SP-OharF**

Ah, Joyce, this is our task. "Hugh MacDiarmid." **SP-MacDH** *Fr.* The World of Words.

Ah! Ken Ye What I Met the Day. John Keats. **CP-KeatJ**

Ah, Lenin, you were right. But I'm a poet. "Hugh MacDiarmid." *Fr.* Second Hymn to Lenin.

"Are my poems spoken in the factories and fields." **SP-MacDH**

Ah, let me look, let me watch, let me wait, unhurried, unprompted! Claude to Eustace. Arthur Hugh Clough. EnVR *Fr.* Amours de Voyage. **SP-ClouA**

Ah life, God, Law, whatever name you have. David Herbert Lawrence. *Fr.* Two Fragments on Sleep. **CP-LawrD**

Ah! little Angel, child of bliss! George Meredith. **CP-MerG2**

Ah! little recks the laborer. Song of the Exposition. Walt Whitman. **CP-WhitW**

Ah, look at all the lonely people. Eleanor Rigby. John Lennon *and* Paul McCartney. **CP-Beatl**

Ah Lord, Lord, if my heart were right with Thine. Christina Georgina Rossetti. **CP-RosC2**

Ah, Lord, we all have pierced Thee: wilt Thou be. One of the Soldiers with a Spear Pierced His Side. Christina Georgina Rossetti. **CP-RosC2**

Ah, love, my love is like a cry in the night. Love Song, A. Paul Laurence Dunbar. **CP-DunbP**

Ah *Lucasta*, why so Bright! To Lucasta. Ode Lyrick. Richard Lovelace. **CP-LoveR**

Ah! *Lycidas*, come tell me why. An Eclogue, or Pastorall between Endimion Porter and Lycidas Herrick. Robert Herrick. **CP-HerrR**

Ah, Madam; you've indeed come back here? A Woman's Fancy. Thomas Hardy. **CP-HardT**

Ah, many, many are the dead. Kathleen Jessie Raine. **SP-RainK**

Ah me, it is cold and chill. The Wraith. Paul Laurence Dunbar. **CP-DunbP**

Ah me, that I should be / Exposed and open evermore to Thee! Thou, God, Seest Me. Christina Georgina Rossetti. **CP-RosC2**

Ah me! the little Tyrant Theefe! Loose Saraband, A. Richard Lovelace. **CP-LoveR**

Ah me! the lowliest children of the spring. *see also translations by* Chapman ("Ye mountain valleys. . . ") *and* Shelley ("Ye Dorian woods and waves. . . "). William Wordsworth. **CP-WorW1**

Ah, Memory—that strange deceiver. Memory. Walter de la Mare. **CP-DeLaW**

Ah, Moon—and Star! Emily Dickinson. **CP-DickE**

Ah, more than any priest, O soul, we too believe in God. Walt Whitman. WGRP *Fr.* Passage to India. **CP-WhitW**

Ah, Muriel! David Herbert Lawrence. **CP-LawrD**

Ah my Anthea! must my heart still break? To Anthea. Robert Herrick. **CP-HerrR**

Ah my craft, it is as Homer says. W. Louis Zukofsky. *Fr.* Chloride of Lime and Charcoal. **CP-ZukLS**

Ah, my darling, when over the purple horizon shall loom. Prophet. David Herbert Lawrence. **CP-LawrD**

Ah my dear[e] angry [*or* angrie] Lord. Bitter-Sweet. George Herbert. **CP-HerbG**

Ah, my heart, ah, what aileth thee. Sir Thomas Wyatt. **CP-WyatT**

Ah, my love, my dear! Sighs. David Herbert Lawrence. *Fr.* Bits. **CP-LawrD**

Ah my Perilla! do'st thou grieve to see. To Perilla. Robert Herrick. **CP-HerrR**

Ah, Necromancy Sweet! Emily Dickinson. **CP-DickE**

Ah non chiamarlo pena. Pitia a Damone. Christina Georgina Rossetti. **CP-RosC3**

Ah, Nora, my Nora, the light fades away. Nora: A Serenade. Paul Laurence Dunbar. **CP-DunbP**

Ah! not by Cam or Isis, famous streams. To a Lady. Samuel Taylor Coleridge. **CP-ColeS**

Ah, not this marble, dead and cold. Washington's Monument, February, 1885. Walt Whitman. **CP-WhitW**

Ah! not to me these dreams belong. Ralph Waldo Emerson. **CP-EmerR**

Ah now great brothers, you two centuries past. Sonnet: The Recollected Actual Voices of Romanticism. Hayden Carruth. **CP-CarHS** *Fr.* Sonnets.

Ah nuts! It's boring reading French newspapers. Les Luths. Frank O'Hara. **SP-OharF**

Ah Posthumus! our year[e]s hence fly[e]. His Age, Dedicated to His Peculiar Friend, Master John Wickes, under the Name of Posthumus. Robert Herrick. **CP-HerrR**

Ah! Posthumus, the years, the years. Horace. *See* 2.14: "Ah, Postumus, fleet-footed are the years!"

Ah, Postumus, fleet-footed are the years! 2.14. Horace. **CP-CummE,** *tr. by* E. E. Cummings; *Fr.* Odes.

Ah Poverties, Wincings, and Sulky Retreats. Walt Whitman. **CP-WhitW**

Ah! quit me not yet, for the wind whistles shrill. Revenge. Percy Bysshe Shelley. *Fr.* Original Poetry by Victor and Cazire. **CP-ShelP**

Ah! reign, wherever Man is found. The Triumph of Heavenly Love Desired. Jeanne Marie Bouvier de la Motte-Guyon, *tr. fr. French by* William Cowper. **CP-CowpW**

Ah, Robin, / Jolly Robin. Sir Thomas Wyatt. **CP-WyatT**

Ah said Sipsop, I only wish Jack [*Hunter*] Tearguts had. William Blake. **CP-BlakW** *Fr.* Chapter Six. *Fr.* An Island in the Moon.

"Ah! say," the fair Louisa cried. Song from the French. *Unknown, tr. fr. French by* Charlotte Smith. **CP-SmitC**

Ah *Serenissa*, from our arms. *in imitation of* Waller. Alexander Pope. **CP-PopeA**

Ah, she was music in herself. How a Little Girl Sang. Nicholas Vachel Lindsay. **CP-LindV**

Ah! so very slowly. Away. John Berryman. **CP-BerrJ**

Ah spring, when with a thaw of blue. Louis Zukofsky. **CP-ZukLS**

Ah, stern, cold man. A Man Who Died. David Herbert Lawrence. **CP-LawrD**

Ah, still Lord, ah sweet Divinity. Psalm II: "Ah, still Lord, ah sweet Divinity." Allen Ginsberg. **CP-GinsA**

Ah strange strange strange. Ralph Waldo Emerson. **CP-EmerR**

Ah, Strephon, how can you despise. Louisa to Strephon. Jonathan Swift. *Fr.* Riddles. **CP-SwifJ**

Ah, Sun-Flower [*or* Ah! Sun-Flower]. William Blake. **CP-BlakW** *Fr.* Songs of Experience.

Ah! sweet kiss the moonbeam that sleeps on yon fountain. Song: To———[Harriet]. Percy Bysshe Shelley. *Fr.* Original Poetry by Victor and Cazire. **CP-ShelP**

Ah, sweetheart, what a pool! Broad, deep, strong, silent, and sedate! "Hugh MacDiarmid." **SP-MacDH** *Fr.* The Kind of Poetry I Want.

Ah, Teneriffe! Emily Dickinson. **CP-DickE**

Ah, That I Were Far Away. Arthur Hugh Clough. **OBNC** *Fr.* Amours de Voyage. **SP-ClouA**

(Upon Apennine Slope.) **FaBoPP**

Ah that the world could use a dream or a flaming truth. Red Wine and Yellow Hair. Kenneth Patchen. **CP-PatcK**

Ah, that Time could touch a form. Peace. William Butler Yeats. **CP-YeatW**

Ah, the bird-like fluting. Flute-Music, with an Accompaniment. Robert Browning. **CP-BroR2**

Ah! the divine infatuation. Hart Crane. *Fr.* Three Locutions Des Pierrots. **CP-CranH**

Ah the great / the venerable. Furniture Mover. Charles Simic. **SP-SimiC**

Ah the people, the people! The People. David Herbert Lawrence. **CP-LawrD**

Ah, The Rule. Jim Morrison. **SP-MorrJ**

Ah—There. Tom Clark. **SP-ClarT**

Ah these are the poor. Street. George Oppen. **CP-OppeG**

Ah these sweet Roman mornings. Roman Morn. Lawrence Ferlinghetti. **SP-FerlL**

Ah, they are passing, passing by. In Praise of Songs That Die. Nicholas Vachel Lindsay. **CP-LindV**

Ah, think how one compelled for life to abide. William Wordsworth. *Fr.* Sonnets upon the Punishment of Death. **CP-WorW2**

Ah, thinks the man, that woman walking. The Woman on Edgehill Road. Stephen Dunn. **SP-DunnS**

Ah! think'st thou, Laura, then, that wealth. Stanzas. Charlotte Smith. **CP-SmitC**

Ah this night, this night mortality wails out. Mercy. James Dickey. **CP-DickJ**

Ah! Thomas, wherefore wouldst thou doubt. St. Thomas. Christopher Smart. **ChIV-2** *Fr.* Hymns and Spiritual Songs for the Fasts and Festivals of the Church of England. **SP-SmarC**

Ah, through the open door. Spring Morning. David Herbert Lawrence. **CP-LawrD**

Ah to be alive. For All. Gary Snyder. **CP-SnydG**

Ah, to be set and printed in. Tune, in American Type. John Updike. **CP-UpdiJ**

Ah. . . to the Villages! Thomas McGrath. **SP-McGrT**

Ah, urged too late! from beauty's bondage free. Verses Addressed to Amanda. James Thomson. **CP-ThomJ**

Ah well! ah well! maybe. Maybe. David Herbert Lawrence. **CP-LawrD**

Ah, well, I abandon you, cherrywood smokestack. The Artist. Kenneth Koch. **SP-KochK**

Ah welladay and wherefore am I here? Christina Georgina Rossetti. **CP-RosC3**

Ah, what a dawn of splendour, when her sowers. George Meredith. *Fr.* France. **CP-MerG1**

Ah! What avails the classic bent. The Benfactors. Rudyard Kipling. **CP-KiplR**

Ah, what can be more stately. Walt Whitman. **AA** *Fr.* Crossing Brooklyn Ferry. **CP-WhitW**

Ah, what is love, our love, she said. Arthur Hugh Clough. **SP-ClouA**

Ah, what shall I be at fifty. Tennyson. **NAEL-2** *Fr.* Morning arises stormy and pale. **EBVVPR** *Fr.* Maud [A Monodrama]. **CP-TennA**

Ah, when the Body, round which in love we clung. Other Influences. William Wordsworth. *Fr.* Ecclesiastical Sonnets. **CP-WorW2**

Ah when you drift hover before you kiss. John Berryman. *Fr.* Sonnets to Chris. **CP-BerrJ**

Ah! where is Palafox? Nor tongue nor pen. 1810. William Wordsworth. **CP-WorW1**

Ah! wherefore do the incurious say. Studies by the Sea. Charlotte Smith. **CP-SmitC**

Ah! wherefore should my weeping maid suppress. On Her Endeavoring to Conceal Her Grief at Parting. William Cowper. **CP-CowpW**

Ah! wherefore with infection should he live. Sonnet 67. William Shakespeare. **PeHV; SCGP** *Fr.* Sonnets. **CP-ShaWS**

Ah, whispering, something again, unseen. To the Sun-set Breeze. Walt Whitman. **CP-WhitW**

Ah! whither, Love, wilt thou now carrie mee? An Hymne in Honour of Beautie. Edmund Spenser. *Fr.* Fowre Hymnes. **CP-Spens**

Ah! why, because the dazzling sun. Emily Brontë. **CP-BronE**

(Stars.) **CP-BronE**

Ah why deceive ourselves! by no mere fit. At Bologna, in Remembrance of the Late Insurrections, 1837. William Wordsworth. **CP-WorW2**

Ah! why will Mem'ry with officious care. To Mrs. G. Charlotte Smith. **CP-SmitC**

Ah, wife, here's one new consequence! Recitation before Bed. David Markson. **CP-MarkD**

Ah, Will the Saviour? Stevie Smith. **CP-SmitS**

Ah, with His Blessing Bright on Thy Mouth and Thy Brow. David Herbert Lawrence. **CP-LawrD**

Ah! without the moon, what white nights. Hart Crane. *Fr.* Three Locutions Des Pierrots. **CP-CranH**

Ah woe is me for pleasure that is vain. Vanity of Vanities. Christina Georgina Rossetti. **CP-RosC3**

Ah, woe is me, my Mother dear! Jeremiah 15th Ch. 10 V. Robert Burns. **CP-BurnR**

Ah! woe is me! poor silver-wing! Faery Song. John Keats. **CP-KeatJ**

Ah, woe, woe, woe, man was created to live by the sweat of his brow. Grasshoppers Are Very Intelligent. Ogden Nash. **CP-NashO**

Ah, would swift ships had never been, for then we ne'er had found. V.A.D. (Mediterranean). Rudyard Kipling. *Fr.* Epitaphs of the War [1914–1918]. **CP-KiplR**

Ah wretched they that worship vanities, *ad. fr. Latin of* Sedulius. Sir Walter Ralegh. **CP-RaleW**

Ah yes, I know you well, a sojourner. Lady Wife. David Herbert Lawrence. **CP-LawrD**

Ah yes, men must learn to serve. Service. David Herbert Lawrence. **CP-LawrD**

Ah, yes, 't is sweet still to remember. Ione. Paul Laurence Dunbar. **CP-DunbP**

Ah, yes, the chapter ends to-day. The End of the Chapter. Paul Laurence Dunbar. **CP-DunbP**

Ah (you say), this is Holy Wisdom. Hilda Doolittle. **NALW; NoAM** *Fr.* Tribute to the Angels. **CP-DoolH**

Ah, you stack of white lilies, all white and gold! Lilies in the Fire. David Herbert Lawrence. **CP-LawrD**

Ah, young man! The Jewess and the V.C. David Herbert Lawrence. *Fr.* Bits. **CP-LawrD**

Ahasuerus. Howard Nemerov. **CP-NemeH**

Ahasuerus in his prime. Nicholas Vachel Lindsay. *Fr.* A Rhyme for All Zionists. **CP-LindV**

Ahasuerus Jenkins of the "Operatic Own." Army Headquarters. Rudyard Kipling. **CP-KiplR**

Ahead, starting from the far north, it wanders. Flowering Death. John Ashbery. **SP-AshbJ**

Ahi culla vuota! ed ahi sepolcro pieno. Christina Georgina Rossetti. **CP-RosC3**

Ai me! I love, give him your hand to kisse. To Mistresse Amie Potter. Robert Herrick. **CP-HerrR**

Ai, they all pass in front of me those girls! The Song of the Young Hawaiian. John Berryman. **CP-BerrJ**

Aid, glorious Martyrs, from your fields of light. General View of the Troubles of the Reformation. William Wordsworth. *Fr.* Ecclesiastical Sonnets. **CP-WorW2**

Aigeltinger. William Carlos Williams. **CP-WilW2**

Ailanthus, goldenrod, scrapiron, what makes you flower? Open-Air Museum. Adrienne Rich. **CP-RicAE; SP-RicA2**

Aim Was Song, The. Robert Frost. **CP-FrosR**

Aimée. George Meredith. **CP-MerG2**

Ain' committed no federal crime. Canto 80. Ezra Pound. *Fr.* Cantos. **CP-PoCan**

Ainsi a-t-on beau. Samuel Beckett. **CP-BeckS**

Ain't Gonna Grieve. "Bob Dylan." **CP-DylaB**

Ain't got a reason. The Slave's Critique of Practical Reason. Rita Dove. **SP-DoveR**

Ain't it hard to stumble. Outlaw Blues. "Bob Dylan." **CP-DylaB**

Ain't it just like the night to play tricks when you're tryin' to be so quiet? Visions of Johanna. "Bob Dylan." **CP-DylaB**

Ain't it nice to have a mammy. Scamp. Paul Laurence Dunbar. **CP-DunbP**

Ain't No Cure for Love. Leonard Cohen. **CP-CoheL**

Ain't No Man Righteous, No Not One. "Bob Dylan." **CP-DylaB**

Ain't nobody better's my Daddy. Little Girl Speakings. Maya Angelou. **SP-AngeM**

Ain't nobody nevah tol' you not a wo'd a-tall. Critters' Dance, De. Paul Laurence Dunbar. **CP-DunbP**

Ain't That Bad. Maya Angelou. **SP-AngeM**

Ain't that something? Why, I knowed old Tom. Hayden Carruth. *Fr.* The Sleeping Beauty. **CP-CarHL**

Air, / be / comes / or. Edward Estlin Cummings. **CP-CummE**

Air. Tom Clark. **SP-ClarT**

Air. Alfonso Cortes, *tr. fr. Spanish by* Thomas Merton. **CP-MertT**

Air / in its brightness. Aer. Hayden Carruth. *Fr.* Journey to a Known Place. **CP-CarHL**

Air. Muriel Rukeyser. **CP-RukeM**

Air. Derek Walcott. **CP-WalcD**

Air. Louis Zukofsky. **CP-ZukLS**

Air a-gittin' cool an' coolah. Signs of the Times. Paul Laurence Dunbar. **CP-DunbP**

Air and Fire. Wendell Berry. **CP-BerrW**

Air at evening thickens with a scent, The. Hay. Charles Tomlinson. **CP-TomlC**

Air can still inspire, The. Rural Mailboxes. Brendan Galvin. **SP-GalvB**

Air: "Cat Bird Singing." Robert Creeley. **CP-CreeR**

Air Circus. Carl Sandburg. **CP-SandC**

Air cool and soft, The. The King watches at Night. Frank Templeton Prince. *Fr.* Chaka. **CP-PrinF**

Air darkened toward morning, The. Letters for the Dead. Philip Levine. **SP-LeviP**

Air deals blows, The: surely too hard, too often? Autumn. Philip Larkin. **CP-LarkP**

Air has no Residence, no Neighbor. Emily Dickinson. **CP-DickE**

Air I breathe in, The. Fifth Mile. James McAuley. *Fr.* Ten-Mile Run. **SP-McAuJ**

Air is a mill of hooks, The. Mystic. Sylvia Plath. **CP-PlatS**

Air is bright with hues of light, The. "Lewis Carroll." *Fr.* Four Riddles. **CP-CarrL**

Air is dark, the night is sad, The. Refrain. Allen Ginsberg. **CP-GinsA**

Air is dark, the sky is gray, The. A Drowsy Day. Paul Laurence Dunbar. **CP-DunbP**

Air is full of a farewell—, The. On Leaving Ullswater. Kathleen Jessie Raine. **SP-RainK**

Air is grey-white as a pigeon-feather, The. Foggy Street. Andrei Voznesensky, *tr. fr. Russian by* Richard Wilbur. **CP-WilbR**

Air is soft as Italy, The. Emily Dickinson. **SP-DickE**

Air is sweetest that a thistle guards, The. Variations: The Air Is Sweetest That a Thistle Guards. James Merrill. **SP-MerrJ**

Air lay softly on the green fur, The. Told. Philip Levine. **SP-LeviP**

Air of an old song's in my head, The. James McAuley. **SP-McAuJ** *Fr.* After the Blizzard.

Air of departures. Silences, An. Coda. Jane Cooper. *Fr.* March. **SP-CoopJ**

Air of Diabelli's. Robert Louis Stevenson. **CP-StevR**

Air of heaven sings. For Allen. Robert Creeley. **CP-CreeR**

Air of lateness blows through the redone bedroom, An. Late Summer at *Milgate.* Robert Lowell. **SP-LoweR**

Air of November. Denise Levertov. **CP-LeveD**

Air one breathes with Smith may be the sharper, The. Couplet for Furnivall on Two Publishers. Robert Browning. **CP-BroR2**

Air Plant, The. Hart Crane. **CP-CranH**

Air Raid across the Bay at Plymouth. Stephen Spender. **CP-SpenS**

Air-Raid Rehearsals. Robinson Jeffers. **CP-JefR2**

Air seeps through alleys and our diaphragms. The ABC of Aerobics. Peter Meinke. **SP-MeinP**

Air Show. John Updike. **CP-UpdiJ**

Air staggers under the sun, and heat-morasses, The. Sun and Air. Richard Wilbur. **CP-WilbR**

Air stiffens to a crust, The. The Wound. Louise Glück. **SP-GlücL**

Air swarms with piranhas, The. Bronchitis on the 14th Floor. Marge Piercy. **SP-PierM**

Air: "The Love of a Woman." Robert Creeley. **CP-CreeR**

Air was full of sun and birds, The. Spring Song. Robert Louis Stevenson. **CP-StevR**

Air was soft, the ground still cold, The. April 5, 1974. Richard Wilbur. **CP-WilbR**

Air without Incense. Adrienne Rich. **CP-RicAE**

Air[e] and Angels. John Donne. **CP-DonnJ**

Aircraft. Rita Dove. **SP-DoveR**

Airey-Force Valley. William Wordsworth. **CP-WorW2**

Airily ice congeals on high. Melting. John Updike. **CP-UpdiJ**

Airman. Stephen Spender. *See* He will watch the hawk with an indifferent eye.

Airman Considers His Power, An. Richard Eberhart. **CP-EberR**

Airport. John Updike. **CP-UpdiJ**

Airport bus from JFK. Queens Cemetery, Setting Sun. Lawrence Ferlinghetti. **SP-FerlL**

Airport coffee tastes less of America, The. The Gulf. Derek Walcott. **CP-WalcD**

Airstrip in Essex, 1960, An. Donald Hall. **CP-HallD**

Airy Christ, The. Stevie Smith. **CP-SmitS**

Airy del Castro was as bold a knight. Anti-Thelyphthora. William Cowper. **CP-CowpW**

Aisle in an eastside department store, The. She Sauntered Most Elegantly Down. Marsden Hartley. *Fr.* City Vignettes. **CP-HartM**

Aisling. Paul Muldoon. **SP-MuldP**

Aix-la-Chapelle. William Wordsworth. *Fr.* Memorials of a Tour of the Continent; 1820. **CP-WorW2**

Ajaccio Violets. James Schuyler. **CP-SchuJ**

Ajanta. Muriel Rukeyser. **CP-RukeM**

Akbar's Bridge. Rudyard Kipling. **CP-KiplR**

Akiba. Muriel Rukeyser. **CP-RukeM**

Al Aaraaf. Edgar Allan Poe. **CP-PoeEd**

  Song: "Young flowers were whispering in melody." **NOBA**

  Song: "Neath blue-bell or streamer." **AmPP; AnAmPo; OxBA**

Alabaster. Gary Snyder. **CP-SnydG**

Alabaster gentry, hacked and battered, The. Compton Wynates, Warwickshire. John Hewitt. **CP-HewiJ**

Alack, what poverty my Muse brings forth. Sonnet 103. William Shakespeare. *Fr.* Sonnets. **CP-ShaWS**

Aladdin and the Jinn. Nicholas Vachel Lindsay. **CP-LindV**

Alarm, The. Thomas Hardy. **CP-HardT**

Alarm, The. James Wright. **CP-WrigJ**

Alas, alas! for the self-destroyed / Vanish as images from a glass. Christina Georgina Rossetti. **CP-RosC2**

Alas, Alas, that I am betrayed. Michelangelo Buonarroti, *tr. fr. Italian by* Ralph Waldo Emerson. **CP-EmerR**

Alas, dear heart! what hap [*or* hope] had I. Sir Thomas Wyatt. **CP-WyatT**

Alas, dear mother, fairest queen and best. A Dialogue between Old England and New. Anne Bradstreet. **CP-BradA**

Alas, dear Mother, fairest queen and best. A Dialogue between Old England and New. Anne Bradstreet. **CP-BradA**

Alas for Man, so stealthily betrayed. Edna St. Vincent Millay. *Fr.* Epitaph for the Race of Man. **CP-MillE**

Alas for obstinate doubt: the dread. A Restless Ghost. Robert Ranke Graves. **CP-GravR**

Alas, Fortune, what aileth thee. Sir Thomas Wyatt. **CP-WyatT**

Alas, good friend, what profit can you see. Lines to a Reviewer. Percy Bysshe Shelley. **CP-ShelP**

Alas, have I not pain enough, my friend. Sonnet 14. Sir Philip Sidney. **NoP; NoSic; OAEL-1** *Fr.* Astrophil and Stella. **SP-SidnP**

Alas, his mind is sunk. Boethius, *tr. fr. Latin.* **MLL,** *tr. by* Helen Waddell; *Fr.* Consolation of Philosophy, The ("De Consolacione Philosophie"). **CP-ChauG**

("Heu Quam Praecipih Mersa Profundo.") **MLL,** *tr. by* Helen Waddell;

Alas, how pleasant are their days. The Unfortunate Lover. Andrew Marvell. **CP-MarvA**

Alas how the wandering mind of man grows weak, driven. Nature Does Not Suffer Decay. John Milton, *tr. fr. Latin by* John T. Shawcross. **CP-MiltJ**

Alas I can't, for tell me how. To his Girles who Would Have Him Sportfull. Robert Herrick. **CP-HerrR**

Alas, it is too late! I can no more. Perjury Excused. Sir John Suckling. **CP-SuckJ**

Alas, madam[e], for stealing [or stelying] of a kiss [or kysse]. Sir Thomas Wyatt. **CP-WyatT**

Alas! my dear, the word thou spakest. Sir Thomas Wyatt. **CP-WyatT**

Alas my Lord, / How should I wrestle all the livelong night. Christina Georgina Rossetti. **CP-RosC3**

Alas, my poor young men. Vitality. David Herbert Lawrence. **CP-LawrD**

Alas, O Lovely One, / Imprisoned here. The Monologue. Walter de la Mare. **CP-DeLaW**

Alas! our Day is forc'd to flye by nighte! The Flight into Egipt. Robert Southwell. **CP-SoutR**

Alas, poor Death, where is thy glory? A Dialogue-Anthem. George Herbert. **CP-HerbG**

Alas, poor man, what hap have I. Sir Thomas Wyatt. **CP-WyatT**

Alas! she would not hear my prayer! Photography Extraordinary. "Lewis Carroll." **CP-CarrL**

Alas, slain is the head of Israel. David's Lamentation for Saul and Jonathan. Anne Bradstreet. **CP-BradA**

Alas, that I ne had English, rhyme or prose. Geoffrey Chaucer. **EPCY** *Fr.* The Legend of Good Women. **CP-ChauG**

Alas, the country! how shall tongue or pen. Byron. **OBSV** *Fr.* The Age of Bronze. **CP-Byron**

Alas, the grief and deadly wo[e]ful smart[!]. Sir Thomas Wyatt. **CP-WyatT**

Alas, the ignorance of unhappy men. Boethius, *tr. fr. Latin.* **MLL,** *tr. by* Helen Waddell; *Fr.* Consolation of Philosophy, The ("De Consolacione Philosophie"). **CP-ChauG**

Alas, there is no still path in my soul. Malcolm Lowry. **CP-LowrM**

Alas! they had been friends in youth. The Scars Remaining. Samuel Taylor Coleridge. **OBNC** *Fr.* Christabel. **CP-ColeS**

Alas! this is not what I thought life was. Fragment. Percy Bysshe Shelley. **CP-ShelP**

Alas! till now I had not known. Hafiz, *tr. by* Ralph Waldo Emerson. **CP-EmerR** *Fr.* Odes.

Alas, 'tis true I have gone here and there. Sonnet 110. William Shakespeare. **EBEV; NoSic; OAEP; OBSC; OXAEP-1; PeHV** *Fr.* Sonnets. **CP-ShaWS**

Alas! what boots the long laborious quest. William Wordsworth. **CP-WorW1**

Alas, when he laughs, it is not he. Helmut. Stephen Spender. **CP-SpenS**

Alas, whence came this change of looks? If I. Sonnet 86. Sir Philip Sidney. *Fr.* Astrophil and Stella. **SP-SidnP**

Alas, young man! your days can ne'er be long. Alexander Pope. **EPCY** *Fr.* The First Satire of the Second Book of Horace [Imitated]. **CP-PopeA**

Alass, dear Friend, the fleeting years. 2.14. Horace. **CP-JohnS,** *tr. by* Samuel Johnson; *Fr.* Odes.

Alastor; or, The Spirit of Solitude. Percy Bysshe Shelley. **CP-ShelP**

"As an eagle grasped." **ChER**

Invocation: "Earth, ocean, air, belovèd brotherhood!" **FiP; NAEL-2**

"Startled by his own thoughts, he looked around." **OxBoS**

"There was a poet whose untimely tomb." **FHYEP; TOF**

"Wildly he wandered on." **TOF**

Alatus. Richard Wilbur. **CP-WilbR**

Alba. Samuel Beckett. **CP-BeckS**

Alba. Robert Creeley. **CP-CreeR**

Alba, The. Charles Olson. **CP-OlsoC**

Alba. Al Young. **CP-YounA**

Alba ("As cool as the pale wet leaves"). Ezra Pound. **SP-PounE**

Alba (1952). Louis Zukofsky. **CP-ZukLS**

Alba ("When the nightingale to his mate"). Ezra Pound. **SP-PounE** *Fr.* Langue d'Oc.

Albany throned in snow! It's winter, Poe. To Poe: Over the Planet, Air Albany–Baltimore. Allen Ginsberg. **CP-GinsA**

Albatross. Martin Edmunds. **SP-EdmuM**

Albeit you're a set book these days oh Keats. More Impatience. Malcolm Lowry. **CP-LowrM**

Albert! / Hey, Albert! Baby. Langston Hughes. **SP-HughL**

Albert Einstein (1879–1955). Siv Cedering Fox. *Fr.* Letters from the Astronomers. **SP-CedeS**

Albert Einstein to Archibald MacLeish. Delmore Schwartz. **SP-SchwD**

Albert Ryder—Moonlightist. Marsden Hartley. **CP-HartM**

Albigenses, The. Robert Duncan. **SP-DuncR**

Albina. Chuck Miller. **SP-MillC**

Albion and Albanius. John Dryden.

Song of the River Thames, A. **SP-DrydJ**

Album Verses. John Greenleaf Whittier. **CP-WhitJ**

Albuquerque. Charles Tomlinson. **CP-TomlC**

Alcaeus to Sappho. William Wordsworth. **CP-WorW1**

Alcaics. Arthur Hugh Clough. **SP-ClouA**

Alcestis. Euripides, *tr. fr. Greek.*

"In heaven-high musings and many." **CP-HousA**

Alcestis on the Poetry Circuit. Erica Jong. **SP-JongE**

Alchemist, The. Louise Bogan. **CP-BogaL**

Alchemist in the City, The. Gerard Manley Hopkins. **CP-HopkG**

Alcohol. Louis MacNeice. **CP-MacNL**

Alcoholic. Malcolm Lowry. **CP-LowrM**

Alcona, in its changing hour. Emily Brontë. **CP-BronE**

Alder Stick, The. John Hewitt. **CP-HewiJ**

Aldershot Crematorium. Sir John Betjeman. **CP-BetjJ**

Alec. John Ciardi. **SP-CiarJ**

Alert Pillow. . . , The. Hart Crane. **CP-CranH**

Alex. Mary Oliver. **SP-OlivM**

Alexander. Walter de la Mare. **CP-DeLaW**

Alexander. Robert Lowell. **SP-LoweR**

Alexander. Frederick Morgan. **SP-MorgF**

Alexander Campbell. Nicholas Vachel Lindsay. **CP-LindV**

My Fathers Came from Kentucky. **AmFN; HBMV**

Rhymed Address to All Renegade Campbellites, Exhorting Them to Return, A.

"As I built cob-houses with small cousins on the floor."

"I walk the forest by the Daniel Boone trail."

"Like the woods of old Kentucky."

"O prodigal son, O recreant daughter."

Written in a Year When Many of My People Died.

Alexander Crummel—Dead. Paul Laurence Dunbar. **CP-DunbP**

Alexander cut the knot. Alexander. Frederick Morgan. **SP-MorgF**

Alexander Selkirk. William Cowper. **CP-CowpW**

Alexander's Feast; or, The Power of Music [or Musique]. John Dryden. **SP-DrydJ**

Alexias, *ad. fr. the Latin* Uxoris Sancti Alexii Querimoniae. Richard Crashaw. **CP-CrasR**

Alexis! ah Alexis! can it be. Amyntor from beyond the Sea to Alexis. Richard Lovelace. **CP-LoveR**

Alfenus from Cremona / forsakes the friendship of friends. Carmen 30. Catullus. *Fr.* Carmina. **CP-Catul**

Alfenus, remember *kind intimacies*? false? They elated us. Catullus. *See* Carmen 30: "Alfenus from Cremona / forsakes the friendship of friends."

Alfenus Varus / buttonholes me. Carmen 10. Catullus. *Fr.* Carmina. **CP-Catul**

Alfred. William Wordsworth. *Fr.* Ecclesiastical Sonnets. **CP-WorW2**

Alfred: A Masque. James Thomson *and* David Mallet.

Contentment. **CP-ThomJ**

"From Those Eternal Regions." **CP-ThomJ**

Rule, Britannia! **CP-ThomJ**

"Sweet Valley, Say." **CP-ThomJ**

To Alfred. **CP-ThomJ**

To Peace. **CP-ThomJ**

Alfred Corning Clark. Robert Lowell. **SP-LoweR**

Alfred the Great. Stevie Smith. **CP-SmitS**

Alfred, this couple here. A Liverpool Epistle. Donald Davie. **CP-DavDo**

Algeria. Hayden Carruth. **CP-CarHS**

Alget honos frondum silvis dependitus, alget. Gerard Manley Hopkins. *Fr.* Elegiacs. **CP-HopkG**

Alhough from then / Steep stands of beech and sugar-maple stem. Fern-Beds in Hampshire County. Richard Wilbur. **CP-WilbR**

Alias to a wand the height lowered. Atque in Perpetuum A.W. Louis Zukofsky. **CP-ZukLS**

Alicante Lullaby. Sylvia Plath. **CP-PlatS**

Alice. Robert Creeley. **CP-CreeR**

Alice. Paul Laurence Dunbar. **CP-DunbP**

Alice. Robert Ranke Graves. **CP-GravR**

Alice. Shel Silverstein. **SP-SilS2**

Alice Corbin Is Gone. Carl Sandburg. **CP-SandC**

Alice, dear, what ails you. A Frosty Night. Robert Ranke Graves. **CP-GravR**

Alice Du Clos. Samuel Taylor Coleridge. **CP-ColeS**

Alice Faye at Ruby Foo's. James Schuyler. **CP-SchuJ**

Alice Fell; or, Poverty. William Wordsworth. **CP-WorW1**

Alice grown lazy, mammoth but not fat. Last Days of Alice. Allen Tate. **CP-TateA**

Alice Miriam. Marsden Hartley. **CP-HartM**

Alice Ordered Me to be Made. Alice Notley. **SP-NotlA**

Alice's Adventures in Wonderland. "Lewis Carroll."

  Alice's Recitation. **CP-CarrL**

  "Beautiful Soup, so rich and green." **CP-CarrL**

  (Turtle Soup.) **CP-CarrL**

  Christmas Greetings. **CP-CarrL**

  Dedication: "All in the golden afternoon." **CP-CarrL**

  Evidence Read at the Trial of the Knave of Hearts. **CP-CarrL**

  Father William. **CP-CarrL**

  " 'You are old,' said the youth, "and your jaws are too weak."" **OxBM**

  "Fury said to a / mouse, That he." **CP-CarrL**

  (Mouse's Tale, The.) **CP-CarrL**

  "How doth the little crocodile." **CP-CarrL**

  "Speak roughly to your little boy." **CP-CarrL**

  (Duchess's Lullaby, The.) **CP-CarrL**

  "Twinkle, twinkle, little bat!" **CP-CarrL**

  (Mad Hatter's Song, The.) **CP-CarrL**

  " 'Will you walk a little faster?' said a [or the] whiting to a [or the] snail." **CP-CarrL**

  (Mock Turtle's Song, The.) **CP-CarrL**

Alice's Recitation. "Lewis Carroll." **CP-CarrL** *Fr.* Alice's Adventures in Wonderland.

Alien Harvest. John Hewitt. **CP-HewiJ**

Aliens, The. Wystan Hugh Auden. **CP-AudeW**

Alighting from my horse to drink with you. William Carlos Williams, *with* David Rafael Wang, *at. to* Wang Wei, *tr. fr. Chinese.* **CP-WilW2**

Alike and Unlike. Thomas Hardy. **CP-HardT**

Alioth. Siv Cedering Fox. *Fr.* Seven Letters to Zakarias. **SP-CedeS**

Alive. Hayden Carruth. **CP-CarHS**

"Alive?"—And I leapt in my wonder. My Cicely. Thomas Hardy. **CP-HardT**

Alive for an Instant. Kenneth Koch. **SP-KochK**

Alive in the World. John Haines. **SP-HainJ**

Alivia sus fatigas. Translations from the Spanish. William Carlos Williams. **CP-WilW1**

Alix. Carl Sandburg. **CP-SandC**

Alkaid. Siv Cedering Fox. *Fr.* Seven Letters to Zakarias. **SP-CedeS**

Alki Beach. Richard Hugo. **CP-HugoR**

Alkor/Mizar. Siv Cedering Fox. *Fr.* Seven Letters to Zakarias. **SP-CedeS**

All after pleasures as I rid one day. Christmas. George Herbert. **CP-HerbG**

All afternoon / the tree shadows, accelerating. Recovery. Archie Randolph Ammons. **SP-AmmoA**

All Afternoon. Charles Tomlinson. **CP-TomlC**

All afternoon cutting bramble blackberries off a tottering brown fence. A Strange New Cottage in Berkeley. Allen Ginsberg. **CP-GinsA**

All afternoon it rained, then. Rain. Mary Oliver. **SP-OlivM**

All afternoon the gramophone. Search for Sound Free from Motion. Wallace Stevens. **CP-StevW**

All All and All the Dry Worlds Lever. Dylan Thomas. **CP-ThomD**

All, All Are Gone, the Old Familiar Quotations. Ogden Nash. **CP-NashO**

All, all of a piece throughout. All, All of a Piece Throughout. John Dryden. **ChTr; CoGr; ELP; ELU; HAP; ImPo; InPS; OxBSP; WeW** *Fr.* The Secular Masque. **SP-DrydJ**

All, All of a Piece Throughout. John Dryden. **ChTr; CoGr; ELP; ELU; HAP; ImPo; InPS** *Fr.* The Secular Masque. **SP-DrydJ**

  (Chorus to the Gods.) **OxBSP**

  (Song: "All, all of a piece throughout.") **WeW**

All alone from his dark sanctum the lingam fronts, affronts the sea. Mahabalipuram. Louis MacNeice. **CP-MacNL**

All along certainly it's been there, waiting before us, waiting to receive us, not to waver. The Past. Charles Kenneth Williams. **SP-WillC**

All along the valley, stream that flashest white. In the Valley of Cauteretz. Tennyson. **CP-TennA**

All Along the Watchtower. "Bob Dylan." **CP-DylaB**

All are but parts of one stupendous whole. Alexander Pope. **FHYEP; WGRP** *Fr.* An Essay on Man. **CP-PopeA**

All are indebted much to thee. Gratitude and Love to God. Jeanne Marie Bouvier de la Motte-Guyon, *tr. fr. French by* William Cowper. **CP-CowpW**

All are limitory, but each has her own. Old People's Home. Wystan Hugh Auden. **CP-AudeW**

All are not ill Plots, that doe sometimes faile. Plots Not Still Prosperous. Robert Herrick. **CP-HerrR**

All are not taken; there are left behind. Consolation. Elizabeth Barrett Browning. **CP-BroEB**

All armies are the same. Ernest Hemingway. **CP-HemiE**

All around / the snow / don't fall. Xmas Poem: Bolinas. Robert Creeley. **CP-CreeR**

All around / the town. Robert Creeley. **CP-CreeR**

All around us things hold together. Keeping the Faith. Leonard Nathan. **SP-NathL**

All as that moth call'd Underwing, alighted. Gerard Manley Hopkins. **CP-HopkG**

All at once I saw them. The Gymnasts. Phoebe Hesketh. **SP-HeskP**

All at once remembering the copses and hills. Unwanted 1943 Chappaqua Flashback. John Clellon Holmes. **SP-HolmJ**

All at Sea. Ezra Pound. **FaBoDD** *Fr.* Canto 12: "And we sit here / under the wall." **NAs** *Fr.* Cantos. **CP-PoCan**

All bags parked / and shelved in our snug bungalow. Swimming Pool Pastoral. Laurence Lieberman. **SP-LiebL**

All beauty, resonance, integrity. Le Livre Est sur la Table. John Ashbery. **SP-AshbJ**

All beginnings start right here. The Move Continuing. Al Young. **CP-YounA**

All beneath the sun hasteth, / All that hath begun wasteth. Christina Georgina Rossetti. **CP-RosC2**

All Bibles or sacred codes have been the causes of the following Errors:. William Blake. *See* The Voice of the Devil.

All Bibles or sacred codes. have been the causes of the following Errors. The Voice of the Devil. William Blake. **NU** *Fr.* The Marriage of Heaven and Hell. **CP-BlakW**

All blue and bright, in glorious light. On the Fall of Zalona. Emily Brontë. **CP-BronE**

All bodies have their yearnings for true evil. True Evil. Robert Ranke Graves. **CP-GravR**

All Bread. Margaret Atwood. **SP-AtwM2**

All breathed in silence, and intensely gazed. Virgil, *tr. by* William Wordsworth. **CP-WorW2** *Fr.* The Aeneid [*or* Eneados, *Aeneis*].

All bubbles travelling. Spring-Shock. James Dickey. **CP-DickJ**

All but Death can be Adjusted. Emily Dickinson. **CP-DickE**

All Catches Alight. Philip Larkin. **CP-LarkP**

All changed now through neglect. The steps dismantled. The House at the Cascades. Adrienne Rich. **CP-RicAE; SP-RicA2**

All Circumstances are the Frame. Emily Dickinson. **CP-DickE**

All cities are open in the hot season. The Topography of History. Thomas McGrath. **SP-McGrT**

All Clear. Marge Piercy. **SP-PierM**

All cries rise, & the three of us. An Ode on Nativity. Charles Olson. **CP-OlsoC; SP-OlsoC**

All crises pass, though not the condition of crisis. John Updike. *Fr.* Spanish Sonnets. **CP-UpdiJ**

All crying, "We will go with you, O Wind!" Misgiving. Robert Frost. **CP-FrosR**

All dark is now no more. Sleeping Out at Easter. James Dickey. **CP-DickJ**

All day, a small mild Negro man with a broom. The Sweeper of Ways. Howard Nemerov. **CP-NemeH**

All day a strong gale rushed north-west by north. Autumn Gale. John Hewitt. **CP-HewiJ**

All day a wounded mountain followed me. Seven Preludes to Silence. Richard Shelton. **SP-ShelR**

All day at the window seat. Charles Wright. **SP-WrigC** *Fr.* Three Poems for the New Year.

  (Three Poems for the New Year [3].) **SP-WrigC**

All-Day Bird, the artist, The. Claritas. Denise Levertov. **CP-LeveD**

All day I bang and bang ar you in thought. Abraham Lincoln. Robert Lowell. **SP-LoweR**

All day I loved you in a fever, holding on to the tail of the horse. At Midocean. Robert Bly. **SP-BlyR**

All day I tried to distinguish. Elms. Louise Glück. **SP-GlücL**

All day—I'm. Communication. Archie Randolph Ammons. **SP-AmmoA**

All Day It Has Rained. Alun Lewis. **CP-LewiA**

All day I've toiled, but not with pain. Emily Brontë. **CP-BronE**

All Day Long. Carl Sandburg. **CP-SandC**

All day long in fog and wind. All Day Long. Carl Sandburg. **CP-SandC**

All day long to the judgement-seat. Gallio's Song. Rudyard Kipling. **CP-KiplR**

All day my husband pounds on the upstairs porch. A Time of Bees. Mona Van Duyn. **SP-VanDM**

All day our eyes could find no resting place. Elegy. Wendell Berry. **CP-BerrW**

All day she plays at chess with the bones of the world. Female Author. Sylvia Plath. **CP-PlatS**

All day the darkness and the cold. On Receiving an Eagle's Quill from Lake Superior. John Greenleaf Whittier. **CP-WhitJ**

All Day the Light Is Clear. Tess Gallagher. **SP-GallT**

All day the opposite house. The Opposite House. Robert Lowell. **SP-LoweR**

All day the rain. Hafiz, tr. by Ralph Waldo Emerson. **CP-EmerR** *Fr.* Odes.

All day the waves assailed the rock. Ralph Waldo Emerson. **CP-EmerR**

All day the wind has made love. On Lake Pend Oreille. Richard Shelton. **SP-ShelR**

All day the yellow elevator cage. The Cathedral Bells. Karl Shapiro. **SP-ShapK**

All day under acrobat. Galway Kinnell. *Fr.* Ruins under the Stars. **SP-KinnG**

All day we watched the gulls. Torn Down from Glory Daily. Anne Sexton. **CP-SextA**

All day we were bent over. Pickers. John Haines. **SP-HainJ**

All de night long twell de moon goes down. Twell de Night Is Pas'. Paul Laurence Dunbar. **CP-DunbP**

All debris ends here at the north end. St. John's Chapel. Richard Hugo. **CP-HugoR**

All devil as I am, a damned wretch. A Penitential Thought, in the Hour of Remorse—Intended for a Tragedy. Robert Burns. **CP-BurnR**

All Do Not All Things Well. Thom Gunn. **CP-GunnT**

All does draw back. The Disposition. Charles Olson. **CP-OlsoC**

All dream, all whim. Joy/Spring. Al Young. **CP-YounA**

All dreams of "imperialism" must be exorcised. "Hugh MacDiarmid." **SP-MacDH** *Fr.* In Memoriam James Joyce.

All dripping in tangles green. The Tuft of Kelp. Herman Melville. **SP-MelvH**

All endeavor to be beautiful. Primer of Plato. Jean Garrigue. **SP-GarrJ**

All ends as all must end. As All Must End. Robert Ranke Graves. **CP-GravR**

All evening, daisies outside the window. The Daisies. Charles Tomlinson. **CP-TomlC**

All Except Hannibal. Robert Ranke Graves. **CP-GravR**

All eyes were on Enceladus's face. Hyperion and Saturn. John Keats. **SeCePo** *Fr.* Hyperion; a Fragment. **CP-KeatJ**

All fables of adventure stress. The History of Science. Wystan Hugh Auden. **CP-AudeW**

All fathers in Western civilization must have. The Father of My Country. Diane Wakoski. **SP-WakoD**

All fears, all doubts and even dreams. To Jane; and in Imitation of Coleridge. Frank O'Hara. **SP-OharF**

All features of the wood are known to me. The Mill (Hempstead). Wystan Hugh Auden. **CP-AudWJ**

All feeling hearts must feel for him. The Coming Storm. Herman Melville. **SP-MelvH**

All fine lads in jest upon the yellow world. It Was a Bomby Evening. Kenneth Patchen. **CP-PatcK**

All Flesh Is Grass. Christina Georgina Rossetti. **CP-RosC2**

All fly away at my approach. Man and Bird. Derek Mahon. *Fr.* Four Walks in the Country Near Saint-Brieuc. **SP-MahoD**

All folk-tales mean by ending. Epithalamium. Wystan Hugh Auden. *Fr.* Eleven Occasional Poems. **CP-AudeW**

All folks who pretend to religion and grace. The Place of the Damned [or Damn'd]. Jonathan Swift. **CP-SwifJ**

All forgot for recollecting. Emily Dickinson. **CP-DickE**

All from the light of the sweet moon. Night. Walter de la Mare. **CP-DeLaW**

All furniture's gone. It hits me in this light. Last Day There. Richard Hugo. **CP-HugoR**

All Gentle Folks Who Owe a Grudge. John Keats. **CP-KeatJ**

All Ghouls' Night. Edwin Rolfe. **CP-RolfE**

All glass may yet be whole. The Scarred Girl. James Dickey. **CP-DickJ**

All goes back to the earth. The Want of Peace. Wendell Berry. **CP-BerrW**

All goes onward and outward, nothing collapses. Walt Whitman. **IMW** *Fr.* Song of Myself. **CP-WhitW**

All good men believe that women would rather get rid of a piece. Don't Even Tell Your Wife, Particularly. Ogden Nash. **CP-NashO**

All Greece hates. Helen. Hilda Doolittle. **CP-DoolH**

All grim and soiled and brown with tan. The Reformer. John Greenleaf Whittier. **CP-WhitJ**

All growth securely grappled to the ground. Winter Park. John Hewitt. **CP-HewiJ**

All had been ordered weeks before the start. Wystan Hugh Auden. *Fr.* The Quest. **CP-AudeW**

All hail! inexorable lord! To Ruin. Robert Burns. **CP-BurnR**

All hail, sweet poet, more full of more strong fire. To Mr. T. W. John Donne. **CP-DonnJ**

"All hail!" the bells of Christmas rang. The Mystic's Christmas. John Greenleaf Whittier. **CP-WhitJ**

All hail to him, the Protean! A tough old chap is he. Our Old Friend Dualism. Thomas Hardy. **CP-HardT**

All Hallows. Louise Glück. **SP-GlücL**

All Hallows. Phoebe Hesketh. **SP-HeskP**

All Hallows' Eve in Kansas. Gary Gildner. **SP-GildG**

All has been plundered from me, but my wit. His Losse. Robert Herrick. **CP-HerrR**

All Havens Astern. Charles Olson. **CP-OlsoC**

All hearts should beat when Cho Fu's orchestra plays "Love." Our Hearts. Kenneth Koch. **SP-KochK**

All heaven is blazing yet / With the meridian sun. Christina Georgina Rossetti. **CP-RosC3**

All heavy minds. Sir Thomas Wyatt. **CP-WyatT**

All her aroused feelings. Up in Here. Tom Clark. **SP-ClarT**

All her charms. Lovely Ad. William Carlos Williams. **CP-WilW1**

All her corn-fields rippled in the sunshine. Thy Brother's Blood Crieth. Christina Georgina Rossetti. *Fr.* The German-French Campaign, 1870–1871. **CP-RosC1**

All her kamikaze friends admired my aunt. A Family Turn. William Stafford. **SP-StafW**

All hills and all interesting—in one field. The Country Was. Randall Jarrell. **CP-JarrR**

All his children in the same house. Job the Father. Richard Shelton. **SP-ShelR**

All holy souls / pray for us fellows. Litany. Thomas Merton. **CP-MertT**

All horns should honk like anything. Iva's Birthday Poem. Marilyn Hacker. **SP-HackM**

All hot and grimy from the road. The Fount of Tears. Paul Laurence Dunbar. **CP-DunbP**

All human kind on earth. Boethius, tr. fr. Latin by Elizabeth I, Queen of England. **NoSic** *Fr.* Consolation of Philosophy, The ("De Consolacione Philosophie"). **CP-ChauG**

All human race would fain be wits. On Poetry: a Rhapsody. Jonathan Swift. **CP-SwifJ**

All human race would fain be wits. Jonathan Swift. **HAP; OBSV; PoEL-3** *Fr.* On Poetry: a Rhapsody. **CP-SwifJ**

All human things are subject to decay. MacFlecknoe; or, A Satire [or Satyr] upon the True-Blue [or -Blew] Protestant Poet T. S. John Dryden. **SP-DrydJ**

All human[e] things are subject to decay. John Dryden. **FiP; NOBE; OBCoV; OBS; SCV; TrGrPo** *Fr.* MacFlecknoe; or, A Satire [or Satyr] upon the True-Blue [or -Blew] Protestant Poet T. S.

(Crown Prince of Dullness, The.) **NOBE**

(Poet Shadwell, The.) **FiP**

(Primacy of Dullness, The.) **OBS**

All hushed and still within the house. Emily Brontë. **CP-BronE**

All *Hybla's* honey, all that sweetnesse can. John 15; Upon Our Lords Last Comfortable Discourse with His Disciples. Bible, *N.T.* **CP-CrasR,** tr. by Richard Crashaw; *Fr.* St. John.

All I Ask. David Herbert Lawrence. **CP-LawrD**

All I believed is true! Mesmerism. Robert Browning. **CP-BroR1**

All I can give you is broken-face gargoyles. Broken-Face Gargoyles. Carl Sandburg. **CP-SandC**

All I can say is—I saw it! Natural Magic. Robert Browning. **CP-BroR2**

All I care about in a man. A Man. David Herbert Lawrence. **CP-LawrD**

All I could see from where I stood. Edna St. Vincent Millay. **FaFP; MoAB; MoAmPo; OHFP; PDV; PFP** *Fr.* Renascence. **CP-MillE**

All I could see from where I stood. Renascence. Edna St. Vincent Millay. **CP-MillE**

All I did wrong, all the Grand Guignol years. John Berryman. *Fr.* Sonnets to Chris. **CP-BerrJ**

All I have is the moment of my life. You. The Offense. James Wright. **CP-WrigJ**

All I have lost, that co'd be rapt from me. The Recompence. Robert Herrick. **CP-HerrR**

All I Know. Charles Bukowski. **SP-BukC2**

All I may, if small. Emily Dickinson. **CP-DickE**

All I met were two birds and the wind. Notes of a Parachute Jumper. Jorge Carrera Andrade, *tr. fr. Spanish by* Thomas Merton. **CP-MertT**

All I planted came up. Annuals. Denise Levertov. **CP-LeveD**

All I Really Want to Do. "Bob Dylan." **CP-DylaB**

All I remember is. Nursery Tale. Philip Larkin. **CP-LarkP**

All I Tell You From My Heart. Robert Ranke Graves. **CP-GravR**

All I will amount to: knowing. Spring. Joseph Ceravolo. **SP-CeraJ**

All ignorance toboggans into know. Edward Estlin Cummings. **CP-CummE; SP-CummE**

All in a dream of the time it was. A Memory of the Sad Chair. John Ciardi. **SP-CiarJ**

All in All. Tennyson. *See* In Love, If Love Be Love.

All in green went my love riding. Edward Estlin Cummings. **CP-CummE; SP-CummE**

All in sattin *Oteny* will be suited. Epigramme. Thomas Campion. *Fr.* Observations in the Art of English Poesie. **CP-CampT**

All in that day that I was born. Last Song. Adrienne Rich. **CP-RicAE**

All in the golden afternoon. Dedication. "Lewis Carroll." **CP-CarrL** *Fr.* Alice's Adventures in Wonderland.

All in thy sight my life doth whole depend. Sir Thomas Wyatt. **CP-WyatT**

All influences return in vain. Robert Louis Stevenson. **CP-StevR**

All is a golden burst, the wind burning. The Flux of Autumn. Jean Garrigue. **SP-GarrJ**

All is a kind of toys, all is a kind of play. Time Passes. Richard Eberhart. **CP-EberR**

All Is Best. John Milton. **NOBE; NOSC; OBEV; OBS; SeCePo** *Fr.* Samson Agonistes. **CP-MiltJ**

All is closed in. Jane Cooper. *Fr.* The Weather of Six Mornings. **SP-CoopJ**

All is far. *tr. fr. the German of* Rilke. Randall Jarrell. **CP-JarrR**

"All is forgiven when guilt is accepted". Delmore Schwartz. **SP-SchwD** *Fr.* Genesis.

All is lithogenesis—or lochia. On a Raised Beach. "Hugh MacDiarmid." **SP-MacDH**

All is nothing, nothing all. Robert Penn Warren. **NOBA** *Fr.* Tiberius on Capri. **SP-WarrR**

All Is Safe. Kenneth Patchen. **CP-PatcK**

All Is Truth. Walt Whitman. **CP-WhitW**

All Is Vanity, Saith the Preacher. Byron. **CP-Byron**

All is well, said the voice from the tiny pulpit. Louis MacNeice. *Fr.* The Kingdom. **CP-MacNL**

All I've ever known are whores, ex-prostitutes. Quiet Clean Girls in Gingham Dresses. . . . Charles Bukowski. **SP-BukC1**

All I've Got to Do. John Lennon *and* Paul McCartney. **CP-Beatl**

All June I bound the rose in sheaves. One Way of Love. Robert Browning. **CP-BroR1**

All kings, and all their favourites [*or* favorites]. The Anniversary [*or* Anniversarie]. John Donne. **CP-DonnJ**

All knew of her as Peter's daughter. Felo de se. Wystan Hugh Auden. **CP-AudWJ**

All-Knowing. David Herbert Lawrence. **CP-LawrD**

All legs and arms and grin. Courting Prosperity. Steve Griffiths. **SP-GrifS**

All life's million conflicting interests and relationships. "Hugh MacDiarmid." **SP-MacDH** *Fr.* Plaited Like the Generations of Men.

All living things. The Will To. Charles Olson. **CP-OlsoC**

All look or [*or* and] likeness caught from earth. Phantom. Samuel Taylor Coleridge, *Unknown, sometimes at. to.* **CP-ColeS**

All looks be pale, hearts [*or* harts] cold as stone. A Lamentation. Thomas Campion. **CP-CampT**

All lovers war, and Cupid hath his tent. 1.9. Ovid. **CP-MarlC,** *tr. by* Christopher Marlowe; *Fr.* Elegies.

All men are born free and unequal. Hard Sayings. John Gould Fletcher. **SP-FletJ** *Fr.* The Parables of Antichrist.

All men are lonely now. Dawn. Edna St. Vincent Millay. **CP-MillE**

All men are worms [*or* wormes]: but this no man. In silk[e]. On Court-Worm[e]. Ben Jonson. **CP-JonsB**

All men are worshippers. Worship. David Herbert Lawrence. **CP-LawrD**

All men for Honor hardest work. Emily Dickinson. **CP-DickE**

All Men throughout the peopled Earth, *see also* "There is no race of men" *tr. by* Helen Waddell *and* "All human kind on earth" *tr. by* Elizabeth I.

Boethius, *tr. by* Samuel Johnson. **CP-JohnS** *Fr.* Consolation of Philosophy, The ("De Consolacione Philosophie"). **CP-ChauG**

All month eating the heart out. The Break. Adrienne Rich. **CP-RicAE**

All morning / rain slowly filled. Making It New. Philip Levine. **SP-LeviP**

All Morning. Theodore Roethke. **CP-RoetT**

All morning the tree men have been taking down the stricken elms skirting the broad sidewalks. Elms. Charles Kenneth Williams. **SP-WillC**

All morning they store suns. Old Age Porch. Grace Paley. **CP-PaleG**

All Mountains. Hilda Doolittle. **CP-DoolH**

All my dark thoughts. Euclid Avenue. Charles Simic. **SP-SimiC**

All my days—. Song Theme. Louis Zukofsky. *Fr.* 29 Poems. **CP-ZukLS**

All my fruit is yours for you are mine. The Vine. Phoebe Hesketh. **SP-HeskP**

All My Life. Leonard Cohen. **CP-CoheL**

All my life. The Rain is My Home. Erica Jong. **SP-JongE**

All my life, / so far, / I have loved. Moccasin Flowers. Mary Oliver. **SP-OlivM**

All my life I have been a prisoner under the Tower. The Tower Struck by Lightning Reversed; the Overturning of the Tower. Marge Piercy. *Fr.* Laying Down the Tower. **SP-PierM**

All my life I have been a witness of things. Two Goes into Two Once, If You Can Get It There. Ogden Nash. **CP-NashO**

All my life that's been / the watchword: Resist! Resist! Hayden Carruth. **CP-CarHS** *Fr.* The Clay Hill Anthology.

All My Loving. John Lennon *and* Paul McCartney. **CP-Beatl**

All my plans for suicide are ridiculous. The Heart's Location. Peter Meinke. **SP-MeinP**

All My Pretty Ones. Anne Sexton. **CP-SextA**

All my universes are the same. Fourth Universe. Diane Wakoski. *Fr.* The Universes. **SP-WakoD**

All my woods are / tangle. Ancient. The Line. Hayden Carruth. **CP-CarHS**

All Nature is a temple where the alive. Correspondences. Charles Baudelaire, *tr. fr. French by* Allen Tate. **CP-TateA**

All Nature is but art, unknown to thee. Alexander Pope. **ECEV** *Fr.* An Essay on Man. **CP-PopeA**

All nature seems at work. Slugs leave their lair. Work without Hope. Samuel Taylor Coleridge. **CP-ColeS**

All nearness pauses, while a star can grow. Edward Estlin Cummings. **CP-CummE**

All night / I float / in the shallow ponds. White Night. Mary Oliver. **SP-OlivM**

All night / in and out the slippery shadows. Nature. Mary Oliver. **SP-OlivM**

All night a wind / drawing cold off the water's. Light from Fundy. Brendan Galvin. **SP-GalvB**

All night above their rocky bed. The Pass of the Sierra. John Greenleaf Whittier. **CP-WhitJ**

All Night, All Night. Delmore Schwartz. **SP-SchwD**

All night and all day the wind roared in the streets. Mid-Country Blow. Theodore Roethke. **CP-RoetT**

All night he lies awake tuning the sky. His Tuning of the Night. Erica Jong. **SP-JongE**

All night he ran, his body air. Transformations. Stanley Jasspon Kunitz. **CP-KuniS**

All night his window / shines in the woods. The Poet. Hayden Carruth. **CP-CarHS**

All night I dream of that which cannot be. A Hopeless Case. Christina Georgina Rossetti. **CP-RosC3**

All night I dream you love me well. Christina Georgina Rossetti. **CP-RosC3**

All night I lay awake beside you. Marthe Away (She is Away). Kenneth Rexroth. **SP-RexrK** *Fr.* Seven Poems for Marthe, My Wife.

All night I sat reading a book. The Reader. Wallace Stevens. **CP-StevW**

All night I spent turning. The Long Goodbye. Gilbert Sorrentino. **SP-SorrG**

All night I weep[e], all day I cry, Ay me[e]. Song 2. Mary Sidney, Countess of Montgomery Wroth. **NOSC** *Fr.* Pamphilia to Amphilanthus. **CP-WrotM**

All night in a thoughtful / mood, she. For Somebody's Marriage. Robert Creeley. **CP-CreeR**

All night in dreams I wrestled with an Uck. El Leon Sends His Greetings. Malcolm Lowry. **CP-LowrM**

All night, in May, dogs barked in the hollow woods. Eidolon. Robert Penn Warren. **SP-WarrR**

All night in the womb I heard the stories. A Little Poem. Randall Jarrell. **CP-JarrR**

All Night, Legs Pointed East. Thom Gunn. **CP-GunnT**

All night long, and every night. Young Night Thought. Robert Louis Stevenson. **CP-StevR**

All night long I hear the sleepers toss. Such Simple Love. Thomas McGrath. **SP-McGrT**

All night long the darling daughter squirms. The Flapper. Allen Tate. **CP-TateA**

All night long the rush and trampling of water. Robinson Jeffers. **CP-JefR3**

All night, snow, then, near dawn, freezing rain, so that by morning the whole city glistens. Snow: I. Charles Kenneth Williams. **SP-WillC**

All night the cocks crew, under a moon like day. Tears in Sleep. Louise Bogan. **CP-BogaL**

All night the crib creaks. During Fever. Robert Lowell. **SP-LoweR**

All night the dreadless Angel unpursu'd. Book VI. John Milton. *Fr.* Paradise Lost. **CP-MiltJ**

All night the sound had. The Rain. Robert Creeley. **CP-CreeR**

All night the wind. History. Thomas McGrath. **SP-McGrT**

All night the wind sings like a surf. The Storm at Night. Thomas Merton. **CP-MertT**

All night, this headland. Sleepless at Crown Point. Richard Wilbur. **CP-WilbR**

All night through, raves or broods. Robert Louis Stevenson. **CP-StevR**

All of a sudden I'm a painter. Artist. Charles Bukowski. **SP-BukC1**

All of December Toward New Year's. Louis Zukofsky. **CP-ZukLS**

All of Roses. David Herbert Lawrence. **CP-LawrD**

"By the Isar, in the twilight."

"Just a few of the roses we gathered from the Isar."

"Now like a rose come tip-toe out of bud."

"When she rises in the morning."

All of the branches / None of the roots. Thomas Merton. **CP-MertT**

All of the Indians are dead. Oklahoma. Ernest Hemingway. **CP-HemiE**

All of the turks are gentlemen and Ismet Pasha is a little. They All Made Peace—What Is Peace? Ernest Hemingway. **CP-HemiE**

All of us are sitting. A Screened Porch in the Country. James Dickey. **CP-DickJ**

All of us believe. Question, The. Wystan Hugh Auden. **CP-AudeW**

All of us delight in dancing and in beholding dances. The Dances and the Dancers. Delmore Schwartz. **SP-SchwD**

All on the mountains, as on tapestries. For Robert Frost, in the Autumn, in Vermont. Howard Nemerov. **CP-NemeH**

All one knows, and knows / upon the possibility of knowing. For Lewis, to Say It. Robert Creeley. **CP-CreeR**

All or None. Randall Jarrell. **CP-JarrR**

All other joys of life he strove to warm. George Meredith. **EnVR** *Fr.* Modern Love. **CP-MerG1**

"All our French poets can turn an inspired line." The Nihilist as Hero. Robert Lowell. **SP-LoweR**

All out of doors [or out-of-doors] looked darkly in at him. An Old Man's Winter Night. Robert Frost. **CP-FrosR**

"All out!" the voices cry in the Park, "All out!" Canto XIX. Louis MacNeice. *Fr.* Autumn Sequel. **CP-MacNL**

All Over Again. Louis MacNeice. **CP-MacNL**

All over America women are burning dinners. What's That Smell in the Kitchen? Marge Piercy. **SP-PierM**

All over the district, on leather couches. Walking through the Upper East Side. Erica Jong. **SP-JongE**

All Over You. "Bob Dylan." **CP-DylaB**

All overgrown by cunning moss. Emily Dickinson. **CP-DickE**

All people that on earth do dwell, *metrical vers. by* William Kethe. Bible, *O.T. See* Psalm 100: "Make a joyful noise unto the Lord, all ye lands."

All Pictures thats Panted with sense & with Thought. William Blake. **CP-BlakW**

All Pink from the Bath She Slept. Charles Olson. **CP-OlsoC**

All plants grow here; the most minute. The Garden of the Gods. Thom Gunn. **CP-GunnT**

All poems can be represented by. Still Lifes. William Carlos Williams. **CP-WilW2**

All power is saved, having no end. Rises. The Dam. Muriel Rukeyser. **CP-RukeM**

All praise the Likeness by thy skill portrayed. To a Painter. William Wordsworth. **CP-WorW2**

All praise to him who hath now turned. On My Son's Return Out of England. Anne Bradstreet. **CP-BradA**

All profits disappear: the gain. The Reckoning. Theodore Roethke. **CP-RoetT**

"All ready?" cried the captain. The Slave-Ships. John Greenleaf Whittier. **CP-WhitJ**

All Religions Are One. William Blake. **CP-BlakW**

All Revelation. Robert Frost. **CP-FrosR**

All revolutions in modern times have led. Sonnet. Hayden Carruth. **CP-CarHS** *Fr.* Sonnets.

All right: and with that wry acceptance you follow the cow-track. The Dogwood. Robert Penn Warren. *Fr.* Dark Woods. **SP-WarrR**

All Right, Edith. Leonard Cohen. **CP-CoheL**

All right, let's go, Professor Pagels. Stepping Out. Robert Pack. **SP-PackR**

All right, let's say you could take a skull and break it. Sonnet: To Eva. Sylvia Plath. **CP-PlatS**

All right, then—next on the pole was Horseman and his friend. Off the Top of My Head. "Bob Dylan." **CP-DylaB**

All right, they're playing Beethoven again; when I was. Sardines in Striped Dresses. Charles Bukowski. **SP-BukC3**

All right. Try this. Northern Pike. James Wright. **CP-WrigJ**

All round about, the clouds encompassed me. To Dr. James Newton Matthews, Mason, Ill. Paul Laurence Dunbar. **CP-DunbP**

All-ruling tyrant of the earth. Jonathan Swift. *Fr.* Riddles. **CP-SwifJ**

All Saints ("As grains of sand"). Christina Georgina Rossetti. **CP-RosC2**

All Saints ("They are flocking from the East"). Christina Georgina Rossetti. **CP-RosC2**

All Saints ("They have brought gold"). Christina Georgina Rossetti. **CP-RosC3**

All Saints. Christopher Smart. *Fr.* Hymns and Spiritual Songs for the Fasts and Festivals of the Church of England. **SP-SmarC**

All Saints: Martyrs. Christina Georgina Rossetti. **CP-RosC2**

All saints revile her, and all sober men. The White Goddess. Robert Ranke Graves. **CP-GravR**

All Seasons Shall Be Sweet. Samuel Taylor Coleridge. **BoTP** *Fr.* Frost at Midnight. **CP-ColeS**

(Silent Icicles, The.) **FaBoRV**

All Seated. Pablo Neruda, *tr. fr. Spanish by* Ben Belitt. **SP-NeruP**

All service ranks the same with God. Service. Robert Browning. **TrGrPo** *Fr.* Pippa Passes. **CP-BroR1**

All shivers, / Dear friends. Peaceful Trees. Charles Simic. **SP-SimiC**

All sixty-three of his years. In Egg Time. Brendan Galvin. **SP-GalvB**

All slumbered whom our rud red tiles. The Elopement. Gerard Manley Hopkins. **CP-HopkG**

All Sorts of Gods. David Herbert Lawrence. **CP-LawrD**

All sorts of singers have this common vice. On Singers. Robert Browning. **CP-BroR2**

All Souls. David Herbert Lawrence. **CP-LawrD**

All Souls. Muriel Rukeyser. **CP-RukeM**

All Souls. May Sarton. **SP-SartM**

All Souls' Day. David Herbert Lawrence. **CP-LawrD**

All Souls' Night. William Butler Yeats. **CP-YeatW** *Fr.* A Vision.

All souls that struggle and aspire. John Greenleaf Whittier. **TrPWD** *Fr.* The Shadow and the Light. **CP-WhitJ**

All Sounds Have Been As Music. Wilfred Owen. **CP-OwenW**

All spine and knotted fin-rays. John Haines. *Fr.* The Fossil. **SP-HainJ**

All spring the birds walked on this wormy world. Elementary Attitudes. Mona Van Duyn. **SP-VanDM**

All stars are(and not one star only)love. Edward Estlin Cummings. **CP-CummE**

All stones have luck built in. Some. Green Stone. Richard Hugo. **CP-HugoR**

All streets are brightly lit; our city is kept clean. The Ship. Wystan Hugh Auden. *Fr.* A Voyage. **CP-AudeW**

All submit to them where they sit, inner, secure, unaproachable to analysis in the soul. Tests. Walt Whitman. **CP-WhitW**

All such proclivities are tabulated. The Quiet Glades of Eden. Robert Ranke Graves. **CP-GravR**

All suddenly a stormy whirlwind blew. The Mask of Cupid. Edmund Spenser. **OBSC** *Fr.* The Faerie Queene. **CP-Spens**

All summer / surrounded by unconditioned air. August. Richard Shelton. **SP-ShelR**

All summer in power, out roaring the bull fiend. On the Orthodoxy and Creed of My Power Mower. John Ciardi. **SP-CiarJ**

All summer long she touched me. Our Lady of Solitude. Leonard Cohen. **CP-CoheL**

All summer neither rain nor wave washes the cormorants. Palinode. Robinson Jeffers. *Fr.* The Broken Balance. **CP-JefR1**

All summer we moved in a villa brimful of echoes. The Other Two. Sylvia Plath. **CP-PlatS**

All summer while the dry winds. And the Greatest of These. Richard Shelton. **SP-ShelR**

All summer's warmth was stored there in the hay. At the Back of the North Wind. Thom Gunn. **CP-GunnT**

All tears done away with the bitter unquiet sea. A Chruchyard Song of Patient Hope. Christina Georgina Rossetti. **CP-RosC2**

All that blazing day, swift-breasted swallows, envious crows, grackles in trees. Thunderstorm in South Dakota. Kay Boyle. **CP-BoylK**

All that blesses the step of the antelope. Else a great Prince in prison lies. Denise Levertov. **CP-LeveD**

All that I do. Emily Dickinson. **CP-DickE**

All that I know / Of a certain star. My Star. Robert Browning. **CP-BroR1**

All that I see is framed. A Fortune. Daniel Gerard Hoffman. **SP-HoffD**

All that I serve will die, all my delights. The Wish to Be Generous. Wendell Berry. **CP-BerrW**

All that is: / The unbroken surface of the sea. Kathleen Jessie Raine. **SP-RainK**

All That Is. Richard Wilbur. **CP-WilbR**

All That Is Lovely in Men. Robert Creeley. **CP-CreeR**

All That is Perfect in Woman. William Carlos Williams. **CP-WilW2**

All that matters is to be at one with the living God. Pax. David Herbert Lawrence. **CP-LawrD**

All that morning in the strawberry field. Bitter Strawberries. Sylvia Plath. **CP-PlatS**

All that night / I prayed for eyes to see again. South: The Name of Home. Alice Walker. **CP-WalkA**

All That Night Lights Were Seen Moving in Every Direction. Kenneth Patchen. **CP-PatcK**

All that passes descends. The Gift of Gravity. Wendell Berry. **CP-BerrW**

All that remains of the garden is the shadow. Late Night Movies IV. John Yau. **SP-YauJo**

All that thy virgin soul can ask be thine. Ralph Waldo Emerson. **CP-EmerR**

All That We Have. Stephen Dunn. **SP-DunnS**

All That We Have Is Life. David Herbert Lawrence. **CP-LawrD**

All that we know is nothing, we are merely crammed waste-paper baskets. All-Knowing. David Herbert Lawrence. **CP-LawrD**

All that we see is penetrated by it. As We Know. John Ashbery. **SP-AshbJ**

All that we see rejoices in the sunshine. Let Everything That Hath Breath Praise the Lord. Christina Georgina Rossetti. **CP-RosC2**

All that which lies outside our sort of why. Objects. Wystan Hugh Auden. **CP-AudeW**

All That's Past. Walter de la Mare. **CP-DeLaW**

All the bad Bauhaus comes to a head. The Humanities Building. Karl Shapiro. **SP-ShapK**

All the Beautiful are Blameless. James Wright. **CP-WrigJ**

All the beer was poisoned and the capt. went down. Love Is a Piece of Paper Torn to Bits. Charles Bukowski. **SP-BukC2**

All the bells were ringing / And all the birds were singing. Christina Georgina Rossetti. **CP-RosC2**

All the bones of five toes are in each of his paddles. Whale Poem. Frederick Morgan. **SP-MorgF**

All the boys are gathered there. On Vulture Peak. Gary Snyder. **CP-SnydG**

All the breath and the bloom of the year in the bag of one bee. Summum Bonum. Robert Browning. **CP-BroR2**

All the Bright Foam of Talk. Kenneth Patchen. **CP-PatcK**

All the buildings in Glasgow are grey. John Maclean (1879-1923). "Hugh MacDiarmid." **SP-MacDH**

All the busted chairs out in the streets. New Year 1970. Jim Carroll. **SP-CarrJ**

All the cants they peddle. Basil Bunting. **CP-BuntB**

All the Casualties. . . . Charles Bukowski. **SP-BukC3**

All the complicated details. Winter Trees. William Carlos Williams. **CP-WilW1**

All the dark hours everywhere repair. Night. Gary Snyder. **CP-SnydG**

All the Day. Kenneth Patchen. **CP-PatcK**

All the Dead Dears. Sylvia Plath. **CP-PlatS**

All the Dead Soldiers. Thomas McGrath. **SP-McGrT**

All the dreary Sunday morning. Ted Hughes. **HAP,** sect. 6; Fr. Skylarks. **SP-HughT**

All the Earth, All the Air. Theodore Roethke. **CP-RoetT**

All the endings in my life. Love Spell: against Endings. Erica Jong. **SP-JongE**

All the essentials were there, the river thin. Old Scene. Richard Hugo. **CP-HugoR**

All the Fancy Things. William Carlos Williams. **CP-WilW1**

All the fantasies that. Robert Creeley. **CP-CreeR**

All the Flowery. Kenneth Patchen. **CP-PatcK**

All the forms are fugitive. Ralph Waldo Emerson. **WGRP** Fr. Woodnotes II ("As sunbeams stream through liberal space"). **CP-EmerR**

All the grass / dies. A Night Sky. Robert Creeley. **CP-CreeR**

All the great & good. Ralph Waldo Emerson. **CP-EmerR**

All the heaven and earth. João Cabral de Melo Neto. **CP-BishE** Fr. The Death and Life of a Severino.

All the heavy days are over. The Countess Cathleen in Paradise. William Butler Yeats. **CP-YeatW**

All the here and all the there. Our Two Worthies. John Crowe Ransom. **SP-RansJ**

All the journeys / To be made for instance, over the seas. James Liddy. Fr. A Munster Song of Love and War. **CP-LiddJ**

All the last lessons of fatigue. The Boathouse. David St. John. **SP-StJoD**

All the letters I can write. Emily Dickinson. **CP-DickE**

All the Little Animals. Muriel Rukeyser. **CP-RukeM**

All the Little Hoof-Prints. Robinson Jeffers. **CP-JefR2**

All the livelong way this day of sweet showers from Portrane on the seashore. Sanies I. Samuel Beckett. **CP-BeckS**

All the lives this place. Wendell Berry. Fr. History. **CP-BerrW**

All the long school-hours, round the irregular hum of the class. A Snowy Day in School. David Herbert Lawrence. **CP-LawrD**

All the lost interpretations. The Return. Louis MacNeice. **CP-MacNL**

All the names I know from nurse. The Flowers. Robert Louis Stevenson. **CP-StevR**

All the night in woe. The Little Girl Found. William Blake. **CP-BlakW** Fr. Songs of Experience.

All the night in woe. The Little Girl Found. William Blake. **CP-BlakW; FHYEP; NOBRP** Fr. Songs of Innocence. **CP-BlakW**

All the night sleep came not upon my eyelids. Sapphics. Algernon Charles Swinburne. **SP-SwinA**

All the old time prophecies about the whites coming to this country. Ghost Dance. Thomas Merton. Fr. West. Fr. The Geography of Lograire. **CP-MertT**

All the others translate: the painter sketches. The Composer. Wystan Hugh Auden. **CP-AudeW**

All the people of the play were there. Landscape with Wave Approaching. Muriel Rukeyser. **CP-RukeM**

All the perversions of the soul. A Small Farm. Michael Hartnett. **SP-HarMi**

All the policemen, saloonkeepers and efficiency experts in Toledo knew. Potomac River Mist. Carl Sandburg. **CP-SandC**

All the Robin Redbreasts. 1885. St. Valentine's Day. Christina Georgina Rossetti. **CP-RosC3**

All the Roses of the World. Kenneth Patchen. **CP-PatcK**

All the Sioux were defeated. Our clan. Report to Crazy Horse. William Stafford. **SP-StafW**

All the Sisters of Mercy. Sisters of Mercy. Leonard Cohen. **CP-CoheL**

All the slow school hours, round the irregular hum of the class. also incl. in The Schoolmaster [B]. David Herbert Lawrence. Fr. The Schoolmaster [A]. **CP-LawrD**

All the slow school hours, round the irregular hum of the class. also incl. in The Schoomaster [A]. David Herbert Lawrence. Fr. The Schoolmaster [B]. **CP-LawrD**

All the soft runs of it, the tin-white gashes. Bougainville. Donald Davie. **CP-DavDo**

All the space under the bridge. Passing Newbridge-on-Wye. Roy Fisher. **SP-FishR**

All the stream that's roaring by. A Needle's Eye. William Butler Yeats. **CP-YeatW**

All the teeth ever I had are worn down and fallen out. Basil Bunting, after Rudaki. **CP-BuntB**

All the toothy Fräuleins are left behind. The Son. Rita Dove. **SP-DoveR**

All the trees all their boughs all their leaves. Out of Sight in the Direction of My Body. Paul Éluard, tr. fr. French by Samuel Beckett. **CP-BeckS**

All the trees are in bloom. Response to a Letter from France. Stephen Dunn. **SP-DunnS**

All the voices of the wood called "Muriel!" Then I Saw What the Calling Was. Muriel Rukeyser. **CP-RukeM**

All the waters of the river Deben. The River Deben. Stevie Smith. **CP-SmitS**

All the way across the Bay Bridge I sang. Buying and Selling. Philip Levine. **SP-LeviP**

All the Way Down. Thomas Merton. **CP-MertT**

All the way from Mexico. An Art. Charles Bukowski. **SP-BukC1**

All the way we heard someone breathing. High Wire. Dabney Stuart. **SP-StuaD**

All the way/ on the road to Gary. The Helmet. Philip Levine. **SP-LeviP**

All the way through the forest, a sound of birdsong. Muriel Rukeyser. **CP-RukeM**

All the way to the city a crying in the air. Grand Central Station. Muriel Rukeyser. **CP-RukeM**

All the While. John Updike. Fr. Living with a Wife. **CP-UpdiJ**

All the while I was. 1968. Tom Clark. **SP-ClarT**

All the while they were talking the new morality. The Encounter. Ezra Pound. **SP-PounE**

All the winter I have lain here. The Stolen Heart. Frank Templeton Prince. **CP-PrinF**

All the wolves of the forest. Lyceia. Robert Ranke Graves. **CP-GravR**

All the women / all their kisses the. A Love Poem. Charles Bukowski. **SP-BukC3**

All the world is out in leaf. Christina Georgina Rossetti. *Fr.* Spring Fancies. **CP-RosC3**

All the world is so sweet, dear. To Alice Dunbar. Paul Laurence Dunbar. **CP-DunbP**

All the world is walking on the Gran Via. Madrid, 1974. Mona Van Duyn. **SP-VanDM**

All the world over, nursing their scars. Rudyard Kipling. **CP-KiplR**

All There Is to Know about Adolph Eichmann. Leonard Cohen. **CP-CoheL**

All These Birds. Richard Wilbur. **CP-WilbR**

All these dormant fields are held beneath the fog. Muscat Pruning. William Everson. **SP-EverW**

All These Dreams. Jane Cooper. **SP-CoopJ**

All these girls licking & sucking. Leaving Syracuse. Al Young. **CP-YounA**

All these illegitimate babies. Valuable. Stevie Smith. **CP-SmitS**

All these love-poems. . . ! Love-Poems: for Mairi MacInnes. Donald Davie. **CP-DavDo**

All these my banners be. Emily Dickinson. **CP-DickE**

All Things. Hayden Carruth. **CP-CarHS**

All things are Atoms: Earth and Water, Air. The Dance of the Solids. John Updike. *Fr.* Midpoint. **CP-UpdiJ**

All things are fair, if we had eyes to see. Behold, It Was Very Good. Christina Georgina Rossetti. **CP-RosC2**

All things are fire. Thomas Merton. *Fr.* The Legacy of Herakleitos. **CP-MertT**

All things are open to these two events. Rewards and Punishments. Robert Herrick. **CP-HerrR**

All things are real. Letter to a Friend: Who Is Nancy Daum? James Schuyler. **CP-SchuJ**

All things are Thine: no gift have we. Hymn for the Opening of Plymouth Church. John Greenleaf Whittier. **CP-WhitJ**

All things are words of some strange tongue, in thrall. Compass. Jorge Luis Borges, *tr. fr. Spanish by* Richard Wilbur. **CP-WilbR**

"All things become thee, being thine," I think sometimes. Woman. Randall Jarrell. **CP-JarrR**

All Things Can Tempt Me. William Butler Yeats. **CP-YeatW**

All things change. / The sun is new everyday. Thomas Merton. *Fr.* The Legacy of Herakleitos. **CP-MertT**

All things compose him. Snow Leopard. Phoebe Hesketh. **SP-HeskP**

All things confirm me in the thought that dust. In Spite of Death. Countee Cullen. **CP-CullC**

All Things Decay and Die. Robert Herrick. **CP-HerrR**

All things decay with Time: The Forrest sees. All Things Decay and Die. Robert Herrick. **CP-HerrR**

All things lay in nature, even the plastic flowers. Hayden Carruth. *Fr.* Paragraphs. **CP-CarHS**

All things lean at you, and some are. Trying to Tell You Something. Robert Penn Warren. **SP-WarrR**

All things new / But I: no shadow. Kathleen Jessie Raine. **SP-RainK**

All things on earth and sea. Robert Louis Stevenson. **CP-StevR**

All things only of earth and water. Basil Bunting. *Fr.* The Spoils. **CP-BuntB**

All things o'r-rul'd are here by Chance. Large Bounds Doe but Bury Us. Robert Herrick. **CP-HerrR**

All Things Pass. Stevie Smith. **CP-SmitS**

All things rehearse. Ralph Waldo Emerson. **CP-EmerR**

All Things Run Well for the Righteous. Robert Herrick. **CP-HerrR**

All things seem mention of themselves. Grand Galop. John Ashbery. **SP-AshbJ**

All things stand out against the sky. Charles Olson. **CP-OlsoC**

All things subjected are to Fate. Change Common to All. Robert Herrick. **CP-HerrR**

All things swept sole away. Emily Dickinson. **CP-DickE**

All things that go deep enough. The Ice Skin. James Dickey. **CP-DickJ**

All things that pass / Are woman's looking-glass. Passing and Glassing. Christina Georgina Rossetti. **CP-RosC2**

All things that Peter saw and felt. Percy Bysshe Shelley. **EPCY** *Fr.* Peter Bell the Third. **CP-ShelP**

All things uncomely and broken, all things worn out and old. The Lover Tells of the Rose in His Heart. William Butler Yeats. **CP-YeatW**

All things within this fading world hath [*or* have] end. Before the Birth of One of Her Children. Anne Bradstreet. **CP-BradA**

All This. . . . Hart Crane. **CP-CranH**

All this and more, though is there more? Emily Dickinson. **SP-DickE**

All This Changing Trouble Luck and Suddenness. John Yau. **SP-YauJo**

All this flesh, meat. Robert Creeley. **CP-CreeR**

All this quiet sweeping round us on the earth's edge. A Small but Brilliant Fire Blazed in the Grate. Kenneth Patchen. **CP-PatcK**

All this stood on her and was the world. *tr. fr. the German of* Rilke. Randall Jarrell. **CP-JarrR**

All this summer fun. / The big waves, and waiting. Lighthouse. Joseph Ceravolo. **SP-CeraJ**

All this talk of equality between the sexes is merely an expression of sex-hate. Men and Women. David Herbert Lawrence. **CP-LawrD**

All this time / You were dead and I did not know. One Month. Muriel Rukeyser. **CP-RukeM**

All those long dead New England farm boys. Snatches for Charles Ives. Daniel Gerard Hoffman. **SP-HoffD**

All those treasures that lie in the little bolted box whose tiny space is. Slow Movement. William Carlos Williams. **CP-WilW1**

All those who have not died have married. The End. Charles Tomlinson. **CP-TomlC**

All those years, alone. You Taught Me. Thomas McGrath. **SP-McGrT**

All thoughts, all passions, all delights. Love. Samuel Taylor Coleridge. **CP-ColeS**

All three are bare. Three. Thom Gunn. **CP-GunnT**

All thro' the livelong night I lay awake. Sonnet from the Psalms. Christina Georgina Rossetti. **CP-RosC3**

All through childhood I never could quite find a place in my family where I fit. Brothers. Stephen Berg. **SP-BergS**

All through that Sunday afternoon. A Kite for Michael and Christopher. Seamus Heaney. **SP-HeanS**

All through the blazing afternoon. Ariadne. Thomas Merton. **CP-MertT; SP-MertT**

All through the damp morning he works, he reads. His Rooms in College. Thom Gunn. **CP-GunnT**

All through the day I, me, mine, I, me, mine. I Me Mine. The Beatles. **CP-Beatl**

All through the night, the leaky faucet. The Leaky Faucet. Ted Kooser. **SP-KoosT**

All through the Rains. Gary Snyder. **CP-SnydG**

"All Thy Works Praise Thee, O Lord": A Processional of Creation. Christina Georgina Rossetti. **CP-RosC2**

All today I lie in the bottom of the wardrobe. Yoko. Thom Gunn. **CP-GunnT**

All Together Now. John Lennon *and* Paul McCartney. **CP-Beatl**

All Tomorrow's Parties. "Lou Reed." **SP-ReedL**

All too often now your voice is too bright. Christmas. Robert Lowell. **SP-LoweR**

All travellers [*or* travelers] at first incline. Stella's Birthday; Written in the Year 1720–21. Jonathan Swift. **CP-SwifJ**

All Trees, all leavy Groves confesse the Spring. Out of Virgil, in the Praise of the Spring. Virgil. **CP-CrasR,** *tr. by* Richard Crashaw; *Fr.* Georgics.

All up and down the avenues. The Condition. Charles Bukowski. **SP-BukC3**

All up and down the street they came back. A Conversation on Morality, Eternity and Copulation. Charles Bukowski. **SP-BukC2**

All visible, visibly. Wystan Hugh Auden. **SD** *Fr.* Runner. *Fr.* Six Commissioned Texts. **CP-AudeW**

All we can dream of loveliness within. Conclusion of a Sonnet on "Keely's Discovery." Robert Browning. **CP-BroR2**

All we do—how old are we? I must be twelve, she a little older; thirteen, fourteen—is hold hands. Still Life. Charles Kenneth Williams. **CP-WillC**

All we have is God's, and yet. Mark 12; (Give to Cæsar————) (And to God————). Bible, *N.T.* **CP-CrasR,** *tr. by* Richard Crashaw; *Fr.* St. Mark.

All we secure of Beauty. Emily Dickinson. **SP-DickE**

All we were going strong last night this time. John Berryman. **FaBoMo** *Fr.* Sonnets to Chris. **CP-BerrJ**

All weareth, all wasteth, / All flitteth, all hasteth. Vigil of the Annunciation. Christina Georgina Rossetti. **CP-RosC2**

All what you are still one, his own to find, *speech of Musidorus.* Sir Philip Sidney. **SP-SidnP** *Fr.* Arcadia.

All wheels; a man breathed fire. The Celebration. James Dickey. **CP-DickJ**

All which isn't singing is mere talking. Edward Estlin Cummings. **CP-CummE**

All winter long. Confession. Alice Walker. **CP-WalkA**

All winter long the huge sad lady. The Duet. Wystan Hugh Auden. **CP-AudeW**

All winter through I bow my head. The Scarecrow. Walter de la Mare. **CP-DeLaW**

All winter you felt nothing. As your body. Song for Making the Birds Come. Stephen Dobyns. **SP-DobyS**

All winter your brute shoulders strained against collars, padding. Names of Horses. Donald Hall. **CP-HallD**

All Wise. Louis Zukofsky. **CP-ZukLS**

All women are pets. Thoughts Thought after a Bridge Party. Ogden Nash. **CP-NashO**

All wonders *Barnzy* speaks, all grosely faind. Epigramme. Thomas Campion. *Fr.* Observations in the Art of English Poesie. **CP-CampT**

All worlds have halfsight,seeing either with. Edward Estlin Cummings. **CP-CummE**

All-worshipp'd Gold! thou mighty mystery! R.S.S. William Cowper. **CP-CowpW**

All ye that know of care and heaviness. Sir Thomas Wyatt. **CP-WyatT**

All year the flax-dam festered in the heart. Death of a Naturalist. Seamus Heaney. **SP-HeanS**

All you are doing and saying is to America dangled mirages. To a President. Walt Whitman. **CP-WhitW**

All you can about animals as persons. What You Should Know to Be a Poet. Gary Snyder. **CP-SnydG**

All You Can Do. Charles Olson. **CP-OlsoC**

All You Need Is Love. John Lennon *and* Paul McCartney. **CP-Beatl**

All you that are enamored of my name. Demos. Edwin Arlington Robinson. **CP-RobiE**

All your two bit psychiatrists are giving you electric shock. Kill Your Sons. "Lou Reed." **SP-ReedL**

Alla Sua Amica. Samuel Taylor Coleridge. **CP-ColeS**

Allan-Bane's Lament. Sir Walter Scott. **SP-ScotW** *Fr.* The Lady of the Lake.

Allan Water. Robert Burns. **CP-BurnR**

"Allas," sche seide, "how that this manis mynde." Heu Quam Precipiti. Boethius, *tr. by* John Walton. **OBMV** *Fr.* Consolation of Philosophy, The ("De Consolacione Philosophie"). **CP-ChauG**

Allbutnotquitemost. Edward Estlin Cummings. **CP-CummE**

All day I lifted stones. Richard Shelton. *Fr.* Dry Season. **SP-ShelR**

"Alle Herrlichkeit Des Menschen." James McAuley. *Fr.* Requiem. **SP-McAuJ**

Allegiance. René Char, *tr. fr. French by* Thomas Merton. **CP-MertT**

Allegiances. William Stafford. **SP-StafW**

Allegory, An. Percy Bysshe Shelley. **CP-ShelP**

Allegory of the Wolf Boy, The. Thom Gunn. **CP-GunnT**

Allegory of Wealth, The. Charles Olson. **CP-OlsoC**

ALLEGORY: *Old Man's Fancy* (Poussin). Jenny Joseph. *Fr.* Altarpiece (A Meditation on Lust, Desire and Love). **SP-JoseJ**

Allegro Moderato. James McAuley. *Fr.* The Exile's Fifth Symphony. **SP-McAuJ**

Allegro Vivace. James McAuley. *Fr.* The Exile's Fifth Symphony. **SP-McAuJ**

Alleluia! or Alas! my heart is crying. Christina Georgina Rossetti. **CP-RosC2**

Allendale. Wystan Hugh Auden. **CP-AudWJ**

Allende at the End. Miller Williams. **SP-WillM**

Alley, The, *in imitation of* Spenser. Alexander Pope. **CP-PopeA**

Alley between the elm trees ends, The. Some Aspects of Immortality. Archibald MacLeish. **CP-MacLa**

Alley ran across the pleasant wood, An. The Mill-House. Robert Louis Stevenson. **CP-StevR**

Alley Rats. Carl Sandburg. **CP-SandC**

Alliance of Education and Government, The. Thomas Gray. **CP-GrayT**

Allie. Robert Ranke Graves. **CP-GravR**

Allie, call the birds in. Allie. Robert Ranke Graves. **CP-GravR**

Allies: According to Herodotus. Charles Kenneth Williams. **SP-WillC**

Alligator Bride, The. Donald Hall. **CP-HallD**

Alligator Poem. Mary Oliver. **SP-OlivM**

Alligator steal your blanket off. Catfish River Lullaby. Kenneth Patchen. **CP-PatcK**

Alligators and Paris and North America. William Dickey. **SP-DickW**

Allow Me, Madam, But It Won't Help. Ogden Nash. **CP-NashO**

Alloy. Muriel Rukeyser. **CP-RukeM**

All's Brillig in Tin Pan Alley. Ogden Nash. **CP-NashO**
    Good Night, Sweet Mind.
    I Saw Euterpe Kissing Santa Claus.

All's over, then: does truth sound bitter. The Lost Mistress. Robert Browning. **CP-BroR1**

All's Well. John Greenleaf Whittier. **CP-WhitJ**

Alma. Frank O'Hara. **SP-OharF**

Alma Mater. Edwin Arlington Robinson. **CP-RobiE**

Almagest, Last Letter to Zakarias. Siv Cedering Fox. **SP-CedeS**

Almanac. Carl Sandburg. **CP-SandC**

Almanac, An. James Schuyler. **CP-SchuJ**

Almanach du Printemps Vivarois. Hayden Carruth. **CP-CarHS**

Almes. Robert Herrick. **CP-HerrR**

Almes. Robert Herrick. **CP-HerrR**

Almighty and al merciable queene. An ABC. Geoffrey Chaucer. **CP-ChauG**

Almighty crowd, thou shorten'st all dispute. John Dryden. **SP-DrydJ** *Fr.* The Medal [*or* Medall].

Almighty Jesu! first and last. The King's Restoration. Christopher Smart. *Fr.* Hymns and Spiritual Songs for the Fasts and Festivals of the Church of England. **SP-SmarC**

Almighty [*or* Almightie] Judge, how shall poor[e] wretches brook. Judgement. George Herbert. **CP-HerbG**

Almighty King! whose wond'rous hand. Grace and Providence. William Cowper. *Fr.* Olney Hymns. **CP-CowpW**

Almighty Lord, who from thy glorious throne. The Church Militant. George Herbert. **CP-HerbG**

Almighty Mammon, make me rich! Modern Prayer. David Herbert Lawrence. **CP-LawrD**

Almond Blossom. David Herbert Lawrence. **CP-LawrD**

Almost always underground, dank. A Lyric Meditation on Sour Locker Rooms. Dabney Stuart. **NGP** *Fr.* The Opposite Field. **SP-StuaD**

Almost at the equator. Once Only. Gary Snyder. **CP-SnydG**

Almost awake? Why, what is this, and whence. Parliamentary Oscillators. Samuel Taylor Coleridge. **CP-ColeS**

Almost Everyone. Stephen Dunn. **SP-DunnS**

Almost happy now, he looked at his estate. Voltaire at Ferney. Wystan Hugh Auden. **CP-AudeW**

Almost I am tempted to essay. Elizabeth Hoar. Ralph Waldo Emerson. **CP-EmerR**

Almost I could prefer. Patience. Robert Ranke Graves. **CP-GravR**

Almost I welcome the dirty subterfuges. In Disguise. Robert Ranke Graves. **CP-GravR**

Almost Made Up Poem, An. Charles Bukowski. **SP-BukC1**

Almost yesterday, those gentle ladies stole. The Lost Ingredient. Anne Sexton. **CP-SextA**

Alms. Edna St. Vincent Millay. **CP-MillE**

Alms-House and Trustees, The. George Crabbe. **SP-CrabG** *Fr.* The Borough.

Alnaschar and the Oxen. Rudyard Kipling. **CP-KiplR** *Fr.* Debits and Credits.

Aloe. Siv Cedering Fox. **SP-CedeS**

Aloe. Louis Zukofsky. **CP-ZukLS**

Aloft, / In the loft. Croft. Stevie Smith. **CP-SmitS**

Alone. "Anna Akhmatova", *tr. fr. Russian by* Stephen Berg. **SP-BergS**

Alone. Maya Angelou. **SP-AngeM**

Alone ("Each lover has a theory. . ."). Wystan Hugh Auden. **CP-AudeW**

Alone ("Soundless is the Winter Darkness"). Wystan Hugh Auden. **CP-AudWJ**

Alone. Walter de la Mare. **CP-DeLaW**

Alone. Walter de la Mare. **CP-DeLaW**

Alone / in that same self where I always was. Nov. 23, 1963: Alone. Allen Ginsberg. **CP-GinsA**

Alone. Richard Shelton. **SP-ShelR**

Alone / With nothing to say / Which is better? Reduced to This. Thomas Merton. **CP-MertT**

Alone again but happeeee. O! Al Young. **CP-YounA**

Alone and in a Circumstance. Emily Dickinson. **CP-DickE**

Alone and Not Alone. Carl Sandburg. **CP-SandC**

Alone at night. 1951. Frank O'Hara. **SP-OharF**

Alone at night in my room. A God. Stephen Berg. **SP-BergS**

Alone at the end of green *allées*, alone. The Statues in the Public Gardens. Howard Nemerov. **CP-NemeH**

Alone far in the wilds and mountains I hunt. Walt Whitman. **SAmP** *Fr.* Song of Myself. **CP-WhitW**

Alone here. Beach, drum out. Two Women. James Dickey. **CP-DickJ**

Alone, I cannot be. Emily Dickinson. **CP-DickE**

Alone I sat; the summer day. Emily Brontë. **CP-BronE**

Alone in Rome! Why Rome is lonely too. Ralph Waldo Emerson. **CP-EmerR**

Alone in the darkling apartment the boy. Messias. Karl Shapiro. **SP-ShapK**

Alone in the Wind, on the Prairie. Nicholas Vachel Lindsay. **CP-LindV**

Alone in the Woods. Stevie Smith. **CP-SmitS**

Alone Lord God, in Whom our trust and peace. Christina Georgina Rossetti. **CP-RosC2**

Alone musing, / Remembering. Sir Thomas Wyatt. **CP-WyatT**

Alone on the jagged rock. November Day at McClure's Beach. Robert Bly. **SP-BlyR**

Alone on the railroad track. Chemin de Fer. Elizabeth Bishop. **CP-BishE**

Alone on the rubble of Earth—all alone—. Life-Force. Louise McNeill. **SP-McNeL**

Alone, one can but toy with imagery. Hourglass. James Merrill. **SP-MerrJ**

Alone, remote, nor witting where I went. The Altar. Edwin Arlington Robinson. **CP-RobiE**

Alone today I mounted that steep hill. Martin and Katherine. William Carlos Williams. **CP-WilW1**

Alone up north, soaking this nutty bulgur for supper. Wheat. Gary Gildner. **SP-GildG**

Alone upon the housetops to the North. The Love Song of Har Dyal. Rudyard Kipling. **CP-KiplR** *Fr.* Beyond the Pale. *Fr.* Plain Tales from the Hills.

Alone with Everybody. Charles Bukowski. **SP-BukC1**

Alone with our madness and favorite flower. Late Echo. John Ashbery. **SP-AshbJ**

Alone, you are no more than many another. Son Altesse. Robert Ranke Graves. **CP-GravR**

Along a leafy lonely river God-shy-eyed fisher boys. James Liddy. *Fr.* Epithalamion I–IV: "Along a leafy lonely river God-shy-eyed fisher boys." **CP-LiddJ**

Along a precipice they wound their way. Fragment of a "Gothic" Tale. William Wordsworth. **CP-WorW1**

Along Aetnaville, where I was born. To the Ohio. James Wright. *Fr.* Many of Our Waters: Variations on a Poem by a Black Child. **CP-WrigJ**

Along an avenue of almond-trees. Mercutio. Walter de la Mare. **CP-DeLaW**

Along and back the creamed arcade. Return to Lahore. Louis MacNeice. **CP-MacNL**

Along by the river of ruin. The River of Ruin. Paul Laurence Dunbar. **CP-DunbP**

Along, come along. The Tinkers Song. Robert Herrick. **CP-HerrR**

Along Crane River's sunny slopes. The Witch of Wenham. John Greenleaf Whittier. **CP-WhitJ**

Along Galeana Street. Octavio Paz, *tr. fr. Spanish by* Elizabeth Bishop. **CP-BishE**

Along History. Muriel Rukeyser. **CP-RukeM**

Along my middle seventies my vision seemed. Bifocal in Gaza. John Hewitt. **CP-HewiJ**

Along Route Two I saw a sign. Route Two. Howard Nemerov. **CP-NemeH**

Along the aisle where prayer was made. The Prayer-Seeker. John Greenleaf Whittier. **CP-WhitJ**

Along the Appian Way / children are playing. Lawrence Ferlinghetti. **SP-FerlL** *Fr.* Canti Romani.

Along the avenue of cypresses. Giorno dei Morti. David Herbert Lawrence. **CP-LawrD**

Along the beach beyond La Boca the Luquillo River. Bridges. Grace Paley. **CP-PaleG**

Along the blushing borders bright with dew. Spring Flowers. James Thomson. **NOBE** *Fr.* Spring. *Fr.* The Seasons. **CP-ThomJ**

Along the brittle treacherous bright streets. Edward Estlin Cummings. **CP-CummE**

Along the coastal waters, signals run. Eastport to Block Island. Adrienne Rich. **CP-RicAE**

Along the dark, and silent night. The Bell-Man. Robert Herrick. **CP-HerrR**

Along the denuded aisles a shadow walks. The Coming of Snow. Hayden Carruth. *Fr.* Contra Mortem. **CP-CarHL**

Along the field as we came by. Alfred Edward Housman. **CP-HousA**

Along the garden terrace, under which. George Meredith. **NOBVV** *Fr.* Modern Love. **CP-MerG1**

Along the highroad the way is too long. Christina Georgina Rossetti. **CP-RosC3**

Along the justexisting road to Roupy. Edward Estlin Cummings. **CP-CummE**

Along the lake, like seals, like seals. August Holidays. David Herbert Lawrence. **CP-LawrD**

Along the mazes of this song I go. William Wordsworth. **CP-WorW1**

Along the red ledge I. All the Flowery. Kenneth Patchen. **CP-PatcK**

Along the Road. Mona Van Duyn. **SP-VanDM**

Along the roadside, like the flowers of gold. Prelude. John Greenleaf Whittier. **AP; APN-1; NAAL-1; NAAL-3; OxBA; PoEL-4** *Fr.* Among the Hills. **CP-WhitJ**

Along the sculptures of the western wall. A Cathedral Façade at Midnight. Thomas Hardy. **CP-HardT**

Along the sprawled body of the derailed. Outside Fargo, North Dakota. James Wright. **CP-WrigJ**

Along the street / In the afternoon. The Empty Days. John Gould Fletcher. **SP-FletJ**

Along the way / He walked that day. Self-Unconscious. Thomas Hardy. **CP-HardT**

Along thy wood-lanes wild, or shrubby lawns. Sonnet to the Forest Ytene. Charlotte Smith. **CP-SmitC**

Along with Youth. Ernest Hemingway. **CP-HemiE**

Alongside the train I labor. Snow on a Southern State. James Dickey. **CP-DickJ**

Aloof. Christina Georgina Rossetti. *See* The Irresponsive silence of the land.

Aloof. Carl Sandburg. **CP-SandC**

Aloof, as if a thing of mood and whim. The Schreckhorn. Thomas Hardy. **CP-HardT**

Aloof in Gaiety. David Herbert Lawrence. **CP-LawrD**

Aloof they crown the foreland lone. Off Cape Colona. Herman Melville. **SP-MelvH**

Álow álow loo no words. Aloe. Louis Zukofsky. **CP-ZukLS**

Alphabet, An. Christina Georgina Rossetti. **CP-RosC3**

Alphabet, The. Karl Shapiro. **SP-ShapK**

Alphabet of, The. The Botticellian Trees. William Carlos Williams. **CP-WilW1**

Alphabet Poem: To the Letter I. Erica Jong. **SP-JongE**

Alphabets. Seamus Heaney. **SP-HeanS**

Alphonso of Castile. Ralph Waldo Emerson. **CP-EmerR**

Alpine. George Oppen. **CP-OppeG**

Alpine Rosy Bells. Louis Zukofsky. **CP-ZukLS**

Alpine Violets. John Gould Fletcher. **SP-FletJ**

Alps on Alps. Alexander Pope. *See* A Little learning is a dangerous [*or* dang'rous] thing.

Already autumn silently / has come to sky and field and tree. John Hewitt. *Fr.* Three Horatian Odes. **CP-HewiJ**

Already blushes on thy cheek. Nemesis. Ralph Waldo Emerson. **CP-EmerR**

Already i am at the end. Combe. Patti Smith. **SP-SmitP**

Already I am no longer looked at with lechery or love. A Sunset of the City. Gwendolyn Brooks. **SP-BrooG**

Already I begin, at morning. The New Place. William Dickey. **SP-DickW**

Already I recognise signs that the trouble has started. Agenda. John Hewitt. **CP-HewiJ**

Already in midsummer / I miss your feet and fur. To a Butterfly. James Merrill. **SP-MerrJ**

Already it's been years. Dancing Together. Al Young. **CP-YounA**

Already running, sprang from the womb; met. The Pacer in the Fresco. John the Baptist. Donald Davie. **CP-DavDo**

Already she seems bone thin. A Poem about Breasts. James Wright. **CP-WrigJ**

Already six years past your age! Dear Keats. Erica Jong. **SP-JongE**

Already summer crested, the decline. Hay. John Hewitt. **CP-HewiJ**

Already the Avenue troughs the light of day. Galway Kinnell. *Fr.* The Avenue Bearing the Initial of Christ into the New World. **SP-KinnG**

Already the father has sent enough of plague. Ad Regem Carolum Parodia [A Parody: To King Charles]. Andrew Marvell, *tr. fr. Latin by* William A. McQueen *and* Kiffin A. Rockwell. **CP-MarvA**

Already, the rain and cold. One Look at the Creation. Martin Edmunds. **SP-EdmuM**

Alright make it a series and call it Marry Nettie. Marry Nettie. Gertrude Stein. **CP-SteiG**

Al's wife claimed I can't be happy. "Bob Dylan." *Fr.* 11 Outlined Epitaphs. **CP-DylaB**

Alsace-Lorraine. George Meredith. **CP-MerG1**

   "Brooding on her deep fall, the many strings."

   "Eastward of Paris morn is high."

   "In Nature is no rearward step allowed."

   "Let but the rational prevail."

   "Mark where a credible ghost pulls bridle to view that bare."

   "Mother who gave birth to Jeanne, The."

   "On her lost arm love bade her look."

   "She hailed him Saint."

   "Sister Hours in circles linked, The."

   "Succourful daughters of men are the rosed and starred."

Also. Roy Fisher. **SP-FishR**

Also he has set the world. George Oppen. *Fr.* Image of the Engine. **CP-OppeG**

Also the headache of / to do right by feeling. Eros. Robert Creeley. **CP-CreeR**

Also there was another story. Also. Roy Fisher. **SP-FishR**

Alston Moor. Wystan Hugh Auden. **CP-AudWJ**

Altar, The, *see also* Commentary—The Altar. Leonard Cohen. **CP-CoheL**

Altar, The. George Herbert. **CP-HerbG**

Altar, The. Edwin Arlington Robinson. **CP-RobiE**

Altarpiece (A Meditation on Lust, Desire and Love). Jenny Joseph. **SP-JoseJ**

ALLEGORY: *Old Man's Fancy* (Poussin).

CENTERPIECE: *St. Sebastian* (Italian).

INTERIOR: *The Man Turns the Sheet for the Musician* (Dutch).

LANDSCAPE: *Jungle Days* (Dutch).

STUDY: *A Lady in her Bedroom* (Bonnard).

Altars in the Street, The. Denise Levertov. **CP-LeveD**

Altarwise by Owl-Light. Dylan Thomas. **CP-ThomD**

"Altarwise by owl-light in the half-way house." **CMoP; FaBoMo; MoAB; Son**

"And from the windy West came two-gunned Gabriel."

"Cartoon of slashes on the tide-traced crater."

"Death is all metaphors, shape in one history." **CMoP; MoAB; Son**

"First there was the lamb on knocking knees." **CMoP**

"From the oracular archives and the parchment." **CMoP**

"Let the tale's sailor from a Christian voyage." **CMoP; FaBoMo; OAEL-2**

"Now stamp the Lord's Prayer on a grain of rice." **FaBoMo**

"This was the crucifixion on the mountain." **CMoP**

"What is the metre of the dictionary?" **CMoP; FaBoMo**

Altarwise by owl-light in the half-way house. Dylan Thomas. **CMoP; FaBoMo; MoAB; Son** *Fr.* Altarwise by Owl-Light. **CP-ThomD**

Alter! When the Hills do. Emily Dickinson. **CP-DickE**

Alteram Partem. Arthur Hugh Clough. **SP-ClouA**

Altercation. David Herbert Lawrence. **CP-LawrD**

Altered from an Old English Song. Robert Burns. **CP-BurnR**

Altered look about the hills, An. Emily Dickinson. **CP-DickE**

Alternate Thoughts from Underground. Margaret Atwood. **SP-AtwM1**

Alternation. George Meredith. **CP-MerG1**

Alternative. Malcolm Lowry. **CP-LowrM**

Alternative Song for the Severed Head in "The King of the Great Clock Tower." William Butler Yeats. **CP-YeatW**

Alternatives to College. "Bob Dylan." **CP-DylaB**

Altgeld. Carl Sandburg. **CP-SandC**

Altham says / they were in a pinnance. The Gulf of Maine. Charles Olson. **SP-OlsoC** *Fr.* The Maximus Poems.

Altho' my bed were in yon muir. Fragment. Robert Burns. **CP-BurnR**

Altho' thy flowers minute, disclose. Ode to the Olive Tree. Charlotte Smith. **CP-SmitC**

Although at first it was single. The Trace. Roy Fisher. **SP-FishR**

Although constructed of the most up-to-date, technically advanced elements of woven glass. Work. Charles Kenneth Williams. **SP-WillC**

Although crowds gathered once if she but showed her face. Fallen Majesty. William Butler Yeats. **CP-YeatW**

Although entangled in prolonged grief. Carmen 65. Catullus. *Fr.* Carmina. **CP-Catul**

Although, great Queen, thou now in silence lie. In Honour of That High and Mighty Princess Queen Elizabeth of Happy Memory. Anne Bradstreet. **CP-BradA**

Although he's apparantly the youngest (his little rasta-beard is barely down and feathers). Instinct. Charles Kenneth Williams. **SP-WillC**

Although [*or* Altho'] I be the basest of mankind. St. Simeon Stylites. Tennyson. **CP-TennA**

Although I can see him still. The Fisherman. William Butler Yeats. **CP-YeatW**

Although I do not hope to turn again. Thomas Stearns Eliot. *Fr.* Ash Wednesday [*or* Ash-Wednesday]. **CP-ElioT**

Although I don't have breath enough. The Last Drowning. Robert Pack. **SP-PackR**

Although I have never learned to mow. The Coney. Paul Muldoon. **SP-MuldP**

Although I mean it, and project the meaning. The Ice-Cream Wars. John Ashbery. **SP-AshbJ**

Although I put away his life. Emily Dickinson. **CP-DickE**

Although I saw before me there the face. Inferential. Edwin Arlington Robinson. **CP-RobiE**

Although I shelter from the rain. The Lamentation of the Old Pensioner. William Butler Yeats. **CP-YeatW**

Although I was tenacious, I never learned. The Maxims of Sisyphus. Delmore Schwartz. **SP-SchwD**

Although I'd lie lapped up in linen. Under the Round Tower. William Butler Yeats. **CP-YeatW**

Although I'm apparently alone, with a pleasant but unextraordinary feeling of self-sufficiency. The Solid. Charles Kenneth Williams. **SP-WillC**

Although it is a cold evening. At the Fishhouses. Elizabeth Bishop. **CP-BishE**

Although it is my native place. Exile. John Hewitt. **CP-HewiJ**

Although it is night, I sit in the bathroom, waiting. Adolescence—II. Rita Dove. **SP-DoveR**

Although [*or* Altho'] my back be at the wa'. Here's His Health in Water. Robert Burns. **CP-BurnR**

Although my house floats on a lawn. Blues for John Coltrane, Dead at 41. William Matthews. **SP-MattW**

Although our suffering meet with no reliefe. Sauce for Sorrowes. Robert Herrick. **CP-HerrR**

Although she be more white. Gerard Manley Hopkins. *Fr.* Fragments. **CP-HopkG**

Although she was beautiful. Woman and Leopard. David St. John. **SP-StJoD**

Although the aepyornis. He "Digesteth Harde Yron." Marianne Craig Moore. **CP-MoorM**

Although the car radio warned that. Tomorrow. Donald Hall. **CP-HallD**

Although the lamp is out, and although it's dusk, late, dull, stifling summer dusk. The Color of Time. Charles Kenneth Williams. **CP-WillC**

Although the letter said. New Readings. Gerard Manley Hopkins. **CP-HopkG**

Although the relatives in the summer house. A Poem for Bhain. John Berryman. **CP-BerrJ**

Although the sky / was bright blue and clarity. Coast of Texas. Gilbert Sorrentino. **SP-SorrG**

Although thou maun never be mine. Here's a Health to Ane I Lo'e Dear. Robert Burns. **CP-BurnR**

Although thou see th'outrageous climb aloft. Bible, *O.T.* *See* Psalm 37: "Fret not thyself because of evildoers."

Although thy hand and faith, and good work[e]s too. Change. John Donne. **CBLP; EBEV** *Fr.* Elegies. **CP-DonnJ**

Although we cannot turne the fervent fit. A Will To Be Working. Robert Herrick. **CP-HerrR**

Although we curse the dreary weather. Flood. Chuck Miller. **SP-MillC**

Although we say we disbelieve. Louis MacNeice. **CP-MacNL** *Fr.* Jigsaws. **CP-MacNL**

Although you fill amethyst cups. Martial, *tr. by* William Matthews. **SP-MattW** *Fr.* Epigrams.

Although you hide in the ebb and flow. The Fish. William Butler Yeats. **CP-YeatW**

Although you know that I denied the sun to you. Daughter. Isabella Gardner. **CP-GardI**

Altitudes. Richard Wilbur. **CP-WilbR**

Always. Robert Ranke Graves. **CP-GravR**

Always / in the middle. Love, Maybe. Audre Lorde. **SP-LordA**

Always a Playground Instructor. Jim Morrison. **SP-MorrJ**

Always Another Viewpoint. Kenneth Patchen. **CP-PatcK**

Always as it holds us in one place, the earth. Immortals. James Dickey. **CP-DickJ**

Always before your voice my soul. Edward Estlin Cummings. **CP-CummE**

Always begins. Emily Dickinson. **SP-DickE**

Always behind my back I hear. Human Life. Tom Clark. **SP-ClarT**

Always day & night. Ralph Waldo Emerson. **CP-EmerR**

Always Ether Comes. Pertussin. Allen Ginsberg. **CP-GinsA**

Always for money, yes, and, yes. Twin Snakes. Leonard Nathan. **SP-NathL**

Always for thirty years now. Fish Peddler and Cobbler. Kenneth Rexroth. **SP-RexrK**

Always—I tell you this they learned. House Fear. Robert Frost. **NTP; VGW; WSC** *Fr.* The Hill Wife. **CP-FrosR**

Always I travelled farther. This House, This Country. Muriel Rukeyser. **CP-RukeM**

Always I wanted to do it myself. Self-Service. John Updike. **CP-UpdiJ**

Always in Late Summer Now, in the City. Gary Gildner. **SP-GildG**

Always in the middle of a kiss. Dirge for a Joker. Sylvia Plath. **CP-PlatS**

Always it happens when we are not there. Metamorphosis. May Sarton. **SP-SartM**

Always it's either. Al Young. **CP-YounA** *Fr.* The Song Turning Back into Itself.

Always Marry an April Girl. Ogden Nash. **CP-NashO**

Always Mine! Emily Dickinson. **CP-DickE**

Always on the horizon someone. History. Richard Shelton. **SP-ShelR**

Always on the point of falling asleep. The Middle Ages. John Haines. **SP-HainJ**

Always, on their generation's breaking wave. The Farmer, Speaking of Monuments. Wendell Berry. **CP-BerrW**

Always our old feuillage! Our Old Feuillage. Walt Whitman. **CP-WhitW**

Always, sweetheart / Carry into your room the blossoming boughs of cherry. Disagreeable Advice. David Herbert Lawrence. **CP-LawrD**

Always that old language for the new. Again, Again. Jean Garrigue. **SP-GarrJ**

Always the generations pass. Nicholas Vachel Lindsay. *Fr.* Shantung[, or The Empire of China is Crumbling Down]. **CP-LindV**

Always the Mob. Carl Sandburg. **CP-SandC**

Always the Same. Adrienne Rich. **CP-RicAE**

Always the same, when on a fated night. The Onset. Robert Frost. **CP-FrosR**

Always the solemnest moment of the year. First Snow. Howard Nemerov. **CP-NemeH**

Always the storm of propaganda blows. Carl Sandburg. *Fr.* The People, Yes. **CP-SandC**

Always This Paying. David Herbert Lawrence. **CP-LawrD**

Always this special / secret feeling, the failure. Hayden Carruth. **CP-CarHS** *Fr.* The Clay Hill Anthology.

Always this waking dream of palmtrees. The Islands. Robert Earl Hayden. **CP-HaydR**

Always too eager for the future, we. Next, Please. Philip Larkin. **CP-LarkP**

Always within me lies. Homage to Ghosts. Jean Garrigue. **SP-GarrJ**

Always you were dancing before the altar of guilt. Marge Piercy. *Fr.* A Shadow Play For Guilt. **SP-PierM**

Alzheimer's Disease. Donald Davie. **CP-DavDo**

Alzheimer's: The Husband. Charles Kenneth Williams. **SP-WillC**

Alzheimer's: The Wife. Charles Kenneth Williams. **SP-WillC**

Am I a fanatic? The opposite. Enough. Marianne Craig Moore. **CP-MoorM**

Am I a stone and not a sheep. Good Friday. Christina Georgina Rossetti. **CP-RosC1**

Am I blind alas. Fragment 41. Hilda Doolittle. **CP-DoolH**

Am I brother to you. Dabney Stuart. *Fr.* The Opposite Field. **SP-StuaD**

Am I despised because you say. To a Gentlewoman Objecting to Him His Grey Hairs. Robert Herrick. **CP-HerrR**

Am I failing? For no longer can I cast. George Meredith. **CABA; EnVR; GBL; OAEP; SCGP** *Fr.* Modern Love. **CP-MerG1**

Am I in your light? / No, go on reading. Three Sides of a Coin. Muriel Rukeyser. **CP-RukeM**

Am I kin to Sorrow. Kin to Sorrow. Edna St. Vincent Millay. **CP-MillE**

Am I My Neighbor's Keeper? Richard Eberhart. **CP-EberR**

Am I obsessed by stone? Life has worn thin here. Almanach du Printemps Vivarois. Hayden Carruth. **CP-CarHS**

Am I the river your white birds fly over? They Ask Each Other Where They Came From. Carl Sandburg. **CP-SandC**

Am I thus conquered [or conquer'd]? have I lost the powers. Sonnet 14. Mary Sidney, Countess of Montgomery Wroth. **NAEL-1; NOSC** *Fr.* Pamphilia to Amphilanthus. **CP-WrotM**

Am I to be cursed forever with becoming. Change of Season. Audre Lorde. **SP-LordA**

Am I to become profligate as if I were a blonde? Meditations in an Emergency. Frank O'Hara. **SP-OharF**

Am I wrong? The roads. Hayden Carruth. **CP-CarHS** *Fr.* The Clay Hill Anthology.

Am told that fasting gives to food. Emily Dickinson. **SP-DickE**

Am was. are leaves few this. is these a or. Edward Estlin Cummings. **CP-CummE**

Amabel. Thomas Hardy. **CP-HardT**

Amadeo— / How can death be beautiful. Modigliani's Death Mask. Marsden Hartley. **CP-HartM**

Amalgams are abundant. Emily Dickinson. **SP-DickE**

Amami, t'amo / Figliolin mio. Christina Georgina Rossetti. **CP-RosC3**

Amang the trees, where humming bees. Robert Burns. **CP-BurnR**

Amaranth, The. Nicholas Vachel Lindsay. **CP-LindV**

Amarantha. A Pastorall. Richard Lovelace. **CP-LoveR**

Amarantha sweet and fair[e]. To Amarantha, That She Would Dishevel[l] Her Hair[e]. Richard Lovelace. **CP-LoveR**

Amaryllis. Edwin Arlington Robinson. **CP-RobiE**

Amatory Lines. Thomas Gray. **CP-GrayT**

Amazing human [or Human] heart [or Heart]. Emily Dickinson. **SP-DickE**

Amazing Tale of Skunkdog, The. Patti Smith. **SP-SmitP**

Amazingly active a toothless old man. Going to Horse Flats. Robinson Jeffers. **CP-JefR2**

Amazingly young beautiful woman poets. Aging Female Poet Reads Little Magazines. Margaret Atwood. **SP-AtwM2**

Amazon chick / with an amazin' pancho villa face, An. "Bob Dylan." *Fr.* Some Other Kinds of Songs. **CP-DylaB**

Amazonian. Donald Davie. **CP-DavDo**

Amazons with Crescent-formed shield, The. Virgil, *tr. by* Sir Walter Ralegh. **CP-RaleW** *Fr.* The Aeneid [*or* Eneados, *Aeneis*].

Ambassador, The. Pablo Neruda, *tr. fr. Spanish by* Ben Belitt. **SP-NeruP**

Ambassador, The. Stevie Smith. **CP-SmitS**

Ambassador, The. Gilbert Sorrentino. **SP-SorrG**

Ambassador Puser the ambassador. Memorial Rain. Archibald MacLeish. **CP-MacLA**

Ambassadors of Grief. Carl Sandburg. **CP-SandC**

Amber Bead, The. Robert Herrick. **CP-HerrR**

Amber husk / fluted with gold. Sea Poppies. Hilda Doolittle. **CP-DoolH**

Amber spray of trees feather-brushed with the dusk, The. Watteau. Derek Walcott. **CP-WalcD** *Fr.* Midsummer.

Ambergris. Stanley Jasspon Kunitz. **CP-KuniS**

Ambience. Robert Ranke Graves. **CP-GravR**

Ambition ("In wayes to greatnesse, think on this"). Robert Herrick. **CP-HerrR**

Ambition: ("In man, ambition is the common'st thing"). Robert Herrick. **CP-HerrR**

Ambition. George Meredith. **CP-MerG2**

Ambition. Walt Whitman. **CP-WhitW**

Ambition Bird, The. Anne Sexton. **CP-SextA**

Ambition cannot find him. Emily Dickinson. **CP-DickE**

Ambition— following down this far famed slope. The Column Intended by Buonaparte for a Triumphal Edifice in Milan, Now Lying by the Way-Side in the Simplon Pass. William Wordsworth. *Fr.* Memorials of a Tour of the Continent; 1820. **CP-WorW2**

Ambition is the Stamp impress'd by Heav'n. Samuel Johnson. **CP-JohnS** *Fr.* Irene.

Ambition, power, and avarice, now have hurled. War. Percy Bysshe Shelley. *Fr.* Posthumous Fragments of Margaret Nicholson. **CP-ShelP**

Ambrosia of Dionysus and Semele, The. Robert Ranke Graves. **CP-GravR**

Ambulance passes / we sit up, The. Midnight. Jim Carroll. **SP-CarrJ**

Ambulances. Philip Larkin. **CP-LarkP**

Ambuscade, The. Sir Walter Scott. **SP-ScotW** *Fr.* The Lady of the Lake.

Ameana pulling, a foot touted high. Catullus. *See* Carmen 41: "Formianus's whore, / long-nosed."

Ameana, that banged-out bitch. Catullus. *See* Carmen 41: "Formianus's whore, / long-nosed."

Amelia Earhart. Patti Smith. **SP-SmitP**

Amen. Christina Georgina Rossetti. **CP-RosC1**

Amen. The casket like a spaceship bears her. Annie Hill's Grave. James Merrill. **SP-MerrJ**

America. Maya Angelou. **SP-AngeM**

America. Robert Creeley. **CP-CreeR**

America. John Gould Fletcher. **SP-FletJ**

America. Allen Ginsberg. **CP-GinsA**

America. Herman Melville. **SP-MelvH**

America. Walt Whitman. **CP-WhitW**

America; a Prophecy. William Blake. **CP-BlakW**
   Empire Is No More. **EnRP**
   Prophecy, A. **FaBoEH**

America, America! Delmore Schwartz. **SP-SchwD**

America As Bullring Arena. Jim Morrison. **SP-MorrJ**

America Is Hard to See. Robert Frost. **CP-FrosR**

America is like Russia. A Poem on America. Allen Ginsberg. **CP-GinsA**

America I've given you all and now I'm nothing. America. Allen Ginsberg. **CP-GinsA**

America was ablaze with lights. The Atlantic Tunnel. Louis MacNeice. **CP-MacNL**

America was always promises. Archibald MacLeish. **AmFN** *Fr.* America Was Promises. **CP-MacLA**

America Was Promises. Archibald MacLeish. **CP-MacLA**
   "America was always promises." **AmFN**

America, when you were born, and when the plains. A Letter to America. Thomas Merton. **CP-MertT**

aMERICA, you caTNip bIN. John Updike. **CP-UpdiJ**
   (ZIP Code Ode.) **CP-UpdiJ**

America, you ode for reality! America. Robert Creeley. **CP-CreeR**

American, An. Rudyard Kipling. **CP-KiplR**

American Aloe on Exhibition, The. Herman Melville. **SP-MelvH**

American Archangel you are going. Moose. Anne Sexton. **CP-SextA**

AMERICAN BANKNOTE FACTORY, THE. This Fall, 1933. Louis Zukofsky. *Fr.* 29 Songs. **CP-ZukLS**

American Boating Song. Louise McNeill. **SP-McNeL**

American Cancer Society Or There Is More Than One Way to Skin a Coon. Audre Lorde. **SP-LordA**

American Change. Allen Ginsberg. **CP-GinsA**

American Citizen. Kay Boyle. **CP-BoylK**

American critic ad 1935. Edward Estlin Cummings. **CP-CummE**

American Eagle, The. David Herbert Lawrence. **CP-LawrD**

American Express. Ted Berrigan. **SP-BerrT**

American Express, Athens, Greece. Charles Bukowski. **SP-BukC2**

American Film, An. Stephen Dunn. **SP-DunnS**

American Glamour. Al Young. **CP-YounA**

American Hakluyt. Richard Eberhart. **CP-EberR**

American Heartbreak. Langston Hughes. **SP-HughL**

American hero must triumph over, The. The Eisenhower's Visit to Franco, 1959. James Wright. **CP-WrigJ**

American horse fast thunder spotted. Ghost Dance: Prologue. Thomas Merton. *Fr.* West. *Fr.* The Geography of Lograire. **CP-MertT**

American Ikon—Lincoln. Marsden Hartley. **CP-HartM**

American Journal. Robert Earl Hayden. **CP-HaydR**

American Letter. Archibald MacLeish. **CP-MacLA**

American Lights, Seen from Off Abroad. John Berryman. **CP-BerrJ**

American papermatch packet, An. Simplex Sigillum Veri: A Catalogue. William Carlos Williams. **CP-WilW1**

American Prayer, An. Jim Morrison. **SP-MorrJ**

American Rebellion, The. Rudyard Kipling. **CP-KiplR**

American Sublime, The. Wallace Stevens. **CP-StevW**

American Time. Al Young. **CP-YounA**

American Tradition. William Wordsworth. *Fr.* The River Duddon [A Series of Sonnets]. **CP-WorW2**

American Twilights, 1957. James Wright. **CP-WrigJ**

American Wedding. James Wright. **CP-WrigJ**

Americans! / The word stands for something. O! Americans. David Herbert Lawrence. **CP-LawrD**

Americans are innocents abroad. Mr Sharp in Florence. Donald Davie. **CP-DavDo**

Americans, The ("Cosmologist says, The"). Charles Olson. **CP-OlsoC**

Americans, The ("What the cosmologist meant by what constitutes"). Charles Olson. **CP-OlsoC**

America's Plutonic Ecstasies. Hart Crane. **CP-CranH**

Ametas and Thestylis Making Hay-Ropes. Andrew Marvell. **CP-MarvA**

Amherst Heart is plain and whole, The. Emily Dickinson. **SP-DickE**

Amiable putrescence carpenters, An. Edward Estlin Cummings. **CP-CummE**

Amicizia: Sirocchia Son D'Amor. Christina Georgina Rossetti. *Fr.* Il Rosseggiar Dell'Oriente Canzoniere. **CP-RosC3**

Amico e Più Che Amico Mio. Christina Georgina Rossetti. *Fr.* Il Rosseggiar Dell'Oriente Canzoniere. **CP-RosC3**

Amico pesce, poiver vorrà. Christina Georgina Rossetti. **CP-RosC3**

Amid a fertile region green with wood. Picture of Daniel in the Lions' Den, at Hamilton Palace. William Wordsworth. **CP-WorW2**

Amid that Platonic statuary, of athletes. The Class Will Come to Order. Stanley Jasspon Kunitz. **CP-KuniS**

Amid the cries of gang walls and surprises the echoes come forward. Thomas Merton. *Fr.* Cables to the Ace. **CP-MertT**

Amid the dark control of lawless sway. Sonnet on Milton. William Wordsworth. **CP-WorW1**

Amid the desolation of a city. The Tower of Famine. Percy Bysshe Shelley. **CP-ShelP**

Amid the doctors in the Temple at twelve, between. The Prayer of the Middle-Aged Man. John Berryman. **CP-BerrJ**

Amid the gray trunks of ancient trees we found. The Lilies. Wendell Berry. **CP-BerrW**

Amid the plash of scarlet mud. George Meredith. *Fr.* The Revolution. **CP-MerG1**

Amid the shade of a deserted hall. Ruin. Christina Georgina Rossetti. **CP-RosC3**

Amid the smoke of cities did you pass. To Joanna. William Wordsworth. **CP-WorW1**

Amid the storms of war, with curious eyes. Lucan, *tr. by* Samuel Johnson. **CP-JohnS** *Fr.* Pharsalia.

Amid these crowded pews must I sit and seem to pray. O Qui Me—! Arthur Hugh Clough. **SP-ClouA**

Amid these days of order, ease, prosperity. The Dying Veteran. Walt Whitman. **CP-WhitW**

Amid this dance of objects sadness steals. In a Carriage, upon the Banks of the Rhine. William Wordsworth. *Fr.* Memorials of a Tour of the Continent; 1820. **CP-WorW2**

Amidst the ample field of things. Reason and Imagination. Christopher Smart. **SP-SmarC**

Amidst the Faltering. Stephen Dunn. **SP-DunnS**

Amidst these glorious works of Thine. Hymn for the Opening of Thomas Starr King's House of Worship. John Greenleaf Whittier. **CP-WhitJ**

Amidst Thuringia's wooded hills she dwelt. The Two Elizabeths. John Greenleaf Whittier. **CP-WhitJ**

Amidst thy sacred effigies. The Emancipation Group. John Greenleaf Whittier. **CP-WhitJ**

Amish, The. John Updike. **CP-UpdiJ**

Amitabha's Vow. Gary Snyder. **CP-SnydG** *Fr.* Burning. *Fr.* Myths and Texts.

Amitites. Ezra Pound. **SP-PounE**

Amnesia. Adrienne Rich. **SP-RicA2**

Amnesiac. Sylvia Plath. **CP-PlatS**

Amnesty. Howard Nemerov. **CP-NemeH**

Amo Ergo Sum. Kathleen Jessie Raine. **SP-RainK**

'Amo!' Four walls constrict great purposes. Quique Amavit. Wystan Hugh Auden. **CP-AudWJ**

Amo Sacrum Vulgus. David Herbert Lawrence. **CP-LawrD**

Amoeba. John Updike. **CP-UpdiJ**

Amoebaean for Daddy. Maya Angelou. **SP-AngeM**

Among / fucks / directly. Poemless Rhymes for the Times. Charles Olson. **CP-OlsoC**

Among / of / green. The Locust Tree in Flower. William Carlos Williams. **CP-WilW1**

Among / the leaves. William Carlos Williams. *See* The Locust Tree in Flower.

Among / these / red pieces of. Edward Estlin Cummings. **CP-CummE**

Among a grave fraternity of Monks. The Foregoing Subject Resumed. William Wordsworth. **CP-WorW2**

Among a hundred windows shining. A Window. Denise Levertov. **CP-LeveD**

Among all lovely things my Love had been. William Wordsworth. **CP-WorW1**

Among all the waste there are the intense stories. Muriel Rukeyser. *Fr.* Letter to the Front. **CP-RukeM**

Among Artisans' Houses. Donald Davie. **CP-DavDo**

Among birches moving their white halfnakedness. The Woman. Hayden Carruth. *Fr.* Contra Mortem. **CP-CarHL**

Among cocoa-nut palms of a far oasis. The Moth That Made God Blind. Hart Crane. **CP-CranH**

Among deep woods is the dismantled scite. Saint Monica. Charlotte Smith. **CP-SmitC**

Among Grass. Muriel Rukeyser. **CP-RukeM**

Among leaf-green / this morning, they. Delta Poems. Muriel Rukeyser. **CP-RukeM**

Among market stalls the pickpockets prowl. Santiago: Market Day in Winter. Stephen Dobyns. **SP-DobyS**

Among my friends love is a great sorrow. Robert Duncan. **SP-DuncR**

Among my own, I'm a figure of fun. The Exile, *En Famille*. James McAuley. **SP-McAuJ**

Among orange-tile rooftops. Prospect. Sylvia Plath. **CP-PlatS**

Among our good deeds of this date. Behavior. Howard Nemerov. **CP-NemeH**

Among [*or* Amang] our young lass[i]es there's [*or* is] Muirland Meg. Muirland Meg. Robert Burns. **CP-BurnR**

Among Ourselves and with All Nations. Kenneth Patchen. **CP-PatcK**

Among pelagian travellers. On the Circuit. Wystan Hugh Auden. **CP-AudeW**

Among School Children. William Butler Yeats. **CP-YeatW**

Among that band of Officers was one. William Wordsworth. **ChER,** *book* 9, *ll.* 288–585; *Fr.* Residence in France ("Even as a river,—partly (it might seem)"). *Fr.* The Prelude; Growth of a Poet's Mind [1850 vers.]. **CP-WorW3**

Among the anthropophagi. Funebrial Reflection. Ogden Nash. **CP-NashO**

Among the beetroots, where we are constrained. Geoffrey Hill. *Fr.* The Mystery of the Charity of Charles Péguy. **CP-HillG**

Among the Brobdingnagians Gulliver. Shaving Mirror. John Updike. **CP-UpdiJ**

Among the bumblebees in red-top hay, a freckled field of brown-eyed. Adelaide Crapsey. Carl Sandburg. **CP-SandC**

Among the changing months, May stands confest. On May. James Thomson. **CP-ThomJ**

Among the disasters that discention brings. Blame the Reward of Princes. Robert Herrick. **CP-HerrR**

Among the dwellers in the silent fields. Grace Darling. William Wordsworth. **CP-WorW2**

Among the dwellings framed by birds. A Wren's Nest. William Wordsworth. **CP-WorW2**

Among the forests of the North. The Caribou. Ogden Nash. **CP-NashO**

Among the Gods. Stanley Jasspon Kunitz. **CP-KuniS**

Among the grassroots. Dogheads. Carl Sandburg. **CP-SandC**

Among the guests who often stayed. Percy Bysshe Shelley. **ChER** *Fr.* Peter Bell the Third. **CP-ShelP**

Among the happy wits this age hath shown. In Honor of Du Bartas, 1641. Anne Bradstreet. **CP-BradA**

Among the heathy hills and ragged woods. Written with a Pencil, Standing by the Fall of Fyers, near Loch-Ness. Robert Burns. **CP-BurnR**

Among the high-branching, leafless boughs. The View from an Attic Window. Howard Nemerov. **CP-NemeH**

Among the Hills. John Greenleaf Whittier. **CP-WhitJ**
Prelude: "Along the roadside, like the flowers of gold." **AP; APN-1; NAAL-1; NAAL-3; OxBA; PoEL-4**

Among the holy Mountains high, *par. by* Milton. Bible, O.T. *See* Psalm 87: "His foundation is in the holy mountains."

Among the iodoform, in twilight-sleep. The Leg. Karl Shapiro. **SP-ShapK**

Among the leaves the small birds sing. Lauds. Wystan Hugh Auden. **TrCP** *Fr.* Horae Canonicae. **CP-AudeW**

Among the legends sung or said. The Wishing Bridge. John Greenleaf Whittier. **CP-WhitJ**

Among the many selves that throng my flesh. Sonnet. John Hewitt. **CP-HewiJ**

Among the men and women the multitude. Among the Multitude. Walt Whitman. **CP-WhitW**

Among the *Mirtles*, as I walkt. Mrs. Eliz. Wheeler, Under the Name of the Lost Shepardesse. Robert Herrick. **CP-HerrR**

Among the more irritating minor ideas. Looking across the Fields and Watching the Birds Fly. Wallace Stevens. **CP-StevW**

Among the mountains I wandered and saw blue haze and red crag and. Masses. Carl Sandburg. **CP-SandC**

Among the mountains were we nursed, loved Stream! To the River Derwent. William Wordsworth. *Fr.* Poems Composed or Suggested During a Tour, in the Summer of 1833. **CP-WorW2**

Among the Multitude. Walt Whitman. **CP-WhitW**

Among the Narcissi. Sylvia Plath. **CP-PlatS**

Among the night-time tribes, in the night-time forest. The Reflection. Frederick Morgan. **CP-MorgF**

Among the numbers who employ. To Lord Harley, since Earl of Oxford, on His Marriage. Jonathan Swift. **CP-SwifJ**

Among the pickled foetuses and bottled bones. Siena Mi Fe'; Disfecemi Maremma. Ezra Pound. **MoAmPo** *Fr.* Hugh Selwyn Mauberley. (Life and Contacts). **SP-PounE**

Among the pines we ran and called. Monologue at Midnight. Robert Penn Warren. **SP-WarrR**

Among the quiet people of the frost. John Haines. *Fr.* The Traveler. **SP-HainJ**

Among the rain. The Great Figure. William Carlos Williams. **CP-WilW1**

Among the Red Guns. Carl Sandburg. **CP-SandC**

Among the Rocks. Robert Browning. **OxBSP** *Fr.* James Lee's Wife. **CP-BroR1**

Among the Ruins of a Convent in the Apennines. William Wordsworth. *Fr.* Memorials of a Tour in Italy, 1837. **CP-WorW2**

Among the serviceable mills and. The Feeders. Donald Davie. **CP-DavDo**

Among the shaded animals. The Cave of Lascaux. Robert Pack. **SP-PackR**

Among the shades and cries of the night. The Indian. Randall Jarrell. **CP-JarrR**

Among the shadows where two streets cross. Trafficker. Carl Sandburg. **CP-SandC**

Among the shapes and shadow-shapes. Carl Sandburg. *Fr.* Timesweep. **CP-SandC**

Among the silvery, the dulled sparkling mica lights of tar roofs. An East Window on Elizabeth Street. James Schuyler. **CP-SchuJ**

Among the smoke and fog of a December afternoon. Portrait of a Lady. Thomas Stearns Eliot. **CP-ElioT**

Among the thousands who with hail and cheer. To Oliver Wendell Holmes. John Greenleaf Whittier. **CP-WhitJ**

Among the wet and sodden grass. The Rain Fell Heavily. Malcolm Lowry. **CP-LowrM**

Among their graven shapes to whom. Fitz-Greene Halleck. John Greenleaf Whittier. **CP-WhitJ**

Among these latter busts we count by scores. Protus. Robert Browning. **CP-BroR1**

Among these North Shore tennis tans I sit. Commencement, Pingree School. John Updike. **CP-UpdiJ**

Among these tempests great and manifold. His Hope or Sheet-Anchor. Robert Herrick. **CP-HerrR**

Among These Turf-Stacks. Louis MacNeice.
(Turf-Stacks.) **CP-MacNL**

Among those I met at Fez, let me mention the celebrated preacher. Ibn Abbad Described by a Friend (Ibn Qunfud). Thomas Merton. *Fr.* Readings from Ibn Abbad. **CP-MertT**

Among Those Killed in the Dawn Raid Was a Man Aged a Hundred. Dylan Thomas. **CP-ThomD**

Among thy fancies, tell me this. The Kisse. Robert Herrick. **CP-HerrR**

Among twenty snowy mountains. Thirteen Ways of Looking at a Blackbird. Wallace Stevens. **CP-StevW**

Among white lilac trusses, green-gold spaces of sunlit grass. May 24th or So. James Schuyler. **CP-SchuJ**

Amor Dormente? Christina Georgina Rossetti. *Fr.* Il Rosseggiar Dell'Oriente Canzoniere. **CP-RosC3**

Amor fati / The love of fate. George Oppen. *Fr.* Of Being Numerous. **CP-OppeG**

Amor Loci. Wystan Hugh Auden. **CP-AudeW**

Amor Mundi. Christina Georgina Rossetti. **CP-RosC1**

Amor Si Sveglia? Christina Georgina Rossetti. *Fr.* Il Rosseggiar Dell'Oriente Canzoniere. **CP-RosC3**

Amor Vincit Omnia. Wystan Hugh Auden. **CP-AudWJ**

Amore E Dispetto. Christina Georgina Rossetti. **CP-RosC3**

Amore E Dovere. Christina Georgina Rossetti. **CP-RosC3**

Amores. Ovid, *tr. fr. Latin.*
"Blest was my reign, retiring Cynthia cry'd." **CP-JohnS**
"Here Tantalus in water seek[e]s for water, and doth miss[e]." **CP-RaleW**, *tr. by* Sir Walter Ralegh;
Ovid in Love. **SP-MahoD**
"Day being humid and my head, The."

Amoretti. Edmund Spenser. **CP-Spens**
I. "Happy ye leaves whenas those lily [*or* lilly] hands." **EBEV; LoBV; NAAL-1; NIP; OAEL-1; PoE; Son;**
III. "Soverayne beauty which I doo admire, The." **PoEL-1**
V. "Rudely thou wrongst my dear heart's desire." **EIL**
VIII. "More than most fair [*or* fayre], full of the living fire [*or* fyre]." **CABA; HBV; NoP; OAEP; PoE; Son; TEP; TrGrPo**
X. "Unrighteous Lord of love, what law is this." **NoP**
XIII. "In That proud port, which her so goodly graceth." **Son**
XV. "Ye tradeful merchants that, with weary toil." **HeIL; HeIP; LiTB; NIP; OAEL-1; Son; TrGrPo**
XVI. "One day as I unwarily did gaze." **OAEL-1**
XIX. "Merry cuckoo, messenger of spring, The." **OBSC**
XXII. "This holy season, fit to fast and pray." **PoE**
XXVI. "Sweet is the rose, but grows upon a brere." **EIL**
XXVII. "Fair proud, now tell me, why should fair be proud." **Son**
XXXIV. "Like as a ship, that through the ocean wide." **NAEL-1; OBSC; PoE**
XXXVII. "What guile [*or* guyle] is this, that those her golden tresses." **NAEL-1; NoP; OBSC; PAI; Son; TrGrPo**
XL. "Mark when she smiles with amiable cheer." **OBSC**
XLIV. "When those renowned noble peers of Greece." **PoE**
XLVII. "Trust not the treason of those smiling looks." **TrGrPo**
LIV. "Of this world's theatre in which we stay." **NAEL-1; NIP; NoP; OAEL-1**
LV. "So oft as I her beauty do behold." **HBV; Son; TrGrPo**
LVI. "Fair ye be sure, but cruel and unkind." **Son**
LXI. "Glorious image of the Maker's beauty, The." **Son**
LXII. "Weary year his race now having run, The." **OBSC**
LXIII. "After long storms and tempests sad assay." **FaBoEn; OAEL-1; OAEP; OBSC**
LXIV. "Coming [*or* Comming] to kiss [*or* kisse] her lips [*or* lyps], (such grace I found)." **EBEV; LoBV; NAEL-1; OAEL-1; Son**
LXV. "Doubt which ye misdeeme, fayre love, is vaine, The." **NAEL-1**
LXX. "Fresh Spring, the herald of love's mighty king." **AWP; CABA; ChTr; EIL; FF; FaBoEn; HAP; HBV; InPS; NoP; OBEV; OBSC; PoE; SeCeV; Son; ViBoPo**
(Fresh Spring, the Herald.) **LiTB**
LXXI. "I joy to see how, in your drawen work." **PoE**
LXXII. "Oft when my spirit doth spread her bolder wings." **OAEP; OBSC; Son**
LXXIV. "Most happy letters framed by skilfull trade." **NAEL-1**
LXXVI. "Fair bosom! fraught with virtue's richest treasure." **NIP**
LXXVII. "Was it a dream, or did I see it plain?" **CBLP; NIP**
LXXIX. "Men call you fair [*or* fayre], and you do[e] credit it." **AWP; FaBoBe; NAEL-1; NoP; Son**
(Sonnet: "Men call you fair, and you do credit it.") **BLPL**
LXXXI. "Fair [*or* Fayre] is my love, when her fair [*or* fayre] golden heares." **EIL; NoP; Son**
LXXXII. "Joy of my life, full oft for loving you." **HeIP**
LXXXIII. "Let not one sparke of filthy lustfull fyre." **TEP**
LXXXIX. "Like as the culver on the bared bough." **FF; GBL; PBBP; PoE**

By Her That Is Most Assured to Her Self. **EnRePo**

"How long shall this like dying life endure." **AAS; EnRePo**

"Lacking my love, I go from place to place." **EiL; NoSic**

Like a huntsman. **EnRePo; GBL; HeIP; NAEL-1; NoP; OAEP; PoE; PoEL-1; SeCePo; Son; TrGrPo**

"Most glorious lord of life that on this day." **CABA; ChIV-2; EBCP; EiL; EnRePo; HAP; HBV; InPS; LiTB; NAEL-1; NOBE; NOCV; NoP; NoSic; OBEV; OHIP; OxBoCh; PoE; SeCeV; Son; TRV; TrPWD**

   (Easter.) **NOBE; OBEV; PeECV**

   (Easter Morning.) **OHIP; TRV**

   ("Most Glorious Lord of lyfe, that on this day.") **PeECV**

My Love Is Like to Ice. **ErPo; FF; FPL; ImPo; LiTB; PAI; TrGrPo**

"New year, forth looking out of Janus' gate." **NoSic**

"One day I wrote her name upon the strand." **AWP; ArLo; BLPL; BoLoP; CABA; CBLP; EBEV; EPCY; EiL; FiP; GBL; HAP; HBV; HeIP; ImPo; InPS; LiTB; NAEL-1; NoP; NoSic; OAEL-1; OAEP; PAI; PBMP; PoE; SeCePo; SeCeV; Son; TFi; WeW**

Panther, knowing that his spotted hide, The. **EnRePo**

Since I Have Lacked the Comfort. **EnRePo**

Amorous Debate, An. Thom Gunn. **CP-GunnT**

Amorous Leander, beautiful and young. Christopher Marlowe. **PeHV** *Fr.* Hero and Leander. **CP-MarlC**

Amorous Neptune. Christopher Marlowe. **NOBE** *Fr.* Hero and Leander. **CP-MarlC**

Amorphous is the mind; its quality. Edna St. Vincent Millay. **CP-MillE**

Amos. John Berryman. **CP-BerrJ**

Amour. David Herbert Lawrence. **CP-LawrD**

Amours de Voyage. Arthur Hugh Clough. **SP-ClouA**

   Ah, That I Were Far Away. **OBNC**

   (Upon Apennine Slope.) **FaBoPP**

   Claude to Eustace. **PeLV**

   Claude to Eustace: "Ah, Let Me Look." **EnVR**

   Claude to Eustace: "I am in love. . . ." **EnVR; FaBoVe**

   Claude to Eustace: "Juxtaposition is great." **CBLP**

   Claude to Eustace: "No, the Christian faith, as at any rate I understood it." **EnVR**

   Claude to Eustace: "Shall we come out of it all. . . ." **EBVVPR**

   Claude to Eustace: "There are two different kinds, I believe, og human attraction." **GTBS-6**

   Claude to Eustace: "These are the facts." **FaBoVe**

   Claude to Eustace: "Tibur is beautiful, too, and the orchard slopes, and the Anio." **GTBS-6**

   Claude to Eustace: "Yes, we are fighting at last, it appears. This morning, as usual." **EBVV; OXAEP-2; PeVV**

   Claude to Eustace—from Bellagio. **FaBoVe**

   "Dear Eustatio, I write that you may write me an answer." **EBVV; EBVVPR; FaBoVe; OBTV; OXAEP-2**

   "Dulce it is, and *decorum*, no doubt, for the country to fall, to." **EBVV; EnVR; FaBoPV; OAEP; OXAEP-2**

   "Farewell, politics, utterly! What can I do? I can not." **FaBoPV**

   Georgina Trevellyn to Luisa: "At last dearest Louisa, I take my pen to address you." **EBVVPR**

   Georgina Trevellyn to Luisa: "Dearest Louisa, Enquire if you please. . . ." **FaBoVe**

   "I cannot stay at Florence, not even to wait for a letter." **EBVVPR,** *canto* 5, 7;

   "Is it illusion? or does there a spirit from perfecter ages." **EBEV; OBNC; OXAEP-2**

   (Spirit from Perfecter Ages.) **OBNC**

   Juxtaposition. **OBNC**

   (Claude to Eustace.) **CBLP**

   "Luther, they say, was unwise; he didn't see how things were going." **FaBoVe**

   Mary Trevellyn to Miss Roper. **FaBoVe**

   "Oh, 'tisn't manly, of course, 'tisin't manly, this method of / wooing;." **EBVVPR,** *canto* 2, 14;

   "Only think, dearest Louisa, what fearful scenes we have witnessed!" **EBVV**

   "Rome disappoints me still; but I shrink and adapt myself to it." **EBVV; EBVVPR; FaBoPP; OBTV; OXAEP-2**

   (Rome.) **FaBoPP**

   Rome ("Rome disappoints me much"). **FaBoPP**

   "Rome will not suit me, Eustace; the priests and soldiers possess / it;." **EBVVPR,** *canto* 5, 10;

   "So, I have seen a man killed!" **EBVV; PeVV**

   "To-morrow we're starting for Florence." **EBVVPR,** *canto* 2, 15;

   "When God makes a great Man he intends all others to crush him." **OBSV**

"Wherefore and how I am certain, I can hardly tell; but it [*or is so*]." **EBVVPR,** *canto* 2, 13;

"You have heard nothing; of course I know you can have heard / nothing." **EBVVPR,** *canto* 5, 11;

Amphibian. Robert Browning. **CP-BroR2**

Amphion the Theban and Arion the Methymnian were both mythical and both singers. The New Song. Clement of Alexandria, *tr. fr. Greek by* Thomas Merton. **CP-MertT**

Ample Garden, The. Robert Ranke Graves. **CP-GravR**

Ample make this Bed. Emily Dickinson. **CP-DickE**

Amplitude. Tess Gallagher. **SP-GallT**

Amplitude,—voltage,—the one friend calls for the one. Message. John Berryman. **CP-BerrJ**

Amputated human hearts pulse in the great glass jars, The. Cowardice. Isabella Gardner. **CP-GardI**

Amru'l Qais and Labīd and Akhtal and blind A'sha and Qais. Basil Bunting, *after* Manuchehri. **CP-BuntB**

Amsterdam. James Merrill. **SP-MerrJ**

Amsterdam Letter. Jean Garrigue. **SP-GarrJ**

Amulet, The. Ralph Waldo Emerson. **CP-EmerR**

Amy Lowell Thoughts. James Schuyler. **CP-SchuJ**

Amy Wentworth. John Greenleaf Whittier. **CP-WhitJ**

   "Her fingers shame the ivory keys." **AnAmPo; BeLS**

Amyntor from beyond the Sea to Alexis. Richard Lovelace. **CP-LoveR**

Amyntor's Grove. Richard Lovelace. **CP-LoveR**

Amy's Cruelty. Elizabeth Barrett Browning. **CP-BroEB**

An "I" can never be a great man. Trigorin. Stephen Spender. **CP-SpenS**

An' O, for ane-and-twenty, Tam! O, for Ane-and-Twenty Tam. Robert Burns. **CP-BurnR**

An somebodie were come again. Carl an the King Come. Robert Burns. **CP-BurnR**

An' that man sweat blood. Canto 22. Ezra Pound. *Fr.* Cantos. **CP-PoCan**

An' that year Metevsky went over to America del Sud. Canto 38. Ezra Pound. *Fr.* Cantos. **CP-PoCan**

Anabasis, The. Allen Tate. **CP-TateA**

Anacortes-Sydney Run, The. Richard Hugo. **CP-HugoR**

Anacreon, *after* Anacreon, Ode 69; *see also* "Painter, by unmatch'd desert." William Wordsworth. **CP-WorW1**

Anacreon's Grave. Johann Wolfgang von Goethe, *tr. fr. German by* James Wright. **CP-WrigJ**

Anacreontic. Robert Herrick. **CP-HerrR**

   (Anacreontike.) **CP-HerrR**

Anacreontike. Robert Herrick. **CP-HerrR**

Anacreontike. Robert Herrick. *See* Anacreontic.

Anacrontik Verse. Robert Herrick. *See* Brisk methinks I am, and fine.

Anactoria. Algernon Charles Swinburne. **SP-SwinA**

Anaemia, dyspepsia and ulcer / affect the chambermaid. Below the Stairs. James Schuyler. **CP-SchuJ**

Anagram, The. John Donne. *Fr.* Elegies. **CP-DonnJ**

Anagram, An. *Unknown.* **CP-BradA**

Anahorish. Seamus Heaney. **SP-HeanS**

Anaktoria. Frederick Morgan. **SP-MorgF**

Analogue. Howard Nemerov. **CP-NemeH**

Analogue of Unity in Multeity. Richard Eberhart. **CP-EberR**

Analysand. Stevie Smith. **CP-SmitS**

Analysis of a Theme. Wallace Stevens. **CP-StevW**

Analyst. Phoebe Hesketh. **SP-HeskP**

Ana(Mary-Army)gram. George Herbert. **CP-HerbG**

Anansi, black busybody of the folktales. Spider. Sylvia Plath. **CP-PlatS**

Anaphora. Elizabeth Bishop. **CP-BishE**

Anaphora, or the Figure of Report. Sir Walter Ralegh. *Fr.* The Arte of English Poesie. **CP-RaleW**

Anaphylactic shock, they talk about. And Is Silent. Howard Nemerov. **CP-NemeH**

Anarchic anger came to beat us down. A Storm of Angels. May Sarton. **SP-SartM**

Anasazi. Gary Snyder. **CP-SnydG**

Anashuya and Vijaya. William Butler Yeats. **CP-YeatW**

Anat and Acbat. The Loves of Anat, I. Charles Olson. **CP-OlsoC**

Anatole Anatole the long jets. Prayer to Saint Anatole. Thomas Merton. *Fr.* Cables to the Ace. **CP-MertT**

Anatomical dishabille. Emily Dickinson. **SP-DickE**

Anatomize their work. Novices. Marianne Craig Moore. **CP-MoorM**

Anatomy. Walter de la Mare. **CP-DeLaW**

Anatomy. Gilbert Sorrentino. **SP-SorrG**

Anatomy of a Cliché. Michael Hartnett. **SP-HarMi**

"Listen, / if I came to you, out of the wind."
Mo Ghrá Thú. **PeIV**

"Some white academy of grace."
Anatomy of Melancholy, The. Thomas Merton. **CP-MertT**

Anatomy of Monotony. Wallace Stevens. **CP-StevW**

Anatomy [or Anatomie] of the World, An[: The First Anniversary]. John Donne. **CP-DonnJ**
First Anniversary [or Anniversarie], The. **AnAnS-1; FaBoRV; MasP; SeCV-1**
("Verse hath a middle nature: heaven keeps souls.") **FaBoRV**, ll. 473–74;
"And new philosophy calls all in doubt." **NOSC**
Doth not a Tenarif[e], or Higher Hill. **ChTr**
"She, she is dead; she's dead: when thou knowest [or know'st] this." **JCP**
Funeral Elegy, A.
"She, she is dead; she's dead: when thou knowest this." **JCP**
To the Praise of the Dead, and the Anatomy.
Verse and Fame. **FaBoRV**

Anaxagoras. David Herbert Lawrence. **CP-LawrD**

Ance mair I hail thee, thou gloomy December! Gloomy December. Robert Burns. **CP-BurnR**

Ance)dance / -ing millions all. Edward Estlin Cummings. **CP-CummE**

Ancestor. John Berryman. **CP-BerrJ**

Ancestors. Tom Clark. **SP-ClarT**

Ancestors. Robert Ranke Graves. **CP-GravR**

Ancestors, The. Allen Tate. **CP-TateA**

Ancestral. Archibald MacLeish. **CP-MacLA**

Ancestral Houses. William Butler Yeats. **CP-YeatW; LiTB; OAEL-2** Fr. Meditations in Time of Civil War. **CP-YeatW**

Ancestral sun, do you remember us. Kathleen Jessie Raine. Fr. To the Sun. **SP-RainK**

Anchor Song. Rudyard Kipling. **CP-KiplR**

Anchorage. Margaret Atwood. **SP-AtwM2**

Anchored. Paul Laurence Dunbar. **CP-DunbP**

Anchored a ways off Buoy Rocks the sailboat. Smalley Bar. Marge Piercy. **SP-PierM**

A(ncient)a / weigh / tless. Edward Estlin Cummings. **CP-CummE**

Ancient and Modern Italy Compared. James Thomson. Fr. Liberty. **CP-ThomJ**

Ancient bridge, and a more ancient tower, An. My House. William Butler Yeats. **CP-YeatW; LiTB** Fr. Meditations in Time of Civil War. **CP-YeatW**

Ancient dame, how wide and vast. Ode on the Death of a Lady. Vincent Bourne, tr. fr. Latin by William Cowper. **CP-CowpW**

Ancient drop of feudal blood, An. Ralph Waldo Emerson. **CP-EmerR**

Ancient forests of China logged, The. Gary Snyder. **CP-SnydG** Fr. Logging. Fr. Myths and Texts.
("But ye shall destroy their altars.") **CP-SnydG**

Ancient Gesture, An. Edna St. Vincent Millay. **CP-MillE**

Ancient lady who dwelt in Rome, An. Ralph Waldo Emerson. **CP-EmerR**

Ancient Mansion, The. George Crabbe. **SP-CrabG** Fr. Posthumous Tales.

Ancient of rivers—called the New—. Ballad of New River. Louise McNeill. **SP-McNeL**

Ancient poets and their learned rhymes [or rimes], The. An Answer to Some Verses Made in His Praise. Sir John Suckling. **CP-SuckJ**

Ancient Proverb, An. William Blake. **CP-BlakW**

Ancient rule prescribed for true knights, An. Absent Crusader. Robert Ranke Graves. **CP-GravR**

Ancient song, reciting, ending, An. Old Chants. Walt Whitman. **CP-WhitW**

Ancient Way Rising. Anne Waldman. **SP-WaldA**

Ancient Speech, The. Kathleen Jessie Raine. **PoSH** Fr. Eileann Chanaidh. **SP-RainK**

Ancient to Ancients, An. Thomas Hardy. **CP-HardT**

Ancient Wars, The. Paul Zimmer. **SP-ZimmP**

Ancient Wisdom Speaks. Hilda Doolittle. **CP-DoolH**

Ancient, world-old Elk paths. Elk Trails. Gary Snyder. **CP-SnydG**

Ancients—all males, of course—, The. Scapegoat. Phoebe Hesketh. **SP-HeskP**

Ancients called me Chaos: my great yeares, ad. fr. Latin of Ovid, Fasti. Sir Walter Ralegh. **CP-RaleW**

And. Robert Creeley. **CP-CreeR**

And / I came here in my young youth. Canto 26. Ezra Pound. Fr. Cantos. **CP-PoCan**

&. Richard Wilbur. **CP-WilbR**

And a family of two is exploring the Student Union. Orientation Week. Ron Koertge. **SP-KoerR**

And a Few More Cargo Songs, sels. Thomas Merton. Fr. East. Fr. The Geography of Lograire. **CP-MertT**

And a girl singing in the symbol air, crossing of gold, a. Muriel Rukeyser. **CP-RukeM**

And a Man Went Out Alone. Kenneth Patchen. **CP-PatcK**

And a poetry in which as in a film. "Hugh MacDiarmid." **SP-MacDH** Fr. The Kind of Poetry I Want.

And a small. To a Mexican Pig-Bank. William Carlos Williams. **CP-WilW1**

And a voice like a voice in dreams cried out in the stone wilderness. An Incident in the Life of a Prophet. Thomas McGrath. **CP-McGrT**

And, after all, it is to them we return. Quaint Mazes. Geoffrey Hill. **NoAM** Fr. An Apology for the Revival of Christian Architecture in England. **CP-HillG**

And after forty years her flowers failed to sing. Saying Goodbye to Mrs. Noraine. Richard Hugo. **CP-HugoR**

And after these the Sea Nymphs marched all. The Sea Nymphs. Edmund Spenser. **CBCK** Fr. The Faerie Queene. **CP-Spens**

And again the screech of the scaffold. Window Washer. Charles Simic. **SP-SimiC**

And Aged Tiriel. stood before the Gates of his beautiful palace. Tiriel. William Blake. **CP-BlakW**

&(all during the / dropsin). Edward Estlin Cummings. **CP-CummE**

And all hours long, the town. Noise of Battle. David Herbert Lawrence. **CP-LawrD**

And all is well, though [or tho'] faith and form. Tennyson. **EBVVPR; OAEL-2** Fr. In Memoriam A. H. H. **CP-TennA**

And All That Came Thereafter. Robert Penn Warren. **SP-WarrR**

And all that is this day. The Hangman's Great Hands. Kenneth Patchen. **CP-PatcK**

And all this here, everything I write, of course. "Hugh MacDiarmid." **SP-MacDH** Fr. In Memoriam James Joyce.

And although that music curved. Allegro Moderato. James McAuley. Fr. The Exile's Fifth Symphony. **SP-McAuJ**

And angling too, that solitary vice. Byron. **SD** Fr. Don Juan. **CP-Byron**

And another regrettable thing about death. Perfection Wasted. John Updike. **CP-UpdiJ**

And answer made King Arthur, breathing hard. Tennyson. **PeECV**, ll. 330–440; Fr. The Passing of Arthur. **FHYEP; NAEL-2; OBNC** Fr. Idylls of the King. **CP-TennA**

And are ye one of the Hermitage. The Inquiry. Thomas Hardy. Fr. At Casterbridge Fair. **CP-HardT**

And arise whatever for? / SUGAR FREE! SUGAR FREE? TAB. I Sit Down to Type. James Schuyler. **CP-SchuJ**

And art thou born, brave babe? Blessed be thy birth! An Epigram on the Prince's Birth. 1630. Ben Jonson. **CP-JonsB**

And art thou cold and lowly laid. Allan-Bane's Lament. Sir Walter Scott. **SP-ScotW** Fr. The Lady of the Lake.

And art thou grieved, sweet and sacred Dove. George Herbert. **CP-HerbG** (Ephesians 4:30. Grieve not the Holy Spirit, etc.) **CP-HerbG**

And as for me, though that I konne [or can] but [or my wit be] lyte. Geoffrey Chaucer. **CH; HeIP; ViBoPo** Fr. The Legend of Good Women. **CP-ChauG**

And as the light divided the dark. Ralph Waldo Emerson. **CP-EmerR**

And as the war in its fifth spring. The Legend of the Dead Soldier. Bertolt Brecht, tr. fr. German by Louis MacNeice. **CP-MacNL**

And as time past when Cato the Severe. Ultimus Heroum: or, To the Most Learned, and to the Right Honourable, Henry, Marquesse of Dorchester. Robert Herrick. **CP-HerrR**

And at these words there rose against the ark. John Gould Fletcher. **SP-FletJ** Fr. Branches of Adam.

And ate so much the bill was five dollars. Two Boys Went Into a Dream Diner. Allen Ginsberg. **CP-GinsA**

And because you love me. Both Sides of the Medal. David Herbert Lawrence. **CP-LawrD**

And bee in his brave court a glorioue light. Sonnet 4. Mary Sidney, Countess of Montgomery Wroth. Fr. A Crowne of Sonetts Dedicated to Love. Fr. Pamphilia to Amphilanthus. **CP-WrotM**

And Bees of Paradise. Hart Crane. **CP-CranH**

And before hell mouth; dry plain. Canto 16. Ezra Pound. Fr. Cantos. **CP-PoCan**

And beneath the star. Fragments from the Alfoxden Note-Book (III). William Wordsworth. **CP-WorW1**

—And blandish me not with the charisma. Open Letter, Returning a Questionnaire Unanswered. Daniel Gerard Hoffman. **SP-HoffD**

And boredom, ennui, depression. Boredom, Ennui, Depression. David Herbert Lawrence. **CP-LawrD**

And buds and blossoms like the rest. Tennyson. **EBVV; FHYEP; FaBoEn; FaBoRV; GTBS-6; GTBS-P; NOBE; OBNC; SeCeV** Fr. In Memoriam A. H. H. **CP-TennA**

And burne, yett burning you will love the smart. Sonnet 5. Mary Sidney, Countess of Montgomery Wroth. *Fr.* A Crowne of Sonetts Dedicated to Love. *Fr.* Pamphilia to Amphilanthus. **CP-WrotM**

And, by that act of giving, my slow hand. John Hewitt. *Fr.* Sonnets for Roberta (1954). **CP-HewiJ**

And call ye this to utter what is just, *par. by* Countess of Pembroke, Mary Sidney Herbert. Bible, *O.T. See* Psalm 58: "Do ye indeed speak righteousness, O congregation?"

And can I ever bid these joys farewell? John Keats. **TOF** *Fr.* Sleep and Poetry. **CP-KeatJ**

And cannot pleasures, while they last. A Valentine. "Lewis Carroll." **CP-CarrL**

And canst thou mock mine agony, thus calm. Despair. Percy Bysshe Shelley. *Fr.* Posthumous Fragments of Margaret Nicholson. **CP-ShelP**

And cruell maid, because I see. The Cruell Maid. Robert Herrick. **CP-HerrR**

And dance this / boneharp tree. "Dance the Orange." Robert Earl Hayden. **CP-HaydR**

And Death Shall Have No Dominion. Dylan Thomas. **CP-ThomD**

And did ever a man go black with sun in a Belgian swamp. Nigger. Karl Shapiro. **SP-ShapK**

And did she dwell in innocence and joy. Randall Jarrell. **CP-JarrR**

And did this all begin, and why am I here. *sl. diff. vers. in sec.1*, The Cantinas line. Malcolm Lowry. *Fr.* The Lighthouse Invites the Storm. **CP-LowrM**

And Did Those Feet. William Blake. *See* And Did Those Feet in Ancient Time.

And Did Those Feet in Ancient Time. William Blake. **AWP; CABA; ClHu; EBEvV; EnRP; FaBV; FaBoCh; FaBoPV; HAP; HeIP; InPS; LoBV; MAT; MeMBP; NAEL-2; NAWM-2; NOBRP; NoP; OAEL-2; OAEP; OBRV; PAI; PeECV; PIP; PoE; PoEL-4; PoRA; PrIm; SCGP; SeCeV; TFi; WGRP** *Fr.* Milton. **CP-BlakW**

(And Did Those Feet.) **ChIV-1**

(Jerusalem.) **BoTP; EaLo; EvOK; FHYEP; FaPoR; NOBE; NOCV; OBEV; OXAEP-2; OtMeF; RB; UV; WaaP**

(New Jerusalem, A.) **CoGr; FSW; FaBoEn; LiTB; SWP; TrGrPo**

(New Jerusalem, The.) **ImPo**

(Prelude: "And did those feet in ancient time.") **OBNC**

"And did you really walk," said I. Canto III: Scarmoges. "Lewis Carroll." *Fr.* Phantasmagoria. **CP-CarrL**

And do I see some cause a hope to feed. Sonnet 66. Sir Philip Sidney. *Fr.* Astrophil and Stella. **SP-SidnP**

And do I waste my time. Ralph Waldo Emerson. **CP-EmerR**

& do what I know best. Anne Waldman. **SP-WaldA**

And do you know a man was born. To Any Dweller in Lewis Street. John Hewitt. **CP-HewiJ**

And do you think that love itself. Edna St. Vincent Millay. *Fr.* Theme and Variations. **CP-MillE**

And does the old wound shudder open? Shall. John Berryman. *Fr.* Sonnets to Chris. **CP-BerrJ**

And Don't Forget Your Corset Cover, Either. Robert Penn Warren. *Fr.* Ballad of a Sweet Dream of Peace. **SP-WarrR**

And Don't Think I Won't Be Waiting. Audre Lorde. **SP-LordA**

And Dost Thou Ask the Reason of My Sadness? Byron. **CP-Byron**

And doun on knes anoon-ryght I me sette. This Fresshe Flour. Geoffrey Chaucer. **SeCePo** *Fr.* The Legend of Good Women. **CP-ChauG**

And dwells there in a female heart. To Miss Macartney. William Cowper. **CP-CowpW**

And earnest to explore within—around—. Matilda Gathering Flowers. Dante Alighieri, *tr. by* Shelley. **CP-ShelP** *Fr.* Purgatorio. *Fr.* Divina Commedia.

And Ebbe. For Ebbe. Robert Creeley. **CP-CreeR**

And Ellen, when the greybeard years. Ralph Waldo Emerson. **CP-EmerR**

And entering towns the guns had missed. Fragment, 1959. Stephen Berg. **SP-BergS**

And ever as he went he swept a lyre. Cancelled Passages of the Poem. Percy Bysshe Shelley. *Fr.* Adonais; An Elegy on the Death of John Keats. **CP-ShelP**

And everything the author knows. Ernest Hemingway. **CP-HemiE**

And everywhere, all over, men have sighed. Night-Piece. Stanley Jasspon Kunitz. **CP-KuniS**

And faces at the glutted shop-windows. Ted Hughes. *Fr.* Boom. **SP-HughT**

And Fall. Phoebe Hesketh. **SP-HeskP**

And Finally. Leonard Nathan. **SP-NathL**

And first an hour of mournful musing. Emily Brontë. **CP-BronE**

And following the poor dead child, the ragazza. Beheld in Naples. Jean Garrigue. **SP-GarrJ**

And for the man with one nightmare, the student of clouds, the bitter. Speech for the Assistant, from Houdini. Muriel Rukeyser. **CP-RukeM**

And for what, except for you, do I feel love? Notes toward a Supreme Fiction. Wallace Stevens. **CP-StevW**

And for what, except for you, do I feel love? Wallace Stevens. **NOBA** *Fr.* Notes toward a Supreme Fiction. **CP-StevW**

And forth from that shadow of a shadow. Kenneth Patchen. *Fr.* Wanderers of the Pale Wood. **CP-PatcK**

& Forty-Second Street. Archibald MacLeish. **CP-MacLA**

And foundry, / (that's art). Picture of a Nude in a Machine Shop. William Carlos Williams. **CP-WilW2**

And from the floating bodies, the incense. Ezra Pound. *See* Canto 20: "Sound slender, quasi tinnula."

And from the windy West came two-gunned Gabriel. Dylan Thomas. *Fr.* Altarwise by Owl-Light. **CP-ThomD**

And from this Mount were blown / seed. Canto 92. Ezra Pound. *Fr.* Cantos. **CP-PoCan**

And glad to find, on again looking at it. A Former Attachment. Robert Ranke Graves. **CP-GravR**

And God created the great whales, and each. John Milton. **MOS** *Fr.* Book VII. *Fr.* Paradise Lost. **CP-MiltJ**

And God, looking out upon earth, said, "Lo, it is time / To create mankind." John Gould Fletcher. **SP-FletJ** *Fr.* Branches of Adam.

And God said, "Let the waters generate." Creation. John Milton. **NOSC,** *ll.* 387–516; **FM** *Fr.* Book VII. *Fr.* Paradise Lost. **CP-MiltJ**

And God the Father Eternal (Boja d'un Dio!). Canto 28. Ezra Pound. *Fr.* Cantos. **CP-PoCan**

And gold and silver are but filthy dross. Gripus. John Keats. **CP-KeatJ**

And had Hafiz. Hafiz, *tr. by* Ralph Waldo Emerson. **CP-EmerR** *Fr.* Odes.

And had no actual / hesitancies, always. On Acid. Robert Creeley. **CP-CreeR**

And haply, bason'd in some unsunn'd cleft. Samuel Taylor Coleridge. **ChER** *Fr.* To a Young Friend. **CP-ColeS**

And has the Sun his flaming chariot driven. Lines Written as a School Exercise at Hawkshead, Anno Aetatis 14. William Wordsworth. **CP-WorW1**

And have they spurned thy word. Massachusetts. John Greenleaf Whittier. **CP-WhitJ**

And he had used love's dream of love before. Archibald MacLeish. **CP-MacLA** *Fr.* The Happy Marriage.

And He Had Wilder Moments. Kenneth Patchen. **CP-PatcK**

And he is an owl. Kafka. Ted Hughes. *Fr.* Boom. **SP-HughT**

And he is risen? Well, be it so. A Drizzling Easter Morning. Thomas Hardy. **CP-HardT**

And he lies dead—. William Dickey. **SP-DickW** *Fr.* Part Song, With Concert of Recorders. **SP-DickW**

And he like me is not too proud. Ralph Waldo Emerson. **CP-EmerR**

And he said to himself. Between Worlds. Carl Sandburg. **CP-SandC**

And he stood at his window and shook his fist at a cloud. Hayden Carruth. *Fr.* The Sleeping Beauty. **CP-CarHL**

And her look touching the air between us like a hand alive to the. Kenneth Patchen. **CP-PatcK**

And here face down beneath the sun. You, Andrew Marvell. Archibald MacLeish. **CP-MacLA**

And here is that part of my dream I would like to forget. Jane Cooper. *Fr.* The Flashboat. **SP-CoopJ**

And here the cross on the window means myself. The Once-in-Passing. Louis MacNeice. **FaBCIP** *Fr.* A Hand of Snapshots. **CP-MacNL**

And here the precious dust is laid [*or* layd]. Maria Wentworth. Thomas Carew. **CP-CareT**

And here we see the invisible boy. Invisible Boy. Shel Silverstein. **SP-SilS2**

And here's a portrait of my granddaughter Una. Granddaughter. Robinson Jeffers. **CP-JefR3**

AND his dark secret love. Print-Out Song. Daniel Gerard Hoffman. **SP-HoffD**

And his legs carried it like a long fork. William Blake. **CP-BlakW**

And how, and how, in faith—a pretty plot. Epilogue. Sir John Suckling. *Fr.* The Goblins. **CP-SuckJ**

And How Keen Was the Vision of Sir Launfal? Ogden Nash. **CP-NashO**

And hungry Debt besieged my door. Ralph Waldo Emerson. **CP-EmerR**

And I am here in Kentucky in the place I have made myself. Wendell Berry. *Fr.* To a Siberian Woodsman. **CP-BerrW**

And I and I / must admit. Belly Song. Etheridge Knight. **SP-KnigE**

And I and your eyes. I And Your Eyes. Etheridge Knight. **SP-KnigE**

And I assemble it as it was when I walked on it. The Release. Thom Gunn. **CP-GunnT**

And I, consign myself to you. Emily Dickinson. **SP-DickE**

. . . and I could see in the clearing. Poem for Beginners. Robert Creeley. **CP-CreeR**

And I declare myself free. Wendell Berry. *Fr.* The Mad Farmer Manifesto: the First Amendment. **CP-BerrW**

And I had it neatly written. Can the Harp Shoot Through Its Propellers? Kenneth Patchen. **CP-PatcK**

And I have come upon this place. L'An Trentiesme de Mon Eage. Archibald MacLeish. **CP-MacLA**

And I have loved thee, Ocean! and my joy. Byron. **OxBoS** *Fr.* The Ocean. **PoEL-4** *Fr.* Childe Harold's Pilgrimage. **CP-Byron**

And I have told you of how things were under Duke Leopold in Siena. Canto 52. Ezra Pound. *Fr.* Cantos. **CP-PoCan**

And I heard the learned astronomer. Olbers' Paradox. Lawrence Ferlinghetti. **SP-FerlL**

And I, I was a good child on the whole. Elizabeth Barrett Browning. **BrRo** *Fr.* Aurora Leigh. **CP-BroEB**

And i imagine. Edward Estlin Cummings. **CP-CummE**

And I lean back into the chair. In the Planetarium. Siv Cedering Fox. **SP-CedeS**

And I Love Her. John Lennon *and* Paul McCartney. **CP-Beatl**

And I remember Spain. Louis MacNeice. **OBWP; OXAEP-2** *Fr.* Autumn Journal. **CP-MacNL**

And, I said, you can take your rich aunts and uncles. The Day I Kicked Away a Bankroll. Charles Bukowski. **SP-BukC2**

And I shout at Iva, whine at you. Easily. Marilyn Hacker. **SP-HackM** *Fr.* Taking Notice.

And I solemnly swear. The Exorcists. Anne Sexton. **CP-SextA**

And I, Too, Am Something of a Stranger Here, My Friend. Kenneth Patchen. **CP-PatcK**

And I was born with you, wasn't I, Blues? The Blues Don't Change. Al Young. **CP-YounA**

And I was past caring so many, too many men. Hayden Carruth. *Fr.* Paragraphs. **CP-CarHS**

And I, who lay so warm and quiet there—. William Dickey. **SP-DickW** *Fr.* Part Song, With Concert of Recorders. **SP-DickW**

And I will bear my vengeful blade. *after the Greek of* Callistratus. William Wordsworth. **CP-WorW1**

And I would have you clad like dominoes. The Mask and Knife. Jean Garrigue. **SP-GarrJ**

And I'd Love You to Be in It. John Ashbery. **SP-AshbJ**

And if an eye may save or slay. Sir Thomas Wyatt. **CP-WyatT**

And if at 80. George Oppen. **APSN** *Fr.* Route. **CP-OppeG**

And if I die, because that part of me. Edna St. Vincent Millay. **CP-MillE**

And if I loved you Wednesday. Thursday. Edna St. Vincent Millay. **CP-MillE**

And, if my grief should still be dearer to me. Percy Bysshe Shelley. *Fr.* Fragments of an Unfinished Drama. **CP-ShelP**

And if no cuckoo sings. If No Cuckoo Sings. Robert Ranke Graves. **CP-GravR**

And if our coming will demand. Communists. Edwin Rolfe. **CP-RolfE**

And if sun comes. Truth. Gwendolyn Brooks. **SP-BrooG** *Fr.* The Womanhood.

And if the cliffs themselves produced the major illusion. Palos Verdes Cliffs. Muriel Rukeyser. **CP-RukeM**

And if the curtain lifts, it is a window-shade. The Victims, a Play for the Home. Muriel Rukeyser. **CP-RukeM**

And if the money be rented. Canto 48. Ezra Pound. *Fr.* Cantos. **CP-PoCan**

And, if the Popocatapetl. Marsden Hartley. **CP-HartM**

And if there can be love again. Weekend Away. John Clellon Holmes. **SP-HolmJ**

And if tonight my soul may find her peace. Shadows. David Herbert Lawrence. **CP-LawrD**

And If You Don't See What You Want, Ask for It. Edwin Rolfe. **CP-RolfE**

And if you will say that this tale teaches. . . . Canto 46. Ezra Pound. *Fr.* Cantos. **CP-PoCan**

And I'll kiss thee yet, yet. Robert Burns. **CP-BurnR**

And in a Glasgow close they found their home. Teetotal Master. John Hewitt. **CP-HewiJ**

And in Another Place Uses the Same Phrase. Kenneth Patchen. **CP-PatcK**

And in Life's noisiest hour. The Presence of Love. Samuel Taylor Coleridge. **CP-ColeS**

And in Melodious Accents I. William Blake. **CP-BlakW**

And in the evening, perilously swathed. Lanes of Death and Birth. Edwin Rolfe. **CP-RolfE**

And in the frosty season, when the sun. William Wordsworth. **FaBoCh; PIP** *Fr.* Introduction—Childhood and School-Time. *Fr.* The Prelude; Growth of a Poet's Mind [1805 vers.]. **CP-WorW3**

(On the Frozen Lake.) **FaBoCh**

And in the midst of all, a fountaine stood. Edmund Spenser. **CH** *Fr.* The Bower of Bliss. **PoEL-1** *Fr.* The Faerie Queene. **CP-Spens**

And in the midst of the Great Assembly Palamabron pray'd. William Blake. **OBF** *Fr.* Milton. **CP-BlakW**

And in the town, in neon-blaring twilight. Hayden Carruth. *Fr.* The Sleeping Beauty. **CP-CarHL**

And is he gone, whom these armes held but now? Luke 2; Quærit Jesum Suum Maria. Bible, *N.T.* **CP-CrasR**, *tr. by* Richard Crashaw; *Fr.* St. Luke.

And is indeed truth beauty?—at the cost. Edna St. Vincent Millay. **CP-MillE**

And is it among rude untutored Dales. William Wordsworth. **CP-WorW1**

And is it stamina / that unseasonably freaks. The Bluet. James Schuyler. **CP-SchuJ**

And is it thus, ye base and blind. An Address to the Mob. William Cowper. **CP-CowpW**

And Is Silent. Howard Nemerov. **CP-NemeH**

And is the water come? Sure't cannot be. Upon Sir John Lawrence's Bringing Water on the Hills [to My L. Middlesex His House at Witten]. Sir John Suckling. **CP-SuckJ**

And is there care in heauen [*or* heaven]? and is there loue [*or* love]. Edmund Spenser. **NOCV; NoSic; OAEL-1; OBSC; OxBoCh** *Fr.* The Faerie Queene. **CP-Spens**

(Guardian Angels.) **OBSC**

And is this all? Can reason do no more. *see also* Horace's Odes 2.10. William Cowper. **CP-CowpW**

And is this August weather? nay not so. Christina Georgina Rossetti. **CP-RosC3**

And is this—Yarrow?—*This* the Stream. Yarrow Visited [September, 1814]. William Wordsworth. **CP-WorW2**

And is thy soul so wrapt in sleep? The World of Dreams. George Crabbe. **SP-CrabG**

And it creams: from under her elbow a suffix of light, a sheen of kept being. William Everson. *Fr.* Tendril in the Mesh. **SP-EverW**

And it seemed, while we waited, he began to walk towards us. Geoffrey Hill. **NoAM; NoP** *Fr.* Mercian Hymns. **CP-HillG**

And it was almost a boy who undid. First Kiss. Rita Dove. **SP-DoveR**

And Jove's right hand approached the ambrosial bowl. *verse tr.fr.* Metamorphoses *by* Apuleius. Elizabeth Barrett Browning. **CP-BroEB**

And Jude the Obscure and His Beloved. David Herbert Lawrence. **CP-LawrD**

And learn O voyager to walk. Seafarer. Archibald MacLeish. **CP-MacLA**

And let thy patriarchs' desire [*or* Patriarches Desire]. The Patriarchs. John Donne. *Fr.* A Litany. **CP-DonnJ**

And lie thou there. Matthew Arnold. **EnVR** *Fr.* Empedocles on Etna. **SP-ArnoM**

And lights a cigarette, noting, far off. Malcolm Lowry. *Fr.* Peter Gaunt and the Canals. **CP-LowrM**

And like a dying lady, lean and pale. The Waning Moon. Percy Bysshe Shelley. **CP-ShelP**

And like myself lone, wholly lone. Emily Brontë. **CP-BronE**

And live I still to see relations gone? To the Memory of My Dear Daughter in Law, Mrs. Mercy Bradstreet. Anne Bradstreet. **CP-BradA**

And long ago, the almond was the symbol of resurrection. Flowers. David Herbert Lawrence. **CP-LawrD**

And looking to where shone Orion. Louis Zukofsky. *Fr.* 29 Poems. **CP-ZukLS**

And Los and Enitharmon builded Jerusalem weeping. Vala, Night the Ninth Being the Last Judgment. William Blake. **OAEL-2** *Fr.* Vala; or The Four Zoas. **CP-BlakW**

And Los beheld the mild Emanation, Jerusalem, eastward bending. In Deadly Fear. William Blake. **SeCePo** *Fr.* Jerusalem; The Emanation of the Giant Albion. **CP-BlakW**

And Love Hung Still. Louis MacNeice. *See* And love hung still as crystal over the bed.

And love hung still as crystal over the bed. Louis MacNeice. **CIP; GBL; MoBrPo** *Fr.* Trilogy for X. **CP-MacNL**

(And Love Hung Still.) **MoBrPo**

And love is then no more than a compromise? To His Cynical Mistress. Thom Gunn. **CP-GunnT**

And man of wit & man. Ralph Waldo Emerson. **CP-EmerR**

And many there were hurt by that strong boy. Love, Hope, Desire and Fear. Percy Bysshe Shelley. **CP-ShelP**

And me that morning Walter showed the house. Sir Walter Vivian's House. Tennyson. **CBCK** *Fr.* Prologue: "Sir Walter Vivian all a summer's day." *Fr.* The Princess. **CP-TennA**

&-moon-He-be-hind-a-mills. Edward Estlin Cummings. **CP-CummE**

And, moon, the darkness you float in. Moon, How Do I Measure Up? Al Young. **CP-YounA**

And moreover, / A gorgeous widgeon. With a Great Goodmorning Kiss and Luck and Love to Our Beloved Harteeste from All the Little Animals. Malcolm Lowry. **CP-LowrM**

And music is still a mystery! Charles Henri Ford. *Fr.* Epigrams. **SP-FordC**

And Must I Sing? What Subject Shall I Choose? Ben Jonson. **CP-JonsB**

And must I then, indeed, Pain, live with you. Edna St. Vincent Millay. **CP-MillE**

And must we part, because some say. The Suspition upon His Over-much Familiarity with a Gentlewoman. Robert Herrick. **CP-HerrR**

And my socks, they are immatcheable. Welcome Home Oh Our Most Beloved Harteebeeste. Malcolm Lowry. **CP-LowrM**

And new philosophy calls all in doubt. John Donne. **NOSC** *Fr.* The First Anniversary [*or* Anniversarie]. **AnAnS-1; FaBoRV; MasP; SeCV-1** *Fr.* Anatomy [*or* Anatomie] of the World, An[: The First Anniversary]. **CP-DonnJ**

And night comes. Siv Cedering Fox. *Fr.* In Search of a Love Poem. **SP-CedeS**

And no night visitors. Charles Henri Ford. **SP-FordC** *Fr.* Secret Haiku.

And, not in vain embodied to the sight. Other Benefits. William Wordsworth. *Fr.* Ecclesiastical Sonnets. **CP-WorW2**

And now / the best of all. Image-Making Love. David Herbert Lawrence. **CP-LawrD**

. . . And now / When the rumble of death. Sunday Morning Prophecy. Langston Hughes. **CP-HughL**

And now and then a loud evangelist. Evangelist. John Hewitt. **CP-HewiJ**

And now as the iron rinds over. Skunk Cabbage. Mary Oliver. **SP-OlivM**

And now creeps down. Imber Nocturnus. Elizabeth Bishop. **CP-BishE**

And now for the Dancing Pants. Dancing Pants. Shel Silverstein. **SP-SilS2**

And now gentlemen. The Base of All Metaphysics. Walt Whitman. **CP-WhitW**

And now, having torn the giant rock from the wall. Any Slave. Edwin Rolfe. **CP-RolfE**

And now I brood on what I think I know. Malcolm Lowry. **CP-LowrM**

And now I will convey thee to thy world. Byron. **NOBRP** *Fr.* Cain: A Mystery. **CP-Byron**

And now in turn see Swinburne bent. Lines on Swinburne. Robert Browning. **CP-BroR2**

And now it is summer. In the Ripeness of the Weed. William Everson. **SP-EverW** *Fr.* The Falling of the Grain.

And now let all the ships come in. Charles Olson. **SP-OlsoC** *Fr.* The Maximus Poems.

And now let pass a week. Once more behold. Robert Browning. **EBVVPR,** *sect.* III; *Fr.* Red Cotton Night-Cap Country. **CP-BroR2**

And now my pampered beast. Epitaph for My Cat. Jean Garrigue. **SP-GarrJ**

And now my spring beauties. Spring Song II. Jean Garrigue. **SP-GarrJ**

And now, outside, the walls. Night Watch. Adrienne Rich. **CP-RicAE; SP-RicA2**

And Now—September. Marsden Hartley. **CP-HartM**

And now September burns the careful tree. September Ode. Donald Hall. **CP-HallD**

And now th'art set wide ope, the Speare's sad art. I Am the Doore. Richard Crashaw. **CP-CrasR**

And now the green household is dark. In the Tree House at Night. James Dickey. **CP-DickJ**

And now the house-dog stretched once more. Emily Brontë. **CP-BronE**

And Now the Leaves Sudddenly Lose Strength. Philip Larkin. **CP-LarkP**

And now the sea-scoured temptress, having failed. The Re-birth of Venus. Geoffrey Hill. **NePoEA** *Fr.* Metamorphoses. **CP-HillG**

And now the seagulls feed on the front porch. Malcolm Lowry. **CP-LowrM**

And now the splendor of your work is here. To Frank O'Hara. James Schuyler. **CP-SchuJ**

And now that sun that through the horizon peeps. Christopher Marlowe. **OAEL-1** *Fr.* Hero and Leander. **CP-MarlC**

And now the vessel skirts the strand. The Lords Strand of Northumberland. Sir Walter Scott. **SP-ScotW** *Fr.* Marmion.

And Now, the Weather. . . . Karl Shapiro. **SP-ShapK**

And now they nigh approachèd to the stead. The Mermaids. Edmund Spenser. **ChTr** *Fr.* The Faerie Queene. **CP-Spens**

And now they turn poor poetry outdoors. What the Gardener Said to Mrs. Trail. Malcolm Lowry. **CP-LowrM**

And now, thirteen centuries later, the flower of man. After Wang Chi. Edwin Rolfe. **CP-RolfE**

"And now to God the Father," he ends. In Church. Thomas Hardy. **IHNG; InPK; MoAB; MoBrPo; SCV** *Fr.* Satires of Circumstance in Fifteen Glimpses. **CP-HardT**

And now to the abyss I pass. Andrew Marvell. **OAEL-1** *Fr.* Upon Appleton House [To My Lord Fairfax]. **CP-MarvA**

And now, unfathomably soon. Outlasting You. Robert Pack. **SP-PackR**

And now, unveiled, the toilet stands displayed. Alexander Pope. **ECEV; NOBE; OBEC; OXAEP-1** *Fr.* The Rape of the Lock[, an Heroi-Comical Poem]. **CP-PopeA**

(Toilet, The.) **NOBE; OBEC**

And now we seek once more the burning breeze. Alun Lewis. *Fr.* Letter From the Cape. **CP-LewiA**

And now when the branches were beginning to be heavy. Bird Talk. Carl Sandburg. **CP-SandC**

And Now Why Tarriest Thou? Christina Georgina Rossetti. **CP-RosC2**

And now you be my guest. The Mysteries. John Berryman. **CP-BerrJ**

And, O beloved voices, upon which. Futurity. Elizabeth Barrett Browning. **CP-BroEB**

And O, ye Fountains, Meadows, Hills, and Groves. William Wordsworth. *Fr.* Ode: Intimations of Immortality [from Recollections of Early Childhood]. **CP-WorW1**

And of Kublai: / "I have told you of that emperor's city in detail"y. Canto 18. Ezra Pound. *Fr.* Cantos. **CP-PoCan**

And of the sixth sense, the infinitesimal suffix. Osip Emilevich Mandelstam. *Fr.* Octets. **CP-DavDo**

And Oh—That the Man I Am Might Cease to Be. David Herbert Lawrence. **CP-LawrD**

And oh what a beautiful child you are. Charles Henri Ford. *Fr.* Epigrams. **SP-FordC**

And on the bridge the wheel turns silently. Fyrbøterer. Malcolm Lowry. *Fr.* The Roar of the Sea and the Darkness. **CP-LowrM**

—And on their brittle green quils. Gerard Manley Hopkins. *Fr.* Fragments. **CP-HopkG**

And One for My Dame. Anne Sexton. **CP-SextA**

And other wond'rous works were done. The Ascension of Our Lord Jesus Christ. Christopher Smart. **NOCV** *Fr.* Hymns and Spiritual Songs for the Fasts and Festivals of the Church of England. **SP-SmarC**

And Others, Vaguer Presences. John Ashbery. **SP-AshbJ**

And Our Eternal Home. Donald Davie. **CP-DavDo**

And Owl. Ted Hughes. **SP-HughT**

And partly they deserve dishonest death. Malcolm Lowry. **CP-LowrM**

And people who talk about faith. Talk of Faith. David Herbert Lawrence. **CP-LawrD**

And Pergamos, / City of the Phrygians. Euripides, *tr.* by Hilda Doolittle ("H.D."). **CP-DoolH** *Fr.* Iphigenia [*or* Iphigeneia] in Aulis.

And Plough-month peters out . its thermal power. John Berryman. *Fr.* Sonnets to Chris. **CP-BerrJ**

And, 'pon my word, before the British came. Granny's Story. Louise McNeill. **SP-McNeL**

And Psyche brought to Venus what was sent. *verse tr.fr.* Metamorphoses *by* Apuleius. Elizabeth Barrett Browning. **CP-BroEB**

And rival Coxcombs with enamored stare. Ralph Waldo Emerson. **CP-EmerR**

And said I that all hope was fled. Song: Hope. Percy Bysshe Shelley. *Fr.* Original Poetry by Victor and Cazire. **CP-ShelP**

And Samson said if yo' shave ma hair. Malcolm Lowry. **CP-LowrM**

And seeing the multitudes, he came down from the mountain. The New Beatitudes. John Gould Fletcher. **SP-FletJ** *Fr.* The Parables of Antichrist.

And shall I prime my children, pray, to pray? Gwendolyn Brooks. **SP-BrooG** *Fr.* The Children of the Poor. **SP-BrooG,** *sect.* I, *pt.* 1-5; *Fr.* The Womanhood.

And shall Love cease? Ask thine own heart, O Woman. Praise of Love. Christina Georgina Rossetti. **CP-RosC3**

"And shall," the Pontiff asks, "profaneness flow." The Council of Clermont. William Wordsworth. *Fr.* Ecclesiastical Sonnets. **CP-WorW2**

And she "like a young year." Lawrence Ferlinghetti. **SP-FerlL**

And, should it be left like this. Marsden Hartley. *Fr.* Un Recuerdo—Hermano—Hart Crane R.I.P. **CP-HartM**

And since he was Master and Servant in all that we asked him. Rudyard Kipling. **FaBoEH** *Fr.* Dead King, The [Edward VII; 1910]. **CP-KiplR**

And since round lines are drawn. Hafiz, *tr.* by Ralph Waldo Emerson. **CP-EmerR** *Fr.* Odes.

And since this life our nonage is. The Angels. John Donne. *Fr.* A Litany. **CP-DonnJ**

And since thou so desirously. The Martyrs. John Donne. *Fr.* A Litany. **CP-DonnJ**

And slowly answered Arthur from the barge. Tennyson. **FaBoEH** *Fr.* The Passing of Arthur. **FHYEP; NAEL-2; OBNC** *Fr.* Idylls of the King. **CP-TennA**

And So. William Matthews. **SP-MattW**

And so / they go back: violin. Da Capo. Charles Tomlinson. **CP-TomlC**

And so an easier life our Cyclops drew, *fr.* Idyl XI. The Cyclops. Theocritus, *tr. fr. Greek* by Elizabeth Barrett Browning. **CP-BroEB.**

And so for all of us. Bits and pieces. Louis MacNeice. **NAs** *Fr.* Turn again, Whittington. Riding the surf. Fr. Day of Renewal. **CP-MacNL**

And so for nights. The Night-Blooming Cereus. Robert Earl Hayden. **CP-HaydR**

And So Goodbye to Cities. Thomas Merton. **CP-MertT**

And so, here happily we meet, fair friend! Red Cotton Night-Cap Country. Robert Browning. **CP-BroR2**

And so I am getting old! Don't Think You Know My Name! Thomas McGrath. **SP-McGrT**

And so I cross into another world. New Heaven and Earth. David Herbert Lawrence. **CP-LawrD**

And so I somehow-nohow played. Robert Browning. **Par** *Fr.* Fifine at the Fair. **CP-BroR2**

And so I'm linked to you. Watchers. Robert Pack. **SP-PackR**

And so return to work—the M.A. gown. Louis MacNeice. *Fr.* Autumn Journal. **CP-MacNL**

And so the days pass. Harmonica Humdrums. Carl Sandburg. **CP-SandC**

And so the flowers grow and are deformed. Roots. Charles Henri Ford. *Fr.* For Djuna Barnes. **SP-FordC**

And so the official archangels. Old Archangels. David Herbert Lawrence. **CP-LawrD**

And so, the retraction. Penelope. Donald Davie. **CP-DavDo**

And so the river moves. The Lost Children. Richard Eberhart. **CP-EberR**

And so these daughters fair of Pandarus. The Daughters of Pandarus. Homer. **CP-BroEB,** *tr.* by Elizabeth Barrett Browning; *Fr.* Odyssey.

And so they cheated and wandered and were loved. The Semi-Lunatics of Kilmuir. Richard Hugo. **CP-HugoR**

And so till we have died. Louis Zukofsky. **CP-ZukLS**

And so to set two brothers by the ears. Epilogue [C] to *What Is She?*. Charlotte Smith. **CP-SmitC** *Fr.* What is She?

And So Today. Carl Sandburg. **CP-SandC**

And so today—they lay him away. And So Today. Carl Sandburg. **CP-SandC**

And so we too [*or* two] came where the rest have come. The Question. Frank Templeton Prince. **CP-PrinF**

And so we wait the tide, and when the dark. Alun Lewis. *Fr.* On Embarkation. **CP-LewiA**

And so with paragraphics. Hayden Carruth. *Fr.* Paragraphs. **CP-CarHS**

And so you found that poor room dull. Appearances. Robert Browning. **CP-BroR2**

And so you might have been. I Have Said, Ye Are Gods. Donald Davie. **CP-DavDo**

And some are sulky, while some will plunge. Rudyard Kipling. **CP-KiplR** *Fr.* Thrown Away. *Fr.* Plain Tales from the Hills.

And something that. . . that is theirs—no longer ours. The Dispossessed. John Berryman. **CP-BerrJ**

And, star and system rolling past. Tennyson. **ImOP** *Fr.* O true and tried, so well and long. **OAEL-2** *Fr.* In Memoriam A. H. H. **CP-TennA**

And still at dawn the fire is lit. Mornings in a New House. James Merrill. **SP-MerrJ**

And still I look for the men who will dare to be. Rose and Cabbage. David Herbert Lawrence. **CP-LawrD**

And still, in spite of all they do, I love the rose of England. A Rose Is Not a Cabbage. David Herbert Lawrence. **CP-LawrD**

And still the heart breaks, wakeful all the night? Alun Lewis. *Fr.* Letter From the Cape. **CP-LewiA**

And still we wear our uniforms, follow. The Progress. Gwendolyn Brooks. **SP-BrooG**

And suddenly the giants tired of play. Thunder. Elizabeth Bishop. **CP-BishE**

And Summer mornings the mute child, rebellious. Eleven. Archibald MacLeish. **CP-MacLA**

& sun & / sil / e / nce. Edward Estlin Cummings. **CP-CummE**

And sun the blear sun straggled forever. Afterword: What the Poet Had Written. Hayden Carruth. *Fr.* North Winter. **CP-CarHL**

And sweet it is to see in summer time. Michelangelo Buonarroti, *tr. fr. Italian* by William Wordsworth. **CP-WorW1**

And take me then! In the dawn under the high window. Louis MacNeice. *Fr.* The Stygian Banks. **CP-MacNL**

And take your time. Charles Henri Ford. **SP-FordC** *Fr.* Emblems of Arachne.

And tallness stood upon the sky like a sparkling mane. O She Is as Lovely-Often as Every Day. Kenneth Patchen. **CP-PatcK**

And Tell Me Poet, Can Love Exist in Slavery? Etheridge Knight. **SP-KnigE**

And that gentle bard. Gentle Spenser. William Wordsworth. **EPCY** *Fr.* Residence at Cambridge. *Fr.* The Prelude; Growth of a Poet's Mind [1850 vers.]. **CP-WorW3**

And that I walk thus proudly crowned withal. Fragment. Percy Bysshe Shelley. **CP-ShelP**

And that inevitable accident. The Next Time. Robert Ranke Graves. **CP-GravR**

And that is our story. Wendell Berry. *Fr.* Rising. **CP-BerrW**

And that night. the white electric storm. Schinden. Patti Smith. **SP-SmitP**

And that was all his life. Kathleen Jessie Raine. **SP-RainK**

And that winter at Valley Forge. George Washington's Camp Cups. Diane Wakoski. **SP-WakoD**

And that you did with said intent procure. Shattered Image. Sir John Betjeman. **CP-BetjJ**

And the / best. To Friends, for Good Health. Louis Zukofsky. **CP-ZukLS**

And the age ended, and the last deliverer died. Wystan Hugh Auden. *See* So an age ended, and its last deliverer died.

And the best gift of God. Ralph Waldo Emerson. **CP-EmerR**

And the blues, I tell you, they blew up. The James Cotton Band at Keystone. Al Young. **CP-YounA**

And the Bordeaux plum / from Marmande (France) in parenthesis with. Camellia Sabina. Marianne Craig Moore. **CP-MoorM**

And the child sitting alone planning her hope. Fourth Elegy. The Refugees. Muriel Rukeyser. **CP-RukeM**

And the Children of Birmingham. Thomas Merton. **CP-MertT; SP-MertT**

And the Clouds Return after the Rain. Stevie Smith. **CP-SmitS**

And the cloven waters like a chasm of mountains. From Vergil's Fourth Georgic. Virgil, *tr.* by Shelley. **CP-ShelP** *Fr.* Georgics.

And the Communists have nothing to offer but fat cheeks and eyeglasses and lying policemen. Kral Majales. Allen Ginsberg. **CP-GinsA**

& the Cool Fluttering. Jim Morrison. **SP-MorrJ**

And the corn singing Millennium! Background with Revolutionaries. Archibald MacLeish. **CP-MacLA**

And the curtain rose in that theatre so long ago. Mood Indigo. James Schuyler. **CP-SchuJ**

And "the earth under our feet." At Kenneth Burke's Place. William Carlos Williams. **CP-WilW2**

And the end of a party is better than the beginning. After Ecclesiastes. Phoebe Hesketh. **SP-HeskP**

And the Falcon Came. Ted Hughes. **SP-HughT**

And the first grey of morning filled the east. Sohrab and Rustum. Matthew Arnold.

And the first owl of. Charles Henri Ford. **SP-FordC** *Fr.* Emblems of Arachne.

And the first, the father, with indomitable will. Richard Eberhart. *Fr.* Orchard. **CP-EberR**

And the first with his hands folded and a money belt for a truss. Vision of Three Angels Viewing the Progress of Socialism. Thomas McGrath. **SP-McGrT**

And the friends of our friends are our friends. La Muerte de Joselito. James Liddy. **CP-LiddJ**

And the Greatest of These. Richard Shelton. **SP-ShelR**

And the hedges wet in the rain, flaking in a sheet of wind. Anthony. Charles Bukowski. **SP-BukC2**

And the keen hound overcomes fortune. A Note in Honor of Machiavelli. Thomas Merton. **CP-MertT**

And the light without: the shade. The Light Within. James Schuyler. **CP-SchuJ**

And the Lord was not in the whirlwind. Louis MacNeice. **EaLo** *Fr.* Visitations. **CP-MacNL**

(And the Lord Was Not in the Whirlwind.) **EaLo**

And the Lord Was Not in the Whirlwind. Louis MacNeice. *See* And the Lord was not in the whirlwind.

And the lovers meet again. Siv Cedering Fox. *Fr.* In Search of a Love Poem. **SP-CedeS**

And the magic law governing our lives. Singleness in Love. Robert Ranke Graves. **CP-GravR**

And the many days and the many nights that I lay as one barren. A Canticle to the Christ in the Holy Eucharist. William Everson. **SP-EverW**

And the mole crept along the garden. Terraces of Rain. David St. John. **SP-StJoD**

And the mountain: each day. Cézanne at Aix. Charles Tomlinson. **CP-TomlC**

And the next day begins. The Munich Agreement. Louis MacNeice. **FaBoEH** *Fr.* Sun shines easy, sun shines gay. *Fr.* Autumn Journal. **CP-MacNL**

And the next I remembered I'm on a table. The Loser. Charles Bukowski. **SP-BukC2**

And the Path of Least. Charles Henri Ford. **SP-FordC** *Fr.* Secret Haiku.

And the Phoenix Has Come. Ted Hughes. **SP-HughT**

And the point in the spectrum. Hilda Doolittle. **NALW** *Fr.* Tribute to the Angels. **CP-DoolH**

And the poor devils dying of cold, outside Sorano. Canto 10. Ezra Pound. *Fr.* Cantos. **CP-PoCan**

And the Rose / Rages. Over the Cross. The Raging of the Rose. William Everson. **SP-EverW** *Fr.* The Rose of Solitude.

And the Scars Will Be Covered. Richard Shelton. **SP-ShelR**

And the Scream. Stephen Berg. **SP-BergS**

And the Spirit said. The Clock of the Years. Thomas Hardy. **CP-HardT**

And the storm swings in from the sea with a smashing of floats. William Everson. *Fr.* Tendril in the Mesh. **SP-EverW**

And the streams here, ledge to ledge. Lights among Redwood. Thom Gunn. **CP-GunnT**

And the subnormal. The Insane Always Loved Me. Charles Bukowski. **SP-BukC1**

And the sun high over horizon hidden in cloud bank. Canto 76. Ezra Pound. *Fr.* Cantos. **CP-PoCan**

And the sun wields mercy. The Sun Wields Mercy. Charles Bukowski. **SP-BukC2**

And the terrible / Pang of the heart unhinged. The Vision of Felicity. William Everson. **SP-EverW** *Fr.* The Rose of Solitude.

And the Trains Go On. Philip Levine. **SP-LeviP**

And the walker sees the sunlit battlefield. Spring Warning. Philip Larkin. **CP-LarkP**

And the water / the rising water. Hayden Carruth. *Fr.* Paragraphs. **CP-CarHS**

And the Wave Sings Because It Is Moving. Philip Larkin. **CP-LarkP**

And the waves / gush pearls. Winter. Mary Oliver. **SP-OlivM**

And the way goes on in the worn earth. Prologue. Archibald MacLeish. **NoAM** *Fr.* Conquistador. **CP-MacLA**

And the world changed. Survival: Infantry. George Oppen. **CP-OppeG**

And the youth free stripling bounding along the Hills of Color. Contest of Bards. Allen Ginsberg. **CP-GinsA**

And their murder towns me sick O it red-streets. The Blind Maidens of Our Homelessness. Kenneth Patchen. **CP-PatcK**

And Their Winter and Night in Disguise. George Oppen. **APSN; NNaP** *Fr.* Some San Francisco Poems. **CP-OppeG**

And Then. Miller Williams. **SP-WillM**

And then a bird that was like a great pale wolf flying down. Kenneth Patchen. *Fr.* Wanderers of the Pale Wood. **CP-PatcK**

And then it was that the Bridegroom beheld the Bride wraith- / like. Kenneth Patchen. *Fr.* Wanderers of the Pale Wood. **CP-PatcK**

And then, one by one, he moved me. Wendell Berry. *Fr.* Elegy: "To be at home on its native ground." **CP-BerrW**

And then that humming. William Everson. **SP-EverW** *Fr.* The Blowing of the Seed.

And then the cow did write. Another Day (And then the cow). Muriel Rukeyser. **CP-RukeM**

And then there was Myrtle's Cousin. Myrtle's Cousin. Theodore Roethke. **CP-RoetT**

And then they pressed the melon. Happy End. Charles Simic. **SP-SimiC**

And then went down to the ship. Canto 1. Ezra Pound. **AmPP; CMoP; LiTA; MeMAP; MoAB; MoAmPo; MoP; NoAM; NoP; OBVE; PoE; SP-PounE; TrGrPo; VGW** *Fr.* Cantos. **CP-PoCan**

And there in the sky is the known face half-hidden. Hayden Carruth. *Fr.* The Sleeping Beauty. **CP-CarHL**

And There Was a Great Calm. Thomas Hardy. **CP-HardT**

And There Was No More Sea. Christina Georgina Rossetti. **CP-RosC2**

And there we were together again. The Return of Morgan and Fingal. Edwin Arlington Robinson. **CP-RobiE**

And there you are again, now as you are. Rembrandt to Rembrandt. Edwin Arlington Robinson. **CP-RobiE**

And therefore if to love can be desert. Sonnet. Elizabeth Barrett Browning. *Fr.* Sonnets from the Portuguese. **CP-BroEB**

And they have to get it right. We just need. A Love Poem. John Ashbery. **SP-AshbJ**

And They Obey. Carl Sandburg. **CP-SandC**

And they walked in the ancient wonder of the morning light. Kenneth Patchen. *Fr.* Wanderers of the Pale Wood. **CP-PatcK**

And they were stronger hands than mine. Dedication, A. Rudyard Kipling. **CP-KiplR**

And think how the nightingale, who is so shy. Paltry-Looking People. David Herbert Lawrence. **CP-LawrD**

And this day Abner lifted a shovel. Canto 77. Ezra Pound. *Fr.* Cantos. **CP-PoCan**

And this day it was Spring. . . .us. Edward Estlin Cummings. **CP-CummE**

And this is the way they ring. Ringing the Bells. Anne Sexton. **CP-SextA**

And this, ladies and gentlemen, whom I am not in fact. The Suicide. Louis MacNeice. **CP-MacNL**

And this of all my Hopes. Emily Dickinson. **CP-DickE**

And this place our forefathers made for man! The Dungeon. Samuel Taylor Coleridge. **CP-ColeS**

And this rest house is that the which he built. On a Ruined House in a Romantic Country. Samuel Taylor Coleridge. **CBNP; FaBoPa; Par** *Fr.* Sonnets Attempted in the Manner of Contemporary Writers. **CP-ColeS**

And this was. The Thirteenth Book. Archibald MacLeish. *Fr.* Conquistador. **CP-MacLA**

And This Will Be All? Carl Sandburg. **CP-SandC**

And tho' my friar's mandate is severe. George Meredith. **CP-MerG2**

And thorns, but did the sculptor spare. Robert Louis Stevenson. **CP-StevR**

And thou, America, / For the scheme's culmination. Walt Whitman. **PGD** *Fr.* Song of the Universal. **CP-WhitW**

And Thou Art Dead, as Young and Fair. Byron. **CP-Byron**

And Thou No Breath at All? Isabella Gardner. **CP-GardI**

And Thou, O Lord! by whom are seen. John Greenleaf Whittier. **TrPWD** *Fr.* The Eternal Goodness. **CP-WhitJ**

And thou shalt not, Firenze 1766, and thou shalt not. Canto 44. Ezra Pound. *Fr.* Cantos. **CP-PoCan**

And thou wert sad—yet I was not with thee. Lines on Hearing That Lady Byron Was Ill. Byron. **CP-Byron**

And though he dearly prized the bards of fame. Ralph Waldo Emerson. **CP-EmerR**

And though it is possible there are many. A Conclusion—Poem. Malcolm Lowry. **CP-LowrM**

And Three Hundred and Sixty-Six in Leap Year. Ogden Nash. **CP-NashO**

And through that bitter agony [*or* agonie]. John Donne. *Fr.* A Litany. **CP-DonnJ**

And thus a poetry which fully understands. "Hugh MacDiarmid." **SP-MacDH** *Fr.* The Kind of Poetry I Want.

And thus declared that Arab lady. Solomon and the Witch. William Butler Yeats. **CP-YeatW**

And thus he spake, each bird and beast behold. John Milton. **OBF** *Fr.* Book VIII. *Fr.* Paradise Lost. **CP-MiltJ**

And thus the people every year. Attack of the Squash People. Marge Piercy. **SP-PierM**

And Thus with All Praise. William Carlos Williams. **CP-WilW1**

And thy illustrious zodiac [*or* Zodiacke]. The Apostles. John Donne. *Fr.* A Litany. **CP-DonnJ**

And "thy true faith can alter never?" On the Quotation "And My True Faith Can Alter Never, Though Thou Art Gone Perhaps Forever." Byron. **CP-Byron**

And to dissolve the heaps. Afternoon lumber water filling. Darjeeling. Thomas Merton. **CP-MertT**

And to Her-Without-Bounds I send. Tribal Memories. Robert Duncan. **SP-DuncR** *Fr.* Passages.

And to paradise which is a port. Louis Zukofsky. *Fr.* 29 Poems. **CP-ZukLS**

And to the kings of the world. Mohammed. Kenneth Patchen. **CP-PatcK**

And to these Rhodians She, the Sharp-eyed One. Translation from Pindar's Seventh Olympian, Epode III. Robert Browning. **CP-BroR2**

And today is Christmas Eve. Once more to work. Canto XXV. Louis MacNeice. *Fr.* Autumn Sequel. **CP-MacNL**

And tomorrow morning at 8 o'clock in Springfield, Massachusetts. Poem. Frank O'Hara. **SP-OharF**

And truth? O, / Truth! George Oppen. *Fr.* A Narrative. **CP-OppeG**

And two women were racing. Sometimes. Two Men. Ron Koertge. **SP-KoerR**

And "Ut Pictura Poesis" Is Her Name. John Ashbery. **SP-AshbJ**

& vanish to Casper, the Grasslands, Otsego County. Throw Matches at the Sun! Anne Waldman. **SP-WaldA**

And war. George Oppen. *Fr.* Blood from the Stone. **CP-OppeG**

And was her daughter like that. Canto 106. Ezra Pound. *Fr.* Cantos. **CP-PoCan**

And was the day of my delight. Tennyson. **OAEL-2** *Fr.* In Memoriam A. H. H. **CP-TennA**

And we came near Corofin through a narrow gate. The Wild Swans of Inverane. Richard Eberhart. **CP-EberR**

And we sit here / under the wall. Canto 12. Ezra Pound. *Fr.* Cantos. **CP-PoCan**

And we were speaking easily and all the light stayed low. In Judgment of the Leaf. Kenneth Patchen. **CP-PatcK**

And were I not, as a man may say, cautious. Robert Browning. **OBCoV** *Fr.* The Flight of the Duchess. **CP-BroR1**

And What About the Children. Audre Lorde. **SP-LordA** ("We've made a child.") **SP-LordA**

And what are you that, wanting you. The Philosopher. Edna St. Vincent Millay. **CP-MillE**

And what costume shall the poor girl wear. All Tomorrow's Parties. "Lou Reed." **SP-ReedL**

And what do I care. What Do I Care? David Herbert Lawrence. **CP-LawrD**

And what do you say. Lightning, Divine Lightning. Al Young. **CP-YounA**

And what does the farmer's daughter think. Husbandry. Barton Sutter. **SP-SuttB**

And what if you were wrong about Albania? Lines for Scott Nearing. Daniel Gerard Hoffman. **SP-HoffD**

And What Is Love? It Is a Doll Dressed Up. John Keats. **CP-KeatJ**

"And what is love?" said Pilate. Kenneth Rexroth. **CP-RexKL** *Fr.* The Dragon and the Unicorn.

"And what is love?" said Pilate. Kenneth Rexroth. **SP-RexrK** *Fr.* "And what is love?" said Pilate. **CP-RexKL** *Fr.* The Dragon and the Unicorn.

" 'And what is love?' said Pilate." **SP-RexrK**

And what is Penance with her knotted thong. Abuse of Monastic Power. William Wordsworth. *Fr.* Ecclesiastical Sonnets. **CP-WorW2**

And what melodious sounds at times prevail! Continued [Other Benefits]. William Wordsworth. *Fr.* Ecclesiastical Sonnets. **CP-WorW2**

And what might that bold man's announcement be. The Sun. Robert Browning. **CP-BroR2**

And what, my thoughtless sons, should fire you more. James Thomson. **ECEV** *Fr.* Summer. *Fr.* The Seasons. **CP-ThomJ**

And what were roses. Perfume?for i do. Edward Estlin Cummings. **CP-CummE**

And what when the glass breaks when the Note sounds? Louis MacNeice. *Fr.* The Stygian Banks. **CP-MacNL**

And What with the Blunders. Kenneth Patchen. **CP-PatcK**

And what would I do in heaven, pray. She of the Dancing Feet Sings. Countee Cullen. **CP-CullC**

And When Freedom Is Achieved. Kenneth Patchen. **CP-PatcK**

And when I am entombed in my place. Ralph Waldo Emerson. **CP-EmerR**

And when I see the heavy red fleece. Erotic. David Herbert Lawrence. **CP-LawrD**

And when I thought, "Our love might end." Daylight. James Schuyler. **CP-SchuJ**

And When in Scenes of Glory. Miller Williams. **SP-WillM**

And when it came down to Negro nights. A Poem for Lena Horne. Al Young. **CP-YounA**

And when KIEN OUEN was throned. Cant 57. Ezra Pound. *Fr.* Cantos. **CP-PoCan**

And when on the dark steel came the roads. We Have Gone Through Great Rooms Together. Carl Sandburg. **CP-SandC**

And when suddenly it hit me. Just Looking, Thank You. Leonard Nathan. **SP-NathL**

And when that ballad lady went. A Road in Kentucky. Robert Earl Hayden. **CP-HaydR**

And When the Green Man Comes. John Haines. **SP-HainJ**

And when the light is exact. Feeling of Time. Giuseppe Ungaretti, *tr. fr. Italian* by Isabella Gardner. **CP-GardI**

And when was dust a thing so harsh? He Remembereth That We Are Dust. Adrienne Rich. **CP-RicAE**

And when we clear away. Louis MacNeice. *Fr.* Autumn Journal. **CP-MacNL**

And when we speak together. Wendell Berry. *Fr.* From the Crest. **CP-BerrW**

And, when you go—much as a meteor. Malcolm Lowry. **CP-LowrM**

And whence and why come you? Lingering Last Drops. Walt Whitman. **CP-WhitW**

And where is truth? On tombs? for such to thee. Fragment: The Sepulchre of Memory. Percy Bysshe Shelley. **CP-ShelP**

And where it falls, a quality. Fire in a Dark Landscape. Charles Tomlinson. **CP-TomlC**

And where now, Bayard, will thy footsteps tend? Bayard Taylor. John Greenleaf Whittier. **CP-WhitJ**

And whilst the outer lake beneath the lash. Percy Bysshe Shelley. **PBBP** *Fr.* The Witch of Atlas. **CP-ShelP**

And whilst [*or* whil'st] this universal choir [*or* universall Quire]. John Donne. *Fr.* A Litany. **CP-DonnJ**

And who art thou? said I to the soft-falling shower. The Voice of the Rain. Walt Whitman. **CP-WhitW**

And Who Do You Think "They" Are? William Carlos Williams. **CP-WilW2**

And who feels discord now or sorrow? Fragment: Love the Universe To-day. Percy Bysshe Shelley. **CP-ShelP**

And who has seen the moon, who has not seen. Moonrise. David Herbert Lawrence. **CP-LawrD**

And who is He that, sculptured in huge stone. The "Moses" of Michael Angelo. Robert Browning. **CP-BroR2**

And who is it that through the watery woods. With Dearest Love Enfolded and Enclosed from *All* the Litle Animals. Malcolm Lowry. **CP-LowrM**

And Who Is It That With Snow-Freaked Antlers Vicariously Museth. Malcolm Lowry. **CP-LowrM**

And who is it through the forest after the. Malcolm Lowry. **CP-LowrM**

And who is this lies prostrate at thy feet? Will These Hands Ne'er Be Clean? Christina Georgina Rossetti. **CP-RosC3**

And whoever forces himself to love anybody. Retort to Jesus. David Herbert Lawrence. **CP-LawrD**

And whoever walks a mile full of false sympathy. Retort to Whitman. David Herbert Lawrence. **CP-LawrD**

And who's this jolly good fellow. A Jolly Good Fellow. Phoebe Hesketh. **SP-HeskP**

And why an honoured [*or* honour'd] ragged shirt, that shows. To a Lady with Child that Asked [*or* Ask'd] an Old Shirt. Richard Lovelace. **CP-LoveR**

And why, Herr Reichsmarschall, is Italy. Reichsmarschall Hermann Göring ("And why, Herr Reichsmarschall, is Italy"). William DeWitt Snodgrass. **SP-SnodW**

And why, in God's name, is that elegant bureau. And Don't Forget Your Corset Cover, Either. Robert Penn Warren. *Fr.* Ballad of a Sweet Dream of Peace. **SP-WarrR**

And why is the sun such a poor friend. Pablo Neruda, *tr. fr. Spanish by* Ben Belitt. **SP-NeruP** *Fr.* Question Book.

And why to me this, thou lame lord of fire. An Execration upon Vulcan. Ben Jonson. **CP-JonsB**

And will you leave me thus alone. Ballad, A. William Wordsworth. **CP-WorW1**

And wilt thou have me fashion into speech. Sonnet. Elizabeth Barrett Browning. **BWW; BrRo; EnVR** *Fr.* Sonnets from the Portuguese. **CP-BroEB**

And wilt [*or* wylt] thou le[a]ve me thus? Sir Thomas Wyatt. **CP-WyatT**

And Wilt Thou Weep When I Am Low? Byron. **CP-Byron**

And Winter. Kay Boyle. **CP-BoylK**

And with what body do they come? Emily Dickinson. **CP-DickE**

And Without. Louis Zukofsky. **CP-ZukLS**

And Wordsworth! Ah, pale ghosts, rejoice! Matthew Arnold. **EPCY** *Fr.* Memorial Verses. **SP-ArnoM**

And Would It Have Been Worth It? Thomas Stearns Eliot. **LPA** *Fr.* The Love Song of J. Alfred Prufrock. **CP-ElioT**

And would you faine the reason know. *At. to* Thomas Campion *and to* Philip Rosseter. **CP-CampT**

And would you gather turds. A History of Love. William Carlos Williams. **CP-WilW2**

And Would You See My Mistress' Face? *At. to* Thomas Campion *and to* Philip Rosseter. **CP-CampT**

And, yeah, brothers. Dark Prophecy: I Sing of Shine. Etheridge Knight. **SP-KnigE**

And yet, because thou overcomest so. Sonnet. Elizabeth Barrett Browning. *Fr.* Sonnets from the Portuguese. **CP-BroEB**

And yet his suffering got involved with all this. Malcolm Lowry. **CP-LowrM**

And yet I am of England too; odi et amo. Malcolm Lowry. **CP-LowrM**

And yet in some very subtle way. Hilda Doolittle. **NALW** *Fr.* Tribute to the Angels. **CP-DoolH**

And yet I've lived like this for years. The Game. Louise Glück. **SP-GlücL**

And yet one arrives somehow. Arrival. William Carlos Williams. **CP-WilW1**

And yet the Sibyl parches, caught and clutched within a fist of dust! Frank Templeton Prince. *Fr.* Apollo and the Sibyl. **CP-PrinF**

—And yet this great wink of eternity. Hart Crane. **AmPP; CoBMV; DTC; GGP; HAP; ImPo; LiTM; MOS; MoAB; MoAmPo; MoPo; MoVE; NePA; OxBA; PPP; PPoe; RaBo; TRP; TwAmPo; UnPo; VGW** *Fr.* Voyages. **CP-CranH**

And "Yonder look! yoho! yoho!" The Doe: A Fragment. George Meredith. **CP-MerG1**

And you as well must die, belovèd dust. Edna St. Vincent Millay. **CP-MillE**

And you have come. The Year of the Child. Robert Earl Hayden. **CP-HaydR**

And You Know. John Ashbery. **SP-AshbJ**

And you may lead a thousand men. Rudyard Kipling. **CP-KiplR** *Fr.* The Light That Failed.

And you my spent heart's treasure. Geoffrey Hill. **HAP** *Fr.* The Pentecost Castle. **CP-HillG**

And you never liked parties. The Table. Carlos Drummond de Andrade, *tr. fr. Portuguese by* Elizabeth Bishop. **CP-BishE**

And you, old woman, are carrying scrub buckets tonight. Heavy and Light. Carl Sandburg. **CP-SandC**

And you play the safe game / the orphan game. Margaret Atwood. *Fr.* The Circle Game. **SP-AtwM1**

And you remember, in the afternoon. Coldness in Love. David Herbert Lawrence. **CP-LawrD**

And you take hold of a handle. Carl Sandburg. *Fr.* The People, Yes. **CP-SandC**

And you too, old man, so we have heard. Eros. George Oppen. **CP-OppeG**

And you, who with your soft but searching voice. Geoffrey Hill. *Fr.* Tenebrae. **CP-HillG**

And Your Bird Can Sing. John Lennon *and* Paul McCartney. **CP-Beatl**

Andante Cantabile. James McAuley. *Fr.* The Exile's Fifth Symphony. **SP-McAuJ**

Andean Flute, The. Derek Mahon. **SP-MahoD**

Andraitx—Pomegranate Flowers. David Herbert Lawrence. **CP-LawrD**

Andrea del Sarto. Robert Browning. **CP-BroR1**

Andrée Rexroth ("Now once more gray mottled buckeye branches"). Kenneth Rexroth. **SP-RexrK**

Andrée Rexroth ("Years have gone. . ."). Kenneth Rexroth. **SP-RexrK** Kings River Canyon. **NaP**

Andrew Jackson was eight feet tall. The Statue of Old Andrew Jackson. Nicholas Vachel Lindsay. **CP-LindV**

Andrew Jones. William Wordsworth. **CP-WorW1**

Andrew Lord Poems. James Schuyler. **CP-SchuJ**

Andrew Rykman's dead and gone. Andrew Rykman's Prayer. John Greenleaf Whittier. **CP-WhitJ**

Andrew Rykman's Prayer. John Greenleaf Whittier. **CP-WhitJ**
   "Make my mortal dreams come true."
   "Pardon, Lord, the lips that dare."

Androcles from his injur'd lord, in dread. Reciprocal Kindness the Primary Law of Nature. Vincent Bourne, *tr. fr. Latin by* William Cowper. **CP-CowpW**

Androgynous child whose hair curls into flowers. The Sun. Marge Piercy. **WPOW** *Fr.* Laying Down the Tower. **SP-PierM**

Androids. William Dickey. **SP-DickW**

Andromache, I think of you! / When the war goes on forever. Charles Henri Ford. *Fr.* Epigrams. **SP-FordC**

Andromeda. Gerard Manley Hopkins. **CP-HopkG**

Androscoggin. Marsden Hartley. **CP-HartM**

Andy it's me, haven't seen you in a while. Hello It's Me. "Lou Reed." **SP-ReedL**

Andy's Chest. "Lou Reed." **SP-ReedL**

Anecdote. Charles Tomlinson. **CP-TomlC**

Anecdote for Fathers. William Wordsworth. **CP-WorW1**

Anecdote of Canna. Wallace Stevens. **CP-StevW**

Anecdote of Hemlock for Two Athenians. Carl Sandburg. **CP-SandC**

Anecdote of Men by the Thousand. Wallace Stevens. **CP-StevW**

Anecdote of the Jar. Wallace Stevens. **CP-StevW**

Anecdote of the Prince of Peacocks. Wallace Stevens. **CP-StevW**

Anecdotes of the Late War. Charles Olson. **CP-OlsoC**

Anelida and Arcite. Geoffrey Chaucer. **CP-ChauG**

Anemone. Muriel Rukeyser. **CP-RukeM**

Anent Socrates, or Somebody. Hayden Carruth. **CP-CarHS**

Aneurin's Harp. George Meredith. **CP-MerG1**

Anew, sun, to fire summer. Louis Zukofsky. **CP-ZukLS**

An(fragrance)Of / (Begins) / millions. Edward Estlin Cummings. **CP-CummE**

Angel, The. William Blake. **CP-BlakW** *Fr.* Songs of Experience.

Angel. James Merrill. **SP-MerrJ**

Angel, The. James Wright. **CP-WrigJ**

Angel and Stone. Howard Nemerov. **CP-NemeH**

Angel and the Anchorite. Richard Shelton. **SP-ShelR**
   "Each morning he rolls over."
   "On the evening of the third day."
   "Stars point in all directions, The."
   "They have lived together for twenty years."
   "When the road forked."

Angel and the Clown, The. Nicholas Vachel Lindsay. **CP-LindV**

Angel asked, as his shoulders were pressed into the stone, The. Statue. Tom Clark. **SP-ClarT**

Angel, be ye ne'er in doubt, An. George Meredith. **CP-MerG2**

Angel begins in the morning, The. Emily Dickinson. **SP-DickE**

Angel Boley. Stevie Smith. **CP-SmitS**

Angel Butcher. Philip Levine. **SP-LeviP**

Angel came to me and said, An. Memorable Fancy, A. William Blake. **NU** *Fr.* The Marriage of Heaven and Hell. **CP-BlakW**

Angel ended, and in *Adams* ear, The. Book VIII. John Milton. *Fr.* Paradise Lost. **CP-MiltJ**

Angel Face. Stevie Smith. **CP-SmitS**

Angel Food Dogs, The. Anne Sexton. **CP-SextA**

Angel from his Paradise drove Adam, An. A Variation on Lines of Landor. Robert Browning. **CP-BroR2**

Angel most cynical. The Violent Hand. Stevie Smith. **CP-SmitS**

Angel of Beach Houses and Picnics. Anne Sexton. *Fr.* Angels of the Love Affair. **CP-SextA**

Angel of Blizzards and Blackouts. Anne Sexton. *Fr.* Angels of the Love Affair. **CP-SextA**

Angel of Clean Sheets. Anne Sexton. *Fr.* Angels of the Love Affair. **CP-SextA**

Angel of Death, The. Siv Cedering Fox. **SP-CedeS**

Angel of death flies, The. Night. Louise Glück. **MoLi** *Fr.* Metamorphosis. **SP-GlücL**

Angel of Fire and Genitals. Anne Sexton. *Fr.* Angels of the Love Affair. **CP-SextA**

Angel of Flight and Sleigh Bells. Anne Sexton. *Fr.* Angels of the Love Affair. **CP-SextA**

Angel of Grace. Stevie Smith. **CP-SmitS**

Angel of Hope and Calendars. Anne Sexton. *Fr.* Angels of the Love Affair. **CP-SextA**

Angel of Patience, The. John Greenleaf Whittier. **CP-WhitJ**

Angel of the Lord sang low, The. The Gift of the Magi. Peter Meinke. **SP-MeinP**

Angel of the Maze, The. James Dickey. **CP-DickJ**

Angel of Tones / flame of accord. Ritornelli. Geoffrey Hill. **CP-HillG**

Angel of Words, in vain I have striven with thee. A Child Asleep. Walter de la Mare. **CP-DeLaW**

Angel, robed in spotless white, An. Dawn. Paul Laurence Dunbar. **CP-DunbP**

Angel Surrounded by Paysans. Wallace Stevens. **CP-StevW**

Angel Syphilis in the circle of Signators, The. In Blood's Domaine. Robert Duncan. **SP-DuncR** *Fr.* Passages.

Angel That Presided o'er My Birth, The. William Blake. **InPK; NAs; OxBSP; RB; TrGrPo** *Fr.* Gnomic Verses. **CP-BlakW**

Angel that rebellion raised, The. Fallen, Fallen. Stevie Smith. **CP-SmitS**

Angel Visitant, An, *ad. fr.* "Die Vögel" *by* Friedrich von Hagedorn. Samuel Taylor Coleridge. **CP-ColeS**

Angela Burdett-Coutts. George Meredith. **CP-MerG2**

Angeli al capo, al piede. Christina Georgina Rossetti. **CP-RosC3**

Angelic Love. George Meredith. **CP-MerG1**

Angelic natures, great in arms. St. Michael and All Angels. Christopher Smart. *Fr.* Hymns and Spiritual Songs for the Fasts and Festivals of the Church of England. **SP-SmarC**

Angelica. Leonard Cohen. **CP-CoheL**

Angelina. Paul Laurence Dunbar. **CP-DunbP**

Angells. Robert Herrick. **CP-HerrR**

Angels, The. John Donne. *Fr.* A Litany. **CP-DonnJ**

Angels, The. Richard Eberhart. **CP-EberR**

Angels, The. John Updike. **CP-UpdiJ**

Angels again / Farmers of the mind. Thomas Merton. *Fr.* Cables to the Ace. **CP-MertT**

Angels are bright still, though the brightest fell. Lucifer. David Herbert Lawrence. **CP-LawrD**

Angels are stooping, The. Cradle Song, A. William Butler Yeats. **CP-YeatW**

Angels at Hamburg, The. Randall Jarrell. **CP-JarrR**

Angels at the foot, / And Angels at the head. Christina Georgina Rossetti. **CP-RosC2**

Angel's Choice. Tom Clark. **SP-ClarT**

Angels coming down the aisles, The. Ascending over Ohio. Lawrence Ferlinghetti. **SP-FerlL**

Angels for Djuna Barnes. Kay Boyle. **CP-BoylK**

Angels gather. / The rush of mad air. Arrival. Maya Angelou. **SP-AngeM**

Angels guide him now, The. In Memory of a Child. Nicholas Vachel Lindsay. **CP-LindV**

Angels have somewhere fought and lost, The. Hymn to Nothingness. David Herbert Lawrence. **CP-LawrD**

Angels, in the early morning. Emily Dickinson. **CP-DickE**

Angels are a-mindin' you, my baby. Jack Frost at Bedtime. Paul Laurence Dunbar. **CP-DunbP**

Angels of Buena Vista, The. John Greenleaf Whittier. **CP-WhitJ**

Angels of the Love Affair. Anne Sexton. **CP-SextA**
   Angel of Beach Houses and Picnics.

Angel of Blizzards and Blackouts.

Angel of Clean Sheets.

Angel of Fire and Genitals.

Angel of Flight and Sleigh Bells.

Angel of Hope and Calendars.

Angels rejoice in, The. Their Rectitude Their Beauty. Donald Davie. **CP-DavDo**

Angels wept to see poor Tolly dead, The. The Toll of the Roads. Stevie Smith. **CP-SmitS**

Angels Wings. Langston Hughes. **SP-HughL**

Angelus. Kathleen Jessie Raine. **SP-RainK**

Angelus Ad Virginem. Gerard Manley Hopkins. **CP-HopkG**

Anger, / as black as a hook. After Auschwitz. Anne Sexton. **CP-SextA**

Anger. Robert Creeley. **CP-CreeR**

Anger. Stephen Dobyns. **SP-DobyS**

Anger. Robert Herrick. **CP-HerrR**

Anger. César Vallejo, *tr. fr. Spanish* by Thomas Merton. **CP-MertT**

Anger against Beasts. Wendell Berry. **CP-BerrW**

Anger & Wrath my bosom rends. William Blake. **CP-BlakW**

Anger at my heart one April morning. Frederick Morgan. **SP-MorgF**

Anger can be transformed. New Mexico. William Carlos Williams. **CP-WilW2**

Anger is a necessary element in the character of God. De Ira Dei. Tom Clark. **SP-ClarT**

Anger of loving, The. Your Fearful Symmetries. Isabella Gardner. **CP-GardI**

Anger shines through me. A Just Anger. Marge Piercy. **SP-PierM**

Anger which breaks a man into children. Anger. César Vallejo, *tr. fr. Spanish* by Thomas Merton. **CP-MertT**

Anger, yes. But God is God. Being Angry with God. Donald Davie. **CP-DavDo**

Anger's Freeing Power. Stevie Smith. **CP-SmitS**

Angie stayed by the victrola. Greenwich 1930's, I. Frederick Morgan. **SP-MorgF**

Angina. James Dickey. **CP-DickJ**

Angkor—on top of the terrace. Angkor Wat. Allen Ginsberg. **CP-GinsA**

Angkor Wat. Allen Ginsberg. **CP-GinsA**

Anglais Mort à Florence. Wallace Stevens. **CP-StevW**

Angle of a Landscape, The. Emily Dickinson. **CP-DickE**

Angler rose, he took his rod, The. Robert Louis Stevenson. **CP-StevR**

Angliae, et unanimis Scotiae pater, anne maritus. *accompanied by English translation.* Thomas Campion. *Fr.* Lord Hay's Mask.

Anglican Lady, An. Donald Davie. **CP-DavDo**

Angling. Robert Lowell. **SP-LoweR**

Anglo-Catholic Congresses. Sir John Betjeman. **CP-BetjJ**

Anglo-Irish Accord, The. John Hewitt. **CP-HewiJ**

Anglo-Latin Verses. Jonathan Swift. **CP-SwifJ**

Anglo-Welshman and his friends, The. Steve Griffiths. **SP-GrifS**

Anglos Have Gone, The. James Liddy. *Fr.* Love Songs of Corca Bascinn. **CP-LiddJ**

Angry and ashamed at. Revulsion. Donald Davie. **CP-DavDo**

Angry, I speak, and pass the hurt to you. Marilyn Hacker. **SP-HackM** *Fr.* Taking Notice.

Angry if Irene be. Upon Irene. Robert Herrick. **CP-HerrR**

Angry men and furious machines. Dutch Graves in Bucks County. Wallace Stevens. **CP-StevW**

Angry nettle and the mild, The. The Plum Gatherer. Edna St. Vincent Millay. **CP-MillE**

Angry Samson. Robert Ranke Graves. **CP-GravR**

Angst, / ennui & angst. Carmen 38. Catullus. *Fr.* Carmina. **CP-Catul**

Anguilla, Adina. A Sea-Chantey. Derek Walcott. **CP-WalcD**

Anguish. The. Edna St. Vincent Millay. **CP-MillE**

Anguish and revenge made visible, her serpents lifted. Medea. Kathleen Jessie Raine. **SP-RainK**

Anguish bloated by the replete scream. Geoffrey Hill. *Fr.* Three Baroque Meditations. **CP-HillG**

Anguish is always there, lurking at night. The Kingdom of Kali. May Sarton. **SRLS** *Fr.* The Invocation to Kali. **SP-SartM**

Anguish of a naked body is more terrible, The. A Prayer to the Lord Ramakrishna. James Wright. **CP-WrigJ**

Anguish sometimes gives a cause. Emily Dickinson. **SP-DickE**

Angutivaun Taina. Rudyard Kipling. **CP-KiplR** *Fr.* Quiquern. *Fr.* The Second Jungle Book.

Anima. Hayden Carruth. **CP-CarHS**

Anima. Richard Eberhart. **CP-EberR**

Anima quodammodo omnia. Translation. Howard Nemerov. **CP-NemeH**

Animal, The. Robert Creeley. **CP-CreeR**

Animal Acts. Charles Simic. **SP-SimiC**

Animal Ball, The. Edna St. Vincent Millay. **CP-MillE**

Animal dwelt, An. Fable for Slumber. Charles Olson. **CP-OlsoC**

Animal I wanted, The. Kenneth Patchen. **CP-PatcK**

Animal, rising at dusk, The. Book of the Jungle. John Haines. **SP-HainJ**

Animal Story, An. Jenny Joseph. **SP-JoseJ**

Animal Trainer, The. John Berryman. **CP-BerrJ**

Animal Tranquility and Decay. William Wordsworth. *See* The Little hedgerow birds.

Animal, Vegetable and Mineral. Louise Bogan. **CP-BogaL**

Animal willows of November. The Willows of Massachusetts. Denise Levertov. **CP-LeveD**

Animals. Robinson Jeffers. **CP-JefR3**

Animals. Frank O'Hara. **SP-OharF**

Animals. Walt Whitman. *See* I think I could turn and live awhile with animals.

Animals. Miller Williams. **SP-WillM**

Animals Are Passing from Our Lives. Philip Levine. **SP-LeviP**

Animals full of light. Meditation. William Stafford. **SP-StafW**

Animals in That Country, The. Margaret Atwood. **SP-AtwM1**

Animals' Last Words. Phoebe Hesketh. **SP-HeskP**

Animals of the morning wood watching in silence as, The. Kenneth Patchen. *Fr.* Wanderers of the Pale Wood. **CP-PatcK**

Animals own a fur world. Adults Only. William Stafford. **SP-StafW**

Animals seem so sad to be themselves. Topsfield Fair. John Updike. **CP-UpdiJ**

Animals Sick of the Plague, The. Marianne Craig Moore. **CP-MoorM** *Fr.* Fables of La Fontaine.

Animate and silent, columns of rain. Fathers. Steve Griffiths. **SP-GrifS**

Animuccia, vagantucccia, morbiduccia. Christina Georgina Rossetti. **CP-RosC3**

Animula. Thomas Stearns Eliot. **CP-ElioT**

Animula. Robinson Jeffers. **CP-JefR3**

Animula. George Oppen. **CP-OppeG**

Animula, Vagula, Blandula. Stevie Smith. **CP-SmitS**

Ann Arbor Song. Ted Berrigan. **SP-BerrT**

Ann Arbor Variations. Frank O'Hara. **SP-OharF**

Ann Burlak. Muriel Rukeyser. **CP-RukeM**

Anna Imroth. Carl Sandburg. **CP-SandC**

Anna Karenina and the Love-sick River. Kenneth Patchen. **CP-PatcK**

Anna, my daughter. Easter. Derek Walcott. **CP-WalcD**

Anna of the Harbor. Patti Smith. **SP-SmitP**

Anna, that sea is tender but the land. With Anna at Camaldoli. Richard Hugo. **CP-HugoR**

Anna, thy charms my bosom fire. Song. Robert Burns. **CP-BurnR**

Anna Who Was Mad. Anne Sexton. **CP-SextA**

Annabel Lee. Edgar Allan Poe. **CP-PoeEd**

Annals of Volusius, cock at his offal. Catullus. *See* Carmen 36: "Volusian sheets / shit-shotten Annals."

Anne. Mary Oliver. **SP-OlivM**

Anne Dick 1. 1936. Robert Lowell. **SP-LoweR**

Anne Dick 2. 1936. Robert Lowell. **SP-LoweR**

Anne-on-Avon. David Markson. **CP-MarkD**

Anne the enigma / Still bears the stigma. Footnotes to "Anne-on-Avon." David Markson. **CP-MarkD**

Anne's Eye is liken'd to the *Sun*. On the Eyes of Miss A——— H———. Byron. **CP-Byron**

Anniad, The. Gwendolyn Brooks. **SP-BrooG**

Annie. Christina Georgina Rossetti. **CP-RosC3**

Annie. Christina Georgina Rossetti. **CP-RosC3**

Annie and Rhoda, sisters twain. The Sisters. John Greenleaf Whittier. **CP-WhitJ**

Annie died the other day. Edward Estlin Cummings. **CP-CummE**

Annie from Miami. Gilbert Sorrentino. **SP-SorrG**

Annie Hill's Grave. James Merrill. **SP-MerrJ**

Annihilation of Nothing, The. Thom Gunn. **CP-GunnT**

Annisquam / Atlantic / river, sea. New England March. Charles Olson. **CP-OlsoC**

Anniversaries. Thomas McGrath. **SP-McGrT**

Anniversary [*or* Anniversarie], The. John Donne. **CP-DonnJ**

Anniversary, An. Wendell Berry. **CP-BerrW**

Anniversary, The. William Dickey. **SP-DickW**

Anniversary. Rita Dove. **SP-DoveR**

Anniversary, An. Thomas Hardy. **CP-HardT**

Anniversary, The. Ogden Nash. **CP-NashO**

Anniversary. Howard Nemerov. **CP-NemeH**

Anniversary. Charles Olson. **CP-OlsoC**

Anniversary Deer, The. Peter Meinke. **SP-MeinP**

Anniversary on the Hymeneals of My Noble Kinsman, Thomas Stanley, Esquire, An. Richard Lovelace. **CP-LoveR**

Anniversary Poem. George Oppen. **APSN; NNaP** *Fr.* Some San Francisco Poems. **CP-OppeG**

Anniversary Poem. John Greenleaf Whittier. **CP-WhitJ**

Annotation for an Epitaph. Adrienne Rich. **CP-RicAE**

Annotations in Verse. Robert Burns. **CP-BurnR**

"Grant me, indulgent Heaven, that I may live."

"Love's records, written on a heart like mine."

"Perish their names, however great or brave."

"Wisdom and Science—honor'd Powers!"

Announced by all the trumpets of the sky. The Snow-Storm. Ralph Waldo Emerson. **CP-EmerR**

Announced by your nakedness you appear. (Sideshow). Bill Knott. **SP-KnotB**

Announced himself Autocrat of all. Essay on Style. Daniel Gerard Hoffman. **SP-HoffD**

Announcement, The. Thomas Hardy. **CP-HardT**

Announcement. Richard Hugo. **CP-HugoR**

Announcer sets the stage, The. Night Games. Ron Koertge. **SP-KoerR**

Annual and Perennial Problem, An. Mona Van Duyn. **SP-VanDM**

Annuals. Denise Levertov. **CP-LeveD**

Annul in Me My Manhood. William Everson. **SP-EverW**

Annunciation, The. Wystan Hugh Auden. *Fr.* For the Time Being; a Christmas Oratorio. **CP-AudeW**

Annunciation. John Donne. **TrCP** *Fr.* La Corona. **ChIV-2; ESCV; OBS; Son** *Fr.* Holy Sonnets. **CP-DonnJ**

Annunciation, The. Thomas Merton. **CP-MertT**

Annunciation. May Sarton. **SP-SartM**

Annunciation of the Blessed Virgin. Christopher Smart. *Fr.* Hymns and Spiritual Songs for the Fasts and Festivals of the Church of England. **SP-SmarC**

Annunciations. Hart Crane. **CP-CranH**

Annunciations. Geoffrey Hill. **CP-HillG**

Annus Memorabilis, 1789. William Cowper. **CP-CowpW**

Annus Mirabilis. John Dryden.

"Cheerful soldiers, with new stores supplied, The." **SP-DrydJ**

Annus Mirabilis. Philip Larkin. **CP-LarkP**

Anointed stone, the coruscated crown, The. The Circumstance. Hart Crane. **CP-CranH**

Anomalous I linger, and ignore. John Berryman. *Fr.* Sonnets to Chris. **CP-BerrJ**

Anomalous structure of the inner ear has been designed as, The. A Lesson in Anatomy. Kay Boyle. **CP-BoylK**

Anon out of the earth a fabric huge. John Milton. **TreFS** *Fr.* Book I. **FHYEP; NAEL-1; OAEL-1; OxAEP-1** *Fr.* Paradise Lost. **CP-MiltJ**

Among the grackles in a half circle on the grass. Seven Eleven. Carl Sandburg. **CP-SandC**

Anonymity has a name. Parable. Thomas McGrath. **SP-McGrT**

Anonymous as cherubs. Two Voices in a Meadow. Richard Wilbur. **CP-WilbR**

Anonymous, she takes her chair. The Page Turner. Gary Gildner. **SP-GildG**

Another [Epigram on Said Occasion]. Robert Burns. **CP-BurnR**

Another [Epitaph on the Lady Mary Villiers] ("Purest soul that e'er was sent, The"). Thomas Carew. **CP-CareT**

Another [On the Duke of Buckingham]. Thomas Carew. **CP-CareT**

Another [Addressed to a Young Lady]. William Cowper. *See* Sweet stream, that winds through [or thro'] yonder glade.

Another [Epitaph]: "Here lies John Trot, the Friend of all mankind." William Blake. **CP-BlakW**

Another ["Thou had'st the wreath before, now take the Tree"], *see also* Upon M. Ben Jonson. Robert Herrick. **CP-HerrR**

Another [To His Booke], *see also* To His Booke ["While thou didst keep thy candor undefil'd"]. Robert Herrick. *See* Who with thy leaves shall wipe (at need).

Another [Epitaph]: "I was buried near this Dike." William Blake. *See* I was buried near this dyke [or Dike].

Another ("The centaur, siren I forgo"), *see also* Snail [or Snayl], The. Richard Lovelace. **CP-LoveR**

Another [To His Booke], *see also* To His Booke ["While thou didst keep thy candor undefil'd"]. Martial. *See* To read my book[e], the virgin shy [or shie].

Another [Epigram]. Alexander Pope. **CP-PopeA**

Another ["Art thou some individual of a kind"], *see also* Treasure. *Unknown, tr. fr.* Greek by William Cowper. **CP-CowpW**

Another ["At three-score winters' end I died"]. *Unknown, tr. fr.* Greek by William Cowper. **CP-CowpW**

Another ["Miser, traversing his house, A"], *see also* Treasure. *Unknown, tr. fr.* Greek by William Cowper. **CP-CowpW**

Another ["Painter, this likeness is too strong"]. *Unknown, tr. fr.* Greek by William Cowper. **CP-CowpW**

Another ["Take to thy bosom, gentle earth, a swain"]. *Unknown, tr. fr.* Greek by William Cowper. **CP-CowpW**

Another ("Phoebus, make haste, the day's too long, be gone"), *see* Letter to Her Husband, Absent upon Public[k] Employment, A. Anne Bradstreet. **CP-BradA**

Another ("As loving hind. . ."). Anne Bradstreet. **CP-BradA**

Another, *see also* Inscription for a Stone. William Cowper. **CP-CowpW**

Another ("Art thou not destin'd? then, with hast, go on"). Robert Herrick. **CP-HerrR**

Another ("As Sun-beames pierce the glasse, and streaming in"). Robert Herrick. **CP-HerrR**

Another ("Bloud of Abel was a thing, The"). Robert Herrick. **CP-HerrR**

Another ("God is *Jehovah* cal'd; which name of His"). Robert Herrick. **CP-HerrR**

Another ("In the morning when ye rise"). Robert Herrick. **CP-HerrR**

Another ("Love he that will; it best likes me"), *see also* Upon Himself ("I dislikt but even now"). Robert Herrick. **CP-HerrR**

Another ("Shame of mans face is no more, The"). Robert Herrick. **CP-HerrR**

Another ("Sin is an act so free, that if we shall"). Robert Herrick. **CP-HerrR**

Another ("Sin is the cause of death"). Robert Herrick. **CP-HerrR**

Another ("That there's a God"). Robert Herrick. **CP-HerrR**

Another ("Thou bidst me come; I cannot come; for why"). Robert Herrick. **CP-HerrR**

Another ("Wassaile the Trees, that they may beare"). Robert Herrick. **CP-HerrR**

Another ("Let the superstitious wife"). Robert Herrick. **CP-HerrR**

Another ("Where love begins, there dead thy first desire"). Robert Herrick. **CP-HerrR**

Another ("If ye fear to be affrighted"). Robert Herrick. *See* If ye fear[e] to be affrighted.

Another ("As I beheld a winters evening air"), *see also* Black Patch on Lucasta's Face, A. Richard Lovelace. **CP-LoveR**

Another ("I Did believe I was in Heav'n"), *see also* Song: "In mine one [or own] monument I lie [or lye]." Richard Lovelace. **CP-LoveR**

Another. Pablo Neruda, *tr. fr.* Spanish by Ben Belitt. **SP-NeruP**

Another ("Artes bred neat *An*"), *see* Anagram, An ("So Bartas-like thy fine spun poems been"). *Unknown.* **CP-BradA**

Another All-Night Party. Thom Gunn. **CP-GunnT**

Another armored animal—scale. The Pangolin. Marianne Craig Moore. **CP-MoorM**

Another Ashtray. Louis Zukofsky. **CP-ZukLS**

Another August. James Merrill. **SP-MerrJ**

Another barrel of insect casings. Texas Sprawl. John Yau. **SP-YauJo**

Another Bed. Charles Bukowski. **SP-BukC1**

Another Beer. William Matthews. **SP-MattW**

Another Border. Daniel Gerard Hoffman. **SP-HoffD**

Another Chain Letter. John Ashbery. **SP-AshbJ**

Another Charme for Stables. Robert Herrick. **CP-HerrR**

Another Christmas wore its sprig of pride. The Carol Singers from the Church. John Hewitt. **CP-HewiJ**

Another Cold May. Louis MacNeice. **CP-MacNL**

Another conscience leaps from a window sill. Obituary for Jan Masaryk. John Clellon Holmes. **SP-HolmJ**

Another Country. Daniel Gerard Hoffman. **SP-HoffD**

Another cove of shale. On the Marginal Way. Richard Wilbur. **CP-WilbR**

Another curious thing about the English middle classes. Middle-Class Children. David Herbert Lawrence. **CP-LawrD**

Another Dark Lady. Edwin Arlington Robinson. **CP-RobiE**

Another dawn, leaden. Words. Philip Levine. **SP-LeviP**

Another Day. A Game of Toys. Paul, Telling the Game. Muriel Rukeyser. **CP-RukeM**

Another Day (And then the cow). Muriel Rukeyser. **CP-RukeM**

Another Day (Child among his powers). Muriel Rukeyser. **CP-RukeM**

Another Day (Day Lilies, Yellow Daisies). Muriel Rukeyser. **CP-RukeM**

Another Day. For a Moment Slipping Back, Again the Unreal King. Muriel Rukeyser. **CP-RukeM**

Another day gone, and still. A Little Vesper. Jane Cooper. **SP-CoopJ**

Another Day (I will now sing). Muriel Rukeyser. **CP-RukeM**

Another Day. In a Field of Peace the Child, Playing. The Child Preparing for Daytime Sleep. Muriel Rukeyser. **CP-RukeM**

Another Day (Miss Lorence). Muriel Rukeyser. **CP-RukeM**

Another Day. Paul in the Mountains of Fantasy. Paul Tells His Adventure. Muriel Rukeyser. **CP-RukeM**

Another Day. The Children Are All Eating. Muriel Rukeyser. **CP-RukeM**

Another Day (You can't come). Muriel Rukeyser. **CP-RukeM**

Another Day (You sit there). Muriel Rukeyser. **CP-RukeM**

Another Descent. Wendell Berry. *See* Through the weeks of deep snow.

Another Dialogue, To Be Sung at the Same Time. Thomas Campion. *Fr.* The Ayres that Were Sung and Played, at *Brougham Castle* in *Westmerland*, in the Kings Entertainment. **CP-CampT**

Another Dog's Death. John Updike. **CP-UpdiJ**

Another Dollar. Charles Kenneth Williams. **CP-WillC**

Another Elegy. Margaret Atwood. **SP-AtwM2**

Another Epitaph on an Army of Mercenaries, *see also* Housman, "Epitaph on an Army of Mercenaries." "Hugh MacDiarmid." **SP-MacDH**

Another [Epitaph on Lady Mary Villiers] ("This little vault, this narrow room"). Thomas Carew. *See* This little vault, this narrow room.

Another evening we sprawled about discussing. Charles on Fire. James Merrill. **SP-MerrJ**

Another Family. Leonard Cohen. **CP-CoheL**

Another four I've left yet to bring on. The Four Seasons of the Year. Anne Bradstreet. **CP-BradA**

Another Fragment to Music. Percy Bysshe Shelley. **CP-ShelP**

Another Girl. John Lennon *and* Paul McCartney. **CP-Beatl**

Another Grace for a Child. Robert Herrick. *See* Here a little child I stand.

Another guest that winter night. Prophetess. John Greenleaf Whittier. **AA** *Fr.* Snow-Bound [*or* Snow-Bound; a Winter Idyl]. **CP-WhitJ**

Another hand is beckoning us. Gone. John Greenleaf Whittier. **CP-WhitJ**

Another hard, hard morning with a hard snow. Hayden Carruth. *Fr.* Paragraphs. **CP-CarHS**

Another Immorality. Malcolm Lowry. **CP-LowrM**

Another. In Defense of Their Inconstancy [*or* Inconstancie]. A Song. Ben Jonson. **CP-JonsB**

Another Lady's [*or* Ladyes] Exception, Present at the Hearing. Ben Jonson. *Fr.* A Celebration of Charis in Ten Lyric[k] Pieces [*or* Peeces]. **CP-JonsB**

Another Language. Erica Jong. **SP-JongE**

Another Leonora captured the poet Torquato. To the Same ["Another Leonora captured the poet Torquato"]. John Milton, *tr. fr. Latin by* John T. Shawcross. **CP-MiltJ**

Another Leonora once inspir'd. John Milton. *See* To the Same ["Another Leonora captured the poet Torquato"].

Another Life. Derek Walcott. **CP-WalcD**

"Fishermen, like thieves, shake out their silver." **PBCV**

"Rain falls like knives, The." **PBCV**

"Well, there you have your seasons, prodigy!" **PBCV**

Another misty one. These opaline. Last Mornings in California. James Merrill. **SP-MerrJ**

Another New-Yeeres Gift, or Song for the Circumcision. Robert Herrick. **CP-HerrR**

Another Night in the Ruins. Galway Kinnell. **SP-KinnG**

Another of God. Robert Herrick. **CP-HerrR**

Another of my new black angels. You Don't Know What Love Is. Al Young. **CP-YounA**

Another of the Same. Sir Walter Ralegh *and* George Clifford. **CP-RaleW** *Fr.* Commendatory Verses to Edmund Spenser's Fairy Queen.

Another of the Same. Edmund Spenser. *Fr.* Astrophel. **CP-Spens**

Another of the Same Nature, Made Since. *Unknown.* **CP-MarlC**

Another old friend, long afterward. Views of Myself. John Berryman. **CP-BerrJ**

Another Old Tale. Jenny Joseph. **SP-JoseJ**

Another Old Woman. William Carlos Williams. **CP-WilW2**

Another on Her, *see also* Upon Julia's Haire Fill'd with Dew. Robert Herrick. **CP-HerrR**

Another on Love ("Love's of it self, too sweet"). Robert Herrick. **CP-HerrR**

Another on [Mr. Herrys]. Richard Crashaw. **CP-CrasR**

Another on the Same, *see also* Obedience. Robert Herrick. **CP-HerrR**

Another on the Same. John Milton. **CP-MiltJ**

Another One. Pablo Neruda, *tr. fr. Spanish by* Ben Belitt. **SP-NeruP**

Another Ophelia. David Herbert Lawrence. **CP-LawrD**

Another Poem for Me (after Recovering from an O.D.) Etheridge Knight. **SP-KnigE**

Another poet, woman and alive. Marilyn Hacker. *Fr.* The Regent's Park Sonnets. **SP-HackM**

Another rape in the trains, a drunk torched in the park. December 27, 1988. Martin Edmunds. **SP-EdmuM**

Another Reply by the Dean. Jonathan Swift. **CP-SwifJ**

Another ribald tale of the good times at Madame Lipsky's. The Pleasures of Peace. Kenneth Koch. **SP-KochK**

Another Room, *see also* Commentary—Another Room. Leonard Cohen. **CP-CoheL**

Another Season. Thomas McGrath. **SP-McGrT**

Another season, proposing a name and a distant resolution. The Ivory Tower. John Ashbery. **SP-AshbJ**

Another side, umbrageous Grots and Caves. Paradise. John Milton. **OBS** *Fr.* Book IV. **OAEL-1** *Fr.* Paradise Lost. **CP-MiltJ**

Another Simple Ballat. Byron. **CP-Byron**

Another Song of a Fool. William Butler Yeats. **CP-YeatW**

Another Spring. Denise Levertov. **CP-LeveD**

Another Spring. Kenneth Rexroth. **SP-RexrK**

Another Spring. Christina Georgina Rossetti. **CP-RosC1**

Another starless night, another novel. The Memoirs of an Imaginary Man. John Clellon Holmes. **SP-HolmJ**

Another story still: a porch with trees. Peterborough. Marilyn Hacker. **SP-HackM**

Another storm, another blizzard. Third Snowfall. Marilyn Hacker. **SP-HackM**

Another summer! Our Independence. Fourth of July in Maine. Robert Lowell. **SP-LoweR**

Another Sunday Morning. Derek Mahon. **SP-MahoD**

Another sunny birthday. I am tormented by poetry and loss. Thomas Merton. *Fr.* Cables to the Ace. **CP-MertT**

Another sword! And what if I could seize. John Keats. **FaBoEH** *Fr.* King Stephen. A Fragment of a Tragedy. **CP-KeatJ**

Another than Wordsworth dropped his live work. Malcolm Lowry. *Fr.* Songs for Second Childhood. **CP-LowrM**

Another Time. Wystan Hugh Auden. **CP-AudeW**

Another to Bring in the Witch. Robert Herrick. **CP-HerrR**

Another, to God ("Lord, do not beat me"). Robert Herrick. **CP-HerrR**

Another, to God ("Though thou beest"). Robert Herrick. **CP-HerrR**

Another to Him. Ben Jonson. **CP-JonsB**

Another, to His Saviour. Robert Herrick. **CP-HerrR**

Another to Mrs. Anne Bradstreet, Author of this Poem. *Unknown, poem signed* "H. S." **CP-BradA**

Another to Neptune. Robert Herrick. **CP-HerrR**

Another to the Maids. Robert Herrick. **CP-HerrR**

Another Translation of the Same Ode. Horace. *See* 1.38: Simplicity.

Another type that England has produced. Little-Boy Brilliant. David Herbert Lawrence. **CP-LawrD**

Another Upon Her, *see also* To His Kinswoman, Mrs. Penelope Wheeler. Robert Herrick. **CP-HerrR**

Another upon Her Weeping. Robert Herrick. **CP-HerrR**

Another, upon the Poems. John Pinchbacke. *Fr.* Commendatory Poems. **CP-LoveR**

Another Version, *see also* Translation of Verses to Lloyd. William Cowper, *ad. fr. the Latin of Vincent Bourne.* **CP-CowpW**

Another Version of the Same, *see also* Bridal Song, A *and* Epithalamium. Percy Bysshe Shelley. **CP-ShelP**

Another Voice. Richard Wilbur. **CP-WilbR**

Another Way of Love. Robert Browning. **CP-BroR1**

Another Weeping Woman. Wallace Stevens. **CP-StevW**

Another Year. William Carlos Williams. **CP-WilW2**

Another year! another deadly blow! November, 1806. William Wordsworth. **CP-WorW1**

Another year of joy & grief. 1884. Christina Georgina Rossetti. **CP-RosC3**

Anseo. Paul Muldoon. **SP-MuldP**

Answer, The. Stephen Berg. **SP-BergS**

Answer, The. Robert Creeley. **CP-CreeR**

Answer, The. William Everson. **SP-EverW**

Answer, An. Robert Frost. **CP-FrosR**

Answer, The. George Herbert. **CP-HerbG**

Answer, The. Robinson Jeffers. **CP-JefR2**

Answer, The. Rudyard Kipling. **CP-KiplR**

Answer, The. Richard Lovelace. **CP-LoveR**

Answer, An. Christina Georgina Rossetti. **CP-RosC3**

Answer, The. Carl Sandburg. **CP-SandC**

Answer, An, *diff. vers.* Jonathan Swift. *See* An Answer to a Scandalous Poem.

Answer, The. John Greenleaf Whittier. **CP-WhitJ**

Answer, The, *see also* "Defamed guiltiness by silence unkempt." Sir Thomas Wyatt. **CP-WyatT**

Answer: how old / is the wind, shakes the trees & moves with the movement of. Hart Crane 2. Robert Creeley. **CP-CreeR**

Answer July. Emily Dickinson. **CP-DickE**

Answer me when I call / God of my righteousness, *par. by* Milton. Bible, *O.T. See* Psalm 4: "Hear me when I call, O God of my righteousness."

Answer that ye made to me, my dear, The [*or* Th']. Sir Thomas Wyatt. **CP-WyatT**

Answer, The [To the Guidwife of Wauchope-House]. Robert Burns. **CP-BurnR**

Answer to ——'s Professions of Affection. Byron. **CP-Byron**

Answer to a Beautiful Poem, Entitled "The Common Lot." Byron. **CP-Byron**

Answer to a Child's Question. Samuel Taylor Coleridge. **CP-ColeS**

Answer to a Scandalous Poem, An. Jonathan Swift. **CP-SwifJ**

Answer to an Invitation. Robert Burns. **CP-BurnR**

Answer to Delany's Riddle, The. Jonathan Swift. **CP-SwifJ**

Answer to Dr. Delany, The. Jonathan Swift. **CP-SwifJ**

Answer to Dr. Delany's Fable of the Pheasant and the Lark, An. Jonathan Swift. **CP-SwifJ**

Answer to "Paulus," The. Jonathan Swift. **CP-SwifJ**

Answer to Prayer. Robert Penn Warren. **SP-WarrR**

Answer to Some Elegant Verses. Byron. **CP-Byron**

Answer to Some Verses Made in His Praise, An. Sir John Suckling. **CP-SuckJ**

Answer to Stanzas Addressed to Lady Hesketh. William Cowper. **CP-CowpW**

Answer to the Ballyspellin Ballad, An. Jonathan Swift. **CP-SwifJ**

Answer to the Following Question of Mrs. Howe. Alexander Pope. **CP-PopeA**

Answer to the Foregoing, Addressed to Miss——. Byron. **CP-Byron**

Answer to the Foregoing—Extempore [Clarinda]. Robert Burns. **CP-BurnR**

Answer to the Parson, An. William Blake. **CP-BlakW**

Answer to Vanessa's Rebus, The. Jonathan Swift. **CP-SwifJ**

Answer to Voznesensky and Evtushenko. Frank O'Hara. **SP-OharF**

Answer Yes or No. Robert Penn Warren. *Fr.* Tale of Time. **SP-WarrR**

Answered when you appeared at the gate. Not always, or even. It Was Being. Kenneth Patchen. **CP-PatcK**

Answering a letter to somebody in Alaska. Love. Charles Bukowski. **SP-BukC3**

Answers. Mary Oliver. **SP-OlivM**

Ant, The. Samuel Johnson. *See* Turn on the prudent Ant, thy heedless eyes.

Ant, The. Richard Lovelace. **CP-LoveR**

Ant! / lugging half an ounce, An. Grace Paley. **CP-PaleG**

Ant, The. Ogden Nash. **CP-NashO**

Ant Dodger. Bill Knott. **SP-KnotB**

Ant Mansion, The. Robert Bly. **SP-BlyR**

Ant on the tablecloth, An. Departmental. Robert Frost. **CP-FrosR**

Antaeus: A Fragment. Wilfred Owen. **CP-OwenW**

Antarctica. Derek Mahon. **SP-MahoD**

Ante-Bellum Sermon, An. Paul Laurence Dunbar. **CP-DunbP**

Ante Mortem. Robinson Jeffers. **CP-JefR1**

Antecedents. Charles Tomlinson. **CP-TomlC**
    Bells: a Period Piece, The.
    Lacunae.
    Milieux.
    Nothing: a Divagation.
    Praeludium.
    Something: a Direction.

Antennae of the race. Somerset. Donald Davie. **CP-DavDo**

Antéros. Gérard de Nerval, *tr. fr. French by* Richard Wilbur. **CP-WilbR**

Anthea bade me tie [*or* tye] her sho[o]e. The Sho[o]e Tying. Robert Herrick. **CP-HerrR**

Anthea I am going hence. To Anthea. Robert Herrick. **CP-HerrR**

Anthea laught, and fearing lest excess[e]. Anthea's Retractation. Robert Herrick. **CP-HerrR**

Anthea, your shy flanks in starlight. Nuda Natens. John Updike. **CP-UpdiJ**

Anthea's Retractation. Robert Herrick. **CP-HerrR**

Anthem: "Birds they sang, The." Leonard Cohen. **CP-CoheL**

Anthem: "Let us praise our Maker, with true passion extol Him." Wystan Hugh Auden. **CP-AudeW**

Anthem for Doomed Youth. Wilfred Owen. **CP-OwenW**

Anthem for St. Cecilia's Day. Wystan Hugh Auden. **CP-AudeW**
    "I cannot grow."
    "In a garden shady this holy lady." **FaBoTw; MP; TwCP**
    "O ear whose creatures cannot wish to fall."

Anthem for the Children of Christ's Hospital. Samuel Taylor Coleridge. **CP-ColeS**

Anthony. Charles Bukowski. **SP-BukC2**

Anthropomorphism Reversed. Jenny Joseph. **SP-JoseJ**

Anthropos apteros for days. The Maze. Wystan Hugh Auden. **CP-AudeW**

Anti-aircraft seen from a certain distance. Dam Neck, Virginia. Richard Eberhart. **CP-EberR**

Anti-Conception. Erica Jong. **SP-JongE**

Anti-Father. Rita Dove. **SP-DoveR**

Anti-master-man, floribund ascetic, An. Landscape with Boat. Wallace Stevens. **CP-StevW**

Anti-Matter. Erica Jong. **SP-JongE**

Anti-Promethean Ode. John Hewitt. **CP-HewiJ**

Anti-Thelyphthora. William Cowper. **CP-CowpW**

Anti-Vietnam War Peace Mobilization. Allen Ginsberg. **CP-GinsA**

Antichrist, playing his lissome flute and merry. Armageddon. John Crowe Ransom. **SP-RansJ**

Anticipation. Emily Brontë. *See* How beautiful the Earth is still.

Anticipation. October, 1803. William Wordsworth. **CP-WorW1**

Antigone. George Meredith. **CP-MerG1**

Antigone. Howard Nemerov. **CP-NemeH**

Antigone. Sophocles, *tr. fr. Ancient Greek*.
    "Happy are those who have never tasted evil." **CP-SpenS**

Antigua. John Updike. **CP-UpdiJ**

Antinoüs: The Diaries. Adrienne Rich. **CP-RicAE; SP-RicA1; SP-RicA2**

Antipas. Christina Georgina Rossetti. **CP-RosC2**

Antipater of Sidon. Hilda Doolittle. **CP-DoolH**

Antiphon: "Let all the world in ev'ry corner sing / My God and King." George Herbert. **CP-HerbG**

Antiphon (2): "Praised be the God of love." George Herbert. **CP-HerbG**

Antipoem 1. Thomas Merton. **CP-MertT**

Antipoetic is the thing. The Entity. William Carlos Williams. **CP-WilW1**

Antipolis. James Dickey. **CP-DickJ**

Antiquarian. Tom Clark. **SP-ClarT**

Antiquary. John Donne. **CP-DonnJ**

Antiquated Grace, An. Emily Dickinson. **CP-DickE**

Antiquated Tree, An. Emily Dickinson. **CP-DickE**

Antique. George Oppen. **CP-OppeG**

Antique Babel, empresse of the East, The. Edmund Spenser. *Fr.* Commendatory Sonnets. **CP-Spens**

Antique Harvesters. John Crowe Ransom. **SP-RansJ**

Antique story comes to me, An. Die Lorelei. Stevie Smith. **CP-SmitS**

Antiques in Ellettsville. Richard Hugo. **CP-HugoR**

Antiquity in blindness praised the son of Iapetus. On the Inventor of Gunpowder. John Milton, *tr. fr. Latin by* John T. Shawcross. **CP-MiltJ**

Antisocial Easter. Richard Hugo. **CP-HugoR**

Antitheses. John Berryman. **CP-BerrJ**

Antiworlds. Andrei Voznesensky, *tr. fr. Russian by* Richard Wilbur. **CP-WilbR**

Antorcha Y Corona, 1968, *spanish vers. of* Torch and Crown, 1968. Robert Ranke Graves. **CP-GravR**

Antrim. Robinson Jeffers. **CP-JefR2**

Antrim April. John Hewitt. **CP-HewiJ**

Ants. Robert Bly. **SP-BlyR**

Ants, The. Charles Bukowski. **SP-BukC2**

Ants. Daniel Gerard Hoffman. **SP-HoffD**

Ants crawl upon paper flowers with all the insect color. Soirée. Charles Bukowski. **SP-BukC2**

Ants of Argos, The. Rita Dove. **SP-DoveR**

Ants, or wise bees, or a gang of wolves. Faith. Robinson Jeffers. **CP-JefR3**

Ants, when they meet each other. Things I Learned Last Week. William Stafford. **SP-StafW**

Anubis, jackal-headed god. The Average Egyptian Faces Death. John Updike. **CP-UpdiJ**

Anubis will stare. Charles Olson. **CP-OlsoC**

Anvil, The. Rudyard Kipling. **CP-KiplR**

Anxia dum natura nimis tibi, Mellea, formam. *acc. by English translation.* Thomas Campion. **CP-CampT**

Anxiety. Archie Randolph Ammons. **SP-AmmoA**

Anxiety. Frank O'Hara. **SP-OharF**

Anxiety I Felt in Guanajuato, The. Richard Eberhart. **CP-EberR**

Anxious eyes loom down the damp-black streets. Dawn Walkers. Jenny Joseph. **SP-JoseJ**

Anxious for verse to come with apt release. October-Born. John Hewitt. **CP-HewiJ**

Anxious milk-blood in the veins of the earth, The. Annunciations. Hart Crane. **CP-CranH**

Anxious Parent, I guess you have just never been around. "My Child Is Phlegmatic. . . "—Anxious Parent. Ogden Nash. **CP-NashO**

Anxious to publicise and pay our dues. Last Will and Testament. Philip Larkin. **CP-LarkP**

Anxious View of a Tree. Hayden Carruth. **CP-CarHS**

Any clear thing that blinds us with surprise. Fishnet. Robert Lowell. **SP-LoweR**

Any contract, tax form, Great Idea. The Loophole. Leonard Nathan. **SP-NathL**

Any fire will do - you who are sleeping. Hayden Carruth. *Fr.* The Sleeping Beauty. **CP-CarHL**

Any Honest Housewife. Robert Ranke Graves. **CP-GravR**

Any hound a porcupine nudges. The Porcupine. Ogden Nash. **CP-NashO**

Any Human to Another. Countee Cullen. **CP-CullC**

Any Husband to Any Wife. Adrienne Rich. **CP-RicAE**

Any Inner City Blues. Al Young. **CP-YounA**

Any Little Old Song. Thomas Hardy. **CP-HardT**

Any man is wonderful. Edward Estlin Cummings. **CP-CummE**

Any man's death could end the story. Wendell Berry. *Fr.* Rising. **CP-BerrW**

Any Milleniums Today, Lady? Ogden Nash. **CP-NashO**

Any Page of Thomas Mann's. Marsden Hartley. **CP-HartM**

Any Rich Suburban Church. John Hewitt. **CP-HewiJ**

Any Size We Please. Robert Frost. **CP-FrosR**

Any Slave. Edwin Rolfe. **CP-RolfE**

Any System. Leonard Cohen. **CP-CoheL**

Any Time. William Stafford. **SP-StafW**

Any Time at All. John Lennon *and* Paul McCartney. **CP-Beatl**

ANY•TRULY•MODERN•STUDY•OF•THE•. HEINRICH•HIMMLER•REICHSFUEHRER•SS—8•APRIL•1945•. William DeWitt Snodgrass. **SP-SnodW**

Any Way for Wealth. Robert Herrick. **CP-HerrR**

Any way you walk. You Have Pissed Your Life. William Carlos Williams. **CP-WilW1**

Any Wife to Any Husband. Robert Browning. **CP-BroR1**

Any woman who says to me. Can't Be Borne. David Herbert Lawrence. **CP-LawrD**

Anybody / Better than. Desert. Langston Hughes. **SP-HughL**

Anybody Else Hate Nicknames? Ogden Nash. **CP-NashO**

Anybody for Money? or, Just Bring Your Own Basket. Ogden Nash. **CP-NashO**

Anyhow, once full Dervish, youngsters came. Shah Abbas. Robert Browning. **CP-BroR2**

Anyone lived in a pretty how town. Edward Estlin Cummings. **CP-CummE; SP-CummE**

Anyone would love to paint from memory. On the Ramblas / A Tree A Girl. Grace Paley. **CP-PaleG**

Anything Is Beautiful If You Say It Is. Wallace Stevens. **CP-StevW**

Anything that moves is white. Hydra 1960. Leonard Cohen. **CP-CoheL**

Anything to have done! Solomon's Mines. Geoffrey Hill. **CP-HillG**

Anyway we are always waking. Souvenirs. Jane Cooper. *Fr.* Dispossessions. **SP-CoopJ**

Anywhere. Robert Creeley. **CP-CreeR**

Anywhere and Everywhere People. Carl Sandburg. **CP-SandC**

Anywhere is conterminous with another. The Return of the Hunters. John Yau. **SP-YauJo**

Aor Against the Bad Reviewer. James McAuley. **SP-McAuJ**

Aor Against the Ingrate Who Abused Our Hospitality. James McAuley. **SP-McAuJ**

"From the burly give-and-take."

"Go on, stir up your tiresome wavelets."

"Here on the vast edges drear."

"Now you lean over suicide's precipice."

"You've mastered the bleak art of Changes."

Aor Against the Philistine Who Destroyed Lovely Dublin Vistas With His Ugly Erections, Then Absconded to London. James McAuley. **SP-McAuJ**

Aor Against the Termagant from California Who Confused Instruction With Indignation. James McAuley. **SP-McAuJ**

Aor Against the Warmonger. James McAuley. **SP-McAuJ**

Apache word for love twists, The. In the Night Desert. William Stafford. **SP-StafW**

Apartment Cats. Thom Gunn. **CP-GunnT**

Apartment space is a butterfly, The. For Jimin in Manchuria II. James Liddy. **CP-LiddJ**

Apartment with a View, An. John Ciardi. **SP-CiarJ**

Apathy and Enthusiasm. Herman Melville. **SP-MelvH**

Ape Experiment Room. Philip Larkin. **CP-LarkP**

Apelles hearing that his boy. The Tears of a Painter. Vincent Bourne, *tr. fr. Latin by* William Cowper. **CP-CowpW**

Apeneck Sweeney spreads his knees. Sweeney among the Nightingales. Thomas Stearns Eliot. **CP-ElioT**

Apes, may I speak to you a moment? Is Wisdom a Lot of Language? Carl Sandburg. **CP-SandC**

Apes yawn and adore their fleas in the sun, The. The Jaguar. Ted Hughes. **SP-HughT**

Aphrodite. Louise Glück. **SP-GlücL**

Aphrodite. Daniel Gerard Hoffman. **SP-HoffD**

Aphrodite, / my Cape Town lady. To Like, to Love. Anne Sexton. **CP-SextA**

Apollo. James Dickey. **CP-DickJ**

Apollo. Jonathan Swift. **CP-SwifJ**

Apollo and Daphne. Christopher Smart. **SP-SmarC**

Apollo and the Fates. Robert Browning. **CP-BroR2**

Apollo and the Sibyl. Frank Templeton Prince. **CP-PrinF**

"And yet the Sibyl parches, caught and clutched within a fist of dust!"

"Sky brims with the ghost of a great rage, The."

"Then came a time of great guilt, that I inhabited."

"Thyme, tufa, sage, anemone."

"White sunlight and the dripping oars!"

Apollo, Christ and God, all three. Sun Up. Phoebe Hesketh. **SP-HeskP**

Apollo, god of light and wit. Apollo. Jonathan Swift. **CP-SwifJ**

Apollo great, whose beams the greater world do light. Sir Philip Sidney. **SP-SidnP** *Fr.* Arcadia.

Apollo Musagete, Poetry, and the Leader of the Muses. Delmore Schwartz. **SP-SchwD**

Apollo of the Physiologists. Robert Ranke Graves. **CP-GravR**

Apollo Outwitted. Jonathan Swift. **CP-SwifJ**

Apollo sings, his harpe resounds; give roome. Upon Master Fletchers Incomparable Playes. Robert Herrick. **CP-HerrR**

Apollo to the Dean. Jonathan Swift. **CP-SwifJ**

Apollo to the Graces. John Keats. **CP-KeatJ**

Apollo's Edict. Jonathan Swift. **CP-SwifJ**

Apologetic Postscript of a Year Later. Robert Louis Stevenson. **CP-StevR**

Apologia Pro Poemate Meo. Wilfred Owen. **CP-OwenW**

Apologia pro Vita Sua. Samuel Taylor Coleridge. **CP-ColeS**

Apologia pro Vita Sua. Alexander Pope. **NOBE** *Fr.* Epistle to Dr. Arbuthnot. **CP-PopeA**

Apologies. Chuang Tzu, *tr. fr. Chinese by* Thomas Merton. **CP-MertT**

Apologies. Marge Piercy. **SP-PierM**

Apologies to Harvard. John Updike. **CP-UpdiJ**

Apologists blame it on the English. In Defense of the English Portrait School. Erica Jong. **SP-JongE**

Apology, An. William Cowper. **CP-CowpW**

Apology, The. Robert Creeley. **CP-CreeR**

Apology, The. Ralph Waldo Emerson. **CP-EmerR**

Apology. Adrienne Rich. **CP-RicAE**

Apology. Adrienne Rich. **CP-RicAE**

Apology, An. Diane Wakoski. **SP-WakoD**

Apology. Richard Wilbur. **CP-WilbR**

Apology. William Carlos Williams. **CP-WilW1**

Apology ("Nor scorn the aid which Fancy oft doth lead"). William Wordsworth. *Fr.* Ecclesiastical Sonnets. **CP-WorW2**

Apology ("Not utterly unworthy to endure"). William Wordsworth. *Fr.* Ecclesiastical Sonnets. **CP-WorW2**

Apology. William Wordsworth. **CP-WorW2**

Apology. William Wordsworth. *Fr.* Sonnets upon the Punishment of Death. **CP-WorW2**

Apology for Apostasy? Etheridge Knight. **SP-KnigE**

Apology for Bad Dreams. Robinson Jeffers. **CP-JefR1**

Apology for Domitian. Robert Penn Warren. **SP-WarrR**

Apology for Her. Emily Dickinson. **CP-DickE**

Apology for Not Invoking the Muse, An. John Ciardi. **SP-CiarJ**

Apology for the Bottle Volcanic, An. Nicholas Vachel Lindsay. **CP-LindV**

Apology [*or* Apologie] for the Foregoing Hymn[e], An. Richard Crashaw. **CP-CrasR**

Apology for the Revival of Christian Architecture in England, An. Geoffrey Hill. **CP-HillG**

Damon's Lament for his Clorinda, Yorkshire 1654.

Eve of St Mark, The.

Fidelities.

Herefordshire Carol, The.

Idylls of the King. **FaBoRV; NoAM; PoE**

Laurel Axe, The. **NAEL-2; NoAM; NoP; PoE**

Loss and Gain.

Quaint Mazes. **NoAM**

Short History of British India (I), A.

Short History of British India (III), A.
Short History of British India (II), A.
Vocations.
Who Are These Coming to the Sacrifice?
Apology for Using the Word "Heart" in Too Many Poems, An. Hayden Carruth. **CP-CarHS**
Apology to the Lady Carteret, An. Jonathan Swift. **CP-SwifJ**
Apostasy is such, if you doubt on. Lost and Found. Archie Randolph Ammons. **SP-AmmoA**
Apostasy of One and But One Lady, The. Richard Lovelace. **CP-LoveR**
Apostles, The. John Donne. *Fr.* A Litany. **CP-DonnJ**
Apostles: Versailles, 1919, The. Geoffrey Hill. *Fr.* Of Commerce and Society: Variations on a Theme. **CP-HillG**
Apostroph. Walt Whitman. **CP-WhitW**
Apostrophe to a Buddhist Monk. David Herbert Lawrence. **CP-LawrD**
Apostrophe to an Old Psalm Tune. Thomas Hardy. **CP-HardT**
Apostrophe to an Old Tree. Charlotte Smith. **CP-SmitC**
Apostrophe to Man. Edna St. Vincent Millay. **CP-MillE**
Apostrophe to the Land. Countee Cullen. **CP-CullC**
Apostrophe to the Ocean. Byron. *See* There is a pleasure in the pathless woods.
Apostrophe to Vincentine, The. Wallace Stevens. **CP-StevW**
Appalachia. Martin Edmunds. **SP-EdmuM**
Apparent Failure. Robert Browning. **CP-BroR1**
Apparently with no surprise. Emily Dickinson. **CP-DickE**
Apparition, The. John Berryman. **CP-BerrJ**
Apparition, An. Donald Davie. **CP-DavDo**
Apparition, The. John Donne. **CP-DonnJ**
Apparition. John Hewitt. **CP-HewiJ**
Apparition, The. Herman Melville. **SP-MelvH**
Apparition, The. Herman Melville. **SP-MelvH**
Apparition. Adrienne Rich. *Fr.* Turning the Wheel. **SP-RicA2**
Apparition, The. Theodore Roethke. **CP-RoetT**
Apparition, The. Charles Tomlinson. **CP-TomlC**
Apparition, The. William Carlos Williams. **CP-WilW2**
Apparition of Splendor. Marianne Craig Moore. **CP-MoorM**
Apparition of these faces in the crowd, The. In a Station of the Metro. Ezra Pound. **SP-PounE**
Apparitions. Walt Whitman. **CP-WhitW**
Apparitions, The. William Butler Yeats. **CP-YeatW**
Apparitions Are Not Singular Occurrences. Diane Wakoski. **SP-WakoD**
Apparuit. Ezra Pound. **SP-PounE**
Appeal, The. Rudyard Kipling. **CP-KiplR**
Appeal, The. David Herbert Lawrence. **CP-LawrD**
Appeal. William Carlos Williams. **CP-WilW1**
Appeal to America on Behalf of the Belgian Destitute, An. Thomas Hardy. **CP-HardT**
Appear far up the cove at low tide. The Clam Diggers and Diggers of Sea Worms. Richard Eberhart. **CP-EberR**
Appearance, An. Sylvia Plath. **CP-PlatS**
Appearance. Charles Tomlinson. **CP-TomlC**
Appearances. Robert Browning. **CP-BroR2**
Appearing unannounced, the moon. Nocturne. Wystan Hugh Auden. **CP-AudeW**
Appeasement of Demeter, The. George Meredith. **CP-MerG1**
Appendicitis is his worst. Hypochondriac Logic. Donald Davie. **CP-DavDo**
Appendix to the Anniad. Gwendolyn Brooks. **SP-BrooG**
Appetite. Stevie Smith. **CP-SmitS**
Appian Way, The. Kenneth Patchen. **CP-PatcK**
Applause. Charles Olson. **CP-OlsoC**
Applause and wondrous gazes of love. S. Miniato: One by Aretino. Richard Hugo. **CP-HugoR**
Applause is a shower. Increment. Archie Randolph Ammons. **SP-AmmoA**
Applaws) / "fell / ow." Edward Estlin Cummings. **CP-CummE**
Apple at Dawn, An. Jim Carroll. **SP-CarrJ**
Apple Blossom. Louis MacNeice. **CP-MacNL**
Apple blossom and / squirrel. What We Think We Know. Thomas McGrath. **SP-McGrT**
Apple blossoms falling o'er thee. Come and Kiss Me Sweet and Twenty. Paul Laurence Dunbar. **CP-DunbP**
Apple Buds. Richard Eberhart. **CP-EberR**
Apple Dumps. Ted Hughes. **SP-HughT**
Apple Gathering, An. Christina Georgina Rossetti. **CP-RosC1**
Apple green chasuble, so, The. The Argonauts. Frank O'Hara. **SP-OharF**
Apple in, The. Alice. Robert Creeley. **CP-CreeR**
Apple Island. Robert Ranke Graves. **CP-GravR**

Apple of islands, Sirmio, & bright peninsulas, set. Carmen 31. Catullus. **OBVE** *Fr.* Carmina. **CP-Catul**
Apple on its bough is her desire, The. Garden Abstract. Hart Crane. **CP-CranH**
Apple orchards, the trees all cover'd with blossoms. Out of May's Shows Selected. Walt Whitman. **CP-WhitW**
Apple Suckling Tree. "Bob Dylan." **CP-DylaB**
Apple Tragedy. Ted Hughes. **SP-HughT**
Apple Tree, The. Galway Kinnell. **SP-KinnG**
Apple-tree, a cedar and an oak, An. A Man's Work. Archibald MacLeish. **CP-MacLA**
Apple Tree in May. May Sarton. **SP-SartM**
Apple Trees, The. Brendan Galvin. **SP-GalvB**
Apple Trees, The. Louise Glück. **SP-GlücL**
Apple-trees bud, but I do not, The. Edna St. Vincent Millay. **CP-MillE**
Apple Uppfle. Robert Creeley. **CP-CreeR**
Apples. Donald Hall. **CP-HallD**
Apples. Jonathan Swift. **AnIV; NCEP; OnYI** *Fr.* Verses Made for the Women Who Cry Apples, etc. **CP-SwifJ**
Apples and Water. Robert Ranke Graves. **CP-GravR**
Apples are still as sweet, The. Everywhere. Al Young. **CP-YounA**
Apples hung until a wind at the equinox, The. Give Your Heart to the Hawks. Robinson Jeffers. **CP-JefR2**
Apples in the garden of Eden. First Spring Dawn. Jenny Joseph. **SP-JoseJ**
Appletreewick. Wystan Hugh Auden. **CP-AudWJ**
Applicant, The. Sylvia Plath. **CP-PlatS**
Applicant for post as literary critic: Here are my credentials, Sir! Editorial Office. David Herbert Lawrence. **CP-LawrD**
Apply for the position (I've forgotten now for what) I had to. In Order to. Kenneth Patchen. **CP-PatcK**
Appointed winners in a long-stretch'd game, The. To-day and Thee. Walt Whitman. **CP-WhitW**
Appointment, An. William Butler Yeats. **CP-YeatW**
Appreciation. Paul Laurence Dunbar. **CP-DunbP**
Appreciation. George Meredith. **CP-MerG1**
Apprehension, An. Elizabeth Barrett Browning. **CP-BroEB**
Apprehensions. Sylvia Plath. **CP-PlatS**
Approach—Calcutta, The. May Sarton. **SP-SartM**
Approach of Autumn. Stanley Jasspon Kunitz. **CP-KuniS**
Approach of Winter. William Carlos Williams. **CP-WilW1**
Approach to a City. William Carlos Williams. **CP-WilW2**
Approach to Thebes, The. Stanley Jasspon Kunitz. **CP-KuniS**
Approached the window as if to see. George Oppen. *Fr.* Of Being Numerous. **CP-OppeG**
Approaching death. William Carlos Williams. **FaBoMo** *Fr.* Asphodel, That Greeny Flower. **CP-WilW2**
Approaching Hour, The. William Carlos Williams. **CP-WilW2**
Approaching my life I am terrified. Jane Cooper. *Fr.* Messages. **SP-CoopJ**
Approaching, nearing, curious. Queries to My Seventieth Year. Walt Whitman. **CP-WhitW**
Approaching Prayer. James Dickey. **CP-DickJ**
Approaching the Castle. Richard Hugo. **CP-HugoR**
Approaching the Walt. On the Industrial Highway. Daniel Gerard Hoffman. **SP-HoffD**
Approved prospect of chairs with visitors to the hero. Thomas Merton. *Fr.* Cables to the Ace. **CP-MertT**
Approximations. Robert Earl Hayden. **CP-HaydR**
Après la Politique, la Haine des Bourbons. Stevie Smith. **CP-SmitS**
Après le Bain. William Carlos Williams. **CP-WilW2**
April. Wystan Hugh Auden. **CP-AudWJ**
April. Walter de la Mare. **CP-DeLaW**
April. Ralph Waldo Emerson. **CP-EmerR**
   Spring. **OtMeF**
April. John Hewitt. **CP-HewiJ**
April, An. Daniel Gerard Hoffman. **SP-HoffD**
April. Thomas Merton. **CP-MertT; SP-MertT**
April. Howard Nemerov. *Fr.* Epigrams: "Wasp, climbing the window pane." **CP-NemeH**
April. Ezra Pound. **SP-PounE**
April. Christina Georgina Rossetti. *Fr.* The Months: A Pageant. **CP-RosC2**
April. Richard Shelton. **SP-ShelR**
April. Charlotte Smith. **CP-SmitC**
April. Gary Snyder. *Fr.* Six Years. **CP-SnydG**
"April" / this letter's dated. Edward Estlin Cummings. **CP-CummE**
April. John Greenleaf Whittier. **CP-WhitJ**
April. William Carlos Williams. **CP-WilW1**

April abomination, that's what I call. *see also* On Canann Mountain Meadow. Hayden Carruth. **CP-CarHS**

April again. Aries comes forth. A Journal of One Significant Landscape. Charles Wright. **SP-WrigC**

April again in Avrillé. The Road to Avrillé. Edna St. Vincent Millay. **CP-MillE**

April and Its Forsythia. James Schuyler. **CP-SchuJ**

April and May. Ralph Waldo Emerson. **GN; OHIP** *Fr.* May-Day. **CP-EmerR**

April, and the last of the plum blossoms. A Sleepless Night. Philip Levine. **SP-LeviP**

April Aubade. Sylvia Plath. **CP-PlatS**

April Awake. John Hewitt. **CP-HewiJ**

April Blue. Al Young. **CP-YounA**

April cold with dropping rain. April and May. Ralph Waldo Emerson. **GN; OHIP** *Fr.* May-Day. **CP-EmerR**

April 18. Sylvia Plath. **CP-PlatS**

April, fair maid, is come with laughter in her eyes. Alston Moor. Wystan Hugh Auden. **CP-AudWJ**

April 5, 1974. Richard Wilbur. **CP-WilbR**

April Fool. Siv Cedering Fox. **SP-CedeS**

April Fool. Louis MacNeice. **CP-MacNL**

April 4th 1968. Thomas Merton. **CP-MertT**

April in a Town. Wystan Hugh Auden. **CP-AudWJ**

April, in another fortnight, metropolitan April. Piano Practice. Derek Walcott. **CP-WalcD**

April in Cerignola. Richard Hugo. **CP-HugoR**

April in November. Archibald MacLeish. **CP-MacLA**

April Interval. Marilyn Hacker. **CP-HackM**

April Inventory. William DeWitt Snodgrass. **SP-SnodW**

April is here but when will Easter come? Sonnet. Wystan Hugh Auden. **CP-AudWJ**

April is the cruellest month, breeding. The Waste Land. Thomas Stearns Eliot. **CP-ElioT**

April is the Saddest Month. William Carlos Williams. **CP-WilW2**

April, like a leopard in the windy woods. April. Thomas Merton. **CP-MertT; SP-MertT**

April Manifesto, An. Louis MacNeice. **CP-MacNL**

April Moon. Walter de la Mare. **CP-DeLaW**

April 1937 In the Oaxaca Train. Malcolm Lowry. *Fr.* The Lighthouse Invites the Storm. **CP-LowrM**

APRIL (*Rowing*). Rudyard Kipling. *Fr.* Verses on Games. **CP-KiplR**

April Sunday Brings the Snow, An. Philip Larkin. **CP-LarkP**

April Thirtieth 1960. Kay Boyle. *Fr.* Two Poems for a Poet. **CP-BoylK**

April this year, not otherwise. Song of a Second April. Edna St. Vincent Millay. **CP-MillE**

April Today Main Street. Charles Olson. **SP-OlsoC** *Fr.* The Maximus Poems.

April Treason. John Crowe Ransom. **SP-RansJ**

April we could hardly tell from May, An. An April. Daniel Gerard Hoffman. **SP-HoffD**

April what an ice-cold promise. Hudson Ferry. James Schuyler. **CP-SchuJ**

April winds are magical, The. April. Ralph Waldo Emerson. **CP-EmerR**

April winds are magical, The. Spring. Ralph Waldo Emerson. **OtMeF** *Fr.* April. **CP-EmerR**

April Woods: Morning. Wendell Berry. **CP-BerrW**

April Yule, Daddy! Ogden Nash. **CP-NashO**

Aprill. Edmund Spenser. **NAEL-1; OBEV; OBSC; PoEL-1** *Fr.* The Shepheardes [*or* Shepeards *or* Shepherd's] Calender. **CP-Spens**

    ("Tell me, good Hobbinoll, what garres thee greete?") **OBEV; OBSC; PoEL-1**

    Ditty, A: In Praise of Eliza, Queen of the Shepherds. **OBEV**

    (Ditty, A: "See where she sits upon the grassy green.") **FaBoCh**

    Elisa ("Ye dainty nymphs, that in this blessed brook"). **OBSC**

    (Lay to Eliza, The.) **NOBE**

April's new apple buds on an old lichened tree. Kathleen Jessie Raine. **SP-RainK**

Apron of Flowers, The. Robert Herrick. **CP-HerrR**

Aprons of Silence. Carl Sandburg. **CP-SandC**

Aqua. Hayden Carruth. *Fr.* Journey to a Known Place. **CP-CarHL**

Aquae Sulis. Thomas Hardy. **CP-HardT**

Aquarian Age. Leonard Cohen. **CP-CoheL**

Aquarium, The. Thom Gunn. *Fr.* Three for Children. **CP-GunnT**

Aquarium. John Hewitt. **CP-HewiJ**

Aquarium. John Hewitt. **CP-HewiJ**

Aquatic Nocturne. Sylvia Plath. **CP-PlatS**

Aqueduct. Thom Gunn. **CP-GunnT**

Aqueduct. Charles Tomlinson. **CP-TomlC**

Arabella. Stevie Smith. **CP-SmitS**

Arabia. Walter de la Mare. **CP-DeLaW**

Arabia. Al Young. **CP-YounA**

Arabia it's so fine so hot. Arabia. Al Young. **CP-YounA**

Arabian Ballad. Johann Wolfgang von Goethe, *tr. fr.* German *by* Ralph Waldo Emerson. **CP-EmerR**

Arabic Poems. George Meredith. **CP-MerG2**

    "As the egg of an ostrich at the bottom [of] a bubbling spring."

    "Her arms two branches of the almond-tree that sway at morn in the."

    "Her cheeks are as a crystal goblet held to the sun."

    "I met at morn a girl of the tribes, bearing a milk-bowl."

    "Let us sing of our beloved, let us sing of that which is sweetest."

    "They that love not—are they not as blind camels that behold no."

    "When I saw the jewelled girdle tied at her waist I thought of."

    "When she laughs there is a glitter as of morning before me."

Arable acres heave. January. Donald Davie. **CP-DavDo**

Aran. Derek Mahon. **SP-MahoD**

Arbatus trees, with their bark like burned skin, The. Galiano Coast: Four Entrances. Margaret Atwood. **SP-AtwM2**

Arbitrary roll-call, An. Norfolk. Donald Davie. **CP-DavDo**

Arbor vitae, whose grooved bole. Message. Denise Levertov. **CP-LeveD**

Arboreal Mystery, An. Grace Paley. **CP-PaleG**

Arcades. John Milton. **CP-MiltJ**

    "Nymphs and Shepherds dance no more." **ELP; FiP**

    (Song from Arcades.) **FiP**

    "O're [*or* O'er] the smooth enamel'd [*or* enameled *or* enamelled] green." **OBEV; OxBSP; TrGrPo**

    (Song: "O'er the smooth enamelled green.") **OxBSP**

Arcades Ambo. Robert Browning. **CP-BroR2**

Arcades of Philadelphia the Past. Wallace Stevens. **CP-StevW**

Arcadia. Sir Philip Sidney.

    "All what you are still one, his own to find." **SP-SidnP**

    "*Apollo* great, whose beams the greater world do light." **SP-SidnP**

    "As I my little flock on Ister Bank." **SP-SidnP**

    "*Aurora*, now thou show'st thy blushing light." **SP-SidnP**

    "Beauty hath force to catch the human sight." **SP-SidnP**

    "Come, *Dorus*, come, let the songs thy sorrows signify." **SP-SidnP**

    "Come shepherd's weeds, become your master's mind." **SP-SidnP**

    "Do not disdain, O straight upraised pine." **SP-SidnP**

    "*Dorus*, tell me, where is thy wonted motion." **OBVE; SP-SidnP**

    "Fair rocks, goodly rivers, sweet woods, when shall I see peace?" **SP-SidnP**

    "Feed on my sheep; my charge, my comfort, feed." **SP-SidnP**

    "Fortune, Nature, Love, long have contended about me." **SP-SidnP**

    "Get hence foul[e] grief[e], the canker of the mind[e]." **SP-SidnP**

    "Hark, plaintful ghosts! Infernal furies, hark." **SP-SidnP**

    Like Those Sick Folks. **OxBSP**

    "Hateful cure with hate to heal, A." **SP-SidnP**

    How Is My Sun. **SP-SidnP**

    This Cave Is Dark. **SiPSBD**

    "I joy in grief, and do detest all joys." **SP-SidnP**

    "If mine eyes can speak to do hearty errand." **SP-SidnP**

    In Vain, Mine Eyes. **SP-SidnP**

    "Lady, reserved by the heav'ns to do pastors' company honour." **SP-SidnP**

    "Leave off my sheep: it is no time to feed." **SP-SidnP**

    "Let mother Earth now deck herself in flowers." **SP-SidnP**

    "Let not old age disgrace my high desire." **SP-SidnP**

    "Like diverse flowers, whose diverse beauties serve." **SP-SidnP**

    "Lock up, fair lids, the treasure of my heart." **SP-SidnP**

    "Love which is imprinted in my soul, The." **SP-SidnP**

    "Loved I am, and yet complain[e] of Love." **SP-SidnP**

    "*speech of Dorus*." **SP-SidnP**

    "Merchant man, whom many seas have taught, The." **SP-SidnP**

    "My lute, within thyself thy tunes enclose." **SP-SidnP**

    "My Muse what ails this ardour." **SP-SidnP**

    "My sheep are thoughts, which I both guide and serve." **SP-SidnP**

    "*speech of Charita*." **SP-SidnP**

    "My words, in hope to blaze my steadfast mind." **SP-SidnP**

    "Now thanked be the great god *Pan*." **SP-SidnP**

    "Now was our heav'nly vault deprived of the light." **SP-SidnP**

    "O night, the ease of care, the pledge of pleasure." **SP-SidnP**

    "O stealing time, the subject of delay." **SP-SidnP**

    "O sweet woods, the delight of solitariness!" **SP-SidnP**

    Sweetly Empty Woods. **CBCK**

    "O words, which fall like summer dew on me!" **SP-SidnP**

"Over these brooks trusting to ease mine eyes." **SP-SidnP**

"Phoebus farewell, a sweeter saint I serve." **SP-SidnP**

"Reason, tell me thy mind, if here be reason." **SP-SidnP**

"Since Nature's works be good, and death doth serve." **SP-SidnP**

"Since so mine eyes are subject to your sight." **SP-SidnP**

"speech of Cleophila." **SP-SidnP**

"Since wailing is a bud of causeful sorrow." **SP-SidnP**

"Sweet glove, the witness of my secret bliss." **SP-SidnP**

"Thy elder care shall from thy careful face." **SP-SidnP**

"Transformed in show, but more transformed in mind." **SP-SidnP**

"Unto the caitiff wretch whom long affliction holdeth." **SP-SidnP**

"Virtue, beauty, and speech, did strike, wound, charm." **SP-SidnP**

"What length of verse can serve brave *Mopsa*'s good to show?" **SP-SidnP**

"What tongue can her perfections tell." **SP-SidnP**

"When two suns do appear." **SP-SidnP**

"Why dost thou haste away." **SP-SidnP**

"With two strange fires of equal heat possessed [*or* possest]." **SP-SidnP**

"Ye [*or* you] goat-herd gods, [that love the grassy mountains]." **SP-SidnP**

"Ye living powers enclosed in stately shrine." **SP-SidnP**

"You goodly pines, which still with brave ascent." **SP-SidnP**

Arcadians the earth inhabited, The, *ad. fr. Latin of* Ovid, *Fasti.* Sir Walter Ralegh. **CP-RaleW**

Arch, The. Herman Melville. **SP-MelvH** *Fr.* Clarel: A Poem and Pilgrimage in the Holy Land.

Arch, The. Charles Tomlinson. **CP-TomlC**

Arch animals' / unearthed faces. Arizona. Louis Zukofsky. *Fr.* 29 Songs. **CP-ZukLS**

Archaeological Picnic, The. Sir John Betjeman. **CP-BetjJ**

Archaeologist's spade, The. Archaeology. Wystan Hugh Auden. **CP-AudeW**

Archaeology. Wystan Hugh Auden. **CP-AudeW**

Archangel Hope / Looks to the azure cope, The. Ralph Waldo Emerson. **CP-EmerR**

Archangel's' Song, The, *tr. fr.* Goethe's *Faust.* Randall Jarrell. **CP-JarrR**

Archbishop Chichely to Henry V. William Wordsworth. *Fr.* Ecclesiastical Sonnets. **CP-WorW2**

Archbishop is away, The. The church is gray. Gray Stones and Gray Pigeons. Wallace Stevens. **CP-StevW**

Archduchess Anne. George Meredith. **CP-MerG1**

Arched corridors. Bare white walls. James McAuley. **SP-McAuJ** *Fr.* Vivaldi in Venice.

Archeology. Robert Pack. **SP-PackR**

Archer. Hilda Doolittle. **CP-DoolH**

Archer, The. Charles Tomlinson. **CP-TomlC**

Archer is wake, The! Peace on Earth. William Carlos Williams. **CP-WilW1**

Arches. James Schuyler. **CP-SchuJ**

Archetype Poem, The. Allen Ginsberg. **CP-GinsA**

Archibald's Example. Edwin Arlington Robinson. **CP-RobiE**

Archie and Tina. Stevie Smith. **CP-SmitS**

Archin' here and arrachin there. "Hugh MacDiarmid." **SP-MacDH** *Fr.* Water Music.

("Wheesht, wheesht, Joyce, and let me hear.") **SP-MacDH**

Archipelago. Louise Glück. **SP-GlückL**

Archipelago, The. Herman Melville. **SP-MelvH**

Architectural Masks. Thomas Hardy. **CP-HardT**

Architecture, An. Wendell Berry. **CP-BerrW**

Architecture, The. Robert Duncan. **SP-DuncR** *Fr.* Passages.

Archival Print, An. William Stafford. **SP-StafW**

Arctic fox / With snow white hocks, The. Malcolm Lowry. **CP-LowrM**

Arctic owl moved across the snowsmooth, The. Hayden Carruth. *Fr.* North Winter. **CP-CarHL**

Arctic Ox (or Goat), The. Marianne Craig Moore. *See* To wear the arctic fox.

Arctic Remembered, The. Edwin Rolfe. **CP-RolfE**

"Arcturus" is his other name. Emily Dickinson. **CP-DickE**

Ardella. Langston Hughes. **SP-HughL**

Arden is not Eden, but Eden's rhyme. In Arden. Charles Tomlinson. **CP-TomlC**

Ardensteil-henarub-izabeth) / this noN. Edward Estlin Cummings. **CP-CummE**

Ardent / yet chill and formal. Gift. Hilda Doolittle. **CP-DoolH**

Are all we have. So count them as they pass. They pass / too quickly. A Few Days. James Schuyler. **CP-SchuJ**

Are built out of the meshing of life and space. And Others, Vaguer Presences. John Ashbery. **SP-AshbJ**

Are eyelids on eyes lying and lifting. Britannia Rules the Waves. Elizabeth Bishop. **CP-BishE**

Are Friends Delight or Pain? Emily Dickinson. **CP-DickE**

Are generally over or around. Pockets. Howard Nemerov. **CP-NemeH**

Are more beautiful than. The Girls at the Green Hotel. Charles Bukowski. **SP-BukC1**

Are my poems spoken in the factories and fields. "Hugh MacDiarmid." **SP-MacDH** *Fr.* Ah, Lenin, you were richt. But I'm a poet. *Fr.* Second Hymn to Lenin.

Are not the joys of morning sweeter. William Blake. **CP-BlakW**

Are planned to make things better and not worse. The Poverty Programs. Howard Nemerov. **CP-NemeH**

Are Poets Ball Players? Isabella Gardner. **CP-GardI**

Are so thin they can stand. The Heroes of Our Times. Richard Shelton. **SP-ShelR**

Are the desolate, dark weeks. These. William Carlos Williams. **CP-WilW1**

Are the living so much use. At the Cenotaph. "Hugh MacDiarmid." **SP-MacDH**

Are the salt and the sugar at work. Pablo Neruda, *tr. fr. Spanish by* Ben Belitt. **SP-NeruP** *Fr.* Question Book.

Are there two things, of all which men possess. To Asra. Samuel Taylor Coleridge. **CP-ColeS**

Are these ashes in my hand. Hilda Doolittle. **AnAn** *Fr.* Sigil. **CP-DoolH**

Are these flowers paint? Back of each bouquet. Bouquets from Corley. Richard Hugo. **CP-HugoR**

Are these mellifluous sheep. Strictly Bucolic. Charles Simic. **SP-SimiC**

Are these your presences, my clan from Heaven? A Prayer to All the Dead Among Mine Own People. Nicholas Vachel Lindsay. **CP-LindV**

Are they blind, the lords of Gaza. Angry Samson. Robert Ranke Graves. **CP-GravR**

Are They Not All Ministering Spirits? Christina Georgina Rossetti. **CP-RosC2**

Are walking towards me. Five Elephants. Rita Dove. **SP-DoveR**

Are we still travelling? The Pillow. Charles Simic. **SP-SimiC**

Are we unfathomable night. Hilda Doolittle. **AnAn** *Fr.* Sigil. **CP-DoolH**

Are we? You murmur "not." What of the night. John Berryman. *Fr.* Sonnets to Chris. **CP-BerrJ**

Are Ye Not Much Better Than They? Christina Georgina Rossetti. **CP-RosC2**

Are You a Snodgrass? Ogden Nash. **CP-NashO**

Are you alive? The Pool. Hilda Doolittle. **CP-DoolH**

Are you awake, / Comrades, this silent night? Haunting Fingers. Thomas Hardy. **CP-HardT**

Are You Born? / I. Muriel Rukeyser. **CP-RukeM**

Are You Born? / II. Muriel Rukeyser. **CP-RukeM**

Are You Content. William Butler Yeats. **CP-YeatW**

"Are you deaf, Father William?" the young man / said. Acrostic: "Are you deaf, Father William?" "Lewis Carroll." **CP-CarrL**

Are you far away? The Familiar. Walter de la Mare. **CP-DeLaW**

Are You groping Your way? Xenophanes, the Monist of Colophon. Thomas Hardy. **CP-HardT**

Are you happy? It's the only. Snatch of Sliphorn Jazz. Carl Sandburg. **CP-SandC**

Are you he who would assume a place to teach or be a poet here in the States? Walt Whitman. **FaBoPV** *Fr.* By Blue Ontario's Shore. **CP-WhitW**

Are you in Eden again, America? The Shout. Anne Sexton. **CP-SextA**

Are you mine my love? Have I lost you to her? Two Sapphics. Isabella Gardner. **CP-GardI**

Are you not weary. Ballet. William Carlos Williams. **CP-WilW1**

Are You Now or Have You Ever Been. Edwin Rolfe. **CP-RolfE**

Are You Pining? David Herbert Lawrence. **CP-LawrD**

Are You Ready? "Bob Dylan." **CP-DylaB**

Are you shaken, are you stirred. Fragment. Robert Ranke Graves. **CP-GravR**

Are You the Lover or Loved? Al Young. **CP-YounA**

Are You the New Person Drawn toward Me? Walt Whitman. **CP-WhitW**

Are You There, Rose Trumbull? Marsden Hartley. **CP-HartM**

Are you what your faire lookes expresse? Thomas Campion. **CP-CampT**

Are you willing to be sponged out, erased, cancelled. Phoenix. David Herbert Lawrence. **CP-LawrD**

Are you You or Me or It? Hello Up There. Marge Piercy. **SP-PierM**

Are your rocks shelter for ships. The Shrine. Hilda Doolittle. **CP-DoolH**

Area— / no test of depth. Emily Dickinson. **SP-DickE**

Arena dust rusted by four bulls' blood to a dull redness. The Goring. Sylvia Plath. **CP-PlatS**

Arènes de Lutèce. Samuel Beckett. **CP-BeckS**

Aren't we nasty little people. Filling the Boxes of Joseph Cornell. Diane Wakoski. **SP-WakoD**

Areopagus. Louis MacNeice. **CP-MacNL**

  "After anemones, after almond."

  "Flying and ravening Curses, bark no more!"

  "Spermologies fallen on stony ground. Stone of relentlessness, stone of crime."

  "Tall story over a dark sanctum, A."

Ares at last has quit the field. Under Which Lyre, a Reactionary Tract for the Times. Wystan Hugh Auden. **CP-AudeW**

Aretemias. Antipater of Sidon. *Fr.* Variations of Greek Themes. **CP-RobiE**

Arethusa. Percy Bysshe Shelley. **CP-ShelP**

Argo. Richard Hugo. **CP-HugoR**

Argonauts, The. David Herbert Lawrence. **CP-LawrD**

Argonauts, The. Frank O'Hara. **SP-OharF**

Arguing over coffee at the station. Between Trains. Robert Ranke Graves. **CP-GravR**

Argument. Elizabeth Bishop. **CP-BishE**

Argument, The, *sels.* William Blake. *Fr.* The Marriage of Heaven and Hell. **CP-BlakW**

Argument, The. Walter de la Mare. **CP-DeLaW**

Argument. Langston Hughes. **SP-HughL**

Argument, An. Nicholas Vachel Lindsay. **CP-LindV**

  Rhymer's Reply: Incense and Splendor, The.

  Voice of the Man Impatient with Visions and Utopias, The.

Argument, Th'. Sir Thomas Wyatt. **CP-WyatT**

Argument. As the true method of knowledge is experiment, The. All Religions Are One. William Blake. **CP-BlakW**

Argument for Suicide. William Wordsworth. **CP-WorW1**

Argument. Man has no notion of moral fitness but from Education, The. There Is No Natural Religion. William Blake. **CP-BlakW**

Argument of His Book, The. Robert Herrick. **CP-HerrR**

Argument: Of the Passion of Christ, An. Thomas Merton. **CP-MertT**

Argus. Alexander Pope. **CP-PopeA**

Aria. Delmore Schwartz. ErPo *Fr.* Two Lyrics from Kilroy's Carnival: A Masque. **SP-SchwD**

Ariadne. Hilda Doolittle. **CP-DoolH**

Ariadne. Thomas Merton. **CP-MertT; SP-MertT**

Ariadne and the Minotaur. Charles Tomlinson. **CP-TomlC**

Ariadne at the Labyrinth. Thomas Merton. **CP-MertT; SP-MertT**

Ariadne To Theseus. Christina Georgina Rossetti. **CP-RosC3**

Ariadne's bird / That lone. In Midsummer Quiet. Charles Simic. **SP-SimiC**

Arid that country and high, anger of sun on the mountains, but. Rattlesnake Country. Robert Penn Warren. **SP-WarrR**

Arides. Ezra Pound. **SP-PounE**

Ariel. Walter de la Mare. **CP-DeLaW**

Ariel. Sylvia Plath. **CP-PlatS**

Ariel to Miranda:—Take. With a Guitar, to Jane. Percy Bysshe Shelley. **CP-ShelP**

Ariel was glad he had written his poems. The Planet on the Table. Wallace Stevens. **CP-StevW**

Arise – arise – the Lord arose. For Sunday. Christopher Smart. *Fr.* Hymns for the Amusement of Children. **SP-SmarC**

Arise, arise, arise! / There is blood on the earth that denies ye bread. An Ode Written October, 1819. Percy Bysshe Shelley. **CP-ShelP**

Arise, arrogant arsemongers / Come! clashing clowns. Malcolm Lowry. **CP-LowrM**

Arise, depart, for this is not your rest. Today's Burden. Christina Georgina Rossetti. **CP-RosC2**

Arise, divine Urania, with new strains. On the Omniscience of the Supreme Being. Christopher Smart. **SP-SmarC**

Arise, dusty shadow, Mars. A Dream at Arles on the Night of the Mistral. Thomas Merton. **CP-MertT**

Arise, up, arise. Now that it is time, shake off slumbers. Elegiac Verses. John Milton, *tr. fr. Latin by* John T. Shawcross. **CP-MiltJ**

Arisen at Last. John Greenleaf Whittier. **CP-WhitJ**

Aristocracy, The. Wendell Berry. **CP-BerrW**

Aristocracy of the Sun. David Herbert Lawrence. **CP-LawrD**

Aristocrat among patriarchs, This. The Copper Beech. Rita Dove. **SP-DoveR**

Aristocratic Area. John Hewitt. **CP-HewiJ**

Aristodemus the Messenian. Thomas Hardy. **CP-HardT**

Aristomenes. Byron. **CP-Byron**

Aristophanes' Apology. Robert Browning. **CP-BroR2**

Arithmetic. John Hewitt. **CP-HewiJ**

Arithmetic. Carl Sandburg. **CP-SandC**

Arithmetic is where numbers fly like pigeons in and out of your head. Arithmetic. Carl Sandburg. **CP-SandC**

Arithmetic on the Frontier. Rudyard Kipling. **CP-KiplR**

Arizona. Louis Zukofsky. *Fr.* 29 Songs. **CP-ZukLS**

Arizona Desert. Charles Tomlinson. **CP-TomlC**

Arizona Highway. Charles Tomlinson. **CP-TomlC**

Arizona Poems. John Gould Fletcher. **SP-FletJ**

  Cliff-dwelling.

  Fuel Vendor, The.

  Mexican Quarter. **BPAW**

  Rain in the Desert.

  Well in the Desert, The.

  Windmills, The.

Ark, The. Robert Ranke Graves. **CP-GravR**

Ark: Angelus: Anvil. Kenneth Patchen. **CP-PatcK**

Ark you're building, The. Etiquette. Leonard Cohen. **CP-CoheL**

Arkansas Traveller. Charles Wright. **SP-WrigC**

Arkansaw's westernmost county. Siloam. Donald Davie. **CP-DavDo**

Arktos. Gary Snyder. **CP-SnydG**

Arles, an arles for my hiring, An. Basil Bunting. **CP-BuntB**

Arlington. John Haines. **SP-HainJ**

Armada of Thirty Whales, An. Daniel Gerard Hoffman. **SP-HoffD**

Armadillo, The. Elizabeth Bishop. **CP-BishE**

Armageddon. John Crowe Ransom. **SP-RansJ**

Armageddon, Armageddon. Paul Muldoon. **SP-MuldP**

Armah: October 12, 1990. Alice Walker. **CP-WalkA**

Arm'd year—year of the struggle. Eighteen Sixty-One. Walt Whitman. **CP-WhitW**

Armed with / a bass-violin. An Old-Fashioned German Christmas Card. William Carlos Williams. **CP-WilW2**

Armenia, Asia's waif, has here. Yerevan. John Updike. *Fr.* Postcards from Soviet Cities. **CP-UpdiJ**

Armenian Lady's Love, The. William Wordsworth. **CP-WorW2**

Armenonville. Edna St. Vincent Millay. **CP-MillE**

Armful, The. Robert Frost. **CP-FrosR**

Armies in the Fire. Robert Louis Stevenson. **CP-StevR**

Armies of the Plain. George Oppen. **CP-OppeG**

Armies of the Wilderness, The. Herman Melville. **SP-MelvH**

Armillaria mellea. Blessing Ode for a Man with Fishbones Around His Neck. Diane Wakoski. **SP-WakoD**

Armistice. Howard Nemerov. **CP-NemeH**

Armistice Day, 1918. Robert Ranke Graves. **CP-GravR**

Armitage of scrap-iron for the radiations of a moon. 7/17/68. Adrienne Rich. **CP-RicAE** *Fr.* Ghazals: Homage to Ghalib. **SP-RicA2**

Armor. James Dickey. **CP-DickJ**

Armored in oxygen. Astronauts. Robert Earl Hayden. **CP-HaydR**

Armored salmon jewel the ice with blood, The. The Market-Place. Howard Nemerov. **CP-NemeH**

Armor's Undermining Modesty. Marianne Craig Moore. **CP-MoorM**

Armour Avenue was the name of this street and door signs on empty. Real Avenue News. Carl Sandburg. **CP-SandC**

Armoury, The. Roy Fisher. **SP-FishR** *Fr.* Inscriptions for Bluebeard's Castle.

Arms and the Boy. Wilfred Owen. **CP-OwenW**

Arms and the Man. Peter Meinke. **SP-MeinP**

Arms, and the Man I sing, the first who bore, *see also* "Now manhood and garbroyls I chaunt, and martial horror" *tr. by* Richard Stanyhurst, "Arms, and the Man I sing, who, forc'd by Fate" *tr. by* John Dryden, "I sing of warfare and a man at war" *tr. by* Robert Fitgerald, *and* "Battellis and the man I will descrive, The" *tr. by* Gavin Douglas. Virgil, *tr. by* William Wordsworth. **CP-WorW2** *Fr.* The Aeneid [*or* Eneados, *Aeneis*].

Army Corps on the March, An. Walt Whitman. **CP-WhitW**

Army Headquarters. Rudyard Kipling. **CP-KiplR**

  ("Old is the song that I sing.") **CP-KiplR**

Army lorry, cold, anonymous, The. Ulster Winter (1942). John Hewitt. **CP-HewiJ**

Army of Clouds! ye wingèd Host in troops. To the Clouds. William Wordsworth. **CP-WorW1**

Around a wild and woody hill. Memorial near the Outlet of the Lake of Thun. William Wordsworth. *Fr.* Memorials of a Tour of the Continent; 1820. **CP-WorW2**

Around, above my bed, the pitch-dark fly. Truth. Howard Nemerov. **CP-NemeH**

Around, around the sun we go. Mother Goose's Garland. Archibald MacLeish. **CP-MacLA**

Around bend after bend. Not of School Age. Robert Frost. **CP-FrosR**

Around Here. Archie Randolph Ammons. **SP-AmmoA**

Around here's a world that we love. Sonnet with X's. Gilbert Sorrentino. **SP-SorrG**

Around herself she wove a rainbow web. The Disenchanted. Isabella Gardner. **CP-GardI**

Around me the images of thirty years. The Municipal Gallery Revisited. William Butler Yeats. **CP-YeatW**

Around my lonely hearth, to-night. Acrostic: Around my lonely hearth, to-night. "Lewis Carroll." **CP-CarrL**

Around Pastor Bonhoeffer. Stanley Jasspon Kunitz. **CP-KuniS**

     Extermination Camp, The.

     Next to Last Things.

     Plot Against Hitler, The.

Around Sebago's lonely lake. Funeral Tree of the Sokokis. John Greenleaf Whittier. **CP-WhitJ**

Around the bend / that tried to loop me home. Stanley Jasspon Kunitz. *Fr.* The Testing-Tree. **CP-KuniS**

Around the cold pool in the metal light. The Hotel Normandie Pool. Derek Walcott. **CP-WalcD**

Around the Fire. Ted Berrigan. **SP-BerrT**

Around the Fire. Leonard Nathan. **SP-NathL**

Around the headland, at the end. The Lives of Gulls and Children. Howard Nemerov. **CP-NemeH**

Around the Horn. Gary Gildner. **SP-GildG**

Around the house the flakes fly faster. Birds at Winter Nightfall. Thomas Hardy. **CP-HardT**

Around the Kitchen Table. Gary Gildner. **SP-GildG**

Around the little park. Back to Life. Thom Gunn. **CP-GunnT**

Around the man who seeks a noble end. Ralph Waldo Emerson. **CP-EmerR**

Around the Mountain. Robert Ranke Graves. **CP-GravR**

Around the old old islands. The Rescue. Frederick Morgan. **SP-MorgF**

Around the smallpox vaccination scar. The Tattooed Lady. Ted Kooser. **SP-KoosT**

Around the Springs of Gray my wild root weaves. William Blake. **CP-BlakW**

Around the time the livingroom. After Losses. Stephen Dunn. **SP-DunnS**

Around the walls pebbled with violent glass. Guardianship. Steve Griffiths. **SP-GrifS**

Around them boomed the rhetoric of time. Kairos and Logos. Wystan Hugh Auden. **CP-AudeW**

Arouse—and let thy foes disperse. Bible, O.T. *See* Psalm 68: "Let God arise, let his enemies be scattered."

Arouse yrself, Bigmans. Bigmans. Charles Olson. **CP-OlsoC**

Arran! a single-crested Teneriffe. On the Firth of Clyde. William Wordsworth. *Fr.* Poems Composed or Suggested During a Tour, in the Summer of 1833. **CP-WorW2**

Arranged by two's as peaches are. Nine Nectarines. Marianne Craig Moore. **CP-MoorM**

Arrangements are changed, The. Wedding Postponed. Carl Sandburg. **CP-SandC**

Arrangements with Earth for Three Dead Friends. James Wright. **CP-WrigJ**

Arrears of Moonlight. Robert Ranke Graves. **CP-GravR**

Arrest of Oscar Wilde at the Cadogan Hotel, The. Sir John Betjeman. **CP-BetjJ**

Arrival. Maya Angelou. **SP-AngeM**

Arrival, The. Wendell Berry. **CP-BerrW**

Arrival, The. Roy Fisher. **SP-FishR** *Fr.* Interiors with Various Figures.

Arrival. Philip Larkin. **CP-LarkP**

Arrival. / The vast crowd on the floor, The. The Big Dance on the Hill. Ernest Hemingway. **CP-HemiE**

Arrival, The. Charles Tomlinson. **CP-TomlC**

Arrival. William Carlos Williams. **CP-WilW1**

Arrival and Departure. Archibald MacLeish. **CP-MacLA**

Arrival at Santos. Elizabeth Bishop. **CP-BishE**

Arrival at the Waldorf. Wallace Stevens. **CP-StevW**

Arrival of the Bee Box, The. Sylvia Plath. **CP-PlatS**

Arrival of the Mail. William Cowper. ECEV *Fr.* The Winter Evening. *Fr.* The Task. **CP-CowpW**

     (Post-Boy, The.) **FiP**

Arrival of the Players, The. George Crabbe. **SP-CrabG** *Fr.* The Borough.

Arrivals, Departures. Philip Larkin. **CP-LarkP**

Arrive / at night. Rustling a Hog. Gary Gildner. **SP-GildG**

Arrive. The Ladies from the Ladies' Betterment League. The Lovers of the Poor. Gwendolyn Brooks. **SP-BrooG**

Arrive to arrive and to arrive here in such thick. If a Poem Can Be Headed into Its Proper Current. Kenneth Patchen. **CP-PatcK**

Arrives and there is. The Age of Elegance. Richard Shelton. *Fr.* The Seven Ages of Man. **SP-ShelR**

Arriving at last. Poem, The. Daniel Gerard Hoffman. **SP-HoffD**

Arriving in the Country Again. James Wright. **CP-WrigJ**

Arrogant Law. Robert Penn Warren. **SP-WarrR**

Arrossisce la rosa: e perchè mai? Christina Georgina Rossetti. **CP-RosC3**

Arrow, The. William Butler Yeats. **CP-YeatW**

Arrow Grasses by Greenbrier River. Louise McNeill. **SP-McNeL**

Arrow in the Wall, An. Andrei Voznesensky, *tr. fr. Russian by* Richard Wilbur. **CP-WilbR**

Arrow on the Vane. Robert Ranke Graves. **CP-GravR**

Arrow Shots. Robert Ranke Graves. **CP-GravR**

Arrows enamored of his Heart. Emily Dickinson. **CP-DickE**

Arroyo Hondo. Charles Tomlinson. **CP-TomlC**

Arroyo Seco. Charles Tomlinson. **CP-TomlC**

Ars Longa. Gilbert Sorrentino. **SP-SorrG**

Ars Longa. Which is crueller. The Peacock Room. Robert Earl Hayden. **CP-HaydR**

Ars Poetica. Donald Davie. **CP-DavDo**

Ars Poetica. John Hewitt. **CP-HewiJ**

Ars Poetica. Archibald MacLeish. **CP-MacLA**

Ars Poetica. Howard Nemerov. **CP-NemeH**

Ars Poetica. Charles Tomlinson. **CP-TomlC**

Ars Poetica. Charles Wright. **SP-WrigC**

Ars Poetica. Al Young. **CP-YounA**

Ars Poetica: Or: Who Lives in the Ivory Tower? Thomas McGrath. **SP-McGrT**

Arsenal at Springfield, The. Henry Wadsworth Longfellow. **SP-LongH** Message of Peace, A. **WBLP**

Arsiero, Asiago, / Half a hundred more. Ernest Hemingway. **CP-HemiE**

Art, An. Charles Bukowski. **SP-BukC1**

Art. Ralph Waldo Emerson. **CP-EmerR**

Art. Herman Melville. **SP-MelvH**

Art. Allen Tate. **CP-TateA**

Art, The. William Carlos Williams. **CP-WilW2**

Art above Nature, to Julia. Robert Herrick. **CP-HerrR**

Art and Cal have made a trade. Martial, *tr. by* William Matthews. **SP-MattW** *Fr.* Epigrams.

Art and Technology. John Hewitt. **CP-HewiJ**

Art begins with a lie. The Lie. Anne Waldman. **SP-WaldA**

Art Is Not for Grown-ups. James Liddy. **CP-LiddJ**

Art is transubstantiation: the bread and wine of life. Fragments of Eternity. John Gould Fletcher. **SP-FletJ** *Fr.* The Parables of Christ.

Art of a Novel, The. Marilyn Hacker. **SP-HackM**

Art of Argument, the Argument of Art, The. David St. John. *Fr.* To Pasolini. **SP-StJoD**

Art of Benny Carter, The. Al Young. **CP-YounA**

Art of Healing, The. Wystan Hugh Auden. **CP-AudeW**

Art of losing isn't hard to master, The. One Art. Elizabeth Bishop. **CP-BishE**

Art of Love, The. Kenneth Koch. **SP-KochK**

     "For there are numerous questions remaining which one must consider."

     "Of course you must stop her. Say anything: 'Hello!' "Good-bye!'"

     "To win the love of women one should first discover." **NNaP**

     "Which cannot be begun, however, until you meet somebody."

Art of Love, The. Ovid, *tr. fr. Latin.*

     "Now *Dædalus*, behold, by fate assign'd." **CP-JohnS**

Art of Poetry, The. Richard Hugo. **CP-HugoR**

Art of Poetry, The. Kenneth Koch. **SP-KochK**

Art of Poetry, The. Alexander Pope. ECEV *Fr.* An Essay on Criticism. **CP-PopeA**

Art of Poetry, The. Charles Tomlinson. **CP-TomlC**

Art of Satire, The. Alexander Pope. *See* Ask you what provocation I have had?

Art of Worldly Wisdom, The. Kenneth Rexroth. **CP-RexKL** *Fr.* The Dragon and the Unicorn.

     "Discursive knowledge, knowledge by." **SP-RexrK**

Art of writing an honest prose, The. The Earthquake in the West. Howard Nemerov. **CP-NemeH**

Art quickens Nature; Care will make a face. Neglect. Robert Herrick. **CP-HerrR**

Art recalls the memory. This Is about Death. Allen Ginsberg. **CP-GinsA**

Art Room in a City School. John Hewitt. **CP-HewiJ**

Art Song. Howard Nemerov. **CP-NemeH**

Art Student. Stephen Spender. **CP-SpenS**

Art, the holy care of life. Richard Eberhart. *Fr.* The Lyric Absolute. **CP-EberR**

Art thou a Statist in the van. A Poet's Epitaph. William Wordsworth. **CP-WorW1**

Art thou asleep? or have thy wings. The Glimpse. Walter de la Mare. **CP-DeLaW**

Art thou indeed forever gone. Melody to a Scene of Former Times. Percy Bysshe Shelley. *Fr.* Posthumous Fragments of Margaret Nicholson. **CP-ShelP**

Art thou not destin'd? then, with hast, go on. Another. Robert Herrick. **CP-HerrR**

Art thou pale for weariness. To the Moon. Percy Bysshe Shelley. **CP-ShelP**

Art thou some individual of a kind. *see also* Treasure. *Unknown, tr. fr. Greek by* William Cowper. **CP-CowpW**

Art Thou That She. *Unknown.* **CP-CampT**

("Art thou that shee then whome noe fayrer is?") **CP-CampT**

Art thou the bird whom Man loves best. The Redbreast Chasing the Butterfly. William Wordsworth. **CP-WorW1**

Art thou the thing I wanted?, vers. 1. Emily Dickinson. **CP-DickE**

Art thou the thing I wanted?, vers. 2. Emily Dickinson. **CP-DickE**

Art thou too fall'n? ere anger could subside, *tr. fr. the Latin of* J.C. Scaliger (Epitaphium in Laudationem Erasmi). Samuel Johnson. **CP-JohnS**

Art thou wise, four things resign. Hafiz, *tr. by* Ralph Waldo Emerson. **CP-EmerR** *Fr.* Odes.

Art to me's hear stellary. Artemisia. Louis Zukofsky. **CP-ZukLS**

Arte of English Poesie, The. Sir Walter Ralegh. **CP-RaleW**

    Anaphora, or the Figure of Report.

    Epizeuxis, the Underlay, or Coocko-spel.

    Ploche, or the Doubler.

Artegal and Elidure. William Wordsworth. **CP-WorW2**

Artegall and Radigund. Edmund Spenser. **OBSC** *Fr.* The Faerie Queene. **CP-Spens**

Artemis. Anne Waldman. **SP-WaldA**

Artemis Prologizes. Robert Browning. **CP-BroR1**

(Artemis speaks.) Orion Dead. Hilda Doolittle. **CP-DoolH**

Artemisia, *in imitation of* the Earl of Dorset. Alexander Pope. **CP-PopeA**

Artemisia. Louis Zukofsky. **CP-ZukLS**

Arterial, *parody of Early Chinese poetry.* Rudyard Kipling. **CP-KiplR** *Fr.* The Muse among the Motors.

Arteries, red lane on lane, The. Bridges. Charles Tomlinson. **CP-TomlC**

Artes bred neat An. *see* Anagram, An ("So Bartas-like thy fine spun poems been"). *Unknown.* **CP-BradA**

Artful Pose. Maya Angelou. **SP-AngeM**

Arthritic gray snowlight hobbles down the valley westward. Hayden Carruth. *Fr.* Paragraphs. **CP-CarHS**

Arthur. Ogden Nash. **CP-NashO**

Arthur Allen, when he lived. Bolyai, the Geometer. Donald Davie. **CP-DavDo**

Arthur Mitchell. Marianne Craig Moore. **CP-MoorM**

Arthur Peyton. Muriel Rukeyser. **CP-RukeM**

Arthure brooks only those that brooke not him. Epigramme. Thomas Campion. *Fr.* Observations in the Art of English Poesie. **CP-CampT**

Arthur's Fight with Orgoglio and Duessa. Edmund Spenser. **EBNV** *Fr.* The Faerie Queene. **CP-Spens**

Arthur's Quoit, Dyffryn. Wystan Hugh Auden. **CP-AudWJ**

Articulacy. Hints from the Koran. Donald Davie. **CP-DavDo**

Artifact. Muriel Rukeyser. **CP-RukeM**

Artifex in Extremis. Donald Davie. **CP-DavDo**

Artificial Intelligence. Adrienne Rich. **CP-RicAE; SP-RicA2**

Artillery [*or* Artillerie]. George Herbert. **CP-HerbG**

Artilleryman's Vision, The. Walt Whitman. **CP-WhitW**

Artist. Charles Bukowski. **SP-BukC1**

Artist. Ralph Waldo Emerson. *Fr.* Quatrains. **CP-EmerR**

Artist, An. Seamus Heaney. **SP-HeanS** *Fr.* Sweeney Redivivus.

Artist, An. Robinson Jeffers. **CP-JefR1**

Artist, The. Kenneth Koch. **SP-KochK**

Artist, The. Stanley Jasspon Kunitz. **CP-KuniS**

Artist, The. William Carlos Williams. **CP-WilW2**

Artist as an Old Man, The. Erica Jong. **SP-JongE**

Artist comes next, The. A Poem About Storytelling. Grace Paley. **CP-PaleG**

Artist of the Beautiful, An. John Greenleaf Whittier. **CP-WhitJ**

Artist, Reclining, The. James McAuley. **SP-McAuJ**

Artist Speaks. . . the Woman Answers, The. Kay Boyle. **CP-BoylK**

Artists. Charles Bukowski. **SP-BukC1**

Artists and writers. The Soul. Charles Olson. **CP-OlsoC**

Artist's Model. Robert Lowell. **SP-LoweR**

Artists, Providers, Places to Go. Roy Fisher. **SP-FishR**

Artists wrestled here! Emily Dickinson. **CP-DickE**

Arts are old, old as the stones, The. Nicholas Vachel Lindsay. *Fr.* Mae Marsh, Motion Picture Actress. **CP-LindV**

Arts Council Meets in Eureka, The. Gary Snyder. **CP-SnydG**

Art's Duped Riddle. John Hewitt. **CP-HewiJ**

Art's the / fruit of. Orchard. Archie Randolph Ammons. **SP-AmmoA**

Artsybashev is a Russian. Foreign. William Carlos Williams. **CP-WilW1**

Arundel Tomb, An. Philip Larkin. **CP-LarkP**

As / we lie side by side. Edward Estlin Cummings. **CP-CummE**

As a boy he was brought to Sulla's villa, The Tombs. Marcus Cato 95–42 B.C. Robert Lowell. **SP-LoweR**

As a boy he was so silent. In Silence Where We Breathe. Jane Cooper. *Fr.* March. **SP-CoopJ**

As a boy I started at the top. The Warehouse Chute. Dabney Stuart. **SP-StuaD**

As a boy my father preached to trees. Barton Sutter. *Fr.* Tools. **SP-SuttB**

As a child holds a pet. Port Bou. Stephen Spender. **CP-SpenS**

As a child I climbed the roof. Roofs. Philip Levine. **SP-LeviP**

As a child showed promise. No need to push him. Louis MacNeice. *Fr.* As In Their Time. **CP-MacNL**

As a child, they could not keep me from wells. Personal Helicon. Seamus Heaney. **SP-HeanS**

As a corpse / Bleeds. Evening. Daniel Gerard Hoffman. **SP-HoffD**

As a dare-gale skylark scanted in a dull cage. The Caged Skylark. Gerard Manley Hopkins. **CP-HopkG**

As a decrepit father takes delight. Sonnet 37. William Shakespeare. *Fr.* Sonnets. **CP-ShaWS**

As a drenched, drowned bee. A Baby Asleep after Pain. David Herbert Lawrence. **CP-LawrD**

As a drenched, drowned bee. *also stands as separate poem* A Baby Asleep after Pain. David Herbert Lawrence. *Fr.* Baby-Movements. **CP-LawrD**

As a gigantic harp in Vermont. The Play. Richard Eberhart. **CP-EberR**

As a girl no one gallantly attends. The Fear of Man. Robert Frost. **CP-FrosR**

As a green thread winds through blue fabric. Geese. Stephen Dobyns. **SP-DobyS**

As a guest who may not stay. In Memory. John Greenleaf Whittier. **CP-WhitJ**

As a horn of the high moon veers in clear skies over Main Street. Idyll. Donald Davie. **CP-DavDo**

As a horse of shell, the water's. Shapes. Kenneth Patchen. **CP-PatcK**

As a King, ...Unto the King. Christina Georgina Rossetti. **CP-RosC2**

As a Less than Robber. Robert Ranke Graves. **CP-GravR**

As a matter of fact, we are better than we know. The Combative Spirit. David Herbert Lawrence. **CP-LawrD**

As a pillar of gnats, moving up and down. Equivalence of Gnats and Mice. Richard Eberhart. **CP-EberR**

As a plant becomes pot-bound. Ego-Bound. David Herbert Lawrence. **CP-LawrD**

As a poet I'm interested in religious ideas. Credo. "Hugh MacDiarmid." **SP-MacDH**

As a queen sits down, knowing that a chair will be there. Walking to Sleep. Richard Wilbur. **CP-WilbR**

As a quiet little seedling. The Seedling. Paul Laurence Dunbar. **CP-DunbP**

As a scurrying snow-flake. Casse-Noisette. Robert Ranke Graves. **CP-GravR**

As a sloop with a sweep of immaculate wing on her delicate spine. Buick. Karl Shapiro. **SP-ShapK**

As a thorn-bush, or oaken bough. On Paddy's Character of "The Intelligencer." Jonathan Swift. **CP-SwifJ**

As a violet's gentle eye. Variation of the Song of the Moon. Percy Bysshe Shelley. *Fr.* Prometheus Unbound. **CP-ShelP**

As a War in Years of Peace. Philip Larkin. **CP-LarkP**

As a woman selecting threads. The Shaping Spirit. Phoebe Hesketh. **SP-HeskP**

As a World Would Have It. Edwin Arlington Robinson. **CP-RobiE**

As Adam, clutching earth, lay stunned within the darkness. John Gould Fletcher. **SP-FletJ** *Fr.* Branches of Adam.

As Adam did in Paradise. Kenoza Lake. John Greenleaf Whittier. **CP-WhitJ**

As Adam Early in the Morning. Walt Whitman. **CP-WhitW**

As Adam lay a-dreaming beneath the Apple Tree. The Four Angels. Rudyard Kipling. **CP-KiplR**

As against now the Gloucester. April Today Main Street. Charles Olson. **SP-OlsoC** *Fr.* The Maximus Poems.

As All Must End. Robert Ranke Graves. **CP-GravR**

As all the pigs have turned back into men. The Supporting Cast, Sotto Voce. Wystan Hugh Auden. *Fr.* The Sea and the Mirror. **CP-AudeW**

As American towns and cities I wander through. Maybe You Can't Take It with You, but Look What Happens When You Leave It Behind. Ogden Nash. **CP-NashO**

As an eagle grasped. Percy Bysshe Shelley. **ChER** *Fr.* Alastor; or, The Spirit of Solitude. **CP-ShelP**

As an intruder I trudged with careful innocence. Old Mansion. John Crowe Ransom. **SP-RansJ**

As an old traveler, I am indebted to paper-bound thrillers. Calling Spring VII-MMMC. Ogden Nash. **CP-NashO**

As an unperfect actor on the stage. Sonnet 23. William Shakespeare. **BiP; HBV; InvP; NoSic; OAEP; Son** *Fr.* Sonnets. **CP-ShaWS**

As Ann came in one summer's day. The Sleeper. Walter de la Mare. **CP-DeLaW**

'As anybody seen Bill 'Awkins? Bill 'Awkins. Rudyard Kipling. **CP-KiplR**

As any(men's hells having wrestled with). Edward Estlin Cummings. **CP-CummE**

As appleblossom to crocus. Basil Bunting. **CP-BuntB**

As, at a railway junction, men. Arthur Hugh Clough. **SP-ClouA**

As at the bottom of a seething well. Song, A. Richard Wilbur. **CP-WilbR**

As at Thy Portals Also Death. Walt Whitman. **CP-WhitW**

As Bad as a Mile. Philip Larkin. **CP-LarkP**

As beautiful as the hands. For Miriam. Kenneth Patchen. **CP-PatcK**

As Befits a Man. Langston Hughes. **SP-HughL**

As birds their infant brood protect. Jehovah-Shammah. William Cowper. *Fr.* Olney Hymns. **CP-CowpW**

As bronze may be much beautified. Fragment. Wilfred Owen. **CP-OwenW**

As by the dead we love to sit. Emily Dickinson. **CP-DickE**

As by the fix'd decrees of Heaven. Pignus Amoris. Byron. **CP-Byron**

As by the streames of *Babilon.* Thomas Campion. **CP-CampT**

As by the streames of Babylon. Bible, *O.T.* See Psalm 137: "By the rivers of Babylon. . . ."

As cauld a wind as ever blew. Lines Written in the Kirk of Lamington. Robert Burns. **CP-BurnR**

As Celia rested in the shade. A Pastoral[l] Dialogue. Thomas Carew. **CP-CareT**

As, certainly, it is not you who sway. A Round & a Canon. Charles Olson. **CP-OlsoC**

As Children bid the Guest "Good Night." Emily Dickinson. **CP-DickE**

As clever Tom Clinch, while the rabble was bawling. Clever Tom Clinch Going to Be Hanged. Jonathan Swift. **CP-SwifJ**

As Cold Water to a Thirsty Soul, So Is Good News from a Far Country. Christina Georgina Rossetti. **CP-RosC2**

As Consequent, Etc. Walt Whitman. **CP-WhitW**

As cool as the pale wet leaves. Alba ("As cool as the pale wet leaves"). Ezra Pound. **SP-PounE**

As Crazy As I Ever Was. Charles Bukowski. **SP-BukC1**

As curly-headed Jemmy was sleeping in bed. "Lewis Carroll." *Fr.* Solutions. *Fr.* Puzzles from Wonderland. **CP-CarrL**

As Daniel, bird-alone, in that far land. Robert Louis Stevenson. *Fr.* Sonnets. **CP-StevR**

As day was born, as night was dying. Impression: Fog Off the Coast of Dorset. Edna St. Vincent Millay. **CP-MillE**

As Devonshire letters, earlier in the year. To Oxford. Gerard Manley Hopkins. **CP-HopkG**

As Doctor Peter said. Hayden Carruth. *Fr.* The Sleeping Beauty. **CP-CarHL**

As down the burn they took their way. Down the Burn Davie. Robert Burns. **CP-BurnR**

As down the stage again. The Dead Tenor. Walt Whitman. **CP-WhitW**

As due by many titles I resign[e]. John Donne. **JCP; MePo; OBS** *Fr.* Divine Meditations. **CP-DonnJ** *Fr.* Holy Sonnets. **CP-DonnJ**

A dying, and behold we live! Christina Georgina Rossetti. **CP-RosC2**

As eager homebound traveller to the goal. After This the Judgement. Christina Georgina Rossetti. **CP-RosC1**

As eons of incalculable strife. Edwin Arlington Robinson. *Fr.* Two Quatrains. **CP-RobiE**

As evening fell the day's oppression lifted. Wystan Hugh Auden. *Fr.* Sonnets from China. **CP-AudeW**

As evening shaped I found me on a moor. A Meeting with Despair. Thomas Hardy. **CP-HardT**

As Expected. Thom Gunn. **CP-GunnT**

As faith thus sanctified the warrior's crest. William Wordsworth. *Fr.* Ecclesiastical Sonnets. **CP-WorW2**

As far as I can see, this autumn haze. The Cocoon. Robert Frost. **CP-FrosR**

As far as statues go, so far there's not. From Trollope's Journal. Elizabeth Bishop. **CP-BishE**

As far from pity, as complaint. Emily Dickinson. **CP-DickE**

As fast as thou shall wane, so fast thou growest. Sonnet 11. William Shakespeare. *Fr.* Sonnets. **CP-ShaWS**

As father Adam first was fool'd. Epitaph on a Henpecked Country Squire. Robert Burns. **CP-BurnR**

As flames that consume the mountains, as winds that coerce the sea. Love Is Strong as Death. Christina Georgina Rossetti. **CP-RosC2**

As Flowers Are. Stanley Jasspon Kunitz. **CP-KuniS**

As flowers have wars that the philosophic eye. As Flowers Are. Stanley Jasspon Kunitz. **CP-KuniS**

As fond mother, when the day is o'er. Nature. Henry Wadsworth Longfellow. **SP-LongH**

As for him who. Fragment. William Carlos Williams. **CP-WilW2**

As for me I am a child of the god of the mountains. This Poem Is for Bear. Gary Snyder. **CP-SnydG** *Fr.* Hunting. *Fr.* Myths and Texts.

As for me, I distrust the commonplace. Vertigo. Adrienne Rich. **CP-RicAE**

As for Me, I'm a Patriot. David Herbert Lawrence. **CP-LawrD**

As for my life, I've led it. A Placid Man's Epitaph. Thomas Hardy. **CP-HardT**

As for ourselves—the ship went out with the evening. The Fifth Book. Archibald MacLeish. *Fr.* Conquistador. **CP-MacLA**

As for Poets. Gary Snyder. **CP-SnydG**

As for the hawk, what grander bird. Sentience. Al Young. **CP-YounA**

As for the liar, fear him less. Sincerity. Thomas Merton. **CP-MertT**

As for the women, who did not. Margaret Atwood. *Fr.* Solstice Poem. **SP-AtwM2**

As freedom is a breakfastfood. Edward Estlin Cummings. **CP-CummE; SP-CummE**

As from afar, / through ringlet of woods. Circle. Robert Creeley. **CP-CreeR**

As from All the Little Animals. Malcolm Lowry. **CP-LowrM**

As from an [or their] ancestral oak. Similes for Two Political Characters of 1819. Percy Bysshe Shelley. **CP-ShelP**

As from the Darkening Gloom a Silver Dove. John Keats. **CP-KeatJ**

As from the earth the light Balloon. Emily Dickinson. **CP-DickE**

As from the fall of candlelight. George Meredith. **CP-MerG2**

As Frost is best conceived. Emily Dickinson. **CP-DickE**

As froth on the face of the deep, / As foam on the crest of the sea. Christina Georgina Rossetti. **CP-RosC2**

As Frothing Wounds of Roses. Kenneth Patchen. **CP-PatcK**

As gay for you to take your father's ax. To a Young Wretch. Robert Frost. **CP-FrosR**

As ghosts peer over a bedroom curtain. Nightfall. Wystan Hugh Auden. **CP-AudWJ**

As Gilly flowers do but stay. Upon a Lady That Dyed in Child-Bed, and Left a Daughter behind Her. Robert Herrick. **CP-HerrR**

As God is my witness where is the difference between. Carmen 97. Catullus. *Fr.* Carmina. **CP-Catul**

As gods sometimes descend from heav'n and deign. *in imitation of* Waller. Alexander Pope. **CP-PopeA**

As good to write as for to lie and groan. Sonnet 40. Sir Philip Sidney. **NoSic** *Fr.* Astrophil and Stella. **SP-SidnP**

As grains of sand, as stars, as drops of dew. All Saints. Christina Georgina Rossetti. **CP-RosC2**

As gray as that slumped. A Fall Day. Charles Simic. **SP-SimiC**

As grit swirls in the wind the word spreads. The Center of Attention. Daniel Gerard Hoffman. **SP-HoffD**

As happiness takes off the tie it borrowed from me. "Unfinished," The. Frank O'Hara. **SP-OharF**

As He Came near Death. Roy Fisher. **SP-FishR**

As he heaved himself backwards. Stopped Frames and Set-Pieces. Roy Fisher. **SP-FishR**

As He Is. Wystan Hugh Auden. **CP-AudeW**

As he is wounded. Geoffrey Hill. *Fr.* The Pentecost Castle. **CP-HillG**

As he lay dead / frost-blue eyes hooded. Dilemma. Phoebe Hesketh. **SP-HeskP**

As he moves the mine detector. Hunting Civil War Relics at Nimblewill Creek. James Dickey. **CP-DickJ**

As he said vanity, so vain say I. The Vanity of All Worldly Things. Anne Bradstreet. **CP-BradA**

As he stood near the plane, they heard him say. Muriel Rukeyser. **CP-RukeM**

As he that sees a dark and shady grove. Holy Baptism (1). George Herbert. **CP-HerbG**

As he was standing below the altars. Ezra Pound. *See* Canto 83: "Hudor / HUDOR et Pax."

As Hermes once took to his feathers light. John Keats. **CP-KeatJ**

(Dream, after Reading Dante's Episode of Paolo and Francesca, A.) **CP-KeatJ**

As honest Jacob on a night. The Patriarch. Robert Burns. **CP-BurnR**

As I am a Rhymer. Samuel Taylor Coleridge. **CP-ColeS**

(On My Joyful Departure from the Same City.) **CP-ColeS**

As I approach the state of pure euphoria. Euphoria. Lawrence Ferlinghetti. **SP-FerlL**

As I beheld a winters evening air. *see also* Black Patch on Lucasta's Face, A. Richard Lovelace. **CP-LoveR**

As I built cob-houses with small cousins on the floor. Nicholas Vachel Lindsay. *Fr.* A Rhymed Address to All Renegade Campbellites, Exhorting Them to Return. *Fr.* Alexander Campbell. **CP-LindV**

As I cam down by Annan side. The Trogger. Robert Burns. **CP-BurnR**

As I cam down by yon castle wa'. Song. Robert Burns. **CP-BurnR**

As I cam in by our gate-end. Bonnie Peg. Robert Burns. **CP-BurnR**

As I came from the. Kenneth Rexroth. **SP-RexrK** *Fr.* Love Poems of Marichiko.

As I Cam[e] O'er [the] Cairney Mount. Robert Burns. **CP-BurnR**

As I came out of the New York Public Library. Nuns in the Wind. Muriel Rukeyser. **CP-RukeM**

As I came over Windy Gap. Running to Paradise. William Butler Yeats. **CP-YeatW**

As I came through the desert on my right. Tiphead. John Hewitt. **CP-HewiJ**

As I came to the edge of the woods. Come In. Robert Frost. **CP-FrosR**

As I climb above the treeline. Difference of Ages. Marge Piercy. *Fr.* Walking into Love. **SP-PierM**

As I descended black impassive rivers. The Drunken Boat. Arthur Rimbaud, *tr. fr. French.*

As I did walk in meadows green. The Vacant Day. Walter de la Mare. **CP-DeLaW**

As I drive to the junction of lane and highway. At Castle Boterel. Thomas Hardy. **CP-HardT**

As I Ebb'd with the Ocean of Life. Walt Whitman. **CP-WhitW**

As I gird on for fighting. Alfred Edward Housman. **CP-HousA**

As I Grew Older. Langston Hughes. **SP-HughL**

As I Grew Up Again. Audre Lorde. **SP-LordA**

As I Grow Older. Richard Shelton. **SP-ShelR**

As I grow older, I must admit with terror:. The Lost Tune. Robert Lowell. **SP-LoweR**

As I grow older I perceive. Poet as Fisherman. Lawrence Ferlinghetti. **SP-FerlL**

As I had seen it practiced in that land. Preparation for the Highest Being. Kenneth Patchen. **CP-PatcK**

As I have known them passionate and fine. The Lost Follower. Robert Frost. **CP-FrosR**

As I have often told. "Hugh MacDiarmid." **SP-MacDH** *Fr.* The Snares of Varuna.

As I have said, I floated to the earth. Percy Bysshe Shelley. **FHYEP** *Fr.* Prometheus Unbound. **CP-ShelP**

As I in hoary [or hoarie] Winter's night stood[e] shivering[e] in the snow[e]. The Burning Babe. Robert Southwell. **CP-SoutR**

As I lay asleep in Italy. The Mask [or Masque] of Anarchy. Percy Bysshe Shelley. **CP-ShelP**

As I lay awake at night-time. The Revisitation. Thomas Hardy. **CP-HardT**

As I Lay Dying. Charles Bukowski. **SP-BukC2**

As I lay sleeping in the park. The Philosophers. Thomas Merton. **CP-MertT**

As I Lay with My Head in Your Lap Camerado. Walt Whitman. **CP-WhitW**

As I leaned to retrieve. The Savage Beast. William Carlos Williams. **CP-WilW2**

As I left my door. James Russell Lowell. Ralph Waldo Emerson. **CP-EmerR**

As I left the Halls at Lumley, rose the vision of a comely. As the Bell Clinks. Rudyard Kipling. **CP-KiplR**

As I lie here in the sun. Jonah. Randall Jarrell. **CP-JarrR**

As I listened from a beach-chair in the shade. Their Lonely Betters. Wystan Hugh Auden. **CP-AudeW**

As I mused by the hearthside. Comfort. Walter de la Mare. **CP-DeLaW**

As I my little flock on Ister Bank. Sir Philip Sidney. **SP-SidnP** *Fr.* Arcadia.

As I one evening [or ev'ning] sat before my cell. Artillery [or Artillerie]. George Herbert. **CP-HerbG**

As I pass through my incarnations in every age and race. The Gods of the Copybook Headings. Rudyard Kipling. **CP-KiplR**

As I passed thru Moscow's grass lots I heard. Two Dreams. Allen Ginsberg. **CP-GinsA**

As I pause at the side of the bath. Grief. David Herbert Lawrence. **CP-LawrD**

As I Ponder'd [or Pondered] in Silence. Walt Whitman. **CP-WhitW**

As I ride, as I ride. Through the Metidja to Abd-el-Kadr. Robert Browning. **CP-BroR1**

As I said before one Saturday night. Jan, the Son of Thomas. Carl Sandburg. **CP-SandC**

As I sat down by Saddle Stream. The Return from Town. Edna St. Vincent Millay. **CP-MillE**

As I sd to my / friend, because I am. I Know a Man. Robert Creeley. **CP-CreeR**

As I sit in twilight late alone by the flickering oak-flame. A Twilight Song. Walt Whitman. **CP-WhitW**

As I sit looking out of a window of the building. The Instruction Manual. John Ashbery. **SP-AshbJ**

As I sit with others at a great feast, suddenly while the music is playing. Thought. Walt Whitman. **CP-WhitW**

As I Sit Writing Here. Walt Whitman. **CP-WhitW**

As I started home after dark. Winter Night Poem for Mary. Wendell Berry. **CP-BerrW**

As I Step over a Puddle at the End of Winter, I Think of an Ancient Chinese Governor. James Wright. **CP-WrigJ**

As I stir this soup my powers come back to me. Modern witches 1: crouching. Jenny Joseph. *Fr.* Life and Turgid Times of A. Citizen. **SP-JoseJ**

As I stood alone on a windy mound. The Last Crusade. John Hewitt. **CP-HewiJ**

As I stood by yon roofless tower. Song. Robert Burns. **CP-BurnR**

As I stroll the city, oft I. A Character, Panegyric, and Description of the Legion Club. Jonathan Swift. **CP-SwifJ**

As I think of yellow. The Intruder. Roy Fisher. **SP-FishR**

As I turn'd into the market-place. George Meredith. **CP-MerG2**

As I Walk These Broad Majestic Days. Walt Whitman. **CP-WhitW**

As I walked in the woods. Ralph Waldo Emerson. **CP-EmerR**

As I Walked Out One Evening. Wystan Hugh Auden. **CP-AudeW**

As I walked out that sultry night. Full Moon. Robert Ranke Graves. **CP-GravR**

As I wandered in the forest. The Wild Flower's Song. William Blake. **CP-BlakW**

As I wandered over the city through the night. John Gould Fletcher. **SP-FletJ** *Fr.* Irradiations.

As I was a wand'ring ae midsummer e'enin. Robert Burns. **CP-BurnR**

As I Was Going to Saint-Ives. Daniel Gerard Hoffman. **SP-HoffD**

As I was out walking on a corner one day. Only a Hobo. "Bob Dylan." **CP-DylaB**

As I was reading the book of nature. The Book of Nature. Richard Eberhart. **CP-EberR**

As I was riding through New England. The Ides of March. Richard Eberhart. **CP-EberR**

As I was spittin' into the Ditch aboard o' the *Crocodile.* Soldier an' Sailor Too. Rudyard Kipling. **CP-KiplR**

As I was travelling toward the city of satisfactions. The City of Satisfactions. Daniel Gerard Hoffman. **SP-HoffD**

As I was walking. Kore. Robert Creeley. **CP-CreeR**

As I was walking among the fires of hell. Memorable Fancy, A. William Blake. **NU** *Fr.* The Marriage of Heaven and Hell. **CP-BlakW**

As I was walking home just now, from seeing. The Departure from Hydra. Kenneth Koch. **SP-KochK**

As I was walking through this parking. A Strange Moment. Charles Bukowski. **SP-BukC3**

As I was walking up the street. O Mally's Meek, Mally's Sweet. Robert Burns. **CP-BurnR**

As I was wandering down the street. Any Milleniums Today, Lady? Ogden Nash. **CP-NashO**

As I Watch'd the Ploughman Ploughing. Walt Whitman. **CP-WhitW**

As I went down our street. Two-Fold. David Herbert Lawrence. **CP-LawrD**

As I went down the hill along the wall. Meeting and Passing. Robert Frost. **CP-FrosR**

As I went down the road to the water, the river to the sea. Asylum Song. Muriel Rukeyser. **CP-RukeM**

As I went down the street in my rose-red pelerine. Casualty. David Herbert Lawrence. *Fr.* Bits. **CP-LawrD**

As I went down to Rotten Lake I remembered. First Elegy. Rotten Lake. Muriel Rukeyser. **CP-RukeM**

As I went in and out I heard pieces. Charles Olson. **CP-OlsoC**

As I went out a crow. The Last Word of a Bluebird. Robert Frost. **CP-FrosR**

As I Went Out Ae May Morning. Robert Burns. **CP-BurnR**

As I Went Out One Morning. "Bob Dylan." **CP-DylaB**

As I went over fossil hill. The Journey. Kathleen Jessie Raine. **SP-RainK**

As I went through the marshes. A Doe at Evening. David Herbert Lawrence. **CP-LawrD**

As I went walking up and down to take the evening air. Macdougal Street. Edna St. Vincent Millay. **CP-MillE**

As I write this letter. P.S. I Love You. The Beatles. **CP-Beatl**

As I write you, discarding for five minutes the names of other women and their destinies. A Poem for Vida Hadjebi Tabrizi. Kay Boyle. **CP-BoylK**

As if a cast of grain leapt back to the hand. An Event. Richard Wilbur. **CP-WilbR**

As if a nail whose wide head. Of Hours. George Oppen. **CP-OppeG**

As If a Phantom Caress'd Me. Walt Whitman. **CP-WhitW**

As if a trespasser. The King of the Ditchbacks. Seamus Heaney. **SP-HeanS**

As if as / if a mys. Edward Estlin Cummings. **CP-CummE**

As if by some fault devine, creating an. For Gaston Lachaise—a Sort of Written Frieze. Marsden Hartley. **CP-HartM**

As if Hallam Movius had placed a grid over it, and plumb-. Charles Olson. **CP-OlsoC**

As if he had been poured. The Graubelle Man. Seamus Heaney. **SP-HeanS**

As if I asked a common Alms. Emily Dickinson. **CP-DickE**

As if I had know you for years drink to me only if. All Over Again. Louis MacNeice. **CP-MacNL**

As if I were composed of dust and air. Master and Mistress. Stanley Jasspon Kunitz. **CP-KuniS**

As if in a presence of an intelligence. The Cold. Charles Simic. **SP-SimiC**

As If It Happened. Tess Gallagher. **SP-GallT**

As if it were a scene made-up by the mind. Often I Am Permitted to Return to a Meadow. Robert Duncan. **SP-DuncR**

As if planted there by giant golfers in the skies. Mt. Gabriel. Derek Mahon. **SP-MahoD**

As if some little Arctic flower. Emily Dickinson. **CP-DickE**

As if that hand. Puñal. Denise Levertov. **CP-LeveD**

As if the ant should fail with desire. Home Thoughts from Abroad. Alun Lewis. **CP-LewiA**

As if the Sea should part. Emily Dickinson. **CP-DickE**

As if the storme meant him. Mark 4; Why Are Yee Afraid, O Yee of Little Faith? Bible, *N.T.* **CP-CrasR**, *tr.* by Richard Crashaw; *Fr.* St. Mark.

As if this light boat had no keel. Sun Boat. May Sarton. **SP-SartM**

As if to take in ocean. Cannibals. Donald Davie. **CP-DavDo**

As if we chewed dry twigs and salt grasses. Robert Lowell. **SP-LoweR** *Fr.* Mexico.

As If You Had Never Been. Richard Eberhart. **CP-EberR**

As imperceptibly as Grief. Emily Dickinson. **CP-DickE**

As in a Swoon. Walt Whitman. **CP-WhitW**

As in Gaugin's *The Loss of Virginity*. The Title. William Carlos Williams. **CP-WilW2**

As in her ancient mistress' lap. Familiarity Dangerous. Vincent Bourne, *tr. fr. Latin* by William Cowper. **CP-CowpW**

As in our clothes, so likewise he who lookes. Lines Have Their Linings, and Bookes Their Buckram. Robert Herrick. **CP-HerrR**

As in poetry. James Liddy. *Fr.* Shore. **CP-LiddJ**

As in some car chase on Sunday-night TV. Miami. John Updike. **CP-UpdiJ**

As in some dim baronial hall restrained. Behind the Arras. Paul Laurence Dunbar. **CP-DunbP**

As in the Aftermath. David Markson. **CP-MarkD**

As in the amusement park they have these streams of water. Small Birds, to Agree with the Leaves, Come in the Fall. Charles Olson. **CP-OlsoC**

As in the green sky. Kenneth Patchen. **CP-PatcK**

As in the hostel by the bridge, I sate. Robert Louis Stevenson. *Fr.* Sonnets. **CP-StevR**

As in the woods, where leathery lichen weaves. Verses Supposed to Have Been Written in the New Forest, in Early Spring. Charlotte Smith. **CP-SmitC**

As in their flight the birds of song. Robert Louis Stevenson. **CP-StevR**

As In Their Time. Louis MacNeice. **CP-MacNL**

"As a child showed promise. No need to push him."

"Citizen of an ever-expanding."

"For what it was worth he had to."

"He had clowned it through. Being born."

"He was the man you thought."

"He was to be found in directories."

"Polyglot, albeit illiterate."

"She believed in love, but was it." **POL**

"She had her mind on the main."

"She was a bundle of statistics, her skin." **POL**

"They were so mean they could not between them." **POL**

"Year by year these old ladies had saved."

As incense smoke thins, a stupendous. God's Measurements. Laurence Lieberman. **SP-LiebL**

As indignation mastered grief, my tongue. After Leaving Italy, Continued. William Wordsworth. *Fr.* Memorials of a Tour in Italy, 1837. **CP-WorW2**

As is the sea marvelous. Edward Estlin Cummings. **CP-CummE**

As is your name, so is your comely face. To the Handsome Mistresse Grace Potter. Robert Herrick. **CP-HerrR**

As Islam's Prophet, when his last day drew. Requital. John Greenleaf Whittier. **CP-WhitJ**

As it fell upon a day. Richard Barnfield. **AWP; CH; CP-ShaWS; EIL; GBL; GTBS; GTBS-P; LoBV; NOBE; OBEV; OBSC; PBBP** *Fr.* The Passionate Pilgrim. **CP-ShaWS**

(Nightingale, The.) **AWP; GTBS; GTBS-P**

(Ode, An.) **EIL; LoBV; OBSC**

(Philomel.) **CH; NOBE; OBEV**

As It Fell upon a Day. "Lewis Carroll." **CP-CarrL**

As it fell upon a day. Gerard Manley Hopkins. **CP-HopkG**

As It Happens. Denise Levertov. **CP-LeveD**

As it is / in my country. We Have a Map of the World. Alice Walker. **CP-WalkA**

As it is, plenty. His Excellency. Wystan Hugh Auden. **CP-AudeW**

As It Moves. Stephen Dunn. **SP-DunnS**

As It Should Be. Derek Mahon. **SP-MahoD**

As It Was. Frederick Morgan. **SP-MorgF**

As it was with Christ, so it is with Malcolm. The Abduction of Saints. Alice Walker. **CP-WalkA**

As It Was Written. Anne Sexton. **CP-SextA**

As Joe Gould says in. Edward Estlin Cummings. **CP-CummE**

As John to Patmos. Derek Walcott. **CP-WalcD**

As Jove will not attend on less. An Epistle upon an Epistle. Jonathan Swift. **CP-SwifJ**

As Julia once a-slumbering lay. The Captived Bee; or, The Little Filcher. Robert Herrick. **CP-HerrR**

As kingdoms after civil broil. Love's Parable. Robert Penn Warren. **SP-WarrR**

As kingfishers catch fire, dragonflies draw flame. Gerard Manley Hopkins. **CP-HopkG**

As late by a sodger I chanced to pass. I'll Mak You Be Fain to Follow Me. Robert Burns. **CP-BurnR**

As late each flower that sweetest blows. The Rose. Samuel Taylor Coleridge. *Fr.* Effusions. **CP-ColeS**

As late I journey'd o'er the extensive plain. Life. Samuel Taylor Coleridge. **CP-ColeS**

As late I lay in slumber's shadowy vale. Burke. Samuel Taylor Coleridge. *Fr.* Effusions. **CP-ColeS**

As late I rambled in the happy fields. To a Friend Who Sent Me Some Roses. John Keats. **CP-KeatJ**

As late in wreaths gay flowers I bound. An Ode in the Manner of Anacreon. Samuel Taylor Coleridge. **CP-ColeS**

As late on Skiddaw's mount I lay supine. A Stanger Minstrel. Samuel Taylor Coleridge. **CP-ColeS**

As lately I a Garland bound. Upon Cupid. Robert Herrick. **CP-HerrR**

As learn'd *Eliza*, sister of the Muse. To Eliza Plucking Laurel in Mr Pope's Gardens. Samuel Johnson. **CP-JohnS**

As leaves are to the tree wheron they grow. At Bologna, in Remembrance of the Late Insurrections, 1837, Continued. William Wordsworth. **CP-WorW2**

As "legal representative." A Circular. Thomas Hardy. **CP-HardT**

As lemmings run into the sea. Running into Things. Miller Williams. **SP-WillM**

As lone I sat one summer's day. Love Despoiled. Paul Laurence Dunbar. **CP-DunbP**

As long as Fame's imperious music rings. Three Quatrains. Edwin Arlington Robinson. **CP-RobiE**

As long as it took fasten it back to a place where after all he. Patriarchal Poetry. Gertrude Stein. **CP-SteiG**

As long as the apple had not been entirely digested, as long as. The Meditation of Simeon. Wystan Hugh Auden. *Fr.* For the Time Being; a Christmas Oratorio. **CP-AudeW**

As long as they trample the sad smiles of guitars. The Long Naked Walk of the Dead. Charles Kenneth Williams. **CP-WillC**

As long as we look forward, all seems free. The Western Approaches. Howard Nemerov. **CP-NemeH**

As long as we looked lay the low country. The Residual Years. William Everson. **SP-EverW**

As Lords. John Milton. **FaBoDD** *Fr.* Samson Agonistes. **CP-MiltJ**

As love / that is. The Bird's Companion. William Carlos Williams. **CP-WilW1**

As Love and Hope together. Love's Vicissitudes. Robert Louis Stevenson. **CP-StevR**

As Lovers Do. "Hugh MacDiarmid." **SP-MacDH**

As loving hind that, hartless, wants her deer. Another Letter to Her Husband Absent upon Public[k] Employment. Anne Bradstreet. **CP-BradA**

"As many as I love,"—Ah Lord, Who lovest all. Whitsun Eve. Christina Georgina Rossetti. **CP-RosC2**

As many Lawes and Lawyers do expresse. A Prognostick. Robert Herrick. **CP-HerrR**

As mastiff dogs in modern phrase are. The Description of a Salamander. Jonathan Swift. **CP-SwifJ**

As men, for fear the stars should sleep and nod. Divinity. George Herbert. **CP-HerbG**

As men from men. William Wordsworth. **EnRP** *Fr.* Despondency Corrected. *Fr.* The Excursion. **CP-WorW2**

As men have loved their lovers in times past. Edna St. Vincent Millay. **CP-MillE**

As mighty thews burst manacles, she went mad. George Meredith. *Fr.* The Revolution. **CP-MerG1**

As movement seen, so is the sound, the singing. Hayden Carruth. *Fr.* The Sleeping Beauty. **CP-CarHL**

As much to blame as Francis Archer seems. To Christopher Marlowe. Charles Henri Ford. **SP-FordC**

As My Blood Was Drawn. Robert Earl Hayden. **CP-HaydR**

As my father, the late star, once told me. Portrait of the Queen in Tears. Louise Glück. **SP-GlücL**

As my first blow against it, I would not stay. The Mad Farmer in the City. Wendell Berry. **CP-BerrW**

As my little Pot doth boyle. To God, His Gift. Robert Herrick. **CP-HerrR**

As my skin wrinkles in warning like. Thermometer. Charles Bukowski. **SP-BukC2**

As newer comers crowd the fore. The Superseded. Thomas Hardy. **CP-HardT**

As night drew on, and, from the crest. Winter Night. John Greenleaf Whittier. **TrGrPo** *Fr.* Snow-Bound [*or* Snow-Bound; a Winter Idyl]. **CP-WhitJ**

As Now It Would Be Snow. Robert Creeley. **CP-CreeR**

As o'er his furrowed fields which lie. Seed-Time and Harvest. John Greenleaf Whittier. **CP-WhitJ**

As o'er the cold sepulchral stone. Lines Written in an Album, at Malta. Byron. **CP-Byron**

As of Bozeman, *sels.* Charles Olson. *Fr.* West. **CP-OlsoC**

As of this date, you are being referred. For My Friend John Lying on the Bed with Morning Heaves. Chuck Miller. **SP-MillC**

As oft as Night's is banish'd by the Morne. Dangers Wait on Kings. Robert Herrick. **CP-HerrR**

As oft mine eye with careless glance. The Silver Thimble. Samuel Taylor Coleridge. *Fr.* Poetical Epistles. **CP-ColeS**

As often as he let himself be seen. The Rat. Edwin Arlington Robinson. **CP-RobiE**

As often as I murmur here. The Poet and the Caged Turtledove. William Wordsworth. **CP-WorW2**

As often as we thought of her. Neighbors. Edwin Arlington Robinson. **CP-RobiE**

As often in a bun. George Meredith. **CP-MerG2**

As oftentimes a river, it might seem. Residence in France. William Wordsworth. *Fr.* The Prelude; Growth of a Poet's Mind [1805 vers.]. **CP-WorW3**

As old as Woe. Emily Dickinson. **CP-DickE**

As on a day Sabina fell asleepe. Thomas Campion. **CP-CampT**

As on a hill-top rude, when closing day. John Milton. *See* Sonnet 3: "As on a rugged mountain at the darkening of evening."

As on a rugged mountain at the darkening of evening. Sonnet 3. John Milton, *tr. fr. Italian by* John T. Shawcross. **CP-MiltJ**

As on a window late I cast mine eye. Love-Joy. George Herbert. **CP-HerbG**

As on Euphrates shady banks we lay. Bible, *O.T. See* Psalm 137: "By the rivers of Babylon. . . ."

As on the first day her first word was *thou*. The Confession. Karl Shapiro. *Fr.* Adam and Eve. **SP-ShapK**

As on the sea-boat shore Brittania sat. Britannia. James Thomson. **CP-ThomJ**

As once I bad good morning to the day. Catullus, *tr. fr. Latin by* Richard Lovelace. **CP-LoveR**

As once in heaven Dante looked back down. The Backward Look. Howard Nemerov. **CP-NemeH**

As one by one withdraw the lofty actors. Death of General Grant. Walt Whitman. **CP-WhitW**

As One does Sickness over. Emily Dickinson. **CP-DickE**

As one of our brightest young intellectuals said to me. What Matters. David Herbert Lawrence. **CP-LawrD**

As one of the secretaries of the moon. Word with José Rodríguez-Feo. Wallace Stevens. **CP-StevW**

As One Put Drunk into the Packet-Boat. John Ashbery. **SP-AshbJ**

As one put drunk into the packet-boat. Tom May's Death. Andrew Marvell. **CP-MarvA**

As one red rose in a garden where all other roses are. As the Apple Tree among the Trees of the Wood. Christina Georgina Rossetti. **CP-RosC2**

As one that strives, being sick, and sick to death. To Celia, upon Love's Ubiquity. Thomas Carew. **CP-CareT**

As one who hangs down-bending from the side. A Dedicated Spirit. William Wordsworth. **SeCePo** *Fr.* Summer Vacation. *Fr.* The Prelude; Growth of a Poet's Mind [1850 vers.]. **CP-WorW3**

As one who having wandered all night long. Robert Louis Stevenson. **CP-StevR**

As one who held herself a part. Sister. John Greenleaf Whittier. **AA** *Fr.* Snow-Bound [*or* Snow-Bound; a Winter Idyl]. **CP-WhitJ**

As one who in his journey bates at Noon. Book XII. John Milton. *Fr.* Paradise Lost. **CP-MiltJ**

As one who, long in thickets and in brakes. The Garden. William Cowper. *Fr.* The Task. **CP-CowpW**

As one who shoots an arrow overhead. Arthur Hugh Clough. **SP-ClouA**

As one who strives a hill to climb. Canto VI: Dyscomfyture. "Lewis Carroll." *Fr.* Phantasmagoria. **CP-CarrL**

As one who(having written). Edward Estlin Cummings. **CP-CummE**

As orange dusk-light falls on an old idea. Sunset S.S. Azemour. Allen Ginsberg. **CP-GinsA**

As our mother the Frigate, bepainted and fine. Cruisers. Rudyard Kipling. **CP-KiplR**

As Parmigianino did it, the right hand. Self-Portrait in a Convex Mirror. John Ashbery. **SP-AshbJ**

As pilot well expert in perilous wave. Edmund Spenser. **OAEL-1; PoEL-1** *Fr.* The Faerie Queene. **CP-Spens**

(Cave of Mammon, The.) **PoEL-1**

"At length they came into a larger space." **FiP**

As pilots pay attention to the air. Morning: I Know Perfectly How in a Minute You Will Stretch and Smile. John Ciardi. **SP-CiarJ**

As plan for Noon and plan for Night. Emily Dickinson. **CP-DickE**

As power and wit will me assist. Sir Thomas Wyatt. **CP-WyatT**

As Puritans they prominently wax. A Certain People. George Meredith. **CP-MerG1**

As quid pro quo for your enchanting verses. Toast, A. Wystan Hugh Auden. *Fr.* Eleven Occasional Poems. **CP-AudeW**

As real as thinking. Robert Creeley. **CP-CreeR**

As rising from the vegetable World. James Thomson. **PoEL-3** *Fr.* Spring. *Fr.* The Seasons. **CP-ThomJ**

As rivers seek the sea. Confluents. Christina Georgina Rossetti. **CP-RosC1**

As Rochefoucauld his maxims drew. Verses on the Death of Dr. Swift, D.S.P.D. Jonathan Swift. **CP-SwifJ**

As Rousseau was another, singing. Hayden Carruth. *Fr.* The Sleeping Beauty. **CP-CarHL**

As salt, keep your savour. In the Hills South of Capernaum, Port. Charles Olson. **CP-OlsoC**

As sharp as in my childhood, still. Edna St. Vincent Millay. **CP-MillE**

As she goes about the homestead. Land-Worker. David Herbert Lawrence. **CP-LawrD** *Fr.* Bits. **CP-LawrD**

As she laughed I was aware of becoming involved in her laughter. Hysteria. Thomas Stearns Eliot. **CP-ElioT**

As she rides to the station. The Traveler. Randall Jarrell. **CP-JarrR**

As She Was Thus Alone in the Clear Moonlight. Kenneth Patchen. **CP-PatcK**

As ships, becalmed at eve, that lay. Qua Cursum Ventus. Arthur Hugh Clough. **SP-ClouA**

As shows [*or* shews] the air[e], when with a rainbow graced. Upon Julia's Ribband. Robert Herrick. **CP-HerrR**

As sickly Plants betray a niggard Earth. The Alliance of Education and Government. Thomas Gray. **CP-GrayT**

As silent as a mirror is believed. Legend. Hart Crane. **CP-CranH**

As sings the pine-tree in the wind. Nature in Leasts. Ralph Waldo Emerson. *Fr.* Quatrains. **CP-EmerR**

As Sir Saltonstall ran over. Buffalo Ode. Charles Olson. **CP-OlsoC**

As Sisyphus against the infernal steep. Byron. **OBSV** *Fr.* English Bards and Scotch Reviewers. **CP-Byron**

As Sleigh Bells seem in summer. Emily Dickinson. **CP-DickE**

As snow lies on the hill love's blackness lies. Charles Olson. **CP-OlsoC; SP-OlsoC**

As solid-seeming as antiquity. A Marriage in the 'Sixties. Adrienne Rich. **CP-RicAE; SP-RicA1; SP-RicA2**

As some bland soul, to whom a debtor says. Her Confession. Thomas Hardy. **CP-HardT**

As some fond virgin, whom her mother's care. Epistle to Miss [*or* Miss Teresa] Blount, on Her Leaving the Town after the Coronation. Alexander Pope. **CP-PopeA**

As some rapt gazer on the lowly earth. Love's Humility. Paul Laurence Dunbar. **CP-DunbP**

As some raw youth in country bred. To Dr. Delany, on the Libels Writ against Him. Jonathan Swift. **CP-SwifJ**

As some vast tropic Tree, itself a Wood. The Tree of Mystery. Samuel Taylor Coleridge. **CP-ColeS**

As some women love jewels. Ode to a Lebanese Crock of Olives. Diane Wakoski. **SP-WakoD**

As sometimes in a dead man's face. Tennyson. **ImPo; LiTB** *Fr.* In Memoriam A. H. H. **CP-TennA**

As soon as / I speak, I. The Pattern. Robert Creeley. **CP-CreeR**

As soon as April pierces to the root. Geoffrey Chaucer. *See* The General Prologue.

As soon as Jesus was dead and buried, the rumors. Mary. Frederick Morgan. **SP-MorgF**

As soon as the blackthorn comes in flower. The Order of Saying. Charles Tomlinson. **CP-TomlC**

As soon as the old man knew he was actually dying, even before anyone else would admit it. When. Charles Kenneth Williams. **SP-WillC**

As spring begins the river rises. March 22, 1968. Wendell Berry. **CP-BerrW**

As spring flowers are promised by. A Quiet Talk with Oneself. Charles Simic. **SP-SimiC**

As spring the winter doth succeed. Anne Bradstreet. **CP-BradA**

As Star that shines dependent upon star. Places of Worship. William Wordsworth. *Fr.* Ecclesiastical Sonnets. **CP-WorW2**

As starts the absent dreamer, when a train. Robert Louis Stevenson. *Fr.* Sonnets. **CP-StevR**

As subtle as tomorrow. Emily Dickinson. **CP-DickE**

As Summer into Autumn slips. Emily Dickinson. **CP-DickE**

As Sun-beams pierce the glasse, and streaming in. Another. Robert Herrick. **CP-HerrR**

As sunbeams stream through liberal space. Woodnotes II ("As sunbeams stream through liberal space"). Ralph Waldo Emerson. **CP-EmerR**

As surely as I hold your hand in mine. Brown Boy to Brown Girl. Countee Cullen. **CP-CullC**

As swallows turning backward. St. Martin's Summer. Robert Louis Stevenson. **CP-StevR**

As swift and dying as the forms of flame. À Constance, This Day. Charles Olson. **CP-OlsoC**

As Tam the chapman on a day. Robert Burns. **CP-BurnR**

(On Tam the Chapman.) **CP-BurnR**

As that named Fred. Edward Estlin Cummings. **CP-CummE**

As the Apple Tree among the Trees of the Wood. Christina Georgina Rossetti. **CP-RosC2**

As the Asian War Begins. Robert Bly. **SP-BlyR**

As the Bell Clinks. Rudyard Kipling. **CP-KiplR**

As the black storm upon the mountain-top. William Wordsworth. **PoEL-4** *Fr.* Residence in London. *Fr.* The Prelude; Growth of a Poet's Mind [1850 vers.]. **CP-WorW3**

As the broken front differential pops and jumps. Hayden Carruth. *Fr.* The Sleeping Beauty. **CP-CarHL**

As the brown mowers strode across the field. The Swathe Uncut. John Hewitt. **CP-HewiJ**

As the Buck Lay Dead. Marsden Hartley. **CP-HartM**

As the builders / Planned, the city trees. Sunnyside Child. George Oppen. **CP-OppeG**

As the cat. Poem. William Carlos Williams. **CP-WilW1**

As the cold aspect of a sunless way. Captivity.—Mary Queen of Scots. William Wordsworth. **CP-WorW2**

As the corn becomes higher. Cricket Match. Carl Sandburg. **CP-SandC**

As the crest of some slow-arching wave. Lincolnshire Shores. Tennyson. **FaBoPP** *Fr.* The Last Tournament. *Fr.* Idylls of the King. **CP-TennA**

As the dawn was breaking the Sambhur belled. Hunting Song of the Seeonee Pack. Rudyard Kipling. **CP-KiplR** *Fr.* Mowgli's Brothers. *Fr.* The Jungle Book.

As the days grow shorter many keys. Keys. Daniel Gerard Hoffman. **SP-HoffD**

As the Dead Prey upon Us. Charles Olson. **CP-OlsoC; SP-OlsoC**

As the dove which found no rest / For the sole of her foot, flew back. Christina Georgina Rossetti. **CP-RosC2**

As the Doves to Their Windows. Christina Georgina Rossetti. **CP-RosC2**

As the drop feeds its fated flower. Ralph Waldo Emerson. **CP-EmerR**

As the earth. Elizabeth Barrett Browning. **EPCY** *Fr.* Aurora Leigh. **CP-BroEB**

As the egg of an ostrich at the bottom [of] a bubbling spring. George Meredith. *Fr.* Arabic Poems. **CP-MerG2**

As the eye fails through age or disease. Robinson Jeffers. **CP-JefR3**

As the eye lifts, the field. Three Sonnets. William Carlos Williams. **CP-WilW2**

As the fireman said. Riding the Elevator into the Sky. Anne Sexton. **CP-SextA**

As the fox, unexpected, / is here, they are still here. Wild Apple Trees. Brendan Galvin. **SP-GalvB**

As the fresh wine the poet pours. Ode to Apollo. William Wordsworth. **CP-WorW1**

As the garbage truck is backing up, one of the garbagemen is absorbed watching a pretty girl pass. Men. Charles Kenneth Williams. **SP-WillC**

As the gods began one world, and man another. Snakecharmer. Sylvia Plath. **CP-PlatS**

As the Greek's Signal Flame. Walt Whitman. **CP-WhitW**

As the hart panteth after the water brooks, *comprises* Psalms 42 *and* 43. Bible, *O.T. See* Psalm 43: "Judge me, O God. . . ."

As the hart panteth after the water brooks. Psalm 42. Bible, *O.T.* **AWP; TRV; TrGrPo; TrJP; WGRP** *Fr.* Psalms. **CP-Psal**

As the hedges, clipt and even. Offering. William Carlos Williams. **CP-WilW1**

As the highway circles the mountain of red mirrors. Dragon's Blood III. John Yau. **SP-YauJo**

As the Human Village Prepares for Its Fate. Tom Clark. **SP-ClarT**

As the Ignorant Savage will sell his own Wife. On the Great Encouragement Given By English Nobility & Gentry to Correggio Rubens Rembrandt Reynolds Gainsborough Catalani Ducrowe & Dilbury Doodle. William Blake. **CP-BlakW**

As the immense dew of Florida. Nomad Exquisite. Wallace Stevens. **CP-StevW**

As the juice ran out on the wooden board. Slicing Oranges for Jeremiah. Diane Wakoski. **SP-WakoD**

As the last light. Whip-Poor-Will. Donald Hall. **CP-HallD**

As the Liberty Lads o'er the Sea. Byron. **CP-Byron**

As the mailman walked up the hill. Pace is the Essence. Charles Bukowski. **SP-BukC3**

As the melting park. At the Park Dance. William DeWitt Snodgrass. **SP-SnodW**

As the mind burns. For G.B.S., Old. William Carlos Williams. **CP-WilW2**

As the Mist Leaves No Scar, *see also* True Love Leaves No Traces. Leonard Cohen. **CP-CoheL**

As the mist leaves no scar. *see also* As the Mist Leaves No Scar. Leonard Cohen. **CP-CoheL**

As the moon sidles up. He and She. William Butler Yeats. **CP-YeatW**

As the player's breath warms the fipple the tone clears. Basil Bunting. **PWE** *Fr.* Grass caught in willow tells the flood's height that has subsided. **FaBoMo** *Fr.* Briggflatts [An Autobiography]. **CP-BuntB**

As the plump squirrel scampers. Today I Was So Happy, So I Made this Poem. James Wright. **CP-WrigJ**

As the poets have mournfully sung. Wystan Hugh Auden. **CBCK; FaBoBl; NBLV; OBAL; OBCoV; PeLi** *Fr.* Shorts [1948–1957] ("At peace under this mandarin, sleep, Lucina"). **CP-AudeW**

(Aesthetic Point of View, The.) **NBLV; OBAL; OBCoV**

(Comprehensive Death.) **CBCK**

(Limerick: "As the poets have mournfully sung.") **FaBoBl; PeLi**

As the poor end of each dead day drew near. Malcolm Lowry. *Fr.* Songs for Second Childhood. **CP-LowrM**

As the rain falls. Rain. William Carlos Williams. **CP-WilW1**

As the seed waits eagerly watching for its flower and fruit. Night VIII (The Eternal Man). William Blake. **PoE** *Fr.* Vala; or The Four Zoas. **CP-BlakW**

As the shield goddess, Mycenae. Charles Olson. **CP-OlsoC**

As the shy Hind, the soft-eyed gentle Brute. The Timorous Hind. Samuel Taylor Coleridge. **CP-ColeS**

As the single pang of the blow, when the metal is mingled well. Tropic Rain. Robert Louis Stevenson. **CP-StevR**

As the snow falls I brush it away. A Snowfall. Richard Eberhart. **CP-EberR**

As the Sparks Fly Upwards. Christina Georgina Rossetti. **CP-RosC2**

As the Starved Maelstrom lap the Navies. Emily Dickinson. **CP-DickE**

As the steady lenses circle. The Light-Keeper. Robert Louis Stevenson. **CP-StevR**

As the sun dims we begin to think. Frederick Morgan. *Fr.* The River. **SP-MorgF**

As the sunbeams stream through liberal space. Ralph Waldo Emerson. **OHIP** *Fr.* Woodnotes II ("As sunbeams stream through liberal space"). **CP-EmerR**

As the sunrise to the night. Fragment: To Italy. Percy Bysshe Shelley. **CP-ShelP**

As the sweet sweat of roses in a still. The Comparison. John Donne. **PeLV** *Fr.* Elegies. **CP-DonnJ**

As the thriftless gold of the *babul* so is the gold that we spend. Rudyard Kipling. *Fr.* Certain Maxims of Hafiz. **CP-KiplR**

As the Time Draws Nigh. Walt Whitman. **CP-WhitW**

As the train chugs past the painting of your face. Dragon's Blood IV. John Yau. **CP-YauJo**

As the vague sun that wrapped the mellow day. Sunset over Glenaan. John Hewitt. **CP-HewiJ**

As the vision of labor grows. Wendell Berry. *Fr.* The Clearing. **CP-BerrW**

As the voice of many waters all saints sing as one. Before the Throne, and Before the Lamb. Christina Georgina Rossetti. **CP-RosC2**

As the wind breaks in from the sea again. Counsel. Charles Bukowski. **SP-BukC2**

As the wise men of old brought gifts. The Gift. William Carlos Williams. **CP-WilW2**

As then, no winde at all there blew. An Elegie, or Friends Passion, for His Astrophill. Edmund Spenser. *Fr.* Astrophel. **CP-Spens**

As these drops fall: so Hope drops now on me. Mary Sidney, Countess of Montgomery Wroth. *Fr.* Part 1. *Fr.* Urania. **CP-WrotM**

As They Draw to a Close. Walt Whitman. **CP-WhitW**

As they grew older. "King and Queen." Donald Hall. **CP-HallD**

As they who, tossing midst the storm at night. The Lost Statesman. John Greenleaf Whittier. **CP-WhitJ**

As they who watch by sick-beds find relief. Amy Wentworth. John Greenleaf Whittier. **CP-WhitJ**

As this comes in. The Lute in the Attic. Kenneth Patchen. **CP-PatcK**

As tho' again—yea, even once again. Rhodes Memorial, Table Mountain. Rudyard Kipling. **CP-KiplR**

As Thomas was cudgelled [*or* cudgell'd *or* cudgel'd] one day by his wife. Three Epigrams. Jonathan Swift. **CP-SwifJ**

As those who are not athletic at breakfast day by day. Nature Morte. Louis MacNeice. **CP-MacNL**

As thou deserv'st, be proud; then gladly let. Pride Allowable in Poets. Robert Herrick. **CP-HerrR**

As though an aged person were to wear. Elegy for the Monastery Barn. Thomas Merton. **CP-MertT; SP-MertT**

As though I'm fooled. That lacy body managed to forget. Nurse's Song. Louise Glück. **SP-GlücL**

As though it were the very soul of rational human intercourse which had been violated. Easter. Charles Kenneth Williams. **SP-WillC**

As though seen among other competing nondescript signs. Shocks Brakes (For Kurt and Yansky). Chuck Miller. **SP-MillC**

As though the skin had been stripped and pulled back onto the skull like a stocking and soldered. Scar. Charles Kenneth Williams. **SP-WillC**

As though there were no flowing. Charles Olson. **CP-OlsoC**

As though they were minting crisp new words. The Poets. Chuck Miller. **SP-MillC**

As through the land at eve we went. Tennyson. **ImPo; LiTB; PoToHe; SCGP** *Fr.* The Princess. **CP-TennA**

(Reconciliation, The.)

(We Kiss'd Again with Tears.) **PoToHe**

As through the wild green hills of Wyre. Alfred Edward Housman. **CP-HousA**

As Thucydides said. A Theory. Thomas McGrath. **SP-McGrT**

As thus the snows arise, and foul and fierce. James Thomson. **ECEV; SeCePo** *Fr.* Winter. *Fr.* The Seasons. **CP-ThomJ**

(Winter Tragedy, A.) **ECEV**

As Thy Days, So Shall Thy Strength Be. Christina Georgina Rossetti. **CP-RosC2**

As Thyself! David Herbert Lawrence. **CP-LawrD**

As time will turn our bodies straight. Religion Is That I Love You. Kenneth Patchen. **CP-PatcK**

A.S. to G.S. Emily Brontë. **CP-BronE**

As to How Much. Louis Zukofsky. **CP-ZukLS**

As to my heart, that may as well be forgotten. Basil Bunting. **CP-BuntB**

As to report, / Within his court. Malcolm Lowry. **CP-LowrM**

As to some lovely temple, tenantless. Edna St. Vincent Millay. **CP-MillE**

As Toilsome I Wander'd Virginia's Woods. Walt Whitman. **CP-WhitW**

As tomorrow as soon as it is day. Thy Gleeman Who Flattered Thee. Charles Olson. **CP-OlsoC**

As 'Twere To-night. Thomas Hardy. **CP-HardT**

As usual i did not find him in cafes, the more dissolute atmosphere. Edward Estlin Cummings. **CP-CummE**

As usual, I was desperate. Coming Home. Tess Gallagher. **SP-GallT**

As usual I'm up before the sun. John Berryman. *Fr.* Sonnets to Chris. **CP-BerrJ**

As usual, legend got it all. Nestor's Bathtub. Rita Dove. **SP-DoveR**

As vain to raise a voice as a sigh. On Going Unnoticed. Robert Frost. **CP-FrosR**

As violets so be I recluse and sweet, / Cheerful as daisies unaccounted rare. Who Hath Despised the Day of Small Things? Christina Georgina Rossetti. **CP-RosC2**

As virtuous men pass [*or* passe] mildly away. Valediction, A: Forbidding Mourning. John Donne. **CP-DonnJ**

As void as clouds that house and harbour none. Fragments. Gerard Manley Hopkins. **CP-HopkG**

As wanton boys, we kill them for our sport. Survivors. Phoebe Hesketh. **SP-HeskP**

As watchers couched beneath a Bantine oak. *after* Horace, Book 5, Ode 31. Rudyard Kipling. **CP-KiplR** *Fr.* Debits and Credits.

As Watchers hang upon the East. Emily Dickinson. **CP-DickE**

As we are so wonderfully done with each other. Kenneth Patchen. **CP-PatcK**

As we came through the gate to look at the few new lambs. Ravens. Ted Hughes. **SP-HughT**

As we came up the brae last night at twelve. Halloweve: A Glensman Speaks. John Hewitt. **CP-HewiJ**

As we came up the steep familiar lane. The Sheep Skull. John Hewitt. **CP-HewiJ**

As we drove back, crossing the hill. A Locked House. William DeWitt Snodgrass. **SP-SnodW**

As we drove down the ramp from the boat. Dover: Believing in Kings. James Dickey. **CP-DickJ**

As we kissed good-bye. Eighteen Days without You. Anne Sexton. **CP-SextA**

As We Know. John Ashbery. **SP-AshbJ**

As we left the garden-party / By the far gate. Leaving. Richard Wilbur. **CP-WilbR**

As we left the highroad and sped dimly. On Leave: Marriage. Alun Lewis. **CP-LewiA**

As we lie down to sleep the world turns half away. Sleeping Standing Up. Elizabeth Bishop. **CP-BishE**

As we live, we are transmitters of life. We Are Transmitters. David Herbert Lawrence. **CP-LawrD**

As we pass Houses musing slow. Emily Dickinson. **CP-DickE**

As We Sit. Robert Creeley. **CP-CreeR**

As we stand talking, his eye. An Old Acquaintance. Lewis Turco. **SP-TurcL**

As we take nature, without permission. Emily Dickinson. **SP-DickE**

As We Walked. Leonard Nathan. **SP-NathL**

As we wandered through the hill of graves. On Castle Hill. Marge Piercy. **SP-PierM**

As wearied pilgrims, once possessed. His Own Epitaph. Robert Herrick. **CP-HerrR**

As weary pilgrim, now at rest. Anne Bradstreet. **CP-BradA**

As, when a beauteous nymph decays. Stella's Birthday (1725). Jonathan Swift. **CP-SwifJ**

As when a breeze / slips off the water. Pollen. Brendan Galvin. **SP-GalvB**

As when a child on some long winter's night. *sometimes at.* to Charles Lamb. Samuel Taylor Coleridge. *Fr.* Effusions. **CP-ColeS**

As when a lofty pile is raised. To Stella, Who Collected and Transcribed His Poems. Jonathan Swift. **CP-SwifJ**

As When a Man, *fr. 1832 vers. of* A Dream of Fair Women; *subsequently deleted.* Tennyson. **ChER** *Fr.* A Dream of Fair Women. **CP-TennA**

As when a ruined face. Grudging Respect. Donald Davie. **CP-DavDo**

As when a Scout / Through dark and desart wayes with peril gone. New Worlds. John Milton. *Fr.* Book III. *Fr.* Paradise Lost. **CP-MiltJ**

As when a ship, that flyes faire under saile. Edmund Spenser. **FHYEP** *Fr.* The Faerie Queene. **CP-Spens**

As, when a storm hath ceased, the birds regain. Recovery. William Wordsworth. *Fr.* Ecclesiastical Sonnets. **CP-WorW2**

As when a tree's cut down the secret root. Prologue to The Tempest [*or* The Enchanted Island]. John Dryden. **SP-DrydJ**

As when far off the warbled strains are heard. La Fayette. Samuel Taylor Coleridge. **EnRP** *Fr.* Effusions. **CP-ColeS**

As when of old some orator renowed. John Milton. **ChIV-1** *Fr.* Book IX. **FHYEP; NAEL-1; NAWM-1; NoP; OAEL-1** *Fr.* Paradise Lost. **CP-MiltJ**

As when of old, some sorceress threw. A Simile. Jonathan Swift. **CP-SwifJ**

As when rooting in a bin. Dick, a Maggot. Jonathan Swift. **CP-SwifJ**

As when someone / You haven't noticed before. Position without a Magnitude. Charles Simic. **SP-SimiC**

As when that Hero, who in each Campaign. A Prologue to a Play for Mr. Dennis's Benefit, in 1733, when He Was Old, Blind, and in Great Distress, a Little before His Death. Alexander Pope. **CP-PopeA**

As when the deluge first began to fall. Ode to the Athenian Society. Jonathan Swift. **CP-SwifJ**

As when the gannet goes deep down. To H. M. Howard Nemerov. **CP-NemeH**

As when the hunt by holt and field. After Reading "Antony and Cleopatra." Robert Louis Stevenson. **CP-StevR**

As When the Mystic. Robert Ranke Graves. **CP-GravR**

As when the new or full moon urges. The Moon and the Waves. Samuel Taylor Coleridge. **CP-ColeS**

As, when the squire and tinker, Wood. Prometheus. Jonathan Swift. **CP-SwifJ**

As when, upon the smooth pacific deep. William Wordsworth. **CP-WorW1**

As white hairs in a silver fox's skin. Schwarzwald. Ernest Hemingway. **CP-HemiE**

As white's the blossom on the rise. The Love-sick Lass. "Hugh MacDiarmid." **SP-MacDH**

As willing lid o'er weary eye. Emily Dickinson. **CP-DickE**

As wishing all about us sweet. On St. Winefred. Gerard Manley Hopkins. **CP-HopkG**

As with a Simple Gesture of the Fingers. Gilbert Sorrentino. **SP-SorrG**

As with heaped bees at hiving time. Robert Louis Stevenson. **NOBVV** *Fr.* Rivers and winds among the twisted hills. **CP-StevR**

As with the dapper terns, or that sole cloud. Trolling for Blues. Richard Wilbur. **CP-WilbR**

As with the Stream our voyage we pursue. Papal Abuses. William Wordsworth. *Fr.* Ecclesiastical Sonnets. **CP-WorW2**

As with torches we go, at wild Christmas. Geoffrey Hill. *Fr.* Funeral Music. **CP-HillG**

As would any sound make. Canzone. Robert Creeley. **CP-CreeR**

As Wulfstan said on another occasion. Speech for the Repeal of the McCarran Act. Richard Wilbur. **CP-WilbR**

As yet a stranger to the gentle fires. John Milton. *See* Elegy 7: "Not yet did I know your laws, enticing Amathusia."

As yet my cheeks were not dry with flowing tears. On the Death of the Bishop of Ely. John Milton, *tr. fr. Latin by* John T. Shawcross. **CP-MiltJ**

As yet this playhouse has no memories. Lines on the Opening of the Belgrade Theatre. John Hewitt. **CP-HewiJ**

As yoked to her by absence as by prescence. Marilyn Hacker. **SP-HackM** *Fr.* Taking Notice.

As you all know, tonight is the night of the full. 12 O'Clock News. Elizabeth Bishop. **CP-BishE**

As You Came from the Holy Land [of Walsingham]. *Unknown, sometimes at. to* Sir Walter Ralegh. **CP-RaleW**

As You Came from the Holy Land. John Ashbery. **SP-AshbJ**

As You Come. Robert Creeley. **CP-CreeR**

As you enter the room a door knob. The Burning of Bustin's Island. Jim Carroll. **SP-CarrJ**

As you face the evening. To a Man Going Blind. John Haines. **SP-HainJ**

As you know, I have not lost you. Orpheus to Eurydice. Frederick Morgan. **SP-MorgF**

As you lay in sleep. Cartography. Louise Bogan. **CP-BogaL**

As You Leave Me. Etheridge Knight. **SP-KnigE**

As You Like It. John Hewitt. **CP-HewiJ**

As you or I, but at least he fights hard to get. Hayden Carruth. *Fr.* The Sleeping Beauty. **CP-CarHL**

As you plaited the harvest bow. The Harvest Bow. Seamus Heaney. **SP-HeanS**

As you read, a white bear leisurely. To the Reader. Denise Levertov. **CP-LeveD**

As you see the large. Jack-Knife. Charles Bukowski. **SP-BukC3**

As you would know, having lived in trouble here at my side. A Plate of Steaming Fish. Kenneth Patchen. **CP-PatcK**

As Zeus sent Hermes / to draw Agenor's cattle. Chronicles. Charles Olson. **SP-OlsoC** *Fr.* The Maximus Poems.

Asbestos. Edwin Rolfe. **CP-RolfE**

Ascend through declension. Geoffrey Hill. *Fr.* Psalms of Assize. **CP-HillG**

Ascending over Ohio. Lawrence Ferlinghetti. **SP-FerlL**

Ascending pile, The. Mulciber. John Milton. **NOSC** *Fr.* Book I. **FHYEP; NAEL-1; OAEL-1; OxAEP-1** *Fr.* Paradise Lost. **CP-MiltJ**

Ascension [*or* Accention]. John Donne. *Fr.* La Corona. **ChIV-2; ESCV; OBS; Son** *Fr.* Holy Sonnets. **CP-DonnJ**

Ascension. Samuel Beckett. **CP-BeckS**

Ascension Day. Christina Georgina Rossetti. **CP-RosC2**

Ascension Day, 1964. Wystan Hugh Auden. **CP-AudeW**

Ascension Eve. Christina Georgina Rossetti. **CP-RosC2**

Ascension has. Emily Dickinson. **SP-DickE**

Ascension of Our Lord Jesus Christ, The. Christopher Smart. **NOCV** *Fr.* Hymns and Spiritual Songs for the Fasts and Festivals of the Church of England. **SP-SmarC**

Ascent of Species. John Milton. **NOSC** *Fr.* Book V. *Fr.* Paradise Lost. **CP-MiltJ**

Ascent to the Sierras. Robinson Jeffers. **CP-JefR1**

Asclepiades the Miser was horrified. Lucilius, *tr. fr. Greek by* Peter Porter. (Miser and the Mouse, The.) **SP-SmarC,** *tr. by* Christopher Smart; ("To a Mouse says a Miser my dear Mr Mouse.") **SP-SmarC,** *tr. by* Christopher Smart;

Ash falls on the roof. Mother. Erica Jong. **SP-JongE**

Ash on an old man's sleeve. Thomas Stearns Eliot. **FaBoTw** *Fr.* Little Gidding. **FaBoMo; FaBoPV; FaBoTw; GTBS-6; GTBS-P; MoP; NAEL-2; NAWM-2; NOBA; NOBE; NoAM; OAEL-2; OXAEP-2; OxBTC; PeECV; PrIm; TAP; TFi** *Fr.* Four Quartets. **CP-ElioT**

Ash tree hides her face, The. The Dark Fiddler. Wystan Hugh Auden. **CP-AudWJ**

Ash Wednesday [*or* Ash-Wednesday]. Thomas Stearns Eliot. **CP-ElioT** "Although I do not hope to turn again." "At the first turning of the second stair." **NOBA** "Blessed sister, holy mother, spirit of the fountain." **EaPr** "If the lost word is lost, if the spent word is spent." **UV**

Ash Wednesday. Thomas Merton. **CP-MertT; SP-MertT**

Ash Wednesday. Christina Georgina Rossetti. **CP-RosC2**

Ash Wednesday. Christina Georgina Rossetti. **CP-RosC3**

Ash Wednesday. First Day of Lent. Christopher Smart. *Fr.* Hymns and Spiritual Songs for the Fasts and Festivals of the Church of England. **SP-SmarC**

Ashamed to be the darling of his grief. Wystan Hugh Auden. *Fr.* The Quest. **CP-AudeW**

Ashboughs. Gerard Manley Hopkins. **CP-HopkG**

Ashen man on ashen cliff above the salt halloo. Statue against a Clear Sky. Wallace Stevens. **EyDe** *Fr.* New England Verses. **CP-StevW**

Ashes. Charles Bukowski. **SP-BukC1**

Ashes. Philip Levine. **SP-LeviP**

Ashes Ashes We All Fall Down. Charles Kenneth Williams. **CP-WillC**

Ashes denote that Fire was. Emily Dickinson. **CP-DickE**

Ashes in the Wind. John Hewitt. **CP-HewiJ**

Ashes of Life. Edna St. Vincent Millay. **CP-MillE**

Ashes of paper, ashes of a world. The Annunciation. Thomas Merton. **CP-MertT**

Ashes of rose. Summer Evening. Marsden Hartley. **CP-HartM**

Ashes of Soldiers. Walt Whitman. **CP-WhitW**

Ashes of Soldiers: Epigraph. Walt Whitman. **CP-WhitW**

Ashes on a Saturday Afternoon. Frank O'Hara. **SP-OharF**

Ashes, the dissonance of unicorns: the edges. Name-Burning. Stephen Dobyns. **SP-DobyS**

Ashes to ashes, dust to dust. Mortality. Paul Laurence Dunbar. **CP-DunbP**

Ashtray. Louis Zukofsky. **CP-ZukLS**

Ashtree on fire, An. Poem for Lara, 10. Michael Hartnett. **SP-HarMi**

Ashurbanipal. Or the stern-view. For Cy Twombly Faced with His First Chicago & N.Y. Shows. Charles Olson. **CP-OlsoC**

Ashurnatsirpal III. Carl Sandburg. **CP-SandC**

Ashville. Richard Hugo. **CP-HugoR**

Asian Peace Offers Rejected without Publication. Robert Bly. **SP-BlyR**

Aside to a Children's Tale. Roy Fisher. **SP-FishR**

Aside to Husbands. Ogden Nash. **CP-NashO**

Asides on the Oboe. Wallace Stevens. **CP-StevW**

Ask Daddy, He Won't Know. Ogden Nash. **CP-NashO**

Ask, is Love divine. George Meredith. **CP-MerG1**

Ask Me. William Stafford. **SP-StafW**

Ask me no more but love. Night Song. John Gould Fletcher. **SP-FletJ**

Ask me no more, for fear I should reply. Alfred Edward Housman. **CP-HousA**

Ask me no more: the moon may draw the sea. Tennyson. **CBLP; GBL; ImPo; LiTB; MeMBP; NAEL-2; OBNC; PoEL-5; TrGrPo** *Fr.* The Princess. **CP-TennA**

Ask[e] Me No More Where Jove Bestow[e]s. Thomas Carew.

(Song, [A]: "Ask[e] me no more where Jove bestows.") **CP-CareT**

Ask Me Why. The Beatles. **CP-Beatl**

Ask[e] me why I send you here. The Primrose. Robert Herrick. **CP-HerrR**

Ask not the cause why sullen Spring. Song to a Fair Young Lady, Going Out of the Town in the Spring. John Dryden. **SP-DrydJ**

Ask not the pallid stranger's woe. Despair. Percy Bysshe Shelley. *Fr.* Original Poetry by Victor and Cazire. **CP-ShelP**

Ask not to know this man. If fame should speak. A Little Shrub Growing By. Ben Jonson. **CP-JonsB**

Ask not why hearts turn magazines of passions. A Funeral Elegy Upon that Pattern and Patron of Virtue. John Norton. **CP-BradA**

Ask of all-healing, all consoling thought. Nicolas-Sébastien Roch Chamfort, *tr. fr. French by* Samuel Beckett. **CP-BeckS**

Ask of the sun. Louis Zukofsky. *Fr.* 29 Poems. **CP-ZukLS**

Ask the Roses. Philip Levine. **SP-LeviP**

Ask what is human life—the sage replies. Hope. William Cowper. **CP-CowpW**

Ask why God made the GEM so small. On Being Asked Why God Had Made Miss D——— So Little and Mrs A——— So Big. Robert Burns. **CP-BurnR**

Ask you what provocation I have had? Alexander Pope. **ECEV; EPCY; NOBE; NOEC; OBSV** *Fr.* Epilogue to the Satires, in Two Dialogues. **CP-PopeA**

   (Art of Satire, The.) **ECEV**

   (Defence of Satire.) **NOEC**

   (Power of Ridicule, The.) **NOBE**

Ask'd in the Country, what I did, I said. Festus Rufius Avienus, *tr. fr. Latin by* Richard Lovelace. **CP-LoveR**

Aske me what hunger is, and Ile reply. Hunger. Robert Herrick. **CP-HerrR**

Aske me, why I do not sing. On Himselfe. Robert Herrick. **CP-HerrR**

Asked a girl what she wanted to be. Drive My Car. John Lennon *and* Paul McCartney. **CP-Beatl**

Asked by a reporter out of questions. On Passion As a Literary Tradition. John Ciardi. **SP-CiarJ**

Askest, "How long thou shalt stay." The Visit. Ralph Waldo Emerson. **CP-EmerR**

Asking is / Dream of deign, *sels.* Kenneth Rexroth. *Fr.* Asking is / Dream of deign. **CP-RexKL** *Fr.* A Prolegomenon to a Theodicy.

Asking is / Dream of deign. Kenneth Rexroth. **CP-RexKL** *Fr.* A Prolegomenon to a Theodicy.

   "Asking is / Dream of deign."

Asking what, asking what?—all a boy's afternoon. Debate: Question, Quarry, Dream. Robert Penn Warren. **SP-WarrR**

Asks anyone—"Where's a tag for steps?" Epps. Robert Browning. **CP-BroR2**

Asleep. Daniel Gerard Hoffman. **SP-HoffD**

Asleep. Wilfred Owen. **CP-OwenW**

Asleep and Awake. Muriel Rukeyser. **CP-RukeM**

Asleep, breathing like an enormous child. Sentry. Edwin Rolfe. **CP-RolfE**

Asleep on the raft and forced far out to sea. The Raft. Robert Ranke Graves. **CP-GravR**

Asleep or waking is it? for her neck. Laus Veneris. Algernon Charles Swinburne. **SP-SwinA**

Asmodaean feat be mine, The. Ralph Waldo Emerson. **CP-EmerR**

Asmodeus. Geoffrey Hill. *See* They, after the slow building of the house.

Asp, The. Ogden Nash. **CP-NashO**

Asparagus. Jonathan Swift. *Fr.* Verses Made for the Women Who Cry Apples, etc. **CP-SwifJ**

Aspasia, yet pursue the sacred Theme. Samuel Johnson. **CP-JohnS** *Fr.* Irene.

Aspect of the Air, An. John Ciardi. **SP-CiarJ**

Aspects of Christianity in America—Concluded—American Episcopacy. William Wordsworth. *Fr.* Ecclesiastical Sonnets. **CP-WorW2**

   (Pilgrim Fathers, The.) **PAH**

Aspects of Christianity in America—Continued. William Wordsworth. *Fr.* Ecclesiastical Sonnets. **CP-WorW2**

   (Pilgrim Fathers, The.) **AiP; PAH**

Aspects of Christianity in America—the Pilgrim Fathers. William Wordsworth. *Fr.* Ecclesiastical Sonnets. **CP-WorW2**

   (Pilgrim Fathers, The.) **AiP; PAH**

Aspen and the Stream, The. Richard Wilbur. **CP-WilbR**

Asperin tree outside told me to say, The. Malcolm Lowry. **CP-LowrM**

Asphodel, An. Allen Ginsberg. **CP-GinsA**

Asphodel, That Greeny Flower. William Carlos Williams. **CP-WilW2**

   "Approaching death." **FaBoMo**

   "Of asphodel, that greeny flower." **CMoP; PP**

Aspirations of the Soul after God. Jeanne Marie Bouvier de la Motte-Guyon, *tr. fr. French by* William Cowper. **CP-CowpW**

Ass[e], The. Robert Herrick. **CP-HerrR**

Ass, The. David Herbert Lawrence. **CP-LawrD**

Ass, The. Stevie Smith. **CP-SmitS**

Ass But No Class. Charles Bukowski. **SP-BukC3**

Ass-eared cross-gartered haloed crowned. Homo Gratia Artis. Isabella Gardner. **CP-GardI**

Ass of Balaam, The. George Meredith. **CP-MerG2**

Assassin, The. Richard Eberhart. **CP-EberR**

Assassin, The. Anne Sexton. **CP-SextA**

Assassin. Charles Tomlinson. **CP-TomlC**

Assassination Raga. Lawrence Ferlinghetti. **SP-FerlL**

Assault. Edna St. Vincent Millay. **CP-MillE**

Assault Convoy, The. Alun Lewis. **CP-LewiA**

Asse Eating the Æneids, The. Quintus Catulus, *tr. fr. Latin by* Richard Lovelace. **CP-LoveR**

Assembling a Street. Brendan Galvin. **SP-GalvB**

Assembly of the Achaians. Homer, *tr. by* George Meredith. **CP-MerG2** *Fr.* The Iliad.

Asses' Out-House, The. Marsden Hartley. **CP-HartM**

Assidue ridet Lycius Clytha ut sua dormit. *acc. by English translation.* Thomas Campion. **CP-CampT**

Assignation, The. Walter de la Mare. **CP-DeLaW**

Assignation, The. James Wright. **CP-WrigJ**

Assignment. Hayden Carruth. **CP-CarHS**

Assis sur la terrasse Café Saint-Séverin. L'Occupation Obsédée. Lawrence Ferlinghetti. **SP-FerlL**

Assisi Fragments, The. Geoffrey Hill. **CP-HillG**

Associate Professor Delivers an Exhortation to His Failing Students, The. Miller Williams. **SP-WillM**

Assorted Chocolates. Ogden Nash. **CP-NashO**

Ass's hoof alone can hold, An. On Burning a Dull Poem. Jonathan Swift. **CP-SwifJ**

Assume, in a bird's eye, the world as a dainty bulge. Two Poems, with Birds. Mona Van Duyn. **SP-VanDM**

Assuming Fine Feathers, W. D. Takes Flight. William DeWitt Snodgrass. **SP-SnodW**

Assuming Our Dominance. Erica Jong. **SP-JongE**

Assuming the Burden. David Herbert Lawrence. **CP-LawrD**

Assuming the Soul Is a Bitch. Charles Olson. **CP-OlsoC**

Assumption of Our Lady, The. Robert Southwell. **CP-SoutR**

Assurance. Robert Frost. **CP-FrosR**

Assurance. George Herbert. **CP-HerbG**

Assurances. Walt Whitman. **CP-WhitW**

Assured by many. Walter Scott. James Schuyler. **CP-SchuJ**

Assured of worthiness we do not dread. Internal Harmony. George Meredith. **CP-MerG1**

Assuredly a lively scene. Arthur Hugh Clough. **SP-ClouA** *Fr.* Dipsychus [and the Spirit].

Assyrian came down like the wolf on the fold, The. The Destruction of Sennacherib. Byron. **CP-Byron**

Aster. Louis Zukofsky. **CP-ZukLS**

Aster, a farewell-summer flower, stays long in the last fall weeks, An. Carl Sandburg. **CP-SandC** *Fr.* The People, Yes. **CP-SandC**

Aster Flower, The. John Gould Fletcher. **SP-FletJ**

Asterisk / Says look below, as a star, The. Games One. Richard Wilbur. **CP-WilbR**

Asthmatic, The, *see also* Commentary—The Asthmatic. Leonard Cohen. **CP-CoheL**

Astigmatic Naturalist, The. Ogden Nash. **CP-NashO**

   Caterpillar, The.

   Hamster, The.

   Platypus, The.

   Toucan, The.

Astigmatism breaks. Hayden Carruth. *Fr.* North Winter. **CP-CarHL**

Astonished Heart, The. Lawrence Ferlinghetti. **SP-FerlL**

Astonished Heaven looked on when man was made. Her Seed; It Shall Bruise Thy Head. Christina Georgina Rossetti. **CP-RosC2**

Astounding subjects are the only ones, the. Emily Dickinson. **SP-DickE**

Astræa. Ralph Waldo Emerson. **CP-EmerR**

Astræa. John Greenleaf Whittier. **CP-WhitJ**

Astræa at the Capitol. John Greenleaf Whittier. **CP-WhitJ**

Astride the boney jointed ridge. Still Life. William Carlos Williams. **CP-WilW2**

Astride the chiffonier of post-oral conductions. Charles Henri Ford. **SP-FordC**

Astrolabes and lexicons. Ballad. George Oppen. **CP-OppeG**

Astrologers' own eyes are set, The. First Song. Andrew Marvell. *Fr.* Two Songs at the Marriage of the Lord Fauconberg and the Lady Mary Cromwell. **CP-MarvA**

Astrologer's Song, An. Rudyard Kipling. **CP-KiplR**

Astrometaphysical. Robert Frost. **CP-FrosR**

Astronauts. Robert Earl Hayden. **CP-HaydR**

Astronomical Changes. David Herbert Lawrence. **CP-LawrD**

Astronomies and slangs to find you, dear. John Berryman. *Fr.* Sonnets to Chris. **CP-BerrJ**

Astronomy. Alfred Edward Housman. **CP-HousA**

Astronomy. James McAuley. **SP-McAuJ**

Astrophel. Edmund Spenser. **CP-Spens**

Astrophel. Edmund Spenser. *Fr.* Astrophel. **CP-Spens**

Another of the Same.

Astrophel.

Elegie, or Friends Passion, for His Astrophill, An.

Epitaph upon the Right Honourable Sir Phillip Sidney, Knight: Lord Governor of Flushing, An.

Mourning Muse of Thestylis, The.

Pastorall Aeglogue upon the Death of Sir Phillip Sidney, Knight, etc, A.

"Such skill, matcht with such courage as he had." **OBWP**

Astrophil and Stella, *often wr. titled* Astrophel and Stella. Sir Philip Sidney. **SP-SidnP**

"Doubt you to whom my Muse these notes intendeth [*or* entendeth]." **EIL; HBV 1-2; OBSC; OxAEP-1; WHA**

(First Song.) **OxAEP-1**

(To Stella.) **EIL; WHA**

Eighth Song. **NoSic; OAEP; OBSC**

Eleventh Song. **NoSic; OxAEP-1**

(Underneath My Window.) **SeCePo**

(Voices at the Window.) **NOBE; OBEV; PoPle**

(Who Is It That This Dark Night.) **EIL; EnRePo; NAEL-1; OBSC; PoE; PoEL-1; SCGP; TEP**

Fifth Song.

Fourth Song. **EIL; EnRePo; GBL; HAP; InvP; NAEL-1; NoP; NoSic; OBSC; UnTE**

I: "Loving in truth, and fain[e] in verse my love to show." **AWP; BLPL; CABA; EBEV; EPCY; FaBoEn; GBL; GGP; HAP; HBV; ImPo; InPS; LiTB; MasP; NAEL-1; NoP; NoSic; OAEL-1; OAEP; OBSC; OXAEP-1; PP; PoE; Poetr; SCGP; SeCePo; SeCeV; Son; TEP; TFi; TrGrPo; TreFT**

Ninth Song. **NoSic**

Sonet 84: "Highway, since you my chief Parnassus be." **EIL; EnRePo; OAEP; OBSC; SCGP**

(Highway, The.) **LiTB; OBEV; OXAEP-1**

Sonnet 10: "Reason, in faith thou art well served, that still." **NAEL-1**

Sonnet 100: "O tears, no tears, but rain from beauty's skies." **Son**

Sonnet 101: "Stella is sick, and in that sick-bed lies."

Sonnet 102: "Where be those roses gone, which sweetened so our eyes?"

Sonnet 103: "O happy Thames, that didst my Stella bear." **OXAEP-1**

Sonnet 104: "Envious wits, what hath been mine offence." **PoE; Son**

Sonnet 105: "Unhappy sight, and hath she vanished by."

Sonnet 106: "O absent presence, Stella is not here."

Sonnet 107: "Stella, since thou so right a Princess art." **HBV; NoP; OXAEP-1**

Sonnet 108: "When sorrow (using mine own fire's might)."

Sonnet 11: "In truth, O Love, with what a boyish kind." **CBLP; EIL; InvP; PoE**

Sonnet 12: "Cupid, because thou shin'st in Stella's eyes."

Sonnet 13: "Phoebus was judge between Jove, Mars, and Love."

Sonnet 14: "Alas, have I not pain enough, my friend." **NoP; NoSic; OAEL-1**

Sonnet 15: "You that do search for every purling spring." **NAEL-1; NoSic; OAEL-1; OBSC; OXAEP-1; Son**

Sonnet 16: "In nature apt to like when I did see." **NAEL-1**

Sonnet 17: "His mother dear Cupid offended late."

Sonnet 18: "With what sharp checks I in myself am shent." **NAEL-1; NoSic**

Sonnet 19: "On Cupid's bow how are my heart-strings bent." **NoSic**

Sonnet 2: "Not at [the] first sight, nor with a dribbed shot." **NAEL-1; OAEL-1**

Sonnet 20: "Fly, fly, my friends, I have my death-wound, fly." **NoSic; OAEL-1; TEP**

Sonnet 21: "Your words my friend (right healthful caustics) blame." **CABA; NAEL-1; NoSic; PoE; TEP**

Sonnet 22: "In highest way of heav'n the sun did ride." **OBSC; Son**

Sonnet 23: "Curious wits,, seeing dull pensiveness, The."

Sonnet 24: "Rich fools there be, whose base and filthy heart."

Sonnet 25: "Wisest scholar of the wight most wise, The." **NoP; OAEL-1**

Sonnet 26: "Though dusty wits dare scorn astrology." **OAEL-1; Son**

Sonnet 27: "Because I oft, in dark abstracted guise." **NoSic**

Sonnet 28: "You that with allegory's curious frame." **InPK; NoSic; OAEL-1**

Sonnet 29: "Like some weak lords, neighboured by mighty kings."

Sonnet 3: "Let dainty wits cry on the sisters nine." **NoSic; OAEL-1; OBSC; Son**

Sonnet 30: "Whether the Turkish new moon minded be." **NoSic; PoE**

Sonnet 31: "With how sad steps, O Moon, thou climb'st the skies." **AWP; BoLoP; CH; ChTr; EIL; EnLoPo; EnRePo; FaBoEn; GBL; HAP; HBV; HeIL; HeIP; InPK; InPS; InvP; MAT; MOON; NAEL-1; NoP; NoSic; OAEP; OBSC; OXAEP-1; PBMP; PPP; PPoe; PoE; PoEL-1; PoRA; SCGP; SeCeV; Son; TEP; TFi; TRP; TrGrPo; WHA; WeW**

(His Lady's Cruelty.) **OBEV**

(Languishing Moon, The.) **BoNaP**

(O the Sad Moon.) **NOBE**

Sonnet 32: "Morpheus, the lively son of deadly sleep."

Sonnet 33: "I might, unhappy word, O me, I might." **OAEL-1; OBSC**

Sonnet 34: "Come, let me write. 'And to what end?' To ease."

Sonnet 35: "What may words say, or what may words not say."

Sonnet 36: "Stella, whence doth this new assault arise."

Sonnet 37: "My mouth doth water, and my breast doth swell." **NAEL-1; Son**

Sonnet 38: "This night, while sleep begins with heavy wings."

Sonnet 39: "Come sleep, O sleep, the certain knot of peace." **CABA; EIL; EnRePo; HBV; NAEL-1; NIP; NoP; NoSic; OAEP; OBSC; OXAEP-1; PPP; PoE; PoRA; SCGP; SCV; Son; TEP; TFi; TrGrPo; TreFS; WHA**

(Sleep.) **LoBV; OBEV**

(To Sleep.) **NOBE**

Sonnet 4: "Virtue, alas, now let me take some rest."

Sonnet 40: "As good to write as for to lie and groan." **NoSic**

Sonnet 41: "Having this day my horse, my hand, my lance." **EnRePo; HAP; NAEL-1; OAEP; OBSC; PoE; Son**

Sonnet 42: "O eyes, which do the spheres of beauty move."

Sonnet 43: "Fair eyes, sweet lips, dear heart, that foolish I."

Sonnet 44: "My words I know do well set forth my mind."

Sonnet 45: "Stella oft sees the very face of woe." **InPS; NAEL-1; NoSic; PoE**

Sonnet 46: "I cursed thee oft, I pity now thy case."

Sonnet 47: "What, have I thus betrayed my liberty?" **GBL; NAEL-1; NIP; NoP; PoEL-1**

(Yoke of Tyranny, The.) **TrGrPo**

Sonnet 48: "Soul's joy, bend not those morning stars from me." **NoP**

Sonnet 49: "I on my horse, and Love on me doth try." **NAEL-1; NoP; OAEL-1; PoE**

Sonnet 5: "It is most true that eyes are formed to serve." **NAEL-1; NoSic; OAEL-1; OBSC; Son**

Sonnet 50: "Stella, the fullness of my thoughts of thee."

Sonnet 51: "Pardon mine ears; both I and they do pray."

Sonnet 52: "Strife is grown between Virtue and Love, A." **NAEL-1; NoP**

Sonnet 53: "In martial sports I had my cunning tried." **NAEL-1; NoSic**

Sonnet 54: "Because I breathe not love to every one." **ImGa; InPS; NoSic; OAEP; OBSC; TrGrPo**

Sonnet 55: "Muses, I oft invoked your holy aid."

Sonnet 56: "Fie, school of Patience, fie; your lesson is." **NAEL-1**

Sonnet 57: "Woe, having made with many fights his own."

Sonnet 58: "Doubt there hath been, when with his golden chain."

Sonnet 59: "Dear, why make you more of a dog than me?" **GBL; OAEP; PrIm**

Sonnet 6: "Some lovers speak, when that their Muses entertain." **NAEL-1; NoSic; Son**

Sonnet 60: "When my good angel guides me to the place."

Sonnet 61: "Oft with true sighs, oft with uncalled tears." **NAEL-1**

Sonnet 62: "Late tired with woe, e'en ready for to pine."

Sonnet 63: "O grammar rules, O now your virtues show."

(Grammar-Rules.) **FaBoUs**

Sonnet 64: "No more, my dear, no more these counsels try." **HBV 1-2; OBSC; SCGP**

Sonnet 65: "Love, by sure proof I may call thee unkind." **Son**

Sonnet 66: "And do I see some cause a hope to feed."

Sonnet 67: "Hope, art thou true, or dost thou flatter me?"

Sonnet 68: "Stella, the only planet of my light." **OBSC**

Sonnet 69: "O joy, too high for my low style to show." **NAEL-1; OXAEP-1; TrGrPo**

Sonnet 7: "When Nature made her chief work, Stella's eyes." **CABA; NAEL-1; NIP; Son**

Sonnet 70: "My Muse may well grudge at my heav'nly joy."

Sonnet 71: "Who will in fairest book of Nature know." **CABA; InPS; NAEL-1; NoP; NoSic; OAEL-1; PoE; Poetr**

Sonnet 72: "Desire, though thou my old companion art." **NAEL-1**

Sonnet 74: "I never drank of Aganippe well." **CABA; EnRePo; HeIP; NAEL-1; NoSic; OBSC; Son**

Sonnet 74: "Love still a boy, and oft a wanton is." **HBV; OAEP; Son**

Sonnet 75: "Of all the kings that ever here did reign." **NoSic**

Sonnet 76: "She comes, and straight therewith her shining twins do move."

Sonnet 77: "Those looks, whose beams be joy, whose motion is delight."

Sonnet 78: "O how the pleasant airs of true love be."

Sonnet 79: "Sweet kiss, thy sweets I fain would sweetly indite."

(Stella's Kiss.) **CBCK; NoSic**

Sonnet 8: "Love, born in Greece, of late fled from his native place."

Sonnet 80: "Sweet swelling lip, well mayst thou swell in pride."

Sonnet 81: "O kiss, which dost those ruddy gems impart." **NAEL-1; Son**

Sonnet 82: "Nymph of the garden where all beauties be." **InvP; PoE**

Sonnet 83: "Good brother Philip, I have borne you long." **PBBP**

Sonnet 85: "I see the house; my heart thyself contain."

Sonnet 86: "Alas, whence came this change of looks? If I."

Sonnet 87: "When I was forced from Stella ever dear." **NAEL-1**

Sonnet 88: "Out, traitor absence: dar'st thou counsel me."

Sonnet 89: "Now that of absence the most irksome night." **NAEL-1**

Sonnet 9: "Queen Virtue's court, which some call Stella's face." **NAEL-1**

Sonnet 90: "Stella, think not that I by verse seek fame." **NoSic; OBSC**

Sonnet 91: "Stella, while now by honour's cruel might." **NAEL-1; PoE**

Sonnet 92: "Be your words made (good sir) of Indian ware." **NoSic**

Sonnet 93: "O fate, O fault, O curse, child of my bliss."

Sonnet 94: "Grief, find the words, for thou hast made my brain."

Sonnet 95: "Yet sighs, dear sighs, indeed true friends you are."

Sonnet 96: "Thought, with good cause thou lik'st so well the night."

Sonnet 97: "Dian, that fain would cheer her friend the Night."

Sonnet 98: "Ah bed, the field where joy's peace some do see." **EnLoPo**

Sonnet 99: "When far-spent night persuades each mortal eye." **CABA; NoSic; OBSC; PoE; Son**

Second Song. **NoSic**

Seventh Song.

Sixth Song. **OBSC**

Tenth Song.

(O Dear Life, When Shall It Be?) **EnRePo**

Third Song. **PoEL-1**

Asylum, The. Hayden Carruth. **CP-CarHL**

"But if the wind should fall and silence spread."

"But once winds lightened, freshening fair from the West."

"Gnarled wind blurs the light, my hurt and another's."

"I came to this place one November day."

"I hurt. Hungrier flowers try my rank ground."

"It was our city too. Chrome and glass."

"Persimmon wind, lost names raining. Thwart."

"Then ultimately asylum is the soul."

"This nation was asylum when we came."

"What does this wind say, plunging upon the land."

"Wind is a stealth of memory. Footsteps fall."

"Winds; words of the wind; rumor of great walls pierced." **SM**

Asylum Song. Muriel Rukeyser. **CP-RukeM**

Asylum under my tread all this day. Samuel Beckett. **CP-BeckS** *Fr.* Echo's Bones.

Asymptotes. Charles Olson. **CP-OlsoC**

At a Bach Concert. Adrienne Rich. **CP-RicAE; SP-RicA2**

At a Bridal. Thomas Hardy. **CP-HardT**

At a bygone Western country fair. At a Country Fair. Thomas Hardy. **CP-HardT**

At a Calvary near the Ancre. Wilfred Owen. **CP-OwenW**

At a certain point every morning. Mirror, Mirror. Jenny Joseph. **SP-JoseJ**

At a Country Fair. Thomas Hardy. **CP-HardT**

At a Country Funeral. Wendell Berry. **CP-BerrW**

At a Country Hotel. Howard Nemerov. **CP-NemeH**

At a Czech Tomb in Tuam. James Liddy. **CP-LiddJ**

At a Deathbed in the Year Two Thousand. Adrienne Rich. **CP-RicAE**

At a Fashionable Dinner. Thomas Hardy. **CP-HardT**

At a Friend's Birthday Party in the Garden at Night. Stephen Berg. **SP-BergS**

At a Glance. Charles Tomlinson. **CP-TomlC**

At a Hasty Wedding. Thomas Hardy. **CP-HardT**

At a House in Hampstead. Thomas Hardy. **CP-HardT**

At a little pond in the woods. William Stafford. *Fr.* Stories to Live in the World With. **SP-StafW**

At a lonely cross where bye-roads met. The Man Who Forgot. Thomas Hardy. **CP-HardT**

At a Loose End. David Herbert Lawrence. **CP-LawrD**

(Dissolute.) **CP-LawrD**

At a Lunar Eclipse. Thomas Hardy. **CP-HardT**

At a March against the Vietnam War. Robert Bly. **SP-BlyR**

At a moment when all the discordant voices of modern society attempt to exorcize the vertigo of man. A Letter to Pablo Antonio Cuadra Concerning Giants. Thomas Merton. **CP-MertT**

At a Parting. Countee Cullen. **CP-CullC**

At a Party. Louise Bogan. **CP-BogaL**

At a Pause in a Country Dance. Thomas Hardy. **CP-HardT**

At a Rehearsal of One of J.M.B.'s Plays. Thomas Hardy. **CP-HardT**

At a Seaside Town in 1869. Thomas Hardy. **CP-HardT**

At a Solemn Music[k]. John Milton. **CP-MiltJ**

"Blest pair of Sirens, pledges of Heaven's joy." **UnS**

At a Summer Hotel. Isabella Gardner. **CP-GardI**

At a VA Hospital in the Middle of the United States of America: An Act in a Play. Etheridge Knight. **SP-KnigE**

At a Vacation Exercise [in the Col[l]e[d]ge [, Part Latin, Part English]]. John Milton. **CP-MiltJ**

"Hail native language, that by sinews weak." **JCP; OBS; PP**

At a Watering-Place. Thomas Hardy. **CMoP** *Fr.* Satires of Circumstance in Fifteen Glimpses. **CP-HardT**

At a Window. Carl Sandburg. **CP-SandC**

At a wolf's wild dugs. Blood. Daniel Gerard Hoffman. **SP-HoffD**

At about 8.15 a.m. / a police reservist called. At the Newsagent's. John Hewitt. **CP-HewiJ**

At Albano. William Wordsworth. *Fr.* Memorials of a Tour in Italy, 1837. **CP-WorW2**

At Algeciras—a Meditation upon Death. William Butler Yeats. **CP-YeatW**

At all thou frankly throwst, while, *Frank,* thy wife. Epigramme. Thomas Campion. *Fr.* Observations in the Art of English Poesie. **CP-CampT**

At an autumn evening bonfire. First Sonata for Karlen Paula. Carl Sandburg. **CP-SandC**

At an Inn. Thomas Hardy. **CP-HardT**

At an Intersection. Thom Gunn. **CP-GunnT**

At Ann's place, even before you arrive. Available Light. Al Young. **CP-YounA**

At another year / I would not boggle. Birthday on the Beach. Ogden Nash. **CP-NashO**

At Apollinaire's Grave. Allen Ginsberg. **CP-GinsA**

At Applethwaite, near Keswick. William Wordsworth. **CP-WorW1**

At Auden's Grave. Karl Shapiro. **SP-ShapK**

At Baia. Hilda Doolittle. **CP-DoolH**

At Bala-Sala, Isle of Man. William Wordsworth. *Fr.* Poems Composed or Suggested During a Tour, in the Summer of 1833. **CP-WorW2**

At Barstow. Charles Tomlinson. **CP-TomlC**

At Beaulieu. Frank Templeton Prince. **CP-PrinF**

At Best, Poets. Robert Ranke Graves. **CP-GravR**

At Beverly Farms, a portly, uncomfortable boulder. Terminal Days at Beverly Farms. Robert Lowell. **SP-LoweR**

At Blackwater Pond. Mary Oliver. **SP-OlivM**

At blond dawn. Jean Sans Terre Circles the Earth Seven Times. Iwan Goll, *tr. fr. French by* William Carlos Williams. **CP-WilW2**

At Bologna, in Remembrance of the Late Insurrections, 1837. William Wordsworth. **CP-WorW2**

At Bologna, in Remembrance of the Late Insurrections, 1837, Continued: "As leaves are to the tree wheron they grow." William Wordsworth. **CP-WorW2**

At Bologna, in Remembrance of the Late Insurrections, 1837, Continued: "Hard task! exclaim the undisciplined, to lean." William Wordsworth. **CP-WorW2**

At break of dawn. Aubade. Wystan Hugh Auden. *Fr.* Three Posthumous Poems. **CP-AudeW**

At breakfast mother sipped her buttermilk. Stanley Jasspon Kunitz. *Fr.* The Magic Curtain. **CP-KuniS**

At breakfast they are sober, subdued. Grenoble Café. Jean Garrigue. **SP-GarrJ**

At Briggflatts Meetinghouse. Basil Bunting. **CP-BuntB**

At Brownhill Inn. Robert Burns. **CP-BurnR**

At Brownhill we always get dainty good cheer. At Brownhill Inn. Robert Burns. **CP-BurnR**

At busy hearts in vain love's arrows fly. Ovid, *tr. by* Samuel Johnson. **CP-JohnS** *Fr.* Remediae Amoris.

At Candle-Lightin' Time. Paul Laurence Dunbar. **CP-DunbP**

At Casterbridge Fair. Thomas Hardy. **CP-HardT**
  After the Club-Dance.
  After the Fair. **CMoP; HAP; VLP**
  Ballad-Singer, The. **BoLoP; OLR; VLP**
  Former Beauties. **CBLP; FaBoEn; NoAM; OBMV; OBNC**
  Inquiry, The.
  Market-Girl, The.
  Wife Waits, A.
At Castle Boterel. Thomas Hardy. **CP-HardT**
At castle shadowed mouth of the / Doonbeg. James Liddy. *Fr.* Birds. **CP-LiddJ**
At castle shadowed mouth of the. James Liddy. *Fr.* Cliffs. **CP-LiddJ**
At Cedros, thudding the dead sand. Tarpon. Derek Walcott. **CP-WalcD**
At Cheshire Cheese. Paul Laurence Dunbar. **CP-DunbP**
At Chinese Checkers. John Berryman. **CP-BerrJ**
At Christmas, my sisters and I. Stille Nacht, Heilege Nacht. Peter Meinke. **SP-MeinP**
At Christmas time / Men make these little boxes lined with velvet. Puppeteer. Jenny Joseph. **SP-JoseJ**
At court I met it, in clothes brave enough. On Something, That Walks [*or*Walkes] Somewhere. Ben Jonson. **CP-JonsB**
At Cronkhite. Richard Hugo. **CP-HugoR**
At Croton. Hilda Doolittle. **CP-DoolH**
At Darien Bridge. James Dickey. **CP-DickJ**
At Darragh's I. James Schuyler. **CP-SchuJ**
At dawn / on the window sill. Poem on My Son's Birthday. Jim Carroll. **SP-CarrJ**
At Dawn. Charles Tomlinson. **CP-TomlC**
At Dawn. William Carlos Williams. **CP-WilW1**
At dawn a knot of sea-lions lies off the shore. Animals. Robinson Jeffers. **CP-JefR3**
At dawn of morn, ere on the brake. The Enchanted Goblet. Sir Walter Scott. **SP-ScotW** *Fr.* The Bridal of Trierman.
At dawn, the crisp goodbye of friends; at night. Long Summer. Robert Lowell. **SP-LoweR**
At dawn the dove croons. California Spring. Charles Wright. **SP-WrigC**
At dawn the Mass. Geoffrey Hill. *Fr.* The Pentecost Castle. **CP-HillG**
At dawn today the spider's web was cold. The End of Summer School. Howard Nemerov. **CP-NemeH**
At Day-Close in November. Thomas Hardy. **CP-HardT**
At daybreak / Little one. School for Dark Thoughts. Charles Simic. **SP-SimiC**
At Delft. Charles Tomlinson. **CP-TomlC**
At Delphi. Donald Hall. **CP-HallD**
At Delphi. May Sarton. **SP-SartM**
At Delphi I prayed. The Prayer. Denise Levertov. **CP-LeveD**
At dinner, because our hosts had been. The Dinner. Stephen Dunn. **SP-DunnS**
At Dinner, She Is Hostess. George Meredith. *See* At dinner, she is hostess, I am host.
At dinner, she is hostess, I am host. George Meredith. **EnVR; HeIP; NOBVV; NoP; OHCV; PoE; Son** *Fr.* Modern Love. **CP-MerG1**
  (At Dinner, She Is Hostess.) **Son**
At dinner we discuss marriage. Good Company. William Matthews. **SP-MattW**
At Dirty Dick's and Sloppy Joe's. Wystan Hugh Auden. **BoLoP; DTC; FaBoTw; MOS** *Fr.* The Supporting Cast, Sotto Voce. *Fr.* The Sea and the Mirror. **CP-AudeW**
  (Song of the Master and Boatswain.) **BoLoP; DTC; MOS**
At Don's Garage. Daniel Gerard Hoffman. **SP-HoffD**
At Dover. William Wordsworth. *Fr.* Memorials of a Tour of the Continent; 1820. **CP-WorW2**
At Draw-Gloves we'l play. Draw Gloves. Robert Herrick. **CP-HerrR**
At Dressing in the Morning. Christopher Smart. *Fr.* Hymns for the Amusement of Children. **SP-SmarC**
At Dublin's high feast sat Primate and Dean. Aye and No. Jonathan Swift. **CP-SwifJ**
At Dunbar, Castle or Arcade. Double Feature. Robert Earl Hayden. **CP-HaydR**
At dusk / from the island in the river. If the Owl Calls Again. John Haines. **SP-HainJ**
At dusk / just when. Edward Estlin Cummings. **CP-CummE**
At dusk Demeter. Demeter at Dusk. Erica Jong. **SP-JongE**
At dusk in my garden the flowers are waiting. Alun Lewis. *Fr.* The Captivity. **CP-LewiA**
At early dawn, or rather when the air. Gordale. William Wordsworth. **CP-WorW2**

At early daybreak, / In the hour when the birds first awaken. Elegy in a Civil War Cemetery. John Gould Fletcher. **SP-FletJ**
At Ease. Walter de la Mare. **CP-DeLaW**
At East Lulworth the dead were friendly and pitiful, I saw them peek. Ghosts in England. Robinson Jeffers. **CP-JefR2**
At eighteen years of age. Jim Carroll. **SP-CarrJ**
At eighteen, you stood for this faded photograph. The Oval Portrait: Jessie Wilkie. Kathleen Jessie Raine. **SP-RainK**
At Eleusis. Hilda Doolittle. **CP-DoolH**
At Eleusis. Algernon Charles Swinburne. **SP-SwinA**
At Evening. Daniel Gerard Hoffman. **SP-HoffD**
At evening, sitting on this terrace. Bat. David Herbert Lawrence. **CP-LawrD**
At evening, something behind me. The Mountain. Elizabeth Bishop. **CP-BishE**
At evening when the lamp is lit. The Land of Story-Books. Robert Louis Stevenson. **CP-StevR**
At Eventide. John Greenleaf Whittier. **CP-WhitJ**
At every stile and hitching post. First Train (1895). Louise McNeill. **SP-McNeL**
At every stroke his brazen fins do take. The Whale. John Donne. **ChTr** *Fr.* The Progress[e] of the Soul[e]. **CP-DonnJ**
At every tempter's first essay. Watching. Christopher Smart. *Fr.* Hymns for the Amusement of Children. **SP-SmarC**
At Farringford. Tennyson. **FaBoPP** *Fr.* To the Rev. F. D. Maurice. **CP-TennA**
At fifty the faces that grin in color. Trouble in Paradise. Gilbert Sorrentino. **SP-SorrG**
At First. Alice Walker. **CP-WalkA**
At First Flower of the Easy Day. John Ciardi. **SP-CiarJ**
At first I thought a pest. Armor's Undermining Modesty. Marianne Craig Moore. **CP-MoorM**
At first I thought she was. Fence. Dabney Stuart. **SP-StuaD**
At first I thought there was a superfine. Fleming Helphenstine. Edwin Arlington Robinson. **CP-RobiE**
At first I was given centuries. Margaret Atwood. **SP-AtwM1**
At first I went just for the girls. Topless. Stephen Dobyns. **SP-DobyS**
At first it came easily, with the knowledge of the shadow line. Punishing the Myth. John Ashbery. **SP-AshbJ**
At first it seemed rather tight. The Daft Little Shoe Clerk Decided It Would Be Fun to Go Up and See What Things Are Like above the Sky. Kenneth Patchen. **CP-PatcK**
At first it·was as though you had passed. Many Wagons Ago. John Ashbery. **SP-AshbJ**
At first light in the shadow, over the roach. The Shaft. John Ciardi. **SP-CiarJ**
At first, not breathed on. Her Room. Kathleen Jessie Raine. **SP-RainK**
At first one might take it. Odradek. Lewis Turco. **SP-TurcL**
At First Sight. Robert Ranke Graves. **CP-GravR**
At first, the euphemistic "blk." Blked. John Updike. **CP-UpdiJ**
At first the game had rules, but in recent centuries they were re-. Why Did What Was When. John Yau. **SP-YauJo**
At first, the mind feels bruised. The Art of Poetry. Charles Tomlinson. **CP-TomlC**
At first the surprise. Dancing with God. Stephen Dunn. **SP-DunnS**
At first when you went away. The Return. Louise Glück. **SP-GlücL**
At five in the morning there were grey voices. Death of an Old Lady. Louis MacNeice. **CP-MacNL**
At 5:00 a.m., in silence, song. Running with the Hyenas. Peter Meinke. **SP-MeinP**
At five precisely in the afternoon. Crossing. Archibald MacLeish. **CP-MacLA**
At Florence. William Wordsworth. **VLP** *Fr.* Memorials of a Tour in Italy, 1837. **CP-WorW2**
At Florence.—From Michaelangelo. William Wordsworth. *Fr.* Memorials of a Tour in Italy, 1837. **CP-WorW2**
At Florence.—From Michelangelo: "Eternal Lord! eased from a cumbrous load." William Wordsworth. *See* Eternal Lord! Eased from a Cumbrous Load.
At Forty. Richard Shelton. **SP-ShelR**
At 42, Simon Rodilla, tile-setter. Nel Mezzo del Cammin di Nostra Vita. Robert Duncan. **SP-DuncR**
At Four A.M. Phoebe Hesketh. **SP-HeskP**
At four in the morning he wakes. The More a Man Has the More a Man Wants. Paul Muldoon. **SP-MuldP**
At four o'clock. Roosters. Elizabeth Bishop. **CP-BishE**
At four this day of June I rise. Four in the Morning. Thomas Hardy. **CP-HardT**
At fourteen, parked / by the depot. Material. Donald Hall. **CP-HallD**

At Francis Allen's on the Christmas Eve. *introduction to* Morte d'Arthur. Tennyson. **NAEL-2** *Fr.* Morte d'Arthur. **CP-TennA**

At Furness Abbey ("Here, where, of havoc tired and rash undoing"). William Wordsworth. **CP-WorW2**

At Furness Abbey ("Well have yon Railway Labourers to THIS ground"). William Wordsworth. **CP-WorW2**

At Galway Races. William Butler Yeats. **CP-YeatW**

At Galway's, such / is the presence of the snows. Continuo. Hayden Carruth. **CP-CarHS**

At gauzy dusk, thin haze like cigarette smoke. Hospital Window. Allen Ginsberg. **CP-GinsA**

At God's word David's kinsmen cast. Abishag. Louise Glück. **SP-GlücL**

At Grandmother's Wake. Kenneth Patchen. **CP-PatcK**

At Grass. Philip Larkin. **CP-LarkP**

At Half Past Anything. Marsden Hartley. **CP-HartM**

At Half past Three, a single Bird. Emily Dickinson. **CP-DickE**

At Hay, or near it, 1944. Herefordshire. Donald Davie. **CP-DavDo**

"At heaven's gate" the larks: have. N.Y. Louis Zukofsky. *Fr.* 29 Songs. **CP-ZukLS**

At Hertford House. Adrienne Rich. **CP-RicAE**

At hest, hendecasyllabics, what is this. Catullus. *See* Carmen 42: "From the quarters of the compass."

At high tide / the sea—they say. Chorus of Troizenian Women. Euripides, *tr. by* Hilda Doolittle ("H.D."). **CP-DoolH** *Fr.* Hippolytus.

At His Execution. Rudyard Kipling. **CP-KiplR**

At his grave ten years after. The Widow. Dabney Stuart. **SP-StuaD**

At his incipient sun. First Love. Stanley Jasspon Kunitz. **CP-KuniS**

At Holwell Farm. Charles Tomlinson. **CP-TomlC**

At home / in the countryside. Pagan. Alice Walker. **CP-WalkA**

At Home. Christina Georgina Rossetti. **CP-RosC1**

At Home in Heaven. Robert Southwell. **CP-SoutR**

At home, in my flannel gown, like a bear to its floe. 90 North. Randall Jarrell. **CP-JarrR; SP-JarrR**

At home with my infirmities I fare. Hawkshead and Dachau in a Christmas Glass. Donald Davie. **CP-DavDo**

At Italo's. David St. John. *Fr.* To Pasolini. **SP-StJoD**

At Ithaca. Hilda Doolittle. **CP-DoolH**

At its margin / the river's double willow. Ode to Arnold Schoenberg. Charles Tomlinson. **CP-TomlC**

At just 5 a / m i hear eng. Edward Estlin Cummings. **CP-CummE**

At Kenneth Burke's Place. William Carlos Williams. **CP-WilW2**

At Knaresborough. Donald Davie. **CP-DavDo**

At Last. David Herbert Lawrence. **CP-LawrD**

At Last. Christina Georgina Rossetti. **CP-RosC2**

At Last. John Greenleaf Whittier. **CP-WhitJ**

At last comes love of such a quality that it would shame me. Gilbert Sorrentino. *Fr.* Elegiacs of Sulpicia. **SP-SorrG**

At last, completed in his rest. Wendell Berry. *Fr.* Elegy: "To be at home on its native ground." **CP-BerrW**

At last, dear friend, your letter has reached me. Elegy 1. John Milton, *tr. fr. Latin by* John T. Shawcross. **CP-MiltJ**

At last, dearest Louisa, I take up my pen to address you. Georgina Trevellyn to Luisa. Arthur Hugh Clough. **EBVVPR** *Fr.* Amours de Voyage. **SP-ClouA**

At last, down in the lane. Wystan Hugh Auden. **CP-AudWJ**

At last I entered a long dark gallery. Fragment. Thomas Hardy. **CP-HardT**

At last I hear the voice well known. A Voice from the World. Gerard Manley Hopkins. **CP-HopkG**

At last I put off love. He Abjures Love. Thomas Hardy. **CP-HardT**

At last! In sight of home again. Song of the Soldiers' Wives and Sweethearts. Thomas Hardy. **CP-HardT**

At last it's still—a gray thaw. Middle Age. Jane Cooper. *Fr.* March. **SP-CoopJ**

At last she calls to mind where hangs a piece. Troy Depicted. William Shakespeare. **OBSC** *Fr.* The Rape of Lucrece. **CP-ShaWS**

At last, so faire a ladie did I spie. Petrarch. *Fr.* The Visions of Petrarch. **CP-Spens**

At last, someone had heard tell of Larry Durrell. Armageddon, Armageddon. Paul Muldoon. **SP-MuldP**

At last the Big Blackfoot river. Making Certain It Goes On. Richard Hugo. **CP-HugoR**

At last the poet spoke. Ralph Waldo Emerson. **CP-EmerR**

"At last! the present darkness! all is known!" Delmore Schwartz. **SP-SchwD** *Fr.* Genesis.

At last the secret is out, as it always must come in the end. Wystan Hugh Auden. *Fr.* Twelve Songs. **CP-AudeW**

At last, to be identified! Emily Dickinson. **CP-DickE**

At last we could keep quiet, each on his own. To Come of Age. Robert Ranke Graves. **CP-GravR**

At last we parley: we so strangely dumb. George Meredith. *Fr.* Modern Love. **CP-MerG1**

At last withdraw your cruelty. Sir Thomas Wyatt. **CP-WyatT**

At last you are tired of being single. Poem Read at Joan Mitchell's. Frank O'Hara. **SP-OharF**

'At last' you think—I read it in your eyes. Waste. Wystan Hugh Auden. **CP-AudWJ**

At last you yielded up the album, which. Lines on a Young Lady's Photograph Album. Philip Larkin. **CP-LarkP**

At least at night, a streetlight. So Long. William Stafford. **SP-StafW**

At least I have the flowers of myself. Hilda Doolittle. **VBLP** *Fr.* Eurydice. **CP-DoolH**

At least I know my peculiar emptiness. Zimmer the Drugstore Cowboy. Paul Zimmer. **SP-ZimmP**

At least, my dear. Edna St. Vincent Millay. **CP-MillE**

At least—to pray—is left—is left. Emily Dickinson. **CP-DickE**

—at least until the 21st century. Stop the Deathwish! Stop It! Stop! Daniel Gerard Hoffman. **SP-HoffD**

At least we cannot live to see it all; no comfort. The World Will Little Note. Kenneth Patchen. **CP-PatcK**

At least, with the dentist / I am aware of the drill. Dissertation II. John Hewitt. **CP-HewiJ**

At leisure is the Soul. Emily Dickinson. **CP-DickE**

At length, even at the time when Morpheus. Joachim Du Bellay. *Fr.* The Visions of Bellay. **CP-Spens**

At length must *Suffolk*'s beauties shine in vain. To Lady Firebrace. Samuel Johnson. **CP-JohnS**

At length, my friend, the far-sent letters come. John Milton. *See* Elegy 1: To Charles Diodati.

At length, my soul! thy fruitless hopes give o'er. Stanzas. François de Malherbe, *tr. fr. French by* Alexander Pope. **CP-PopeA**

At length nigh to the sea they drew. Edmund Spenser. **NoP** *Fr.* The Faerie Queene. **CP-Spens**

At length they came into a larger space. Edmund Spenser. **FiP** *Fr.* As pilot well expert in perilous wave. **OAEL-1; PoEL-1** *Fr.* The Faerie Queene. **CP-Spens**

At length to hospital. Hospital Visits. Philip Larkin. **CP-LarkP**

At length with jostling, elbowing, and the aid. Byron. **OBRV; OBSV** *Fr.* The Vision of Judgment. **CP-Byron**

At Lindos. May Sarton. **SP-SartM**

At Loafing-Holt. Paul Laurence Dunbar. **CP-DunbP**

At low cost woodlands con. Lily-of-the-Valley. Louis Zukofsky. **CP-ZukLS**

At low tide like this how sheer the water is. The Bight. Elizabeth Bishop. **CP-BishE**

At Lulworth Cove a Century Back. Thomas Hardy. **CP-HardT**

At Madame Tussaud's in Victorian Years. Thomas Hardy. **CP-HardT**

At Maganosc / in the stone bedroom. William Dickey. **SP-DickW** *Fr.* In The Dreaming. **SP-DickW**

At Majority. Adrienne Rich. **CP-RicAE**

At Malcolm Lowry's Grave. David Markson. **CP-MarkD**

At Market Hill, as well appears. On Cutting Down the Old Thorn at Market Hill. Jonathan Swift. **CP-SwifJ**

At Mass. Nicholas Vachel Lindsay. **CP-LindV**

At Mayfair Lodgings. Thomas Hardy. **CP-HardT**

At Melville's Tomb. Hart Crane. **CP-CranH**

At mid-morning her wheel-chair seems to rock. The Angel of the Maze. James Dickey. **CP-DickJ**

At Middle-Field Gate in February. Thomas Hardy. **CP-HardT**

At Midnight. David Herbert Lawrence. **CP-LawrD**

At midnight, after hours of love, I ate. Charles Olson. **CP-OlsoC**

At midnight by the stream I roved. Lewti. Samuel Taylor Coleridge. **CP-ColeS**

At midnight, in the month of June. The Sleeper. Edgar Allan Poe. **CP-PoeEd**

At midnight, in the room where he lay dead. His Heart. Thomas Hardy. **CP-HardT**

At midnight on the next balcony. Lawrence Ferlinghetti. **SP-FerlL** *Fr.* Canti Romani.

At midnight tears. Solitary Observation Brought Back from a Sojourn in Hell. Louise Bogan. **CP-BogaL**

At midnight the teacher lectures on his throne. Reflections at Lake Louise. Allen Ginsberg. **CP-GinsA**

At midnight the world is a mediate / perspective. Two Ways of Looking in a Mirror. Robert Creeley. **CP-CreeR**

At midnight they roused us. In the distance we heard. City of Anguish. Edwin Rolfe. **CP-RolfE**

At Midocean. Robert Bly. **SP-BlyR**

At Moonrise and Onwards. Thomas Hardy. **CP-HardT**

At morn, at noon, at eve, and middle night. The Poet. John Keats. **CP-KeatJ**

At morn—at noon—at twilight dim. Hymn. Edgar Allan Poe. **CP-PoeEd**

At morn I plucked a rose and gave it Thee. A Rose Plant in Jericho. Christina Georgina Rossetti. **CP-RosC1**

At morn I prayed, "I fain would see." Trinitas. John Greenleaf Whittier. **CP-WhitJ**

At morn we placed on his funeral bier. By Callimachus. Callimachus, *tr. fr. Greek by* William Cowper. **CP-CowpW**

At morning on the garden seat. Robert Louis Stevenson. **CP-StevR**

At morning we all look out. Hedge Life. James Dickey. **CP-DickJ**

At mo[o]st mischief. Sir Thomas Wyatt. **CP-WyatT**

At Muzot. May Sarton. **SP-SartM**

At my age my father. The Gathering. Wendell Berry. **CP-BerrW**

At my Command yon' Iron Gates unfold. Samuel Johnson. **CP-JohnS** *Fr.* Irene.

At My Father's Grave. "Hugh MacDiarmid." **SP-MacDH**

At my homely Country-seat. Larr's Portion, and the Poets Part. Robert Herrick. **CP-HerrR**

At Night. Paul Laurence Dunbar. **CP-DunbP**

At Night. Richard Eberhart. **CP-EberR**

At Night. William Carlos Williams. **CP-WilW1**

At night, by the fire. Domination of Black ("At night, by the fire"). Wallace Stevens. **CP-StevW**

At night Chinamen jump. Poem. Frank O'Hara. **SP-OharF**

At night I lay with you. Ernest Hemingway. **CP-HemiE**

At night, in the fish-light of the moon, the dead wear our white shirts. Charles Wright. *Fr.* Homage to Paul Cézanne. **SP-WrigC**

At night make me one with the darkness. Wendell Berry. **EaPr** *Fr.* Prayers and Sayings of the Mad Farmer. **CP-BerrW**

At night, passing the open door. Fontenelle. Howard Nemerov. **CP-NemeH**

At night the factories. Varick Street. Elizabeth Bishop. **CP-BishE**

At night—the light turned off, the filament. Burning Trash. John Updike. **CP-UpdiJ**

At night the mountains look like huge. Moving Again. William Matthews. **SP-MattW**

At night the paintings roll up their colors. Talk of the Paintings. Peter Meinke. **SP-MeinP**

At Night the States. Alice Notley. **SP-NotlA**

At night the wind dies. March Heat. William Matthews. **SP-MattW**

At night they move from room to room glinting. The Exiles. Frederick Morgan. **SP-MorgF**

At night, toward dawn, all the lights of the shore have died. Hooded Night. Robinson Jeffers. **CP-JefR2**

At night when each dark shape in the desert. The Great Gulf. Richard Shelton. **SP-ShelR**

At night, when I can't sleep. Career for a Child of Five. Kenneth Patchen. **CP-PatcK**

At Nightfall. Siv Cedering Fox. **SP-CedeS**

At nightfall, as the sea darkens. Ghost Crabs. Ted Hughes. **SP-HughT**

At nine in the morning there passed a church. Faintheart in a Railway Train. Thomas Hardy. **CP-HardT**

At nine years a sickly boy lay down. Records. Allen Tate. **CP-TateA**

At ninety-seven my uncle found God heavy. Alec. John Ciardi. **SP-CiarJ**

At No Distance. Roy Fisher. **SP-FishR**

At noon I passed and saw you there. Paper Banners. John Hewitt. **CP-HewiJ**

At noon in the desert a panting lizard. At the Bomb Testing Site. William Stafford. **SP-StafW**

At noon, the furry girls stretch out and talk about fucking. The Oppositions. Frederick Morgan. **SP-MorgF**

At noon the sky goes off like a gun. Tropics. Thomas Merton. **CP-MertT; SP-MertT**

At noontime under the very tall pines. In Tobey Woods. Hayden Carruth. **CP-CarHS**

At North Farm. John Ashbery. **SP-AshbJ**

At Once. Roy Fisher. **SP-FishR**

At once, from hence, my lines and I depart. To Mr. T. W. John Donne. **CP-DonnJ**

At once on th' Eastern cliff of Paradise. John Milton. **PeECV** *Fr.* Book V. *Fr.* Paradise Lost. **CP-MiltJ**

At once whatever happened starts receding. Whatever Happened? Philip Larkin. **CP-LarkP**

At once with him they rose. Hell. John Milton. **OBS** *Fr.* Book II. **FHYEP; NAEL-1; OxAEP-1** *Fr.* Paradise Lost. **CP-MiltJ**

At one of those bars where they weigh you at the door. A Glass Darkly. Miller Williams. **SP-WillM**

At one the wind rose. Night-Music. Philip Larkin. **CP-LarkP**

At one they hurry in to eat. Waitress. Thom Gunn. **CP-GunnT**

At Our Best. Richard Hugo. **CP-HugoR**

At Our House. William Stafford. **SP-StafW**

At Parting. Wystan Hugh Auden. **CP-AudWJ**

At Parting. Wystan Hugh Auden. **CP-AudWJ**

At Pavia, a visitation of some sorrow. Boethius'. Geoffrey Hill. *Fr.* Mercian Hymns. **CP-HillG**

At peace here—I feel you about me. To the Outer World. William Carlos Williams. **CP-WilW1**

At peace under this mandarin, sleep, Lucina. In Memoriam L. K.-A. 1950–1952. Wystan Hugh Auden. *Fr.* Shorts [1948–1957] ("At peace under this mandarin, sleep, Lucina"). **CP-AudeW**

At Père Lachaise. Mona Van Duyn. **SP-VanDM**

At pet stores in Detroit, you can buy. Poem With One Fact. Donald Hall. **CP-HallD**

At Plymouth in the friendly crowd. Ralph Waldo Emerson. **CP-EmerR**

At Pompeii. Percy Bysshe Shelley. **FaBoPP** *Fr.* Ode to Naples. **CP-ShelP**

At Port Royal. John Greenleaf Whittier. **CP-WhitJ**
Song of the Negro Boatmen. **GN**

At Post and Paire, or Slam, Tom Tuck would play. Upon Tuck. Robert Herrick. **CP-HerrR**

At present I am a blank, and I admit it. Blank. David Herbert Lawrence. **CP-LawrD**

At Provincetown. Daniel Gerard Hoffman. **SP-HoffD**

At Rome ("Is this, ye Gods, the Capitolian Hill?"). William Wordsworth. *Fr.* Memorials of a Tour in Italy, 1837. **CP-WorW2**

At Rome ("They—who have seen the noble Roman's scorn"). William Wordsworth. *Fr.* Memorials of a Tour in Italy, 1837. **CP-WorW2**

At Rome.—Regrets.—In Allusion to Niebuhr and Other Modern Historians. William Wordsworth. *Fr.* Memorials of a Tour in Italy, 1837. **CP-WorW2**

At Rome.—Regrets.—In Allusion to Niebuhr and Other Modern Historians, Continued. William Wordsworth. *Fr.* Memorials of a Tour in Italy, 1837. **CP-WorW2**

At Roslin Inn. Robert Burns. **CP-BurnR**

At Runnymede, at Runnymede. The Reeds of Runnymede. Rudyard Kipling. **CP-KiplR**

At Rushy-Pond. Thomas Hardy. **CP-HardT**

At Saint Mary's Church. Charles Tomlinson. **CP-TomlC**

At San Miguel de los Baños. Attempt to Discover Life. Wallace Stevens. **CP-StevW**

At Sant' Antimo. Charles Tomlinson. **CP-TomlC**

At Sarray, in the land of Tartarye. The Squire's Tale. Geoffrey Chaucer. *Fr.* The Canterbury Tales. **CP-ChauG**

At School. Stevie Smith. **CP-SmitS**

At School-Close. John Greenleaf Whittier. **CP-WhitJ**

At school, his anxious dream was poetry. Borrowed Line. David Markson. **CP-MarkD**

At school I always walk with Elwyn. At School. Stevie Smith. **CP-SmitS**

At sea in the dome of St. Paul's. Homage to Wren. Louis MacNeice. **CP-MacNL**

At Sea off the Isle of Man. William Wordsworth. *Fr.* Poems Composed or Suggested During a Tour, in the Summer of 1833. **CP-WorW2**

At Sea, September 1833. Ralph Waldo Emerson. **CP-EmerR**

At secret daybreak they had met. Martins: September. Walter de la Mare. **CP-DeLaW**

At seventeen women were strange & forbidden phenomenons. For Irving. Robert Creeley. **CP-CreeR**

At Shag's Heath. Thomas Hardy. **CP-HardT**

At Shottery, Anne Hathaway's Cottage. John Hewitt. **CP-HewiJ**

At sight of sparkling Bowls or beauteous Dames. Samuel Johnson. **CP-JohnS**
(Reply to Impromptu Verses by Baretti, A.) **CP-JohnS**

At six / I lived in a graveyard full of dolls. Those Times. Anne Sexton. **CP-SextA**

At six A.M. the log cabins. Moose in the Morning, Northern Maine. Mona Van Duyn. **SP-VanDM**

At six in the morning you scratched at my porthole. A Rhapsody on Irish Themes. Randall Jarrell. **CP-JarrR**

At Six O'Clock. John Berryman. *See* I lift—lift you five States away your glass.

At six o'clock we were waiting for coffee. A Miracle for Breakfast. Elizabeth Bishop. **CP-BishE**

At six, when April chills our hands and feet. Elektra on Third Avenue. Marilyn Hacker. **SP-HackM**

At sixteen I came West, riding. A Living Pearl. Kenneth Rexroth. **SP-RexrK**

At Slim's River. John Haines. **SP-HainJ**

At Some Lone Alehouse. Matthew Arnold. **FaBoDD** *Fr.* The Scholar-Gipsy. **SP-ArnoM**

At sound as of rushing wind, and sight as of fire. Whitsun Day. Christina Georgina Rossetti. **CP-RosC2**

At start of spring I open a trench. Wendell Berry. **CP-BerrW** (Purification, A.) **CP-BerrW**

At Stoke. Charles Tomlinson. **CP-TomlC**

At Stool-ball, Lucia, let us play. Stool-Ball. Robert Herrick. **CP-HerrR**

At such a time, in such a spot. Emily Brontë. **CP-BronE**

At sun up I am up. Angel Butcher. Philip Levine. **SP-LeviP**

At sunrise on a pin. Radiometer. James Merrill. **SP-MerrJ**

At sunset, only to his true love. Bird of Paradise. Robert Ranke Graves. **CP-GravR**

At sunset over the water. Roy Fisher. **SP-FishR** *Fr.* Glenthorne Poems.

At sunset the hills turn purple. Frederick Morgan. *Fr.* Moments. **SP-MorgF**

At Sunset Time. Paul Laurence Dunbar. **CP-DunbP**

At Tea. Thomas Hardy. *Fr.* Satires of Circumstance in Fifteen Glimpses. **CP-HardT**

At ten A.M. the young housewife. The Young Housewife. William Carlos Williams. **CP-WilW1**

At 10 o'clock Haydon. I'm With You. Charles Olson. **CP-OlsoC**

At ten o'clock on Christmas Eve. Christmas Eve. John Hewitt. **CP-HewiJ**

At The Abbey Theatre. William Butler Yeats. **CP-YeatW**

At the Airport. Howard Nemerov. **CP-NemeH**

At the airport, ready to leave on my little trip. The Fear of Flying. Mona Van Duyn. **SP-VanDM**

At the alder-darkened brink. Hamlen Brook. Richard Wilbur. **CP-WilbR**

At the Altar. Robert Lowell. **InPK** *Fr.* Between the Porch and the Altar. **SP-LoweR**

At the Altar-Rail. Thomas Hardy. **MoAB; MoBrPo** *Fr.* Satires of Circumstance in Fifteen Glimpses. **CP-HardT**

At the Annual Clay Nursing Home White Elephant Sale and Picnic. The Clay Nursing Home. John Yau. **SP-YauJo**

At the Aquatic Sports. Thomas Hardy. **CP-HardT**

At the back of the houses there is the wood. The House in the Wood. Randall Jarrell. **CP-JarrR**

At the Back of the North Wind. Thom Gunn. **CP-GunnT**

At the Bait Stand. Ted Kooser. **SP-KoosT**

At the Ball Game. William Carlos Williams. **CP-WilW1**

At the Bank in Spain. David Herbert Lawrence. **CP-LawrD**

At the Bar. Malcolm Lowry. *Fr.* The Cantinas. **CP-LowrM**

At the Bar. William Carlos Williams. **CP-WilW1**

At the Barriers. Thom Gunn. **CP-GunnT**

At the Battery. Grace Paley. **CP-PaleG**

At the Beach. James Schuyler. **CP-SchuJ**

At the beginning of a street some say never ends. Rumors. John Yau. **SP-YauJo**

At the big round table in the university. Marge Piercy. *Fr.* Excursions, Incursions. **SP-PierM**

At the Birth of an Age. Robinson Jeffers. **CP-JefR2**

At the blackboard I had missed. Zimmer's Head Thudding against the Blackboard. Paul Zimmer. **SP-ZimmP**

At the Bomb Testing Site. William Stafford. **SP-StafW**

At the bottom of the Arctic sea, they say. Ted Hughes. **SP-HughT** *Fr.* Gaudete.

"At the boundary of the mighty world" H. (T) 620 foll. Charles Olson. **SP-OlsoC** *Fr.* The Maximus Poems.

At the Brink of the Winter. William Carlos Williams. **CP-WilW2**

At the Bus Stop Next to the Funeral Home. Ted Kooser. **SP-KoosT**

At the Cabin. Richard Hugo. **CP-HugoR**

At the Café de la Terrasse. Morlaix: Into the Future with Neil Young. Lawrence Ferlinghetti. **SP-FerlL**

At the Café Parnasse. Donald Davie. **CP-DavDo**

At the Cannon's Mouth. Herman Melville. **SP-MelvH**

At The Canoe Club. Richard Eberhart. **CP-EberR**

At the Cearne. David Herbert Lawrence. **CP-LawrD**

At the Cenotaph. "Hugh MacDiarmid." **SP-MacDH**

At the Centre. Thom Gunn. **CP-GunnT**

At the Chiming of Light upon Sleep. Philip Larkin. **CP-LarkP**

At the clear core, morning. The Bead. Charles Tomlinson. **CP-TomlC**

At the clear heart of the paperweight in green. The Visit. Stephen Berg. **SP-BergS**

At the Close. George Meredith. **CP-MerG1**

At the close of a winter day. The Rhyme of the Three Captains. Rudyard Kipling. **CP-KiplR**

At the Coke plant, toting empties. Hard Work 1956. Stephen Dunn. **SP-DunnS**

At the coming up of Phoebus the all-luminous charioteer. Phaéthôn. George Meredith. **CP-MerG1**

At the Consecration. Steve Griffiths. *Fr.* Hymns and Backward Glances. **SP-GrifS**

At the Convent of Camaldoli. William Wordsworth. *Fr.* Memorials of a Tour in Italy, 1837. **CP-WorW2**

At the Convent of Camaldoli, Continued. William Wordsworth. *Fr.* Memorials of a Tour in Italy, 1837. **CP-WorW2**

At the Core. Marge Piercy. **SP-PierM**

At the corner / of Forty-second and Broadway. This Street Never Sleeps. Carl Sandburg. **CP-SandC**

At the corner of Wood Street, when daylight appears. The Reverie of Poor Susan. William Wordsworth. **CP-WorW1**

At the cottage door, in the fat black pot. The Iron Pot. John Hewitt. **CP-HewiJ**

At the Cradle of Genius. Donald Davie. **CP-DavDo**

At the creation of the Earth. The Birth of Pleasure. Percy Bysshe Shelley. **CP-ShelP**

At the crossing, wind-stricken in blow, I saw. Only the Irresistible Abides. Jean Garrigue. **SP-GarrJ**

At the Crossroads. Bill Knott. **SP-KnotB**

At the day's end I found. Kathleen Jessie Raine. *Fr.* Three Poems of Incarnation. **SP-RainK**

At the demolishing, this seat. To My Lord Fairfax. Andrew Marvell. **NOSC** *Fr.* Upon Appleton House [To My Lord Fairfax]. **CP-MarvA**

At the Dinner-Table. Thomas Hardy. **CP-HardT**

At the dinner table, before the baked eggplant. The Boast. Rita Dove. **SP-DoveR**

At the Door. Stephen Berg. **SP-BergS** *Fr.* For My Father.

At the door. Standing at the Door. Diane Wakoski. **SP-WakoD**

At the Draper's. Thomas Hardy. **MoAB; MoBrPo; OBD; OxBM** *Fr.* Satires of Circumstance in Fifteen Glimpses. **CP-HardT**

At the earliest ending of winter. Not Ideas about the Thing but the Thing Itself. Wallace Stevens. **CP-StevW**

At the edge. The Outdoor Concert. Thom Gunn. **CP-GunnT**

At the Edge. Charles Tomlinson. **CP-TomlC**

At the edge of a beautiful gulf of gloom and stillness. Lake Shore at Night. John Gould Fletcher. **SP-FletJ**

At the edge of conversations. The Insistence of Things. Charles Tomlinson. **CP-TomlC**

At the Edge of the Body. Erica Jong. **SP-JongE**

At the edge of the city the pickerel. The Wreckage. Donald Hall. **CP-HallD**

At the edge of the mariner's. Primer for the Nuclear Age. Rita Dove. **SP-DoveR**

At the Edge of the Suburbs. Siv Cedering Fox. **SP-CedeS**

At the eleventh hour he came. The Vineyard. Rudyard Kipling. **CP-KiplR** *Fr.* Debits and Credits.

At the end a / "The Prisoner of Zenda." The Prisoner of Zenda. Richard Wilbur. **CP-WilbR**

At the end, he listened only to. Late Stravinsky Listening to Late Beethoven. Stephen Spender. **CP-SpenS**

At the end of a freight train rolling away. Late Lights in Minnesota. Ted Kooser. **SP-KoosT**

At the end of a long-walled garden. The Cottage Hospital. Sir John Betjeman. **CP-BetjJ**

At the end of an unending war. Urlicht. Charles Tomlinson. **CP-TomlC**

At the end of October. The Snake. Wendell Berry. **CP-BerrW**

At the end of our Ruegen holiday, that night. The Sign *Faehre nach Wilm.* Stephen Spender. **CP-SpenS**

At the end of Tarriers' Lane, which was the street. Wm. Brazier. Robert Ranke Graves. **CP-GravR**

At the end of the familiar. Roy Fisher. **SP-FishR** *Fr.* Handsworth Liberties.

At the End of the Passage. Rudyard Kipling. *Fr.* Life's Handicap. "Sky is lead, and our faces are red, The." **CP-KiplR**

At the End of the Rainbow. John Updike. **CP-UpdiJ**

At the end of the row. The Objection to Being Stepped On. Robert Frost. **CP-FrosR**

At the end of the street. A Summer Night. Ted Kooser. **SP-KoosT**

At the End of the War. Richard Eberhart. **CP-EberR**

At the end of the war I arose. The Driver. James Dickey. **CP-DickJ**

At the End of the Weekend. Ted Kooser. **SP-KoosT**

At the end of this sentence, rain will begin. Map of the New World. Derek Walcott. **CP-WalcD**

At the Entering of the New Year. Thomas Hardy. **CP-HardT**

At the Entrance to the Other World. Kenneth Patchen. **CP-PatcK**

At the equinox when the earth was veiled in a late rain, wreathed with wet poppies, waiting spring. Continent's End. Robinson Jeffers. **CP-JefR1**

At the Eremite or Upper Convent of Camaldoli. William Wordsworth. *Fr.* Memorials of a Tour in Italy, 1837. **CP-WorW2**

At the Executed Murderer's Grave. James Wright. **CP-WrigJ**

At the Fall of an Age. Robinson Jeffers. **CP-JefR2**

At the far end of a trip north. Nooksack Valley. Gary Snyder. **CP-SnydG**

At the Faucet of June. William Carlos Williams. **CP-WilW1**

At the feet o' Jesus. Feet o' Jesus. Langston Hughes. **SP-HughL**

At the ferocious phenomenon of 5 o'clock i find myself gently decompos. Edward Estlin Cummings. **CP-CummE**

At the Fillmore. Philip Levine. **SP-LeviP**

At the first ball his wicket fell, and sins. George Meredith. **CP-MerG2**

At the first strokes of the fiddle bow. The Wheel. Wendell Berry. **CP-BerrW**

At the first turning of the second stair. Thomas Stearns Eliot. **NOBA** *Fr.* Ash Wednesday [*or* Ash-Wednesday]. **CP-ElioT**

At the Fishhouses. Elizabeth Bishop. **CP-BishE**

At the foot of every steep cliff or precipice in high Alpine regions. James Fenton. *Fr.* Exempla. **SP-FentJ**

At the foot of his long shadow. The New House. Wendell Berry. *Fr.* The Handing Down. **CP-BerrW**

At the foot of the playground slide. The Play of Memory. John Updike. *Fr.* Midpoint. **CP-UpdiJ**

At the Front. David Herbert Lawrence. **CP-LawrD**

At the frontier the long train slows to a stop. The Frontier. John Hewitt. **CP-HewiJ**

At the Funeral. George Meredith. **CP-MerG2**

At the furthermost reach of the sea. The Surgery of the Sea. Erica Jong. **SP-JongE**

At the *Gare Bruxelles-Midi*. Lawrence Ferlinghetti. **SP-FerlL**

At the Gate. Geoffrey Chaucer. SeCePo *Fr.* Troilus and Criseyde [*or* Criseide]. **CP-ChauG**

At the Gate. Robert Ranke Graves. **CP-GravR**

At the Gates of Aerea. René Char, *tr. fr. French by* Thomas Merton. **CP-MertT**

At the Gates of Tombs. Carl Sandburg. **CP-SandC**

At the gay at the apple at the white sun. Winter at the Inn. Kenneth Patchen. **CP-PatcK**

At the German Writers Conference in Munich. Rita Dove. **SP-DoveR**

At the golden gate of song. Inspiration. Paul Laurence Dunbar. **CP-DunbP**

At the Grave of Burns (1803, Seven Years After His Death). William Wordsworth. **CP-WorW1**

At the Grave of Henry James. Wystan Hugh Auden. **CP-AudeW**

At the half-way house the pony died. Half Way. Carl Sandburg. **CP-SandC**

At the head of this street a gasping organ is waving moth-eaten. Edward Estlin Cummings. **CP-CummE**

At the height of love. Mistrust of the Beloved. William Carlos Williams. **CP-WilW2**

At the Hill Fort. Charles Tomlinson. **CP-TomlC**

At the hole where he went in. Rudyard Kipling. **CP-KiplR** *Fr.* Rikki-Tikki-Tavi. *Fr.* The Jungle Book.

At the Home for Unwed Mothers. James Dickey. **CP-DickJ**

At the hospital where I had the echocardiagram. Sonnet. Hayden Carruth. **CP-CarHS** *Fr.* Sonnets.

At the Hour of the Breaking of the Rocks. Robert Penn Warren. *Fr.* Kentucky Mountain Farm. **SP-WarrR**

At the hour when the first symptoms of mental viduity makes themselves felt. Scene. Paul Éluard, *tr. fr. French by* Samuel Beckett. **CP-BeckS**

At the Indian Killer's Grave. Robert Lowell. **SP-LoweR**

At the Inn. John Ashbery. **SP-AshbJ**

At the Isle of Wight. 1793. William Wordsworth. **CP-WorW1**

At the Jewish New Year. Adrienne Rich. **CP-RicAE; SP-RicA2**

At the last moment you decided. The Thrifty Lover. Marge Piercy. **SP-PierM**

At the last, tenderly. The Last Invocation. Walt Whitman. **CP-WhitW**

At the last turn in the path. Saying Farewell at the Monastery After Hearing the Old Master Lecture on "Return to the Source." Gary Snyder. **CP-SnydG**

At the Lincoln Memorial. Archibald MacLeish. **CP-MacLA**

At the Lion's Head. David Markson. **CP-MarkD**

At the long meadow's end, where the road runs. The Pond. Howard Nemerov. **CP-NemeH**

At the Maison Lyons. Wystan Hugh Auden. **CP-AudWJ**

At the Manger. Wystan Hugh Auden. *Fr.* For the Time Being; a Christmas Oratorio. **CP-AudeW**

"Led by the light of an unusual star." **PChr**

At the Meeting of the Days. John Gould Fletcher. **SP-FletJ**

At the "Mermaid." Robert Browning. **CP-BroR2**

At the midnight in the silence of the sleep-time. Epilogue. Robert Browning. **CP-BroR2**

At the Mill. Thomas Hardy. **CP-HardT**

At the Moment of Victory. Edwin Rolfe. **CP-RolfE**

At the morning break. The College Fence. John Hewitt. **CP-HewiJ**

(At The Museum). Bare Sheets III. John Yau. **SP-YauJo**

At the Museum of Natural History. Erica Jong. **SP-JongE**

At the near approach of a star. . . huge tides. Robinson Jeffers. **CP-JefR3**

At the New Year. Kenneth Patchen. **LiTM** *Fr.* Eight Early Poems. **CP-PatcK**

At the Newsagent's. John Hewitt. **CP-HewiJ**

At the next table, two carry on. Carrying On. Leonard Nathan. **SP-NathL**

At the next vacancy for God, if I am elected. In Place of a Curse. John Ciardi. **SP-CiarJ**

At the open door of the room I stand and look at the night. Restlessness. David Herbert Lawrence. **CP-LawrD**

At the outset, hysteria. Cholera. Rita Dove. **SP-DoveR**

At the Park Dance. William DeWitt Snodgrass. **SP-SnodW**

At the Party. Wystan Hugh Auden. **CP-AudeW**

At the penultimate move, their saga nearly sung. Chess. Louis MacNeice. **CP-MacNL**

At the Piano. Thomas Hardy. **CP-HardT**

At the Piano. John Updike. *Fr.* Living with a Wife. **CP-UpdiJ**

At the Poem Society a black-haired man stands up to say. Fresh Air. Kenneth Koch. **SP-KochK**

At the Poem Society a black-haired man stands up to say. Kenneth Koch. *Fr.* Fresh Air. **SP-KochK**

At the Porch of the Caryatids. Stanley Jasspon Kunitz. *Fr.* Signs and Portents. **CP-KuniS**

At the present rate it must come to pass. Something for Hope. Robert Frost. **CP-FrosR**

At the Publix counter, she lifts the plastic. Arms and the Man. Peter Meinke. **SP-MeinP**

At the Queen's Park Hotel, with its white, high-ceilinged rooms. Derek Walcott. **CP-WalcD** *Fr.* Midsummer.

At the Railway Station, Upway. Thomas Hardy. **CP-HardT**

At the Roman Wall, 1956. Daniel Gerard Hoffman. **SP-HoffD**

At the round earth's imagined corners, blow. John Donne. **BLPL; CABA; ChIV-2; ChTr; ClHu; EBCP; EBEV; EaLo; EnRePo; FHYEP; FaBoEn; FaBoRV; HAP; HeIL; HeIP; ImPo; InPS; JCP; LiTB; LoBV; MeLP; MePo; NAEL-1; NAWM-1; NOBE; NOSC; NoP; OAEL-1; OAEP; OBD; OBS; OxAEP-1; OxBoCh; PAI; PFP; PPP; PPoe; PeECV; PoE; PoEL-2; PoPle; QFR; SCGP; SeCP; SeCV-1; SeCeV; Son; TEP; TFi; TOF; TreFT** *Fr.* Divine Meditations. **CP-DonnJ** *Fr.* Holy Sonnets. **CP-DonnJ**

(Blow Your Trumpets.) **ChTr; EBCP**

At the Royal Academy. Thomas Hardy. **CP-HardT**

At the sea at the beach in the dark there was somebody. On a Night You Don't Sleep. Charles Bukowski. **SP-BukC2**

At the Seaside [*or* Sea-Side]. Robert Louis Stevenson. **CP-StevR**

At the shiver of morning, a little before the false dawn. Honeymoon Time at an Inn. Thomas Hardy. **CP-HardT**

At the shower's head, high over the porcelain moonscape. Adultery At Forty. Donald Hall. **CP-HallD**

At the sign "Fred Muffin's Antiques" they turned off the road into a. On the Towpath. John Ashbery. **SP-AshbJ**

At the Slackening of the Tide. James Wright. **CP-WrigJ**

At the small end of an illness. The World Contracted to a Recognizable Image. William Carlos Williams. **CP-WilW2**

At the Smithville Methodist Church. Stephen Dunn. **SP-DunnS**

At the Stilli's Mouth. Richard Hugo. **CP-HugoR**

At the stoplight waiting for the light. Two Scavengers in a Truck, Two Beautiful People in a Mercedes. Lawrence Ferlinghetti. **SP-FerlL**

At the street corner, hunched up. Market at Turk. Thom Gunn. **CP-GunnT**

At the Synod in St Patrick's. Donald Davie. **CP-DavDo**

At the tangled heart of a wood I fell asleep. The Home-Coming. Robert Ranke Graves. **CP-GravR**

At the Tavern. Paul Laurence Dunbar. **CP-DunbP**

At the tide-pool pocketed in broken granite. Frederick Morgan. *Fr.* Blue Hill Poems. **SP-MorgF**

At the time of evening when cars run sweetly. Oxford: Sudden Illness at the Bus-stop. Sir John Betjeman. **CP-BetjJ**

At the time of nougats, the peer yellow. Forces, the Will & the Weather. Wallace Stevens. **CP-StevW**

At the Time of Peony Blossoming. Robert Bly. **SP-BlyR**

At the top of a low hill. Hampstead; the Horse Chestnut Trees. Thom Gunn. **CP-GunnT**

At the Tourist Centre in Boston. Margaret Atwood. **SP-AtwM1**

At the Trade Center. Charles Tomlinson. **CP-TomlC**

At the Un-National Monument along the Canadian Border. William Stafford. **SP-StafW**

At the Wailing Wall in Jerusalem. Countee Cullen. **CP-CullC**

At the War Office, London. Thomas Hardy. **CP-HardT**

At the Water's Edge. Seamus Heaney. *Fr.* Triptych. **SP-HeanS**

At the Wedding March. Gerard Manley Hopkins. **CP-HopkG**

At the Well. Robert Ranke Graves. **CP-GravR**

At the Well. Leonard Nathan. **SP-NathL**

At the Wicket-Gate. Thomas Hardy. **CP-HardT**

At the Window. David Herbert Lawrence. **CP-LawrD**

At the wood's mouth. The Gibber. Theodore Roethke. **NAAL-2** *Fr.* The Lost Son. **CP-RoetT**

At the Word "Farewell." Thomas Hardy. **CP-HardT**

At the worst place in the hills above the city. The Birthday Dream. James Dickey. **CP-DickJ**

At the Y on Fridays. When the Retarded Swim. Gary Gildner. **SP-GildG**

At the Zoo. Isabella Gardner. **CP-GardI**

At thirteen they were known as the inseparables. Cézanne and Zola. Stephen Dobyns. **SP-DobyS**

At 38,000 feet you had better. The Wart. Robert Penn Warren. **SP-WarrR**

At Thirty-One, When Some Are Rich. Philip Larkin. **CP-LarkP**

At Thirty Years. Byron. **FiP** *Fr.* Canto the First. **EnRP; NAEL-2; NoP; OAEL-2; PoE** *Fr.* Don Juan. **CP-Byron**

At this moment lava travels / down the long Sicilian slope. Disaster on the Box. John Hewitt. **CP-HewiJ**

At This Moment of Time. Delmore Schwartz. **SP-SchwD**

At This Precise Moment of History. Thomas Merton. *Fr.* West. *Fr.* The Geography of Lograire. **CP-MertT**

At this west-most U.S. point. Cape Alava. Richard Hugo. **CP-HugoR**

At this wharf there are no grand landings to speak of. A Winter Ship. Sylvia Plath. **CP-PlatS**

At th'Ivory Tribunall of your hand. [With Some Poems Sent to a Gentlewoman. I]. Richard Crashaw. **CP-CrasR**

At Thomas Hardy's Birthplace, 1953. James Wright. **CP-WrigJ**

At three in the afternoon on a clear day. A Newspaper Picture of Spectators at a Hotel Fire. Miller Williams. **SP-WillM**

At 3 o'clock in the afternoon. Nones. Donald Davie. *Fr.* Horae Canonicae. **CP-DavDo**

At three-score winters' end I died. Another ["At three-score winters' end I died"]. *Unknown, tr. fr. Greek by* William Cowper. **CP-CowpW**

At 3:30 a.m. in the morning. 3:30 A.M. Conversation. Charles Bukowski. **SP-BukC2**

At thy nativity a glorious quire. John Milton. **PChr** *Fr.* Book I. *Fr.* Paradise Regained [*or* Regain'd]. **CP-MiltJ**

At times our Britain cannot rest. To the Marquis of Dufferin and Ava. Tennyson. **CP-TennA**

At times we had a run of servant girls. Domestic Help. John Hewitt. **CP-HewiJ**

At times when under cover I 've said. The Instructor. Rudyard Kipling. **CP-KiplR**

At Timon's Villa. Alexander Pope. *See* At Timon's villa let us pass a day.

At Timon's villa let us pass a day. Alexander Pope. **NOEC; OBSV; PoE** *Fr.* Epistle IV, to Richard Boyle, Earl of Burlington. **CP-PopeA**

  (At Timon's Villa.) **OBSV**, *ll.* 99–168;

  (Timon's Villa.) **PoE**, *ll.* 99–180;

At Topsham, / winter-swept. The Bend of the Androscoggin. Marsden Hartley. **CP-HartM**

At Tower Peak. Gary Snyder. **CP-SnydG**

At Trotsky's House. Charles Tomlinson. **CP-TomlC**

At Trumpyngtoun, nat fer fro Cantebrigge. The Reeve's Tale. Geoffrey Chaucer. *Fr.* The Canterbury Tales. **CP-ChauG**

At tu quisquis eris, miseri qui cruda poetæ. Verses on the Death of His Mother. Samuel Johnson. **CP-JohnS**

At twelve, the disintegration of afternoon. What We See Is What We Think. Wallace Stevens. **CP-StevW**

At twelve the rain had gone and left a windy star-splashed sky. A Labour Victory. John Hewitt. **CP-HewiJ**

At 28 I was still faithless. 28. Philip Levine. **SP-LeviP**

At twenty-five a man is on his way. A Point of Age. John Berryman. **CP-BerrJ**

At twenty-five or a little later he had decided. Mauberly's Son: A Summary. John Hewitt. **CP-HewiJ**

At twenty love disintegrates. Gilbert Sorrentino. **SP-SorrG**

At twenty, stooping round about. With Age Wisdom. Archibald MacLeish. **CP-MacLA**

At twenty-three, he's pierced with ache for Christ. Sister's Son. David Markson. **CP-MarkD**

At Twenty we find our friends for ourselves, but it takes Heaven. Wystan Hugh Auden. *Fr.* Shorts I ("Watch upon my wrist, The"). **CP-AudeW**

At twilight I went into the street. Descending Figure. Louise Glück. **SP-GlücL**

At two after noon for our Psyche inquire. On Psyche. Jonathan Swift. **CP-SwifJ**

At two in the morning, when the moon. Highway 30. Ted Kooser. **SP-KoosT**

At two o'clock in the morning, if you open your window and listen. The Dawn Wind. Rudyard Kipling. **CP-KiplR**

At two, the barnyard settled. Pamela. Rita Dove. **SP-DoveR**

At two thousand feet the sea wrinkles like an old man's hand. Encounter. Thomas McGrath. **SP-McGrT**

At Undressing in the Evening. Christopher Smart. *Fr.* Hymns for the Amusement of Children. **SP-SmarC**

At Vallombrosa. William Wordsworth. *Fr.* Memorials of a Tour in Italy, 1837. **CP-WorW2**

At Viscount Nelson's lavish funeral. 1805. Robert Ranke Graves. **CP-GravR**

At Waking. Thomas Hardy. **CP-HardT**

At Washington. John Greenleaf Whittier. **CP-WhitJ**

At Wells: Polyphony. Charles Tomlinson. **CP-TomlC**

At Westminster, hid from the light of day. The Coronation. Thomas Hardy. **CP-HardT**

At whatver page the book fell open. The Tattooed Desert. Richard Shelton. **SP-ShelR**

At Whigham's Inn, Sanquar. Robert Burns. **CP-BurnR**

At White River Roadhouse in the Yukon. Gary Snyder. **CP-SnydG**

At whom is the rice grinning. Pablo Neruda, *tr. fr. Spanish by* Ben Belitt. **SP-NeruP** *Fr.* Question Book.

At Woodlawn I heard the dead cry. The Flight. Theodore Roethke. **NAAL-2; RB; TRP; TrGrPo** *Fr.* The Lost Son. **CP-RoetT**

At Woodward's Gardens. Robert Frost. **CP-FrosR**

At Wynard's Gap. Thomas Hardy. **CP-HardT**

At Yorktown. Charles Olson. **CP-OlsoC; SP-OlsoC**

At Your Old House. William Dickey. **SP-DickW**

  "Do they remember me?" **SP-DickW**

  "Fretful and sick, you ask." **SP-DickW**

  "Fretful and sick, you long." **SP-DickW**

  "Nevertheless, sleep / And as your eyes close." **SP-DickW**

  "No, the night has gone." **SP-DickW**

  "Yes, they remember you." **SP-DickW**

Atalanta. Charles Olson. **CP-OlsoC**

Atalanta in Calydon. Algernon Charles Swinburne.

  Before the Beginning of Years. **SP-SwinA**

  Hounds of Spring, The. **SP-SwinA**

  Not as with Sundering of the Earth. **SP-SwinA**

  O That I Now. **SP-SwinA**

  We Have Seen Thee, O Love. **SP-SwinA**

  Who Hath Given Man Speech? **SP-SwinA**

Atalanta in Camden-Town. "Lewis Carroll." **CP-CarrL**

Atheist, Laodicean or. Widowers. Donald Davie. **CP-DavDo**

Athelstan King / Lord among Earls. *see other translations:* Brunanburg *and* Battle of Brunanburh. *Unknown, tr. fr. Anglo-Saxon by* Alfred, Lord Tennyson. **CP-TennA**

Athena in the Front Lines. Marge Piercy. **SP-PierM**

Athenians mark the moss-grown gate, The. The Garden of Metrodorus. Herman Melville. **SP-MelvH**

Athens. John Milton. *See* Look once more ere we leave this specular Mount.

Athens. Percy Bysshe Shelley. **GrIP** *Fr.* Ode to Liberty. **CP-ShelP**

Athens rose: a city such as vision. Athens. Percy Bysshe Shelley. **GrIP** *Fr.* Ode to Liberty. **CP-ShelP**

Atherton's Gambit. Edwin Arlington Robinson. **CP-RobiE**

Atkins. George Meredith. **CP-MerG2**

Atlanta sped him on his journey north. Homecoming (August 7, 1934). Edwin Rolfe. **CP-RolfE**

Atlantic, The. Charles Tomlinson. **CP-TomlC**

Atlantic City. Stephen Dunn. **SP-DunnS**

Atlantic City Convention, The. William Carlos Williams. **CP-WilW1**

Atlantic City Waiter. Countee Cullen. **CP-CullC**

Atlantic is a stormy moat; and the Mediterranean, The. The Eye. Robinson Jeffers. **CP-JefR3**

Atlantic Review misspelled Kokoschka, The. Irreversible. Roy Fisher. **SP-FishR**

Atlantic Tunnel, The. Louis MacNeice. **CP-MacNL**

Atlantis. Wystan Hugh Auden. **CP-AudeW**

Atlantis. Hart Crane. **HoFi; LiTM; MoPo; NYP; NePA; TwAmPo** *Fr.* The Bridge. **CP-CranH**

Atlas. John Hewitt. **CP-HewiJ**

Atlas. George Meredith. **CP-MerG2**

Atlas. Jonathan Swift. **CP-SwifJ**

Atlas and the Fatman. Thomas Merton. **CP-MertT**

Atlas cedar from Africa and. Exposing Fox and Artifice. Siv Cedering Fox. *Fr.* Onna-E, Pictures of Women. **SP-CedeS**

Atlas, How Have You Been? Carl Sandburg. **CP-SandC**

Atlas of the Difficult World, An. Adrienne Rich. **SP-RicA1**

Atmosphere. Robert Frost. **CP-FrosR**

Atmospheric acquaintance, The. Emily Dickinson. **SP-DickE**

Atom bellies like a cauliflower, The. Jane Cooper. *Fr.* After the Bomb Tests. **SP-CoopJ**

Atom displaces all atoms beside, The. Ralph Waldo Emerson. **CP-EmerR**

Atom from atom yawns as far. Ralph Waldo Emerson. **CP-EmerR**

Atom is a crystal, The. To Crystallization. John Updike. *Fr.* Seven Odes to Seven Natural Processes. **CP-UpdiJ**

Atomic Pantoum. Peter Meinke. **SP-MeinP**

Atonement, The. John Milton. **OBS** *Fr.* Book III. *Fr.* Paradise Lost. **CP-MiltJ**

Atop each stem. End of May. Mona Van Duyn. **SP-VanDM**

Atop the down pasture. Enniscorthy Suite. Charles Olson. **CP-OlsoC**

Atque in Perpetuum A.W. Louis Zukofsky. **CP-ZukLS**

Atque tribus primum quod flumen fontibus exit. Gerard Manley Hopkins. *Fr.* Fragments on St. Winefred. **CP-HopkG**

Atropos to Ophelia. Alun Lewis. **CP-LewiA**

Attack, The. David Herbert Lawrence. **CP-LawrD**

Attack of the Squash People. Marge Piercy. **SP-PierM**

Attar of Roses. Donald Davie. **CP-DavDo**

Attempt at the Manner of Waller, An. William Cowper. **CP-CowpW**

Attempt the end, and never stand to doubt. Seek[e] and Find[e]. Robert Herrick. **CP-HerrR**

Attempt to be a painter and nothing but a painter finding AM so difficult, The. The Painter Speaks—the Woman Answers. Kay Boyle. **CP-BoylK**

Attempt to Discover Life. Wallace Stevens. **CP-StevW**

Attempted Departure. James Dickey. **CP-DickJ**

Attempting to Persuade You to Go for a Walk in the Public Gardens. Jean Garrigue. **SP-GarrJ**

Attend to the music divine. Bible, *O.T. See* Psalm 134: "Behold, bless ye the Lord, all ye servants of the Lord."

Attention. Archie Randolph Ammons. **SP-AmmoA**

Attention. Adrienne Rich. **CP-RicAE; SP-RicA2**

Attention: First Lady of the Festival. James Liddy. **CP-LiddJ**

Attention Makes Infinity. Richard Wilbur. **CP-WilbR**

Attentive eyes, fantastic heed. A Poet. Thomas Hardy. **CP-HardT**

Attentiveness. Alice Walker. **CP-WalkA**

Attic, The. Richard Eberhart. *Fr.* Burr Oaks. **CP-EberR**

Attic, The. Derek Mahon. **SP-MahoD**

Attic, The. Lewis Turco. **SP-TurcL**

Attic and the cedar closet—nostalgia!, The. The Attic. Richard Eberhart. *Fr.* Burr Oaks. **CP-EberR**

Attic maid! with honey fed. To the Swallow. Euenus, *tr. fr. Greek by* William Cowper. **CP-CowpW**

Attic Poem. Lewis Turco. **SP-TurcL**

Attic Which Is Desire, The. William Carlos Williams. **CP-WilW1**

Attics cleared; shelves and drawers emptied. Preparing to Leave. Phoebe Hesketh. **SP-HeskP**

Atticus ("How did they fume, and stamp, and roar, and chafe"). Alexander Pope. **InPK; OBEC; TW; WHA** *Fr.* Epistle to Dr. Arbuthnot. **CP-PopeA**

Atticus ("Peace to all such! but were there one whose fires"). Alexander Pope. **AWP; InPK; NOBE; SeCePo; TRP; WHA** *Fr.* Epistle to Dr. Arbuthnot. **CP-PopeA**

(On Addison.) **IHNG**

Attila. William Everson. **SP-EverW**

Attila. David Herbert Lawrence. **CP-LawrD**

Attila. Kenneth Patchen. **CP-PatcK**

Attila, Hitler. Robert Lowell. **SP-LoweR**

Attis. Catullus. *See* Carmen 63: "Plunging towards Phrygia over violent water."

Attis: Or, Something Missing. Basil Bunting. **CP-BuntB**

"I thought I saw my late wife (a very respectable woman)."

"Out of puff / noonhot in tweeds and gray felt."

"What mournful stave, what bellow shakes the grove?"

Attitudes. Richard Eberhart. **CP-EberR**

Irish Catholic.

New England Protestant.

Atun-Re / the sun disk. Reaching Out with the Hands of the Sun. Diane Wakoski. **SP-WakoD**

Atypical Affair, An. Allen Ginsberg. **CP-GinsA**

Atys. Alfred Edward Housman. **CP-HousA**

Au clair de la lune. Malcolm Lowry. **CP-LowrM**

Au Clair de la Lune. "Hugh MacDiarmid." **SP-MacDH**

Au Clair de la Lune. "Hugh MacDiarmid." *Fr.* Au Clair de la Lune. **SP-MacDH**

Au Clair de la Lune.

Huntress and Her Dogs, The.

Man in the Moon, The. **NeBP**

Moonstruck.

(Munestruck.) **NeBP**

Au voleur, au voleur, au voleur!—. George Meredith. **CP-MerG2**

Aubade: "At break of dawn." Wystan Hugh Auden. *Fr.* Three Posthumous Poems. **CP-AudeW**

Aubade: "Beckoned anew to a World." Wystan Hugh Auden. **CP-AudeW**

Aubade: "Cool and beautiful as the blossom of the wild carrot." Edna St. Vincent Millay. **CP-MillE**

Aubade: "Having bitten on life like a sharp apple." Louis MacNeice. **CP-MacNL**

Aubade: "I wish for you that when you wake." Donald Davie. **CP-DavDo**

Aubade: "I work all day, and get half-drunk at night." Philip Larkin. **CP-LarkP**

Aubade: "My dove, my doe." Stevie Smith. **CP-SmitS**

Aubade: "Today above the gull's call." Louise Glück. **SP-GlücL**

Aubade: "Truck gears grinding up Marin." Tom Clark. **SP-ClarT**

Aubade: "Weaned from moon." Daniel Gerard Hoffman. **SP-HoffD**

Aubade: "Who has hold of Juliet's nipples." Frederick Morgan. *Fr.* Enigmas. **SP-MorgF**

Aubade: Bermuda. Thomas Merton. **CP-MertT**

Aubade for Infants. Louis MacNeice. **CP-MacNL**

Aubade—Harlem. Thomas Merton. **CP-MertT; SP-MertT**

Aubade: Lake Erie. Thomas Merton. **CP-MertT; SP-MertT**

Aubade, 1925. Louis Zukofsky. *Fr.* 29 Poems. **CP-ZukLS**

Aubade—the Annunciation. Thomas Merton. **CP-MertT**

Aubade—the City. Thomas Merton. **CP-MertT; SP-MertT**

Aubade to Fear (Heavy with Child). Louise McNeill. **SP-McNeL**

Aube Provençale. Marilyn Hacker. **SP-HackM**

Auburn. Carl Sandburg. **CP-SandC**

Auburn autumn leaves, will you come back? Auburn. Carl Sandburg. **CP-SandC**

Auction, The. Theodore Roethke. **CP-RoetT**

Auction. William DeWitt Snodgrass. **SP-SnodW**

Auctioneer. Carl Sandburg. **CP-SandC**

Auctioneer of Parting, The. Emily Dickinson. **CP-DickE**

Audacities and fetes of the drunken weeks! John Berryman. *Fr.* Sonnets to Chris. **CP-BerrJ**

Audacity of Bliss, said Jacob to the Angel. Emily Dickinson. **SP-DickE**

Auden at Milwaukee. Stephen Spender. **CP-SpenS**

Auden's Funeral. Stephen Spender. **CP-SpenS**

Audible trout, / Notional midges. Beds. Girls on the Bridge. Derek Mahon. **SP-MahoD**

Audience cheers as the monkey correctly, The. Avenue of Americans. John Yau. **SP-YauJo**

Audit. Leonard Nathan. **SP-NathL**

Audition. Dabney Stuart. **SP-StuaD**

Audley Court. Tennyson. **CP-TennA**

"Sleep, Ellen Aubrey, sleep, and dream of me." **CBLP**

Audubon. Robert Penn Warren. **SP-WarrR**

Dream He Never Knew the End of, The.

Love and Knowledge.

Sign Whereby He Knew, The.

Sound of That Wind, The.

Tell Me a Story. **MT**

Was Not the Lost Dauphin.

We Are Only Ourselves.

Auf wiedersehen! We part a little while. T.A.M. Edward Estlin Cummings. **CP-CummE**

Aufilena—*bonnie, simple,* laud and they're amicable. Catullus. *See* Carmen 110: "Men always praise an honest whore."

Aufilena, virile content him weave her her solo. Catullus. *See* Carmen 111: "In constancy content with one man, there."

Augment of Re-Birth. Jim Morrison. **SP-MorrJ**

Augsburg Adoration, The. Randall Jarrell. **CP-JarrR**

Auguries of Innocence. William Blake. **CP-BlakW**

"Bat that flits at close of eve, The." **UV**

"God appears, and God is Light." **TRV**

"Robin Redbreast in a cage, A." **FaPON; MoShBr; OxBoLi**

(Three Things to Remember.) **FaPON; MoShBr**

"To see a World in a Grain of Sand." **EnlH; HoFi; ImOP; InPK; NTP; TRV; TreFS,** *ll.* 1–4;

August. Jim Carroll. **SP-CarrJ**

August. Hayden Carruth. **CP-CarHS**

August. John Clare. **SP-ClarJ** *Fr.* The Shepherd's [*or* Shepheards] Calendar.

August. William Everson. **SP-EverW**

August. Ted Kooser. **SP-KoosT**

August. Louis MacNeice. **CP-MacNL**

August. Mary Oliver. **SP-OlivM**

August. Adrienne Rich. **SP-RicA2**

August. Christina Georgina Rossetti. *Fr.* The Months: A Pageant. **CP-RosC2**

August. Richard Shelton. **SP-ShelR**

August. Gary Snyder. *Fr.* Six Years. **CP-SnydG**

August. Edmund Spenser. **GN** *Fr.* The Faerie Queene. **CP-Spens**

August. Edmund Spenser. *Fr.* The Shepheardes [*or* Shepeards *or* Shepherd's] Calender. **CP-Spens**

It Fell upon a Holy [*or* Holly] Eve. **CBLP; InvP**

(Roundelay, A: "It fell upon a holy eve.") **EIL**

August. Algernon Charles Swinburne. **SP-SwinA**

August and laurelled have been content to speak for an age, and the ages that follow. Soliloquy. Robinson Jeffers. **CP-JefR1**

AUGUST (*Coaching*). Rudyard Kipling. *Fr.* Verses on Games. **CP-KiplR**

August 8th. Anne Sexton. **CP-SextA**

8/8/68: i. Adrienne Rich. **CP-RicAE** *Fr.* Ghazals: Homage to Ghalib. **SP-RicA2**

8/8/68: ii. Adrienne Rich. **CP-RicAE** *Fr.* Ghazals: Homage to Ghalib. **SP-RicA2**

August Evening Outside of Nashville, An. Miller Williams. **SP-WillM**

August First, *see also* Essay on Marriage. Hayden Carruth. **CP-CarHS**

August first: it was a year ago. For K.J., Leaving and Coming Back. Marilyn Hacker. **SP-HackM**

August First, 1974. James Schuyler. **CP-SchuJ**

8/1/68. Adrienne Rich. **CP-RicAE** *Fr.* Ghazals: Homage to Ghalib. **SP-RicA2**

August 14, 1961. Hayden Carruth. **CP-CarHS**

8/4/68. Adrienne Rich. **CP-RicAE** *Fr.* Ghazals: Homage to Ghalib. **SP-RicA2**

August, goldenrod blowing. We walk. Maple Syrup. Donald Hall. **CP-HallD**

August. Hear / the cicadas. Speaking for Them. Hayden Carruth. **CP-CarHS**

August Holidays. David Herbert Lawrence. **CP-LawrD**

August is nearly over, the people. Louis MacNeice. **CMoP** *Fr.* Autumn Journal. **CP-MacNL**

August Midnight, An. Thomas Hardy. **CP-HardT**

August Night. James Schuyler. **CP-SchuJ**

August, 1940. John Gould Fletcher. **SP-FletJ**

August, 1945. Howard Nemerov. **CP-NemeH**

August 1968. Wystan Hugh Auden. **CP-AudeW**

August 1939. John Hewitt. **CP-HewiJ**

August on Sourdough, a Visit from Dick Brewer. Gary Snyder. **CP-SnydG**

August Rain. Robert Bly. **SP-BlyR**

August. Render to Caesar. Speak parrot: a gimmick for Poll. Canto I. Louis MacNeice. *Fr.* Autumn Sequel. **CP-MacNL**

August 17th. Anne Sexton. **CP-SextA**

August, tasting of ripe grapes and afternoon sleep. Sonnet. James Schuyler. **CP-SchuJ**

August 22, 1939. Kenneth Rexroth. **SP-RexrK**

August Voice, An. Elizabeth Barrett Browning. **CP-BroEB**

Augustus Observes the Sunset. Rita Dove. *Fr.* A Suite for Augustus. **SP-DoveR**

Augustus still survives in Maro's strain. Epigram on Colley Cibber. Samuel Johnson. **CP-JohnS**

Auld chuckie Reekie's sair distrest. To William Creech. Robert Burns. **CP-BurnR**

Auld com'rade dear and brither sinner. Letter to J———s T———t, Gl—nc———r. Robert Burns. **CP-BurnR**

Auld Farmer's New-Year-Morning Salutation to His Auld Mare, Maggie, on Giving Her the Accustomed Ripp of Corn to Hansel in the New-Year, The. Robert Burns. **CP-BurnR**

Auld Lang Syne. Robert Burns. **CP-BurnR**

Auld Man's Mare's Dead, The. Robert Burns. **CP-BurnR**

Auld Man's Winter Thought, The. Robert Burns. **CP-BurnR**

AULD NIBOR I'm three times, doubly, o'er your debtor. Second Epistle to Davie. Robert Burns. **CP-BurnR**

Auld Rob Morris. Robert Burns. **CP-BurnR**

Auld wumman cam' in, a mere rickle o' banes, in a faded black dress, An. Old Wife in High Spirits. "Hugh MacDiarmid." **SP-MacDH**

Aulder than mammoth or than mastodon. Gairmscoile. "Hugh MacDiarmid." **SP-MacDH**

Aunt. Al Young. **CP-YounA**

Aunt Cis and Uncle Tom. John Hewitt. **CP-HewiJ**

Aunt Edith married Sam, an amateur. Uncle Sam and Aunt Edie. John Hewitt. **CP-HewiJ**

Aunt Elsie hears / Singing in the night. Aunt Elsie's Night Music. Mary Oliver. **SP-OlivM**

Aunt Elsie's Night Music. Mary Oliver. **SP-OlivM**

Aunt Gertrud. Peter Meinke. **SP-MeinP**

Aunt Helen. Thomas Stearns Eliot. **CP-ElioT**

Aunt Imogen. Edwin Arlington Robinson. **CP-RobiE**

Aunt Jemima of the Ocean Waves. Robert Earl Hayden. **CP-HaydR**

Aunt Jennifer's Tigers. Adrienne Rich. **CP-RicAE; SP-RicA1; SP-RicA2**

Aunt Leaf. Mary Oliver. **SP-OlivM**

Aunt Mabel. William Stafford. **SP-StafW**

Aunt Mary. John Ciardi. **SP-CiarJ**

Aunt Mary. Peter Meinke. **SP-MeinP**

Aunt, my down-to-earth father's sibling, went to stay, An. A Relative and an Absolute. Mona Van Duyn. **SP-VanDM**

Aunt Rose—now—might I see you. To Aunt Rose. Allen Ginsberg. **CP-GinsA**

Aunt Sue has a head full of stories. Aunt Sue's Stories. Langston Hughes. **SP-HughL**

Aunt Sue's Stories. Langston Hughes. **SP-HughL**

Auntie's Skirts. Robert Louis Stevenson. **CP-StevR**

Aura. Erica Jong. **SP-JongE**

Aura dolcissima, ma donde siete? Christina Georgina Rossetti. **CP-RosC3**

Aurelius, father, assure that the o numb. Catullus. *See* Carmen 21: "Impresario of nediness."

Aureng-Zebe. John Dryden. **SP-DrydJ**

Prologue: "Our author by experience finds it true." **FiP; OBS; OxBoLi; SeCV-2**

When I Consider Life. **FiP**

Auricle's Oracle. Daniel Gerard Hoffman. **SP-HoffD**

Aurora and Tithonus. Euripides. **CP-BroEB** *tr. by* Elizabeth Barrett Browning; *Fr.* Troades.

Aurora Borealis. Rita Dove. **SP-DoveR**

Aurora Est Musis Amica. Samuel Johnson. **CP-JohnS**

Aurora is the effort. Emily Dickinson. **CP-DickE**

Aurora Leigh. Elizabeth Barrett Browning. **CP-BroEB**

"And I, I was a good child on the whole." **BrRo**

"As the earth." **EPCY**

"Books, books, books!" **WPOW**

"By Keats's soul, the man who never stepped." **EPCY**

"Critics say that epics have died out, The." **NALW; PBWP; PeVV**

"I had a little chamber in the house." **FaBoPP**

"I just knew it when we swept above the old roofs of Dijon." **PeVV**

"I learnt the collects and the catechism." **EnVR; TEP**

"I mused/ Up and down, up and down, the terraced streets." **OBTV**

"I think I see my father's sister stand." **NALW**

"My mother was a Florentine." **NALW**

"Of writing many books there is no end!" **NOBVV**

Olives and Mountains. **FaBoPP; OBTV**

Reading. **GN**

Sweetness of England, The. **OXAEP-2**

"Then, land!--then, England! oh, the frosty cliffs." **FaBoPP; NAEL-2**

" 'Then, must it be'." **NALW**

" 'There it is!/ You play beside a death-bed like a child'." **BrRo**

"Truth, so far, in my book; the truth which draws." **WGRP**

Tuscan Life. **FaBoPP**

"Without considering whether they were fit." **PFP**

Aurora, now thou show'st thy blushing light, *speech of Cleophila*. Sir Philip Sidney. **SP-SidnP** *Fr.* Arcadia.

Auroras of Autumn, The. Wallace Stevens. **CP-StevW**

"Farewell to an idea. . . A cabin stands." **CMoP; HCAP; PoE**

"Farewell to an idea. . . The mother's face." **HCAP; PoE**
"Is there an imagination that sits enthroned." **HCAP**
"It is a theatre floating through the clouds." **HCAP**
"This is where the serpent lives, the bodiless." **CMoP; PoE**
"Unhappy people in a happy world, An." **CMoP; PoE**
Aus Dem Zweiten Reich. Basil Bunting. **CP-BuntB**
"Herr Lignitz knows Old Berlin. It is near the Post Office."
"Renowned author of, The."
"Women swarm in Tauentsienstrasse."
Aus Einem April. Frank O'Hara. **SP-OharF**
Aus Einer Kindheit. Kenneth Koch. **SP-KochK**
Auspex. Robert Frost. **CP-FrosR**
Auspicious Reverence! Hush all meaner song. The Destiny of Nations.
    Samuel Taylor Coleridge. **CP-ColeS**
Austere Poem. Richard Eberhart. **CP-EberR**
Austerities. Charles Simic. **SP-SimiC**
Austin! accept a grateful verse from me! To Dr. Austin. William Cowper.
    CP-CowpW
Austin is a Poet, Austin writes a psalm. Emily Dickinson. **SP-DickE**
Australian mounted infantryman now teaches, The. Carl Sandburg. *Fr.* The
    People, Yes. **CP-SandC**
Authentic! Shadows of it, The. Matins. Denise Levertov. **CP-LeveD**
Author ad Librum. Ben Jonson. **CP-JonsB**
Author Apologizes to a Lady, for His Being a Little Man, The. Christopher
    Smart. **SP-SmarC**
Author of light, revive my dying spright. Thomas Campion. **CP-CampT**
Author of the Jesus Papers Speaks, The. Anne Sexton. **CP-SextA**
Author to Her Book, The. Anne Bradstreet. **CP-BradA**
Author to the Reader, The. Randall Jarrell. **CP-JarrR**
Author to the Reader, The ("Deare eye, that daynest to let fall a looke").
    Robert Southwell. **CP-SoutR**
Author to the Reader, The ("Deare eye that doost peruse my Muses stile").
    Robert Southwell. **CP-SoutR**
Author upon Himself, The. Jonathan Swift. **CP-SwifJ**
Authority of Krajova, The. Kenneth Patchen. **CP-PatcK**
Authors are judg'd by strange capricious Rules. Prologue to the *Three Hours
    after Marriage*. Alexander Pope. **CP-PopeA**
Author's Earnest Cry and Prayer, to the Right Honorable and Honorable, the
    Scotch Representatives in the House of Commons, The. Robert Burns.
    CP-BurnR
Author's Manner of Living, The. Jonathan Swift. **CP-SwifJ**
Authors Motto, The. Richard Crashaw. **CP-CrasR**
Author's Prologue. Dylan Thomas. **CP-ThomD**
Authors' Residences. John Updike. **CP-UpdiJ**
Author's Voyage down the Rhine (Thirty Years Ago). William
    Wordsworth. **CP-WorW2**
Authours Epitaph, Made by Himself, The. Sir Walter Ralegh. **CP-RaleW**
Auto-Da-Fé. David Herbert Lawrence. **CP-LawrD**
Auto Poesy: On the Lam from Bloomington. Allen Ginsberg. **CP-GinsA**
Auto Wreck. Karl Shapiro. **SP-ShapK**
Autobiographia Literaria. Frank O'Hara. **SP-OharF**
Autobiographical Note. Kenneth Patchen. **CP-PatcK**
Autobiographies. Derek Mahon. **SP-MahoD**
    Bicycle, The.
    Home Front, The. **FaBCIP**
    Last Resort, The.
    Lost Girls, The. **FaBCIP**
Autobiographies. Frederick Morgan. **SP-MorgF**
Autobiography, *See also* Autobiography ("I am leading a quiet life") by Sonja
    [dA]kesson. Lawrence Ferlinghetti. **SP-FerlL**
Autobiography. Thom Gunn. **CP-GunnT**
Autobiography. Archibald MacLeish. **CP-MacLA**
Autobiography. Louis MacNeice. **CP-MacNL**
Autobiography at an Air-Station. Philip Larkin. **CP-LarkP**
Autobiography of the Impotent Man, The. James McAuley. **SP-McAuJ**
    "But old Lares with the rest forgot in time."
    "Child of ten, no more, A."
    "My earliest memory? why, the lassitude!"
    "To feel at my heels the smooth stones."
Autograph, An. John Greenleaf Whittier. **CP-WhitJ**
Autograph, An. John Greenleaf Whittier. **CP-WhitJ**
Autolycus. Louis MacNeice. **CP-MacNL**
Automaton, The. Randall Jarrell. **CP-JarrR**
Autopsy on this childhood then reveals, An. Malcolm Lowry. **CP-LowrM**
Autorotation without Gravity. Tom Clark. **SP-ClarT**
Autumn. Wystan Hugh Auden. **CP-AudWJ**
Autumn. Walter de la Mare. **CP-DeLaW**

Autumn. James Dickey. **CP-DickJ**
Autumn. Philip Larkin. **CP-LarkP**
Autumn. Archibald MacLeish. **CP-MacLA**
Autumn. Raissa Maritain, *tr. fr. French by* Thomas Merton. **CP-MertT**
Autumn. Grace Paley. **CP-PaleG**
Autumn. Christina Georgina Rossetti. **CP-RosC1**
Autumn. Christina Georgina Rossetti. **CP-RosC3**
Autumn. Stevie Smith. *See* He Told His Life Story to Mrs. Courtly.
Autumn. Edmund Spenser. **GN** *Fr.* The Faerie Queene. **CP-Spens**
Autumn. James Thomson. *Fr.* The Seasons. **CP-ThomJ**
    "Cormorant on high, The." **OxBoS**
Autumn. Charles Tomlinson. **CP-TomlC**
Autumn. William Carlos Williams. **CP-WilW1**
Autumn: A Dirge. Percy Bysshe Shelley. **CP-ShelP**
Autumn. A haze is gold. The Gossamers. Charles Tomlinson. **CP-TomlC**
Autumn Air. Charles Simic. **SP-SimiC**
Autumn at Taos. David Herbert Lawrence. **CP-LawrD**
Autumn at Whitewell. Phoebe Hesketh. **SP-HeskP**
Autumn Begins in Martins Ferry, Ohio. James Wright. **CP-WrigJ**
Autumn Break. Joseph Ceravolo. **SP-CeraJ**
Autumn Burning, An. Wendell Berry. **CP-BerrW**
Autumn Chant. Edna St. Vincent Millay. **CP-MillE**
Autumn Chapter in a Novel. Thom Gunn. **CP-GunnT**
Autumn Day. Rainer Maria Rilke, *tr. fr. German by* C. F. MacIntyre. **CP-
    SpenS**
    ("Lord, it is time. The summer was so great.") **CP-SpenS,** *tr.* by Stephen
    Spender;
Autumn Daybreak. Edna St. Vincent Millay. **CP-MillE**
Autumn departs; but still his mantle's fold. Autumn on Tweedside. Sir
    Walter Scott. **SP-ScotW** *Fr.* The Lord of the Isles.
Autumn Drives (Early 1800s), The. Louise McNeill. **SP-McNeL**
Autumn: Early Morning. Isabella Gardner. **CP-GardI**
Autumn Equinox. Adrienne Rich. **CP-RicAE**
Autumn Even-Song. George Meredith. **CP-MerG1**
Autumn Evening. Wystan Hugh Auden. **CP-AudWJ**
Autumn Evening. Robinson Jeffers. **CP-JefR1**
Autumn feels slowed down, the. Paula Becker to Clara Westhoff. Adrienne
    Rich. **SP-RicA2**
Autumn Fires. Robert Louis Stevenson. **CP-StevR**
Autumn Floods. Chuang Tzu, *tr. fr. Chinese by* Thomas Merton. **CP-
    MertT**
Autumn Gale. John Hewitt. **CP-HewiJ**
Autumn Gold: New England Fall. Allen Ginsberg. **CP-GinsA**
Autumn Has Caught Us in Our Summer Wear. Philip Larkin. **CP-LarkP**
Autumn has emptied heaven of its birds. Autumn Song. Thomas McGrath.
    SP-McGrT
Autumn Imagined. Donald Davie. **CP-DavDo**
Autumn in California. Kenneth Rexroth. **SP-RexrK**
Autumn in King's Hintock Park. Thomas Hardy. **CP-HardT**
Autumn is among us. Emily Dickinson. **SP-DickE**
Autumn is come, dear kindly dame. Autumn. Wystan Hugh Auden. **CP-
    AudWJ**
Autumn is over the long leaves that love us. The Falling of the Leaves.
    William Butler Yeats. **CP-YeatW**
Autumn Is the Crows' Time. Kenneth Patchen. **CP-PatcK**
Autumn is very wild though. In My Crib. Joseph Ceravolo. **SP-CeraJ**
Autumn is:that between there and here. Edward Estlin Cummings. **CP-
    CummE**
Autumn Journal. Louis MacNeice. **CP-MacNL**
    "And I remember Spain." **OBWP; OXAEP-2**
    "And so return to work—the M.A. gown."
    "And when we clear away."
    "August is nearly over, the people." **CMoP**
    "But work is alien; what do I care for the Master."
    "Close and slow, summer is ending in Hampshire."
    "Conferences, adjournments, ultimatums." **FaBoPV; OxBTC; WaP**
    "December the nineteenth: over the black roofs."
    "From the second floor up, looking north, having breakfast."
    "In the days that were early the music came easy."
    "Nelson stands on a black pillar."
        Week to Christmas, A. **TIRV**
    "Next day I drove by night, The."
    "Nightmare leaves fatigue." **AnIL; BIrV; CIP; FaBCIP; PNI**
    "Now we are back to normal, now the mind is." **CMoP; OXAEP-2**
    "Pigeons riddle the London air, The."
    "Road ran downhill into Spain, The."

"September has come and I wake."

"Shelley and jazz and lieder and love and hymn-tunes." **NOBL**

"Sleep, my body, sleep, my ghost."

"Sleep serene, avoid the backward." **CMoP**

"Spider, spider, twisting tight."

"Sun shines easy, sun shines gay."
Munich Agreement, The. **FaBoEH**

"These days are misty, insulated, mute." **CMoP**

"To-day was a beautiful day, the sky was a brilliant." **CP-MacNL**

"Which things being so, as we said when we studied."
"I ought to be glad." **OBCoV**

Autumn Journey. Frank Templeton Prince. **CP-PrinF**

Autumn Leaves. James Schuyler. **CP-SchuJ**

Autumn leaves blow from my hand. Ezra Pound. *See* Canto 93: "A man's paradise his good nature."

Autumn! Leaves in symphonic tumult. Lacunae. Charles Tomlinson. *Fr.* Antecedents. **CP-TomlC**

Autumn Morning in Shokoku-ji, An. Gary Snyder. **HAP; VGW; WeW** *Fr.* Four Poems for Robin. **CP-SnydG**

Autumn Movement. Carl Sandburg. **CP-SandC**

Autumn 1980. Marilyn Hacker. **SP-HackM**

Autumn 1964. Sir John Betjeman. **CP-BetjJ**

Autumn, 1939. Alun Lewis. **CP-LewiA**

Autumn of Many Years, The. Kenneth Rexroth. **CP-RexKL** *Fr.* The Homestead Called Damascus.
"How short a time for a life to last." **SP-RexrK**

Autumn on Tweedside. Sir Walter Scott. **SP-ScotW** *Fr.* The Lord of the Isles.

Autumn—overlooked my Knitting. Emily Dickinson. **CP-DickE**

Autumn Perspective. Erica Jong. **SP-JongE**

Autumn Piece. Charles Tomlinson. **CP-TomlC**

Autumn Rain. David Herbert Lawrence. **CP-LawrD**

Autumn Rain-Scene, An. Thomas Hardy. **CP-HardT**

Autumn Refrain. Wallace Stevens. **CP-StevW**

Autumn resumes the land, ruffles the woods. The Laurel Axe. Geoffrey Hill. **NAEL-2; NoAM; NoP; PoE** *Fr.* An Apology for the Revival of Christian Architecture in England. **CP-HillG**

Autumn seems ending: there is lassitude. October. Charles Tomlinson. **CP-TomlC**

Autumn Sequel. Louis MacNeice. **CP-MacNL**

Canto I: "August. Render to Caesar. Speak parrot: a gimmick for Poll."

Canto II: "On the other hand," said Gavin—or could have said.

Canto III: "To work—To Beaconsfield. A suburban train."

Canto IV: "To work. To my own office, my own job."
(From Autumn Sequel.) **FaBCIP**

CantoV: "Hence these arrears, this filing cabinet crammed."

Canto VI: "Everydayness is good; particular-dayness."

Canto VII: "Cloud of witnesses. To whom? To what?, A."
(Fanfare for the Makers, A.) **NOBE**

Canto VIII: "Fair; not to say radiant. The Twentyfifth of September."

Canto IX: "Master closed the door. The unmodern words, The."

Canto X: "Daily news. And today? There is not so much to note."

Canto XI: "Golden guineas filter through the mist, The."

Canto XII: "Now to dissolve in port. I take the train."

Canto XIII: "Leaving the colleges then and their half-remembered."

Canto XIV: "Battle? That is one way of looking at the matter, A."

Canto XV: "Been here before? Whether he has or no."

Canto XVI: "Young man cannot answer. Is this life?, The."

Canto XVII: "This was the night that specially we went down."

Canto XVIII: "Lament for the Makers. Monday comes: at noon."

Canto XIX: "All out!" the voices cry in the Park, "All out!"

Canto XX: "To Wales once more, though not on holiday now."

Canto XXI: "Thirtieth inst., too soon the thirtieth ult, The."

Canto XXII: "So this is Glastonbury. A green hill far away."

Canto XXIII: "December continues mild. The rose garden."

Canto XXIV: "December the Twenty-third: I visit the Ancient East."

Canto XXV: "And today is Christmas Eve. Once more to work."

Canto XXVI: "Morning bright as summer. The job on hand, A."

Autumn Sequence. Adrienne Rich. **CP-RicAE**

Autumn Song. Wystan Hugh Auden. *Fr.* Twelve Songs. **CP-AudeW**

Autumn Song. Thomas McGrath. **SP-McGrT**

Autumn Sonnets, The. May Sarton.
"If I could let you go as trees let go." **SP-SartM**

Autumn Sunshine. David Herbert Lawrence. **CP-LawrD**

Autumn surrounds the valley, iniquity. The Wanderings of the Tribe. Alí Chumacero, *tr. fr. Spanish by* William Carlos Williams. **CP-WilW2**

Autumn, the Third Pastoral, or Hylas and Ægon. Alexander Pope. *Fr.* Pastorals. **CP-PopeA**

Autumn Thoughts. John Greenleaf Whittier. **CP-WhitJ**

Autumn-time has come, The. My Triumph. John Greenleaf Whittier. **CP-WhitJ**

Autumn-Time, Wind and the Planet Pluto. Joseph Ceravolo. **SP-CeraJ**

Autumn torture. The old signs. Antinoüs: The Diaries. Adrienne Rich. **CP-RicAE; SP-RicA1; SP-RicA2**

Autumn Valley. John Hewitt. **CP-HewiJ**

Autumn Violets. Christina Georgina Rossetti. **CP-RosC1**

Autumn Warmth. Robert Pack. **SP-PackR**

Autumn was the heavy mood of the human. The Man of Summer. Richard Eberhart. *Fr.* The Seasons. **CP-EberR**

Autumnal[l], The. John Donne. **InPS; JCP; NOSC; OAEP; PoEL-2; SeCV-1; TEP** *Fr.* Elegies. **CP-DonnJ**

Autumnal. Richard Eberhart. **CP-EberR**

Autumnal. Louise Glück. **SP-GlücL**

Autumnal. John Hewitt. **CP-HewiJ**

Autumnal. Howard Nemerov. **CP-NemeH**

Autumnal. James Wright. **CP-WrigJ**

Autumnal gales had wreaked their will, The. On the Esplanade. Walter de la Mare. **CP-DeLaW**

Aux Imagistes. William Carlos Williams. **CP-WilW1**

Available Light. Al Young. **CP-YounA**

Avalanche. Leonard Cohen. **CP-CoheL**

Avalanche. William Dickey. **SP-DickW**

Avarice. George Herbert. **CP-HerbG**

Avarice and Ambition Only Were the First Builders of Towns and Founders of Empire. Kenneth Patchen. **CP-PatcK**

Avarice, the noose that lets oil, oh my dear oh. Invincibility. Frank O'Hara. **SP-OharF**

Avarus et Plutus. John Gay, *tr. fr. English by* William Cowper. **CP-CowpW**

Avast, the Pileated Woodpecker. On the Extinction of a Species. Daniel Gerard Hoffman. **SP-HoffD**

Avaunt all specious pliancy of mind. William Wordsworth. **CP-WorW1**

Avaunt this economic rage! To the Utilitarians. William Wordsworth. **CP-WorW2**

[—] avaunt! with tenfold pleasure. The Vale of Esthwaite. William Wordsworth. **CP-WorW1**

Ave atque Vale. Gilbert Sorrentino. **SP-SorrG**

Ave Caesar. Robinson Jeffers. **CP-JefR2**

Ave Imperatrix! Rudyard Kipling. **CP-KiplR**

Ave Maria. Hart Crane. **HoFi; MoPo; NOBA; NePA; NoAM** *Fr.* The Bridge. **CP-CranH**

Ave Maria. Frank O'Hara. **SP-OharF**

'Ave you 'eard o' the Widow at Windsor. The Widow at Windsor. Rudyard Kipling. **CP-KiplR**

Avec Ardeur. Marianne Craig Moore. **CP-MoorM**

Avec Merci, Mother. Maya Angelou. **SP-AngeM**

Avenge O Lord thy slaughtered [*or* slaughter'd] Saints, whose bones. John Milton. **CP-MiltJ**
(Sonnet 18: "Avenge O Lord thy slaughter'd Saints, whose bones.") **CP-MiltJ**

Avenue A. Frank O'Hara. **SP-OharF**

Avenue Bearing the Initial of Christ into the New World, The. Galway Kinnell. **SP-KinnG**

"Already the Avenue troughs the light of day."

"Behind the Power Station on 14th, the held breath." **NaP**

"Children set fires in ashbarrels." **NaP**

"First Sun Day of the year. Tonight." **NaP**

"Fishmarket closed, the fishes gone into flesh, The." **NaP**

"From the Station House."

"Garbage-disposal truck, The."

"In sunlight on the Avenue." **LiTM**

"In the pushcart market, on Sunday." **NaP**

"It was Gold's junkhouse, the one the clacking."

"Next door, outside the pink-fronted Bodega Hispano."

"Pcheek pcheek pcheek pcheek pcheek." **LiTM; NePoEA-2**

"Promise was broken too freely, The." **NaP**

"That violent song of the twilight!"

Avenue of Americans. John Yau. **SP-YauJo**

Avenue of Poplars, The. William Carlos Williams. **CP-WilW1**

Avenue rises toward a city of white marble, The. Sleeping. Donald Hall. **CP-HallD**

Avenue was green and long, and green, The. A Visit to Castletown House. Michael Hartnett. **SP-HarMi**

Avenues, The. David St. John. **SP-StJoD**

Average Egyptian Faces Death, The. John Updike. **CP-UpdiJ**

Average Guy. "Lou Reed." **SP-ReedL**

Avert, High Wisdom, never vainly wooed. On the Danger of War. George Meredith. **CP-MerG1**

Avising the bright beams of these fair eyes. Sir Thomas Wyatt. **CP-WyatT**

Avoid extremes; and shun the fault of such. Alexander Pope. **FHYEP** *Fr.* An Essay on Criticism. **CP-PopeA**

Avoid three kinds of Master. To a Novice. Thomas Merton. *Fr.* Readings from Ibn Abbad. **CP-MertT**

Avoid, you strollers in the dark street. Against Illuminations. Archibald MacLeish. **CP-MacLA**

Avon, The. William Wordsworth. **CP-WorW2**

Avon—a precious, an immortal name! The Avon. William Wordsworth. **CP-WorW2**

Avondale. Stevie Smith. **CP-SmitS**

Avondall. Stevie Smith. **CP-SmitS**

Avon's Harvest. Edwin Arlington Robinson. **CP-RobiE**

Avowal, The. Richard Wilbur. **CP-WilbR**

Aw, Dylan, have you left us? Have you gone? Hayden Carruth. **CP-CarHS** *Fr.* The Bloomingdale Papers.

Aw, piss, and sing, be. A Po-sy, a Po-sy. Charles Olson. **CP-OlsoC**

Aw right then. Chillens, I know you. How To. Hayden Carruth. **CP-CarHS**

Awa Whigs Awa. Robert Burns. **CP-BurnR**

Awa wi' your witchcraft o' beauty's alarms. Hey for a Lass wi' a Tocher. Robert Burns. **CP-BurnR**

Await. James Schuyler. **CP-SchuJ**

Awaiting the Swimmer. James Dickey. **CP-DickJ**

Awake — arise — lift up thy voice. Easter Day. Christopher Smart. *Fr.* Hymns and Spiritual Songs for the Fasts and Festivals of the Church of England. **SP-SmarC**

Awake! Walter de la Mare. **CP-DeLaW**

Awake, Aeolian lyre, awake. The Progress of Poesy. Thomas Gray. **CP-GrayT**

Awake, Aeolian lyre, awake. The Progress of Poesy. Thomas Gray. **CP-GrayT**

Awake again in Asia, Lord of peace. To Buddha. Nicholas Vachel Lindsay. *Fr.* Poems Speaking of Buddha, Prince Siddartha. **CP-LindV**

Awake all night with loving. Fired. Langston Hughes. **SP-HughL**

Awake alone in the house. Sleepless. Stephen Spender. **CP-SpenS**

Awake at Night. Wendell Berry. **CP-BerrW**

Awake, Awake! [Thou Heavy Sprite]. Thomas Campion. **CP-CampT**

Awake! awake! how loud the stormy morning. Song by Julius Angora. Emily Brontë. **CP-BronE**

Awake, awake, my little Boy! The Land of Dreams. William Blake. **CP-BlakW**

AWAKE! For the morning. Boston 5:00 A.M.—10/74. Etheridge Knight. **SP-KnigE**

Awake, great Sir, the Sun shines here [*or* heer]. On New-Year's Day 1640, to the King. Sir John Suckling. **CP-SuckJ**

Awake! I'm off to cities far away. Chimes Play "Life's a Bumper!"The. Thomas Hardy. **CP-HardT**

Awake in a giant night. Giant Night. Anne Waldman. **SP-WaldA**

Awake, my St. John! leave all meaner things. Alexander Pope. **NAEL-1; NoP; OAEP; PoEL-3** *Fr.* An Essay on Man. **CP-PopeA** Wild Garden, The. **PrIm**

Awake, my St. John! leave all meaner things. The Wild Garden. Alexander Pope. **PrIm** *Fr.* Awake, my St. John! leave all meaner things. **NAEL-1; NoP; OAEP; PoEL-3** *Fr.* An Essay on Man. **CP-PopeA**

Awake or sleeping (for I know not which). An Old-World Thicket. Christina Georgiana Rossetti. **CP-RosC2**

Awake sad heart, whom sorrow ever drowns. The Dawning. George Herbert. **CP-HerbG**

Awake, thou spring of speaking grace, mute rest becomes not thee. Thomas Campion. **CP-CampT**

Awake, Thou That Sleepest. Christina Georgina Rossetti. **CP-RosC2**

Awake to the cold light. March. Hart Crane. **CP-CranH**

Awake ye muses nine, sing me a strain divine. Emily Dickinson. **CP-DickE**

Awaken, Bells Falling. Lewis Turco. **SP-TurcL**

Awakened by the clarity of dream. The Dreamer. Daniel Gerard Hoffman. **SP-HoffD**

Awakening. Robert Bly. **SP-BlyR**

Awakening, The. Robert Creeley. **CP-CreeR**

Awakening, The. Paul Laurence Dunbar. **CP-DunbP**

Awakening, The. Robert Ranke Graves. **CP-GravR**

Awakening, The. Charles Tomlinson. **CP-TomlC**

Awakening, The. Alice Walker. **CP-WalkA**

Awakening of Man, The. Robert Browning. **WGRP** *Fr.* Paracelsus. **CP-BroR1**

Awakes for me and leaps from shroud. The Night-Walk. George Meredith. **CP-MerG1**

Awaking. Stephen Spender. **CP-SpenS**

Awaking in New York. Maya Angelou. **SP-AngeM**

Awaking morning laughs from heaven. Emily Brontë. **CP-BronE**

Aware. Wystan Hugh Auden. **CP-AudWJ**

Aware. David Herbert Lawrence. **CP-LawrD**

Aware that summer baked the water clear. Skykomish River Running. Richard Hugo. **CP-HugoR**

Aware to the dry throat of the wide hell in the world. King David Dances. John Berryman. **CP-BerrJ**

Awareness of Time. John Hewitt. **CP-HewiJ**

Away. John Berryman. **CP-BerrJ**

Away. Robert Creeley. **CP-CreeR**

Away. Walter de la Mare. **CP-DeLaW**

Away! Robert Frost. **CP-FrosR**

Away above a harborful. Lawrence Ferlinghetti. **SP-FerlL**

Away, and leave me, thou thing most abhorred. To My Muse. Ben Jonson. **CP-JonsB**

Away, away, it is the air. William Wordsworth. **CP-WorW1**

Away, away, resign me now. Emily Brontë. **CP-BronE**

Away away this allure. Late Morning Talk. James McAuley. **SP-McAuJ**

Away, Away, Ye Notes of Woe! Byron. **CP-Byron**

Away, away, your flattering arts. Written in "Letters to an Italian Nun and an English Gentleman: by J.J. Rousseau: Founded on Facts." Byron. **CP-Byron**

Away by the lands of the Japanee. The Rhyme of the Three Sealers. Rudyard Kipling. **CP-KiplR**

Away despair; my gracious Lord doth hear[e]. The Bag. George Herbert. **CP-HerbG**

Away from Home are some and I. Emily Dickinson. **CP-DickE**

Away from It All. Ogden Nash. **CP-NashO**

Away goes Sussex William with his pack. William Cowper. **CP-CowpW**

Away, haunt not thou me. Arthur Hugh Clough. **SP-ClouA**

Away Match: June 1924. John Hewitt. **CP-HewiJ**

Away, Melancholy. Stevie Smith. **CP-SmitS**

Away! the moor is dark beneath the moon. Stanzas—April, 1814. Percy Bysshe Shelley. **CP-ShelP**

Away, those cloudy looks, that lab'ring sigh. To a Friend, in Answer to a Melancholy Letter. Samuel Taylor Coleridge. *Fr.* Poetical Epistles. **CP-ColeS**

Away thou fondling motley humourist. Satire 1. John Donne. **NoSic** *Fr.* Satires. **CP-DonnJ**

Away, through bramble, bush, and trees. Love of the Woods. Johann N. Vogl, *tr. fr.* German *by* George Meredith. **CP-MerG2**

Away with funeral music—set. Robert Louis Stevenson. **CP-StevR**

Away with silks, away with lawn. Clothes Do But Cheat and Cozen [*or* Cousen] Us. Robert Herrick. **CP-HerrR**

Away with your fictions of flimsy romance. The First Kiss of Love. Byron. **CP-Byron**

Away, ye gay landscapes, ye gardens of roses! Lachin y Gair. Byron. **CP-Byron**

Awed I behold once more. Ralph Waldo Emerson. **CP-EmerR**

Awful darkness of the town, The. Edward Estlin Cummings. **CP-CummE**

Awful rushes at times. Flesh. Robert Creeley. **CP-CreeR**

Awful shadow of some unseen Power, The. Hymn to Intellectual Beauty. Percy Bysshe Shelley. **CP-ShelP**

Awful Tempest mashed the air, An. Emily Dickinson. **CP-DickE**

AWFULMUSICAW. Thomas Merton. *Fr.* A Selection of Concrete Poems. **CP-MertT**

Awhile caught in the bog of politics. To Be Used in an Address Delivered at the Unveiling of a Plaque Commemorating "George A. Birmingham." John Hewitt. **CP-HewiJ**

Awkward as the homely are. Emily Dickinson. **SP-DickE**

Awkwardness, the grace. Siena. Charles Olson. **CP-OlsoC**

Awoke. James Schuyler. **CP-SchuJ**

Awoke into a Dream of Singing. Daniel Gerard Hoffman. **SP-HoffD**

Ax. Charles Simic. **SP-SimiC**

Ax God:Sea Pursuit, The. James Dickey. **CP-DickJ**

Axe angles / from my neighbor's ashcan, An. Junk. Richard Wilbur. **CP-WilbR**

Axe Handles. Gary Snyder. **CP-SnydG**

Axe-Helve, The. Robert Frost. **CP-FrosR**

Axes / After whose stroke the wood rings. Words. Sylvia Plath. **CP-PlatS**

Axes has been ringin' in de woods de blessid day, De. A Back-Log Song. Paul Laurence Dunbar. **CP-DunbP**

Axiom. Margaret Atwood. **SP-AtwM1**

Ay, ay, Oay--the winds that bend the brier! Tristram's Song. Tennyson. **FaBoRV** *Fr.* The Last Tournament. *Fr.* Idylls of the King. **CP-TennA**

"Ay, but, Ferishtah,"—a disciple smirked. Plot-Culture. Robert Browning. **CP-BroR2**

Ay, lay him 'neath the Simla pine. Possibilities. Rudyard Kipling. **CP-KiplR**

Ay, man is manly. Here you see. On the Photograph of Corps Commander. Herman Melville. **SP-MelvH**

Ay me, how many perils doe unfold [*or* enfold]. Edmund Spenser. **FHYEP; OAEL-1** *Fr.* The Faerie Queene. **CP-Spens**

Ay me! whilst thee the shores and sounding seas. John Milton. **Prf** *Fr.* Lycidas. **CP-MiltJ**

Ay, note that Potter's wheel. Why Time Spins Fast. Robert Browning. **FaBoDD** *Fr.* Rabbi Ben Ezra. **CP-BroR1**

Ay, sure, this is most brave. Archibald MacLeish. **CP-MacLA** *Fr.* Hamlet of A. Macleish. **CP-MacLA**

Ay, this same midnight, by this chair of mine. With Bernard de Mandeville. Robert Browning. **CP-BroR2**

Ay, Trochu, in Paris which Prussians environ. Mettle and Metal. Robert Browning. **CP-BroR2**

Ay, 'twas here, on this spot. Atalanta in Camden-Town. "Lewis Carroll." **CP-CarrL**

Ay Waukin O. Robert Burns. *See* Simmer's a Pleasant Time.

Aye and No. Jonathan Swift. **CP-SwifJ**

Aye and No: A Fable. Jonathan Swift. **CP-SwifJ**

Aye, but she? Ode to Silence. Edna St. Vincent Millay. **CP-MillE**

Aye, lay him in his grave, the old dead year! The King is Dead. Paul Laurence Dunbar. **CP-DunbP**

Aye me, an eunuch keeps my mistress chaste. 2.3. Ovid. **CP-MarlC,** *tr. by* Christopher Marlowe; *Fr.* Elegies.

Aye me, that love should natures workes accuse! At. to Thomas Campion *and to* Philip Rosseter. **CP-CampT**

Aye mon, it's true; I'm no' that weel. Robert Louis Stevenson. **CP-StevR**

Aye, there it is! It wakes to-night. Emily Brontë. **CP-BronE**

Aye, well I know 'tis ghastly to descend that valley. On the Same Picture. Walt Whitman. **CP-WhitW**

Ayee! Ai! This is heavy earth on our shoulders. Burying Ground by the Ties. Archibald MacLeish. **CP-MacLA**

Ayers Rock / Uluru Song. Allen Ginsberg. **CP-GinsA**

Ayr. Richard Hugo. **CP-HugoR**

Ayres that Were Sung and Played, at *Brougham Castle* in *Westmerland*, in the Kings Entertainment, The. Thomas Campion. **CP-CampT**

    Another Dialogue, To Be Sung at the Same Time.

    Ballad, A: "Dido was the Carthage Queene."

    "Come follow me, my wandring mates."

    Dance, The. **CP-CampT; EllL; FaBoCh; LoBV**

    Dialogue Sung the First Night, A.

    Farewell Song, The.

    Kings Good-night, The.

    Lords Welcome, sung before the Kings Good-night, The.

    Song: "Shadowes darkning our intents, The."

    "Truth, sprung from heaven, shall shine."

Azalea. Louis Zukofsky. **CP-ZukLS**

Azalea is grown while we sleep, The. Canto 107. Ezra Pound. *Fr.* Cantos. **CP-PoCan**

Azaleas. Peter Meinke. **SP-MeinP**

Aziola, The. Percy Bysshe Shelley. **CP-ShelP**

Azores. John Updike. **CP-UpdiJ**

Azrael's Count. Rudyard Kipling. **CP-KiplR**

Aztec. Carl Sandburg. **CP-SandC**

Aztec Mask. Carl Sandburg. **CP-SandC**

Aztec sacrifice, / beside the head of Pope, An. Le Musée Imaginaire. Charles Tomlinson. **CP-TomlC**

Aztec sandstone waterholes known by Moapa've. Las Vegas: Verses Improvised for El Dorado H.S. Newspaper. Allen Ginsberg. **CP-GinsA**

Azure striation swirls beyond the stones. Marilyn Hacker. **SP-HackM** *Fr.* La Fontaine de Vaucluse.

Azure yielder, The. Naked. Alvaro Figueredo, *tr. by* William Carlos Williams. **CP-WilW2**

B

B———. Robert Creeley. **CP-CreeR**

B / eLl / s? / bE. Edward Estlin Cummings. **CP-CummE**

B / et / wee / n no / w dis. Edward Estlin Cummings. **CP-CummE**

B. is for Bach—. Marsden Hartley. **CP-HartM**

Babahak. Ussin Kerim, *tr. fr. Bulgarian by* William Matthews. **SP-MattW**

Babe, The. Charles Olson. **CP-OlsoC**

Babe is at peace within the womb, The. Fragment: Life Rounded with Sleep. Percy Bysshe Shelley. **CP-ShelP**

Babe was laid in the Manger, The. A Nativity. Rudyard Kipling. **CP-KiplR**

Babel. Louis MacNeice. **CP-MacNL**

Babelfield. Patti Smith. **SP-SmitP**

Babelogue. Patti Smith. **SP-SmitP**

Babe's Riddle, The. Archibald MacLeish. *Fr.* Songs for Eve. **CP-MacLA**

Babiaantje, The. Frank Templeton Prince. **CP-PrinF**

Babies in their mothers' arms. Wystan Hugh Auden. *Fr.* Shorts [1939–1947] ("Motionless, deep in his mind, lies the past the poet's forgotten"). **CP-AudeW**

Babies insurance. I dont love nobody. that's my policy. Gibralto. Patti Smith. **SP-SmitP**

Baboon and the State, The. John Ciardi. **SP-CiarJ**

Baby. Langston Hughes. **SP-HughL**

Baby & the Gypsy. Anne Waldman. **SP-WaldA**

Baby Asleep after Pain, A. David Herbert Lawrence. **CP-LawrD**

Baby black's / been had. "Bob Dylan." *Fr.* Some Other Kinds of Songs. **CP-DylaB**

Baby black's / been had. Some Other Kinds of Songs. "Bob Dylan." **CP-DylaB**

Baby Book Fate Dream. Tom Clark. **SP-ClarT**

Baby Breakdown. Anne Waldman. **SP-WaldA**

Baby cry— / Oh fie! Christina Georgina Rossetti. **CP-RosC2**

Baby Face. Carl Sandburg. **CP-SandC**

Baby got here once who before, A. The Rampage. Charles Kenneth Williams. **CP-WillC; SP-WillC**

Baby, how come you can't see me. Ultimatum. Langston Hughes. **SP-HughL**

Baby, I don't want. Charles Kenneth Williams. **CP-WillC**

Baby, if you love me. Down and Out. Langston Hughes. **SP-HughL**

Baby, I'm in the Mood for You. "Bob Dylan." **CP-DylaB**

Baby is a harmless thing / And wins our hearts with one accord, A. Christmas Day. Christina Georgina Rossetti. **CP-RosC2**

Baby, I've been waiting. Waiting for the Miracle. Leonard Cohen. **CP-CoheL**

Baby lies so fast asleep / That we cannot wake her. Christina Georgina Rossetti. **CP-RosC2**

Baby moon, a canoe, a silver papoose canoe sails and sails in the, The. Early Moon. Carl Sandburg. **CP-SandC**

Baby-Movements. David Herbert Lawrence. **CP-LawrD**

    Running Barefoot.

    Trailing Clouds.

Baby New to Earth and Sky, The. Tennyson. **MeMBP** *Fr.* In Memoriam A. H. H. **CP-TennA**

Baby on the way! Charles Henri Ford. **SP-FordC** *Fr.* Secret Haiku.

Baby picked from an ash barrel by the night police, The. Chicago Boy Baby. Carl Sandburg. **CP-SandC**

Baby Picture. Anne Sexton. **CP-SextA**

Baby Pictures of Famous Dictators. Charles Simic. **SP-SimiC**

Baby Running Barefoot. David Herbert Lawrence. **CP-LawrD**

Baby Song. Thom Gunn. **CP-GunnT** *Fr.* Three Songs.

Baby Song of the Four Winds. Carl Sandburg. **CP-SandC**

Baby Songs Ten Months Old. David Herbert Lawrence. **CP-LawrD**

Baby, Stop Crying. "Bob Dylan." **CP-DylaB**

Baby Toes. Carl Sandburg. **CP-SandC**

Baby Tortoise. David Herbert Lawrence. **CP-LawrD**

Baby Vamps. Carl Sandburg. **CP-SandC**

Baby vamps, is it harder work than it used to be? Baby Vamps. Carl Sandburg. **CP-SandC**

Baby Villon. Philip Levine. **SP-LeviP**

Baby watched a ford, whereto, A. Wagtail and Baby. Thomas Hardy. **CP-HardT**

Baby-Witch. Erica Jong. **SP-JongE**

Baby You're a Rich Man. John Lennon *and* Paul McCartney. **CP-Beatl**

Babylon, Babylon, Babylon the Great. Nicholas Vachel Lindsay. **CP-LindV**

Babylon slim / -ness of / evenslicing. Edward Estlin Cummings. **CP-CummE**

Babylon the Great. Christina Georgina Rossetti. **CP-RosC2**

Baby's cradle with no baby in it, A. Christina Georgina Rossetti. **CP-RosC2**

Baby's flight will embellish History. Emily Dickinson. **SP-DickE**

Baby's good to me you know. I Feel Fine. The Beatles. **CP-Beatl**

Baby's in Black. John Lennon *and* Paul McCartney. **CP-Beatl**

Baby's in Jail; the Animal Day Plays Alone. Charles Henri Ford. **SP-FordC**

Baby's Pantoum. Anne Waldman. **SP-WaldA**

Babysitters, The. Sylvia Plath. **CP-PlatS**

Bacardi Spreads the Eagle's Wing. Hart Crane. **CP-CranH**

Baccalaureate. Archibald MacLeish. **CP-MacLA**

Baccalaureate Hymn. Edna St. Vincent Millay. **CP-MillE**, *ar. by with music*;

Bacchae. Euripides, *tr. fr. Greek.*
   Choros Translations. **CP-DoolH**

Bacchanalian Verse, A. Robert Herrick. **CP-HerrR**

Bacchus. Ralph Waldo Emerson. **CP-EmerR**

Bacchus. John Milton. **FaBoDD** *Fr.* Comus; a Masque Presented at Ludlow Castle.

Bacchus and Ariadne. Hesiod. **CP-BroEB,** *tr. by* Elizabeth Barrett Browning; *Fr.* Theogony.

Bacchus, let me drink no more. A Hymn[e] to Bacchus. Robert Herrick. **CP-HerrR**

Bacchus, that first from out the purple grape. Bacchus. John Milton. **FaBoDD** *Fr.* Comus; a Masque Presented at Ludlow Castle.

Bach and the Lady. Wystan Hugh Auden. **CP-AudWJ**

Bach is spreading softly down. A Musical Offering. Leonard Nathan. **SP-NathL**

Bachanalian Ode, A. "Lewis Carroll." **CP-CarrL**

Bachanalian Verse, A. Robert Herrick. **CP-HerrR**

Bachelor 'e fights for one, The. The Married Man. Rudyard Kipling. **CP-KiplR**

Bachelour I will, A. No Spouse but a Sister. Robert Herrick. **CP-HerrR**

Back. John Berryman. **CP-BerrJ**

Back. Jane Cooper. *Fr.* March. **SP-CoopJ**

Back. Rita Dove. *Fr.* A Suite for Augustus. **SP-DoveR**

Back. James Schuyler. **CP-SchuJ**

Back, The. Karl Shapiro. **SP-ShapK**

Back-Again, The. Louis MacNeice. *Fr.* A Hand of Snapshots. **CP-MacNL**

Back and forth across / time, lots of things. You. Robert Creeley. **CP-CreeR**

Back and forth, back and forth. Fall 1961. Robert Lowell. **SP-LoweR**

Back Bay. John Updike. **CP-UpdiJ**

Back broad and straight from crop to hocks. Draft Board. Malcolm Lowry. **CP-LowrM**

Back for his holiday from across the water. The Back-Again. Louis MacNeice. *Fr.* A Hand of Snapshots. **CP-MacNL**

Back from Australia. Sir John Betjeman. **CP-BetjJ**

Back from the cordial Grave I drag thee. Emily Dickinson. **CP-DickE**

Back from Vacation. John Updike. **CP-UpdiJ**

Back; gone country around, / like wind in hollow rabbit. Pain Songs. Joseph Ceravolo. **SP-CeraJ**

Back Home. Jim Carroll. **SP-CarrJ**

Back Home. Martin Edmunds. **SP-EdmuM**

Back in '15, when life was harsh. The Field-Postcard. Robert Ranke Graves. **CP-GravR**

Back in the Seventeen-Seventies to Birmingham he came. Louis MacNeice. *Fr.* Our Sister Water. **CP-MacNL**

Back in the USSR. John Lennon *and* Paul McCartney. **CP-Beatl**

Back-Log Song, A. Paul Laurence Dunbar. **CP-DunbP**

Back-looking memory / And prophet hope both sprang from out. Memory and Hope. Elizabeth Barrett Browning. **CP-BroEB**

Back of Affluence. Donald Davie. **CP-DavDo**

Back of Budbill's where it dreens offn the ledges. Snugger. Hayden Carruth. *Fr.* The Sleeping Beauty. **CP-CarHL**

Back of Gino's Place. Richard Hugo. **CP-HugoR**

Back of the dam, under. The Town of Hill. Donald Hall. **CP-HallD**

Back on Times Square, Dreaming of Times Square. Allen Ginsberg. **CP-GinsA**

Back out of all this now too much for us. Directive. Robert Frost. **CP-FrosR**

Back Road Country. Marsden Hartley. **CP-HartM**

Back roads I've traveled late, The. Beyond Hammonton. Stephen Dunn. **SP-DunnS**

Back Stairs, The. John Gould Fletcher. **SP-FletJ** *Fr.* The Ghosts of an Old House.

Back then, before we came. On Freedom's Ground. Richard Wilbur. **CP-WilbR**

Back then when so much was clear. Tenderness. Stephen Dunn. **SP-DunnS**

Back through clouds. Train Tune. Louise Bogan. **CP-BogaL**

Back through the Looking Glass to This Side. John Ciardi. **SP-CiarJ**

Back to Base. Jenny Joseph. **SP-JoseJ**

Back to Carrick, the castle as plumb assured. Carrick Revisited. Louis MacNeice. **CP-MacNL**

Back to Life. Thom Gunn. **CP-GunnT**

Back to my native place. Welcome Home. Thomas Hardy. **CP-HardT**

Back to the Army Again. Rudyard Kipling. **CP-KiplR**

Back to the breast of thy mother. Alexander Crummel—Dead. Paul Laurence Dunbar. **CP-DunbP**

Back to the figure. Robert Duncan. **SP-DuncR** *Fr.* The Structure of Rime.

Back to the great music, Scottish Gaels. Too long. "Hugh MacDiarmid." **SP-MacDH** *Fr.* Good-bye Twilight.

Back To The Palace. Lines to a Girl 5 Days After Her 21st Birthday. Ernest Hemingway. **CP-HemiE**

Back to the streets always, ravaged and wet. Jim Carroll. **SP-CarrJ**

Back Tooth. Muriel Rukeyser. **CP-RukeM**

Back up in the room they snap on. Making Love After Hours. Al Young. **CP-YounA**

Back wings, The. Between Walls. William Carlos Williams. **CP-WilW1**

Back Yard. Carl Sandburg. **CP-SandC**

Backcountry Blues. Kenneth Patchen. **CP-PatcK**

Backdrop Addresses Cowboy. Margaret Atwood. **SP-AtwM1**

Backdrop With Lovers, 1931. Tess Gallagher. **SP-GallT**

Background and the Figure, The. Thomas Hardy. **CP-HardT**

Background with Revolutionaries. Archibald MacLeish. **CP-MacLA**

Backs twist with the kiss, The. "Kiss, The." Donald Hall. **CP-HallD**

Backside of the Academy, The. Muriel Rukeyser. **CP-RukeM**

Backtalk. Brendan Galvin. **SP-GalvB**

Backtrack of sea, the baywater goes; flats. Conjuration. Richard Wilbur. **CP-WilbR**

Backtracking. Al Young. **CP-YounA**

Backward among the dusky years. Compassion. Thomas Hardy. **CP-HardT**

Backward Flight. Louise McNeill. **SP-McNeL**

Backward Look, The. Howard Nemerov. **CP-NemeH**

Backward Spring, A. Thomas Hardy. **CP-HardT**

Backwards. Robert Creeley. **CP-CreeR**

Backyard. Alice Notley. **SP-NotlA**

Backyard in California, A. Hayden Carruth. **CP-CarHS**

Bacterial War, The. Howard Nemerov. **CP-NemeH**

Bad. William Matthews. **SP-MattW**

Bad Action. Charles Bukowski. **SP-BukC3**

Bad among the Good are here mixt ever, The. Good, and Bad. Robert Herrick. **CP-HerrR**

Bad Angels, The. Stephen Dunn. **SP-DunnS**

Bad are all surfeits: but Physicitians call. Surfeits. Robert Herrick. **CP-HerrR**

Bad are the times. *Sil.* And wors then they are we. A Pastorall Sung to the King: Montano, Silvio, and Mirtillo, Shepards. Robert Herrick. **CP-HerrR**

Bad Beginning, A. David Herbert Lawrence. **CP-LawrD**

Bad die old, The. Triolet. Isabella Gardner. **CP-GardI**

Bad Dream. Louis MacNeice. **CP-MacNL**

Bad Dream, A. Kathleen Jessie Raine. **SP-RainK**

Bad Dreams I. Robert Browning. **CP-BroR2**

Bad Dreams II. Robert Browning. **CP-BroR2**

Bad Dreams III. Robert Browning. **CP-BroR2**

Bad Dreams IV. Robert Browning. **CP-BroR2**

Bad Example, The. Thomas Hardy. **CP-HardT**

Bad Eyes Spinning the Rock. Richard Hugo. **CP-HugoR**

Bad Habit, The. Charles Henri Ford. **SP-FordC**

Bad Island, The—Easter. Robert Frost. **CP-FrosR**

Bad Lord Byron went to the firing, helmet and dogs and all. Louis MacNeice. *Fr.* Cock o' the North. **CP-MacNL**

Bad Luck Card. Langston Hughes. **SP-HughL**

Bad May Be Better. Robert Herrick. **CP-HerrR**

Bad Morning. Langston Hughes. **SP-HughL**

Bad Mouth. Margaret Atwood. **SP-AtwM2**

Bad Mouth. Charles Kenneth Williams. **CP-WillC**

Bad Music, The. Randall Jarrell. **CP-JarrR**

Bad News. John Crowe Ransom. *Fr.* Two Gentlemen in Bonds. **SP-RansJ**

Bad news, bad news / Come to me where I sleep. Percy's Song. "Bob Dylan." **CP-DylaB**

Bad Night, A. Wystan Hugh Auden. **CP-AudeW**

Bad Old Days, The. Kenneth Rexroth. **SP-RexrK**

Bad Princes Pill Their People. Robert Herrick. **CP-HerrR**

Bad Season Makes the Poet Sad, The. Robert Herrick. **CP-HerrR**

Bad Thing came in the night, and, this time, ate away part of my. The Story of an Olson, and Bad Thing. Charles Olson. **CP-OlsoC**

Bad Times Song. Jean Garrigue. **SP-GarrJ**

Bad Turn, A. John Clellon Holmes. **SP-HolmJ**

Bad Vision at the Skagit. Richard Hugo. **CP-HugoR**

Bad Wages for Good Service. Robert Herrick. **CP-HerrR**

Badger ("When midnight comes a host of dogs and men"). John Clare. **SP-ClarJ**

Badger grunting on his woodland track, The. John Clare. Untitled. **SP-ClarJ**

Badger grunting on his woodland track, The. Untitled. John Clare. **SP-ClarJ** *Fr.* The Badger grunting on his woodland track.

Badgers, The. Seamus Heaney. **SP-HeanS**

Baffled / by the choreography of the season. Autumn Piece. Charles Tomlinson. **CP-TomlC**

Baffled for just a day or two. Emily Dickinson. **CP-DickE**

Bag, The. George Herbert. **CP-HerbG**

Bag of the Bee, The. Robert Herrick. **CP-HerrR**

Bag of tricks—is it?, A. Honey and Salt. Carl Sandburg. **CP-SandC**

Bag-Snatching in Dublin. Stevie Smith. **CP-SmitS**

Bagatelles the Madrigals, The. Wallace Stevens. **CP-StevW**

Bagatto. Charles Olson. **CP-OlsoC**

Baggage King, The. James Dickey. **CP-DickJ**

Bagous, whose care doth thy mistress bridle. 2.2. Ovid. **CP-MarlC**, *tr. by* Christopher Marlowe; *Fr.* Elegies.

Bagpipe Music. "Hugh MacDiarmid." **SP-MacDH**

Bagpipe Music. Louis MacNeice. **CP-MacNL**

Bagpipe Who Didn't Say No, The. Shel Silverstein. **SP-SilS2**

Bags of Meat. Thomas Hardy. **CP-HardT**

Bah! I have sung women in three cities. Cino. Ezra Pound. **SP-PounE**

Bahamas. Archibald MacLeish. **CP-MacLA**

Bahamas. George Oppen. **CP-OppeG**

Bahá'u'lláh in the Garden of Ridwan. Robert Earl Hayden. **CP-HaydR**

Baile and Aillinn. William Butler Yeats. **CP-YeatW**

Bailing the Boat. Mary Oliver. **SP-OlivM**

Baillie Swan, Baillie Swan. Epigram on James Baillie Swan. Robert Burns. *Fr.* Dumfries Epigrams. **CP-BurnR**

Bairns gat out wi' an unco shout, The. The Deuks Dang o'er My Daddie. Robert Burns. **CP-BurnR**

Bait[e], The. John Donne. **CP-DonnJ**; **CP-MarlC**

Baited / bear / on / the ashtray, The. Ashtray. Louis Zukofsky. **CP-ZukLS**

Baja Beatitudes. Lawrence Ferlinghetti. **SP-FerlL**

Baja Revisited. Lawrence Ferlinghetti. **SP-FerlL**

Baked and cleaned. Grandmother. Siv Cedering Fox. **SP-CedeS**

Baker's Tale, The. "Lewis Carroll." **EBEV; NAEL-2; OXAEP-2** *Fr.* The Hunting of the Snark. **CP-CarrL**

Bal Masqué. Edwin Rolfe. **CP-RolfE**

Bala Krishna's voice. Charles Henri Ford. **SP-FordC** *Fr.* Emblems of Arachne.

Balade of Complaint, A. Geoffrey Chaucer. **CP-ChauG**

Balance. Patti Smith. **SP-SmitP**

Balance checkbook. / Rid lawn of onion grass. Things to Do. James Schuyler. **CP-SchuJ**

Balance is preserved by the snails climbing the, The. One for the Shoeshine Man. Charles Bukowski. **SP-BukC1**

Balance of Europe, The. Alexander Pope. **CP-PopeA**

Balancing spaces are not disturbed, The. The Known Soldier. Kenneth Patchen. **CP-PatcK**

Balaustion's Adventure. Robert Browning. **CP-BroR1**

Bald heads forgetful of their sins. The Scholars. William Butler Yeats. **CP-YeatW**

Bald man in plaid playing the harpsichord, The. San Jose Symphony Reception. Lawrence Ferlinghetti. **SP-FerlL**

Bald this, hunched, jaw on fist. The Geriatric Ward. John Hewitt. **CP-HewiJ**

Balder. Frederick Morgan. **SP-MorgF**

Baldungan Castle. James McAuley. **SP-McAuJ**

Baldur Was Beautiful Too. Isabella Gardner. **CP-GardI**

Bale-Fire, The. Sir Walter Scott. **SP-ScotW** *Fr.* The Lay of the Last Minstrel.

Baler, The. Hayden Carruth. **CP-CarHS**

Balieff's actors from The Bat. When Fresh, It Was Sweet. William Carlos Williams. **CP-WilW1**

Balin and Balan. Tennyson. **CP-TennA** *Fr.* Idylls of the King. Vivien's Song. **OAEL-2**

Ball Game, The. Robert Creeley. **CP-CreeR**

Ball Game. Richard Eberhart. **CP-EberR**

Ball Poem, The. John Berryman. **CP-BerrJ**

Ball whizzed by,—It grazed his Ear, The. Epigram on an Event in Col. Evans's Redoubted Performances in Spain. William Wordsworth. **CP-WorW2**

Ball will bounce, but less and less. It's not, A. Juggler. Richard Wilbur. **CP-WilbR**

Ballad[e] [upon a Wedding], A. Sir John Suckling. **CP-SuckJ** Bride, The. **TrGrPo**

Ballad: "Astrolabes and lexicons." George Oppen. **CP-OppeG**

Ballad: "He offered her his paucity." Wystan Hugh Auden. **CP-AudWJ**

Ballad, The. John Hewitt. **CP-HewiJ**

Ballad, The. John Hewitt. **CP-HewiJ**

Ballad: "I know my love is true." Paul Laurence Dunbar. **CP-DunbP**

Ballad: "Of all the twice ten thousand bards." Byron. **CP-Byron**

Ballad: "Soft white lamb in the daisy meadow." Christina Georgina Rossetti. **CP-RosC3**

Ballad: "Summer morning is risen." John Clare. **SP-ClarJ** *Fr.* Child Harold.

Ballad: "Though it may seem rude." Ben Jonson. **CP-JonsB** *Fr.* The Masque of Augurs.

Ballad: "To a man and his wife." William Carlos Williams. **CP-WilW2**

Ballad: "Twas in the springtime of the year." Malcolm Lowry. **CP-LowrM**

Ballad: "What are we having for dinner tonight?" Edwin Rolfe. **CP-RolfE**

Ballad: "What's that approaching like dust like poverty." Charles Simic. **SP-SimiC**

Ballad, A: "And will you leave me thus alone." William Wordsworth. **CP-WorW1**

Ballad, A: "Dido was the Carthage Queene." Thomas Campion. *Fr.* The Ayres that Were Sung and Played, at *Brougham Castle* in *Westmerland*, in the Kings Entertainment. **CP-CampT**

Ballad, A: "There was a lass and she was fair." Robert Burns. **CP-BurnR**

Ballad, A: "We have a song for the death in her body." Robert Creeley. **CP-CreeR**

Ballad, A: "While Prose-work and rhymes." Robert Burns. **CP-BurnR**

Ballad: Between the Boxcars. Robert Penn Warren. **SP-WarrR**
    He Was Formidable. **LiSp**
    I Can't Even Remember the Name. **CRP**

Ballad for a Friend. "Bob Dylan." **CP-DylaB**

Ballad for Americans. Charles Olson. **CP-OlsoC**

Ballad for Baudelaire. Charles Henri Ford. **SP-FordC**

Ballad from Childhood. Audre Lorde. **SP-LordA**

Ballad in Plain D. "Bob Dylan." **CP-DylaB**

Ballad of a Bad Boy. Patti Smith. **SP-SmitP**

Ballad of a Sweet Dream of Peace. Robert Penn Warren. **SP-WarrR**
    And Don't Forget Your Corset Cover, Either.
    Friends of the Family, or Bowling a Sticky Cricket.
    Go it, Granny—Go it, Hog!
    I Guess You Ought to Know Who You Are.
    Keepsakes.
    Rumor Unverified Stop Can You Confirm Stop.
    You Never Knew Her Either, Though You Thought You Did.

Ballad of a Thin Man. "Bob Dylan." **CP-DylaB**

Ballad of a Wilful Woman. David Herbert Lawrence. **CP-LawrD**

Ballad of an Intellectual. Edward Estlin Cummings. **CP-CummE**

Ballad of Another Ophelia. David Herbert Lawrence. **CP-LawrD**

Ballad of Ballymote, The. Tess Gallagher. **SP-GallT**

Ballad of Barnaby, The. Wystan Hugh Auden. **OBNV** *Fr.* Six Commissioned Texts. **CP-AudeW**

Ballad of Billie Potts, The. Robert Penn Warren. **SP-WarrR**

Ballad of Blossom, The. Mona Van Duyn. **SP-VanDM**

Ballad of Boding, A. Christina Georgina Rossetti. **CP-RosC2**

Ballad of Boh Da Thone, The. Rudyard Kipling. **CP-KiplR** ("This is the ballad of Boh Da Thone.") **CP-KiplR**

Ballad of Burdens, A. Algernon Charles Swinburne. **SP-SwinA**

Ballad of Chaldon Down, The. Edna St. Vincent Millay. **CP-MillE**

Ballad of Chocolate Mabbie, The. Gwendolyn Brooks. **CAPP** *Fr.* A Street in Bronzeville. **SP-BrooG**

Ballad of Christmas, A. Walter de la Mare. **CP-DeLaW**

Ballad of Death, A. Algernon Charles Swinburne. **SP-SwinA**

Ballad of Donald White. "Bob Dylan." **CP-DylaB**

Ballad of East and West, The. Rudyard Kipling. **CP-KiplR**

Ballad of Fair Ladies in Revolt, A. George Meredith. **CP-MerG1**

Ballad of Faith. William Carlos Williams. **CP-WilW2**

Ballad of Father Gilligan, The. William Butler Yeats. **CP-YeatW**

Ballad of Father O'Hart, The. William Butler Yeats. **CP-YeatW**

Ballad of Fisher's Boardinghouse, The. Rudyard Kipling. **CP-KiplR**

("That night, when through the mooring-chains.") CP-KiplR

Ballad of Frankie Lee and Judas Priest, The. "Bob Dylan." CP-DylaB

Ballad of Hagan Waker, The. Patti Smith. SP-SmitP

Ballad of Hollis Brown. "Bob Dylan." CP-DylaB

Ballad of Isabelle Eberhardt. Patti Smith. SP-SmitP

Ballad of Joe Bittner. Louise McNeill. SP-McNeL

Ballad of John and Yoko, The. John Lennon *and* Paul McCartney. CP-Beatl

Ballad of Johnny, The. May Sarton. SP-SartM

Ballad of Ladies Lost and Found. Marilyn Hacker. SP-HackM

Ballad of Life, A. Algernon Charles Swinburne. SP-SwinA

Ballad of Love. Edward Estlin Cummings. CP-CummE

Ballad of Love's Skeleton, The. Thomas Hardy. CP-HardT

Ballad of Minepit Shaw, The. Rudyard Kipling. CP-KiplR

Ballad of Miss Sally. Louise McNeill. SP-McNeL

Ballad of Mister Dutcher and the Last Lynching in Gupton. Robert Penn Warren. SP-WarrR

Ballad of Moll Magee, The. William Butler Yeats. CP-YeatW

Ballad of Nat Turner, The. Robert Earl Hayden. CP-HaydR

Ballad of New River. Louise McNeill. SP-McNeL

Ballad of Orange and Grape. Muriel Rukeyser. CP-RukeM

Ballad of Past Meridian, A. George Meredith. CP-MerG1

Ballad of Remembrance, A. Robert Earl Hayden. CP-HaydR

Ballad of Rudolph Reed, The. Gwendolyn Brooks. SP-BrooG

Ballad of Sue Ellen Westerfield, The. Robert Earl Hayden. CP-HaydR

Ballad of the Absent Mare. Leonard Cohen. CP-CoheL

Ballad of the "Bolivar", The. Rudyard Kipling. CP-KiplR

Ballad of the Brown Girl, The. Countee Cullen. CP-CullC

Ballad of the Brown Girl. Alice Walker. CP-WalkA

Ballad of the Cars, The, *parody of a Border Ballad.* Rudyard Kipling. CP-KiplR *Fr.* The Muse among the Motors.

Ballad of the Clairvoyant Widow. Theodore Roethke. CP-RoetT

Ballad of the *Clampherdown*, The. Rudyard Kipling. CP-KiplR

Ballad of the Corn-Cob and the Lie, The. Archibald MacLeish. CP-MacLA

Ballad of the Dark Ladié, The. Samuel Taylor Coleridge. CP-ColeS

Ballad of the Despairing Husband. Robert Creeley. CP-CreeR

Ballad of the Enamord Image, The. Robert Duncan. SP-DuncR

Ballad of the Fortune Teller. Langston Hughes. SP-HughL

Ballad of the Foxhunter, The. William Butler Yeats. CP-YeatW

Ballad of the Girl Whose Name Is Mud. Langston Hughes. SP-HughL

Ballad of the Goodly Fere. Ezra Pound. SP-PounE

Ballad of the Gypsy. Langston Hughes. SP-HughL

Ballad of the Harp-Weaver, The. Edna St. Vincent Millay. CP-MillE

Ballad of the Investiture 1969, A. Sir John Betjeman. CP-BetjJ

Ballad of the King's Jest, The. Rudyard Kipling. CP-KiplR

Ballad of the King's Mercy, The. Rudyard Kipling. CP-KiplR

Ballad of the Lady Eglantine, The. George Meredith. CP-MerG2

Ballad of the Landlord. Langston Hughes. SP-HughL

Ballad of the Late Annie, The. Gwendolyn Brooks. *Fr.* Notes from the Childhood and the Girlhood. SP-BrooG

Ballad of the Light-Eyed Little Girl, The. Gwendolyn Brooks. SP-BrooG *Fr.* The Womanhood.

Ballad of the Lonely Masturbator, The. Anne Sexton. CP-SextA

Ballad of the Long-legged Bait. Dylan Thomas. CP-ThomD

Ballad of the Man Who's Gone. Langston Hughes. SP-HughL

Ballad of the Noble Intentions. Edwin Rolfe. CP-RolfE

Ballad of the Red Earl, The. Rudyard Kipling. CP-KiplR

Ballad of the Rest Home. Louise McNeill. SP-McNeL

Ballad of the Scarecrow, The. Dabney Stuart. SP-StuaD

Ballad of the Scholar's Lament. Edward Estlin Cummings. CP-CummE

Ballad of the Sixties. May Sarton. SP-SartM

Ballad of the Three Birds. Dabney Stuart. SP-StuaD

Ballad of the Upper Bumping. Richard Hugo. CP-HugoR

Ballad of the Wheel, The. Charles Simic. SP-SimiC

Ballad of Will, The. Sir Thomas Wyatt. CP-WyatT

Ballad on the Game of Traffic, A. Jonathan Swift. CP-SwifJ

Ballad-Singer, The. Thomas Hardy. BoLoP; OLR; VLP *Fr.* At Casterbridge Fair. CP-HardT

Ballad Theme, A. Muriel Rukeyser. CP-RukeM

Ballad to the Tune of the Cutpurse [*or* "The Cut-Purse"], A. Jonathan Swift. CP-SwifJ

Ballade: "By Mystic's banks I held my dream." Paul Laurence Dunbar. CP-DunbP

Ballade: "Does something lie who'd rather stand." Edward Estlin Cummings. CP-CummE

Ballade: "Lady of Heaven, Queen of nature." François Villon, *tr. fr. French by* Isabella Gardner. CP-GardI

Ballade: "My heart's felt no wounds big or small." Anne Waldman. SP-WaldA

Ballade: "White night roared with a huge north-wind, The." Edward Estlin Cummings. CP-CummE

Ballade: "You who outlive us, you, our mortal brothers." François Villon, *tr. fr. French by* Isabella Gardner. CP-GardI

Ballade by the Fire. Edwin Arlington Robinson. CP-RobiE

Ballade for the Duke of Orléans. Richard Wilbur. CP-WilbR

Ballade in Old French. François Villon, *tr. fr. French by* Richard Wilbur. CP-WilbR

Ballade of Broken Flutes. Edwin Arlington Robinson. CP-RobiE

Ballade of Burial, A. Rudyard Kipling. CP-KiplR

Ballade of Forgiveness. François Villon, *tr. fr. French by* Richard Wilbur. CP-WilbR

Ballade of Jakko Hill, A. Rudyard Kipling. CP-KiplR

Ballade of Poisons. Allen Ginsberg. CP-GinsA

Ballade of Soul. Edward Estlin Cummings. CP-CummE

Ballade of the Ladies of Time Past. François Villon, *tr. fr. French by* Richard Wilbur. CP-WilbR

Ballade to End With, A. François Villon, *tr. fr. French by* Richard Wilbur. CP-WilbR

Ballet, The. Thomas Hardy. CP-HardT

Ballet. William Carlos Williams. CP-WilW1

Balloon Faces. Carl Sandburg. CP-SandC

Balloon of the Mind, The. William Butler Yeats. CP-YeatW

Balloons. Sylvia Plath. CP-PlatS

Balloons and Wooden Guns. John Hewitt. CP-HewiJ

Balloons hang on wires in the Marigold Gardens, The. Balloon Faces. Carl Sandburg. CP-SandC

Ball's Bluff. Herman Melville. SP-MelvH

Bally *Power Play*. Thom Gunn. CP-GunnT

Balm in Gilead. Christina Georgina Rossetti. CP-RosC2

Balme. Edmund Spenser. CH *Fr.* The Faerie Queene. CP-Spens

Baltic Fog Notes. Carl Sandburg. CP-SandC

Baltimore bones groan maliciously under sidewalk. Haunting Poe's Baltimore. Allen Ginsberg. CP-GinsA

Balustrade along my balcony, The. Beaded Balustrade. James Schuyler. CP-SchuJ

Bamberg. Randall Jarrell. CP-JarrR

Bambini picking daisies in the new spring grass. Daisies of Florence. Kathleen Jessie Raine. SP-RainK

Banal machines are exposing themselves, The. Ashes on a Saturday Afternoon. Frank O'Hara. SP-OharF

Banal Sojourn. Wallace Stevens. CP-StevW

Banana Dwarf, The. Laurence Lieberman. SP-LiebL

Banana Madonna, The. Laurence Lieberman. SP-LiebL

Banana-stuffed, the ape behind the brain. After Sunday Dinner We Uncles Snooze. John Ciardi. SP-CiarJ

Bananas down at the Safeway, The. The High-Class Bananas. Gary Gildner. SP-GildG

Bancroft, the message-bearing wire. Suggestion for a Telegraphic Birthday Greeting. Robert Browning. CP-BroR2

Band-Aids. Shel Silverstein. SP-SilS2

Band Concert. Carl Sandburg. CP-SandC

Band concert public square Nebraska city. Flowing and circling dresses. Band Concert. Carl Sandburg. CP-SandC

Band played *Idomeneo*, The. Charles Dodgson's Song. Randall Jarrell. CP-JarrR

Bandage. Stephen Berg. SP-BergS

Bandit to prince was his advance one night. The Right Possessor. Thom Gunn. CP-GunnT

Bandol (Var). Stevie Smith. CP-SmitS

Bandstand. John Hewitt. CP-HewiJ

Bandusian Spring than glass more brightly clear. *see also* "O fountain of Bandusia" *tr. by* Eugene Field. Horace. CP-WorW1, *tr. by* William Wordsworth; *Fr.* Odes.

Bang—a burning, A. Ted Hughes. SP-HughT *Fr.* Gaudete.

Bang-Klang. Shel Silverstein. SP-SilS2

Banging around in a cigarette she isn't "in love." Ted Berrigan. SP-BerrT *Fr.* The Sonnets.

Banging around in a cigarette she isn't "in love" / She murmurs of signs to her fingers. Ted Berrigan. SP-BerrT *Fr.* The Sonnets.

Bangor, Spring 1916. John Hewitt. CP-HewiJ

Banish Air from Air. Emily Dickinson. CP-DickE

Banished. Daniel Gerard Hoffman. SP-HoffD

Banished from Massachusetts. John Greenleaf Whittier. **CP-WhitJ**

Banishment, The. John Milton. *See* So spake our Mother Eve, and Adam heard.

Banjo done commence de shune, De. A Virginia Reel. Paul Laurence Dunbar. **CP-DunbP**

Banjo Song, A. Paul Laurence Dunbar. **CP-DunbP**

Bank Account. Robert Ranke Graves. **CP-GravR**

Bank feels no lameness of his knotty gout. On Bank the Usurer. Ben Jonson. **CP-JonsB**

Bank Fraud, A. Rudyard Kipling. *Fr.* Plain Tales from the Hills. "He drank strong waters and his speech was coarse." **CP-KiplR**

Bank Holiday. Wystan Hugh Auden. **CP-AudWJ**

Bank is a matter of columns, The. A Woman in Front of a Bank. William Carlos Williams. **CP-WilW2**

Bank swallows veer and dip, The. The Siskins. Theodore Roethke. **CP-RoetT**

Bank Thrown Down, The. Jonathan Swift. **CP-SwifJ**

Banked oars fell an hundred strong, The. The Rowers. Rudyard Kipling. **CP-KiplR**

Banked winter cloud. Kathleen Jessie Raine. **SP-RainK**

Bankers Are Just Like Anybody Else, Except Richer. Ogden Nash. **CP-NashO**

Banking to land, as readily as birds. The Landing. Charles Tomlinson. **CP-TomlC**

Banks. Max Jacob, *tr. fr. French by* Elizabeth Bishop. **CP-BishE**

Banks O' Doon, The. Robert Burns. *See* Ye banks and braes o' Bonnie Doon.

Banks o' Doon, The: "Ye flowery banks o' bonie Doon." Robert Burns. *See* Ye flowery banks o' bonie Doon.

Banks of a Stream Where Creatures Bathe. James Merrill. **SP-MerrJ**

Banks of Cree. Robert Burns. **CP-BurnR**

Banks of Nith, The. Robert Burns. **CP-BurnR**

Banks of the Devon, The. Robert Burns. **CP-BurnR**

Banneker. Rita Dove. **SP-DoveR**

Banner Bearer, The. William Carlos Williams. **CP-WilW2**

Bannerman's Island. Richard Hugo. **CP-HugoR**

Banners, The. Robert Duncan. **SP-DuncR**

Banners! Bunting! The engine throbs. A Special Train. Daniel Gerard Hoffman. **SP-HoffD**

Banners from East, from South. George Meredith. *Fr.* The Revolution. **CP-MerG1**

Banners from South, from East. George Meredith. *Fr.* The Revolution. **CP-MerG1**

Bannocks o' Bear-Meal. Robert Burns. **CP-BurnR**

Banquet. The. Dante Alighieri, *tr. fr. Italian by* Howard Nemerov. **CP-NemeH** *Fr.* Convito.

Banquet, The. George Herbert. **CP-HerbG**

Banquet, The. John Keats. **SeCePo** *Fr.* Lamia. **CP-KeatJ**

Banquet, The. John Milton. **NOSC** *Fr.* Book II. *Fr.* Paradise Regained [*or* Regain'd]. **CP-MiltJ**

Banquet, The. Ogden Nash. **CP-NashO**

Banquet Night. Rudyard Kipling. **CP-KiplR** *Fr.* Debits and Credits.

Banquo. Walter de la Mare. **CP-DeLaW**

Bantams in Pine-Woods. Wallace Stevens. **CP-StevW**

Banyan Tree, Old Year's Night, The. Derek Walcott. **CP-WalcD**

Baptism. Alice Walker. **CP-WalkA**

Baptism. William Wordsworth. *Fr.* Ecclesiastical Sonnets. **CP-WorW2**

Baptisme. Robert Herrick. **CP-HerrR**

Baptist Childhood, A. Donald Davie. *Fr.* A Dissentient Voice. **CP-DavDo**

Baptist might have been ordained to cry, The. Before the Picture of the Baptist, by Raphael, in the Gallery at Florence. William Wordsworth. *Fr.* Memorials of a Tour in Italy, 1837. **CP-WorW2**

Bar. Langston Hughes. **SP-HughL**

Bar[re] close as you can, and bolt fast too your door[e]. No Lock against Lechery. Robert Herrick. **CP-HerrR**

Bar Games. Gilbert Sorrentino. **SP-SorrG**

Bar Giamaica, 1959-60. Charles Wright. **SP-WrigC**

Bar Not the Door. Thomas Campion. **CP-CampT**

Bar of steel--it is only, A. Carl Sandburg. **AiP** *Fr.* Smoke and Steel. **CP-SandC**

Bar-Room Matins. Louis MacNeice. **CP-MacNL**

Bar-Room TV. Ted Hughes. *Fr.* Boom. **SP-HughT**

Barbara Frietchie. John Greenleaf Whittier. **CP-WhitJ**

Barbara's eyes are blue as azure. Won't You? Shel Silverstein. **SP-SilS2**

Barbed seeds in double ranks. Sours of the Hills. Gary Snyder. **CP-SnydG**

Barbed seeds in double ranks. Sours of the Hills. Gary Snyder. **CP-SnydG**

Barber, A. Sir John Suckling. **CP-SuckJ**

Barber, barber, come and get me. I'll Get One Tomorrow. Ogden Nash. **CP-NashO**

Barber is cutting the hair, A. Self-Portrait at Thirty-Nine. Ted Kooser. **SP-KoosT**

Barberry-Tree, The, Sometimes att. to Wordsworth. Samuel Taylor Coleridge. **CP-ColeS; CP-WorW1**

Barbie Doll. Marge Piercy. **SP-PierM**

Barcelona in Wartime. Louis MacNeice. *Fr.* Entered in the Minutes. **CP-MacNL**

Barclay of Ury. John Greenleaf Whittier. **CP-WhitJ**

Bard. William Everson. **SP-EverW**

Bard & mystic held me for their own, The. Rex. Ralph Waldo Emerson. **CP-EmerR**

Bard, if e'er he feel at all, The. To Mrs. King. William Cowper. **CP-CowpW**

Bard of the Fleece, whose skilful genius made. To the Poet, John Dyer. William Wordsworth. **CP-WorW1**

Bard or dunce is blest, but hard. Ralph Waldo Emerson. **CP-EmerR**

Bard, The [A Pindaric Ode]. Thomas Gray. **CP-GrayT**
  Pindaric Ode, A. **SeCePo**
  "Ruin seize thee, ruthless King!" **FaBoEH**

Bard whom pilf'red pastorals reknown, The. Alexander Pope. **OBSV** *Fr.* Epistle to Dr. Arbuthnot. **CP-PopeA**

Bard—whose soul is meek as dawning day, The. Occasioned by the Battle of Waterloo February, 1816. William Wordsworth. **CP-WorW2**

Bards, The. Robert Ranke Graves. **CP-GravR**

Bard's Epitaph, A. Robert Burns. **CP-BurnR**

Bards falter in shame, their running verse, The. The Bards. Robert Ranke Graves. **CP-GravR**

Bards of passion and of mirth. Ode. John Keats. **CP-KeatJ**

Bards of the island city!—where of old. To a Poetical Trio in the City of Gotham. John Greenleaf Whittier. **CP-WhitJ**

Bards wha hae for Hellas bled—. Louis MacNeice. **CP-MacNL** *Fr.* Cock o' the North. **CP-MacNL**

Bare Almond-Trees. David Herbert Lawrence. **CP-LawrD**

Bare bulb on a frayed cord, bad. Monday. Martin Edmunds. **SP-EdmuM**

Bare cherry tree, The. The Bare Tree. William Carlos Williams. **CP-WilW2**

Bare Fig-trees. David Herbert Lawrence. **CP-LawrD**

Bare-handed, I had the combs. Stings. Sylvia Plath. **CP-PlatS**

Bare Sheets I. John Yau. **SP-YauJo**

Bare Sheets II. John Yau. **SP-YauJo**

Bare Sheets III. John Yau. **SP-YauJo**

Bare skin is my wrinkled sack. The Shrouded Stranger. Allen Ginsberg. **CP-GinsA**

Bare thin, The. Fifth Universe. Diane Wakoski. *Fr.* The Universes. **SP-WakoD**

Bare Tree, The. Gilbert Sorrentino. **SP-SorrG**

Bare Tree, The. William Carlos Williams. **CP-WilW2**

Bare tree holds the fog in place, A. Testament. Daniel Gerard Hoffman. **SP-HoffD**

Bare tree reaches over, A. Fluidity, Charmouth. Steve Griffiths. **SP-GrifS**

Bare white marble room. Tunisian Nostalgia. Lawrence Ferlinghetti. **SP-FerlL**

Barefoot. Anne Sexton. **CP-SextA**

Barefoot Boy, The. John Greenleaf Whittier. **CP-WhitJ**
  "Blessings on thee, little man." **FaPON**
  "Oh for boyhood's painless play." **AiP**

Barefoot in purple pants. At the Piano. John Updike. *Fr.* Living with a Wife. **CP-UpdiJ**

Barefoot in purple pants. Living with a Wife. John Updike. **CP-UpdiJ**

Bareheaded / The hair blond in tight curls. The Swaggering Gait. William Carlos Williams. **CP-WilW2**

Barely and *widely*. Louis Zukofsky. **CP-ZukLS**

Barely Aware of the Insistent Loud Roars. Gilbert Sorrentino. **SP-SorrG**

Barely tolerated, living on the margin. Soonest Mended. John Ashbery. **SP-AshbJ**

Barj made all things, the wild. Creation Myth. Frank Templeton Prince. **CP-PrinF**

Bark of a fox rings, sonorous and long, The. Winter Night in Woodland. Thomas Hardy. **CP-HardT**

Bark smells like pineapple: Jeffries. Foxtail Pine. Gary Snyder. **CP-SnydG**

Barker, The. Dabney Stuart. **SP-StuaD**

Barking sound the shepherd hears, A. Fidelity. William Wordsworth. **CP-WorW1**

Barley-Break; or, Last in Hell. Robert Herrick. **CP-HerrR**

Barley or rye / blue and white green. Charles Olson. **CP-OlsoC**

Barlow. Stevie Smith. **CP-SmitS**

Barmaids Are Diviner Than Mermaids. Ogden Nash. **CP-NashO**

Barn, The. Richard Eberhart. *Fr.* Burr Oaks. **CP-EberR**

Barn, The. Stephen Spender. **CP-SpenS**

Barn, The. Lewis Turco. **SP-TurcL**

Barn Burnt in Ohio, A. Daniel Gerard Hoffman. **SP-HoffD**

Barn in Wisconsin. Edwin Rolfe. **CP-RolfE**

Barn, you have leaned too far. Old Farm in Northern Michigan. Gary Gildner. **SP-GildG**

Barnardine, given his life back. Barnardine's Reply. Roy Fisher. **SP-FishR**

Barnardine's Reply. Roy Fisher. **SP-FishR**

Barney Hung Over. Paul Zimmer. **SP-ZimmP**

Barnfloor and Winepress. Gerard Manley Hopkins. **CP-HopkG**

Barnsley and District. Donald Davie. **CP-DavDo**

Barnsley Cricket Club. Donald Davie. *Fr.* Two Dedications. **CP-DavDo**

Barnsley, 1966. Donald Davie. **CP-DavDo**

Barnzy stiffly vowes that hees no Cuckold. Epigramme. Thomas Campion. *Fr.* Observations in the Art of English Poesie. **CP-CampT**

Barometer, The. Charles Tomlinson. **CP-TomlC**

Barometer of my moods today, mayfly. Mayfly. Louis MacNeice. **CP-MacNL**

Baron Baedeker Blew His Nose and, Sighing, Departed, The. Howard Nemerov. **CP-NemeH**

Baroque Comment. Louise Bogan. **CP-BogaL**

Baroque Gravure, A. Thomas Merton. **CP-MertT**

Baroque Image. May Sarton. **SP-SartM**

Baroque night advances in its clouds, A. Second Elegy. Age of Magicians. Muriel Rukeyser. **CP-RukeM**

Baroque Wall-Fountain in the Villa Sciarra, A. Richard Wilbur. **CP-WilbR**

Barque Nornen. Charles Tomlinson. **CP-TomlC**

Barque of phosphor / On the palmy beach. Fabliau of Florida. Wallace Stevens. **CP-StevW**

Barrel-organ / assails the suburb, A. At Trotsky's House. Charles Tomlinson. **CP-TomlC**

Barren. Audre Lorde. **SP-LordA**

Barren Leaves. Thom Gunn. **CP-GunnT**

Barren Woman. Sylvia Plath. **CP-PlatS**

Barrier, The. Paul Laurence Dunbar. **CP-DunbP**

Bars. Carl Sandburg. **CP-SandC**

Bars are thick with drops that show, The. At Middle-Field Gate in February. Thomas Hardy. **CP-HardT**

Barthélémon at Vauxhall. Thomas Hardy. **CP-HardT**

Bartholdi Statue, The. John Greenleaf Whittier. **CP-WhitJ**

Bartholomew Fair. Ben Jonson.
"My masters and friends, and good people draw near." **CP-JonsB**

Bas-Relief. Carl Sandburg. **CP-SandC**

Base of All Metaphysics, The. Walt Whitman. **CP-WhitW**

Base words are uttered only by the base. Wystan Hugh Auden. **OxBSP; PeLV** *Fr.* Shorts [1939–1947] ("Motionless, deep in his mind, lies the past the poet's forgotten"). **CP-AudeW**
(Words.) **PeLV**

Base yourself on these. Tapicer. Roy Fisher. **SP-FishR** *Fr.* Five Pilgrims in the Prologue to the Canterbury Tales.

Baseball and Classicism. Tom Clark. **SP-ClarT**

Baseball and Writing. Marianne Craig Moore. **CP-MoorM**

Baseball Canto. Lawrence Ferlinghetti. **SP-FerlL**

Baseball Players, The. Donald Hall. **CP-HallD**

Basement of a church, The. Free Clinic. Chuck Miller. **SP-MillC**

Bashful Arides, The. Arides. Ezra Pound. **SP-PounE**

Bashfulnesse. Robert Herrick. **CP-HerrR**

Bashing the Babies. John Ciardi. **SP-CiarJ**

Bashō, coming / To the city of Nagoya. The Snow Party. Derek Mahon. **SP-MahoD**

Basic hatred / sometimes has a flower. Love Poem, A. William Carlos Williams. **CP-WilW2**

Basic ones don't seem to change much, The. Semantic Drift. Chuck Miller. **SP-MillC**

Basics. James Dickey. **CP-DickJ**

Basket. Carl Sandburg. **CP-SandC**

Basket broad of woven white rods, A. Gerard Manley Hopkins. **CP-HopkG**

Baskets. Louise Glück. **SP-GlücL**

Bass. Richard Hugo. **CP-HugoR**

Bassetti's Lions. Richard Hugo. **CP-HugoR**

Basta! David Herbert Lawrence. **CP-LawrD**

Basta una notte a maturare il fungo. Christina Georgina Rossetti. **CP-RosC3**

Bastard Peace, A. William Carlos Williams. **CP-WilW1**

Bastards. Robert Herrick. **CP-HerrR**

Bat. David Herbert Lawrence. **CP-LawrD**

Bat, The. Ogden Nash. **CP-NashO**

Bat, The. Theodore Roethke. **CP-RoetT**

Bat. Anne Sexton. **CP-SextA**

Bat is born, A. Bats. Randall Jarrell. **CP-JarrR**

Bat is dun, with wrinkled Wings, The. Emily Dickinson. **CP-DickE**

Bat that flits at close of eve, The. William Blake. **UV** *Fr.* Auguries of Innocence. **CP-BlakW**

Bath. Carl Sandburg. **CP-SandC**

Bath, The. Gary Snyder. **CP-SnydG**

Bath after Sailing. John Updike. **CP-UpdiJ**

Bath House, The. Thom Gunn. *Fr.* The Geysers. **CP-GunnT**

Bath Room, The. Richard Eberhart. *Fr.* Suite in Prison. **CP-EberR**

Bathe me O God in thee, mounting to thee. Walt Whitman. **TrPWD** *Fr.* Passage to India. **CP-WhitW**

Bathed. Tom Clark. **SP-ClarT**

Bathed in War's Perfume. Walt Whitman. **CP-WhitW**

Bathers, The. Hart Crane. **CP-CranH**

Bathing Resort. David Herbert Lawrence. **CP-LawrD**

Bathroom tiles are very pink and new, The. 1976. Marilyn Hacker. **SP-HackM**

Bathtub is white and full of strips, The. The Stones of Time. Kenneth Koch. **NoAM** *Fr.* Days and Nights. **SP-KochK**

Bathtub Thoughts. Wystan Hugh Auden. **CP-AudeW**

Bats, The. Brendan Galvin. **SP-GalvB**

Bats. Randall Jarrell. **CP-JarrR**

Bats at play taunt us with "guess how many." Above the Edge of Doom. Robert Ranke Graves. **CP-GravR**

Batt he gets children, not for love to reare 'em. Upon Batt. Robert Herrick. **CP-HerrR**

Batter my heart, three-personed [*or* three person'd] God; for you. John Donne. **BLPL; BiP; CABA; ClHu; EBEV; EBEvV; EaLo; EnRePo; FF; FHYEP; FaFP; GoBC; HAP; HelP; HoPM; ImPo; InPK; InPS; JCP; LiTB; MeLP; MePo; NAEL-1; NIP; NOBE; NOSC; NoP; OAEL-1; OAEP; OBS; OxAEP-1; OxBoCh; PAI; PPP; PPoe; PeECV; PoE; PoEL-2; Poetr; PrIm; SeCP; SeCV-1; SeCePo; SeCeV; SoSe; Son; TEP; TFi; TOF; TrCP; TrGrPo; TrPWD; TreFT** *Fr.* Divine Meditations. **CP-DonnJ** *Fr.* Holy Sonnets. **CP-DonnJ**

Batter'd, wrecked old man, A. Prayer of Columbus. Walt Whitman. **CP-WhitW**

Battered pail of ash, A. Doña Sebastiana. Martin Edmunds. **SP-EdmuM**

Battered Wife, The. Donald Davie. **CP-DavDo**

Batteries Out of Ammunition. Rudyard Kipling. **MMA** *Fr.* Epitaphs of the War [1914–1918]. **CP-KiplR**

Battery. Anne Waldman. **SP-WaldA**

Battle. Robinson Jeffers. *See* Foreseen for so many years: these evils, this monstrous violence.

Battle, The. Shel Silverstein. **SP-SilS2**

Battle Autumn of 1862, The. John Greenleaf Whittier. **CP-WhitJ**

Battle Continues, The. "Hugh MacDiarmid."
Major Road Ahead. **SP-MacDH**
"One loves the temporal, some unique manifestation." **SP-MacDH**

Battle fought between the Soul, The. Emily Dickinson. **CP-DickE**

Battle had passed from the height, The. Emily Brontë. **CP-BronE**

Battle of Brunanburh, see other translations: Brunanburg *and* Battle of Brunanburh. *Unknown, tr. fr.* Anglo-Saxon *by* Alfred, Lord Tennyson. **CP-TennA**

Battle of Copenhagen, The. Ernest Hemingway. **CP-HemiE**

Battle of Hastings, The. Daniel Gerard Hoffman. **SP-HoffD**

Battle'd of Life. David Herbert Lawrence. **CP-LawrD**

Battle of Murfreesboro. Allen Tate. **CP-TateA**

Battle of Sherra-Moor, The. Robert Burns. **CP-BurnR**

Battle of Stone River, Tennessee. Herman Melville. **SP-MelvH**

Battle of the *Bonhomme Richard* and the *Serapis*. Walt Whitman. *See* Would You Hear of an Old-Time [*or* Old-Fashioned] Sea fight?

Battle of Unameit, The. Kenneth Patchen. **CP-PatcK**

Battle of Waterloo, The. Byron. *See* There was a sound of revelry by night.

Battle rent a cobweb diamond-strung, The. Range-finding. Robert Frost. **CP-FrosR**

Battle-Scene. Sylvia Plath. **CP-PlatS**

Battle? That is one way of looking at the matter, A. Canto XIV. Louis MacNeice. *Fr.* Autumn Sequel. **CP-MacNL**

Battle, The ("Not far advanc'd was morning day"). Sir Walter Scott. *Fr.* Marmion.
(Douglas and Marmion.) **SP-ScotW**

Battlefield, The. Kay Boyle. **CP-BoylK**

Battlefield, A. Donald Davie. **CP-DavDo**

Battles tucked away in padded cells. Cyriaque d'Etremont: Bluenose Portrait Effect #1. Marsden Hartley. **CP-HartM**

Battles whose names I do not know. Looking. Muriel Rukeyser. **CP-RukeM**

Battleship Newsreel. Allen Ginsberg. **CP-GinsA**

Batxóca. Robert Ranke Graves. **CP-GravR**

Baucis and Philemon, *ad. fr.* Ovid, Metamorphoses, 8.626–724. Jonathan Swift. **CP-SwifJ**

  ("In antient Time, as Story tells.") **CP-SwifJ**

  (Story of Baucis & Philemon, The.) **CP-SwifJ**

Baudelaire in Cythera. Basil Bunting, *after the French of* Baudelaire. **CP-BuntB**

Baudelaire took the train. Radiant Silhouette III. John Yau. **SP-YauJo**

Baudelaire, who once explained. Give Them Blood. Gilbert Sorrentino. **SP-SorrG**

Bavarian Gentians. David Herbert Lawrence. **CP-LawrD**

Bawbee. Wystan Hugh Auden. **CP-AudWJ**

Bawdy Can Be Sane. David Herbert Lawrence. **CP-LawrD**

Bay Bank. Archie Randolph Ammons. **SP-AmmoA**

Bay horse is fitted with a white jade saddle, The. The March. Li Po, *tr. fr. Chinese by* William Carlos Williams *with* David Rafael Wang. **CP-WilW2**

Bay in Anglesey, A. Sir John Betjeman. **CP-BetjJ**

Bay is not blue but sombre yellow, The. Self-Criticism in February. Robinson Jeffers. **CP-JefJ**

Bay of Recovery. Richard Hugo. **CP-HugoR**

Bay of Resolve. Richard Hugo. **CP-HugoR**

Bay of Sad Loss. Richard Hugo. **CP-HugoR**

Bay of Seven Islands, The. John Greenleaf Whittier. **CP-WhitJ**

Bay today breaks, The. Today. James Schuyler. **CP-SchuJ**

Bayard Taylor. John Greenleaf Whittier. **CP-WhitJ**

Bayberry. Louis Zukofsky. **CP-ZukLS**

Bayonet. Anne Sexton. **CP-SextA**

Bayonet Charge. Ted Hughes. **SP-HughT**

Bayonne Entering NYC. Allen Ginsberg. **CP-GinsA**

Bayonne Turnpike to Tuscarora. Allen Ginsberg. **CP-GinsA**

Be a Demon! David Herbert Lawrence. **CP-LawrD**

Be a lone dog / Little brother. To Sons: Not to Be Numb. Thomas Merton. *Fr.* Cables to the Ace. **CP-MertT**

Be a son of this instant. To a Novice. Thomas Merton. *Fr.* Readings from Ibn Abbad. **CP-MertT**

Be advised by me, darling. Advice from a Mother. Robert Ranke Graves. **CP-GravR**

Be Angry at the Sun. Robinson Jeffers. **CP-JefR3**

Be angry now no more! Walter de la Mare. **CP-DeLaW**

Be angry yourself, as well you may. No Letter. Robert Ranke Graves. **CP-GravR**

Be assured, the Dragon is not dead. Vanity. Robert Ranke Graves. **CP-GravR**

Be awake mornings. See light spread across the lawn. Crystal. Ted Berrigan. **SP-BerrT**

Be bold my Booke, nor be abasht, or feare. To His Booke. Robert Herrick. **CP-HerrR**

Be-Bop Boys. Langston Hughes. **SP-HughL**

Be calm? And was I frantic? The Clinging Vine. Edwin Arlington Robinson. **CP-RobiE**

Be calm, collected, easy. The Unknown War. Carl Sandburg. **CP-SandC**

Be careful not to cross the gander. The Gander. Ogden Nash. **CP-NashO**

Be careful of words. Words. Anne Sexton. **CP-SextA**

Be careful, then, and be gentle about death. All Souls' Day. David Herbert Lawrence. **CP-LawrD**

Be composed—be at ease with me—I am Walt Whitman, liberal and lusty as Nature. To a Common Prostitute. Walt Whitman. **CP-WhitW**

Be earnest, Earth,—and kind. To Earth. Hart Crane. **CP-CranH**

Be faithful unto death. Christ proffers thee. That No Man Take Thy Crown. Christina Georgina Rossetti. **CP-RosC2**

Be fixed, you rapid orbs, that bear. The Fourth Song. Thomas Carew. **CP-CareT** *Fr.* Carew's Masque. **CP-CareT**

Be flip with us if you want to, spring wind. Spring Wind. Carl Sandburg. **CP-SandC**

Be gay now. Spring Carries Surprises. Carl Sandburg. **CP-SandC**

Be gentle, O hands of a child. Dreams. Walter de la Mare. **CP-DeLaW**

Be gentle with it—Coax it. Emily Dickinson. **SP-DickE**

Be gone ye blockheads, *Heraclitus* cries, *fr.* Vitae. Diogenes Laertius, *tr. fr. Greek by* Samuel Johnson. **CP-JohnS**

Be happy you two. A Marriage Song for Florence and Harry. Louis Zukofsky. **CP-ZukLS**

Be in me as the eternal moods. Doria. Ezra Pound. **SP-PounE**

Be It So. David Herbert Lawrence. **CP-LawrD**

Be it so, for I submit; his doom is fair. John Milton. **NAWM-1** *Fr.* Book X. **FHYEP** *Fr.* Paradise Lost. **CP-MiltJ**

Be it the summer-noon: a sandy space. The Sea: A Summer and Winter View. George Crabbe. **SP-CrabG** *Fr.* The Borough.

Be kind to yourself, it is only one. Who Be Kind To. Allen Ginsberg. **CP-GinsA**

Be land ready. Be Ready. Carl Sandburg. **CP-SandC**

Be loose. Be easy. Be ready. Forgotten Wars. Carl Sandburg. **CP-SandC**

Be me a Pharaoh. For Us, Who Dare Not Dare. Maya Angelou. **SP-AngeM**

Be merciful unto me, O God, be merciful unto me. Psalm 57. Bible, *O.T. Fr.* Psalms. **CP-Psal**

Be merciful unto me, O God: for man would swallow me up. Psalm 56. Bible, *O.T. Fr.* Psalms. **CP-Psal**

Be Mine the Doom. Emily Dickinson. **CP-DickE**

Be music, night, / That her sleep may go. Kenneth Patchen. **CP-PatcK**

Be My Defender, *ad. fr.* Psalm 4. Thomas Merton. **CP-MertT**

Be natural, / wise / as you can be. The Name. Robert Creeley. **CP-CreeR**

Be near me when my light is low. Tennyson. **EBVV; EBVVPR; ELP; EnVR; HAP; HelP; LiTB; MeMBP; NOCV; NoP; OAEL-2; PeECV; PoEL-5; SCGP; SCV** *Fr.* In Memoriam A. H. H. **CP-TennA**

Be Nobody's Darling. Alice Walker. **CP-WalkA**

Be not dismaid[e], though crosses cast thee down[e]. Comforts in Crosses. Robert Herrick. **CP-HerrR**

Be not obedient of the excellent, do not prize the silly with an exceptionally pushy person or orphan. Day and Night in 1952. Frank O'Hara. **SP-OharF**

Be not proud, but now incline. The Changes to Corinna. Robert Herrick. **CP-HerrR**

Be not sparing. Herrings. Jonathan Swift. **AnIV; NCEP; OnYI** *Fr.* Verses Made for the Women Who Cry Apples, etc. **CP-SwifJ**

Be not thou silent now at length, *par. by* Milton. Bible, *O.T. See* Psalm 83: "Keep not thou silence, O God."

Be not too wildly amorous of the far. The Imagination's Pride. Walter de la Mare. **CP-DeLaW**

Be of good cheer, brave spirit; steadfastly. Ralph Waldo Emerson. **CP-EmerR**

Be of good cheer, for I, ev'n I. Immortality. Christopher Smart. *Fr.* Hymns for the Amusement of Children. **SP-SmarC**

Be of love(a little). Edward Estlin Cummings. **CP-CummE**

Be Off! Stevie Smith. **CP-SmitS**

Be patient, solemn nose. Precious Five. Wystan Hugh Auden. **CP-AudeW**

Be perpendicular to the basket. Foul Shots: A Clinic. William Matthews. **SP-MattW**

Be private / let no one but strangers touch you. Coda. Richard Shelton. **SP-ShelR**

Be proud[,] as Spaniards! [and] Leap for Pride[,] ye Fleas[!]. On Donne's First Poem. Samuel Taylor Coleridge. **CP-ColeS**

Be proud New-York of your prize domes. & Forty-Second Street. Archibald MacLeish. **CP-MacLA**

Be proud you people of these graves. City of Monuments. Muriel Rukeyser. **CP-RukeM**

Be proud, young rejoicers, jesters, poets. Bequest. Edwin Rolfe. **CP-RolfE**

Be, rather than be called, a child of God. On an Infant Which Died before Baptism. Samuel Taylor Coleridge. **CP-ColeS**

Be Ready. Carl Sandburg. **CP-SandC**

Be sad, be cool, be kind. The Long Shadow of Lincoln: A Litany. Carl Sandburg. **CP-SandC**

Be safe, nor fear thyself so good a fame. To One that Desired Me Not to Name Him. Ben Jonson. **CP-JonsB**

Be showtime again. Somebody will paint beautiful faces all over. Soon It Will. Kenneth Patchen. **CP-PatcK**

Be Silence from your dismal cave abroad. Ode to Silence. Richard Eberhart. **CP-EberR**

Be slowly lifted up, thou long black arm. Sonnet. Wilfred Owen. **CP-OwenW**

Be somber with those in smoke garments. If So Hap May Be. Carl Sandburg. **CP-SandC**

Be Something Else. Robert Penn Warren. **SP-WarrR**

Be still / as we— / keep measure. Stones to Wind. Marsden Hartley. **CP-HartM**

Be Still! David Herbert Lawrence. **CP-LawrD**

Be still / Listen to the stones of the wall. In Silence. Thomas Merton. **CP-MertT**

Be still as before oh pool. Old Music for Quiet Hearts. Carl Sandburg. **CP-SandC**

Be still, heart, cease those measured strokes. The Foolish Heart. Countee Cullen. **CP-CullC**

Be still—listen to the wind! Mistral Over the Graves. Archibald MacLeish. **CP-MacLA**

Be still, my soul, be still; the arms you bear are brittle. Alfred Edward Housman. **CP-HousA**

Be sure my coming was a sharp offense. Edna St. Vincent Millay. **CP-MillE**

Be suspicious, / I say. A Warning to the Man in Receiving at Sears. Diane Wakoski. **SP-WakoD**

Be Thankful unto Him. Bible, *O.T. See* Psalm 100: "Make a joyful noise unto the Lord, all ye lands."

Be the mistress[e] of my choice. What Kind of Mistress[e] He Would Have. Robert Herrick. **CP-HerrR**

Be the proud Thames of trade the busy mart! To the River Arun. Charlotte Smith. **CP-SmitC**

Be this the chosen site; the virgin sod. Church to Be Erected. William Wordsworth. *Fr.* Ecclesiastical Sonnets. **CP-WorW2**

Be those few hours, which I have yet to spend. His Meditation upon Death. Robert Herrick. **CP-HerrR**

Be thou then my beauty named. Thomas Campion. **CP-CampT**

Be to her, Persephone. Prayer to Persphone. Edna St. Vincent Millay. *Fr.* Memorial to D. C. **CP-MillE**

Be uncovered! / Hoe with look life! Sun rises. Wild Provoke of the Endurance Sky. Joseph Ceravolo. **SP-CeraJ**

Be unto love as rain is unto colour;create. Edward Estlin Cummings. **CP-CummE**

Be warned of steps retrieved in pain. Mentor and Pupils. George Meredith. **CP-MerG2**

Be well assured that on our side. A Song in Storm. Rudyard Kipling. **CP-KiplR**

Be who you are and will be. For Each of You. Audre Lorde. **SP-LordA**

Be Wise, and Fly Not. Thomas Campion. **CP-CampT**
    ("Your faire lookes urge my desire.") **CP-CampT**

Be wise as thou art cruel; do not press. Sonnet 140. William Shakespeare. **NoSic** *Fr.* Sonnets. **CP-ShaWS**

Be with Me. Leonard Cohen. **CP-CoheL**

Be with me, Luis de San Angel, now. Ave Maria. Hart Crane. **HoFi; MoPo; NOBA; NePA; NoAM** *Fr.* The Bridge. **CP-CranH**

Be[e] you all pleased [*or* pleas'd]? your pleasures grieve not[t] me[e]. Sonnet 9. Mary Sidney, Countess of Montgomery Wroth. **BWW; NOSC** *Fr.* Pamphilia to Amphilanthus. **CP-WrotM**

Be you still, be you still, trembling heart. To His Heart, Bidding It Have No Fear. William Butler Yeats. **CP-YeatW**

Be your words made (good sir) of Indian ware. Sonnet 92. Sir Philip Sidney. **NoSic** *Fr.* Astrophil and Stella. **SP-SidnP**

Beach, The. Robert Ranke Graves. **CP-GravR**

Beach, The. Robinson Jeffers. **CP-JefR1**

Beach / On. / Ourselves alone are walking, The. Song about Sinn Fein for Serena. James Liddy. *Fr.* Shore. **CP-LiddJ**

Beach Head, The. Thom Gunn. **CP-GunnT**

Beach holds and sifts us through her dreaming fingers, The. Poem. Bill Knott. **SP-KnotB**

Beach Trip. Charles Bukowski. **SP-BukC1**

Beach was crowded, The. The Sea Corpse. Anne Sexton. **CP-SextA**

Beaches; it is true: they go on on. Circuit. James Dickey. **CP-DickJ**

Beachhead. Derek Walcott. **CP-WalcD**

Beachthieves. Richard Hugo. **CP-HugoR**

Beachy Head. Charlotte Smith. **CP-SmitC**
    ("I once was happy, when, while yet a child.") **WPE**

Beacon, The. Richard Wilbur. **CP-WilbR**

Bead, The. Charles Tomlinson. **CP-TomlC**

Beaded Balustrade. James Schuyler. **CP-SchuJ**

Beads around / my neck / Mt. Kenya away. African Images, Glimpses from a Tiger's Back. Alice Walker. **CP-WalkA**

Beaks of Eagles, The. Robinson Jeffers. **CP-JefR2**

Beale Street. Langston Hughes. **SP-HughL**

Beams of April, ere it goes, The. The Silk Worm. Vincent Bourne, *tr. fr. Latin by* William Cowper. **CP-CowpW**

Beams of noon, like burning lances, through the tree-tops flash and glisten. The Slaves of Martinique. John Greenleaf Whittier. **CP-WhitJ**

Bean Eaters, The. Gwendolyn Brooks. **SP-BrooG**

Bean-Feast, The. Robert Browning. **CP-BroR2**

Bean Field, The. John Clare. **SP-ClarJ**

Bean Spasms. Ted Berrigan. **SP-BerrT**

Bean-Stalk, The. Edna St. Vincent Millay. **CP-MillE**

Bean-Stripe: also, Apple-Eating, A. Robert Browning. **CP-BroR2**

Beanfield full in blossom smells as sweet, A. The Bean Field. John Clare. **SP-ClarJ**

Bear, The. Robert Frost. **CP-FrosR**

Bear, The. Galway Kinnell. **SP-KinnG**

Bear and the Garden-Lover, The. Marianne Craig Moore. **CP-MoorM** *Fr.* Fables of La Fontaine.

Bear and the Last Person to Remember, The. Robert Penn Warren. *Fr.* Fall Comes in Back-Country Vermont. **SP-WarrR**

Bear came out of night, The. The History of Bears. Paul Zimmer. **SP-ZimmP**

Bear Gulch Road. Al Young. **CP-YounA**

Bear Hamlet, like a soldier, to the stage. Orphic Scenario. Howard Nemerov. **CP-NemeH**

Bear him, comrades, to his grave. Burial of Barber. John Greenleaf Whittier. **CP-WhitJ**

Bear in mind. Drum. Langston Hughes. **SP-HughL**

Bear in mind these dead: / I can find no plainer words. Neither an Elegy Nor a Manifesto. John Hewitt. **CP-HewiJ**

Bear loped before me, A. John Haines. *Fr.* The Turning. **SP-HainJ**

Bear me to Dictaeus. Acon. Hilda Doolittle. **CP-DoolH**

Bear on the Unicycle, The. Robert Pack. **SP-PackR**

Bear part with me most straight and pleasant tree. Mary Sidney, Countess of Montgomery Wroth. *See* Beare part with me most straight and pleasant Tree.

Bear Paw. Richard Hugo. **CP-HugoR**

Bear puts both arms around the tree above her, The. The Bear. Robert Frost. **CP-FrosR**

Bear sleeps in a cellarhole; pine needles, A. New Hampshire. Donald Hall. **CP-HallD**

Bear Track Plantation: Shortly after Shiloh. Robert Penn Warren. *Fr.* Two Studies in Idealism: Short Survey of American and Human History. **SP-WarrR**

Bear under the snow, A. March. James Wright. **CP-WrigJ**

Bear who eats with a silver spoon, A. Animal Acts. Charles Simic. **SP-SimiC**

Bear with fur that appeared to have been licked backward, A. The Bear and the Garden-Lover. Marianne Craig Moore. **CP-MoorM** *Fr.* Fables of La Fontaine.

Bear witness, Erin! when thine injured isle. To Ireland. Percy Bysshe Shelley. **CP-ShelP**

Bearded goldfish move about the bowl, The. Goldfish. Howard Nemerov. **CP-NemeH**

Bearded Iris. Louis Zukofsky. **CP-ZukLS**

Bearded Oaks. Robert Penn Warren. **SP-WarrR**

Bearded Woman, by Ribera, The. Paul Muldoon. **SP-MuldP**

Beardless then on the old oak benches. Letter to Sainte-Beuve. James Liddy. **CP-LiddJ**

Beards of the grain, gray-green: the lances. The Girl Dreams That She Is Giselle. Randall Jarrell. **CP-JarrR**

Beare part with me most straight and pleasant Tree. Mary Sidney, Countess of Montgomery Wroth. *Fr.* Part 1. *Fr.* Urania. **CP-WrotM**
    ("Bear part with me most straight and pleasant tree.") **WPE**
    (Morea's Sonnet.) **WPE**

Bearer, The. Hayden Carruth. **CP-CarHS**

Bearer of Evil Tidings, The. Robert Frost. **CP-FrosR**

Bearer of Freedom's holy light. Democracy. John Greenleaf Whittier. **CP-WhitJ**

Bearing and giving are different, it appears. Witness. Donald Davie. **CP-DavDo**

Bearing the long lance, their banners before them. Archibald MacLeish. *Fr.* Hamlet of A. Macleish. **CP-MacLA**

Bears. Adrienne Rich. **CP-RicAE; SP-RicA2**

Bears and Waterfalls. May Sarton. **SP-SartM**

Bears at Raspberry Time. Hayden Carruth. **CP-CarHS**

Bears gash the forest trees. To Be Called A Bear. Robert Ranke Graves. **CP-GravR**

Beast, The. Charles Bukowski. **SP-BukC2**

Beast, The. Theodore Roethke. **CP-RoetT**

Beast. Alice Walker. **CP-WalkA**

Beast and bird must bow aside. Epilogue for a Masque of Purcell. Adrienne Rich. **CP-RicAE**

Beast, Book, Body. Erica Jong. **SP-JongE**

Beast-head in the mirror. The Whiskey Priest Recites His Holy Office. James McAuley. **SP-McAuJ** *Fr.* The Exile's Recurring Nightmare.

Beast in View. Muriel Rukeyser. **CP-RukeM**

Beast stands at my eye, A. The Naked Land. Kenneth Patchen. **CP-PatcK**

Beastie, The. John Hewitt. **CP-HewiJ**

Beasts. Richard Wilbur. **CP-WilbR**

Beasts Are Very Wise, The. Rudyard Kipling. **CP-KiplR**

Beasts' Confession to the Priest, The. Jonathan Swift. **CP-SwifJ**

Beasts Have Entered, The. Siv Cedering Fox. **SP-CedeS**

Beasts in the schoolroom, whose transparent faces, The. Blues for Warren. Thomas McGrath. **SP-McGrT**

Beasts in their major freedom. Beasts. Richard Wilbur. **CP-WilbR**

Beasts of each kind their fellows spare. Juvenal, *tr. by* Samuel Johnson. **CP-JohnS** *Fr.* Satires.

Beasts of the field, fowls likewise of the air. The Ark. Robert Ranke Graves. **CP-GravR**

Beat at the bars. Bars. Carl Sandburg. **CP-SandC**

Beat! Beat! Drums! Walt Whitman. **CP-WhitW**

Beat hell out of it. Episode 17. William Carlos Williams. **CP-WilW1** *Fr.* Paterson.

Beat off in our last fight were we? Rudyard Kipling. **CP-KiplR** *Fr.* The Naulahka.

Beat, Old Heart. Carl Sandburg. **CP-SandC**

Beat, old heart, these are the old bars. Beat, Old Heart. Carl Sandburg. **CP-SandC**

Beat out continuance in the choking veins. The Blood is Justified. Muriel Rukeyser. **CP-RukeM**

Beat the drums of tragedy for me. Fantasy in Purple. Langston Hughes. **SP-HughL**

Beat-up datsun idling in the road. Kisiabaton. Gary Snyder. **CP-SnydG**

Beating asphalt into highway potholes. The Spring. Gary Snyder. **CP-SnydG**

Beating Time. Robert Pack. **SP-PackR**

Beatrice. "Lewis Carroll." **CP-CarrL**

Beatrice and Dante. Robert Ranke Graves. **CP-GravR**

Beatrice Signorini. Robert Browning. **CP-BroR2**

Beatrice's Last Words. Percy Bysshe Shelley. **FiP** *Fr.* The Cenci. **CP-ShelP**

Beau of the Dead. Donald Hall. **CP-HallD**

Beaucaire. Jean Garrigue. **SP-GarrJ**

Beauharnois ("bronze clock"). Margaret Atwood. *Fr.* Four Small Elegies. **SP-AtwM2**

Beauharnois ("is the man"). Margaret Atwood. *Fr.* Four Small Elegies. **SP-AtwM2**

Beauharnois, Glengarry. Margaret Atwood. *Fr.* Four Small Elegies. **SP-AtwM2**

Beaumaris, December 21, 1963. Sir John Betjeman. **CP-BetjJ**

Beaumont! it was thy wish that I should rear. At Applethwaite, near Keswick. William Wordsworth. **CP-WorW1**

Beau's Reply. William Cowper. **CP-CowpW**

Beau's Reply to the Five Ladies' Answer, The. Jonathan Swift. **CP-SwifJ**

Beauteous rose-bud, young and gay. To Miss C*********, a Very Young Lady. Robert Burns. **CP-BurnR**

Beauteous, Yea Beauteous More than These. Christopher Smart. **EaLo** *Fr.* A Song to David. **SP-SmarC**

Beauti-ful. Charles Bukowski. **SP-BukC3**

Beautician, The. Thom Gunn. **SP-GunnT**

Beautie Without Love Deformitie, *see also* Thou Art Not Fair. Thomas Campion. **CP-CampT**

Beautie's no other but a lovely Grace. Beauty. Robert Herrick. **CP-HerrR**

Beautiful / is the / unmea. Edward Estlin Cummings. **CP-CummE**

Beautiful Aeroplane, The. Charles Tomlinson. **CP-TomlC**

Beautiful and happy girl, A. Memories. John Greenleaf Whittier. **CP-WhitJ**

Beautiful as a tiered cloud, skysails set and shrouds twanging. Clipper-Ships. John Gould Fletcher. **SP-FletJ**

Beautiful as the flying legend of some leopard. Judith of Bethulia. John Crowe Ransom. **SP-RansJ**

Beautiful Berta aboard a bewildering barque. Waltz of the Empty Roadhouse. Gilbert Sorrentino. *Fr.* Twelve Études for Voice and Kazoo. **SP-SorrG**

Beautiful Bowel Movement, The. John Updike. **CP-UpdiJ**

Beautiful Captive, The. Robinson Jeffers. **CP-JefR3**

Beautiful cashier's white face has risen once more, The. Before a Cashier's Window in a Department Store. James Wright. **CP-WrigJ**

Beautiful Changes, The. Richard Wilbur. **CP-WilbR**

Beautiful dive, then floating, A. The Whole Creation Groans to Be Delivered. Marsden Hartley. *Fr.* Un Recuerdo—Hermano—Hart Crane R.I.P. **CP-HartM**

Beautiful Dove, come back to us in April. Song. Edna St. Vincent Millay. **CP-MillE**

Beautiful Evelyn Hope is dead! Evelyn Hope. Robert Browning. **CP-BroR1**

Beautiful floors and a lively. Hope. William Matthews. **SP-MattW**

Beautiful For Situation. Christina Georgina Rossetti. **CP-RosC2**

Beautiful Funerals. James Schuyler. **CP-SchuJ**

Beautiful girl said something in your praise, A. To a Friend on His Marriage. Frank Templeton Prince. **CP-PrinF**

Beautiful lady, / in reverence. Geoffrey Hill. *Fr.* Scenes with Harlequins. **CP-HillG**

Beautiful Lawn Sprinkler, The. Howard Nemerov. **CP-NemeH**

Beautiful little children. Kyoto Born in Spring Song. Gary Snyder. **CP-SnydG**

Beautiful Lofty Things. William Butler Yeats. **CP-YeatW**

Beautiful, my delight. To Be Sung on the Water. Louise Bogan. **CP-BogaL**

Beautiful new / Character may enter the, A. Charles Henri Ford. **SP-FordC** *Fr.* Emblems of Arachne.

Beautiful New / York sky harder. Blue. James Schuyler. **CP-SchuJ**

Beautiful Old Age. David Herbert Lawrence. **CP-LawrD**

Beautiful Parsi woman in your pale silk veil. The Parsi Woman. Edna St. Vincent Millay. **CP-MillE**

Beautiful rush, The. Marsden Hartley. **CP-HartM**

Beautiful Soup. Gilbert Sorrentino. **SP-SorrG**

Beautiful Soup, so rich and green. "Lewis Carroll." **CP-CarrL** *Fr.* Alice's Adventures in Wonderland.

(Turtle Soup.) **CP-CarrL**

Beautiful, tame, and wild / Sad, pathetic, eating starfish on the window. Love of a Seagull. Malcolm Lowry. **CP-LowrM**

Beautiful, tender, wasting away for sorrow. Luscious and Sorrowful. Christina Georgina Rossetti. **CP-RosC2**

Beautiful, the fair, the elegant, The. Beauty. Wilfred Owen. **CP-OwenW**

Beautiful the hanging cliff and the wind-thrown cedars, but they have no. On an Anthology of Chinese Poems. Robinson Jeffers. **CP-JefR3**

Beautiful Toilet, The. Ezra Pound, *tr. fr. Mei Sheng, 140 B.C.* **SP-PounE**

Beautiful Women. Stephen Dunn. **SP-DunnS**

Beautiful Women. Walt Whitman. **CP-WhitW**

Beautiful years when she was by me and we visited. Morro Bay. Robinson Jeffers. **CP-JefR3**

Beautiful You Are. Kenneth Patchen. **CP-PatcK**

Beautiful Young Girl Walking Past the Graveyard—, The. Charles Bukowski. **SP-BukC1**

Beautiful Young Nymph Going to Bed, A. Jonathan Swift. **CP-SwifJ**

Beautifully Janet slept. Janet Waking. John Crowe Ransom. **SP-RansJ**

Beauty. Stephen Dobyns. **SP-DobyS**

Beauty. Ralph Waldo Emerson. **CP-EmerR**

Beauty, The. Thomas Hardy. **CP-HardT**

Beauty. Robert Herrick. **CP-HerrR**

Beauty / is to lay hold of Love. Charles Olson. **CP-OlsoC**

Beauty. Wilfred Owen. **CP-OwenW**

Beauty. Christopher Smart. *Fr.* Hymns for the Amusement of Children. **SP-SmarC**

Beauty. *Unknown. See* Beauty is but a vain and doubtful good.

Beauty and Beauty's son and rosemary. Rosemary. Marianne Craig Moore. **CP-MoorM**

Beauty and Moonlight. William Wordsworth. **CP-WorW1**

Beauty and the Beast. Rita Dove. **SP-DoveR**

Beauty and youth, with manners sweet, and friends. On the Grave. Herman Melville. **SP-MelvH**

Beauty be not caused—It Is. Emily Dickinson. **CP-DickE**

Beauty cannot be shown. Adam in the Evening. Archibald MacLeish. *Fr.* Songs for Eve. **CP-MacLA**

Beauty crowds me till I die. Emily Dickinson. **CP-DickE**

Beauty hath force to catch the human sight, *speech of Cleophila.* Sir Philip Sidney. **SP-SidnP** *Fr.* Arcadia.

Beauty I Would Suffer For. Marge Piercy. **SP-PierM**

Beauty in Trouble. Robert Ranke Graves. **CP-GravR**

Beauty is a shell. Song. William Carlos Williams. **CP-WilW2**

Beauty Is But a Painted Hell. Thomas Campion. **CP-CampT**

Beauty is but a vain and doubtful good. *Unknown.* **CP-ShaWS; OBSC** *Fr.* The Passionate Pilgrim. **CP-ShaWS**

(Beauty.) **OBSC**

Beauty is often timidity. Emily Dickinson. **SP-DickE**

Beauty is sometimes personified. On Beauty. Kenneth Koch. **SP-KochK**

Beauty is that Medusa's head. Archibald MacLeish. **CP-MacLA** *Fr.* The Happy Marriage.

Beauty Is Vain. Christina Georgina Rossetti. **CP-RosC1**

Beauty, no other thing is, than a beam[e]. The Definition of Beauty. Robert Herrick. **CP-HerrR**

Beauty of a maiden is coveted by the world, The. Ce-Lia The Immortal Beauty. William Carlos Williams, *with* David Rafael Wang, *at. to* Wang Wei, *tr. fr. Chinese.* **CP-WilW2**

Beauty of manhole covers—what of that? The. Manhole Covers. Karl Shapiro. **SP-ShapK**

Beauty of Milwaukee Cold with Rain, The. Al Young. **CP-YounA**

Beauty of my table, The. *see also* Commentary—The Café. Leonard Cohen. **CP-CoheL**

Beauty of the earth is a resilient wonderful thing, The. Metamorphosis. Robinson Jeffers. **CP-JefR3**

Beauty of the Ship, The. Walt Whitman. **CP-WhitW**

Beauty of Things, The. Robinson Jeffers. **CP-JefR3**

Beauty Rohtraut. Eduard Friedrich Mörike, *tr. fr. German by* George Meredith. **CP-MerG1**

Beauty, Since You So Much Desire. Thomas Campion. **CP-CampT**

Beauty's Soliloquy during Her Honeymoon, A. Thomas Hardy. **CP-HardT**

Beaver cut his timber, The. Cobbler Keezar's Vision. John Greenleaf Whittier. **CP-WhitJ**

Beaverbank. Richard Hugo. **CP-HugoR**

Beaverhouse Downriver, The. Barton Sutter. **SP-SuttB**

Bebopper in his soul, he sends, A. Dexter Gordon at Keystone Korner. Al Young. **CP-YounA**

Because / an obstreperous grin minutely floats. Edward Estlin Cummings. **CP-CummE**

Because / death is so lovely. Because. Peter Meinke. **SP-MeinP**

Because. John Lennon *and* Paul McCartney. **CP-Beatl**

Because. Peter Meinke. **SP-MeinP**

Because / you go away i give roses who. Edward Estlin Cummings. **CP-CummE**

Because a Lady chose to say. Arthur Hugh Clough. **SP-ClouA**

Because a woman. All You Can Do. Charles Olson. **CP-OlsoC**

Because altruists are the least sexy. From the Manifesto of the Selfish. Stephen Dunn. **SP-DunnS**

Because finally the personal. Essay on the Personal. Stephen Dunn. **SP-DunnS**

Because Flat-foot is the favourite of the white leghorn cock, and. Flat-Foot's Song. David Herbert Lawrence. **CP-LawrD**

Because Great Pan is dead, Astraea gone. From the Desk of the Laureate: For Immediate Release. Howard Nemerov. **CP-NemeH**

Because he could not face. The Founder. George Oppen. **CP-OppeG**

Because He First Loved Us. Christina Georgina Rossetti. **CP-RosC2**

Because he had spoken harshly to his mother. Revelation. Robert Penn Warren. **SP-WarrR**

Because he has bright white teeth, Eg- / natius whips out a. Carmen 39. Catullus. *Fr.* Carmina. **CP-Catul**

Because he loves Her. Emily Dickinson. **CP-DickE**

Because he played games seriously. Competition. Stephen Dunn. **SP-DunnS**

Because he puts the compromising chart. Zola. Edwin Arlington Robinson. **CP-RobiE**

Because he was a butcher and thereby. Reuben Bright. Edwin Arlington Robinson. **CP-RobiE**

Because his wife refused to miss a dress fitting. Cézanne and the Love of Color. Stephen Dobyns. **SP-DobyS**

Because I am a fraud / Because I am afraid. Mr. Lowry's Good Friday under a Real Cactus. Malcolm Lowry. **CP-LowrM**

Because I am bewildered, because I must decide, because my. The Massacre of the Innocents. Wystan Hugh Auden. *Fr.* For the Time Being; a Christmas Oratorio. **CP-AudeW**

Because I am by nature blind. Jonathan Swift. *Fr.* Riddles. **CP-SwifJ**

Because I am drunk, this Independence Night. The Fourth of July. Howard Nemerov. **CP-NemeH**

Because I am here. Gazing Out, Gazing In. Erica Jong. **SP-JongE**

"Because I am mad about women." The Wild Old Wicked Man. William Butler Yeats. **CP-YeatW**

Because I am the bullet. What the White Had to Say. Charles Simic. **SP-SimiC**

Because I breathe not love to every one. Sonnet 54. Sir Philip Sidney. **ImGa; InPS; NoSic; OAEP; OBSC; TrGrPo** *Fr.* Astrophil and Stella. **SP-SidnP**

Because I chose to hear a special thunder in my head. The Originators. Thomas Merton. **CP-MertT**

Because I could not stop for Death. Emily Dickinson. **CP-DickE**

Because I don't have spit. Fast Speaking Woman. Anne Waldman. **SP-WaldA**

Because I feel that, in the Heavens above. To My Mother. Edgar Allan Poe. **CP-PoeEd**

Because I had loved so deeply. Compensation. Paul Laurence Dunbar. **CP-DunbP**

Because I have called to you. Calls. Carl Sandburg. **CP-SandC**

Because I have thee still kept from lies and blame. Sir Thomas Wyatt. **CP-WyatT**

Because I lay my. Why Is God Love, Jack? Allen Ginsberg. **CP-GinsA**

Because I liked you better. Alfred Edward Housman. **CP-HousA**

Because I love / The sun pours out its rays of living gold. Amo Ergo Sum. Kathleen Jessie Raine. **SP-RainK**

Because I love you more than any. Interlude: Hephaestion's Prayer. David St. John. **SP-StJoD**

Because i love you)last night. Edward Estlin Cummings. **CP-CummE**

Because I oft, in dark abstracted guise. Sonnet 27. Sir Philip Sidney. **NoSic** *Fr.* Astrophil and Stella. **SP-SidnP**

Because I Paced My Thought. John Hewitt. **CP-HewiJ**

Because I see these mountains they are brought low. Shadow. Kathleen Jessie Raine. *Fr.* Eileann Chanaidh. **SP-RainK**

Because I sought it far from men. Rudyard Kipling. **CP-KiplR** *Fr.* The Naulahka.

Because I was content with these poor fields. Musketaquid. Ralph Waldo Emerson. **CP-EmerR**

Because I was slow with girls. Not the Occult. Stephen Dunn. **SP-DunnS**

Because I'd seen you not believe your lover. John Berryman. *Fr.* Sonnets to Chris. **CP-BerrJ**

Because in December when the gifts fly—. Martial, *tr. by* William Matthews. **SP-MattW** *Fr.* Epigrams.

Because in the deepnesses of night you smoulder as a ray that does not violate the dark but solemnly defines it. The Canticle of the Rose. William Everson. **SP-EverW** *Fr.* The Rose of Solitude.

Because in the heart / of darkness I could not see. Hayden Carruth. **CP-CarHS** *Fr.* The Clay Hill Anthology.

Because it could do it well. It Is Writing. Roy Fisher. **SP-FishR**

Because it's / Spring / thingS. Edward Estlin Cummings. **CP-CummE**

Because man is not virtuous in himself. Tribute. Countee Cullen. **CP-CullC**

Because my Brook is fluent. Emily Dickinson. **CP-DickE**

Because my cousin the priest. Inventing Ballygalvin. Brendan Galvin. **SP-GalvB**

Because my grandmother's hours. Woman Enough. Erica Jong. **SP-JongE**

Because my will is simple as a window. The Blessed Virgin Mary Compared to a Window. Thomas Merton. **CP-MertT**

Because of a coolness in the air. The Day. James Schuyler. **CP-SchuJ**

Because of love's infallibility. The Crab-Tree. Robert Ranke Graves. **CP-GravR**

Because of me, because of you. Randall Jarrell. **CP-JarrR**

Because of the memory of one we held dear. In a Province. Frank Templeton Prince. **CP-PrinF**

Because of the silent snow, we are all hushed. Winter-Lull. David Herbert Lawrence. **CP-LawrD**

Because of the stink of the dungeons: 1344. Ezra Pound. *See* Canto 25: "Book of the council major."

Because of the way one thing. Confirmation. Dabney Stuart. **SP-StuaD**

Because one loves you, Helen Grey. Helen Grey. Christina Georgina Rossetti. **CP-RosC3**

Because one's husband is different from one's self. Causes. Mona Van Duyn. **SP-VanDuyn**

Because our young were drab. Think Tank. James Merrill. **SP-MerrJ**

Because poor PUER's both unsure and vain. Gemini. Richard Wilbur. **CP-WilbR**

Because sap fell away. Wystan Hugh Auden. **CP-AudWJ**

Because she lost her father. The Heidelberg Landlady. Erica Jong. **SP-JongE**

Because she wanted me, I slipped out of my skin. The Angel of Death. Siv Cedering Fox. **SP-CedeS**

Because she wants to touch him. Parable of the Four-Poster. Erica Jong. **SP-JongE**

Because, straying through the wine-gardens with the grace and. Often Was It. Kenneth Patchen. **CP-PatcK**

Because that stealing immortalitie, *ad. fr. Greek of* Pindar. Sir Walter Ralegh. **CP-RaleW**

Because that you are going. Emily Dickinson. **CP-DickE**

Because the Bee may blameless hum. Emily Dickinson. **CP-DickE**

Because the cockpit, like the snowy village in a paperweight. Black Box. William Matthews. **SP-MattW**

Because the known and the unknown. George Oppen. *Fr.* Of Being Numerous. **CP-OppeG**

Because the mind will defend anything. Under the Black Oaks. Stephen Dunn. **SP-DunnS**

Because the moon burns a bright orange. Cemetery Nights II. Stephen Dobyns. **SP-DobyS**

Because the moon comes. Whatever Became of Me. Richard Shelton. **SP-ShelR**

Because the Pleasure-Bird Whistles. Dylan Thomas. **CP-ThomD**

Because the snow is deep. The Fox. Kenneth Patchen. **CP-PatcK**

Because the velvet image. To Hedli. Louis MacNeice. **CP-MacNL**

Because the wind has changed, because I guess. Clearing the Title. James Merrill. **SP-MerrJ**

Because there is safety in derision. The Apparitions. William Butler Yeats. **CP-YeatW**

Because there was a man somewhere in a candystripe silk shirt. Homage to the Empress of the Blues. Robert Earl Hayden. **CP-HaydR**

Because there was no other place. Flee on Your Donkey. Anne Sexton. **CP-SextA**

"Because They Are Desiring. . . ." Tom Clark. **SP-ClarT**

Because they are not. The Deceptrices. William Carlos Williams. **CP-WilW2**

Because they could not give it too much ground. In a Bird Sanctuary. Richard Wilbur. **CP-WilbR**

Because they were crude and easy and without fixed expectation. Prologue: Letter to an Indolent Norn. John Ciardi. **SP-CiarJ**

Because this world is on the wing and what cometh no man can know. Magic Psalm. Allen Ginsberg. **CP-GinsA**

Because thou hast the power and own'st the grace. Sonnet. Elizabeth Barrett Browning. *Fr.* Sonnets from the Portuguese. **CP-BroEB**

Because Thy Love hath sought me, / All mine is Thine and Thine is mine. Christina Georgina Rossetti. **CP-RosC2**

Because 'twas Riches I could own. Emily Dickinson. **CP-DickE**

Because we always said Toity-toid Street and. Myrtle the Turtle. Peter Meinke. **SP-MeinP**

Because we Are Not Taken Seriously. Stephen Dunn. **SP-DunnS**

Because we couldn't sleep we went on. A Morning. Margaret Atwood. **SP-AtwM1**

Because we have no type of earth for everyone. All the Day. Kenneth Patchen. **CP-PatcK**

Because we lived our several lives. The House. Mary Oliver. **SP-OlivM**

Because we love bare hills and stunted trees. Hound Voice. William Butler Yeats. **CP-YeatW**

Because we met at dusk. To an Old Poet in Peru. Allen Ginsberg. **CP-GinsA**

Because we rage inside. Why We Are Truly a Nation. William Matthews. **SP-MattW**

Because What I Want Most Is Permanence. May Sarton. **SP-SartM**

Because when our clothes hung from the slanting alders. Reasons. Daniel Gerard Hoffman. **SP-HoffD**

Because with bought books, Sir, your study's fraught. Ausonius, *tr. fr. Latin* by Richard Lovelace. **CP-LoveR**

Because women are expected to keep silent about. On Stripping Bark from Myself. Alice Walker. **CP-WalkA**

Because you are. Against Silence. Marilyn Hacker. **SP-HackM**

Because you are simple people, kindly and romantic. Fourth Act. Robinson Jeffers. **CP-JefR3**

Because you did, I too arrange flowers. Still Life with Tulips. Erica Jong. **SP-JongE**

Because you have found me in the pitch-dark night. Ribh at the Tomb of Baile and Aillinn. William Butler Yeats. **CP-YeatW**

Because you have thrown off your Prelate Lord. John Milton. **CP-MiltJ** (On the Forcers of Conscience.) **CP-MiltJ**

Because you intoxicate like all the drinks. Louis MacNeice. *Fr.* Flowers in the Interval. **CP-MacNL**

Because you love me I have much achieved. Encouraged. Paul Laurence Dunbar. **CP-DunbP**

Because you never yet have loved me, dear. Touching "Never." Christina Georgina Rossetti. **CP-RosC2**

Because you take life in your stride(instead. Edward Estlin Cummings. **CP-CummE**

Because you were foolish enough to love one place. Adult Grief. Louise Glück. **SP-GlückL**

Because you will not overthrow your life. *see also* Commentary—The Asthmatic. Leonard Cohen. **CP-CoheL**

Because you're sweet and lovely girl I love you. For You Blue. George Harrison. **CP-BeatI**

Beckon to me to come. Lover to Mistress. Thomas Hardy. **CP-HardT**

Beckoned anew to a world. Aubade. Wystan Hugh Auden. **CP-AudeW**

Becoming a Nun. Erica Jong. **SP-JongE**

Becoming Somebody Else. Charles Kenneth Williams. **CP-WillC**

Becoming the river, we are the river. Refusing the Necessary. Stephen Dobyns. **SP-DobyS**

Bec's Birthday. Jonathan Swift. **CP-SwifJ**

Bed, The. Robert Creeley. **CP-CreeR**

Bed, The. Thom Gunn. **CP-GunnT**

Bed, The. Archibald MacLeish. **CP-MacLA**

Bed, The. "Lou Reed." **SP-ReedL**

Bed by the Window, The. Robinson Jeffers. **CP-JefR2**

Bed frames them. Their eyes, The. Lovers. Lewis Turco. **SP-TurcL**

Bed, glasses off, and all's. Myopia: a Night. Robert Lowell. **SP-LoweR**

Bed in Summer. Robert Louis Stevenson. **CP-StevR**

Bed in the Sky, The. Gary Snyder. **CP-SnydG**

Bed is not very big, The. Edward Estlin Cummings. **CP-CummE**

Bed-Man, or Grave-Maker, The. Robert Herrick. **CP-HerrR**

Bed of Forget-Me-Nots, A. Christina Georgina Rossetti. **CP-RosC3**

Bed of Old John Zeller, The. Wallace Stevens. **CP-StevW**

Bed of the World, The. Erica Jong. **SP-JongE**

Bed the inter- / loping grass. In the Round. James Schuyler. **CP-SchuJ**

Bed was made, the room was fit, The. A Camp. Robert Louis Stevenson. **CP-StevR**

Beddybye. Bill Knott. **SP-KnotB**

Bedfordshire. Donald Davie. **CP-DavDo**

Bedlam Revisited. John Ciardi. **SP-CiarJ**

Bedpans. Charles Bukowski. **SP-BukC1**

Bedraggled rose, The. Charles Henri Ford. **SP-FordC** *Fr.* Secret Haiku.

Bedridden Peasant, The. Thomas Hardy. **CP-HardT**

Bedroom. John Gould Fletcher. **SP-FletJ** *Fr.* The Ghosts of an Old House.

Bedroom Farce. Geoffrey Chaucer. **FaBoDD** *Fr.* The Reeve's Tale. *Fr.* The Canterbury Tales. **CP-ChauG**

Beds of Grainne and Diarmuid, The. Robert Ranke Graves. **CP-GravR**

Beds that are mirrors. Marge Piercy. *Fr.* Doing It Differently. **SP-PierM**

Beds, Toilets, You and Me—. Charles Bukowski. **SP-BukC1**

Bedside. Margaret Atwood. **SP-AtwM2**

Bedtime. Denise Levertov. **CP-LeveD**

Bedtime Stories. Mona Van Duyn. **SP-VanDM**

Bedtime Story. Charles Simic. **SP-SimiC**

Bedtime's come fu' little boys. Lullaby. Paul Laurence Dunbar. **CP-DunbP**

Bee, The. Charles Bukowski. **SP-BukC1**

Bee, The. James Dickey. **CP-DickJ**

Bee! / drowning in, A. Grace Paley. **CP-PaleG**

Bee allur'd by the perfume, A. The Bee and the Pine-Apple. William Cowper. **CP-CowpW**

Bee and the Pine-Apple, The. William Cowper. **CP-CowpW**

Bee-Boy's Song, The. Rudyard Kipling. **CP-KiplR** *Fr.* Dymchurch Flit. *Fr.* Puck of Pook's Hill.

Bee from court of Love, and reason torne. Sonnet 10. Mary Sidney, Countess of Montgomery Wroth. *Fr.* A Crowne of Sonetts Dedicated to Love. *Fr.* Pamphilia to Amphilanthus. **CP-WrotM**

Bee given to him who triumphs in his right. Sonnet 12. Mary Sidney, Countess of Montgomery Wroth. *Fr.* A Crowne of Sonetts Dedicated to Love. *Fr.* Pamphilia to Amphilanthus. **CP-WrotM**

Bee his burnished Carriage, A. Emily Dickinson. **CP-DickE**

Bee hit sip some honey f'om de matermony vine, De. Song. Paul Laurence Dunbar. **CP-DunbP**

Bee! I'm expecting you! Emily Dickinson. **CP-DickE**

Bee is not afraid of me, The. Emily Dickinson. **CP-DickE**

Bee Meeting, The. Sylvia Plath. **CP-PlatS**

Bee Song. Carl Sandburg. **CP-SandC**

Bee that was searching for sweets one day, A. Two Songs. Paul Laurence Dunbar. **CP-DunbP**

Beech. Robert Frost. **CP-FrosR**

Beech, The. Charles Tomlinson. **CP-TomlC**

Beech, The. Charles Tomlinson. **CP-TomlC**

Beech boles whiten in the swollen stream, The. Autumn, 1939. Alun Lewis. **CP-LewiA**

Beech leaves which might have clung. March. Richard Wilbur. **CP-WilbR**

Beehold this sacred fire. Mary Sidney, Countess of Montgomery Wroth. *Fr.* Part 2. *Fr.* Urania. **CP-WrotM**

Beeing past the paines of love. Song. Mary Sidney, Countess of Montgomery Wroth. *Fr.* Pamphilia to Amphilanthus. **CP-WrotM**

Beekeeper Speaks. . . , The, *see also* And Is Silent. Howard Nemerov. **CP-NemeH**

Beekeeper's Daughter, The. Sylvia Plath. **CP-PlatS**

Been here before? Whether he has or no. Canto XV. Louis MacNeice. *Fr.* Autumn Sequel. **CP-MacNL**

Been so long since a strange woman has slept in my bed. I and I. "Bob Dylan." **CP-DylaB**

Beeny Cliff. Thomas Hardy. **CP-HardT**

Beeny did not quiver. A Death-Day Recalled. Thomas Hardy. **CP-HardT**

Beer. Charles Bukowski. **SP-BukC1**

Beer Bottle. Ted Kooser. **SP-KoosT**

Bees, The. Audre Lorde. **SP-LordA**

Bees and a honeycomb in the dried head of a horse in a pasture corner—. In Tall Grass. Carl Sandburg. **CP-SandC**

Bees and lilies there were. Bring the Day! Theodore Roethke. **CP-RoetT**

Bees and Morning Glories. John Ciardi. **SP-CiarJ**

Bees and the Flies, The. Rudyard Kipling. **CP-KiplR**

Bees are Black, with Gilt Surcingles. Emily Dickinson. **CP-DickE**

Bees are eating the candy, The. An Indian Market in Mexico. Randall Jarrell. **CP-JarrR**

Bees aren't humble, they don't notably bumble. *see also* And Is Silent. Howard Nemerov. **CP-NemeH**

Bees at the six-pointed junkweed blooms. A Journal of Three Questions. Charles Wright. **SP-WrigC**

Bees! Bees! Hark to your bees! The Bee-Boy's Song. Rudyard Kipling. **CP-KiplR** *Fr.* Dymchurch Flit. *Fr.* Puck of Pook's Hill.

Bees build in the crevices, The. The Stare's Nest by My Window. William Butler Yeats. **BIrV; CP-YeatW; GTBS-6; GTBS-P; InPS; LiTB; NOBE** *Fr.* Meditations in Time of Civil War. **CP-YeatW**

Bee's 5th. Charles Bukowski. **SP-BukC1**

Bee's fixed hexagon, The. Come, Sleep. Louise Bogan. **CP-BogaL**

Bees forage where the blue ajuga's grown. Nature Morte. Howard Nemerov. **CP-NemeH**

Bees in the crevices, The. William Butler Yeats. *See* The Stare's Nest by My Window.

Bees in the late summer sun. Bee Song. Carl Sandburg. **CP-SandC**

Bees love grass, The. Thomas Merton. **CP-MertT**

Beethoven. Robert Lowell. **SP-LoweR**

Beethoven Attends the C Minor Seminar. Charles Tomlinson. **CP-TomlC**

Beethoven during breakfast? The human soul. C Minor. Richard Wilbur. **CP-WilbR**

Beethoven Triumphant. John Berryman. **CP-BerrJ**

Beethoven's Death Mask. Stephen Spender. **CP-SpenS**

Beetle, The, *see also* Commentary—The Beetle. Leonard Cohen. **CP-CoheL**

Beetle loves his unpretending track, The. William Wordsworth. **FaBoCo; FiBHP; Par** *Fr. sequel to* Gold and Silver Fishes in a Vase. **CP-WorW2**

Beetle near my foot, The. Providence 2. John Hewitt. **CP-HewiJ**

Beetle soars, the beetle spins, The. George Meredith. **CP-MerG2**

Before. Wystan Hugh Auden. **CP-AudWJ**

Before. Wystan Hugh Auden. **CP-AudWJ**

Before. Robert Browning. **CP-BroR1**

Before. Miller Williams. **SP-WillM**

Before a Cashier's Window in a Department Store. James Wright. **CP-WrigJ**

Before a Midnight Breaks in Storm. Rudyard Kipling. **CP-KiplR**

Before a world of tremulous green baize. Motley. George Meredith. **CP-MerG2**

Before and after Summer. Thomas Hardy. **CP-HardT**

Before and after the eye, grasses go over the long fields. *second vers.* James Dickey. **CP-DickJ**

Before breakfast you drew down the blind. The Steam Crane. Roy Fisher. **SP-FishR** *Fr.* Interiors with Various Figures.

Before Danger. Muriel Rukeyser. **CP-RukeM**

Before Dark. Wendell Berry. **CP-BerrW**

"Before Dawn. . . ." Tom Clark. **SP-ClarT**

Before Dawn. Walter de la Mare. **CP-DeLaW**

Before dawn the coyotes. Manzanita. Gary Snyder. **CP-SnydG**

Before Dinner, *sels.* Robert Burns. *Fr.* Graces————at the Globe Tavern. **CP-BurnR**

Before Even This. Leonard Nathan. **SP-NathL**

Before God died, shot while running away. Knobs and Levers. Robert Ranke Graves. **CP-GravR**

Before He comes we weigh the Time! Emily Dickinson. **CP-DickE**

Before he made me what I am. Robot. Robert Pack. **SP-PackR**

Before he sails a man may go on leave. Alun Lewis. *Fr.* On Embarkation. **CP-LewiA**

Before he went to live with owls and bats. Nebuchadnezzar's Dream. John Keats. **CP-KeatJ**

Before his father. Charles Henri Ford. **SP-FordC** *Fr.* Secret Haiku.

Before I am completely shriven. Single Vision. Stanley Jasspon Kunitz. **CP-KuniS**

Before I began life this time. Last Poem. Ted Berrigan. **SP-BerrT**

Before I die. Four. Robert Creeley. **CP-CreeR**

Before I got my eye put out. Emily Dickinson. **CP-DickE**

Before I Knocked. Dylan Thomas. **CP-ThomD**

Before I offer the wood. Ritual. James McAuley. **SP-McAuJ**

Before I see another day. The Complaint of a Forsaken Indian Woman. William Wordsworth. **CP-WorW1**

Before I sigh my last gasp, let me breathe. The Will. John Donne. **CP-DonnJ**

Before infinity drinks the sun, Sleepwalker rambles in the desert. Culebra Cascabel. Tom Clark. **SP-ClarT**

Before Invasion, 1940. Sir John Betjeman. **CP-BetjJ**

Before it came inside. What's That. Anne Sexton. **CP-SextA**

Before Knowledge. Thomas Hardy. **CP-HardT**

Before Life and After. Thomas Hardy. **CP-HardT**

Before man came to blow it right. The Aim Was Song. Robert Frost. **CP-FrosR**

Before Mans fall, the Rose was born. The Rose. Robert Herrick. **CP-HerrR**

Before March. Archibald MacLeish. **CP-MacLA**

Before Marching and After. Thomas Hardy. **CP-HardT**

Before me a far-off time arises. Some Future Moon. Donald Davie. **CP-DavDo**

Before morning you shall be here. Alba. Samuel Beckett. **CP-BeckS**

Before my closing eyes, dear Cynthia, stand. Tibullus, *tr. by* Samuel Johnson. **CP-JohnS** *Fr.* Elegies.

Before my drift-wood fire I sit. Burning Drift-Wood. John Greenleaf Whittier. **CP-WhitJ**

Before my face the picture hangs. Robert Southwell. **NoSic; OBD** *Fr.* Upon the Image of Death. **CP-SoutR**

Before my feet the ploughshare rolls the earth. Winter Ploughing. William Everson. **SP-EverW**

Before My Friend Arrived. Thomas Hardy. **CP-HardT**

Before my Spring I garnered Autumn's gain. Rudyard Kipling. **CP-KiplR** *Fr.* Without Benefit of Clergy. *Fr.* Life's Handicap.

Before Our Lady's on Des Peres Boulevard. One Moment in Eternity. Howard Nemerov. **CP-NemeH**

Before our lives divide for ever. The Triumph of Time. Algernon Charles Swinburne. **SP-SwinA**

Before our lunch, lovely G tries to explain. The Art of Argument, the Argument of Art. David St. John. *Fr.* To Pasolini. **SP-StJoD**

Before Parting. Algernon Charles Swinburne. **SP-SwinA**

Before Plato told the great lie of ideals. For the Heroes Are Dipped in Scarlet. David Herbert Lawrence. **CP-LawrD**

Before she has her floor swept. Portrait by a Neighbour. Edna St. Vincent Millay. **CP-MillE**

Before Sunrise, ere Colour sprang. Fall'n Is Lucifer. George Meredith. **CP-MerG2**

Before supper we had seen three grazing deer. The President's Speech. Hayden Carruth. **CP-CarHS**

Before that thundercloud breaks from its hawsers. Derek Walcott. **CP-WalcD** *Fr.* Midsummer.

Before the Anæsthetic; or, A Real Fright. Sir John Betjeman. **CP-BetjJ**

Before the Beginning. Christina Georgina Rossetti. **CP-RosC2**

Before the beginning of things. Prelude. John Gould Fletcher. **SP-FletJ**

Before the beginning of Years. Algernon Charles Swinburne. **SP-SwinA** *Fr.* Atalanta in Calydon.

Before the beginning Thou hast foreknown the end. Before the Beginning. Christina Georgina Rossetti. **CP-RosC2**

Before the Birth of One of Her Children. Anne Bradstreet. **CP-BradA**

Before the braces give, the cripple eased to earth. This Early Day. Kenneth Patchen. **CP-PatcK**

Before the Carnival. Thom Gunn. **CP-GunnT**

Before the chipmunks filch. Cherry Robbers. Richardson Pack. **SP-PackR**

Before the cock in the barnyard spoke. Hangman's Oak. Edna St. Vincent Millay. **CP-MillE**

Before the Dance. Charles Tomlinson. **CP-TomlC**

Before the dark-brow'd sons of Spain. The Inca's Daughter. Walt Whitman. **CP-WhitW**

Before the dawn men dream of shapes of ships. Port Caradoc. Frederick Morgan. **SP-MorgF**

Before the dusk grows deeper. Dusk. Joseph Ceravolo. **SP-CeraJ**

Before the Fall. John Milton. *See* She as a veil down to the slender waist.

Before the first visitor comes the spring. The Chinese Restaurant in Portrush. Derek Mahon. **SP-MahoD**

Before the fragile gradual throne of night. Edward Estlin Cummings. **CP-CummE**

Before the grass could be planted. Building in Nova Scotia. Stephen Dunn. **SP-DunnS**

Before the grass is out the people are out. Paterson. William Carlos Williams. **CP-WilW1**

Before the great resumption. Frederick Morgan. *Fr.* Meditations for Autumn. **SP-MorgF**

Before the greenish door she stood. Window Washer—Avenue C. Marsden Hartley. **CP-HartM**

Before the ice is in the pools. Emily Dickinson. **CP-DickE**

Before the ice the convulsions of. The Double Hellas. Kenneth Rexroth. **CP-RexKL** *Fr.* The Homestead Called Damascus.

Before the Judgment. Robert Duncan. **SP-DuncR** *Fr.* Passages.

Before the knowledge in me, he, beautiful, down in the dirt, kneels. Robert Penn Warren. *Fr.* Saul at Gilboa. **SP-WarrR**

Before the light radiates, where do you place it. Energy of the Pre-World as a Bungee Cable Jumper. Tom Clark. **SP-ClarT**

Before the mountains were brought forth, before. Christina Georgina Rossetti. **Son** *Fr.* Later Life: A Double Sonnet of Sonnets. **CP-RosC2**

Before the Paling of the Stars. Christina Georgina Rossetti. **CP-RosC3**

Before the Picture of the Baptist, by Raphael, in the Gallery at Florence. William Wordsworth. *Fr.* Memorials of a Tour in Italy, 1837. **CP-WorW2**

Before the Press scarce one co'd see. To His Book ("Before the Press scarce one co'd see"). Robert Herrick. **CP-HerrR**

[Before the Rape]. William Shakespeare. **NoSic** *Fr.* The Rape of Lucrece. **CP-ShaWS**

Before the shutter blinks. The Portrait. William Matthews. **SP-MattW**

Before the six[t]h day of the next new year. On the Card[e]s, and Dice. Sir Walter Ralegh. **CP-RaleW**

Before the starry threshold of *Jove[']s* court. Comus; a Masque Presented at Ludlow Castle. John Milton. **CP-MiltJ**

Before the Throne, and Before the Lamb. Christina Georgina Rossetti. **CP-RosC2**

Before the War. Marilyn Hacker. **SP-HackM**

Before the world had past her time of youth. William Wordsworth. *Fr.* Sonnets upon the Punishment of Death. **CP-WorW2**

Before the World Was Made, *fr.* A Woman Young and Old. William Butler Yeats. **CP-YeatW**

Before their journeys men have dreams. Returning to Europe. Howard Nemerov. **CP-NemeH**

Before there was in Egypt any sound. Monadnock through the Trees. Edwin Arlington Robinson. **CP-RobiE**

Before This. Charles Kenneth Williams. **CP-WillC**

Before this cooling planet shall be cold. Edna St. Vincent Millay. *Fr.* Epitaph for the Race of Man. **CP-MillE**

Before this dance is through I think I'll love you too. I'm Happy Just to Dance with You. The Beatles. **CP-Beatl**

Before this little gift was come. Robert Louis Stevenson. **CP-StevR**

Before this longing. Her Longing. Theodore Roethke. **CP-RoetT**

Before this loved one. This Loved One. Wystan Hugh Auden. **CP-AudeW**

Before, though, Paris was wonderful. Wanderers. Years of the Dog. Archibald MacLeish. **CP-MacLA**

Before thy betters with suspense. Silence. Christopher Smart. *Fr.* Hymns for the Amusement of Children. **SP-SmarC**

Before train-time they swept across the track. Gestures. Daniel Gerard Hoffman. **SP-HoffD**

Before we could call / America home. A Child's Japan. May Sarton. **SP-SartM**

Before we part to alien thoughts and aims. Lines. Thomas Hardy. **CP-HardT**

Before word of his painting got around. Before. Miller Williams. **SP-WillM**

Before you can learn the trees, you have to learn. Learning the Trees. Howard Nemerov. **CP-NemeH**

Before you filled the dark eye. Weave a Circle Round Me Thrice. Brendan Galvin. **SP-GalvB**

Before you, I was living on an island. Celebration for June 24. Thomas McGrath. **SP-McGrT**

Before you leave her, the woman who though you lavish. Advice to a God. Mona Van Duyn. **SP-VanDM**

Before you thought of Spring. Emily Dickinson. **CP-DickE**

Before you will it so. Beloved Beware. Alun Lewis. **CP-LewiA**

Began and end with a double. He places his feet. Darts. Louis MacNeice. *Fr.* Indoor Sports. **CP-MacNL**

Began with swirling, blind, unstilled oh still. John Berryman. *Fr.* Sonnets to Chris. **CP-BerrJ**

Begat. Anne Sexton. *Fr.* The Death of the Fathers. **CP-SextA**

Beggar at the Door for Fame, The. Emily Dickinson. **CP-DickE**

Beggar in Sapri. Richard Hugo. **CP-HugoR**

Beggar Lad—dies early, The. Emily Dickinson. **CP-DickE**

Beggar Maid and King Cophetua, The. Robert Ranke Graves. **CP-GravR**

Beggar Speaks, The. Nicholas Vachel Lindsay. **CP-LindV**

Beggar to Beggar Cried. William Butler Yeats. **CP-YeatW**

Beggar to Mab, the Fairy [or Fairie] Queen, The. Robert Herrick. **CP-HerrR**

Beggar, when I hurried to the door, The. Scissors For a One-Armed Tailor. John Hewitt. **CP-HewiJ**

Beggars. Robert Herrick. **CP-HerrR**

Beggars, The. Sylvia Plath. **CP-PlatS**

Beggars. William Wordsworth. **CP-WorW1**

Beggar's Soliloquy, The. George Meredith. **CP-MerG1**

Beggar's Valentine, The. Nicholas Vachel Lindsay. **CP-LindV**

Begger, The. Robert Herrick. **CP-HerrR**

Begging Another, on Colour of Mending the Former. Ben Jonson. **CBLP; OAEP; PoEL-2; UnTE** *Fr.* A Celebration of Charis in Ten Lyric[k] Pieces [*or* Peeces]. **CP-JonsB**

Begging on North Main. Dabney Stuart. **SP-StuaD**

Begin a song. A Lion upon the Floor. Charles Olson. **CP-OlsoC**

Begin by dipping your brush into clear light. Midsummer Mobile. Sylvia Plath. **CP-PlatS**

Begin. Carnation underfoot, tea splashing stars. Komboloi. James Merrill. **SP-MerrJ**

Begin, ephebe, by perceiving the idea. Wallace Stevens. **NOBA** *Fr.* It Must Be Abstract. *Fr.* Notes toward a Supreme Fiction. **CP-StevW**

Begin right here. The Campground Road. Some calls it the. Hayden Carruth. *Fr.* Paragraphs. **CP-CarHS**

Begin to charm, and as thou strok'st mine ears. To Music. Robert Herrick. **CP-HerrR**

Begin with a kiss[e]. Up Tail[e]s All. Robert Herrick. **CP-HerrR**

Begin with a pool. The deepening. The Existing Pool. Hayden Carruth. **CP-CarHS**

Begin with a Victorian cottage in a Rhode Island. Wind Chimes. Stephen Dobyns. **SP-DobyS**

Beginne with Jove; then is the worke halfe done. Evensong. Robert Herrick. **CP-HerrR**

Beginner, The, *parody of* Robert Browning. Rudyard Kipling. **CP-KiplR** *Fr.* The Muse among the Motors.

Beginner, The. Rudyard Kipling. **FaBoTw** *Fr.* Epitaphs of the War [1914–1918]. **CP-KiplR**

Beginner, / Perpetual beginner. What Can I Tell My Bones? Theodore Roethke. **AmPP; NOBA** *Fr.* Meditations of an Old Woman. **CP-RoetT**

Beginners. Walt Whitman. **CP-WhitW**

Beginner's Guide. Howard Nemerov. **CP-NemeH**

Beginner's Guide to the Ocean, A. Ogden Nash. **CP-NashO**

Beginning, A. Wendell Berry. *Fr.* Work Song. **CP-BerrW**

Beginning, A. Charles Bukowski. **SP-BukC3**

Beginning, The. Louise Glück. *Fr.* Marathon. **SP-GlücL**

Beginning, The. Wallace Stevens. **CP-StevW**

Beginning. James Wright. **CP-WrigJ**

Beginning and end. Wendell Berry. *Fr.* From the Crest. **CP-BerrW**

Beginning at five o'clock, just before dawn rises. My Friend Felix. Donald Hall. **CP-HallD**

Beginning, Difficult. Robert Herrick. **CP-HerrR**

Beginning is a cold wind, The. Frederick Morgan. *Fr.* Poems of the Two Worlds. **SP-MorgF**

Beginning My Studies. Walt Whitman. **CP-WhitW**

Beginning of a Great Adventure. "Lou Reed." **SP-ReedL**

Beginning of a Poem of These States. Allen Ginsberg. **CP-GinsA**

Beginning of April, The. Charles Kenneth Williams. **CP-WillC; SP-WillC**

Beginning of Heliodorus, The. Heliodorus, *tr. fr. Classical Greek by* Richard Crashaw. **CP-CrasR**

Beginning of the Armadilloes, The. Rudyard Kipling. *Fr.* Just-So Stories. "I've never sailed the Amazon." **CP-KiplR**

Beginning of the End, The. Gerard Manley Hopkins. **CP-HopkG**

Beginning of Writing, The. Robert Duncan. **SP-DuncR**

Beginning—or, The. Primavera Transportata al Morale. William Carlos Williams. **CP-WilW1**

Beginning to dangle beneath. In the Marble Quarry. James Dickey. **CP-DickJ**

Beginning to know / how the die. The Tomb of Stéphane Mallarmé. Charles Simic. **SP-SimiC**

Beginning to Say No. Tess Gallagher. **SP-GallT**

Beginning with the palest and softest lavender. Hayden Carruth. *Fr.* North Winter. **CP-CarHL**

Beginnings. Robert Earl Hayden. **CP-HaydR** "Plowdens, Finns." **CNA**

Beginnings, The. Rudyard Kipling. **CP-KiplR**

Beginnings and Endings. Robert Herrick. **CP-HerrR**

Begins with the *ooo ooo* of a mourning dove. Holy Thursday. Charles Wright. **SP-WrigC**

Begone, thou fond presumptuous Elf. The Waterfall and the Eglantine. William Wordsworth. **CP-WorW1**

Begot like other children, he. T the Great. Wystan Hugh Auden. **CP-AudeW**

Begotten of the Spleen. Charles Simic. **SP-SimiC**

Beguiled into forgetfulness of care. Lines Suggested By a Portrait from the Pencil of F. Stone. William Wordsworth. **CP-WorW2**

Begun in Cuautla, July, 1937, Finished in the Farolita Jan. 1938, *sl. diff. vers., incl. in* Lighthouse Invites the Storm. Malcolm Lowry. *See* Thirty Five Mescals in Cuautla.

Behavior. Howard Nemerov. **CP-NemeH**

Behaviour. David Herbert Lawrence. **CP-LawrD**

Beheaded in the middle of the. 12:18 A.M. Charles Bukowski. **SP-BukC1**

Beheld in Naples. Jean Garrigue. **SP-GarrJ**

Behind a brightening cloud. James McAuley. **SP-McAuJ** *Fr.* After the Blizzard.

Behind a large truck. Chuck Miller. **SP-MillC**

Behind each garage a ladder. Late September. Ted Kooser. **SP-KoosT**

Behind glass in Mexico / this clay doll draws. Five Poems for Dolls. Margaret Atwood. **SP-AtwM2**

Behind him the hotdogs split and drizzled. Suicide off Egg Rock. Sylvia Plath. **SP-PlatS**

Behind his back, the first wave passes over. The Agent. Richard Wilbur. **CP-WilbR**

Behind its snout like a huge button. Photo of the Author with a Favorite Pig. William Matthews. **SP-MattW**

Behind King's Chapel what the earth has kept. At the Indian Killer's Grave. Robert Lowell. **SP-LoweR**

Behind Me—dips Eternity. Emily Dickinson. **CP-DickE**

Behind me the woods fill with the clashing. Waking to My Name. Robert Pack. **SP-PackR**

Behind New York there's a face. For the Chinese New Year & for Bill Berkson. Frank O'Hara. **SP-OharF**

Behind our back the golden woods. A Winter Sky. Galway Kinnell. **SP-KinnG**

Behind shut doors, in shadowy quarantine. The First Time. Karl Shapiro. **SP-ShapK**

Behind Stowe. Elizabeth Bishop. **CP-BishE**

Behind that white brow. To a Dead Journalist. William Carlos Williams. **CP-WilW1**

Behind the Arras. Paul Laurence Dunbar. **CP-DunbP**

Behind the barn the lady from the city. The Admiral Fan. Charles Kenneth Williams. **CP-WillC**

Behind the church in the Isleta Pueblo, there is a courtyard. Ants. Robert Bly. **SP-BlyR**

Behind the grid, the radiant. Death of a Painter. Donald Davie. **CP-DavDo**

Behind the hills, from the city of an Etrascan gateway. Metals. Donald Davie. **CP-DavDo**

Behind the house the upland falls. After the Pleasure Party. Herman Melville. **SP-MelvH**

Behind the Knight. Stevie Smith. **CP-SmitS**

Behind the lids of sleep. Kathleen Jessie Raine. **SP-RainK**

Behind the locked doors. The Barn. Lewis Turco. **SP-TurcL**

Behind the Mirror. Thom Gunn. **CP-GunnT**

Behind the mountain's belly-button. Pirate Poem. Frederick Morgan. **SP-MorgF**

Behind the North Wind. Donald Davie. **CP-DavDo**

Behind the Northern curtain-folds he passed. George Meredith. *Fr.* Napoléon. **CP-MerG1**

Behind the Power Station on 14th, the held breath. Galway Kinnell. **NaP** *Fr.* The Avenue Bearing the Initial of Christ into the New World. **SP-KinnG**

Behind the radio's altarlight. Compline. Philip Larkin. **CP-LarkP**

Behind the thin / Grey cloud that cover'd but not hid the sky. Samuel Taylor Coleridge. *Fr.* Some Fragments, Mainly from Manuscripts of 1797–8. **CP-ColeS**

Behind the thorn-trees thin smoke, scutch-grass or. Geoffrey Hill. *Fr.* Mercian Hymns. **CP-HillG**

Behind their house, behind the back porch. George Oppen. *Fr.* Of Being Numerous. **CP-OppeG**

Behind these pulsing lips. Queen Nefertiti–Small Fragment of Nose and Mouth Only. Marsden Hartley. **SP-HartM**

Behind this mirror no new world. After the Funeral: Cleaning Out the Medicine Cabinet. Ted Kooser. **SP-KoosT**

Behind Us. Stephen Berg. **SP-BergS**

Behind us at our evening meal. The Common Question. John Greenleaf Whittier. **CP-WhitJ**

Behind us, the blank world; in front of us, what we see. Music. Stephen Berg. **SP-BergS**

Behind What Little Mirror. . . . May Sarton. **SP-SartM**

Behind yon hills where Lugar flows. Song. Robert Burns. **CP-BurnR**

Behold—a mere like a madonna's head. Water-Lilies. Edward Estlin Cummings. **CP-CummE**

Behold a parable. A fished for B. MAY (*Fishing*). Rudyard Kipling. *Fr.* Verses on Games. **CP-KiplR**

Behold! a proof of Irish sense! Jonathan Swift, *authorship disputed.* **CP-SwifJ**

Behold a pupil of the monkish gown. Alfred. William Wordsworth. *Fr.* Ecclesiastical Sonnets. **CP-WorW2**

Behold: A Relationship. Marge Piercy. *Fr.* Walking into Love. **SP-PierM**

Behold a Shaking. Christina Georgina Rossetti. **CP-RosC2**
  "Blessed that flock safe penned in Paradise."
  "Man rising to the doom that shall not err."

Beho[u]ld, a silly [*or* sely *or* little] tender babe. New Prince, New Pomp[e]. Robert Southwell. **CP-SoutR**

Behold an emblem of our human mind. On the Banks of a Rocky Stream. William Wordsworth. **CP-WorW2**

Behold an Israelite indeed. St. Bartholomew. Christopher Smart. *Fr.* Hymns and Spiritual Songs for the Fasts and Festivals of the Church of England. **SP-SmarC**

Behold around us pomp and pride. The End of All. Walt Whitman. **CP-WhitW**

Behold, as goblins dark of mien. Robert Louis Stevenson. **CP-StevR**

Behold best-selling Mr. Furneval. Lecturer in Bookstore. Ogden Nash. **CP-NashO**

Behold, bless ye the Lord, all ye servants of the Lord. Psalm 134. Bible, *O.T. Fr.* Psalms. **CP-Psal**

Behold, four Kings in majesty rever'd. The Playing Cards. Alexander Pope. **ChTr** *Fr.* The Rape of the Lock[, an Heroi-Comical Poem]. **CP-PopeA**

Behold, Friends, once more the Revolution has performed its famous. A Note on the Late Elections. Thomas McGrath. **SP-McGrT**

Behold her, single in the field. The Solitary Reaper. William Wordsworth. **CP-WorW1**

Behold, how good and how pleasant it is. Psalm 133. Bible, *O.T.* **AWP; TrJP** *Fr.* Psalms. **CP-Psal**

Behold, I have taken at thy hands immortal wine. S.F.D. Edward Estlin Cummings. **CP-CummE**

Behold I make partition. The Pilgrims. Ralph Waldo Emerson. **CP-EmerR**

Behold I see the haven nigh at hand. Edmund Spenser. **FHYEP** *Fr.* The Faerie Queene. **CP-Spens**

Behold, I stand at the door and knock. Christina Georgina Rossetti. **CP-RosC3**

Behold in heaven a floating dazzling cloud. Thou Knewest. . . Thou Oughtest Therefore. Christina Georgina Rossetti. **CP-RosC2**

Behold! in various throngs the scribbling crew. Byron. **EnRP; OAEL-2** *Fr.* English Bards and Scotch Reviewers. **CP-Byron**

Behold, It Was Very Good. Christina Georgina Rossetti. **CP-RosC2**

Behold, love, thy power how she despiseth! Sir Thomas Wyatt. **CP-WyatT**

Behold my fair, where-e'er we rove. The Winter's Walk. Samuel Johnson. **CP-JohnS**

Behold, my Love, how green the groves. Scotish Song. Robert Burns. **CP-BurnR**

Behold, O Man. Edmund Spenser. **EIL** *Fr.* The Faerie Queene. **CP-Spens**

Behold, One of Several Little Christs. Kenneth Patchen. **CP-PatcK**

Behold that great Plotinus swim. *fr.* Words for Music Perhaps. William Butler Yeats. **CP-YeatW**

Behold the blessings of a lucky lot! Elegy. Byron. **CP-Byron**

Behold, the Bridegroom cometh: go ye out. Advent Sunday. Christina Georgina Rossetti. **CP-RosC2**

Behold the child among his new-born blisses. William Wordsworth. *Fr.* Ode: Intimations of Immortality [from Recollections of Early Childhood]. **CP-WorW1**

Behold the child, by Nature's kindly law. Alexander Pope. **ECEV; FaBoRV; POL** *Fr.* An Essay on Man. **CP-PopeA**

Behold the critic, pitched like the *castrati*. Pipling. Theodore Roethke. **OBCoV; TW** *Fr.* Three Epigrams. **CP-RoetT**

Behold the duck. / It does not cluck. The Duck. Ogden Nash. **CP-NashO**

Behold the fatal day arrive! Jonathan Swift. **PeLV; SCV** *Fr.* Verses on the Death of Dr. Swift, D.S.P.D. **CP-SwifJ**

Beho[u]ld the father is His daughter's son[ne]. The Nativity of Christ[e]. Robert Southwell. **CP-SoutR**

Behold the fire and the wood but where is the lamb. Abraham and Isaac. Isabella Gardner. **CP-GardI**

Behold the genial boy who promised much. Two Views of a Philosopher. Howard Nemerov. **CP-NemeH**

Behold, the Gods are with her, and are known. George Meredith. *Fr.* France. **CP-MerG1**

Behold the hippopotamus! The Hippopotamus. Ogden Nash. **CP-NashO**

Behold the hour, the boat arrive. Song. Robert Burns. **CP-BurnR**

Behold the Man! Christina Georgina Rossetti. **CP-RosC2**

Behold the manly mesomorph. Wystan Hugh Auden. **OxBSP** *Fr.* Shorts [1948–1957] ("At peace under this mandarin, sleep, Lucina"). **CP-AudeW**

Behold the shades of afternoon have fallen. William Wordsworth. **EnRP** *Fr.* Discourse of the Wanderer and an Evening Visit to the Lake. *Fr.* The Excursion. **CP-WorW2**

Behold the sky. A Moment. Wystan Hugh Auden. **CP-AudWJ**

Behold the woes of matrimonial life. *see also* Wife of Bath's Tale, The. Geoffrey Chaucer. **CP-PopeA** *Fr.* The Canterbury Tales. **CP-ChauG**

Behold the Woman. Thomas McGrath. **SP-McGrT**

Behold this little Bane. Emily Dickinson. **CP-DickE**

Behold This Swarthy Face. Walt Whitman. **CP-WhitW**

Behold those monarch oaks that rise. A Copy of Verses upon Two Celebrated Modern Poets. Jonathan Swift. **CP-SwifJ**

Behold! three Sister wonders, in whom met. Paris's Second Judgement. Richard Lovelace. **CP-LoveR**

Behold, where Dryden's less presumptuous car. Thomas Gray. **EPCY** *Fr.* The Progress of Poesy. **CP-GrayT**

Behold, within the leafy shade. The Sparrow's Nest. William Wordsworth. **CP-WorW1**

Behold yon breathing prospect bids the Muse. James Thomson. **PoE** *Fr.* Spring. *Fr.* The Seasons. **CP-ThomJ**

Behold your Cross, Christians! The Cross. David Herbert Lawrence. **CP-LawrD**

Beholde, how good and joyfull a thinge it is, brethren to dwell to gether in unitye. Bible, *O.T. See* Psalm 133: "Behold, how good and how pleasant it is."

Beholders, The. James Dickey. **CP-DickJ**

Beholding element, in whose pure eye. The Aspen and the Stream. Richard Wilbur. **CP-WilbR**

Bei Hennef. David Herbert Lawrence. **CP-LawrD**

Beige sailors with large noses. Seashore through Dark Glasses (Atlantic City). Langston Hughes. **SP-HughL**

Bein' Back Home. Paul Laurence Dunbar. **CP-DunbP**

Being, The. Hayden Carruth. **PoA** *Fr.* Contra Mortem. **CP-CarHL**

Being, The. James Dickey. **CP-DickJ**

Being / twelve / who hast merely. Edward Estlin Cummings. **CP-CummE**

Being a father / Is quite a bother. Soliloquy in Circles. Ogden Nash. **CP-NashO**

Being a Seven-Year-Old Boy's Elaborate Memory of the Day of His Birth. Nicholas Vachel Lindsay. *Fr.* Doctor Mohawk. **CP-LindV**

Being Alive. David Herbert Lawrence. **CP-LawrD**

Being Alone. Charles Kenneth Williams. **CP-WillC; SP-WillC**

Being alone has always been very necessary to me. At one time I. Charles Bukowski. *Fr.* Horsemeat. **SP-BukC3**

Being Altogether Literal, & Specific, and Seeking at the Same Time to be Successfully Explicit. Charles Olson. **CP-OlsoC**

Being Angry with God. Donald Davie. **CP-DavDo**

Being as Memory, The. Hayden Carruth. *Fr.* Contra Mortem. **CP-CarHL**

Being as Moment, The. Hayden Carruth. *Fr.* Contra Mortem. **CP-CarHL**

Being as none is, I do complain. Sir Thomas Wyatt. **CP-WyatT**

Being as Prevision, The. Hayden Carruth. *Fr.* Contra Mortem. **CP-CarHL**

Being Asked To Define Bourgeois Individuality. William Dickey. **SP-DickW**

Being away from you I have to feel you like some people feel god. Thread. Patti Smith. **SP-SmitP**

Being black, you merged with the night. War. Charles Henri Ford. **SP-FordC**

Being Born. Thom Gunn. **CP-GunnT**

Being Called. John Ciardi. **SP-CiarJ**

Being Country Bred. Mary Oliver. **SP-OlivM**

Being drawn again. Some Loss. Roy Fisher. **SP-FishR**

Being driven after the hearse thru suburbs. H.T. Louis Zukofsky. **CP-ZukLS**

Being for the Benefit of Mr. Kite. John Lennon *and* Paul McCartney. **CP-Beatl**

Being Here. Miller Williams. **SP-WillM**

Being his resting place. A Dog Sleeping on My Feet. James Dickey. **CP-DickJ**

Being in this stage. Wide Awake, Full of Love. William Carlos Williams. **CP-WilW2**

Being *incontentabile* / Like Foscolo, in making verse. Frank Templeton Prince. *Fr.* Memoirs in Oxford. **CP-PrinF**

Being kissed on the back. Knee Song. Anne Sexton. **CP-SextA**

Being My Notion, as a Ferocious Small-Boy, of My Ancestral Protector. Nicholas Vachel Lindsay. *Fr.* Doctor Mohawk. **CP-LindV**

Being new inside—so that outside, the outside. Marsden Hartley. **CP-HartM**

Being nor whim nor. Charles Henri Ford. **SP-FordC** *Fr.* Emblems of Arachne.

Being now three or four years more than sixty. The World's Wonders. Robinson Jeffers. **CP-JefR3**

Being of Three Minds. Howard Nemerov. **CP-NemeH**

Being old and gray, I can now remember my school days in Switzerland. I. After Lake Leman. Robinson Jeffers. **CP-JefR3**

Being Once Blind, His Request to Biancha. Robert Herrick. **CP-HerrR**

Being, I. Frederick Morgan. **SP-MorgF**

Being one day at my window all alone. Petrarch. *Fr.* The Visions of Petrarch. **CP-Spens**

Being out of heart with government. An Appointment. William Butler Yeats. **CP-YeatW**

Being set on the idea. Atlantis. Wystan Hugh Auden. **CP-AudeW**

Being so hideous that the air weeps blood. Kenneth Patchen. **CP-PatcK**

Being so young he feels the weight of history. The Conscript. Louis MacNeice. **CP-MacNL**

Being the Dedication of a Morning. Nicholas Vachel Lindsay. **CP-LindV**

Being to timelessness as it's to time. Edward Estlin Cummings. **CP-CummE**

Being together is knowing. Bridging. Marge Piercy. **SP-PierM**

Being Treated to Ellinda. Richard Lovelace. **CP-LoveR**

Being, II. Frederick Morgan. **SP-MorgF**

Being, whose flesh dissolves. To the Unseeable Animal. Wendell Berry. **CP-BerrW**

Being with you / here, in this room. Margaret Atwood. *Fr.* The Circle Game. **SP-AtwM1**

Being without quality. Vox Humana. Thom Gunn. **CP-GunnT**

Being Young and Green. Edna St. Vincent Millay. **CP-MillE**

Being your slave, what should I do[e] but tend. Sonnet 57. William Shakespeare. **GTBS; GTBS-6; GTBS-P; HAP; NoSic; OBEV; PeHV; PoEL-2** *Fr.* Sonnets. **CP-ShaWS**

Being(just a little). Edward Estlin Cummings. **CP-CummE**

Belated Birthday Poem, A. James Schuyler. **CP-SchuJ**

Belated Palinode for Dylan Thomas. Lawrence Ferlinghetti. **SP-FerlL**

Belated wanderer of the ways of spring. To a Violet Found on All Saints' Day. Paul Laurence Dunbar. **CP-DunbP**

Belbroughton Road is bonny, and pinkly bursts the spray. May-Day Song for North Oxford. Sir John Betjeman. **CP-BetjJ**

Belfast. Louis MacNeice. **CP-MacNL**

Belfast on a Sunday Afternoon. Donald Davie. **CP-DavDo**

Belfastman, The. John Hewitt. **CP-HewiJ**

Belfastman Abroad Argues with Himself. John Hewitt. **CP-HewiJ**

Belgium. Edward Estlin Cummings. **CP-CummE**

Belgrade Moon. Al Young. **CP-YounA**

Belief / As unbelief before, Shakes us by fits. Belief and Unbelief. Robert Browning. **FaBV** *Fr.* Bishop Blougram's Apology. **CP-BroR1**

Belief. Wystan Hugh Auden. **CP-AudWJ**

Belief. David Herbert Lawrence. **CP-LawrD**

Belief. Philip Levine. **SP-LeviP**

Belief. Alun Lewis. **CP-LewiA**

Belief and Unbelief. Robert Browning. **FaBV** *Fr.* Bishop Blougram's Apology. **CP-BroR1**

Belief in God is an inclination to listen. No Hearing. Robert Lowell. **SP-LoweR**

Believe, if ever the bridges of this town. Edna St. Vincent Millay. **CP-MillE**

Believe in this couple this day who come. Glen Uig. Richard Hugo. **CP-HugoR**

Believe it or not, as you choose. Catharina, the Second Part. William Cowper. **CP-CowpW**

Believe Me, Edith. Leonard Cohen. **CP-CoheL**

Believe me, I have studied men. George Meredith. **CP-MerG2**

Believe me, knot of gristle, I bleed like a tree. Give Way, Ye Gates. Theodore Roethke. **CP-RoetT**

Believe me, Lucy Larcom, it gives me real sorrow. Letter to Lucy Larcom. John Greenleaf Whittier. **CP-WhitJ**

Believe the automatic righteousness. Against the War in Vietnam. Wendell Berry. **CP-BerrW**

Believe't, young man, I can as eas'ly tell. Upon Two Sisters. Sir John Suckling. **CP-SuckJ**

Believing in Symbols. Miller Williams. **SP-WillM**

Believing in Those Inexorable Laws. Muriel Rukeyser. **CP-RukeM**

Believing something will happen. Crisis on the Savannah. Tom Clark. **SP-ClarT**

Believing that we are to have no Face. Emily Dickinson. **SP-DickE**

Belinda lived in a little white house. The Tale of Custard the Dragon. Ogden Nash. **CP-NashO**

Belinda's Petition. Rita Dove. **SP-DoveR**

Bell, The. John Hewitt. **CP-HewiJ**

Bell / Too softly and too slowly tolled, The. Kenneth Rexroth. **SP-RexrK** *Fr.* The Bell / Too softly and too slowly tolled. **CP-RexKL** *Fr.* A Prolegomenon to a Theodicy. "They were in an unstable condition." **SP-RexrK**

Bell Buoy, The. Rudyard Kipling. **CP-KiplR**

Bell dipthonging in an atmosphere, A. A Dubious Night. Richard Wilbur. **CP-WilbR**

Bell doth toll, The. The Knell. George Herbert. **CP-HerbG**

Bell-looking-glass upright leaf-shells ring the. Venus's Looking-glass. Louis Zukofsky. **CP-ZukLS**

Bell-Man, The. Robert Herrick. **CP-HerrR**

Bell-man of night, if I about shall go. Cock-Crow. Robert Herrick. **CP-HerrR**

Bell-Ringer, The. Pablo Neruda, *tr. fr. Spanish by* Ben Belitt. **SP-NeruP**

Bell rings once and then the woods are still, The. The Tollhouse. Lewis Turco. **SP-TurcL**

Bell-rope that gathers God at dawn, The. The Broken Tower. Hart Crane. **CP-CranH**

Bell Speech. Richard Wilbur. **CP-WilbR**

Bell struck one, and shook the silent tower, The. Fair Elenor. William Blake. **CP-BlakW**

Bell to sore knees vestigial crowds, let crush. John Berryman. *Fr.* Sonnets to Chris. **CP-BerrJ**

Bell Tower of Authenay, The. Pablo Neruda, *tr. fr. Spanish by* Ben Belitt. **SP-NeruP**

Bell went heavy to-day, The. Premonitions. Thomas Hardy. **CP-HardT**

Bella Donna Iu. Li Yü, *tr. fr. Chinese by* William Carlos Williams *with* David Rafael Wang. **CP-WilW2**

Bella Roma. Martin Edmunds. **SP-EdmuM**

Belle Isle, 1949. Philip Levine. **SP-LeviP**

Bellerophon. George Meredith. **CP-MerG1**

Bellis perennis daisy of history. Daisy. Louis Zukofsky. **CP-ZukLS**

Bellisle! that is a fabling name, but we. Gerard Manley Hopkins. **CP-HopkG**

Bellman, The. Robert Herrick. **CP-HerrR**

Bellman himself they all praised to the skies—, The. "Lewis Carroll." **OBCoV** *Fr.* The Hunting of the Snark. **CP-CarrL**

Bellman looked uffish, and wrinkled his brow. Fit the Fourth: The Hunting. "Lewis Carroll." *Fr.* The Hunting of the Snark. **CP-CarrL**

Bells, The. Walter de la Mare. **CP-DeLaW**

Bells. David Herbert Lawrence. **CP-LawrD**

Bells, The. Edgar Allan Poe. **CP-PoeEd**

Bells, The. Anne Sexton. **CP-SextA**

Bells: a Period Piece, The. Charles Tomlinson. *Fr.* Antecedents. **CP-TomlC**

Bells and Queen Victoria, The. Rudyard Kipling. **CP-KiplR**

Bells are booming down the bohreens. Ireland with Emily. Sir John Betjeman. **CP-BetjJ**

Bells for John Whiteside's Daughter. John Crowe Ransom. **SP-RansJ**

Bells have quit their clanging, The; here beneath. New Year Morning. Adrienne Rich. **CP-RicAE**

Bells in tower at evening toll. Alfred Edward Housman. **CP-HousA**

Bells of a Chinese Temple, The. Richard Eberhart. **CP-EberR**

Bells of waiting Advent ring, The. Christmas. Sir John Betjeman. **CP-BetjJ**

Bells, the cannons, the houses black with crepe, The. The Abduction. Rita Dove. **SP-DoveR**

Belly, The. Stephen Dobyns. **SP-DobyS**

Belly Dancer. Diane Wakoski. **SP-WakoD**

Belly Dancer at the Hotel Jerome. Stephen Dunn. **SP-DunnS**

Belly Locks Shnooks Oakie. Louis Zukofsky. **CP-ZukLS**

Belly puts on a bright red wig, The. The Belly. Stephen Dobyns. **SP-DobyS**

Belly Song. Etheridge Knight. **SP-KnigE**

Belly's full. Sick. Robert Creeley. **CP-CreeR**

Belonging. Steve Griffiths. **SP-GrifS**

Beloved, / In what other lives or lands. Refusal. Maya Angelou. **SP-AngeM**

Beloved, *sl. diff. vers.* David Herbert Lawrence. *See* Land-Worker.

Beloved! amid the earnest woes. To F——. Edgar Allan Poe. **CP-PoeEd**

Beloved Beware. Alun Lewis. **CP-LewiA**

Beloved friend, who living many years. Hugh Stuart Boyd [His Death, 1848]. Elizabeth Barrett Browning. **CP-BroEB**

Beloved, gaze in thine own heart. The Two Trees. William Butler Yeats. **CP-YeatW**

"Beloved, let us love one another," says St. John. Christina Georgina Rossetti. **CP-RosC2**

Beloved, may your sleep be sound. *fr.* Words for Music Perhaps. William Butler Yeats. **CP-YeatW**

Belovéd, my Belovéd, when I think. Sonnet. Elizabeth Barrett Browning. **OAEP; Son; WPE** *Fr.* Sonnets from the Portuguese. **CP-BroEB**

Beloved Pupil! Tamed by thee. To My Pupil. "Lewis Carroll." **CP-CarrL**

Belovèd, thou hast brought me many flowers. Sonnet. Elizabeth Barrett Browning. **EBVV; EnVR; OAEP; OBNC; WPE** *Fr.* Sonnets from the Portuguese. **CP-BroEB**

"Beloved Vale!" I said, "when I shall con." William Wordsworth. **CP-WorW1**

Beloved, yield thy time to God, for He / Will make eternity thy recompense. Christina Georgina Rossetti. **CP-RosC2**

Belovéd you are. For Viola: De Gustibus. William Carlos Williams. **CP-WilW1**

Below. Wendell Berry. **CP-BerrW**

Below me, a pool gathers. To the August Fallen. James Wright. **CP-WrigJ**

Below me Ticknall lay but in the light. Wystan Hugh Auden. **CP-AudWJ**

Below the Mournes in May. John Hewitt. **CP-HewiJ**

Below the ridge a raven flew. Love in Barrenness. Robert Ranke Graves. **CP-GravR**

Below, the river scrambled like a goat. God's Little Mountain. Geoffrey Hill. **CP-HillG**

Below the Stairs. James Schuyler. **CP-SchuJ**

Below the ten thousand billionth of a centimeter. The First Day. Howard Nemerov. **CP-NemeH**

Below the thunders of the upper deep. The Kraken. Tennyson. **CP-TennA**

Below the wall in the lake-garden. Meben. Kenneth Patchen. **CP-PatcK**

Below thir stanes lie Jamie's banes. On a Noisy Polemic. Robert Burns. **CP-BurnR**

Below Tintern. Charles Tomlinson. **CP-TomlC**

Below what we think we are. Underneath. David Herbert Lawrence. **CP-LawrD**

Belsen, Day of Liberation. Robert Earl Hayden. **CP-HaydR**

Belshazzar! from the banquet turn. To Belshazzar. Byron. **CP-Byron**

Belshazzar had a Letter. Emily Dickinson. **CP-DickE**

Belt. Richard Hugo. **CP-HugoR**

Belts. Rudyard Kipling. **CP-KiplR**

Belvoir thy coat was not more golden than thy heart. Death of the Dog Belvoir. Stevie Smith. **CP-SmitS**

Ben. Paul Muldoon. *Fr.* 7, Middagh Street. **SP-MuldP**

Ben Jonson Entertains a Man from Stratford. Edwin Arlington Robinson. **CP-RobiE**

Ben Jonson said he was? O I could still. No Better Than a "Withered Daffodil." Marianne Craig Moore. **CP-MoorM**

Ben Jonson's Grace before King James. Ben Jonson. **CP-JonsB**

Ben Karshook's Wisdom. Robert Browning. **CP-BroR2**

Ben Trovato. Edwin Arlington Robinson. **CP-RobiE**

Benath yon eastern ridge, the craggy bound. For a Seat in the Groves of Coleorton. William Wordsworth. **CP-WorW1**

Bench of Boors, The. Herman Melville. **SP-MelvH**

Bend low again, night of summer stars. Summer Stars. Carl Sandburg. **CP-SandC**

Bend of the Androscoggin, The. Marsden Hartley. **CP-HartM**

Bended to fops who bent to him. Ralph Waldo Emerson. **CP-EmerR**

Bending over like this to get my hands empty. An Obsolescent and His Deity (Polyptych). Bill Knott. **SP-KnotB**

Bending staff I would not break, A. Questions of Life. John Greenleaf Whittier. **CP-WhitJ**

Bending the Bow. Robert Duncan. **SP-DuncR**

Bendix. John Updike. **CP-UpdiJ**

Beneath a hundred years of thaw and freeze. The Turnpike. Louise McNeill. **SP-McNeL**

Beneath a knap where flown. Ditty. Thomas Hardy. **CP-HardT**

Beneath a motionless yew. Walter de la Mare. **CP-DeLaW**

Beneath Blessington's eyes. Impromptu. Byron. **CP-Byron**

Beneath him with new wonder now he views. John Milton. **PPP** *Fr.* Book IV. **OAEL-1** *Fr.* Paradise Lost. **CP-MiltJ**

Beneath My Hand and Eye the Distant Hills, Your Body. Gary Snyder. **CP-SnydG**

Beneath My Hands. Leonard Cohen. **CP-CoheL**

Beneath my palm-trees, by the riverside. Song of the Indian Maid, The ("Beneath my palm-trees, by the riverside"). John Keats. **NOBE** *Fr.* Endymion: Poetic Romance. **CP-KeatJ**

Beneath sky's broken tiles, ancient barns are embedded in plaster. John Yau. **SP-YauJo** *Fr.* Predella.

Beneath that loved and celebrated breast. O Breath. Elizabeth Bishop. *Fr.* Four Poems. **CP-BishE**

Beneath the blaze of a tropical sun the mountain peaks are the Thrones of Frost. The Blossoming of the Solitary Date-Tree. Samuel Taylor Coleridge. **CP-ColeS**

Beneath the carving drag the wood. Oaxaca. Audre Lorde. **SP-LordA**

Beneath the concave of an April sky. Vernal Ode. William Wordsworth. **CP-WorW2**

Beneath the deep verandah's shade. The Moon of Other Days. Rudyard Kipling. **CP-KiplR**

Beneath the grain. No Strings Attached. Al Young. **CP-YounA**

Beneath the hedge, or near the stream. The Glow-worm. Vincent Bourne, *tr. fr. Latin by* William Cowper. **CP-CowpW**

Beneath the low-hung night cloud. The Three Bells. John Greenleaf Whittier. **CP-WhitJ**

Beneath the Malebolge lies Hastings street. Malcolm Lowry. **CP-LowrM**

Beneath the moonlight and the snow. My Birthday. John Greenleaf Whittier. **CP-WhitJ**

Beneath the sagging roof. Ezra Pound. **MoAmPo** *Fr.* Hugh Selwyn Mauberley. (Life and Contacts). **SP-PounE**

Beneath the shade a spreading Beech displays. Autumn, the Third Pastoral, or Hylas and Ægon. Alexander Pope. *Fr.* Pastorals. **CP-PopeA**

Beneath the Sidewalk. Stephen Dunn. **SP-DunnS**

Beneath the vans of doom did men pass in. Forest History. George Meredith. **CP-MerG1**

Beneath the waters of the sea. Mock Turtle's Song, The. "Lewis Carroll." **CP-CarrL**

Beneath the white thorn lovely May, *see also* The Golden Net. William Blake. **CP-BlakW**

Beneath their flames, cities of candelabra. The Chestnut Avenue: at Alton House. Charles Tomlinson. **CP-TomlC**

Beneath these fruit-tree boughs that shed. The Green Linnet. William Wordsworth. **CP-WorW1**

Beneath this slab. Lather as You Go. Ogden Nash. **CP-NashO**

Beneath this stone a Berry is planted. Wendell Berry. *Fr.* Testament. **CP-BerrW**

Beneath this stone does William Hazlitt lie. W. H. *Eheu!.* Samuel Taylor Coleridge. **CP-ColeS**

Beneath this thorn when I was young. *Part 1 and stanzas 1–5 of part 2 sometimes at. to* Coleridge. William Wordsworth. **CP-WorW1**

Beneath thy skies, November! Song, A. John Greenleaf Whittier. **CP-WhitJ**

Beneath Time's roaring cannon. When the Mississippi Flowed in Indiana. Nicholas Vachel Lindsay. **CMoP** *Fr.* Three Poems About Mark Twain. **CP-LindV**

Beneath yon birch with silver bark. The Ballad of the Dark Ladié. Samuel Taylor Coleridge. **CP-ColeS**

Benedicite. John Greenleaf Whittier. **CP-WhitJ**

Benedictine Echard, The. The Vision of Echard. John Greenleaf Whittier. **CP-WhitJ**

Benediction. Stanley Jasspon Kunitz. **CP-KuniS**

Benedictus. Donald Davie. **CP-DavDo**

Benefits of an Education, The. John Ciardi. **SP-CiarJ**

Benevolence. John Greenleaf Whittier. **CP-WhitJ**

Benfactors, The. Rudyard Kipling. **CP-KiplR**

Beni Hasan. Louis MacNeice. **CP-MacNL**

Benison given. Unused, A. The Singer Will Not Sing. Maya Angelou. **SP-AngeM**

Benjamin Bunnn. Shel Silverstein. **SP-SilS2**

Ben's Last Fight. Thomas Merton. **CP-MertT**

Bent. The. Donald Davie. **CP-DavDo**

Bent double, like old beggars under sacks. Dulce Et Decorum Est. Wilfred Owen. **CP-OwenW**

Bent a laboring oar, that toils in the surf of the ocean. Henry Wadsworth Longfellow. *Fr.* Part the First. *Fr.* Evangeline, a Tale of Acadie. **SP-LongH**

Bent over the railing in the back woodlot. So Near—And Yet. Kenneth Patchen. **CP-PatcK**

Beowulf. Richard Wilbur. **CP-WilbR**

Beowulf may have killed Grendel and. The Beast. Charles Bukowski. **SP-BukC2**

Beppo; a Venetian Story. Byron. **CP-Byron**

"England! with all thy faults I love thee still." **PlP; UnPo**

Italy. **OBRV; PlP; SeCePo**

(Italy versus England.) **NOBE**

"'Tis know, at least it should be, that throughout." **NOBRP**

Bequest. Alun Lewis. **CP-LewiA**

Bequest. Edwin Rolfe. **CP-RolfE**

Berceuse: to end the sorrow of mortals. Thomas Merton. **CP-MertT**

Berck-Plage. Sylvia Plath. **CP-PlatS**

Bereaved of all, I went abroad. Emily Dickinson. **CP-DickE**

Bereaved Swan, The. Stevie Smith. **CP-SmitS**

Bereavement. Elizabeth Barrett Browning. **CP-BroEB**

Bereavement. David Herbert Lawrence. **CP-LawrD**

Bereavement. Percy Bysshe Shelley. *Fr.* Poems from St. Irvyne, or, The Rosicrucian. **CP-ShelP**

Bereavement. Stevie Smith. **CP-SmitS**

Bereavement in their death to feel. Emily Dickinson. **CP-DickE**

Bereft. Robert Frost. **CP-FrosR**

Bereft. Thomas Hardy. **CP-HardT**

Bereft of Its Great Poets, *after the Irish of* David O'Bruadair. Michael Hartnett. **SP-HarMi**

Bereft, She Thinks She Dreams. Thomas Hardy. **CP-HardT**

Berg, The. Herman Melville. **SP-MelvH**

Berkeley did not forsee such misty weather. A Chronic Condition. Richard Wilbur. **CP-WilbR**

Berkeley Pome. Al Young. **CP-YounA**

Berket and the Stars. William Carlos Williams. **CP-WilW1**

Berkshire. Donald Davie. **CP-DavDo**

Berlin: First Night & Early Morning. Robert Creeley. **CP-CreeR**

Berlin in Ruins. Thom Gunn. **CP-GunnT**

Bermuda. Jane Cooper. **SP-CoopJ**

Bermudas. Andrew Marvell. **CP-MarvA**

Bernál Díaz' Preface to his Book. Archibald MacLeish. *Fr.* Conquistador. **CP-MacLA**

Bernstein! Can you still hear me? Are you conscious? Thomas Merton. *Fr.* Cables to the Ace. **CP-MertT**

Berried brake and reedy island. We Have Loved of Yore. Robert Louis Stevenson. **CP-StevR**

Berry Feast, A. Gary Snyder. **CP-SnydG**

Berry House, The. Marsden Hartley. **CP-HartM**

Berry Territory. Gary Snyder. **CP-SnydG**

Berrying. Ralph Waldo Emerson. **CP-EmerR**

Berryman's Dead. John Clellon Holmes. **SP-HolmJ**

Bertha in the Lane. Elizabeth Barrett Browning. **CP-BroEB**

Beshrew that heart that makes my heart to groan. Sonnet 133. William Shakespeare. **InvP; OXAEP-1** *Fr.* Sonnets. **CP-ShaWS**

Beside a narrow trail in the blue. Dream of the Lynx. John Haines. **SP-HainJ**

Beside a stricken field I stood. The Watchers. John Greenleaf Whittier. **CP-WhitJ**

Beside her in the dark the chime. Archibald MacLeish. **CP-MacLA** *Fr.* The Happy Marriage.

Beside her, she a limpid brook, I took. Day Song. Charles Olson. **CP-OlsoC**

Beside herself (and me, too, so help me), & she. Day Song, the Day After. Charles Olson. **CP-OlsoC**

Beside me,—in the car,—she sat. Natura Naturans. Arthur Hugh Clough. **SP-ClouA**

Beside me in this garden. Korean Mums. James Schuyler. **CP-SchuJ**

Beside My Son, *see also* Commentary—Beside My Son. Leonard Cohen. **CP-CoheL**

Beside Oneself. Malcolm Lowry. **CP-LowrM**

Beside our way the streams are dried. To Booker T. Washington. Paul Laurence Dunbar. **CP-DunbP**

Beside that milestone where the level sun. Response. John Greenleaf Whittier. **CP-WhitJ**

Beside the bridge's photogen- / ic lapse into air you'll. Letter from Provence. Louise Glück. **SP-GlücL**

Beside the Brokenstraw or Licking Creek. John Chapman. Richard Wilbur. **CP-WilbR**

Beside the confines of the Ægean main. Fragment from the "Monk of Athos." Byron. **CP-Byron**

Beside the crater and the tattered palm. The Dead in Melanesia. Randall Jarrell. **CP-JarrR**

Beside the door / She stood whom I had known before. A Friend Revisited. Donald Hall. **CP-HallD**

Beside the fall, the moonlight spills. The Death of Elizabeth Grieve. Charles Tomlinson. **CP-TomlC**

Beside the fruitfull shore of muddie Nile. Edmund Spenser. *Fr.* Visions of the World's Vanity [*or* Vanitie]. **CP-Spens**

Beside the Mare Crisium, that sea. The Explorers. Adrienne Rich. **CP-RicAE**

Beside the Mead of Memories. The Dead Quire. Thomas Hardy. **CP-HardT**

Beside the pleasant Mill of Trompington. Wordsworth Reading Chaucer. William Wordsworth. **EPCY** *Fr.* Residence at Cambridge. *Fr.* The Prelude; Growth of a Poet's Mind [1850 vers.]. **CP-WorW3**

Beside the pleasant Mills of Trompington. William Wordsworth. **OBRV** *Fr.* Residence at Cambridge. *Fr.* The Prelude; Growth of a Poet's Mind [1805 vers.]. **CP-WorW3**

Beside the river Eden. Kathleen Jessie Raine. *Fr.* By the River Eden. **SP-RainK**

Beside the Seaside. Sir John Betjeman. **CP-BetjJ**
   "Green shutters, shut your shutters! Windyridge." **OxBTC**

Beside the sultry stream he curbs amain his smoking mare. Iconia. George Meredith. **CP-MerG2**

Beside the waterfall / by the lichen face of rock. Rondo of the Familiar. Robert Pack. **SP-PackR**

Beside this door a January tree. Purely Local. Adrienne Rich. **CP-RicAE**

Beside this lake / where there are no other people. Younger Sister, Going Swimming. Margaret Atwood. **SP-AtwM1**

Beside those spires so spick and span. Distant View of a Provincial Town. Sir John Betjeman. **CP-BetjJ**

Beside you, prone. Prelude to a Parting. Maya Angelou. **SP-AngeM**

Besides the autumn poets sing. Emily Dickinson. **CP-DickE**

Besides this May. Emily Dickinson. **CP-DickE**

Besides us two, i'th'Temple here's not one. To Julia in the Temple. Robert Herrick. **CP-HerrR**

Bespoke for weeks, he turned up some morning. Thatcher. Seamus Heaney. **SP-HeanS**

Bess[y] and Her Spinning-Wheel. Robert Burns. **CP-BurnR**

Best and brightest, come away! Percy Bysshe Shelley. **CP-ShelP**
   (To Jane: The Invitation.) **CP-ShelP**

Best Beast of the Fat-Stock Show at Earls Court, The. Stevie Smith. **CP-SmitS**

Best Beast of the Show, The. The Best Beast of the Fat-Stock Show at Earls Court. Stevie Smith. **CP-SmitS**

Best Defense is Offensive, The. Marge Piercy. **SP-PierM**

Best dream I ever. Nice Try. Charles Bukowski. **SP-BukC3**

Best Friends. Erica Jong. **SP-JongE**

Best Gains—must have the Losses' Test. Emily Dickinson. **CP-DickE**

Best House They Was Ever In (Retired Coal Operator). Louise McNeill. **SP-McNeL**

Best ideal is the true, The. Summa. Gerard Manley Hopkins. **CP-HopkG**

Best is, in war or faction or ordinary vindictive life, not to take sides. Time of Disturbance. Robinson Jeffers. **CP-JefR3**

Best of life is presence of a muse, The. Ralph Waldo Emerson. **CP-EmerR**

Best of School, The, *also stands as separate poem and inc. in* The Schoolmaster [A]. David Herbert Lawrence. *Fr.* The Schoolmaster [B]. **CP-LawrD**

Best of School, The, *also stands as sl. diff. separate poem and incl. in* The Schoolmaster [B]. David Herbert Lawrence. *Fr.* The Schoolmaster [A]. **CP-LawrD**

Best of School, The. David Herbert Lawrence. **CP-LawrD**

Best of ways. That there be a law the Earth gives and the Mountain. Robert Duncan. **SP-DuncR** *Fr.* The Structure of Rime.

Best party of all is when, The. The Party. Phoebe Hesketh. **SP-HeskP**

Best She Could, The. Thomas Hardy. **CP-HardT**

Best slave, The. Alcestis on the Poetry Circuit. Erica Jong. **SP-JongE**

Best Society. Philip Larkin. **CP-LarkP**

Best sprig of the clan. Carmen 24. Catullus. *Fr.* Carmina. **CP-Catul**

Best Thing in the World, The. Elizabeth Barrett Browning. **CP-BroEB**

Best thing in the world but I better be quick about it, The. Biotherm [for Bill Berkson]. Frank O'Hara. **SP-OharF**

Best Things dwell out of Sight. Emily Dickinson. **CP-DickE**

Best Times. Thomas Hardy. **CP-HardT**

Best To Be Merry. Robert Herrick. **CP-HerrR**

Best way in (not that I've checked the map), The. Worcestershire. Donald Davie. **CP-DavDo**

Best Way to Get Famous Is to Run Away, The. Charles Bukowski. **SP-BukC2**

Best were last in the school marathon, The. Poem Inspired By Auden and Clare's Snail. Malcolm Lowry. **CP-LowrM**

Best, who could, went back—because they nursed, The. Depravity: Two Sermons. Donald Davie. **CP-DavDo**

Best Witchcraft is Geometry. Emily Dickinson. **CP-DickE**

Bestiaries Are Out. Wystan Hugh Auden. **CP-AudeW**

Bestiary, A. Kenneth Rexroth. **SP-RexrK**
   Aardvark. **SP-RexrK**
   Cat. **SP-RexrK**
   Deer. **HoPM; PBBP**
   Fox. **NNaP; SP-RexrK**
   Goat. **SP-RexrK**
   Herring. **HoPM; SP-RexrK**
   Horse. **NNaP**
   I. **SP-RexrK**
   Lion. **HoPM; SP-RexrK**
   Man. **SP-RexrK**
   Raccoon. **NNaP; SP-RexrK; ZA**
   (Racoon.) **FiBHP**
   Uncle Sam. **SP-RexrK**
   Unicorn. **SP-RexrK**
   Vulture. **NNaP; SP-RexrK**
   Wolf. **NNaP; SP-RexrK**
   You. **HoPM**

Bestiary for the Fingers of My Right Hand. Charles Simic. **SP-SimiC**

Bestow, dear Lord, upon our youth. Prayer for a Blessing. William Cowper. *Fr.* Olney Hymns. **CP-CowpW**

Bethesda: A Sequel. Arthur Hugh Clough. **SP-ClouA**

Bethink, poor heart, what bitter kind of jest. Epitaph. Hafiz, *tr. fr. Persian by* Ralph Waldo Emerson. **CP-EmerR**

Bethou me, said sparrow, to the crackled blade. Wallace Stevens. **LiTM; MoPo** *Fr.* It Must Change. *Fr.* Notes toward a Supreme Fiction. **CP-StevW**

Betrayal. Walter de la Mare. **CP-DeLaW**

"Betrayal?" / he asked me / the. Recognizing That My Wrists Always Have Salmon Leaping for Spring in Them. Diane Wakoski. **SP-WakoD**

Betrayal. John Hewitt. **CP-HewiJ**

Betrayal, The. Thomas Merton. **CP-MertT**

Betrayed. "Lou Reed." **SP-ReedL**

Betrayed by his five mechanic agents, falling. The Little Odyssey of Jason Quint, of Science, Doctor. Thomas McGrath. **SP-McGrT**

Betrothal, The. Edna St. Vincent Millay. **CP-MillE**

Betrothed. Louise Bogan. **CP-BogaL**

Betrothed, The. Rudyard Kipling. **CP-KiplR**

Betrothed to Righteousness might be. Emily Dickinson. **CP-DickE**

Better, / despite the worms talking to. Suicide Note. Anne Sexton. **CP-SextA**

Better born than married, misled. The Grandmother. Wendell Berry. **CP-BerrW**

Better for the widow, that she should not live in fear of surprise, The. James Fenton. **SCBI** *Fr.* A German Requiem. **SP-FentJ**

Better, goddamn it. Why, whenever I see folks. Hayden Carruth. *Fr.* The Sleeping Beauty. **CP-CarHL**

Better on your arse than on your feet. Nicolas-Sébastien Roch Chamfort, *tr. fr. French by* Samuel Beckett. **SP-BeckS**

Better Resurrection, A. Christina Georgina Rossetti. **CP-RosC1**

Better So. Christina Georgina Rossetti. **CP-RosC3**

Better stuffed in a bag; drowned. Adolf Hitler ("Better stuffed in a bag; drowned"). William DeWitt Snodgrass. **SP-SnodW**

Better than flowers. William Carlos Williams. **CP-WilW1** *Fr.* Paterson.

Better—than Music! For I—who heard it. Emily Dickinson. **CP-DickE**

Better that every fiber crack. Monologue at 3 A.M. Sylvia Plath. **CP-PlatS**

Better the big NOW, singular. James McAuley. **SP-McAuJ** *Fr.* Studies for a Self-Portrait at Forty.

Better the wind, the sea, the salt. The Look-out. Hilda Doolittle. **CP-DoolH**

Better to be the rock above the river. La Crosse at Ninety Miles an Hour. Richard Eberhart. **CP-EberR**

Better we all were in our graves. On a Printer's Being Sent to Newgate. Jonathan Swift. **CP-SwifJ**

Betterwear Man, The. Phoebe Hesketh. **SP-HeskP**

Betterwear man / stands at the backdoor and knocks, The. The Betterwear Man. Phoebe Hesketh. **SP-HeskP**

Bettine, friend of Goethe. To Bettine. Elizabeth Barrett Browning. **CP-BroEB**

Betting on how many leaves cover a birch. Cemetery Nights IV. Stephen Dobyns. **SP-DobyS**

Betty and Gerald Noxon. Malcolm Lowry. **CP-LowrM**

Between. John Ciardi. **SP-CiarJ**

Between / slats of the garden. During Rain. Charles Tomlinson. **CP-TomlC**

Between / the image of it. Face and Image. Charles Tomlinson. **CP-TomlC**

Between a sea and a sea where the combers meet. The Being as Moment. Hayden Carruth. *Fr.* Contra Mortem. **CP-CarHL**

Between a smoking fire and a tolling bell. Half Truth from Cape Town. Louis MacNeice. **CP-MacNL**

Between Adventure. Wystan Hugh Auden. **CP-AudeW**

Between air and the water, glows Puente Curvo. To Puente Curvo on the Maldonado Spit in Uruguay. Pablo Neruda, *tr. fr. Spanish by* Ben Belitt. **SP-NeruP**

Between Angels. Stephen Dunn. **SP-DunnS**

Between attention and attention. Easy Knowledge. Wystan Hugh Auden. **CP-AudeW**

Between death and the celebration of death. On Reading "The Love and Death of Cornet Christopher Rilke." Howard Nemerov. **CP-NemeH**

Between 1850 and 1855. What Happened. Diane Wakoski. **SP-WakoD**

Between extremities. Vacillation. William Butler Yeats. **CP-YeatW**

Between five and fifty. Praise. Jane Cooper. **SP-CoopJ**

Between green / mountains. Edward Estlin Cummings. **CP-CummE**

Between her breasts is my home, between her breasts. Song of a Man Who Is Loved. David Herbert Lawrence. **CP-LawrD**

Between identity and difference. Being of Three Minds. Howard Nemerov. **CP-NemeH**

Between March and April when barrows of daffodils butter the pavement. Street Scene. Louis MacNeice. **CP-MacNL**

Between me and the sunset, like a dome. The Man against the Sky. Edwin Arlington Robinson. **CP-RobiE**

Between Moon and Moon. Robert Ranke Graves. **CP-GravR**

Between My Country—and the Others. Emily Dickinson. **CP-DickE**

Between my finger and my thumb. Digging. Seamus Heaney. **SP-HeanS**

Between my husband & my people, Samson. Dalila. George Meredith. **CP-MerG2**

Between Myself and Death. Kenneth Rexroth. **SP-RexrK**

Between Namur and Liege. William Wordsworth. *Fr.* Memorials of a Tour of the Continent; 1820. **CP-WorW2**

Between Nose and Eyes a strange contest arose. Report of an Adjudged Case. William Cowper. **CP-CowpW**

Between nose-red gross. Edward Estlin Cummings. **CP-CummE**

Between painting a roof yesterday and the hay. Independence Day. Wendell Berry. **CP-BerrW**

Between plunging valleys, on a bareback of hill. Football at Slack. Ted Hughes. **SP-HughT**

Between pond and sheepbarn, by maples and watery birches. A Sister on the Tracks. Donald Hall. **CP-HallD**

Between the Acts. Stanley Jasspon Kunitz. **CP-KuniS**

Between the breasts / of bestial. Edward Estlin Cummings. **CP-CummE**

Between the Bridges. Richard Hugo. **CP-HugoR**

Between the brown hands of a server-lad. Maundy Thursday. Wilfred Owen. **CP-OwenW**

"Between the Clock and the Bed." Donald Hall. **CP-HallD**

Between the clod and the midnight. The Interim. Robert Penn Warren. *Fr.* Tale of Time. **SP-WarrR**

Between the dark and the daylight. The Children's Hour. Henry Wadsworth Longfellow. **SP-LongH**

Between the event and the word, golden. Composition in Gold and Red-Gold. Robert Penn Warren. **SP-WarrR**

Between the folding sea-downs. The Re-Enactment. Thomas Hardy. **CP-HardT**

Between the form of Life and Life. Emily Dickinson. **CP-DickE**

Between the fountain and the rill. Alternation. George Meredith. **CP-MerG1**

Between the freeway / and the gray conning towers. A Walk with Tom Jefferson. Philip Levine. **SP-LeviP**

Between the Gates. John Greenleaf Whittier. **CP-WhitJ**

Between the illuminations of great mornings. The Seeming. Muriel Rukeyser. **CP-RukeM**

Between the living world. The Cold Pane. Wendell Berry. **CP-BerrW**

Between the long wars. Peace Between Wars. Carl Sandburg. **CP-SandC**

Between the mountains of spices. Isaiah. Leonard Cohen. **CP-CoheL**

Between the pastel boutiques. Thom Gunn. *Fr.* Talbot Road. **CP-GunnT**

Between the Porch and the Altar. Robert Lowell. **SP-LoweR**

  At the Altar. **InPK**

Between the red-top and the rye. The Hawkweed. Edna St. Vincent Millay. **CP-MillE**

Between the river and the sea. Purgatory Blind. Charles Olson. **CP-OlsoC**

Between the stones the human animal. Genus: Homo. Jenny Joseph. **SP-JoseJ**

Between the swimming-pool and cricket-ground. Aldershot Crematorium. Sir John Betjeman. **CP-BetjJ**

Between the usurer and any man who / wants to do a good job. Canto 87. Ezra Pound. *Fr.* Cantos. **CP-PoCan**

Between the violet and the void. Nor Good Red Herring. Isabella Gardner. **CP-GardI**

Between the waving tufts of jungle-grass. Rudyard Kipling. **CP-KiplR**

Between the Window and the Screen. Howard Nemerov. **CP-NemeH**

Between those happenings that prefigure it. Wystan Hugh Auden. *Fr.* Shorts I ("Watch upon my wrist, The"). **CP-AudeW**

Between Trains. Robert Ranke Graves. **CP-GravR**

Between 2 and 5 p.m. and day and any time on Sunday and. Eating My Senior Citizen's Dinner at the Sizzler. Charles Bukowski. **SP-BukC3**

Between two burrs on the map. A Serious Step Taken Lightly. Robert Frost. **CP-FrosR**

Between Two Hills. Carl Sandburg. **CP-SandC**

Between Two Prisoners. James Dickey. **CP-DickJ**

Between two rivers, / North of the park. Island. Langston Hughes. **SP-HughL** *Fr.* Lenox Avenue Mural.

Between two sister moorland rills. The Danish Boy; A Fragment. William Wordsworth. **CP-WorW1**

Between Two Wars. Kenneth Rexroth. **SP-RexrK**

Between Us. Stephen Berg. **SP-BergS**

Between Us Now. Thomas Hardy. **SP-HardT**

Between us on our wide bed we cuddle an incubus. Marilyn Hacker. **SP-HackM** *Fr.* The Navigators.

Between waking and sleep / I am alone in a bright field. The Horses. Phoebe Hesketh. **SP-HeskP**

Between Walls. William Carlos Williams. **CP-WilW1**

Between Worlds. Carl Sandburg. **CP-SandC**

Betwixt mine eye and heart a league is took. Sonnet 47. William Shakespeare. EyDe *Fr.* Sonnets. **CP-ShaWS**

Beucolick, or Discourse of Neatherds, A. Robert Herrick. **CP-HerrR**

Beverly / who wished his mother wanting a girl again. On the Death of a Middle-Aged Man. Miller Williams. **SP-WillM**

Beverly Hills, Chicago. Gwendolyn Brooks. **SP-BrooG** *Fr.* The Womanhood.

Bewail my chance: the sad book is returnéd. 1.12. Ovid. **CP-MarlC**, *tr. by* Christopher Marlowe; *Fr.* Elegies.

Bewail not much, my parents! me, the prey. Lucianus, *tr. fr. Latin by* William Cowper. **CP-CowpW**

  (On an Infant.) **CP-CowpW**

Beware! Walter de la Mare. **CP-DeLaW**

Beware beware beware / because because because. Edward Estlin Cummings. **CP-CummE**

Beware!—breathes the faint evening wind? Shadow. Walter de la Mare. **CP-DeLaW**

Beware, Madam! Robert Ranke Graves. **CP-GravR**

Beware, madam, of the witty devil. Beware, Madam! Robert Ranke Graves. **CP-GravR**

Beware, my friend! of crystal brook. On an Ugly Fellow. *Unknown, tr. fr. Greek by* William Cowper. **CP-CowpW**

Beware, my words have teeth. Display. Robert Pack. **SP-PackR**

Beware o' Bonie Ann. Robert Burns. **CP-BurnR**

Beware, O My Dear Young Men. David Herbert Lawrence. **CP-LawrD**

Beware of building! I intended. Epigrams on His Garden Shed. William Cowper. **CP-CowpW**

Beware of the machinery of longevity. When a man's life is over. Wendell Berry. *Fr.* Prayers and Sayings of the Mad Farmer. **CP-BerrW**

Beware of the man who denounces ambition. Seventeen Warnings in Search of a Feminist Poem. Erica Jong. **SP-JongE**

Beware of the trumpeting swine. Nicholas Vachel Lindsay. *Fr.* The Tale of the Tiger Tree. **CP-LindV**

Beware of what comes out of Montreal. Montreal. Leonard Cohen. **CP-CoheL**

Beware the ball-point lens. New Year Wishes for the English. Donald Davie. **CP-DavDo**

Beware the giddy spell, ground fallen away. An East Wind. Robert Ranke Graves. **CP-GravR**

Beware! The Israelite of old, who tore. The Warning. Henry Wadsworth Longfellow. **SP-LongH**

Beware the Man. Stevie Smith. **CP-SmitS**

Beware the man who's crossed in love. Rudyard Kipling. **CP-KiplR** *Fr.* The Naulahka.

Beware the Unhappy Dead! David Herbert Lawrence. **CP-LawrD**

Beware writing of freedom: the idea is political. Many Handles. Carl Sandburg. **CP-SandC**

Bewcastle now must keep the Hold. The Defenceless Border. Sir Walter Scott. **SP-ScotW** *Fr.* The Bridal of Trierman.

Bewick Finzer. Edwin Arlington Robinson. **CP-RobiE**

Bewildered with the broken tongue. Words in Time. Archibald MacLeish. **CP-MacLA**

Beyond. Charles Kenneth Williams. **CP-WillC**

Beyond all this, the wish to be alone. Wants. Philip Larkin. **CP-LarkP**

Beyond and farther and yet from every vantage. The Mountain Fastness. Hayden Carruth. *Fr.* Contra Mortem. **CP-CarHL**

Beyond Descartes. Jenny Joseph. **SP-JoseJ**

Beyond Hammonton. Stephen Dunn. **SP-DunnS**

Beyond Howth Head. Derek Mahon. **SP-MahoD**

Beyond Magdalen and by the Bridge, on a place called there the Plain. Cheery Beggar. Gerard Manley Hopkins. **CP-HopkG**

Beyond me the common daylight. The Portcullis. Roy Fisher. **SP-FishR** *Fr.* Inscriptions for Bluebeard's Castle.

Beyond my terrace and its five stone steps. The Observer. Stephen Dunn. **SP-DunnS**

Beyond Nagel's Funeral Parlor. The Elizabethans Called It Dying. James Schuyler. **CP-SchuJ**

Beyond Reason. Stanley Jasspon Kunitz. **CP-KuniS**

Beyond Seattle. Thomas McGrath. **SP-McGrT**

Beyond th' old Pillars many have travelled. Sir John Wingfield. John Donne. **CP-DonnJ**

Beyond that stand of firs. A Late Answer. Philip Levine. **SP-LeviP**

Beyond the Alps. Robert Lowell. **SP-LoweR**

Beyond the brassy sun-stare where each shade. Giraffes. Phoebe Hesketh. **SP-HeskP**

Beyond the bright cartoons. Far Out. Philip Larkin. **CP-LarkP**

Beyond the brittle towns asleep. Edward Estlin Cummings. **CP-CummE**

Beyond the Broken House. Marsden Hartley. **CP-HartM**

Beyond the brown hill. Vigo County. Etheridge Knight. *Fr.* Indiana Haiku—2. **SP-KnigE**

Beyond the cornfields and the wood. Parted. Paul Laurence Dunbar. **CP-DunbP**

Beyond the crowding spires of pine, the hill. James McAuley. **SP-McAuJ** *Fr.* Sunflowers: An Ode.

Beyond the Dark Cedars. Kenneth Patchen. **CP-PatcK**

Beyond the end of the world. Reunion. John Gould Fletcher. **SP-FletJ**

Beyond the eye, grasses go over the long fields. *first vers.* James Dickey. **CP-DickJ**

Beyond the gates thou gav'st a field to till. In Lupum. Robert Louis Stevenson. **CP-StevR**

Beyond the great valley an odd instinctive rising. Ascent to the Sierras. Robinson Jeffers. **CP-JefR1**

Beyond the hour we counted rain that fell. Old Countryside. Louise Bogan. **CP-BogaL**

Beyond the Hudson's. The Undertaking in New Jersey. George Oppen. **CP-OppeG**

Beyond the Last Lamp. Thomas Hardy. **CP-HardT**

Beyond the meadow still where sweeps. George Meredith. **CP-MerG2**

Beyond the Moon. Nicholas Vachel Lindsay. **CP-LindV**

Beyond the moor and mountain crest. The West. Alfred Edward Housman. **CP-HousA**

Beyond the narrows of the Inner Hebrides. Now Returned Home. Robinson Jeffers. **CP-JefR1**

Beyond the Pale. Rudyard Kipling. *Fr.* Plain Tales from the Hills. Love Song of Har Dyal, The. **CP-KiplR**

Beyond the Pale, *after* Corbière. Derek Mahon. **SP-MahoD**

Beyond the path of the outmost sun through utter darkness hurled. Dedication from "Barrack-Room Ballads." Rudyard Kipling. **CP-KiplR**

Beyond the Pleasure Principle. Howard Nemerov. **CP-NemeH**

Beyond the Red River. Thomas McGrath. **SP-McGrT**

Beyond the Rockies. David Herbert Lawrence. **CP-LawrD**

Beyond the sea, in a green land. How One Chose. Christina Georgina Rossetti. **CP-RosC3**

Beyond the seas we know, stretch seas unknown. Christina Georgina Rossetti. *Fr.* Later Life: A Double Sonnet of Sonnets. **CP-RosC2**

Beyond the Sierras, and sage-brush Nevada ranges. Red Mountain. Robinson Jeffers. **CP-JefR2**

Beyond the Snow Belt. Mary Oliver. **SP-OlivM**

Beyond the stolid iron pond. Edward Estlin Cummings. **CP-CummE**

Beyond the white hill which maroons us. Margaret Atwood. *Fr.* Solstice Poem. **SP-AtwM2**

Beyond the windows, past the fern. He Looks out the Window at the Town. Wendell Berry. *Fr.* The Handing Down. **CP-BerrW**

Beyond the wrack and eucharist of snow. At the Hour of the Breaking of the Rocks. Robert Penn Warren. *Fr.* Kentucky Mountain Farm. **SP-WarrR**

Beyond the Years. Paul Laurence Dunbar. **CP-DunbP**

Beyond them, hill and field. Wyeth's Mild Cans. Richard Wilbur. **CP-WilbR**

Beyond this final house. Boone. Wendell Berry. **CP-BerrW**

Beyond this road the blackness bends. Sanine to Leda. Robert Creeley. **CP-CreeR**

Beyond this shadow and this turbulent sea. Christina Georgina Rossetti. *Fr.* Faint, Yet Pursuing. **CP-RosC3**

Beyond truth, / tenacity: of those. Margaret Atwood. **SP-AtwM1**

Beyond What. Alice Walker. **CP-WalkA**

Beyond Words. Robert Frost. **CP-FrosR**

Bheinn Naomh. Kathleen Jessie Raine. **SP-RainK**

Golden Flowers.
Loch, The.
Man.
Summit, The.
Sun.

Bi-Focal. William Stafford. **SP-StafW**

Bianca. Frederick Morgan. **SP-MorgF**

Bianca among the Nightingales. Elizabeth Barrett Browning. **CP-BroEB**

Biancha, Let / Me pay the debt. Kissing Usurie. Robert Herrick. **CP-HerrR**

Bias of the father runs on through the son, The. Endless Cycle. "Lou Reed." **SP-ReedL**

Bibber besotted, with scowl of a cur, having heart of a deer, thou! Homer, *tr. by* George Meredith. **CP-MerG1** *Fr.* The Iliad.

Bibbles. David Herbert Lawrence. **CP-LawrD**

Bible is an antique Volume, The. Emily Dickinson. **CP-DickE**

Bibliographers, The. Geoffrey Hill. **CP-HillG**

Bibulous Compound Of. Jim Morrison. **SP-MorrJ**

Bice laughs, when no man speaks; and doth protest. Upon Bice. Robert Herrick. **CP-HerrR**

Bicentennial. John Ciardi. **SP-CiarJ**

Bicentennial Words for the Liberal Magistrates of 1798. James Liddy. **CP-LiddJ**

Bicoastal Journal. Charles Wright. **SP-WrigC**

Bicycle, The. Derek Mahon. *Fr.* Autobiographies. **SP-MahoD**

Bicycle Chain, A. John Updike. **CP-UpdiJ**

Bicycles and the Apex, The. George Oppen. **CP-OppeG**

Bid a strong ghost stand at the head. A Prayer for My Son. William Butler Yeats. **CP-YeatW**

Bid adieu, my sad heart, bid adieu to thy peace. William Cowper. **CP-CowpW**

Bid all profane away. Ben Jonson. **CP-JonsB** *Fr.* Masque of Hymen.

Bid me to live, and I will live. To Anthea, Who May Command Him Anything. Robert Herrick. **CP-HerrR**

Bid toad sits in my writing room, The. March 7th. Anne Sexton. **CP-SextA**

Bidden Guest, The. Geoffrey Hill. **CP-HillG**

Bideford! Nothing will do. Fare Thee Well. Donald Davie. **CP-DavDo**

Bifocal in Gaza. John Hewitt. **CP-HewiJ**

Bifurcation. Robert Browning. **CP-BroR2**

Big Bang. Robert Pack. **SP-PackR**

Big Bastard with a Sword. Charles Bukowski. **SP-BukC2**

Big Beat. Allen Ginsberg. **CP-GinsA**

Big Bessie Throws Her Son into the Street. Gwendolyn Brooks. **VGW** *Fr.* A Catch of Shy Fish. **SP-BrooG**

Big Billie Potts was big and stout. The Ballad of Billie Potts. Robert Penn Warren. **SP-WarrR**

Big black beard. Guru. Charles Bukowski. **SP-BukC1**

Big Boots of Pain, The. Anne Sexton. **CP-SextA**

Big Boy came. Catch. Langston Hughes. **SP-HughL**

Big Brown Eyes. Gilbert Sorrentino. **SP-SorrG**

Big bud of moon hangs out of the twilight, A. Liaison. David Herbert Lawrence. **CP-LawrD**

Big Daddy Lipscomb, who used to help them up. Say Good-bye to Big Daddy. Randall Jarrell. **CP-JarrR**

Big Dance on the Hill, The. Ernest Hemingway. **CP-HemiE**

Big family, The. Mutchmore and Not-So. Stevie Smith. **CP-SmitS**

Big Fat Fly, A. Charles Olson. **CP-OlsoC**

Big fish eat the little fish, The. Carl Sandburg. *Fr.* The People, Yes. **CP-SandC**

Big guns again. / No speakee well. Imperator Victus. Hart Crane. **CP-CranH**

Big Harpe, Little Harpe. Theory of Evil. Robert Earl Hayden. **CP-HaydR**

Big Heart, The. Anne Sexton. **CP-SextA**

Big House, The. Paul Muldoon. **SP-MuldP**

Big John of Echo Park. Charles Bukowski. **SP-BukC3**

Big lad with too much face, The. Lunch Wagon on Highway 57. Kenneth Patchen. **CP-PatcK**

Big Max. Charles Bukowski. **SP-BukC1**

Big mercy and little mercy big mercy. Cracks. Charles Kenneth Williams. **CP-WillC**

Big missal splayed, The. In Illo Tempore. Seamus Heaney. **SP-HeanS** *Fr.* Sweeney Redivivus.

Big mountains sit still in the afternoon light, The. Sinners. David Herbert Lawrence. **CP-LawrD**

Big Ocean-Waving, Woman-Pulling Moon. Al Young. **CP-YounA**

Big oil tanks squat next the railroad. Carl Sandburg. *Fr.* The People, Yes. **CP-SandC**

Big People, The. César Vallejo, *tr. fr. Spanish by* James Wright. **CP-WrigJ**

Big Rock. Richard Eberhart. **CP-EberR**

Big Room, The. John Hewitt. **CP-HewiJ**

Big sloppy wounded dog. Winter. Charles Bukowski. **SP-BukC1**

Big star, and that other, The. Leaflets. Adrienne Rich. **CP-RicAE; SP-RicA2**

Big Steamers. Rudyard Kipling. **CP-KiplR**

Big stones of the cistern behind the barn, The. Twilights. James Wright. **CP-WrigJ**

Big Sur. Al Young. **CP-YounA**

Big Tent Under the Roof, The. Ogden Nash. **CP-NashO**

Big-uddered piebald cattle low. Christmas Holiday. Alun Lewis. **CP-LewiA**

Big Wind. Theodore Roethke. **CP-RoetT**

Big wings dawns dark. Eagle. Ted Hughes. **SP-HughT**

Big, wise / man. The happy. Indians. Robert Creeley. **CP-CreeR**

Big wood, small wood, little wood, bark. Welcome Home Oh Most Loved and Famed Harteebeeste. Malcolm Lowry. **CP-LowrM**

Big World, The. Leonard Cohen. **CP-CoheL**

Big young bareheaded woman, A. Proletarian Portrait. William Carlos Williams. **CP-WilW1**

Bigger the box the more it holds, The. Boxes and Bags. Carl Sandburg. **CP-SandC**

Biggest bore in town, The. Pain. Richard Shelton. **SP-ShelR**

Bight, The. Elizabeth Bishop. **CP-BishE**

Bigmans. Charles Olson. **CP-OlsoC**

Bigmans II. Charles Olson. **CP-OlsoC**

Bigness of cannon, The. Edward Estlin Cummings. **CP-CummE**

Bigotry's Victim. Percy Bysshe Shelley. **CP-ShelP**

Bilbea. Carl Sandburg. **CP-SandC**

Bilbea, I was in Babylon on Saturday night. Bilbea. Carl Sandburg. **CP-SandC**

Bill, The. Muriel Rukeyser. **CP-RukeM**

Bill 'Awkins. Rudyard Kipling. **CP-KiplR**

Bill Burroughs in Tangiers slowly transfiguring into sanctity season after. Fragment: The Names II. Allen Ginsberg. **CP-GinsA**

Bill, Kath and family gone. Personal. Malcolm Lowry. **CP-LowrM**

Billboards and Galleons. Nicholas Vachel Lindsay. **CP-LindV**

   "Buzzing autos, like black bees."

   "Each day is Biloxi's birthday party."

   "There were open boxes of fine cigars."

Billboards and the street car signs told the people, The. Bitter Summer Thoughts—No. XXII. Carl Sandburg. **CP-SandC**

Billet to the Company of Players. Jonathan Swift. **CP-SwifJ**

Billetin. Malcolm Lowry. **CP-LowrM**

Billets, biglietti, as coin was too heavy for transport. Canto 56. Ezra Pound. *Fr.* Cantos. **CP-PoCan**

Billets Doux for the Harteebeeste. Malcolm Lowry. **CP-LowrM**

Billfold. Robert Creeley. **CP-CreeR**

Billiard Table, The. Roy Fisher. **SP-FishR** *Fr.* Interiors with Various Figures.

Billie. Al Young. **CP-YounA**

Billie Holiday. Hayden Carruth. **CP-CarHS**

Billings and Cooings from "The Berkeley Barb." Mona Van Duyn. **SP-VanDM**

Billion Freedoms, The. Kenneth Patchen. **CP-PatcK**

Billows on the beach are leaping around it, The. To William Shelley ("Billows on the beach are leaping around it, The"). Percy Bysshe Shelley. **CP-ShelP**

Billows swell, the winds are high, The. Temptation. William Cowper. *Fr.* Olney Hymns. **CP-CowpW**

Billy. "Bob Dylan." **CP-DylaB**

Billy Budd, Foretopman. Herman Melville.

   Billy in the Darbies. **SP-MelvH**

Billy in the Darbies. Herman Melville. **SP-MelvH** *Fr.* Billy Budd, Foretopman.

Billy McCoy. Gilbert Sorrentino. **SP-SorrG**

Billy Shears / What would you think if I sang out of tune would you stand up and walk out on me. With a Little Help from My Friends. The Beatles. **CP-Beatl**

Binah. Kathleen Jessie Raine. **SP-RainK**

Bind fast my hands, they have deservéd chains. 1.7. Ovid. **CP-MarlC,** *tr. by* Christopher Marlowe; *Fr.* Elegies.

Bind me but to thee with thine haire. The Bondman. Robert Herrick. **CP-HerrR**

Bind me—I still can sing. Emily Dickinson. **CP-DickE**

Bind up thy tresses, thou beautiful one. Stanzas. John Greenleaf Whittier. **CP-WhitJ**

Binding the Dragon. May Sarton. **SP-SartM**

Bindweed, The. Walter de la Mare. **CP-DeLaW**

Bindweed. John Updike. **CP-UpdiJ**

Binnacle, The. Charles Olson. **CP-OlsoC**

Binsey Poplars (Felled 1879). Gerard Manley Hopkins. **CP-HopkG**

Biography, The. Thomas Merton. **CP-MertT; SP-MertT**

Biography. Edwin Rolfe. **CP-RolfE**

Biography. Carl Sandburg. **CP-SandC**

Biography first convinces us. Emily Dickinson. **SP-DickE**

Biography in the First Person. Stephen Dunn. **SP-DunnS**

Biography of Southern Rain. Kenneth Patchen. **CP-PatcK**

Biography of the Author: A Cento, A. Charles Tomlinson. **CP-TomlC**

Biography, sirs, should begin—with the breath of a man, A. Biography. Carl Sandburg. **CP-SandC**

Biological Reflection. Ogden Nash. **CP-NashO**

Biotherm [for Bill Berkson]. Frank O'Hara. **SP-OharF**

Birch begins to crack its outer sheath, The. A Young Birch. Robert Frost. **CP-FrosR**

Birchbrook Mill. John Greenleaf Whittier. **CP-WhitJ**

Birches. Robert Frost. **CP-FrosR**

Birches. David Markson. **CP-MarkD**

Birches are mad with green points, The. Portrait of the Author. William Carlos Williams. **CP-WilW1**

Birches birches birches true and white. The Trees. Hayden Carruth. *Fr.* Contra Mortem. **CP-CarHL**

Birchington Churchyard. Christina Georgina Rossetti. **CP-RosC2**

Bird, The. Robert Creeley. **CP-CreeR**

Bird / flies / out the / window. She / flies, The. 3 in 1. Robert Creeley. **CP-CreeR**

Bird. Pablo Neruda, *tr. fr. Spanish by* Ben Belitt. **SP-NeruP**

Bird, The. Charles Simic. **SP-SimiC**

Bird. William Carlos Williams. **CP-WilW2**

Bird, bird don't edge me in. The Reply. Theodore Roethke. **CP-RoetT**

Bird book says, common, conspicuous, The. Patch Work. Thom Gunn. **CP-GunnT**

Bird calls me, A. The Bird. Charles Simic. **SP-SimiC**

Bird came down the Walk, A. Emily Dickinson. **CP-DickE**

Bird-Catcher's Boy, The. Thomas Hardy. **CP-HardT**

Bird did prance—the Bee did play, The. Emily Dickinson. **CP-DickE**

Bird-dream and peeling wallpaper. The Night They Took Whitey. Charles Bukowski. **SP-BukC2**

Bird fish and man / I cannot fly into the sun. Man Fish and Bird. John Hewitt. **CP-HewiJ**

Bird flew down from a tall tree, A. A Version of the Phoenix Story. Jenny Joseph. **SP-JoseJ**

Bird flew out of a cloud, A. Woman and Emblems. Muriel Rukeyser. **CP-RukeM**

Bird Footprint. Carl Sandburg. **CP-SandC**

Bird Frau, The. Rita Dove. **SP-DoveR**

Bird half wakened in the lunar moon, A. On a Bird Singing in its Sleep. Robert Frost. **CP-FrosR**

Bird her punctual music brings, The. Emily Dickinson. **CP-DickE**

Bird, in Soliloquizing Voices a Woman's Wish, The. Marsden Hartley. **CP-HartM**

Bird in the Hand: Two Solos, A. Richard Shelton. **SP-ShelR**

Bird in the Tree, The. Malcolm Lowry. **CP-LowrM**

Bird in Whatever Name, The. John Ciardi. **SP-CiarJ**

Bird kept saying that birds had once been men, The. On an Old Horn. Wallace Stevens. **CP-StevW**

Bird Killer, The. Wendell Berry. **CP-BerrW**

Bird-Language. Wystan Hugh Auden. **CP-AudeW**

Bird must sing to earn the Crumb, The. Emily Dickinson. **CP-DickE**

Bird of Night. Ernest Hemingway. **CP-HemiE**

Bird of Night, The. Randall Jarrell. **CP-JarrR**

Bird of Paradise. Robert Ranke Graves. **CP-GravR**

Bird of the spray, the tree of bones. Loss. Randall Jarrell. **CP-JarrR**

Bird on the Wire. Leonard Cohen. **CP-CoheL**

Bird or Beast? Christina Georgina Rossetti. **CP-RosC1**

Bird-Queen, The. Kenneth Patchen. **CP-PatcK**

Bird Raptures. Christina Georgina Rossetti. **CP-RosC1**

Bird sails from the hole in that high stone, A. The Colors of a Bird. Richard Hugo. **CP-HugoR**

Bird sat on a red handle, The. Understandings in Blue. Carl Sandburg. **CP-SandC**

Bird-Scene at a Rural Dwelling, A. Thomas Hardy. **CP-HardT**

Bird sighs for the air. The Lover's Song. William Butler Yeats. **CP-YeatW**

Bird sings the selfsame song, A. The Selfsame Song. Thomas Hardy. **CP-HardT**

Bird Song, A. Christina Georgina Rossetti. **CP-RosC1**

Bird Song. William Carlos Williams. **CP-WilW2**

Bird song is flute song and a glory. Thrush Song at Dawn. Richard Eberhart. **CP-EberR**

Bird-soul was ashamed, The. From "Bird Conversations." Farid-uddin Attar, *tr. fr. Persian by* Ralph Waldo Emerson. **CP-EmerR**

Bird Talk. Carl Sandburg. **CP-SandC**

Bird that cries like a baby, The. Louis Zukofsky. **CP-ZukLS**

Bird that I don't know, A. A Country Life. Randall Jarrell. **CP-JarrR**

Bird, that's fetch't from Phasis floud, The. Out of Petronius. Petronius Arbiter, *tr. fr. Latin by* Richard Crashaw. **CP-CrasR**

Bird, the Bird, the Bird, The. Robert Creeley. **CP-CreeR**

Bird was gone the ghastly trees, The. Ralph Waldo Emerson. **CP-EmerR**

Bird watchers top my honors list. Up from the Egg; the Confessions of a Nuthatch Avoider. Ogden Nash. **CP-NashO**

Bird, who for his other sins, A. A Character. Samuel Taylor Coleridge. **CP-ColeS**

Bird who watches me, The. Peaceful Kingdom. Charles Simic. **SP-SimiC**

Bird-Window-Flying. Tess Gallagher. **SP-GallT**

Bird with a name it does not itself, A. The Bird in Whatever Name. John Ciardi. **SP-CiarJ**

Bird with outstretched. Bird. William Carlos Williams. **CP-WilW2**

Bird with the Coppery, Keen Claws, The. Wallace Stevens. **CP-StevW**

Bird with the Dark Plumes, The. Robinson Jeffers. **CP-JefR1**

Bird-witted. Marianne Craig Moore. **CP-MoorM**

Bird would be a soundless thing, The. Emily Dickinson. **SP-DickE**

Birdbrain. Allen Ginsberg. **CP-GinsA**

Birdbrain runs the World! Birdbrain. Allen Ginsberg. **CP-GinsA**

Birdcage Walk. David Herbert Lawrence. **CP-LawrD**

Birdcage Walk. Thomas Merton. **CP-MertT; SP-MertT**

Birdie with a yellow bill, A. Time to Rise. Robert Louis Stevenson. **CP-StevR**

Birdies, Don't Make Me Laugh. Ogden Nash. **CP-NashO**

Birdless, the bush yet shakes. Encounter. Charles Tomlinson. **CP-TomlC**

Birds, The. William Blake. **CP-BlakW**

Birds. Tom Clark. **SP-ClarT**

Birds, The. Robert Creeley. **CP-CreeR**

Birds(/ here,inven / ting air). Edward Estlin Cummings. **CP-CummE**

Birds. Robinson Jeffers. **CP-JefR1**

Birds. James Liddy. **CP-LiddJ**
    At castle shadowed mouth of the / Doonbeg.
    "Cormorants / By the pollock holes diving."
    "Hesperian evenings certainly."
    "Night / We went running to the garden."
    "Sea / Is not distinguished by."
    "Wild curlew whistle I offer my death to."

Birds, The. Ogden Nash. **CP-NashO**

Birds. James Schuyler. **CP-SchuJ**

Birds, The. Dabney Stuart. **SP-StuaD**

Birds, The. William Carlos Williams. **CP-WilW1**

Birds about the house pretend to be, The. The Return of the Evening Grosbeaks. Adrienne Rich. **CP-RicAE**

Birds against the April wind, The. What the Birds Said. John Greenleaf Whittier. **CP-WhitJ**

Birds all the sunny day. Nest Eggs. Robert Louis Stevenson. **CP-StevR**

Birds and Fishes. Robinson Jeffers. **CP-JefR3**

Birds and Flowers. William Carlos Williams. **CP-WilW1**

Birds and periodic blood. 5:30 A.M. Adrienne Rich. **CP-RicAE; SP-RicA1; SP-RicA2**

Birds are flowers flying. Mirrorment. Archie Randolph Ammons. **SP-AmmoA**

Birds are on fire, The. Singing Is Fire. Charles Bukowski. **SP-BukC2**

Birds are our friends, The. Nor did the prophet. Louis Zukofsky. *Fr.* Songs of Degrees. **CP-ZukLS**

Birds—are they worth remembering?, The. Wingtip. Carl Sandburg. **CP-SandC**

Birds are very bold this Morning, The. Emily Dickinson. **SP-DickE**

Birds at Winter Nightfall. Thomas Hardy. **CP-HardT**

Birds begin as an isolated shower, The. Elizabeth. Paul Muldoon. **SP-MuldP**

Birds begun at Four o'clock, The. Emily Dickinson. **CP-DickE**

Birds build but not I build, no, but wipe, Time's wife. Caring for Surfaces. Mona Van Duyn. **SP-VanDM**

Bird's Companion, The. William Carlos Williams. **CP-WilW1**

Birds doe sing, day doth apeere, The. Song. Mary Sidney, Countess of Montgomery Wroth. *Fr.* Pamphilia to Amphilanthus. **CP-WrotM**

Birds everywhere are talking, The. For George (II). Grace Paley. **CP-PaleG**

Bird's-Eye View, A. Christina Georgina Rossetti. **CP-RosC1**

Bird's-Eye View of the Tool and Die Co. John Ashbery. **SP-AshbJ**

Birds' feet and baby feet. Writing on Sand. Charles Tomlinson. **CP-TomlC**

Birds flitting in and out of the barn. On the Venerable Bede. Louis MacNeice. *Fr.* Dark Age Glosses. **CP-MacNL**

Birds from Parnassus, / swift. Euripides, *tr. fr. Greek by* Hilda Doolittle ("H.D."). **CP-DoolH** *Fr.* Ion.

Birds have a finer body and tinier brain—. Das ewig Weibliche. Robert Lowell. **SP-LoweR**

Birds have flown away from the mountains, The. Chung Yuan Liu, *tr. fr. Chinese by* William Carlos Williams *with* David Rafael Wang. **CP-WilW2**

Birds have flown their summer skies to the south, The. Beyond the Red River. Thomas McGrath. **SP-McGrT**

Birds here should have names so hard to say. Montgomery Hollow. Richard Hugo. **CP-HugoR**

Birds in a whirl, drift to the rooftops. This Poem Is for Birds. Gary Snyder. **CP-SnydG** *Fr.* Hunting. *Fr.* Myths and Texts.

Birds in Snow. Hilda Doolittle. **CP-DoolH**

Birds in the gardens of Avignon, The. Voyage en Provence. Archibald MacLeish. **CP-MacLA**

Birds in the high Hall-garden. Tennyson. **EBVVPR; NAEL-2; PeVV** *Fr.* Maud [A Monodrama]. **CP-TennA**

Birds, Like Thoughts. John Ciardi. **SP-CiarJ**

Birds meet above the new Moon. Edward Estlin Cummings. **CP-CummE**

Birds of Killingworth, The (The Poet's Tale). Henry Wadsworth Longfellow. *Fr.* Tales of a Wayside Inn.
    (Poet's Tale: The Birds of Killingworth, The.) **SP-LongH**
    "Do you ne'er think what wondrous beings these?" **WBLP**

Birds of Paradise Being Very Plain Birds, The. Diane Wakoski. **SP-WakoD**

"Birds of Prey" March. Rudyard Kipling. **CP-KiplR**

Birds of Vietnam, The. Hayden Carruth. **CP-CarHS**

Birds put off their ev'ry hue, The. On Mrs. Montagu's Feather-Hangings. William Cowper. **CP-CowpW**

Birds reported from the South, The. Emily Dickinson. **CP-DickE**

Birds' Rondel, The, *mod. vers. by* Louis Untermeyer. Geoffrey Chaucer. *See* Now Welcom[e], Somer [*or* Summer].

Birds they sang, The. Anthem. Leonard Cohen. **CP-CoheL**

Birds whistled, all. An Amorous Debate. Thom Gunn. **CP-GunnT**

Birdsnest built on the palm of the high, A. Lightness. Richard Wilbur. **CP-WilbR**

Birdsong, The. William Carlos Williams. **CP-WilW2**

Birdsong. May. Tuscany. A house. Sunset. Bronze. James Merrill. **SP-MerrJ**

Birks of Aberfeldy, The [Composed on the Spot]. Robert Burns. **CP-BurnR**

Birmingham. Louis MacNeice. **CP-MacNL**

Birmingham, October '80. A man. Pete Brown's Old Eggs Still Hatch. Roy Fisher. **SP-FishR**

Birth, A. James Dickey. **CP-DickJ**

Birth, A. Muriel Rukeyser. **CP-RukeM**

Birth, The. William Carlos Williams. **CP-WilW2**

Birth and Death. Richard Eberhart. **CP-EberR**

Birth and Death. Robinson Jeffers. **CP-JefR3**

Birth and Death of the Sun, The. Jim Carroll. **SP-CarrJ**

Birth Comes to the Archbishop. Ogden Nash. **CP-NashO**

Birth-Day Ode. December 31st 1787, A. Robert Burns. **CP-BurnR**

Birth-Dues. Robinson Jeffers. **CP-JefR1**

Birth is the starting point of passion. Fog Numbers. Carl Sandburg. **CP-SandC**

Birth (Near Port William), The. Wendell Berry. **CP-BerrW**

Birth Night. David Herbert Lawrence. **CP-LawrD**

Birth of a Goddess. Robert Ranke Graves. **CP-GravR**

Birth of Angels. Robert Ranke Graves. **CP-GravR**

Birth of Christ, The. John Gould Fletcher. **SP-FletJ** *Fr.* The Parables of Christ.

Birth of color / out of night and the ground. April Woods: Morning. Wendell Berry. **CP-BerrW**

Birth of Love. Robert Penn Warren. **SP-WarrR**

Birth of Love, The. William Wordsworth. **CP-WorW1**

Birth of Pleasure, The. Percy Bysshe Shelley. **CP-ShelP**

Birth of Rainbow. Ted Hughes. **SP-HughT**

Birth of the Spirit, The. Richard Eberhart. **CP-EberR**

Birth of the Sun, The. Pablo Antonio Cuadra, *tr. fr. Spanish by* Thomas Merton. **CP-MertT**

Birth of the Water Baby, The. Erica Jong. **SP-JongE**

Birth of Venus, The. Hayden Carruth. **CP-CarHS**

Birth of Venus, The. Randall Jarrell. **CP-JarrR**

Birth of Venus, The. Muriel Rukeyser. **CP-RukeM**

Birth of Venus, The. William Carlos Williams. **CP-WilW2**

Birth Report. Stephen Dobyns. **SP-DobyS**

Birthday. John Ciardi. **SP-CiarJ**

Birthday, A. Robert Creeley. **CP-CreeR**

Birthday. Richard Hugo. **CP-HugoR**

Birthday. Robinson Jeffers. **CP-JefR3**

Birthday. Ted Kooser. **SP-KoosT**

Birthday. David Herbert Lawrence. **CP-LawrD**

Birthday. John Lennon *and* Paul McCartney. **CP-Beatl**

Birthday, A. Christina Georgina Rossetti. **CP-RosC1**

Birthday (Autobiography). Robinson Jeffers. **CP-JefR3**

Birthday Book, A. Gertrude Stein. **CP-SteiG**

Birthday Card for a Psychiatrist. Mona Van Duyn. **SP-VanDM**

Birthday Dream, The. James Dickey. **CP-DickJ**

Birthday Greeting. Basil Bunting. **CP-BuntB**

Birthday Memorial to Seventh Street, A. Audre Lorde. **SP-LordA**

Birthday of an Aging Seer. John Crowe Ransom. *Fr.* Sixteen Poems in Eight Pairings. **SP-RansJ**

Birthday of but a single pang. Emily Dickinson. **CP-DickE**

Birthday on the Acropolis. May Sarton. **SP-SartM**

Birthday on the Beach. Ogden Nash. **CP-NashO**

Birthday Poem. Jim Carroll. **SP-CarrJ**
   "But everything has worked out fine."
   "I hope that George enjoys the gifts."
   "It's still gray and wet almost pink."
   "Ron Padgett is holding two birthday gifts."
   "3 hours into the afternoon of March 9th."

Birthday Poem. Thom Gunn. **CP-GunnT**

Birthday Poem. Jenny Joseph. **SP-JoseJ**

Birthday Poem. Etheridge Knight. **SP-KnigE**

Birthday Poem. Al Young. **CP-YounA**

Birthday Present, A. Sylvia Plath. **CP-PlatS**

Birthday Rhyme for Roberta, A. John Hewitt. **CP-HewiJ**

Birthday Wreath, The. John Greenleaf Whittier. **CP-WhitJ**

Birthdays from the ocean one desert april noon. That "Craning of the Neck." Isabella Gardner. **CP-GardI**

Birthnight: To F., The. Walter de la Mare. **CP-DeLaW**

Birthplace, The. Robert Frost. **CP-FrosR**

Birthplace: New Rochelle. George Oppen. **CP-OppeG**

Birthpalce of Mr. William Shakespeare author, The. Verses for a Centennial. Archibald MacLeish. **CP-MacLA**

Birthright, The. Rudyard Kipling. **CP-KiplR** *Fr.* Debits and Credits.

Birthright. Louis MacNeice. **CP-MacNL**

Birth's Obituary. Charles Olson. **CP-OlsoC**

Bisara of Pooree, The. Rudyard Kipling. *Fr.* Plain Tales from the Hills. "Little Blind Fish, thou art marvellous wise!" **CP-KiplR**

Biscuits with honey running down into the deep crevices. Overweight Poem. Diane Wakoski. **SP-WakoD**

Bishop Blougram's Apology. Robert Browning. **CP-BroR1**
   Belief and Unbelief. **FaBV**

Bishop Orders His Tomb at Saint Praxed's Church, The. Robert Browning. **CP-BroR1**

Bishop Tutu's Visit to the White House: 1984. Charles Kenneth Williams. **SP-WillC**

Bishops and Priests, blessèd are ye, if deep. William Wordsworth. *Fr.* Ecclesiastical Sonnets. **CP-WorW2**

Bishops of the Church of England, The. Stevie Smith. **CP-SmitS**

Bison first surveyed this track, The. The Autumn Drives (Early 1800s). Louise McNeill. **SP-McNeL**

Bit of talcum, A. Reflection on Babies. Ogden Nash. **CP-NashO**

Bit of yarrow and then of rue, A. Bouquet in Dog Time. Hayden Carruth. **CP-CarHS**

Bitch that was full pregnant grown, A. The Fable of the Bitches. Jonathan Swift. **CP-SwifJ**

Bitcheries of Madison Avenue, The. Hayden Carruth. **CP-CarHS** *Fr.* The Bloomingdale Papers.

Bites and Kisses. Robert Ranke Graves. **CP-GravR**

Biting of Beggars. Robert Herrick. **CP-HerrR**

Bits. David Herbert Lawrence. **CP-LawrD**
   Casualty.
   Child and the Soldier, The.
   Daughter of the Great Man, The.
   Drill in the Heat.
   Dust in the East.
   Foreign Sunset.
   Girl in Cairo, The.
   Grey Nurse, The.
   Jewess and the V.C., The.
   Land-Worker.
   Last Minute, The.
   Litany of Grey Nurses.
   Maiden's Prayer.
   Man Hauling a Wagon.
   Mesopotamia.
   Message to Perfidious Soldier.
   Mother's Son in Salonika.
   Mourning.
   Munitions.
   Neither Moth Nor Rust.
   Pietá.
   Prisoner at Work in a Turkish Garden.
   Prisoners at Work in the Rain.
   Sighs.
   "Sisters, I am sorry for this foreign man."
   Swing Song of a Girl and a Soldier.
   Tales.
   Vicar's Son.
   Well in Africa, The.
   Zeppelin Nights.

Bitten and burned into mirrors of thin gold. The Weathercocks. Charles Tomlinson. **CP-TomlC**

Bitter, bitter jewel. Hilda Doolittle. **NALW** *Fr.* Tribute to the Angels. **CP-DoolH**

Bitter blue fingers. The Firing. Gary Snyder. **CP-SnydG**

Bitter cold winter night, A. Who Will Take Over the Universe? Allen Ginsberg. **CP-GinsA**

Bitter for Sweet. Christina Georgina Rossetti. **CP-RosC1**

Bitter Herb. Erica Jong. **SP-JongE**

Bitter Life, A. John Updike. **SP-UpdiJ**

Bitter Reflection, A. Samuel Taylor Coleridge. **CP-ColeS**

Bitter Spring Again, The. Al Young. **CP-YounA**

Bitter Strawberries. Sylvia Plath. **CP-PlatS**

Bitter Summer Thoughts. Carl Sandburg. **CP-SandC**

Bitter Summer Thoughts—No. 3. Carl Sandburg. **CP-SandC**

Bitter Summer Thoughts—No. XXII. Carl Sandburg. **CP-SandC**

Bitter-Sweet. George Herbert. **CP-HerbG**

Bitter upon conviction. Interstitial Office. John Berryman. **CP-BerrJ**

Bitter veins reject the dream, dismiss the fire, The. Farewell to the Bluewoman. Kenneth Patchen. **CP-PatcK**

Bitter Waters. Walter de la Mare. **CP-DeLaW**

Bitter winter / Rain. The Winter After. Charles Olson. **CP-OlsoC**

Bitter World of Spring, The. William Carlos Williams. **CP-WilW2**

Bitter year it was. What woman ever, A. The Wreath. Robert Ranke Graves. **CP-GravR**

Bitterly, England, must thou grieve. How Sleep the Brave. Walter de la Mare. **CP-DeLaW**

Bitterness, A. Mary Oliver. **SP-OlivM**

Bivouac. Alun Lewis. **CP-LewiA**

Bivouac on a Mountain Side. Walt Whitman. **CP-WhitW**

Bix to Buxtehude to Boulez. The Victor Dog. James Merrill. **SP-MerrJ**

Bixby Canyon. Allen Ginsberg. **CP-GinsA**

Bixby Canyon Ocean Path Word Breeze. Allen Ginsberg. **CP-GinsA**

Bixby's Landing. Robinson Jeffers. **CP-JefR1**

Bizarre. Allen Tate. **CP-TateA**

!blac / k / agains / t. Edward Estlin Cummings. **CP-CummE**

Black / Blue Black / Blue. Kenneth Rexroth. **CP-RexKL** *Fr.* A Prolegomenon to a Theodicy.

Black. Robert Ranke Graves. **CP-GravR**

Black and White. John Hewitt. **CP-HewiJ**

Black and white dog, A. Crown Hill Cemetary, Indianapolis. Etheridge Knight. *Fr.* Indiana Haiku—2. **SP-KnigE**

Black Angel's Death Song. "Lou Reed." **SP-ReedL**

Black Art, The. Anne Sexton. **CP-SextA**

Black-Ass Poem After Talking to Pamela Churchill. Ernest Hemingway. **CP-HemiE**

Black at that depth. Pacific Lament. Charles Olson. **CP-OlsoC**

Black Beast, The. Ted Hughes. **SP-HughT**

Black Berry—wears a Thorn in his side, The. Emily Dickinson. **CP-DickE**

Black Birch in Winter, A. Richard Wilbur. **CP-WilbR**

Black bird scudding. The Bobolink. Edna St. Vincent Millay. **CP-MillE**

Black Book, The. John Berryman.

"Grandfather, sleepless in a room upstairs." **CP-BerrJ**

"Lover & child, a little sing." **CP-BerrJ**

"Luftmenschen dream, the men who live on air." **CP-BerrJ**

Black Box. William Matthews. **SP-MattW**

Black Brook. Charles Tomlinson. **CP-TomlC**

Black Bull, The. Martin Edmunds. **SP-EdmuM**

Black bull bellowed before the sea, The. The Bull of Bendylaw. Sylvia Plath. **CP-PlatS**

Black bull of enormous power, A. Llangefni Market. Steve Griffiths. **SP-GrifS**

Black bull, square and strong. Bull Alone. Phoebe Hesketh. **SP-HeskP**

Black cat, sweet brother. For James Baldwin. Kay Boyle. **CP-BoylK**

Black chest hairs, soft sudden mass. Lines Muttered in Sleep. Rita Dove. **SP-DoveR**

Black Christ, The. Countee Cullen. **CP-CullC**

Black clippers, tarred with whales' blood, fold their sails. Old New England. Derek Walcott. **CP-WalcD**

Black cloud / is a happy portent, The. For a Moment of Darkness over the Nations. John Hewitt. **CP-HewiJ**

Black Cottage, The. Robert Frost. **CP-FrosR**

Black Crow Blues. "Bob Dylan." **CP-DylaB**

Black Day, The. Archibald MacLeish. **CP-MacLA**

Black Demons hovering o'er his mitred head. Scene in Venice. William Wordsworth. *Fr.* Ecclesiastical Sonnets. **CP-WorW2**

Black Diamond Bay. "Bob Dylan" *and* Jacques Levy. **CP-DylaB**

Black dog barking at the moon. Alun Lewis. *Fr.* Songs for the Night. **CP-LewiA**

Black dog in a, A. Charles Henri Ford. **SP-FordC** *Fr.* Emblems of Arachne.

Black Dog, Red Dog. Stephen Dobyns. **SP-DobyS**

Black drinks the sun and draws all colours to it. Black. Robert Ranke Graves. **CP-GravR**

Black eyed susan. The Wildflower. William Carlos Williams. **CP-WilW1**

Black Faced Sheep, The. Donald Hall. **CP-HallD**

Black from sun and the stain of hemlock bark. Kapowsin. Richard Hugo. **CP-HugoR**

Black girl going, A. Generation II. Audre Lorde. **SP-LordA**

Black Goddess, The. Robert Ranke Graves. **CP-GravR**

Black hair you'd say she had, or rather. Edna St. Vincent Millay. **CP-MillE**

Black Hills, The. William Everson. **SP-EverW**

Black Hole, The. Robert Pack. **SP-PackR**

Black Horizons. Carl Sandburg. **CP-SandC**

Black horizons, come up. Black Horizons. Carl Sandburg. **CP-SandC**

Black Hoyden. Donald Davie. **CP-DavDo**

Black Humor. Archibald MacLeish. **CP-MacLA**

Black, ice-grey, white, azure, orange. Homage to Arnaut. Gilbert Sorrentino. **SP-SorrG**

Black in blazonry means. The Buffalo. Marianne Craig Moore. **CP-MoorM**

Black Jackets. Thom Gunn. **CP-GunnT**

Black lady, / two eyes. KE 6-8018. Anne Sexton. **CP-SextA**

Black lake, black boat, two black, cut-paper people. Crossing the Water. Sylvia Plath. **CP-PlatS**

Black, long-tailed, The. The Yellow Season. William Carlos Williams. **CP-WilW2**

Black Lotus of the Links. Laurence Lieberman. **SP-LiebL**

Black Magdalens. Countee Cullen. **CP-CullC**

Black Magicians / Come home: the pink meat image. The Change: *Kyoto-Tokyo Express.* Allen Ginsberg. **CP-GinsA**

Black Mail. Alice Walker. **CP-WalkA**

Black Majesty. Countee Cullen. **CP-CullC**

Black man, bright nouveautés leave one, at best, pseudonymous. Nudity in the Colonies. Wallace Stevens. **CP-StevW**

Black marble mantelpiece, The. Evening. James Schuyler. **CP-SchuJ**

Black March. Stevie Smith. **CP-SmitS**

Black Maria. Langston Hughes. **SP-HughL**

Black Mesa, The. James Merrill. **SP-MerrJ**

Black Money. Tess Gallagher. **SP-GallT**

Black mood, away! Winter Carol. May Sarton. **SP-SartM**

Black Mother Woman. Audre Lorde. **SP-LordA**

Black Mt. College Has a Few Words for a Visitor. Charles Olson. **CP-OlsoC**

Black November. Chuck Miller. **SP-MillC**

Black November Turkey, A. Richard Wilbur. **CP-WilbR**

Black Nude. Charles Tomlinson. **CP-TomlC**

Black Ode. Maya Angelou. **SP-AngeM**

Black on flat water past the jonquil lawns. The Black Swan. James Merrill. **SP-MerrJ**

Black Panther and the Little Boy, The. Kenneth Patchen. **CP-PatcK**

Black Patch on Lucasta's Face, A. Richard Lovelace. **CP-LoveR**

Black Pierrot, A. Langston Hughes. **SP-HughL**

Black Pine Tree in an Orange Light. Sylvia Plath. **CP-PlatS**

Black Poet Leaps to His Death, A. Etheridge Knight. **SP-KnigE**

Black poets should live—not leap. For Black Poets Who Think of Suicide. Etheridge Knight. **SP-KnigE**

Black Poppy (At the Temple). David St. John. **SP-StJoD**

Black Prince, The. Alice Walker. **CP-WalkA**

Black Queen for More Than a Day. Al Young. **CP-YounA**

Black queen on the red king. Solitaire. John Updike. **CP-UpdiJ**

Black queen treading the night. The Panther and the Antelope. Phoebe Hesketh. **SP-HeskP**

Black relatives / you are always. Some Things I Like about My Triple Bloods. Alice Walker. **CP-WalkA**

Black Richard. George Meredith. **CP-MerG2**

Black Rock, The. John Gould Fletcher. **SP-FletJ**

Black Rook in Rainy Weather. Sylvia Plath. **CP-PlatS**

Black Samson of Brandywine. Paul Laurence Dunbar. **CP-DunbP**

Black screen. the glittering lights of the river, The. Suite. Patti Smith. **SP-SmitP**

Black ship of night. January in New York. Erica Jong. **SP-JongE**

Black Silk. Tess Gallagher. **SP-GallT**

Black Snake, The. Mary Oliver. **SP-OlivM**

Black sticks poke out of the back-garden. Hodge Looks toward London. Wystan Hugh Auden. **CP-AudWJ**

Black Stone on Top of a White Stone. César Vallejo, *tr. fr. Spanish by* Thomas Merton. **CP-MertT**

Black Stones of Iona, The. William Wordsworth. *Fr.* Poems Composed or Suggested During a Tour, in the Summer of 1833. **CP-WorW2**

Black summer, black Vermont. Who sees. The Mountain. Hayden Carruth. **CP-CarHS**

Black Swan, The. Randall Jarrell. **CP-JarrR; SP-JarrR**

Black Swan, The. James Merrill. **SP-MerrJ**

Black Tambourine. Hart Crane. **CP-CranH**

Black teenager strapped to, A. Manhattan March, The 1970s. Al Young. **CP-YounA**

Black teeth / Seek the pale ropes which bind life. Lives of the Swan. Kenneth Patchen. **CP-PatcK**

Black thunderclouds mass up against the wind. Malcolm Lowry. *Fr.* The Roar of the Sea and the Darkness. **CP-LowrM**

Black Tower, The. William Butler Yeats. **CP-YeatW**

Black Train, The. Thomas McGrath. **SP-McGrT**

Black trees. The banks fill with shadow. At the Door. Stephen Berg. **SP-BergS** *Fr.* For My Father.

Black village of gravestones. Heptonstall. Ted Hughes. **SP-HughT**

Black Walnut Tree, The. Mary Oliver. **SP-OlivM**

Black water. White waves. Furrows snowcapped. Seamus Heaney. **NoAM** *Fr.* Station Island. **SP-HeanS**

Black waters' / Novemeber / clouds. Hill. Louis Zukofsky. **CP-ZukLS**

Black windows. Her arms, The. Six/Nine/Forty-Four. David St. John. **SP-StJoD**

Black Winds, The. William Carlos Williams. **CP-WilW1**

Black-winged gull, The. Song. William Carlos Williams. **CP-WilW1**

Blackberry Eating. Galway Kinnell. **SP-KinnG**

Blackberry-Picking. Seamus Heaney. **SP-HeanS**

Blackberry, white, The. Sobieski's Shield. Geoffrey Hill. **CP-HillG**

Blackberry Winter ("If there be a power of sweetness, let it lie"), *see also* Blackberry Winter ("If the lady hath any loveliness, let it die"). John Crowe Ransom. **SP-RansJ**

Blackberrying. Sylvia Plath. **CP-PlatS**

Blackbird. John Lennon *and* Paul McCartney. **CP-Beatl**

Blackbird, The. Derek Mahon. **SP-MahoD**

Blackbird flew to a hawthorn bush, A. Black and White. John Hewitt. **CP-HewiJ**

Blackbird in a wicker cage, A. The Two Blackbirds. George Meredith. **CP-MerG1**

Blackbird of Avondale sang the Anglo-Gaelic as, The. Taking One's Students to Avondale. James Liddy. **CP-LiddJ**

Blackbird of Derrycairn. 1969, Ireland of the Bombers. Donald Davie. *Fr.* Two from Ireland. **CP-DavDo**

Blackbird singing in the dead of night. Blackbird. John Lennon *and* Paul McCartney. **CP-Beatl**

Blackbird used to come each day, The. Dead Blackbird. Phoebe Hesketh. **SP-HeskP**

Blackbirds Are Rough Today, The. Charles Bukowski. **SP-BukC2**

Blackbird's song the blackbird's song, The. Ralph Waldo Emerson. **CP-EmerR**

Blackburn's Dream. Gilbert Sorrentino. **SP-SorrG**

Blacked-out on a wagon, part of my life cut out forever. 7/16/68: i. Adrienne Rich. **CP-RicAE** *Fr.* Ghazals: Homage to Ghalib. **SP-RicA2**

Blackened and firescarred, / Up from the stokehole. Number 8 Fireman. Malcolm Lowry. **CP-LowrM**

Blackening Sky. Robert Ranke Graves. **CP-GravR**

Blacker and whiter than the pages of his ledger. Hymn to Commerce. Thomas Merton. **CP-MertT**

Blackfoot bends, pools deep around, The. Where Jennie Used to Swim. Richard Hugo. **CP-HugoR**

Blackfriars. Sir John Betjeman. **CP-BetjJ**

Blackie, the Electric Rembrandt. Thom Gunn. **CP-GunnT**

Blacklisted. Carl Sandburg. **CP-SandC**

Blackness / Was a building blocking my birth moon. Mount Zion. Ted Hughes. **SP-HughT**

Black'on frowns east on Maidon. After the Club-Dance. Thomas Hardy. *Fr.* At Casterbridge Fair. **CP-HardT**

Blacksmith's Serenade, The. Nicholas Vachel Lindsay. **CP-LindV**

Blackstone is gone. Law. Charles Olson. **CP-OlsoC**

Blackstudies. Audre Lorde. **SP-LordA**

Bladder Song. Leonard Nathan. **SP-NathL**

Blades. Charles Kenneth Williams. **CP-WillC; SP-WillC**

Blades sway. They ride, The. Reeds. Charles Tomlinson. **CP-TomlC**

Blair Purves: Bluenose Portrait Effect #2. Marsden Hartley. **CP-HartM**

Blake drew the guilt of God. The Elohim Creating Adam. Roy Fisher. **SP-FishR**

Blakes apology for His Catalogue. William Blake. **CP-BlakW**
("Who cries all art is a fraud & Genius a trick.") **CP-BlakW**

Blame. Robert Herrick. **CP-HerrR**

Blame. Charles Kenneth Williams. **SP-WillC**

Blame me not dearest, though grieved for your sake. Mary Sidney, Countess of Montgomery Wroth. *Fr.* Part 1. *Fr.* Urania. **CP-WrotM**

Blame me not that I refuse. George Meredith. **CP-MerG2**

Blame me not that this epistle. To Charles Baxter. Robert Louis Stevenson. **CP-StevR**

Blame me not thou hoarse preacher. Hafiz, *tr.* by Ralph Waldo Emerson. **CP-EmerR** *Fr.* Odes.

Blame Not My Cheekes. Thomas Campion. **CP-CampT**

Blame not my lute, for he must sound [*or* sssnd *or* Sownde]. Sir Thomas Wyatt. **CP-WyatT**

"Blame not thyself too much," I said, "nor blame." Tennyson. **NAEL-2** *Fr.* So was their sanctuary violated. *Fr.* The Princess. **CP-TennA**

Blame the Reward of Princes. Robert Herrick. **CP-HerrR**

Blame the Thought, Cling to the Bummer. Allen Ginsberg. **CP-GinsA**

Blameless as daylight I stood looking. The Eye-Mote. Sylvia Plath. **CP-PlatS**

Blanc de Blanc. Siv Cedering Fox. *Fr.* Onna-E, Pictures of Women. **SP-CedeS**

Blanch swears her Husband's lovely; when a scald. Upon Blanch. Robert Herrick. **CP-HerrR**

Blanched tree livid behind, The. Iowa. Donald Davie. **CP-DavDo**

Bland as the morning breath of June. A Dream of Summer. John Greenleaf Whittier. **CP-WhitJ**

Blandly mother. Wild Orphan. Allen Ginsberg. **CP-GinsA**

Blandly she lies. Marsden Hartley. *Fr.* Ironies out of St. George's. **CP-HartM**

Blandula, Tenella, Vagula. Ezra Pound. **SP-PounE**

Blank, A. Thom Gunn. **CP-GunnT**

Blank. David Herbert Lawrence. **CP-LawrD**

Blank Misgivings of a Creature Moving About in Worlds Not Realized. Arthur Hugh Clough. **SP-ClouA**
"Here am I yet, another twelvemonth spent."
"How often sit I, poring o'er."
"I have seen higher holier things than these."
"Like a child."
"O kind protecting Darkness! as a child."
"Once more the wonted road I tread."
"Roused by importunate knocks."

"Though to the vilest things beneath the moon."
"Well, well,—Heaven bless you all from day to day!"
"Yes, I have lied, and so must walk my way."

Blank of the Wall, The. Donald Davie. **CP-DavDo**

Blanket Charge. Robert Ranke Graves. **CP-GravR**

Blasphemies, The. Louis MacNeice. **CP-MacNL**

Blast—1875, The. Robert Louis Stevenson. **CP-StevR**

Blast from Freedom's Northern hills, upon its Southern way, The. Massachusetts to Virginia. John Greenleaf Whittier. **CP-WhitJ**

Blasted with sighs, and surrounded with tears. Twicknam [*or* Twickenham] Garden. John Donne. **CP-DonnJ**

Blasting from Heaven. Philip Levine. **SP-LeviP**

Blasts of Autumn as they scatter round, The. Written in October. Charlotte Smith. **CP-SmitC**

Blasts rip Newspaper Gray [*or* grey] Mannahatta's mid day Air Spires. Friday the Thirteenth. Allen Ginsberg. **CP-GinsA**

Blazing in Gold and quenching in Purple. Emily Dickinson. **CP-DickE**

Blazing shark, The. 99 to One. Charles Bukowski. **SP-BukC1**

Bleakness in the town. Hayden Carruth. *Fr.* The Sleeping Beauty. **CP-CarHL**

Bleasdale: The Wooden Circle. Phoebe Hesketh. **SP-HeskP**

Bleecker Street. Jean Garrigue. **SP-GarrJ**

Bleecker Street, Summer. Derek Walcott. **CP-WalcD**

Bleeder. Stephen Dobyns. **SP-DobyS**

Bleeding Gums. James Schuyler. **CP-SchuJ**

Bleeding Hand: or, The Sprig of Eglantine Given to a Maid, The. Robert Herrick. **CP-HerrR**

Bleeding of the mountains. Martin Luther King, Malcolm X. Muriel Rukeyser. **CP-RukeM**

Bleeze. John Hewitt. **CP-HewiJ**

Blemish. Paul Muldoon. **SP-MuldP**

Bleow us all day, a mile away, in a flashing. Skelpick. Donald Davie. **CP-DavDo**

Blepharipappus Glandulosus or White Tidy-Tips. Malcolm Lowry. *Fr.* The Moon in Scandinavia. **CP-LowrM**

Bless / something small. A Pryaer. Robert Creeley. **CP-CreeR**

Bless God, he went as soldiers. Emily Dickinson. **CP-DickE**

Bless J-s-s Ch———, O Cardoness. [On] Maxwell of Cardoness. Robert Burns. **CP-BurnR**

Bless the Lord, O my soul: and all that is within me. Psalm 103. Bible, *O.T.* **AWP** *Fr.* Psalms. **CP-Psal**

Bless the Lord, O my soul. O Lord my God. Psalm 104. Bible, *O.T.* **NAWM-1; OHIP; TrJP; WGRP** *Fr.* Psalms. **CP-Psal**

Bless Thee, O Lord, for the living arc of the sky over me this morning. Glass House Canticle. Carl Sandburg. **CP-SandC**

Bless Zeruah Higley Guernsey of Castleton, Vermont. A Blessing of Women. Stanley Jasspon Kunitz. *Fr.* Words for the Unknown Makers: A Garland of Commemorative Verses. **CP-KuniS**

Blessed, The. William Butler Yeats. **CP-YeatW**

Blessed Are the Angels in Heaven. Richard Eberhart. **CP-EberR**

Blessed are the man and the woman, *par.* by Stephen Mitchell. Bible, *O.T.* *See* Psalm 1: "Blessed is the man that walketh. . . "

Blessed are the undefiled in the way. Psalm 119. Bible, *O.T.* *Fr.* Psalms. **CP-Psal**

Blessed are those who have not seen. In Stratis Viarum III. Arthur Hugh Clough. **SP-ClouA**

Blessed Are You. Leonard Cohen. **CP-CoheL**

Blessed [*or* Blesst] are your north parts, for all this long time. To Mr I. L. John Donne. **CP-DonnJ**

Blessed be the dancers! The dancers. Praise for All Dancers. Robert Bly. **SP-BlyR**

Blessèd be the English and all their ways and works. Jobson's Amen. Rudyard Kipling. **CP-KiplR**

Blessed be the Lord my strength. Psalm 144. Bible, *O.T.* *Fr.* Psalms. **CP-Psal**

Blessed Be the Muses. Allen Ginsberg. **CP-GinsA**

Blessed be the Paps which Thou hast Sucked. Bible, *N.T.*, *tr.* by Richard Crashaw. *Fr.* St. Luke.
(Luke 11; Blessed Be the Paps Which Thou Hast Sucked.) **CP-CrasR**

Blessed be this place. Blood and the Moon. William Butler Yeats. **CP-YeatW**

Blessed Dear & heart's Delight. 1878. Christina Georgina Rossetti. **CP-RosC3**

Blessed Event. Wystan Hugh Auden. **CP-AudeW**

Blessed Event. Marsden Hartley. **CP-HartM**

Blessed flagellants set forth, mounted on tatters of flaming horses, The. John Yau. **SP-YauJo** *Fr.* Predella.

Blessed is every one that feareth the Lord. Psalm 128. Bible, *O.T.* **TRV** *Fr.* Psalms. **CP-Psal**

Blessed is he that considereth the poor. Psalm 41. Bible, *O.T.* *Fr.* Psalms. **CP-Psal**

Blessed is he whose transgression is forgiven, whose sin is covered. Psalm 32. Bible, *O.T.* *Fr.* Psalms. **CP-Psal**

Blessed Is the Man. Marianne Craig Moore. **CP-MoorM**

Blessed is the man that walketh not in the counsel of the ungodly [*or* wicked]. Psalm 1. Bible, *O.T.* **AWP; BiP; TrJP; WGRP** *Fr.* Psalms. **CP-Psal**

Blessed land of Judæa! thrice hallowed of song. Palestine. John Greenleaf Whittier. **CP-WhitJ**

Blessed lot hath he, who having passed. To the Rev. George Coleridge. Samuel Taylor Coleridge. **CP-ColeS**

Blessed moon / noon. Full Moon. William Carlos Williams. **CP-WilW1**

Blessed sister, holy mother, spirit of the fountain. Thomas Stearns Eliot. **EaPr** *Fr.* Ash Wednesday [*or* Ash-Wednesday]. **CP-ElioT**

Blessed Sun. Robert Ranke Graves. **CP-GravR**

Blessed that flock safe penned in Paradise. Christina Georgina Rossetti. *Fr.* Behold a Shaking. **CP-RosC2**

Blessed Virgin Compared to the Air We Breathe, The. Gerard Manley Hopkins. **CP-HopkG**

Blessed Virgin Mary Compared to a Window, The. Thomas Merton. **CP-MertT**

Blessèd was our first age and morning-time. *parody of* Boethius. Rudyard Kipling. **CP-KiplR** *Fr.* The Muse among the Motors.

Blessèd water, blessèd man. . . . Robert Creeley. **CP-CreeR**

Blessed with a joy that only she. The Gift of God. Edwin Arlington Robinson. **CP-RobiE**

Blessing. John Hewitt. **CP-HewiJ**

Blessing. James McAuley. *Fr.* Requiem. **SP-McAuJ**

Blessing, The. John Updike. **CP-UpdiJ**

Blessing, A. James Wright. **CP-WrigJ**

Blessing in Disguise, A. John Ashbery. **SP-AshbJ**

Blessing in this conscious fruit, the hurt, The. Beyond Reason. Stanley Jasspon Kunitz. **SP-KuniS**

Blessing Ode for a Man with Fishbones Around His Neck. Diane Wakoski. **SP-WakoD**

Blessing of the Worms, The. John Gould Fletcher. **SP-FletJ** *Fr.* The Parables of Antichrist.

Blessing of Women, A. Stanley Jasspon Kunitz. *Fr.* Words for the Unknown Makers: A Garland of Commemorative Verses. **CP-KuniS**

Blessings in abundance come. The Good-Night, or Blessing. Robert Herrick. **CP-HerrR**

Blessings of a Country Life, The. Jonathan Swift. *Fr.* Verses from Quilica. **CP-SwifJ**

Blessings on thee, little man. The Barefoot Boy. John Greenleaf Whittier. **CP-WhitJ**

Blessings on thee, little man. John Greenleaf Whittier. **FaPON** *Fr.* The Barefoot Boy. **CP-WhitJ**

Blest as th'immortal Gods is he. Translation of Horace "Epode the 2d" ("Beatus Ille"). Horace, *tr. by* Samuel Johnson. **CP-JohnS** *Fr.* Epodes.

Blest be McMurdo to his latest day! On John McMurdo. Robert Burns. **CP-BurnR**

Blest be the God of love. Evensong [*or* Even-Song]. George Herbert. **CP-HerbG**

Blest be thy name, who didst restore. Upon My Daughter Hannah Wiggin her Recovery from a Dangerous Fever. Anne Bradstreet. **CP-BradA**

Blest is the man who hath not walk'd astray, *par. by* Milton. Bible, *O.T.* *See* Psalm 1: "Blessed is the man that walketh. . . ."

Blest is the sword that leaps from sheath. George Meredith. **CP-MerG2**

Blest is this Isle—our native Land. To the Lady Fleming on Seeing the Foundation Preparing for the Erection of Rydal Chapel, Westmoreland. William Wordsworth. **CP-WorW2**

Blest is yon shepherd, on the turf reclined. Charlotte Smith. **CP-SmitC**

Blest Order, which in power dost so excel[l]. The Priesthood. George Herbert. **CP-HerbG**

Blest pair of Sirens, pledges of Heaven's joy. John Milton. **UnS** *Fr.* At a Solemn Music[k]. **CP-MiltJ**

Blest pair of *Sirens*, pledges of Heav'ns [*or* Heaven's] joy. At a Solemn Music[k]. John Milton. **CP-MiltJ**

Blest Statesman He, Whose Mind's Unselfish Will. William Wordsworth. **CP-WorW2**

Blest the infant Babe. William Wordsworth. **TOF** *Fr.* School-Time. **FHYEP** *Fr.* The Prelude; Growth of a Poet's Mind [1850 vers.]. **CP-WorW3**

Blest was my reign, retiring Cynthia cry'd. Ovid, *tr. by* Samuel Johnson. **CP-JohnS** *Fr.* Amores.

Blest! who far from all mankind. Repose in God. Jeanne Marie Bouvier de la Motte-Guyon, *tr. fr. French by* William Cowper. **CP-CowpW**

Blight. Ralph Waldo Emerson. **CP-EmerR**

Blight. Edna St. Vincent Millay. **CP-MillE**

Blind Always Come as Such a Surprise, The. Ted Kooser. **SP-KoosT**

Blind are their own brothers; we, The. Like Owls. Robert Ranke Graves. **CP-GravR**

Blind Arrow, A. Robert Ranke Graves. **CP-GravR**

Blind Boy, The. Walter de la Mare. **CP-DeLaW**

Blind form birth, they do not know, The. Some Lines Finished Just Before Dawn at the Bedside of a Dying Student / It has Snowed All Night. Miller Williams. **SP-WillM**

Blind from my birth, / Where flowers are springing. Christina Georgina Rossetti. **CP-RosC2**

Blind Girl. Jane Cooper. **SP-CoopJ**

Blind Highland Boy, The; A Tale Told by the Fire-side, After Returning to the Vale of Grasmere. William Wordsworth. **CP-WorW1**

Blind Horses. Robinson Jeffers. **CP-JefR2**

Blind Lead the Blind, The. Wystan Hugh Auden. **CP-AudWJ**

Blind Love. William Shakespeare. *See* Sonnet 148: "O me, what eyes hath Love put in my head."

Blind Maidens of Our Homelessness, The. Kenneth Patchen. **CP-PatcK**

Blind man, A. I can stare at him. A Solitude. Denise Levertov. **CP-LeveD**

Blind man draws his curtains for the night, The. Boarding House. Ted Kooser. **SP-KoosT**

Blind man loves you with his eyes, The. Petitions. Leonard Cohen. **CP-CoheL**

Blind man to the maiden said, The. Robert Browning. **CP-BroR2**

Blind-Man's Buff. William Blake. **CP-BlakW**

Blind Man's Song, The, *tr. from the German of* Rilke. Randall Jarrell. **CP-JarrR**

Blind Sheep, The. Randall Jarrell. **CP-JarrR**

Blind with love, my daughter. Pain for a Daughter. Anne Sexton. **CP-SextA**

Blind'd be the last of men. Kenneth Patchen. **CP-PatcK**

Blinded Bird, The. Thomas Hardy. **CP-HardT**

Blindest buzzard that I know, The. A Sketch. Christina Georgina Rossetti. **CP-RosC3**

Blindman by the name of La Fontaine, A. Haec Fabula Docet. Robert Frost. **CP-FrosR**

Blindness of Samson, The. John Milton. **ImPO; LiTB** *Fr.* Samson Agonistes. **CP-MiltJ**

"I, dark in light, exposed." **TrGrPo**

Blinds are drawn because of the sun, The. *also stands as separate poem and inc. in* The Schoolmaster [A]. David Herbert Lawrence. *Fr.* The Schoolmaster [B]. **CP-LawrD**

Blinds are drawn because of the sun, The. *also stands as sl. diff. separate poem and incl. in* The Schoolmaster [B]. David Herbert Lawrence. *Fr.* The Schoolmaster [A]. **CP-LawrD**

Blinds are drawn because of the sun, The. The Best of School. David Herbert Lawrence. **CP-LawrD**

Blinds me / like the light of that surf. Your Letter. Adrienne Rich. **CP-RicAE**

Blisful lyf, a paisible and a swete, A. The Former Age. Geoffrey Chaucer. **CP-ChauG**

Bliss fell "in love with us" (Knox). I know it, I'm super-hype too. James Liddy. *Fr.* Epithalamion I–IV: "Along a leafy lonely river God-shy-eyed fisher boys." **CP-LiddJ**

Bliss is the plaything of the child. Emily Dickinson. **CP-DickE**

Bliss it is at break of day. Sunrise. Walter de la Mare. **CP-DeLaW**

Bliss of man, The (could pride that blessing find). Alexander Pope. **NOEC; NU** *Fr.* An Essay on Man. **CP-PopeA**

Blisse (last night drunk) did kisse his mothers knee. Upon Blisse. Robert Herrick. **CP-HerrR**

Blister we not for *bursati*? So when the heart is vext. Rudyard Kipling. *Fr.* Certain Maxims of Hafiz. **CP-KiplR**

Blizzard. Louise McNeill. **SP-McNeL**

Blizzard. James Schuyler. **CP-SchuJ**

Blizzard. William Carlos Williams. **CP-WilW1**

Blizzard in the mountains. Dusk. The cabin's light. Hayden Carruth. *Fr.* The Sleeping Beauty. **CP-CarHL**

Blizzard Notes. Carl Sandburg. **CP-SandC**

Blizzard sun upturn tulips chances. Tulip. Louis Zukofsky. **CP-ZukLS**

Blizzard trampling past has left. Hayden Carruth. *Fr.* North Winter. **CP-CarHL**

Blizzards have brought down the beech tree. The Beech. Charles Tomlinson. **CP-TomlC**

Blizzards of paper. Unlearning to Not Speak. Marge Piercy. **SP-PierM**

Blked. John Updike. **CP-UpdiJ**

Bloath, The. Shel Silverstein. **SP-SilS2**

Block. Hayden Carruth. **CP-CarHS**

Block City. Robert Louis Stevenson. **CP-StevR**

Block is bare except for this five-story, The. What the Brand New Freeway Won't Go By. Richard Hugo. **CP-HugoR**

Blocked-out Tree, The. A Quilt-Pattern. Randall Jarrell. **CP-JarrR**

Blocking the sidewalk so. The Gossips. William Carlos Williams. **CP-WilW2**

Blocks. Frank O'Hara. **SP-OharF**

Blond boy wearing thick glasses, A. The Window. Leonard Cohen. **CP-CoheL**

Blond cowl terse as a blunt threat to injure, The. Love among the Manichees. William Dickey. **SP-DickW**

Blond Road, The. Richard Hugo. **CP-HugoR**

Blonde hair flows over her shoulders. Siren. James McAuley. *Fr.* Ten-Mile Run. **SP-McAuJ**

Blood. James Dickey. **CP-DickJ**

Blood. Daniel Gerard Hoffman. **SP-HoffD**

Blood a rarest oil. Oleo Strut. Gilbert Sorrentino. **SP-SorrG**

Blood & Honey. Erica Jong. **SP-JongE**

Blood and the Moon. William Butler Yeats. **CP-YeatW**

Blood began to waste into the clods, The. The Book of the Dead. Thom Gunn. **CP-GunnT**

Blood blister over my thumb-moon. Fox Blood. James Dickey. **CP-DickJ**

Blood Bridge. Jim Carroll. **SP-CarrJ**

Blood Deeper than Night. Lewis Turco. **SP-TurcL**

Blood Flows Back, The. Stevie Smith. **CP-SmitS**

Blood flows in me, but what does it have to do. Living by the Red River. James Wright. **CP-WrigJ**

Blood from the Stone. George Oppen. **CP-OppeG**

"And war."

"Fifty years / Sidereal time."

"In the door, / Long legged, tall."

"Thirties. And / A spectre, The."

Blood goes through your neck veins with a noise they call singing, The. Machine. Gun. Nest. Margaret Atwood. **SP-AtwM2**

Blood-Guilt, The. Robinson Jeffers. **CP-JefR3**

Blood has been harder to dam back than water. The Flood. Robert Frost. **CP-FrosR**

Blood I foresaw. I had put by. Assassin. Charles Tomlinson. **CP-TomlC**

Blood is blood and bone is bone. Mummy. Carl Sandburg. **CP-SandC**

Blood is Justified, The. Muriel Rukeyser. **CP-RukeM**

Blood is more showy (gaudy) than the Breath, The. Emily Dickinson. **SP-DickE**

Blood is thicker than water. Ernest Hemingway. **CP-HemiE**

Blood Lake, The. John Haines. **SP-HainJ**

Blood-Money. Walt Whitman. **CP-WhitW**

Blood of all men of all nations being red, The. Carl Sandburg. *Fr.* The People, Yes. **CP-SandC**

Blood of the Poet, The. William Everson. **SP-EverW**

Blood of the Sun. Kenneth Patchen. **CP-PatcK**

Blood-red and blue glass. Roy Fisher. **SP-FishR** *Fr.* Matrix.

Blood-red bird with one green eye, A. Roundelay. Isabella Gardner. **CP-GardI**

Blood-Sister. Adrienne Rich. **SP-RicA2**

Blood strepped, The. Memo #2. Etheridge Knight. **SP-KnigE**

Blood we give the dead to drink, The. Didactic Poem. Denise Levertov. **CP-LeveD**

Bloodbirth. Audre Lorde. **SP-LordA**

Bloodhounds look like sad old judges, The. Nice Day for a Lynching. Kenneth Patchen. **CP-PatcK**

Bloodroot is white, The. Wendell Berry. *Fr.* Window Poems. **CP-BerrW**

Bloody and a sudden end, A. John Kinsella's Lament for Mrs. Mary Moore. William Butler Yeats. **CP-YeatW**

Bloody Brae, The. John Hewitt. **CP-HewiJ**

Bloody Mary's venomous flames can curl. The Martyrdom of Bishop Farrar. Ted Hughes. **SP-HughT**

Bloody Sire, The. Robinson Jeffers. **CP-JefR3**

Bloom—is Result—to meet a Flower. Emily Dickinson. **CP-DickE**

Bloom upon the Mountain—stated. Emily Dickinson. **CP-DickE**

Bloomingdale Papers, The. Hayden Carruth.

"Aw, Dylan, have you left us? Have you gone?" **CP-CarHS**

"Bitcheries of Madison Avenue, The." **CP-CarHS**

"December now. Winter deepens and darkens. Stars." **CP-CarHS**

"Diagnosis is / Anxiety psychoneurosis, The." **CP-CarHS**

"Expectantly and fearfully I sing." **CP-CarHS**

"For thon demgeorne dreorigne oft." **CP-CarHS**

Hall Five. **CP-CarHS**

"I know there is a country where we go." **CP-CarHS**

"In deep winter the sea roams." **CP-CarHS**

"In the hot high summer I came." **CP-CarHS**

"Once on a night in spring." **CP-CarHS**

"Rule of the majority is / strictly enforced in all matters, The." **CP-CarHS**

"This all begins on a November day." **CP-CarHS**

"'Tis a fine deceit." **CP-CarHS**

"To dig at Luxor, to peer." **CP-CarHS**

Blossom [*or* Blossome], The. John Donne. **CP-DonnJ**

Blossom, The. William Blake. **FHYEP; GoJo; PB; PBBP** *Fr.* Songs of Innocence. **CP-BlakW**

Blossom. Mary Oliver. **SP-OlivM**

Blossom and greenness, making all. The Birthday Wreath. John Greenleaf Whittier. **CP-WhitJ**

Blossom perhaps is an introduction, A. Emily Dickinson. **SP-DickE**

Blossom Themes. Carl Sandburg. **CP-SandC**

Blossomed Thorn, The. John Hewitt. **CP-HewiJ**

Blossoming are people / nimbler than Really. Edward Estlin Cummings. **CP-CummE**

Blossoming Oakwood. James Schuyler. **CP-SchuJ**

Blossoming of the Solitary Date-Tree, The. Samuel Taylor Coleridge. **CP-ColeS**

Blossoms burgeon sumptuously, The. The Happy Tree. Wystan Hugh Auden. **CP-AudWJ**

Blossoms of babies. Handfuls. Carl Sandburg. **CP-SandC**

Blossoms will run away. Emily Dickinson. **CP-DickE**

Blotch of pallor stirs beneath the high, A. In the Dark. David Herbert Lawrence. **CP-LawrD**

Bloud of Abel was a thing, The. Another. Robert Herrick. **CP-HerrR**

Blow, The. Thomas Hardy. **CP-HardT**

Blow, blow your trumpets till they crack. Fame's Penny-Trumpet. "Lewis Carroll." **CP-CarrL**

Blow, Bugle, Blow. Tennyson. *See* The Splendor falls on castle walls.

Blow is Creation, / & the Trumpet the Nasturtium, The. Charles Olson. **SP-OlsoC** *Fr.* The Maximus Poems.

Blow out the candles of your cake. For K. R. on Her Sixtieth Birthday. Richard Wilbur. **CP-WilbR**

Blow, West Wind. Robert Penn Warren. **SP-WarrR**

Blow Your Trumpets. John Donne. *See* At the round earth's imagined corners, blow.

Blowgun and Rattlesnake. James Dickey. **CP-DickJ**

Blowin' in the Wind. "Bob Dylan." **CP-DylaB**

Blowing of the Seed, The. William Everson.

"And then that humming." **SP-EverW**

"If you were to try to say." **SP-EverW**

"Of such touch given." **SP-EverW**

Blown sand heaps on me, that none may learn, The. Pelicans in the Wilderness (A Grave near Halfa). Rudyard Kipling. **PeFWW** *Fr.* Epitaphs of the War [1914–1918]. **CP-KiplR**

Blows the wind today, and the sun and the rain are flying. To S. R. Crockett. Robert Louis Stevenson. **CP-StevR**

Blowsy geraniums, clay pots stained here. Writer-in-Residence. William Matthews. **SP-MattW**

Blude-red rose at Yule may blaw, The. To Daunton Me. Robert Burns. **CP-BurnR**

Bludius et Corona [Blood and the Crown]. Andrew Marvell. **CP-MarvA**

Blue. Robert Creeley. **CP-CreeR**

Blue. Paul Laurence Dunbar. **CP-DunbP**

Blue. James Schuyler. **CP-SchuJ**

Blue Anchor, The. Jane Cooper. **SP-CoopJ**

Blue and dark. *ink version.* David Herbert Lawrence. **CP-LawrD**

Blue and white came out. Lake Michigan Morning. Carl Sandburg. **CP-SandC**

Blue anemone with a dark core, The. Mediterranean in January. David Herbert Lawrence. **CP-LawrD**

Blue Angel, The. Allen Ginsberg. **CP-GinsA**

Blue Bayou. Langston Hughes. **SP-HughL**

Blue bell is the sweetest flower, The. Emily Brontë. **CP-BronE**

Blue-bell springs upon the ledge, A. Spring Song. Paul Laurence Dunbar. **CP-DunbP**

Blue, blue is the grass about the river. The Beautiful Toilet. Ezra Pound, *tr. fr. Mei Sheng, 140 B.C.* **SP-PounE**

Blue Bug. Marianne Craig Moore. **CP-MoorM**

Blue Buildings in the Summer Air, The. Wallace Stevens. **CP-StevW**

Blue butterflies' eyed wings. Kathleen Jessie Raine. **SP-RainK**

Blue-Butterfly Day. Robert Frost. **CP-FrosR**

Blue Cheese and Chili Peppers. Charles Bukowski. **SP-BukC1**

Blue crabs come to the brown pond's edge, The. Crab Crack. John Updike. **CP-UpdiJ**

Blue dark of early morn. From Oslo. Chuck Miller. **SP-MillC**

Blue-dark, still. Winter Dawn. Chuck Miller. **SP-MillC**

Blue devils' / Bluest. Thus. Charles Simic. **SP-SimiC**

Blue Dress, The. Siv Cedering Fox. **SP-CedeS**

Blue Dress. Tom Clark. **SP-ClarT**

Blue Dwarfs. Margaret Atwood. **SP-AtwM2**

Blue exhaust speeds parting's litany, The. Malcolm Lowry. *Fr.* The Canadian Turned Back at the Border. **CP-LowrM**

Blue Eye, The. James Merrill. **SP-MerrJ**

Blue-Eyed Lassie, The. Robert Burns. **CP-BurnR**

Blue-eyed phantom far before, A. Fata Morgana. Christina Georgina Rossetti. **CP-RosC1**

Blue-Flag in the Bog, The. Edna St. Vincent Millay. **CP-MillE**

Blue flags, yellow flags, flags all freckled. July. Christina Georgina Rossetti. *Fr.* The Months: A Pageant. **CP-RosC2**

Blue Flower, The. Muriel Rukeyser. **CP-RukeM**

Blue-Fly, The. Robert Ranke Graves. **CP-GravR**

Blue from Heaven, The. Stevie Smith. **CP-SmitS**

Blue-geese, white-geese, you may say. Hilda Doolittle. **NOBA** *Fr.* The Flowering of the Rod. **CP-DoolH**

Blue Ghazals, The. Adrienne Rich. **CP-RicAE; SP-RicA2**

Blue Girls. John Crowe Ransom. **SP-RansJ**

Blue go up & blue go down. American Lights, Seen from Off Abroad. John Berryman. **CP-BerrJ**

Blue-grained line circles a fragment of the mind, A. For L.G.: Unseen for Twenty Years. Adrienne Rich. **SP-RicA2**

Blue Grotto, The. James Merrill. **SP-MerrJ**

Blue Hill Poems. Frederick Morgan. **SP-MorgF**

   "At the tide-pool pocketed in broken granite."

   "Cricket in the kitchen."

   "Do not wait for the owl to come out."

   "Eyes looked at me from the old stone wall."

   "Green men march along the ground, The."

   "In the deep afternoon."

   "Nothing is better than seaweed on rocks."

   "October in Maine. The human touch."

   "Oh, unapproachable One."

   "We have acquaintances."

   "Worm beneath the grass, The."

Blue in the green trees, what are they climbing? Boys in the Branches. Muriel Rukeyser. **CP-RukeM**

Blue in the west the mountain stands. Vickery's Mountain. Edwin Arlington Robinson. **CP-RobiE**

Blue Is the Sky. George Meredith. **CP-MerG2**

Blue Island Intersection. Carl Sandburg. **CP-SandC**

Blue Jay, The. David Herbert Lawrence. **CP-LawrD**

Blue jay scuffling in the bushes follows, The. On the Move. Thom Gunn. **CP-GunnT**

Blue Jay Way. George Harrison. **CP-Beatl**

Blue July, bright July. July. George Meredith. **CP-MerG1**

Blue leather harness slips off glistening shoulders. Radiant Silhouette I. John Yau. **SP-YauJo**

Blue Lias Inn, The. John Hewitt. **CP-HewiJ**

Blue light is the night harbor-slip. Louis Zukofsky. **PoE** *Fr.* 29 Poems. **CP-ZukLS**

Blue light, morning. This Decoration. Hayden Carruth. **CP-CarHS**

Blue-lights sent up by ship forlorn. The Arch. Herman Melville. **SP-MelvH** *Fr.* Clarel: A Poem and Pilgrimage in the Holy Land.

Blue Like the Heavens. Gary Gildner. **SP-GildG**

Blue Maroons. Carl Sandburg. **CP-SandC**

Blue Mask, The. "Lou Reed." **SP-ReedL**

Blue Moles. Sylvia Plath. **CP-PlatS**

Blue Monday. Langston Hughes. **SP-HughL**

Blue Monday. Diane Wakoski. **SP-WakoD**

Blue Morning Glories. Peter Meinke. **SP-MeinP**

Blue Mountain. James Liddy. **CP-LiddJ**

Blue mountains to the north of the walls. *fr. the Chinese of* Li Po (701-62). Ezra Pound. **SP-PounE**

Blue mountains with snow and blue cold rough water. Happiness. Malcolm Lowry. **CP-LowrM**

Blue Movie. John Ciardi. **SP-CiarJ**

Blue Notes. William Matthews. **SP-MattW**

Blue of morning glory climbs fences and houses, The. Morning Glory Blue. Carl Sandburg. **CP-SandC**

Blue of the heaps of beads poured into her breasts. Blue Monday. Diane Wakoski. **SP-WakoD**

Blue pencil of the wave, The. Social. Charles Bukowski. **SP-BukC1**

Blue pick / up truck, A. Boone County. Etheridge Knight. *Fr.* Missouri Haiku. **SP-KnigE**

Blue Pill, The. Jim Carroll. **SP-CarrJ**

Blue Poles. Jim Carroll. **SP-CarrJ**

Blue preacher / flew toward the swamp, A. Some Herons. Mary Oliver. **SP-OlivM**

Blue Ribbon at Amesbury, A. Robert Frost. **CP-FrosR**

Blue Rider rode over The Bridge into the Bauhaus, The. Expressionist History of German Expressionism. Lawrence Ferlinghetti. **SP-FerlL**

Blue Ridge. Carl Sandburg. **CP-SandC**

Blue Roses. Rudyard Kipling. **CP-KiplR** *Fr.* The Light That Failed.

Blue shot dawn, A. Themes in Contrast. Carl Sandburg. **CP-SandC**

Blue Skies. Archie Randolph Ammons. **SP-AmmoA**

Blue Sky, The. Gary Snyder. **CP-SnydG**

Blue sky to the south, clouds to the north. This Life. Stephen Dobyns. **SP-DobyS**

Blue sky upon the horizon. If I Don't Be There by Morning. "Bob Dylan" *and* Helena Springs. **CP-DylaB**

Blue Sonata. John Ashbery. **SP-AshbJ**

Blue Spruce. Muriel Rukeyser. **CP-RukeM**

Blue Stone. Richard Hugo. **CP-HugoR**

Blue Suburban. Howard Nemerov. **CP-NemeH**

Blue sun in his red cockade, The. The News and the Weather. Wallace Stevens. **CP-StevW**

Blue Swallows, The. Howard Nemerov. **CP-NemeH**

Blue Symphony. John Gould Fletcher. **SP-FletJ**

Blue Teal's Mother. James Wright. **CP-WrigJ**

Blue That Reminds Me of the Boat When She Left, The. Anne Waldman. **SP-WaldA**

Blue, the most beautiful of afternoons. Falling Asleep in a Darkening Room. Al Young. **CP-YounA**

Blue the triangular why. Edward Estlin Cummings. **CP-CummE**

Blue! 'Tis the Life of Heaven, the Domain. John Keats. **CP-KeatJ**

Blue took you, a wing of ash, The. At Dawn. Charles Tomlinson. **CP-TomlC**

Blue Towel, A. James Schuyler. **CP-SchuJ**

Blue Turning Grey. Gilbert Sorrentino. **SP-SorrG**

Blue, unstirrable, dreaming. The Change. James Dickey. **CP-DickJ**

Blue water, and behind. After-Glow. Edward Estlin Cummings. **CP-CummE**

Blue Waves. David St. John. **SP-StJoD**

Blue wave's slumber and the rocky brow, The. Olive Grove. James Merrill. **SP-MerrJ**

Blue windows, blue rooftops. On Rachmaninoff's Birthday. Frank O'Hara. **SP-OharF**

Blue Wing, The. Donald Hall. **CP-HallD**

Blue woman with sticking out breasts hanging, A. Edward Estlin Cummings. **CP-CummE**

Blue woolen glove folded over like an old one dollar bill someone keeps. Predella. John Yau. **SP-YauJo**

Bluebeard. Edna St. Vincent Millay. **CP-MillE**

Bluebeard. Sylvia Plath. **CP-PlatS**

Bluebeard. Let the gentle wife prepare. Ralph Waldo Emerson. **CP-EmerR**

Bluebeard's Wife. Howard Nemerov. *Fr.* Seven Macabre Songs. **CP-NemeH**

Bluebells. Louis MacNeice. **CP-MacNL**

Bluebells come crowding a fellside. The Metamorphosis. Charles Tomlinson. **CP-TomlC**

Blueberries. Robert Frost. **CP-FrosR**

Bluebird, What Do You Feed On? Carl Sandburg. **CP-SandC**

Blueblack swallows with their saffron breasts, The. Swallows. Marsden Hartley. **CP-HartM**

Bluebonnets in Texas in a cold spring. Deux Morceaux en Forme de Banane. Gilbert Sorrentino. **SP-SorrG**

Bluefin may nose / up to a window, glum, A. This Fog. Brendan Galvin. **SP-GalvB**

Blueflags. William Carlos Williams. **CP-WilW1**

Blueness. David Herbert Lawrence. **CP-LawrD**

Blues, The. Byron. **CP-Byron**

Blues, The. William Matthews. **SP-MattW**

Blues, The. Jim Morrison. **SP-MorrJ**

Blues. Edwin Rolfe. **CP-RolfE**

Blues. Derek Walcott. **CP-WalcD**

Blues at Dawn. Langston Hughes. **SP-HughL**

Blues Don't Change, The. Al Young. **CP-YounA**

Blues for Jimmy. Thomas McGrath. **SP-McGrT**

Blues for John Coltrane, Dead at 41. William Matthews. **SP-MattW**

Blues for the Old Revolutionary Woman. Thomas McGrath. **SP-McGrT**

Blues for Warren. Thomas McGrath. **SP-McGrT**

Blues in December. Al Young. **CP-YounA**

Blues may be the life you've led, The. A Good Woman Feeling Bad. Maya Angelou. **SP-AngeM**

Bluet, The. James Schuyler. **CP-SchuJ**

Bluet is a small flower, creamy-throated, that grows in patches, The. Footnote. James Schuyler. **CP-SchuJ**

Bluewhite birdlight. Monday Beach, Cold Day. Charles Bukowski. **SP-BukC2**

"Blumine" Risponde. Christina Georgina Rossetti. *Fr.* Il Rosseggiar Dell'Oriente Canzoniere. **CP-RosC3**

Blunder is an estimate, The. Emily Dickinson. **CP-DickE**

Blush as of roses, A. Le Marais du Cygne. John Greenleaf Whittier. **CP-WhitJ**

Blush as you stroke the curves—. Food of the Dead. Robert Ranke Graves. **CP-GravR**

Blush, folly, blush: here's none that fears. Ben Jonson. **CP-JonsB** *Fr.* The Poetaster.

Blythe hae I been on yon hill. Song. Robert Burns. **CP-BurnR**

Blythe Was She. Robert Burns.
  ("By Oughtertyre grows the aik.") **CP-BurnR**
  (Song.—Composed at Auchtertyre on Miss Euphemia Murray of Lentrose.) **CP-BurnR**

Bo, may you someday. Of Brook and Stone. Hayden Carruth. **CP-CarHS**

Bo was three when we slugged through Arizona, The. Sonnet. Hayden Carruth. **CP-CarHS** *Fr.* Sonnets.

Boa Constrictor. Shel Silverstein. **SP-SilS2**

Boadicea: An Ode. William Cowper. **CP-CowpW**

Boanerges Blitzen, servant of the Queen. The Man Who Could Write. Rudyard Kipling. **CP-KiplR**

Boar. Daniel Gerard Hoffman. **SP-HoffD**

Boarding House. Ted Kooser. **SP-KoosT**

Boardwalks are empty, the cafés closed, The. Elegy of Last Resort. Howard Nemerov. **CP-NemeH**

Boast, The. Rita Dove. **SP-DoveR**

Boast of heraldry, the pomp of pow'r, The. Thomas Gray. **OBD** *Fr.* Elegy Written in a Country Churchyard. **CP-GrayT**

Boasts time mocks cumber Rome. Wren. At Briggflatts Meetinghouse. Basil Bunting. **CP-BuntB**

Boat, A. Margaret Atwood. **SP-AtwM2**

Boat, The. Charles Olson. **CP-OlsoC**

Boat, The. Anne Sexton. *Fr.* The Death of the Fathers. **CP-SextA**

Boat, The. Stevie Smith. **CP-SmitS**

Boat amid the ripples, drifting, rocking, A. Pastime. Christina Georgina Rossetti. **CP-RosC2**

Boat, beneath a sunny sky, A. Acrostic: A boat, beneath a sunny sky. "Lewis Carroll." **CP-CarrL** *Fr.* Through the Looking-Glass.

Boat-Builder's Caulking Irons, The. John Hewitt. **CP-HewiJ**

Boat moves slowly through the fens, The. Slow Boat Ride. Richard Eberhart. **CP-EberR**

Boat of Ra-Set moves with the sun, The. Canto 98. Ezra Pound. *Fr.* Cantos. **CP-PoCan**

Boat on the Serchio, The. Percy Bysshe Shelley. **CP-ShelP**
  "Our boat is asleep on Serchio's stream." **Mes**

Boat Ride. Tess Gallagher. **SP-GallT**

Boat Song. Sir Walter Scott. *See* Hail to the Chief Who in Triumph Advances.

Boat Stealing. William Wordsworth. *See* One evening (surely I was led by her).

Boat that sails upon the sea, A. The Way of the World. Christina Georgina Rossetti. **CP-RosC3**

Boat that took my love away, The. The Boat. Stevie Smith. **CP-SmitS**

Boathouse, The. David St. John. **SP-StJoD**

Boating party, The. The Magic Morning. Stevie Smith. **CP-SmitS**

Boatman rowed into, The. The Blue Grotto. James Merrill. **SP-MerrJ**

Boatmen of Santorin, The. Archibald MacLeish. **CP-MacLA**

Boatmen on the bay of Santorin, The. The Boatmen of Santorin. Archibald MacLeish. **CP-MacLA**

Boatmen swing their lanterns on the Caribbean, The. Malcolm Lowry. **CP-LowrM**

Boats in a Fog. Robinson Jeffers. **CP-JefR1**

Boats' lights in the dawn going so swiftly the, The. Charles Olson. **SP-OlsoC** *Fr.* The Maximus Poems.

Boats of Newhaven and Folkestone and Dover. The French Wars. Rudyard Kipling. **CP-KiplR**

Boats sail on the rivers, / And ships sail on the seas. Christina Georgina Rossetti. **CP-RosC2**

Bob. Charles Kenneth Williams. **CP-WillC; SP-WillC**

Bob and I / in different rooms. Quarrel. Grace Paley. **CP-PaleG**

Bob Dylan's Blues. "Bob Dylan." **CP-DylaB**

Bob Dylan's Dream. "Bob Dylan." **CP-DylaB**

Bob Dylan's New Orleans Rag. "Bob Dylan." **CP-DylaB**

Bob Dylan's 115th Dream. "Bob Dylan." **CP-DylaB**

Bob o' Dumblane, The. Robert Burns. **CP-BurnR**

Bob Southey! You're a poet—poet-laureate. Dedication. Byron. **CTC; EnRP; FiP; OAEL-2; OBSV** *Fr.* Don Juan. **CP-Byron**

Bob Southey! You're a poet—poet-laureate. Southey and Wordsworth. Byron. **TrGrPo** *Fr.* Dedication: "Bob Southey! You're a poet--poet-laureate." **CTC; EnRP; OAEL-2; OBSV** *Fr.* Don Juan. **CP-Byron**

Bob Visits Friends. Grace Paley. **CP-PaleG**

Bobbie. Robert Creeley. **CP-CreeR**

Bobbing in the waters of the womb. The Buddha in the Womb. Erica Jong. **SP-JongE**

Bobby Delano. Robert Lowell. **SP-LoweR**

Bobò is dead, but don't take off your hat. The Funeral of Bobò. Joseph Brodsky, *tr. fr. Russian by* Richard Wilbur. **CP-WilbR**

Bobolink! / Bobolink! / Spink! Max Schling, Max Schling, Lend Me Your Green Thumb. Ogden Nash. **CP-NashO**

Bobolink, The. Edna St. Vincent Millay. **CP-MillE**

Bobolink is gone, The. Emily Dickinson. **CP-DickE**

Bobs. Rudyard Kipling. **CP-KiplR**

Boccaccio: The Plague Years. Rita Dove. **SP-DoveR**

Bodiless God. David Herbert Lawrence. **CP-LawrD**

Body / Eternal Shadow of the finite Soul, The. Body Imaging Soul. Samuel Taylor Coleridge. **CP-ColeS**

Body, The. Robert Herrick. **CP-HerrR**

Body, The. Frederick Morgan. **SP-MorgF**

Body / the endless dunes, The. Easter. Patti Smith. **SP-SmitP**

Body, The. Charles Kenneth Williams. **SP-WillC**

Body and Soul. "Anvari", *tr. fr. Persian by* Ralph Waldo Emerson. **CP-EmerR**

Body and Soul. Hilda Doolittle. **CP-DoolH**

Body and Spirit I surrendered whole. The Wonder. Rudyard Kipling. *Fr.* Epitaphs of the War [1914–1918]. **CP-KiplR**

Body Beside the Ties, The. Kenneth Patchen. **CP-PatcK**

Body, blind with sleep, A. Statue. Gerrit Achterberg, *tr. fr. Dutch by* Adrienne Rich. **CP-RicAE**

Body cannot lie, but its betrayals, The. Handclap. Muriel Rukeyser. **CP-RukeM**

Body Count. Leonard Nathan. **SP-NathL**

Body dies / little by little, The. The Deaths of the Other Children. Margaret Atwood. **SP-AtwM1**

Body frozen in the lake, The. The Body. Frederick Morgan. **SP-MorgF**

Body grows without, The. Emily Dickinson. **CP-DickE**

Body Imaging Soul. Samuel Taylor Coleridge. **CP-ColeS**

Body is like a November birch facing the full moon, The. Solitude Late at Night in the Woods. Robert Bly. **SP-BlyR**

Body is the Soul's [*or* Soules] poor[e] house, or home, The. The Body. Robert Herrick. **CP-HerrR**

Body of a child lay in the pool, The. Round. Jenny Joseph. **SP-JoseJ**

Body of a sick world hung on a lofty cross. The Last Judgment. John Gould Fletcher. **SP-FletJ** *Fr.* The Parables of Christ.

Body of Desire, The. David St. John. *Fr.* Study for the World's Body. **SP-StJoD**

Body of God, The. David Herbert Lawrence. **CP-LawrD**

Body of itself is clean, but the caged mind, The. Obscenity. David Herbert Lawrence. **CP-LawrD**

Body of Jesus taken down from the cross. Loin Cloth. Carl Sandburg. **CP-SandC**

Body of Romulus, The. Stephen Dobyns. **SP-DobyS**

Body Politic, The. Donald Hall. **CP-HallD**

Body's Curse, The. Stephen Dobyns. **SP-DobyS**

Body's Hope, The. Stephen Dobyns. **SP-DobyS**

Body's Journey, The. Stephen Dobyns. **SP-DobyS**

Body's salt, the soule is; which when gon, The. The Soul Is the Salt. Robert Herrick. **CP-HerrR**

Body's Strength, The. Stephen Dobyns. **SP-DobyS**

Body's Weight, The. Stephen Dobyns. **SP-DobyS**

Boeotian. Robert Frost. **CP-FrosR**

Boer War Bread Strike. James Schuyler. **CP-SchuJ**

'Boes. Carl Sandburg. **CP-SandC**

Bog cotton and whin. A stone. Donegal. Brendan Galvin. **SP-GalvB**

Bog-Face. Stevie Smith. **CP-SmitS**

Bog Oak. Seamus Heaney. **SP-HeanS**

Bog Queen. Seamus Heaney. **SP-HeanS**

Bogland. Seamus Heaney. **SP-HeanS**

Bogside, Derry, 1971. John Hewitt. **CP-HewiJ**

Boh Da Thone was a warrior bold. The Ballad of Boh Da Thone. Rudyard Kipling. **CP-KiplR**

Bohemian, The. Paul Laurence Dunbar. **CP-DunbP**

Bohemian Hymn. Ralph Waldo Emerson. **CP-EmerR**

Boil. John Updike. **CP-UpdiJ**

Boilermakers. Gilbert Sorrentino. **SP-SorrG**

Boiling Water, The. Kenneth Koch. **SP-KochK**

Bois seul. Samuel Beckett. **CP-BeckS**

Bokardo. Edwin Arlington Robinson. **CP-RobiE**

Bold be the critic, zealous to his trust. 2.2. Horace, *tr.* by Samuel Johnson. **CP-JohnS** *Fr.* Epistles.

Bold encroachers on the deep, The. The Run upon the Bankers. Jonathan Swift. **CP-SwifJ**

Bold Horatius. Wilfred Owen. **CP-OwenW**

Bold is the man who, in this nicer age. Prologue to Tancred and Sigismunda. James Thomson. **CP-ThomJ**

Bold words affirmed, in days when faith was strong. At Sea off the Isle of Man. William Wordsworth. *Fr.* Poems Composed or Suggested During a Tour, in the Summer of 1833. **CP-WorW2**

Boldness[e] in Love. Thomas Carew. **CP-CareT**

Bolero, silk-tassled, the fuchsia, The. For Kazuko. Rita Dove. **SP-DoveR**

"Bolinas and Me. . . ." Robert Creeley. **CP-CreeR**

Bolivar. John Greenleaf Whittier. **CP-WhitJ**

Bolsheviks. Aba Shtoltsenberg, *tr. fr. Yiddish* by Stanley Kunitz. **CP-KuniS**

Bolt and bar the shutter. *fr.* Words for Music Perhaps. William Butler Yeats. **CP-YeatW**

Bolt-hole of brigandage, old keep. *after* Corbière. Derek Mahon. **SP-MahoD**

Bolton-Le-Moors, 1960. Phoebe Hesketh. **SP-HeskP**

Bolyai, the Geometer. Donald Davie. **CP-DavDo**

Bomb Test. Gary Snyder. **CP-SnydG**

Bomb (II). Pablo Neruda, *tr. fr. Spanish* by Ben Belitt. **SP-NeruP**

Bombarded City, The. Thomas Merton. **CP-MertT**

Bombardment. David Herbert Lawrence. **CP-LawrD**

Bombed in London. Rudyard Kipling. *Fr.* Epitaphs of the War [1914–1918]. **CP-KiplR**

Bombed Public House, The. John Hewitt. **CP-HewiJ**

Bombers spread out, temperature steady, The. War and Silence. Robert Bly. **SP-BlyR**

Bon bon il est un pays. Samuel Beckett. **CP-BeckS**

"Bon soir, monsieur," they called to me. The Street Called Crooked. Countee Cullen. **CP-CullC**

Bon Voyage. Edwin Arlington Robinson. **CP-RobiE**

Bon Voyage. Edwin Rolfe. **CP-RolfE**

Bond and Free. Robert Frost. **CP-FrosR**

Bondman, The. Robert Herrick. **CP-HerrR**

Bone. Thom Gunn. **CP-GunnT**

Bone. Charles Tomlinson. **CP-TomlC**

Bone Dreams. Seamus Heaney. **SP-HeanS**

Bone-Flower Elegy. Robert Earl Hayden. **CP-HaydR**

Bone Hunting. Richard Hugo. **CP-HugoR**

Bone-idle, I lie listening to the rain. Dejection. Derek Mahon. **SP-MahoD**

Bone Poem. Mary Oliver. **SP-OlivM**

Bone that has no Marrow, The. Emily Dickinson. **CP-DickE**

Bone to his bone, grain to his grain of dust. To Every Seed His Own Body. Christina Georgina Rossetti. **CP-RosC2**

Bones. Frederick Morgan. **SP-MorgF**

Bones. Carl Sandburg. **CP-SandC**

Bones a-gittin' achy. Chrismus Is A-Comin'. Paul Laurence Dunbar. **CP-DunbP**

Bones go under the soil, under the soil, The. Bones. Frederick Morgan. **SP-MorgF**

Bones of Coleridge, The. Richard Eberhart. **CP-EberR**

Bones of My Father, The. Etheridge Knight. **SP-KnigE**

Bones of saints are praised above their flesh, The. Reliquary. Adrienne Rich. **CP-RicAE**

Bones wrenched, weak whimper, lids wrinkled, first dazzle known. Aware. Wystan Hugh Auden. **CP-AudWJ**

Bonfire, The. Robert Frost. **CP-FrosR**

Bonfire. Tess Gallagher. **SP-GallT**

Bonfires, The. Wystan Hugh Auden. **CP-AudeW**

Bonfires, The. Rudyard Kipling. **CP-KiplR**

Bonhoeffer in his skylit cell. Christmas Trees. Geoffrey Hill. **CP-HillG**

Bonie Bell. Robert Burns. **CP-BurnR**

Bonie Dundee. Robert Burns. **CP-BurnR**

Bonie Lad That's Far Awa, The. Robert Burns. **CP-BurnR**

Bonie Laddie, Highland Laddie. Robert Burns. **CP-BurnR**

Bonie Lass Made the Bed to Me, The. Robert Burns. *See* When Januar' wind war blawing cauld.

Bonie Mary. Robert Burns. **CP-BurnR**

Bonnie Broukit Bairn, The. "Hugh MacDiarmid." **SP-MacDH**

Bonnie Peg. Robert Burns. **CP-BurnR**

Bonnie [*or* Bonny] Wee Thing, The. Robert Burns. **CP-BurnR** ("Wishfully I look and languish.") **CP-BurnR**

Bonniest lad that e'er I saw, The. Highland Laddie. Robert Burns. **CP-BurnR**

Bonny and stout and brown, without a hat. Merry Maid. John Clare. **SP-ClarJ**

Bononian, sis Rufa, Rufus' lum fell at. Catullus. *See* Carmen 59: "Menenius' wife, / a red-headed cat from Bologna."

Bonsai tree / in the attractive pot, The. A Work of Artifice. Marge Piercy. **SP-PierM**

Boobyhatch's bars, the guards, the nurses, The. Ontological Episode of the Asylum. Hayden Carruth. **CP-CarHS**

Boogah Man, The. Paul Laurence Dunbar. **CP-DunbP**

Boogie: 1 A.M. Langston Hughes. **SP-HughL**

Boogie With O.O. Gabugah. Al Young. **CP-YounA**

Boojum Tree, The. Richard Shelton. **SP-ShelR**

Book, The. Hayden Carruth. *Fr.* Contra Mortem. **CP-CarHL**

Book, The. Frank Templeton Prince. **CP-PrinF**

Book, The. Adrienne Rich. **CP-RicAE; SP-RicA2**

Book, The. John Greenleaf Whittier. **CP-WhitJ**

Book, The. Miller Williams. **SP-WillM**

Book came forth of late, called PETER BELL, A. On the Detraction Which Followed the Publication of a Certain Poem. William Wordsworth. **CP-WorW2**

Book Club. Ted Kooser. **SP-KoosT**

Book goes fluttering crazily through the space of my room toward the wall like a bird, The. My Book, My Book. Charles Kenneth Williams. **SP-WillC**

Book is golden with an orange spine, and the girl, The. Katia Reading. Stephen Dobyns. **SP-DobyS**

Book is only the Heart's Portrait, A. Emily Dickinson. **SP-DickE**

Book of Ahania, The. William Blake. **CP-BlakW**

Book of Ancestors. Margaret Atwood. **SP-AtwM1**

Book of Annandale, The. Edwin Arlington Robinson. **CP-RobiE**

Book of Ephraim, The. James Merrill. Lost in Translation. **SP-MerrJ**

Book of Job and a Draft of a Poem to Praise the Paths of the Living, The. George Oppen. **CP-OppeG**

Book of Kells, The. Howard Nemerov. **CP-NemeH**

Book of Los, The. William Blake. **CP-BlakW** Immortal, The. **LiTB; LoBV; MeMBP**

Book of Nature, The. Richard Eberhart. **CP-EberR**

Book of Resemblances, A. Robert Duncan. **SP-DuncR**

Book of the council major. Canto 25. Ezra Pound. *Fr.* Cantos. **CP-PoCan**

Book of the Dead, The. Thom Gunn. **CP-GunnT**

Book of the Dead, The. Muriel Rukeyser. **CP-RukeM**

Book of the Duchesse, The. Geoffrey Chaucer. **CP-ChauG** Dream, The. **FiP; PBBP**

Book of the Jungle. John Haines. **SP-HainJ**

Book of Thel, The. William Blake. **CP-BlakW** " 'O little cloud,' the virgin said, "I charge thee tell to me."" **OBD** Secrets of the Earth, The. **NOBE** Thel. Thel's Motto. **ChTr** "Then Thel astonish'd view'd the Worm upon its dewy bed."

Book of Urizen [*or* First Book of Urizen], The. William Blake. **CP-BlakW**

Book of Wild Flowers, The. Joseph Ceravolo. **SP-CeraJ**

Book Our Mothers Read, The. John Greenleaf Whittier. **BLRP** *Fr.* Miriam. **CP-WhitJ** (Knowledge.) **PoToHe**

Book thou givest, dear as such, The. The Little Friend. Elizabeth Barrett Browning. **CP-BroEB**

Book was writ[t] of late called [*or* call'd] *Tetrachordon*, A. John Milton. **CP-MiltJ** (Sonnet 12: "Book was writt of late call'd Tetrachordon, A.") **CP-MiltJ**

Book-Worms, The. Robert Burns. **CP-BurnR**

Bookcase has its books, a horse supports its rider, A. The Body's Weight. Stephen Dobyns. **SP-DobyS**

Booker T. Washington. Paul Laurence Dunbar. **CP-DunbP**

Booker Washington Trilogy, The. Nicholas Vachel Lindsay. **CP-LindV**
  John Brown. **MoAmPo**
  King Solomon and the Queen of Shiba.
  "Lady's in return may grasp as much, The." **DIP**
  Simon Legree—A Negro Sermon. **HBMV; InMe; LiTA; MeMAP;**
    MoVE; NePA; TAP
  (Negro Sermon—Simon Legree, A.) **MoAmPo**
Bookful Blockhead, The. Alexander Pope. **OBSV** *Fr.* An Essay on
  Criticism. **CP-PopeA**
Books. Erica Jong. **SP-JongE**
Books. William Wordsworth. *Fr.* The Prelude; Growth of a Poet's Mind
  [1805 vers.]. **CP-WorW3**
Books. William Wordsworth. *Fr.* The Prelude; Growth of a Poet's Mind
  [1850 vers.]. **CP-WorW3**
  "Gracious spirit o'er this earth presides, A." **OBRV**
  "He, who in his youth." **TOF**
  There Was a Boy. **CP-WorW1; ChER; FHYEP; FaBoRV; MeMBP;**
    NOBRP; OBRV; PoEL-4, *book* 5, *ll.* 364–397;
  (Boy of Winander, The.) **PoE,** *book* 5, *ll.* 364–388;
  (Winander Lake.) **FiP,** *book* 5, *ll.* 364–388;
  There Was a Boy. **RB,** *book* 5, *ll.* 389–422;
  "These mighty workmen of our later age." **EnRP**
  "Thirteen years / Or haply less, I might have seen, when first." **OxAEP-2**
  "When Contemplation, like the night-calm felt." **OAEL-2**
  "Wherupon I told, / That once in the stillness of a summer's moon."
  PoEL-4
Books and the Man I sing, the first who brings. Alexander Pope. *See* To
  Dr. Jonathan Swift.
Books, books, books! Elizabeth Barrett Browning. **WPOW** *Fr.* Aurora
  Leigh. **CP-BroEB**
Books, do not look at me. Sand in the Air. Louis MacNeice. **CP-MacNL**
Books In the Running Brooks. Christina Georgina Rossetti. **CP-RosC3**
Books litter the bed, / leaves the lawn. It. October. James Schuyler. **CP-**
  SchuJ
Books Men Die For. Carl Sandburg. **CP-SandC**
Books which are stitched up the center with coarse white thread. Books.
  Erica Jong. **SP-JongE**
Booleys, The. John Hewitt. **CP-HewiJ**
Boom. Ted Hughes. **SP-HughT**
  "And faces at the glutted shop-windows."
  Bar-Toom TV.
  Kafka.
  Tutorial.
  Wino.
Boom! Howard Nemerov. **CP-NemeH**
Boon Nature yields each day a brag which we now first behold. Nature.
  Ralph Waldo Emerson. *Fr.* Quatrains. **CP-EmerR**
Boone. Wendell Berry. **CP-BerrW**
Boone County. Etheridge Knight. *Fr.* Missouri Haiku. **SP-KnigE**
Boop-Boop-Adieup, Little Group! Ogden Nash. **CP-NashO**
Boot and Saddle. Robert Browning. **HBV; OAEP; SoSe** *Fr.* Cavalier
  Tunes. **CP-BroR1**
Boot, saddle, to horse, and away! Boot and Saddle. Robert Browning.
  HBV; OAEP; SoSe *Fr.* Cavalier Tunes. **CP-BroR1**
Bootblack, The. Charles Tomlinson. **CP-TomlC**
Booth led boldly with his big bass drum. General William Booth Enters into
  Heaven. Nicholas Vachel Lindsay. **CP-LindV**
Boots. Rudyard Kipling. **CP-KiplR**
Boots of Spanish Leather. "Bob Dylan." **CP-DylaB**
Bop Lyrics. Allen Ginsberg. **CP-GinsA**
Bordello. Lewis Turco. **SP-TurcL**
  Envoi: The Wind Carol.
  (Wind Carol, The.) **SM**
  Hank Fedder.
  Jason Potter.
  Jasper Olson.
  Jonathan Hawkins.
  Lafe Grat.
  Rick De Travaille. **SM**
  Simon Judson. **SM**
  Will Somers.
Border Ballad, A. Paul Laurence Dunbar. **CP-DunbP**
Border is what creates illegal aliens, The. Hayden Carruth. *Fr.* The
  Sleeping Beauty. **CP-CarHL**
Border Line. Langston Hughes. **SP-HughL**
Border with no country. Sleep. William Matthews. **SP-MattW**
Borderers, The. A Tragedy. William Wordsworth. **CP-WorW1**

Bored to Choresis. Allen Tate. **CP-TateA**
Boredom, Ennui, Depression. David Herbert Lawrence. **CP-LawrD**
Boreman takes tole, cheats, flatters, lyes, yet Boreman. Upon Boreman.
  Epig. Robert Herrick. **CP-HerrR**
Borges Death Mask. Jim Carroll. **SP-CarrJ**
Borinage receded, at last, like a bad dream, The. Vincent. Edwin Rolfe.
  CP-RolfE
Boris Pasternak. "Anna Akhmatova", *tr. fr. Russian by* Stanley Kunitz *with*
  Max Hayward. **CP-KuniS**
Born a million years ago you stay here a million years. . . watching the.
  Blue Ridge. Carl Sandburg. **CP-SandC**
Born a poor young country boy. Mother Nature's Son. The Beatles. **CP-**
  Beatl
Born ailing on a hemisphere apart, *sl. diff. vers. incl. in* Perhaps for
  Eridanus. Malcolm Lowry. **CP-LowrM**
Born & lost in a throw of time. Romance. Anne Waldman. **SP-WaldA**
Born at "The Bell" in Gloucester. Homage to George Whitefield. Donald
  Davie. **CP-DavDo**
Born for this world. Tendril. Leonard Nathan. **SP-NathL**
Born from ignoble stock on a day of dearth. Lack. Robert Ranke Graves.
  CP-GravR
Born green we were. Firesong. Sylvia Plath. **CP-PlatS**
Born I was to be old. Anacreontic. Robert Herrick. **CP-HerrR**
Born[e] I was to meet with Age. On Himselfe. Robert Herrick. **CP-HerrR**
Born in a sour waste lot. Nasturtium. Thom Gunn. **CP-GunnT**
Born in December. Muriel Rukeyser. **CP-RukeM**
Born in Red Hook, Brooklyn, in the year of who knows when. Joey. "Bob
  Dylan" *and* Jacques Levy. **CP-DylaB**
Born in the garret, in the kitchen bred. A Sketch from Private Life.
  Byron. **CP-Byron**
Born in this island, maimed by history. The Dilemma. John Hewitt. **CP-**
  HewiJ
Born in this world. Gospel Noble Truths. Allen Ginsberg. **CP-GinsA**
Born, it's not good for much, a vehicle. The Body's Journey. Stephen
  Dobyns. **SP-DobyS**
Born like a dwarf. Speaking Bitterness. Anne Sexton. **CP-SextA**
Born of mobs, born of steam. Nicholas Vachel Lindsay. *Fr.* The Kallyope
  Yell. **CP-LindV**
Born of the sorrowful of heart. For Paul Laurence Dunbar. Countee
  Cullen. **CP-CullC** *Fr.* Four Epitaphs.
Born salesman, am I. And One for My Dame. Anne Sexton. **CP-SextA**
Born to be. born to be me. Balance. Patti Smith. **SP-SmitP**
Born Yesterday. Philip Larkin. **CP-LarkP**
Borne down by bitter misfortune. Carmen 68. Catullus. *Fr.* Carmina. **CP-**
  Catul
Borne down by the inability to lift the heaviness. Charles Olson. **CP-OlsoC**
Borne on the warm wing of the western gale. The Return of the Nightingale.
  Written in May 1791. Charlotte Smith. **CP-SmitC**
Borough, The, *sels.* George Crabbe.
  Alms-House and Trustees, The. **SP-CrabG**
  Arrival of the Players, The. **SP-CrabG**
  Condemned Felon, The. **SP-CrabG**
  Election, The. **SP-CrabG**
  Poor and Their Dwellings, The. **SP-CrabG**
  Sea: A Summer and Winter View, The. **SP-CrabG**
  Vicar, The. **SP-CrabG**
  "But let applause be dealt in all we may." **OBNC**
Borrow Urania's subtile wings. Ralph Waldo Emerson. **CP-EmerR**
Borrowed Line. David Markson. **CP-MarkD**
Borrowed Ones, The. Tess Gallagher. **SP-GallT**
Borrowed wings on his ankles. Perseus. Louis MacNeice. **CP-MacNL**
Borrowing from the French. Ralph Waldo Emerson. *Fr.* Quatrains. **CP-**
  EmerR
  (Needless Worry.) **TreFT**
Boss came around at Christmas, The. A Little Song about Charity. Thomas
  McGrath. **SP-McGrT**
Boss, the crane operator, one of the workers, a friend of somebody in the
  junkyard, The. Fire. Charles Kenneth Williams. **SP-WillC**
Boston. Ralph Waldo Emerson. **CP-EmerR**
Boston. Edwin Arlington Robinson. **CP-RobiE**
Boston Ballad, A [*or* A Boston Ballad *1854*]. Walt Whitman. **CP-WhitW**
Boston College team has gold helmets, under which the, The. The Hockey
  Poem. Robert Bly. **SP-BlyR**
Boston Common. John Berryman. **CP-BerrJ**
Boston Common—Long Time Ago. Marsden Hartley. **CP-HartM**
Boston Evening Transcript, The. Thomas Stearns Eliot. **CP-ElioT**
Boston 5:00 A.M.—10/74. Etheridge Knight. **SP-KnigE**

Boston: From the Embankment. Dabney Stuart. *Fr.* The Charles River. **SP-StuaD**

Boston has a festival. In the Public Garden. Marianne Craig Moore. **CP-MoorM**

Boston Hymn. Ralph Waldo Emerson. **CP-EmerR**

Boston Lying-In. John Updike. *Fr.* Waiting Rooms. **CP-DickE**

Boston Portrait Projections. Marsden Hartley. **CP-HartM**

Corillyn is Dark.

Rapture.

This Lady Rides a Languid Dromedary toward Her Dear-God.

Boston's used bookshops, anachronisms from London. Napoleon. Robert Lowell. **SP-LoweR**

Bosun is a pimp as white as snow, The. Visiting the Wreck: An Able Seaman Explains. Malcolm Lowry. **CP-LowrM**

Bosun's Song. Malcolm Lowry. **CP-LowrM**

Boswell: Sir, what is the chief. Kenneth Rexroth. **SP-RexrK** *Fr.* Zoraster long ago / Said poetry presents us. **CP-RexKL** *Fr.* The Dragon and the Unicorn.

Boswell—you old rake—I have tried to imitate. To James Boswell in London. Erica Jong. **SP-JongE**

Bosworth Field. Robert Lowell. **SP-LoweR**

Botanist. Ralph Waldo Emerson. *Fr.* Quatrains. **CP-EmerR**

Botanist on Alp (No. 1). Wallace Stevens. **CP-StevW**

Botanist on Alp (No. 2). Wallace Stevens. **CP-StevW**

Botched job, / the blindfold slipped, he sees, A. Newsreel: Man and Firing Squad. Margaret Atwood. **SP-AtwM1**

Both. Stephen Berg. **SP-BergS**

Both beautiful, one a gazebo. Louis. Paul Muldoon. *Fr.* 7, Middagh Street. **SP-MuldP**

Both eaching come ghostlike. Edward Estlin Cummings. **CP-CummE**

Both Hansel and Jack hated their mothers. Hidden Meanings. Dabney Stuart. **SP-StuaD**

Both lurks and shines hid in an Amber-tear. Martial, *tr. fr. Latin by* Richard Lovelace. **CP-LoveR**

Both robbed of air, we both lie in one ground. Hero and Leander. John Donne. **CP-DonnJ**

Both Sides of the Medal. David Herbert Lawrence. **CP-LawrD**

Both, the company of men. The Company of Men. Charles Olson. **CP-OlsoC**

Both were jailbirds; no speechmakers at all. Jack London and O. Henry. Carl Sandburg. **CP-SandC**

Both you two have. To the Yew and Cypress to Grace His Funeral. Robert Herrick. **CP-HerrR**

Bother, The, *parody of* Arthur Clough. Rudyard Kipling. **CP-KiplR** *Fr.* The Muse among the Motors.

Bothwell Castle. William Wordsworth. **CP-WorW2**

Botticellian Trees, The. William Carlos Williams. **CP-WilW1**

Bottle, The. Walter de la Mare. **CP-DeLaW**

Bottle Is Drunk Out by One, The. Philip Larkin. **CP-LarkP**

Bottle of Aspirins, The. Stevie Smith. **CP-SmitS**

Bottled up for days, mostly. Charles Olson. **SP-OlsoC** *Fr.* The Maximus Poems.

Bottleneck. Louis MacNeice. **CP-MacNL**

Bottom drops off quickly, The. A Primer for Swimming at Black Point. Stephen Dunn. **SP-DunnS**

Bottom Line, The. Richard Shelton. **SP-ShelR**

Bottom of the air is disturbed as with an undertow, The. She, Thus. Charles Olson. **CP-OlsoC**

Bottom of the Glass, The. Stanley Jasspon Kunitz. **CP-KuniS**

Bottom of the sea accomodates mountain ranges, The. Carl Sandburg. *Fr.* The People, Yes. **CP-SandC**

Bottom of the sea has come, The. Song. Thomas Merton. **CP-MertT; SP-MertT**

Bottom of the universe and, The. Crawl. Charles Kenneth Williams. **CP-WillC**

Bottoming Out. "Lou Reed." **SP-ReedL**

Bottommost. Archie Randolph Ammons. **SP-AmmoA**

Bottoms *milfoil yarrow* holm seas. Yarrow. Louis Zukofsky. **CP-ZukLS**

Bougainville. Donald Davie. **CP-DavDo**

Boughs being pruned, birds preenèd, show more fair. Gerard Manley Hopkins. **CP-HopkG**

Boughs, the boughs are bare enough, The. Winter with the Gulf Stream. Gerard Manley Hopkins. **CP-HopkG**

Bought a three-bedroom house in 1948 so that. He. Ron Koertge. **SP-KoerR**

Bounce to Fop. Alexander Pope. **CP-SwifJ**

Bound—a trouble. Emily Dickinson. **CP-DickE**

Bound (almost) now of my book I see, The. On His Booke. Robert Herrick. **CP-HerrR**

Bound and free. Eudaimon. Kathleen Jessie Raine. **SP-RainK**

Bound, blinded, stymied, with bared blades for walls. The Eight of Swords. Marge Piercy. *Fr.* Laying Down the Tower. **SP-PierM**

Bound No'th Blues. Langston Hughes. **SP-HughL**

Bound upon a Wheel. Jenny Joseph. **SP-JoseJ**

Bound with baling wire to the tubular jerry-built bumper of a beat-up old dump truck. Souls. Charles Kenneth Williams. **SP-WillC**

Boundaries, fought clear, are abandoned, The. Nearing Equinox. Archie Randolph Ammons. **SP-AmmoA**

Boundary. Adrienne Rich. **CP-RicAE**

Boundary Commission, The. Paul Muldoon. **SP-MuldP**

Boundary Stone, The. David Herbert Lawrence. **CP-LawrD**

Boundless Moment, A. Robert Frost. **CP-FrosR**

Bounty. Robert Pack. **SP-PackR**

Bouquet, The. Wallace Stevens. **CP-StevW**

Bouquet in Dog Time. Hayden Carruth. **CP-CarHS**

Bouquet of Belle Scavoir. Wallace Stevens. **CP-StevW**

Bouquet of Roses in Sunlight. Wallace Stevens. **CP-StevW**

Bouquet of Ten Roses, A. Robert Bly. **SP-BlyR**

Bouquets from Corley. Richard Hugo. **CP-HugoR**

Bour-Tree Den, The. Robert Louis Stevenson. **CP-StevR**

Bourgeois and Bolshevist. David Herbert Lawrence. **CP-LawrD**

Bourgeois and the bolshevist are both quite blind, The. The Half-Blind. David Herbert Lawrence. **CP-LawrD**

Bourgeois asserts the he owns his property by divine right, The. Property and No-Property. David Herbert Lawrence. **CP-LawrD**

Bourgeois cowardice produces bolshevist impudence. Cowardice and Impudence. David Herbert Lawrence. **CP-LawrD**

Bourgeois produces the bolshevist, inevitably, The. Bourgeois and Bolshevist. David Herbert Lawrence. **CP-LawrD**

Bourne, The. Christina Georgina Rossetti. **CP-RosC1**

B.O.W. John Hewitt. **CP-HewiJ**

Bow both your heads at once, and hearts. Ben Jonson. **CP-JonsB** *Fr.* The Irish Masque.

Bow down thine ear, O Lord, hear me. Psalm 86. Bible, *O.T. Fr.* Psalms. **CP-Psal**

Bow to me, bow to me. The Dance of Death. Robert Browning. **CP-BroR2**

Bow to me, bow to me. Fever. Robert Browning. **FL** *Fr.* The Dance of Death. **CP-BroR2**

Bower, The. Richard Eberhart. **CP-EberR**

Bower-Bird. Robert Ranke Graves. **CP-GravR**

Bower-bird improvised a cool retreat, The. Bower-Bird. Robert Ranke Graves. **CP-GravR**

Bower of Bliss, The. Edmund Spenser. **PoEL-1** *Fr.* The Faerie Queene. **CP-Spens**

"And in the midst of all, a fountaine stood." **CH**

"Eftsoones they heard a most melodious sound." **EBEvV; NOBE; OBSC; SCV**

"Thence passing forth, they shortly do arrive." **FiP**

Bowers whereat, in dreams, I see, The. To ———. Edgar Allan Poe. **CP-PoeEd**

Bowing he asks her the favor. Dancers. Donald Hall. **CP-HallD**

Bowing the Head. Donald Davie. **CP-DavDo**

Bowl of Blood, The. Robinson Jeffers. **CP-JefR3**

Bowled Over. Ted Hughes. **SP-HughT**

Bowlers Anonymous. Stephen Dobyns. **SP-DobyS**

Bowles and Campbell. Byron. **CP-Byron**

Bowls. David Herbert Lawrence. **CP-LawrD**

Bowls. Marianne Craig Moore. **CP-MoorM**

Bows glided down, and the coast, The. Ballad of the Long-legged Bait. Dylan Thomas. **CP-ThomD**

Box, The. Robert Creeley. **CP-CreeR**

Box cars run by a mile long. Work Gangs. Carl Sandburg. **CP-SandC**

Box Comes Home, A. John Ciardi. **SP-CiarJ**

Box mountain of hardened tears is hoisted up the scaffold, two, A. John Yau. **SP-YauJo** *Fr.* Predella.

Box of teak, a box of sandalwood, A. Plymouth. Philip Larkin. **CP-LarkP**

Box was set in a hole in the ground, The. How It Was at the End. Stephen Dobyns. **SP-DobyS**

Boxer bitch is pregnant, The. Geisha. Gary Gildner. **SP-GildG**

Boxers Hit Harder When Women Are Around. Kenneth Patchen. **CP-PatcK**

Boxes and Bags. Carl Sandburg. **CP-SandC**

Boxing. Rudyard Kipling. *See* NOVEMBER (*Boxing*).

Boy, A. John Ashbery. **SP-AshbJ**

Boy. John Ciardi. **SP-CiarJ**

Boy, the. Robert Creeley. **CP-CreeR**

Boy / with the / finger in, The. Hero. Robert Creeley. **CP-CreeR**

Boy accepted them, The. Daedalus: The Dirge. George Oppen. **CP-OppeG**

Boy Alexander understands his father to be a famous lawyer, The. Boy and Father. Carl Sandburg. **CP-SandC**

Boy and Father. Carl Sandburg. **CP-SandC**

Boy and girl are picking irises. On Iona. Phoebe Hesketh. **SP-HeskP**

Boy and the Angel, The. Robert Browning. **CP-BroR1**

Boy and the Bush, The. Theodore Roethke. **CP-RoetT**

Boy and the Man, The. Edward Estlin Cummings. **CP-CummE**

Boy at the Window. Richard Wilbur. **CP-WilbR**

Boy bring the bowl full of wine. Hafiz, tr. by Ralph Waldo Emerson. **CP-EmerR** *Fr.* Odes.

Boy came up the street and there was a girl, A. For Instance. John Ciardi. **SP-CiarJ**

Boy, Cat, Canary. Stephen Spender. **CP-SpenS**

Boy, don't come around here telling me you. Talking to My Mailbox. . . . Charles Bukowski. **SP-BukC3**

Boy Drowning. Phoebe Hesketh. **SP-HeskP**

Boy has never known her not to cheat, The. The Card Game. Stephen Dobyns. **SP-DobyS**

Boy, he rode with telegrams / A man, delivered postcards and letters, A. S.S.K. John Hewitt. **CP-HewiJ**

Boy heart of Johnny Jones—aching today? Buffalo Bill. Carl Sandburg. **CP-SandC**

Boy! I detest all Persian fopperies. Horace. *See* 1.38: Simplicity.

Boy, I hate their empty shows. 1.38. Horace. **CP-CowpW**, tr. by William Cowper; *Fr.* Odes.

Boy in a New York room spellbound by the snow, A. Poem of the Gold Coin. Frederick Morgan. **SP-MorgF**

Boy in the Roman Zoo. Archibald MacLeish. **CP-MacLA**

Boy is as old as the stars, A. To My God in His Sickness. Philip Levine. **SP-LeviP**

Boy is driving nails into the dirt, A. The Highlands 1966. Martin Edmunds. **SP-EdmuM**

Boy, is it crowded here in the arms of Morpheus. Sleep. Ron Koertge. **SP-KoerR**

Boy Johnny. Christina Georgina Rossetti. **CP-RosC2**

Boy Made of Meat, The; A Poem for Children. William DeWitt Snodgrass. **SP-SnodW**

Boy-Man. Karl Shapiro. **SP-ShapK**

Boy must learn the man, The. Wendell Berry. *Fr.* Rising. **CP-BerrW**

Boy of Winander, The. William Wordsworth. *See* There Was a Boy.

Boy planted a bean, The. Jack and the Beanstalk. Jenny Joseph. *Fr.* Fables. **SP-JoseJ**

Boy, presuming on his intellect, A. At Woodward's Gardens. Robert Frost. **CP-FrosR**

Boy Scouts' Patrol Song, A. Rudyard Kipling. **CP-KiplR**

Boy Seen in a Bus Journey. John Hewitt. **CP-HewiJ**

Boy sits in the classroom, The. Learning Experience. Marge Piercy. **SP-PierM**

Boy steadies the air rifle on his arm, The. Peter's Diary in Goodentown. Kenneth Patchen. **CP-PatcK**

Boy turned to a newt!, A. The Fountain of Arethusa. Donald Davie. **CP-DavDo**

Boy twenty-one, in Donne, shied like a blow. John Berryman. *Fr.* Sonnets to Chris. **CP-BerrJ**

Boy waits on the top step, his hand on the door, The. Black Dog, Red Dog. Stephen Dobyns. **SP-DobyS**

Boy was in the hallway drinking a glass of tea, The. Land. Patti Smith. **SP-SmitP**

Boy who climbed the creaking stairs, The. Alun Lewis. *Fr.* Threnody for a Starry Night. **CP-LewiA**

Boy who had Gumption and Push, A. The Boy and the Bush. Theodore Roethke. **CP-RoetT**

Boy with Book of Knowledge. Howard Nemerov. **CP-NemeH**

Boy with His Hair Cut Short. Muriel Rukeyser. **CP-RukeM**

Boy with the frail romantic grace. Boy Seen in a Bus Journey. John Hewitt. **CP-HewiJ**

Boy, you're gonna Carry That Weight. Carry That Weight. John Lennon *and* Paul McCartney. **CP-Beatl**

Boyg, Peer Gynt, the One Only One, The. Randall Jarrell. **CP-JarrR**

Boyne at Navan swam in light, The. Evening on the Boyne. Donald Davie. **CP-DavDo**

Boys and girls, / Come out to play. The Passionate Pagan and the Dispassionate Public. Ogden Nash. **CP-NashO**

Boys and girls held her dear. Dirge. Edna St. Vincent Millay. *Fr.* Memorial to D. C. **CP-MillE**

Boys and girls, we pledge allegiance. Catullus. *See* Carmen 34: "Moving in her radiant care."

Boys come, each year more gallant, playing chicken, The. 1930's. Robert Lowell. **SP-LoweR**

Boy's Death, The. Ludwig Uhland, tr. fr. German by George Meredith. **CP-MerG2**

Boy's Dream, The. Thomas Hardy. **CP-HardT**

Boys dream of native girls who bring breadfruit. Breadfruit. Philip Larkin. **CP-LarkP**

Boys from Saint Bernard's, The. Grace Paley. **CP-PaleG**

Boys i mean are not refined, The. Edward Estlin Cummings. **CP-CummE**

Boys in sporadic but tenacious droves. The Horse Chestnut Tree. Richard Eberhart. **CP-EberR**

Boys in the Branches, The. Muriel Rukeyser. **CP-RukeM**

Boys of These Men Full Speed. Muriel Rukeyser. **CP-RukeM**

Boy's Room. George Oppen. **CP-OppeG**

Boy's Summer Song, A. Paul Laurence Dunbar. **CP-DunbP**

Boys Then and Now. Thomas Hardy. **CP-HardT**

Boy's Will is the Wind's Will?, A. Ogden Nash. *Fr.* Posies from a Second Childhood, or, Hark How Gaffer Do Chaffer. **CP-NashO**

Boy's Will, Joyful Labor without Pay, and Harvest Home (1918). Robert Penn Warren. **SP-WarrR**

  Hands Are Paid.

  Morning.

  Snake, The.

  Work. **SaC**

Br-r-r-am-m-m, rackety-am-m, OM, *Am*. What the Motorcycle Said. Mona Van Duyn. **SP-VanDM**

Bracelet, The. John Donne. *Fr.* Elegies. **CP-DonnJ**

Bracelet, A. Robert Ranke Graves. **CP-GravR**

Bracelet invisible, A. A Bracelet. Robert Ranke Graves. **CP-GravR**

Bracelet of Pearle: To Silvia, The. Robert Herrick. **CP-HerrR**

Bracelet; to Julia, The. Robert Herrick. **CP-HerrR**

Bracken Hills in Autumn. "Hugh MacDiarmid." **SP-MacDH**

Brackish reach of shoal off Madaket—, A. The Quaker Graveyard in Nantucket. Robert Lowell. **SP-LoweR**

Bradford Millionaire. John Hewitt. **CP-HewiJ**

Braes, The. Richard Hugo. **CP-HugoR**

Braes o' Ballochmyle, The. Robert Burns. **CP-BurnR**

Braes O' Layde, The. John Hewitt. **CP-HewiJ**

Brag, sweet tenor bull. Basil Bunting. **NoAM; PoE** *Fr.* Briggflatts [An Autobiography]. **CP-BuntB**

Braggart. John Clare. **SP-ClarJ**

Braggart, The, *parody of* Matthew Prior. Rudyard Kipling. **CP-KiplR** *Fr.* The Muse among the Motors.

Brahma. Ralph Waldo Emerson. **CP-EmerR**

Brain, be ice, / A frozen bowl of thought. Mens Creatrix. Stanley Jasspon Kunitz. **CP-KuniS**

Brain Child. Phoebe Hesketh. **SP-HeskP**

Brain constructs its systems to enclose, The. Organic Bloom. Stanley Jasspon Kunitz. **CP-KuniS**

Brain—is wider than the Sky, The. Emily Dickinson. **CP-DickE**

Brain itself in its skull, The. Harsh Climate. Charles Simic. **SP-SimiC**

Brain, within its Groove, The. Emily Dickinson. **CP-DickE**

Brainstorm. Howard Nemerov. **CP-NemeH**

Brainwashing. Carl Sandburg. **CP-SandC**

Brainwaves. Daniel Gerard Hoffman. **SP-HoffD**

Braised Leeks & Framboise. Diane Wakoski. **SP-WakoD**

Bran. Paul Muldoon. **SP-MuldP**

Branch on bird / Singing and losing leaves. Autumn. Raissa Maritain, *tr. fr. French by* Thomas Merton. **CP-MertT**

Branches. Carl Sandburg. **CP-SandC**

Branches murmur with soft thunder, The. The Patrol. Alun Lewis. **CP-LewiA**

Branches of Adam. John Gould Fletcher. **SP-FletJ**

  "And at these words there rose against the ark." **SP-FletJ**

  "And God, looking out upon earth, said, 'Lo, it is time / To create mankind'." **SP-FletJ**

  "As Adam, clutching earth, lay stunned within the darkness." **SP-FletJ**

  "Cain and Abel in the meantime had grown." **SP-FletJ**

  Epilogue: "By the glare of the guttering torch." **SP-FletJ**

  "Fourfold is made the divine nature of man." **SP-FletJ**

  "In the still evening of the sixth long day." **SP-FletJ**

  "Night lay upon the ocean like a sword." **SP-FletJ**

  "Now it was noonday, fortieth of the flood." **SP-FletJ**

  "Now it was the ninth morning and the unseen God." **SP-FletJ**

  "Out of the waves they clomb, plant, insect, fish, and bird." **SP-FletJ**

"Six long days was the unseen God in labour with the earth." **SP-FletJ**

"Then the archangels all together abandoned the black menacing sky." **SP-FletJ**

"There was a pool that rippled in the silence of the north." **SP-FletJ**

"They buried Abel at sunset in the red wet earth." **SP-FletJ**

Branching head of, The. The Lily. William Carlos Williams. **CP-WilW1**

Brancusi. Carl Sandburg. **CP-SandC**

Brancusi is a galoot; he saves tickets to take him nowhere; a galoot with. Brancusi. Carl Sandburg. **CP-SandC**

Brand. John Haines. **SP-HainJ**

Brand New Morning Love Song, A. Al Young. **CP-YounA**

Branded for Slaughter. Kay Boyle. **CP-BoylK**

Branded Hand, The. John Greenleaf Whittier. **CP-WhitJ**

Brandish's sword of God before them blaz'd, The. Expulsion from Paradise. John Milton. ChTr *Fr.* Book XII. *Fr.* Paradise Lost. **CP-MiltJ**

Brandons Both. Christina Georgina Rossetti. **CP-RosC2**

Brandy Glass, The. Louis MacNeice. **CP-MacNL**

Branksome Hall. Sir Walter Scott. **SP-ScotW** *Fr.* The Lay of the Last Minstrel.

Brantôme. Donald Davie. **CP-DavDo**

Brasen tower [*or* Tower] with doors [*or* dores] close barred [*or* bar'd], The. Horace, *tr. by* Sir Walter Ralegh. **CP-RaleW** *Fr.* Odes.

Brasilia. Sylvia Plath. **CP-PlatS**

Brass-green bird with grass-, A. Smooth Gnarled Crape Myrtle. Marianne Craig Moore. **CP-MoorM**

Brass Keys. Carl Sandburg. **CP-SandC**

Brass medallion profile of your face I keep always, The. Medallion. Carl Sandburg. **CP-SandC**

Brassiere Factory, The. Kenneth Koch. **SP-KochK**

Bravado. Stephen Dobyns. **SP-DobyS**

Bravado. Robert Frost. *Fr.* Five Nocturnes. **CP-FrosR**

Brave / to keep as captive. Prisoners. Michael Hartnett. **SP-HarMi**

Brave, brave were the soldiers (high named to-day) who lived through the fight. The Bravest Soldiers. Walt Whitman. **CP-WhitW**

Brave Bull. Charles Bukowski. **SP-BukC2**

Brave Champions! Go On with the Farce. Byron. **CP-Byron**

Brave Empedocles defying fools, The. Ralph Waldo Emerson. **CP-EmerR**

Brave Geraint, a knight of Arthur's court, The. The Marriage of Geraint. Tennyson. *Fr.* Idylls of the King. **CP-TennA**

Brave infant of Saguntum, clear[e]. To the Immortal[l] Memory [*or* Memorie] and Friendship of That Noble Pair[e], Sir Lucius Cary and Sir H. [*or* Henry] Morison. Ben Jonson. **CP-JonsB**

Brave is the sight when a champion tall. Sonnet to J.M. George Meredith. **CP-MerG2**

Brave lads in olden musical centuries. To H.F. Brown. Robert Louis Stevenson. **CP-StevR**

Brave Man, The. Wallace Stevens. **CP-StevW**

Brave New World. Archibald MacLeish. **CP-MacLA**

Brave rose, (alas!) where art thou? in the chair. Church-Rents and Schisms. George Herbert. **CP-HerbG**

Brave Schill! by death delivered, take thy flight. William Wordsworth. **CP-WorW1**

Brave youth, to whom Fate in one hour. For a Picture Where a Queen Laments over the Tomb of a Slain Knight. Thomas Carew. **CP-CareT**

Bravely deckt, come forth, bright day. Thomas Campion. **CP-CampT**

Bravely from Fairyland he rode, on furlough. The Broken Girth. Robert Ranke Graves. **CP-GravR**

Bravery runs in my family. Coward. Archie Randolph Ammons. **SP-AmmoA**

Bravest Soldiers, The. Walt Whitman. **CP-WhitW**

Bravo. Charles Bukowski. **SP-BukC3**

Bravo, Paris Exposition! Walt Whitman. **CP-WhitW**

Braw, braw lads on Yarrow braes. Galla Water. Robert Burns. **CP-BurnR**

Brawling of a sparrow in the eaves, The. *see also* The Sorrow of Love ("The quarrel of the sparrows in the eaves"). William Butler Yeats. **CP-YeatW**

Brazed city / reorders its own, The. Geoffrey Hill. *Fr.* Churchill's Funeral. **CP-HillG**

Brazen hynotics glitter here. Hart Crane. *Fr.* For the Marriage of Faustus and Helen. **CP-CranH**

Braziers, It Seems, Are Preparing to Pass, The. Byron. **CP-Byron**

Brazil. John Updike. **CP-UpdiJ**

Brazil, January 1, 1502. Elizabeth Bishop. **CP-BishE**

Brazilian butterflies, static and perfect as. Butterfly Piece. Robert Earl Hayden. **CP-HaydR**

Brazilian Tragedy. Manuel Bandeira, *tr. fr. Portuguese by* Elizabeth Bishop. **CP-BishE**

Breach, The. John Hewitt. **CP-HewiJ**

Bread. Stephen Berg. **SP-BergS**

Bread. James Dickey. **CP-DickJ**

Bread. Michael Hartnett. *See* Her iron beats.

Bread. Charles Kenneth Williams. **CP-WillC; SP-WillC**

Bread and Milk for Breakfast. Christina Georgina Rossetti. **CP-RosC2**

Bread of this World; Praises III, The. Thomas McGrath. **SP-McGrT**

Bread upon the Waters. David Herbert Lawrence. **CP-LawrD**

Breadfruit. Philip Larkin. **CP-LarkP**

Break, The. Donald Davie. **CP-DavDo**

Break, The. Adrienne Rich. **CP-RicAE**

Break, The. Anne Sexton. **CP-SextA**

Break Away, The. Anne Sexton. **CP-SextA**

Break, Break, Break. Tennyson. **CP-TennA**

Break, Fant'sy, from thy cave of cloud. Ben Jonson. **CP-JonsB** *Fr.* The Vision of Delight.

Break me my bounds, and let me fly. A Career. Paul Laurence Dunbar. **CP-DunbP**

Break me no bread however white it be. Hunger. Countee Cullen. **CP-CullC**

Break not the slumbers of the bride. Hymneal Song, on the Nuptials of the Lady Ann Wentworth and the Lord Lovelace. Thomas Carew. **CP-CareT**

Break of Morning. Walter de la Mare. **CP-DeLaW**

Break off / fallen Catullus. Carmen 8. Catullus. *Fr.* Carmina. **CP-Catul**

Break off Delay, since we but read of one. Delay. Robert Herrick. **CP-HerrR**

Break the box and shed the nard. Easter. Gerard Manley Hopkins. **CP-HopkG**

Break up conventional. Charles Henri Ford. **SP-FordC** *Fr.* Secret Haiku.

Breake now my heart and dye! Oh no, she may relent. Thomas Campion. **CP-CampT**

Breakfast. Diane Wakoski. **SP-WakoD**

Breakfast. William Carlos Williams. **CP-WilW1**

Breakfast in a Bowling Alley in Utica, New York. Adrienne Rich. **CP-RicAE**

Breakfast is an institution that I don't know who commenced it. The Eight O'Clock Peril. Ogden Nash. **CP-NashO**

Breakfast is drunk now. . . Damp earth. Our Daily Bread. César Vallejo, *tr. fr. Spanish by* James Wright. **CP-WrigJ**

Breakfast peremptorily closes. Breakfast Table. Robert Ranke Graves. **CP-GravR**

Breakfast Table. Robert Ranke Graves. **CP-GravR**

Breakfasting alone in Karachi, Delhi, Calcutta. Solitary Travel. Louis MacNeice. **CP-MacNL**

Breaking. Wendell Berry. **CP-BerrW**

Breaking Camp. Marge Piercy. **SP-PierM**

Breaking Ground. Thom Gunn. **CP-GunnT**

Kent.

Monterey.

Breaking of Rainbows, The. Howard Nemerov. **CP-NemeH**

Breaking Open. Muriel Rukeyser. **CP-RukeM**

Breaking the Charm. Paul Laurence Dunbar. **CP-DunbP**

Breaking the nets of the world, in glimpses going. Muriel Rukeyser. **CP-RukeM**

Breaking Webs. Louis MacNeice. **CP-MacNL**

Break[e] of Day. John Donne. **CP-DonnJ**

Breakout. Charles Bukowski. **SP-BukC2**

Breaks from the blue-black. The Turtle. Mary Oliver. **SP-OlivM**

Breaks in splendor on / the window glass of. The Morning. James Schuyler. **CP-SchuJ**

Breakwater. Dabney Stuart. **SP-StuaD**

Breast, The. Anne Sexton. **CP-SextA**

Breast under breast when you shall lie. Ghosts. Countee Cullen. **CP-CullC**

Breastplate. John Hewitt. **CP-HewiJ**

Breasts. Tess Gallagher. **SP-GallT**

Breasts. Charles Simic. **SP-SimiC**

Breasts of the loving mothers flow with milk, The. Frederick Morgan. *Fr.* Death Mother. **SP-MorgF**

Breath. James Dickey. **CP-DickJ**

Breath. Philip Levine. **SP-LeviP**

Breath of Air, A. James Wright. **CP-WrigJ**

Breath of Life, The. David Herbert Lawrence. **CP-LawrD**

Breath of Life, The. David Herbert Lawrence. **CP-LawrD**

Breath of Nature, The. Chuang Tzu, *tr. fr. Chinese by* Thomas Merton. **CP-MertT**

Breath of Night, The. Randall Jarrell. **CP-JarrR; SP-JarrR**

Breath of the Briar. George Meredith. **CP-MerG1**

Breath of the mountains, fresh born in the regions majestic, A. The Poetry of Wordsworth. George Meredith. **CP-MerG1**

Breath of What's-Out-There sags, The. Night Journal II. Charles Wright. **SP-WrigC**

Breath within us is the wind without, The. Equations of a Villanelle. Howard Nemerov. **CP-NemeH**

Breath you now, while Io Hymen. Thomas Campion. *Fr.* The Lords Mask[e].

Breathe. . . / open fields / like tipping your hat to the sun. Highway Report. Jim Carroll. **SP-CarrJ**

Breathe deep of the / freshly gray morning air, mild. Three Meditations. Denise Levertov. **CP-LeveD**

Breathe from the gentle South, O Lord. The Waiting Soul. William Cowper. *Fr.* Olney Hymns. **CP-CowpW**

Breathe in experience, breathe out poetry. Poem Out of Childhood. Muriel Rukeyser. **CP-RukeM**

Breathe, Julia, breathe, and Ile protest. On Julia's Breath. Robert Herrick. **CP-HerrR**

Breathe not, hid Heart: cease silently. To an Unborn Pauper Child. Thomas Hardy. **CP-HardT**

Breathe on the living. Kenneth Patchen. **CP-PatcK**

Breathe with me this fear. Edward Estlin Cummings. **CP-CummE**

Breathes there a bard who isn't moved. On Being Chosen Poet of Vermont. Robert Frost. **CP-FrosR**

Breathes there the [or a] Man [with Soul So Dead]. Sir Walter Scott. **SP-ScotW** *Fr.* The Lay of the Last Minstrel.

  (Caledonia.)

  O Caledonia! **FaBoPP**

Breathing, The. Denise Levertov. **CP-LeveD**

Breathing Exercises. Leonard Nathan. **SP-NathL**

Breathing in morning. Song Turning Back Into Itself 1. Al Young. **CP-YounA**

Breathing in morning. Al Young. **CP-YounA** *Fr.* The Song Turning Back into Itself.

Breathing Landscape. Muriel Rukeyser. **CP-RukeM**

Breathing of the earth, The. Carl Sandburg. *Fr.* The People, Yes. **CP-SandC**

Breathing Purely. Daniel Gerard Hoffman. **SP-HoffD**

Breathless, The. Richard Eberhart. **CP-EberR**

Brecht in Svendborg. Derek Mahon. **SP-MahoD**

Bred up at home, full early I begun. Alexander Pope. *Fr.* The Second Epistle of the Second Book of Horace Imitated. **CP-PopeA**

"Brederode" / (to Rush, Ap 4. 1790). Canto 94. Ezra Pound. *Fr.* Cantos. **CP-PoCan**

Bredon Hill. Alfred Edward Housman. **CP-HousA**

Breeze came to the aid of that wilted day, A. The Other Cindy. John Ashbery. **SP-AshbJ**

Breeze discovered my open book, A. A Cloud Shadow. Robert Frost. **CP-FrosR**

Breeze is blowin' 'cross de bay, De. Parted. Paul Laurence Dunbar. **CP-DunbP**

Breeze keeps fleshing the flag, A. Embassy. Charles Tomlinson. **CP-TomlC**

Breeze of the night in gentler sighs. Song. Byron. **CP-Byron**

Breeze ruffles the rain-pool, A. From the Japanese, IV. John Gould Fletcher. **SP-FletJ**

Breezes blowin' middlin' brisk. Speakin' o' Christmas. Paul Laurence Dunbar. **CP-DunbP**

Brekekekex? / The frogs of upstate speak. Poolville, N.Y. Charles Tomlinson. **CP-TomlC**

Brennbaum. Ezra Pound. **MoAmPo** *Fr.* Hugh Selwyn Mauberley. (Life and Contacts). **SP-PounE**

Brennende Liebe. Louise Glück. **SP-GlücL**

Brennoralt. Sir John Suckling. **CP-SuckJ**

  "Bright star o' th' lower orb, twinkling inviter."

  "Come, let the State stay."

  "Hall, a hall, A."

  "She's pretty to walk with."

  "That box, fair mistress, which thou gavest to me."

  "This moiety war."

Breslau, November-December 1917. Jane Cooper. *Fr.* Threads: Rosa Luxemburg from Prison. **SP-CoopJ**

Breslau, Spring 1918. Jane Cooper. *Fr.* Threads: Rosa Luxemburg from Prison. **SP-CoopJ**

Brethren, how shall it fare with me. The Question. Rudyard Kipling. **CP-KiplR**

Breughel. Stevie Smith. **CP-SmitS**

Breughel's Winter. Walter de la Mare. **CP-DeLaW**

Brewing of Soma, The. John Greenleaf Whittier. **CP-WhitJ**

  "Dear Lord and Father of Mankind." **AH; NOCV; TRV; TrPWD**

Briar Rose (Sleeping Beauty). Anne Sexton. **CP-SextA**

Bribes and Gifts Get All. Robert Herrick. **CP-HerrR**

Brick distinguishes this country. Amsterdam Letter. Jean Garrigue. **SP-GarrJ**

Brickenden, Hertfordshire. Stevie Smith. **CP-SmitS**

Bricklayer Love. Carl Sandburg. **CP-SandC**

Bricklayer's Lunch Hour, The. Allen Ginsberg. **CP-GinsA**

Bricks, The. Kenneth Koch. **SP-KochK**

Bricks in a wall, The. The Bricks. Kenneth Koch. **SP-KochK**

Bricks of the wall. The Garden Wall. Denise Levertov. **CP-LeveD**

Brickyards at Beacon. Edwin Rolfe. **CP-RolfE**

Bridal Ballad. Edgar Allan Poe. **CP-PoeEd**

Bridal Measure, A. Paul Laurence Dunbar. **CP-DunbP**

Bridal of Pennacook, The. John Greenleaf Whittier. **CP-WhitJ**

Bridal of Trierman, The. Sir Walter Scott.

  Defenceless Border, The. **SP-ScotW**

  Enchanted Goblet, The. **SP-ScotW**

  Magic Castle, The. **SP-ScotW**

Bridal Photo, 1906. John Ciardi. **SP-CiarJ**

Bridal Piece. Louise Glück. **SP-GlücL**

Bridal Song: "O come, soft rest of cares, come Night." George Chapman. **NOBE; OBEV** *Fr.* Hero and Leander.

Bridal Song, A: "Golden gates of Sleep unbar, The", *see also* Epithalamium *and* Another Version of the Same. Percy Bysshe Shelley. **CP-ShelP**

Bride. Archie Randolph Ammons. **SP-AmmoA**

Bride, The. David Herbert Lawrence. **CP-LawrD**

Bride, The. Charles Olson. **CP-OlsoC**

Bride, The. Sir John Suckling. **TrGrPo** *Fr.* A Ballad[e] [upon a Wedding]. **CP-SuckJ**

Bride and Groom Lie Hidden for Three Days. Ted Hughes. **SP-HughT**

Bride-Cake, The. Robert Herrick. **CP-HerrR**

Bride disappears. After twenty minutes of searching, The. The Impossible Marriage. Donald Hall. **SP-HallD**

Bride in the 30's, A. Wystan Hugh Auden. **CP-AudeW**

Bride leaves her father's house, The. The Bride. Charles Olson. **CP-OlsoC**

Bride-Night Fire, The. Thomas Hardy. **CP-HardT**

Bride of Abydos, The. Byron. **CP-Byron**

Bride of Reason, The. Donald Davie. **CP-DavDo**

Bride of the Bear. William Everson. **SP-EverW**

Bride Song, A. Christina Georgina Rossetti. **CP-RosC1**

Bride Song. Christina Georgina Rossetti. **OBEV; OBVV; WPE** *Fr.* The Prince's Progress. **CP-RosC1**

  (Too Late.) **OtMeF**

Bride the groom the small grin, The. A Hit Album. Gilbert Sorrentino. **SP-SorrG**

Bride-to-be lies in her bed, The. The Wedding-Dress. Jim Morrison. **SP-MorrJ**

Bride to Groom. Jenny Joseph. **SP-JoseJ**

Bridegroom, The. Rudyard Kipling. **FaBoEE** *Fr.* Epitaphs of the War [1914–1918]. **CP-KiplR**

Bridge, The. Hart Crane. **CP-CranH**

  Atlantis. **HoFi; LiTM; MoPo; NYP; NePA; TwAmPo**

  Ave Maria. **HoFi; MoPo; NOBA; NePA; NoAM**

  Cape Hatteras. **InPS; MoAB; MoAmPo**

    "Nasal whine of power whips a new universe." **MoAB; MoAmPo**

    (Power.) **MoAmPo**

  Cutty Sark. **FaBoMo**

  Powhatan's Daughter.

    Dance, The. **LiTM; MoAB; MoAmPo; OxBA**

    Harbor Dawn, The. **AP; AmPP; CMoP; CoBMV; CrMA; FaBV; GOA; LiTM; MoAB; MoAmPo; MoPo; NOBA; NYP; NePA; NoAM; OxBA; PrIm; SeCeV; TrGrPo; TwAmPo**

    Indiana.

    River, The. **AmPP; CMoP; GOA; MoAB; MoAmPo; NOBA; OxBA; PrIm**

    "Down, down—born pioneers in time's despite." **TrGrPo**

    Van Winkle. **AmPP; FaBV; MoAB; MoAmPo**

  Quaker Hill. **LiTM**

  Three Songs. **NAAL-2**

    National Winter Garden. **ErPo; InPS; LiTM; NAAL-2; OxBA**

    Southern Cross.

    Virginia.

  To Brooklyn Bridge. **AP; AiP; AmPP; BLPL; CABA; CMoP; ChIV-1; ClHu; CoBMV; CrMA; EyDe; FaBoEn; HAP; HelP; HoFi; ImPo; InPS; LiTA; LiTM; MeMAP; MoAB; MoAmPo; MoPo; NOBA;**

NYP; NePA; NoAM; NoP; OxBA; PoE; PoPl; PrIm; SeCeV; TAP; TFi; TRP; WeW

(Poem: To Brooklyn Bridge.) AmFP; AmPP; CMoP; HAP; HeIP; NoAM; NoP; TAP; WeW

Tunnel, The. CMoP; HoFi; MAT; MoAB; MoAmPo; OxBA

Bridge, The. Walter de la Mare. **CP-DeLaW**

Bridge for the Living. Philip Larkin. **CP-LarkP**

Bridge-Guard in the Karroo. Rudyard Kipling. **CP-KiplR**

Bridge of Estador, The. Hart Crane. **CP-CranH**

Bridge of Lodi, The. Thomas Hardy. **CP-HardT**

Bridge of Sighs, The. Richard Hugo. **CP-HugoR**

Bridge says: Come across, try me; see how good I am, The. Potomac Town in February. Carl Sandburg. **CP-SandC**

Bridge Through My Window. Audre Lorde. **SP-LordA**

Bridged and forgot, the river. The River Bridged and Forgot. Wendell Berry. **CP-BerrW**

Bridges. Grace Paley. **CP-PaleG**

Bridges. Charles Tomlinson. **CP-TomlC**

Bridging. Marge Piercy. **SP-PierM**

Brief Encounter. Phoebe Hesketh. **SP-HeskP**

Brief Guide to New York, A. Ogden Nash. **CP-NashO**

Brief Guide to Rhyming, or, How Be the Little Busy Doth?, A. Ogden Nash. **CP-NashO**

Brief harp of the larches. To Friend-Tree of Counted Days. René Char, *tr. fr. French by* William Carlos Williams. **CP-WilW2**

Brief History. Richard Hugo. **CP-HugoR**

Brief Innocence. Maya Angelou. **SP-AngeM**

Brief Journey West, The. Howard Nemerov. **CP-NemeH**

Brief Lief. William Carlos Williams. **CP-WilW2**

Brief Lives. Donald Hall. **CP-HallD**

Brief Message. Allen Tate. **CP-TateA**

Brief Reunion. Robert Ranke Graves. **CP-GravR**

Briefcases. Stephen Dunn. **SP-DunnS**

Briefly they are amazed. The marigold-fields. Terribilis Est Locus Iste; *Gaugin and the Pont-Aven School.* Geoffrey Hill. **CP-HillG**

Brigadas Internacionales. Edwin Rolfe. **CP-RolfE**

Briggflatts [An Autobiography]. Basil Bunting. **CP-BuntB**

  "Brag, sweet tenor bull." **NoAM; PoE**

  "Down into dust and reeds."

  "Drip—icicle's gone."

    "Light lifts from the water." **OAEL-2; PoPo**

  "Grass caught in willow tells the flood's height that has subsided." **FaBoMo**

  "As the player's breath warms the fipple the tone clears." **PWE**

  "Poet appointed dare not decline."

  "Loaded with mail of linked lies." **FaBoEH**

  "Strong song tows, A." **OAEL-2**

BrIght / bRight s??? big / (soft). Edward Estlin Cummings. **CP-CummE**

Bright as the Pleiades Upon the Soul. Malcolm Lowry. **CP-LowrM**

Bright Babe! whose awfull beautyes [*or* beauties] make. Richard Crashaw. **CP-CrasR**

(Hymn in the Glorious Epiphanie.) **CP-CrasR**

Bright baffling Soul, least capturable of themes. To Shakespeare. Thomas Hardy. **CP-HardT**

Bright ball of flame that through the gloom of even. Sonnet: To a Balloon Laden with Knowledge. Percy Bysshe Shelley. **CP-ShelP**

Bright Be the Place of Thy Soul! Byron. **CP-Byron**

Bright Bindings. Countee Cullen. **CP-CullC**

Bright bird with one wing. The Future. Richard Shelton. **SP-ShelR**

Bright clasp of her whole hand around my finger. To My Daughter. Stephen Spender. **CP-SpenS**

Bright cloud, / Bringer of rain to far fields. Kathleen Jessie Raine. **SP-RainK**

Bright clouds of reverence, sufferably bright. The Veil of Light. Samuel Taylor Coleridge. **CP-ColeS**

Bright Conversation with Saint-Ex. Carl Sandburg. **CP-SandC**

Bright Crown of Freedom, The. James Liddy. **CP-LiddJ**

Bright drop quivering on a thorn, The. Penshurst Place. Derek Mahon. **SP-MahoD**

Bright Flower! whose home is everywhere. To the Daisy. William Wordsworth. **CP-WorW1**

Bright from the shell of that much limited man. George Meredith. *Fr.* Napoléon. **CP-MerG1**

Bright Goddesse, whether Jove thy father be. *fr. the Latin of* Euphormio. Richard Crashaw. **CP-CrasR**

Bright-haired company of youthful slaves, A. Casual Incitement. William Wordsworth. *Fr.* Ecclesiastical Sonnets. **CP-WorW2**

Bright is the moon on the deep, *alt. vers. of* "Sweet and low, sweet and low." Tennyson. **PlP** *Fr.* The Princess. **CP-TennA**

Bright is the ring of words. Robert Louis Stevenson. **CP-StevR**

Bright Life. Walter de la Mare. **CP-DeLaW**

Bright light, swift-winged winds, springs of the rivers, numberless. Aeschylus, *tr. by* David Grene. **GrIP** *Fr.* Prometheus Bound. **CP-BroEB**

Bright Martial Maid, Queen of the frozen zone. In Eandem Reginae Sueciae Transmissam [To Christina, Queen of Sweden]. Andrew Marvell, *tr. fr. Latin by* William A. McQueen *and* Kiffin A. Rockwell. **CP-MarvA**

Bright mirror I braved: the devil in it, The. Cleopatra to the Asp. Ted Hughes. **SP-HughT**

Bright Nightgown. Gilbert Sorrentino. **SP-SorrG**

Bright ran thy line, O Galloway. Lord Galloway. Robert Burns. **DBV; OxBoLi** *Fr.* Epigrams on Lord Galloway. **CP-BurnR**

Bright scene; a summer morning, A. A Minor Victorian Painter. John Hewitt. **CP-HewiJ**

Bright Sirius! that when Orion pales. The Star Sirius. George Meredith. **CP-MerG1**

Bright soul, of whom if any country known. To the Lady Elizabeth Queen of Bohemia. George Herbert. **CP-HerbG**

Bright spark, shot from a brighter place. The Star[re]. George Herbert. **CP-HerbG**

Bright star o' th' lower orb, twinkling inviter. Sir John Suckling. *Fr.* Brennoralt. **CP-SuckJ**

Bright Star! Would I Were Steadfast as Thou Art. John Keats. **CP-KeatJ**

Bright starre of Majesty, oh shedd on mee. Upon the birth of the Princesse Elizabeth. Richard Crashaw. **CP-CrasR**

Bright Stella, form'd for universal Reign. To Miss Hickman Playing on the Spinet. Samuel Johnson. **CP-JohnS**

Bright tulips, we do know. To a Bed of Tulips. Robert Herrick. **CP-HerrR**

Bright vocabularies are transient as rainbows. Precious Moments. Carl Sandburg. **CP-SandC**

Bright wanderer, fair coquette of Heaven. Fragment: To the Moon. Percy Bysshe Shelley. **CP-ShelP**

Bright was the summer's noon when quickening steps. Summer Vacation. William Wordsworth. *Fr.* The Prelude; Growth of a Poet's Mind [1850 vers.]. **CP-WorW3**

Brightest and best are the sons of morning. Tableau de l'Inconstance des Mauvais Anges. Stevie Smith. **CP-SmitS**

Brightness of Distance. Robert Penn Warren. *Fr.* Infant Boy at Midcentury. **SP-WarrR**

Brighton Beach. Derek Mahon. **SP-MahoD**

Brighton Rock by Graham Greene. Bill Knott. **SP-KnotB**

Brignall Banks. Sir Walter Scott. **EnRP; HBV 1-2; OAEP; OBEV; OBRV** *Fr.* Edmund's Songs. **SP-ScotW** *Fr.* Rokeby.

(Edmund's Song.) **PoRA**

(Outlaw, The.) **GTBS; GTBS-6; GTBS-P; OtMeF**

(Song: Brignal Banks.) **OxAEP-2**

Brigs of Ayr, a Poem. Inscribed to J. B*********, Esq; Ayr, The. Robert Burns. **CP-BurnR**

Brilliance. Donald Davie. **CP-DavDo**

Brilliance, The. William Carlos Williams. **CP-WilW2**

Brilliant as oiled plumage in hollows of sand. The Chiming at Trwyn Du. Steve Griffiths. **SP-GrifS**

Brilliant network-lights tentacle dim suburbs. Rising Over Night-Blackened Detroit Streets. Allen Ginsberg. **CP-GinsA**

Brilliant Sad Sun. William Carlos Williams. **CP-WilW1**

Brilliant Silence. Charles Tomlinson. **CP-TomlC**

Brilliant, the full-bodied, the real of the world in their powers, The. Muriel Rukeyser. **CP-RukeM**

Brim. Carl Sandburg. **CP-SandC**

Brim Beauvais. Gertrude Stein. **CP-SteiG**

Brim's hammer hit a wheelbarrow; a silver of iron sent itself through the. Brim. Carl Sandburg. **CP-SandC**

Bring away this Sacred Tree. Thomas Campion. *Fr.* Description of a Maske: Presented in the Banqueting Roome at *Whitehall*, on Saint Stephens Night Last, at the Marriage of the Right Honourable the Earle of *Somerset:* and the Right Noble the Lady FRANCES *Howard.* **CP-CampT**

Bring away / straight things. Horse on Fire. Charles Bukowski. **SP-BukC2**

Bring Down the Beams. Charles Bukowski. **SP-BukC2**

Bring in the steaming bowl, my lads. A Wassail for the New Year. George Meredith. **CP-MerG2**

Bring, in this timeless grave to throw. Alfred Edward Housman. **CP-HousA**

Bring It Up from the Dark. Robert Duncan. **SP-DuncR**

Bring me my rose-buds, drawer, come. A Frolic[k]. Robert Herrick. **CP-HerrR**

Bring me now the bright flower. Nightsong. Carl Sandburg. **CP-SandC**

"Bring me soft song," said Aladdin. Aladdin and the Jinn. Nicholas Vachel Lindsay. **CP-LindV**

Bring me the livery of no other man. The Bohemian. Paul Laurence Dunbar. **CP-DunbP**

Bring me the sunset in a cup. Emily Dickinson. **CP-DickE**

Bring me to see, Lord, bring me yet to see. The General Assembly and Church of the Firstborn. Christina Georgina Rossetti. **CP-RosC2**

Bring me to the blasted oak. *fr.* Words for Music Perhaps. William Butler Yeats. **CP-YeatW**

Bring me wine, but wine which never grew. Bacchus. Ralph Waldo Emerson. **CP-EmerR**

Bring not bright candles, for his eyes. Reverie. Walter de la Mare. **CP-DeLaW**

Bring on a pail of smoke. Impasse. Carl Sandburg. **CP-SandC**

"Bring out your dead!" The midnight street. The Female Martyr. John Greenleaf Whittier. **CP-WhitJ**

Bring the comb and play upon it! Marching Song. Robert Louis Stevenson. **CP-StevR**

Bring the Day! Theodore Roethke. **CP-RoetT**

Bring the holy crust of Bread. Charmes. Robert Herrick. **CP-HerrR**

Bring up from the dark water. Bring It Up from the Dark. Robert Duncan. **SP-DuncR**

Bring wine release me. Hafiz, *tr.* by Ralph Waldo Emerson. **CP-EmerR** *Fr.* Odes.

Bringers. Carl Sandburg. **CP-SandC**

Bringing. Muriel Rukeyser. **CP-RukeM**

Bringing a Turtle Home. Robert Lowell. **SP-LoweR**

Bringing It All Back Home. "Bob Dylan." **CP-DylaB**

Bringing It Down. Stephen Dunn. **SP-DunnS**

Bringing It Home. Charles Kenneth Williams. **CP-WillC**

Bringing our love to the zoo to see what species. Marriage, with Beasts. Mona Van Duyn. **SP-VanDM**

Bringing their frozen swords, their salt-bleached eyes, their salt-bleached hair. The Warriors of the North. Ted Hughes. **SP-HughT**

Bringing to Light. Thom Gunn. **CP-GunnT**

Bringing you back here—. Robert Creeley. **CP-CreeR**

Brise Marine. Derek Walcott. **CP-WalcD**

Brisk from the autumn of the sunlit square. Municipal Gallery Revisited, October 1954. John Hewitt. **CP-HewiJ**

Brisk methinks I am, and fine. Robert Herrick. **CP-HerrR** (Anacrontik Verse.) **CP-HerrR**

Bristol. Sir John Betjeman. **CP-BetjJ**

Bristol and Clifton. Sir John Betjeman. **CP-BetjJ**

Britain. George Meredith. **CP-MerG2**

Britain. James Thomson. *Fr.* Liberty. **CP-ThomJ**

Britannia. James Thomson. **CP-ThomJ**

Britannia. James Thomson. *See* Happy Britannica.

Britannia Rules the Waves. Elizabeth Bishop. **CP-BishE**

British Boy, The. David Herbert Lawrence. *Fr.* Songs I Learnt at School. **CP-LawrD**

British Church, The. George Herbert. **CP-HerbG**

British Museum Reading Room, The. Louis MacNeice. **CP-MacNL**

British puss demurely mews, The. Philological. John Updike. **CP-UpdiJ**

British-Roman Song, A. Rudyard Kipling. **CP-KiplR** *Fr.* A Centurion of the Thirtieth. *Fr.* Puck of Pook's Hill.

British Sincerity. David Herbert Lawrence. **CP-LawrD**

British Song, A. Stevie Smith. **CP-SmitS**

British Stripling's War-Song, The, *ad. fr.* German of Stolberg. Samuel Taylor Coleridge. **CP-ColeS**

British Workman and the Government, The. David Herbert Lawrence. **CP-LawrD**

Britomart at Isis' Church. Edmund Spenser. **PoE** *Fr.* The Faerie Queene. **CP-Spens**

Britomart in the House of Busirane. Edmund Spenser. **FiP** *Fr.* The Legend of Britomartis, or of Chastitie. **NAEL-1** *Fr.* The Faerie Queene. **CP-Spens**

Britons! when last ye met, with distant streak. Verses Addressed to J. Horne Tooke and the Company Who Met on 28 June 1796 to Celebrate His Poll at the Westminster Election. Samuel Taylor Coleridge. **CP-ColeS**

Brittaine, the mighty Oceans lovely Bride. Upon the Duke of *Yorke* his Birth a Panegyricke. Richard Crashaw. **CP-CrasR**

Brittannia's Baby. David Herbert Lawrence. **CP-LawrD**

"Broad acres, sir." You hear them in my talk. At Knaresborough. Donald Davie. **CP-DavDo**

Broad-Ax, The. Walt Whitman. **MoAmPo** *Fr.* Song of the Broad-Axe [*or* Broad-Ax]. **CP-WhitW**

Broad-backed hippopotamus, The. The Hippopotamus. Thomas Stearns Eliot. **CP-ElioT**

Broad bald moon edged up where the sea was wide, The. On the Esplanade. Thomas Hardy. **CP-HardT**

Broad-bottomed Sealea. Romatic Portrait. Louis Zukofsky. *Fr.* Michtam. **CP-ZukLS**

Broad-breasted Pollards with broad-branching head. Samuel Taylor Coleridge. *Fr.* Some Fragments, Mainly from Manuscripts of 1797–8. **CP-ColeS**

Broad field darkens, but, still moving round, The. Central Park. Howard Nemerov. **CP-NemeH**

Broad-hipped, this earth-mother twists to check. Gaea. Martin Edmunds. **SP-EdmuM**

Broad of Church and broad of mind. The Wykehamist. Sir John Betjeman. **CP-BetjJ**

Broad sun, The. The Far-Farers. Robert Louis Stevenson. **CP-StevR**

Broad sun-stoned beaches. Midsummer, Tobago. Derek Walcott. **CP-WalcD**

Broadcast. Philip Larkin. **CP-LarkP**

Broadcasting to the G.B.P. David Herbert Lawrence. **CP-LawrD**

Broadstone, The. Robinson Jeffers. **CP-JefR2**

Broadway. Carl Sandburg. **CP-SandC**

Broadway. Walt Whitman. **CP-WhitW**

Broadway! Broadway! Gilbert Sorrentino. **SP-SorrG**

Broadway Pageant, A. Walt Whitman. **CP-WhitW**

Broagh. Seamus Heaney. **SP-HeanS**

Brocado's and damasks, and tabbies, and gauzes. An Excellent New Song on a Seditious Pamphlet. Jonathan Swift. **CP-SwifJ**

Broke to every known mischance, lifted over all. France. Rudyard Kipling. **CP-KiplR**

Broken ALTAR, Lord, thy servant rear[e]s, A. The Altar. George Herbert. **CP-HerbG**

Broken Appointment, A. Thomas Hardy. **CP-HardT**

Broken arm of the black oak, The. Oak Arms. Carl Sandburg. **CP-SandC**

Broken Back Blues. Robert Creeley. **CP-CreeR**

Broken Balance, The. Robinson Jeffers. **CP-JefR1**

"Mourning the broken balance, the hopeless prostration of the earth." Palinode.

"Rain, hail and brutal sun, the plow in the roots." Reference to a Passage in Plutarch's Life of Sulla. **CrMA**

"That light blood-loving weasel, a tongue of yellow." To the Children.

"Under my windows, between the road and the sea-cliff, bitter wild grass." Broken blood, the hunting flame, The. The Machine-Gun. Randall Jarrell. **CP-JarrR**

Broken bollard, rusted hawser. Louis MacNeice. *Fr.* Donegal Triptych. **CP-MacNL**

Broken Bowl, The. James Merrill. **SP-MerrJ**

Broken Christall, The. Robert Herrick. **CP-HerrR**

Broken Compact. Robert Ranke Graves. **CP-GravR**

Broken Dark, The. Robert Earl Hayden. **CP-HaydR**

Broken dike, the levee washed away, The. Edna St. Vincent Millay. *Fr.* Epitaph for the Race of Man. **CP-MillE**

Broken Dreams. William Butler Yeats. **CP-YeatW**

Broken Drought, The. Robert Frost. **CP-FrosR**

Broken-Face Gargoyles. Carl Sandburg. **CP-SandC**

Broken Friendship, The. Stevie Smith. **CP-SmitS**

Broken Girth, The. Robert Ranke Graves. **CP-GravR**

Broken Ground, The. Wendell Berry. **CP-BerrW**

Broken Heart, The. John Donne. **CP-DonnJ**

Broken Heart, The. Stevie Smith. **CP-SmitS**

"Broken heart.". but *can* a heart break, now?, A. John Berryman. *Fr.* Sonnets to Chris. **CP-BerrJ**

Broken heart, you / timeless wonder. Echo. Robert Creeley. **CP-CreeR**

Broken Hearted Soprano. Carl Sandburg. **CP-SandC**

Broken Home, The. James Merrill. **SP-MerrJ**

Broken in fortune, but in mind entire. At Bala-Sala, Isle of Man. William Wordsworth. *Fr.* Poems Composed or Suggested During a Tour, in the Summer of 1833. **CP-WorW2**

Broken in pieces all asunder. Affliction (4). George Herbert. **CP-HerbG**

Broken ivories / playing. The Keys. Erica Jong. **SP-JongE**

Broken-Link Handicap, The. Rudyard Kipling. *Fr.* Plain Tales from the Hills.

"While the snaffle holds or the long-neck stings." **CP-KiplR**

Broken Men, The. Rudyard Kipling. **CP-KiplR**

Broken Neck. Robert Ranke Graves. **CP-GravR**

Broken Off by the Music. John Yau. **SP-YauJo**

("With the first gray light of dawn.") **SP-YauJo**

Broken part heals even stronger than the rest, The. Consolations. William Stafford. **SP-StafW**

Broken Pen, The. Richard Eberhart. **CP-EberR**

Broken pillar of the wing jags from the clotted shoulder, The. Hurt Hawks. Robinson Jeffers. **CP-JefR1**

Broken Promise. Archibald MacLeish. **CP-MacLA**

Broken Sky. Carl Sandburg. **CP-SandC**

Broken snow should leave the traces, The. The Snow. Robert Creeley. **CP-CreeR**

Broken Sonnet. Carl Sandburg. **CP-SandC**

Broken Tabernacles. Carl Sandburg. **CP-SandC**

Broken Tower, The. Hart Crane. **CP-CranH**

Broken Wing Theory. Richard Eberhart. **CP-EberR**

Bronchitis at the Chelsea—or Salud Raul. Isabella Gardner. **CP-GardI**

Bronchitis on the 14th Floor. Marge Piercy. **SP-PierM**

Broncho That Would Not Be Broken, The. Nicholas Vachel Lindsay. **CP-LindV**

Bronkhorst Divorce Case, The. Rudyard Kipling. *Fr.* Plain Tales from the Hills.
"In the daytime, when she moved about me." **CP-KiplR**

Bronze. James Merrill. **SP-MerrJ**

Bronze clock brought, The. Beauharnois. Margaret Atwood. *Fr.* Four Small Elegies. **SP-AtwM2**

Bronze David of Donatello, The. Randall Jarrell. **CP-JarrR; SP-JarrR**

BRONze fasHIONs / RONZEfa shIONS BR. Thomas Merton. *Fr.* A Selection of Concrete Poems. **CP-MertT**

Bronze General Grant riding a bronze horse in Lincoln Park, The. Bronzes. Carl Sandburg. **CP-SandC**

Bronze Head, A. William Butler Yeats. **CP-YeatW**

Bronze soldier hitches a bronze cape, The. In Memoriam Francis Ledwidge. Seamus Heaney. **SP-HeanS**

Bronzes. Carl Sandburg. **CP-SandC**

Bronzes. Carl Sandburg. **CP-SandC**

Bronzeville Man with a Belt in the Back. Gwendolyn Brooks. **SP-BrooG**

Bronzeville Mother Loiters in Mississippi. Meanwhile, a Mississippi Mother Burns Bacon, A. Gwendolyn Brooks. **SP-BrooG**

Bronzeville Woman in a Red Hat. Gwendolyn Brooks. **SP-BrooG**

Brooch of Lorn, The. Sir Walter Scott. **SP-ScotW** *Fr.* The Lord of the Isles.

Brooding and seated at the summit. Why Some Look up to Planets and Heroes. Thomas Merton. **CP-MertT; SP-MertT**

Brooding Grief. David Herbert Lawrence. **CP-LawrD**

Brooding Likeness. Louise Glück. **SP-GlücL**

Brooding on her deep fall, the many strings. George Meredith. *Fr.* Alsace-Lorraine. **CP-MerG1**

Brooding on the eightieth letter of *Fors Clavigera*. Geoffrey Hill. **HAP; PoE** *Fr.* Mercian Hymns. **CP-HillG**

Brook, The. Hayden Carruth. *Fr.* Contra Mortem. **CP-CarHL**

Brook, The. Jean Garrigue. **SP-GarrJ**

Brook and road. The Simplon Pass. William Wordsworth. **CP-WorW1**

Brook and road, The. William Wordsworth. **OBRV** *Fr.* Cambridge and the Alps. *Fr.* The Prelude; Growth of a Poet's Mind [1805 vers.]. **CP-WorW3**

Brook beneath the water mill, The. Mark Van Doren and the Brook. Archibald MacLeish. **CP-MacLA**

Brook contains its landing under water, The. The Brook. Jean Garrigue. **SP-GarrJ**

Brook glancing under green leaves, self-delighting, exulting, A. The Poetry of Coleridge. George Meredith. **CP-MerG1**

Brook had been frozen almost everywhere Mounds, The. The Water. Hayden Carruth. *Fr.* Contra Mortem. **CP-CarHL**

Brook has holes in its cover, The. Hayden Carruth. *Fr.* North Winter. **CP-CarHL**

Brook in the City, A. Robert Frost. **CP-FrosR**

Brook sings on the selfsame strain, The. Old Age. Ralph Waldo Emerson. **CP-EmerR**

Brook! whose society the Poet seeks. William Wordsworth. **CP-WorW1**

Brooke whose streame so great, so good. An Epitaph. Upon Doctor Brooke. Richard Crashaw. **CP-CrasR**

Brookland Road. Rudyard Kipling. **CP-KiplR**

Brooklyn College Brain. Allen Ginsberg. **CP-GinsA**

Brooks are bristling in the field, The. Poesie Abrutie. Wallace Stevens. **CP-StevW**

Brooks Atkinson. Archibald MacLeish. **CP-MacLA**

Broom Besoms ["I maun hae a wife, whatsoe'er she be"]. Robert Burns. **CP-BurnR**

Broom Besoms ["Young and souple was I, when I lap the dyke"]. Robert Burns. **CP-BurnR**

Broom, its straws bleached, tips bent, leans. To Charlie. Stephen Berg. **SP-BergS**

Broom trees twirped by our rosewood bungalow, The. Harriet's Dream. Robert Lowell. **SP-LoweR**

Brooms. Charles Simic. **SP-SimiC**

Broomstead a lamenesse got by cold and Beere. Upon One-Ey'd Broomsted. Robert Herrick. **CP-HerrR**

Brose and Butter. Robert Burns. **CP-BurnR**

Brother. Robert Ranke Graves. **CP-GravR**

Brother, The. Thomas Hardy. **CP-HardT**

Brother. Richard Shelton. **SP-ShelR**

Brother and Sister. "Lewis Carroll." **CP-CarrL**

Brother and Sister. Walter de la Mare. **CP-DeLaW**

Brother and Sister. David Herbert Lawrence. **CP-LawrD**

Brother, brother, best avoid your workmate. Little Ballad for Americans—1954. Edwin Rolfe. **CP-RolfE**

Brother Bruin. Christina Georgina Rossetti. **CP-RosC2**

Brother Bulleys, let us sing. The Bullfinches. Thomas Hardy. **CP-HardT**

Brother, consider as you go your way. Somebody and Somebody Else and You. Edwin Rolfe. **CP-RolfE**

Brother Fire. Louis MacNeice. **CP-MacNL**

Brother hopping down the stairs. Cantico Per Lo Tuo Amore V. James Liddy. **CP-LiddJ**

Brother, I am fire. Kin. Carl Sandburg. **CP-SandC**

Brother, joy to you! / I've brought some snowdrops; only just a few. February. Christina Georgina Rossetti. *Fr.* The Months: A Pageant. **CP-RosC2**

Brother, my brother, whither do you pass? To a Face in a Crowd. Robert Penn Warren. **SP-WarrR**

Brother, no decrepitude. Ralph Waldo Emerson. **CP-EmerR**

Brother of Ingots—Ah Peru. Emily Dickinson. **CP-DickE**

Brother of Mercy, The. John Greenleaf Whittier. **CP-WhitJ**

Brother of Ophir. Emily Dickinson. **CP-DickE**

Brother Paul! look! Suzanne. William Carlos Williams. **CP-WilW2**

Brother, that breathe the August air. If Still Your Orchards Bear. Edna St. Vincent Millay. **CP-MillE**

Brother, the scent of your clothing. Swing Song of a Girl and a Soldier. David Herbert Lawrence. *Fr.* Bits. **CP-LawrD**

Brotherhood. George Meredith. **CP-MerG2**

Brotherhood in Pain. Robert Penn Warren. **SP-WarrR**

Brotherhood is not by the blood certainly, The. Speech to Those Who Say Comrade. Archibald MacLeish. **CP-MacLA**

Brotherhood of Men. Richard Eberhart. **CP-EberR**
"Came lassitude and despair of the mind."
"Caught there, then, on the Rock. At Corregidor."
"My mind was heavy and my luck was dark."
"Rumors of liberation. We could not believe it."

Brothers. Stephen Berg. **SP-BergS**

Brothers, The. John Hewitt. **CP-HewiJ**

Brothers. Gerard Manley Hopkins. **CP-HopkG**

Brothers. Langston Hughes. **SP-HughL**

Brothers, The. William Wordsworth. **CP-WorW1**

Brothers and sisters, Celestine. Ballade of Forgiveness. François Villon, *tr. fr.* French by Richard Wilbur. **CP-WilbR**

Brothers! between you and me. To the Republicans of North America. Percy Bysshe Shelley. **CP-ShelP**

Brothers spoke of Ghosts,—a favourite theme, The. Lady Barbara; or, The Ghost. George Crabbe. **SP-CrabG** *Fr.* Tales of the Hall.

Brothers, the curving grasses and their daughters. The Trappist Cemetery—Gethsemani. Thomas Merton. **CP-MertT; SP-MertT**

Brought almost to tears. Toward the End of Winter. Gilbert Sorrentino. **SP-SorrG**

Brought in tame from the. Charles Henri Ford. **SP-FordC** *Fr.* Secret Haiku.

Brought up never getting punched. He/She. Stephen Dunn. **SP-DunnS**

Brow / so far receded now, The. A. Lincoln—Odd, or Even. Marsden Hartley. **CP-HartM**

Brow is that of Deity, The. Emily Dickinson. **SP-DickE**

Brown and furry / Caterpillar in a hurry. Christina Georgina Rossetti. **CP-RosC2**

Brown and furry. Christina Georgina Rossetti. **BoTP; FaBoVe; FaPON; GoJo; OxBChV; RHPC; SUS; SiSoPo; SoPo** *Fr.* Sing-Song. **CP-RosC2**

(Caterpillar, The.) **BoTP; FaPON; GoJo; OxBChV; RHPC; SUS; SiSoPo; SoPo**

Brown and silver, the tufted. For Floss. Denise Levertov. **CP-LeveD**

Brown Bess. Rudyard Kipling. **CP-KiplR**

Brown Boy to Brown Girl. Countee Cullen. **CP-CullC**

Brown bread Tom Pennie eates, and must of right. Upon Pennie. Robert Herrick. **CP-HerrR**

Brown-checked, neat as new spring tweed. The Mallard. Phoebe Hesketh. **SP-HeskP**

Brown dominates this bar. Décor. John Updike. **CP-UpdiJ**

Brown Dwarf of Rügen, The. John Greenleaf Whittier. **CP-WhitJ**

Brown enormous odor he lived by, The. The Prodigal. Elizabeth Bishop. **CP-BishE**

Brown Girl Dead, A. Countee Cullen. **CP-CullC**

Brown Gold. Carl Sandburg. **CP-SandC**

Brown Gulls. Marsden Hartley. **CP-HartM**

Brown lived at such a lofty farm. Brown's Descent; or, The Willy-Nilly. Robert Frost. **CP-FrosR**

Brown Menace or Poem to the Survival of Roaches, The. Audre Lorde. **SP-LordA**

Brown oak tree leans, A. Riverside Park. Etheridge Knight. *Fr.* Indiana Haiku. **SP-KnigE**

Brown of Ossawatomie. John Greenleaf Whittier. **CP-WhitJ**

Brown old man with a green thumb, A. He Was. Richard Wilbur. **CP-WilbR**

Brown Penny. William Butler Yeats. **CP-YeatW**

Brown piano in diamond, A. Portland Coliseum. Allen Ginsberg. **CP-GinsA**

Brown Stone. Richard Hugo. **CP-HugoR**

Brown stonepeaks—rockstumps. Sonora Desert-Edge. Allen Ginsberg. **CP-GinsA**

Brown tents are staked upon the slopes of Gauley. Reforestation. Louise McNeill. **SP-McNeiL**

Brown woman with watermarked eyes. On Susan's Birthday. Jim Carroll. **SP-CarrJ**

Brownie, The. William Wordsworth. **CP-WorW2**

Brownie, Brownie, let down your milk. Christina Georgina Rossetti. **CP-RosC2**

Brownie sits in the Scotchman's room, The. The Demon of the Study. John Greenleaf Whittier. **CP-WhitJ**

Brownie's Cell, The. William Wordsworth. **CP-WorW2**

Brown's Bay, Islandmagee, Spring 1917. John Hewitt. **CP-HewiJ**

Brown's Descent; or, The Willy-Nilly. Robert Frost. **CP-FrosR**

Browns, the olives, and the yellows died, The. Winter Song. Wilfred Owen. **CP-OwenW**

Brueghel in the Doria. Richard Hugo. **CP-HugoR**

Brueghel: The Triumph of Time. Howard Nemerov. **CP-NemeH**

Bruges ("Bruges I saw attired with golden light"). William Wordsworth. *Fr.* Memorials of a Tour of the Continent; 1820. **CP-WorW2**

Bruges ("Spirit of Antiquity—enshrined, The"). William Wordsworth. *Fr.* Memorials of a Tour of the Continent; 1820. **CP-WorW2**

Bruges I saw attired with golden light. Bruges . William Wordsworth. *Fr.* Memorials of a Tour of the Continent; 1820. **CP-WorW2**

Bruise is not there, The. The Answer. William Everson. **SP-EverW**

Bruised Reed Shall He Not Break, A. Christina Georgina Rossetti. **CP-RosC1**

Bruised Titans, The. John Keats. **OBNC; OBRV** *Fr.* Hyperion; a Fragment. **CP-KeatJ**

Brunhilde, with the young Norn soul. With a Rose, to Brunhilde. Nicholas Vachel Lindsay. **CP-LindV**

Bruno's Song. "Lewis Carroll." **CP-CarrL** *Fr.* Sylvie and Bruno.

Brush Fire. James Wright. **CP-WrigJ**

Brush of a raven's, not an eagle's wing! Thyestes. Donald Davie. **CP-DavDo**

Brussels in Winter. Wystan Hugh Auden. **CP-AudeW**

Brutal lips, slasher lips—as a stunned toddler. Fatal Kisses. Stephen Dobyns. **SP-DobyS**

Brutal the wind, a Bronze Age. Epiphany. Jim Carroll. **SP-CarrJ**

Brutally sheared-off cliff, A. Wiltshire. Donald Davie. **CP-DavDo**

Brutish are coming; the Brutish, The. W. D. Tries to Warn Cock Robin. William DeWitt Snodgrass. **SP-SnodW**

Bryan, Bryan, Bryan, Bryan. Nicholas Vachel Lindsay. **CP-LindV**
   "Election night at midnight."
   "In a nation of one hundred fine, mob-hearted, lynching, relenting, repenting millions."
   "July, August, suspense. / Wall Street lost to sense."
   "Then we stood where we could see."
   "When Bryan came to Springfield, and Altgeld gave him greeting."
   "Where is McKinley, that respectable McKinley."

Bryant on His Birthday. John Greenleaf Whittier. **CP-WhitJ**

Bubble; a Song, The. Robert Herrick. **CP-HerrR**

Bubble breaking, The. Shot. Robert Creeley. **CP-CreeR**

Bubble of Air. Muriel Rukeyser. **CP-RukeM**

Bubbles. Carl Sandburg. **CP-SandC**

Bubbs Creek Haircut. Gary Snyder. **CP-SnydG**

Buck in the Snow, The. Edna St. Vincent Millay. **CP-MillE**

Buck Moon—From the Field Guide to Insects. Mary Oliver. **SP-OlivM**

Buckdancer's Choice. James Dickey. **CP-DickJ**

Buckets of Rain. "Bob Dylan." **CP-DylaB**

Buckhounds went on under the rain, The. Hunt. Kay Boyle. **CP-BoylK**

Buckinghamshire. Donald Davie. **CP-DavDo**

Buckles glitter, billies lean, The. American Twilights, 1957. James Wright. **CP-WrigJ**

Buckwheat. Carl Sandburg. **CP-SandC**

Bucolick betwixt Two: Lacon and Thyrsis, A. Robert Herrick. **CP-HerrR**

Bucolics. Wystan Hugh Auden. **CP-AudeW**
   Islands.
   Lakes. **NePA; NePoAm**
   Mountains. **FaBoPV**
   Plains. **NePA**
   Streams.
   Winds.
   Woods.

Bucolics. Sylvia Plath. **CP-PlatS**

Bud / stands for all things, The. Saint Francis and the Sow. Galway Kinnell. **SP-KinnG**

Bud Powell, Paris, 1959. William Matthews. **SP-MattW**

Buddha. Herman Melville. **SP-MelvH**

Buddha and Christ. John Gould Fletcher. **SP-FletJ**

Buddha at Kamakura. Rudyard Kipling. **CP-KiplR**

Buddha died and. Land O'Lakes, Wisc. Allen Ginsberg. **CP-GinsA**

Buddha in the Womb, The. Erica Jong. **SP-JongE**

Buddha in the Woodpile, A. Lawrence Ferlinghetti. **SP-FerlL**

Buddha Inherits 6 Cars on His Birthday, The. Diane Wakoski. **SP-WakoD**

Buddha is dying, The. Pictures From Tofukuji. Anne Waldman. **SP-WaldA**

Buddhas and engines serve us undersea. The Mermen. Hart Crane. **CP-CranH**

Buddha's Last Instruction, The. Mary Oliver. **SP-OlivM**

Buddhist Painter Prepares to Paint, The. Hayden Carruth. **CP-CarHS**

Buddy. Langston Hughes. **SP-HughL**

Budgerigar is baby blue, The. Budgie. Louis MacNeice. **CP-MacNL**

Budgie. Louis MacNeice. **CP-MacNL**

Budging the sluggard ripples of the Somme. Hospital Barge at Cérisy. Wilfred Owen. **CP-OwenW**

Budmouth Dears. Thomas Hardy. **CP-HardT** *Fr.* The Dynasts.

Buds and Babies. Christina Georgina Rossetti. **CP-RosC2**

Bud(spiggy nuvduh fienus). Edward Estlin Cummings. **CP-CummE**

Buenos Aires. Robert Lowell. **SP-LoweR**

Buffalo, The. Marianne Craig Moore. **CP-MoorM**

Buffalo Bill. Charles Bukowski. **SP-BukC2**

Buffalo Bill. Carl Sandburg. **CP-SandC**

Buffalo Bill's / defunct / who used to. Edward Estlin Cummings. **CP-CummE; SP-CummE**

Buffalo Coat, The. Thomas McGrath. **SP-McGrT**

Buffalo Days I was asleep when you waked up the buffalo. Collected Poems. Kenneth Koch. **SP-KochK**

Buffalo Dusk. Carl Sandburg. **CP-SandC**

Buffalo in Compound: Alberta. Margaret Atwood. **SP-AtwM1**

Buffalo Ode. Charles Olson. **CP-OlsoC**

Buffaloes are gone, The. Buffalo Dusk. Carl Sandburg. **CP-SandC**

Buffe loves fat vians, fat ale, fat all things. Epigramme. Thomas Campion. *Fr.* Observations in the Art of English Poesie. **CP-CampT**

Bufo. Alexander Pope. **OBEC; OBSV** *Fr.* Epistle to Dr. Arbuthnot. **CP-PopeA**

Bug, flower, bird on slipware fired and fluted. Syrinx. James Merrill. **SP-MerrJ**

Bug Spots. Carl Sandburg. **CP-SandC**

Buggins is Drunk[e] all night, all day he sleepes. Upon Buggins. Robert Herrick. **CP-HerrR**

Bugle Song. Tennyson. *See* The Splendor falls on castle walls.

Bugler boy from barrack (it is over the hill), A. The Bugler's First Communion. Gerard Manley Hopkins. **CP-HopkG**

Bugler named Dougal MacDougal, A. Edouard. Ogden Nash. **CP-NashO**

Bugler's First Communion, The. Gerard Manley Hopkins. **CP-HopkG**

Bugles Sang. Wilfred Owen. **CP-OwenW**

Bugs. Ogden Nash. **CP-NashO**

Bugs lived in her hair. Irene Gogle. Paul Zimmer. **SP-ZimmP**

Buick. Karl Shapiro. **SP-ShapK**

Build a man of straw and rags. Chipping Away at Death. Stephen Dunn. **SP-DunnS** *Fr.* Sympathetic Magic.

Build at Kallundborg by the sea. Kallundborg Church. John Greenleaf Whittier. **CP-WhitJ**

Build Soil. Robert Frost. **CP-FrosR**

Builder, in building the little house. The Kitchen Chimney. Robert Frost. **CP-FrosR**

Builder left one narrow rent, The. Samuel Taylor Coleridge. *See* Wedded Love.

Builder of heaven, The. Hafiz, *tr.* by Ralph Waldo Emerson. **CP-EmerR** *Fr.* Odes.

Builder of Houses, The. Jane Cooper. **SP-CoopJ**

Builders, The. Kenneth Patchen. **CP-PatcK**

Building, The. Philip Larkin. **CP-LarkP**

Building. Richard Shelton. *Fr.* Three Poems For A Twenty-Fifth Anniversary. **SP-ShelR**

Building. Gary Snyder. **CP-SnydG**

Building had better days, The. Chez Macadam. Gilbert Sorrentino. **SP-SorrG**

Building in Nova Scotia. Stephen Dunn. **SP-DunnS**

Building is a telescope of wood, The. The Ropewalk. Lewis Turco. **SP-TurcL**

Building of the Skyscraper, The. George Oppen. **CP-OppeG**

Building Site, The. Jenny Joseph.

"Walk in the woods at the hour when the fuddled sun." **SP-JoseJ**

Building up / in any way. Poet at Carpenter's Bench. Diane Wakoski. **SP-WakoD**

Buildings. James Schuyler. **CP-SchuJ**

Buildings embankment parkway grass and river. Buildings. James Schuyler. **CP-SchuJ**

Buildings to the horizon, an accretion. São Paulo. John Updike. **CP-UpdiJ**

Built for quoting in a tight corner. Roy Fisher. **SP-FishR** *Fr.* Diversions.

Built long ago, old / sills rotting in mud. My Hut. Hayden Carruth. **CP-CarHS**

Bulbs are in the sod, The. Emily Dickinson. **SP-DickE**

Bulbs burn phosphorescent, white, The. Ted Berrigan. **SP-BerrT** *Fr.* The Sonnets.

Bulk of it / In air, The. Chartres. George Oppen. **CP-OppeG**

Bulks where the barley blew, time out of mind. The Long Home. John Berryman. **CP-BerrJ**

Bull, The. William Carlos Williams. **CP-WilW1**

Bull Alone. Phoebe Hesketh. **SP-HeskP**

Bull Moses, The. Ted Hughes. **SP-HughT**

Bull of Bendylaw, The. Sylvia Plath. **SP-PlatS**

Bull-roarers cannot keep up the annual rain. Wystan Hugh Auden. *Fr.* Shorts [1948–1957] ("At peace under this mandarin, sleep, Lucina"). **CP-AudeW**

Bull Song. Margaret Atwood. *Fr.* Songs of the Transformed. **SP-AtwM1**

Bull, the Fleece are crammed [*or* cramm'd], and not a room, The. Audley Court. Tennyson. **CP-TennA**

Bulldog on the Roof—Avenue C. Marsden Hartley. **CP-HartM**

Bulldoze all memories and sanctuaries: our birthright. New Jerusalem. Louis MacNeice. **CP-MacNL**

Bulldozers come, they rip, The. The Development. Marge Piercy. **SP-PierM** *Fr.* Sand Roads.

Bullet from the back of a bush took Medgar Evers' blood, A. Only a Pawn in Their Game. "Bob Dylan." **CP-DylaB**

Bulletin. Archie Randolph Ammons. **SP-AmmoA**

!Bulletin! Malcolm Lowry. **CP-LowrM**

Bulletin from the Stadium, A. Thom Gunn. **CP-GunnT**

Bulletin Has Just Come In, A. Ogden Nash. **CP-NashO**

Bullfinches, The. Thomas Hardy. **CP-HardT**

Bulwark. Laurence Lieberman. **SP-LiebL**

Bum & zoom. leaving & yet never this awful old. September's Book. Alice Notley. **SP-NotlA**

Bumble Bee—the Bumble Bee, The. George Meredith. **CP-MerG2**

Bumblebee / is less than a stack of, The. Poem for Liz. Charles Bukowski. **SP-BukC2**

Bump d'Bump. Maya Angelou. **SP-AngeM**

Bumpity Road to Mutual Devotion, The. Marge Piercy. **SP-PierM**

Bums, on Waking. James Dickey. **CP-DickJ**

Bunch of Grapes, The. George Herbert. **CP-HerbG**

Bunch of wrack was hung inside the porch, A. The Witch. John Hewitt. **CP-HewiJ**

Buncha hardboil guys frum duh A.C. fulla. Edward Estlin Cummings. **CP-CummE**

Bundle of Myrrh Is My Well-Beloved unto Me, A. Christina Georgina Rossetti. **CP-RosC2**

Bundles. Carl Sandburg. **CP-SandC**

Bungalows, The. John Ashbery. **SP-AshbJ**

Bungie do's fast; looks pale; puts Sack-cloth on. Upon Bungie. Robert Herrick. **CP-HerrR**

Bunk Johnson Blowing. Muriel Rukeyser. **CP-RukeM**

Bunyan, of course. But Potton it was, or Sandy. Bedfordshire. Donald Davie. **CP-DavDo**

Buona Notte. Percy Bysshe Shelley. **CP-ShelP**

"Buona notte, buona notte!"—come mai. Buona Notte. Percy Bysshe Shelley. **CP-ShelP**

Buoy—no, how. Louis Zukofsky. *Fr.* 29 Poems. **CP-ZukLS**

Buoys begin clanging like churches. The River That Is East. Galway Kinnell. **CP-KinnG**

Bura and Helice on Achaian ground. Ovid, *tr.* by Sir Walter Ralegh. **CP-RaleW** *Fr.* Metamorphoses.

Burbank crossed a little bridge. Burbank with a Baedeker: Beistein with a Cigar. Thomas Stearns Eliot. **CP-ElioT**

Burbank with a Baedeker: Beistein with a Cigar. Thomas Stearns Eliot. **CP-ElioT**

Burden. Richard Eberhart. **CP-EberR**

Burden, The. Rudyard Kipling. **CP-KiplR** *Fr.* Debits and Credits.

Burden Baskets. Adrienne Rich. *Fr.* Turning the Wheel. **SP-RicA2**

Burden of fair women. Vain delight, The. A Ballad of Burdens. Algernon Charles Swinburne. **SP-SwinA**

Burden of Strength, The. George Meredith. **CP-MerG1**

Burdened heart that bleeds and bears, A. When I Was in Trouble I Called upon the Lord. Christina Georgina Rossetti. **CP-RosC2**

Burdens of the world, The. Correction. Archie Randolph Ammons. **SP-AmmoA**

Burdock—clawed my Gown, A. Emily Dickinson. **CP-DickE**

Bureaucrats: Diggers. Thomas Merton. **CP-MertT**

Burghers, The. Thomas Hardy. **CP-HardT**

Burghers of Petty Death. Wallace Stevens. **CP-StevW**

Burglar, The. Ron Koertge. **SP-KoerR**

Burglar of Babylon, The. Elizabeth Bishop. **CP-BishE**

Burglary. William Matthews. **SP-MattW**

Burial, The. Rudyard Kipling. **CP-KiplR**

Burial, The. Archibald MacLeish. **CP-MacLA**

Burial. Edna St. Vincent Millay. **CP-MillE**

Burial. May Sarton. **SP-SartM**

Burial. Alice Walker. **CP-WalkA**

Burial Anthem. Christina Georgina Rossetti. **CP-RosC3**

Burial Ground. Charles Olson. **CP-OlsoC**

Burial of Barber. John Greenleaf Whittier. **CP-WhitJ**

Burial Place of Ibn Abbad, The. Thomas Merton. *Fr.* Readings from Ibn Abbad. **CP-MertT**

Buriall. Robert Herrick. **CP-HerrR**

Buried among white rooms. Ape Experiment Room. Philip Larkin. **CP-LarkP**

Buried at Springs. James Schuyler. **CP-SchuJ**

Buried Lake, The. Allen Tate. **CP-TateA**

Buried Life, The. Matthew Arnold. **SP-ArnoM**

Burke. Samuel Taylor Coleridge. *Fr.* Effusions. **CP-ColeS**

Burlesque. Muriel Rukeyser. **CP-RukeM**

Burlesque for Palgrave on the Pronunciation of "Metamorphosis." Robert Browning. **CP-BroR2**

Burlesque Translation of Lines from Lope de Vega's *Arcadia.* Samuel Johnson. *See* The Turnip Vendor.

Burly and clean, with bark in umber scrolled. The Return. Robert Penn Warren. *Fr.* Kentucky Mountain Farm. **SP-WarrR**

Burly, dozing, humble-bee. The Humble-Bee. Ralph Waldo Emerson. **CP-EmerR**

Burly driver at my side, The. The Hill-Top. John Greenleaf Whittier. **CP-WhitJ**

Burly Fading One, The. Robert Earl Hayden. **CP-HaydR**

Burly major they denied, The. On the Grettir Saga. Louis MacNeice. *Fr.* Dark Age Glosses. **CP-MacNL**

Burly, provincial France. Brantôme. Donald Davie. **CP-DavDo**

Burma Casualty. Alun Lewis. **CP-LewiA**

"Lying in the hospital he often thought."

"Mending, with books and papers and a fan."

"Three endless weeks of sniping all the way."

" 'Your leg must go. Okay?' the surgeon said."

Burn, The. Galway Kinnell. **SP-KinnG**

Burn-Out. Gary Gildner. **SP-GildG**

Burn this shot. That gray is what it is. A Snapshot of 15th S.W. Richard Hugo. **CP-HugoR**

Burn your literary verses. Ralph Waldo Emerson. **CP-EmerR**

Burne, or drowne me, choose ye whether. Song. Robert Herrick. **CP-HerrR**

Burned out, there was no road back. Glyndŵr Subdued. Steve Griffiths. **SP-GrifS**

Burning / burning / burning / there was finally something. Crow's Last Stand. Ted Hughes. **SP-HughT**

Burning. Gary Snyder. *Fr.* Myths and Texts.
    Amitabha's Vow. **CP-SnydG**
    "Face in the crook of her neck." **CP-SnydG**
    John Muir on Mt. Ritter. **CP-SnydG**
    Maitreya the Future Buddha. **CP-SnydG**
    Maudgalyâyana Saw Hell. **CP-SnydG**
    Second Shaman Song. **CP-SnydG**
    "Spikes of new smell driven up nostrils." **CP-SnydG**
    "Stone-flake and salmon." **CP-SnydG**
    Text, The. **CP-SnydG**
    "Wash me on home, mama." **CP-SnydG**

Burning Babe, The. Robert Southwell. **CP-SoutR**

Burning Book [or the Contented Metaphysician], The. Edwin Arlington Robinson. **CP-RobiE**

Burning Book, The. William Everson. **SP-EverW** *Fr.* The Falling of the Grain.

Burning Bush. Daniel Gerard Hoffman. **SP-HoffD**

Burning Bush. Muriel Rukeyser. **CP-RukeM**

Burning Dawn. Hayden Carruth. **CP-CarHS**

Burning Drift-Wood. John Greenleaf Whittier. **CP-WhitJ**

Burning fire shakes in the night, The. Invocation. Walter de la Mare. **CP-DeLaW**

Burning Graves at Netherton, The. Roy Fisher. **SP-FishR**

Burning Island. Gary Snyder. **CP-SnydG**

Burning Mountain, The. John Gould Fletcher. **SP-FletJ**

Burning Mystery of Anna in 1951, The. Kenneth Koch. **SP-KochK**

Burning of Bustin's Island, The. Jim Carroll. **SP-CarrJ**

Burning of Paper instead of Children, The. Adrienne Rich. **SP-RicA1; SP-RicA2**

Burning Oneself In. Adrienne Rich. **SP-RicA2**

Burning Oneself Out. Adrienne Rich. **SP-RicA2**

Burning Roses. Patti Smith. **SP-SmitP**

Burning the Christmas Greens. William Carlos Williams. **CP-WilW2**

Burning the Holly. Thomas Hardy. **CP-HardT**

Burning the Leaves. Howard Nemerov. **CP-NemeH**

Burning the Letters. Randall Jarrell. **CP-JarrR**

Burning the Letters. Sylvia Plath. **CP-PlatS**

Burning the News. Lewis Turco. **SP-TurcL**

Burning the Small Dead. Gary Snyder. **CP-SnydG**

Burning Trash. John Updike. **CP-UpdiJ**

Burnished, burned-out, still burning as the year. The Public Garden. Robert Lowell. **SP-LoweR**

Burnished-head / By burnished-head. Euripides, *tr.* by Hilda Doolittle ("H.D."). **CP-DoolH** *Fr.* Iphigenia [*or* Iphigeneia] in Aulis.

Burnishing, Oakland. Muriel Rukeyser. **CP-RukeM**

Burns. John Greenleaf Whittier. **CP-WhitJ**

Burns Grace at Kirkudbright. Robert Burns. *See* Some have [*or* hae] meat and cannot [*or* canna] eat.

Burnt Bridge, The. Louis MacNeice. **CP-MacNL**

Burnt Norton. Thomas Stearns Eliot. **CMoP; LiTM; MoAB; MoAmPo; NAAL-2; PoE** *Fr.* Four Quartets. **CP-ElioT**
    "Words move, music moves." **UnS**

Burnt-Out Spa, The. Sylvia Plath. **CP-PlatS**

Burnt pier: the last passenger: the farewells, The. Malcolm Lowry. **CP-LowrM**

Burnt Post, The. John Hewitt. **CP-HewiJ**

Burnt Ship, A. John Donne. **CP-DonnJ**

Burnt year. Trick riders blunder about the concrete, A. Roy Fisher. **SP-FishR** *Fr.* New Diversions.

Burr is a smell-feast, and a man alone. Upon Burr. Robert Herrick. **CP-HerrR**

Burr Oaks. Richard Eberhart. **CP-EberR**
    Attic, The.
    Barn, The.
    Cemetery, The.
    Grove, The.
    Jungle, The. **MoAB**
    Orchard, The.
    Pasture, The.

Burra-Boo—Shirra Sha! Song of the New Zealander among the Ruins of Old London. George Meredith. **CP-MerG2**

Burros are all heehawed out, The. Going Back Home. Al Young. **CP-YounA**

Bursting Rapture. Robert Frost. **CP-FrosR**

Bursts from a rending East in flaws. Hard Weather. George Meredith. **CP-MerG1**

Bury Hope out of sight, / No book for it and no bell. Christina Georgina Rossetti. **CP-RosC2**

Bury me on a Sunday. Farmer Dunman's Funeral. Thomas Hardy. **CP-HardT**

Bury the Great Duke. Ode on the Death of the Duke of Wellington. Tennyson. **CP-TennA**

Bury the Great Duke. Tennyson. **EBVVPR** *Fr.* Ode on the Death of the Duke of Wellington. **CP-TennA**

Bury this old Illinois farmer with respect. Illinois Farmer. Carl Sandburg. **CP-SandC**

Bury thy dead, dear friend. Ye Have Forgotten the Exhortation. Christina Georgina Rossetti. **CP-RosC3**

Bury thy sorrows, and they shall rise. Sorrows and Joys. George Meredith. **CP-MerG1**

Burying Blues for Janis. Marge Piercy. **SP-PierM**

Burying Field. Louise McNeill. **SP-McNeL**

Burying Ground by the Ties. Archibald MacLeish. **CP-MacLA**

Bus along St Clair: December, A. Margaret Atwood. **SP-AtwM1**

Bus driver / went gently on the bends, The. Still Too Quick to Hold. Steve Griffiths. **SP-GrifS**

Bus has gone by, The. Fernando Pessoa. *Fr.* Twelve Poems from *The Keeper of the Flocks*. **CP-MertT**

Bus is crammed with laden passengers, The. On a Country Bus Forty Years Ago. John Hewitt. **CP-HewiJ**

Bus is waiting at the southern gate, The. James Fenton. **SCBI** *Fr.* A German Requiem. **SP-FentJ**

Bus jolts on defunctive gasoline, The. Last Bus, Saturday Night. Wystan Hugh Auden. **CP-AudWJ**

Bus Stop. Alice Notley. **SP-NotlA**

Bus to Alliston, Ontario, The. Margaret Atwood. **SP-AtwM2**

Bus to Veracruz, The. Richard Shelton. **SP-ShelR**

Busbound out of New York. Accumulation. John Updike. **CP-UpdiJ**

Buses Headed for Scranton, The. Ogden Nash. **CP-NashO**

Business, The. Robert Creeley. **CP-CreeR**

Business. George Herbert. **CP-HerbG**

Business, The. Charles Olson. **CP-OlsoC**

Business Acquaintances. John Updike. **CP-UpdiJ**

Business enough indeed. Emily Dickinson. **SP-DickE**

Business Girls. Sir John Betjeman. **CP-BetjJ**

Business man the acquirer vast, The. My Legacy. Walt Whitman. **CP-WhitW**

Business man, the acquirer vast, The. *earlier vers. of* My Legacy. Walt Whitman. **CP-WhitW**

Business Men. Louis MacNeice. *Fr.* Entered in the Minutes. **CP-MacNL**

Business men with awkward hips. The City. Sir John Betjeman. **CP-BetjJ**

Business Personals. John Ashbery. **SP-AshbJ**

Busload of Faith. "Lou Reed." **SP-ReedL**

Busride along waterfront down Yessler under street bridge to the old red wobbly hall. Afternoon Seattle. Allen Ginsberg. **CP-GinsA**

Bustle in a House, The. Emily Dickinson. **CP-DickE**

Busy day has hurried by , The. Written on Returning to the P. of I. on the 10th of January, 1827. Emily Brontë. **CP-BronE**

Busy inquiring heart, what wouldst thou know? The Discharge. George Herbert. **CP-HerbG**

Busy missing you. Emily Dickinson. **SP-DickE**

Busy [*or* Busie] old fool[e], unruly sun[ne]. The Sun[ne] Rising. John Donne. **CP-DonnJ**

But. Robert Creeley. **CP-CreeR**

But. Robert Creeley. **CP-CreeR**

"But / he" i / staring / into winter twi. Edward Estlin Cummings. **CP-CummE**

But a chappie needs diverting. A Chappie. Paul Laurence Dunbar. **CP-DunbP**

But also dying / (as well as). Edward Estlin Cummings. **CP-CummE**

But anxious cares the pensive nymph oppressed. Alexander Pope. **EBNV; OXAEP-1** *Fr.* The Rape of the Lock[, an Heroi-Comical Poem]. **CP-PopeA**

But as this fugitive sunlight. Ralph Waldo Emerson. **CP-EmerR**

But at night the park. George Oppen. *Fr.* A Narrative. **CP-OppeG**

But be contented: when that fell arrest. Sonnet 74. William Shakespeare. **NAEL-1; OBSC; OXAEP-1; Son** *Fr.* Sonnets. **CP-ShaWS**

But being not amazing:without love. Edward Estlin Cummings. **CP-CummE**

But borne, and like a short Delight. Upon a Child. An Epitaph. Robert Herrick. **CP-HerrR**

But can see better there, and laughing there. *Quote fr. Edward Young.* Gwendolyn Brooks. **PoNe** *Fr.* Notes from the Childhood and the Girlhood. **SP-BrooG**

But cause thou hear'st the mighty king of Spain. To Inigo, Marquess Would Be, a Corollary. Ben Jonson. **CP-JonsB**

But come. Grief must have its term? Guilt too, then. James Fenton. **SCBI** *Fr.* A German Requiem. **SP-FentJ**

But desire is a kind of leisure. Lust Acts. William Matthews. **SP-MattW**

But did not Adam, Eve's appointed playmate. History of the Fall. Robert Ranke Graves. **CP-GravR**

But did you ever know the whole world was once held prisoner in a bank? Thomas Merton. *Fr.* The Early Legend. **CP-MertT**

But do not let us quarrel any more. Andrea del Sarto. Robert Browning. **CP-BroR1**

But do not let your ignorance. Wendell Berry. *Fr.* Testament. **CP-BerrW**

But do thy worst to steal thyself away. Sonnet 92. William Shakespeare. *Fr.* Sonnets. **CP-ShaWS**

But don't you know it, my dear. Looking at a Picture on an Anniversary. Thomas Hardy. **CP-HardT**

But even so, he said, daily I hanker, daily. Louis MacNeice. *Fr.* Day of Returning. **CP-MacNL**

But everything has worked out fine. Jim Carroll. *Fr.* Birthday Poem. **SP-CarrJ**

But evil is a third thing. Doors. David Herbert Lawrence. **CP-LawrD**

But few they were who came to see. The American Aloe on Exhibition. Herman Melville. **SP-MelvH**

But for a brief / Moment, a poised minute. A Grasshopper. Richard Wilbur. **CP-WilbR**

But for the Grace of God. Edwin Arlington Robinson. **CP-RobiE**

But for the wits of either Charles's days. Alexander Pope. **EPCY** *Fr.* The First Epistle of the Second Book of Horace Imitated. **CP-PopeA**

But Fortune governed all their works[,] till when. Aeschylus. **CP-RaleW; SiPSBD**, *tr. by* Sir Walter Ralegh; *Fr.* Prometheus Bound. **CP-BroEB**

But from these years I can remember still. Those Morning Walks. John Hewitt. **CP-HewiJ**

But give them me, the mouth, the eyes, the brow! Eurydice to Orpheus. Robert Browning. **CP-BroR1**

But God will keep his promise yet. Ralph Waldo Emerson. **CP-EmerR**

But God's Own Descent. Robert Frost. **EaLo** *Fr.* Kitty Hawk. **CP-FrosR**

But grant I may relapse, for want of grace. Alexander Pope. *Fr.* The Second Epistle of the Second Book of Horace Imitated. **CP-PopeA**

But grant, the virtues of a temp'rate prime. Life's Last Scene. Samuel Johnson. **OBEC; SeCePo** *Fr.* The Vanity of Human Wishes [The Tenth Satire of Juvenal Imitated]. **CP-JohnS**

But granted that it's nothing paradoxically enough beyond mere personal. Edward Estlin Cummings. **CP-CummE**

But Greece and her foundations are. Percy Bysshe Shelley. **GrIP** *Fr.* Hellas. **CP-ShelP**

But hark! the Curfew tolls! and lo! the night. A Winter's Evening. William Wordsworth. **CP-WorW1**

But he his wonted pride. Satan and His Host. John Milton. **OBS** *Fr.* Book I. **FHYEP; NAEL-1; OAEL-1; OxAEP-1** *Fr.* Paradise Lost. **CP-MiltJ**

But He Says I Misunderstood. Alice Notley. **SP-NotlA**

But hear. If you stay, and the child be born. In the Restaurant. Thomas Hardy. **MoAB; MoBrPo** *Fr.* Satires of Circumstance in Fifteen Glimpses. **CP-HardT**

But here no cannon thunders to the gale. Conclusion. William Wordsworth. *Fr.* The River Duddon [A Series of Sonnets]. **CP-WorW2**

But I am not lost. The Way Back. Leonard Cohen. **CP-CoheL**

But I am not of the King's table; nor his stable. Misanthrope. John Crowe Ransom. *Fr.* Two Gentlemen in Bonds. **SP-RansJ**

But I came back, after the last bus. Thom Gunn. *Fr.* Talbot Road. **CP-GunnT**

But I Say unto You: Love One Another. David Herbert Lawrence. **CP-LawrD**

But I shall live when you are dead and damned. Malcolm Lowry. *Fr.* The Comedian. **CP-LowrM**

But I would rather be horizontal. I Am Vertical. Sylvia Plath. **CP-PlatS**

But I'd go today. Ultimatum. Philip Larkin. **FL** *Fr.* Poetry of Departures. **CP-LarkP**

But if a living dance upon dead minds. Edward Estlin Cummings. **CP-CummE; SP-CummE**

But if as (not by that the soul desired). Arthur Hugh Clough. *Fr.* Seven Sonnets. **SP-ClouA**

But if i should say. Edward Estlin Cummings. **CP-CummE**

But if that Cerberus, my mind, should be. The Utter Rim. Robert Ranke Graves. **CP-GravR**

But if the wind should fall and silence spread. Hayden Carruth. *Fr.* The Asylum. **CP-CarHL**

But if there be a power too just and strong. John Dryden. **NOCV** *Fr.* Religio Laici. **SP-DrydJ**

But if thou do thy best. Ralph Waldo Emerson. **CP-EmerR**

But in the dome of mighty Mars the red. Geoffrey Chaucer. **OBWP** *Fr.* The Knight's Tale. *Fr.* The Canterbury Tales. **CP-ChauG**

But in the end one tires of the high-flown. About the Phoenix. James Merrill. **SP-MerrJ**

But in these years, what is free, what is strong? Muriel Rukeyser. **CP-RukeM**

But Islands of the Blessed, bless you, son. An Answer. Robert Frost. **CP-FrosR**

But isn't talking. The Hill Has Something to Say. Rita Dove. **SP-DoveR**

But it won't be that way. Hilda Doolittle. **AnAn** *Fr.* Sigil. **CP-DoolH**

But, it's because the liquor of summer nights. Here Everything Is Still Floating. John Ashbery. **SP-AshbJ**

But it's falling already. Apple Tree in May. May Sarton. **SP-SartM**

But Joan, where is Bessy?—She. George Meredith. *Fr.* Fragments for "The Harvest Home" and "The Doe." **CP-MerG2**

But lately seen in gladsome green. The Auld Man's Winter Thought. Robert Burns. **CP-BurnR**

But let applause be dealt in all we may. George Crabbe. **OBNC** *Fr.* The Vicar. **SP-CrabG** *Fr.* The Borough.

But liberty, and triumphs on the Main. New Churches. William Wordsworth. *Fr.* Ecclesiastical Sonnets. **CP-WorW2**

But little Carmine hath her face. Emily Dickinson. **CP-DickE**

But lose patience. Louis Zukofsky. *Fr.* Sequence 1944-6. **CP-ZukLS**

But lovelier far than this, the paradise. William Wordsworth. **OAEL-2** *Fr.* Retrospect Love of Nature Leading to Love of Mankind. *Fr.* The Prelude; Growth of a Poet's Mind [1850 vers.]. **CP-WorW3**

But masked of the self. William Everson. *Fr.* In the Fictive Wish. **SP-EverW**

But men have known. Archibald MacLeish. *Fr.* Hamlet of A. Macleish. **CP-MacLA**

But Men loved Darkness[e] Rather Than [*or* Then] Light. Richard Crashaw. **CP-CrasR**

But mind, but thought / If these have been the master part of us. Life and Thought. Matthew Arnold. **FiP** *Fr.* Empedocles on Etna. **SP-ArnoM**

But mr can you maybe listen there's. Edward Estlin Cummings. **CP-CummE**

But most by numbers judge a poet's song. Alexander Pope. **FiP; NIP**, *ll.* 337-383; **SeCePo** *Fr.* An Essay on Criticism. **CP-PopeA** (Poetical Numbers.) **SeCePo**, *ll.* 337-383;

But Murderous. Stevie Smith. **CP-SmitS**

But nakedness, woolen massa, concerns an innermost atom. Nudity at the Capital. Wallace Stevens. **CP-StevW**

But Nature whistled with all her winds. Ralph Waldo Emerson. **CP-EmerR**

But nearer than Guardian Angel. Hilda Doolittle. **NALW** *Fr.* Tribute to the Angels. **CP-DoolH**

But never fall from fealty to light. Malcolm Lowry. *Fr.* The Cantinas. **CP-LowrM**

But never yet the man was found. Ralph Waldo Emerson. **CP-EmerR**

But no screen would show. Travelogue. George Oppen. **CP-OppeG**

But not for a king's daughter? Here where Sir Patrick Spens. The North Sea. Louis MacNeice. **CP-MacNL**

But not on a shell, she starts. The Paltry Nude Starts on a Spring Voyage. Wallace Stevens. **CP-StevW**

But now at thirty years my hair is grey. Growing Old. Byron. **NOBE; SCV** *Fr.* Canto the First. **EnRP; NAEL-2; NoP; OAEL-2; PoE** *Fr.* Don Juan. **CP-Byron**

But now farewell. I am going a long way. Tennyson. **FaBoRV** *Fr.* The Passing of Arthur. **FHYEP; NAEL-2; OBNC** *Fr.* Idylls of the King. **CP-TennA**

But now having seen. William Everson. *Fr.* In the Fictive Wish. **SP-EverW**

But now I see myself a fool. Villaknell. Malcolm Lowry. **CP-LowrM**

But now my oat proceeds. John Milton. **OxBoS** *Fr.* Lycidas. **CP-MiltJ**

But now the gentle dew-fall sends abroad. Looking Down on Nether Stowey. Samuel Taylor Coleridge. **FaBoPP** *Fr.* Fears in Solitude. **CP-ColeS**

But now the salmon-fishers moist. Carrying Their Coracles. Andrew Marvell. **ChTr** *Fr.* Upon Appleton House [To My Lord Fairfax]. **CP-MarvA**

But now the wholesome music of the wood. Vivien's Song. Tennyson. **OAEL-2** *Fr.* Balin and Balan. *Fr.* Idylls of the King. **CP-TennA**

But Now They Have Seen, and Hated. Richard Crashaw. **CP-CrasR**

But, O immortals! What had I to plead. Christopher Smart. **NOEC** *Fr.* Hymn to the Supreme Being. **SP-SmarC**

But O to see his solar eyes. Ralph Waldo Emerson. **CP-EmerR**

But observe;although / once is never the beginning of. Edward Estlin Cummings. **CP-CummE**

But of course the poem is not an assertion. Do you see? When I wrote. The Impossible Indispensability of the Ars Poetica. Hayden Carruth. **CP-CarHS**

But of Life? Kenneth Patchen. **CP-PatcK**

But often now the youthful eye cuts down its. God Works in a Mysterious Way. Gwendolyn Brooks. **SP-BrooG**

But oil on plaster yet again? Dialogue in Milan. David Markson. **CP-MarkD**

But old Lares with the rest forgot in time. James McAuley. *Fr.* The Autobiography of the Impotent Man. **SP-McAuJ**

But once I dared to lift my eyes. To ———. Byron. **CP-Byron**

But once winds lightened, freshening fair from the West. Hayden Carruth. *Fr.* The Asylum. **CP-CarHL**

But one stood up and said: I love. Votaries of Both Sexes Cry First to Venus. Stevie Smith. **CP-SmitS**

But Only Mine. James Wright. **CP-WrigJ**

But only three in all God's universe. Sonnet. Elizabeth Barrett Browning. *Fr.* Sonnets from the Portuguese. **CP-BroEB**

But Oothoon is not so; a virgin filled with virgin fancies. Desire and Jealousy. William Blake. **ECEV** *Fr.* Visions of the Daughters of Albion. **CP-BlakW**

But our escape: to what god did we owe it. Pandora. Robert Ranke Graves. **CP-GravR**

But outer Space. Robert Frost. **CP-FrosR**

But peaceful was the night. John Milton. **FaBoCh** *Fr.* Hymn on the Morning of Christ's Nativity [*or* On the Morning of Christ's Nativity]. **FiP; NAEL-1; NOBE; OBEV; OtMeF** *Fr.* On the Morning of Christs Nativity. **CP-MiltJ**

But please walk softly as you do. Enter This Deserted House. Shel Silverstein. **SP-SilS2**

But ran from such wondering as I ran. And All That Came Thereafter. Robert Penn Warren. **SP-WarrR**

But rarely seen since Nature's birth. Robert Burns. *Fr.* On Jessy Lewars. **CP-BurnR**

But rumors hung about the country-side. At Some Lone Alehouse. Matthew Arnold. **FaBoDD** *Fr.* The Scholar-Gipsy. **SP-ArnoM**

But scarce observ'd, the knowing and the bold. On Gold. Samuel Johnson. **IHNG** *Fr.* The Vanity of Human Wishes [The Tenth Satire of Juvenal Imitated]. **CP-JohnS**

But see here comes thy reverend Sire. John Milton. **EBEV** *Fr.* Samson Agonistes. **CP-MiltJ**

But see what living glory floods the west. George Meredith. **CP-MerG2**

But shairly, shairly, there maun be. "Hugh MacDiarmid." **SP-MacDH** *Fr.* Esplumeoir.

But she is wise and waits until I sleep. She Comes To Him in the Night. Alun Lewis. *Fr.* War Wedding. **CP-LewiA**

But she was both,—she was both loved and love. Archibald MacLeish. **CP-MacLA** *Fr.* The Happy Marriage.

But should I not pity that poor devil. Man of Evil. Robert Ranke Graves. **CP-GravR**

But since I have feet I can walk. I Have No Wings. Richard Shelton. **SP-ShelR**

But, sires, o word forgat I in my tale. Geoffrey Chaucer. **EBEV** *Fr.* The Pardoner's Tale. **FHYEP; NAEL-1; NAWM-1; NoP; OAEL-1; PoE** *Fr.* The Canterbury Tales. **CP-ChauG**

But sithens you it assay to kill. Sir Thomas Wyatt. **CP-WyatT**

But So As by Fire. George Oppen. **NNaP** *Fr.* Some San Francisco Poems. **CP-OppeG**

But so to be the denizen stingaree. Euclid Avenue. Hart Crane. **CP-CranH**

But sovran Jove's rapacious Bird, the regal. *verse tr. fr.* Metamorphoses *by* Apuleius. Elizabeth Barrett Browning. **CP-BroEB**

But still, still. . . / In stillness mystery calls. Sonnet. Hayden Carruth. **CP-CarHS** *Fr.* Sonnets.

But still the thunder of Los peals loud and thus the thunder's cry. William Blake. **OAEL-2** *Fr.* Jerusalem; The Emanation of the Giant Albion. **CP-BlakW**

But tell me, child, your choice, your fancy; what to buy, *sl. diff. vers.* Gerard Manley Hopkins. *See* The Handsome Heart.

But that from slow dissolving pomps of dawn. Arthur Hugh Clough. **SP-ClouA**

But that Thou art my wisdom, Lord. Submission. George Herbert. **CP-HerbG**

But that was nothing to what things came out. Welsh Incident. Robert Ranke Graves. **CP-GravR**

But the Beast of the Wood came as a smiling man. Kenneth Patchen. *Fr.* Wanderers of the Pale Wood. **CP-PatcK**

But the hearts that once adored me. Emily Brontë. **CP-BronE**

But the Images of His Former Dreams Still Haunted Him. Kenneth Patchen. **CP-PatcK**

But the light is imagined. Gilbert Sorrentino. **SP-SorrG**

But the little more: the little more. The Little More. James Dickey. **CP-DickJ**

But the majestic river floated on. Matthew Arnold. **SP-ArnoM** *Fr.* Sohrab and Rustum.

But the other / day i was passing a certain. Edward Estlin Cummings. **CP-CummE**

—But the street is the river—. Butterton Ford. Roy Fisher. **SP-FishR**

But the surf is white, down the long strange coast. St. Francis of San Francisco. Nicholas Vachel Lindsay. *Fr.* Golden Whales of California. **CP-LindV**

But the Wine-press of Los is eastward of Golgonooza, before the Seat. William Blake. **NOBRP** *Fr.* Milton. **CP-BlakW**

But there was one who was the paragon. The One I Loved. John Hewitt. **CP-HewiJ**

But these are not my hills, they are too high. Mourne Mountains. John Hewitt. **CP-HewiJ**

But they are accurate. That is a target. A Game of Darts at the Chesterfield Arms. Muriel Rukeyser. **CP-RukeM**

But they are telling stories. Frank Templeton Prince. *Fr.* Drypoints of the Hasidim. **CP-PrinF**

But they could *do* something about that. Jenny Joseph. *Fr.* Life and Turgid Times of A. Citizen. **SP-JoseJ**

But this is our desire, and of its worth. The Gyroscope. Muriel Rukeyser. **CP-RukeM**

But thou, false infidel! shall writhe. Byron. **VVA** *Fr.* The Giaour. **CP-Byron**

But Thy Commandment Is Exceeding Broad. Christina Georgina Rossetti. **CP-RosC2**

But to advise thee, Ben, in this strict age. On the Magnetic Lady. Ben Jonson. **CP-JonsB**

But, to outweigh all harm, the sacred Book. Translation of the Bible. William Wordsworth. *Fr.* Ecclesiastical Sonnets. **CP-WorW2**

But to reach the archimedean point. Mysticism Has Not the Patience To Wait for God's Revelation. Richard Eberhart. **CP-EberR**

But, to remote Northumbria's royal Hall. Paulinus. William Wordsworth. *Fr.* Ecclesiastical Sonnets. **CP-WorW2**

But to turn in on the world, you are all the places. Louis MacNeice. *Fr.* Flowers in the Interval. **CP-MacNL**

But true expression, like th' unchanging sun. Alexander Pope. **FHYEP** *Fr.* An Essay on Criticism. **CP-WorW2**

But   turning   a corner   ,i. Edward Estlin Cummings. **CP-CummE**

But turning toward Ololon in terrible majesty Milton. William Blake. **OXAEP-2** *Fr.* Milton. **CP-BlakW**

But 'twas a time when France was rejoiced. William Wordsworth. **FaBoPV** *Fr.* Cambridge and the Alps. *Fr.* The Prelude; Growth of a Poet's Mind [1805 vers.]. **CP-WorW3**

But under the carpeting, / past the pavement's end, and. Oliverio Girondo. Pablo Neruda, *tr. fr. Spanish by* Ben Belitt. **SP-NeruP**

But we cannot go back to Charles V. Charles V by Titian. Robert Lowell. **SP-LoweR**

But we little animaux have gone. Malcolm Lowry. **CP-LowrM**

But we must build our walls, for what we are. Ultimatum. Philip Larkin. **CP-LarkP**

But we've the may / (for you are in love). Song. Edward Estlin Cummings. **CP-CummE**

But what avail inadequate words to reach. Utterance. John Greenleaf Whittier. **CP-WhitJ**

But what if One, through grove or flowery mead. Reproof. William Wordsworth. *Fr.* Ecclesiastical Sonnets. **CP-WorW2**

But what indeed is ask'd of me? Gerard Manley Hopkins. **CP-HopkG**

But what is love? Tell me, dear heart, I beg you. What is Love? Robert Ranke Graves. **CP-GravR**

But what is strength without a double share. John Milton. **ChIV-1** *Fr.* Samson Agonistes. **CP-MiltJ**

But what is the earthquake's cry at last. The Voice of the Earthquake. Nicholas Vachel Lindsay. *Fr.* Golden Whales of California. **CP-LindV**

But when I waked, I saw that I saw not. A Storm at Sea. John Donne. **NOBE** *Fr.* The Storm[e]. **CP-DonnJ**

But when so many had died, so many and at such speed. James Fenton. **SCBI** *Fr.* A German Requiem. **SP-FentJ**

But when the next day brake from underground. Percivale's Quest. Tennyson. **OAEL-2** *Fr.* The Holy Grail. *Fr.* Idylls of the King. **CP-TennA**

But when to mischief mortals bend their will. Alexander Pope. **OXAEP-1** *Fr.* The Rape of the Lock[, an Heroi-Comical Poem]. **CP-PopeA**

But whence came they who for the Saviour Lord. The Vaudois. William Wordsworth. *Fr.* Ecclesiastical Sonnets. **CP-WorW2**

But wher they may returne with honors grace. Sonnet 9. Mary Sidney, Countess of Montgomery Wroth. *Fr.* A Crowne of Sonetts Dedicated to Love. *Fr.* Pamphilia to Amphilanthus. **CP-WrotM**

But where began the change; and what's my crime? George Meredith. **NBM; PoEL-5** *Fr.* Modern Love. **CP-MerG1**

But wherefore do not you a mightier way. Sonnet 16. William Shakespeare. **FaBoEn** *Fr.* Sonnets. **CP-ShaWS**

But where's the man who counsel can bestow. Alexander Pope. **OXAEP-1,** *ll.* 631–744; *Fr.* An Essay on Criticism. **CP-PopeA**

But whether in the uncoloured light of truth. Arthur Hugh Clough. *Fr.* Seven Sonnets. **CP-ClouA**

But who died here. It's Not Who Lived Here. Charles Bukowski. **SP-BukC2**

But who is it that through the salmonberry wobbleth. With Sweet Sweet Love from All Your Amused Little Animals. Malcolm Lowry. **CP-LowrM**

But who is it who the forest leapeth. With Sweet Devotion and True from All the Little Animals. Malcolm Lowry. **CP-LowrM**

But who is this, what thing of sea or land? Delilah. John Milton. **SeCePo** *Fr.* Samson Agonistes. **CP-MiltJ**

But who shall parcel out. William Wordsworth. **TOF** *Fr.* School-Time. **FHYEP** *Fr.* The Prelude; Growth of a Poet's Mind [1850 vers.]. **CP-WorW3**

But whom those errant moans accused. George Meredith. *Fr.* Napoléon. **CP-MerG1**

But whoso may, thrice happy man him hold. Edmund Spenser. **WGRP** *Fr.* An Hymne of Heavenly Beautie. **PeECV** *Fr.* Fowre Hymnes. **CP-Spens**

"But why did he do it, Grandpa?" I said. A Confederate Veteran Tries to Explain the Event. Robert Penn Warren. **SP-WarrR**

But why do I feel so strangely about you? Sphinx. David Herbert Lawrence. **CP-LawrD**

"But why do you go?" said the lady, while both sat[e] under the yew. Lord Walter's Wife. Elizabeth Barrett Browning. **CP-BroEB**

"but why should" / the / greatest. Edward Estlin Cummings. **CP-CummE**

But why so solemn when the bell tolled? Tolling Bell. Robert Ranke Graves. **CP-GravR**

But women pass as if I were a urinal. I Wanted My Name on the Side of a Building I Wanted to Be as Feared as the Word Biopsy. Ron Koertge. **SP-KoerR**

But work is alien; what do I care for the Master. Louis MacNeice. *Fr.* Autumn Journal. **CP-MacNL**

But ye shall destroy their altars. Gary Snyder. *See* The Ancient forests of China logged.

But Yet Again, We Fought. David Markson. **CP-MarkD**

But You. Robert Creeley. **CP-CreeR**

But you *have* disturbed my heart. *see also* Another Room. Leonard Cohen. **CP-CoheL**

But, you see, said the handsome young man with the chamois gloves. Natural Complexion. David Herbert Lawrence. **CP-LawrD**

But you, Thomas Jefferson. Brave New World. Archibald MacLeish. **CP-MacLA**

Butcher glances through a bank window and sees, A. Inappropriate Gestures. Stephen Dobyns. **SP-DobyS**

Butcher knife was there, The. Clash. William Stafford. **SP-StafW**

Butcher Shop. Charles Simic. **SP-SimiC**

Butcher's. Jenny Joseph. *Fr.* Life and Turgid Times of A. Citizen. **SP-JoseJ**

Butler, fetch the ruby wine. From the Persian of Hafiz. Hafiz, *tr. fr. Persian* by Ralph Waldo Emerson. **CP-EmerR**

Butt of Winter, The. Marge Piercy. **SP-PierM**

Butter-and-Eggs. Louis Zukofsky. **CP-ZukLS**

Butter Colors. Carl Sandburg. **CP-SandC**

Butterandeggs. William Carlos Williams. **CP-WilW1**

Buttercup Children, The. Phoebe Hesketh. **SP-HeskP**

Buttercup is like a golden cup, The. Golden Glories. Christina Georgina Rossetti. **CP-RosC2**

Buttered Greens. James Schuyler. **CP-SextA**

Butterflies. Rudyard Kipling. **CP-KiplR**

Butterflies are white and blue. Mariposa. Edna St. Vincent Millay. **CP-MillE**

Butterflies over the Map. Robert Penn Warren. *Fr.* Mexico Is a Foreign Country: Four Studies in Naturalism. **SP-WarrR**

Butterfly. David Herbert Lawrence. **CP-LawrD**

Butterfly / or falling leaf. The Dancer. Philip Larkin. **CP-LarkP**

Butterfly. Nicanor Parra, *tr. fr. Spanish* by Thomas Merton. **CP-MertT**

Butterfly, a [*or* the] cabbage-white, The. Flying Crooked. Robert Ranke Graves. **CP-GravR**

Butterfly and the Bull, The. Charles Henri Ford. **SP-FordC**

Butterfly-girl of the Mussulman, all. Osip Emilevich Mandelstam. *Fr.* Octets. **CP-DavDo**

Butterfly in honored Dust, The. Emily Dickinson. **CP-DickE**

Butterfly is dainty flippant fragile, The. Jenny Joseph. *Fr.* Fables. **SP-JoseJ**

Butterfly obtains, The. Emily Dickinson. **CP-DickE**

Butterfly Piece. Robert Earl Hayden. **CP-HaydR**

Butterfly That Stamped, The. Rudyard Kipling. *Fr.* Just-So Stories. "There was never a queen like Balkis." **CP-KiplR**

Butterfly the ancient Grecians made, The. Psyche. Samuel Taylor Coleridge. **CP-ColeS**

Butterfly, the wind blows sea-ward, strong beyond the garden wall! Butterfly. David Herbert Lawrence. **CP-LawrD**

Butterfly upon the Sky, The. Emily Dickinson. **CP-DickE**

Butterfly's Assumption Gown, The. Emily Dickinson. **CP-DickE**

Butterfly's Numidian Gown, The. Emily Dickinson. **CP-DickE**

Butterton Ford. Roy Fisher. **SP-FishR**

Buttons. Carl Sandburg. **CP-SandC**

Buttons for Swallows. Marsden Hartley. **CP-HartM**

Buy Braw Troggin. An Excellent New Song. Robert Burns. **CP-BurnR** *Fr.* The Heron Ballads, 1795.

Buy, buy, buy, / Is the Peace-markt cry. Song. George Meredith. **CP-MerG2**

Buy me an ounce and i'll sell you a pound. Edward Estlin Cummings. **CP-CummE**

Buy my English posies! The Flowers. Rudyard Kipling. **CP-KiplR**

Buyers and Sellers. Carl Sandburg. **CP-SandC**

Buying and Selling. Philip Levine. **SP-LeviP**

Buying the Whore. Anne Sexton. **CP-SextA**

Buzz [*or* buz], quoth the blue fly [*or* flie]. Ben Jonson. **CP-JonsB** *Fr.* Oberon, the Fairy Prince.

Buzz saw snarled and rattled in the yard, The. Out, Out —. Robert Frost. **CP-FrosR**

Buzzards. Wystan Hugh Auden. **CP-AudWJ**

Buzzards bring out their young one. High Summer. Charles Tomlinson. **CP-TomlC**

Buzzards over Pondy Woods, The. Pondy Woods. Robert Penn Warren. **SP-WarrR**

Buzzard's two-note cry falls plaintively, The. Translating the Birds. Charles Tomlinson. **CP-TomlC**

Buzzing autos, like black bees. Nicholas Vachel Lindsay. *Fr.* Billboards and Galleons. **CP-LindV**

Bweteen Hyssop and Axe. Robert Ranke Graves. **CP-GravR**

B.W.I. John Updike. **CP-UpdiJ**

By a Blest Husband Guided, Mary Came. William Wordsworth. **CP-WorW2**

By a departing light. Emily Dickinson. **CP-DickE**

By a flower—By a letter. Emily Dickinson. **CP-DickE**

By a Lake in Minnesota. James Wright. **CP-WrigJ**

By a mad miracle I go intact. Street Song. Sylvia Plath. **CP-PlatS**

By a peninsula the wanderer sat and sketched. Emblems of Conduct. Hart Crane. **CP-CranH**

By a pleasant rivers side. Mary Sidney, Countess of Montgomery Wroth. *Fr.* Love's Victorie. **CP-WrotM**

By a Retired Mariner (A Friend of the Author). William Wordsworth. *Fr.* Poems Composed or Suggested During a Tour, in the Summer of 1833. **CP-WorW2**

By a River in the Osage Country. William Stafford. **SP-StafW**

By a route obscure and lonely. Dream-Land [*or* Dreamland]. Edgar Allan Poe. **CP-PoeEd**

By a street-organ stands a minstrel bawling. Joy. John Gould Fletcher. **SP-FletJ**

By a wall the stranger now calls his. A Kiss. Thomas Hardy. **CP-HardT**

By a window in the west. The Weaver. John Haines. **SP-HainJ**

By Air to Birmingham on a Mid-June Evening. John Hewitt. **CP-HewiJ**

"By all I am misunderstood!" if the Matron shall say, or the Maid. Rudyard Kipling. *Fr.* Certain Maxims of Hafiz. **CP-KiplR**

By all means sing of love, but if you do. Truest Poetry Is the Most Feigning, The [or, Ars Poetica for Hard Times]. Wystan Hugh Auden. **CP-AudeW**

By Allan-side I chanc'd to rove. Allan Water. Robert Burns. **CP-BurnR**

By an alley lined with tumble-down shacks. Mexican Quarter. John Gould Fletcher. **BPAW** *Fr.* Arizona Poems. **SP-FletJ**

By an old red-pate, murdering hag pursued. The Author upon Himself. Jonathan Swift. **CP-SwifJ**

By and large there is no blood. Homewreck. Karl Shapiro. **SP-ShapK**

By antique Fancy trimmed—though lowly, bred. The Town of Schwytz. William Wordsworth. *Fr.* Memorials of a Tour of the Continent; 1820. **CP-WorW2**

By art, by music, overthrilled. Ralph Waldo Emerson. **CP-EmerR**

By Art's bold privilege Warrior and War-horse stand. On a Portrait of the Duke of Wellington upon the Field of Waterloo, by Haydon. William Wordsworth. **CP-WorW2**

By Blue Ontario's Shore. Walt Whitman. **CP-WhitW**

"Are you he who would assume a place to teach or be a poet here in the States?" **FaBoPV**

Poet, The. **MoAmPo**

By bolstered words I am borne in hand. Sir Thomas Wyatt. **CP-WyatT**

By breakfast time the bustle's on. Morning. Robert Penn Warren. *Fr.* Boy's Will, Joyful Labor without Pay, and Harvest Home (1918). **SP-WarrR**

By breath of beds of roses drawn. Hafiz, *tr.* by Ralph Waldo Emerson. **CP-EmerR** *Fr.* Odes.

By Broad Potomac's Shore. Walt Whitman. **CP-WhitW**

By Callimachus. Callimachus, *tr. fr. Greek by* William Cowper. **CP-CowpW**

By Candlelight. Sylvia Plath. **CP-PlatS**

By Canoe through the Fir Forest. James Dickey. **NYBP** *Fr.* On the Coosawattee. **CP-DickJ**

By chain yet stronger must the Soul be tied. Sacrament. William Wordsworth. *Fr.* Ecclesiastical Sonnets. **CP-WorW2**

By chance my fingers, resting on my face. Anatomy. Walter de la Mare. **CP-DeLaW**

By chance the minister when I was born. Outside the Creeds. John Hewitt. **CP-HewiJ**

By chapel bare, with walls sea-beat. The Haglets. Herman Melville. **SP-MelvH**

By children's birth, and death, I am become. Niobe. John Donne. **CP-DonnJ**

By Chivalries as tiny. Emily Dickinson. **CP-DickE**

By constantly tormenting them. The Poor. William Carlos Williams. **CP-WilW1**

By Cure of—Sulfa. Charles Olson. **CP-OlsoC**

By dark severance the apparition head. Painted Head. John Crowe Ransom. **SP-RansJ**

By Day, a Lifted Study-Storehouse. Philip Larkin. **CP-LarkP**

By day, American bomb flights. Dr. Joseph Goebbels, Minister for Propaganda. William DeWitt Snodgrass. **SP-SnodW**

By day and night dream about happy death. Give Your Wish Light. Robinson Jeffers. **CP-JefR2**

By day she woos me, soft, exceeding fair. The World. Christina Georgina Rossetti. **CP-RosC1**

By day the bat is cousin to the mouse. The Bat. Theodore Roethke. **CP-RoetT**

By day the skyscraper looms in the smoke and sun and has a soul. Skyscraper. Carl Sandburg. **CP-SandC**

By day the sun ranted. Chanson Triste. Alun Lewis. **CP-LewiA**

By day these men ask nothing, and obey. Infantry. Alun Lewis. **CP-LewiA**

By day. . . tireless smokestacks. . . hungry smoky shanties hanging to. Five Towns on the B. and O. Carl Sandburg. **CP-SandC**

By Disposition of Angels. Marianne Craig Moore. **CP-MoorM**

By dream I saw, one of the three. The Dreame. Robert Herrick. **CP-HerrR**

By duty bound, and not by custom led. To the Memory of My Dear and Ever Honored Father Thomas Dudley Esq. Who Deceased July 31, 1653, and of His Age 77. Anne Bradstreet. **CP-BradA**

By easy stations where time crossed and left. The River. John Ciardi. **SP-CiarJ**

By fate exalted high in place. Jonathan Swift. *Fr.* Riddles. **CP-SwifJ**

By fate, not option, frugal Nature gave. Xenophanes. Ralph Waldo Emerson. **CP-EmerR**

By fire and cloud, across the desert sand. The New Exodus. John Greenleaf Whittier. **CP-WhitJ**

By following many a color-coded corridor. Aerie. John Updike. **CP-UpdiJ**

By force I live, in will I wish to dye. Life is But Losse. Robert Southwell. **CP-SoutR**

By Frazier Creek Falls. Gary Snyder. **CP-SnydG**

By gifts the Macedon clave Gates a-sunder. 3.16. Horace. **CP-RaleW,** *tr. by* Sir Walter Ralegh; *Fr.* Odes.

By God, I don't know what to. Prayer in Bad Weather. Charles Bukowski. **SP-BukC1**

By god i want above fourteenth. Edward Estlin Cummings. **CP-CummE**

By goodness and by evil so surrounded, how can the heart. Edna St. Vincent Millay. **CP-MillE**

By Heart. Al Young. **CP-YounA**

By Henstridge Cross at the Year's End. Thomas Hardy. **CP-HardT**

By Her Aunt's Grave. Thomas Hardy. **MoAB; MoBrPo** *Fr.* Satires of Circumstance in Fifteen Glimpses. **CP-HardT**

By Her That Is Most Assured to Her Self. Edmund Spenser. **EnRePo** *Fr.* Amoretti. **CP-Spens**

By her the heaven is in his course contained. Scudamor in the Temple of Venus. Edmund Spenser. **PoE** *Fr.* The Faerie Queene. **CP-Spens**

By Heraclides. *Unknown, tr. fr. Greek by* William Cowper. **CP-CowpW**

By holding one's head stock-still and measuring. Thin Air. John Updike. **CP-UpdiJ**

By holy zeal inspired, and led by fame. Verses Occasioned by the Sudden Drying Up of St. Patrick's Well near Trinity College, Dublin. Jonathan Swift. **CP-SwifJ**

By homely gift and hindered Words. Emily Dickinson. **CP-DickE**

By houres we all live here, in Heaven is known. No Time in Eternity. Robert Herrick. **CP-HerrR**

By June our brook's run out of song and speed. Hyla Brook. Robert Frost. **CP-FrosR**

By Keats's soul, the man who never stepped. Elizabeth Barrett Browning. **EPCY** *Fr.* Aurora Leigh. **CP-BroEB**

By kinds I keep my kinds in check. Ralph Waldo Emerson. **CP-EmerR**

By kiss of death, bullet on brow. Bowled Over. Ted Hughes. **SP-HughT**

By Lamplight. Stanley Jasspon Kunitz. **CP-KuniS**

By landscape reminded once of his mother's figure. Adolescence. Wystan Hugh Auden. **CP-AudeW**

By little accurate saints thickly which tread. Edward Estlin Cummings. **CP-CummE**

By long observation I have understood. Wood, an Insect. Jonathan Swift. **CP-SwifJ**

By Love, and by Beauty. My Eppie. Robert Burns. **CP-BurnR**

By Lyne and Tyne, by Thames and Tees. To Doctor John Brown. Robert Louis Stevenson. **CP-StevR**

By me, says Wisdom, monarchs reign. The Accession of King George III. Christopher Smart. *Fr.* Hymns and Spiritual Songs for the Fasts and Festivals of the Church of England. **SP-SmarC**

By miracles exceeding power of man. Crucifying. John Donne. *Fr.* La Corona. **ChIV-2; ESCV; OBS; Son** *Fr.* Holy Sonnets. **CP-DonnJ**

By Morning Twilight. George Meredith. **CP-MerG1**

By Moschus. Moschus, *tr. fr. Greek by* William Cowper. **CP-CowpW**

By Moscow Self-Devoted to a Blaze. William Wordsworth. **CP-WorW2**

By Mrs. Hopley. Gerard Manley Hopkins. **CP-HopkG**

By my Window have I for Scenery. Emily Dickinson. **CP-DickE**

By Mystic's banks I held my dream. Ballade. Paul Laurence Dunbar. **CP-DunbP**

By night: by darkness: turning from the sun. The Fourteenth Book. Archibald MacLeish. *Fr.* Conquistador. **CP-MacLA**

By night they haunted a thicket of April mist. Spectral Lovers. John Crowe Ransom. **SP-RansJ**

By night we lingered [*or* linger'd] on the lawn. Tennyson. **EBVV; EnVR; FHYEP; HAP; LoBV; NoP; OAEL-2; OBNC; PeECV; PoEL-5; TOF** *Fr.* In Memoriam A. H. H. **CP-TennA**

"Till now the doubtful dusk reveal'd." **GTBS-6; GTBS-P**

By night, when others soundly slept. Occasional Meditations: "By night, when others soundly slept." Anne Bradstreet. **CP-BradA**

By Nilus Once I Knew. Hart Crane. **CP-CranH**

By No Means Native. Adrienne Rich. **CP-RicAE**

By no specific dart of gold. Dark Path. Malcolm Lowry. **CP-LowrM**

By now I bet he's dead which suits me fine. Bleeder. Stephen Dobyns. **SP-DobyS**

By One of the Old School Who Was Bid to Follow Mr. Browning's Flights. Gerard Manley Hopkins. *Fr.* Seven Epigrams. **CP-HopkG**

By order of hunger the starving stood in line. Song Contest. Geoffrey Hill. **CP-HillG**

By Oughtertyre grows the aik. Robert Burns. *See* Blythe Was She.

By our first strange and fatal [*or* fatall] interview. On His Mistress [*or* Mistris]. John Donne. **AnAnS-1; BoLoP; CBLP; EBEV; ESCV; GBL; LiTB; LoBV; MeLP; MePo; NAEL-1; NOBE; NoSic; OXAEP-1; PoEL-2; SCGP; SeCP; SeCV-1; SeCeV** *Fr.* Elegies. **CP-DonnJ**

By Palladas. Palladas, *tr. fr. Greek by* William Cowper. **CP-CowpW**

By Philemon. Philemon, *tr. fr. Greek by* William Cowper. **CP-CowpW**

By playful smiles, (alas! too oft). Epitaph in the Chapel Yard of Langdale, Westmoreland. William Wordsworth. **CP-WorW2**

By rocky shores / We have heard of thy fame. A Tibute to the Renowned Harteebeeste. Malcolm Lowry. **CP-LowrM**

By Rome's dim relics there walks a man. The Roman Gravemounds. Thomas Hardy. **CP-HardT**

By Rufus' hall, where Thames polluted flows. On the Report that a Wooden Bridge. James Thomson. **CP-ThomJ**

By Rugged Ways. Paul Laurence Dunbar. **CP-DunbP**

By Saturday I said you would be better on Sunday. The Operation. Robert Creeley. **CP-CreeR**

By September 3rd I had made my bundle. Victory. James Dickey. **CP-DickJ**

By shores and woods and steeples. Alfred Edward Housman. **CP-HousA**

By sin and Satan un-intic't. Patience. Christopher Smart. *Fr.* Hymns for the Amusement of Children. **SP-SmarC**

By sloth on sorrow fathered. Lollocks. Robert Ranke Graves. **CP-GravR**

By snails, by leaps of frog, I came here, spirit. Unfold! Unfold! Theodore Roethke. **CP-RoetT**

By so much, vertue is the lesse. Vertue Best United. Robert Herrick. **CP-HerrR**

By such and such an offering. Emily Dickinson. **CP-DickE**

By such examples moved to unbought pains. Saxon Monasteries, and Lights and Shades of the Religion. William Wordsworth. *Fr.* Ecclesiastical Sonnets. **CP-WorW2**

By sunny market-place and street. Prelude. Robert Louis Stevenson. **CP-StevR**

By That Long Scan of Waves. Walt Whitman. **NAAL-1; NAAL-3** *Fr.* Fancies at Navesink. **CP-WhitW**

By that the Manciple hadde his tale ended. The Introduction to the Parson's Tale. Geoffrey Chaucer. **NAEL-1** *Fr.* The Canterbury Tales. **CP-ChauG**

By that the Maunciple hadde his tale al ended. The Parson's Prologue. Geoffrey Chaucer. *Fr.* The Canterbury Tales. **CP-ChauG**

By the Barrows. Thomas Hardy. **CP-HardT**

By the Bivouac's Fitful Flame. Walt Whitman. **CP-WhitW**

By the brilliant ramp. 3 A.M. John Updike. **CP-UpdiJ**

By the city dead-house by the gate. The City Dead-House. Walt Whitman. **CP-WhitW**

by the customs on Baggot bridge. To the Memory of Sylvia Plath: A Personal Note. James Liddy. **CP-LiddJ**

By the Deep Sea. Byron. *See* The Ocean.

By the Denali road, facing. Denali Road. John Haines. **SP-HainJ**

By the dry road the fathers cough and spit. The Brief Journey West. Howard Nemerov. **CP-NemeH**

By the Earth's Corpse. Thomas Hardy. **CP-HardT**

By the eleven. I Mean, No. Charles Olson. **CP-OlsoC**

By the excellence of his work the workman is a neighbor. By. Wendell Berry. *Fr.* Prayers and Sayings of the Mad Farmer. **CP-BerrW**

By the Exeter River. Donald Hall. **CP-HallD**

By the fall of years I learn how it has been. A Lineage. Wendell Berry. *Fr.* Work Song. **CP-BerrW**

By the Fire. Wystan Hugh Auden. **CP-AudWJ**

By the Fire-Side. Robert Browning. **CP-BroR1**

By the first of August. I Remember. Anne Sexton. **CP-SextA**

By the fourth (or is it the fifth?). Poisoned in Nassau. John Updike. **CP-UpdiJ**

By the gas-fire, kneeling. Olga Poems. Denise Levertov. **CP-LeveD**

By the Gasworks, Solihull. Wystan Hugh Auden. **CP-AudWJ**

By the gate with star and moon. Medallion. Sylvia Plath. **CP-PlatS**

By the Gateway of India: Bombay. Alun Lewis. **CP-LewiA**

By the glare of the guttering torch. Epilogue. John Gould Fletcher. **SP-FletJ** *Fr.* Branches of Adam.

By the great oak logs that yet burn. Grandfather's Grave. John Gould Fletcher. **SP-FletJ**

By the great river Deschutes. Wild Life Cameo, Early Morn. Lawrence Ferlinghetti. **SP-FerlL**

By the Hoof of the Wild Goat. Rudyard Kipling. **CP-KiplR** *Fr.* To Be Filed for Reference. *Fr.* Plain Tales from the Hills.

By the Isar, in the twilight, *also stands as sl. diff. separate poem* River Roses. David Herbert Lawrence. *Fr.* All of Roses. **CP-LawrD**

By the Isar, in the twilight. River Roses. David Herbert Lawrence. **CP-LawrD**

By the just vengeance of incensed skies. Judas. Jonathan Swift. **CP-SwifJ**

By the lake at Armenonville in the Bois de Boulogne. Armenonville. Edna St. Vincent Millay. **CP-MillE**

By the Laws of the Family Circle 'tis written in letters of brass. Public Waste. Rudyard Kipling. **CP-KiplR**

By the light of insomnia, truths. John Updike. *Fr.* Spanish Sonnets. **CP-UpdiJ**

By the mossy brink. On a Fête at Carlton House: Fragment. Percy Bysshe Shelley. **CP-ShelP**

By the next kindling of the day. To Julia, in Her Dawn, or Day-breake. Robert Herrick. **CP-HerrR**

By the Ninth Green, St. Enodoc. Sir John Betjeman. **CP-BetjJ**

By the North Gate, the wind blows full of sand. *fr. the Chinese of* Li Po (701-62). Ezra Pound. **SP-PounE**

By the Ocean. John Haines. **SP-HainJ**

By the old Moulmein Pagoda, lookin' lazy at [*or* eastward to] the sea. Mandalay. Rudyard Kipling. **CP-KiplR**

By the pale light of languorous lamps. Delphine and Hippolyta. James Liddy. **CP-LiddJ**

By the Passeyr. George Meredith. **CP-MerG2**

By the Pond. Roy Fisher. *Fr.* City. **SP-FishR**

By the pool that I see in my dreams, dear love. The Pool. Paul Laurence Dunbar. **CP-DunbP**

By the river. Embankment at Night, before the War: Charity. David Herbert Lawrence. **CP-LawrD**

By the River Eden. Kathleen Jessie Raine. **SP-RainK**

"Beside the river Eden."

"Lapwing's wavering flight, The."

"Never twice that river."

By the rivers of Babel we sate. Bible, *O.T.* *See* Psalm 137: "By the rivers of Babylon. . . "

By the rivers of Babylon, there we sat down, yea, we wept, when [*or* then] we remembered Zion. Psalm 137. Bible, *O.T.* **AWP; NAWM-1; OAEL-1; TrGrPo; TrJP** *Fr.* Psalms. **CP-Psal**

By the Rivers of Babylon We Sat Down and Wept. Byron. **CP-Byron**

By the road to church, Shaker Village. Religious Articles. Donald Hall. **CP-HallD**

By the road to the contagious hospital. Spring and All. William Carlos Williams. **CP-WilW1**

By the Road to Upper Midhope. Donald Davie. **CP-DavDo**

By the roots of my hair some god got hold of me. The Hanging Man. Sylvia Plath. **CP-PlatS**

By the Rosanna. George Meredith. **CP-MerG1**

By the rude bridge that arched the flood. Ralph Waldo Emerson. **CP-EmerR**

(Hymn[:] Sung at the Completion of the Concord Monument, April 19, 1836.) **CP-EmerR**

By the ruined arch, where the bougainvillea bled. The World Comes Galloping: A True Story. Robert Penn Warren. *Fr.* Mexico Is a Foreign Country: Four Studies in Naturalism. **SP-WarrR**

By the Runic Stone. Thomas Hardy. **CP-HardT**

By the rushy-fringed bank. Sabrina's Song. John Milton. **NOSC** *Fr.* Comus; a Masque Presented at Ludlow Castle.

By the Same. Charlotte Smith. **CP-SmitC**

By the Same. Just before His Death. Charlotte Smith. **CP-SmitC**

By the Same. To Solitude. Charlotte Smith. **CP-SmitC**

By the Same. To the North Star. Charlotte Smith. **CP-SmitC**

By the Sea. Christina Georgina Rossetti. **CP-RosC1**

By the sea it was, the Pacific. Whatever Becomes of the Living. Al Young. **CP-YounA**

By the sea loch the island cattle. The Thrush in the Gaelic Islands. Archibald MacLeish. **CP-MacLA**

By the Sea-Shore, Isle of Man. William Wordsworth. *Fr.* Poems Composed or Suggested During a Tour, in the Summer of 1833. **CP-WorW2**

By the Sea-Side. William Wordsworth. **CP-WorW2**

By the sea's edge, on gravel and on sand. Sonnet. John Hewitt. **CP-HewiJ**

By the shores of Gitche[e] Gumee. Henry Wadsworth Longfellow. **EBEvV; FaPON; FaPoB; OHFP; PFP; WBLP** *Fr.* Hiawatha's Childhood. **SP-LongH** *Fr.* The Song of Hiawatha.

By the shot tower near the chimneys. Blackfriars. Sir John Betjeman. **CP-BetjJ**

By the Side of Rydal Mere. William Wordsworth. **CP-WorW2**

By the singed maple tree, the gate unlatches. A Cord of Wood. Robert Pack. **SP-PackR**

By the Spring at Sunset. Nicholas Vachel Lindsay. **CP-LindV**

By the square elm of Ida. Canto 78. Ezra Pound. *Fr.* Cantos. **CP-PoCan**

By the Stream. Paul Laurence Dunbar. **CP-DunbP**

By the Stream. Richard Eberhart. **CP-EberR**

By the unacknowledged tie. Ralph Waldo Emerson. **CP-EmerR**

By the Waters of Babylon. Christina Georgina Rossetti. **CP-RosC3**

By the Waters of Babylon. B.C. 570. Christina Georgina Rossetti. **CP-RosC1**

By the waters of Babylon we sat downe and weapte, when we remembered the, O Syon. Bible, *O.T.* *See* Psalm 137: "By the rivers of Babylon. . . ."

By the way its every. Everywhere. William Matthews. *Fr.* Flood. **SP-MattW**

By the weak'st means things mighty are o'rethrown. Meane Things Overcome Mighty. Robert Herrick. **CP-HerrR**

By the well in the desert I sat for long. The Well in the Desert. John Gould Fletcher. *Fr.* Arizona Poems. **SP-FletJ**

By the well, where the bullocks go. What the People Said. Rudyard Kipling. **CP-KiplR**

By their floating mill. Stray Pleasures. William Wordsworth. **CP-WorW1**

By Their Works. John Greenleaf Whittier. **CP-WhitJ**

By this exchange of eyes, this encirclement. Everywhere Is Here. Robert Ranke Graves. **CP-GravR**

By this he knew she wept with waking eyes. George Meredith. **EnLoPo; EnVR; HBV; HeIP; HoPM; NAEL-2; NBM; NOBVV; NoP; OAEL-2; OAEP; OHCV; OxBM; PBMP; PoE; PoEL-5; Son** *Fr.* Modern Love. **CP-MerG1**

(End of Love, The.) **HoPM**

By this he knew she wept with waking eyes. Modern Love. George Meredith. **CP-MerG1**

By this, Leander, being near the land. Christopher Marlowe. **EBEV; ErPo** *Fr.* Hero and Leander. **CP-MarlC**

By this the Northerne wagoner had set. Edmund Spenser. **FHYEP; NoSic** *Fr.* The Faerie Queene. **CP-Spens**

By this time had they reached the Stygian pool. Ben Jonson. **NOSC** *Fr.* On the Famous Voyage. **CP-JonsB**

By those bright eyes, at whose immortal fires. Elegy, An. Ben Jonson. **CP-JonsB**

By those soft Tods of wool[l]. A Conjuration, to Electra. Robert Herrick. **CP-HerrR**

By thy fault is my mind brought to that pass. Catullus. *See* Carmen 75: "Reason blinded by sin, Lesbia."

By Thy long-drawn anguish to atone. Tuesday in Holy Week. Christina Georgina Rossetti. **CP-RosC2**

By time and after, where the guessed-at dead. The Graph. John Ciardi. **SP-CiarJ**

By Time, and Counsell, doe the best we can. Event of Things Not in Our Power. Robert Herrick. **CP-HerrR**

By Train from Berlin. Erica Jong. **SP-JongE**

By Use Comes Easinesse. Robert Herrick. **CP-HerrR**

By vain affections unenthralled. Cenotaph. William Wordsworth. **CP-WorW2**

By way of Fishguard, all the lying devils. Single Fare. Richard Graves. **CP-GravR**

By Way of Remembrance. Christina Georgina Rossetti. **CP-RosC3**

By ways remote and distant waters sped. Catullus. *See* Carmen 101: "Journeying over many seas and through many countries."

By what power was love confined. Incommunicality of Love. Thomas Carew. *Fr.* Four Songs, by Way of Chorus To a Play. **CP-CareT**

By what serene malevolence of names. Theophilus. Edwin Arlington Robinson. **CP-RobiE**

By whom was David taught. Jehovah-Nissi. William Cowper. *Fr.* Olney Hymns. **CP-CowpW**

By Word of Mouth. Rudyard Kipling. *Fr.* Plain Tales from the Hills. "Not though you die to-night, O Sweet, and wail." **CP-KiplR**

By yon castle wa' at the close of the day. There'll Never Be Peace Till Jamie Comes Hame. Robert Burns. **CP-BurnR**

By your knees they rightly clasp you. Woman of Greece. Robert Ranke Graves. **CP-GravR**

By your leave! The Pious Cat. Basil Bunting. **CP-BuntB**

Bye Baby Bother. Stevie Smith. **CP-SmitS**

Bye-Child. Seamus Heaney. **SP-HeanS**

Bygone Occasion, A. Thomas Hardy. **CP-HardT**

Byrnies, The. Thom Gunn. **CP-GunnT**

Byron, how sweetly sad thy melody! To Lord Byron. John Keats. **CP-KeatJ**

Byron-Shelley Conversation, A. Frank Templeton Prince. **CP-PrinF**

Byron vs. DiMaggio. Peter Meinke. **SP-MeinP**

Bystanders. William Matthews. **SP-MattW**

Byways and bygone. The Traveler. Maya Angelou. **SP-AngeM**

Byzantium. Charles Tomlinson. **CP-TomlC**

Byzantium. William Butler Yeats. **CP-YeatW**

Byzantium: Or Where the Great Life Begins. Malcolm Lowry. **CP-LowrM**

C

C B M. George Meredith. **CP-MerG2**

'c-hommodating he'd bait, seeking *accomodating* willed. Catullus. *See* Carmen 84: " '*H*advantageous' breathes Arrius heavily."

C Minor. Richard Wilbur. **CP-WilbR**

C 33. Hart Crane. **CP-CranH**

Ca' the Ewes [*or* Yowes] [to the Knowes]. Robert Burns. **CP-BurnR**

Ca' the Yowes [to the Knowes]. Robert Burns. **CP-BurnR**

Cabaret Voltaire. Peter Meinke. **SP-MeinP**

Cabbage catch the moon. Nocturn Cabbage. Carl Sandburg. **CP-SandC**

Cabbage in History, The. Dabney Stuart. **SP-StuaD**

Cabbage-Roses. David Herbert Lawrence. **CP-LawrD**

Cabby said: "Hey, what do you think that does", The. Tanck's Song About the Transportation Business. Hayden Carruth. **CP-CarHS** *Fr.* Songs About What Comes Down: The Complete Works of Mr. Septic Tanck.

Cabin. Anne Waldman. **SP-WaldA**

Cabin in the Clearing, A. Robert Frost. **CP-FrosR**

Cabin in the Rockies. Allen Ginsberg. **CP-GinsA**

Cabin Site Christmas Island, N.S. Martin Edmunds. **SP-EdmuM**

Cabin Tale, A. Paul Laurence Dunbar. **CP-DunbP**

Cabinet of Seeds Displayed, A. Howard Nemerov. **CP-NemeH**

Cable bows downward, The. The Ferry. Lewis Turco. **SP-TurcL**

Cable Hymn, The. John Greenleaf Whittier. **CP-WhitJ**

Cable rises / up the midtown, The. Music Television. Jim Carroll. **SP-CarrJ**

Cables To Rage Or I've Been Talking On This Street Corner. . . . Audre Lorde. **SP-LordA**

Cables to the Ace. Thomas Merton. **CP-MertT**

"Abandon your body and soul into the abundance of light sent from above."

"Adventure of Giomar: Castilian footbsll / Minding doctrines."

"After that we'll meet in some Kingdom they forgot."

"Amid the cries of gang walls and surprises the echoes come forward."

"Angels again / Farmers of the mind."

"Another sunny birthday. I am tormented by poetry and loss."

"Approved prospect of chairs with visitors to the hero."

"Bernstein! Can you still hear me? Are you conscious?"

"Corporate posture: variables of fat."

"Decoding the looks of opposites. Writing down their silences."

"Determined to love / Lured by the barbarous fowl."

"Don't go unhappy / To the ultraviolet home."

Dramas of the Evening.

"Each ant has his appointed task."

"Edifying cables can be made musical if played and sung by full-armed societies doomed to an electric war."

"Elastic programs to draft nonspecialist energy and rotate."

"Eve moves: golden Mother of baroque lights."

"Finally the public sender of this island shuts down its trance."

"Flash of falling metals. The shower of parts, cameras, guns of experience, The."

"Follow the ways of no man, not even your own."

"Formerly we knew / Years of peaceable system."

"Future of transgression. It is in the homes of Caliban."

"Gellasenheit: / Desert and void. The Uncreated is waste and emptiness."

"Gem notes / Of the examiner."

"Give me a cunning dollar that tells me no lie."

"Good morning! Address more inspections."

Harmonies of Excess, The.

" 'Hats off,' cried the midget."

"He speaks cautiously to the Tea phone when it invites."

"How can it be done / Without delay."

"I am about to make my home."

"I am doubted, therefore I am."

"I seek you in the hospital where you work."

"I think poetry must / I think it must."

"I will get up and go to Marble country."

"It rained dark and cold on the Day of St. Theresa of the Heart."

"It was already raining. They discovered all the bags were empty."

"Je vous lis les sonnets d'un capitaine aveugle."

"Let choirs of educated men compose."

"Let us cool your bitter sweet charm with incense and verse."

"Letters to a corridor: 'Put the whole family out into the hall'."

"Listen with a tremor to the aero-captain."

"Lone train alarms the summer silence with a contralto trident, A."

"Look! The Engineer! He thinks he has caught something!"

"Milton's fiends—Republican, bituminous—begin their scenarios."

"Morning / The chatter of meats."

"Morning. Good for foliage to resist the faithful wind."

Newscast.

"Next! The Guards hitch up their belts and look around."

"No man can see God except he be blind."

"Not to be without words in a season of effort."

"Note to subversives: Uncle has two extreme right hands and means business!"

"Now leaning over the salt nerve of our wave length we have decided to send you the frozen exports of a compromised musician."

"Now the unruly knowing."

"O God do I have to be Wordsworth."

"O it is not lazy to be a messenger or to live out of the shadow of some town."

"Oh, said the discontented check, you will indeed win like it says in the papers."

"Oh yes it is intelligence."

"On the long road of winding steel."

Original Sin.

"Our infantry is combing the hideouts."

"Outcry. A circus on another planet. The hero does not trust the evidence of verbs."

"Pencil continues to grieve with long questions in the same lounge full of sea walkers, The."

"Perfect act is empty. Who can see it?, The."

Planet over Eastern Parkway, The.

Prayer to Saint Anatole.

Prospects of Nostradamus, The.

"Rock shot chasms / Promise unplanned flight."

"Sartre said Francis Ponge had a moss-complex."

"Seer interprets the ministry of the stars, the broken gear of a bird, A."

"Since you and I became engines."

"Slowly slowly / Comes Christ through the garden."

Solemn Music.

"Some may say that the electric world."

"Studies of man's friendly competitor the rat have shown."

"Sweetgum avenue leads to a college of charm, The."

"That's the girl in the middle, the one who will show you."

"They improve their inimitable wire."

"This is how to / This is with imperatives."

To Daughters: To Study History.

To Sons: Not to Be Numb.

"True word of eternity is spoken only in the spirit of that man who is himself a wilderness, The."

"Twelve smoky gates flame with mass-demonstrations."

"Uncle Sam with a knife at his throat."

Vital Imperatives for Chester.

"Warm sun. Perhaps these yellow wild-flowers have the minds of little girls."

"What do you teach me / Mama my cow?"

"Wounded football hero / Is nominated to share / In the human condition, The."

"Write a prayer to a computer?"

"You, Reader, need no prologue. Do you think these Horatian Odes are all about you?"

"You taught me language and my profit on't."

Caboose Factory, The. Ron Koertge. **SP-KoerR**

Caboose Thoughts. Carl Sandburg. **CP-SandC**

Cactus has grown young leaves, The. The Flatterers. Marsden Hartley. **CP-HartM**

Cactus rose-mauve and gray, twin overturned. Louis Zukofsky. *Fr.* 29 Poems. **CP-ZukLS**

Cadenced in chromatic space. Incantate the Cockatrice. Isabella Gardner. **CP-GardI**

Cadenus and Vanessa. Jonathan Swift. **CP-SwifJ**

Cadenza. Isabella Gardner. **CP-GardI**

Cadenza. Ted Hughes. **SP-HughT**

Cadenza. Carl Sandburg. **CP-SandC**

Cadenza on Garnette. John Berryman. **CP-BerrJ**

Cadwaller-Smiths, The. Pride Goeth Before a Raise or Ah, There, Mrs. Cadwallader-Smith. Ogden Nash. **CP-NashO**

Caelius Aufilenus' mate, Quintius Aufilena's *am.* Catullus. *See* Carmen 100: "Undone or done up with love."

Caelius, Lesbia new star, Lesbia a light. Catullus. *See* Carmen 058: "Lesbia, our Lesbia, the same old Lesbia."

Caelius, my Lesbia, that one, that only Lesbia. Catullus. *See* Carmen 058: "Lesbia, our Lesbia, the same old Lesbia."

Caesar Knifed Again, or, Culture Biz Gets Hep, Boffs Profs. Ogden Nash. **CP-NashO**

Caesar Mamurraque! / A peerless pair of brazen buggers. Carmen 57. Catullus. Fr. Carmina. CP-Catul

Caesar, when that the traitor of Egypt. Sir Thomas Wyatt. **CP-WyatT**

Caesarion. James Merrill. *Fr.* Topics. **SP-MerrJ**

Café, The, *see also* Commentary—The Café. Leonard Cohen. **CP-CoheL**

Café du Pont. Peter Meinke. **SP-MeinP**

Café in Warsaw. Allen Ginsberg. **CP-GinsA**

Café Notre Dame. Lawrence Ferlinghetti. **SP-FerlL**

Café: 3 A.M. Langston Hughes. **SP-HughL**

Café Vue des Alpes. Peter Meinke. **SP-MeinP**

Cafeteria in Boston. Thom Gunn. **CP-GunnT**

Cage, The. Walter de la Mare. **CP-DeLaW**

Cage, The. Walter de la Mare. **CP-DeLaW**

Cage, The. Richard Eberhart. **CP-EberR**

Cage of myself clamps shut, The. The Prisoner. Erica Jong. **SP-JongE**

Caged Bird. Maya Angelou. **SP-AngeM**

Caged Bird, The. May Sarton. **SP-SartM**

Caged Goldfinch, The. Thomas Hardy. **CP-HardT**

Caged in the carnal canvas like a sea. On Rico LeBrun's Crucifixion. Edwin Rolfe. **CP-RolfE**

Caged Skylark, The. Gerard Manley Hopkins. **CP-HopkG**

Caged Thrush Freed and Home Again, The. Thomas Hardy. **CP-HardT**

Cageing of Ares, The. George Meredith. **CP-MerG1**

Cages do not suit the Swiss. Emily Dickinson. **SP-DickE**

Cage's quartet no. 1—really it's a. Listen. Hayden Carruth. **CP-CarHS**

Cahokia. Carl Sandburg. **CP-SandC**

Cahoots. Carl Sandburg. **CP-SandC**

Cain. Howard Nemerov. **CP-NemeH**

Cain: A Mystery. Byron. **CP-Byron**

"And now I will convey thee to thy world." **NOBRP**

"Hear, Jehovah! / May the eternal serpent's curse be on him!" **NOBRP**

"Oh! thou dead / And everlasting witness! whose unsinking." **ChIV-1**

Cain and Abel. Rudyard Kipling. **CP-KiplR**

Cain and Abel in the meantime had grown. John Gould Fletcher. **SP-FletJ** *Fr.* Branches of Adam.

Cain shall not slay Abel today on our good ground. A Poem of God's Mercy. Malcolm Lowry. *Fr.* The Roar of the Sea and the Darkness. **CP-LowrM**

Caird prevail'd—th' unblushing fair, The. Robert Burns. *Fr.* The Jolly Beggars.

Cairn, The. Edna St. Vincent Millay. **CP-MillE**

Cairn in Loch An Duin, The. Richard Hugo. **CP-HugoR**

Cairo 1326. Thomas Merton. *Fr.* East with Ibn Battuta. *Fr.* East. *Fr.* The Geography of Lograire. **CP-MertT**

Cal Coolidge and the Co. John Ciardi. **SP-CiarJ**

Calais, August, 1802. William Wordsworth. **CP-WorW1**

Calais, August 15, 1802. William Wordsworth. **CP-WorW1**

Calcium days, days when we feed our bones! Desire for Spring. Kenneth Koch. **SP-KochK**

Calder, A. Karl Shapiro. **SP-ShapK**

Calder's Hands. John Updike. **CP-UpdiJ**

Caledonia. Robert Burns. **CP-BurnR**

Caledonia. Sir Walter Scott. *See* Breathes there the [*or* a] Man [with Soul So Dead].

Caledonian Antisyzygy, The. "Hugh MacDiarmid." **SP-MacDH**

Calef in Boston. John Greenleaf Whittier. **CP-WhitJ**

Calendar, The. John Haines. **SP-HainJ**

Calendar. John Updike. **CP-UpdiJ**

Calendar behind my father's chair, The. Portraits on the Walls. John Hewitt. **CP-HewiJ**

Calendar in the Attic, The. John Gould Fletcher. **SP-FletJ** *Fr.* The Ghosts of an Old House.

Calendar-Watchers, or, What's So Wonderful about Being a Patriarch, The. Ogden Nash. **CP-NashO**

Cales and Guiana. John Donne. **CP-DonnJ**

Calf, The. Robert Burns. **CP-BurnR**

Calf, The. Thomas Hardy. **CP-HardT**

Calf, The. Ogden Nash. **CP-NashO**

Caliban to the Audience. Wystan Hugh Auden. *Fr.* The Sea and the Mirror. **CP-AudeW**

Caliban upon Setebos; or, Natural Theology in the Island. Robert Browning. **CP-BrowR**

Calicut. Thomas Merton. *Fr.* East with Ibn Battuta. *Fr.* East. *Fr.* The Geography of Lograire. **CP-MertT**

Calidore. A Fragment. John Keats. **CP-KeatJ**

Calidus Juventa? Allen Tate. **CP-TateA**

California. Wystan Hugh Auden. **CP-AudWJ**

California. "Bob Dylan." **CP-DylaB**

California. George Oppen. **CP-OppeG**

California Dreaming. Charles Wright. **SP-WrigC**

California Peninsula: El Camino Real. Al Young. **CP-YounA**

California Petrarchan. Karl Shapiro. **SP-ShapK**

California Poem. Jim Carroll. **SP-CarrJ**

California Prodigal. Maya Angelou. **SP-AngeM**

California rolls into. Delia Rexroth. Kenneth Rexroth. **SP-RexrK**

California shakes its petals / poppies. On the Subject of Roses. Diane Wakoski. **SP-WakoD**

California song, A. Song of the Redwood-Tree. Walt Whitman. **CP-WhitW**

California Spring. Charles Wright. **SP-WrigC**

Caligari. Carl Sandburg. **CP-SandC**

Caligula's Dream. John Updike. **CP-UpdiJ**

Call, The. James Dickey. **CoPo; NePoEA-2** *Fr.* The Owl King. **CP-DickJ**

Call, The. George Herbert. **CP-HerbG**

Call, The. George Meredith. **CP-MerG2**

Call, The. Charles Kenneth Williams. **SP-WillC**

Call down a blessing. Song: Olive Tree. Robert Ranke Graves. **CP-GravR**

Call down the hawk from the air. The Hawk. William Butler Yeats. **CP-YeatW**

Call exalted green leap spider. Spider or Ribbon Plant. Louis Zukofsky. **CP-ZukLS**

Call for Clues. William DeWitt Snodgrass. **SP-SnodW**

Call him deluded, say that he. Homage to Paul Robeson. Robert Earl Hayden. **CP-HaydR**

Call him not heretic whose works attest. By Their Works. John Greenleaf Whittier. **CP-WhitJ**

Call Him the Lover and call me the Bride. The Song the Body Dreamed in the Spirit's Mad Behest. William Everson. **SP-EverW**

Call himself unbegun, for the sea made him; assemblages of. Ryder. Muriel Rukeyser. **CP-RukeM**

Call into Death. David Herbert Lawrence. **CP-LawrD**

Call It a Good Marriage. Robert Ranke Graves. **CP-GravR**

Call it love. It's the Way You Play the Game. Charles Bukowski. **SP-BukC1**

Call it to mind, O my love. Air of Diabelli's. Robert Louis Stevenson. **CP-StevR**

Call Letters: Mrs. V.B. Maya Angelou. **SP-AngeM**

Call Martha Corey. The Trial. Henry Wadsworth Longfellow. **PAH** *Fr.* Act IV. *Fr.* Giles Corey of the Salem Farms. **SP-LongH**

Call me / your deepest urge. The Brown Menace or Poem to the Survival of Roaches. Audre Lorde. **SP-LordA**

Call me no more. His Lachrimae or Mirth, Turn'd to Mourning. Robert Herrick. **CP-HerrR**

Call me not false, beloved. The Bridegroom. Rudyard Kipling. **FaBoEE** *Fr.* Epitaphs of the War [1914–1918]. **CP-KiplR**

Call me not rebel, though in what I sing. Ad Olum. Robert Louis Stevenson. **CP-StevR**

Call me to you / at siesta. Carmen 32. Catullus. *Fr.* Carmina. **CP-Catul**

Call not the royal Swede unfortunate. William Wordsworth. **CP-WorW1**

Call of the Christian, The. John Greenleaf Whittier. **CP-WhitJ**

Call of the North. Phoebe Hesketh. **SP-HeskP**

Call of the Wild, The. Gary Snyder. **CP-SnydG**

Call off your eyes from care. A Young Man's Exhortation. Thomas Hardy. **CP-HardT**

Call out, celebrate the beam. The Tears of a Muse in America. Frank Templeton Prince. **CP-PrinF**

Call that the Public Voice which is their Error. William Blake. **CP-BlakW**

Call the Next Witness. Carl Sandburg. **CP-SandC**

Call the roller of big cigars. The Emperor of Ice-Cream. Wallace Stevens. **CP-StevW**

Call to National Service, A. Thomas Hardy. **CP-HardT**

Call us back, call us with your sliding silver. Spring Cries. Carl Sandburg. **CP-SandC**

Calla lily in a tulip skirt, A. Thirteen Years. Martin Edmunds. **SP-EdmuM**

Callacanthus / out again (the golden fury seen), The. For a Man Gone to Stuttgart Who Left an Automobile Behind Him. Charles Olson. **CP-OlsoC**

Called Back. Charles Wright. **SP-WrigC**

Called death, is darkness. Sans Name. Charles Olson. **CP-OlsoC**

Called dog men. Royals. James Schuyler. **CP-SchuJ**

Called him "Big Joe" yes and Joe Turner it was his name. Hayden Carruth. *Fr.* The Sleeping Beauty. **CP-CarHL**

Called *Niobe* high more callous. Lilies. Louis Zukofsky. **CP-ZukLS**

Called out on Christmas Eve for a working-party. Devil on Ice. Donald Davie. **CP-DavDo**

Called To Be Saints. Christina Georgina Rossetti. **CP-RosC2**

Callers, The. Marilyn Hacker. **SP-HackM**

Callicles' Song. Matthew Arnold. *See* Song of Callicles, The ("Through the black, rushing smoke-burst").

Calling. Archie Randolph Ammons. **SP-AmmoA**

Calling all butterflies of every race. Robert Frost. **CP-FrosR** (Pod of the Milkweed.) **CP-FrosR**

Calling, and Correcting. Robert Herrick. **CP-HerrR**

Calling and the melody all night long, The. Chapultepec Park / I. Muriel Rukeyser. **CP-RukeM**

Calling Dr. Dunninger. Gilbert Sorrentino. **SP-SorrG**

Calling Infinity. Tom Clark. **SP-ClarT**

Calling Lucasta from Her Retirement. Richard Lovelace. **CP-LoveR**

Calling of Names, The. Maya Angelou. **SP-AngeM**

Calling Spring VII-MMMC. Ogden Nash. **CP-NashO**

Calling to mind[e], mine eie long went about [*or* my eyes went long about]. The Excuse. Sir Walter Ralegh. **CP-RaleW**

Calliope. Hilda Doolittle. **CP-DoolH**

Callisto, Ganymede, Europa, Io. The Moons of Jupiter. John Updike. **CP-UpdiJ**

Calls, The. Wilfred Owen. **CP-OwenW**

Calls. Carl Sandburg. **CP-SandC**

Calls on the Heart. Elizabeth Barrett Browning. **CP-BroEB**

Calm[e], The. John Donne. **CP-DonnJ**

Calm, The. John Gould Fletcher. *Fr.* Sand and Spray: A Sea-Symphony. **SP-FletJ**

Calm, The. Tess Gallagher. **SP-GallT**

Calm and Full the Ocean. Robinson Jeffers. **CP-JefR3**

Calm as an under-current, strong to draw. William the Third. William Wordsworth. *Fr.* Ecclesiastical Sonnets. **CP-WorW2**

Calm before the Storm, The. "Lou Reed." **SP-ReedL**

Calm Day at Drake's Bay. Robert Bly. **SP-BlyR**

Calm is all nature as a resting wheel. Written in Very Early Youth. William Wordsworth. **CP-WorW1**

Calm Is the Fragrant Air, and Loth to Lose. William Wordsworth. **CP-WorW2**

Calm is the morn without a sound. Tennyson. **ChTr; EBEV; EBVV; ELP; EnVR; FHYEP; FaBoEn; FaBoPP; FaBoRV; FiP; HeIP; LiTB; NOBE; NoP; OBNC; PeECV; PlP; PoEL-5; SeCeV; TrGrPo** *Fr.* In Memoriam A. H. H. **CP-TennA** (Lincolnshire Wolds and Lincolnshire Sea.) **FaBoPP**

Calm on his charger black and tall. Richard Lionheart. George Meredith. **CP-MerG2**

Calm on the breast of Loch Maree. The Well of Loch Maree. John Greenleaf Whittier. **CP-WhitJ**

Calm, The / Cool face of the river. Suicide's Note. Langston Hughes. **SP-HughL**

Calm Under Fire. Jim Carroll. **SP-CarrJ**

Calm was Half-Moon Bay; we lay at anchor there. Dream of Saba. Edna St. Vincent Millay. **CP-MillE**

Calm[e] was the day, and through the trembling air [*or* ayre]. Prothalamion. Edmund Spenser. **SP-Spens**

Calm was the day, and through the trembling air. Edmund Spenser. **EBEvV; EnRePo; ImPo; SCGP** *Fr.* Prothalamion. **CP-Spens** ("Calme was the day, and through the trembling ayre.") **OXAEP-1**

Calm was the evening, as if asleep. The Spark. Walter de la Mare. **CP-DeLaW**

Calme was the day, and through the trembling ayre. Edmund Spenser. *See* Calm was the day, and through the trembling air.

Calming Thought of All, The. Walt Whitman. **CP-WhitW**

Calmly the night came down. The Earthquake. John Greenleaf Whittier. **CP-WhitJ**

Calvary. Edwin Arlington Robinson. **CP-RobiE**

Calverly's. Edwin Arlington Robinson. **CP-RobiE**

Calvert! it must not be unheard by them. To the Memory of Raisley Calvert. William Wordsworth. **CP-WorW1**

Calves harshly parted from their mamas. Ted Hughes. **SP-HughT** *Fr.* Gaudete.

Calvinistic Evensong. Sir John Betjeman. **CP-BetjJ**

Calybes plough not their barren soile, The, *ad. fr. Latin of* Apollon. Sir Walter Ralegh. **CP-RaleW**

Calypso. Wystan Hugh Auden. *Fr.* Ten Songs. **CP-AudeW**

Calypso. Hilda Doolittle. **CP-DoolH**

Calypsos. William Carlos Williams. **CP-WilW2**

Calypso's Island. Archibald MacLeish. **CP-MacLA**

Calypso's Island. Thomas Merton. **CP-MertT; SP-MertT**

Camaradas Y Compañeras. John Hewitt. **CP-HewiJ**

Camas Prairie School. Richard Hugo. **CP-HugoR**

Camberley. Sir John Betjeman. **CP-BetjJ**

Cambodia. James Fenton. **SP-FentJ**

Cambridge and the Alps. William Wordsworth. *Fr.* The Prelude; Growth of a Poet's Mind [1805 vers.]. **CP-WorW3**

Cambridge and the Alps. William Wordsworth. *Fr.* The Prelude; Growth of a Poet's Mind [1850 vers.]. **CP-WorW3**

"Brook and road, The." **OBRV**

"But 'twas a time when Europe was rejoiced." **FaBoPV**

Coleridge's Mind a Life Unto Itself. **EPCY**

"Far different dejection once was mine." **OBTV,** *book* 6, *ll.* 491–657; **RB** (Crossing the Alps.) **RB,** *book* 6, *ll.* 491–572;

"I, too, have been a Wanderer; but, alas!" **OxAEP-2**

Imagination. **FiP**

"Melancholy slackening that ensued." **PoEL-4**

"Poet's soul was with me at that time, The." **EnRP**

"Single tree, A." **OBRV**

"'Tis told by one whom stormy waters threw." **ImOP**

Types and Symbols of Eternity. **CBCK**

"When from the Vallais we had turned, and clomb." **TOF**

"When the third summer freed us from restraint." **OAEL-2**

Cambridge friend put in,—one whom I used, A. John Berryman. *Fr.* Sonnets to Chris. **CP-BerrJ**

Cambridge: From the Cowley Fathers Monastery. Dabney Stuart. *Fr.* The Charles River. **SP-StuaD**

Cambridge ladies who live in furnished souls, The. Edward Estlin Cummings. **CP-CummE; SP-CummE**

Cambridgeshire. Donald Davie. **CP-DavDo**

Camden, most reverend head, to whom I owe. To William Camden. Ben Jonson. **CP-JonsB**

Camden nights dire with honeysuckle. Too-Late Words to My Father. John Clellon Holmes. **SP-HolmJ**

Came gift wrapped from the liquor store. A bum. October 18: Boston. John Ciardi. **SP-CiarJ**

Came in my full youth to the midnight cave. Ajanta. Muriel Rukeyser. **CP-RukeM**

Came in upon him once how he might find. Hayden Carruth. *Fr.* The Sleeping Beauty. **CP-CarHL**

Came lassitude and despair of the mind. Richard Eberhart. *Fr.* Brotherhood of Men. **CP-EberR**

Came Neptunus / his mind leaping / like dolphins. Canto 116. Ezra Pound. **APSN** *Fr.* Cantos. **CP-PoCan**

Came So Far for Beauty. Leonard Cohen. **CP-CoheL**

Came to lakes; came to dead water. A Field of Light. Theodore Roethke. **CP-RoetT**

Came to me— / Who? Basil Bunting, *after the Persian of* Rudaki. **CP-BuntB**

Camel, The. Ogden Nash. **CP-NashO**

Camel-Driver, A. Robert Browning. **CP-BroR2**

Camellia Sabina. Marianne Craig Moore. **CP-MoorM**

Camels. Archie Randolph Ammons. **SP-AmmoA**

Camel's hump is an ugly lump, The. Rudyard Kipling. **CP-KiplR** *Fr.* How the Camel Got His Hump. *Fr.* Just-So Stories.

Camelus Saltat. George Meredith. **CP-MerG1**

Camelus Saltat: Continued. George Meredith. **CP-MerG1**

Cameo, The. Edna St. Vincent Millay. **CP-MillE**

Cameo of a Chinese Woman on Mulberry Street. John Yau. **SP-YauJo**

Camera. John Updike. **CP-UpdiJ**

Camera at the crossing sees the city. Gauley Bridge. Muriel Rukeyser. **CP-RukeM**

Camoëns. Herman Melville. **SP-MelvH**

Camoëns, he the accomplished and the good. Torquato Tasso, *tr. fr. Italian by* William Wordsworth. **CP-WorW1**

Camp, A. Robert Louis Stevenson. **CP-StevR**

Camp in the Prussian Forest, A. Randall Jarrell. **CP-JarrR; SP-JarrR**

Camp-stool for chair once more and packing case for table. Work-Room. Robert Ranke Graves. **CP-GravR**

Camp Wakonda, 1940. Robert Pack. **SP-PackR**

Campanella. Frank Templeton Prince. **CP-PrinF**

Campanula. Kathleen Jessie Raine. **CP-RainK**

Campbells Are Comin, The. Robert Burns. **CP-BurnR**

Camperdown Elm, The. Marianne Craig Moore. **CP-MoorM**

Campions. David Herbert Lawrence. **CP-LawrD**

Camps hold [*or* held] their distance— [of] brown chestnuts and grey smoke, The. Derek Walcott. **CP-WalcD** *Fr.* Midsummer.

Camps of Green. Walt Whitman. **CP-WhitW**

Campus oakgrove is, The. Grove's Way. Archie Randolph Ammons. **SP-AmmoA**

Campus on the Hill, The. William DeWitt Snodgrass. **SP-SnodW**

Can a bell ring in the heart. When Death Came April Twelve 1945. Carl Sandburg. **CP-SandC**

Can a mote of sunlight defeat its purpose. Louis Zukofsky. **CP-ZukLS**

Can another love be born. Hilda's Morning and Evening Dose of Rhyme. George Meredith. **CP-MerG2**

Can anyone lend me. Drats. Shel Silverstein. **SP-SilS2**

Can anything avail / Beldame, for my hid grief? The Husband's View. Thomas Hardy. **CP-HardT**

Can bare fact make the cloth of a shining poem? Waiting for the Chariot. Carl Sandburg. **CP-SandC**

Can beauty that did prompt me first to write. Elegy, An. Ben Jonson. **CP-JonsB**

Can Death Be Sleep, When Life Is But a Dream. John Keats. **CP-KeatJ**

Can feel it in the pushing. Robert Creeley. **CP-CreeR**

Can flame beget white steel. She Contrasts with Herself Hippolyta. Hilda Doolittle. **CP-DoolH**

Can historical materialism, which is only a historical method. To My Friend the Late Beatrice Hastings. "Hugh MacDiarmid." **SP-MacDH**

Can I cease to care. Song—(On Chloris Being Ill). Robert Burns. **CP-BurnR**

Can I easily say, / I know you of course now. Sisters. Adrienne Rich. **CP-RicAE; SP-RicA2**

Can I Get You a Glass of Water? or, Please Close the Glottis after You. Ogden Nash. **CP-NashO**

Can I know it?—Nay.— / Shall I know it?—Yea. Christina Georgina Rossetti. **CP-RosC2**

Can I not come to Thee, my God, for these. To His Ever-Loving God. Robert Herrick. **CP-HerrR**

Can I not sin, but thou wilt be. To His Conscience. Robert Herrick. **CP-HerrR**

Can I see another's woe. On Another's Sorrow. William Blake. **AWP; EBCP; EnRP; FHYEP; FaBV; OXAEP-2; PoEL-4** *Fr.* Songs of Innocence. **CP-BlakW**

Can It Be? Stevie Smith. **CP-SmitS**

Can it be growing colder when I begin. Adrienne Rich. **NAAL-2** *Fr.* Twenty-one Love Poems. **SP-RicA1; SP-RicA2**

Can it be right to give what I can give? Sonnet. Elizabeth Barrett Browning. **CTC; HBV; OHCV; Son** *Fr.* Sonnets from the Portuguese. **CP-BroEB**

Can it be so? It must be so. Her Haunting-Ground. Thomas Hardy. **CP-HardT**

Can it be speech itself. Closer. Robert Pack. **SP-PackR**

Can Life be a blessing. John Dryden. **SP-DrydJ** *Fr.* Troilus and Cressida. (Song: "Can life be a blessing.") **SP-DrydJ**

Can man rejoice who lives in hourly fear? Let Patience Have Her Perfect Work. Christina Georgina Rossetti. **CP-RosC2**

Can peach renew lost blossom, / Or violet lost perfume. Go In Peace. Christina Georgina Rossetti. **CP-RosC2**

Can pleasing sight, misfortune ever bring? Sonnet 5. Mary Sidney, Countess of Montgomery Wroth. *Fr.* Pamphilia to Amphilanthus. **CP-WrotM**

Can ratt-rime and ragments o' quenry. A Drunk Man Looks at the Thistle. "Hugh MacDiarmid." **SP-MacDH**

Can rules or tutors educate. Culture. Ralph Waldo Emerson. **CP-EmerR**

Can the Harp Shoot Through Its Propellers? Kenneth Patchen. **CP-PatcK**

Can the lov'd Image of thy deerest face. Sonnet. Mary Sidney, Countess of Montgomery Wroth. *Fr.* Pamphilia to Amphilanthus. **CP-WrotM**

Can there be anything more mean. William Blake. **CP-BlakW**

Can these movements which move themselves. Belly Dancer. Diane Wakoski. **SP-WakoD**

Can those old dusty learned men. Mathematics. John Hewitt. **CP-HewiJ**

Can we believe—by an effort. Cities. Hilda Doolittle. **CP-DoolH**

Can we not force from widowed poetry. An Elegy upon the Death of the Dean of [St.] Paul's, Dr. John Donne. Thomas Carew. **CP-CareT**

Can We Resolve the Past. Jim Morrison. **SP-MorrJ**

Can white birds sing? An ornithologist. No White Bird Sings. John Ciardi. **SP-CiarJ**

Can Ye Labor Lea, *see also* The Plowman: "I paid a man at Martinmass." Robert Burns. **CP-BurnR**

Can you, after dark, bcome a darkie? After Dark. David Herbert Lawrence. **CP-LawrD**

Can you believe it? Barton Sutter. *Fr.* Cedarhome. **SP-SuttB**

Can You Leave Me Thus, My Katy. Robert Burns. **CP-BurnR** ("Canst thou leave me thus, my Katy.") **CP-BurnR**

Can you match with me. Jonathan Swift. **CP-SwifJ**

Can You Please Crawl Out Your Window? "Bob Dylan." **CP-DylaB**

Can you still love, having once shared love's secret. Unposted Letter. Robert Ranke Graves. **CP-GravR**

Can you still stand on the edge of the Neva. Roses. Stephen Berg. **SP-BergS**

Can you, the Author of our joy, / So soone depart? Thomas Campion. *Fr.* A Relation of the Late Royall Entertainment Given by the Right

Honourable the Lord *Knowles*, at *Cawsome*-House neere *Redding:* to Our Most *Gracious Queene, Queene* ANNE, *in her* Progresse toward the *Bathe*, upon the *Seven and Eight and Twentie Dayes of Aprill.* **CP-CampT**

Cana. Thomas Merton. **CP-MertT; SP-MertT**

Canaan. Geoffrey Hill. **CP-HillG**

Canada. Robert Creeley. **CP-CreeR**

Canada some wars are waiting for you. Cherry Orchards. Leonard Cohen. **CP-CoheL**

Canadaigua. Frederick Morgan. **SP-MorgF**

Canadian Pacific. Derek Mahon. **SP-MahoD**

Canadian Turned Back at the Border, The. Malcolm Lowry. **CP-LowrM**
  "Blue exhaust speeds parting's litany, The."
  "Helpless submarine is left aglow, The."
  "Inspectors here crunched bags on injured locks."
  "Packed bus that brought me back glared and stunk, The."
  "Pathos broods, a desolation glowers, A."
  "Singing smell of tar, of the highway, A."
  "Well, the redwin's a public charge! Over."
  "White gulls blow from the Rockies like Norway."

Canadians and Pottawatomies. Carl Sandburg. **CP-SandC**

Canal. Muriel Rukeyser. **CP-RukeM**

Canal. Charles Tomlinson. **CP-TomlC**

Canal, Froghall, The. Wystan Hugh Auden. **CP-AudWJ**

Canapés, my Fabullus, at home any. Catullus. *See* Carmen 13: "I shall expect / you in to dine."

Canaries in the morning, orchestras. Academic Discourse at Havana. Wallace Stevens. **CP-StevW**

Canary, The. Ogden Nash. **CP-NashO**

Canary-birds feed on sugar and seed. The Song of the Camel. Charles Edward Carryl. *Fr.* The Admiral's Caravan.

Cancel, Catullus, the expectancies of friendship. Carmen 72. Catullus. *Fr. Carmina.* **CP-Catul**

Cancelled Fragments of the Ode to Heaven, *see also* Ode to Heaven. Percy Bysshe Shelley. **CP-ShelP**

Cancelled Passage. Percy Bysshe Shelley. **CP-ShelP**

Cancelled Passages of the Poem. Percy Bysshe Shelley. *Fr.* Adonais; An Elegy on the Death of John Keats. **CP-ShelP**

Cancelled Stanza. Percy Bysshe Shelley. **CP-ShelP**

Cancelled Stanza of the Mask of Anarchy. Percy Bysshe Shelley. *Fr.* The Mask [*or* Masque] of Anarchy. **CP-ShelP**

Cancer. Lewis Turco. **SP-TurcL**

Cancer Cells, The. Richard Eberhart. **CP-EberR**

Cancer Match, The. James Dickey. **CP-DickJ**

Candid and generous and just. William Cowper. **OBF** *Fr.* Friendship. **CP-CowpW**

Candid Friend who strikes because he loves, The. George Meredith. **CP-MerG2**

Candle, A. Sir John Suckling. **CP-SuckJ**

Candle a Saint, The. Wallace Stevens. **CP-StevW**

Candle in his white grave-clothes, always turning his cowled head, The. Louis MacNeice. *Fr.* Candles. **CP-MacNL**

Candle Indoors, The. Gerard Manley Hopkins. **CP-HopkG**

Candle, Lamp & Firefly. Tess Gallagher. **SP-GallT**

Candle light blue banners incense. Land O'Lakes, Wisconsin: Vajrayana Seminary. Allen Ginsberg. **CP-GinsA**

Candleberry bayberry spice resinwax green. Bayberry. Louis Zukofsky. **CP-ZukLS**

Candlemas Dialogue, A. Christina Georgina Rossetti. **CP-RosC2**

Candlemas Procession, The. Thomas Merton. **CP-MertT; SP-MertT**

Candles. Louis MacNeice. **CP-MacNL**
  "Candle in his white grave-clothes, always turning his cowled head, The."
  "I have no clock, yet I can hear."

Candles. Sylvia Plath. **CP-PlatS**

Candles and / Here Comes a glass box. Edward Estlin Cummings. **CP-CummE**

Candles Gutter Low, The. Wystan Hugh Auden. **CP-AudWJ**

Candles now gutter low; there is no priest to bless. The Candles Gutter Low. Wystan Hugh Auden. **CP-AudWJ**

Candor—my tepid friend. Emily Dickinson. **CP-DickE**

Candor of Julias Teeth, The. Robert Herrick. **CP-HerrR**

Candour compels me, Becher! to commend. Answer to Some Elegant Verses. Byron. **CP-Byron**

Candy / Is dandy. Reflections on Ice-breaking. Ogden Nash. **CP-NashO**

Candy Darling. Charles Henri Ford. *Fr.* Four Elegies. **SP-FordC**

Candy Says. "Lou Reed." **SP-ReedL**

Candy screen wrappers of. The Murder Mystery. "Lou Reed." **SP-ReedL**

Canis Major. Robert Frost. **CP-FrosR**

Canna's Basalt Crags. Kathleen Jessie Raine. **SP-RainK**

Cannas shiny as slag. Flower Dump. Theodore Roethke. **CP-RoetT**

Canned Goods. Dabney Stuart. **SP-StuaD**

Cannibal. Thom Gunn. *Fr.* Three for Children. **CP-GunnT**

Cannibal Bratuscha. Muriel Rukeyser. **CP-RukeM**

Cannibals. Donald Davie. **CP-DavDo**

Cannon Beach. Diane Wakoski. **SP-WakoD**

Cannon his name. George Meredith. *Fr.* Napoléon. **CP-MerG1**

Cannon his name. Napoléon. George Meredith. **CP-MerG1**

Cannoneer is dead, The. On Seeing an Old Civil War Painting with My Love. Charles Bukowski. **SP-BukC2**

Cannon's brazen lips are cold, The. To Pius IX. John Greenleaf Whittier. **CP-WhitJ**

Cannot Sweeten. Christina Georgina Rossetti. **CP-RosC3**

Canny Castor, Punching Pollux. Malcolm Lowry. **CP-LowrM**

Canoe Speaks, The. Robert Louis Stevenson. **CP-StevR**
  "On the great streams the ships may go." **SD**

Canonization, The. John Donne. **CP-DonnJ**

Canon's Yeoman's Prologue, The. Geoffrey Chaucer. *Fr.* The Canterbury Tales. **CP-ChauG**

Canon's Yeoman's Tale, The. Geoffrey Chaucer. *Fr.* The Canterbury Tales. **CP-ChauG**

Canossa. Howard Nemerov. **CP-NemeH**

Canst be idle? canst thou play? Business. George Herbert. **CP-HerbG**

Canst thou imagine where those spirits live. Percy Bysshe Shelley. **WSC** *Fr.* Prometheus Unbound. **CP-ShelP**

Canst thou leave me thus, my Katy. Robert Burns. *See* Can You Leave Me Thus, My Katy.

Canst thou, O cruel! say I love thee not. Sonnet 149. William Shakespeare. *Fr.* Sonnets. **CP-ShaWS**

Can't Be Borne. David Herbert Lawrence. **CP-LawrD**

Can't Buy Me Love. John Lennon *and* Paul McCartney. **CP-Beatl**

Can't cut it (night). February Air. Ted Berrigan. **SP-BerrT**

Cant first attacked as such, 1596, Count Fransesco Cenci (source:). Being Altogether Literal, & Specific, and Seeking at the Same Time to be Successfully Explicit. Charles Olson. **CP-OlsoC**

Can't give you up, can't stop. Musical Garden. Anne Waldman. **SP-WaldA**

Can't myself / lett off this. Echo Of. Robert Creeley. **CP-CreeR**

Can't seem to wake you, kid, guess it. The Body Beside the Ties. Kenneth Patchen. **CP-PatcK**

Can't you hear that rooster crowin'? New Morning. "Bob Dylan." **CP-DylaB**

Can't you think death lives. Pablo Neruda, *tr. fr. Spanish by* Ben Belitt. **SP-NeruP** *Fr.* Question Book.

Canta Naranja. Gilbert Sorrentino. **SP-SorrG**

Cantab, The. Vincent Bourne, *tr. fr. Latin by* William Cowper. **CP-CowpW**

Cantabat Veneres meras Catullus. *acc. by English translation.* Thomas Campion. **CP-CampT**

Cantaloupe, The. Ogden Nash. **CP-NashO**

Cantata, A. Jonathan Swift. **CP-SwifJ**

Cantata, from Metastasio. William Wordsworth. **CP-WorW1**

Canterbury Tales, The, *Line numbers in diff. anthologies may refer to diff. manuscript sources.* Geoffrey Chaucer. **CP-ChauG**
  Canon's Yeoman's Prologue, The.
  Canon's Yeoman's Tale, The.
  Chaucer's Retraction.
  Clerk's Prologue, The.
  Clerk's Tale, The.
    Patient Griselda. **PoRA**
  Cook's Prologue, The.
  Cook's Tale, The. **BXAP**
  Epilogue to the Man of Laws' Tale, The.
    Shipman, The ("Parson him answered, 'Benedcite!,' The"). **ACP**
  Epilogue to the Merchant's Tale.
  Epilogue to the Nun's Priest's Tale.
  Franklin's Prologue, The. **NAEL-1; OAEL-1**
  Franklin's Tale, The. **NAEL-1; OAEL-1**
  Friar's Prologue, The. **PoE**
  Friar's Tale, The. **PoE**
  General Prologue, The. **FHYEP; NAWM-1; OAEL-1; PoE**
    ("As soon as April pierces to the root.") **NAWM-1**
    "A-morwe, whan that day bigan to springe." **FiP**
    "Clerk ther was of Oxenford also, A." **InPS**
    (Seven Pilgrims: A Clerk.) **TrGrPo**
    "Good man ther[e] was of religioun [*or* religion], A." **ACP; NOCV**
    "Good Wyf [*or* Wif] was ther of bisyde [*or* biside] Bathe, A." **EBEV; InPS**

(Seven Pilgrims: A Wyf of Bathe.) **TrGrPo**

"Knight [*or* Knyght] ther[e] was, and that a worthy man, A." **UV**, *ll.* 43–72; **InPS**, *ll.* 43–78; **FaBoEH; TrGrPo**

(Knighthood, The.) **FaBoEH**

(Seven Pilgrims: A Knight.) **TrGrPo**

"Marchant was ther with a forked berd, A." **CTC**

"Monk ther was, a fair for the maistrye [*or* maistrie], A." **OBCoV; TrGrPo**

("Monk there was, a monk of mastery, A.") **TrGrPo**

(Seven Pilgrims: A Monk.) **TrGrPo**

"Monk ther was, a fair for the maistrie, A." **CTC**

"Sergeant of the Lawe, war and wys, A." **CTC**

Seven Pilgrims: A Miller. **TrGrPo**

Seven Pilgrims: A Squire [*or* Squyer]. **TrGrPo**

Shipman, The ("Shipman was ther, woning fer by weste, A"). **MOS**

"Somonour was ther with us in that place, A." **OBCoV**

"Ther[e] was also a Nonne [*or* nun], a Prioress[e]." **CTC; NOBE; TrGrPo**

(Madame Eglantine.) **NOBE**

(Seven Pilgrims: A Prioress[e].) **TrGrPo**

("There also was a nun, a Prioress.") **TrGrPo**

"This Pardoner had hair as yellow as wax." **SCV**

"Whan that Aprille [*or* April, *or* Aprill] with his[e] shoures [*or* showres] sote [*or* soote]." **ChTr; TRP**, *ll.* 1–18; **TrGrPo**, *ll.* 1–18, *incl. mod. vers. by* Louis Untermeyer; **PPP**, *ll.* 1–271; **FiP**, *ll.* 1–34; **CTC**, *ll.* 1–37; **SCV**, *ll.* 1–42, *incl. mod. vers. by* Nevill Coghill; **EBEvV**, *ll.* 1–78; **PrIm**

(When April with Its Sweet Showers.) **PrIm**, *ll.* 1–18;

("When April with its sweet showers.") **TFi**, *ll.* 1–42, *mod. vers. by* William Harmon;

("When in April the sweet showers fall.") **TEP**, *ll.* 1–34, *mod. vers. by* Nevill Coghill;

("When the sweet showers of April fall and shoot.") **SCV**, *ll.* 1–42, *mod. vers. by* Nevill Coghill;

("When the sweet showers of April follow March.") **TrGrPo**, *ll.* 1–18, *mod. vers. by* Louis Untermeyer;

Introduction to the Franklin's Prologue and Tale. **NAEL-1**

Introduction to the Man of Law's Tale. **FiP**

Introduction to the Pardoner's Tale.

(Introduction to the Pardoner's Prologue and Tale.) **FHYEP; NAEL-1; NoP; PoE**

Introduction to the Parson's Tale, The. **NAEL-1**

Introduction to the Squire's Tale.

January and May, or the Merchant's Tale. **CP-PopeA**

Knight's Tale, The.

"But in the dome of mighty Mars the red." **OBWP**

"This Palamon gan knytte his browes tweye." **OBF**

Man of Law's Tale, The.

Manciple's Prologue, The.

Manciple's Tale, The.

Controlling the Tongue. **OxBChV**

"Lat take a cat, and fostre him wel[l] with milk." **OFC**, *ll.* 71–78; **ChTr**

Manciple's Tale—A Modernization, The. **CP-WorW1**

Merchant's Prologue, The.

Merchant's Tale, The.

"Fresh-hearted May on hearing what he said." **OxBM**

Miller's Prologue, The. **NAEL-1; NAWM-1; OAEL-1**

("When the knight had finished, no one, young or old.") **NAWM-1**

Miller's [*or* Milleres] Tale, The. **FaBoBl; NAEL-1; NAWM-1; OAEL-1; OxBoLi; PeLV; TEP**

("There used to be a rich old oaf.") **NAWM-1**

"Fair was this yonge wyf, and therwithal." **EBEV**

Monk's Tale, The.

Nun's Priest's Tale, The. **FHYEP; NAEL-1; NAWM-1; NoP; OAEL-1; TrGrPo**

("Once a poor widow, aging year by year.") **NAWM-1**

("Poore widwe [*or* widow], somdeel [*or* somedeal] stape in age, A.") **NAEL-1; NoP**

"His comb was redder than the fine coral." **PBBP**

"There liv'd, as Authors tell, in Days of Yore." **OBVE**

"This Chauntecleer stood hye up-on his toos." **FiP**

Pardoner's Prologue, The. **FHYEP; NAEL-1; NAWM-1; NoP; OAEL-1; PoE**

(" 'In churches,' said the Pardoner, 'when I preach'.") **NAWM-1**

Pardoner's Tale, The. **FHYEP; NAEL-1; NAWM-1; NoP; OAEL-1; PoE**

("There was a company of young folk living.") **NAWM-1**

"But, sires, o word forgat I in my tale." **EBEV**

Death and the Three Revellers. **OBNV**

"It's of three rioters I have to tell." **SCV**

"This olde man gan looke in his visage." **OBD**

Three Rioters, The. **EBNV**

Parson's Prologue, The.

Parson's Tale, The.

Physician's Tale, The.

Prioress' Tale—A Modernization, The. **CP-WorW1**

Prioress's Prologue, The.

Two Invocations of the Virgin, II. **ACP**

Prioress's Tale, The. **ACP**

Prologue of the Monk's Tale, The.

Prologue of the Nun's Priest's Tale, The.

(" 'Stop!' cried the Knight. 'No more of this, good sir!' ") **NAWM-1**

Prologue of the Prioress's Tale.

Prologue to Sir Thopas. **NAEL-1; Par**

Reeve's Prologue, The.

Reeve's Tale, The.

Bedroom Farce. **FaBoDD**

Second Nun's Prologue, The.

Two Invocations of the Virgin, I. **ACP**

Second Nun's Tale, The.

Shipman's Tale, The.

Sir Thopas.

(Tale of Sir Thopas, The.) **Par**, *ll.* 1–247; **BXAP**, *ll.* 1–248; **NAEL-1**, *ll.* 1–252;

Squire's Tale, The.

Summoner's Prologue, The.

Summoner's Tale, The.

Tale of Melibee, The.

Wife of Bath, The. **CP-PopeA**

"If poor (you say) she drains her husband's purse." **OBSV**

Wife of Bath's Prologue, The. **FHYEP; NAEL-1; OAEL-1**, *ll.* 1–862 *complete;*

"Experience, though noon auctoritee." **OxBoLi; PeLV**

"If there were no authority on earth." **OxBM**

"My fifth housebonde, god his soule blesse!" **FiP**

"Tell me to what conclusion or in aid." **OxBM**

Wife of Bath's Tale, The. **FHYEP; NAEL-1; OAEL-1**

Canterbury thought / The bargain fair enough. Ecumenical Exchange, 1989. Frank Templeton Prince. **CP-PrinF**

Canthara. William Carlos Williams. **CP-WilW1**

Canti Romani. Lawrence Ferlinghetti.

"Along the Appian Way / children are playing." **SP-FerlL**

"At midnight on the next balcony." **SP-FerlL**

Canticle. Wendell Berry. **CP-BerrW**

Canticle, A. Herman Melville. **SP-MelvH**

Canticle for Good Friday. Geoffrey Hill. **CP-HillG**

Canticle for October. Marsden Hartley. **CP-HartM**

Canticle for the Blessed Virgin. Thomas Merton. **CP-MertT**

Canticle for the Feast of the Most Precious Blood, 1954, A. William Everson. **SP-EverW** *Fr.* The Cross Tore a Hole.

Canticle of Jack Kerouac, The. Lawrence Ferlinghetti. **SP-FerlL**

Canticle of the Rose, The. William Everson. **SP-EverW** *Fr.* The Rose of Solitude.

Canticle to Apollo, A. Robert Herrick. **CP-HerrR**

Canticle to the Christ in the Holy Eucharist, A. William Everson. **SP-EverW**

Canticle to the Waterbirds, A. William Everson. **SP-EverW**

Cantico. James Liddy. **CP-LiddJ**

Cantico Per Lo Tuo Amore V. James Liddy. **CP-LiddJ**

Cantico Per Lo Tuo Amore IV. James Liddy. **CP-LiddJ**

Cantico Per Lo Tuo Amore III. James Liddy. **CP-LiddJ**

Cantico Per Lo Tuo Amore II. James Liddy. **CP-LiddJ**

Cantilena Politica-Jocunda Facta Post Principis Discessum In Hispaniam. Sir John Suckling. **CP-SuckJ**

Cantina Iannini. Richard Hugo. **CP-HugoR**

Cantinas, The, *same poetry, sts. arr. differently, in* Lighthouse Invites the Storm. Malcolm Lowry. **CP-LowrM**

"Above all, absent yourself from that affair."

At the Bar.

"But never fall from fealty to light."

Delirium in Vera Cruz. **FaBoTw; OxBTC**

Doctor Usquebaugh.

"How did all this begin, and why am I here."

"I have known a city of dreadful night."

Last Man in the Dôm, The.

Memory of the Hospitality of American Barmen.

"Most nauseous of all drinks, what is your spell?"

"Shakespeare should have come to Acapulco."

Thirty Five Mescals in Cuautla.

"When you were starving, you waited—how long?"

Canto I: "August. Render to Caesar. Speak parrot: a gimmick for Poll." Louis MacNeice. *Fr.* Autumn Sequel. **CP-MacNL**

Canto II: "On the other hand," said Gavin—or could have said. Louis MacNeice. *Fr.* Autumn Sequel. **CP-MacNL**

Canto III: "To work—To Beaconsfield. A suburban train." Louis MacNeice. *Fr.* Autumn Sequel. **CP-MacNL**

Canto IV: "To work. To my own office, my own job." Louis MacNeice. *Fr.* Autumn Sequel. **CP-MacNL**

(From Autumn Sequel.) **FaBCIP**

Canto V: "Hence these arrears, this filing cabinet crammed." Louis MacNeice. *Fr.* Autumn Sequel. **CP-MacNL**

Canto VI: "Everydayness is good; particular-dayness." Louis MacNeice. *Fr.* Autumn Sequel. **CP-MacNL**

Canto VII: "Cloud of witnesses. To whom? To what?, A." Louis MacNeice. *Fr.* Autumn Sequel. **CP-MacNL**

(Fanfare for the Makers, A.) **NOBE**

Canto VIII: "Fair; not to say radiant. The Twentyfifth of September." Louis MacNeice. *Fr.* Autumn Sequel. **CP-MacNL**

Canto IX: "Master closed the door. The unmodern words, The." Louis MacNeice. *Fr.* Autumn Sequel. **CP-MacNL**

Canto X: "Daily news. And today? There is not so much to note." Louis MacNeice. *Fr.* Autumn Sequel. **CP-MacNL**

Canto XI: "Golden guineas filter through the mist, The." Louis MacNeice. *Fr.* Autumn Sequel. **CP-MacNL**

Canto XII: "Now to dissolve in port. I take the train." Louis MacNeice. *Fr.* Autumn Sequel. **CP-MacNL**

Canto XIII: "Leaving the colleges then and their half-remembered." Louis MacNeice. *Fr.* Autumn Sequel. **CP-MacNL**

Canto XIV: "Battle? That is one way of looking at the matter, A." Louis MacNeice. *Fr.* Autumn Sequel. **CP-MacNL**

Canto XV: "Been here before? Whether he has or no." Louis MacNeice. *Fr.* Autumn Sequel. **CP-MacNL**

Canto XVI: "Young man cannot answer. Is this life?, The." Louis MacNeice. *Fr.* Autumn Sequel. **CP-MacNL**

Canto XVII: "This was the night that specially we went down." Louis MacNeice. *Fr.* Autumn Sequel. **CP-MacNL**

Canto XVIII: "Lament for the Makers. Monday comes; at noon." Louis MacNeice. *Fr.* Autumn Sequel. **CP-MacNL**

Canto XIX: "All out!" the voices cry in the Park, "All out!" Louis MacNeice. *Fr.* Autumn Sequel. **CP-MacNL**

Canto XX: "To Wales once more, though not on holiday now." Louis MacNeice. *Fr.* Autumn Sequel. **CP-MacNL**

Canto XXI "Thirtieth inst., too soon the thirtieth ult, The." Louis MacNeice. *Fr.* Autumn Sequel. **CP-MacNL**

Canto XXII: "So this is Glastonbury. A green hill far away." Louis MacNeice. *Fr.* Autumn Sequel. **CP-MacNL**

Canto XXIII: "December continues mild. The rose garden." Louis MacNeice. *Fr.* Autumn Sequel. **CP-MacNL**

Canto XXIV: "December the Twenty-third: I visit the Ancient East." Louis MacNeice. *Fr.* Autumn Sequel. **CP-MacNL**

Canto XXV: "And today is Christmas Eve. Once more to work." Louis MacNeice. *Fr.* Autumn Sequel. **CP-MacNL**

Canto XXVI: "Morning bright as summer. The job on hand, A." Louis MacNeice. *Fr.* Autumn Sequel. **CP-MacNL**

Canto Amor. John Berryman. **CP-BerrJ**

Canto I: The Trystyng. "Lewis Carroll." *Fr.* Phantasmagoria. **CP-CarrL**

Canto II: Hys Fyve Rules. "Lewis Carroll." *Fr.* Phantasmagoria. **CP-CarrL**

Canto III: Scarmoges. "Lewis Carroll." *Fr.* Phantasmagoria. **CP-CarrL**

Canto IV: Hys Nouryture. "Lewis Carroll." *Fr.* Phantasmagoria. **CP-CarrL**

Canto One Hundred and One. Charles Olson. **CP-OlsoC**

Canto Primo. Thomas Campion. *See* Hark, All You Ladies [That Do Sleep].

Canto Quarto. Thomas Campion. **CP-CampT**

Canto Quinto. Thomas Campion. *See* Content.

Canto Secundo. Thomas Campion. *See* What Fair[e] Pomp[e].

Canto Tertio. Thomas Campion. *See* My Love bound me with a kiss[e].

Canto the Fourth. Byron. *Fr.* Childe Harold's Pilgrimage. **CP-Byron**

"Egeria! sweet creation of some heart." **NOBRP**

"Roll on, thou deepand dark blue ocean—roll!" **NOBRP**

"What from this barren being do we reap?" **FHYEP**

"What from this barren being do we reap?" **NOBRP**

Canto V: Byckerment. "Lewis Carroll." *Fr.* Phantasmagoria. **CP-CarrL**

Canto VI: Dyscomfyture. "Lewis Carroll." *Fr.* Phantasmagoria. **CP-CarrL**

Canto VII: Sad Souvenaunce. "Lewis Carroll." *Fr.* Phantasmagoria. **CP-CarrL**

Cantos, The. Robert Creeley. **CP-CreeR**

Cantos. Ezra Pound. **CP-PoCan**

Addendum for C: "Evil is Usury, *neschek*, The."

Addendum for C: "Now sun rises in Ram sign."

Fragment (1966): "That her acts / Olga's acts / of beauty."

Canto 1: "And then went down to the ship." AmPP; CMoP; LiTA; MeMAP; MoAB; MoAmPo; MoP; NoAM; NoP; OBVE; PoE; SP-PounE; TrGrPo; VGW

Canto 2: "Hang it all, Robert Browning." AmPP; CoBMV; HAP; MeMAP; MoAB; MoAmPo; NOBA; NePA; NoAM; OxBA; PoA; SP-PounE; TwAmPo

(Dionysus.) **FaBoDD**

Canto 4: "I sat on the Dogana's steps." MeMAP; SP-PounE; TAP

Canto 5: "Palace in smoky light."

Canto 6: "Great bulk, huge mass, thesaurus."

Canto 7: "Eleanor (she spoiled in a British climate)." NOBA; NoAM

Canto 8: "These fragments you have shelved (shored)."

Canto 9: "One year floods rose." SP-PounE

Canto 10: "And the poor devils dying of cold, outside Sorano."

Canto 11: "Egradment li antichi cavaler romanj."

Canto 12: "And we sit here / under the wall." NAs

("Said Jim X. . . .") NAs

All at Sea. FaBoDD

Canto 13: "Kung walked / by the dynastic temple." CMoP; FaBoMo; PoE; SP-PounE

Canto 14: "Io venni luogo d'ogni luce muto."

(Canto 14: "Slough of unamiable liars, The.") SP-PounE

("Slough of unamiable liars, The.") SP-PounE

Canto 15: "Saccharescent, lying in glucose, The."

Canto 16: "And before hell mouth; dry plain."

Canto 17: "So that the vines burst from my fingers." InPS; MeMAP; NAAL-2; OBMV; SP-PounE

Canto 18: "And of Kublai: / 'I have told you of that emperor's city in detail.' "

Canto 19: "Sabotage? Yes, he took it up to Manhattan."

Canto 20: "Sound slender, quasi tinnula."

("And from the floating bodies, the incense.") SP-PounE

(Canto 20: "And from the floating bodies, the incense.") SP-PounE

Canto 21: " 'Keep the peace, Borso!' Where are we?"

Canto 22: "An' that man sweat blood."

Canto 23: " 'Et omniformis,' Psellos, 'omnis.' "

Canto 24: "Thus the book of the mandates."

Canto 25: "Book of the council major."

("Because of the stink of the dungeons: 1344.") SP-PounE

(Canto 25: "Because of the stink of the dungeons: 1344.") SP-PounE

Canto 26: "And / I came here in my young youth."

Canto 27: "Formando di disio nuova persona."

Canto 28: "And God the Father Eternal (Boja d'un Dio!)."

Canto 29: "Pearl, great sphere, and hollow."

Canto 30: "Compleynt, compleynt I hearde upon a day."

Canto 31: "Tempus loquendi, tempus tacendi."

Canto 32: " 'Revolution,' said Mr. Adams, The."

Canto 33: "Is that despotism."

Canto 34: "Oils, beasts, grasses, petrifactions, birds, incrustations."

Canto 35: "So this is (may we take it) Mitteleuropa."

Canto 36: "Lady asks me, A / I speak in season."

(Canzone: Donna Mi Priegha.) CTC

(Donna Mi Priegha.) OBVE

Canto 37: " 'Thou shalt not covet,' said Martin Van Buren, 'jail 'em for debt.' "

Canto 38: "An' that year Metevsky went over to America del Sud."

Canto 39: "Desolate is the room where the cat sat."

Canto 40: "Esprit de corps in permanent bodies."

Canto 41: " 'Ma questo,' / said the Boss, 'è divertente.' "

Canto 42: "We ought, I think, to say in civil terms: You be damned."

Canto 43: "To the serenissimo Dno (pronounced Domino)."

Canto 44: "And thou shalt not, Firenze 1766, and thou shalt not."

Canto 45: "With Usura." CMoP; LiTM; MeMAP; MoPo; NAAL-2;

NOBA; NePA; PoE; SP-PounE; TW

Canto 46: "And if you will say that this tale teaches. . . ."

Canto 47: "Who even dead, yet hath his mind entire!" **CMoP; PoE; SP-PounE; VGW**

Canto 48: "And if the money be rented."

Canto 49: "For the seven lakes, and by no man these verses." **SP-PounE**

Canto 50: " 'Revolution' said Mr Adams 'took place in the.' "

Canto 51: "Shines / in the mind of heaven God [*or* heaven God]." **SP-PounE**

Canto 52: "And I have told you of how things were under Duke Leopold in Siena."

Canto 53: "Yeou taught men to break branches." **SP-PounE**

Canto 54: "So that Tien-tan chose bulls, a thousand."

Canto 55: "Orbem bellis, urbem gabellis."

Canto 56: "Billets, biglietti, as coin was too heavy for transport."

Canto 57: "And when KIEN OUEN was throned."

Canto 58: "Sinbu put order in Sun land, Nippon, in the beginning of all things."

Canto 59: "De libro CHI-KING sic censeo."

Canto 60: "So the Jesuits brought in astronomy."

Canto 61: "YONG TCHING / his fourth son, to honour his forebears."

Canto 62: "Acquit of evil intention."

Canto 63: "Towards sending of Ellsworth."

Canto 64: "To John's bro, the sheriff, we lay a kind word in passing."

Canto 65: "Jurors refuse to take oath."

Canto 66: "Could not let us bring their sugar to Europe."

Canto 67: "Whereof memory of man runneth not to the contrary."

Canto 68: "Philosophers say, The: one, the few, the many."

Canto 69: "In which case a minister here from Congress wd / be useful."

Canto 70: "My situation almost the only one in the world."

Canto 71: "German ambassador once told me he cdn't bear St Paul, A."

Canto 72: "Purché si cominci a ricordare la guerra di merda."

Canto 73: "E poi dormii."

Canto 74: "Enormous tragedy of the dream in the peasant's bent shoulders, The." **PoE; SP-PounE**

Canto 75: "Out of Phlegethon!"

Canto 76: "And the sun high over horizon hidden in cloud bank." **SP-PounE**

("L'ara sul rostro / 20 years of the dream.") **SP-PounE**

Canto 77: "And this day Abner lifted a shovel."

Canto 78: "By the square elm of Ida."

Canto 79: "Moon, cloud, tower, a patch of the battistero all of a whiteness." **SP-PounE**

("Moon has a swollen cheek, The.") **SP-PounE**

Canto 80: "Ain' committed no federal crime." **FaBoTw; IHNG; PoA; SP-PounE**

("Nancy where art thou?") **SP-PounE**

("Tudor indeed is gone and every rose.") **FaBoTw**

Canto 81: "Zeus lies in Ceres' bosom." **CMoP; FaBoMo; FaBoTw; HAP; MoAB; MoP; NAAL-2; NOBA; NOBE; NePA; NoAM; OxBA; PoE; RaBo; SP-PounE; SeCeV; VGW**

("Yet / Ere the season died a-cold.") **SP-PounE**

Canto 82: "When with his hunting dog I see a cloud."

Canto 83: "Hudor / HUDOR et Pax." **SP-PounE**

("As he was standing below the altars.") **SP-PounE**

Canto 84: "8th October: / Si tuit li dolh elh plor."

Canto 85: "LING / Our dynasty came in because of a great sensibility."

Canto 86: "WITH solicitude / that mirrored turbationem."

Canto 87: "Between the usurer and any man who / wants to do a good job."

Canto 88: "It was Saturday the 1st day of April, toward noon."

Canto 89: "To know the histories / to know good from evil."

Canto 90: "From the colour the nature." **APSN; VGW**

Canto 91: "Ab lo dolchor qu'al cor mi vai."

Canto 92: "And from this Mount were blown / seed."

Canto 93: "A man's paradise is his good nature." **SP-PounE**

("Autumn leaves blow from my hand.") **SP-PounE**

Canto 94: " 'Brederode' / (to Rush, Ap 4. 1790)."

Canto 95: "LOVE, gone as lightning."

Canto 96: "Kredemon . . . / kredemon . . . / and the wave concealed her."

Canto 97: "Melik & Edward struck coins-with-a-sword."

Canto 98: "Boat of Ra-Set moves with the sun, The."

Canto 99: "Till the blue grass turn yellow."

Canto 100: "Has packed the Supreme Court."

Canto 101: "Finding scarcely anyone save Monsieur de Rémusat."

Canto 102: "This I had from Kalupso."

Canto 103: "1850: gt objection to any honesty in the White House."

Canto 104: "Na Khi talk made out of wind noise."

Canto 105: "Feb. 1956 / Is this a divagation."

Canto 106: "And was her daughter like that."

Canto 107: "Azalea is grown while we sleep, The."

Canto 108: "COMMINUIT / there is frost on the rock's face."

Canto 109: "Pro Veritate. . . / curtiliagia teneant."

Canto 110: "Thy quiet house / The crozier's curve runs in the wall."

Canto 111, Notes for: "I, one thing, as relation to one thing."

Canto 112, From: "Owl, and wagtail / and huo-hu, the fire-fox."

Canto 113: "Thru the 12 Houses of Heaven." **NYBP**

Canto 114: "Pas même Fréron / hais personne / pas même Fréron."

Canto 115, From: "Scientists are in terror, The." **FaBoMo**

(From CXV: "Scientists are in terror, The.") **APSN; CP-PoCan; FaBoMo**

Canto 116: "Came Neptunus / his mind leaping / like dolphins." **APSN**

Canto 117 et seq., Notes for: "For the blue flash and the moments / benedetta."

Canute. William Wordsworth. *Fr.* Ecclesiastical Sonnets. **CP-WorW2**

Canvassing for the Election. David Herbert Lawrence. **CP-LawrD**

Canyon is choked with stones and undergrowth, The. Cliff-dwelling. John Gould Fletcher. *Fr.* Arizona Poems. **SP-FletJ**

Canyon Wren, The. Gary Snyder. **CP-SnydG**

Canzone: "As would any sound make." Robert Creeley. **CP-CreeR**

Canzone: "Consider the three functions of the tongue." Marilyn Hacker. **SP-HackM**

Canzone: "On the tropical coast of Java." Gilbert Sorrentino. **SP-SorrG**

Canzone: "Scoffing, amorous maidens and young men." John Milton, *tr. fr. Italian by* John T. Shawcross. **CP-CowpW; CP-MiltJ**

("They mock my toil—the nymphs and am'rous swains.") **CP-CowpW,** *tr. by* William Cowper;

Canzone: "When shall we learn, what should be clear as day." Wystan Hugh Auden. **CP-AudeW**

Canzone: Donna Mi Priegha. Ezra Pound. *See* Canto 36: "Lady asks me, A / I speak in season."

Canzonetta. Isabella Gardner. **CP-GardI**

Cap, The. Phoebe Hesketh. **SP-HeskP**

Cap and Bells, The. William Butler Yeats. **CP-YeatW**

Cap and Bells; or, The Jealousies, The. John Keats. **CP-KeatJ**

Cap and gown instead of a sweatrag, A. Malcolm Lowry. **CP-LowrM**

Cap D'Antibes. Edna St. Vincent Millay. **CP-MillE**

Cap of Lead across the sky, A. Emily Dickinson. **CP-DickE**

Capacity. John Updike. **CP-UpdiJ**

Cape Alava. Richard Hugo. **CP-HugoR**

Cape Ann. Thomas Stearns Eliot. **GoJo; NAEL-2; NoAM** *Fr.* Landscapes. **CP-ElioT**

Cape Breton. Elizabeth Bishop. **CP-BishE**

Cape Hatteras. Hart Crane. **InPS; MoAB; MoAmPo** *Fr.* The Bridge. **CP-CranH**

"Nasal whine of power whips a new universe." **MoAB; MoAmPo** (Power.) **MoAmPo**

Cape Nothing. Richard Hugo. **CP-HugoR**

Cape Sunion. John Hewitt. **CP-HewiJ**

Capital, The. Wystan Hugh Auden. **CP-AudeW**

Capital, The. Adrienne Rich. **CP-RicAE**

Capital letters prompting every line. Poem: A Reminder. Robert Ranke Graves. **CP-GravR**

Capitalist, The. George Meredith. **CP-MerG2**

Capitalist was I, A. The Capitalist. George Meredith. **CP-MerG2**

Capitallett. Poem: A Reminder. Robert Ranke Graves. **CP-GravR**

Capitals. Howard Nemerov. **CP-NemeH**

Capitán profundo, capitán geloso. The Revolutionists Stop for Orangeade. Wallace Stevens. **CP-StevW**

Capitol Air, *with music.* Allen Ginsberg. **CP-GinsA**

Cap'n never drawls, *We're seven miles,* The. 39,000 Feet. William Matthews. **SP-MattW**

Capo che chinasi, / Occhi che chiudonsi. Christina Georgina Rossetti. **CP-RosC3**

Capone-face, fish, / flabbergaasted at being dumped. Tautog. Brendan Galvin. **SP-GalvB**

Cappadocian Song. Hayden Carruth. **CP-CarHS**

Capped arbiter of beauty in this street. Hart Crane. **FaBoMo; ImPo; LiTM** *Fr.* For the Marriage of Faustus and Helen. **CP-CranH**

Capper Kaplinski at the North Side Cue Club. Hayden Carruth. **CP-CarHS**

Caprice. Sir John Betjeman. **CP-BetjJ**

Capricious fortune ever joys. Seneca, *tr. by* Samuel Johnson. **CP-JohnS** *Fr.* Hercules Furens.

Capricorn (of sizable thirst). The Year Is a Great Circle or the Year Is a Great Mistake. Charles Olson. **CP-OlsoC**

Capricornus / Manifest exemplary cussedness if you wish to get through this quarter with. Your Horoscope. Charles Henri Ford. **SP-FordC**

Captain, The. Leonard Cohen. **CP-CoheL**

Captain Ahab's desire was the White Whale. Why the Postman Has to Ring Twice, or, Yellow Envelope, Where Have You Gone? Ogden Nash. **CP-NashO**

Captain Bada. Frank O'Hara. **SP-OharF**

Captain Blaze. Frederick Morgan. **SP-MorgF**

Captain called me to his bed, The. The Captain. Leonard Cohen. **CP-CoheL**

Captain Carpenter. John Crowe Ransom. **SP-RansJ**

Captain Craig. Edwin Arlington Robinson. **CP-RobiE**

"I doubt if ten men in all Tilbury Town." **PoEL-5**

Captain Hook. Shel Silverstein. **SP-SilS2**

Captain in Time of Peace. Thom Gunn. **CP-GunnT**

Captain John Smith. Ogden Nash. **CP-NashO**

Captain Marvell. Gilbert Sorrentino. **SP-SorrG**

Captain or Colonel, or Knight in Arms. John Milton. **CP-MiltJ**

(Sonnet 8: "Captain or Colonel, or Knight in Arms.") **CP-MiltJ**

Captain paces the bridge in lofty scorn, The. The Stowaway. Malcolm Lowry. **CP-LowrM**

Captain's Lady, The. Robert Burns. **CP-BurnR**

Captains of industry, your aimless power. Allen Tate. *Fr.* Sonnets of the Blood. **CP-TateA**

Captain's Song, The. John Berryman. **CP-BerrJ**

Captain's Well, The. John Greenleaf Whittier. **CP-WhitJ**

Captive, The. Walter de la Mare. **CP-DeLaW**

Captive, The. Walter de la Mare. **CP-DeLaW**

Captive, The. Rudyard Kipling. **CP-KiplR**

Captive Bird was gone;— to cliff or moor, The. On Revisiting Dunlolly Castle. William Wordsworth. *Fr.* Poems Composed or Suggested During a Tour, in the Summer of 1833. **CP-WorW2**

Captive Escaped in the Wilds of America. Addressed to the Hon. Mrs. O'Neill, The. Charlotte Smith. **CP-SmitC**

Captive on a foreign shore. Cassandra. George Meredith. **CP-MerG1**

Captived Bee; or, The Little Filcher, The. Robert Herrick. **CP-HerrR**

Captives. Ernest Hemingway. **CP-HemiE**

Captives—a Psalm, The. Thomas Merton. **CP-MertT; SP-MertT**

Captivity, The. Alun Lewis. **CP-LewiA**

"At dusk in my garden the flowers are waiting."

"Fishes inhabit the deep rock crannies, the worm the dry."

"Gates of my palace are opened wide, The."

"Pharaoh has seen me in the hovels of Israel."

"Swallows are nesting in the hovels of Israel, The."

"They have clipped the wings of my doves, my messengers."

Captivity.—Mary Queen of Scots. William Wordsworth. **CP-WorW2**

Captivity of the Fly. Archibald MacLeish. **CP-MacLA**

Capture. Archie Randolph Ammons. **SP-AmmoA**

Capture, The. Paul Laurence Dunbar. **CP-DunbP**

Caput Mortuum. Edwin Arlington Robinson. **CP-RobiE**

Car, The. Robert Creeley. **RR** *Fr.* The Car / moving / the hill / down. **CP-CreeR**

Car / moving / the hill / down, The. Robert Creeley. **CP-CreeR**

Car, The. **RR**

Car Cemetery. Jim Morrison. **SP-MorrJ**

Car coughing moves with. The Car. Robert Creeley. **RR** *Fr.* The Car / moving / the hill / down. **CP-CreeR**

Car Crash. Allen Ginsberg. **CP-GinsA**

Car is heavy with children, The. The Road Back. Anne Sexton. **CP-SextA**

Car parked on gravel near the Castle Gate. A Country Walk in May. John Hewitt. **CP-HewiJ**

Car turned over three times, The. For Mike and Jeannie: Resisters Fifteen Years Later. Grace Paley. **CP-PaleG**

Car wheels roar over freeway concrete. Guru Om. Allen Ginsberg. **CP-GinsA**

Car with ten headless dead bodies in the back, A. Omen. Frederick Morgan. **SP-MorgF**

Caradoc. Thomas Gray. **CP-GrayT**

Caravan. John Berryman. **CP-BerrJ**

Caravan of Silence. Richard Eberhart. **CP-EberR**

Caraway Seed, The. Ogden Nash. **CP-NashO**

Card, A. William Cowper. **CP-CowpW**

Card Game, The. Stephen Dobyns. **SP-DobyS**

Card-house over the fault, The. The Rising Sun. Randall Jarrell. **CP-JarrR**

Card Island or Cod Island? Isabella Gardner. **CP-GardI**

Card-Players, The. Philip Larkin. **CP-LarkP**

Card table in the library stands ready, A. Lost in Translation. James Merrill. **SP-MerrJ** *Fr.* The Book of Ephraim.

Cardin o't, The. Robert Burns. **CP-BurnR**

Cardinal, A. James Schuyler. **CP-SchuJ**

Cardinal, A. William DeWitt Snodgrass. **SP-SnodW**

Cardinal and the Dog, The. Robert Browning. **CP-BroR2**

Cardinal Bembo's Epitaph on Raphael. Thomas Hardy, *after* Pietro Bembo. **CP-HardT**

Cardinal Newman. Christina Georgina Rossetti. **CP-RosC3**

Cards. Gilbert Sorrentino. **SP-SorrG**

Cards that brighten the New Year, The. For the Visitors' Book. Kathleen Jessie Raine. **SP-RainK**

Cardtable is black, the cards are played face down, The. Draw. Robert Lowell. **SP-LoweR**

Care a Good Keeper. Robert Herrick. **CP-HerrR**

Care and Generosity. Christopher Smart. **SP-SmarC**

Care flieth, / Hope and fear together. Christina Georgina Rossetti. **CP-RosC3**

Care keepes the Conquest; 'tis no lesse renown[e]. Care a Good Keeper. Robert Herrick. **CP-HerrR**

Career. Kay Boyle. **CP-BoylK**

Career, A. Paul Laurence Dunbar. **CP-DunbP**

Career for a Child of Five. Kenneth Patchen. **CP-PatcK**

Career of flowers differs from ours, The. Emily Dickinson. **SP-DickE**

Careers. Stephen Dobyns. **SP-DobyS**

Careful observers may foretell the hour. A Description of a City Shower. Jonathan Swift. **CP-SwifJ**

Careful text-books measure, The. Hymn of Breaking Strain. Rudyard Kipling. **CP-KiplR**

Careful, they said: don't slip. The Danger. Pablo Neruda, *tr. fr. Spanish by* Ben Belitt. **SP-NeruP**

Carefully / the leaves of autumn. Late October. Maya Angelou. **SP-AngeM**

Carefully as a man tying up tomato plants. Ars Longa. Gilbert Sorrentino. **SP-SorrG**

Careless and still. The Rabbit Hunter. Robert Frost. **CP-FrosR**

Careless Love. Stanley Jasspon Kunitz. **CP-KuniS**

Careless Lover, The. Sir John Suckling. **CP-SuckJ**

Careless Night. Robert Lowell. **SP-LoweR**

Cares o' love are sweeter far, The. Robert Burns. **CP-BurnR**

Carew's Masque. Thomas Carew. **CP-CareT**

Coelum Britannicum. **CP-CareT**

First Song, The.

Fourth Song, The.

Second Song, The.

Third Song, The.

Cargo Catechism. Thomas Merton. *Fr.* East. *Fr.* The Geography of Lograire. **CP-MertT**

Cargo Songs. Thomas Merton. *Fr.* East. *Fr.* The Geography of Lograire. **CP-MertT**

Caria and Philistia considered. Cry Faugh! Robert Ranke Graves. **CP-GravR**

Caribbean Wind. "Bob Dylan." **CP-DylaB**

Caribou, The. Ogden Nash. **CP-NashO**

Caricature, The. Thomas Hardy. **CP-HardT**

Caridad para los pobrecitos. Los Pobrecitos. Charles Tomlinson. **CP-TomlC**

Caring for Surfaces. Mona Van Duyn. **SP-VanDM**

C[h]aritas Nimia; or, The Dear[e] Bargain. Richard Crashaw. **CP-CrasR**

Carkanet, The. Robert Herrick. **CP-HerrR**

Carl an the King Come. Robert Burns. **CP-BurnR**

Carlos, keep calm, love. Don't Kill Yourself. Carlos Drummond de Andrade, *tr. fr. Portuguese by* Elizabeth Bishop. **CP-BishE**

Carlos Trujillo / killed this mountain wolf. Anecdote. Charles Tomlinson. **CP-TomlC**

Carlos, your art is embryos. For a Mexican Painter. Muriel Rukeyser. **CP-RukeM**

Carlotta's Confession. Donald Hall. **CP-HallD**

Carlovingian Dreams. Carl Sandburg. **CP-SandC**

Carloway Broch. Richard Hugo. **CP-HugoR**

Carly Simon / on the juke. Mike. James Schuyler. **CP-SchuJ**

Carmel. Robinson Jeffers. **CP-JefR3**

Carmel Point. Robinson Jeffers. **CP-JefR3**

Carmel Valley. Allen Ginsberg. **CP-GinsA**

Carmen 1: "To whom should I present this." Catullus. **CP-ZukLS** *Fr.* Carmina. **CP-Catul**

("Whom do I give my neat little volume.") **CP-ZukLS,** *tr. by* Louis Zukofsky *and* Celia Zukofsky.

Carmen 2: "Lesbia's sparrow! / Lesbia's plaything!" Catullus. **CP-ZukLS** *Fr.* Carmina. **CP-Catul**

("Sparrow, my girl's pleasure, delight of my girl.") **CP-ZukLS,** *tr. by* Louis Zukofsky *and* Celia Zukofsky.

Carmen 3: "Who loves beauty / veil her statues." Catullus. **CP-ZukLS** *Fr.* Carmina. **CP-Catul**

(Death of a Starling, The.) **CP-WorW1,** *tr. by* William Wordsworth.

(Death of Lesbia's Bird, The.) **AWP,** *tr. by* Samuel Taylor Coleridge.

(Death of the Starling, The.) **PBBP,** *tr. by* Samuel Taylor Coleridge.

("Lament, o graces of Venus, and Cupids.") **CP-ZukLS,** *tr. by* Louis Zukofsky *and* Celia Zukofsky.

("Pity! mourn in plaintive tone.") **AWP; PBBP,** *tr. by* Samuel Taylor Coleridge.

("Pity mourns in plaintive tone.") **CP-WorW1,** *tr. by* William Wordsworth.

(Translation from Catullus ("Ye Cupids, droop each little head").) **CP-Byron,** *tr. by* Byron.

("Ye Cupids, droop each little head.") **CP-Byron,** *tr. by* Byron.

Carmen 4: "My bean-pod boat you see here." Catullus. **CP-ZukLS** *Fr.* Carmina. **CP-Catul**

(*Carmina,* IV.) **OBVE**

("Facile as can be the boat you see, my guests, says.") **CP-ZukLS,** *tr. by* Louis Zukofsky *and* Celia Zukofsky.

("Stranger, the bark you see before you says.") **AWP; OBVE,** *tr. by* John Hookham Frere.

("This racer of the watry plain.") **OBVE**

(Yacht, The.) **AWP; OBVE,** *tr. by* John Hookham Frere.

Carmen 5: "Lesbia / live with me", *see also sts. 1-3,* Stomping with Catullus (*by* Robert Creeley *in his* Collected Poems 1945-1975. Catullus. **CP-ZukLS; NAWM 1-2; STV** *Fr.* Carmina. **CP-Catul**

(*Carmina,* V.) **OBVE,** *tr. by* Richard Crashaw. **OBVE,** *tr. by* Walter Savage Landor. **OBVE,** *tr. by* William Wordsworth.

(Catullus: *Carmen v.*) **SP-MorgF,** *tr. by* Frederick Morgan.

(Catullus to Lesbia.) **ErPo,** *tr. by* James Reeves.

("Come and let us live my Deare.") **CavP; OBVE,** *tr. by* Richard Crashaw.

("Come, Lesbia, let us live and love.") **NAWM 1-2,** *tr. by* Horace Gregory.

("Come, my Celia, let us prove.") **EnRePo; ErPo; OBVE,** *tr. by* Ben Jonson.

(Courtship.) **CavP,** *tr. by* Alexander Brome.

("I tell you, Lesbia, life is love.") **ErPo,** *tr. by* James Reeves.

(Kiss-Fest, The.) **InMe,** *tr. by* Irwin Edman.

(Lesbia.) **PrIm,** *tr. by* Sheridan Baker. **CP-WorW1,** *tr. by* William Wordsworth.

("Lesbia, my love, let's be gay and enjoy ourselves.") **InMe,** *tr. by* Irwin Edman.

("Let's live, my Lesbia, and love.") **PrIm,** *tr. by* Sheridan Baker.

("Let's live, my Lesbia, and make love.") **SP-MorgF,** *tr. by* Frederick Morgan.

("May we live, my Lesbia, love while we may.") **CP-ZukLS,** *tr. by* Louis Zukofsky *and* Celia Zukofsky.

("My Lesbia let us love and live.") **CavP,** *tr. by* Alexander Brome. **CP-WorW1; OBVE,** *tr. by* William Wordsworth.

(My Sweetest Lesbia [Let Us Live and Love].) **AAS; AWP; BiP; CABA; CP-CampT; EIL; EnRePo; FF; GBL; HAP; HeIP; InPS; LoBV; NAEL-1; NIP; NoP; NoSic; OAEL-1; OBSC; PoE; PoRA; PrIm; SCGP; TEP; TFi; TrGrPo; UnTE; WeW,** *tr. by* Thomas Campion.

("My sweetest Lesbia, let us live and love.") **AAS; AWP; BiP; CABA; CP-CampT; EBEV; ELP; EIL; EnRePo; FF; GBL; HAP; HBV 1-2; HeIP; InPS; LoBV; NAEL-1; NIP; NoP; NoSic; OAEL-1; OBSC; OBVE; PoE; PoRA; PrIm; SCGP; SeCeV; TEP; TFi; TrGrPo; UnTE; WeW,** *tr. by* Thomas Campion.

(Out of Catullus.) **CavP,** *tr. by* Richard Crashaw.

(So Let's Live—Really Live!) **ArLo,** *tr. by* John Frederick Nims.

("So let's live—really live!—for love and loving.") **ArLo; STV,** *tr. by* John Frederick Nims.

(Song to Celia.) **EnRePo; ErPo,** *tr. by* Ben Jonson.

(To Celia.) **OBVE,** *tr. by* Ben Jonson.

(To Lesbia.) **ELP; HBV 1-2,** *tr. by* Thomas Campion.

(Vivamos, Mea Lesbia, atque Amemus.) **EBEV; SeCeV,** *tr. by* Thomas Campion.

("Yes! my Lesbia! let us prove.") **OBVE,** *tr. by* Walter Savage Landor.

"Sunne may set and rise, The." **CP-RaleW; FaBoEE; NoSic; OBVE,** *tr. by* Sir Walter Ralegh. **EnRePo; FaBoRV; SiPS**

(Lines from Catullus.) **EnRePo; SiPS,** *tr. by* Sir Walter Ralegh.

(Sun May Set, The.) **FaBoRV,** *tr. by* Sir Walter Raligh.

Carmen 6: "Your most recent acquisition, Flavius." Catullus. **CP-ZukLS; ErPo** *Fr.* Carmina. **CP-Catul**

("Flavius, if your girl friend.") **ErPo,** *tr. by* Horace Gregory.

("Flavius—that delicate lass—to Catullus.") **CP-ZukLS,** *tr. by* Louis Zukofsky *and* Celia Zukofsky.

Carmen 7: "Curious to learn / how may kiss- / es of your lips." Catullus. **CP-ZukLS** *Fr.* Carmina. **CP-Catul**

(*Ad Lesbiam.*) **OxBI,** *tr. by* Niall Sheridan.

("How many kisses, Lesbia, you ask.") **OxBI,** *tr. by* Niall Sheridan.

("Queries, you ask how many times must I kiss.") **CP-ZukLS,** *tr. by* Louis Zukofsky *and* Celia Zukofsky.

("Thy kisses dost thou bid me count.") **UnTE,** *tr. by* George Lamb.

(To Lesbia.) **UnTE,** *tr. by* George Lamb.

Carmen 8: "Break off / fallen Catullus." Catullus. **AAS; CP-CampT; CP-ZukLS; NAWM 1-2; NCEP; STV** *Fr.* Carmina. **CP-Catul**

(*Carmina,* VIII.) **OBVE,** *tr. by* Louis Zukofsky *and* Celia Zukofsky. **OBVE,** *tr. by* Thomas Campion.

(Catullus Talks to Himself.) **UnTE,** *tr. by* Louis Untermeyer.

("Catullus, you're a fool. I said.") **UnTE,** *tr. by* Louis Untermeyer.

("Harden now thy tyred hart, with more than flinty rage.") **AAS; CP-CampT; NCEP; OBVE,** *tr. by* Thomas Campion.

("Miss her, Catullus? don't be so inept to rail.") **CP-ZukLS; OBVE,** *tr. by* Louis Zukofsky *and* Celia Zukofsky.

("O poor Catullus, stupid long enough!") **STV,** *tr. by* John Frederick Nims.

("Poor damned Catullus, here's no time for nonsense.") **NAWM 1-2,** *tr. by* Horace Gregory.

(To Himself.) **AWP,** *tr. by* William Ellery Leonard.

("Wretched Catullus, play the fool no more.") **AWP,** *tr. by* William Ellery Leonard.

Carmen 9: "Veraniolus, / first of friends." Catullus. **CP-ZukLS; PeHV** *Fr.* Carmina. **CP-Catul**

("Veranius, my dear friend, the friend worth.") **PeHV,** *tr. by* James Michie.

("Veranius of all my beloved friends.") **CP-ZukLS,** *tr. by* Louis Zukofsky *and* Celia Zukofsky.

Carmen 10: "Alfenus Varus / buttonholes me." Catullus. **CP-ZukLS** *Fr.* Carmina. **CP-Catul**

(*Carmina,* X.) **OBVE,** *tr. by* John Hookham Frere.

(Fib Detected, A.) **AWP,** *tr. by* John Hookham Frere.

("Varus old crony had me visit his love.") **CP-ZukLS,** *tr. by* Louis Zukofsky *and* Celia Zukofsky.

("Varus, whom I chanced to meet.") **AWP; OBVE,** *tr. by* John Hookham Frere.

Carmen 11: "Furius, Aurelius, friends of my youth." Catullus. **CP-ZukLS** *Fr.* Carmina. **CP-Catul**

(Catullus: *Carmen xi.*) **SP-MorgF,** *tr. by* Frederick Morgan.

("Furius and Aurelius, loyal friends.") **SP-MorgF,** *tr. by* Frederick Morgan.

("Furius, Aurelius: comities—Catullus.") **CP-ZukLS,** *tr. by* Louis Zukofsky *and* Celia Zukofsky.

Carmen 12: "While everyone else is laughing & drinking." Catullus. **CP-ZukLS** *Fr.* Carmina. **CP-Catul**

("Marrucinus Asinius, that sinister.") **CP-ZukLS,** *tr. by* Louis Zukofsky *and* Celia Zukofsky.

Carmen 13: "I shall expect / you in to dine." Catullus. **CP-LoveR; CP-ZukLS** *Fr.* Carmina. **CP-Catul**

("Canapés, my Fabullus, at home any.") **CP-ZukLS,** *tr. by* Louis Zukofsky *and* Celia Zukofsky.

(*Carmina,* XIII.) **OBVE,** *tr. by* Richard Lovelace.

("Fabullus I will treat you handsomely.") **CP-LoveR; OBVE,** *tr. by* Richard Lovelace.

Carmen 14: "If, my irrepressible Calvus, I didn't." Catullus. **CP-ZukLS** *Fr.* Carmina. **CP-Catul**

("Not that I look to my eyes more than your love.") **CP-ZukLS,** *tr. by* Louis Zukofsky *and* Celia Zukofsky.

Carmen 15: "*My love & I* are yours to command." Catullus. **CP-ZukLS; FaBoBl; PeHV** *Fr.* Carmina. **CP-Catul**

("Commend to you my cares for the love I love.") **CP-ZukLS,** *tr. by* Louis Zukofsky *and* Celia Zukofsky.

("I entrust my all to you, Aurelius.") **PeHV**

("I'm placing in your hands my lover and myself.") **FaBoBl,** *tr. by* Rodney Pybus.

Carmen 16: "Pedicabo et irrumabo." Catullus. **CP-ZukLS; PeHV** *Fr.* Carmina. **CP-Catul**

("I'll have you by the short and curly hair.") **PeHV,** *tr. by* James Michie.

("Piping, beaus, I'll go *whoosh* and I'll rumble you.") **CP-ZukLS,** *tr. by* Louis Zukofsky *and* Celia Zukofsky.

Carmen 17: "Cologna Veneta - / where the good folk." Catullus.
    CP-ZukLS *Fr.* Carmina. **CP-Catul**
("O Colonia, whose wishes build a long bridge to dance on.") **CP-ZukLS,**
    tr. by Louis Zukofsky *and* Celia Zukofsky.
Carmen 18: "I dedicate, I consecrate this grove to thee." Catullus. *Fr.*
    Carmina. **CP-Catul**
Carmen 21: "Impresario of neediness." Catullus. **CP-ZukLS** *Fr.*
    Carmina. **CP-Catul**
("Aurelius, father, assure that the o numb.") **CP-ZukLS,** *tr. by* Louis
    Zukofsky *and* Celia Zukofsky.
Carmen 22: "I must, Varus, tell you." Catullus. **CP-ZukLS** *Fr.* Carmina.
    CP-Catul
(*Carmina, XXII.*) **OBVE,** *tr. by* Matthew Prior.
("Suffenus is, stay Varus,—whom you've proven—is the.") **CP-ZukLS,** *tr.
    by* Louis Zukofsky *and* Celia Zukofsky.
("Suffenus, whom so well you know.") **AWP,** *tr. by* Walter Savage
    Landor.
("Suffenus whom you know, the Witty.") **OBVE,** *tr. by* Matthew Prior.
(To Varus.) **AWP,** *tr. by* Walter Savage Landor.
Carmen 23: "Friend Furius, / who has no slaves & no money." Catullus.
    CP-ZukLS *Fr.* Carmina. **CP-Catul**
("Furius, with no key to service, no key.") **CP-ZukLS,** *tr. by* Louis
    Zukofsky *and* Celia Zukofsky.
Carmen 24: "Best sprig of the clan." Catullus. **CP-ZukLS** *Fr.* Carmina.
    CP-Catul
("O quick floss silk of the Juventii, form.") **CP-ZukLS,** *tr. by* Louis
    Zukofsky *and* Celia Zukofsky.
Carmen 25: "From Thallus the pederast." Catullus. **CP-ZukLS** *Fr.*
    Carmina. **CP-Catul**
("Conniving Thallus, mulley, you, cony cully, cop below.") **CP-ZukLS,**
    tr. by Louis Zukofsky *and* Celia Zukofsky.
Carmen 26: "Your cottage, Furius, sheltered." Catullus. **CP-ZukLS** *Fr.*
    Carmina. **CP-Catul**
("Furius, 'Little Villa' has no nod for Auster.") **CP-ZukLS,** *tr. by* Louis
    Zukofsky *and* Celia Zukofsky.
Carmen 27: "Falernian, / old Falernian!" Catullus. **CP-ZukLS** *Fr.*
    Carmina. **CP-Catul**
("Minister wet to lee, pour the Falernian.") **CP-ZukLS,** *tr. by* Louis
    Zukofsky *and* Celia Zukofsky.
Carmen 28: "In Piso's suite / are empty pockets." Catullus. **CP-ZukLS**
    Fr. Carmina. **CP-Catul**
("Piso's own comates, his, corps an inane as.") **CP-ZukLS,** *tr. by* Louis
    Zukofsky *and* Celia Zukofsky.
Carmen 29: "What man could stomach the sight." Catullus. **CP-ZukLS**
    Fr. Carmina. **CP-Catul**
("Whose hoax to put up with, outstare, protest patience.") **CP-ZukLS,** *tr.
    by* Louis Zukofsky *and* Celia Zukofsky.
Carmen 30: "Alfenus from Cremona / forsakes the friendship of friends."
    Catullus. **CP-ZukLS** *Fr.* Carmina. **CP-Catul**
("Alfenus, remember *kind* intimacies? false? They elated us.") **CP-ZukLS,**
    tr. by Louis Zukofsky *and* Celia Zukofsky.
Carmen 31: "Apple of islands, Sirmio, & bright peninsulas, set." Catullus.
    CP-ZukLS; STV *Fr.* Carmina. **CP-Catul**
(*Carmina,* XXXI.) **OBVE,** *tr. by* Thomas Hardy.
(Catullus: XXXI.) **CP-HardT,** *tr. by* Thomas Hardy.
(Dear Little Sirmio.) **CP-SmitS,** *tr. by* Stevie Smith.
("Dear little Sirmio / Of all capes and islands.") **CP-SmitS,** *tr. by* Stevie
    Smith.
("Gem of all isthmuses and isles that lie.") **AWP,** *tr. by* Charles Stuart
    Calverley.
("Jewel of the almost islands and the isles.") **STV,** *tr. by* John Frederick
    Nims.
("Peninsular arm, Sirmio, insular arm, well.") **CP-ZukLS,** *tr. by* Louis
    Zukofsky *and* Celia Zukofsky.
(Sirmio.) **AWP,** *tr. by* Charles Stuart Calverley.
("Sirmio, thou dearest dear of strands.") **CP-HardT,** *tr. by* Thomas Hardy.
Carmen 32: "Call me to you / at siesta." Catullus. **CP-ZukLS** *Fr.*
    Carmina. **CP-Catul**
(Dearest Ipsitilla.) **FaBoBl,** *tr. by* Rodney Pybus.
("Dearest Ipsitilla, I'd absolutely love it.") **FaBoBl,** *tr. by* Rodney Pybus.
("Hypsithilla, ask me over.") **ErPo,** *tr. by* Gardner E. Lewis.
("I'm a bow, my dual kiss, Ipsithilla.") **CP-ZukLS,** *tr. by* Louis Zukofsky
    and Celia Zukofsky.
(Invitation to an Invitation, An.) **ErPo,** *tr. by* Gardner E. Lewis.
Carmen 33: "Vibennius & son, renowned." Catullus. **CP-ZukLS; PeHV**
    Fr. Carmina. **CP-Catul**
("Of all our bath-house thieves the cleverest one.") **PeHV,** *tr. by* James
    Michie.
("Offer 'em up to me—bullneck crook of the baths.") **CP-ZukLS,** *tr. by*
Louis Zukofsky *and* Celia Zukofsky.
Carmen 34: "Moving in her radiant care." Catullus. **CP-ZukLS** *Fr.*
    Carmina. **CP-Catul**
("Boys and girls, we pledge allegiance.") **Moon,** *tr. by* Horace Gregory.
("Diana guardeth our estate.") **AWP,** *tr. by* Richard Claverhouse Jebb.
("Diana, sum us in faith a.") **CP-ZukLS,** *tr. by* Louis Zukofsky *and* Celia
    Zukofsky.
(Dianae Sumus in Fide.) **Moon,** *tr. by* Horace Gregory.
(Hymn to Diana.) **AWP,** *tr. by* Richard Claverhouse Jebb.
Carmen 35: "Fetch, papyrus, / our soft-measured poet." Catullus.
    CP-ZukLS *Fr.* Carmina. **CP-Catul**
("Poet I'm too near your and my sod daily.") **CP-ZukLS,** *tr. by* Louis
    Zukofsky *and* Celia Zukofsky.
Carmen 36: "Volusian sheets / shit-shotten Annals." Catullus. **CP-ZukLS**
    Fr. Carmina. **CP-Catul**
("*Annals* of Volusius, cock at his offal.") **CP-ZukLS,** *tr. by* Louis
    Zukofsky *and* Celia Zukofsky.
Carmen 37: "Nine posts, five doors, up the Clivus." Catullus. **CP-ZukLS**
    Fr. Carmina. **CP-Catul**
("Salt hacks, tavern boys, what skews, can't you burn alleys.") **CP-
    ZukLS,** *tr. by* Louis Zukofsky *and* Celia Zukofsky.
Carmen 38: "Angst, / ennui & angst." Catullus. **CP-ZukLS; PeHV** *Fr.*
    Carmina. **CP-Catul**
("My last—Cornificius—your Catullus'.") **CP-ZukLS,** *tr. by* Louis
    Zukofsky *and* Celia Zukofsky.
("Your Catullus is depressed, Cornificus.") **PeHV**
Carmen 39: "Because he has bright white teech, Eg- / natius whips out a."
    Catullus. **CP-ZukLS** *Fr.* Carmina. **CP-Catul**
(*Carmina,* XXXIX.) **OBVE,** *tr. by* Walter Savage Landor.
("Egnatius, candid as his horse-bit white dentures.") **CP-ZukLS,** *tr. by*
    Louis Zukofsky *and* Celia Zukofsky.
("Egnatius has fine teeth, and those.") **OBVE,** *tr. by* Walter Savage
    Landor.
Carmen 40: "Whatever could have possessed you." Catullus. **CP-ZukLS**
    Fr. Carmina. **CP-Catul**
(*Carmina,* XL.) **OBVE,** *tr. by* Louis Zukofsky *and* Celia Zukofsky.
("What demented malice, my silly Ravidus.") **CP-ZukLS; OBVE,** *tr. by*
    Louis Zukofsky *and* Celia Zukofsky.
Carmen 41: "Formianus's whore, / long-nosed." Catullus. **CP-ZukLS** *Fr.*
    Carmina. **CP-Catul**
("Ameana pulling, a foot touted high.") **CP-ZukLS,** *tr. by* Louis Zukofsky
    and Celia Zukofsky.
("Ameana, that banged-out bitch.") **SP-MorgF,** *tr. by* Frederick Morgan.
(Catullus: *Carmen xli.*) **SP-MorgF,** *tr. by* Frederick Morgan.
Carmen 42: "From the quarters of the compass." Catullus. **CP-ZukLS;
    DBV** *Fr.* Carmina. **CP-Catul**
("At hest, hendecasyllabics, what is this.") **CP-ZukLS,** *tr. by* Louis
    Zukofsky *and* Celia Zukofsky.
("Hendecasyllables, help! Come to my call.") **DBV,** *tr. by* James Michie.
Carmen 43: "O elegant whore!" Catullus. **CP-ZukLS** *Fr.* Carmina. **CP-
    Catul**
("Salvé, next, minimal, poor little nosey.") **CP-ZukLS,** *tr. by* Louis
    Zukofsky *and* Celia Zukofsky.
Carmen 44: "It depends who's talking if you're a 'Sabine.' " Catullus.
    CP-ZukLS *Fr.* Carmina. **CP-Catul**
("O farm, dear nest, or say Sabine, ah say Tibur's.") **CP-ZukLS,** *tr. by*
    Louis Zukofsky *and* Celia Zukofsky.
Carmen 45: "Phyllis Corydon clutched to him." Catullus. **BoLoP;
    CP-ZukLS** *Fr.* Carmina. **CP-Catul**
(Acme and Septimius.) **AWP; OBVE; UnTE,** *tr. by* Abraham Cowley.
("Acme, Septimius, sighs so amorous.") **CP-ZukLS,** *tr. by* Louis
    Zukofsky *and* Celia Zukofsky.
(Septimius and Acme.) **CP-WorW1,** *tr. by* William Wordsworth.
("Septimius thus his love addressed.") **CP-WorW1,** *tr. by* William
    Wordsworth.
("Whilst on Septimius' panting Breast.") **AWP; OBVE; UnTE,** *tr. by*
    Abraham Cowley.
Carmen 46: "Now spring bursts." Catullus. **CP-ZukLS; PoPl** *Fr.*
    Carmina. **CP-Catul**
("Now Spring brings back the tepid breeze.") **PoPl,** *tr. by* L.R. Lind.
("Warm gale, a dose of spring—revert to the pores.") **CP-ZukLS,** *tr. by*
    Louis Zukofsky *and* Celia Zukofsky.
Carmen 47: "Lucius Calpurnius Piso Caesoninus." Catullus. **CP-ZukLS**
    Fr. Carmina. **CP-Catul**
("Porky and Socration, two-eye sins as try.") **CP-ZukLS,** *tr. by* Louis
    Zukofsky *and* Celia Zukofsky.
Carmen 48: "Iuventius, / were I allowed." Catullus. **CP-Byron; CP-
    ZukLS; PeHV** *Fr.* Carmina. **CP-Catul**
("If I could go on kissing your honeyed eyes.") **PeHV**

("Juvencius, thy fair sweet Eyes.") **CP-LoveR**, *tr.* by Richard Lovelace.

("Mellowed *those*, I call *those* eyes, Juventius.") **CP-ZukLS**, *tr.* by Louis Zukofsky *and* Celia Zukofsky.

("Oh! might I kiss those eyes of fire.") **CP-Byron; TSF**, *tr.* by Byron.

(To Ellen.) **TSF**, *tr.* by Byron.

(To Juvencius.) **CP-LoveR**

Carmen 49: "Silver-tongued among the sons of Rome." Catullus. **CP-ZukLS** *Fr.* Carmina. **CP-Catul**

(Disertissime Romuli Nepotum.) **SP-SmarC**, *tr.* by Christopher Smart.

("Master of eloquence and Rome's potent line.") **CP-ZukLS**, *tr.* by Louis Zukofsky *and* Celia Zukofsky.

("O Thou, of British Orators the chief.") **SP-SmarC**, *tr.* by Christopher Smart.

(To Marcus T. Cicero.) **CP-LoveR**, *tr.* by Richard Lovelace.

("Tully to thee Rome's eloquent Sole Heir.") **CP-LoveR**, *tr.* by Richard Lovelace.

Carmen 50: "Other day we spent, The." Catullus. **CP-ZukLS** *Fr.* Carmina. **CP-Catul**

("Yesterday, Licinius, what a day it was.") **CP-ZukLS**, *tr.* by Louis Zukofsky *and* Celia Zukofsky.

Carmen 51: "Godlike the man who." Catullus. **CP-ZukLS** *Fr.* Carmina. **CP-Catul**

("Equal to Jove that youth must be.") **CP-Byron**, *tr.* by Byron.

("He'll hie me, par *is* he? the God divide her.") **CP-ZukLS**, *tr.* by Louis Zukofsky *and* Celia Zukofsky.

("Like to a god he seems to me.") **AWP**, *tr.* by William Ellery Leonard.

(Sappho.) **AWP**, *tr.* by William Ellery Leonard.

(Translation from Catullus ("Equal to Jove that youth must be").) **CP-Byron**, *tr.* by Byron.

Carmen 52: "Drop dead, Catullus, lie right down & die." Catullus. **CP-ZukLS** *Fr.* Carmina. **CP-Catul**

("Quick death, Catullus! what more horrors may hurry!") **CP-ZukLS**, *tr.* by Louis Zukofsky *and* Celia Zukofsky.

Carmen 53: "I laughed. Calvus. I laughed today." Catullus. **CP-ZukLS** *Fr.* Carmina. **CP-Catul**

("Risible nice go when from mud a crony.") **CP-ZukLS**, *tr.* by Louis Zukofsky *and* Celia Zukofsky.

Carmen 54: "If not by all that his friends boast." Catullus. **CP-ZukLS** *Fr.* Carmina. **CP-Catul**

("Otho's scooped nut its pusillanimity.") **CP-ZukLS**, *tr.* by Louis Zukofsky *and* Celia Zukofsky.

Carmen 55: "Where / if it's not too much to ask." Catullus. **CP-ZukLS** *Fr.* Carmina. **CP-Catul**

(*Carmina*, LV.) **OBVE**, *tr.* by Nahum Tate.

("Now if thou hast one dram of Grace.") **OBVE**, *tr.* by Nahum Tate.

("Rum asks—see, fortune won't molest you.") **CP-ZukLS**, *tr.* by Louis Zukofsky *and* Celia Zukofsky.

Carmen 56: "Matter for mirth, Cato, & a smile, A." Catullus. **CP-ZukLS; PeHV** *Fr.* Carmina. **CP-Catul**

("I have something for you to laugh at, Cato.") **PeHV**

("O ram ridicule home, Cato, the jokes some.") **CP-ZukLS**, *tr.* by Louis Zukofsky *and* Celia Zukofsky.

Carmen 57: "*Caesar Mamurraque!* / A peerless pair of brazen buggers." Catullus. **CP-ZukLS; DBV** *Fr.* Carmina. **CP-Catul**

(" 'Pull! crew' 's convenient to reprobate kin hides.") **CP-ZukLS**, *tr.* by Louis Zukofsky *and* Celia Zukofsky.

("They make a pretty pair of debauchees.") **DBV**, *tr.* by James Michie.

Carmen 58: "Lesbia, our Lesbia, the same old Lesbia." Catullus. **CP-ZukLS; NAWM 1-2** *Fr.* Carmina. **CP-Catul**

("Caelius, Lesbia new star, Lesbia a light.") **CP-ZukLS**, *tr.* by Louis Zukofsky *and* Celia Zukofsky.

("Caelius, my Lesbia, that one, that only Lesbia.") **NAWM 1-2**, *tr.* by Horace Gregory.

Carmen 59: "Menenius' wife, / a red-headed cat from Bologna." Catullus. **CP-ZukLS** *Fr.* Carmina. **CP-Catul**

("Bononian, sis Rufa, Rufus' lum fell at.") **CP-ZukLS**, *tr.* by Louis Zukofsky *and* Celia Zukofsky.

Carmen 60: "Hard. Hard. As she-cat whelped in desert mountains." Catullus. **CP-ZukLS; NAWM 1-2** *Fr.* Carmina. **CP-Catul**

("None but a lioness moaned this, Libya's mountains.") **CP-ZukLS**, *tr.* by Louis Zukofsky *and* Celia Zukofsky.

("Were you born of a lioness in the Libyan Mountains.") **NAWM 1-2**, *tr.* by Horace Gregory.

Carmen 61: "Hill (breeder) of Helicon." Catullus. **CP-ZukLS; OxBM** *Fr.* Carmina. **CP-Catul**

("Guardian of Helicon, Urania's son.") **OxBM**, *tr.* by Frederic Raphael *and* Kenneth McLeish.

("Who lives o on Helicon hill.") **CP-ZukLS**, *tr.* by Louis Zukofsky *and* Celia Zukofsky.

Hymeneal. **PeHV**, *tr.* by James Michie.

Carmen 62: "Gather young men as the twilight gathers." Catullus. **CP-ZukLS** *Fr.* Carmina. **CP-Catul**

("Vesper out there, you vain knees can sure get up: Vesper, Olympus.") **CP-ZukLS**, *tr.* by Louis Zukofsky *and* Celia Zukofsky.

Carmen 63: "Plunging towards Phrygia over violent water." Catullus. **CP-ZukLS** *Fr.* Carmina. **CP-Catul**

(Attis.) **OBVE; STV**, *tr.* by Peter Whigham.

("Over oceans sped he, Attis, in the speediest of ships.") **STV**, *tr.* by John Frederick Nims.

("Spurred altering wake toss Attis his craft racing till marled in the.") **CP-ZukLS**, *tr.* by Louis Zukofsky *and* Celia Zukofsky.

Carmen 64: "In old days / driving through soft waters." Catullus. **APSN; CP-ZukLS** *Fr.* Carmina. **CP-Catul**

("Left hand holding distaff and wool retained on it (ah mixture).") **APSN**, *tr.* by Louis Zukofsky *and* Celia Zukofsky.

("Pelion could one time prong its top worthy keel in pines.") **CP-ZukLS**, *tr.* by Louis Zukofsky *and* Celia Zukofsky.

Carmen 65: "Although entangled in prolonged grief." Catullus. **CP-ZukLS** *Fr.* Carmina. **CP-Catul**

(Grief.) **RaBo**, *tr.* by Jacob Rabinowitz.

("Grief reached across the world to get me.") **RaBo**, *tr.* by Jacob Rabinowitz.

("Yet see (may as I do) a confect of my cure—a dolor.") **CP-ZukLS**, *tr.* by Louis Zukofsky *and* Celia Zukofsky.

Carmen 66: "Who scans the bright machinery of the skies." Catullus. **CP-ZukLS** *Fr.* Carmina. **CP-Catul**

("Human all key mog knee this pecks it loom in a moon the.") **CP-ZukLS**, *tr.* by Louis Zukofsky *and* Celia Zukofsky.

Carmen 67: "Sweet entrance to a husband's pleasure." Catullus. **CP-ZukLS** *Fr.* Carmina. **CP-Catul**

(Dialogue with a Door.) **UnTE**, *tr.* by John Nott.

("Hail, door, to husband and to father dear!") **UnTE**, *tr.* by John Nott.

("O dear cool you couldn't be virile—you couldn't a parent he.") **CP-ZukLS**, *tr.* by Louis Zukofsky *and* Celia Zukofsky.

Carmen 68: "Borne down by bitter misfortune." Catullus. **CP-ZukLS** *Fr.* Carmina. **CP-Catul**

("Cold how mean, fortune consuming you oppresses your care, your.") **CP-ZukLS**, *tr.* by Louis Zukofsky *and* Celia Zukofsky.

Carmen 69: "Do not wonder when the wench declines." Catullus. **CP-ZukLS** *Fr.* Carmina. **CP-Catul**

(*Carmina*, LXIX.) **OBVE**, *tr.* by Richard Lovelace.

("No lift odd mere horror, harrowed (why boy?) that no woman will.") **CP-ZukLS**, *tr.* by Louis Zukofsky *and* Celia Zukofsky.

("That no fair woman will, wonder not why.") **CP-LoveR; OBVE**, *tr.* by Richard Lovelace.

(To Rufus.) **CP-LoveR**

Carmen 70: "Lesbia says she'd rather marry me", *see also sts. 1-3*, Stomping with Catullus (*by* Robert Creeley). Catullus. **CP-ZukLS; NAWM 1-2; STV** *Fr.* Carmina. **CP-Catul**

(*Carmina*, LXX.) **OBVE**, *tr.* by Philip Sidney. **OBVE**, *tr.* by Richard Lovelace.

(Female Inconstancy.) **CP-LoveR**, *tr.* by Richard Lovelace.

("My fair says, she no spouse but me.") **PV**, *tr.* by George Lamb.

("My girl says she'll take no one else as a lover.") **STV**, *tr.* by John Frederick Nims.

("My Mistresse sayes she'll marry none but me.") **CP-LoveR; OBVE**, *tr.* by Richard Lovelace.

(My Woman.) **ArLo; PoPl**, *tr.* by Gilbert Highet.

("My woman says she wants no other lover.") **ArLo; PoPl**, *tr.* by Gilbert Highet.

("My woman says that she would rather wear the wedding-veil for me.") **NAWM 1-2**, *tr.* by Horace Gregory.

("Newly say dickered my love air my own would marry me all.") **CP-ZukLS**, *tr.* by Louis Zukofsky *and* Celia Zukofsky.

(On the Inconstancy of Women.) **PV**, *tr.* by George Lamb.

("Unto no body my woman saith she had rather a wife be.") **OBVE**, *tr.* by Philip Sidney.

Carmen 71: "If ever anyone / was deservedly plagued by a goat under his armpits." Catullus. **CP-ZukLS** *Fr.* Carmina. **CP-Catul**

("Securer a bo? no sacred armpits lair hops as that he-goat's.") **CP-ZukLS**, *tr.* by Louis Zukofsky *and* Celia Zukofsky.

Carmen 72: "There was a time, Lesbia, when." Catullus. **CP-LoveR; CP-ZukLS; FMP** *Fr.* Carmina. **CP-Catul**

(*Carmina*, LXXII.) **OBVE**, *tr.* by Richard Lovelace. **OBVE**, *tr.* by William Walsh.

("Decay bars one time, 'solely to know, see Catullus'.") **CP-ZukLS**, *tr.* by Louis Zukofsky *and* Celia Zukofsky.

("That me alone you lov'd, you once did say.") **CP-LoveR; FMP; OBVE**, *tr.* by Richard Lovelace.

("Thou saidst that I alone thy Heart cou'd move.") **OBVE,** *tr. by* William Walsh.

("Thou saidst that I alone thy heart could move.") **OxBSP,** *tr. by* William Walsh.

(To His False Mistress.) **OxBSP,** *tr. by* William Walsh.

Carmen 73: "Cancel, Catullus, the expectancies of friendship." Catullus. **CP-ZukLS; DBV** *Fr.* Carmina. **CP-Catul**

("Day, see no day—choke, qualm, quick qualm—benevolence, merit are.") **CP-ZukLS,** *tr. by* Louis Zukofsky *and* Celia Zukofsky.

("Expect no thanks ever from anyone.") **DBV,** *tr. by* James Michie.

Carmen 74: "Gellius, / hearing his uncle anathematise the mere mention." Catullus. **CP-ZukLS** *Fr.* Carmina. **CP-Catul**

("Gellius how he'd rare at pot true uncle objurgate soul array.") **CP-ZukLS,** *tr. by* Louis Zukofsky *and* Celia Zukofsky.

Carmen 75: "Reason blinded by sin, Lesbia." Catullus. **CP-LoveR; CP-ZukLS; NAWM 1-2; STV; WeW** *Fr.* Carmina. **CP-Catul**

("By thy fault is my mind brought to that pass.") **CP-LoveR**

(*Carmina,* LXXV.) **OBVE,** *tr. by* Walter Savage Landor.

("How cast down is the mind that took to my Lesbia, culprit.") **CP-ZukLS,** *tr. by* Louis Zukofsky *and* Celia Zukofsky.

("None could ever say that she.") **AWP; OBVE,** *tr. by* Walter Savage Landor.

("Now my mind's been brought to such a state—and it's your fault.") **STV,** *tr. by* John Frederick Nims.

("Now my mind's been brought to such extremes—and it's your fault.") **WeW,** *tr. by* John Frederick Nims.

(True or False.) **AWP,** *tr. by* Walter Savage Landor.

("You are the cause of this destruction, Lesbia.") **NAWM 1-2,** *tr. by* Horace Gregory.

Carmen 76: "If evocations of past kindness shed." Catullus. **CP-ZukLS; NAWM 1-2** *Fr.* Carmina. **CP-Catul**

("If a man can find rich consolation, remembering his good deeds and.") **NAWM 1-2,** *tr. by* Horace Gregory.

("Seek or record then the benefactor—pree or voluptuous.") **CP-ZukLS,** *tr. by* Louis Zukofsky *and* Celia Zukofsky.

Carmen 77: "Whom I have trusted to no end (Rufus)." Catullus. **CP-ZukLS** *Fr.* Carmina. **CP-Catul**

("Rufey my how frustrate unquickened and craved the tie I'm equal.") **CP-ZukLS,** *tr. by* Louis Zukofsky *and* Celia Zukofsky.

Carmen 78: "Gallus's brothers possess / one, the most attractive of wives." Catullus. **CP-ZukLS** *Fr.* Carmina. **CP-Catul**

("Gallus ha' but brothers: bro one's lady slip's make so young she's.") **CP-ZukLS,** *tr. by* Louis Zukofsky *and* Celia Zukofsky.

Carmen 79: "They nickname Lesbia's brother 'pulcher.' " Catullus. **CP-ZukLS** *Fr.* Carmina. **CP-Catul**

("Lesbius has pooled her: kidney? whom Lesbia my—lit.") **CP-ZukLS,** *tr. by* Louis Zukofsky *and* Celia Zukofsky.

Carmen 80: "How is it, Gellius." Catullus. **CP-ZukLS; PeHV** *Fr.* Carmina. **CP-Catul**

("Gellius, what reason can you give why those ruddy lips of yours.") **PeHV**

("Quiddity, Gelli, quarry, rosy as these too lips belie.") **CP-ZukLS,** *tr. by* Louis Zukofsky *and* Celia Zukofsky.

Carmen 81: "Surely, Iuventius, one of this throng in Rome." Catullus. **CP-ZukLS; PeHV** *Fr.* Carmina. **CP-Catul**

("Juventius, could you not find in this great crowd of men.") **PeHV**

("Not many enchant you (put to it) popular is he, Juventi.") **CP-ZukLS,** *tr. by* Louis Zukofsky *and* Celia Zukofsky.

Carmen 82: "My eyes in your pledge, Quintius." Catullus. **CP-ZukLS** *Fr.* Carmina. **CP-Catul**

("Quinti, see if't be wish of cool eyes day bear your Catullus.") **CP-ZukLS,** *tr. by* Louis Zukofsky *and* Celia Zukofsky.

("Quintius if you'll endear Catullus eyes.") **CP-LoveR,** *tr. by* Richard Lovelace.

(To Quintius.) **CP-LoveR,** *tr. by* Richard Lovelace.

Carmen 83: "Lesbia is extraordinarily vindictive." Catullus. **CP-ZukLS; NAWM 1-2** *Fr.* Carmina. **CP-Catul**

("Lesbia (my price scent t'her hero) mauls and deplores me, '*dig it*'.") **CP-ZukLS,** *tr. by* Louis Zukofsky *and* Celia Zukofsky.

("Lesbia speaks evil of me with her husband near and he (damned.") **NAWM 1-2,** *tr. by* Horace Gregory.

Carmen 84: " 'Hadvantageous' breathes Arrius heavily." Catullus. **CP-ZukLS** *Fr.* Carmina. **CP-Catul**

("'c-hommodating' he'd bait, seeking *accomodating* willed.") **CP-ZukLS,** *tr. by* Louis Zukofsky *and* Celia Zukofsky.

Carmen 85: "I hate and I love. And if you ask me how." Catullus. **CP-LoveR; CP-ZukLS; NAWM 1-2; STV; WeW** *Fr.* Carmina. **CP-Catul**

(*Carmina,* LXXXV.) **OBVE,** *tr. by* Ezra Pound. **OBVE,** *tr. by* Richard Lovelace. **OBVE,** *tr. by* Walter Savage Landor.

("Her that I love, I hate! 'How's that, do you know?' they wonder.") **STV; WeW,** *tr. by* John Frederick Nims.

("I hate and love. / And if you ask me why.") **NAWM 1-2,** *tr. by* Horace Gregory.

("I hate and love. Why? You may ask but.") **CTC; OBVE,** *tr. by* Ezra Pound.

("I hate and love, wouldst thou the reason know?") **CP-LoveR; OBVE,** *tr. by* Richard Lovelace.

("I hate, and yet I love thee too.") **PoPl,** *tr. by* Abraham Cowley.

("I love and hate. Ah! never asky why so!") **OBVE,** *tr. by* Walter Savage Landor.

("O th'hate I move love. Quarry if fact I am, for that's so re queries.") **CP-ZukLS,** *tr. by* Louis Zukofsky *and* Celia Zukofsky.

(Ode et Amo.) **CTC,** *tr. by* Ezra Pound.

(To Lesbia.) **PoPl,** *tr. by* Abraham Cowley.

Carmen 86: "We have heard of Quintia's beauty. To me she is tall, slender." Catullus. **CP-LoveR; CP-ZukLS; NAWM 1-2** *Fr.* Carmina. **CP-Catul**

("Quintia is handsome, fair, tall, straight, all these.") **CP-LoveR,** *tr. by* Richard Lovelace.

("Quintia's *foremost* to multitudes; my eye can deed her *long, e—*.") **CP-ZukLS,** *tr. by* Louis Zukofsky *and* Celia Zukofsky.

("There are many who think of Quintia in terms of beauty.") **NAWM 1-2,** *tr. by* Horace Gregory.

Carmen 87: "No woman loved, in truth, Lesbia." Catullus. **CP-LoveR; CP-ZukLS; NAWM 1-2** *Fr.* Carmina. **CP-Catul**

("No love by test, my love, 'll air then, time, say the care of all my time.") **CP-ZukLS,** *tr. by* Louis Zukofsky *and* Celia Zukofsky.

("No one can boast herself so much belov'd.") **CP-LoveR,** *tr. by* Richard Lovelace.

("No woman, if she is honest, can say that she's.") **NAWM 1-2,** *tr. by* Horace Gregory.

Carmen 88: "What, Gellius, of the man." Catullus. **CP-ZukLS** *Fr.* Carmina. **CP-Catul**

("Quid, fact it is Gelli? quick'ning mother, at (queer) sis, all three.") **CP-ZukLS,** *tr. by* Louis Zukofsky *and* Celia Zukofsky.

Carmen 89: "Gellius is thin. / So?" Catullus. **CP-ZukLS** *Fr.* Carmina. **CP-Catul**

("Gellius is thin why yes: kiddin'? quite a bonny mater.") **CP-ZukLS,** *tr. by* Louis Zukofsky *and* Celia Zukofsky.

Carmen 90: "Let there stem (Gellius)." Catullus. **CP-ZukLS** *Fr.* Carmina. **CP-Catul**

("Now seed their Magus (of Gelli's mother wrestling confounded.") **CP-ZukLS,** *tr. by* Louis Zukofsky *and* Celia Zukofsky.

Carmen 91: "In this hopeless & wasting love of mine." Catullus. **CP-ZukLS** *Fr.* Carmina. **CP-Catul**

("No idea, Gelli, spurred me to mirror you faithful.") **CP-ZukLS,** *tr. by* Louis Zukofsky *and* Celia Zukofsky.

Carmen 92: "Lesbia loads me night & day with her curses." Catullus. **CP-ZukLS** *Fr.* Carmina. **CP-Catul**

(*Carmina,* XCII.) **OBVE,** *tr. by* Jonathan Swift. **OBVE,** *tr. by* Tom Brown. **OBVE,** *tr. by* William Walsh.

(Catullus.) **BoLoP,** *tr. by* Peter Whigham.

("Each Moment of the long-liv'd Day.") **OBVE,** *tr. by* Tom Brown.

(Lesbia.) **CP-SwifJ,** *tr. by* Jonathan Swift.

("Lesbia forever on me rails.") **AWP; CP-SwifJ; OBVE,** *tr. by* Jonathan Swift.

("Lesbia may dicker simper maul or nag talk at whom, come.") **CP-ZukLS,** *tr. by* Louis Zukofsky *and* Celia Zukofsky.

(Lesbia Railing.) **AWP,** *tr. by* Jonathan Swift.

("Thou saidst that I alone thy Heart cou'd move.") **OBVE; OxBSP,** *tr. by* William Walsh.

(To His False Mistress.) **OxBSP,** *tr. by* William Walsh.

Carmen 93: "Utter indifference to your welfare, Caesar." Catullus. **CP-ZukLS** *Fr.* Carmina. **CP-Catul**

("Nil, not my aim to study you, Caesar, to be—well, a placater.") **CP-ZukLS,** *tr. by* Louis Zukofsky *and* Celia Zukofsky.

Carmen 94: "Stuffing, O'Toole naturally stuffs with his tool." Catullus. **CP-ZukLS** *Fr.* Carmina. **CP-Catul**

("Meantool amuck with her. Muck with her mean tool ah? Geared I.") **CP-ZukLS,** *tr. by* Louis Zukofsky *and* Celia Zukofsky.

Carmen 95: "Nine harvests & nine winters since its inception." Catullus. **CP-ZukLS** *Fr.* Carmina. **CP-Catul**

("*Zmyrna,* my own Cinna, nine harvests passed making his hymn.") **CP-ZukLS,** *tr. by* Louis Zukofsky *and* Celia Zukofsky.

Carmen 96: "If, Calvus, effects of grief." Catullus. **CP-ZukLS** *Fr.* Carmina. **CP-Catul**

("Friend, if the mute and shrouded dead.") **AWP,** *tr. by* H.W. Garrod.

(Love and Death.) **AWP,** *tr. by* H.W. Garrod.

("See quick calm moot as gratifying the tombed—sepulchres.") **CP-**

ZukLS, *tr.* by Louis Zukofsky *and* Celia Zukofsky.

Carmen 97: "As God is my witness where is the difference between." Catullus. **CP-ZukLS; DBV; FaBoBl** *Fr.* Carmina. **CP-Catul**

("No it would not mean a damn (quick whim referred to pure.") **CP-ZukLS**, *tr.* by Louis Zukofsky *and* Celia Zukofsky.

("So help me God, I couldn't choose between.") **DBV; FaBoBl**, *tr.* by James Michie.

Carmen 98: "Same can be said of you, Victius, The." Catullus. **CP-ZukLS; DBV** *Fr.* Carmina. **CP-Catul**

("In the, same in (when qualm?) thick wee poetry, putrid Victi.") **CP-ZukLS**, *tr.* by Louis Zukofsky *and* Celia Zukofsky.

("Of you, if anyone, it can be said.") **DBV**, *tr.* by James Michie.

Carmen 99: "Purloining while you played in honeyed youth." Catullus. **CP-ZukLS; PeHV** *Fr.* Carmina. **CP-Catul**

("Juventus, my honey, while you played.") **PeHV**, *tr.* by James Michie.

("Surreptitious you at bay doom loot is, my little Juventi.") **CP-ZukLS**, *tr.* by Louis Zukofsky *and* Celia Zukofsky.

Carmen 100: "Undone or done up with love." Catullus. **CP-ZukLS** *Fr.* Carmina. **CP-Catul**

("Caelius Aufilenus' mate, Quintius Aufilena's *am.*") **CP-ZukLS**, *tr.* by Louis Zukofsky *and* Celia Zukofsky.

Carmen 101: "Journeying over many seas and through many countries." Catullus. **CP-ZukLS** *Fr.* Carmina. **CP-Catul**

(Adaption of a Theme from Catullus.) **CP-TateA**, *tr.* by Allen Tate.

("By ways remote and distant waters sped.") **AWP; IMW**, *tr.* by Aubrey Beardsley.

(Catullus: *Carmen ci.*) **SP-MorgF**, *tr.* by Frederick Morgan.

("Mulled hosts their countries yet mulled there by a core of wake tossed.") **CP-ZukLS**, *tr.* by Louis Zukofsky and Celia Zukofsky.

(On the Burial of His Brother.) **AWP; IMW**, *tr.* by Aubrey Beardsley.

("Past towns, states, deserts, hills, and rivers borne.") **CP-TateA**, *tr.* by Allen Tate.

("Travelling many nations, many seas.") **SP-MorgF**, *tr.* by Frederick Morgan.

Carmen 102: "If, Cornelius, we entrust our secrets." Catullus. **CP-ZukLS** *Fr.* Carmina. **CP-Catul**

("Secret I take it a commitment hushed to feed amic—.") **CP-ZukLS**, *tr.* by Louis Zukofsky *and* Celia Zukofsky.

Carmen 103: "Either give me my hundred pounds back, Silo." Catullus. **CP-LoveR; CP-ZukLS** *Fr.* Carmina. **CP-Catul**

("*Out*—so this means you render them, ten sestertia, Silo.") **CP-ZukLS**, *tr.* by Louis Zukofsky *and* Celia Zukofsky.

("Sylo pray pay me my ten Sesterces.") **CP-LoveR**, *tr.* by Richard Lovelace.

Carmen 104: "Do you really believe I could blacken my life." Catullus. **CP-ZukLS** *Fr.* Carmina. **CP-Catul**

("Credit me poor to say of my life *maledictory weed die.*") **CP-ZukLS**, *tr.* by Louis Zukofsky *and* Celia Zukofsky.

Carmen 105: "O'Toole / attempting an entry of the *mons Parnassus.*" Catullus. **CP-ZukLS** *Fr.* Carmina. **CP-Catul**

("Meantool reconnoiters Pipléa scanning Their mountain.") **CP-ZukLS**

Carmen 106: "When an auctioneer's seen with a good-looking boy." Catullus. **CP-ZukLS** *Fr.* Carmina. **CP-Catul**

("Cute boy arm in elbow prize con man, kid, what do we see.") **CP-ZukLS**, *tr.* by Louis Zukofsky *and* Celia Zukofsky.

Carmen 107: "If ever anyone anywhere, Lesbia, is looking." Catullus. **CP-ZukLS; NAWM 1-2** *Fr.* Carmina. **CP-Catul**

("See could we quit coveting hope taunting where hope hid and.") **CP-ZukLS**, *tr.* by Louis Zukofsky *and* Celia Zukofsky.

("When at last after long despair, our hopes ring true again.") **NAWM 1-2**, *tr.* by Horace Gregory.

Carmen 108: "If, by general consent, it should be decided." Catullus. **CP-ZukLS; DBV** *Fr.* Carmina. **CP-Catul**

("Cominius, you reprobate old goat.") **DBV**, *tr.* by James Michie.

("See, Comini, popular arbitrer turned on uncanny senescence.") **CP-ZukLS**, *tr.* by Louis Zukofsky *and* Celia Zukofsky.

Carmen 109: "Joy of my life! you tell me this." Catullus. **CP-ZukLS; NAWM 1-2** *Fr.* Carmina. **CP-Catul**

("My life, my love, you say our love will last forever.") **NAWM 1-2**, *tr.* by Horace Gregory.

("You could then, my heart, wit, eye, mean in proposing love our aim.") **CP-ZukLS**, *tr.* by Louis Zukofsky *and* Celia Zukofsky.

Carmen 110: "Men always praise an honest whore." Catullus. **CP-ZukLS** *Fr.* Carmina. **CP-Catul**

("Aufilena—*bonnie, simple,* laud and they're amicable.") **CP-ZukLS**, *tr.* by Louis Zukofsky *and* Celia Zukofsky.

Carmen 111: "In constancy content with one man, there." Catullus. **CP-ZukLS** *Fr.* Carmina. **CP-Catul**

("Aufilena, virile content him weave her her solo.") **CP-ZukLS**, *tr.* by Louis Zukofsky *and* Celia Zukofsky.

Carmen 112: "Naso! an elevated personage." Catullus. **CP-ZukLS** *Fr.* Carmina. **CP-Catul**

("Mool 'tis homos,' Naso 'n' queer take 'im mool 'tis ho most *he.*") **CP-ZukLS**, *tr.* by Louis Zukofsky *and* Celia Zukofsky.

("Naso, you are many men's man; and yet.") **ErPo**, *tr.* by Jack Lindsay.

(To Naso.) **ErPo**, *tr.* by Jack Lindsay.

Carmen 113: "In The Year of Pompey's First Consulate, Cinna." Catullus. **CP-ZukLS** *Fr.* Carmina. **CP-Catul**

("Consul (ere) Pompei O preened a duo, Cinna, so lay bound.") **CP-ZukLS**, *tr.* by Louis Zukofsky *and* Celia Zukofsky.

Carmen 114: "O'Toole is generally accounted." Catullus. **CP-ZukLS** *Fr.* Carmina. **CP-Catul**

("Firmum is all too known fails so Meantool a Dives.") **CP-ZukLS**, *tr.* by Louis Zukofsky *and* Celia Zukofsky.

Carmen 115: "O'Toole is the proud master of." Catullus. **CP-ZukLS** *Fr.* Carmina. **CP-Catul**

("Meantool inhabits in style three times ten hewed acres, forty.") **CP-ZukLS**, *tr.* by Louis Zukofsky *and* Celia Zukofsky.

Carmen 116: "Conscientiously bringing my mind to bear on this problem." Catullus. **CP-ZukLS** *Fr.* Carmina. **CP-Catul**

("Sigh paid to be studious when I moved went on to (queer) once.") **CP-ZukLS**, *tr.* by Louis Zukofsky *and* Celia Zukofsky.

Carmen Circulare, *parody of* Horace. Rudyard Kipling. **CP-KiplR** *Fr.* The Muse among the Motors.

Carmen de Boheme. Hart Crane. **CP-CranH**

Carmen Saeculare. Charles Hubert Sisson, *after the Latin of* Horace.

("Phoebus and Dian, queen of bow'rs.") **SP-SmarC**, *tr.* by Christopher Smart.

(Secular Ode, The.) **SP-SmarC**, *tr.* by Christopher Smart.

Carmencita's tawny paps. Basil Bunting. **CP-BuntB**

Carmina. Catullus, *tr. fr. Latin* by Peter Whigham. **CP-Catul**

Carmen 1: "To whom should I present this." **CP-ZukLS**

("Whom do I give my neat little volume.") **CP-ZukLS**, *tr.* by Louis Zukofsky *and* Celia Zukofsky.

Carmen 2: "Lesbia's sparrow! / Lesbia's plaything!" **CP-ZukLS**

("Sparrow, my girl's pleasure, delight of my girl.") **CP-ZukLS**, *tr.* by Louis Zukofsky *and* Celia Zukofsky.

Carmen 3: "Who loves beauty / veil her statues." **CP-ZukLS**

(Death of a Starling, The.) **CP-WorW1**, *tr.* by William Wordsworth.

(Death of Lesbia's Bird, The.) **AWP**, *tr.* by Samuel Taylor Coleridge.

(Death of the Starling, The.) **PBBP**, *tr.* by Samuel Taylor Coleridge.

("Lament, o graces of Venus, and Cupids.") **CP-ZukLS**, *tr.* by Louis Zukofsky *and* Celia Zukofsky.

("Pity! mourn in plaintive tone.") **AWP; PBBP**, *tr.* by Samuel Taylor Coleridge.

("Pity mourns in plaintive tone.") **CP-WorW1**, *tr.* by William Wordsworth.

(Translation from Catullus ("Ye Cupids, droop each little head").) **CP-Byron**, *tr.* by Byron.

("Ye Cupids, droop each little head.") **CP-Byron**, *tr.* by Byron.

Carmen 4: "My bean-pod boat you see here." **CP-ZukLS**

(*Carmina,* IV.) **OBVE**

("Facile as can be the boat you see, my guests, says.") **CP-ZukLS**, *tr.* by Louis Zukofsky *and* Celia Zukofsky.

("Stranger, the bark you see before you says.") **AWP; OBVE**, *tr.* by John Hookham Frere.

("This racer of the watry plain.") **OBVE**

(Yacht, The.) **AWP; OBVE**, *tr.* by John Hookham Frere.

Carmen 5: "Lesbia / live with me." **CP-ZukLS; NAWM 1-2; STV**

(*Carmina,* V.) **OBVE**, *tr.* by Richard Crashaw. **OBVE**, *tr.* by Walter Savage Landor. **OBVE**, *tr.* by William Wordsworth.

(Catullus: *Carmen v.*) **SP-MorgF**, *tr.* by Frederick Morgan.

(Catullus to Lesbia.) **ErPo**, *tr.* by James Reeves.

("Come and let us live my Deare.") **CavP; OBVE**, *tr.* by Richard Crashaw.

("Come, Lesbia, let us live and love.") **NAWM 1-2**, *tr.* by Horace Gregory.

("Come, my Celia, let us prove.") **EnRePo; ErPo; OBVE**, *tr.* by Ben Jonson.

(Courtship.) **CavP**, *tr.* by Alexander Brome.

("I tell you, Lesbia, life is love.") **ErPo**, *tr.* by James Reeves.

(Kiss-Fest, The.) **InMe**, *tr.* by Irwin Edman.

(Lesbia.) **PrIm**, *tr.* by Sheridan Baker. **CP-WorW1**, *tr.* by William Wordsworth.

("Lesbia, my love, let's be gay and enjoy ourselves.") **InMe**, *tr.* by Irwin Edman.

("Let's live, my Lesbia, and love.") **PrIm**, *tr.* by Sheridan Baker.

("Let's live, my Lesbia, and make love.") **SP-MorgF**, *tr.* by Frederick Morgan.

("Dearest Ipsitilla, I'd absolutely love it.") **FaBoBl,** *tr. by* Rodney Pybus.

("Hypsithilla, ask me over.") **ErPo,** *tr. by* Gardner E. Lewis.

("I'm a bow, my dual kiss, Ipsithilla.") **CP-ZukLS,** *tr. by* Louis Zukofsky *and* Celia Zukofsky.

(Invitation to an Invitation, An.) **ErPo,** *tr. by* Gardner E. Lewis.

Carmen 33: "Vibennius & son, renowned." **CP-ZukLS; PeHV**

("Of all our bath-house thieves the cleverest one.") **PeHV,** *tr. by* James Michie.

("Offer 'em up to me—bullneck crook of the baths.") **CP-ZukLS,** *tr. by* Louis Zukofsky *and* Celia Zukofsky.

Carmen 34: "Moving in her radiant care." **CP-ZukLS**

("Boys and girls, we pledge allegiance.") **Moon,** *tr. by* Horace Gregory.

("Diana guardeth our estate.") **AWP,** *tr. by* Richard Claverhouse Jebb.

("Diana, sum us in faith a.") **CP-ZukLS,** *tr. by* Louis Zukofsky *and* Celia Zukofsky.

(Dianae Sumus in Fide.) **Moon,** *tr. by* Horace Gregory.

(Hymn to Diana.) **AWP,** *tr. by* Richard Claverhouse Jebb.

Carmen 35: "Fetch, papyrus, / our soft-measured poet." **CP-ZukLS**

("Poet I'm too near your and my sod daily.") **CP-ZukLS,** *tr. by* Louis Zukofsky *and* Celia Zukofsky.

Carmen 36: "Volusian sheets / shit-shotten Annals." **CP-ZukLS**

("*Annals* of Volusius, cock at his offal.") **CP-ZukLS,** *tr. by* Louis Zukofsky *and* Celia Zukofsky.

Carmen 37: "Nine posts, five doors, up the Clivus." **CP-ZukLS**

("Salt hacks, tavern boys, what skews, can't you burn alleys.") **CP-ZukLS,** *tr. by* Louis Zukofsky *and* Celia Zukofsky.

Carmen 38: "Angst, / ennui & angst." **CP-ZukLS; PeHV**

("My last—Cornificius—your Catullus'.") **CP-ZukLS,** *tr. by* Louis Zukofsky *and* Celia Zukofsky.

("Your Catullus is depressed, Cornificus.") **PeHV**

Carmen 39: "Because he has bright white teech, Eg- / natius whips out a." **CP-ZukLS**

(*Carmina,* XXXIX.) **OBVE,** *tr. by* Walter Savage Landor.

("Egnatius, candid as his horse-bit white dentures.") **CP-ZukLS,** *tr. by* Louis Zukofsky *and* Celia Zukofsky.

("Egnatius has fine teeth, and those.") **OBVE,** *tr. by* Walter Savage Landor.

Carmen 40: "Whatever could have possessed you." **CP-ZukLS**

(*Carmina,* XL.) **OBVE,** *tr. by* Louis Zukofsky *and* Celia Zukofsky.

("What demented malice, my silly Ravidus.") **CP-ZukLS; OBVE,** *tr. by* Louis Zukofsky *and* Celia Zukofsky.

Carmen 41: "Formianus's whore, / long-nosed." **CP-ZukLS**

("Ameana pulling, a foot touted high.") **CP-ZukLS,** *tr. by* Louis Zukofsky *and* Celia Zukofsky.

("Ameana, that banged-out bitch.") **SP-MorgF,** *tr. by* Frederick Morgan.

(Catullus: *Carmen xli.*) **SP-MorgF,** *tr. by* Frederick Morgan.

Carmen 42: "From the quarters of the compass." **CP-ZukLS; DBV**

("At hest, hendecasyllabics, what is this.") **CP-ZukLS,** *tr. by* Louis Zukofsky *and* Celia Zukofsky.

("Hendecasyllables, help! Come to my call.") **DBV,** *tr. by* James Michie.

Carmen 43: "O elegant whore!" **CP-ZukLS**

("Salvé, next, minimal, poor little nosey.") **CP-ZukLS,** *tr. by* Louis Zukofsky *and* Celia Zukofsky.

Carmen 44: "It depends who's talking if you're a 'Sabine.'" **CP-ZukLS**

("O farm, dear nest, or say Sabine, ah say Tibur's.") **CP-ZukLS,** *tr. by* Louis Zukofsky *and* Celia Zukofsky.

Carmen 45: "Phyllis Corydon clutched to him." **BoLoP; CP-ZukLS**

(Acme and Septimius.) **AWP; OBVE; UnTE,** *tr. by* Abraham Cowley.

("Acme, Septimius, sighs so amorous.") **CP-ZukLS,** *tr. by* Louis Zukofsky *and* Celia Zukofsky.

(Septimius and Acme.) **CP-WorW1,** *tr. by* William Wordsworth.

("Septimius thus his love addressed.") **CP-WorW1,** *tr. by* William Wordsworth.

("Whilst on Septimius' panting Breast.") **AWP; OBVE; UnTE,** *tr. by* Abraham Cowley.

Carmen 46: "Now spring bursts." **CP-ZukLS; PoPl**

("Now Spring brings back the tepid breeze.") **PoPl,** *tr. by* L.R. Lind.

("Warm gale, a dose of spring—revert to the pores.") **CP-ZukLS,** *tr. by* Louis Zukofsky *and* Celia Zukofsky.

Carmen 47: "Lucius Calpurnius Piso Caesoninus." **CP-ZukLS**

("Porky and Socration, two-eye sins as try.") **CP-ZukLS,** *tr. by* Louis Zukofsky *and* Celia Zukofsky.

Carmen 48: "Iuventius, / were I allowed." **CP-Byron; CP-ZukLS; PeHV**

("If I could go on kissing your honeyed eyes.") **PeHV**

("Juvencius, thy fair sweet Eyes.") **CP-LoveR,** *tr. by* Richard Lovelace.

("Mellowed *those,* I call *those* eyes, Juventius.") **CP-ZukLS,** *tr. by*

Louis Zukofsky *and* Celia Zukofsky.

("Oh! might I kiss those eyes of fire.") **CP-Byron; TSF,** *tr. by* Byron.

(To Ellen.) **TSF,** *tr. by* Byron.

(To Juvencius.) **CP-LoveR**

Carmen 49: "Silver-tongued among the sons of Rome." **CP-ZukLS**

(Disertissime Romuli Nepotum.) **SP-SmarC,** *tr. by* Christopher Smart.

("Master of eloquence and Rome's potent line.") **CP-ZukLS,** *tr. by* Louis Zukofsky *and* Celia Zukofsky.

("O Thou, of British Orators the chief.") **SP-SmarC,** *tr. by* Christopher Smart.

(To Marcus T. Cicero.) **CP-LoveR,** *tr. by* Richard Lovelace.

("Tully to thee Rome's eloquent Sole Heir.") **CP-LoveR,** *tr. by* Richard Lovelace.

Carmen 50: "Other day we spent, The." **CP-ZukLS**

("Yesterday, Licinius, what a day it was.") **CP-ZukLS,** *tr. by* Louis Zukofsky *and* Celia Zukofsky.

Carmen 51: "Godlike the man who." **CP-ZukLS**

("Equal to Jove that youth must be.") **CP-Byron,** *tr. by* Byron.

("He'll hie me, par *is* he? the God divide her.") **CP-ZukLS,** *tr. by* Louis Zukofsky *and* Celia Zukofsky.

("Like to a god he seems to me.") **AWP,** *tr. by* William Ellery Leonard.

(Sappho.) **AWP,** *tr. by* William Ellery Leonard.

(Translation from Catullus ("Equal to Jove that youth must be").) **CP-Byron,** *tr. by* Byron.

Carmen 52: "Drop dead, Catullus, lie right down & die." **CP-ZukLS**

("Quick death, Catullus! what more horrors may hurry!") **CP-ZukLS,** *tr. by* Louis Zukofsky *and* Celia Zukofsky.

Carmen 53: "I laughed. Calvus. I laughed today." **CP-ZukLS**

("Risible nice go when from mud a crony.") **CP-ZukLS,** *tr. by* Louis Zukofsky *and* Celia Zukofsky.

Carmen 54: "If not by all that his friends boast." **CP-ZukLS**

("Otho's scooped nut its pusillanimity.") **CP-ZukLS,** *tr. by* Louis Zukofsky *and* Celia Zukofsky.

Carmen 55: "Where / if it's not too much to ask." **CP-ZukLS**

(*Carmina,* LV.) **OBVE,** *tr. by* Nahum Tate.

("Now if thou hast one dram of Grace.") **OBVE,** *tr. by* Nahum Tate.

("Rum asks—see, fortune won't molest you.") **CP-ZukLS,** *tr. by* Louis Zukofsky *and* Celia Zukofsky.

Carmen 56: "Matter for mirth, Cato, & a smile, A." **CP-ZukLS; PeHV**

("I have something for you to laugh at, Cato.") **PeHV**

("O ram ridicule home, Cato, the jokes some.") **CP-ZukLS,** *tr. by* Louis Zukofsky *and* Celia Zukofsky.

Carmen 57: "*Caesar Mamurraque!* / A peerless pair of brazen buggers." **CP-ZukLS; DBV**

(" 'Pull! crew' 's convenient to reprobate kin hides.") **CP-ZukLS,** *tr. by* Louis Zukofsky *and* Celia Zukofsky.

("They make a pretty pair of debauchees.") **DBV,** *tr. by* James Michie.

Carmen 58: "Lesbia, our Lesbia, the same old Lesbia." **CP-ZukLS; NAWM 1-2**

("Caelius, Lesbia new star, Lesbia a light.") **CP-ZukLS,** *tr. by* Louis Zukofsky *and* Celia Zukofsky.

("Caelius, my Lesbia, that one, that only Lesbia.") **NAWM 1-2,** *tr. by* Horace Gregory.

Carmen 59: "Menenius' wife, / a red-headed cat from Bologna." **CP-ZukLS**

("Bononian, sis Rufa, Rufus' lum fell at.") **CP-ZukLS,** *tr. by* Louis Zukofsky *and* Celia Zukofsky.

Carmen 60: "Hard. Hard. As she-cat whelped in desert mountains." **CP-ZukLS; NAWM 1-2**

("None but a lioness moaned this, Libya's mountains.") **CP-ZukLS,** *tr. by* Louis Zukofsky *and* Celia Zukofsky.

("Were you born of a lioness in the Libyan Mountains.") **NAWM 1-2,** *tr. by* Horace Gregory.

Carmen 61: "Hill (breeder) of Helicon." **CP-ZukLS; OxBM**

("Guardian of Helicon, Urania's son.") **OxBM,** *tr. by* Frederic Raphael *and* Kenneth McLeish.

("Who lives o on Helicon hill.") **CP-ZukLS,** *tr. by* Louis Zukofsky *and* Celia Zukofsky.

Hymeneal. **PeHV,** *tr. by* James Michie.

Carmen 62: "Gather young men as the twilight gathers." **CP-ZukLS**

("Vesper out there, you vain knees can sure get up: Vesper, Olympus.") **CP-ZukLS,** *tr. by* Louis Zukofsky *and* Celia Zukofsky.

Carmen 63: "Plunging towards Phrygia over violent water." **CP-ZukLS**

(Attis.) **OBVE; STV,** *tr. by* Peter Whigham.

("Over oceans sped he, Attis, in the speediest of ships.") **STV,** *tr. by* John Frederick Nims.

("Spurred altering wake toss Attis his craft racing till marled in the.") **CP-ZukLS,** *tr. by* Louis Zukofsky *and* Celia Zukofsky.

Carmina, LXX. Catullus. *See* Carmen 70: "Lesbia says she'ld rather marry me."

Carmina, LXXII. Catullus. *See* Carmen 72: "There was a time, Lesbia, when."

Carmina, LXXV. Catullus. *See* Carmen 75: "Reason blinded by sin, Lesbia."

Carmina, LXXXV. Catullus. *See* Carmen 85: "I hate and I love. And if you ask me how."

Carmina, XCII. Catullus. *See* Carmen 92: "Lesbia loads me night & day with her curses."

Carmine defunctum, Breto, caute inducis Amorem. *acc. by English translation*. Thomas Campion. **CP-CampT**

Carnal Knowledge. Thom Gunn. **CP-GunnT**

Carnality, the organic ruffles of / opening pink and white and red. Carnations. Hayden Carruth. **CP-CarHS**

Carnations. Hayden Carruth. **CP-CarHS**

Carnations. John Hewitt. **CP-HewiJ**

Carnations. Theodore Roethke. **CP-RoetT**

Carnations and Butterflies. Alexander Pope. **NOEC** *Fr.* Yet, yet a moment, one dim ray of light. **NAEL-1; OAEL-1; PoEL-3** *Fr.* The Dunciad. **CP-PopeA**

Carnegie Hall: Rescued. Marianne Craig Moore. **CP-MoorM**

Carnegie Library, Juvenile Division, The. Randall Jarrell. **CP-JarrR; SP-JarrR**

Carnival, The. Robert Creeley. **CP-CreeR**

Carnival Inside, The. Richard Hugo. **CP-HugoR**

Carnival 1927. Kay Boyle. **CP-BoylK**

Caro Mimo mio: My first trip south. It's not what. Letter to Hanson from Miami. Richard Hugo. **CP-HugoR**

Carol: "Flocks feed by darkness with a noise of whispers." Thomas Merton. **CP-MertT; SP-MertT**

Carol, A. Donald Hall. **CP-HallD**

Carol: "Now is the world withdrawn all." Howard Nemerov. **CP-NemeH**

Carol: "To end all carols, darling." Louis MacNeice. **CP-MacNL**

Carol, A: "Our Lord Who did the Ox command." Rudyard Kipling. **CP-KiplR**

Carol, A: "When Jesus got my broken back for Christmas, Juniors." Thomas Merton. **CP-MertT**

Carol Closing Sixty-Nine. Walt Whitman. **CP-WhitW**

Carol for Children, A. Ogden Nash. **CP-NashO**

Carol of Death, The. Walt Whitman. *See* Come lovely and soothing death.

Carol of Jack Frost, A. George Meredith. **CP-MerG2**

Carol of Patience. Robert Ranke Graves. **CP-GravR**

Carol Singers. John Hewitt. **CP-HewiJ**

Carol Singers from the Church, The. John Hewitt. **CP-HewiJ**

Carole, si quid habes longo quod tempore coctum. *acc. by English translation*. Thomas Campion. **CP-CampT**

Carolina Moon. Al Young. **CP-YounA**

Caroline Herschel (1750–1848). Siv Cedering Fox. *Fr.* Letters from the Astronomers. **SP-CedeS**

Caroline Says II. "Lou Reed." **SP-ReedL**

Carols nature, counsel men. The Three Singers to Young Blood. George Meredith. **CP-MerG1**

Carp and Goldfish. John Yau.
   "Some fish we peel back, leaving only the bones. Others devour us." **SP-YauJo**
   "To the young boy standing in front of the large glass tanks, each." **SP-YauJo**

Carp are secrets, The. Lifting Illegal Nets by Flashlight. James Wright. **CP-WrigJ**

Carpe Diem. Robert Frost. **CP-FrosR**

Carpe Diem. Horace. *Fr.* Three Odes of Horace. **CP-MacNL**

Carpenter called Joseph Love, it's true, A. My Aunt Sarah and Uncle Joe. John Hewitt. **CP-HewiJ**

Carpentered hen, The. A Wooden Darning Egg. John Updike. **CP-UpdiJ**

Carpenter's Boat. George Oppen. **CP-OppeG**

Carpenter's made a hole, The. A Hole in the Floor. Richard Wilbur. **CP-WilbR**

Carpenter's Son, The. Alfred Edward Housman. **CP-HousA**

Carpenter's Song, The. Stephen Dunn. **SP-DunnS**

Carpet Not Bought, A. James Merrill. **SP-MerrJ**

Carpet raveling on the loom a girl, A. The Being as Memory. Hayden Carruth. *Fr.* Contra Mortem. **CP-CarHL**

Carrara, Looking Seaward. Lawrence Ferlinghetti. **SP-FerlL**

Carriage from Sweden, A. Marianne Craig Moore. **CP-MoorM**

Carriages slow, / And a name I should know, The. In a Train. Wystan Hugh Auden. **CP-AudWJ**

Carrick Revisited. Louis MacNeice. **CP-MacNL**

Carrickfergus. Louis MacNeice. **CP-MacNL**

Carrie. Ted Kooser. **SP-KoosT**

Carried her unprotesting out the door. The Rites for Cousin Vit. Gwendolyn Brooks. **SP-BrooG** *Fr.* The Womanhood.

Carried this morning in the dodge and swoop. Cougar Meat. Tess Gallagher. **SP-GallT**

Carrier, The. Thomas Hardy. **CP-HardT**

Carrier Letter. Hart Crane. **CP-CranH**
   (Exile.) **CP-CranH**
   ("My hands have not touched pleasure since your hands.") **CP-CranH**

Carrion, A. Charles Baudelaire, *tr. fr. French by* Allen Tate. **CP-TateA**

Carrion Comfort. Gerard Manley Hopkins. **CP-HopkG**

Carrion Crow, The. Archibald MacLeish. **CP-MacLA**

Carrion Spring, The. Archibald MacLeish. *Fr.* The Pot of Earth. **CP-MacLA**

Carrowkeel. Brendan Galvin. **SP-GalvB**

Carry her over the water. Wystan Hugh Auden. **FaBoTw; RB** *Fr.* Ten Songs. **CP-AudeW**

Carry me back to Ole Virginny. First Families Move Over! Ogden Nash. **CP-NashO**

Carry That Weight. John Lennon *and* Paul McCartney. **CP-Beatl**

Carrying a bunch of marigolds. A Negro Woman. William Carlos Williams. **CP-WilW2**

Carrying Food Home in Winter. Margaret Atwood. **SP-AtwM1**

Carrying On. Leonard Nathan. **SP-NathL**

Carrying Their Coracles. Andrew Marvell. **ChTr** *Fr.* Upon Appleton House [To My Lord Fairfax]. **CP-MarvA**

Carrying their deckhands' bicycles. The Tugs of Hull. George Oppen. **CP-OppeG**

Carrying water to the Youth in Honor of Sappho Jane Harrison & Miss Duncan if She Had. Charles Olson. **CP-OlsoC**

Cars in Caracas, The. John Updike. **CP-UpdiJ**

Cars line up over the buried Fleet. Rivers Are Running Beneath Us. Steve Griffiths. **SP-GrifS**

Cars on the highway filled with speech. George Oppen. **APSN** *Fr.* Route. **CP-OppeG**

Cars once steel and green, now old. Louis Zukofsky. **VGW** *Fr.* 29 Poems. **CP-ZukLS**
   (Cars Once Steel and Green, Now Old.) **VGW**

Cars Once Steel and Green, Now Old. Louis Zukofsky. *See* Cars once steel and green, now old.

Cars run in a void of utensils, The. George Oppen. **APSN** *Fr.* Route. **CP-OppeG**

Cars slide minute down asphalt lanes in front of. Thoughts on a Breath. Allen Ginsberg. **CP-GinsA**

Carscape. Charles Tomlinson. **CP-TomlC**

Carson. Paul Muldoon. *Fr.* 7, Middagh Street. **SP-MuldP**

Carson at Six Road Ends. John Hewitt. **CP-HewiJ**

Cartagena. Gary Snyder. **CP-SnydG**

Carteret was welcomed to the shore. An Epigram on Wood's Brass Money. Jonathan Swift. **CP-SwifJ**

Carter's Funeral, The. Wystan Hugh Auden. **CP-AudWJ**

Carter's trophy, A. Bog Oak. Seamus Heaney. **SP-HeanS**

Cartographies of Silence. Adrienne Rich. **SP-RicA2**

Cartography. Louise Bogan. **CP-BogaL**

Cartoon. Carl Sandburg. **CP-SandC**

Cartoon of slashes on the tide-traced crater. Dylan Thomas. *Fr.* Altarwise by Owl-Light. **CP-ThomD**

Carts of the wee blind lass, The. Kenneth Patchen. **CP-PatcK**

Caruso. James McAuley. **SP-McAuJ**

Caruso: a voice. Sleeping with Women. Kenneth Koch. **SP-KochK**

Carver, having loved too long in vain, A. The Carver. To His Mistress. Thomas Carew. **CP-CareT**

Carver. To His Mistress, The. Thomas Carew. **CP-CareT**

Carving on the jamb of an embrasure, A. The Priory of St Saviour, Glendalough. Donald Davie. **CP-DavDo**

Casa felice ove più volte omai. Non Son Io La Rosa Ma Vi Stetti Appresso. Christina Georgina Rossetti. *Fr.* Il Rosseggiar Dell'Oriente Canzoniere. **CP-RosC3**

Casa Guidi Windows. Elizabeth Barrett Browning. **CP-BroEB**

Casabianca. Elizabeth Bishop. **CP-BishE**

Casarola. Charles Tomlinson. **CP-TomlC**

Cascade. John Yau. **SP-YauJo**

Cascando. Samuel Beckett. **CP-BeckS**

Case for Jefferson, A. Robert Frost. **CP-FrosR**

Case is a Lawyer, that near pleads alone. Upon Case. Robert Herrick. **CP-HerrR**

Case of Mistaken Identity, A. John Hewitt. **CP-HewiJ**

Case of The, The. Mona Van Duyn. **SP-VanDM**

Casella. Ralph Waldo Emerson. *Fr.* Quatrains. **CP-EmerR**

Caserta Garden. Richard Wilbur. **CP-WilbR**

Casino. Wystan Hugh Auden. **CP-AudeW**

Cass and Me. Paul Muldoon. **SP-MuldP**

Cassandra. Louise Bogan. **CP-BogaL**

Cassandra. Hilda Doolittle. **CP-DoolH**

Cassandra. Robinson Jeffers. **CP-JefR3**

Cassandra. Louise McNeill. **SP-McNeL**

Cassandra. George Meredith. **CP-MerG1**

Cassandra. Edwin Arlington Robinson. **CP-RobiE**

Cassandra Southwick. John Greenleaf Whittier. **CP-WhitJ**

Casse-Noisette. Robert Ranke Graves. **CP-GravR**

Cassinus and Peter. Jonathan Swift. **CP-SwifJ**

Cast a bronze of my head and legs and put them on the king's street. Savoir Faire. Carl Sandburg. **CP-SandC**

Cast a cold eye. William Butler Yeats. **FaBoEE** *Fr.* Under Ben Bulben. **CP-YeatW**

Cast down but not destroyed, chastened not slain. Christina Georgina Rossetti. **CP-RosC2**

Cast Off, The. Marge Piercy. **SP-PierM**

Cast the bantling on the rocks. Power. Ralph Waldo Emerson. **APN-1** *Fr.* Quatrains. **CP-EmerR**

Castara Victrix, Fragments. Gerard Manley Hopkins. **CP-HopkG**

Castaway, The. William Cowper. **CP-CowpW**

Castaway, The. Derek Walcott. **CP-WalcD**

Castel Sant'Angelo. Richard Hugo. **CP-HugoR**

Casterbridge Captains, The. Thomas Hardy. **CP-HardT**

Casting. Howard Nemerov. **CP-NemeH**

Casting. Dabney Stuart. **SP-StuaD**

Casting from the Miami causeway. The Osprey Suicides. Laurence Lieberman. **SP-LiebL**

Casting the times with their stong signes. Sospetto d'Herode. Giovanni Battista Marino. **CP-CrasR** *Fr.* Strage degli innocenti, La.

Castle, The. Roy Fisher. **SP-FishR** *Fr.* Inscriptions for Bluebeard's Castle.

Castle, The. Robert Ranke Graves. **CP-GravR**

Castle, The. Stevie Smith. **CP-SmitS**

Castle, The. Charles Tomlinson. **CP-TomlC**

Castle-Builder's World, A. Christina Georgina Rossetti. **CP-RosC2**

Castle Gordon—*Intended to Be Sung to Morag.* Robert Burns. **CP-BurnR**

Castle has gone into the cliff, The. Near Ceibwr. Charles Tomlinson. **CP-TomlC**

Castle mad with decay, intimate streets, The. Viva La Resistènza. Richard Hugo. **CP-HugoR**

Castle of Indolence, The. James Thomson. **CP-ThomJ**

"In lowly dale, fast by a river's side." **EnRP; NOEC; SeCePo**

(Land of Indolence, The.) **SeCePo**

"O mortal man, who livest here by toil." **LAuP**

"Sometimes the pencil, in cool airy halls." **PoEL-3**

Castle Rock. Frederick Morgan. **SP-MorgF**

Castle Wood. Emily Brontë. **CP-BronE**

Castles and Distances. Richard Wilbur. **CP-WilbR**

Casts aside the two-arm two-leg article—. The Swift Comes the Swift. Ted Hughes. **SP-HughT**

Casual Acquaintance, The. Thomas Hardy. **CP-HardT**

Casual Incitement. William Wordsworth. *Fr.* Ecclesiastical Sonnets. **CP-WorW2**

Casual reverberation is not restitution, The. Kenneth Rexroth. *Fr.* A Prolegomenon to a Theodicy. **CP-RexKL**

Casual solitude that is beyond casualness, A. John Yau. **SP-YauJo** *Fr.* Scenes from the Life of Boullee.

Casual Wear. James Merrill. **NIP** *Fr.* Topics. **SP-MerrJ**

Casualties. Robert Herrick. **CP-HerrR**

Casualty. Seamus Heaney. **SP-HeanS**

Casualty, A. Daniel Gerard Hoffman. **SP-HoffD**

Casualty. Langston Hughes. **SP-HughL**

Casualty. David Herbert Lawrence. *Fr.* Bits. **CP-LawrD**

Casualty, The. Louis MacNeice. **CP-MacNL**

Casualty. Edwin Rolfe. **CP-RolfE**

Cat, The. Wystan Hugh Auden. **CP-AudWJ**

Cat, The. Charles Baudelaire, *tr. fr.* French by Countee Cullen. **CP-CullC**

Cat, The. Lawrence Ferlinghetti. **SP-FerlL**

Cat / licks its paw and, The. The Cat. Lawrence Ferlinghetti. **SP-FerlL**

Cat, The. William Matthews. **SP-MattW**

Cat. Kenneth Rexroth. **SP-RexrK** *Fr.* A Bestiary. **SP-RexrK**

Cat, The. Lewis Turco. **SP-TurcL**

Cat and Mouse. Ted Hughes. **SP-HughT**

Cat and the Moon, The. William Butler Yeats. **CP-YeatW**

Cat and the Wind, The. Thom Gunn. **CP-GunnT**

Cat as Cat, The. Denise Levertov. **CP-LeveD**

Cat Asks Mouse Out. Stevie Smith. **CP-SmitS**

Cat bird singing / makes music like sounds coming. Air: "Cat Bird Singing." Robert Creeley. **CP-CreeR**

Cat-Goddesses. Robert Ranke Graves. **CP-GravR**

Cat has fallen asleep, The. Sitting All Evening Alone in the Kitchen. Ted Kooser. **SP-KoosT**

Cat in distress, A. Verses on a Cat. Percy Bysshe Shelley. **CP-ShelP**

Cat in the Wood, The. Archibald MacLeish. **CP-MacLA**

Cat in the wood cried farewell cried farewell, The. The Cat in the Wood. Archibald MacLeish. **CP-MacLA**

Cat Naps Are Too Good for Cats. Ogden Nash. **CP-NashO**

Cat on my bosom, The. The Cat as Cat. Denise Levertov. **CP-LeveD**

Cat sits on the pavement by the house, A. The Lonely Man. Randall Jarrell. **CP-JarrR**

Cat stirs in the material world, A. From the Japanese. Louise Glück. **SP-GlücL**

Cat That Walked by Himself, The. Rudyard Kipling. *Fr.* Just-So Stories. "Pussy can sit by the fire and sing." **CP-KiplR**

Cat went here and there, The. The Cat and the Moon. William Butler Yeats. **CP-YeatW**

Cat! who hast passed [*or* pass'd] thy grand climacteric. John Keats. **CP-KeatJ**

(To Mrs. Reynolds's Cat.) **CP-KeatJ**

Cat with yellow eyes doesn't yet realize, The. Getting Up. Stephen Dobyns. **SP-DobyS**

Cataldo Mission. Richard Hugo. **CP-HugoR**

Catalogue. Edwin Rolfe. **CP-RolfE**

Catalogue of I. Edwin Rolfe. **CP-RolfE**

Catalpa, The. John Ciardi. **SP-CiarJ**

Catalpa's white week is ending there, The. The Catalpa. John Ciardi. **SP-CiarJ**

Catarina to Camoens. Elizabeth Barrett Browning. **CP-BroEB**

Catastrophic Birth. William Carlos Williams. **CP-WilW2**

Catch. Archie Randolph Ammons. **SP-AmmoA**

Catch. Langston Hughes. **SP-HughL**

Catch, The. Erica Jong. **SP-JongE**

Catch. Jenny Joseph. **SP-JoseJ**

Catch, The. Stanley Jasspon Kunitz. **CP-KuniS**

Catch, The. Richard Wilbur. **CP-WilbR**

Catch not my breath, O clamorous heart. Tennyson. **NAEL-2** *Fr.* This lump of earth has left his estate. *Fr.* Maud [A Monodrama]. **CP-TennA**

Catch of Shy Fish, A. Gwendolyn Brooks. **SP-BrooG**

Big Bessie Throws Her Son into the Street. **VGW**

Garbageman: the Man with the Orderly Mind. **CAPP**

Old People Working (Garden, Car). **SaC**

Old Tennis Player. **LiSp; SD**

Sick Man Looks at Flowers.

Spaulding and Francois.

Surrealist and Omega, A.

Weaponed Woman.

Catch phrase "Nothing human to me is alien", The. Period II. Ogden Nash. *Fr.* Period Period. **CP-NashO**

Catch What You Can. Jean Garrigue. **SP-GarrJ**

Catcher holds a kangaroo fetus in his, The. Mitts and Gloves. Bill Knott. **SP-KnotB**

Catching Ballet of the Wedding Clothes, The. Thomas Hardy. **CP-HardT**

Catechism, The. Walter de la Mare. **CP-DeLaW**

Catechism, A. William Stafford. **SP-StafW**

Catechizing. William Wordsworth. *Fr.* Ecclesiastical Sonnets. **CP-WorW2**

Caterpillar, A. Robert Bly. **SP-BlyR**

Caterpillar, The. Ogden Nash. *Fr.* The Astigmatic Naturalist. **CP-NashO**

Caterpillar, The. Christina Georgina Rossetti. *See* Brown and furry.

Caterpillar, The. Miller Williams. **SP-WillM**

Catfish. "Bob Dylan" *and* Jacques Levy. **CP-DylaB**

Catfish River Lullaby. Kenneth Patchen. **CP-PatcK**

Catharina. William Cowper. **CP-CowpW**

Catharina, the Second Part. William Cowper. **CP-CowpW**

Cathedral Bells, The. Karl Shapiro. **SP-ShapK**

Cathedral evening, tinkle of candles. Beautiful You Are. Kenneth Patchen. **CP-PatcK**

Cathedral Façade at Midnight, A. Thomas Hardy. **CP-HardT**

Cathedrals, etc. William Wordsworth. *Fr.* Ecclesiastical Sonnets. **CP-WorW2**

Catherine of Alexandria. Rita Dove. **SP-DoveR**

Catherine of Siena. Rita Dove. **SP-DoveR**

Catholic / Each week. Mother Was a Good. Siv Cedering Fox. **SP-CedeS**

Catholic Bells, The. William Carlos Williams. **CP-WilW1**

Catnap, with Nightmare. James McAuley. **SP-McAuJ** *Fr.* Meditations of Afternoon.

Catprints, dogprints, marks. Roominghouse, Winter. Margaret Atwood. **SP-AtwM1**

Catrine woods were yellow seen, The. The Braes o' Ballochmyle. Robert Burns. **CP-BurnR**

Cats, *See also* Lovers, Scholars—the fervent, the austere. Charles Baudelaire, *tr. fr. French by* Countee Cullen. **CP-CullC**

Cats. Phoebe Hesketh. **SP-HeskP**

Cats. Louis MacNeice. *Fr.* Nature Notes. **CP-MacNL**

Cats and a Cock. Muriel Rukeyser. **CP-RukeM**

Cats are contradictions: tooth and claw. Cats. Phoebe Hesketh. **SP-HeskP**

Cat's asleep; I whisper *kitten*, The. The Happy Cat. Randall Jarrell. **CP-JarrR**

Cat's eye marble is green, The. Backyard. Alice Notley. **SP-NotlA**

Cat's glinting face as it stared, The. Roy Fisher. **SP-FishR** *Fr.* Metamorphoses.

Cats Like Angels. Marge Piercy. **SP-PierM**

Cats' Month, The. William Carlos Williams. **CP-WilW1**

Cats of Greece, The. Marge Piercy. **SP-PierM**

Cats. One ashen, head and neck of a mantis, The. Aor Against the Termagant from California Who Confused Instruction With Indignation. James McAuley. **SP-McAuJ**

Cats walk the floor at midnight; that enemy of fog. Retroduction to American History. Allen Tate. **CP-TateA**

Cattail fluff / blows in. Porous. William Carlos Williams. **CP-WilW1**

Cattails. Richard Hugo. **CP-HugoR**

Cattivo Tempo. Wystan Hugh Auden. **CP-AudeW**

Cattle are crowding the salt-lick. In December. Charles Tomlinson. **CP-TomlC**

Cattle crowding round this beverage clear, The. Nun's Well, Brigham. William Wordsworth. **CP-WorW2**

Cattle crowding round this beverage clear, The. Nun's Well, Brigham. William Wordsworth. *Fr.* Poems Composed or Suggested During a Tour, in the Summer of 1833. **CP-WorW2**

Cattle in the slaughter-pens, laboratory dogs. The King of Beasts. Robinson Jeffers. **CP-JefR3**

Catullian Hendecasyllables. Samuel Taylor Coleridge. **CP-ColeS**

Catullus. Catullus. *See* Carmen 92: "Lesbia loads me night & day with her curses."

Catullus: *Carmen xi*. Catullus. *See* Carmen 11: "Furius, Aurelius, friends of my youth."

Catullus: *Carmen v*. Catullus. *See* Carmen 5: "Lesbia / live with me."

Catullus: *Carmen xli*. Catullus. *See* Carmen 41: "Formianus's whore, / long-nosed."

Catullus: *Carmen ci*. Catullus. *See* Carmen 101: "Journeying over many seas and through many countries."

Catullus viii. Louis Zukofsky. **CP-ZukLS**

Catullus on Friendship. Donald Davie. **CP-DavDo**

Catullus Talks to Himself. Catullus. *See* Carmen 8: "Break off / fallen Catullus."

Catullus: XXXI. Catullus. *See* Carmen 31: "Apple of islands, Sirmio, & bright peninsulas, set."

Catullus to Lesbia. Catullus. *See* Carmen 5: "Lesbia / live with me."

Catullus, you're a fool. I said. Catullus. *See* Carmen 8: "Break off / fallen Catullus."

Caught between the twisted stars the plotted lines the faulty map. Romeo Had Juliette. "Lou Reed." **SP-ReedL**

Caught by the lure of marriage. Name. Robert Ranke Graves. **CP-GravR**

Caught in a Net. Nicholas Vachel Lindsay. **CP-LindV**

Caught in a wedge of clanging trams and cars. Stallion. John Hewitt. **CP-HewiJ**

Caught in my prime in pitiful disaster. Minor Poet's Dilemma, 1940. John Hewitt. **CP-HewiJ**

Caught in the briary stars. Hayden Carruth. *Fr.* North Winter. **CP-CarHL**

Caught in the centre of a soundless field. Myxomatosis. Philip Larkin. **CP-LarkP**

Caught in the Swamp. Joseph Ceravolo. **SP-CeraJ**

Caught off first, he leaped to run to second, but. Ball Game. Richard Eberhart. **CP-EberR**

Caught Susanner whistlin'; well. Breaking the Charm. Paul Laurence Dunbar. **CP-DunbP**

Caught—the bubble. Sonnet. Elizabeth Bishop. **CP-BishE**

Caught there, then, on the Rock. At Corregidor. Richard Eberhart. *Fr.* Brotherhood of Men. **CP-EberR**

Caught upon a thousand thorns, I sing. 1934. Richard Eberhart. **CP-EberR**

Caul Gate, Farewell, that hath me bound. Lese-Wiat, from Caul Gate. Louis Zukofsky. *Fr.* Michtam. **CP-ZukLS**

Caul Gate, Farewell, that hath me bound. Michtam. Louis Zukofsky. **CP-ZukLS**

Cauld blaws the wind frae east to west. Up in the Morning Early. Robert Burns. **CP-BurnR**

Cauld Frosty Morning. Robert Burns. **CP-BurnR**

Cauld Is the E'enin Blast. Robert Burns. **CP-BurnR**

Cauliflower, The. John Haines. **SP-HainJ**

Cauliflower-eared Spartan. Reading and Talking. Louis Zukofsky. **CP-ZukLS**

Cause, the Cause, The. Charles Olson. **CP-OlsoC**

Cause Won, The. Vincent Bourne, *tr. fr. Latin by* William Cowper. **CP-CowpW**

Cause you don't love me. Bad Luck Card. Langston Hughes. **SP-HughL**

Causerie. Allen Tate. **CP-TateA**

Causes. Mona Van Duyn. **SP-VanDM**

Causes are in Time; only their issue, The. The Allegory of the Wolf Boy. Thom Gunn. **CP-GunnT**

Caution, A. Robert Herrick. **CP-HerrR**

Caution in Councell. Robert Herrick. **CP-HerrR**

Caution to Everybody, A. Ogden Nash. **CP-NashO**

Cautionary, The. Charles Kenneth Williams. **SP-WillC**

Cautious Circumspection Does Not Win the West. Gilbert Sorrentino. **SP-SorrG**

Cavalier Tunes. Robert Browning. **CP-BroR1**
  Boot and Saddle. **HBV; OAEP; SoSe**

Cavalli marittimi / Urtansi in guerra. Christina Georgina Rossetti. **CP-RosC3**

Cavalry Crossing a Ford. Walt Whitman. **CP-WhitW**

Cavatina of broken parlando utterances, A. *Firenze*, a Lifetime Later. Lawrence Ferlinghetti. **SP-FerlL**

Cave, The. Louise McNeill. **SP-McNeL**

Cave, The. Charles Kenneth Williams. **CP-WillC; SP-WillC**

Cave Canem. Edna St. Vincent Millay. **CP-MillE**

Cave downstairs, The. Above the Cave. Denise Levertov. **CP-LeveD**

Cave of Despair, The. Edmund Spenser. **OBNV** *Fr.* The Faerie Queene. **CP-Spens**
  "Ere long they come, where that same wicked wight." **NOBE; OAEL-1**

Cave of Lascaux, The. Robert Pack. **SP-PackR**

Cave of Making, The. Wystan Hugh Auden. *Fr.* Thanksgiving for a Habitat. **CP-AudeW**

Cave of Mammon, The. Edmund Spenser. *See* As pilot well expert in perilous wave.

Cave of Nakedness, The. Wystan Hugh Auden. *Fr.* Thanksgiving for a Habitat. **CP-AudeW**

Cave of Staffa ("Thanks for the lessons of this Spot—fit school"). William Wordsworth. *Fr.* Poems Composed or Suggested During a Tour, in the Summer of 1833. **CP-WorW2**

Cave of Staffa ("We saw, but surely, in the motley crowd"). William Wordsworth. **VLP** *Fr.* Poems Composed or Suggested During a Tour, in the Summer of 1833. **CP-WorW2**

Cave of Staffa ("Ye shadowy Beings, that have rights and claims"). William Wordsworth. **VLP** *Fr.* Poems Composed or Suggested During a Tour, in the Summer of 1833. **CP-WorW2**

Cave Painting. Hayden Carruth. **CP-CarHS**

Cave/wall the cave lion's, The. On All Sides. Charles Olson. **CP-OlsoC**

Cavern, The. Charles Tomlinson. **CP-TomlC**

Caverns of the Grave Ive seen, The. William Blake. **CP-BlakW**

Caves, The. Jim Carroll. **SP-CarrJ**

Caw Caw Caw / on a far shingle long ago. The Sea and Ourselves at Cape Ann. Lawrence Ferlinghetti. **SP-FerlL**

Cawdor. Robinson Jeffers. **CP-JefR1**

C————d faithful likeness, friend Painter, would'st seize? Robert Burns. *Fr.* Dumfries Epigrams. **CP-BurnR**

Ce bruit da la mer. Denise Levertov. **CP-LeveD**

Ce-Lia the Immortal Beauty. William Carlos Williams, *with* David Rafael Wang, *at. to* Wang Wei, *tr. fr. Chinese.* **CP-WilW2**

Ce qu'a de pis. Samuel Beckett. **CP-BeckS**

Ce qu'ont les yeux. Samuel Beckett. **CP-BeckS**

Ce Xochitl: The Sign of Flowers. Thomas Merton. *Fr.* South. *Fr.* The Geography of Lograire. **CP-MertT**

Cease, fond wretch, to love, so oft deluded. Epigramme. Thomas Campion. *Fr.* Observations in the Art of English Poesie. **CP-CampT**

Cease, thou afflicted soul, to mourn. A Lover, in the Disguise of an Amazon, Is Dearly Beloved of His Mistress. Thomas Carew. **CP-CareT**

Cease, ye prudes, your envious railing. Written under the Picture of the Celebrated Miss Burns. Robert Burns. **CP-BurnR**

Ceaselessly from grey skies fell the rain. A Rainy Afternoon. Wystan Hugh Auden. **CP-AudWJ**

Ceci est digne de gens sans dieu. Stevie Smith. **CP-SmitS**

Ceci n'est pas une Pipe. Charles Tomlinson. **CP-TomlC**

Cecil Sliding Away from the Memory of Wanda. Paul Zimmer. **SP-ZimmP**

Cecil, Zimmer, and the Man-Made Lake. Paul Zimmer. **SP-ZimmP**

Cedarhome. Barton Sutter. **SP-SuttB**
  "Can you believe it?"
  "I didn't used to care much."
  "Just learning to talk, I watched."
  "Make no mistake. The cedar."

Cedars and the westward sun. The Curse. John Berryman. **CP-BerrJ**

Cefalù. Frank Templeton Prince. **CP-PrinF**

Ceilidhe, The. John Hewitt. **CP-HewiJ**

Ceiling, The. Theodore Roethke. **CP-RoetT**

Ceiling is carried on corbels laid, The. Chapel-at-Ease. Frank Templeton Prince. **CP-PrinF**

Celebrants came chanting "God is dead!", The. The Death of God. Howard Nemerov. **CP-NemeH**

Celebrating Giacometti. René Char, tr. fr. French by Thomas Merton. **CP-MertT**

Celebration, The. James Dickey. **CP-DickJ**

Celebration. Thomas McGrath. **SP-McGrT**

Celebration, A. William Carlos Williams. **CP-WilW1**

Celebration for George Sarton, A. May Sarton. **SP-SartM**

Celebration for June 24. Thomas McGrath. **SP-McGrT**

Celebration in the Plaza, The. Adrienne Rich. **CP-RicAE**

Celebration of Charis in Ten Lyric[k] Pieces [or Peeces], A. Ben Jonson. **CP-JonsB**
  Another Lady's [or Ladyes] Exception, Present at the Hearing.
  Begging Another, on Colour of Mending the Former. **CBLP; OAEP; PoEL-2; UnTE**
  Claiming [or Clayming] a Second Kiss[e] by Desert.
  Her Man Described by Her Own[e] Dictamen.
  Her Triumph. **CBLP; CTC; EBEV; EIL; InvP; JCP; NOSC; OPOP; PoEL-2; PrIm; SeCV-1**
    (Triumph of Charis, The.) **ELP; LiTB; NOBE; NoP; TFi**
  His Discourse with Cupid.
  His Excuse for Loving. **EnRePo; JCP; NOSC; PoEL-2; QFR; SeCV-1**
  How He Saw Her. **EnRePo; OAEP; QFR; SeCV-1**
  Urging Her of a Promise.
  What He[e] Suffered.

Celebration of Rust, A. Barton Sutter. **SP-SuttB**

Celebration of Sorts, A. Gilbert Sorrentino. **SP-SorrG**

Celebration of the Lizard. Jim Morrison. **SP-MorrJ**

Celery. Ogden Nash. **CP-NashO**

Celery. John Updike. **CP-UpdiJ**

Celestial Circus, The. Nicholas Vachel Lindsay. **CP-LindV**

Celestial Dealings. Archie Randolph Ammons. **SP-AmmoA**

Celestial Evening, October 1967. Charles Olson. **SP-OlsoC** Fr. The Maximus Poems.

Celestial Globe. Howard Nemerov. **CP-NemeH**

Celestial pow'rs! that piety regard, ad. fr. Dionysus' Periegesis. Samuel Johnson, tr. fr. Greek. **CP-JohnS**

Celestial Surgeon, The. Robert Louis Stevenson. **CP-StevR**

Celia Bleeding, to the Surgeon. Thomas Carew. **CP-CareT**

Celia Singing ("You that think Love can convey"). Thomas Carew. **CP-CareT**

Celia Singing ("Hark, how my Celia, with the choice"). Thomas Carew. **CP-CareT**

Celia's Birthday Poem. Louis Zukofsky. **CP-ZukLS**

Cell, The. Louise Glück. **SP-GlücL**

Cell, The. Edwin Rolfe. **CP-RolfE**

Cell by cell the baby made herself, the cells. Sara in Her Father's Arms. George Oppen. **CP-OppeG**

Cell Song. Etheridge Knight. **SP-KnigE**

Cellaphon–a Favorite Word with Picabia. Marsden Hartley. **CP-HartM**

Cellar underneath the house, though not lived in, A. Down There. Wystan Hugh Auden. Fr. Thanksgiving for a Habitat. **CP-AudeW**

Celle Qui Fût Héaulmiette. Wallace Stevens. **CP-StevW**

Celles. Marilyn Hacker. **SP-HackM**

Cellophane. Charles Kenneth Williams. **CP-WillC**

Cells. Rudyard Kipling. **CP-KiplR**

Celluloid of a photograph holds them well, The. Six Young Men. Ted Hughes. **SP-HughT**

Celt in all his variants from Builth to Ballyhoo, The. The Puzzler. Rudyard Kipling. **CP-KiplR**

Celtic Fringe, The. Stevie Smith. **CP-SmitS**

Celtic genius—Cornwall, Scotland, Ireland, Wales—, The. "Hugh MacDiarmid." **SP-MacDH** Fr. Cornish Heroic Song for Valda Trevlyn.

Celtic spearman forcing the cromlech-builder's brown daughter, A. Second-Best. Robinson Jeffers. **CP-JefR2**

Celts, The. Stevie Smith. **CP-SmitS**

Cemaes Songs. Steve Griffiths. **SP-GrifS**

Cemetery, The. Richard Eberhart. Fr. Burr Oaks. **CP-EberR**

Cemetery at Academy, California, The. Philip Levine. **SP-LeviP**

Cemetery Nights, with music. Stephen Dobyns. **SP-DobyS**

Cemetery Nights II. Stephen Dobyns. **SP-DobyS**

Cemetery Nights IV. Stephen Dobyns. **SP-DobyS**

Cemetery Nights V. Stephen Dobyns. **SP-DobyS**

Cemetery of Childhood. Joaquim Cardozo, tr. fr. Portuguese by Elizabeth Bishop. **CP-BishE**

Cenci, The. Percy Bysshe Shelley. **CP-ShelP**
  Beatrice's Last Words. **FiP**
  Cenci's Curse upon His Daughter, The. **TW**

Cenciaja. Robert Browning. **CP-BroR2**

Cenci's Curse upon His Daughter, The. Percy Bysshe Shelley. **TW** Fr. The Cenci. **CP-ShelP**

Cenotaph, The. James Schuyler. **CP-SchuJ**
  Edge in the Morning, The.
  Moneses Uniflora.
  We See Seals. Boats Go By.

Cenotaph. William Wordsworth. **CP-WorW2**

Cenotaph. John Yau. **SP-YauJo**

Cenotaph of Snow. John Yau. **SP-YauJo**

Censer-Moon, The. Nicholas Vachel Lindsay. **CP-LindV**

Censers are swinging / Over the town. The Soul of the City Receives the Gift of the Holy Spirit. Nicholas Vachel Lindsay. **CP-LindV**

Censors. David Herbert Lawrence. **CP-LawrD**

Censors. David Herbert Lawrence. **CP-LawrD**

Censorship. John Ciardi. **SP-CiarJ**

Censure not sharply then, but me advise. Epistle to a Friend, An. Ben Jonson. **CP-JonsB**

Census man, The. Madam and the Census Man. Langston Hughes. **SP-HughL**

Census of murdered, A. Last Lynx. Daniel Gerard Hoffman. **SP-HoffD**

Census-Taker, The. Robert Frost. **CP-FrosR**

Centaur, The. Theodore Roethke. Fr. Three Epigrams. **CP-RoetT**

Centaur does not need a Horse, The. The Centaur. Theodore Roethke. Fr. Three Epigrams. **CP-RoetT**

Centaur, siren [or syren], I forgo[e], The. see also Snail [or Snayl], The. Richard Lovelace. **CP-LoveR**

Centaur Song. Hilda Doolittle. **CP-DoolH**

Centaurs, The. Rudyard Kipling. **CP-KiplR** Fr. Debits and Credits.

Centaurs. Frederick Morgan. **SP-MorgF**

Centaurs' habits are not of the nicest. Centaurs. Frederick Morgan. **SP-MorgF**

Centenarian, The. William Carlos Williams. **CP-WilW1**

Centenarian's Story, The. Walt Whitman. **CP-WhitW**

Centenary Note: Inscribed to Little Crow, Leader of the Sioux Rebellion in Minnesota, 1862, A. James Wright. **CP-WrigJ**

Centenary of Garibaldi, The. George Meredith. **CP-MerG2**

Centennial Bell that will not ring. Conversation in a Belfry. Archibald MacLeish. **CP-MacLA**

Centennial For Whitman. Richard Eberhart. **CP-EberR**

Centennial Hymn. John Greenleaf Whittier. **CP-WhitJ**

Center is known weak sighted, and he sells. Upon Center a Spectacle-Maker with a Flat Nose. Robert Herrick. **CP-HerrR**

Center of Attention, The. Daniel Gerard Hoffman. **SP-HoffD**

CENTERPIECE: St. Sebastian (Italian). Jenny Joseph. Fr. Altarpiece (A Meditation on Lust, Desire and Love). **SP-JoseJ**

Centipede. Rita Dove. **SP-DoveR**

Centipede, The. Ogden Nash. **CP-NashO**

Cento Made By Wordsworth, A. William Wordsworth. **CP-WorW2**

Central Park. Robert Lowell. **SP-LoweR**

Central Park. Howard Nemerov. **CP-NemeH**

"Centre of Earth!" a Chinaman he said. The Chinaman. Christina Georgina Rossetti. **CP-RosC3**

Centre of equal daughters, equal sons. America. Walt Whitman. **CP-WhitW**

Centuries near Spinnazola. Richard Hugo. **CP-HugoR**

Centuries of life have passed. On Seeing Some Dutch Pictures. Wystan Hugh Auden. **CP-AudWJ**

Centurion of the Thirtieth, A. Rudyard Kipling. *Fr.* Puck of Pook's Hill. British-Roman Song, A. **CP-KiplR**

Cities and Thrones and Powers. **CP-KiplR**

Century Dying, A. Pablo Neruda, *tr. fr. Spanish by* Ben Belitt. **SP-NeruP**

Century-plant has flowered, its golden blossom, The. The Flowering Aloe. Robert Ranke Graves. **CP-GravR**

Cerebral Emotions. David Herbert Lawrence. **CP-LawrD**

Ceremonial. Richard Eberhart. **CP-EberR**

Ceremonial rose in the lapel, A. Bridal Photo, 1906. John Ciardi. **SP-CiarJ**

Ceremonies for Candlemas[se] Eve. Robert Herrick. **CP-HerrR**

Ceremonies for Candlemasse Day, The. Robert Herrick. **CP-HerrR**

Ceremonies for Christmas[se]. Robert Herrick. **CP-HerrR**

"Wassail the trees, that they may bear." **PChr**

Ceremony. William Stafford. **SP-StafW**

Ceremony. Richard Wilbur. **CP-WilbR**

Ceremony after a Fire Raid. Dylan Thomas. **CP-ThomD**

Ceremony and Vision. John Berryman. **CP-BerrJ**

Ceremony By the Sea, A. Richard Eberhart. **CP-EberR**

Ceremony for Edward Dahlberg. Thomas Merton. **CP-MertT**

Ceremony upon Candlemas Eve. Robert Herrick. **CP-HerrR**

Cerinthus, don't you have some soft thought for your girl. Gilbert Sorrentino. *Fr.* Elegiacs of Sulpicia. **SP-SorrG**

Cernis ut eoi descendat gemmula roris. *see also* On a Drop of Dew. Andrew Marvell. **CP-MarvA**

Certain branches cut. October. Denise Levertov. **CP-LeveD**

Certain Choices. Richard Shelton. **SP-ShelR**

Certain colors got lodged under. The Reading of an Ever-Changing Tale. John Yau. **SP-YauJo**

Certain Dead. John Haines. **SP-HainJ**

Certain figures seem to control. A Poem for My Wife. Gilbert Sorrentino. **SP-SorrG**

Certain Maxims of Hafiz. Rudyard Kipling. **CP-KiplR**

"As the thriftless gold of the *babul* so is the gold that we spend."

"Blister we not for *bursati?* So when the heart is vext."

" 'By all I am misunderstood!' if the Matron shall say, or the Maid."

"Does the woodpecker flit round the young *ferash?* Does the grass clothe a new-built wall?"

"If it be pleasant to look on, stalled in the packed *serai.*"

"If She grow suddenly gracious—reflect. Is it all for thee?"

"If She have spoken a word, remember thy lips are sealed."

"If we fall in the race, though we win, the hoof-slide is scarred on the course."

"In public Her face turneth to thee, and pleasant Her smile when ye meet." Maxim. **OtMeF**

"My Son, if a maiden deny thee and scuffingly bid thee give o'er."

"My son if I, Hafiz, thy father, take hold of thy knees in my pain."

"Pleasant the snaffle of Courtship, improving the manners and carriage."

"Seek not for favour of women. So shall you find it indeed."

"Temper of chums, the love of your wife, and a new piano's tune, The."

"Ways of man with a maid be strange, yet simple and tame, The."

"Who are the rulers of Ind—to whom shall we bow the knee?"

"With a 'weed' among men or horses verily this is the best."

"Yea, though a Kafir die, to him is remitted Jehannum."

Certain melodies can break your heart. Minuet in G. Peter Meinke. **SP-MeinP**

Certain Mercies. Robert Ranke Graves. **CP-GravR**

Certain Music, A. Muriel Rukeyser. **CP-RukeM**

Certain neighbour lying sick to death, A. The Family. Robert Browning. **CP-BroR2**

Certain old emblems are needed. Marvellous. Gilbert Sorrentino. **SP-SorrG**

Certain People, A. George Meredith. **CP-MerG1**

Certain Phenomena of Sound. Wallace Stevens. **CP-StevW**

Certain poet in outlandish clothes, A. The Old Age of Queen Maeve. William Butler Yeats. **CP-YeatW**

Certain portions of the heart. Anatomy. Gilbert Sorrentino. **SP-SorrG**

Certain Prospects and Spectacular Diversions. Leonard Nathan. **SP-NathL**

Certain Sharpness in the Morning Air, A. Mary Oliver. **SP-OlivM**

Certain Slant of Sunlight, A. Ted Berrigan. **SP-BerrT**

Certain things here are quietly American. Derek Walcott. **CP-WalcD** *Fr.* Midsummer.

Certain trees. Epitaph: Lorine Niedecker. Roy Fisher. **SP-FishR**

Certain Type of Scientist Speaks, A. Alexander Pope. **ECEV** *Fr.* Yet, yet a moment, one dim ray of light. **NAEL-1; OAEL-1; PoEL-3** *Fr.* The Dunciad. **CP-PopeA**

Certain waters are as blue as metal. On the Anniversary of My Baptism. Thomas Merton. **CP-MertT; SP-MertT**

Certain Weathers. Jenny Joseph. **SP-JoseJ**

Certainly, Lean-shanks, you have forced the pace. Mens Sana in Corpore Sano. Donald Davie. **CP-DavDo**

Certainly praise: let song mount again and again. Wystan Hugh Auden. *Fr.* Sonnets from China. **CP-AudeW**

Certainly sought: one quiet time. The Dogs. Charles Bukowski. **SP-BukC2**

Certainty Before Lunch. John Berryman. **CP-BerrJ**

Certainty of being part of the atmosphere, The. John Yau. **SP-YauJo** *Fr.* Scenes from the Life of Boullee.

Certes, it is a noble sport. JANUARY (*Hunting*). Rudyard Kipling. *Fr.* Verses on Games. **CP-KiplR**

Ces morts / cette lesbos. Semiotic Poem from Racine's "Iphigenie." Thomas Merton. *Fr.* A Selection of Concrete Poems. **CP-MertT**

'Cession's stahted on de gospel way, De. A Spiritual. Paul Laurence Dunbar. **CP-DunbP**

C'est un grand Monsieur Pussy-Cat. Monsieur Pussy-Cat, Blackmailer. Stevie Smith. **CP-SmitS**

Cetus, a Letter from Jonah. Siv Cedering Fox. **SP-CedeS**

Ceux Qui Luttent. Stevie Smith. **CP-SmitS**

Cézanne. William Carlos Williams. **CP-WilW2**

Cézanne and the Love of Color. Stephen Dobyns. **SP-DobyS**

Cézanne and Zola. Stephen Dobyns. **SP-DobyS**

Cézanne at Aix. Charles Tomlinson. **CP-TomlC**

Cézanne's Ambition. Stephen Dobyns. **SP-DobyS**

Cézanne's Doubts. Stephen Dobyns. **SP-DobyS**

Cézanne's Love of Poetry. Stephen Dobyns. **SP-DobyS**

Cézanne's Outrageousness. Stephen Dobyns. **SP-DobyS**

Cézanne's Ports. Allen Ginsberg. **CP-GinsA**

Chaconne for Unaccompanied Violin. Charles Tomlinson. **CP-TomlC**

Chacun à Son Berlitz. Ogden Nash. **CP-NashO**

Chagall. Raissa Maritain, *tr. fr. French by* Thomas Merton. **CP-MertT**

Chagall's sweet lovers mounting into blue. Lovers Are like Children. Adrienne Rich. **CP-RicAE**

Chain I Gave, The. Byron. **CP-Byron**

Chain is on the door, The. One Hundred and Ninety-Nine Pounds of Clay Leaning Forward. Charles Bukowski. **SP-BukC2**

Chain of memory is resurrection I am a vain man, The. Charles Olson. **CP-OlsoC; SP-OlsoC**

Chain Saw at Dawn in Vermont in Time of Drouth. Robert Penn Warren. **SP-WarrR**

Chains of Mountains. Joseph Ceravolo. **SP-CeraJ**

Chair, The. Theodore Roethke. **CP-RoetT**

Chair she sat in, like a burnished throne, The. A Game of Chess. Thomas Stearns Eliot. **SCV** *Fr.* The Waste Land. **CP-ElioT**

Chair squeaks in a high wind, The. Nostalgias. Derek Mahon. **SP-MahoD**

Chaka. Frank Templeton Prince. **CP-PrinF**

He Bathes in the Morning.

He Compares Old Customs with Those of His Kingdom.

How Festivals Were Celebrated.

King watches at Night, The.

People Rest after Conquests, The.

Chakora bird / Like a partridge. It is said, The. Charles Henri Ford. **SP-FordC** *Fr.* Emblems of Arachne.

Chalk Blue. Stephen Spender. *Fr.* Lost Days. **CP-SpenS**

Chalk-white, light dazzled on the stone. Twice Lovely. Walter de la Mare. **CP-DeLaW**

Chalkley Hall. John Greenleaf Whittier. **CP-WhitJ**

Challenge, The. William Everson. **SP-EverW**

Challenge: A Court Ballad, The. Alexander Pope. **CP-PopeA**

Challenge to my verbalising mind, A. Aquarium. John Hewitt. **CP-HewiJ**

Challenged once more to reunite. Song: Twinned Heart. Robert Ranke Graves. **CP-GravR**

Challenger, The. Mona Van Duyn. **SP-VanDM**

Chambermaid's First Song, The. William Butler Yeats. **CP-YeatW**

Chambermaid's Second Song, The. William Butler Yeats. **CP-YeatW**

Chambers of my heart are many, dear, The. George Meredith. **CP-MerG2**

Chameleons feed on light and air. An Exhortation. Percy Bysshe Shelley. **CP-ShelP**

Chamfort. Carl Sandburg. **CP-SandC**

Champ. Robert Pack. **SP-PackR**

Champagne. Rita Dove. **SP-DoveR**

Champion of those who groan beneath. To William Lloyd Garrison. John Greenleaf Whittier. **CP-WhitJ**

Champion smiles, The—What Personality! Wystan Hugh Auden. *Fr.* Shorts [1939–1947] ("Motionless, deep in his mind, lies the past the poet's forgotten"). **CP-AudeW**

Champs d'Honneur. Ernest Hemingway. **CP-HemiE**

Chance, The. Robert Creeley. **CP-CreeR**

Chance. Hilda Doolittle. **CP-DoolH**

Chance, an external compulsion. Moira's Messages. Tom Clark. **SP-ClarT**

Chance and chance and thereby starlit. Animula. George Oppen. **CP-OppeG**

Chance is the remotest, The. Some Science Fiction. Robert Frost. **CP-FrosR**

Chance Meeting. Hilda Doolittle. **CP-DoolH**

Chance of a few morning sprinkles, A. October 5, 1981. James Schuyler. **CP-SchuJ**

Chancellor once was a tree full of fruit, The. On Thurlow. William Cowper. **CP-CowpW**

Chances, The. Wilfred Owen. **CP-OwenW**

Chances are we will sink quietly back. Clay out of Silence. Charles Kenneth Williams. **CP-WillC; SP-WillC**

Chances of Rhyme, The. Charles Tomlinson. **CP-TomlC**

Chances "R." Allen Ginsberg. **CP-GinsA**

Change. Tom Clark. **SP-ClarT**

Change, The, *see also* Commentary—The Change. Leonard Cohen. **CP-CoheL**

Change. Robert Creeley. **CP-CreeR**

Change, The. James Dickey. **CP-DickJ**

Change. John Donne. **CBLP; EBEV** *Fr.* Elegies. **CP-DonnJ**

Change, The. Paul Laurence Dunbar. **CP-DunbP**

Change. Robert Ranke Graves. **CP-GravR**

Change, The. Thomas Hardy. **CP-HardT**

Change. Stanley Jasspon Kunitz. **CP-KuniS**

Change. David Herbert Lawrence. **CP-LawrD**

Change and chancefulness in my flowering youthtime. The Temporary the All. Thomas Hardy. **CP-HardT**

Change Common to All. Robert Herrick. **CP-HerrR**

Change Gives Content. Robert Herrick. **CP-HerrR**

Change Has Come, The. Paul Laurence Dunbar. **CP-DunbP**

Change Here for Wichita Falls, or, Has Anybody Seen My Wanderlust? Ogden Nash. **CP-NashO**

Change in Recurrence. George Meredith. **CP-MerG1**

Change: *Kyoto-Tokyo Express*, The. Allen Ginsberg. **CP-GinsA**

Change Me, Some God, Into That Breathing Rose! William Wordsworth. **Son** *Fr.* The River Duddon [A Series of Sonnets]. **CP-WorW2**

Change of Address. William Matthews. **SP-MattW**

Change of Air, A. Wystan Hugh Auden. **CP-AudeW**

Change of Government. David Herbert Lawrence. **CP-LawrD**

Change of Habit, A. Charles Bukowski. **SP-BukC1**

Change of Life. David Herbert Lawrence. **CP-LawrD**

Change of Season. Audre Lorde. **SP-LordA**

Change of World, A. Adrienne Rich. **CP-RicAE**

Change Upon Change. Elizabeth Barrett Browning. **CP-BroEB**

Changed by this last enchantment of our kind. Men of My Century Loved Mozart. Archibald MacLeish. **CP-MacLA**

Changed Woman, The. Louise Bogan. **CP-BogaL**

Changelessness / is Nature's change. Emily Dickinson. **SP-DickE**

Changeling, The. Thomas McGrath. **SP-McGrT**

Changeling, The. Theodore Roethke. **CP-RoetT**

Changeling, The. John Greenleaf Whittier. **CP-WhitJ**

Changelings, The. Rudyard Kipling. **CP-KiplR** *Fr.* Debits and Credits.

Changes. Maya Angelou. **SP-AngeM**

Changes, The. Robert Creeley. **CP-CreeR**

Changes. John Haines. **SP-HainJ**

Changes at Meridian. Richard Hugo. **CP-HugoR**

Changes in Policy at Taholah. Richard Hugo. **CP-HugoR**

Changes to Corinna, The. Robert Herrick. **CP-HerrR**

Changing Chimes. Christina Georgina Rossetti. **CP-RosC2**

Changing Colour. Phoebe Hesketh. **SP-HeskP**

Changing Diapers. Gary Snyder. **CP-SnydG**

Changing figures The dionysian child. The Wheel of Being I. Hayden Carruth. *Fr.* Contra Mortem. **CP-CarHL**

Changing, he walks the changing avenue. La Promenade de Protée. Charles Tomlinson. *Fr.* Two Poems on titles proposed by Octavio and Marie José Paz. **CP-TomlC**

Changing Light Winds. Carl Sandburg. **CP-SandC**

Changing of the Guards. "Bob Dylan." **CP-DylaB**

Changing skyline, A. A Sequence. Denise Levertov. **CP-LeveD**

Changing Time. Paul Laurence Dunbar. **CP-DunbP**

Channel Crossing. Sylvia Plath. **CP-PlatS**

Channel Firing. Thomas Hardy. **CP-HardT**

Channel 13. James Merrill. **SP-MerrJ**

Channing. John Greenleaf Whittier. **CP-WhitJ**

Chanson. Robert Creeley. **CP-CreeR**

Chanson. William Carlos Williams. **CP-WilW2**

Chanson Pour Billie. Charles Henri Ford. **SP-FordC**

Chanson Triste. Alun Lewis. **CP-LewiA**

Chanson un Peu Naïve. Louise Bogan. **CP-BogaL**

Chant for the Five-Year Plan. John Hewitt. **CP-HewiJ**

Chant of the Frontiersman. Wang Ch'ang-ling, *tr. fr.* Chinese by William Carlos Williams *with* David Rafael Wang. **CP-WilW2**

Chant-Pagan. Rudyard Kipling. **CP-KiplR**

Chant to Be Used in Processions around a Site with Furnaces. Thomas Merton. **CP-MertT; SP-MertT**

Chant we the story now. Eden in Winter. Nicholas Vachel Lindsay. **CP-LindV**

Chanting of the Whales, The. Nicholas Vachel Lindsay. *Fr.* Golden Whales of California. **CP-LindV**

Chanting the Square Deific. Walt Whitman. **CP-WhitW**

Chaos. Alexander Pope. *See* The Reign of Chaos.

Chaos! Cosmos! Cosmos, Chaos! who can tell how all will end? Tennyson. **FaBoEH** *Fr.* Locksley Hall Sixty Years After. **CP-TennA**

Chaos in Motion and Not in Motion. Wallace Stevens. **CP-StevW**

Chaotic pile of barren stone. A Descriptive Ode, Supposed to have Been Written under the Ruins of Rufus's Castle. Charlotte Smith. **CP-SmitC**

Chapel, A. James Schuyler. **CP-SchuJ**

Chapel-at-Ease. Frank Templeton Prince. **CP-PrinF**

Chapel Further West than Most, A. Richard Hugo. **CP-HugoR**

Chapel of the Hermits, The. John Greenleaf Whittier. **CP-WhitJ**

Chapel-Organist, The. Thomas Hardy. **CP-HardT**

Chapel's cowbell, The. Crusoe's Island. Derek Walcott. **CP-WalcD**

Chaplet for Judith Landry, A. Marilyn Hacker. **SP-HackM**

Chaplinesque. Hart Crane. **CP-CranH**

Chapman. Muriel Rukeyser. **CP-RukeM**

Chappie, A. Paul Laurence Dunbar. **CP-DunbP**

Chapter Forever. David St. John. **SP-StJoD**

Chapter Heading. Ernest Hemingway. **CP-HemiE**

Chapter Six. William Blake. *Fr.* An Island in the Moon. "Ah said Sipsop, I only wish Jack [*Hunter*] Tearguts had." **CP-BlakW**

Chapultepec Park / I. Muriel Rukeyser. **CP-RukeM**

Chapultepec Park / II. Muriel Rukeyser. **CP-RukeM**

Chaque jour envie. Samuel Beckett. **CP-BeckS**

Character, A. Samuel Taylor Coleridge. **CP-ColeS**

Character. Ralph Waldo Emerson. **CP-EmerR**

Character, A. Tennyson. **CP-TennA**

Character, A. William Wordsworth. **CP-WorW1**

Character of Charles Brown. John Keats. *See* He is to weet a melancholy carle.

Character of Holland, The. Andrew Marvell. **CP-MarvA** "Holland, that scarce deserves the name of land." **OBSV** "Holland, that scarce deserves the name of land." **ChTr**

Character of Love Seen as a Search for the Lost, The. Kenneth Patchen. **CP-PatcK**

Character of Marlborough, A, *extended vers.* Alexander Pope. **CP-PopeA** *Fr.* An Essay on Man. **CP-PopeA**

Character of Sir Robert Walpole, The. Jonathan Swift. **CP-SwifJ**

Character of the Happy Warrior. William Wordsworth. **CP-WorW1**

Character of Wallenstein, The. Samuel Taylor Coleridge. **CP-ColeS** *Fr.* The Death of Wallenstein.

Character, Panegyric, and Description of the Legion Club, A. Jonathan Swift. **CP-SwifJ**

Characteristic, nevertheless strange. The Strayed Message. Robert Ranke Graves. **CP-GravR**

Characteristic of the mind, The. Mind and Nature. Richard Eberhart. **CP-EberR**

Characteristically. Robert Creeley. **CP-CreeR**

Characteristics of a Child Three Years Old. William Wordsworth. **CP-WorW1**

Charade. Christina Georgina Rossetti. **CP-RosC3**

Charade on Dr Thomas Barnard. Samuel Johnson. **CP-JohnS**

Charades. Christina Georgina Rossetti. **CP-RosC3**

Charge of the Light Brigade, The. Tennyson. **CP-TennA** "Stormed at with shot and shell." **Poetr**

Charges Against Cock Robin, The. William DeWitt Snodgrass. **SP-SnodW**

Chariot so strict chariot. Day. Allen Tate. **CP-TateA**

Charioteer. Hilda Doolittle. **CP-DoolH**

Charioteer of Delphi, The. James Merrill. **SP-MerrJ**

Charis, guess[e], and do[e] not miss[e]. Claiming [or Clayming] a Second Kiss[e] by Desert. Ben Jonson. Fr. A Celebration of Charis in Ten Lyric[k] Pieces [or Peeces]. **CP-JonsB**

Charis one day in discourse. Urging Her of a Promise. Ben Jonson. Fr. A Celebration of Charis in Ten Lyric[k] Pieces [or Peeces]. **CP-JonsB**

Charity. William Cowper. **CP-CowpW**

Charity. Paul Laurence Dunbar. **CP-DunbP**

Charity. Christina Georgina Rossetti. **CP-RosC3**

Charity. Christopher Smart. Fr. Hymns for the Amusement of Children. **SP-SmarC**

Charity in Thought. Samuel Taylor Coleridge. **CP-ColeS**

Charity Never Faileth. Christina Georgina Rossetti. **CP-RosC2**

Charity Overcoming Envy. Marianne Craig Moore. **CP-MoorM**

Charivari. Margaret Atwood. **SP-AtwM1**

Charles and Arthur. Gilbert Sorrentino. **SP-SorrG**

Charles—and I say it wond'ring—thou must know. John Milton. See Sonnet 4: "Diodati, and I will say it to you with wonder."

Charles Carville's Eyes. Edwin Arlington Robinson. **CP-RobiE**

Charles Cavendish to His Posterity. Ben Jonson. **CP-JonsB**

Charles Dodgson's Song. Randall Jarrell. **CP-JarrR**

Charles II. Andrew Marvell. See Paint last the King, and a dead shade of night.

Charles Ives, I have heard. Ives. Richard Eberhart. **CP-EberR**

Charles! my slow heart was only sad, when first. Sonnet to a Friend Who Asked[,] How I Felt When the Nurse First Presented My Infant to Me. Samuel Taylor Coleridge. **CP-ColeS**

Charles on Fire. James Merrill. **SP-MerrJ**

Charles on the Trevisan, night bridge. Self-Portrait. Charles Wright. **SP-WrigC**

Charles River, The. Dabney Stuart. **SP-StuaD**
  Boston: From the Embankment.
  Cambridge: From the Cowley Fathers Monastery.

Charles Simic. Charles Simic. **SP-SimiC**

Charles V by Titian. Robert Lowell. **SP-LoweR**

Charles the First. Percy Bysshe Shelley. **CP-ShelP**
  "Heigho! the lark and the owl!" **PBBP**
  "Widow bird sate mourning for her love, A." **BoTP; CH; CoGr; ELP; FaBoEn; FaPON; GTBS; GTBS-6; GTBS-P; LO; LoBV; MeMBP; NOBE; OBNC; OxBSP; PoEL-4**
  (Song, A: "Widow bird sate mourning for her love, A.") **MeMBP; NOBE; OBNC; OxBSP; PoEL-4**
  (Widow Bird, A.) **BoTP; CH; FaPON**

Charles the Second. William Wordsworth. Fr. Ecclesiastical Sonnets. **CP-WorW2**

Charles XII of Sweden. Samuel Johnson. See On what foundation stands the warrior's pride.

Charleston. John Updike. **CP-UpdiJ**

Charleston in the Eighteen-Sixties. Adrienne Rich. **CP-RicAE; SP-RicA2**

Charleston Plantations. May Sarton. **SP-SartM**

Charlie He's My Darling. Robert Burns. **CP-BurnR**

Charlock per Winkle. Louis Zukofsky. **CP-ZukLS**

Charlotte Corday. Charles Tomlinson. **CP-TomlC**

Charlotte, "the angel of / assassination," is unrelaxed. "Marat's Death." Donald Hall. **CP-HallD**

Charm, The. Robert Creeley. **CP-CreeR**

Charm, The. Rita Dove. **SP-DoveR**

Charm[e]. Ben Jonson. **CP-JonsB** Fr. The Witches' Charms. Fr. The Masque of Queens.

Charm, A. Rudyard Kipling. **CP-KiplR**

Charm, The. Gilbert Sorrentino. **SP-SorrG**

Charm for Cantinflas, A. Muriel Rukeyser. **CP-RukeM**

Charm for Sound Sleeping, A. Robert Ranke Graves. **CP-GravR**

Charm invests a face, A. Emily Dickinson. **CP-DickE**

Charm me asleep, and melt me so. Robert Herrick. **UnS** Fr. To Music, to Becalm His Fever. **CP-HerrR**

Charm me asleep, and melt me so. To Music, to Becalm His Fever. Robert Herrick. **CP-HerrR**

Charm with your stainlessness these winter nights. Advent. Thomas Merton. **CP-MertT; SP-MertT**

Charm'd and instructed by thy powerful song. To Mr. Thomson. Douglas Malloch. **CP-ThomJ**

Charm'd by thy suffrage, shall I yet aspire. To a Friend. Charlotte Smith. **CP-SmitC**

Charme, or an Allay for Love, A. Robert Herrick. **CP-HerrR**

Charmes. Robert Herrick. **CP-HerrR**

Charmes. Robert Herrick. **CP-HerrR**

Charming lady, she whose beautiful name honors. Sonnet 2. John Milton, tr. fr. Italian by John T. Shawcross. **CP-MiltJ**

Charming oysters I cry. Oysters. Jonathan Swift. Fr. Verses Made for the Women Who Cry Apples, etc. **CP-SwifJ**

Charming, the movement of girls about a May-pole in May. Men Working. Edna St. Vincent Millay. **CP-MillE**

Charms and Knots. George Herbert. **CP-HerbG**

Charms, that call down the moon from out her sphere. To Music, to Becalm a Sweet-sick Youth. Robert Herrick. **CP-HerrR**

Charon. Louis MacNeice. **CP-MacNL**

Charon. Christina Georgina Rossetti. **CP-RosC3**

Charon and Phylomel, a Dialogue Sung. Robert Herrick. **CP-HerrR**

Charon, indeed, your dreaded oar. Sappho Crosses the Dark River into Hades. Edna St. Vincent Millay. **CP-MillE**

Charon, O Charon, draw thy Boat to th'shore. The New Charon. Robert Herrick. **CP-HerrR**

Charon! O gentle Charon! let us wooe thee. Charon and Phylomel, a Dialogue Sung. Robert Herrick. **CP-HerrR**

Charon! receive a family on board. On Niobe. Unknown, tr. fr. Greek by William Cowper. **CP-CowpW**

Charon! Thou slave! Thou foul! Thou Cavalier [or Cavaleer]! A Mock Charon. Richard Lovelace. **CP-LoveR**

Charon's Cosmology. Charles Simic. **SP-SimiC**
  ("With only his dim lantern.") **SP-SimiC**

Charred hansom is discovered on Bubbling Well Road. In the shade. John Yau. **SP-YauJo** Fr. Predella.

Charred Voice of Max Ernst, The. John Yau. **SP-YauJo**

Charroll Presented to Dr. Williams Bp. of Lincolne as a Newyears Guift, A. Robert Herrick. **CP-HerrR**

Chartist's Complaint, The. Ralph Waldo Emerson. **CP-EmerR**

Chartres. Archibald MacLeish. **CP-MacLA**

Chartres. George Oppen. **CP-OppeG**

Chartres Annunciation, The. Kathleen Jessie Raine. **SP-RainK**

Chartres Windows. Rudyard Kipling. **CP-KiplR**

Chas sing does(who). Edward Estlin Cummings. **CP-CummE**

Chase, The. Paul Laurence Dunbar. **CP-DunbP**

Chase, The. Sir Walter Scott. Fr. The Lady of the Lake.
  Invocation: "Harp of the North! that mouldering long hast hung." **SP-ScotW**

Chase in Spring, The. Hayden Carruth. **CP-CarHS**

Chasers. Carl Sandburg. **CP-SandC**

Chasing the Bird. Robert Creeley. **CP-CreeR**

Chasm. Archie Randolph Ammons. **SP-AmmoA**

Chast as Creation meant us, and more bright. To His Honoured and Ingenious Friend Col. Richard Lovelace, on His Lucasta. Thomas Rawlins. Fr. Commendatory Poems. **CP-LoveR**

Chaste and kind. . . "a pattern." Master & Man. Donald Davie. **CP-DavDo**

Chastity. David Herbert Lawrence. **CP-LawrD**

Chastity. John Milton. **OBS** Fr. Comus; a Masque Presented at Ludlow Castle.

Chastity ("I Mean That Too, But Yet a Hidden Strength"). John Milton. **NOSC** Fr. Comus; a Masque Presented at Ludlow Castle.

Château de Muzot. Charles Tomlinson. **CP-TomlC**

Chateau Hardware, The. John Ashbery. **SP-AshbJ**

Château Jackson. Louis MacNeice. **CP-MacNL**

Chatham was my depot. Kent. Donald Davie. **CP-DavDo**

Chatsworth! thy stately mansion, and the pride. 1830. William Wordsworth. **CP-WorW2**

Chatter of birds two by two raises a night song joining a litany of running water. Prairie Waters by Night. Carl Sandburg. **CP-SandC**

"Chattering, gum snapping audience," A. Miss Moore at Assembly. John Updike. **CP-UpdiJ**

Chaucer. Edward Estlin Cummings. **CP-CummE**

Chaucer, Langland, Douglas, Dunbar, with all your. Ode to the Medieval Poets. Wystan Hugh Auden. **CP-AudeW**

Chaucer's Retraction. Geoffrey Chaucer. Fr. The Canterbury Tales. **CP-ChauG**

Chaucer's Wishes for his 'Troilus'. Geoffrey Chaucer. See Go, Little Book ("Go, litel book, go litel myn tragedy").

Chaucer's Wordes unto Adam, his Owne Scriveyn. Geoffrey Chaucer. **CP-ChauG**

Che. Derek Walcott. **CP-WalcD**

Che Di Lor Suona Su Nella Tua Vita. Louis Zukofsky. **CP-ZukLS**

Che fai lontan da me. Sapessi Pure! Christina Georgina Rossetti. Fr. Il Rosseggiar Dell'Oriente Canzoniere. **CP-RosC3**

Che Farò; Senza Euridice. Randall Jarrell. **CP-JarrR**

Che Ti darò Gesù Signor mio buono? Oh Forza Irresistibile Dell'umile Preghiera. Christina Georgina Rossetti. *Fr.* Il Rosseggiar Dell'Oriente Canzoniere. **CP-RosC3**

Cheap Blue. Carl Sandburg. **CP-SandC**

Cheap little rhymes. Sliver. Langston Hughes. **SP-HughL**

Cheap Rent. Carl Sandburg. **CP-SandC**

Chearful sage, when solemn dictatees fail. Horace. *See* 2.6: "This was the summit of my views."

Cheat of Cupid; or, The Ungentle Guest, The. Robert Herrick. **CP-HerrR**

Checkers, checkmate and checkerboard. Louis Zukofsky. *Fr.* 29 Songs. **CP-ZukLS**

Checklist. Stephen Dunn. **SP-DunnS**

Cheered with this hope, to Paris I returned. William Wordsworth. **EnRP,** book 10, *ll.* 48–480, *abr*; *Fr.* Residence in France and French Revolution. *Fr.* The Prelude; Growth of a Poet's Mind [1850 vers.]. **CP-WorW3**

Cheerfu' supper done, wi' serious face, The. Robert Burns. **WGRP** *Fr.* The Cotter's Saturday Night [Inscribed to Robert Aiken [*or* R. A****], Esq.]. **CP-BurnR**

Cheerful soldiers, with new stores supplied, The. John Dryden. **SP-DrydJ** *Fr.* Annus Mirabilis.

Cheerful youth joined Coleridge on his walk, A. Keats at Highgate. Thom Gunn. **CP-GunnT**

Cheerfulness in lordly. Sing unto the Lord a New Song. Donald Davie. **CP-DavDo**

Cheerfulness Taught by Reason. Elizabeth Barrett Browning. **CP-BroEB**

Cheerfulness in Charitie: or, The Sweet Sacrifice. Robert Herrick. **CP-HerrR**

Cheery Beggar. Gerard Manley Hopkins. **CP-HopkG**

Chee$e. Thomas Merton. **CP-MertT**

Cheever's People. Erica Jong. **SP-JongE**

Cheiron. James McAuley.
    "I became a single sinew." **SP-McAuJ**
    "To learn those powers, I surrendered." **SP-McAuJ**
    "When I was a Curragh stableboy." **SP-McAuJ**
    "Young broke ribs and thighs, holding, The." **SP-McAuJ**

Chekhov on Sakhalin. Seamus Heaney. **SP-HeanS**

Cheliuskin. Edwin Rolfe. **CP-RolfE**

Chelsea Girls. "Lou Reed." **SP-ReedL**

Chelsea Hotel. Leonard Cohen. **CP-CoheL**

Chelsea May. Jim Carroll. **SP-CarrJ**

Cheltenham. Sir John Betjeman. **CP-BetjJ**

Chemical conviction, The. Emily Dickinson. **CP-DickE**

Chemicals ripen the citrus. In California. Donald Davie. **CP-DavDo**

Chemin de Fer. Elizabeth Bishop. **CP-BishE**

Chemist of love, The. Hafiz, *tr.* by Ralph Waldo Emerson. **CP-EmerR** *Fr.* Odes.

Chemistry. Al Young. **CP-YounA**

Chenille. James Dickey. **CP-DickJ**

Cheops, to sail eternity. Ship in the Tomb. Archibald MacLeish. **CP-MacLA**

Cher Maître: / Neither my explication. Letter to William Frohock. Daniel Gerard Hoffman. **SP-HoffD**

Chérie / the very,picturesque,last Day. Edward Estlin Cummings. **CP-CummE**

Cherish the Ladies. Paul Muldoon. **SP-MuldP**

Cherish you then the hope I shall forget. Edna St. Vincent Millay. **CP-MillE**

Cherishing that is speechless, The. Emily Dickinson. **SP-DickE**

Cherrie-Ripe. Robert Herrick. **CP-HerrR**

Cherrie-Ripe, Ripe, Ripe, I cry. Cherrie-Ripe. Robert Herrick. **CP-HerrR**

Cherries. Stephen Berg. **SP-BergS**

Cherries. Robert Browning. **CP-BroR2**

Cherries. Pablo Neruda, *tr. fr. Spanish by* Ben Belitt. **SP-NeruP**

Cherry. Jenny Joseph. *Fr.* Derivations. **SP-JoseJ**

Cherry and I were going up the clubhouse elevator. Last-Minute Change of Plans. Ron Koertge. **SP-KoerR**

Cherry Blossoms at Evening. William Carlos Williams. **CP-WilW2**

Cherry-colored picture hat, A. Hats. James Schuyler. **CP-SchuJ**

Cherry Orchards. Leonard Cohen. **CP-CoheL**

Cherry-Pit. Robert Herrick. **CP-HerrR**

Cherry red chrome dazzle, A. Craft. John Ciardi. **SP-CiarJ**

Cherry-red her mouth was. Eleanor. Christina Georgina Rossetti. **CP-RosC3**

Cherry Ripe. Donald Davie. **CP-DavDo**

Cherry Robbers. David Herbert Lawrence. **CP-LawrD**

Cherry Robbers. Richardson Pack. **SP-PackR**

Cherry Saplings. William DeWitt Snodgrass. **SP-SnodW**

Cherry Tree, The. Thom Gunn. **CP-GunnT**

Cherry Tree, The. Howard Nemerov. **CP-NemeH**

Cherry Trees, The. Walter de la Mare. **CP-DeLaW**

Cherrylog Road. James Dickey. **CP-DickJ**

Cherub, The. Ogden Nash. **CP-NashO**

Cheshire. Donald Davie. **CP-DavDo**

Chess. Louis MacNeice. **CP-MacNL**

Chester. Paul Muldoon. *Fr.* 7, Middagh Street. **SP-MuldP**

Chester. Shel Silverstein. **SP-SilS2**

Chestnut and beech / sycamore and willow. Lyric. John Hewitt. **CP-HewiJ**

Chestnut Avenue: at Alton House, The. Charles Tomlinson. **CP-TomlC**

Chestnut casts his flambeaux, and the flowers, The. Alfred Edward Housman. **CP-HousA**

Chestnut Orchard. Louise McNeill. **SP-McNeL**

Cheval-Glass, The. Thomas Hardy. **CP-HardT**

Cheval-glass is empty, The. Montage. Charles Tomlinson. **CP-TomlC**

Cheveril cries out, my verses libels are. On Cheveril. Ben Jonson. **CP-JonsB**

Cheville. "Hugh MacDiarmid." **SP-MacDH**

Chewing [of] the Cud, The. Robert Herrick. **CP-HerrR**

Chez Jane. Frank O'Hara. **SP-OharF**

Chez Macadam. Gilbert Sorrentino. **SP-SorrG**

Chi Hsing Tzu was a trainer of fighting cocks. The Fighting Cock. Chuang Tzu, *tr. fr. Chinese by* Thomas Merton. **CP-MertT**

Chiami il mio core / Crudele, altero. A Tirsi. Christina Georgina Rossetti. **CP-RosC3**

Chiami il mio core / Crudele, altero. Amore E Dovere. Christina Georgina Rossetti. **CP-RosC3**

Chic Freedom's Reflection. Alice Walker. **CP-WalkA**

Chicago. Charles Bukowski. **SP-BukC1**

Chicago. Robert Creeley. **CP-CreeR**

Chicago. John Greenleaf Whittier. **CP-WhitJ**

Chicago Airport / O'Hare, The. Illegal Aliens. Grace Paley. **CP-PaleG**

Chicago Boy Baby. Carl Sandburg. **CP-SandC**

Chicago Defender Sends a Man to Little Rock, The. Gwendolyn Brooks. **SP-BrooG**

Chicago English Afternoon. Ted Berrigan. **SP-BerrT**

Chicago Morning. Ted Berrigan. **SP-BerrT**

Chicago Poet. Carl Sandburg. **CP-SandC**

Chicago seems all fox and swine. Carl Sandburg. *Fr.* The People, Yes. **CP-SandC**

Chicago to Salt Lake by Air. Allen Ginsberg. **CP-GinsA**

Chicago Train, The. Louise Glück. **SP-GlücL**

Chicago's avenues, as white as Poland. Derek Walcott. **CP-WalcD** *Fr.* Midsummer.

Chickadee. Brendan Galvin. **SP-GalvB**

Chicken. How shall I tell you what it is. A Presentation of Two Birds to My Son. James Wright. **CP-WrigJ**

Chicken-Licken. Maya Angelou. **SP-AngeM**

Chicken, she chided early, should not wait. Sunday Chicken. Gwendolyn Brooks. *Fr.* Notes from the Childhood and the Girlhood. **SP-BrooG**

Chicken Unlimited. Peter Meinke. **SP-MeinP**

Chicken Without a Head, The. Charles Simic. **SP-SimiC**

Chicks. Carl Sandburg. **CP-SandC**

Chicks in the egg picks at the shell, cracks open one oval world, and, The. Chicks. Carl Sandburg. **CP-SandC**

Chicory. Hayden Carruth. **CP-CarHS**

Chicory. Louis Zukofsky. **CP-ZukLS**

Chicory and Daisies. William Carlos Williams. **CP-WilW1**

Chiddingly, pronounced. Sussex. Donald Davie. **CP-DavDo**

Chide not; let me breathe a little. Death's Chill Between. Christina Georgina Rossetti. **CP-RosC3**

Chief is silent, The. Urn with a Political Profile. Pablo Antonio Cuadra, *tr. fr. Spanish by* Thomas Merton. **CP-MertT**

Chief Mystery, The. David Herbert Lawrence. **CP-LawrD**

Chief of all. Samson's Complaint. John Milton. **NOSC** *Fr.* Samson Agonistes.

Chief of organic numbers! On Seeing a Lock of Milton's Hair. John Keats. **CP-KeatJ**

Chief of our aunts—not only I. To Auntie. Robert Louis Stevenson. **CP-StevR**

Chief of the civil administration, The. Pilate. Donald Davie. **CP-DavDo**

Chief Standing Water. Charles Tomlinson. **CP-TomlC**

Chiefest among Ten Thousand, The. Christina Georgina Rossetti. **CP-RosC2**

Chiefest among Ten Thousand, The. Christina Georgina Rossetti. *See* I Will Lift Up Mine Eyes unto the Hills.

Chiefly I prize this loss of patience, deep. Among Ourselves and with All Nations. Kenneth Patchen. **CP-PatcK**

Chieftain Iffucan of Azcan in caftan. Bantams in Pine-Woods. Wallace Stevens. **CP-StevW**

Chiesa E Signore. Christina Georgina Rossetti. **CP-RosC3**

Chilam Balam. Thomas Merton. *Fr.* South. *Fr.* The Geography of Lograire. **CP-MertT**

Child, The. Hayden Carruth. *Fr.* Contra Mortem. **CP-CarHL**

Child, The. Richard Eberhart. **CP-EberR**

Child, The. Donald Hall. **CP-HallD**

Child, The, *tr. fr. the German of* Rilke. Randall Jarrell. **CP-JarrR**

Child. Sylvia Plath. **CP-PlatS**

Child. Carl Sandburg. **CP-SandC**

Child (a boy) bouncing, A. To. William Carlos Williams. **CP-WilW1**

Child among his powers gathering, The. Another Day (Child among his powers). Muriel Rukeyser. **CP-RukeM**

Child and girl each morning summer winter or dismay. Of Flesh and Bone. Isabella Gardner. **CP-GardI**

Child and Mother. Muriel Rukeyser. **CP-RukeM**

Child and the Sage, The. Thomas Hardy. **CP-HardT**

Child and the Soldier, The. David Herbert Lawrence. *Fr.* Bits. **CP-LawrD**

Child and Vegetables. William Carlos Williams. **CP-WilW1**

Child Asleep, A. Elizabeth Barrett Browning. **CP-BroEB**

Child Asleep, A. Walter de la Mare. **CP-DeLaW**

Child Asleep, The. Muriel Rukeyser. *Fr.* Night-Music. **CP-RukeM**

Child Bearers, The. Anne Sexton. **CP-SextA**

Child Called *Morte*, A. Siv Cedering Fox. **SP-CedeS**

Child comes sometimes with his mother's needle, The. The Voyage of the Needle. James Dickey. **CP-DickJ**

Child crying in the night, A. Charles Simic. **SP-SimiC**

Child Dead in Old Seas. Maya Angelou. **SP-AngeM**

Child dear to my eye, God's blessing is on thy service. Vicar's Son. David Herbert Lawrence. *Fr.* Bits. **CP-LawrD**

Child disturbs our view, The. Tow-head bent, she. Three Valentines to the Wide World. Mona Van Duyn. **SP-VanDM**

Child draws the outline of a body, A. Portrait. Louise Glück. **SP-GlücL**

Child dreaming along a crowded street, The. The Sweet-Shop Round The Corner. Robert Ranke Graves. **CP-GravR**

Child Face. Carl Sandburg. **CP-SandC**

Child Growing Up with the Sun, A. Jim Carroll. **SP-CarrJ**

Child Harold. John Clare.
  Ballad: "Summer morning is risen." **SP-ClarJ**
  Song: "Dying gales of sweet even." **SP-ClarJ**
  Song: "Say What Is Love—To Live In Vain." **SP-ClarJ**

Child, I have counted. Trinacria. Basil Bunting. **CP-BuntB**

Child, I thought summer would solve all things, A. Poem Influenced By John Davenport and Cervantes. Malcolm Lowry. **CP-LowrM**

Child Ill, A. Sir John Betjeman. **CP-BetjJ**

Child in a little boat. Kathleen Jessie Raine. *Fr.* Three Poems of Incarnation. **CP-RainK**

Child in the Great Wood. Muriel Rukeyser. **CP-RukeM**

Child in the Sabbath peace, there, A. A Sunday. Walter de la Mare. **CP-DeLaW**

Child in the womb. How to Sleep. Philip Larkin. **CP-LarkP**

Child is born, they cry, a child, A. Christmas. Stevie Smith. **CP-SmitS**

Child is Father to the Man, The. Gerard Manley Hopkins. **FaBoCo; NOBVV; NTP** *Fr.* A Trio of Triolets. **CP-HopkG** (Triolet.) **NOBL**

Child Is Father to the Man, But with More Authority, The. Ogden Nash. **CP-NashO**

Child is sleeping in His golden house, The. Song for the Blessed Sacrament. Thomas Merton. **CP-MertT**

Child is speaking to the father, The. On the Subway Station. Grace Paley. **CP-PaleG**

Child like mustard seed, The. War-Baby. David Herbert Lawrence. **CP-LawrD**

Child looked in the pool, A. Here Lies Treasure: Here Be Monsters. Jenny Joseph. **SP-JoseJ**

Child Margaret. Carl Sandburg. **CP-SandC**

Child Margaret begins to write numbers on a Saturday morning, the, The. Child Margaret. Carl Sandburg. **CP-SandC**

Child may find no words for its sorrow, A. Malcolm Lowry. **CP-LowrM**

Child Moon. Carl Sandburg. **CP-SandC**

Child most infantine, A. A Child of Twelve. Percy Bysshe Shelley. **GN** *Fr.* The Revolt of Islam. **CP-ShelP**

Child[e] My Choice [*or* Choyse], A. Robert Southwell. **CP-SoutR**

Child Next Door, The. Robert Penn Warren. *Fr.* To a Little Girl, One Year Old, in a Ruined Fortress. **SP-WarrR**

Child of a line accurst / And old as Troy. Bon Voyage. Edwin Arlington Robinson. **CP-RobiE**

Child of Delight! with sunbright hair. R.C. Emily Brontë. *Fr.* The Two Children. **CP-BronE**

Child of God Longing To See Him Beloved, A. Jeanne Marie Bouvier de la Motte-Guyon, *tr. fr. French by* William Cowper. **CP-CowpW**

Child of loud-throated War! the mountain Stream. Address to Kilchurn Castle, upon Loch Awe. William Wordsworth. **CP-WorW1**

Child of Mary Queen of Scots, The. James I. Rudyard Kipling. **CP-KiplR**

Child of my winter, born. Heart's Needle. William DeWitt Snodgrass. **SP-SnodW**

Child of My Winter Born. William DeWitt Snodgrass. **MoAmPo** *Fr.* Heart's Needle. **SP-SnodW**

Child of patient industry. Invitation to the Bee. Charlotte Smith. **CP-SmitC**

Child of ten, no more, A. James McAuley. *Fr.* The Autobiography of the Impotent Man. **SP-McAuJ**

Child of the Aztec gods. Dusty Doors. Carl Sandburg. **CP-SandC**

Child of the clouds! remote from every taint. William Wordsworth. *Fr.* The River Duddon [A Series of Sonnets]. **CP-WorW2**

Child of the Moon. Pablo Neruda, *tr. fr. Spanish by* Ben Belitt. **SP-NeruP**

Child of the Nineties considers with laughter, The. JULY (*Archery*). Rudyard Kipling. *Fr.* Verses on Games. **CP-KiplR**

Child of the pure unclouded brow. Dedication. "Lewis Carroll." **CP-CarrL** *Fr.* Through the Looking-Glass.

Child of the Romans. Carl Sandburg. **CP-SandC**

Child of the root, among your apples and forests. Muriel Rukeyser. **CP-RukeM**

Child of the sunlight in the tower room. Hero with Girl and Gorgon. Howard Nemerov. **CP-NemeH**

Child of Twelve, A. Percy Bysshe Shelley. **GN** *Fr.* The Revolt of Islam. **CP-ShelP**

Child on Top of a Greenhouse. Theodore Roethke. **CP-RoetT**

Child played being a gravedigger, A. The Game. Charles Simic. **SP-SimiC**

Child Poems. Hilda Doolittle. **CP-DoolH**
  Dedication: "When everything was over."
  Dream.
  Grown Up.
  If Your Eyes Had Been Blue.
  No.
  Socratic. **HoPM**

Child Psychology. Charles Kenneth Williams. **SP-WillC**

Child riding the stormy mane of noon, A. Are You Born? / II. Muriel Rukeyser. **CP-RukeM**

Child said *What is the grass?*, A. Walt Whitman. **AA; BLPL; NoP; SAmP** *Fr.* Song of Myself. **CP-WhitW**
  (Grass.) **BLPL; ImPo**

Child said: "Pretty bird, The". Three Moments. Christina Georgina Rossetti. **CP-RosC3**

Child saw the bombers skate like stones across the fields, The. Come to the Stone. Randall Jarrell. **CP-JarrR**

Child should always say what's true, A. Whole Duty of Children. Robert Louis Stevenson. **CP-StevR**

Child-Songs. John Greenleaf Whittier. **CP-WhitJ**

Child / Is bathing in the mud, The. Three Generations. K'o Chia Tsang, *tr. fr. Chinese by* William Carlos Williams *with* David Rafael Wang. **CP-WilW2**

Child, the Chair, the Leaf, The. John Hewitt. **CP-HewiJ**

Child, the current of your breath is six days long. Unknown Girl in the Maternity Ward. Anne Sexton. **CP-SextA**

Child, the poems, the child, the poems, the journeys, The. Gift. Muriel Rukeyser. **CP-RukeM**

Child, the temptation please resist. If Fun Is Fun, Isn't That Enough? Ogden Nash. **CP-NashO**

Child wakes in the morning to enter a country, The. Muriel Rukeyser. **CP-RukeM**

Child, were I king, I'd yield my royal rule. From Victor Hugo. Thomas Hardy. **CP-HardT**

Child, what can those old men bring you? Let Them Ask Your Pardon. Carl Sandburg. **CP-SandC**

Child: What is the destination of the sunlight's. Mother & Child. Anne Waldman. **SP-WaldA**

Child with a chip of mirror in his eye. The Snow Queen. Adrienne Rich. **CP-RicAE; SP-RicA2**

Child with Veteran. Robert Ranke Graves. **CP-GravR**

Childe Harold to the Round Tower Came. William Carlos Williams. **CP-WilW2**

Childe Harold's Farewell to England. Byron. **OHFP** *Fr.* Childe Harold's Pilgrimage. **CP-Byron**

Childe Harold's Pilgrimage. Byron. **CP-Byron**

    Canto the Fourth.

      "Egeria! sweet creation of some heart." **NOBRP**

      "Roll on, thou deepand dark blue ocean—roll!" **NOBRP**

      "What from this barren being do we reap?" **FHYEP; NOBRP**

    Childe Harold's Farewell to England. **OHFP**

      "Come, blue-eyed maid of heaven!—but thou, alas!" **NOBRP**

    Dying Gladiator, The. **NOBE**

    Fame. **FiP**

    "He that has sail'd upon the dark blue sea." **MOS**

    "He who, grown aged in this world of woe." **EPCY**

    "I stood in Venice on the Bridge of Sighs." **EnRP; FaBoPP; OBTV**

      (On the Bridge of Sighs.) **FaBoPP**

    "Is thy face like thy mother's, my fair child!" **ChER; EnRP; OAEL-2**

    "In my youth's summer I did sing of One." **NOBRP**

    "Lake Leman woos me with its crystal face." **NOBRP**

    "Sky is changed!—and such a change! Oh night, The." **NOBRP**

    "There is a very life in our despair." **NOBRP**

    It Is the Hush of Night. **LiTB; MeMBP**

    Lake Leman ("Clear, placid Leman! thy contrasted lake"). **OBNC**

    "Lake Leman woos me with its crystal face." **InPS; PoEL-4**

      (Lake Leman.) **PoEL-4**

    Ocean, The. **PoEL-4**

      (By the Deep Sea.) **OBNC**

    "And I have loved thee, Ocean! and my joy." **OxBoS**

    "Roll on, thou deep and dark blue ocean—roll!" **FaPON; GN; OxBoS; UV; WGRP**

      (Roll On, Thou Deep and Dark Blue Ocean.) **FaPON**

      (To the Ocean.) **GN; WGRP**

    "There is a pleasure in the pathless woods." **BLPL; ChTr; FaBV; FaBoBe; FiP; GGP; ImPo; LiTB; MOS; MeMBP; OHFP; OXAEP-2; OxBoS; TFi; TrGrPo; WBLP**

      (Apostrophe to the Ocean.) **OHFP; WBLP**

      (Deep and Dark Blue Ocean.) **ChTr**

      (Ocean, The.) **FaBV; MeMBP; TFi; TrGrPo**

      (Roll On, Thou Deep and Dark Blue Ocean.) **FiP**

      (Sea, The.) **BLPL; FaBoBe; GGP; ImPo; LiTB**

    "Thou glorious mirror, where the Almighty's form." **OxBoS**

    "Oh love! no habitant of earth thou art." **CBLP; OBNC**

      (Fatal Spell, The.) **OBNC**

    "Oh, thou! in Hellas deemed of heavenly birth." **NAEL-2**

    "On, on the vessel flies, the land is gone." **OBTV**

    "Once more upon the waters! yet once more!" **FHYEP**

    Poet and the World, The. **SeCePo**

    Rome by Metella's Tomb. **FaBoPP**

    "Stop! for thy tread is on an empire's dust!" **InPS**

    "There was a sound of revelry by night." **BeLS; EBEV; EBEvV; FaBV; FaBoBe; FaBoCh; FaBoEH; FaBoEn; FaFP; FiP; GN; HBV; NOBE; OBNC; OBWP; OXAEP-2; OtMeF; TFi; TrGrPo; TreF; WBLP; WaaP**

      (Battle of Waterloo, The.) **FaFP; TreF**

      (Eve of Waterloo, The.) **BeLS; EBEvV; FaBV; FaBoBe; FaBoCh; FaBoEn; HBV; NOBE; OBNC; OtMeF**

      (Night before the Battle of Waterloo, The.) **WBLP**

      (Night before Waterloo, The.) **GN**

      (There Was a Sound of Revelry by Night.) **TFi**

      (Waterloo.) **FiP; TrGrPo; WaaP**

    To Eddleston. **PeHV**

    To Ianthe.

      (Dedication: To Ianthe.) **FaBoEn; OBNC**

    Wandering Outlaw, The. **FiP**

    "Where'er we tread 'tis haunted, holy ground." **GrIP**

Childe Horvald to the Dark Tower Came. John Ciardi. **SP-CiarJ**

Childe Roland to the Dark Tower Came. Robert Browning. **CP-BroR1**

Childe Rolandine. Stevie Smith. **CP-SmitS**

Childhood, *ad. fr. the German of* Rilke. Randall Jarrell. **CP-JarrR**

Childhood. Kathleen Jessie Raine. **SP-RainK**

Childhood. Rainer Maria Rilke, *tr. fr. German by* Howard Nemerov. **CP-NemeH**

Childhood among the Ferns. Thomas Hardy. **CP-HardT**

Childhood Is the Kingdom Where Nobody Dies. Edna St. Vincent Millay. **CP-MillE**

Childhood Memory. Kathleen Jessie Raine. **SP-RainK**

Childhood of Parmenides, The. Charles Simic. **SP-SimiC**

Childhood of the Hero. Kenneth Patchen. **CP-PatcK**

Childhood's Body. Charles Wright. **SP-WrigC**

Childish God of Love did sweare, The. Love Conquer'd. Richard Lovelace. **CP-LoveR**

Childish Prank, A. Ted Hughes. **SP-HughT**

Childish Recollections. Byron. **CP-Byron**

Childless Father, The. William Wordsworth. **CP-WorW1**

Childless Woman. Sylvia Plath. **CP-PlatS**

Childlessness. James Merrill. **SP-MerrJ**

    ("Weather of this winter night, my dream-wife, The.") **SP-MerrJ**

Children, The. Rudyard Kipling. **CP-KiplR**

Children, The. Anne Sexton. **CP-SextA**

Children, The. William Carlos Williams. **CP-WilW2**

Children and Sir Nameless, The. Thomas Hardy. **CP-HardT**

Children are all crying in their pens, The. The Children. Anne Sexton. **CP-SextA**

Children are dumb to say how hot the day is. The Cool Web. Robert Ranke Graves. **CP-GravR**

Children Are Game. Isabella Gardner. **CP-GardI**

Children are healthy, The. Note to Grandparents. Grace Paley. **CP-PaleG**

Children are off somewhere, The. Lights I Have Seen Before. Philip Levine. **SP-LeviP**

Children aren't happy with nothing to ignore. The Parent. Ogden Nash. **CP-NashO**

Children at play in a field. Stanley Jasspon Kunitz. *Fr.* Signs and Portents. **CP-KuniS**

Children begin at green dawn nimbly to build. The Altars in the Street. Denise Levertov. **CP-LeveD**

Children brave by day have strange fears at night. *also appears in* The Lighthouse Invites the Storm, *sl. diff. vers.* Malcolm Lowry. *Fr.* The Moon in Scandinavia. **CP-LowrM**

Children, come to my knee. News. Randall Jarrell. **CP-JarrR**

Children dear, was it yesterday. Matthew Arnold. **BoTP** *Fr.* The Forsaken Merman. **SP-ArnoM**

Children do not always mean. Christmas Carols. Margaret Atwood. **SP-AtwM2**

Children go forward with their little satchels, The. The School Children. Louise Glück. **SP-GlücL**

Children, I come back today. The Negro Mother. Langston Hughes. **SP-HughL**

Children, I crave your kind forbearance. A Child's Guide to Parents. Ogden Nash. **CP-NashO**

Children I told you I tell you our sun was a hail of gold! Summers Ago. Isabella Gardner. **CP-GardI**

Children, if you dare to think. Warning to Children. Robert Ranke Graves. **CP-GravR**

Children in a Walled Garden. Steve Griffiths. **SP-GrifS**

Children in Exile. James Fenton. **SP-FentJ**

Children in the street play hard, The. Warning: Children at Play. Howard Nemerov. **CP-NemeH**

Children like the block, The. Margaret Atwood. *Fr.* The Circle Game. **SP-AtwM1**

Children nurs'd woods tilled rock. Yaupon. Louis Zukofsky. **CP-ZukLS**

Children of Darkness. Robert Ranke Graves. **CP-GravR**

Children of Darkness. Richard Wilbur. **CP-WilbR**

Children of large nervous furs. Newscast. Thomas Merton. *Fr.* Cables to the Ace. **CP-MertT**

Children of my happier prime. Immolated. Herman Melville. **SP-MelvH**

Children of Stare, The. Walter de la Mare. **CP-DeLaW**

Children of the Cross, The. Stevie Smith. **CP-SmitS**

Children of the early / Countryside. Penobscot. George Oppen. **CP-OppeG**

Children of the future Age. A Little Girl Lost. William Blake. **CP-BlakW** *Fr.* Songs of Experience.

Children of the Poor, The. Gwendolyn Brooks. **SP-BrooG**, *sect.* I, *pt.* 1-5; *Fr.* The Womanhood.

    "And shall I prime my children, pray, to pray?" **SP-BrooG**

    "First fight. Then fiddle. Ply the slipping string." **SP-BrooG**

    "People who have no children can be hard." **SP-BrooG**

    "What shall I give my children? who are poor?" **SP-BrooG**

    "When my dears die, the festival-colored brightness." **SP-BrooG**

Children on the lawn / joined hand to hand, The. Margaret Atwood. *Fr.* The Circle Game. **SP-AtwM1**

Children on the lawn / joined hand to hand, The. The Circle Game. Margaret Atwood. **SP-AtwM1**

Children picking up our bones. A Postcard from the Volcano. Wallace Stevens. **CP-StevW**

Children play on into. Hide and Seek. Thom Gunn. **CP-GunnT**

Children remembering sadness grieve, they grieve. Facing Sentencing. Muriel Rukeyser. **CP-RukeM**

Children Selecting Books in a Library. Randall Jarrell. **CP-JarrR; SP-JarrR**

Children set fires in ashbarrels. Galway Kinnell. **NaP** *Fr.* The Avenue Bearing the Initial of Christ into the New World. **SP-KinnG**

Children Singing in School. David Herbert Lawrence. **CP-LawrD**

Children take longer to die. A Snapshot of Uig in Montana. Richard Hugo. **CP-HugoR**

Children, the Sandbar, That Summer. Muriel Rukeyser. **CP-RukeM**

Children the time of angry fathers. A Round and a Hope for Smithgirls. Thomas Merton. **CP-MertT**

Children walking with their grandmothers. The Nature of This City. Grace Paley. **CP-PaleG**

Children warned against the Mandrake—. Mayapple Hill. Louise McNeill. **SP-McNeL**

Children we have not borne. To My Daughter the Junkie on a Train. Audre Lorde. **SP-LordA**

Children who explored the brook and found, The. To Walter de la Mare. Thomas Stearns Eliot. **CP-ElioT**

Children who paddle where the ocean bed shelves steeply. Advice to Young Children. Stevie Smith. **CP-SmitS**

Children, you are very little. Good and Bad Children. Robert Louis Stevenson. **CP-StevR**

Children's Arms. Randall Jarrell. *Fr.* The Lost World. **CP-JarrR; SP-JarrR**

Children's Crusade, The. Philip Levine. **SP-LeviP**

Children's eyes were like lakes of the sea, The. The Triumph of Education. Howard Nemerov. **CP-NemeH**

Children's Games. Louis MacNeice. **CP-MacNL**

Children's Hour, The. Henry Wadsworth Longfellow. **SP-LongH**

Children's Orchard, The. Muriel Rukeyser. **CP-RukeM**

Children's Party. Ogden Nash. **CP-NashO**

Children's Rhymes. Langston Hughes. **SP-HughL**

Children's voices in the orchard. New Hampshire. Thomas Stearns Eliot. **FaBoCh; GTBS-6; GTBS-P; NoAM; WeW** *Fr.* Landscapes. **CP-ElioT**

Child's Amaze, A. Walt Whitman. **CP-WhitW**

Child's Being, The. Hayden Carruth. *Fr.* Contra Mortem. **CP-CarHL**

Child's Evening Prayer, A. Samuel Taylor Coleridge. **CP-ColeS**

Child's faith is new, The. Emily Dickinson. **CP-DickE**

Child's Garden, A. Donald Hall. **CP-HallD**

Child's Garden, A, *parody of* Robert Louis Stevenson. Rudyard Kipling. **CP-KiplR** *Fr.* The Muse among the Motors.

Child's Grave at Florence, A. Elizabeth Barrett Browning. **CP-BroEB**

Child's Guide to Parents, A. Ogden Nash. **CP-NashO**

Child's Guide to Philosophy, A. Phoebe Hesketh. **SP-HeskP**

Child's Japan, A. May Sarton. **CP-SartM**

Child's Park Stones. Sylvia Plath. **CP-PlatS**

Child's Prayer, A. George Meredith. **CP-MerG2**

Child's Song. Robert Lowell. **SP-LoweR**

Child's song sounds behind the mud walls, A. Air. Alfonso Cortes, *tr. fr. Spanish by* Thomas Merton. **CP-MertT**

Child's Talk in April. Christina Georgina Rossetti. **CP-RosC1**

Child's Thought of God, A. Elizabeth Barrett Browning. **CP-BroEB**

Child's wonder, The. The Child Moon. Carl Sandburg. **CP-SandC**

Chile, these steps is hard to climb. Dime. Langston Hughes. **SP-HughL**

Chill, A. Christina Georgina Rossetti. **CP-RosC1**

Chill and mirk is the nightly blast. Stanzas. Byron. **CP-Byron**

Chill blank world. Yet over the utmost sea, A. Christina Georgina Rossetti. **CP-RosC2**

Chill to the marrow. Sparrow. Thom Gunn. **CP-GunnT** *Fr.* Three Songs.

Chill waves whiten in the sharp North-east, The. Written at Weymouth in Winter. Charlotte Smith. **CP-SmitC**

Chill wind sweeps the high places, A. Blackstudies. Audre Lorde. **SP-LordA**

Chilled by the Present, its gloom and its noise. Wystan Hugh Auden. **PPP** *Fr.* Sonnets from China. **CP-AudeW**

Chilled cricket calls rasp dwindling in the night. It Comes to This. Robert Pack. **SP-PackR**

Chillianwallah. George Meredith. **CP-MerG2**

Chillicothe. Carl Sandburg. **CP-SandC**

Chilliwack. Malcolm Lowry. **CP-LowrM**

Chilly Night, A. Christina Georgina Rossetti. **CP-RosC3**

Chilly Peace infests the Grass, A. Emily Dickinson. **CP-DickE**

Chilly,murky night, A. Edward Estlin Cummings. **CP-CummE**

Chil's Song. Rudyard Kipling. **CP-KiplR** *Fr.* Red Dog. *Fr.* The Second Jungle Book.

Chimaera. David Herbert Lawrence. **CP-LawrD**

Chimaeras, The. Wystan Hugh Auden. **CP-AudeW**

Chime of the bells, and the church clock striking eight, The. The Little Town at Evening. David Herbert Lawrence. **CP-LawrD**

Chimes, The. Thomas Hardy. **CP-HardT**

Chimes called midnight, just at interlune, The. Aquae Sulis. Thomas Hardy. **CP-HardT**

Chimes for Yahya. James Merrill. **SP-MerrJ**

Chimes of Freedom. "Bob Dylan." **CP-DylaB**

Chimes Play "Life's a Bumper!" The. Thomas Hardy. **CP-HardT**

Chiming at Trwyn Du, The. Steve Griffiths. **SP-GrifS**

Chimney, breathing a little smoke, A. February. James Schuyler. **CP-SchuJ**

Chimney Sweeper, The ("A little black thing among the snow"). William Blake. **CP-BlakW** *Fr.* Songs of Experience.

Chimney Sweeper, The ("When my mother died I was very young"). William Blake. **CH; EnRP; FF; FHYEP; FaBoPV; HelP; HoFi; InPK; LAuP; NAEL-2; NAWM-2; NOEC; OAEL-2; OXAEP-2; OxBChV; PAI; PPP; PPoe; PoE; Poetr; SCGP; SaC; SoSe; TEP; TFi** *Fr.* Songs of Innocence. **CP-BlakW**

China-going P. & O.'s. Rudyard Kipling. **CP-KiplR** *Fr.* The Crab That Played with the Sea. *Fr.* Just-So Stories.

China Journal. Charles Wright. **SP-WrigC**

Chinaberries / Change from green to rosy. In, The. Charles Henri Ford. **SP-FordC** *Fr.* Emblems of Arachne.

Chinaman, The. Christina Georgina Rossetti. **CP-RosC3**

Chinaman said don't take the hardware, The. Hello, Willie Shoemaker. Charles Bukowski. **SP-BukC2**

Chinese Benevolent Association's Annual Christmas Party, The. Toy Trucks and Fried Rice. John Yau. **SP-YauJo**

Chinese Fluteplayer. John Hewitt. **CP-HewiJ**

Chinese Journal. Charles Wright. **SP-WrigC**

Chinese moon, / I knew it once, The. Dancing Pierrot. Al Young. **CP-YounA**

Chinese Nightingale. Ted Berrigan. **SP-BerrT**

Chinese Nightingale, The. Nicholas Vachel Lindsay. **CP-LindV**

Chinese Nightingale. William Carlos Williams. **CP-WilW1**

Chinese Poets. John Clellon Holmes. **SP-HolmJ**

Chinese Restaurant in Portrush, The. Derek Mahon. **SP-MahoD**

Chinese Tomb Guardians. Robert Bly. **SP-BlyR**

Chinese Toy, A. William Carlos Williams. **CP-WilW1**

Chinese vessels at anchor in the harbor. Calicut. Thomas Merton. *Fr.* East with Ibn Battuta. *Fr.* East. *Fr.* The Geography of Lograire. **CP-MertT**

Chink, The. Robert Ranke Graves. **CP-GravR**

Chinook. Paul Muldoon. **SP-MuldP**

Chipmunk, The. Ogden Nash. **CP-NashO**

Chipmunk chewing the Chippendale. Exit, Pursued by a Bear. Ogden Nash. **CP-NashO**

Chipmunk: slash with quick teeth. Dark Waters. William Everson. **SP-EverW**

Chipmunk's Day, The. Randall Jarrell. **CP-JarrR**

Chipping Away at Death. Stephen Dunn. **SP-DunnS** *Fr.* Sympathetic Magic.

Chips. Steve Griffiths. **SP-GrifS**

Chirico. Roy Fisher. **SP-FishR**

Chirico—and There are Blue and White. Marsden Hartley. **CP-HartM**

Chitter of chipmunk. Marsden Hartley. **CP-HartM**

Chivalry. George Meredith. **CP-MerG2**

Chladni strewed on glass the sand. Ralph Waldo Emerson. **CP-EmerR**

Chloe and the Roué. Ogden Nash. *Fr.* Fables Bullfinch Forgot. **CP-NashO**

Chloe behold! againe I bowe. To Chloe, Courting Her for His Friend. Richard Lovelace. **CP-LoveR**

Chloe to Daphnis in Hyde Park. Wystan Hugh Auden. **CP-AudWJ**

Chloë's Poem. John Updike. **CP-UpdiJ**

Chloride of Lime and Charcoal. Louis Zukofsky. **CP-ZukLS**

"Homer's Argos hearing."

"There when the water was not potable."

"How sweet is the sun, is the sun."

"There when the water was not potable."

"Zinnias you look so much like Gentiles."

W.

Chloridia. Ben Jonson.

"Come forth, come forth, the gentle Spring." **CP-JonsB**

Chocorua to Its Neighbor. Wallace Stevens. **CP-StevW**

Choice, A. Paul Laurence Dunbar. **CP-DunbP**

Choice, The. Rudyard Kipling. **CP-KiplR**

Choice. David Herbert Lawrence. **CP-LawrD**

Choice, The. Frederick Morgan. **SP-MorgF**

Choice, The. William Butler Yeats. **CP-YeatW**

Choice of Evils. David Herbert Lawrence. **CP-LawrD**

Choice of Flowers, The. Steve Griffiths. **SP-GrifS**

Choice of Weapons, A. Stanley Jasspon Kunitz. **CP-KuniS**

Choice of you shuts up that peacock-fan. To My Wife. Philip Larkin. **CP-LarkP**

Choice proposed: ascends, the nervy conductor, The. Trophies. Muriel Rukeyser. **CP-RukeM**

Choices. Carl Sandburg. **CP-SandC**

Choir and Music of Solitude and Silence, The. Delmore Schwartz. **SP-SchwD**

Choir of bright beauties in spring did appear, A. The Lady's Song. John Dryden. **SP-DrydJ**

Choir of Day, The. William Blake. *See* Thou hearest the nightingale begin the song of spring.

Choir Singing, The. Grace Paley. **CP-PaleG**

Choirmaster's Burial, The. Thomas Hardy. **CP-HardT**

Choke cherry blossoms on the Back. On the Shore. Charles Olson. **CP-OlsoC**

Chokecherry. Louis Zukofsky. **CP-ZukLS**

Cholera. Rita Dove. **SP-DoveR**

Cholera Camp. Rudyard Kipling. **CP-KiplR**

Chomei at Toyama. Basil Bunting. **CP-BuntB**

Choose. Carl Sandburg. **CP-SandC**

Choose Flowers that have no Fang, Dear. Emily Dickinson. **SP-DickE**

Choose for the Best. Robert Herrick. **CP-HerrR**

Choose me your Valentine. To His Mistress[e]. Robert Herrick. **CP-HerrR**

Choose One From Among Them. Richard Shelton. **SP-ShelR**

Choose your own difference between surgery. Differences. John Ciardi. **SP-CiarJ**

Choosers, The. Stevie Smith. **CP-SmitS**

Choosing a Stone. John Haines. **SP-HainJ**

Chop-Cherry. Robert Herrick. **CP-HerrR**

Chop Chop. Jim Carroll. **SP-CarrJ**

Chopin Bukowski. Charles Bukowski. **SP-BukC1**

Choral Amphisbaena. John Yau. **SP-YauJo**

Choral: The Pink Church. William Carlos Williams. **CP-WilW2**

Chorale. Jenny Joseph. *Fr.* Life and Turgid Times of A. Citizen. **SP-JoseJ**

Chord. Langston Hughes. **SP-HughL**

Chords. Carl Sandburg. **CP-SandC**

Choric Song: "There is sweet music here that softer falls." Tennyson. *See* There is sweet music here that softer falls.

Choric Song of the Lotos-Eaters. Tennyson. *See* There is sweet music here that softer falls.

Choric Song of the Lotus-Eaters. Tennyson. *See* There is sweet music here that softer falls.

Choros Sequence. Hilda Doolittle. **CP-DoolH**

Choros Translations. Euripides, *tr. fr. Greek by* Hilda Doolittle ("H.D."). **CP-DoolH** *Fr.* Bacchae.

Chorus: "Give away her gowns." Edna St. Vincent Millay. *Fr.* Memorial to D. C. **CP-MillE**

Chorus: "Let the Priests of the Raven of dawn, no longer in deadly black." William Blake. *Fr.* The Marriage of Heaven and Hell. **CP-BlakW**

Chorus? / Words and silence, standing face to face. A Responsory. Thomas Merton. **CP-MertT**

Chorus (androgynous): "Find me". George Oppen. *Fr.* Of Being Numerous. **CP-OppeG**

Chorus for One Voice. Charles Simic. **SP-SimiC**

Chorus from "Hellas." Percy Bysshe Shelley. *See* The World's great age begins anew.

Chorus from "The Rock." Thomas Stearns Eliot. **LiTB** *Fr.* Choruses from "The Rock." **CP-ElioT**

Chorus of Athenians. Alexander Pope. *Fr.* Two Chorus's to the Tragedy of Brutus. **CP-PopeA**

Chorus of Furies. Basil Bunting. **CP-BuntB**

Chorus of Old Men in "Ægeus", The. Edwin Arlington Robinson. **CP-RobiE**

Chorus of Satyrs, Driving Their Goats. Euripides. **AWP** *Fr.* The Cyclops. **CP-ShelP**

Chorus of the Archangels, The. Johann Wolfgang von Goethe. *See* The Sun makes music as of old.

Chorus of the Pities. Thomas Hardy. **CP-HardT** *Fr.* The Dynasts.

Chorus of the Women of Chalkis. Euripides, *tr. by* Hilda Doolittle ("H.D."). **CP-DoolH** *Fr.* Iphigenia [*or* Iphigeneia] in Aulis.

Chorus of Troizenian Women. Euripides, *tr. by* Hilda Doolittle ("H.D."). **CP-DoolH** *Fr.* Hippolytus.

Chorus of Youths and Virgins. Alexander Pope. *Fr.* Two Chorus's to the Tragedy of Brutus. **CP-PopeA**

Chorus to the Gods. John Dryden. *See* All, All of a Piece Throughout.

Chorus: "To throw away the key and walk away." Wystan Hugh Auden. *See* To throw away the key and walk away.

Chorus: "World's great age begins anew, The." Percy Bysshe Shelley. *See* The World's great age begins anew.

Chorus: "Worlds on worlds are rolling ever." Percy Bysshe Shelley. *See* Worlds on worlds are rolling ever.

Choruses from "The Rock." Thomas Stearns Eliot. **CP-ElioT**

Chorus from "The Rock." **LiTB**

"Eagle soars in the summit of heaven, The." **OBMV**

"I journeyed to the suburbs, and there I was told." **UV**

"O Light Invisible, we praise Thee!" **ILwL; OxBoCh; TrPWD**

Chosen, The. Thomas Hardy. **CP-HardT**

Chosen, The. Daniel Gerard Hoffman. **SP-HoffD**

Chosen, The. Leonard Nathan. **SP-NathL**

Chosen, *fr.* A Woman Young and Old. William Butler Yeats. **CP-YeatW**

Chosun. James Fenton. **SP-FentJ**

Chrismus Is A-Comin'. Paul Laurence Dunbar. **CP-DunbP**

Chrismus on the Plantation. Paul Laurence Dunbar. **CP-DunbP**

Christ. Robert Herrick. **CP-HerrR**

Christ bids the dumbe tongue speake, it speakes; the sound. Mark 7; The Dumbe Healed, and the People Enjoyed Silence. Bible, *N.T.* **CP-CrasR**, *tr. by* Richard Crashaw; *Fr.* St. Mark.

Christ but they're few. Edward Estlin Cummings. **CP-CummE**

Christ but this earth goes over to the squall of time! The Sunset Piece. Archibald MacLeish. **CP-MacLA**

Christ! Christ! Christ! that the world. Kenneth Patchen. **CP-PatcK**

Christ Church Meadows, [Oxford]. Donald Hall. **CP-HallD**

Christ-cut: the cedar. Passion Week. William Everson. **SP-EverW**

Christ died for God and me. Conviction (i). Stevie Smith. **CP-SmitS**

Christ God who savest man, save most. Count Gismond. Robert Browning. **CP-BroR1**

Christ harrowed Hell in pity for all damned souls. Descent into Hell. Robert Ranke Graves. **CP-GravR**

Christ, He requires still, wheresoere He comes. Christs Part. Robert Herrick. **CP-HerrR**

Christ I am tired of fruit in poetry. Malcolm Lowry. **CP-LowrM**

Christ, I have read, did to His chaplains say. Salutation. Robert Herrick. **CP-HerrR**

Christ in Hades. Wystan Hugh Auden. **CP-AudWJ**

Christ is walking in your blood today. Villanelle. Richard Eberhart. **CP-EberR**

Christ, keep me from the self-survey. Beauty. Christopher Smart. *Fr.* Hymns for the Amusement of Children. **SP-SmarC**

Christ never did so great a work, but there. Christs Action. Robert Herrick. **CP-HerrR**

Christ passed before my shop, and as I spat. Ahasuerus. Howard Nemerov. **CP-NemeH**

Christ, slashed with an axe, in the humped church. Malcolm Lowry. *Fr.* The Roar of the Sea and the Darkness. **CP-LowrM**

Christ that as the maggot. Vision and Prayer. Miller Williams. **SP-WillM**

Christ the dew in the clod. Johnny Appleseed's Hymn to the Sun. Nicholas Vachel Lindsay. **CP-LindV**

Christ took our Nature on Him, not that He. Christs Incarnation. Robert Herrick. **CP-HerrR**

Christ was not sad, i'th garden, for His own. Christs Sadnesse. Robert Herrick. **CP-HerrR**

Christ when he dy'd. Christs Victory. Richard Crashaw. **CP-CrasR**

Christ, when He hung the dreadfull Crosse upon. Christs Words on the Crosse, My God, My God. Robert Herrick. **CP-HerrR**

Christabel. Samuel Taylor Coleridge. **CP-ColeS**

Christabel and Geraldine. **PeHV**

In the Touch of This Bosom There Worketh a Spell. **RB**

Scars Remaining, The. **OBNC**

"'Tis the middle of night by the castle clock." **OBRV; WHA**

"'Tis the middle of night by the castle clock." **CH**

"'Tis the middle of night by the castle clock." **FaBoVe; OAEP**

"'Tis the middle of night by the castle clock." **FiP**

"'Tis the middle of night by the castle clock." **SeCePo**

Christabel and Geraldine. Samuel Taylor Coleridge. **PeHV** *Fr.* Christabel. **CP-ColeS**

In the Touch of This Bosom There Worketh a Spell. **RB**

Christall Violl Cupid brought, A. Upon Love. Robert Herrick. **CP-HerrR**

Christening, A. Donald Davie. **CP-DavDo**

Christening, The. Thomas Hardy. **CP-HardT**

Christe's Retorne out of Egipt. Robert Southwell. **CP-SoutR**

Christe's Sleeping Frendes. Robert Southwell. **CP-SoutR**

Christian, The. William Cowper. *Fr.* Olney Hymns. **CP-CowpW**

Christian and Jew. A Dialogue. Christina Georgina Rossetti. **CP-RosC1**

Christian coin, The. Threnody. William Carlos Williams. **CP-WilW2**

Christian Fearing the Sky. Paul Zimmer. **SP-ZimmP**

Christian Forbearance. William Blake. *See* A Poison Tree.

Christian! going, gone!, A. The Christian Slave. John Greenleaf Whittier. **CP-WhitJ**

Christian Hero, A. Donald Davie. **CP-DavDo**

Christian Militant. Robert Herrick. **CP-HerrR**

Christian Slave, The. John Greenleaf Whittier. **CP-WhitJ**

Christian to Try: "I am so coxed in it." John Berryman. *Fr.* Sonnets to Chris. **CP-BerrJ**

Christian Tourists, The. John Greenleaf Whittier. **CP-WhitJ**

Christina. Louis MacNeice. *Fr.* Novelettes. **CP-MacNL**

Christina. Thomas Merton. **CP-MertT**

Christina, maiden of heroic mien! To Christina. John Milton, *tr. fr. Latin by* William Cowper. **CP-CowpW**

Christine is the girl I adore. Charles Henri Ford. *Fr.* Epigrams. **SP-FordC**

Christmas. Sir John Betjeman. **CP-BetjJ**

Christmas. Paul Laurence Dunbar. **CP-DunbP**

Christmas. George Herbert. **CP-HerbG**

Christmas. Robert Lowell. **SP-LoweR**

Christmas. Robert Lowell. **SP-LoweR**

Christmas. Charles Olson. **CP-OlsoC**

Christmas. Stevie Smith. **CP-SmitS**

Christmas as to People. Thomas Merton. **CP-MertT**

Christmas at Sea. Robert Louis Stevenson. **CP-StevR**

Christmas Blackmail. Phoebe Hesketh. **SP-HeskP**

Christmas Canticle. Edna St. Vincent Millay. **CP-MillE**

Christmas Card, A. Thomas Merton. **CP-MertT**

Christmas Card, After the Assassinations, A. Mona Van Duyn. **SP-VanDM**

Christmas Carmen, A. John Greenleaf Whittier. **CP-WhitJ**

Christmas Carol: "Ring out, ye bells!" Paul Laurence Dunbar. **CP-DunbP**

Christmas Carol, A. Algernon Charles Swinburne. *See* Three damsels in the queen's chamber.

Christmas Carol, A: "In the bleak mid-winter." Christina Georgina Rossetti. **CP-RosC1**

  My Gift. **FaPON; PChr; SiSoSe**

Christmas Carol, A: "Shepherds went their hasty way, The." Samuel Taylor Coleridge. **CP-ColeS**

Christmas Carol, A: "Thank God, thank God, we do believe." Christina Georgina Rossetti. **CP-RosC3**

Christmas Carol for Emanuel Carnevali, A. Kay Boyle. **CP-BoylK**

Christmas Carol, for My Godchildren, A. Christina Georgina Rossetti. *See* The Shepherds Had an Angel.

Christmas Caroll Sung to the King in the Presence at White-Hall, A. Robert Herrick. **CP-HerrR**

  "Darling of the world is come, The." **PChr**

Christmas Carols. Margaret Atwood. **SP-AtwM2**

Christmas Carols. Christina Georgina Rossetti. **CP-RosC2**

  "Holy, heavenly chime / Rings fulness in of time, A."

  "Lo! newborn Jesus / Soft and weak and small."

  "Whoso hears a chiming for Christmas at the nighest."

Christmas Crown, A. Marilyn Hacker. **SP-HackM**

Christmas Day. Christina Georgina Rossetti. **CP-RosC2**

Christmas Day. Christopher Smart. **ChTr; OBCP** *Fr.* The Nativity of Our Lord and Saviour Jesus Christ. **NOCV; SBVL** *Fr.* Hymns and Spiritual Songs for the Fasts and Festivals of the Church of England. **SP-SmarC**

Christmas Eve. Wystan Hugh Auden. **CP-AudWJ**

Christmas-Eve. Robert Browning. **CP-BroR1**

  Earth Breaks Up. **TrCP**

Christmas Eve. John Hewitt. **CP-HewiJ**

Christmas Eve. Ted Kooser. **SP-KoosT**

Christmas Eve. Christina Georgina Rossetti. **CP-RosC2**

Christmas Eve. Muriel Rukeyser. **CP-RukeM**

Christmas Eve. Anne Sexton. **CP-SextA**

Christmas Eve, Alone. Charles Bukowski. **SP-BukC1**

Christmas Eve, and twelve of the clock. The Oxen. Thomas Hardy. **CP-HardT**

Christmas Eve in Whitneyville, 1955. Donald Hall. **CP-HallD**

Christmas Eve, night of nights, and Big Creek. Storm-Surge. William Everson. **SP-EverW**

Christmas Eve Service at Midnight at St. Michael's. Robert Bly. **SP-BlyR**

Christmas Folksong, A. Paul Laurence Dunbar. **CP-DunbP**

Christmas Ghost-Story, A. Thomas Hardy. **CP-HardT**

Xmas Gift. Allen Ginsberg. *See* Xmas Gift.

Christmas Gifts. Elizabeth Barrett Browning. **CP-BroEB**

Christmas Greeting, A. Walt Whitman. **CP-WhitW**

Christmas Greeting, A. James Wright. **CP-WrigJ**

Christmas Greetings. "Lewis Carroll." **CP-CarrL** *Fr.* Alice's Adventures in Wonderland.

Christmas hath a darkness / Brighter than the blazing noon. Christmas Eve. Christina Georgina Rossetti. **CP-RosC2**

Christmas His Masque. Ben Jonson.

  "Hum drum, sauce for a cony." **CP-JonsB**

  "Nor do you think that their legs is all." **CP-JonsB**

Christmas Holiday. Alun Lewis. **CP-LewiA**

Christmas Hymn, A. Richard Wilbur. **CP-WilbR**

Xmas in February. "Lou Reed." **SP-ReedL**

Christmas in India. Rudyard Kipling. **CP-KiplR**

Christmas in the Elgin Room. Thomas Hardy. **CP-HardT**

Christmas in the Heart. Paul Laurence Dunbar. **CP-DunbP**

Christmas is as Christmas does. Christmas as to People. Thomas Merton. **CP-MertT**

Christmas Letter to a Psychiatrist. May Sarton. **SP-SartM**

Christmas: May 10, 1970. Robert Creeley. **CP-CreeR**

Christmas Morning. Howard Nemerov. **CP-NemeH**

Christmas Night. Steve Griffiths. *Fr.* Hymns and Backward Glances. **SP-GrifS**

Christmas night: the solstice storm. The Narrows of Birth. William Everson. **SP-EverW**

Christmas 1950. William Carlos Williams. **CP-WilW2**

Christmas 1944. Hilda Doolittle. **CP-DoolH**

Christmas: 1924. Thomas Hardy. **CP-HardT**

Christmas of 1888, The. John Greenleaf Whittier. **CP-WhitJ**

Christmas Poem for Nancy. Delmore Schwartz. *Fr.* Occasional Poems. **SP-SchwD**

Christmas Rhymers, Ballynure, 1941, The. John Hewitt. **CP-HewiJ**

Christmas Robin, The. Robert Ranke Graves. **CP-GravR**

Christmas Roses, The. Randall Jarrell. **CP-JarrR**

Christmas Shopping. Louis MacNeice. **CP-MacNL**

Christmas Syllabics for a Wife. Donald Davie. **CP-DavDo**

Christmas: three tourist / liners in port, two more at anchor. Island Trashfires. Laurence Lieberman. **SP-LiebL**

Christmas Tree. Richard Eberhart. **CP-EberR**

Christmas Tree. Robert Lowell. **SP-LoweR**

Christmas Tree, The. Frederick Morgan. **SP-MorgF**

Christmas Trees. Robert Frost. **CP-FrosR**

Christmas Trees. Geoffrey Hill. **CP-HillG**

Christmas with Shepherds in Brefaro. Richard Hugo. **CP-HugoR**

Christmasse-Eve, Another Ceremonie. Robert Herrick. **CP-HerrR**

Christmastide. Thomas Hardy. **CP-HardT**

Christmastide. Christina Georgina Rossetti. **CP-RosC2**

Christofo Colombo was a hungry man. Mysterious Biography. Carl Sandburg. **CP-SandC**

Christopher Columbus. Thomas Merton. **CP-MertT**

Christo's. Paul Muldoon. **SP-MuldP**

Christs Action. Robert Herrick. **CP-HerrR**

Christs Birth. Robert Herrick. **CP-HerrR**

Christ's Bloody Sweate. Robert Southwell. **CP-SoutR**

Christ[e]'s Childhood[e]. Robert Southwell. **CP-SoutR**

Christ's first portrait was a donkey's head. Words. Robert Lowell. **SP-LoweR**

Christ's Heart was wrung for me, if mine is sore. Surely He Hath Borne Our Griefs. Christina Georgina Rossetti. **CP-RosC2**

Christs Incarnation. Robert Herrick. **CP-HerrR**

Christs Part. Robert Herrick. **CP-HerrR**

Christs Sadnesse. Robert Herrick. **CP-HerrR**

Christs Suffering. Robert Herrick. **CP-HerrR**

Christs Twofold Coming. Robert Herrick. **CP-HerrR**

Christs Victory. Richard Crashaw. **CP-CrasR**

Christ's white laughter runs across the world. The Birth of Christ. John Gould Fletcher. **SP-FletJ** *Fr.* The Parables of Christ.

Christs Words on the Crosse, My God, My God. Robert Herrick. **CP-HerrR**

Christus Natus Est. Countee Cullen. **CP-CullC**

Chromatism in Red. Marsden Hartley. **CP-HartM**

Chromium-Plated Hat. Inlaid with Scenes from Siegfried, A. Howard Nemerov. **CP-NemeH**

Chromo. Martin Edmunds. **SP-EdmuM**

Chromo. Carl Sandburg. **CP-SandC**

Chronic Condition, A. Richard Wilbur. **CP-WilbR**

"Chronic Kicker," The. Paul Laurence Dunbar. **CP-DunbP**

Chronicle of Division. William Everson.
  "Sea: / And in its flaw the sprung silence." **SP-EverW**
Chronicles. Charles Olson. **SP-OlsoC** *Fr.* The Maximus Poems.
Chronological. Hayden Carruth. *Fr.* Poetical Abstracts. **CP-CarHS**
Chronometer fell in the bilge and was useless, The. The Voyage of Kevin O'Riordine. Malcolm Lowry. **CP-LowrM**
Chronos, Chronos, mend thy pace. John Dryden. *See* The Secular Masque.
Chronos, Chronos, mend thy ways. The Secular Masque. John Dryden.
Chruchyard Song of Patient Hope, A. Christina Georgina Rossetti. **CP-RosC2**
Chrysanth. Jenny Joseph. *Fr.* Life and Turgid Times of A. Citizen. **SP-JoseJ**
Chrysanthemum, The. William Carlos Williams. **CP-WilW2**
Chrysanthemum. Louis Zukofsky. **CP-ZukLS**
Chrysanthemums. Donald Davie. **CP-DavDo**
Chrysanthemums last too long for these ravenous ladies. Starved Lovers. Archibald MacLeish. **CP-MacLA**
Chuang Tzu and Hui Tzu. The Joy of Fishes. Chuang Tzu, *tr. fr. Chinese by* Thomas Merton. **CP-MertT**
Chuang Tzu with his bamboo pole. The Turtle. Chuang Tzu, *tr. fr. Chinese by* Thomas Merton. **CP-MertT**
Chuff, lately rich in name, in chattels, goods. On Chuff, Banks the Usurer's Kinsman. Ben Jonson. **CP-JonsB**
Ch'ui the draftsman / Could draw more perfect circles freehand. When the Shoe Fits. Chuang Tzu, *tr. fr. Chinese by* Thomas Merton. **CP-MertT**
Chums, The. Theodore Roethke. **CP-RoetT**
Church, The. David Herbert Lawrence. **CP-LawrD**
Church, The. Lewis Turco. **SP-TurcL**
Church and State. William Butler Yeats. **CP-YeatW**
Church and the Wedding, The. Thomas Hardy. **CP-HardT**
Church bells toll a melancholy round, The. Written in Disgust of Vulgar Superstition. John Keats. **CP-KeatJ**
Church-Builder, The. Thomas Hardy. **CP-HardT**
Church Cemetery in St. Mary's, A. Peter Meinke. **SP-MeinP**
Church flings forth a battled shade, The. The Church-Builder. Thomas Hardy. **CP-HardT**
Church-Floor[e], The. George Herbert. **CP-HerbG**
Church Going. Philip Larkin. **CP-LarkP**
Church I hate, and have good reason, The. Verses on the Upright Judge. Jonathan Swift. **CP-SwifJ**
Church is a business, and the rich, The. After Lorca. Robert Creeley. **CP-CreeR**
Church is an iceberg, The. Winter Night. Charles Simic. **SP-SimiC**
Church is small and well designed, The. Mass. John Hewitt. **CP-HewiJ**
Church-Lock and Key. George Herbert. **CP-HerbG**
Church mice had been bombed out of Albert, The. The Only Bird That Sang. Kay Boyle. **CP-BoylK**
Church Militant. Donald Davie. **CP-DavDo**
Church Militant, The. George Herbert. **CP-HerbG**
Church Monuments. George Herbert. **CP-HerbG**
Church-Music[k]. George Herbert. **CP-HerbG**
Church of England Thoughts Occasioned by Hearing the Bells of Magdalen Tower from the Botanic Garden, Oxford on St. Mary Magdalen's Day. Sir John Betjeman. **CP-BetjJ**
Church of Ireland. Donald Davie. **CP-DavDo**
Church of San Salvador Seen from the Lake of Lugano. William Wordsworth. *Fr.* Memorials of a Tour of the Continent; 1820. **CP-WorW2**
Church of Vico-Morcote [*or* Vice-Morcate], The. View by Color Photography on a Commercial Calendar. William Carlos Williams. **CP-WilW2**
Church on Comiaken Hill, The. Richard Hugo. **CP-HugoR**
Church-Porch, The. George Herbert. **CP-HerbG**
  "Drink not the third glass, which thou canst not tame." **FaBoDD**
  "Wit's an unruly engine, wildly striking." **OBF**
Church-Rents and Schisms. George Herbert. **CP-HerbG**
Church Romance, A. Thomas Hardy. **CP-HardT**
Church to Be Erected. William Wordsworth. *Fr.* Ecclesiastical Sonnets. **CP-WorW2**
Church was locked, so I went to the incumbent, The. Exchange of Livings. Sir John Betjeman. **CP-BetjJ**
Churches are best for prayer, that have least light. Dark Churches. John Donne. **FaBoRV** *Fr.* A Hymn [*or* Hymne] to Christ, at the Author's Last Going into Germany. **CP-DonnJ**
Churchill's Funeral. Geoffrey Hill. **CP-HillG**
  "Brazed city / reorders its own, The."
  "Copper clouds / are not of this light, The."
  "Endless London / mourns for that knowledge."

  "Innocent soul / ghosting for its lost."
  "Stone Pietà / for which the city."
Churchill's Grave. Byron. **CP-Byron**
Church's Restoration, The. Sir John Betjeman. **CP-BetjJ**
Churchyard among the Mountains, The. William Wordsworth. *Fr.* The Excursion. **CP-WorW2**
Churchyard among the Mountains (Continued), The. William Wordsworth. *Fr.* The Excursion. **CP-WorW2**
Churchyard Wall, The. Charles Tomlinson. **CP-TomlC**
Churl in spirit, up or down, The. Tennyson. *Fr.* In Memoriam A. H. H. **CP-TennA**
Churros. James Liddy. **CP-LiddJ**
Chysauster. Richard Hugo. **CP-HugoR**
Ci-gît l Foetus(unborn to not die). Edward Estlin Cummings. **CP-CummE**
Cibber! write all thy Verses upon Glasses. Alexander Pope. *Fr.* Epigrams Occasioned by Cibber's Verses in Praise of Nash. **CP-PopeA**
Cicada. John Haines. **SP-HainJ**
  "I sank past bitten leaves."
  "It was late summer."
  "Whisper, dry and insane, A."
Cicada. Marsden Hartley. **CP-HartM**
Cicada fill up the bamboo thickets. Rainbow Body. Gary Snyder. **CP-SnydG**
Cicada rubs its wings and makes a. Cicada. Marsden Hartley. **CP-HartM**
Cicada shell, The. August. Ted Kooser. **SP-KoosT**
Cicadas. Richard Wilbur. **CP-WilbR**
Cicadas are singing in the mulberry forest, The. Chant of the Frontiersman. Wang Ch'ang-ling, *tr. fr. Chinese by* William Carlos Williams *with* David Rafael Wang. **CP-WilW2**
Cicadas blur the ear as the blue heat haze. The Summer. Hayden Carruth. *Fr.* Contra Mortem. **CP-CarHL**
Cicero, the Sacrificial Killing. Robert Lowell. **SP-LoweR**
Cider 5[dc] A Glass. Donald Hall. **CP-HallD**
Cider in the rain barrel, corn in the popper. Faldang. Louise McNeill. **SP-McNeL**
Cigarettes and Whiskey and Wild, Wild Women. Anne Sexton. **CP-SextA**
Cigarettes wetted with beer from. Coupons. Charles Bukowski. **SP-BukC1**
Cin Cin Cin Cinzaaaano, pow. Madrid 1963: Some Changes. Al Young. **CP-YounA**
Cinco de Mayo. Jim Carroll. *Fr.* 3 Short Poems. **SP-CarrJ**
Cinderella. Randall Jarrell. **CP-JarrR; SP-JarrR**
Cinderella. Sylvia Plath. **CP-PlatS**
Cinderella. Anne Sexton. **CP-SextA**
Cinderella's Story. Mona Van Duyn. **SP-VanDM**
Cinders. Wystan Hugh Auden. **CP-AudWJ**
Cindy, I've used my writing all my life. Sonnet. Hayden Carruth. **CP-CarHS** *Fr.* Sonnets.
Cindy, the secret's out. Yes, you're addict-. Sonnet. Hayden Carruth. **CP-CarHS** *Fr.* Sonnets.
Cinema is cruel, The. An Image of Leda. Frank O'Hara. **SP-OharF**
Cinema of a Man. Archibald MacLeish. **CP-MacLA**
Cinematic blossoming of love gasoline. Slow Life. Tom Clark. **SP-ClarT**
Cinna seems poor in show. Martial, *tr. fr. Latin by* Richard Lovelace. **CP-LoveR**
Cinnamon and rayon. Graduation. Langston Hughes. **SP-HughL**
Cinnamon rose doth, The. Nature. Marsden Hartley. **CP-HartM**
Cino. Ezra Pound. **SP-PounE**
Cinos. Charles Olson. **CP-OlsoC**
Cinquefoil. Louis Zukofsky. **CP-ZukLS**
Circe. Wystan Hugh Auden. **CP-AudeW**
Circe. Hilda Doolittle. **CP-DoolH**
Circe. Louis MacNeice. **CP-MacNL**
Circe / Mud Poems. Margaret Atwood. **SP-AtwM1**
  "Fist, withered and strung, The."
  "Here are the holy birds."
  "Holding my arms down."
  "I made no choice / I decided nothing." **NALW**
  "It was not my fault, these animals."
  "It's the story that counts." **NALW**
  "Last year I abstained / this year I devour."
  "Men with the heads of eagles." **NoAM**
  "My face, my other faces."
  "Not you I fear but that other."
  "Now it is winter. / By winter I mean: white, silent."
  "People come from all over to consult me, bringing their limbs." **NALW**
  "There are so many things I want."
  "There are two islands / at least, they do not exclude each other."

"There must be more for you to do."
"This is not something that can be renounced."
"This story was told to me by another traveller." **NALW**
"Through this forest / burned and sparse, the tines."
"We walk in the cedar groves."
"When you look at nothing."
"You may wonder why I'm not describing the landscape for you."
"You stand at the door / bright as an icon."
"You think you are safe at last."
"Your flawed body, sickle."
Circle, The. Robert Creeley. **CP-CreeR**
Circle. Robert Creeley. **CP-CreeR**
Circle, The. Jean Garrigue. **SP-GarrJ**
Circle, a Square, a Triangle and a Ripple of Water, A. Jane Cooper. **SP-CoopJ**
Circle Game, The. Margaret Atwood. **SP-AtwM1**
  "And you play the safe game / the orphan game."
  "Being with you / here, in this room."
  "Children like the block, The."
  "Children on the lawn / joined hand to hand, The."
  "However, / in all their games."
  "Returning to the room: / I notice how."
  "Summer again; / in the mirrors of this room."
Circle is broken, one seat is forsaken, The. Lament, A. John Greenleaf Whittier. **CP-WhitJ**
Circle of Doors. Carl Sandburg. **CP-SandC**
Circle of saints, all, A. Weeper in Jalisco. Charles Tomlinson. **CP-TomlC**
Circles and Squares. John Haines. **CP-HainJ**
Circling Splinters. Archie Randolph Ammons. **SP-AmmoA**
Circling the Daughter. Etheridge Knight. **SP-KnigE**
Circling the Sun, at a respectful distance. Problems of Gender. Robert Ranke Graves. **CP-GravR**
Circuit. James Dickey. **CP-DickJ**
Circular, A. Thomas Hardy. **CP-HardT**
Circular moon saw-wheels through the oak-grove. 1930's. Robert Lowell. **SP-LoweR**
Circulations of the Song. Robert Duncan. **SP-DuncR**
Circumambulating Arunachala. Gary Snyder. **CP-SnydG**
Circumcision. Christopher Smart. *Fr.* Hymns and Spiritual Songs for the Fasts and Festivals of the Church of England. **SP-SmarC**
Circumcision, The. Robert Southwell. **CP-SoutR**
Circumference thou Bride of Awe. Emily Dickinson. **CP-DickE**
Circumstance, The. Hart Crane. **CP-CranH**
Circumstance. *Unknown, tr. fr. Greek by* Shelley. **CP-ShelP**
Circumstances Alter Cases. Paul Laurence Dunbar. **CP-DunbP**
Circus, The. Wystan Hugh Auden. **CP-AudWJ**
Circus, The. Kenneth Koch. **SP-KochK**
Circus, The. Kenneth Koch. **SP-KochK**
Circus. Louis MacNeice. **CP-MacNL**
  Clowns. **VoGa**
  Elephants.
  Horses. **VoGa**
  Trapezists. **VoGa**
Circus Animals' Desertion, The. William Butler Yeats. **CP-YeatW**
Circus in Three Rings. Sylvia Plath. **CP-PlatS**
Circus-Rider to Ringmaster. Thomas Hardy. **CP-HardT**
Circus Ring. Robert Ranke Graves. **CP-GravR**
Cirque d'Hiver. Elizabeth Bishop. **CP-BishE**
Cisma de Inglaterra. Pedro Calderón de la Barca, *tr. fr. Spanish.*
  "Hast thou not seen, officious with delight." **CP-ShelP**
Cistercians might crack their sides. Hernani. George Meredith. **CP-MerG1**
Cistertian Monastery. William Wordsworth. *Fr.* Ecclesiastical Sonnets. **CP-WorW2**
Citation for Horace Gregory. Muriel Rukeyser. **CP-RukeM**
Citation on Retirement. John Ciardi. **SP-CiarJ**
Cities. Hilda Doolittle. **CP-DoolH**
Cities and Thrones and Powers. Rudyard Kipling. **CP-KiplR** *Fr.* A Centurion of the Thirtieth. *Fr.* Puck of Pook's Hill.
Cities are full of pride, The. To the City of Bombay. Rudyard Kipling. **CP-KiplR**
Cities arise. . . . The Underground. Thomas McGrath. **SP-McGrT**
Cities of the Plain, The. Mona Van Duyn. **SP-VanDM**
Cities of the Plain, The. John Greenleaf Whittier. **CP-WhitJ**
Citizen. Robert Creeley. **CP-CreeR**
Citizen CB. Al Young. **CP-YounA**
Citizen Dreaming, The. Thomas McGrath. **SP-McGrT**

Citizen, myself, or personal friend. Allen Tate. *See* Gay citizen, myself, and thoughtful friend.
Citizen of an ever-expanding. Louis MacNeice. *Fr.* As In Their Time. **CP-MacNL**
City. Gerrit Achterberg, *tr. fr. Dutch by* Adrienne Rich. **CP-RicAE**
City, The. Sir John Betjeman. **CP-BetjJ**
City. Sir John Betjeman. **CP-BetjJ**
City, The. Robert Creeley. **CP-CreeR**
City. Roy Fisher. **SP-FishR**
  By the Pond.
  City.
  Entertainment of War, The.
  Hill behind the Town, The.
  Lullaby and Exhortation for the Unwilling Hero.
  North Area.
  Park, The.
  Poplars, The.
  Starting to Make a Tree.
  Sun Hacks, The.
  Wind at Night, The.
City, The. Ogden Nash. **CP-NashO**
City after Noon, The. Thomas Merton. **CP-MertT**
City, City! Randall Jarrell. **CP-JarrR**
City Dead-House, The. Walt Whitman. **CP-WhitW**
City Dog goes to the drinking trough, The. The Wild Dog. Stevie Smith. **CP-SmitS**
City Flats, Coal yards and brown rivers. Wings Lifted over the Black Pit. Allen Ginsberg. **CP-GinsA**
City floats no longer like a bait, The. Late Autumn in Venice. Rainer Maria Rilke, *tr. fr. German by* Delmore Schwartz. **SP-SchwD**
City gleams with lights this evening, The. City Lights. John Gould Fletcher. **SP-FletJ**
City had withdrawn into itself, The. Christmas Trees. Robert Frost. **CP-FrosR**
City has tits in rows, The. Grotesque. William Carlos Williams. **CP-WilW1**
City Home Detroit. Al Young. **CP-YounA**
City in the Sea, The. Edgar Allan Poe. **CP-PoeEd**
City lies grey and sopping like a dead rat, The. The Butt of Winter. Marge Piercy. **SP-PierM**
City-Life. David Herbert Lawrence. **CP-LawrD**
City Life. James Liddy. *Fr.* Ossie Esmonde. *Fr.* His Resplendent Neighbours. **CP-LiddJ**
City lifts toward heaven from the continent of sleep, The. Dawn Song. Thomas McGrath. **SP-McGrT**
City Lights. John Gould Fletcher. **SP-FletJ**
City Lights. "Lou Reed." **SP-ReedL**
City Midnight Junk Strains. Allen Ginsberg. **CP-GinsA**
City Morning. John Hewitt. **CP-HewiJ**
City Mouse and the Garden Mouse, The. Christina Georgina Rossetti. **BoTP; FaBoBe; FaPON; HBV; HBVY; NTCP** *Fr.* Sing-Song. **CP-RosC2**
City mouse lives in a house, The. Christina Georgina Rossetti. **CP-RosC2**
City Number. Carl Sandburg. **CP-SandC**
City of Anguish. Edwin Rolfe. **CP-RolfE**
City of Brass, The. Rudyard Kipling. **CP-KiplR**
City of Dreadful Knight, The. James Liddy. *Fr.* Glass after Oblivion. **CP-LiddJ**
City of eternal flowers. Out and In. Kenneth Koch. *Fr.* Days and Nights. **SP-KochK**
City of God, The. Thomas Merton. *Fr.* The Tower of Babel—A Morality. **CP-MertT**
City of Keansburg, The. George Oppen. **CP-OppeG**
City of Monuments. Muriel Rukeyser. **CP-RukeM**
City of Orgies. Walt Whitman. **CP-WhitW**
City of Satisfactions, The. Daniel Gerard Hoffman. **SP-HoffD**
City of Ships. Walt Whitman. **CP-WhitW**
City of Sleep, The. Rudyard Kipling. **CP-KiplR**
City of the corporations, A. George Oppen. *Fr.* A Language of New York. **CP-OppeG**
City of the heart, The. Chapultepec Park / II. Muriel Rukeyser. **CP-RukeM**
City Planners, The. Margaret Atwood. **SP-AtwM1**
City plum is not a plum, A. Christina Georgina Rossetti. **CP-RosC2**
City Psalm. Denise Levertov. **CP-LeveD**
City squats on my back, The. Route Six. Stanley Jasspon Kunitz. **CP-KuniS**
City That Will Not Repent, The. Nicholas Vachel Lindsay. **CP-LindV**

City Trees. Edna St. Vincent Millay. **CP-MillE**

City Vignettes. Marsden Hartley. **CP-HartM**
   Musicologist—Preference, Prokofieff.
   She Sauntered Most Elegantly Down.

City we shared without knowing. Poem about Oxford. Philip Larkin. **CP-LarkP**

City, when we see you coming down. The Heavenly City. Thomas Merton. **SP-MertT** *Fr.* Figures for an Apocalypse. **CP-MertT**

City which thou seest no other deem, The. Rome. John Milton. **OBS** *Fr.* Book IV. *Fr.* Paradise Regained [*or* Regain'd]. **CP-MiltJ**

City will see him no more at important meetings, The. Variation on a Theme by Newbolt. Sir John Betjeman. **CP-BetjJ**

City without Walls. Wystan Hugh Auden. **CP-AudeW**

City's Death by Fire, A. Derek Walcott. **CP-WalcD**

City's Spring, The. Thomas Merton. **CP-MertT**

Ciudadela, 1991. Steve Griffiths. **SP-GrifS**

Civic water / with lilies and flies. Roy Fisher. **SP-FishR** *Fr.* Studies.

Civil Servant, The. Alun Lewis. *Fr.* Poems from the Chinese. **CP-LewiA**

Civil War, The. Charles Olson. **CP-OlsoC**

Civil War, The. Anne Sexton. **CP-SextA**

Civil world will much forgive, The. Ralph Waldo Emerson. **CP-EmerR**

Civilisation is hooped together, brought. Meru. William Butler Yeats. **CP-YeatW**

Civilities of Lamplight. Charles Tomlinson. **CP-TomlC**

Civility of nature overthrown, The. Autumn. Charles Tomlinson. **CP-TomlC**

Civilization. Diane Wakoski. **SP-WakoD**

Civilization and Its Discontents. William Matthews. **SP-MattW**

Civilization Constantly Worrying about Itself as It Goes on Doing What It Is Worrying About That It Is Doing, A. Jean Garrigue. **SP-GarrJ**

Civilization—spurns—the Leopard! Emily Dickinson. **CP-DickE**

Civilizations are set up and knocked down. At the Gates of Tombs. Carl Sandburg. **CP-SandC**

Civilized, crying how to be human again: this will tell you how. Sign-Post. Robinson Jeffers. **CP-JefR2**

Clachard. Richard Hugo. **CP-HugoR**

Clack, clack, clack, went the mill-wheel as I came. The Second Visit. Thomas Hardy. **CP-HardT**

Clack your beaks you cormorants and kittiwakes. A Canticle to the Waterbirds. William Everson. **SP-EverW**

Clad All in Brown. Jonathan Swift. **CP-SwifJ**

Claim, The. Elizabeth Barrett Browning. **CP-BroEB**

Claiming [*or* Clayming] a Second Kiss[e] by Desert. Ben Jonson. *Fr.* A Celebration of Charis in Ten Lyric[k] Pieces [*or* Peeces]. **CP-JonsB**

Claims. Louis Zukofsky. **CP-ZukLS**

Claims of the sea, of the tide, move out, The. Nocturn IV. Carl Sandburg. **CP-SandC**

Clairvaux. Thomas Merton. **CP-MertT**

Clairvaux Prison. Thomas Merton. **CP-MertT**

Clam Diggers and Diggers of Sea Worms, The. Richard Eberhart. **CP-EberR**

Clam Man. Mary Oliver. **SP-OlivM**

Clambering up the Cold Mountain path. Han-shan, *tr. fr. Chinese by* Gary Snyder. **CP-SnydG**

Clamminess hangs all over like a clout, A. Suspense. Thomas Hardy. **CP-HardT**

Clamor of gulls, A / outside the French windows. Triste Corbiére. Lawrence Ferlinghetti. **SP-FerlL**

Clams, The. Daniel Gerard Hoffman. **SP-HoffD**

Clams and barnacles clatter. Alki Beach. Richard Hugo. **CP-HugoR**

Clan, The. John Updike. **CP-UpdiJ**

Clan of imps—morose and ugly things, A. The Paper Palace. Edward Estlin Cummings. **CP-CummE**

Clanging along in A-flat. The Home Pianist's Companion. Roy Fisher. **SP-FishR**

Clapper hovers, but why run so hard?, The. Surviving Love. John Berryman. **CP-BerrJ**

Clapping blackness of the wings of pointed cormorants, the great indolent planes, The. The Cycle. Robinson Jeffers. **CP-JefR1**

Clara Ducum soboles, superis nova sedibus hospes. Laments for a Noble Lady. Robert Southwell. **CP-SoutR**

Clara walked in the garden with the children. Memories of the Ancient World. Carlos Drummond de Andrade, *tr. fr. Portuguese by* Thomas Merton. **CP-MertT**

Clare De Lughnasa. James Liddy. **CP-LiddJ**

Clare, the Butterflies. James Liddy. **CP-LiddJ**

Clarel: A Poem and Pilgrimage in the Holy Land. Herman Melville.
   Arch, The. **SP-MelvH**
   Empty Stirrups. **SP-MelvH**
   Epilogue: "If Luther's day expand to Darwin's year." **SP-MelvH**
   Inscription, The: "While yet Rolfe's foot in stirrup stood." **SP-MelvH**
   Mortmain Reappears. **SP-MelvH**
   Of Wickedness the Word. **SP-MelvH**
   Prelusive. **SP-MelvH**
   Sketch, A. **SP-MelvH**
   Ungar and Rolfe. **SP-MelvH**
   Via Crucis. **SP-MelvH**
   Vine and Clarel. **SP-MelvH**

Clarifications. Archie Randolph Ammons. **SP-AmmoA**

Clarinda. Robert Burns. **CP-BurnR**

Clarinda, mistress of my soul. Clarinda. Robert Burns. **CP-BurnR**

Claritas. Denise Levertov. **CP-LeveD**

Clarities, The. Stephen Dunn. **SP-DunnS**

Clarity / In the sense of *transparence*. George Oppen. *Fr.* Of Being Numerous. **CP-OppeG**

Clarity! clarity! a semblance of motion, omniscience. / There is no such thing as a breakdown. Ted Berrigan. **SP-BerrT** *Fr.* The Sonnets.

Clark Street Bridge. Carl Sandburg. **CP-SandC**

Clarkson! it was an obstinate hill to climb. To Thomas Clarkson, on the Final Passing of the Bill for the Abolition of the Slave Trade. March, 1807. William Wordsworth. **CP-WorW1**

Clash. William Stafford. **SP-StafW**

Clash in Arms of the Achaians and Trojans. Homer, *tr. by* George Meredith. **CP-MerG1** *Fr.* The Iliad.

Clash of salutation. As keels thrust into shingle. Geoffrey Hill. **NoAM; NoP** *Fr.* Mercian Hymns. **CP-HillG**

Clash went the Billiard Balls. Sir John Betjeman. **CP-BetjJ**

Clasped Skeleton, The. Thomas Hardy. **CP-HardT**

Clasping her magic. After the ball. James Merrill. **SP-MerrJ**

Clasping like bucklers to their bodies, books. Little Rock Arkansas 1957. Isabella Gardner. **CP-GardI**

Clasping of Hands. George Herbert. **CP-HerbG**

Class. Charles Tomlinson. **CP-TomlC**

Class-children are singing in school. Children Singing in School. David Herbert Lawrence. **CP-LawrD**

Class of 1934. Kenneth Patchen. **CP-PatcK**

Class Will Come to Order, The. Stanley Jasspon Kunitz. **CP-KuniS**

Classes. David Herbert Lawrence. **CP-LawrD**

Classic Ballroom Dances. Charles Simic. **SP-SimiC**

Classic Case, A. Gilbert Sorrentino. **SP-SorrG**

Classic Picture. William Carlos Williams. **CP-WilW2**

Classic Scene. William Carlos Williams. **CP-WilW1**

Classical. Hayden Carruth. *Fr.* Poetical Abstracts. **CP-CarHS**

Classical Optical. John Updike. **CP-UpdiJ**

Classicality Applied to Tea-Dealing: A Fancy Inspired by Westbourne Grove. Robert Browning. **CP-BroR2**

Classmate, The. Adrienne Rich. **CP-RicAE**

Claude to Eustace: "Ah, Let Me Look." Arthur Hugh Clough. **EnVR** *Fr.* Amours de Voyage. **SP-ClouA**

Claude to Eustace. Arthur Hugh Clough. **PeLV** *Fr.* Amours de Voyage. **SP-ClouA**

Claude to Eustace. Arthur Hugh Clough. *See* Juxtaposition.

Claude to Eustace: "I am in love. . . ." Arthur Hugh Clough. **EnVR; FaBoVe** *Fr.* Amours de Voyage. **SP-ClouA**

Claude to Eustace: "Juxtaposition is great." Arthur Hugh Clough. **CBLP** *Fr.* Amours de Voyage. **SP-ClouA**

Claude to Eustace: "No, the Christian faith, as at any rate I understood it." Arthur Hugh Clough. **EnVR** *Fr.* Amours de Voyage. **SP-ClouA**

Claude to Eustace: "Shall we come out of it all. . . ." Arthur Hugh Clough. **EBVVPR** *Fr.* Amours de Voyage. **SP-ClouA**

Claude to Eustace: "There are two different kinds, I believe, og human attraction." Arthur Hugh Clough. **GTBS-6** *Fr.* Amours de Voyage. **SP-ClouA**

Claude to Eustace: "These are the facts." Arthur Hugh Clough. **FaBoVe** *Fr.* Amours de Voyage. **SP-ClouA**

Claude to Eustace: "Tibur is beautiful, too, and the orchard slopes, and the Anio." Arthur Hugh Clough. **GTBS-6** *Fr.* Amours de Voyage. **SP-ClouA**

Claude to Eustace: "Yes, we are fighting at last, it appears. This morning, as usual." Arthur Hugh Clough. **EBVV; OXAEP-2; PeVV** *Fr.* Amours de Voyage. **SP-ClouA**

Claude to Eustace—*from Bellagio*. Arthur Hugh Clough. **FaBoVe** *Fr.* Amours de Voyage. **SP-ClouA**

Claus von Stauffenberg. Thom Gunn. **CP-GunnT**

Clavering. Edwin Arlington Robinson. **CP-RobiE**

Clavichord. Walter de la Mare. **CP-DeLaW**

Clavichord, The. May Sarton. **SP-SartM**

Claw at his eyes, O carrion crow. The Carrion Crow. Archibald MacLeish. **CP-MacLA**

Clay County. Etheridge Knight. *Fr.* Missouri Haiku. **SP-KnigE**

Clay Hill Anthology, The. Hayden Carruth.

   "Again on dark looms." **CP-CarHS**

   "Against the wall he / gropes like ivy, you pray, I." **CP-CarHS**

   "All my life that's been / the watchword: Resist! Resist!" **CP-CarHS**

   "Always this special / secret feeling, the failure." **CP-CarHS**

   "Am I wrong? The roads." **CP-CarHS**

   "Because in the heart / of darkness I could not see." **CP-CarHS**

   "Coarse leaf, alder leaf." **CP-CarHS**

   "Dawn. Hoar on the grass." **CP-CarHS**

   "Ducks, waking at sea." **CP-CarHS**

   " 'Ecstasy is the / disaster of pleasure': this." **CP-CarHS**

   "Electroshock. Bang—." **CP-CarHS**

   "Emptiness—you know." **CP-CarHS**

   "Excellence requires / leaf-rakers to sweep one spot." **CP-CarHS**

   "Fathers die, but sons." **CP-CarHS**

   "For your love given." **CP-CarHS**

   "Forward! You must. Keep." **CP-CarHS**

   "Hard journey—yes, A." **CP-CarHS**

   "Have you ever seen." **CP-CarHS**

   "He: Life is an old / casino in the park. I." **CP-CarHS**

   "Hey, Basho, you there!" **CP-CarHS**

   "I live where Frost lived." **CP-CarHS**

   "Ideas hit life like / planks hitting water. Some skim." **CP-CarHS**

   "Imagine bird bones." **CP-CarHS**

   "Last year of youth, The." **CP-CarHS**

   "Let my snow-tracks lead." **CP-CarHS**

   "Look, a cypress tree." **CP-CarHS**

   "Mansion burned. Maids, The." **CP-CarHS**

   "Niobe, your tears." **CP-CarHS**

   "No, I was wrecked here." **CP-CarHS**

   "October. Twilight / flutters like cloth of silver." **CP-CarHS**

   "Of course make love not." **CP-CarHS**

   "One ant turns backward." **CP-CarHS**

   "Out of the garden." **CP-CarHS**

   "Over and over." **CP-CarHS**

   "Parting up / down from / one on the shore, two egrets—." **CP-CarHS**

   "Reversions, always." **CP-CarHS**

   "Sanskrit root word, The." **CP-CarHS**

   "Shadow sprang out, The." **CP-CarHS**

   "She lay like a book." **CP-CarHS**

   "Shirt, britches, paper." **CP-CarHS**

   "Sigh, you seven seas." **CP-CarHS**

   "Steeple bush, hardhack." **CP-CarHS**

   "There! Whitman's skull—." **CP-CarHS**

   "Therefore to us, time's / final lesson: be content." **CP-CarHS**

   "They gave me in trust." **CP-CarHS**

   "Today my poems seem / only the spells I muttered." **CP-CarHS**

   "Trees, the naked trees." **CP-CarHS**

   "True, I happen. So." **CP-CarHS**

   "Tsar, who knew you? Who." **CP-CarHS**

   "Well, beat on, beat on." **CP-CarHS**

   "Why speak of the use / of poetry? Poetry." **CP-CarHS**

   "Wise child is born, The." **CP-CarHS**

   "Women like new brooms." **CP-CarHS**

   "You—Spanish-speaking." **CP-CarHS**

Clay Nursing Home, The. John Yau. **SP-YauJo**

Clay out of Silence. Charles Kenneth Williams. **CP-WillC; SP-WillC**

Clay somnambule returned / after many years away. Paris Transformations. Lawrence Ferlinghetti. **SP-FerlL**

Clay tone your purple arrives. Grassflower. Louis Zukofsky. **CP-ZukLS**

Clayfeld Among the Quarks. Robert Pack. **SP-PackR**

Clayfeld believed indulging in one's whims. Clayfeld's Glove. Robert Pack. **SP-PackR**

Clayfeld considered Rita the most gifted student. Clayfeld's Operatic Debut. Robert Pack. **SP-PackR**

Clayfeld Prunes His Apple Trees. Robert Pack. **SP-PackR**

Clayfeld recalls his hobby as a boy. Clayfeld's Microscope. Robert Pack. **SP-PackR**

Clayfeld Renews His Vow to Evelyn. Robert Pack. **SP-PackR**

Clayfeld sat up in bed at 3:00 A.M. Clayfeld Among the Quarks. Robert Pack. **SP-PackR**

Clayfeld was working on a bust of Freud. Clayfeld's Infancy. Robert Pack. **SP-PackR**

Clayfeld's Anniversary Song, *with music*. Robert Pack. **SP-PackR**

Clayfeld's Campaign. Robert Pack. **SP-PackR**

Clayfeld's Daughter Reveals Her Plans. Robert Pack. **SP-PackR**

Clayfeld's Duck. Robert Pack. **SP-PackR**

Clayfeld's father died after two strokes. Clayfeld's Duck. Robert Pack. **SP-PackR**

Clayfeld's Glove. Robert Pack. **SP-PackR**

Clayfeld's Infancy. Robert Pack. **SP-PackR**

Clayfeld's Metamorphosis. Robert Pack. **SP-PackR**

Clayfeld's Microscope. Robert Pack. **SP-PackR**

Clayfeld's Operatic Debut. Robert Pack. **SP-PackR**

Clayfeld's Son Selects His Specialty. Robert Pack. **SP-PackR**

Clayfeld's Twin, *with music*. Robert Pack. **SP-PackR**

Cle— / 1600 men to a stone. Please mention. Egypt. Kenneth Patchen. **CP-PatcK**

Clean Conscience Never Relaxes, A. Ogden Nash. **CP-NashO**

Clean Curtains. Carl Sandburg. **CP-SandC**

Clean-Cut Kid. "Bob Dylan." **CP-DylaB**

Clean-cut pirate meets and befriends priceless stolen owl. Dramas of the Evening. Thomas Merton. *Fr.* Cables to the Ace. **CP-MertT**

Clean Hands. Carl Sandburg. **CP-SandC**

Clean Old Man. Charles Bukowski. **SP-BukC1**

Clean Platter, The. Ogden Nash. **CP-NashO**

Clean used ones, of course. Also a dresser scarf, woven with a pattern. "Used Handkerchiefs 5[dc]." James Schuyler. **CP-SchuJ**

Cleanliness. Stephen Dunn. **SP-DunnS**

Clear air said, "I was your home once," The. Words in the Air. Philippe Jaccottet. *Fr.* Three Poems by Phillipe Jaccottet. **SP-MahoD**

Clear and Colder. Robert Frost. **CP-FrosR**

Clear [*or* Cleere] are her eyes. Upon Her Eyes. Robert Herrick. **CP-HerrR**

Clear Days, The. Wendell Berry. **CP-BerrW**

Clear Eyes. Walter de la Mare. **CP-DeLaW**

Clear green stars / Rise and set: / Peaceful dragon. Submerged Dragon. Thomas Merton. **CP-MertT**

Clear knowledge having come. Logic. Robert Ranke Graves. **CP-GravR**

Clear Midnight, A. Walt Whitman. **CP-WhitW**

Clear objects / one grows to love. The clarity, The. Poem. Gilbert Sorrentino. **SP-SorrG**

Clear, placid Leman! thy contrasted lake. Lake Leman . Byron. **OBNC**
Fr. It Is the Hush of Night. **LiTB; MeMBP** *Fr.* Childe Harold's Pilgrimage. **CP-Byron**

Clear running stream. Running Water Music II. Gary Snyder. **CP-SnydG**

Clear sky may tell it wrong, A. The Choice. Frederick Morgan. **SP-MorgF**

Clear smoke, / a fire in the far off. Fire. Robert Creeley. **CP-CreeR**

Clear the music, clear the message, the mind clear. Placation of Reality. Richard Eberhart. **CP-EberR**

Clear Vision, The. John Greenleaf Whittier. **CP-WhitJ**

Clear water in a brilliant bowl. The Poems of Our Climate. Wallace Stevens. **CP-StevW**

Clear weather of juniper, The. Sloe Gin. Seamus Heaney. **SP-HeanS**

Clearances. Seamus Heaney. **SP-HeanS**

   "Cool that came off sheets just off the line, The."

   "Fear of affectation made her affect."

   "I thought of walking round and round a space."

   "In the last minutes he said more to her." **PNI**

   "When all the rooms were away at Mass." **PNI**

Clearances, The. Richard Hugo. **CP-HugoR**

Cleared. Rudyard Kipling. **CP-KiplR**

Clearing, The. Wendell Berry. **CP-BerrW**

   "As the vision of labor grows."

   "Evening comes / when we finish work and go, An."

   "February. A cloudy day."

   "In the predicament of other lives."

   "Man who does not ask too much, A."

   "Streets, guns, machines."

   "Through elm, buckeye, thorn."

   "Vision must have severity."

   "Vision reaches the ground."

   "We don't bother nobody."

   "We pile the brush high."

Clearing. Tess Gallagher. **SP-GallT**

Clearing, The. Louise McNeill. **SP-McNeL**

Clearing the Title. James Merrill. **SP-MerrJ**

Clearly about You. Robert Penn Warren. **SP-WarrR**

Clearly my ruined garden as it stood. Edna St. Vincent Millay. **CP-MillE**

Clearness. Richard Wilbur. **CP-WilbR**

Cleavage. Archie Randolph Ammons. **SP-AmmoA**

Clefs. Carl Sandburg. **CP-SandC**

Cleft, as the top of the inspired Hill. To my Dear Friend Mr. E.R. Richard Lovelace. **CP-LoveR**

Cleggan. Richard Hugo. **CP-HugoR**

Clemency. Robert Herrick. **CP-HerrR**

Clemency in Kings. Robert Herrick. **CP-HerrR**

Clemente (1934-1972). Tom Clark. **SP-ClarT**

Cleon. Robert Browning. **CP-BroR1**
  Greece. **OtMeF**

Cleon the poet (from the sprinkled isles). Cleon. Robert Browning. **CP-BroR1**

Cleon the poet, (from the sprinkled isles). Greece. Robert Browning. **OtMeF** Fr. Cleon. **CP-BroR1**

Cleopatra. "Anna Akhmatova", tr. fr. Russian by Stanley Kunitz. **CP-KuniS**

Cleopatra. George Meredith. **CP-MerG2**

Cleopatra built / like a smooth arrow or. Edward Estlin Cummings. **CP-CummE**

Cleopatra dead and famous, / Wanton Helen, bane of Greece. Motives. John Hewitt. **CP-HewiJ**

Cleopatra to the Asp. Ted Hughes. **SP-HughT**

Clepsydra. John Ashbery. **SP-AshbJ**

Clergyman's Second Tale, The. Arthur Hugh Clough. **SP-ClouA** Fr. Mari Magno.

Cleric, The. Seamus Heaney. **SP-HeanS** Fr. Sweeney Redivivus.

Clerical Integrity. William Wordsworth. Fr. Ecclesiastical Sonnets. **CP-WorW2**

Clerical Oppressors. John Greenleaf Whittier. **CP-WhitJ**

Clerihew for Alan Gaylord, A. Richard Eberhart. **CP-EberR**

Clerk Bukashkin is our neighbor, The. Antiworlds. Andrei Voznesensky, tr. fr. Russian by Richard Wilbur. **CP-WilbR**

Clerk ther was of Oxenford also, A. Geoffrey Chaucer. **InPS** Fr. The General Prologue. **FHYEP; NAWM-1; OAEL-1; PoE** Fr. The Canterbury Tales. **CP-ChauG**

  (Seven Pilgrims: A Clerk.) **TrGrPo**

Clerks, The. Edwin Arlington Robinson. **CP-RobiE**

Clerks and the Bells, The. Rudyard Kipling. **CP-KiplR**

Clerk's Prologue, The. Geoffrey Chaucer. Fr. The Canterbury Tales. **CP-ChauG**

Clerk's Tale, The. Geoffrey Chaucer. Fr. The Canterbury Tales. **CP-ChauG**
  Patient Griselda. **PoRA**

Cleveland, Oh? Kenneth Patchen. **CP-PatcK**

Cleveland, the Flats. Allen Ginsberg. **CP-GinsA**

Clever, defensive, seasoned animals. A Winter Day in Ohio. James Wright. **CP-WrigJ**

Clever little Willie wee, / Bright eyed, blue eyed little fellow. Christina Georgina Rossetti. **CP-RosC2**

Clever Strategem: Or, How to Handle Mystics, A. Thomas Merton. Fr. South. Fr. The Geography of Lograire. **CP-MertT**

Clever Tom Clinch Going to Be Hanged. Jonathan Swift. **CP-SwifJ**

Click and clatter. Water off for heaven. From the Rain Forest Down. Richard Hugo. **CP-HugoR**

Cliff and Wave. Robert Ranke Graves. **CP-GravR**

Cliff-dwelling. John Gould Fletcher. Fr. Arizona Poems. **SP-FletJ**

Cliff Dwelling, A. Robert Frost. **CP-FrosR**

Cliff Edge, The. Robert Ranke Graves. **CP-GravR**

Cliff Klingenhagen. Edwin Arlington Robinson. **CP-RobiE**

Cliff Temple, The. Hilda Doolittle. **CP-DoolH**

Cliffs. James Liddy. **CP-LiddJ**
  "At castle shadowed mouth of the."
  "Cliffs with sea breaking at their."
  "Island / Of the hungry bishop, The."
  "Mistress on her white horse at, The."
  "Since the splendour of MacDonnell of the cliffs."

Cliffs come sheering down into woodland here. Casarola. Charles Tomlinson. **CP-TomlC**

Cliffs with sea breaking at their. James Liddy. Fr. Cliffs. **CP-LiddJ**

Climacteric. Ralph Waldo Emerson. Fr. Quatrains. **CP-EmerR**

Climate of Thought, The. Robert Ranke Graves. **CP-GravR**

Climate of War, The. Kenneth Patchen. **CP-PatcK**

Climb / into a jar. Pithos. Rita Dove. **SP-DoveR**

Climb at court for me that will. The Second Chorus from Seneca's Tragedy "Thyestes." Seneca, tr. fr. Latin by Andrew Marvell. **CP-MarvA** Fr. Thyestes.

Climb Down, O Lordly Mind. David Herbert Lawrence. **CP-LawrD**

Climb to Snowdon, The. William Wordsworth. See In one of these excursions, travelling then.

Climbed from the road and found. Latitude, Longitude. George Oppen. **CP-OppeG**

Climbed uphill to the seashore summerhouse. The Summerhouse. Daniel Gerard Hoffman. **SP-HoffD**

Climber. Steve Griffiths. **SP-GrifS**

Climbing. Tom Clark.

Climbing a path which leads back never more. O. W. Holmes on His Eightieth Birthday. John Greenleaf Whittier. **CP-WhitJ**

Climbing Down. David Herbert Lawrence. **CP-LawrD**

Climbing Katahdin. Daniel Gerard Hoffman. **SP-HoffD**

Climbing Katahdin in 1964. Katahdin. Frederick Morgan. Fr. Eight Triolets. **SP-MorgF**

Climbing the heights of Berkeley. The City That Will Not Repent. Nicholas Vachel Lindsay. **CP-LindV**

Climbing the Hill within the Deafening Wind. Philip Larkin. **CP-LarkP**

Climbing the peak of Tamalpais the loose. The Impossible Poem. George Oppen. **NNaP** Fr. Some San Francisco Poems. **CP-OppeG**

Climbing through the January snow, into the Lobo canyon. Mountain Lion. David Herbert Lawrence. **CP-LawrD**

Climbing to Colonnata past ravines. Above Carrara. Charles Tomlinson. **CP-TomlC**

Climbing to reach the costly Hearts. Emily Dickinson. **CP-DickE**

Climbing Up. David Herbert Lawrence. **CP-LawrD**

Cling to the long. Dead Farms, Dead Leaves. Ted Hughes. **SP-HughT**

Clinging Vine, The. Edwin Arlington Robinson. **CP-RobiE**

Clings to the shadows, a wan silhouette. Frost. Charles Tomlinson. **CP-TomlC**

Clink of Rhyme, The. John Hewitt. **CP-HewiJ**

Clinkum-clank in the rain they ride. The Bour-Tree Den. Robert Louis Stevenson. **CP-StevR**

Clinkum-clank o' Sabbath bells. A Lowden Sabbath Morn. Robert Louis Stevenson. **CP-StevR**

Clinton South of Polk. Carl Sandburg. **CP-SandC**

Clipper-Ships. John Gould Fletcher. **SP-FletJ**

Clitophon and Lucippe. Achilles Tatius, tr. fr. Greek by Richard Lovelace. **CP-LoveR**

Clive. Robert Browning. **CP-BroR2**

Cloak, The. Robert Ranke Graves. **CP-GravR**

Cloak for a Man Who Has No Need for Winter, A. Kay Boyle. **CP-BoylK**

Cloak, the Boat, and the Shoes, The. William Butler Yeats. **CP-YeatW**

Cloakroom pegs are empty now, The. The School in August. Philip Larkin. **CP-LarkP**

Cloathes, Are Conspirators. Robert Herrick. **CP-HerrR**

Cloaths for Continuance. Robert Herrick. **CP-HerrR**

Clock, The. Thom Gunn. **CP-GunnT**

Clock beneath the Cupola. The Song of the Ackworth Clock. Basil Bunting. **CP-BuntB**

Clock in the Square, A. Adrienne Rich. **CP-RicAE**

Clock in the Tower of the Church, The. Randall Jarrell. **CP-JarrR**

Clock is getting ready to strike forever o'clock, A. Forever O'Clock. Robert Penn Warren. **SP-WarrR**

Clock of my days winds down, The. The Alligator Bride. Donald Hall. **CP-HallD**

Clock of the Years, The. Thomas Hardy. **CP-HardT**

Clock of the Years, The. William Carlos Williams. **CP-WilW2**

Clock on the parlor wall, stout as a mariner's clock, The. The Day I Was Older. Donald Hall. **CP-HallD**

Clock stopped, A. Emily Dickinson. **CP-DickE**

Clock strikes one that just struck two, The. Emily Dickinson. **CP-DickE**

Clock-Winder, The. Thomas Hardy. **CP-HardT**

Clock With No Hands, A. Howard Nemerov. **CP-NemeH**

Clocks. Carl Sandburg. **CP-SandC**

Clocks begin, civicly simultaneous, The. At Delft. Charles Tomlinson. **CP-TomlC**

Clocks belled twelve. Main Street showed otherwise. Owl. Sylvia Plath. **CP-PlatS**

Clocks blue seconds fold over me. Paregoric Babies. Jim Carroll. **SP-CarrJ**

Clocks cannot tell our time of day. Wystan Hugh Auden. **CP-AudeW**

Clocks cry: stillness is a lie, my dear. To Eva Descending the Stair. Sylvia Plath. **CP-PlatS**

Clocks of time divide us, The. Song: The Clocks of Time. Robert Ranke Graves. **CP-GravR**

Clock's untiring fingers wind the wool of darkness, The. Louis MacNeice. **CP-MacNL**

(Cradle Song for Miriam.) **CP-MacNL**

Clod and [or &] the Pebble, The. William Blake. **CP-BlakW** *Fr.* Songs of Experience.

Cloe [or Chloe]. Alexander Pope. *See* Yet Cloe [or Chloe] sure was form'd without a Spot—.

Clogged and soft and sloppy eyes. The Parents: People Like Our Marriage Maxie and Andrew. Gwendolyn Brooks. *Fr.* Notes from the Childhood and the Girlhood. **SP-BrooG**

Clogh-Oir: September 1971. John Hewitt. **CP-HewiJ**

Cloister (khanqahs) of Darvishes. Cairo 1326. Thomas Merton. *Fr.* East with Ibn Battuta. *Fr.* East. *Fr.* The Geography of Lograire. **CP-MertT**

Cloistered. Seamus Heaney. **SP-HeanS**

Cloistered as the snail and conch. The Lady in the Single. Louise Glück. **SP-GlücL**

Clonking up the cobbled roadway, I bob. Kimono. Laurence Lieberman. **SP-LiebL**

Clora, come view my soul, and tell. The Gallery. Andrew Marvell. **CP-MarvA**

Clorinda and Damon. Andrew Marvell. **CP-MarvA**

Close and slow, summer is ending in Hampshire. Louis MacNeice. *Fr.* Autumn Journal. **CP-MacNL**

Close as I ever came to seeing things. Seeing Things. Howard Nemerov. **CP-NemeH**

Close bound in a familiar bed. Prometheus. Robert Ranke Graves. **CP-GravR**

Close by the threshold of a door nail'd fast. The Colubriad. William Cowper. **CP-CowpW**

Close by those meads, for ever crowned with flow'rs. Alexander Pope. **EBEvV; EBNV; FaBoEH; FaBoPP; FiP; OBSV; OxBoLi** *Fr.* The Rape of the Lock[, an Heroi-Comical Poem]. **CP-PopeA**

(Hampton Court.) **FaBoPP; OBSV**

Close Echo hears the woodman's axe. Woodman and Echo. George Meredith. **CP-MerG1**

Close, eyes, and soul, come home! Lent. Thomas Merton. **CP-MertT**

Close keep your lips, if that you meane. To Women, to Hide Their Teeth, if They Be Rotten or Rusty. Robert Herrick. **CP-HerrR**

Close-mouthed you sat five thousand years and never let out a whisper. A Sphinx. Carl Sandburg. **CP-SandC**

Close of Summer, The. Charlotte Smith. **CP-SmitC**

Close Relations. Archie Randolph Ammons. **SP-AmmoA**

Close the shutters. Let the ceiling fly. La Foce. Archibald MacLeish. **CP-MacLA**

Close the vein! It is Easter Eve. Louis MacNeice. *Fr.* Cock o' the North. **CP-MacNL**

Close to the best known Author, *Umbra* sits. Umbra. Alexander Pope. **CP-PopeA**

Close to the gates a spacious garden lies, *see also* "Without the hall, and close upon the gates" *and* "To left and right, outside, he saw an orchard." *see also* Alkinoos'Garden. Homer, *tr.* by Alexander Pope. **CP-PopeA** *Fr.* Odyssey.

Close up the casement, draw the blind. Shut Out That Moon. Thomas Hardy. **CP-HardT**

Close-woven words my care / I praised where praise seems due. Style. John Hewitt. **CP-HewiJ**

Close your eyes. Louis Zukofsky. *Fr.* 29 Poems. **CP-ZukLS**

Close your eyes and I'll kiss you. All My Loving. John Lennon *and* Paul McCartney. **CP-Beatl**

Close your eyes, close the door. I'll Be Your Baby Tonight. "Bob Dylan." **CP-DylaB**

Close your eyes, my love, let me make you blind! These Clever Women. David Herbert Lawrence. **CP-LawrD**

Closed for Good. Robert Frost. **CP-FrosR**

Closed Gentian Distances. James Schuyler. **CP-SchuJ**

Closed House, The. Frederick Morgan. **SP-MorgF**

Closed like confessionals, they thread. Ambulances. Philip Larkin. **CP-LarkP**

Closed Pub, The. Malcolm Lowry. **CP-LowrM**

Closed then an open meeting, A. The Necessity of Writing in This Tongue. James Liddy. **CP-LiddJ**

Closed World, The. Denise Levertov. **CP-LeveD**

Closer. Robert Pack. **SP-PackR**

Closest at lampfall. Lampfall. Derek Walcott. **CP-WalcD**

Closet, The. Bill Knott. **SP-KnotB**

Closet, The. Gilbert Sorrentino. **SP-SorrG**

Closing Album, The. Louis MacNeice. **CP-MacNL**

Cushendun. **FaBCIP**

Dublin. **CIP; FaBoPP; IIP; OBTV; OxBTC**

Galway. **OxBI**

Sligo and Mayo. **FaBoPP**

"Why, now it has happened."

Closing the sacred Book which long has fed. Rural Ceremony. William Wordsworth. *Fr.* Ecclesiastical Sonnets. **CP-WorW2**

Closing Time. Leonard Cohen. **CP-CoheL**

Closure. Leonard Nathan. **SP-NathL**

Cloth of the Tempest, The. Kenneth Patchen. **CP-PatcK**

Clothed with the wind, light in the light. *tr. fr. the German of* Rilke. Randall Jarrell. **CP-JarrR**

Clother of the lily, Feeder of the sparrow. They Toil Not, Neither Do They Spin. Christina Georgina Rossetti. **CP-RosC2**

Clothes. Anne Sexton. **CP-SextA**

Clothes Do But Cheat and Cozen [or Cousen] Us. Robert Herrick. **CP-HerrR**

Clothes Line. "Bob Dylan." **CP-DylaB**

Clots of age, grovel and palsy, crave, The. John Berryman. *Fr.* Sonnets to Chris. **CP-BerrJ**

Cloud, The. Robert Herrick. **CP-HerrR**

Cloud. Jenny Joseph. *Fr.* Derivations. **SP-JoseJ**

Cloud, The. Raissa Maritain, *tr. fr. French by* Thomas Merton. **CP-MertT**

Cloud, The. William Matthews. **SP-MattW**

Cloud. Kathleen Jessie Raine. **SP-RainK**

Cloud, The. Percy Bysshe Shelley. **CP-ShelP**

Cloud and Flame. John Berryman. **CP-BerrJ**

Cloud Change. Charles Tomlinson. **CP-TomlC**

Cloud—cloud—cloud— hurls. It. Gary Snyder. **CP-SnydG**

Cloud fell down from the heavens, A. A Starry Night. Paul Laurence Dunbar. **CP-DunbP**

Cloud, Florida, 1985, The. Peter Meinke. **SP-MeinP**

Cloud in the sky, A. The Cloud. Raissa Maritain, *tr. fr. French by* Thomas Merton. **CP-MertT**

Cloud is free only, The. The Law That Marries All Things. Wendell Berry. **CP-BerrW**

Cloud, like that the old-time Hebrew saw, A. Storm on Lake Asquam. John Greenleaf Whittier. **CP-WhitJ**

Cloud looked in at the window, The. Changing Time. Paul Laurence Dunbar. **CP-DunbP**

Cloud moved close, A. The bulk of the wind shifted. The Visitant. Theodore Roethke. **CP-RoetT**

Cloud of witnesses. To whom? To what?, A. Canto VII. Louis MacNeice. **NOBE** *Fr.* Autumn Sequel. **CP-MacNL**

Cloud-puffball, torn tufts, tossed pillows flaunt forth, then chevy on an air. That Nature Is a Heraclitean Fire and of the Comfort of the Resurrection. Gerard Manley Hopkins. **CP-HopkG**

Cloud rack drifts across the sun, A. Progress. Wystan Hugh Auden. **CP-AudWJ**

Cloud Seeding. Howard Nemerov. **CP-NemeH**

Cloud Shadow, A. Robert Frost. **CP-FrosR**

Cloud Shadows. John Updike. **CP-UpdiJ**

Cloud upon cloud / Clouds after rain. Ralph Waldo Emerson. **CP-EmerR**

Cloud upon cloud / The world is seeming. Ralph Waldo Emerson. **CP-EmerR**

Cloud withdrew from the Sky, A. Emily Dickinson. **CP-DickE**

Cloudburst and steady downpour now. Gifts of Rain. Seamus Heaney. **SP-HeanS**

Clouded with snow / The cold winds blow. Winter. Walter de la Mare. **CP-DeLaW**

Cloudless night like this, A. A Walk After Dark. Wystan Hugh Auden. **CP-AudeW**

Clouds. Stephen Dobyns. **SP-DobyS**

Clouds. Robert Herrick. **CP-HerrR**

Clouds. Denise Levertov. **CP-LeveD**

Clouds. Philip Levine. **SP-LeviP**

Clouds, The. Charles Olson. **CP-OlsoC**

Clouds. Charles Tomlinson. **CP-TomlC**

Clouds, The. William Carlos Williams. **CP-WilW2**

Cloud's a clue. O cloud!, The. Solving the Riddle. Charles Simic. **SP-SimiC**

Clouds, Airs, Carried me Away. Muriel Rukeyser. **CP-RukeM**

Clouds and the stars didn't wage this war, The. For the Record. Adrienne Rich. **SP-RicA2**

Clouds are electric in this university, The. 7/12/68. Adrienne Rich. **CP-RicAE** *Fr.* Ghazals: Homage to Ghalib. **SP-RicA2**

Clouds are panting. / There is a subequal brightness, The. Chains of Mountains. Joseph Ceravolo. **SP-CeraJ**

Clouds are pushing in grey reluctance slowly northward to you, The. Letter from Town: On a Grey Morning in March. David Herbert Lawrence. **CP-LawrD**

Clouds are withdrawn, The. Sunrise. George Meredith. **CP-MerG1**

Clouds as I see them, rising, The. Clouds. Denise Levertov. **CP-LeveD**

Clouds before the sun when the sun rose, The. Meditation. John Berryman. **CP-BerrJ**

Clouds blown together, like ragged whorls of smoke, The. Midwinter Sunset. John Gould Fletcher. **SP-FletJ**

Clouds continued swelling like poisoned fish, The. Modern Love. John Yau. **SP-YauJo**

Clouds covered it, The. Charles Henri Ford. **SP-FordC** *Fr.* Emblems of Arachne.

Clouds do not always viel the skies. 2.9. Horace. **CP-JohnS,** *tr. by* Samuel Johnson; *Fr.* Odes.

Clouds drape moon in striped appeals. Recoil. John Yau. **SP-YauJo**

Clouds dripped poisonous dew to spite, The. Poisoned Day. Robert Ranke Graves. **CP-GravR**

Clouds fly fast across the moon, The. Marian. George Meredith. **CP-MerG2**

Clouds from the west have covered the sun. The Thresher. John Hewitt. **CP-HewiJ**

Clouds glow like coals just fresh from fire, a flare. The Unextinguished. Theodore Roethke. **CP-RoetT**

Clouds, gold and purple, o'er the westering ray. Written at the Same Place, on Seeing a Seaman Return Who Had Been Imprisoned at Rochfort. Charlotte Smith. **CP-SmitC**

Clouds, lingering yet, extend in solid bars. Composed by the Side of Grasmere Lake. William Wordsworth. **CP-WorW1**

Clouds moved in another hundred feet, The. Clouds. Stephen Dobyns. **SP-DobyS**

Clouds of dissipation hang like wars, The. Poem for Paul Eluard. Charles Henri Ford. **SP-FordC**

Clouds of Evening. Robinson Jeffers. **CP-JefR1**

Clouds of Uig, The. Richard Hugo. **CP-HugoR**

Clouds' silent shadows passing across the Sun above Teton's mountaintop. What's Dead? Allen Ginsberg. **CP-GinsA**

Clouds so swift / Rain won't lift. You Ain't Goin' Nowhere. "Bob Dylan." **CP-DylaB**

Clouds spout upon her. Rain on a Grave. Thomas Hardy. **CP-HardT**

Clouds stand lordly over Fenwick. Chinese Poets. John Clellon Holmes. **SP-HolmJ**

Clouds, the source of rain, one stormy night, The. Lost in Heaven. Robert Frost. **CP-FrosR**

Clouds their Backs together laid, The. Emily Dickinson. **CP-DickE**

Clouds took me by the hand. Stanley Jasspon Kunitz. *Fr.* Meditations on Death. **CP-KuniS**

Clouds were moving to the east, The. After. Frederick Morgan. **SP-MorgF**

Clouds, which rise with thunder, slake, The. All's Well. John Greenleaf Whittier. **CP-WhitJ**

Clouds within the Milky Way, The. Skyey Developments. John Updike. **CP-UpdiJ**

Clover. Herman Melville. **SP-MelvH**

Clover. Louis Zukofsky. **CP-ZukLS**

Clovers, The. Jean Garrigue. **SP-GarrJ**

Clover's simple Flame, The. Emily Dickinson. **CP-DickE**

Clown, The. Siv Cedering Fox. **SP-CedeS**

Clown, The. John Clare. **SP-ClarJ**

Clown, The. Donald Hall. **CP-HallD**

Clown. Phoebe Hesketh. **SP-HeskP**

Clown Flowers. Phoebe Hesketh. **SP-HeskP**

Clownlike, happiest on your hands. You're. Sylvia Plath. **CP-PlatS**

Clowns. Louis MacNeice. **VoGa** *Fr.* Circus. **CP-MacNL**

Clowns, Clowns and / Clowns. Clowns. Louis MacNeice. **VoGa** *Fr.* Circus. **CP-MacNL**

Clown's smirk in the skull of a baboon, A. Edward Estlin Cummings. **CP-CummE; SP-CummE**

Clown's Song. John Gould Fletcher. **SP-FletJ**

Cloy'd with the torments of a tedious night. Sonnet 12. Mary Sidney, Countess of Montgomery Wroth. *Fr.* Pamphilia to Amphilanthus. **CP-WrotM**

Club Car, The. Ogden Nash. **CP-NashO**

Clues. Muriel Rukeyser. **CP-RukeM**

Clues to what they remembered had been pasted into an album, The. Cenotaph. John Yau. **SP-YauJo**

Clump of jessamine / Softly beneath the rain, The. Bedroom. John Gould Fletcher. **SP-FletJ** *Fr.* The Ghosts of an Old House.

Clumsy at first, fitting together. Kentucky River Junction. Wendell Berry. **CP-BerrW**

Clumsy futility, drown yourself. Calypso. Hilda Doolittle. **CP-DoolH**

Clunton and Clunbury. Alfred Edward Housman. **CP-HousA**

Cluster of morning glories erupted from his skull, A. Sohl. Patti Smith. **SP-SmitP**

Clutching his cross, St. Vladimir. Kiev. John Updike. *Fr.* Postcards from Soviet Cities. **CP-UpdiJ**

Clutter-up People. Alice Walker. **CP-WalkA**

Clydesider. David Herbert Lawrence. **CP-LawrD**

C'mon Jack. Allen Ginsberg. **CP-GinsA**

C'mon said the pilot and. Small Plane in Kansas. Thom Gunn. **CP-GunnT**

Coach is at the door at last, The. Farewell to the Farm. Robert Louis Stevenson. **CP-StevR**

Coal. Audre Lorde. **SP-LordA**

("I is the total black.") **SP-LordA**

Coal Fern. Louise McNeill. **SP-McNeL**

Coal Fire, The. Donald Hall. **CP-HallD**

Coal fire burned in a basket grate, A. The Coal Fire. Donald Hall. **CP-HallD**

Coal Fire in Winter, A. Thomas McGrath. **SP-McGrT**

Coal was blacker than coal, The. The Fights. Gilbert Sorrentino. **SP-SorrG**

Coarse leaf, alder leaf. Hayden Carruth. **CP-CarHS** *Fr.* The Clay Hill Anthology.

Coast hills at Sovranes Creek, The. The Place for No Story. Robinson Jeffers. **CP-JefR2**

Coast-Nightmare, A. Christina Georgina Rossetti. **CP-RosC3**

Coast of Maine. Richard Eberhart. **CP-EberR**

Coast of Texas. Gilbert Sorrentino. **SP-SorrG**

Coast-Road, The. Robinson Jeffers. **CP-JefR2**

Coast-road was being straightened and repaired again, The. Thurso's Landing. Robinson Jeffers. **CP-JefR2**

Coastal Moon. Al Young. **CP-YounA**

Coastal Strip. George Oppen. **CP-OppeG**

Coasters, The. John Hewitt. **CP-HewiJ**

Coastwise Lights, The. Rudyard Kipling. **CP-KiplR**

Coat, The. Stephen Berg. **SP-BergS**

Coat, A. William Butler Yeats. **CP-YeatW**

Coats, The. Tess Gallagher. **SP-GallT**

Cob clouts his shooes, and as the story tells. Upon Cob. Robert Herrick. **CP-HerrR**

Cob, thou nor soldier, thief, nor fencer art. To Pertinax Cob. Ben Jonson. **CP-JonsB**

Cobble thrown a hundred years ago, A. Clearances. Seamus Heaney. **SP-HeanS**

Cobbler Keezar's Vision. John Greenleaf Whittier. **CP-WhitJ**

Coblers Catch, The. Robert Herrick. **CP-HerrR**

Cobra, The. Ogden Nash. **CP-NashO**

Cobra Lilies in the Supermarket. Diane Wakoski. **SP-WakoD**

Cobweb. John Hewitt. **CP-HewiJ**

Cobwebs. Christina Georgina Rossetti. **CP-RosC3**

Cobwebs and Ratholes. Marsden Hartley. **CP-HartM**

Cochiti. Charles Tomlinson. **CP-TomlC**

Cock-a-Doo. Stevie Smith. **CP-SmitS**

Cock-a-doodle-doo the brass-lined rooster goes [*or* says]. Dog. John Crowe Ransom. **SP-RansJ**

Cock-a-Hoop. Isabella Gardner. **CP-GardI**

Cock and cunt. Hymn to the Word. Charles Olson. **CP-OlsoC**

Cock and the Fox, The. Geoffrey Chaucer. *See* The Nun's Priest's Tale.

Cock and the Hen, The. Stevie Smith. **CP-SmitS**

Cock calls his Wife his Hen: when Cock goes too't. Upon Cock. Robert Herrick. **CP-HerrR**

Cock-Crow. Robert Herrick. **CP-HerrR**

Cock crows, The / But no queen rises. Depression before Spring. Wallace Stevens. **CP-StevW**

Cock-Fighters Garland. William Cowper. **CP-CowpW**

Cock in Pullet's Feathers. Robert Ranke Graves. **CP-GravR**

Cock is crowing, The. Written in March [While Resting on the Bridge at the Foot of Brother's Water]. William Wordsworth. **CP-WorW1**

Cock o' the North. Louis MacNeice. **CP-MacNL**

"Bad Lord Byron went to the firing, helmet and dogs and all."

"Bards wha hae for Hellas bled—."

"Close the vein! It is Easter Eve."

"Flattest place, it seems, in Hellas. A bad dream, The."

Cock of the North, The. The Cock and the Hen. Stevie Smith. **CP-SmitS**

Cock on the weather vane, The. The Weathercock on the Cathedral of Quito. Jorge Carrera Andrade, *tr. fr. Spanish by* Thomas Merton. **CP-MertT**

Cock-pit. Jim Morrison. **SP-MorrJ**

Cock shall crow, The. Ditty. Robert Louis Stevenson. **CP-StevR**

Cock the right eyebrow: Heredity. James McAuley. **SP-McAuJ** *Fr. Studies for a Self-Portrait at Forty.*

Cock up Your Beaver. Robert Burns. **CP-BurnR**

Cockchafer. Isabella Gardner. **CP-GardI**

Cockle. Louis Zukofsky. **CP-ZukLS**

Cockleburs came on the burdocks, The. Suburban Sicilian Sketches. Carl Sandburg. **CP-SandC**

Cockle's Antibilious Pills. Gerard Manley Hopkins. *Fr. A Trio of Triolets.* **CP-HopkG**

Cocklorel would needs have the devil his guest. Ben Jonson. **CP-JonsB** *Fr. The Gypsies Metamorphosed.*

Cockney Amorist, The. Sir John Betjeman. **CP-BetjJ**

Cockroach. Charles Bukowski. **SP-BukC1**

Cockroach. Anne Sexton. **CP-SextA**

Cockroach crouched, The. Cockroach. Charles Bukowski. **SP-BukC1**

Cock's clear voice into the clearer air, The. Robert Louis Stevenson. **CP-StevR**

Cocks crow / Dogs bark / This all men know. Tao. Chuang Tzu, *tr. fr. Chinese by* Thomas Merton. **CP-MertT**

Cocktails / and signs of. Louis Zukofsky. *Fr. 29 Poems.* **CP-ZukLS**

Cocoa-nut naught. On the High Price of Fish. William Cowper. **CP-CowpW**

Cocoa Tree. Jorge Carrera Andrade, *tr. fr. Spanish by* Thomas Merton. **CP-MertT**

Cocoon, The. Robert Frost. **CP-FrosR**

Cocoon above! Cocoon below! Emily Dickinson. **CP-DickE**

Cocooned in Time, at this inhuman height. Back from Australia. Sir John Betjeman. **CP-BetjJ**

Cod Head, The. William Carlos Williams. **CP-WilW1**

Cod Summer. Marge Piercy. **SP-PierM**

Coda. Jim Carroll. **SP-CarrJ**

Coda. Jane Cooper. *Fr. March.* **SP-CoopJ**

Coda. Marilyn Hacker. *Fr. The Regent's Park Sonnets.* **SP-HackM**

Coda. Louis MacNeice. **CP-MacNL**

Coda. Ezra Pound. **SP-PounE**

Coda. Richard Shelton. **SP-ShelR**

Coda: Song. Ted Berrigan. **SP-BerrT**

Code, The. Robert Frost. **CP-FrosR**

Code, The. John Updike. **CP-UpdiJ**

Code of Morals, A. Rudyard Kipling. **CP-KiplR**
("Lest you should think this story true.") **CP-KiplR**

Codicil. Derek Walcott. **CP-WalcD**

Coelum Britannicum. Thomas Carew. **CP-CareT** *Fr. Carew's Masque.* **CP-CareT**

Coeur de Lion. Frank Templeton Prince. **CP-PrinF**

Coeur Simple. Stevie Smith. **CP-SmitS**

Coffee Cup, The. Donald Hall. **CP-HallD**

Coffee leaps in a crystal knob. Louis MacNeice. *Fr. Country Week-End.* **CP-MacNL**

Coffee with the Meal. Ogden Nash. **CP-NashO**

Coffin—is a small Domain, A. Emily Dickinson. **CP-DickE**

Cogimur; invitis (Clarissime) parce quaerelis. Illustrissimo, Potentissimoque Principi, *Frederico* Quinto, Rheni Comiti Palatino, Duci Bavariae, &c. Thomas Campion. **CP-CampT**

Cogis ut inspidus sapiat, damnose Cupido. *acc. by English translation.* Thomas Campion. **CP-CampT**

Coheires. Robert Herrick. **CP-HerrR**

Cohorts of charabancs fanfared Offa's province and. Geoffrey Hill. *Fr. Mercian Hymns.* **CP-HillG**

Coign of Vantage. Ron Koertge. **SP-KoerR**

Coil of space the cones of light, The. Ralph Waldo Emerson. **CP-EmerR**

Coiled in the azimuth, Vipère. Mix the Ingredients. Hayden Carruth. **CP-CarHS**

Coin, A. Carl Sandburg. **CP-SandC**

Coin the daydawn into lines. Ralph Waldo Emerson. **CP-EmerR**

Coincidence. Robert Pack. **SP-PackR**

Coincidences undeniably imply meaning. Relevance. David Markson. **CP-MarkD**

Coiner, The. Rudyard Kipling. **CP-KiplR**

Coins and Coffins under My Bed. Diane Wakoski. **SP-WakoD**

Coins handsome as Nero's; of good substance and. Geoffrey Hill. **FaBoMo; HAP; NoAM** *Fr. Mercian Hymns.* **CP-HillG**

Coitus. Ezra Pound. **SP-PounE**

Cold, The. Wendell Berry. **CP-BerrW**

Cold / cold / on the bold. Other Than. Charles Olson. **CP-OlsoC**

Cold / like Grandfather's icehouse. God's Backside. Anne Sexton. **CP-SextA**

Cold. Pablo Neruda, *tr. fr. Spanish by* Ben Belitt. **SP-NeruP**

Cold, The. Charles Simic. **SP-SimiC**

Cold, The. Barton Sutter. **SP-SuttB**

Cold and clear-cut face, why come you so cruelly meek. Tennyson. **EBVVPR** *Fr. Maud [A Monodrama].* **CP-TennA**

Cold and final, the imagination. Two Lovers and a Beachcomber by the Real Sea. Sylvia Plath. **CP-PlatS**

Cold and the cranes. / Cranes in the. Migratory Noon. Joseph Ceravolo. **SP-CeraJ**

Cold as no love, and wild with all negation. Quand on n'a pas ce que l'on aime, il faut aimer ce que l'on a—. Stevie Smith. **CP-SmitS**

Cold as No Plea. The Death Sentence. Stevie Smith. **CP-SmitS**

Cold as the breath of winds that blow. Lucasta's World. Richard Lovelace. **CP-LoveR**

Cold Blood. David Herbert Lawrence. **CP-LawrD**

Cold blood or warm, crawling or fluttering. Pet Shop. Louis MacNeice. **CP-MacNL**

Cold Blue Tinge. Charles Simic. **SP-SimiC**

Cold came. It has photographed the scene, The. In the Balance. Charles Tomlinson. **CP-TomlC**

Cold, clear, and blue, the morning heaven. Emily Brontë. **CP-BronE**

Cold-cold-are the sabre wings of the Jaeger. A Simple Seabird's Tribute to Her Harteebeeste. Malcolm Lowry. **CP-LowrM**

Cold cold cold of a special night. Rock-Study with Wanderer. John Berryman. **CP-BerrJ**

Cold, cold is the blast when December is howling. Song. Percy Bysshe Shelley. *Fr. Original Poetry by Victor and Cazire.* **CP-ShelP**

Cold coming we had of it, A. Journey of the Magi. Thomas Stearns Eliot. **CP-ElioT**

Cold Divinities, The. James Wright. **CP-WrigJ**

Cold earth slept below, The. Lines. Percy Bysshe Shelley. **CP-ShelP**

Cold-eyed, in Naples once. Stanley Jasspon Kunitz. *Fr. The Lincoln Relics.* **CP-KuniS**

Cold Faces. Jim Carroll. **SP-CarrJ**

Cold felt cold until our blood, The. Phantasia for Elvira Shatayev. Adrienne Rich. **SP-RicA1; SP-RicA2**

Cold Front, A. William Carlos Williams. **CP-WilW2**

Cold Heaven, The. William Butler Yeats. **CP-YeatW**

Cold holds everything in abeyance, The. Commas in Wintertime. Richard Eberhart. **CP-EberR**

Cold how mean, fortune consuming you oppresses your care, your. Catullus. *See* Carmen 68: "Borne down by bitter misfortune."

Cold hunger tripped her but her years. Hayden Carruth. *Fr. North Winter.* **CP-CarHL**

Cold in cathedral the old women pray. The Old Country. Howard Nemerov. **CP-NemeH**

Cold in the earth, and the deep snow piled above thee! Remembrance. Emily Brontë. **CP-BronE**

Cold Iron. Rudyard Kipling. **CP-KiplR**

Cold is here. Impossible to wake, The. The Rocks. Stephen Berg. **SP-BergS**

Cold moon hangs to the sky by its horn, The. The Night of the Dance. Thomas Hardy. **CP-HardT**

Cold moonlight / Is it you stopping my marrow seeds from growing? Moon. Jenny Joseph. *Fr. Derivations.* **SP-JoseJ**

Cold moons withdraw, refusing to come to terms. Metamorphoses of the Moon. Sylvia Plath. **CP-PlatS**

Cold Mountain is a house, *after* Han-shan. Gary Snyder. **CP-SnydG**

Cold Night, The. William Carlos Williams. **CP-WilW1**

Cold night, the sidewalk we walk on icy, A. Christmas Eve Service at Midnight at St. Michael's. Robert Bly. **SP-BlyR**

Cold on my narrow cot I lie. To a Jilted Lover. Sylvia Plath. **CP-PlatS**

Cold opal eyes gleaming. The Silence of the Lambs. Tom Clark. **SP-ClarT**

Cold Pane, The. Wendell Berry. **CP-BerrW**

Cold Pastoral. Allen Tate. **CP-TateA**

Cold Plums. Charles Bukowski. **SP-BukC1**

Cold remote islands, The. Night. Louise Bogan. **CP-BogaL**

Cold rewards trail in, when the man is blind, The. John Berryman. *Fr. Sonnets to Chris.* **CP-BerrJ**

Cold Rheum. Archie Randolph Ammons. **SP-AmmoA**

Cold rises around / our house, the wind, The. Midwinter, Presolstice. Margaret Atwood. **SP-AtwM1**

Cold Roast Hamlet Blues, Blubberhouses Blues, Ugley Blues. Malcolm Lowry. **CP-LowrM**

Cold rosy dawn in New York City. American Express. Ted Berrigan. **SP-BerrT**

Cold, slow, silent, but returning, after so many hours. A Prayer at Morning. Randall Jarrell. **CP-JarrR**

Cold so keen, A. Nightgown. James Merrill. **SP-MerrJ**

Cold Spring, A. Elizabeth Bishop. **CP-BishE**

Cold Spring Harbor. Derek Walcott. **CP-WalcD**

Cold Spring in Essex. Donald Davie. **CP-DavDo**

Cold Sunbeams. Nicholas Vachel Lindsay. **CP-LindV**

Cold the day and cold the drifted snow. January. Christina Georgina Rossetti. *Fr.* The Months: A Pageant. **CP-RosC2**

Cold the day and cold the drifted snow. The Months: A Pageant. Christina Georgina Rossetti. **CP-RosC2**

Cold Warrior: Anzac Day, 1946. John Hewitt. **CP-HewiJ**

Cold Water. Donald Hall. **CP-HallD**

Cold whip-adder unespied, The. Gerard Manley Hopkins. **CP-HopkG**

Cold white snowy [or snowie] nunnery, The. The Virgins. John Donne. *Fr.* A Litany. **CP-DonnJ**

Cold wind of autumn, blowing loud. Autumn Daybreak. Edna St. Vincent Millay. **CP-MillE**

Cold wind stirs the blackthorn, A. Endure Hardness. Christina Georgina Rossetti. **CP-RosC2**

Cold Window. John Clellon Holmes. **SP-HolmJ**

Colder Fire. Robert Penn Warren. **LiTM** *Fr.* To a Little Girl, One Year Old, in a Ruined Fortress. **SP-WarrR**

Colder than land is the random sea, shriveling. Aqua. Hayden Carruth. *Fr.* Journey to a Known Place. **CP-CarHL**

Colder the Air, The. Elizabeth Bishop. **CP-BishE**

Coldly, bleakly, drearily. Emily Brontë. **CP-BronE**

Coldly we spake. The Saxons, overpowered. William Wordsworth. *Fr.* Ecclesiastical Sonnets. **CP-WorW2**

Coldness in Love. David Herbert Lawrence. **CP-LawrD**

Coleridge. Robert Lowell. **SP-LoweR**

Coleridge and Richard II. Robert Lowell. **SP-LoweR**

Coleridge received the Person from Porlock. Thoughts about the Person from Porlock. Stevie Smith. **CP-SmitS**

Coleridge stands, he flamed for the one friend. . . . Coleridge. Robert Lowell. **SP-LoweR**

Coleridge wasn't flatter-blinded by. Coleridge and Richard II. Robert Lowell. **SP-LoweR**

Coleridge's Mind a Life Unto Itself. William Wordsworth. **EPCY** *Fr.* Cambridge and the Alps. *Fr.* The Prelude; Growth of a Poet's Mind [1850 vers.]. **CP-WorW3**

Cole's Island. Charles Olson. **SP-OlsoC** *Fr.* The Maximus Poems.

Coleus. Louis Zukofsky. **CP-ZukLS**

Colin Clouts Come Home Againe. Edmund Spenser. **CP-Spens**

Colin, my deare, when shall it please thee sing. November. Edmund Spenser. **PoEL-1** *Fr.* The Shepheardes [or Shepeards or Shepherd's] Calender. **CP-Spens**

Colin, well fits thy sad cheare this sad stownd. A Pastorall Aeglogue upon the Death of Sir Phillip Sidney, Knight, etc. Edmund Spenser. *Fr.* Astrophel. **CP-Spens**

Coliseum, The. Edgar Allan Poe. **CP-PoeEd**

Collage of Echoes. Isabella Gardner. **CP-GardI**

Collar, The. George Herbert. **CP-HerbG**

Collarbone [or Collar-Bone] of a Hare, The. William Butler Yeats. **CP-YeatW**

Collected, Harry stood awee. Robert Burns. *Fr.* Extempore, in the Court of S——. **CP-BurnR**

Collected Poems. Kenneth Koch. **SP-KochK**

Collected Poems of, The. Charles Olson. **CP-OlsoC**

Collector Cleans His Picture, The. Thomas Hardy. **CP-HardT**

Collector's Choice. John Hewitt. **CP-HewiJ**

College, The. Lewis Turco. **SP-TurcL**

College Colonel, The. Herman Melville. **SP-MelvH**

College Fence, The. John Hewitt. **CP-HewiJ**

College Formal: Renaissance Casino. Langston Hughes. **SP-HughL**

College of cocktails, a few gentlemen. John Berryman. *Fr.* Sonnets to Chris. **CP-BerrJ**

College Under Water. Anne Waldman. **SP-WaldA**

Collier's Wife, The. David Herbert Lawrence. **CP-LawrD**

Collision with the earth has finally come—. Ted Hughes. **SP-HughT** *Fr.* Gaudete.

Colloque Sentimental. Frank O'Hara. **SP-OharF**

Colloquy for the States. Archibald MacLeish. **CP-MacLA**

Colloquy in Black Rock. Robert Lowell. **SP-LoweR**

Colloquy with a Polish Aunt. Wallace Stevens. **CP-StevW**

Colmcille. John Hewitt. *Fr.* Two Irish Saints. **CP-HewiJ**

Colney Hatch. John Hewitt. **CP-HewiJ**

Cologna Veneta. - / where the good folk. Carmen 17. Catullus. *Fr.* Carmina. **CP-Catul**

Cologne. Samuel Taylor Coleridge. **CP-ColeS**

Colonel Martin. William Butler Yeats. **CP-YeatW**

Colonel to be shot at dawn, The. Wystan Hugh Auden. **CP-AudWJ**

Colonel went out sailing, The. Colonel Martin. William Butler Yeats. **CP-YeatW**

Colonel's Soliloquy, The. Thomas Hardy. **CP-HardT**

Colonial Consequence. John Hewitt. **CP-HewiJ**

Colonist's "they" that needs no antecedent, The. Monmouthshire. Donald Davie. **CP-DavDo**

Colonus' Praise. Sophocles, *tr. by* W. B. Yeats. **CP-YeatW** *Fr.* Oedipus at Colonus.

Colony, The. John Hewitt. **CP-HewiJ**

Colony, The. Lewis Turco. **SP-TurcL**

Colony of the Sun, The. Kenneth Patchen. **CP-PatcK**

Colony's so old and it's out of touch, The. Colonial Consequence. John Hewitt. **CP-HewiJ**

Colophon. Robert Ranke Graves. **CP-GravR**

Colophon. Adrienne Rich. **CP-RicAE**

Color-bearers facing death, The. Rebel Color-Bearers at Shiloh. Herman Melville. **SP-MelvH**

Color, Caste, Denomination. Emily Dickinson. **CP-DickE**

Color floods to the spot, dull purple. Contusion. Sylvia Plath. **CP-PlatS**

Color is image. Charles Olson. **CP-OlsoC**

Color of lemon, mango, peach. Southern Sunrise. Sylvia Plath. **CP-PlatS**

Color of Snow, The. Erica Jong. **SP-JongE**

Color of Stepped on Gum, The. Tom Clark. **SP-ClarT**

Color of the Grave is Green, The. Emily Dickinson. **CP-DickE**

Color of Time, The. Charles Kenneth Williams. **CP-WillC**

Color, taste, and smell, smaragdus, sugar, and musk. Abu Nadhar 'Abdu'l 'Aziz, *tr. fr. Persian by* Ralph Waldo Emerson. **CP-EmerR**

Colorado. Mona Van Duyn. **SP-VanDM**

Colored Band, The. Paul Laurence Dunbar. **CP-DunbP**

Colored Blues Singer. Countee Cullen. **CP-CullC**

Colored Soldiers, The. Paul Laurence Dunbar. **CP-DunbP**

Colors. Robert Creeley. **CP-CreeR**

Colors. Countee Cullen. **CP-CullC**

Colors. Shel Silverstein. **SP-SilS2**

Colors. Anne Waldman. **SP-WaldA**

Colors are more complicated than a state. Colors. Anne Waldman. **SP-WaldA**

Colors of a Bird, The. Richard Hugo. **CP-HugoR**

Colors of stars. Colors. Robert Creeley. **CP-CreeR**

Colossians 3:3. George Herbert. *See* My words and thoughts do both express this notion.

Colossus, The. Sylvia Plath. **CP-PlatS**

Colour, The. Thomas Hardy. **CP-HardT**

Colour. John Hewitt. **CP-HewiJ**

Colour fulfills where Music has no power. Chartres Windows. Rudyard Kipling. **CP-KiplR**

Colour Machine, The. Thom Gunn. **CP-GunnT**

Colour Supplement Pages. Roy Fisher. **SP-FishR**

Colours drain, shapes blur, resisting. The Kiss at Bayreuth. Thom Gunn. **CP-GunnT**

Colours of Night, The. Robert Ranke Graves. **CP-GravR**

Colubriad, The. William Cowper. **CP-CowpW**

Columbian Ode. Paul Laurence Dunbar. **CP-DunbP**

Columbian's Song, The. Walt Whitman. **CP-WhitW**

Columbines. Kathleen Jessie Raine. **SP-RainK**

Columbus. Thomas McGrath. **SP-McGrT**

Columbus. Ogden Nash. **CP-NashO**

Columbus may have worked the wind. America Is Hard to See. Robert Frost. **CP-FrosR**

Columbus said the world is round? The Edge of the World. Shel Silverstein. **SP-SilS2**

Columbus, wearing a night-gown made from a treasure map. Columbus. Thomas McGrath. **SP-McGrT**

Column Intended by Buonaparte for a Triumphal Edifice in Milan, Now Lying by the Way-Side in the Simplon Pass, The. William Wordsworth. *Fr.* Memorials of a Tour of the Continent; 1820. **CP-WorW2**

Columns. Rudyard Kipling. **CP-KiplR**

Columns glow faintly white, The. These Unreturning Destinies. Kenneth Patchen. **CP-PatcK**

Columns of the Parthenon, The. Donald Hall. **CP-HallD**

Comanches. Daniel Gerard Hoffman. **SP-HoffD**

Comanding Asker, if it be. The Faire Begger. Richard Lovelace. **CP-LoveR**

Combat. Charles Kenneth Williams. **CP-WillC; SP-WillC**

Combat Cultural. Marianne Craig Moore. **CP-MoorM**

Combative Spirit, The. David Herbert Lawrence. **CP-LawrD**

Combe. Patti Smith. **SP-SmitP**

Combed thru the piers the wind. The Translucent Mechanics. George Oppen. **NNaP** *Fr.* Some San Francisco Poems. **CP-OppeG**

Combination of blind drive and accident which make up what, The. Out of Darkness I Came. Tom Clark. **SP-ClarT**

Come, / Let us roam the night together. Harlem Night Song. Langston Hughes. **SP-HughL**

Come. Stevie Smith. **CP-SmitS**

Come [Harriet]! sweet is the hour. Song. Percy Bysshe Shelley. *Fr.* Original Poetry by Victor and Cazire. **CP-ShelP**

Come / this evening. The End. Frederick Morgan. **SP-MorgF**

Come, / tired old thing. Marsden Hartley. **CP-HartM**

Come a little further—why be afraid. Edward Estlin Cummings. **CP-CummE**

Come a shore, come, merrie mates. Thomas Campion. *Fr.* Description of a Maske: Presented in the Banqueting Roome at *Whitehall*, on Saint Stephens Night Last, at the Marriage of the Right Honourable the Earle of *Somerset*: and the Right Noble the Lady FRANCES *Howard*. **CP-CampT**

"Come aboard" the old man used to say. Rosy, It Was. Charles Olson. **CP-OlsoC**

Come again to the place. After the Visit. Thomas Hardy. **CP-HardT**

Come All Ye Brave Boys. Allen Ginsberg. **CP-GinsA**

Come all ye Sons of Art. Gilbert Sorrentino. **SP-SorrG**

Come all you young men that proudly display. Come All Ye Brave Boys. Allen Ginsberg. **CP-GinsA**

Come along, everybody, see the pretty baby. After the Christening. Ogden Nash. **CP-NashO**

Come along in then, little girl! From a Very Little Sphinx. Edna St. Vincent Millay. **CP-MillE**

Come, And Be My Baby. Maya Angelou. **SP-AngeM**

Come and come forth and come up from the cup of. Words for a Trumpet Chorale Celebrating the Autumn. Delmore Schwartz. **SP-SchwD**

Come and eat your Pablum. James Fenton. *Fr.* Exempla. **SP-FentJ**

Come and Kiss Me Sweet and Twenty. Paul Laurence Dunbar. **CP-DunbP**

Come and let us live my Deare. Catullus. *See* Carmen 5: "Lesbia / live with me."

Come and let us live my Deare. Out of Catullus. Ausonius, *tr. fr. Latin by* Richard Crashaw. **CP-CrasR**

Come and let's in solemn wise. The Sacrifice, by Way of Discourse betwixt Himselfe and Julia. Robert Herrick. **CP-HerrR**

Come Anthea, know thou this. To Anthea. Robert Herrick. **CP-HerrR**

Come Anthea let us two. The Wake. Robert Herrick. **CP-HerrR**

Come Arabella, fetch the cake. The Party. Ogden Nash. **CP-NashO**

Come around you rovin' gamblers and a story I will tell. Rambling, Gambling Willie. "Bob Dylan." **CP-DylaB**

Come as my doctor. Invitation to Bristol. Robert Ranke Graves. **CP-GravR**

Come away, / Make no delay. Doomsday. George Herbert. **CP-HerbG**

Come away, arm'd with loves delights. Thomas Campion. **CP-CampT**

Come away; bring thy golden theft. Song, A. Thomas Campion. *Fr.* The Lords Mask[e].

Come away! come away! there's a frost along the marshes. The Wilderness. Edwin Arlington Robinson. **CP-RobiE**

Come away to dreamin' town. Dreamin' Town. Paul Laurence Dunbar. **CP-DunbP**

Come baby, find me, come baby, remind me of where I once begun. Emotionally Yours. "Bob Dylan." **CP-DylaB**

Come back and you will find me just the same. Randall Jarrell, Office Hours 10-11. Randall Jarrell. **CP-JarrR**

Come back Mother, come back from. An Eternity. William Carlos Williams. **CP-WilW2**

Come back, Peter. Come back, Ben Britten. Ben. Paul Muldoon. *Fr.* 7, Middagh Street. **SP-MuldP**

Come back to me, who wait and watch for you. Christina Georgina Rossetti. *Fr.* Monna Innominata. **CP-RosC2**

Come back when fog drifts out over the city. He Was Alone (As in Reality) Upon His Humble Bed. Kenneth Patchen. **CP-PatcK**

Come balmy sleep! tired Nature's soft resort! To Sleep. Charlotte Smith. **CP-SmitC**

Come, be content, since out it must. To Charles Ford, Esq. on His Birthday. Jonathan Swift. **CP-SwifJ**

Come, be happy!—sit near me. Invocation to Misery. Percy Bysshe Shelley. **CP-ShelP**

Come blessed sleep, most full, most perfect, come. There Remaineth Therefore a Rest for the People of God. Christina Georgina Rossetti. **CP-RosC3**

Come blithefull Neatherds, let us lay. A Beucolick, or Discourse of Neatherds. Robert Herrick. **CP-HerrR**

Come, blue-eyed maid of heaven!—but thou, alas! Byron. **NOBRP** *Fr.* Childe Harold's Pilgrimage. **CP-Byron**

Come, blunt your spear with us. Huntress. Hilda Doolittle. **CP-DoolH**

Come boat me o'er, come row me o'er. O'er the Water to Charlie. Robert Burns. **CP-BurnR**

Come, brave soldiers, come, and see. In Cicatrices Domini Jesu. Richard Crashaw. **CP-CrasR**

Come, Break with Time. Louise Bogan. **CP-BogaL**

Come, bring thy gift. If blessings were as slow. An Offering. George Herbert. **CP-HerbG**

Come, bring with a noise. Ceremonies for Christmas[se]. Robert Herrick. **CP-HerrR**

Come bring your sampler, and with Art. The Wounded Heart. Robert Herrick. **CP-HerrR**

Come, bumpers high, express your joy. You're Welcome, Willie Stewart. Robert Burns. **CP-BurnR**

Come, buy my fine oranges, sauce for your veal. Oranges. Jonathan Swift. *Fr.* Verses Made for the Women Who Cry Apples, etc. **CP-SwifJ**

Come buy my fine wares. Apples. Jonathan Swift. **AnIV; NCEP; OnYI** *Fr.* Verses Made for the Women Who Cry Apples, etc. **CP-SwifJ**

Come, Capsicum, cast off thy membranous pods. The Sensualist. John Updike. **CP-UpdiJ**

Come, Celia, fix thine eyes on mine. To a Lady, Not Yet Enjoyed by Her Husband. Thomas Carew. **CP-CareT**

Come, chearfull day, part of my life, to mee. Thomas Campion. *See* Come, Cheerful Day!

Come cheer up, my lads, 'tis to glory we steer! Christina Georgina Rossetti. **CP-RosC3**

Come, Cheerful Day! Thomas Campion. **CP-CampT**

("Come, chearfull day, part of my life, to mee.") **CP-CampT**

Come, child, while rambling through the nation. The Club Car. Ogden Nash. **CP-NashO**

Come children, gather round my knee. Good Riddance, but Now What? Ogden Nash. **CP-NashO**

Come close to me, dear friends; still closer; thus! Paracelsus. Robert Browning. **CP-BroR1**

Come closer, hat in the dust. The Wars. Pablo Neruda, *tr. fr. Spanish by* Ben Belitt. **SP-NeruP**

Come closer yet, my honeysuckle, my sweetheart Jinny. The Land of Whipperginny. Robert Ranke Graves. **CP-GravR**

Come, come away / Or let me go. Upon a Delaying Lady. Robert Herrick. **CP-HerrR**

Come, come dear Night! Love's mart of kisses. Epithalamion Teratos. George Chapman. **ElL; LoBV; NoSic** *Fr.* Hero and Leander. **CP-MarlC**

Come, come, no time for lamentation now. John Milton. **ChTr; FaBoRV; FiP** *Fr.* Samson Agonistes. **CP-MiltJ**

(Death of Samson.) **ChTr**

(No Time for Lamentation Now.) **FaBoRV**

Come, come, thou bleak December Wind. A Death Wish. Samuel Taylor Coleridge. **CP-ColeS**

Come, come with emulative strife. Learning. Christopher Smart. *Fr.* Hymns for the Amusement of Children. **SP-SmarC**

Come crown my brows with leaves of myrtle. The Tortoise. Ogden Nash. **CP-NashO**

Come, cuckoo, come; / Come again, swift swallow. Summer. Christina Georgina Rossetti. **CP-RosC3**

Come Dance in Baronies. René Char, *tr. fr. French by* Thomas Merton. **CP-MertT**

Come darkest night, be[e]coming sorrow best. Sonnet 19. Mary Sidney, Countess of Montgomery Wroth. **NOSC** *Fr.* Pamphilia to Amphilanthus. **CP-WrotM**

Come, dear Amanda, quit the town. To Amanda. James Thomson *and* David Mallet. **CP-ThomJ**

Come, dear children, let us away. The Forsaken Merman. Matthew Arnold. **SP-ArnoM**

Come, Death (1). Stevie Smith. **CP-SmitS**

Come, Death (2). Stevie Smith. **CP-SmitS**

Come death, come bands, nor do you shrink, my eares. Acts 21; I Am Ready Not Onely To Be Bound but To Dye. Richard Crashaw. **CP-CrasR**

Come, Death, I'd have a word with thee. Motley. Walter de la Mare. **CP-DeLaW**

Come deere, lett's waulke into this spring. Mary Sidney, Countess of Montgomery Wroth. *Fr.* Part 2. *Fr.* Urania. **CP-WrotM**

Come, Doctor, we must fly someotherwhere. William Dickey. **SP-DickW** *Fr.* Part Song, With Concert of Recorders. **SP-DickW**

Come, *Dorus,* come, let the songs thy sorrows signify, *dialogue of Lalus and Dorus.* Sir Philip Sidney. **SP-SidnP** *Fr.* Arcadia.

Come down, and dance ye in the toyle. A Song to the Maskers. Robert Herrick. **CP-HerrR**

Come down Canyon Creek trail on a summer afternoon. How to Regain Your Soul. William Stafford. **SP-StafW**

Come down, come down Beloved. Thomas Merton. *Fr.* Figures for an Apocalypse. **CP-MertT**

Come down, O maid, from yonder mountain height. Tennyson. **EBVV; FF; GTBS-P; MeMBP; NAEL-2; NOBVV; OAEL-2; OBEV; OBNC; PIP; SCGP; TrGrPo** *Fr.* So was their sanctuary violated. *Fr.* The Princess. **CP-TennA**

(Idyl, An: "Come down, O maid, from yonder mountain height.") **TrGrPo**

Come down to my room. My Room. Leonard Cohen. **CP-CoheL**

Come, drink a stirrup cup with me. The Stirrup Cup. Paul Laurence Dunbar. **CP-DunbP**

Come, drunks and drug-takers; come, perverts unnerved! Several Voices Out of a Cloud. Louise Bogan. **CP-BogaL**

Come, eat the bread of idleness. The Beggar Speaks. Nicholas Vachel Lindsay. **CP-LindV**

Come, *Espilus,* come now declare thy skill, *dialogue of Therion and Espilus.* Sir Philip Sidney. **SP-SidnP** *Fr.* The Lady of May.

Come, essay a sprightly measure. A Bridal Measure. Paul Laurence Dunbar. **CP-DunbP**

Come evening once again, season of peace. William Cowper. **NAEL-1** *Fr.* The Winter Evening. *Fr.* The Task. **CP-CowpW**

Come, fair muse of Grub Street, the dialogue write. A Dialogue between Captain Tom and Sir Henry Dutton Colt. Jonathan Swift. **CP-SwifJ**

Come, follow me by the smell. Onyons. Jonathan Swift. **BIrV; CP-SwifJ; FaBoUs** *Fr.* Verses Made for the Women Who Cry Apples, etc. **CP-SwifJ**

Come, follow me into the realms of music. Here is the gate. "Hugh MacDiarmid." **SP-MacDH** *Fr.* Plaited Like the Generations of Men.

Come follow me, my wandring mates. Thomas Campion. *Fr.* The Ayres that Were Sung and Played, at *Brougham Castle* in *Westmerland,* in the Kings Entertainment. **CP-CampT**

Come Forth. James Wright. **CP-WrigJ**

Come forth, come forth, the gentle Spring. Ben Jonson. **CP-JonsB** *Fr.* Chloridia.

Come forth, ye Nymphes, come forth, forsake your watry bowres. The Mourning Muse of Thestylis. Edmund Spenser. *Fr.* Astrophel. **CP-Spens**

Come friend / I have an old story to tell you. Wallflower. Anne Sexton. **CP-SextA**

Come, friendly bombs, and fall on Slough. Slough. Sir John Betjeman. **CP-BetjJ**

Come from his gal's. Edward Estlin Cummings. **CP-CummE**

Come from the whirling zodiac. Gilbert Sorrentino. **SP-SorrG**

Come gather 'round friends. North Country Blues. "Bob Dylan." **CP-DylaB**

Come Gather Round Me Parnellites. William Butler Yeats. **CP-YeatW**

Come gather 'round people. The Times They Are A-Changin'. "Bob Dylan." **CP-DylaB**

Come, gaze with me upon this dome. Edward Estlin Cummings. **CP-CummE**

Come, gentle Air! th' Æolian shepherd said. *in imitation of* Waller. Alexander Pope. **CP-PopeA**

Come, Gentle God. James Thomson. **CP-ThomJ**

Come, gentle sleep, death's image though thou art. Thomas, the Younger Warton, tr. *fr. Latin by* William Wordsworth. **CP-WorW1**

Come, gentle Spring, ethereal Mildness come. Spring. James Thomson. *Fr.* The Seasons. **CP-ThomJ**

Come, gentle Venus! and assuage. A Nuptial song. James Thomson. **CP-ThomJ**

Come, George. Champagne and oysters. No Comment! John Hewitt. **CP-HewiJ**

Come guard this night the Christmas-Pie. Christmasse-Eve, Another Ceremonie. Robert Herrick. **CP-HerrR**

Come, healing god! Apollo, come and aid. Verses to Amanda. In Imitation of Tibullus. James Thomson. **CP-ThomJ**

Come heavenly Muse a suppliant asks thine aid. Lines on the Death of Miss M. B. Farnham. Ralph Waldo Emerson. **CP-EmerR**

Come heavenly Muse my voice inspire. No. 13 Hymn Written in Concord Sept. 1814. Ralph Waldo Emerson. **CP-EmerR**

Come here, I want to show you something. Sightseeing. Rita Dove. **SP-DoveR**

Come, here is adieu to the city. Robert Louis Stevenson. **CP-StevR**

Come hither all sweet maidens soberly. On a Leander Gem which Miss Reynolds, My Kind Friend, Gave Me. John Keats. **CP-KeatJ**

Come hither and behold the fruits. The Gulf of All Human Possessions. Jonathan Swift. *Fr.* Riddles. **CP-SwifJ**

Come hither, child—who gifted thee. Emily Brontë. **CP-BronE**

Come hither, gently rowing. Water Ballad. Samuel Taylor Coleridge. **CP-ColeS**

Come hither my boy tell me what thou seest here. Lacedemonian Instruction. William Blake. **CP-BlakW**

Come hither my sparrows. The Fairy. William Blake. **CP-BlakW**

Come hither, my sweet Rosalind. Rosalind and Helen; A Modern Eclogue. Percy Bysshe Shelley. **CP-ShelP**

Come, holy Silence, come. Silence. David Herbert Lawrence. **CP-LawrD**

Come home, come home! and where an home hath he. Arthur Hugh Clough. **SP-ClouA**

Come home, victorious wounded!—let the dead. Edna St. Vincent Millay. **CP-MillE**

Come, I will make the continent indissoluble. For You O Democracy. Walt Whitman. **CP-WhitW**

Come In. Robert Frost. **CP-FrosR**

Come in a week. Return of Returns. David Herbert Lawrence. **CP-LawrD**

Come in, dear guests, we've got a treat for you. Out Is Out. Ogden Nash. **CP-NashO**

Come in, the ford is roaring on the plain. Enid's Song. Tennyson. **FaBoRV** *Fr.* Geraint and Enid. *Fr.* Idylls of the King. **CP-TennA**

Come into Animal Presence. Denise Levertov. **CP-LeveD**

Come into the garden, Maud. Tennyson. **AWP; EBEvV; EBVV; EBVVPR; EnVR; FHYEP; FaBV; FiP; NOBE; NOBVV; OAEL-2; OXAEP-2; PIP; PoE; UV; VPP** *Fr.* Maud [A Monodrama]. **CP-TennA**

(Come into the Garden, Maud.) **PIP**

(Song: "Come into the garden, Maud.") **AWP**

Come into the Garden, Maud. Tennyson. *See* Come into the garden, Maud.

Come, Kings, and listen to my song. Gwin, King of Norway. William Blake. **CP-BlakW**

Come knock your heads against this stone. Epitaph, An. William Blake. **CP-BlakW**

Come lady, bring that pot. Tinker Jack and the Tidy Wives. Sylvia Plath. **CP-PlatS**

Come laughing when the wind. Folly of Clowns. Kenneth Patchen. **CP-PatcK**

Come learn with me the fatal song. The Mighty Heart. Ralph Waldo Emerson. **AA** *Fr.* Woodnotes II ("As sunbeams stream through liberal space"). **CP-EmerR**

Come leave the loathèd stage. Ode to Himself. Ben Jonson. **CP-JonsB**

Come, leave this loathed Country-life, and then. Upon Hinmself. Robert Herrick. **CP-HerrR**

Come, lecturer on love, resume your rostrum. Last Letter to the Scholar. Jean Garrigue. **SP-GarrJ**

Come, Lesbia, let us live and love. Catullus. *See* Carmen 5: "Lesbia / live with me."

Come, let me sing into your ear. *fr.* Words for Music Perhaps. William Butler Yeats. **CP-YeatW**

Come, let me write. 'And to what end?' To ease. Sonnet 34. Sir Philip Sidney. *Fr.* Astrophil and Stella. **SP-SidnP**

Come, let the State stay. Sir John Suckling. *Fr.* Brennoralt. **CP-SuckJ**

Come, let us build a temple to oblivion. Tabernacle. David Herbert Lawrence. **CP-LawrD**

Come, let us here enjoy the shade. Song, A. Ben Jonson. **CP-JonsB**

Come Let Us Mock at the Great. William Butler Yeats. **IHNG** *Fr.* Nineteen Hundred and Nineteen. **CP-YeatW**

Come, let us pity those who are better off than we are. The Garret. Ezra Pound. **SP-PounE**

Come, let us plant our love as farmers plant. The Love Tree. Countee Cullen. **CP-CullC**

Come let us pray to the Lord of the sky. Nicholas Vachel Lindsay. *Fr.* Johnny Appleseed's Wife of the Mind. **CP-LindV**

Come, let us rejoice in James Joyce, in the greatness of this poet. Delmore Schwartz. **SP-SchwD** *Fr.* A King of Kings, A King among the Kings.

Come Let Us Sound With Melodie. Thomas Campion. **CP-CampT**

Come let us strew roses. Hafiz, tr. by Ralph Waldo Emerson. **CP-EmerR** *Fr.* Odes.

Come, let us tell the weeds in ditches. Last Hill in a Vista. Louise Bogan. **CP-BogaL**

Come, let's to Culliford Hill and Wood. The Ballad of Love's Skeleton. Thomas Hardy. **CP-HardT**

Come lie with me and be my love. Lawrence Ferlinghetti. **SP-FerlL**

Come Little Birds. Robinson Jeffers. **CP-JefR3**

Come, little infant, love me now. Young Love. Andrew Marvell. **CP-MarvA**

Come, live in Now and occupy it well. Non Cogunt Astra. Robert Ranke Graves. **CP-GravR**

Come live with me and be my dear. Another of the Same Nature, Made Since. *Unknown.* **CP-MarlC**

Come live with me and be my love. A Further Proposal. Allen Ginsberg. **CP-GinsA**

Come live with me[e] and be my Love. The Passionate Shepherd to His Love. Christopher Marlowe. **CP-MarlC**

Come live with me and be my love. War Resisters' Song. Thomas McGrath. **SP-McGrT**

Come live with me[e], and be[e] my love. The Bait[e]. John Donne. **CP-DonnJ; CP-MarlC**

Come look they said. In San Salvador (I). Grace Paley. **CP-PaleG**

Come Lord, my head doth burn, my heart is sick. Home. George Herbert. **CP-HerbG**

Come lovely and soothing death. Walt Whitman. **DL; SCV** *Fr.* When Lilacs Last in the Dooryard Bloom'd. **OFD,** *sect.* 1, 2, and 6; **AP; APN-1; AWP; AmPP; BiP; CABA; CBCWP; FPL; FaBoEn; HAP; HBV; LiTA; LoBV; MasP; MeMAP; MoAmPo; NAAL-1; NAAL-3; NIP; NOBA; NoP; OxBA; PAI; PAL; PPP; PPoe; PoEL-5; PoRA; SAmP; SeCeV; TAP; TFi; TrGrPo; TreF** *Fr.* Memories of President Lincoln. **CP-WhitW**

(Carol of Death, The.) **DL**

Come, lovely cat, to this adoring breast, *See also* Come, lovely cat, to this adoring breast. The Cat. Charles Baudelaire, *tr. fr. French by* Countee Cullen. **CP-CullC**

Come lusty gamesters of the sea. Mary Sidney, Countess of Montgomery Wroth. *Fr.* Part 2. *Fr.* Urania. **CP-WrotM**

Come, Madam, come, all rest my powers defy [*or* defie]. To His Mistress Going to Bed. John Donne. **BoLoP; CBLP; EnRePo; ErPo; FaBoBl; JCP; MePo; NoP; NoSic; OAEL-1; OXAEP-1; OxBM; PoE; SeCP; TEP; UnTE** *Fr.* Elegies. **CP-DonnJ**

Come, megrims, mollygrubs and collywobbles! So Penseroso. Ogden Nash. **CP-NashO**

Come, merry May, on this first day. May Song. George Meredith. **CP-MerG2**

Come merry spring delight us. Song 3. Mary Sidney, Countess of Montgomery Wroth. *Fr.* Pamphilia to Amphilanthus. **CP-WrotM**

Come moo, dear moo, let's you and me. Due Respect. John Updike. **CP-UpdiJ**

Come Morning. John Ciardi. **SP-CiarJ**

Come, Muse, migrate from Greece and Ionia. The Muse in the New World. Walt Whitman. **MoAmPo** *Fr.* Song of the Exposition. **CP-WhitW**

Come, my beloved. From the Garden. Anne Sexton. **CP-SextA**

Come, my beloved, hear from me. Robert Louis Stevenson. **CP-StevR**

Come, my Celia, let us prove. Catullus. *See* Carmen 5: "Lesbia / live with me."

Come my Celia, let us prove, *after* Catullus, Carmen 5. Song. To Celia. Ben Jonson. **CP-JonsB** *Fr.* Volpone.

Come, my little children, here are songs for you. Robert Louis Stevenson. **CP-StevR**

Come, my little one, closer up against me. Wedlock. David Herbert Lawrence. **CP-LawrD**

Come, my sheep, my goats, graze where the shoots are tender. Louis MacNeice. *Fr.* Suite for Recorders. **CP-MacNL**

Come, my songs, let us speak of perfection. Salvationists. Ezra Pound. **SP-PounE**

Come, my tan-faced children. Pioneers! O Pioneers! Walt Whitman. **CP-WhitW**

Come, my Way, my Truth, my Life. The Call. George Herbert. **CP-HerbG**

Come, noble nymphs, and do not hide. Ben Jonson. **CP-JonsB** *Fr.* Neptune's Triumph.

Come not with kisses. Leda. David Herbert Lawrence. **CP-LawrD**

Come Not; Yet Come! Thomas Hardy. **CP-HardT**

Come nothing to my comparable soul. Edward Estlin Cummings. **CP-CummE**

"Come now," I said, "put off these webs of death". Bright Life. Walter de la Mare. **CP-DeLaW**

Come, O come, my life's delight. My Life's Delight. Thomas Campion. **CP-CampT**

Come October, if I close my eyes. The House Fly. James Merrill. **SP-MerrJ**

Come On! William Carlos Williams. **CP-WilW2**

Come On, Come Back. Stevie Smith. **CP-SmitS**

Come on, come on! And where you go. Ben Jonson. **CP-JonsB** *Fr.* Pleasure Reconciled to Virtue.

Come on come on come on come on. Everybody's Got Something to Hide Except Me and My Monkey. John Lennon *and* Paul McCartney. **CP-Beatl**

Come on! Come on! This hillock hides the spire. Sunday Afternoon Service in St. Enodoc Church, Cornwall. Sir John Betjeman. **CP-BetjJ**

Come On In, the Senility Is Fine. Ogden Nash. **CP-NashO**

Come on, superstition, and get my goat. Carl Sandburg. *Fr.* The People, Yes. **CP-SandC**

Come on walkin' wid me, Lucy. A Spring Wooing. Paul Laurence Dunbar. **CP-DunbP**

Come out, come out, wherever you are. Sarajevo Moon. Al Young. **CP-YounA**

Come out of the dark earth. Invocation. May Sarton. **SP-SartM**

Come over to my window, my little darling. So Long, Marianne. Leonard Cohen. **CP-CoheL**

Come, peace of mind, delightful guest! Ode to Peace. William Cowper. **CP-CowpW**

Come, Philomele, that sing'st of ravishment. William Shakespeare. **PBBP** *Fr.* The Rape of Lucrece. **CP-ShaWS**

Come pity [*or* pitie] us, all ye, who see. The Widow's Tears [*or* Widdowes Teares]: or, Dirge of Dorcas. Robert Herrick. **CP-HerrR**

Come play with me. To a Squirrel at Kyle-na-no. William Butler Yeats. **CP-YeatW**

Come pleasant thoughts; sweet thoughts, at will. Arthur Hugh Clough. **SP-ClouA**

Come, ponder well, for 'tis no jest. The Yearly Distress. William Cowper. **CP-CowpW**

Come praise Colonus' horses, and come praise. Colonus' Praise. Sophocles, *tr. by* W. B. Yeats. **CP-YeatW** *Fr.* Oedipus at Colonus.

Come rain down words as does. The God of Details. Donald Davie. **CP-DavDo**

Come rede me, dame, come tell me, dame. Robert Burns. **CP-BurnR**

Come, Rosie Angel, clasp. W. D. Is Concerned About the Character Assassination of Cock Robin. William DeWitt Snodgrass. **SP-SnodW**

Come, Rosie Angel, faced with blues. Disguised as Cock Robin, W. D. Escapes. William DeWitt Snodgrass. **SP-SnodW**

Come round me, little childer. The Ballad of Moll Magee. William Butler Yeats. **CP-YeatW**

Come, said my soul. Walt Whitman. **CP-WhitW**

Come said the Muse. Song of the Universal. Walt Whitman. **CP-WhitW**

Come shepherd's weeds, become your master's mind, *speech of Dorus.* Sir Philip Sidney. **SP-SidnP** *Fr.* Arcadia.

Come show thy Durham Breast. Emily Dickinson. **CP-DickE**

Come sing the name that brings all hearts. Fireside. George Meredith. **CP-MerG2**

Come sit beneath the tariff walls. The Economist's Song. Stanley Jasspon Kunitz. **CP-KuniS**

Come sit by my side, while this picture I draw. A Portrait from the Life. Jonathan Swift. **CP-SwifJ**

Come sit we by the fires side. The Coblers Catch. Robert Herrick. **CP-HerrR**

Come sit we under yonder Tree. To the Maids to Walke Abroad. Robert Herrick. **CP-HerrR**

Come, skilfull Lupo, now, and take. To the Painter, To Draw Him a Picture. Robert Herrick. **CP-HerrR**

Come, Sleep. Louise Bogan. **CP-BogaL**

Come sleep, O sleep, the certain knot of peace. Sonnet 39. Sir Philip Sidney. **CABA; EIL; EnRePo; HBV; LoBV; NAEL-1; NIP; NOBE; NoP; NoSic; OAEP; OBEV; OBSC; OXAEP-1; PPP; PoE; PoRA; SCGP; SCV; Son; TEP; TFi; TrGrPo; TreFS; WHA** *Fr.* Astrophil and Stella. **SP-SidnP**

Come slowly—Eden! Emily Dickinson. **CP-DickE**

Come small creatures of low estate, friskily moving. To the Field Mice. Richard Eberhart. **CP-EberR**

Come something come blood sunlight come and they break. The Eye-Beaters. James Dickey. **CP-DickJ**

Come, sons of summer, by whose toil[e]. The Hock-Cart, or Harvest Home. Robert Herrick. **CP-HerrR**

Come, spread foam rubber on the floor. I Can't Have a Martini, Dear, but You Take One, or, Are You Going to Sit THere Guzzling All Night? Ogden Nash. **CP-NashO**

Come Spring, Come Sorrow. David Herbert Lawrence. **CP-LawrD**

Come, surly fellow, come: a song! The Haunted House. Robert Ranke Graves. **CP-GravR**

Come swish around my pretty punk. A Drunken Man's Praise of Sobriety. William Butler Yeats. **CP-YeatW**

Come!—the palace of heaven rests on aëry pillars. Hafiz, *tr. by* Ralph Waldo Emerson. **CP-EmerR** *Fr.* Odes.

Come, the wind may never again. D.G.C. to J.A. Emily Brontë. **CP-BronE**

Come then in robe of darkest blue. To Melpomene. William Wordsworth. **CP-WorW1**

Come then Poet, and sing. And Tell Me Poet, Can Love Exist in Slavery? Etheridge Knight. **SP-KnigE**

Come Then to Prayers. Philip Larkin. **CP-LarkP**

Come, then, with showers; I love thy cloudy face. April. Walter de la Mare. **CP-DeLaW**

Come, thou awakener of the spirit's ocean. Fragment: Zephyrus the Awakener. Percy Bysshe Shelley. **CP-ShelP**

Come thou, but lead out of the inmost cave. Percy Bysshe Shelley. *Fr.* Ode to Liberty. **CP-ShelP**

"Come," thou dost say to Angels. Advent. Christina Georgina Rossetti. **CP-RosC3**

Come thou not neere those men, who are like Bread. To His Booke. Robert Herrick. **CP-HerrR**

Come thou, who art the wine and wit. His Winding-Sheet. Robert Herrick. **CP-HerrR**

Come to me darling little Ben. Farewell Rehearsed. Allen Tate. **CP-TateA**

Come to me God; but do not come. To God. Robert Herrick. **CP-HerrR**

Come to me in any shape! Song. George Meredith. **CP-MerG1**

Come to me in the silence of the night. Echo. Christina Georgina Rossetti. **CP-RosC1**

Come to me only with playthings now. . . . Murmurings in a Field Hospital. Carl Sandburg. **CP-SandC**

Come to my room off the street, come into the greasy shadows. Sister Ann. Stephen Berg. **SP-BergS**

Come to Sunny Prestatyn. Sunny Prestatyn. Philip Larkin. **CP-LarkP**

Come to the pane, draw the curtain apart. My Little March Girl. Paul Laurence Dunbar. **CP-DunbP**

Come to the Stone. Randall Jarrell. **CP-JarrR**

Come to your heaven, you [or yowe] heavenly choirs [or quires]. New Heaven, New War[re]. Robert Southwell. **CP-SoutR**

Come to your windows, rich women. Thomas Merton. *Fr.* Figures for an Apocalypse. **CP-MertT**

Come Together. John Lennon *and* Paul McCartney. **CP-Beatl**

Come Unto Me. Christina Georgina Rossetti. **CP-RosC3**

Come Unto These Yellow Sands. Gerard Manley Hopkins. *Fr.* Songs from Shakespeare, in Latin and Greek. **CP-HopkG**

Come Up from the Fields Father. Walt Whitman. **CP-WhitW**

Come up here, O dusty feet! Fairy Bread. Robert Louis Stevenson. **CP-StevR**

"Come up now into / the world" no need to light. To the Poets: To Make Much of Life. George Oppen. **CP-OppeG**

Come up, thou red thing. Southern Night. David Herbert Lawrence. **CP-LawrD**

Come upon this heap. It Uses Us! Leonard Cohen. **CP-CoheL**

Come virgin Tapers of pure waxe. Epithalamium. Richard Crashaw. **CP-CrasR**

Come, walk with me. Emily Brontë. **CP-BronE**

Come walk with me, my love, to Neasden Lane. In Willesden Churchyard. Sir John Betjeman. **CP-BetjJ**

Come, wander forth with me! the orange flowers. Serenade. Christina Georgina Rossetti. **CP-RosC3**

Come (we say) Clemenceau. The Dead to Clemenceau: November 1929. Robinson Jeffers. **CP-JefR2**

Come we shepheards whose blest sight. In the Holy Nativity of Our Lord God. Richard Crashaw. **CP-CrasR**

Come, wed me, Lady Singleton. Lady "Rogue" Singleton. Stevie Smith. **CP-SmitS**

Come were Shepheards who have seene. A Hymne of the Nativity, Sung by the Shepheards. Richard Crashaw. **CP-CrasR**

Come were the times of Ceres' sacrifice. 3.9. Ovid. **CP-MarlC,** *tr.* by Christopher Marlowe; *Fr.* Elegies.

Come, when no graver cares employ. To the Rev. F. D. Maurice. Tennyson. **CP-TennA**

Come when the nights are bright with stars. Invitation to Love. Paul Laurence Dunbar. **CP-DunbP**

Come where the grieving rivers of the night. Song. Thomas Merton. **CP-MertT**

Come wind an Easter lily peace in your hair. Fragment from "A Schoolboy's Odyssey." Kenneth Patchen. *Fr.* Eight Early Poems. **CP-PatcK**

Come with me / into the field of sunflowers. The Sunflowers. Mary Oliver. **SP-OlivM**

Come with our voices, let us war. The Musical Strife; in a Pastoral Dialogue. Ben Jonson. **CP-JonsB**

Come with rain, O loud Southwester! To the Thawing Wind. Robert Frost. **CP-FrosR**

Come with the cannon-wheel. Hatton's "God of War." George Meredith. **CP-MerG2**

Come with the Spring-time, forth fair maid, and be. The Meddow Verse; or, Aniversary to Mistris Bridget Lowman. Robert Herrick. **CP-HerrR**

Come with us and play! From "The Birth of Venus," Song. William Carlos Williams. **CP-WilW1**

Come ye hither all, whose taste. The Invitation. George Herbert. **CP-HerbG**

Come ye that are disturbed, this steady voice. William Wordsworth. **CP-WorW1**

Come ye—who, if (which Heaven avert!) the Land. Lines on the Expected Invasion 1803. William Wordsworth. **CP-WorW1**

Come you, cartoonists. Halsted Street Car. Carl Sandburg. **CP-SandC**

Come you ladies and you gentlemen, a-listen to my song. Hard Times in New York Town. "Bob Dylan." **CP-DylaB**

Come you masters of war. Masters of War. "Bob Dylan." **CP-DylaB**

Come, you pretty false-eyed wanton [or false-ey'd wanton]. Thomas Campion. **CP-CampT**

Come(all your mischief- / hatchers hatch). Edward Estlin Cummings. **CP-CummE**

Comeallye for Robert Carlton Brown, A. Kay Boyle. **CP-BoylK**

Comedian, The. Malcolm Lowry. **CP-LowrM**

"But I shall live when you are dead and damned."

"Darkness has its compensations, both." **CPA**

Dried Up River is like the Soul, A.

"I met a man who suffered more than I."

"Love which comes too late is like that black storm."

"Poem about a poem that can't be written, A."

"Resurgent sorrow is a sea in the cave."

"Searching in a ravaged heart for anguish."

"There is a tide in the affairs of men."

"This is the end but since it is the end."

"Wounded voice over the telephone, A."

"You gave yourself to death but never to me."

"You were in hell fire? had been all your life?"

Comedian as the Letter C, The. Wallace Stevens. **CP-StevW**

Comedian stands on a corner, the sky is, The. Edward Estlin Cummings. **CP-CummE**

Comedy. Charles Tomlinson. **CP-TomlC**

Comedy Card for a Serious Case. Thomas Merton. **CP-MertT**

Comedy like That, A. Gertrude Stein. **CP-SteiG**

Comedy of Belief. Charles Henri Ford. **SP-FordC**

Comely Acts well; and when he speaks his part. Upon Comely a Good Speaker but an Ill Singer. Robert Herrick. **CP-HerrR**

Comely and capable one of our race. On the Portrait of a Woman About to Be Hanged. Thomas Hardy. **CP-HardT**

Comes a big slow fish with tailfins erect in light smog. Day Six O'Hare Telephane. Thomas Merton. *Fr.* West. *Fr.* The Geography of Lograire. **CP-MertT**

Comes home dull with coal-dust deliberately. Her Husband. Ted Hughes. **SP-HughT**

Comes the time when it's later. A Wicker Basket. Robert Creeley. **CP-CreeR**

Comes to mind as another small upheaval. The Frog. Paul Muldoon. **SP-MuldP**

Comes walking barefoot. Sojourner Truth. Robert Earl Hayden. **CNA** *Fr.* Stars. **CP-HaydR**

Comet at Yell'ham, The. Thomas Hardy. **CP-HardT**

Comet of Prophecy, The. Nicholas Vachel Lindsay. **CP-LindV**

Comfort. Elizabeth Barrett Browning. **CP-BroEB**

Comfort. Robert Creeley. **CP-CreeR**

Comfort. Walter de la Mare. **CP-DeLaW**

Comfort. Malcolm Lowry. **CP-LowrM**

Comfort. Richard Shelton. **SP-ShelR**

Comfort. William Carlos Williams. **CP-WilW2**

Comfort at hand! Pluck up thy heart. Sir Thomas Wyatt. **CP-WyatT**

Comfort In Calamity. Robert Herrick. **CP-HerrR**

Comfort thyself, my wo[e]ful heart. Sir Thomas Wyatt. **CP-WyatT**

Comfort to a Lady Upon the Death of Her Husband. Robert Herrick. **CP-HerrR**

Comfort to a Youth That Had Lost His Love. Robert Herrick. **CP-HerrR**

Comfort with a purring cat. Ralph Waldo Emerson. **CP-EmerR**

Comfortable craggy slope, The. Going. Richard Eberhart. **CP-EberR**

Comforter, The. Donald Davie. **CP-DavDo**

Comforters, The. Rudyard Kipling. **CP-KiplR**

Comforts in Contentions. Robert Herrick. **CP-HerrR**

Comforts in Crosses. Robert Herrick. **CP-HerrR**

Comic Books vs. History. Margaret Atwood. **SP-AtwM1**

Comin[g] thro' [or through] the Rye. Robert Burns. **CP-BurnR**

Coming. Philip Larkin. **CP-LarkP**

Coming about / When the squall knocked her. Squall. George Oppen. **CP-OppeG**

Coming across a letter. Letter. Frank Templeton Prince. **CP-PrinF**

Coming & Going. James McAuley. **SP-McAuJ**

Coming around the corner of the dark trail . . . what was wrong with the. The Inquisitors. Robinson Jeffers. **CP-JefR3**

Coming at Last to Night's Most Thankful Springs. Philip Larkin. **CP-LarkP**

Coming Awake. David Herbert Lawrence. **CP-LawrD**

Coming Back. Pablo Neruda, tr. fr. Spanish by Ben Belitt. **SP-NeruP**

Coming Back to America. James Dickey. **CP-DickJ**

Coming Back to You. Leonard Cohen. **CP-CoheL**

Coming by evening through the wintry city. At a Bach Concert. Adrienne Rich. **CP-RicAE; SP-RicA2**

Coming by noon to all the branches. What Troubles I Have Seen in Birdlegged Spring. Thomas Merton. **CP-MertT**

Coming down / out of the freezing sky. White Owl Flies Into and Out of the Field. Mary Oliver. **SP-OlivM**

Coming Down from the Acropolis. William DeWitt Snodgrass. **SP-SnodW**

Coming down the mountain in the twilight. Where the Hayfields Were. Archibald MacLeish. **CP-MacLA**

Coming Down through Somerset. Ted Hughes. **SP-HughT**

Coming Down to the Desert at Lordsburg, N.M. Hayden Carruth. **CP-CarHS**

Coming Fall, The. Denise Levertov. **CP-LeveD**

Coming from a country where we never fail. One Son North to Naples. Richard Hugo. **CP-HugoR**

Coming from the deli / a block away today I. This Dark Apartment. James Schuyler. **CP-SchuJ**

Coming from the Heart (The Road Is Long). "Bob Dylan" and Helena Springs. **CP-DylaB**

Coming Home. Tess Gallagher. **SP-GallT**

Coming Home, Detroit, 1968. Philip Levine. **SP-LeviP**

Coming Home, Garden State Parkway. Stephen Dunn. **SP-DunnS**

Coming home on a summer night. Small Moon. Howard Nemerov. **CP-NemeH**

Coming home with the last load I ride standing. Emergency Haying. Hayden Carruth. **CP-CarHS**

Coming into the world. A Poem to Be Watched. Roy Fisher. **SP-FishR**

Coming of Arthur, The. Tennyson. Fr. Idylls of the King. **CP-TennA**
  Merlin's Riddling. **FaBoRV**

Coming of Good Luck, The. Robert Herrick. **CP-HerrR**

Coming of Love, The. Wystan Hugh Auden. **CP-AudWJ**

Coming of May, The. Edward Estlin Cummings. **CP-CummE**

Coming of Quetzalcoatl, The. David Herbert Lawrence. **CP-LawrD**

Coming of Snow, The. Hayden Carruth. Fr. Contra Mortem. **CP-CarHL**

Coming of the Cold, The. Theodore Roethke. **CP-RoetT**

Coming of the End, The. Thomas Hardy. **CP-HardT**

Coming of War, The; Actaeon. Ezra Pound. **SP-PounE**

Coming of winter / is a beech sapling. Hayden Carruth. Fr. North Winter. **CP-CarHL**

Coming of Wisdom with Time, The. William Butler Yeats. **CP-YeatW**

Coming Out. Ron Koertge. **SP-KoerR**

Coming Right Up. Archie Randolph Ammons. **SP-AmmoA**

"Coming!" she calls out from the doorway. Drowning. Robert Pack. **SP-PackR**

Coming Storm, The. Herman Melville. **SP-MelvH**

Coming To. Archie Randolph Ammons. **SP-AmmoA**

Coming To. Dabney Stuart. **SP-StuaD**

Coming to a cavern in a valley. Another Country. Daniel Gerard Hoffman. **SP-HoffD**

Coming to Christ. Robert Herrick. **CP-HerrR**

Coming to Spain on the first day of the fighting. Sestina. Muriel Rukeyser. Fr. Letter to the Front. **CP-RukeM**

Coming together at night, in rented halls, in bedrooms. Unit Meeting. Edwin Rolfe. **CP-RolfE**

Coming toward you in my red coat. Jean Sans Terre Wraps Himself in a Red Coat. Iwan Goll, tr. fr. French by Isabella Gardner. **CP-GardI**

Coming up England by a different line. I Remember, I Remember. Philip Larkin. **CP-LarkP**

Coming Up Oxford Street: Evening. Thomas Hardy. **CP-HardT**

Coming up the green lane from the sea. Tryst. John Hewitt. **CP-HewiJ**

Cominius, you reprobate old goat. Catullus. See Carmen 108: "If, by general consent, it should be decided."

Command the Roofe great Genius, and from thence. To the Genius of His House. Robert Herrick. **CP-HerrR**

Command the stones in a loud voice. How to Amuse a Stone. Richard Shelton. **SP-ShelR**

Commander, The. Sir John Betjeman. **CP-BetjJ**

Commander Lowell. Robert Lowell. **SP-LoweR**

Commanders, The. Tom Clark. **SP-ClarT**

Commandments, The. Erica Jong. **SP-JongE**

Commandments. David Herbert Lawrence. **CP-LawrD**

Commas in Wintertime. Richard Eberhart. **CP-EberR**

Commemorative of a Naval Victory. Herman Melville. **SP-MelvH**

Commencement. Dabney Stuart. **SP-StuaD**

Commencement, Pingree School. John Updike. **CP-UpdiJ**

Commend to you my cares for the love I love. Catullus. See Carmen 15: "My love & I are yours to command."

Commendatory Poems. Var. authors. **CP-LoveR**
  AD EUNDEM.
  Another, upon the Poems.
  De Domino Richardo Lovelacio, Armigero & Chiliarcha, Viro Incomparabili.
  Exastichon.
  On the Poems.
  Peri Tou Autou.
  To Colonel Richard Lovelace, on the Publishing of His Ingenious Poems.
  To His Honoured and Ingenious Friend Col. Richard Lovelace, on His Lucasta.
  To His Much Honoured Friend Mr. Richard Lovelace, on His Poems.
  To His Noble Friend Mr. Richard Lovelace upon His Poems.
  To my best Brother on his Poems, called Lucasta.
  To My Deare Brother, Colonel Richard Lovelace.
  To My Much Loved Friend, Richard Lovelace Esq.
  To My Noble and Most Ingenious Friend, Col. Richard Lovelace, upon His Lucasta.
  To the Honorable, Valiant, and Ingenious Colonel Richard Lovelace, on His Exquisite Poems.
  "World shall now no longer mourne, nor vex, The."

Commendatory Sonnets. Edmund Spenser. **CP-Spens**
  "Antique Babel, empresse of the East, The."
  To the Right Worshipfull, My Singular Good Frend, Master Gabriell Harvey, Doctor of the Lawes. **NoSic**
  "Wherefore doth vaine Antiquitie so vaunt."
  "Who so wil seeke by right deserts t'attaine."

Commendatory Verses to Edmund Spenser's Fairy Queen. Sir Walter Ralegh.
  Another of the Same. **CP-RaleW**
  Vision upon This Concei[p]t of the Faerie [orFaery] Queen[e], A. **CP-RaleW**

Commendo tibi, Nashe, Puritanum. acc. by English translation. Thomas Campion. **CP-CampT**

Comment on Curb. Langston Hughes. **SP-HughL** Fr. Lenox Avenue Mural.

Comment on Verse. John Hewitt. **CP-HewiJ**

Commentary—A Working Man, see also Working Man, A. Leonard Cohen. **CP-CoheL**

Commentary—Another Room, see also Another Room. Leonard Cohen. **CP-CoheL**

Commentary—Beside My Son, see also Beside My Son. Leonard Cohen. **CP-CoheL**

Commentary—Death to This Book, see also Death to This Book. Leonard Cohen. **CP-CoheL**

Commentary—Final Examination, see also Final Examination. Leonard Cohen. **CP-CoheL**

Commentary—How to Speak Poetry, see also How to Speak Poetry. Leonard Cohen. **CP-CoheL**

Commentary—Hurry to Your Dinner, see also Hurry to Your Dinner. Leonard Cohen. **CP-CoheL**

Commentary—It's Probably Spring. Leonard Cohen. **CP-CoheL**

Commentary—My Wife and I, see also My Wife and I. Leonard Cohen. **CP-CoheL**

Commentary—She Has Given Me the Bullet, see also She Has Given Me the Bullet. Leonard Cohen. **CP-CoheL**

Commentary—The Altar, see also Altar, The. Leonard Cohen. **CP-CoheL**

Commentary—The Asthmatic, see also Asthmatic, The. Leonard Cohen. **CP-CoheL**

Commentary—The Beetle, see also Beetle, The. Leonard Cohen. **CP-CoheL**

Commentary—The Café, see also Café, The. Leonard Cohen. **CP-CoheL**

Commentary—The Change, see also Change, The. Leonard Cohen. **CP-CoheL**

Commentary—The News You Really Hate, *see also* News You Really Hate, The. Leonard Cohen. **CP-CoheL**

Commentary—This Marriage, *see also* This Marriage *and* Commentary Two—This Marriage. Leonard Cohen. **CP-CoheL**

Commentary II—This Marriage, *see also* This Marriage *and* Commentary—This Marriage. Leonard Cohen. **CP-CoheL**

Commercial Variations. Frank O'Hara. **SP-OharF**

Commination Service, The. William Wordsworth. *Fr.* Ecclesiastical Sonnets. **CP-WorW2**

Commingling sky, A. Freely Espousing. James Schuyler. **CP-SchuJ**

COMMINUIT / there is frost on the rock's face. Canto 108. Ezra Pound. *Fr.* Cantos. **CP-PoCan**

Commitment, A. Richard Eberhart. **CP-EberR**

Committee, The—now a permanent body. Dream. Marianne Craig Moore. **CP-MoorM**

Commodore Barry. Donald Davie. **CP-DavDo**

Common Cold, The. Ogden Nash. **CP-NashO**

Common Form. Rudyard Kipling. **FaBoEE; FaBoTw; PV; PeFWW** *Fr.* Epitaphs of the War [1914–1918]. **CP-KiplR**

Common Grave, The. James Dickey. **CP-DickJ**

Common Ground, A. Denise Levertov. **CP-LeveD**

Common Ground. Dabney Stuart. **SP-StuaD**

Common Holly bears a berry. Golden Holly. Christina Georgina Rossetti. **CP-RosC3**

Common Life, The. Wystan Hugh Auden. *Fr.* Thanksgiving for a Habitat. **CP-AudeW**

Common Life, The. Wallace Stevens. **CP-StevW**

Common Moth feeds on woolen cloths, The. That Common Moth. Isabella Gardner. **CP-GardI**

Common Place. Charles Olson. **CP-OlsoC**

Common Question, The. John Greenleaf Whittier. **CP-WhitJ**

Common rain had come again, The. The First Night of Fall and Falling Rain. Delmore Schwartz. **SP-SchwD**

Common Saw, A. Howard Nemerov. **CP-NemeH**

Common Things. Paul Laurence Dunbar. **CP-DunbP**

Common Wisdom, The. Howard Nemerov. **CP-NemeH**

Commonplace, The. Walt Whitman. **CP-WhitW**

Commonplace Day, A. Thomas Hardy. **CP-HardT**

Communal Message. Malcolm Lowry. **CP-LowrM**

Communication. Archie Randolph Ammons. **SP-AmmoA**

Communication I. Maya Angelou. **SP-AngeM**

Communication to Nancy Cunard, A. Kay Boyle. **CP-BoylK**

Communication II. Maya Angelou. **SP-AngeM**

Communion. Charles Bukowski. **SP-BukC1**

Communion. Paul Laurence Dunbar. **CP-DunbP**

Communion, The. Thomas Merton. **CP-MertT**

Communist. John Berryman. **CP-BerrJ**

Communist, The. Malcolm Lowry. **CP-LowrM**

Communists. Edwin Rolfe. **CP-RolfE**

Community, The. Stephen Dobyns. **SP-DobyS**

Community. John Donne. **CP-DonnJ**

Community. Marge Piercy. **SP-PierM**

Commuted Sentence, The. Stevie Smith. **CP-SmitS**

Commuter. Roy Fisher. **SP-FishR**

Comp. Religion. John Updike. **CP-UpdiJ**

Compact. Robert Ranke Graves. **CP-GravR**

Compact: at Volterra, The. Charles Tomlinson. **CP-TomlC**

Companion, The. Marilyn Hacker. **SP-HackM**

Companion, The. Daniel Gerard Hoffman. **SP-HoffD**

Companion, The. Edwin Arlington Robinson. **CP-RobiE**

Companion! by whose buoyant Spirit cheered. To Henry Crabbe Robinson. William Wordsworth. *Fr.* Memorials of a Tour in Italy, 1837. **CP-WorW2**

Companion in Rome, whom Rome makes as old as Rome. Derek Walcott. **CP-WalcD** *Fr.* Midsummer.

Companion to the Foregoing [Love Lies Bleeding]. William Wordsworth. **CP-WorW2**

Companion without news, A. Plagues of a Country Life. Jonathan Swift. *Fr.* Verses from Quilica. **CP-SwifJ**

Companionable Ills, The. Sylvia Plath. **CP-PlatS**

Companionless / Without trace you are. Wind. Kathleen Jessie Raine. **SP-RainK**

Companions, The. Wendell Berry. **CP-BerrW**

Companions. Archibald MacLeish. **CP-MacLA**

Companions, The. Howard Nemerov. **CP-NemeH**

Companions, all day long we've stood. Emily Brontë. **CP-BronE**

Companion's Progress, A. Paul Laurence Dunbar. **CP-DunbP**

Company. Rita Dove. **SP-DoveR**

Company. John Hewitt. **CP-HewiJ**

Company. Stevie Smith. **CP-SmitS**

Company (Coal Miner), The. Louise McNeill. **SP-McNeL**

Company of Men, The. Charles Olson. **CP-OlsoC**

Company owned the houses, The. The Company (Coal Miner). Louise McNeill. **SP-McNeL**

Comparative Iconography. Hayden Carruth. **CP-CarHS**

Compari. David Herbert Lawrence. **CP-LawrD**

Comparison, The. Thomas Carew. **CP-CareT**

Comparison, A. William Cowper. **CP-CowpW**

Comparison, The. John Donne. **PeLV** *Fr.* Elegies. **CP-DonnJ**

Comparison. Paul Laurence Dunbar. **CP-DunbP**

Comparison with a Sunflower. Phoebe Hesketh. **CP-HeskP**

Compass. Jorge Luis Borges, *tr. fr. Spanish by* Richard Wilbur. **CP-WilbR**

Compassion. Jim Carroll. *Fr.* 3 Short Poems. **SP-CarrJ**

Compassion. Thomas Hardy. **CP-HardT**

Compassion. Alun Lewis. **CP-LewiA**

Compassion in the world again is bred. Ralphius. John Donne. **CP-DonnJ**

Compassion is pungent / & sharply aromatic. Small. Flowers of the Foothills & Mountain Valleys. Alice Notley. **SP-NotlA**

Compelled by calamity's magnet. Aftermath. Sylvia Plath. **CP-PlatS**

Compendium. Rita Dove. **SP-DoveR**

Compensation. Paul Laurence Dunbar. **CP-DunbP**

Compensation ("Why should I keep holiday"). Ralph Waldo Emerson. **CP-EmerR**

Compensation ("Wings of Time are black and white, The"). Ralph Waldo Emerson. **CP-EmerR**

Competition. Stephen Dunn. **SP-DunnS**

Competitions of the sky, The. Emily Dickinson. **CP-DickE**

Complacencies of the peignoir, and late. Sunday Morning. Wallace Stevens. **CP-StevW**

Complacency! My Father! Emily Dickinson. **SP-DickE**

Complacent Fictions were they, yet the same. At Rome.—Regrets.—In Allusion to Niebuhr and Other Modern Historians, Continued. William Wordsworth. *Fr.* Memorials of a Tour in Italy, 1837. **CP-WorW2**

Complaining. George Herbert. **CP-HerbG**

Complaining, alas, without redress. Sir Thomas Wyatt. **CP-WyatT**

Complaint, A. Gerard Manley Hopkins. **CP-HopkG**

Complaint. Richard Wilbur. **CP-WilbR**

Complaint. William Carlos Williams. **CP-WilW1**

Complaint, A. William Wordsworth. **CP-WorW1**

Complaint. James Wright. **CP-WrigJ**

Complaint and Reply. Robert Ranke Graves. **CP-GravR**

Complaint for Mary and Marcel, A. Kay Boyle. **CP-BoylK**

Complaint of a Forsaken Indian Woman, The. William Wordsworth. **CP-WorW1**

Complaint of Annelida to False Arcite, The. Geoffrey Chaucer. **CP-BroEB**

Complaint of Chaucer to His Purse, The. Geoffrey Chaucer. *See* To you [*or* yow], my purse [*or* purs], and to non [*or* no *or* noon] other wight.

Complaint of Mars, The. Geoffrey Chaucer. **CP-ChauG**

Complaint of Ninathóma, The. Samuel Taylor Coleridge. *Fr.* Effusions. **CP-ColeS**

Complaint of the Fair Armoress [*or* Armouress], The. François Villon, *tr. fr. French by* Algernon Charles Swinburne. **SP-SwinA**

Complaint of the Morpethshire Farmer, The. Basil Bunting. **CP-BuntB**

Complaint of the Skeleton to Time. Allen Ginsberg. **CP-GinsA**

Complaint of Troilus, The. Geoffrey Chaucer. **NOBE; OBEV** *Fr.* Troilus and Criseyde [*or* Criseide]. **CP-ChauG**

Complaint of Venus, The. Geoffrey Chaucer. **CP-ChauG**

Complaint on the Miseries of Life, A. James Thomson. **CP-ThomD**

Complaint to Four Angels. Ogden Nash. **CP-NashO**

Complaint unto His Lady, A. Geoffrey Chaucer. **CP-ChauG**

Complaint unto Pity, The. Geoffrey Chaucer. **CP-ChauG**

Complaints of Poverty, The, *sels.* Nicholas James. Deathwatch. **SP-SuttB**

"When loons laugh he does not."

Complaynt. Anne Waldman. **SP-WaldA**

Complaynt d'Amours. Geoffrey Chaucer. **CP-ChauG**

Compleat Anglers, The. Isabella Gardner. **CP-GardI**

Complement, The. Thomas Carew. **CP-CareT**

Complete Destruction. William Carlos Williams. **CP-WilW1**

Completely New Set of Objects, A. Wallace Stevens. **CP-StevW**

Completely protected on all sides. The Observer. Adrienne Rich. **CP-RicAE; SP-RicA2**

Complexity, The. William Carlos Williams. **CP-WilW2**

Compleyne ne koude, ne might myn herte never. A Balade of Complaint. Geoffrey Chaucer. **CP-ChauG**

Complaynt Blossoms April to July. Charles Olson. **CP-OlsoC**

Compleynt, compleynt I hearde upon a day. Canto 30. Ezra Pound. *Fr. Cantos.* **CP-PoCan**

Complimentary Pieces to Milton. *Various Authors, tr. fr. Italian by* William Cowper. **CP-CowpW**

   Epigram, An: "Meles and Mincio, both your urns depress."

   Neapolitan John Baptist Manso, The.

   Ode, An: "Exalt me, Clio, to the skies."

   To John Milton.

   To Mr. John Milton of London.

Compliments of a Friend. Ogden Nash. **CP-NashO**

Compline. Wystan Hugh Auden. *Fr. Horae Canonicae.* **CP-AudeW**

Compline. John Berryman. **CP-BerrJ**

Compline. Richard Crashaw. **CP-CrasR**

Compline. Donald Davie. *Fr. Horae Canonica.* **CP-DavDo**

Compline. Philip Larkin. **CP-LarkP**

Compose for Red a proper verse. For Malcolm, a Year After. Etheridge Knight. **SP-KnigE**

Composed / solely of carbon and soot-roses. The Night-Train. Charles Tomlinson. **CP-TomlC**

Composed after a Journey across the Hamilton Hills, Yorkshire. William Wordsworth. **CP-WorW1**

Composed after Reading a Newspaper of the Day. William Wordsworth. **CP-WorW2**

Composed among the Ruins of a Castle in North Wales. William Wordsworth. **CP-WorW2**

Composed at Cora Linn in Sight of Wallace's Tower. William Wordsworth. **CP-WorW2**

Composed at Rydal on May Morning, 1838. William Wordsworth. *Fr. Memorials of a Tour in Italy, 1837.* **CP-WorW2**

Composed at the Same Time and on the Same Occasion. William Wordsworth. *See* I dropped my pen; and listened to the Wind.

Composed by the Sea-Shore. William Wordsworth. **CP-WorW2**

Composed by the Sea-Side, near Calais, August, 1802. William Wordsworth. **CP-WorW1**

Composed by the Side of Grasmere Lake. William Wordsworth. **CP-WorW1**

Composed During a Storm. William Wordsworth. **CP-WorW2**

Composed During a Walk on the Downs, in November 1787. Charlotte Smith. **CP-SmitC**

Composed in One of the Catholic Cantons. William Wordsworth. *Fr. Memorials of a Tour of the Continent; 1820.* **CP-WorW2**

Composed in One of the Valleys of Westmoreland, on Easter Sunday. William Wordsworth. **CP-WorW2**

Composed in Roslin Chapel, During a Storm. William Wordsworth. **CP-WorW2**

Composed in the Glen of Loch Etive. William Wordsworth. **CP-WorW2**

Composed in the Valley near Dover, on the Day of Landing. William Wordsworth. **CP-WorW1**

Composed Near Calais on the Road Leading to Ardres, August 7, 1802. William Wordsworth. **CP-WorW1**

Composed of horny, jagged blacks. Tropical Beetles. John Updike. **CP-UpdiJ**

Composed on a May Morning. William Wordsworth. **CP-WorW2**

Composed on the Banks of a Rocky Stream. William Wordsworth. **CP-WorW2**

Composed on the Eve of the Marriage of a Friend in the Vale of Grasmere, 1812. William Wordsworth. **CP-WorW1**

Composed upon an Evening of Extraordinary Splendour and Beauty. William Wordsworth. **CP-WorW2**

Composed upon Westminster Bridge, September 3, 1802. William Wordsworth. **CP-WorW1**

Composed When a Probability Existed of Our Being Obliged to Quit Rydal Mount as a Residence. William Wordsworth. **CP-WorW2**

Composed While the Author Was Engaged in Writing a Tract, Occasioned by the Convention of Cintra. William Wordsworth. **CP-WorW1**

Composer, The. Wystan Hugh Auden. **CP-AudeW**

Composition / Beginning to write. Continuing finally to write. Writing finally to continue beginning, A. The Beginning of Writing. Robert Duncan. **SP-DuncR**

Composition. May Sarton. **SP-SartM**

Composition. Charles Tomlinson. **CP-TomlC**

Composition. William Carlos Williams. **CP-WilW1**

Composition in Gold and Red-Gold. Robert Penn Warren. **SP-WarrR**

Composition in Grey and Pink. Charles Wright. **SP-WrigC**

Compra? Compra?—the street cry. Teotihuacán. Charles Tomlinson. **CP-TomlC**

Comprehensive Death. Wystan Hugh Auden. *See* As the poets have mournfully sung.

Compton Wynates, Warwickshire. John Hewitt. **CP-HewiJ**

Compulsive preacher, large, and loud of voice. Demagogue. John Hewitt. **CP-HewiJ**

Compulsory Chapel. Alice Walker. **CP-WalkA**

Compunction at presumption. Woe unto Thee! Donald Davie. **CP-DavDo**

Computation, The. John Donne. **CP-DonnJ**

Comrade. Paul Laurence Dunbar. **CP-DunbP**

Comrade D.R.—. Two Dedications: D.R. Louis Zukofsky. *Fr.* 29 Poems. **CP-ZukLS**

Comrade locust sings / With a splinter in his throat. Radicals. Jorge Carrera Andrade, *tr. fr. Spanish by* Thomas Merton. **CP-MertT**

Comrade of the snow & wind. Ralph Waldo Emerson. **CP-EmerR**

Comrade or the book is good, The. Ralph Waldo Emerson. **CP-EmerR**

Comrades, leave me here a little, while as yet 'tis early morn. Locksley Hall. Tennyson. **CP-TennA**

Comus; a Masque Presented at Ludlow Castle. John Milton.

   (Mask, A.) **CP-MiltJ**

   Bacchus. **FaBoDD**

   Chastity. **OBS**

   Chastity ("I Mean That Too, But Yet a Hidden Strength"). **NOSC**

   Comus's Praise of Nature. **PoEL-3**

   Echo. **ELP; LoBV; OBEV; OBS; SeCeV**

      (Lady Sings, The.) **NOBE**

      (Lady's Song.) **TrGrPo**

   Mask, A. **OxAEP-1**

      "Nay, lady, sit; if I but wave this wand." **OxAEP-1**

   Resources. **FaBoDD**

   Sabrina. **OBS**

   Sabrina Fair. **EBEV; ELP; FaBoCh; GN; PoEL-3**

      (Sabrina.) **CH; NOBE; OBEV**

      (Song.) **OXAEP-1**

   Sabrina's Song. **NOSC**

   Star That Bids the Shepherd Fold, The. **FaBoCh; OBEV; PPoe; WHA**

      (Comus' Invocation to His Readers.) **TrGrPo**

      (Comus Speaks.) **NOBE**

      (Comus' Summons.) **NOSC**

      (Invocation of Comus, The.) **OBS**

      (Light Fantastic Round, A.) **FaBoDD**

      (Mask, A.) **FiP**

   Temperance and Virginity. **OBS**

   "To the ocean now I fly." **NOBE; NOSC; OBEV; OBS; OXAEP-1; TrGrPo**

      (Farewell of the Attendant Spirit.) **TrGrPo**

      (Spirit Epiloguizes, The.) **NOBE**

      (Spirit's Epilogue, The.) **NOSC**

Comus' Invocation to His Readers. John Milton. *See* The Star That Bids the Shepherd Fold.

Comus Speaks. John Milton. *See* The Star That Bids the Shepherd Fold.

Comus' Summons. John Milton. *See* The Star That Bids the Shepherd Fold.

Comus's Praise of Nature. John Milton. **PoEL-3** *Fr.* Comus; a Masque Presented at Ludlow Castle.

Con Brio. William Carlos Williams. **CP-WilW1**

Con the dead page as 'twere live love: press on! Her Reproach. Thomas Hardy. **CP-HardT**

Con/tin/u/way/shun Blues. Etheridge Knight. **SP-KnigE**

Conacre. John Hewitt. **CP-HewiJ**

Conan. Thomas Gray. **CP-GrayT**

Concealment: Ishi, the Last Wild Indian, The. William Stafford. **SP-StafW**

Conceit, A. Maya Angelou. **SP-AngeM**

Conceit. David Herbert Lawrence. **CP-LawrD**

Conceit. Lewis Turco. **SP-TurcL**

Concei[p]t begotten by the eyes. A Poesie to Prove Affection is Not Love. Sir Walter Ralegh. **CP-RaleW**

Conceive a man,should he have anything. Edward Estlin Cummings. **CP-CummE; SP-CummE**

Concentration Camps, The. May Sarton. **BTR; SRLS** *Fr.* The Invocation to Kali. **SP-SartM**

Concentrical, the universe and I. Geometry of Moods. Stanley Jasspon Kunitz. **CP-KuniS**

Concept is interesting, The: to see, as though reflected. Wet Casements. John Ashbery. **SP-AshbJ**

Concept Self-Conceived, A. Robert Frost. **CP-FrosR**

Conception. "Hugh MacDiarmid." **SP-MacDH**

Conception of our Ladie, The. Robert Southwell. **CP-SoutR**

Congratulation. William Wordsworth. *Fr.* Ecclesiastical Sonnets. **CP-WorW2**

Congress of Nations, The. George Meredith. **CP-MerG2**

Conjectural First Draft of the Petition to Queen Anne. Sir Walter Ralegh. **CP-RaleW**

Conjecture. Thomas Hardy. **CP-HardT**

Conjectures. William Wordsworth. *Fr.* Ecclesiastical Sonnets. **CP-WorW2**

Conjecturing a Climate. Emily Dickinson. **CP-DickE**

Conjugation of the Paramecium, The. Muriel Rukeyser. **CP-RukeM**

Conjugations of the verb "to be." Firesticks. Stanley Jasspon Kunitz. **CP-KuniS**

Conjunction. Robert Ranke Graves. **CP-GravR**

Conjunctions. William Butler Yeats. **CP-YeatW**

Conjuration. Richard Wilbur. **CP-WilbR**

Conjuration, to Electra. A. Robert Herrick. **CP-HerrR**

Conjure away the blue and the dim and the dark cloths. Cadenza. Isabella Gardner. **CP-GardI**

Connais-Tu le Pays? Richard Shelton. **SP-ShelR**

Connais-tu peut-être la chanson ancienne "C'était un étranger." Petit Poème en Prose. Frank O'Hara. **SP-OharF**

Connecticut River in Flood, The. Brendan Galvin. **SP-GalvB**

Connection, The. Charles Olson. **CP-OlsoC**

Connections. Stephen Dobyns. **SP-DoveR**

Connections: Vermont Vietnam (I). Grace Paley. **CP-PaleG**

Connections: Vermont Vietnam (II). Grace Paley. **CP-PaleG**

Conniving Thallus, mulley, you, cony cully, cop below. Catullus. *See* Carmen 25: "From Thallus the pederast."

Connoisseur of Chaos. Wallace Stevens. **CP-StevW**

Connotation of infinity, A. Edward Estlin Cummings. **CP-CummE**

Connubii Flores, or the Well-Wishes at Weddings. Robert Herrick. **CP-HerrR**

Conquer we shall, but we must first contend. The End. Robert Herrick. **CP-HerrR**

Conqueror. Charles Olson. **CP-OlsoC**

Conqueror Worm, The. Edgar Allan Poe. **CP-PoeEd**

Conquerors, The. Paul Laurence Dunbar. **CP-DunbP**

Conquest, The. Byron. **CP-Byron**

Conquest. William Carlos Williams. **CP-WilW1**

Conquest by Flight. Thomas Carew. **CP-CareT**

Conquest of Finland, The. John Greenleaf Whittier. **CP-WhitJ**

Conquest of Granada, The. John Dryden.
  Epilogue to the Second Part of *The Conquest of Granada.* **SP-DrydJ**
  Song: "Wherever I am, and whatever I do." **SP-DrydJ**

Conquistador. . . . / And we marched against them there in the next spring. The Fifteenth Book. Archibald MacLeish. *Fr.* Conquistador. **CP-MacLA**

Conquistador. Archibald MacLeish. **CP-MacLA**
  Bernál Díaz' Preface to his Book.
  Prologue: "And the way goes on in the worn earth." **NoAM**
  First Book, The.
  Second Book, The.
  Third Book, The.
  Fourth Book, The.
  Fifth Book, The.
  Sixth Book, The.
  Seventh Book, The.
  Eighth Book, The.
  Ninth Book, The.
  Tenth Book, The.
  Eleventh Book, The.
  Twelfth Book, The.
  Thirteenth Book, The.
  Fourteenth Book, The.
  Fifteenth Book, The.
  True History of Bernál Díaz.

Conquistador! Live dangerously, my Byron. To Thom Gunn in Los Altos, California. Donald Davie. **CP-DavDo**

Conrad, Conrad, aren't you old. Conrad Sits in Twilight. John Crowe Ransom. **MeMAP; OxBA** *Fr.* Sixteen Poems in Eight Pairings. **SP-RansJ**

Conrad in Twilight. John Crowe Ransom. *See* Conrad Sits in Twilight.

Conrad Sits in Twilight. John Crowe Ransom. *Fr.* Sixteen Poems in Eight Pairings. **SP-RansJ**
  (Conrad in Twilight.) **MeMAP; OxBA**

Conscience. George Herbert. **CP-HerbG**

Conscience. David Herbert Lawrence. **CP-LawrD**

Conscience. Charles Kenneth Williams. **SP-WillC**

Conscience and Remorse. Paul Laurence Dunbar. **CP-DunbP**

Conscientious Objector. Edna St. Vincent Millay. **CP-MillE**

Conscientious Objector, The. Karl Shapiro. **SP-ShapK**

Conscientiously bringing my mind to bear on this problem. Carmen 116. Catullus. *Fr.* Carmina. **CP-Catul**

Conscious. Wilfred Owen. **CP-OwenW**

Conscious am I in my Chamber. Emily Dickinson. **CP-DickE**

Consciousness / in itself. Who Shall Doubt. George Oppen. **CP-OppeG**

Consciousness. Robinson Jeffers. **CP-JefR1**

Consciousness is the only home. Emily Dickinson. **SP-DickE**

Consciousness, said Don Miguel, *is a disease.* Poem. Edwin Rolfe. **CP-RolfE**

Conscript. Philip Larkin. **CP-LarkP**

Conscript, The. Louis MacNeice. **CP-MacNL**

Conscript, The. Stephen Spender. **CP-SpenS**

Conscript's Song. Edwin Rolfe. **CP-RolfE**

Consecrating Mother, The. Anne Sexton. **CP-SextA**

Consent, The. Howard Nemerov. **CP-NemeH**

Consequences. Wystan Hugh Auden. **CP-AudWJ**

Consequences. Steve Griffiths. **SP-GrifS**

Consequences. John Hewitt. **CP-HewiJ**

Consequences. Rudyard Kipling. *Fr.* Plain Tales from the Hills. "Rosicrucian subtleties / In the Orient had risen." **CP-KiplR**

Conservatrix of Milesien. Ezra Pound. *Fr.* Hugh Selwyn Mauberley. (Life and Contacts). **SP-PounE**

Consider / a girl who keeps slipping off. Briar Rose (Sleeping Beauty). Anne Sexton. **CP-SextA**

Consider. Wystan Hugh Auden. *See* Consider this and in our time.

Consider. Christina Georgina Rossetti. **CP-RosC1**

Consider a fact: an olive. How the Elephant Got His Hump. Miller Williams. **SP-WillM**

Consider greatness. Great Men. Robinson Jeffers. **CP-JefR3**

Consider her now, glowing, light-worn. A Sunday Sonnet for My Mother's Mother. Al Young. **CP-YounA**

Consider how the seed lost by a bird. Howard Nemerov. *Fr.* Runes. **CP-NemeH**

Consider Icarus, pasting those sticky wings on. To a Friend Whose Work Has Come to Triumph. Anne Sexton. **CP-SextA**

Consider, if you will, how lovers lie. Extract. Wystan Hugh Auden. **CP-AudWJ**

Consider Me. Langston Hughes. **SP-HughL**

Consider now, stranger, how the new land lies. New Land. Mona Van Duyn. **SP-VanDM**

Consider now that Troy has burned. The Second-Best Bed. Howard Nemerov. **CP-NemeH**

Consider O / woman this / my body. Edward Estlin Cummings. **CP-CummE**

Consider sorrowes, how they are aright. Griefe. Robert Herrick. **CP-HerrR**

Consider the auk. A Caution to Everybody. Ogden Nash. **CP-NashO**

Consider the banker. / He was once a financial anchor. Anybody for Money? or, Just Bring Your Own Basket. Ogden Nash. **CP-NashO**

Consider the breaking of waves on a shore. The measure. The Measure of Poetry. Howard Nemerov. **CP-NemeH**

Consider the case of Mr. Suggs. The Strange Case of the Entomologist's Heart. Ogden Nash. **CP-NashO**

Consider the Lapel, Sir. Ogden Nash. **CP-NashO**

Consider the Lilies of the Field. ("Flowers preach to us..."). Christina Georgina Rossetti. **CP-RosC1**

Consider the Lilies of the Field. ("Solemn and most glorious..."). Christina Georgina Rossetti. **CP-RosC2**

Consider the man without a watch. I Had No Idea It Was So Late. Ogden Nash. **CP-NashO**

Consider: the mind's a mirror of. Reflections. Daniel Gerard Hoffman. **SP-HoffD**

Consider the mysterious salt. In Time Like Air. May Sarton. **SP-SartM**

Consider the sound. Charles Henri Ford. **SP-FordC** *Fr.* Emblems of Arachne.

Consider the three functions of the tongue. Canzone. Marilyn Hacker. **SP-HackM**

Consider them both in paradise. W. H. Auden & Mantan Moreland. Al Young. **CP-YounA**

Consider this and in our time. Wystan Hugh Auden. **CP-AudeW**
  (Consider.) **CP-AudeW**

Consider this silent disciplined assembly. Alun Lewis. *Fr.* On Embarkation. **CP-LewiA**

Consider what you have lost by lack of faith. Malcolm Lowry. **CP-LowrM**

Consider Wordsworth in his withered age. Poem. John Hewitt. **CP-HewiJ**

Considerable Speck, A. Robert Frost. **CP-FrosR**

Consideration for Others. Christopher Smart. *See* Mutual Subjection.

Considered by the logical brief clock. Strange Calendar. Stanley Jasspon Kunitz. **CP-KuniS**

Considering stars, / sand-grains, shells. I Am. Phoebe Hesketh. **SP-HeskP**

Considering the Snail. Thom Gunn. **CP-GunnT**

Consistency is terrific. A Killer. Charles Bukowski. **SP-BukC1**

Consolation. Elizabeth Barrett Browning. **CP-BroEB**

Consolation. Malcolm Lowry. **CP-LowrM**

Consolation, A. William Shakespeare. *See* Sonnet 29: "When, in disgrace with fortune and men's eyes."

Consolation, fr. A Woman Young and Old. William Butler Yeats. **CP-YeatW**

Consolation of Philosophy, The ("De Consolacione Philosophie"). Boethius, *tr. fr.* Latin *to* Middle English by Geoffrey Chaucer. **CP-ChauG**

  "Alas, his mind is sunk." **MLL,** *tr. by* Helen Waddell;

  ("Heu Quam Praeciph Mersa Profundo.") **MLL,** *tr. by* Helen Waddell;

  "Alas, the ignorance of unhappy men." **MLL,** *tr. by* Helen Waddell;

  "All human kind on earth." **NoSic**

  "All Men throughout the peopled Earth." **CP-JohnS**

  "Give me, O Father! to thy throne access." **CP-JohnS**

  "Happy he whose eyes have view'd." **CP-JohnS; OBVE**

  "Happy that first white age! when wee." **NOSC; OBVE; PAI**

  "Happy, too happy was the world." **MLL,** *tr. by* Helen Waddell; Happy Too Much. **CTC**

  "He that hath set his headlong heart." **MLL,** *tr. by* Helen Waddell;

  "He who has made his reckoning with life." **MLL,** *tr. by* Helen Waddell; Heu Quam Precipiti. **OBMV**

  "Hither, O captives, hither let you come." **MLL,** *tr. by* Helen Waddell; Huc omnes pariter. **OBMV**

  "Man who pants for ample Sway, The." **CP-JohnS** New Year's Eve. **MLL,** *tr. by* Helen Waddell;

  "O Father, give the spirit power to climb." **MLL,** *tr. by* Helen Waddell;

  "O Maker of the starry world." **MLL,** *tr. by* Helen Waddell;

  "O thou, whose all-creating hands sustain." **CP-PopeA**

  "O thou whose pow'r o'er moving worlds presides." **CP-JohnS; OBVE; TrPWD**

  "O Thou whose reason guides the universe." **MLL,** *tr. by* Helen Waddell;

  "Prudent Hind intent on Gain, The." **CP-JohnS**

  "Songs I wrote when I was young and ardent, The." **MLL,** *tr. by* Helen Waddell;

  "Stars hidden by dark clouds." **MLL,** *tr. by* Helen Waddell;

  "Then night was shaken from me." **MLL,** *tr. by* Helen Waddell;

  "There is no race of men." **MLL,** *tr. by* Helen Waddell;

  "This bird was happy once in the high trees." **MLL,** *tr. by* Helen Waddell;

  "This concord tempers then the elements." **MLL,** *tr. by* Helen Waddell;

  "Though countless as the Grains of Sand." **CP-JohnS; OBVE**

  "Through Gripus Grounds let rich Pactolus roll." **CP-JohnS**

  "Truth in platonic ornaments bedeck'd." **CP-JohnS**

  "Unless the soul, to vice a thrall." **CP-JohnS**

  "Vainly the Tyrian Purple bright." **CP-JohnS**

  "What pleasure in such vehement commotion." **MLL,** *tr. by* Helen Waddell;

  "Who thought in high midsummer." **MLL,** *tr. by* Helen Waddell;

  "Wouldst thou to some stedfast Seat." **CP-JohnS**

Consolation Sonata. Carl Sandburg. **CP-SandC**

Consolations. William Stafford. **SP-StafW**

Consolations for Double Bass. Charles Tomlinson. **CP-TomlC**

Consolations of Memory, The, *parody of* Boethius. Rudyard Kipling. **CP-KiplR** *Fr.* The Muse among the Motors.

Consolations of Philosophy. Derek Mahon. **SP-MahoD**

Consolations of Sociobiology, The. Bill Knott. **SP-KnotB**

Consolidation / of voices in the street, A. The Square. Charles Tomlinson. **CP-TomlC**

Consorting with Angels. Anne Sexton. **CP-SextA**

Consortium of Stones. Robert Ranke Graves. **CP-GravR**

Conspiracy, The. Robert Creeley. **CP-CreeR**

Conspiracy, The. Charles Tomlinson. **CP-TomlC**

Constancy. George Herbert. **CP-HerbG**

Constancy to an Ideal Object. Samuel Taylor Coleridge. **CP-ColeS**

Constant. Louis MacNeice. **CP-MacNL**

Constant Bridegrooms, The. Kenneth Patchen. **CP-PatcK**

Constant Lover, A [*or* The]. Sir John Suckling. *See* Out upon it! I have loved [*or* lov'd].

Constant singing / Of the radios, and the art, The. George Oppen. *Fr.* A Narrative. **CP-OppeG**

Constant the waterman. A Late Anniversary. Donald Davie. **CP-DavDo**

Constant to none, but ever false to me. Elegye, An. Thomas Campion. **AAS** *Fr.* Observations in the Art of English Poesie.

Constantly near you, I never in my entire. The Horse Show. William Carlos Williams. **CP-WilW2**

Constantly risking absurdity. Lawrence Ferlinghetti. **SP-FerlL**

Constellation Orion, The. Ted Kooser. **SP-KoosT**

Constitution Day. Charles Tomlinson. **CP-TomlC**

Constricted by my tortured thought. Prayer before Study. Theodore Roethke. **CP-RoetT**

Construction. William Carlos Williams. **CP-WilW2**

Consul (ere) Pompei O preened a duo, Cinna, so lay bound. Catullus. *See* Carmen 113: "In The Year of Pompey's First Consulate, Cinna."

Consult ere thou begin'st, that done, go on. Consultation. Robert Herrick. **CP-HerrR**

Consultation. Robert Herrick. **CP-HerrR**

Consulting I Ching Smoking Pot Listening to the Fugs Sing Blake. Allen Ginsberg. **CP-GinsA**

Consulting summer's clock. Emily Dickinson. **CP-DickE**

Consumed. Eaten away. And love across the street. Arthur Peyton. Muriel Rukeyser. **CP-RukeM**

Consumer, The. Marge Piercy. **SP-PierM**

Consummate Happiness. William Wordsworth. **OBNC** *Fr.* Summer Vacation. *Fr.* The Prelude; Growth of a Poet's Mind [1805 vers.]. **CP-WorW3**

Consummation is the hurry of fools. Emily Dickinson. **SP-DickE**

Cont)- / in / this / crazily. Edward Estlin Cummings. **CP-CummE**

Contact. Steve Griffiths. **SP-GrifS**

Contact, A. Louis MacNeice. **CP-MacNL**

Contained in this short Life. Emily Dickinson. **CP-DickE**

Contemplate all this work of Time. Tennyson. **EBVV; EnVR; FF; OAEL-2; SBVL; SeCeV** *Fr.* In Memoriam A. H. H. **CP-TennA**

Contemplate, when the sun declines. Sunset and Sunrise. William Cowper, *tr. fr. the Latin of* Owen. **CP-CowpW**

Contemplation of Dead Reckoning. Malcolm Lowry. **CP-LowrM**

Contemplation of Our State in Our Deathbed. John Donne. **OBS** *Fr.* The Second Anniversary [*or* Anniversarie]. **ESCV; SeCP** *Fr.* Of the Progres[se] of the Soule; the Second Anniversarie. **CP-DonnJ**

Contemplation of the Sword. Robinson Jeffers. **CP-JefR2**

Contemplation would make a good life, keep it strict, only. The Cruel Falcon. Robinson Jeffers. **CP-JefR2**

Contemplations. Anne Bradstreet. **CP-BradA**

  "I wist not what to wish, yet sure thought I." **PBWP**

  "Mariner that on smooth waves doth glide, The." **WPOW**

  "O Time the fatal wrack of mortal things." **PBWP; WPOW**

  "Shall I then praise the heavens, the trees, the earth." **NOSC; PBWP**

  "Silent alone, where none or saw, or heard." **PBWP**

  "So he that saileth in this world of pleasure." **WPOW**

  "When I behold the heavens as in their prime." **PBWP**

Contemporania. Ezra Pound.

Tenzone. **SP-PounE**

Contemporania. William Carlos Williams. **CP-WilW1**

Contemporaries all surpassed, see one. William Cowper. **EPCY** *Fr.* Table Talk. **CP-CowpW**

Contemporary Announcement. Maya Angelou. **SP-AngeM**

Contemporary Portrait. Archibald MacLeish. **CP-MacLA**

Contempt and pangs and haunting fears— / Too late for hope, too late for ease. An Exceeding Bitter Cry. Christina Georgina Rossetti. **CP-RosC2**

Contempt of Poetry, The. Edmund Spenser. *See* October.

Contemptuous of his home beyond. Christina Georgina Rossetti. **CP-RosC3**

Contend in a sea which the land partly encloses. The Yachts. William Carlos Williams. **CP-WilW1**

Contend with steepness, the dark air. Richard Eberhart. *Fr.* Four Lakes' Days. **CP-EberR**

Contender, The. Ted Hughes. **SP-HughT**

Contending with the demon doubt. Doubts before Dreaming. Erica Jong. **SP-JongE**

Content. Thomas Campion.

  (Canto Quinto.) **CP-CampT**

  ("Daie, a night, an houre of sweete content, A.") **CP-CampT**

Content. Paul Laurence Dunbar. **CP-DunbP**

Content. George Herbert. **CP-HerbG**

Content and Ri[t]ch[e]. Robert Southwell. **CP-SoutR**

  "I wrastle not with rage." **OBF**

Content in you. New Legends. Robert Ranke Graves. **CP-GravR**

Content, Not Cates. Robert Herrick. **CP-HerrR**

Content thee, greedy heart. The Size. George Herbert. **CP-HerbG**

Content to come, content to go, / Content to wrestle or to race. Do This, and He Doeth It. Christina Georgina Rossetti. **CP-RosC2**

Contented Peasant, The. George Crabbe. **SP-CrabG** *Fr.* The Parish Register.

Contented wi' Little. Robert Burns. (Song: "Contented wi' little, and cantie wi' mair.") **CP-BurnR**

Contention. Robert Herrick. **CP-HerrR**

Contentment. William Cowper. **ChIV-2** *Fr.* Olney Hymns. **CP-CowpW**

Contentment. James Thomson *and* David Mallet. **CP-ThomJ** *Fr.* Alfred: A Masque.

Contest, The. Hilda Doolittle. **CP-DoolH**

Contest of Bards. Allen Ginsberg. **CP-GinsA**

Continent's a tamed ox, with all its mountains, The. July Fourth by the Ocean. Robinson Jeffers. **CP-JefR1**

Continent's End. Robinson Jeffers. **CP-JefR1**

Contingencies. Stephen Dobyns. **SP-DobyS**

Continual Conversation with a Silent Man. Wallace Stevens. **CP-StevW**

Continual Ministry of Thy Anger, The. Kenneth Patchen. **CP-PatcK**

Continually is continuously. Over and Done With. Archie Randolph Ammons. **SP-AmmoA**

Continuation of a Long Poem of These States. Allen Ginsberg. **CP-GinsA** S.F. Southward. **NAAL-2**

Continuation of R. Garnett's *Nix*. Gerard Manley Hopkins. **CP-HopkG**

Continuation of the Landscape. Kenneth Patchen. **CP-PatcK**

Continued [Church to Be Erected]. William Wordsworth. *Fr.* Ecclesiastical Sonnets. **CP-WorW2**

Continued [Dissolution of the Monasteries]. William Wordsworth. *Fr.* Ecclesiastical Sonnets. **CP-WorW2**

Continued [Inside of King's College Chapel, Cambridge]. William Wordsworth. *Fr.* Ecclesiastical Sonnets. **CP-WorW2**

Continued [Other Benefits]. William Wordsworth. *Fr.* Ecclesiastical Sonnets. **CP-WorW2**

Continued [Seclusion]. William Wordsworth. *Fr.* Ecclesiastical Sonnets. **CP-WorW2**

Continuing. Al Young. **CP-YounA**

Continuing forward with a trembling. Robert Creeley. **CP-CreeR**

Continuing Story of Bungalow Bill, The. John Lennon *and* Paul McCartney. **CP-Beatl**

Continuing to Live. Philip Larkin. **CP-LarkP**

Continuities. Walt Whitman. **CP-WhitW**

Continuity. Roy Fisher. **SP-FishR**

Continuity. Steve Griffiths. **SP-GrifS**

Continuo. Hayden Carruth. **CP-CarHS**

Continuum. Adrienne Rich. **CP-RicAE**

Contours and the shine, The. Sea-Trout and Butterfish. William Carlos Williams. **CP-WilW1**

Contra Blake. Wystan Hugh Auden. *Fr.* Shorts I ("Watch upon my wrist, The"). **CP-AudeW**

Contra Mortem. Hayden Carruth. **CP-CarHL**

  Being, The. **PoA**

  Being as Memory, The.

  Being as Moment, The.

  Being as Prevision, The.

  Book, The.

  Brook, The.

  Child, The.

  Child's Being, The.

  Coming of Snow, The.

  Ecstasy, The.

  Fall, The.

  Great Death, The.

  Leaves, The.

  Little Death, The.

  Moon, The.

  Mountain Fastness, The.

  Nothing I, The.

  Nothing II, The.

  Primavera, The.

  Stone, The.

  Summer, The.

  Sun, The.

  Thaw, The.

  Trees, The.

  Village, The.

  Water, The.

  Wheel of Being I, The.

  Wheel of Being II, The.

Woman, The.

Woman's Genitals, The.

Contractions. Steve Griffiths. **SP-GrifS**

Contradiction. David Markson. **CP-MarkD**

Contradictions, *parody of* Henry Wadsworth Longfellow. Rudyard Kipling. **CP-KiplR** *Fr.* The Muse among the Motors.

Contradictions: Tracking Poems. Adrienne Rich.

  "Dear Adrienne, / I feel signified by pain." **SP-RicA1**

  "Dear Adrienne: / I'm calling you up tonight." **SP-RicA1**

  "My mouth hovers across your breasts." **SP-RicA1**

  "Problem, unstated until now, is how, The." **SP-RicA1**

  "This high summer we love will pour its light." **SP-RicA1**

  "You: air-driven reft from the tuber-bitten soil." **SP-RicA1**

  "You who think I find words for everything." **SP-RicA1**

Contrapuntalist, A / composer of chorales. Melchior Vulpius. Marianne Craig Moore. **CP-MoorM**

Contrariness of the Mad Farmer, The. Wendell Berry. **CP-BerrW**

Contrary Theses (I). Wallace Stevens. **CP-StevW**

Contrary Theses (II). Wallace Stevens. **CP-StevW**

Contrary to / tales you told us. Anti-Father. Rita Dove. **SP-DoveR**

Contrast, A. Wystan Hugh Auden. **CP-AudeW**

Contrast. Joseph Ceravolo. **SP-CeraJ**

Contrast. Robinson Jeffers. **CP-JefR1**

Contrast; the Parrot and the Wren, The. William Wordsworth. **CP-WorW2**

Contretemps, The. Thomas Hardy. **CP-HardT**

Contrite Heart, The. William Cowper. *See* The Lord Will Happiness Divine.

Control Burn. Gary Snyder. **CP-SnydG**

Control of the passes was, he saw, the key. Wystan Hugh Auden. **CP-AudWJ; CP-AudeW**

  (Secret Agent, The.) **CP-AudeW**

Controlling the Tongue. Geoffrey Chaucer. **OxBChV** *Fr.* The Manciple's Tale. *Fr.* The Canterbury Tales. **CP-ChauG**

Controversy, The. William Carlos Williams. **CP-WilW2**

Contusion. Sylvia Plath. **CP-PlatS**

Conundrum of the Workshops, The. Rudyard Kipling. **CP-KiplR**

Conundrums. David Herbert Lawrence. **CP-LawrD**

Convalescence, The. Charles Henri Ford. **SP-FordC**

Convalescence in Summer 1949. Isabella Gardner. **CP-GardI**

Convalescent / to get along the shop fronts. Roy Fisher. **SP-FishR** *Fr.* Studies.

Convent Threshold, The. Christina Georgina Rossetti. **CP-RosC1**

  "I tell you what I dreamed last night." **PeVV**

Conventional Ballad. William Carlos Williams. **CP-WilW2**

Conventionalist, The. Stevie Smith. **CP-SmitS**

Convergence of the Many. René Char, *tr. fr. French by* Thomas Merton. **CP-MertT**

Convergence of the Twain, The. Thomas Hardy. **CP-HardT**

Conversation, A. Margaret Atwood. **SP-AtwM2**

Conversation, The. Wendell Berry. *Fr.* The Handing Down. **CP-BerrW**

Conversation. John Berryman. **CP-BerrJ**

Conversation. Elizabeth Bishop. *Fr.* Four Poems. **CP-BishE**

Conversation, A. Robert Bly. **SP-BlyR**

Conversation. William Cowper. **CP-CowpW**

Conversation, The. Thom Gunn. **CP-GunnT**

Conversation. Louis MacNeice. **CP-MacNL**

Conversation. John Updike. **CP-UpdiJ**

Conversation among the Ruins. Sylvia Plath. **CP-PlatS**

Conversation at Dawn, A. Thomas Hardy. **CP-HardT**

Conversation at Midnight with Oscar Williams. Isabella Gardner. **CP-GardI**

Conversation begins / with a lie. And each, A. Cartographies of Silence. Adrienne Rich. **SP-RicA2**

Conversation by the Body's Light. Jane Cooper. **SP-CoopJ**

Conversation Galante. Thomas Stearns Eliot. **CP-ElioT**

Conversation Galante. Charles Olson. **CP-OlsoC**

Conversation in a Belfry. Archibald MacLeish. **CP-MacLA**

Conversation in a Cheap Room. Charles Bukowski. **SP-BukC2**

Conversation of Old Men, The. Thom Gunn. **CP-GunnT**

Conversation of Prayer, The. Dylan Thomas. **CP-ThomD**

Conversation on Morality, Eternity and Copulation, A. Charles Bukowski. **SP-BukC2**

Conversation Piece. Leonard Nathan. **SP-NathL**

Conversation with a Fireman from Brooklyn. Tess Gallagher. **SP-GallT**

Conversation with a Holy Woman Not Seen for Many Years. Robert Bly. **SP-BlyR**

Conversation with Leonardo, A. John Ciardi. **SP-CiarJ**

Conversation with my friend is particularly. Edward Estlin Cummings. **CP-CummE**

Conversation with the Devil, A. Randall Jarrell. **CP-JarrR**

Conversation with the Kid. Patti Smith. **SP-SmitP**

Conversations. Thomas Merton. **CP-MertT**

Conversations are simple: about food, The. Under the Window: Ouro Prêto. Elizabeth Bishop. **CP-BishE**

Conversations in Crisis. Audre Lorde. **SP-LordA**

Conversations in Hungary, August 1969. John Hewitt. **CP-HewiJ**

Conversations With Goethe. Malcolm Lowry. **CP-LowrM**

Conversing with Paradise. Howard Nemerov. **CP-NemeH**

Conversion. William Wordsworth. *Fr.* Ecclesiastical Sonnets. **CP-WorW2**

Conversion of Aurelian McGoggin, The. Rudyard Kipling. *Fr.* Plain Tales from the Hills.

"Ride with an idle whip, ride with an unused heel." **CP-KiplR**

Conversion of St. Paul. Christina Georgina Rossetti. **CP-RosC2**

Conversion of St. Paul. Christopher Smart. *Fr.* Hymns and Spiritual Songs for the Fasts and Festivals of the Church of England. **SP-SmarC**

Conveyor belts bearing hubcaps and loneliness, The. Introduction to the 20th Century. Stephen Dunn. **SP-DunnS**

Convict, The. William Wordsworth. **CP-WorW1**

Convict strolled into the prison administration building to, The. Rehabilitation & Treatment in the Prisons of America. Etheridge Knight. **SP-KnigE**

Conviction (i). Stevie Smith. **CP-SmitS**

Conviction (ii). Stevie Smith. **CP-SmitS**

Conviction (iii). Stevie Smith. **CP-SmitS**

Conviction (iv). Stevie Smith. **CP-SmitS**

Convinced by Sorrow. Elizabeth Barrett Browning. **BLRP; WBLP** *Fr.* The Cry of the Human. **CP-BroEB**

Convito. Dante Alighieri.

Banqauet, The. **CP-NemeH**

Conviviality of Cows, The. Stephen Dobyns. **SP-DobyS**

Convivio. William Carlos Williams. **CP-WilW2**

Convoy. Louis MacNeice. **CP-MacNL**

Convoy Escort. Rudyard Kipling. *Fr.* Epitaphs of the War [1914–1918]. **CP-KiplR**

Convulsions came; and, where the field. The Apparition. Herman Melville. **SP-MelvH**

Conway Burying Ground. Archibald MacLeish. **CP-MacLA**

Coo-saw kin-ens sees seas season. Dogwood. Louis Zukofsky. **CP-ZukLS**

Cook. Roy Fisher. **SP-FishR** *Fr.* Five Pilgrims in the Prologue to the Canterbury Tales.

Cook County. Archibald MacLeish. **CP-MacLA**

Cook in the Galley, The. Malcolm Lowry. **CP-LowrM**

Cook named McMurray, A. Second Limick. Ogden Nash. **CP-NashO**

Cook of Londoun, while the Reve spak, The. The Cook's Prologue. Geoffrey Chaucer. *Fr.* The Canterbury Tales. **CP-ChauG**

Cooking Egg, A. Thomas Stearns Eliot. **CP-ElioT**

Cook's Prologue, The. Geoffrey Chaucer. *Fr.* The Canterbury Tales. **CP-ChauG**

Cook's Tale, The. Geoffrey Chaucer. **BXAP** *Fr.* The Canterbury Tales. **CP-ChauG**

Cool and beautiful as the blossom of the wild carrot. Aubade. Edna St. Vincent Millay. **CP-MillE**

Cool and Plain. Stevie Smith. **CP-SmitS**

Cool around the Fire, The. Gary Snyder. **CP-SnydG**

Cool as a Cucumber. Stevie Smith. **CP-SmitS**

Cool beneath melon-colored cloth, your belly. For Arl in Her Sixth Month. Al Young. **CP-YounA**

Cool Breeze. Joseph Ceravolo. **SP-CeraJ**

Cool is the wind, for the summer is waning. To the Road. Paul Laurence Dunbar. **CP-DunbP**

Cool northern waters. The Engine Room, S.S. Sappa Creek. Gary Snyder. **CP-SnydG**

Cool of an oak's unchequered shade, The. Last Hours. David Herbert Lawrence. **CP-LawrD**

Cool small evening shrunk to a dog bark and the clank of a bucket, A. Full Moon and Little Frieda. Ted Hughes. **SP-HughT**

Cool Stream, The. Thom Gunn. *Fr.* The Geysers. **CP-GunnT**

Cool that came off sheets just off the line, The. Seamus Heaney. *Fr.* Clearances. **SP-HeanS**

Cool Tombs. Carl Sandburg. **CP-SandC**

Cool Web, The. Robert Ranke Graves. **CP-GravR**

Cool whisper of the trees. Nightfall. Wystan Hugh Auden. **CP-AudWJ**

Cool with the touch of autumn, waters break. Lament for My Brother on a Hayrake. James Wright. **CP-WrigJ**

Cool you proceed at speed. George Meredith. **CP-MerG2**

Cool your heels on the rail of an observation car. Still Life. Carl Sandburg. **CP-SandC**

Coole Park and Ballylee, 1931. William Butler Yeats. **CP-YeatW**

Coole Park, 1929. William Butler Yeats. **CP-YeatW**

Coolgreany. James Liddy. **CP-LiddJ**

Coomb-Firtrees say that Life is a moan. Yell'ham-Wood's Story. Thomas Hardy. **CP-HardT**

Coon, why did you come to this dance. Raccoon. Anne Sexton. **CP-SextA**

Cootchie. Elizabeth Bishop. **CP-BishE**

Cootchie, Miss Lula's servant, lies in marl. Cootchie. Elizabeth Bishop. **CP-BishE**

Cop-Out Session. Etheridge Knight. **SP-KnigE**

Coplas. Geoffrey Hill. *Fr.* The Songbook of Sebastian Arrurruz. **CP-HillG**

Copper Beech, The. Rita Dove. **SP-DoveR**

Copper clouds / are not of this light, The. Geoffrey Hill. *Fr.* Churchill's Funeral. **CP-HillG**

Cops and Robbers. Donald Hall. **CP-HallD**

Cops want me to come down and identify, The. She Came Out of the Bathroom With Her Flaming Red Hair and Said—. Charles Bukowski. **SP-BukC1**

Copy of Verses upon Two Celebrated Modern Poets, A. Jonathan Swift. **CP-SwifJ**

Copying Architecture in an Old Minster. Thomas Hardy. **CP-HardT**

Coquette, and After, The. Thomas Hardy. **CP-HardT**

Coquette Conquered, A. Paul Laurence Dunbar. **CP-DunbP**

Cor Cordium. Countee Cullen. **CP-CullC**

Cor cordium is written there. Cor Cordium. Countee Cullen. **CP-CullC**

Cor Mio. Christina Georgina Rossetti. **CP-RosC3**

Cor mio a cui si volge l'altro mio core. Amico e Più Che Amico Mio. Christina Georgina Rossetti. *Fr.* Il Rosseggiar Dell'Oriente Canzoniere. **CP-RosC3**

Cor mio, cor mio / Più non ti veggo, ma mi rammento. Christina Georgina Rossetti. **CP-RosC3**

Cora. Langston Hughes. **SP-HughL**

Coral. Tom Clark. **SP-ClarT**

Coral. Derek Walcott. **CP-WalcD**

Coral and clear emerald. The Spirit of Air. Walter de la Mare. **CP-DeLaW**

Coral Reef, The. Laurence Lieberman. **SP-LiebL**

Coral worm beneath the sea, The. Ralph Waldo Emerson. **CP-EmerR**

Cord of Wood, A. Robert Pack. **SP-PackR**

Corduroy Road. Rita Dove. **SP-DoveR**

Core of conversations we never had, A. Sister, Morning Is a Time for Miracles. Audre Lorde. **SP-LordA**

Core of the strong hill: not understood, The. Natural Resources. Adrienne Rich. **SP-RicA2**

Corfe Castle. Alun Lewis. **CP-LewiA**

Corillyn is Dark. Marsden Hartley. *Fr.* Boston Portrait Projections. **CP-HartM**

Corillyn will come, with her accustomed tricks. Corillyn is Dark. Marsden Hartley. *Fr.* Boston Portrait Projections. **CP-HartM**

Corinna. Jonathan Swift. **CP-SwifJ**

Corinna foots it in bare feet. Young Matrons Dancing. John Updike. **CP-UpdiJ**

Corinna, pride of Drury Lane. A Beautiful Young Nymph Going to Bed. Jonathan Swift. **CP-SwifJ**

Corinna's Going a-Maying. Robert Herrick. **CP-HerrR**

Coriolan. Thomas Stearns Eliot. **CP-ElioT**

Difficulties of a Statesman.

Triumphal March. **OBWP; WaaP**

Cormorant on high, The. James Thomson. **OxBoS** *Fr.* Autumn. *Fr.* The Seasons. **CP-ThomJ**

Cormorant still screams, The. Late. Louise Bogan. **CP-BogaL**

Cormorants / By the pollock holes diving. James Liddy. *Fr.* Birds. **CP-LiddJ**

Corn and Beans. Carl Sandburg. **CP-SandC**

Corn Harvest, The. William Carlos Williams. **ArNa; PPP** *Fr.* Pictures from Brueghel. **CP-WilW2**

Corn Hut Talk. Carl Sandburg. **CP-SandC**

Corn is coming along, The. Cain. Howard Nemerov. **CP-NemeH**

Corn Prattlings. Carl Sandburg. **CP-SandC**

Corn-Song, A. Paul Laurence Dunbar. **CP-DunbP**

Corn-Song, The. John Greenleaf Whittier. **GN; OHIP** *Fr.* The Huskers. **CP-WhitJ**

Corn-Stalk Fiddle, The. Paul Laurence Dunbar. **CP-DunbP**

Corncrake. John Hewitt. **CP-HewiJ**

Corncrakes. Louis MacNeice. *Fr.* Nature Notes. **CP-MacNL**

Cornelian, The. Byron. **CP-Byron**

Cornelius Verner. Louise McNeill. **SP-McNeL**

Corner. Roy Fisher. **SP-FishR**

Corner, The. Donald Hall. **CP-HallD**

Corner Meeting. Langston Hughes. **SP-HughL**

Corner of a great rain, The. Contemporania. William Carlos Williams. **CP-WilW1**

Corner of the sun, A. Coolgreany. James Liddy. **CP-LiddJ**

Corner Seat. Louis MacNeice. **CP-MacNL**

Corner Stone, The. Walter de la Mare. **CP-DeLaW**

Corner Tree. Louise McNeill. **SP-McNeL**

Corners. Stephen Dunn. **SP-DunnS**

Corners. Laurence Lieberman. **SP-LiebL**

Cornet Cornelius Rilke. Stephen Spender. **CP-SpenS**

Cornfield, The. Muriel Rukeyser. **CP-RukeM**

Cornfield Ridge and Stream. Carl Sandburg. **CP-SandC**

Cornfields, The. Nicholas Vachel Lindsay. **CP-LindV**

Cornflowers. James Schuyler. **CP-SchuJ**

Corniche—Marseille. Marsden Hartley. **CP-HartM**

Cornish Cliffs. Sir John Betjeman. **CP-BetjJ**

Cornish Heroic Song for Valda Trevlyn. "Hugh MacDiarmid."
  "Celtic genius—Cornwall, Scotland, Ireland, Wales—, The." **SP-MacDH**
  "His attitude towards woman is the basic point." **SP-MacDH**
  "I sing of Cornwall." **SP-MacDH**

Cornkind. Frank O'Hara. **SP-OharF**

Cornpicker Poem. Robert Bly. **SP-BlyR**

Corns, heartburn, sinus headaches, such minor ailments. A Change of Air. Wystan Hugh Auden. **CP-AudeW**

Cornucopia. Carl Sandburg. **CP-SandC**

Cornwall. Donald Davie. **CP-DavDo**

Cornwall, Touring. Richard Hugo. **CP-HugoR**

Corona. Tess Gallagher. **SP-GallT**

Corona Virginum. Sigebert of Liege. *Fr.* Four Medieval Latin Poems. **CP-MacNL**

Coronach. "Lewis Carroll." **CP-CarrL**

Coronach. Sir Walter Scott. **BSV; CH; EnRP; GTBS; GTBS-6; GTBS-P; HBV 1-2; NOBRP; OAEP; OBRV; OHIP; OxAEP-2; SCGP; SP-ScotW; TrGrPo; TrefS; WHA** *Fr.* The Lady of the Lake.

Coronal, A. William Carlos Williams. **CP-WilW1**

Coronation, The. Thomas Hardy. **CP-HardT**

Coronation Murder, The. Robert Ranke Graves. **CP-GravR**

Coroner's Inquest. William DeWitt Snodgrass. **SP-SnodW**

Coroner's merry little children, The. Hic Jacet. William Carlos Williams. **CP-WilW1**

Coronet, The. Andrew Marvell. **CP-MarvA**

Coronet of Moonlight. Robert Ranke Graves. **CP-GravR**

Corot. David Herbert Lawrence. **CP-LawrD**

Corporal, The. Thom Gunn. **CP-GunnT**

Corporate Entity. Archibald MacLeish. **CP-MacLA**

Corporate posture: variables of fat. Thomas Merton. *Fr.* Cables to the Ace. **CP-MertT**

Corps de Plane. Patti Smith. **SP-SmitP**

Corpse and Mirror I. John Yau.
  "When one of our citizens dies, his corpse is placed in his chariot." **SP-YauJo**
  "When one of our citizens dies, his head is cut off and placed inside." **SP-YauJo**

Corpse and Mirror II. John Yau.
  "When a comet passes over the town, whoever sees it knows a corpse." **SP-YauJo**
  "When you break a mirror, you must count up the pieces to see if." **SP-YauJo**

Corpse and Mirror III. John Yau.
  "When the movie ends and the lights come on, the audience is puzzled." **SP-YauJo**
  "When the movie ends, the lights come on. The audience is puzzled." **SP-YauJo**

Corpse has walked across my shadow, A. Into the Known. Tess Gallagher. **SP-GallT**

Corpse is in the central square, in the spring sun, The. Mystery. Edwin Rolfe. **CP-RolfE**

Corpse my mother made, The. Addio. John Ciardi. **SP-CiarJ**

Corpse-Plant, The. Adrienne Rich. **CP-RicAE; SP-RicA2**

Corpse Song. Margaret Atwood. *Fr.* Songs of the Transformed. **SP-AtwM1**

Corpses are cold in the tomb. Lines Written During the Castlereagh Administration. Percy Bysshe Shelley. **CP-ShelP**

Corral. Lewis Turco. **SP-TurcL**

Correct death is written in, The. The Assassin. Anne Sexton. **CP-SextA**

Correcting Manuscript. Malcolm Lowry. **CP-LowrM**

Correction. Archie Randolph Ammons. **SP-AmmoA**

Correction. Robert Herrick. **CP-HerrR**

Correction: *Eve* Delved and *Adam* Span. Ogden Nash. **CP-NashO**

Correspondence. Roy Fisher. **SP-FishR**

Correspondence between Mr. Harrison in Newcastle and Mr. Sholto Peach Harrison in Hull. Stevie Smith. **CP-SmitS**

Correspondence in After Years. David Herbert Lawrence. **CP-LawrD**

Correspondence School Instructor Says Goodbye to His Poetry Students, The. Galway Kinnell. **CP-KinnG**

Correspondences. Charles Baudelaire, *tr. fr.* French by Allen Tate. **CP-TateA**

Correspondences. James Liddy. **CP-LiddJ**

Correspondences. James Liddy. **CP-LiddJ**

Correspondences. Muriel Rukeyser. **CP-RukeM**

Corrib: An Emblem. Donald Davie. **CP-DavDo**

Corridor, The. Thom Gunn. **CP-GunnT**

Corridor. John Hewitt. **CP-HewiJ**

Corridor, The. Edwin Arlington Robinson. **CP-RobiE**

Corrina, Corrina. "Bob Dylan." **CP-DylaB**

Corrugated roof, The. Everybody Lying on Their Stomachs, Head toward the Candle, Reading, Sleeping, Drawing. Gary Snyder. **CP-SnydG**

Corruptible if all things are. Tricked by Eternity to the Heart. Archibald MacLeish. **CP-MacLA**

Corruption reaps the young; you dread. Feud. Theodore Roethke. **CP-RoetT**

Corruptions of the Higher Clergy. William Wordsworth. *Fr.* Ecclesiastical Sonnets. **CP-WorW2**

Corruptions of war and peace, the public and wholesale crimes that, The. Skunks. Robinson Jeffers. **CP-JefR3**

Corsair, The. Byron. **CP-Byron**
  "O'er the glad waters of the dark blue sea."
  "Unlike the heroes of each ancient race." **NOBRP**
Sunset over the Aegean. **OBNC; OBRV**

Cortège. Edwin Arlington Robinson. **CP-RobiE**

Cortege. Richard Shelton. **SP-ShelR**

Cortège for Colette. Jean Garrigue. **SP-GarrJ**
  ("Minister of birds, / Keeper of islands and pools.") **SP-GarrJ**

Cortege for Rosenbloom. Wallace Stevens. **CP-StevW**

Coruscating in her bones. Spendthrift. Isabella Gardner. **CP-GardI**

Corydon's Lament and Resolution. Christina Georgina Rossetti. **CP-RosC3**

Coryphée gravefooted precise, dance to the gracious music. Basil Bunting. **CP-BuntB**

Cosmic Comics. Howard Nemerov. **CP-NemeH**

Cosmic Gall. John Updike. **CP-UpdiJ**

Cosmologist says, The. Americans, The ("Cosmologist says, The"). Charles Olson. **CP-OlsoC**

Cosmopolitan Sense, The. Jim Carroll. **SP-CarrJ**

Cosmopolites without a plea. Emily Dickinson. **CP-DickE**

Cosmos has played, The. The Xylophone of the Spine. Erica Jong. **SP-JongE**

Costa Blanca, The. Sir John Betjeman. **CP-BetjJ**

Cosway Frazer & Baldwin of Egypts Lake. William Blake. **CP-BlakW**

Cot of an old lady. At Grandmother's Wake. Kenneth Patchen. **CP-PatcK**

Cottage by the Bridge. James Liddy. **CP-LiddJ**

Cottage garden owned a boxwood maze, The. Summer Arcady. John Hewitt. **CP-HewiJ**

Cottage Hospital, The. Sir John Betjeman. **CP-BetjJ**

Cottage Street, 1953. Richard Wilbur. **CP-WilbR**

Cottager and His Landlord, The. John Milton. *See* The Fable of the Peasant and the Overlord.

Cottager to Her Infant, (By My Sister), The. Dorothy Wordsworth, *Third and fourth stanzas by* William Wordsworth. **CP-WorW1**

Cotter's Saturday Night [Inscribed to Robert Aiken [*or* R. A****], Esq.], The. Robert Burns. **CP-BurnR**
  "Cheerfu' supper done, wi' serious face, The." **WGRP**
  "November chill blaws loud wi' angry sugh." **OBEC**

Cotton Mather died when I was a boy. The books. The Blue Buildings in the Summer Air. Wallace Stevens. **CP-StevW**

Cotton rows crisscross the world. The Memory. Maya Angelou. **SP-AngeM**

Cottonmouth Country. Louise Glück. **SP-GlücL**

Cottum perfidiae haud satis pudenter. *acc. by English translation.* Thomas Campion. **CP-CampT**

Cougar Meat. Tess Gallagher. **SP-GallT**

Cough Syrup. Jim Carroll. **SP-CarrJ**

Coughing in the Morning. Autumn Gold: New England Fall. Allen Ginsberg. **CP-GinsA**

Could all this be forgotten? Yes, a schism. John Keats. **ChER** *Fr.* Sleep and Poetry. **CP-KeatJ**

Could all we little folks that wait. A Panegyric on the Reverend Dean Swift. Jonathan Swift. **SP-SwifJ**

Could Be. Langston Hughes. **SP-HughL**

Could he have made Priscilla share. Llewellyn and the Tree. Edwin Arlington Robinson. **CP-RobiE**

Could he possess an idea? The Difficulty of Ideas. Richard Eberhart. **CP-EberR**

Could Homer come himself, distressed and poor. Epigram on the Refusal of the University of Oxford to Subscribe to His Translation of Homer. William Cowper. **CP-CowpW**

Could Hope inspect her Basis. Emily Dickinson. **CP-DickE**

Could I be sure that I shall see the day. Sonnet. Allen Tate. **CP-TateA**

Could I but live again. Pisgah-Sights. II. Robert Browning. **CP-BroR2**

Could I but ride indefinite. Emily Dickinson. **CP-DickE**

Could I but Will. Thomas Hardy. **CP-HardT**

Could—I do more—for Thee. Emily Dickinson. **CP-DickE**

Could I, from heav'n inspir'd, as sure presage. On a Similar Occasion for the Year 1788. William Cowper. **CP-CowpW**

Could I have said while he was here. Tennyson. *Fr.* In Memoriam A. H. H. **CP-TennA**

Could I, heart-broken, reach his place of birth. On Correggio. Robert Browning. **CP-BroR2**

Could I remount the river of my years. Fragment, A. Byron. **CP-Byron**

Could I the priest's consent have gained. William Wordsworth. **CP-WorW1**

Could I—then—shut the door. Emily Dickinson. **CP-DickE**

Could I unthink you. Anti-Conception. Erica Jong. **SP-JongE**

Could I visit the Beds. Emily Dickinson. **SP-DickE**

Could live—did live. Emily Dickinson. **CP-DickE**

Could Love for ever. Stanzas. Byron. **CP-Byron**

Could man be drunk for ever. Alfred Edward Housman. **CP-HousA**

Could mortal lip divine. Emily Dickinson. **CP-DickE**

Could my heart more tongues imploy. Thomas Campion. **CP-CampT**

Could my poore hart whole worlds of toungs employ. Thomas Campion. **CP-CampT**

Could not let us bring their sugar to Europe. Canto 66. Ezra Pound. *Fr.* Cantos. **CP-PoCan**

Could not once blinding me, cruel[l], suffice? Samson to His De[or a]lilah. Richard Crashaw. **CP-CrasR**

Could She See the Whole Real World with Her Ghost Breast Eyes Shut under a Blouse Lid? Gary Snyder. **CP-SnydG**

Could some descending escalator. The Snark Was a Boojum Was a Prawn. Ogden Nash. **CP-NashO**

Could that be a babe crawling there in night's black? I Guess You Ought to Know Who You Are. Robert Penn Warren. *Fr.* Ballad of a Sweet Dream of Peace. **SP-WarrR**

Could that sweet Darkness where they dwell. Emily Dickinson. **CP-DickE**

"Could that"i marveled"be / you?" Edward Estlin Cummings. **CP-CummE**

Could we forget the widowed hour. Tennyson. *Fr.* In Memoriam A. H. H. **CP-TennA**

Could we know how kin we are. George Meredith. **CP-MerG2**

Could we like youth consume the stolen night? Horologikos. Hayden Carruth. **CP-CarHS**

Could write of fucking—. Robert Creeley. **CP-CreeR**

Could ye be very blest in hearkening. Vanities. Elizabeth Barrett Browning. **CP-BroEB**

Could you tell me how to grow. Emily Dickinson. **SP-DickE**

Council, The. Wystan Hugh Auden. **CP-AudeW**

Council of Clermont, The. William Wordsworth. *Fr.* Ecclesiastical Sonnets. **CP-WorW2**

Council of Satan, The. John Milton. **PoEL-3** *Fr.* Book I. **FHYEP; NAEL-1; OAEL-1; OxAEP-1** *Fr.* Paradise Lost. **CP-MiltJ**

Councils. Marge Piercy. **SP-PierM**

Counsel. Charles Bukowski. **SP-BukC2**

Counsel, A. Christina Georgina Rossetti. **CP-RosC3**

Counsell. Robert Herrick. **CP-HerrR**

Count Flanders / Was eaten up with pride. Après la Politique, la Haine des Bourbons. Stevie Smith. **CP-SmitS**

Count Gismond. Robert Browning. **CP-BroR1**

Count it anyway he wants. Variation on Guilt. Rita Dove. **SP-DoveR**

Count not that far that can be had. Emily Dickinson. **CP-DickE**

Count them unclean, these tears that turn no mill. Edna St. Vincent Millay. **CP-MillE**

Count these reminiscences like money. Carlovingian Dreams. Carl Sandburg. **CP-SandC**

Countenance, A. Thomas Hardy. **CP-HardT**

Counter, The. William Carlos Williams. **CP-WilW2**

Counter and Clubb were men in trade, whose pains. The Wager. George Crabbe. **SP-CrabG** *Fr.* Tales.

Counter Mood. Countee Cullen. **CP-CullC**

Counterblast—1886, The. Robert Louis Stevenson. **CP-StevR**

Counterblast Ironical, The. Robert Louis Stevenson. **CP-StevR**

Counterblast on Penny Trumpet. Christina Georgina Rossetti. **CP-RosC3**

Counterfeit—a Plated Person, A. Emily Dickinson. **CP-DickE**

Counterfeit bucolic scene, A. Roy Fisher. **SP-FishR** *Fr.* New Diversions.

Counterparts. Stephen Dobyns. **SP-DobyS**

Counterpoint, A. Robert Creeley. **CP-CreeR**

Countess, The. John Greenleaf Whittier. **CP-WhitJ**

Countess Cathleen in Paradise, The. William Butler Yeats. **CP-YeatW**

Countess' Pillar. William Wordsworth. **CP-WorW2**

Counting. Philip Larkin. **CP-LarkP**

Counting. Carl Sandburg. **CP-SandC**

Counting-out Rhyme. Edna St. Vincent Millay. **CP-MillE**

Counting-Out Song, A. Rudyard Kipling. **CP-KiplR** *Fr.* Land and Sea Tales.

Counting Small-boned Bodies. Robert Bly. **SP-BlyR**

Counting the Beats. Robert Ranke Graves. **CP-GravR**

Counting the times as if they added up. John Yau. **SP-YauJo** *Fr.* Scenes from the Life of Boullee.

Countless gold of a merry heart, The. Riches. William Blake. **CP-BlakW**

Countless these crosses and these ruinous stones. The Taciturn. Walter de la Mare. **CP-DeLaW**

Countries we depart will manage without us, The. Goodbye, Göteborg. John Updike. **CP-UpdiJ**

Country & Western. Marilyn Hacker. **SP-HackM**

Country & Western II. Marilyn Hacker. **SP-HackM**

Country beneath / the earth has a green sun, The. Procedures for Underground. Margaret Atwood. **SP-AtwM1**

Country Burying (1919). Robert Penn Warren. **SP-WarrR**

Country Excursion. Kenneth Patchen. **CP-PatcK**

Country Gentleman, The. Alun Lewis. *Fr.* Poems from the Chinese. **CP-LewiA**

Country is a funny place, The. Nine Miles to the Railroad. Ogden Nash. **CP-NashO**

Country is not named, The. Dürer's Vision. John Haines. **SP-HainJ**

Country kid in Mississippi I drew water, A. A Little More Traveling Music. Al Young. **CP-YounA**

Country Lassie. Robert Burns. **CP-BurnR**

Country Life, A. Randall Jarrell. **CP-JarrR**

Country Life. James Liddy. *Fr.* Ossie Esmonde. *Fr.* His Resplendent Neighbours. **CP-LiddJ**

Country Life: To His Brother, M. Tho. Herrick. Robert Herrick. **CP-HerrR**

Country Life, to the Honored Mr. Endymion Porter[, Groome of the Bed-Chamber to His Maj.], The. Robert Herrick. **CP-HerrR**

Country Lover. Maya Angelou. **SP-AngeM**

Country Mansion, A. Robert Ranke Graves. **CP-GravR**

Country of a Thousand Years of Peace, The. James Merrill. **SP-MerrJ**

Country of hunchbacks!—where the strong, straight spine. Sonnet to Gath. Edna St. Vincent Millay. **CP-MillE**

Country of Marriage, The. Wendell Berry. **CP-BerrW**

  "How many times have I come to you out of my head."

  "I dream of you walking at night along the streams."

  "I give you what is unbounded, passing from dark to dark."

  "Our bond is no little economy based on the exchange."

  "Sometimes our life reminds me."

  "This comes after silence. Was it something I said."

  "What I am learning to give you is my death."

Country of the Camisards, The. Robert Louis Stevenson. **CP-StevR** *Fr.* Travels with a Donkey.

Country Pie. "Bob Dylan." **CP-DylaB**

Country Poem with Little Country. Ernest Hemingway. **CP-HemiE**

Country Squire and the Mandrake, The. Christopher Smart. **SP-SmarC**

Country surrounds the city, The. Revolution in the Revolution in the Revolution. Gary Snyder. **CP-SnydG**

Country Talk. John Hewitt. **CP-HewiJ**

Country Villa. Jean Garrigue. **SP-GarrJ**

Country Walk in March, A. John Hewitt. **CP-HewiJ**

Country Walk in May, A. John Hewitt. **CP-HewiJ**

Country Was, The. Randall Jarrell. **CP-JarrR**

Country Wedding, The. Thomas Hardy. **CP-HardT**

Country Week-End. Louis MacNeice. **CP-MacNL**
  "Coffee leaps in a crystal knob."
  "Forth from a sack of fishing-reels and deck-quoits."
  "Here too, as in my childhood, twilight."
  "Wild grass in spate in a rainy wind."
Country where he lives, The. Wendell Berry. *Fr.* Window Poems. **CP-BerrW**
Country Words. Wallace Stevens. **CP-StevW**
Countryman, The. Wallace Stevens. **CP-StevW**
'Country's love- / liness', it said, The. Hyphens. Charles Tomlinson. **CP-TomlC**
Countryside. Charles Bukowski. **SP-BukC2**
Countryside a long vaguely troubled sleep, The. Little Song for Ivy Day, 1991. James Liddy. **CP-LiddJ**
County. Sir John Betjeman. **CP-BetjJ**
County Durham. Donald Davie. **CP-DavDo**
County Guy. Sir Walter Scott. *See* Serenade, A: "Ah! County Guy, the hour is nigh."
Coup. Leonard Nathan. **SP-NathL**
Coup de Grace. Anne Waldman. **SP-WaldA**
Couper o' Cuddy cam here awa, The. We'll Hide the Couper behint the Door. Robert Burns. **CP-BurnR**
Couple, The. Maya Angelou. **SP-AngeM**
Couple, The. Robert Lowell. **SP-LoweR**
Couple, A. Carl Sandburg. **CP-SandC**
Couple in the Next Room, The. John Ashbery. **SP-AshbJ**
Couple of women is one too many, A. The Fool. Stevie Smith. **CP-SmitS**
Couple we know were into everything, A. The Quiz. Ron Koertge. **SP-KoerR**
Couples. Carl Sandburg. **CP-SandC**
Couples on the boat to the Isola di Giglio. The Light. Lawrence Ferlinghetti. **SP-FerlL**
Couples sought (enclose photographs please). Billings and Cooings from "The Berkeley Barb." Mona Van Duyn. **SP-VanDM**
Couples Under Cover. Ted Hughes. **SP-HughT**
Couplet. Charles Tomlinson. **CP-TomlC**
Couplet about Birds. Thomas Gray. *See* There pipes the woodlark, and the song[-]thrush there.
Couplet for Furnivall on Two Publishers. Robert Browning. **CP-BroR2**
Couplings buckled, cracked, collapsed. The Wreck of the Circus Train. Hayden Carruth. **CP-CarHS**
Coupons. Charles Bukowski. **SP-BukC1**
Courage. Walter de la Mare. **CP-DeLaW**
Courage. Steve Griffiths. **SP-GrifS**
Courage. David Herbert Lawrence. **CP-LawrD**
Courage. Anne Sexton. **CP-SextA**
Courage. Richard Shelton. **SP-ShelR**
Courage, a Tale. Thom Gunn. **CP-GunnT**
Courage Cool'd. Robert Herrick. **CP-HerrR**
Courage for Lost Poems. Marsden Hartley. **CP-HartM**
"Courage!" he said, and pointed toward the land. The Lotus-Eaters. Tennyson. **CP-TennA**
Courage is not standing on the crosstrees. Malcolm Lowry. **CP-LowrM**
Courage, my chieftain, and strike the blow. Field-Marshal Radetzky. Franz Grillparzer, *tr. fr. German by* George Meredith. **CP-MerG2**
Courage, my Soul, now learn to wield. A Dialogue between the Resolved Soul and Created Pleasure. Andrew Marvell. **CP-MarvA**
Courage of Shutting-Up, The. Sylvia Plath. **CP-PlatS**
Courage of the shut mouth, in spite of artillery!, The. The Courage of Shutting-Up. Sylvia Plath. **CP-PlatS**
Courage, poor heart of stone! Tennyson. *Fr.* Maud [A Monodrama]. **CP-TennA**
Courage that my mother had, The. Edna St. Vincent Millay. **CP-MillE**
Courage to Be New, The. Robert Frost. **CP-FrosR**
Courage yet, my brother or my sister! To a Foil'd European Revolutionaire. Walt Whitman. **CP-WhitW**
Courante Monsieur. Richard Lovelace. **CP-LoveR**
Courbet might have painted this. Composition. Charles Tomlinson. **CP-TomlC**
Couriers, The. Sylvia Plath. **CP-PlatS**
Course. Muriel Rukeyser. **CP-RukeM**
Course Work. Archie Randolph Ammons. **SP-AmmoA**
Court is far away, The. Emily Dickinson. **CP-DickE**
Court Lady, A. Elizabeth Barrett Browning. **CP-BroEB**
Court Lady Standing under Cherry Tree. John Gould Fletcher. **SP-FletJ**
Court-Martial. Robert Penn Warren. **SP-WarrR**
Court of First Appeal. Kenneth Patchen. **CP-PatcK**

Court of Love, A. Robert Ranke Graves. **CP-GravR**
Court Revolt, The. Thom Gunn. **CP-GunnT**
Courteously self-assured, although alone. Charlotte Corday. Charles Tomlinson. **CP-TomlC**
Courtesies of good-morning and good-evening. On Dwelling. Robert Ranke Graves. **CP-GravR**
Courtesies of the Interregnum. Thom Gunn. **CP-GunnT**
Courtesy Call. John Updike. **CP-UpdiJ**
Courthouse, The. Lewis Turco. **SP-TurcL**
Courting a widow, briefly, Grandfather. The Breach. John Hewitt. **CP-HewiJ**
Courting of Dinah Shadd, The. Rudyard Kipling. *Fr.* Life's Handicap. Private Ortheris's Song. **CP-KiplR**
Courting Prosperity. Steve Griffiths. **SP-GrifS**
Courtling, I rather thou shouldst utterly. To Censorious Courtling. Ben Jonson. **CP-JonsB**
Courtroom is quiet, but who will confess?, The. A Singer Must Die. Leonard Cohen. **CP-CoheL**
Courtship. Catullus. *See* Carmen 5: "Lesbia / live with me."
Courtship, The. James Dickey. **CP-DickJ**
Courtship. Rita Dove. **SP-DoveR**
Courtship, Diligence. Rita Dove. **SP-DoveR**
Courtship of Miles Standish, The. Henry Wadsworth Longfellow. **SP-LongH**
John Alden.
  "Into the open air John Alden, perplexed and bewildered." **TreFS**
War-Token, The. **PAH**
Love and Friendship. **TreFS**
Lover's Errand, The. **TreFS**
March of Miles Standish, The.
  "Meanwhile the stalwart Miles Standish was marching steadily northward." **TreFS**
Miles Standish.
  "In the Old Colony days, in Plymouth the land of the Pilgrims." **AiP; TreFS**
Priscilla. **TreFS**
Sailing of the Mayflower, The.
  Expedition to Wessagusset, The. **PAH**
  "There with his boat was the Master, already a little impatient." **TreFS**
Spinning-Wheel, The.
  "Month after month passed away, and in autumn the ships of the merchants." **TreFS**
Wedding-Day, The.
  "This was the wedding morn of Priscilla the Puritan Maiden." **TreFS**
Courtship of the Jersey Lineman. Laurence Lieberman. **SP-LiebL**
Courtyard Thaw, A. Richard Wilbur. **CP-WilbR**
Courtyards in Delft. Derek Mahon. **SP-MahoD**
Cousin, The. Stevie Smith. **CP-SmitS**
Cousin Euphemia Knows Best, or, Physician, Heal Somebody Else. Ogden Nash. **CP-NashO**
Cousin Florence. Richard Eberhart. **CP-EberR**
Cousin, it's of you I always dream. El Sueño de la Razón. Jane Cooper. **FaBoWP** *Fr.* March. **SP-CoopJ**
Cousin Kate. Christina Georgina Rossetti. **CP-RosC1**
Cousin Nancy. Thomas Stearns Eliot. **CP-ElioT**
Cousins. Archie Randolph Ammons. **SP-AmmoA**
Covenant, The. William Cowper. *Fr.* Olney Hymns. **CP-CowpW**
Covenant, The. Rudyard Kipling. **CP-KiplR**
Covenant, The. Charles Kenneth Williams. **SP-WillC**
Covenant Woman. "Bob Dylan." **CP-DylaB**
Covenanters, The. "Hugh MacDiarmid." **SP-MacDH**
Covenanter's Grave, The. John Hewitt. **CP-HewiJ**
Cover him over with daisies white. The Death of the First Born. Paul Laurence Dunbar. **CP-DunbP**
Cover me over. Bringers. Carl Sandburg. **CP-SandC**
Cover Me Over. Richard Eberhart. **CP-EberR**
Cover my eyes with your pinions. Bird of Night. Ernest Hemingway. **CP-HemiE**
Cover that infant's mouth and eyes. Adam's Jealousy: Eve's Answer. Archibald MacLeish. *Fr.* Songs for Eve. **CP-MacLA**
Covered Bridge, The. Lewis Turco. **SP-TurcL**
Covered the flowered linen. Home, and I've. Marilyn Hacker. **SP-HackM**
Covered with yellow leaves. Memory Gardens. Allen Ginsberg. **CP-GinsA**
Covetous Still Captives, The. Robert Herrick. **CP-HerrR**
Covetousness. Stephen Dobyns. **SP-DobyS**
Cow, The. Ogden Nash. **CP-NashO**
Cow, The. Theodore Roethke. **CP-RoetT**

Cow, The. Robert Louis Stevenson. **CP-StevR**

Cow in Apple Time, The. Robert Frost. **CP-FrosR**

Cow of morning spurted, The. The Last Vision of Eoghan Rua Ó Súilleabháin. Michael Hartnett. **SP-HarMi**

Cow wandering in the bare field, The. Randall Jarrell. **CP-JarrR**

Cowan Bridge; At the Site of 'Lowood School'. Geoffrey Hill. **CP-HillG**

Coward. Archie Randolph Ammons. **SP-AmmoA**

Coward, The. Rudyard Kipling. **FaBoEE; FaBoTw; OAEP; PeFWW** *Fr.* Epitaphs of the War [1914–1918]. **CP-KiplR**

Coward, The. Stephen Spender. **CP-SpenS**

Cowardice. Isabella Gardner. **CP-GardI**

Cowardice and Impudence. David Herbert Lawrence. **CP-LawrD**

Cowards. David Herbert Lawrence. **CP-LawrD**

Cowards fear to die, but Courage stout. Sir Walter Ralegh. **CP-RaleW**
(Sir W. Ralegh, on the Snuff of a Candle the Night Before He Died.) **CP-RaleW**

Cowboy gear hangs from smoky beams: the Colt. Signs. James McAuley. **SP-McAuJ**

Cowboy, where's your class-conscious horse? Dicty Glide in Central Park Menagerie. Charles Henri Ford. **SP-FordC**

Cowdung-colored mud, The. Five Poems from Mexico. Denise Levertov. **CP-LeveD**

Cowhorn-crowned, shockheaded, cornshuck-bearded. The Knight, Death, and the Devil. Randall Jarrell. **CP-JarrR**

Cowper had sinn'd with some excuse. On a Mistake in His Translation of Homer. William Cowper. **CP-CowpW**

Cowper, whose silver voice, task'd sometimes hard. Sonnet to Henry Cowper. William Cowper. **CP-CowpW**

Cowper's Grave. Elizabeth Barrett Browning. **CP-BroEB**

Cows, a Vision. Tess Gallagher. **SP-GallT**

Cows at Night, The. Hayden Carruth. **CP-CarHS**

Cows go around saying Moo. A Word on Wind. Ogden Nash. **CP-NashO**

Cows in Art Class. Charles Bukowski. **SP-BukC2**

Cowshed Blues, The. Hayden Carruth. **CP-CarHS**

Coxcomb bird, so talkative and grave, The. Alexander Pope. **ImPo** *Fr.* Epistle I, to Sir Richard Temple, Lord Cobham. **CP-PopeA**

Coyotes know it's just, The. About the Elk and the Coyotes That Killed Her Calf. Stephen Dunn. **SP-DunnS**

Coyote's Song. William Dickey. **SP-DickW**

Crab Crack. John Updike. **CP-UpdiJ**

Crab faces gownes with sundry Furres; 'tis known. Upon Crab. Robert Herrick. **CP-HerrR**

Crab That Played with the Sea, The. Rudyard Kipling. *Fr.* Just-So Stories. "China-going P. & O.'s." **CP-KiplR**

Crab-Tree, The. Robert Ranke Graves. **CP-GravR**

Crabapple Blossoms. Carl Sandburg. **CP-SandC**

Crabapples. Carl Sandburg. **CP-SandC**

Crabbed Age and Youth. William Shakespeare. *See* Crabbed age and youth cannot live together.

Crabbed age and youth cannot live together. William Shakespeare. **CP-ShaWS; EBEvV; EIL; FaBoEn; GBL; GTBS; GTBS-P; HBV 1-2; InPS; LiTB; NIP; NoSic; OBEV; OBSC; TreFS; UnTE** *Fr.* The Passionate Pilgrim. **CP-ShaWS**
(Age and Youth.) **EIL; FaBoEn**
(Crabbed Age and Youth.) **EBEvV; GBL; HBV 1-2; InPS; LiTB; NIP; NoSic; OBEV; TreFS; UnTE**
(Madrigal, A: "Crabbed age and youth.") **GTBS; GTBS-P; InPS**
(Youth and Age.) **OBSC**

Crabs. Marge Piercy. **SP-PierM**

Crack! Daniel Gerard Hoffman. **SP-HoffD**

Crack, The. Denise Levertov. **CP-LeveD**

Crack in the stone, the black filament, The. The Compact: at Volterra. Charles Tomlinson. **CP-TomlC**

Crack in the World. Anne Waldman. **SP-WaldA**

Crack of a starting pistol. Jean Jaurès. Geoffrey Hill. *Fr.* The Mystery of the Charity of Charles Péguy. **CP-HillG**

Cracked Apple Tree, The. Robert Pack. **SP-PackR**

Cracked Looking Glass. Jean Garrigue. **SP-GarrJ**

Cracked walk in the garden, A. Flesh and Blood. Adrienne Rich. **CP-RicAE**

Cracking a Few Hundred Million Years. Archie Randolph Ammons. **SP-AmmoA**

Cracking the Safe. Chuang Tzu, *tr. fr.* Chinese by Thomas Merton. **CP-MertT**

Crackling on burnt whin, springing over moss. The Booleys. John Hewitt. **CP-HewiJ**

Cracks. Charles Kenneth Williams. **CP-WillC**

Cracks in eight log buildings, counting sheds. Montana Ranch Abandoned. Richard Hugo. **CP-HugoR**

Cracks in the Pavement. James Liddy. **CP-LiddJ**

Cradle Song, A: "Angels are stooping, The." William Butler Yeats. **CP-YeatW**

Cradle Song, A: "Sleep, sleep, beauty bright." William Blake. **CP-BlakW** ("Sleep Sleep; in thy sleep.") **CP-BlakW**

Cradle Song, A: "Sweet dreams, form a shade." William Blake. **EnRP; FHYEP; LAuP; OAEP; OBCP; SBVL** *Fr.* Songs of Innocence. **CP-BlakW**

Cradle Song for Eleanor. Louis MacNeice. *See* Sleep, my darling, sleep.

Cradle Song for Miriam. Louis MacNeice. *See* The Clock's untiring fingers wind the wool of darkness.

Cradled in the smiling moon. *They Part at Daybreak, Returning Their Inevitable Ways.* Alun Lewis. *Fr.* War Wedding. **CP-LewiA**

Cradock Newton: From an Epitaph. Charles Tomlinson. **CP-TomlC**

Craft. John Ciardi. **SP-CiarJ**

Craftsman, The. Rudyard Kipling. **CP-KiplR**

Crafty boy that had full oft assay'd, The. Song. Sir John Suckling. **CP-SuckJ**

Craig-y-Don. Steve Griffiths. **SP-GrifS**

Craigdarroch, fam'd for speaking art. Sketch for an Elegy. Robert Burns. **CP-BurnR**

Craigieburn-Wood—A Song. Robert Burns. **CP-BurnR**

Craigvara House. Derek Mahon. **SP-MahoD**

Cramm'd to the throat with wholesome moral stuff. Epilogue to Tancred and Sigismunda. James Thomson. **CP-ThomJ**

Cramped in that funnelled hole, they watched the dawn. Fragment. Wilfred Owen. **CP-OwenW**

Crane, The. Robert Ranke Graves. **CP-GravR**

Crane, The. Charles Tomlinson. **CP-TomlC**

Crane lounes loudly in his need, The. The Crane. Robert Ranke Graves. **CP-GravR**

Crane over seas and forests seeks her home, The. Malcolm Lowry. **CP-LowrM**

Cranefly in September, A. Ted Hughes. **SP-HughT**

Cranes. John Haines. **SP-HainJ**

Cranes along the scaffolding are gorged, The. Man. Randall Jarrell. **CP-JarrR**

Cranmer. William Wordsworth. *Fr.* Ecclesiastical Sonnets. **CP-WorW2**

Cranston Near the City Line. Ted Berrigan. **SP-BerrT**

Crapshooters. Carl Sandburg. **CP-SandC**

Crash. Allen Ginsberg. **CP-GinsA**

Crash. Gary Snyder. **CP-SnydG**

Crash / Take Valium Sleep. Things to Do in Providence. Ted Berrigan. **SP-BerrT**

Crash on crash of the sea. Sea Heroes. Hilda Doolittle. **CP-DoolH**

Crash on the levee, mama. Down in the Flood. "Bob Dylan." **CP-DylaB**

Crashed through the woods that lumbering Coach. The dust. The Last Coachload. Walter de la Mare. **CP-DeLaW**

Crassis invideo tenuis nimis ipse, videtur. *acc. by English translation.* Thomas Campion. **CP-CampT**

Crate of Sterling Loving Cups, A. John Ciardi. **SP-CiarJ**

Craters. James Dickey. **CP-DickJ**

Craved, having so long gone. Seconds. Louise Glück. **SP-GlücL**

Craving for infinity, The. A Singular Yen. Al Young. **CP-YounA**

Craving for Spring. David Herbert Lawrence. **CP-LawrD**

Craw cracks in sirrop; and do's stinking say. Upon Craw. Robert Herrick. **CP-HerrR**

Crawl. Charles Kenneth Williams. **CP-WillC**

Crawling black transgressor, A. Oil Field. Louise McNeill. **SP-McNeL**

Crawling glaciers pierce me with the spears. Percy Bysshe Shelley. **FHYEP** *Fr.* Prometheus Unbound. **CP-ShelP**

Crawling out from under the hedgerow. For Barbara. Chuck Miller. **SP-MillC**

Crawls through the yard fence. Depression Wind (Winter 1930). Louise McNeill. **SP-McNeL**

Crayon House. Muriel Rukeyser. **CP-RukeM**

Crazed. Walter de la Mare. **CP-DeLaW**

Crazed Girl, A. William Butler Yeats. **CP-YeatW**

Crazed Moon, The. William Butler Yeats. **CP-YeatW**

Crazed through much child-bearing. The Crazed Moon. William Butler Yeats. **CP-YeatW**

Crazy Carlson cleared this meadow alone. Crazy Carlson's Meadow. Robert Bly. **SP-BlyR**

Crazy Carlson's Meadow. Robert Bly. **SP-BlyR**

Crazy clock two hours astray / defies the angle of the sun, The. Second Front: Double Summertime, July 1943. John Hewitt. **CP-HewiJ**

Crazy, girls, crazy. Don is gone. Epitaph. Howard Nemerov. **CP-NemeH**

Crazy Jane and Jack the Journeyman, *fr.* Words for Music Perhaps. William Butler Yeats.

Crazy Jane and the Bishop, *fr.* Words for Music Perhaps. William Butler Yeats. **CP-YeatW**

Crazy Jane Grown Old Looks at the Dancers, *fr.* Words for Music Perhaps. William Butler Yeats. **CP-YeatW**

Crazy Jane on God, *fr.* Words for Music Perhaps. William Butler Yeats. **CP-YeatW**

Crazy Jane on the Day of Judgment, *fr.* Words for Music Perhaps. William Butler Yeats. **CP-YeatW**

Crazy Jane Reproved, *fr.* Words for Music Perhaps. William Butler Yeats. **CP-YeatW**

Crazy Jane Talks with the Bishop, *fr.* Words for Music Perhaps. William Butler Yeats. **CP-YeatW**

Crazy jay blue) / demon laughshriek. Edward Estlin Cummings. **CP-CummE**

Crazy kid-face. B———. Robert Creeley. **CP-CreeR**

Crazy man that found a cup, A. The Empty Cup. William Butler Yeats. *Fr.* A Man Young and Old. **CP-YeatW**

Crazy Spiritual, A. Allen Ginsberg. **CP-GinsA**

Crazy Weather. John Ashbery. **SP-AshbJ**

Crazy Woman, The. Gwendolyn Brooks. **SP-BrooG**

Creak, little wood thing, creak. The Little Old Table. Thomas Hardy. **CP-HardT**

Creamcheese babies square and downy as bolsters. The Peaceable Kingdom. Marge Piercy. **SP-PierM**

Creams. Charles Kenneth Williams. **CP-WillC**

Created by the poet to sing my song. The Reaper. Robert Duncan. **SP-DuncR**

Created purely from glass the saint stands. In Piam Memoriam. Geoffrey Hill. **CP-HillG**

Creation. John Milton. **NOSC,** *ll.* 387–516; *Fr.* Book VII. *Fr.* Paradise Lost. **CP-MiltJ**

(Creation of the Animals.) **FM,** *ll.* 387–505;

Creation. Kenneth Patchen. **CP-PatcK**

Creation, The. Mona Van Duyn. **SP-VanDM**

Creation and the Prophet. George Meredith. **CP-MerG2**

Creation Myth. Wendell Berry. **CP-BerrW**

Creation Myth. Frank Templeton Prince. **CP-PrinF**

Creation Myth on a Moebius Band. Howard Nemerov. **CP-NemeH**

Creation of Anguish. Howard Nemerov. **CP-NemeH**

Creation of the Animals. John Milton. *See* Creation.

Creations of Sound, The. Wallace Stevens. **CP-StevW**

Creator. Archibald MacLeish. **CP-MacLA**

Creator of world and of birth, The. Special Starlight. Carl Sandburg. **CP-SandC**

Creature David, The. Donald Davie. **CP-DavDo**

Creature of God, thy coat. Hymn to the Seal. Stevie Smith. **CP-SmitS**

Credea di rivederti e ancor ti aspetto. Ripetizione. Christina Georgina Rossetti. *Fr.* Il Rosseggiar Dell'Oriente Canzoniere. **CP-RosC3**

Credences of Summer. Wallace Stevens. **CP-StevW**

Credibility. John Ciardi. **SP-CiarJ**

Credit me poor to say of my life *maledictory weed die.* Catullus. *See* Carmen 104: "Do you really believe I could blacken my life."

Credit of the Conquerer, The. Robert Herrick. **CP-HerrR**

Creditor, The. Louis MacNeice. **CP-MacNL**

Credo. Phoebe Hesketh. **SP-HeskP**

Credo. Robinson Jeffers. **CP-JefR1**

Credo. "Hugh MacDiarmid." **SP-MacDH**

Credo. Edwin Arlington Robinson. **CP-RobiE**

Credo. Edwin Rolfe. **CP-RolfE**

Credo in Intellectum Videntem. Allen Tate. **CP-TateA**

Creed. James McAuley. *Fr.* Requiem. **SP-McAuJ**

Creed. George Meredith. **CP-MerG2**

Creed. Leonard Nathan. **SP-NathL**

Creeks. Mary Oliver. **SP-OlivM**

Creep up, moon, on the south sky. Moon Path. Carl Sandburg. **CP-SandC**

Creeps and Crawls. Ogden Nash. **CP-NashO**

Creme tangerine and montelimar. Savoy Truffle. George Harrison. **CP-Beatl**

Creole Mephistopheles, The. Laurence Lieberman. **SP-LiebL**

Creon's Muse. Donald Davie. **CP-DavDo**

Crêpes Flambeau. Tess Gallagher. **SP-GallT**

Crépuscule Provençale. Marilyn Hacker. **SP-HackM**

Crescent blade with its snake, The. The Scythe. Lewis Turco. **SP-TurcL**

Crescent Moon Like a Canoe. Marge Piercy. **SP-PierM**

Crescent-Moon, the Star of Love, The. William Wordsworth. **CP-WorW2**

Crescenzio, the Pope's Legate at the High Council, Trent. The Cardinal and the Dog. Robert Browning. **CP-BroR2**

Cretaceous bird, your giant claw no lime. Edna St. Vincent Millay. *Fr.* Epitaph for the Race of Man. **CP-MillE**

Cretan Woman, The. Robinson Jeffers. **CP-JefR3**

Cretians ever lyars were, they care not what they say, The, *ad. fr. Latin of* Callimachus. Sir Walter Ralegh. **CP-RaleW**

Crewcut et Ux. have raised their long-haired pup. History of Hair from World War II to the Present. Howard Nemerov. **CP-NemeH**

Cri / C / k / et / in. Edward Estlin Cummings. **CP-CummE**

Crib stock fothered, horses suppered up, The. Winter Evening. John Clare. **SP-ClarJ**

Cribs loaded with roughage huddle together. From a Bus Window in Central Ohio, Just before a Thunder Shower. James Wright. **CP-WrigJ**

Cricket, The. Vincent Bourne, *tr. fr. Latin by* William Cowper. **CP-CowpW**

Cricket in the kitchen. Frederick Morgan. *Fr.* Blue Hill Poems. **SP-MorgF**

Cricket in the telephone is still, The. Certain Phenomena of Sound. Wallace Stevens. **CP-StevW**

Cricket Master. Sir John Betjeman. **CP-BetjJ**

Cricket Match. Carl Sandburg. **CP-SandC**

Crickets' / thickets / light, / delight. Louis Zukofsky. *Fr.* 29 Songs. **CP-ZukLS**

Crickets call through the long, long night, The. Johnny Appleseed's Wife from the Palace of Eve. Nicholas Vachel Lindsay. **CP-LindV**

Crickets on a Strike. Nicholas Vachel Lindsay. **CP-LindV**

Crickets sang, The. Emily Dickinson. **CP-DickE**

Cried Innocence, "Mother, my thumbs, my thumbs!" The Tortured. May Sarton. **SP-SartM**

Cried Out with Tears. Christina Georgina Rossetti. **CP-RosC2**

Cries of the eagle / dancers at Cochiti, The. Cochiti. Charles Tomlinson. **CP-TomlC**

Cries from Chiapas. Muriel Rukeyser. **CP-RukeM**

Cries of gold or men about to hang. Helena, Where Homes Go Mad. Richard Hugo. **CP-HugoR**

Crime. Robert Penn Warren. **SP-WarrR**

Crime, The. Charles Kenneth Williams. **SP-WillC**

Crime. Charles Kenneth Williams. **SP-WillC**

Criminal possession of a controlled substance. News Bulletin. Allen Ginsberg. **CP-GinsA**

Crimson. Carl Sandburg. **CP-SandC**

Crimson as the rubies, crimson as the roses, / Crimson as the sinking sun. Let Them Rejoice in Their Beds. Christina Georgina Rossetti. **CP-RosC2**

Crimson blossom charms the bee, The. To Miss Isabella Macleod. Robert Burns. **CP-BurnR**

Crimson Changes People. Carl Sandburg. **CP-SandC**

Crimson curtains round my mother's bed. Christina Georgina Rossetti. **CP-RosC2**

Crimson Cyclamen, The. William Carlos Williams. **CP-WilW1**

Crimson flames tied through my ears. My Back Pages. "Bob Dylan." **CP-DylaB**

Crimson is the slow smolder of the cigar end I hold. Crimson. Carl Sandburg. **CP-SandC**

Crimson Rambler. Carl Sandburg. **CP-SandC**

Crinan Canal. Richard Hugo. **CP-HugoR**

Crinkled paper makes a brilliant sound, A. Extracts from Addresses to the Academy of Fine Ideas. Wallace Stevens. **CP-StevW**

Crinkling Trails. Archie Randolph Ammons. **SP-AmmoA**

Cripple. Carl Sandburg. **CP-SandC**

Cripple aches in his lost limb, The. Spring Cleaning. Louis MacNeice. **CP-MacNL**

Cripple every step Drudges & labours, The. William Blake. **CP-BlakW**

Cripple in the Subway, The. Louise Glück. **SP-GlücL**

Cripples, The. Richard Hugo. **CP-HugoR**

Cripples and Other Stories. Anne Sexton. **CP-SextA**

Crippling, The. Marge Piercy. **SP-PierM**

Crisis. John Berryman. **CP-BerrJ**

Crisis, The. Robert Creeley. **CP-CreeR**

Crisis, The. Paul Laurence Dunbar. **CP-DunbP**

Crisis, The. George Meredith. **CP-MerG2**

Crisis, The. Gilbert Sorrentino. **SP-SorrG**

Crisis, The. John Greenleaf Whittier. **CP-WhitJ**

Crisis is a Hair. Emily Dickinson. **CP-DickE**

Crisis is sweet and yet the Heart. Emily Dickinson. **CP-DickE**

Crisis on the Savannah. Tom Clark. **SP-ClarT**

Crispus Attucks. Robert Earl Hayden. **CP-HaydR**

Crisscross. Carl Sandburg. **CP-SandC**

Cristina. Robert Browning. **CP-BroR1**

Cristina and Monaldeschi. Robert Browning. **CP-BroR2**

Critic. Howard Nemerov. **CP-NemeH**

Critic, The. Frank O'Hara. **SP-OharF**

Critic, The. Charles Kenneth Williams. **SP-WillC**

Critic With His Pained Eye, The. Richard Eberhart. **CP-EberR**

Critics. Jonathan Swift. *See* Hobbes clearly proves that every creature.

Critics and Connoisseurs. Marianne Craig Moore. **CP-MoorM**

Critics!—appalled, I venture on the name. On Critics. Robert Burns.
DBV; IHNG *Fr.* To R***** G***** of F*****, Esq. **CP-BurnR**

Critics Can Bleed. Roy Fisher. **SP-FishR**

Critics on the Lawn. Archibald MacLeish. **CP-MacLA**

Critics, right honourable Bard, decree. Two Epigrams on Byron's *Cain*.
William Wordsworth. **CP-WorW2**

Critics say that epics have died out, The. Elizabeth Barrett Browning.
NALW; PBWP; PeVV *Fr.* Aurora Leigh. **CP-BroEB**

Critters' Dance, De. Paul Laurence Dunbar. **CP-DunbP**

Crivelli, dead four hundred years and more. The Humanist. Alun Lewis.
CP-LewiA

Cro-Magnons. Lawrence Ferlinghetti. **SP-FerlL**

Croak, croak, croak. A Bird's-Eye View. Christina Georgina Rossetti. **CP-RosC1**

Croce e Delizia al Cor. Tess Gallagher. **SP-GallT**

Crocodile. John Crowe Ransom. *See* In due season the amphibious
crocodile.

Crocodile / Went to the dentist, The. The Crocodile's Toothache. Shel
Silverstein. **SP-SilS2**

Crocodile at the Ancient Tombs. Howard Nemerov. **CP-NemeH**

Crocodile's Toothache, The. Shel Silverstein. **SP-SilS2**

Crocus. Louis Zukofsky. **CP-ZukLS**

Crocus armies from the dead, The. Veni Coronaberis. Geoffrey Hill. **CP-HillG**

Crocus Night. James Schuyler. **CP-SchuJ**

Crocus stars the border, The. Wystan Hugh Auden. **CP-AudWJ**

Crocuses and snowdrops wither. Seasons. Christina Georgina Rossetti. **CP-RosC3**

Croft. Stevie Smith. **CP-SmitS**

Cr[omek] loves artists as he loves his Meat. William Blake. **CP-BlakW**

Cromek Speaks. William Blake. **CP-BlakW**

Cromlech, The. Louis MacNeice. **CP-MacNL**

Cromwell Dead. Andrew Marvell. *See* I saw him dead, a leaden slumber
lyes [*or* lies].

Cromwell, our chief [*or* cheif] of men, who through a cloud. John Milton.
CP-MiltJ

(Sonnet 16: "Cromwell, our cheif of men, who through a cloud.") **CP-MiltJ**

Cronkhite Beach. Charles Tomlinson. **CP-TomlC**

Crooked-angle wings. Roy Fisher. **SP-FishR** *Fr.* Diversions.

Crooked, black tree. Trees. William Carlos Williams. **CP-WilW1**

Crooked, crawling tide with long wet fingers. Tide of Storms. John Gould
Fletcher. *Fr.* Sand and Spray: A Sea-Symphony. **CP-FletJ**

Crooked you are, but that dislikes not me. Upon a Crooked Maid. Robert
Herrick. **CP-HerrR**

Crool Time. Gilbert Sorrentino. **SP-SorrG**

Croon. Langston Hughes. **SP-HughL**

Crop-Dusting. Daniel Gerard Hoffman. **SP-HoffD**

Crops were made, the leaves, The. History. Wendell Berry. *Fr.* History.
CP-BerrW

Cross, The. John Donne. **CP-DonnJ**

Cross[e], The. George Herbert. **CP-HerbG**

Cross. Phoebe Hesketh. **SP-HeskP**

Cross. Langston Hughes. **SP-HughL**

Cross, The. David Herbert Lawrence. **CP-LawrD**

Cross, The. Allen Tate. **CP-TateA**

Cross, The. John Greenleaf Whittier. **CP-WhitJ**

Cross begot me on the stone, The. Ah, Will the Saviour? Stevie Smith.
CP-SmitS

Cross-country, out of sea fog. The Message. Denise Levertov. **CP-LeveD**

Cross-Currents. Thomas Hardy. **CP-HardT**

Cross Didn't Fall on Me, A. Leonard Cohen. **CP-CoheL**

Cross-fade of grief to nothingness. The Unoccupied Zone. Louis Aragon, *tr.*
fr. French by Louis MacNeice. **CP-MacNL**

Cross Fire. Joseph Ceravolo. **SP-CeraJ**

Cross-hatching technique which allowed our ancestors to exchange, The.
Whatever It Is, Wherever You Are. John Ashbery. **SP-AshbJ**

Cross-Legged, the Spider and the Web. Charles Olson. **CP-OlsoC; SP-OlsoC**

Cross My Heart and Hope to Die, It Was the Very Same Song Exactly.
Hayden Carruth. **CP-CarHS**

Cross not, cross not, merry men of France. To the Merry Men of France.
George Meredith. **CP-MerG2**

Cross of Snow, The. Henry Wadsworth Longfellow. **SP-LongH**

Cross staggered him. At the cliff-top, The. Canticle for Good Friday.
Geoffrey Hill. **CP-HillG**

Cross, the Cross, The. Tortoise-Shell. David Herbert Lawrence. **CP-LawrD**

Cross the hands over the breaest here—so. Anna Imroth. Carl Sandburg.
CP-SandC

Cross Tore a Hole, The. William Everson.
Canticle for the Feast of the Most Precious Blood, 1954, A. **SP-EverW**

Crossbow wanted a child. The Children's Crusade. Philip Levine. **SP-LeviP**

Crosse and Pile. Robert Herrick. **CP-HerrR**

Crossed Apple, The. Louise Bogan. **CP-BogaL**

Crossed Numbers. Carl Sandburg. **CP-SandC**

Crossed-over dreams, or infertile. He, Who, in His Abandnoned Infancy,
Spoke of Jesus, Caesar, Those Who Beg, and Hell. Charles Olson.
CP-OlsoC

Crossed Wires. Jim Carroll. **SP-CarrJ**

Crosses. Robert Herrick. **CP-HerrR**

Crosses. Robert Herrick. **CP-HerrR**

Crosses on the convent roofs, The. Botanist on Alp (No. 2). Wallace
Stevens. **CP-StevW**

Crossing, The. John Hewitt. **CP-HewiJ**

Crossing. Langston Hughes. **SP-HughL**

Crossing. Archibald MacLeish. **CP-MacLA**

Crossing, The. Howard Nemerov. **CP-NemeH**

Crossing, The. Richard Shelton. **SP-ShelR**

Crossing alone the nighted ferry. Alfred Edward Housman. **CP-HousA**

Crossing at rush hour the Walt Whitman Bridge. A Modern Poet. Howard
Nemerov. **CP-NemeH**

Crossing Brooklyn Ferry. Charles Tomlinson. **CP-TomlC**

Crossing Brooklyn Ferry. Walt Whitman. **CP-WhitW**
"Ah, what can be more stately." **AA**

Crossing from a chore as the day. Long Shadow. John Updike. **CP-UpdiJ**

Crossing Lady-Stanley, Here, 1868. Steve Griffiths. **SP-GrifS**

Crossing Nation. Allen Ginsberg. **CP-GinsA**

Crossing on Staten Island Ferry. Kenneth Patchen. **CP-PatcK**

Crossing the Alps. William Wordsworth. *See* Far different dejection once
was mine.

Crossing the Atlantic. Anne Sexton. **CP-SextA**

Crossing the Bar. Tennyson. **CP-TennA**

Crossing the Border. Ogden Nash. **CP-NashO**

Crossing the Ohio When Poppies Bloom in Ashtabula. Carl Sandburg. **CP-SandC**

Crossing the Paces. Carl Sandburg. **CP-SandC**

Crossing the sound I summoned you in thought. Kathleen Jessie Raine. **SP-RainK**

Crossing the street. The Broken Home. James Merrill. **SP-MerrJ**

Crossing the Swamp. Mary Oliver. **SP-OlivM**

Crossing the Water. Sylvia Plath. **CP-PlatS**

Crossing Walt Whitman Bridge. Daniel Gerard Hoffman. **SP-HoffD**

Crossroads. Stephen Dobyns. **SP-DobyS**

Crossroads, The. Jim Morrison. **SP-MorrJ**

Crossword Puzzles. Louis MacNeice. *Fr.* Indoor Sports. **CP-MacNL**

Crosswords. Thom Gunn. *Fr.* Transients and Residents. **CP-GunnT**

Crouched beneath a snowbound sky. The Grey Ones. Louis MacNeice.
CP-MacNL

Crouched down by a roadside windbreak. Listening to the Mourners. James
Wright. **CP-WrigJ**

Crouched on a ridge sloping to where you pour. John Berryman. *Fr.*
Sonnets to Chris. **CP-BerrJ**

Crouched on wet shingle at the cove. The Judges. Robert Ranke Graves.
CP-GravR

Crouched upon sea-chiselled gravel, staring out and up at the sea. Louis
MacNeice. *Fr.* Day of Returning. **CP-MacNL**

Crow, The. Kay Boyle. **CP-BoylK**

Crow, The. Robert Creeley. **CP-CreeR**

Crow. Ted Hughes.
Dawn's Rose. **SP-HughT**
Littleblood. **SP-HughT**
That Moment. **SP-HughT**

Crow. Charles Tomlinson. **CP-TomlC**

Crow and the Birds. Ted Hughes. **SP-HughT**

Crow Hill. Ted Hughes. **SP-HughT**
("Farms are oozing craters in, The.") **SP-HughT**
Crow in the cage in the dining-room, The. The Crow. Robert Creeley. **CP-CreeR**
Crow is only an anvil, The. Chickadee. Brendan Galvin. **SP-GalvB**
Crow pecking a patch of last ice. Cold Window. John Clellon Holmes. **SP-HolmJ**
Crow Ride. Archie Randolph Ammons. **SP-AmmoA**
Crow sits in the pine tree, The. The Crow. Kay Boyle. **CP-BoylK**
Crow Song. Margaret Atwood. *Fr.* Songs of the Transformed. **SP-AtwM1**
Crowd and Company, The. Robert Herrick. **CP-HerrR**
Crowd at the ball game, The. At the Ball Game. William Carlos Williams. **CP-WilW1**
Crowd moves forward on the midway, back, The. World's Fair. John Berryman. **CP-BerrJ**
Crowd of the Greek force, The. Euripides, *tr. by* Hilda Doolittle ("H.D."). **CP-DoolH** *Fr.* Iphigenia [*or* Iphigeneia] in Aulis.
Crowded Countries of the Bomb, The. George Oppen. **CP-OppeG**
Crowded Net, The. Kenneth Patchen. **CP-PatcK**
Crowdieknowe. "Hugh MacDiarmid." **SP-MacDH**
Crowding this beach / are milkstones, white. Stone Speech. Charles Tomlinson. **CP-TomlC**
Crowing of the cock, The. Wystan Hugh Auden. **CP-AudWJ**
Crown, The. John Donne. *See* Deign[e] at my hands this crown[e] of prayer and praise.
Crown, The. Gilbert Sorrentino. **SP-SorrG**
Crown, a crown for Love's bright head, A. Ben Jonson. **CP-JonsB** *Fr.* Love Freed from Ignorance and Folly.
Crown Hill Cemetary, Indianapolis. Etheridge Knight. *Fr.* Indiana Haiku—2. **SP-KnigE**
Crown of Bays, The. Stevie Smith. **CP-SmitS**
Crown of Gold, The. Stevie Smith. **CP-SmitS**
Crown of Love, The. George Meredith. **CP-MerG1**
Crown Prince of Dullness, The. John Dryden. *See* All human[e] things are subject to decay.
Crown'd with the sickle and the wheaten sheaf. Autumn. James Thomson. *Fr.* The Seasons. **CP-ThomJ**
Crowne of Sonetts Dedicated to Love, A. Mary Sidney, Countess of Montgomery Wroth. *Fr.* Pamphilia to Amphilanthus. **CP-WrotM**
   Sonnet 1: "In this strang labourinth how shall I turne?"
   Sonnet 2: "Is to leave all, and take the thread of love."
   Sonnet 3: "His flames ar joyes, his bands true lovers might."
   Sonnet 4: "And bee in his brave court a gloriouse light."
   Sonnet 5: "And burne, yett burning you will love the smart."
   Sonnet 6: "Hee may owr profitt, and out Tuter prove."
   Sonnet 7: "How blest bee they then, who his favors prove."
   Sonnet 8: "Hee that shunns love doth love him self the less."
   Sonnet 9: "But wher they may returne with honors grace."
   Sonnet 10: "Bee from court of Love, and reason torne."
   Sonnet 11: "Unprofitably pleasing, and unsound."
   Sonnet 12: "Bee given to him who triumphs in his right."
   Sonnet 13: "Free from all fogs butt shining faire, and cleere."
   Sonnet 14: "Except my hart which you beestow'd before."
Crowned and Buried. Elizabeth Barrett Browning. **CP-BroEB**
Crowned and Wedded. Elizabeth Barrett Browning. **CP-BroEB**
Crowned king, A. William Blake. **CP-BlakW** *Fr.* An Island in the Moon.
Crowning a bluff where gleams the lake below. Pontoosuce. Herman Melville. **SP-MelvH**
Crowning hour when bodies vie with souls, The. Ralph Waldo Emerson. **CP-EmerR**
Crows, The. Louise Bogan. **CP-BogaL**
Crows. Tom Clark. **SP-ClarT**
Crows. Mary Oliver. **SP-OlivM**
Crows. Marge Piercy. **SP-PierM**
Crows. Charles Simic. **SP-SimiC**
Crows are flying above the foyer of summer, The. The Novel. Wallace Stevens. **CP-StevW**
Crow's First Lesson. Ted Hughes. **SP-HughT**
Crows in the fog, dogs. Charles Henri Ford. **SP-FordC** *Fr.* Emblems of Arachne.
Crow's Last Stand. Ted Hughes. **SP-HughT**
Crow's Mark. Hayden Carruth. **CP-CarHS**
Crows, mingled, The. Clarifications. Archie Randolph Ammons. **SP-AmmoA**
Crows see me. / They stretch their glossy necks, The. Entering the Kingdom. Mary Oliver. **SP-OlivM**
Croydon. Sir John Betjeman. **CP-BetjJ**

Crucible. Carl Sandburg. **CP-SandC**
Crucibles of Love. Robert Ranke Graves. **CP-GravR**
Crucified Lord, however much I burn. Lachrimae Coactae. Geoffrey Hill. *Fr.* Lachrimae; or Seven Tears Figured in Seven Passionate Pavans. **CP-HillG**
Crucified lord, so naked to the world. Lachrimae Antiquae Novae. Geoffrey Hill. *Fr.* Lachrimae; or Seven Tears Figured in Seven Passionate Pavans. **CP-HillG**
Crucified Lord, you swim upon your cross. Lachrimae Verae. Geoffrey Hill. **NAEL-2; NoAM; NoP** *Fr.* Lachrimae; or Seven Tears Figured in Seven Passionate Pavans. **CP-HillG**
Crucifix in the Filing Cabinet, The. Karl Shapiro. **SP-ShapK**
Crucifixion. Hayden Carruth. **CP-CarHS**
Crucifixion, The. John Gould Fletcher. **SP-FletJ** *Fr.* The Parables of Christ.
Crucifixion, The. Alun Lewis. **CP-LewiA**
Crucifixion, The. John Greenleaf Whittier. **CP-WhitJ**
Crucifixion of Noel, The. Marsden Hartley. **CP-HartM**
Crucifixion of Our Blessed Lord. Christopher Smart. **ChIV-2** *Fr.* Hymns and Spiritual Songs for the Fasts and Festivals of the Church of England. **SP-SmarC**
Crucifixion of the Skyscraper. John Gould Fletcher. **SP-FletJ**
Crucifying. John Donne. *Fr.* La Corona. **ChIV-2; ESCV; OBS; Son** *Fr.* Holy Sonnets. **CP-DonnJ**
Crude Foyer. Wallace Stevens. **CP-StevW**
Crude Lament. William Carlos Williams. **CP-WilW1**
Crudely continues what has been begun. Captain in Time of Peace. Thom Gunn. **CP-GunnT**
Cruel Cerinthus! does the fell disease. Imitation of Tibullus. Byron. **CP-Byron**
Cruel, cruel is the presence of weather. Weather. Kay Boyle. **CP-BoylK**
Cruel Experiments Continue! Gilbert Sorrentino. **SP-SorrG**
Cruel Falcon, The. Robinson Jeffers. **CP-JefR2**
Cruel Mistress, A. Thomas Carew. **CP-CareT**
Cruel Mistress, The. Robert Louis Stevenson. **CP-StevR**
Cruel of heart, lay down my song. To Those Without Pity. Edna St. Vincent Millay. **CP-MillE**
Cruelkind Swans, The. Kenneth Patchen. **CP-PatcK**
Cruell Maid, The. Robert Herrick. **CP-HerrR**
Cruell Remembrance alas now be still. Mary Sidney, Countess of Montgomery Wroth. *Fr.* Urania. **CP-WrotM**
Crueller than owl or eagle. Ted Hughes. **HAP** *Fr.* Skylarks. **SP-HughT**
Cruelly, love / walk the autumn long. Edward Estlin Cummings. **CP-CummE**
Cruelties. Robert Herrick. **CP-HerrR**
Cruelties of the Sportive Power. Kenneth Patchen. **CP-PatcK**
Cruelty. Robert Herrick. **CP-HerrR**
Cruelty and rain could be expected. The House on 15th S.W. Richard Hugo. **CP-HugoR**
Cruelty Base in Commanders. Robert Herrick. **CP-HerrR**
Cruelty is rarely conscious. The Photograph of the Unmade Bed. Adrienne Rich. **CP-RicAE; SP-RicA2**
Cruise, The. Muriel Rukeyser. **CP-RukeM**
Cruisers. Rudyard Kipling. **CP-KiplR**
Cruising these residential Sunday / streets in dry August sunlight. The City Planners. Margaret Atwood. **SP-AtwM1**
Crumb, a Crumb, and a Little Seed, A. Paul Laurence Dunbar. **CP-DunbP**
Crumbling elms and evergreens, The. Emily Dickinson. **SP-DickE**
Crumbling is not an instant's Act. Emily Dickinson. **CP-DickE**
Crumbs or the Loaf. Robinson Jeffers. **CP-JefR2**
Crumpled clothes come slowly off. Roy Fisher. **SP-FishR** *Fr.* Metamorphoses.
Crumpled paper, little stick. The Stick. Anne Waldman. **SP-WaldA**
Crunch, The. Charles Bukowski. **SP-BukC1**
Crusaders. William Wordsworth. *Fr.* Ecclesiastical Sonnets. **CP-WorW2**
Crusades. William Wordsworth. *Fr.* Ecclesiastical Sonnets. **CP-WorW2**
Crusoe. Thomas Merton. **CP-MertT; SP-MertT**
Crusoe in England. Elizabeth Bishop. **CP-BishE**
Crusoe's Island. Derek Walcott. **CP-WalcD**
Crusoe's Journal. Derek Walcott. **CP-WalcD**
Crust of bread and a corner to sleep in, A. Life. Paul Laurence Dunbar. **CP-DunbP**
Crustaceous / wedge / of sweaty kitchens. The Agonized Spires. William Carlos Williams. **CP-WilW1**
Crutches. Stephen Berg. **SP-BergS**
Crutches. Robert Herrick. **CP-HerrR**
Cry Baby Cry. John Lennon *and* Paul McCartney. **CP-Beatl**
Cry Faugh! Robert Ranke Graves. **CP-GravR**

Cry for me, ladies, your servant. Guillaume de Machault (1300-1377)
Ballade: Plourès, dames. Louis Zukofsky. **CP-ZukLS**

Cry from the green-grained sticks of the fire, A. Surview [or Surview:
Cogitavi Vias Meas]. Thomas Hardy. **CP-HardT**

Cry Going Out over Pastures, The. Robert Bly. **SP-BlyR**

Cry in Distress, A. Bible, O.T. *See* Psalm 22: "My God, my God, why hast
thou forsaken me?"

Cry "Murder" in the market-place, and each. Rudyard Kipling. **CP-KiplR**
Fr. His Wedded Wife. *Fr.* Plain Tales from the Hills.

Cry of a Lost Soul, The. John Greenleaf Whittier. **CP-WhitJ**

Cry of the Children, The. Elizabeth Barrett Browning. **CP-BroEB**
"They look up with their pale and sunken faces." NBM; OBD

Cry of the Homeless. Thomas Hardy. **CP-HardT**

Cry of the Human, The. Elizabeth Barrett Browning. **CP-BroEB**
Convinced by Sorrow. **BLRP; WBLP**

Cry of the Masses. David Herbert Lawrence. **CP-LawrD**

Cry pain, & the dogs of yrself devour. Charles Olson. **CP-OlsoC**

CRY what shall I cry? Difficulties of a Statesman. Thomas Stearns Eliot.
Fr. Coriolan. **CP-ElioT**

Crying from exile, I. Elegy. Marilyn Hacker. **SP-HackM**

Crying, my little one, footsore and weary? Christina Georgina Rossetti. **CP-RosC2**

Cryopexy. Charles Wright. **SP-WrigC**

Crystal. Ted Berrigan. **SP-BerrT**

Crystal, The. Robert Ranke Graves. **CP-GravR**

Crystal. Thom Gunn. *Fr.* Transients and Residents. **CP-GunnT**

Crystal Cabinet, The. William Blake. **CP-BlakW**

Crystal Cage, The. Stanley Jasspon Kunitz. **CP-KuniS**

Crystal Gazer. Sylvia Plath. **CP-PlatS**

Crystal Lithium, The. James Schuyler. **CP-SchuJ**

Crystal Maze, A. William Carlos Williams. **CP-WilW1**

Crystals like Blood. "Hugh MacDiarmid." **SP-MacDH**

Cuba. Paul Muldoon. **SP-MuldP**

Cuban Doctor, The. Wallace Stevens. **CP-StevW**

Cuccurucù! Cuccurucù! / All'alba il gallo canta. Christina Georgina
Rossetti. **CP-RosC3**

Cuchulain. William Carlos Williams. **CP-WilW2**

Cuchulain Comforted. William Butler Yeats. **CP-YeatW**

Cuchulain's Fight with the Sea, *diff. vers.* William Butler Yeats. *See* A
Man came slowly from the setting sun.

Cuckold's Song, The. Leonard Cohen. **CP-CoheL**

Cuckoo. Louis MacNeice. **CP-MacNL**

Cuckoo, The. Ogden Nash. **CP-NashO**

Cuckoo across the poppies. Cuckoo. Louis MacNeice. **CP-MacNL**

Cuckoo and the coo-dove's ceaseless calling, The. Sigh No More. David
Herbert Lawrence. **CP-LawrD**

Cuckoo and the Nightingale, The. William Wordsworth. **CP-WorW1**

Cuckoo at Laverna May 25, 1837, The. William Wordsworth. *Fr.*
Memorials of a Tour in Italy, 1837. **CP-WorW2**

Cuckoo-Clock, The. William Wordsworth. **CP-WorW2**

Cuckoo King, The. Howard Nemerov. **CP-NemeH**

Cuckoo Song. Hilda Doolittle. **CP-DoolH**

Cuckoo Song. Rudyard Kipling. **CP-KiplR**

Cucumber impaled upon a picket, The. Mysteries Sacred and Profane.
Gilbert Sorrentino. **SP-SorrG**

Cucumbers are thirsty, their big leaves turn away from, The. Glimpse of the
Waterer. Robert Bly. **SP-BlyR**

Cuddie [or Cuddy], for shame hold up thy heavy[e] head. October.
Edmund Spenser. NAEL-1; OAEL-1; OBSC *Fr.* The Shepheardes [or
Shepeards or Shepherd's] Calender. **CP-Spens**

Cuffe comes to Church much; but he keeps his bed. Upon Cuffe. Epig.
Robert Herrick. **CP-HerrR**

Cuidadores de Autos. Stephen Dobyns. **SP-DobyS**

Cuirassiers of the Frontier, The. Robert Ranke Graves. **CP-GravR**

Cuisine Bourgeoise. Wallace Stevens. **CP-StevW**

Cujus pulchritudinem / Sol et luna mirantur. St. Agnes: A Responsory.
Thomas Merton. **CP-MertT; SP-MertT**

Cul-de-Sac. Allen Tate. **CP-TateA**

Culebra Cascabel. Tom Clark. **SP-ClarT**

Culled from the brambled ceiling of my wide. Marilyn Hacker.
SP-HackM *Fr.* Separations.

Culloden. Richard Hugo. **CP-HugoR**

Culprit, The. Alfred Edward Housman. **CP-HousA**

Cultivation of Christmas Trees, The. Thomas Stearns Eliot. **CP-ElioT**

Cultra Manor: The Ulster Folk Museum. John Hewitt. **CP-HewiJ**

Culture. Ralph Waldo Emerson. **CP-EmerR**

Culture and Anarchy. Adrienne Rich. **SP-RicA2**

Cum caelum et tellus et vasti machina mundi. Poema de assumptione
b.v.m. Robert Southwell. **CP-SoutR**

Cum caput Hesperiis attollit Phœbus ab undis. Aurora Est Musis Amica.
Samuel Johnson. **CP-JohnS**

Cum tibi vilescat doctus lepidusque Catullus. *acc. by English translation.*
Thomas Campion. **CP-CampT**

Cum tot sustineat reges et tanta, neque ulla. On Loyalty. William Cowper.
CP-CowpW

Cumaean Sibyl, charming Ogress. Our Doom to Bloom. Robert Frost. **CP-FrosR**

Cumberland. Donald Davie. **CP-DavDo**

Cumberland Water Authority. William Wordsworth. FaBoDD *Fr.* The
Waggoner. **CP-WorW1**

Cumhal called out, bending his head. The Blessed. William Butler Yeats.
CP-YeatW

Cummings. Archibald MacLeish. **CP-MacLA**

Cummings. David Markson. **CP-MarkD**

Cumulatives. Carl Sandburg. **CP-SandC**

Cunctation in Correction. Robert Herrick. **CP-HerrR**

Cunning sures & the Aim at yours, The. William Blake. **CP-BlakW**

Cunts. John Updike. **CP-UpdiJ**

Cup for hope! she said, A. Three Seasons. Christina Georgina Rossetti.
CP-RosC1

Cup, ignorant and cruel. To Wine. Louise Bogan. **CP-BogaL**

Cup of Cold Water. Siv Cedering Fox. **SP-CedeS**

Cup of life is not so shallow, The. Ralph Waldo Emerson. **CP-EmerR**

Cup with a Jaguar for the Drinking of Health. Pablo Antonio Cuadra, *tr. fr.
Spanish by* Thomas Merton. **CP-MertT**

Cupid as he lay among. The Wounded Cupid. Robert Herrick. **CP-HerrR**

Cupid, because thou shin'st in Stella's eyes. Sonnet 12. Sir Philip Sidney.
Fr. Astrophil and Stella. **SP-SidnP**

Cupid blessed bee thy might. Mary Sidney, Countess of Montgomery
Wroth. *Fr.* Love's Victorie. **CP-WrotM**

Cupid Far Gone. Richard Lovelace. **CP-LoveR**

Cupid, if storying Legends tell aright. Kisses. Samuel Taylor Coleridge.
Fr. Effusions. **CP-ColeS**

Cupid laid by his brand, and fell asleep. Sonnet 153. William
Shakespeare. *Fr.* Sonnets. **CP-ShaWS**

Cupido. Ralph Waldo Emerson. **CP-EmerR**

Cupid's Arrows. Rudyard Kipling. *Fr.* Plain Tales from the Hills.
"Pit where the buffalo cooled his hide." **CP-KiplR**

Cupola, The. Louise Bogan. **CP-BogaL**

Cups. David Herbert Lawrence. **CP-LawrD**

Cups of Coffee. Carl Sandburg. **CP-SandC**

Curate and churchwarden, The. Tom Raban. William Cowper. **CP-CowpW**

Curate's Kindness, The. Thomas Hardy. **CP-HardT**

Curative Powers of Silence, The. Al Young. **CP-YounA**

Curb Science? Robinson Jeffers. **CP-JefR3**

Cure, The. Robert Ranke Graves. **CP-GravR**

Curé, The. Rudyard Kipling. **CP-KiplR**

Cure, The. Anne Waldman. **SP-WaldA**

Cure, The. William Carlos Williams. **CP-WilW2**

Curé and pastor, dead at the one time. The Jesuits in North America.
Donald Davie. **CP-DavDo**

Cure for Warts, The. Paul Muldoon. **SP-MuldP**

Cure of Souls, A. Denise Levertov. **CP-LeveD**

Curfew. Paul Éluard, *tr. fr. French by* William Carlos Williams. **CP-WilW2**

Curfew tolls the knell of parting day, The. Elegy Written in a Country
Churchyard. Thomas Gray. **CP-GrayT**

Curfew tolls the knell of parting day, The. Thomas Gray. UV *Fr.* Elegy
Written in a Country Churchyard. **CP-GrayT**

Curfew Tower, The. John Hewitt. **CP-HewiJ**

Curiosity. Paul Laurence Dunbar. **CP-DunbP**

Curious child, who dwelt upon a tract, A. William Wordsworth. WGRP
Fr. Despondency Corrected. *Fr.* The Excursion. **CP-WorW2**

Curious Cloud surprised the Sky, A. Emily Dickinson. **CP-DickE**

Curious heart plays with its fears:, The. The Shot. Robert Ranke Graves.
CP-GravR

Curious reticence afflicts my generation, faced with the holocaust, A. The
Event Itself. Hayden Carruth. **CP-CarHS**

Curious to learn / how many kiss- / es of your lips. Carmen 7. Catullus.
Fr. Carmina. **CP-Catul**

Curious to see oneself irresistibly alive in the middle of death. Prologo.
Thomas Merton. **CP-MertT**

Curious upward stumbling motion, The. Thoughts to a Concerto of
Telemann. Lawrence Ferlinghetti. **SP-FerlL**

Curious wits, seeing dull pensiveness, The. Sonnet 23. Sir Philip Sidney. *Fr.* Astrophil and Stella. **SP-SidnP**

Curiously enough. actual revolutions are made by robots. Revolutions as Such! David Herbert Lawrence. **CP-LawrD**

Curl Up and Diet. Ogden Nash. **CP-NashO**

Curled red locks looped back over the shoe-sole parabola. Saltcod Red. Laurence Lieberman. **SP-LiebL**

Curled, too much curled, he was sleeping. Fathers and Sons. James Dickey. **CP-DickJ**

Curlews in April. Ted Hughes. *Fr.* Curlews Lift. **SP-HughT**

Curlews Lift. Ted Hughes. **SP-HughT**

    "Curlews in April."

    "Out of the maternal watery blue lines."

Curly Blue Buppo, The. Kenneth Patchen. **CP-PatcK**

Curly-head, / Plump little mother's girl. To the Thin and Elegant Woman Who Resides Inside of Alix Nelson. Diane Wakoski. **SP-WakoD**

Currants on a bush, / And figs upon a stem. Christina Georgina Rossetti. **CP-RosC2**

Current, The. Wendell Berry. **CP-BerrW**

Current, The. James Merrill. **SP-MerrJ**

Current murmured northward, warmth, The. Cheliuskin. Edwin Rolfe. **CP-RolfE**

Currente Calamo. Arthur Hugh Clough. **SP-ClouA** *Fr.* Mari Magno.

Currents rage deep inside us, The. Video Violence. "Lou Reed." **SP-ReedL**

Curs'd be the man, the poorest wretch in life. The Henpeck'd Husband. Robert Burns. **CP-BurnR**

Curse, A. Wystan Hugh Auden. **CP-AudeW**

Curse, The. John Berryman. **CP-BerrJ**

Curse. Robert Creeley. **CP-CreeR**

Curse, The. John Donne. **CP-DonnJ**

Curse, A. Malcolm Lowry. **CP-LowrM**

Curse. Malcolm Lowry. *Fr.* Songs for Second Childhood. **CP-LowrM**

Curse, The. Edna St. Vincent Millay. **CP-MillE**

Curse. A Song, The. Robert Herrick. **CP-HerrR**

Curse against Elegies, A. Anne Sexton. **CP-SextA**

Curse for Kings, A. Nicholas Vachel Lindsay. **CP-LindV**

Curse for the War Machine, A. Charles Henri Ford. **SP-FordC**

Curse not the mice, no grist of thine they eat. Upon Ralph. Robert Herrick. **CP-HerrR**

Curse of a Rich Polish Peasant on His Sister Who Ran Away with a Wild Man. Carl Sandburg. **CP-SandC**

Curse of Cromwell, The. William Butler Yeats. **CP-YeatW**

Curse of Minerva, The. Byron. **CP-Byron**

Curse of the Charter-Breakers, The. John Greenleaf Whittier. **CP-WhitJ**

Curse of the Earth Magician on a Metal Land. Marge Piercy. **SP-PierM**

Curse of the Frogs, The. Paul Zimmer. **SP-ZimmP**

Curse on ungrateful man, that can be pleas'd. On Fergusson. Robert Burns. **CP-BurnR**

Curse thee, Life, I will live with thee no more! The Suicide. Edna St. Vincent Millay. **CP-MillE**

Curse upon each king who leads his state, A. A Curse for Kings. Nicholas Vachel Lindsay. **CP-LindV**

Curses & Invocations. Jim Morrison. **SP-MorrJ**

Cursing rogue with a merry face, A. The Hour before Dawn. William Butler Yeats. **CP-YeatW**

Cursing this mistral. Crépuscule Provençale. Marilyn Hacker. **SP-HackM**

Cursive crawl, the squared-off characters, The. Writing. Howard Nemerov. **CP-NemeH**

Curtain. Paul Laurence Dunbar. **CP-DunbP**

Curtain Call. Charles Tomlinson. **CP-TomlC**

Curtains! Donald Davie. **CP-DavDo**

Curtains forcing their will. Awaking in New York. Maya Angelou. **SP-AngeM**

Curtains in the House of the Metaphysician, The. Wallace Stevens. **CP-StevW**

Curtains Now Are Drawn, The. Thomas Hardy. **CP-HardT**

Curtains part) / the peacockappareled. Edward Estlin Cummings. **CP-CummE**

Curtains were half drawn, the floor was swept, The. After Death. Christina Georgina Rossetti. **CP-RosC1**

Curtis and I sit drinking auburn sherry. Five O'Clock, Beacon Hill. Adrienne Rich. **CP-RicAE**

Curtis, you've been American too long. A Letter to Curtis Bradford. Donald Davie. **CP-DavDo**

Curvd lines toe-drawn, round cornerd squares, The. Hop, Skip, and Jump. Gary Snyder. **CP-SnydG**

Curve of lamps that climbs into the dark, The. The Question. Charles Tomlinson. **CP-TomlC**

Curve of the two steel spring-up prongs on. The Wild Edge. Gary Snyder. **CP-SnydG**

Cushendun. Louis MacNeice. **FaBCIP** *Fr.* The Closing Album. **CP-MacNL**

Cushkib Fair. John Hewitt. **CP-HewiJ**

Custard, The. Robert Herrick. **CP-HerrR**

Customs Collector's Report, The. Stanley Jasspon Kunitz. **CP-KuniS**

Cut. Sylvia Plath. **CP-PlatS**

Cut a cane that once. In the Bulrush. Rita Dove. **SP-DoveR**

Cut down that timber! Bells, too many and strong. The Planster's Vision. Sir John Betjeman. **CP-BetjJ**

Cut Flower, A. Karl Shapiro. **SP-ShapK**

Cut Grass. Philip Larkin. **CP-LarkP**

Cut if you will, with Sleep's dull knife. Midnight Oil. Edna St. Vincent Millay. **CP-MillE**

Cut into by doors. Venice. Charles Tomlinson. **CP-TomlC**

Cut off from the great rebus of stars. Millennial Icon. Tom Clark. **SP-ClarT**

Cut out for the river on an October morn. So Long It's Been Good to Know You. Chuck Miller. **SP-MillC**

Cut-rate goods for cut-rate people. A Spade a Spade (Grocery for the Poor). Chuck Miller. **SP-MillC**

Cut the bank for the fill. The Defective Record. William Carlos Williams. **CP-WilW1**

Cut Worm. Roy Fisher. **SP-FishR**

Cute boy arm in elbow prize con man, kid, what do we see. Catullus. *See* Carmen 106: "When an auctioneer's seen with a good-looking boy."

Cutting across a vacant lot. The House in the Vacant Lot. Miller Williams. **SP-WillM**

Cutting an alder branch to shape a stick. The Alder Stick. John Hewitt. **CP-HewiJ**

Cutting Off One's Ears for Someone Else Is Wrong. Jenny Joseph. *Fr.* Fables. **SP-JoseJ**

Cutting the Firebreak. William Everson. **SP-EverW**

Cutting up an Ox. Chuang Tzu, *tr. fr. Chinese* by Thomas Merton. **CP-MertT**

Cuttings ("Sticks-in-a-drowse droop over sugary loam"). Theodore Roethke. **CP-RoetT**

Cuttings ("This urge, wrestle, resurrection of dry sticks"). Theodore Roethke. **CP-RoetT**

Cutty Sark. Hart Crane. **FaBoMo** *Fr.* The Bridge. **CP-CranH**

Cwa een like milk-wort and bog-cotton hair! Milk-Wort and Bog Cotton. "Hugh MacDiarmid." **SP-MacDH**

Cy Est Pourtraicte, Madame Ste Ursule, et Les Unze Mille Vierges. Wallace Stevens. **CP-StevW**

Cybernetics. Howard Nemerov. **CP-NemeH**

Cycle. Geoffrey Hill. **CP-HillG**

Cycle, The. Robinson Jeffers. **CP-JefR1**

Cycle, The. Theodore Roethke. **CP-RoetT**

Cycle begins anew, The. Augment of Re-Birth. Jim Morrison. **SP-MorrJ**

Cyclist. Louis MacNeice. **CP-MacNL**

Cyclist, The. Marge Piercy. **SP-PierM**

Cyclops. Margaret Atwood. **SP-AtwM1**

Cyclops, The. Euripides, *tr. fr. Greek* by Shelley. **CP-ShelP**

    Chorus of Satyrs, Driving Their Goats. **AWP**

    Love Song: "One with eyes the fairest." **AWP**

Cyclops, The. Theocritus, *tr. fr. Greek* by Elizabeth Barrett Browning. **CP-BroEB**

Cydonian Spring with her attendant train. The Spring. Ezra Pound. **SP-PounE**

Cygnets dark; their black feet. The Menagerie at Versailles in 1775. John Updike. **CP-UpdiJ**

Cymochles and Phaedria. Edmund Spenser. **OBSC** *Fr.* The Faerie Queene. **CP-Spens**

Cynical. Gilbert Sorrentino. **SP-SorrG**

Cynicks narrow houshold stuffe of Crutch, The. Ausonius, *tr. fr. Latin* by Richard Lovelace. **CP-LoveR**

Cynic's Epitaph. Thomas Hardy. **CP-HardT**

Cynthia's Revels. Ben Jonson.

    "O, that joy so soon should waste!" **CP-JonsB**

    "Queen and huntress, chaste and fair." **CP-JonsB**

    "Slow, slow, fresh fount, keep time with my salt tears." **CP-JonsB**

    "Thou more than most sweet glove." **CP-JonsB**

Cynthius pluck ye by the eare. Disswasions from Idlenesse. Robert Herrick. **CP-HerrR**

Cypassis, that a thousand ways trim'st hair. 2.8. Ovid, *tr.* by Christopher Marlowe. **CP-MarlC** *Fr.* Elegies.

Cypress Avenue, The. Donald Davie. **CP-DavDo**

Cypress stood up like a church, The. Bianca among the Nightingales. Elizabeth Barrett Browning. **CP-BroEB**

Cypress-Tree of Ceylon, The. John Greenleaf Whittier. **CP-WhitJ**

Cypresses. David Herbert Lawrence. **CP-LawrD**

Cyriack, this three years['] day these eyes, though clear. John Milton. **CP-MiltJ**

   (Sonnet 22: "Cyriack, this three years day these eyes, though clear.") **CP-MiltJ**

Cyriack, whose Grandsire on the Royal Bench. John Milton. **CP-MiltJ**

   (Sonnet 21: "Cyriack, whose Grandsire on the Royal Bench.") **CP-MiltJ**

Cyriaque d'Etremont: Bluenose Portrait Effect #1. Marsden Hartley. **CP-HartM**

Cyril Connolly. Stephen Spender. **CP-SpenS**

Cythera's pearls were dim. Psyche. Hilda Doolittle. **CP-DoolH**

Cywydd. Gerard Manley Hopkins. **CP-HopkG**

Czecho-Slovakia. Edna St. Vincent Millay. **CP-MillE**

D

D. C. Rita Dove. *Fr.* A Suite for Augustus. **SP-DoveR**

D-re-A-mi-N-gl-Y / leaves / (sEe). Edward Estlin Cummings. **CP-CummE**

Da Boyg. Charles Olson. **CP-OlsoC**

Da Capo. Charles Tomlinson. **CP-TomlC**

Da Tagte Es. Samuel Beckett. **CP-BeckS**

D'abord / à plat sur du dur. Samuel Beckett. **CP-BeckS**

Daddy, / don't let your dog. *See also* Hughes's Warning: Augmented. Langston Hughes. **SP-HughL**

Daddy. Sylvia Plath. **CP-PlatS**

Daddy-Do-Nothing. David Herbert Lawrence. **CP-LawrD**

Daddy-o / Buddy-o. Migrant. Langston Hughes. **SP-HughL**

"Daddy" Warbucks. Anne Sexton. **CP-SextA**

Daddy's Home, See You Tomorrow. Ogden Nash. *Fr.* Posies from a Second Childhood, or, Hark How Gaffer Do Chaffer. **CP-NashO**

Dae what ye wull ye canna parry. "Hugh MacDiarmid." **EBEV; OXAEP-2** *Fr.* A Drunk Man Looks at the Thistle. **SP-MacDH**

Daedalus: The Dirge. George Oppen. **CP-OppeG**

Daemon, The. Louise Bogan. **CP-BogaL**

Daemon initiate, spirit. Euripides, *tr.* by Hilda Doolittle ("H.D."). **CP-DoolH** *Fr.* Hippolytus.

Daemon of the World, The; A Fragment. Percy Bysshe Shelley. **CP-ShelP**

Dæmonic and the Celestial Love, The. Ralph Waldo Emerson. **APN-1** *Fr.* Initial, Dæmonic, and Celestial Love. **CP-EmerR**

Daemons. John Ciardi. **SP-CiarJ**

Daffy Duck in Hollywood. John Ashbery. **SP-AshbJ**

Hollywood Everything, A. **CBCK**

Daft Little Shoe Clerk Decided It Would Be Fun to Go Up and See What Things Are Like above the Sky, The. Kenneth Patchen. **CP-PatcK**

Daft things people do, The. High life. Jenny Joseph. *Fr.* Life and Turgid Times of A. Citizen. **SP-JoseJ**

Dago shovelman sits by the railroad track, The. Child of the Romans. Carl Sandburg. **CP-SandC**

Dagonet, the fool, whom Gawain in his mood. The Last Tournament. Tennyson. *Fr.* Idylls of the King. **CP-TennA**

Daguerreotype Taken in Old Age. Margaret Atwood. **SP-AtwM1**

Dagwood and Blondie. Charles Bukowski. **SP-BukC3**

Dahlia. Louis Zukofsky. **CP-ZukLS**

Dahlias, The. John Gould Fletcher. **SP-FletJ**

Daibutsu. Laurence Lieberman. **SP-LiebL**

Daie, a night, an houre of sweete content, A. Thomas Campion. *See* Content.

Daih's a moughty soothin' feelin'. 'Long To'ds Night. Paul Laurence Dunbar. **CP-DunbP**

Daily Bread. Wystan Hugh Auden. **CP-AudWJ**

Daily Globe, The. Howard Nemerov. **CP-NemeH**

Daily Library Visitor. Marsden Hartley. **CP-HartM**

Daily Life of the Worker Bee, The. Marge Piercy. **SP-PierM**

Daily news. And today? There is not so much to note. Canto X. Louis MacNeice. *Fr.* Autumn Sequel. **CP-MacNL**

Daily Reviewer-Haupt. David Markson. **CP-MarkD**

Daily the / sledgehammers and the. Sad-Eyed Mules of Men. Charles Bukowski. **SP-BukC2**

Daily Things We Do, The. Philip Larkin. **CP-LarkP**

Daily, though no ears attended. The Obedient. Rudyard Kipling. *Fr.* Epitaphs of the War [1914–1918]. **CP-KiplR**

Daimyo and the courtesan / Compliment each other, The. Scene from a Drama. John Gould Fletcher. **SP-FletJ**

Dainty Davie. Robert Burns. **CP-BurnR**

Daisies, The. Charles Tomlinson. **CP-TomlC**

Daisies are broken. Love Song. William Carlos Williams. **CP-WilW1**

Daisies of Florence. Kathleen Jessie Raine. **SP-RainK**

Daisy, The. Walter de la Mare. **CP-DeLaW**

Daisy, The. Tennyson. **CP-TennA**

Daisy. William Carlos Williams. **CP-WilW1**

Daisy. Louis Zukofsky. **CP-ZukLS**

Daisy and dandelion, speedwell, daffodil. Demi-Exile. Howth. Donald Davie. **CP-DavDo**

Daisy follows soft the Sun, The. Emily Dickinson. **CP-DickE**

Daisy now is out upon the green, The. Song. George Meredith. **CP-MerG1**

Dakar Doldrums. Allen Ginsberg. **CP-GinsA**

Da'kest hour, dey allus say, De. Joggin' Erlong. Paul Laurence Dunbar. **CP-DunbP**

Dalila. George Meredith. **CP-MerG2**

Dalliance of the Eagles, The. Walt Whitman. **CP-WhitW**

Dam, The. Muriel Rukeyser. **CP-RukeM**

Dam Neck, Virginia. Richard Eberhart. **CP-EberR**

Dam was built in, The. Cecil, Zimmer, and the Man-Made Lake. Paul Zimmer. **SP-ZimmP**

Damaetas. Byron. **CP-Byron**

Dame, dame! the watch is set. The Witches' Charms. Ben Jonson. *Fr.* The Masque of Queens.

Dame Kind. Wystan Hugh Auden. **CP-AudeW**

Dame Nature. Edmund Spenser. **PoEL-1** *Fr.* The Faerie Queene. **CP-Spens**

Dame of Athelhall, The. Thomas Hardy. **CP-HardT**

Dames du Temps Jadis. Robert Lowell. **SP-LoweR**

Damming Stream. Wystan Hugh Auden. **CP-AudWJ**

Damn it all! all this our South stinks peace. Sestina: Altaforte. Ezra Pound. **SP-PounE**

Damn it, one shouts, but there is no echo in the forest. A Short Poem in Color. Kay Boyle. **CP-BoylK**

Damn near where'er you look, a writer's ghost. Literary Dublin. John Updike. **CP-UpdiJ**

Damn that celibate farm, that cracker-box house. Censorship. John Ciardi. **SP-CiarJ**

Damn You, Jim D., You Woke Me Up. John Berryman. **CP-BerrJ**

"Damn!" you would say if I were to write the best. The Casualty. Louis MacNeice. **CP-MacNL**

Damned. John Berryman. **CP-BerrJ**

Damned. Lost & *damned*. And I find I'm pregnant. Damned. John Berryman. **CP-BerrJ**

Damned ugly things. Tanck's Song About Brains. Hayden Carruth. **CP-CarHS** *Fr.* Songs About What Comes Down: The Complete Works of Mr. Septic Tank.

Damon & Pythias. Robert Creeley. **CP-CreeR**

Damon, come drive thy flocks this way. Clorinda and Damon. Andrew Marvell. **CP-MarvA**

Damon the Mower. Andrew Marvell. **CP-MarvA**

Damon's Epitaph. John Milton, *tr. fr. Latin* by John T. Shawcross. **CP-MiltJ**

   (On the Death of Damon.) **CP-CowpW**, *tr.* by William Cowper;

   ("Ye nymphs of Himera (for ye have shed).") **CP-CowpW**, *tr.* by William Cowper;

Damon's Lament for his Clorinda, Yorkshire 1654. Geoffrey Hill. *Fr.* An Apology for the Revival of Christian Architecture in England. **CP-HillG**

Damp[e], The. John Donne. **CP-DonnJ**

Dampness in the air. Charles Henri Ford. **SP-FordC** *Fr.* Emblems of Arachne.

Dan. Carl Sandburg. **CP-SandC**

Dan Jackson's Reply. Jonathan Swift. **CP-SwifJ**

Danaan children laugh, in cradles of wrought gold, The. The Unappeasable Host. William Butler Yeats. **CP-YeatW**

Danaë. Jenny Joseph. **SP-JoseJ**

Dance, A. Wendell Berry. **CP-BerrW**

Dance, The. Wendell Berry. **CP-BerrW**

Dance, The. Elizabeth Barrett Browning. **CP-BroEB**

Dance, The. Thomas Campion. **CP-CampT; EIL; FaBoCh; LoBV** *Fr.* The Ayres that Were Sung and Played, at Brougham Castle in Westmerland, in the Kings Entertainment. **CP-CampT**

Dance, The. Hart Crane. **LiTM; MoAB; MoAmPo; OxBA** *Fr.* Powhatan's Daughter. *Fr.* The Bridge. **CP-CranH**

Dance, The. Paul Laurence Dunbar. **CP-DunbP**

Dance / is not yet / and when it will begin, The. Before the Dance. Charles Tomlinson. **CP-TomlC**

Dance, The. Philip Larkin. **CP-LarkP**

Dance, The. Theodore Roethke. **DIP** *Fr.* Four for Sir John Davies. **CP-RoetT**

Dance, The. Edmund Spenser. *See* The Dance of the Graces.

Dance, The ("In Brueghel's great picture"). William Carlos Williams. **CP-WilW2**

Dance, The ("When the snow falls"). William Carlos Williams. **CP-WilW2**

Dance at the Phoenix, The. Thomas Hardy. **CP-HardT**

Dance begins: to end about a form, The. The Desert Music. William Carlos Williams. **CP-WilW2**

Dance begins with the sun descending, The. Marrakech. Richard Eberhart. **CP-EberR**

Dance, dance, and visit now the shadowes of our joy. Thomas Campion. *Fr.* The Lords Mask[e].

Dance, Domingo, dance! The Festival of the Corn. Marsden Hartley. **CP-HartM**

Dance Figure. Ezra Pound. **SP-PounE**

"Dance for a year and a day!" he cried. The Priest's Curse on Dancing. Howard Nemerov. **CP-NemeH**

Dance for Aging Hipsters, A. Al Young. **CP-YounA**

Dance for Li Po, A. Al Young. **CP-YounA**

Dance for Ma Rainey, A. Al Young. **CP-YounA**

Dance for Militant Dilettantes, A. Al Young. **CP-YounA**

Dance in Jinoteca, The. Grace Paley. **CP-PaleG**

Dance like a jackrabbit. The Inside Chance. Marge Piercy. **SP-PierM**

Dance Me to the End of Love. Leonard Cohen. **CP-CoheL**

Dance now and sing the joy and love we owe. Thomas Campion. *Fr.* A Relation of the Late Royall Entertainment Given by the Right Honourable the Lord *Knowles*, at *Cawsome-House neere Redding:* to Our Most *Gracious Queene, Queene* ANNE, *in her* Progresse toward the *Bathe*, upon *the Seven and Eight and Twentie Dayes of Aprill.* **CP-CampT**

Dance of Death, The. Robert Browning. **CP-BroR2**

    Fever. **FL**

    Madness. **FL**

Dance of the Graces, The. Edmund Spenser. **OBSC** *Fr.* The Faerie Queene. **CP-Spens**

    (Dance, The.) **TrGrPo**

Dance, of the Grizzly Bear, The. Charles Olson. **CP-OlsoC**

Dance of the Infidels. Al Young. **CP-YounA**

Dance of the Macabre Mice. Wallace Stevens. **CP-StevW**

Dance of the Solids, The. John Updike. *Fr.* Midpoint. **CP-UpdiJ**

Dance of Words. Robert Ranke Graves. **CP-GravR**

Dance on, dance on, we see, we see. Arthur Hugh Clough. **SP-ClouA**

Dance passes beyond us, The. Wendell Berry. *Fr.* Passing the Strait. **CP-BerrW**

"Dance the Orange." Robert Earl Hayden. **CP-HaydR**

Dance there upon the shore. To a Child Dancing in the Wind. William Butler Yeats. **CP-YeatW**

Dance Unmacabre. Ogden Nash. **CP-NashO**

Dancer, The. Hilda Doolittle. **CP-DoolH**

Dancer. Langston Hughes. **SP-HughL**

Dancer, The. Philip Larkin. **CP-LarkP**

Dancer, The. Alun Lewis. **CP-LewiA**

Dancer. Carl Sandburg. **CP-SandC**

Dancer, The. Al Young. **CP-YounA**

Dancer at Cruachan and Cro-Patrick, The, *fr.* Words for Music Perhaps. William Butler Yeats. **CP-YeatW**

Dancer at Kozani's. Richard Hugo. **CP-HugoR**

Dancers. Donald Hall. **CP-HallD**

Dancers at the Moy. Paul Muldoon. **SP-MuldP**

Dancer's Reply, The, *see also* Steps for a Dancer. Howard Nemerov. **CP-NemeH**

Dances and the Dancers, The. Delmore Schwartz. **SP-SchwD**

Dancin' the funky chicken. Ain't That Bad. Maya Angelou. **SP-AngeM**

Dancing. Robert Creeley. **CP-CreeR**

Dancing. Al Young. **CP-YounA** .

Dancing All Alone. Al Young. **CP-YounA**

Dancing & Thrashing. Jim Morrison. **SP-MorrJ**

Dancing Bear grotesque and funny, A. Brother Bruin. Christina Georgina Rossetti. **CP-RosC2**

Dancing Day to Day. Al Young. **CP-YounA**

Dancing Flame. Robert Ranke Graves. **CP-GravR**

Dancing for a Prize. Nicholas Vachel Lindsay. **CP-LindV**

Dancing girls here. . . after a long night of it. . . , The. Branches. Carl Sandburg. **CP-SandC**

Dancing in the Laundromat [or] Dust: an Ordinary Song. Al Young. **CP-YounA**

Dancing in the Street. Al Young. **CP-YounA**

Dancing in Vacationland. Stephen Dobyns. **SP-DobyS**

Dancing Measures. Donald Davie. **CP-DavDo**

Dancing Naked. Al Young. **CP-YounA**

Dancing on the Grave of a Son of a Bitch. Diane Wakoski. **SP-WakoD**

Dancing on the hill-tops, / Singing in the valleys. Christina Georgina Rossetti. **CP-RosC2**

Dancing Pants. Shel Silverstein. **SP-SilS2**

Dancing Pierrot. Al Young. **CP-YounA**

Dancing Together. Al Young. **CP-YounA**

Dancing with God. Stephen Dunn. **SP-DunnS**

Dandelion, The. Nicholas Vachel Lindsay. **CP-LindV**

Dandelion. Louis Zukofsky. **CP-ZukLS**

Dandelion Sermon, The. James Merrill. *Fr.* Five Old Favorites. **SP-MerrJ**

Dandelions. Louis MacNeice. *Fr.* Nature Notes. **CP-MacNL**

Dandelions. Howard Nemerov. **CP-NemeH**

Dandelion's pallid tube, The. Emily Dickinson. **CP-DickE**

Dane-Geld. Rudyard Kipling. **CP-KiplR**

Danes were here. The forts above the road, The. The Braes O' Layde. John Hewitt. **CP-HewiJ**

Danger, The. Pablo Neruda, *tr. fr. Spanish by* Ben Belitt. **SP-NeruP**

Danger, danger of dying. Winter Landscapes. Donald Davie. **CP-DavDo**

Danger in the Air, The. Archibald MacLeish. **CP-MacLA**

Danger is not at first. Emily Dickinson. **SP-DickE**

Danger not an inch outside, The. Assurance. Robert Frost. **CP-FrosR**

Danger of Loss, The. Robert Bly. **SP-BlyR**

Dangerous Gift, The. Robert Ranke Graves. **CP-GravR**

Dangerous gift & grace is mine, A. Ralph Waldo Emerson. **CP-EmerR**

Dangerous Little Boy Fairies, The. Nicholas Vachel Lindsay. **CP-LindV**

Dangerous Year, The. John Berryman. **CP-BerrJ**

Dangers of the Journey to the Happy Land. Joseph Ceravolo. **SP-CeraJ**

Dangers Wait on Kings. Robert Herrick. **CP-HerrR**

Daniel. Nicholas Vachel Lindsay. **CP-LindV**

Daniel Boone, the father of Kentucky. Poem. William Carlos Williams. **CP-WilW1**

Daniel Neall. John Greenleaf Whittier. **CP-WhitJ**

Daniel Wheeler. John Greenleaf Whittier. **CP-WhitJ**

Danish Boy; A Fragment, The. William Wordsworth. **CP-WorW1**

Danish Conqueror, on his royal chair, The. A Fact, and an Imagination or, Canute and Alfred, on the Sea-Shore. William Wordsworth. **CP-WorW2**

Danish Conquests. William Wordsworth. *Fr.* Ecclesiastical Sonnets. **CP-WorW2**

Danish native, The. A Smiling Dane. William Carlos Williams. **CP-WilW2**

Danish Sailor's Song. Malcolm Lowry. **CP-LowrM**

D'Annunzio. Ernest Hemingway. **CP-HemiE**

Danny dead of heart attack. Landed Fish. Marge Piercy. **SP-PierM**

Danny Deever. Rudyard Kipling. **CP-KiplR**

Dans le Restauramt. Thomas Stearns Eliot. **CP-ElioT**

Dans un Seul Lit. Robert Ranke Graves. **CP-GravR**

Danse Africaine. Langston Hughes. **SP-HughL**

Danse Macabre. Wystan Hugh Auden. **CP-AudeW**

Danse Macabre. William Everson. **SP-EverW**

Danse Macabre. Sylvia Plath. **CP-PlatS**

Danse Manhattanique. Stephen Dunn. **SP-DunnS**

Danse Russe. William Carlos Williams. **CP-WilW1**

Dante. "Anna Akhmatova", *tr. fr. Russian by* Stanley Kunitz. **CP-KuniS**

Dante Études. Robert Duncan.

    Everything Speaks to Me. **SP-DuncR**

    Household, The. **SP-DuncR**

Dante Gabriel. David Markson. **CP-MarkD**

Dante himself endured. Her Wrath. Theodore Roethke. **CP-RoetT**

Dante 3. Buonconte. Robert Lowell. **SP-LoweR**

Dante's Tomb. John Berryman. **CP-BerrJ**

Dante's Vita Nuova, *See also* La Vita Nuova *tr. by*Dante Gabriel Rossetti. Dante Alighieri, *tr. fr. Italian by* Ralph Waldo Emerson. **CP-EmerR**

Danube to the Severn gave, The. Tennyson. **EBVV; EBVVPR; EnVR; FF; FaBoPP; GTBS-6; GTBS-P; LoBV; NoP** *Fr.* In Memoriam A. H. H. **CP-TennA**

    (Hushing of the Wye, The.) **FaBoPP**

Daphnaïda. Edmund Spenser. **CP-Spens**

    "She fell away in her first ages spring." **OBEV; PoPle**

Daphne. John Haines. **SP-HainJ**
  "I know three women that are you."
  "Of yourself and your beginnings."
  "You rise from your sleep."

Daphne. Gerard Manley Hopkins. **CP-HopkG**

Daphne. George Meredith. **CP-MerG1**

Daphne. Edna St. Vincent Millay. **CP-MillE**

Daphne. Jonathan Swift. **CP-SwifJ**

Daphne knows, with equal ease. Daphne. Jonathan Swift. **CP-SwifJ**

Daphne with her thighs in bark, *sels.* Ezra Pound. *Fr.* Hugh Selwyn Mauberley. (Life and Contacts). **SP-PounE**

Daphnis and Chloe. Andrew Marvell. **CP-MarvA**

Daphnis must from Chloe part. Daphnis and Chloe. Andrew Marvell. **CP-MarvA**

Dappled die-away, The. Morning, Midday, and Evening Sacrifice. Gerard Manley Hopkins. **CP-HopkG**

Dare you dispute / You saucy brute. An Answer to the Ballyspellin Ballad. Jonathan Swift. **CP-SwifJ**

Dare you see a Soul at the White Heat? Emily Dickinson. **CP-DickE**

Dared and done: at last I stand upon the summit, Dear and True! La Saisiaz. Robert Browning. **CP-BroR2**

Dares the lama, most fleet of the sons of the wind. Bigotry's Victim. Percy Bysshe Shelley. **CP-ShelP**

Darest Thou Now O Soul. Walt Whitman. **CP-WhitW**

Darien. Robert Ranke Graves. **CP-GravR**

Daring as the noon-tide ray. St. Barnabas. Christopher Smart. *Fr.* Hymns and Spiritual Songs for the Fasts and Festivals of the Church of England. **SP-SmarC**

Daring to Be the Same. Tom Clark. **SP-ClarT**

Darius the Mede was a king and a wonder. Daniel. Nicholas Vachel Lindsay. **CP-LindV**

Darjeeling. Thomas Merton. **CP-MertT**

Dark / days are past. The Mysteries. Hilda Doolittle. **CP-DoolH**

Dark accurate plunger down the successive knell. The Subway. Allen Tate. **CP-TateA**

Dark Age Glosses. Louis MacNeice. **CP-MacNL**
  "After long trouble in a taedious way." **KTR**
  On the Four Masters.
  On the Grettir Saga.
  On the Njal Saga.
  On the Venerable Bede.

Dark ages, calm and merry. The North Sea, in a Snowstorm. Donald Davie. **CP-DavDo**

Dark American Sunset, The. Jim Morrison. **SP-MorrJ**

Dark ancestral fields. Northern Heather. Robinson Jeffers. **CP-JefR2**

Dark and conceal'd art thou, soft Evening's Queen. To the Invisible Moon. Charlotte Smith. **CP-SmitC**

Dark and intent, you sit. Confidence. William Dickey. **SP-DickW**

Dark and more dark the shades of evening fell. Composed after a Journey across the Hamilton Hills, Yorkshire. William Wordsworth. **CP-WorW1**

Dark and pillowy cloud, the sallow trees, The. Composed During a Walk on the Downs, in November 1787. Charlotte Smith. **CP-SmitC**

Dark and the Fair, The. Stanley Jasspon Kunitz. **CP-KuniS**

Dark as a gypsy, berry. Old Meg. Thom Gunn. **CP-GunnT**

Dark as if cloven from darkness. Mountains. Robert Earl Hayden. *Fr.* An Inference of Mexico. **CP-HaydR**

Dark at Four O'Clock. Leonard Cohen. **CP-CoheL**

Dark August. Derek Walcott. **CP-WalcD**

Dark bell leadens the hour, A. The Hospital in Winter. Roy Fisher. **SP-FishR**

Dark blood of night-time, The. Nocturne. Louis MacNeice. **CP-MacNL**

Dark blue wind of early autumn, The. Sleep Impression. Carl Sandburg. **CP-SandC**

Dark brown is the river. Where Go the Boats? Robert Louis Stevenson. **CP-StevR**

Dark brown pinstripe, the trousers. The Suit. Philip Levine. **SP-LeviP**

Dark Château, The. Walter de la Mare. **CP-DeLaW**

Dark child in my arms, eyes. To a Child in Calcutta. Galway Kinnell. **SP-KinnG**

Dark children of the mere and marsh. Rudyard Kipling. **CP-KiplR**

Dark Churches. John Donne. **FaBoRV** *Fr.* A Hymn [*or* Hymne] to Christ, at the Author's Last Going into Germany. **CP-DonnJ**

Dark Clack of Morays, The. Diane Wakoski. **SP-WakoD** *Fr.* Fifteen Poems for a Lunar Eclipse None of Us Saw. **SP-WakoD**

Dark Continent. Tom Clark. **SP-ClarT**

Dark day / hard, swarming. Flashes. James Schuyler. **CP-SchuJ**

Dark Day, The. William Carlos Williams. **CP-WilW1**

Dark, deeply. A red. Inside the River. James Dickey. **CP-DickJ**

Dark eleventh hour, The. Ulster. Rudyard Kipling. **CP-KiplR**

Dark Encounter, The. Thomas Merton. **CP-MertT**

Dark eyed, / O woman of my dreams. Dance Figure. Ezra Pound. **SP-PounE**

Dark-Eyed Gentleman, The. Thomas Hardy. **CP-HardT**

Dark Eyes. "Bob Dylan." **CP-DylaB**

Dark Fiddler, The. Wystan Hugh Auden. **CP-AudWJ**

Dark Flower of Cheshire garden. Ralph Waldo Emerson. **CP-EmerR**

Dark frost was in the air without. Winter Dusk. Walter de la Mare. **CP-DeLaW**

Dark gathering clouds involve the threatening skies. Elegy. Charlotte Smith. **CP-SmitC**

Dark geese treading blowing Dakota snows, The. Snow Geese. Robert Bly. **SP-BlyR**

Dark God of Eros, Christ of the buried brood. William Everson. *Fr.* Tendril in the Mesh. **SP-EverW**

Dark-green upon distant heights. Prologue at Sixty. Wystan Hugh Auden. **CP-AudeW**

Dark gypsies have convened on the square. Babahak. Ussin Kerim, *tr. fr. Bulgarian by* William Matthews. **SP-MattW**

Dark Hills, The. Edwin Arlington Robinson. **CP-RobiE**

Dark hollow faces under caps. Frank Templeton Prince. *Fr.* Drypoints of the Hasidim. **CP-PrinF**

Dark House, The. Edwin Arlington Robinson. **CP-RobiE**

Dark House. Tennyson. *See* Dark house, by which once more I stand.

Dark house, by which once more I stand. Tennyson. **EBEV; EBVV; EBVVPR; EnVR; FHYEP; FaBoEn; GTBS-6; GTBS-P; HAP; HeIP; ImPo; InPK; LiTB; MeMBP; NOBE; NoP; OAEL-2; OBD; OBNC; PPoe; PeHV; PoEL-5; SCGP; SCV; SeCeV; SoSe; UnPo** *Fr.* In Memoriam A. H. H. **CP-TennA**

  (Dark House.) **ImPo; LiTB; SCGP**

Dark is dividing, the sun is coming past the wall, The. The Dawn Verse. David Herbert Lawrence. **CP-LawrD**

Dark is in my throat, The. Getting Up in Winter. Jenny Joseph. **SP-JoseJ**

Dark is the night. Vigil. Walter de la Mare. **CP-DeLaW**

Dark lean face, a narrow, slanting eye, A. Iago. Walter de la Mare. **CP-DeLaW**

Dark lintels, the blue and foreign stones, The. Adrienne Rich. **NALW; NoAM** *Fr.* Twenty-one Love Poems. **SP-RicA1; SP-RicA2**

Dark men are speaking to dark men. Chuck Miller. **SP-MillC**

Dark mind dark soul dark age. History of the World: a TV Docu-Drama. Lawrence Ferlinghetti. **SP-FerlL**

Dark Morning, The. Thomas Merton. **CP-MertT**

Dark Night of the Soul. Robert Penn Warren. **SP-WarrR**

Dark night, pale, spare image. They Die Over and Over. In the Movies. Gilbert Sorrentino. **SP-SorrG**

Dark of primaeval pine encircles me. By the Ninth Green, St. Enodoc. Sir John Betjeman. **CP-BetjJ**

Dark of the Moon. Daniel Gerard Hoffman. **SP-HoffD**

Dark on Dark. Roy Fisher. **SP-FishR**

Dark on the ridge of the cold salt wave. George Meredith. **CP-MerG2**

Dark one crouching in his cave alone, The. Frederick Morgan. *Fr.* Poems of the Two Worlds. **SP-MorgF**

Dark Ones. James Dickey. **CP-DickJ**

Dark-out Lucifer detesting this, The. Gerard Manley Hopkins. **CP-HopkG**

Dark Path. Malcolm Lowry. **CP-LowrM**

Dark plume fetch me from yon blasted yew, A. Return. William Wordsworth. **HAP** *Fr.* The River Duddon [A Series of Sonnets]. **CP-WorW2**

Dark Portrait, A. Lawrence Ferlinghetti. **SP-FerlL**

Dark projecting corner. Corner. Roy Fisher. **SP-FishR**

Dark Prophecy: I Sing of Shine. Etheridge Knight. **SP-KnigE**

Dark rose grew in the desert, A. Saint Anthony and the Rose of Life. Stevie Smith. **CP-SmitS**

Dark Satanic Mills. David Herbert Lawrence. **CP-LawrD**

Dark Shades. Charles Bukowski. **SP-BukC1**

Dark specks whirr like lint alive in the sunlight. Ephemeridae. Daniel Gerard Hoffman. **SP-HoffD**

Dark steel, the muffled flash. Strafford. Frank Templeton Prince. **CP-PrinF**

Dark stone statue of Goya, The. Goya & the Sleep of Reason. Lawrence Ferlinghetti. **SP-FerlL**

Dark struggles broken westward. Men blink out. Encounter. Wystan Hugh Auden. **CP-AudWJ**

Dark Summer. Louise Bogan. **CP-BogaL**

Dark swallows will doubtless come back killing. Will Not Come Back. Robert Lowell. **SP-LoweR**

Dark the halls, and cold the feast. The New Wife and the Old. John Greenleaf Whittier. **CP-WhitJ**

Dark theme keeps me here, A. In Evening Air. Theodore Roethke. **CP-RoetT**

Dark things of the wood, The. The Family. Mary Oliver. **SP-OlivM**

Dark, underground, is furnished with the bone. Sonnet. Louise Bogan. **CP-BogaL**

Dark was that day when Diesel. A Curse. Wystan Hugh Auden. **CP-AudeW**

Dark was the day for Childe Rolandine the artist. Childe Rolandine. Stevie Smith. **CP-SmitS**

Dark was the day when Diesel. A Curse. Wystan Hugh Auden. **CP-AudeW**

Dark was the day for Childe Rolandine the artist. Childe Rolandine. Stevie Smith. **CP-SmitS**

Dark was thick, The. A boy he seemed at that time. The Seven Times. Thomas Hardy. **CP-HardT**

Dark water, underground. The Cycle. Theodore Roethke. **CP-RoetT**

Dark Waters. William Everson. **SP-EverW**

Dark will come, I said, The. Moonset. Hayden Carruth. **CP-CarHS**

Dark with power. Wendell Berry. **CP-BerrW**

Dark within dark I cling to sleep. Kenneth Rexroth. **CP-RexKL; SP-RexrK** *Fr.* The Phoenix and the Tortoise.

Dark woman, head bent, listening for something, A. An Atlas of the Difficult World. Adrienne Rich. **SP-RicA1**

Dark Wood, Dark Water. Sylvia Plath. **CP-PlatS**

Dark Woods. Robert Penn Warren. **SP-WarrR**

    Dogwood, The.

    Hazel Leaf, The.

    Tonight the Woods Are Darkened.

Dark woods, I give myself entirely over. December Trees. Charles Simic. **SP-SimiC**

Dark Years, The. Wystan Hugh Auden. **CP-AudeW**

Darkening the edges of the land. Suggestions for the Improvement of a Sunset. Charles Tomlinson. **CP-TomlC**

Darker than night; and, oh, much darker, she. The Shade. Walter de la Mare. **CP-DeLaW**

Darklight. Adrienne Rich.

    "When heat leaves the walls at last." **SP-RicA1**

Darkling Alphabet, A. William DeWitt Snodgrass. **SP-SnodW**

Darkling I listen; and for many a time. John Keats. **OBD** *Fr.* Ode to a Nightingale. **CP-KeatJ**

Darkling Thrush, The. Thomas Hardy. **CP-HardT**

Darkly against the winter's white. Fall Song. Howard Nemerov. **CP-NemeH**

Darkness / above all things. A Prayer to the Sun. Geoffrey Hill. **PRA** *Fr.* Four Poems Regarding the Endurance of Poets. **CP-HillG**

Darkness / as black as your eyelid. The Fury of Sunrises. Anne Sexton. *Fr.* The Furies. **CP-SextA**

Darkness. Byron. **CP-Byron**

Darkness and light are both alike to Thee. Christina Georgina Rossetti. **CP-RosC2**

Darkness and snow descend. Advent. Wystan Hugh Auden. *Fr.* For the Time Being; a Christmas Oratorio. **CP-AudeW**

Darkness at the break of noon. It's Alright, Ma (I'm Only Bleeding). "Bob Dylan." **CP-DylaB**

Darkness comes out of the earth. Twilight. David Herbert Lawrence. **CP-LawrD**

Darkness falls like a wet sponge. The Picture of Little J. A. in a Prospect of Flowers. John Ashbery. **SP-AshbJ**

Darkness gathering in the branches. Grandmother in Heaven. Philip Levine. **SP-LeviP**

Darkness, giving us dream's black unity. Seventh Elegy. Dream-Singing Elegy. Muriel Rukeyser. **CP-RukeM**

Darkness had fallen. I opened the door. Unforeseen. Walter de la Mare. **CP-DeLaW**

Darkness has dawned in the east. Percy Bysshe Shelley. **EnRP** *Fr.* Hellas. **CP-ShelP**

Darkness has its compensations, both. Malcolm Lowry. **CPA** *Fr.* The Comedian. **CP-LowrM**

Darkness lifts, imagine, in your lifetime, The. The Undertaking. Louise Glück. **SP-GlücL**

Darkness Music. Muriel Rukeyser. **CP-RukeM**

Darkness of the year begins, The. Political Song for the Year's End. Thomas McGrath. **SP-McGrT**

Darkness of trees, The. But So As by Fire. George Oppen. **NNaP** *Fr.* Some San Francisco Poems. **CP-OppeG**

Darkness rolls upward, The. Blue Symphony. John Gould Fletcher. **SP-FletJ**

Darkness steals the forms of all the queens, The. Firelight and Nightfall. David Herbert Lawrence. **CP-LawrD**

Darkness surrounds us; seeking, we are lost. Uncertainty. William Wordsworth. *Fr.* Ecclesiastical Sonnets. **CP-WorW2**

Darkness waits apart from any occasion for it. Interlunar. Margaret Atwood. **SP-AtwM2**

Darkness was bad as weariness, till Grimes said. Puncture. John Crowe Ransom. **SP-RansJ**

Darkness was overtraced on every face. Emily Brontë. **CP-BronE**

Darlene's Hospital. John Ashbery. **SP-AshbJ**

Darling / you are not at all. Surfaces. Peter Meinke. **SP-MeinP**

Darling, darling, by narrow ambages. Postscript. Stanley Jasspon Kunitz. **CP-KuniS**

Darling Daughter of Babylon. Nicholas Vachel Lindsay. **CP-LindV**

Darling Daughters. Stevie Smith. **CP-SmitS**

Darling I wait O in my upstairs box. John Berryman. *Fr.* Sonnets to Chris. **CP-BerrJ**

Darling, if ever on some night of fever. First Love. Robert Ranke Graves. **CP-GravR**

Darling little baby child. The Sad Mother. Stevie Smith. **CP-SmitS**

Darling little Cousin, / With your thoughtful look. To Lalla, Reading My Verses Topsy-Turvy. Christina Georgina Rossetti. **CP-RosC3**

Darling, my darling, my heart is on the wing. Morning Song of Love. Paul Laurence Dunbar. **CP-DunbP**

Darling of Gods and Men, beneath the gliding stars. Basil Bunting, *after the Latin of* Lucretius. **CP-BuntB**

Darling of Milton—when that marble man. To Eve, Man's Dream of Wifehood as Described by Milton. Nicholas Vachel Lindsay. **CP-LindV**

Darling of our hearts, drowning. Elegy for Margaret. Stephen Spender. **CP-SpenS**

Darling of the world is come, The. Robert Herrick. **PChr** *Fr.* A Christmas Caroll Sung to the King in the Presence at White-Hall. **CP-HerrR**

Darling, splitting the wood can wait until. Prayer for Prayer. Robert Pack. **SP-PackR**

Darling, the plates have been cleared away. Beauty and the Beast. Rita Dove. **SP-DoveR**

Darling, what is that? The Drop of a Hat. Ogden Nash. **CP-NashO**

Darling!because my blood can sing. Edward Estlin Cummings. **CP-CummE; SP-CummE**

Darlings. Charles Bukowski. **SP-BukC3**

Dar'st thou amid the varied multitude. The Solitary. Percy Bysshe Shelley. **CP-ShelP**

Dart, The. Thomas Carew. **CP-CareT**

Darting fear, a pomp, a tear, A. Emily Dickinson. **CP-DickE**

Darts. Louis MacNeice. *Fr.* Indoor Sports. **CP-MacNL**

Daruma. Louis Zukofsky. **CP-ZukLS**

Darzee's Chaunt. Rudyard Kipling. **CP-KiplR** *Fr.* Rikki-Tikki-Tavi. *Fr.* The Jungle Book.

Das ewig Weibliche. Robert Lowell. **SP-LoweR**

Dashing in glass we race. Eccentric Motion. Muriel Rukeyser. **CP-RukeM**

Dat Ol' Mare o' Mine. Paul Laurence Dunbar. **CP-DunbP**

Data. Joseph Ceravolo. **SP-CeraJ**

Dates. Gertrude Stein. **CP-SteiG**

Dates: Penkhull New Road. Charles Tomlinson. **CP-TomlC**

Datura stramonium / of the poisonous flowers. Thorn Apple. Erica Jong. **SP-JongE**

Daughter. James Dickey. **CP-DickJ**

Daughter. Isabella Gardner. **CP-GardI**

Daughter. John Updike. **CP-UpdiJ**

Daughter is mad, and so, The. Anne. Mary Oliver. **SP-OlivM**

Daughter Moves Out, A. Lewis Turco. **SP-TurcL**

Daughter of Chaos' doting years. Ode to the Departed Regency-Bill—1789. Robert Burns. **CP-BurnR**

Daughter of earth and child of the wave be appeased. William Everson. **NoAM** *Fr.* Tendril in the Mesh. **SP-EverW**

Daughter of Eve, A. Christina Georgina Rossetti. **CP-RosC1**

Daughter of Heaven and Earth, coy Spring. May-Day. Ralph Waldo Emerson. **CP-EmerR**

Daughter of Herodias, The. Robert Louis Stevenson. **CP-StevR**

Daughter of Jove, relentless Power. Hymn to Adversity. Thomas Gray. **CP-GrayT**

Daughter of music. A Song for the Year's End. Louis Zukofsky. **CP-ZukLS**

Daughter of the Great Man, The. David Herbert Lawrence. *Fr.* Bits. **CP-LawrD**

Daughter Returns, A. Thomas Hardy. **CP-HardT**

Daughter, Teuila, Native Name for Adorner, The. Robert Louis Stevenson. *Fr.* The Family. **CP-StevR**

Daughter, this is our laughing-box. Inside the Gyroscope. Laurence Lieberman. **SP-LiebL**

"Daughter, thou art come to die." A Very Old Song. "William Laird." **CP-HerrR**

Daughter to that good Earl[e], once President. John Milton. **CP-MiltJ**
   (Sonnet 10: "Daughter to that good Earle, once President.") **CP-MiltJ**

Daughters, The. Stephen Berg. **SP-BergS**

Daughters of Beulah! Muses who inspire the Poets Song. William Blake. **PeECV** *Fr.* Milton. **CP-BlakW**

Daughters of Jove, whose voice is melody. Hymn to Selene. *Unknown.* **CP-ShelP** *Fr.* Homeric Hymns.

Daughters of Mne [*or* The] Seraphim led round their sunny flocks, The. Thel. William Blake. *Fr.* The Book of Thel. **CP-BlakW**

Daughters of Pandarus, The. Homer. **CP-BroEB,** *tr.* by Elizabeth Barrett Browning; *Fr.* Odyssey.

Daughters of the Horseleech, The. Stanley Jasspon Kunitz. **CP-KuniS**

Daughters of the horseleech crying "Give! Give!", The. The Daughters of the Horseleech. Stanley Jasspon Kunitz. **CP-KuniS**

Daughters of the subtle flood. Ben Jonson. **CP-JonsB** *Fr.* The Masque of Blackness.

Daughters of Time, the hypocritic Days. Days. Ralph Waldo Emerson. **CP-EmerR**

David / (Rave-id). Lines on the Poet Being Informed That His Epic About the Philistines Etc. Needed Cutting. Malcolm Lowry. **CP-LowrM**

David. Diane Wakoski. *Fr.* Fifteen Poems for a Lunar Eclipse None of Us Saw. **SP-WakoD**

David Dancing. Donald Davie. **CP-DavDo**

David has said and sung it sweet. Plenteous Redemption. Christopher Smart. *Fr.* Hymns for the Amusement of Children. **SP-SmarC**

David Walker (1785–1830). Rita Dove. **SP-DoveR**

David was my brother. Some Brilliant Sky. Diane Wakoski. **SP-WakoD**

David's Folly. Daniel Gerard Hoffman. **SP-HoffD**

David's Lamentation for Saul and Jonathan. Anne Bradstreet. **CP-BradA**

David's Night in Veliès. James Merrill. **SP-MerrJ**

David's Peccavi. Robert Southwell. **CP-SoutR**

Dawdling into glory; / or with hammer-strokes. Antitheses. John Berryman. **CP-BerrJ**

Dawn. / A white sail. Landing in Cairo. Martin Edmunds. **SP-EdmuM**

Dawn / and now.begins / feeling. Edward Estlin Cummings. **CP-CummE**

Dawn. Wystan Hugh Auden. **CP-AudWJ**

Dawn. Wystan Hugh Auden. **CP-AudWJ**

Dawn. Walter de la Mare. **CP-DeLaW**

Dawn. Paul Laurence Dunbar. **CP-DunbP**

Dawn. Gerard Manley Hopkins. **CP-HopkG**
   "Dawn that the pebbly low-down East."
   "In more precision now of light and dark."
   "Now more precisely touched in light and gloom."

Dawn. Robinson Jeffers. **CP-JefR3**

Dawn. Philip Larkin. **CP-LarkP**

Dawn. William Matthews. **SP-MattW**

Dawn. Edna St. Vincent Millay. **CP-MillE**

Dawn. Chuck Miller. **SP-MillC**

Dawn. Robert Penn Warren. *Fr.* Penological Study: Southern Exposure. **SP-WarrR**

Dawn. Robert Penn Warren. *Fr.* Two Poems about Suddenly and a Rose. **SP-WarrR**

Dawn. Charles Kenneth Williams. **SP-WillC**

Dawn. William Carlos Williams. **CP-WilW1**

Dawn, The. William Butler Yeats. **CP-YeatW**

Dawn—a smouldering fume of dry frost. Earth-Numb. Ted Hughes. **SP-HughT**

Dawn after the Dance, The. Thomas Hardy. **CP-HardT**

Dawn alps, The. Perspectives. Denise Levertov. **CP-LeveD**

Dawn an unsympathetic yellow. Electrical Storm. Elizabeth Bishop. **CP-BishE**

Dawn and a high film; the sun burned it. We in the Fields. William Everson. **SP-EverW**

Dawn and Dew my Bearers be. Emily Dickinson. **SP-DickE**

Dawn and, distant, the steel-snarl and lyric. Chain Saw at Dawn in Vermont in Time of Drouth. Robert Penn Warren. **SP-WarrR**

Dawn and Sunrise. Sir Walter Scott. **SP-ScotW** *Fr.* Rokeby.

Dawn; and the jew's-harp's sawing seesaw song. Pilots, Man Your Planes. Randall Jarrell. **CP-JarrR**

Dawn at Saint Patrick's. Derek Mahon. **SP-MahoD**

Dawn birds at noon. Roy Fisher. **SP-FishR** *Fr.* New Diversions.

Dawn Bombardment. Robert Ranke Graves. **CP-GravR**

Dawn brings with it, The. Juan Ramón Jiménez. *Fr.* Ten Short Poems. **CP-WrigJ**

Dawn came at six today. To the Man in the Yellow Terry. Alice Walker. **CP-WalkA**

Dawn Chorus, The. Derek Mahon. **SP-MahoD**

Dawn coming / the roosters call in the distance. Start Up the Music Again. Chuck Miller. **SP-MillC**

Dawn creeping gray from offshore. Long Pond Summer. Brendan Galvin. **SP-GalvB**

Dawn cried out: the brutal voice of a bird. In All These Acts. William Everson. **SP-EverW**

Dawn. First light tearing. Clouds. Philip Levine. **SP-LeviP**

Dawn. Hoar on the grass. Hayden Carruth. **CP-CarHS** *Fr.* The Clay Hill Anthology.

Dawn in Threshing Time. Robert Bly. **SP-BlyR**

Dawn is no longer in the house of the Fish. Astronomical Changes. David Herbert Lawrence. **CP-LawrD**

Dawn off the Foreland—the young flood making. Mine Sweepers. Rudyard Kipling. **CP-KiplR**

Dawn offers / innocence to a half-mad city. Brief Innocence. Maya Angelou. **SP-AngeM**

Dawn on the East Coast. Alun Lewis. **CP-LewiA**

Dawn rose for hunting, trampling on the hills. Humpty Dumpty. Wystan Hugh Auden. **CP-AudWJ**

Dawn Song. Thomas McGrath. **SP-McGrT**

Dawn Song. Edwin Rolfe. **CP-RolfE**

Dawn that the pebbly low-down East. Gerard Manley Hopkins. *Fr.* Dawn. **CP-HopkG**

Dawn. The Hour of Lauds. Thomas Merton. *Fr.* Hagia Sophia. **CP-MertT**

Dawn this morning burned all red. Yankee Doodle. Nicholas Vachel Lindsay. **CP-LindV**

Dawn Verse, The. David Herbert Lawrence. **CP-LawrD**

Dawn Walkers. Jenny Joseph. **SP-JoseJ**

Dawn was apple-green, The. Green. David Herbert Lawrence. **CP-LawrD**

Dawn will be the time and the forest will be the place. The Ecstasy. Hayden Carruth. *Fr.* Contra Mortem. **CP-CarHL**

Dawn Wind, The. Rudyard Kipling. **CP-KiplR**

Dawnbreaker. Robert Earl Hayden. **CP-HaydR**

Dawning, The. George Herbert. **CP-HerbG**

Dawnlight freezes against the east-wire. I Had Hope When Violence Was Ceas't. Geoffrey Hill. **CP-HillG**

Dawn's cold imperative compels. Alun Lewis. *Fr.* Indian Day. **CP-LewiA**

Dawn's orb orange-raw shining over Palisades. We Rise on Sun Beams and Fall in the Night. Allen Ginsberg. **CP-GinsA**

Dawn's Rose. Ted Hughes. **SP-HughT** *Fr.* Crow.

Day / diminutive / Night is the Mother, is the / Fixer of Change. Littleton, N.H. Robert Creeley. **CP-CreeR**

Day, A. Stephen Berg. **SP-BergS**

Day. William Blake. **CP-BlakW**

Day / drunk with the nectar of, A. Wonder. Maya Angelou. **SP-AngeM**

Day. Paul Laurence Dunbar. **CP-DunbP**

Day! / Faster and more fast. Pippa Passes. Robert Browning. **CP-BroR1**

Day / my father's heart attacked, The. Heart Attack. Gary Gildner. **SP-GildG**

Day, The. James Schuyler. **CP-SchuJ**

Day, The. James Schuyler. **CP-SchuJ**

Day. Allen Tate. **CP-TateA**

Day, A. John Greenleaf Whittier. **CP-WhitJ**

Day after day alone on a hill. The Fool on the Hill. John Lennon. **CP-Beatl**

Day after day, day after still day. Summer's Elegy. Howard Nemerov. **CP-NemeH**

Day after day in a high room between. Winter Words. Philip Levine. **SP-LeviP**

Day after day, night on bombarded night. Radio Madrid—1937. Edwin Rolfe. **CP-RolfE**

Day after somber day. Plaint. Theodore Roethke. **CP-RoetT**

Day after you left, The. Disintegration. Richard Shelton. **SP-ShelR**

Day Alvero Pineda Was Killed, The. Ron Koertge. **SP-KoerR**

Day and Night Handball. Stephen Dunn. **SP-DunnS**

Day and Night in 1952. Frank O'Hara. **SP-OharF**

Day and night the Accuser makes no pause. Christina Georgina Rossetti. **CP-RosC2**

Day arrives of the autumn fair, The. A Sheep Fair. Thomas Hardy. **CP-HardT**

Day astonishes and the night fills me with fear, The. A Wolf. Paul Éluard, *tr. fr. French by* William Carlos Williams. **CP-WilW2**

Day-Bed, The. Richard Eberhart. **CP-EberR**

Day before divorce, I take my children, The. My Children at the Dump. John Updike. **CP-UpdiJ**

Day before he died, a burnet moth, The. In Memory of Boris Pasternak. Denise Levertov. **CP-LeveD**

Day before I died, The. Tragic Detail. William Carlos Williams. **CP-WilW2**

Day Before Thanksgiving, a Call Comes to Me Concerning Insulation, The. Gary Gildner. **SP-GildG**

Day Begins, A. Denise Levertov. **CP-LeveD**

Day being humid and my head, The. Ovid. *Fr.* Ovid in Love. **SP-MahoD** *Fr.* Amores.

Day being Whitsun we had pigeon for dinner, The. Basil Bunting. **CP-BuntB**

Day Born Without a Mouth. Chuck Miller. **SP-MillC**

Day by day for her darlings to her much she added more. Nature. Ralph Waldo Emerson. **CP-EmerR**

Day by day, such rewards. The Prolific Spell. Donald Davie. **CP-DavDo**

Day by day the acacia tree. Acacia Tree. Kathleen Jessie Raine. **SP-RainK**

Day by day your estimation clocks up. Administration. Philip Larkin. **CP-LarkP**

Day came slow—till Five o'clock, The. Emily Dickinson. **CP-DickE**

Day changes from cannon to morning glory. Prell. Jim Carroll. **SP-CarrJ**

Day clacks and birds, The. Geoffrey Hill. *Fr.* Scenes with Harlequins. **CP-HillG**

Day comes and goes, The. Robert Creeley. **CP-CreeR**

Day creeps down. The moon is creeping up. The Man on the Dump. Wallace Stevens. **CP-StevW**

Day Detail—Low Light of Afternoon. Tom Clark. **SP-ClarT**

Day Dream, A. Emily Brontë. **CP-BronE**

Day-Dream, A ("My eyes make pictures, when they are shut"). Samuel Taylor Coleridge. **CP-ColeS**

Day-Dream, The ("If thou wert here, these tears were tears of light"). Samuel Taylor Coleridge. **CP-ColeS**

Day-dreams of a Tourist. Wystan Hugh Auden. **CP-AudWJ**

Day for Anne Frank, A. Charles Kenneth Williams. **CP-WillC; SP-WillC**

Day grew small, surrounded tight, The. Emily Dickinson. **CP-DickE**

Day hangs heavy, The. Greyday. Maya Angelou. **SP-AngeM**

Day has turned to a silver mirror. The Lake of Tears. Roy Fisher. **SP-FishR** *Fr.* Inscriptions for Bluebeard's Castle.

Day has twenty-four hours, The. Charles Henri Ford. **SP-FordC** *Fr.* Secret Haiku.

Day! hast thou two faces. The Chartist's Complaint. Ralph Waldo Emerson. **CP-EmerR**

Day he brought that old clock from the mill, The. The Mill Clock. Phoebe Hesketh. **SP-HeskP**

Day! Help! Help! Another Day!, A. Emily Dickinson. **CP-DickE**

Day hot in the terror of her head. Dusk. Allen Tate. **CP-TateA**

Day I Kicked Away a Bankroll, The. Charles Bukowski. **SP-BukC2**

Day I Was Older, The. Donald Hall. **CP-HallD**

Day in Late October, A. Mona Van Duyn. **SP-VanDM**

Day in the Life, A. John Lennon *and* Paul McCartney. **CP-Beatl**

Day is a Poem, The. Robinson Jeffers. **CP-JefR3**

Day is a woman who loves you. Open, The. Driving Montana. Richard Hugo. **CP-HugoR**

Day Is At Hand, The. Christina Georgina Rossetti. **CP-RosC2**

Day is awake. The bark calls to the rain still in the cloud, The. July Morning. Robert Bly. **SP-BlyR**

Day is closing dark and cold, The. The Legend of St. Mark. John Greenleaf Whittier. **CP-WhitJ**

Day is curl'd [*or* curl'd] about again [*or.* agen], The. An Anniversary on the Hymeneals of My Noble Kinsman, Thomas Stanley, Esquire. Richard Lovelace. **CP-LoveR**

Day is dark—the night, The. Marsden Hartley. **CP-HartM**

Day Is Done, The. Henry Wadsworth Longfellow. **SP-LongH**

Day is done, the winter sun, The. Castle Wood. Emily Brontë. **CP-BronE**

Day is drawing to its fall, A. First Sight of Her and After. Thomas Hardy. **CP-HardT**

Day is ending, the night descending, The. Old Song. David Herbert Lawrence. **CP-LawrD**

Day is going, now 'tis noon, The. George Meredith. **CP-MerG2**

Day Is Gone and All Its Sweets Are Gone, The. John Keats. **CP-KeatJ**

Day is gone, the night is come, The. A Child's Prayer. George Meredith. **CP-MerG2**

Day is gray / as stone: the stones, The. The Day. James Schuyler. **CP-SchuJ**

Day is great and strong—, The. World without Peculiarity. Wallace Stevens. **CP-StevW**

Day is spent, and hath his will on me, The. Evensong. George Herbert. **CP-HerbG**

Day is the children's friend. The Prejudice against the Past. Wallace Stevens. **CP-StevW**

Day is turning ghost, The. A Commonplace Day. Thomas Hardy. **CP-HardT**

Day John Kennedy Died, The. "Lou Reed." **SP-ReedL**

Day Kennedy Died. Al Young. **CP-YounA**

Day Lady Died, The. Frank O'Hara. **SP-OharF**

Day lilies, yellow daisies, Queen Anne's lace. A barrel, a box of. Another Day (Day Lilies, Yellow Daisies). Muriel Rukeyser. **CP-RukeM**

Day Marked with a Small White Stone, A. Charles Simic. **SP-SimiC**

Day? Memorial, The. Grape Sherbet. Rita Dove. **SP-DoveR**

Day my parents tried to wean me, The. Wean Poem. Gary Gildner. **SP-GildG**

Day of Battle, The. Alfred Edward Housman. **CP-HousA**

Day of fire is coming, the thrush, The. The Fury of Earth. Anne Sexton. *Fr.* The Furies. **CP-SextA**

Day of life and death offers its flowers, The. All Souls. Muriel Rukeyser. **CP-RukeM**

Day of mist: day of tarnish. Resolve. Sylvia Plath. **CP-PlatS**

Day of Rabblement. Kenneth Patchen. **CP-PatcK**

Day of Renewal. Louis MacNeice. **CP-MacNL**

　"Do I prefer to forget it? This middle stretch." **NAs**

　"Milestones. My own; small things lost in a vast." **NAs**

　"This year, last year, one time, ever."

　"Turn again, Whittington. Riding the surf."

　"And so for all of us. Bits and pieces." **NAs**

Day of Returning. Louis MacNeice. **CP-MacNL**

　"But even so, he said, daily I hanker, daily."

　"Crouched upon sea-chiselled gravel, staring out and up at the sea."

　"Home beyond this life? Or through it? If through, how?"

　"They call me crafty, I robbed my brother."

Day of sunlight and swallows, A. Hostage. Malcolm Lowry. **CP-LowrM**

Day of sunny face and temper, A. Big Bessie Throws Her Son into the Street. Gwendolyn Brooks. **VGW** *Fr.* A Catch of Shy Fish. **SP-BrooG**

Day of the cloud in fleets! O day. The South-Wester. George Meredith. **CP-MerG1**

Day of the Daughter of Hades, The. George Meredith. **CP-MerG1**

　"He tells it, who knew the law."

　"He who has looked upon Earth."

　"Him loved she. Lo, now was he veiled."

　"Noise of the hollow ground, A."

　"Nor had saffron and sapphire and red."

　"Now the meadows with crocus besprent."

　"Now the valley in ruin of fields."

　"Now the youth footed swift to the dawn."

　"Now the youth was not ware of the beams."

　"Then again in disorderly woods."

　"Then said she, quick as the cries."

　"This, no more, doth Callistes recall."

Day of the Dead (Tehuantepec). Robert Earl Hayden. *Fr.* An Inference of Mexico. **CP-HaydR**

Day of the funeral we noticed, The. A Neighbor's Funeral. John Hewitt. **CP-HewiJ**

Day of the Locusts. "Bob Dylan." **CP-DylaB**

Day of the Sentry, The. David St. John. **SP-StJoD**

Day on the Big Branch, A. Howard Nemerov. **CP-NemeH**

Day on the boulevards chosen out of ten years of, A. Berket and the Stars. William Carlos Williams. **CP-WilW1**

Day on which the world ends will, The. The Day the World Ends. Stephen Dobyns. **SP-DobyS**

Day red like the cardinal, The. Said Adam. Charles Olson. **CP-OlsoC**

Day returns, my bosom burns, The. Robert Burns. **CP-BurnR**

　(Seventh of November, The.) **CP-BurnR**

Day says nothing, and lacks for nothing. . . God; The. Robert Lowell. *Fr.* Fall Weekend at *Milgate*. **SP-LoweR**

Day, see no day—choke, qualm, quick qualm—benevolence, merit are. Catullus. *See* Carmen 72: "Cancel, Catullus, the expectancies of friendship."

Day seemed suddenly to give to black-&-white, The. Meridian. David St. John. **SP-StJoD**

Day set on Norham's castled steep. Norham Castle. Sir Walter Scott. **SP-ScotW** *Fr.* Marmion.

Day she goes, The. Emily Dickinson. **CP-DickE**

Day she visited the dissecting room, The. Two Views of a Cadaver Room. Sylvia Plath. **CP-PlatS**

Day Six O'Hare Telephone. Thomas Merton. *Fr.* West. *Fr.* The Geography of Lograire. **CP-MertT**

Day Song. Charles Olson. **CP-OlsoC**

Day Song, the Day After. Charles Olson. **CP-OlsoC**

Day that hath no tinge of night. As Thy Days, So Shall Thy Strength Be. Christina Georgina Rossetti. **CP-RosC2**

Day that I was crowned, The. Emily Dickinson. **CP-DickE**

Day that is the night of days, The. England before the Storm. George Meredith. **CP-MerG1**

Day that passes. Que J'ay Dit Devant. Louis Zukofsky. **CP-ZukLS**

Day that she put on white for good, The. Nurse. Leonard Nathan. **SP-NathL**

Day the brook went out, The. Hayden Carruth. *Fr.* North Winter. **CP-CarHL**

Day the Epileptic Spoke, The. Charles Bukowski. **SP-BukC3**

Day the Perfect Speakers Left, The. Leonard Nathan. **SP-NathL**

Day the World Ends, The. Stephen Dobyns. **SP-DobyS**

Day they cut my tongue out, The. The Poet to His Tongue. Peter Meinke. **SP-MeinP**

Day They Eulogized Mahalia, The. Audre Lorde. **SP-LordA**

Day Trip to Donegal. Derek Mahon. **SP-MahoD**

Day Tripper. John Lennon *and* Paul McCartney. **CP-Beatl**

Day turning to night. Eternal City. Hayden Carruth. **CP-CarHS**

Day undressed—Herself, The. Emily Dickinson. **CP-DickE**

Day very solid February 12th, 1944, A. Hayden Carruth. Jaz *Fr.* Paragraphs. **CP-CarHS**

Day was gathered on waking, The. Robert Creeley. **CP-CreeR**

Day was here when it was his to know, The. The New Tenants. Edwin Arlington Robinson. **CP-RobiE**

Day was not, the morning died of heat, The. Heat Wave. Malcolm Lowry. **CP-LowrM**

Day was unbearably mild, The. A Mourning. Jean Garrigue. **SP-GarrJ**

Day was wet, the rain fell souse, The. Lays of Sorrow, No. 1. "Lewis Carroll." **CP-CarrL**

Day when Charmus ran with five, The. A Mighty Runner. Nicarchus of Alexandria. **MeMAP; OBAL; SD** *Fr.* Variations of Greek Themes. **CP-RobiE**

Day when the under-cover writings, The. And Who Do You Think "They" Are? William Carlos Williams. **CP-WilW2**

Day which never could be yesterday, A. The Impossible Day. Robert Ranke Graves. **CP-GravR**

Day Without Night. Louise Glück. **SP-GlücL**

Day without rain is like, A. Weathering. Archie Randolph Ammons. **SP-AmmoA**

Day works on, The. Mexican Valley. James Dickey. **CP-DickJ**

Day you came, The. Breasts. Tess Gallagher. **SP-GallT**

Day you died I went into the dirt, The. Electra on Azalea Path. Sylvia Plath. **CP-PlatS**

Day you told me you had a bank acount, The. A Poem of Love. Kay Boyle. **CP-BoylK**

Day Zimmer Lost Religion, The. Paul Zimmer. **SP-ZimmP**

Daybreak. James Dickey. **CP-DickJ**

Daybreak. Galway Kinnell. **SP-KinnG**

Daybreak. James McAuley. **SP-McAuJ**

Daybreak. Carl Sandburg. **CP-SandC**

Daybreak. Barton Sutter. **SP-SuttB**

Daybreak. William Carlos Williams. **CP-WilW1**

Daybreak comes first. Daybreak. Carl Sandburg. **CP-SandC**

Daybreak in Alabama. Langston Hughes. **SP-HughL**

Daylight. James Schuyler. **CP-SchuJ**

Daylong, light, gold, leans on the land. The Snake. Robert Penn Warren. *Fr.* Boy's Will, Joyful Labor without Pay, and Harvest Home (1918). **SP-WarrR**

Daylong this tomcat lies stretched flat. Esther's Tomcat. Ted Hughes. **SP-HughT**

Days. Ralph Waldo Emerson. **CP-EmerR**

Days, The. Donald Hall. **CP-HallD**

Days. Phoebe Hesketh. **SP-HeskP**

Days. Philip Larkin. **CP-LarkP**

Days and Days. Robert Creeley. **CP-CreeR**

Days and Nights. Kenneth Koch. **SP-KochK**

Days and Nights. Kenneth Koch. *Fr.* Days and Nights. **SP-KochK**
  Days and Nights.
    "I certainly have lost something." **NoAM**
    "I certainly have lost something." **NoAM**
    Invention of Poetry, The.
    Out and In.
    Secret, The.
    Stones of Time, The. **NoAM**

Days are bright. Seesaw. Thom Gunn. **CP-GunnT**

Days are clear, / Day after day, The. Christina Georgina Rossetti. **CP-RosC2**

Days are cold, the nights are long, The. The Cottager to Her Infant, (By My Sister). Dorothy Wordsworth, *Third and fourth stanzas by* William Wordsworth. **CP-WorW1**

Days are incestuous, each with its yesterday, The. Sundays, They Sleep Late. Muriel Rukeyser. **CP-RukeM**

Days are over, I leave after breakfast, The. Purgatory. John Berryman. **CP-BerrJ**

Day's at end and there's nowhere to go. Allen Tate. *Fr.* More Sonnets at Christmas. **CP-TateA**

Days git wa'm an' wa'mah. Wadin' in de Crick. Paul Laurence Dunbar. **CP-DunbP**

Days grow and the stars cross over, The. Darkness Music. Muriel Rukeyser. **CP-RukeM**

Days in the train, a. Robert Creeley. **CP-CreeR**

Day's Journey, A. John Greenleaf Whittier. **CP-WhitJ**

Days later—neither having. Robert Creeley. **CP-CreeR**

Days, like sand, run through the hour-glass. Days. Phoebe Hesketh. **SP-HeskP**

Days Like Smitten Cymbals of Brass, The. Malcolm Lowry. **CP-LowrM**

Days of Kindness. Leonard Cohen. **CP-CoheL**

Days of 1959. Marilyn Hacker. **SP-HackM**

Days of 1944: Three Friends. Marilyn Hacker. **SP-HackM**

Days of 1941 and '44. James Merrill. **SP-MerrJ**

Days of 1971. James Merrill. **SP-MerrJ**

Days of 1964. James Merrill. **SP-MerrJ**

Days of 1935. James Merrill. **SP-MerrJ**

Days of the dead men, Danny. Drumnotes. Carl Sandburg. **CP-SandC**

Days of Vanity. Christina Georgina Rossetti. **CP-RosC1**

Days of Yore, The. Stevie Smith. **CP-SmitS**

Days pass over me, The. Ralph Waldo Emerson. **CP-EmerR**

Days passed—and Monte Calvo would not clear. At Albano. William Wordsworth. *Fr.* Memorials of a Tour in Italy, 1837. **CP-WorW2**

Day's Ration, The. Ralph Waldo Emerson. **CP-EmerR**

Day's sharp strife is ended now, The. After Election. John Greenleaf Whittier. **CP-WhitJ**

Days she looks at floors, a thick degrading cloud. Indian Girl. Richard Hugo. **CP-HugoR**

Days shorten, the south blows wide for showers now, The. Salmon Fishing. Robinson Jeffers. **CP-JefR1**

Days: Spring, The. Adrienne Rich. **CP-RicAE**

Days that cannot bring you near. Argument. Elizabeth Bishop. **CP-BishE**

Days that we can spare, The. Emily Dickinson. **CP-DickE**

Days to come are a watershed, The. We Hesitate. John Ashbery. **SP-AshbJ**

Days to Recollect. Thomas Hardy. **CP-HardT**

Days undefiled by luxury or sloth. To the Pennsylvanians. William Wordsworth. **CP-WorW2**

Days went by, The. I took up the old days. Tuscan Life. Elizabeth Barrett Browning. **FaBoPP** *Fr.* Aurora Leigh. **CP-BroEB**

Days, when the ball of our vision. Youth in Memory. George Meredith. **CP-MerG1**

Dayseye hugging the earth, The. Daisy. William Carlos Williams. **CP-WilW1**

Daystar. Rita Dove. **SP-DoveR**

Daytime / wonder at / the quieter possibilities. The Plan. Robert Creeley. **CP-CreeR**

Dazzle of Darkness. Robert Ranke Graves. **CP-GravR**

Dazzle on the sea, my darling, The. Leaving Barra. Louis MacNeice. **CP-MacNL**

Dazzled blood, The. Faustus Triumphant. Thom Gunn. **CP-GunnT**

Dazzling Burden, The. Kenneth Patchen. **CP-PatcK**

D.D. Byrde Callyng Jennie Wrenn. William DeWitt Snodgrass. **SP-SnodW**

De / on one, The. Archie Randolph Ammons. **SP-AmmoA**

De Anima. Howard Nemerov. **CP-NemeH**

De Arte Poetica. Robert Ranke Graves. **CP-GravR**

De Carlo Lots, The. Anne Waldman. **SP-WaldA**

De Catullo et Martiale, *acc. by English translation.* Thomas Campion. **CP-CampT**

De Cœnatione Micae. Martial, *tr. fr. Latin by* Robert Louis Stevenson. **CP-StevR**

De Domino Richardo Lovelacio, Armigero & Chiliarcha, Viro Incomparabili. *Unknown. Fr.* Commendatory Poems. **CP-LoveR**

De Epigrammate, *acc. by English translation.* Thomas Campion. **CP-CampT**

De Erotio Puella. Robert Louis Stevenson. **CP-StevR**

De Fran. Draco, *acc. by English translation.* Thomas Campion. **CP-CampT**

De Gustibus. Robert Browning. **CP-BroR1**
  "Italy, my Italy?" **PlP**

"What I love best in all the world." **FaBoPP; OBTV**
   (Italy of the South.) **FaBoPP**
"Your ghost will walk, you lover of trees." **PlP**
De horologio portabili, *acc. by English translation.* Thomas Campion. **CP-CampT**
De Hortis Julii Martialis. Robert Louis Stevenson. **CP-StevR**
De Ira Dei. Tom Clark. **SP-ClarT**
De Jure Belli ac Pacis. Geoffrey Hill. **CP-HillG**
De là où nous sommes assis plus haut que les gradins. Arènes de Lutèce. Samuel Beckett. **CP-BeckS**
De Lesseps, he said, was not the only one. Malcolm Lowry. *Fr.* Peter Gaunt and the Canals. **CP-LowrM**
De libro CHI-KING sic censeo. Canto 59. Ezra Pound. *Fr.* Cantos. **CP-PoCan**
De Los Cantares. Charles Olson. **CP-OlsoC**
De M. Antonio. Robert Louis Stevenson. **CP-StevR**
De minimus curat non Lex, utcumque poetica. De Arte Poetica. Robert Ranke Graves. **CP-GravR**
De Mortuis. James McAuley. **SP-McAuJ** *Fr.* Meditations of Afternoon.
De obitu Phil. Sydnaei equitis aurati generosissimi, *acc. by English translation.* Thomas Campion. **CP-CampT**
De pied ferme. Samuel Beckett. **CP-BeckS**
De Pré Est Vénéneux Mais Joli en Automne. Gilbert Sorrentino. **SP-SorrG**
De Profundis. Elizabeth Barrett Browning. **CP-BroEB**
   "Whatever's lost, it first was won." **TrPWD**
De Profundis. Christina Georgina Rossetti. **CP-RosC2**
De Profundis. Georg Trakl, *tr. fr. German by* James Wright. **CP-WrigJ**
De Profundis ("From depth of grief"). Bible, *O.T. See* Psalm 130: "Out of the depths have I cried unto thee, O Lord."
De Profundis ("Out of the depths have I cried unto thee, O Lord"). Bible, *O.T. See* Psalm 130: "Out of the depths have I cried unto thee, O Lord."
De Quincey in Later Life. Derek Mahon. **SP-MahoD**
De Regis reditu e Scotia, *acc. by English translation.* Thomas Campion. **CP-CampT**
De Rerum Natura (On the Nature of Things). Lucretius, *tr. fr. Latin.*
   "If all this world had no original[l]." **CP-RaleW,** *tr. by* Sir Walter Ralegh;
De Rerum Virtute. Robinson Jeffers. **CP-JefR3**
De Sade's rent walls let in. Lacoste. Charles Tomlinson. **CP-TomlC**
De shepherd shrieves in Egyptian light. Pocomania. Derek Walcott. **CP-WalcD**
De Sole. Charles Tomlinson. **CP-TomlC**
De Votre Bonheur Il ne Reste Que Vos Photos. Archibald MacLeish. **CP-MacLA**
Dea ex Machina. John Updike. **CP-UpdiJ**
Deacon Jones' Grievance. Paul Laurence Dunbar. **CP-DunbP**
Deacon thought. "I know them," he began, The. Ben Trovato. Edwin Arlington Robinson. **CP-RobiE**
Deacon, you are to recognize in this. A Gathered Church. Donald Davie. *Fr.* A Dissentient Voice. **CP-DavDo**
Dead! / And the Muses cried with a stormy cry. The Dead Prophet. Tennyson. **CP-TennA**
Dead / are the departed therefrom. Whose, The. The Human Communion. Traces. Robert Duncan. **SP-DuncR**
Dead. Paul Laurence Dunbar. **CP-DunbP**
Dead, The. Randall Jarrell. **CP-JarrR**
Dead, The. Sylvia Plath. **CP-PlatS**
Dead, The. Kathleen Jessie Raine. **SP-RainK**
Dead again, The. A Historian. Daniel Gerard Hoffman. **SP-HoffD**
Dead and the Living One, The. Thomas Hardy. **CP-HardT**
Dead are a cadmium blue, The. Charles Wright. **HCAP** *Fr.* Homage to Paul Cézanne. **SP-WrigC**
Dead are dreaming of breathing, The. Snow. William Matthews. **SP-MattW**
Dead are hidden from the sea. The sea, The. Graves in Uig. Richard Hugo. **CP-HugoR**
Dead are hovering on the air, The. Nexus. Richard Eberhart. **CP-EberR**
Dead are on their journey, the way is dark, The. Song of the Dead. David Herbert Lawrence. **CP-LawrD**
Dead are waiting for us in our rooms, The. Charles Wright. *Fr.* Homage to Paul Cézanne. **SP-WrigC**
Dead are with us to stay, The. Charles Wright. *Fr.* Homage to Paul Cézanne. **SP-WrigC**
Dead as a doornail, / live as the wind. Lawrence in Taos. John Clellon Holmes. **SP-HolmJ**
Dead Baby. Stephen Dobyns. **SP-DobyS**
Dead Baby, The. William Carlos Williams. **CP-WilW1**

Dead Bastard, The. Thomas Hardy. **CP-HardT**
Dead-Beat, The. Wilfred Owen. **CP-OwenW**
Dead before Death. Christina Georgina Rossetti. **CP-RosC1**
Dead Beggar, an Elegy Addressed to a Lady, The. Charlotte Smith. **CP-SmitC**
Dead birds fell, but no one had seen them fly, The. Some Dreams They Forgot. Elizabeth Bishop. **CP-BishE**
Dead Blackbird. Phoebe Hesketh. **SP-HeskP**
Dead Boy. John Crowe Ransom. **SP-RansJ**
Dead boy living among men as a man, A. A Head. James Schuyler. **CP-SchuJ**
Dead Bride, The. Geoffrey Hill. **TW** *Fr.* Three Baroque Meditations. **CP-HillG**
Dead Bride, The. Christina Georgina Rossetti. **CP-RosC3**
Dead brood over Europe, the cloud and vision descends over chearful France, The. The French Revolution. William Blake. **CP-BlakW**
Dead by the Side of the Road, The. Gary Snyder. **CP-SnydG**
Dead child lay in the shroud, The. The Gift of the Sea. Rudyard Kipling. **CP-KiplR**
Dead City, The. Christina Georgina Rossetti. **CP-RosC3**
Dead Color. Charles Wright. **SP-WrigC**
Dead, dead, dead, dead. Winter. Adrienne Rich. **CP-RicAE**
Dead do not need, The. Everything. Charles Bukowski. **SP-BukC2**
Dead Dog. Pablo Neruda, *tr. fr. Spanish by* Ben Belitt. **SP-NeruP**
Dead Dog (For Goo). Chuck Miller. **SP-MillC**
Dead Emperor, The. Walt Whitman. **CP-WhitW**
Dead-ends at 19th one / block over from Dolores. Blossoming Oakwood. James Schuyler. **CP-SchuJ**
Dead every enormous piece. Edward Estlin Cummings. **CP-CummE**
Dead fall around us like rain, The. Charles Wright. *Fr.* Homage to Paul Cézanne. **SP-WrigC**
Dead falls the Cause, if once the Hand be mute. Bribes and Gifts Get All. Robert Herrick. **CP-HerrR**
Dead Farms, Dead Leaves. Ted Hughes. **SP-HughT**
Dead Feast of the Kol-Folk, The. John Greenleaf Whittier. **CP-WhitJ**
Dead grasshoppers' / bone-white. Desert Autumn. Charles Tomlinson. **CP-TomlC**
Dead Hand. Robert Ranke Graves. **CP-GravR**
Dead have been awaken'd—shall I sleep?, The. Journal in Cephalonia. Byron. **CP-Byron**
Dead Heart, The. Anne Sexton. **CP-SextA**
Dead Hope. Christina Georgina Rossetti. **CP-RosC1**
Dead in Melanesia, The. Randall Jarrell. **CP-JarrR**
Dead in the cold, a song-singing thrush. Christina Georgina Rossetti. **CP-RosC2**
Dead in the year—. Robert Creeley. **CP-CreeR**
Dead in their dressing rooms, The. Curtain Call. Charles Tomlinson. **CP-TomlC**
Dead in There. Langston Hughes. **SP-HughL**
Dead in via, The. La Préface. Charles Olson. **CP-OlsoC**
Dead King, The. Robert Pack. **SP-PackR**
Dead King, The [Edward VII; 1910]. Rudyard Kipling. **CP-KiplR**
   "And since he was Master and Servant in all that we asked him." **FaBoEH**
Dead Language: Circa 1885, A. Robert Penn Warren. *Fr.* Mortmain. **SP-WarrR**
Dead lemon like a cowled old woman crouching in the cold, A. For *Under the Volcano.* Malcolm Lowry. **CP-LowrM**
Dead Liebknecht, The. "Hugh MacDiarmid." **SP-MacDH**
Dead, long dead. Tennyson. **EBVVPR** *Fr.* Maud [A Monodrama]. **CP-TennA**
Dead man, A/ who never caused others to die. Wystan Hugh Auden. **OAEL-2** *Fr.* Marginalia. **CP-AudeW**
Dead Man, Dead Man. "Bob Dylan." **CP-DylaB**
Dead man in his cave beginning to sweat, The. Ted Hughes. *Fr.* Out. **SP-HughT**
Dead man sat in the sun, The. Malcolm Lowry. *Fr.* Songs for Second Childhood. **CP-LowrM**
Dead Man Walking, The. Thomas Hardy. **CP-HardT**
Dead men are wisest, for they know. The Wise. Countee Cullen. **CP-CullC**
Dead men tell cryptic tales and this is one. Malcolm Lowry. **CP-LowrM**
Dead Men's Child, The. Robinson Jeffers. **CP-JefR1**
Dead mosquito, flattened against a door, A. 7/26/68: II. Adrienne Rich. **CP-RicAE** *Fr.* Ghazals: Homage to Ghalib. **SP-RicA2**
Dead Now. Charles Bukowski. **SP-BukC2**
Dead of Night. Jenny Joseph. **SP-JoseJ**
Dead on one side. Walking the Fire Line. James Dickey. **CP-DickJ**

Dead! One of them shot by the sea in the east. Mother and Poet. Elizabeth Barrett Browning. **CP-BroEB**

Dead Pan, The. Elizabeth Barrett Browning. **CP-BroEB**

Dead People. David Herbert Lawrence. **CP-LawrD**

Dead Petra in her hill-tomb sleeps. The "Rock" in El Ghor. John Greenleaf Whittier. **CP-WhitJ**

Dead Priestess Speaks, A. Hilda Doolittle. **CP-DoolH**

Dead Prophet, The. Tennyson. **CP-TennA**

Dead Quire, The. Thomas Hardy. **CP-HardT**

Dead River. Howard Nemerov. **CP-NemeH**

Dead Rose, A. Elizabeth Barrett Browning. **CP-BroEB**

Dead Salamander's Song. Jim Carroll. **SP-CarrJ**

Dead Seal [near McClure's Beach], The. Robert Bly. **SP-BlyR**

Dead Shall Be Raised Incorruptible, The. Galway Kinnell. **SP-KinnG**
     "Few bones, A."
     "I ran / my neck broken I ran."
     "In the ditch."
     "In the Twentieth Century of my trespass on earth." **TW**
     "On the television screen."
     "Piece of flesh gives off, A."
     "That you Captain? Sure."

Dead shalt thou lie; and nought. fr. the Greek of Sappho. Thomas Hardy. **CP-HardT**

Dead, she became space-earth. Ted Hughes. **SP-HughT** *Fr.* Seven Dungeon Songs.

Dead Ship of Harpswell, The. John Greenleaf Whittier. **CP-WhitJ**

Dead Skunk. Richard Eberhart. **CP-EberR**

Dead Soldiers. James Fenton. **SP-FentJ**

Dead Statesman, A. Rudyard Kipling. **FaBoEE; IHNG; NBLV; OPOU; PoWW** *Fr.* Epitaphs of the War [1914–1918]. **CP-KiplR**

Dead Still. Andrei Voznesensky, *tr. fr. Russian* by Richard Wilbur. **CP-WilbR**

Dead Tenor, The. Walt Whitman. **CP-WhitW**

Dead! Thirteen a month ago! Little Mattie. Elizabeth Barrett Browning. **CP-BroEB**

Dead to Clemenceau: November 1929, The. Robinson Jeffers. **CP-JefR2**

Dead Tree, The. Peter Meinke. **SP-MeinP**

Dead tree that, frozen, utters at the top, The. Fragment. Malcolm Lowry. **CP-LowrM**

Dead Village, The. Edwin Arlington Robinson. **CP-RobiE**

Dead "Wessex" the Dog to the Household. Thomas Hardy. **CP-HardT**

Dead Wingman, The. Randall Jarrell. **CP-JarrR; SP-JarrR**

Dead woman lay in her first night's grave, The. The Dead and the Living One. Thomas Hardy. **CP-HardT**

Dead Women. Siv Cedering Fox. **SP-CedeS**

Deader they die here, or at least. One Voter out of Sixteen. Robert Penn Warren. *Fr.* Fall Comes in Back-Country Vermont. **SP-WarrR**

Deadly Nightshade. Erica Jong. **SP-JongE**

Deadly Victorians, The. David Herbert Lawrence. **CP-LawrD**

Deadness was threatening us—15 Nigerians and 1 Mississippi nigger, The. Ilu, the Talking Drum. Etheridge Knight. **SP-KnigE**

Deaf and Dumb. Robert Browning. **CP-BroR1**

Deaf children were monkey-nimble, fish-tremulous and sudden, The. Deaf School. Ted Hughes. **SP-HughT**

Deaf, giddy, odious to my friends. On His Own Deafness. Jonathan Swift. **CP-SwifJ**

Deaf School. Ted Hughes. **SP-HughT**

Deaf Zone. Archie Randolph Ammons. **SP-AmmoA**

Deal not with me God as I have dealt with Man. Death-Bed of a Financier. Stevie Smith. **CP-SmitS**

Deal was here, / Oh love alas, The. Malcolm Lowry. **CP-LowrM**

Dean, adult education may seem silly. Lucretius versus the Lake Poets. Robert Frost. **CP-FrosR**

Dean and the Duke, The. Jonathan Swift. **CP-SwifJ**

Dean-Bourn, farewell; I never look to see. To Dean-bourn, a Rude River in Devon, by Which Sometimes He Lived. Robert Herrick. **CP-HerrR**

Dean of Faculty—a New Ballad, The. Robert Burns. **CP-BurnR**

Dean of St. Patrick's to Thomas Sheridan, The. Jonathan Swift. **CP-SwifJ**

Dean Smedley Gone to Seek His Fortune. Jonathan Swift. **CP-SwifJ**

Dean Swift's Answer to the Reverend Dr. Sheridan. Jonathan Swift. **CP-SwifJ**

Dean to Himself on St. Cecilia's Day, The. Jonathan Swift. **CP-SwifJ**

Dean to Thomas Sheridan, The. Jonathan Swift. **CP-SwifJ**

Dean would visit Market Hill, The. Lady Acheson Weary of the Dean. Jonathan Swift. **CP-SwifJ**

Dean's Answer to "Upon Stealing a Crown," The. Jonathan Swift. **CP-SwifJ**

Dean's Reasons for Not Building at Drapier's Hill, The. Jonathan Swift. **CP-SwifJ**

Dear . . . . John Yau. **SP-YauJo**

Dear, The. Thomas Hardy. **CP-HardT**

Dear Adrienne, / I feel signified by pain. Adrienne Rich. **SP-RicA1** *Fr.* Contradictions: Tracking Poems.

Dear Adrienne: / I'm calling you up tonight. Adrienne Rich. **SP-RicA1** *Fr.* Contradictions: Tracking Poems.

Dear Albert. This is a wholesome town. Really. Cherries grow. Letter to Goldbarth from Big Fork. Richard Hugo. **CP-HugoR**

Dear, all benevolence of fingering lips. In Sickness and in Health. Wystan Hugh Auden. **CP-AudeW**

Dear An: This will be your first widow Christmas. Such a young. Letter to Annick from Boulder. Richard Hugo. **CP-HugoR**

Dear and great Angel, wouldst thou only leave. The Guardian-Angel. Robert Browning. **CP-BroR1**

Dear and most Loved wife it is with pleasure. Gary Gildner. *Fr.* Letters from Vicksburg. **SP-GildG**

Dear and Mutch Loved One with pleasure I take. Gary Gildner. *Fr.* Letters from Vicksburg. **SP-GildG**

Dear Andrew, with the brindled hair. To Andrew Lang. Robert Louis Stevenson. **CP-StevR**

Dear Angels and dear disembodied Saints. Christina Georgina Rossetti. **CP-RosC2**

Dear Anima, Show These Words. James Liddy. **CP-LiddJ**

Dear Anna—between friend and friend. Epistle to Lady Austen. William Cowper. **CP-CowpW**

Dear Anne Sexton, I. Erica Jong. **SP-JongE**

Dear Anne Sexton, II. Erica Jong. **SP-JongE**

Dear Antigone, / after going over all the arguments. Letter. Leonard Nathan. **SP-NathL**

Dear Archie: I hope the boat trip home wasn't long. Letter to Ammons from Maratea. Richard Hugo. **CP-HugoR**

Dear architect of fine *Chateaux en l'air*. To William Hayley, Esq.: In Reply to His Solicitation to Write with Him in a Literary Work. William Cowper. **CP-CowpW**

Dear are the pleasant memories. Ralph Waldo Emerson. **CP-EmerR**

Dear Arl. Al Young. **CP-YounA**

Dear arrears of tenderness. Emily Dickinson. **SP-DickE**

Dear Arthur: In a country where a wealthy handful. Letter to Oberg from Pony. Richard Hugo. **CP-HugoR**

Dear Arthur Symons, a lily. The Debt. James Liddy. **CP-LiddJ**

Dear Azura, my alpha through omega. Ode to October Mist. Robert Pack. **SP-PackR**

Dear be still! Time's start of us lengthens slowly. Basil Bunting. **CP-BuntB**

Dear be the Church that, watching o'er the needs. Baptism. William Wordsworth. *Fr.* Ecclesiastical Sonnets. **CP-WorW2**

Dear Becher, you tell me to mix with mankind. Lines. Byron. **CP-Byron**

Dear Bill, / When I search the past for you. A Letter to William Carlos Williams. Kenneth Rexroth. **SP-RexrK**

Dear Bill: This is where the Nisei farmed, here where the blacktop. Letter to Matthews from Barton Street Flats. Richard Hugo. **CP-HugoR**

Dear Bill: We don't know the new heavy kind of wolf. Letter to Stafford from Polson. Richard Hugo. **CP-HugoR**

Dear Bob: I'll be damned. The good, oh so utterly sweet. Letter to Peterson from the Pike Place Market. Richard Hugo. **CP-HugoR**

Dear Bobbi: God, it's cold. Unpredicted, of course, by forecast. Letter to Hill from St. Ignatius. Richard Hugo. **CP-HugoR**

Dear boy, you will not hear me speak. Pangloss's Song: A Comic-Opera Lyric. Richard Wilbur. **CP-WilbR**

Dear brother, would you know the life. Ralph Waldo Emerson. **CP-EmerR**

Dear Cecelia we hav hat some warm times. Gary Gildner. *Fr.* Letters from Vicksburg. **SP-GildG**

Dear Cecelia well its shel and shel and. Gary Gildner. *Fr.* Letters from Vicksburg. **SP-GildG**

Dear Charles: And so we meet once in San Francisco and I. Letter to Simic from Boulder. Richard Hugo. **CP-HugoR**

Dear CHARLES, My Muse, Asleep or Dead. Philip Larkin. **CP-LarkP**

Dear Charles! whilst yet thou wert a babe, I ween. To a Friend [Charles Lamb] Who Had Declared His Intention of Writing No More Poetry. Samuel Taylor Coleridge. **CP-ColeS**

Dear Child of God. Stevie Smith. **CP-SmitS**

Dear Child of Nature, let them rail! To a Young Lady Who Had Been Reproached for Taking Long Walks in the Country. William Wordsworth. **CP-WorW1**

DEAR CHRIS / It is 3:17 a.m. in New York city, yes, it is. Ted Berrigan. **SP-BerrT** *Fr.* The Sonnets.

Dear Cimon Gray, / The other day. Robert Burns. *Fr.* To Symon Gray. **CP-BurnR**

Dear Colette. Erica Jong. **SP-JongE**

Dear Col'nel, COBHAM's and your country's Friend! The Second Epistle of the Second Book of Horace Imitated. Alexander Pope. **CP-PopeA**

Dear Condor: Much thanks for that telephonic support. Letter to Kizer from Seattle. Richard Hugo. **CP-HugoR**

Dear Cousin Nancy: / You probably never heard of me or Cousin Beauregard. Ms. Found under a Serviette in a Lovely Home. Ogden Nash. **CP-NashO**

Dear Craoibhin Aoibhin, look into our case. At The Abbey Theatre. William Butler Yeats. **CP-YeatW**

Dear critic, who my lightness so deplores. To a Captious Critic. Paul Laurence Dunbar. **CP-DunbP**

Dear, damn'd, distracting Town, farewell! A Farewell to London in the Year 1715. Alexander Pope. **CP-PopeA**

Dear Dark Continent. Alice Notley. **SP-NotlA**

Dear Dave: Rain five days and I love it[. A relief]. Letter to Wagoner from Port Townsend. Richard Hugo. **CP-HugoR**

Dear Dean, if e'er again you write. A Letter from Dean Swift to Dean Smedley. Jonathan Swift. **CP-SwifJ**

Dear Denise: Long way from, long time since Boulder[. I hope]. Letter to Levertov from Butte. Richard Hugo. **CP-HugoR**

Dear Dennice: I'm this close but the pass is tough this year. Letter to Scanlon from Whitehall. Richard Hugo. **CP-HugoR**

Dear Dick, prithee tell by what passion you move? On the Archbishop of Cashel and Bettesworth. Jonathan Swift. **CP-SwifJ**

Dear Dick, This kind of travel is cheap enough. Letter to Richard Hugo From Drumcliff. James McAuley. **SP-McAuJ**

Dear Dick: You know all that pissing and moaning around I've. Letter to Blessing from Missoula. Richard Hugo. **CP-HugoR**

Dear Doctor, I Have Read Your Play. Byron. **CP-Byron**

Dear Dorothy. Robert Creeley. **CP-CreeR**

Dear Eavan, / Just yesterday afternoon. Late August Letter. Marilyn Hacker. **SP-HackM**

Dear Ed: I get the sad news from Des Moines no doubt not sad. Letter to Mayo from Missoula. Richard Hugo. **CP-HugoR**

Dear Ellen, many a golden year. Ralph Waldo Emerson. **CP-EmerR**

Dear Eustatio, I write that you may write me an answer. Arthur Hugh Clough. **EBVV; EBVVPR; FaBoVe; OBTV; OXAEP-2** *Fr.* Amours de Voyage. **SP-ClouA**

Dear fellow-artist, why so free. To a Young Beauty. William Butler Yeats. **CP-YeatW**

Dear Fellow-travellers! think not that the Muse. Dedication (Sent with These Poems, in Ms., To ...). William Wordsworth. *Fr.* Memorials of a Tour of the Continent; 1820. **CP-WorW2**

Dear Female Heart. Stevie Smith. **CP-SmitS**

Dear Fred: I hope this finds you, Marge and children O.K. Letter to Garber from Skye. Richard Hugo. **CP-HugoR**

Dear Friend. Charles Bukowski. **SP-BukC2**

Dear friend, although the stamps are oddly beautiful. The Glory Set. Edwin Rolfe. **CP-RolfE**

Dear friend, can you walk. Emily Dickinson. **SP-DickE**

Dear friend, far off, my lost desire. Tennyson. **EBVVPR; FHYEP; OAEL-2** *Fr.* In Memoriam A. H. H. **CP-TennA**

Dear[e] friend, sit down: the tale is long and sad. Love Unknown. George Herbert. **CP-HerbG**

Dear Friends. Edwin Arlington Robinson. **CP-RobiE**

Dear Friends and Gentle Hearts. Countee Cullen. **CP-CullC**

Dear friends, stay! / Lamplit wafts of wit keep sorrow. Queen Caroline to Her Guests. Thomas Hardy. **CP-HardT**

Dear friends, the moment's come to ask. Reichsmarschall Hermann Göring ("Dear friends, the moment's come to ask"). William DeWitt Snodgrass. **SP-SnodW**

Dear friends, who read the world aright. Wordsworth. John Greenleaf Whittier. **CP-WhitJ**

Dear Gary: As soon as you'd gone winter snapped shut again. Letter to Snyder from Montana. Richard Hugo. **CP-HugoR**

Dear Gary: The houses in Wallace are closed after 94 years. Letter to Gildner from Wallace. Richard Hugo. **CP-HugoR**

Dear George, behold the portentous day. Advice outside a Church. Ogden Nash. **CP-NashO**

Dear girl, dream daughter of the childless years. For Jean. John Hewitt. **CP-HewiJ**

Dear God (safe ambiguity). Timeo. Isabella Gardner. **CP-GardI**

Dear golden eyes / Are bold and wise. A Little Ditty for This Day to the Beloved Harteebeeste. Malcolm Lowry. **CP-LowrM**

Dear good God, we've blundered into some musical. Manet: "The Execution of the Emperor Maximilian." William DeWitt Snodgrass. **SP-SnodW**

Dear grandpapa, / To be obedient. Lines to My Grandfather. Christina Georgina Rossetti. **CP-RosC3**

Dear, had the world in its caprice. Respectability. Robert Browning. **CP-BroR1**

Dear heart, good-night! Premonition. Paul Laurence Dunbar. **CP-DunbP**

Dear Heaven! for this sweet pledge of life. George Meredith. **CP-MerG2**

Dear, heavn-designing [or heavn-designed] soul! Richard Crashaw. **CP-CrasR**

(To [Mrs. M. R.] Councel Concerning Her Choise.) **CP-CrasR**

Dear Henley, with a pig's snout on. To W.E. Henley. Robert Louis Stevenson. **CP-StevR**

Dear Herries, let's hope, by impounding your Pope. The Dogma Triumphant. Robert Browning. **CP-BroR2**

Dear home, thou scene of earliest hopes and joys. Fragment: Home. Percy Bysshe Shelley. **CP-ShelP**

Dear Hosmer; or still dearer Hatty. A Round Robin. Robert Browning. **CP-BroR2**

Dear, I must be gone. *fr.* A Woman Young and Old. William Butler Yeats. **CP-YeatW**

Dear If I with Guile. Thomas Campion. **CP-CampT**

Dear————, I'll gie ye some advice. Robert Burns. **CP-BurnR**

(To a Painter.) **CP-BurnR**

Dear Imbellis. The Ancient Wars. Paul Zimmer. **SP-ZimmP**

Dear J.D.: One should think of Chief Joseph here[, coming soft]. Letter to Reed from Lolo. Richard Hugo. **CP-HugoR**

Dear Jim: The Bedfords are not to be found. Maybe. Letter to Wright from Gooseprairie. Richard Hugo. **CP-HugoR**

Dear Jim: This is as far as I ever chased a girl. Letter to Welch from Browning. Richard Hugo. **CP-HugoR**

Dear Joe. James Schuyler. **CP-SchuJ**

Dear John: Great to see your long-coming, well-crafted book. Letter to Haislip from Hot Springs. Richard Hugo. **CP-HugoR**

Dear John: This is a Dear John letter from booze. Letter to Logan from Milltown. Richard Hugo. **CP-HugoR**

Dear Jonno / there are pigeons who nest. A Trip on the Staten Island Ferry. Audre Lorde. **CP-LordA**

Dear Jool, I Miss You in Saint-Saturnin. Marilyn Hacker. **SP-HackM**

Dear Joseph—five and twenty years ago. Epistle to Hill. William Cowper. **CP-CowpW**

Dear Judas. Robinson Jeffers. **CP-JefR2**

Dear Judith: In sincerest gratitude. A Chaplet for Judith Landry. Marilyn Hacker. **SP-HackM**

Dear Karl. Stevie Smith. **CP-SmitS**

Dear Keats. Erica Jong. **SP-JongE**

Dear Kelly, when I was a kid. To Kelly Miller, Jr. Paul Laurence Dunbar. **CP-DunbP**

Dear Kenward. A Stone Knife. James Schuyler. **CP-SchuJ**

Dear Lady, tapping at your door. From Wishing-Land. Robert Louis Stevenson. **CP-StevR**

Dear Landlord. "Bob Dylan." **CP-DylaB**

Dear language, English, whose. Strathnaver. Donald Davie. **CP-DavDo**

Dear Life. Richard Shelton. **SP-ShelR**

Dear little Bog-Face. Bog-Face. Stevie Smith. **CP-SmitS**

Dear Little Sirmio. Catullus. *See* Carmen 31: "Apple of islands, Sirmio, & bright peninsulas, set."

Dear little Sirmio / Of all capes and islands. Catullus. *See* Carmen 31: "Apple of islands, Sirmio, & bright peninsulas, set."

Dear Liz: Here's where I degraded myself for the last time. Letter to Libbey from St. Regis. Richard Hugo. **CP-HugoR**

Dear Lizbie Browne. To Lizbie Browne. Thomas Hardy. **CP-HardT**

Dear Long, in this sequstr'd scene. To Edward Noel Long, Esq. Byron. **CP-Byron**

Dear Lord, accept a sinful heart. Self-Acquaintance. William Cowper. **NOCV** *Fr.* Olney Hymns. **CP-CowpW**

Dear Lord and Father of Mankind. John Greenleaf Whittier. **AH; NOCV; TRV; TrPWD** *Fr.* The Brewing of Soma. **CP-WhitJ**

Dear Lord, let me recount to Thee. It Is Finished. Christina Georgina Rossetti. **CP-RosC2**

Dear Lord, observe this bended knee. Prayer at the End of a Rope. Ogden Nash. **CP-NashO**

Dear lords of life, stump-toothed, with ragged breath. Geoffrey Hill. **DiPo** *Fr.* The Mystery of the Charity of Charles Péguy. **CP-HillG**

Dear [or Deare] love, for nothing less[e] than thee. The Dream[e]. John Donne. **CP-DonnJ**

Dear love, since the impossible proves. The Impossible. Robert Ranke Graves. **CP-GravR**

"Dear love, why should you weep." A Lost World. Robert Ranke Graves. **CP-GravR**

Dear loved one did I mention General Grants. Gary Gildner. *Fr.* Letters from Vicksburg. **SP-GildG**

Dear loved one well the last 2 days I spent. Gary Gildner. *Fr.* Letters from Vicksburg. **SP-GildG**

Dear Madeline: I'm getting strange when I drink. In Solon. Letter to Sister Madeline from Iowa City. Richard Hugo. **CP-HugoR**

Dear Mama, / Time I pay rent and get my food. Letter. Langston Hughes. **SP-HughL** *Fr.* Lenox Avenue Mural.

Dear man with the accurate mafia. Song of the Fox. Margaret Atwood. *Fr.* Songs of the Transformed. **SP-AtwM1**

Dear March, Come in. Emily Dickinson. **CP-DickE**

Dear Margie, hello. It is 5:15 a.m. Ted Berrigan. **SP-BerrT** *Fr.* The Sonnets.

Dear Marvin: Months since I left broke down and sobbing. Letter to Bell from Missoula. Richard Hugo. **CP-HugoR**

Dear Mary, / Yes, it will be bliss. A Mind's Journey to Diss. Sir John Betjeman. **CP-BetjJ**

Dear Marys, Dear Mother, Dear Daughter. Erica Jong. **SP-JongE**

Dear matted squirrel tongue. Radiant Silhouette V. John Yau. **SP-YauJo**

Dear Michele: Once, according to a native, this town. Letter to Birch from Deer Lodge. Richard Hugo. **CP-HugoR**

Dear Mike: We didn't have a chance. Our starter had no change. Letter to Mantsch from Havre. Richard Hugo. **CP-HugoR**

Dear Miss Dix, I am a young lady of Scandinavian origin, and I. The Strange Case of the Lovelorn Letter Writer. Ogden Nash. **CP-NashO**

Dear Miss Dix, I am a young man of half-past thirty-seven. Two and One Are a Problem. Ogden Nash. **CP-NashO**

Dear Miss Lucy: I been 'tinkin' dat I'd write you long fo' dis. A Letter. Paul Laurence Dunbar. **CP-DunbP**

Dear Miss Miller. Letter to a Substitute Teacher. Gary Gildner. **SP-GildG**

Dear Miss Roper, It seems, George Vernon, before we left Rome, said. Mary Trevelyn to Miss Roper. Arthur Hugh Clough. **FaBoVe** *Fr.* Amours de Voyage. **SP-ClouA**

Dear Miss Unger. To Miss Unger. Robert Browning. **CP-BroR2**

Dear Mr. Bowles found out too late. Emily Dickinson. **SP-DickE**

Dear Mr Fisher I am writing. Paraphrases. Roy Fisher. **SP-FishR**

Dear mother cease complaints, and wipe your eyes. New England. Anne Bradstreet. **KTR** *Fr.* A Dialogue between Old England and New. **CP-BradA**

Dear Mother, dear Mother, the Church is cold. The Little Vagabond. William Blake. **CP-BlakW** *Fr.* Songs of Experience.

Dear Muse. Stevie Smith. **CP-SmitS**

Dear my friend and fellow-student, I would lean my spirit o'er you! Lady Geraldine's Courtship. Elizabeth Barrett Browning. **CP-BroEB**

Dear, my friend & honour'd madam! of hard facts I'm not a hoarder. George Meredith. **CP-MerG2**

Dear native Brook! wild streamlet of the West! Sonnet to the River Otter. Samuel Taylor Coleridge. **CP-ColeS**

Dear native regions, I foretell. Extract from the Conclusion of a Poem, Composed in Anticipation of Leaving School. William Wordsworth. **CP-WorW1**

Dear nut / Uncrackable by nuance or debate. To My Greek. James Merrill. **SP-MerrJ**

Dear object of defeated care! Lines Written beneath a Picture. Byron. **CP-Byron**

Dear Obour / Our crossing was without. A Letter from Phillis Wheatley. Robert Earl Hayden. **CP-HaydR**

Dear Old Stockholm. Al Young. **CP-YounA**

Dear Old Village, The. Sir John Betjeman. **CP-BetjJ**

Dear old woman in the lane, The. Christina Georgina Rossetti. **CP-RosC2**

Dear ones in the house of the dead. Kathleen Jessie Raine. **SP-RainK**

Dear ones, in those days it was otherwise. The Woman Who Raised Goats. Tess Gallagher. **SP-GallT**

Dear Pa and Ma. Charles Bukowski. **SP-BukC3**

Dear Partie—. To Partridge Merrithew. Marsden Hartley. **CP-HartM**

Dear Peter, Dear Peter. To Peter Stuart. Robert Burns. **CP-BurnR**

Dear Philip: "Thank God for boozy godfathers." Epistle to a Godson. Wystan Hugh Auden. **CP-AudeW**

Dear President whose art sublime. To Sir Joshua Reynolds. William Cowper. **CP-CowpW**

Dear Prudence. John Lennon *and* Paul McCartney. **CP-Beatl**

Dear queen and mother—what do the archers now! Niobe. Kenneth Patchen. **CP-PatcK**

Dear Ralph, to your Great Stone Face. Emerson's Concord. Richard Eberhart. **CP-EberR**

Dear Ravi Shankar. Al Young. **CP-YounA**

Dear Reader. Peter Meinke. **SP-MeinP**

Dear relatives and friends, when my last breath. Wendell Berry. *Fr.* Testament. **CP-BerrW**

Dear Reliques! from a pit of vilest mould. Feelings of a French Royalist, on the Disinterment of the Remains of the Duke D'Enghien. William Wordsworth. **CP-WorW2**

Dear Reliques of a dislodg'd Soul, whose lack. Death's Lecture. Richard Crashaw. **CP-CrasR**

Dear Reynolds! as last night I lay in bed. To J. H. Reynolds, Esq. John Keats. **CP-KeatJ**

Dear Robert / Lots of whales cavort and spout. Letter to Bly from La Push. Richard Hugo. **CP-HugoR**

Dear Ron: hello. Your name is now a household name. Ted Berrigan. **SP-BerrT** *Fr.* The Sonnets.

Dear Ron: Keats was a baiter of bears etc. Ted Berrigan. **SP-BerrT** *Fr.* The Sonnets.

Dear Sam weeps a cold. Vir VII. James Liddy. *Fr.* Vir I–XII. **CP-LiddJ**

Dear San: Everybody doesn't write poetry. Feeling and Form. Marilyn Hacker. **SP-HackM**

Dear Scipio Sprague / sans plague sans blague. Epitaph. Malcolm Lowry. **CP-LowrM**

"Dear! Shall I see thy face," she said. The Dame of Athelhall. Thomas Hardy. **CP-HardT**

Dear Sheridan, a loving pair. George Nim-Dan-Dean, Esq. to Mr. Sheridan. Jonathan Swift. **CP-SwifJ**

Dear, simple girl, those flattering arts. Answer to the Foregoing, Addressed to Miss———. Byron. **CP-Byron**

Dear Sir, / our Lucky humbly begs. To Alexander Findlater. Robert Burns. **CP-BurnR**

Dear Sir, at ony time or tide. Reply to Robert Riddell. Robert Burns. **CP-BurnR**

Dear sir, good-morrow! Five years back. Ad Se Ipsum. Robert Louis Stevenson. **CP-StevR**

Dear Sir, of late delighted with the sight. To Her Most Honored Father Thomas Dudley, Esquire, These Humbly Presented. Anne Bradstreet. **CP-BradA**

Dear Sir: the summum bonum is. A Letter to the Denouncers. Edwin Rolfe. **CP-RolfE**

Dear Sister! while the wise and sage. To My Sister. John Greenleaf Whittier. **CP-WhitJ**

Dear Smed, I read thy brilliant lines. His Grace's Answer to Jonathan. Jonathan Swift. **CP-SwifJ**

Dear Smith [*or* S****], the sleest, paukie thief. Robert Burns. **CP-BurnR** (To J. S****.) **CP-BurnR**

Dear Thamson class, whaure'er I gang. Their Laureate to an Academy Class Dinner Club. Robert Louis Stevenson. **CP-StevR**

Dear, think not that they will forget you. Her Temple. Thomas Hardy. **CP-HardT**

Dear tho' unseen! tho' I have left behind. To Mary Pridham. Samuel Taylor Coleridge. **CP-ColeS**

Dear, though the night is gone. Wystan Hugh Auden. *Fr.* Twelve Songs. **CP-AudeW**

Dear[e], though to part it be a hell. To Dianeme. Robert Herrick. **CP-HerrR**

Dear to the Loves, and to the Graces vowed. Mary Queen of Scots. William Wordsworth. *Fr.* Poems Composed or Suggested During a Tour, in the Summer of 1833. **CP-WorW2**

Dear Tom, / When my next volume (granted: slender). Riposte. Marilyn Hacker. **SP-HackM**

Dear Tom, I'm surprised that your verse did not jingle. To Thomas Sheridan. Jonathan Swift. **CP-SwifJ**

Dear Tom, this verse, which however the beginning may appear. George Nim-Dan-Dean's Invitation to Mr. Thomas Sheridan. Jonathan Swift. **CP-SwifJ**

Dear Tom: / Tom, I will do anything you recommend. December 1989. Kay Boyle. **CP-BoylK**

Dear Tomasito. In Dream Time. Thomas McGrath. **SP-McGrT**

Dear Toni Instead of a Letter of Congratulation. Audre Lorde. **SP-LordA**

Dear Uncle Jim, this garden ground. Historical Associations. Robert Louis Stevenson. **CP-StevR**

Dear Vi: You were great at the Roethke festival this summer. Letter to Gale from Ovando. Richard Hugo. **CP-HugoR**

Dear Voyager: / This is to thank you for. An Open Letter to Voyager II. John Updike. **CP-UpdiJ**

Dear Wanda, / I go out in the long nights to. I Go Out in the Long Nights. Paul Zimmer. **SP-ZimmP**

Dear Wanda, / Worrying about you all the time. Worrying About You All the Time. Paul Zimmer. **SP-ZimmP**

Dear Wanderer, on your unimagined journey. Nocturne. Frederick Morgan. **SP-MorgF**

Dear water, clear water, playful in all your streams. Streams. Wystan Hugh Auden. *Fr.* Bucolics. **CP-AudeW**

Dear welcomer, I think you must agree. An Invitation. Thom Gunn. **CP-GunnT**

Dear Whizz, I remember you at St. Mark's in '39. To Auden on His Fiftieth. Richard Eberhart. **CP-EberR**

Dear, why make you more of a dog than me? Sonnet 59. Sir Philip Sidney. **GBL; OAEP; PrIm** *Fr.* Astrophil and Stella. **SP-SidnP**

Dear wife after less than half an hour. Letter. Edwin Rolfe. **CP-RolfE**

Dear wife and bosom friend I hat seen hart. Gary Gildner. *Fr.* Letters from Vicksburg. **SP-GildG**

Dear wife and friend I dozed but now will try. Gary Gildner. *Fr.* Letters from Vicksburg. **SP-GildG**

Dear wife and friend I hav not mutch to write. Gary Gildner. *Fr.* Letters from Vicksburg. **SP-GildG**

Dear wife I feal prety rested now. Gary Gildner. *Fr.* Letters from Vicksburg. **SP-GildG**

Dear woman I again take pen in hand. Gary Gildner. *Fr.* Letters from Vicksburg. **SP-GildG**

Dear woman I am sor a littel bit. Gary Gildner. *Fr.* Letters from Vicksburg. **SP-GildG**

Dear woman I am well and hope you ar. Gary Gildner. *Fr.* Letters from Vicksburg. **SP-GildG**

Dear woman I was glat to hear from you. Gary Gildner. *Fr.* Letters from Vicksburg. **SP-GildG**

Dear X, you wouldn't believe how curious. To a Dead Flame. John Updike. **CP-UpdiJ**

Dear you and I are two who this year blessed. The Grocery Bouquet. Isabella Gardner. **CP-GardI**

Deare cherish this, and with it[t] my soules will. Sonnet 26. Mary Sidney, Countess of Montgomery Wroth. **BWW** *Fr.* Pamphilia to Amphilanthus. **CP-WrotM**

Deare eye, that daynest to let fall a looke. Author to the Reader, The ("Deare eye, that daynest to let fall a looke"). Robert Southwell. **CP-SoutR**

Deare eye that doost peruse my Muses stile. Author to the Reader, The ("Deare eye that doost peruse my Muses stile"). Robert Southwell. **CP-SoutR**

Deare eyes farewell, my Sunne once, now my end. Lindamira's Complaint. Mary Sidney, Countess of Montgomery Wroth. *Fr.* Part 1. *Fr.* Urania. **CP-WrotM**

Deare eyes farewell, my Sunne once, now my end. Sonnet 1. Mary Sidney, Countess of Montgomery Wroth. *Fr.* Lindamira's Complaint. *Fr.* Part 1. *Fr.* Urania. **CP-WrotM**

Deare eyes how well (indeed) you doe adorne. Sonnet 2. Mary Sidney, Countess of Montgomery Wroth. *Fr.* Pamphilia to Amphilanthus. **CP-WrotM**

Deare fammish nott what you your self gave food. Sonnet 13. Mary Sidney, Countess of Montgomery Wroth. *Fr.* Pamphilia to Amphilanthus. **CP-WrotM**

Deare how doe thy wining eyes. Dialogue: Sheapherd, and Sheapherdess. Mary Sidney, Countess of Montgomery Wroth. *Fr.* Part 1. *Fr.* Urania. **CP-WrotM**

Deare, if I with guile would guild a true intent. Dear If I with Guile. Thomas Campion. **CP-CampT**

Deare Love, alas, how have I wronged thee. Mary Sidney, Countess of Montgomery Wroth. *Fr.* Part 1. *Fr.* Urania. **CP-WrotM**

Deare Lovelace, I am now about to prove. To My Much Loved Friend, Richard Lovelace Esq. John Jephson. *Fr.* Commendatory Poems. **CP-LoveR**

Deare Perenna, prethee come. To Perenna, A Mistresse. Robert Herrick. **CP-HerrR**

Deare, though unconstant, these I send to you. Mary Sidney, Countess of Montgomery Wroth. *Fr.* Urania. **CP-WrotM**

Deare wee Browne Byrdie, dare wee too. D.D. Byrde Callyng Jennie Wrenn. William DeWitt Snodgrass. **SP-SnodW**

Dearest, best and brightest. The Pine Forest of the Cascine Near Pisa. Percy Bysshe Shelley. **CP-ShelP**

Dearest Dimpling, we believe. George Meredith. **CP-MerG2**

Dearest Evelyn, I often think of you. The Jungle Husband. Stevie Smith. **CP-SmitS**

Dearest Foxxy, / I am in a crate. Love Letter Written in a Burning Building. Anne Sexton. **CP-SextA**

Dearest, I never knew such loving. There. Sonnet. Hayden Carruth. **CP-CarHS** *Fr.* Sonnets.

Dearest Ipsitilla. Catullus. *See* Carmen 32: "Call me to you / at siesta."

Dearest Ipsitilla, I'd absolutely love it. Catullus. *See* Carmen 32: "Call me to you / at siesta."

Dearest, it was a night. The Birthnight: To F. Walter de la Mare. **CP-DeLaW**

Dearest Louisa, Enquire if you please about Mr. Claude. Georgina Trevellyn to Luisa. Arthur Hugh Clough. **FaBoVe** *Fr.* Amours de Voyage. **SP-ClouA**

Dearest love: The roses are in bloom again. Brennende Liebe. Louise Glück. **SP-GlücL**

Dearest Man-in-the-Moon. Erica Jong. **SP-JongE**

Dearest of thousands, now the time drawes neere. His Charge to Julia at His Death. Robert Herrick. **CP-HerrR**

Dearest one, daughter! at glance of your brow-shaded eye. The Glance. Walter de la Mare. **CP-DeLaW**

Dearest, thy tresses are not threads of gold. The Comparison. Thomas Carew. **CP-CareT**

Dearest was the one to whom it fell, The. Hilda. John Crowe Ransom. **SP-RansJ**

Dearest, where thy shadow falls. Hafiz, *tr. fr. Persian by* Ralph Waldo Emerson. **CP-EmerR**

Dearly-beloved Mr Squire. Mr Squire. David Herbert Lawrence. **CP-LawrD**

Death. Emily Brontë. *See* Death, that struck when I was most confiding.

Death, The. Hayden Carruth. *Fr.* Mother. **CP-CarHL**

Death. Paul Laurence Dunbar. **CP-DunbP**

Death. George Herbert. **CP-HerbG**

Death, *tr. fr. the German of* Rilke. Randall Jarrell. **CP-JarrR**

Death. Bill Knott. **SP-KnotB**

Death. David Herbert Lawrence. **CP-LawrD**

Death. Thomas Merton. **CP-MertT**

Death. Christina Georgina Rossetti. **CP-RosC3**

Death. Percy Bysshe Shelley. **CP-ShelP**

Death. Percy Bysshe Shelley. **CP-ShelP**

Death. Richard Shelton. **SP-ShelR**

Death. Robert Louis Stevenson. **CP-StevR**

Death. Lewis Turco. **SP-TurcL**

Death. William Carlos Williams. **CP-WilW1**

Death. William Carlos Williams. **CP-WilW2**

Death. William Butler Yeats. **CP-YeatW**

Death also is trying to be life. Life Is Trying to Be Life. Ted Hughes. **SP-HughT**

Death and Burial of McDonald Clarke, a Parody, The. Walt Whitman. **CP-WhitW**

Death & Co. Sylvia Plath. **CP-PlatS**

Death and Daphne. Jonathan Swift. **CP-SwifJ**

Death and Doctor Hornbook [A True Story]. Robert Burns. **CP-BurnR**

Death and Dying Words of Poor Mailie, the Author's Only Pet Yowe, an Unco Mournfu' Tale, The. Robert Burns. **CP-BurnR**

Death, and it is broken. The Instrument. Kathleen Jessie Raine. *Fr.* Three Poems on Illusion. **SP-RainK**

Death and Life of a Severino, The. João Cabral de Melo Neto, *tr. fr. Portuguese by* Elizabeth Bishop.

 "All the heaven and earth." **CP-BishE**

 "My name is Severino." **CP-BishE**

 "Whom are you carrying." **CP-BishE**

Death and the Bridge. Robert Lowell. **SP-LoweR**

Death and the Lovers. May Sarton. **SP-SartM**

Death and the Maiden. Howard Nemerov. **CP-NemeH**

Death and the Sun. Derek Mahon. **SP-MahoD**

Death and the Three Revellers. Geoffrey Chaucer. **OBNV** *Fr.* The Pardoner's Tale. **FHYEP; NAEL-1; NAWM-1; NoP; OAEL-1; PoE** *Fr.* The Canterbury Tales. **CP-ChauG**

Death at the Office, A. Ted Kooser. **SP-KoosT**

Death Baby, The. Anne Sexton. **CP-SextA**

Death Ballad. John Berryman. **CP-BerrJ**

Death[,] be not proud, though some have called thee. John Donne. **BiP; CABA; ChTr; DL; EBEvV; EIL; EnRePo; FF; FHYEP; FPL; FaBV; FaBoEn; FaBoRV; FaFP; GoBC; HAP; HBV 1-2; HeIL; HeIP; ImPo; InPK; InPS; InvP; JCP; LiTB; LoBV; MeLP; MePo; NAEL-1; NAWM-1; NIP; NOBE; NOSC; NoP; OAEL-1; OAEP; OBD; OBS; OPOU; OxAEP-1; PAI; PBMP; PPP; PPoe; PoE; PoEL-2; PoRA; Poetr; PrIm; SCGP; SCV; SeCP; SeCV-1; SeCeV; SoSe; TEP; TRP; TRV; TrCP; TrGrPo; TreFS; WHA; WeW** *Fr.* Divine Meditations. **CP-DonnJ** *Fr.* Holy Sonnets. **CP-DonnJ** (Holy Sonnet.) **OPOU**

Death-Bed, A. Rudyard Kipling. **CP-KiplR**

Death-Bed of a Financier. Stevie Smith. **CP-SmitS**

Death-bell beats!—, The. Sister Rosa: A Ballad. Percy Bysshe Shelley. *Fr.* Poems from St. Irvyne, or, The Rosicrucian. **CP-ShelP**

Death Bereaves Our Common Mother Nature Grieves for My Dead Brother. Stevie Smith. **CP-SmitS**

Death blow is a Life blow to Some, A. Emily Dickinson. **CP-DickE**

Death By Aesthetics. Mona Van Duyn. **SP-VanDM**

Death by Drums. Robert Ranke Graves. **CP-GravR**

Death by Radio. William Carlos Williams. **CP-WilW2**

Death by Water. Thomas Stearns Eliot. **OBVE** *Fr.* The Waste Land. **CP-ElioT**

Death by Water. Edwin Rolfe. **CP-RolfE**

Death by Water. Patti Smith. **SP-SmitP**

Death Came to Me. Stevie Smith. **CP-SmitS**

Death can have no alternative but Love. Song: Cherries or Lilies. Robert Ranke Graves. **CP-GravR**

Death cannot plunder half so fast. Emily Dickinson. **SP-DickE**

Death comes once, let it be easy. Finish. Carl Sandburg. **CP-SandC**

Death-Day Recalled, A. Thomas Hardy. **CP-HardT**

Death Demonstrates His Presence to Zimmer. Paul Zimmer. **SP-ZimmP**

Death devours all lovely things. Passer Mortuus Est. Edna St. Vincent Millay. **CP-MillE**

Death Drag (The Elegist). John Clellon Holmes. **SP-HolmJ**

Death-Dream, The. Walter de la Mare. **CP-DeLaW**

Death Ends All Woe. Robert Herrick. **CP-HerrR**

Death favoured me from the first, well knowing I could not endure. The Favour. Rudyard Kipling. *Fr.* Epitaphs of the War [1914–1918]. **CP-KiplR**

Death for the Dark Stranger. Thomas McGrath. **SP-McGrT**

Death, from a Distance. Jorge Guillén, *tr. fr. Spanish by* Richard Wilbur. **CP-WilbR**

Death from Cancer. Robert Lowell. **SP-LoweR** *Fr.* In Memory of Arthur Winslow.

Death, from where we stand, is nonexistence. The Vantage. Frederick Morgan. **SP-MorgF**

Death gallops up the bridge of red railtie girders. Death and the Bridge. Robert Lowell. **SP-LoweR**

Death goes far around. Emily Dickinson. **SP-DickE**

Death Grapple, The. Robert Ranke Graves. **CP-GravR**

Death-grip of the chalky clouds lets slip, The. Landing in the Rain at La Guardia. John Updike. **CP-UpdiJ**

Death has a look of finality. Louis MacNeice. *Fr.* The Trolls. **CP-MacNL**

Death has a younger brother. Waiting Room Only. Leonard Nathan. **SP-NathL**

Death has only to touch a trifle. Emily Dickinson. **SP-DickE**

Death, he thinks. In fact he has thought it every day. Hayden Carruth. *Fr.* The Sleeping Beauty. **CP-CarHL**

Death himself. L M F B R. Gary Snyder. **CP-SnydG**

Death I have entered is a death, The. Robert Penn Warren. *Fr.* Saul at Gilboa. **SP-WarrR**

Death I recant, and say, unsaid by me. Elegy on Mistress Boulstred. John Donne. **CP-DonnJ**

Death, I repent. Kathleen Jessie Raine. **MoAB; OxBTC** *Fr.* Two Invocations of Death. **SP-RainK**

(Invocation of Death.) **MoAB**

Death, I say, my heart is bowed. The Shroud. Edna St. Vincent Millay. **CP-MillE**

Death in all its forms. Charles Henri Ford. *Fr.* Epigrams. **SP-FordC**

Death in Leamington. Sir John Betjeman. **CP-BetjJ**

Death In Moonlight. Stanley Jasspon Kunitz. **CP-KuniS**

Death in the Aquarium. Richard Hugo. **CP-HugoR**

Death in the Desert, A. Robert Browning. **CP-BroR1**

Death in the Desert, A. Charles Tomlinson. **CP-TomlC**

Death in the Mines. Richard Eberhart. **CP-EberR**

Death in the Rose Garden. Stevie Smith. **CP-SmitS**

Death in the West, A. Donald Davie. **CP-DavDo**

Death in Venice. Charles Tomlinson. **CP-TomlC**

Death is a dead, at least that's what Freud said. Einstein & Freud & Jack. Howard Nemerov. **CP-NemeH**

Death is a Dialogue between. Emily Dickinson. **CP-DickE**

Death is all metaphors, shape in one history. Dylan Thomas. **CMoP; MoAB; Son** *Fr.* Altarwise by Owl-Light. **CP-ThomD**

Death is here and death is there. Death. Percy Bysshe Shelley. **CP-ShelP**

Death is like the insect. Emily Dickinson. **CP-DickE**

Death is more than. Edward Estlin Cummings. **CP-CummE**

Death is no escape, ah no! only a doorway to the inevitable. Death. David Herbert Lawrence. **CP-LawrD**

Death is only a technical correction of the market. Answer Yes or No. Robert Penn Warren. *Fr.* Tale of Time. **SP-WarrR**

Death is perhaps an intimate friend. Emily Dickinson. **SP-DickE**

Death is potential to that Man. Emily Dickinson. **CP-DickE**

Death is serious. Small Moment. Howard Nemerov. **CP-NemeH**

Death is stronger than all the governments. Death Snips Proud Men. Carl Sandburg. **CP-SandC**

Death Is Swallowed Up in Victory. Christina Georgina Rossetti. **CP-RosC3**

Death is the least of things to be feared. Frederick Morgan. *Fr.* Death Mother. **SP-MorgF**

Death is the supple Suitor. Emily Dickinson. **CP-DickE**

Death is the tranquil night. From Heine. Louise Bogan. **CP-BogaL**

Death is the twin of Sleep, they say. The Twin of Sleep. Robert Ranke Graves. **CP-GravR**

Death King, The. Anne Sexton. **CP-SextA**

Death knell is ringing, The. Percy Bysshe Shelley. **CP-ShelP**

Death leaves Us homesick, who behind. Emily Dickinson. **CP-DickE**

Death loves rich people. Funny Poem. Bill Knott. **SP-KnotB**

Death makes his / obeisance. The Festival. Robert Creeley. **CP-CreeR**

Death Mother. Frederick Morgan. **SP-MorgF**

"Breasts of the loving mothers flow with milk, The."

"Death is the least of things to be feared."

"I cornered the thief in the garage at dusk."

"Is it useful to have a mythology of death."

"Lady, when you were born."

"One sweltering Sunday afternoon in August."

"There was no bulldozer handy, so."

"Who will laugh / in coldest glee."

"You came as sleep, warily."

"You cast me from your filthy womb."

Death music sounds for a boy by a stream. Roy Fisher. *Fr.* Five Morning Poems from a Picture by Manet. **SP-FishR**

Death News. Allen Ginsberg. **CP-GinsA**

Death obtains the Rose. Emily Dickinson. **SP-DickE**

Death of / one is, The. Robert Creeley. **CP-CreeR**

Death of a First-Born, A. Christina Georgina Rossetti. **CP-RosC3**

Death of a Gardener. Phoebe Hesketh. **SP-HeskP**

Death of a Lady's Man. Leonard Cohen. **CP-CoheL**

Death of a Naturalist. Seamus Heaney. **SP-HeanS**

Death of a Painter. Donald Davie. **CP-DavDo**

Death of a Romantic. Erica Jong. **SP-JongE**

Death of a Soldier, The. Wallace Stevens. **CP-StevW**

Death of a Starling, The. Catullus. *See* Carmen 3: "Who loves beauty / vel her statues."

Death of a Toad, The. Richard Wilbur. **CP-WilbR**

Death of a Voice. Donald Davie. **CP-DavDo**

Death of a Young Son by Drowning. Margaret Atwood. **SP-AtwM1**

Death Of A.G.A., The. Emily Brontë. **CP-BronE**

Death of Alexander. Robert Lowell. **SP-LoweR**

Death of an Actress. Louis MacNeice. **CP-MacNL**

Death of an Irishwoman. Michael Hartnett. **SP-HarMi**

Death of an Oaxaqueñian. Malcolm Lowry. **CP-LowrM**

Death of an Old Lady. Louis MacNeice. **CP-MacNL**

Death of Anne Boleyn. Robert Lowell. **SP-LoweR**

Death of Argentine, The. Sir Walter Scott. **SP-ScotW** *Fr.* The Lord of the Isles.

Death of Artists, The. James Liddy. **CP-LiddJ**

Death of Autumn, The. Edna St. Vincent Millay. **CP-MillE**

Death of Buckingham, The. Alexander Pope. *See* The Duke of Buckingham.

Death of Count Roland. Robert Lowell. **SP-LoweR**

Death of Elizabeth Grieve, The. Charles Tomlinson. **CP-TomlC**

Death of Emmett Till, The. "Bob Dylan." **CP-DylaB**

Death of Europe, The. Charles Olson. **CP-OlsoC; SP-OlsoC**

Death of Fathers. James McAuley. **SP-McAuJ**

Death of Franco of Cologne, The: His Prophecy of Beethoven. William Carlos Williams. **CP-WilW1**

Death of General Grant. Walt Whitman. **CP-WhitW**

Death of God, The. Howard Nemerov. **CP-NemeH**

Death of Haidée, The. Byron. **FiP** *Fr.* Canto the Fourth. *Fr.* Don Juan. **CP-Byron**

Death of Hoel, The. Thomas Gray. **CP-GrayT**

Death of King George V. Sir John Betjeman. *See* Spirits of well-shot woodcock, partridge, snipe.

Death of Lesbia's Bird, The. Catullus. *See* Carmen 3: "Who loves beauty / vel her statues."

Death of Little Boys. Allen Tate. **CP-TateA**

Death of love comes from reiteration, The. The Reiteration. Robert Ranke Graves. **CP-GravR**

Death of Lovers, The. James Liddy. **CP-LiddJ**

Death of Marmion, The. Sir Walter Scott. **SP-ScotW** *Fr.* Marmion.

Death of Mathmaticians, The. James Liddy. **CP-LiddJ**

Death of Mr. Mounsel. Stevie Smith. **CP-SmitS**

Death of Myth-making, The. Sylvia Plath. **CP-PlatS**

Death of Our Era, The. David Herbert Lawrence. **CP-LawrD**

Death of our Ladie, The. Robert Southwell. **CP-SoutR**

Death of Regret, The. Thomas Hardy. **CP-HardT**

Death of Samson. John Milton. *See* Come, come, no time for lamentation now.

Death of See, The. William Carlos Williams. **CP-WilW1**

Death of Shelley, The. Geoffrey Hill. *Fr.* Of Commerce and Society: Variations on a Theme. **CP-HillG**

"Rivers bring down. The sea."

"Slime; the residues of refined tears."

Death of Sir Nihil, book the *nth*. Tywater. Richard Wilbur. **CP-WilbR**

Death of the Ball Turret Gunner, The. Randall Jarrell. **CP-JarrR; SP-JarrR**

Death of the Baron, The. David Herbert Lawrence. **CP-LawrD**

Death of the Dog Belvoir. Stevie Smith. **CP-SmitS**

Death of the Fathers, The. Anne Sexton. **CP-SextA**

Begat.

Boat, The.

Friends.

How We Danced. **DIP**

Oysters.

Santa.

Death of the First Born, The. Paul Laurence Dunbar. **CP-DunbP**

Death of the Hare, The. William Butler Yeats. *Fr.* A Man Young and Old. **CP-YeatW**

Death of the Hired Man, The. Robert Frost. **CP-FrosR**

Death of the Hired Zimmer. Paul Zimmer. **SP-ZimmP**

Death of the Horses by Fire. Tess Gallagher. **SP-GallT**

Death of the Infanta, The. Charles Tomlinson. **CP-TomlC**

Death of the Kapowsin Tavern. Richard Hugo. **CP-HugoR**

Death of the Nature-Lover, The, *for earlier vers. see* My Departure. Walt Whitman. **CP-WhitW**

Death of the Pilot Whales, The. Peter Meinke. **SP-MeinP**

Death of the Poor. James Liddy. **CP-LiddJ**

Death of the Sheriff, The. Robert Lowell. **SP-LoweR**

Death of the Small Commune, The. Marge Piercy. **SP-PierM**

Death of the Starling, The. Catullus. *See* Carmen 3: "Who loves beauty / vel her statues."

Death of the Virgin, The. David Markson. **CP-MarkD**

Death of Venus, The. Robert Creeley. **CP-CreeR**

Death of Wallenstein, The. Samuel Taylor Coleridge. Character of Wallenstein, The. **CP-ColeS**

Death of Will, The. Charles Tomlinson. **CP-TomlC**

Death of Winter, The. George Meredith. **CP-MerG1**

Death on All Fronts. Allen Ginsberg. **CP-GinsA**

Death Piece. Theodore Roethke. **CP-RoetT**

Death Room, The. Robert Ranke Graves. **CP-GravR**

Death Row. Richard Shelton. **SP-ShelR**

Death Scene, A. Emily Brontë. **CP-BronE**

(From a D— W— in the N. C.) **CP-BronE**

Death sent / To fetch you, but you had no idle care. On a Greek Tomb Relief. Wystan Hugh Auden. **CP-AudWJ**

Death Sentence, The. Stevie Smith. **CP-SmitS**

Death sets a Thing significant. Emily Dickinson. **CP-DickE**

Death Snips Proud Men. Carl Sandburg. **CP-SandC**

Death Song[, A]. Paul Laurence Dunbar. **CP-DunbP**

Death stands straight in her cart. The Morada La Muerte. Martin Edmunds. *Fr.* The High Road to Taos. **SP-EdmuM**

Death, that struck when I was most confiding. Emily Brontë. **CP-BronE**

(Death.) **CP-BronE**

Death the Barber. William Carlos Williams. **CP-WilW1**

Death, thou wast once an uncouth hideous thing. Death. George Herbert. **CP-HerbG**

Death, to the dead for evermore. Robert Louis Stevenson. **CP-StevR**

Death to the Poor. Charles Baudelaire, *tr. fr. French by* Countee Cullen. **CP-CullC**

Death to This Book, *see also* Commentary—Death to This Book. Leonard Cohen. **CP-CoheL**

Death to Van Gogh's Ear! Allen Ginsberg. **CP-GinsA**

Death took my father. Manos Karastefanís. James Merrill. **SP-MerrJ**

Death underlines our loss. The man who moved. Essay on Dreiser (1871-1945). Edwin Rolfe. **CP-RolfE**

Death, unduly undoing. Songlet. Archie Randolph Ammons. **SP-AmmoA**

Death Wants More Death. Charles Bukowski. **SP-BukC2**

Death warrants are supposed to be. Emily Dickinson. **CP-DickE**

Death-Watches. Christina Georgina Rossetti. **CP-RosC2**

Death went upon a solemn day. Death and Daphne. Jonathan Swift. **CP-SwifJ**

Death, what dost? ô hold thy Blow. Upon the Death of the Most Desired Mister Herrys. Richard Crashaw. **CP-CrasR**

Death! where is thy victory? To Death. Percy Bysshe Shelley. **CP-ShelP**

Death Will Amuse Them. Kenneth Patchen. **CP-PatcK**

Death will come and it will have your eyes. Homage to Cesare Pavese. Charles Wright. **SP-WrigC**

Death Wish, A. Samuel Taylor Coleridge. **CP-ColeS**

Death-Wish, The. Louis MacNeice. **CP-MacNL**

Death(having lost)put on his universe. Edward Estlin Cummings. **CP-CummE; SP-CummE**

Deathly Child, The. Stevie Smith. **CP-SmitS**

Deaths. Denise Levertov. **CP-LeveD**

Deaths. Derek Mahon. **SP-MahoD**

Deaths and Electrocutions. James Liddy. *Fr.* Glass after Oblivion. **CP-LiddJ**

Deaths and Entrances. Dylan Thomas. **CP-ThomD**

Death's Chill Between. Christina Georgina Rossetti. **CP-RosC3**

Death's Chimney. Edward Estlin Cummings. **CP-CummE**

Death's Door. Thom Gunn. **CP-GunnT**

Death's Echo. Wystan Hugh Auden. **CP-AudeW**

Death's-head moth, A. Charles Henri Ford. **SP-FordC** *Fr.* Secret Haiku.

Death's head of realism, The. Fyodor. Allen Ginsberg. **CP-GinsA**

Death's Lecture. Richard Crashaw. **CP-CrasR**

Deaths of the Goddesses, The. Erica Jong. **SP-JongE**

Deaths of the Other Children, The. Margaret Atwood. **SP-AtwM1**

Death's Ostracism. Stevie Smith. **CP-SmitS**

Death's taxi crackles through the mist. The cheeks. To the Airport. Adrienne Rich. **CP-RicAE**

Death's Valley. Walt Whitman. **CP-WhitW**

Death's Waylaying not the sharpest. Emily Dickinson. **CP-DickE**

Deathsong for a Maiden. Kenneth Patchen. **CP-PatcK**

Deathwatch. Barton Sutter. **SP-SuttB** *Fr.* The Complaints of Poverty.

"When loons laugh he does not."

Débâcle. Louis MacNeice. **CP-MacNL**

Debate: Question, Quarry, Dream. Robert Penn Warren. **SP-WarrR**

Debate with the Rabbi. Howard Nemerov. **CP-NemeH**

Debet multa tibi veneranda (Bacone) poesis. *acc. by English translation.* Thomas Campion. **CP-CampT**

Debetur alto iure Principium Iovi, *accompanied by English translation.* Thomas Campion. *Fr.* The Lords Mask[e].

Debits and Credits. Rudyard Kipling.

Alnaschar and the Oxen. **CP-KiplR**

Banquet Night. **CP-KiplR**

Birthright, The. **CP-KiplR**

Burden, The. **CP-KiplR**

Centaurs, The. **CP-KiplR**

Changelings, The. **CP-KiplR**

Gipsy Vans. **CP-KiplR**

Jane's Marriage. **CP-KiplR**

Last Ode, The. **CP-KiplR**

Late Came the God. **CP-KiplR**

Legend of Truth, A. **CP-KiplR**

Portent, The. **CP-KiplR**

Rahere. **CP-KiplR**

Supports, The. **CP-KiplR**

To the Companions. **CP-KiplR**

Untimely. **CP-KiplR**

Vineyard, The. **CP-KiplR**

We and They. **CP-KiplR**

Deborah as Scion. James Dickey. **CP-DickJ**

Debris. Walt Whitman. **CP-WhitW**

Debris of Life and Mind. Wallace Stevens. **CP-StevW**

Debt, The. Paul Laurence Dunbar. **CP-DunbP**

Debt, The. James Liddy. **CP-LiddJ**

Debt. George Oppen. **CP-OppeG**

Debt. Allen Tate. **CP-TateA**

Debt for Tomorrow, A. Roy Fisher. **SP-FishR**

Debt is paid, The. The Past. Ralph Waldo Emerson. **CP-EmerR**

Debts writing me letters. Suite. Jean Garrigue. **SP-GarrJ**

Decade only meaningful (decimal death). The Lie of 10, or the Concept of Zero. Charles Olson. **CP-OlsoC**

Decadent people, they fight, A. Who. Charles Olson. **CP-OlsoC**

Decay. George Herbert. **CP-HerbG**

Decay bars one time, 'solely to know, see Catullus'. Catullus. *See* Carmen 72: "There was a time, Lesbia, when."

Decay of cathedrals, The. Light Becomes Darkness. William Carlos Williams. **CP-WilW1**

Decay of Piety. William Wordsworth. **CP-WorW2**

Decaying Lambskins. Robinson Jeffers. **CP-JefR2**

Dedication to the Poet Laureate. Byron. *See* Dedication: "Bob Southey! You're a poet--poet-laureate."

Dedication To the Right Honorable John Lovelace. The. Richard Lovelace. **CP-LoveR**

Dedicatory Poem. Robert Louis Stevenson. **CP-StevR**

Deed knocks first at Thought, A. Emily Dickinson. **CP-DickE**

Deed of Gift. Robert Ranke Graves. **CP-GravR**

Deed took all my heart, The. The Return. Mary Oliver. **SP-OlivM**

Deem as ye list. Upon good cause. Sir Thomas Wyatt. **CP-WyatT**

Deemed this an outpost, I. Wystan Hugh Auden. **CP-AudWJ**

Deep Analysis. Philip Larkin. **CP-LarkP**

Deep and Dark Blue Ocean. Byron. *See* There is a pleasure in the pathless woods.

Deep as the winter plain, two armies. Stephen Spender. *See* Two Armies.

Deep asleep, perfect immobility, no apparent evidence of consciousness or of dream. Waking Jed. Charles Kenneth Williams. **CP-WillC; SP-WillC**

Deep Chess. Lawrence Ferlinghetti. **SP-FerlL**

Deep, deep below our violences. Winds. Wystan Hugh Auden. *Fr.* Bucolics. **CP-AudeW**

Deep, deep down in the silent grave. Emily Brontë. **CP-BronE**

Deep, deep, under the sea. Lied von Castelli. George Meredith. **CP-MerG2**

Deep dish. Lumps in it, A. I Need, I Need. Theodore Roethke. **CP-RoetT**

Deep Fishing. Richard Eberhart. **CP-EberR**

Deep Happiness, A. Leonard Cohen. **CP-CoheL**

Deep in a forest where the kestrel screamed. The Dwelling-Place. Walter de la Mare. **CP-DeLaW**

Deep in a time that cannot come again. Lines & Circularities. Howard Nemerov. **CP-NemeH**

Deep in earth's opaque mirror. Symmetries & Asymmetries. Wystan Hugh Auden. **CP-AudeW**

Deep in English country lanes I walk. An Exile in Devon. Jenny Joseph. **SP-JoseJ**

Deep in liquid indigo. Aquatic Nocturne. Sylvia Plath. **CP-PlatS**

Deep in my heart that aches with the repression. Unexpressed. Paul Laurence Dunbar. **CP-DunbP**

Deep in that black water where you tossed a book. Lake Byron, Maybe Gordon Lord. Richard Hugo. **CP-HugoR**

Deep in the air the past appears. The Greeks. Tom Clark. **SP-ClarT**

Deep in the back ways of my mind I see them. My Great-Grandfather's Slaves. Wendell Berry. **CP-BerrW**

Deep in the Century of Opposites. Muriel Rukeyser. **CP-RukeM**

Deep in the dusty chattels of the tombs. Carl Sandburg. *Fr.* The People, Yes. **CP-SandC**

Deep in the heart of the lake. Water Music. Alun Lewis. **CP-LewiA**

Deep in the man sits fast his fate. Fate. Ralph Waldo Emerson. **CP-EmerR**

Deep in the muck of unregarded doom. Edna St. Vincent Millay. **CP-MillE**

Deep in the shady sadness of a vale. Hyperion; a Fragment. John Keats. **CP-KeatJ**

Deep in the shady sadness of a vale. John Keats. **OXAEP-2,** *book* I–III; **ChER; FHYEP; FaBoEn; FiP; NOBRP; OAEP; OBNC; OBRV; PoEL-4; TrGrPo** *Fr.* Hyperion; a Fragment. **CP-KeatJ**

(Saturn.) **OBNC; TrGrPo**

Deep in the soul a strong delusion dwells. Idealism. Ralph Waldo Emerson. **CP-EmerR**

Deep in the still mysterious waters of the lake a world lies drowned. The Abominable Lake. Stevie Smith. **CP-SmitS**

Deep in the study / of Eugenics. The Phœnix. Ogden Nash. **CP-NashO**

Deep in this earth. Epitaph. Edwin Rolfe. **CP-RolfE**

Deep in woodland dell. My Lady of the Wood. Wystan Hugh Auden. **CP-AudWJ**

Deep is the lamentaion! Not alone. Imaginative Regrets. William Wordsworth. *Fr.* Ecclesiastical Sonnets. **CP-WorW2**

Deep pools of shade beneath dense maples. July. John Updike. **CP-UpdiJ**

Deep Religious Faith. William Carlos Williams. **CP-WilW2**

Deep roots moving in lush soil to send a silver-gray beech tree. Carl Sandburg. *Fr.* Timesweep. **CP-SandC**

Deep Sam deeply circumcised. Vir X. James Liddy. *Fr.* Vir I–XII. **CP-LiddJ**

Deep-Sea Cables, The. Rudyard Kipling. **CP-KiplR**

Deep-sea frost, and. A Lily at Noon. Donald Davie. **CP-DavDo**

Deep-sea salmon far at sea, The. Old Man's Journey. Archibald MacLeish. **CP-MacLA**

Deep Sea Wandering. Carl Sandburg. **CP-SandC**

Deep sea was the wandering. Deep Sea Wandering. Carl Sandburg. **CP-SandC**

Deep South. Thomas McGrath. **SP-McGrT**

Deep sunk in floods of grief. Bible, *O.T. See* Psalm 130: "Out of the depths have I cried unto thee, O Lord."

Deep-sworn Vow, A. William Butler Yeats. **CP-YeatW**

Deep Winter. James Schuyler. **CP-SchuJ**

Deep wooden note, A. Overheard. Denise Levertov. **CP-LeveD**

Deep Woods. Howard Nemerov. **CP-NemeH**

Deeper Than Love. David Herbert Lawrence. **CP-LawrD**

Deeper Than Love. David Herbert Lawrence. **CP-LawrD**

Deeper than sleep but not so deep as death. Night Feeding. Muriel Rukeyser. **CP-RukeM**

Deepest Sensuality, The. David Herbert Lawrence. **CP-LawrD**

Deepest sleep holds us, The. Wendell Berry. *Fr.* From the Crest. **CP-BerrW**

Deeply Morbid. Stevie Smith. **CP-SmitS**

Deer. Kenneth Rexroth. **HoPM; PBBP** *Fr.* A Bestiary. **SP-RexrK**

Deer. Dabney Stuart. **SP-StuaD**

Deer among Cattle. James Dickey. **CP-DickJ**

Deer and the dachshund are one, The. Loneliness in Jersey City. Wallace Stevens. **CP-StevW**

Deer and the Snake, The. Kenneth Patchen. **CP-PatcK**

Deer are gentle and graceful. Deer. Kenneth Rexroth. **HoPM; PBBP** *Fr.* A Bestiary. **SP-RexrK**

Deer [*or* Dear] God, / If thy smart Rod. An Ode, or Psalme, to God. Robert Herrick. **CP-HerrR**

Deer is humble, lovely as God made her, The. The Deer and the Snake. Kenneth Patchen. **CP-PatcK**

Deer Lay Down Their Bones, The. Robinson Jeffers. **CP-JefR3**

Deer were bounding like blown leaves, The. Fire on the Hills. Robinson Jeffers. **CP-JefR2**

Deerest if I by my deserving. Song. Mary Sidney, Countess of Montgomery Wroth. *Fr.* Pamphilia to Amphilanthus. **CP-WrotM**

Defamed guiltiness by silence unkempt, *see also* Answer, The ("Even when you lust, ye may refrain"). Sir Thomas Wyatt. **CP-WyatT**

Defeat. Charles Bukowski. **SP-BukC1**

Defeat. Walter de la Mare. **CP-DeLaW**

Defeat. John Hewitt. **CP-HewiJ**

Defeat. Alun Lewis. *Fr.* Two Legends: for Greece. **CP-LewiA**

Defeated. Robert Bly. **SP-BlyR**

Defeated, The. Alfred Edward Housman. **CP-HousA**

Defeated: for Wales, The. Alun Lewis. **CP-LewiA**

Defeathered. Phoebe Hesketh. **SP-HeskP**

Defective Record, The. William Carlos Williams. **CP-WilW1**

Defence for Women, A. Robert Herrick. **CP-HerrR**

Defence of Satire. Alexander Pope. *See* Ask you what provocation I have had?

Defenceless Border, The. Sir Walter Scott. **SP-ScotW** *Fr.* The Bridal of Trierman.

Defending the Faith. Allen Ginsberg. **CP-GinsA**

Defending the Provinces. Brendan Galvin. **SP-GalvB**

Defense. William Carlos Williams. **CP-WilW2**

Defense of Luxembourg. Ernest Hemingway. **CP-HemiE**

Defense of the Islands. Thomas Stearns Eliot. **CP-ElioT**

Defensio in Extremis. John Berryman. **CP-BerrJ**

Deferred. Langston Hughes. **SP-HughL**

Defiance to Cupid. William Carlos Williams. **CP-WilW2**

Define. So the drum commands. Hayden Carruth. *Fr.* Michigan Water: a Few Riffs before Dawn. **CP-CarHL**

Definite motion is accomplished. Continuation of the Landscape. Kenneth Patchen. **CP-PatcK**

Definition. Grace Paley. **CP-PaleG**

Definition. Edwin Rolfe. **CP-RolfE**

Definition in the Face of Unnamed Fury. Rita Dove. **SP-DoveR**

Definition of Beauty, The. Robert Herrick. **CP-HerrR**

Definition of Beauty is, The. Emily Dickinson. **CP-DickE**

Definition of Love, The. Andrew Marvell. **CP-MarvA**

Definition of the Frontiers. Archibald MacLeish. **CP-MacLA**

Definitions of Old Age. Archibald MacLeish. **CP-MacLA**

Deflowering. Lawrence Ferlinghetti. **SP-FerlL**

Deformed Mistress, The. Sir John Suckling. **CP-SuckJ**

Deformed Transformed, The. Byron. **CP-Byron**

Defrauded I a Butterfly. Emily Dickinson. **CP-DickE**

Deftly, admiral, cast your fly. Wystan Hugh Auden. **GTBS-6; GTBS-P** *Fr.* Five Songs ("Deftly, admiral, cast your fly"). **CP-AudeW**

(Song: "Deftly, admiral, cast your fly.") **GTBS-6; GTBS-P**

Degenerate Douglas! O [*or* oh,] the unworthy lord! William Wordsworth. **CP-WorW1**

(Sonnet Composed at—Castle.) **CP-WorW1**

Degrade first the Arts if you'd Mankind degrade. Advice of the Popes Who Succeeded the Age of Rafael. William Blake. **CP-BlakW**

Degrees of Gray in Philipsburg. Richard Hugo. **CP-HugoR**

Deign, Sovereign Mistress! to accept a Lay. Lines Inscribed in a Copy of His Poems Sent to the Queen for the Royal Library at Windsor. William Wordsworth. **CP-WorW2**

Deign[e] at my hands this crown[e] of prayer and praise. John Donne. **ChIV-2; ESCV; OBS; Son** *Fr.* La Corona. **ChIV-2; ESCV; OBS; Son** *Fr.* Holy Sonnets. **CP-DonnJ**

   (Crown, The.) **ChIV-2**

   (La Corona.) **ESCV; OBS; Son**

Deil [*or* De'il] cam fiddling through the town, The. The De'il's [*or* Deil's] Awa wi' th' [*or the*] Exciseman. Robert Burns. **CP-BurnR**

De'il's [*or* Deil's] Awa wi' th' [*or the*] Exciseman, The. Robert Burns. **CP-BurnR**

Deities and Beasts. John Updike. **CP-UpdiJ**

Deity, The. John Greenleaf Whittier. **CP-WhitJ**

Déjà, Indeed. John Updike. **CP-UpdiJ**

   ("I sometimes fear that I shall never view.") **CP-UpdiJ**

Déja Vu. Louis MacNeice. **CP-MacNL**

Dejection. Derek Mahon. **SP-MahoD**

Dejection; an Ode. Samuel Taylor Coleridge. **CP-ColeS**

Delay. Robert Herrick. **CP-HerrR**

Delay, well, travellers must expect. Autobiography at an Air-Station. Philip Larkin. **CP-LarkP**

Delayed till she had ceased to know. Emily Dickinson. **CP-DickE**

Delaying Bride, The. Robert Herrick. **CP-HerrR**

Delectable Duchy. Sir John Betjeman. **CP-BetjJ**

Delft. Rita Dove. **SP-DoveR**

Delhi. Thomas Merton. *Fr.* East with Ibn Battuta. *Fr.* East. *Fr.* The Geography of Lograire. **CP-MertT**

Delia. Robert Burns. **CP-BurnR**

Delia Rexroth. Kenneth Rexroth. **SP-RexrK**

Delia Rexroth. Kenneth Rexroth. **SP-RexrK**

Delia, th' unkindest girl on earth. William Cowper. **CP-CowpW**

Deliberate motion and the blue sound. The Soldier Who Lived Through the War. Howard Nemerov. **CP-NemeH**

Deliberately, long ago / the carcasses. From an Old House in America. Adrienne Rich. **SP-RicA1; SP-RicA2**

Delicacies, The. William Carlos Williams. **CP-WilW1**

Delicate border. A nonexistent country, A. By Train from Berlin. Erica Jong. **SP-JongE**

Delicate Cluster. Walt Whitman. **CP-WhitW**

Delicate eyes that blinked blue Rockies all ash. On Neal's Ashes. Allen Ginsberg. **CP-GinsA**

Delicate french girl jukebox husky lament, The. Growing Old Again. Allen Ginsberg. **CP-GinsA**

Delicate lepidopteran tongue, The. Hearts' and Flowers'. Archibald MacLeish. **CP-MacLA**

Delicate omens traced in air. Motto to "Fate." Ralph Waldo Emerson. **CP-EmerR**

Delicate, Plummeting Bodies, The. Stephen Dobyns. **SP-DobyS**

Delicate the syllables that release the repression. The Gentle. Theodore Roethke. **CP-RoetT**

Delicious, white, refined. Domino. James Merrill. **SP-MerrJ**

Delight—becomes pictorial. Emily Dickinson. **CP-DickE**

Delight dances. Robert Creeley. **CP-CreeR**

Delight has no Competitor. Emily Dickinson. **SP-DickE**

Delight in Disorder. Robert Herrick. **CP-HerrR**

Delight is as the flight. Emily Dickinson. **CP-DickE**

Delight is not to be trusted. Not to Be Trusted. Robert Penn Warren. **SP-WarrR**

Delight it is in youth and May. Alfred Edward Housman. **CP-HousA**

Delight of Being Alone. David Herbert Lawrence. **CP-LawrD**

Delighted excited journeying youward. Betty and Gerald Noxon. Malcolm Lowry. **CP-LowrM**

Delighted with Bluepink. Kenneth Patchen. **CP-PatcK**

Delightful Evening. Wallace Stevens. **CP-StevW**

Delight's Despair at setting. Emily Dickinson. **CP-DickE**

Delilah. Rudyard Kipling. **CP-KiplR**

   ("We have another Viceroy now,—those days are dead and done.") **CP-KiplR**

Delilah. John Milton. **SeCePo** *Fr.* Samson Agonistes. **CP-MiltJ**

Delilah Aberyswith was a lady—not too young. Delilah. Rudyard Kipling. **CP-KiplR**

Delinquent, The. Paul Laurence Dunbar. **CP-DunbP**

Delinquent. Langston Hughes. **SP-HughL**

Delinquent Travellers, The. Samuel Taylor Coleridge. **CP-ColeS**

Delirium in Los Angeles, *sl. diff. vers. incl. in* Pijijiapan. Malcolm Lowry. *Fr.* Songs for Second Childhood. **CP-LowrM**

Delirium in Vera Cruz, *also appears independently of* Cantinas *in* CP-LOWRY. Malcolm Lowry. **FaBoTw; OxBTC** *Fr.* The Cantinas. **CP-LowrM**

Deliver me from mine enemies, O my God. Psalm 59. Bible, *O.T.* *Fr.* Psalms. **CP-Psal**

Deliver me, O Lord, from the evil man. Psalm 140. Bible, *O.T.* *Fr.* Psalms. **CP-Psal**

Deliver us for thy descent. John Donne. *Fr.* A Litany. **CP-DonnJ**

Deliverance. Robert Ranke Graves. **CP-GravR**

Deliverance from a Fit of Fainting. Anne Bradstreet. **CP-BradA**

Deliverance of Jehovah, The. Bible, *O.T.* *See* Psalm 27: "Lord is my light and my salvation, The. . . ."

Deliverer, The. John Milton. *See* Oh [*or* O] how comely it is and how reviving.

Delivery to the Secular Arm, The: A Scene During the Existence of the Spanish Inquisition at Antwerp, 1570. Robert Browning. **CP-BroR2**

Della Primavera Transportata al Morale. William Carlos Williams. **CP-WilW1**

Dellius, that car which, night and day. *parody of* Horace. Rudyard Kipling. **CP-KiplR** *Fr.* The Muse among the Motors.

Delos. John Hewitt. **CP-HewiJ**

Delphi. Hilda Doolittle. **CP-DoolH**

Delphic Oracle upon Plotinus, The, *fr.* Words for Music Perhaps. William Butler Yeats. **CP-YeatW**

Delphine and Hippolyta. James Liddy. **CP-LiddJ**

Delphinium flings a shadow, A. Out of the Rainbow End. Carl Sandburg. **CP-SandC**

Delphiniums are born. Crossed Numbers. Carl Sandburg. **CP-SandC**

Delta. Adrienne Rich. **SP-RicA1**

Delta Poems. Muriel Rukeyser. **CP-RukeM**

Deluded mortals, whom the great. Libel on the Reverend Dr. Delany and His Excellency John, Lord Carteret. Jonathan Swift. **CP-SwifJ**

Deluge, The. Robert Herrick. **CP-HerrR**

Delusion of Saints. Robinson Jeffers. **CP-JefR2**

Delusions of the days that once have been. Prologue. Henry Wadsworth Longfellow. **PAH** *Fr.* Giles Corey of the Salem Farms. **SP-LongH**

Deluxe Assorted. Gilbert Sorrentino. **SP-SorrG**

Dely. Paul Laurence Dunbar. **CP-DunbP**

Demagogue. John Hewitt. **CP-HewiJ**

Demand. Langston Hughes. **SP-HughL**

Demand me again what Kafka's riddles mean. John Berryman. *Fr.* Sonnets to Chris. **CP-BerrJ**

DeMarco said the special bus. The Knot Hole Gang. Brendan Galvin. **SP-GalvB**

Demerol. Al Young. **CP-YounA**

Demeter. Hilda Doolittle. **CP-DoolH**

Demeter at Dusk. Erica Jong. **SP-JongE**

Demeter devastated our good land. The Appeasement of Demeter. George Meredith. **CP-MerG1**

Demi-Exile. Howth. Donald Davie. **CP-DavDo**

Demiurge. David Herbert Lawrence. **CP-LawrD**

Demiurge's Laugh, The. Robert Frost. **CP-FrosR**

Democracy. Leonard Cohen. **CP-CoheL**

Democracy. Langston Hughes. **SP-HughL**

Democracy. David Herbert Lawrence. **CP-LawrD**

Democracy. John Greenleaf Whittier. **CP-WhitJ**

Democracy Is Serivce. David Herbert Lawrence. **CP-LawrD**

Democratic Order, The: Such Things in Twenty Years I Understood. Alice Walker. **CP-WalkA**

Democrats. Donald Davie. **CP-DavDo**

Democritus laughed when he. Correspondences. Muriel Rukeyser. **CP-RukeM**

Demon. Anne Sexton. **CP-SextA**

Demon and Beast. William Butler Yeats. **CP-YeatW**

Demon Came to Me, A. Jean Garrigue. **SP-GarrJ**

Demon Justice. David Herbert Lawrence. **CP-LawrD**

Demon Lover, The. Erica Jong. **SP-JongE**

Demon Lover, The. Adrienne Rich. **CP-RicAE; SP-RicA1; SP-RicA2**

Demon of the Study, The. John Greenleaf Whittier. **CP-WhitJ**

Demon who throughout our late estrangement, The. This Holy Month. Robert Ranke Graves. **CP-GravR**

Demonstration, The. Frederick Morgan. **SP-MorgF**

Demonstration. Kenneth Patchen. **CP-PatcK**

Demonstrations in the streets. Stanley Jasspon Kunitz. *Fr.* Journal for My Daughter. **CP-KuniS**

Demos. Edwin Arlington Robinson. **CP-RobiE**

Demure apothecary / Whose early reverend genius my young eye. S. R. Ralph Waldo Emerson. **CP-EmerR**

Denali Road. John Haines. **SP-HainJ**

Denial, A. Elizabeth Barrett Browning. **CP-BroEB**

Denial[l]. George Herbert. **CP-HerbG**

Denial—is the only fact. Emily Dickinson. **CP-DickE**

Deniall in Women No Disheartning to Men. Robert Herrick. **CP-HerrR**

Denied night's face / have shadowless they? Edward Estlin Cummings. **CP-CummE**

Denis, / Whose motionable, alert, most vaulting wit. Gerard Manley Hopkins. **CP-HopkG**

Denise. "Bob Dylan." **CP-DylaB**

Denner's Old Woman. Vincent Bourne, *tr. fr. Latin by* William Cowper. **CP-CowpW**

Denouement. Sylvia Plath. **CP-PlatS**

Dense dark day, two sun chairs. A Held Breath. James Schuyler. **CP-SchuJ**

Dense, low, irregular overcast is flowing rapidly in over the city from the middle South, A. The Storm. Charles Kenneth Williams. **SP-WillC**

Denver tower blocks group'd under gray haze. Flying Elegy. Allen Ginsberg. **CP-GinsA**

Deny yourself all. The Thoughtful Lover. William Carlos Williams. **CP-WilW2**

Departed, The. Donald Davie. **CP-DavDo**

Departed Child! I could forget thee once. Maternal Grief. William Wordsworth. **CP-WorW1**

Departed—to the Judgment. Emily Dickinson. **CP-DickE**

Departing summer hath assumed. September, 1819. William Wordsworth. **CP-WorW2**

Departing Words to a Son, *with music.* Robert Pack. **SP-PackR**

Department of Plants and Structures— obsolete, the old name. George Oppen. **APSN** *Fr.* Route. **CP-OppeG**

Departmental. Robert Frost. **CP-FrosR**

Departure. Louise Glück. **SP-GlücL**

Departure. Thomas Hardy. **CP-HardT**

Departure, A. Rudyard Kipling. **CP-KiplR** *Fr.* Land and Sea Tales.

Departure. David Herbert Lawrence. **CP-LawrD**

Departure, The. Alun Lewis. **CP-LewiA**

Departure. Edna St. Vincent Millay. **CP-MillE**

Departure. Sylvia Plath. **CP-PlatS**

Departure. Charles Tomlinson. **CP-TomlC**

Departure from Hydra, The. Kenneth Koch. **SP-KochK**

Departure from the Bush. Margaret Atwood. **SP-AtwM1**

Departure from the Vale of Grasmere. August, 1803. William Wordsworth. **CP-WorW1**

Departure of the Good Daemon, The. Robert Herrick. **CP-HerrR**

Departure of the Ships. Howard Nemerov. **CP-NemeH**

Dependance. William Cowper. *Fr.* Olney Hymns. **CP-CowpW**

Dependence! heavy, heavy are thy chains. To Dependence. Charlotte Smith. **CP-SmitC**

Dependencies, The. Howard Nemerov. **CP-NemeH**

Deplorable his lot who tills the ground. William Wordsworth. *Fr.* Ecclesiastical Sonnets. **CP-WorW2**

Depose your finger of that Ring. Sonnet. Richard Lovelace. **CP-LoveR**

Deposition, The. Howard Nemerov. **CP-NemeH**

Deposition from Love, A. Thomas Carew. **CP-CareT**

Depot, The. Lewis Turco. **SP-TurcL**

Depravity: Two Sermons. Donald Davie. **CP-DavDo**

Depressed by a Book of Bad Poetry, I Walk toward an Unused Pasture and Invite the Insects to Join Me. James Wright. **CP-WrigJ**

Depression before Spring. Wallace Stevens. **CP-StevW**

Depression in Early Spring. Erica Jong. **SP-JongE**

Depression Wind (Winter 1930). Louise McNeill. **SP-McNeL**

Depressionism. Bill Knott. **SP-KnotB**

Deprivation. Thomas McGrath. **SP-McGrT**

Deprived of learning and. Catherine of Alexandria. Rita Dove. **SP-DoveR**

Deprived of other Banquet. Emily Dickinson. **CP-DickE**

Deprived of root, and branch, and rind. Jonathan Swift. *Fr.* Riddles. **CP-SwifJ**

Depth of Love. Robert Ranke Graves. **CP-GravR**

Depths, The. Denise Levertov. **CP-LeveD**

Der Abschied. May Sarton. **SP-SartM**

Der gute Herr Gott. Ode to Rot. John Updike. *Fr.* Seven Odes to Seven Natural Processes. **CP-UpdiJ**

Der Tag. Malcolm Lowry. **CP-LowrM**

Derbyshire. Donald Davie. **CP-DavDo**

Derbyshire Turf. Donald Davie. **CP-DavDo**

Derelict, The. Rudyard Kipling. **CP-KiplR**

Derivations. Jenny Joseph. **SP-JoseJ**
  Cherry.
  Cloud.
  Geranium.
  Lady.
  Moon.
  Rose.
  Story.
  Translation.
  Watching a child watching a witch. **AIW**
  X marks the spot. A postcard from home.

Derne. John Greenleaf Whittier. **CP-WhitJ**

Derry Morning. Derek Mahon. **SP-MahoD**

Dervish—(though yet un-dervished, call him so). The Eagle. Robert Browning. **CP-BroR2**

Dervish whined to *Said*, The. Ralph Waldo Emerson. **CP-EmerR**

Descartes and the Stove. Charles Tomlinson. **CP-TomlC**

Descartes—You There? Jenny Joseph. **SP-JoseJ**

Descend from Heaven [*or* Heav'n], Urania, by that name. John Milton. **EPCY,** *ll.* 1–31; **EBEV; NAEL-1; NOSC; OAEL-1; TOF,** *ll.* 1–39; **FiP; OBS** *Fr.* Book VII. *Fr.* Paradise Lost. **CP-MiltJ**
  (Invocation to Urania.) **FiP; OBS,** *ll.* 1–39;

Descend from Heav'n *Urania*, by that name. Book VII. John Milton. *Fr.* Paradise Lost. **CP-MiltJ**

Descend O radiant God!—the plains are thirsting. Evening, after a Picture. Johann Christoph Friedrich von Schiller, *tr. fr. German by* George Meredith. **CP-MerG2**

Descend, silent spirit. Prayer to the Snowy Owl. John Haines. **SP-HainJ**

Descend, Ye Nine. Alexander Pope. **GN** *Fr.* Ode for Music on St. Cecilia's Day. **CP-PopeA**

Descend, ye Nine! descend and sing. Ode for Music on St. Cecilia's Day. Alexander Pope. **CP-PopeA**

Descendants stretching beyond her reach. Violet at Ninety. Phoebe Hesketh. **SP-HeskP**

Descended, Adam to the bower where Eve. Adam Fallen. John Milton. **NOCV** *Fr.* Book XII. *Fr.* Paradise Lost. **CP-MiltJ**

Descending Figure. Louise Glück. **SP-GlücL**

Descending hillsides in. Across Lamarck Col. Gary Snyder. **CP-SnydG**

Descending out of the grey. Elephant Trunk. Louis MacNeice. **CP-MacNL**

Descent, The. John Hewitt. **CP-HewiJ**

Descent, The. William Carlos Williams. **CP-WilW2**

Descent. William Carlos Williams. **CP-WilW2**

Descent beckons, the. The Descent. William Carlos Williams. **CP-WilW2**

Descent from the Cross, The. Christina Georgina Rossetti. **CP-RosC2**

Descent Into Hades. Kathleen Jessie Raine. **SP-RainK**

Descent into Hell. Robert Ranke Graves. **CP-GravR**

Descent of Alette, The. Alice Notley.
  From *The Descent of Alette*, Book 3. **SP-NotlA**

Descent of Mr. Aldez, The. John Updike. **CP-UpdiJ**

Descent of Odin, The. Thomas Gray. **CP-GrayT**

Descent of Winter, The. William Carlos Williams. **CP-WilW1**
  "To freight cars in the air." **InPK**

Describe: The Rain on Dasaswamedh Ghat. Allen Ginsberg. **CP-GinsA**

Descripcion; of a Woman, The. Robert Herrick. **CP-HerrR**

Description. Charles Simic. **SP-SimiC**

Description of a City Shower, A. Jonathan Swift. **CP-SwifJ**

Description of a Maske: Presented in the Banqueting Roome at *Whitehall*, on Saint Stephens Night Last, at the Marriage of the Right Honourable the Earle of *Somerset*: and the Right Noble the Lady FRANCES *Howard*. Thomas Campion. **CP-CampT**
  "Bring away this Sacred Tree."
  "Come a shore, come, merrie mates."
  "Goe, happy man, like th' Evening Starre."
  "Let us now sing of Loves delight."
  "Pulchro pulchra datur, sociali foedere amanti."
  "Uni eqo mallem placuisse docto."
  "Vanish, vanish hence, confusion."
  "Verae ut supersint nuptiae."
  "While dancing rests, fit place to musicke graunting."

Description of a Religious House and Condition of Life, *ad. fr. the Latin* Domus non Auratae Descriptio. Richard Crashaw. **CP-CrasR**

Description of a Salamander, The. Jonathan Swift. **CP-SwifJ**

Description of an Irish Feast, The, *with music.* Hugh MacGowran, *tr. fr. Irish by* Jonathan Swift. **CP-SwifJ**

Description of an Irish Feast, The. Jonathan Swift. **CP-SwifJ**

Description of Love, A. Sir Walter Ralegh. **CP-RaleW**

Description of Mother Ludwell's Cave, A. Jonathan Swift. **CP-SwifJ**

Description of Some Confederate Soldiers, A. Randall Jarrell. **CP-JarrR**

Description of the Morning, A. Jonathan Swift. **CP-SwifJ**

Description of the sensuous, A. The Question. Robert Creeley. **CP-CreeR**

Description, Speeches, and Songs, of the Lords Maske, Presented in the Banquetting-House on the Marriage Night of the High and Mightie Count Palatine, *and the Royally Descended the Ladie* ELISABETH. Thomas Campion. *See* The Lords Mask[e].

Description without Place. Wallace Stevens. **CP-StevW**

Descriptions of Imaginary Poetries. Robert Duncan. **SP-DuncR**

Descriptive Ode, Supposed to Have Been Written under the Ruins of Rufus's Castle, A. Charlotte Smith. **CP-SmitC**

Descriptive Sketches Taken During a Pedestrian Tour among the Alps. William Wordsworth. **CP-WorW1**

Desdain ("A quoy servent tant d'artifices"), *see also* Desdain ("To what end serve the promises"). Sir John Suckling. **CP-SuckJ**

Desdain ("To what end serve the promises"), *see also* Desdain ("A quoy servent tant d'artifices"). Sir John Suckling. **CP-SuckJ**

Desdichada. Muriel Rukeyser. **CP-RukeM**

Desert / —roseate metallic blue, The. The Desert. Jim Morrison. **SP-MorrJ**

Desert. Langston Hughes. **SP-HughL**

Desert, The. Jim Morrison. **SP-MorrJ**

Desert. Richard Shelton. **SP-ShelR**

Desert as Garden of Paradise, The. Adrienne Rich. **SP-RicA1**

Desert Autumn. Charles Tomlinson. **CP-TomlC**

Desert Casino, The. Jim Carroll. **SP-CarrJ**

Desert for All of Music to Take Place. Alice Notley. **SP-NotlA**

Desert Fringe. Robert Ranke Graves. **CP-GravR**

Desert moves out on half the horizon, The. The Supper after the Last. Galway Kinnell. **SP-KinnG**

Desert Music, The. William Carlos Williams. **CP-WilW2**

Desert of Melancholy, The. Lewis Turco. **SP-TurcL**

Desert of weed and water-darkened stone under my western windows, A. People and a Heron. Robinson Jeffers. **CP-JefR1**

Desert Places. Robert Frost. **CP-FrosR**

Desert vulture / jealousy, The. George Meredith. **CP-MerG2**

Desert Wars. Tom Clark. **SP-ClarT**

Desert Water. Richard Shelton. **SP-ShelR**

Deserted Cabin. John Haines. **SP-HainJ**

Deserted Garden, The. Elizabeth Barrett Browning. **CP-BroEB**

Deserted Lumber Yard. Louise McNeill. **SP-McNeL**

Deserted Parks, The. "Lewis Carroll." **CP-CarrL**

Deserted Plantation, The. Paul Laurence Dunbar. **CP-DunbP**

Deserter, The. Alfred Edward Housman. **CP-HousA**

Deserter. Malcolm Lowry. **CP-LowrM**

Deserter, The. Stevie Smith. **CP-SmitS**

Design. Robert Frost. **CP-FrosR**

Design for November. William Carlos Williams. **CP-WilW2**

Design in Living Colors. Adrienne Rich. **CP-RicAE**

Design of a House, The. Wendell Berry. **CP-BerrW**

Desire. Samuel Taylor Coleridge. **CP-ColeS**

Desire. Stephen Dobyns. **SP-DobyS**

Desire. Stephen Dunn. **SP-DunnS**

Desire. Langston Hughes. **SP-HughL**

Desire. David Herbert Lawrence. **CP-LawrD**

Desire. David St. John. **SP-StJoD**

Desire / The. The. Louis Zukofsky. **CP-ZukLS**

Desire, alas, my master and my foe. Sir Thomas Wyatt. **CP-WyatT**

Desire and / All the sweet pulsing aches. Killed Piave—July 8—1918. Ernest Hemingway. **CP-HemiE**

Desire and Jealousy. William Blake. **ECEV** *Fr.* Visions of the Daughters of Albion. **CP-BlakW**

Desire and Possession. Jonathan Swift. **CP-SwifJ**

Desire and terror then had each of each. George Meredith. *Fr.* Napoléon. **CP-MerG1**

Desire, first, by a natural miracle. The Snapped Thread. Robert Ranke Graves. **CP-GravR**

Desire for Spring. Kenneth Koch. **SP-KochK**

Desire Goes Down into the Sea. David Herbert Lawrence. **CP-LawrD**

Desire has failed, desire has failed. Grasshopper Is a Burden. David Herbert Lawrence. **CP-LawrD**

Desire Is a World by Night. John Berryman. **CP-BerrJ**

Desire Is Dead. David Herbert Lawrence. **CP-LawrD**

Desire (Liner Notes). "Bob Dylan." **CP-DylaB**

Desire no bread, forsake the guest hall of the earth. Hafiz, *tr. by* Ralph Waldo Emerson. **CP-EmerR** *Fr.* Odes.

Desire of Wine. John Milton. **FaBoDD** *Fr.* Samson Agonistes. **CP-MiltJ**

Desire, though thou my old companion art. Sonnet 72. Sir Philip Sidney. **NAEL-1** *Fr.* Astrophil and Stella. **SP-SidnP**

Desire to sorrow doth me constrain. Sir Thomas Wyatt. **CP-WyatT**

Desire we past illusions to recall? William Wordsworth. *Fr.* Poems Composed or Suggested During a Tour, in the Summer of 1833. **CP-WorW2**

Desired as Summer rain. George Meredith. **CP-MerG2**

Desires of Men and Women. John Berryman. **CP-BerrJ**

Desist Cockchafers: You Kamikaze Beetles of June. Cockchafer. Isabella Gardner. **CP-GardI**

Desist, thou analytic wretch! Memo to His Lady's Therapist. David Markson. **CP-MarkD**

Desmond has a barrow in the market place. Ob-La-Di Ob-La-Da. The Beatles. **CP-BeatI**

Desmond, what of the blue nights. The Sea in Winter. Derek Mahon. **SP-MahoD**

Desnos Reading the Palms of Men on Their Way to the Gas Chambers. Stephen Berg. **SP-BergS**

Desolate and lone. Lost. Carl Sandburg. **CP-SandC**

Desolate Field, The. William Carlos Williams. **CP-WilW1**

Desolate is the room where the cat sat. Canto 39. Ezra Pound. *Fr.* Cantos. **CP-PoCan**

Desolate lemons, hold. Sunday Lemons. Derek Walcott. **CP-WalcD**

Desolation. Wendell Berry. **CP-BerrW**

Desolation, A. Allen Ginsberg. **CP-GinsA**

Desolation. Thomas Merton. *Fr.* Readings from Ibn Abbad. **CP-MertT**

Desolation Dreamed Of. Edna St. Vincent Millay. **CP-MillE**

Desolation Row. "Bob Dylan." **CP-DylaB**

Despair. John Berryman. **CP-BerrJ**

Despair. Samuel Taylor Coleridge. **CP-ColeS**

Despair. Paul Laurence Dunbar. **CP-DunbP**

Despair. Richard Eberhart. **CP-EberR**

Despair. Christina Georgina Rossetti. **CP-RosC3**

Despair. Anne Sexton. **CP-SextA**

Despair. Percy Bysshe Shelley. *Fr.* Original Poetry by Victor and Cazire. **CP-ShelP**

Despair. Percy Bysshe Shelley. *Fr.* Posthumous Fragments of Margaret Nicholson. **CP-ShelP**

Despair. Edmund Spenser. **SeCePo** *Fr.* The Faerie Queene. **CP-Spens**

Despair that is silent, A. Day Born Without a Mouth. Chuck Miller. **SP-MillC**

Despair was what I called. Sticks. Stephen Berg. **SP-BergS**

Despaire takes heart, when ther's no hope to speed. Fear[e] Gets Force. Robert Herrick. **CP-HerrR**

Despairing Man Draws a Serpent, The. Pablo Antonio Cuadra, *tr. fr. Spanish by* Thomas Merton. **CP-MertT**

Despair's advantage is achieved. Emily Dickinson. **CP-DickE**

Desperate, The. Alun Lewis. **CP-LewiA**

Desperate, The. Chuck Miller. **SP-MillC**

Desperate young man. The Halfworld. William Carlos Williams. **CP-WilW1**

Desperately my spirit wiled me. A Dream. Wystan Hugh Auden. **CP-AudWJ**

Despisals. Muriel Rukeyser. **CP-RukeM**

Despised and Rejected. Christina Georgina Rossetti. **CP-RosC1** "Then I cried out upon him: Cease." **PeVV**

Despite and Still. Robert Ranke Graves. **CP-GravR**

Despite his nightly cup of chicken soup. Clayfeld's Metamorphosis. Robert Pack. **SP-PackR**

Despite strangulated cries. Slick. Daniel Gerard Hoffman. **SP-HoffD**

Despite the darkened / pews and cloisters, I see—at once. The Mural of Wakeful Sleep. Laurence Lieberman. **SP-LiebL**

Despite the lonesome look. On the London Train. John Berryman. **CP-BerrJ**

Despite this learned cult's official. Apollo of the Physiologists. Robert Ranke Graves. **CP-GravR**

Despite us / there is only one universe, the sun. Margaret Atwood. *Fr.* Two-Headed Poems. **SP-AtwM2**

Despond who will—*I heard a voice exclaim.* William Wordsworth. *Fr.* Poems Composed or Suggested During a Tour, in the Summer of 1833. **CP-WorW2**

Despondency, *sels.* William Wordsworth. *Fr.* The Excursion. **CP-WorW2**

Despondency, an Ode. Robert Burns. **CP-BurnR**

Despondency Corrected. William Wordsworth. *Fr.* The Excursion. **CP-WorW2**

"As men from men." **EnRP**

"Curious child, who dwelt upon a tract, A." **WGRP**

Desponding Father! Mark This Altered Bough. William Wordsworth. **CP-WorW2**

Desponding Phyllis was endued. Phyllis [*or* Phillis *or* Progress of Love, The]. Jonathan Swift. **CP-SwifJ**

Despots of Manchester, Oligarchs! George Meredith. **CP-MerG2**

Destined lover, whom his stars, The. The Lover's Stars. Gerard Manley Hopkins. **CP-HopkG**

Destined Pair, The. Thomas Hardy. **CP-HardT**

Destined to war from very infancy. Gabriello Chiabrera, *tr. fr.* Italian by William Wordsworth. **CP-WorW1**

Destinies, destinations: In Morrisville. Hayden Carruth. *Fr.* The Sleeping Beauty. **CP-CarHL**

Destiny. David Herbert Lawrence. **CP-LawrD**

Destiny of Nations, The. Samuel Taylor Coleridge. **CP-ColeS**

" 'Even so' (the exulting Maiden said)." **ChER**

"For what is Freedom, but the unfettered use." **EnRP**

Destroyers, The. Rudyard Kipling. **CP-KiplR**

Destroyers. Carl Sandburg. **CP-SandC**

Destroyers in Collision. Rudyard Kipling. *Fr.* Epitaphs of the War [1914–1918]. **CP-KiplR**

Destroying Beauty. Charles Bukowski. **SP-BukC2**

Destruction. Alun Lewis. **CP-LewiA**

Destruction of Carthage, The. Kenneth Patchen. **CP-PatcK**

Destruction of Grief. Muriel Rukeyser. **CP-RukeM**

Destruction of Sennacherib, The. Byron. **CP-Byron**

Destruction of the Bastile. Samuel Taylor Coleridge. **CP-ColeS**

Desultory Stanzas, upon Receiving the Preceding Sheets from the Press. William Wordsworth. *Fr.* Memorials of a Tour of the Continent; 1820. **CP-WorW2**

Detached, The. Maya Angelou. **SP-AngeM**

Detail, A. Gilbert Sorrentino. **SP-SorrG**

Detail. William Carlos Williams. **CP-WilW2**

Detail. William Carlos Williams. **CP-WilW2**

Detail. William Carlos Williams. **CP-WilW2**

Detail. William Carlos Williams. **CP-WilW2**

Details for Paterson. William Carlos Williams. **CP-WilW2**

Detective, The. Sylvia Plath. **CP-PlatS**

Detective Story. Wystan Hugh Auden. **CP-AudeW**

Detectives from the vice squad. Café: 3 A.M. Langston Hughes. **SP-HughL**

Determined to love / Lured by the barbarous fowl. Thomas Merton. *Fr.* Cables to the Ace. **CP-MertT**

Detestable race, continue to expunge yourself, die out. Apostrophe to Man. Edna St. Vincent Millay. **CP-MillE**

Dethroned. Wystan Hugh Auden. **CP-AudWJ**

Detraction Execrated. Sir John Suckling. **CP-SuckJ**

Detroit Grease Shop Poem. Philip Levine. **SP-LeviP**

Detroit 1958. Al Young. **CP-YounA**

Deuks Dang o'er My Daddie, The. Robert Burns. **CP-BurnR**

Deutsch durch Freud. Randall Jarrell. **CP-JarrR; SP-JarrR**

Deutzia. Louis Zukofsky. **CP-ZukLS**

Deux Morceaux en Forme de Banane. Gilbert Sorrentino. **SP-SorrG**

Devastation / of being, The. Song. Frederick Morgan. **SP-MorgF**

Development. Robert Browning. **CP-BroR2**

Development, The. Marge Piercy. **SP-PierM** *Fr.* Sand Roads.

Devereaux wakes this morning with a dream of mountains. Gliding. Jim Carroll. **SP-CarrJ**

Deviation, The. Louise Glück. *Fr.* Dedication to Hunger. **SP-GlücL**

Devil believes that the Lord will come, The. The Two Round Spaces on the Tombstone. Samuel Taylor Coleridge. **CP-ColeS**

Devil crept in eden wood. Edward Estlin Cummings. **CP-CummE**

Devil got notice that Grose was a-dying, The. Epigram on Capt. Francis Grose, the Celebrated Antiquary. Robert Burns. **CP-BurnR**

Devil, had he fidelity, The. Emily Dickinson. **CP-DickE**

Devil is a gentleman, The. Malcolm Lowry. **CP-LowrM**

Devil-My-Wife, The. Stevie Smith. **CP-SmitS**

Devil now knew his proper cue, The. Percy Bysshe Shelley. **OBSV** *Fr.* Peter Bell the Third. **CP-ShelP**

Devil on Ice. Donald Davie. **CP-DavDo**

Devil return'd to hell by two, The. The Devil's Drive. Byron. **CP-Byron**

Devil was a Gentleman, The. Malcolm Lowry. *Fr.* Songs for Second Childhood. **CP-LowrM**

Devilish and the dark, the dying and diseas'd, The. The Rounded Catalogue Divine Complete. Walt Whitman. **CP-WhitW**

Devil's Advice to Story-Tellers, The. Robert Ranke Graves. **CP-GravR**

Devil's Drive, The. Byron. **CP-Byron**

Devil's Thoughts, The. Samuel Taylor Coleridge. **CP-ColeS**

Devil's Walk, The. Percy Bysshe Shelley. **CP-ShelP**

Devonshire. Donald Davie. **CP-DavDo**

Devonshire Road, A. Samuel Taylor Coleridge. **CP-ColeS**

Devonshire Street W.1. Sir John Betjeman. **CP-BetjJ**

Devotion. Robert Frost. **CP-FrosR**

Devotion, A. Kenneth Patchen. **CP-PatcK**

Devotion Makes the Deity. Robert Herrick. **CP-HerrR**

Devotion should always wear a fence. Emily Dickinson. **SP-DickE**

Devotion: That It Flow; That There Be Concentration. Tess Gallagher. **SP-GallT**

Devotional Incitements. William Wordsworth. **CP-WorW2**

Devotions. James Wright. **CP-WrigJ**

Devouring Time, blunt thou the lion's paws. Sonnet 19. William Shakespeare. **AWP; ChTr; EBEV; HeIP; ImPo; MAT; NAEL-1; NoSic; OAEL-1; OBSC; OXAEP-1; PoE; PoEL-2; SCGP; TrGrPo; WHA** *Fr.* Sonnets. **CP-ShaWS**

Devout Fits. John Donne. *See* Oh, to vex me, contraries [*or* conrraryes] meet in one.

Dew falls but the, The. Charles Henri Ford. **SP-FordC** *Fr.* Emblems of Arachne.

Dew is drying fast, a last drop glistens, The. John Berryman. *Fr.* Sonnets to Chris. **CP-BerrJ**

Dew—is the Freshet in the Grass. Emily Dickinson. **CP-DickE**

Dew Sat on Julia's Hair. Robert Herrick.

(Upon Julia's Haire Fill'd with Dew.) **CP-HerrR**

Dew steams off the thatches, The. Wystan Hugh Auden. **CP-AudWJ**

Dew suffced itself, A. Emily Dickinson. **CP-DickE**

Dew, sweat, grass-prickle, tantrums. Bad. William Matthews. **SP-MattW**

Dew, the rain and moonlight, The. A Net to Snare the Moonlight. Nicholas Vachel Lindsay. **CP-LindV**

Dew was falling fast, the stars began to blink, The. Pet Lamb, The; A Pastoral. William Wordsworth. **CP-WorW1**

Dews drop slowly and dreams gather, The: unknown spears. The Valley of the Black Pig. William Butler Yeats. **CP-YeatW**

Dewy fields in the morning under the sun. Gerard Manley Hopkins. *Fr.* Fragments. **CP-HopkG**

Dexter Gordon at Keystone Korner. Al Young. **CP-YounA**

Dey been speakin' at de cou't-house. Speakin' at de Cou't-House. Paul Laurence Dunbar. **CP-DunbP**

Dey had a gread big pahty down to Tom's de othah night. The Party. Paul Laurence Dunbar. **CP-DunbP**

Dey is snow upon de meddahs. Snowin'. Paul Laurence Dunbar. **CP-DunbP**

Dey is times in life when Nature. When de Co'n Pone's Hot. Paul Laurence Dunbar. **CP-DunbP**

Dey was onct a awful quoil. Trouble in de Kitchen. Paul Laurence Dunbar. **CP-DunbP**

Dey was talkin' in de cabin, dey was talkin' in de hall. When Dey 'Listed Colored Soldiers. Paul Laurence Dunbar. **CP-DunbP**

Dey's a so't o' threatenin' feelin' in de blowin' of de breeze. Soliloquy of a Turkey. Paul Laurence Dunbar. **CP-DunbP**

Dezembrum. Wallace Stevens. **CP-StevW**

D.G.C. to J.A. Emily Brontë. **CP-BronE**

Diabetes. James Dickey. **CP-DickJ**

Diabolo. Marsden Hartley. **CP-HartM**

Diaghilev Did Not Say "Étonnez-Moi." Gilbert Sorrentino. **SP-SorrG**

Diagnosis is / Anxiety psychoneurosis, The. Hayden Carruth. **CP-CarHS** *Fr.* The Bloomingdale Papers.

Diagonal white city dreamed by a Frenchman. Washington. John Updike. **CP-UpdiJ**

Diagram. Robinson Jeffers. **CP-JefR3**

Diagrams. Thom Gunn. **CP-GunnT**

Diagrams, The. Frederick Morgan. **SP-MorgF**

Dial Tone, The. Howard Nemerov. **CP-NemeH**

Dialectic. Charles Tomlinson. **CP-TomlC**

Dialectical Songs. Howard Nemerov. **CP-NemeH**

"Let sin be preordained."

Lucifer.

"Now that the salt has lost its savor."

Dialog with Mister Clapcott. Thomas Merton. *Fr.* East. *Fr.* The Geography of Lograire. **CP-MertT**

Dialogue, A. George Herbert. **CP-HerbG**

Dialogue. Frederick Morgan. *Fr.* Eight Triolets. **SP-MorgF**

Dialogue. Howard Nemerov. **CP-NemeH**

Dialogue, A. Alexander Pope. **CP-PopeA**

Dialogue. Adrienne Rich. **SP-RicA2**

Dialogue. Carl Sandburg. **CP-SandC**

Dialogue, A. Percy Bysshe Shelley. **CP-ShelP**

Dialogue. Charles Tomlinson. **CP-TomlC**

Dialogue-Anthem, A. George Herbert. **CP-HerbG**

Dialogue between an Eminent Lawyer and Dr. Swift, Dean of St. Patrick's. Jonathan Swift. **CP-SwifJ**

Dialogue between Captain Tom and Sir Henry Dutton Colt, A. Jonathan Swift. **CP-SwifJ**

Dialogue between Father and Daughter. Robert Browning. **CP-BroR2**

Dialogue between Ghost and Priest. Sylvia Plath. **CP-PlatS**

Dialogue between Old England and New, A. Anne Bradstreet. **CP-BradA**

Dialogue between Old England and New, A. Anne Bradstreet. **CP-BradA**
New England. **KTR**
Old England. **KTR**

Dialogue between Soul and Body, A. Randall Jarrell. **CP-JarrR**

Dialogue between the Resolved Soul and Created Pleasure, A. Andrew Marvell. **CP-MarvA**

Dialogue Between the Self & the Soul. Anne Waldman. **SP-WaldA**

Dialogue between the Soul and [the] Body, A. Andrew Marvell. **CP-MarvA**

Dialogue between Thyrsis and Dorinda, A. Andrew Marvell. **CP-MarvA**

Dialogue Betwixt Himselfe and Mistresse Eliza: Wheeler, Under the Name of Amarillis, A. Robert Herrick. **CP-HerrR**

Dialogue En Route. Sylvia Plath. **CP-PlatS**

Dialogue in Milan. David Markson. **CP-MarkD**

Dialogue. Lucasta, Alexis. Richard Lovelace. **CP-LoveR**

Dialogue. Lute and Voice, A. Richard Lovelace. **CP-LoveR**

Dialogue of Birds for Howard Nemerov, A. Kay Boyle. **CP-BoylK**

Dialogue of Self and Soul, A. William Butler Yeats. **CP-YeatW**

Dialogue of Watching, A. Kenneth Rexroth. **SP-RexrK** *Fr.* Seven Poems for Marthe, My Wife.

Dialogue on the Headland. Robert Ranke Graves. **CP-GravR**

Dialogue: Sheapherd, and Sheapherdess. Mary Sidney, Countess of Montgomery Wroth. *Fr.* Urania. **CP-WrotM**

Dialogue Sung the First Night, A. Thomas Campion. *Fr.* The Ayres that Were Sung and Played, at *Brougham Castle* in *Westmerland*, in the Kings Entertainment. **CP-CampT**

Dialogue with a Door. Catullus. *See* Carmen 67: "Sweet entrance to a husband's pleasure."

Dialogue with Outer Space. John Ciardi. **SP-CiarJ**

Diamond Cutters, The. Adrienne Rich. **CP-RicAE; SP-RicA1; SP-RicA2**

Diamond grand, The. Why My Mother Likes Liberace. Diane Wakoski. **SP-WakoD**

Diamond on the Hand, A. Emily Dickinson. **CP-DickE**

Diamond or a coal? / A diamond, if you please, A. Christina Georgina Rossetti. **CP-RosC2**

Diamonds in the Mine. Leonard Cohen. **CP-CoheL**

Diamonds on Liz's Bosom, The. Alice Walker. **CP-WalkA**

Dian, that fain would cheer her friend the Night. Sonnet 97. Sir Philip Sidney. *Fr.* Astrophil and Stella. **SP-SidnP**

Diana guardeth our estate. Catullus. *See* Carmen 34: "Moving in her radiant care."

Diana, sum us in faith a. Catullus. *See* Carmen 34: "Moving in her radiant care."

Dianae Sumus in Fide. Catullus. *See* Carmen 34: "Moving in her radiant care."

Diana's Hunting-Song. John Dryden. **NOBE; SeCePo** *Fr.* The Secular Masque. **SP-DrydJ**

Diaries. Anne Waldman. **SP-WaldA**

Diaries of Death. Charles Olson. **CP-OlsoC**

Diary. Jenny Joseph. **SP-JoseJ**

Diary of a Church Mouse. Sir John Betjeman. **CP-BetjJ**

Diary of Desert War. Tom Clark. **SP-ClarT**

Diaspora. Wystan Hugh Auden. **CP-AudeW**

Diatribe Against the Old Gods. Clement of Alexandria, *tr. fr. Greek.*
Idol of Sarapis, The. **CP-MertT**
Priests of the Old Gods, The. **CP-MertT**
Zeus Is Dead. **CP-MertT**

Dic ubi nunc quod amo est! ubinam quod semper amavi? Elegia VIII. Robert Southwell. **CP-SoutR**

Dice, The. Frank Templeton Prince. **CP-PrinF**

Dichotomy. John Hewitt. **CP-HewiJ**

Dichtung und Wahrheit. Wystan Hugh Auden. **CP-AudeW**

Dick, a Maggot. Jonathan Swift. **CP-SwifJ**

Dick, I went back to those rocks today. Note from Capri to Richard Ryan on the Adriatic Floor. Richard Hugo. **CP-HugoR**

Dick Mid's large bluish face without eyebrows. Edward Estlin Cummings. **CP-CummE**

Dick, thou'rt resolved, as I am told. The First Ode of the Second Book of Horace Paraphrased and Addressed to Richard Steele, Esq. Jonathan Swift. **CP-SwifJ**

Dick's Variety. Jonathan Swift. **CP-SwifJ**

"Dicky the Stick"—. Robert Creeley. **CP-CreeR**

Dictatorial Owl, The. Charlotte Smith. **CP-SmitC**

Dictic, *one-word poem.* One Word as the Complete Poem. Charles Olson. **CP-OlsoC**

Diction. Robert Creeley. **CP-CreeR**

Dictum. Countee Cullen. **CP-CullC**

Dicty Glide in Central Park Menagerie. Charles Henri Ford. **SP-FordC**

Did all the lets and bars appear. The March into Virginia. Herman Melville. **SP-MelvH**

Did any bird come flying. Bird or Beast? Christina Georgina Rossetti. **CP-RosC1**

Did Cytherea to the skies. On a Bath. Plato, *tr. fr. Greek by* William Cowper. **CP-CowpW**

Did ever problem thus perplex. The Problem. Jonathan Swift. **CP-SwifJ**

Did he who drew her in the years ago. To an Imposter of Rosalind. Thomas Hardy. **CP-HardT**

Did Helen steal my love from me? Gerard Manley Hopkins. **CP-HopkG**

Did I believe I had a clear mind? Breaking. Wendell Berry. **CP-BerrW**

Did I boast of liberty? Mary Sidney, Countess of Montgomery Wroth. *Fr.* Urania. **CP-WrotM**

Did I come from this, a hardware store. Iowa Déjà Vu. Richard Hugo. **CP-HugoR**

Did I hear it half in a doze. Tennyson. *Fr.* Maud [A Monodrama]. **CP-TennA**

Did I or love, or could I others draw. To His Honoured Friend, M. John Weare, Councellour. Robert Herrick. **CP-HerrR**

Did I see a crucifix in your eyes. Crimson Changes People. Carl Sandburg. **CP-SandC**

Did I see it go by. A Wish to Comply. Robert Frost. **CP-FrosR**

Did I tell you of a strange dream I had? The Inland Sea. Jenny Joseph. **SP-JoseJ**

Did I write this. Charles Kenneth Williams. **SP-WillC**

Did it come from. Kušiwoqqóbī. Gary Snyder. **CP-SnydG**

Did it once issue from the carver's hand. The Sphinx. Wystan Hugh Auden. *Fr.* A Voyage. **CP-AudeW**

Did life's penurious length. Emily Dickinson. **CP-DickE**

Did no one else, then, see them, man. The Single Witness. Thomas Hardy. **CP-HardT**

Did not my muse (what can she less?). An Apology. William Cowper. **CP-CowpW**

Did not the heavenly rhetoric of thine eye, *sl. diff. vers. also in* Love's Labours Lost, IV, iii. *Various Authors.* **CP-ShaWS** *Fr.* The Passionate Pilgrim. **CP-ShaWS**

Did not thy reason and thy sense. An Attempt at the Manner of Waller. William Cowper. **CP-CowpW**

Did not want the air. Song, The. Ted Hughes. **SP-HughT**

Did one look at what one saw. Hieroglyphic. Hart Crane. **CP-CranH**

Did Our Best Moment last. Emily Dickinson. **CP-DickE**

Did pangs of grief for lenient time too keen. Isle of Man. William Wordsworth. *Fr.* Poems Composed or Suggested During a Tour, in the Summer of 1833. **CP-WorW2**

Did she suffer—except to leave you? Emily Dickinson. **SP-DickE**

Did someone say that there would be an end. All Souls. May Sarton. **SP-SartM**

Did ter notice that lass, sister, as stood away back. Violets for the Dead. David Herbert Lawrence. **CP-LawrD**

Did the fingers of the hand. Odi et Amo. Alun Lewis. **CP-LewiA**

Did the Harebell loose her girdle. Emily Dickinson. **CP-DickE**

Did the people of Viet Nam. What Were They Like? Denise Levertov. **CP-LeveD**

Did these night-hung houses. The Suicide. Walter de la Mare. **CP-DeLaW**

Did they catch as it were in a Vision at shut of the day. Jezreel. Thomas Hardy. **CP-HardT**

Did they send me away from my cat and my wife. Gunner. Randall Jarrell. **CP-JarrR**

Did This Happen to Your Mother? Did Your Sister Throw Up a Lot? Alice Walker. **CP-WalkA**

Did We abolish Frost. Emily Dickinson. **CP-DickE**

Did we count great, O soul, to penetrate the themes of mighty books. My Canary Bird. Walt Whitman. **CP-WhitW**

Did we disobey Him? Emily Dickinson. **CP-DickE**

Did you ask dulcet rhymes from me? To a Certain Civilian. Walt Whitman. **CP-WhitW**

Did you bring the bottle, Mr. J.? And in Another Place Uses the Same Phrase. Kenneth Patchen. **CP-PatcK**

Did you ever go down to the river. Reverie on the Harlem River. Langston Hughes. **SP-HughL**

Did you ever stand in a Cavern's Mouth. Emily Dickinson. **CP-DickE**

Did you hear? The Old Warrior Terror. Alice Walker. **CP-WalkA**

Did you notice all the water. Knokke. Robert Creeley. **CP-CreeR**

Did you see something within the house. She Who Saw Not. Thomas Hardy. **CP-HardT**

Did you see the streetcars. Streetcars. Leonard Cohen. **CP-CoheL**

Did you stay up last night (the Magi did). A Loose Mountain. Robert Frost. **CP-FrosR**

Did you think I was talking about my life? 7/14/68: i. Adrienne Rich. **CP-RicAE** *Fr.* Ghazals: Homage to Ghalib. **SP-RicA2**

Didactic Laurel, loose your reasoning leaf. The Maimed Man. Allen Tate. **CP-TateA**

Didactic Piece. Louise Bogan. **CP-BogaL**

Didactic Poem. Denise Levertov. **CP-LeveD**

Didn't own much. George. Barton Sutter. **SP-SuttB**

Dido am I, the founder first of Carthage. Sir Thomas Wyatt. **CP-WyatT**

Dido My Dear, Alas, Is Dead. Edmund Spenser. **ChTr** *Fr.* November. **PoEL-1** *Fr.* The Shepheardes [*or* Shepeards *or* Shepherd's] Calender. **CP-Spens**

Dido was the *Carthage* Queene. Ballad, A. Thomas Campion. *Fr.* The Ayres that Were Sung and Played, at *Brougham Castle* in *Westmerland*, in the Kings Entertainment. **CP-CampT**

Dido's Farewell to Aeneas. Stevie Smith. **CP-SmitS**

Didst thou not find the place inspired [*or* inspir'd]. Upon My Lady Carlisle's Walking in Hampton Court Garden. Sir John Suckling. **CP-SuckJ**

Didymus. Louis MacNeice. **CP-MacNL**

Didymus. Louis MacNeice. **EaLo** *Fr.* Entered in the Minutes. **CP-MacNL**

"Last light purples the mirrors of paddy, the tracks, The."

"Million simmering kettles: in the Destroyer's shrine, A."

"Nothing more simple. Among the tarnished."

"Oh but my doubt is a sea harsher than this that I see."

Die Älte Frau, Die Älte Marschallin. William Dickey. **SP-DickW**

Die, Boreas, / And drown your ruins in the gaudy sea. Canticle for the Blessed Virgin. Thomas Merton. **CP-MertT**

Die ere long I'm sure, I shall. After Autumne, Winter. Robert Herrick. **CP-HerrR**

Die Gold Orangen. Robert Lowell. *Fr.* Eight Months Later. **SP-LoweR**

Die in the grain. King of the Wood / King of the Dead. Charles Olson. **CP-OlsoC**

Die Lorelei. Stevie Smith. **CP-SmitS**

Die Neuen Heiligen. John Updike. **CP-UpdiJ**

Died. . . . Elizabeth Barrett Browning. **CP-BroEB**

Died in the meadow, there. The Green Fires. Kenneth Patchen. **CP-PatcK**

Dien Bien Phu. Adrienne Rich. **SP-RicA2**

Dieppe, Dieppe ("Again the last ebb"). Samuel Beckett. **CP-BeckS**

Dieppe, Dieppe ("Encore le dernier reflux"). Samuel Beckett. **CP-BeckS**

Dies Illa. David Herbert Lawrence. **CP-LawrD**

Dies Irae. David Herbert Lawrence. **CP-LawrD**

Dies Irae. Thomas of Celano, *tr. fr. Latin by* Richard Crashaw. **CP-CrasR**

Diet. Robert Herrick. **CP-HerrR**

Difference, A. Tom Clark. **SP-ClarT**

Difference, The. Thomas Hardy. **CP-HardT**

Difference, The. David Herbert Lawrence. **CP-LawrD**

Difference between / me &, The. Imaginary Number. Archie Randolph Ammons. **SP-AmmoA**

Difference between Despair, The. Emily Dickinson. **CP-DickE**

Difference between you and her, The. Song: Dew-Drop and Diamond. Robert Ranke Graves. **CP-GravR**

Difference Betwixt King and Subjects, The. Robert Herrick. **CP-HerrR**

Difference of Ages. Marge Piercy. *Fr.* Walking into Love. **SP-PierM**

Difference of Opinion with Lygdamus. Ezra Pound. **MeMAP** *Fr.* Homage to Sextus Propertius. **SP-PounE**

Differences. John Ciardi. **SP-CiarJ**

Differences. Paul Laurence Dunbar. **CP-DunbP**

Differences, The. Thom Gunn. **CP-GunnT**

Different. Phoebe Hesketh. **SP-HeskP**

Different Cereal, A. John Yau. **SP-YauJo**

Different Clare, as foam-whipped as line-edged by poor men, A. Clare, the Butterflies. James Liddy. **CP-LiddJ**

Different Drum, A. Leonard Cohen. **CP-CoheL**

Different kind of thought, A. Come On! William Carlos Williams. **CP-WilW2**

Different Kinds of Good-by. Carl Sandburg. **CP-SandC**

Different Prince, A. John Yau. **SP-YauJo**

Different Ship, A. Pablo Neruda, *tr. fr. Spanish by* Ben Belitt. **SP-NeruP**

Difficult achievement for true lovers, A. The Starred Coverlet. Robert Ranke Graves. **CP-GravR**

Difficult Death. David Herbert Lawrence. **CP-LawrD**

Difficult friend, I would have preferred. Tristia: 1891–1938. Geoffrey Hill. *Fr.* Four Poems Regarding the Endurance of Poets. **CP-HillG**

Difficult Man, A. John Hewitt. **CP-HewiJ**

"Difficult ordinary happiness," / no one nowadays believes in you. In the Woods. Adrienne Rich. **CP-RicAE; SP-RicA1; SP-RicA2**

Difficult part of love, The. Love. Philip Larkin. **CP-LarkP**

Difficult Resolution, The. Randall Jarrell. **CP-JarrR**

Difficult to think of a stone's gratitude. The Stone. Hayden Carruth. *Fr.* Contra Mortem. **CP-CarHL**

Difficulties of a Statesman. Thomas Stearns Eliot. *Fr.* Coriolan. **CP-ElioT**

Difficulties, the impossibilities, The. Robert Lowell. **SP-LoweR** *Fr.* Mexico.

Difficulty of Ideas, The. Richard Eberhart. **CP-EberR**

Difficulty to think at the end of day, The. A Rabbit as King of the Ghosts. Wallace Stevens. **CP-StevW**

Diffidently, when asked who might I be. Powers Unconfessed. Robert Ranke Graves. **CP-GravR**

Diffugere Nives. Alfred Edward Housman. **CP-HousA**

Diffuse the outpourings of the spiritual coward. Prognosis. Theodore Roethke. **CP-RoetT**

Dig a Pony. John Lennon *and* Paul McCartney. **CP-Beatl**

Dig It. The Beatles. **CP-Beatl**

Digger Indians were too primitive, The. Marge Piercy. *Fr.* Doing It Differently. **SP-PierM**

Digging. Margaret Atwood. **SP-AtwM1**

Digging. Donald Hall. **CP-HallD**

Digging. Seamus Heaney. **SP-HeanS**

Digging for China. Richard Wilbur. **CP-WilbR**

Digging for Indians. Gary Gildner. **SP-GildG**

Digging In. Marge Piercy. **SP-PierM**

Digging Is an Art. Richard Hugo. **CP-HugoR**

Digging Wonder. Archie Randolph Ammons. **SP-AmmoA**

Digging Worms. Robert Bly. **SP-BlyR**

Dignissimo Suo Amico Doctori Witty, *see also* To His Worthy Friend Doctor Witty upon His Translation of the "Popular Errors." Andrew Marvell. **CP-MarvA**

Dijon. Daniel Gerard Hoffman. **SP-HoffD**

Dilemma, The. Robert Ranke Graves. **CP-GravR**

Dilemma. Phoebe Hesketh. **SP-HeskP**

Dilemma, The. John Hewitt. **CP-HewiJ**

Dilemma in the Delta. John Updike. **CP-UpdiJ**

Dilettante, The: A Modern Type. Paul Laurence Dunbar. **CP-DunbP**

Dillingham, Alaska, the Willow Tree Bar. Gary Snyder. **CP-SnydG**

Dilton Marsh Halt. Sir John Betjeman. **CP-BetjJ**

Diluculo surgit Sapiens, et per juga nigra. Philosophus et Phasiani. John Gay, *tr. fr. English by* William Cowper. **CP-CowpW**

Dim / i / nu / tiv / e this park is e. Edward Estlin Cummings. **CP-CummE**

Dim, as the borrow's beam of moon and stars. John Dryden. **FiP; NOSC; OAEL-1; OBS; OxBoCh** *Fr.* Religio Laici. **SP-DrydJ**

(Reason and Religion.) **FiP**

(Reason and Revelation.) **OBS**

Dim, as the borrowed beam of moon and stars. Religio Laici. John Dryden. **SP-DrydJ**

Dim-berried is the mistletoe. Before Dawn. Walter de la Mare. **CP-DeLaW**

Dim boy claps because the others clap, The. The Freaks at Spurgin Road Field. Richard Hugo. **CP-HugoR**

Dim dawn behind the tamarisks—the sky is saffron-yellow. Christmas in India. Rudyard Kipling. **CP-KiplR**

Dim deep of a yellow evening slides, The. Vision. Edward Estlin Cummings. **CP-CummE**

Dim Hour! that sleep'st on pillowing clouds afar. The Hour When We Shall Meet Again. Samuel Taylor Coleridge. **CP-ColeS**

Dim House, Bright Face. Tess Gallagher. **SP-GallT**

Dim in the glimmering room. My Father's Honour. Donald Davie. **CP-DavDo**

Dim vales—and shadowy floods. Fairyland [*or* Fairy-Land]. Edgar Allan Poe. **CP-PoeEd**

Dim-winged spirits of the night, The. What the Scarecrow Said. Nicholas Vachel Lindsay. **CP-LindV**

Dime. Langston Hughes. **SP-HughL**

Dime Store Mystery. "Lou Reed." **SP-ReedL**

Dimensions. Robert Creeley. **CP-CreeR**

Dimensions. Charles Kenneth Williams. **CP-WillC; SP-WillC**

Dimly Outlined by a Police Artist. Charles Simic. *See* An Especially forlorn human specimen.

Dimple in the Tomb, A. Emily Dickinson. **CP-DickE**

Din of work is subdued, The. Lullaby. Wystan Hugh Auden. **CP-AudeW**

Dinah in Heaven. Rudyard Kipling. **CP-KiplR**

Dinah Kneading Dough. Paul Laurence Dunbar. **CP-DunbP**

Dinah stan' befo' de glass. The Looking-Glass. Paul Laurence Dunbar. **CP-DunbP**

Dined with Auden. He'd been at Milwaukee. Auden at Milwaukee. Stephen Spender. **CP-SpenS**

"Ding a ding," / The sweet bells sing. Christina Georgina Rossetti. **CP-RosC2**

Ding-dong, ding-dong, ding-dong. A Dirge for a Righteous Kitten. Nicholas Vachel Lindsay. **CP-LindV**

Dingley and Brent. Jonathan Swift. **CP-SwifJ**

Dining Out with Doug and Frank. James Schuyler. **CP-SchuJ**

Dinky. Theodore Roethke. **CP-RoetT**

Dinner, The. Stephen Dunn. **SP-DunnS**

Dinner at George & Katie Schneeman's. Ted Berrigan. **SP-BerrT**

Dinner Menu a Burnt Offering, A. James Liddy. *Fr.* Glass after Oblivion. **CP-LiddJ**

Dinosaur Bones, The. Carl Sandburg. **CP-SandC**

Dinosaur bones are dusted every day, The. The Dinosaur Bones. Carl Sandburg. **CP-SandC**

Dinosaur died, and small, The. The Naked Ape. John Updike. **CP-UpdiJ**

Diodati, and I will say it to you with wonder. Sonnet 4. John Milton, *tr. fr. Italian by* John T. Shawcross. **CP-MiltJ**

Dion. William Wordsworth. **CP-WorW2**

Dionysiaca. Nonnus.
How Bacchus Comforts Ariadne. **CP-BroEB**

Dionysus. Ezra Pound. *See* Canto 2: "Hang it all, Robert Browning."

Dioscuri guardyou in this passing, The. The Self Prepares for an Unwilling Journey. William Dickey. **SP-DickW**

Dip down upon the northern shore. Tennyson. **EBVV** *Fr.* In Memoriam A. H. H. **CP-TennA**

Diplomacy. Paul Laurence Dunbar. **CP-DunbP**

Diplomacy: The Father. William DeWitt Snodgrass. **SP-SnodW**

Dipped myself in a future night. A Future Night. Leonard Cohen. **CP-CoheL**

Dipper, small dust-colored bird with robin, The. Three Praises. Margaret Atwood. **SP-AtwM2**

Dipsychus [and the Spirit]. Arthur Hugh Clough.
"Assuredly a lively scene." **SP-ClouA**
" 'There is no God,' the wicked saith." **SP-ClouA**

Diptera. John Hewitt. **CP-HewiJ**

Dire Coasts. John Clellon Holmes. **SP-HolmJ**

Dire was the hate at old Harlaw. The Dean of Faculty—a New Ballad. Robert Burns. **CP-BurnR**

Dìreadh III. "Hugh MacDiarmid." **SP-MacDH**

Directions for a Birthday Song. Jonathan Swift. **CP-SwifJ**

Directive. Robert Frost. **CP-FrosR**

Director of Alienation. Lawrence Ferlinghetti. **SP-FerlL**

Dirge: "Boys and girls that held her dear." Edna St. Vincent Millay. *Fr.* Memorial to D. C. **CP-MillE**

Dirge: "From a friend's friend I taste friendship." Stevie Smith. **CP-SmitS**

Dirge: "He has hid his face, and he's gone!" George Meredith. **CP-MerG2**

Dirge: "I hate myself for lovin' you and the weakness that it showed." "Bob Dylan." **CP-DylaB**

Dirge: "Knows he who tills this lonely field." Ralph Waldo Emerson. **CP-EmerR**

Dirge: "Place this bunch of mignonette." Paul Laurence Dunbar. **CP-DunbP**

Dirge, A: "She was as sweet as violets. . ." Christina Georgina Rossetti. **CP-RosC3**

Dirge: "Some one who hears the bugle neigh will know." Thomas Merton. **CP-MertT**

Dirge, A: "Rough wind, that moanest loud." Percy Bysshe Shelley. **CP-ShelP**

Dirge, A: "Why were you born when the snow was falling?" Christina Georgina Rossetti. **CP-RosC1**

Dirge for a Joker. Sylvia Plath. **CP-PlatS**

Dirge for a Righteous Kitten, A. Nicholas Vachel Lindsay. **CP-LindV**

Dirge for a Soldier. Paul Laurence Dunbar. **CP-DunbP**

Dirge for a Town in France. Thomas Merton. **CP-MertT; SP-MertT**

Dirge for the City of Miami. Thomas Merton. **CP-MertT**

Dirge for the Proud World. Thomas Merton. **CP-MertT**

Dirge for the World Joyce Died In. Thomas Merton. **CP-MertT**

Dirge for the Year. Percy Bysshe Shelley. **CP-ShelP**

Dirge for Two Veterans. Walt Whitman. **CP-WhitW**

Dirge in Woods. George Meredith. **CP-MerG1**

Dirge is wailing from the Gulf of storm-vexed Mexico, A. Bolivar. John Greenleaf Whittier. **CP-WhitJ**

Dirge of Dead Sisters. Rudyard Kipling. **CP-KiplR**

Dirge of Jephthah's Daughter, The. Robert Herrick. **CP-HerrR**

Dirge Sung by a Minstrel. William Wordsworth. **CP-WorW1**

Dirge upon the Death of the Right Valiant Lord, Bernard Stuart, A. Robert Herrick. **CP-HerrR**

Dirge Without Music. Edna St. Vincent Millay. **CP-MillE**

Dirt. "Lou Reed." **SP-ReedL**

Dirtiest Man in the World, The. Shel Silverstein. **SP-SilS2**

Dirty Blvd. "Lou Reed." **SP-ReedL**

Dirty Christmas / which Origen. Christmas. Charles Olson. **CP-OlsoC**

Dirty colours of her kiss have just, The. Edward Estlin Cummings. **CP-CummE**

Dirty dogs of Egypt stride down my bones, The. The Dogs of Egypt. Charles Bukowski. **SP-BukC2**

Dirty Dozen, The. Roy Fisher. **SP-FishR**

Dirty Laundry Poem, The. Erica Jong. **SP-JongE**

Dirty Nature, / Dirty sea. The Dirty Dozen. Roy Fisher. **SP-FishR**

Dirty picture, a photograph, possibly a tintype, from the turn of the century, even before:, A. Floor. Charles Kenneth Williams. **CP-WillC; SP-WillC**

Dirty socks in dirty sneakers. Sorting, Wrapping, Packing, Stuffing. James Schuyler. **CP-SchuJ**

Dirty Souls. Alfonso Cortes, *tr. fr. Spanish by* Thomas Merton. **CP-MertT**

Dirty Talker: D Line, Boston, The. Charles Kenneth Williams. **SP-WillC**

Dirty Word, The. Karl Shapiro. **SP-ShapK**

Dirty word hops in the cage of the mind like the Pondicherry vulture, The. The Dirty Word. Karl Shapiro. **SP-ShapK**

Dîs Aliter Visum; or, Le Byron de Nos Jours. Robert Browning. **CP-BroR1**

Dis is gospel weathah sho'. Song of Summer. Paul Laurence Dunbar. **CP-DunbP**

Disabled. Wilfred Owen. **CP-OwenW**

Disagreeable Advice. David Herbert Lawrence. **CP-LawrD**

Disancred from a blisful shore. The Prodigall Chyld's Soule Wracke. Robert Southwell. **CP-SoutR**

Disappearance begins with you. The Tunnel. John Haines. **SP-HainJ**

Disappearance of Oilcloth, The. Gilbert Sorrentino. **SP-SorrG**

Disappearances in the Guarded Sector. Tess Gallagher. **SP-GallT**

Disappearing around the corner. Foggy Morning. Al Young. **CP-YounA**

Disappearing Island, The. Seamus Heaney. **SP-HeanS**

Disappointed. Paul Laurence Dunbar. **CP-DunbP**

Disappointment, The. Robert Creeley. **CP-CreeR**

Disappointment I am talking of now, The. George Washington: The Whole Man. Diane Wakoski. **SP-WakoD**

Disarmament. John Greenleaf Whittier. **CP-WhitJ**

Disaster on the Box. John Hewitt. **CP-HewiJ**

Disasters numb within us, The. Life at War. Denise Levertov. **CP-LeveD**

Disbeliever walked the moonlit place, The. Palace of the Babies. Wallace Stevens. **CP-StevW**

Discard the fear and what. The Couple. Maya Angelou. **SP-AngeM**

Discarded Love Poem, The. Robert Ranke Graves. **CP-GravR**

Discharge, The. George Herbert. **CP-HerbG**

Discharged upon the body of the world. Devonshire. Donald Davie. **CP-DavDo**

Disciple, The. John Berryman. **CP-BerrJ**

Disciple, The. Rudyard Kipling. **CP-KiplR**

Disciple complained to Keng, A. Keng's Disciple. Chuang Tzu, *tr. fr. Chinese by* Thomas Merton. **CP-MertT**

Discipline, A. Wendell Berry. **CP-BerrW**

Discipline. George Herbert. **CP-HerbG**

Discipline. David Herbert Lawrence. **CP-LawrD**

Discipline of Wisdom, The. George Meredith. **CP-MerG1**

Disciplined as we lab technicians are. The Ecstasy of the Rat. Robert Pack. **SP-PackR**

Disclosure, The. Denise Levertov. **CP-LeveD**

Discoloured lights slant from the high rose window. Westminster Abbey. Alun Lewis. **CP-LewiA**

Discontent. Elizabeth Barrett Browning. **CP-BroEB**

Discontent. John Gould Fletcher. **SP-FletJ**

Discontent with that first draft. Where one's own. Before the Judgment. Robert Duncan. **SP-DuncR** *Fr.* Passages.

Discontented Poet: A Masque, The. Ralph Waldo Emerson. **CP-EmerR**

Discontents in Devon. Robert Herrick. **CP-HerrR**

Discord in Childhood. David Herbert Lawrence. **CP-LawrD**

Discord Not Disadvantageous. Robert Herrick. **CP-HerrR**

Discouragement. Thomas Hardy. **CP-HardT**

Discourse / of sun and moon. Wrestling. Thom Gunn. **CP-GunnT**

Discourse of the Wanderer and an Evening Visit to the Lake. William Wordsworth. *Fr.* The Excursion. **CP-WorW2**

  "Behold the shades of afternoon have fallen." **EnRP**

  "To every Form of being is assigned." **EnRP**

Discourse was deemed Man's noblest attribute. Illustrated Books and Newspapers. William Wordsworth. **CP-WorW2**

Discovered. Paul Laurence Dunbar. **CP-DunbP**

Discovering, discovering trees light up green at night. No Hearing. Robert Lowell. **SP-LoweR**

Discovering My Daughter. Dabney Stuart. **SP-StuaD**

Discovering the Form. Roy Fisher. **SP-FishR**

Discovery / Angels & Sailors (rich girls). Tales of the American Night. Jim Morrison. **SP-MorrJ**

Discovery, The. Paul Laurence Dunbar. **CP-DunbP**

Discovery, The. Thomas Hardy. **CP-HardT**

Discovery. Edwin Arlington Robinson. **CP-RobiE**

Discovery, A. Christina Georgina Rossetti. **CP-RosC3**

Discovery, The. Jonathan Swift. **CP-SwifJ**

Discovery of Honey, The. John Yau. **SP-YauJo**

Discovery of the Madeiras, The. Robert Frost. **CP-FrosR**

Discovery of the Pacific, The. Thom Gunn. **CP-GunnT**

Discreet and prudent we that Discord call. Contention. Robert Herrick. **CP-HerrR**

Discreet householder exclaims on the grandsire, A. Old Man Playing with Children. John Crowe Ransom. **SP-RansJ**

Discrepancies. Charles Tomlinson. **CP-TomlC**

Discrete Gloss, A. Charles Olson. **CP-OlsoC**

Discription of a Maske, Presented before the Kinges Majestie *at Whitehall, on Twelfth Night* Last, in Honour of the Lord HAYES, and His Bride, Daughter and Heire to the *Honourable the Lord* Dnnye, *their* Marriage Having Been the Same Day at Court Solemnized, The. Thomas Campion. *See* Lord Hay's Mask.

Discursive knowledge, knowledge by. Kenneth Rexroth. **SP-RexrK** *Fr. Art of Worldly Wisdom, The.* **CP-RexKL** *Fr.* The Dragon and the Unicorn.

Disdain me not without desert. Sir Thomas Wyatt. **CP-WyatT**

Disdain not, madam, on him to look. Sir Thomas Wyatt. **CP-WyatT**

Disdain Punished. John Dryden. **EBNV; NOSC** *Fr.* Theodore and Honoria, From [Fables Ancient and Modern from] Boccace. **SP-DrydJ**

Disdain Returned. Thomas Carew. **CP-CareT**

  True Beauty, The. **GTBS; GTBS-6; GTBS-P**

  (Disdain Returned.) **PFP**

Disdain Returned. Thomas Carew. *See* The True Beauty.

Disease, The. Muriel Rukeyser. **CP-RukeM**

Disease: After-Effects, The. Muriel Rukeyser. **CP-RukeM**

Diseased or unwanted / trees, cut into pieces, thrown. Marsh, Hawk. Margaret Atwood. **SP-AtwM2**

Diseases, famine, enemies, in us no change have wrought, *ad. fr. Latin of* Marius Victor. Sir Walter Ralegh. **CP-RaleW**

Disembarking at Quebec. Margaret Atwood. **SP-AtwM1**

Disenchanted, The. Isabella Gardner. **CP-GardI**

Disenthralled, The. John Greenleaf Whittier. **CP-WhitJ**

Disertissime Romuli Nepotum. Catullus. *See* Carmen 49: "Silver-tongued among the sons of Rome."

Disguise, The. Walter de la Mare. **CP-DeLaW**

Disguised as an Arab, the bouzouki player. Belly Dancer at the Hotel Jerome. Stephen Dunn. **SP-DunnS**

Disguised as Cock Robin, W. D. Escapes. William DeWitt Snodgrass. **SP-SnodW**

Disguised as Humpty-Dumpty, W. D. Practices Tumbling. William DeWitt Snodgrass. **SP-SnodW**

Disguised bravado all doors open revise or polish. George Sand. Anne Waldman. **SP-WaldA**

Disguises. Leonard Cohen. **CP-CoheL**

Dish of Fruit, The. William Carlos Williams. **CP-WilW2**

Dish of Peaches in Russia, A. Wallace Stevens. **CP-StevW**

Dishes are apples are guitars. Still Life II. Howard Nemerov. **CP-NemeH**

Dishevelled leaves creep down. Where They Lived. Thomas Hardy. **CP-HardT**

Dishonest Mailmen, The. Robert Creeley. **CP-CreeR**

Dishonoured Rock and Ruin! that, by law. Eagles. William Wordsworth. **CP-WorW2**

Disillusion with the French Revolution. Charlotte Smith. **ECWP** *Fr.* Long wintry months are past; the Moon that now. *Fr.* The Emigrants. **CP-SmitC**

Disillusionment of Ten O'Clock. Wallace Stevens. **CP-StevW**

Disindividuating Chaos. The Passage. Richard Eberhart. **CP-EberR**

Disinherited. John Donne. **CP-DonnJ**

Disintegration. Philip Larkin. **CP-LarkP**

Disintegration. Richard Shelton. **SP-ShelR**

Disjunctive conjunction, severing, The. Or. Tom Clark. **SP-ClarT**

Dislocado. Chuck Miller. **SP-MillC**

Dismal bell hung in the belfry, A. The Fairy Bell. Stevie Smith. **CP-SmitS**

Dismal fog-hoarse siren howls at dawn, A. The Calls. Wilfred Owen. **CP-OwenW**

Dismantled Ship, The. Walt Whitman. **CP-WhitW**

Dismantling the Silence. Charles Simic. **SP-SimiC**

Dismissing reports and men, he put pressure on the. Geoffrey Hill. **HAP** *Fr.* Mercian Hymns. **CP-HillG**

Displaced by sandy distances. Southwest of True North. Isabella Gardner. **CP-GardI**

Display. Robert Pack. **SP-PackR**

Display thy breasts, my Julia: there let me. Upon Julia's Breasts. Robert Herrick. **CP-HerrR**

Disposal. William DeWitt Snodgrass. **SP-SnodW**

Disposings of the heart in man, The. The Creature David. Donald Davie. **CP-DavDo**

Disposition, The. Charles Olson. **CP-OlsoC**

Dispossessed, The. John Berryman. **CP-BerrJ**

Dispossessed, The. Sylvia Plath. **CP-PlatS**

Dispossessions. Jane Cooper. **SP-CoopJ**

  Inheritances.

  Souvenirs.

  Things.

Disputants, The. William Carlos Williams. **CP-WilW1**

Disquieting Muses, The. Sylvia Plath. **CP-PlatS**

Disquieting muses again: what are "leftovers?", The. Business Personals. John Ashbery. **SP-AshbJ**

Disruption has become my secret cause. Statements in a Personal Winter. John Clellon Holmes. **SP-HolmJ**

Dissecto Nervae capite, haud (chirurge) cerebrum. *acc. by English translation.* Thomas Campion. **CP-CampT**

Dissemblers, The. Thomas Hardy. **CP-HardT**

Dissensions. William Wordsworth. *Fr.* Ecclesiastical Sonnets. **CP-WorW2**

Dissent. A Fable. Donald Davie. *Fr.* A Dissentient Voice. **CP-DavDo**

Dissentient Voice, A. Donald Davie. **CP-DavDo**

  Baptist Childhood, A.

  Dissent. A Fable.

  Gathered Church, A.

  Portrait of the Artist as a Farmyard Fowl.

Dissertation I. John Hewitt. **CP-HewiJ**

Dissertation II. John Hewitt. **CP-HewiJ**

Dissolute. David Herbert Lawrence. *See* At a Loose End.

Dissolution, The. John Donne. **CP-DonnJ**

Dissolution of the Monasteries. William Wordsworth. *Fr.* Ecclesiastical Sonnets. **CP-WorW2**

Dissolving in the chemic vat. Change. Stanley Jasspon Kunitz. **CP-KuniS**

Dissolving, the coals shift. Rain swaddles us. The Ruin. Charles Tomlinson. **CP-TomlC**

Disswasions from Idlenesse. Robert Herrick. **CP-HerrR**

Distance. Robert Creeley. **CP-CreeR**

Distance / Dappled with diminish'd trees. Gerard Manley Hopkins. **CP-HopkG**

Distance Betters Dignities. Robert Herrick. **CP-HerrR**

Distance Between Us. Chuck Miller. **SP-MillC**

Distance beyond / Sky's reach, membrane, A. A Night Outing. Jim Carroll. **SP-CarrJ**

Distance brings proportion. From here. Tao in the Yankee Stadium Bleachers. John Updike. **CP-UpdiJ**

Distance—is not the Realm of Fox. Emily Dickinson. **CP-DickE**

Distance is on edge. Geoffrey Hill. *Fr.* Scenes with Harlequins. **CP-HillG**

Distance that lies from here, The. Space Song. Alfonso Cortes, *tr. fr. Spanish by* Thomas Merton. **CP-MertT**

Distance that the dead have gone, The. Emily Dickinson. **CP-DickE**

Distance Traveled. Anne Waldman. **SP-WaldA**

Distances, The. Jim Carroll. **SP-CarrJ**

Distances, The. John Hewitt. **CP-HewiJ**

Distances. Richard Hugo. **CP-HugoR**

Distances, The. Charles Olson. **CP-OlsoC; SP-OlsoC**

Distances They Keep, The. Howard Nemerov. **CP-NemeH**

Distant Fury of Battle, The. Geoffrey Hill. **CP-HillG**

Distant Rainfall. Robinson Jeffers. **CP-JefR2**

Distant View of a Provincial Town. Sir John Betjeman. **CP-BetjJ**

Distinction. Paul Laurence Dunbar. **CP-DunbP**

Distinctions. Charles Tomlinson. **CP-TomlC**

Distraction. Howard Nemerov. **CP-NemeH**

Distraction is the panacea, Sir! George Meredith. *Fr.* Modern Love. **CP-MerG1**

Distractions. William Wordsworth. *Fr.* Ecclesiastical Sonnets. **CP-WorW2**

Distractions and the Human Crowd. Stevie Smith. **CP-SmitS**

Distressed Travellers, The. William Cowper. **CP-CowpW**

Distressful gift! this Book receives. William Wordsworth. **CP-WorW1**

District in the City, A. Richard Hugo. **CP-HugoR**

Distrust ("To safeguard man from wrongs, there nothing must"). Robert Herrick. **CP-HerrR**

Distrust ("What ever men for Loyalty pretend"). Robert Herrick. **CP-HerrR**

Distrustful of the Gentian. Emily Dickinson. **CP-DickE**

Disturb the balance, broken bird. The Birdsong. William Carlos Williams. **CP-WilW2**

Disturber, The. Paul Laurence Dunbar. **CP-DunbP**

Disunited Scithians, when they sought, The. To the Most Puisant and Gratious James King of Great Britaine. Thomas Campion. *Fr.* Lord Hay's Mask.

Disused Shed in Co. Wexford, A. Derek Mahon. **SP-MahoD**

Ditch is dear to the Drunken man, The. Emily Dickinson. **CP-DickE**

Ditty: "Beneath a knap where flown." Thomas Hardy. **CP-HardT**

Ditty: "Cock shall crow, The." Robert Louis Stevenson. **CP-StevR**

Ditty: "Moon will run all consciences to cover, The." Allen Tate. **CP-TateA**

Ditty, A: In Praise of Eliza, Queen of the Shepherds. Edmund Spenser. **OBEV** *Fr.* Aprill. **NAEL-1; OBEV; OBSC; PoEL-1** *Fr.* The Shepheardes *or* Shepeards *or* Shepherd's] Calender.

(Ditty, A: "See where she sits upon the grassy green.") **FaBoCh**

Ditty, A: "See where she sits upon the grassy green." Edmund Spenser. *See* Ditty, A: In Praise of Eliza, Queen of the Shepherds.

Divagation. Allen Tate. *Fr.* The Progress of Œnia. **CP-TateA**

Dive. Langston Hughes. **SP-HughL**

Dive for dreams / or a slogan may topple you. Edward Estlin Cummings. **CP-CummE**

Dive, mermaids, with sharp swords. Nicholas Vachel Lindsay. *Fr.* The Sea Serpent Chantey. **CP-LindV**

Diver, The. Robert Earl Hayden. **CP-HaydR**

Diver, The. Leonard Nathan. **SP-NathL**

Divers[e] [*or* Dyvers] doth[e] use, as I have heard and kno[w]. Sir Thomas Wyatt. **CP-WyatT**

Diversions. Roy Fisher.

"Build for quoting in a tight corner." **SP-FishR**

"Crooked-angle wings." **SP-FishR**

"Everything cast in iron." **SP-FishR**

"Grey weather beating across the upland." **SP-FishR**

"Here comes the modulation." **SP-FishR**

"I saw what there was to write and I wrote it." **SP-FishR**

"Just beside my track through the dark." **SP-FishR**

"Kites are the best sort of gods, The." **SP-FishR**

"Leaden August with the life gone out of it." **SP-FishR**

"Out to one side." **SP-FishR**

"Outlines / start to appear." **SP-FishR**

"Periodicity: the crack." **SP-FishR**

"Pilgrim disposition—, The." **SP-FishR**

"Roused from a double." **SP-FishR**

"Sliding the tongue-leaved." **SP-FishR**

"Then some calm and formal portrait." **SP-FishR**

"Trouble coming, on a Saturday or a Monday." **SP-FishR**

"Walk through, minding the nettles." **SP-FishR**

"Woman across the lane, The." **SP-FishR**

"World / arranged in zones, A." **SP-FishR**

Divertimiento. William Carlos Williams. **CP-WilW1**

Divided Destinies. Rudyard Kipling. **CP-KiplR**

Divided, the Man is Dreaming. John Haines. **SP-HainJ**

Divina Commedia, sels. Dante Alighieri, *tr. fr. Italian.*

Inferno.

Francesca of Rimini. **CP-Byron**

Ugolino. **CP-ShelP**

Purgatorio.

Matilda Gathering Flowers. **CP-ShelP**

Divination by a Daffadill [*or* Daffodil]. Robert Herrick. **CP-HerrR**

Divine and Human Pleading. Christina Georgina Rossetti. **CP-RosC3**

Divine Compassion. John Greenleaf Whittier. **CP-WhitJ**

Divine destroyer, pit[t]y me no more. A La Bourbon. Richard Lovelace. **CP-LoveR**

Divine Falling of Leaves, A. César Vallejo, *tr. fr. Spanish by* James Wright. **CP-WrigJ**

Divine Image, The ("To Mercy, Pity, Peace, and Love"). William Blake. **BoTP; CoGr; EBCP; EnRP; FHYEP; FaBoEn; HoFi; LAuP; LO; MeMBP; NAEL-2; NOBE; NOBRP; NOEC; NoP; OAEL-2; OAEP; OBEC; OBNC; OxBoCh; PFP; PPP; PeECV; PoE; PoEL-4; TEP; TRV; WGRP** *Fr.* Songs of Innocence. **CP-BlakW**

Divine Inviters! I accept. Ralph Waldo Emerson. **CP-EmerR**

Divine Justice Amiable. Jeanne Marie Bouvier de la Motte-Guyon, *tr. fr. French by* William Cowper. **CP-CowpW**

Divine Love, A. Thomas Carew. **CP-CareT**

Divine Love Endures No Rival. Jeanne Marie Bouvier de la Motte-Guyon, *tr. fr. French by* William Cowper. **CP-CowpW**

Divine Meditations, *This collection of 19 sonnets is often titled* Holy Sonnets. John Donne. **CP-DonnJ** *Fr.* Holy Sonnets. **CP-DonnJ**

(Holy Sonnets.) **AnAnS-1; ESCV; MasP**

"As due by many titles I resign[e]." **JCP; MePo; OBS**

"At the round earth's imagined corners, blow." **BLPL; CABA; ChIV-2; ChTr; ClHu; EBCP; EBEV; EaLo; EnRePo; FHYEP; FaBoEn; FaBoRV; HAP; HeLL; HeIP; ImPo; InPS; JCP; LiTB; LoBV; MeLP; MePo; NAEL-1; NAWM-1; NOBE; NOSC; NoP; OAEL-1; OAEP; OBD; OBS; OxAEP-1; OxBoCh; PAI; PFP; PPP; PPoe; PeECV; PoE; PoEL-2; PoPle; QFR; SCGP; SeCP; SeCV-1; SeCeV; Son; TEP; TFi; TOF; TreFT**

(Blow Your Trumpets.) **ChTr; EBCP**

"Batter my heart, three-personed [*or* three person'd] God; for you." **BLPL; BiP; CABA; ClHu; EBEV; EBEvV; EaLo; EnRePo; FF; FHYEP; FaFP; GoBC; HAP; HeIP; HoPM; ImPo; InPK; InPS; JCP; LiTB; MeLP; MePo; NAEL-1; NIP; NOBE; NOSC; NoP; OAEL-1; OAEP; OBS; OxAEP-1; OxBoCh; PAI; PPP; PPoe; PeECV; PoE; PoEL-2; Poetr; PrIm; SeCP; SeCV-1; SeCePo; SeCeV; SoSe; Son; TEP; TFi; TOF; TrCP; TrGrPo; TrPWD; TreFT**

"Death[,] be not proud, though some have called thee." **BiP; CABA; ChTr; DL; EBEvV; EIL; EnRePo; FF; FHYEP; FPL; FaBV; FaBoEn; FaBoRV; FaFP; GoBC; HAP; HBV 1-2; HeLL; HeIP; ImPo; InPK; InPS; InvP; JCP; LiTB; LoBV; MeLP; MePo; NAEL-1; NAWM-1; NIP; NOBE; NOSC; NoP; OAEL-1; OAEP; OBD; OBS; OPOU; OxAEP-1; PAI; PBMP; PPP; PPoe; PoE; PoEL-2; PoRA; Poetr; PrIm; SCGP; SCV; SeCP; SeCV-1; SeCeV; SoSe; TEP; TRP; TRV; TrCP; TrGrPo; TreFS; WHA; WeW**

(Holy Sonnet.) **OPOU**

"Father, part of his double interest." **JCP; OBS**

"I am a little world made cunningly." **CABA; ChIV-1; EnRePo; NAEL-1; NIP; NoP; OBS; OxBoCh; PoE; SeCP; Son; TEP**

"If faithful soul[e]s be alike glorified [*or* glorifi'd]." **OBS**

"If poisonous [*or* poysonous] mineral[l]s, and if that tree." **EBEV; EnRePo; FaBoVe; ImPo; JCP; LiTB; MePo; NAEL-1; NoP; OAEL-1; OBS; OxAEP-1; PFP; PPP; PoEL-2; SCGP; SeCP; Son; UnPo; WHA**

"O might those sigh[e]s and tear[e]s return[e] again[e]." **BiP; OBS**

"Oh my black[e] soul[e]! now thou art summoned." **EBEV; JCP; OAEL-1; OBS; OxAEP-1; Poetr; Son; TEP; TOF**

"Oh, to vex me, contraries [*or* conraryes] meet in one." **NOSC; OAEL-1; PoEL-2; SeCePo; Son**

(Devout Fits.) **SeCePo**

("Oh, to vex me, two contraries meet in one.") **ChIV-2**

"Show me dear[e] Christ, thy spouse, so bright and clear." **MeLP; NAEL-1; NOSC; NoP; OAEP; OBS; PoE; Son**

("Show me, dear Christ, Thy Spouse, so bright and clear.") **PeECV**

"Since she whom I loved [*or* lov'd] hath paid [*or* payd] her last debt." **JCP; MePo; NAEL-1; NOSC; OAEP; Son**

"Spit in my face ye [*or* you] Jew[e]s, and pierce my side." **JCP; OBS; OxBoCh; Son; TOF**

"This is my play's [*or* playes] last scene, here heavens appoint." **EBEV; FaBoVe; JCP; LoBV; MeLP; MePo; NIP; OAEP; OBS; OxBoCh; PAI; SeCP; Son; TEP**

"Thou hast made me, and shall thy work[e] decay?" **AnAnS-1; EBEV; EnRePo; FaBoEn; MasP; MeLP; NAEL-1; NOBE; NOCV; NOSC; NoP; OAEP; OBS; OxAEP-1; OxBoCh; PoEL-2; SCGP; SeCP; Son; TEP**

"What if this present were the world's last night?" **EBEV; HeIP; ImPo; InPS; JCP; LiTB; MeLP; NAEL-1; NOCV; NOSC; OAEP; OBS;**

OxAEP-1; PeECV; PoE; SeCeV; Son; TEP

"Why are we[e] by all creatures waited on?" **CABA; JCP; NOCV; OBS; PoE; PoEL-2; TrCP**

"Wilt thou love God, as he thee? [or thee!] then digest." **JCP; OBS; TrCP**

Divine Mistress, A. Thomas Carew. **CP-CareT**

Divinely Superfluous Beauty. Robinson Jeffers. **CP-JefR1**

Diving / through bedrooms. The Moon. William Carlos Williams. **CP-WilW1**

Diving Ballet, The. Laurence Lieberman. **SP-LiebL**

Diving board trembles, The. Walk in Canada. Malcolm Lowry. **CP-LowrM**

Diving into the Wreck. Adrienne Rich. **SP-RicA1; SP-RicA2**

Divining Water. Muriel Rukeyser. **CP-RukeM**

Divinity. George Herbert. **CP-HerbG**

Divinity of air, fleet-feather'd gales. Aeschylus, *tr.* by Gerard Manley Hopkins. *Fr.* Prometheus Bound. **CP-BroEB**

Division. Louise Bogan. **CP-BogaL**

Division, The. Thomas Hardy. **CP-HardT**

Division of Parts, The. Anne Sexton. **CP-SextA**

Divisions. Robert Creeley. **CP-CreeR**

Divorce. Erica Jong. **SP-JongE**

Divorce. Anne Sexton. **CP-SextA**

Divorce. Miller Williams. **SP-WillM**

Divorce of Lovers, A. May Sarton.
"I shall not see the end of this unweaving." **SP-SartM**

Divorce, Thy Name Is Woman. Anne Sexton. **CP-SextA**

Divorce Work. Anne Waldman. **SP-WaldA**

Divorced, Husband Demolishes Home. John Ciardi. **SP-CiarJ**

Dixon. Richard Hugo. **CP-HugoR**

Do. / omful / relaxing. Edward Estlin Cummings. **CP-CummE**

Do' a-stan'in' on a jar, fiah a-shinin' thoo. Howdy, Honey, Howdy! Paul Laurence Dunbar. **CP-DunbP**

Do all men wait like this for breaking light. Expectancy. John Hewitt. **CP-HewiJ**

Do any of you old fogies remember Mrs. Hauksbee? How to Be Married without a Spouse, or, Mr. Kipling, What Have You Done with Mr. Hauksbee? Ogden Nash. **CP-NashO**

Do birds need to fly so much. Charles Henri Ford. *Fr.* Epigrams. **SP-FordC**

Do[e] but consider this small dust. The Hour-Glass [or Houre-Glasse]. Ben Jonson. **CP-JonsB**

Do, Do, Do What You Done, Done, Done Before, Before, Before. Ogden Nash. **CP-NashO**

Do duty feeling nought and truth believe. Arthur Hugh Clough. **SP-ClouA**

Do I hear them? Yes, I hear the children singing—and what of it? London Bridge. Edwin Arlington Robinson. **CP-RobiE**

Do I know these, slack-shaped and wan. In a Former Resort after Many Years. Thomas Hardy. **CP-HardT**

Do I not deal with angels. For Miriam. Kenneth Patchen. **CP-PatcK**

Do I not know what savage blossom only under the pitting hail. What Savage Blossom. Edna St. Vincent Millay. **CP-MillE**

Do I prefer to forget it? This middle stretch. Louis MacNeice. **NAs** *Fr.* Day of Renewal. **CP-MacNL**

Do it *just right*, anything will grow. Now If You. Kenneth Patchen. **CP-PatcK**

Do me that love. Kenneth Patchen. **CP-PatcK**

Do Not! Stevie Smith. **CP-SmitS**

Do not, at this high time, desert. Quatrain. Charles Olson. **CP-OlsoC**

Do not bake bread in an oven that is not made of stone. Some General Instructions. Kenneth Koch. **SP-KochK**

Do not be afraid / O my people. *ad. fr.* Isaiah 43:1. Thomas Merton. **CP-MertT**

Do not be afraid. Stranger. Richard Shelton. **SP-ShelR**

Do not be afraid / though the light is far. Night Music. John Clellon Holmes. **SP-HolmJ**

Do Not Be Afraid of No. Gwendolyn Brooks. *Fr.* Notes from the Childhood and the Girlhood. **SP-BrooG**

Do Not Be Ashamed. Wendell Berry. **CP-BerrW**

Do not be eager, spring, to come. For a Mild Season. John Hewitt. **CP-HewiJ**

Do not be frightened. *see also* Commentary—The Beetle. Leonard Cohen. **CP-CoheL**

Do not because this day I have grown saturnine. Under Saturn. William Butler Yeats. **CP-YeatW**

Do not beguile my heart. Complaining. George Herbert. **CP-HerbG**

Do not call to her there. The Hill. Charles Tomlinson. **CP-TomlC**

Do not disdain, O straight upraised pine, *speech of Pamela.* Sir Philip Sidney. **SP-SidnP** *Fr.* Arcadia.

Do not enforce the tired wolf. *"A" version.* John Crowe Ransom. **AP; CoBMV; EAS; MoAB; MoAmPo; MoPo; MoVE; NePA; OxBA; PoCh** *Fr.* Sixteen Poems in Eight Pairings. **SP-RansJ**

Do not enforce the tired wolf. *"B" version.* John Crowe Ransom. *Fr.* Sixteen Poems in Eight Pairings. **SP-RansJ**

Do not enquire from the centurion nodding. The Silver Age. Thom Gunn. **CP-GunnT**

Do not ever let the door of the old garret creak. Cobwebs and Ratholes. Marsden Hartley. **CP-HartM**

Do not go gentle into that good night. Dylan Thomas. **CP-ThomD**

Do not guard this as rich stuff without mark. Memory. Louise Bogan. **CP-BogaL**

Do not hold me, Siegmund. A Love-Passage. David Herbert Lawrence. **CP-LawrD**

Do not hold my few years / against me. So We've Come at Last to Freud. Alice Walker. **CP-WalkA**

Do not imagine his father lying. Voice of America. Miller Williams. **SP-WillM**

Do not imagine that Jack and Rose apart. Jack's Letter. John Crowe Ransom. **SP-RansJ**

Do not leave me. Louis Zukofsky. *Fr.* 29 Songs. **CP-ZukLS**

Do not lecture me, doctor, about your science. Ekstase, Alptraum, Schlaf in einem Nest von Flammen. Hayden Carruth. **CP-CarHS**

Do not, Leúconoé, seek to inquire what is forbidden, what. Carpe Diem. Horace. *Fr.* Three Odes of Horace. **CP-MacNL**

Do not lie there in the darkness silent. Thunderhead. Archibald MacLeish. **CP-MacLA**

Do not mistake me: I was never a rival. To the Teumessian Vixen. Robert Ranke Graves. **CP-GravR**

Do not, O do not prize thy beauty at too high a rate. *Unknown. See* Do Not, Oh, Do Not Prize.

Do Not, Oh, Do Not Prize. *Unknown.* **CP-CampT**
("Do not, O do not prize thy beauty at too high a rate.") **CP-CampT**

Do Not Pick Up the Telephone. Ted Hughes. **SP-HughT**

Do not presume to bury me with them. Words on a Grave. Malcolm Lowry. **CP-LowrM**

Do not sing those old songs here tonight. October Tragedy. William Everson. **SP-EverW**

Do not sneer, stranger, if one by one. Bach and the Lady. Wystan Hugh Auden. **CP-AudWJ**

Do not speak of yourself (for God's sake) even when asked. Advice to the Old. Kay Boyle. **CP-BoylK**

Do not stab my heart like this, scabby vagrants, garbage hounds, waiting. The Lost Dogs of Phnom Penh. Kay Boyle. **CP-BoylK**

Do not suddenly break the branch, or. Usk. Thomas Stearns Eliot. **FaBoCh; NOCV; PeECV** *Fr.* Landscapes. **CP-ElioT**

Do not think I am not grateful for your small. Gratitude. Louise Glück. **SP-GlücL**

Do not think me gentle. A Warning to My Readers. Wendell Berry. **CP-BerrW**

Do not try to adopt me. I'm on an Island. Tom Clark. **SP-ClarT**

Do not wait for the owl to come out. Frederick Morgan. *Fr.* Blue Hill Poems. **SP-MorgF**

Do not wonder when the wench declines. Carmen 69. Catullus. *Fr.* Carmina. **CP-Catul**

Do not worry. Comfort. Richard Shelton. **SP-ShelR**

Do nothing to injure the living. Marsden Hartley. **CP-HartM**

Do People moulder equally. Emily Dickinson. **CP-DickE**

Do poets really suffer more. The Words Continue Their Journey. Margaret Atwood. **SP-AtwM2**

Do Right to Me Baby (Do Unto Others). "Bob Dylan." **CP-DylaB**

Do Sphinxes Think? Dorothy Nash. **CP-NashO**

Do squamous and squiggling fish. Nocturne. Wystan Hugh Auden. **CP-AudeW**

"Do such, wait so," you said; I waited. Did you wait? Randall Jarrell. **CP-JarrR**

Do Take Muriel Out. Stevie Smith. **CP-SmitS**

Do that which you can do. Ralph Waldo Emerson. **CP-EmerR**

Do the Dead Know What Time It Is? Kenneth Patchen. **CP-PatcK**

Do the wife and baby travelling to see. The Sick Nought. Randall Jarrell. **CP-JarrR**

Do they block the way? Softly, Then, Softly. David Herbert Lawrence. **CP-LawrD**

Do they remember me? William Dickey. **SP-DickW** *Fr.* At Your Old House. **SP-DickW**

Do This, and He Doeth It. Christina Georgina Rossetti. **CP-RosC2**

Do way, do way, ye little wily prat! Sir Thomas Wyatt. **CP-WyatT**

Do we indeed desire the dead. Tennyson. **EBVVPR; EnVR; OAEL-2; OBD** *Fr.* In Memoriam A. H. H. **CP-TennA**

Do We Understand Each Other? Allen Ginsberg. **CP-GinsA**

Do we want to return to the womb? Not at all. Wystan Hugh Auden. *Fr.* Shorts [1939–1947] ("Motionless, deep in his mind, lies the past the poet's forgotten"). **CP-AudeW**

Do what you come for, captain, with your news. To Captain Hungry. Ben Jonson. **CP-JonsB**

Do with me, God! as Thou didst deal with John. To God. Robert Herrick. **CP-HerrR**

Do words make up the majesty. Geoffrey Hill. *Fr.* Three Baroque Meditations. **CP-HillG**

Do ye hear the children weeping, O my brothers. The Cry of the Children. Elizabeth Barrett Browning. **CP-BroEB**

Do ye indeed speak righteousness, O congregation? Psalm 58. Bible, *O.T. Fr.* Psalms. **CP-Psal**

Do you? / Yes. / *Do you what?.* Dialogue with Outer Space. John Ciardi. **SP-CiarJ**

Do you ask what the birds say? The Sparrow, the Dove. Answer to a Child's Question. Samuel Taylor Coleridge. **CP-ColeS**

Do you believe in a God. Ordinary God. Donald Davie. **CP-DavDo**

"Do you delude yourself?" a neighbor asks. Troughs of Sea. Robert Ranke Graves. **CP-GravR**

Do you exist. The Unknown. William Carlos Williams. **CP-WilW2**

Do you forget the shifting hole. To a Defeated Savior. James Wright. **CP-WrigJ**

Do you hanker for April showers. Here We Go Quietly Nuts in May. Ogden Nash. **CP-NashO**

Do You Have. Jim Morrison. **SP-MorrJ**

Do you hear the low winds singing. For Rosaline's Album. Christina Georgina Rossetti. **CP-RosC3**

Do you hear yellow detonations. Pablo Neruda, *tr. fr. Spanish by* Ben Belitt. **SP-NeruP** *Fr.* Question Book.

Do you imagine, wakeful late in bed. Partial Analysis. Marilyn Hacker. **SP-HackM**

Do you know Dr. Nott? The New Vicar of Bray. Byron. **CP-Byron**

Do you know Hitler? Does he like you? Muriel Rukeyser. **CP-RukeM**

Do you know how much pain is left. After That. Charles Kenneth Williams. **CP-WillC**

Do you know how the dream looms? how if summer misses one of us. Silver Wind. Carl Sandburg. **CP-SandC**

Do you know Mr. Ganderdonk, he is no Einstein, he has no. Slow Down, Mr. Ganderdonk, You're Late. Ogden Nash. **CP-NashO**

Do you know my friend Mr. Betts? Mr. Betts's Mind a Kingdom Is. Ogden Nash. **CP-NashO**

Do you know that sad journey is lifted from your darling's heart? Gilbert Sorrentino. *Fr.* Elegiacs of Sulpicia. **SP-SorrG**

Do you know the name of the average animal? Drunken Girl. Muriel Rukeyser. **CP-RukeM**

Do you know the warm progress. An American Prayer. Jim Morrison. **SP-MorrJ**

Do you know what. Fancy. Robert Creeley. **CP-CreeR**

Do you know what I play to be, in bed at night? Muriel Rukeyser. **CP-RukeM**

Do you like me? Lessons in Hunger. Anne Sexton. **CP-SextA**

Do you like your life? Three A.M. and Then Five. John Ciardi. **SP-CiarJ**

Do you love me, or are you just extending goodwill? Is Your Love in Vain? "Bob Dylan." **CP-DylaB**

Do you ne'er think what wondrous beings these? Henry Wadsworth Longfellow. **WBLP** *Fr.* Birds of Killingworth, The (The Poet's Tale). *Fr.* Tales of a Wayside Inn.

Do You Not Father Me. Dylan Thomas. **CP-ThomD**

Do you not hear me calling, white deer with no horns? William Butler Yeats. **CP-YeatW**

(He Mourns for the Change That Has Come upon Him and His Beloved, and Longs for the End of the World.) **CP-YeatW**

Do you not hear the Aziola cry? The Aziola. Percy Bysshe Shelley. **CP-ShelP**

Do You Plan to Speak Bantu? or Abbreviation is the Thief of Sanity. Ogden Nash. **CP-NashO**

Do you really believe I could blacken my life. Carmen 104. Catullus. *Fr.* Carmina. **CP-Catul**

Do you recall / That day in Fall. Days to Recollect. Thomas Hardy. **CP-HardT**

Do you recall how we sat by the smokily-burning. Memory of Cassis. Edna St. Vincent Millay. **CP-MillE**

Do you recall the night we flung. Night Transfigured. Charles Tomlinson. **CP-TomlC**

Do you remember. Reminder. David Herbert Lawrence. **CP-LawrD**

Do you remember—can we e'er forget? To My Old Familiars. Robert Louis Stevenson. **CP-StevR**

Do you remember how last year we walked. Bizarre. Allen Tate. **CP-TateA**

Do you remember how the rocket went on. Two Tales of Liadoff. Wallace Stevens. **CP-StevW**

Do you remember learning to tie your shoes? The Spirit the Triumph. Charles Kenneth Williams. **CP-WillC; SP-WillC**

Do you remember me, Cass. Cass and Me. Paul Muldoon. **SP-MuldP**

Do you remember the first raw winter. The Bumpity Road to Mutual Devotion. Marge Piercy. **SP-PierM**

Do you remember when the fluttering dusk. Edward Estlin Cummings. **CP-CummE**

Do you remember when we dreamed about the owl. The Hard Part. Charles Kenneth Williams. **CP-WillC**

Do you remember, when you were first a child. Message from Home. Kathleen Jessie Raine. **SP-RainK**

Do you see the sea, breaking itself to bits against the islands. Mana of the Sea. David Herbert Lawrence. **CP-LawrD**

"Do You Think. . . ." Robert Creeley. **CP-CreeR**

Do you think / Death is an answer then? Interrogate the Stones. Archibald MacLeish. **CP-MacLA**

Do you think it is easy to change? Change. David Herbert Lawrence. **CP-LawrD**

Do you think of me as I think of you. L. E. L.'s Last Question. Elizabeth Barrett Browning. **CP-BroEB**

Do you think of me at all. Dead "Wessex" the Dog to the Household. Thomas Hardy. **CP-HardT**

Do you think old people should be put away. Question. Grace Paley. **CP-PaleG**

Do You Want Affidavits? Carl Sandburg. **CP-SandC**

Do You Want to Know a Secret? John Lennon *and* Paul McCartney. **CP-Beatl**

Doc, I bin lookin' for you. Detail. William Carlos Williams. **CP-WilW2**

Dock Song Crazy. Al Young. **CP-YounA**

Dockery and Son. Philip Larkin. **CP-LarkP**

Dockery was junior to you. Dockery and Son. Philip Larkin. **CP-LarkP**

Docking at Palermo. Richard Hugo. **CP-HugoR**

Docks. Carl Sandburg. **CP-SandC**

Doctor———. Robert Browning. **CP-BroR2**

Doctor, The. Stevie Smith. **CP-SmitS**

Doctor and Dean, Pope, Parnell and Gay, The. Scriblerian Verses. Jonathan Swift. **CP-SwifJ**

Doctor arrives to inject the movie star against, The. A Conversation. Robert Bly. **SP-BlyR**

Doctor asked her what she wanted done, The. Edna St. Vincent Millay. *Fr.* Sonnets from an Ungrafted Tree. **CP-MillE**

Doctor calls it "revenge of the nerves," the. Emily Dickinson. **SP-DickE**

Doctor Faustus. Geoffrey Hill. **CP-HillG**

Doctor Faustus. Christopher Marlowe. **CP-JefR2**

("In front of.") **CP-JefR2**

"Ah, Faustus,/ Now hast thou but one bare hour [*or* hower] to live." **FaBoVe; HeIP; ILwL; PeECV; PoEL-2; TrGrPo**

(End of Doctor Faustus, The.) **PoEL-2**

(End of Faustus, The.) **TrGrPo**

Was This the Face. **EBEV; EBEvV; GBL; HeIP; LPA; NIP; TrGrPo; TreF**

(Face of Helen, The.) **FaBV**

(Helen.) **BLPL; FaFP; ImPo; LiTB; WHA**

(Helen of Troy.) **FF**

"Where are you damn'd?" **OBD**

Dr. Fell and Points West. Ogden Nash. **CP-NashO**

Doctor Fell? I Thought So. Ogden Nash. **CP-NashO**

Dr. Fell is at the door and my *mens sana* is about to depart from. A Visit From Dr. Fell. Ogden Nash. **CP-NashO**

Doctor gets you when you're born, The. I Yield to My Learned Brother or Is There a Candlestick Maker in the House? Ogden Nash. **CP-NashO**

Doctor Gliedschirm, skin specialist, surgeries 14–16 hours or by appointment. James Fenton. **SP-FentJ** *Fr.* A German Requiem. **SP-FentJ**

Doctor, I did not see that you were there. William Dickey. **SP-DickW** *Fr.* Part Song, With Concert of Recorders. **SP-DickW**

Dr. Joseph Goebbels, Minister for Propaganda. William DeWitt Snodgrass. **SP-SnodW**

Doctor Love. Patti Smith. **SP-SmitP**

Doctor Meinière—. Roy Fisher. **SP-FishR** *Fr.* Matrix.

Doctor Mohawk. Nicholas Vachel Lindsay. **CP-LindV**

Being a Seven-Year-Old Boy's Elaborate Memory of the Day of His Birth.

Being My Notion, as a Ferocious Small-Boy, of My Ancestral Protector. One Brief Hour of Grown-up Glory on the Gulf of Mexico.

Doctor Muses, The. John Hewitt. **CP-HewiJ**

Doctor of Billiards. Edwin Arlington Robinson. **CP-RobiE**

Doctor of Geneva, The. Wallace Stevens. **CP-StevW**

Doctor of the Heart, The. Anne Sexton. **CP-SextA**

Doctor punched my vein, The. Scyros. Karl Shapiro. **SP-ShapK**

Doctor Robert. John Lennon *and* Paul McCartney. **CP-Beatl**

Dr. Sigmund Freud Discovers the Sea Shell. Archibald MacLeish. **CP-MacLA**

Dr. Swift to Mr. Pope. Jonathan Swift. **CP-SwifJ**

Dr. Swift's Answer to Dr. Sheridan. Jonathan Swift. **CP-SwifJ**

Doctor Trustus: Man of Good Will. John Clellon Holmes. **SP-HolmJ**

Doctor Usquebaugh. Malcolm Lowry. *Fr.* The Cantinas. **CP-LowrM**

Doctors, The. John Donne. *Fr.* A Litany. **CP-DonnJ**

Doctors. Rudyard Kipling. **CP-KiplR**

Doctors, The. Muriel Rukeyser. **CP-RukeM**

Doctors. Anne Sexton. **CP-SextA**

Doctor's Bag, The. John Hewitt. **CP-HewiJ**

Doctors, in the Talmud, say The. Penitence. Robert Herrick. **CP-HerrR**

Doctor's intellectual wife, The. Exeter. Sir John Betjeman. **CP-BetjJ**

Doctors tell me that some people wonder who they are, they don't. You Bet Travel Is Broadening. Ogden Nash. **CP-NashO**

Doctors tender of their fame, The. Jonathan Swift. **NOBL** *Fr.* Verses on the Death of Dr. Swift, D.S.P.D. **CP-SwifJ**

Documenting It. Miller Williams. **SP-WillM**

Dodder, The. Malcolm Lowry. **CP-LowrM**

Dodona. Hilda Doolittle. **CP-DoolH**

Doe: A Fragment, The. George Meredith. **CP-MerG1**

Doe at Evening, A. David Herbert Lawrence. **CP-LawrD**

Doeg, though without knowing how or why. John Dryden *and* Nahum Tate. **SP-DrydJ** *Fr.* Absalom and Achitophel, Pt. II.

Does anybody mind if I don't live in a house that is quaint? No Wonder Our Fathers Died. Ogden Nash. **CP-NashO**

Does anyone know, says Eve, that fable. Eve's Child. Archibald MacLeish. *Fr.* Songs for Eve. **CP-MacLA**

Does anything get more tangled and higgeldy-piggeldy than the days as they drop. A Post-Impressionist Susurration for the First of November, 1983. Hayden Carruth. **CP-CarHS**

Does haughty Gaul invasion threat. The Dumfires Volunteers. Robert Burns. **CP-BurnR**

Does he want you down there. To My Father's Violin. Thomas Hardy. **CP-HardT**

Does love end here? Or a man's work? Sharp Words in the Men's Room. Dabney Stuart. **SP-StuaD**

Does No Love Last? Stevie Smith. **CP-SmitS**

Does No One at All Ever Feel This Way in the Least? Robert Frost. **CP-FrosR**

Does not show his. His Shirt. Rita Dove. **SP-DoveR**

Does Pity give, tho' Fate denies. Song. Charlotte Smith. **CP-SmitC**

Does something lie who'd rather stand. Ballade. Edward Estlin Cummings. **CP-CummE**

Does that lamp still burn in my Father's house. A Prodigal Son. Christina Georgina Rossetti. **CP-RosC2**

Does the court pucell then so censure me. An Epigram on the Court Pucell. Ben Jonson. **CP-JonsB**

Does the Eagle know what is in the pit? Thel's Motto. William Blake. **ChTr** *Fr.* The Book of Thel. **CP-BlakW**

Does the road wind up-hill all the way? Uphill [*or* Up-Hill]. Christina Georgina Rossetti. **CP-RosC1**

Does the Wild Rose? Robert Penn Warren. **SP-WarrR**

Does the woodpecker flit round the young *ferash?* Does the grass clothe a new-built wall? Rudyard Kipling. *Fr.* Certain Maxims of Hafiz. **CP-KiplR**

Does this water. At the Well. Leonard Nathan. **SP-NathL**

Does yesterday's perfection seem not quite. Edward Estlin Cummings. **CP-CummE**

Doesn't he *see* / in the tree / something of *me*? Look. Robert Creeley. **CP-CreeR**

Doesn't, when we touch it, that sheen of infinitesimally pebbled steel, doesn't it, perhaps. New Car. Charles Kenneth Williams. **SP-WillC**

Doeth Well. . . Doeth Better. Christina Georgina Rossetti. **CP-RosC2**

Dog. Charles Bukowski. **SP-BukC1**

Dog. Lawrence Ferlinghetti. **SP-FerlL**

Dog. John Crowe Ransom. **SP-RansJ**

Dog, The. Charles Kenneth Williams. **CP-WillC; SP-WillC**

Dog—An Idyllium, The. William Wordsworth. **CP-WorW1**

Dog and the Thief, The. Jonathan Swift. **CP-SwifJ**

Dog and the Water-Lily, The. William Cowper. **CP-CowpW**

Dog barked; then the woman stood in the doorway, and hearing iron strike stone down the steep road, The. Roan Stallion. Robinson Jeffers. **CP-JefR1**

Dog barks far out, A. Ernesto Cardenal, *tr. by* Thomas Merton. **CP-MertT** *Fr.* Gethsemani, KY.

Dog Body and Cat Mind. Jenny Joseph. **SP-JoseJ**

Dog came loping to his side, A. Pot-Luck among the Casuals. Marsden Hartley. **CP-HartM**

Dog Crunch. Jim Carroll. **SP-CarrJ**

Dog Day Vespers. Charles Wright. **SP-WrigC**

Dog Days. Siv Cedering Fox. **SP-CedeS**

Dog days of marriage have come, The. The Boojum Tree. Richard Shelton. **SP-ShelR**

Dog disappears / across a small lake, A. A Song of Autumn. Joseph Ceravolo. **SP-CeraJ**

Dog Dream. Patti Smith. **SP-SmitP**

Dog go howlin' 'long de road, De. Hope. Paul Laurence Dunbar. **CP-DunbP**

Dog in a Cornfield. James Wright. **CP-WrigJ**

Dog in the Sky, The. Robinson Jeffers. **CP-JefR3**

Dog Lake with Paula. Richard Hugo. **CP-HugoR**

Dog lies in his kennel, The. Christina Georgina Rossetti. **CP-RosC2**

Dog Life. William Matthews. **SP-MattW**

Dog Love. Brendan Galvin. **SP-GalvB**

Dog Poem. Philip Levine. **SP-LeviP**

Dog Sleeping on My Feet, A. James Dickey. **CP-DickJ**

Dog snout puzzles out the look of a man, A. The Baboon and the State. John Ciardi. **SP-CiarJ**

Dog surroundingly howls, A. A Morning. James Dickey. **CP-DickJ**

Dog that spoke, a monster born of sheep, A. Mongolian Idiot. Karl Shapiro. **SP-ShapK**

Dog-Tired. David Herbert Lawrence. **CP-LawrD**

Dog-tired, suisired, will now my body down. The Poet's Final Instructions. John Berryman. **CP-BerrJ**

Dog trots freely in the street, The. Dog. Lawrence Ferlinghetti. **SP-FerlL**

Dog Under False Pretences. William Dickey. **SP-DickW**

Dog Wants His Dinner, The. James Schuyler. **CP-SchuJ**

Dog Yoga. Charles Wright. **SP-WrigC**

Dogfish. Daniel Gerard Hoffman. **SP-HoffD**

Dogfish. Mary Oliver. **SP-OlivM**

Doggerel. Malcolm Lowry. **CP-LowrM**

Doggerel by a Senior Citizen. Wystan Hugh Auden. **CP-AudeW**

"Doggerel," he thought, "will do for churchwardens." Shakespeare's Grave. Robinson Jeffers. **CP-JefR2**

Doggerel of a Diehard Who Sleeps in a Nest of Newspapers. Jean Garrigue. **SP-GarrJ**

Dogheads. Carl Sandburg. **CP-SandC**

Dogma Triumphant, The. Robert Browning. **CP-BroR2**

Dogmatic Teachers, of the snow-white fur! Composed on the Banks of a Rocky Stream. William Wordsworth. **CP-WorW2**

Dogs, The. Charles Bukowski. **SP-BukC2**

Dogs. Charles Bukowski. **SP-BukC3**

Dogs and angels are not. A Plate Glass Window. Charles Bukowski. **SP-BukC1**

Dogs bark at everyone they do not know. Thomas Merton. *Fr.* The Legacy of Herakleitos. **CP-MertT**

Dog's Best Friend Is His Illiteracy, A. Ogden Nash. **CP-NashO**

Dog's Death. John Updike. **CP-UpdiJ**

Dogs greet me, I descend, The. I Come Home Wanting to Touch Everyone. Stephen Dunn. **SP-DunnS**

Dogs have nothing better, The. Three Days of Forest, a River, Free. Rita Dove. **SP-DoveR**

Dogs in the Park. Louis MacNeice. **CP-MacNL**

Dogs of Egypt, The. Charles Bukowski. **SP-BukC2**

Dogs of hell have claws like cats, The. How Do They Get Your Number? Charles Bukowski. **SP-BukC3**

Dogs of indecision, The. The Clear Days. Wendell Berry. **CP-BerrW**

Dogs of Zimmer, The. Paul Zimmer. **SP-ZimmP**

Dogs ran in the woods today, The. The Hunt Goes By. Howard Nemerov. *Fr.* Epigrams: "Wasp, climbing the window pane." **CP-NemeH**

Dogs, Sheep, Cows, Goats. Gary Snyder. **SP-SnydG**

Dog's still jerking on his chain, The. For a Little Girl of Pompeii. Brendan Galvin. **SP-GalvB**

Dogs' tails tick like metronomes, The. The Lugubrious, Salubrious Seaside. Louis MacNeice. **CP-MacNL**

Dogwood. John Gould Fletcher. **SP-FletJ**

Dogwood, The. Robert Penn Warren. *Fr.* Dark Woods. **SP-WarrR**

Dogwood. Louis Zukofsky. **CP-ZukLS**

Dogwood Comes Out Yellow, The. Charles Olson. **CP-OlsoC**

Dogwood flakes / what is green. Variations Done for Gerald Van de Wiele. Charles Olson. **CP-OlsoC; SP-OlsoC**

Dogwood Trees, The. Robert Earl Hayden. **CP-HaydR**

Doin' the Things That We Want To. "Lou Reed." **SP-ReedL**

Doing, a filthy pleasure is, and short. Fragmentum Petron. Arbitr. The Same Translated. Petronius Arbiter, *tr. fr. Latin* by Ben Jonson. **CP-JonsB**

Doing It Differently. Marge Piercy. **SP-PierM**

  "Beds that are mirrors."

  "Digger Indians were too primitive, The."

  "In the pit of the night our bodies merge."

  "Trying to enter each other."

  "We will be equal, we say, new man and new woman."

  "When we mesh badly, with scraping and squeaking."

  "You are an opening in me."

  "You lay in bed depressed, passive as butter."

Doing the House. Richard Hugo. **CP-HugoR**

Dolce cor mio perduto e non perduto. Lassù Fia Caro Il Rivederci. Christina Georgina Rossetti. *Fr.* Il Rosseggiar Dell'Oriente Canzoniere. **CP-RosC3**

Dole of Jarl Thorkell, The. John Greenleaf Whittier. **CP-WhitJ**

Doll in the doll-maker's house, A. The Dolls. William Butler Yeats. **CP-YeatW**

Doll-like, strangely gamin, limbs small and delicate. Swinburne on the Playing Fields. James Liddy. **CP-LiddJ**

Doll she so soone began the wanton trade. Upon Doll. Robert Herrick. **CP-HerrR**

Doll Upon the Topmost Bough, The. Nicholas Vachel Lindsay. *Fr.* This Section Is a Christmas Tree. **CP-LindV**

Dollarton Bus Stop, The. Malcolm Lowry. **CP-LowrM**

Dolls, / by the thousands. The Falling Dolls. Anne Sexton. **CP-SextA**

Dolls, The. Thomas Hardy. **CP-HardT**

Dolls. David St. John. **SP-StJoD**

Dolls, The. William Butler Yeats. **CP-YeatW**

Doll's "Arabian Nights," A. Nicholas Vachel Lindsay. **CP-LindV**

Doll's boy's asleep / under a stile. Edward Estlin Cummings. **CP-CummE**

Doll's hair concealing, A. Partial Resemblance. Denise Levertov. **CP-LeveD**

Dolls Play at Hansel and Gretel, The. William Dickey. **SP-DickW**

Dolly. Thom Gunn. **CP-GunnT**

Dolly sits a-quilting by her mother, stitch by stitch. The Quilting. Paul Laurence Dunbar. **CP-DunbP**

Dolor. Theodore Roethke. **CP-RoetT**

Dolour of Autumn. David Herbert Lawrence. **CP-LawrD**

Dolphin. Robert Lowell. **SP-LoweR**

Dolphin / walked upon the land a little while, The. Living on the Surface. Miller Williams. **SP-WillM**

Dolphin plunge, fountain play. Invocation. Louis MacNeice. **CP-MacNL**

Dolphins play, The. The Aquarium. Thom Gunn. *Fr.* Three for Children. **CP-GunnT**

Dolus. Thomas Campion. **CP-CampT**

Domaine Public. Geoffrey Hill. **OxBC** *Fr.* Four Poems Regarding the Endurance of Poets. **CP-HillG**

Dome of Sunday, The [*or* A]. Karl Shapiro. **SP-ShapK**

Dome of the capitol looks to the Potomac river, The. Smoke Rose Gold. Carl Sandburg. **CP-SandC**

Domesday Song. Wystan Hugh Auden. *Fr.* Ten Songs. **CP-AudeW**

Domestic Help. John Hewitt. **CP-HewiJ**

Domestic Life of Ghosts, The. Tom Clark. **SP-ClarT**

Domestic Peace. Samuel Taylor Coleridge. *Fr.* Effusions. **CP-ColeS**

Domicilium. Thomas Hardy. **CP-HardT**

Domimie's Log, A. John Hewitt. **CP-HewiJ**

Dominant marble, neither will I yield! Don Juan to the Statue. Howard Nemerov. **CP-NemeH**

Dominant Woman. David Herbert Lawrence. **CP-LawrD**

Domination of Black ("At night, by the fire"). Wallace Stevens. **CP-StevW**

Domine Deus, *par. by* Countess of Pembroke, Mary Sidney Herbert. Bible, *O.T. See* Psalm 88: "O God of my salvation."

Dominic has / a doll wired. Edward Estlin Cummings. **CP-CummE**

Dominion: Depression. Charles Kenneth Williams. **SP-WillC**

Dominion lasts until obtained. Emily Dickinson. **CP-DickE**

Domino. James Merrill. **SP-MerrJ**

Dominoes. Gilbert Sorrentino. **SP-SorrG**

Don Baty, the Draft Resister. Muriel Rukeyser. **CP-RukeM**

Don Carlos in a merry spite. Stella at Woodpark. Jonathan Swift. **CP-SwifJ**

Don Juan. Byron. **CP-Byron**

  "And angling too, that solitary vice." **SD**

  Dedication: "Bob Southey! You're a poet—poet-laureate." **CTC; EnRP; OAEL-2; OBSV**

  (Dedication to the Poet Laureate.) **FiP**

  "If, fallen in evil days on evil tongue." **EPCY**

  Southey and Wordsworth. **TrGrPo**

  "You gentlemen, by dint of long seclusion." **EPCY**

  Fragment: "I would to heaven that I were so much clay." **CTC; FiP; NAEL-2; NOBL; NoP; OAEL-2; OxBSP; PrIm**

  "In her first passion woman loves her lover." **ErPo**

  Canto the First. **EnRP; NAEL-2; NoP; OAEL-2; PoE**

    At Thirty Years. **FiP**

    Donna Julia. **PoEL-4**

    Growing Old. **NOBE; SCV**

    "I want a hero: an uncommon want." **FHYEP**

    My Days of Love Are Over. **OBNC**

    Poetical Commandments. **FiP; OBRV; OxBoLi; PeLV,** *canto* 1, *stanzas* 204–206;

    (Poet's Credo.) **SeCePo,** *canto* 1, *stanzas* 204–207;

    "Poor Julia's heart was in an awkward state." **NOBRP**

    "Sagest of women, even of widows, she." **NOBL; PeLV**

    "They tell me 'tis decided you depart." **CBLP**

    "They tell me 'tis decided; you depart." **NOBRP**

    "'Tis sweet to see the evening star appear." **MeMBP**

    "'Twas on a summer's day—the sixth of June." **PPP**

    "What is the end of fame? 'Tis but to fill." **OBCoV**

    "Young Juan wandered by the glassy brooks." **OBCoV,** *canto* 1, *stanzas* 90–96;

  Canto the Second.

    "Fourth day came, but not a breath of air, The." **ChER**

    Haidée and Don Juan. **OBNC**

    Hock and Soda Water. **FaBoDD**

    Juan and Haidée. **EBNV**

    "Juan embark'd--the ship got under way." **MOS**

    "Oh ye! who teach the ingenuous youth of nations." **EnRP**

    "Ship, called the most holy *Trinidada*, The." **OxBoS**

    "Shore looked wild, without a trace of man, The." **HAP**

    "There, breathless, with his digging nails he clung." **OxAEP-2**

    "'Tis thus with people in an open boat." **FaBoPV**

  Canto the Third.

    Evening. **TrGrPo**

    (Hesperus the Bringer.) **AWP**

    "Haidée and Juan carpeted their feet." **NOBRP**

    "Hail, Muse! et caetera.--We left Juan sleeping." **OAEL-2**

    "I know that what our neighbours call *longueurs*." **OBSV**

    "Isles of Greece, the isles of Greece!, The." **AWP; ChTr; FaBoEn; FaPoB; FaPoR; FiP; HBV; LiTB; NOBE; OBEV; OBRV; OBTV; OXAEP-2; RoGo; SeCeV; TreFS; WHA**

    "Fill high the bowl with Samian wine!" **GrIP**

    "Isles of Greece, the isles of Greece!, The." **GrIP**

    "Milton's the prince of poets—so we say." **NOBL**

    "Old Lambro pass'd unseen a private gate." **EnRP**

    "We learn from Horace, Homer sometimes sleep." **EPCY**

  Canto the Fourth.

    Death of Haidée, The. **FiP**

    Haidee. **SeCePo**

    "I leave Don Juan for the present, safe." **NOBRP**

    "Nothing so difficult as a beginning." **EnRP,** *canto* 4, *stanzas* 1–73; **FiP**

    (Romantic to Burlesque.) **FiP,** *canto* 4, *stanzas* 1–3;

    "They were alone once more; for them to be." **EBEV**

  Canto the Fifth.

    Gulbeyaz. **PoEL-4**

    "I wonder if his appetite was good?" **OAEL-2**

  Canto the Sixth.

    "I love the sex, and sometimes would reverse." **CBLP**

  Canto the Seventh.

    " 'Let there be light!' said God, and there was light!" **OBWP**

    "O Love! O Glory! what are you who fly." **OAEL-2**

  Canto the Ninth.

    "Oh, Wellington! (or 'Villainton') for fame." **FiP; OBSV; OxAEP-2; OxBoLi**

    (On Wellington.) **FiP**

    "Though somewhat large, exuberant, and truculent." **OAEL-2**

    "To be or not to be! That is the question." **OBCoV**

"You are 'the best of cut-throats:'—do not start." **FaBoEH; IHNG**

(On Wellington ("You are 'the best of cut-throats' ").) **IHNG**

Canto the Eleventh. **NOBRP**

"In the great world—which, being interpreted." **OxBoLi; PeLV**

Juan in England. **FaBoVe**, *canto* 11, *stanza* 8–20;

"Juan knew several languages—as well." **OAEL-2**

"Over the stones still rattling, up Pall Mall." **NOBL**

"To our theme. The man who has stood on the Acropolis." **InPS; OBSV**

" 'Where is the world!' cries Young at eighty." **FaBoPV**

Canto the Twelfth.

"Why call the miser miserable? as." **UnPo**

"Young unmarried man, with a good name, A." **NOBL**

Canto the Thirteenth. **MeMBP**

(Lady Adeline Amundeville.) **PoEL-4**

Canto the Fourteenth.

"You know, or you don't know, that great Bacon saith." **NOBL**

Canto the Fifteenth.

"I perch upon a humbler promontory." **EPCY**

Don Juan. John Clare.

" 'Poets are born'—and so are whores—the trade is." **SP-ClarJ**

Don Juan. David Herbert Lawrence. **CP-LawrD**

Don Juan had got out on Shooter's Hill. Juan in England. Byron. **FaBoVe**, *canto* 11, *stanza* 8–20; *Fr.* Canto the Eleventh. **NOBRP** *Fr.* Don Juan. **CP-Byron**

Don Juan needs no bed, being far too impatient to undress. The Cave of Nakedness. Wystan Hugh Auden. *Fr.* Thanksgiving for a Habitat. **CP-AudeW**

Don Juan to the Statue. Howard Nemerov. **CP-NemeH**

Don Ramón don't drink, don't smoke. Song to the Tune of *La Cucaracha*. David Herbert Lawrence. **CP-LawrD**

Don Sebastian. John Dryden.

Prologue to *Don Sebastian*. **SP-DrydJ**

Don Surly, to aspire the glorious name. On Don Surly. Ben Jonson. **CP-JonsB**

Don, the divinest women that have walked. With Daniel Bartoli. Robert Browning. **CP-BroR2**

Doña Sebastiana. Martin Edmunds. **SP-EdmuM**

Donaghadee. Thomas Hardy. **CP-HardT**

Donahue's Sister. Thom Gunn. **CP-GunnT**

Donald. Robert Browning. **CP-BroR2**

Done are the toils and the wearisome marches. Ode for Memorial Day. Paul Laurence Dunbar. **CP-DunbP**

Done, Finished with the Biggest Cock. Allen Ginsberg. **CP-GinsA**

Donegal. Brendan Galvin. **SP-GalvB**

Donegal Triptych. Louis MacNeice. **CP-MacNL**

"Acid and ignorant voice, desist."

"Broken bollard, rusted hawser."

"Which being so, which beauties being evanescent but also recurrent."

Donkey, The. Theodore Roethke. **CP-RoetT**

Donkey, The. Stevie Smith. **CP-SmitS**

Donkey's tail is very nice, A. The Monotony Song. Theodore Roethke. **CP-RoetT**

Donn, / though you are cousin. James Liddy. *Fr.* Sandhills. **CP-LiddJ**

Donn na Duimche. James Liddy. *Fr.* Sandhills. **CP-LiddJ**

Donna. Diane Wakoski. *Fr.* Fifteen Poems for a Lunar Eclipse None of Us Saw. **SP-WakoD**

Donna Julia. Byron. **PoEL-4** *Fr.* Canto the First. **EnRP; NAEL-2; NoP; OAEL-2; PoE** *Fr.* Don Juan. **CP-Byron**

Donna MacElmain. Louise McNeill. **SP-McNeL**

Donna Mi Priegha. Ezra Pound. *See* Canto 36: "Lady asks me, A / I speak in season."

Donne He's Regular. Malcolm Lowry. **CP-LowrM**

Donne, the delight of Phoebus, and each Muse. To John Donne. Ben Jonson. **CP-JonsB**

Donnez à manger aux affamées. The Film Star. Stevie Smith. **CP-SmitS**

Don't / ever refuse / the. Easter. Robert Creeley. **CP-CreeR**

Don't. Charles Kenneth Williams. **CP-WillC**

Don't Ask. Roy Fisher. **SP-FishR**

Don't ask for the true story. True Stories. Margaret Atwood. **SP-AtwM2**

Don't be alarmed! Let me sit here with you. Coincidence. Robert Pack. **SP-PackR**

Don't Be Cross, Amanda. Ogden Nash. **CP-NashO**

Don't believe yourself sterile, although, an exile from women. Upon an Eunuch: A Poet. Andrew Marvell, *tr. fr. Latin by* William A. McQueen *and* Kiffin A. Rockwell. **CP-MarvA**

Don't Bother Me. George Harrison. **CP-Beatl**

Don't bother me. / I've just / been born. One or Two Things. Mary Oliver. **SP-OlivM**

Don't Break It. Joseph Ceravolo. **SP-CeraJ**

Don't care for it. Berkshire. Donald Davie. **CP-DavDo**

Don't come any of that Byzantium stuff. Byzantium: Or Where the Great Life Begins. Malcolm Lowry. **CP-LowrM**

Don't cries to please my. Edward Estlin Cummings. **CP-CummE**

Don't Cry, Darling, It's Blood All Right. Ogden Nash. **CP-NashO**

Don't Even Tell Your Wife, Particularly. Ogden Nash. **CP-NashO**

Don't expect smiles on all my faces. Notes Towards an Autobiography. Richard Shelton. **CP-ShelR**

Don't Fall Apart on Me Tonight. "Bob Dylan." **CP-DylaB**

Don't Forget. Stephen Berg. **SP-BergS**

Don't get me wrong oblivion. Edward Estlin Cummings. **CP-CummE**

Don't Go Home with Your Hard-on. Leonard Cohen. **CP-CoheL**

Don't go unhappy / To the ultraviolet home. Thomas Merton. *Fr.* Cables to the Ace. **CP-MertT**

Don't Grin, or You'll Have to Bear It. Ogden Nash. **CP-NashO**

Don't Grow Old. Allen Ginsberg. **CP-GinsA**

Don't Grow Old. Allen Ginsberg. **CP-GinsA**

Father Death Blues. **SM**

Don't Guess, Let Me Tell You. Ogden Nash. **CP-NashO**

Don't hate your parents, or your children will hire. The Hard Way. Robert Lowell. **SP-LoweR**

Don't, Have One for the Road. Malcolm Lowry. **CP-LowrM**

Don't hurt the radio for. Radio. Tom Clark. **SP-ClarT**

Don't kid yourself: / something kills them all—. A Kind of Lecture on a Dull Day When There Isn't Even a Fly Around to Kill. Charles Bukowski. **SP-BukC2**

Don't Kill Yourself. Carlos Drummond de Andrade, *tr. fr. Portuguese by* Elizabeth Bishop. **CP-BishE**

Don't let it mean anything. Rifkin Movement. Richard Eberhart. **CP-EberR**

Don't Let Me Down. John Lennon *and* Paul McCartney. **CP-Beatl**

Don't let that horse. Lawrence Ferlinghetti. **SP-FerlL**

Don't let your dog curb you! *See also* Hughes's Warning. Langston Hughes. **SP-HughL**

Don't lock me in wedlock, I want. About Marriage. Denise Levertov. **CP-LeveD**

Don't Look at Me. David Herbert Lawrence. **CP-LawrD**

Don't Look Back. Dabney Stuart. **SP-StuaD**

Don't Look for the Silver Lining, Just Wait for It. Ogden Nash. **CP-NashO**

Don't Look Now. Ogden Nash. **CP-NashO**

Don't look now, God, we're all right. May 30th. Anne Sexton. **CP-SextA**

Don't own so much clutter that you will be relieved to see your. Wendell Berry. *Fr.* Prayers and Sayings of the Mad Farmer. **CP-BerrW**

Don't Pass Me By. "Ringo Starr." **CP-Beatl**

Don't play too much, don't play. The Accompanist. William Matthews. **SP-MattW**

Don't play with sharp tools, these are edge 'uns. Rhyme on Edward Burne-Jones. Robert Browning. **CP-BroR2**

Don't pray for the rain to stop. Wendell Berry. *Fr.* Prayers and Sayings of the Mad Farmer. **CP-BerrW**

Don't put up my Thread and Needle. Emily Dickinson. **CP-DickE**

Don't say, don't say there is no water. The Fountain. Denise Levertov. **CP-LeveD**

Don't say, "humbly." Graph for Action. William Carlos Williams. **CP-WilW1**

Don't scream at me you God damn' wops. Kennedy *Ucciso*. Richard Hugo. **CP-HugoR**

Don't Sign Anything. Robert Creeley. **CP-CreeR**

Don't spill the salt, for it is the landmark. Spilling the Salt. David Herbert Lawrence. **CP-LawrD**

Don't stand out there, man, in all that howlllllllll. A Six Inch Chapter—in Verse. Charles Olson. **CP-OlsoC**

Don't Start That. Jim Morrison. **SP-MorrJ**

Don't tell him about the beauty of losing. Revival Meeting for Wheelchairs and Stretchers. Leonard Nathan. **SP-NathL**

Don't these city lights light these streets to life. City Lights. "Lou Reed." **SP-ReedL**

Don't they consult the 'Victims,' though? Canto V: Byckerment. "Lewis Carroll." *Fr.* Phantasmagoria. **CP-CarrL**

Don't think / because her petal thighs. Girl in White. Marge Piercy. **SP-PierM**

Don't think it won't come to you. Watching a child watching a witch. Jenny Joseph. **AIW** *Fr.* Derivations. **SP-JoseJ**

Don't think of it. Praise. Wendell Berry. **CP-BerrW**

Don't Think Twice, It's All Right. "Bob Dylan." **CP-DylaB**

Don't Think You Know My Name! Thomas McGrath. **SP-McGrT**

Don't Touch the Girls. Charles Bukowski. **SP-BukC1**

Don't trot trot to Bost-. Reveille for a Rockinghorse Poet. Isabella Gardner. **CP-GardI**

Don't undress my love. Trapped. Charles Bukowski. **SP-BukC1**

Don't Wait, Hit Me Now! Ogden Nash. **CP-NashO**

Don't wanna judge nobody, don't wanna be judged. Do Right to Me Baby (Do Unto Others). "Bob Dylan." **CP-DylaB**

Don't Wash Your Hair in the Streetcar, Nora Dear. Kenneth Patchen. **CP-PatcK**

Don't waste your time, Leuconoé, living in fear and hope. 1.2. Horace. **SP-MahoD,** tr. by Derek Mahon; *Fr.* Odes.

Don't worry about rejections, pard. For Al—. Charles Bukowski. **SP-BukC1**

Don't worry and fret about the crops. After you have done all you can for them, let them stand in the weather on their own. Wendell Berry. *Fr.* Prayers and Sayings of the Mad Farmer. **CP-BerrW**

Don't Ya Tell Henry. "Bob Dylan." **CP-DylaB**

Don't you also feel danger. Pablo Neruda, tr. fr. *Spanish* by Ben Belitt. **SP-NeruP** *Fr.* Question Book.

Don't you care for my love? she said bitterly. Intimates. David Herbert Lawrence. **CP-LawrD**

Don't you dream of a world, a society, with no coercion? Wystan Hugh Auden. *Fr.* Shorts [1939–1947] ("Motionless, deep in his mind, lies the past the poet's forgotten"). **CP-AudeW**

Don'ts. David Herbert Lawrence. **CP-LawrD**

Doodler, The. James Merrill. **SP-MerrJ**

Doom and She. Thomas Hardy. **CP-HardT**

Doom and Siesta Time. Charles Bukowski. **SP-BukC1**

Doom is dark and deeper than any sea-dingle. The Wanderer. Wystan Hugh Auden. **CP-AudeW**

Doom is the House without the Door. Emily Dickinson. **CP-DickE**

Doom of each, said Doctor Usquebaugh, The. Doctor Usquebaugh. Malcolm Lowry. *Fr.* The Cantinas. **CP-LowrM**

Doom of Exiles. Sylvia Plath. **CP-PlatS**

Doom of Fruit without the Bloom, A. Emily Dickinson. **SP-DickE**

Doom'd as I am in solitude to waste. On the Death of Russell. William Cowper. **CP-CowpW**

Doomed as we are our native dust. Composed in One of the Catholic Cantons. William Wordsworth. *Fr.* Memorials of a Tour of the Continent; 1820. **CP-WorW2**

Doomed—regard the Sunrise, The. Emily Dickinson. **CP-DickE**

Doomes-Day. Robert Herrick. **CP-HerrR**

Dooms menace from tumults. Who's immune. Beethoven Triumphant. John Berryman. **CP-BerrJ**

Doomsday. George Herbert. **CP-HerbG**

Doomsday. Sylvia Plath. **CP-PlatS**

Doomsday Books, The. Howard Nemerov. **CP-NemeH**

Door, The. Wystan Hugh Auden. *See* Out of it steps our future, through this door.

Door, The. Jane Cooper. **SP-CoopJ**

Door, The. ("It is hard"). Robert Creeley. **CP-CreeR**

Door, The. ("Thump. Thump."). Robert Creeley. **CP-CreeR**

Door, The. Robert Ranke Graves. **CP-GravR**

Door, The. Frederick Morgan. **SP-MorgF**

Door: / PER L'UNIVERSO / is what it says, A. Idyll. Charles Tomlinson. **CP-TomlC**

Door, The. Charles Tomlinson. **CP-TomlC**

Door, The. Lewis Turco. **SP-TurcL**

Door-bell jangled in evening's peace, The. The Owl. Walter de la Mare. **CP-DeLaW**

Door Gunner to the Moment, (A Shau Valley 1968), The. Tom Clark. **SP-ClarT**

Door in the Dark, The. Robert Frost. **CP-FrosR**

Door is shut. / The red rider, The. A Sense of Distance. Charles Tomlinson. **CP-TomlC**

Door it opened slowly, The. Story of Isaac. Leonard Cohen. **CP-CoheL**

Door just opened on a street, A. Emily Dickinson. **CP-DickE**

Door of Death, The. William Blake. **ChTr** *Fr.* Dedication of the Illustrations to Blair's "Grave."

Door of Death is made of Gold, The. Dedication of the Illustrations to Blair's "Grave." William Blake. **CP-BlakW**

Door of the shed, The. The Turn. Frederick Morgan. **SP-MorgF**

Door opens, The. Thom Gunn. *Fr.* Jack Straw's Castle. **CP-GunnT**

Door sunk in a hillside, with a bolt, A. The Icehouse in Summer. Howard Nemerov. **CP-NemeH**

Door that opens on, A. Gilbert Sorrentino. **SP-SorrG**

Door to the Forest, The. Tom Clark. **SP-ClarT**

Door turned its white face, A. John Haines. *Fr.* The Mirror. **SP-HainJ**

Door was bolted and the windows of my porch, The. The Milkman. Isabella Gardner. **CP-GardI**

Door was shut. I looked between, The. Shut Out. Christina Georgina Rossetti. **CP-RosC1**

Doorkeepers of Zion, The. Zion. Rudyard Kipling. **CP-KiplR**

Doors. David Herbert Lawrence. **CP-LawrD**

Doors. Carl Sandburg. **CP-SandC**

Doors, The. David St. John. **SP-StJoD**

Doors are down before the ancient tombs, The. The Pride of the Dead. Thomas Merton. **CP-MertT**

Doors, Doors, Doors. Anne Sexton. **CP-SextA**

Doors in the Wind and the Water. Marge Piercy. **SP-PierM**

Doors of the morning must open, The. Pass, Friend. Carl Sandburg. **CP-SandC**

Doors of the Year, Well Done, The. Steve Griffiths. **SP-GrifS**

Doors open, The. In the Beach House. Anne Sexton. **CP-SextA**

Doors open in the mind. Doors in the Wind and the Water. Marge Piercy. **SP-PierM**

Doors were oak, massive, The. The Doors. David St. John. **SP-StJoD**

Doors were wide, the story saith, The. Rudyard Kipling. **CP-KiplR** *Fr.* The Return of Imray. *Fr.* Life's Handicap.

Doors, where my heart was used to beat. Tennyson. **EnVR; FHYEP; NoP; OBNC; PoEL-5; SCV** *Fr.* In Memoriam A. H. H. **CP-TennA**

Doorstep, Lightning, Waif-Dreaming. James Dickey. **CP-DickJ**

Doorways to everywhere the poet said. Lady/Lord in Doorway. James Liddy. **CP-LiddJ**

Dorabella's Naples Watercolor. James Schuyler. **CP-SchuJ**

Dora's gone to Ireland. How She Went to Ireland. Thomas Hardy. **CP-HardT**

Dorcas. James Liddy. **CP-LiddJ**

Doria. Ezra Pound. **SP-PounE**

Doricha. Posidippus. **AWP; FaBoEE; OBVE** *Fr.* Variations of Greek Themes. **CP-RobiE**

Dorinda dreams of dress abed. Jonathan Swift. **CP-SwifJ**

Dormi, Jesu! Mater ridet, *Latin vers. tr. by* Coleridge. Samuel Taylor Coleridge. *See* The Virgin's Cradle-Hymn.

Dornröschen, princess. Hayden Carruth. *Fr.* The Sleeping Beauty. **CP-CarHL**

Dorothy Wordsworth, dying, did not want to read. My Sisters, O My Sisters. May Sarton. **SP-SartM**

Dorset. Sir John Betjeman. **CP-BetjJ**

Dorset. Donald Davie. **CP-DavDo**

Dorset, the Grace of Courts, the Muses' Pride. Epitaph on Charles Earl of Dorset. Alexander Pope. **CP-PopeA**

Dorset! whose early steps with mine have stray'd. To the Duke of Dorset. Byron. **CP-Byron**

Dortmunder. Samuel Beckett. **CP-BeckS**

Dorus, tell me, where is thy wonted motion, *dialogue of Dicus and Dorus.* Sir Philip Sidney. **OBVE; SP-SidnP** *Fr.* Arcadia.

Do's Fortune rend thee? Beare with thy hard Fate. Suffer Thou that Canst not Shift. Robert Herrick. **CP-HerrR**

Dosn't thou 'ear my 'erse's legs, as they canters awaäy? Northern Farmer: New Style. Tennyson. **CP-TennA**

Dost ask, dear Captain, why from Syme. To Captain G————, on Being Asked Why I Was Not to Be of the Party with Him and His Brother K-nm-re at Syme's. Robert Burns. **CP-BurnR**

Dost ask me, why I send thee here. The Primrose. Robert Burns. **CP-BurnR**

Dost blush, my dear Billy, asham'd of thyself. Robert Burns. *Fr.* On an Old Acquaintance Who Seemed to Pass the Bard without Notice. *Fr.* Dumfries Epigrams. **CP-BurnR**

Dost hang thy head, Billy, asham'd that thou knowest me? Robert Burns. *Fr.* On an Old Acquaintance Who Seemed to Pass the Bard without Notice. *Fr.* Dumfries Epigrams. **CP-BurnR**

Dost me of new crimes always guilty frame? 2.7. Ovid. **CP-MarlC,** tr. by Christopher Marlowe; *Fr.* Elegies.

Dost see how unregarded now. Sonnet. Sir John Suckling. **CP-SuckJ**

Dost tha hear my horse's feet, as he canters away? Lord Tennyson and Lord Melchett. David Herbert Lawrence. **CP-LawrD**

Dost thou behold some woeful soul. George Meredith. **CP-MerG2**

Dost thou look back on what hath been. Tennyson. *Fr.* In Memoriam A. H. H. **CP-TennA**

Dost thou love me, my Belovèd? Proof and Disproof. Elizabeth Barrett Browning. **CP-BroEB**

Dost Thou Not Care? Christina Georgina Rossetti. **CP-RosC1**

Dost thou not hear me Ellen. Ralph Waldo Emerson. **CP-EmerR**

Dost thou not rise, indignant Shade. Extempore—on Some Commemorations of Thomson. Robert Burns. **CP-BurnR**

Dost thou weep, mourning mother. The Mourning Mother. Elizabeth Barrett Browning. **CP-BroEB**

Dostoievsky Warns W. D. about Wearing Raskolnikov's Hat. William DeWitt Snodgrass. **SP-SnodW**

Dostoyevsky. Kenneth Patchen. **CP-PatcK**

Dotage. George Herbert. **CP-HerbG**

Doth most humbly show it. The Humble Petition of Poor Ben to the Best of Monarchs, Masters, Men, King Charles. Ben Jonson. **CP-JonsB**

Doth not a Tenarif[e], or Higher Hill. John Donne. **ChTr** *Fr.* The First Anniversary [*or* Anniversarie]. **AnAnS-1; FaBoRV; MasP; SeCV-1** *Fr.* Anatomy [*or* Anatomie] of the World, An[: The First Anniversary]. **CP-DonnJ**

D'où / la voix qui dit. Samuel Beckett. **CP-BeckS**

Double Acrostic: I sing a place wherein agree. "Lewis Carroll." **CP-CarrL**

Double Acrostic: Two little girls near London dwell. "Lewis Carroll." **CP-CarrL**

Double Axe, The. Robinson Jeffers. **CP-JefR3**

  Inhumanist, The.

  Love and the Hate, The.

Double Bass. Robert Ranke Graves. **CP-GravR**

Double Dialogue: *Homage to Robert Frost.* Muriel Rukeyser. **CP-RukeM**

Double, diverse, sullen, and strange. Sir Thomas Wyatt. **CP-WyatT**

Double, double, root and branch. Charles Olson. **CP-OlsoC**

Double, double, twice the face. Bagatto. Charles Olson. **CP-OlsoC**

Double-Ended Dory, A. Brendan Galvin. **SP-GalvB**

Double-Ended Tram, The. John Hewitt. **CP-HewiJ**

Double Exposure. Archie Randolph Ammons. **SP-AmmoA**

Double Feature. Robert Earl Hayden. **CP-HaydR**

Double Feature. Theodore Roethke. **CP-RoetT**

Double-Headed Snake of Newbury, The. John Greenleaf Whittier. **CP-WhitJ**

Double helix and the triple star, The. Peter Meinke. *Fr.* Mendel's Laws. **SP-MeinP**

Double Hellas, The. Kenneth Rexroth. **CP-RexKL** *Fr.* The Homestead Called Damascus.

  "World is composed of a pair of, The." **SP-RexrK**

Double Image, The. Anne Sexton. **CP-SextA**

Double Monologue. Adrienne Rich. **CP-RicAE**

Double moon, one on the high backdrop of the west, one on the, The. River Moons. Carl Sandburg. **CP-SandC**

Double Ode. Muriel Rukeyser. **CP-RukeM**

Double Rainbow, The. Charles Tomlinson. **CP-TomlC**

Double Shame, The. Stephen Spender. **CP-SpenS**

Double-Tail Dog. Shel Silverstein. **SP-SilS2**

Double Vision. Robert Lowell. **SP-LoweR**

Double Vision of Michael Robartes, The. William Butler Yeats. **CP-YeatW**

Double Voice, The. Margaret Atwood. **SP-AtwM1**

Doubling and doubling with laborious walk. Rest and Be Thankful! William Wordsworth. **CP-WorW2**

Doubt. Tennyson. *See* You say, but with no touch of scorn.

Doubt and the passion, The. The Oath. Robert Ranke Graves. **CP-GravR**

Doubt if it be Us, A. Emily Dickinson. **CP-DickE**

Doubt Me! My Dim Companion! Emily Dickinson. **CP-DickE**

Doubt No More that Oberon. Edna St. Vincent Millay. **CP-MillE**

Doubt there hath been, when with his golden chain. Sonnet 58. Sir Philip Sidney. *Fr.* Astrophil and Stella. **SP-SidnP**

Doubt to which a wavering hope had clung, The. Composed When a Probability Existed of Our Being Obliged to Quit Rydal Mount as a Residence. William Wordsworth. **CP-WorW2**

Doubt you fought so long, The. The Whip. Edwin Arlington Robinson. **CP-RobiE**

Doubt you to whom my Muse these notes intendeth [*or* entendeth]. Sir Philip Sidney. **EIL; HBV 1-2; OBSC; OxAEP-1; WHA** *Fr.* Astrophil and Stella. **SP-SidnP**

  (First Song.) **OxAEP-1**

  (To Stella.) **EIL; WHA**

Doubtless he saw some path clear, having found. Geoffrey Hill. *Fr.* Metamorphoses. **CP-HillG**

Doubtless, sweet girl! the hissing lead. Lines Addressed to a Young Lady. Byron. **CP-Byron**

Doubts before Dreaming. Erica Jong. **SP-JongE**

Douglas and Marmion. Sir Walter Scott. *See* Battle, The ("Not far advanc'd was morning day").

Douglass. Paul Laurence Dunbar. **CP-DunbP**

Douglas's Ride. Emily Brontë. **CP-BronE**

Dove, The. Leonard Cohen. **CP-CoheL**

Dove, The. Walter de la Mare. **CP-DeLaW**

Dove, The. Paul Laurence Dunbar. **CP-DunbP**

Dove alone expresses, The. Thomas Campion. **PBBP** *Fr.* What Harvest Half So Sweet Is. **CP-CampT**

Dove Came, The. Ted Hughes. **SP-HughT**

Dove flew with an Olive Branch, A. The Olive Branch. George Meredith. **CP-MerG1**

Dove in the Belly, The. Wallace Stevens. **CP-StevW**

Dove-melting mountains, ridges gashed with water. No More Sea. Louis MacNeice. **CP-MacNL**

Dove of Dacca, The. Rudyard Kipling. **CP-KiplR**

Dove of liberty sat on an egg, The. The American Eagle. David Herbert Lawrence. **CP-LawrD**

Dove sta amore / Where lies love. Lawrence Ferlinghetti. **SP-FerlL**

Dove that lets the silence answer. The Wood Dove at Sandy Spring. Archibald MacLeish. **CP-MacLA**

Dove walks with sticky feet, The. Pastoral. Kenneth Patchen. **CP-PatcK**

Dove-white gulls / on the wet lawn in Washington Square, The. I Genitori Perduti. Lawrence Ferlinghetti. **SP-FerlL**

Doveglion. Edward Estlin Cummings. **CP-CummE**

Dover. Wystan Hugh Auden. **CP-AudeW**

Dover Beach. Matthew Arnold. **SP-ArnoM**

"Dover Beach"—a Note to That Poem. Archibald MacLeish. **CP-MacLA**

Dover: Believing in Kings. James Dickey. **CP-DickJ**

Doves, The. William Cowper. **CP-CowpW**

Doves the speckled doves, The. In Aix. Grace Paley. **CP-PaleG**

Dow Jones: Down. Charles Bukowski. **SP-BukC2**

Down. Joseph Ceravolo. **SP-CeraJ**

Down. Robert Ranke Graves. **CP-GravR**

(Down, / to my soul. Love. Charles Olson. **CP-OlsoC**

Down a rope of. The Plunge. Thom Gunn. **CP-GunnT**

Down a swift Stream, thus far, a bold design. William Wordsworth. *Fr.* Ecclesiastical Sonnets. **CP-WorW2**

Down Along the Cove. "Bob Dylan." **CP-DylaB**

Down among strict roots and rocks. Danse Macabre. Sylvia Plath. **CP-PlatS**

Down & Back. John Berryman. **CP-BerrJ**

Down and Out. Langston Hughes. **SP-HughL**

Down at the bottom of a well. Doggerel. Malcolm Lowry. **CP-LowrM**

Down at the Docks. Kenneth Koch. **SP-KochK**

Down at the Hotel Sherlock Holmes. Thomas Merton. *Fr.* Figures for an Apocalypse. **CP-MertT**

Down between the walls of shadow. Subway. Carl Sandburg. **CP-SandC**

Down by a shining water well. My Kingdom. Robert Louis Stevenson. **CP-StevR**

Down by the bay I. Attention. Archie Randolph Ammons. **SP-AmmoA**

Down by the Nile water. Moses. Howard Nemerov. **CP-NemeH**

Down by the Salley Gardens. William Butler Yeats. **CP-YeatW**

Down by the waters of the sea. Never-To-Be. Walter de la Mare. **CP-DeLaW**

"Down cellar," said the cricket. Nicholas Vachel Lindsay. *Fr.* The Potatoes' Dance. **CP-LindV**

Down comes the winter rain. Unrealized. Thomas Hardy. **CP-HardT**

Down, down beneath the daisy beds. The Song of the Garden-Toad. Nicholas Vachel Lindsay. **CP-LindV**

Down, down—born pioneers in time's despite. Hart Crane. **TrGrPo** *Fr.* The River. **AmPP; CMoP; GOA; MoAB; MoAmPo; NOBA; OxBA; PrIm** *Fr.* Powhatan's Daughter. *Fr.* The Bridge. **CP-CranH**

Down, down, down! Finding Your Level. David Herbert Lawrence. **CP-LawrD**

Down drop of the blackbird, The. Three Spring Notations on Bipeds. Carl Sandburg. **CP-SandC**

Down from Chicago Bryan came. Muriel Rukeyser. **CP-RukeM**

Down from Gerlachovka. After Hal'amová. James Liddy. **CP-LiddJ**

Down Home. Robert Creeley. **CP-CreeR**

Down home / he sets on a stoop. Neighbor. Langston Hughes. **SP-HughL**

Down in Ol' Dontcaradama. Kenneth Patchen. **CP-PatcK**

Down in the bass / That steady beat. Easy Boogie. Langston Hughes. **SP-HughL**

Down in the cellars, nothing is visible. Thom Gunn. *Fr.* Jack Straw's Castle. **CP-GunnT**

Down in the dark cave. Pocket Song. Leonard Nathan. **SP-NathL**

Down in the engine room again. Envoy to Six Years. Gary Snyder. *Fr.* Six Years. **CP-SnydG**

Down in the Flood. "Bob Dylan." **CP-DylaB**

Down in the Lone Valley. Kenneth Patchen. **CP-PatcK**

Down in the orchard. Geoffrey Hill. **HAP** *Fr.* The Pentecost Castle. **CP-HillG**

Down in the river-garden a grey-gold. Geoffrey Hill. *Fr.* The Mystery of the Charity of Charles Péguy. **CP-HillG**

Down in the street there are ice-cream parlors to go to. Thank You for Not Cooperating. John Ashbery. **SP-AshbJ**

Down in this bone-bare, borrowed basement flat. Monody. David Markson. **CP-MarkD**

Down in West Texas where the sun. West Texas. Langston Hughes. **SP-HughL**

Down into dust and reeds. Basil Bunting. *Fr.* Briggflatts [An Autobiography]. **CP-BuntB**

Down lay Karl Onyx for his end of time. Karl Onyx. George Meredith. **CP-MerG2**

Down Low. Archie Randolph Ammons. **SP-AmmoA**

Down on the ancient wharf, the sand, I sit with a new-comer chatting. Twenty Years. Walt Whitman. **CP-WhitW**

Down panic, down. The castle is still here. Thom Gunn. *Fr.* Jack Straw's Castle. **CP-GunnT**

Down. Shovelled. Can hear. Alternate Thoughts from Underground. Margaret Atwood. **SP-AtwM1**

Down some mud alley / in back of a Kansas town. Vignette. John Clellon Holmes. **SP-HolmJ**

Down stucco sidestreets. Dublinesque. Philip Larkin. **CP-LarkP**

Down the Burn Davie. Robert Burns. **CP-BurnR**

Down the close, darkening lanes they sang their way. The Send-Off. Wilfred Owen. **CP-OwenW**

Down the dark Bardol corridors. Room in a Penitentiary. Chuck Miller. **SP-MillC**

Down the dawn-brown. The Current. James Merrill. **SP-MerrJ**

Down the dusty lane of summer. The Buttercup Children. Phoebe Hesketh. **SP-HeskP**

Down the façade lean statues listening. Thunder in Tuscany. Charles Tomlinson. **CP-TomlC**

Down the Highway. "Bob Dylan." **CP-DylaB**

Down the Lanes and Paths (For Stack). Chuck Miller. **SP-MillC**

Down the Mississippi. John Gould Fletcher. **SP-FletJ**

Down the Mousehole, and What Science Missed There. Ogden Nash. **CP-NashO**

Down the river, on rafts you came. The Rafts. Adrienne Rich. **CP-RicAE**

Down the road someone is practising scales. Sunday Morning. Louis MacNeice. **CP-MacNL**

Down the rock chute into the tombs of the kings they grope these battling sandalled. This Is the Life. Louis MacNeice. **CP-MacNL**

Down the small and crooked road. Poem. Thomas McGrath. **SP-McGrT**

Down the stairs flying, looks at the surfaces. Muriel Rukeyser. **CP-RukeM**

Down the stone stairs. After the Opera. David Herbert Lawrence. **CP-LawrD**

Down the street the dogs are barkin'. One Too Many Mornings. "Bob Dylan." **CP-DylaB**

Down the track of a Philippine Island. The Enclosure. James Dickey. **CP-DickJ**

Down the turning stairway. John Haines. *Fr.* The Mirror. **SP-HainJ**

Down There. Wystan Hugh Auden. *Fr.* Thanksgiving for a Habitat. **CP-AudeW**

Down there in those islands. Bahamas. Archibald MacLeish. **CP-MacLA**

Down there like. Maybe not the same, of course. Hayden Carruth. *Fr.* The Sleeping Beauty. **CP-CarHL**

Down this old well. The Well. Adrienne Rich. **CP-RicAE**

Down, throw down his like who eat. Cinos. Charles Olson. **CP-OlsoC**

Down Time's quaint stream. Emily Dickinson. **CP-DickE**

Down to the Dregs. César Vallejo, *tr. fr. Spanish by* James Wright. **CP-WrigJ**

Down-town / Swarms. Surely the oldest city. George Oppen. *Fr.* Tourist Eye. **CP-OppeG**

Down valley a smoke haze. Mid-August at Sourdough Mountain Lookout. Gary Snyder. **CP-SnydG**

Down Wall Street. The Workers Rose on May Day or Postcript to Karl Marx. Audre Lorde. **SP-LordA**

Down, Wanton, Down! Robert Ranke Graves. **CP-GravR**

Down went the grand "Queen Mary." The Sea Fight. Thomas Hardy. **CP-HardT**

Down Wessex way, when spring's a-shine. The Spring Call. Thomas Hardy. **CP-HardT**

Down where the dog-toothed tide. Art Song. Howard Nemerov. **CP-NemeH**

Down where the stone's cold shadow. News from the Low Country. Leonard Nathan. **SP-NathL**

Down with the Rosemary and Bay[e]s. Ceremonies for Candlemas[se] Eve. Robert Herrick. **CP-HerrR**

Down with the rosemary, and so. Ceremony upon Candlemas Eve. Robert Herrick. **CP-HerrR**

Down, you mongrel, Death! The Poet and His Book. Edna St. Vincent Millay. **CP-MillE**

Downhill. James McAuley. *Fr.* Ten-Mile Run. **SP-McAuJ**

Downpour that subdued everybody and, The. Roy Fisher. **SP-FishR** *Fr.* New Diversions.

Downstairs a clock had chimed, two o'clock only. Down. Robert Ranke Graves. **CP-GravR**

Downstairs I laugh, I sport and jest with all. L. E. L. Christina Georgina Rossetti. **CP-RosC1**

Downstream on impassive rivers suddenly. Arthur Rimbaud. *See* The Drunken Boat.

Downtown, an office tower is going up. Diagrams. Thom Gunn. **CP-GunnT**

Downtown at the Front St. Bi-jo (spelt Bijou). Stanley Jasspon Kunitz. *Fr.* The Magic Curtain. **CP-KuniS**

Downward through the evening twilight. Hiawatha's Childhood. Henry Wadsworth Longfellow. **SP-LongH** *Fr.* The Song of Hiawatha.

Downward you cast your eyes. To a Small Buddha. Wystan Hugh Auden. **CP-AudWJ**

Downwards. Charles Kenneth Williams. **CP-WillC; SP-WillC**

Downwind, he caught the scent. Hunter, Prey. Dabney Stuart. **SP-StuaD**

Dowser, The. Louis MacNeice. **CP-MacNL**

Doze o blk / capitalists. Memo #9. Etheridge Knight. **SP-KnigE**

Dozen years have passed since then, A. To the Memory of James Connolly. John Hewitt. **CP-HewiJ**

Dozens, The. Audre Lorde. **SP-LordA**

Dozens of blue relics slip from their envelopes, rise and turn toward. La Brea. John Yau. **SP-YauJo**

Dozing on the Lawn. Archibald MacLeish. **CP-MacLA**

Dr. Joseph Goebbels ("Say goodbye to the help, the ranks"). William DeWitt Snodgrass. **CAPP** *Fr.* The Führer Bunker. **SP-SnodW**

"Stand back, make way, you mindless scum." **TW**

Dr. Joseph Goebbels ("Stand back, make way, you mindless scum"). William DeWitt Snodgrass. **SP-SnodW** *Fr.* The Führer Bunker. **SP-SnodW**

Dr. Ramsden cannot read *The Times* obituary to-day. I.M. Walter Ramsden, Ob. March 26, 1947, Pembroke College, Oxford. Sir John Betjeman. **CP-BetjJ**

Dr. Y / I need a thin hot wire. Letters to Dr. Y. Anne Sexton. **CP-SextA**

Drab Habitation of Whom? Emily Dickinson. **CP-DickE**

Drab look'd long at his neighbour's note. The Song of Drab. George Meredith. **CP-MerG2**

Draft Balance Sheet. James McAuley. **SP-McAuJ**

Draft Board. Malcolm Lowry. **CP-LowrM**

Draft Horse, The. Robert Frost. **CP-FrosR**

Draft of love was cool and sweet, The. Love's Draft. Paul Laurence Dunbar. **CP-DunbP**

Dragging his hunger through the sky. The Vulture. Samuel Beckett. **CP-BeckS** *Fr.* Echo's Bones.

Dragon, The. Edmund Spenser. **SeCePo** *Fr.* The Faerie Queene. **CP-Spens**

Dragon and the Unicorn, The, *sels.* Kenneth Rexroth.
  " 'And what is love?' said Pilate." **CP-RexKL**
  " 'And what is love?' said Pilate." **SP-RexrK**
  "Art of Worldly Wisdom, The." **CP-RexKL**
  "Discursive knowledge, knowledge by." **SP-RexrK**
  "New York a grey haze with flights of." **CP-RexKL**
  "I come back to the cottage in." **SP-RexrK**
  "Over Switzerland broods the." **CP-RexKL**
  "Zoraster long ago / Said poetry presents us." **CP-RexKL**
  "Boswell: Sir, what is the chief." **SP-RexrK**

Dragon Country: To Jacob Boehme. Robert Penn Warren. **SP-WarrR**

Dragon-fly, The. Wystan Hugh Auden. **CP-AudWJ**

Dragon-Fly, The. Charles Olson. **CP-OlsoC**

Dragonfly, The. Louise Bogan. **CP-BogaL**

Dragonfly, The. Stanley Jasspon Kunitz. **CP-KuniS**

Dragonfly, The. Edna St. Vincent Millay. **CP-MillE**

Dragonfly, The. Howard Nemerov. **CP-NemeH**

Dragons Are Too Seldom. Ogden Nash. **CP-NashO**

Dragon's Blood I. John Yau. **SP-YauJo**

Dragon's Blood II. John Yau. **SP-YauJo**

Dragon's Blood III. John Yau. **SP-YauJo**

Dragon's Blood IV. John Yau. **SP-YauJo**

Dragon's Proteus. He must be fought, The. Binding the Dragon. May Sarton. **SP-SartM**

Dragoons, I tell you the white hydrangeas turn rust and go soon. Carl Sandburg. **CP-SandC**

Drained Cup, The. David Herbert Lawrence. **CP-LawrD**

Drake in the Southern Sea. Ernesto Cardenal, *tr. fr. Spanish by* Thomas Merton. **CP-MertT**

Drake's Drum. Geoffrey Hill. *Fr.* Metamorphoses. **CP-HillG**

Drama, A. David Herbert Lawrence. **CP-LawrD**

Drama. Howard Nemerov. **CP-NemeH**

Drama of Exile, A. Elizabeth Barrett Browning. **CP-BroEB**

"Drama of politics doesn't interest me," said a news rewrite man, The. Carl Sandburg. *Fr.* The People, Yes. **CP-SandC**

Dramas of the Evening. Thomas Merton. *Fr.* Cables to the Ace. **CP-MertT**

Drama's Vitallest Expression is the Common Day. Emily Dickinson. **CP-DickE**

Dramatis Personae. Charles Olson. **CP-OlsoC**

Drapier's Hill. Jonathan Swift. **CP-SwifJ**

Drats. Shel Silverstein. **SP-SilS2**

Draw. Robert Lowell. **SP-LoweR**

Draw a green cedar over the peeping sky. *Marriage Bed, The.* Alun Lewis. *Fr.* War Wedding. **CP-LewiA**

Draw, and Drinke. Robert Herrick. **CP-HerrR**

Draw as you will there are no images. In a Room with Picassos. Jane Cooper. **SP-CoopJ**

Draw Gloves. Robert Herrick. **CP-HerrR**

Draw over and dig. Roots. Gary Snyder. **CP-SnydG**

Drawer's Condition on November 28, 1961, The. Leonard Cohen. **CP-CoheL**

Drawing. George Oppen. **CP-OppeG**

Drawing. Al Young. **CP-YounA**

Drawing Details in an Old Church. Thomas Hardy. **CP-HardT**

Drawing Lessons. Howard Nemerov. **CP-NemeH**

Drawing-Room. David Herbert Lawrence. **CP-LawrD**

Drawing the Triangle. Charles Simic. **SP-SimiC**

Drawn by the annual call, we now behold. The Arrival of the Players. George Crabbe. **SP-CrabG** *Fr.* The Borough.

Drawn daily in the dragnet of a horde. A Great Headmaster. John Hewitt. **CP-HewiJ**

Drawn to Perspective. Charles Simic. **SP-SimiC**

Drayman, The. Walt Whitman. PoNe *Fr.* Song of Myself. **CP-WhitW** "Oxen that rattle the yoke and chain or halt in the leafy shade." **FM**

Dread, A. Daniel Gerard Hoffman. **SP-HoffD**

Dread hour! when, upheaved by war's sulphurous blast. Fort Fuentes. William Wordsworth. *Fr.* Memorials of a Tour of the Continent; 1820. **CP-WorW2**

Dread Mother of Forgetfulness. Hymn to Physical Pain. Rudyard Kipling. **CP-KiplR**

Dread Nay. Samuel Beckett. **CP-BeckS**

Dread not the shackles: on with thine intent. Wit Punisht, Prospers Most. Robert Herrick. **CP-HerrR**

Dread of an impending umptieth. Ouzo for Robin. James Merrill. **SP-MerrJ**

Dread spirit in me that I ever try. Vision 1948. Allen Ginsberg. **CP-GinsA**

Dreadful. Shel Silverstein. **SP-SilS2**

Dreadful burden of our sins we feel, The. Fragment, A. John Greenleaf Whittier. **CP-WhitJ**

Dreadful hour with leaden pace approached, The. Lisy's Parting with Her Cat. James Thomson. **CP-ThomJ**

Dream, A. Wystan Hugh Auden. **CP-AudWJ**

Dream, The. Wendell Berry. **CP-BerrW**

Dream, A. William Blake. **CH; EnRP; FHYEP; HoFi; LAuP; NOBRP; PoPle** *Fr.* Songs of Innocence. **CP-BlakW**

Dream, The. Louise Bogan. **CP-BogaL**

Dream, A. Robert Burns. **CP-BurnR**

Dream, The. Byron. **CP-Byron**

Dream, The. Geoffrey Chaucer. FiP; PBBP *Fr.* The Book of the Duchesse. **CP-ChauG**

Dream, The. Leonard Cohen. **CP-CoheL**

Dream, The. ("A lake"). Robert Creeley. **CP-CreeR**

Dream, The. ("Such perfection"). Robert Creeley. **CP-CreeR**

Dream, A. Walter de la Mare. **CP-DeLaW**

Dream, The. John Donne. *Fr.* Elegies. **CP-DonnJ**

Dream[e], The. John Donne. **CP-DonnJ**

Dream. Hilda Doolittle. *Fr.* Child Poems. **CP-DoolH**

Dream, A. Richard Eberhart. **CP-EberR**

Dream, The. Richard Eberhart. **CP-EberR**

Dream, A. Allen Ginsberg. **CP-GinsA**

Dream, The. Robert Earl Hayden. **CP-HaydR**

Dream, The. Robert Herrick. **CP-HerrR**

Dream. Langston Hughes. **SP-HughL**

Dream, The. Randall Jarrell. **CP-JarrR**

Dream[e], The. Ben Jonson. **CP-JonsB**

Dream, A. John Keats. OBNC *Fr.* The Fall of Hyperion. **CP-KeatJ** "Methought I stood where trees of every clime." **OBRV**

Dream / like a fire truck, A. The Dream. Diane Wakoski. *Fr.* Fifteen Poems for a Lunar Eclipse None of Us Saw. **SP-WakoD**

Dream, The. Louise McNeill. **SP-McNeL**

Dream. Edna St. Vincent Millay. **CP-MillE**

Dream. Marianne Craig Moore. **CP-MoorM**

Dream, A. Howard Nemerov. *Fr.* Seven Macabre Songs. **CP-NemeH**

Dream, The. Sylvia Plath. **CP-PlatS**

Dream, A. Edgar Allan Poe. **CP-PoeEd**

Dream. Kathleen Jessie Raine. **SP-RainK**

Dream, A. "Lou Reed." **SP-ReedL**

Dream, The. Theodore Roethke. **CP-RoetT**

Dream, A. Christina Georgina Rossetti. **CP-RosC3**

Dream, The. Christina Georgina Rossetti. **CP-RosC3**

Dream. Stevie Smith. **CP-SmitS**

Dream, The. Stephen Spender. **CP-SpenS**

Dream, A. Charles Tomlinson. **CP-TomlC**

Dream, The. Charles Tomlinson. **CP-TomlC**

Dream, The. Lewis Turco. **SP-TurcL**

Dream, The. Diane Wakoski. *Fr.* Fifteen Poems for a Lunar Eclipse None of Us Saw. **SP-WakoD**

Dream / we dreamed, A. Perpetuum Mobile: The City. William Carlos Williams. **CP-WilW1**

Dream, The. Charles Kenneth Williams. **SP-WillC**

Dream, after Reading Dante's Episode of Paolo and Francesca, A. John Keats. *See* As Hermes once took to his feathers light.

Dream and Reality. John Updike. **CP-UpdiJ**

Dream at Arles on the Night of the Mistral, A. Thomas Merton. **CP-MertT**

Dream Boogie. Langston Hughes. **SP-HughL**

Dream Boogie: Variation. Langston Hughes. **SP-HughL**

Dream-Confused. David Herbert Lawrence. **CP-LawrD**

Dream Days. Derek Mahon. *See* When you stop to consider.

Dream days of fond delight and hours. Madrigal, A. Paul Laurence Dunbar. **CP-DunbP**

Dream-Drumming. Muriel Rukeyser. **CP-RukeM**

Dream Dust. Langston Hughes. **SP-HughL**

Dream (Escape from the Sculpture Museum) and Waking. James Merrill. **SP-MerrJ**

Dream Flood, The. James Dickey. **CP-DickJ**

Dream-flowers. Kathleen Jessie Raine. **SP-RainK**

Dream fluently, still brothers, who when young. To the Etruscan Poets. Richard Wilbur. **CP-WilbR**

Dream-Follower, The. Thomas Hardy. **CP-HardT**

Dream Forest. Donald Davie. **CP-DavD0**

Dream Girl. Carl Sandburg. **CP-SandC**

Dream He Never Knew the End of, The. Robert Penn Warren. *Fr.* Audubon. **SP-WarrR**

Dream in a dream the heavy soul somewhere. Canto Amor. John Berryman. **CP-BerrJ**

Dream is a cocktail at Sloppy Joe's, The. Havana Dreams. Langston Hughes. **SP-HughL**

"Dream is the thought in the ghost, The." George Meredith. WGRP *Fr.* A Faith on Trial. **CP-MerG1**

Dream is vague, The. Beale Street. Langston Hughes. **SP-HughL**

Dream Is—Which? The. Thomas Hardy. **CP-HardT**

Dream Journey of the Head and Heart. Richard Eberhart. **CP-EberR**

Dream-Land [*or* Dreamland]. Edgar Allan Poe. **CP-PoeEd**

Dream Land. Christina Georgina Rossetti. **CP-RosC1**

Dream Life of a Coffin Factory in Lynn, Massachussetts, The. John Yau. **SP-YauJo**

Dream-Love. Christina Georgina Rossetti. **CP-RosC1**

Dream not, O Soul, that easy is the task. Help. John Greenleaf Whittier. **CP-WhitJ**

Dream Objects. John Updike. **CP-UpdiJ**

Dream of a Brother, A. Robert Bly. **SP-BlyR**

Dream of a Strange One. James Liddy. **CP-LiddJ**

Dream of All the Springfield Writers, The. Nicholas Vachel Lindsay. **CP-LindV**

Dream of Burial, A. James Wright. **CP-WrigJ**

Dream of Comparison, A. Stevie Smith. **CP-SmitS**

Dream of Death, A. William Butler Yeats. **CP-YeatW**

Dream of Fair Women, A. Tennyson. **CP-TennA**
  As When a Man. **ChER**
Dream of fantastic horses, A. The Horse from Hell. Erica Jong. **SP-JongE**
Dream of Flying Comes of Age, The. Howard Nemerov. **CP-NemeH**
Dream of Frances Speedwell, A. Robert Ranke Graves. **CP-GravR**
Dream of Hell, A. Robert Ranke Graves. **CP-GravR**
Dream of Jealousy, A. Seamus Heaney. **SP-HeanS**
Dream of limestone in sea-light, A. Thinking of Inis Oírr in Cambridge, Mass. Derek Mahon. **SP-MahoD**
Dream of mine flew over the mead, A. The Dream-Follower. Thomas Hardy. **CP-HardT**
Dream of Mourning, The. Louise Glück. **SP-GlücL**
Dream of Nourishment, A. Stevie Smith. **CP-SmitS**
Dream of Old Vienna, A. James Merrill. *Fr.* Five Old Favorites. **SP-MerrJ**
Dream of Pio Nono, The. John Greenleaf Whittier. **CP-WhitJ**
Dream of Retarded Children, A. Robert Bly. **SP-BlyR**
Dream of Rimbaud. Patti Smith. **SP-SmitP**
Dream of Roses, A. Kathleen Jessie Raine. **SP-RainK**
Dream of Saba. Edna St. Vincent Millay. **CP-MillE**
Dream of Summer, A. John Greenleaf Whittier. **CP-WhitJ**
Dream of the City Shopwoman. Thomas Hardy. **CP-HardT**
Dream of the Departing Soldier. Malcolm Lowry. **CP-LowrM**
Dream of the Lynx. John Haines. **SP-HainJ**
Dream of the Police, The. John Haines. **SP-HainJ**
  "About the hour the December moon."
  "I saw in that glittering distance."
  "People fell back, a field of wheat, The."
Dream of the world / speaking to me. Recovering. Muriel Rukeyser. **CP-RukeM**
Dream of Trees, A. Mary Oliver. **SP-OlivM**
Dream of Waking, The. Randall Jarrell. **CP-JarrR**
Dream of What Is Missing, A. Robert Bly. **SP-BlyR**
Dream of Whitman Paraphrased, Recognized and Made More Vivid by Renoir, A. Delmore Schwartz. **SP-SchwD**
Dream on, for dreams are sweet. Dreams. Paul Laurence Dunbar. **CP-DunbP**
Dream on the Night of First Snow, A. Robert Bly. **SP-BlyR**
Dream 1: the Bush Garden. Margaret Atwood. **SP-AtwM1**
Dream or No, A. Thomas Hardy. **CP-HardT**
Dream Pang, A. Robert Frost. **CP-FrosR**
Dream: pigeon— / rooftop, water. For Walter Chappell. Robert Creeley. **CP-CreeR**
Dream please / no favors. The Long Bells. Charles Kenneth Williams. **CP-WillC**
Dream Question, A. Thomas Hardy. **CP-HardT**
Dream Range, The. Thomas McGrath. **SP-McGrT**
Dream Recalled on Waking. Robert Ranke Graves. **CP-GravR**
Dream Record: June 8, 1955. Allen Ginsberg. **CP-GinsA**
Dream Report. John Yau. **SP-YauJo**
Dream: she is learning to fly, A. Holding Pattern. Leonard Nathan. **SP-NathL**
Dream Song I. Paul Laurence Dunbar. **CP-DunbP**
Dream Song II. Paul Laurence Dunbar. **CP-DunbP**
Dream sponsors: / Charles Manson, tongue. Thom Gunn. *Fr.* Jack Straw's Castle. **CP-GunnT**
Dream Take: 22. Al Young. **CP-YounA**
Dream that waketh, A. Days of Vanity. Christina Georgina Rossetti. **CP-RosC1**
Dream there is wherein we are fain to scream, A. Christina Georgina Rossetti. *Fr.* Later Life: A Double Sonnet of Sonnets. **CP-RosC2**
Dream 3: Night Bear Which Frightened Cattle. Margaret Atwood. **SP-AtwM1**
Dream Time, The. Ted Hughes. *Fr.* Out. **SP-HughT**
Dream tree, Polly's tree, A. Polly's Tree. Sylvia Plath. **CP-PlatS**
Dream 2: Brian the Still-Hunter. Margaret Atwood. **SP-AtwM1**
Dream Variation[s]. Langston Hughes. **SP-HughL**
Dream went on like a rake of sliced bamboo, The. Randall Jarrell 3. Robert Lowell. **SP-LoweR**
Dream with Clam-Diggers. Sylvia Plath. **CP-PlatS**
Dream within a Dream, A. Edgar Allan Poe. **CP-PoeEd**
  "I stand amid the roar." **ChTr**
Dreame, The. Robert Herrick. **CP-HerrR**
Dreamer, The. ("O Thou who"). Walter de la Mare. **CP-DeLaW**
Dreamer, The. ("Woods were still"). Walter de la Mare. **CP-DeLaW**
Dreamer, The. Paul Laurence Dunbar. **CP-DunbP**
Dreamer, The. Daniel Gerard Hoffman. **SP-HoffD**

Dreamers, The. Robert Duncan. **SP-DuncR**
Dreamin' Town. Paul Laurence Dunbar. **CP-DunbP**
Dreaming. Juan Ramón Jiménez. *Fr.* Ten Short Poems. **CP-WrigJ**
Dreaming Children. Robert Ranke Graves. **CP-GravR**
Dreaming Fool. Carl Sandburg. **CP-SandC**
Dreaming in marble all the castle lay. Of Nicolette. Edward Estlin Cummings. **CP-CummE**
Dreaming of Africa. To a Slave Named Job. Stanley Jasspon Kunitz. *Fr.* Words for the Unknown Makers: A Garland of Commemorative Verses. **CP-KuniS**
Dreaming of apples on a wall. "Lewis Carroll." *Fr.* Puzzles. *Fr.* Puzzles from Wonderland. **CP-CarrL**
Dreaming of grips at her heart. Rain Winds Blow Doors Open. Carl Sandburg. **CP-SandC**
Dreaming of walking. Charles Henri Ford. **SP-FordC** *Fr.* Secret Haiku.
Dreaming the actual world. Morning Song. Leonard Nathan. **SP-NathL**
Dreaming the Breasts. Anne Sexton. **CP-SextA**
Dreaming Trader, The, *sl. diff.* Thomas Merton. *See* Hymn to Commerce.
Dreaming we were awake, we heard the rivers. Muriel Rukeyser. **CP-RukeM**
Dreaming with a Friend. Stephen Berg. **SP-BergS**
Dreamjot: 1962. Al Young. **CP-YounA**
Dreamland. "Lewis Carroll." **CP-CarrL**
Dreams. Robert Creeley. **CP-CreeR**
Dreams. ("Be gentle"). Walter de la Mare. **CP-DeLaW**
Dreams. ("Ev'n one"). Walter de la Mare. **CP-DeLaW**
Dreams. Paul Laurence Dunbar. **CP-DunbP**
Dreams. Paul Laurence Dunbar. **CP-DunbP**
Dream[e]s. Robert Herrick. **CP-HerrR**
Dreams. Randall Jarrell. **CP-JarrR**
Dreams. Mary Oliver. **SP-OlivM**
Dreams. Edgar Allan Poe. **CP-PoeEd**
  "Oh! that my young life were a lasting dream!" **AmPP; MeMAP; OxBA; Poetr; TAP,** *ll.* 1–12;
Dreams. Kathleen Jessie Raine. **SP-RainK**
Dreams. James Schuyler. **CP-SchuJ**
Dreams About Clothes. James Merrill. **SP-MerrJ**
Dreams are rare visitors now, The. Children in a Walled Garden. Steve Griffiths. **SP-GrifS**
Dreams are the subtle Dower. Emily Dickinson. **CP-DickE**
Dreams—are well—but Waking's better. Emily Dickinson. **CP-DickE**
Dreams Bite. Audre Lorde. **SP-LordA**
Dreams Dreamed. Kay Boyle. **CP-BoylK**
Dreams, graves, pools, growing. So to Speak. Carl Sandburg. **CP-SandC**
Dreams in Middle Age. Louis MacNeice. **CP-MacNL**
Dreams in the Dusk. Carl Sandburg. **CP-SandC**
Dreams of Paradise. Al Young. **CP-YounA**
Dreams of the Animals. Margaret Atwood. **SP-AtwM1**
Dreams of Wild Horses, The. Thomas McGrath. **SP-McGrT**
Dreams Old and Nascent, *sl. diff version of poems* Drams Old and Nascent: Old *and* Dreams Old and Nascent: Nascent. David Herbert Lawrence. **CP-LawrD**
Dreams Old and Nascent: Nascent. David Herbert Lawrence. **CP-LawrD**
Dreams Old and Nascent: Old. David Herbert Lawrence. **CP-LawrD**
Dreams, that elude the Waker's frenzied grasp. Acrostic: Dreams, that elude the Waker's frenzied grasp—. "Lewis Carroll." **CP-CarrL** *Fr.* Sylvie and Bruno Concluded.
Dreamwood. Adrienne Rich. **SP-RicA1**
Drear and desolate shore!, A. The Rock-Tomb of Bradore. John Greenleaf Whittier. **CP-WhitJ**
Dreary, heavy / accumulation. Robert Creeley. **CP-CreeR**
Drenched with purple. Simaetha. Hilda Doolittle. **CP-DoolH**
Dresden to Chesapeake Bay. Jim Carroll. **SP-CarrJ**
Dress was a suspicious madder, importing the cruelty of roses, The. Edward Estlin Cummings. **CP-CummE**
Dressing. Dabney Stuart. **SP-StuaD**
Dribble lights a shelf, A. Aqueduct. Thom Gunn. **CP-GunnT**
Dried Sturgeon, The. Robert Bly. **SP-BlyR**
Dried Up River is like the Soul, A, *sl. diff. vers. incl. in* Pijijiapan. Malcolm Lowry. *Fr.* The Comedian. **CP-LowrM**
Drift, drift, do not lift. American Boating Song. Louise McNeill. **SP-McNeL**
Drift of Petals, The. John Hewitt. **CP-HewiJ**
Drifter off Tarentum, A. Rudyard Kipling. **FaBoEE; MMA; NSI; PeFWW; PoPle; PoWW** *Fr.* Epitaphs of the War [1914–1918]. **CP-KiplR**
Drifter's Escape. "Bob Dylan." **CP-DylaB**

Drifting. James Dickey. **CP-DickJ**

Drifting night in the Georgia pines. O Daedalus, Fly Away Home. Robert Earl Hayden. **CP-HaydR**

Drifting Off. Seamus Heaney. **SP-HeanS** *Fr.* Sweeney Redivivus.

Drifting smoke is gone, today, The. Fourth of July. William DeWitt Snodgrass. **SP-SnodW**

Drifting South. Gilbert Sorrentino. **SP-SorrG**

Driftrose. Barton Sutter. **SP-SuttB**

Driftwood. Richard Wilbur. **CP-WilbR**

Driftwood gathered here and there. To Pfrimmer. Paul Laurence Dunbar. **CP-DunbP**

Driftwood I have become. Waiting. Phoebe Hesketh. **SP-HeskP**

Drill, The. Charles Bukowski. **SP-BukC1**

Drill holes in small rocks, then press your lips. Spring Rain. Stephen Dobyns. **SP-DobyS**

Drill in the Heat. David Herbert Lawrence. *Fr.* Bits. **CP-LawrD**

Drills chatter full of mud and compressed air. Dillingham, Alaska, the Willow Tree Bar. Gary Snyder. **CP-SnydG**

Drink. William Carlos Williams. **CP-WilW1**

Drink black coffee from a thermos. The Cool around the Fire. Gary Snyder. **CP-SnydG**

Drink, hear my counsel, my son, that the world fret thee not. Hafiz, *tr. by* Ralph Waldo Emerson. **CP-EmerR** *Fr.* Odes.

Drink not the third glass, which thou canst not tame. George Herbert. **FaBoDD** *Fr.* The Church-Porch.

Drink of Water, A. Seamus Heaney. **SP-HeanS**

Drink, sex and jazz all sweet things, brother: far. The Dance. Philip Larkin. **CP-LarkP**

Drink till the turbans are all unbound. Hafiz, *tr. by* Ralph Waldo Emerson. **CP-EmerR** *Fr.* Odes.

Drink[e] to me, only, [or onely] with thine eyes, *adapted from the Greek of Philostratus.* Song. To Celia. Ben Jonson. **CP-JonsB**

Drink Wine, and live here blithefull, while ye may. To Youth. Robert Herrick. **CP-HerrR**

Drink wine and the heaven. Hafiz, *tr. by* Ralph Waldo Emerson. **CP-EmerR** *Fr.* Odes.

Drink with Something in It, A. Ogden Nash. **CP-NashO**

Drinke up / Your cup. A Bachanalian Verse. Robert Herrick. **CP-HerrR**

Drinker, The. Robert Lowell. **SP-LoweR**

Drinking 15 dollar champagne—. The Price. Charles Bukowski. **SP-BukC1**

Drinking from a Helmet. James Dickey. **CP-DickJ**

Drinking German beer. Ah. . . . Charles Bukowski. **SP-BukC1**

Drinking Song. Robert Burns. *See* See the smoking bowl before us.

Drinking Song. Thomas Hardy. **CP-HardT**

Drinking Song, A. William Butler Yeats. **CP-YeatW**

Drinking the seconal dissolved in bourbon. The Case of The. Mona Van Duyn. **SP-VanDM**

Drinking Together. Li Po, *tr. fr. Chinese by* William Carlos Williams *with* David Rafael Wang. **CP-WilW2**

Drinking versus Thinking. Samuel Taylor Coleridge. **CP-ColeS**

Drip—icicle's gone. Basil Bunting. *Fr.* Briggflatts [An Autobiography]. **CP-BuntB**

"Light lifts from the water." **OAEL-2; PoPo**

Dripping / words / off. (Ryokan's scroll). Louis Zukofsky. **CP-ZukLS**

Drive. Charles Tomlinson. **CP-TomlC**

"Drive All Blames into One." Allen Ginsberg. **CP-GinsA**

Drive, fast kisses. Louis Zukofsky. **CP-ZukLS**

Drive in the Country, A. Ted Kooser. **SP-KoosT**

Drive My Car. John Lennon *and* Paul McCartney. **CP-Beatl**

Drive to Los Alamos, A. Thom Gunn. **CP-GunnT**

Driven, at midnight, to growth, the city's wistful turnings. Lover as Fox. Muriel Rukeyser. **CP-RukeM**

Driven by desire, I did this deed. Sir Thomas Wyatt. **CP-WyatT**

Driven by desire to set affection. Sir Thomas Wyatt. **CP-WyatT**

Driven in by Autumn's sharpening air. Redbreast, The [Suggested in a Westmoreland Cottage]. William Wordsworth. **CP-WorW2**

Driven in by autumn's sharpening air. William Wordsworth. **PBBP** *Fr.* Redbreast, The [Suggested in a Westmoreland Cottage]. **CP-WorW2**

Driven out of Paradise. To the Babylonians. Howard Nemerov. **CP-NemeH**

Driver, The. James Dickey. **CP-DickJ**

Drĭver drive fáster and máke a good rún. Calypso. Wystan Hugh Auden. *Fr.* Ten Songs. **CP-AudeW**

Driver, Driver. Robert Penn Warren. **SP-WarrR**

Drives sheep through ravine. The Maid. *Unknown, tr. fr. Chinese by* William Carlos Williams *with* David Rafael Wang. **CP-WilW2**

Driveway. Muriel Rukeyser. **CP-RukeM**

Driving a prairie, we see a mill far off. Distances. Richard Hugo. **CP-HugoR**

Driving across the American Desert and Thinking of the Sahara. John Ciardi. **SP-CiarJ**

Driving along the coast road. Mobile Homes. Robert Creeley. **CP-CreeR**

Driving along the road and looking. Driving through Snow. Stephen Spender. **CP-SpenS**

Driving along the unfenced road / in August dusk, the sun gone from. The Distances. John Hewitt. **CP-HewiJ**

Driving Alongside the Housatonic River Alone on a Rainy April Night. William Matthews. **SP-MattW**

Driving back from the market. The Green Shelf. Donald Hall. **CP-HallD**

Driving Gloves. Diane Wakoski. **SP-WakoD**

Driving in for a wash and. Charles Bukowski. *Fr.* Horsemeat. **SP-BukC3**

Driving Me Away. Erica Jong. **SP-JongE**

Driving Montana. Richard Hugo. **CP-HugoR**

Driving North from Savannah on My Birthday. Paul Zimmer. **SP-ZimmP**

Driving north, I catch the hillshapes, Gurney. To Ivor Gurney. Charles Tomlinson. **CP-TomlC**

Driving northward in February once. The Running Changes. Roy Fisher. **SP-FishR**

Driving once more / on Central—though what. Albuquerque. Charles Tomlinson. **CP-TomlC**

Driving Out Again at Night. Stephen Berg. *Fr.* For My Father.

Driving south on U.S. 71. The Muse. Miller Williams. **SP-WillM**

Driving the team, he came up over. Grandfather. Ted Kooser. **SP-KoosT**

Driving through Minnesota during the Hanoi Bombings. Robert Bly. **SP-BlyR**

Driving through Oregon (Dec. 1973). John Haines. **SP-HainJ**

Driving through Snow. Stephen Spender. **CP-SpenS**

Driving through Tennessee. Charles Wright. **SP-WrigC**

Driving to desire, adread also to dare. Sir Thomas Wyatt. **CP-WyatT**

Driving to Long Buckby down the byroads. The Riders. John Hewitt. **CP-HewiJ**

Driving to Passalacqua, 1960. Charles Wright. **SP-WrigC**

Driving toward Boston I Run across One of Robert Bly's Old Poems. Thomas McGrath. **SP-McGrT**

Driving toward the Lac Qui Parle River. Robert Bly. **SP-BlyR**

Driving up from Tees-side. County Durham. Donald Davie. **CP-DavDo**

Drizzle. Paul Laurence Dunbar. **CP-DunbP**

Drizzling Easter Morning, A. Thomas Hardy. **CP-HardT**

Droning a drowsy syncopated tune. The Weary Blues. Langston Hughes. **SP-HughL**

Droop, droop no more, or hang the head. Upon Julias Recovery. Robert Herrick. **CP-HerrR**

Drooping, the labourer-ox. James Thomson. **FM** *Fr.* Winter. *Fr.* The Seasons. **CP-ThomJ**

Drop dead, Catullus, lie right down where you are & die. Carmen 52. Catullus. *Fr.* Carmina. **CP-Catul**

Drop fell on the Apple Tree, A. Emily Dickinson. **CP-DickE**

Drop of a Hat, The. Ogden Nash. **CP-NashO**

Drop on the window, once, twice, A. November. Archibald MacLeish. **CP-MacLA**

Drop, one drop, how sweetly one fair[e] drop, A. Luke 16; Dives *Asking a Drop.* Bible, *N.T.* **CP-CrasR,** *tr. by* Richard Crashaw; *Fr.* St. Luke.

Drop, that wrestles in the Sea, The. Emily Dickinson. **CP-DickE**

Dropped into the Ether Acre. Emily Dickinson. **CP-DickE**

Drops of water bead. Love Poems. Dabney Stuart. **SP-StuaD**

Dross of verse. Rhyme!, The. I, Mencius, Pupil of the Master. Charles Olson. **CP-OlsoC**

Drought. Charles Kenneth Williams. **SP-WillC**

Drought. Grey spirals into hard blue. Dust-Devils. James McAuley. **SP-McAuJ**

Drove a school bus for the extra money. He. Ron Koertge. **SP-KoerR**

Drovers, The. John Greenleaf Whittier. **CP-WhitJ**

Drowne me not you cruell teares. Mary Sidney, Countess of Montgomery Wroth. *Fr.* Part 1. *Fr.* Urania. **CP-WrotM**

Drowned Children, The. Louise Glück. **SP-GlücL**

Drowned Lover, The. Percy Bysshe Shelley. *Fr.* Poems from St. Irvyne, or, The Rosicrucian. **CP-ShelP**

Drowned Man: Death Between Two Rivers, The. Thomas McGrath. **SP-McGrT**

Drowned moon plunges, The. Kenneth Rexroth. **SP-RexrK** *Fr.* The Silver Swan.

Drowned under Grass. Stephen Spender. *Fr.* Lost Days. **CP-SpenS**

Drowning. Robert Pack. **SP-PackR**

Drowning, drowning, I espie. The Deluge. Robert Herrick. **CP-HerrR**

Drowning is not so pitiful. Emily Dickinson. **CP-DickE**

Drowning is pushing through. Boy Drowning. Phoebe Hesketh. **SP-HeskP**

Drowning (I). Grace Paley. **CP-PaleG**

Drowning (II). Grace Paley. **CP-PaleG**

Drowning with Others. James Dickey. **CP-DickJ**

Drowning Young Man, The. Muriel Rukeyser. **CP-RukeM**

Drowse Murmurs. Allen Ginsberg. **CP-GinsA**

Drowsiness, identity, drifting / some kind of white. Nodding. Tom Clark. **SP-ClarT**

Drowsing in my chair of disbelief. The Visitation. Robert Ranke Graves. **CP-GravR**

Drowsy. Carl Sandburg. **CP-SandC**

Drowsy carrier sways, The. *parody of* Henry Wadsworth Longfellow. Rudyard Kipling. **CP-KiplR** *Fr.* The Muse among the Motors.

Drowsy Day, A. Paul Laurence Dunbar. **CP-DunbP**

Drowsy with beauty, I bathe &. The Afternoon After. Al Young. **CP-YounA**

Drue feasts no Puritans; the churles, he saith. Epigramme. Thomas Campion. *Fr.* Observations in the Art of English Poesie. **CP-CampT**

Drue gives thee money, yet thou thankst not him. Epigramme. Thomas Campion. *Fr.* Observations in the Art of English Poesie. **CP-CampT**

Drug of the incomprehensible. The Bad Habit. Charles Henri Ford. **SP-FordC**

Drug Store. Karl Shapiro. **SP-ShapK**

Drugged. Walter de la Mare. **CP-DeLaW**

Drugs Alcohol Little Sister. John Berryman. **CP-BerrJ**

Drugs Made Pauline Vague. Stevie Smith. **CP-SmitS**

Drugstore Library. William Carlos Williams. **CP-WilW2**

Druid Love. Robert Ranke Graves. **CP-GravR**

Druid Stones at Kensaleyre. Richard Hugo. **CP-HugoR**

Druidic Rimes. Howard Nemerov. **CP-NemeH**

Druidical Excommunication. William Wordsworth. *Fr.* Ecclesiastical Sonnets. **CP-WorW2**

Drum, The. Louise Bogan. **CP-BogaL**

Drum. Langston Hughes. **SP-HughL**

Drum is played. / From here a rose, A. June. James Schuyler. **CP-SchuJ**

Drum on your drums, batter on your banjos. Jazz Fantasia. Carl Sandburg. **CP-SandC**

Drum roars up, The. The Drum. Louise Bogan. **CP-BogaL**

Drum upon the table you drum. For My Friend. Charles Olson. **CP-OlsoC**

Drum World, The. Charles Olson. **CP-OlsoC**

Drumlin Woodchuck, A. Robert Frost. **CP-FrosR**

Drummed their boots on the camion floor. Riparto d'Assalto. Ernest Hemingway. **CP-HemiE**

Drummer Hodge. Thomas Hardy. **CP-HardT**

Drummond Hadley / TWO POEMS. West 4 and 5. Charles Olson. *Fr.* West. **CP-OlsoC**

Drumnotes. Carl Sandburg. **CP-SandC**

Drums, The. Robert Creeley. **CP-CreeR**

Drums in Scotland. Richard Hugo. **CP-HugoR**

Drums of the early evening wake. La Comparsa en Oriente. Thomas Merton. **CP-MertT**

Drunk. David Herbert Lawrence. **CP-LawrD**

'Drunk again! Where do you think you are?'. Louis MacNeice. **CP-MacNL** *Fr.* The Kingdom. **CP-MacNL**

Drunk and the Sailor, The. William Carlos Williams. **CP-WilW2**

Drunk and writing poems. As Crazy As I Ever Was. Charles Bukowski. **SP-BukC1**

Drunk at 3 a.m. at the bottom of my 2nd bottle. Here I Am. Charles Bukowski. **SP-BukC3**

Drunk, drunk, drunk, amid the blaze of noon. Folly on Royal Street before the Raw Face of God. Robert Penn Warren. **SP-WarrR**

Drunk Man Looks at the Thistle, A. "Hugh MacDiarmid." **FaBoDD** *Fr.* A Drunk Man Looks at the Thistle. **SP-MacDH**

Drunk Man Looks at the Thistle, A. "Hugh MacDiarmid." **SP-MacDH**

"Dae what ye wull ye canna parry." **EBEV; OXAEP-2**

Drunk Man Looks at the Thistle, A. **FaBoDD**

Farewell to Dostoevski. **NAEL-2**

Yet Ha'e I Silence Left. **NAEL-2**

Drunk who lives across the street from us, The. Neighbor. Richard Hugo. **CP-HugoR**

Drunkard. Langston Hughes. **SP-HughL**

Drunkard, The. Louis MacNeice. **CP-MacNL**

Drunkard, The. William Carlos Williams. **CP-WilW1**

Drunkard cannot meet a Cork, A. Emily Dickinson. **CP-DickE**

Drunkard to His Bottle, The. John Greenleaf Whittier. **CP-WhitJ**

Drunkards, The. Malcolm Lowry.

"Noise of death is in this desolate bar, The." **CP-LowrM**

"Notions of freedom are tied up with drink." **CP-LowrM**

Drunkard's Funeral, The. Nicholas Vachel Lindsay. **CP-LindV**

Drunkards in the Street, The. Nicholas Vachel Lindsay. **CP-LindV**

Drunkards of salt water, thirsty for disaster. At the Bar. Malcolm Lowry. *Fr.* The Cantinas. **CP-LowrM**

Drunken Boat, The. Arthur Rimbaud, *tr. fr.* French.

("Downstream on impassive rivers suddenly.") **CP-BeckS**, *tr. by* Samuel Beckett;

(Drunken Boat.) **CP-BeckS**, *tr. by* Samuel Beckett;

"Hearing the thunder of the intransitive weirs." **SP-MahoD**

Drunken Boat. Arthur Rimbaud. *See* The Drunken Boat.

Drunken Charlie. Robinson Jeffers. **CP-JefR3**

Drunken Fisherman, The. Robert Lowell. **SP-LoweR**

Drunken Girl. Muriel Rukeyser. **CP-RukeM**

Drunken man / On an old pier, The. Night Scene. George Oppen. **CP-OppeG**

Drunken Man's Praise of Sobriety, A. William Butler Yeats. **CP-YeatW**

Drunken night in my house with a, A. Dream Record: June 8, 1955. Allen Ginsberg. **CP-GinsA**

Drunken Winter. Joseph Ceravolo. **SP-CeraJ**

Drunks. John Berryman. **CP-BerrJ**

Drusilla. Ogden Nash. **CP-NashO**

Dry August Burned. Walter de la Mare. **CP-DeLaW**

Dry birch logs. Near Pah-Gotzin-Kay. Thomas McGrath. **SP-McGrT**

Dry brown coughing beneath their feet, The. Beverly Hills, Chicago. Gwendolyn Brooks. **SP-BrooG** *Fr.* The Womanhood.

Dry Loaf. Wallace Stevens. **CP-StevW**

Dry Ode, The. Charles Olson. **CP-OlsoC**

Dry Places. Thomas Merton. **CP-MertT; SP-MertT**

Dry Rot, The. Richard Eberhart. **CP-EberR**

Dry rot intruding where the wood is wet. Enemies of a House. John Updike. **CP-UpdiJ**

Dry Salvages, The. Thomas Stearns Eliot. **AiP; LiTB; NoP; OxBA; SeCePo** *Fr.* Four Quartets. **CP-ElioT**

"River is within us, the sea is all about us, The." **OxBoS**

Dry Season. Richard Shelton. **SP-ShelR**

"All day I lifted stones."

"I have chosen this place."

"I who was promised."

"Now while the moon pulls darkness."

"Some years the birds."

"There is a bird."

"When a man loves the desert."

Dry season. Block. So, rain. . . . Though Dry, Not Dry. Donald Davie. **CP-DavDo**

Dry Summer, Islandmagee, 1921. John Hewitt. **CP-HewiJ**

Dry the tears for holy Eva. Eva. John Greenleaf Whittier. **CP-WhitJ**

Dry they call him, and dry is what he hopes. John Dryden. Hayden Carruth. **CP-CarHS**

Dry thy tears / My pretty dears. Communal Message. Malcolm Lowry. **CP-LowrM**

Dry timber under that rich foliage. *fr.* A Woman Young and Old. William Butler Yeats. **CP-YeatW**

Dry walls, and nettles battered by the dust. Fantasia on 'Horbury'; John Bacchus Dykes, 1859. Geoffrey Hill. **CP-HillG**

Dry Winter Letter to Friends, A. Ted Kooser. **SP-KoosT**

Dry your sweet cheek, long drown'd with sorrows raine. Comfort to a Lady Upon the Death of Her Husband. Robert Herrick. **CP-HerrR**

Drying Their Wings. Nicholas Vachel Lindsay. **CP-LindV**

Dryness is upon the house, A. In Honor of David Anderson Brooks, My Father. Gwendolyn Brooks. **SP-BrooG**

Drypoint. John Hewitt. **CP-HewiJ**

Drypoints of the Hasidim. Frank Templeton Prince. **CP-PrinF**

"But they are telling stories."

"Dark hollow faces under caps."

"Reading their story I follow and agree."

"Same grey path covered with last year's leaves, The."

"To believe is above all to be in love."

Dtran of Return. Richard Shelton. **SP-ShelR**

Du rêve, de la mathématique, et de la mort. Howard Nemerov. **CP-NemeH**

Duan First. Robert Burns. *Fr.* The Vision. **CP-BurnR**

"Sun had clos'd the winter-day, The." **BSV**

"Sun had clos'd the winter-day, The." **OxBS**

Duan Second. Robert Burns. *Fr.* The Vision. **CP-BurnR**

Dubhe. Siv Cedering Fox. *Fr.* Seven Letters to Zakarias. **SP-CedeS**

Dubiety. Robert Browning. **CP-BroR2**

Dubious daylight ended, The. The Two Rosalinds. Thomas Hardy. **CP-HardT**

Dubious light sad glimmers o'er the sky, The. A Lover's Complaint to His Mistress. Samuel Taylor Coleridge. **CP-ColeS**

Dubious Night, A. Richard Wilbur. **CP-WilbR**

Dublin. Louis MacNeice. **CIP; FaBoPP; IIP; OBTV; OxBTC** *Fr.* The Closing Album. **CP-MacNL**

Dublin Georgian. Donald Davie. **CP-DavDo**

Dublin Georgian (2). Donald Davie. **CP-DavDo**

Dublinesque. Philip Larkin. **CP-LarkP**

Duchamp and Man Ray. Roy Fisher. **SP-FishR** *Fr.* New Diversions.

Duchess Potatoes, The. Diane Wakoski. **SP-WakoD**

Duchess's Lullaby, The. "Lewis Carroll." *See* Speak roughly to your little boy.

Duck, The. Ogden Nash. **CP-NashO**

Duck come switchin' 'cross de lot. The Capture. Paul Laurence Dunbar. **CP-DunbP**

Duck fats rot in the roasting pan, The. Throwing Out the Flowers. Gwendolyn Brooks. *Fr.* Notes from the Childhood and the Girlhood. **SP-BrooG**

Duck Train—Vocal Arctic Fox-Trot. Malcolm Lowry. **CP-LowrM**

Ducks, at first, except they didn't. Seals in the Inner Harbor. Brendan Galvin. **SP-GalvB**

Ducks in the pond. The Picnic. Robert Creeley. **CP-CreeR**

Ducks of oak, ducks of distinction. With Devotion Entire from All Your Little Animals We Thought Fit to Revive the Following Ditty. Malcolm Lowry. **CP-LowrM**

Ducks require no ship and sail. What Ducks Require. John Crowe Ransom. **SP-RansJ**

Ducks, waking at sea. Hayden Carruth. **CP-CarHS** *Fr.* The Clay Hill Anthology.

Duckturne. Malcolm Lowry. **CP-LowrM**

Duddingstone. Robert Louis Stevenson. **CP-StevR**

Dude in Denver. Al Young. **CP-YounA**

Dudley from the Castle keep. In the Black Country. Roy Fisher. **SP-FishR**

Dudwood. Donald Davie. **CP-DavDo**

Due Respect. John Updike. **CP-UpdiJ**

Due to the working success of the. Fourth Printing. Marsden Hartley. **CP-HartM**

Due to weekend conditions, and although there's. Sundays Kill More Men Than Bombs. Charles Bukowski. **SP-BukC2**

Duel, The. Byron. **CP-Byron**

Duel, The. Thomas Hardy. **CP-HardT**

Duel between Marsyas and Apollo was one of those, The. Marsyas, Midas and the Barber. Stephen Dobyns. **SP-DobyS**

Dueling the Monkey. Jim Carroll. **SP-CarrJ**

Duet, The. Wystan Hugh Auden. **CP-AudeW**

Duet. Theodore Roethke. **CP-RoetT**

Duet, with Muffled Brake Drums. John Updike. **CP-UpdiJ**

Duettist to her Pianoforte, A. Thomas Hardy. **CP-HardT**

Dufferin, Simcoe, Grey. Margaret Atwood. **AMV-81** *Fr.* Four Small Elegies. **SP-AtwM2**

Duffy's Circus. Paul Muldoon. **SP-MuldP**

Duke Ellington Dream, The. Paul Zimmer. **SP-ZimmP**

Duke Hwan and the Wheelwright. Chuang Tzu, *tr. fr. Chinese by* Thomas Merton. **CP-MertT**

Duke insists you stay; you could do worse, The. The Tuscan Brutus. Donald Davie. **CP-DavDo**

Duke of Buckingham, The. Alexander Pope. **NOBE; OBEC** *Fr.* Epistle III, to Allen Lord Bathurst. **CP-PopeA**

(Death of Buckingham, The.) **FiP**

(Villers.) **FaBoDD**

Duke Valentine had been in Lombardy with the King. Basil Bunting, *after the Italian of* Machiavelli. **CP-BuntB**

Duke's Song, The. Mary Sidney, Countess of Montgomery Wroth. *See* If a clear [*or* cleere] fountain[e] still keeping a sad course.

Dulce Et Decorum Est. Wilfred Owen. **CP-OwenW**

Dulce it is, and, *decorum,* no doubt, for the country to fall, to. Arthur Hugh Clough. **EBVV; EnVR; FaBoPV; OAEP; OXAEP-2** *Fr.* Amours de Voyage. **SP-ClouA**

Dule of a Dewsbury Matron. Donald Davie. **CP-DavDo**

Dull as I was, to think that a Court Fly. A Black Patch on Lucasta's Face. Richard Lovelace. **CP-LoveR**

Dull conclave of crows'-footed faces, The. Hitch Your Wagon to a Star. Allen Tate. **CP-TateA**

Dull-headed, with dull fingers. To Judith, Taking Leave. Adrienne Rich. **CP-RicAE; SP-RicA2**

Dull knife cuts our hand, The. Deprivation. Thomas McGrath. **SP-McGrT**

Dull masses of dense green. Down the Mississippi. John Gould Fletcher. **SP-FletJ**

Dull, sluggish, Ile! what more than Lethargy. On the Gunpowder-Treason. Richard Crashaw. **CP-CrasR**

Dull, Sullen Prisoners. Alexander Pope. *See* Most souls, 'tis true, but peep out once an age.

Dull to myself and almost dead to these. The Bad Season Makes the Poet Sad. Robert Herrick. **CP-HerrR**

Dull uncertain brain, A. Ralph Waldo Emerson. **CP-EmerR**

Dull uniformity in fools. Dick's Variety. Jonathan Swift. **CP-SwifJ**

Dullness in February: Japan. Gary Snyder. **CP-SnydG**

Dulness[e]. George Herbert. **CP-HerbG**

Dulness, with redoubted sway. Robert Burns. *Fr.* To Symon Gray. **CP-BurnR**

Duluth's an iron ore shipping town in Minnesota. My Life in a Stolen Moment. "Bob Dylan." **CP-DylaB**

Duly with knees that feign to quake. Rimmon. Rudyard Kipling. **CP-KiplR**

Dumb Friend, A. Christina Georgina Rossetti. **CP-RosC3**

Dumb Soldier, The. Robert Louis Stevenson. **CP-StevR**

Dumfires Volunteers, The. Robert Burns. **CP-BurnR**

Dumfries Epigrams. Robert Burns. **CP-BurnR**

   "C———d faithful likeness, friend Painter, would'st seize?"

   Epigram on James Baillie Swan.

   "Friend Commissar, since we're met and are happy."

   On an Old Acquaintance Who Seemed to Pass the Bard without Notice.

   "Dost blush, my dear Billy, asham'd of thyself."

   "Dost hang thy head, Billy, asham'd that thou knowest me?"

   On Mr. Burke by an Opponent and a Friend to Mr. Hastings.

   "Pray who are these *Natives* the Rabble so ven'rate."

   "Should he escape the slaughter of thine Eyes."

Dummies. Randall Jarrell. **CP-JarrR**

Dump, The. Donald Hall. **CP-HallD**

D'un sonno profondissimo. Christina Georgina Rossetti. **CP-RosC3**

Dunbarton. Robert Lowell. **SP-LoweR**

Duncan Davison. Robert Burns. **CP-BurnR**

Duncan Gibb o' Focherty's. Focherty. "Hugh MacDiarmid." **SP-MacDH**

Duncan Gray ["Weary fa' you, Duncan Gray"]. Robert Burns. **CP-BurnR**

Duncan Gray. Robert Burns. **CP-BurnR**

Dunciad, The. Alexander Pope. **CP-PopeA**

   "High on a gorgeous seat, that far out-shone."

   "This labour passed, by Bridewell all descend." **FHYEP**

   "Three college sophs, and three pert templars came." **FHYEP**

   To Dr. Jonathan Swift. **OxAEP-1**, *book* I, *ll.* 1–330; **CBNP**

   ("Books and the Man I sing, the first who brings.") **CBNP**, *book* I, *ll.* 1–84, *first edition vers.*;

   "Here she beholds the chaos dark and deep." **FHYEP**

   "Yet, yet a moment, one dim ray of light." **NAEL-1; OAEL-1; PoEL-3**

   Carnations and Butterflies. **NOEC**

   Certain Type of Scientist Speaks, A. **ECEV**

   "More had she spoke, but yawn'd—All nature nods." **FHYEP**

   "Next, bidding all draw near on bended knees." **ECEV; OBSV**

   (Idle Pursuits.) **ECEV**, *book* IV, *ll.* 565–604;

   "Oh (cry'd the Goddess) for some pedant Reign!" **FaBoEH**

   Reign of Chaos, The. **EBEV; FaBoPV; SCV**

   (Chaos.) **LoBV**

   (Reign of Chaos, The.) **FiP**

   (Triumph of Dullness [*or* Dulness], The.) **NOBE; NoP**

   "She comes! she comes! the sable throne behold." **ECEV**

   Triumph of Dullness, The. **NOEC**

   Young Traveller Is Presented to the Goddess Dulness, A. **NOEC**

Dundrige his Issue hath; but is not styl'd. Upon Dundrige. Robert Herrick. **CP-HerrR**

Dunes. Carl Sandburg. **CP-SandC**

Dungannon Cattle Market. John Hewitt. **CP-HewiJ**

Dungeon, The. Samuel Taylor Coleridge. **CP-ColeS**

Dungeon Amorist, The. Laurence Lieberman. **SP-LiebL**

Dungeon horrible, on all sides round, A. John Milton. **OBD** *Fr.* Book I. **FHYEP; NAEL-1; OAEL-1; OxAEP-1** *Fr.* Paradise Lost. **CP-MiltJ**

Dungeon where they keep me is of rock, The. Campanella. Frank Templeton Prince. **CP-PrinF**

Dunkirk to be Let. Jonathan Swift. **CP-SwifJ**

   "Old Lewis thus the terms of peace to burnish." **CP-SwifJ**

Dunlolly Eagle, The. William Wordsworth. *Fr.* Poems Composed or Suggested During a Tour, in the Summer of 1833. **CP-WorW2**

Dunna thee tell me it's his'n, mother. Whether or Not. David Herbert Lawrence. **CP-LawrD**

Duns Scotus. Thomas Merton. **CP-MertT; SP-MertT**

Duns Scotus's Oxford. Gerard Manley Hopkins. **CP-HopkG**

Duntulm Castle. Richard Hugo. **CP-HugoR**

Dupont's Round Fight. Herman Melville. **SP-MelvH**

Dura. Charles Olson. **CP-OlsoC**

Dürer, I like that horse of yours. Travelling Slaughterhouse. Charles Simic. **SP-SimiC**

Dürer would have seen a reason for living. The Steeple-Jack. Marianne Craig Moore. **CP-MoorM** *Fr.* Part of a Novel, Part of a Poem, Part of a Play.

Dürer's Vision. John Haines. **SP-HainJ**

Duress of pains and grievous smart. Sir Thomas Wyatt. **CP-WyatT**

During a lull at dinner the vampire frankly. A Narrow Escape. James Merrill. **SP-MerrJ**

During a war the poets turn to war. Ordonnance. Thomas McGrath. **SP-McGrT**

During an Absence. Thom Gunn. **CP-GunnT**

During Fever. Robert Lowell. **SP-LoweR**

During Menstruation. John Updike. *Fr.* Living with a Wife. **CP-UpdiJ**

During Rain. Charles Tomlinson. **CP-TomlC**

During summer in these latitudes. San Juan's Day. Richard Shelton. **SP-ShelR**

During that long time, in those places. The Wedding. James Dickey. **CP-DickJ**

During the eastering of untainted morns. Gerard Manley Hopkins. **CP-HopkG**

During the Eichmann Trial. Denise Levertov. **CP-LeveD** When We Look Up. **BTR**

During the first pogrom they. Lovers. Leonard Cohen. **CP-CoheL**

During the journey there come moments of waking. Muriel Rukeyser. **CP-RukeM**

During the Passaic Strike of 1926. Louis Zukofsky. *Fr.* 29 Poems. **CP-ZukLS**

During this silence, innocent of song. Sonnet in Autumn. John Hewitt. **CP-HewiJ**

During Wind and Rain. Thomas Hardy. **CP-HardT**

Dusk. Joseph Ceravolo. **SP-CeraJ**

Dusk, The. William Everson. **SP-EverW**

Dusk. Roy Fisher. **SP-FishR**

Dusk. Chuck Miller. **SP-MillC**

Dusk. Stephen Spender. **CP-SpenS**

Dusk. Allen Tate. **CP-TateA**

Dusk dark / On Railroad Avenue. Railroad Avenue. Langston Hughes. **SP-HughL**

Dusk in the Woods. Chuck Miller. **SP-MillC**

Dusk, iridescent gasoline floats on the. Going Back to the River. Marilyn Hacker. **SP-HackM**

Dusk of dawn, the prophet called it, The. Dawn Song. Edwin Rolfe. **CP-RolfE**

Dusk of Horses, The. James Dickey. **CP-DickJ**

Dusk of the Revolutionaries. John Haines. **SP-HainJ**

Dusk of this box wood, The. Hoof Dusk. Carl Sandburg. **CP-SandC**

Dusk so dark woodsmoke, A. One for the Road. Martin Edmunds. **SP-EdmuM**

Dusk so thick, swarming, earthlike, The. Summer Evening. Chuck Miller. **SP-MillC**

Dust. Stephen Berg. **SP-BergS**

Dust. James Dickey. **CP-DickJ**

Dust. Carl Sandburg. **CP-SandC**

Dust always blowing about the town. A Peck of Gold. Robert Frost. **CP-FrosR**

Dust as we are, the immortal spirit grows. William Wordsworth. **SCV** *Fr.* Introduction—Childhood and School-Time. **EnRP; FHYEP** *Fr.* The Prelude; Growth of a Poet's Mind [1850 vers.]. **CP-WorW3**

Dust behind I strove to join, The. Emily Dickinson. **CP-DickE**

Dust-Devils. James McAuley. **SP-McAuJ**

Dust flies smothering, as on clatt'ring Wheels. Perspiration: A Travelling Eclogue. Samuel Taylor Coleridge. **CP-ColeS**

Dust in a cloud, blinding weather. Apples and Water. Robert Ranke Graves. **CP-GravR**

Dust in the East. David Herbert Lawrence. *Fr.* Bits. **CP-LawrD**

Dust in the Eyes. Robert Frost. **CP-FrosR**

Dust is the only Secret. Emily Dickinson. **CP-DickE**

Dust like the Mosquito, The. Emily Dickinson. **SP-DickE**

Dust Now Is. . . . Hart Crane. **CP-CranH**

Dust of man's trouble rises, The. Kenneth Rexroth. **CP-RexKL** *Fr.* The Heart's Garden, the Garden's Heart.

Dust of Snow. Robert Frost. **CP-FrosR**

Dust of the feet / And dust of the wheels. Clark Street Bridge. Carl Sandburg. **CP-SandC**

Dust of Timas, The. Sappho. **AWP** *Fr.* Variations of Greek Themes. **CP-RobiE**

"Dust," she said. "What is it? Where does it come from?" How Lewisburg, Pa., Escaped the Avenging Angel. Hayden Carruth. **CP-CarHS**

Dust that clouded your last drunk dream. Ovando. Richard Hugo. **CP-HugoR**

Dust to Dust. Walter de la Mare. **CP-DeLaW**

Dust unto dust! and shall no more be said. Ralph Waldo Emerson. **CP-EmerR**

Dust was too thick every summer. Every winter. Brief History. Richard Hugo. **CP-HugoR**

Dustcart, The. John Hewitt. **CP-HewiJ**

Dustcart anchored in our cinder field, A. The Dustcart. John Hewitt. **CP-HewiJ**

Dusting. Rita Dove. **SP-DoveR**

Dusty Answer, A. George Meredith. *See* Thus piteously Love closed what he begat.

Dusty Doors. Carl Sandburg. **CP-SandC**

Dusty Miller. Robert Burns. **CP-BurnR**

Dusty Old Fairgrounds. "Bob Dylan." **CP-DylaB**

Dusty olive trees. Marsden Hartley. **CP-HartM**

Dusty Roads. John Hewitt. **CP-HewiJ**

Dutch Cleanser. John Updike. **CP-UpdiJ**

Dutch Courtyard, A. Richard Wilbur. **CP-WilbR**

Dutch Graves in Bucks County. Wallace Stevens. **CP-StevW**

Dutch in the Medway, The. Rudyard Kipling. **CP-KiplR**

Dutch in the Medway, The. Andrew Marvell. **FaBoEH; OBS** *Fr.* The Last Instructions to a Painter. **CP-MarvA**

Dutch Interior. May Sarton. **SP-SartM**

Dutch White Iris. May Sarton. **CP-ZukLS**

Duties of the Wind are few, The. Emily Dickinson. **CP-DickE**

Dutifully I close this book. Colophon. Robert Ranke Graves. **CP-GravR**

Duty. Ralph Waldo Emerson. **FaFP; GN; HBV 1-2; HBVY; TRV; TreF; TreFS; YaD** *Fr.* In an Age of Fops and Toys. **FPL; LiTA; PoLF** *Fr.* Voluntaries. **CP-EmerR**

Duty shunned, signals drunk. Prelude to Consternation. John Hewitt. **CP-HewiJ**

Duty Surviving Self-Love. Samuel Taylor Coleridge. **CP-ColeS**

Duty—that's to say, complying. Arthur Hugh Clough. **SP-ClouA**

Duty to Tyrants. Robert Herrick. **CP-HerrR**

Duty Was His Lodestar. Stevie Smith. **CP-SmitS**

Duty was my Lobster, my Lobster was she. Duty Was His Lodestar. Stevie Smith. **CP-SmitS**

Duwamish. Richard Hugo. **CP-HugoR**

Duwamish Head. Richard Hugo. **CP-HugoR**

Duwamish No. 2. Richard Hugo. **CP-HugoR**

Dwarf, The. Wallace Stevens. **CP-StevW**

Dwarf and Doctor Freud, The. Robert Pack. **SP-PackR**

Dwarf barefooted, chanting, The. The Peasants. Alun Lewis. **CP-LewiA**

Dwarf in the Woods. Mona Van Duyn. **SP-VanDM**

Dwarf pine and yellow moonshine grass. Burying Field. Louise McNeill. **SP-McNeL**

Dwarfcypress silva evergreen spineranks branchlets. Lavender Cotton. Louis Zukofsky. **CP-ZukLS**

Dwarfs, The. Siv Cedering Fox. **SP-CedeS**

Dwarfs shuffle up the white steps, The. We Are Not Worthy, Lord. Kenneth Patchen. **CP-PatcK**

Dweller in yon dungeon dark. Ode, Sacred to the Memory of Mrs. ——— of ———. Robert Burns. **CP-BurnR**

Dwelling. Richard Hugo. **CP-HugoR**

Dwelling-Place, The. Walter de la Mare. **CP-DeLaW**

Dwindled creeks of summer, The. Creeks. Mary Oliver. **SP-OlivM**

Dwindling body of ageing fish, A. Friends of the River Trent. Stevie Smith. **CP-SmitS**

Dwindling pole, / Tall perpendicular in air, The. Eagle. Stanley Jasspon Kunitz. **CP-KuniS**

Dwingelo. Gerrit Achterberg, *tr. fr. Dutch by* Adrienne Rich. **CP-RicAE**

Dybbuk. Lewis Turco. **SP-TurcL**

D'ye know your man that's come to live at Layde? The Fairy-Man at Layde. John Hewitt. **CP-HewiJ**

Dyere. Roy Fisher. **SP-FishR** *Fr.* Five Pilgrims in the Prologue to the Canterbury Tales.

Dyer's Phancy Turned to a Sinner's Complainte. Robert Southwell. **CP-SoutR**

Dying. Robert Creeley. **CP-CreeR**

Dying. Pablo Neruda, *tr. fr. Spanish by* Ben Belitt. **SP-NeruP**

Dying Art, A. Derek Mahon. **SP-MahoD**

Dying at my music! Emily Dickinson. **CP-DickE**

Dying away as of trees, A. Louis Zukofsky. *Fr.* 29 Poems. **CP-ZukLS**

Dying Chauffer, The, *parody of* Adam Lindsay Gordon. Rudyard Kipling. **CP-KiplR** *Fr.* The Muse among the Motors.

Dying Child, The. John Clare. **SP-ClarJ**

Dying! Dying in the night! Emily Dickinson. **CP-DickE**

Dying Earth, The. "Hugh MacDiarmid." **SP-MacDH**

Dying embers glowed in the grate. By the Fire. Wystan Hugh Auden. **CP-AudWJ**

Dying gales of sweet even. Song. John Clare. **SP-ClarJ** *Fr.* Child Harold.

Dying Gladiator, The. Byron. **NOBE** *Fr.* Childe Harold's Pilgrimage. **CP-Byron**

Dying House, The. Wystan Hugh Auden. **CP-AudWJ**

Dying is a wild Night. Emily Dickinson. **SP-DickE**

Dying is fine)but Death. Edward Estlin Cummings. **CP-CummE**

Dying Lawrence. John Clellon Holmes. **SP-HolmJ**

Dying man / Lifts his head, The. People Are So Busy: Or: That's Life! Thomas McGrath. **SP-McGrT**

Dying Man, The. Theodore Roethke. **CP-RoetT**

Dying man on his pillow, The. The Satire. Walter de la Mare. **CP-DeLaW**

Dying Man to His Betrothed, The. Christina Georgina Rossetti. **CP-RosC3**

Dying need but little, Dear, The. Emily Dickinson. **CP-DickE**

Dying now, or already dead. Paul Blackburn. Ted Berrigan. **SP-BerrT**

Dying of the day in the dying of the year, The. The Return. Charles Olson. **CP-OlsoC**

Dying Phobiac Takes His Fears with Him, The. John Updike. *Fr.* Two Sonnets Whose Titles Came to Me Simultaneously. **CP-UpdiJ**

Dying sun, shine warm a little longer! Lament for Pasiphaë. Robert Ranke Graves. **CP-GravR**

Dying Swan, The. James McAuley. **SP-McAuJ**

Dying Swan, The. Tennyson. **CP-TennA**

Dying Tiger—moaned for Drink, A. Emily Dickinson. **CP-DickE**

Dying! To be afraid of thee. Emily Dickinson. **CP-DickE**

Dying Veteran, The. Walt Whitman. **CP-WhitW**

Dykes, The. Rudyard Kipling. **CP-KiplR**

Dylan. David Markson. **CP-MarkD**

Dylan Thomas, and Now Matthew Mead—as He Himself, "To Edward Thomas." Charles Olson. **CP-OlsoC**

Dymchurch Flit. Rudyard Kipling. *Fr.* Puck of Pook's Hill.

  Bee-Boy's Song, The. **CP-KiplR**

  Three-Part Song, A. **CP-KiplR**

Dynamiter. Carl Sandburg. **CP-SandC**

Dynasts, The. Thomas Hardy.

  Budmouth Dears. **CP-HardT**

  Chorus of the Pities. **CP-HardT**

  Epilogue: "We have now set forth, in our imperfect way." **CP-HardT**

  Eve of Waterloo, The. **CP-HardT**

  Last Chorus. **CP-HardT**

  My Love's Gone a-Fighting. **CP-HardT**

  Night of Trafalgar, The. **CP-HardT**

  Prologue: "In these stern times of ours, when crimson strife." **CP-HardT**

Dytiscus. "Hugh MacDiarmid." **SP-MacDH**

Dzules, *sels.* Thomas Merton. *Fr.* South. *Fr.* The Geography of Lograire. **CP-MertT**

E

E / cco the uglies / t. Edward Estlin Cummings. **CP-CummE**

E babbo e mamma ha il nostro figliolino. Christina Georgina Rossetti. **CP-RosC3**

E multis aliquos si non despexit amantes. *acc. by English trnaslation.* Thomas Campion. **CP-CampT**

E Nihilo Nihil. Byron. **CP-Byron**

E. P. Ode Pour l'Election de Son Sepulchre. Ezra Pound. *See* For three years, out of key with his time.

"E Pluribus Unum." John Yau. **SP-YauJo**

E poi dormii. Canto 73. Ezra Pound. *Fr.* Cantos. **CP-PoCan**

'E was warned agin 'er. The Sergeant's Weddin'. Rudyard Kipling. **CP-KiplR**

Each act of criticism is general. Their Day. John Ashbery. **SP-AshbJ**

Each afternoon the world goes by above it. Remote Farm on the Dubrovnik-Sarajevo Run. Richard Hugo. **CP-HugoR**

Each and All. Ralph Waldo Emerson. **CP-EmerR**

Each ant has his appointed task. Thomas Merton. *Fr.* Cables to the Ace. **CP-MertT**

Each argument begets its counterpart. The Pull of Memory. Richard Eberhart. *Fr.* Aesthetics after War. **CP-EberR**

Each barge on the river easily tows. Quai d'Orléans. Elizabeth Bishop. **CP-BishE**

Each bead of the mist is burning. A Stillness. Daniel Gerard Hoffman. **SP-HoffD**

Each Bird Walking. Tess Gallagher. **SP-GallT**

Each blest drop, on each blest limb [*or* limme]. On the Water of Our Lord's Baptism[e]. Richard Crashaw. **CP-CrasR**

Each body has its art, its precious prescribed. Still Do I Keep My Look, My Identity. Gwendolyn Brooks. **SP-BrooG**

Each creature holds an insular point in space. Life. Elizabeth Barrett Browning. **CP-BroEB**

Each dawn is clear. Gary Snyder. **CP-SnydG** *Fr.* Logging. *Fr.* Myths and Texts.

Each day another installment of the old. The Daily Globe. Howard Nemerov. **CP-NemeH**

Each day brings its toad, each night its dragon. Jerome. Randall Jarrell. **CP-JarrR**

Each day is Biloxi's birthday party. Nicholas Vachel Lindsay. *Fr.* Billboards and Galleons. **CP-LindV**

Each day just goes so fast. Love You To. George Harrison. **CP-Beatl**

Each day the terror wagon. War. Richard Shelton. **SP-ShelR**

Each day the tide withdraws; chills us; pastes. Wreaths. Geoffrey Hill. **CP-HillG**

Each day with so much ceremony. Anaphora. Elizabeth Bishop. **CP-BishE**

Each day's tour, I gather sandy castles. John Updike. *Fr.* Spanish Sonnets. **CP-UpdiJ**

Each evening the man whose wife has gone. Footstep. Stephen Dobyns. **SP-DobyS**

Each evening the sea casts starfish up on the beach. Poem (the Starfish One). Bill Knott. **SP-KnotB**

Each for himself is still the rule. Arthur Hugh Clough. **SP-ClouA** (In Stratis Viarum I.) **SP-ClouA**

Each from Different Heights. Stephen Dunn. **SP-DunnS**

Each gesture / is a common one, a. A Reason. Robert Creeley. **CP-CreeR**

Each hurt swallowed. Promises. Rita Dove. **SP-DoveR**

Each inly murm'ring at th'unequal meed. 2.1. Horace, *tr. by* Samuel Johnson. **CP-JohnS** *Fr.* Epistles.

Each Is Alone, Each Is Everything. Kenneth Patchen. **CP-PatcK**

Each July, an evening arrives. The First Night of Fall. Brendan Galvin. **SP-GalvB**

Each Life Converges to some Centre. Emily Dickinson. **CP-DickE**

Each lover has a theory of his own. Alone. Wystan Hugh Auden. **CP-AudeW**

Each Man is in His Spectres power. William Blake. **CP-BlakW**

Each man me telleth I change most my device [*or* devise]. Sir Thomas Wyatt. **CP-WyatT**

Each man pictures his hell or heaven different. Hells and Heavens. Carl Sandburg. **CP-SandC**

Each minute what I hear is you—. You. Stephen Berg. **SP-BergS**

Each Moment of the long-liv'd Day. Catullus. *See* Carmen 92: "Lesbia loads me night & day with her curses."

Each morning a woman opens the door. Milk. Stephen Berg. **SP-BergS**

Each morning he rolls over. Richard Shelton. *Fr.* Angel and the Anchorite. **SP-ShelR**

Each morning in the soft prismatic light. Vida, Mykonos. John Hewitt. **CP-HewiJ**

Each morning my characters. Marching through a Novel. John Updike. **CP-UpdiJ**

Each morning the man rises from bed because the invisible. It's Like This. Stephen Dobyns. **SP-DobyS**

Each morning when Carmina's crippled rooster. Jabón. Gary Gildner. **SP-GildG**

Each morning when I break my buttered toast. Keeping Informed in D.C. Howard Nemerov. **CP-NemeH**

Each movement of the Mozart has a soloist and as each appears the conductor tunes her instrument. Junior High School Concert: Salle Rossini. Charles Kenneth Williams. **SP-WillC**

Each must, in vertue, strive to excell. Vertue. Robert Herrick. **CP-HerrR**

Each night / I work late. Reminded of One of Those Girls I Never Was. Diane Wakoski. **SP-WakoD**

Each night another room. On Tour. Jim Carroll. **SP-CarrJ**

Each night for seven nights beyond the gulf. The Oleaster. Robert Ranke Graves. **CP-GravR**

Each night, this adroit young lady. Aerialist. Sylvia Plath. **CP-PlatS**

Each of them must have terrified. In Memory of the Utah Stars. William Matthews. **SP-MattW**

Each of us has the time. Treviso, the Pescheria. Donald Davie. **CP-DavDo**

Each of us like you. Adonis. Hilda Doolittle. **CP-DoolH**

Each of us waking to the window's light. Exile. Donald Hall. **CP-HallD**

Each One, Pull One. Alice Walker. **CP-WalkA**

Each one shall sit at table with his own cup and spoon. A Practical Program for Monks. Thomas Merton. **CP-MertT; SP-MertT**

Each person's own particular angel (so believe, nations). To Leonora Singing in Rome. John Milton, tr. fr. Latin by John T. Shawcross. **CP-MiltJ**

Each red seed bursts. Hymn to Proserpine. Charles Olson. **CP-OlsoC**

Each Scar I'll keep for Him. Emily Dickinson. **CP-DickE**

Each Second is the last. Emily Dickinson. **CP-DickE**

Each servant stamps the reader with a look. Sonnet. John Ashbery. **SP-AshbJ**

Each shift you make in the sunlight somewhere. Sunlight Is Imagination. Richard Wilbur. **CP-WilbR**

Each soul I might have succoured, may have slain. Christina Georgina Rossetti. Fr. If Thou Sayest, Behold, We Knew It Not. **CP-RosC2**

Each spot where tulips prank their state. From Omar Chiam. Omar Khayyám, tr. fr. Persian by Ralph Waldo Emerson. **CP-EmerR**

Each Summer's Swallows. John Updike. **CP-UpdiJ**

Each that we lose takes part of us. Emily Dickinson. **CP-DickE**

Each thing, / you didn't even taste it. Post Cards. Robert Creeley. **CP-CreeR**

Each thing in the clean morning light. New Year's Day. Ted Kooser. **SP-KoosT**

Each time a perishable shadow fell. On the Death of My Student, the Poet Serafin. Kay Boyle. **CP-BoylK**

Each time I order her to go. Forgiveness. Alice Walker. **CP-WalkA**

Each time it happened recklessly. The Moon's Tear. Robert Ranke Graves. **CP-GravR**

Each time it rings. The Thing. William Carlos Williams. **CP-WilW2**

Each traveller prays, "Let me be far from any." Journey to Iceland. Wystan Hugh Auden. **CP-AudeW**

Each tree stands alone in stillness. Ted Berrigan. **SP-BerrT** Fr. The Sonnets.

Each vast block in its batter. The Icehouse, Pointe au Baril, Ontario. William Matthews. **SP-MattW**

Each voice which was asked. The Hero. Robert Creeley. **CP-CreeR**

Each way the turn. The Turn. Robert Creeley. **CP-CreeR**

Each year at this time I shall be telling you of the Lord. May Day Sermon to the Women of Gilmer County, Georgia, by a Woman Preacher Leaving the Baptist Church. James Dickey. **CP-DickJ**

Each year, just as the blossoms. All or None. Randall Jarrell. **CP-JarrR**

Each year the dead grow less dead, and nudge. Charles Wright. Fr. Homage to Paul Cézanne. **CP-WrigC**

Each year you came jogging or loping down that hall. Testament for My Students, 1968–1969. Kay Boyle. **CP-BoylK**

Eager hours and unreluctant years, The. Percy Bysshe Shelley. Fr. Ode to Liberty. **CP-ShelP**

Eager Journey. John Hewitt. **CP-HewiJ**

Eager note on my door said "Call me", The. Poem. Frank O'Hara. **SP-OharF**

Eager Youths to a Dead Girl. Allen Tate. **CP-TateA**

Eagerly, Musician. United Nations Hymn. Wystan Hugh Auden. Fr. Six Commissioned Texts. **CP-AudeW**

Eagerness of objects to, The. Interior (With Jane). Frank O'Hara. **SP-OharF**

Eagle, The. Robert Browning. **CP-BroR2**

Eagle, The. Edward Estlin Cummings. **CP-CummE**

Eagle. Ted Hughes. **SP-HughT**

Eagle. Stanley Jasspon Kunitz. **CP-KuniS**

Eagle, The. Allen Tate. **CP-TateA**

Eagle, The. Tennyson. **CP-TennA**

Eagle and hawk with their great claws and hooked heads. Robinson Jeffers. **CP-JefR3**

Eagle and the Dove, The. William Wordsworth. **CP-WorW2**

Eagle and the Tortoise, The. Samuel Taylor Coleridge. **CP-ColeS**

Eagle carries / Off a single sheep. Carry, An. Charles Henri Ford. **SP-FordC** Fr. Emblems of Arachne.

Eagle in New Mexico. ("On a low"). David Herbert Lawrence. **CP-LawrD**

Eagle in New Mexico. ("Towards the sun"). David Herbert Lawrence. **CP-LawrD**

"Towards the sun, towards the south-west." **RB**

Eagle of the Inner Eye. Marsden Hartley. Fr. Word Arrangements for Pictures by Morris Graves. **CP-HartM**

Eagle Rock. Alice Walker. **CP-WalkA**

Eagle so caught in some bursting cloud, An. Percy Bysshe Shelley. **PBBP** Fr. Prometheus Unbound. **CP-ShelP**

Eagle soars in the summit of heaven, The, fr. sect. 1. Thomas Stearns Eliot. **OBMV** Fr. Choruses from "The Rock." **CP-ElioT**

Eagle, stooping from yon snow-blown peaks, The. Inscription. John Greenleaf Whittier. **CP-WhitJ**

Eagle That Is Forgotten, The. Nicholas Vachel Lindsay. **CP-LindV**

Eagle Valor, Chicken Mind. Robinson Jeffers. **CP-JefR3**

Eagle wants no friends, The. Marsden Hartley. **CP-HartM**

Eagle! why soarest thou above that tomb? Spirit of Plato. Unknown, tr. fr. Greek by Shelley. **CP-ShelP**

Eagles. James Dickey. **CP-DickJ**

Eagles. Daniel Gerard Hoffman. **SP-HoffD**

Eagles. William Wordsworth. **CP-WorW2**

Eagle's Mile, The. James Dickey. **CP-DickJ**

Eagle's nest on the head of an old redwood on one of the, An. The Beaks of Eagles. Robinson Jeffers. **CP-JefR2**

Ear, The. Robert Creeley. **CP-CreeR**

Ear, The. Louis MacNeice. **CP-MacNL**

Ear threading, The. The Stream. Charles Simic. **SP-SimiC**

Eare-rings. Robert Herrick. **CP-HerrR**

Earl of Breadalbane's Ruined Mansion, and Family Burial-Place, near Killin, The. William Wordsworth. **CP-WorW2**

Earlier in the century it was not unusual to spend an evening. The Dream Life of a Coffin Factory in Lynn, Massachussetts. John Yau. **SP-YauJo**

Earlier in the evening the moon. The Moon. Robert Creeley. **CP-CreeR**

Earlier Lovers. Robert Ranke Graves. **CP-GravR**

Earlier than I could learn. The Reincarnation of Captain Cook. Margaret Atwood. **SP-AtwM1**

Earliest morning, switching all the tracks. Love Lies Sleeping. Elizabeth Bishop. **CP-BishE**

Earliest recorded citing, The. Champ. Robert Pack. **SP-PackR**

Earliest sportsman in the earliest dawn, The. The Worst Sinner, Jonathan Edwards' God. Robert Lowell. **SP-LoweR**

Earliest words for it are transparent, The. Fate. Tom Clark. **SP-ClarT**

Early / bird catches, The. Layabout. Archie Randolph Ammons. **SP-AmmoA**

Early after the night long revel. Hafiz, tr. by Ralph Waldo Emerson. **CP-EmerR** Fr. Odes.

Early and Late. Robert Pack. **SP-PackR**

Early April on Broadway, south of Union Square. Seeing Off a Friend. Stephen Dobyns. **SP-DobyS**

Early, before the soldiers are awake. The Swimmer. Alun Lewis. **CP-LewiA**

Early Bird. Shel Silverstein. **SP-SilS2**

Early Blizzard. Thomas Merton. **CP-MertT**

Early blue evening. Wonder. Langston Hughes. **SP-HughL**

Early Butterfly, The. Charlotte Smith. **CP-SmitC**

Early Copper. Carl Sandburg. **CP-SandC**

Early December in Croton-on-Hudson. Louise Glück. **SP-GlücL**

Early, early in the morning, even before five o'clock, the. The Hanging of the Mouse. Elizabeth Bishop. **CP-BishE**

Early Electric! With what radiant hope. The Metropolitan Railway. Sir John Betjeman. **CP-BetjJ**

Early Evening Quarrel. Langston Hughes. **SP-HughL**

Early flowered everlasting, The. The Dodder. Malcolm Lowry. **CP-LowrM**

Early frost, and a lone cricket, An. A Petty Thing. Stephen Dunn. **SP-DunnS**

Early Hours. Carl Sandburg. **CP-SandC**

Early in the mornin'. Obviously Five Believers. "Bob Dylan." **CP-DylaB**

Early in the Morning. Kenneth Patchen. **CP-PatcK**

Early in the morning I hear on your piano. Robert Louis Stevenson. **CP-StevR**

Early Legend, The. Thomas Merton. **CP-MertT**

"But did you ever know the whole world was once held prisoner in a bank?"

"My birthday was in March, when the weather was furious."

"Out of the rain and the darkness and the depths, the bottomless holes in the green sea."

"Take thought, man, tonight."

"When night falls / beat one drum / in honor of night."

"With great speed I set the young man free."

Early Losses: a Requiem. Alice Walker. **CP-WalkA**

Early Lynching. Carl Sandburg. **CP-SandC**

Early Martyr, An. William Carlos Williams. **CP-WilW1**

Early Mass. Thomas Merton. **CP-MertT**

Early May (a late spring) a field. Industrial Archaeology. James Schuyler. **CP-SchuJ**

Early May, after cold rain the sun baffling cold wind. Dan. Carl Sandburg. **CP-SandC**

Early Moon. Carl Sandburg. **CP-SandC**

Early Morning. Wystan Hugh Auden. **CP-AudWJ**

Early Morning. Wystan Hugh Auden. **CP-AudWJ**

Early Morning Bathing. Wystan Hugh Auden. **CP-AudWJ**

Early Morning Crucifixion, An. Jim Carroll. **SP-CarrJ**

Early Morning on the Tel Aviv-Haifa Freeway. Rita Dove. **SP-DoveR**

Early Morning. The Hour of Prime. Thomas Merton. *Fr.* Hagia Sophia. **CP-MertT**

Early Morning Walk to Work. James McAuley. **SP-McAuJ**

Early one mornin' the sun was shinin'. Tangled Up in Blue. "Bob Dylan." **CP-DylaB**

Early Pompeian. Derek Walcott. **CP-WalcD**

Early Spring, *sl. diff. vers.* David Herbert Lawrence. *See* Amour.

Early Spring Between Madison and Bellingham. Robert Bly. **SP-BlyR**

Early Summer Sketch. Edward Estlin Cummings. **CP-CummE**

Early sun on Beaulieu water. Youth and Age on Beaulieu River, Hants. Sir John Betjeman. **CP-BetjJ**

Early the day before she had heard gulls. Danaë. Jenny Joseph. **SP-JoseJ**

Early violets we saw together, The. Approach of Autumn. Stanley Jasspon Kunitz. **CP-KuniS**

Earnest, earthless, equal, attuneable, vaulty, voluminous,. . . stupendous. Spelt from Sibyl's Leaves. Gerard Manley Hopkins. **CP-HopkG**

Earnest Liberal's Lament, The. Ernest Hemingway. **CP-HemiE**

Earnest man, in long-forgotten years, An. The Story of Sir Arnulph. George Meredith. **CP-MerG2**

Earnest scholar skilled to weigh, An. On the Choice of a Title. John Hewitt. **CP-HewiJ**

Ears beringed with fuzz. Louis Zukofsky. *Fr.* 29 Songs. **CP-ZukLS**

Ears in the Turrets Hear. Dylan Thomas. **CP-ThomD**

Ears of the forest, The. What Splendid Birthdays. Kenneth Patchen. **CP-PatcK**

Ears stung with cold, The. The Finches. Wendell Berry. **CP-BerrW**

Earth, The. Ralph Waldo Emerson. **CP-EmerR**

Earth. Pablo Neruda, *tr. fr. Spanish by* Ben Belitt. **SP-NeruP**

Earth, The. Anne Sexton. **CP-SextA**

Earth a flower. For Nothing. Gary Snyder. **CP-SnydG**

Earth again like a ship steams out of the dark sea over, The. The Shadow of Death. David Herbert Lawrence. **CP-LawrD**

Earth and a Wedded Woman. George Meredith. **CP-MerG1**

Earth and Fire. Wendell Berry. **CP-BerrW**

Earth and Heaven. Christina Georgina Rossetti. **CP-RosC3**

Earth and heaven, so little known, The. Gerard Manley Hopkins. **CP-HopkG**

Earth and Her Praisers. Elizabeth Barrett Browning. **CP-BroEB**

Earth and Man. George Meredith. **CP-MerG1**

Earth-animal tastes, The. In the Courtyard of Secret Life. Kenneth Patchen. **CP-PatcK**

Earth, bind us close, and time ; nor, sky, deride. Preamble. Muriel Rukeyser. **CP-RukeM**

Earth Breaks Up. Robert Browning. **TrCP** *Fr.* Christmas-Eve. **CP-BroR1**

Earth cannot bar flame from ascending, / Hell cannot bind light from descending. St. John, Apostle. Christina Georgina Rossetti. **CP-RosC2**

Earth does not understand her child. The Return. Edna St. Vincent Millay. **CP-MillE**

Earth Dweller. William Stafford. **SP-StafW**

Earth, earth, / riding your merry-go-round. As It Was Written. Anne Sexton. **CP-SextA**

Earth Falls Down, the. Anne Sexton. **CP-SextA**

Earth feels old tonight, The. Greeting. May Sarton. **SP-SartM**

Earth fills her lap with pleasures of her own. William Wordsworth. *Fr.* Ode: Intimations of Immortality [from Recollections of Early Childhood]. **CP-WorW1**

Earth gave me body; strong through fire am I. Some Riddles from Symphosius. Richard Wilbur. **CP-WilbR**

Earth gave up her dead that tide, The. Rudyard Kipling. **CP-KiplR** *Fr.* The Man Who Was. *Fr.* Life's Handicap.

Earth grown old, yet still so green. Advent. Christina Georgina Rossetti. **CP-RosC2**

Earth has been unkind to him, The. Toothache Man. John Updike. **CP-UpdiJ**

Earth has clear call of daily bells, / A chancel-vault of gloom and star. Christina Georgina Rossetti. **CP-RosC2**

Earth has covered Sicilian Syracuse, there asphodel grows, The. What are Cities For? Robinson Jeffers. **CP-JefR2**

Earth has many keys, The. Emily Dickinson. **CP-DickE**

Earth has not anything to show [*or* shew] more fair. Composed upon Westminster Bridge, September 3, 1802. William Wordsworth. **CP-WorW1**

Earth has turned over; our side feels the cold. Through the Looking-Glass. Wystan Hugh Auden. **CP-AudeW**

Earth in beauty dressed. Her Anxiety. William Butler Yeats. **CP-YeatW**

Earth is a forgotten cinder, The. Carl Sandburg. *Fr.* Timesweep. **CP-SandC**

Earth is become the seat of a new sea. Mist. Edward Estlin Cummings. **CP-CummE**

Earth is bright though the boughs of the moon like a, The. Cinema of a Man. Archibald MacLeish. **CP-MacLA**

Earth is for the living OR, The. Canto One Hundred and One. Charles Olson. **CP-OlsoC**

Earth is full of anger, The. Hymn before Action. Rudyard Kipling. **CP-KiplR**

Earth is God's, with all she bears, The. Bible, *O.T.* *See* Psalm 24: "Earth is the Lord's and the fulness thereof, The."

Earth is near tonight; O slow, The. The Other Side: The Green Home. Kenneth Patchen. **CP-PatcK**

Earth is old, The. Earth and Her Praisers. Elizabeth Barrett Browning. **CP-BroEB**

Earth is the Lord's and the fulness thereof, The. Psalm 24. Bible, *O.T.* **AWP; EaLo; FaPON; TrGrPo; TrJP; TreFT** *Fr.* Psalms. **CP-Psal**

Earth lay golden green, The. Going from Battle to Battle. Charles Olson. **CP-OlsoC**

Earth like a tipsy. Edward Estlin Cummings. **CP-CummE**

Earth locked out the light, The. Ted Hughes. **SP-HughT** *Fr.* Seven Dungeon Songs.

Earth loves her young: a preference manifest. Earth's Preference. George Meredith. **CP-MerG1**

Earth-meaning, The. Fulfilment. Langston Hughes. **SP-HughL**

Earth, My Likeness. Walt Whitman. **CP-WhitW**

Earth-Numb. Ted Hughes. **SP-HughT**

Earth, ocean, air, belovèd brotherhood! Alastor; or, The Spirit of Solitude. Percy Bysshe Shelley. **CP-ShelP**

Earth, ocean, air, belovèd brotherhood! Invocation. Percy Bysshe Shelley. **FiP; NAEL-2** *Fr.* Alastor; or, The Spirit of Solitude. **CP-ShelP**

Earth orbits on the sun and has no sign. Howard Nemerov. *Fr.* Four Sonnets. **CP-NemeH**

Earth owls in ancient burrows clumpt. The Sentinels. Robert Duncan. **SP-DuncR**

Earth Psalm. Denise Levertov. **CP-LeveD**

Earth rais'd up her head. Earth's Answer. William Blake. **CP-BlakW** *Fr.* Songs of Experience.

Earth, receive an honoured guest. Wystan Hugh Auden. **ChMP; ChTr; FaBoRV; FaBoTw; Mes** *Fr.* In Memory of W. B. Yeats. **CP-AudeW**

Earth rolls these houses out into the sun. Early Morning. Wystan Hugh Auden. **CP-AudWJ**

Earth Shall Tremble at the Look of Him, The. Christina Georgina Rossetti. **CP-RosC2**

Earth spins to my finger-tips and, The. The Globe in North Carolina. Derek Mahon. **SP-MahoD**

Earth-spirit, wood-spirit, stone. Flute Song. Jane Cooper. **SP-CoopJ**

Earth, still heavy and warm with afternoon, The. Nocturne. Archibald MacLeish. **CP-MacLA**

Earth, sweet Earth, sweet landscape, with leavès throng. Ribblesdale. Gerard Manley Hopkins. **CP-HopkG**

Earth, the rock and the oil of the earth, the slippery frozen places of, The. Four Steichen Prints. Carl Sandburg. **CP-SandC**

Earth! thou mother of numberless children, the nurse and the mother. *ad. fr. the German of* Stolberg's "Hymne an die Erde." Samuel Taylor Coleridge. **CP-ColeS**

Earth Tremors Felt in Missouri. Mona Van Duyn. **SP-VanDM**

Earth was certain for all that; in spite, The. Ebes Anthos Apollumenon. Wystan Hugh Auden. **CP-AudWJ**

Earth was form'd, but in the womb as yet, The. John Milton. **MOS** *Fr.* Book VII. *Fr.* Paradise Lost. **CP-MiltJ**

Earth was grateful for a day of rain, The. Friendship. Wystan Hugh Auden. **CP-AudWJ**

Earth was green, the sky was blue, The. A Green Cornfield. Christina Georgina Rossetti. **CP-RosC1**

Earth was my home, but even there I was a stranger. Stanley Jasspon Kunitz. *Fr.* The Flight of Apollo. **CP-KuniS**

Earth was not Earth before her sons appeared. Appreciation. George Meredith. **CP-MerG1**

Earth water stars and flesh—the seamless coat. Place of a Skull. Louis MacNeice. **CP-MacNL**

Earth will be going on a long time, The. Lute Music. Kenneth Rexroth. **SP-RexrK**

Earth Worm, The. Denise Levertov. **CP-LeveD**

Earth would not seem homelike without. Emily Dickinson. **SP-DickE**

Earthly doctor fiddled with his beard, The. Fables of the Moscow Subway. Howard Nemerov. **CP-NemeH**

Earthquake, The. Jane Cooper. **SP-CoopJ**

Earthquake, *ad. fr.* Isaiah 52. Thomas Merton. **CP-MertT**

Earthquake, The. John Greenleaf Whittier. **CP-WhitJ**

Earthquake in the West, The. Howard Nemerov. **CP-NemeH**

Earth's Answer. William Blake. **CP-BlakW** *Fr.* Songs of Experience.

Earth's Holocaust. James Schuyler. **CP-SchuJ**

Earth's Immortalities. Robert Browning. **CP-BroR1**

    Fame. **PP; SoSe**

    Love. **ArLo; EnLoPo**

Earth's littered wi' larochs o' Empires. Au Clair de la Lune. "Hugh MacDiarmid." *Fr.* Au Clair de la Lune. **SP-MacDH**

Earth's Praises. Wystan Hugh Auden. **CP-AudWJ**

Earth's Preference. George Meredith. **CP-MerG1**

Earth's Secret. George Meredith. **CP-MerG1**

Earthworm. Anne Sexton. **CP-SextA**

Earthworm. John Updike. **CP-UpdiJ**

Earthy Anecdote. Wallace Stevens. **CP-StevW**

Ease. William Cowper. **TEP** *Fr.* The Sofa. *Fr.* The Task. **CP-CowpW**

Ease. Robert Herrick. **CP-HerrR**

Ease is the weary merchant's pray'r. Horace. *See* 2.16: To Grosphus.

Eased into the succession / by the ailing aged consul. The Well-Intentioned Consul. John Hewitt. **CP-HewiJ**

Easier to encapsulate your lives. Granddaughter. Adrienne Rich. *Fr.* Grandmothers. **SP-RicA2**

Easily, almost matter-of-factly they step. The Performers. Robert Earl Hayden. **CP-HaydR**

Easily you move, easily your head. A Bride in the 30's. Wystan Hugh Auden. **CP-AudeW**

East, The. Alun Lewis. **CP-LewiA**

East. Louis MacNeice. *Fr.* Sleeping Winds. **CP-MacNL**

East, *sels.* Thomas Merton. *Fr.* The Geography of Lograire. **CP-MertT**

    And a Few More Cargo Songs.

    Cargo Catechism.

    Cargo Songs.

    Dialog with Mister Clapcott.

    East with Ibn Battuta.

        Cairo 1326.

        Calicut.

        Delhi.

        Isfahan.

        Mecca.

        Nusayris, The.

        Syria.

    East with Malinowski.

    John the Volcano.

    Place Names. **ChIV-1**

    Sewende (Seven Day).

    Tibud Maclay.

East Anglian Bathe. Sir John Betjeman. **CP-BetjJ**

East Antrim Winter. John Hewitt. **CP-HewiJ**

East Boston. Al Young. **CP-YounA**

East Coker. Thomas Stearns Eliot. **HAP; PPP; VGW** *Fr.* Four Quartets. **CP-ElioT**

East Coocoo. William Carlos Williams. **CP-WilW2**

East-End Curate, An. Thomas Hardy. **CP-HardT**

East European Cooking. Charles Simic. **SP-SimiC**

East from Glacier Park. John Haines. *Fr.* News from the Glacier. **SP-HainJ**

East Hampton—Boston by Air. John Updike. **CP-UpdiJ**

East is the time of stars. From the Kuan-Tzu. Frederick Morgan. **SP-MorgF**

East of Los Angeles in a small town. The Lion Farm. Leonard Nathan. **SP-NathL**

East Wind, An. Robert Ranke Graves. **CP-GravR**

East wind finds the gap bringing rain, The. The Return: An Elegy. Robert Penn Warren. **SP-WarrR**

East winde with Aurora hath abiding, The. Ovid, *tr. by* Sir Walter Ralegh. **CP-RaleW** *Fr.* Metamorphoses.

East Window on Elizabeth Street, An. James Schuyler. **CP-SchuJ**

East with Ibn Battuta. Thomas Merton. *Fr.* East. *Fr.* The Geography of Lograire. **CP-MertT**

    Cairo 1326.

    Calicut.

    Delhi.

    Isfahan.

    Mecca.

    Nusayris, The.

    Syria.

East with Malinowski. Thomas Merton. *Fr.* East. *Fr.* The Geography of Lograire. **CP-MertT**

Easter. Robert Creeley. **CP-CreeR**

Easter. George Herbert. **CP-HerbG**

Easter. Gerard Manley Hopkins. **CP-HopkG**

Easter. Frank O'Hara. **SP-OharF**

Easter. Charles Olson. **CP-OlsoC**

Easter. Patti Smith. **SP-SmitP**

Easter. Edmund Spenser. *See* Most glorious lord of life that on this day.

Easter. Derek Walcott. **CP-WalcD**

Easter. Charles Kenneth Williams. **SP-WillC**

Easter again, and a small rain falls. The Other Side of the River. Charles Wright. **SP-WrigC**

Easter and the resurrection. Good Friday. Charles Tomlinson. *Fr.* Three Wagnerian Lyrics. **CP-TomlC**

Easter at Christmas. Alun Lewis. **CP-LewiA**

Easter Carol, An. Christina Georgina Rossetti. **CP-RosC2**

Easter Communion. Gerard Manley Hopkins. **CP-HopkG**

Easter-Day. Robert Browning. **CP-BroR1**

Easter Day. Richard Crashaw. **CP-CrasR**

Easter Day. Christina Georgina Rossetti. **CP-RosC2**

Easter Day. Christopher Smart. *Fr.* Hymns and Spiritual Songs for the Fasts and Festivals of the Church of England. **SP-SmarC**

Easter Day II. Arthur Hugh Clough. **SP-ClouA**

Easter Day. Naples, 1849. Arthur Hugh Clough. **SP-ClouA**

Easter Eve 1945. Muriel Rukeyser. **CP-RukeM**

Easter Even. Christina Georgina Rossetti. **CP-RosC2**

Easter Even. Christina Georgina Rossetti. **CP-RosC3**

Easter Flock. John Hewitt. **CP-HewiJ**

Easter Flower Gift, An. John Greenleaf Whittier. **CP-WhitJ**

Easter has come around. William DeWitt Snodgrass. **CAPP; ConAP; NMP; NePoEA; VCAP** *Fr.* Heart's Needle. **SP-SnodW**

Easter Hymn. Alfred Edward Housman. **CP-HousA**

Easter in Neuchâtel. Peter Meinke. **SP-MeinP**

Easter Monday. Wystan Hugh Auden. **CP-AudWJ**

Easter Monday. Christina Georgina Rossetti. **CP-RosC2**

Easter Morning. Christina Georgina Rossetti. **CP-RosC3**

Easter Morning. May Sarton. **SP-SartM**

Easter Morning. Edmund Spenser. *See* Most glorious lord of life that on this day.

Easter, 1916. William Butler Yeats. **CP-YeatW**

Easter, 1968. May Sarton. **SP-SartM**

Easter Ode, An. Paul Laurence Dunbar. **CP-DunbP**

Easter Returns. Louis MacNeice. **CP-MacNL**

Easter Season. Louise Glück. **SP-GlücL**

Easter stars are shining, The. Flight to the City. William Carlos Williams. **CP-WilW1**

Easter Sunday. Tom Clark. **SP-ClarT**

Easter Sunday. Allen Ginsberg. **CP-GinsA**

Easter Tuesday. John Hewitt. **CP-HewiJ**

Easter Tuesday. Christina Georgina Rossetti. **CP-RosC2**

Easter Wings. George Herbert. **CP-HerbG**

Eastern Ballad, An. Allen Ginsberg. **CP-GinsA**

Eastern European Eclogues. Rita Dove. **SP-DoveR**

Eastern guard tower. Haiku. Etheridge Knight. **SP-KnigE**

Eastern sky at sunset taking, The. The Coming Fall. Denise Levertov. **CP-LeveD**

Eastern War Time. Adrienne Rich.

    "Memory says: Want to do right? Don't count on me." **SP-RicA1**

Easters of childhood heaped in motley shards. Easter Returns. Louis MacNeice. **CP-MacNL**

Eastport to Block Island. Adrienne Rich. **CP-RicAE**

E[e]astrich, thou feather[e]d fool[e] and easy [*or* easie] prey. Lucasta's Fan[ne], with a Looking-Glass[e] in It. Richard Lovelace. **CP-LoveR**

Eastward from here. The Blue Sky. Gary Snyder. **CP-SnydG**

Eastward of Paris morn is high. George Meredith. *Fr.* Alsace-Lorraine. **CP-MerG1**

Eastward the armies. William Everson. **SP-EverW**

Easy. Stevie Smith. **CP-SmitS**

Easy as cove-water rustles its pebbles and shells. Part of a Letter. Richard Wilbur. **CP-WilbR**

Easy Boogie. Langston Hughes. **SP-HughL**

Easy Decision, An. Kenneth Patchen. **CP-PatcK**

Easy-Goin' Feller, An. Paul Laurence Dunbar. **CP-DunbP**

Easy Humanism plagues the land, An. Conclusion. John Updike. *Fr.* Midpoint. **CP-UpdiJ**

Easy in their ugly skins. Easy. Stevie Smith. **CP-SmitS**

Easy Knowledge. Wystan Hugh Auden. **CP-AudeW**

Easy lazy length of limb, An. Portraits. Christina Georgina Rossetti. **CP-RosC3**

Easy Rider. Kenneth Patchen. **CP-PatcK**

Easy to match what others do. Ralph Waldo Emerson. **CP-EmerR**

Eat. Charles Bukowski. **SP-BukC2**

Eat Helen B Happy (a Found Poem). Etheridge Knight. **SP-KnigE**

Eat like a Turk. Jonathan Swift. *Fr.* Verses from Quilica. **CP-SwifJ**

Eat the bit of cake in your garden. Emily Dickinson. **SP-DickE**

Eat Your Heart Out. Charles Bukowski. **SP-BukC1**

Eat your Rose Hips, C'est La Vie. Diane Wakoski. *Fr.* Fifteen Poems for a Lunar Eclipse None of Us Saw. **SP-WakoD**

Eaten by Butterflies. Charles Bukowski. **SP-BukC2**

Eaten I have; and though I had good cheere. Meat without Mirth. Robert Herrick. **CP-HerrR**

'Eathen, The. Rudyard Kipling. **CP-KiplR**

Eating a sandwich. We Make Our Vows Together with All Beings. Gary Snyder. **CP-SnydG**

Eating cold plums in bed. Cold Plums. Charles Bukowski. **SP-BukC1**

Eating Fire. Margaret Atwood. **SP-AtwM1**

Eating My Senior Citizen's Dinner at the Sizzler. Charles Bukowski. **SP-BukC3**

Eating Outside. Stephen Berg. **SP-BergS**

Eating Snake. Margaret Atwood. **SP-AtwM2**

Eating the living germs of grasses. Song of the Taste. Gary Snyder. **CP-SnydG**

Eating the Pig. Donald Hall. **CP-HallD**

Eavesdropper. Sylvia Plath. **CP-PlatS**

Ebb. Edna St. Vincent Millay. **CP-MillE**

Ebb slips from the rock, the sunken, The. Night. Robinson Jeffers. **CP-JefR1**

Eben Haëzer. Gerrit Achterberg, *tr. fr. Dutch* by Adrienne Rich. **CP-RicAE**

Ebes Anthos Apollumenon. Wystan Hugh Auden. **CP-AudWJ**

Ecce Homo. John Berryman. **CP-BerrJ**

Ecce Homo. John Hewitt. **CP-HewiJ**

Ecce quam leve et quam jocosum. Psalm 132: A Modern Monastic Revision. Thomas Merton. **CP-MertT**

Ecce Sponsus. Hilda Doolittle. **CP-DoolH**

Ecce Tibi Heroem claris natalibus ortum. De Domino Richardo Lovelacio, Armigero & Chiliarcha, Viro Incomparabili. *Unknown. Fr.* Commendatory Poems. **CP-LoveR**

Eccentric Motion. Muriel Rukeyser. **CP-RukeM**

Ecclesiast, The. John Ashbery. **SP-AshbJ**

Ecclesiastes. Derek Mahon. **SP-MahoD**

Ecclesiastical Sonnets. William Wordsworth. **CP-WorW2**
　　Abuse of Monastic Power.
　　Acquittal of the Bishops.
　　Afflictions of England.
　　Alfred.
　　Apology ("Nor scorn the aid which Fancy oft doth lead").
　　Apology ("Not utterly unworthy to endure").
　　Archbishop Chichely to Henry V.
　　"As faith thus sanctified the warrior's crest."
　　Aspects of Christianity in America—Concluded—American Episcopacy. (Pilgrim Fathers, The.) **PAH**
　　Aspects of Christianity in America—Continued. (Pilgrim Fathers, The.) **AiP; PAH**
　　Aspects of Christianity in America—the Pilgrim Fathers. (Pilgrim Fathers, The.) **AiP; PAH**
　　Baptism.
　　"Bishops and Priests, blessèd are ye, if deep."
　　Canute.
　　Casual Incitement.
　　Catechizing.
　　Cathedrals, etc.
　　Charles the Second.
　　Church to Be Erected.
　　Cistertian Monastery.
　　Clerical Integrity.
　　"Coldly we spake. The Saxons, overpowered."
　　Commination Service, The.
　　Conclusion: "Why Sleeps the future, as a snake enrolled."
　　Confirmation.
　　Confirmation Continued.
　　Congratulation.
　　Conjectures.
　　Continued [Church to Be Erected].
　　Continued [Dissolution of the Monasteries].
　　Continued [Inside of King's College Chapel, Cambridge].
　　Continued [Other Benefits].
　　Continued [Seclusion].
　　Conversion.
　　Corruptions of the Higher Clergy.
　　Council of Clermont, The.
　　Cranmer.
　　Crusaders.
　　Crusades.
　　Danish Conquests.
　　"Deplorable his lot who tills the ground."
　　Dissensions.
　　Dissolution of the Monasteries.
　　Distractions.
　　"Down a swift Stream, thus far, a bold design."
　　Druidical Excommunication.
　　Edward Signing the Warrant for the Execution of Joan of Kent.
　　Edward VI. **EPCY**
　　Ejaculation.
　　Elizabeth.
　　Emigrant French Clergy.
　　Eminent Reformers.
　　English Reformers in Exile.
　　Forms of Prayer at Sea.
　　"From false assumption rose, and fondly hailed."
　　Funeral Service.
　　General View of the Troubles of the Reformation.
　　Glad Tidings.
　　Gunpowder Plot.
　　His Descendents.
　　"How soon—alas! did Man, created pure."
　　"I saw the figure of a lovely Maid."
　　Illustration; the Jung-Frau and the Fall of the Rhine near Schaffhausen.
　　Imaginative Regrets.
　　Influence Abused.
　　Inside of King's College Chapel, Cambridge. **EnRP; OBNC** (Within King's College Chapel, Cambridge.) **GTBS; GTBS-6; GTBS-P**
　　Interdict, An.
　　Introduction: "I, who accompanied with faithful pace."
　　Latimer and Ridley.
　　Latitudinarianism.
　　Laud.
　　Liturgy, The.
　　Marriage Ceremony, The.
　　Missions and Travels.
　　Monastery of Old Bangor.
　　Monastic Voluptuousness.
　　Monks and Schoolmen.
　　Mutability. **EBEV; EnRP; HeIP; InPK; LiTB; MeMBP; NOBE; NoP; OAEL-2; OBEV; PoEL-4; PrIm**
　　New Church-Yard.
　　New Churches.
　　Norman Conquest, The.
　　Obligations of Civil to Religious Liberty.
　　Old Abbeys.
　　Other Benefits.
　　Other Influences.
　　Papal Abuses.
　　Papal Dominion.
　　Pastoral Character.
　　Patriotic Sympathies.
　　Paulinus.
　　Persecution.
　　Persecution of the Scottish Covenanters.
　　Persuasion.

Places of Worship.

Point at Issue, The.

"Praised be the Rivers, from their mountain springs."

Primitive Saxon Clergy.

Recovery.

Reflections.

Regrets.

Reproof.

Revival of Popery.

Richard I.

Rural Ceremony.

Sacheverel.

Sacrament.

Saints.

Same Subject, The [Dissolution of the Monasteries].

Same, The [Eminent Reformers].

Same, The [Inside of King's College Chapel, Cambridge].

Saxon Conquest.

Saxon Monasteries, and Lights and Shades of the Religion.

Scene in Venice.

Seclusion.

Sponsors.

Struggle of the Britons against the Barbarians.

Temptations from Roman Refinements.

Thanksgiving after Childbirth.

Translation of the Bible.

Transubstantiation.

Trepidation of the Druids. **Son**

Troubles of Charles the First.

Uncertainty.

Vaudois, The.

Virgin, The. **GoBC**

  (Sonnet to the Virgin.) **ISi**

Visitation of the Sick.

Waldenses.

Walton's Book of Lives.

Wars of York and Lancaster.

"Where long and deeply hath been fixed the root."

Wicliffe.

William the Third.

Ecco a letter starting "dearest we." Edward Estlin Cummings. **CP-CummE**

Echetlos. Robert Browning. **CP-BroR2**

Echo. Robert Creeley. **CP-CreeR**

Echo. Robert Creeley. **CP-CreeR**

Echo. Robert Creeley. **CP-CreeR**

Echo. Walter de la Mare. **CP-DeLaW**

Echo. Audre Lorde. **SP-LordA**

Echo. John Milton. **ELP; LoBV; OBEV; OBS; SeCeV** *Fr.* Comus; a Masque Presented at Ludlow Castle.

  (Lady Sings, The.) **NOBE**

  (Lady's Song.) **TrGrPo**

Echo. Christina Georgina Rossetti. **CP-RosC1**

Echo-Elf Answers, The. Thomas Hardy. **CP-HardT**

Echo for the Promise of Georg Trakl's Life. James Wright. **CP-WrigJ**

Echo from Willowwood, An. Christina Georgina Rossetti. **CP-RosC3**

Echo Of. Robert Creeley. **CP-CreeR**

Echo, the beating of the tide. Prophecy on Lethe. Stanley Jasspon Kunitz. **CP-KuniS**

Echo, upon the Gemmi. William Wordsworth. *Fr.* Memorials of a Tour of the Continent; 1820. **CP-WorW2**

Echoed aria of threat opera. Somnambulism. Tom Clark. **SP-ClarT**

Echoes. "Lewis Carroll." **CP-CarrL**

Echoes. Hart Crane. **CP-CranH**

Echoes. Robert Creeley. **CP-CreeR**

Echoes of voices stilled may linger on. The Assignation. Walter de la Mare. **CP-DeLaW**

Echoing [or Ecchoing] Green, The. William Blake. **BoTP; CABA; CH; FHYEP; HoFi; LAuP; NAEL-2; NTP; OBEC; OXAEP-2; PoE; PoSC; UnPo; WiR** *Fr.* Songs of Innocence. **CP-BlakW**

Echo's Bones. Samuel Beckett.

  "Asylum under my tread all this day." **CP-BeckS**

  Vulture, The. **CP-BeckS**

Eclipse, The. Robert Herrick. **CP-HerrR**

Eclipse of the Sun, 1820, The. William Wordsworth. *Fr.* Memorials of a Tour of the Continent; 1820. **CP-WorW2**

Eclogue: "JANE SNEED BEGAN IT: My poor John, alas." John Crowe Ransom. **SP-RansJ**

Eclogue: "Men talking / Near the room's center. They have said, The." George Oppen. **CP-OppeG**

Eclogue at Nash's Grove. James Wright. **CP-WrigJ**

Eclogue between the Motherless. Louis MacNeice. **CP-MacNL**

Eclogue by a Five-Barred Gate. Louis MacNeice. **CP-MacNL**

Eclogue for Christmas, An. Louis MacNeice. **CP-MacNL**

Eclogue from Iceland. Louis MacNeice. **CP-MacNL**

Eclogue of the Liberal and the Poet. Allen Tate. **CP-TateA**

Eclogue, or Pastorall between Endimion Porter and Lycidas Herrick, An. Robert Herrick. **CP-HerrR**

Eclogue 1613. December 26. John Donne. **CP-DonnJ**

Eclogues. Virgil, *tr. fr.* Latin.

  From Vergil's Tenth Eclogue. **CP-ShelP**

  "With me retire and leave the pomp of courts." **CP-JohnS**

Ecologue. Allen Ginsberg. **CP-GinsA**

"Economic secu / rity" is a cu. Edward Estlin Cummings. **CP-CummE**

Economics. Wystan Hugh Auden. *Fr.* Shorts I ("Watch upon my wrist, The"). **CP-AudeW**

Economics. Mona Van Duyn. **SP-VanDM**

Economist's Song, The. Stanley Jasspon Kunitz. **CP-KuniS**

Écoute-les / s'ajouter. Samuel Beckett. **CP-BeckS**

Ecquis Binas. Gerard Manley Hopkins. **CP-HopkG**

Ecstasies of Dialectic, The. Howard Nemerov. **CP-NemeH**

Ecstasy, The. Hayden Carruth. *Fr.* Contra Mortem. **CP-CarHL**

Ecstasy, The. John Donne. **CP-DonnJ**

"Ecstasy is the / disaster of pleasure": this. Hayden Carruth. **CP-CarHS** *Fr.* The Clay Hill Anthology.

Ecstasy of Chaos. Robert Ranke Graves. **CP-GravR**

Ecstasy of the Pure. Kenneth Patchen. **CP-PatcK**

Ecstasy of the Rat, The. Robert Pack. **SP-PackR**

Ecstasy to guess, The. Emily Dickinson. **CP-DickE**

Ecstatic bird songs pound. Dawn. William Carlos Williams. **CP-WilW1**

Ecumenical Exchange, 1989. Frank Templeton Prince. **CP-PrinF**

Ed ascoltando al leggier mormorio, *subsel.* Ezra Pound. *See* Canto 81: "Zeus lies in Ceres' bosom."

Ed Stiles and old Tom Birnam went up to their cattle on the bare hills. The Wind-Struck Music. Robinson Jeffers. **CP-JefR2**

Edain came out of Midhir's hill, and lay. The Harp of Aengus. William Butler Yeats. **CP-YeatW**

Eddi, priest of St. Wilfrid. Eddi's Service. Rudyard Kipling. **CP-KiplR**

Eddie's on the mound. Around the Horn. Gary Gildner. **SP-GildG**

Eddi's Service. Rudyard Kipling. **CP-KiplR**

Eden. Donald Davie. **CP-DavDo**

Eden. John Milton. *See* Thus was this place, / A happy rural seat of various view.

Eden. Charles Tomlinson. **CP-TomlC**

Eden in Winter. Nicholas Vachel Lindsay. **CP-LindV**

Eden is that old-fashioned House. Emily Dickinson. **CP-DickE**

Eden! till now thy beauty had I viewed. The River Eden, Cumberland. William Wordsworth. *Fr.* Poems Composed or Suggested During a Tour, in the Summer of 1833. **CP-WorW2**

Eden was an endless place. Eve's Exile. Archibald MacLeish. *Fr.* Songs for Eve. **CP-MacLA**

Edgar Lee Masters. Richard Eberhart. **CP-EberR**

Edge, The. Robert Creeley. **CP-CreeR**

Edge, The. Louise Glück. **SP-GlücL**

Edge. Sylvia Plath. **CP-PlatS**

Edge in the Morning, The. James Schuyler. *Fr.* The Cenotaph. **CP-SchuJ**

Edge of the cancer, The. Front Lines. Gary Snyder. **CP-SnydG**

Edge of the River, The. Thomas McGrath. **SP-McGrT**

Edge of the World, The. Shel Silverstein. **SP-SilS2**

Edgehill Fight. Rudyard Kipling. **CP-KiplR**

Edges, The. Gilbert Sorrentino. **SP-SorrG**

Edges. Allen Tate. **CP-TateA**

Edgy, perhaps. *Not* on the point of bursting-forth. How Do You Do, Dr Berryman, Sir? John Berryman. **CP-BerrJ**

Edifying cables can be made musical if played and sung by full-armed societies doomed to an electric war. Thomas Merton. *Fr.* Cables to the Ace. **CP-MertT**

Edina! *Scotia's* darling seat! Address to Edinburgh. Robert Burns. **CP-BurnR**

Edinburgh From Blackford Hill. Sir Walter Scott. *See* Edinburgh from the Pentland Hills.

Edinburgh from the Pentland Hills. Sir Walter Scott. *Fr.* Marmion.

  (Edinburgh From Blackford Hill.) **SP-ScotW**

Edison. Robinson Jeffers. **CP-JefR2**

Editorial Office. David Herbert Lawrence. **CP-LawrD**

Edmonton, Thy Cemetery. . . . Stevie Smith. **CP-SmitS**

Edmund! thy grave with aking eye I scan. Lines on a Friend. Samuel Taylor Coleridge. **CP-ColeS**

Edmund's Song. Sir Walter Scott. *See* Brignall Banks.

Edmund's Songs. Sir Walter Scott. **SP-ScotW** *Fr.* Rokeby.

Brignall Banks. **EnRP; HBV 1-2; OAEP; OBEV; OBRV**

(Edmund's Song.) **PoRA**

(Outlaw, The.) **GTBS; GTBS-6; GTBS-P; OtMeF**

(Song: Brignal Banks.) **OxAEP-2**

Edouard. Ogden Nash. **CP-NashO**

Education. Steve Griffiths. **SP-GrifS**

Education a Failure. William Carlos Williams. **CP-WilW2**

Education of a Novelist. Adrienne Rich. **SP-RicA2**

Education of Nature, The. William Wordsworth. *See* Three years she grew in sun and shower.

Edward. Gary Gildner. **SP-GildG**

Edward and Jane a married couple were. The Clergyman's Second Tale. Arthur Hugh Clough. **SP-ClouA** *Fr.* Mari Magno.

Edward Lear. Wystan Hugh Auden. **CP-AudeW**

Edward Shore. George Crabbe. **SP-CrabG** *Fr.* Tales.

Edward Signing the Warrant for the Execution of Joan of Kent. William Wordsworth. *Fr.* Ecclesiastical Sonnets. **CP-WorW2**

Edward VI. William Wordsworth. **EPCY** *Fr.* Ecclesiastical Sonnets. **CP-WorW2**

Edward Thomas. Phoebe Hesketh. **SP-HeskP**

Edwardian pillar boxes wait for Edwardian letters; the Museum. October in Bloomsbury. Louis MacNeice. **CP-MacNL**

Edwardian Sunday, Broomhill, Sheffield, An. Sir John Betjeman. **CP-BetjJ**

Edward's Anecdote. Donald Hall. **CP-HallD**

Edwards' great millstone and rock. Jonathan Edwards in Western Massachusetts. Robert Lowell. **SP-LoweR**

Edwin Booth. Nicholas Vachel Lindsay. *Fr.* Epitaphs for Two Players. **CP-LindV**

Edwin Morris. Tennyson. **CP-TennA**

Edwin Muir. Archibald MacLeish. **CP-MacLA**

Eel, The. Ogden Nash. **CP-NashO**

Eel. Muriel Rukeyser. **CP-RukeM**

Eel-Grass. Edna St. Vincent Millay. **CP-MillE**

Eeles winds and turnes. and cheats and steales; yet Eeles. Upon Eeles. Robert Herrick. **CP-HerrR**

Eels. Malcolm Lowry. **CP-LowrM**

Eemis-Stane, The. "Hugh MacDiarmid." **SP-MacDH**

E'en all Religious courses to be rich. Any Way for Wealth. Robert Herrick. **CP-HerrR**

Eeny, Meeny, Miney, Mo, Miss Beech. Gary Gildner. **SP-GildG**

E'er bribes convince you whom to choose. The Elephant. Jonathan Swift. **CP-SwifJ**

Ef dey's anyt'ing dat riles me. Possum. Paul Laurence Dunbar. **CP-DunbP**

Ef you's only got de powah fe' to blow a little whistle. Limitations. Paul Laurence Dunbar. **CP-DunbP**

Effeminate Englishmen. William Cowper. **EBEvV; ECEV** *Fr.* The Timepiece. *Fr.* The Task. **CP-CowpW**

(England.) **FiP**

Effigy vessels shapes of apes. The Ladies of Tlatilco. Thomas Merton. *Fr.* South. *Fr.* The Geography of Lograire. **CP-MertT**

Effort at Speech between Two People. Muriel Rukeyser. **CP-RukeM**

Effort of Love, The. David Herbert Lawrence. **CP-LawrD**

Efforts of Affection. Marianne Craig Moore. **CP-MoorM**

Effusion in the Pleasure-Ground on the Banks of the Bran, Near Dunkeld. William Wordsworth. **CP-WorW2**

Effusion in the Presence of the Painted Tower of Tell, at Altorf. William Wordsworth. *Fr.* Memorials of a Tour of the Continent; 1820. **CP-WorW2**

Effusions. Samuel Taylor Coleridge. **CP-ColeS**

Burke.

Complaint of Ninathóma, The.

Domestic Peace.

Eolian Harp, The. **EnRP; FHYEP; NAEL-2; NOBRP; NoP; OAEL-2**

Genevieve.

Gentle Look, The.

Imitated from Ossian.

Imitated from the Welch.

Kiss, The.

Kisses.

Koskiusko. **EnRP**

La Fayette.

(LaFayette.) **EnRP**

Lines Composed While Climbing the Left Ascent of Brockley Coomb, in the County of Somerset, May, 1795.

Lines in the Manner of Spenser.

Mrs. Siddons.

On a Discovery Made Too Late. **EnRP; Son**

Outcast, The.

Pitt.

Pity.

Priestley.

Rose, The.

Sigh, The.

To a Friend [Charles Lamb] Together with an Unfinished Poem.

To a Young Ass. **EnRP; OBEC; OxAEP-2**

To an Infant.

To Earl Stanhope.

To Richard Brinsley Sheridan, Esq.

To the Author of "The Robbers."

To the Autumnal Moon.

To the Honourable Mr. Erskine.

To the Nightingale.

To the Rev. [*or* Reverend] W. L. Bowles. **EnRP; Son**

Written in Early Youth, the Time an Autumnal Evening.

Effusions of a School-Patriarch, The. Arthur Hugh Clough. **SP-ClouA**

Eftsoones they heard a most melodious sound. Edmund Spenser. **EBEvV; NOBE; OBSC; SCV** *Fr.* The Bower of Bliss. **PoEL-1** *Fr.* The Faerie Queene. **CP-Spens**

Eftsoons they saw an hideous host array'd. Sea Monsters. Edmund Spenser. **ChTr; FaBoEn** *Fr.* The Faerie Queene. **CP-Spens**

E.G. to M.R. Emily Brontë. **CP-BronE**

Egeria! sweet creation of some heart. Byron. **NOBRP** *Fr.* Canto the Fourth. *Fr.* Childe Harold's Pilgrimage. **CP-Byron**

Egg, The. Louise Glück. **SP-GlücL**

Egg. Daniel Gerard Hoffman. **SP-HoffD**

Egg, The. Gary Snyder. **CP-SnydG**

Egg and the Machine, The. Robert Frost. **CP-FrosR**

Egg-Head. Ted Hughes. **SP-HughT**

Egg-Shell, The. Rudyard Kipling. **CP-KiplR**

Eggplant Epithalamion, The. Erica Jong. **SP-JongE**

Eggs. Stephen Dunn. **SP-DunnS**

Eggs boiling in a pot. Divorce. Erica Jong. **SP-JongE**

Eggs. Dates and camel's milk. From Dread in the Eyes of Horses. Tess Gallagher. **SP-GallT**

Eggs of Pheasants wrie-nos'd Tooly sells, The. Upon Tooly. Robert Herrick. **CP-HerrR**

Egnatius, candid as his horse-bit white dentures. Catullus. *See* Carmen 39: "Because he has bright white teech, Eg- / natius whips out a."

Egnatius has fine teeth, and those. Catullus. *See* Carmen 39: "Because he has bright white teech, Eg- / natius whips out a."

Ego. John Greenleaf Whittier. **CP-WhitJ**

Ego-Bound. David Herbert Lawrence. **CP-LawrD**

Ego-Bound Women. David Herbert Lawrence. **CP-LawrD**

Ego Confession. Allen Ginsberg. **CP-GinsA**

Ego Dominus Tuus. William Butler Yeats. **CP-YeatW**

Egocentric. Stevie Smith. **CP-SmitS**

Egoist. Pablo Neruda, *tr. fr. Spanish* by Ben Belitt. **SP-NeruP**

Egoists, The. David Herbert Lawrence. **CP-LawrD**

Ego's county he inheritied, The. Conscript. Philip Larkin. **CP-LarkP**

Egotism. A Letter to J.T. Becher. Byron. **CP-Byron**

Egradment li antichi cavaler romanj. Canto 011. Ezra Pound. *Fr.* Cantos. **CP-PoCan**

Egregious was the egret's error, very. Even Egrets Err. John Updike. **CP-UpdiJ**

Egret, The. Mary Oliver. **SP-OlivM**

Egrets. Mary Oliver. **SP-OlivM**

Egypt. Hilda Doolittle. **CP-DoolH**

Egypt. Martin Edmunds. **SP-EdmuM**

Egypt. Kenneth Patchen. **CP-PatcK**

Egypt, divided buy the river Nile. John Milton. **FaBoPV** *Fr.* Book XII. *Fr.* Paradise Lost. **CP-MiltJ**

Egypt, Everything. Tom Clark. **SP-ClarT**

Egypt, Tobago. Derek Walcott. **CP-WalcD**

Egyptian Maid; or, The Romance of the Water Lilly, The. William Wordsworth. **CP-WorW2**

Egyptian Night. John Hewitt. **CP-HewiJ**

Egyptian Pulled Glass Bottle in the Shape of a Fish, An. Marianne Craig Moore. **CP-MoorM**

Egyptians [*or Aegyptians*] think[e] it sin[ne] to root[e] up, or to bite. Juvenal, *tr. by* Sir Walter Ralegh. **CP-RaleW** *Fr.* Satires.

Egyptology. Erica Jong. **SP-JongE**

Egypts Pyramids inclose their Kings. Mary Sidney, Countess of Montgomery Wroth. *Fr.* Part 1. *Fr.* Urania. **CP-WrotM**

E.H. John Hewitt. **CP-HewiJ**

"Eh bien! Marche!," fit le Majeur Ydow. Le Majeur Ydow. Stevie Smith. **CP-SmitS**

Eh, man Henley, you're a Don! Robert Louis Stevenson. **CP-StevR**

Eheu! Fugaces, or, What a Difference a Lot of Days Make. Ogden Nash. **CP-NashO**

Ei Men Een Mathein. Sir John Suckling. **CP-SuckJ**

Eia ergo. For this is Sion's twin city. Geoffrey Hill. *Fr.* Hymns to Our Lady of Chartres. **CP-HillG**

Eia, with handbells, jews' harps, risible. Geoffrey Hill. **DiPo** *Fr.* Hymns to Our Lady of Chartres. **CP-HillG**

Eider afloat in the bay. Kathleen Jessie Raine. **SP-RainK**

Eidolon. Robert Penn Warren. **SP-WarrR**

Eidolons, Eidólons. Walt Whitman. **CP-WhitW**

8/22/38–8/22/68. Gary Gildner. **SP-GildG**

Eight Days a Week. John Lennon *and* Paul McCartney. **CP-Beatl**

Eight Early Poems. Kenneth Patchen. **CP-PatcK**

At the New Year. **LiTM**

Fragment from "A Schoolboy's Odyssey."

Geography of Music. **UnAS**

"I know the hair, tissue, skin."

"It is a lonely walk into the mind's retreat."

Sea Has Caves and Urns, The.

"This room has mystery like trance."

"Your name includes the shadow flight of birds."

Eight hours between us, eight. England. Donald Davie. **CP-DavDo**

Eight Months Later, title same as that of the first sel. Robert Lowell. **SP-LoweR**

Eight Months Later, title same as that of the longer work. Robert Lowell. *Fr.* Eight Months Later. **SP-LoweR**

Die Gold Orangen.

Eight Months Later.

VIII. "More than most fair [*or* fayre], full of the living fire [*or* fyre]." Edmund Spenser. **CABA; HBV; NoP; OAEP; PoE; Son; TEP; TrGrPo** *Fr.* Amoretti. **CP-Spens**

Eight Observations on the Nature of Eternity. Charles Tomlinson. **CP-TomlC**

Eight O'Clock. Alfred Edward Housman. **CP-HousA**

Eight o'clock; / The postman's knock! Christina Georgina Rossetti. **CP-RosC2**

Eight o'clock, no later. The Lamps. Mary Oliver. **SP-OlivM**

Eight O'Clock Peril, The. Ogden Nash. **CP-NashO**

Eight of 'em hyeah all tol' an' yet. Puttin' the Baby Away. Paul Laurence Dunbar. **CP-DunbP**

Eight of Swords, The. Marge Piercy. *Fr.* Laying Down the Tower. **SP-PierM**

Eight or nine yards. Roy Fisher. **SP-FishR** *Fr.* Matrix.

Eight Riddles from Symphosius. Richard Wilbur. **CP-WilbR**

Eight times the autumn weather. Frank Templeton Prince. *Fr.* Yüan Chên Variations. **CP-PrinF**

Eight Triolets. Frederick Morgan. **SP-MorgF**

Adamson.

Dialogue.

"I have been here before."

"I'll say goodbye to the hope of fame."

Katahdin.

Leviathan.

1928.

Two.

8/12/70. James Schuyler. **CP-SchuJ**

8 Words. Marsden Hartley. **CP-HartM**

Eight Years After. Donald Davie. **CP-DavDo**

Eight years ago this May. A Spring Night in Shokoku-ji. Gary Snyder. **ArLo; VGW** *Fr.* Four Poems for Robin. **CP-SnydG**

Eight years difference in age seems now, The. Terminal. Thom Gunn. **CP-GunnT**

Eight years removed from them, I sit among. Widener Library, Reading Room. John Updike. **CP-UpdiJ**

8/9. Anne Waldman. **SP-WaldA**

Eighteen below: the black-capped chickadee. Rage. Peter Meinke. **SP-MeinP**

Eighteen Days in a Tuscan World. Richard Hugo. **CP-HugoR**

Eighteen Days without You. Anne Sexton. **CP-SextA**

1880. Christina Georgina Rossetti. *See* More shower than shine.

1885. St. Valentine's Day. Christina Georgina Rossetti. **CP-RosC3**

1884. Christina Georgina Rossetti. **CP-RosC3**

1887. Alfred Edward Housman. **CP-HousA**

1886, St. Valentine's Day. Christina Georgina Rossetti. **CP-RosC3**

1811 ("Power of Armies is a visible thing, The"). William Wordsworth. **CP-WorW1**

1850: gt objection to any honesty in the White House. Canto 103. Ezra Pound. *Fr.* Cantos. **CP-PoCan**

1805. Robert Ranke Graves. **CP-GravR**

Eighteen Flavors. Shel Silverstein. **SP-SilS2**

1847. Brendan Galvin. **SP-GalvB**

1811 ("Here pause: the poet claims at least this praise"). William Wordsworth. *See* Here pause: the poet claims at least this praise.

1801. William Wordsworth. **CP-WorW1**

1810. ("Ah! Where is Pala fox?"). William Wordsworth. **CP-WorW1**

1810. ("O'erweening Statesman . . ."). William Wordsworth. **CP-WorW1**

Eighteen luscious, scrumptious flavors. Eighteen Flavors. Shel Silverstein. **SP-SilS2**

1892—19—. Archibald MacLeish. **CP-MacLA**

1892-1941. Louis Zukofsky. **CP-ZukLS**

1878. Christina Georgina Rossetti. **CP-RosC3**

1879. Christina Georgina Rossetti. **CP-RosC3**

Eighteen Sixty-One. Walt Whitman. **CP-WhitW**

1830. William Wordsworth. **CP-WorW2**

1837 War in Retrospect. Margaret Atwood. **SP-AtwM1**

18 West 11th Street. James Merrill. **SP-MerrJ**

Eighteenth-Century Calvinistic Hymn, An. Sir John Betjeman. **CP-BetjJ**

Eighth Air Force. Randall Jarrell. **CP-JarrR; SP-JarrR**

Eighth Book, The. Archibald MacLeish. *Fr.* Conquistador. **CP-MacLA**

Eighth Elegy. Children's Elegy. Muriel Rukeyser. **CP-RukeM**

"That is what they say, who were broken off from love." **LCAP**

8th October: / Si tuit li dolh elh plor. Canto 84. Ezra Pound. *Fr.* Cantos. **CP-PoCan**

Eighth Psalm. Anne Sexton. *Fr.* O Ye Tongues. **CP-SextA**

Eighth Song. Sir Philip Sidney. **NoSic; OAEP; OBSC** *Fr.* Astrophil and Stella. **SP-SidnP**

Eighty-eight thousand six-hundred. Buck Moon—From the Field Guide to Insects. Mary Oliver. **SP-OlivM**

LXXXIX. "Like as the culver on the bared bough." Edmund Spenser. **FF; GBL; PBBP; PoE** *Fr.* Amoretti. **CP-Spens**

'Eighty-nine was bad. At least a hundred. Graves at Elkhorn. Richard Hugo. **CP-HugoR**

LXXXI. "Fair [*or* Fayre] is my love, when her fair [*or* fayre] golden heares." Edmund Spenser. **EIL; NoP; Son** *Fr.* Amoretti. **CP-Spens**

86'd. Charles Bukowski. **SP-BukC2**

LXXXIII. "Let not one sparke of filthy lustfull fyre." Edmund Spenser. **TEP** *Fr.* Amoretti. **CP-Spens**

LXXXII. "Joy of my life, full oft for loving you." Edmund Spenser. **HeIP** *Fr.* Amoretti. **CP-Spens**

82 X 48. Laurence Lieberman. **SP-LiebL**

Eileann Chanaidh. Kathleen Jessie Raine. **SP-RainK**

Ancient Speech, The. **PoSH**

Highland Graveyard.

Island Cross, The.

Nameless Islets.

Shadow.

Stone on High Crag.

Eileen. Richard Hugo. **CP-HugoR**

Eilshemius. Marsden Hartley. **CP-HartM**

Ein Feste Burg Ist Unser Gott. John Greenleaf Whittier. **CP-WhitJ**

Eine Kleine Nachtmusik. Randall Jarrell. **CP-JarrR**

Eine Kleine Snailmusik. May Sarton. **SP-SartM**

Einstein. Archibald MacLeish. **CP-MacLA**

Einstein & Freud & Jack. Howard Nemerov. **CP-NemeH**

Einstein's Pegasus. Robert Pack. **SP-PackR**

Eisenhower Years, The. Paul Zimmer. **SP-ZimmP**

Eisenhower's Visit to Franco, 1959. James Wright. **CP-WrigJ**

Either give me my hundred pounds back, Silo. Carmen 103. Catullus. *Fr.* Carmina. **CP-Catul**

Either heard or taught. Song for a Thin Sister. Audre Lorde. **SP-LordA**

Either in or out of. The Finger. Robert Creeley. **CP-CreeR**

Either it's her sister or an apparition, and she hopes. The Room. Stephen Dobyns. **SP-DobyS**

Either she was foul, or her attire was bad. 3.6. Ovid, *tr. by* Christopher Marlowe. **CP-MarlC**　*Fr.* Elegies.

Either we lodge diurnally here together. Elsewhere. Robert Ranke Graves. **CP-GravR**

Either you will / go through this door. Prospective Immigrants Please Note. Adrienne Rich. **CP-RicAE; SP-RicA1; SP-RicA2**

Eiusdem ad Authorem, *accompanied by Eng. translation.* Thomas Campion. **CP-CampT**

Ejaculation. William Wordsworth. *Fr.* Ecclesiastical Sonnets. **CP-WorW2**

Ejected Indians haunt the lawns. West Virginia's Auburn. Donald Davie. **CP-DavDo**

Ekstase, Alptraum, Schlaf in einem Nest von Flammen. Hayden Carruth. **CP-CarHS**

El-Hajj Malik El-Shabazz. Robert Earl Hayden. **CP-HaydR**

El Hombre. William Carlos Williams. **CP-WilW1**

El Hombre del Ombre. Jim Carroll. **SP-CarrJ**

El Leon is swimming. !Bulletin! Malcolm Lowry. **CP-LowrM**

El Leon Sends His Greetings. Malcolm Lowry. **CP-LowrM**

El Leon's mane is a mythical mane. Just a Merry Little Ditty of Welcome for the Most Beloved Harteebeeste on Easter Sunday. Malcolm Lowry. **CP-LowrM**

El Niño. Martin Edmunds. **SP-EdmuM**

El Santuario de Chimayó. Martin Edmunds. *Fr.* The High Road to Taos. **SP-EdmuM**

El Sueño de la Razón. Jane Cooper. **FaBoWP** *Fr.* March. **SP-CoopJ**

El toro / From the blind kingdom. La Corrida. Robert Earl Hayden. *Fr.* An Inference of Mexico. **CP-HaydR**

Elaine. Edna St. Vincent Millay. **CP-MillE**

Elaine the fair, Elaine the loveable. Lancelot and Elaine. Tennyson. *Fr.* Idylls of the King. **CP-TennA**

Elastic programs to draft nonspecialist energy and rotate. Thomas Merton. *Fr.* Cables to the Ace. **CP-MertT**

Elate of heart and confidence of fame, *fr.* 1790 *vers.* Samuel Taylor Coleridge. **EPCY** *Fr.* Monody on the Death of Chatterton. **CP-ColeS**

Elbows on dry books, we dreamed. Spring in the Classroom. Mary Oliver. **SP-OlivM**

Elder folks shook hands at last, The. The Meeting. John Greenleaf Whittier. **CP-WhitJ**

Elderly Discontented Women. David Herbert Lawrence. **CP-LawrD**

Elderly gentle clean-shaven man, An. Roseblade's Visitants and Mine. John Hewitt. **CP-HewiJ**

Elderly Sex. John Updike. **CP-UpdiJ**

Eldest-born of pow'rs divine! To Health. *Unknown, tr. fr. Greek by* William Cowper. **CP-CowpW**

Eldest son bestrides him, The. The Undertaker's Horse. Rudyard Kipling. **CP-KiplR**

Eldorado. Edgar Allan Poe. **CP-PoeEd**

Eleanor. Christina Georgina Rossetti. **CP-RosC3**

Eleanor Rigby. John Lennon *and* Paul McCartney. **CP-Beatl**

Eleanor (she spoiled in a British climate). Canto 7. Ezra Pound. **NOBA; NoAM** *Fr.* Cantos. **CP-PoCan**

Eleanor's Letters. Donald Hall. **CP-HallD**

Elect, The. Donald Davie. **CP-DavDo**

Elect, The. Dabney Stuart. **SP-StuaD**

Elected Silence, sing to me. The Habit of Perfection. Gerard Manley Hopkins. **CP-HopkG**

Election, The. George Crabbe. **SP-CrabG** *Fr.* The Borough.

Election, The. Leonard Nathan. **SP-NathL**

Election: A New Song, The. Robert Burns. **CP-BurnR** *Fr.* The Heron Ballads, 1795.

Election Day. William Carlos Williams. **CP-WilW2**

Election Day Is a Holiday. Ogden Nash. **CP-NashO**

Election Day, November, 1884. Walt Whitman. **CP-WhitW**

Election night at midnight. Nicholas Vachel Lindsay. *Fr.* Bryan, Bryan, Bryan, Bryan. **CP-LindV**

Election Night Pome. Al Young. **CP-YounA**

Elections to the Hebdomadal Council, The. "Lewis Carroll." **CP-CarrL**

Electra Becomes Morbid. Ogden Nash. **CP-NashO**

Electra on Azalea Path. Sylvia Plath. **CP-PlatS**

Electra-Orestes. Hilda Doolittle.
　"He marked the pattern of the sky." **CP-DoolH**
　"Lovers may come and go." **CP-DoolH**
　"Never let it be said." **CP-DoolH**
　"No one knows, / the heart of a child." **CP-DoolH**
　"She is dead." **CP-DoolH**
　"To love, one must slay." **CP-DoolH**

Electric Drills. John Yau. **SP-YauJo**

Electric Sign Goes Dark, An. Carl Sandburg. **CP-SandC**

Electric Storm. Jim Morrison. **SP-MorrJ**

Electrical Storm. Elizabeth Bishop. **CP-BishE**

Electrical Storm. Robert Earl Hayden. **CP-HaydR**

Electroshock. Bang—. Hayden Carruth. **CP-CarHS** *Fr.* The Clay Hill Anthology.

Elegance. Christopher Smart. **NOCV** *Fr.* Hymns for the Amusement of Children. **SP-SmarC**

Elegant bird— / delicate claws, An. Bird. Pablo Neruda, *tr. fr. Spanish by* Ben Belitt. **SP-NeruP**

Elegeia I (1595), *acc. by English translation.* Thomas Campion. **CP-CampT**

Elegia. Edwin Rolfe, *tr. fr. Spanish by* Jose Rubia Barcia. **CP-RolfE**

Elegia. Edwin Rolfe. **CP-RolfE**

Elegia VIII. Robert Southwell. **CP-SoutR**

Elegia I (1619), *acc. by English translation.* Thomas Campion. **CP-CampT**

Elegia IX. Robert Southwell. **CP-SoutR**

Elegiac Musings in the Grounds of Coleorton Hall, the Seat of the Late Sir G.H. Beaumont, BART. William Wordsworth. **CP-WorW2**

Elegiac Stanzas. William Wordsworth. *Fr.* Memorials of a Tour of the Continent; 1820. **CP-WorW2**

Elegiac Stanzas (Addressed to Sir G.H.B. upon the Death of His Sister-in-Law). William Wordsworth. **CP-WorW2**

Elegiac Stanzas Composed in the Churchyard of Grasmere. William Wordsworth. **CP-WorW1**

Elegiac Stanzas: On a Visit to Dove Cottage. Geoffrey Hill. **CP-HillG**

Elegiac Stanzas on the Death of Sir Peter Parker, Bart. Byron. **CP-Byron**

Elegiac Stanzas Suggested by a Picture of Peele Castle, in a Storm [Painted by Sir George Beaumont]. William Wordsworth. **CP-WorW1**

Elegiac Verses. John Milton, *tr. fr. Latin by* John T. Shawcross. **CP-MiltJ**

Elegiac Verses in Memory of My Brother, John Wordsworth. William Wordsworth. **CP-WorW1**

Elegiacs. Gerard Manley Hopkins. **CP-HopkG**
　"Alget honos frondum silvis dependitus, alget."
　"Quo rubeant dulcesve rosae vel pomifer aestas?"
　Tristi Tu, Memini.

Elegiacs of Sulpicia. Gilbert Sorrentino. **SP-SorrG**
　"At last comes love of such a quality that it would shame me."
　"Cerinthus, don't you have some soft thought for your girl."
　"Do you know that sad journey is lifted from your darling's heart?"
　"Light, my light, let me never be again."
　"My hated birthday looms. In the rude and wretched country."
　"That you allow yourself this vast neglect of me."

Elegie, An: "Me thinks when Kings, Prophets, and Poets dye." Samuel Holland. *Fr.* Elegies, 1660. **CP-LoveR**

Elegie V: His Picture. John Donne. *See* His Picture.

Elegie: Going to Bed. John Donne. *See* To His Mistress Going to Bed.

Elegie: His Parting from Her. John Donne. *See* His Parting from Her.

Elegie: "Nature's lay ideot, I taught thee to love." John Donne. *See* Nature's lay idiot [or Ideot], I taught thee to love.

Elegie on the Death of Doctor Porter, An. Richard Crashaw. **CP-CrasR**

Elegie. On the Death of Mrs. Cassandra Cotton, An. Richard Lovelace. **CP-LoveR**

Elegie, or Friends Passion, for His Astrophill, An. Edmund Spenser. *Fr.* Astrophel. **CP-Spens**

Elegie. Princesse Katherine, An. Richard Lovelace. **CP-LoveR**

Elegie XVI: On His Mistress. John Donne. *See* On His Mistress [or Mistris].

Elegie upon the Untimely Death of Prince *Henry*, An. Thomas Campion. **CP-CampT**

Elegies. John Donne. **CP-DonnJ**
　Anagram, The.
　Autumnall[l], The. **InPS; JCP; NOSC; OAEP; PoEL-2; SeCV-1; TEP**
　Bracelet, The.
　Change. **CBLP; EBEV**
　Comparison, The. **PeLV**
　Dream, The.
　Expostulation, The.
　His Parting from Her. **EBEV**
　　(Elegie: His Parting from Her.) **OBS**
　His Picture. **EnRePo; FaBoEn; MePo**
　　(Elegie V: His Picture.) **MeLP; OBS; OXAEP-1**
　Jealousy. **FF**
　　(Jealosie.) **CBLP; ESCV**
　Julia.
　Love's Progress. **LiTB; OAEL-1**
　Love's War.
　"Nature's lay idiot [or Ideot], I taught thee to love." **CBLP; NoP; OXAEP-1; PeLV; SeCP**

(Elegie: "Nature's lay ideot, I taught thee to love.") **OXAEP-1; SeCP**

"Oh, let me not serve so, as those men serve."

On His Mistress [or Mistris]. **AnAnS-1; BoLoP; CBLP; EBEV; ESCV; LiTB; NAEL-1; NoSic; PoEL-1; SeCeV**

  (Elegie XVI: On His Mistress.) **OXAEP-1; SeCP**

  (Elegy on His Mistress.) **GBL; LoBV; MeLP; MePo; SCGP; SeCV-1**

  (To His Mistress Desiring to Travel with Him as His Page.) **NOBE**

Perfume, The. **AnAnS-1; ESCV; NoSic; SeCP**

Sappho to Philaenis. **FaBoBl**

Tale of a Citizen and His Wife, A.

To His Mistress Going to Bed. **BoLoP; FaBoBl; JCP; NoSic; OAEL-1; PoE; TEP; UnTE**

  (Elegie: Going to Bed.) **EnRePo; MePo; OxBM**

  (Elegy XIX. To His Mistris Going to Bed.) **NoP**

  (To His Mistris Going to Bed.) **CBLP; ErPo; OXAEP-1; SeCP**

Variety.

Elegies. Ovid, *tr. fr. Latin.*

I, 13. Elegy: Ad Auroram, ne properet. **CP-MarlC,** *tr. by* Christopher Marlowe.

1.1: Quemadmodum a Cupidine pro bellis amoris scribere coactus sit. **CP-MarlC,** *tr. by* Christopher Marlowe.

1.2: Quod primo amore correptus, in triumphium duci se a Cupidine patiatur. **CP-MarlC,** *tr. by* Christopher Marlowe.

1.3: Ad amicam. **CP-MarlC**

1.4: Amicam, qua arte, quibusve nutibus in caena, presente viro uti debeat, admonet. **CP-MarlC,** *tr. by* Christopher Marlowe.

1.5: Corinnae concubitus. **CP-MarlC**

1.6: Ad Janitorem, ut fores sibi aperiat. **CP-MarlC,** *tr. by* Christopher Marlowe.

1.7: Ad pacandam amicam, quam verberaverat. **CP-MarlC,** *tr. by* Christopher Marlowe.

1.8: Execratur lenam, quae puellam suam meretricia arte instituebat. **CP-MarlC,** *tr. by* Christopher Marlowe.

1.9: Ad Atticum, amantem non oportere desidiosum esse, sicuti nec militem. **CP-MarlC,** *tr. by* Christopher Marlowe.

1.10: Ad puellam, ne pro amore praemia poscat. **CP-MarlC,** *tr. by* Christopher Marlowe.

1.11: Napen alloquitur, ut paratas tabellas ad Corinnam perferat. **CP-MarlC,** *tr. by* Christopher Marlowe.

1.12: Tabellas quas miserat execratur, quod amica noctem negabat. **CP-MarlC,** *tr. by* Christopher Marlowe.

1.14: Puellam consolatur cui prae nimia cura comae deciderant. **CP-MarlC,** *tr. by* Christopher Marlowe.

1.15: Ad invidos, quod fama poetarum sit perennis. **CP-MarlC,** *tr. by* Christopher Marlowe.

2.1: Quod pro gigantomachia amores scribere sit coactus. **CP-MarlC**

2.2: Ad Bagoum, ut custodiam puellae sibi commissae laxiorem habeat. **CP-MarlC,** *tr. by* Christopher Marlowe.

2.3: Ad Eunuchum servantem dominam. **CP-MarlC,** *tr. by* Christopher Marlowe.

2.4: Quod amet mulieres, cuiuscunque formae sint. **CP-MarlC,** *tr. by* Christopher Marlowe.

2.5: Ad amicam corruptam. **CP-MarlC,** *tr. by* Christopher Marlowe.

2.6: In mortem psittaci. **CP-MarlC,** *tr. by* Christopher Marlowe.

2.7: Amicae se purgat quod ancillam non amet. **CP-MarlC,** *tr. by* Christopher Marlowe.

2.8: Ad Cypassim ancillam Corinnae. **CP-MarlC**

2.9: Ad Cupidinem. **CP-MarlC,** *tr. by* Christopher Marlowe.

2.10: Ad Graecinum quod eodem tempore duas amet. **CP-MarlC**

2.11: Ad amicam navigantem. **CP-MarlC,** *tr. by* Christopher Marlowe.

2.12: Exultat, quod amica potitus sit. **CP-MarlC,** *tr. by* Christopher Marlowe.

2.13: Ad Isidem, ut parientem Corinnam iuvet. **CP-MarlC,** *tr. by* Christopher Marlowe.

2.14: In amicam, quod abortivum ipsa fecerit. **CP-MarlC,** *tr. by* Christopher Marlowe.

2.15: Ad annulum, quem dono amicae dedit. **CP-MarlC,** *tr. by* Christopher Marlowe.

2.16: Ad amicam, ut ad rura sua veniat. **CP-MarlC,** *tr. by* Christopher Marlowe.

2.17: Quod Corinnae soli sit serviturus. **CP-MarlC,** *tr. by* Christopher Marlowe.

2.18: Ad Macrum, quod de amoribus scribat. **CP-MarlC,** *tr. by* Christopher Marlowe.

2.19: Ad rivalem, cui uxor curae non erat. **CP-MarlC,** *tr. by* Christopher Marlowe.

3.1: Deliberatio poetae, utrum elegos pergat scribere an potius tragedias. **CP-MarlC,** *tr. by* Christopher Marlowe.

3.2: Ad amicam cursum equorum spectantem. **CP-MarlC,** *tr. by* Christopher Marlowe.

3.3: De amica, quae periuraverat. **CP-MarlC,** *tr. by* Christopher Marlowe.

3.4: Ad virum servantem coniugem. **CP-MarlC,** *tr. by* Christopher Marlowe.

3.5: Ad amnem, dum iter faceret ad amicam. **CP-MarlC,** *tr. by* Christopher Marlowe.

3.6: Quod ab amica receptus cum ea coire non potuit, conqueritur. **CP-MarlC**

3.7: Quod ab amica non recipiatur, dolet. **CP-MarlC,** *tr. by* Christopher Marlowe.

3.8: Tibulli mortem deflet. **CP-MarlC,** *tr. by* Christopher Marlowe.

3.9: Ad Cererem, conquerens quod eius sacris cum amica concumbere non permittatur. **CP-MarlC,** *tr. by* Christopher Marlowe.

3.10: Ad amicam, a cuius amore discedere non potest. **CP-MarlC,** *tr. by* Christopher Marlowe.

3.11: Dolet amicam suam ita suis carminibnus innotuisse ut rivales multos sibi pararit. **CP-MarlC,** *tr. by* Christopher Marlowe.

3.12: De Iunonis festo. **CP-MarlC,** *tr. by* Christopher Marlowe.

3.13: Ad amicam, si peccatura est, ut occulte peccet. **CP-MarlC,** *tr. by* Christopher Marlowe.

3.14: Ad Venerem, quod elegis finem imponat. **CP-MarlC,** *tr. by* Christopher Marlowe.

5.12: "You bid me write t' amuse the tedious hours." **CP-CowpW**

Elegies. Tibullus, *tr. fr. Latin.*

"Before my closing eyes, dear Cynthia, stand." **CP-JohnS**

"How sweet in sleep to pass the careless hours." **CP-JohnS**

Elegies for Paradise Valley. Robert Earl Hayden. **CP-HaydR**

Elegies for Walker Dabney Stuart, Jr. Dabney Stuart. **SP-StuaD**

Elegies, 1660. *Var. authors.* **CP-LoveR**

Elegie, An: "Me thinks when Kings, Prophets, and Poets dye."

On My Brother.

On the Death of My Dear Brother.

On the Truly Honourable Coll. Richard Lovelace, Occasioned by the Publication of His Posthume-Poems.

Sacred to the Memory of My Late Honoured Friend, Collonell Richard Lovelace.

To His Noble Friend Capt. Dudley Lovelace, upon His Edition of His Brother's Poems.

To the Memory of My Worthy Friend, Coll. Richard Lovelace.

Upon the Posthume and Precious Poems of the Nobly Extracted Gentleman Mr. R.L.

Elegy: "All day our eyes could find no resting place." Wendell Berry. **CP-BerrW**

Elegy: "Behold the blessings of a lucky lot!" Byron. **CP-Byron**

Elegy: "Crying from exile, I." Marilyn Hacker. **SP-HackM**

Elegy: "Dark gathering clouds involve the threatening skies." Charlotte Smith. **CP-SmitC**

Elegy: "Good morning!" Al Young. **CP-YounA**

Elegy: "Her face like a rain-beaten stone on the day she rolled off." Theodore Roethke. **CP-RoetT**

Elegy: "I can almost see it." Thom Gunn. **CP-GunnT**

Elegy: "I expected him to look dead in the casket." Richard Hugo. **CP-HugoR**

Elegy: "I lay down in my grave." Maya Angelou. **SP-AngeM**

Elegy: "Let them bury your big eyes." Edna St. Vincent Millay. **CMoP; MoAB; MoAmPo; OxBA; PoRA** *Fr.* Memorial to D. C. **CP-MillE**

Elegy: "Liebe Frau Emma." Wystan Hugh Auden. *Fr.* Eleven Occasional Poems. **CP-AudeW**

Elegy: "My father was born with a spade in his hand and traded it." John Ciardi. **SP-CiarJ**

Elegy: "No more the white refulgent streets." Allen Tate. **CP-TateA**

Elegy: "Note / as it gets darker." Charles Simic. **SP-SimiC**

Elegy: "Our hammock swung between Americas." Derek Walcott. **CP-WalcD**

Elegy: "Should every creature be as I have been." Theodore Roethke. **CP-RoetT**

Elegy: "Since louely sweete, much like unto a Dewe." Robert Herrick. **CP-HerrR**

Elegy: "Sun immense and rosy, The." David Herbert Lawrence. **CP-LawrD**

Elegy: "To be at home on its native ground." Wendell Berry. **CP-BerrW**

  "And then, one by one, he moved me."

  "At last, completed in his rest."

  "Finally, he brought me to a hill."

  "I saw one standing aside, alone."

  "My mind was overborne with questions."

  "To be at home on its native ground."

  "We came then to his time of pain."

"We stood on a height."

Elegy: "Too proud to die; broken and blind he died." Dylan Thomas. **CP-ThomD**

Elegy: "Wagtail splutters in the stream, A." Wystan Hugh Auden. **CP-AudWJ**

Elegy: "Who keeps the owl's breath? Whose eyes desire?" David St. John. **SP-StJoD**

Elegy: "Why was it that you gave us no warning." Wystan Hugh Auden. **CP-AudWJ**

Elegy, An: "By those bright eyes, at whose immortal fires." Ben Jonson. **CP-JonsB**

Elegy, An: "Can beauty that did prompt me first to write." Ben Jonson. **CP-JonsB**

Elegy [or Elegie], An: "Let me be what I am, as Virgil cold." Ben Jonson. **CP-JonsB**

Elegy, An: "Since you must go, and I must bid farewell." Ben Jonson. **CP-JonsB**

Elegy, An: "That love's a bitter sweet, I ne'er conceive." Ben Jonson. **CP-JonsB**

Elegy, An: "Though beauty be the mark of praise." Ben Jonson. **CP-JonsB**

Elegy [or Elegie], An: "'Tis true, I'm broke! Vows, oaths, and all I had." Ben Jonson. **CP-JonsB**

Elegy before Death. Edna St. Vincent Millay. **CP-MillE**

Elegy Before the Time. William Dickey. **SP-DickW**

Elegy Che Guevara. Allen Ginsberg. **CP-GinsA**

Elegy 5: On the Coming of Spring. John Milton, *tr. fr. Latin by* John T. Shawcross. **CP-CowpW; CP-MiltJ**

("Time, never wand'ring from his annual round.") **CP-CowpW,** *tr. by* William Cowper;

Elegy for a Diver. Peter Meinke. **SP-MeinP**

Elegy for a Nature Poet. Howard Nemerov. **CP-NemeH**

Elegy for a Trappist. Thomas Merton. **CP-MertT**

Elegy for a Whale. Erica Jong. **SP-JongE**

Elegy for D.H. Lawrence, An. William Carlos Williams. **CP-WilW1**

Elegy for Ernest Hemingway, An. Thomas Merton. **CP-MertT; SP-MertT**

Elegy for Eugenesis. Allen Tate. **CP-TateA**

Elegy for Five Old Ladies, An. Thomas Merton. **CP-MertT; SP-MertT**

Elegy for Henry Street. Charles Tomlinson. **CP-TomlC**

Elegy for James Thurber. Thomas Merton. **CP-MertT; SP-MertT**

Elegy for Jane. Theodore Roethke. **CP-RoetT**

Elegy for J.F.K. Wystan Hugh Auden. *Fr.* Eleven Occasional Poems. **CP-AudeW**

Elegy for John Tripp. Steve Griffiths. **SP-GrifS**

Elegy for Margaret. Stephen Spender. **CP-SpenS**

Elegy for Maria Alves. Joaquim Cardozo, *tr. fr. Portuguese by* Elizabeth Bishop. **CP-BishE**

Elegy for Minor Poets. Louis MacNeice. **CP-MacNL**

Elegy for Neal Cassady. Allen Ginsberg. **CP-GinsA**

Elegy for Our Dead. Edwin Rolfe. **CP-RolfE**

Elegy for the Giant Tortoises. Margaret Atwood. **SP-AtwM1**

Elegy for the Monastery Barn. Thomas Merton. **CP-MertT; SP-MertT**

Elegy for the Poet Morgan Blum, An. James Wright. **CP-WrigJ**

Elegy for the Silent Voices and the Joiners of Everything. Kenneth Patchen. **CP-PatcK**

Elegy for Wesley Wells. Donald Hall. **CP-HallD**

Elegy 4: To Thomas Young. John Milton, *tr. fr. Latin by* John T. Shawcross. **CP-CowpW; CP-MiltJ**

("Hence my epistle—skim the deep—fly o'er.") **CP-CowpW,** *tr. by* William Cowper;

Elegy Imitated from One of Akenside's Blank-Verse Inscriptions. Samuel Taylor Coleridge. **CP-ColeS**

Elegy in a Civil War Cemetery. John Gould Fletcher. **SP-FletJ**

Elegy in a Firelit Room. James Wright. **CP-WrigJ**

Elegy in April and September. Wilfred Owen. **CP-OwenW**

Elegy in the Classroom. Anne Sexton. **CP-SextA**

Elegy Just in Case. John Ciardi. **SP-CiarJ**

Elegy XIX. To His Mistris Going to Bed. John Donne. *See* To His Mistress Going to Bed.

Elegy? No muse, it asks a strain, An. Proludium. Ben Jonson. **CP-JonsB**

Elegy of Last Resort. Howard Nemerov. **CP-NemeH**

Elegy on a Nordic White Protestant. John Gould Fletcher. **SP-FletJ**

Elegy on an Empty Skyscraper. John Gould Fletcher. **SP-FletJ**

Elegy on Captain Matthew Henderson [*or* Capt. M————— H———] [A *Gentleman* Who Held the Patent for His Honours Immediately from Almighty God!]. Robert Burns. **CP-BurnR**

"Mourn, ye wee songsters o' the wood." **PBBP**

Elegy on Dicky and Dolly, An. Jonathan Swift. **CP-SwifJ**

Elegy on His Mistress. John Donne. *See* On His Mistress [*or* Mistris].

Elegy on London. John Gould Fletcher. **SP-FletJ**

Elegy on Mister William Cruikshank A. M. Robert Burns. **CP-BurnR**

Elegy on Mistress Boulstred. John Donne. **CP-DonnJ**

Elegy on My Muse. Ben Jonson. *Fr.* Eupheme. **CP-JonsB**

(Lady Venetia Digby, The.) **GoBC**

Elegy on Newstead Abbey. Byron. **CP-Byron**

Elegy on Parting, An. James Thomson. **CP-ThomJ**

Elegy on Peg Nicholson. Robert Burns. **CP-BurnR**

Elegy on the Death of John Keats, An. Percy Bysshe Shelley. *See* Peace, peace! he is not dead, he doth not sleep.

Elegy on the Death of Kenneth Patchen, An. Lawrence Ferlinghetti. **SP-FerlL**

Elegy on the Death of Robert Ruisseaux. Robert Burns. **CP-BurnR**

Elegy on the Dust. Thom Gunn. **NoAM** *Fr.* Misanthropos. **CP-GunnT**

Elegy on the L. C. John Donne. **CP-DonnJ**

Elegy on the La: Pen: Sent to My Mistress Out of France, An. Thomas Carew. **CP-CareT**

Elegy [or Elegie] on the Lady Jane Pawlet [or Paulet], [Marchioness of Winton], An. Ben Jonson. **CP-JonsB**

"How did she leave the world? with what contempt?" **OBD**

Elegy on the Lady Markham. John Donne. **CP-DonnJ**

Elegy on the Much Lamented Death of Mr. Demar, the Famous Rich Usurer, An. Jonathan Swift. **CP-SwifJ**

Elegy On the Supposed Death of Mr. Partridge, the Almanac Maker. Jonathan Swift. **CP-SwifJ**

Elegy on the Year 1788. Robert Burns. **CP-BurnR**

Elegy on Tintern Abbey. John Gould Fletcher. **SP-FletJ**

Elegy 1: To Charles Deodati. John Milton, *tr. fr. Latin by* John T. Shawcross. **CP-CowpW; CP-MiltJ**

("At length, my friend, the far-sent letters come.") **CP-CowpW,** *tr. by* William Cowper;

Elegy 2: On the Death of the Beadle of Cambridge University. John Milton, *tr. fr. Latin by* John T. Shawcross. **CP-CowpW; CP-MiltJ**

("Thee, whose refulgent staff, and summons clear.") **CP-CowpW,** *tr. by* William Cowper;

Elegy 3: On the Death of the Bishop of Winchester. John Milton, *tr. fr. Latin by* John T. Shawcross. **CP-CowpW; CP-MiltJ**

("Silent I sat, dejected, and alone.") **CP-CowpW,** *tr. by* William Cowper;

Elegy 6: To Charles Deodati. John Milton, *tr. fr. Latin by* John T. Shawcross. **CP-CowpW; CP-MiltJ**

("With no rich viands overcharg'd, I send.") **CP-CowpW,** *tr. by* William Cowper;

Elegy 7: "Not yet did I know your laws, enticing Amathusia." John Milton, *tr. fr. Latin by* John T. Shawcross. **CP-CowpW; CP-MiltJ**

("As yet a stranger to the gentle fires.") **CP-CowpW,** *tr. by* William Cowper;

Elegy to Dispel Gloom, An. Lawrence Ferlinghetti. **SP-FerlL**

Elegy to the Memory of an Unfortunate Lady. Alexander Pope. **CP-PopeA**

"Most souls, 'tis true, but peep out once an age." **CH; FaBoRV**

(Dull, Sullen Prisoners.) **FaBoRV**

Elegy upon James Therburn, An. James Thomson. **CP-ThomJ**

Elegy Upon that Honorable and Reknowned Knight Sir Philip Sydney, An. Anne Bradstreet. **CP-BradA**

Elegy upon the Death of Doctor [*or* Dr.] Donne, Dean of Paul's, An. Thomas Carew. *See* An Elegy upon the Death of the Dean of [St.] Paul's, Dr. John Donne.

Elegy upon the Death of Mistress Boulstred, An. John Donne. **CP-DonnJ**

Elegy upon the Death of Mr. Stanninow Fellow of Queenes Colledge. Richard Crashaw. **CP-CrasR**

Elegy upon the Death of My Lord Francis Villiers, An. Andrew Marvell. **CP-MarvA**

Elegy upon the Death of the Dean of [St.] Paul's, Dr. John Donne, An. Thomas Carew.

(Elegy upon the Death of Doctor [*or* Dr.] Donne, Dean of Paul's, An.) **CP-CareT**

On the Death of Donne. **NOBE**

Elegy upon the Untimely Death of the Incomparable Prince Henry. John Donne. **CP-DonnJ**

Elegy VII. Ezra Pound. *See* Me happy, night, night full of brightness.

Elegy Written in a Country Churchyard. Thomas Gray. **CP-GrayT**

"Boast of heraldry, the pomp of pow'r, The." **OBD**

"Curfew tolls the knell of parting day, The." **UV**

Epitaph: "Here rests his head upon the lap of earth." **FHYEP; FaBoPV; SCGP**

Elegy Written in the Same Place upon the Same Occasion. William Wordsworth. **CP-WorW1**

Elegye, An: "Constant to none, but ever false to me." Thomas Campion. **AAS** *Fr.* Observations in the Art of English Poesie. **CP-CampT**

Elektra on Third Avenue. Marilyn Hacker. **SP-HackM**

Element Fire Boasts of the Constellations, The. Anne Bradstreet. **CBCK** *Fr.* The Four Elements. **CP-BradA**

Element in which they live, The. The Skeleton. Robert Creeley. **CP-CreeR**

Element of air was out of hand, The. Interlude. Theodore Roethke. **CP-RoetT**

Element of Elegy, The. Emily Dickinson. **SP-DickE**

Element of mischief contributed, An. Summer Breezes. Frank O'Hara. **SP-OharF**

Elemental. David Herbert Lawrence. **CP-LawrD**

Elemental. Charles Tomlinson. **CP-TomlC**

Elemental murmur, The. The Falls. Galway Kinnell. **SP-KinnG**

Elementals, The. Kathleen Jessie Raine. **SP-RainK**

Elementary Attitudes. Mona Van Duyn. **SP-VanDM**

Elementary Cosmogony. Charles Simic. **SP-SimiC**

Elementary Scene, The. Randall Jarrell. **CP-JarrR**

Elementary School Classroom in a Slum, An. Stephen Spender. **CP-SpenS**

Elements, The. David Herbert Lawrence. **CP-LawrD**

Elements have merged into solicitude, The. The Racer's Widow. Louise Glück. **SP-GlücL**

Elements of clothes, an arm and hand the head of a cock. Charles Olson. **CP-OlsoC**

Elements on my table. A Ghost May Come. Allen Ginsberg. **CP-GinsA**

Elements respect their Maker's seal!, The. Fragment from the Wandering Jew. Percy Bysshe Shelley. **CP-ShelP**

Elephant. David Herbert Lawrence. **CP-LawrD**

Elephant, The. Jonathan Swift. **CP-SwifJ**

Elephant Is Slow to Mate, The. David Herbert Lawrence. **CP-LawrD**

Elephant made of cotton, An. The Grand Palace of Versailles. Kenneth Patchen. **CP-PatcK**

Elephant, say, scraping its dry sides. West. George Oppen. **CP-OppeG**

Elephant, the huge old beast, The. The Elephant Is Slow to Mate. David Herbert Lawrence. **CP-LawrD**

Elephant Trunk. Louis MacNeice. **CP-MacNL**

Elephants. Louis MacNeice. *Fr.* Circus. **CP-MacNL**

Elephants. Marianne Craig Moore. **CP-MoorM**

Elephants Are Different to Different People. Carl Sandburg. **CP-SandC**

Elephant's Child, The. Rudyard Kipling. *Fr.* Just-So Stories.
  "I keep six honest serving-men." **CP-KiplR**

Elephants in the Circus. David Herbert Lawrence. **CP-LawrD**

Elephants Plodding. David Herbert Lawrence. **CP-LawrD**

Eleutheria. James Wright. **CP-WrigJ**

Elevator Boy. Langston Hughes. **SP-HughL**

Elevator music from a Tokyo radio. The Sad Hour of Your Peace. Al Young. **CP-YounA**

Eleven. Archibald MacLeish. **CP-MacLA**

Eleven Addresses to the Lord. John Berryman. **CP-BerrJ**
  "After a Stoic, a Peripatetic, a Pythagorean."
  "Fearful I peer upon the mountain path."
  "Germanicus leapt upon the wild lion in Smyrna."
  "Holy, & holy. The damned are said to say."
  "Holy, as I suppose I dare to call you."
  "If I say Thy name, art Thou there? It may be so."
  "Master of beauty, craftsman of the snowflake." **PAI; UnPo**
  Prayer for the Self, A. **PPP**
  "Sole watchman of the flying stars, guard me." **UnPo**
  "Surprise me on some ordinary day."
  "Under new management, Your Majesty."

Eleven Occasional Poems. Wystan Hugh Auden. **CP-AudeW**
  Elegy: "Liebe Frau Emma."
  Elegy for J.F.K.
  Epithalamium: "All folk-tales mean by ending."
  Eulogy.
  Josef Weinheber.
  Lines for Elizabeth Mayer.
  Lines to Dr Walter Birk On His Retiring from General Practice.
  Mosaic for Marianne Moore, A.
  Short Ode to a Philologist, A.
  Toast, A ("As quid pro quo for your enchanting verses").
  Toast, A ("What on earth does one say at a Gaudy").

11 Outlined Epitaphs. "Bob Dylan." **CP-DylaB**
  "Al's wife claimed I can't be happy."
  "I end up then."
  "In times behind, I too."
  "Jim Jim / where is our party?"
  "Night passes fast for me now, The."

"Oh where were these magazines."

"Russian has three an' a half red eyes, A."

"So at last at least."

"Town I was born in holds no memories, The."

"Woody Guthrie was my last idol."

"Yes, I am a thief of thoughts."

Eleven rogues and he to judge a fool. Mr. High-Mind. John Updike. **CP-UpdiJ**

Eleven-thirty and hot. The Cyclist. Marge Piercy. **SP-PierM**

11:02 A.M. The Bird Disappeared. John Ciardi. **SP-CiarJ**

Elevens. Marilyn Hacker. **SP-HackM**

11th: and Last Booke of the Ocean to Scinthia, The. Sir Walter Ralegh. **CP-RaleW** *Fr.* The Ocean's Love to Cynthia.

Eleventh Avenue Racket. Carl Sandburg. **CP-SandC**

Eleventh Book, The. Archibald MacLeish. *Fr.* Conquistador. **CP-MacLA**

Eleventh Hour, The. Christina Georgina Rossetti. **CP-RosC3**

Eleventh Night, The. John Hewitt. **CP-HewiJ**

Eleventh Song. Sir Philip Sidney. **NoSic; OxAEP-1** *Fr.* Astrophil and Stella. **SP-SidnP**
  (Underneath My Window.) **SeCePo**
  (Voices at the Window.) **NOBE; OBEV; PoPle**
  (Who Is It That This Dark Night.) **EIL; EnRePo; NAEL-1; OBSC; PoE; PoEL-1; SCGP; TEP**

Elias Gove—or, The Second Coming. Marsden Hartley. **CP-HartM**

Elias—Variations on a Theme. Thomas Merton. **CP-MertT**

Elijah on Mount Carmel. Robert Penn Warren. **SP-WarrR**

Elijah's Wagon knew no thill. Emily Dickinson. **CP-DickE**

Elinda's [or Ellinda's] Glove. Richard Lovelace. **CP-LoveR**

Elisa ("Ye dainty nymphs, that in this blessed brook"). Edmund Spenser. **OBSC** *Fr.* Aprill. **NAEL-1; OBEV; OBSC; PoEL-1** *Fr.* The Shepheardes [or Shepeards or Shepherd's] Calender. **CP-Spens**
  (Lay to Eliza, The.) **NOBE**

Elixir [or Elixer], The. George Herbert. **CP-HerbG**

Elixir. David Herbert Lawrence. **CP-LawrD**

Eliza, what fools are the Mussulman sect. To Eliza. Byron. **CP-Byron**

Elizabeth. Robert Lowell. **SP-LoweR**

Elizabeth. Paul Muldoon. **SP-MuldP**

Elizabeth. William Wordsworth. *Fr.* Ecclesiastical Sonnets. **CP-WorW2**

Elizabeth and the Golden Oranges. Diane Wakoski. **SP-WakoD**

Elizabeth Gone. Anne Sexton. **CP-SextA**

Elizabeth Hoar. Ralph Waldo Emerson. **CP-EmerR**

Elizabeth told Essex. Emily Dickinson. **CP-DickE**

Elizabethans Called It Dying, The. James Schuyler. **CP-SchuJ**

Elk Trails. Gary Snyder. **CP-SnydG**

Ella Mason and Her Eleven Cats. Sylvia Plath. **CP-PlatS**

Ellen. George Crabbe. **SP-CrabG** *Fr.* Tales of the Hall.

Ellen Irwin; or, The Braes of Kirtle. William Wordsworth. **CP-WorW1**

Ellen Middleton. Christina Georgina Rossetti. **CP-RosC3**

Ellendene. John Hewitt. **CP-HewiJ**

Ellen's Song. Sir Walter Scott. **SP-ScotW** *Fr.* The Lady of the Lake.

Elles viennent, *Author's own French vers. of his* "They come." Samuel Beckett. **CP-BeckS**

Elliott. John Greenleaf Whittier. **CP-WhitJ**

Ellora. Leonard Nathan. **SP-NathL**

Elm. Sylvia Plath. **CP-PlatS**

Elm. John Updike. **CP-UpdiJ**

Elm Buds. Carl Sandburg. **CP-SandC**

Elm buds are out. Elm Buds. Carl Sandburg. **CP-SandC**

Elm Tree, An. William DeWitt Snodgrass. **SP-SnodW**

Elm tree is our highest mountain peak, The. In Praise of Prairie. Theodore Roethke. **CP-RoetT**

Elms. Louise Glück. **SP-GlücL**

Elms. Charles Kenneth Williams. **SP-WillC**

Elms' silhouettes, The. Late January. John Updike. **CP-UpdiJ**

Elohim Creating Adam, The. Roy Fisher. **SP-FishR**

Eloi, Eloi, Lama Sabachthani? David Herbert Lawrence. **CP-LawrD**

Eloisa. Alexander Pope. **SeCePo** *Fr.* Eloisa to Abelard. **CP-PopeA**

Eloisa to Abelard. Alexander Pope. **CP-PopeA**
  Eloisa. **SeCePo**
  Vestal, The. **ACP**
    (Life of a Nun.) **ECEV**

Elopement, The. Thomas Hardy. **CP-HardT**

Elopement, The. Gerard Manley Hopkins. **CP-HopkG**

Else a great Prince in prison lies. Denise Levertov. **CP-LeveD**

Elsewhere. Robert Ranke Graves. **CP-GravR**

Elsie Flimmerwon, you got a job now with a jazz outfit in vaudeville.
Vaudeville Dancer. Carl Sandburg. **CP-SandC**
Elsinore was the battlements of Oaxaca. Malcolm Lowry. **CP-LowrM**
Elusive / This godfather who mostly forgets one's birthday. Godfather.
Louis MacNeice. **CP-MacNL**
Elves, The. Denise Levertov. **CP-LeveD**
Elves are no smaller. The Elves. Denise Levertov. **CP-LeveD**
Elvira, by love's grace. Homage. William Carlos Williams. **CP-WilW1**
Elvis Presley. Thom Gunn. **CP-GunnT**
Elysium. David Herbert Lawrence. **CP-LawrD**
Elysium is as far as to. Emily Dickinson. **CP-DickE**
Emancipation. Paul Laurence Dunbar. **CP-DunbP**
Emancipation Group, The. John Greenleaf Whittier. **CP-WhitJ**
Emancipation of Mr. Poplin, or, Skoal to the Skimmerless. Ogden Nash.
CP-NashO
Emancipators, The. Randall Jarrell. **CP-JarrR**
Emasculation. David Herbert Lawrence. **CP-LawrD**
Embankment at Night, before the War: Charity. David Herbert Lawrence.
CP-LawrD
Embankment at Night, before the War: Outcasts. David Herbert Lawrence.
CP-LawrD
Embarcation. Thomas Hardy. **CP-HardT**
Embarkation, The. Henry Wadsworth Longfellow. **PAH** *Fr.* Part the First.
Fr. Evangeline, a Tale of Acadie. **SP-LongH**
Embarrassment of one another. Emily Dickinson. **CP-DickE**
Embassy. Charles Tomlinson. **CP-TomlC**
Embers of the day are red, The. Evensong. Robert Louis Stevenson. **CP-StevR**
Embertide. Christina Georgina Rossetti. **CP-RosC2**
Emblem. Richard Eberhart. **CP-EberR**
Emblem. Roy Fisher. **SP-FishR**
Emblem, The. Geoffrey Hill. *Fr.* Locust Songs. **CP-HillG**
Emblem of blasted hope and lost desire. Sonnet. Paul Laurence Dunbar.
CP-DunbP
Emblems. Allen Tate. **CP-TateA**
Emblems of Arachne. Charles Henri Ford.
"And take your time." **SP-FordC**
"And the first owl of." **SP-FordC**
"Bala Krishna's voice." **SP-FordC**
"Beautiful new / Character may enter the, A." **SP-FordC**
"Being nor whim nor." **SP-FordC**
"Black dog in a, A." **SP-FordC**
"Chakora bird / Like a partridge. It is said, The." **SP-FordC**
"Chinaberries / Change from green to yellow. In, The." **SP-FordC**
"Clouds covered it, The." **SP-FordC**
"Consider the sound." **SP-FordC**
"Crows in the fog, dogs." **SP-FordC**
"Dampness in the air." **SP-FordC**
"Dew falls but the, The." **SP-FordC**
"Eagle carries / Off a single sheep. Carry, An." **SP-FordC**
"Forms and flowers." **SP-FordC**
"Human kites, fantastic." **SP-FordC**
"I am Mantra." **SP-FordC**
"In a dream you had." **SP-FordC**
"In struggling to get." **SP-FordC**
"In the maze of the." **SP-FordC**
"In the playpen of." **SP-FordC**
"In the tentacles." **SP-FordC**
"Indra; my house; the." **SP-FordC**
"Invisible envelopes, / A standstill afternoon." **SP-FordC**
"Juggernaut chanting." **SP-FordC**
"Krishna climbs up there." **SP-FordC**
"Large bead on the." **SP-FordC**
"Masks without faces." **SP-FordC**
"Mount Stavros sits on." **SP-FordC**
"Neurotic demon, / Trying to convince himself." **SP-FordC**
"No beings but." **SP-FordC**
"Not locking onto." **SP-FordC**
"Nubian in / Tangerine, carrying a, A." **SP-FordC**
"Oh, a patch of green." **SP-FordC**
"On a high branch two." **SP-FordC**
"Peaks of pleasure, peaks." **SP-FordC**
"Place in which to, A." **SP-FordC**
"Pre-puberty boys." **SP-FordC**
"Prevalence of the." **SP-FordC**
"Ram wears a cowboy." **SP-FordC**

"Real dreams. More real than." **SP-FordC**
"Realization / Of fantasy, yes. This, A." **SP-FordC**
"Sharp eyes, hoodlum skin." **SP-FordC**
"Shaven heads, rubber." **SP-FordC**
"Small black goat with, A." **SP-FordC**
"Soldiers walk around." **SP-FordC**
"Soleil d'automne. Do." **SP-FordC**
"Some flowers come up." **SP-FordC**
"Sorer the joints, The." **SP-FordC**
"Standing on the garden." **SP-FordC**
"There's that praying." **SP-FordC**
"They need no other." **SP-FordC**
"This same sea, there." **SP-FordC**
"Tonguless crocodile / Meets eyeless tiger darted." **SP-FordC**
"Trees with white perfumed." **SP-FordC**
"Untouched ones, the, The." **SP-FordC**
"Wall ritual. These." **SP-FordC**
"We each play our roles." **SP-FordC**
"Weather is mild, The." **SP-FordC**
"When the coolie blew." **SP-FordC**
"Whole family weeping." **SP-FordC**
"Yes, wave your magic." **SP-FordC**
Emblems of Conduct. Hart Crane. **CP-CranH**
Emblems of Exile. Thomas McGrath. **SP-McGrT**
Embowering rose, the acacia, and the pine, The. Inscription in the Grounds of
Coleorton. William Wordsworth. **CP-WorW1**
Embrace, The. Leonard Cohen. **CP-CoheL**
Embrace, The. Louise Glück. **SP-GlücL**
Embracing in the road. Hawk's Shadow. Louise Glück. **SP-GlücL**
Embro Hie Kirk. Robert Louis Stevenson. **CP-StevR**
Embroidered in a tapestry of green. Design in Living Colors. Adrienne
Rich. **CP-RicAE**
Embryonic or symphonic. Hot House. Al Young. **CP-YounA**
Emerald Ice. Diane Wakoski. **SP-WakoD**
Emerald is as green as grass, An. Flint. Christina Georgina Rossetti.
OxBChV; RHPC; TiPo *Fr.* Sing-Song. **CP-RosC2**
Emerald is as green as grass, An. Christina Georgina Rossetti. **CP-RosC2**
Emerald mosque / in motion, The. Ah—There. Tom Clark. **SP-ClarT**
Emergency Haying. Hayden Carruth. **CP-CarHS**
Emerges daintily, the skunk. The Wood Weasel. Marianne Craig Moore.
CP-MoorM
Emerging from aeons of ocean on to the shore. Vistas. Louis MacNeice.
CP-MacNL
Emerson's Concord. Richard Eberhart. **CP-EberR**
Emerson's intimacy with his "Bee." Emily Dickinson. **SP-DickE**
Emigrant French Clergy. William Wordsworth. *Fr.* Ecclesiastical Sonnets.
CP-WorW2
Emigrant Mother, The. William Wordsworth. **CP-WorW1**
Emigrant, to the Receding Shore. Donald Davie. **CP-DavDo**
Emigrants, The. Charlotte Smith. **CP-SmitC**
"Long wintry months are past; the Moon that now."
Disillusion with the French Revolution. **ECWP**
"Slow in the Wintry Morn, the struggling light."
Émigrée from the Bronx, a married child. Nights of 1962: The River
Merchant's Wife. Marilyn Hacker. **SP-HackM**
Emily and Kate. The Cage. Richard Eberhart. **CP-EberR**
Emily Brontë. Ted Hughes. **SP-HughT**
Emily Dickenson: / You gave us the bumblebee who has a soul. Letters to
Dead Imagists. Carl Sandburg. **CP-SandC**
Emily Dickinson. Richard Eberhart. **CP-EberR**
Emily Dickinson. Phoebe Hesketh. **SP-HeskP**
Emily Dickinson. John Hewitt. **CP-HewiJ**
Emily Hardcastle, Spinster. John Crowe Ransom. **SP-RansJ**
Emily Writes Such a Good Letter. Stevie Smith. **CP-SmitS**
Emily, you were sick. North & South. Donald Davie. **CP-DavDo**
Eminent Reformers. William Wordsworth. *Fr.* Ecclesiastical Sonnets. **CP-WorW2**
Emlyn reads in Dickens' clothes. The Clan. John Updike. **CP-UpdiJ**
Emotional Friend, The. David Herbert Lawrence. **CP-LawrD**
Emotional Lies. David Herbert Lawrence. **CP-LawrD**
Emotionally Yours. "Bob Dylan." **CP-DylaB**
Emotions are engaged, The. George Oppen. *Fr.* Of Being Numerous. **CP-OppeG**
Emp Lace. Gertrude Stein. **CP-SteiG**
Empathy. Robert Pack. **SP-PackR**
Empathy and New Year. James Schuyler. **CP-SchuJ**

Empedocles. George Meredith. **CP-MerG1**

Empedocles on Etna. Matthew Arnold. **SP-ArnoM**

  "And lie thou there." **EnVR**

  "Far far from here." **FiP; GTBS-6; GTBS-P**

    (Song of Callicles, The ("Far, far from here").) **FiP**

  "It is so small a thing." **OBEV; OBVV**

    (Hymn of Empedocles.) **OBEV**

  Life and Thought. **FiP**

  Song of Callicles, The ("Through the black, rushing smoke-burst").

    NOBE; OAEL-2; OBEV; OBVV

    (Callicles' Song.) **ChTr; LoBV**

    (Not Here, O Apollo.) **FaBoRV**

    (Song for Apollo.) **FiP**

    (Song of the Muses, The.) **WiR**

Emperor, The. Marge Piercy. *Fr.* Laying Down the Tower. **SP-PierM**

Emperor / sleeps in a palace of porphyry, The. Edward Estlin Cummings. **CP-CummE**

Emperor, Emperor! Napoleon III in Italy. Elizabeth Barrett Browning. **CP-BroEB**

Emperor Frederick of Our Time, The. George Meredith. **CP-MerG1**

Emperor of Ice-Cream, The. Wallace Stevens. **CP-StevW**

Emperors and Kings, How Oft Have Temples Rung. William Wordsworth. **CP-WorW2**

Emperor's favorite concubine, The. Wystan Hugh Auden. *Fr.* Five Songs ("Deftly, admiral, cast your fly"). **CP-AudeW**

Emperors' heads around the Sheldonian, The. Oxford, Thirty Years After. John Updike. **CP-UpdiJ**

Empire Builders. Archibald MacLeish. **CP-MacLA**

Empire Is No More. William Blake. **EnRP** *Fr.* America; a Prophecy. **CP-BlakW**

Empire of Coins, An. Charles Bukowski. **SP-BukC2**

Empire of Dreams. Charles Simic. **SP-SimiC**

Empire of Persia, The. Kenneth Patchen. **CP-PatcK**

Empires. Robert Herrick. **CP-HerrR**

Empires of Kings, are now, and ever were. Empires. Robert Herrick. **CP-HerrR**

Employment (1). George Herbert. **CP-HerbG**

Employment (2). George Herbert. *See* He that is weary, let him sit.

Empress of Art, for thee I twine. "Lewis Carroll." *Fr.* Four Riddles. **CP-CarrL**

Emptied.hills.listen. Edward Estlin Cummings. **CP-CummE**

Emptiness. Stephen Dunn. **SP-DunnS**

Emptiness in my eyes had begged her question. Confession. Leonard Nathan. **SP-NathL**

Emptiness—you know. Hayden Carruth. **CP-CarHS** *Fr.* The Clay Hill Anthology.

Empty. Erica Jong. **SP-JongE**

Empty battlefields keep their phantoms. New Feet. Carl Sandburg. **CP-SandC**

Empty Boat, The. Chuang Tzu, *tr. fr. Chinese by* Thomas Merton. **CP-MertT**

Empty Boats, The. Nicholas Vachel Lindsay. **CP-LindV**

Empty Cup, The. William Butler Yeats. *Fr.* A Man Young and Old. **CP-YeatW**

Empty Days, The. John Gould Fletcher. **SP-FletJ**

Empty House, The. Walter de la Mare. **CP-DeLaW**

Empty House. Stephen Spender. **CP-SpenS**

Empty house on a horizon. A Heap of Broken Images. Lawrence Ferlinghetti. **SP-FerlL**

Empty, I echo to the least footfall. Barren Woman. Sylvia Plath. **CP-PlatS**

Empty my Heart, of Thee. Emily Dickinson. **CP-DickE**

Empty Place, An. Robert Bly. **SP-BlyR**

Empty Place, An. Ted Kooser. **SP-KoosT**

Empty Purse: A Sermon to our Later Prodigal Son, The. George Meredith. **CP-MerG1**

Empty Shoes. Louis MacNeice. *Fr.* Out of the Picture. **CP-MacNL**

Empty stage-set on the headland. Cape Sunion. John Hewitt. **CP-HewiJ**

Empty Stirrups. Herman Melville. **SP-MelvH** *Fr.* Clarel: A Poem and Pilgrimage in the Holy Land.

Empty the last drop. Plunger. Carl Sandburg. **CP-SandC**

Empty Threat, An. Robert Frost. **CP-FrosR**

Empty vast days built in the waste memory seem a jail for. Basil Bunting. **CP-BuntB**

Empty Vessel. "Hugh MacDiarmid." **SP-MacDH**

Empty Woman, The. Gwendolyn Brooks. **SP-BrooG**

Emptying his bowel. Roy Fisher. **SP-FishR** *Fr.* The Six Deliberate Acts.

Emptying his bowel. Roy Fisher. **SP-FishR** *Fr.* The Six Deliberate Acts.

En Amérique, professeur; / En Angleterre, journaliste. Mélange Adultère de Tout. Thomas Stearns Eliot. **CP-ElioT**

En-dor. Rudyard Kipling. **CP-KiplR**

En face. Samuel Beckett. **CP-BeckS**

En ma Provence le blé est toujours vert. Ma Provence. Kenneth Koch. **SP-KochK**

En Masse. David Herbert Lawrence. **CP-LawrD**

En peur Idalius tremulis circumvolat alis. AD EUNDEM. Thomas Hamersley. *Fr.* Commendatory Poems. **CP-LoveR**

En route to Roseau / Valley Church, we pass defunct. The Banana Madonna. Laurence Lieberman. **SP-LiebL**

En Route to Southampton. James Schuyler. **CP-SchuJ**

Enacting someone's notion of themselves. Aunt Jemima of the Ocean Waves. Robert Earl Hayden. **CP-HaydR**

Enamour'd, artless, young, on foreign ground. John Milton. *See* Sonnet 6: "Young, gentle, and candid lover that I am."

Enamoured by / Brevity in method. Epitaph. Charles Tomlinson. **CP-TomlC**

Encase your legs in nylons. Inexpensive Progress. Sir John Betjeman. **CP-BetjJ**

Encased in talent like a uniform. The Novelist. Wystan Hugh Auden. **CP-AudeW**

Enchanted Goblet, The. Sir Walter Scott. **SP-ScotW** *Fr.* The Bridal of Trierman.

Enchanter of Yellow Gold to the Old Friend, The. James Liddy. **CP-LiddJ**

Encinctured with a twine of leaves. Samuel Taylor Coleridge. **CP-ColeS**

Encirclement. Alun Lewis. **CP-LewiA**

Encircling ground, in native turf arrayed, The. New Church-Yard. William Wordsworth. *Fr.* Ecclesiastical Sonnets. **CP-WorW2**

Enclave / Filled with their own, An. George Oppen. *Fr.* A Narrative. **CP-OppeG**

Enclave, The. Robert Penn Warren. *Fr.* The True Nature of Time. **SP-WarrR**

Enclave where new mythologies. Zeus over Redeye. Robert Earl Hayden. **CP-HaydR**

Enclosed in this disturbing mutual wood. The Prisoners. Adrienne Rich. **CP-RicAE; SP-RicA2**

Enclosure, The. James Dickey. **CP-DickJ**

Encomium Balnei. Wystan Hugh Auden. *Fr.* Thanksgiving for a Habitat. **CP-AudeW**

Encompassed. Marsden Hartley. **CP-HartM**

Encore le dernier reflux. *Author's own French vers. of his* Dieppe. Samuel Beckett. **CP-BeckS**

Encounter, An. Wystan Hugh Auden. **CP-AudeW**

Encounter. Wystan Hugh Auden. **CP-AudWJ**

Encounter. John Ciardi. **SP-CiarJ**

Encounter, The. Walter de la Mare. **CP-DeLaW**

Encounter. William Everson. **SP-EverW**

Encounter, An. Robert Frost. **CP-FrosR**

Encounter, The. Louise Glück. *Fr.* Marathon. **SP-GlücL**

Encounter, The. Robert Ranke Graves. **CP-GravR**

Encounter, The. Alun Lewis. **CP-LewiA**

Encounter. Thomas McGrath. **SP-McGrT**

Encounter. Frederick Morgan. **SP-MorgF**

Encounter. Mary Oliver. **SP-OlivM**

Encounter, The. Charles Olson. **CP-OlsoC**

Encounter, The. Ezra Pound. **SP-PounE**

Encounter. Richard Shelton. **SP-ShelR**

Encounter. Charles Tomlinson. **CP-TomlC**

Encounter at Nightfall. Kenneth Patchen. **CP-PatcK**

Encounter in the Cage Country. James Dickey. **CP-DickJ**

Encounter Nineteen Twenty. John Hewitt. **CP-HewiJ**

Encounter With R.J. Welch, The Antiquary. John Hewitt. **CP-HewiJ**

Encouraged. Paul Laurence Dunbar. **CP-DunbP**

Encouragement. Paul Laurence Dunbar. **CP-DunbP**

Encouragements to a Lover. Sir John Suckling. *See* Why so pale and wan, fond lover?

Encyclopædia, The. Nicholas Vachel Lindsay. **CP-LindV**

End, The. Charles Bukowski. **SP-BukC2**

End, The. Robert Creeley. **CP-CreeR**

End, The. Allen Ginsberg. **CP-GinsA**

End, The. Robert Herrick. **CP-HerrR**

End, The. Robert Herrick. **CP-HerrR**

End. Langston Hughes. **SP-HughL**

End, The. David Herbert Lawrence. **CP-LawrD**

End, The. John Lennon *and* Paul McCartney. **CP-Beatl**

End, The. Frederick Morgan. **SP-MorgF**

End, The. Jim Morrison. **SP-MorrJ**

End, The. Wilfred Owen. **CP-OwenW**

End, An. Christina Georgina Rossetti. **CP-RosC1**

End, The. Charles Tomlinson. **CP-TomlC**

End came suddenly for him, The. The Suicide. Alun Lewis. **CP-LewiA**

End Decreed, An. Robert Herrick. **CP-HerrR**

End fond jealousie alas I know, An. Sonnet 7. Mary Sidney, Countess of Montgomery Wroth. *Fr.* Pamphilia to Amphilanthus. **CP-WrotM**

End has come, as come it must, The. At School-Close. John Greenleaf Whittier. **CP-WhitJ**

End Is Not Yet, The. Christina Georgina Rossetti. **CP-RosC2**

End, Middle, Beginning. Anne Sexton. **CP-SextA**

End now the White-loafe, & the Pye. Upon Candlemasse Day. Robert Herrick. **CP-HerrR**

End of a road. The Son. Louise McNeill. **SP-McNeL**

End of a Short Affair, The. Charles Bukowski. **SP-BukC1**

End of All, The. Walt Whitman. **CP-WhitW**

End of all things is at hand. We all, The. Sunday Before Advent. Christina Georgina Rossetti. **CP-RosC2**

End of Another Home Holiday. David Herbert Lawrence. **CP-LawrD**

End of Camp Alamoosook. Robert Lowell. **SP-LoweR**

End of Doctor Faustus, The. Christopher Marlowe. *See* Ah, Faustus,/ Now hast thou but one bare hour [*or* hower] to live.

End of Drought. Charles Kenneth Williams. **SP-WillC**

End of Faustus, The. Christopher Marlowe. *See* Ah, Faustus,/ Now hast thou but one bare hour [*or* hower] to live.

End of His Work, The. Robert Herrick. **CP-HerrR**

End of Job, The. John Gould Fletcher. **SP-FletJ** *Fr.* The Parables of Antichrist.

End of Krim's Pad, The. Richard Hugo. **CP-HugoR**

End of Love, The. George Meredith. *See* By this he knew she wept with waking eyes.

End of March, The. Elizabeth Bishop. **CP-BishE**

End of May. Mona Van Duyn. **SP-VanDM**

End of My Life in Art. Leonard Cohen. **CP-CoheL**

End of Play. Robert Ranke Graves. **CP-GravR**

End of Season. Robert Penn Warren. **SP-WarrR**

End of Summer. Stanley Jasspon Kunitz. **CP-KuniS**

End of Summer School, The. Howard Nemerov. **CP-NemeH**

End of the affair is always death, The. The Ballad of the Lonely Masturbator. Anne Sexton. **CP-SextA**

End of the Boo[c]k[e]s, of the Ocean's Love to Cynthia [*or* Scinthia], and the Beginning[e] of the 12 [*or* 22] Boo[c]k, Entreating of Sorrow, The. Sir Walter Ralegh. **CP-RaleW** *Fr.* The Ocean's Love to Cynthia.

End of the Chapter, The. Paul Laurence Dunbar. **CP-DunbP**

End of the Day, The. Robert Creeley. **CP-CreeR**

End of the Dream, The. Jim Morrison. **SP-MorrJ**

End of the Episode, The. Thomas Hardy. **CP-HardT**

End of the Line, The. Thomas McGrath. **SP-McGrT**

End of the Negotiable Beggar Bond Banquet, The. Chuck Miller. **SP-MillC**

End of the Parade, The. William Carlos Williams. **CP-WilW2**

End of the Rainbow, The. Randall Jarrell. **CP-JarrR**

End of the Rainbow, The. Jim Morrison. **SP-MorrJ**

End of the Rope, The. William Carlos Williams. **CP-WilW2**

End of the Street, The. John Haines. **SP-HainJ**

End of the Summer, The. John Haines. **SP-HainJ**

"Let the inhuman, drab machines."

"Subversive leaves, you fall."

"Sun keeps its promises, The."

End of the World, The. Louise Glück. **SP-GlücL**

End of the World, The. John Hewitt. **CP-HewiJ**

End of the World / is the Turn-About, The. Charles Olson. **CP-OlsoC**

End of the World. Robinson Jeffers. **CP-JefR3**

End of the World, The. Archibald MacLeish. **CP-MacLA**

End of the World, The. Thomas McGrath. **SP-McGrT**

End of the year fell chilly, The. New Year's Eve. Alfred Edward Housman. **CP-HousA**

End of the Year 1912. Thomas Hardy. **CP-HardT**

End of the year wears its face in the moon against the disguises one would otherwise put upon it. New Year's. Robert Creeley. **CP-CreeR**

End of Time, The. Christina Georgina Rossetti. **CP-RosC3**

End of Travel, An. Robert Louis Stevenson. **CP-StevR**

End of winter seeped up, The. Julian Barely Misses Zimmer's Brains. Paul Zimmer. **SP-ZimmP**

End, The Beginning, The. David Herbert Lawrence. **CP-LawrD**

End was more of a melting, The. The Death of Will. Charles Tomlinson. **CP-TomlC**

Endanger it, and the Demand. Emily Dickinson. **CP-DickE**

Endearing Waltz!—to thy more melting tune. Byron. **DIP** *Fr.* The Waltz. **CP-Byron**

Ended, a story is history. Wendell Berry. *Fr.* Rising. **CP-BerrW**

Ended Day, An. Walt Whitman. **CP-WhitW**

Ended, ere it begun. Emily Dickinson. **CP-DickE**

Endegeeste. Howard Nemerov. **CP-NemeH**

Ending, An. Howard Nemerov. **CP-NemeH**

Ending. Alice Walker. **CP-WalkA**

Endings. Stephen Berg. **SP-BergS**

Endings. Derek Walcott. **CP-WalcD**

Endless. Muriel Rukeyser. **CP-RukeM**

Endless and flooded, An. Sunday, 4 A.M. Elizabeth Bishop. **CP-BishE**

Endless Anxiety. David Herbert Lawrence. **CP-LawrD**

Endless Cycle. "Lou Reed." **SP-ReedL**

Endless generations of mankind swarming together. The Procession. John Gould Fletcher. **SP-FletJ** *Fr.* The Parables of Christ.

Endless Life. Lawrence Ferlinghetti. **SP-FerlL**

Endless line of splendor, An. Foreign Missions in Battle Array. Nicholas Vachel Lindsay. **CP-LindV**

Endless London / mourns for that knowledge. Geoffrey Hill. *Fr.* Churchill's Funeral. **CP-HillG**

Endless part of disintegration, The. The Wisdom of Insecurity. Richard Eberhart. **CP-EberR**

Endless Pavement. Robert Ranke Graves. **CP-GravR**

Endless the splendid life of the world. Endless Life. Lawrence Ferlinghetti. **SP-FerlL**

Endlessly, endlessly, / The definition of mortality. George Oppen. *Fr.* Image of the Engine. **CP-OppeG**

Endlessly to no end wending. Me and the Rock. Stanley Jasspon Kunitz. **CP-KuniS**

Endor. Howard Nemerov. **CP-NemeH**

Endorsement to the Deed of Separation, in the April of 1816. Byron. **CP-Byron**

Endow the Living—with the Tears. Emily Dickinson. **CP-DickE**

Ends. Robert Frost. **CP-FrosR**

Ends of the crisp buds she chips, The. Gerard Manley Hopkins. *Fr.* Fragments. **CP-HopkG**

Endure friend-parting yet, old soldier. To a Friend Parting. Robert Penn Warren. **SP-WarrR**

Endure Hardness. Christina Georgina Rossetti. **CP-RosC2**

Endure what life God gives and ask no longer span. From "Oedipus at Colonus." William Butler Yeats. *Fr.* A Man Young and Old. **CP-YeatW**

Endymion: Poetic Romance. John Keats. **CP-KeatJ**

Hymn to Pan. **ChER; MeMBP; OBRV; PoEL-4**

Life Again. **SeCePo**

"Muse of native land! loftiest Muse!" **EnRP**

"O Moon! the oldest shades 'mong oldest trees." **EnRP**

"O sovereign power of love! O grief! O balm!" **EnRP; OBNC**

Sleeping Youth, A. **SeCePo**

Song of the Indian Maid. **NOBE; OAEP; OBEV**

(O Sorrow!) **CH**

Song of the Indian Maid, The ("Beneath my palm-trees, by the riverside"). **NOBE**

Thing of Beauty, A. **BLPL; CTC; EBEvV; EnRP; FHYEP; FaBV; FaFP; FiP; ImPo; LiTB; MeMBP; NIP; NOBRP; NTP; OAEP; OBNC; OBRV; OXAEP-2; PoPl; PrIm; TRV; TreF**

Endymion, your star is steadfast now. To Endymion. Countee Cullen. **CP-CullC**

Enemies of a House. John Updike. **CP-UpdiJ**

Enemies of the Angels, The. John Berryman. **CP-BerrJ**

Enemy, The. Thomas McGrath. **SP-McGrT**

Enemy, The. Alice Walker. **CP-WalkA**

Enemy Number One. Carl Sandburg. **CP-SandC**

Enemy [*or* en'my] of life, decayer of all kind, The [*or* Th']. Sir Thomas Wyatt. **CP-WyatT**

Enemy of Those Who Are Enemies of Sleep. Jean Garrigue. **SP-GarrJ**

Enemy's not poverty. It's wind, The. South Italy, Remote and Stone. Richard Hugo. **CP-HugoR**

Enemy's Portrait, The. Thomas Hardy. **CP-HardT**

Energetic Women. David Herbert Lawrence. **CP-LawrD**

Energy: A Villanelle. John Updike. **CP-UpdiJ**

Energy of the Pre-World as a Bungee Cable Jumper. Tom Clark. **SP-ClarT**

"Enforced lapse . . . . The." Tom Clark. **SP-ClarT**

Enfranchising cable, silvered by the sea. Granite and Steel. Marianne Craig Moore. **CP-MoorM**

Eng. Stevie Smith. **CP-SmitS**

Engelberg, the Hill of Angels. William Wordsworth. *Fr.* Memorials of a Tour of the Continent; 1820. **CP-WorW2**

Engine and tender, old loaf-shaped Pullman. The Old Trip by Dream Train. Brendan Galvin. **SP-GalvB**

Engine and transmission and the wheels, The. The Great Society, Mark X. Howard Nemerov. **CP-NemeH**

Engine Drain, The. Stevie Smith. **CP-SmitS**

Engine House, The. Wystan Hugh Auden. **CP-AudWJ**

Engine is killing the track, the track is silver, The. Totem. Sylvia Plath. **CP-PlatS**

Engine Room, S.S. Sappa Creek, The. Gary Snyder. **CP-SnydG**

Engine tells the knell of parting day, The. With Midsummer Devotion from All the Little Animals to Their Beloved Harteebeeste. Malcolm Lowry. **CP-LowrM**

Engines of Gloom and Affection. John Yau. **SP-YauJo**

("Sky is green, and there is no book to tell us what it means, The.") **SP-YauJo**

England. William Cowper. *See* Effeminate Englishmen.

England. Donald Davie. **CP-DavDo**

England. Walter de la Mare. **CP-DeLaW**

England. Marianne Craig Moore. **CP-MoorM**

England Again. John Gould Fletcher. **SP-FletJ**

England! awake! awake! awake! William Blake. **EnRP; FHYEP; NoP; OBNC; OBRV** *Fr.* Jerusalem; The Emanation of the Giant Albion. **CP-BlakW**

(Prelude: "England! awake! awake! awake!") **OBNC**

England before the Storm. George Meredith. **CP-MerG1**

England, confess your sins! toward the poor. An Exultation. William Carlos Williams. **CP-WilW2**

England in 1929. David Herbert Lawrence. **CP-LawrD**

England is a cosy little country. The Open Door. Rudyard Kipling. **CP-KiplR**

England Is Our Enemy. "Hugh MacDiarmid."

"It is possible that a change may come." **SP-MacDH**

"To distinctly English writers in England." **SP-MacDH**

England, my England--you have been my tutrix. Wystan Hugh Auden. **OBSV** *Fr.* Letter to Lord Byron. **CP-AudeW**

England seems full of graves to me. Spirits Summoned West. David Herbert Lawrence. **CP-LawrD**

England! the time is come when thou shouldst wean. William Wordsworth. **CP-WorW1**

England to Germany in 1914. Thomas Hardy. **CP-HardT**

England was always a country of men. England in 1929. David Herbert Lawrence. **CP-LawrD**

England! with all thy faults I love thee still. Byron. **PlP; UnPo** *Fr.* Beppo; a Venetian Story. **CP-Byron**

England, with all thy faults, I love thee still. Effeminate Englishmen. William Cowper. **EBEvV; ECEV; FiP** *Fr.* The Time-piece. *Fr.* The Task. **CP-CowpW**

England yet sleeps: was she not called of old? Percy Bysshe Shelley. *Fr.* Ode to Liberty. **CP-ShelP**

England, you had better go. Voices against England in the Night. Stevie Smith. **CP-SmitS**

England's Answer. Rudyard Kipling. **CP-KiplR**

England's Difficulty. Seamus Heaney. **SP-HeanS**

England's Double Knavery. "Hugh MacDiarmid."

"Left-wing poetry represents a rise in the price of bread." **SP-MacDH**

England's lads are miniature men. Boy-Man. Karl Shapiro. **SP-ShapK**

England's on the anvil—hear the hammers ring. The Anvil. Rudyard Kipling. **CP-KiplR**

English, The. Stevie Smith. **CP-SmitS**

English Advance at Flodden, The. Sir Walter Scott. **SP-ScotW** *Fr.* Marmion.

English Are So Nice!, The. David Herbert Lawrence. **CP-LawrD**

English Bards and Scotch Reviewers. Byron. **CP-Byron**

"As Sisyphus against the infernal steep." **OBSV**

"Behold! in various throngs the scribbling crew." **EnRP; OAEL-2**

"Illustrious Holland! hard would be his lot." **OBRV; OBSV**

"Next comes the dull disciple of thy school." **EPCY**

"Shall gentle Coleridge pass unnoticed here." **EPCY**

"There be who say, in these enlightened days." **EPCY**

"Thus Lays of Minstrels—may they be the last! -." **EPCY**

"Time has been, when yet the muse was young, The." **FHYEP**

"Time was, ere yet in these degenerate days." **EPCY; FHYEP**

"When some brisk youth, the tenant of a stall." **PF**

"When Vice triumphant holds her sov'reign sway." **FHYEP**

William Lisle Bowles. **OBNC**

English Breeze, An. Robert Louis Stevenson. **CP-StevR**

English Downs. Walter de la Mare. **CP-DeLaW**

English Encouragement of Art Cromeks Opinions Put Into Rhyme. William Blake. **CP-BlakW**

English Flag, The. Rudyard Kipling. **CP-KiplR**

English Garden in Austria, An. Randall Jarrell. **CP-JarrR**

English heart, my commandant, An. To Colonel Charles. George Meredith. **CP-MerG1**

English is a language than which none is sublimer. A Brief Guide to Rhyming, or, How Be the Little Busy Doth? Ogden Nash. **CP-NashO**

English Reformers in Exile. William Wordsworth. *Fr.* Ecclesiastical Sonnets. **CP-WorW2**

English Revenant, An. Donald Davie. **CP-DavDo**

English *Sapphick*, The. Thomas Campion. *Fr.* Observations in the Art of English Poesie. **CP-CampT**

English Song. Robert Burns. **CP-BurnR**

English Song. Robert Burns. **CP-BurnR**

("O wert thou, Love, but near me.") **CP-BurnR**

English Sparrows. Edna St. Vincent Millay. **CP-MillE**

English Train Compartment. John Updike. **CP-UpdiJ**

English Visitor, The. Stevie Smith. **CP-SmitS**

English Way, The. Rudyard Kipling. **CP-KiplR**

Englishman in Italy, The. Robert Browning. **CP-BroR1**

Piano di Sorrento. **FaBoPP; SeCePo**

(Englishman in Italy, The ["Time for rain! for your long hot dry autumn"].) **SeCePo**

Englishman in Italy, The ["Time for rain! for your long hot dry autumn"]. Robert Browning. *See* Piano di Sorrento.

Englishman in the old days, An. Carl Sandburg. **FYAP** *Fr.* The People, Yes. **CP-SandC**

Enhanced in a tower, asleep, dreaming about him. The Garden. Robert Ranke Graves. **CP-GravR**

Enid's Song. Tennyson. **FaBoRV** *Fr.* Geraint and Enid. *Fr.* Idylls of the King. **CP-TennA**

Enigma, The. Richard Eberhart. **CP-EberR**

Enigma, An. Edgar Allan Poe. **CP-PoeEd**

Enigmas. Frederick Morgan. **SP-MorgF**

Aubade: "Who has hold of Juliet's nipples."

Mirror.

Shame.

Thaw.

Enion Replies from the Caverns of the Grave. William Blake. **OBNC** *Fr.* Vala; or The Four Zoas. **CP-BlakW**

Enitharmon Revives with Los. William Blake. **OBNC** *Fr.* Vala; or The Four Zoas. **CP-BlakW**

(Enitharmon's Song.) **ChTr**

Enitharmon's Song. William Blake. *See* Enitharmon Revives with Los.

Enjoyable clouds, and a man comes. Expanses. James Dickey. **CP-DickJ**

Enkindled Spring, The. David Herbert Lawrence. **CP-LawrD**

Enlightened Teacher, gladly from thy hand. To the Rev. Christopher Wordsworth, D.D., Master of Harrow School. William Wordsworth. **CP-WorW2**

Enniscorthy Suite. Charles Olson. **CP-OlsoC**

Ennui. Langston Hughes. **SP-HughL**

Eno aged Mother. The Book of Los. William Blake. **CP-BlakW**

Enoch Arden. Tennyson. **CP-TennA**

November in the Isle of Wight. **FaBoPP**

Enormous and solid. The Grove. Octavio Paz, *tr. fr. Spanish by* Elizabeth Bishop. **CP-BishE**

Enormous cloud-mountains that form over Point Lobos and into the sunset. Clouds of Evening. Robinson Jeffers. **CP-JefR1**

Enormous head of a bison, The. The Head on the Table. John Haines. **SP-HainJ**

Enormous heat has encircled the garden, The. Zenith. Jenny Joseph. **SP-JoseJ**

Enormous Love, it's no good asking. Randall Jarrell. **CP-JarrR**

Enormous moon, that rise behind these hills. Edna St. Vincent Millay. **CP-MillE**

Enormous mortgage must be paid somehow, The. The Dispossessed. Sylvia Plath. **CP-PlatS**

Enormous tragedy of the dream in the peasant's bent shoulders, The. Canto 74. Ezra Pound. **SP-PounE** *Fr.* Cantos. **CP-PoCan**

Enough. Archie Randolph Ammons. **SP-AmmoA**

Enough. Robert Creeley. **CP-CreeR**

Enough. Marianne Craig Moore. **CP-MoorM**

Enough. Marianne Craig Moore. **CP-MoorM**

Enough: and leave the rest to fame. An Epitaph upon —. Andrew Marvell. **CP-MarvA**

Enough! for see, with dim association. Transubstantiation. William Wordsworth. *Fr.* Ecclesiastical Sonnets. **CP-WorW2**

Enough is done highminded friend go sleep. Ralph Waldo Emerson. **CP-EmerR**

Enough is enough. If you got. Tanck's Epilogue. Hayden Carruth. **CP-CarHS** *Fr.* Songs About What Comes Down: The Complete Works of Mr. Septic Tank.

Enough is so vast a sweetness. Emily Dickinson. **SP-DickE**

Enough of climbing toil!—Ambition treads. Ode to Lycoris. William Wordsworth. **CP-WorW2**

Enough of garlands, of the Arcadian crook. Suggested at Tyndrum in a Storm. William Wordsworth. **CP-WorW2**

Enough of rose-bud lips, and eyes. The Russian Fugitive. William Wordsworth. **CP-WorW2**

Enough of Thought, Philosopher. Emily Brontë. **CP-BronE**
(Philosopher, The.) **CP-BronE**
"O for the time when I shall sleep." **OBD**

Enough, small Room,—though all too true. Arthur Hugh Clough. **SP-ClouA**

Enough! we're tired, my heart and I. My Heart and I. Elizabeth Barrett Browning. **CP-BroEB**

Enquiring fields, courtesies, The. Pastoral. Allen Tate. **CP-TateA**

Enrica, 1865. Christina Georgina Rossetti. **CP-RosC1**

Enrich My Resignation. Hart Crane. **CP-CranH**

Enriching the Earth. Wendell Berry. **CP-BerrW**

Ensamhet. Chuck Miller. **SP-MillC**

Ensenada. Jim Morrison. **SP-MorrJ**

Enter into His gates with thanksgiving, *sel., v. 4.* Bible, *O.T. See* Psalm 100: "Make a joyful noise unto the Lord, all ye lands."

"Enter my palace," if a prince should say. The Founder of the Feast. Robert Browning. **CP-BroR2**

Enter no(silence is the blood whose flesh). Edward Estlin Cummings. **CP-CummE**

Enter the chilly no-man's land of about. The Ghost's Leavetaking. Sylvia Plath. **CP-PlatS**

Enter the ruined hacienda: see Christ. Prophecy in Stone. Edwin Rolfe. **CP-RolfE**

Enter the Slip. Jim Morrison. **SP-MorrJ**

Enter these enchanted woods. George Meredith. *Fr.* The Woods of Westermain. **CP-MerG1**

Enter these enchanted woods. The Woods of Westermain. George Meredith. **CP-MerG1**

Enter This Deserted House. Shel Silverstein. **SP-SilS2**

Enter with him. Legend. Wystan Hugh Auden. **CP-AudeW**

Entered in an event. Jogger. Daniel Gerard Hoffman. **SP-HoffD**

Entered in the Minutes. Louis MacNeice. **CP-MacNL**
Barcelona in Wartime.
Business Men.
Didymus. **EaLo**
Night Club. **FaBoDD; OxBSP**

Entering, I find friends everywhere. Saturday Night at the Elk's Club. Richard Shelton. **SP-ShelR**

Entering Minetta's soft yellow chrome, to the acrid bathroom. The Old Village before I Die. Allen Ginsberg. **CP-GinsA**

Entering the Kingdom. Mary Oliver. **SP-OlivM**

Entering the midnight. Talking Late with the Governor about the Budget. Gary Snyder. **CP-SnydG**

Entering the Storm, Unable to Swim, Zimmer, Rollo, and Cecil Are Saved. Paul Zimmer. **SP-ZimmP**

Enters give / whose lost is his found. Edward Estlin Cummings. **CP-CummE**

Entertainment of War, The. Roy Fisher. *Fr.* City. **SP-FishR**

Entertainment, or Porch-Verse, at the Marriage of Mr. Henry Northleigh [*or* Hen. Northly] and the Most Witty Mrs. Lettice Yard, The. Robert Herrick. **CP-HerrR**

Enthroned in plastic, shrouded in wool, diamond crowned. To the Body. Allen Ginsberg. **CP-GinsA**

Enthroned upon the mighty truth. Justice. Paul Laurence Dunbar. **CP-DunbP**

Enthused I went to Yale, enthused. The Story of My Life. John Updike. **CP-UpdiJ**

"Enthusiasm", An. Charles Olson. **CP-OlsoC**

Enthusiasm for Hats. Howard Nemerov. **CP-NemeH**

Enthusiast, The. Herman Melville. **SP-MelvH**

Enthusiast Is a Devotee Is a Rooter, or, Mr. Hemingway, Meet Mr. Stengel, An. Ogden Nash. **CP-NashO**

Entire Surrender, The. Jeanne Marie Bouvier de la Motte-Guyon, *tr. fr. French by* William Cowper. **CP-CowpW**

Entirely. Louis MacNeice. **CP-MacNL**

Entity, The. William Carlos Williams. **CP-WilW1**

Entraining to Southampton in the parlor car with Jap and Vincent, I. Joe's Jacket. Frank O'Hara. **SP-OharF**

Entre deux belles femmes dans un seul lit. Dans un Seul Lit. Robert Ranke Graves. **CP-GravR**

Entre la scène et moi. La Mouche. Samuel Beckett. **CP-BeckS**

Entre Nous. Robert Creeley. **CP-CreeR**

Entropy. Miller Williams. **SP-WillM**

Entry. Edwin Rolfe. **CP-RolfE**

Enueg II. Samuel Beckett. **CP-BeckS**

Enueg I. Samuel Beckett. **CP-BeckS**

Enviable Isles, The. Herman Melville. **SP-MelvH**

Envious and foul disease, could there not be. An Epigram. To the Small-Pox. Ben Jonson. **CP-JonsB**

Envious wits, what hath been mine offence. Sonnet 104. Sir Philip Sidney. **PoE; Son** *Fr.* Astrophil and Stella. **SP-SidnP**

Envisage it: the Atlantic. Behind the North Wind. Donald Davie. **CP-DavDo**

Envoi: "From the red chimneys smoke climbs slow and straight." Wystan Hugh Auden. **CP-AudWJ**

Envoi: "Particulars they want." Robert Creeley. **CP-CreeR**

Envoi: "Take up your load and go, lad." Wystan Hugh Auden. **CP-AudWJ**

Envoi: "There is no now for us but always." Robert Ranke Graves. **CP-GravR**

Envoi: "You go / Now you are glad." Wystan Hugh Auden. **CP-AudWJ**

Envoi: "Go, dumb-born book." Ezra Pound. *See* Envoi (1919).

Envoi (1919). Ezra Pound. **HAP; MoP; UnPo; VGW** *Fr.* Hugh Selwyn Mauberley. (Life and Contacts). **SP-PounE**
(Envoi: "Go, dumb-born book.") **MoAB; MoAmPo; OxBA**

Envoi No. 2. Wystan Hugh Auden. **CP-AudWJ**

Envoi: The Wind Carol. Lewis Turco. *Fr.* Bordello. **SP-TurcL**
(Wind Carol, The.) **SM**

Envoi to the Reader. Basil Bunting. **CP-BuntB**

Envoi to the Same. Another, *see also* To the Lady Elizabeth Queen of Bohemia. George Herbert. **CP-HerbG**

Envoy, The. Geoffrey Chaucer. *See* Go, Little Book ("Go, litel book, go litel myn tragedy").

Envoy: "Go, little book, and wish to all." Robert Louis Stevenson. **CP-StevR**

Envoy: "Love, all day there has been at the edge of my mind." Wendell Berry. **CP-BerrW**

Envoy to Six Years. Gary Snyder. *Fr.* Six Years. **CP-SnydG**

Envy. Stephen Dobyns. **SP-DobyS**

Envy, sl. diff. vers. Hilda Doolittle. *See* Fragment 68: "I envy you your chance of death."

Envy. Edmund Spenser. **TW** *Fr.* The Faerie Queene. **CP-Spens**

Envy, if thy jaundiced eye. At Whigham's Inn, Sanquar. Robert Burns. **CP-BurnR**

Envy the mad killer who lies in the ditch and grieves. Crime. Robert Penn Warren. **SP-WarrR**

Envy, why carp'st thou my time is spent so ill. 1.15. Ovid. **CP-MarlC**, *tr. by* Christopher Marlowe; *Fr.* Elegies.

Enzyme Poem for Suzanne, An. Paul Zimmer. **SP-ZimmP**

Eolian Harp, The. Samuel Taylor Coleridge. **EnRP; FHYEP; NAEL-2; NOBRP; NoP; OAEL-2** *Fr.* Effusions. **CP-ColeS**

Eons gone by the sea. Hayden Carruth. *Fr.* North Winter. **CP-CarHL**

Eos. Tom Clark. **SP-ClarT**

Epeisodia. Thomas Hardy. **CP-HardT**

Ephemera. William Butler Yeats. **CP-YeatW**

Ephemeridae. Daniel Gerard Hoffman. **SP-HoffD**

Ephesians 4:30. Grieve not the Holy Spirit, etc. George Herbert. *See* And art thou grieved, sweet and sacred Dove.

Ephraim Repenting. William Cowper. **ChIV-1** *Fr.* Olney Hymns. **CP-CowpW**

Epi-Strauss-ium. Arthur Hugh Clough. **SP-ClouA**

Epic Expands, The. Robert Creeley. **CP-CreeR**

Epic Stars, The. Robinson Jeffers. **CP-JefR3**

Epic, The [Morte d'Arthur], *conclusion to* Morte d'Arthur. Tennyson. **NAEL-2** *Fr.* Morte d'Arthur. **CP-TennA**

Epic, The [Morte d'Arthur], *introduction to* Morte d'Arthur. Tennyson. **NAEL-2** *Fr.* Morte d'Arthur. **CP-TennA**

Epicoene; or, The Silent Woman. Ben Jonson.
"Modest, and fair, for fair and good are near." **CP-JonsB**
"Still to be neat, still to be dressed [*or* Drest]." **CP-JonsB**

Epidermal Macabre. Theodore Roethke. **CP-RoetT**

Epigon. Charles Olson. **CP-OlsoC**

Epigoni, The. Wystan Hugh Auden. **CP-AudeW**

Epigram: "Golden one is gone from the banquets, The." Hilda Doolittle. **CP-DoolH**

Epigram: "Lord Pam in the church (could [*or* cou'd] you think it) kneeled [*or* kneel'd] down." Jonathan Swift. **CP-SwifJ**

Epigram: "My Lord complains, that Pope, stark mad with gardens." Alexander Pope. **CP-PopeA**

Epigram: "None then should through thy beawty, Lawra, pine." Thomas Campion. *Fr.* Observations in the Art of English Poesie. **CP-CampT**

Epigram: "Peter complains, that God has given." Alexander Pope. **CP-PopeA**

Epigram: "To purify their wine some people bleed." William Cowper. **CP-CowpW**

Epigram: "When other Ladies to the Groves go down." Alexander Pope. **CP-PopeA**

Epigram: "Whoe'er he be that sojourns here." Robert Burns. **CP-BurnR**

Epigram, An: "Friend Rundle fell with grievous bump." Jonathan Swift. **CP-SwifJ**

Epigram, An: "In your indignation what mercy appears." Jonathan Swift. **CP-SwifJ**

Epigram, An: "Meles and Mincio, both your urns depress." *Unknown. Fr.* Complimentary Pieces to Milton. **CP-CowpW**

Epigram, An: "Merlin, the great King Arthur being slaine." Thomas Campion. *Fr.* Lord Hay's Mask.

Epigram, An: "That you have seen the pride, beheld the sport." Ben Jonson. **CP-JonsB**

Epigram from the French: "Sir, I admit your general [*or* gen'ral] Rule." Alexander Pope, *also at. to* Matthew Prior *and to* Samuel Taylor Coleridge. **CP-PopeA**

Epigram in a Maid of Honour's Prayer-Book. Alexander Pope. **CP-PopeA**

Epigram is but a feeble thing, An. William Cowper. **CP-CowpW**

Epigram of Homer, An. Homer, *tr. fr. Greek by* William Cowper. **CP-CowpW**

Epigram on a Painting of Golgotha. Allen Ginsberg. **CP-GinsA**

Epigram on an Event in Col. Evans's Redoubted Performances in Spain. William Wordsworth. **CP-WorW2**

Epigram on an Old Lady Who Had Some Curious Notions Respecting the Soul. Byron. **CP-Byron**

Epigram on Capt. Francis Grose, the Celebrated Antiquary. Robert Burns. **CP-BurnR**

Epigram on Colley Cibber. Samuel Johnson. **CP-JohnS**

Epigram on Doctor Babington. Robert Burns. *See* That there is falsehood in his looks.

Epigram on Fasting. Jonathan Swift. **CP-SwifJ**

Epigram on James Baillie Swan. Robert Burns. *Fr.* Dumfries Epigrams. **CP-BurnR**

Epigram on Rough Roads. Robert Burns. **CP-BurnR**

Epigram on Said Occasion. Robert Burns. **CP-BurnR**

Epigram on School Days. Robert Browning. **CP-BroR2**

Epigram on Scolding, An. Jonathan Swift. **CP-SwifJ**

Epigram on Sir Edward Coke, when He Was Lord Chief Justice of England, An. Ben Jonson. **CP-JonsB**

Epigram on the Court Pucell, An. Ben Jonson. **CP-JonsB**

Epigram on the Hermitage at Richmond. Jonathan Swift. **CP-SwifJ**

Epigram on the Prince's Birth. 1630, An. Ben Jonson. **CP-JonsB**

Epigram on the Refusal of the University of Oxford to Subscribe to His Translation of Homer. William Cowper. **CP-CowpW**

Epigram on the Toasts of the Kit-Cat Club, Anno 1716. Alexander Pope. **CP-PopeA**

Epigram on William, Lord Burl[eigh], Lo[rd] High Treasurer of England, An. Ben Jonson. **CP-JonsB**

Epigram on Wood's Brass Money, An. Jonathan Swift. **CP-SwifJ**

Epigram: Political Reflexion. Howard Nemerov. *See* Political Reflexion [*or* Reflection].

Epigram. To a Friend and Son. Ben Jonson. **CP-JonsB**

Epigram. To K[ing] Charles for a[n] Hundred Pounds He Sent Me in My Sickness. 1629. An. Ben Jonson. **CP-JonsB**

Epigram to My Bookseller. Ben Jonson. **CP-JonsB**

Epigram to My Jovial Good Friend Mr Robert Dover, on His Great Instauration of His Hunting and Dancing at Cotswold, An. Ben Jonson. **CP-JonsB**

Epigram to My Muse, the Lady Digby, on Her Husband, Sir Kenelm Digby, An. Ben Jonson. **CP-JonsB**

Epigram. To our Great and Good K[ing] Charles on his Anniversary Day. 1629, An. Ben Jonson. **CP-JonsB**

Epigram to the Coucillor That Pleaded and Carried the Cause, An. Ben Jonson. **CP-JonsB**

Epigram. To the Honoured———, Countess of———, An. Ben Jonson. **CP-JonsB**

Epigram. To the Household. 1630, An. Ben Jonson. **CP-JonsB**

Epigram to the Queen, Then Lying In. 1630, An. Ben Jonson. **CP-JonsB**

Epigram. To the Small-Pox, An. Ben Jonson. **CP-JonsB**

Epigram. To Thomas Lo[rd] Ellsmere, the Last Term He Sat Chancellor, An. Ben Jonson. **CP-JonsB**

Epigram. To William, Earl of Newcastle, An. Ben Jonson. **CP-JonsB**

Epigram. To William, Earl of Newcastle, An. Ben Jonson. **CP-JonsB**

Epigramma: "Haeredem (ut spes est) pariet nova nupta Scot Anglum", *accompanied by English translation.* Thomas Campion. *Fr.* Lord Hay's Mask.

Epigramma: "Quid tu te numeris immisces? anne medentem", *accompanied by English translation.* Thomas Campion. *Fr.* Lord Hay's Mask.

Epigramma in Duos Montes Amosclivium et Bilboreum: Farfacio [Epigram on Two Mountains, Almscliff and Bilbrough: To Fairfax]. Andrew Marvell, *tr. fr. Latin by* William A. McQueen *and* Kiffin A. Rockwell. **CP-MarvA**

Epigramma Martialis. Lib. VIII. lxxvii. The Same Translated. Ben Jonson, *tr. fr. the Latin of* Martial. **CP-JonsB**

Epigramme: "All in sattin Oteny will be suited." Thomas Campion. *Fr.* Observations in the Art of English Poesie. **CP-CampT**

Epigramme: "All wonders Barnzy speakes, all grosely faind." Thomas Campion. *Fr.* Observations in the Art of English Poesie. **CP-CampT**

Epigramme: "Arthure brooks only those that brooke not him." Thomas Campion. *Fr.* Observations in the Art of English Poesie. **CP-CampT**

Epigramme: "At all thou frankly throwst, while, Frank, thy wife." Thomas Campion. *Fr.* Observations in the Art of English Poesie. **CP-CampT**

Epigramme: "Barnzy stiffly vowes that hees no Cuckold." Thomas Campion. *Fr.* Observations in the Art of English Poesie. **CP-CampT**

Epigramme: "Buffe loves fat vians, fat ale, fat all things." Thomas Campion. *Fr.* Observations in the Art of English Poesie. **CP-CampT**

Epigramme: "Cease, fond wretch, to love, so oft deluded." Thomas Campion. *Fr.* Observations in the Art of English Poesie. **CP-CampT**

Epigramme: "Drue feasts no Puritans; the churles, he saith." Thomas Campion. *Fr.* Observations in the Art of English Poesie. **CP-CampT**

Epigramme: "Drue gives thee money, yet thou thankst not him." Thomas Campion. *Fr.* Observations in the Art of English Poesie. **CP-CampT**

Epigramme: "Hast ever seen a man." William Carlos Williams. **CP-WilW1**

Epigramme: "His late losse the Wireless Higs in order." Thomas Campion. *Fr.* Observations in the Art of English Poesie. **CP-CampT**

Epigramme: "If fancy can not erre which vertue guides." Thomas Campion. *Fr.* Observations in the Art of English Poesie. **CP-CampT**

Epigramme: "Kate can fancy only berdles husbands." Thomas Campion. *Fr.* Observations in the Art of English Poesie. **CP-CampT**

Epigramme: "Lockly spits apace, the rhewme he cals it." Thomas Campion. *Fr.* Observations in the Art of English Poesie. **CP-CampT**

Epigramme: "Phoebe all the rights Elisa claymeth." Thomas Campion. *Fr.* Observations in the Art of English Poesie. **CP-CampT**

Epigramme: "Smith, by sute divorst, the knowne adultres." Thomas Campion. *Fr.* Observations in the Art of English Poesie. **CP-CampT**

Epigramme: "Thou telst me, Barnzy, Dawson hath a wife." Thomas Campion. *Fr.* Observations in the Art of English Poesie. **CP-CampT**

Epigramme: "Tosts as snakes or as the mortall Henbane." Thomas Campion. *Fr.* Observations in the Art of English Poesie. **CP-CampT**

Epigramme: "What though Harry braggs, let him be noble." Thomas Campion. *Fr.* Observations in the Art of English Poesie. **CP-CampT**

Epigramme: "Why droopst thou, Trefeild? Will Hurst the Banker." Thomas Campion. *Fr.* Observations in the Art of English Poesie. **CP-CampT**

Epigramme: "Wiseman wary lives, yet most secure, A." Thomas Campion. *Fr.* Observations in the Art of English Poesie. **CP-CampT**

Epigrams. Hilda Doolittle. **CP-DoolH**
  "O ruthless, perilous, imperious hate."
  "Torture me not with this or that or this."

Epigrams. Charles Henri Ford. **SP-FordC**
  "And music is still a mystery!"
  "And oh what a beautiful child you are."
  "Andromache, I think of you! / When the war goes on forever."
  "Christine is the girl I adore."
  "Death in all its forms."
  "Do birds need to fly so much."
  "Even when the heart of the world is found."
  "Feet of his days have been mangled, The."
  "Glass violin is broken, The."
  "Hair of her head could be a bed, The."
  "Happy? The very eye of the world."
  "I love my animal heart."
  "If someone asked you to be happy."
  "Let us make of day a delirium."
  "Little lamb who made thee? / Ho but the egg is growing hair."
  "Not everyone has plenty of time to die in."
  "Pleasure boat, pleasure boat where has it gone?"

"Sandman, I'd tear you limb from limb."
"Simple is madness, like a kick in the pants."
"So you'd eat the ear of Van Gogh!"
"Tender blows the leaf, tender drops the eye."
"What hard work it takes."
"Will of the weed to startle, The."
"Wind is the breath of it."
"World's a mirror. Break it and you die!, The."
Epigrams. Martial, *tr. fr. Latin.*
"Although you fill amethyst cups." **SP-MattW**
"Art and Cal have made a trade." **SP-MattW**
"Because in December when the gifts fly—." **SP-MattW**
"*Gaurus* pretends to *Cato's* fame." **CP-JohnS**
"Here he is whom you read and clamor for." **SP-MattW**
" 'It's nothing,' whatever." **SP-MattW**
"Long year I squeezed out a tiny book, The." **SP-MattW**
"Not him I prize who poorly gains." **CP-JohnS**
"Old friend, suppose luck grants to us." **SP-MattW**
"Papylus had a dong so long." **SP-MattW**
"Slave that Cinna's named his cook, The." **SP-MattW**
"Someone we both know, Rufus, looked me." **SP-MattW**
"Surrounded by eunuchs and limp as a tissue." **SP-MattW**
"Ted's studio burnt down, with all his poems." **SP-MattW**
" 'Tell me the truth, Mark,' you insist." **SP-MattW**
"Ten times a year you're ill, Malingerus." **SP-MattW**
"That plush hair Fabulla wears?" **SP-MattW**
"Why is it modern poets are ignored." **SP-MattW**
"You announce that you are beautiful." **SP-MattW**
"You lie and I concur. You 'give'." **SP-MattW**
"You sold a slave just yesterday." **SP-MattW**
"You wonder, Lupus, who's the best schoolmaster." **SP-MattW**
"You're hot to trot? Well then I'm not." **SP-MattW**
Epigrams: "Oh, Castlereagh! thou art a patriot now." Byron. **CP-Byron**
Epigrams: "Wasp, climbing the window pane." Howard Nemerov. **CP-NemeH**
Absent-Minded Professor. **ELU**
April.
Hunt Goes By, The.
Invocation: "Wasp, climbing the window pane."
Lucilius.
Mythological Beast.
Old Story, An.
Political Reflexion [*or* Reflection]. **ELU**
    (Epigram: Political Reflexion.) **NIP**
    (Sparrow in the Zoo, The.) **MoP**
Spiral Shell, A.
Epigrams Occasion'd by an Invitation to Court. Alexander Pope. **CP-PopeA**
"*Adam* had fallen twice, if for an apple."
"In the *lines* that you sent, are the *Muses* and *Graces.*"
"On Sunday at six, in the street that's call'd *Gerrard.*"
"They may talk of the *goddesses* in *Ida* veils."
"They say *Argyll*'s a wit, for what?"
"You *Bellenden, Griffin,* and little *Lepell.*"
Epigrams Occasioned by Cibber's Verses in Praise of Nash. Alexander Pope. **CP-PopeA**
"*Cibber!* write all thy Verses upon Glasses."
"O *Nash!* more blest in ev'ry other thing."
Epigrams on His Garden Shed. William Cowper. **CP-CowpW**
Epigrams on Lord Galloway. Robert Burns. **CP-BurnR**
Lord Galloway. **DBV; OxBoLi**
On Lord Galloway. **FaBoEE**
    (On the Same Nobleman.)
On Seeing the Beautiful County-Seat of Lord G———.
To the Same, on the Author Being Threatened with His Resentment.
Epigraph. William Blake. *See* I give you the end of a golden string.
Epigraph: "Lot's wife, / married to chance." Robert Creeley. **CP-CreeR**
Epigraph to *Call Me Ishmael.* Charles Olson. **CP-OlsoC**
Epigraph to "The Woodlanders." Thomas Hardy. **CP-HardT**
Epilogue: "And how, and how, in faith—a pretty plot." Sir John Suckling. *Fr.* The Goblins. **CP-SuckJ**
Epilogue: "At the midnight in the silence of the sleep-time." Robert Browning. **CP-BroR2**
Epilogue: "By the glare of the guttering torch." John Gould Fletcher. **SP-FletJ** *Fr.* Branches of Adam.

Epilogue: "He died in December. He must descend." John Berryman. **CP-BerrJ**
Epilogue: "If Luther's day expand to Darwin's year." Herman Melville. **SP-MelvH** *Fr.* Clarel: A Poem and Pilgrimage in the Holy Land.
Epilogue: "Lily, being white not red, The." Countee Cullen. **CP-CullC**
Epilogue: "Oh, Love—no, Love! All the noise below, Love." Robert Browning. **CP-BroR2**
Epilogue: "On the first of the Feast of Feasts." Robert Browning. **CP-BroR1**
Epilogue: "Our play is done; and yours doth now begin." Sir John Suckling. *Fr.* Aglaura. **CP-SuckJ**
Epilogue: "Plays are like feasts; and every act should be." Sir John Suckling. *Fr.* The Fifth Act of Aglaura As Presented to the Court. *Fr.* Aglaura. **CP-SuckJ**
Epilogue: "Poets pour us wine, The." Robert Browning. **CP-BroR2**
Epilogue: "There's something in a stupid ass." Byron. **CP-Byron**
Epilogue: "Truly my Satan thou art but a dunce." William Blake. **HAP; ImPo; OAEL-2; OBNC; PeECV; PoE; WeW** *Fr.* The Gates of Paradise.
    (To the Accuser Who Is the God of This World.) **FHYEP; NoP; OxBSP; SCGP; TrGrPo**
Epilogue: "We have now set forth, in our imperfect way." Thomas Hardy. **CP-HardT** *Fr.* The Dynasts.
Epilogue [A] to *What Is She?.* Charlotte Smith. **CP-SmitC** *Fr.* What is She?
Epilogue [B] to *What Is She?.* Charlotte Smith. **CP-SmitC** *Fr.* What is She?
Epilogue [C] to *What Is She?.* Charlotte Smith. **CP-SmitC** *Fr.* What is She?
Epilogue for a Masque of Purcell. Adrienne Rich. **CP-RicAE**
Epilogue for the Court, *sels.* Sir John Suckling. *Fr.* Aglaura. **CP-SuckJ**
Epilogue: " 'O where are you going?' said reader to rider." Wystan Hugh Auden. *See* "O where are you going?" said reader to rider.
Epilogue, The: "It was a dream delivered the epilogue." Charles Tomlinson. **CP-TomlC**
Epilogue, The: "Stubborne Author of the trifle, Crime, The." Richard Lovelace. **CP-LoveR**
Epilogue: The Burial of the Last Elder. John Ciardi. **SP-CiarJ**
Epilogue to a Human Drama. Stephen Spender. **CP-SpenS**
Epilogue to a Play for the Benefit of the Weavers in Ireland, An. Jonathan Swift. **CP-SwifJ**
Epilogue to Agamemnon. James Thomson. **CP-ThomJ**
Epilogue to Horace's *Carmen Seculare.* Samuel Johnson. **CP-JohnS**
Epilogue to Mr. Rowe's *Jane Shore.* Alexander Pope. **CP-PopeA**
Epilogue to Mother's Day, Which Is To Be Published on Any Day But Mother's Day. Ogden Nash. **CP-NashO**
Epilogue to Œnia. Allen Tate. *Fr.* The Progress of Œnia. **CP-TateA**
Epilogue to Tancred and Sigismunda. James Thomson. **CP-ThomJ**
Epilogue to the Adventures While Preaching the Gospel of Beauty. Nicholas Vachel Lindsay. **CP-LindV**
Epilogue to *The Distrest Mother,* An. Samuel Johnson. **CP-JohnS**
Epilogue to the Man of Laws' Tale, The. Geoffrey Chaucer. *Fr.* The Canterbury Tales. **CP-ChauG**
Shipman, The ("Parson him answered, 'Benedcite!,' The"). **ACP**
Epilogue to the Merchant's Tale. Geoffrey Chaucer. *Fr.* The Canterbury Tales. **CP-ChauG**
Epilogue to the Nun's Priest's Tale. Geoffrey Chaucer. *Fr.* The Canterbury Tales. **CP-ChauG**
Epilogue to the Satires, in Two Dialogues. Alexander Pope. **CP-PopeA**
"Ask you what provocation I have had?" **ECEV; EPCY; NOBE; NOEC; OBSV**
    (Art of Satire, The.) **ECEV**
    (Defence of Satire.) **NOEC**
    (Power of Ridicule, The.) **NOBE**
"Spare then the person, and expose the vice." **OBSV**
"Virtue may choose the high or low degree." **NOBE; OBSV**
    (Triumph of Vice, The.) **NOBE; OBSV**
Epilogue to the Second Part of *The Conquest of Granada.* John Dryden. **SP-DrydJ** *Fr.* The Conquest of Granada.
Epilogue to the University of Oxford, 1674. John Dryden. *See* Oft has our Poet wisht [*or* wished], this happy Seat.
Epilogue to *Tyrannic[k] Love.* John Dryden. **SP-DrydJ** *Fr.* Tyrannic Love.
Epiphany. Jim Carroll. **SP-CarrJ**
Epiphany. Christina Georgina Rossetti. **CP-RosC2**
Epiphany. Christopher Smart. **NOCV** *Fr.* Hymns and Spiritual Songs for the Fasts and Festivals of the Church of England. **SP-SmarC**
Epiphanye, The. Robert Southwell. **CP-SoutR**
Epiphanytide. Christina Georgina Rossetti. **CP-RosC2**

Epipsychidion, *see also* Fragments Connected with Epipsychdion. Percy Bysshe Shelley. **CP-ShelP**

"Let us become the overhanging day." **OAEL-2**

Longest Journey, The. **OtMeF; OxBM**

"Spouse! Sister! Angel! Pilot of the Fate." **CBLP; ChER**

"Thy wisdom speaks in me, and bids me dare." **OAEL-2**

"True Love in this differs from gold and clay." **FHYEP; OBNC**

Episode, An. Wystan Hugh Auden. **CP-AudWJ**

Episode of Hands. Hart Crane. **CP-CranH**

Episode of Nisus and Euryalus, The. Byron. **CP-Byron**

Episode of Sarpedon, The. Homer, *tr.* by Alexander Pope. **CP-PopeA** *Fr.* The Iliad.

"Thus *Hector*, great in Arms, contends in vain."

Episode 17. William Carlos Williams. **CP-WilW1** *Fr.* Paterson.

Episodes. Walter de la Mare. **CP-DeLaW**

Episodes for a Panel. James McAuley. **SP-McAuJ** *Fr.* Studies for a Self-Portrait at Forty.

Epistemology. Richard Wilbur. **CP-WilbR**

Epistle: "Jesus loved the sunsets on Galilee." Carl Sandburg. **CP-SandC**

Epistle Answering to One That Asked to Be Sealed of the Tribe of Ben, An. Ben Jonson. **CP-JonsB**

Epistle Containing the Strange Medical Experience of Karshish, the Arab Physician, An. Robert Browning. **CP-BroR1**

Epistle V, to Mr. Addison. Alexander Pope. **CP-PopeA**

Epistle IV, to Richard Boyle, Earl of Burlington. Alexander Pope. **CP-PopeA**

"At Timon's villa let us pass a day." **NOEC; OBSV; PoE**

(At Timon's Villa.) **OBSV,** *ll.* 99–168;

(Timon's Villa.) **PoE,** *ll.* 99–180;

Epistle I, to Sir Richard Temple, Lord Cobham. Alexander Pope. **CP-PopeA**

"Coxcomb bird, so talkative and grave, The." **ImPo**

Epistle III, to Allen Lord Bathurst. Alexander Pope. **CP-PopeA**

Duke of Buckingham, The. **NOBE; OBEC**

(Death of Buckingham, The.) **FiP**

(Villers.) **FaBoDD**

Epistle to a Friend. Byron. **CP-Byron**

Epistle to a Friend ("They are not, sir, worst owers, that do pay"). Ben Jonson. **CP-JonsB**

Epistle to a Friend, An ("Censure not sharply then, but me advise"). Ben Jonson. **CP-JonsB**

Epistle to a Friend, An ("Sir, I am thankful, first, to heaven, for you"). Ben Jonson. **CP-JonsB**

Epistle to a Friend, to Persuade Him to the Wars, An. Ben Jonson. **CP-JonsB**

"Whole world here, leavened with madness, swells, The." **JCP**

Epistle to a Godson. Wystan Hugh Auden. **CP-AudeW**

Epistle to a Patron, An. Frank Templeton Prince. **CP-PrinF**

Epistle to a Protestant Lady in France, An. William Cowper. **CP-CowpW**

Epistle to a Young Friend. Robert Burns. **CP-BurnR**

Epistle to Albert Dew-Smith. Robert Louis Stevenson. **CP-StevR**

Epistle to Augusta. Byron. **CP-Byron**

Epistle to Be Left in the Earth. Archibald MacLeish. **CP-MacLA**

Epistle to Captn Willm Logan at Park. Robert Burns. **CP-BurnR**

Epistle to Charles Baxter. Robert Louis Stevenson. **CP-StevR**

Epistle to Davie, a Brother Poet. Robert Burns. **CP-BurnR**

Epistle to Dr. Arbuthnot, *in imitation of* Horace (*Satires*, Prologue). Alexander Pope. **CP-PopeA**

Apologia pro Vita Sua. **NOBE**

Atticus ("How did they fume, and stamp, and roar, and chafe"). **InPK; OBEC; TW; WHA**

Atticus ("Peace to all such! but were there one whose fires"). **AWP; InPK; NOBE; SeCePo; TRP; WHA**

(On Addison.) **IHNG**

"Bard whom pilf'red pastorals reknown, The." **OBSV**

Bufo. **OBEC; OBSV**

"Let Sporus tremble--'What? That thing of silk'." **AWP; ChTr; NOBE; OBSV; SCV**

(Sporus.) **AWP; ChTr; NOBE; OBSV**

"Shut, shut the door, good *John!* fatigu'd, I said." **OBCoV**

"There are, who to my person pay their court." **OBF**

"Why did [*or* do] I write? what sin to me unknown." **ChTr; EBEV; EPCY; FiP; TOF**

"Yet let me flap this bug with gilded wings." **ECEV**

Epistle to Dr. Nares. Christopher Smart. **SP-SmarC**

Epistle to Elizabeth, Countess of Rutland. Ben Jonson. **CP-JonsB**

Epistle. To Enrique Caracciolo Trejo. Donald Davie. **CP-DavDo**

Epistle to Hill. William Cowper. **CP-CowpW**

Epistle to Hugh Parker. Robert Burns. **CP-BurnR**

Epistle to J. L*****k, an Old Scotch Bard. Robert Burns. *See* While briers an' woodbines budding green.

Epistle to J. R******, Enclosing Some Poems. Robert Burns. **CP-BurnR**

Epistle to James Craggs, Esq., Secretary of State. Alexander Pope. **CP-PopeA**

Epistle to John Goldie in Kilmarnock, Author of, the Gospel Recovered. Robert Burns. **CP-BurnR**

Epistle to John Hamilton Reynolds. John Keats. **OBNC** *Fr.* To J. H. Reynolds, Esq. **CP-KeatJ**

Epistle to John Sherratt, Esq., An. Christopher Smart. **SP-SmarC**

Epistle. To Katharine, Lady Aubigny. Ben Jonson. **CP-JonsB**

Epistle to Lady Austen. William Cowper. **CP-CowpW**

Epistle to Léon-Paul Fargue. Archibald MacLeish. **CP-MacLA**

Epistle to Master Arth[ur] Squib, An. Ben Jonson. **CP-JonsB**

"Turn him, and see his threads; look if he be." **OBF**

Epistle to Master John Selden, An. Ben Jonson. **CP-JonsB**

"I know to whom I write. Here, I am sure." **OBF,** *ll.* 1–14;

Epistle to Miss [*or* Miss Teresa] Blount, on Her Leaving the Town after the Coronation. Alexander Pope. **CP-PopeA**

Epistle to Miss Blount, with the Works of Voiture. Alexander Pope. **CP-PopeA**

Epistle to Mr Arthur Squib. Ben Jonson. **CP-JonsB**

Epistle to Mr. Jervas, with Dryden's Translation of Fresnoy's *Art of Painting*. Alexander Pope. **CP-PopeA**

Epistle to Mr Tytler of Woodhouselee, Author of a Defence of Mary Queen of Scots. Robert Burns. **CP-BurnR**

Epistle. To My Lady Covell. Ben Jonson. **CP-JonsB**

Epistle to Robert Earl of Oxford and Earl Mortimer. Alexander Pope. **CP-PopeA**

Epistle to Robt. Graham Esq: of Fintry on the Election for the Dumfries String of Boroughs, Anno 1790. Robert Burns. **CP-BurnR**

Epistle to Robert Lloyd, Esq., An. William Cowper. **CP-CowpW**

Epistle to Sir Edward Sackville, now Earl of Dorset, An. Ben Jonson. **CP-JonsB**

Epistle to Sir George Howland Beaumont, BART. William Wordsworth. **CP-WorW1**

Epistle [II,] to a Lady[: Of the Characters of Women]. Alexander Pope. **CP-PopeA**

Epistle [II,] to a Lady[: Of the Characters of Women]. Alexander Pope. **CP-PopeA**

Ghosts of Beauty, The. **OBSV**

"Nothing so true as what you once let fall." **OxBoLi**

"Yet Cloe [*or* Chloe] sure was form'd without a Spot—." **AWP; ErPo; NOBE; OBSV**

(Cloe [*or* Chloe].) **AWP; NOBE; OBSV**

Epistle upon an Epistle, An. Jonathan Swift. **CP-SwifJ**

Epistles. Horace, *tr. fr.* Latin.

1.4: "Tibullus, whom I love and praise." **SP-SmarC,** *tr.* by Christopher Smart.

1.20: "You seem to cast, my vent'rous book." **SP-SmarC,** *tr.* by Christopher Smart.

2.1: "Each inly murm'ring at th'unequal meed." **CP-JohnS**

2.2: "Bold be the critic, zealous to his trust." **CP-JohnS**

Epistles: "I am writing you." Lewis Turco. **SP-TurcL**

Epitaph: "Again, traveller, you have come a long way led by that star." Thomas McGrath. **SP-McGrT**

Epitaph: "Bethink, poor heart, what bitter kind of jest." Hafiz, *tr. fr.* Persian by Ralph Waldo Emerson. **CP-EmerR**

Epitaph: "Crazy, girls, crazy. Don is gone." Howard Nemerov. **CP-NemeH**

Epitaph: "Dear Scipio Sprague / sans plague sans blague." Malcolm Lowry. **CP-LowrM**

Epitaph: "Deep in this earth." Edwin Rolfe. **CP-RolfE**

Epitaph: Enamoured by / Brevity in method. Charles Tomlinson. **CP-TomlC**

Epitaph: "Grieve not for happy Claudius, he is dead." Edna St. Vincent Millay. **CP-MillE**

Epitaph: "Heap not on this mound." Edna St. Vincent Millay. **CP-MillE** *Fr.* Memorial to D. C. **CP-MillE**

Epitaph: "Here rests his head upon the lap of earth", *see also* Shelley's "Hic sinu fessum caput hospitali." Thomas Gray. **FHYEP; FaBoPV; SCGP** *Fr.* Elegy Written in a Country Churchyard. **CP-GrayT**

Epitaph: "I never cared for Life: Life cared for me." Thomas Hardy. **CP-HardT**

Epitaph: "Lo worms enjoy the seat of bliss." Robert Burns. *See* Lo worms enjoy the seat of bliss.

Epitaph: "Of the Great World he knew not much." Howard Nemerov. **CP-NemeH**

Epitaph: "She leans across a golden table." Countee Cullen. **CP-CullC**

Epitaph: "Six months to six years added he remained." William Wordsworth. **CP-WorW1**

Epitaph: "Slave yet wearing on my head a crown, A." Christina Georgina Rossetti. **CP-RosC3**

Epitaph: "So I may say." Hilda Doolittle. **CP-DoolH**

Epitaph: "Stop, Christian passer-by!—Stop, child of God." Samuel Taylor Coleridge. **CP-ColeS**

Epitaph: "These are two friends whose lives / were undivided." Percy Bysshe Shelley. **CP-ShelP**

Epitaph: "Well then, poor G——— lies under ground!" Alexander Pope. **CP-PopeA**

Epitaph; "Old willow with hollow branches, An." William Carlos Williams. **CP-WilW1**

Epitaph, An: "Come knock your heads against this stone." William Blake. **CP-BlakW**

Epitaph, An: "Here lies a most beatiful lady." Walter de la Mare. **CP-DeLaW**

Epitaph, An: "Here lies one, who never drew." William Cowper. **CP-CowpW**

Epitaph, An: "Last, Stone, a little yet." Walter de la Mare. **CP-DeLaW**

Epitaph, An: "Stay, if you list, O passer by the way." Alfred Edward Housman. **CP-HousA**

Epitaph, An: "What beauty would have lovely styled." Ben Jonson. **CP-JonsB**

Epitaph, An: "My name—my country—what are they to thee." Paulus Silentiarius. *See* My name—my country—what are they to thee?

Epitaph Extempore, on a Person Nicknamed the Marquis, Who Desired Burns to Write One on Him. Robert Burns. **CP-BurnR**

Epitaph for a Conscript, 1940. John Hewitt. **CP-HewiJ**

Epitaph for a Gardener. John Hewitt. **CP-HewiJ**

Epitaph for a Public Servant. Thomas Merton. **CP-MertT**

Epitaph for Fire and Flower. Sylvia Plath. **CP-PlatS**

Epitaph for G. K. Chesterton. Thomas Hardy. **CP-HardT**

Epitaph for George Moore. Thomas Hardy. **CP-HardT**

Epitaph for H——— L———, Esq., of L———. Robert Burns. **CP-BurnR**

Epitaph for John Bunny, Motion-Picture Comedian. Nicholas Vachel Lindsay. *Fr.* Epitaphs for Two Players. **CP-LindV**

Epitaph for J. H. Writer in Ayr. Robert Burns. **CP-BurnR**

Epitaph for John McCutcheon. Archibald MacLeish. **CP-MacLA**

Epitaph for Joseph Blacket. Byron. **CP-Byron**

Epitaph for Liberal Poets. Louis MacNeice. **CP-MacNL**

Epitaph for My Cat. Jean Garrigue. **SP-GarrJ**

Epitaph for One Who Would Not Be Buried in Westminster Abbey ("Heroes, and Kings! your distance keep"), *see also* Epitaph for One Who Would Not Be Buried in Westminster Abbey ("Under this Marble, or under this Sill"). Alexander Pope. **CP-PopeA**

Epitaph for One Who Would Not Be Buried in Westminster Abbey ("Under this Marble, or under this Sill"), *see also* Epitaph for One Who Would Not Be Buried in Westminster Abbey ("Heroes, and Kings! your distance keep"). Alexander Pope. **CP-PopeA**

Epitaph for the Race of Man. Edna St. Vincent Millay. **CP-MillE**

"Alas for Man, so stealthily betrayed."

"Before this cooling planet shall be cold."

"Broken dike, the levee washed away, The."

"Cretaceous bird, your giant claw no lime."

"He heard the coughing tiger in the night." **CP-MillE**

"He woke in terror to a sky more bright."

"Here lies, and none to mourn him but the sea." **HeIP**

"Him not the golden fang of furious heaven."

"His heatless room the watcher of the stars."

"Now forth to meadow as the farmer goes."

"Now sets his foot upon the eastern sill."

"O Earth, unhappy planet born to die." **HeIP; WoWa**

"Observe how Miyanoshita cracked in two."

"Only the diamond and the diamond's dust."

"See where Capella with her golden kids." **CMoP; MoAB; MoAmPo**

"Sweeter was loss than silver coins to spend."

"When Death was young and bleaching bones were few."

"When Man is gone and only gods remain."

Epitaph for the Unknown Soldier. Wystan Hugh Auden. **FaBoCo** *Fr.* Shorts [1948–1957] ("At peace under this mandarin, sleep, Lucina"). **CP-AudeW**

Epitaph for William Nicol. Robert Burns. *See* Ye maggots, feed on Willie's brains.

Epitaph. Here Lies Robert Fergusson, Poet. Robert Burns. **CP-BurnR**

Epitaph in Form of a Ballad, The. François Villon, *tr. fr.* French by Algernon Charles Swinburne. **SP-SwinA**

Epitaph in Grasmere Church. William Wordsworth. **CP-WorW2**

Epitaph in the Chapel Yard of Langdale, Westmoreland. William Wordsworth. **CP-WorW2**

Epitaph in the Imperative Mode. Louise McNeill. **SP-McNeL**

Epitaph in Three Parts. Sylvia Plath. **CP-PlatS**

Epitaph Intended for Mr. Rowe, in Westminster Abbey. Alexander Pope. **CP-PopeA**

Epitaph Intended for Sir Isaac Newton, in Westminster Abbey. Alexander Pope. *See* Nature and Nature's Laws lay hid in Night.

Epitaph: Lorine Niedecker. Roy Fisher. **SP-FishR**

Epitaph (of By-Words). Alexander Pope. **CP-PopeA**

Epitaph of Sir Thomas Gravener, [Knight], An. Sir Thomas Wyatt. **CP-WyatT**

Epitaph on a Child. Thomas Gray. **CP-GrayT**

Epitaph on a Free but Tame Redbreast. William Cowper. **CP-CowpW**

Epitaph on a Friend. Byron. **CP-Byron**

Epitaph on a Hare. William Cowper. **CP-CowpW**

Epitaph on a Henpecked Country Squire. Robert Burns. **CP-BurnR**

Epitaph on a Man who Had a Scold to His Wife. Robert Herrick. **CP-HerrR**

Epitaph on a Pessimist. Thomas Hardy. **CP-HardT**

Epitaph on a Philosopher the Reports of Whose Death Have Been Grossly Minimized. Howard Nemerov. **CP-NemeH**

Epitaph on a Tyrant. Wystan Hugh Auden. **CP-AudeW**

Epitaph on a Wag in Mauchline. Robert Burns. **CP-BurnR**

Epitaph on an Army of Mercenaries. Alfred Edward Housman. **CP-HousA**

Epitaph on an Infant. Samuel Taylor Coleridge. **CP-ColeS**

Epitaph on an Infant. Samuel Taylor Coleridge. **CP-ColeS**

Epitaph on Charles Earl of Dorset. Alexander Pope. **CP-PopeA**

Epitaph on Chartres, *see also* Epitaph on the Count of Mirandula. Alexander Pope. **CP-PopeA**

Epitaph on Claudy Phillips, a Musician, An. Samuel Johnson. *See* Phillips, whose touch harmonious could remove.

Epitaph on D——— C———. Robert Burns. **CP-BurnR**

Epitaph on Dr. Francis Atterbury, Bishop of Rochester, Who Died in Exile at Paris, 1732; a Dialogue. Alexander Pope. **CP-PopeA**

Epitaph on Dr. Johnson. William Cowper. **CP-CowpW**

Epitaph on Edmund Duke of Buckingham, Who Died in the Nineteenth Year of His Age, 1735. Alexander Pope. **CP-PopeA**

Epitaph on Elizabeth, L. H. Ben Jonson. **CP-JonsB**

Epitaph on Fop. William Cowper. **CP-CowpW**

Epitaph on General Henry Withers, in Westminster-Abbey, 1729. Alexander Pope. **CP-PopeA**

Epitaph on Henry Fielding, Esq. Christopher Smart. **SP-SmarC**

Epitaph, on Henry L[ord] La-ware. To the Passer-By, An. Ben Jonson. **CP-JonsB**

Epitaph on Himself. John Donne. **CP-DonnJ**

Epitaph on Holy Willie. Robert Burns. **CP-BurnR**

Epitaph on James Craggs, Esq., in Westminster Abbey. Alexander Pope. **CP-PopeA**

Epitaph on John Adams, of Southwell. Byron. **CP-Byron**

Epitaph on J-hn B-shby. Robert Burns. **CP-BurnR**

Epitaph on John Dove [Innkeeper, Mauchline]. Robert Burns. **CP-BurnR**

Epitaph on John Knight, Who Died Oct. 2, 1733. Alexander Pope. **CP-PopeA**

Epitaph on Katherine, Lady Ogle. Ben Jonson. **CP-JonsB**

Epitaph on Master Philip Gray, An. Ben Jonson. **CP-JonsB**

Epitaph on Master Vincent Corbet[t], An. Ben Jonson. **CP-JonsB**

Epitaph on Miss Stanley. James Thomson. **CP-ThomJ**

Epitaph on Mr. Burton. Robert Burns. *See* Here cursing swearing Burton lies.

Epitaph on Mr. Chester. William Cowper. **CP-CowpW**

Epitaph on Mr. Elijah Fenton, at Easthamstead in Berks, 1730. Alexander Pope. **CP-PopeA**

Epitaph on Mrs. Corbet, Who Died of a Cancer in Her Breast. Alexander Pope. **CP-PopeA**

Epitaph on Mrs. Higgins. William Cowper. **CP-CowpW**

Epitaph on Mrs Jane Clarke. Thomas Gray. **CP-GrayT**

Epitaph on my Dear and Ever Honored Mother Mrs. Dorothy Dudley. Anne Bradstreet. **CP-BradA**

Epitaph on My Own Friend, and My Father's Friend, Wm Muir in Tarbolton Miln. Robert Burns. **CP-BurnR**

Epitaph on Our Gardener, Dead Near Liverpool. Malcolm Lowry. **CP-LowrM**

Epitaph on R. Muir. Robert Burns. **CP-BurnR**

Epitaph on Sir Godfrey Kneller, in Westminster-Abbey, 1723. Alexander Pope. **CP-PopeA**

Epitaph on Sir William Trumbal. Alexander Pope. **CP-PopeA**

Epitaph on Sir William Williams. Thomas Gray. **CP-GrayT**

Epitaph on S.P. [Salomon *or* Salathiel Pavy], a Child of Q[ueen] El[izabeth's] Chapel. Ben Jonson. **CP-JonsB**

Epitaph on the Count of Mirandula, *see also* Epitaph on Chartres. Alexander Pope. **CP-PopeA**

Epitaph on the Earl of Leicester [*or* Leceister]. Sir Walter Ralegh. **CP-RaleW**

Epitaph on the Earl of Salisbury. *Unknown, sometimes at. to* Sir Walter Ralegh. **CP-RaleW**

Epitaph on the Hon. Simon Harcourt. Alexander Pope. **CP-PopeA**

Epitaph on the Lady Mary Villiers. Thomas Carew. **CP-CareT**

Epitaph on the Lady S.: Wife of Sir W.S. Thomas Carew. **CP-CareT**

Epitaph on the Marchioness of Winchester, An. John Milton. **CP-MiltJ**

Epitaph on the Monument of the Honourable Robert Digby, and of his Sister Mary, erected by their Father the Lord Digby, in the Church of Sherborne in Dorsetshire, 1727. Alexander Pope. **CP-PopeA**

Epitaph on the Tomb of Sir Edward Giles and His Wife in the South Aisle of Dean Prior Church. Robert Herrick. **CP-HerrR**

Epitaph on the Tombstone of James Christopher Wilson. George Meredith. **CP-MerG2**

Epitaph on William Hogarth, An. Samuel Johnson. **CP-JohnS**

Epitaph to a Man Not Dead. John Hewitt. **CP-HewiJ**

Epitaph upon —, An. Andrew Marvell. **CP-MarvA**

Epitaph upon a Child, An. Robert Herrick. **CP-HerrR**

Epitaph upon a Sober Matron, An. Robert Herrick. **CP-HerrR**

Epitaph upon a Virgin, An. Robert Herrick. **CP-HerrR**

Epitaph upon a Young Married Couple, An. Richard Crashaw. *See* To these, whom death again did wed.

Epitaph. Upon Doctor Brooke, An. Richard Crashaw. **CP-CrasR**

Epitaph upon Mr. Ashton, a Conformable Citizen, An. Richard Crashaw. **CP-CrasR**

Epitaph upon the Right Hono[u]rable Sir Philip Sidney Knight, Lord Governor of Flushing, An. Sir Walter Ralegh. *See* To praise thy life[,] or wail[e] thy worthy[orwoorthie] death.

Epitaph upon the Right Honourable Sir Phillip Sidney, Knight: Lord Governor of Flushing, An. Edmund Spenser. *Fr.* Astrophel. **CP-Spens**

Epitaphium, *Latin vers. of epitaph in* Gray's Elegy Written in a Country Churchyard; *see also* "Here rests his head upon the lap of earth." Percy Bysshe Shelley. **CP-ShelP**

Epitaphium Alterum, *see also* Epitaph on a Hare. William Cowper. **CP-CowpW**

Epitaphium Erotii. Robert Louis Stevenson. **CP-StevR**

Epitaphium Testamentarium. Samuel Taylor Coleridge. **CP-ColeS**

Epitaphs: "Fu I loved the high cloud and the hill." Ezra Pound. **SP-PounE**

Epitaphs for Two Players. Nicholas Vachel Lindsay. **CP-LindV**
> Edwin Booth.
> Epitaph for John Bunny, Motion-Picture Comedian.

Epitaphs of the War [1914–1918]. Rudyard Kipling. **CP-KiplR**
> Actors.
> Batteries Out of Ammunition. **MMA**
> Beginner, The. **FaBoTw**
> Bombed in London.
> Bridegroom, The. **FaBoEE**
> Common Form. **FaBoEE; FaBoTw; PV; PeFWW**
> Convoy Escort.
> Coward, The. **FaBoEE; FaBoTw; OAEP; PeFWW**
> Dead Statesman. **FaBoEE; IHNG; NBLV; OPOU; PoWW**
> Destroyers in Collision.
> Drifter off Tarentum, A. **FaBoEE; MMA; NSI; PeFWW; PoPle; PoWW**
> Equality of Sacrifice. **FaBoTw; OAEP**
> Ex-Clerk.
> Favour, The.
> Grave Near Cairo, A.
> Hindu Sepoy in France.
> Journalists.
> Native Water-Carrier (M.E.F.)
> Obedient, The.
> Only Son, An.
> Pelicans in the Wilderness (A Grave near Halfa). **PeFWW**
> R.A.F. (Aged Eighteen). **PoWW**
> Raped and Revenged.
> Rebel, The.
> Refined Man, The. **FaBoEE; FaBoTw; MMA; PeFWW**
> Salonikan Grave.
> Servant, A. **PeFWW**
> Shock.
> Sleepy Sentinel, The.
> Son, A. **ChMP; FaBoEE; PeFWW**
> Two Canadian Memorials.
> Unknown Female Corpse. **PoWW**
> V.A.D. (Mediterranean).
> Wonder, The.

Epithalamion: "Glad time is at his point arrived." Ben Jonson. **CP-JonsB** *Fr.* Masque of Hymen.

Epithalamion: "Hark, hearer, hear what I do; lend a thought now, make believe." Gerard Manley Hopkins. **CP-HopkG**

Epithalamion: "O who will share with me." John Hewitt. **CP-HewiJ**

Epithalamion: "Pussy put her paw into the pail of paint." Ted Berrigan. **SP-BerrT**

Epithalamion: "Thou aged unreluctant earth who dost." Edward Estlin Cummings. **CP-CummE**

Epithalamion: "Up, youths and virgins, up, and praise." Ben Jonson. **CP-JonsB** *Fr.* The Haddington Masque.

Epithalamion: "Ye learned sisters, which have oftentimes." Edmund Spenser. **CP-Spens**
> "Now al is done; bring home the bride againe." **FiP**
> "Wake, now my love, awake; for it is time." **GBL**
> Who Is the Same, Which at My Window Peepes? **NAs**

Epithalamion, An, or Marriage Song on the Lady Elizabeth and Count Palatine Being Married on St. Valentine's Day. John Donne. **CP-DonnJ**

Epithalamion Made at Lincoln's Inn [*or* Lincolnes Inne]. John Donne. **CP-DonnJ**

Epithalamion of a Peach. John Crowe Ransom. *Fr.* Two Gentlemen in Bonds. **SP-RansJ**

Epithalamion I–IV: "Along a leafy lonely river God-shy-eyed fisher boys." James Liddy. **CP-LiddJ**
> "Along a leafy lonely river God-shy-eyed fisher boys."
> "Bliss fell 'in love with us' (Knox). I know it, I'm super-hype too."
> "I know nothing but this scene." **BiHa**
> "Lest the hoar frost grip the iridescent tent of your marriage."

Epithalamion: or, a Song. Ben Jonson. **CP-JonsB**

Epithalamion Teratos. George Chapman. **EIL; LoBV; NoSic** *Fr.* Hero and Leander. **CP-MarlC**

Epithalamium: "All folk-tales mean by ending." Wystan Hugh Auden. *Fr.* Eleven Occasional Poems. **CP-AudeW**

Epithalamium: "Come virgin Tapers of pure waxe." Richard Crashaw. **CP-CrasR**

Epithalamium: "He is here, Urania's son." Alfred Edward Housman. **CP-HousA**

Epithalamium: "Night, with all thine eyes look down!", *see also* Bridal Song, A *and* Another Version of the Same. Percy Bysshe Shelley. **CP-ShelP**

Epithalamium: "There were others; their bodies." Louise Glück. **SP-GlücL**

Epithalamium at St. Michael's Cemetary. John Ciardi. **SP-CiarJ**

Epithalamy to Sir Thomas Southwell and His Lady, An. Robert Herrick. **CP-HerrR**

Epizeuxis, the Underlay, or Coocko-spel. Sir Walter Ralegh. *Fr.* The Arte of English Poesie. **CP-RaleW**

Eplenor. Archibald MacLeish. **CP-MacLA**

Epoch of a streetcar drawn by horses, The. Baby Pictures of Famous Dictators. Charles Simic. **SP-SimiC**

Epode: "Not to know vice at all, and keep[e] true state." Ben Jonson. **CP-JonsB**

Epodes. Horace, *tr. fr. Latin.*
> Praises of a Country Life, The. **CP-JonsB**
> Translation of Horace "Epode the 2d" ("Beatus Ille"). **CP-JohnS**
> Translation of Horace: Epode xi. **CP-JohnS**

Eppie McNab. Robert Burns. **CP-BurnR**

Epps. Robert Browning. **CP-BroR2**

Eppure Allora Venivi. Christina Georgina Rossetti. *Fr.* Il Rosseggiar Dell'Oriente Canzoniere. **CP-RosC3**

Epstein, Spare That Yule Log! Ogden Nash. **CP-NashO**

Equal to Jove that youth must be. Catullus. *See* Carmen 51: "Godlike the man who."

Equality. John Hewitt. **CP-HewiJ**

Equality of Sacrifice. Rudyard Kipling. **FaBoTw; OAEP** *Fr.* Epitaphs of the War [1914–1918]. **CP-KiplR**

Equalizer, An. Robert Frost. **CP-FrosR**

Equally innocent. Song: Victims of Calumny. Robert Ranke Graves. **CP-GravR**

Equations of a Villanelle. Howard Nemerov. **CP-NemeH**

Equestrian Sestina. Donald Davie. **CP-DavDo**

Equilibrations. Archie Randolph Ammons. **SP-AmmoA**

Equilibrists, The. John Crowe Ransom. **SP-RansJ**

Equinox. Audre Lorde. **SP-LordA**

Equipment. Paul Laurence Dunbar. **CP-DunbP**

Equipoise: becalmed / Trees, a dome of kindness. Evening in Connecticut. Louis MacNeice. **CP-MacNL**

Equivalence of Gnats and Mice. Richard Eberhart. **CP-EberR**

Er-Heb beyond the Hills of Ao-Safai. The Sacrifice of Er-Heb. Rudyard Kipling. **CP-KiplR**

Eras do not end when great poets die. The Poet as Mastercraftsman. Michael Hartnett. *Fr.* Notes on My Contemporaries. **SP-HarMi**

Erase the lines: I pray you not to love classifications. Monument. Robinson Jeffers. **CP-JefR3**

Eraser. Charles Simic. **SP-SimiC**

Erasmus. Edwin Arlington Robinson. **CP-RobiE**

Erasure. Marge Piercy. **SP-PierM**

Erat Hora. Ezra Pound. **SP-PounE**

Erato popped in. What a talent for suspicion! An Apology for Not Invoking the Muse. John Ciardi. **SP-CiarJ**

Ere cherries ripe, and strawberries be gone. The New Cry. Ben Jonson. **CP-JonsB**

Ere down yon blue Carpathian hills. The Knight of St. John. John Greenleaf Whittier. **CP-WhitJ**

Ere elfish Night shall sift another day. Sonnet. Hart Crane. **CP-CranH**

Ere God had built the mountains. Wisdom. William Cowper. **ChIV-1** *Fr.* Olney Hymns. **CP-CowpW**

Ere he was born, the stars of fate. Horoscope. Ralph Waldo Emerson. *Fr.* Quatrains. **CP-EmerR**

Ere I goe hence and bee noe more. Mr. Hericke his Daughter's Dowrye. Robert Herrick. **CP-HerrR**

Ere I had told / Ten birthdays when among the mountain-slopes. William Wordsworth. **TOF** *Fr.* Introduction—Childhood and School-Time. **EnRP; FHYEP** *Fr.* The Prelude; Growth of a Poet's Mind [1850 vers.]. **CP-WorW3**

Ere long they come, where that same wicked wight. Edmund Spenser. **NOBE; OAEL-1** *Fr.* The Cave of Despair. **OBNV** *Fr.* The Faerie Queene. **CP-Spens**

Ere Mor the Peacock flutters, ere the Monkey People cry. The Song of the Little Hunter. Rudyard Kipling. **CP-KiplR** *Fr.* The King's Ankus. *Fr.* The Second Jungle Book.

Ere on my bed my limbs I lay. A Child's Evening Prayer. Samuel Taylor Coleridge. **CP-ColeS**

Ere on my bed my limbs I lay, / It hath not been my use to pray. The Pains of Sleep. Samuel Taylor Coleridge. **CP-ColeS**

Ere Sin could blight or Sorrow fade. Epitaph on an Infant. Samuel Taylor Coleridge. **CP-ColeS**

Ere Sleep Comes Down to Soothe the Weary Eyes. Paul Laurence Dunbar. **CP-DunbP**

Ere stopping or turning, to put forth a hande. *parody of* Thoams Tusser. Rudyard Kipling. **CP-KiplR** *Fr.* The Muse among the Motors.

Ere the birth of my life, if I wished it or no. The Suicide's Argument. Samuel Taylor Coleridge. **CP-ColeS**

Ere the Brothers through the gateway. The Horn of Egremont Castle. William Wordsworth. **CP-WorW1**

Ere the cock has crowed. *after* Eduard Mörike. Randall Jarrell. **CP-JarrR**

Ere the daughter of Brunswick is cold in her grave. The Irish Avatar. Byron. **CP-Byron**

Ere the mother's milk had dried. The Totem. Rudyard Kipling. **CP-KiplR**

Ere the steamer bore him Eastward, Sleary was engaged to marry. The Post That Fitted. Rudyard Kipling. **CP-KiplR**

Ere-while of Musick, and Ethereal mirth. The Passion. John Milton. **CP-MiltJ**

Ere with Cold Beads of Midnight Dew. William Wordsworth. **CP-WorW2**

Ere yet our course was graced with social trees. Flowers. William Wordsworth. *Fr.* The River Duddon [A Series of Sonnets]. **CP-WorW2**

Erecting beyond the boundaries of all government. Robert Duncan. **SP-DuncR** *Fr.* The Structure of Rime.

Eric Dolphy can't wake up. The Door to the Forest. Tom Clark. **SP-ClarT**

Eric—we used to call him Eric. The Men of Sheepshead. George Oppen. **CP-OppeG**

Erice, Western Sicily. John Hewitt. **CP-HewiJ**

Erige Cor Tuum ad Me in Caelum. Hilda Doolittle. **CP-DoolH**

Eringo root in the north. Isle of Man Wildflowers. Malcolm Lowry. **CP-LowrM**

Erinna to Sappho. James Wright. **CP-WrigJ**

Erinnyes. David Herbert Lawrence. **CP-LawrD**

Eroica. Allen Ginsberg. **CP-GinsA**

Eros. Robert Creeley. **CP-CreeR**

Eros. Hilda Doolittle. **CP-DoolH**

Eros. Ralph Waldo Emerson. **CP-EmerR**

Eros. Louise Glück. *Fr.* Dedication to Hunger. **SP-GlücL**

Eros. Denise Levertov. **CP-LeveD**

Eros. George Oppen. **CP-OppeG**

Eros aei lalethros hetairos. Samuel Taylor Coleridge. **CP-ColeS**

Eros at Temple Stream. Denise Levertov. **CP-LeveD**

Eros at the World Kite Pageant. Laurence Lieberman. **SP-LiebL**

Eros in May at MacDowell. Isabella Gardner. **CP-GardI**

Eros to Howard Nemerov. Mona Van Duyn. **SP-VanDM**

Eros Turannos. Edwin Arlington Robinson. **CP-RobiE**

Erosong. Al Young. **CP-YounA**

Erotic. David Herbert Lawrence. **CP-LawrD**

Erotic Epigrams. John Updike. **CP-UpdiJ**

Err shall they not, who resolute explore. Translations from the *Medea* of Euripedes. Euripides, *tr. by* Samuel Johnson. **CP-JohnS** *Fr.* Medea. **CP-JefR3,** *tr. by* Robinson Jeffers;

Errand, The. Anne Sexton. **CP-SextA**

Errat adhuc vitreus per prata virentia rivus. In Rivum a Mola Stoana Lichfeldiæ Diffluentem. Samuel Johnson. **CP-JohnS**

Errata. Charles Simic. **SP-SimiC**

Error, disease, snow, sudden weather. The Cornfield. Muriel Rukeyser. **CP-RukeM**

Errors. John Ashbery. **SP-AshbJ**

Errors of a Wise Man make your Rule, The. William Blake. **CP-BlakW**

Eruptive lightnings flutter to and fro. Summer Silence. Edward Estlin Cummings. **CP-CummE**

Es War Einmal. Stevie Smith. **CP-SmitS**

Es war einmal. . . No, it's too heavy. Märchenbilder. John Ashbery. **SP-AshbJ**

Escape, The. Charles Bukowski. **SP-BukC1**

Escape, The. Leonard Cohen. **CP-CoheL**

Escape, The. James Dickey. **CP-DickJ**

Escape. David Herbert Lawrence. *See* When we get out of the glass bottles of our ego.

Escape at Bedtime. Robert Louis Stevenson. **CP-StevR**

Escape from the black widow spider. The Escape. Charles Bukowski. **SP-BukC1**

Escape had gravely dulled our gear. The Survivors. John Clellon Holmes. **SP-HolmJ**

Escape is such a thankful Word. Emily Dickinson. **CP-DickE**

Escape me? / Never. Life in a Love. Robert Browning. **CP-BroR1**

Escape to the Mountain. Christina Georgina Rossetti. **CP-RosC2**

Escaped thy place of wintry rest. To a Butterfly in a Window. Charlotte Smith. **CP-SmitC**

Escaping backward to perceive. Emily Dickinson. **CP-DickE**

Escaping from allegories / in the misty east, where inherited events. Migration: C.P.R. Margaret Atwood. **SP-AtwM1**

Escapist—Never. Robert Frost. **CP-FrosR**

Escorial, The. Gerard Manley Hopkins. **CP-HopkG**

Eskimo Tales. John Yau. **SP-YauJo**

Eskimo Villanelle. John Yau. **SP-YauJo**

Eskimos in Manitoba. Recital. John Updike. **CP-UpdiJ**

Especially forlorn human specimen, An. Charles Simic. **SP-SimiC** *Fr.* Rosalia. **SP-SimiC**

  (Dimly Outlined by a Police Artist.) **PPR**

  ("Especially forlorn specimen, An.") **PPR**

Especially forlorn specimen, An. Charles Simic. *See* An Especially forlorn human specimen.

Especially in rain my faith. Solemn Music. Leonard Nathan. **SP-NathL**

Especially When the October Wind. Dylan Thomas. **CP-ThomD**

Esplumeoir. "Hugh MacDiarmid."

  "But shairly, shairly there maun be." **SP-MacDH**

Esprit de corps in permanent bodies. Canto 40. Ezra Pound. *Fr.* Cantos. **CP-PoCan**

Esquimos Have No Word for "War," The. Mary Oliver. **SP-OlivM**

Essay. Hayden Carruth. **CP-CarHS**

Essay on Chess. Karl Shapiro. **SP-ShapK**

Essay on Criticism, An. Alexander Pope. **CP-PopeA**

  Art of Poetry, The. **ECEV**

  "Avoid extremes; and shun the fault of such." **FHYEP**

  Bookful Blockhead, The. **OBSV**

  "But most by numbers judge a poet's song." **FiP; NIP,** *ll.* 337–383; **SeCePo**

  (Poetical Numbers.) **SeCePo,** *ll.* 337–383;

  "But true expression, like th' unchanging sun." **FHYEP**

"But where's the man who counsel can bestow." **OXAEP-1**, *ll.* 631–744;

"First follow Nature, and your judgment frame." **FiP**, *ll.* 68–91;

"In wit, as nature, what affects our hearts." **HAP**

"Little learning is a dangerous [*or* dang'rous] thing, A." **EBEvV; FPL; HAP; HoPM; PoLF; TrGrPo**, *ll.* 215–232; **ChTr; FaFP; ImPo; LiTB; NOBE; SeCePo**

    (Alps on Alps.) **FaFP**, *ll.* 215–232;

    (Little Learning, A.) **ChTr; NOBE; SeCePo**, *ll.* 215–232; **ImPo; LiTB**, *ll.* 215–252;

"Of all the causes which conspire to blind." **OxAEP-1**

Plain Fools. **OBSV**

"Pride, Malice, Folly, against Dryden rose." **EPCY**

Servile Herd, The. **OBSV**

"Some beauties yet no precepts can declare." **HAP**

"Some to Conceit alone their taste confine." **OxAEP-1**, *ll.* 289–393;

"Still green with bays each ancient altar stands." **EPCY**

"Thus critics, of less judgment than caprice." **OAEL-1**

"'Tis hard to say, if greater want of skill." **OAEL-1**, *ll.* 1–266;

"True ease in writing comes from art, not chance." **InPK; TrGrPo**, *ll.* 362–383;

"True wit is Nature to advantage dressed." **HAP**

"Unhappy wit, like most mistaken things." **EPCY**

"Where'er you find the cooling western breeze." **OBCoV**

"Yet, if we look more closely, we shall find." **FiP**

Essay on Criticism, An. Mona Van Duyn. **SP-VanDM**

Essay on Death. Hayden Carruth. **CP-CarHS**

Essay on Dreiser (1871-1945). Edwin Rolfe. **CP-RolfE**

Essay on Liberation, An. David St. John. **SP-StJoD**

Essay on Love. Hayden Carruth. **CP-CarHS**

Essay on Man, An. Alexander Pope. **CP-PopeA**

    "All are but parts of one stupendous whole." **FHYEP; WGRP**

    "All Nature is but art, unknown to thee." **ECEV**

    "Awake, my St. John! leave all meaner things." **NAEL-1; NoP; OAEP; PoEL-3**

    Wild Garden, The. **PrIm**

    "Behold the child, by Nature's kindly law." **ECEV; FaBoRV; POL**

    "Bliss of man, The (could pride that blessing find)." **NOEC; NU**

Character of Marlborough, A. **CP-PopeA**

Faith. **WGRP**

    "Far as creation's ample range extends." **ECEV; FM; ImOP**

    "For forms of government let fools contest." **ECEV**

    "Honor and shame from no condition rise." **TrGrPo**

    "Hope humbly then; with trembling pinions soar." **EBEvV; TrGrPo**

    "Know then thyself, presume not God to scan." **BLPL; ECEV; NOEC; OAEL-1; SeCePo; TrGrPo**, *ll.* 1–18; **TFi**, *ll.* 1–42; **ACP; EBEvV; FHYEP; FaFP; FiP; GoBC; ImPo; LiTB; NAEL-1; NOBE; NoP; OBEC; PAI; PPoe; PoEL-3; PrIm; TRV**

    (Know Then Thyself.) **ImPo**, *ll.* 1–66;

    (Know Thyself.) **NOBE**, *ll.* 1–18;

    (Man.) **PrIm**, *ll.* 1–18;

    (Paragon of Animals, The.) **ACP**, *ll.* 1–30;

    (Proper Study of Mankind, The.) **FiP**, *ll.* 1–30;

    (Riddle of the World.) **FaFP**, *ll.* 1–18;

    Life's Poor Play. **OBEC; SeCePo**

    "Lo, the poor Indian! whose untutor'd mind." **NU**

    "Look round our world; behold the chain of love." **FHYEP; OBD**

    "Nor think, in nature's state they blindly trod." **OAEL-1**

    "Placed on this isthmus of a middle state." **WeW**

    Pleasure of Hope, The. **ACP**

    Soul's Calm Sunshine, The. **FaBoRV**

    "What if the foot, ordain'd the dust to tread." **FaBoPV**

    "What would this Man? Now upward will he soar." **HeIP**

    "Whate'er the passion--knowledge, fame, or pelf." **FiP; TrGrPo**

    (Human Folly.) **FiP**

    "What's fame? A fancied life in others' breath." **FHYEP**

Essay on Marriage. Hayden Carruth. **CP-CarHS**

Essay on Sanity. Stephen Dunn. **SP-DunnS**

Essay on Stone, *see also* On Canann Mountain Meadow. Hayden Carruth. **CP-CarHS**

Essay on Style. Daniel Gerard Hoffman. **SP-HoffD**

Essay on Style. Frank O'Hara. **SP-OharF**

Essay on the Human Will, An. Randall Jarrell. **CP-JarrR**

Essay on the Personal. Stephen Dunn. **SP-DunnS**

Essential Beauty. Philip Larkin. **CP-LarkP**

Essential oils—are wrung. Emily Dickinson. **CP-DickE**

Essential poem at the centre [*or* center] of things, The. A Primitive like an Orb. Wallace Stevens. **CP-StevW**

Essential Resources. Adrienne Rich. **SP-RicA2**

Essex. Sir John Betjeman. **CP-BetjJ**

Essex. Donald Davie. **CP-DavDo**

Establishment is shocked. Stir no adventure. Edna St. Vincent Millay. **CP-MillE**

Estais Muertos. César Vallejo, *tr. fr. Spanish by* Thomas Merton. **CP-MertT**

Esther say I drink too much. Various Protestations From Various People. Etheridge Knight. **SP-KnigE**

Esther's Tomcat. Ted Hughes. **SP-HughT**

Esthetic Theories: Art as Expression. Randall Jarrell. **CP-JarrR**

Esthétique du Mal. Wallace Stevens. **CP-StevW**

    "He was at Naples writing letters home." **CMoP; MeMAP; NOBA**

    "How red the rose that is the soldier's wound." **CMoP; NOBA; WaP; WaaP**

    (Soldier's Wound, The.) **WaaP**

    "Life is a bitter aspic. We are not." **CMoP**

    "Sun, in clownish yellow, but not a clown, The." **NOBA**

Estivation means passing the summer in a torpid condition, which is why I love to estivate. I Always Say There's No Place Like New York in the Summer, or, That Cottage Small by a Waterfall Was Snapped Up Last February. Ogden Nash. **CP-NashO**

Estocada stuck well stuck. They run round in circles. Ernest Hemingway. **CP-HemiE** *Fr.* The Soul of Spain with McAlmon and Bird the Publishers.

Estranged. Walter de la Mare. **CP-DeLaW**

Estranged from Beauty, none can be. Emily Dickinson. **CP-DickE**

Estranged in site. The Parthenon. Herman Melville. **SP-MelvH**

Estuary silted up, The. The Raid. Alun Lewis. **CP-LewiA**

Et Dona Ferentes. Rudyard Kipling. **CP-KiplR**

Et in Arcadia Ego. Wystan Hugh Auden. **CP-AudeW**

Et là être là encore là. Mort de A.D. Samuel Beckett. **CP-BeckS**

Et miser atque vorax optat sibi Nerva podagram. *acc. by English translation.* Thomas Campion. **CP-CampT**

"Et omniformis," Psellos, "omnis." Canto 23. Ezra Pound. *Fr.* Cantos. **CP-PoCan**

Et Tu In Arcadia Vixisti. John Hewitt. **CP-HewiJ**

Et Tu In Arcadia Vixisti. Robert Louis Stevenson. **CP-StevR**

Etcher of the secret wrinkles. Stanley Jasspon Kunitz. *Fr.* Meditations on Death. **CP-KuniS**

Eternal Child, The. Kathleen Jessie Raine. **SP-RainK**

Eternal Circle. "Bob Dylan." **CP-DylaB**

Eternal City. Hayden Carruth. **CP-CarHS**

Eternal Dice, The. César Vallejo, *tr. fr. Spanish by* James Wright. **CP-WrigJ**

Eternal Female ground! [*or* groan'd!] it was heard all over the Earth, The. A Song of Liberty. William Blake. *Fr.* The Marriage of Heaven and Hell. **CP-BlakW**

Eternal gates' terrific porter lifted the northern bar, The. The Secrets of the Earth. William Blake. **NOBE** *Fr.* The Book of Thel. **CP-BlakW**

Eternal God[,] (for whom who ever [*or* whoever] dare). Upon the Translation of the Psalms by Sir Philip Sidney, and the Countess of Pembroke His Sister. John Donne. **CP-DonnJ**

Eternal Goodness, The. John Greenleaf Whittier. **CP-WhitJ**

    "And Thou, O Lord! by whom are seen." **TrPWD**

    "I know not what the future hath." **BLRP; NOCV**

Eternal Lord! Eased from a Cumbrous Load, *ad. fr. the Italian of* Michelangelo Buonarotti. William Wordsworth. **TrPWD** *Fr.* Memorials of a Tour in Italy, 1837. **CP-WorW2**

    (At Florence.—From Michelangelo: "Eternal Lord! eased from a cumbrous load.")

Eternal Spirit of the chainless Mind! The Prisoner of Chillon. Byron. **CP-Byron**

Eternal Spirit of the chainless mind! Sonnet on Chillon. Byron. **FiP; GTBS; GTBS-6; GTBS-P; LiTB; LoBV; MeMBP; OAEP; OBRV; PBMP; SeCeV; TrGrPo; TreFS** *Fr.* The Prisoner of Chillon. **CP-Byron**

Eternal tiger, fretting in the dark. The Tiger of Camden Town. Alun Lewis. **CP-LewiA**

Eternal Vernal, or, In All My Dreams My Fair Face Beams, The. Ogden Nash. **CP-NashO**

Eternal Watcher, who doth wake, The. Fayzi, *tr. fr. Persian by* Ralph Waldo Emerson. **CP-EmerR**

Eternally given. Seek / The flowers of the. To Be Holy, Be Wholly Your Own. Kenneth Patchen. **CP-PatcK**

Eternally Undismayed Are the Poolshooters. William Matthews. **SP-MattW**

Eternity [*or* Eternitie]. Robert Herrick. **CP-HerrR**

Eternity ("He who binds [*or* bends] to himself a joy"). William Blake. **AWP; ArNa; EBEV; EnlH; FaBoEE; ImPo; LAuP; LoBV; MeMBP; NOBE; NTP; NoP; OBNC; OxBSP; PFP; Poetr; RB; SCGP; SoSe; Spl; TrGrPo** *Fr.* Several Questions Answered. **CP-BlakW**

Eternity. Tom Clark. **SP-ClarT**

Eternity. Hart Crane. **CP-CranH**

Eternity, An. Archibald MacLeish. **CP-MacLA**

Eternity, An. William Carlos Williams. **CP-WilW2**

Eternity. William Carlos Williams. **CP-WilW2**

Eternity. Al Young. **CP-YounA**

Eternity Blues. Hayden Carruth. **CP-CarHS**

Eternity is passion, girl or boy. Whence Had They Come? William Butler Yeats. **CP-YeatW**

Eternity may imitate. Emily Dickinson. **SP-DickE**

Eternity of Love Protested. Thomas Carew. **CP-CareT**

Ethereal minstrel! pilgrim of the sky! To a Skylark. William Wordsworth. **CP-WorW2**

Ethereal race, inhabitants of air. An Ode on Æolus's Harp. James Thomson. **CP-ThomJ**

Etherealizing. Robert Frost. **CP-FrosR**

Ethics. Charles Kenneth Williams. **SP-WillC**

Ethinthus, Queen of Waters. William Blake. **ChTr** *Fr.* Europe; A Prophecy. **CP-BlakW**

Ethiopia Saluting the Colors. Walt Whitman. **CP-WhitW**

Ethnobotany. Gary Snyder. **CP-SnydG**

Etienne de la Boéce. Ralph Waldo Emerson. **CP-EmerR**

Etiquette. Leonard Cohen. **CP-CoheL**

Être là sans mâchoires sans dents. Samuel Beckett. **CP-BeckS**

Etruria Vale. Charles Tomlinson. **CP-TomlC**

Etude. Frederick Morgan. **SP-MorgF**

Études de Plusiers Paysages de l'Âme. Hayden Carruth. **CP-CarHS**

Eucharist, The. Robert Herrick. **CP-HerrR**

Euclia's Hymn. Ben Jonson. **CP-JonsB** *Fr.* Love's Triumph through Callipolis.

Euclid. Nicholas Vachel Lindsay. **CP-LindV** *Fr.* Poems about the Moon.

Euclid alone has looked on Beauty bare. Edna St. Vincent Millay. **CP-MillE**

Euclid Avenue. Hart Crane. **CP-CranH**

Euclid Avenue. Charles Simic. **SP-SimiC**

Eudaimon. Kathleen Jessie Raine. **SP-RainK**

Eugene Connolly. James Liddy. **CP-LiddJ**

Eugene, Orgeon. Jim Carroll. **SP-CarrJ**

Euglena. Miller Williams. **SP-WillM**

Eulalie—A Song. Edgar Allan Poe. **CP-PoeEd**

Eulenspiegelei. Stevie Smith. **CP-SmitS**

Eulogy. Wystan Hugh Auden. *Fr.* Eleven Occasional Poems. **CP-AudeW**

Eulogy to a Hell of a Dame—. Charles Bukowski. **SP-BukC3**

Eunice. Sir John Betjeman. **CP-BetjJ**

Eunice. Thomas Hardy. **CP-HardT**

Eunuch and the unicorn, The. The Primrose Bed. Robert Ranke Graves. **CP-GravR**

Eunuch is a silly fat, The. Still Life I. Howard Nemerov. **CP-NemeH**

Eupheme. Ben Jonson. **CP-JonsB**
  Elegy on My Muse.
    (Lady Venetia Digby, The.) **GoBC**
  Mind, The.
    (Picture of Her Mind, The.) **GoBC**
  Picture of the Body, The. **NOSC**

Euphoria. Lawrence Ferlinghetti. **SP-FerlL**

Euphrasy. Walter de la Mare. **CP-DeLaW**

Europa. Derek Walcott. **CP-WalcD**

Europa, / your red-haired. For the West. Gary Snyder. **CP-SnydG**

Europe. Howard Nemerov. **CP-NemeH**

Europe; A Prophecy. William Blake. **CP-BlakW**
  Ethinthus, Queen of Waters. **ChTr**

Europe! Europe! Allen Ginsberg. **CP-GinsA**

Europe has run its course, and whether to fall by its own sickness or ours. Invasion. Robinson Jeffers. **CP-JefR3**

Europe 1953. For Ethel Rosenberg. Adrienne Rich. **SP-RicA1; SP-RicA2**

Europe, the 72d and 73d Year of These States. Walt Whitman. **CP-WhitW**

Europe, the much-scarred, much-scoured terrain. The Lowlands of Holland. Geoffrey Hill. *Fr.* Of Commerce and Society: Variations on a Theme. **CP-HillG**

European Trib. boy's face photo'd eyes opened. Elegy Che Guevara. Allen Ginsberg. **CP-GinsA**

Europeans, The. Robert Creeley. **CP-CreeR**

Euryclea's Tale. Adrienne Rich. **CP-RicAE**

Eurydice. Margaret Atwood. **SP-AtwM2**

Eurydice. Hilda Doolittle. **CP-DoolH**
  "At least I have the flowers of myself." **VBLP**
  "So you have swept me back." **NALW; VBLP; VGW**

Eurydice. Robert Ranke Graves. **CP-GravR**

Eurydice. Raissa Maritain, *tr. fr. French by* Thomas Merton. **CP-MertT**

Eurydice. John Updike. **CP-UpdiJ**

Eurydice—it concerned thee, O Lord, The. The Loss of the Eurydice. Gerard Manley Hopkins. **CP-HopkG**

Eurydice to Orpheus. Robert Browning. **CP-BroR1**

Eurydice to Orpheus. Jenny Joseph. **SP-JoseJ**

Euthanasia. Byron. **CP-Byron**

Euthanasia. Allen Tate. **CP-TateA**

Eutychides. Lucilius. **OBAL** *Fr.* Variations of Greek Themes. **CP-RobiE**

Ev erythingex Cept: / that / 's what she's. Edward Estlin Cummings. **CP-CummE**

Eva. Christina Georgina Rossetti. **CP-RosC3**

Eva. John Greenleaf Whittier. **CP-WhitJ**

Eva B Hitler, geb. Braun. William DeWitt Snodgrass. **SP-SnodW**

Eva Braun. William DeWitt Snodgrass. **CAPP** *Fr.* The Führer Bunker. **SP-SnodW**

Evadne. Hilda Doolittle. **CP-DoolH**

Evaluation Under a Pine Tree, Lying On Pine Needles, An. Richard Eberhart. **CP-EberR**

Evangelie, or, The Figure of Literary Corruption, Seeking Glory Not Truth. Stevie Smith. **CP-SmitS**

Evangeline, a Tale of Acadie. Henry Wadsworth Longfellow. **SP-LongH**
  Part the First.
    "Bent like a laboring oar, that toils in the surf of the ocean."
    Embarkation, The. **PAH**
    "In the Acadian land, on the shores of the Basin of Minas."
    Evangeline in Acadie. **AA**
    "Now had the seasons returned, when the nights grow colder and longer."
    "In-doors, warm by the wide mouthed fireplace, idly the farmer." **APN-1**
    "Pleasantly rose next morn the sun on the village of Grand-Pré."
  Part the Second.
    "Far in the West there lies a desert land, where the mountains."
    "Far in the West there lies a desert land, where the mountains." **APN-1**
    "In that delightful land which is washed by the Delaware's waters."
    Finding of Gabriel, The. **AA**
    "It was the month of May. Far down the Beautiful River."
    Lakes of the Atchafalaya, The. **PoEL-5**
    On the Atchafalaya. **AA**
    "Softly the evening came. The sun from the western horizon." **APN-1**
    "Many a weary night had passed since the burning of Grand-Pré."
    "Near to the bank of the river, o'ershadowed by oaks, from whose branches."
  Tale of Acadie, A. **MeMAP**
    "This is the forest primeval. The murmuring pines and the hemlocks." **APN-1; UV**

Evangeline in Acadie. Henry Wadsworth Longfellow. **AA** *Fr.* In the Acadian land, on the shores of the Basin of Minas. *Fr.* Part the First. *Fr.* Evangeline, a Tale of Acadie. **SP-LongH**

Evangelist, The. Donald Davie. **CP-DavDo**

Evangelist. John Hewitt. **CP-HewiJ**

Evangelist St John my patron was, The. William Wordsworth. **HAP,** *book 3, ll. 46–63;* **FaBoRV** *Fr.* Residence at Cambridge. *Fr.* The Prelude; Growth of a Poet's Mind [1850 vers.]. **CP-WorW3**

  (Newton's Statue.) **FaBoRV,** *book 3, ll. 46–63;*

Evangelist's Wife, An. Edwin Arlington Robinson. **CP-RobiE**

Evarra and His Gods. Rudyard Kipling. **CP-KiplR**

Evasive souls, of whom the wise lose track. The Imaginative Life. Geoffrey Hill. **CP-HillG**

Eve. Jane Cooper. **SP-CoopJ**

Eve. David Herbert Lawrence. **CP-LawrD**

Eve. John Milton. *See* In bower and field he sought, where any tuft.

Eve. Howard Nemerov. **CP-NemeH**

Eve. Christina Georgina Rossetti. **CP-RosC1**

Eve. William Carlos Williams. **CP-WilW1**

Eve & her envy roving slammed me down. Gislebertus' Eve. John Berryman. **CP-BerrJ**

Eve Answers the Burdock. Archibald MacLeish. *Fr.* Songs for Eve. **CP-MacLA**

Eve Explains Everything to the Thrush Who Repeats Everything. Archibald MacLeish. *Fr.* Songs for Eve. **CP-MacLA**

Eve has just succumbed to the serpent. He is quite. Excerpts from God's Secret Diary. Ron Koertge. **SP-KoerR**

Eve in the Dawn. Archibald MacLeish. *Fr.* Songs for Eve. **CP-MacLA**

Eve is a twofold mystery. The Poet's Vow. Elizabeth Barrett Browning. **CP-BroEB**

Eve moves: golden Mother of baroque lights. Thomas Merton. *Fr.* Cables to the Ace. **CP-MertT**

Eve of Ch'ing Ming—Clear Bright, The. Kenneth Rexroth. **CP-RexKL; SP-RexrK** *Fr.* The Heart's Garden, the Garden's Heart.

Eve of Election, The. John Greenleaf Whittier. **CP-WhitJ**

Eve of St. Agnes, The. John Keats. **CP-KeatJ**

Eve of St. Agony, or the Middle Class Was Sitting on Its Fat. Kenneth Patchen. **CP-PatcK**

Eve of St. Mark, The. John Keats. **CP-KeatJ**

Eve of St Mark, The. Geoffrey Hill. *Fr.* An Apology for the Revival of Christian Architecture in England. **CP-HillG**

Eve of Waterloo, The. Byron. *See* There was a sound of revelry by night.

Eve of Waterloo, The. Thomas Hardy. **CP-HardT** *Fr.* The Dynasts.

Eve Old. Archibald MacLeish. *Fr.* Songs for Eve. **CP-MacLA**

Eve, our mother, care and keep! Eve Quiets Her Children. Archibald MacLeish. *Fr.* Songs for Eve. **CP-MacLA**

Eve Penitent. John Milton. **OBS** *Fr.* Book X. **FHYEP** *Fr.* Paradise Lost. **CP-MiltJ**

Eve Quiets Her Children. Archibald MacLeish. *Fr.* Songs for Eve. **CP-MacLA**

Eve roved in Paradise, I've heard. Ralph Waldo Emerson. **CP-EmerR**

Eve said: / From tree to tree. What Eve Said. Archibald MacLeish. *Fr.* Songs for Eve. **CP-MacLA**

Eve Speaks to Adam. John Milton. *See* With thee conversing I forget all time.

Eve to Adam. John Milton. *See* With thee conversing I forget all time.

Eve to the Storm of Thunder. Archibald MacLeish. *Fr.* Songs for Eve. **CP-MacLA**

Evelyn G. of Christminster. Thomas Hardy. **CP-HardT**

Evelyn Hope. Robert Browning. **CP-BroR1**

Even a hair. Sea Level. Al Young. **CP-YounA**

Even a pencil has fear to. Edward Estlin Cummings. **CP-CummE**

Even a thing like this takes pathos. An Old Warplane. Howard Nemerov. **CP-NemeH**

Even a tree has inclination. Roots. Phoebe Hesketh. **SP-HeskP**

Even after his death he did not return. Dante. "Anna Akhmatova", *tr. fr. Russian by* Stanley Kunitz. **CP-KuniS**

Even after the letters, there is work. Juanita Tinsley. Muriel Rukeyser. **CP-RukeM**

Even as a dragon's eye that feels the stress. William Wordsworth. **CP-WorW1**

Even as a river,—partly (it might seem). Residence in France. William Wordsworth. *Fr.* The Prelude; Growth of a Poet's Mind [1850 vers.]. **CP-WorW3**

Even as children they were late sleepers. The Undead. Richard Wilbur. **CP-WilbR**

Even as I Hold You. Alice Walker. **CP-WalkA**

Even as I seem to see. Snorkeling in the Caribbean. Dabney Stuart. **SP-StuaD**

Even as lame things thirst their perfection, so. To Mr E. G. John Donne. **CP-DonnJ**

Even as she slides down the ways. The Schooner. Lewis Turco. **SP-TurcL**

Even as the street becomes familiar to you. After Moving. John Yau. **SP-YauJo**

Even as the sun with purple-colour'd face. Venus and Adonis. William Shakespeare. **CP-ShaWS**

Even as when you behold hot swarms of the tribes of the wild bees. Assembly of the Achaians. Homer, *tr. by* George Meredith. **CP-MerG2** *Fr.* The Iliad.

Even at night the air rang and rang. Boccaccio: The Plague Years. Rita Dove. **SP-DoveR**

Even at school he was different. Different. Phoebe Hesketh. **SP-HeskP**

Even before his book came out. Ars Poetica. Howard Nemerov. **CP-NemeH**

Even being able to get a glimpse of moon. Fun City Samba. Al Young. **CP-YounA**

Even culture / ought to. The Whole World. Charles Olson. **CP-OlsoC**

Even during war, moments of delicate peace. Muriel Rukeyser. **TrJP** *Fr.* Letter to the Front. **CP-RukeM**

Even Egrets Err. John Updike. **CP-UpdiJ**

Even from the train the hill looked empty. A Story. Randall Jarrell. **CP-JarrR**

Even here, in a forest in the foothills of a range of mountains, lucent air, the purest dawn. The Insult. Charles Kenneth Williams. **SP-WillC**

Even if all desires things moments be. Edward Estlin Cummings. **CP-CummE**

Even If I Could. Charles Kenneth Williams. **CP-WillC; SP-WillC**

Even if love convey. Louis Zukofsky. **CP-ZukLS**

Even if we knew the children were all asleep. Poetry: III. Adrienne Rich. **SP-RicA1**

Even in a country you know by heart. Traveling at Home. Wendell Berry. **CP-BerrW**

Even in barbarian countries they would take us for. You Came By on Bamboo Stilts, Playing Horse. . . . James Liddy. **CP-LiddJ**

Even in bed I pose: desire may grow. Carnal Knowledge. Thom Gunn. **CP-GunnT**

Even in childhood. Liadan and Curithir. Robert Ranke Graves. **CP-GravR**

Even in death they prosper; even in the death. Necropolis. Karl Shapiro. **SP-ShapK**

Even in July, from this point north. Point No Point. Richard Hugo. **CP-HugoR**

Even in spring, even in first. April in November. Archibald MacLeish. **CP-MacLA**

Even in steadiest mood of reason, when. Books. William Wordsworth. *Fr.* The Prelude; Growth of a Poet's Mind [1805 vers.]. **CP-WorW3**

Even in the bluest noonday of July. To Mrs. Will H. Low. Robert Louis Stevenson. **CP-StevR**

Even In The Grave. Walter de la Mare. **CP-DeLaW**

Even in the moment of our earliest kiss. Edna St. Vincent Millay. **CP-MillE**

Even in the pink crib. One-Eye, Two-Eyes, Three-Eyes. Anne Sexton. **CP-SextA**

Even in the pools. Dyere. Roy Fisher. **SP-FishR** *Fr.* Five Pilgrims in the Prologue to the Canterbury Tales.

Even in the time when as yet. The Wanderer. William Carlos Williams. **CP-WilW1**

Even in the time when still I. Wanderer, The: A Rococo Study. William Carlos Williams. **CP-WilW1**

Even iron can put forth. Almond Blossom. David Herbert Lawrence. **CP-LawrD**

Even love must pass through loneliness. Setting Out. Wendell Berry. **CP-BerrW**

Even now one is amazed. Geoffrey Hill. *Fr.* Scenes with Harlequins. **CP-HillG**

Even now there are places where a thought might grow. A Disused Shed in Co. Wexford. Derek Mahon. **SP-MahoD**

Even now this landscape is assembling. All Hallows. Louise Glück. **SP-GlücL**

Even now, when I patrol my thoughts of you. Prophet in a Landscape of Immemorial Time. Bill Knott. **SP-KnotB**

Even Now You Are Leaving. Tess Gallagher. **SP-GallT**

Even Numbers. Carl Sandburg. **CP-SandC**

Even on the quietest days the distant. Ford Manor. Derek Mahon. **SP-MahoD**

Even Over the Flat Land. Jenny Joseph. **SP-JoseJ**

Even she too dead! all languor on her brow. Imogen. Walter de la Mare. **CP-DeLaW**

Even so—as a man at the end tries no more. The Wreck of the *Swan*. "Hugh MacDiarmid." **SP-MacDH**

Even so bewails, the poplar groves among. Translation of Virgil's Georgic IV. 511–15. Virgil, *tr. by* William Wordsworth. **CP-WorW2** *Fr.* Georgics.

Even so distant, I can taste the grief. Deceptions. Philip Larkin. **CP-LarkP**

Even so for me a Vision sanctified. November, 1836. William Wordsworth. **CP-WorW2**

Even so it was. From Flodden ridge. The English Advance at Flodden. Sir Walter Scott. **SP-ScotW** *Fr.* Marmion.

"Even so" (the exulting Maiden said). Samuel Taylor Coleridge. **ChER** *Fr.* The Destiny of Nations. **CP-ColeS**

Even such is time, which takes in trust. The Authours Epitaph, Made by Himself. Sir Walter Ralegh. **CP-RaleW**

Even such the contrast that, where'er we move. Troubles of Charles the First. William Wordsworth. *Fr.* Ecclesiastical Sonnets. **CP-WorW2**

Even sunlight dares. Prisoner. Maya Angelou. **SP-AngeM**

Even the barnacle has certain rights. This Octopus Exploits Women. James Fenton. **SP-FentJ**

Even the beauty of the rose doth cast. Shadow. Walter de la Mare. **CP-DeLaW**

Even the bravest that are slain. The Trial by Existence. Robert Frost. **CP-FrosR**

Even the dignity of Christ. The Red Branch. Donald Hall. **CP-HallD**

Even the mountaineer came back. The Bell-Ringer. Pablo Neruda, *tr. fr. Spanish by* Ben Belitt. **SP-NeruP**

Even the old emotions are finished. Dies Irae. David Herbert Lawrence. **CP-LawrD**

Even the old priest, in his long black robe and silvery hair. At the Bank in Spain. David Herbert Lawrence. **CP-LawrD**

Even the rainbow has a body. The Rainbow. David Herbert Lawrence. **CP-LawrD**

Even the shrewd and bitter. Prologue to "Rhymes to be Traded for Bread." Nicholas Vachel Lindsay. **CP-LindV**

Even the sun-clouds this morning cannot manage such skirts. Poppies in October. Sylvia Plath. **CP-PlatS**

Even the walls are flowing, even the ceiling. Variation on Heraclitus. Louis MacNeice. **CP-MacNL**

Even the wide Heath, where the unequal ground. The Heath. Charlotte Smith. **CP-SmitC**

Even these stones I placed crudely once. The Little Fire in the Woods. Hayden Carruth. **CP-CarHS**

Even they that have no murdrous will, *ad. fr. Latin of* Juvenal. Sir Walter Ralegh. **CP-RaleW**

Even though you outwit me, I'm not going back to you. A Woman's Decision. Leonard Cohen. **CP-CoheL**

Even to think / of installing an air-conditioner. Song: Luxury. Hayden Carruth. **CP-CarHS**

Even tomorrow he may leave his room. WW I. Miller Williams. **SP-WillM**

Even when death has taken. For Dudley. Richard Wilbur. **CP-WilbR**

Even when first her face. Someone Talking to Himself. Richard Wilbur. **CP-WilbR**

Even when I thought I prayed, I was talking to myself; when I. Ghazal V. Adrienne Rich. **SP-RicA2** *Fr.* Shooting Script. **CP-RicAE**

Even when the heart of the world is found. Charles Henri Ford. *Fr.* Epigrams. **SP-FordC**

Even when you lust, ye may refrain. *see also* "Defamed guiltiness by silence unkempt." Sir Thomas Wyatt. **CP-WyatT**

Even while I speak, the sacred roofs of France. Emigrant French Clergy. William Wordsworth. *Fr.* Ecclesiastical Sonnets. **CP-WorW2**

Even with its own ax to grind, sometimes. The Mind, Intractable Thing. Marianne Craig Moore. **CP-MoorM**

Even you, Sweet Basil: even you. Steepletop. Edna St. Vincent Millay. **CP-MillE**

Even your odds and ends. I Love Your Crazy Bones. Barton Sutter. **SP-SuttB**

Evening. Byron. **TrGrPo** *Fr.* Canto the Third. *Fr.* Don Juan. **CP-Byron** (Hesperus the Bringer.) **AWP**

Evening. John Clare. **SP-ClarJ**

Evening. John Clare. **SP-ClarJ**

Evening. Walter de la Mare. **SP-DeLaW**

Evening. Walter de la Mare. **CP-DeLaW**

Evening. Hilda Doolittle. **CP-DoolH**

Evening. Paul Laurence Dunbar. **CP-DunbP**

Evening. Daniel Gerard Hoffman. **SP-HoffD**

Evening, *tr. fr. the German of* Rilke. Randall Jarrell. **CP-JarrR**

Evening, *also stands as a sl. diff. separate poem,* Rondeau of a Conscientious Objector. David Herbert Lawrence. *Fr.* The Schoolmaster [A]. **CP-LawrD**

Evening. Thomas Merton. **CP-MertT; SP-MertT**

Evening. James Schuyler. **CP-SchuJ**

Evening. Sir Walter Scott. **SP-ScotW** *Fr.* Rokeby.

Evening. Charles Simic. **SP-SimiC**

Evening. Charlotte Smith. **CP-SmitC**

Evening. James Wright. **CP-WrigJ**

Evening: A Studio in Rome. Miller Williams. **SP-WillM**

Evening, after a Picture. Johann Christoph Friedrich von Schiller, *tr. fr. German by* George Meredith. **CP-MerG2**

Evening at Axel's. James Liddy. **CP-LiddJ**

Evening at the calm. Sea Storm. Richard Eberhart. **CP-EberR**

Evening bird is singing, The. Duckturne. Malcolm Lowry. **CP-LowrM**

Evening Bird Song. Richard Eberhart. **CP-EberR**

Evening, blue, voluptuous, of June, The. Memory: The Walk on the Beach. John Gould Fletcher. **SP-FletJ**

Evening, bringing me out of the government building. Muriel Rukeyser. *Fr.* Letter to the Front. **CP-RukeM**

Evening came, a paw, to the gray hut by the river. Fall Journey. William Stafford. **SP-StafW**

Evening Clouds, The. John Gould Fletcher. **SP-FletJ**

Evening comes / when we finish work and go, An. Wendell Berry. *Fr.* The Clearing. **CP-BerrW**

Evening comes early, and soon discovers. Master's in the Garden Again. John Crowe Ransom. *Fr.* Sixteen Poems in Eight Pairings. **SP-RansJ**

Evening comes on and the hills thicken. A Boat. Margaret Atwood. **SP-AtwM2**

Evening day is churning, The. Afternoon Nocturne. Malcolm Lowry. **CP-LowrM**

Evening Ebb. Robinson Jeffers. **CP-JefR2**

Evening faultless interval when, An. Sanctuary. John Berryman. **CP-BerrJ**

Evening folds about itself the dark, The. *tr. fr. the German of* Rilke. Randall Jarrell. **CP-JarrR**

Evening Grass, The. Kay Boyle. **CP-BoylK**

Evening Hawk. Robert Penn Warren. **SP-WarrR**

Evening in a Sugar Orchard. Robert Frost. **CP-FrosR**

Evening in angelus has blessed the land, The. Evening in Spring. John Hewitt. **CP-HewiJ**

Evening in Burmah. John Greenleaf Whittier. **CP-WhitJ**

Evening in Connecticut. Louis MacNeice. **CP-MacNL**

Evening in Galilee, An. Thomas Hardy. **CP-HardT**

Evening in Paradise. John Milton. *See* Now came still Ev'ning [*or* evening *or* Eevning] on, and Twilight gray [*or* grey].

Evening in Spring. John Hewitt. **CP-HewiJ**

Evening in the Sanitarium. Louise Bogan. **CP-BogaL**

Evening Indoors. Louis MacNeice. **CP-MacNL**

Evening is the Fourth of July. Summer. Al Young. **CP-YounA**

Evening isnt so much a playland as it is. Groupie. Al Young. **CP-YounA**

Evening Land, The. David Herbert Lawrence. **CP-LawrD**

Evening Lull, An. Walt Whitman. **CP-WhitW**

Evening moth / sips at mouth. Go Lightly. Marsden Hartley. **CP-HartM**

Evening Music. May Sarton. **SP-SartM**

Evening News. Jim Carroll. **SP-CarrJ**

Evening News, The. Audre Lorde. **SP-LordA**

Evening News, The. Gilbert Sorrentino. **SP-SorrG**

Evening Ode, An. Samuel Johnson. **CP-JohnS**

Evening of the Visitation, The. Thomas Merton. **CP-MertT**

Evening on Lesbos. Edna St. Vincent Millay. **CP-MillE**

Evening on the Boyne. Donald Davie. **CP-DavDo**

Evening Out, The. Ogden Nash. **CP-NashO**

Evening passes fast away, The. Emily Brontë. **CP-BronE** (Self-Interrogation.) **CP-BronE**

Evening Plaza, San Miguel. Muriel Rukeyser. **CP-RukeM**

Evening: Ponte al Mare, Pisa. Percy Bysshe Shelley. **CP-ShelP**

Evening Prayer, *ad. fr.* Psalm 140, 141. Thomas Merton. **CP-MertT**

Evening Questions. Carl Sandburg. **CP-SandC**

Evening Sea Wind. Carl Sandburg. **CP-SandC**

Evening Shadows. Thomas Hardy. **CP-HardT**

Evening Song. Langston Hughes. **SP-HughL**

Evening-Star. Louise Bogan. **CP-BogaL**

Evening Star, The, *tr. fr. the German of* Rilke. Randall Jarrell. **CP-JarrR**

Evening Star. Edgar Allan Poe. **CP-PoeEd**

Evening Stroll in the Suburbs. Mona Van Duyn. **SP-VanDM**

Evening sulks along the shore, the reddening sun, The. Forte Dei Marmi. David Herbert Lawrence. **CP-LawrD**

Evening sun was sinking down, The. Emily Brontë. **CP-BronE**

Evening Sunsets Witness and Pass On, The. Carl Sandburg. **CP-SandC**

Evening: To Harriet. Percy Bysshe Shelley. **CP-ShelP**

Evening Walk Addressed to a Young Lady, An. William Wordsworth. **CP-WorW1**

Evening Walk by the Sea-Side, An. Charlotte Smith. **CP-SmitC**

Evening Walk in France. May Sarton. **SP-SartM**

Evening Waterfall. Carl Sandburg. **CP-SandC**

Evening When the Full Moon Rose as the Sun Set, An. Robert Bly. **SP-BlyR**

Evening Wind. James Schuyler. **CP-SchuJ**

Evening with the Master, An. Charles Simic. **SP-SimiC**

Evening without Angels. Wallace Stevens. **CP-StevW**

Evening: Zero Weather. Thomas Merton. **CP-MertT; SP-MertT**

Evenings I hear. A Plague of Starlings. Robert Earl Hayden. **CP-HaydR**

Evenings in Vermont. James Schuyler. **CP-SchuJ**

Evening's Love, An. John Dryden. Song: "You charmed me not with that fair face." **SP-DrydJ**

Evenings seem endless, now. Roots. Adrienne Rich. **CP-RicAE; SP-RicA2**

Eveningsong at Bellosguardo. Erica Jong. **SP-JongE**

Evensong [*or* Even-Song]. George Herbert. **CP-HerbG**

Evensong. Richard Crashaw. **CP-CrasR**

Evensong. George Herbert. **CP-HerbG**

Evensong. Robert Herrick. **CP-HerrR**

Evensong. Robert Louis Stevenson. **CP-StevR**

Event / a reflection. Shenandoah. Charles Olson. **CP-OlsoC**

Event, The. Hayden Carruth. *Fr.* Mother. **CP-CarHL**

Event, The. Leonard Cohen. **CP-CoheL**

Event, The. Rita Dove. **SP-DoveR**

Event. Sylvia Plath. **CP-PlatS**

Event. Charles Tomlinson. **CP-TomlC**

Event, The. Robert Penn Warren. **SP-WarrR**

Event, The. Robert Penn Warren. *See Nigger:* as if it were not.

Event, An. Richard Wilbur. **CP-WilbR**

Event at Konna, The. Kenneth Patchen. **CP-PatcK**

Event Itself, The. Hayden Carruth. **CP-CarHS**

Event of Things Not in Our Power. Robert Herrick. **CP-HerrR**

Event was directly behind Him, The. Emily Dickinson. **CP-DickE**

Event Without Particulars. James Merrill. *Fr.* Five Old Favorites. **SP-MerrJ**

Events in a Rustic Mirror. George Meredith. **CP-MerG2**

Events in my native province now. Parallels Never Meet. John Hewitt. **CP-HewiJ**

Events reported by the ear. Heard and Seen. Wystan Hugh Auden. **CP-AudeW**

Eventual Proteus. Margaret Atwood. **SP-AtwM1**

Eventually one finds / There is no environment. The Place. Richard Eberhart. **CP-EberR**

Ever a Seeker. Carl Sandburg. **CP-SandC**

Ever After. Tess Gallagher. **SP-GallT**

Ever again to breathe pure happiness. Happiness. Wilfred Owen. **CP-OwenW**

Ever as now with Love and Virtue's glow. Fragment of a Sonnet: To Harriet. Percy Bysshe Shelley. **CP-ShelP**

Ever as We Sailed. Percy Bysshe Shelley. **SeCePo** *Fr.* The Revolt of Islam. **CP-ShelP**

Ever before my face there went. Vain Finding. Walter de la Mare. **CP-DeLaW**

Ever exulting in thyself, on fire. Humanity. Walter de la Mare. **CP-DeLaW**

Ever invoking fire from heaven, the fire. George Meredith. *Fr.* France. **CP-MerG1**

Ever let the Fancy roam. Fancy. John Keats. **CP-KeatJ**

Ever mine [*or* myn] hap[pe] is slack and slo[w] in coming [*or* commyng]. Petrarch, *tr. fr. Italian by* Sir Thomas Wyatt. **CP-WyatT**

Ever perilous / And precious, like an ember from the fire. To the Stormy Petrel. Robert Louis Stevenson. **CP-StevR**

Ever restless, restless, craving rest. Camoëns. Herman Melville. **SP-MelvH**

Ever Since. Archibald MacLeish. **CP-MacLA**

Ever since he arrived in this country. A Casualty. Daniel Gerard Hoffman. **SP-HoffD**

Ever since observation taught me temptation. Song of the Devil. Wystan Hugh Auden. *Fr.* Two Songs. **CP-AudeW**

Ever since our lunch of cheese. Dearest Man-in-the-Moon. Erica Jong. **SP-JongE**

Ever since the old days. Lament of a Maiden for the Warrior's Death. Pablo Antonio Cuadra, *tr. fr. Spanish by* Thomas Merton. **CP-MertT**

Ever since they'd left the Tennessee ridge. The Event. Rita Dove. **SP-DoveR**

Ever that Everest. Time. James Merrill. **SP-MerrJ**

Ever the poet *from* the land. Poet. Ralph Waldo Emerson. *Fr.* Quatrains. **CP-EmerR**

Ever the Rock of Ages melts. Ralph Waldo Emerson. **CP-EmerR**

Ever the same, forever new! Awaking. Stephen Spender. **CP-SpenS**

Ever the undiscouraged, resolute, struggling soul of man. Life. Walt Whitman. **CP-WhitW**

Everest. Wystan Hugh Auden. **CP-AudWJ**

Evergreen. Phoebe Hesketh. **SP-HeskP**

Everlasting Arms, The, *Moulton,* Modern Reader's Bible. Bible, *O.T. See* Psalm 91: "He that dwelleth in the secret place. . . ."

Everlasting Contenders, The. Kenneth Patchen. **CP-PatcK**

Everlasting Flowers. David Herbert Lawrence. **CP-LawrD**

Everlasting Gospel, The. William Blake. **CP-BlakW**

   "Vision of Christ that thou dost see, The." **ChIV-2**

   "Was Jesus Chaste? or did he." **ChIV-2**

   "Was Jesus Humble? or did he." **ChIV-2**

Everlasting layers / Of ideas, images, feelings. "Hugh MacDiarmid." **SP-MacDH** *Fr.* Plaited Like the Generations of Men.

Everlasting Monday, The. Sylvia Plath. **CP-PlatS**

Everlasting universe of things, The. Mont Blanc. Percy Bysshe Shelley. **CP-ShelP**

Everlasting Voices, The. William Butler Yeats. **CP-YeatW**

Everness. Jorge Luis Borges, *tr. fr. Spanish by* Richard Wilbur. **CP-WilbR**

Every Artemisia. Thomas Hardy. **CP-HardT**

Every branch big with it. Snow in the Suburbs. Thomas Hardy. **CP-HardT**

Every choice is always the wrong choice. Whole Love. Robert Ranke Graves. **CP-GravR**

Every created thing has ways of pronouncing its ownhood. Natural Linguistics. Wystan Hugh Auden. **CP-AudeW**

Every Day. Tom Clark. **SP-ClarT**

Every Day. Robert Creeley. **CP-CreeR**

Every Day. William Carlos Williams. **CP-WilW2**

Every day a wilderness—no. Dusting. Rita Dove. **SP-DoveR**

Every day alone whittles me. Going In. Marge Piercy. **SP-PierM**

Every day became a slow July. Sweat, it was clear. Leaving the Dream. Richard Hugo. **CP-HugoR**

Every day brings a ship. Letters. Ralph Waldo Emerson. **CP-EmerR**

Every day he went out, forsaking. Grace Paley. *Fr.* Stanzas: Old Age and the Conventions of Retirement Have Driven My Friends from the Work They Love. **CP-PaleG**

Every day I peruse the box scores for hours. Baseball and Classicism. Tom Clark. **SP-ClarT**

Every Day Is Monday. Ogden Nash. **CP-NashO**

Every day is the last day. The Wind on the Way. Carl Sandburg. **CP-SandC**

Every day our bodies separate. Villanelle. Marilyn Hacker. **SP-HackM**

Every evening / in this old valley. Quebec Suite. Mona Van Duyn. **SP-VanDM**

Every Evening in Axel's. James Liddy. **CP-LiddJ**

Every evening the L & N. Ernesto Cardenal, *tr. by* Thomas Merton. **CP-MertT** *Fr.* Gethsemani, KY.

Every fear is a desire. Every desire is fear. A Staffordshire Murderer. James Fenton. **SP-FentJ**

Every few years, down at the Florida Keys. The Death of the Pilot Whales. Peter Meinke. **SP-MeinP**

Every good wind he hangs over the field. Hawk in Uig. Richard Hugo. **CP-HugoR**

Every Grain of Sand. "Bob Dylan." **CP-DylaB**

Every heavy in every afternoon. Mr. Big. Ron Koertge. **SP-KoerR**

Every hour, every moment. Hilda Doolittle. **NALW; NoAM** *Fr.* Tribute to the Angels. **CP-DoolH**

Every Little Thing. John Lennon *and* Paul McCartney. **CP-Beatl**

Every Lovely Limb's a Desolation. Stevie Smith. **CP-SmitS**

Every man / is his own clock. The Clock of the Years. William Carlos Williams. **CP-WilW2**

Every Man His Own Matador; or for That Matter Any Member of the Family. Charles Olson. **CP-OlsoC**

Every man spins a web of light circles. Webs. Carl Sandburg. **CP-SandC**

Every month, / the reminder of emptiness. Empty. Erica Jong. **SP-JongE**

Every moon every year every wind must travel and pass on. Dzules. Thomas Merton. *Fr.* South. *Fr.* The Geography of Lograire. **CP-MertT**

Every morn I lift my head. Ralph Waldo Emerson. **APN-1** *Fr.* Monadnoc. **CP-EmerR**

Every morning / the world / is created. Morning Poem. Mary Oliver. **SP-OlivM**

Every Morning. Alice Walker. **CP-WalkA**

Every morning I forget how it is. Poem. Charles Simic. **SP-SimiC**

Every morning I wash the slate clean. By the Stream. Richard Eberhart. **CP-EberR**

Every night / the owl / with his wild monkey-face. Lonely, White Fields. Mary Oliver. **SP-OlivM**

Every night at sleepy-time. Complaint to Four Angels. Ogden Nash. **CP-NashO**

Every night my prayers I say. System. Robert Louis Stevenson. **CP-StevR**

Every now and then we went out to dinner. Life on the Edge of the Continent. Ron Koertge. **SP-KoerR**

Every October millions of little fish come along the shore. Birds and Fishes. Robinson Jeffers. **CP-JefR3**

"Every one". Bobbie. Robert Creeley. **CP-CreeR**

Every one of the red roses opened. Edward Estlin Cummings. **CP-CummE**

Every One That Is Perfect Shall Be as His Master. Christina Georgina Rossetti. **CP-RosC2**

Every peak is a crater. This is the law of volcanoes. Adrienne Rich. **NAAL-2; NALW; NoAM** *Fr.* Twenty-one Love Poems. **SP-RicA1; SP-RicA2**

Every Pebble. Leonard Cohen. **CP-CoheL**

Every poet is a sacrificial spirit. The Sacrifice. Richard Eberhart. **CP-EberR**

Evil Tendencies Cancel. Robert Frost. *Fr.* Ten Mills. **CP-FrosR**

Evil World-Soul, The. David Herbert Lawrence. **CP-LawrD**

Evill. Robert Herrick. **CP-HerrR**

Evill no Nature hath; the losse of good. Evill. Robert Herrick. **CP-HerrR**

Evils of the City. Gilbert Sorrentino. **SP-SorrG**

Ev'n exactors of the toll. St. Matthew. Christopher Smart. *Fr.* Hymns and Spiritual Songs for the Fasts and Festivals of the Church of England. **SP-SmarC**

Ev'n one who has little travelled in. Dreams. Walter de la Mare. **CP-DeLaW**

Ev'n yet his voice from Hell's dread shades we hear. Virgil, *tr. by* Samuel Johnson. **CP-JohnS** *Fr.* The Aeneid [*or* Eneados, *Aeneis*].

Ev'ning, now, from purple wings. An Evening Ode. Samuel Johnson. **CP-JohnS**

Evolution. Leonard Nathan. **SP-NathL**

Evolution of the Dragon, The. Wystan Hugh Auden. **CP-AudWJ**

Evolutionary Poem No. 1. Etheridge Knight. **SP-KnigE**

Evolutionary Poem No. 2. Etheridge Knight. **SP-KnigE**

Ev'ry Dame affects good fame, what ere her doings be. Thomas Campion. **CP-CampT**

Ev'rybody's building the big ships and the boats. Quinn the Eskimo. "Bob Dylan." **CP-DylaB**

E.W. to A.G.A. Emily Brontë. **CP-BronE**

Ewes are in the shed, The. Couples Under Cover. Ted Hughes. **SP-HughT**

Ewigkeit. Jorge Luis Borges, *tr. fr. Spanish by* Richard Wilbur. **CP-WilbR**

Ex-Basketball Player. John Updike. **CP-UpdiJ**

Ex-Clerk. Rudyard Kipling. *Fr.* Epitaphs of the War [1914–1918]. **CP-KiplR**

Ex luctu populus, redditur ipse chalybs. Fragment of a Series of Elegies. Robert Southwell. **CP-SoutR**

Ex nihilo, Owen imagines, then contrives. Owen at Play. James McAuley. **SP-McAuJ**

Ex-Poet, The. Malcolm Lowry. **CP-LowrM**

Ex-Serviceman, The. John Hewitt. **CP-HewiJ**

Ex Vermibus. "Hugh MacDiarmid." **SP-MacDH**

Exact beat from—, The. Hayden Carruth. **Jaz** *Fr.* Paragraphs. **CP-CarHS**

Exactly at one o'clock your arms broach. Tarquin. Frank O'Hara. **SP-OharF**

Exactly like a rain cloud. Ever After. Tess Gallagher. **SP-GallT**

Exaggeration. Elizabeth Barrett Browning. **CP-BroEB**

Exalt me, Clio to the skies. Ode, An. *Unknown. Fr.* Complimentary Pieces to Milton. **CP-CowpW**

Exaltation of larks arising, An. The Larks. Daniel Gerard Hoffman. **SP-HoffD**

Exam Dream, The. Erica Jong. **SP-JongE**

Examination, The. James McAuley. **SP-McAuJ**

Examination, The. William DeWitt Snodgrass. **SP-SnodW**

Examination at the Womb-Door. Ted Hughes. **SP-HughT**

Examination into Life and Death, An. Kenneth Patchen. **CP-PatcK**

Examination of Psyche: Thoughts of Home. Richard Eberhart. **CP-EberR**

Examination of the Hero in a Time of War. Wallace Stevens. **CP-StevW**

Examination Statute. "Lewis Carroll." **CP-CarrL**

Examples—for Richard Bridgeman. Charles Olson. **CP-OlsoC**

Examples, or Like Prince, Like People. Robert Herrick. **CP-HerrR**

Exasperated, worn, you conjure a mansion. Desires of Men and Women. John Berryman. **CP-BerrJ**

Exasperations of a Novelist. Howard Nemerov. **CP-NemeH**

Exastichon. Villiers Harington. *Fr.* Commendatory Poems. **CP-LoveR**

Excavation of Troy. Archibald MacLeish. **CP-MacLA**

Exceeding Bitter Cry, An. Christina Georgina Rossetti. **CP-RosC2**

Exceeding brightness of this early sun, The. The Sun This March. Wallace Stevens. **CP-StevW**

Excellence is a gift: among mankind. Runner. Wystan Hugh Auden. *Fr.* Six Commissioned Texts. **CP-AudeW**

Excellence is sparse. Ezra Pound in Pisa. Donald Davie. **CP-DavDo**

Excellence requires / leaf-rakers to sweep one spot. Hayden Carruth. **CP-CarHS** *Fr.* The Clay Hill Anthology.

Excellent herbs had our fathers of old. Our Fathers of Old. Rudyard Kipling. **CP-KiplR**

Excellent New Ballad, An. Jonathan Swift. **CP-SwifJ**

Excellent New Song, An. Jonathan Swift. **CP-SwifJ**

Excellent New Song on a Seditious Pamphlet, An. Jonathan Swift. **CP-SwifJ**

Excellent New Song upon His Grace Our Good Lord Archbishop of Dublin, An. Jonathan Swift. **CP-SwifJ**

Excelsior. Ralph Waldo Emerson. *Fr.* Quatrains. **CP-EmerR**

Excelsior. Walt Whitman. **CP-WhitW**

Except. Wendell Berry. **CP-BerrW**

Except for the dog, that she wouldn't have him put away, wouldn't let him die, I'd have liked her. The Dog. Charles Kenneth Williams. **CP-WillC; SP-WillC**

Except for the little girl. Even If I Could. Charles Kenneth Williams. **CP-WillC; SP-WillC**

Except for the undeniable flash of envy I feel, the reflexive competitiveness, he's inconsequential. Love: Youth. Charles Kenneth Williams. **SP-WillC**

Except in idea, perfection is as wild. The Design of a House. Wendell Berry. **CP-BerrW**

Except in your / honour. Edward Estlin Cummings. **CP-CummE; SP-CummE**

Except my hart which you beestow'd before. Sonnet 14. Mary Sidney, Countess of Montgomery Wroth. *Fr.* A Crowne of Sonetts Dedicated to Love. *Fr.* Pamphilia to Amphilanthus. **CP-WrotM**

Except that through the wet panes. Variant on a Scrap of Conversation. Charles Tomlinson. **CP-TomlC**

Except the Heaven had come so near. Emily Dickinson. **CP-DickE**

Except the Lord Build the House. Donald Davie. **CP-DavDo**

Except the Lord build the house. Psalm 127. Bible, *O.T.* **BiP; TRV; TrJP; TreF** *Fr.* Psalms. **CP-Psal**

Except the occasional auxilary horse or hound. The Silent Shepherds. Robinson Jeffers. **CP-JefR3**

Except the smaller size. Emily Dickinson. **CP-DickE**

Except to Heaven, she is nought. Emily Dickinson. **CP-DickE**

Except when he enters my son. The String. James Dickey. **CP-DickJ**

Except where blast-furnaces and generating-stations. Forty Years On. Wystan Hugh Auden. **CP-AudeW**

Exceptional / even deviant / you draw your long skirts. Heroines. Adrienne Rich. **SP-RicA2**

Excerpts from God's Secret Diary. Ron Koertge. **SP-KoerR**

Excerpts from the Notebook of the Poet of Santo Tomas. Richard Shelton. **SP-ShelR**

Excesse. Robert Herrick. **CP-HerrR**

Excesses of God, The. Robinson Jeffers. **CP-JefR1**

Exchange, The. Samuel Taylor Coleridge. **CP-ColeS**

Exchange in greed the ungraceful signs. Thrust. The Violent Space. Etheridge Knight. **SP-KnigE**

Exchange of Gifts, An. May Sarton. **SP-SartM**

Exchange of Livings. Sir John Betjeman. **CP-BetjJ**

Exchanges. James Dickey. **CP-DickJ**

Exchanging gentle grips, the men retire. An Imaginable Conference. John Updike. **CP-UpdiJ**

Exchanging Hats. Elizabeth Bishop. **CP-BishE**

Excursion, The. William Wordsworth. **CP-WorW2**

  Churchyard among the Mountains, The.

  Churchyard among the Mountains (Continued), The.

  Despondency.

  Despondency Corrected.

    "As men from men." **EnRP**

    "Curious child, who dwelt upon a tract, A." **WGRP**

  Discourse of the Wanderer and an Evening Visit to the Lake.

    "Behold the shades of afternoon have fallen." **EnRP**

    "To every Form of being is assigned." **EnRP**

  "Oft, through thy fair domains, illustrious Peer!"

  Parsonage, The.

  Pastor, The.

  identical to lines 754–860 of The Recluse; Home at Grasmere. **EnRP; FHYEP; NoP; PoE**

  Solitary, The.

    "Homeward the / Shepherds moved." **EnRP**

    "I could not, ever and anon, forbear." **EnRP**

  Wanderer, The. **EnRP**

    "Supine the Wanderer lay." **NOBRP**

  Wanderer Recalls the Past, The. **OBNC**

Excursion: Or: O Columbus!, The. Thomas McGrath. **SP-McGrT**

Excursion Train. David Herbert Lawrence. **CP-LawrD**

Excursions, Incursions. Marge Piercy. **SP-PierM**

  "At the big round table in the university."

  "I am sitting on a kitchen chair."

  "Learning to manage the process."

  "Men are laughing as I approach, The."

Excursus of Reassurance in Begonia Time, An. Hayden Carruth. **CP-CarHS**

Excuse, The. Sir Walter Ralegh. **CP-RaleW**

Excuse. Alice Walker. **CP-WalkA**

Excuse is needless when with love sincere. To S.H. William Wordsworth. **CP-WorW2**

Excuse me, but are you a superior person? Canvassing for the Election. David Herbert Lawrence. **CP-LawrD**

Excuse, my lord, the liberty I take. Letter to Lord Byron. Wystan Hugh Auden. **CP-AudeW**

Exeat. Stevie Smith. **CP-SmitS**

Execration upon Vulcan, An. Ben Jonson. **CP-JonsB**

Executioner, The. Ted Hughes. **SP-HughT**

Executions in Moscow, The. Kenneth Patchen. **CP-PatcK**

Executive. Sir John Betjeman. **CP-BetjJ**

Executive Discovers Poetry, The. Dabney Stuart. **SP-StuaD**

Executive speed is poetry! Whereas. Savannah. Donald Davie. **CP-DavDo**

Executive's Death, The. Robert Bly. **SP-BlyR**

Executives Third Tier. John Hewitt. **CP-HewiJ**

Exempla. James Fenton. **SP-FentJ**

"Adult: That's a tattooed man."

"At the foot of every steep cliff or precipice in high Alpine regions."

"Come and eat your Pablum."

"For the context of the basidiocarp Singer states." **PeLV**

"Frog hunts on land by vision. He escapes, A."

Fruit-Grower in War-time (and Some of His Enemies), The.

"Genus Stephanoma, The."

"GIRL ATTACKED."

"In September greasebands are put on standard apple."

"Obsolete Oxfordshire game of 'A-All,' The."

Pitt-Rivers Museum, Oxford, The. **FaBoMo**

"Psychopharmacological drugs."

South Parks Road.

"Sweden. Lapp. Pouch made from a blackthroated diver."

Terminal Moraine, A. **SCBI**

"Voice disguiser with membrane of a spider's egg-case, A."

Exeo in a spasm. Enueg I. Samuel Beckett. **CP-BeckS**

Exercise, The. Thom Gunn. **CP-GunnT**

Exercise, An. William Carlos Williams. **CP-WilW2**

Exercise. William Carlos Williams. **CP-WilW2**

Exercise No. 2. William Carlos Williams. **CP-WilW2**

Exercises on Themes from Life. Alice Walker. **CP-WalkA**

Exeter. Sir John Betjeman. **CP-BetjJ**

Exeunt. Richard Wilbur. **CP-WilbR**

Exeunt Omnes. Thomas Hardy. **CP-HardT**

Exeunt the Viols. Rita Dove. **SP-DoveR**

Exhaustion among rocks. The Mirages. Robert Earl Hayden. **CP-HaydR**

Exhiliration is the Breeze. Emily Dickinson. **CP-DickE**

Exhiliration—is within. Emily Dickinson. **CP-DickE**

Exhortation. Louise Bogan. **CP-BogaL**

Exhortation, An. Percy Bysshe Shelley. **CP-ShelP**

Exhortation to Prayer. William Cowper. **NOCV** *Fr.* Olney Hymns. **CP-CowpW**

Exile, An. Samuel Taylor Coleridge. **CP-ColeS**

Exile. Hart Crane. *See* Carrier Letter.

Exile, The. Walter de la Mare. **CP-DeLaW**

Exile. Walter de la Mare. **CP-DeLaW**

Exile. Louise Glück. **SP-GlücL**

Exile. Donald Hall. **CP-HallD**

Exile. John Hewitt. **CP-HewiJ**

Exile, The. Khvaju of Kerman, *tr. fr. Persian by* Ralph Waldo Emerson. **CP-EmerR**

Exile. John Milton. *See* So spake our Mother Eve, and Adam heard.

Exile. Frederick Morgan. **SP-MorgF**

Exile. Kathleen Jessie Raine. *Fr.* Three Poems on Illusion. **SP-RainK**

Exile. Karl Shapiro. **CRP** *Fr.* Adam and Eve. **SP-ShapK**

Exile. Derek Walcott. **CP-WalcD**

Exile, *En Famille*, The. James McAuley. **SP-McAuJ**

Exile in Devon, An. Jenny Joseph. **SP-JoseJ**

Exile is the luckiest of men, The. Malcolm Lowry. *Fr.* The Moon in Scandinavia. **CP-LowrM**

Exile of Music. Muriel Rukeyser. **CP-RukeM**

Exile on His Failing Vision, The. James McAuley. **SP-McAuJ**

"Hup! I come to a halt, facing the sea. Count."

"Overgrown roses have speckled the granite sill, The."

"Returned to desk and book, pad and pen, the eyes."

Exile Takes Stock of His Surroundings, The. James McAuley. **SP-McAuJ**

Exiled. Edna St. Vincent Millay. **CP-MillE**

Exiles, The. Wystan Hugh Auden. **CP-AudeW**

Exiles. Marilyn Hacker. **SP-HackM**

Exiles, The. Frederick Morgan. **SP-MorgF**

Exiles, The. Stephen Spender. **CP-SpenS**

Exiles, The. John Greenleaf Whittier. **CP-WhitJ**

Exile's Departure, The. John Greenleaf Whittier. **CP-WhitJ**

Exile's Fifth Symphony, The. James McAuley. **SP-McAuJ**

Allegro Moderato.

Allegro Vivace.

Andante Cantabile.

Scherzo.

fr. the Chinese of Li Po (701-62). Li Po. **SP-PounE**

Exiles' Line, The. Rudyard Kipling. **CP-KiplR**

Exile's Recurring Nightmare, The. James McAuley.

Journey With a Conjuror. **SP-McAuJ**

Memoirs of a Son of Erin. **SP-McAuJ**

Prologue: "Not for me, the crusader cross." **SP-McAuJ**

Whiskey Priest Recites His Holy Office, The. **SP-McAuJ**

Exile's Return, The. Elizabeth Barrett Browning. **CP-BroEB**

Exile's Return, The. Robert Lowell. **SP-LoweR**

Exile's Return. Malcolm Lowry. **CP-LowrM**

Exiles, the proverb says, subsist on hope. Euripides, *tr.* by Samuel Johnson. **CP-JohnS** *Fr.* Phœnissae.

Existence Before Essence. Hayden Carruth. **CP-CarHS**

Existing Pool, The. Hayden Carruth. **CP-CarHS**

Exit. Edwin Arlington Robinson. **CP-RobiE**

Exit a kind of unkindness exit. Edward Estlin Cummings. **CP-CummE**

Exit from Eden, The. John Milton. *See* So spake our Mother Eve, and Adam heard.

Exit Line. John Ciardi. **SP-CiarJ**

Exit Molloy. Derek Mahon. **POL** *Fr.* Four Walks in the Country Near Saint-Brieuc. **SP-MahoD**

Exit, Pursued by a Bear. Ogden Nash. **CP-NashO**

Exodus. George Oppen. **CP-OppeG**

Exodus 1947. Edwin Rolfe. **CP-RolfE**

Exodus with Children. Peter Meinke. **SP-MeinP**

Exorcism. Jenny Joseph. **SP-JoseJ**

Exorcism. Diane Wakoski. **SP-WakoD**

Exorcists, The. Anne Sexton. **CP-SextA**

Exotic. Archie Randolph Ammons. **SP-AmmoA**

Exotica. Frederick Morgan. **SP-MorgF**

Expanse cannot be lost. Emily Dickinson. **CP-DickE**

Expanses. James Dickey. **CP-DickJ**

Expatiation on the Combining of Weathers at Thirty-Seventh and Indiana Where the Southern More or Less Crosses the Dog, An. Hayden Carruth. **CP-CarHS**

Expatriates, The. Anne Sexton. **CP-SextA**

Expect na, Sir, in this narration. A Dedication to G**** H******* Esq. Robert Burns. **CP-BurnR**

Expect no thanks ever from anyone. Catullus. *See* Carmen 72: "Cancel, Catullus, the expectancies of friendship."

Expect not here a curious river fine. A Prologue of the Author's to a Masque at Witten. Sir John Suckling. **CP-SuckJ**

Expect Nothing. Robert Ranke Graves. **CP-GravR**

Expect Nothing. Alice Walker. **CP-WalkA**

Expect nothing. Live frugally. Expect Nothing. Alice Walker. **CP-WalkA**

Expectancy. John Hewitt. **CP-HewiJ**

Expectant faces brimmed the waiting square. Rome Sunday[,] June 1960. John Hewitt. **CP-HewiJ**

Expectant Shelters, The. Kenneth Patchen. **CP-PatcK**

Expectant yet relaxed, he. Hotblood on Friday. Thom Gunn. **CP-GunnT**

Expectantly and fearfully I sing. Hayden Carruth. **CP-CarHS** *Fr.* The Bloomingdale Papers.

Expectation. Paul Laurence Dunbar. **CP-DunbP**

Expectation and Experience. Thomas Hardy. **CP-HardT**

Expectation—is Contentment. Emily Dickinson. **CP-DickE**

Expectations. Steve Griffiths. **SP-GrifS**

Expecting rain, the profile of a day. Frontispiece. John Ashbery. **SP-AshbJ**

Expecting Silence. Donald Davie. **CP-DavDo**

Expecting your arrival tomorrow, I find myself thinking I love You. Dichtung und Wahrheit. Wystan Hugh Auden. **CP-AudeW**

Expedient, An—Leonardo da Vinci's—and a Query. Marianne Craig Moore. **CP-MoorM**

Expedition to Wessagusset, The. Henry Wadsworth Longfellow. **PAH** *Fr.* The Sailing of the Mayflower. *Fr.* The Courtship of Miles Standish. **SP-LongH**

Expense of spirit in a waste of shame, The [*or* Th']. Sonnet 129. William Shakespeare. **AWP; BiP; CABA; CoGr; EBEV; EnRePo; ErPo;**

FaBoEn; GBL; HAP; HeIP; ImPo; InPS; LiTB; LoBV; MasP; NAEL-1; NIP; NOBE; NoP; NoSic; OAEL-1; OBEV; OBSC; OXAEP-1; OtMeF; PAI; PPP; PPoe; PIP; PoE; PoEL-2; Poetr; QFR; SCGP; SCV; SeCePo; SeCeV; Son; TEP; TFi; TrGrPo; UnPo; WHA; WeW *Fr.* Sonnets. **CP-ShaWS**

Expenses Exhaust. Robert Herrick. **CP-HerrR**

Experience. Charles Bukowski. **SP-BukC2**

Experience. Ralph Waldo Emerson. **CP-EmerR**

Experience, An. Thomas Hardy. **CP-HardT**

Experience. Charles Kenneth Williams. **SP-WillC**

Experience bows a sweet contented face. Christina Georgina Rossetti. **CP-RosC2**

Experience Evoked. Richard Eberhart. **CP-EberR**

Experience is the Angled Road. Emily Dickinson. **CP-DickE**

Experience, like a pale musician, holds. Perplexed Music. Elizabeth Barrett Browning. **CP-BroEB**

Experience, though noon auctoritee. Geoffrey Chaucer. **OxBoLi; PeLV** *Fr.* The Wife of Bath's Prologue. **FHYEP; NAEL-1; OAEL-1,** *ll.* 1–862 *complete; Fr.* The Canterbury Tales. **CP-ChauG**

Experience, though noon auctoritee. The Wife of Bath's Prologue. Geoffrey Chaucer. **FHYEP; NAEL-1; OAEL-1,** *ll.* 1–862 *complete; Fr.* The Canterbury Tales. **CP-ChauG**

Experience to Let. Ogden Nash. **CP-NashO**

Experiment escorts us last. Emily Dickinson. **CP-DickE**

Experiment to me. Emily Dickinson. **CP-DickE**

Experimenting. Roy Fisher. **SP-FishR** *Fr.* Interiors with Various Figures.

Expert, The. Rudyard Kipling. **CP-KiplR**

Expert coachdog when other things go slack. He Is an. Kenneth Patchen. **CP-PatcK**

Experts say for me to do it well. Running. Brendan Galvin. **SP-GalvB**

Expiration, The. John Donne. **CP-DonnJ**

"Explain the joke," he said. The Joke. Phoebe Hesketh. **SP-HeskP**

Explaining the Nature of Evidence. Stephen Dobyns. **SP-DobyS**

Explanation, The. Rudyard Kipling. **CP-KiplR**

Explanation. Leonard Nathan. **SP-NathL**

Explanation. Wallace Stevens. **CP-StevW**

Explanation of the Grasshopper, An. Nicholas Vachel Lindsay. **CP-LindV**

Explanations of Love. Carl Sandburg. **CP-SandC**

Exploits of a Machine Age. Thomas Merton. **CP-MertT**

Exploration. Daniel Gerard Hoffman. **SP-HoffD**

Explorations. Louis MacNeice. **CP-MacNL**

Explorer, The. Rudyard Kipling. **CP-KiplR**

Explorer on Main Street, The. Richard Eberhart. **CP-EberR**

Explorers, The. Margaret Atwood. **SP-AtwM1**

Explorers, The. Adrienne Rich. **CP-RicAE**

Explorers. Charles Simic. **SP-SimiC**

Explorers will come, The. The Explorers. Margaret Atwood. **SP-AtwM1**

Explosion. Robinson Jeffers. **CP-JefR3**

Explosion, The. Philip Larkin. **CP-LarkP**

Explosion of a bomb, The. Perhaps. Stephen Spender. **CP-SpenS**

Exposé. John Updike. **CP-UpdiJ**

Exposed Nest, The. Robert Frost. **CP-FrosR**

Exposed to grief too long. Reprieve and Admixture. Charles Bukowski. **SP-BukC2**

Exposing Fox and Artifice. Siv Cedering Fox. *Fr.* Onna-E, Pictures of Women. **SP-CedeS**

Expostulation. William Cowper. **CP-CowpW**

Expostulation, The. John Donne. *Fr.* Elegies. **CP-DonnJ**

Expostulation, An. Thomas Hardy. **CP-HardT**

Expostulation, The. Sir John Suckling. **CP-SuckJ**

Expostulation. John Greenleaf Whittier. **CP-WhitJ**

Expostulation and Reply. William Wordsworth. **CP-WorW1**

Expostulation with Inigo Jones, An. Ben Jonson. **CP-JonsB**

Exposure. Wilfred Owen. **CP-OwenW**

Exposure. John Updike. **CP-UpdiJ**

Exposure to this page can induce. *see also* Asthmatic, The. Leonard Cohen. **CP-CoheL**

Express, The. Stephen Spender. **CP-SpenS**

Expression. Thom Gunn. **CP-GunnT**

Expressionist History of German Expressionism. Lawrence Ferlinghetti. **SP-FerlL**

Expulsion from Eden, The. John Milton. **OPOU** *Fr.* Book XII. *Fr.* Paradise Lost. **CP-MiltJ**

Expulsion from Eden grows indistinct. Emily Dickinson. **SP-DickE**

Expulsion from Paradise. John Milton. **ChTr** *Fr.* Book XII. *Fr.* Paradise Lost. **CP-MiltJ**

Extemporaneous Effusion on Being Appointed to the Excise, An. Robert Burns. **CP-BurnR**

Extempore [on the *Loyal Natives'* Verses]. Robert Burns. **CP-BurnR**

Extempore. Robert Burns. **CP-BurnR**

Extempore Effusion upon the Death of James Hogg. William Wordsworth. **CP-WorW2**
   London, from Hampstead Heath. **FaBoPP**

Extempore Elegy, An. Samuel Johnson. **CP-JohnS**

Extempore Epistle to Mr. McAdam of Craigengillian, (Wrote in Nanse Tinnock's, Mauchline) in Answer to an Obliging Letter He Sent in the Commencement of My Poetic Career. Robert Burns. **CP-BurnR**

Extempore, in the Court of S———. Robert Burns. **CP-BurnR**
   "Collected, Harry stood awee."
   "He clench'd his pamphlets in his fist."

Extempore—On Being Shown a Beautiful County Seat Belonging to the Same [Maxwell of Cardoness]. Robert Burns. **CP-BurnR**

Extempore—on Some Commemorations of Thomson. Robert Burns. **CP-BurnR**

Extempore Reply to an Invitation. Robert Burns. **CP-BurnR**

Extempore—To Mr. Gavin Hamilton. Robert Burns. **CP-BurnR**

Extempore Verses on Dining with Lord Daer. Robert Burns. **CP-BurnR**

Extended and always uncentered which is why it scares. The Child's Being. Hayden Carruth. *Fr.* Contra Mortem. **CP-CarHL**

Extermination Camp, The. Stanley Jasspon Kunitz. *Fr.* Around Pastor Bonhoeffer. **CP-KuniS**

Extinct stars, The / look down. To the Horned God. Erica Jong. **SP-JongE**

Extinct Vertebrate, An. Robinson Jeffers. **CP-JefR3**

Extol thee—could I? Then I will. Emily Dickinson. **CP-DickE**

Extract. Wystan Hugh Auden. **CP-AudWJ**

Extract from "A New England Legend." John Greenleaf Whittier. **CP-WhitJ**

Extract from Memoirs. Howard Nemerov. **CP-NemeH**

Extract from the Conclusion of a Poem, Composed in Anticipation of Leaving School. William Wordsworth. **CP-WorW1**

Extracts from Addresses to the Academy of Fine Ideas. Wallace Stevens. **CP-StevW**

Extracts from an Opera. John Keats. **CP-KeatJ**

Extraordinary patience of things!, The. Carmel Point. Robinson Jeffers. **CP-JefR3**

Extraordinary References. Wallace Stevens. **CP-StevW**

Extravagance of nature took his mind, The. Malcolm Lowry. *Fr.* Peter Gaunt and the Canals. **CP-LowrM**

Extreme delicacy of this Easter morning, The. Easter Morning. May Sarton. **SP-SartM**

Extreme fatigue, down to the marrow bone. Orchid. Robert Pack. **SP-PackR**

Extremity. Richard Eberhart. **CP-EberR**

Exultantly he drives his screaming pinnace. Alun Lewis. *Fr.* The Madman. **CP-LewiA**

Exultate Deo. Christina Georgina Rossetti. **CP-RosC2**

Exultation, An. William Carlos Williams. **CP-WilW2**

Exultation is the going. Emily Dickinson. **CP-DickE**

"Ey! Goddes mercy!"seyde oure Hooste tho. Epilogue to the Merchant's Tale. Geoffrey Chaucer. *Fr.* The Canterbury Tales. **CP-ChauG**

Eye, The. Robert Creeley. **CP-CreeR**

Eye, The. Robert Creeley. **CP-CreeR**

Eye / drinks the dry orange ground. Arizona Desert. Charles Tomlinson. **CP-TomlC**

Eye, The. Robert Herrick. **CP-HerrR**

Eye, The. Robert Herrick. **CP-HerrR**

Eye, The. Robinson Jeffers. **CP-JefR3**

Eye, The. Allen Tate. **CP-TateA**

Eye, The. Richard Wilbur. **CP-WilbR**

Eye Altering Alters All, The. Allen Ginsberg. **CP-GinsA**

Eye and Tooth. Robert Lowell. **SP-LoweR**

Eye ascending / is gone up, The. Roy Fisher. **SP-FishR** *Fr.* New Diversions.

Eye-Beaters, The. James Dickey. **CP-DickJ**

Eye can hardly pick them out, The. At Grass. Philip Larkin. **CP-LarkP**

Eye follows, the land, The. California Prodigal. Maya Angelou. **SP-AngeM**

Eye for Color, An. John Hewitt. **CP-HewiJ**

Eye Hath Not Seen. Christina Georgina Rossetti. **CP-RosC3**

"Eye hath not seen:"—yet man hath known and weighed. That Which Hath Been Is Named Already, and It Is Known That It Is Man. Christina Georgina Rossetti. **CP-RosC2**

Eye I look out of, The. The Eye. Robert Creeley. **CP-CreeR**

Eye in the Rock, The. John Haines. **SP-HainJ**

Eye Is a Dog Howling in the Distance, The. Pablo Antonio Cuadra, *tr. fr. Spanish by* Thomas Merton. **CP-MertT**

Eye-Mote, The. Sylvia Plath. **CP-PlatS**

Eye of / the hut, The. Hayden Carruth. *Fr.* North Winter. **CP-CarHL**

Eye of looking back were well, An. Ben Jonson. **CP-JonsB** *Fr.* Pleasure Reconciled to Virtue.

Eye on the object, eye on the congeries. Warwickshire. Donald Davie. **CP-DavDo**

Eye-Opener. Malcolm Lowry. **CP-LowrM**

EYE•PATCH•THATS•THE•ANSWER•, AN. HEINRICH•HIMMLER, FORMER•REICHSFUEHRER•SS—1•MAY•1945•. William DeWitt Snodgrass. **SP-SnodW**

Eye unacquitted by whatever it holds in allegiance, The. Didactic Piece. Louise Bogan. **CP-BogaL**

Eye which made this saw no pallor, The. Museum Piece. Hayden Carruth. **CP-CarHL**

Eyeglasses, The. William Carlos Williams. **CP-WilW1**

Eyeing the grass for mushrooms, you will find. Mushrooms. Charles Tomlinson. **CP-TomlC**

Eyelashes did their job. Fear of Domesticity. Bill Knott. **SP-KnotB**

Eyelids. Stephen Dobyns. **SP-DobyS**

Eyelids glowing, some chill morning, the. Monet: "Les Nymphéas." William DeWitt Snodgrass. **SP-SnodW**

Eyelids meet. / He'll catch a little nap, The. In the Smoking-Car. Richard Wilbur. **CP-WilbR**

Eyelids of eve fall together at last, The. The Eve of Waterloo. Thomas Hardy. **CP-HardT** *Fr.* The Dynasts.

Eyes. Walter de la Mare. **CP-DeLaW**

Eyes, The. Robert Herrick. **CP-HerrR**

Eyes. William Matthews. **SP-MattW**

Eyes. James Schuyler. **CP-SchuJ**

Eyes: A Fragment. Percy Bysshe Shelley. **CP-ShelP**

Eyes aloft, over dangerous places. Butterflies. Rudyard Kipling. **CP-KiplR**

Eyes and Tears. Andrew Marvell. **CP-MarvA**

Eyes are clouded where, The. Squince. Derek Mahon. **SP-MahoD**

Eyes are drawn to the dusty ground in fall, The. An Empty Place. Robert Bly. **SP-BlyR**

Eyes at the Window. James Schuyler. **CP-SchuJ**

Eyes at the window are Norma Shearer's, The. Eyes at the Window. James Schuyler. **CP-SchuJ**

Eyes before the Eares, The. Robert Herrick. **CP-HerrR**

Eyes, calm beside thee, (Lady couldst thou know!). Sonnet. Robert Browning. **CP-BroR2**

Eyes, can you tell mee wher my hart remaines? Sonnet. Mary Sidney, Countess of Montgomery Wroth. *Fr.* Pamphilia to Amphilanthus. **CP-WrotM**

Eyes closed, half waking, that first morning. The Departure. Alun Lewis. **CP-LewiA**

Eyes Fastened with Pins. Charles Simic. **SP-SimiC**

Eyes in All Heads to Be Looked out Of. Anne Waldman. **SP-WaldA**

Eyes look into the well. Wystan Hugh Auden. *Fr.* Ten Songs. **CP-AudeW**

Eyes looked at me from the old stone wall. Frederick Morgan. *Fr.* Blue Hill Poems. **SP-MorgF**

EYES: Medium. All There Is to Know about Adolph Eichmann. Leonard Cohen. **CP-CoheL**

Eyes of a Blind Man. Edwin Rolfe. **CP-CareT; CP-RolfE**

Eyes of a Boy. Edwin Rolfe. **CP-RolfE**

Eyes of grey—a sodden quay. The Lovers' Litany. Rudyard Kipling. **CP-KiplR**

Eyes of Night-Time. Muriel Rukeyser. **CP-RukeM**

Eyes of others, The. A Little Scandal. Marge Piercy. *Fr.* Walking into Love. **SP-PierM**

Eyes of strangers, The. Strangers. Philip Larkin. **CP-LarkP**

Eyes of the crow and the eye of the camera open, The. Memorial for the City. Wystan Hugh Auden. **CP-AudeW**

Eyes of the eagle are yours, eyes of the dove are yours. Being the Dedication of a Morning. Nicholas Vachel Lindsay. **CP-LindV**

Eyes open to a cry of pulleys, The. Love Calls Us to the Things of This World. Richard Wilbur. **CP-WilbR**

Eye's plain version is a thing apart, The. An Ordinary Evening in New Haven. Wallace Stevens. **CP-StevW**

Eyes shined. Permanence. Archie Randolph Ammons. **SP-AmmoA**

Eyes that glass fear, though fear on furtive foot. A Hare. Walter de la Mare. **CP-DeLaW**

Eyes That Last I Saw in Tears. Thomas Stearns Eliot. **CP-ElioT**

Ezekiel. John Greenleaf Whittier. **CP-WhitJ**

Ezekiel's Rabbit. William Dickey. **SP-DickW**

Ezra Æsop, at eighty-eight. A Parable for Sports Writers, Society Columnists, Bond Salesmen, and Poets or Go Get a Reputation. Ogden Nash. **CP-NashO**

Ezra Pound in Pisa. Donald Davie. **CP-DavDo**

Ezry. Archibald MacLeish. **CP-MacLA**

F

F / eeble a blu / r of cr. Edward Estlin Cummings. **CP-CummE**

F. de Samara to A. G. A. Emily Brontë. **CP-BronE**

$F = ci^2$ Keats: the intensity of object The trouble. The Post Virginal. Charles Olson. **CP-OlsoC**

F is for foetus(a). Edward Estlin Cummings. **CP-CummE**

F. (Missive & Walk) I. #53. Frank O'Hara. **SP-OharF**

Fabergé. James Schuyler. **CP-SchuJ**

Fabian Bell—His Last Visit to Cuernavaca. Marsden Hartley. **CP-HartM**

Fable: "Mountain and the squirrel, The." Ralph Waldo Emerson. **CP-EmerR**

Fable: "Once upon a today and yesterday and nevermore there were 7 men." Etheridge Knight. **SP-KnigE**

Fable, A. Richard Wilbur. **CP-WilbR**

Fable: "Yes it was the prince's kiss." Muriel Rukeyser. **CP-RukeM**

Fable, A: "Raven, while with glossy breast, A." William Cowper. **CP-CowpW**

Fable for a War. Thomas Merton. **CP-MertT**

Fable for Slumber. Charles Olson. **CP-OlsoC**

Fable of Dryope, The. Ovid, *tr. by* Alexander Pope. **CP-PopeA** *Fr.* Metamorphoses.

Fable of Midas, The. Jonathan Swift. **CP-SwifJ**

Fable of the Bitches, The. Jonathan Swift. **CP-SwifJ**

Fable of the Peasant and the Overlord, The. John Milton, *tr. fr. Latin by* John T. Shawcross. **CP-MiltJ**

(Cottager and His Landlord, The.) **CP-CowpW**, *tr. by* William Cowper;

("Peasant to his lord pay'd yearly court, A.") **CP-CowpW**, *tr. by* William Cowper;

Fable of the Rhododendron Stealers. Sylvia Plath. **CP-PlatS**

Fable of the War, A. Howard Nemerov. **CP-NemeH**

Fable of the Water Merchants. Stephen Dunn. **SP-DunnS**

Fable of the Widow and Her Cat, A. Jonathan Swift. **CP-SwifJ**

Fables. Jenny Joseph. **SP-JoseJ**

  "Butterfly is dainty flippant fragile, The."

  Cutting Off One's Ears for Someone Else Is Wrong.

  "Fifty-thousand cats cross our garden—."

  "Gentleman that my black hen lays eggs for, The."

  Jack and the Beanstalk.

  Muse.

  "Stay close, little tortoise, dig in."

  "Think of the minute amount a mouse eats." **SP-JoseJ**

  "This nut withering on the shelf."

  "To achieve knowledge, salting away Faust's stock—."

  "Washing is jerked from shade into the sun, The."

Fables Bullfinch Forgot. Ogden Nash. **CP-NashO**

  Chloe and the Roué.

  Leda's Fortunate Gaffe.

  Medusa and the Mot Juste.

  Thirteenth Labor of Hercules, The.

Fables for Stormont. John Hewitt. **CP-HewiJ**

Fables of La Fontaine. Marianne Craig Moore.

  Animals Sick of the Plague, The. **CP-MoorM**

  Bear and the Garden-Lover, The. **CP-MoorM**

  Fox and the Grapes, The. **CP-MoorM**

  Lion In Love, The. **CP-MoorM**

  Mouse Metamorphosed Into a Maid, The. **CP-MoorM**

Fables of the Moon. Richard Eberhart. **CP-EberR**

Fables of the Moscow Subway. Howard Nemerov. **CP-NemeH**

Fabliau of Florida. Wallace Stevens. **CP-StevW**

Fabulae. Phaedrus, *tr. fr. Latin.*

  "Let those whom folly prompts to sneer." **CP-JohnS**

  "Through all the town the busy triflers swarm." **CP-JohnS**

  "Tinsel glitter, and the specious mein, The." **CP-JohnS**

  "Two-fold gift in this my volume lies, A." **CP-JohnS**

  "Wretch that often has deceiv'd, The." **CP-JohnS**

Fabulists, The. Rudyard Kipling. **CP-KiplR**

Fabullus I will treat you handsomely. Catullus. *See* Carmen 13: "I shall expect / you in to dine."

Fabulous against ,a,fathoming jelly. Edward Estlin Cummings. **CP-CummE**

Face, A. Robert Browning. **CP-BroR1**

Face, The. Randall Jarrell. **CP-JarrR; SP-JarrR**

Face, The. Philip Levine. **SP-LeviP**

Face, A. Marianne Craig Moore. **CP-MoorM**

Face. Adrienne Rich. **CP-RicAE**

Face. Carl Sandburg. **CP-SandC**

Face. Richard Shelton. **SP-ShelR**

Face, The. Stevie Smith. **CP-SmitS**

Face / was / beautiful, The. Was. Robert Creeley. **CP-CreeR**

Face and Image. Charles Tomlinson. **CP-TomlC**

Face at the Casement, The. Thomas Hardy. **CP-HardT**

(Face) (Autumn) (En Face). Bill Knott. **SP-KnotB**

Face devoid of love or grace, A. Emily Dickinson. **CP-DickE**

Face I carry with me—last, The. Emily Dickinson. **CP-DickE**

Face in evanescence lain, The. Emily Dickinson. **CP-DickE**

Face in stone and / Stone in face. Portrait in Stone. Charles Tomlinson. **CP-TomlC**

Face in the crook of her neck. Gary Snyder. **CP-SnydG** *Fr.* Burning. *Fr.* Myths and Texts.

Face in the Mirror, The. Robert Ranke Graves. **CP-GravR**

Face in the quiet night, The. Long Gone Blues. Gilbert Sorrentino. **SP-SorrG**

Face Lift. Sylvia Plath. **CP-PlatS**

Face like a chocolate bar. 125th Street. Langston Hughes. **SP-HughL**

Face looks out at me, A. When You Throw Amber into the Well of the Moon. Diane Wakoski. **SP-WakoD**

Face, Ocean. Richard Eberhart. **CP-EberR**

Face of all the world is changed, I think, The. Sonnet. Elizabeth Barrett Browning. **CTC; HBV; OAEP; VLP** *Fr.* Sonnets from the Portuguese. **CP-BroEB**

Face of Helen, The. Christopher Marlowe. *See* Was This the Face.

Face of the Dam: Vivian Jones. Muriel Rukeyser. **CP-SpenS**

Face of the Earth, The. Charles Henri Ford. **SP-FordC**

Face of the Precipice is Black with Lovers, The. Thomas McGrath. **SP-McGrT**

Face-Paintings of the Caduveo Indians. William Dickey. **SP-DickW**

Face that should content me wonders [or wondrous] well, A. Sir Thomas Wyatt. **CP-WyatT**

Face the moon. Ask: is it less, now that man. At Our Best. Richard Hugo. **CP-HugoR**

Face the Orient. Anne Waldman. **SP-WaldA**

Face to Face. Denise Levertov. **CP-LeveD**

Face to Face. Adrienne Rich. **CP-RicAE; SP-RicA1; SP-RicA2**

Face to face in my chamber, my silent chamber, I saw her. Confessions. Elizabeth Barrett Browning. **CP-BroEB**

Face to the wall and behind him. The Wall. Louis MacNeice. **CP-MacNL**

Face was necessary—I found face. Ted Hughes. **SP-HughT** *Fr.* Seven Dungeon Songs.

Face we choose to miss, The. Emily Dickinson. **CP-DickE**

Face While Shaving. Charles Bukowski. **SP-BukC2**

Faced to the island, Mackinnon's boat. Mackinnon's Boat. Charles Tomlinson. **CP-TomlC**

Faced with furnace demands during its education. Burning Bush. Muriel Rukeyser. **CP-RukeM**

Faces. Maya Angelou. **SP-AngeM**

Faces. John Ciardi. **SP-CiarJ**

Faces. Stephen Dobyns. **SP-DobyS**

Faces. Walt Whitman. **CP-WhitW**

Faces and more remember. Faces. Maya Angelou. **SP-AngeM**

Faces greying faster than loam-crumbs on a harrow. Judge Not. Theodore Roethke. **CP-RoetT**

Faces in the Fire. "Lewis Carroll." **CP-CarrL**

Faces No Longer White. Edwin Rolfe. **CP-RolfE**

Faces of Doom and Sterility. Gilbert Sorrentino. **SP-SorrG**

Faces of Girls Looking at Themselves in the River. Pablo Antonio Cuadra, *tr. fr. Spanish by* Thomas Merton. **CP-MertT**

Faces of two eternities keep looking at me. Two Neighbors. Carl Sandburg. **CP-SandC**

Faces of women long dead, of our family, The. Kadya Molodovsky, *tr. fr. Yiddish by* Adrienne Rich. **SP-RicA2**

(Poem of Women.) **SP-RicA2**

Faces Seen Once. James Dickey. **CP-DickJ**

Faces seen once are seen. Faces Seen Once. James Dickey. **CP-DickJ**

Faces there at the center, ruinous, The. The Island (VIII). Pablo Neruda, *tr. fr. Spanish by* Ben Belitt. **SP-NeruP** *Fr.* The Separate Rose.

Facile as can be the boat you see, my guests, says. Catullus. *See* Carmen 4: "My bean-pod boat you see here."

Facing Africa. James Dickey. **CP-DickJ**

Facing Sentencing. Muriel Rukeyser. **CP-RukeM**

Facing the Chair. "Hugh MacDiarmid." **SP-MacDH**

Facing the humping flatfaced banks. Tenor Solo on St. Cecilia's Day. James McAuley. **SP-McAuJ**

Facing the Way. Alice Walker. **CP-WalkA**

Facing the wind of the avenues. The Sweater of Vladimir Ussachevsky. John Haines. **SP-HainJ**

Facing West from California's Shores. Walt Whitman. **CP-WhitW**

Fact. Langston Hughes. **SP-HughL**

Fact, and an Imagination or, Canute and Alfred, on the Sea-Shore, A. William Wordsworth. **CP-WorW2**

Fact of a Doorframe, The. Adrienne Rich. **SP-RicA1**

Fact of the Act. Robert Ranke Graves. **CP-GravR**

Fact of the Matter, The. Hayden Carruth. **CP-CarHS**

Fact that Earth is Heaven, The. Emily Dickinson. **CP-DickE**

Fact that the sun has once again with sharp claws, The. A Waking. Daniel Gerard Hoffman. **SP-HoffD**

Faction du Muet. René Char, *tr. tr. French by* Thomas Merton. **CP-MertT**

Factions. Robert Herrick. **CP-HerrR**

Factory Cities, The. David Herbert Lawrence. **CP-LawrD**

Factory off Santa Fe Ave. was, The. Sparks. Charles Bukowski. **SP-BukC3**

Factory Windows Are Always Broken. Nicholas Vachel Lindsay. **CP-LindV**

Facts. "Lewis Carroll." **CP-CarrL**

Facts & Issues, The. John Berryman. **CP-BerrJ**

Facts by our side are never sudden. Emily Dickinson. **CP-DickE**

Facts have no eyes. One must. Observation of Facts. Charles Tomlinson. **CP-TomlC**

Fade tender lily, / Fade O crimson rose. Autumn. Christina Georgina Rossetti. **CP-RosC3**

Faded, *tr. fr. the German of* Rilke. Randall Jarrell. **CP-JarrR**

Faded Boy—in sallow Clothes, A. Emily Dickinson. **CP-DickE**

Faded Face, The. Thomas Hardy. **CP-HardT**

Faded Leaf: A Chapter of Family History, The. John Hewitt. **CP-HewiJ**

Faded mind, / fading colors. Place. Robert Creeley. **CP-CreeR**

Fading of the Sun, A. Wallace Stevens. **CP-StevW**

Fading Rose, The. Thomas Hardy. **CP-HardT**

Faerie Queene, The. Edmund Spenser. **CP-Spens**

  Address to Venus. **AWP**

  (Prayer to Venus.) **EIL**

  "And is there care in heauen [or heaven]? and is there loue [or love]." **NOCV; NoSic; OAEL-1; OBSC; OxBoCh**

  (Guardian Angels.) **OBSC**

  Artegall and Radigund. **OBSC**

  Arthur's Fight with Orgoglio and Duessa. **EBNV**

  "As pilot well expert in perilous wave." **OAEL-1; PoEL-1**

  (Cave of Mammon, The.) **PoEL-1**

  "At length they came into a larger space." **FiP**

  "As when a ship, that flyes faire vnder saile." **FHYEP**

  "At length nigh to the sea they drew." **NoP**

  August. **GN**

  Autumn. **GN**

  "Ay me, how many perils doe unfold [or enfold]." **FHYEP; OAEL-1**

  Balme. **CH**

  "Behold I see the haven nigh at hand." **FHYEP**

  Behold, O Man. **EIL**

  Bower of Bliss, The. **PoEL-1**

  "And in the midst of all, a fountaine stood." **CH**

  "Eftsoones they heard a most melodious sound." **EBEvV; NOBE; OBSC; SCV**

  "Thence passing forth, they shortly do arrive." **FiP**

  Britomart at Isis' Church. **PoE**

  "By this the Northerne wagoner had set." **FHYEP; NoSic**

  Cave of Despair, The. **OBNV**

  "Ere long they come, where that same wicked wight." **NOBE; OAEL-1**

  Cymochles and Phaedria. **OBSC**

  Dame Nature. **PoEL-1**

  Dance of the Graces, The. **OBSC**

  (Dance, The.) **TrGrPo**

  Despair. **SeCePo**

  Dragon, The. **SeCePo**

  Envy. **TW**

  "Faire knight (quoth he) Hierusalem that is." **FaBoPV**

" 'Faire sir,' quoth she, 'be not displeasd at all'." **MOS**

Fight of the Red Cross Knight and the Heathen Sansjoy, The. **FHYEP; FiP; NoSic**

"From thence into the open fields he fled." **OBSC**

Garden of Adonis, The. **NOBE; PoEL-1**

"In that same gardin all the goodly flowres." **NOBE**

Garden of Proserpina, The. **ChTr**

"Gentle knight was pricking on the plaine, A." **EBEV; FHYEP; NAEL-1; OAEL-1; Poetr**

Guyon's Voyage to the Bower of Bliss. **NoSic**

"Two dayes now in that sea he sayled has." **OxBoS**

Happy Isle. **OBSC**

"Hard is the doubt, and difficult to deeme." **OAEL-1**

"He making speedy way through spersed ayre." **NoSic**

"He there now does enjoy eternal rest." **ChTr; MOS**

(Sleep after Toil.) **ChTr**

"He was to weet a man of full ripe years." **UV**, *sect.* 4, *canto* 3;

"High time now gan it wex for Una faire." **FHYEP**

Hill of the Graces, The. **NOBE**

House of Ate, The. **OBSC**

House of Busyrane, The. **NoSic**

House of Richesse, The. **CH**

"In such luxurious plentie of all pleasure." **OAEL-1**

"It fortuned (as faire it then befell)." **OAEL-1**

"It often falss (as here it erst befell)." **OBF**

Kinds of Trees to Plant. **OHIP**

Legend of Britomartis, or of Chastitie, The. **NAEL-1**

Britomart in the House of Busirane. **FiP**

Legend of the Knight of the Red Crosse, or of Holinesse, The. **EPCY; FHYEP; NAEL-1; OAEL-1**

(Invocation to the Faerie Queene.) **FiP**

"Like as a ship, that through the ocean wyde." **EtS; MOS**

"Like as the tide that comes from th' Ocean main." **HoPM**

Mask of Cupid, The. **OBSC**

(Masque of Cupid, The.)

"First was Fancy, like a lovely boy, The." **NOBE**

"Noble Mayde, still standing, all this vewd, The." **PoEL-1**

Mask of Mutability, The. **OBSC**

(Pageant of the Seasons and the Months, The.) **OXAEP-1**

(Seasons, The.) **GN**

May. **GN**

Mermaids, The. **ChTr**

Mutability. **PoEL-1**

Mutability Claims to Rule the World. **NoSic**

Nature's Reply to Mutability. **NOBE**

Nought is on earth more sacred or divine. **OAEL-1**

"Nought is there under heav'ns wide hollownesse." **FHYEP**

"Nought vnder heauen so strongly doth allure." **NoSic**

"Now, at the time that was before agreed." **OAEL-1**

"Now strike your sailes, ye jolly mariners." **EtS; MOS**

Nymphs and Graces Dancing, The. **DIP**

"O goodly golden chaine, wherewith yfere." **FHYEP**

"O what an endelesse worke have I in hand." **MOS**

Prince Arthur. **OBSC**

"Redoubted knights, and honorable Dames." **NoP**

"Right well I wote [*or* wrote] most mighty Soueraine [*or* soveraine]." **NoSic; OAEL-1**

Rivers Come to the Hall of Proteus for the Marriage of the Thames and the Medway, The. **FaBoPP**

Rivers of Ireland, The. **CBCK**

"Rugged forhead that with grave foresight, The." **OAEL-1; OBSC**

(Love.) **OBSC**

Scudamor in the Temple of Venus. **PoE**

Sea Monsters. **ChTr; FaBoEn**

Sea Nymphs, The. **CBCK**

"So as they travelled, the drouping night." **OAEL-1**

"So forth she comes, and to her coche does clyme." **NAEL-1; OAEL-1**

"So oft as I with state of present time." **OAEL-1**

"Sudden upriseth from her stately palace." **PPP**

Summer. **GN**

Temple of Venus, The. **EIL; WHA**

"Then said that royall Pere in sober wise." **OAEL-1**

"Thence forward by that painfull way they pas." **OAEL-1**

"There the most daintie Paradise on ground." **EBEV**

"They sate to meat, and Satyrane his chaunce." **OAEL-1**

"Tho when as chearelesse night ycovered had." **OAEL-1**

"Thus being entered, they behold around." **OAEL-1**

Vision of the Graces, The. **NoSic**

"Well may I weene, faire ladies, all this while." **OAEL-1**

What If Some Little Paine the Passage Have. **CH; EtS**

"What man is he, that boasts of fleshly might." **FHYEP**

"What man so wise, what earthly wit so ware." **FHYEP**

"When I bethinke me on that speech whyleare." **NoSic; OAEL-1; OxBoCh**

"Whiles someone did chant this lovely lay, The." **EIL; FF; OBVE**

(Gather the Rose.) **EIL**

(Song of Bliss.) **FF**

"Whilom, as antique stories tellen us." **EPCY**

"Who now does follow the foule Blatant Beest." **OAEL-1**

"Who travels [*or* trauels] by the wearie wandring way." **OBD; OXAEP-1**

Winter. **GN**

"Young knight, what ever that dost armes professe." **FHYEP**

Faery Bird's Song. John Keats. *See* Shed no tear! O, shed no tear!

Faery Chasm, The. William Wordsworth. *Fr.* The River Duddon [A Series of Sonnets]. **CP-WorW2**

Faery Song. John Keats. **CP-KeatJ**

Faery Song, A. William Butler Yeats. **CP-YeatW**

Fafnir and the Knights. Stevie Smith. **CP-SmitS**

Faggot, The. Jonathan Swift. **CP-SwifJ**

Fagots blazed, the caldron's smoke, The. The Brewing of Soma. John Greenleaf Whittier. **CP-WhitJ**

Fags and their gay dogs are patrolling, The. Sunday in Boston. John Updike. **CP-UpdiJ**

Fahrenheit *Gesundheit.* Ogden Nash. **CP-NashO**

Failed Fathers. Lewis Turco. **SP-TurcL**

Failed Image. John Hewitt. **CP-HewiJ**

Failed Spirit, The. Stevie Smith. **CP-SmitS**

Failed Suicide, The. Ted Kooser. **SP-KoosT**

Failing impartial measure to dispense. A Plea for Authors, May, 1838. William Wordsworth. **CP-WorW2**

Failure, A. David Herbert Lawrence. **CP-LawrD**

Failure. Charles Kenneth Williams. **SP-WillC**

Failure of a Secular Life, The. Leonard Cohen. **CP-CoheL**

Failure, worse failure, nothing seen. World, World—. George Oppen. **CP-OppeG**

Failures. One after the. 35 Seconds. Charles Bukowski. **SP-BukC2**

Fain would I kiss my Julia's dainty leg. Her Legs. Robert Herrick. **CP-HerrR**

Fain Would I Wed. Thomas Campion. **CP-CampT**

("Faine would I wed a faire yong man that day and night could please mee.") **CP-CampT**

Fain would my Muse the flow'ry Treasures sing. *in imitation of* Cowley. Alexander Pope. **CP-PopeA**

Faine would I my love disclose. Thomas Campion. **CP-CampT**

Faine would I wed a faire yong man that day and night could please mee. Thomas Campion. *See* Fain Would I Wed.

Faint and worn and aged. The Eleventh Hour. Christina Georgina Rossetti. **CP-RosC3**

Faint blue circles underneath your eyes, The. De Pré Est Vénéneux Mais Joli en Automne. Gilbert Sorrentino. **SP-SorrG**

Faint Music. Walter de la Mare. **CP-DeLaW**

Faint now the colours in the West. The Tryst. Walter de la Mare. **CP-DeLaW**

Faint Praise. Charles Kenneth Williams. **CP-WillC**

Faint, sickening scent of irises, A. Scent of Irises. David Herbert Lawrence. **CP-LawrD**

Faint sighings sounded, not of wind, amid. The Image. Walter de la Mare. **CP-DeLaW**

Faint white pillars that seem to fade. Fragment. Edwin Arlington Robinson. **CP-RobiE**

Faint with love, the Lady of the South. Fragment: The Lady of the South. Percy Bysshe Shelley. **CP-ShelP**

Faint, Yet Pursuing. Christina Georgina Rossetti. **CP-RosC3**

"Beyond this shadow and this turbulent sea."

"Press onward, quickened souls, who mounting move."

Faintheart in a Railway Train. Thomas Hardy. **CP-HardT**

Faintly the ne'er-do-well. The Flute of the Lonely. Nicholas Vachel Lindsay. **CP-LindV**

Fair Amy of the terraced house. Amy's Cruelty. Elizabeth Barrett Browning. **CP-BroEB**

Fair and false! No dawn will greet. Song. George Meredith. **CP-MerG1**

Fair Bedfellow, The. George Meredith. **CP-MerG2**

Fair below Helvellyn, The. William Wordsworth. **FaBoPP** *Fr.* Retrospect Love of Nature Leading to Love of Mankind. *Fr.* The Prelude; Growth of a Poet's Mind [1805 vers.]. **CP-WorW3**

Fair, but of fairness as a vision dream'd. A Fragment of Anything You Like. Gerard Manley Hopkins. **CP-HopkG**

Fair Caroline, I wonder what. To C.F.H. Thomas Hardy. **CP-HardT**

Fair Charmer, cease, nor make your voice's prize. *in imitation of* Waller. Alexander Pope. **CP-PopeA**

Fair copy of my Celia's face. To T. H., a Lady Resembling My Mistress. Thomas Carew. **CP-CareT**

Fair Cuirass Shattered. Allen Tate. **CP-TateA**

Fair[e] daffodils [*or* daffadills], we weep to see. To Daffodils [*or* Daffadills]. Robert Herrick. **CP-HerrR**

Fair[e] Days; or, Dawn[e]s Deceitful[l]. Robert Herrick. **CP-HerrR**

Fair Doris, break thy glass, it hath perplex'd. To A.D., Unreasonable, Distrustful of Her Own Beauty. Thomas Carew. **CP-CareT**

Fair Elenor. William Blake. **CP-BlakW**

Fair Eliza. Robert Burns. **CP-BurnR**

Fair Ellen Irwin, when she sate. Ellen Irwin; or, The Braes of Kirtle. William Wordsworth. **CP-WorW1**

Fair Empress of the Poet's soul. To Clarinda. Robert Burns. **CP-BurnR**

Fair eyes, sweet lips, dear heart, that foolish I. Sonnet 43. Sir Philip Sidney. *Fr.* Astrophil and Stella. **SP-SidnP**

Fair fa' your honest, sonsie face. To a Haggis. Robert Burns. **CP-BurnR**

Fair fall thy soft heart! Hafiz, *tr. by* Ralph Waldo Emerson. **CP-EmerR** *Fr.* Odes.

Fair friend, 'tis true, your beauties move. Ben Jonson. **CP-JonsB**

Fair Game. John Hewitt. **CP-HewiJ**

Fair, great, and good, since seeing you, we see. To the Countess of Salisbury. John Donne. **CP-DonnJ**

Fair Head in Antrim, long dark waves of wet heather to the black lips of the height. An Irish Headland. Robinson Jeffers. **CP-JefR2**

Fair in the Woods, The. Thom Gunn. **CP-GunnT**

Fair is Middle-Earth nor changes, though to Age. Wystan Hugh Auden. *Fr.* Shorts [1948–1957] ("At peace under this mandarin, sleep, Lucina"). **CP-AudeW**

Fair is My Love. William Shakespeare. *See* Fair is my love, but not so fair as fickle.

Fair is my love, but not so fair as fickle. William Shakespeare. **CP-ShaWS; EIL** *Fr.* The Passionate Pilgrim. **CP-ShaWS**

(Fair is My Love.) **EIL**

Fair is our lot—O goodly is our heritage! A Song of the English. Rudyard Kipling. **CP-KiplR**

Fair Isabel, poor simple Isabel! Isabella; or, The Pot of Basil. John Keats. **CP-KeatJ**

Fair Isle at Sea—thy lovely name. Robert Louis Stevenson. **CP-StevR**

Fair isle, that from the fairest of all flowers. Sonnet to Zante. Ugo Foscolo, *tr. fr. Greek by* Edgar Allen Poe. **CP-PoeEd**

Fair Jenny. Robert Burns. **CP-BurnR**

Fair ladies, number five. On the Five Ladies at Sot's Hole, with the Doctor at Their Head. Jonathan Swift. **CP-SwifJ**

Fair ladies tall lovers / riding are through the. Edward Estlin Cummings. **CP-CummE**

Fair Lady! can I sing of flowers. To a Lady. William Wordsworth. **CP-WorW2**

Fair Lady! whose harmonious name the Rhine. John Milton. *See* Sonnet 2: "Charming lady, she whose beautiful name honors."

Fair lady works at shuttles, The. Dueling the Monkey. Jim Carroll. **SP-CarrJ**

Fair Land! Thee all men greet with joy; how few. After Leaving Italy. William Wordsworth. *Fr.* Memorials of a Tour in Italy, 1837. **CP-WorW2**

Fair land where all is brave and kind. Appletreewick. Wystan Hugh Auden. **CP-AudWJ**

Fair maid, you need not take the hint. Robert Burns. **CP-BurnR**
   (To Miss Ainslie, in Church.) **CP-BurnR**

Fair Margaret. Christina Georgina Rossetti. **CP-RosC3**

Fair Marg'ret sat in her bower. Lord Thomas and Fair Margaret. Christina Georgina Rossetti. **CP-RosC3**

Fair Mother Earth lay on her back last night. Ode to the Spirit of Earth in Autumn. George Meredith. **CP-MerG1**

Fair Nature's priestesses! to whom. To ———. John Greenleaf Whittier. **CP-WhitJ**

Fair; not to say radiant. The Twentyfifth of September. Canto VIII. Louis MacNeice. *Fr.* Autumn Sequel. **CP-MacNL**

Fair of face, full of pride. A Lyke-Wake Song. Algernon Charles Swinburne. **SP-SwinA**

Fair[e] pledges of a fruitful tree. To Blossoms. Robert Herrick. **CP-HerrR**

Fair Pomona flourish'd in his reign, The. Vertumnus and Pomona. Ovid, *tr. by* Alexander Pope. **CP-PopeA** *Fr.* Metamorphoses.

Fair Prime of Life! Were It Enough to Gild. William Wordsworth. **CP-WorW2**

Fair princess[e] of the spacious air. The Falcon. Richard Lovelace. **CP-LoveR**

Fair Quakeress, The. John Greenleaf Whittier. **CP-WhitJ**

Fair rising from her icy couch. Wild Flowers. Charlotte Smith. **CP-SmitC**

Fair river! in thy bright, clear flow. To the River———. Edgar Allan Poe. **CP-PoeEd**

Fair rocks, goodly rivers, sweet woods, when shall I see peace? Sir Philip Sidney. **SP-SidnP** *Fr.* Arcadia.

Fair seed time had my soul, and I grew up. William Wordsworth. **NoP,** *book* 1, *ll.* 301–646; *Fr.* Introduction—Childhood and School-Time. **EnRP; FHYEP** *Fr.* The Prelude; Growth of a Poet's Mind [1850 vers.]. **CP-WorW3**

Fair seed-time had my soul, and I grew up. William Wordsworth. **OBNC; OxAEP-2,** *book* 1, *ll.* 305–489; **FaBoPP** *Fr.* Introduction—Childhood and School-Time. *Fr.* The Prelude; Growth of a Poet's Mind [1805 vers.]. **CP-WorW3**

   (On the Solitary Fells around Hawkshead.) **FaBoPP,** *book* 1, *ll.* 305–350;

Fair ship, that from the Italian shore. Tennyson. **EBVV; EBVVPR; EnVR; OAEL-2; PeHV** *Fr.* In Memoriam A. H. H. **CP-TennA**

Fair Singer, The. Andrew Marvell. **CP-MarvA**

Fair sinks the summer evening now. Emily Brontë. **CP-BronE**

Fair soul, which wast, not only, as all souls be. Obsequies to the Lord Harrington, Brother to the Lady Lucy, Countess of Bedford. John Donne. **CP-DonnJ**

Fair, square Harvard, crib of the pilgrim mind. Apologies to Harvard. John Updike. **CP-UpdiJ**

Fair stands the ancient Rectory. Lays of Sorrow, No. 2. "Lewis Carroll." **CP-CarrL**

Fair Star of evening, Splendo[u]r of the west. Composed by the Sea-Side, near Calais, August, 1802. William Wordsworth. **CP-WorW1**

Fair, sweet and young, receive a prize. Song. John Dryden. **SP-DrydJ**

Fair the face of orient day. Delia. Robert Burns. **CP-BurnR**

Fair the sun riseth, / Bright as bright can be. Moonshine. Christina Georgina Rossetti. **CP-RosC3**

Fair[e] was the dawn[e], and but e'ne now the skies. Fair[e] Days; or, Dawn[e]s Deceitful[l]. Robert Herrick. **CP-HerrR**

Fair was the morn when the fair queen of love. *Various Authors.* **CP-ShaWS** *Fr.* The Passionate Pilgrim. **CP-ShaWS**

Fair was this yonge wyf, and therwithal. Geoffrey Chaucer. **EBEV** *Fr.* The Miller's [*or* Milleres] Tale. **FaBoBl; NAEL-1; NAWM-1; OAEL-1; OxBoLi; PeLV; TEP** *Fr.* The Canterbury Tales. **CP-ChauG**

Fair waved the golden corn. In Canaan's Happy Land. Stevie Smith. **CP-SmitS**

Fair weather for your journey! whither away. Jack & Harry. George Meredith. **CP-MerG2**

Fair World Tho' a Fallen, A. Christina Georgina Rossetti. **CP-RosC3**

Fairbanks Under the Solstice. John Haines. **SP-HainJ**

Faire after Foule. Robert Herrick. **CP-HerrR**

Faire and foule dayes trip Crosse and Pile; The faire. Crosse and Pile. Robert Herrick. **CP-HerrR**

Faire Begger, The. Richard Lovelace. **CP-LoveR**

Faire If You Expect Admiring. Thomas Campion. **CP-CampT**

Faire knight (quoth he) Hierusalem that is. Edmund Spenser. **FaBoPV** *Fr.* The Faerie Queene. **CP-Spens**

Faire Shewes Deceive. Robert Herrick. **CP-HerrR**

"'Faire sir,' quoth she, 'be not displeasd at all.'" Edmund Spenser. **MOS** *Fr.* The Faerie Queene. **CP-Spens**

Faire [*or* fayre] soule, how long shall veyles thy graces shroud? At Home in Heaven. Robert Southwell. **CP-SoutR**

Fairer than younger beauties, more beloved. Valentines From C.G.R. Christina Georgina Rossetti. **CP-RosC3**

Fairer through Fading—as the Day. Emily Dickinson. **CP-DickE**

Fairest and foremost of the train, that wait. Charity. William Cowper. **CP-CowpW**

Fairest, and still truest eyes. Song. Mary Sidney, Countess of Montgomery Wroth. *Fr.* Pamphilia to Amphilanthus. **CP-WrotM**

Fairest, brightest, hues of ether fade, The. William Wordsworth. **CP-WorW1**

Fairest flowers are gone! for tempests fell, The. Charlotte Smith. **CP-SmitC**

Fairest Home I ever knew, The. Emily Dickinson. **CP-DickE**

Fairest isle, all isles excelling. Song of Venus. John Dryden. **SP-DrydJ** *Fr.* King Arthur.

Fairest maid on Devon banks. Robert Burns. *See* Song: "Full well thou knowest I love thee dear."

Fairest of the Destinies. Fragments Written for Hellas. Percy Bysshe Shelley. **CP-ShelP**

Fairfax, whose name in armes through Europe rings. John Milton. **CP-MiltJ**

(Sonnet 15: "Fairfax, whose name in armes through Europe rings.") **CP-MiltJ**

Fairfield. Richard Hugo. **CP-HugoR**

Fairground. Wystan Hugh Auden. **CP-AudeW**

Fairies, The. Robert Herrick. **CP-HerrR**

Fairies break their dances, The. Alfred Edward Housman. **CP-HousA**

Fairies' Siege, The. Rudyard Kipling. **CP-KiplR** *Fr.* Kim.

Fairy, The. William Blake. **CP-BlakW**

Fairy and the soul proceeded, The. The Magic Car Moved On. Percy Bysshe Shelley. **GN** *Fr.* Queen Mab. **CP-ShelP**

Fairy [or Faery or Faiery] beam[e] upon you, The. Ben Jonson. **CP-JonsB** *Fr.* The Gypsies Metamorphosed.

Fairy Bell, The. Stevie Smith. **CP-SmitS**

Fairy Bread. Robert Louis Stevenson. **CP-StevR**

Fairy Bridal Hymn, The. Nicholas Vachel Lindsay. **CP-LindV**

Fairy came to my window last night, A. A Tale. Wystan Hugh Auden. **CP-AudWJ**

Fairy from the Apple-Seed, The. Nicholas Vachel Lindsay. **CP-LindV**

Fairy in Winter, The. Walter de la Mare. **CP-DeLaW**

Fairy-Man at Layde, The. John Hewitt. **CP-HewiJ**

Fairy skipd [or leapt] upon my knee, A. William Blake. **CP-BlakW**

Fairy Song. Randall Jarrell. **CP-JarrR**

Fairy Story. Stevie Smith. **CP-SmitS**

Fairy Tale. Stephen Dunn. **SP-DunnS**

Fairy Temple; or, Oberon's Chapel, The. Robert Herrick. **CP-HerrR**

Fairy Thresher, The. John Hewitt. **CP-HewiJ**

Fairyland [or Fairy-Land]. Edgar Allan Poe. **CP-PoeEd**

Fait Accompli. John Crowe Ransom. *Fr.* Two Gentlemen in Bonds. **SP-RansJ**

Faith. Paul Laurence Dunbar. **CP-DunbP**

Faith. Ralph Waldo Emerson. *See* Sacrifice.

Faith. George Herbert. **CP-HerbG**

Faith. Robert Herrick. **CP-HerrR**

Faith. Robinson Jeffers. **CP-JefR3**

Faith. Alexander Pope. **WGRP** *Fr.* An Essay on Man. **CP-PopeA**

Faith. Christopher Smart. **ChIV-1** *Fr.* Hymns for the Amusement of Children. **SP-SmarC**

Faith and Hope are wings to Love. Christina Georgina Rossetti. **CP-RosC3**

Faith Four-square. Robert Herrick. **CP-HerrR**

Faith Healing. Philip Larkin. **CP-LarkP**

Faith, Hope, and Charity. Samuel Taylor Coleridge. **CP-ColeS**

"Faith" is a fine invention. Emily Dickinson. **CP-DickE**

Faith is a thing that's four-square; let it fall. Faith Four-square. Robert Herrick. **CP-HerrR**

Faith—is the Pierless Bridge. Emily Dickinson. **CP-DickE**

Faith like the warrior ant swarming, enslaving. John Berryman. *Fr.* Sonnets to Chris. **CP-BerrJ**

Faith of years is broken. Fair Margaret. Christina Georgina Rossetti. **CP-RosC3**

Faith on Trial, A. George Meredith. **CP-MerG1**

" 'Dream is the thought in the ghost, The'." **WGRP**

Faith struck Sebastian, got him. CENTERPIECE: St. Sebastian (Italian). Jenny Joseph. *Fr.* Altarpiece (A Meditation on Lust, Desire and Love). **SP-JoseJ**

Faithful, The. Jane Cooper. **SP-CoopJ**

Faithful Friend, The. William Cowper. **CP-CowpW**

Faithful "I am sorry", A. Emily Dickinson. **SP-DickE**

Faithful Swallow, The. Thomas Hardy. **CP-HardT**

"Faithful to the end" Amended, vers. 1. Emily Dickinson. **CP-DickE**

"Faithful to the end" Amended, vers. 2. Emily Dickinson. **CP-DickE**

"Faithful to the end" Amended, vers. 2. Emily Dickinson. **CP-DickE**

Faithful to your commandments, o consciousness, o. Philology Recapitulates Ontology, Poetry Is Ontology. Delmore Schwartz. **SP-SchwD**

Faithful to your commands, o consciousness, o. Poem. Delmore Schwartz. **SP-SchwD**

Faithful Wilson. Thomas Hardy. **CP-HardT**

Faithful youth, A. A Crazy Spiritual. Allen Ginsberg. **CP-GinsA**

Faithfull lovers keepe from hence. Mary Sidney, Countess of Montgomery Wroth. *Fr.* Part 1. *Fr.* Urania. **CP-WrotM**

Faithfully tinying at twilight voice. Edward Estlin Cummings. **CP-CummE**

Faithless. Walter de la Mare. **CP-DeLaW**

Faithless Shepherdess, The. Christina Georgina Rossetti. **CP-RosC3**

Faithless the watch that I kept: now I have none to keep. The Sleepy Sentinel. Rudyard Kipling. *Fr.* Epitaphs of the War [1914–1918]. **CP-KiplR**

Faithlesse and fond mortality. Upon the Death of a Gentleman. Richard Crashaw. **CP-CrasR**

Faiths pure shield, the Christian *Diana*. The English *Sapphick*. Thomas Campion. *Fr.* Observations in the Art of English Poesie. **CP-CampT**

Fake poet sat down in his gilt, The. The Plagiarist. Malcolm Lowry. **CP-LowrM**

Faking was three times married to Faking. Malcolm Lowry. **CP-LowrM**

Falcon, The. Richard Lovelace. **CP-LoveR**

Falcon Woman, The. Robert Ranke Graves. **CP-GravR**

Falcons have come to the city, The. Sky Sign. Charles Bukowski. **SP-BukC3**

Faldang. Louise McNeill. **SP-McNeL**

Falernian, / old Falernian! Carmen 27. Catullus. *Fr.* Carmina. **CP-Catul**

Fall. Wendell Berry. **CP-BerrW**

Fall, The. Hayden Carruth. *Fr.* Contra Mortem. **CP-CarHL**

Fall. Robert Creeley. **CP-CreeR**

Fall!, The. Archibald MacLeish. *Fr.* Songs for Eve. **CP-MacLA**

Fall, The. Thomas Merton. **CP-MertT; SP-MertT**

Fall, The. John Milton. **PoEL-3** *Fr.* Book IX. **FHYEP; NAEL-1; NAWM-1; NoP; OAEL-1** *Fr.* Paradise Lost. **CP-MiltJ**

(Fall, The.)

Fall, The. John Milton. *See* The Fall.

Fall. John Updike. **CP-UpdiJ**

Fall. Mona Van Duyn. **SP-VanDM**

Fall Again, The. Howard Nemerov. **CP-NemeH**

Fall and rise of her midriff bells. I watch. John Berryman. *Fr.* Sonnets to Chris. **CP-BerrJ**

Fall Comes in Back-Country Vermont. Robert Penn Warren. **SP-WarrR**

Afterwards.

Bear and the Last Person to Remember, The.

Human Fabric, The.

One Voter out of Sixteen.

Fall Day, A. Charles Simic. **SP-SimiC**

Fall, dews of Heaven, upon my burning breast. Written at Exmouth, Midsummer, 1795. Charlotte Smith. **CP-SmitC**

Fall—dust of / decaying. October. Tom Clark. **SP-ClarT**

Fall has come, clear as the eyes of chickens, The. Robert Bly. **SP-BlyR**

(Uneasiness in Fall.) **SP-BlyR**

Fall in Corrales. Richard Wilbur. **CP-WilbR**

Fall in Massachusetts. Isabella Gardner. **CP-GardI**

Fall Journey. William Stafford. **SP-StafW**

Fall, leaves, fall; die, flowers, away. Emily Brontë. **CP-BronE**

Fall 1961. Robert Lowell. **SP-LoweR**

Fall of a Wall. John Donne. **CP-DonnJ**

Fall of Day, The. David Herbert Lawrence. **CP-LawrD**

Fall of Hyperion, The. John Keats. **CP-KeatJ**

Dream, A. **OBNC**

"Methought I stood where trees of every clime." **OBRV**

"Fanatics have their dreams, wherewith they weave." **TOF**

Prest her cold finger closer to her lips. **EnRP**

"Towards the altar sober-paced I went." **TOF**

Fall of Jock Gillespie, The. Rudyard Kipling. **CP-KiplR**

Fall of Night, The. Thomas Merton. **CP-MertT**

Fall of Rome, The. Wystan Hugh Auden. **CP-AudeW**

Fall of the Aar—Handec, The. William Wordsworth. *Fr.* Memorials of a Tour of the Continent; 1820. **CP-WorW2**

Fall of the Angels, The. John Milton. *See* Is this the region, this the soil, the clime.

Fall of the Evening Star. Kenneth Patchen. **CP-PatcK**

Fall Out. Charles Bukowski. **SP-BukC3**

Fall '66. Thomas Merton. **CP-MertT**

Fall Song. Howard Nemerov. **CP-NemeH**

Fall Squashes. Brendan Galvin. **SP-GalvB**

Fall stream from Heaven to bless: return as well. Inscription on a Well in Memory of the Martyrs of the War. Ralph Waldo Emerson. **CP-EmerR**

Fall the deep curtains. Archer. Hilda Doolittle. **CP-DoolH**

Fall we moved to the farm, I was thirteen, The. The Solitary Pond. John Updike. **CP-UpdiJ**

Fall Weekend at *Milgate*. Robert Lowell. **SP-LoweR**

"Day says nothing, and lacks for nothing. . . God; The."

"Milgate kept standing for four centuries."

"Soaking leaves, green yellow, hold like rubber, The."

Fall with me / Through the frigid stars. Medusa. Hart Crane. **CP-CranH**

Fall work almost done. . . . Another Season. Thomas McGrath. **SP-McGrT**

Fallen, and diffused into a shapeless heap. William Wordsworth. *Fr.* The River Duddon [A Series of Sonnets]. **CP-WorW2**

Fallen Angels, The. John Milton. *See* Satan Defiant.

Fallen Angels, The. Anne Sexton. **CP-SextA**

Fallen, Fallen. Stevie Smith. **CP-SmitS**

Fallen from the clouds, well-met. Days of 1971. James Merrill. **SP-MerrJ**

Fallen in between the tendons and bones. Hand. Robinson Jeffers. **CP-JefR3**

Fallen Leaves. David Herbert Lawrence. **CP-LawrD**

Fallen Majesty. William Butler Yeats. **CP-YeatW**

Fallen one, your private ghosts are. Heroes. Jim Carroll. **SP-CarrJ**

Fallen, so freshly fallen. The Dragonfly. Stanley Jasspon Kunitz. **CP-KuniS**

Fallen star / Cooled from the sun to the brink of death we are, A. Reclaimed. Phoebe Hesketh. **SP-HeskP**

Fallen Tower of Siloam, The. Robert Ranke Graves. **CP-GravR**

Fallgrief's Girlfriends. Ted Hughes. **SP-HughT**

Falling. Robert Creeley. **CP-CreeR**

Falling. James Dickey. **CP-DickJ**

Falling / from grace—. Falling. Robert Creeley. **CP-CreeR**

Falling Asleep. Wendell Berry. **CP-BerrW**

Falling Asleep. Robert Bly. **SP-BlyR**

Falling asleep can be quite lovely. Calling Dr. Dunninger. Gilbert Sorrentino. **SP-SorrG**

Falling Asleep in a Darkening Room. Al Young. **CP-YounA**

Falling Asleep in America. Allen Ginsberg. **CP-GinsA**

Falling away, A. Roy Fisher. **SP-FishR** *Fr.* Handsworth Liberties.

Falling Dolls, The. Anne Sexton. **CP-SextA**

Falling downhill—. Robert Creeley. **CP-CreeR**

Falling in love is never as simple. Randall Jarrell. **CP-JarrR**

Falling Leaves. Kathleen Jessie Raine. **SP-RainK**

Falling of Sally, The. George Meredith. **CP-MerG2**

Falling of the Grain, The. William Everson.
  Burning Book, The. **SP-EverW**
  In the Ripeness of the Weed. **SP-EverW**

Falling of the Leaves, The. William Butler Yeats. **CP-YeatW**

Falling Out, A. Michael Hartnett. **SP-HarMi**

Falling out of love. Erasure. Marge Piercy. **SP-PierM**

Falling plummeting unexpectedly sickeningly. The Little Death. Hayden Carruth. *Fr.* Contra Mortem. **CP-CarHL**

Falling snow has made her thoughtful, The. My Mother Remembers That She Was Beautiful. Tess Gallagher. **SP-GallT**

Fall'n Is Lucifer. George Meredith. **CP-MerG2**

Fallow between the horny trees. Dog in a Cornfield. James Wright. **CP-WrigJ**

Fallow Deer at the Lonely House, The. Thomas Hardy. **CP-HardT**

Falls, The. Galway Kinnell. **SP-KinnG**

Falls apart / when he takes his glasses off. My Father's Face. Siv Cedering Fox. **SP-CedeS**

Falltime. Carl Sandburg. **CP-SandC**

False Achitophel, The. John Dryden. *See* Of these the false Achitophel was first.

False Bay. Frank Templeton Prince. **CP-PrinF**

False Country of the Zoo. Jean Garrigue. **SP-GarrJ**

False, cruel, disappointed, stung to th' heart. In Seditionem Horrendum. William Cowper. **CP-CowpW**

False Dawn. Rudyard Kipling. *Fr.* Plain Tales from the Hills.
  "To-night, God knows what thing shall tide." **CP-KiplR**

False Democracy and Real. David Herbert Lawrence. **CP-LawrD**

False glozing pleasures, casks of happiness. Dotage. George Herbert. **CP-HerbG**

False Gods, The. Edwin Arlington Robinson. **CP-RobiE**

False history gets made all day, any day. Burden Baskets. Adrienne Rich. *Fr.* Turning the Wheel. **SP-RicA2**

False [or Faulce] hope which feeds but[t] to destroy, and spill. Sonnet 35. Mary Sidney, Countess of Montgomery Wroth. **KTR; NAEL-1** *Fr.* Pamphilia to Amphilanthus. **CP-WrotM**

False Mourning. Robert Herrick. **CP-HerrR**

False Postulate. Jenny Joseph. **SP-JoseJ**

False Security. Sir John Betjeman. **CP-BetjJ**

False Solomon's Seal. Howard Nemerov. **CP-NemeH**

False Step, A. Elizabeth Barrett Browning. **CP-BroEB**

False strawberry is. Grace Paley. **CP-PaleG**

False world, good night: since thou hast brought. To the World [A Farewell for a Gentlewoman, Virtuous and Noble]. Ben Jonson. **CP-JonsB**

False Youth: Autumn: Clothes of the Age. James Dickey. **CP-DickJ**

False Youth: Two Seasons. James Dickey. **CP-DickJ**

Falsehood of Thee could I suppose. Emily Dickinson. **CP-DickE**

Falsifiers of things seen!, The. The Eighth Book. Archibald MacLeish. *Fr.* Conquistador. **CP-MacLA**

Falstaff. Walter de la Mare. **CP-DeLaW**

Falstaff. Thom Gunn. *Fr.* Transients and Residents. **CP-GunnT**

Faltering and sad the unhappy Pilgrim roves. The Pilgrim. Charlotte Smith. **CP-SmitC**

Famam, posteritas quam dedit Orpheo. *accompanied by Eng. translation.* Thomas Campion. **CP-CampT**

Fame. Robert Browning. **PP; SoSe** *Fr.* Earth's Immortalities. **CP-BroR1**

Fame. Byron. **FiP** *Fr.* Childe Harold's Pilgrimage. **CP-Byron**

Fame. Ralph Waldo Emerson. **CP-EmerR**

Fame. Robert Herrick. **CP-HerrR**

Fame. John Hewitt. **CP-HewiJ**

Fame If Not Fortune. Carl Sandburg. **CP-SandC**

Fame is a bee. Emily Dickinson. **CP-DickE**

Fame is a fickle food. Emily Dickinson. **CP-DickE**

Fame is the one that does not stay. Emily Dickinson. **CP-DickE**

Fame is the tint that Scholars leave. Emily Dickinson. **CP-DickE**

Fame, like a wayward girl, will still be coy. John Keats. **CP-KeatJ** *Fr.* Two Sonnets on Fame.
  (On Fame ("Fame, like a wayward girl, will still be coy").) **CP-KeatJ**

Fame Makes Us Forward. Robert Herrick. **CP-HerrR**

Fame of Myself, to justify. Emily Dickinson. **CP-DickE**

Fame Speaks. Edward Estlin Cummings. **CP-CummE**

Fame tells of groves—from England far away. June, 1820. William Wordsworth. **CP-WorW2**

Fame, wisdom, love, and power were mine. All Is Vanity, Saith the Preacher. Byron. **CP-Byron**

"Fame!" Yes, I said it and you read it. First. The Two Poets of Croisic. Robert Browning. **CP-BroR2**

Famed for contemptuous breach of sacred ties. Windsor Poetics. Byron. **CP-Byron**

Famed for their civil and domestic quarrels. On a Royal Visit to the Vaults. Byron. **CP-Byron**

Fame's Boys and Girls, who never die. Emily Dickinson. **CP-DickE**

Fame's Penny-Trumpet. "Lewis Carroll." **CP-CarrL**

Fame's pillar here, at last, we set. The Pillar of Fame. Robert Herrick. **CP-HerrR**

Fame's Vanity. Walt Whitman. **CP-WhitW**

Familial. William Matthews. **SP-MattW**

Familiar, The. Wendell Berry. **CP-BerrW**

Familiar, The. Walter de la Mare. **CP-DeLaW**

Familiar Things. George Meredith. **CP-MerG2**

Familiarity Dangerous. Vincent Bourne, *tr. fr. Latin by* William Cowper. **CP-CowpW**

Families. Grace Paley. **CP-PaleG**

Families. "Lou Reed." **SP-ReedL**

Familist's Hymn, The. John Greenleaf Whittier. **CP-WhitJ**

Family, The. Robert Browning. **CP-BroR2**

Family, The. Robert Creeley. **CP-CreeR**

Family, The. Donald Hall. **CP-HallD**

Family [or Familie], The. George Herbert. **CP-HerbG**

Family, The. Mary Oliver. **SP-OlivM**

Family. Grace Paley. **CP-PaleG**

Family, The. Robert Louis Stevenson. **CP-StevR**
  "About my fields, in the broad sun."
  "The Adorner of the uncomely—Those."
  Daughter, Teuila, Native Name for Adorner, The.
  "I meanwhile in the populous house apart."
  Mother and Daughter.
  "Old lady (so they say) but I, The."
  "Tall as a guardsman, pale as the east at dawn."
  "These rings, O my beloved pair."
  "What glory for a boy of ten."

Family Affairs. Maya Angelou. **SP-AngeM**

Family Album in Red Plush. Marsden Hartley. **CP-HartM**

Family Circle. Leonard Nathan. **SP-NathL**

Family clambered into the crowded bus, The. An Incident. John Hewitt. **CP-HewiJ**

Family Court. Ogden Nash. **CP-NashO**

Family decides to have a party, A. White Pig. Stephen Dobyns. **SP-DobyS**

Family Ghosts. Wystan Hugh Auden. **CP-AudeW**

Family Group. Archibald MacLeish. **CP-MacLA**

Family had buried him, The. After the Burial. Thomas Hardy. **CP-HardT**

Family Mottoes. Frank Templeton Prince. **CP-PrinF**

Family Of. Alice Walker. **CP-WalkA**

Family Portrait. Carlos Drummond de Andrade, *tr. fr. Portuguese by* Elizabeth Bishop. **CP-BishE**

Family Portrait. Kenneth Patchen. **CP-PatcK**

Family Portraits. Thomas Hardy. **CP-HardT**

Family Resemblance, A. Audre Lorde. **SP-LordA**

Family Reunion. Hayden Carruth. **CP-CarHS**

Family Reunion. Sylvia Plath. **CP-PlatS**

Family story tells, and it was told true, The. The Funnel. Anne Sexton. **CP-SextA**

Family Tree, The. Laurence Lieberman. **SP-LiebL**

Family Turn, A. William Stafford. **SP-StafW**

Family will hate most, The. Burglary. William Matthews. **SP-MattW**

Famous Blue Raincoat. Leonard Cohen. **CP-CoheL**

Famous doctor held up Grandma's stomach, The. I Wanted to Be a Doctor. Leonard Cohen. **CP-CoheL**

Famous engines support type B network. Thomas Merton. **CP-MertT**

Famous kingdom of the birds, The. Somewhere Is Such a Kingdom. John Crowe Ransom. **SP-RansJ**

Famous man is Robin Hood, A. Rob Roy's Grave. William Wordsworth. **CP-WorW1**

Famous Poet. Ted Hughes. **SP-HughT**

Famous Prediction of Merlin, A. Jonathan Swift. "Seven and Ten addyd to nyne." **CP-SwifJ**

Famous Resort in Late Autumn, The. Delmore Schwartz. **SP-SchwD**

Famous torturer takes a walk, The. Rough Outline. Charles Simic. **SP-SimiC**

Famous Writer, The. Charles Bukowski. **SP-BukC3**

Fan Sketched with Silver Egrets, A. David St. John. **SP-StJoD**

Fanaticism? No. Writing is exciting. Baseball and Writing. Marianne Craig Moore. **CP-MoorM**

Fanatics have their dreams, wherewith they weave. The Fall of Hyperion. John Keats. **CP-KeatJ**

Fanatics have their dreams, wherewith they weave. John Keats. **TOF** *Fr.* The Fall of Hyperion. **CP-KeatJ**

Fanatics have their dreams, wherewith they weave. Prest her cold finger closer to her lips. John Keats. **EnRP** *Fr.* The Fall of Hyperion. **CP-KeatJ**

Fancies at Navesink. Walt Whitman. **CP-WhitW**
  By That Long Scan of Waves. **NAAL-1; NAAL-3**
  Had I the Choice. **PP; Poetr; SoSe**

Fancy, A. Thomas Carew. **CP-CareT**

Fancy. Robert Creeley. **CP-CreeR**

Fancy. John Keats. **CP-KeatJ**

Fancy and Tradition. William Wordsworth. **CP-WorW2**

Fancy I had today, The. Amphibian. Robert Browning. **CP-BroR2**

Fancy in Nubibus. Samuel Taylor Coleridge. **CP-ColeS**

Fancy, who leads the pastimes of the glad. A Morning Exercise. William Wordsworth. **CP-WorW2**

Fancy's Knell. Alfred Edward Housman. **CP-HousA**

Fanfare for the Makers, A. Louis MacNeice. *See* Canto VII: "Cloud of witnesses. To whom? To what?, A."

Fanny's Cold Blue Eyes. Diane Wakoski. **SP-WakoD**

Fans and the beltings they roar round me, The. The Song of the Lathes. Rudyard Kipling. **CP-KiplR**

Fantasia on 'Horbury'; John Bacchus Dykes, 1859. Geoffrey Hill. **CP-HillG**

Fantasia on "The Nut-Brown Maid." John Ashbery. "Unless this is the shelf of whatever happens?" **SP-AshbJ**

Fantasies / indulged, great. Robert Creeley. **CP-CreeR**

Fantasy. Robinson Jeffers. **CP-JefR3**

Fantasy. Frank O'Hara. **SP-OharF**

Fantasy and Conversation. Audre Lorde. **SP-LordA**

Fantasy and phantom—. Marsden Hartley. **CP-HartM**

Fantasy holds the child in the man, the lover in the monk, the monk in the lover. Louis MacNeice. *Fr.* The Stygian Banks. **CP-MacNL**

Fantasy in Purple. Langston Hughes. **SP-HughL**

Fantasy of a Small Idea. Richard Eberhart. **CP-EberR**

Far above the dome. It Pleases. Gary Snyder. **CP-SnydG**

Far are the shades of Arabia. Arabia. Walter de la Mare. **CP-DeLaW**

Far are those tranquil hills. The Three Strangers. Walter de la Mare. **CP-DeLaW**

Far as creation's ample range extends. Alexander Pope. **ECEV; FM; ImOP** *Fr.* An Essay on Man. **CP-PopeA**

Far away, I suppose you could say. What Is the Blues? Al Young. **CP-YounA**

Far away in the twilight time. The Double-Headed Snake of Newbury. John Greenleaf Whittier. **CP-WhitJ**

Far away is close at hand. Song of Contrariety. Robert Ranke Graves. **CP-GravR**

Far away is the land of rest. Lines. Emily Brontë. **CP-BronE**

Far away under us, they are mowing on the green steps. The Beholders. James Dickey. **CP-DickJ**

Far back, in the time of ice. The Ghost Hunter. John Haines. **SP-HainJ**

Far back, related on my mother's side. Old Salt Kossabone. Walt Whitman. **CP-WhitW**

Far back the shouting Briton in foray. Ulsterman. John Hewitt. **CP-HewiJ**

Far back when I went zig-zagging. Orion. Adrienne Rich. **CP-RicAE; SP-RicA1; SP-RicA2**

Far between sundown's finish an' midnight's broken toll. Chimes of Freedom. "Bob Dylan." **CP-DylaB**

Far Cry from Africa, A. Derek Walcott. **CP-WalcD**

Far different dejection once was mine. William Wordsworth. **OBTV,** *book* 6, *ll.* 491–657; **RB** *Fr.* Cambridge and the Alps. *Fr.* The Prelude; Growth of a Poet's Mind [1805 vers.]. **CP-WorW3**
  (Crossing the Alps.) **RB,** *book* 6, *ll.* 491–572;

Far down in the sweltering guts of the ship. The Worker. Ernest Hemingway. **CP-HemiE**

Far down the purple wood. The Constant Bridegrooms. Kenneth Patchen. **CP-PatcK**

"Far enough down is China," somebody said. Digging for China. Richard Wilbur. **CP-WilbR**

Far-Far-Away. Tennyson. **CP-TennA**

Far, far away is mirth withdrawn. Emily Brontë. **CP-BronE**

Far, far away, O ye. Lines. Percy Bysshe Shelley. **CP-ShelP**

Far far from gusty waves these children's faces. An Elementary School Classroom in a Slum. Stephen Spender. **CP-SpenS**

Far far from here. Matthew Arnold. **FiP; GTBS-6; GTBS-P** *Fr.* Empedocles on Etna. **SP-ArnoM**
  (Song of Callicles, The ("Far, far from here").) **FiP**

Far far the least of all, in want. The Prisoners. Stephen Spender. **CP-SpenS**

Far-Farers, The. Robert Louis Stevenson. **CP-StevR**

Far Field, The. Theodore Roethke. **NAAL-2; NoAM; NoP; PrIm; SeCeV** *Fr.* North American Sequence. **CP-RoetT**

Far from a cultural centre he was used. Wystan Hugh Auden. **CMoP; NoAM** *Fr.* Sonnets from China. **CP-AudeW**

Far from from my dearest Friend, 'tis mine to rove. An Evening Walk Addressed to a Young Lady. William Wordsworth. **CP-WorW1**

Far from his close and noisome cell. The Human Sacrifice. John Greenleaf Whittier. **CP-WhitJ**

Far from Love the Heavenly Father. Emily Dickinson. **CP-DickE**

Far from normal far from normal far from normal I am. I Am. Stevie Smith. **CP-SmitS**

Far from our debtors. The Blessings of a Country Life. Jonathan Swift. *Fr.* Verses from Quilica. **CP-SwifJ**

Far from our home by Grasmere's quiet Lake. Epistle to Sir George Howland Beaumont, BART. William Wordsworth. **CP-WorW1**

Far from the age of my Spanish ancestor. One Brief Hour of Grown-up Glory on the Gulf of Mexico. Nicholas Vachel Lindsay. *Fr.* Doctor Mohawk. **CP-LindV**

Far from the clams and fogs and bogs. The End of the Rainbow. Randall Jarrell. **CP-JarrR**

Far from the French countryside. The Story of Toile. Siv Cedering Fox. *Fr.* Onna-E, Pictures of Women. **SP-CedeS**

Far from the loud sea beaches. A Visit from the Sea. Robert Louis Stevenson. **CP-StevR**

Far from the Rappahannock, the silent. Into the Dusk-Charged Air. John Ashbery. **SP-AshbJ**

Far from the sea far from the sea. The Canticle of Jack Kerouac. Lawrence Ferlinghetti. **SP-FerlL**

Far from the Soil. Leonard Cohen. **CP-CoheL**

Far from the steamy parlors of the north. The Little Robber Girl Considers the Wide World. Marilyn Hacker. **SP-HackM**

Far from the sun and summer gale. Thomas Gray. **EPCY** *Fr.* The Progress of Poesy. **CP-GrayT**

Far from the world, O Lord, I flee. Retirement. William Cowper. *Fr.* Olney Hymns. **CP-CowpW**

Far from these stones, in my country wind shouts. Confederate Graves in Little Rock. Richard Hugo. **CP-HugoR**

Far happier are the dead, methinks, than they. On Invalids. *Unknown, tr. fr. Greek by* William Cowper. **CP-CowpW**

Far have you come, my lady, from the town. Robert Louis Stevenson. *Fr.* Rondels. **CP-StevR**

Far hence amid an isle of wondrous beauty. Old Ireland. Walt Whitman. **CP-WhitW**

Far I hear the bugle blow. The Day of Battle. Alfred Edward Housman. **CP-HousA**

Far in a western brookland. Alfred Edward Housman. **CP-HousA**

Far in the chambers of the west. Dawn and Sunrise. Sir Walter Scott. **SP-ScotW** *Fr.* Rokeby.

Far in the West there lies a desert land, where the mountains. Henry Wadsworth Longfellow. **APN-1** *Fr.* Far in the West there lies a desert land, where the mountains. *Fr.* Part the Second. *Fr.* Evangeline, a Tale of Acadie. **SP-LongH**

Far in the West there lies a desert land, where the mountains. Henry Wadsworth Longfellow. *Fr.* Part the Second. *Fr.* Evangeline, a Tale of Acadie. **SP-LongH**

"Far in the West there lies a desert land, where the mountains." **APN-1**

Far in the woods my stealthy flute. William DeWitt Snodgrass. **SP-SnodW**

Far inland here Death's pinions mocked the roar. Truce. Walter de la Mare. **CP-DeLaW**

Far into moonlight he tries. The Mockingbird. Brendan Galvin. **SP-GalvB**

Far into the vast the mists grow dim. Dawn. Wystan Hugh Auden. **CP-AudWJ**

Far islands. . . veiled by cold rain. Beyond Seattle. Thomas McGrath. **SP-McGrT**

Far known to sea and shore. Alfred Edward Housman. **CP-HousA**

Far moon maketh lovers wise, The. Moonlight. Walter de la Mare. **CP-DeLaW**

Far-off / at the core of space. Swan. David Herbert Lawrence. **CP-LawrD**

Far off, above the plain the summer dries. Second Air Force. Randall Jarrell. **CP-JarrR**

Far off, from the burned fields. Ashes. Philip Levine. **SP-LeviP**

Far-Off Light. Daniel Gerard Hoffman. **SP-HoffD**

Far-off, most secret, and inviolate Rose. The Secret Rose. William Butler Yeats. **CP-YeatW**

Far Off-Shore. Herman Melville. **SP-MelvH**

Far-off the lily-statues stand white-ranked in the garden at home. At the Front. David Herbert Lawrence. **CP-LawrD**

Far off, two fields away. Dark Night of the Soul. Robert Penn Warren. **SP-WarrR**

Far off we saw them in the upland field. Salute. John Hewitt. **CP-HewiJ**

Far on the sands, the low, retiring tide. Charlotte Smith. **CP-SmitC**

Far Out. Philip Larkin. **CP-LarkP**

Far over seas an island is. Robert Louis Stevenson. **CP-StevR**

Far overhead—the glass set fair. The Omen. Walter de la Mare. **CP-DeLaW**

Far-removed Mountain Men, The. Hayden Carruth. **CP-CarHS**

Far Rockaway Night Till Morning. Carl Sandburg. **CP-SandC**

Far seen the river glides below. Ralph Waldo Emerson. **CP-EmerR**

Far side of your moon is black, The. Song: The Far Side of Your Moon. Robert Ranke Graves. **CP-GravR**

Far star that tickles for me my sensitive plate. Skeptic. Robert Frost. **CP-FrosR**

Far up into the amethystine vapours. Everest. Wystan Hugh Auden. **CP-AudWJ**

Far 'yont amang the years to be. The Maker to Posterity. Robert Louis Stevenson. **CP-StevR**

Farallones seals clubbed, The. Visiting the Farallones. Robert Bly. **SP-BlyR**

Fare Thee Well. Byron. **CP-Byron**

Fare Thee Well. Donald Davie. **CP-DavDo**

Fare Well. John Berryman. **CP-BerrJ**

Fare Well. Walter de la Mare. **CP-DeLaW**

Fareweel to a' our Scotish fame. Such a Parcel of Rogues in a Nation. Robert Burns. **CP-BurnR**

Farewel, Aruna!—on whose varied shore. On Leaving a Part of Sussex. Charlotte Smith. **CP-SmitC**

Farewel D.r Friend! may Guid-luck hit you. To John Kennedy. Robert Burns. **CP-BurnR**

Farewel, ye lawns!—by fond remembrance blest. Charlotte Smith. **CP-SmitC**

Farewell: "Farewell, and when forth." Robert Louis Stevenson. **CP-StevR**

Farewell: "Farewell dear friends." Stevie Smith. **CP-SmitS**

Farewell: "Farewell, my love, goodbye." Martin Edmunds. **SP-EdmuM**

Farewell: "Oh it's fare thee well my darlin' true." "Bob Dylan." **CP-DylaB**

Farewell. Sir Walter Scott. *See* Harp of the North, Farewell! The Hills Grow Dark.

Farewell, A: "Farewell, thou little Nook of mountain-ground." William Wordsworth. **CP-WorW1**

Farewell, A: "Flow down, cold rivulet, to the sea." Tennyson. **CP-TennA**

Farewell, A: "My horse's feet beside the lake." Matthew Arnold. **SP-ArnoM** *Fr.* Switzerland.

Farewell, A: "What shall I say, dear friends, to whom I owe." John Greenleaf Whittier. **CP-WhitJ**

Farewell, all my welfare. Sir Thomas Wyatt. **CP-WyatT**

Farewell and adieu to you, Harwich Ladies. Rudyard Kipling. **CP-KiplR**

Farewell and adieu to you noble hearties. Tom Deadlight. Herman Melville. **SP-MelvH**

Farewell, and when forth. Farewell. Robert Louis Stevenson. **CP-StevR**

Farewell Angelina. "Bob Dylan." **CP-DylaB**

Farewell!—But not for ever, Hope replies. Translation of Epitaph to Northcot. William Cowper, *tr. fr. the Latin of Morley Unwin.* **CP-CowpW**

Farewell, dear babe, my heart's too much content! In Memory of My Dear Grandchild Elizabeth Bradstreet Who Deceased August, 1665, Being a Year and a Half Old. Anne Bradstreet. **CP-BradA**

Farewell dear friends. Farewell. Stevie Smith. **CP-SmitS**

Farewell, dear scenes, for ever closed to me. Lines Written upon a Window-Shutter at Weston. William Cowper. **CP-CowpW**

Farewell, deep Valley, with thy one rude House. The Pastor. William Wordsworth. *Fr.* The Excursion. **CP-WorW2**

Farewell! endued with all that could engage. Lines for a Memorial of Ashley Cowper. William Cowper. **CP-CowpW**

Farewell fair Arminda, my joy and my grief. Song. John Dryden. **SP-DrydJ**

Farewell, fair day and fading light! The Lost Occasion. Robert Louis Stevenson. **CP-StevR**

Farewell fair Saint, may not the seas and wind. On His Mistress[e] Going to Sea. Thomas Cary. **CP-CareT**

Farewell, false hearts! whose best affections fail. Valediction, The. William Cowper. **CP-CowpW**

Farewell, false love, the oracle of lies. A Farewell to False Love. Sir Walter Ralegh. **CP-RaleW**

Farewell, farewell! but this I tell. Samuel Taylor Coleridge. **PFP** *Fr.* The Rime of the Ancient Mariner. **CP-ColeS**

Farewell, Farewell, *Despedida!*. Jesus' Farewell. David Herbert Lawrence. **CP-LawrD**

Farewell, farewell, my love Irene. My Love Irene. Paul Laurence Dunbar. **CP-DunbP**

Farewell, Foolish Objects. Charles Bukowski. **SP-BukC2**

Farewell for ever, well for ever fare. Murder. Stevie Smith. **CP-SmitS**

Farewell Frost; or, Welcome the Spring. Robert Herrick. **CP-HerrR**

Farewell! If Ever Fondest Prayer. Byron. **CP-Byron**

Farewell Lines. William Wordsworth. **CP-WorW2**

Farewell, love, and all thy law[e]s forever. Sir Thomas Wyatt. **CP-WyatT**

Farewell, my Highland lassie! when the year returns around. O Theos Meta Sou. Arthur Hugh Clough. **SP-ClouA**

Farewell, my love, goodbye. Farewell. Martin Edmunds. **SP-EdmuM**

Farewell, my tender brother. Think. Beatrice's Last Words. Percy Bysshe Shelley. **FiP** *Fr.* The Cenci. **CP-ShelP**

Farewell of the Attendant Spirit. John Milton. *See* To the ocean now I fly.

Farewell, old Scotia's bleak domains. Farewell, The. Robert Burns. **CP-BurnR**

Farewell parental scenes! a sad farewell! Sonnet on Quitting Christ's Hospital. Samuel Taylor Coleridge. **CP-ColeS**

Farewell Petition to J.C.H., Esq. Byron. **CP-Byron**

Farewell, politics, utterly! What can I do? I can not. Arthur Hugh Clough. **FaBoPV** *Fr.* Amours de Voyage. **SP-ClouA**

Farewell Rehearsed. Allen Tate. **CP-TateA**

"Farewell, Romance!" the Cave-men said. The King. Rudyard Kipling. **CP-KiplR**

Farewell sadness. Scarcely Disfigured. Paul Éluard, *tr. fr. French by Samuel Beckett.* **CP-BeckS**

Farewell Song, The. Thomas Campion. *Fr.* The Ayres that Were Sung and Played, at *Brougham Castle* in *Westmerland*, in the Kings Entertainment. **CP-CampT**

Farewell Song. Paul Laurence Dunbar. **CP-DunbP**

Farewell, sweet Love! yet blame you not my truth. Farewell to Love. Samuel Taylor Coleridge. **CP-ColeS**

Farewell Symphony, The. Randall Jarrell. **CP-JarrR**

Farewell, The: "Farewell, old Scotia's bleak domains." Robert Burns. **CP-BurnR**

Farewell, The: "Gone, gone,—sold and gone." John Greenleaf Whittier. **CP-WhitJ**

Farewell, The: "Sweetest Loue since wee must part." Robert Herrick. **CP-HerrR**

Farewell, the reign of cruelty! Sir Thomas Wyatt. **CP-WyatT**

Farewell Thing While Breathing, A. Charles Bukowski. **SP-BukC2**

Farewell! Thou art too dear[e] for my possessing. Sonnet 87. William Shakespeare. **CBLP; EBEV; EBEvV; EIL; GTBS; GTBS-6; GTBS-P; ImPo; InPS; InvP; LiTB; MasP; NAEL-1; NOBE; NoSic; OAEL-1; OAEP; OBEV; OBSC; OXAEP-1; PeHV; PoEL-2; QFR; Son; TFi; TrGrPo** *Fr.* Sonnets. **CP-ShaWS**

Farewell, thou child of my right hand, and joy. On My First Son [*or* Sonne]. Ben Jonson. **CP-JonsB**

Farewell, thou fair day; thou green earth; and ye skies. Orananaoig, or, the Song of Death. Robert Burns. **CP-BurnR**

Farewell, thou little Nook of mountain-ground. Farewell, A. William Wordsworth. **CP-WorW1**

Farewell, thou stream that winding flows. Song. Robert Burns. **CP-BurnR**

Farewell, thou Thing, time-past so knowne, so dear. His Farewell [*or* Farewell] to Sack. Robert Herrick. **CP-HerrR**

Farewell to a name and a number. Alfred Edward Housman. **CP-HousA**

Farewell To Alexandria, A. Emily Brontë. **CP-BronE**

Farewell to an idea. . . A cabin stands. Wallace Stevens. **CMoP; HCAP; PoE** *Fr.* The Auroras of Autumn. **CP-StevW**

Farewell to an idea. . . The mother's face. Wallace Stevens. **HCAP; PoE** *Fr.* The Auroras of Autumn. **CP-StevW**

Farewell to Anactoria. Sappho, *tr. fr. Greek by* Allen Tate. **CP-TateA**

Farewell to Arcady. Paul Laurence Dunbar. **CP-DunbP**

Farewell to barn and stack and tree. Alfred Edward Housman. **CP-HousA**

Farewell to Dostoevski. "Hugh MacDiarmid." **NAEL-2** *Fr.* A Drunk Man Looks at the Thistle. **SP-MacDH**

Farewell to English, A. Michael Hartnett.
   "I say farewell to English verse." **SP-HarMi**
   "This road is not new." **SP-HarMi**

Farewell to False Love, A. Sir Walter Ralegh. **CP-RaleW**

Farewell to Florida. Wallace Stevens. **CP-StevW**

Farewell to London in the Year 1715, A. Alexander Pope. **CP-PopeA**

Farewell to Love. Samuel Taylor Coleridge. **CP-ColeS**

Farewell to Love. John Donne. **CP-DonnJ**

Farewell to Love. Sir John Suckling. **CP-SuckJ**
   ("Well, shadow'd landskip, fare ye well.") **CP-SuckJ**

Farewell to Malta. Byron. **CP-Byron**

Farewell to Melancholy. Lewis Turco. **SP-TurcL**

Farewell to Miles. John Berryman. **CP-BerrJ**

Farewell to the Bluewoman. Kenneth Patchen. **CP-PatcK**

Farewell. To the Brethren of St. James' Lodge, Tarbolton, The. Robert Burns. **CP-BurnR**

Farewell to the Court. Sir Walter Ralegh. **CP-RaleW**

Farewell to the Farm. Robert Louis Stevenson. **CP-StevR**

Farewell to the Land where the gloom of my Glory. Napoleon's Farewell. Byron. **CP-Byron**

Farewell to the Muse. Byron. **CP-Byron**

Farewell to the Shopping District of Antibes. John Updike. **CP-UpdiJ**

Farewell to Van Gogh. Charles Tomlinson. **CP-TomlC**

Farewell, too little and too lately known. To the Memory of Mr Oldham. John Dryden. **SP-DrydJ**

Farewell ungrateful[l] traitor [*or* traytor], / Farewell my perjured swain. John Dryden. **SP-DrydJ** *Fr.* The Spanish Friar [*or* Fryar].
   (Song: "Farewell ungrateful[l] traitor [*or* traytor].") **SP-DrydJ**

Farewell ye banks, where late the primrose growing. The Close of Summer. Charlotte Smith. **CP-SmitC**

Farewell, ye dungeons dark and strong. Robert Burns. **CP-BurnR**
   (McPherson's Farewell.) **CP-BurnR**

Farewell, ye lofty spires. The Last Farewell. Edward Bliss Emerson. **CP-EmerR**

Farewell ye sequent graces. Basil Bunting. **CP-BuntB**

Farewell,runaway snows! For the meadow is green,and the tree stands. 4.7. Horace. **CP-CummE**, *tr. by* E. E. Cummings; *Fr.* Odes.

Farglow. Wystan Hugh Auden. **CP-AudWJ**

Fargo. John Updike. **CP-UpdiJ**

Faridun watched the road. Firdausi. **CP-BuntB** *Fr.* Faridun's Sons.

Faridun's Sons. Firdausi, *tr. fr. Persian by* Basil Bunting.
   "Faridun watched the road." **CP-BuntB**

Faring, The. Charles Tomlinson. **CP-TomlC**

Faring, The. Robert Penn Warren. *Fr.* The True Nature of Time. **SP-WarrR**

Farm, The. Robert Creeley. **CP-CreeR**

Farm, The. Gary Gildner. **SP-GildG**

Farm, The. Donald Hall. **CP-HallD**

Farm, The. Archibald MacLeish. **CP-MacLA**

Farm afternoons, there's much too much blue air. Sonnet of Intimacy. Vinícius de Moraes, *tr. fr. Portuguese by* Elizabeth Bishop. **CP-BishE**

Farm boy lost in the snow, A. Or, Solitude. Donald Davie. **CP-DavDo**

Farm boy, only older than myself, The. The Hired Lad's Farewell. John Hewitt. **CP-HewiJ**

Farm boys wild to couple. The Sheep Child. James Dickey. **CP-DickJ**

Farm Child's Lullaby, The. Paul Laurence Dunbar. **CP-DunbP**

Farm Country. Mary Oliver. **SP-OlivM**

Farm Implements and Rutabagas in a Landscape. John Ashbery. **SP-AshbJ**

Farm on the Great Plains, The. William Stafford. **SP-StafW**

Farm Picture, A. Walt Whitman. **CP-WhitW**

Farm travels in snow, The. Wendell Berry. *Fr.* From the Crest. **CP-BerrW**

Farm Walk, A. Christina Georgina Rossetti. *See* The Year stood at its equinox.

Farm-Woman's Winter, The. Thomas Hardy. **CP-HardT**

Farmer, The. William Carlos Williams. **CP-WilW1**

Farmer among the Tombs, The. Wendell Berry. **CP-BerrW**

Farmer and the Queen, The. Shel Silverstein. **SP-SilS2**

Farmer and the Sea, The. Wendell Berry. **CP-BerrW**

Farmer Dunman's Funeral. Thomas Hardy. **CP-HardT**

Farmer, Dying. Richard Hugo. **CP-HugoR**

Farmer in deep thought, The. The Farmer. William Carlos Williams. **CP-WilW1**

Farmer, in the pride of sea-won acres, The. Sunday in October. Richard Eberhart. **CP-EberR**

Farmer of the Augustan Age, A. The Bees and the Flies. Rudyard Kipling. **CP-KiplR**

Farmer of Tilsbury Vale, The. William Wordsworth. **CP-WorW1**

Farmer, Speaking of Monuments, The. Wendell Berry. **CP-BerrW**

Farmers. James Dickey. **CP-DickJ**

Farmer's goose, who in the stubble, The. The Progress of Poetry. Jonathan Swift. **CP-SwifJ**

Farmers in Vermont, The. Dog Days. Siv Cedering Fox. **SP-CedeS**

Farmer's Second Son, The. John Hewitt. **CP-HewiJ**

Farmer's Testimony, The. Richard Shelton. **SP-ShelR**

Farmer's Wife, The. Anne Sexton. **CP-SextA**

Farmer's Wife: at Fostons Ash, The. Charles Tomlinson. **CP-TomlC**

Farmhouse curtained neat, The. The Neglected Lane. John Hewitt. **CP-HewiJ**

Farmhouse lingers, though averse to square, The. A Brook in the City. Robert Frost. **CP-FrosR**

Farms are oozing craters in, The. Ted Hughes. *See* Crow Hill.

Farms of home lie lost in even, The. Alfred Edward Housman. **CP-HousA**

Farr off from these a slow and silent stream. The Place of the Damned. John Milton. **FaBoEn** *Fr.* Book II. **FHYEP; NAEL-1; OxAEP-1** *Fr.* Paradise Lost. **CP-MiltJ**

Farther and farther and far apart. When the Scientists Told Me of the Expanding Universe. Louise McNeill. **SP-McNeL**

Farther than I have been. The Summit. Kathleen Jessie Raine. *Fr.* Bheinn Naomh. **SP-RainK**

Farther up the gorge the sea's voice fainted and ceased. All the Little Hoof-Prints. Robinson Jeffers. **CP-JefR2**

Farthest Thunder that I heard, The. Emily Dickinson. **CP-DickE**

Fascinating chill that music leaves, The. Emily Dickinson. **CP-DickE**

Fascination / o' jack-o'-lanterns. Metaphysical. Hayden Carruth. *Fr.* Poetical Abstracts. **CP-CarHS**

Fascination of What's Difficult, The. William Butler Yeats. **CP-YeatW**

Fashions are changing in the sphere. A Change of World. Adrienne Rich. **CP-RicAE**

Fast-Anchor'd Eternal O Love! Walt Whitman. **CP-WhitW**

Fast As You Can Count to Ten. John Ciardi. **SP-CiarJ**

Fast asleep, mine own familiar friend. Better So. Christina Georgina Rossetti. **CP-RosC3**

Fast Bound Together. Robert Ranke Graves. **CP-GravR**

Fast Food. Charles Kenneth Williams. **SP-WillC**

Fast, or Lent, The. Robert Herrick. **CP-HerrR**

Fast Speaking Woman. Anne Waldman. **SP-WaldA**

Fast this Life of mine was dying. Life and Love. Elizabeth Barrett Browning. **CP-BroEB**

Fasten black eyes on me. Spanish. Carl Sandburg. **CP-SandC**

Fasten your hair with a golden pin. He Gives His Beloved Certain Rhymes. William Butler Yeats. **CP-YeatW**

Faster, faster with no loss of ritual. Procession. Allen Tate. **CP-TateA**

Faster than fairies, faster than witches. From a Railway Carriage. Robert Louis Stevenson. **CP-StevR**

Fastness, *parody of* Alfred, Lord Tennyson. Rudyard Kipling. **CP-KiplR** *Fr.* The Muse among the Motors.

Fat. Charles Kenneth Williams. **SP-WillC**

Fat, aging, the child clinging to her hand. Randall Jarrell. **CP-JarrR**

Fat be my Hinde; unlearned be my wife. His Wish . Robert Herrick. **CP-HerrR**

Fat black bucks in a wine-barrel room. The Congo. Nicholas Vachel Lindsay. **CP-LindV**

Fat-kneed god! Feeder of mangy leopards! You Also, Gaius Valerius Catullus. Archibald MacLeish. **CP-MacLA**

Fat Lady, The. Hayden Carruth. **CP-CarHS**

Fat lady sings to Der Rosenkavalier, The. Chester. Paul Muldoon. *Fr.* 7, Middagh Street. **SP-MuldP**

Fat Man in the Mirror, The, after Werfel. Robert Lowell. **SP-LoweR**

Fat Mexican woman in front of me in line, A. Charles Bukowski. *Fr.* Horsemeat. **SP-BukC3**

Fat pine boughs. Eating Outside. Stephen Berg. **SP-BergS**

Fat sixty-year-old man woke me. "Hello", A. Birthday. John Ciardi. **SP-CiarJ**

Fat time of the year is also time, The. Howard Nemerov. *Fr.* Runes. **CP-NemeH**

Fat Woman, The. Walter de la Mare. **CP-DeLaW**

Fata Morgana. Siv Cedering Fox. **SP-CedeS**

Fata Morgana. Christina Georgina Rossetti. **CP-RosC1**

Fatal Interview. Edna St. Vincent Millay. **CP-MillE**

Fatal Kisses. Stephen Dobyns. **SP-DobyS**

Fatal Sisters, The. Thomas Gray, *after the Icelandic.* **CP-GrayT**

Fatal Spell, The. Byron. *See* Oh love! no habitant of earth thou art.

Fatality. David Herbert Lawrence. **CP-LawrD**

Fate. Tom Clark. **SP-ClarT**

Fate ("Deep in the man sits fast his fate"). Ralph Waldo Emerson. **CP-EmerR**

Fate ("Her planted eye to-day controls"). Ralph Waldo Emerson. **APN-1** *Fr.* Quatrains. **CP-EmerR**

Fate ("That you are fair or wise is vain"). Ralph Waldo Emerson. **CP-EmerR**

Fate. Kenneth Koch. **SP-KochK**

Fate. Carl Sandburg. **CP-SandC**

Fate and the Younger Generation. David Herbert Lawrence. **CP-LawrD**

Fate comes with pennies or dollars. Fate. Carl Sandburg. **CP-SandC**

Fate gave the word, the arrow sped. Robert Burns. **CP-BurnR**

(Mother's Lament for the Loss of Her Only Son, A.) **CP-BurnR**

Fate, heat, the strike of the night. The Strike of the Night. Jean Garrigue. **SP-GarrJ**

Fate hired me once to play a villain's part. Between the Acts. Stanley Jasspon Kunitz. **CP-KuniS**

Fate is dead. God is in man. The Truth. Alfonso Cortes, *tr. fr. Spanish by* Thomas Merton. **CP-MertT**

Fate lifts us up so she can hurl. In Memoriam. John Updike. **CP-UpdiJ**

Fate slew Him, but He did not drop. Emily Dickinson. **CP-DickE**

Fate Spinners in Time-Editing Studio, Eternity Blvd., 2 A.M. Tom Clark. **SP-ClarT**

Fate succumbs. Marginalia. Wystan Hugh Auden. **CP-AudeW**

Fate summoned, in gray-bearded age, to act. Thiers. John Greenleaf Whittier. **CP-WhitJ**

Fateless Ones, The. Kathleen Jessie Raine. **SP-RainK**

Fately alone with you once more. That Other World. Robert Ranke Graves. **CP-GravR**

Fates, The. Wilfred Owen. **CP-OwenW**

Fate's now grown merciful to men. The Tooth-Ache Cured by a Kiss. Thomas Carew. **CP-CareT**

Father / and mother / and sister. The Family. Robert Creeley. **CP-CreeR**

Father, The. John Donne. NOCV *Fr.* A Litany. **CP-DonnJ**

Father, / I wait for you in oceans. Child Dead in Old Seas. Maya Angelou. **SP-AngeM**

Father. Robert Lowell. **SP-LoweR**

Father. Peter Meinke. **SP-MeinP**

Father, / the Santa Claus suit. Santa. Anne Sexton. *Fr.* The Death of the Fathers. **CP-SextA**

Father, / who were all those friends. Friends. Anne Sexton. *Fr.* The Death of the Fathers. **CP-SextA**

Father. James Wright. **CP-WrigJ**

Father and Child, *fr.* A Woman Young and Old. William Butler Yeats. **CP-YeatW**

Father and daughter marched between. Soldiers with Green Leggings. Peter Meinke. **SP-MeinP**

Father and I drove to the sand-quarry across the ruined marshlands. Sand-Quarry with Moving Figures. Muriel Rukeyser. **CP-RukeM**

Father and mother sat, and the sister beside her, The. Four in a Family. Muriel Rukeyser. **CP-RukeM**

Father and Son. Stanley Jasspon Kunitz. **CP-KuniS**

Father Animus and Zimmer. Paul Zimmer. **SP-ZimmP**

Father Animus asked who broke. Father Animus and Zimmer. Paul Zimmer. **SP-ZimmP**

Father-confessor / Of the fat hen. Knife. Charles Simic. **SP-SimiC**

Father dead, land lost, stepmother haggard with kids. A Dead Language: Circa 1885. Robert Penn Warren. *Fr.* Mortmain. **SP-WarrR**

Father, Dear Father, Go Jump in the Lake, or, You're Costlier than You Think. Ogden Nash. **CP-NashO**

Father Death Blues. Allen Ginsberg. **SM** *Fr.* Don't Grow Old. **CP-GinsA**

Father dreams that he was hid in a tree, The. Muriel Rukeyser. **CP-RukeM**

Father Explains, A. John Hewitt. **CP-HewiJ**

Father, Father, I am overwhelmed. A Prayer After All. John Berryman. **CP-BerrJ**

Father, father, where are you going? Little Boy Lost, The. William Blake. **EnRP; FHYEP; LAuP; NoP; TiPo** *Fr.* Songs of Innocence. **CP-BlakW**

Father for a Fool, A. Stevie Smith. **CP-SmitS**

Father gets a bullet in the eye, killing him, The. Beauty. Stephen Dobyns. **SP-DobyS**

Father Guru. Allen Ginsberg. **CP-GinsA**

Father Guru unforlorn. Father Guru. Allen Ginsberg. **CP-GinsA**

Father has given his year-old son *Le Monde* to play with in his stroller and the baby does, The. Reading: Early Sorrow. Charles Kenneth Williams. **SP-WillC**

Father has his arm around Tereze. Still Life. Louise Glück. **SP-GlücL**

Father, he cried, after the critics' chewing. A Sacrificed Author. Howard Nemerov. *Fr.* Gnomes. **CP-NemeH**

Father I am burning roses. Burning Roses. Patti Smith. **SP-SmitP**

Father, I fear your trade. The Bird-Catcher's Boy. Thomas Hardy. **CP-HardT**

Father, I scarcely could believe you dead. From an Asian Tent. Thom Gunn. **CP-GunnT**

Father in a Dream. Robert Lowell. **SP-LoweR**

Father-in-Law. Derek Mahon. **SP-MahoD**

Father is the Void, The. No Matter, Never Mind. Gary Snyder. **CP-SnydG**

Father John Burges, / Necessity urges. To Master John Burges. Ben Jonson. **CP-JonsB**

Father me not. Begat. Anne Sexton. *Fr.* The Death of the Fathers. **CP-SextA**

Father, Mother, and me. We and They. Rudyard Kipling. **CP-KiplR** *Fr.* Debits and Credits.

Father Neptune one day to Freedom did say. Neptune's Little Affair with Freedom. David Herbert Lawrence. *Fr.* Songs I Learnt at School. **CP-LawrD**

Father of All! In every [*or* ev'ry] Age. The Universal Prayer [Deo Opt. Max.]. Alexander Pope. **CP-PopeA**

Father of heaven, and him, by whom. The Father. John Donne. **NOCV** *Fr.* A Litany. **CP-DonnJ**

Father of Light! great God of Heaven! The Prayer of Nature. Byron. **CP-Byron**

Father of My Country, The. Diane Wakoski. **SP-WakoD**

Father of Night. "Bob Dylan." **CP-DylaB**

Father of the Faithful said, The. Faith. Christopher Smart. **ChIV-1** *Fr.* Hymns for the Amusement of Children. **SP-SmarC**

"Father O'Haire," said the girl to the priest. An Island Folk Tale. John Hewitt. **CP-HewiJ**

Father out Walking on the Lawn, A. Rita Dove. **SP-DoveR**

Father, part of his double interest. John Donne. **JCP; OBS** *Fr.* Divine Meditations. **CP-DonnJ** *Fr.* Holy Sonnets. **CP-DonnJ**

Father sees a son nearing manhood, A. Carl Sandburg. *Fr.* The People, Yes. **CP-SandC**

Father shall shine. The father shall stand at home. Now, The. Another Day. A Game of Toys. Paul, Telling the Game. Muriel Rukeyser. **CP-RukeM**

Father Son and Holy Ghost. Audre Lorde. **SP-LordA**

Father, the Cavalier. Donald Davie. **CP-DavDo**

Father, the Year Has Fallen. Audre Lorde. **SP-LordA**

Father, this year's jinx rides us apart. All My Pretty Ones. Anne Sexton. **CP-SextA**

Father, Thy word is past, man shall find grace. The Atonement. John Milton. **OBS** *Fr.* Book III. *Fr.* Paradise Lost. **CP-MiltJ**

Father! to God himself we cannot give. Sponsors. William Wordsworth. *Fr.* Ecclesiastical Sonnets. **CP-WorW2**

Father! to Thy suffering poor. The Familist's Hymn. John Greenleaf Whittier. **CP-WhitJ**

Father was a man, The. Two Ways of Love. Marsden Hartley. **CP-HartM**

Father, who designs his babe a priest, The. William Cowper. **OBSV** *Fr.* Tirocinium; or, A Review of Schools. **CP-CowpW**

Father William. "Lewis Carroll." **CP-CarrL** *Fr.* Alice's Adventures in Wonderland.

" 'You are old,' said the youth, 'and your jaws are too weak'." **OxBM**

Father, you must have been. Offering. Thomas McGrath. **SP-McGrT**

Father, you seem to have been sleeping fair? A Last Journey. Thomas Hardy. **CP-HardT**

Fathering the Map. Robert Pack. **SP-PackR**

Fathers. Steve Griffiths. **SP-GrifS**

Fathers, The. Charles Olson. **CP-OlsoC**

Fathers and Sons. James Dickey. **CP-DickJ**

Fathers and Sons. Donald Hall. **CP-HallD**

Father's Bedroom. Robert Lowell. **SP-LoweR**

Father's Death, A. John Hewitt. **CP-HewiJ**

Fathers die, but sons. Hayden Carruth. **CP-CarHS** *Fr.* The Clay Hill Anthology.

Father's letter to your father said. Anne Dick 1. 1936. Robert Lowell. **SP-LoweR**

Fathers of all the pretty children, The. Cabaret Voltaire. Peter Meinke. **SP-MeinP**

Father's Thought of His Daughter, The. John Gould Fletcher. **SP-FletJ**

Father's Voice. William Stafford. **SP-StafW**

Fatigue. David Herbert Lawrence. **CP-LawrD**

Fatigue of Objects, The. Thomas McGrath. **SP-McGrT**

Fatigue, regrets. The lights. The Demon Lover. Adrienne Rich. **CP-RicAE; SP-RicA1; SP-RicA2**

Fatima. Tennyson. **CP-TennA**

Fatt soyle, full springe, sweete olive, grape of blesse. Christ's Bloody Sweate. Robert Southwell. **CP-SoutR**

Fatted / on herbs, swollen on crabapples. The Porcupine. Galway Kinnell. **SP-KinnG**

Fault was mine, the fault was mine, The. Tennyson. *Fr.* Maud [A Monodrama]. **CP-TennA**

Faun. Sylvia Plath. **CP-PlatS**

Fauré Ballade, The. James Schuyler. **CP-SchuJ**

Fauré's Second Piano Quartet. James Schuyler. **CP-SchuJ**

Faust. John Ashbery. **SP-AshbJ**

Faust, *sels.* Johann Wolfgang von Goethe, *tr. fr. German.*
Prologue in Heaven. **CP-ShelP**
   "Sun makes music as of old, The." **AWP; OBVE**
   (Chorus of the Archangels, The.) **OBVE**
   "Would you not like a broomstick? As for me." **CP-ShelP**

Faustina, or Rock Roses. Elizabeth Bishop. **CP-BishE**

Faustus and I. Anne Sexton. **CP-SextA**

Faustus Triumphant. Thom Gunn. **CP-GunnT**

Favorite, The. Theodore Roethke. **CP-RoetT**

Favorite Iraqi Soldier. Stephen Dobyns. **SP-DobyS**

Favour, The. Rudyard Kipling. *Fr.* Epitaphs of the War [1914–1918]. **CP-KiplR**

Favourite pleasure hath it been with me, A. William Wordsworth. **OBRV** *Fr.* Summer Vacation. *Fr.* The Prelude; Growth of a poet's Mind [1805 vers.]. **CP-WorW3**

Fawn, The. Edna St. Vincent Millay. **CP-MillE**

Fawn's Foster-Mother. Robinson Jeffers. **CP-JefR1**

Fayette beside King Lewis stood. William Blake. **CP-BlakW**

Fayetteville Dawn (1). John Clellon Holmes. **SP-HolmJ**

Fayetteville Dawn (2). John Clellon Holmes. **SP-HolmJ**

Fayne Would I But I Dare Not. Sir Walter Ralegh. **CP-RaleW**

Fayre Mayd, you did but cast your eyes erewhile. To a Mayd. Robert Herrick. **CP-HerrR**

Fea / therr / ain / :dreamin. Edward Estlin Cummings. **CP-CummE**

Feacie (some say) doth wash her clothes i'th'Lie. Upon a Cheap Laundresse: Epigram. Robert Herrick. **CP-HerrR**

Fear. Charles Bukowski. **SP-BukC1**

Fear. Hart Crane. **CP-CranH**

Fear. Walter de la Mare. **CP-DeLaW**

Fear. Stephen Dobyns. **SP-DobyS**

Fear, The. Robert Frost. **CP-FrosR**

Fear, The. Geoffrey Hill. *Fr.* Metamorphoses. **CP-HillG**

Fear. Randall Jarrell. **CP-JarrR**

Fear / of drowning. Imitations of Drowning. Anne Sexton. **CP-SextA**

Fear. Grace Paley. **CP-PaleG**

Fear. Charles Simic. **SP-SimiC**

Fear. Robert Southwell. **CBCK** *Fr.* Saint Peter's Complaint. **CP-SoutR**

Fear and Trembling. Jim Carroll. **SP-CarrJ**

Fear death?—to feel the fog in my throat. Prospice. Robert Browning. **CP-BroR1**

Fear-dulled eyes in the pallid face, The. In Disgrace. Walter de la Mare. **CP-DeLaW**

Fear, Faith, and Hope have sent their hearts above. Ye Are Come unto Mount Sion. Christina Georgina Rossetti. **CP-RosC2**

Fear God — obey his just decrees. The Conclusion of the Matter. Christopher Smart. **ChIV-1** *Fr.* Hymns for the Amusement of Children. **SP-SmarC**

Fear hath a hundred eyes that all agree. Gunpowder Plot. William Wordsworth. *Fr.* Ecclesiastical Sonnets. **CP-WorW2**

Fear in the Afternoon. John Clellon Holmes. **SP-HolmJ**

Fear is a Porch. Jim Morrison. **SP-MorrJ**

Fear Is What Quickens Me. James Wright. **CP-WrigJ**

Fear, jealousy and murder are the same. Gamecock. James Dickey. **CP-DickJ**

Fear, like a living fire that only death. Avon's Harvest. Edwin Arlington Robinson. **CP-RobiE**

Fear—like Dying, dilates trust. Emily Dickinson. **SP-DickE**

Fear no more, thou timid Flower! The Snow-Drop. Samuel Taylor Coleridge. **CP-ColeS**

Fear Not. Gary Snyder. **CP-SnydG**

Fear not / That nobody knows. Finis. Wystan Hugh Auden. **CP-AudWJ**

Fear not, dear friend, but freely live your days. Robert Louis Stevenson. **CP-StevR**

Fear not, dear love, that I'll reveal. Secrecy [*or* Secresie] Protested. Thomas Carew. **CP-CareT**

Fear of affectation made her affect. Seamus Heaney. *Fr.* Clearances. **SP-HeanS**

Fear of Angels, The. May Sarton. **SP-SartM**

Fear of Darkness, The. Wendell Berry. **CP-BerrW**

Fear of Domesticity. Bill Knott. **SP-KnotB**

Fear of Dreaming. Jim Carroll. **SP-CarrJ**

Fear of falling is why the old men walk. Sonnet. Hayden Carruth. **CP-CarHS** *Fr.* Sonnets.

Fear of Flying, The. Mona Van Duyn. **SP-VanDM**

Fear of God, The. Robert Frost. **CP-FrosR**

Fear of *Gray's Anatomy*. Brendan Galvin. **SP-GalvB**

Fear of Love, The. Wendell Berry. **CP-BerrW**

Fear of Man, The. Robert Frost. **CP-FrosR**

Fear of poetry is the, The. Reading Time : 1 Minute 26 Seconds. Muriel Rukeyser. **CP-RukeM**

Fear of Society Is the Root of All Evil. David Herbert Lawrence. **CP-LawrD**

Fear of the Waldorf Cafeteria. Brendan Galvin. **SP-GalvB**

Fear ringed by doubt is my eternal moon. Malcolm Lowry. **CP-LowrM**

Fear. Three bears / are not fear, mother. Bears at Raspberry Time. Hayden Carruth. **CP-CarHS**

Fear was on the cattle, for the gale was on the sea, The. Mulholland's Contract. Rudyard Kipling. **CP-KiplR**

Feare. Robert Herrick. **CP-HerrR**

Fearful, The. Sylvia Plath. **CP-PlatS**

Fearful I peer upon the mountain path. John Berryman. *Fr.* Eleven Addresses to the Lord. **CP-BerrJ**

Fearful with them gathered about my bed on that dreary autumn. Rising a Little. Kenneth Patchen. **CP-PatcK**

Fear[e] Gets Force. Robert Herrick. **CP-HerrR**

Fearing that Albion should turn his back against the Divine Vision. William Blake. **OAEL-2** *Fr.* Jerusalem; The Emanation of the Giant Albion. **CP-BlakW**

Fearlessandbosomy / this / grand:gal. Edward Estlin Cummings. **CP-CummE**

Fears and Scruples. Robert Browning. **CP-BroR2**

Fears in Solitude. Samuel Taylor Coleridge. **CP-ColeS**
   Looking Down on Nether Stowey. **FaBoPP**
   O My Mother Isle! **FaBoPP**
   "On the green sheep-track, up the heathy hill." **OBNC**

Feast, The. Jenny Joseph. **SP-JoseJ**

Feast, The. Galway Kinnell. **SP-KinnG**

Feast. Edna St. Vincent Millay. **CP-MillE**

Feast and noon grew high, and Sacrifice, The. John Milton. **EBEV** *Fr.* Samson Agonistes. **CP-MiltJ**

Feast Green Beast. Jim Morrison. **SP-MorrJ**

Feast of Famine: Marquesan Manners, The. Robert Louis Stevenson. **CP-StevR**

"Feast of light!" Clayfield proclaimed, A. Clayfield's Daughter Reveals Her Plans. Robert Pack. **SP-PackR**

Feast of the Annunciation. Christina Georgina Rossetti. **CP-RosC2**

Feast of the Presentation. Christina Georgina Rossetti. **CP-RosC2**

Feast was over in Branksome tower, The. Branksome Hall. Sir Walter Scott. **SP-ScotW** *Fr.* The Lay of the Last Minstrel.

Feasts. John Ciardi. **SP-CiarJ**

Feather from the Whippoorwill, A. Emily Dickinson. **CP-DickE**

Feather Lights. Carl Sandburg. **CP-SandC**

Feather'd battalions, squadrons on the wing. Translation of Addison's Pugmaiogeranomachia; The Battle of the Pygmies and Cranes. Samuel Johnson, *tr. from the Latin of Joseph Addison.* **CP-JohnS**

Feathered Robe, The. Gary Snyder. **CP-SnydG**

Feathers. Jane Cooper. *Fr.* March. **SP-CoopJ**

Feathers are thick and look sculptured, The. Removed from Natural Habitat. Diane Wakoski. **SP-WakoD**

Feathers on Turf. John Hewitt. *Fr.* Freehold. **CP-HewiJ**

Feathers up fast, and steeples; then in clods. The Fountain. Donald Davie. **CP-DavDo**

Featureless ghost under the wall cannot jerk out at us, The. Elegy for the Silent Voices and the Joiners of Everything. Kenneth Patchen. **CP-PatcK**

Feb. 1956 / Is this a divagation. Canto 105. Ezra Pound. *Fr.* Cantos. **CP-PoCan**

February. John Clare. *Fr.* The Shepherd's [*or* Shepheards] Calendar. (February: A Thaw.) **SP-ClarJ**

    ("Snow is gone from cottage tops, The.") **SP-ClarJ**

February. Daniel Gerard Hoffman. **SP-HoffD**

February. Christina Georgina Rossetti. *Fr.* The Months: A Pageant. **CP-RosC2**

February. James Schuyler. **CP-SchuJ**

February. Charles Simic. **SP-SimiC**

February. Gary Snyder. *Fr.* Six Years. **CP-SnydG**

February. Edmund Spenser. *Fr.* The Shepheardes [*or* Shepeards *or* Shepherd's] Calender. **CP-Spens**

    Oak and the Brere, The. **OBSC**

February. A cloudy day. Wendell Berry. *Fr.* The Clearing. **CP-BerrW**

February: A Thaw. John Clare. *See* February.

February Air. Ted Berrigan. **SP-BerrT**

FEBRUARY (*Coursing*). Rudyard Kipling. *Fr.* Verses on Games. **CP-KiplR**

February Dawn, A. Wystan Hugh Auden. **CP-AudWJ**

February 11, 1977, *with music.* Frederick Morgan. **SP-MorgF**

February 11th. Anne Sexton. **CP-SextA**

February Floods, 1953. Jenny Joseph. **SP-JoseJ**

February 14. 1883. Christina Georgina Rossetti. **CP-RosC3**

February 4th. Anne Sexton. **CP-SextA**

February is the shortest month, and good. The Inn. Frank Templeton Prince. **CP-PrinF**

February of the merely real, A. Marilyn Hacker. **SP-HackM** *Fr.* Separations.

February 17th. Ted Hughes. **SP-HughT**

February 17th. Anne Sexton. **CP-SextA**

February 10, One Year Too Late. Charles Olson. **CP-OlsoC**

February 3rd. Anne Sexton. **CP-SextA**

February 13, 1975. James Schuyler. **CP-SchuJ**

February 20th. Anne Sexton. **CP-SextA**

February 21st. Anne Sexton. **CP-SextA**

February 22. John Updike. **CP-UpdiJ**

February 2, 1968. Wendell Berry. **CP-BerrW**

February: water and sky a gape. Winter Oysters. Brendan Galvin. **SP-GalvB**

Feckless Dinner Party, The. Walter de la Mare. **CP-DeLaW**

Fee, faw, fum! bubble and squeak! Holy-Cross Day. Robert Browning. **CP-BroR1**

Fee Fi Ho Hum, No Wonder Baby Sucks Her Thumb. Ogden Nash. **CP-NashO**

Feeble Caligula! To say. August, 1945. Howard Nemerov. **CP-NemeH**

Feed on my sheep; my charge, my comfort, feed, *speech of Dorus.* Sir Philip Sidney. **SP-SidnP** *Fr.* Arcadia.

Feeders, The. Donald Davie. **CP-DavDo**

Feeding the Ducks. Leonard Nathan. **SP-NathL**

Feeding the Sun. Bill Knott. **SP-KnotB**

Feel for the Wrongs of Universal Ken. William Wordsworth. **CP-WorW2**

Feel for your bad fall how could I fail. A Sympathy, a Welcome. John Berryman. **CP-BerrJ**

Feel of Hands, The. Thom Gunn. **CP-GunnT**

Feeling and Form. Marilyn Hacker. **SP-HackM**

Feeling chilled in that cold country. Poem. Kenneth Patchen. **CP-PatcK**

Feeling comes, The. The Few Silver Scales. Diane Wakoski. **SP-WakoD**

Feeling Fucked Up. Etheridge Knight. **SP-KnigE**

Feeling good, green light, the earthly paradise. Poet Redeemed & Dead. Donald Davie. **CP-DavDo**

Feeling it with me. Walking on Water. James Dickey. **CP-DickJ**

Feeling of Time. Giuseppe Ungaretti, *tr. fr. Italian by* Isabella Gardner. **CP-GardI**

Feeling the icy kick, the endless waves. The Swimming Lesson. Mary Oliver. **SP-OlivM**

Feelings I don't have I don't have, The. To Women, as Far as I'm Concerned. David Herbert Lawrence. **CP-LawrD**

Feelings of a French Royalist, on the Disinterment of the Remains of the Duke D'Enghien. William Wordsworth. **CP-WorW2**

Feelings of a Noble Biscayan at One of Those Funerals 1810. William Wordsworth. **CP-WorW1**

Feelings of a Republican on the Fall of Bonaparte. Percy Bysshe Shelley. **CP-ShelP**

Feelings of the Tyrolese. William Wordsworth. **CP-WorW1**

Feet clap roadmetal: lakes. Downhill. James McAuley. *Fr.* Ten-Mile Run. **SP-McAuJ**

Feet have left the wormholed flooring, The. Song to an Old Burden. Thomas Hardy. **CP-HardT**

Feet o' Jesus. Langston Hughes. **SP-HughL**

Feet of Cheese. Love Is a Dog from Hell. Charles Bukowski. **SP-BukC1**

Feet of his days have been mangled, The. Charles Henri Ford. *Fr.* Epigrams. **SP-FordC**

Feet of people walking home, The. Emily Dickinson. **CP-DickE**

Feet of the Young Men, The. Rudyard Kipling. **CP-KiplR**

Feh! You call this pumpernickel. Pumpernickel. Leonard Nathan. **SP-NathL**

Felice la tua madre. Per Preferenza. Christina Georgina Rossetti. *Fr.* Il Rosseggiar Dell'Oriente Canzoniere. **CP-RosC3**

Felicia Hemans. Elizabeth Barrett Browning. **CP-BroEB**

Felicitie Knowes No Fence. Robert Herrick. **CP-HerrR**

Felicity of Grief!—even Death being kind. Edna St. Vincent Millay. **CP-MillE**

Felicity, Quick of Flight. Robert Herrick. **CP-HerrR**

Felicity's Fourth Order. Donald Davie. **CP-DavDo**

Feliksowa has gone again from our house and this time for good, I hope. Curse of a Rich Polish Peasant on His Sister Who Ran Away with a Wild Man. Carl Sandburg. **CP-SandC**

Felix Baran / Hugo Gerlot. Gary Snyder. **CP-SnydG** *Fr.* Logging. *Fr.* Myths and Texts.

Felix Randal. Gerard Manley Hopkins. **CP-HopkG**

Felixstowe, or, The Last of Her Order. Sir John Betjeman. **CP-BetjJ**

Fellatio. John Updike. **CP-UpdiJ**

Felled Elm and She, The. Thomas Hardy. **CP-HardT**

Felled in my tracks by your tremendous horse. Lines to Mr Frost. John Berryman. **CP-BerrJ**

Felled Tree, A. Daniel Gerard Hoffman. **SP-HoffD**

Fellow Citizens. Carl Sandburg. **CP-SandC**

Fellow-Men. David Herbert Lawrence. **CP-LawrD**

Fellow Oddballs. William Matthews. **SP-MattW**

Fellow Soul, Sound Hunting to Thy Immeasurable Heart. Kenneth Patchen. **CP-PatcK**

Fells sweep upward to drag down the sun, The. Lead's the Best. Wystan Hugh Auden. **CP-AudWJ**

Felo de se. Wystan Hugh Auden. **CP-AudWJ**

Female Author. Sylvia Plath. **SP-PlatS**

Female Coercion. David Herbert Lawrence. **CP-LawrD**

Female Exile. Written at Brighthelmstone in November 1792, The. Charlotte Smith. **CP-SmitC**

Female Glory. Richard Lovelace. **CP-LoveR**

Female Inconstancy. Catullus. *See* Carmen 70: "Lesbia says she'ld rather marry me."

Female Martyr, The. John Greenleaf Whittier. **CP-WhitJ**

Female of the Species, The. Rudyard Kipling. **CP-KiplR**

Feminine Charm. Stevie Smith. **CP-SmitS**

Feminine Ending or, Abandoned, She Died. Isabella Gardner. **CP-GardI**

Feminine Honour. Thomas Carew. *Fr.* Four Songs, by Way of Chorus To a Play. **CP-CareT**

Femmes Damnees. Philip Larkin. **CP-LarkP**

Fence, A. Carl Sandburg. **CP-SandC**

Fence. Dabney Stuart. **SP-StuaD**

Fence Between. Marsden Hartley. **CP-HartM**

Fence Posts. Gary Snyder. **CP-SnydG**

Fence Wire. James Dickey. **CP-DickJ**

Fenced in by need his youth had passed. Cornelius Verner. Louise McNeill. **SP-McNeL**

Fencing a rough place on the mountain. The Gap. John Hewitt. **CP-HewiJ**

Fennel. Thom Gunn. **CP-GunnT**

Fergus and the Druid. William Butler Yeats. **CP-YeatW**

Fergus Falling. Galway Kinnell. **SP-KinnG**

Fern, The. Wendell Berry. *Fr.* The Handing Down. **CP-BerrW**

Fern. Ted Hughes. **SP-HughT**

Fern-Beds in Hampshire County. Richard Wilbur. **CP-WilbR**

Fern coming up shyly, A. Velvet Rocks. Richard Eberhart. **CP-EberR**

Fern Hill. Dylan Thomas. **CP-ThomD**

Fernery, The. Hart Crane. **CP-CranH**

Ferniehirst Castle. Richard Hugo. **CP-HugoR**

Ferns. Robert Bly. **SP-BlyR**

Ferns are in the fiddlehead, fiddlehead, The. Hill Song. Louise McNeill. **SP-McNeL**

Ferocious as a Bee without a wing. Emily Dickinson. **SP-DickE**

Ferrini—I. Charles Olson. **CP-OlsoC**

Ferry, The. Lewis Turco. **SP-TurcL**

Ferry. Louis Zukofsky. *Fr.* 29 Poems. **CP-ZukLS**

Ferry Me across the Water. Christina Georgina Rossetti. **BiP; ChTr; GoJo; NTP; OxBChV; PDV; SUS; TLR** *Fr.* Sing-Song. **CP-RosC2** (Ferryman, The.) **BoTP; SoPo**

Ferry Me across the Water. Christina Georgina Rossetti. **CP-RosC2**

Ferryboat Bill. "Lou Reed." **SP-ReedL**

Ferryman, The. Christina Georgina Rossetti. *See* Ferry Me across the Water.

Fertile. William Carlos Williams. **CP-WilW2**

Fertillest soil this side of the Tigris, The. Fargo. John Updike. **CP-UpdiJ**

Fervor parches you sometimes, A. Between Myself and Death. Kenneth Rexroth. **SP-RexrK**

Festina Lentè. Samuel Johnson. **CP-JohnS**

Festival, The. Robert Creeley. **CP-CreeR**

Festival lights go on. Fête. Donald Hall. **CP-HallD**

Festival of the Corn, The. Marsden Hartley. **CP-HartM**

Festival was over, the boys were all plannin' for a fall, The. Lily, Rosemary, and the Jack of Hearts. "Bob Dylan." **CP-DylaB**

Festivals, The. Robert Duncan. **SP-DuncR**

Festivals have I seen that were not names. Calais, August 15, 1802. William Wordsworth. **CP-WorW1**

Fetch. Lewis Turco. **SP-TurcL**

Fetch, papyrus, / our soft-measured poet. Carmen 35. Catullus. *Fr.* Carmina. **CP-Catul**

Fetching Her. Thomas Hardy. **CP-HardT**

Fête. Donald Hall. **CP-HallD**

Fête Champetre, The. Robert Burns. **CP-BurnR**

Fetter, The. Robert Ranke Graves. **CP-GravR**

Fetters of winter are shattered,shatter, The. 1.4. Horace. **CP-CummE,** *tr. by* E. E. Cummings; *Fr.* Odes.

Feud. Theodore Roethke. **CP-RoetT**

Feudal Keep, the bastions of Cohorn, The. On Entering Douglas Bay, Isle of Man. William Wordsworth. *Fr.* Poems Composed or Suggested During a Tour, in the Summer of 1833. **CP-WorW2**

Feuer-Nacht. Louise Bogan. **CP-BogaL**

Fever. Robert Browning. **FL** *Fr.* The Dance of Death. **CP-BroR2**

Fever. Hendrick De Vries, *tr. fr. Dutch by* Adrienne Rich. **CP-RicAE**

Fever, A. John Donne. **CP-DonnJ**

Fever. Martin Edmunds. **SP-EdmuM**

Fever. Thom Gunn. **CP-GunnT**

Fever. Alun Lewis. **CP-LewiA**

Fever. John Updike. **CP-UpdiJ**

Fever 103°. Sylvia Plath. **CP-PlatS**

Few and Simple. Wystan Hugh Auden. **CP-AudeW**

Few are free / All might be. Ralph Waldo Emerson. **CP-EmerR**

Few are my fellow-men, A. Fellow-Men. David Herbert Lawrence. **CP-LawrD**

Few Ashes for Sunday Morning, A. Marge Piercy. **SP-PierM**

Few Bars Over Again, A. Steve Griffiths. **SP-GrifS**

Few bold Patriots, Reliques of the Fight, A. Pelayo. William Wordsworth. **CP-WorW1**

Few bones, A. Galway Kinnell. *Fr.* The Dead Shall Be Raised Incorruptible. **SP-KinnG**

Few brief years have passed away, A. The Freed Islands. John Greenleaf Whittier. **CP-WhitJ**

Few come this way; not that the darkness. Edna St. Vincent Millay. **CP-MillE**

Few Days, A. James Schuyler. **CP-SchuJ**

Few days after her baptism Catherine Tekakwitha, A. A Great Feast in Quebec. Leonard Cohen. **CP-CoheL**

Few days ago, A. A Wife Talks to Herself. Stephen Berg. **SP-BergS**

Few days come your way, A. For Dr. Dewey. Chuck Miller. **SP-MillC**

Few Drops Known, The. Walt Whitman. **CP-WhitW**

Few footsteps stray when dusk droops o'er. The Tailor. Walter de la Mare. **CP-DeLaW**

Few Fortunate. Robert Herrick. **CP-HerrR**

Few have the gramophone that. Clare De Lughnasa. James Liddy. **CP-LiddJ**

Few leaves remain, A. Long Goodbye. Thomas McGrath. **SP-McGrT**

Few light flakes of snow, A. Kyoto: March. Gary Snyder. **CP-SnydG**

Few may see. Loki's Song. Frederick Morgan. **SP-MorgF**

Few miles ago, a year, a year, A. The Farewell Symphony. Randall Jarrell. **CP-JarrR**

Few nights ago I was half-watching the news on television and half-reading to my daughter, A. The Last Deaths. Charles Kenneth Williams. **CP-WillC; SP-WillC**

Few roads grassen quicker than Lovers' Lane. Lovers' Lane. Wystan Hugh Auden. **CP-AudWJ**

Few Silver Scales, The. Diane Wakoski. **SP-WakoD**

Few Sirens, A. Alice Walker. **CP-WalkA**

Few things are duller. When the Devil Was Sick Could He Prove It? Ogden Nash. **CP-NashO**

Few things are less endearing than a personal comparison. The Nymph and the Shepherd, or She Went That-a-Way. Ogden Nash. **CP-NashO**

Few things for themselves, A. O Florida, Venereal Soil. Wallace Stevens. **CP-StevW**

Few things surpass old wine; and they may preach. Hock and Soda Water. Byron. **FaBoDD** *Fr.* Canto the Second. *Fr.* Don Juan. **CP-Byron**

Few years have pass'd since thou and I. To a Youthful Friend. Byron. **CP-Byron**

Few, yet enough. Emily Dickinson. **CP-DickE**

Fiammetta Breaks Her Peace. Rita Dove. **SP-DoveR**

Fiascherino. Charles Tomlinson. **CP-TomlC**

Fiat Voluntas Tua. The Oaxaca Bus. Charles Tomlinson. **CP-TomlC**

Fib Detected, A. Catullus. *See* Carmen 10: "Alfenus Varus / buttonholes me."

Fickle comfort steals away. Changes. Maya Angelou. **SP-AngeM**

Fickle crowd with fortune comes and goes, The. Juvenal, *tr. by* Samuel Johnson. **CP-JohnS** *Fr.* Satires.

Fiction. Howard Nemerov. **CP-NemeH**

Fiction, The. Gilbert Sorrentino. **SP-SorrG**

Fiction and the Reading Public. Philip Larkin. **CP-LarkP**

Fiddlehead ferns down by our pond, The. Spring Song. John Updike. **CP-UpdiJ**

Fiddler, The. Thomas Hardy. **CP-HardT**

Fiddler. Louise McNeill. **SP-McNeL**

Fiddler of Dooney, The. William Butler Yeats. **CP-YeatW**

Fidelities. Geoffrey Hill. *Fr.* An Apology for the Revival of Christian Architecture in England. **CP-HillG**

Fidelity. David Herbert Lawrence. **CP-LawrD**

Fidelity. William Wordsworth. **CP-WorW1**

Fidelity never flickers. Emily Dickinson. **SP-DickE**

Fie, Aphrodite, shamming you are no mother. The Bad Example. Thomas Hardy. **CP-HardT**

Fie, Mr. Coleridge!—and can this be you? The Reproof and Reply. Samuel Taylor Coleridge. **CP-ColeS**

Fie My Fum. Allen Ginsberg. **CP-GinsA**

Fie, (quoth my Lady) what a stink is here? Upon a Sowre-Breath Lady. Robert Herrick. **CP-HerrR**

Fie, school of Patience, fie; your lesson is. Sonnet 56. Sir Philip Sidney. **NAEL-1** *Fr.* Astrophil and Stella. **SP-SidnP**

Fie [*or* Fy] tedious Hope, why do[e] you still rebel[l]? Sonnet 27. Mary Sidney, Countess of Montgomery Wroth. **NOSC** *Fr.* Pamphilia to Amphilanthus. **CP-WrotM**

Fie upon hearts that burn with mutual fire[!]. Against Fruition. Sir John Suckling. **CP-SuckJ**

Field and Forest. Randall Jarrell. **CP-JarrR; SP-JarrR**

Field Asters. Herman Melville. **SP-MelvH**

Field Commander Cohen. Leonard Cohen. **CP-CoheL**

Field Hospital, A. Randall Jarrell. **CP-JarrR; SP-JarrR**

Field Hospital, The. Paul Muldoon. **SP-MuldP**

Field-Marshal Radetzky. Franz Grillparzer, *tr. fr. German by* George Meredith. **CP-MerG2**

Field Mouse at My Fishing Hole, A. Gary Gildner. **SP-GildG**

Field mouse flickers, The. Where. Wendell Berry. **CP-BerrW**

Field near Linden, Alabama. Mary Oliver. **SP-OlivM**

Field of Glory, The. Edwin Arlington Robinson. **CP-RobiE**

Field of Inheritance, The. Brendan Galvin. **SP-GalvB**

Field of Light, A. Theodore Roethke. **CP-RoetT**

Field of Stubble, lying sere, A. Emily Dickinson. **CP-DickE**

Field of the Caribou, The. John Haines. **SP-HainJ**

Field of wind gave license for defeat, A. Spinazzola: *Quella Cantina Là.* Richard Hugo. **CP-HugoR**

Field People. Carl Sandburg. **CP-SandC**

Field-Postcard, The. Robert Ranke Graves. **CP-GravR**

Field Sports. Alexander Pope. *See* When milder autumn summer's heat succeeds.

Field tipped over pleasantly and he, The. Nap. Mona Van Duyn. **SP-VanDM**

Field Work. Seamus Heaney. **SP-HeanS**

Fields are black once more, The. Reading in Fall Rain. Robert Bly. **SP-BlyR**

Fields are white to harvest, look and see, The. When My Heart Is Vexed I Will Complain ("Fields are white to harvest, look and see, The"). Christina Georgina Rossetti. **CP-RosC2**

Fields from Islington to Marybone, The. William Blake. **ChTr; FaBoPV; OBNV; OBRV** *Fr.* Jerusalem; The Emanation of the Giant Albion. **CP-BlakW**

(Prelude: "Fields from Islington to Marybone, The.") **OBNC**

Fields of Earth. Kenneth Patchen. **CP-PatcK**

Fields of the sky, The. Thoughts of the Time. Charles Olson. **CP-OlsoC**

Fields parched, the leaves, The. The Words Lying Idle. William Carlos Williams. **CP-WilW2**

Fields rattle / with red birds, The. 4:30 A.M. Charles Bukowski. **SP-BukC2**

Fields where we slept. Muriel Rukeyser. **CP-RukeM**

Fields which with covetous spirit we sold, The. Repentance; A Pastoral Ballad. William Wordsworth. **CP-WorW1**

Fiend, The. James Dickey. **CP-DickJ**

Fiend / Saw undelighted all delight, all kind, The. John Milton. **FaBoPV** *Fr.* Book IV. **OAEL-1** *Fr.* Paradise Lost. **CP-MiltJ**

Fiend fallen are the rich from dives. Hospitality. Malcolm Lowry. **CP-LowrM**

Fiend slays the children of the messenger, A. The Intimate Guest. Kenneth Patchen. **CP-PatcK**

Fiend's Weather. Louise Bogan. **CP-BogaL**

Fierce and stupid all dogs are. Dog Poem. Philip Levine. **SP-LeviP**

Fierce beasts of the woods and wildernesses, The. Fragment: The Lake's Margin. Percy Bysshe Shelley. **CP-ShelP**

Fierce bodily control, constant routine. Two Disciplines. Robert Ranke Graves. **CP-GravR**

Fierce love, alas yett lett mee rest. Mary Sidney, Countess of Montgomery Wroth. *Fr.* Part 2. *Fr.* Urania. **CP-WrotM**

Fierce musical cries of a couple of sparrowhawks hunting on the headland, The. Birds. Robinson Jeffers. **CP-JefR1**

Fierce passions discompose the mind. Contentment. William Cowper. **ChIV-2** *Fr.* Olney Hymns. **CP-CowpW**

Fierce roars the midnight storm. Song. Percy Bysshe Shelley. *Fr.* Original Poetry by Victor and Cazire. **CP-ShelP**

Fierce though your love of her may be. To Myrto About Herself. Robert Ranke Graves. **CP-GravR**

Fierceness of Female, The. Anne Sexton. **CP-SextA**

Fiery Cross, The. Sir Walter Scott. **SP-ScotW** *Fr.* The Lady of the Lake.

Fiery mountains answer each other, The. Liberty. Percy Bysshe Shelley. **CP-ShelP**

Fiesta. Malcolm Lowry. **CP-LowrM**

Fiesta Melons. Sylvia Plath. **CP-PlatS**

Fife and Drum. John Dryden. **GN** *Fr.* A Song for St Cecilia's Day [1687]. **SP-DrydJ**

Fifine at the Fair. Robert Browning. **CP-BroR2**

"And so I somehow-nohow played." **Par**

Fifteen. William Stafford. **SP-StafW**

Fifteen. Charles Kenneth Williams. **SP-WillC**

1500 crimes have you committed. The Soul's Pentonville. Malcolm Lowry. **CP-LowrM**

Fifteen Poems for a Lunar Eclipse None of Us Saw. Diane Wakoski. **SP-WakoD**

Dark Clack of Morays, The. **SP-WakoD**

David.

Donna.

Dream, The.

Eat your Rose Hips, C'est La Vie.

For Michael, Armoured with Roses.

Lady Who Sang, The.

Light.

Not the Blood a Dreamer Kissed from My Mouth.

Poetry, the Unpredictable.

Roses Were Talking, The.

Sun with Hands for Rays.

Water.

Western Music.

Write.

Fifteen to Eighteen. Marilyn Hacker. **SP-HackM**

XV. "Ye tradeful merchants that, with weary toil." Edmund Spenser. **HeIL; HeIP; LiTB; NIP; OAEL-1; Son; TrGrPo** *Fr.* Amoretti. **CP-Spens**

Fifteen years ago I found my father's. Briefcases. Stephen Dunn. **SP-DunnS**

15 Years Later. William Carlos Williams. **CP-WilW2**

Fifteen years and my tongue's still flapping. Not Her, She Aint No Gypsy. Al Young. **CP-YounA**

Fifteenth Book, The. Archibald MacLeish. *Fr.* Conquistador. **CP-MacLA**

Fifteenth Farewell. Louise Bogan. **CP-BogaL**

Fifteenth of May. Cherry blossom. The swifts. Swifts. Ted Hughes. **SP-HughT**

Fifth Act of Aglaura As Presented to the Court, The. Sir John Suckling. *Fr.* Aglaura. **CP-SuckJ**

Epilogue: "Plays are like feasts; and every act should be."

Prologue: "'Fore love, a mighty session; and (I fear)."

Prologue to the Court ("'Tis strange, perchance you'll think, that she, that died").

Fifth Book, The. Archibald MacLeish. *Fr.* Conquistador. **CP-MacLA**

Fifth Dimension. Kenneth Patchen. **CP-PatcK**

Fifth Elegy. A Turning Wind. Muriel Rukeyser. **CP-RukeM**

Fifth Epistle. Donald Davie. *Fr.* Six Epistles to Eva Hesse. **CP-DavDo**

Fifth Mile. James McAuley. *Fr.* Ten-Mile Run. **SP-McAuJ**

Fifth Ode of Horace, The. Horace. *See* 1.5: "What slender youth bedewed [*or* bedew'd] with liquid odours" ("Quis multa gracilis").

Fifth of November, The. Christopher Smart. *Fr.* Hymns and Spiritual Songs for the Fasts and Festivals of the Church of England. **SP-SmarC**

Fifth Psalm. Anne Sexton. *Fr.* O Ye Tongues. **CP-SextA**

Fifth Song. Sir Philip Sidney. *Fr.* Astrophil and Stella. **SP-SidnP**

Fifth Universe. Diane Wakoski. *Fr.* The Universes. **SP-WakoD**

Fifth Version, The. Hayden Carruth. *Fr.* The Mythology of Dark and Light. **CP-CarHL**

Her Dream.

His Dream.

50–50. Langston Hughes. **SP-HughL**

Fifty-Fifty. Carl Sandburg. **CP-SandC**

LV. "So oft as I her beauty do behold." Edmund Spenser. **HBV; Son; TrGrPo** *Fr.* Amoretti. **CP-Spens**

LIV. "Of this world's theatre in which we stay." Edmund Spenser. **NAEL-1; NIP; NoP; OAEL-1** *Fr.* Amoretti. **CP-Spens**

Fifty Males Sitting Together. Robert Bly. **SP-BlyR**

Fifty miles down the road you can give. Stealing the Christmas Greens. Brendan Galvin. **SP-GalvB**

50 on 50. Peter Meinke. **SP-MeinP**

56 and *tomato*. History in a Minor Key. Kenneth Patchen. **CP-PatcK**

LVI. "Fair ye be sure, but cruel and unkind." Edmund Spenser. **Son** *Fr.* Amoretti. **CP-Spens**

56 Year Old Poem, A. Charles Bukowski. **SP-BukC1**

Fifty-thousand cats cross our garden—. Jenny Joseph. *Fr.* Fables. **SP-JoseJ**

Fifty years / Sidereal time. George Oppen. *Fr.* Blood from the Stone. **CP-OppeG**

Fifty years' flight! Wherein should he rejoice. Lines for the Jubilee Window. Robert Browning. **CP-BroR2**

Fig, The. May Sarton. **SP-SartM**

Fig flames inward on the bough, and I, The. The Red Mullet. Robert Penn Warren. **SP-WarrR**

Fig for 6-par-T-pak ginger ale!, A. Malcolm Lowry. *Fr.* The Moon in Scandinavia. **CP-LowrM**

Fig for those by law protected!, A. Robert Burns. *See* See the smoking bowl before us.

Fig-trees, weird fig-trees. Bare Fig-trees. David Herbert Lawrence. **CP-LawrD**

Fight. Carl Sandburg. **CP-SandC**

Fight, The. William Carlos Williams. **CP-WilW2**

Fight at the welfare office again, A. The End of the Negotiable Beggar Bond Banquet. Chuck Miller. **SP-MillC**

Fight! O My Young Men. David Herbert Lawrence. **CP-LawrD**

Fight of the Red Cross Knight and the Heathen Sansjoy, The. Edmund Spenser. **FHYEP; FiP; NoSic** *Fr.* The Faerie Queene. **CP-Spens**

Fight on Durnover Moor, The. Thomas Hardy. **CP-HardT**

Fight thou with shafts of silver, and o'[e]rcome. Money Gets the Mastery [*or* Masterie]. Robert Herrick. **CP-HerrR**

Fight your little fight, my boy. Don'ts. David Herbert Lawrence. **CP-LawrD**

Fighters. René Char, *tr. fr. French by* Thomas Merton. **CP-MertT**

Fighting Cock, The. Chuang Tzu, *tr. fr. Chinese by* Thomas Merton. **CP-MertT**

Fighting for Roses. Muriel Rukeyser. **CP-RukeM**

Fights, The. Gilbert Sorrentino. **SP-SorrG**

Figlia, la madre disse. Versi. Christina Georgina Rossetti. **CP-RosC3**

Figs. David Herbert Lawrence. **CP-LawrD**

Figs on the fig tree in the yard are green, The. Departure. Sylvia Plath. **CP-PlatS**

Figueras Castle. William Carlos Williams. **CP-WilW2**

Figurative Description of the Procedure of Divine Love, A. Jeanne Marie Bouvier de la Motte-Guyon, *tr. fr. French by* William Cowper. **CP-CowpW**

Figure Eights. Siv Cedering Fox. **SP-CedeS**

Figure for J.V. Meer, A. Jean Garrigue. **SP-GarrJ**

Figure in a Landscape. Jenny Joseph. **SP-JoseJ**

Figure in the Doorway, The. Robert Frost. **CP-FrosR**

Figure in the Scene, The. Thomas Hardy. **CP-HardT**

Figure me to yourself, I pray. Epistle to Albert Dew-Smith. Robert Louis Stevenson. **CP-StevR**

Figure Motioned with Its Mangled Hand Toward the Wall Behind It, The. Kenneth Patchen. **CP-PatcK**

Figure of Eight. Louis MacNeice. **CP-MacNL**

Figure of the Witch. Erica Jong. **SP-JongE**

Figure of Time, A. Denise Levertov. **CP-LeveD**

Figure or figures unknown. Grocery. Charles Simic. **SP-SimiC**

Figure, The / of tall. The Province. William Carlos Williams. **CP-WilW2**

Figurehead, The. Karl Shapiro. **SP-ShapK**

Figures, The. Robert Creeley. **CP-CreeR**

Figures for an Apocalypse. Thomas Merton. **CP-MertT**

"Come down, come down Beloved."

"Come to your windows, rich women."

"Down at the Hotel Sherlock Holmes."

Heavenly City, The. **SP-MertT**

In the Ruins of New York.

Landscape: Beast. **SP-MertT**

Landscape, Prophet and Wild-dog. **SP-MertT**

"Look in the night, look, look in the night."

Figures of Thought. Howard Nemerov. **CP-NemeH**

Figures on a silent screen. Woman-Enough. Tess Gallagher. **SP-GallT**

Figuring. Charles Simic. **SP-SimiC**

Figuring Belief. Archie Randolph Ammons. **SP-AmmoA**

Filament carrying morning through the waves, A. Muriel Rukeyser. **CP-RukeM**

File into yellow candle light, fair choristers of King's. Sunday Morning, King's Cambridge. Sir John Betjeman. **CP-BetjJ**

Files— / The Files— / Office Files! The Files. Rudyard Kipling. **CP-KiplR**

Files, The. Rudyard Kipling. **CP-KiplR**

Files on files of Prairie Maize. Trophies of Peace. Herman Melville. **SP-MelvH**

Filial Piety. William Wordsworth. **CP-WorW2**

Filii prodigi porcos pascentis ad patrem epistola. Robert Southwell. **CP-SoutR**

Filippo Baldinucci on the Privilege of Burial. Robert Browning. **CP-BroR2**

Fill and Illumined. Joseph Ceravolo. **SP-CeraJ**

Fill for Me a Brimming Bowl. John Keats. **CP-KeatS**

Fill high the bowl with Samian wine! Byron. **GrIP** *Fr.* The Isles of Greece, the isles of Greece! **AWP; ChTr; FaBoEn; FaPoB; FaPoR; FiP; HBV; LiTB; NOBE; OBEV; OBRV; OBTV; OXAEP-2; RoGo; SeCeV; TreFS; WHA** *Fr.* Canto the Third. *Fr.* Don Juan. **CP-Byron**

Fill me a mighty Bowle. A Bacchanalian Verse. Robert Herrick. **CP-HerrR**

Fill me my Wine in Christall; thus, and thus. How He Would Drinke His Wine. Robert Herrick. **CP-HerrR**

Fill me with the rosy wine. Robert Burns. *Fr.* On Jessy Lewars. **CP-BurnR**

Fill the Goblet. Byron. **CP-Byron**

Filled here with contempt. Blue Turning Grey. Gilbert Sorrentino. **SP-SorrG**

Filled Stocking, The. John Hewitt. **CP-HewiJ**

Filling in the Dots. Archie Randolph Ammons. **SP-AmmoA**

Filling Station. Elizabeth Bishop. **CP-BishE**

Filling the Boxes of Joseph Cornell. Diane Wakoski. **SP-WakoD**

Filling the grooves of his name. A Hill Village. Martin Edmunds. *Fr.* The High Road to Taos. **CP-EdmuM**

Filling the mind. The Clouds. William Carlos Williams. **CP-WilW2**

Filling us with such bowels of. Sext. Donald Davie. *Fr.* Horae Canonicae. **CP-DavDo**

Fills up / Sun, moon, stars, he fills them up. The Executioner. Ted Hughes. **SP-HughT**

Film, The. Denise Levertov. **CP-LeveD**

Film is gray and wobbly, and shot through with jots of tarnished, The. Picture Book. John Yau. **SP-YauJo**

Film Passion. David Herbert Lawrence. **CP-LawrD**

Film Star, The. Stevie Smith. **CP-SmitS**

Films. Carl Sandburg. **CP-SandC**

Fin fond du néant. Samuel Beckett. **CP-BeckS**

Final. Pablo Neruda, *tr. fr. Spanish by* Ben Belitt. **SP-NeruP**

Final Affection, A. Paul Zimmer. **SP-ZimmP**

Final Chorus, The. Percy Bysshe Shelley. *See* The World's great age begins anew.

Final Curve. Langston Hughes. **SP-HughL**

Final Examination, *see also* Commentary—Final Examination. Leonard Cohen. **CP-CoheL**

Final Notations. Adrienne Rich. **SP-RicA1**

Final Soliloquy of the Interior Paramour. Wallace Stevens. **CP-StevW**

Final Sonnet, A. Ted Berrigan. **SP-BerrT** *Fr.* The Sonnets.

Final Version, The. Hayden Carruth. *Fr.* The Mythology of Dark and Light. **CP-CarHL**

Final-year student at the Art School, A. Drypoint. John Hewitt. **CP-HewiJ**

Finale. Alun Lewis. **CP-LewiA**

Finale. Louis MacNeice. *Fr.* Out of the Picture. **CP-MacNL**

Finality broods upon the things that pass. A Walk by the Charles. Adrienne Rich. **CP-RicAE; SP-RicA2**

Finally a Valentine. Louis Zukofsky. **CP-ZukLS**

Finally, he brought me to a hill. Wendell Berry. *Fr.* Elegy: "To be at home on its native ground." **CP-BerrW**

Finally, he decided there was too much pain. 21st Century Man. Richard Eberhart. **CP-EberR**

Finally I have a house. Homesick. Marge Piercy. **SP-PierM**

Finally, in the last year of her age. A Pastoral Nun. Wallace Stevens. **CP-StevW**

Finally in white innocence. Fantasy. Robinson Jeffers. **CP-JefR3**

Finally the public sender of this island shuts down its trance. Thomas Merton. *Fr.* Cables to the Ace. **CP-MertT**

Finally, the remaining distinctions begin. Medusa. John Yau. **SP-YauJo**

Finally you sit. Poem with Orange. Al Young. **CP-YounA**

Finches, The. Wendell Berry. **CP-BerrW**

Find Meat on Bones. Dylan Thomas. **CP-ThomD**

Find the Face. Marsden Hartley. **CP-HartM**

Finding in a friend's garden columbines. Columbines. Kathleen Jessie Raine. **SP-RainK**

Finding is the first Act. Emily Dickinson. **CP-DickE**

Finding of Gabriel, The. Henry Wadsworth Longfellow. **AA** *Fr.* In that delightful land which is washed by the Delaware's waters. *Fr.* Part the Second. *Fr.* Evangeline, a Tale of Acadie. **SP-LongH**

Finding of Love, The. Robert Ranke Graves. **CP-GravR**

Finding One of the Ghosts. Dabney Stuart. **SP-StuaD**

Finding scarcely anyone save Monsieur de Rémusat. Canto 101. Ezra Pound. *Fr.* Cantos. **CP-PoCan**

Finding the Andromeda Nebula. Siv Cedering Fox. **SP-CedeS**

Finding the Father. Robert Bly. **SP-BlyR**

Finding Your Level. David Herbert Lawrence. **CP-LawrD**

"Fine China". Robert Creeley. **CP-CreeR**

Fine cloth of your love might be a fabric of Egypt. They Buy with an Eye to Looks. Carl Sandburg. **CP-SandC**

Fine clouds open their outfits. T'ang Notebook. Charles Wright. **SP-WrigC**

Fine delight that fathers thought; the strong, The. To R. B. Gerard Manley Hopkins. **CP-HopkG**

Fine evening may I have. Courtship. Rita Dove. **SP-DoveR**

Fine evenings always bring their thoughts of her. The Sunken Lane. Wystan Hugh Auden. **CP-AudWJ**

Fine flame of silver birches flickers. A Welsh Night. Alun Lewis. **CP-LewiA**

Fine Madam Would-be, wherefore should you fear. To Fine Lady Would-Be. Ben Jonson. **CP-JonsB**

Fine old house with the Georgian Door, The. Population Explosion. Archibald MacLeish. **CP-MacLA**

Fine powder of the dry rot, The. The Dry Rot. Richard Eberhart. **CP-EberR**

Fine presentiments controlled him. Ralph Waldo Emerson. **CP-EmerR**

Fine Work with Pitch and Copper. William Carlos Williams. **CP-WilW1**

Finest / lad of all is Mr, The. It Depends on Whose Science. Kenneth Patchen. **CP-PatcK**

Finestra Mia Orientale. Christina Georgina Rossetti. *Fr.* Il Rosseggiar Dell'Oriente Canzoniere. **CP-RosC3**

Finger, The. Robert Creeley. **CP-CreeR**

Fingerprints. Leonard Cohen. **CP-CoheL**

Fingers of the Light, The. Emily Dickinson. **CP-DickE**

Fingers turn the pages, The. Ever a Seeker. Carl Sandburg. **CP-SandC**

Finis. Wystan Hugh Auden. **CP-AudWJ**

Finis. Edward Estlin Cummings. **CP-CummE**

Finis, apparent on an earlier page. Leaving the Rest Unsaid. Robert Ranke Graves. **CP-GravR**

Finis Coronat Opus. Frank Templeton Prince. **CP-PrinF**

Finish, The. Daniel Gerard Hoffman. **SP-HoffD**

Finish. Carl Sandburg. **CP-SandC**

Finished Man, A. Richard Wilbur. **CP-WilbR**

Finisterre. Sylvia Plath. **CP-PlatS**

Finite and Infinite. Elizabeth Barrett Browning. **CP-BroEB**

Finite life, little sister, A. Emily Dickinson. **SP-DickE**

Finite—to fail, but infinite to Venture. Emily Dickinson. **CP-DickE**

Finn, Finn / Tribal and double. To Daughters: To Study History. Thomas Merton. *Fr.* Cables to the Ace. **CP-MertT**

Fins. Carl Sandburg. **CP-SandC**

Fintry, my stay in worldly strife. Epistle to Robt. Graham Esq: of Fintry on the Election for the Dumfries String of Boroughs, Anno 1790. Robert Burns. **CP-BurnR**

Fiordispina. Percy Bysshe Shelley. **CP-ShelP**

Fire, The. Robert Creeley. **CP-CreeR**

Fire. Robert Creeley. **CP-CreeR**

Fire, The. Robert Duncan. **SP-DuncR** *Fr.* Passages.

Fire, The. Martin Edmunds. **SP-EdmuM**

Fire, The. Louise Glück. **SP-GlücL**

Fire. Langston Hughes. **SP-HughL**

Fire. Robinson Jeffers. **CP-JefR3**

Fire. David Herbert Lawrence. **CP-LawrD**

Fire. David Herbert Lawrence. **CP-LawrD**

Fire. Charles Kenneth Williams. **SP-WillC**

Fire a few years before had skinned the hills' faces. The Love and the Hate. Robinson Jeffers. *Fr.* The Double Axe. **CP-JefR3**

Fire advances along the log, The. Logs on the Hearth. Thomas Hardy. **CP-HardT**

Fire and Deluge, rival pretenders. Mist. Robert Ranke Graves. **CP-GravR**

Fire and Ice. Robert Frost. **CP-FrosR**

Fire and wings, De Bosis, soaring above. Poem in the Form of a Letter: to Lauro de Bosis. Kenneth Patchen. **CP-PatcK**

Fire at the Waxworks, The, *after* Henrikas Radauskas. Randall Jarrell. **CP-JarrR**

Fire Dreams. Carl Sandburg. **CP-SandC**

Fire-Eater. Ted Hughes. **SP-HughT**

Fire, Famine, and Slaughter. Samuel Taylor Coleridge. **CP-ColeS**

Fire, fire, fire, fire! Thomas Campion. **CP-CampT**

Fire flickers on the deep hearth in the dark hall. Fire. Robinson Jeffers. **CP-JefR3**

Fire from a fixèd star. The World of the Perfect Tear. Thomas McGrath. **SP-McGrT**

Fire I praise was once perduring flame, The. Allen Tate. **PoA** *Fr.* Sonnets of the Blood. **CP-TateA**

Fire in a Dark Landscape. Charles Tomlinson. **CP-TomlC**

Fire in her ashes Ireland feels. Ireland. George Meredith. **CP-MerG2**

Fire in leaf and grass, The. Living. Denise Levertov. **CP-LeveD**

Fire in the Hole. Gary Snyder. **CP-SnydG**

Fire Is. Charles Olson. **CP-OlsoC**

Fire is ash, The: the early morning sun. Femmes Damnees. Philip Larkin. **CP-LarkP**

Fire is eating, The. Burning the News. Lewis Turco. **SP-TurcL**

Fire-Logs. Carl Sandburg. **CP-SandC**

Fire makes noises like snow on wet panes, The. Li Po. Charles Olson. **CP-OlsoC**

Fire of Despair Has Been Our Savior, The. Robert Bly. **SP-BlyR**

Fire of Drift-Wood, The. Henry Wadsworth Longfellow. **SP-LongH**

Fire of Hell this strange condition hath, The. Hell Fire. Robert Herrick. **CP-HerrR**

Fire of Myself. Joseph Ceravolo. **SP-CeraJ**

Fire of the seed is in her pose, The. Child and Vegetables. William Carlos Williams. **CP-WilW1**

Fire of Unknown Origin, A. Patti Smith. **SP-SmitP**

Fire of winter sunset. Aloof. Carl Sandburg. **CP-SandC**

Fire on the Hills. Robinson Jeffers. **CP-JefR2**

Fire Pages. Carl Sandburg. **CP-SandC**

Fire Spirit. William Carlos Williams. **CP-WilW1**

Fire stop thief help murder save the world. Edward Estlin Cummings. **CP-CummE**

Fire that must flame is with apt fuell fed. Thomas Campion. **CP-CampT**

Fire Thief, The. Anne Sexton. **CP-SextA**

Fire took the house. Black bricks. Salvaged Parts. William Stafford. **SP-StafW**

Fire-Truck, A. Richard Wilbur. **CP-WilbR**

Fire Walker. Robert Ranke Graves. **CP-GravR**

Firebombers, The. Anne Sexton. **CP-SextA**

Firebombing, The. James Dickey. **CP-DickJ**

Fireborn Are at Home in Fire, The. Carl Sandburg. **CP-SandC**

Firebreathers at the Café Deux Magots, The. Miller Williams. **SP-WillM**

Firecrackers came from China. Bitter Summer Thoughts—No. 3. Carl Sandburg. **CP-SandC**

Fired. Langston Hughes. **SP-HughL**

Fired in sanguine clay, the model head. The Lady and the Earthenware Head. Sylvia Plath. **CP-PlatS**

Fireflies. Tom Clark. **SP-ClarT**

Fireflies. Charles Tomlinson. **CP-TomlC**

Fireflies and the stars our only light, The. The Spinning Heart. John Berryman. **CP-BerrJ**

Fireflies in the Corn. David Herbert Lawrence. **CP-LawrD**

Fireflies in the Garden. Robert Frost. **CP-FrosR**

Firelight. Edwin Arlington Robinson. **CP-RobiE**

Firelight. John Greenleaf Whittier. *See* Shut in from all the world without.

Firelight and Nightfall. David Herbert Lawrence. **CP-LawrD**

Firelight gleams upon your hair, The. Vision. Wystan Hugh Auden. **CP-AudWJ**

Firelight in Sunlight. Howard Nemerov. *See* Firelight in sunlight, silver-pale.

Firelight in sunlight, silver-pale. Howard Nemerov. **CP-NemeH** (Firelight in Sunlight.) **CP-NemeH**

Firemen's Ball, The. Nicholas Vachel Lindsay. *Fr.* Poems Speaking of Buddha, Prince Siddartha. **CP-LindV**

Firenze, a Lifetime Later. Lawrence Ferlinghetti. **SP-FerlL**

Fires, The. Rudyard Kipling. **CP-KiplR**

Fire's gone down: burnt pine, The. James McAuley. **SP-McAuJ** *Fr.* Habitations.

Fireside. George Meredith. **CP-MerG2**

Fireside Reverie. George Meredith. **CP-MerG2**

Firesong. Sylvia Plath. **CP-PlatS**

Firesticks. Stanley Jasspon Kunitz. **CP-KuniS**

Firewood under the eaves. Aged Tamba Temple Plum Tree Song. Gary Snyder. **CP-SnydG**

Firework bangs echo up the valley. April. Gary Snyder. *Fr.* Six Years. **CP-SnydG**

Fireworks. Dabney Stuart. **SP-StuaD**

Fireworks. John Updike. **CP-UpdiJ**

Firing, The. Kenneth Patchen. **CP-PatcK**

Firing, The. Gary Snyder. **CP-SnydG**

Firm-footed, small, she thrust my pram. The Drift of Petals. John Hewitt. **CP-HewiJ**

Firm-lipped, high-bosomed, slender Queen of Beanstalk Land. Batxóca. Robert Ranke Graves. **CP-GravR**

Firmament breaks up. In black eclipse, The. A Word for the Hour. John Greenleaf Whittier. **CP-WhitJ**

Firmum is all too known fails so Meantool a Dives. Catullus. *See* Carmen 114: "O'Tool is generally accounted."

First, The. Wendell Berry. **CP-BerrW**

First / bury your hands. Ritual. Bill Knott. **SP-KnotB**

First / time is / the first, The. Robert Creeley. **CP-CreeR**

First a sea: soft sands, muds, and marls. What Happened Here Before. Gary Snyder. **CP-SnydG**

First a word was fuzzy, and was nothing. Words. Richard Eberhart. **CP-EberR**

First Advent of Love. Samuel Taylor Coleridge. **CP-ColeS**

First age of the world was counterpoint, The. The Four Ages. Howard Nemerov. **CP-NemeH**

First Anniversary [*or* Anniversarie], The. John Donne. **AnAnS-1; FaBoRV; MasP; SeCV-1** *Fr.* Anatomy [*or* Anatomie] of the World, An[: the First Anniversary]. **CP-DonnJ**

("Verse hath a middle nature: heaven keeps souls.") **FaBoRV,** *ll.* 473–74; "And new philosophy calls all in doubt." **NOSC**

Doth not a Tenarif[e], or Higher Hill. **ChTr**

"She, she is dead; she's dead: when thou knowest [*or* know'st] this." **JCP**

First Anniversary of the Government under His Highness the Lord Protector, 1655, The. Andrew Marvell. **CP-MarvA**

First, apologies, as usual. Questions for my Grandfather. James McAuley. **SP-McAuJ**

First, April, she with mellow show[e]rs. Robert Herrick. **CP-HerrR**

(Succession of the Foure Sweet Months, The.) **CP-HerrR**

First, are you our sort of a person? The Applicant. Sylvia Plath. **CP-PlatS**

First Autumn, The. May Sarton. **SP-SartM**

First blossom was the best blossom, The. Apple Blossom. Louis MacNeice. **CP-MacNL**

First Book, The. Archibald MacLeish. *Fr.* Conquistador. **CP-MacLA**

First-Born, The. George Meredith. **CP-MerG2**

First-Born of Egypt, The. Robert Browning. **CP-BroR2**

First came fine words softening our souls for magic. Earlier Lovers. Robert Ranke Graves. **CP-GravR**

First came the legions, then the colonists. The Colony. John Hewitt. **CP-HewiJ**

First came the Lion-Rider, across the green fields of the morning. Kenneth Patchen. **CP-PatcK**

First Canzone of the Convito, The. Dante Alighieri, *tr. fr. Italian by* Shelley. **CP-ShelP**

First chainsaw I owned was years ago, The. Regarding Chainsaws. Hayden Carruth. **CP-CarHS**

First Chantey, The. Rudyard Kipling. **CP-KiplR**

First Chime. Ogden Nash. *Fr.* Ring out the Old, Ring in the New, but Don't Get Caught in Between. **CP-NashO**

First-class brains of a senior civil servant, The. Mortality. Sir John Betjeman. **CP-BetjJ**

First cocks begin clearing the throat of morning—, The. A Valley Where I Don't Belong. Marge Piercy. **SP-PierM**

First Cold. Stephen Berg. **SP-BergS**

"First cold winter twilights. . . ." Tom Clark. **SP-ClarT**

First commandment of the wind. From the Inside. Paul Éluard, *tr. fr. French by* William Carlos Williams. **CP-WilW2**

First Confession, A, *fr.* A Woman Young and Old. William Butler Yeats. **CP-YeatW**

First Corncrake. John Hewitt. **CP-HewiJ**

First Crusades, The! Kenneth Patchen. **CP-PatcK**

First Dances. Frank O'Hara. **SP-OharF**

First Dandelion, The. Walt Whitman. **CP-WhitW**

First Day, The. Phoebe Hesketh. **SP-HeskP**

First Day, The. Howard Nemerov. **CP-NemeH**

First Day, The. Christina Georgina Rossetti. *See* I wish I could remember the [or that] first day.

First day and night alarmed child's salt eye. Periodicity. John Hewitt. **CP-HewiJ**

First Day that I was a Life, The. Emily Dickinson. **CP-DickE**

First-Day Thoughts. John Greenleaf Whittier. **CP-WhitJ**

First Day's Night had come, The. Emily Dickinson. **CP-DickE**

First Death in Nova Scotia. Elizabeth Bishop. **CP-BishE**

First Desires. Charles Kenneth Williams. **SP-WillC**

First Elegy. Rotten Lake. Muriel Rukeyser. **CP-RukeM**

First Epistle. Donald Davie. *Fr.* Six Epistles to Eva Hesse. **CP-DavDo**

First Epistle of the First Book of Horace Imitated, The. Alexander Pope. **CP-PopeA**

"Well, if a King's a lion, at the least." **ECEV; OBSV**

(Profiteers.) **ECEV**

First Epistle of the Second Book of Horace Imitated, The. Alexander Pope. **CP-PopeA**

"But for the wits of either Charles's days." **EPCY**

Ideals of Satire, The. **FiP**

"Milton's strong pinion now not heaven can bound." **EPCY**

"Of little use the man you may suppose." **EBEV**

"Shakespeare (whom you and every playhouse bill)." **EPCY**

"We conquered France, but felt our captive's charms." **EPCY**

"Who now reads Cowley? if he pleases yet." **EPCY**

First Families Move Over! Ogden Nash. **CP-NashO**

First few wounds are nearly invisible, The. Shooting a Farmhouse. Ted Kooser. **SP-KoosT**

First Fig. Edna St. Vincent Millay. **CP-MillE**

First fight. Then fiddle. Ply the slipping string. Gwendolyn Brooks. **SP-BrooG** *Fr.* The Children of the Poor. **SP-BrooG**, sect. I, pt. 1-5; *Fr.* The Womanhood.

First fire since the summer is lit, and is smoking into the room, The. Shortening Days at the Homestead. Thomas Hardy. **CP-HardT**

First fish / I ever caught, The. The Fish. Mary Oliver. **SP-OlivM**

First Flight, The. Seamus Heaney. **SP-HeanS** *Fr.* Sweeney Redivivus.

First Flight. Daniel Gerard Hoffman. **SP-HoffD**

First Flight. Louise McNeill. **SP-McNeL**

First Flight. Mona Van Duyn. **SP-VanDM**

First flower, / Fields' document, The. Palms for a Catholic Child. Kenneth Patchen. **CP-PatcK**

First Flowers, The. John Greenleaf Whittier. **CP-WhitJ**

First flowret of the year is that which shows. In the First Page of an Album by One Whose Handwriting Is Wretchedly Bad. William Wordsworth. **CP-WorW2**

First follow Nature, and your judgment frame. Alexander Pope. **FiP**, *ll.* 68–91; *Fr.* An Essay on Criticism. **CP-PopeA**

First, for effusions due unto the dead. Upon His Sister-in-Law, Mistress Elizabeth Herrick. Robert Herrick. **CP-HerrR**

First, for your shape, the curious cannot shew. *see also* To His Kinswoman, Mrs. Penelope Wheeler. Robert Herrick. **CP-HerrR**

First frost, and I walk among the rose-fruit, the marble toes. Private Ground. Sylvia Plath. **CP-PlatS**

First Funeral. John Hewitt. **CP-HewiJ**

First Goodbye. Louise Glück. *Fr.* Marathon. **SP-GlücL**

First Grade. William Stafford. **SP-StafW**

First Hard Frost, The. Barton Sutter. **SP-SuttB**

First having read the book of myths. Diving into the Wreck. Adrienne Rich. **SP-RicA1; SP-RicA2**

First he could not remember. Documenting It. Miller Williams. **SP-WillM**

First he drew a strike zone. The Hummer. William Matthews. **SP-MattW**

First he gave me. Pomegranate. Louise Glück. **SP-GlücL**

First he must go where / Not even the birds will brave his solitude. The Buddhist Painter Prepares to Paint. Hayden Carruth. **CP-CarHS**

First he said. Transitional. William Carlos Williams. **CP-WilW1**

First heaven is a flowery plain, The. The Green Castle. Robert Ranke Graves. **CP-GravR**

First Honey. John Hewitt. **CP-HewiJ**

First horn lifts its arm over the dew-lit grass, The. The House Slave. Rita Dove. **SP-DoveR**

First I looked on, after a long time far from home, The. American Change. Allen Ginsberg. **CP-GinsA**

First I salute this soil of the blessed, river and rock! Pheidippides. Robert Browning. **CP-BroR2**

First I saw it in colour, then I killed it. The Sign. Roy Fisher. **SP-FishR**

First I will tell you something of these two. Archibald MacLeish. **CP-MacLA** *Fr.* The Happy Marriage.

First, I would have her be beautiful. Selecting a Reader. Ted Kooser. **SP-KoosT**

First I would like to write for you a poem to be shouted in the teeth. Horse Fiddle. Carl Sandburg. **CP-SandC**

First idea was not our own, The. Adam. Wallace Stevens. **NOBA** *Fr.* It Must Be Abstract. *Fr.* Notes toward a Supreme Fiction. **CP-StevW**

First in these fields I try the sylvan strains. Spring, the First Pastoral, or Damon. Alexander Pope. *Fr.* Pastorals. **CP-PopeA**

First Invention on the Theme of the Adam. Robert Duncan. **SP-DuncR**

First is female, The. Terminal Tramps. Charles Tomlinson. **CP-TomlC**

First Jock he / was kilt a handsome. Edward Estlin Cummings. **CP-CummE**

First, Jollies wife is lame; then next, loose-hipt. Upon Jollies Wife. Robert Herrick. **CP-HerrR**

First Kingdom, The. Seamus Heaney. **SP-HeanS** *Fr.* Sweeney Redivivus.

First Kiss. Rita Dove. **SP-DoveR**

First Kiss of Love, The. Byron. **CP-Byron**

First kiss was with stumbling fingertips, The. The Kiss. Karl Shapiro. *Fr.* Adam and Eve. **SP-ShapK**

First, last, and dearest, / My love, mine own. From Mestastasio. Christina Georgina Rossetti. **CP-RosC3**

First Leaf, The. Howard Nemerov. **CP-NemeH**

First Leaf, The. William DeWitt Snodgrass. **SP-SnodW**

First Lesson about Man. Thomas Merton. **CP-MertT**

First lesson: Don't. Articulacy. Hints from the Koran. Donald Davie. **CP-DavDo**

First Letters. John Hewitt. **CP-HewiJ**

First light—call it. Cloud Change. Charles Tomlinson. **CP-TomlC**

First light of day in Mississippi. Birthday Poem. Al Young. **CP-YounA**

First light strikes / across a landmass. Drive. Charles Tomlinson. **CP-TomlC**

First Limick. Ogden Nash. **CP-NashO**

First Love. Thomas Campion. **CP-CampT**

First Love. Robert Ranke Graves. **CP-GravR**

First Love. Stanley Jasspon Kunitz. **CP-KuniS**

First Love. Robert Lowell. **SP-LoweR**

First Love. "Hugh MacDiarmid." **CP-MacDH**

First Love. Edwin Rolfe. **CP-RolfE**

First Love. William Butler Yeats. *Fr.* A Man Young and Old. **CP-YeatW**

First make the mouthpiece classic. Sisters. Anne Waldman. **SP-WaldA**

First Man, The. Thom Gunn. *Fr.* Misanthropos. **CP-GunnT**

First man who whistled, The. The First. Wendell Berry. **CP-BerrW**

First Marrs or Makes, The. Robert Herrick. **CP-HerrR**

First, may the hand of bounty bring. Happinesse to Hospitalitie, or a Hearty Wish to Good House-Keeping. Robert Herrick. **CP-HerrR**

First Meditation. Theodore Roethke. **LCAP; NOBA** *Fr.* Meditations of an Old Woman. **CP-RoetT**

First Meeting. Wystan Hugh Auden. **CP-AudWJ**

First Meeting with a Possible Mother-in-Law. Thom Gunn. **CP-GunnT**

First Mile. James McAuley. *Fr.* Ten-Mile Run. **SP-McAuJ**

First month of his absence, The. Song (On Seeing Dead Bodies Floating Off the Cape). Alun Lewis. **CP-LewiA**

First Morning. David Herbert Lawrence. **CP-LawrD**

First morning of mist after days of draining, unwavering heat along the shore: a *breath*, The. Dawn. Charles Kenneth Williams. **SP-WillC**

First morning of Three Mile Island: those first disquieting, uncertain, mystifying hours, The. Tar. Charles Kenneth Williams. **CP-WillC; SP-WillC**

First movie I ever saw was the Walt Disney Cartoon *The Three Little Pigs* , The. The Lonedale Operator. John Ashbery. **SP-AshbJ**

First Mute Coming, A. Emily Dickinson. **CP-DickE**

First name cut on a rock, a King's, The. Uncalendared Love. Robert Ranke Graves. **CP-GravR**

First Neighbours. Margaret Atwood. **SP-AtwM1**

First News from Villafranca. Elizabeth Barrett Browning. **CP-BroEB**

First Night at Sea. John Berryman. **CP-BerrJ**

First Night of Fall, The. Brendan Galvin. **SP-GalvB**

First Night of Fall and Falling Rain, The. Delmore Schwartz. **SP-SchwD**

First O Songs for a Prelude. Walt Whitman. **CP-WhitW**

First Ode of the Fourth Book of Horace Imitated, The. Alexander Pope. **CP-PopeA**

First Ode of the Second Book of Horace Paraphrased and Addressed to Richard Steele, Esq., The. Jonathan Swift. **CP-SwifJ**

First of all is God, and the same last is he, The, *ad. fr. Latin of* Proclus. Sir Walter Ralegh. **CP-RaleW**

First of all my dreams was of, The. The . Edward Estlin Cummings. **CP-CummE**

First of April, The. Jonathan Swift. **CP-SwifJ**

First of Jealousy. Dialogue, The. Thomas Carew. *Fr.* Four Songs, by Way of Chorus To a Play. **CP-CareT**

First of May, The. Alfred Edward Housman. **CP-HousA**

First of the undecoded messages read: "Popeye sits in thunder," The. Farm Implements and Rutabagas in a Landscape. John Ashbery. **SP-AshbJ**

First off, I have to say I can't talk good. Marvin McCabe. Hayden Carruth. **CP-CarHS**

First offer Incense, then thy field and meads. Pray and Prosper. Robert Herrick. **CP-HerrR**

First one was for the clock, The. Another Beer. William Matthews. **SP-MattW**

First or Last. Thomas Hardy. **CP-HardT**

First owl of the evening. Charles Henri Ford. **SP-FordC** *Fr.* Secret Haiku.

First page only for you, The. Slowly. Anne Waldman. **SP-WaldA**

First Pantomime. John Hewitt. **CP-HewiJ**

First Payment Deferred. Ogden Nash. **CP-NashO**

First Poem to Mary in London. Ernest Hemingway. **CP-HemiE**

First Point of Aries, The. Howard Nemerov. **CP-NemeH**

First Practice. Gary Gildner. **SP-GildG**

First Praise. William Carlos Williams. **CP-WilW1**

First president to be loved by his, The. Edward Estlin Cummings. **CP-CummE**

First Psalm, The. Robert Burns. **CP-BurnR**

First Psalm. Anne Sexton. *Fr.* O Ye Tongues. **CP-SextA**

First real job I had was delivering drugs, The. Getting Experience. Miller Williams. **SP-WillM**

First retainer / he gave to her, The. A Marriage. Robert Creeley. **CP-CreeR**

First Ride. John Hewitt. **CP-HewiJ**

First robin the; / you say something. Edward Estlin Cummings. **CP-CummE**

First rose on my rose-tree, The. Three Songs of Shattering. Edna St. Vincent Millay. **CP-MillE**

First runner reached us, The. The Finish. Daniel Gerard Hoffman. **SP-HoffD**

First Satire of the Second Book of Horace [Imitated], The. Alexander Pope. **CP-PopeA**

"Alas, young man! your days can ne'er be long;." **EPCY**

Question of Libel, A. **PrIm**

"With all a woman's virtues but the pox." **OBSV**

First, scattering rain on the Polish cities, The. 1 September 1939. John Berryman. **CP-BerrJ**

First Shaman Song. Gary Snyder. **CP-SnydG** *Fr.* Hunting. *Fr.* Myths and Texts.

First she like a piece of ill-oiled. Edward Estlin Cummings. **CP-CummE**

First: She's a listener. Learning From Barbara Deming. Grace Paley. **CP-PaleG**

First Sight. Philip Larkin. **CP-LarkP**

First Sight of Her and After. Thomas Hardy. **CP-HardT**

First signs of the death of the boom came in the summer, The. Tampa Stomp. John Berryman. **CP-BerrJ**

First Six Verses of the Ninetieth Psalm, The. Robert Burns. **CP-BurnR**

First Snow. Ted Kooser. **SP-KoosT**

First Snow. Howard Nemerov. **CP-NemeH**

First Snow. Mary Oliver. **SP-OlivM**

First Snow. May Sarton. **SP-SartM**

First Snow in Alsace. Richard Wilbur. **CP-WilbR**

First Snow in the Glens. John Hewitt. **CP-HewiJ**

First Sonata for Karlen Paula. Carl Sandburg. **CP-SandC**

First Song, The. Thomas Carew. **CP-CareT** *Fr.* Carew's Masque. **CP-CareT**

First Song. Galway Kinnell. **SP-KinnG**

First Song. Andrew Marvell. *Fr.* Two Songs at the Marriage of the Lord Fauconberg and the Lady Mary Cromwell. **CP-MarvA**

First Song. Sir Philip Sidney. *See* Doubt you to whom my Muse these notes intendeth [*or* entendeth].

First Song of Huitzilopochtli. David Herbert Lawrence. **CP-LawrD**

First South and Cambridge. Richard Hugo. **CP-HugoR**

First Spring Dawn. Jenny Joseph. **SP-JoseJ**

First Spring Day, The. Christina Georgina Rossetti. **CP-RosC1**

First, suicide notes should be. Suicide. Alice Walker. **CP-AudeW**

First Sun Day of the year. Tonight. Galway Kinnell. **NaP** *Fr.* The Avenue Bearing the Initial of Christ into the New World. **SP-KinnG**

First Sunday I missed Mass on purpose, The. The Day Zimmer Lost Religion. Paul Zimmer. **SP-ZimmP**

First that beautiful mad exploration. Journey toward Poetry. May Sarton. **SP-SartM**

First that broke silence was good old Ben, The. Sir John Suckling. **EPCY** *Fr.* A Session[s] of the Poets. **CP-SuckJ**

First the distant cocks. A hairfine. Louis MacNeice. *Fr.* The Island. **CP-MacNL**

First the fish must be caught. The White Queen's Riddle. "Lewis Carroll." **CP-CarrL** *Fr.* Through the Looking-Glass.

First—the sun coming closer, growing by the minute. Notes for a Little Play. Ted Hughes. **SP-HughT**

First the warmth, variability. The Rose. William Carlos Williams. **CP-WilW1**

First then made he a big strong shield, with his cunningest craft-skill. The Shield of Achilles. Homer, *tr. by* George Meredith. **CP-MerG2** *Fr.* The Iliad.

First then the *Prunus* and the Japanese cherry. Suburban Spring in Warwickshire. John Hewitt. **CP-HewiJ**

First there is the wind but not like the familiar wind but long. Definition of the Frontiers. Archibald MacLeish. **CP-MacLA**

First there was putting hot-water bottles to it. Inevitable. Sir John Betjeman. **CP-BetjJ**

First there was the lamb on knocking knees. Dylan Thomas. **CMoP** *Fr.* Altarwise by Owl-Light. **CP-ThomD**

First there were those who died. Living among the Dead. William Matthews. **SP-MattW**

First, They Said. Alice Walker. **CP-WalkA**

First thing in the morning, The. Pocoangelini 8. Lewis Turco. **SP-TurcL**

First Things. Robert Lowell. **SP-LoweR**

First Things. Adrienne Rich. **CP-RicAE**

First Things First. Wystan Hugh Auden. **CP-AudeW**

First three deer bounding. Three Deer One Coyote Running in the Snow. Gary Snyder. **CP-SnydG**

First three roses / opened up today, the outer petals, The. For Bob Dash. James Schuyler. **CP-SchuJ**

First Time, The. Robert Creeley. **CP-CreeR**

First Time, The. Karl Shapiro. **SP-ShapK**

First time ever I saw Johnny Spain was, The. Johnny Spain's White Heifer. Hayden Carruth. **CP-CarHS**

First time he kissed me, he but only kissed. Sonnet. Elizabeth Barrett Browning. **BLPA; BLPL; CTC; FaBoBe; HBV; PoPl** *Fr.* Sonnets from the Portuguese. **CP-BroEB**

First time I met him Henry Moore was sixty. Before tea, The. Notes For Nobody. Donald Hall. **CP-HallD**

First time I went, The. Gregory Corso's Story. Allen Ginsberg. **CP-GinsA**

First time out. Lives. Derek Mahon. **SP-MahoD**

First time that I dreamed, we were in flight, The. The Lesson. Wystan Hugh Auden. **CP-AudeW**

First time that Peter denièd his Lord, The. A Song at Cock-Crow. Rudyard Kipling. **CP-KiplR**

First time that the sun rose on thine oath, The. Sonnet. Elizabeth Barrett Browning. **EnVR; NAEL-2; WPE** *Fr.* Sonnets from the Portuguese. **CP-BroEB**

First to go was William. I recall, The. My Uncle Willy. John Hewitt. **CP-HewiJ**

First Train (1895). Louise McNeill. **SP-McNeL**

First Travels of Max. John Crowe Ransom. **SP-RansJ**

First under up and then again down under. On Our Sympathy with the Under Dog. Robert Frost. **CP-FrosR**

First Universe. Diane Wakoski. *Fr.* The Universes. **SP-WakoD**

First Version, The. Hayden Carruth. *Fr.* The Mythology of Dark and Light. **CP-CarHL**

First Voice, The. "Lewis Carroll." *Fr.* The Three Voices. **CP-CarrL**

First warm day, The. Late February. Ted Kooser. **SP-KoosT**

First warm summer afternoon I ask my [*or* a] friend, The. To the Same Place. Stephen Berg. **SP-BergS** *Fr.* For My Father.

First was Fancy, like a lovely boy, The. Edmund Spenser. **NOBE** *Fr.* The Mask of Cupid. **OBSC** *Fr.* The Faerie Queene. **CP-Spens**

First was like a dream thro' summer heat, The. From House to Home. Christina Georgina Rossetti. **CP-RosC1**

First was the world as one great cymbal made. Music's Empire. Andrew Marvell. **CP-MarvA**

First we carried out the faggot of steel stakes. Starting to Make a Tree. Roy Fisher. *Fr.* City. **SP-FishR**

First We knew of Him was Death, The. Emily Dickinson. **CP-DickE**

First We Take Manhattan. Leonard Cohen. **CP-CoheL**

First week the soil was clean, The. Digging for Indians. Gary Gildner. **SP-GildG**

First when Maggie [*or* Maggy] was my care. Whistle o'er the Lave o't. Robert Burns. **CP-BurnR**

First white hair coils in my hand, The. Sign. Marge Piercy. **SP-PierM**

First Winter. Pablo Neruda, *tr. fr. Spanish* by Ben Belitt. **SP-NeruP**

First Word at Last, The. Robert Pack. **SP-PackR**

First Work, and Then Wages. Robert Herrick. **CP-HerrR**

First year was like icing, The. More Pleasant Adventures. John Ashbery. **SP-AshbJ**

First, you think they are dead. Lobsters in the Window. William DeWitt Snodgrass. **SP-SnodW**

Firstborn. Louise Glück. **SP-GlücL**

Firste stok, fader of gentilesse, The. Geoffrey Chaucer. **CP-ChauG** (Gentilesse.) **CP-ChauG**

Firstly Inclined to Take What It Is Told. Gwendolyn Brooks. **SP-BrooG**

Fish. / Bequeath fish. Dates. Gertrude Stein. **CP-SteiG**

Fish, The. Elizabeth Bishop. **CP-BishE**

Fish, / Firelight, A. Lullaby and Exhortation for the Unwilling Hero. Roy Fisher. *Fr.* City. **SP-FishR**

Fish. David Herbert Lawrence. **CP-LawrD**

Fish, The. Marianne Craig Moore. **CP-MoorM**

Fish, The. Ogden Nash. **CP-NashO**

Fish, The. Mary Oliver. **SP-OlivM**

Fish? Shel Silverstein. **SP-SilS2**

Fish. William Carlos Williams. **CP-WilW1**

Fish, The. William Butler Yeats. **CP-YeatW**

Fish are staying here, The. Heart Feels the Water. Joseph Ceravolo. **SP-CeraJ**

Fish are very good at swimming. Barmaids Are Diviner Than Mermaids. Ogden Nash. **CP-NashO**

Fish bones walked the waves off Hatteras. Cottonmouth Country. Louise Glück. **SP-GlücL**

Fish Crier. Carl Sandburg. **CP-SandC**

Fish, Fish. Stevie Smith. **CP-SmitS**

Fish float belly-up, for real—, The. Bomb Test. Gary Snyder. **CP-SnydG**

Fish flopped on my shoes, / turned up a chilly eye, The. Providence 3. John Hewitt. **CP-HewiJ**

Fish has laid her succulent eggs. Vicissitudes of the Creator. Archibald MacLeish. **CP-MacLA**

Fish have no clothes. Afterword. James Liddy. **CP-LiddJ**

Fish in the Stone, The. Rita Dove. **SP-DoveR**

Fish in the unruffled lakes. Wystan Hugh Auden. **BoLoP; CBLP; CMoP; ChMP; MoAB; MoBrPo; MoP** *Fr.* Twelve Songs. **CP-AudeW**

Fish is speech, or see, The. Abstract #1, Yucatan. Charles Olson. **CP-OlsoC**

Fish is the Flower of Water, A. Charles Olson. **CP-OlsoC**

Fish Peddler and Cobbler. Kenneth Rexroth. **SP-RexrK**

Fish-Scale Sunrise, A. Wallace Stevens. **CP-StevW**

Fish scales, old newspapers, unopened cans. Sources. Philip Levine. **SP-LeviP**

Fish-sky at morning. *see also* True Confessional. Lawrence Ferlinghetti. **SP-FerlL**

Fish swim onto sand in error. La Push. Richard Hugo. **CP-HugoR**

Fish That Walked, The. Anne Sexton. **CP-SextA**

Fish-Women.—On Landing at Calais. William Wordsworth. *Fr.* Memorials of a Tour of the Continent; 1820. **CP-WorW2**

Fisher Cat, The. Richard Eberhart. **CP-EberR**

Fisher Child's Lullaby, The. Paul Laurence Dunbar. **CP-DunbP**

Fisher-Wife, A. Christina Georgina Rossetti. **CP-RosC2**

Fisherman, The. William Butler Yeats. **CP-YeatW**

Fisherman Poet. Phoebe Hesketh. **SP-HeskP**

Fisherman's Return. Malcolm Lowry. **CP-LowrM**

Fisherman's swapping a yarn for a yarn, The. The Flower Boat. Robert Frost. **CP-FrosR**

Fishermen, The. John Greenleaf Whittier. **CP-WhitJ**

Fishermen, The. James Wright. **CP-WrigJ**

Fishermen at Ballyshannon. Limbo. Seamus Heaney. **SP-HeanS**

Fishermen, like thieves, shake out their silver. Derek Walcott. **PBCV** *Fr.* Another Life. **CP-WalcD**

Fishermen on Lake Michigan, sometimes, The. Kicks. Howard Nemerov. **CP-NemeH**

Fishermen rowing homeward in the dusk, The. The Harbour. Derek Walcott. **CP-WalcD**

Fishermen's Last Supper. Marsden Hartley. **CP-HartM**

Fishes are born in water. Man Is Born in Tao. Chuang Tzu, *tr. fr. Chinese* by Thomas Merton. **CP-MertT**

Fishes inhabit the deep rock crannies, the worm the dry. Alun Lewis. *Fr.* The Captivity. **CP-LewiA**

Fishing. Paul Laurence Dunbar. **CP-DunbP**

Fishing. William Wordsworth. **SD** *Fr.* Introduction—Childhood and School-Time. **EnRP; FHYEP** *Fr.* The Prelude; Growth of a Poet's Mind [1850 vers.]. **CP-WorW3**

Fishing at Forty. Barton Sutter. **SP-SuttB**

Fishing for Eel Totems. Margaret Atwood. **SP-AtwM1**

Fishmarket closed, the fishes gone into flesh, The. Galway Kinnell. **NaP** *Fr.* The Avenue Bearing the Initial of Christ into the New World. **SP-KinnG**

Fishmonger. Marsden Hartley. **CP-HartM**

Fishnet. Robert Lowell. **SP-LoweR**

Fist. Philip Levine. **SP-LeviP**

Fist, The. Derek Walcott. **CP-WalcD**

Fist, withered and strung, The. Margaret Atwood. *Fr.* Circe / Mud Poems. **SP-AtwM1**

Fisted, bitten by blizzards. Lava Bed. William Everson. **SP-EverW**

Fit against the Country, A. James Wright. **CP-WrigJ**

Fit for the Pleiads' azure chord. Hafiz, *tr. by* Ralph Waldo Emerson. **CP-EmerR** *Fr.* Odes.

Fit of Rhyme [*or* Rime] against Rhyme [*or* Rime], A. Ben Jonson. **CP-JonsB**

Fit retribution, by the moral code. William Wordsworth. *Fr.* Sonnets upon the Punishment of Death. **CP-WorW2**

Fit the Fifth: The Beaver's Lesson. "Lewis Carroll." *Fr.* The Hunting of the Snark. **CP-CarrL**

Fit the First: The Landing. "Lewis Carroll." *See* "Just the place for a Snark!" the Bellman cried.

Fit the Fourth: The Hunting. "Lewis Carroll." *Fr.* The Hunting of the Snark. **CP-CarrL**

Fit the Seventh: The Banker's Fate. "Lewis Carroll." *Fr.* The Hunting of the Snark. **CP-CarrL**

Fit the Sixth: The Barrister's Dream. "Lewis Carroll." **EBNV** *Fr.* The Hunting of the Snark. **CP-CarrL**

Fitful alternations of the rain, The. Fragment: Rain. Percy Bysshe Shelley. **CP-ShelP**

Fitter to see Him, I may be. Emily Dickinson. **CP-DickE**

Fitting, The. Edna St. Vincent Millay. **CP-MillE**

Fitting of the Mask, The. Stanley Jasspon Kunitz. **CP-KuniS**

Fitz-Eustace's Song. Sir Walter Scott. **SP-ScotW** *Fr.* Marmion.

Fitz-Greene Halleck. John Greenleaf Whittier. **CP-WhitJ**

5 / derbies-with-men-in-them smoke Helmar. Edward Estlin Cummings. **CP-CummE**

Five, *English vers. of* Quinque. Robert Ranke Graves. **CP-GravR**

Five / jays / discuss / goodandevil. Hayden Carruth. *Fr.* North Winter. **CP-CarHL**

Five / Senses gone, The. Ozymandias. George Oppen. **CP-OppeG**

Five A.M. in the Pinewoods. Mary Oliver. **SP-OlivM**

Five Americans. Edward Estlin Cummings. **CP-CummE**
  Fran.
  Gert.
  Liz.
  Mame.
  Marj.
Five-and-twenty years have gone. In Memory of Alfred Pollexfen. William Butler Yeats. **CP-YeatW**
Five beringed fingers of Creation. *English vers. of* Quinque. Robert Ranke Graves. **CP-GravR**
Five breaths pray in me: sun moon. Thomas Merton. **CP-MertT**
Five brick panels, three small windows, six lions' heads with. The Backside of the Academy. Muriel Rukeyser. **CP-RukeM**
Five Carlins—A Ballad—Tune, Chevy Chase, The. Robert Burns. **CP-BurnR**
Five Cent Balloons. Carl Sandburg. **CP-SandC**
Five circus clowns dying this year, morning newspapers told their lives. Legends. Carl Sandburg. **CP-SandC**
Five Day Week, The. Grace Paley. **CP-PaleG**
Five-day week was set like a firecracker, The. The Five Day Week. Grace Paley. **CP-PaleG**
Five Elephants. Rita Dove. **SP-DoveR**
Five Enemies, The. Chuang Tzu, *tr. fr. Chinese by* Thomas Merton. **CP-MertT**
515 Madison Avenue. Rhapsody. Frank O'Hara. **SP-OharF**
Five-Finger Exercises. Thomas Stearns Eliot. **CP-ElioT**
  Lines for Cuscuscaraway and Mirza Murad Ali Beg. **FiBHP; NBLV; NTP; OBAL; OBCoV; PeLV; PoPl; SpRo; UV; VoGa**
  Lines to a Duck in a Park.
  Lines to a Persian Cat.
  Lines to a Yorkshire Terrier.
  Lines to Ralph Hodgson Esqre. **NBLV; OBAL; PeLV**
Five Flights Up. Elizabeth Bishop. **CP-BishE**
Five. . . four. . . three. . . two. . . one. Stanley Jasspon Kunitz. *Fr.* The Magic Curtain. **CP-KuniS**
Five geese deploy mysteriously. Bas-Relief. Carl Sandburg. **CP-SandC**
Five hours, (and who can do it less in?). The Lady's Dressing Room. Jonathan Swift. **CP-SwifJ**
Five Lies About the Moon. Richard Shelton. **SP-ShelR**
  Full Daytime Moon, The.
  Full Harvest Moon, The.
  Gibbous Moon, The.
  Half-Moon, The.
  Waning Crescent Moon, The.
Five lines, not four. And keep the song. Tanck's Prolegomenon. Hayden Carruth. **CP-CarHS** *Fr.* Songs About What Comes Down: The Complete Works of Mr. Septic Tank.
Five little girls, of Five, Four, Three, Two, One. A Game of Fives. "Lewis Carroll." **CP-CarrL**
Five little roses spoke. Public Letter to Emily Dickinson. Carl Sandburg. **CP-SandC**
Five lone clangs from the house-clock nigh. The Shiver. Thomas Hardy. **CP-HardT**
Five miles to my mother's house. That Saturday Without a Car. Stephen Dunn. **SP-DunnS**
Five months ago the stream did flow. Change Upon Change. Elizabeth Barrett Browning. **CP-BroEB**
Five Morning Poems from a Picture by Manet. Roy Fisher. **SP-FishR**
  "Death music sounds for a boy by a stream."
  "Looking for life, I lost my mind."
  "Nowhere. Hear the stormy spring."
  "Walking beside the wall towards the stream."
  "Wells of shadow by the stream."
Five Nocturnes. Robert Frost. **CP-FrosR**
  Bravado.
  In the Long Night.
  Night Light, The.
  On Making Certain Anything Has Happened.
  Were I in Trouble. **OxBSP**
Five O'Clock, Beacon Hill. Adrienne Rich. **CP-RicAE**
Five o'clock prairie sunset is a strong man going to sleep after a long, The. Rusty Crimson. Carl Sandburg. **CP-SandC**
Five O'Clock Shadow. Sir John Betjeman. **CP-BetjJ**
Five old bells, The. Weeknight Service. David Herbert Lawrence. **CP-LawrD**
Five Old Favorites. James Merrill. **SP-MerrJ**
  Dandelion Sermon, The.
  Dream of Old Vienna, A.
  Event Without Particulars.
  Midnight Snack, The.
  Sundown and Starlight.
Five or four whippoorwhills. A Nature Note. Robert Frost. **CP-FrosR**
Five Pilgrims in the Prologue to the Canterbury Tales. Roy Fisher.
  Cook. **SP-FishR**
  Dyere. **SP-FishR**
  Knight. **SP-FishR**
  Tapicer. **SP-FishR**
  Webbe. **SP-FishR**
Five planets and a brilliant young moon. Moon and Five Planets. Robinson Jeffers. **CP-JefR3**
Five P.M. Ted Kooser. **SP-KoosT**
Five Poems about Poetry. George Oppen. **CP-OppeG**
  From Virgil. **NNaP**
  Gesture, The. **NNaP**
  Little Hole, The.
  Parousia.
  That Land.
Five Poems for Dolls. Margaret Atwood. **SP-AtwM2**
Five Poems for Grandmothers. Margaret Atwood. **SP-AtwM2**
  "Goodbye, mother / of my mother, old bone."
  "How little I know / about you finally." **CrSp**
  "In the house on the cliff."
  "It is not the things themselves."
  "Some kind of ritual / for your dwindling."
Five Poems from Mexico. Denise Levertov. **CP-LeveD**
Five rings light your approach across. A Father out Walking on the Lawn. Rita Dove. **SP-DoveR**
V. "Rudely thou wrongst my dear heart's desire." Edmund Spenser. **EIL** *Fr.* Amoretti. **CP-Spens**
Five seeing, and seven blind. "Lewis Carroll." *Fr.* Solutions. *Fr.* Puzzles from Wonderland. **CP-CarrL**
Five sessions of God willing lethal x. Santorini: Stopping the Leak. James Merrill. **SP-MerrJ**
Five shadows in heavy motion, lumbering half-seen. Tarpon. Laurence Lieberman. **SP-LiebL**
Five slender birches grouped in peace. *Poet, The.* Alun Lewis. *Fr.* Poems from the Chinese. **CP-LewiA**
Five soldiers fixed by Mathew Brady's eye. Looking into History. Richard Wilbur. **CP-WilbR**
Five Songs ("Deftly, admiral, cast your fly"). Wystan Hugh Auden. **CP-AudeW**
Five Songs ("What's in your mind, my dove, my coney"). Wystan Hugh Auden. **CP-AudeW**
  "Deftly, admiral, cast your fly." **GTBS-6; GTBS-P**
  (Song: "Deftly, admiral, cast your fly.") **GTBS-6; GTBS-P**
  "Emperor's favorite concubine, The."
  "For what as easy." **NoP; PeLV**
  (Love Song: "For what as easy.") **PeLV**
  "Make this night loveable." **TW**
  (Song: "Make this night loveable.") **TW**
  " 'O where are you going?' said reader to rider." **CMoP; CoGr; FaBoCh; LiTB; LiTM; MeMAP; NOBE; NoAM; OAEL-2; SoSe; UV**
  (Epilogue: " 'O where are you going?' said reader to rider.") **FaBoCh**
  (Song: " 'O where are you going?' said reader to rider.") **OAEL-2**
  "Seen when nights are silent."
  "Starling and a willow-wren, A." **FaBoMo**
  "That night when joy began." **OxBTC; PAI; SoSe**
  "What's in your mind, my dove, my coney."
  "When rites and melodies begin." **NePA; OAEL-2**
  (Proof, The.) **NePA; OAEL-2**
Five Stanzas for My Two Brothers. Siv Cedering Fox. **SP-CedeS**
Five Students, The. Thomas Hardy. **CP-HardT**
Five summer days, five summer nights. The Blue-Fly. Robert Ranke Graves. **CP-GravR**
5:30 A.M. Adrienne Rich. **CP-RicAE; SP-RicA1; SP-RicA2**
Five thousand lovers I would have taken. Madness. Al Young. **CP-YounA**
Five thousand souls are here, and all are bounded. A Troopship in the Tropics. Alun Lewis. **CP-LewiA**
Five Towns on the B. and O. Carl Sandburg. **CP-SandC**
Five Virgins, The, *English tr. of* Les Cinq Vierges. Thomas Merton, *tr. fr. French by* William Davis. **CP-MertT**
Five windows light the cavern'd Man; thro' one he breathes the air. Europe; A Prophecy. William Blake. **CP-BlakW**
Five Women. Marsden Hartley. **CP-HartM**
Five Women Bathing in Moonlight. Richard Wilbur. **CP-WilbR**

Five-Year Step, A. John Ciardi. **SP-CiarJ**

Five years are vanished since I first poured out. Residence in London. William Wordsworth. *Fr.* The Prelude; Growth of a Poet's Mind [1805 vers.]. **CP-WorW3**

Five years have passed [*or* past]; five summers, with the length. Lines Composed a Few Miles above Tintern Abbey on Revisiting the Banks of the Wye during a Tour, July 13, 1798. William Wordsworth. **CP-WorW1**

Five years of cringing child small. The Child. Richard Eberhart. **CP-EberR**

Five years since you died and I am. Letter to a Dead Father. Richard Shelton. **SP-ShelR**

Fix this pothook of beauty on this palette. Serena III. Samuel Beckett. **CP-BeckS**

Fix your eyes on any chance object. For instance. Brotherhood in Pain. Robert Penn Warren. **SP-WarrR**

Fixed is the doom; and to the last of years. Robert Louis Stevenson. **CP-StevR**

Fixed Stars. Peter Meinke. **SP-MeinP**

Fixing a Hole. The Beatles. **CP-Beatl**

Fixing the Clock. Isabella Gardner. **CP-GardI**

Fixture, A. Gilbert Sorrentino. **SP-SorrG**

Fl / a / tt / ene / d d. Edward Estlin Cummings. **CP-CummE**

Flaccus, there are creatures for you over-Gothic. Louis MacNeice. *Fr.* Memoranda to Horace. **CP-MacNL**

Flag, The. Richard Eberhart. **CP-EberR**

Flag. Shel Silverstein. **SP-SilS2**

Flag of Ecstasy. Charles Henri Ford. **SP-FordC**

Flag that hung half-mast to-day, The. The Hon. Sec. Sir John Betjeman. **CP-BetjJ**

Flags are up again along the coast, The. Coast of Maine. Richard Eberhart. **CP-EberR**

Flags beyond those dunes are roaring, The. One by Twachtman at the Frye. Richard Hugo. **CP-HugoR**

Flags in the water, The. Flushing Meadows. Louis Zukofsky. *Fr.* Sequence 1944-6. **CP-ZukLS**

Flags of the Pacific. The Wedding of the Rose and the Lotus. Nicholas Vachel Lindsay. **CP-LindV**

Flags of war like storm-birds fly, The. The Battle Autumn of 1862. John Greenleaf Whittier. **CP-WhitJ**

Flailed from the heart of water in a bow. Ballade for the Duke of Orléans. Richard Wilbur. **CP-WilbR**

Flake the Wind exasperate, The. Emily Dickinson. **CP-DickE**

Flakes pour to the black dead. In the Camp There Was One Alive. Randall Jarrell. **CP-JarrR**

Flame, The. Louise McNeill. **SP-McNeL**

Flame. Charles Tomlinson. **CP-TomlC**

Flame at my footfall, Parnassus! Apollo. Apollo and the Fates. Robert Browning. **CP-BroR2**

Flame blue wisps in the west. October Paint. Carl Sandburg. **CP-SandC**

Flame crept up the prtrait line by line, The. The Photograph. Thomas Hardy. **CP-HardT**

Flame from each finger, A. I Am A Light You Could Read By. Marge Piercy. **SP-PierM**

Flame guttered, flared impossibly high, The. Dazzle of Darkness. Robert Ranke Graves. **CP-GravR**

Flame in the pit, flame. Last Judgement. Charles Tomlinson. **CP-TomlC**

Flame of a Candle, The. Howard Nemerov. **CP-NemeH**

Flame of rushlight in the cell, A. Saint Cadoc. Sir John Betjeman. **CP-BetjJ**

Flame-red moon, the harvest moon, The. The Harvest Moon. Ted Hughes. **SP-HughT**

Flames of a blasted escape. Long Enough. Thomas Merton. **CP-MertT**

Flaming / They seem / To come, sometimes. The Secret. Kenneth Koch. *Fr.* Days and Nights. **SP-KochK**

Flaming Heart, The. Richard Crashaw. **CP-CrasR**

  "Live here, great heart; and love and dy and kill." **OBS**

  "Live in these conquering leaves; live all the same." **OXAEP-1**

  "O Heart! that equal poise of love's both parts." **GeHe; TrGrPo**

  "O thou undaunted daughter of desires!" **HAP; NOBE; OBEV**

  (Upon the Book and Picture of the Seraphical Saint Teresa.) **NOBE; OBEV**

Flaming sighs that boil within my breast, The. Sir Thomas Wyatt. **CP-WyatT**

Flamingos of the Soda Lakes. Laurence Lieberman. **SP-LiebL**

Flammonde. Edwin Arlington Robinson. **CP-RobiE**

Flanders. Carl Sandburg. **CP-SandC**

Flanders, the name of a place, a country of people. Flanders. Carl Sandburg. **CP-SandC**

Flanking the place, / a cypress. At Sant' Antimo. Charles Tomlinson. **CP-TomlC**

Flapper. David Herbert Lawrence. **CP-LawrD**

Flapper, The. Allen Tate. **CP-TateA**

Flapper Vote. David Herbert Lawrence. **CP-LawrD**

Flash, The. James Dickey. **CP-DickJ**

Flash Back. Allen Ginsberg. **CP-GinsA**

Flash Crimson. Carl Sandburg. **CP-SandC**

Flash Flood. William DeWitt Snodgrass. **SP-SnodW**

Flash of falling metals. The shower of parts, cameras, guns of experience, The. Thomas Merton. *Fr.* Cables to the Ace. **CP-MertT**

Flash of lightning and we see enameled, The. Girl at Sixteen with Lightning. Gilbert Sorrentino. *Fr.* Twelve Études for Voice and Kazoo. **SP-SorrG**

Flashboat, The. Jane Cooper. **SP-CoopJ**

  "And here is that part of my dream I would like to forget."

  "High deck. Blue skies overhead. White distance, A."

  "I did not protest. I spoke nothing but the truth."

  "Now it's our turn. Three a.m."

Flashes. James Schuyler. **CP-SchuJ**

Flashing Cliff, A. Muriel Rukeyser. **CP-RukeM**

Flat. Charles Kenneth Williams. **CP-WillC; SP-WillC**

Flat as to an eagle's eye. George Meredith. **PeVV** *Fr.* The Nuptials of Attila. **CP-MerG1**

Flat as to an eagle's eye. The Nuptials of Attila. George Meredith. **CP-MerG1**

Flat Earth folk will lift their eyes, The. Orientations. John Hewitt. **CP-HewiJ**

Flat, eventless afternoon. To a Fish Head Found on the Beach Near Málaga. Philip Levine. **SP-LeviP**

Flat-Foot's Song. David Herbert Lawrence. **CP-LawrD**

Flat gray banana store front, The. Unintentional Paint. Carl Sandburg. **CP-SandC**

Flat land lies under water, The. Basil Bunting. **CP-BuntB**

Flat Lands. Carl Sandburg. **CP-SandC**

Flat One, A. William DeWitt Snodgrass. **SP-SnodW**

Flat Roofs. Ernest Hemingway. **CP-HemiE**

Flat Suburbs, S.W., in the Morning. David Herbert Lawrence. **CP-LawrD**

Flat Waters of the West in Kansas. Carl Sandburg. **CP-SandC**

Flat with variations. Not. Delft. Rita Dove. **SP-DoveR**

Flat year, when summer never arrived, The. Graves. Richard Hugo. **CP-HugoR**

Flatbush. Peter Meinke. **SP-MeinP**

Flatfish. Dabney Stuart. **SP-StuaD**

Flatness is all. The sunfish lives in it. Post-Therapy Room. William Dickey. **SP-DickW**

Flatted Fifths. Langston Hughes. **SP-HughL**

Flattened shape / the first shape, The. Andrew Lord Poems. James Schuyler. **CP-SchuJ**

Flattening dough for pastry. Labor and Tribulation. James McAuley. *Fr.* Requiem. **SP-McAuJ**

Flattered at having no. An Anglican Lady. Donald Davie. **CP-DavDo**

Flattered by grief, the changeable spirit. Muriel Rukeyser. *Fr.* Night-Music. **CP-RukeM**

Flattered with promise of escape. Thoughts on the Seasons. William Wordsworth. **CP-WorW2**

Flatterers, The. Marsden Hartley. **CP-HartM**

Flatterie. Robert Herrick. **CP-HerrR**

Flattery. William Carlos Williams. **CP-WilW2**

Flattest place, it seems, in Hellas. Bad Dream. Louis MacNeice. *Fr.* Cock o' the North. **CP-MacNL**

Flatting Mill, The. William Cowper. **CP-CowpW**

Flaubert in Egypt. Robert Penn Warren. **SP-WarrR**

Flaubert wanted to write a novel. Style. Howard Nemerov. **CP-NemeH**

Flaunt of the sunshine I need not your bask. Walt Whitman. **TrGrPo** *Fr.* Song of Myself. **CP-WhitW**

Flavius, if your girl friend. Catullus. *See* Carmen 6: "Your most recent acquisition, Flavius."

Flavius—that delicate lass—to Catullus. Catullus. *See* Carmen 6: "Your most recent acquisition, Flavius."

Flaw, The. Robert Lowell. **SP-LoweR**

Flea, The. John Donne. **CP-DonnJ**

Fleas, too, / have fled, The. Charles Kenneth Williams. **CP-WillC**

Flèche d'Or. James Merrill. **SP-MerrJ**

Fleck of sky you are. Mother to Babe. George Meredith. **CP-MerG1**

Fleckings, The. John Updike. **CP-UpdiJ**

Flecknoe, an English Priest at Rome. Andrew Marvell. **CP-MarvA**

Fled are the frosts, and now the fields appear[e]. Farewell Frost; or, Welcome the Spring. Robert Herrick. **CP-HerrR**

Fled are those times, when, in harmonious strains. Truth in Poetry. George Crabbe. **SP-CrabG** *Fr.* The Village.

Fledgling, The. Edna St. Vincent Millay. **CP-MillE**

Fle[e] fro[m] the pres[s] [or prees] and dwelle with soothfastnesse [or soth[e]fastnesse]. Geoffrey Chaucer. **CP-ChauG** (Truth.) **CP-ChauG**

Flee into some forgotten night and be. The Tryst. Walter de la Mare. **CP-DeLaW**

Flee on Your Donkey. Anne Sexton. **CP-SextA**

Fleeing from short-haired mad executives. Two Climbs. Wystan Hugh Auden. **CP-AudeW**

Fleet Astronomer can bore, The. Vanity [or Vanitie] (1). George Herbert. **CP-HerbG**

Fleet of Deer, A. Patti Smith. **SP-SmitP**

Fleet ships encountering on the high seas. Good Ships. John Crowe Ransom. **SP-RansJ**

Fleet Visit. Wystan Hugh Auden. **CP-AudeW**

Fleeting, The. Walter de la Mare. **CP-DeLaW**

Fleg. Charles Bukowski. **SP-BukC2**

Fleming Helphenstine. Edwin Arlington Robinson. **CP-RobiE**

Flesh. Robert Creeley. **CP-CreeR**

Flesh and Blood. Adrienne Rich. **CP-RicAE**

Flesh and the Spirit, The. Anne Bradstreet. **CP-BradA**

Flesh covers the bone, The. Alone with Everybody. Charles Bukowski. **SP-BukC1**

Flesh has knowledge of the flesh, The. Regard of Tangents. Stanley Jasspon Kunitz. **CP-KuniS**

Flesh, of a sudden, gone nameless in music, flesh. Old Nigger on One-Mule Cart Encountered Late at Night When Driving Home from Party in the Back Country. Robert Penn Warren. **SP-WarrR**

Flesh of Her. Jim Morrison. **SP-MorrJ**

Flesh of our flesh—bone of our bone. Burial Anthem. Christina Georgina Rossetti. **CP-RosC3**

Flesh of the house is heavy sea-orphaned stone, the imagination of, The. Winged Rock. Robinson Jeffers. **CP-JefR2**

Flesh they say is stronger, The. What the Lion Said to the Child. Archibald MacLeish. *Fr.* Songs for Eve. **CP-MacLA**

Flesh's / signals. Robert Creeley. **CP-CreeR**

Fleuves et océans. Samuel Beckett. **CP-BeckS**

Flew in from Miami Beach BOAC. Back in the USSR. John Lennon *and* Paul McCartney. **CP-Beatl**

Flicker / of *this* light / on consciousness—a. Christmas: May 10, 1970. Robert Creeley. **CP-CreeR**

Flickering / in the buildings. Rock Flow, River Mix. Muriel Rukeyser. **CP-RukeM**

Flickering of incessant rain. John Gould Fletcher. **SP-FletJ** *Fr.* Irradiations.

Flickering shades, / Stick figures, lithe game. The Hunt by Night. Derek Mahon. **SP-MahoD**

Flies. Donald Hall. **CP-HallD**

Flight, The. Walter de la Mare. **CP-DeLaW**

Flight, The. John Haines. **SP-HainJ**

Flight, The. Marsden Hartley. **CP-HartM**

Flight. John Hewitt. **CP-HewiJ**

Flight, The. Rudyard Kipling. **CP-KiplR**

Flight. Robert Lowell. **SP-LoweR**

Flight. George Oppen. **CP-OppeG**

Flight, The. Theodore Roethke. **NAAL-2; RB; TRP; TrGrPo** *Fr.* The Lost Son. **CP-RoetT**

Flight. Anne Sexton. **CP-SextA**

Flight, The. Charles Tomlinson. **CP-TomlC**

Flight. Charles Kenneth Williams. **CP-WillC**

Flight from Bootle, The. Sir John Betjeman. **CP-BetjJ**

Flight into Egipt, The. Robert Southwell. **CP-SoutR**

Flight into Egypt, The. Wystan Hugh Auden. **CP-AudeW** *Fr.* For the Time Being; a Christmas Oratorio. **CP-AudeW**

"He is the Way." **EaLo**

"Well, so that is that. Now we must dismantle the tree." **LiTA; MeMAP; MoAB; MoBrPo; OAEL-2; OBCP**

(After Christmas.) **MoAB; MoBrPo**

(Narrator.) **MeMAP**

Flight into Egypt, The. Thomas Merton. **CP-MertT; SP-MertT**

Flight of Apollo, The. Stanley Jasspon Kunitz. **CP-KuniS**

"Earth was my home, but even there I was a stranger."

"I was stranger on earth."

Flight of Lin Hui, The. Chuang Tzu, *tr. fr. Chinese by* Thomas Merton. **CP-MertT**

Flight of six heavy-motored bombing-planes, A. The Great Sunset. Robinson Jeffers. **CP-JefR2**

Flight of Swans. Robinson Jeffers. **CP-JefR2**

Flight of the bird—any bird—measuring, The. The Flight. Marsden Hartley. **CP-HartM**

Flight of the Duchess, The. Robert Browning. **CP-BroR1**

Flight of the Duchess, The. Robert Browning. **CP-BroR1**

"And were I not, as a man may say, cautious." **OBCoV**

Flight of the Heart. Louis MacNeice. **CP-MacNL**

Flight to Catalina. Erica Jong. **SP-JongE**

Flight to the City. William Carlos Williams. **CP-WilW1**

Flightily falling words like yellow. Idle Talk. Louis MacNeice. **CP-MacNL**

Fling out your banners, your honors be bringing. Emancipation. Paul Laurence Dunbar. **CP-DunbP**

Fling your red scarf faster and faster, dancer. Mask. Carl Sandburg. **CP-SandC**

Flint. Christina Georgina Rossetti. **OxBChV; RHPC; TiPo** *Fr.* Sing-Song. **CP-RosC2**

Flint and Steel. Thomas McGrath. **SP-McGrT**

Flintlike, her feet struck. Hardcastle Crags. Sylvia Plath. **CP-PlatS**

Flippancies. Richard Wilbur. **CP-WilbR**

Star System, The. **NBLV**

What's Good for the Soul is Good for Sales. **NBLV**

Flirt. John Updike. **CP-UpdiJ**

Flirt. Al Young. **CP-YounA**

Flirtation. Rita Dove. **SP-DoveR**

Flirt's Tragedy, The. Thomas Hardy. **CP-HardT**

Float / ing / ly) / i / (in Khoury's warm). Edward Estlin Cummings. **CP-CummE**

FloatfloaflofIf / lloloa. Edward Estlin Cummings. **CP-CummE**

Floating. Kenneth Rexroth. **SP-RexrK**

Floating cloud follows the sun, The. To Li Po. Tu Fu, *tr. fr. Chinese by* William Carlos Williams *with* David Rafael Wang. **CP-WilW2**

Floating Gardens. Joseph Ceravolo. **SP-CeraJ**

Floating of a leaf that fell, The. The Golden Leaf. Kathleen Jessie Raine. **SP-RainK**

Floating Poem, Unnumbered, The. Adrienne Rich. **NALW; NoAM** *Fr.* Twenty-one Love Poems. **SP-RicA1; SP-RicA2**

Floating thru morning. Friday the 12th. Al Young. **CP-YounA**

Floats. A masked soul listening for death. And Owl. Ted Hughes. **SP-HughT**

Flock, The. Derek Walcott. **CP-WalcD**

Flock of seagulls on a field—, A. False Postulate. Jenny Joseph. **SP-JoseJ**

Flock of sheep that leisurely pass by, A. To Sleep. William Wordsworth. **CP-WorW1**

Flocks feed by darkness with a noise of whispers. Carol. Thomas Merton. **CP-MertT; SP-MertT**

Flood, The. Elizabeth Bishop. **CP-BishE**

Flood, The. Robert Frost. **CP-FrosR**

Flood. William Matthews. **SP-MattW**

Everywhere.

Flood Light.

Flood Peak.

Flood Plain.

Record Flood.

Taken at the Flood.

Waters, The.

Flood. Chuck Miller. **SP-MillC**

Flood, The. John Milton. **NOSC** *Fr.* Book XI. *Fr.* Paradise Lost. **CP-MiltJ**

Flood, The. Charles Tomlinson. **CP-TomlC**

Flood, if he has for him and his a bit. Upon Flood, Or a Thankfull Man. Robert Herrick. **CP-HerrR**

Flood Light. William Matthews. *Fr.* Flood. **SP-MattW**

Flood Peak. William Matthews. *Fr.* Flood. **SP-MattW**

Flood Plain. William Matthews. *Fr.* Flood. **SP-MattW**

Flood Symphony, The. John Gould Fletcher. **SP-FletJ**

Flood that swept her to be slave, The. George Meredith. *Fr.* Napoléon. **CP-MerG1**

Flood-tide below me! I see you face to face! Crossing Brooklyn Ferry. Walt Whitman. **CP-WhitW**

Flood waters in Brigantine. The Landscape. Stephen Dunn. **SP-DunnS**

Flood with reed-grown slime banks, till I be past. 3.5. Ovid. **CP-MarlC,** *tr. by* Christopher Marlowe; *Fr.* Elegies.

Flooded Meadows. Thom Gunn. **CP-GunnT**

Floods, The. Rudyard Kipling. **CP-KiplR**

Floods are roused, and will not soon be weary, The. Nunnery. William Wordsworth. *Fr.* Poems Composed or Suggested During a Tour, in the Summer of 1833. **CP-WorW2**

Floods Clap Their Hands, The. Bible, *O.T. See* Psalm 98: "O sing unto the Lord a new song. . . ."

Floor / of the temple, the. Trance. Hilda Doolittle. **CP-DoolH**

Floor. Charles Kenneth Williams. **CP-WillC; SP-WillC**

Flora. Charlotte Smith. **CP-SmitC**

Floral Decorations for Bananas. Wallace Stevens. **CP-StevW**

Floral Teaching. Christina Georgina Rossetti. **CP-RosC3**

Florence, for Mary McCarthy. Robert Lowell. **SP-LoweR**

Florence. Patti Smith. **SP-SmitP**

Florence, Bologna, Parma, Modena. Italy and the World. Elizabeth Barrett Browning. **CP-BroEB**

Florentine Ingratitude. William Blake. **CP-BlakW**

Florentine mosquito / Afloat on black air. Mosquito in Florence. Stephen Spender. *Fr.* Lost Days. **CP-SpenS**

Florentines. Geoffrey Hill. **CP-HillG**

Florida. Elizabeth Bishop. **CP-BishE**

Florida Night, A. Paul Laurence Dunbar. **CP-DunbP**

Floris in Italy, Fragments. Gerard Manley Hopkins. **CP-HopkG**

Florist Rose, The. Robert Ranke Graves. **CP-GravR**

Florists, who have fondly watch'd. A Walk in the Shrubbery. Charlotte Smith. **CP-SmitC**

Floruit, floret, floreat! Cheltenham. Sir John Betjeman. **CP-BetjJ**

Floss won't save you from an Abyss. Emily Dickinson. **CP-DickE**

Flossie put the velvet pansies. The Modest Achievement. William Carlos Williams. **CP-WilW2**

Flotsam. Walter de la Mare. **CP-DeLaW**

Flotsam and jetsam / are gentlemen poeds. Edward Estlin Cummings. **CP-CummE; SP-CummE**

Flounder. Robert Lowell. **SP-LoweR**

Flounderlike, poetry. Double Exposure. Archie Randolph Ammons. **SP-AmmoA**

Flourishing vine, whose kindling clusters glow. Fragment: The Vine-Shroud. Percy Bysshe Shelley. **CP-ShelP**

Flow down, cold rivulet, to the sea. Farewell, A. Tennyson. **CP-TennA**

Flow, Flow, Flow. Stevie Smith. **CP-SmitS**

Flow, flow the waves hated. Ralph Waldo Emerson. **CP-EmerR**
    (Motto to "Illusions.") **CP-EmerR**

Flow Gently, Sweet Afton. Robert Burns.
    (Afton Water.) **CP-BurnR**

Flow of Thought. Richard Eberhart. **CP-EberR**

Flow was toward the land, The. Soul. Richard Eberhart. **CP-EberR**

Flow, water, the blue water. All Is Safe. Kenneth Patchen. **CP-PatcK**

Flower, The. Robert Creeley. **CP-CreeR**

Flower, The. Robert Creeley. **CP-CreeR**

Flower, The. Walter de la Mare. **CP-DeLaW**

Flower, The. George Herbert. **CP-HerbG**

Flower / lovingly pressed in an album. A Very Small Casualty. Phoebe Hesketh. **SP-HeskP**

Flower, The. Robert Penn Warren. *Fr.* To a Little Girl, One Year Old, in a Ruined Fortress. **SP-WarrR**

Flower, The. William Carlos Williams. **CP-WilW1**

Flower, The. William Carlos Williams. **CP-WilW1**

Flower Arrangements. Howard Nemerov. **CP-NemeH**

Flower-Arranging Summer, A. May Sarton. **SP-SartM**

Flower asked: "Will my scent, / Perhaps, survive me?", The. Meditation before an Ancient Poem. Pablo Antonio Cuadra, *tr. fr. Spanish by* Thomas Merton. **CP-MertT**

Flower Boat, The. Robert Frost. **CP-FrosR**

Flower Dump. Theodore Roethke. **CP-RoetT**

Flower Garden at Coleorton Hall, Leicestershire, A. William Wordsworth. **CP-WorW2**

Flower-Gathering. Robert Frost. **CP-FrosR**

Flower god, god of the spring, beautiful, bountiful. Robert Louis Stevenson. **CP-StevR**

Flower grows, The. Charles Olson. **CP-OlsoC**

Flower Herding on Mount Monadnock. Galway Kinnell. **SP-KinnG**

Flower—I never fancied, jewel—I profess you! Magical Nature. Robert Browning. **CP-BroR2**

Flower I took away and wither and fear—, The. title same as that of the longer work. Robert Lowell. *Fr.* Eight Months Later. **SP-LoweR**

Flower in a Letter, A. Elizabeth Barrett Browning. **CP-BroEB**

Flower in the crannied wall. Tennyson. **CP-TennA**

Flower in the glass peanut bottle formerly in the kitchen crooked to take. Transcription of Organ Music. Allen Ginsberg. **CP-GinsA**

Flower it blaws, it fades, it fa's, The. Lovely Polly Stewart. Robert Burns. **CP-BurnR**

Flower keeps it's appointment. Emily Dickinson. **SP-DickE**

Flower, memory—. Kathleen Jessie Raine. **SP-RainK**

Flower must not blame the Bee, The. Emily Dickinson. **CP-DickE**

Flower of Mending, The. Nicholas Vachel Lindsay. **CP-LindV**

Flower of the Fruit, The. Alfonso Cortes, *tr. fr. Spanish by* Thomas Merton. **CP-MertT**

Flower of the Ruins, The. George Meredith. **CP-MerG1**

Flower Show. Louis MacNeice. **CP-MacNL**

Flower that smiles to-day, The. Mutability. Percy Bysshe Shelley. **CP-ShelP**

Flower, The / fallen / she saw it. The Loving Dexterity. William Carlos Williams. **CP-WilW2**

Flower unfolds its dawning cup, The. Song. George Meredith. **CP-MerG1**

Flower was offered [*or* offerd] to me, A. My Pretty Rose Tree. William Blake. **CP-BlakW** *Fr.* Songs of Experience.

Flower will not trouble her, it has so small a Foot, A. Emily Dickinson. **CP-DickE**

Flowering, The. Jim Morrison. **SP-MorrJ**

Flowering / of god-like people, The. The Flowering. Jim Morrison. **SP-MorrJ**

Flowering Aloe, The. Robert Ranke Graves. **CP-GravR**

Flowering breaker detonates its surf, The. Origins. Derek Walcott. **CP-WalcD**

Flowering Death. John Ashbery. **SP-AshbJ**

Flowering of the Rod, The. Hilda Doolittle. **CP-DoolH**
    "Blue-geese, white-geese, you may say." **NOBA**
    "It is no madness to say." **FaBoMo**

Flowering Plum. Louise Glück. **SP-GlücL**

Flowering stomach / scroll of leaf. Yellow Pitcher Plant. Thom Gunn. **CP-GunnT**

Flowerlike, The / animal perfume. Eros. Denise Levertov. **CP-LeveD**

Flowers. Robert Creeley. **CP-CreeR**

Flowers, The. Rudyard Kipling. **CP-KiplR**

Flowers. David Herbert Lawrence. **CP-LawrD**

Flowers, The. Robert Louis Stevenson. **CP-StevR**

Flowers. William Wordsworth. *Fr.* The River Duddon [A Series of Sonnets]. **CP-WorW2**

Flowers achieve their own floweriness and it is a miracle. Flowers and Men. David Herbert Lawrence. **CP-LawrD**

Flowers Alone, The. William Carlos Williams. **CP-WilW1**

Flowers and Men. David Herbert Lawrence. **CP-LawrD**

Flowers and Stationmaster. Wystan Hugh Auden. **CP-AudWJ**

Flowers Appear on the Earth, The. Christina Georgina Rossetti. **CP-RosC2**

Flowers are yours, The. A Rosebush in an Unlikely Garden. William Carlos Williams. **CP-WilW2**

Flowers by the Sea. William Carlos Williams. **CP-WilW1**

Flowers by the Sea. William Carlos Williams. **CP-WilW1**

Flowers can be cousins of the stars. There Are Different Gardens. Carl Sandburg. **CP-SandC**

Flowers in the Interval. Louis MacNeice. **CP-MacNL**
    "Because you intoxicate like all the drinks."
    "But to turn in on the world, you are all the places."
    "In still grey dawn a delicate tendril."
    "With you, pray not without you, trapped on the edge of the world."

Flowers in Winter. John Greenleaf Whittier. **CP-WhitJ**

Flowers like a gangster's funeral. Viewing the Body. William DeWitt Snodgrass. **SP-SnodW**

Flowers! My friend, be delighted with what you like; but with. Delighted with Bluepink. Kenneth Patchen. **CP-PatcK**

Flower's Name, The. Robert Browning. **CTC** *Fr.* Garden Fancies. **CP-BroR1**

Flowers of air / With lilac defining air. Air. Muriel Rukeyser. **CP-RukeM**

Flowers of the field, The. The Hawthorn Hath a Deathly Smell. Walter de la Mare. **CP-DeLaW**

Flowers of the Foothills & Mountain Valleys. Alice Notley. **SP-NotlA**

Flowers of the sea are brief, The. The Carrion Spring. Archibald MacLeish. *Fr.* The Pot of Earth. **CP-MacLA**

Flowers of the willow-herb are wool. Seed-Time. George Meredith. **CP-MerG1**

Flowers on the Top of the Pillars at the Entrance of the Cave. William Wordsworth. *Fr.* Poems Composed or Suggested During a Tour, in the Summer of 1833. **CP-WorW2**

Flowers preach to us if we will hear. Consider the Lilies of the Field. Christina Georgina Rossetti. **CP-RosC1**

Flowers remind of jewels. Song: Three Rings for Her. Robert Ranke Graves. **CP-GravR**

Flowers Tell Months. Carl Sandburg. **CP-SandC**

Flowers that a friend brings twice a week, The. Flower Arrangements. Howard Nemerov. **CP-NemeH**

Flowers that bloom in sun and shade / And glitter in the dew, The. Patience of Hope. Christina Georgina Rossetti. **CP-RosC2**

Flowers That I Left in the Ground, The. Leonard Cohen. **CP-CoheL**

Flowers through the window. Nantucket. William Carlos Williams. **CP-WilW1**

Flowers to the House. Kenneth Patchen. **CP-PatcK**

Flower's Tragedy, The. Thomas Hardy. **CP-HardT**

Flowers—Well—if anybody. Emily Dickinson. **CP-DickE**

Flowers with the ragged names. Companions. Archibald MacLeish. **CP-MacLA**

Flowing edge to edge. The Winds. William Carlos Williams. **CP-WilW1** *Fr.* A Folded Skyscraper.

Flowing River, A. William Carlos Williams. **CP-WilW2**

Floyd O'Brien, Teagardens Charlie & Jack. Who Cares, Long as It's B-Flat. Hayden Carruth. **CP-CarHS**

Flu. Al Young. **CP-YounA**

Fluidity, Charmouth. Steve Griffiths. **SP-GrifS**

Flukum couldn't stand the strain. Flukum. A Poem for Black Relocation Centers. Etheridge Knight. **SP-KnigE** *Fr.* Two Poems for Black Relocation Centers.

Flumen Tenebrarum. Richard Wilbur. **CP-WilbR**

Flung / far down, / as the / gull rises. Gull. Charles Tomlinson. **CP-TomlC**

Flung from demonic wombs. Gary Snyder. **CP-SnydG** *Fr.* Hunting. *Fr.* Myths and Texts.

Flung with door-slam and whistle-blow. Limbo. Phoebe Hesketh. **SP-HeskP**

Flunked out and laid-off. The Eisenhower Years. Paul Zimmer. **SP-ZimmP**

Flurry. John Updike. **CP-UpdiJ**

Flush or Faunus. Elizabeth Barrett Browning. **CP-BroEB**

Flush pink runner of the sun, The. Yellow Evening Star. Carl Sandburg. **CP-SandC**

Flushed by the spirit of the genial year. James Thomson. **OxAEP-1** *Fr.* Spring. *Fr.* The Seasons. **CP-ThomJ**

Flushing Meadows. Louis Zukofsky. *Fr.* Sequence 1944-6. **CP-ZukLS**

Flushing Meadows, 1939. Daniel Gerard Hoffman. **SP-HoffD**

Flute, The. Jelaluddin Rumi, *sometimes at. to* Hilali, *tr. fr.* Persian by Ralph Waldo Emerson. **CP-EmerR**

Flute Music. Charles Tomlinson. **CP-TomlC**

Flute-Music, with an Accompaniment. Robert Browning. **CP-BroR2**

Flute of the Lonely, The. Nicholas Vachel Lindsay. **CP-LindV**

Flute of water. . . green deep and hearing, The. The Crowded Net. Kenneth Patchen. **CP-PatcK**

Flute Song. Jane Cooper. **SP-CoopJ**

Flute Song. Hilda Doolittle. **CP-DoolH**

Flutesong willow winding weather. World War. Richard Eberhart. **CP-EberR**

Flutter of blue pigeon's wings, The. Pigeon. Carl Sandburg. **CP-SandC**

Fluttered Wings. Christina Georgina Rossetti. **CP-RosC2**

Fluttering spread thy purple pinions. A Love Song in the Modern Taste. Jonathan Swift. **CP-SwifJ**

Flux. Richard Eberhart. **CP-EberR**

Flux. Carl Sandburg. **CP-SandC**

Flux abalze flog a new. Phlox. Louis Zukofsky. **CP-ZukLS**

Flux cause. Samuel Beckett. **CP-BeckS**

Flux of Autumn, The. Jean Garrigue. **SP-GarrJ**

Fly, The. William Blake. *See* Little Fly.

Fly. Joseph Ceravolo. **SP-CeraJ**

Fly, The. Leonard Cohen. **CP-CoheL**

Fly, The. Galway Kinnell. **SP-KinnG**

Fly, The. Ogden Nash. **CP-NashO**

Fly, The. Karl Shapiro. **SP-ShapK**

Fly. John Updike. **CP-UpdiJ**

Fly about a Glass[e] of Burnt Claret, A. Richard Lovelace. **CP-LoveR**

Fly against the window pane, The. Captivity of the Fly. Archibald MacLeish. **CP-MacLA**

Fly Away, Fly Away. Christina Georgina Rossetti. **CP-RosC2**

Fly Caught in a Cobweb, A. Richard Lovelace. **CP-LoveR**

Fly, crane—your wing assumes no weight—. Lone Cheer from the Stands for a Bitter Crane. Richard Hugo. **CP-HugoR**

Fly down, Death: call me. Madboy's Song. Muriel Rukeyser. **CP-RukeM**

Fly envious Time, till thou run out thy race. On Time. John Milton. **CP-MiltJ**

Fly, fly, my friends, I have my death-wound, fly. Sonnet 20. Sir Philip Sidney. **NoSic; OAEL-1; TEP** *Fr.* Astrophil and Stella. **SP-SidnP**

Fly hence O! joy noe longer heere abide. Sonnet 29. Mary Sidney, Countess of Montgomery Wroth. **KTR** *Fr.* Pamphilia to Amphilanthus. **CP-WrotM**

Fly hence Pale Care, noe more remember. A Charroll Presented to Dr. Williams Bp. of Lincolne as a Newyears Guift. Robert Herrick. **CP-HerrR**

Fly in Amber. Isabella Gardner. **CP-GardI**

Fly into the Sun. "Lou Reed." **SP-ReedL**

Fly is not a nuisance to itself, The. Trying to Understand Violence. Jenny Joseph. **SP-JoseJ**

Fly me not, though I be gray. Upon His Gray Haires. Robert Herrick. **CP-HerrR**

Fly Me to the Moon. Miller Williams. **SP-WillM**

Fly not from him whose silent misery. To His Mistress Retiring in Affection. Thomas Carew. **CP-CareT**

Fly on into my poem. The John Coltrane Dance. Al Young. **CP-YounA**

Fly sleeps on the field of a green curtain, A. Flies. Donald Hall. **CP-HallD**

Fly, some kind Harbinger, to Grasmere-dale! William Wordsworth. **CP-WorW1**

Fly That Flew into My Mistress'[s] Eye, A. Thomas Carew. **CP-CareT**

Fly to my Mistresse, pretty pilfring Bee. The Present: or, The Bag of the Bee. Robert Herrick. **CP-HerrR**

Fly traiter joye whose end brings butt dispaire. Sonnet. Mary Sidney, Countess of Montgomery Wroth. *Fr.* Pamphilia to Amphilanthus. **CP-WrotM**

Flyer's Fall. Wallace Stevens. **CP-StevW**

Flying Above California. Thom Gunn. **CP-GunnT**

Flying and ravening Curses, bark no more! Louis MacNeice. *Fr.* Areopagus. **CP-MacNL**

Flying at night, above the clouds, all earthmarks spurned. The Star. Wendell Berry. **CP-BerrW**

Flying away to Milan / I look down and back at Paris. Plan du Centre de Paris à Vol D'Oiseau. Lawrence Ferlinghetti. **SP-FerlL**

Flying below Sea Level. Laurence Lieberman. **SP-LiebL**

Flying Crooked. Robert Ranke Graves. **CP-GravR**

Flying Dutchman, The. Edwin Arlington Robinson. **CP-RobiE**

Flying Elegy. Allen Ginsberg. **CP-GinsA**

Flying Festoon, The. Shel Silverstein. **SP-SilS2**

Flying Fish. Carl Sandburg. **CP-SandC**

Flying Home. Galway Kinnell. **SP-KinnG**

Flying House, and the May Queen Eternal, The. Nicholas Vachel Lindsay. **CP-LindV**

Flying Inland. John Yau. **SP-YauJo**

Flying Inside Your Own Body. Margaret Atwood. **SP-AtwM2**

Flying into a strange town, being met at the. On and Off the Road. Charles Bukowski. **SP-BukC3**

'Flying mare'—that / Throw in wrestling, The. The Wrestlers on the Vase. Charles Tomlinson. **CP-TomlC**

Flying Red Horse, The. Muriel Rukeyser. **CP-RukeM**

Flying, Reflying, Farming. Richard Hugo. **CP-HugoR**

Flying south-west—say Washington to Albuquerque. Sight and Flight. Charles Tomlinson. **CP-TomlC**

Flying to Hanoi. Muriel Rukeyser. **CP-RukeM**

Flying word from here and there, A. The Master. Edwin Arlington Robinson. **CP-RobiE**

Flying You Home. Erica Jong. **SP-JongE**

Foal of generous breed along the plains, The. The Horse. William Wordsworth. **CP-WorW1**

Foam lips / waters / in following folds. The Flight. Charles Tomlinson. **CP-TomlC**

Focherty. "Hugh MacDiarmid." **SP-MacDH**

Focus. Adrienne Rich. **CP-RicAE; SP-RicA1; SP-RicA2**

Focus. Charles Tomlinson. *Fr.* In Winter Woods. **CP-TomlC**

Foemineos dea quae nigro sub Limine manes. *acc. by English translation.* Thomas Campion. **CP-CampT**

Fog. Walter de la Mare. **CP-DeLaW**

Fog. Robinson Jeffers. **CP-JefR1**

Fog. Kenneth Patchen. **CP-PatcK**

Fog. Carl Sandburg. **CP-SandC**

Fog. Robert Penn Warren. **SP-WarrR**

Fog, and orchid sun. Signs. Charles Olson. **CP-OlsoC**

Fog, as it enters the lowland, is smoothing away, The. In December. Charles Tomlinson. **CP-TomlC**

Fog blows, The. The Mind's Notice. Charles Olson. **CP-OlsoC**

Fog burns off and the crowd mingles promiscuously, The. At the Barriers. Thom Gunn. **CP-GunnT**

Fog comes / on little cat feet, The. Fog. Carl Sandburg. **CP-SandC**

Fog drifts slowly down the hill, The. The Night Piece. Thom Gunn. **CP-GunnT**

Fog Envelops the Animals. James Dickey. **CP-DickJ**

Fog fills the little square. La Vie En Rose. Kenneth Rexroth. **SP-RexrK**

Fog has sealed in the house. On Cape Cod a Child Is Stolen. William Matthews. **SP-MattW**

Fog is departing, let it go. Odor, The. To Artemis. Hayden Carruth. **CP-CarHS**

Fog Numbers. Carl Sandburg. **CP-SandC**

Fog over the base: the beams ranging. A Front. Randall Jarrell. **CP-JarrR; SP-JarrR**

Fog Over the Sea and the Sun Going Down. Kenneth Patchen. **CP-PatcK**

Fog Portrait. Carl Sandburg. **CP-SandC**

Fog Township. Brendan Galvin. **SP-GalvB**

Fogged hill-scene on an enormous continent, A. Hunger. Adrienne Rich. **SP-RicA2**

Foggy Morning. Al Young. **CP-YounA**

Foggy Street. Andrei Voznesensky, *tr. fr. Russian by* Richard Wilbur. **CP-WilbR**

Foghorn in Horror. Muriel Rukeyser. **CP-RukeM**

Foil, The. George Herbert. **CP-HerbG**

Fold now thine armes; and hang the head. To Myrrha Hard-Hearted. Robert Herrick. **CP-HerrR**

Folded Skyscraper, A. William Carlos Williams.
    Hemmed-in Males. **CP-WilW1**
    Winds, The. **CP-WilW1**

Folding away my tools with the dead parts of. Bring Down the Beams. Charles Bukowski. **SP-BukC2**

Folds on your shirt lie like shadows. The Blue That Reminds Me of the Boat When She Left. Anne Waldman. **SP-WaldA**

Foliage has dropped, The. Wendell Berry. *Fr.* Window Poems. **CP-BerrW**

Folk Custom. John Hewitt. **CP-HewiJ**

Folk for Tea. John Hewitt. **CP-HewiJ**

Folk Singer of the Thirties, A. James Dickey. **CP-DickJ**

Folk Song, A: "Hitch up honey for the / market race all." Robert Creeley. **CP-CreeR**

Folk Tale. Daniel Gerard Hoffman. **SP-HoffD**

Folk Tune. Richard Wilbur. **CP-WilbR**

Folkestone Limerick. Robert Browning. **CP-BroR2**

Folks ain't got no right to censuah othah [*or* uthah] folks about dey habits. Accountability. Paul Laurence Dunbar. **CP-DunbP**

Folks built that barn, your great grandfather, and them, The. Mona Van Duyn. **SP-VanDM**

Folks, I'm telling you. Advice. Langston Hughes. **SP-HughL**

Folks is talkin' 'bout de money. The Real Question. Paul Laurence Dunbar. **CP-DunbP**

Folks, we'd have zero'd in to a big break-thru. Personal Packaging, Inc. Robert Ranke Graves. **CP-GravR**

Folks with no titles in front of their names, The. In Explanation of Our Times. Langston Hughes. **SP-HughL**

Folkways. Isabella Gardner. **CP-GardI**

Follen. John Greenleaf Whittier. **CP-WhitJ**

Follies. Carl Sandburg. **CP-SandC**

Follies of Adam, The. Theodore Roethke. **CP-RoetT**

Follow a shadow [*or* shaddow], it still flies you. Song. That Women Are But Men's Shadows. Ben Jonson. **CP-JonsB**

Follow, follow[e] / Though with mischiefe. Thomas Campion. **EnLoPo** *Fr.* Observations in the Art of English Poesie. **CP-CampT**

Follow its lazy main street lounging. Hawthorne. Robert Lowell. **SP-LoweR**

Follow me, follow me. Will o' the Wisp. George Meredith. **CP-MerG1**

Follow Me 'Ome. Rudyard Kipling. **CP-KiplR**

Follow That Stagecoach. Diane Wakoski. **SP-WakoD**

"Follow the Drinking Gourd. . . ." Robert Creeley. **CP-CreeR**

Follow the train full of bodies. Judge Every One with Perfect Calm. Alice Walker. **CP-WalkA**

Follow the ways of no man, not even your own. Thomas Merton. *Fr.* Cables to the Ace. **CP-MertT**

Follow Thy Fair Sun[ne] [Unhappy Shadow]. Thomas Campion. **CP-CampT**
    ("Followe thy faire sunne, unhappy shaddowe.") **CP-CampT**

Follow to the deep wood's weeds. Fragment. Percy Bysshe Shelley. **CP-ShelP**

Follow wise Orion. Emily Dickinson. **CP-DickE**

Follow Your Saint [Follow with Accents Sweet]. Thomas Campion. **CP-CampT**

Followe thy faire sunne, unhappy shaddowe. Thomas Campion. *See* Follow Thy Fair Sun[ne] [Unhappy Shadow].

Followed by garrulous hunters, the soft children grovel. All the Bright Foam of Talk. Kenneth Patchen. **CP-PatcK**

Follower. Seamus Heaney. **SP-HeanS**

Following day was overcast, each street, The. Pity. Richard Wilbur. **CP-WilbR**

Following It. Stephen Berg. **SP-BergS**

Following the white horse of the famous legend we shall cross. The Crossing. John Hewitt. **CP-HewiJ**

Folly of Being Comforted, The. William Butler Yeats. **CP-YeatW**

Folly of Clowns. Kenneth Patchen. **CP-PatcK**

Folly on Royal Street before the Raw Face of God. Robert Penn Warren. **SP-WarrR**

Folly would needs make mee a lover bee. Sonnet 10. Mary Sidney, Countess of Montgomery Wroth. *Fr.* Pamphilia to Amphilanthus. **CP-WrotM**

F.O.M. Muriel Rukeyser. **CP-RukeM**

Fond aged man, why doe you on me gaze. Mary Sidney, Countess of Montgomery Wroth. *Fr.* Part 1. *Fr.* Urania. **CP-WrotM**

Fond credos, plaster ecstasies! The Stranger. Adrienne Rich. **CP-RicAE**

Fond Farewell, A. William Carlos Williams. **CP-WilW2**

Fond man, that canst believe [*or* beleeve] her blood. Celia Bleeding, to the Surgeon. Thomas Carew. **CP-CareT**

Fond man, that hop'st to catch that face. To the Painter. Thomas Carew. **CP-CareT**

Fond scenes, which delighted my youthful existence. The Exile's Departure. John Greenleaf Whittier. **CP-WhitJ**

Fond woman, which wouldst [*or* would'st] have thy husband die. Jealousy. John Donne. **CBLP; ESCV; FF** *Fr.* Elegies. **CP-DonnJ**

Fond words have oft been spoken to thee, sleep! To Sleep. William Wordsworth. **CP-WorW1**

Fond youth! who dream'st that hoarded gold. From Menander. Menander, *tr. fr. Greek by* William Cowper. **CP-CowpW**

Fondling only to throttle the nuzzling moment. Restaurant Car. Louis MacNeice. **CP-MacNL**

Fone sayes, those mighty whiskers he do's weare. Upon Fone a Schoolmaster. Epigram. Robert Herrick. **CP-HerrR**

Font of Type, A. Walt Whitman. **CP-WhitW**

Font, the flint, the ammonite, The. Stone. John Hewitt. **CP-HewiJ**

Fontaine, Je Ne Boirai Pas De Ton Eau! Edna St. Vincent Millay. **CP-MillE**

Fontaine-les-Dijon Revisited. Daniel Gerard Hoffman. **SP-HoffD**

Fontanel. John Hewitt. **CP-HewiJ**

Fontenelle. Howard Nemerov. **CP-NemeH**

Food. Anne Sexton. **CP-SextA**

Food. John Updike. **CP-UpdiJ**

Food of the Dead. Robert Ranke Graves. **CP-GravR**

Food of the North. David Herbert Lawrence. **CP-LawrD**

Food on the walls of the dark tombs, The. Réchauffé. Louis MacNeice. **CP-MacNL**

Fool, The. "Hugh MacDiarmid." **SP-MacDH**

Fool, The. Charles Olson. **CP-OlsoC**

Fool, / put your adventures. Hero. William Carlos Williams. **CP-WilW1**

Fool, The. Stevie Smith. **CP-SmitS**

Fool by the Roadside, The. William Butler Yeats. **CP-YeatW**

Fool hath said in his heart, The, There is no God. Psalm 14. Bible, *O.T.* **TrJP** *Fr.* Psalms. **CP-Psal**

Fool hath said in his heart, The, There is no God. Psalm 53. Bible, *O.T. Fr.* Psalms. **CP-Psal**

Fool I was to sleep at noon, A. A Daughter of Eve. Christina Georgina Rossetti. **CP-RosC1**

Fool, if to keep thy wife thou hast no need. 2.19. Ovid. **CP-MarlC,** *tr. by* Christopher Marlowe; *Fr.* Elegies.

Fool is one, The. To a Novice. Thomas Merton. *Fr.* Readings from Ibn Abbad. **CP-MertT**

Fool much bit by fleas put out the light, A. Richard Lovelace, *after the Greek of* Lucian. **CP-LoveR**

Fool on the Hill, The. John Lennon. **CP-Beatl**

Fool there was and he made his prayer, A. The Vampire. Rudyard Kipling. **CP-KiplR**

Fooles are they, who never know. Best To Be Merry. Robert Herrick. **CP-HerrR**

Foolin' wid de Seasons. Paul Laurence Dunbar. **CP-DunbP**

Foolish About Windows. Carl Sandburg. **CP-SandC**

Foolish Heart, The. Countee Cullen. **CP-CullC**

Foolish poet wonders, The. The Poet Hin. Stevie Smith. **CP-SmitS**

Foolish queen of fairyland, The. Crickets on a Strike. Nicholas Vachel Lindsay. **CP-LindV**

Foolishnesse. Robert Herrick. **CP-HerrR**

Fools. Robert Ranke Graves. **CP-GravR**

Fool's Cap, The. John Hewitt. **CP-HewiJ**

Fool's Song, The. Walter de la Mare. **CP-DeLaW**

Fool's Song, The. William Carlos Williams. **CP-WilW1**

Fools, they are the only nation. Ben Jonson. **CP-JonsB** *Fr.* Volpone.

Foot-Note, A. William Carlos Williams. **CP-WilW1**

Foot of / a dog, The. Dog Crunch. Jim Carroll. **SP-CarrJ**

Foot of death has printed on my chest, The. Shudder [, The]. Donald Hall. **CP-HallD**

Football at Slack. Ted Hughes. **SP-HughT**

Football with white eyebrows the, A. Edward Estlin Cummings. **CP-CummE**

Footing Turf. John Hewitt. **CP-HewiJ**

Footlights cannot improve the grave. Emily Dickinson. **SP-DickE**

Footnote. James Schuyler. **CP-SchuJ**

Footnote, A. Stephen Spender. **CP-SpenS**

Footnote to Howl. Allen Ginsberg. **CP-GinsA**

Footnotes to "Anne-on-Avon." David Markson. **CP-MarkD**

Footnotes to "The Autobiography of Bertrand Russell." Mona Van Duyn. **SP-VanDM**

   "Once out of Eden, love learned its deviousness."

   "This seems, in a world where love must take its chances." **HAP**

Footprint and eye fringe. All Wise. Louis Zukofsky. **CP-ZukLS**

Footprint of a bird in sand brought your face, The. Bird Footprint. Carl Sandburg. **CP-SandC**

Footstep. Stephen Dobyns. **SP-DobyS**

For a Birthday. Thom Gunn. **CP-GunnT**

For a Boy Born in Wartime. Jane Cooper. **SP-CoopJ**

For a Brookline Lady I Love. Etheridge Knight. **SP-KnigE**

For a Bus on Its Side and the Man Inside It. Robert Creeley. **CP-CreeR**

For a countryman the living landscape is. Landscape. John Hewitt. **CP-HewiJ**

For a Critic Who Tries to Write Poems. Thomas McGrath. **SP-McGrT**

For a Dead Citizen. Allen Tate. **CP-TateA**

For a Dead Lady. Edwin Arlington Robinson. **CP-RobiE**

For a Fatherless Son. Sylvia Plath. **CP-PlatS**

For a Friend. Robert Creeley. **CP-CreeR**

For a Friend. Robert Creeley. **CP-CreeR**

For a Friend. Ted Kooser. **SP-KoosT**

For a Good Dog. Ogden Nash. **CP-NashO**

For a Heracles in his fighting ire there is never the glory that follows. The Labourer. George Meredith. **CP-MerG2**

For a kiss or two, confesse. A Bucolick betwixt Two: Lacon and Thyrsis. Robert Herrick. **CP-HerrR**

For a Lady I Know. Countee Cullen. **CP-CullC** *Fr.* Four Epitaphs.

For a Lady of Whom I Speak. Charles Olson. **CP-OlsoC**

For a Lamb. Richard Eberhart. **CP-EberR**

For a Little Girl of Pompeii. Brendan Galvin. **SP-GalvB**

For a long day and a night we read the names. Reading the Names of the Vietnam War Dead. Thomas McGrath. **SP-McGrT**

For a long time I used to get up early. Bird's-Eye View of the Tool and Die Co. John Ashbery. **SP-AshbJ**

For a long time now. Rolling Back. John Haines. **SP-HainJ**

For a long time unhappy. The Truce between the Sexes. Erica Jong. **SP-JongE**

For a long time, we shall have only to listen. The Time of Burning. May Sarton. **SRLS** *Fr.* The Invocation to Kali. **SP-SartM**

For a Lost Child. William Stafford. **SP-StafW**

For a Low Voice. William Carlos Williams. **CP-WilW2**

For a Man Gone to Stuttgart Who Left an Automobile Behind Him. Charles Olson. **CP-OlsoC**

For a man to come out of the sea, they. Evil. Charles Olson. **CP-OlsoC**

For a Market-Clock. Samuel Taylor Coleridge. **CP-ColeS**

For a Marriage. Louise Bogan. **CP-BogaL**

For a Mercy Received. Christina Georgina Rossetti. **CP-RosC3**

For a Mexican Painter. Muriel Rukeyser. **CP-RukeM**

For a Mild Season. John Hewitt. **CP-HewiJ**

For a Moment. David Herbert Lawrence. **CP-LawrD**

For a Moment of Darkness over the Nations. John Hewitt. **CP-HewiJ**

For a moment pause. The Mound. Thomas Hardy. **CP-HardT**

For a Mouthy Woman. Countee Cullen. **CP-CullC**

For a Muse Meant. Robert Duncan. **SP-DuncR**

For a New Year. Jenny Joseph. **SP-JoseJ**

For a night and a day. Wendell Berry. *Fr.* Window Poems. **CP-BerrW**

For a Northern Woman. Richard Hugo. **CP-HugoR**

For a Pessimist. Countee Cullen. **CP-CullC**

For a Picture of Saint Dorothea, *Shorter and diff. vers. of* Lines for a Picture of St. Dorothea; *see also* St. Dorothea. Gerard Manley Hopkins. **CP-HopkG**

For a Picture Where a Queen Laments over the Tomb of a Slain Knight. Thomas Carew. **CP-CareT**

For a Poet. Countee Cullen. **CP-CullC**

For a Russian Poet. Adrienne Rich. **CP-RicAE; SP-RicA2**

For a Screaming Lady. Robert Creeley. **CP-CreeR**

For a season there must be pain. The Widower. Rudyard Kipling. **CP-KiplR**

For a Seat in the Groves of Coleorton. William Wordsworth. **CP-WorW1**

For a September Afternoon of Unexpected Brightness. John Hewitt. **CP-HewiJ**

For a Sister. Adrienne Rich. **SP-RicA2**

For a Song of the Languagers. Robert Duncan. **SP-DuncR**

For a Stone Girl at Sanchi. Gary Snyder. **CP-SnydG**

For a Time and Place. James Dickey. **CP-DickJ**

For a time it is part of the machinery. Death and the Lovers. May Sarton. **SP-SartM**

For a week now our bodies have whispered. Sestina. Marilyn Hacker. **SP-HackM**

For a woman named Gorrel. Poor Gorrel. Kenneth Patchen. **CP-PatcK**

For a woman's face remembered as a spot of quick light on the flat land. Remembered Women. Carl Sandburg. **CP-SandC**

For a Young Artist. Robert Earl Hayden. **CP-HaydR**

For action born, existing to be tried. Near the Same Lake [Thrasymene]. William Wordsworth. *Fr.* Memorials of a Tour in Italy, 1837. **CP-WorW2**

For Advent. Christina Georgina Rossetti. **CP-RosC3**

For age is opportunity no less. Henry Wadsworth Longfellow. **PoToHe** *Fr.* Morituri Salutamus. **SP-LongH**

For ages, on our river borders. The First Flowers. John Greenleaf Whittier. **CP-WhitJ**

For Al—. Charles Bukowski. **SP-BukC1**

For Alexander there was no Far East. Worlds. Richard Wilbur. **CP-WilbR**

For All. Christina Georgina Rossetti. **CP-RosC2**

For All. Gary Snyder. **CP-SnydG**

For all his vehemence & hydraulic opinions. The Heroes. John Berryman. **CP-BerrJ**

For all night sins, with others' wives, unknown. On Old Colt. Ben Jonson. **CP-JonsB**

For all our workes, a recompence is sure. Satisfaction for Sufferings. Robert Herrick. **CP-HerrR**

For All That. David Herbert Lawrence. **CP-LawrD**

For All the Grief. Walter de la Mare. **CP-DeLaW**

For all they said, / I could not see the waterfall. The Waterfall. Mary Oliver. **SP-OlivM**

For all those who died. Erica Jong. **SP-JongE**

For all thy many courtesies to me. To his Faithfull Friend, Master John Crofts, Cup-bearer to the King. Robert Herrick. **CP-HerrR**

For All We Have and Are [1914]. Rudyard Kipling. **CP-KiplR**

For All Who Ever Sent Lace Valentines. Nicholas Vachel Lindsay. **CP-LindV**

For all who trod / Golden North American streets. James Liddy. *Fr.* A Munster Song of Love and War. **CP-LiddJ**

For Allen. Robert Creeley. **CP-CreeR**

For America is a lady rocking on a porch in an unpainted house. Sixth Psalm. Anne Sexton. *Fr.* O Ye Tongues. **CP-SextA**

For an Age of Plastics. [Plymouth]. Donald Davie. **CP-DavDo**

("With the effect almost of carving the hillside.") **CP-DavDo**

For an American. Kay Boyle. **CP-BoylK**

For an Amorous Lady. Theodore Roethke. **CP-RoetT**

For an Anarchist. Countee Cullen. **CP-CullC**

For an Anniversary. Robert Creeley. **CP-CreeR**

For an Atheist. Countee Cullen. **CP-CullC**

For an Autumn Festival. John Greenleaf Whittier. **CP-WhitJ**
   Harvest Hymn. **OHIP**

For an Earth-Landing. Erica Jong. **SP-JongE**

For an Evolutionist and His Opponent. Countee Cullen. **CP-CullC**

For an Exchange of Rings. Donald Hall. **CP-HallD**

For an hour he wonders what the girl could be thinking. The White Skirt. Stephen Dobyns. **SP-DobyS**

For an Orchard Tree. Jean Garrigue. **SP-GarrJ**

For Anne. Leonard Cohen. **CP-CoheL**

For Anne, at a Little Distance. John Haines. **SP-HainJ**

For Anne Gregory. William Butler Yeats. **CP-YeatW**

For Annie. Edgar Allan Poe. **CP-PoeEd**

For any Irishman. John Hewitt. **CP-HewiJ**

For any ruffian of the sky. Edward Estlin Cummings. **CP-CummE**

For any save a lover. George Meredith. **CP-MerG2**

For Any Women Who Pass This House. John Hewitt. **CP-HewiJ**

For Anybody. Robert Creeley. **CP-CreeR**

For Anybody's Martyr's Song. Jean Garrigue. **SP-GarrJ**

For Arl in Her Sixth Month. Al Young. **CP-YounA**

For Arthur Okamura. Robert Creeley. **CP-CreeR**

For Arvia. Edwin Arlington Robinson. **CP-RobiE**

For as many nights as there are. Jonathan Hawkins. Lewis Turco. *Fr.* Bordello. **SP-TurcL**

For as the baby springs out like a starfish into her million light. Tenth Psalm. Anne Sexton. *Fr.* O Ye Tongues. **CP-SextA**

For asking, why is there something. The Childhood of Parmenides. Charles Simic. **SP-SimiC**

For authorities whose hopes. The Paper Nautilus. Marianne Craig Moore. **CP-MoorM**

For awhile I thought I had gotten. The Cripple in the Subway. Louise Glück. **SP-GlücL**

For Barbara. ("Crawling out"). Chuck Miller. **SP-MillC**

For Barbara. ("Standing up"). Chuck Miller. **SP-MillC**

For Barbara. ("Wandering in"). Chuck Miller. **SP-MillC**

For being comely, consonant, and free. To His Brother in Law Master John Wingfield. Robert Herrick. **CP-HerrR**

For Benny and Sabina. Robert Creeley. **CP-CreeR**

For Betsy and Tom. Robert Creeley. **CP-CreeR**

For Billy Holt. Ted Hughes. **SP-HughT**

For Black Poets Who Think of Suicide. Etheridge Knight. **SP-KnigE**

For blocks the derelicts. Spokane Perspective. James McAuley. **SP-McAuJ**

For Bob Dash. James Schuyler. **CP-SchuJ**

For brave comportment, wit without offence. To His Honoured and Most Ingenious Friend, Mr. Charles Cotton. Robert Herrick. **CP-HerrR**

For Bryher and Perdita. Hilda Doolittle. *Fr.* Hymen. **CP-DoolH**

For Busha. John Hewitt. **CP-HewiJ**

For centuries only painters, poets and sculptors. The Aging Actress Sees Herself at the Late Show. Miller Williams. **SP-WillM**

For centuries sadhus live and die. Circumambulating Arunachala. Gary Snyder. **CP-SnydG**

For certain minutes at the least. Demon and Beast. William Butler Yeats. **CP-YeatW**

For Certain Subscribers to the Miners' Fund. John Hewitt. **CP-HewiJ**

For César Vallejo and his Profound Oxides of Sadness. Chuck Miller. **SP-MillC**

For Cherries plenty, and for Coran's. Being Treated to Ellinda. Richard Lovelace. **CP-LoveR**

For Children When They Grow Up. Charles Kenneth Williams. **CP-WillC**

For Christ's sake and for mine and last for a child's god gone. Malcolm Lowry. *Fr.* The Moon in Scandinavia. **CP-LowrM**

For Chuck Hinman. Robert Creeley. **CP-CreeR**

For civill, cleane, and circumcised wit. To His Honoured Friend, Sir John Mynts. Robert Herrick. **CP-HerrR**

For cosmos, which has too much to live up to. A Garland for Christopher Smart. Mona Van Duyn. **SP-VanDM**

For Creely's Ear. Allen Ginsberg. **CP-GinsA**

For C.W.B. Elizabeth Bishop. **CP-BishE**

For Cy Twombly Faced with His First Chicago & N.Y. Shows. Charles Olson. **CP-OlsoC**

For Danny. Grace Paley. **CP-PaleG**

For Danton. Charles Tomlinson. **CP-TomlC**

For Daphne at Lone Lake. John Haines. **SP-HainJ**

For Daughters of Magdalen. Countee Cullen. **CP-CullC**

For days neglected. Robert Creeley. **CP-CreeR**

For days the good old bitch had been dying, her back. Another Dog's Death. John Updike. **CP-UpdiJ**

For Death—or rather. Emily Dickinson. **CP-DickE**

For deathless powers to verse belong. Ralph Waldo Emerson. **CP-EmerR**

For Deirdre. John Hewitt. **CP-HewiJ**

For Deliverance from a Fever. Anne Bradstreet. **CP-BradA**

For Djuna Barnes. Charles Henri Ford. **SP-FordC**

    Jeweled Bat, The.

    Roots.

    Seis Hermanos.

For Dr. Dewey. Chuck Miller. **SP-MillC**

For Doreen. A Voice from the Garden. Donald Davie. **CP-DavDo**

For Doyle Fosso. Archie Randolph Ammons. **SP-AmmoA**

For Dudley. Richard Wilbur. **CP-WilbR**

For E. J. P. Leonard Cohen. **CP-CoheL**

For Each. Christina Georgina Rossetti. **CP-RosC2**

For each ecstatic instant. Emily Dickinson. **CP-DickE**

For Each of You. Audre Lorde. **SP-LordA**

For each one Body, that i'th earth is sowne. The Resurrection, Possible, and Probable. Robert Herrick. **CP-HerrR**

For ease of heart and mind / I estimate each stride. A Birthday Rhyme for Roberta. John Hewitt. **CP-HewiJ**

For Ebbe. Robert Creeley. **CP-CreeR**

For Eleanor and Bill Monahan. William Carlos Williams. **CP-WilW2**

For Eleanor Boylan Talking with God. Anne Sexton. **CP-SextA**

For Elektra. Marilyn Hacker. **SP-HackM**

For Eli Jacobson. Kenneth Rexroth. **SP-RexrK**

For Elizabeth. Jim Carroll. **SP-CarrJ**

For Ellen. Richard Wilbur. **CP-WilbR**

For Ethel Rosenberg. Adrienne Rich. **SP-RicA1; SP-RicA2**

For Eugene McCarthy. Robert Lowell. **SP-LoweR**

For Ever. Robert Ranke Graves. **CP-GravR**

For ever, Fortune, wilt thou prove. James Thomson. **CP-ThomJ** (To Fortune.) **CP-ThomJ**

For ever hallowed be this morning fair. Glad Tidings. William Wordsworth. *Fr.* Ecclesiastical Sonnets. **CP-WorW2**

For every Bird a Nest. Emily Dickinson. **CP-DickE**

For every god. Ralph Waldo Emerson. **CP-EmerR**

For every hour that thou wilt spare me now. Love's Usury. John Donne. **CP-DonnJ**

For Every Last Batch When the Next One Comes Along. William Dickey. **SP-DickW**

For every parcel I stoop down to seize. The Armful. Robert Frost. **CP-FrosR**

For exactly six seconds riding to work. One of Those Rare Occurrences on a City Bus. Miller Williams. **SP-WillM**

For Example. Gary Snyder. **CP-SnydG**

For Ezra Pound. Jim Carroll. **SP-CarrJ**

For Fathers of Girls. Stephen Dunn. **SP-DunnS**

For Fear. Robert Creeley. **CP-CreeR**

For fear strangers might intrude upon us. Fortunate Child. Robert Ranke Graves. **CP-GravR**

For February 14th. Marianne Craig Moore. **CP-MoorM**

For fifteen days my cobweb spun. Cobweb. John Hewitt. **CP-HewiJ**

For fifteen winter days. Ralph Waldo Emerson. **CP-EmerR**

"For fifteen years he never knew I never". Hayden Carruth. *Fr.* The Sleeping Beauty. **CP-CarHL**

For fifty thousand years man has been dreaming of powers. Robinson Jeffers. **CP-JefR3**

For fifty years the bubbles marked. Bay of Sad Loss. Richard Hugo. **CP-HugoR**

For five years the swallows did not build. The Swallows Return. Richard Eberhart. **CP-EberR**

For Floss. Denise Levertov. **CP-LeveD**

For Fog and Fate no charm is found. Destroyers in Collision. Rudyard Kipling. *Fr.* Epitaphs of the War [1914–1918]. **CP-KiplR**

For forms of government let fools contest. Alexander Pope. **ECEV** *Fr.* An Essay on Man. **CP-PopeA**

For fortunes favours you your riches bring. Mr Stothard to Mr Cromek. William Blake. **CP-BlakW**

For forty days the Lord abstain'd. Temperance. Christopher Smart. *Fr.* Hymns for the Amusement of Children. **SP-SmarC**

For Fran. Philip Levine. **SP-LeviP**

For francoise hardy / at the seine's edge. "Bob Dylan." *Fr.* Some Other Kinds of Songs. **CP-DylaB**

For Freckle-Faced Gerald. Etheridge Knight. **SP-KnigE**

For Friends Only. Wystan Hugh Auden. *Fr.* Thanksgiving for a Habitat. **CP-AudeW**

For Friendship. Robert Creeley. **CP-CreeR**

For Fugitives. Frank Templeton Prince. **CP-PrinF**

For Fun. Muriel Rukeyser. **CP-RukeM**

For Gail, When I Was Five. Charles Kenneth Williams. **CP-WillC; SP-WillC**

For Gaston Lachaise—a Sort of Written Frieze. Marsden Hartley. **CP-HartM**

For G. H. Esq. Robert Burns. **CP-BurnR**

For G.B.S., Old. William Carlos Williams. **CP-WilW2**

For gear your typewriter and an old rugby boot. Homage to Malcolm Lowry. Derek Mahon. **SP-MahoD**

For Genius made his cabin wide. Ralph Waldo Emerson. **CP-EmerR**

For gentlest uses, oft-times Nature takes. Engelberg, the Hill of Angels. William Wordsworth. *Fr.* Memorials of a Tour of the Continent; 1820. **CP-WorW2**

For George (I). Grace Paley. **CP-PaleG**

For George Santayana. Robert Lowell. **SP-LoweR**

For George (II). Grace Paley. **CP-PaleG**

For God While Sleeping. Anne Sexton. **CP-SextA**

For God's sake [*or* Godsake] hold your tongue, and let me love. The Canonization. John Donne. **CP-DonnJ**

For God's sake, let us be men. Let Us Be Men. David Herbert Lawrence. **CP-LawrD**

For God's sake, let us stop, oh you who stand behind us. Munitions. David Herbert Lawrence. *Fr.* Bits. **CP-LawrD**

For Grace, after a Party. Frank O'Hara. **SP-OharF**

For Han Shan on His Cold Mountain. Chuck Miller. **CP-MillC**

For having left the birds that left me. Poem. James Dickey. **CP-DickJ**

For healthful indigence in vain they pray. Virgil, *tr.* by Samuel Johnson. **CP-JohnS** *Fr.* The Aeneid [*or* Eneados, *Aeneis*].

For Helen. Robert Creeley. **CP-CreeR**

For Helen Keller. Countee Cullen. **CP-CullC**

For her size the moor hen. Wild Eggs. James Schuyler. **CP-SchuJ**

For her who owns this splendid toy. The Horologe of the Fields. Charlotte Smith. **CP-SmitC**

For here indeed was the unassailable kingdom of the heart itself. Kenneth Patchen. *Fr.* Wanderers of the Pale Wood. **CP-PatcK**

For him alone life's worse than worst. Edward Estlin Cummings. **CP-CummE**

For Him I Sing. Walt Whitman. **CP-WhitW**

For him who struck thy foreign string. Emily Brontë. **CP-BronE**

For his constant dwelling place has Hafiz. Hafiz, *tr.* by Ralph Waldo Emerson. **CP-EmerR** *Fr.* Odes.

For his long working life an engineer. The Volunteer. John Hewitt. **CP-HewiJ**

For his mind, I do[e] not care. Another Lady's [*or* Ladyes] Exception, Present at the Hearing. Ben Jonson. *Fr.* A Celebration of Charis in Ten Lyric[k] Pieces [*or* Peeces]. **CP-JonsB**

For his o'erarching and last lesson the greybeard sufi. A Persian Lesson. Walt Whitman. **CP-WhitW**

For hours / they float in the distance. Field near Linden, Alabama. Mary Oliver. **CP-OlivM**

For H.P. Christina Georgina Rossetti. **CP-RosC3**

For I am an orphan with two death masks on the mantel and. Fourth Psalm. Anne Sexton. *Fr.* O Ye Tongues. **CP-SextA**

For I am not without authority in my jeopardy, which I derive inevitably from the glory of the name of the Lord. God Hath Sent Me to Sea for Pearls. Christopher Smart. **CBCK** *Fr.* Let Elizur Rejoice with the Partridge. **PoEL-3** *Fr.* Fragment B. *Fr.* Jubilate Agno. **SP-SmarC**

For I am rightful fellow of their band. Mentors. Gwendolyn Brooks. **SP-BrooG**

For I bless the PRINCE of PEACE and pray that all the guns may be nail'd up, save such as are for the rejoicing days. Christopher Smart. **InPS** *Fr.* Fragment B. *Fr.* Jubilate Agno. **SP-SmarC**

For I can snore like a bullhorn. After Making Love We Hear Footsteps. Galway Kinnell. **SP-KinnG**

For I Dipped [*or* Dipt] into the Future. Tennyson. **PGD; PoLF; TRV** *Fr.* Locksley Hall. **CP-TennA**

(Lines.) **PAW**

(Prophecy.) **TreF; WBLP**

For I have got another girl— another girl. Another Girl. John Lennon *and* Paul McCartney. **CP-Beatl**

For I have learned. William Wordsworth. **NU** *Fr.* Lines Composed a Few Miles above Tintern Abbey on Revisiting the Banks of the Wye during a Tour, July 13, 1798. **CP-WorW1**

For I have lov'd the rural walk through lanes. William Cowper. **EnRP; NOEC** *Fr.* The Sofa. *Fr.* The Task. **CP-CowpW**

(Rural Sights and Sounds.) **NOEC,** *book* 1, *ll.* 109–210; God Made the Country. **FiP; PoEL-3**

For I pray there is an almighty to bless the piss oak that surrounds me. Second Psalm. Anne Sexton. *Fr.* O Ye Tongues. **CP-SextA**

For I prophesy that they will understand the blessing and virtue of the rain. Christopher Smart. **ECEV** *Fr.* Fragment C. *Fr.* Jubilate Agno. **SP-SmarC**

For I prophesy that we shall have our horns again. Christopher Smart. **ChIV-1** *Fr.* Fragment C. *Fr.* Jubilate Agno. **SP-SmarC**

For I will consider my Cat Jeoffry. Christopher Smart. **CTC; ChTr; FM; FaBoCh; HAP; HeIP; InPK; LAuP; LiTB; NAEL-1; NOEC; NTP; NU; NoP; OBF; OBWVE; OFC; OxAEP-1; PAI; PCat; PPP; PoE; PoEL-3; PrIm; Prf; RB; SCV; SeCePo; SeCeV; SoCa; TRP; TTTS; WeW; WiR** *Fr.* Fragment B. *Fr.* Jubilate Agno. **SP-SmarC**

(My Cat Jeoffry.) **ChTr; FaBoCh; LiTB; PoE; RB; SeCePo; SoCa; WiR**

(Of Jeoffry, His Cat.) **NU; PrIm**

For I will consider my Cat Jeoffry. Christopher Smart. **UV** *Fr.* For I will consider my Cat Jeoffry. **CTC; ChTr; FM; FaBoCh; HAP; HeIP; InPK; LAuP; LiTB; NAEL-1; NOEC; NTP; NU; NoP; OBF; OBWVE; OFC; OxAEP-1; PAI; PCat; PPP; PoE; PoEL-3; PrIm; Prf; RB; SCV; SeCePo; SeCeV; SoCa; TRP; TTTS; WeW; WiR** *Fr.* Fragment B. *Fr.* Jubilate Agno. **SP-SmarC**

"For I will consider my Cat Jeoffry." **UV**

For I will consider my dog Poochkin. Jubilate Canis. Erica Jong. **SP-JongE**

For I would walk alone. William Wordsworth. **OBRV** *Fr.* School-Time. *Fr.* The Prelude; Growth of a Poet's Mind [1805 vers.]. **CP-WorW3**

For if the sun breed maggots in a dead. Archibald MacLeish. *Fr.* The Pot of Earth. **CP-MacLA**

For Instance. John Ciardi. **SP-CiarJ**

For instance you walk in and faint. Mozart Chemisier. Frank O'Hara. **SP-OharF**

For Irving. Robert Creeley. **CP-CreeR**

For it did come to that. And a Man Went Out Alone. Kenneth Patchen. **CP-PatcK**

For J. Jean Garrigue. **SP-GarrJ**

For J.A. As Dusk Deepens Canyon. Anne Waldman. **SP-WaldA**

For James Baldwin. Kay Boyle. **CP-BoylK**

For James Dean. Frank O'Hara. **SP-OharF**

For James Schevill. Kay Boyle. **CP-BoylK**

For Jane Myers. Louise Glück. **SP-GlückL**

For Janet Kafka, Dead at 30. Al Young. **CP-YounA**

For Jean. John Hewitt. **CP-HewiJ**

For Jean Migrenne. Marilyn Hacker. **SP-HackM**

For Jennifer, 6, on the Teton. Richard Hugo. **CP-HugoR**

For Jeriann's Hands. Marge Piercy. **SP-PierM**

For Jimin in Manchuria II. James Liddy. **CP-LiddJ**

For Joanne in Poland. Al Young. **CP-YounA**

For Joel. Robert Creeley. **CP-CreeR**

For John Chappell. Gary Snyder. **CP-SnydG**

For John Clare. John Ashbery. **SP-AshbJ**

For John Donne. Jim Carroll. **SP-CarrJ**

For John F. Kennedy; His Inauguration. Robert Frost. **CP-FrosR**

For John Keats, Apostle of Beauty. Countee Cullen. **CP-CullC** *Fr.* Four Epitaphs.

For John, Who Begs Me Not to Enquire Further. Anne Sexton. **CP-SextA**

For Johnny Pole on the Forgotten Beach. Anne Sexton. **CP-SextA**

For Joseph Conrad. Countee Cullen. **CP-CullC**

For joy & beauty planted it. Ralph Waldo Emerson. **CP-EmerR**

For Juan Rulfo. Chuck Miller. **SP-MillC**

For Judy. Gary Gildner. **SP-GildG**

For Judy. Chuck Miller. **SP-MillC**

For Judy. Chuck Miller. **SP-MillC**

For Julia in Nebraska. Adrienne Rich. **SP-RicA2**

For K. R. on Her Sixtieth Birthday. Richard Wilbur. **CP-WilbR**

For Kayle Boyle. Muriel Rukeyser. **CP-RukeM**

For Kazuko. Rita Dove. **SP-DoveR**

For Kenneth & Miriam Patchen. Al Young. **CP-YounA**

For King, for Robert Kennedy. Robert Earl Hayden. **CNA** *Fr.* Words in the Mourning Time. **CP-HaydR**

For King, for Robert Kennedy. Words in the Mourning Time. Robert Earl Hayden. **CP-HaydR**

For K.J., Leaving and Coming Back. Marilyn Hacker. **SP-HackM**

For Langston Hughes. Etheridge Knight. **SP-KnigE**

For largest Woman's Heart I knew. Emily Dickinson. **CP-DickE**

For Leslie. Robert Creeley. **CP-CreeR**

For let the impediment be what it may. Fragment. William Wordsworth. **CP-WorW1**

For Lew Welch in a Snowfall. Gary Snyder. **CP-SnydG**

For Lewis, to Say It. Robert Creeley. **CP-CreeR**

For L.G.: Unseen for Twenty Years. Adrienne Rich. **SP-RicA2**

For Life I Had Never Cared Greatly. Thomas Hardy. **CP-HardT**

For lo! the board with cups and spoons is crown'd. Alexander Pope. **UV** *Fr.* The Rape of the Lock[, an Heroi-Comical Poem]. **CP-PopeA**

For lofty sense. Wild Shakespeare. James Thomson. **EPCY** *Fr.* Summer. *Fr.* The Seasons. **CP-ThomJ**

For Lois. Richard Shelton. **SP-ShelR**

For long the cruel wish I knew. The Coquette, and After. Thomas Hardy. **CP-HardT**

For Lords or kings I dinna mourn. Elegy on the Year 1788. Robert Burns. **CP-BurnR**

For losing her love all would I profane. Kenneth Patchen. **CP-PatcK**

For Louise and Tom Gossett. Archie Randolph Ammons. **SP-AmmoA**

For Love. Robert Creeley. **CP-CreeR**

For love—I would. The Warning. Robert Creeley. **CP-CreeR**

For love of lovely words, and for the sake. Skerryvore. Robert Louis Stevenson. **CP-StevR**

For love we all go. The People, the People. George Oppen. **CP-OppeG**

For Love's sake, kiss[e] me once again[e]. Begging Another, on Colour of Mending the Former. Ben Jonson. **CBLP; OAEP; PoEL-2; UnTE** *Fr.* A Celebration of Charis in Ten Lyric[k] Pieces [*or* Peeces]. **CP-JonsB**

For Love's Sake Only. Elizabeth Barrett Browning. *See* Sonnet: "If thou must love me, let it be for nought."

For Lucifer, that old athlete. Ralph Waldo Emerson. **CP-EmerR**

For Lucinda, Robert, and Karyn. Miller Williams. **SP-WillM**

For Lucy, on Her Birthday. Miller Williams. **SP-WillM**

For Lycidas the laurel is not sere. In Memorium: D.H. Lawrence. John Hewitt. **CP-HewiJ**

For Lyra yet shall be the pole. Ralph Waldo Emerson. **CP-EmerR**

For Mac Hammond. Charles Olson. **CP-OlsoC**

For Malcolm, a Year After. Etheridge Knight. **SP-KnigE**

For man is between the pinchers while his soul is shaping and purifying. Christopher Smart. **ChIV-1** *Fr.* Fragment B. *Fr.* Jubilate Agno. **SP-SmarC**

For man to tell how human life began. John Milton. **ChIV-1** *Fr.* Book VIII. *Fr.* Paradise Lost. **CP-MiltJ**

For Marianne Moore's Birthday. Kay Boyle. **CP-BoylK**

For Marisol. Robert Creeley. **CP-CreeR**

For Martin. Robert Creeley. **CP-CreeR**

For Mary Ellen McAnally. Etheridge Knight. **SP-KnigE**

For me, my friend, if not that tears did tremble. Fragment: To a Friend Released from Prison. Percy Bysshe Shelley. **CP-ShelP**

For me the Muse a simple band design'd. To Mr. Hayley, on Receiving Some Elegant Lines from Him. Charlotte Smith. **CP-SmitC**

For me, the naked and the nude. The Naked and the Nude. Robert Ranke Graves. **CP-GravR**

For me there was no audience. Bull Song. Margaret Atwood. *Fr.* Songs of the Transformed. **SP-AtwM1**

For Mélisande / flower-child of the forest. Mélisande. Charles Tomlinson. **CP-TomlC**

For Memory. Adrienne Rich. **SP-RicA1; SP-RicA2**

For Memory. Muriel Rukeyser. **CP-RukeM**

For Michael, Armoured with Roses. Diane Wakoski. *Fr.* Fifteen Poems for a Lunar Eclipse None of Us Saw. **SP-WakoD**

For Mickey. Chuck Miller. **SP-MillC**

For Mike and Jeannie: Resisters Fifteen Years Later. Grace Paley. **CP-PaleG**

For Mike and Kim. Chuck Miller. **SP-MillC**

For Miriam. Kenneth Patchen. **CP-PatcK**

For Miriam. Kenneth Patchen. **CP-PatcK**

For Miriam. Kenneth Patchen. **CP-PatcK**

For Miriam. Kenneth Patchen. **CP-PatcK**

For Miriam. Kenneth Patchen. **CP-PatcK**

For Miriam. Charles Tomlinson. **CP-TomlC**

For Mrs. Jones. Chuck Miller. **SP-MillC**

For modes of faith let graceless Zealots fight. Faith. Alexander Pope. **WGRP** *Fr.* An Essay on Man. **CP-PopeA**

For Molly, Concerning God. Erica Jong. **SP-JongE**

For months my hand had been sealed off. The Touch. Anne Sexton. **CP-SextA**

For more than five thousand years. At the Jewish New Year. Adrienne Rich. **CP-RicAE; SP-RicA2**

For Mr. Death Who Stands with His Door Open. Anne Sexton. **CP-SextA**

For My Brother: Reported Missing In Action, 1943. Thomas Merton. **CP-MertT; SP-MertT**

For my dagger is bathed in the blood of the brave. A Dialogue. Percy Bysshe Shelley. **CP-ShelP**

For My Daughter. Ron Koertge. **SP-KoerR**

For my embalming, Julia, do but this. His Embalming to Julia. Robert Herrick. **CP-HerrR**

For My Father. Stephen Berg.

At the Door. **SP-BergS**

Driving Out Again at Night.

Red Weed. **SP-BergS**

To the Same Place. **SP-BergS**

For My Father. Louise Glück. **MoLi** *Fr.* Metamorphosis. **SP-GlücL**

For My Friend. Charles Olson. **CP-OlsoC**

For My Friend John Lying on the Bed with Morning Heaves. Chuck Miller. **SP-MillC**

For My Friend Who Planted a Tree for His Daughter Jane. Grace Paley. **CP-PaleG**

For My Funeral. Alfred Edward Housman. **CP-HousA**

For My Grandmother. Countee Cullen. **CP-CullC** *Fr.* Four Epitaphs.

For My Grandmother, Bridget Halpin. Michael Hartnett. **SP-HarMi**

For My Husband. Erica Jong. **SP-JongE**

For My Lover, Returning to His Wife. Anne Sexton. **CP-SextA**

For My Mother. Louise Glück. **SP-GlücL**

For My Mother: Genevieve Jules Creeley. Robert Creeley. **CP-CreeR**

For My Mother in Her First Illness, from a Window Overlooking Notre Dame. Jane Cooper. **SP-CoopJ**

For my neighbour Ile not know. Safety To Look to Ones Selfe. Robert Herrick. **CP-HerrR**

For my part. Northwood Path. Louise Glück. **SP-GlücL**

For my part, I never care. Lips Tongueless[e]. Robert Herrick. **CP-HerrR**

For My Singing Sister. Audre Lorde. **SP-LordA**

For my sins I live in the city of New York. Whitman in Black. Ted Berrigan. **SP-BerrT**

For My Sister, against Narrowness. Erica Jong. **SP-JongE**

For My Sister Molly Who in the Fifties. Alice Walker. **CP-WalkA**

For My Son. Muriel Rukeyser. **CP-RukeM**

For My Son Noah, Ten Years Old. Robert Bly. **SP-BlyR**

For My Young Friends Who Are Afraid. William Stafford. **SP-StafW**

For Myra out of the Album. John Ciardi. **SP-CiarJ**

For Myself. Countee Cullen. **CP-CullC**

For nations vague as weed. Nothing to Be Said. Philip Larkin. **CP-LarkP**

For Nature true & like in every place. Ralph Waldo Emerson. **CP-EmerR**

For Nineteenth-Century Burials. Sir John Betjeman. **CP-BetjJ**

For No Clear Reason. Robert Creeley. **CP-CreeR**

For No One. John Lennon *and* Paul McCartney. **CP-Beatl**

For Nordahl Grieg Ship's Fireman. Malcolm Lowry. **CP-LowrM**

For not the brave, or wise, or great. Pindar. **CP-JohnS** *Fr.* Pythian Odes.

For Nothing. Gary Snyder. **CP-SnydG**

For now too nigh / The archangel stood, and from the other hill. Their Banishmnet. John Milton. SeCePo *Fr.* Book XII. *Fr.* Paradise Lost. **CP-MiltJ**

For Oh, her lanely nights are lang. Robert Burns. *See* How lang and dreary is the night.

For old New England. Seeking. James Schuyler. **CP-SchuJ**

For once she gets to go with big Cousin Beatie. Speak, Memory! Mona Van Duyn. **SP-VanDM**

For Once, Then, Something. Robert Frost. **CP-FrosR**

For One Sake. Christina Georgina Rossetti. **CP-RosC3**

For one season, much laughter: we learned to take. James McAuley. *Fr.* Three Acts from a Play. **SP-McAuJ**

For one so rarely tun'd to fit all parts. To the Most Accomplisht Gentleman, Master Edward Norgate, Clark of the Signet to His Majesty. Robert Herrick. **CP-HerrR**

For one throb of the artery. A Meditation in Time of War. William Butler Yeats. **CP-YeatW**

For One Who Did Not March. John Hewitt. **CP-HewiJ**

For one who watches with too little rest. Sacred Heart. Thom Gunn. **CP-GunnT**

For Orford and for Waldegrave. Byron. **CP-Byron**

For other beds the priests there used none. Britomart at Isis' Church. Edmund Spenser. **PoE** *Fr.* The Faerie Queene. **CP-Spens**

For Our Sweethearteebeeste on Hartebeeste Day. Malcolm Lowry. **CP-LowrM**

For our white and our excellent nights—for the nights of swift running. Rudyard Kipling. **CP-KiplR** *Fr.* Red Dog. *Fr.* The Second Jungle Book.

For over forty years I'd paid it atlas homage. Hammerfest. Wystan Hugh Auden. **CP-AudeW**

For Pao-Chin, a Boatman on the Yellow Sea. Edna St. Vincent Millay. **CP-MillE**

For Papa. Hayden Carruth. **CP-CarHS**

For papers I think I need, we bump off. On the Way Home From Nowhere, New Year's Eve. Miller Williams. **SP-WillM**

For parents, the only way. The Way of Pain. Wendell Berry. **CP-BerrW**

For Patrick, Aetat: LXX. Sir John Betjeman. **CP-BetjJ**

For Paul Laurence Dunbar. Countee Cullen. **CP-CullC** *Fr.* Four Epitaphs.

For pearls, plunge in the sea. *Unknown, tr. fr.* Persian *by* Jean Chardin *and fr.* French *by* Ralph Waldo Emerson. **CP-EmerR**

For Phil. Chuck Miller. **SP-MillC**

For pity's sake. Pity's Sake. Archibald MacLeish. **CP-MacLA**

For Poets. Al Young. **CP-YounA**

For prodigal read generous. Edward Estlin Cummings. **CP-CummE**

For Proserpine. Stanley Jasspon Kunitz. **CP-KuniS**

For Proust. James Merrill. **SP-MerrJ**

For punishment in warre, it will suffice. Clemency. Robert Herrick. **CP-HerrR**

For Queen Victoria's Birthday. Walt Whitman. **CP-WhitW**

For R. John Hewitt. **CP-HewiJ**

For Rainer Gerhardt. Robert Creeley. **CP-CreeR**

For reading I can recommend. Domaine Public. Geoffrey Hill. **OxBC** *Fr.* Four Poems Regarding the Endurance of Poets. **CP-HillG**

For Realism. Roy Fisher. **SP-FishR**

For reasons of their own the red-winged blackbirds. Wherever. Daniel Gerard Hoffman. **SP-HoffD**

For Reuben, at Twelve Months. Miller Williams. **SP-WillM**

For Richard Hopper (Dies 1978). Chuck Miller. **SP-MillC**

For Richard Wilbur. James Dickey. **CP-DickJ**

For Richmond's Garden Wall. Robert Louis Stevenson. **CP-StevR**

For Righteousness' Sake. John Greenleaf Whittier. **CP-WhitJ**

For rigorous teachers seized my youth. Matthew Arnold. **FHYEP** *Fr.* Stanzas from the Grande Chartreuse. **SP-ArnoM**

For R. A. Esq. Robert Burns. **CP-BurnR**

For Robert Bhain Campbell. James Dickey. **CP-DickJ**

For Robert Frost. Galway Kinnell. **SP-KinnG**

For Robert Frost, in the Autumn, in Vermont. Howard Nemerov. **CP-NemeH**

For Robert Kennedy Nineteen Twenty-Five to Sixty-Eight. Robert Lowell. **SP-LoweR**

For Robert Smithson. Jim Carroll. **SP-CarrJ**

For Roberta in the Garden. John Hewitt. **CP-HewiJ**

For ropes of pearle, first Madam Ursly showes. Upon Madam Ursly. Robert Herrick. **CP-HerrR**

For Rosaline's Album. Christina Georgina Rossetti. **CP-RosC3**

For R.S. Thomas. John Hewitt. **CP-HewiJ**

For safety on the expedition. The Ballad of Johnny. May Sarton. **SP-SartM**

For Sale. Robert Lowell. **SP-LoweR**

For Sale. Shel Silverstein. **SP-SilS2**

For sale: by order of the remaining heirs. Sale. Theodore Roethke. **CP-RoetT**

For Sappho, Back. Charles Olson. **CP-OlsoC; SP-OlsoC**

For Saturday. Christopher Smart. **FaBoCh; LAuP; NOEC; OxBChV** *Fr.* Hymns for the Amusement of Children. **SP-SmarC**

(Hymn for Saturday.) **OxBChV**

(Lark's Nest, A.) **FaBoCh**

For Schnu. Chuck Miller. **SP-MillC**

For second course, last night, a Custard came. The Custard. Robert Herrick. **CP-HerrR**

For security against robbers who snatch purses, rifle luggage, and crack safes. Cracking the Safe. Chuang Tzu, *tr. fr. Chinese by* Thomas Merton. **CP-MertT**

For Selma Gubin's Umbrellas. Louis Zukofsky. **CP-ZukLS**

For seven days it rained that June. Wash. John Updike. **CP-UpdiJ**

For several weeks I have been reading. Expression. Thom Gunn. **CP-GunnT**

For shame! / Let Folly and Knavery. On Johnson's Opinion of Hampden. Robert Burns. **CP-BurnR**

For shame! deny that thou bear'st love to any. Sonnet 10. William Shakespeare. **MasP** *Fr.* Sonnets. **CP-ShaWS**

For shamefast harm of great and hateful need. Sir Thomas Wyatt. **CP-WyatT**

For Shoshana Rihn—Pat Swinton. Marge Piercy. **SP-PierM**

For Sidney Bechet. Philip Larkin. **CP-LarkP**

For Signs. Thom Gunn. **CP-GunnT**

For Sir W. Trumbull. Alexander Pope. **CP-PopeA**

For sixty years the pine lumber barn. Carl Sandburg. *Fr.* The People, Yes. **CP-SandC**

"For Some Weeks. . . ." Robert Creeley. **CP-CreeR**

For some weeks / now, caught in my. "For Some Weeks. . . ." Robert Creeley. **CP-CreeR**

For Somebody's Marriage. Robert Creeley. **CP-CreeR**

For something out of sight. The Summons. James Dickey. **CP-DickJ**

For sport my Julia threw a lace. The Silken Snake. Robert Herrick. **CP-HerrR**

For Stonecutters. John Hewitt. **CP-HewiJ**

For Strong Women. Marge Piercy. **SP-PierM**

For Such a Bird He Had No Convenient Cage. Jean Garrigue. **SP-GarrJ**

For such a theme (atrocities) you find. Method. For Ronald Gaskell. Donald Davie. **CP-DavDo**

For Sue's Birthday. Jim Carroll. **SP-CarrJ**

For Sunday. Christopher Smart. *Fr.* Hymns for the Amusement of Children. **SP-SmarC**

For Sunday's play he never makes excuse. Lout, The. John Clare. **SP-ClarJ**

For surely the flower, as Williams. An Excursus of Reassurance in Begonia Time. Hayden Carruth. **CP-CarHS**

For ten years I have been rooted in these hills. Gestalt at Sixty. May Sarton. **SP-SartM**

For that a man is a mark. Ralph Waldo Emerson. **CP-EmerR**

For that fair[e] blessed mother-maid. The Virgin Mary. John Donne. *Fr.* A Litany. **CP-DonnJ**

For that free Grace bringing us past great risks. John Berryman. *See* Minnesota Thanksgiving.

For that I have forgot the world these days. Sonnet. Edward Estlin Cummings. **CP-CummE**

For that I never knew you, I only learned to dread you. St. Roach. Muriel Rukeyser. **CP-RukeM**

For that it is love and covers us. Love I. Charles Olson. **CP-OlsoC**

For that tree with no fruit but its flower. For an Orchard Tree. Jean Garrigue. **SP-GarrJ**

For that you never acknowledged me, I acknowledge. Desdichada. Muriel Rukeyser. **CP-RukeM**

For the aging hipster. A Dance for Aging Hipsters. Al Young. **CP-YounA**

For the Air is purified by prayer which is made aloud and with all our might. Christopher Smart. **Prf** *Fr.* Fragment B. *Fr.* Jubilate Agno. **SP-SmarC**

For the angels who inhabit this town. Locked Doors. Anne Sexton. **CP-SextA**

For the Anniversary of my Mother's Death. Archibald MacLeish. **CP-MacLA**

For the Author's Father. Robert Burns. **CP-BurnR**

For the benefit of Mister Kite there will be a show tonight on trampoline. Being for the Benefit of Mr. Kite. John Lennon *and* Paul McCartney. **CP-Beatl**

For the blue flash and the moments / benedetta. Canto 117 et seq., Notes for. Ezra Pound. *Fr.* Cantos. **CP-PoCan**

For the Boy Who Was Dodger Point Lookout Fifteen Years Ago. Gary Snyder. **CP-SnydG**

For the Children. Gary Snyder. **CP-SnydG**

For the Chinese New Year & for Bill Berkson. Frank O'Hara. **SP-OharF**

For the comprehension of Suffering. Emily Dickinson. **SP-DickE**

For the Conjunction of Two Planets. Adrienne Rich. **CP-RicAE; SP-RicA2**

For the context of the basidiocarp Singer states. James Fenton. **PeLV** *Fr.* Exempla. **SP-FentJ**

For the Dead. Adrienne Rich. **SP-RicA1; SP-RicA2**

For the Death of Vince Lombardi. James Dickey. **CP-DickJ**

For the Deserted. Frank Templeton Prince. **CP-PrinF**

For the discipline nothing had changed. The mood was still. The Lament upon the Waters. John Ashbery. **SP-AshbJ**

For the doubling of flowers is the improvement of the gard'ner's talent. Christopher Smart. **ChIV-2; LAuP; NOEC** *Fr.* Fragment B. *Fr.* Jubilate Agno. **SP-SmarC**

For the fairest maid in Hampton. The Changeling. John Greenleaf Whittier. **CP-WhitJ**

For the Felling of an Elm in the Harvard Yard. Adrienne Rich. **CP-RicAE**

For the first time today. Willkie—Stopless Falling through Air. Muriel Rukeyser. **CP-RukeM**

For the first twenty years [or yeares], since yesterday. The Computation. John Donne. **CP-DonnJ**

For the Fountains and Fountaineers of Villa d'Este. Jean Garrigue. **SP-GarrJ**

For the Future. Wendell Berry. **CP-BerrW**

For *The Garland of Rachel.* "Lewis Carroll." *Fr.* Two Poems to Rachel Daniel. **CP-CarrL**

For the gay tailfeathers, say, what'll you pay?—. Auction. William DeWitt Snodgrass. **SP-SnodW**

For the Ghost of Li Po. Stephen Berg. **SP-BergS**

For the gladness here where the sun is shining at evening on the weeds at. Our Prayer of Thanks. Carl Sandburg. **CP-SandC**

For the Graduation. Robert Creeley. **CP-CreeR**

For the Graduation. Robert Creeley. **CP-CreeR**

For the Graduation: Bolinas, 1972. Robert Creeley. **CP-CreeR**

FOR THE HARLOT HAS A HARDLOT. Ernest Hemingway. **CP-HemiE**

For the heart, willing and not willing. The Clovers. Jean Garrigue. **SP-GarrJ**

For the Heroes Are Dipped in Scarlet. David Herbert Lawrence. **CP-LawrD**

For the historical ache, the ache passed down. To a Terrorist. Stephen Dunn. **SP-DunnS**

For the Hog Killing. Wendell Berry. **CP-BerrW**

For the Hour of Prime. Richard Crashaw. **CP-CrasR**

For the Humanism Class at Fairchild Airforce Base, in Place of a Session on the Book of Job. James McAuley. **SP-McAuJ**

For the Irish Sea. Steve Griffiths. **SP-GrifS**

For the lands and for these passionate days and for myself. The Return of the Heroes. Walt Whitman. **CP-WhitW**

For the Last Wolverine. James Dickey. **CP-DickJ**

For the long nights you lay awake. To Alison Cunningham. Robert Louis Stevenson. **CP-StevR**

For the Madrid Road. Randall Jarrell. **CP-JarrR**

For the Man Who Fails. Paul Laurence Dunbar. **CP-DunbP**

For the Marriage of Faustus and Helen. Hart Crane. **CP-CranH**

   "Brazen hynotics glitter here."

   "Capped arbiter of beauty in this street." **FaBoMo; ImPo; LiTM**

   "Mind has shown itself at times, The."

For the Marsh's Birthday. James Wright. **CP-WrigJ**

For the Mother of My Mother's Mother. Kenneth Patchen. **CP-PatcK**

For the New Railway Station in Rome. Richard Wilbur. **CP-WilbR**

For the New Year. Robert Creeley. **CP-CreeR**

For the Nightly Ascent of the Hunter Orion over a Forest Clearing. James Dickey. **CP-DickJ**

For the people of that flow. George Oppen. *Fr.* Of Being Numerous. **CP-OppeG**

For the pleasures of the many. Variations, Calypso and Fugue on a Theme of Ella Wheeler Wilcox. John Ashbery. **SP-AshbJ**

For the Poor. William Cowper. *Fr.* Olney Hymns. **CP-CowpW**

For the Rebuilding of a House. Wendell Berry. **CP-BerrW**

For the Record. Adrienne Rich. **SP-RicA2**

For the Restoration of My Dear Husband from a Burning Ague. Anne Bradstreet. **CP-BradA**

For the Running of the New York City Marathon. James Dickey. **CP-DickJ**

For the Sake o' Somebody. Robert Burns. *See* My heart is sair—I dare na tell.

For the sake of him who showed. Outsong in the Jungle. Rudyard Kipling. **CP-KiplR** *Fr.* The Spring Running. *Fr.* The Second Jungle Book.

For the sake of some things. Rosemary. Edna St. Vincent Millay. **CP-MillE**

For the sake of the record. The Customs Collector's Report. Stanley Jasspon Kunitz. **CP-KuniS**

For the scaffold spreads its gray flower. A Devotion. Kenneth Patchen. **CP-PatcK**

For the second time in a year this lady with the white hands is brought. White Hands. Carl Sandburg. **CP-SandC**

For the servant of God. Desolation. Thomas Merton. *Fr.* Readings from Ibn Abbad. **CP-MertT**

For the seven lakes, and by no man these verses. Canto 49. Ezra Pound. **SP-PounE** *Fr.* Cantos. **CP-PoCan**

For the Sexes the Gates of Paradise. William Blake. *See* The Gates of Paradise.

For the Shut Eye. Marsden Hartley. **CP-HartM**

For the Spanish Poet Miguel Hernandez. Thomas Merton. **CP-MertT**

For the spiritual musick is as follows. Christopher Smart. **NOEC** *Fr.* Fragment B. *Fr.* Jubilate Agno. **SP-SmarC**

For the Spot Where the Hermitage Stood on St Herbert's Island, Derwent-Water. William Wordsworth. **CP-WorW1**

For the Squadron. Howard Nemerov. **CP-NemeH**

For the Student Strikers. Richard Wilbur. **CP-WilbR**

For the sweet sake of inscapes. Since You Asked Me. Mona Van Duyn. **SP-VanDM**

For the Time Being; a Christmas Oratorio. Wystan Hugh Auden. **CP-AudeW**

   Advent.

      "If, on account of the political situation." **LiTA; WaP**

   Annunciation, The.

   At the Manger.

      "Led by the light of an unusual star." **PChr**

   Flight into Egypt, The. **CP-AudeW**

      "He is the Way." **EaLo**

      "Well, so that is that. Now we must dismantle the tree." **LiTA; MeMAP; MoAB; MoBrPo; OAEL-2; OBCP**

      (After Christmas.) **MoAB; MoBrPo**

      (Narrator.) **MeMAP**

   Massacre of the Innocents, The.

   Meditation of Simeon, The.

   Summons, The.

      "Great is Caesar: He has conquered Seven Kingdoms." **LiTM**

      "Our Father, whose creative Will." **TrPWD**

   Temptation of St. Joseph, The.

   Vision of the Shepherds, The.

For the Union Dead. Robert Lowell. **SP-LoweR**

For the Visitors' Book. Kathleen Jessie Raine. **SP-RainK**

For the way they fan their wings. Sengekontacket. Brendan Galvin. **SP-GalvB**

For the West. Gary Snyder. **CP-SnydG**

For the Word Is Flesh. Stanley Jasspon Kunitz. **CP-KuniS**

For the wrongs that women do. Nun's Song. William Carlos Williams. **CP-WilW2**

For the Year of the Insane. Anne Sexton. **CP-SextA**

For the Young Who Want To. Marge Piercy. **SP-PierM**

For their descent, / dancing round my desk. Blessed Be the Muses. Allen Ginsberg. **CP-GinsA**

For Theodore Roosevelt. Paul Laurence Dunbar. **CP-DunbP**

For there are numerous questions remaining which one must consider. Kenneth Koch. *Fr.* The Art of Love. **SP-KochK**

For there is no friend like a sister. Christina Georgina Rossetti. **OBF** *Fr.* Goblin Market. **CP-RosC1**

For There's Bishop's Teign. John Keats. **CP-KeatJ**

For these are sacred fishes all. Ad Piscatorem. Robert Louis Stevenson. **CP-StevR**

For these of old the trader. Alfred Edward Housman. **CP-HousA**

For Thieves and Beggars. Frank Templeton Prince. **CP-PrinF**

For thine is the kingdom. Lord's Prayer. David Herbert Lawrence. **CP-LawrD**

For Thine Own Sake, O My God. Christina Georgina Rossetti. **CP-RosC2**

For things we never mention. The Broken Men. Rudyard Kipling. **CP-KiplR**

For thirst of power that Heaven disowns. Ode on the Installation of His Royal Highness Prince Albert as Chancellor of the University of Cambridge, July, 1847. William Wordsworth. **CP-WorW2**

For thirty yeares, Tubbs has been proud and poor. Upon Tubbs. Robert Herrick. **CP-HerrR**

For this—accepted Breath. Emily Dickinson. **CP-DickE**

For this agility chance found. The Age Demanded. Ezra Pound. *Fr.* Mauberly (1920). *Fr.* Hugh Selwyn Mauberley. (Life and Contacts). **SP-PounE**

For this and for all enclosures like it the archetype. The Cave of Making. Wystan Hugh Auden. *Fr.* Thanksgiving for a Habitat. **CP-AudeW**

For this generation, / infected with too many antidotes. Nightclubbing. Jim Carroll. **SP-CarrJ**

For this man shed no tear. Ballad for Baudelaire. Charles Henri Ford. **SP-FordC**

For this present, hard. Woodnotes I ("For this present, hard"). Ralph Waldo Emerson. **CP-EmerR**

For this ring upon my finger. Bride to Groom. Jenny Joseph. **SP-JoseJ**

For this your mother sweated in the cold. To Jesus on His Birthday. Edna St. Vincent Millay. **CP-MillE**

For thon demgeorne dreorigne oft. Hayden Carruth. **CP-CarHS** *Fr.* The Bloomingdale Papers.

For Those my unbaptized Rhymes [*or* Rhimes]. His Prayer for Absolution. Robert Herrick. **CP-HerrR**

For Those Who Pray for the Souls of Broken Dolls. Chuck Miller. **SP-MillC**

For thou art with me here upon the banks. William Wordsworth. **Prf** *Fr.* Lines Composed a Few Miles above Tintern Abbey on Revisiting the Banks of the Wye during a Tour, July 13, 1798. **CP-WorW1**

For though our disapproval / Shakes every wing and finlet. Welcome Home, Oh Our Sweetest Harteebeeste Beloved. Malcolm Lowry. **CP-LowrM**

For thought & not praise. Terminus. Ralph Waldo Emerson. **CP-EmerR**

For three insane things evil, and for four. Amos. John Berryman. **CP-BerrJ**

For three years at evening. The Sleeping Brute. William Carlos Williams. **CP-WilW2**

For three years, diabolus in the scale. Ezra Pound. *Fr.* Mauberly (1920). *Fr.* Hugh Selwyn Mauberley. (Life and Contacts). **SP-PounE**

For three years, out of key with his time. Ezra Pound. Hugh Selwyn Mauberley. (Life and Contacts). **SP-PounE**

For thus, since the body's death is quick, seems less. The Sequel, the Conclusion, the Endlessness. Delmore Schwartz. **SP-SchwD**

For thus the royal *Mandate* ran. Robert Burns. **OBF** *Fr.* Second Epistle to John Lapraik.

For to Admire. Rudyard Kipling. **CP-KiplR**

For to love her for her looks lovely. Sir Thomas Wyatt. **CP-WyatT**

For Tom. Robert Creeley. **CP-CreeR**

For truth I may this sentence tell. A Good Death. Robert Herrick. **CP-HerrR**

For two days I have dug around a rock. Rock. Miller Williams. **SP-WillM**

For two rewards, & nought beside. Ibn-i-Yamin, *tr. fr. Persian by* Ralph Waldo Emerson. **CP-EmerR**

For two straight days. The Man and the Goshawk. Gary Gildner. **SP-GildG**

For two who. Alice Walker. **CP-WalkA**

  (Dedication.) **CP-WalkA**

For two years I broke from these cycles, simply. Marge Piercy. *Fr.* The Homely War. **SP-PierM**

For Una. Robinson Jeffers. **CP-JefR3**

For *Under the Volcano.* Malcolm Lowry. **CP-LowrM**

For us like any other fugitive. Another Time. Wystan Hugh Auden. **CP-AudeW**

For Us Two, Reader Dear. Walt Whitman. **CP-WhitW**

For Us, Who Dare Not Dare. Maya Angelou. **SP-AngeM**

For us who, from the moment. Address to the Beasts. Wystan Hugh Auden. **CP-AudeW**

For Victor Jara. Miller Williams. **SP-WillM**

For Viola: De Gustibus. William Carlos Williams. **CP-WilW1**

For W——— Who Commanded Well. Howard Nemerov. **CP-NemeH**

For W. H. Auden. Richard Wilbur. **CP-WilbR**

For Walker Evans. John Clellon Holmes. **SP-HolmJ**

For Walter Chappell. Robert Creeley. **CP-CreeR**

For want of [or I] will in woe I plain. Sir Thomas Wyatt. **CP-WyatT**

For Warmth Alone, for Shelter Only. Edna St. Vincent Millay. **CP-MillE**

For wars his life and half a world away. Lullaby, A. Randall Jarrell. **CP-JarrR**

For W.C.W. ("Pleasure of the wit sustains, The"). Robert Creeley. **CP-CreeR**

For W.C.W. ("Rhyme is after, The"). Robert Creeley. **CP-CreeR**

For we have gone a curious way from there. William Dickey. **SP-DickW** *Fr.* Part Song, With Concert of Recorders. **SP-DickW**

For we have thought the longer thoughts. Chapter Heading. Ernest Hemingway. **CP-HemiE**

For what as easy. Wystan Hugh Auden. **NoP; PeLV** *Fr.* Five Songs ("What's in your mind, my dove, my coney"). **CP-AudeW**

  (Love Song: "For what as easy.") **PeLV**

For what contend the wise?—for nothing less. The Point at Issue. William Wordsworth. *Fr.* Ecclesiastical Sonnets. **CP-WorW2**

For what is Freedom, but the unfettered use. Samuel Taylor Coleridge. **EnRP** *Fr.* The Destiny of Nations. **CP-ColeS**

For what it was worth he had to. Louis MacNeice. *Fr.* As In Their Time. **CP-MacNL**

For what need I of book or priest. Ralph Waldo Emerson. **CP-EmerR**

For what we owe to other days. Exit. Edwin Arlington Robinson. **CP-RobiE**

For whatever is let go. May Song. Wendell Berry. **CP-BerrW**

For whatever, it could / be done, simply. The Chance. Robert Creeley. **CP-CreeR**

For when it dawn'd—they dropp'd their arms. Samuel Taylor Coleridge. **UnS** *Fr.* The Rime of the Ancient Mariner. **CP-ColeS**

For when they meet, the tensile air. The Paradigm. Allen Tate. **CP-TateA**

For who can human back? Autumn Break. Joseph Ceravolo. **SP-CeraJ**

For whom do we scrape our tribute of pain. Geoffrey Hill. *Fr.* Funeral Music. **CP-HillG**

For whom the possessed sea littered, on both shores. Requiem for the Plantagenet Kings. Geoffrey Hill. **CP-HillG**

For whose adornment the mouths. Kenneth Patchen. **CP-PatcK**

For wine, they drank the ocean—. Fishermen's Last Supper. Marsden Hartley. **CP-HartM**

For X. Louis MacNeice. *See* When clerks and navvies fondle.

For years I explored the pharmacopoeia. On the Threshold of His Greatness, the Poet Comes Down With a Sore Throat. Howard Nemerov. **CP-NemeH**

For years I mustered on our biggest table. Lead Soldiers and Regimental Uniforms. John Hewitt. **CP-HewiJ**

For years I thought I knew, at the bottom of the dream. The Meeting. Louise Bogan. **CP-BogaL**

For years I thought the birds meant, well. Mocking Bird Song. Leonard Nathan. **SP-NathL**

For years it was land working me, oil fields. 3 A.M. Kitchen: My Father Talking. Tess Gallagher. **SP-GallT**

For years, so long, I had imagined. West Pitch at the Falls. Marsden Hartley. **CP-HartM**

For years the old Italians have been dying. The Old Italians Dying. Lawrence Ferlinghetti. **SP-FerlL**

For years we shared the same pillow, and nothing knew. Offering. Siv Cedering Fox. **SP-CedeS**

For years we've had a little dog. Two Dogs Have I. Ogden Nash. **CP-NashO**

For You. Ted Berrigan. **SP-BerrT**

For You. Robert Creeley. **CP-CreeR**

For You. Carl Sandburg. **CP-SandC**

For you am I collared to quit my dear. John Berryman. *Fr.* Sonnets to Chris. **CP-BerrJ**

For you an idyl, was it not, so far. John Berryman. *Fr.* Sonnets to Chris. **CP-BerrJ**

For you and I are bathed in silence. We Must Be Slow. Kenneth Patchen. **CP-PatcK**

For You Blue. George Harrison. **CP-Beatl**

For you I have emptied the meaning. Louis Zukofsky. **CP-ZukLS**

For You O Democracy. Walt Whitman. **CP-WhitW**

For you there ought. For Leslie. Robert Creeley. **CP-CreeR**

For you who loved me too. For Fugitives. Frank Templeton Prince. **CP-PrinF**

For Your Birthday. Jim Carroll. **SP-CarrJ**

For your letter, dear—[Hattie], accept my best thanks. To Miss — — [Harriet Grove] from Miss — — [Elizabeth Shelley]. Percy Bysshe Shelley. *Fr.* Original Poetry by Victor and Cazire. **CP-ShelP**

For your love given. Hayden Carruth. **CP-CarHS** *Fr.* The Clay Hill Anthology.

For Zadkine. Louis Zukofsky. **CP-ZukLS**

For / From Lew. Gary Snyder. **CP-SnydG**

Forage Sestina. Marilyn Hacker. **SP-HackM**

Foraminiferal millennia. Undersea. Archie Randolph Ammons. **SP-AmmoA**

Forbear this liquid fire, fly. A Fly about a Glass[e] of Burnt Claret. Richard Lovelace. **CP-LoveR**

Forbear, thou great good husband, little ant. The Ant. Richard Lovelace. **CP-LoveR**

Forbear to deem the Chronicler unwise. Plea for the Historian. William Wordsworth. *Fr.* Memorials of a Tour in Italy, 1837. **CP-WorW2**

Forbear to tempt me, Prowl, I will not show. To Prowl the Plagiary. Ben Jonson. **CP-JonsB**

Forbearance. Samuel Taylor Coleridge. **CP-ColeS**

Forbearance. Ralph Waldo Emerson. **CP-EmerR**

Forbeare darke night, my joyes now budd againe. Sonnet 4. Mary Sidney, Countess of Montgomery Wroth. *Fr.* Pamphilia to Amphilanthus. **CP-WrotM**

Forbecause a prisoner lies. Coeur de Lion. Frank Templeton Prince. **CP-PrinF**

Forbidden Banns, The. Thomas Hardy. **CP-HardT**

Forbidden Fruit a flavor has. Emily Dickinson. **CP-DickE**

Forbidden Things. Alice Walker. **CP-WalkA**

Forbidden Words. Robert Ranke Graves. **CP-GravR**

Forbore the ant hill, shunned to tread. Ralph Waldo Emerson. **CP-EmerR**

Forc'd from home, and all its pleasures. The Negro's Complaint. William Cowper. **CP-CowpW**

Force and His Master. George Meredith. **CP-MerG2**

Force is my lot and not pink-clustered. Examination of the Hero in a Time of War. Wallace Stevens. **CP-StevW**

Force of Prayer, The; or, The Founding of Bolton Priory; A Tradition. William Wordsworth. **CP-WorW1**

Force that through the green fuse drives the flower, The. The . Dylan Thomas. **CP-ThomD**

Forced as I was, I ran a race with death. Track. Richard Eberhart. **CP-EberR**

Forced Recruit, The. Elizabeth Barrett Browning. **CP-BroEB**

Forced yellow spring before crenated. Forsythia. Louis Zukofsky. **CP-ZukLS**

Forces, the Will & the Weather. Wallace Stevens. **CP-StevW**

Forcing House. Theodore Roethke. **CP-RoetT**

Ford Madox Ford ("Lobbed ball plops, then dribbles to the cup, The"). Robert Lowell. **SP-LoweR**

Ford Manor. Derek Mahon. **SP-MahoD**

Ford o' Kabul River. Rudyard Kipling. **CP-KiplR**

'Fore love, a mighty session; and (I fear). Prologue. Sir John Suckling. *Fr.* The Fifth Act of Aglaura As Presented to the Court. *Fr.* Aglaura. **CP-SuckJ**

Foreboding. Walter de la Mare. **CP-DeLaW**

Foreboding. Walter de la Mare. **CP-DeLaW**

Foreboding, The. Robert Ranke Graves. **CP-GravR**

Foreboding. John Haines. **SP-HainJ**

Forebodings are the fiends of Recreance. Edwin Arlington Robinson. *Fr.* Octaves. **CP-RobiE**

Forecast. David Herbert Lawrence. **CP-LawrD**

Forefinger of stone, dreamed by a sculptor, points to the sky, The. Slants at Buffalo, New York. Carl Sandburg. **CP-SandC**

Foregoing Subject Resumed, The. William Wordsworth. **CP-WorW2**

Foreguarded and unfevered and serene. The Sage. Edwin Arlington Robinson. **CP-RobiE**

Foreign. William Carlos Williams. **CP-WilW1**

Foreign Affairs. Stanley Jasspon Kunitz. **CP-KuniS**

Foreign Children. Robert Louis Stevenson. **CP-StevR**

Foreign hands and feet that tear my window shades, The. Wrong Number. Charles Bukowski. **SP-BukC2**

Foreign Lands. Robert Louis Stevenson. **CP-StevR**

Foreign Missions in Battle Array. Nicholas Vachel Lindsay. **CP-LindV**

Foreign Shore, Old Woman, Slaughter of Octopus. Robert Penn Warren. **SP-WarrR**

Foreign Sunset. David Herbert Lawrence. *Fr.* Bits. **CP-LawrD**

Foreigners are people somewhere else. Goody for Our Side and Your Side Too. Ogden Nash. **CP-NashO**

Foreknown. The victor / sees the disaster through and through. Letters: March 1969. Adrienne Rich. **CP-RicAE; SP-RicA2**

Foreman of quarries in Cyprus. On Reading Edmund Wilson's Remarks about Rimbaud. Malcolm Lowry. *Fr.* The Moon in Scandinavia. **CP-LowrM**

Forerunners. Ralph Waldo Emerson. **CP-EmerR**

Forerunners, The. George Herbert. **CP-HerbG**

Forerunners. Muriel Rukeyser. **CP-RukeM**

Foreseen for so many years: these evils, this monstrous violence. Robinson Jeffers. **CP-JefR3**

(Battle.) **CP-JefR3**

Foresight. William Wordsworth. **CP-WorW1**

Foresight and Patience. George Meredith. **CP-MerG1**

Forest. Jean Garrigue. **SP-GarrJ**

Forest Beyond the Glass, The. Lewis Turco. **SP-TurcL**

Forest Birds. Charles Simic. **SP-SimiC**

Forest Boy, The. Charlotte Smith. **CP-SmitC**

Forest Greeting, The. Paul Laurence Dunbar. **CP-DunbP**

Forest History. George Meredith. **CP-MerG1**

Forest huge of ancient Caledon, The. Suggested by a View from an Eminence in Inglewood Forest. William Wordsworth. **CP-WorW2**

Forest is multitude. Kathleen Jessie Raine. **SP-RainK**

Forest Murmurs, *after Eduard Mörike*. Randall Jarrell. **CP-JarrR**

Forest of Europe. Derek Walcott. **CP-WalcD**

Forest of pine darkness. Shadows, A. The Chase in Spring. Hayden Carruth. **CP-CarHS**

Forest Thought, A. Robert Browning. **CP-BroR2**

Forester. Ralph Waldo Emerson. *Fr.* Quatrains. **CP-EmerR**

Forests. Walter de la Mare. **CP-DeLaW**

Forever. Paul Laurence Dunbar. **CP-DunbP**

Forever at His side to walk. Emily Dickinson. **CP-DickE**

Forever at war news I am. Mary Sheffield. James Dickey. **CP-DickJ**

Forever honored be the Tree. Emily Dickinson. **CP-DickE**

Forever—is composed of Nows. Emily Dickinson. **CP-DickE**

Forever, it comes from the head. / Where does it end?. Venom. James Dickey. **CP-DickJ**

Forever nameless / Forever unknown. Belief. David Herbert Lawrence. **CP-LawrD**

Forever O'Clock. Robert Penn Warren. **SP-WarrR**

Forever over now, forever, forever gone. The Cameo. Edna St. Vincent Millay. **CP-MillE**

Forever Young. "Bob Dylan." **CP-DylaB**

Forewarned of madness. The Halls of Bedlam. Robert Ranke Graves. **CP-GravR**

Forger, The. Derek Mahon. **SP-MahoD**

Forget. David Herbert Lawrence. **CP-LawrD**

Forget Me Not. Christina Georgina Rossetti. **CP-RosC3**

Forget not yet the tried intent. Sir Thomas Wyatt. **CP-WyatT**

Forget the foolishness with which I vexed you. Superstition. Robert Ranke Graves. **CP-GravR**

Forget the keep-off sign. That cow. Houses Lie, Believe the Lying Sea. Richard Hugo. **CP-HugoR**

Forget! The lady with the Amulet. Emily Dickinson. **CP-DickE**

Forget the rest: my heart is true. The Leap. Robert Ranke Graves. **CP-GravR**

Forget the tube of bark. Very Tree. Stanley Jasspon Kunitz. **CP-KuniS**

Forget What Did. Philip Larkin. **CP-LarkP**

Forgetfulness. Hart Crane. **CP-CranH**

Forgetfulness! I would thy hand could close. To Oblivion. Charlotte Smith. **CP-SmitC**

Forgetting I am alive, the tent comes over me. The Jewel. James Dickey. **CP-DickJ**

Forgetting to Forget. Robert Pack. **SP-PackR**

Forgive, illustrious Country! these deep sighs. From the Alban Hills, Looking towards Rome. William Wordsworth. *Fr.* Memorials of a Tour in Italy, 1837. **CP-WorW2**

Forgive Me, Forgive Me. Stevie Smith. **CP-SmitS**

Forgive me if I come too much. Emily Dickinson. **SP-DickE**

Forgive Me If My Praises. Alice Walker. **CP-WalkA**

Forgive me, love, if I withdraw awhile. Her Brief Withdrawal. Robert Ranke Graves. **CP-GravR**

Forgive me, my delight. To Tanya at Christmas. Wendell Berry. **CP-BerrW**

Forgive, O Lord, my little jokes on Thee. Robert Frost. **CP-FrosR**

Forgive this nerve. I walked here up the long hill. Why I Think of Dumar Sadly. Richard Hugo. **CP-HugoR**

Forgive this singsong, / It's just my spring song. The Eternal Vernal, or, In All My Dreams My Fair Face Beams. Ogden Nash. **CP-NashO**

Forgive what I give you. Though nightmare and cinders. To Mary. Louis MacNeice. **CP-MacNL**

Forgiveness, A. Robert Browning. **CP-BroR2**

Forgiveness. Walter de la Mare. **CP-DeLaW**

Forgiveness. Alice Walker. **CP-WalkA**

Forgiveness. John Greenleaf Whittier. **CP-WhitJ**

Forgot! Stevie Smith. **CP-SmitS**

Forgotten Language. Shel Silverstein. **SP-SilS2**

Forgotten Miniature, A. Thomas Hardy. **CP-HardT**

Forgotten Rock, The. Richard Eberhart. **CP-EberR**

Forgotten Wars. Carl Sandburg. **CP-SandC**

Fork. Charles Simic. **SP-SimiC**

Fork of Annie, The. Marsden Hartley. **CP-HartM**

Forlorn and white, / Whorls of purity about a golden chalice. White Symphony. John Gould Fletcher. **SP-FletJ**

Forlorn indeed Hope on these shores. Killala. Donald Davie. **CP-DavDo**

Forlorn, my love, no comfort near. English Song. Robert Burns. **CP-BurnR**

Forlorn Sea, The. Stevie Smith. **CP-SmitS**

Form, The. John Berryman. **CP-BerrJ**

Form. James Dickey. **CP-DickJ**

Form and Theory of Poetry. Miller Williams. **SP-WillM**

Form Is an Angel, The. Jim Morrison. **SP-MorrJ**

Form of Adaptation, A. Robert Creeley. **CP-CreeR**

Form of Christ cut from dark wood, the pale, A. Sonnet. Howard Nemerov. **CP-NemeH**

Form of the grasses against, The. The Total Parts of a World. Robert Creeley. **CP-CreeR**

Form of Women, A. Robert Creeley. **CP-CreeR**

Form upon the quilted, A. Threshold. Denise Levertov. **CP-LeveD**

Formal as minuet or sonnet. Mystery Story. Howard Nemerov. **CP-NemeH**

Formal Auctioneer, The. Ted Hughes. **SP-HughT**

Formal Design, A. William Carlos Williams. **CP-WilW2**

Formal Elegy. John Berryman. **CP-BerrJ**

Formal, informal, by a country's cast. Homage to Edward Thomas. Derek Walcott. **CP-WalcD**

Formal World relaxes her cold chain, The. Apology. William Wordsworth. *Fr.* Sonnets upon the Punishment of Death. **CP-WorW2**

Formando di disio nuova persona. Canto 27. Ezra Pound. *Fr.* Cantos. **CP-PoCan**

Formative Mastership. Richard Eberhart. **CP-EberR**

Formed a new beast today: eye of hawk. Eyes in All Heads to Be Looked out Of. Anne Waldman. **SP-WaldA**

Former Age, The. Geoffrey Chaucer. **CP-ChauG**

Former Attachment, A. Robert Ranke Graves. **CP-GravR**

Former Beauties. Thomas Hardy. **CBLP; FaBoEn; NoAM; OBMV; OBNC** *Fr.* At Casterbridge Fair. **CP-HardT**

Former four now ending their discourse, The. Of the Four Humors in Man's Constitution. Anne Bradstreet. **CP-BradA**

Former gave with eloquent characters, The. In the French Translation of Lucan by Monsieur De Brebeuf Are These Verses: Lib 3. Lucan, *tr. fr. Latin of* Andrew Marvell, *fr. the French of* de Brebeuf by William A. McQueen *and* Kiffin A. Rockwell. **CP-MarvA** *Fr.* Pharsalia.

Formerly a Slave. Herman Melville. **SP-MelvH**

Formerly we knew / Years of peaceable system. Thomas Merton. *Fr.* Cables to the Ace. **CP-MertT**

Formianus's whore, / long-nosed. Carmen 41. Catullus. *Fr.* Carmina. **CP-Catul**

Formosa. Muriel Rukeyser. **CP-RukeM**

Forms and flowers. Charles Henri Ford. **SP-FordC** *Fr.* Emblems of Arachne.

Forms of Knowledge, The. Kenneth Patchen. **CP-PatcK**

Forms of Love, The. George Oppen. **CP-OppeG**

Forms of Prayer at Sea. William Wordsworth. *Fr.* Ecclesiastical Sonnets. **CP-WorW2**

Forms of the Human. Richard Eberhart. **CP-EberR**

Forms' passage as. Robert Creeley. **CP-CreeR**

Forms, qualities, lives, humanity, language, thoughts. Germs. Walt Whitman. **CP-WhitW**

Fornicator. A New Song, The. Robert Burns. **CP-BurnR**

Forsake me not thus, Adam, witness Heav'n. Eve Penitent. John Milton. **OBS** *Fr.* Book X. **FHYEP** *Fr.* Paradise Lost. **CP-MiltJ**

Forsaken, The. William Wordsworth. **CP-WorW1**

Forsaken and Forlorn. David Herbert Lawrence. **CP-LawrD**

Forsaken Girl, The, *after* Eduard Mörike. Randall Jarrell. **CP-JarrR**

Forsaken Lady to Her False Servant, A. Richard Lovelace. **CP-LoveR**

Forsaken Merman, The. Matthew Arnold. **SP-ArnoM**
  "Children dear, was it yesterday." **BoTP**

Forsaking all others, we. Wendell Berry. *Fr.* Passing the Strait. **CP-BerrW**

Forsythia. Louis Zukofsky. **CP-ZukLS**

Fort, The. Lewis Turco. **SP-TurcL**

Fort Benton. Richard Hugo. **CP-HugoR**

Fort Casey, without Guns. Richard Hugo. **CP-HugoR**

Fort Collins, Colorado. Al Young. **CP-YounA**

Fort Fuentes. William Wordsworth. *Fr.* Memorials of a Tour of the Continent; 1820. **CP-WorW2**

Fort Robinson. Ted Kooser. **SP-KoosT**

Forte Dei Marmi. David Herbert Lawrence. **CP-LawrD**

Forth from a Jutting Ridge, Around Whose Base. William Wordsworth. **CP-WorW2**

Forth from a sack of fishing-reels and deck-quoits. Louis MacNeice. *Fr.* Country Week-End. **CP-MacNL**

Forth from ages thick in mystery. Sine Prole. Thomas Hardy. **CP-HardT**

Forth from her land to mine she goes. To Princess Kaiulani. Robert Louis Stevenson. **CP-StevR**

Forth from the curtain of clouds, from the tent of purple and scarlet. The Wedding-Day. Henry Wadsworth Longfellow. *Fr.* The Courtship of Miles Standish. **SP-LongH**

Forth from the glaring heat. By the Passeyr. George Meredith. **CP-MerG2**

Forth rushed from Envy sprung and Self-conceit. Protest against the Ballot. William Wordsworth. **CP-WorW2**

Forthwith readily swathing her head in a sheeny fine linen. Helen on the Skaian Gates. Homer, *tr.* by George Meredith. **CP-MerG2** *Fr.* The Iliad.

Forthwith the sounds and seas, each creek and bay. John Milton. **ChIV-1** *Fr.* Book VII. *Fr.* Paradise Lost. **CP-MiltJ**

Forties Flick. John Ashbery. **SP-AshbJ**

Fortification, A. Margaret Atwood. **SP-AtwM1**

Fortified in their front parlours, at Yuletide men. Geoffrey Hill. *Fr.* Mercian Hymns. **CP-HillG**

Fortitude. Archie Randolph Ammons. **SP-AmmoA**

Fortitude. Christopher Smart. **ChIV-2** *Fr.* Hymns for the Amusement of Children. **SP-SmarC**

Fortitude incarnate. Emily Dickinson. **CP-DickE**

Fortitude of the North, The. Herman Melville. **SP-MelvH**

Fortress, The. Louise Glück. **SP-GlücL**

Fortress, The. Anne Sexton. **CP-SextA**

Fortù, fortù, my beloved one. The Englishman in Italy. Robert Browning. **CP-BroR1**

Fortunate Child. Robert Ranke Graves. **CP-GravR**

Fortunate land, that Egypt, where / From time to time the phoenix comes. The Fact of the Matter. Hayden Carruth. **CP-CarHS**

Fortunate man it is not too late. The Woodthrush. William Carlos Williams. **CP-WilW2**

Fortunate sheer a mile's upmost. Lily-of-the-Valley Fortunei. Louis Zukofsky. **CP-ZukLS**

Fortunate Traveller, The. Derek Walcott. **CP-WalcD**

Fortune. Geoffrey Chaucer. **CP-ChauG**

Fortune. Robert Herrick. **CP-HerrR**

Fortune, A. Daniel Gerard Hoffman. **SP-HoffD**

Fortune and Glory may be lost and woone. To the Most High and Mighty Prince Charles. Thomas Campion. **CP-CampT**

Fortune and Hope! I've made my port. Prudentius, *tr. fr. Latin by* Ralph Waldo Emerson. **CP-EmerR**

Fortune did never favour one. Fortune Favours. Robert Herrick. **CP-HerrR**

Fortune doth frown. Sir Thomas Wyatt. **CP-WyatT**

Fortune Favours. Robert Herrick. **CP-HerrR**

Fortune favours the Brave, old Proverbs say. Mr Cromek to Mr Stothard. William Blake. **CP-BlakW**

Fortune! I thank thee: gentle Goddess! thanks! Verses Written at Bath on Finding the Heel of a Shoe. William Cowper. **CP-CowpW**

Fortune, Nature, Love, long have contended about me, *speech of Dorus.* Sir Philip Sidney. **SP-SidnP** *Fr.* Arcadia.

Fortune no higher Project can devise. Discord Not Disadvantageous. Robert Herrick. **CP-HerrR**

Fortune Teller, The. Howard Nemerov. **CP-NemeH**

Fortune teller looked in my hand. Madam and the Fortune Teller. Langston Hughes. **SP-HughL**

Fortune, what aileth thee. Sir Thomas Wyatt. **CP-WyatT**

Fortune's a blind profuser of her own. Fortune. Robert Herrick. **CP-HerrR**

Fortune's Falsehoode. Robert Southwell. **CP-SoutR**

Fortune's Mist. Richard Eberhart. **CP-EberR**

Fortune's Wheel. In the. Charles Henri Ford. **SP-FordC** *Fr.* Secret Haiku.

Forty Augusts—aye, and several more—ago. The Voice of Things. Thomas Hardy. **CP-HardT**

Forty Days. Tom Clark. **SP-ClarT**

Forty feet long sixty feet high hotel. Heat. Allen Ginsberg. **CP-GinsA**

45 Mercy Street. Anne Sexton. **CP-SextA**

"Forty-Four Hours" Strike, 1919, The. John Hewitt. **CP-HewiJ**

XLIV. "When those renowned noble peers of Greece." Edmund Spenser. **PoE** *Fr.* Amoretti. **CP-Spens**

44th Birthday Evening, at Harris's. Ted Berrigan. **SP-BerrT**

XL. "Mark when she smiles with amiable cheer." Edmund Spenser. **OBSC** *Fr.* Amoretti. **CP-Spens**

40 odd year old Para 10, A. The Birth. William Carlos Williams. **CP-WilW2**

Forty-odd years ago—. Anniversaries. Thomas McGrath. **SP-McGrT**

XLVII. "Trust not the treason of those smiling looks." Edmund Spenser. **TrGrPo** *Fr.* Amoretti. **CP-Spens**

Forty-some years—and so far away. The Runaway Team (Written a Few Days After John Glenn's Space Flight). Louise McNeill. **SP-McNeL**

Forty springs back, I recall. The Opportunity. Thomas Hardy. **CP-HardT**

Forty-two years ago (to me if to no one else). Star-Gazer. Louis MacNeice. **CP-MacNL**

Forty Years. Wendell Berry. **CP-BerrW**

Forty years back, when much had place. George Meredith (1828-1909). Thomas Hardy. **CP-HardT**

Forty years I lived. Garden Moment. Louise McNeill. **SP-McNeL**

Forty Years On. Wystan Hugh Auden. **CP-AudeW**

Forward rush by the lamp in the gloom, A. The Contretemps. Thomas Hardy. **CP-HardT**

Forward she leans, with hollowing back, stock-still. Io. Gerard Manley Hopkins. **CP-HopkG**

Forward violet thus did I chide, The. Sonnet 99. William Shakespeare. **OAEP; OBSC; OXAEP-1** *Fr.* Sonnets. **CP-ShaWS**

Forward! You must. Keep. Hayden Carruth. **CP-CarHS** *Fr.* The Clay Hill Anthology.

Forward youth that would appear, The. An Horatian Ode upon Cromwell's Return from Ireland. Andrew Marvell. **CP-MarvA**

Fossil, The. John Haines. **SP-HainJ**
  "All spine and knotted fin-rays."
  "Inside the shell of our skulls."
  "Sometimes in our sleep."

Fossil, fuchsia, mantis, man. Theme and Variation. Robert Earl Hayden. **CP-HaydR**

Fossil, yet I'm here, Professor Pagels, A. Autumn Warmth. Robert Pack. **SP-PackR**

Foss'io regina / Tu re saresti. Christina Georgina Rossetti. **CP-RosC3**

Foster-Mother's Tale, The. Samuel Taylor Coleridge. **CP-ColeS**

Foster the Light. Dylan Thomas. **CP-ThomD**

Foul is she and ill-favoured, set askew. Babylon the Great. Christina Georgina Rossetti. **CP-RosC2**

Foul, or Twenty-Five. Malcolm Lowry. **CP-LowrM**

Foul Shots: A Clinic. William Matthews. **SP-MattW**

Foul weather sighs old time. Azalea. Louis Zukofsky. **CP-ZukLS**

Foules Rondel. Geoffrey Chaucer. *See* Now Welcom[e], Somer [*or* Summer].

Foulest brute that stinks below. Clad All in Brown. Jonathan Swift. **CP-SwifJ**

Found a family, build a state. Fragments of a Lost Gnostic Poem of the Twelfth [*or* 12th] Century. Herman Melville. **SP-MelvH**

Found in a Storm. William Stafford. **SP-StafW**

Found it once more in the ocean's rush. Jim Carroll. *Fr.* The New Death. **SP-CarrJ**

Found Macaronic Antipoem. Thomas Merton, *tr. fr. Latin and German by* Thomas Merton. *Fr.* A Selection of Concrete Poems. **CP-MertT**

Foundations of American Industry, The. Donald Hall. **CP-HallD**

Founded on rock and facing the night-fouled sea. The Beacon. Richard Wilbur. **CP-WilbR**

Founder, The. George Oppen. **CP-OppeG**

Founder of the Feast, The. Robert Browning. **CP-BroR2**

Founderous wilding weeds endear paradise. Weeds. Louis Zukofsky. **CP-ZukLS**

Founding Fathers, Nineteenth-Century Style, Southeast U.S.A. Robert Penn Warren. **SP-WarrR**

Foundling, A. Margaret Atwood. **SP-AtwM1**

Fount of Tears, The. Paul Laurence Dunbar. **CP-DunbP**

Fountain, The. William Cowper. *See* Praise for the Fountain Opened.

Fountain, The. Donald Davie. **CP-DavDo**

Fountain, The. Denise Levertov. **CP-LeveD**

Fountain, The. John Greenleaf Whittier. **CP-WhitJ**

Fountain, The. William Wordsworth. **CP-WorW1**

Fountain, a Bottle, a Donkey's Ears and Some Books, A. Robert Frost. **CP-FrosR**

Fountain—from four blocks away—can look like ice, A. The Gate Is Prouti. Charles Olson. **CP-OlsoC**

Fountain from Wilderness Stone, A, *par. by* David Rosenberg. Bible, *O.T.* *See* Psalm 114: "When Israel went out of Egypt."

Fountain in its source, The. Living Water. Jeanne Marie Bouvier de la Motte-Guyon, *tr. fr. French by* William Cowper. **CP-CowpW**

Fountain of Arethusa, The. Donald Davie. **CP-DavDo**

Fountain of Cyanë, The. Donald Davie. **CP-DavDo**

Fountain of our sweetest, quick to spring, A. J. C. M. George Meredith. **CP-MerG1**

Fountain plays / through summer dusk in gaunt shadows, The. The Memorial Fountain. Roy Fisher. **SP-FishR**

Fountains are dry and the roses over, The. The Manor Garden. Sylvia Plath. **CP-PlatS**

Fountains mingle with the river, The. Love's Philosophy. Percy Bysshe Shelley. **CP-ShelP**

Four. Robert Creeley. **CP-CreeR**

Four, The. David Herbert Lawrence. **CP-LawrD**

Four Ages, The. William Cowper. **CP-CowpW**

Four Ages, The. Howard Nemerov. **CP-NemeH**

Four Ages of Man, The. William Butler Yeats. **CP-YeatW**

Four Angels, The. Rudyard Kipling. **CP-KiplR**

Four Archangels, so the legends tell, The. The Legend of Mirth. Rudyard Kipling. **CP-KiplR**

Four Auguries. Margaret Atwood. **SP-AtwM1**

Four boards of the coffin lid, The. After Death. Algernon Charles Swinburne. **SP-SwinA**

Four bright steel crosses. Detroit Grease Shop Poem. Philip Levine. **SP-LeviP**

Four Brothers, The. Carl Sandburg. **CP-SandC**

Four climbed High-Stoy from Ivelwards. Under High-Stoy Hill. Thomas Hardy. **CP-HardT**

Four close but several trees, each green, none equal. Democrats. Donald Davie. **CP-DavDo**

Four Dancers at an Irish Wedding. Tess Gallagher. **SP-GallT**

Four days with you, my father three months dead. The Stream. Mona Van Duyn. **SP-VanDM**

Four Elegies. Charles Henri Ford. **SP-FordC**
  Candy Darling.
  Max Ernst.
  Mishima.
  St.-John Perse.

Four Elements, The. Anne Bradstreet. **CP-BradA**
  Element Fire Boasts of the Constellations, The. **CBCK**

Four Epitaphs. Countee Cullen. **CP-CullC**
  For a Lady I Know. **CP-CullC**
  For John Keats, Apostle of Beauty. **CP-CullC**
  For My Grandmother. **CP-CullC**
  For Paul Laurence Dunbar. **CP-CullC**

Four Exposures. Richard Eberhart. **CP-EberR**

Four-Feet. Rudyard Kipling. **CP-KiplR**

Four fellows in orange uniforms. Santiago: Five Men in the Street: Number One. Stephen Dobyns. **SP-DobyS**

Four Fiery Steed Impatient of the Rein. William Wordsworth. **CP-WorW2**

Four-footed, silent, resilient, feathered. Mythological Beast. Howard Nemerov. *Fr.* Epigrams: "Wasp, climbing the window pane." **CP-NemeH**

Four Footprints. Thomas Hardy. **CP-HardT**

Four for Sir John Davies. Theodore Roethke. **CP-RoetT**
  Dance, The. **DIP**

Four greens / the poplar trunk. Hayden Carruth. *Fr.* North Winter. **CP-CarHL**

Four Haiku. Allen Ginsberg. **CP-GinsA**

Four hundred years ago a tangled waste. Columbian Ode. Paul Laurence Dunbar. **CP-DunbP**

Four in a Family. Muriel Rukeyser. **CP-RukeM**

Four in the Morning. Thomas Hardy. **CP-HardT**

Four Kantian Lyrics. Charles Tomlinson. **CP-TomlC**
  How It Happened.
  Insufficiency of Earth, An.
  On a Theme of Pasternak.
  What It Was Like.

Four Lakes' Days. Richard Eberhart. **CP-EberR**
  "Contend with steepness, the dark air."
  "Labour them, these drenched heights."
  "Point-pushed by the wind, rain."
  "Summery Windermere, sweet lake!" **MiAP**
  (Four Lakes' Days, The.) **MiAP**, *sect.* 1;

Four Lakes' Days, The. Richard Eberhart. *See* Summery Windermere, sweet lake!

Four Medieval Latin Poems. *Various Authors, tr. fr. Latin by* Louis MacNeice. **CP-MacNL**
  Corona Virginum.
  Jam Lucis Orto Sidere.
  Meum Est Propositum.
  Ut Quid Iubes, Pusiole.

Four men got in discussion. Each one said. Metamorphosis. Chuang Tzu, *tr. fr. Chinese by* Thomas Merton. **CP-MertT**

Four[e] Monarchies, The. Anne Bradstreet. **CP-BradA**
  Semiramis. **KTR**

Four-o'clock. Louis Zukofsky. **CP-ZukLS**

Four o'clock this afternoon. Cortège. Edwin Arlington Robinson. **CP-RobiE**

4 Other Countries. Louis Zukofsky. **CP-ZukLS**

Four oval shadows, paired, ringed each by sun. John Berryman. *Fr.* Sonnets to Chris. **CP-BerrJ**

Four pelicans went over the house. Pelicans. Robinson Jeffers. **CP-JefR1**

Four Poems. Elizabeth Bishop. **CP-BishE**
  Conversation.
  O Breath.
  Rain Towards Morning.
  While Someone Telephones. **NMP**

Four Poems. James Schuyler. **CP-SchuJ**
  Frank! Frank!
  "It's 4:30 in Cambridge."
  Mass. Ave., Cambridge, Mass.
  "We must observe the amenities."

Four Poems for Robin. Gary Snyder. **CP-SnydG**
  Autumn Morning in Shokoku-ji, An. **HAP; VGW; WeW**
  December at Yase.
  Siwashing It Out Once in Siuslaw Forest.
  Spring Night in Shokoku-ji, A. **ArLo; VGW**

Four Poems Regarding the Endurance of Poets. Geoffrey Hill. **CP-HillG**
  Domaine Public. **OxBC**
  Men Are a Mockery of Angels.
  Prayer to the Sun, A. **PRA**
  Tristia: 1891–1938.

Four Points, The, *parody of* Thomas Tusser. Rudyard Kipling. **CP-KiplR** *Fr.* The Muse among the Motors.

Four Preludes on Playthings of the Wind. Carl Sandburg. **CP-SandC**

Four Quartets. Thomas Stearns Eliot. **CP-ElioT**
  Burnt Norton. **CMoP; LiTM; MoAB; MoAmPo; NAAL-2; PoE**
    "Words move, music moves." **UnS**
  Dry Salvages, The. **AiP; LiTB; NoP; OxBA; SeCePo**
    "River is within us, the sea is all about us, The." **OxBoS**
  East Coker. **HAP; PPP; VGW**
  Little Gidding. **FaBoMo; FaBoPV; FaBoTw; GTBS-6; GTBS-P; MoP; NAEL-2; NAWM-2; NOBA; NOBE; NoAM; OAEL-2; OXAEP-2;**

OxBTC; PeECV; PrIm; TAP; TFi
"Ash on an old man's sleeve." **FaBoTw**
"We shall not cease from exploration." **ImOP**
Four Quartz Crystal Clocks. Marianne Craig Moore. **CP-MoorM**
Four Riddles. "Lewis Carroll." **CP-CarrL**
"Air is bright with hues of light, The."
"Empress of Art, for thee I twine."
"My First is singular at best."
"There was an ancient City, stricken down."
Four-room shack aspiring high. Robert Frost. **CP-FrosR**
Four Sambas. Unknown, tr. fr. Portuguese by Elizabeth Bishop. **CP-BishE**
Four sat on in the bare room, The. Wystan Hugh Auden. **CP-AudWJ**
Four seasons fill the measure of the year. The Human Seasons. John Keats. **CP-KeatJ**
Four Seasons in American Woods. Robert Bly.
"Spring has come; I look up and see." **SP-BlyR**
Four Seasons of the Year, The. Anne Bradstreet. **CP-BradA**
Four shells on four yards. Survivors. James McAuley. Fr. Requiem. **SP-McAuJ**
462-0614. Charles Bukowski. **SP-BukC1**
Four Small Elegies. Margaret Atwood. **SP-AtwM2**
Beauharnois.
Beauharnois.
Beauharnois, Glengarry.
Dufferin, Simcoe, Grey. **AMV-81**
4 Sniffs & I'm High. Aether. Allen Ginsberg. **CP-GinsA**
Four Songs, by Way of Chorus To a Play. Thomas Carew. **CP-CareT**
Feminine Honour.
First of Jealousy. Dialogue, The.
Incommunicability of Love.
Separation of Lovers.
Four Songs the Night Nurse Sang. Robert Duncan. **SP-DuncR**
Four Sonnets. Howard Nemerov. **CP-NemeH**
"Earth orbits on the sun and has no sign."
"Of fire and of lust proceeds the world."
"You too will cool, though from your distance light."
"Your beauty once the profit of your scorn."
Four Steichen Prints. Carl Sandburg. **CP-SandC**
Four sweaters are woven upon me. Springer Mountain. James Dickey. **CP-DickJ**
Four[e] Things Make Us Happy Here. Robert Herrick. **CP-HerrR**
4:30 A.M. Charles Bukowski. **SP-BukC2**
Four-thirty in the morning. Fragment of New York, 1929. Richard Eberhart. **CP-EberR**
Four times the sun had risen and set; and now on the fifth day. The Embarkation. Henry Wadsworth Longfellow. **PAH** Fr. Part the First. Fr. Evangeline, a Tale of Acadie. **SP-LongH**
Four Trees—upon a solitary Acre. Emily Dickinson. **CP-DickE**
Four Walks in the Country Near Saint-Brieuc. Derek Mahon. **SP-MahoD**
After Midnight.
Exit Molloy. **POL**
Man and Bird.
Morning.
Four walls are drawn tight round the crew of us. Cinders. Wystan Hugh Auden. **CP-AudWJ**
Four Ways of Knowledge. Robert Bly. **SP-BlyR**
Four white heifers with sprawling hooves. The Orotava Road. Basil Bunting. **CP-BuntB**
Four white towers slowly glide, The. She Remains. Alun Lewis. Fr. War Wedding. **CP-LewiA**
Four years ago I met your death here. Letter from Chicago. May Sarton. **SP-SartM**
Foure Teeth thou had'st that ranck'd in goodly state. Out of Martiall. Martial, tr. fr. Latin by Richard Crashaw. **CP-CrasR**
Fourfold Aspect, The. Elizabeth Barrett Browning. **CP-BroEB**
Fourfold is made the divine nature of man. John Gould Fletcher. **SP-FletJ** Fr. Branches of Adam.
Fourteen. Marilyn Hacker. **SP-HackM**
Fourteen, a sonneteer thy praises sings. A Sonnet upon Sonnets. Robert Burns. **CP-BurnR**
Fourteen centuries fall away, The. The Shadow and the Light. John Greenleaf Whittier. **CP-WhitJ**
14 November, 1973. Sir John Betjeman. **CP-BetjJ**
Fourteen people have been known to come again. One came. A Little Novel. Gertrude Stein. **CP-SteiG**
Fourteen-year-old, why must you giggle and dote. The Conventionalist. Stevie Smith. **CP-SmitS**
Fourteenth Anniversary, The. Richard Shelton. **SP-ShelR**

Fourteenth Book, The. Archibald MacLeish. Fr. Conquistador. **CP-MacLA**
Fourth. Hayden Carruth. **CP-CarHS**
Fourth, The. Shel Silverstein. **SP-SilS2**
Fourth Act. Robinson Jeffers. **CP-JefR3**
4th Base. Gary Gildner. **SP-GildG**
Fourth Book, The. Archibald MacLeish. Fr. Conquistador. **CP-MacLA**
Fourth day came, but not a breath of air, The. Byron. **ChER** Fr. Canto the Second. Fr. Don Juan. **CP-Byron**
Fourth Dimension, The. Leonard Nathan. **SP-NathL**
Fourth Elegy. The Refugees. Muriel Rukeyser. **CP-RukeM**
Fourth Epistle. Donald Davie. Fr. Six Epistles to Eva Hesse. **CP-DavDo**
Fourth Floor, Dawn, Up All Night Writing Letters. Allen Ginsberg. **CP-GinsA**
Fourth in a five-house terrace, stucco-faced. 96 Clifton Park Avenue and the Robinsons. John Hewitt. **CP-HewiJ**
Fourth Limick. Ogden Nash. **CP-NashO**
4th May Morning. Christina Georgina Rossetti. **CP-RosC3**
Fourth Meditation. Theodore Roethke. Fr. Meditations of an Old Woman. **CP-RoetT**
Fourth of July. Ted Hughes. **SP-HughT**
Fourth of July. Peter Meinke. **SP-MeinP**
Fourth of July, The. Howard Nemerov. **CP-NemeH**
Fourth of July. William DeWitt Snodgrass. **SP-SnodW**
Fourth of July, The. Richard Wilbur. **CP-WilbR**
4th of July. William Carlos Williams. **CP-WilW1**
Fourth of July in Maine. Robert Lowell. **SP-LoweR**
Fourth of July Night. Carl Sandburg. **CP-SandC**
Fourth Printing. Marsden Hartley. **CP-HartM**
Fourth Psalm. Anne Sexton. Fr. O Ye Tongues. **CP-SextA**
Fourth Song, The. Thomas Carew. **CP-CareT** Fr. Carew's Masque. **CP-CareT**
Fourth Song. Sir Philip Sidney. **ElL; EnRePo; GBL; HAP; InvP; NAEL-1; NoP; NoSic; OBSC; UnTE** Fr. Astrophil and Stella. **SP-SidnP**
Fourth Time Around. "Bob Dylan." **CP-DylaB**
Fourth Universe. Diane Wakoski. Fr. The Universes. **SP-WakoD**
Fourth Version, The, sels. Hayden Carruth. Fr. The Mythology of Dark and Light. **CP-CarHL**
Fous qui disiez. Samuel Beckett. **CP-BeckS**
Fowls of heaven, The. James Thomson. **PBBP** Fr. Winter. Fr. The Seasons. **CP-ThomJ**
Fowls speak and sing, settling for the night, The. Winter Nightfall. Wendell Berry. **CP-BerrW**
Fowre Hymnes. Edmund Spenser. **CP-Spens**
Hymne in Honour of Beautie, An.
Hymne in Honour of Love, An.
Hymne of Heavenly Beautie, An. **PeECV**
"But whoso may, thrice happy man him hold." **WGRP**
Hymne of Heavenly Love, An.
Fox, The. Phoebe Hesketh. **SP-HeskP**
Fox / is so quiet, The. The Snowshoe Hare. Mary Oliver. **SP-OlivM**
Fox, The. Philip Levine. **SP-LeviP**
Fox, The. Paul Muldoon. **SP-MuldP**
Fox, The. Kenneth Patchen. **CP-PatcK**
Fox. Kenneth Rexroth. **NNaP; SP-RexrK** Fr. A Bestiary. **SP-RexrK**
Fox, The. Charles Tomlinson. **CP-TomlC**
Fox and Geese. Louise McNeill. **SP-McNeL**
Fox and Geese is shut; the Fox and Geese, The. The Closed Pub. Malcolm Lowry. **CP-LowrM**
Fox and the Grapes, The. Marianne Craig Moore. **CP-MoorM** Fr. Fables of La Fontaine.
Fox Blood. James Dickey. **CP-DickJ**
Fox-Fire: 1956. Robert Penn Warren. Fr. Mortmain. **SP-WarrR**
Fox Gallery, The. Charles Tomlinson. **CP-TomlC**
Fox-Hunting. Rudyard Kipling. **CP-KiplR**
Fox is very clever, The. Fox. Kenneth Rexroth. **NNaP; SP-RexrK** Fr. A Bestiary. **SP-RexrK**
Fox lifts his head from the feathers, The. A Ghost Story. Randall Jarrell. **CP-JarrR**
Fox of Gascon, though some say of Norman descent, A. The Fox and the Grapes. Marianne Craig Moore. **CP-MoorM** Fr. Fables of La Fontaine.
Fox, the owl, the spider, and the mole, The. William Blake. **CP-BlakW**
Foxes' Moon. Charles Tomlinson. **CP-TomlC**
Foxfur. Robert Lowell. **SP-LoweR**
Foxgloves. Carl Sandburg. **CP-SandC**
Foxtail Pine. Gary Snyder. **CP-SnydG**
Foyer, The. Roy Fisher. **SP-FishR** Fr. Interiors with Various Figures.
Foyer's revolving doors are fixed open to let the dull heat, The. The Foyer. Roy Fisher. **SP-FishR** Fr. Interiors with Various Figures.

Fra Lippo Lippi. Robert Browning. **CP-BroR1**
  "I shall paint/ God in the midst." **Prf**
Frae Anither Window in Thrums. "Hugh MacDiarmid."
  "Gin but the oor 'ud chop and set me free." **SP-MacDH**
  "Here in the hauf licht hoo I've grown!" **SP-MacDH**
  "Here in the hauf licht waitin' till the clock." **SP-MacDH**
  "I'm weary o' the shapes mere chance can thraw." **SP-MacDH**
  "That's the condition o't or near." **SP-MacDH**
Frae nirly, nippin', Eas'lan' breeze. Ille Terrarum. Robert Louis Stevenson. **CP-StevR**
Frae the friends and Land I love. Robert Burns. **CP-BurnR**
Fragile! Charles Bukowski. **SP-BukC2**
Fragment: "Alas! this is not what I thought life was." Percy Bysshe Shelley. **CP-ShelP**
Fragment: "Altho' my bed were in yon muir." Robert Burns. **CP-BurnR**
Fragment: "And that I walk thus proudly crowned withal." Percy Bysshe Shelley. **CP-ShelP**
Fragment: "Are you shaken, are you stirred." Robert Ranke Graves. **CP-GravR**
Fragment: "As bronze may be much beautified." Wilfred Owen. **CP-OwenW**
Fragment: "As for him who." William Carlos Williams. **CP-WilW2**
Fragment: "At last I entered a long dark gallery." Thomas Hardy. **CP-HardT**
Fragment: "Cramped in that funnelled hole, they watched the dawn." Wilfred Owen. **CP-OwenW**
Fragment: "Dead tree that, frozen, utters at the top, The." Malcolm Lowry. **CP-LowrM**
Fragment: "Faint white pillars that seem to fade." Edwin Arlington Robinson. **CP-RobiE**
Fragment: "Follow to the deep wood's weeds." Percy Bysshe Shelley. **CP-ShelP**
Fragment: "For let the impediment be what it may." William Wordsworth. **CP-WorW1**
Fragment: "Gentle story of two lovers young, A." Percy Bysshe Shelley. **CP-ShelP**
Fragment: "Great Spirit." Percy Bysshe Shelley. **CP-ShelP**
Fragment: "He came to him in the extasy of pray'r." William Cowper. **CP-CowpW**
Fragment: "Her flowing locks, the raven's wing." Robert Burns. **CP-BurnR**
Fragment: "I faint, I perish with my love! I grow." Percy Bysshe Shelley. **CP-ShelP**
Fragment: "I saw his round mouth's crimson deepen as it fell." Wilfred Owen. **CP-OwenW**
Fragment: "I stood upon a heaven-cleaving turret." Percy Bysshe Shelley. **CP-ShelP**
Fragment: "I would not be a king—enough." Percy Bysshe Shelley. **CP-ShelP**
Fragment: "I would to heaven that I were so much clay." Byron. **CTC; FiP; NAEL-2; NOBL; NoP; OAEL-2; OxBSP; PrIm** *Fr.* Don Juan. **CP-Byron**
Fragment: "Is it that in some brighter sphere." Percy Bysshe Shelley. **CP-ShelP**
Fragment: "Methought I was a billow in the crowd." Percy Bysshe Shelley. **CP-ShelP**
Fragment: "My God, Bill, what have you done?" William Carlos Williams. **CP-WilW2**
Fragment: "My head is wild with weeping for a grief." Percy Bysshe Shelley. **CP-ShelP**
Fragment: "Not one corner of a foreign field." Wilfred Owen. **CP-OwenW**
Fragment: "Now health forsakes that angel face." Robert Burns. **CP-BurnR**
Fragment: "O thou immortal deity." Percy Bysshe Shelley. **CP-ShelP**
Fragment: "O'er the raised earth the gales of evening sigh." Samuel Taylor Coleridge. **CP-ColeS**
Fragment: "Rude wind is singing, The." Percy Bysshe Shelley. **CP-ShelP**
Fragment: "Such hope, as is the sick despair of good." Percy Bysshe Shelley. **CP-ShelP**
Fragment: " 'Tis midnight now—athwart the murky air." Percy Bysshe Shelley. *Fr.* Posthumous Fragments of Margaret Nicholson. **CP-ShelP**
Fragment: "To the laboratory then I went. What little." John Ciardi. **SP-CiarJ**
Fragment: "Unrisen splendour of the brightest sun." Percy Bysshe Shelley. **CP-ShelP**
Fragment: "Viewless and invisible Consequence, The." Percy Bysshe Shelley. **CP-ShelP**
Fragment: "Wake the serpent not—lest he." Percy Bysshe Shelley. **CP-ShelP**
Fragment: "What men gain fairly—that they should possess." Percy Bysshe Shelley. **CP-ShelP**

Fragment: "When a lover clasps his fairest." Percy Bysshe Shelley. **CP-ShelP**
Fragment: "When soft winds and sunny skies." Percy Bysshe Shelley. **CP-ShelP**
Fragment: "Who can know more deeply than I your loneliness there?" Hayden Carruth. **CP-CarHS**
Fragment: "Why, why tell thy lover." Robert Burns. **CP-BurnR**
Fragment: "Witness Thou." William Wordsworth. **CP-WorW1**
Fragment: "Ye gentle visitations of calm thought." Percy Bysshe Shelley. **CP-ShelP**
Fragment: "Yes! all is past—swift time has fled away." Percy Bysshe Shelley. *Fr.* Posthumous Fragments of Margaret Nicholson. **CP-ShelP**
Fragment 36: "I know not what to do." Hilda Doolittle. **CP-DoolH**
Fragment 41: "Am I blind alas." Hilda Doolittle. **CP-DoolH**
Fragment, A: "Could I remount the river of my years." Byron. **CP-Byron**
Fragment, A: "Dreadful burden of our sins we feel, The." John Greenleaf Whittier. **CP-WhitJ**
Fragment, A: "Green grow the rashes, O; / Green grow the rashes, O; / The lasses they hae wimble bores." Robert Burns. *See* Green Grow[s] the Rashes.
Fragment, A: "On the street I am met with constant hostility." Robert Creeley. **CP-CreeR**
Fragment, A: "One night as I did wander." Robert Burns. **CP-BurnR**
Fragment A, *sels.* Christopher Smart. *Fr.* Jubilate Agno. **SP-SmarC**
  "Let Anaiah bless with the Dragon-fly, who sails over the pond by the wood-side and feedeth on the cresses." **FaBoVe,** *ll.* 100–113;
  "Rejoice in God, O ye Tongues; give the glory to the Lord, and the Lamb." **FaBoVe,** *ll.* 1–22;
  "Rejoice in God, O ye Tongues; give the glory to the Lord, and the Lamb." **PoE,** *ll.* 1–11;
Fragment, A: "When first I came to Stewart Kyle." Robert Burns. **CP-BurnR**
Fragment, A: "When *Guilford* good our Pilot stood." Robert Burns. **CP-BurnR**
Fragment, A: "When I see a rabbit." Jim Carroll. **SP-CarrJ**
Fragment, A: "When, to their airy hall, my fathers' voice." Byron. **CP-Byron**
Fragment, A: "Where aloneness fiercely." Alun Lewis. **CP-LewiA**
Fragment: A Roman's Chamber. Percy Bysshe Shelley. **CP-ShelP**
Fragment: A Serpent-Face. Percy Bysshe Shelley. **CP-ShelP**
Fragment: A Somersetshire Tragedy. William Wordsworth. **CP-WorW1**
Fragment: A Tale Untold. Percy Bysshe Shelley. **CP-ShelP**
Fragment: A Wanderer. Percy Bysshe Shelley. **CP-ShelP**
Fragment: Amor Aeternus. Percy Bysshe Shelley. **CP-ShelP**
Fragment: Apostrophe to Silence. Percy Bysshe Shelley. **CP-ShelP**
Fragment B, *sels.* Christopher Smart. *Fr.* Jubilate Agno. **SP-SmarC**
  "For I bless the PRINCE of PEACE and pray that all the guns may be nail'd up, save such as are for the rejoicing days." **InPS**
  "For I will consider my Cat Jeoffry." **CTC; ChTr; FM; FaBoCh; HAP; HelP; InPK; LAuP; LiTB; NAEL-1; NOEC; NTP; NU; NoP; OBF; OBWVE; OFC; OxAEP-1; PAI; PCat; PPP; PoE; PoEL-3; PrIm; Prf; RB; SCV; SeCePo; SeCeV; SoCa; TRP; TTTS; WeW; WiR** (My Cat Jeoffry.) **ChTr; FaBoCh; LiTB; PoE; RB; SeCePo; SoCa; WiR**
  (Of Jeoffry, His Cat.) **NU; PrIm**
  "For I will consider my Cat Jeoffry." **UV**
  "For man is between the pinchers while his soul is shaping and purifying." **ChIV-1**
  "For the Air is purified by prayer which is made aloud and with all our might." **Prf**
  "For the doubling of flowers is the improvement of the gard'ner's talent." **ChIV-2; LAuP; NOEC**
  "For the spiritual musick is as follows." **NOEC**
  Let Elizur Rejoice with the Partridge. **PoEL-3**
    God Hath Sent Me to Sea for Pearls. **CBCK**
    "Let Elizur[e] rejoice with the Partridge." **OAEL-1**
  "Let Ephah rejoice with Buprestis, the Lord endue us with temperance and humanity, till every cow have her mate!" **NOEC**
  "Let Peter rejoice with the Moon Fish who keeps up the life in the waters by night." **ChIV-1**
  "Let Shobi rejoice with the Kastrel—blessed be the name JESUS in falconry and in the MALL." **NOEC**
Fragment: Beauty's Halo. Percy Bysshe Shelley. **CP-ShelP**
Fragment C. Christopher Smart. *Fr.* Jubilate Agno. **SP-SmarC**
  "For I prophesy that they will understand the blessing and virtue of the rain." **ECEV**
  "For I prophesy that we shall have our horns again." **ChIV-1**
Fragment D. Christopher Smart. *Fr.* Jubilate Agno. **SP-SmarC**
  Mineral Rejoicings. **CBCK**

Fragment: Death in Life. Percy Bysshe Shelley. **CP-ShelP**

Fragment—Epistle from Esopus to Maria. Robert Burns. **CP-BurnR**

Fragment 40: "Keep love and he wings." Hilda Doolittle. **CP-DoolH**

Fragment from a Journal. Leonard Cohen. **CP-CoheL**

Fragment from a "Schoolboy's Odyssey." Kenneth Patchen. *Fr.* Eight Early Poems. **CP-PatcK**

Fragment from Correspondence. Howard Nemerov. **CP-NemeH**

Fragment from Dove Cottage Manuscript 44 (I). William Wordsworth. **CP-WorW1**

Fragment from May. Philip Larkin. **CP-LarkP**

Fragment from the "Monk of Athos." Byron. **CP-Byron**

Fragment from the Wandering Jew. Percy Bysshe Shelley. **CP-ShelP**

Fragment: Home. Percy Bysshe Shelley. **CP-ShelP**

Fragment: Igniculus Desiderii. Percy Bysshe Shelley. **CP-ShelP**

Fragment: "In vain did Time and Nature. . . ." William Wordsworth. **CP-WorW1**

Fragment: Life Rounded with Sleep. Percy Bysshe Shelley. **CP-ShelP**

Fragment: Little N.Y. Ode. Jim Carroll. **SP-CarrJ**

Fragment: Love the Universe To-day. Percy Bysshe Shelley. **CP-ShelP**

Fragment: Love's Tender Atmosphere. Percy Bysshe Shelley. **CP-ShelP**

Fragment: May the Limner. Percy Bysshe Shelley. **CP-ShelP**

Fragment: Milton's Spirit. Percy Bysshe Shelley. **CP-ShelP**

Fragment: Music and Sweet Poetry. Percy Bysshe Shelley. **CP-ShelP**

Fragment 1956. Allen Ginsberg. **CP-GinsA**

Fragment (1966): "That her acts / Olga's acts / of beauty." Ezra Pound. *Fr.* Cantos. **CP-PoCan**

Fragment, 1959. Stephen Berg. **SP-BergS**

Fragment of a *Bas Relief.* John Ciardi. **SP-CiarJ**

Fragment of a Ghost Story. Percy Bysshe Shelley. **CP-ShelP**

Fragment of a "Gothic" Tale. William Wordsworth. **CP-WorW1**

Fragment of a Lost Poem. Robert Ranke Graves. **CP-GravR**

Fragment of a Meditation. Allen Tate. **CP-TateA**

Fragment of a Poem on the Works and Wonders of Almighty Power. James Thomson. **CP-ThomJ**

Fragment of a Satire on Satire. Percy Bysshe Shelley. **CP-ShelP**

Fragment of a Series of Elegies. Robert Southwell. **CP-SoutR**

Fragment of a Sonnet: Farewell to North Devon. Percy Bysshe Shelley. **CP-ShelP**

Fragment of a Sonnet: To Harriet. Percy Bysshe Shelley. **CP-ShelP**

Fragment of an Agon. Thomas Stearns Eliot. **LiTB** *Fr.* Sweeney Agonistes. **CP-ElioT**

Fragment of an Epistle to Thomas Moore. Byron. **CP-Byron**

Fragment of an Intended Poem on Milton, Written in the Copy of *Paradise Lost* Which Belonged to Wordsworth at Cambridge. William Wordsworth. **CP-WorW1**

Fragment of Anything You Like, A. Gerard Manley Hopkins. **CP-HopkG**

Fragment of *Brutus*, an Epic. Alexander Pope. **CP-PopeA**

Fragment of New York, 1929. Richard Eberhart. **CP-EberR**

Fragment of the "Castle Builder." John Keats. **CP-KeatJ**

Fragment of the Elegy on the Death of Adonis. Bion, *tr. fr. Greek by* Shelley. **CP-ShelP**

Fragment of the Elegy on the Death of Bion, *see also translations by* Chapman ("Ye mountain valleys. . . ") *and* Wordsworth ("Ah me! the lowliest children. . . "). Moschus, *tr. fr. Greek by* Shelley. **CP-ShelP**

Fragment of weak flesh that circles round, A. A Plan of Self-Subjection. Thom Gunn. **CP-GunnT**

Fragment: Omens. Percy Bysshe Shelley. **CP-ShelP**

Fragment—on Glenriddel's Fox Breaking His Chain, A. Robert Burns. **CP-BurnR**

Fragment on Keats. Percy Bysshe Shelley. **CP-ShelP**

Fragment 113: "Not honey, / not the plunder of the bee." Hilda Doolittle. **CP-DoolH**

Fragment, or The Triumph of Conscience, *for diff. vers., see* Victoria. Percy Bysshe Shelley. *Fr.* Original Poetry by Victor and Cazire. **CP-ShelP**

Fragment: Pater Omnipotens. Percy Bysshe Shelley. **CP-ShelP**

Fragment: Rain ("Fitful alternations of the rain, The"). Percy Bysshe Shelley. **CP-ShelP**

Fragment: Rain ("Gentleness of rain was in the wind, The"). Percy Bysshe Shelley. **CP-ShelP**

Fragment: Redundance. William Wordsworth. **CP-WorW1**

Fragment: Rome and Nature. Percy Bysshe Shelley. **CP-ShelP**

Fragment: Satan Broken Loose. Percy Bysshe Shelley. **CP-ShelP**

Fragment 68: "I envy you your chance of death." Hilda Doolittle. **CP-DoolH**

Fragment: Sufficient Unto the Day. Percy Bysshe Shelley. **CP-ShelP**

Fragment: The Baker's Cart. William Wordsworth. **CP-WorW1**

Fragment: The Deserts of Dim Sleep. Percy Bysshe Shelley. **CP-ShelP**

Fragment: The False Laurel and the True. Percy Bysshe Shelley. **CP-ShelP**

Fragment: The Lady of the South. Percy Bysshe Shelley. **CP-ShelP**

Fragment: The Lake's Margin. Percy Bysshe Shelley. **CP-ShelP**

Fragment: The Names II. Allen Ginsberg. **CP-GinsA**

Fragment: The Sepulchre of Memory. Percy Bysshe Shelley. **CP-ShelP**

Fragment: The Vine-Shroud. Percy Bysshe Shelley. **CP-ShelP**

Fragment: Thoughts Come and Go in Solitude. Percy Bysshe Shelley. **CP-ShelP**

Fragment: To a Friend Released from Prison. Percy Bysshe Shelley. **CP-ShelP**

Fragment: To Byron. Percy Bysshe Shelley. **CP-ShelP**

Fragment: To Italy. Percy Bysshe Shelley. **CP-ShelP**

Fragment: To Music, A. Percy Bysshe Shelley. **CP-ShelP**

Fragment: To One Singing. Percy Bysshe Shelley. **CP-ShelP**

Fragment: To the Mind of Man. Percy Bysshe Shelley. **CP-ShelP**

Fragment: To the Moon. Percy Bysshe Shelley. **CP-ShelP**

Fragment: To the People of England. Percy Bysshe Shelley. **CP-ShelP**

Fragment: Wedded Souls. Percy Bysshe Shelley. **CP-ShelP**

Fragment, Which Was Meant for the Beginning of an Elegy on the Late Miss Burnet of Monboddo, A. Robert Burns. **CP-BurnR**

Fragment: Wine of the Fairies. Percy Bysshe Shelley. **CP-ShelP**

Fragment Written Shortly after the Marriage of Miss Chaworth. Byron. **CP-Byron**

Fragment: "Yet once again." William Wordsworth. *See* Yet once again do I behold the forms.

Fragment: Zephyrus the Awakener. Percy Bysshe Shelley. **CP-ShelP**

Fragmentary Blue. Robert Frost. **CP-FrosR**

Fragmentation of good gear is sad, The. But they could *do* something about that. Jenny Joseph. *Fr.* Life and Turgid Times of A. Citizen. **SP-JoseJ**

Fragments. Stephen Dobyns. **SP-DobyS**

Fragments. Gerard Manley Hopkins. **CP-HopkG**

Fragments. Gerard Manley Hopkins. **CP-HopkG**

Fragments. Gerard Manley Hopkins. **CP-HopkG**

Fragments. Gerard Manley Hopkins. **CP-HopkG**

Fragments. Gerard Manley Hopkins. **CP-HopkG**

"Although she be more white."

"—And on their brittle green quils."

"Dewy fields in the morning under the sun."

"Ends of the crisp buds she chips, The."

"His gilded rowels."

"How looks the night? There does not miss a star." **OxBSP** (How Looks the Night?) **OxBSP**

"In her cheeks that dwell."

"Night's lantern / Pointed with piercèd lights, and breaks of rays."

"Now the rain."

"Or ever the early stirrings of skylark."

"Pure gold lily, but by the pure gold lily, A."

"Sky minted into golden sequins, The."

"Sparky air, The."

"Star most spiritual, principal, preeminent, A."

"Stars waving their indivisible rays."

"Sun just risen, The."

"There is an island, wester'd in the main."

"They came / Next to meadows abundant, pierced with flowers."

"Thick-fleeced bushes like a heifer's ear."
("Out-fleeced bushes like a spaniel's ear.")

"Time was late and the wet yellow woods, The."

"We live to see."

"When cuckoo calls and I may hear."

"Whose braggart 'scutcheon, whose complaisant crest."

"Wind, that passes by so fleet, The."

Fragments; "Locke sank into a swoon." William Butler Yeats. **CP-YeatW**

Fragments Connected with Epipsychidion, *see also* Epipsychidion. Percy Bysshe Shelley. **CP-ShelP**

Fragments: "Decorous, and forbearing further correction." Robert Creeley. **CP-CreeR**

Fragments: Drafts, Mostly or All for a Poem on a Heroic Theme. William Wordsworth. **CP-WorW1**

Fragments for "The Harvest Home" and "The Doe." George Meredith. **CP-MerG2**

"But Joan, where is Bessy?—She."

"Full loud & fresh crows Chaunticlere!"

"Poor things! we know not what they suffer."

Fragments from Dove Cottage Manuscript 44 (II). William Wordsworth. **CP-WorW1**

Fragments from the Alfoxden Note-Book (II). William Wordsworth. **CP-WorW1**

Fragments from the Alfoxden Note-Book (III). William Wordsworth. **CP-WorW1**

Fragments from the Alfoxden Notebook (I). William Wordsworth. **CP-WorW1**

Fragments from the "Christabel" Note-book. William Wordsworth. **CP-WorW1**

Fragments from the Duck Anthology to Greet Our Beloved Harteebeeste in the Morning Watch. Malcolm Lowry. **CP-LowrM**

Fragments of a Lost Gnostic Poem of the Twelfth [*or* 12th] Century. Herman Melville. **SP-MelvH**

Fragments of an Old Song 1. Gilbert Sorrentino. **SP-SorrG**

Fragments of an Old Song 2. Gilbert Sorrentino. **SP-SorrG**

Fragments of an Unfinished Drama. Percy Bysshe Shelley. **CP-ShelP**

"And, if my grief should still be dearer to me."

"He came like a dream in the dawn of life."

Fragments of Eternity. John Gould Fletcher. **SP-FletJ** *Fr.* The Parables of Christ.

Fragments on St. Winefred. Gerard Manley Hopkins. **CP-HopkG**

"Atque tribus primum quod flumen fontibus exit."

"Iam si rite sequor prisci vestigia facti."

"Quin etiam nostros non aspernata labores."

Fragments Supposed to Be Parts of Otho, *see also* Otho. Percy Bysshe Shelley. **CP-ShelP**

Fragments Written for Hellas. Percy Bysshe Shelley. **CP-ShelP**

Fragmentum Petron. Arbitr. The Same Translated. Petronius Arbiter, *tr. fr. Latin* by Ben Jonson. **CP-JonsB**

Fragonard. Ogden Nash. **CP-NashO**

Fragrance is, The. Of Mathilde. Charles Olson. **CP-OlsoC**

Fragrant sag of fruit distinctly grouped, A. Edward Estlin Cummings. **CP-CummE**

Frail as the leaves that quiver on the sprays. Homer, *tr. by* Samuel Johnson. **CP-JohnS** *Fr.* The Iliad.

Frail creatures are we all! To be the best. Humility the Mother of Charity. Samuel Taylor Coleridge. **CP-ColeS**

Frailty. George Herbert. **CP-HerbG**

Frailty, Thy Name Is a Misnomer. Ogden Nash. **CP-NashO**

Fram Pharos I have seen her white. Song from "Cleopatra." John Berryman. **CP-BerrJ**

Frame. Adrienne Rich. **SP-RicA2**

Framed in a jagged window of grey stones. Corfe Castle. Alun Lewis. **CP-LewiA**

Framed in her phoenix fire-screen, Edna Ward. Cottage Street, 1953. Richard Wilbur. **CP-WilbR**

Fran. Edward Estlin Cummings. *Fr.* Five Americans. **CP-CummE**

France. Rudyard Kipling. **CP-KiplR**

France. George Meredith. **CP-MerG1**

"Ah, what a dawn of splendour, when her sowers."

"Behold, the Gods are with her, and are known."

"Ever invoking fire from heaven, the fire."

"Henceforth of her the Gods are known."

"Look not for spreading boughs."

"O she that made the brave appeal."

"She shall rise worthier of her prototype."

"She snatched at heaven's flame of old."

"Swift fall the blows, and men upbraid."

"They are with her now, and in her ears, and known."

"We look for her that sunlike stood."

France; an Ode. Samuel Taylor Coleridge. **CP-ColeS**

France (Concluded). William Wordsworth. *Fr.* The Prelude; Growth of a Poet's Mind [1850 vers.]. **CP-WorW3**

"It hath been told." **EnRP**

Noble, The. **ChTr**

"O[h!] pleasant exercise of hope and joy!" **HAP; PoEL-4**, book 11, *ll.* 105–144; **FiP**

(French Revolution, The.) **FiP**, *book 11, ll.* 105–144;

France! How shall we call her belle again? La Belle, La Douce, La Grande. Countee Cullen. **CP-CullC**

France lured me forth; the realm that I had crossed. William Wordsworth. **FaBoPV** *Fr.* Residence in France ("Even as a river,—partly (it might seem)"). *Fr.* The Prelude; Growth of a Poet's Mind [1850 vers.]. **CP-WorW3**

France of the poujadiste! Right Wing Sympathies. Donald Davie. **CP-DavDo**

France, one of the great modes of the human mind and heart. Letter to Pierre Emmanuel. Kathleen Jessie Raine. **SP-RainK**

France, The 18th Year of These States. Walt Whitman. **CP-WhitW**

Francesca in Winter. Stevie Smith. **CP-SmitS**

Francesca of Rimini. Dante Alighieri, *tr. by* Byron. **CP-Byron** *Fr.* Inferno. *Fr.* Divina Commedia.

Francesco and Clare. David St. John. **SP-StJoD**

Francisco, I'll Bring You Red Carnations. Philip Levine. **SP-LeviP**

Francisco on his shelf. Santo. James Merrill. **SP-MerrJ**

Franck ne'r wore silk she sweares; but I reply. Upon Franck. Robert Herrick. **CP-HerrR**

Franck wo'd go scoure her teeth; and setting to't. Upon Franck. Robert Herrick. **CP-HerrR**

François Villon Forgotten. Carl Sandburg. **CP-SandC**

Frank Courtship, The. George Crabbe. **SP-CrabG** *Fr.* Tales.

Frank! Frank! James Schuyler. *Fr.* Four Poems. **CP-SchuJ**

Frank O'Hara. Ted Berrigan. **SP-BerrT**

Frank, will['] t live handsomely? Trust not too far. Advice to My Best Brother, Colonel Francis Lovelace. Richard Lovelace. **CP-LoveR**

Frankie Laine was singing "Jezebel." Memories. Leonard Cohen. **CP-CoheL**

Frankie's Trade. Rudyard Kipling. **CP-KiplR**

Frankincense, The. Robert Herrick. **CP-HerrR**

Franklin Square. William Carlos Williams. **CP-WilW2**

Franklin's Prologue, The. Geoffrey Chaucer. **NAEL-1; OAEL-1** *Fr.* The Canterbury Tales. **CP-ChauG**

Franklin's Tale, The. Geoffrey Chaucer. **NAEL-1; OAEL-1** *Fr.* The Canterbury Tales. **CP-ChauG**

Frantic throb of the train, The. A Train at Night. David Herbert Lawrence. **CP-LawrD**

Franz, a Goose. May Sarton. **SP-SartM**

Frater Ave Atque Vale. Tennyson. **CP-TennA**

Fraternal Rage, the guilty Thebes alarms. Publius Papinius Statius, *tr. by* Alexander Pope. **CP-PopeA** *Fr.* Thebais.

Fratricide, The. John Greenleaf Whittier. **CP-WhitJ**

Frau Bauman, Frau Schmidt, and Frau Schwartze. Theodore Roethke. **CP-RoetT**

Frau Doktor / Mama Brundig. The Frog Prince. Anne Sexton. **CP-SextA**

Freak but moist flower, A. The Love Plant. Anne Sexton. **CP-SextA**

Freaks at Spurgin Road Field, The. Richard Hugo. **CP-HugoR**

Freaks of Fashion. Christina Georgina Rossetti. **CP-RosC2**

Fred? Shel Silverstein. **SP-SilS2**

Fred and the Holy Grail. William Dickey. **SP-DickW**

Fred, where is north? West-running Brook. Robert Frost. **CP-FrosR**

Freddy. Stevie Smith. **CP-SmitS**

Frederick Alexander Pott. Time's Fool. John Updike. **CP-UpdiJ**

Frederick Douglass. Paul Laurence Dunbar. **CP-DunbP**

Frederick Douglass. Robert Earl Hayden. **CP-HaydR**

FREE / To the World. Man! Archibald MacLeish. **CP-MacLA**

Free as a thistle, white hair blowing. Second Childhood. Phoebe Hesketh. **SP-HeskP**

Free bird leaps / on the back of the wind, A. Caged Bird. Maya Angelou. **SP-AngeM**

Free Clinic. Chuck Miller. **SP-MillC**

Free evening fades, outside the windows fastened with decorative iron grilles, The. Evening in the Sanitarium. Louise Bogan. **CP-BogaL**

Free Fantasia: Tiger Flowers. Robert Earl Hayden. **CP-HaydR**

Free Foot, The. John Hewitt. **CP-HewiJ**

Free from all fogs butt shining faire, and cleere. Sonnet 13. Mary Sidney, Countess of Montgomery Wroth. *Fr.* A Crowne of Sonetts Dedicated to Love. *Fr.* Pamphilia to Amphilanthus. **CP-WrotM**

Free from the proud, the pompous, and the vain. To My Worthy Friend, Mr. T.B. One of the People Called Quakers. Christopher Smart. **SP-SmarC**

Free heart, that singest to-day. Calls on the Heart. Elizabeth Barrett Browning. **CP-BroEB**

Free Mason. John Hewitt. **CP-HewiJ**

Free One, A. Wystan Hugh Auden. *See* Watch any day his nonchalant pauses, see.

Free thyself from wo. Hafiz, *tr. by* Ralph Waldo Emerson. **CP-EmerR** *Fr.* Odes.

Free to travel, he still couldn't be shown how lucky. David Walker (1785–1830). Rita Dove. **SP-DoveR**

Free Welcome. Robert Herrick. **CP-HerrR**

Free! while in the cathedral at Seville. Heaven. John Berryman. **CP-BerrJ**

Free Will. David Herbert Lawrence. **CP-LawrD**

Freed dove flew to the Rajah's tower, The. The Dove of Dacca. Rudyard Kipling. **CP-KiplR**

Freed Islands, The. John Greenleaf Whittier. **CP-WhitJ**

Freed the Fret of Thinking. Thomas Hardy. **CP-HardT**

Freediving thirty to forty feet, only a few seconds to spare. Lobsters in the Brain Coral. Laurence Lieberman. **SP-LiebL**

Freedom. Ralph Waldo Emerson. **CP-EmerR**

Freedom and Discipline. Hayden Carruth. **CP-CarHS**

Freedom as Experience. Thomas Merton. **CP-MertT; SP-MertT**

Freedom, farewell! Or so the soldiers say. Port of Embarkation. Randall Jarrell. **CP-JarrR**

Freedom in Brazil. John Greenleaf Whittier. **CP-WhitJ**

Freedom in love? It has been questioned. Think. Sonnet. Hayden Carruth. **CP-CarHS** *Fr.* Sonnets.

Freedom is a Habit. Carl Sandburg. **CP-SandC**

Freedom, New Hampshire. Galway Kinnell. **SP-KinnG**

Freedom of Loving, The. Wendell Berry. *Fr.* The Handing Down. **CP-BerrW**

Freedom of the Moon, The. Robert Frost. **CP-FrosR**

Freedom of the wholly mad, The. The Phenomenology of Anger. Adrienne Rich. **SP-RicA1; SP-RicA2**

Freedom: The Unmolested Eagle of Myself. Charles Bukowski. **SP-BukC2**

Freedom Train. Langston Hughes. **SP-HughL**

Freedoms / out of contrivance. Roy Fisher. **SP-FishR** *Fr.* Glenthorne Poems.

Freedom's Plow. Langston Hughes. **SP-HughL**

Freehold. Robert Ranke Graves. **CP-GravR**

Freehold. John Hewitt. **CP-HewiJ**

    Feathers on Turf.

    Glittering Sod, The.

    Lonely Heart, The.

    Townland of Peace.

Freely Espousing. James Schuyler. **CP-SchuJ**

Freewheeling down the escarpment past the unpassing horse. The Cyclist. Louis MacNeice. **CP-MacNL**

Freezing convict wanted, The. A Thanksgiving for My Father. William Stafford. **SP-StafW**

Freight Cars. Stephen Dobyns. **SP-DobyS**

Freight train rattles and jars through sleep, A. The Soundings. Leonard Nathan. **SP-NathL**

Freight trains, / when I was fifteen, The. Then. Frederick Morgan. **SP-MorgF**

Freighter, gay with rust, The. Jews at Haifa. Randall Jarrell. **CP-JarrR; SP-JarrR**

Freighter 1940. Malcolm Lowry. **CP-LowrM**

Frémont Campaign Song, A. John Greenleaf Whittier. **CP-WhitJ**

French and English. Leonard Cohen. **CP-CoheL**

French and the Spanish Guerrillas, The. William Wordsworth. **CP-WorW1**

French Army in Russia 1812–1813, The. William Wordsworth. **CP-WorW2**

French Distichs. Samuel Johnson. **CP-JohnS**

French Hill. Hayden Carruth. **CP-CarHS**

French is easy. Chacun à Son Berlitz. Ogden Nash. **CP-NashO**

French Pronunciation Simplified for Julian Trevelyan. Malcolm Lowry. **CP-LowrM**

French Revolution, The. William Blake. **CP-BlakW**

    Louis XVI. **ChER**

French Revolution, The. William Wordsworth. *See* O[h!] pleasant exercise of hope and joy!

French Revolution as It Appeared to Enthusiasts at Its Commencement. Reprinted from "The Friend." William Wordsworth. **CP-WorW1**

French Wars, The. Rudyard Kipling. **CP-KiplR**

Frenchie. Stephen Dobyns. **SP-DobyS**

Frenzy. George Crabbe. **NOBE** *Fr.* Sir Eustace Grey. **SP-CrabG**

Frenzy. Anne Sexton. **CP-SextA**

Frenzy softens the air. Radiant Silhouette IV. John Yau. **SP-YauJo**

Frequency of images of the moon. Study of Images II. Wallace Stevens. **CP-StevW**

Frequently the woods are pink. Emily Dickinson. **CP-DickE**

Frequently when the night. The Apparition. John Berryman. **CP-BerrJ**

Fresco: Departure for an Imperialist War. Thomas McGrath. **SP-McGrT**

Fresh addenda are published every day. Wystan Hugh Auden. *Fr.* The Quest. **CP-AudeW**

Fresh Air. Kenneth Koch. **SP-KochK**

    "At the Poem Society a black-haired man stands up to say."

    "Oh to be seventeen years old."

    "Summer in the trees! 'It is time to strangle several bad poets'."

    "Supposing that one walks out into the air." **OBCoV**

Fresh as the day, and new as are the hours. A Song of Welcome to King Charles. Ben Jonson. **CP-JonsB**

Fresh Cheese and Cream. Robert Herrick. **CP-HerrR**

Fresh from the dewy hill, the merry year. Song. William Blake. **CP-BlakW**

Fresh from the knife and coming to. Louis MacNeice. **CP-MacNL** *Fr.* Jigsaws. **CP-MacNL**

Fresh-hearted May on hearing what he said. Geoffrey Chaucer. **OxBM** *Fr.* The Merchant's Tale. *Fr.* The Canterbury Tales. **CP-ChauG**

Fresh June morning, A. Frederick Morgan. *Fr.* The River. **SP-MorgF**

Fresh morning gusts have blown away all fear. To a Young Lady Who Sent Me a Laurel Crown. John Keats. **CP-KeatJ**

Fresh Spring has come with flower and leaf to warn. George Meredith. **CP-MerG2**

Fresh Spring, the Herald. Edmund Spenser. *See* LXX. "Fresh Spring, the herald of love's mighty king."

Fresh strewings [or strowings] allow. The Peter-penny. Robert Herrick. **CP-HerrR**

Fresh Water. David Herbert Lawrence. **CP-LawrD**

Freshly, gaily, the rivulet flows. A Shout to the Sheperds. Ralph Waldo Emerson. **CP-EmerR**

Freshman Blues. John Berryman. **CP-BerrJ**

Fret not thyself because of evildoers. Psalm 37. Bible, *O.T.* *Fr.* Psalms. **CP-Psal**

Fretful and sick, you ask. William Dickey. **SP-DickW** *Fr.* At Your Old House. **SP-DickW**

Fretful and sick, you long. William Dickey. **SP-DickW** *Fr.* At Your Old House. **SP-DickW**

Fretted discoloured towers and domes. Frank Templeton Prince. *Fr.* Memoirs in Oxford. **CP-PrinF**

Freya. Frederick Morgan. **SP-MorgF**

Friar had said his paternosters duly, The. Necrological. John Crowe Ransom. **SP-RansJ**

Friar uxorious! George Meredith. **CP-MerG2**

Friar's Prologue, The. Geoffrey Chaucer. **PoE** *Fr.* The Canterbury Tales. **CP-ChauG**

Friar's Tale, The. Geoffrey Chaucer. **PoE** *Fr.* The Canterbury Tales. **CP-ChauG**

Friday arrives with all its attendant ecstasies. Called Back. Charles Wright. **SP-WrigC**

Friday first's the day appointed. To Dr. John MacKenzie. Robert Burns. **CP-BurnR**

Friday, Good Friday, which. Charles Olson. **CP-OlsoC**

Friday Night. Robert Ranke Graves. **CP-GravR**

Friday Night. Robert Ranke Graves. **CP-GravR**

Friday Night in the Royal Station. Philip Larkin. **CP-LarkP**

Friday the Thirteenth. Allen Ginsberg. **CP-GinsA**

Friday the 12th. Al Young. **CP-YounA**

Friday's Child. Wystan Hugh Auden. **CP-AudeW**

Friend, The. Robert Creeley. **CP-CreeR**

Friend, The. Charles Olson. **CP-OlsoC**

Friend, The. Marge Piercy. **SP-PierM**

Friend, The. Stevie Smith. **CP-SmitS**

Friend, A. William DeWitt Snodgrass. **SP-SnodW**

Friend, The. Miller Williams. **SP-WillM**

Friend Anguish reveals is, The. Emily Dickinson. **SP-DickE**

Friend by enemy I call you out. To Others than You. Dylan Thomas. **CP-ThomD**

Friend, call it bad karma if you're. Tanck's Song About the Jinx. Hayden Carruth. **CP-CarHS** *Fr.* Songs About What Comes Down: The Complete Works of Mr. Septic Tanck.

Friend Commissar, since we're met and are happy. Robert Burns. *Fr.* Dumfries Epigrams. **CP-BurnR**

Friend Furius, / "who has no slaves & no money." Carmen 23. Catullus. *Fr.* Carmina. **CP-Catul**

Friend I can trust is the one who will let me have my death, The. Adrienne Rich. **CP-RicAE**

Friend I commend to thee the narrow way. Then They That Feared the Lord Spake Often One to Another. Christina Georgina Rossetti. **CP-RosC3**

Friend, if the mute and shrouded dead. Catullus. *See* Carmen 96: "If, Calvus, effects of grief."

Friend in a tipi in the, A. Two Fawns That Didn't See the Light This Spring. Gary Snyder. **CP-SnydG**

Friend, in my mountain-side demesne. To A Gardener. Robert Louis Stevenson. **CP-StevR**

Friend is a / solemnity, A. Emily Dickinson. **SP-DickE**

Friend is he, who, hunted as a foe, A. Nuru'ddin Abdu 'R-Rahman Jami, *tr. fr. Persian by* Ralph Waldo Emerson. **CP-EmerR**

Friend, Lover, Husband, Sister, Brother! An Exile. Samuel Taylor Coleridge. **CP-ColeS**

Friend o' the Poet, tired and leal. Poem. Robert Burns. **CP-BurnR**

Friend of mine! whose lot was cast. Remembrance. John Greenleaf Whittier. **CP-WhitJ**

Friend of my many years! A Legacy. John Greenleaf Whittier. **CP-WhitJ**

Friend of my soul! as with moist eye. Follen. John Greenleaf Whittier. **CP-WhitJ**

Friend of my winter, yesterday's friend. Winter. Pablo Neruda, *tr. fr. Spanish* by Ben Belitt. **SP-NeruP**

Friend of my youth! when young we roved. To the Earl of Clare. Byron. **CP-Byron**

Friend of the Fourth Decade, The. James Merrill. **SP-MerrJ**

Friend of the Slave, and yet the friend of all. Daniel Neall. John Greenleaf Whittier. **CP-WhitJ**

Friend of the wise! and teacher of the good! Samuel Taylor Coleridge. **CP-ColeS**

Friend of the wretched! wherefore should the eye. Ode to Death. Charlotte Smith. **CP-SmitC**

Friend Revisited, A. Donald Hall. **CP-HallD**

Friend Rundle fell with grievous bump. Epigram, An. Jonathan Swift. **CP-SwifJ**

Friend saw the rooms, A. Boy's Room. George Oppen. **CP-OppeG**

Friend, then, whatever has become of us. Rhetoric. Marilyn Hacker. **SP-HackM**

Friend (this is an imaginary letter). Marilyn Hacker. **SP-HackM** *Fr.* Separations.

Friend, thou beholdest the lightning? Who has the charge of it. A Song in the Desert. Rudyard Kipling. **CP-KiplR**

Friend, when the thundercloud is low. George Meredith. **CP-MerG2**

Friend, When You Speak. Leonard Cohen. **CP-CoheL**

Friend who calls up over the telephone, The. The Sport of Kings. Ernest Hemingway. **CP-HemiE**

Friend who wild from Wisdom's way, The. To Mr. S. McKenzie. Robert Burns. **CP-BurnR**

Friend, with regard to this same hare. To the Rev. Mr. Powell. Christopher Smart. **SP-SmarC**

Friend writes / How's the prince?, A. Sunburst. Dabney Stuart. **SP-StuaD**

Friendless. John Berryman. **CP-BerrJ**

Friendless and faint, with martyred steps and slow. Calvary. Edwin Arlington Robinson. **CP-RobiE**

Friendless in Clare, except Brian Boydell. Friendless. John Berryman. **CP-BerrJ**

Friendly Advice to a Lot of Young Men. Charles Bukowski. **SP-BukC2**

Friendly cow, all red and white, The. The Cow. Robert Louis Stevenson. **CP-StevR**

Friendly, ripe old man, full-charged with tales, A. J.B. Shelton (1876–1958), The Coventry Antiquarian. John Hewitt. **CP-HewiJ**

Friendly Touch, The. Ogden Nash. **CP-NashO**

Friends. John Ashbery. **SP-AshbJ**

Friends, The. Robert Creeley. **CP-CreeR**

Friends, The. Rudyard Kipling. **CP-KiplR**

Friends. Anne Sexton. *Fr.* The Death of the Fathers. **CP-SextA**

Friends. Charles Kenneth Williams. **CP-WillC**

Friends. William Butler Yeats. **CP-YeatW**

Friends & Relatives. White Eyes. Anne Waldman. **SP-WaldA**

Friends are nations in themselves. Emily Dickinson. **SP-DickE**

Friends Beyond. Thomas Hardy. **CP-HardT**

Friend's Burial, The. John Greenleaf Whittier. **CP-WhitJ**

Friends, cousins, strangers saluted. Rite. John Hewitt. **CP-HewiJ**

Friends have all in common. Found Macaronic Antipoem. Thomas Merton, *tr. fr. Latin and German* by Thomas Merton. *Fr.* A Selection of Concrete Poems. **CP-MertT**

Friends, I commend to you the narrow way. Thy Friend and Thy Father's Friend Forget Not. Christina Georgina Rossetti. **CP-RosC2**

Friend's Illness, A. William Butler Yeats. **CP-YeatW**

Friends make / the most of it. For Tom. Robert Creeley. **CP-CreeR**

Friends of faces unknown and a land. Only a Curl. Elizabeth Barrett Browning. **CP-BroEB**

Friends of his Youth, The. William Butler Yeats. *Fr.* A Man Young and Old. **CP-YeatW**

Friends of the born nurse, The. Wystan Hugh Auden. *Fr.* Shorts [1927–1932] ("Pick a quarrel, go to war"). **CP-AudeW**

Friends of the Family, or Bowling a Sticky Cricket. Robert Penn Warren. *Fr.* Ballad of a Sweet Dream of Peace. **SP-WarrR**

Friends of the River Trent. Stevie Smith. **CP-SmitS**

Friends to me are frozen wine. Ralph Waldo Emerson. **CP-EmerR**

Friends warned of moose that. The Moose Wallow. Robert Earl Hayden. **CP-HaydR**

Friends who come to see you, The. Sleep. James Schuyler. **CP-SchuJ**

Friendship. Wystan Hugh Auden. **CP-AudWJ**

Friendship. William Cowper. **CP-CowpW**

"Candid and generous and just." **OBF**

Friendship ("Ruddy drop of manly blood, A"). Ralph Waldo Emerson. **CP-EmerR**

Friendship ("Thou foolish Hafiz! Say, do churls"). Hafiz, *tr. fr. Persian* by Ralph Waldo Emerson. **CP-EmerR**

Friendship agony! words came to me. A Postscript. Hart Crane. **CP-CranH**

Friendship, as some sage poet sings. On the Aphorism "L'Amitié est l'Amour sans Ailes." Charlotte Smith. **CP-SmitC**

Friendship, peculiar Gift of Heav'n. An Ode on Friendship. Samuel Johnson. **CP-JohnS**

Friendship turns. And turns again. Another name. No Yellow Jackets on the Mountain. Dabney Stuart. **SP-StuaD**

Friendship, when a friend meant a helping sword. No Resurrection. Robinson Jeffers. **CP-JefR2**

Frigate Pelican, The. Marianne Craig Moore. **CP-MoorM**

Frigg. Frederick Morgan. **SP-MorgF**

Fright among the Runes. Isabella Gardner. **CP-GardI**

Frightened fearful afraid. Age. Grace Paley. **CP-PaleG**

Frightened Man, The. Louise Bogan. **CP-BogaL**

Frightened Men. Robert Ranke Graves. **CP-GravR**

Frightening the blood in its tunnel. Sunstroke. Ted Hughes. **SP-HughT**

Frigid and sweet Her parting Face. Emily Dickinson. **CP-DickE**

Friskers, or, Gods and Men. Stevie Smith. **CP-SmitS**

Frisky Lamb, A. Christina Georgina Rossetti. **CP-RosC2**

Fritillary, The. John Updike. **CP-UpdiJ**

Frock. James Schuyler. **CP-SchuJ**

Frog, The. Paul Muldoon. **SP-MuldP**

Frog and the Golden Ball, The. Robert Ranke Graves. **CP-GravR**

Frog Autumn. Sylvia Plath. **CP-PlatS**

Frog hunts on land by vision. He escapes, A. James Fenton. *Fr.* Exempla. **SP-FentJ**

Frog Prince, The. Anne Sexton. **CP-SextA**

Frog Prince, The. Stevie Smith. **CP-SmitS**

Frog Songs. Carl Sandburg. **CP-SandC**

Frog, that Naked Creature, The. May Sarton. **SP-SartM**

Frogs are croaking in every pond, The. March Song. Wystan Hugh Auden. **CP-AudWJ**

Frogs Eat Butterflies. Snakes Eat Frogs. Hogs Eat Snakes. Men Eat Hogs. Wallace Stevens. **CP-StevW**

Frogs' eggs in globular clusters. Tommy's Pond. John Ciardi. **SP-CiarJ**

Frolic, A. Paul Laurence Dunbar. **CP-DunbP**

Frolic[k], A. Robert Herrick. **CP-HerrR**

Frollick Virgins once these were. How Pansies or Hearts-Ease Came First. Robert Herrick. **CP-HerrR**

From a / highway below a face. View of a Lake. William Carlos Williams. **CP-WilW1**

From a Book. William Carlos Williams. **CP-WilW1**

From a Buick 6. "Bob Dylan." **CP-DylaB**

From a Bus Window in Central Ohio, Just before a Thunder Shower. James Wright. **CP-WrigJ**

From a Chapter on Literature. Adrienne Rich. **CP-RicAE**

From a College Window. David Herbert Lawrence. **CP-LawrD**

From a Diary. Frederick Morgan. **SP-MorgF**

From a dream of armor collapsing. The Grackles. Brendan Galvin. **SP-GalvB**

From a D— W— in the N. C. Emily Brontë. *See* A Death Scene.

From a Dungeon Wall in the Southern College. Emily Brontë. **CP-BronE**

From a far mountain creeping down. Ralph Waldo Emerson. **CP-EmerR**

From a Forgotten Book. Frederick Morgan. **SP-MorgF**

From a friend's friend I taste friendship. Dirge. Stevie Smith. **CP-SmitS**

From A Go to B, If You Can Find It. Diane Wakoski. **SP-WakoD**

From a libation cup. Shang Cup. Louis Zukofsky. **CP-ZukLS**

From a long way, and Pilgrimage for Love. Mary Sidney, Countess of Montgomery Wroth. *Fr.* Part 1. *Fr.* Urania. **CP-WrotM**

From a Long Way Out of Pah-Gatzin-Kay. Thomas McGrath. **SP-McGrT**

From a magician's midnight sleeve. Late Air. Elizabeth Bishop. **CP-BishE**

From a Manhattan Tomb. Ogden Nash. **CP-NashO**

From a Museum Man's Album. John Hewitt. **CP-HewiJ**

From a Notebook. James Merrill. **SP-MerrJ**

From a Paris Window—High. Marsden Hartley. **CP-HartM**

From a Photograph. George Oppen. **CP-OppeG**

From a Phrase of Simone Weil's and Some Words of Hegel's. George Oppen. **CP-OppeG**

From a place I came. Kathleen Jessie Raine. **OxBTC** *Fr.* Two Invocations of Death. **SP-RainK**

From a Play. Alun Lewis. **CP-LewiA**

From a Play. William Carlos Williams. **CP-WilW2**

From a Play: Publisher's Song. Muriel Rukeyser. **CP-RukeM**

From a Railway Carriage. Robert Louis Stevenson. **CP-StevR**

From a Record of Disappointment. Howard Nemerov. **CP-NemeH**

From a Schuylkill in mid-earth there came emerging. A Completely New Set of Objects. Wallace Stevens. **CP-StevW**

From a single grain they have multiplied. Crows. Mary Oliver. **SP-OlivM**

From a Survivor. Adrienne Rich. **SP-RicA1; SP-RicA2**

From a Train Window. Edna St. Vincent Millay. **CP-MillE**

From a Very Little Sphinx. Edna St. Vincent Millay. **CP-MillE**

From a view to a kill in pursuit. Leicestershire. Donald Davie. **CP-DavDo**

From a Window. William Carlos Williams. **CP-WilW2**

From Above. John Updike. **CP-UpdiJ**

From above the moon. Envoi to the Reader. Basil Bunting. **CP-BuntB**

From air seen fathom-deep. Island in the Works. James Merrill. **SP-MerrJ**

From Alcuin. Alcuin, *tr. fr. Latin by* Ralph Waldo Emerson. *Fr.* Quatrains. **CP-EmerR**

From all the Jails the Boys and Girls. Emily Dickinson. **CP-DickE**

From all the rest I single you out, having a message for you. To One Shortly to Die. Walt Whitman. **CP-WhitW**

From Altitude, the Diamonds. Richard Hugo. **CP-HugoR**

From Alton Bay to Sandwich Dome. The Wood Giant. John Greenleaf Whittier. **CP-WhitJ**

From an Asian Tent. Thom Gunn. **CP-GunnT**

From an empty sky. Object in a Setting. Charles Tomlinson. **CP-TomlC**

From an English Sensibility. Roy Fisher. **SP-FishR**

From an Old House in America. Adrienne Rich. **SP-RicA1; SP-RicA2**

From Anacreon ("'Twas now the hour when Night had driven"), *Fr. the Greek of Anacreon*. Byron. **CP-Byron**

From Anacreon ("I wish to tune my quivering lyre"), *Fr. the Greek of Anacreon*. Byron. **CP-Byron**

From Another Sore Fit. Anne Bradstreet. **CP-BradA**

From any hedgerow, any copse. Gerard Manley Hopkins. **CP-HopkG**

From art, from nature, from the schools. Tennyson. **OAEL-2** *Fr.* In Memoriam A. H. H. **CP-TennA**

From Autumn Sequel. Louis MacNeice. *See* Canto IV: "To work. To my own office, my own job."

From bad lands where eggs are small and dear. Wystan Hugh Auden. *Fr.* Shorts [1948–1957] ("At peace under this mandarin, sleep, Lucina"). **CP-AudeW**

From Bangor I once went to Six Road Ends. Carson at Six Road Ends. John Hewitt. **CP-HewiJ**

From barren coldness birds. Games Two. Richard Wilbur. **CP-WilbR**

From behind he takes her waist. First Dances. Frank O'Hara. **SP-OharF**

From being anxious, or secure. John Donne. *Fr.* A Litany. **CP-DonnJ**

From below, the waist-thick pine. Yggdrasil. Paul Muldoon. **SP-MuldP**

From Bermondsey to Wandsworth. South London Sketch, 1944. Sir John Betjeman. **CP-BetjJ**

From "Bird Conversations." Farid-uddin Attar, *tr. fr. Persian by* Ralph Waldo Emerson. **CP-EmerR**

From blackhearted water colder. Castles and Distances. Richard Wilbur. **CP-WilbR**

From Blank to Blank. Emily Dickinson. **CP-DickE**

From Bowling Green. Al Young. **CP-YounA**

From breakfast on through all the day. The Land of Nod. Robert Louis Stevenson. **CP-StevR**

From brightening fields of ether fair-disclosed. Summer. James Thomson. *Fr.* The Seasons. **CP-ThomJ**

From Brooklyn Heights one sees the bay. With a Photograph to Zell, Now Bound for Spain. Hart Crane. **CP-CranH**

From Brooklyn, over the Brooklyn Bridge, on this fine morning. Invitation to Miss Marianne Moore. Elizabeth Bishop. **CP-BishE**

From China contra-boom-bang water. Mendocino, Like You Said. Richard Hugo. **CP-HugoR**

From Clee to heaven the beacon burns. 1887. Alfred Edward Housman. **CP-HousA**

From Cocoon forth a Butterfly. Emily Dickinson. **CP-DickE**

From commissars of daylight. The Marriage Portion. Adrienne Rich. **CP-RicAE**

From Cratetos. William Blake. **CP-BlakW**

From death and dark oblivion (near the Same). The Mind of the Frontispiece to a Book. Ben Jonson. **CP-JonsB**

From depth of grief / Where drowned I lie, *par. by* Countess of Pembroke, Mary Sidney Herbert. Bible, *O.T. See* Psalm 130: "Out of the depths have I cried unto thee, O Lord."

F[f]rom depth of[f] sin[n] and from a deep despair [*or* diepe dispaire]. Bible, *O.T. See* Psalm 130: "Out of the depths have I cried unto thee, O Lord."

From depth to height, from height to loftier height. Resurgam. Christina Georgina Rossetti. **CP-RosC2**

From Disaster. George Oppen. **CP-OppeG**

From disorder (a chaos). Descent. William Carlos Williams. **CP-WilW2**

From distant regions, Fortune sends. The Revolution at Market Hill. Jonathan Swift. **CP-SwifJ**

From Dr. Swift to Dr. Sheridan. Jonathan Swift. **CP-SwifJ**

From Dread in the Eyes of Horses. Tess Gallagher. **SP-GallT**

From early dawn until the flush of noon. Christina Georgina Rossetti. **CP-RosC3**

From early youth I ploughed the restless Main. By a Retired Mariner (A Friend of the Author). William Wordsworth. *Fr.* Poems Composed or Suggested During a Tour, in the Summer of 1833. **CP-WorW2**

From east and west across the horizon's edge. Old Age's Ship & Crafty Death's. Walt Whitman. **CP-WhitW**

From easterly crepuscular arrivals. An English Revenant. Donald Davie. **CP-DavDo**

From empty windows / Voice of dead eyes. Rafael Alberti, *tr. by* Thomas Merton. **CP-MertT** *Fr.* Roman Nocturnes.

From epigram to epic is the course. Strange Metamorphosis of Poets. Howard Nemerov. **CP-NemeH**

From every quarter of your land. Ave Imperatrix! Rudyard Kipling. **CP-KiplR**

From everywhere else (Ceylon, Orinoco, Valdivia). The Island (XX). Pablo Neruda, *tr. fr. Spanish by* Ben Belitt. **SP-NeruP** *Fr.* The Separate Rose.

From fabrication springs the spiral stair. The Princess and the Goblins. Sylvia Plath. **CP-PlatS**

From fairest creatures we desire increase. Sonnet 1. William Shakespeare. **CTC; FaBoEn; HeIP; ImPo; LiTB; MasP; OAEP; OBSC; TrGrPo** *Fr.* Sonnets. **CP-ShaWS**

From fall to spring the russet acorn. Holidays. Ralph Waldo Emerson. **CP-EmerR**

From false assumption rose, and fondly hailed. William Wordsworth. *Fr.* Ecclesiastical Sonnets. **CP-WorW2**

From famine, pestilence and persecution. Canadian Pacific. Derek Mahon. **SP-MahoD**

From far and near / He drew the scattered ciphers. Arthur Hugh Clough. **SP-ClouA**

From Far Dakota's Cañons (June 25, 1876). Walt Whitman. **CP-WhitW**

From far, from eve and morning. Alfred Edward Housman. **CP-HousA**

From far out in the center of the naked lake. The Loon's Cry. Robert Bly. **SP-BlyR**

From feather-stuffed bolsters of cloud. Cold Spring Harbor. Derek Walcott. **CP-WalcD**

From Fortune's Reach. Robert Southwell. **CP-SoutR**

From Frodmer's Drama "The Friends." Ralph Waldo Emerson. **CP-EmerR**

From gallery-grave and the hunt of a wren-king. Wystan Hugh Auden. **EyDe** *Fr.* Prologue: The Birth of Architecture. *Fr.* Thanksgiving for a Habitat. **CP-AudeW**

From gallery-grave and the hunt of a wren-king. Prologue: The Birth of Architecture. Wystan Hugh Auden. *Fr.* Thanksgiving for a Habitat. **CP-AudeW**

From gold to gray. The Eve of Election. John Greenleaf Whittier. **CP-WhitJ**

From Great Consciousness vision Harlem 1948 buildings standing in Eternity. Who. Allen Ginsberg. **CP-GinsA**

From Hafiz. Hafiz. **CP-EmerR** *Fr.* I said to heaven that glowed above. *Fr.* Odes.

From harmony, from heavenly [*or* heav'nly] harmony. A Song for St Cecilia's Day [1687]. John Dryden. **SP-DrydJ**

From Heine. Louise Bogan. **CP-BogaL**

From Helsinki to Liverpool with Lumber. Malcolm Lowry. *Fr.* The Roar of the Sea and the Darkness. **CP-LowrM**

From hence began that Plot, the nation's curse. John Dryden. **FaBoEH** *Fr.* Absalom and Achitophel, Pt. I. **SP-DrydJ**

From Her in the Country. Thomas Hardy. **CP-HardT**

From her perch of beauty. Avec Merci, Mother. Maya Angelou. **SP-AngeM**

From here on, all of us will be living. 8/8/68: i. Adrienne Rich. **CP-RicAE** *Fr.* Ghazals: Homage to Ghalib. **SP-RicA2**

From here, the quay, one looks above to mark. The Harbour Bridge. Thomas Hardy. **CP-HardT**

From here through tunnelled gloom the track. The Railway Junction. Walter de la Mare. **CP-DeLaW**

From here to there—. Roy Fisher. **SP-FishR** *Fr.* Handsworth Liberties.

From high to higher forces. Ralph Waldo Emerson. **CP-EmerR**

From his brimstone bed at break of day. The Devil's Thoughts. Samuel Taylor Coleridge. **CP-ColeS**

From his shoulder Hiawatha. Hiawatha's Photographing. "Lewis Carroll." **CP-CarrL**

From his slim Palace in the Dust. Emily Dickinson. **CP-DickE**

From his tall masted Tree. A Canticle for the Feast of the Most Precious Blood, 1954. William Everson. **SP-EverW** *Fr.* The Cross Tore a Hole.

From House to Home. Christina Georgina Rossetti. **CP-RosC1**

From Ibn Jemin. Ibn-i-Yamin, *tr. fr. Persian by* Ralph Waldo Emerson. **CP-EmerR**

From Illinois and Indiana came a later myth. Carl Sandburg. *Fr.* The People, Yes. **CP-SandC**

From Iron. Robert Frost. **CP-FrosR**

From Julianus. Emperor Julian, *tr. fr. Greek by* William Cowper. **CP-CowpW**

From Kansas City, the. Elegy Before the Time. William Dickey. **SP-DickW**

From labours through the night, outworn. George Meredith. **CP-MerG2**

From lamplight and an aged leaf. George Meredith. **CP-MerG2**

From landscape the color of lions. Robert Penn Warren. *Fr.* Saul at Gilboa. **SP-WarrR**

From leaf to leaf in silence. Ascension Day, 1964. Wystan Hugh Auden. **CP-AudeW**

From left to right, she leads the eye. Myth on Mediterranean Beach: Aphrodite as Logos. Robert Penn Warren. **SP-WarrR**

From Little down to Least, in due degree. Catechizing. William Wordsworth. *Fr.* Ecclesiastical Sonnets. **CP-WorW2**

From looking at things Navajo. Process. Al Young. **CP-YounA**

From loud sound and still chance. Baroque Comment. Louise Bogan. **CP-BogaL**

From love one takes. The Necessity. Denise Levertov. **CP-LeveD**

From Love's First Fever to Her Plague. Dylan Thomas. **CP-ThomD**

From low to high doth dissolution climb. Mutability. William Wordsworth. **EBEV; EnRP; HelP; InPK; LiTB; MeMBP; NOBE; NoP; OAEL-2; OBEV; PoEL-4; PrIm** *Fr.* Ecclesiastical Sonnets. **CP-WorW2**

From many morning-glories. How the Wings Were Made. Nicholas Vachel Lindsay. *Fr.* The Tree of Laughing Bells or The Wings of the Morning. **CP-LindV**

From Matlock Bath's half-timbered station. Matlock Bath. Sir John Betjeman. **CP-BetjJ**

From me my Silvia ranne away. A Song upon Silvia. Robert Herrick. **CP-HerrR**

From me, Professor Pagels, it's. The First Word at Last. Robert Pack. **SP-PackR**

From Me to You. The Beatles. **CP-Beatl**

From Menander. Menander, *tr. fr. Greek by* William Cowper. **CP-CowpW**

From Mestastasio. Christina Georgina Rossetti. **CP-RosC3**

From mighty wrongs to petty perfidy. Fame. Byron. **FiP** *Fr.* Childe Harold's Pilgrimage. **CP-Byron**

From Molepolole and Morogoro. Reflexions on the Seizure of the Suez, and on a Proposal to Line the Banks of That Canal with Billboard Advertisements. Howard Nemerov. **CP-NemeH**

From Montauk Point. Walt Whitman. **CP-WhitW**

From Morning-Glory to Petersburg. Adrienne Rich. **CP-RicAE; SP-RicA2**

From My Diary. Stephen Spender. **CP-SpenS**

From My Diary, July 1914. Wilfred Owen. **CP-OwenW**

From my great-grandmother on. The Escape. James Dickey. **CP-DickJ**

From my high love I look at that poor world there. Kenneth Patchen. **CP-PatcK**

From my journal, March Eight, Nineteen Sixty-nine: Garnie's whisper to me, while we were. Many of Our Waters: Variations on a Poem by a Black Child. James Wright. **CP-WrigJ**

From My Last Years. Walt Whitman. **CP-WhitW**

From my mother's sleep I fell into the State. The Death of the Ball Turret Gunner. Randall Jarrell. **CP-JarrR; SP-JarrR**

From My Notes for a Series of Lectures on Murder. Stevie Smith. **CP-SmitS**

From my propped radio. Mixed Signals. Chuck Miller. **SP-MillC**

From my rented attic with no earth. Landowners. Sylvia Plath. **CP-PlatS**

From my wife and household and fields. Air and Fire. Wendell Berry. **CP-BerrW**

From My Window. Charles Kenneth Williams. **CP-WillC; SP-WillC**

From narrow provinces. The Moose. Elizabeth Bishop. **CP-BishE**

From Nature doth emotion come, and moods. Same Subject (Continued) [Imagination and Taste, How Impaired and Restored]. William Wordsworth. *Fr.* The Prelude; Growth of a Poet's Mind [1850 vers.]. **CP-WorW3**

From Nature doth emotion come, and moods. Same Subject (Continued) [Imagination]. William Wordsworth. *Fr.* The Prelude; Growth of a Poet's Mind [1805 vers.]. **CP-WorW3**

From Nature doth emotion come, and moods. William Wordsworth. **EnRP** *Fr.* Same Subject (Continued) [Imagination and Taste, How Impaired and Restored]. *Fr.* The Prelude; Growth of a Poet's Mind [1850 vers.]. **CP-WorW3**

From Nature doth emotion come, and moods. William Wordsworth. **OBNC** *Fr.* Same Subject (Continued) [Imagination]. *Fr.* The Prelude; Growth of a Poet's Mind [1805 vers.]. **CP-WorW3**

From Nature's beginning. Ralph Waldo Emerson. **CP-EmerR**

From near the sea, like Whitman my great predecessor, I call. Ode: Salute to the French Negro Poets. Frank O'Hara. **SP-OharF**

From needing danger, to be[e] good. John Donne. *Fr.* A Litany. **CP-DonnJ**

From nine o'clock till morning light. The Nightingale. Gerard Manley Hopkins. **CP-HopkG**

From noise of scare-fires rest ye free. The Bellman. Robert Herrick. **CP-HerrR**

From noiseful arms, and acts of prowess done. The Holy Grail. Tennyson. *Fr.* Idylls of the King. **CP-TennA**

From Now On. Charles Kenneth Williams. **CP-WillC**

From "Oedipus at Colonus." William Butler Yeats. *Fr.* A Man Young and Old. **CP-YeatW**

From off a hill whose concave wombe reworded. A Lover's Complaint. William Shakespeare. **CP-ShaWS**

From old Fort Walla Walla and the Klickitats. In the Oregon Country. William Stafford. **SP-StafW**

From Omar Chiam. Omar Khayyám, *tr. fr. Persian by* Ralph Waldo Emerson. **CP-EmerR**

From CXII: "Owl, and wagtail / and huo-hu, the fire-fox", *See* Canto 112, From. Ezra Pound. *See* Canto 112, From: "Owl, and wagtail / and huo-hu, the fire-fox."

From one to two. To My Valentines. Louis Zukofsky. **CP-ZukLS**

From Orford Ness to Shingle Street. Dawn on the East Coast. Alun Lewis. **CP-LewiA**

From Oslo. Chuck Miller. **SP-MillC**

From our evening fireside now. Emily Brontë. **CP-BronE**

From our shoved up bank. Welcome Home, Oh Sweetest Harteebeeste. Malcolm Lowry. **CP-LowrM**

From our very high window at the Sheraton. Sonnet. Hayden Carruth. **CP-CarHS** *Fr.* Sonnets.

From out of the cold Caribbean. Fred? Shel Silverstein. **SP-SilS2**

From out the Queen's Highcliffe for weeks at a stretch. Margate, 1940. Sir John Betjeman. **CP-BetjJ**

From pain and peril, by land and main. The Captain's Well. John Greenleaf Whittier. **CP-WhitJ**

From Paumanok Starting I Fly Like a Bird. Walt Whitman. **CP-WhitW**

From Pent-up Aching Rivers. Walt Whitman. **CP-WhitW**

From Perugia. John Greenleaf Whittier. **CP-WhitJ**

From Petrarch ("Oh! place me where the burning noon"). Petrarch, *tr. fr. Italian by* Charlotte Smith. **CP-SmitC**

From Pico & the Women: A Life. Robert Creeley. **CP-CreeR**

From plane of light to plane, wings dipping through. Evening Hawk. Robert Penn Warren. **SP-WarrR**

From Plane to Plane. Robert Frost. **CP-FrosR**

From pleasure of the bed. The Chambermaid's Second Song. William Butler Yeats. **CP-YeatW**

From Portofino Point. John Gould Fletcher. **SP-FletJ**

From powdery Palmyre, the tireless wind. The Waters. Richard Wilbur. **CP-WilbR**

From purest wells of English undefiled. James Russell Lowell. John Greenleaf Whittier. **CP-WhitJ**

From reality's flowing flurry. Turning. Archie Randolph Ammons. **SP-AmmoA**

From right to left, and to and fro. The Maze. Vincent Bourne, *tr. fr. Latin by* William Cowper. **CP-CowpW**

From Rite and Ordinance abused they fled. Aspects of Christianity in America—Continued. William Wordsworth. **AiP; PAH** *Fr.* Ecclesiastical Sonnets. **CP-WorW2**

From sand he pours himself into deep water. The Life of the Otter. Thom Gunn. **CP-GunnT**

From scars where kestrels hover. Missing. Wystan Hugh Auden. **CP-AudeW**

From school to Cam or Isis, and thence home. William Cowper. **OBTV** *Fr.* The Progress of Error. **CP-CowpW**

From sleep, before first light. Phaedra in the Farm House. Thom Gunn. **CP-GunnT**

From solitary flowerstalk some fingers. Snow-Wreath. Louis Zukofsky. **CP-ZukLS**

From some abiding central source of power. Music at the Villa Marina. Robert Louis Stevenson. **CP-StevR**

From something in the trees. For the New Year. Robert Creeley. **CP-CreeR**

From spiralling ecstatically this. Edward Estlin Cummings. **CP-CummE**

From stainless steel basins of water. The Operation. William DeWitt Snodgrass. **SP-SnodW**

From Stirling Castle we had seen. Yarrow Unvisited [1803]. William Wordsworth. **CP-WorW1**

From summer and the wheel-shaped city. Washington Cathedral. Karl Shapiro. **SP-ShapK**

From sunlight, the obvious and the lush. A Worker's Creed. Stephen Dunn. **SP-DunnS**

From Sunset to Star Rise. Christina Georgina Rossetti. **CP-RosC1**

From tempting Satan to tempt us. John Donne. *Fr.* A Litany. **CP-DonnJ**

From ten to five we whacked the waves. Bath after Sailing. John Updike. **CP-UpdiJ**

From Thallus the pederast. Carmen 25. Catullus. *Fr.* Carmina. **CP-Catul**

From that blest bed the hero came. Andrew Marvell. **JCP** *Fr.* Upon Appleton House [To My Lord Fairfax]. **CP-MarvA**

From that day[e] thee Hart strokes [*or* strokys]. Sums. Donald Hall. **CP-HallD**

From that deep shelter'd solitude. The Wheat-Ear. Charlotte Smith. **CP-SmitC**

From that time forth, Authority in France. France (Concluded). William Wordsworth. *Fr.* The Prelude; Growth of a Poet's Mind [1850 vers.]. **CP-WorW3**

From the Alban Hills, Looking towards Rome. William Wordsworth. *Fr.* Memorials of a Tour in Italy, 1837. **CP-WorW2**

From the "Antigone", *fr.* A Woman Young and Old. William Butler Yeats. **CP-YeatW**

From the Antique. Christina Georgina Rossetti. **CP-RosC3**

From the Antique. Christina Georgina Rossetti. **CP-RosC3**

From the Arabic: An Imitation. Percy Bysshe Shelley. **CP-ShelP**

From the archaic ships the green and red. Mathilde in Normandy. Adrienne Rich. **CP-RicAE**

From the bad eye and early morning. Lost Souls. Charles Wright. **SP-WrigC**

From the balcony of the seaside hotel you can see the jeweled towers. Missing Pages. John Yau. **SP-YauJo**

From the balcony of the Thetford Hill. The Choir Singing. Grace Paley. **CP-PaleG**

From the Baptismal hour, through weal and woe. Funeral Service. William Wordsworth. *Fr.* Ecclesiastical Sonnets. **CP-WorW2**

From the bare planks the reflected sun lights up. Nest of Vampires. James Fenton. **SP-FentJ**

From the bed where I lay. John Haines. *Fr.* The Mirror. **SP-HainJ**

From the beginning, SIN. There Was a Youth Whose Name Was Thomas Granger. Charles Olson. **CP-OlsoC**

From the being borne to the dying. Frederick Morgan. *Fr.* Meditations for Autumn. **SP-MorgF**

From the besieged Ardea all in post. The Rape of Lucrece. William Shakespeare. **CP-ShaWS**

From "The Birth of Venus," Song. William Carlos Williams. **CP-WilW1**

From the bonny bells of heather. Heather Ale: A Galloway Legend. Robert Louis Stevenson. **CP-StevR**

From the breach to the iron explosion. Pablo Neruda, *tr. fr. Spanish by* Ben Belitt. **SP-NeruP** *Fr.* Skystones.

From the Bridge. Stephen Berg. **SP-BergS**

From the burly give-and-take. James McAuley. *Fr.* Aor Against the Ingrate Who Abused Our Hospitality. **SP-McAuJ**

From the Canton of Expectation. Seamus Heaney. **SP-HeanS**

From the Chinese. John Gould Fletcher. **SP-FletJ**

From the Chinese of Wang Li Shi. John Hewitt. **CP-HewiJ**

From the cities where from caves. Cancelled Stanza of the Mask of Anarchy. Percy Bysshe Shelley. *Fr.* The Mask [*or* Masque] of Anarchy. **CP-ShelP**

From the closed garden. Hymen. Hilda Doolittle. **CP-DoolH**

From the cognoscenti. Edward Estlin Cummings. **CP-CummE**

From the colour the nature. Canto 90. Ezra Pound. **APSN; VGW** *Fr.* Cantos. **CP-PoCan**

From the contamination / Of laudation. Arthur Hugh Clough. **SP-ClouA**

From the Coptic. Stevie Smith. **CP-SmitS**

From the Corpse Woodpiles, from the Ashes. Robert Earl Hayden. **CP-HaydR**

From the Country to the City. Elizabeth Bishop. **CP-BishE**

From the County Lunatic Asylum. Stevie Smith. **CP-SmitS**

From the Crab's whirl. Frederick Morgan. *Fr.* Poems of the Two Worlds. **SP-MorgF**

From the Crest. Wendell Berry. **CP-BerrW**
   "And when we speak together."
   "Beginning and end."
   "Deepest sleep holds us, The."
   "Farm travels in snow, The."
   "Going into the city, coming."
   "Let the great song come."

   "Little farm, motherland, made."
   "My life's wave is at its crest."
   "What we leave behind to sleep."
   "When I think of death I see."

From the Cupola. James Merrill. **SP-MerrJ**

From the Dark Chambers of Dejection Freed. William Wordsworth. **CP-WorW2**

From the dark side, feet first, breech birth, the fighter falls. Paratrooper. Mona Van Duyn. **SP-VanDM**

From the Dark Tower. Countee Cullen. **CP-CullC**

From the dark yard by the sheepbarn the cock crowed. The Henyard Round. Donald Hall. **CP-HallD**

From the date that the doors of his prep-school close. The Waster. Rudyard Kipling. **CP-KiplR**

From the Day Room. Phoebe Hesketh. **SP-HeskP**

From the derelict garden creeps the cat. Shadows Coming. Jenny Joseph. **SP-JoseJ**

From *The Descent of Alette*, Book 3. Alice Notley. **SP-NotlA** *Fr.* The Descent of Alette.

From the Desk of the Laureate: For Immediate Release. Howard Nemerov. **CP-NemeH**

From the Diary of John Manningham of the Middle Temple. Sir Walter Ralegh. **CP-RaleW**

From the dire monument of thy black room[e]. Calling Lucasta from Her Retirement. Richard Lovelace. **CP-LoveR**

From the Distance. Wendell Berry. **CP-BerrW**

From the dithyramb to the root of the sea. Search. Pablo Neruda, *tr. fr. Spanish by* Ben Belitt. **SP-NeruP**

From the drama of horror and despair. The Gesture. Richard Eberhart. **CP-EberR**

From the dress-box's plashing tis–. The Catch. Richard Wilbur. **CP-WilbR**

From the Duck-Pond to the Carousel. Muriel Rukeyser. **CP-RukeM**

From the dull confines of the drooping West. His Return to London. Robert Herrick. **CP-HerrR**

From the Earth, and from thy bloud, O heaven, they came, *ad. fr. Latin of* John Cassam. Sir Walter Ralegh. **CP-RaleW**

From the Embassy. Robert Ranke Graves. **CP-GravR**

From the famous Peak of Derby. Ben Jonson. **CP-JonsB** *Fr.* The Gypsies Metamorphosed.

From the fierce aspect of this River, throwing. The Fall of the Aar—Handec. William Wordsworth. *Fr.* Memorials of a Tour of the Continent; 1820. **CP-WorW2**

From the first he would not avoid it. The Crucifixion. Alun Lewis. **CP-LewiA**

From the first it had been like a. A Bronzeville Mother Loiters in Mississippi. Meanwhile, a Mississippi Mother Burns Bacon. Gwendolyn Brooks. **SP-BrooG**

From the first light when in the upland field. Winter Day. John Hewitt. **CP-HewiJ**

From the forests and highlands. Hymn of Pan. Percy Bysshe Shelley. **CP-ShelP**

From the four corners of the earth. Carl Sandburg. **CMoP** *Fr.* The People, Yes. **CP-SandC**

From the French. Byron. **CP-Byron**

From the French. Byron. **CP-Byron**

From the French (1). Stevie Smith. **CP-SmitS**

From the French (2). Stevie Smith. **CP-SmitS**

From the Frick. The weather. Back. James Schuyler. **CP-SchuJ**

From the Frontier of Writing. Seamus Heaney. **SP-HeanS**

From the Garden. Anne Sexton. **CP-SextA**

From the geyser ventilators. Business Girls. Sir John Betjeman. **CP-BetjJ**

From *The Gleanings of a Gadwall*. Malcolm Lowry. **CP-LowrM**

From the Great Western. Sir John Betjeman. **CP-BetjJ**

From the Greek. Stevie Smith. **CP-SmitS**

From the Greek of Moschus. Moschus. *See* When winds that move not its calm surface sweep.

From the green Amesbury hill which bears the name. The Bay of Seven Islands. John Greenleaf Whittier. **CP-WhitJ**

From the heart of Waumbek Methma. Mary Garvin. John Greenleaf Whittier. **CP-WhitJ**

From the heel / Of a half loaf. Austerities. Charles Simic. **SP-SimiC**

From the high senate of the gods, to you. Coelum Britannicum. Thomas Carew. **CP-CareT** *Fr.* Carew's Masque. **CP-CareT**

From the high stream the water poured and forced. The Old Mill-Race. John Hewitt. **CP-HewiJ**

From the Highest Camp. Thom Gunn. **CP-GunnT**

From the hills of home forth looking, far beneath the tent-like span. The Garrison of Cape Ann. John Greenleaf Whittier. **CP-WhitJ**

From the hilltop we could overlook. Westport. Galway Kinnell. **SP-KinnG**

From the hodge porridge. The Farmer's Wife. Anne Sexton. **CP-SextA**

From the Inca. Charles Olson. **CP-OlsoC**

From the Inside. Paul Éluard, *tr. fr. French by* William Carlos Williams. **CP-WilW2**

From the Italian. Stevie Smith. **CP-SmitS**

From the Japanese. Louise Glück. **SP-GlücL**

From the Japanese, I. John Gould Fletcher. **SP-FletJ**

From the Japanese, II. John Gould Fletcher. **SP-FletJ**

From the Japanese, III. John Gould Fletcher. **SP-FletJ**

From the Japanese, IV. John Gould Fletcher. **SP-FletJ**

From the Japanese, V. John Gould Fletcher. **SP-FletJ**

From the Japanese, VI. John Gould Fletcher. **SP-FletJ**

From the Journal of Immutable Truths. Gilbert Sorrentino. **SP-SorrG**

From the Kuan-Tzu. Frederick Morgan. **SP-MorgF**

From the Last Dream of a Dying Woman Aged Eighty. Howard Nemerov. *Fr.* Seven Macabre Songs. **CP-NemeH**

From the last hill that looks on thy once holy dome. On the Day of the Destruction of Jerusalem by Titus. Byron. **CP-Byron**

From the Latin. Geoffrey Hill. *Fr.* The Songbook of Sebastian Arrurruz. **CP-HillG**

From the Legend of St. Clement. Thomas Merton. **CP-MertT**

From The Life and Character of Dean Swift. Jonathan Swift. **NOBL** *Fr.* The Life and Genuine Character of Dr Swift. **CP-SwifJ**

From the life held back in secret. Poem About Birch Trees. John Haines. **SP-HainJ**

From the Lookout Rock. Richard Wilbur. **CP-WilbR**

From the low eighteenth-century window—its thicknesses. Kapuzinerberg (Salzburg). Pierre Jean Jouve, *tr. fr. French by* Louise Bogan. **CP-BogaL**

From the Manifesto of the Selfish. Stephen Dunn. **SP-DunnS**

From the Misery of Don Joost. Wallace Stevens. **CP-StevW**

From the Motorway. Charles Tomlinson. **CP-TomlC**

From the Move to California. William Stafford. **SP-StafW**

From the New World. Donald Davie. **CP-DavDo**

"From the next . . . ." James Schuyler. **CP-SchuJ**

From the open market with its tangy smell. If Blood Were Not as Powerful as It Is. Tess Gallagher. **SP-GallT**

From the oracular archives and the parchment. Dylan Thomas. **CMoP** *Fr.* Altarwise by Owl-Light. **CP-ThomD**

From the Original Draft of the Poem to William Shelley, *see also* To William Shelley ("Billows on the beach are leaping around it, The"). Percy Bysshe Shelley. **CP-ShelP**

From the Outside. Paul Éluard, *tr. fr. French by* William Carlos Williams. **CP-WilW2**

From the Packet of Anacharsis. Wallace Stevens. **CP-StevW**

From the Past and Unavailing. The Pilot. Edwin Arlington Robinson. **CP-RobiE**

From the people the countries get their names. Carl Sandburg. *Fr.* The People, Yes. **CP-SandC**

From the Persian of Hafiz. Hafiz, *tr. fr. Persian by* Ralph Waldo Emerson. **CP-EmerR**

From the Pier's head, musing, and with increase. At Dover. William Wordsworth. *Fr.* Memorials of a Tour of the Continent; 1820. **CP-WorW2**

From the porch at dusk I watched. Before Dark. Wendell Berry. **CP-BerrW**

From the Porch at Runnymede. Paul Laurence Dunbar. **CP-DunbP**

From the porch; from the hayrick where her prickled. Mood Indigo. William Matthews. **SP-MattW**

From the Prison House. Adrienne Rich. **SP-RicA2**

From the private ease of Mother's womb. Baby Song. Thom Gunn. **CP-GunnT** *Fr.* Three Songs.

From the Prometheus Vinctus of Aeschylus. Byron. **CP-Byron**

From the quarters of the compass. Carmen 42. Catullus. *Fr.* Carmina. **CP-Catul**

From the Rain Forest Down. Richard Hugo. **CP-HugoR**

From the red chimneys smoke climbs slow and straight. Envoi. Wystan Hugh Auden. **CP-AudWJ**

From the Republic of Conscience. Seamus Heaney. **SP-HeanS**

From the roadside the undersides. Running in Snow. James McAuley. **SP-McAuJ**

From the Roof. Denise Levertov. **CP-LeveD**

From the roof of Burford Church. Shooting of Levellers, Burford, 1649. Steve Griffiths. **SP-GrifS**

From the salt age, yes from the salt age. Old snapshot from Venice 1952. Robert Lowell. **SP-LoweR**

From the scorch and poverty, from the cumin and opulence. Scenic View. William Matthews. **SP-MattW**

From the scratchy past his voice. Caruso. James McAuley. **SP-McAuJ**

From the sea came a hand. Two Hands. Anne Sexton. **CP-SextA**

From the sea-coast, from the bleak ravines of the hills. America. John Gould Fletcher. **SP-FletJ**

From the Second Chapter of a Verse History of the World. Thomas Merton. **CP-MertT**

From the second floor up, looking north, having breakfast. Louis MacNeice. *Fr.* Autumn Journal. **CP-MacNL**

From the Shore. Carl Sandburg. **CP-SandC**

From the shrivelling gray. The Disclosure. Denise Levertov. **CP-LeveD**

From the slow march and muffled drum. A King's Soliloquy. Thomas Hardy. **CP-HardT**

From *The Song of Ullikummi, tr. fr.* Hurrian and Hittite. Charles Olson. **CP-OlsoC**

From the soothing distance. The Orchard at Night in Rain Light. Al Young. **CP-YounA**

From the spent dream behind me. John Haines. *Fr.* Homestead. **SP-HainJ**

From the Station House. Galway Kinnell. *Fr.* The Avenue Bearing the Initial of Christ into the New World. **SP-KinnG**

From the stores of eldest Matter. Ralph Waldo Emerson. **CP-EmerR**

From the Suburbs. Louise Glück. **FaBoWP; GeTw; NALW** *Fr.* Dedication to Hunger. **SP-GlücL**

From the Temple to your home. Connubii Flores, or the Well-Wishes at Weddings. Robert Herrick. **CP-HerrR**

From the Terrace. Frederick Morgan. **SP-MorgF**

From the throat he can rally strength. Remembering. Muriel Rukeyser. **CP-RukeM**

From the Tibetan. John Hewitt. **CP-HewiJ**

From the time he knew. Growing a Ghost. Howard Nemerov. **CP-NemeH**

From the time of the early radishes. Weeds. Carl Sandburg. **CP-SandC**

From the top of. Pine River. Gary Snyder. **CP-SnydG**

From *The Touchstone of Truth.* Ben Jonson. **CP-JonsB**

From the 'Town Guide'. Roy Fisher. **SP-FishR**

From the very first coming down. Wystan Hugh Auden. **CP-AudWJ**

From the very first coming down. The Letter. Wystan Hugh Auden. **CP-AudeW**

From the wan dream that was her waking day. Edna St. Vincent Millay. *Fr.* Sonnets from an Ungrafted Tree. **CP-MillE**

From the wash the laundress sends. Alfred Edward Housman. **CP-HousA**

From the Wave. Thom Gunn. **CP-GunnT**

From the well-springs of Hudson, the sea-cliffs of Maine. The Quaker Alumni. John Greenleaf Whittier. **CP-WhitJ**

From the wheel and the drift of Things. The Prayer of Miriam Cohen. Rudyard Kipling. **CP-KiplR**

From the white-blossom'd sloe, my dear Chloris requested. On Chloris Requesting Me to Give Her a Spray of a Sloe-Thorn in Full Blossom. Robert Burns. **CP-BurnR**

From the window of your sister's house. For Daphne at Lone Lake. John Haines. **SP-HainJ**

From the wrecked byre. Roy Fisher. **SP-FishR** *Fr.* Glenthorne Poems.

From the years. Things Kept. William Dickey. **SP-DickW**

From thee, ELIZA, I must go. Song. Robert Burns. **CP-BurnR**

From their grave lion-mouths, oracles. Oracles. Kathleen Jessie Raine. **SP-RainK**

From thence into the open fields he fled. Edmund Spenser. **OBSC** *Fr.* The Faerie Queene. **CP-Spens**

From thence our kinde hard-hearted is, enduring paine and care. Ovid, *tr. by* Sir Walter Ralegh. **CP-RaleW** *Fr.* Metamorphoses.

From these drear solitudes and frowzy Cells. Fragment—Epistle from Esopus to Maria. Robert Burns. **CP-BurnR**

From these high [*or* hie] hill[e]s as when a spring doth fall. Sir Thomas Wyatt. **CP-WyatT**

From these night fields and waters do men raise. Archibald MacLeish. *Fr.* Hamlet of A. Macleish. **CP-MacLA**

From these wild rocks I look to-day. The Laurels. John Greenleaf Whittier. **CP-WhitJ**

From thirty years back my grandmother with us boys. Housekeeping. Donald Davie. **CP-DavDo**

From This Acceptance, Sir, We Might Proceed. Malcolm Lowry. **CP-LowrM**

From this bleeding hand of mine. The Bleeding Hand: or, The Sprig of Eglantine Given to a Maid. Robert Herrick. **CP-HerrR**

From this deep chasm, where quivering sunbeams play. William Wordsworth. *Fr.* The River Duddon [A Series of Sonnets]. **CP-WorW2**

From This Distance: The Last Poem of the Clare Bards in Praise of the MacDonnells of Kilkee. James Liddy. **CP-LiddJ**

From this emblem what variance your motto evinces. Ich Dien. Byron. **CP-Byron**

From This Far. Derek Walcott. **CP-WalcD**

From this high quarried ledge I see. The Mountain over Aberdare. Alun Lewis. **CP-LewiA**

From this hill they are clear, the people. In Your Good Dream. Richard Hugo. **CP-HugoR**

From this hospital bed. The Injury. William Carlos Williams. **CP-WilW2**

From this new culture of the air we finally see. Ode to Gaea. Wystan Hugh Auden. **CP-AudeW**

From thorny wilds a Monster came. Self-Love and Truth Incompatible. Jeanne Marie Bouvier de la Motte-Guyon, tr. fr. French by William Cowper. **CP-CowpW**

"From Those Eternal Regions." James Thomson *and* David Mallet. **CP-ThomJ** *Fr.* Alfred: A Masque.

From thought to thought, from hill to hill love doth me lead. Sir Thomas Wyatt. **CP-WyatT**

From thy far sources 'mid mountains airily climbing. Arthur Hugh Clough. **SP-ClouA**

From thy worth and weight the stars gravitate. To the Shah, from Enweri. "Anvari", tr. fr. Persian by Ralph Waldo Emerson. **CP-EmerR**

From Time. James Dickey. **CP-DickJ**

From time one I've been reading slaughter. On Hearing a New Escalation. Richard Hugo. **CP-HugoR**

From trivia of froth and pollen. The Cromlech. Louis MacNeice. **CP-MacNL**

From Trollope's Journal. Elizabeth Bishop. **CP-BishE**

From twig to twig the spider weaves. Outer and Inner. George Meredith. **CP-MerG1**

From under crunch of my man's boot. Ode for Ted. Sylvia Plath. **CP-PlatS**

From us, of course, you want gristly bones. Talking to Dogs. Wystan Hugh Auden. **CP-AudeW**

From Us She wandered now a Year. Emily Dickinson. **CP-DickE**

From vague regions of sleep I come again. Kathleen Jessie Raine. **SP-RainK**

From Venice Was That Afternoon. Jean Garrigue. **SP-GarrJ**

From Venus born, thy beauty shows. Pethox the Great. Jonathan Swift. **CP-SwifJ**

From Vergil's Fourth Georgic. Virgil, tr. by Shelley. **CP-ShelP** *Fr.* Georgics.

From Vergil's Tenth Eclogue. Virgil, tr. by Shelley. **CP-ShelP** *Fr.* Eclogues.

From Vernon Street in Bolton. Bolton-Le-Moors, 1960. Phoebe Hesketh. **SP-HeskP**

From Victor Hugo. Thomas Hardy. **CP-HardT**

From victory in love I now am come. Mary Sidney, Countess of Montgomery Wroth. *Fr.* Part 1. *Fr.* Urania. **CP-WrotM**

From Vienna it's picture postcard all the way. At Auden's Grave. Karl Shapiro. **SP-ShapK**

From Virgil. George Oppen. NNaP *Fr.* Five Poems about Poetry. **CP-OppeG**

From Walden. Phoebe Hesketh. **SP-HeskP**

From Water-Tower Hill to the brick prison. Point Shirley. Sylvia Plath. **CP-PlatS**

From Waterloo Bridge, Ensuing Dark. Steve Griffiths. **SP-GrifS**

From wayward flight, I wake to dwell. Quasars. Robert Pack. **SP-PackR**

From what graveyards and sepulchers have they come. Carl Sandburg. *Fr.* The People, Yes. **CP-SandC**

From what hardened hands / the tool comes to us. The Gift. Pablo Neruda, tr. fr. Spanish by Ben Belitt. **SP-NeruP**

From what Hyrcanian glen or frozen hill. Percy Bysshe Shelley. *Fr.* Ode to Liberty. **CP-ShelP**

From whence arrived the praying mantis. The Praying Mantis. Ogden Nash. *Fr.* Nature-Walks, or, Not to Mention a Dopping of Sheldrakes. **CP-NashO**

From whence cometh song? Song. Theodore Roethke. **CP-RoetT**

From whence was first this fury hurl'd. The First of Jealousy. Dialogue. Thomas Carew. *Fr.* Four Songs, by Way of Chorus To a Play. **CP-CareT**

From where do poems come? Crucibles of Love. Robert Ranke Graves. **CP-GravR**

From where I lingered in a lull in March. Evening in a Sugar Orchard. Robert Frost. **CP-FrosR**

From where I stand, Professor Pagels. Proton Decay. Robert Pack. **SP-PackR**

From where she stood the air she craved, *see also* "He rode across like a cavalier." Two Who Croseed a Line (She Crosses). Countee Cullen. **CP-CullC**

From where you are at any moment you. The Step. Frederick Morgan. **SP-MorgF**

From wisedome Fortune differs farre, ad. fr. Athenaeus. Sir Walter Ralegh. **CP-RaleW**

From Wishing-Land. Robert Louis Stevenson. **CP-StevR**

From Wynyard's Gap the livelong day. A Trampwoman's Tragedy. Thomas Hardy. **CP-HardT**

From Yellow Lake: An Interval. Mona Van Duyn. **SP-VanDM**

From Yorktown's ruins, ranked and still. Yorktown. John Greenleaf Whittier. **CP-WhitJ**

From you have I been absent in the spring. Sonnet 98. William Shakespeare. **AWP; ChTr; EBEV; EIL; ImPo; LiTB; NAEL-1; NOBE; NoSic; OBEV; OBSC; OXAEP-1; PoPle; TEP** *Fr.* Sonnets. **CP-ShaWS**

Frondes Agrestes. Charles Tomlinson. **CP-TomlC**

Fronleichnam. David Herbert Lawrence. **CP-LawrD**

Front, A. Randall Jarrell. **CP-JarrR; SP-JarrR**

Front Door Soliloquy. Robert Ranke Graves. **CP-GravR**

Front Lawn. Leonard Cohen. **CP-CoheL**

Front lawn is littered with young men, The. Aging Female Poet Sits on the Balcony. Margaret Atwood. **SP-AtwM2**

Front Lines. Gary Snyder. **CP-SnydG**

Frontenac. Donald Davie. **CP-DavDo**

Frontier, The. John Hewitt. **CP-HewiJ**

Frontier, The. James Wright. **CP-WrigJ**

Frontispiece. John Ashbery. **SP-AshbJ**

Frost. Wystan Hugh Auden. **CP-AudWJ**

Frost. John Hewitt. **CP-HewiJ**

Frost. Charles Tomlinson. **CP-TomlC**

Frost. John Updike. **CP-UpdiJ**

Frost, and a leaf has quit the tulip tree. Of Margaret. John Crowe Ransom. *Fr.* Sixteen Poems in Eight Pairings. **SP-RansJ**

Frost at Midnight. Samuel Taylor Coleridge. **CP-ColeS**
    All Seasons Shall Be Sweet. **BoTP**
    (Silent Icicles, The.) **FaBoRV**
    "Frost performs its secret ministry, The." **OPOU**

Frost Flowers. David Herbert Lawrence. **CP-LawrD**

Frost has settled down upon the trees, The. Winter in the Boulevard. David Herbert Lawrence. **CP-LawrD**

Frost is beautiful, The. Diary. Jenny Joseph. **SP-JoseJ**

Frost Lay White on California, A. William Everson. **SP-EverW**

Frost-locked all the winter. Spring. Christina Georgina Rossetti. **CP-RosC1**

Frost of Death was on the Pane, The. Emily Dickinson. **CP-DickE**

Frost performs its secret ministry, The. Samuel Taylor Coleridge. **OPOU** *Fr.* Frost at Midnight. **CP-ColeS**

Frost performs its secret ministry, The. Frost at Midnight. Samuel Taylor Coleridge. **CP-ColeS**

Frost-rime edges blades of grass. Kathleen Jessie Raine. **SP-RainK**

Frost Spirit, The. John Greenleaf Whittier. **CP-WhitJ**

Frost upon small rain—the ebony lacquered avenue. *parody of Early Chinese poetry.* Rudyard Kipling. **CP-KiplR** *Fr.* The Muse among the Motors.

Frost was never seen, The. Emily Dickinson. **CP-DickE**

Frosty Morning, A. William Cowper. *See* Tis morning' and the sun with ruddy orb.

Frosty Night, A. Robert Ranke Graves. **CP-GravR**

Froth. Richard Eberhart. **CP-EberR**

Frown there like Cressy or like Agincourt. Landscape: Wheatfields. Thomas Merton. **CP-MertT**

Frowned the Laird on the Lord: "So, red-handed I catch thee?" Muckle-Mouth Meg. Robert Browning. **CP-BroR2**

Frowns are on every Muse's face. On Seeing a Needlecase in the Form of a Harp; the Work of E.M.S. William Wordsworth. **CP-WorW2**

Frozen / brook sprawls, The. Hayden Carruth. *Fr.* North Winter. **CP-CarHL**

Frozen City, The. Howard Nemerov. **CP-NemeH**

Frozen-faced, by the stripped trees. Cold. Pablo Neruda, tr. fr. Spanish by Ben Belitt. **SP-NeruP**

Frozen Food Section. Charles Bukowski. **SP-BukC3**

Frozen Greenhouse, The. Thomas Hardy. **CP-HardT**

Frozen Heart, The. Robert Herrick. **CP-HerrR**

Frozen in a grimace, all cavernous threat. Tiger Skull. Charles Tomlinson. **CP-TomlC**

Frozen Lake, The. Stevie Smith. **CP-SmitS**

Frozen rain of the first November days, The. Without Notice Beforehand. Carl Sandburg. **CP-SandC**

Frozen Stream, A. Ted Kooser. **SP-KoosT**

Frozen Zone; or, Julia Disdainful, The. Robert Herrick. **CP-HerrR**

Fruit. Sir John Betjeman. **CP-BetjJ**

Fruit, The. William Carlos Williams. **CP-WilW2**

Fruit, for sculpture. Charles Tomlinson. **CP-TomlC**

Fruit-Gift, The. John Greenleaf Whittier. **CP-WhitJ**

Fruit-Grower in War-time (and Some of His Enemies), The. James Fenton. *Fr.* Exempla. **SP-FentJ**

Fruit machines and pin tables. Yours Next. Louis MacNeice. **CP-MacNL**

Fruit of all the service that I serve, The. Sir Thomas Wyatt. **CP-WyatT**

Fruit of Aurora's tears, fair Rose. Song. François-Joachim Pierre de, Cardinal Bernis, *tr. fr. French by* Charlotte Smith. **CP-SmitC**

Fruit of the Flower. Countee Cullen. **CP-CullC**

Fruit rolled by all day, The. Pickle Belt. Theodore Roethke. **CP-RoetT**

Fruits & Vegetables. Erica Jong. **SP-JongE**

Fruits breaking the branches. Basil Bunting. **CP-BuntB**

Fruits of Virtue. Steve Griffiths. **SP-GrifS**

Fry's Cocoa! The word / means food of the gods. Adverts. James Schuyler. **CP-SchuJ**

Fu' de peace o' my eachin' heels, set down. Itching Heels. Paul Laurence Dunbar. **CP-DunbP**

Fu I loved the high cloud and the hill. Epitaphs. Ezra Pound. **SP-PounE**

Fuchsia and ragweed and the distant hills. Cushendun. Louis MacNeice. **FaBCIP** *Fr.* The Closing Album. **CP-MacNL**

Fuck. Charles Bukowski. **SP-BukC1**

FUCK COMMUNISM / it's red white and blue. Tambourine Life. Ted Berrigan. **SP-BerrT**

Fucked the Mountain. *tr. fr. Hurrian and Hittite.* Charles Olson. **CP-OlsoC**

Fucker, you might at least send me a couple of your. . . . American Express, Athens, Greece. Charles Bukowski. **SP-BukC2**

Fuel Vendor, The. John Gould Fletcher. *Fr.* Arizona Poems. **SP-FletJ**

Fugitive. Thomas Merton. **CP-MertT**

Fugitive firs and larches for a moment. Advocates. Robert Ranke Graves. **CP-GravR**

Fugitives, The. Percy Bysshe Shelley. **CP-ShelP**

Fugitive's Ride, The. Stevie Smith. **CP-SmitS**

Fugue. Howard Nemerov. **CP-NemeH**

Führer Bunker, The. William DeWitt Snodgrass. **SP-SnodW**
  Dr. Joseph Goebbels ("Say goodbye to the help, the ranks"). **CAPP**
  "Stand back, make way, you mindless scum." **TW**
  Dr. Joseph Goebbels ("Stand back, make way, you mindless scum"). **SP-SnodW**
  Eva Braun. **CAPP**

Fuite d'Enfance. Stevie Smith. **CP-SmitS**

Fulfilment. Paul Laurence Dunbar. **CP-DunbP**

Fulfilment. Langston Hughes. **SP-HughL**

Full cloves / Of your buttocks, the convex, The. A Shallot. Richard Wilbur. **CP-WilbR**

Full Daytime Moon, The. Richard Shelton. *Fr.* Five Lies About the Moon. **SP-ShelR**

Full faith I have she holds that rarest gift. George Meredith. *Fr.* Modern Love. **CP-MerG1**

Full Fathom Five. Gerard Manley Hopkins. *Fr.* Songs from Shakespeare, in Latin and Greek. **CP-HopkG**

Full Fathom Five. Sylvia Plath. **CP-PlatS**

Full fed Rose on meals of Tint, A. Emily Dickinson. **CP-DickE**

Full Harvest Moon, The. Richard Shelton. *Fr.* Five Lies About the Moon. **SP-ShelR**

Full in the hand, heavy. September Afternoon at Four O'Clock. Marge Piercy. **SP-PierM**

Full Life. David Herbert Lawrence. **CP-LawrD**

Full loud & fresh crows Chaunticlere! George Meredith. *Fr.* Fragments for "The Harvest Home" and "The Doe." **CP-MerG2**

Full many a dreary hour have I passed. To My Brother George. John Keats. **CP-KeatJ**

Full Many a Glorious Morning. William Shakespeare. *See* Sonnet 33: "Full many a glorious morning have I seen[e]."

Full many a glorious morning have I seen[e]. Sonnet 33. William Shakespeare. **AWP; EBEV; EBEvV; EIL; FaBoEn; FaFP; HAP; HBV; ImPo; LiTB; LoBV; NIP; NoP; NoSic; OAEL-1; OAEP; OBSC; OXAEP-1; OtMeF; PPP; PoRA; SCGP; SeCeV; Son; TEP; TFi; TrGrPo; TreFS; WeW** *Fr.* Sonnets. **CP-ShaWS**

Full Moon. Robert Ranke Graves. **CP-GravR**

Full Moon. Robert Earl Hayden. **CP-HaydR**

Full moon, / On fresh snow, and the fox vixen, The. My Love Has Been. Martin Edmunds. **SP-EdmuM**

Full Moon. William Carlos Williams. **CP-WilW1**

Full Moon and Little Frieda. Ted Hughes. **SP-HughT**

Full moon, as she tipped the hill, rising, The. Common Place. Charles Olson. **CP-OlsoC**

Full moon easterly rising, furious, The. A Love Story. Robert Ranke Graves. **CP-GravR**

Full moon glazes the city, A. Following It. Stephen Berg. **SP-BergS**

Full moon is partly hidden by cloud, The. A Fable of the War. Howard Nemerov. **CP-NemeH**

Full moon is so fierce that I can count the, The. Europa. Derek Walcott. **CP-WalcD**

Full moon is the Shield of faith, The. The Shield of Faith. Nicholas Vachel Lindsay. **CP-LindV**

Full moon over the shopping mall. Spring Fashions. Allen Ginsberg. **CP-GinsA**

Full moon tilts over the lawns and trees, A. Driving Out Again at Night. Stephen Berg. *Fr.* For My Father.

Full moon was shining upon the broad sea, The. The Shy Man. Theodore Roethke. **CP-RoetT**

Full nine years old my cellar stows. 4.11. Horace. **SP-SmarC**, *tr. by* Christopher Smart; *Fr.* Odes.

Full of her long white arms and milky skin. The Equilibrists. John Crowe Ransom. **SP-RansJ**

Full of Joy Do Not Know; They Need Not, The. Richard Eberhart. **CP-EberR**

Full of Life Now. Walt Whitman. **CP-WhitW**

Full of passion and giggles. A Young Poet. Frank O'Hara. **SP-OharF**

Full of rebellion, I would die. Nature. George Herbert. **CP-HerbG**

Full of the moon. In pine woods a snowlight, The. Hayden Carruth. *Fr.* The Sleeping Beauty. **CP-CarHL**

Full of thy glory am I. Song. George Meredith. **CP-MerG2**

Full of wickedness, I—of many a smutch'd deed reminiscent—of worse deeds capable. Of Many a Smutch'd Deed Reminiscent. Walt Whitman. **CP-WhitW**

Full Professor, A. Howard Nemerov. **CP-NemeH**

Full Song, A. Thomas Campion. *Fr.* The Lords Mask[e]. *Fr.* Prestige. **CP-MerG2**

Full sooth he was a jewel bird to own. George Meredith. *Fr.* Prestige. **CP-MerG2**

FULL SPEED ASTERN). Edward Estlin Cummings. **CP-CummE**

Full thirty foot she towered from waterline to rail. The Three-Decker. Rudyard Kipling. **CP-KiplR**

Full thirty frosts since thou wert young. Upon a Venerable Rival. William Cowper. **CP-CowpW**

Full Well I Know. Stevie Smith. **CP-SmitS**

Full well I know that she is there. Gertrude Stein. **PoA** *Fr.* Stanzas in Meditation. **CP-SteiG**

Full well it may be seen. Sir Thomas Wyatt. **CP-WyatT**

Full well thou knowest I love thee dear. Song. Robert Burns. **CP-BurnR**

Full year since, I took this eager city, A. An Irishman in Coventry. John Hewitt. **CP-HewiJ**

Fullness of love sleeps in us like a sea. George Meredith. **CP-MerG2**

Fun City Samba. Al Young. **CP-YounA**

Function. John Hewitt. **CP-HewiJ**

Fund Appeal. Grace Paley. **CP-PaleG**

Fundamental question about revolution, The. Facing the Way. Alice Walker. **CP-WalkA**

Funebrial Reflection. Ogden Nash. **CP-NashO**

Funeral[1], The. John Donne. **CP-DonnJ**

Funeral. David Markson. **CP-MarkD**

Funeral, The. Dabney Stuart. **SP-StuaD**

Funeral Elegy, A. John Donne. *Fr.* Anatomy [*or* Anatomie] of the World, An[: The First Anniversary]. **CP-DonnJ**

Funeral Elegy Upon that Pattern and Patron of Virtue, A. John Norton. **CP-BradA**

Funeral Homes. William Matthews. **SP-MattW**

Funeral in Hungary. Kay Boyle. **CP-BoylK**

Funeral Music. Geoffrey Hill. **CP-HillG**
  "As with torches we go, at wild Christmas."
  "For whom do we scrape our tribute of pain."
  "Let mind be more precious than soul; it will not."
  "My little son, when you could command marvels." **NoAM**
  "Not as we are but as we must appear." **NoAM**
  "Processionals in the exemplary cave."
  "Prowess, vanity, mutual regard."
  "They bespoke doomsday and they meant it by."

Funeral of Bobò, The. Joseph Brodsky, *tr. fr. Russian by* Richard Wilbur. **CP-WilbR**

Funeral paths are hung with snow, The. Night-Time in the Cemetery. Stevie Smith. **CP-SmitS**

Funeral Rites. Seamus Heaney. **SP-HeanS**

Funeral[l] Rites of the Rose, The. Robert Herrick. **CP-HerrR**

Funeral Service. William Wordsworth. *Fr.* Ecclesiastical Sonnets. **CP-WorW2**

Funeral Tree of the Sokokis. John Greenleaf Whittier. **CP-WhitJ**

Funeral[l] stone, A. To Laurels. Robert Herrick. **CP-HerrR**

Funky blues / Keen toed shoes. Country Lover. Maya Angelou. **SP-AngeM**

Funnel. Anne Sexton. **CP-SextA**

Funny. Charles Bukowski. **SP-BukC3**

Funny. Robert Creeley. **CP-CreeR**

Funny. Stephen Dobyns. **SP-DobyS**

Funny Death. Allen Ginsberg. **CP-GinsA**

Funny Poem. Bill Knott. **SP-KnotB**

Funny thing about a chair, A. The Chair. Theodore Roethke. **CP-RoetT**

Funny—to be a Century. Emily Dickinson. **CP-DickE**

Fur the color of mud, the smooth loper. A Berry Feast. Gary Snyder. **CP-SnydG**

Furies, The. May Sarton. **SP-SartM**

Furies, The. Anne Sexton. **CP-SextA**

　Fury of Abandonment, The.

　Fury of Beautiful Bones, The.

　Fury of Cocks, The.

　Fury of Cooks, The.

　Fury of Earth, The.

　Fury of Flowers and Worms, The.

　Fury of God's Good-bye, The.

　Fury of Guitars and Sopranos, The.

　Fury of Hating Eyes, The.

　Fury of Jewels and Coal, The.

　Fury of Overshoes, The.

　Fury of Rain Storms, The.

　Fury of Sundays, The.

　Fury of Sunrises, The.

　Fury of Sunsets, The.

Furies, The. Stephen Spender. **CP-SpenS**

Furious gun in his raging ire, The. Sir Thomas Wyatt. **CP-WyatT**

Furious prisoner of the womb, The. An Argument: Of the Passion of Christ. Thomas Merton. **CP-MertT**

Furious Voyage, The. Robert Ranke Graves. **CP-GravR**

Furius and Aurelius, loyal friends. Catullus. *See* Carmen 11: "Furius, Aurelius, friends of my youth."

Furius, Aurelius: comities—Catullus. Catullus. *See* Carmen 11: "Furius, Aurelius, friends of my youth."

Furius, Aurelius, friends of my youth. Carmen 11. Catullus. *Fr.* Carmina. **CP-Catul**

Furius, "Little Villa" has no nod for Auster. Catullus. *See* Carmen 26: "Your cottage, Furius, sheltered."

Furius, with no key to service, no key. Catullus. *See* Carmen 23: "Friend Furius, / who has no slaves & no money."

Furl of fresh-leaved dogrose down, The. Gerard Manley Hopkins. **CP-HopkG**

Furl we the sails, and pass with tardy oars. Crusaders. William Wordsworth. *Fr.* Ecclesiastical Sonnets. **CP-WorW2**

Furnace. Ted Kooser. **SP-KoosT**

Furnished and clean, this room does not betray. Succession. Howard Nemerov. **CP-NemeH**

Furnished Rooms. Marsden Hartley. **CP-HartM**

Furniture. David Herbert Lawrence. **CP-LawrD**

Furniture, The. John Updike. **CP-UpdiJ**

Furniture Mover. Charles Simic. **SP-SimiC**

Furniture of a Woman's Mind, The. Jonathan Swift. **CP-SwifJ**

'Furrow' is inexact: / no ship could be. On Water. Charles Tomlinson. **CP-TomlC**

Further Arrivals. Margaret Atwood. **SP-AtwM1**

Further in Summer than the Birds. Emily Dickinson. **CP-DickE**

Further-off people are the smaller. Grandparents, The. Perspectives. Louis MacNeice. **CP-MacNL**

Further Passages from The Kind of Poetry I Want, *see also* Kind of Poetry I Want, The. "Hugh MacDiarmid."

　"Greatest poets undergo a kind of crisis in their art, The." **SP-MacDH**

　"Poetry like a lance at rest, A." **SP-MacDH**

　"Poetry like the barrel of a gun, A." **SP-MacDH**

Further Proposal, A. Allen Ginsberg. **CP-GinsA**

Further Reflection on Parsley. Ogden Nash. **CP-NashO**

"Further than." Louis Zukofsky. **CP-ZukLS**

Furthest journey is the journey that stays till, The. The Castle. Roy Fisher. **SP-FishR** *Fr.* Inscriptions for Bluebeard's Castle.

Furtively sounding / In the high. It Is Big Inside a Man. Kenneth Patchen. **CP-PatcK**

Fury and counter fury! The volcano! Catastrophic Birth. William Carlos Williams. **CP-WilW2**

Fury of Abandonment, The. Anne Sexton. *Fr.* The Furies. **CP-SextA**

Fury of Aerial Bombardment, The. Richard Eberhart. **CP-EberR**

Fury of Beautiful Bones, The. Anne Sexton. *Fr.* The Furies. **CP-SextA**

Fury of Cocks, The. Anne Sexton. *Fr.* The Furies. **CP-SextA**

Fury of Cooks, The. Anne Sexton. *Fr.* The Furies. **CP-SextA**

Fury of Earth, The. Anne Sexton. *Fr.* The Furies. **CP-SextA**

Fury of Flowers and Worms, The. Anne Sexton. *Fr.* The Furies. **CP-SextA**

Fury of God's Good-bye, The. Anne Sexton. *Fr.* The Furies. **CP-SextA**

Fury of Guitars and Sopranos, The. Anne Sexton. *Fr.* The Furies. **CP-SextA**

Fury of Hating Eyes, The. Anne Sexton. *Fr.* The Furies. **CP-SextA**

Fury of Jewels and Coal, The. Anne Sexton. *Fr.* The Furies. **CP-SextA**

Fury of Overshoes, The. Anne Sexton. *Fr.* The Furies. **CP-SextA**

Fury of Rain Storms, The. Anne Sexton. *Fr.* The Furies. **CP-SextA**

Fury of Sundays, The. Anne Sexton. *Fr.* The Furies. **CP-SextA**

Fury of Sunrises, The. Anne Sexton. *Fr.* The Furies. **CP-SextA**

Fury of Sunsets, The. Anne Sexton. *Fr.* The Furies. **CP-SextA**

Fury said to a / mouse, That he. "Lewis Carroll." **CP-CarrL** *Fr.* Alice's Adventures in Wonderland.

　(Mouse's Tale, The.) **CP-CarrL**

Fusion. George Meredith. **CP-MerG2**

Fusion is miracle and there is no other way, it is necessary. The Magician. Marge Piercy. *Fr.* Laying Down the Tower. **SP-PierM**

Fust and His Friends. Robert Browning. **CP-BroR2**

Futile, now, in our days of grief. Catalogue. Edwin Rolfe. **CP-RolfE**

Futility. Walter de la Mare. **CP-DeLaW**

Futility. Wilfred Owen. **CP-OwenW**

Future, The. Leonard Cohen. **CP-CoheL**

Future, The. Ralph Waldo Emerson. **CP-EmerR**

Future, The. Richard Shelton. **SP-ShelR**

Future—never spoke, The. Emily Dickinson. **CP-DickE**

Future Night, A. Leonard Cohen. **CP-CoheL**

Future of religion lies in the mystery of touch, The. Future Religion. David Herbert Lawrence. **CP-LawrD**

Future of transgression. It is in the homes of Caliban. Thomas Merton. *Fr.* Cables to the Ace. **CP-MertT**

Future Peace and Glory of the Church, The. William Cowper. *Fr.* Olney Hymns. **CP-CowpW**

　(Hymn 10.) **ChIV-1**

Future Relationships. David Herbert Lawrence. **CP-LawrD**

Future Religion. David Herbert Lawrence. **CP-LawrD**

Future States. David Herbert Lawrence. **CP-LawrD**

Future sucks, The. Hustings, The ("Future sucks, The"). Charles Olson. **CP-OlsoC**

Future War. David Herbert Lawrence. **CP-LawrD**

Future weighs down on me, The. The Blue Anchor. Jane Cooper. **SP-CoopJ**

Futurity. Elizabeth Barrett Browning. **CP-BroEB**

Fuzon, on a chariot iron-wing'd. The Book of Ahania. William Blake. **CP-BlakW**

Fuzzed snow browning in lastyear's haystubble, the pasture's winter-starved moss. Thaw. Hayden Carruth. **CP-CarHS**

Fuzzy fellow, without feet, A. Emily Dickinson. **CP-DickE**

Fuzzy-Wuzzy. Rudyard Kipling. **CP-KiplR**

Fy let us a' to K[IRKUDBRIGHT]. The Election: A New Song. Robert Burns. **CP-BurnR** *Fr.* The Heron Ballads, 1795.

Fyodor. Allen Ginsberg. **CP-GinsA**

Fyrbøterer. Malcolm Lowry. *Fr.* The Roar of the Sea and the Darkness. **CP-LowrM**

G

G / ra / D / ua / lLy &. Edward Estlin Cummings. **CP-CummE**

G. I. Graves in Tuscany. Richard Hugo. **CP-HugoR**

G. M. B. Donald Davie. **CP-DavDo**

G stands for goat and also. Goat. Kenneth Rexroth. **SP-RexrK** *Fr.* A Bestiary. **SP-RexrK**

Gabriel. Adrienne Rich. **CP-RicAE**

Gabriel, from heaven's king. Angelus Ad Virginem. Gerard Manley Hopkins. **CP-HopkG**

Gabriel MacElmain, Pioneer. Louise McNeill. **SP-McNeL**

Gaea. Martin Edmunds. **SP-EdmuM**

Gaelic bard they praise who in fourteen adjectives, A. The Ancient Speech. Kathleen Jessie Raine. **PoSH** *Fr.* Eilean Chanaidh. **SP-RainK**

Gagarin says, in ecstasy. Heel & Toe to the End. William Carlos Williams. **CP-WilW2**

Gaily bedight, / A gallant knight. Eldorado. Edgar Allan Poe. **CP-PoeEd**

Gaily into Ruislip Gardens. Middlesex. Sir John Betjeman. **CP-BetjJ**

Gain and Gettings. Robert Herrick. **CP-HerrR**

Gainst Fate no counsell can prevaile. Ovid, *tr.* by Sir Walter Ralegh. **CP-RaleW** *Fr.* Tristium.

Gairmscoile. "Hugh MacDiarmid." **SP-MacDH**

Gal; many a thing I've seen her lift without strain or hurry of. Sturdy Legs, That. Kenneth Patchen. **CP-PatcK**

Gala, holding on. Zinnias. Robert Earl Hayden. **CP-HaydR**

Galahad, Knight Who Perished. Nicholas Vachel Lindsay. **CP-LindV**

Galahad. . . soldier that perished. . . ages ago. Galahad, Knight Who Perished. Nicholas Vachel Lindsay. **CP-LindV**

Galán. Archibald MacLeish. **CP-MacLA**

Gale, The. John Gould Fletcher. *Fr.* Sand and Spray: A Sea-Symphony. **SP-FletJ**

Gale in April. Robinson Jeffers. **CP-JefR1**

Gale that wrecked you on the sand, The. Northman. Ralph Waldo Emerson. *Fr.* Quatrains. **CP-EmerR**

Galiano Coast: Four Entrances. Margaret Atwood. **SP-AtwM2**

Galilee Shore. Allen Ginsberg. **CP-GinsA**

Galileo Galilei (1564–1642). Siv Cedering Fox. *Fr.* Letters from the Astronomers. **SP-CedeS**

Galileo's Chair. Richard Hugo. **CP-HugoR**

Galla Water. Robert Burns. **CP-BurnR**

Gallant Château. Wallace Stevens. **CP-StevW**

Gallant Weaver, The. Robert Burns. **CP-BurnR**

Gallant Youth, who may have gained, The. Yarrow Revisited. William Wordsworth. **CP-WorW2**

Gallant's Song. Thomas Hardy. **CP-HardT**

(Galleons in sea-pomp) sails. An Armada of Thirty Whales. Daniel Gerard Hoffman. **SP-HoffD**

Galleria Umberto I. Richard Hugo. **CP-HugoR**

Gallery, The. Andrew Marvell. **CP-MarvA**

Gallery of sacred pictures manifold. The Book. John Greenleaf Whittier. **CP-WhitJ**

Galley-Slave, The. Rudyard Kipling. **CP-KiplR**

Galliass, The. Walter de la Mare. **CP-DeLaW**

Gallio's Song. Rudyard Kipling. **CP-KiplR**

Galloping Cat, The. Stevie Smith. **CP-SmitS**

Galloping collection of boards, The. Somewhere. Robert Creeley. **CP-CreeR**

Galloway Tam. Robert Burns. **CP-BurnR**

Gallows, The. John Greenleaf Whittier. **CP-WhitJ**

Gallows Etiquette. Charles Simic. **SP-SimiC**

Gallowstree drops, The. Jesus Unborn. Anne Sexton. **CP-SextA**

Gallus ha' but brothers: bro one's lady slip's make so young she's. Catullus. *See* Carmen 78: "Gallus's brothers possess / one, the most attractive of wives."

Gallus's brothers possess / one, the most attractive of wives. Carmen 78. Catullus. *Fr.* Carmina. **CP-Catul**

Galoots. Carl Sandburg. **CP-SandC**

Galoots, you hairy, hankering. Galoots. Carl Sandburg. **CP-SandC**

Galway. Louis MacNeice. **OxBI** *Fr.* The Closing Album. **CP-MacNL**

Galway Jack, Dublin Moira, wild swans. Inchiquin Lake, Penobscot Bay. Richard Eberhart. **CP-EberR**

Gambel quail looks like a medieval knight, The. Territorial Rights. Richard Shelton. **SP-ShelR**

Gambit, The. Richard Shelton. **SP-ShelR**

Gamblers, The. Nicholas Vachel Lindsay. **CP-LindV**

Gambling at Reno. William Dickey. **SP-DickW**

Gambling in Stateline, Nevada. James Wright. **CP-WrigJ**

Gambol and song and jubilee are done. Valedictory Poem. Ralph Waldo Emerson. **CP-EmerR**

Game, The. Louise Glück. **SP-GlücL**

Game, The. Stanley Jasspon Kunitz. **CP-KuniS**

Game, The. Charles Simic. **SP-SimiC**

Game, The. Charles Kenneth Williams. **SP-WillC**

Game after Supper. Margaret Atwood. **SP-AtwM1**

Game at Salzburg, A. Randall Jarrell. **CP-JarrR; SP-JarrR**

Game of Ball, A. Muriel Rukeyser. **CP-RukeM**

Game of Chess, A. Thomas Stearns Eliot. **SCV** *Fr.* The Waste Land. **CP-ElioT**

Game of Darts at the Chesterfield Arms, A. Muriel Rukeyser. **CP-RukeM**

Game of Fives, A. "Lewis Carroll." **CP-CarrL**

Gamecock. James Dickey. **CP-DickJ**

Games in the Field, The. Paul Zimmer. **SP-ZimmP**

Games One. Richard Wilbur. **CP-WilbR**

Games Two. Richard Wilbur. **CP-WilbR**

Gamut, The. Maya Angelou. **SP-AngeM**

Gamut. Louis Zukofsky. **CP-ZukLS**

Gander, The. Ogden Nash. **CP-NashO**

Gane is the day and mirk's the night. Then Guidwife Count the Lawin. Robert Burns. **CP-BurnR**

Gang in its working clothes, The. Carl Sandburg. *Fr.* The People, Yes. **CP-SandC**

Gang of labourers on the piled wet timber, A. Morning Work. David Herbert Lawrence. **CP-LawrD**

Gangster. Robert Creeley. **CP-CreeR**

Gangway or Curtain Up! Then forth. Sailing Orders. Louis MacNeice. **CP-MacNL**

Gannets. Mary Oliver. **SP-OlivM**

Gap, The. John Hewitt. **CP-HewiJ**

Gap. Leonard Nathan. **SP-NathL**

Gap, The. Charles Tomlinson. **CP-TomlC**

Gap, The. Charles Kenneth Williams. *See* So often and with such cruel fascination I have dreamed the implacable void that contains dream.

Gap in the White, The. Thomas Hardy. **CP-HardT**

Gap where the quarry is keeps moving away, The. The Quarry. Charles Tomlinson. **CP-TomlC**

Gape, gape, gorlin'. Ex Vermibus. "Hugh MacDiarmid." **SP-MacDH**

Garage in Co. Cork, A. Derek Mahon. **SP-MahoD**

Garbage-disposal truck, The. Galway Kinnell. *Fr.* The Avenue Bearing the Initial of Christ into the New World. **SP-KinnG**

Garbageman: the Man with the Orderly Mind. Gwendolyn Brooks. **CAPP** *Fr.* A Catch of Shy Fish. **SP-BrooG**

Garda at my window, tipping, The. In Ireland I Remebered the Foxes of Truro, Massachusetts. Brendan Galvin. **SP-GalvB**

Garden, The. William Cowper. *Fr.* The Task. **CP-CowpW**

  How to Grow Cucumbers. **FaBoUs**

  "I was a stricken deer, that left the herd." **EnRP; FaBoRV; FiP; LoBV; NAEL-1; OAEP; OxBoCh; PAI; PoE**

  ("Morning finds the self-sequestr'd man, The.") **PoE**

  (Stricken Deer, The.) **FiP; LoBV**

  "Philosophy, baptised." **EPCY**

Garden. Hilda Doolittle. **CP-DoolH**

Garden, The. Roy Fisher. **SP-FishR** *Fr.* Inscriptions for Bluebeard's Castle.

Garden, The. Louise Glück. **SP-GlücL**

Garden, The. Robert Ranke Graves. **CP-GravR**

Garden. Langston Hughes. **SP-HughL**

Garden, The, *see also* Hortus. Andrew Marvell. **CP-MarvA**

Garden, A. Andrew Marvell. *See* See how the flowers, as at parade.

Garden, The, *in imitation of* Cowley. Alexander Pope. **CP-PopeA**

Garden, The. Ezra Pound. **SP-PounE**

Garden, The. Edwin Arlington Robinson. **CP-RobiE**

Garden, The. Shel Silverstein. **SP-SilS2**

Garden, The. Robert Penn Warren. **SP-WarrR**

Garden. John Greenleaf Whittier. **CP-WhitJ**

Garden Abstract. Hart Crane. **CP-CranH**

Garden called Gethsemane, The. Gethsemane. Rudyard Kipling. **CP-KiplR**

Garden Fancies. Robert Browning. **CP-BroR1**

  Flower's Name, The. **CTC**

  Sibrandus Schafnaburgensis. **CTC; EBVV; TEP**

Garden flew round with the angel, The. The Pleasures of Merely Circulating. Wallace Stevens. **CP-StevW**

Garden flooded with. Charles Henri Ford. **SP-FordC** *Fr.* Secret Haiku.

Garden God, The. Richard Eberhart. **CP-EberR**

Garden Idyl, A. George Meredith. **CP-MerG1**

Garden in a garden; a green spot, A. On Keats, 18 January, 1948 (Eve of St Agnes). Christina Georgina Rossetti. **CP-RosC3**

Garden Moment. Louise McNeill. **SP-McNeL**

Garden of Adonis, The. Edmund Spenser. **NOBE; PoEL-1** *Fr.* The Faerie Queene. **CP-Spens**

  "In that same gardin all the goodly flowres." **NOBE**

Garden of Amour, The. Guillaume de Lorris *and* Jean de Meun, *tr.* by Geoffrey Chaucer. **PoEL-1** *Fr.* The Romance [*or* Romaunt] of the Rose. **CP-ChauG**

Garden of Appleton House, The ("When in the east the morning ray"). Andrew Marvell. **NOBE** *Fr.* Upon Appleton House [To My Lord Fairfax]. **CP-MarvA**

Garden of Boccaccio, The. Samuel Taylor Coleridge. **CP-ColeS**

Garden of Childhood, The. May Sarton. **SP-SartM**

Garden of Disorder, The. Charles Henri Ford. **SP-FordC**

Garden of Epicurus, The. George Meredith. **CP-MerG1**

Garden of Love, The. William Blake. **CP-BlakW** *Fr.* Songs of Experience.

Garden of Metrodorus, The. Herman Melville. **SP-MelvH**

Garden of mouthings, A. Purple, scarlet-speckled, black. The Beekeeper's Daughter. Sylvia Plath. **CP-PlatS**

Garden of Proserpina, The. Edmund Spenser. **ChTr** *Fr.* The Faerie Queene. **CP-Spens**

Garden of the Gods, The. Thom Gunn. **CP-GunnT**

Garden Party, The. Donald Davie. **CP-DavDo**

Garden Seat, The. Thomas Hardy. **CP-HardT**

Garden State. Allen Ginsberg. **CP-GinsA**

Garden Wall, The. Denise Levertov. **CP-LeveD**

Garden was, by mesuring, The. The Garden of Amour. Guillaume de Lorris and Jean de Meun, tr. by Geoffrey Chaucer. **PoEL-1** *Fr.* The Romance [or Romaunt] of the Rose. **CP-ChauG**

Garden we walked in, The. Green Grass and Yellow Balloons. Etheridge Knight. **SP-KnigE**

Garden Wireless. Carl Sandburg. **CP-SandC**

Gardener, The. Stephen Dobyns. **SP-DobyS**

Gardener. Ralph Waldo Emerson. **OxBA** *Fr.* Quatrains. **CP-EmerR**

Gardener. Robert Ranke Graves. **CP-GravR**

Gardener. Erica Jong. **SP-JongE**

Gardener, The. Louis MacNeice. **FaBCIP; IIP** *Fr.* Novelettes. **CP-MacNL**

Gardener, The. Robert Louis Stevenson. **CP-StevR**

Gardener does not love to talk, The. The Gardener. Robert Louis Stevenson. **CP-StevR**

Gardener in Haying-Time, The. Edna St. Vincent Millay. **CP-MillE**

Gardener to His God, The. Mona Van Duyn. **SP-VanDM**

Gardener wi' His Paddle—or, The Gardener's March, The. Robert Burns. **CP-BurnR**

Gardening. Archie Randolph Ammons. **SP-AmmoA**

Gardens No Emblems. Donald Davie. **CP-DavDo**

Gardens of Alcinous, The, *see also* Alkinoos'Garden. Homer, tr. by Alexander Pope. **CP-PopeA** *Fr.* Odyssey.

Gare du Midi. Wystan Hugh Auden. **CP-AudeW**

Gareth and Lynette. Tennyson. *Fr.* Idylls of the King. **CP-TennA**

Gargoyle. Carl Sandburg. **CP-SandC**

Garibaldi. Elizabeth Barrett Browning. **CP-BroEB**

Garibaldi. John Greenleaf Whittier. **CP-WhitJ**

Garish room—oil-lamped; a stove's warm blaze, A. Of a Son. Walter de la Mare. **CP-DeLaW**

Garland for Christopher Smart, A. Mona Van Duyn. **SP-VanDM**

Garland for Ivor Gurney, A. Donald Davie. **CP-DavDo**

Garland for Ronsard, A. Donald Davie. **CP-DavDo**

Garland for Thomas Eakins, A. Charles Tomlinson. **CP-TomlC**

Garland of Red, A. Tom Clark. **SP-ClarT**

Garland [or Ghyrlond] of the Blessèd Virgin Mary [or Marie], The. Ben Jonson. **CP-JonsB**

Garlands fade that Spring so lately wove, The. Charlotte Smith. **CP-SmitS** (Written at the Close of Spring.) **CP-SmitS**

Garlands for Queens, may be. Emily Dickinson. **CP-DickE**

Garnie, I wish I was a seagull. A Poem by Garnie Braxton. James Wright. **CP-WrigJ**

Garret, The. Paul Laurence Dunbar. **CP-DunbP**

Garret, The. Ezra Pound. **SP-PounE**

Garrison, The. Wystan Hugh Auden. **CP-AudeW**

Garrison. John Greenleaf Whittier. **CP-WhitJ**

Garrison of Cape Ann, The. John Greenleaf Whittier. **CP-WhitJ**

Garron Top. John Hewitt. **CP-HewiJ**

Gas fire, The. The Persian. Stevie Smith. **CP-SmitS**

Gas lamps flared yellow in the muddy street. The Blind Lead the Blind. Wystan Hugh Auden. **CP-AudWJ**

Gas Station, The. Charles Kenneth Williams. **CP-WillC; SP-WillC**

Gas was on in the Institute, The. A Shropshire Lad. Sir John Betjeman. **CP-BetjJ**

Gasholders, russet among fields. Mildams, marpools. Geoffrey Hill. **HAP; NoAM; NoP** *Fr.* Mercian Hymns. **CP-HillG**

Gasman Invites the Skyscrapers to Dance. Marge Piercy. **SP-PierM**

Gasoline makes game scarce. From the Move to California. William Stafford. **SP-StafW**

Gat ye me, O gat ye me. The Lass of Ecclefechan. Robert Burns. **CP-BurnR**

Gate, The. Charles Tomlinson. **CP-TomlC**

Gate City Breakdown. Charles Wright. **SP-WrigC**

Gate-crashing ghost, aggressive. Loneliness. Wystan Hugh Auden. **CP-AudeW**

Gate Is Prouti, The. Charles Olson. **CP-OlsoC**

Gates, The. Muriel Rukeyser. **CP-RukeM**

Gates clanged and they walked you into jail, The. The Conscientious Objector. Karl Shapiro. **SP-ShapK**

Gates of Eden. "Bob Dylan." **CP-DylaB**

Gates of my palace are opened wide, The. Alun Lewis. *Fr.* The Captivity. **CP-LewiA**

Gates of Paradise, The. William Blake.
(For the Sexes the Gates of Paradise.) **CP-BlakW**
Epilogue: "Truly my Satan thou art but a dunce." **HAP; ImPo; OAEL-2; OBNC; PeECV; PoE; WeW**
(To the Accuser Who Is the God of This World.) **FHYEP; NoP; OxBSP; SCGP; TrGrPo**

Gateway, The. Robert Ranke Graves. **CP-GravR**

Gateway, Grove, / and Dover say. A Rack of Paperbacks. John Updike. **CP-UpdiJ**

Gather a body to me. The Telesphere. Charles Olson. **SP-OlsoC** *Fr.* The Maximus Poems.

Gather for festival. Hilda Doolittle. **MoAmPo** *Fr.* Songs from Cyprus. **CP-DoolH**

Gather, O gather, / Foeman and friend in love and peace! Cancelled Stanza. Percy Bysshe Shelley. **CP-ShelP**

Gather out of star-dust. Dream Dust. Langston Hughes. **SP-HughL**

Gather the Rose. Edmund Spenser. *See* The Whiles someone did chant this lovely lay.

Gather the stars if you wish it so. Stars, Songs, Faces. Carl Sandburg. **CP-SandC**

Gather up / In the arms of your pity. Litany. Langston Hughes. **SP-HughL**

Gather while you may. Rose. Kathleen Jessie Raine. **SP-RainK**

Gather ye rosebuds, while ye may. To [the] Virgins, to Make Much of Time. Robert Herrick. **CP-HerrR**

Gather ye roses while ye may. Robert Louis Stevenson. **CP-StevR**

Gather young men as the twilight gathers. Carmen 62. Catullus. *Fr.* Carmina. **CP-Catul**

Gathered at random, like extras, the figures effect. What the Recent Survey Has Revealed. James McAuley. **SP-McAuJ**

Gathered at the time of thanks; and the harvest. Family Reunion. Hayden Carruth. **CP-CarHS**

Gathered Church, A. Donald Davie. *Fr.* A Dissentient Voice. **CP-DavDo**

Gathered in the dark pub at the Basin. The Word. John Hewitt. **CP-HewiJ**

Gathered into the Earth. Emily Dickinson. **CP-DickE**

Gatherers of wild seed and froststained fruit. Kenneth Patchen. *Fr.* The Hunted City. **CP-PatcK**

Gathering, The. Wendell Berry. **CP-BerrW**

Gathering early morning / Mushrooms, the music of the. Kenneth Rexroth. **CP-RexKL** *Fr.* The Heart's Garden, the Garden's Heart.

Gathering Leaves. Robert Frost. **CP-FrosR**

Gathering Mushrooms. Paul Muldoon. **SP-MuldP**

Gathering Praties. John Hewitt. **CP-HewiJ**

Gathering Wood. Philip Larkin. **CP-LarkP**

Gaudete. Ted Hughes.
"At the bottom of the Arctic sea, they say." **SP-HughT**
"Bang—a burning, A." **SP-HughT**
"Calves harshly parted from their mamas." **SP-HughT**
"Collision with the earth has finally come—." **SP-HughT**
"Grass-blade is not without, The." **SP-HughT**
"I know well / You are not infallible." **SP-HughT**
"I see the hawk's bride in the oak's grasp." **SP-HughT**
"Once I said lightly." **SP-HughT**
"Primrose petal's edge, A." **SP-HughT**
"Sometimes it comes, a gloomy flap of lightning." **SP-HughT**
"Swallow—rebuilding, The." **SP-HughT**
"This is the maneater's skull." **SP-HughT**
"Waving goodbye, from your banked hospital bed." **SP-HughT**
"Your tree—your oak." **SP-HughT**

Gauge. Langston Hughes. **SP-HughL**

Gauger walked with willing foot, The. A Song of the Road. Robert Louis Stevenson. **CP-StevR**

Gauley Bridge. Muriel Rukeyser. **CP-RukeM**

Gauley Bridge is a good town for Negroes, they let us stand. George Robinson: Blues. Muriel Rukeyser. **CP-RukeM**

Gauley fox can scent the maddened rattler, The. Timber Boom. Louise McNeill. **SP-McNeL**

Gauley mail was overdue, The. Jed Kane. Louise McNeill. **SP-McNeL**

Gaunt, my hope, horse-wise. Min Schleppner. William Carlos Williams. **CP-WilW1**

Gaunt tentacles in greedy disarray. Portrait of a Death. Edwin Rolfe. **CP-RolfE**

Gaurus pretends to *Cato's* fame. Martial, *tr.* by Samuel Johnson. **CP-JohnS** *Fr.* Epigrams.

Gautama in the Deer Park at Benares. Kenneth Patchen. **CP-PatcK**

Gave me 50 dollars for Christmas one year. He. Ron Koertge. **SP-KoerR**

Gave me his car. He. Ron Koertge. **SP-KoerR**

Gavel hammered. The sentence tore my ear, The. Reading at the Old Federal Courts Building, St. Paul. Richard Hugo. **CP-HugoR**

Gawain. Frederick Morgan. **SP-MorgF**

Gawaine, aware again of Lancelot. Lancelot. Edwin Arlington Robinson. **CP-RobiE**

Gawaine, Gawaine, what look ye for to see. Merlin. Edwin Arlington Robinson. **CP-RobiE**

Gawky lad strides round the auction pen, The. Sheep Fair. John Hewitt. **CP-HewiJ**

Gay Chaps at the Bar. Gwendolyn Brooks. **SP-BrooG**

Gay citizen, myself, and thoughtful friend. Allen Tate. *Fr.* More Sonnets at Christmas. **CP-TateA**
("Citizen, myself, or personal friend.") **WaP**

Gay go up and gay go down. The Bells and Queen Victoria. Rudyard Kipling. **CP-KiplR**

"Gay" is the captivating cognomen of a Young Woman of cambridge,mass. Edward Estlin Cummings. **CP-CummE**

Gay ore gook con candlelows. Bearded Iris. Louis Zukofsky. **CP-ZukLS**

Gayest of Bright Flowers, The. William Carlos Williams. **CP-WilW1**

Gaza. Jane Cooper. **SP-CoopJ**

Gaze at a fire till it grow cold and far. Practical Mysticism. John Hewitt. **CP-HewiJ**

Gazelle Calf, The. David Herbert Lawrence. **CP-LawrD**

Gazelle-calf, oh my children, The. Tales. David Herbert Lawrence. *Fr.* Bits. **CP-LawrD**

Gazing Grain, The. John Ashbery. **SP-AshbJ**

Gazing Out, Gazing In. Erica Jong. **SP-JongE**

Gazing thro' her chamber window. Reflection. Christina Georgina Rossetti. **CP-RosC3**

Gazing upon him now, severe and dead. Edna St. Vincent Millay. **SBG** *Fr.* Sonnets from an Ungrafted Tree. **CP-MillE**

Gee, I know / a lovely girl. Person. Robert Creeley. **CP-CreeR**

Gee i like to think of dead it means nearer because deeper firmer. Edward Estlin Cummings. **CP-CummE**

Geek, The. Ted Kooser. **SP-KoosT**

Geese. Stephen Dobyns. **SP-DobyS**

Gehazi. Rudyard Kipling. **CP-KiplR**

Geisha. Gary Gildner. **SP-GildG**

Gellasenheit: / Desert and void. The Uncreated is waste and emptiness. Thomas Merton. *Fr.* Cables to the Ace. **CP-MertT**

Gellius / hearing his uncle anathematise the mere mention. Carmen 74. Catullus. *Fr.* Carmina. **CP-Catul**

Gellius how he'd rare at pot true uncle objurgate soul array. Catullus. *See* Carmen 74: "Gellius, / hearing his uncle anathematise the mere mention."

Gellius is thin. / So? Carmen 89. Catullus. *Fr.* Carmina. **CP-Catul**

Gellius is thin why yes: kiddin'? quite a bonny mater. Catullus. *See* Carmen 89: "Gellius is thin. / So?"

Gellius, what reason can you give why those ruddy lips of yours. Catullus. *See* Carmen 80: "How is it, Gellius."

Gem notes / Of the examiner. Thomas Merton. *Fr.* Cables to the Ace. **CP-MertT**

Gem of all isthmuses and isles that lie. Catullus. *See* Carmen 31: "Apple of islands, Sirmio, & bright peninsulas, set."

Gemela. James Wright. *Fr.* Many of Our Waters: Variations on a Poem by a Black Child. **CP-WrigJ**

Gemini. Robert Creeley. **CP-CreeR**

Gemini. Louise Glück. **SP-GlücL**

Gemini. Audre Lorde. **SP-LordA**

Gemini. Richard Wilbur. **CP-WilbR**

Gemona-del-Friuli, 1961–1976. Donald Davie. **CP-DavDo**

Gems and jewels let them heap. In a Garret. Herman Melville. **SP-MelvH**

Gen. Gary Snyder. **CP-SnydG**

Genealogical Reflection. Ogden Nash. **CP-NashO**

General and the Tango Singer, The. Stephen Dobyns. **SP-DobyS**

General Assembly and Church of the Firstborn, The. Christina Georgina Rossetti. **CP-RosC2**

General commits his emptiness to God, The. Wit's End. Ted Hughes. *Fr.* Scapegoats and Rabies. **SP-HughT**

General 'eard the firin' on the flank, The. Stellenbosch. Rudyard Kipling. **CP-KiplR**

General Joubert. Rudyard Kipling. **CP-KiplR**

General Martinet Gem Coughed A-hem, and A-hem, and A-hem. Motet. Louis Zukofsky. **CP-ZukLS**

General Matthei Drives Home through Santiago. Stephen Dobyns. **SP-DobyS**

General Prologue, The. Geoffrey Chaucer. **FHYEP; NAWM-1; OAEL-1; PoE** *Fr.* The Canterbury Tales. **CP-ChauG**
("As soon as April pierces to the root.") **NAWM-1**
"A-morwe, whan that day bigan to springe." **FiP**
"Clerk ther was of Oxenford also, A." **InPS**
(Seven Pilgrims: A Clerk.) **TrGrPo**
"Good man ther[e] was of religioun [*or* religion], A." **ACP; NOCV**
"Good Wyf [*or* Wif] was ther of bisyde [*or* biside] Bathe, A." **EBEV; InPS**
(Seven Pilgrims: A Wyf of Bathe.) **TrGrPo**
"Knight [*or*Knyght] ther[e] was, and that a worthy man, A." **UV**, *ll.* 43–72; **InPS**, *ll.* 43–78; **FaBoEH; TrGrPo**
(Knighthood, The.) **FaBoEH**
(Seven Pilgrims: A Knight.) **TrGrPo**
"Marchant was ther with a forked berd, A." **CTC**
"Monk ther was, a fair for the maistrye [*or* maistrie], A." **OBCoV; TrGrPo**
("Monk there was, a monk of mastery, A.") **TrGrPo**
(Seven Pilgrims: A Monk.) **TrGrPo**
"Monk ther was, a fair for the maistrie, A." **CTC**
"Sergeant of the Lawe, war and wys, A." **CTC**
Seven Pilgrims: A Miller. **TrGrPo**
Seven Pilgrims: A Squire [*or* Squyer]. **TrGrPo**
Shipman, The ("Shipman was ther, woning fer by weste, A"). **MOS**
"Somonour was ther with us in that place, A." **OBCoV**
"Ther[e] was also a Nonne [*or* nun], a Prioress[e]." **CTC; NOBE; TrGrPo**
(Madame Eglantine.) **NOBE**
(Seven Pilgrims: A Prioress[e].) **TrGrPo**
("There also was a nun, a Prioress.") **TrGrPo**
"This Pardoner had hair as yellow as wax." **SCV**
"Whan that Aprille [*or* April, *or* Aprill] with his[e] shoures [*or* showres] sote [*or* soote]." **ChTr; TRP**, *ll.* 1–18; **TrGrPo**, *ll.* 1–18, *incl. mod. vers. by* Louis Untermeyer; **PPP**, *ll.* 1–271; **FiP**, *ll.* 1–34; **CTC**, *ll.* 1–37; **SCV**, *ll.* 1–42, *incl. mod. vers. by* Nevill Coghill; **EBEvV**, *ll.* 1–78; **PrIm**
(When April with Its Sweet Showers.) **PrIm**, *ll.* 1–18;
("When April with its sweet showers.") **TFi**, *ll.* 1–42, *mod. vers. by* William Harmon;
("When in April the sweet showers fall.") **TEP**, *ll.* 1–34, *mod. vers. by* Nevill Coghill;
("When the sweet showers of April fall and shoot.") **SCV**, *ll.* 1–42, *mod. vers. by* Nevill Coghill;
("When the sweet showers of April follow March.") **TrGrPo**, *ll.* 1–18, *mod. vers. by* Louis Untermeyer;

General Song of Humanity, The. Lawrence Ferlinghetti. **SP-FerlL**

General Summary, A. Rudyard Kipling. **CP-KiplR**

General View of the Troubles of the Reformation. William Wordsworth. *Fr.* Ecclesiastical Sonnets. **CP-WorW2**

General William Booth Enters into Heaven. Nicholas Vachel Lindsay. **CP-LindV**

Generally, reading palms or handwriting or faces. The Model. Wystan Hugh Auden. **CP-AudeW**

Generals, The. Shel Silverstein. **SP-SilS2**

Generals came to the president, The. Connections: Vermont Vietnam (II). Grace Paley. **CP-PaleG**

Generation. Audre Lorde. **SP-LordA**

Generation II. Audre Lorde. **SP-LordA**

Generations of Men, The. Robert Frost. **CP-FrosR**

Generic College. John Updike. **CP-UpdiJ**

Generosity. Christopher Smart. *Fr.* Hymns for the Amusement of Children. **SP-SmarC**

Generous Days, The. Stephen Spender. **CP-SpenS**

Genesis. Geoffrey Hill. **CP-HillG**

Genesis. Etheridge Knight. **SP-KnigE**

Genesis. Nicholas Vachel Lindsay. **CP-LindV**

Genesis. Louis MacNeice. **CP-MacNL**

Genesis. Theodore Roethke. **CP-RoetT**

Genesis. Delmore Schwartz.

" 'All is forgiven when guilt is accepted'." **SP-SchwD**

" 'At last! the present darkness! all is known!'." **SP-SchwD**

" 'Interpretation! that's the act of mind'." **SP-SchwD**

" 'Lo, we descend like light. Light. Light'." **SP-SchwD**

" 'Now we approach the darkness of to-night!'." **SP-SchwD**

" 'O Death, great captain, lift anchor!'." **SP-SchwD**

" 'O New York boy, this is Life, Life in which'." **SP-SchwD**

" 'O what a mess of judgment we have made'." **SP-SchwD**

"Sand upon the Red Sea shore, or on the beach, The." **SP-SchwD**

Genesis. William Carlos Williams. **CP-WilW1**

Genesis 11. Etheridge Knight. **SP-KnigE**

Genesis tells us of Jubal and Jabal. Efforts of Affection. Marianne Craig Moore. **CP-MoorM**

Geneva. Barton Sutter. **SP-SuttB**

Geneva Restored. Charles Tomlinson. **CP-TomlC**

Genevieve. Samuel Taylor Coleridge. *Fr.* Effusions. **CP-ColeS**

Genevieve / what are you seeing. Memorial II. Audre Lorde. **SP-LordA**

Genghis Chan: Private Eye I. John Yau. *See* I was floating through a cross section.

Genghis Chan: Private Eye II. John Yau. **SP-YauJo**

Genghis Chan: Private Eye III. John Yau. **SP-YauJo**

Genghis Chan: Private Eye IV. John Yau. **SP-YauJo**

Genghis Chan: Private Eye V. John Yau. **SP-YauJo**

Genghis Chan: Private Eye VI. John Yau. **SP-YauJo**

Genghis Chan: Private Eye VII. John Yau. **SP-YauJo**

Genial hearth, a hospitable board, A. Pastoral Character. William Wordsworth. *Fr.* Ecclesiastical Sonnets. **CP-WorW2**

Genial spark the poet felt, The. Ralph Waldo Emerson. **CP-EmerR**

Genitrix Laesa. Thomas Hardy. **CP-HardT**

Genius. Philip Levine. **SP-LeviP**

Genius, The. William Carlos Williams. **CP-WilW2**

Genius Child. Langston Hughes. **SP-HughL**

Genius is the ignition of affection. Emily Dickinson. **SP-DickE**

Genius mixt too strong a cup, The. The Dreamers. Robert Duncan. **SP-DuncR**

Genius of Burke! forgive the pen seduced. William Wordsworth. **FaBoPV** *Fr.* Residence in London. *Fr.* The Prelude; Growth of a Poet's Mind [1850 vers.]. **CP-WorW3**

Genius of Raphael! if thy wings. A Jewish Family (in a Small Valley Opposite St Goar, upon the Rhine). William Wordsworth. **CP-WorW2**

Genius of th' Augustan age, The. On the Author of Letters on Literature. William Cowper. **CP-CowpW**

Genius of the Crowd, The. Charles Bukowski. **SP-BukC2**

Genius! Thou gift of Heaven! thou light divine! Edward Shore. George Crabbe. **SP-CrabG** *Fr.* Tales.

Genoa and the Mediterranean. Thomas Hardy. **CP-HardT**

Genocide doesn't only mean bombs. Vietnam Addenda. Audre Lorde. **SP-LordA**

Gentian has a parched Corolla, The. Emily Dickinson. **CP-DickE**

Gentian weaves her fringes, The. Emily Dickinson. **CP-DickE**

Gentile night and the white stars in congress, The. Poem for Jacques Maritain and Leon Trotzky. Delmore Schwartz. **SP-SchwD**

Gentilesse. Geoffrey Chaucer. *See* The Firste stok, fader of gentilesse.

Gentle, The. Theodore Roethke. **CP-RoetT**

"Gentle and Giving" and Other Sayings. Kenneth Patchen. **CP-PatcK**

Gentle and smiling as before. The Wheel. Robert Earl Hayden. **CP-HaydR**

Gentle as breathing. Sleep by the Hot Stream. Thom Gunn. *Fr.* The Geysers. **CP-GunnT**

Gentle as the Lamb of God Made into Mad Cutlets. Chuck Miller. **SP-MillC**

Gentle Bush, The. John Hewitt. **CP-HewiJ**

Gentle, gentle river / Hurrying along. The Rose. Christina Georgina Rossetti. **CP-RosC3**

Gentle knight was pricking on the plaine, A. Edmund Spenser. **EBEV; FHYEP; NAEL-1; OAEL-1; Poetr** *Fr.* The Faerie Queene. **CP-Spens**

Gentle knights, / Know some measure of your nights. Ben Jonson. **CP-JonsB** *Fr.* Oberon, the Fairy Prince.

Gentle Look, The. Samuel Taylor Coleridge. *Fr.* Effusions. **CP-ColeS**

Gentle Love, be not dismayed. Ben Jonson. **CP-JonsB** *Fr.* Love Freed from Ignorance and Folly.

Gentle Man, The. William Carlos Williams. **CP-WilW1**

Gentle Negress, The. William Carlos Williams. **CP-WilW2**

Gentle Negress, The. William Carlos Williams. **CP-WilW2**

Gentle Rejoinder, The. William Carlos Williams. **CP-WilW2**

Gentle River, in her Cupid's honor, The. *verse tr. fr.* Metamorphoses *by* Apuleius. Elizabeth Barrett Browning. **CP-BroEB**

Gentle Snorer, The. Mona Van Duyn. **SP-VanDM**

Gentle Spenser. William Wordsworth. **EPCY** *Fr.* Residence at Cambridge. *Fr.* The Prelude; Growth of a Poet's Mind [1850 vers.]. **CP-WorW3**

Gentle Spring has charmed the earth. Ralph Waldo Emerson. **CP-EmerR**

Gentle story of two lovers young, A. Fragment. Percy Bysshe Shelley. **CP-ShelP**

Gentle wind blows in from the water, A. The Great Birds. Kenneth Patchen. **CP-PatcK**

Gentle youth, forbear. Hero Feels the Shaft of Love. Christopher Marlowe. **GBL** *Fr.* Hero and Leander. **CP-MarlC**

Gentleman, The. Robert Ranke Graves. **CP-GravR**

Gentleman, The. David Herbert Lawrence. **CP-LawrD**

Gentleman and the Bastard, The. Charles Bukowski. **SP-BukC3**

Gentleman of Shalott, The. Elizabeth Bishop. **CP-BishE**

Gentleman that my black hen lays eggs for, The. Jenny Joseph. *Fr.* Fables. **SP-JoseJ**

Gentleman to give us somewhat new, A. A Prologue to the Scholars. Richard Lovelace. **CP-LoveR**

Gentlemanly gentleman, as mild as May, A. Coffee with the Meal. Ogden Nash. **CP-NashO**

Gentleman's coming, A. The Catching Ballet of the Wedding Clothes. Thomas Hardy. **CP-HardT**

Gentleman's Epitaph on Himself and a Lady, Who Were Buried Together, A. Thomas Hardy. **CP-HardT**

Gentleman's Second-Hand Suit, A. Thomas Hardy. **CP-HardT**

Gentlemen, gentlemen, these / are the waiters I mentioned in my friend's work. The Insane Waiters. Gilbert Sorrentino. **SP-SorrG**

Gentlemen, I give you the British Empire. Scram, Lion! Ogden Nash. **CP-NashO**

Gentlemen-Rankers. Rudyard Kipling. **CP-KiplR**

Gentleness and starvation tame. Lady with a Falcon. May Sarton. **SP-SartM**

Gentleness for my dog, A. The Red Front. Edward Estlin Cummings, *tr. from the French of Louis Aragon.* **CP-CummE**

Gentleness of Death, The. George Meredith. **CP-MerG2**

Gentleness of rain is in the wind, The. Malcolm Lowry. *Fr.* Songs for Second Childhood. **CP-LowrM**

Gentleness of rain was in the wind, The. Fragment: Rain. Percy Bysshe Shelley. **CP-ShelP**

Gentlenesse. Robert Herrick. **CP-HerrR**

Gentlest Poet, with free thoughts endowed, The. Suggested by a Picture of the Bird of Paradise. William Wordsworth. **CP-WorW2**

Gentlest Shade that walked Elysian plains, The. Departure from the Vale of Grasmere. August, 1803. William Wordsworth. **CP-WorW1**

Gently I took that which ungently came. Forbearance. Samuel Taylor Coleridge. **CP-ColeS**

Genus: Homo. Jenny Joseph. **SP-JoseJ**

Genus Stephanoma, The. James Fenton. *Fr.* Exempla. **SP-FentJ**

Geographer. Marilyn Hacker. **SP-HackM**

Geographical Knowledge. Thomas Hardy. **CP-HardT**

Geography. Kenneth Koch. **SP-KochK**

Geography comes to an end. Sacred Heart 2. Thomas Merton. **CP-MertT**

Geography of Lograire, The. Thomas Merton. **CP-MertT**

East.

And a Few More Cargo Songs.

Cargo Catechism.

Cargo Songs.

Dialog with Mister Clapcott.

East with Ibn Battuta.

Cairo 1326.

Calicut.

Delhi.

Isfahan.

Mecca.

Nusayris, The.

Syria.

East with Malinowski.

John the Volcano.

Place Names. **ChIV-1**

Sewende (Seven Day).

Tibud Maclay.

North.

Kane Relief Expedition.

Prologue: Why I Have a Wet Footprint on Top of My Mind.

Queens Tunnel.

Ranter and Their Pleads, The.

"There is a grain of sand in Lambeth which Satan cannot find."

Prologue: The Endless Inscription.

South.

Ce Xochitl: The Sign of FLowers.

Chilam Balam.

Clever Strategem: Or, How to Handle Mystics, A.

Dzules.

Hymns of Lograire.

Ladies of Tlatilco, The.

Miami You Are About to Be Surprised.

Notes for a New Liturgy.

"Roar of red wood racer eats field. Green breakaway go cars light lanes."

Two Moralities.

Hare's Message.

Thonga Lament.

"Will a narrow lane / Save Cain?"

West.

At This Precise Moment of History.

Day Six O'Hare Telephane.

Ghost Dance.

Ghost Dance: Prologue.

Geography of Music. Kenneth Patchen. **UnAS** *Fr.* Eight Early Poems. **CP-PatcK**

Geography of the House, The. Wystan Hugh Auden. *Fr.* Thanksgiving for a Habitat. **CP-AudeW**

Geography of the Near Past. Al Young. **CP-YounA**

Geography of this Time. Archibald MacLeish. **CP-MacLA**

Geometric Death. Marsden Hartley. **CP-HartM**

Geometry. Rita Dove. **SP-DoveR**

Geometry of Moods. Stanley Jasspon Kunitz. **CP-KuniS**

Geordie [An Old Ballad]. *Unknown.* **CP-BurnR**

George. Barton Sutter. **SP-SuttB**

George C. Tilyou Smiles. Gilbert Sorrentino. **SP-SorrG**

George Crabbe. Edwin Arlington Robinson. **CP-RobiE**

George hadn't gone down to the canyon mouth for a whole week and so. Resurrection. Robinson Jeffers. **CP-JefR2**

George III. Byron. **TW** *Fr.* The Vision of Judgment. **CP-Byron**

George III. Byron. *See* George the Third.

George Jackson. "Bob Dylan." **CP-DylaB**

George L. Stearns. John Greenleaf Whittier. **CP-WhitJ**

George Meredith (1828-1909). Thomas Hardy. **CP-HardT**

George Nim-Dan-Dean, Esq. to Mr. Sheridan. Jonathan Swift. **CP-SwifJ**

George Nim-Dan-Dean's Invitation to Mr. Thomas Sheridan. Jonathan Swift. **CP-SwifJ**

George Robinson: Blues. Muriel Rukeyser. **CP-RukeM**

George Sand. Anne Waldman. **SP-WaldA**

George Sterling. Robinson Jeffers. **CP-JefR1**

George Sterling's Death. Robinson Jeffers. **CP-JefR1**

George Stubbs at Yale. Richard Hugo. **CP-HugoR**

George the Third. Byron. **FiP** *Fr.* The Vision of Judgment. **CP-Byron** (George III.) **TW**

George Trakl Journal. Charles Wright. **SP-WrigC**

George Washington. Louis Zukofsky. **CP-ZukLS**

George Washington Slept Here. Diane Wakoski. **SP-WakoD**

George Washington: The Whole Man. Diane Wakoski. **SP-WakoD**

George Washington Writes Home About Harvesting His Hemp. Diane Wakoski. **SP-WakoD**

George Washington, your name is on my lips. Patriotic Poem. Diane Wakoski. **SP-WakoD**

George Washington's Camp Cups. Diane Wakoski. **SP-WakoD**

Georgia Beach. Margaret Atwood. **SP-AtwM2**

Georgia Dusk. Langston Hughes. **SP-HughL**

Georgia Nightmare. Edwin Rolfe. **CP-RolfE**

Georgia O'Keeffe. Patti Smith. **SP-SmitP**

Georgia Song, A. Maya Angelou. **SP-AngeM**

Georgics. Virgil, *tr. fr. Latin.*

From Vergil's Fourth Georgic. **CP-ShelP**

"On vent'rous wing in quest of praise I go." **CP-JohnS**

Orpheus and Eurydice. **CP-WorW1**

Out of Virgil, in the Praise of the Spring. **CP-CrasR,** *tr. by* Richard Crashaw;

Translation of Virgil's Georgic IV. 511–15. **CP-WorW2**

Georgina Trevellyn to Louisa: "At last dearest Louisa, I take my pen to address you." Arthur Hugh Clough. **EBVVPR** *Fr.* Amours de Voyage. **SP-ClouA**

Georgina Trevellyn to Luisa: "Dearest Louisa, Enquire if you please. . . ." Arthur Hugh Clough. **FaBoVe** *Fr.* Amours de Voyage. **SP-ClouA**

Geraint and Enid. Tennyson. *Fr.* Idylls of the King. **CP-TennA**

Enid's Song. **FaBoRV**

Geraldine. Emily Brontë. **CP-BronE**

Geraldine, the moon is shining. Song By Julius Brenzaida To G.S. Emily Brontë. **CP-BronE**

Geranium. Jenny Joseph. *Fr.* Derivations. **SP-JoseJ**

Geranium, The. Theodore Roethke. **CP-RoetT**

Gerd sits spindle-shanked in her dark tent. Crystal Gazer. Sylvia Plath. **CP-PlatS**

Gerda in the Aerie. Marilyn Hacker. **SP-HackM**

Geriatric Ward, The. John Hewitt. **CP-HewiJ**

Geriatrics. Steve Griffiths. **SP-GrifS**

Germ, The. Ogden Nash. **CP-NashO**

Germ-Destroyer, A. Rudyard Kipling. *Fr.* Plain Tales from the Hills. "Pleasant it is for the Little Tin Gods." **CP-KiplR**

German ambassador once told me he cdn't bear St Paul, A. Canto 71. Ezra Pound. *Fr.* Cantos. **CP-PoCan**

German-French Campaign, 1870–1871, The. Christina Georgina Rossetti. **CP-RosC1**

Thy Brother's Blood Crieth.

Today For Me.

German Girls! The German Girls!, The. Archibald MacLeish. **CP-MacLA**

German Lairdie, The. Robert Burns. **CP-BurnR**

German Requiem, A. James Fenton. **SP-FentJ**

"Better for the widow, that she should not live in fear of surprise, The." **SCBI**

"Bus is waiting at the southern gate, The." **SCBI**

"But come. Grief must have its term? Guilt too, then." **SCBI**

"But when so many had died, so many and at such speed." **SCBI**

"Doctor Gliedschirm, skin specialist, surgeries 14–16 hours or by appointment." **SP-FentJ**

"His wife nods, and a secret smile." **SCBI**

"How comforting it is, once or twice a year." **SCBI**

"It is not what they built. It is what they knocked down." **SCBI**

"Would come down, would ever come down."

Germanicus leapt upon the wild lion in Smyrna. John Berryman. *Fr.* Eleven Addresses to the Lord. **CP-BerrJ**

Germans Are Lunatics, The. Randall Jarrell. **CP-JarrR**

Germans on the Heights of Hochheim, The. William Wordsworth. **CP-WorW2**

Germans, she said, were sometimes independent. Middlesex. Donald Davie. **CP-DavDo**

Germs. Walt Whitman. **CP-WhitW**

Gerontion. Thomas Stearns Eliot. **CP-ElioT**

Gerontion. Thomas Stearns Eliot. **CP-ElioT**

"Vacant shuttles / Weave the wind. I have no ghosts." **UV**

Gerousios Oinos. Robert Browning. **CP-BroR2**

Gert. Edward Estlin Cummings. *Fr.* Five Americans. **CP-CummE**

Gertie Gitana's hymn to waltzing. Basil Bunting. **CP-BuntB**

Gertrude's Prayer. Rudyard Kipling. **CP-KiplR**

Gestalt at Sixty. May Sarton. **SP-SartM**

Gesture, The. Robert Creeley. **CP-CreeR**

Gesture, The. Richard Eberhart. **CP-EberR**

Gesture, A. James McAuley. **SP-McAuJ**

Gesture, The. George Oppen. **NNaP** *Fr.* Five Poems about Poetry. **CP-OppeG**

Gesture, A. Dabney Stuart. **SP-StuaD**

Gesture by a Lady with an Assumed Name, A. James Wright. **CP-WrigJ**

Gesture she makes is the fear, The. The Gesture. Robert Creeley. **CP-CreeR**

Gestures. Daniel Gerard Hoffman. **SP-HoffD**

Get Back. The Beatles. **CP-Beatl**

Get hence foul[e] grief[e], the canker of the mind[e]. Sir Philip Sidney. **SP-SidnP** *Fr.* Arcadia.

Get it anyway. Robert Creeley. **CP-CreeR**

Get out. / stop draggin your feet through my veins. Exorcism. Diane Wakoski. **SP-WakoD**

Get Out of Town. Thomas McGrath. **SP-McGrT**

Get out the lunch-box of your dreams. Lunch in a Jim Crow Car. Langston Hughes. **SP-HughL**

Get that feeling sometimes. Al Young. **CP-YounA** *Fr.* The Song Turning Back into Itself.

Get up, get up for shame! The blooming morn. Corinna's Going a-Maying. Robert Herrick. **CP-HerrR**

Get up thou lazy lump thou log get up. Lament of a Slug-a-Bed's Wife. Stevie Smith. **CP-SmitS**

Get used to it then. Successions. Pablo Neruda, *tr. fr. Spanish by* Ben Belitt. **SP-NeruP**

Get ye up from the wrath of God's terrible day! The Cities of the Plain. John Greenleaf Whittier. **CP-WhitJ**

Get Your Rocks Off! "Bob Dylan." **CP-DylaB**

Gethsemane. Rudyard Kipling. **CP-KiplR**

Gethsemani, KY. Ernesto Cardenal, *tr. fr. Spanish.*
"Dog barks far out, A." **CP-MertT**
"Every evening the L & N." **CP-MertT**
"I do not know who is out in the snow." **CP-MertT**
"I turned out the light to see the snow." **CP-MertT**
"Like empty beer cans, like cigarette butts." **CP-MertT**
"Like the flights of ducks." **CP-MertT**
"Long freight train / Wakes me in my cell, The." **CP-MertT**
"Sound of passing cars, (if a car comes), The." **CP-MertT**
"Spring has come with its smell of Nicaragua." **CP-MertT**
"That auto horn sounds familiar." **CP-MertT**
"When the first signs go on." **CP-MertT**
"Zinc roofs in the moonlight, The." **CP-MertT**

Gethsemene and Cana. Emily Dickinson. **SP-DickE**

Getting a grip on the leash. A Goodbye. Mona Van Duyn. **SP-VanDM**

Getting Better. The Beatles. **CP-Beatl**

Getting dressed, in the mirror. The Public Bath. Gary Snyder. **CP-SnydG**

Getting Experience. Miller Williams. **SP-WillM**

Getting in the Wood. Gary Snyder. **CP-SnydG**

Getting It Wrong, Again. Steve Griffiths. **SP-GrifS**

Getting the License. Ron Koertge. **SP-KoerR**

Getting the Message. Miller Williams. **SP-WillM**

Getting There. Sylvia Plath. **CP-PlatS**

Getting through with the world. Approach to a City. William Carlos Williams. **CP-WilW2**

Getting Up. Stephen Dobyns. **SP-DobyS**

Getting Up Ahead of Someone (Sun). Frank O'Hara. **SP-OharF**

Getting Up in Winter. Jenny Joseph. **SP-JoseJ**

Getting Up Late. Robert Bly. **SP-BlyR**

Getty. Richard Hugo. **CP-HugoR**

Geyser, The. Thom Gunn. *Fr.* The Geysers. **CP-GunnT**

Geysers, The. Thom Gunn. **CP-GunnT**
Bath House, The.
Cool Stream, The.
Geyser, The.
Sleep by the Hot Stream.

G.F. Died 1954, Aged 27. William Dickey. **SP-DickW**

Ghaselle. Hafiz, *tr. fr. Persian* by Ralph Waldo Emerson. **CP-EmerR**

Ghasta; or, The Avenging Demon!!! Percy Bysshe Shelley. *Fr.* Original Poetry by Victor and Cazire. **CP-ShelP**

Ghazal V. Adrienne Rich. **SP-RicA2** *Fr.* Shooting Script. **CP-RicAE**

Ghazals: Homage to Ghalib. Adrienne Rich. **SP-RicA2**
7/12/68. **CP-RicAE**
7/13/68. **CP-RicAE**
7/14/68: i. **CP-RicAE**
7/14/68: i. **CP-RicAE**
7/16/68: i. **CP-RicAE**
7/16/68: ii. **CP-RicAE**
7/17/68. **CP-RicAE**
7/26/68: i. **CP-RicAE**
8/1/68. **CP-RicAE**
8/4/68. **CP-RicAE**
8/8/68: i. **CP-RicAE**
8/8/68: ii. **CP-RicAE**
7/26/68: II. **CP-RicAE**

Ghost, The. Walter de la Mare. **CP-DeLaW**

Ghost, The. Walter de la Mare. **CP-DeLaW**

Ghost. Robinson Jeffers. **CP-JefR3**

Ghost, The, after Sextus Propertius. Robert Lowell. **SP-LoweR**

Ghost, The. Frederick Morgan. **SP-MorgF**

Ghost, The. James Wright. **CP-WrigJ**

Ghost, a Real Ghost, A. Randall Jarrell. **CP-JarrR**

Ghost Crabs. Ted Hughes. **SP-HughT**

Ghost Dance. Thomas Merton. *Fr.* West. *Fr.* The Geography of Lograire. **CP-MertT**

Ghost Dance: Prologue. Thomas Merton. *Fr.* West. *Fr.* The Geography of Lograire. **CP-MertT**

Ghost-grey the fall of night. A Robin. Walter de la Mare. **CP-DeLaW**

Ghost House. Robert Frost. **CP-FrosR**

Ghost Hunter, The. John Haines. **SP-HainJ**

Ghost in a Field of Mint. Richard Hugo. **CP-HugoR**

Ghost is someone: death has left a hole, A. after Sextus Propertius. Robert Lowell. **SP-LoweR**

Ghost May Come, A. Allen Ginsberg. **CP-GinsA**

Ghost of a Chance. Adrienne Rich. **CP-RicAE; SP-RicA1; SP-RicA2**

Ghost of Abel, The. William Blake. **CP-BlakW**

Ghost of His Wife Comes to Tell Him How It Is. Miller Williams. **SP-WillM**

Ghost of Ninon would be sorry now, The. Veteran Sirens. Edwin Arlington Robinson. **CP-RobiE**

Ghost of Roger Casement, The. William Butler Yeats. **CP-YeatW**

Ghost of the Buffaloes, The. Nicholas Vachel Lindsay. *See* Last night at black midnight I woke with a cry.

Ghost of the Past, The. Thomas Hardy. **CP-HardT**

Ghost of Ware, The. Stevie Smith. **CP-SmitS**

Ghost Story, A. Randall Jarrell. **CP-JarrR**

Ghost Story, *with music.* Robert Pack. **SP-PackR**

Ghosts. Countee Cullen. **CP-CullC**

Ghosts. John Hewitt. **CP-HewiJ**

Ghosts. Mary Oliver. **SP-OlivM**

Ghosts. Anne Sexton. **CP-SextA**

Ghosts. Miller Williams. **SP-WillM**

Ghosts as Cocoons. Wallace Stevens. **CP-StevW**

Ghosts at Garnet. Richard Hugo. **CP-HugoR**

Ghosts in England. Robinson Jeffers. **CP-JefR2**

Ghosts in Love. Nicholas Vachel Lindsay. **CP-LindV**

Ghosts in New Houses. Malcolm Lowry. **CP-LowrM**

Ghost's Leavetaking, The. Sylvia Plath. **CP-PlatS**

Ghosts of an Old House, The. John Gould Fletcher.
Back Stairs, The. **SP-FletJ**
Bedroom. **SP-FletJ**
Calendar in the Attic, The. **SP-FletJ**
Old Nursery. **SP-FletJ**
Vision. **SP-FletJ**
Well, The. **SP-FletJ**

Ghosts of Beauty, The. Alexander Pope. **OBSV** *Fr.* Epistle [II,] to a Lady[: Of the Characters of Women]. **CP-PopeA**

Ghosts of the dead! have I not heard your yelling. On the Dark Height of Jura. Percy Bysshe Shelley. *Fr.* Poems from St. Irvyne, or, The Rosicrucian. **CP-ShelP**

Ghost's Petition, The. Christina Georgina Rossetti. **CP-RosC1**

Ghosts there must be with me in this old house. Solitude. Walter de la Mare. **CP-DeLaW**

Gi' me a reefer, Lawd. The Wrong Door. William Carlos Williams. **CP-WilW2**

Giacometti. Richard Wilbur. **CP-WilbR**

Giant and Saint. Marsden Hartley. **CP-HartM**

Giant in the Garden. May Sarton. **SP-SartM**

Giant Night. Anne Waldman. **SP-WaldA**

Giant Norway spruce from Podunk, its lower branches bound, The. December. James Schuyler. **CP-SchuJ**

Giant Snail. Elizabeth Bishop. *Fr.* Rainy Season; Sub-Tropics. **CP-BishE**

Giant Toad. Elizabeth Bishop. *Fr.* Rainy Season; Sub-Tropics. **CP-BishE**

Giant whispering and coughing from. Broadcast. Philip Larkin. **CP-LarkP**

Giantess, *see also tr. by* Roy Campbell, "Of old when Nature, in her verve defiant." Charles Baudelaire, *tr. fr. French* by Karl Shapiro. **SP-ShapK**

Giantess, The. Richard Eberhart. **CP-EberR**

Giants did advance their wicked hand, The, *ad. fr. Latin of* Cornelius Severus. Sir Walter Ralegh. **CP-RaleW**

Giant's Ring, The. Robinson Jeffers. **CP-JefR2**

Giaour, The. Byron. **CP-Byron**
"But thou, false infidel! shall writhe." **VVA**

Giaour and the Pacha, The. Richard Wilbur. **CP-WilbR**

Gibber, The. Theodore Roethke. **NAAL-2** *Fr.* The Lost Son. **CP-RoetT**

Gibbous Moon, The. Richard Shelton. *Fr.* Five Lies About the Moon. **SP-ShelR**

Gibbous moon hangs out of the twilight, A. The Yew-Tree on the Downs. David Herbert Lawrence. **CP-LawrD**

Gibbs. Muriel Rukeyser. **CP-RukeM**
"It was much later in his life he rose." **ImOP**

Gibralto. Patti Smith. **SP-SmitP**

Giddiness. George Herbert. **CP-HerbG**

Gie the Lass her Fairin'. Robert Burns. **CP-BurnR**

Gif Ye Wol Stonden Hardie Wight. John Keats. **CP-KeatJ**

Giffen's Debt. Rudyard Kipling. **CP-KiplR**

Gift. The. Charles Bukowski. **CP-BukC2**

Gift, The. John Ciardi. **SP-CiarJ**

Gift. Leonard Cohen. **CP-CoheL**

Gift, The. Robert Creeley. **CP-CreeR**

Gift, The. Hilda Doolittle. **CP-DoolH**

Gift. Hilda Doolittle. **CP-DoolH**

Gift, The. Louise Glück. **SP-GlücL**

Gift, The. Pablo Neruda, *tr. fr. Spanish by* Ben Belitt. **SP-NeruP**

Gift, The. "Lou Reed." **SP-ReedL**

Gift. Muriel Rukeyser. **CP-RukeM**

Gift. Alice Walker. **CP-WalkA**

Gift. Alice Walker. **CP-WalkA**

Gift, The. Charles Kenneth Williams. **CP-WillC; SP-WillC**

Gift, The. William Carlos Williams. **CP-WilW2**

Gift for a Believer. Philip Levine. **SP-LeviP**

Gift from the cold and silent Past! The Norsemen. John Greenleaf Whittier. **CP-WhitJ**

Gift is small, The. Lines for a Gift. Robert Browning. **CP-BroR2**

Gift of God, The. Edwin Arlington Robinson. **CP-RobiE**

Gift of Gravity, The. Wendell Berry. **CP-BerrW**

Gift of Great Value, A. Robert Creeley. **CP-CreeR**

Gift of Harun Al-Rashid, The. William Butler Yeats. **CP-YeatW**

Gift of Light, A. Marge Piercy. **SP-PierM**

Gift of neither Heaven nor Earth, The. Emily Dickinson. **SP-DickE**

Gift of Prophecy Lost, The. Miller Williams. **SP-WillM**

Gift of Sight. Robert Ranke Graves. **CP-GravR**

Gift of speech is a very terrible thing O man, The. Speech. Wystan Hugh Auden. **CP-AudWJ**

Gift of the Magi, The. Peter Meinke. **SP-MeinP**

Gift of the Sea, The. Rudyard Kipling. **CP-KiplR**

Gift of Tongue. Tom Clark. **SP-ClarT**

Gift of Tritemius, The. John Greenleaf Whittier. **CP-WhitJ**

Gift Outright, The. Robert Frost. **CP-FrosR**

Gift-Poem ("December steel done . . . "). Muriel Rukeyser. **CP-RukeM**

Gift-Poem ("Year in its cold beginning"). Muriel Rukeyser. **CP-RukeM**

Gifts, The. Richard Wilbur. **CP-WilbR**

Gifts of one who loved me. Motto to "Gifts." Ralph Waldo Emerson. **CP-EmerR**

Gifts of Rain. Seamus Heaney. **SP-HeanS**

Gigantic Beauty of a Stallion, A. Walt Whitman. **ASP; ImGa; PDV** *Fr.* Song of Myself. **CP-WhitW**

Gigantic beauty of a stallion, fresh and responsive to my caresses, A. A Gigantic Beauty of a Stallion. Walt Whitman. **ASP; ImGa; PDV** *Fr.* Song of Myself. **CP-WhitW**

Gigantomachia. Wallace Stevens. **CP-StevW**

Gigolo. Sylvia Plath. **CP-PlatS**

Gila Bend. James Dickey. **CP-DickJ**

Gilbert had sailed to India's shore. The Vampirine Fair. Thomas Hardy. **CP-HardT**

Gilded hummingbirds are whizzing. An Oiran and Her Kamuso. John Gould Fletcher. **SP-FletJ**

Gilded phaloi of the crocuses, The. Coitus. Ezra Pound. **SP-PounE**

Giles Corey of the Salem Farms. Henry Wadsworth Longfellow. **SP-LongH**

Act IV.

Trial, The. **PAH**

Prologue: "Delusions of the days that once have been." **PAH**

Gimboling. Isabella Gardner. **CP-GardI**

Gimlet. Gilbert Sorrentino. **SP-SorrG**

Gimme $25.00. Request. Langston Hughes. **SP-HughL**

Gin. David St. John. **SP-StJoD**

Gin but the oor 'ud chop and set me free. "Hugh MacDiarmid." **SP-MacDH** *Fr.* Frae Anither Window in Thrums.

Gin-drenched, negotiating New York night. Lowry. David Markson. **CP-MarkD**

Gin the Goodwife Stint. Basil Bunting. **CP-BuntB**

Gina, I saw you walk. An Apparition. Donald Davie. **CP-DavDo**

Ginevra. Percy Bysshe Shelley. **CP-ShelP**

"She is still, she is cold." **ChER**

Ginger, who are you going with? Basil Bunting, *after the Latin of* Horace. **CP-BuntB**

Ginkgoes in Fall. Howard Nemerov. **CP-NemeH**

Gino hummed an epithalamium. Marilyn Hacker. *Fr.* The Regent's Park Sonnets. **SP-HackM**

Ginsberg? Charles Bukowski. **SP-BukC3**

Giordano, verily thy Pencil's skill. To Lucca Giordano. William Wordsworth. **CP-WorW2**

Giorno dei Morti. David Herbert Lawrence. **CP-LawrD**

Giovanni Diodati. Charles Tomlinson. **CP-TomlC**

Giovanni's *Rape of the Sabine Women* at Wildenstein's. George Oppen. **CP-OppeG**

Gipsies: "Gipsies seek wide sheltering woods again, The." John Clare. **SP-ClarJ**

Gipsies. Derek Mahon. **SP-MahoD**

Gipsies: "Snow falls deep; the forest lies alone, The." John Clare. **SP-ClarJ**

Gipsies seek wide sheltering woods again, The. Gipsies. John Clare. **SP-ClarJ**

Gipsy. David Herbert Lawrence. **CP-LawrD**

Gipsy Girl, The. Wystan Hugh Auden. **CP-AudWJ**

Gipsy Trail, The. Rudyard Kipling. **CP-KiplR**

Gipsy Vans. Rudyard Kipling. **CP-KiplR** *Fr.* Debits and Credits.

Giraffes. Phoebe Hesketh. **SP-HeskP**

Giralda, The. Jean Garrigue. **SP-GarrJ**

Girard, Girard. Laurence Lieberman. **SP-LiebL**

Girl. The Beatles. **CP-Beatl**

Girl, The. William Carlos Williams. **CP-WilW1**

Girl, The. William Carlos Williams. **CP-WilW2**

Girl and Baby Florist Sidewalk Pram Nineteen Seventy Something. Kenneth Koch. **SP-KochK**

Girl and Her Fawn, The. Andrew Marvell. *See* The Nymph and Her Fawn.

Girl and Horse, 1928. Margaret Atwood. **SP-AtwM1**

Girl at Play. Dabney Stuart. **SP-StuaD**

Girl at Sixteen with Lightning. Gilbert Sorrentino. *Fr.* Twelve Études for Voice and Kazoo. **SP-SorrG**

Girl at the Play. Muriel Rukeyser. **CP-RukeM**

GIRL ATTACKED. James Fenton. *Fr.* Exempla. **SP-FentJ**

Girl being chosen stood in her naked room, The. Mortal Girl. Muriel Rukeyser. **CP-RukeM**

Girl do you think. Excavation of Troy. Archibald MacLeish. **CP-MacLA**

Girl Dreams That She Is Giselle, The. Randall Jarrell. **CP-JarrR**

Girl goes dancing there, The. Sweet Dancer. William Butler Yeats. **CP-YeatW**

Girl grown woman fire mother of fire. Waterlily Fire. Muriel Rukeyser. **CP-RukeM**

Girl in a Cage. Carl Sandburg. **CP-SandC**

Girl in a Library, A. Randall Jarrell. **CP-JarrR; SP-JarrR**

Girl in a Nightgown. Wallace Stevens. **CP-StevW**

Girl in a Window, A. James Wright. **CP-WrigJ**

Girl in Cairo, The. David Herbert Lawrence. *Fr.* Bits. **CP-LawrD**

Girl in the bikini, my / wife, the lady—she sits on, The. An Obscene Poem. Robert Creeley. **CP-CreeR**

Girl in the Red Convertible, The. Gary Gildner. **SP-GildG**

Girl in the tea shop, The. The Tea Shop. Ezra Pound. **SP-PounE**

Girl in White. Marge Piercy. **SP-PierM**

Girl lashed to the stake, The. Poem. Edwin Rolfe. **CP-RolfE**

Girl of Cadiz, The. Byron. **CP-Byron**

Girl of My Dreams, The. Dabney Stuart. **SP-StuaD**

Girl of My Dreams Is Dying. Dabney Stuart. **SP-StuaD**

Girl of the North Country. "Bob Dylan." **CP-DylaB**

Girl on the Bus Stop Bench, The. Charles Bukowski. **SP-BukC1**

Girl this evening regrets her surrender with tears, A. Somewhere. Howard Nemerov. **CP-NemeH**

Girl Walking into a Shadow, A. James Wright. **CP-WrigJ**

Girl Who Died #1, The. Alice Walker. **CP-WalkA**

Girl Who Died #2, The. Alice Walker. **CP-WalkA**

Girl Who Has Drowned Herself Speaks, A. Stephen Spender. **CP-SpenS**

Girl who, in 1971, when I was living by myself, painfully lonely, bereft, depressed, A. Shame. Charles Kenneth Williams. **SP-WillC**

Girl whose arms are leaves, The. The Yellow Tree Peony. William Carlos Williams. **CP-WilW2**

Girl whose cheeks are covered with paint, A. Biological Reflection. Ogden Nash. **CP-NashO**

Girl with all that raising, A. Ballad of the Girl Whose Name Is Mud. Langston Hughes. **SP-HughL**

Girl with 'Cello. May Sarton. **SP-SartM**

Girl with Sampler. Stanley Jasspon Kunitz. *Fr.* Words for the Unknown Makers: A Garland of Commemorative Verses. **CP-KuniS**

Girl with the burning golden eyes. To Gloriana. Nicholas Vachel Lindsay. **CP-LindV**

Girl You Thought You Loved, The. Lewis Turco. **SP-TurcL**

Girls. Charles Bukowski. **SP-BukC3**

Girls! Stevie Smith. **CP-SmitS**

Girls, The. Diane Wakoski. **SP-WakoD**

Girls are coming home in their cars, The. Girls Coming Home. Charles Bukowski. **SP-BukC1**

Girls at the Green Hotel, The. Charles Bukowski. **SP-BukC1**

Girls buck the wind in the grooves toward work. The Morning Half-Life Blues. Marge Piercy. **SP-PierM**

Girls Coming Home. Charles Bukowski. **SP-BukC1**

Girls Fighting, Broadway. Karl Shapiro. **SP-ShapK**

Girls From Nowhere. Charles Bukowski. **SP-BukC3**

Girl's Garden, A. Robert Frost. **CP-FrosR**

Girls in Pantyhose. Charles Bukowski. **SP-BukC1**

Girls Next Door, The. Thom Gunn. **CP-GunnT**

Girls of St. Mary's school, The. Harold Fogel Could Be Anywhere. Gary Gildner. **SP-GildG**

Girls on the Bridge. Derek Mahon. **SP-MahoD**

Girls, protected by gold wire from the gaze, The. And You Know. John Ashbery. **SP-AshbJ**

Girl's Ring, A. Edward Estlin Cummings. **CP-CummE**

Girl's Song. Louise Bogan. **CP-BogaL**

Girl's Song, *fr.* Words for Music Perhaps. William Butler Yeats. **CP-YeatW**

Girls wake, stretch, and pad up to the door, The. Apartment Cats. Thom Gunn. **CP-GunnT**

Girls who found themselves in blue stories. Où Sont Ils, Où, Vïerge Souvrain? Gilbert Sorrentino. **SP-SorrG**

Girls with eyes of wicks of lights, The. The Oracle. Thomas Merton. **CP-MertT**

Girt with a boyish grab for boyish task. Dedication. "Lewis Carroll." *Fr.* The Hunting of the Snark. **CP-CarrL**

Gislebertus' Eve. John Berryman. **CP-BerrJ**

Give a dime to a beggar for I have seen a sight. Adventures, Midnight. Muriel Rukeyser. *Fr.* Night-Music. **CP-RukeM**

. . . *give a man his*. Wait for Me. Robert Creeley. **CP-CreeR**

Give All to Love. Ralph Waldo Emerson. **CP-EmerR**

Give, ask for nothing, hope for nothing. Expect Nothing. Robert Ranke Graves. **CP-GravR**

Give away her gowns. Chorus. Edna St. Vincent Millay. *Fr.* Memorial to D. C. **CP-MillE**

Give beauty all her right. Thomas Campion. **CP-CampT**

Give ear, O my people, to my law. Psalm 78. Bible, *O.T. Fr.* Psalms. **CP-Psal**

Give ear, O Shepherd of Israel, thou that leadest Joseph like a flock. Psalm 80. Bible, *O.T. Fr.* Psalms. **CP-Psal**

Give ear to my prayer, O God. Psalm 55. Bible, *O.T.* **AWP** *Fr.* Psalms. **CP-Psal**

Give ear to my words, O Lord, consider my meditation. Psalm 5. Bible, *O.T. Fr.* Psalms. **CP-Psal**

Give end unto thy pastimes, Love. Ben Jonson. **CP-JonsB** *Fr.* Love Restored.

Give her but a least excuse to love me! Song. Robert Browning. **ViBoPo** *Fr.* Pippa Passes. **CP-BroR1**

Give him the darkest inch your shelf allows. George Crabbe. Edwin Arlington Robinson. **CP-RobiE**

Give house-roome to the best; 'Tis never known. Choose for the Best. Robert Herrick. **CP-HerrR**

Give, if thou canst, an Almes; if not, afford. Almes. Robert Herrick. **CP-HerrR**

Give it what name you choose. Comparative Iconography. Hayden Carruth. **CP-CarHS**

Give little Anguish. Emily Dickinson. **CP-DickE**

Give Lucinda pearl nor stone. To the New Year [For the Countess of Carlisle]. Thomas Carew. **CP-CareT**

Give me a Cell. His Wish to Privacie. Robert Herrick. **CP-HerrR**

Give me a cunning dollar that tells me no lie. Thomas Merton. *Fr.* Cables to the Ace. **CP-MertT**

Give Me A Doctor. Wystan Hugh Auden. *See* Give me a doctor, partridge-plump.

Give me a doctor, partridge-plump. Wystan Hugh Auden. **OBCoV** *Fr.* Shorts [1948–1957] ("At peace under this mandarin, sleep, Lucina"). **CP-AudeW**

(Give Me A Doctor.) **OBCoV**

Give me a golden pen, and let me lean. On Leaving Some Friends at an Early Hour. John Keats. **CP-KeatJ**

Give me a land of boughs in leaf. Alfred Edward Housman. **CP-HousA**

Give me a man that is not dull. His Desire. Robert Herrick. **CP-HerrR**

Give me a poem / To wring the hearts of men. Malcolm Lowry. **CP-LowrM**

Give me a reason why men call. Upon Punchin. Robert Herrick. **CP-HerrR**

Give Me A Sponge. David Herbert Lawrence. **CP-LawrD**

Give me a thrill, says the reader. Fiction and the Reading Public. Philip Larkin. **CP-LarkP**

Give me all mountains. All Mountains. Hilda Doolittle. **CP-DoolH**

Give me back my broken night. The Future. Leonard Cohen. **CP-CoheL**

Give me back my fingerprints. Fingerprints. Leonard Cohen. **CP-CoheL**

Give me Honours: what are these. Honours Are Hindrances. Robert Herrick. **CP-HerrR**

Give me hunger / O you gods that sit and give. At a Window. Carl Sandburg. **CP-SandC**

Give me more love or more disdain. Mediocrity in Love Rejected. Thomas Carew. **CP-CareT**

Give me my Scallop[-]shell of quiet. The Passionate Man[']s Pilgrimage. Sir Walter Ralegh. **CP-RaleW**

Give me no days more brilliant than I know. Content. Paul Laurence Dunbar. **CP-DunbP**

Give me, O Father! to thy throne access. Boethius, *tr. by* Samuel Johnson. **CP-JohnS** *Fr.* Consolation of Philosophy, The ("De Consolacione Philosophie"). **CP-ChauG**

Give me one kiss. To Dianeme. Robert Herrick. **CP-HerrR**

Give me that man that dares bestride. His Cavalier. Robert Herrick. **CP-HerrR**

Give me the food that satisfies a Guest. Kisses. Robert Herrick. **CP-HerrR**

Give me the lowest place: not that I dare. The Lowest Place. Christina Georgina Rossetti. **CP-RosC1**

Give me the money, / Give me the money. Malcolm Lowry. **CP-LowrM**

Give me the moon at my feet. Prayer. David Herbert Lawrence. **CP-LawrD**

Give Me the Splendid Silent Sun. Walt Whitman. **CP-WhitW**

Give me the thing I need the most. Prayer. Wystan Hugh Auden. **CP-AudWJ**

Give me this day a faith not personal. Allen Tate. *Fr.* More Sonnets at Christmas. **CP-TateA**

Give me truths; / For I am weary of the surfaces. Blight. Ralph Waldo Emerson. **CP-EmerR**

Give me wine, and give me meate. To Sir Clipseby Crew. Robert Herrick. **CP-HerrR**

Give Me Women, Wine, and Snuff. John Keats. **CP-KeatJ**

Give me your anathema. Whiffletree. Carl Sandburg. **CP-SandC**

Give me your hand. A Conceit. Maya Angelou. **SP-AngeM**

Give me your hand old Revolutionary. The Centenarian's Story. Walt Whitman. **CP-WhitW**

Give me your patience, sister, while I frame. Acrostic. John Keats. **CP-KeatJ**

Give me your poppies. Choros Sequence. Hilda Doolittle. **CP-DoolH**

Give over seeking bastard joy. Exhortation. Louise Bogan. **CP-BogaL**

Give pensions to the Learned Pig. William Blake. **CP-BlakW**

Give place all ye that doth rejoice. Sir Thomas Wyatt. **CP-WyatT**

Give the engines room. The Firemen's Ball. Nicholas Vachel Lindsay. *Fr.* Poems Speaking of Buddha, Prince Siddartha. **CP-LindV**

Give the king thy judgments, O God. Psalm 72. Bible, *O.T. Fr.* Psalms. **CP-Psal**

Give Them Blood. Gilbert Sorrentino. **SP-SorrG**

Give them my regards when you go to the school reunion. More of a Corpse than a Woman. Muriel Rukeyser. **CP-RukeM**

Give thy tongue no tho'ts. A Modern Version of Polonius' Advice. Ernest Hemingway. **CP-HemiE**

Give to barrows, trays, and pans. Art. Ralph Waldo Emerson. **CP-EmerR**

Give to imagination some pure light. George Meredith. *Fr.* Modern Love. **CP-MerG1**

Give to me the life I love. The Vagabond. Robert Louis Stevenson. **CP-StevR**

Give unto all, lest he, whom thou deni'st. Almes. Robert Herrick. **CP-HerrR**

Give unto the Lord, O ye mighty. Psalm 29. Bible, *O.T.* **AWP** *Fr.* Psalms. **CP-Psal**

Give us back, Oh give us back. Cry of the Masses. David Herbert Lawrence. **CP-LawrD**

Give Us Gods. David Herbert Lawrence. **CP-LawrD**

Give us the grace to be men. Thus Far So Nobly Advanced. Kenneth Patchen. **CP-PatcK**

Give Us the Thebaïd. David Herbert Lawrence. **CP-LawrD**

Give Want her welcome if she comes; we find. Poverty and Riches. Robert Herrick. **CP-HerrR**

Give way, and be ye ravished by the sun. To Marygolds. Robert Herrick. **CP-HerrR**

Give way, give way, now, now my Charles shines here. To the King. Robert Herrick. **CP-HerrR**

Give way, give way ye Gates, and win. The Wassaile. Robert Herrick. **CP-HerrR**

Give Way, Ye Gates. Theodore Roethke. **CP-RoetT**

Give way, you fiends, and give that man some happiness. *incl. in* Perhaps for Eridanus. Malcolm Lowry. *Fr.* The Moon in Scandinavia. **CP-LowrM**

Give you a lantern. Kenneth Patchen. **CP-PatcK**

Give Your Heart to the Hawks. Robinson Jeffers. **CP-JefR2**

Give Your Wish Light. Robinson Jeffers. **CP-JefR2**

Given a crisp leaf or a lichened strip. Dichotomy. John Hewitt. **CP-HewiJ**

Given Grace, A. Charles Tomlinson. **CP-TomlC**

Given in Marriage unto Thee. Emily Dickinson. **CP-DickE**

Given the choice of blowing up the Empire. Teacher Answering Young Radicals. Stephen Dunn. **SP-DunnS**

Given the rock to hew, and split. The Sister. Marsden Hartley. **CP-HartM**

Giver of Gifts, The. Stephen Dobyns. **SP-DobyS**

Giving and Taking. John Greenleaf Whittier. **CP-WhitJ**

Giving It Up. Charles Kenneth Williams. **CP-WillC; SP-WillC**

Giving oneself to the dentist or doctor who is a good one. The Kind of Act Of. Robert Creeley. **CP-CreeR**

Giving Thanks, *sel., v. 4.* Bible, *O.T. See* Psalm 100: "Make a joyful noise unto the Lord, all ye lands."

Giving Them What For. Steve Griffiths. **SP-GrifS**

Glacials. Archie Randolph Ammons. **SP-AmmoA**

Glacier, The. Louis MacNeice. **CP-MacNL**

Glacier, The. Charles Tomlinson. **CP-TomlC**

Glad. Wystan Hugh Auden. *Fr.* Three Posthumous Poems. **CP-AudeW**

Glad Day for Laurence Vail, A. Kay Boyle. **CP-BoylK**

Glad old house of lichened stonework. To a Well-Named Dwelling. Thomas Hardy. **CP-HardT**

Glad Sight Wherever New with Old. William Wordsworth. **CP-WorW2**

Glad they were there. Louis Zukofsky. **CP-ZukLS**

Glad Tidings. William Wordsworth. *Fr.* Ecclesiastical Sonnets. **CP-WorW2**

Glad time is at his point arrived. Epithalamion. Ben Jonson. **CP-JonsB** *Fr.* Masque of Hymen.

Gladeth, ye foules, of the morrowe gray. The Complaint of Mars. Geoffrey Chaucer. **CP-ChauG**

Gladiators, The. Stanley Jasspon Kunitz. **CP-KuniS**

Gladly I would be again. High Summer. Kathleen Jessie Raine. **SP-RainK**

Gladness of Death. David Herbert Lawrence. **CP-LawrD**

Gladstone Street. Charles Tomlinson. **CP-TomlC**

Gladstone was still respected. Yeux Glauques. Ezra Pound. **MoAmPo** *Fr.* Hugh Selwyn Mauberley. (Life and Contacts). **SP-PounE**

Glamorous and difficult friend. Thom Gunn. *Fr.* Talbot Road. **CP-GunnT**

Glamour of the end attic, the smell of old, The. Perdita. Louis MacNeice. **CP-MacNL**

Glamour of this moment too will pass, The. Demerol. Al Young. **CP-YounA**

Glance, The. Walter de la Mare. **CP-DeLaW**

Glance, The. George Herbert. **CP-HerbG**

Glance—and instantly the small meek flower, A. A Pot Of Musk. Walter de la Mare. **CP-DeLaW**

Glance back four years (yes, nearly four years now). A Poem for February First 1975. Kay Boyle. **CP-BoylK**

Glance drops here like a hawk falling, The. Morwenna's Cliff. Charles Tomlinson. **CP-TomlC**

Glance from the Bridge, A. Richard Wilbur. **CP-WilbR**

Glanders. Paul Muldoon. **SP-MuldP**

Glands for the financier. Robert Graves. Ernest Hemingway. **CP-HemiE**

Glanmore Sonnets. Seamus Heaney. **SP-HeanS**
  "I dreamt we slept in a moss in Donegal." **NoP**
  "This evening the cuckoo and the corncrake." **IPY**
  "Thunderlight on the split logs: big raindrops." **IPY**
  "Vowels plowed into other: opened ground." **NoP**

Glare goes down. The metal of a molten pane, The. Glass Grain. Charles Tomlinson. **CP-TomlC**

Glasco had none, but now some teeth has got. Upon Glasco. Epig. Robert Herrick. **CP-HerrR**

Glasgow, 1960. "Hugh MacDiarmid." **SP-MacDH**

Glass. Brendan Galvin. **SP-GalvB**

Glass after Oblivion. James Liddy. **CP-LiddJ**
  City of Dreadful Knight, The.
  Deaths and Electrocutions.
  Dinner Menu a Burnt Offering, A.
  Jours-Fixes.
  Mothermas.
  Orpheus as a Christian Scientist.
  Orpheus in Connaught.
  Wave of the Nineties, The.

Your Pleasure in my Cemetery.

Glass, air, ice, light. Waiting on the Corners. Donald Hall. **CP-HallD**

Glass Darkly, A. Miller Williams. **SP-WillM**

Glass Dialectic. Howard Nemerov. **CP-NemeH**

Glass Falling. Louis MacNeice. **CP-MacNL**

Glass gauds from Murano. Death in Venice. Charles Tomlinson. **CP-TomlC**

Glass Globe. Archie Randolph Ammons. **SP-AmmoA**

Glass Grain. Charles Tomlinson. **CP-TomlC**

Glass has been falling all the afternoon, The. Storm Warnings. Adrienne Rich. **CP-RicAE; SP-RicA1; SP-RicA2**

Glass House Canticle. Carl Sandburg. **CP-SandC**

Glass in a Liverpool drawing room cracked across, A. Nineteen-Seventeen. Donald Davie. **CP-DavDo**

Glass is going down. The sun, The. Glass Falling. Louis MacNeice. **CP-MacNL**

Glass of Pure Water, The. "Hugh MacDiarmid." **SP-MacDH**

Glass of sweet milk, A. Rediscovered Diary Entry. Al Young. **CP-YounA**

Glass of Water, A. May Sarton. **SP-SartM**

Glass of Water, The. Wallace Stevens. **CP-StevW**

Glass Onion. The Beatles. **CP-Beatl**

Glass Orchard. Raissa Maritain, *tr. fr. French by* Thomas Merton. **CP-MertT**

Glass, out of deep[e] and out of desperate [*or* desp'rate] want. Upon Glass: Epigram. Robert Herrick. **CP-HerrR**

Glass Poem. Karl Shapiro. **CP-ShapK**

Glass ponds astound the juicy grass, the air is wild. It Rained Last Night. Isabella Gardner. **CP-GardI**

Glass Speciality. Archie Randolph Ammons. **SP-AmmoA**

Glass violin is broken, The. Charles Henri Ford. *Fr.* Epigrams. **SP-FordC**

Glass was the Street—in tinsel Peril. Emily Dickinson. **CP-DickE**

Glasses. John Updike. **CP-UpdiJ**

Glassy water, glassy water. Translation of the Beginning of *Rio Verde*. Samuel Johnson. **SP-JohnS**

Glastonbury Thorn, The. George Meredith. **CP-MerG2**

Glaucous Winged Gull, The. Malcolm Lowry. **CP-LowrM**

Glaze of ice glistens in the manure, A. The Kiss. Robert Pack. **SP-PackR**

Glazed mind layed in a, A). Edward Estlin Cummings. **CP-CummE**

Glazunoviana. John Ashbery. **SP-AshbJ**

Gleam of an heroic Act, The. Emily Dickinson. **CP-DickE**

Gleaming head of one fine friend, The. In Praise of Gloriana's Remarkable Golden Hair. Nicholas Vachel Lindsay. *Fr.* This Section Is a Christmas Tree. **CP-LindV**

Gleams, a green lamp. Ferry. Louis Zukofsky. *Fr.* 29 Poems. **CP-ZukLS**

Gleaner (Suggested By a Picture), The. William Wordsworth. **CP-WorW2**

Gleaning. Randall Jarrell. **CP-JarrR; SP-JarrR**

Glee. George Meredith. **CP-MerG2**

Glee—The great storm is over. Emily Dickinson. **CP-DickE**

Glen-Almain; Or, the Narrow Glen. William Wordsworth. **CP-WorW1**

Glen of Light, The. John Hewitt. **CP-HewiJ**

Glen of Silence, The. "Hugh MacDiarmid." **SP-MacDH**

Glen Uig. Richard Hugo. **CP-HugoR**

Glenaan. John Hewitt. **CP-HewiJ**

Glenarriffe and Parkmore. John Hewitt. **CP-HewiJ**

Glendun. John Hewitt. **CP-HewiJ**

Glendun on a Wet July Day. John Hewitt. **CP-HewiJ**

Gleneden's Dream. Emily Brontë. **CP-BronE**

Glengormley. Derek Mahon. **SP-MahoD**

Glens, The. John Hewitt. **CP-HewiJ**

Glens of Atrim, The. John Hewitt. **CP-HewiJ**

Glenthorne Poems. Roy Fisher.
  "At sunset over the water." **SP-FishR**
  "Freedoms / out of contrivance." **SP-FishR**
  "From the wrecked byre." **SP-FishR**
  "Gone down / from the upper air." **SP-FishR**
  "Hills lie thick, The." **SP-FishR**
  "I have slept shallow a long while." **SP-FishR**
  "Real things move." **SP-FishR**
  "Steep turn down, A." **SP-FishR**
  "Straight into the sea fog." **SP-FishR**
  "Walking at dusk often." **SP-FishR**

Gli Scafari. Charles Tomlinson. **CP-TomlC**

Glide gentle streams, and beare. The Teare Sent to Her from Stanes. Robert Herrick. **CP-HerrR**

Glide gently, thus for ever glide. Remembrance of Collins, Composed upon the Thames near Richmond. William Wordsworth. **CP-WorW1**

Gliding. Jim Carroll. **SP-CarrJ**

Gliding o'er All. Walt Whitman. **CP-WhitW**

Glimmer. Carl Sandburg. **CP-SandC**

Glimmer of the limes, sun-heavy, sleeping, The. From a College Window. David Herbert Lawrence. **CP-LawrD**

Glimmer'd along the square-cut steep. Gerard Manley Hopkins. **CP-HopkG**

Glimpse, The. Walter de la Mare. **CP-DeLaW**

Glimpse, The. Thomas Hardy. **CP-HardT**

Glimpse, The. George Herbert. **CP-HerbG**

Glimpse, A. Walt Whitman. **CP-WhitW**

Glimpse of the Waterer. Robert Bly. **SP-BlyR**

Glimpse through an interstice caught, A. A Glimpse. Walt Whitman. **CP-WhitW**

Glimpses. David Herbert Lawrence. **CP-LawrD**

Glistening field has survived its battles, The. Near York. Charles Tomlinson. **CP-TomlC**

Glittering leaves of the rhododendrons, The. Green Symphony. John Gould Fletcher. **SP-FletJ**

Glittering Sod, The. John Hewitt. *Fr.* Freehold. **CP-HewiJ**

Globe in North Carolina, The. Derek Mahon. **SP-MahoD**

Gloire de Dijon. David Herbert Lawrence. **CP-LawrD**

Gloom in my mind: I leaned. On a May Night. Charles Tomlinson. **CP-TomlC**

Gloom of death is on the raven's wing, The. The Raven. Nicarchus of Alexandria. **AWP; FaBoEE; OBAL** *Fr.* Variations of Greek Themes. **CP-RobiE**

Gloomy December. Robert Burns. **CP-BurnR**

Gloomy grammarians in golden gowns. On the Manner of Addressing Clouds. Wallace Stevens. **CP-StevW**

Gloomy hulls, in armour [*or* armor] grim, The. The *Temeraire*. Herman Melville. **SP-MelvH**

Gloomy is this weary scrimmage. Foul, or Twenty-Five. Malcolm Lowry. **CP-LowrM**

Gloomy Lady. Charles Bukowski. **SP-BukC1**

Gloomy night embraced the place. The Shepherds' Hymn. Richard Crashaw. **NOBE** *Fr.* In the Holy Nativity of Our Lord God.

Gloomy night is gath'ring fast, The. Song. Robert Burns. **CP-BurnR**

Gloria in Excelsis, The, *see also* "Glory be to God on high, and on earth peace, good-will towards men." Saint Ambrose, *tr. fr. Latin by* Thomas Merton. **CP-MertT**

Gloria Mundi. Walter de la Mare. **CP-DeLaW**

Glorie. Robert Herrick. **CP-HerrR**

Glories, The. Rudyard Kipling. **CP-KiplR**

Glorious, nourishing, flourishing moon, swollen with. The Moon, the Whole Moon, and Nothing but the Moon. Al Young. **CP-YounA**

Glorious people vibrated again, A. Ode to Liberty. Percy Bysshe Shelley. **CP-ShelP to David. SP-SmarC**

Glorious vision hovers o'er his soul, A. Tasso and Leonora. Christina Georgina Rossetti. **CP-RosC3**

Glory. Robert Herrick. **CP-HerrR**

Glory. David Herbert Lawrence. **CP-LawrD**

Glory. James McAuley. *Fr.* Requiem. **SP-McAuJ**

Glory and loveliness have passed away. To Leigh Hunt, Esq. John Keats. **CP-KeatJ**

Glory be to God for dappled things. Pied Beauty. Gerard Manley Hopkins. **CP-HopkG**

Glory be to the Graces! A Psalme or Hymne to the Graces. Robert Herrick. **CP-HerrR**

Glory! Hallelujah! / The dawn's a-comin'! Prayer Meeting. Langston Hughes. **SP-HughL**

Glory is a flame off exploit, so we say. In Honour of St. Alphonsus Rodriguez. Gerard Manley Hopkins. **CP-HopkG**

Glory is fallen out of, The. Edward Estlin Cummings. **CP-CummE**

Glory is that bright tragic thing. Emily Dickinson. **CP-DickE**

Glory no ther thing is (Tullie sayes). Glory. Robert Herrick. **CP-HerrR**

Glory of Darkness, *ink version*. David Herbert Lawrence. **CP-LawrD**

Glory of evening was spread through the west, The. The Convict. William Wordsworth. **CP-WorW1**

Glory of God, The, *sl. diff. vers.* Bible, *O.T. See* Psalm 19: "Heavens declare the glory of God, The."

Glory of the Garden, The. Rudyard Kipling. **CP-KiplR**

"Then seek your job with thankfulness and work till further orders." **EBCP**

Glory of the Sea, The. Malcolm Lowry. **CP-LowrM**

Glory Set, The. Edwin Rolfe. **CP-RolfE**

Glory to God Alone. Jeanne Marie Bouvier de la Motte-Guyon, *tr. fr. French by* William Cowper. **CP-CowpW**

Glory to God! and to the Power who came. Ejaculation. William Wordsworth. *Fr.* Ecclesiastical Sonnets. **CP-WorW2**

Glory to God in the highest. *see also* "Glory be to God on high, and on earth peace, good-will towards men." Saint Ambrose, *tr. fr. Latin by* Thomas Merton. **CP-MertT**

Glory Trumpeter, The. Derek Walcott. **CP-WalcD**

Gloss, A. Charles Olson. **CP-OlsoC**

Gloss, on the Difficulties of Translation. John Hewitt. **CP-HewiJ**

Gloss on the Sin of Ixion. Thomas Merton. **CP-MertT**

Glossina Morsitans, or, the Tsetse. Ogden Nash. **CP-NashO**

Gloucestershire. Donald Davie. **CP-DavDo**

Glove, The. Robert Browning. **CP-BroR1**

Glove, The. Raissa Maritain, *tr. fr. French by* Thomas Merton. **CP-MertT**

Glow of cells in the warm Sea, A. Caesarion. James Merrill. *Fr.* Topics. **SP-MerrJ**

Glow of my campfire is dark red and flameless, The. Toward An Organic Philosophy. Kenneth Rexroth. **SP-RexrK**

Glow-worm, The. Vincent Bourne, *tr. fr. Latin by* William Cowper. **CP-CowpW**

Glow-Worm, The. Charlotte Smith. **CP-SmitC**

Glowing is her Bonnet. Emily Dickinson. **CP-DickE**

Glum Clayfeld was defeated three to one. Clayfeld's Campaign. Robert Pack. **SP-PackR**

Glutton, The. Sylvia Plath. **CP-PlatS**

Gluttony. Stephen Dobyns. **SP-DobyS**

Glycine's Song. Samuel Taylor Coleridge. *Fr.* Zapolya. (Song: "Sunny shaft did I behold, A.") **CP-ColeS**

Glyndŵr Subdued. Steve Griffiths. **SP-GrifS**

Gnädiges Fräulein. Stevie Smith. **CP-SmitS**

Gnarled wind blurs the light, my hurt and another's. Hayden Carruth. *Fr.* The Asylum. **CP-CarHL**

Gnat on My Paper. Richard Eberhart. **CP-EberR**

Gnat-Psalm. Ted Hughes. **SP-HughT**

Gnats. Richard Eberhart. **CP-EberR**

Gnawing the highway's edges, its black mouth. The Swamp. Derek Walcott. **CP-WalcD**

Gnome. Samuel Beckett. **CP-BeckS**

Gnomes. Howard Nemerov. **CP-NemeH**

Love.

Minim.

Sacrificed Author, A.

Gnomic Verses. William Blake. **CP-BlakW**

"Abstinence sows sand all over." **EBEV; FF; FaBoEE; GBL; MeMBP; OxBM; TrGrPo**

Angel That Presided o'er My Birth, The. **InPK; NAs; OxBSP; RB; TrGrPo**

Great Things [Are Done]. **ArNa; OxBSP**

"He has observed the golden rule." **TrGrPo**

"Sword sang [*or* sung] on the barren heath, The." **ChTr; FaBoEE; TrGrPo**

(Sword and the Sickle, The.) **ChTr**

"They said this mystery shall never cease." **TrGrPo**

Gnomons. Richard Wilbur. **CP-WilbR**

Γνωθι Σεαυτον. Ralph Waldo Emerson. **CP-EmerR**

Gnothi seauton—and is this the prime. Self-Knowledge. Samuel Taylor Coleridge. **CP-ColeS**

Gnothi Seauton (Post Lexicon Anglicanum Auctum et Emendatum). Samuel Johnson. **CP-JohnS**

Gnu, The. Theodore Roethke. **CP-RoetT**

Go / Make a Bridge. Charles Olson. **CP-OlsoC**

Go and ask Robin to bring the girls over. Vision by Sweetwater. John Crowe Ransom. **SP-RansJ**

Go, and catch a falling star. Song. John Donne. **CP-DonnJ**

Go Ask the Dead. Thomas McGrath. **SP-McGrT**

Go away. Leave the high winds of May. Crossing the Ohio When Poppies Bloom in Ashtabula. Carl Sandburg. **CP-SandC**

Go back in your mind to that Middlesex height. Meditation on a Constable Picture. Sir John Betjeman. **CP-BetjJ**

Go Back to Antique Ages, If Thine Eyes. William Wordsworth. **CP-WorW2**

Go back to Egypt and the Greeks. A Mad Gleam. Allen Ginsberg. **CP-GinsA**

Go Back to Square One. Jenny Joseph. **SP-JoseJ**

Go boldly forth, and feast on being's banquet, *after the Arabic*. Ralph Waldo Emerson. **CP-EmerR**

Go, burning sighs, unto the frozen heart. Sir Thomas Wyatt. **CP-WyatT**

Go, cruel tyrant of the human breast! Supposed To Be Written by Werter. Charlotte Smith. **CP-SmitC**

Go deeper than love, for the soul has greater depths. Know Deeply, Know Thyself More Deeply. David Herbert Lawrence. **CP-LawrD**

Go, dumb-born book. Envoi (1919). Ezra Pound. **HAP; MoAB; MoAmPo; MoP; OxBA; UnPo; VGW** *Fr.* Hugh Selwyn Mauberley. (Life and Contacts). **SP-PounE**

Go! fair Example of untainted youth. Epitaph on the Monument of the Honourable Robert Digby, and of his Sister Mary, erected by their Father the Lord Digby, in the Church of Sherborne in Dorsetshire, 1727. Alexander Pope. **CP-PopeA**

Go, faithful Portrait! and where long hath knelt. To the Author's Portrait. William Wordsworth. **CP-WorW2**

Go fetch to me a pint o'wine. Robert Burns. **CP-BurnR** (My Bonnie [or Bony] Mary.) **CP-BurnR**

Go, fool, and hatch of the air. The Green Man. Charles Olson. **CP-OlsoC**

Go foolish thoughts, and join the throng. Arthur Hugh Clough. **SP-ClouA**

Go, for they call you, Shepherd, from the hill. The Scholar-Gipsy. Matthew Arnold. **SP-ArnoM**

Go forward, sun, do not torment us. Drill in the Heat. David Herbert Lawrence. *Fr.* Bits. **CP-LawrD**

Go from me, summer friends, and tarry not. From Sunset to Star Rise. Christina Georgina Rossetti. **CP-RosC1**

Go from me. Yet I feel that I shall stand. Sonnet. Elizabeth Barrett Browning. **BLPL; BWW; CBLP; HBV; OBEV; OBVV; OXAEP-2; TrGrPo; TreFS** *Fr.* Sonnets from the Portuguese. **CP-BroEB**

Go Get the Goodly Squab. Sylvia Plath. **CP-PlatS**

Go hang yourself, you old M.D.! The Common Cold. Ogden Nash. **CP-NashO**

Go hence, and with this parting kisse. The Parting Verse, Or Charge to His Supposed Wife When He Travelled. Robert Herrick. **CP-HerrR**

Go I must; when I am gone. To His Tomb-Maker. Robert Herrick. **CP-HerrR**

Go if thou wilt ambrosial Flower. Ralph Waldo Emerson. **CP-EmerR**

Go in Green. Gertrude Stein. **CP-SteiG**

Go in Manhattan. I Heard Brew Moore Say, One Day. Ted Berrigan. **SP-BerrT**

Go In Peace. Christina Georgina Rossetti. **CP-RosC2**

Go in peace my Beloved; tho' never again. Young Men Aye Were Fickle Found Since Summer Trees Were Leafy. Christina Georgina Rossetti. **CP-RosC3**

Go inside a stone. Stone. Charles Simic. **SP-SimiC**

Go, intercept some fountain in the vein. Upon the Death of the Lord Hastings. Andrew Marvell. **CP-MarvA**

Go into the garden. Ralph Waldo Emerson. **CP-EmerR**

Go it, Granny—Go it, Hog! Robert Penn Warren. *Fr.* Ballad of a Sweet Dream of Peace. **SP-WarrR**

Go Lightly. Marsden Hartley. **CP-HartM**

Go, litel book, go litel myn tragedye. Go, Little Book ("Go, litel book, go litel myn tragedy"). Geoffrey Chaucer. **EPCY; FiP; OAEL-1; OxBM; ViBoPo** *Fr.* Troilus and Criseyde [or Criseide]. **CP-ChauG**

Go, little book, and find our Friend. Sent to George Lyttleton, Esq., Soon After the Death of His Wife. James Thomson. **CP-ThomJ**

Go, little book, and wish to all. Envoy. Robert Louis Stevenson. **CP-StevR**

Go, Little Book ("Go, litel book, go litel myn tragedy"). Geoffrey Chaucer. **OAEL-1; OxBM; ViBoPo** *Fr.* Troilus and Criseyde [or Criseide]. **CP-ChauG** (Chaucer's Wishes for his 'Troilus'.) **EPCY** (Envoy, The.) **FiP**

Go little book, go little fable. Author ad Librum. Ben Jonson. **CP-JonsB**

Go, little book—the ancient phrase. Robert Louis Stevenson. **CP-StevR**

Go look for beauty where you least. More Than a Fool's Song. Countee Cullen. **CP-CullC**

Go Mary I would say to thee. Travel Poem. Ernest Hemingway. **CP-HemiE**

Go, my flock, go get you hence. Ninth Song. Sir Philip Sidney. **NoSic** *Fr.* Astrophil and Stella. **SP-SidnP**

Go, my songs, seek your praise from the young and from the intolerant. Ité. Ezra Pound. **SP-PounE**

Go not, happy day. Tennyson. **EBVV** *Fr.* Maud [A Monodrama]. **CP-TennA**

Go not too near a House of Rose. Emily Dickinson. **CP-DickE**

Go now, ingenuous Youth!—The trying hour. To a Young Man Entering the World. Charlotte Smith. **CP-SmitC**

Go on brave Hopton, to effectuate that. To the Lord Hopton, on His Fight in Cornwall. Robert Herrick. **CP-HerrR**

Go on, high ship, since now, upon the shore. Farewell to Florida. Wallace Stevens. **CP-StevW**

Go on, stir up your tiresome wavelets. James McAuley. *Fr.* Aor Against the Ingrate Who Abused Our Hospitality. **SP-McAuJ**

Go on, sweet bird, and soothe my care. Revision for Clarinda. Robert Burns. **CP-BurnR**

Go out into Nature and plant trees. Ralph Waldo Emerson. **CP-EmerR**

Go[e], perjured [or perjur'd] man, and if thou e'er [or ere] return. The Curse. A Song. Robert Herrick. **CP-HerrR**

Go pretty [or prettie] child and bear[e] this flower. To His Saviour, a Child; a Present, by a Child. Robert Herrick. **CP-HerrR**

Go, roads, to the four quarters of our quiet distance. The Evening of the Visitation. Thomas Merton. **CP-MertT**

Go Round. Gary Snyder. **CP-SnydG**

Go, rural Naiad! wind thy stream along. To the Naiad of the Arun. Charlotte Smith. **CP-SmitC**

Go slow, my soul, to feed thyself. Emily Dickinson. **CP-DickE**

Go[e], smiling soul[e]s, your new-built cages break[e]. To the Infant Martyrs. Richard Crashaw. **CP-CrasR**

Go, Soul [or Goe soule], the body's[orbodies] guest. The Lie. Sir Walter Ralegh. **CP-RaleW**

Go, speed the stars of thought. Ralph Waldo Emerson. **CP-EmerR** (Motto to "Intellect.") **CP-EmerR**

Go, stalk the red dear o'er the heather. Rudyard Kipling. **CP-KiplR** *Fr.* Pig. Fr. Plain Tales from the Hills.

Go talk with those who are rumored to be unlike you. For the Student Strikers. Richard Wilbur. **CP-WilbR**

Go tell Amynta, gentle swain. Song. John Dryden. **SP-DrydJ** *Fr.* Sylvae.

"Go tell it." What a Message. Emily Dickinson. **CP-DickE**

Go tell the earth to shake. *ad. fr.* Isaiah 52. Thomas Merton. **CP-MertT**

Go—thou art all unfit to share. On a Mischievous Bull. William Cowper. **CP-CowpW**

Go, thou gentle whispering wind. A Prayer to the Wind. Thomas Carew. **CP-CareT**

Go Thou to Rome. Percy Bysshe Shelley. **ChTr** *Fr.* Adonais; An Elegy on the Death of John Keats. **CP-ShelP** (Grave of Keats, The.) **FaBoPP**

Go thou to thy learned task. Botanist. Ralph Waldo Emerson. *Fr.* Quatrains. **CP-EmerR**

Go thy great way! Emily Dickinson. **CP-DickE**

Go to Glenarriffe if you'd know this Antrim. Glenarriffe and Parkmore. John Hewitt. **CP-HewiJ**

Go to sleep—though of course you will not. A Goodnight. William Carlos Williams. **CP-WilW1**

Go to the depths of willing. American Hakluyt. Richard Eberhart. **CP-EberR**

Go to the patch some afternoon. How to Make Rhubarb Wine. Ted Kooser. **SP-KoosT**

Go to the Shine That's on a Tree. Richard Eberhart. **CP-EberR**

Go to the western gate, Luke Havergal. Luke Havergal. Edwin Arlington Robinson. **CP-RobiE**

Go to Tibet. / Ride a camel. Friendly Advice to a Lot of Young Men. Charles Bukowski. **SP-BukC2**

Go traveling with us! Emily Dickinson. **CP-DickE**

Go tuneful bird, forbear to soar. *in imitation of* Cowley. Alexander Pope. **CP-PopeA**

Go, wash thyself in Jordan—go, wash thee and be clean! Naaman's Song. Rudyard Kipling. **CP-KiplR**

Go 'way from my window. It Ain't Me, Babe. "Bob Dylan." **CP-DylaB**

Go where you will. No Fixed Place. Alice Walker. **CP-WalkA**

Go wooe young Charles no more to looke. To His Muse. Robert Herrick. **CP-HerrR**

Goaded by outraged Soul. All Ghouls' Night. Edwin Rolfe. **CP-RolfE**

Goal in sight! Look up and sing, / Set faces full against the light, The. Christina Georgina Rossetti. **CP-RosC2**

Goal of Intellectual Man, The. Richard Eberhart. **CP-EberR**

Goat. Kenneth Rexroth. **SP-RexrK** *Fr.* A Bestiary. **SP-RexrK**

Goat, The. William Carlos Williams. **CP-WilW2**

Goats and Monkeys. Derek Walcott. **CP-WalcD**

Goats go past the house like dry leaves in the dawn. She-Goat. David Herbert Lawrence. **CP-LawrD**

Goatsucker. Sylvia Plath. **CP-PlatS**

Gob Music. Theodore Roethke. **CP-RoetT**

Goblets all are broken, The. Have Patience. Christina Georgina Rossetti. **CP-RosC3**

Goblin Market. Christina Georgina Rossetti. **CP-RosC1**
    "For there is no friend like a sister." **OBF**
    " 'Good folk,' said Lizzie." **FaBoVe**
    "Laughed every goblin." **BrRo**
    Laura and Lizzie Asleep. **PeHV**
    "Morning and evening." **BoTP; CBCK; EBEvV**
    (Worrying Fruit.) **CBCK**

Goblins, The. Sir John Suckling. **CP-SuckJ**
    Epilogue: "And how, and how, in faith—a pretty plot."
    "Health to the nut-brown lass, A."

Prologue: "Wit in a prologue poets justly may."

"Some drink! what, boy, some drink!"

"Welcome, welcome, mortal wight."

God, A. Stephen Berg. **SP-BergS**

God. Edward Estlin Cummings. **CP-CummE**

God, The. Hilda Doolittle. **CP-DoolH**

God ("God (as the learned Damascen write)"). Robert Herrick. **CP-HerrR**

God ("God is more here, then in another place"). Robert Herrick. **CP-HerrR**

God ("God, in the *holy Tongue*, they call"). Robert Herrick. **CP-HerrR**

God ("In God there's nothing, but 'tis known to be"). Robert Herrick. **CP-HerrR**

God, A. Ted Hughes. **SP-HughT**

God. David Herbert Lawrence. **CP-LawrD**

God / sitting at midday outside the cafe at Aix. Being, I. Frederick Morgan. **SP-MorgF**

God! / The I-killer! In the Breach. William Everson. **SP-EverW**

God, A Poem. James Fenton. **SP-FentJ**

God always was. Being, II. Frederick Morgan. **SP-MorgF**

God and all angels sing the world to sleep. The Men That Are Falling. Wallace Stevens. **CP-StevW**

God, and Lord. Robert Herrick. **CP-HerrR**

God and Man. Richard Eberhart. **CP-EberR**

God and Man. Stevie Smith. **CP-SmitS**

God and the Devil. Stevie Smith. **CP-SmitS**

God and the devil still are wrangling. For a Mouthy Woman. Countee Cullen. **CP-CullC**

God and the Holy Ghost. David Herbert Lawrence. **CP-LawrD**

God, and the King. Robert Herrick. **CP-HerrR**

God answers with my doom! I am annulled. The Reply. Allen Ginsberg. **CP-GinsA**

God appears, and God is Light. William Blake. **TRV** *Fr.* Auguries of Innocence. **CP-BlakW**

God, as He is most Holy knowne. God is One. Robert Herrick. **CP-HerrR**

God, as He's potent, so He's likewise known. Gods Bounty. Robert Herrick. **CP-HerrR**

God, awful and powerful beyond the sky's acre. At the End of the War. Richard Eberhart. **CP-EberR**

God banish from your house. Benediction. Stanley Jasspon Kunitz. **CP-KuniS**

God be merciful unto us, and bless us. Psalm 67. Bible, *O.T.* **FaPON** *Fr.* Psalms. **CP-Psal**

'God be praised that made. A Garland for Ivor Gurney. Donald Davie. **CP-DavDo**

God be with thee, gladsome Ocean! On Revisiting the Sea-Shore, after Long Absence. Samuel Taylor Coleridge. **CP-ColeS**

God be with thee, my beloved,—God be with thee! Valediction, A. Elizabeth Barrett Browning. **CP-BroEB**

God bless New Hampshire! from her granite peaks. New Hampshire. John Greenleaf Whittier. **CP-WhitJ**

God bless the little Island! Song. George Meredith. **CP-MerG2**

God bless ye, brothers! in the fight. To the Reformers of England. John Greenleaf Whittier. **CP-WhitJ**

God bought man here with his hearts blood expense. Gods Price, and Mans Price. Robert Herrick. **CP-HerrR**

God called the nearest angels who dwell with Him above. The Two Angels. John Greenleaf Whittier. **CP-WhitJ**

God can do all things, save but what are known. His Power. Robert Herrick. **CP-HerrR**

God can't be wrathfull; but we may conclude. Gods Anger. Robert Herrick. **CP-HerrR**

God co'd [*or* could] have made all rich, or all men poor[e]. Riches and Poverty. Robert Herrick. **CP-HerrR**

God created alcohol. Io Baccho! William Carlos Williams. **CP-WilW2**

God created his image. Fill and Illumined. Joseph Ceravolo. **SP-CeraJ**

God damn it. Dancing on the Grave of a Son of a Bitch. Diane Wakoski. **SP-WakoD**

God did forbid the Israelites, to bring. The Ass[e]. Robert Herrick. **CP-HerrR**

God don't make no promises that He don't keep. When You Gonna Wake Up? "Bob Dylan." **CP-DylaB**

God doth embrace the good with love; & gaines. Pittie, and Punishment. Robert Herrick. **CP-HerrR**

God doth not promise here to man, that He. Gods Time Must End Our Trouble. Robert Herrick. **CP-HerrR**

God-Forgotten. Thomas Hardy. **CP-HardT**

God from our eyes all teares hereafter wipes. Teares. Robert Herrick. **CP-HerrR**

God gave a Loaf to every Bird. Emily Dickinson. **CP-DickE**

God gave all men all earth to love. Sussex. Rudyard Kipling. **CP-KiplR**

God gave to me a child in part. Robert Louis Stevenson. **CP-StevR**

God gave us fingers—Ma says, "Use your fork." Ma and God. Shel Silverstein. **SP-SilS2**

God Germed in Raw Granite. William Everson. **SP-EverW**

God gets up in the morning. God Is No Gentleman. Carl Sandburg. **CP-SandC**

God give those drunkards drink who wake at dawn. A Prayer. Malcolm Lowry. **CP-LowrM**

God give you pardon from gratitude. Song. Robert Creeley. **CP-CreeR**

God gives his mercies to be spent. Vanity of the World. William Cowper. *Fr.* Olney Hymns. **CP-CowpW**

God gives not onely corne, for need. To God. Robert Herrick. **CP-HerrR**

God gives to none so absolute an Ease. Ease. Robert Herrick. **CP-HerrR**

God gloats upon Her stunning flesh. Upon. Edward Estlin Cummings. **CP-CummE**

God grant a blessing on this tower and cottage. Prayer on Going into My House. William Butler Yeats. **CP-YeatW**

God guard me from those thoughts men think. A Prayer for Old Age. William Butler Yeats. **CP-YeatW**

God had but one Son free from sin; but none. Correction. Robert Herrick. **CP-HerrR**

God had called us, and we came. The Blue-Flag in the Bog. Edna St. Vincent Millay. **CP-MillE**

God has a brown voice. For Eleanor Boylan Talking with God. Anne Sexton. **CP-SextA**

God has a Right Hand, but is quite bereft. The Right Hand. Robert Herrick. **CP-HerrR**

God Has a Twofold Part. Robert Herrick. **CP-HerrR**

God has foure keyes, which He reserves alone. Gods Keyes. Robert Herrick. **CP-HerrR**

God has his plans, and what if we. To the Memory of Mary Young. Paul Laurence Dunbar. **CP-DunbP**

God has his whips here to a twofold end. Whips. Robert Herrick. **CP-HerrR**

God hates the Duall Number; being known. The Number of Two. Robert Herrick. **CP-HerrR**

God Hath Sent Me to Sea for Pearls. Christopher Smart. **CBCK** *Fr.* Let Elizur Rejoice with the Partridge. **PoEL-3** *Fr.* Fragment B. *Fr.* Jubilate Agno. **SP-SmarC**

God hath this world for many made; 'tis true. This, and the Next World. Robert Herrick. **CP-HerrR**

God hath two wings, which He doth ever move. Mercy and Love. Robert Herrick. **CP-HerrR**

God He refuseth no man; but makes way. Free Welcome. Robert Herrick. **CP-HerrR**

God He rejects all prayers that are sleight. Prayers Must Have Poise. Robert Herrick. **CP-HerrR**

God Heares Us. Robert Herrick. **CP-HerrR**

God heares us when we pray, but yet defers. Gods Gifts Not Soon[e] Granted. Robert Herrick. **CP-HerrR**

God help that country where informers thrive! The Black Day. Archibald MacLeish. **CP-MacLA**

God help those and others who. Malcolm Lowry. *Fr.* The Moon in Scandinavia. **CP-LowrM**

God hides from man the reck'ning Day, that He. The Judgment-Day. Robert Herrick. **CP-HerrR**

God Hides His People. Jeanne Marie Bouvier de la Motte-Guyon, *tr. fr. French by* William Cowper. **CP-CowpW**

God i had forgotten how. New York—Albany. Lawrence Ferlinghetti. **SP-FerlL**

God, I know nothing, my sense is all nonsense. A Grace. Donald Hall. **CP-HallD**

God, if this were enough. If This Were Faith. Robert Louis Stevenson. **CP-StevR**

God in Heaven, forgive my death, it lies. Death in the Rose Garden. Stevie Smith. **CP-SmitS**

God in His own Day will be then severe. Sin Severely Punisht. Robert Herrick. **CP-HerrR**

God in his wisdom made the fly. The Fly. Ogden Nash. **CP-NashO**

God in the great assembly stands, *par. by* Milton. Bible, *O.T. See* Psalm 82: "God standeth in the congregation of the mighty."

God, in the *holy Tongue*, they call. God. Robert Herrick. **CP-HerrR**

God is a distant—stately Lover. Emily Dickinson. **CP-DickE**

God is above the sphere of our esteem. What God Is. Robert Herrick. **CP-HerrR**

God is all fore-part; for, we never see. Upon God. Robert Herrick. **CP-HerrR**

God is all-present to what e'er we do. Gods Presence. Robert Herrick. **CP-HerrR**

God is all-sufferance here; here He doth show. To God. Robert Herrick. **CP-HerrR**

God is away for the summer. Ernest Hemingway. **CP-HemiE**

God Is Born. David Herbert Lawrence. **CP-LawrD**

God is day and night, winter and summer, conflict and peace. Thomas Merton. *Fr.* The Legacy of Herakleitos. **CP-MertT**

God is Good. It Is a Beautiful Night. Wallace Stevens. **CP-StevW**

God, is His Name of Nature; but that word. God, and Lord. Robert Herrick. **CP-HerrR**

God is indeed a jealous God. Emily Dickinson. **CP-DickE**

God is *Jehovah* cal'd; which name of His. Another. Robert Herrick. **CP-HerrR**

God is kept in this box of pine. The Meetinghouse. Lewis Turco. **SP-TurcL**

God is more here, then in another place. God. Robert Herrick. **CP-HerrR**

God Is No Gentleman. Carl Sandburg. **CP-SandC**

God is not offered to the senses. December Journal. Charles Wright. **SP-WrigC**

God is not on[e]ly merciful, to call. Calling, and Correcting. Robert Herrick. **CP-HerrR**

God is not only [*or* onely] said to be. Upon God. Robert Herrick. **CP-HerrR**

God is older than the sun and moon. Maximus. David Herbert Lawrence. **CP-LawrD**

God is One. Robert Herrick. **CP-HerrR**

God Is Our Hope and Strength. Christina Georgina Rossetti. **CP-RosC2**

God is our refuge and strength, a very present help in trouble. *see also* Coleridge's "God is our strength and our refuge: therefore will we not tremble." Bible, *O.T.* **AWP; TRV; TrGrPo; TreFT** *Fr.* Psalms. **CP-Psal**

God is simpler than you are. For Children When They Grow Up. Charles Kenneth Williams. **CP-WillC**

God is so potent, as His Power can. Gods Power. Robert Herrick. **CP-HerrR**

God is the great urge that has not yet found a body. The Body of God. David Herbert Lawrence. **CP-LawrD**

God is the one. For Molly, Concerning God. Erica Jong. **SP-JongE**

God is then said for to descend, when He. Gods Descent. Robert Herrick. **CP-HerrR**

God, Jack of all trades. Praying to Big Jack. Anne Sexton. **CP-SextA**

God knows / We have our troubles too. High to Low. Langston Hughes. **SP-HughL**

God knows how our neighbor managed to breed. Sow. Sylvia Plath. **CP-PlatS**

God knows, my Martial, if we two could be. Ad Martialem. Robert Louis Stevenson. **CP-StevR**

God loads, and unloads, (thus His work begins). Loading and Unloading. Robert Herrick. **CP-HerrR**

God loafs around heaven. The Earth. Anne Sexton. **CP-SextA**

God love you now, if no one else will ever. Thomas McGrath. **SP-McGrT** (Ode for the American Dead in Asia.) **SP-McGrT**

God Maddens Him Whom 'T Is His Will to Lose. Byron. **CP-Byron**

God made a little Gentian. Emily Dickinson. **CP-DickE**

God made no act without a cause. Emily Dickinson. **CP-DickE**

God Made the Country. William Cowper. **FiP; PoEL-3** *Fr.* For I have lov'd the rural walk through lanes. **EnRP; NOEC** *Fr.* The Sofa. *Fr.* The Task. **CP-CowpW**

God make me the poet of simplicity. My Prayer. Edward Estlin Cummings. **CP-CummE**

God makes not good men wantons, but doth bring. Good Men Afflicted Most. Robert Herrick. **CP-HerrR**

God-Monger, The. Anne Sexton. **CP-SextA**

God moves in a mysterious way. Light Shining out of Darkness. William Cowper. **EBEV; EBEvV; ECEV; ELP; EaLo; EnRP; FHYEP; FPL; FaBoCh; FiP; HBV 1-2; HelP; ImPo; LiTB; NOBE; NOCV; NOEC; NoP; OBEC; PWR; PoEL-3; SCGP; SeCePo; TFi; TOF; TRV; TrGrPo; WGRP** *Fr.* Olney Hymns. **CP-CowpW**

God, namèd Love, whose fount Thou art. A Supplication for Love. Elizabeth Barrett Browning. **CP-BroEB**

God Neither Known Nor Loved by the World. Jeanne Marie Bouvier de la Motte-Guyon, *tr. fr. French by* William Cowper. **CP-CowpW**

God n'ere afflicts us more then our desert. Affliction. Robert Herrick. **CP-HerrR**

God Not To Be Comprehended. Robert Herrick. **CP-HerrR**

God of being demoralized, The. Distraction. Howard Nemerov. **CP-NemeH**

God of Details, The. Donald Davie. **CP-DavDo**

God of Fair Beginnings, The. The Song of Diego Valdez. Rudyard Kipling. **CP-KiplR**

God of Love—*ah, benedicite!*, The. The Cuckoo and the Nightingale. William Wordsworth. **CP-WorW1**

God of love my Shepherd is, The. The Twenty-third Psalm. George Herbert. **CP-HerbG**

God of my childhood. "Alle Herrlichkeit Des Menschen." James McAuley. *Fr.* Requiem. **SP-McAuJ**

God of my father discovered at midnight. Oya. Audre Lorde. **SP-LordA**

God of my life, to thee I call. Looking Upwards in a Storm. William Cowper. *Fr.* Olney Hymns. **CP-CowpW**

God of our fathers, known of old. Recessional. Rudyard Kipling. **CP-KiplR**

God of the golden bow. Ode to Apollo. John Keats. **CP-KeatJ**

God of the Meridian. John Keats. **CP-KeatJ**

God of the people. Dodona. Hilda Doolittle. **CP-DoolH**

God of the right, arise. To Miss Mary Britton. Paul Laurence Dunbar. **CP-DunbP**

God of the river leans, The. Observance. Wendell Berry. **CP-BerrW**

God of the World, all dread things suddenly make. Petition Concerning the Death-Wish. John Clellon Holmes. **SP-HolmJ**

God of This World, The. Howard Nemerov. **CP-NemeH**

God of war assured King Arsounas, Do not be fooled by. Eternity. Tom Clark. **SP-ClarT**

God on our Youth bestowes but little ease. Youth, and Age. Robert Herrick. **CP-HerrR**

God, only God is eternal. Moth and Rust. David Herbert Lawrence. **CP-LawrD**

God, only God is eternally. Neither Moth Nor Rust. David Herbert Lawrence. *Fr.* Bits. **CP-LawrD**

God only knew how Saadi dined. Ralph Waldo Emerson. **CP-EmerR**

God pardons those, who do through frailty sin. Pardon. Robert Herrick. **CP-HerrR**

God permits industrious Angels. Emily Dickinson. **CP-DickE**

God pity me whom(god distinctly has). Edward Estlin Cummings. **CP-CummE**

God prosper, speed, and save. A New National Anthem. Percy Bysshe Shelley. **CP-ShelP**

God Reigns. Paul Laurence Dunbar. **CP-DunbP**

God Rest Ye Merry, Gentlemen. Derek Walcott. **CP-WalcD**

God rest you, merry Innocents. A Carol for Children. Ogden Nash. **CP-NashO**

God rest you, peaceful gentlemen, let nothing you dismay. Russia to the Pacifists. Rudyard Kipling. **CP-KiplR**

God Said "They Did Not Hear. . . ." Thomas Merton. **CP-MertT**

God save me from the Porkers. County. Sir John Betjeman. **CP-BetjJ**

God Saves the King. Donald Davie. **CP-DavDo**

God scourgeth some severely, some He spares. No Escaping the Scourging. Robert Herrick. **CP-HerrR**

God seems much more friendly. Emily Dickinson. **SP-DickE**

God shook thy roundness in His finger's cup, *sl. diff. vers.* David Herbert Lawrence. *See* Michael Angelo.

God snaps your picture—don't look away—. An Archival Print. William Stafford. **SP-StafW**

God Sparing in Scourging. Robert Herrick. **CP-HerrR**

God Speaks. Stevie Smith. **CP-SmitS**

God. Spell dawns / Drained of all light. A Frost Lay White on California. William Everson. **SP-EverW**

God standeth in the congregation of the mighty. Psalm 82. Bible, *O.T. Fr.* Psalms. **CP-Psal**

God still rewards us more then our desert. God Sparing in Scourging. Robert Herrick. **CP-HerrR**

God strengthen me to bear myself. Who Shall Deliver Me? Christina Georgina Rossetti. **CP-RosC1**

God strikes His Church, But 'tis to this intent. Persecutions Purifie. Robert Herrick. **CP-HerrR**

God suffers not his Saints, and Servants deere. Paine and Pleasure. Robert Herrick. **CP-HerrR**

God the Creator, with a pulseless hand. The Measure. Elizabeth Barrett Browning. **CP-BroEB**

God the Drinker. Stevie Smith. **CP-SmitS**

God the Eater. Stevie Smith. **CP-SmitS**

God, the Eternal! Infinite! All-wise! Cain: A Mystery. Byron. **CP-Byron**

God The Lord save Massachusetts. Ralph Waldo Emerson. **CP-EmerR**

God then confounds mans face, when He not hears. Confusion of Face. Robert Herrick. **CP-HerrR**

God, though to Thee our psalm we raise. Nondum. Gerard Manley Hopkins. **CP-HopkG**

God to Be First Served. Robert Herrick. **CP-HerrR**

God! to my little meale and oyle. To God. Robert Herrick. **CP-HerrR**

God took a crayon in his hand. Cul-de-Sac. Allen Tate. **CP-TateA**

God tried to teach Crow how to talk. Crow's First Lesson. Ted Hughes. **SP-HughT**

God turne us every drem to goode! The House of Fame. Geoffrey Chaucer. **CP-ChauG**

God went out of me. The Sickness unto Death. Anne Sexton. **CP-SextA**

God when for sin He makes His Children smart. God Has a Twofold Part. Robert Herrick. **CP-HerrR**

God when He takes my goods and chattels hence. Upon God. Robert Herrick. **CP-HerrR**

God when He's angry here with any one. Gods Anger without Affection. Robert Herrick. **CP-HerrR**

God, whether by unconscious instinct, or waking, or in a dream, I do. What Odd Expedients. Robinson Jeffers. **CP-JefR3**

God who made the garden green. Eve's First Prophecy. Archibald MacLeish. *Fr.* Songs for Eve. **CP-MacLA**

God, who me gives a will for to repent. To God. Robert Herrick. **CP-HerrR**

God, who with the thunders and great voices. Heaven and Earth. Elizabeth Barrett Browning. **CP-BroEB**

God, who's in Heav'n, will hear from thence. God Heares Us. Robert Herrick. **CP-HerrR**

God will have all, or none; serve Him, or fall. Neutrality Loathsome. Robert Herrick. **CP-HerrR**

God with honour hang your head. At the Wedding March. Gerard Manley Hopkins. **CP-HopkG**

God Works in a Mysterious Way. Gwendolyn Brooks. **SP-BrooG**

God would not let the spheric Lights accost. Hugh Stuart Boyd [His Blindness]. Elizabeth Barrett Browning. **CP-BroEB**

God, you could grow to love it, God-fearing, God. Ecclesiastes. Derek Mahon. **SP-MahoD**

Goddamn / tuition &, The. Accepted. David Markson. **CP-MarkD**

Goddamned animals might know more than we do about some things, The. Ribbons. Charles Kenneth Williams. **CP-WillC**

Goddess, The. Thom Gunn. **CP-GunnT**

Goddess, I come to you. To the Goddess. Erica Jong. **SP-JongE**

Goddess of Nature's Diatribe to her People, The. Jenny Joseph. **SP-JoseJ**

Goddess stands in front of her cave, The. In Anselm Hollo's Poems. Ted Berrigan. **SP-BerrT**

Goddess Who Created This Passing World, The. Alice Notley. **SP-NotlA**

Goddesse, I begin an Art. A Vow to Minerva. Robert Herrick. **CP-HerrR**

Goddesse, I do love a girle. A Short Hymne to Venus. Robert Herrick. **CP-HerrR**

Goddesse of Youth, and Lady of the Spring. To the Queene. Robert Herrick. **CP-HerrR**

Godfather. Louis MacNeice. **CP-MacNL**

Godfather Death. Anne Sexton. **CP-SextA**

Godhead as Lynx, The. May Sarton. **SP-SartM**

Godhead, I adore thee fast in hiding; thou. S. Thomae Aquinatis Rhythmus ad SS. Sacramentum. Gerard Manley Hopkins. **CP-HopkG**

Godhulivela. Hayden Carruth. **CP-CarHS**

Godlike the man who. Carmen 51. Catullus. *Fr.* Carmina. **CP-Catul**

Godly Girzie. Robert Burns. **CP-BurnR**

Gods. Hayden Carruth. **CP-CarHS**

Gods, The. David Herbert Lawrence. **CP-LawrD**

Gods. David Herbert Lawrence. **CP-LawrD**

Gods. Anne Sexton. **CP-SextA**

Gods. Walt Whitman. **CP-WhitW**

God's Acre. Alfred Edward Housman. **CP-HousA**

God's Acre. Christina Georgina Rossetti. **CP-RosC2**

Gods Anger. Robert Herrick. **CP-HerrR**

Gods Anger without Affection. Robert Herrick. **CP-HerrR**

God's angry with the world again. Electrical Storm. Robert Earl Hayden. **CP-HaydR**

Gods are less, The. The Hidden Singer. Wendell Berry. **CP-BerrW**

Gods are too airy: feathery as the snow, The. The Skier and the Mountain. Richard Eberhart. **CP-EberR**

God's Backside. Anne Sexton. **CP-SextA**

Gods Blessing. Robert Herrick. **CP-HerrR**

Gods boundlesse mercy is (to sinfull man). Gods Mercy. Robert Herrick. **CP-HerrR**

Gods Bounty ("God, as He's potent, so He's likewise known"). Robert Herrick. **CP-HerrR**

Gods Bounty ("Gods Bounty, that ebbs lesse and lesse"). Robert Herrick. **CP-HerrR**

God's child in Christ adopted—Christ my all. My Baptismal Birthday [*or* Birth-Day]. Samuel Taylor Coleridge. **CP-ColeS**

Gods Commands. Robert Herrick. **CP-HerrR**

God's counsel còlumnar-severe. Margaret Clitheroe. Gerard Manley Hopkins. **CP-HopkG**

Gods Descent. Robert Herrick. **CP-HerrR**

Gods drift down to drink your brew, The. Aegir. Frederick Morgan. **SP-MorgF**

Gods Dwelling. Robert Herrick. **CP-HerrR**

God's Education. Thomas Hardy. **CP-HardT**

God's evident, and may be said to be. Gods Presence. Robert Herrick. **CP-HerrR**

God's Funeral. Thomas Hardy. **CP-HardT**

Gods Gifts Not Soon[e] Granted. Robert Herrick. **CP-HerrR**

God's Glory. Bible, *O.T. See* Psalm 19: "Heavens declare the glory of God, The."

God's Glory and my country's shame. The Black Christ. Countee Cullen. **CP-CullC**

Gods Grace. Robert Herrick. **CP-HerrR**

God's Grandeur. Gerard Manley Hopkins. **CP-HopkG**

Gods Hands. Robert Herrick. **CP-HerrR**

Gods Keyes. Robert Herrick. **CP-HerrR**

God's Little Mountain. Geoffrey Hill. **CP-HillG**

God's love and peace be with thee, where. Benedicite. John Greenleaf Whittier. **CP-WhitJ**

God's Measurements. Laurence Lieberman. **SP-LiebL**

Gods Mercy. Robert Herrick. **CP-HerrR**

Gods Mirth, Mans Mourning. Robert Herrick. **CP-HerrR**

Gods of Hellas, gods of Hellas. The Dead Pan. Elizabeth Barrett Browning. **CP-BroEB**

Gods of old are silent on their shore, The. Aristomenes. Byron. **CP-Byron**

Gods of the Copybook Headings, The. Rudyard Kipling. **CP-KiplR**

Gods of the Nile, should this stout fellow here. A Grave Near Cairo. Rudyard Kipling. *Fr.* Epitaphs of the War [1914–1918]. **CP-KiplR**

Gods of the sea. Hermonax. Hilda Doolittle. **CP-DoolH**

Gods of Washington, D.C., The. Richard Eberhart. **CP-EberR**

Gods Pardon. Robert Herrick. **CP-HerrR**

Gods Power. Robert Herrick. **CP-HerrR**

God's Precepts Perfect, *vv. 7–9 of sl. diff. vers.* Bible, *O.T. See* Psalm 19: "Heavens declare the glory of God, The."

Gods Prescience makes none sinfull; but th'offence. Prescience. Robert Herrick. **CP-HerrR**

Gods Presence ("God is all-present to what e'er we do"). Robert Herrick. **CP-HerrR**

Gods Presence ("God's evident, and may be said to be"). Robert Herrick. **CP-HerrR**

Gods Presence ("God's present ev'ry where; but most of all"). Robert Herrick. **CP-HerrR**

God's present ev'ry where; but most of all. Gods Presence. Robert Herrick. **CP-HerrR**

Gods Price, and Mans Price. Robert Herrick. **CP-HerrR**

Gods Providence. Robert Herrick. **CP-HerrR**

Gods Prt. Robert Herrick. **CP-HerrR**

Gods require the thighes, The. The Smell of the Sacrifice. Robert Herrick. **CP-HerrR**

Gods Rod doth watch while men do sleep; & then. The Rod. Robert Herrick. **CP-HerrR**

God's said our hearts to harden them. Hardning of Hearts. Robert Herrick. **CP-HerrR**

God's said to dwell there, wheresoever He. Gods Dwelling. Robert Herrick. **CP-HerrR**

God's said to leave this place, and for to come. Another of God. Robert Herrick. **CP-HerrR**

Gods that are wiser than Learning, The. A Rector's Memory. Rudyard Kipling. **CP-KiplR**

Gods! The Gods!, The. David Herbert Lawrence. **CP-LawrD**

Gods Time Must End Our Trouble. Robert Herrick. **CP-HerrR**

Gods to Kings the Judgement give to sway, The. Obedience in Subjects. Robert Herrick. **CP-HerrR**

God's undivided, One in Persons Three. To God. Robert Herrick. **CP-HerrR**

Gods walk in the breath of the woods, The. Ralph Waldo Emerson. **CP-EmerR**

God's World. Edna St. Vincent Millay. **CP-MillE**

Godspeed. John Greenleaf Whittier. **CP-WhitJ**

God,Thine the hand that doth extend. Edward Estlin Cummings. **CP-CummE**

Goe, happy man, like th' Evening Starre. Thomas Campion. *Fr.* Description of a Maske: Presented in the Banqueting Roome at *Whitehall*, on Saint Stephens Night Last, at the Marriage of the Right Honourable the Earle

of *Somerset:* and the Right Noble the Lady FRANCES *Howard.* **CP-CampT**

Goe, happy Rose, and, enterwove. To the Rose; a Song. Robert Herrick. **CP-HerrR**

Goe hence away, and in thy parting know. Upon Parting. Robert Herrick. **CP-HerrR**

Goe now; and with some dar[e]ing drugg. Temperance or the Cheap Physitian upon the Translation of Lessius. Richard Crashaw. **CP-CrasR**

Goe, numbers, boldly passe, stay not for ayde. Thomas Campion. *Fr.* Observations in the Art of English Poesie. **CP-CampT**

Goe thou forth my booke, though late. To His Booke. Robert Herrick. **CP-HerrR**

Goes by at 1:00 a.m. two nights of the week. I can. The Streetsweeper. Ron Koertge. **SP-KoerR**

Goes by below. A Sun Cab. James Schuyler. **CP-SchuJ**

Goes the world now, it will with thee goe hard. Once Poore, Still Penurious. Robert Herrick. **CP-HerrR**

Goethe and Pose. David Herbert Lawrence. **CP-LawrD**

Goethe in Weimar sleeps, and Greece. Memorial Verses. Matthew Arnold. **SP-ArnoM**

Goethe, they say, was a great poet, Pindar, perhaps, was a great poet. Robinson Jeffers. **CP-JefR3**

Goffle brook of a May day. Spring is Here Again, Sir. William Carlos Williams. **CP-WilW2**

Gog. Ted Hughes. **SP-HughT**

Goin' Back. Paul Laurence Dunbar. **CP-DunbP**

Goin' down the road, Lawd. Bound No'th Blues. Langston Hughes. **SP-HughL**

Goin' Home. Paul Laurence Dunbar. **CP-DunbP**

Goin' to Acapulco. "Bob Dylan." **CP-DylaB**

Going. Robert Creeley. **CP-CreeR**

Going. Richard Eberhart. **CP-EberR**

Going, The. Thomas Hardy. **CP-HardT**

Going. Philip Larkin. **CP-LarkP**

Going. James Schuyler. **CP-SchuJ**

Going and Staying. Thomas Hardy. **CP-HardT**

Going Away. Howard Nemerov. **CP-NemeH**

Going Back. David Herbert Lawrence. **CP-LawrD**

Going Back Home. Al Young. **CP-YounA**

Going back to D.F. Mexico City Lover. Al Young. **CP-YounA**

Going Back to the River. Marilyn Hacker. **SP-HackM**

Going backward / All of me and some. In the Pocket. James Dickey. **CP-DickJ**

Going Backward Going Forward. Richard Eberhart. **CP-EberR**

Going for Water. Robert Frost. **CP-FrosR**

Going from a world we know, The. Emily Dickinson. **CP-DickE**

Going from Battle to Battle. Charles Olson. **CP-OlsoC**

Going, Going. Philip Larkin. **CP-LarkP**

Going, Going, Gone. "Bob Dylan." **CP-DylaB**

Going Gone. Anne Sexton. **CP-SextA**

Going his rounds one day in Ispahan. The Melon-Seller. Robert Browning. **CP-BroR2**

Going Home. Derek Mahon. **SP-MahoD**

Going home by lamplight across Boston Common. A Revivalist in Boston. Adrienne Rich. **CP-RicAE**

Going In. Marge Piercy. **SP-PierM**

Going In. Anne Waldman. **SP-WaldA**

Going into the city, coming. Wendell Berry. *Fr.* From the Crest. **CP-BerrW**

Going Man, A. Marsden Hartley. **CP-HartM**

Going of the Battery, The. Thomas Hardy. **CP-HardT**

Going of the glade-boat, The. The Load of Sugar-Cane. Wallace Stevens. **CP-StevW**

Going Out to Look at the Year's First Blossoms. Martin Edmunds. **SP-EdmuM**

Going Somewhere. Walt Whitman. **CP-WhitW**

Going through me, the roman sun. Via appia. James Dickey. **CP-DickJ**

Going to bed / And when we have done. She Had Concealed Him in a Deep Dark Cave. Kenneth Patchen. **CP-PatcK**

Going to Bed. Robert Creeley. **CP-CreeR**

Going to Chicago. Allen Ginsberg. **CP-GinsA**

Going to Church. John Hewitt. **CP-HewiJ**

Going to Heaven! Emily Dickinson. **CP-DickE**

Going—to—Her!, vers. 2; see also *Going to Him! Happy letter!.* Emily Dickinson. **CP-DickE**

Going to Him! Happy letter!, vers. 1; see also *Going—to—Her!.* Emily Dickinson. **CP-DickE**

Going to Horse Flats. Robinson Jeffers. **CP-JefR2**

Going to Italy. Donald Davie. **CP-DavDo**

Going to Maine. Richard Eberhart. **CP-EberR**

Going to sleep, I cross my hands on my chest. Death. Bill Knott. **SP-KnotB**

Going to Sylvie's. Jenny Joseph. *Fr.* Life and Turgid Times of A. Citizen. **SP-JoseJ**

Going to the Bakery. Elizabeth Bishop. **CP-BishE**

Going to Walden. Mary Oliver. **SP-OlivM**

Going up or coming down. Colorado. Mona Van Duyn. **SP-VanDM**

Going up to Dublin. John Hewitt. **CP-HewiJ**

Gold. Walter de la Mare. **CP-DeLaW**

Gold. Donald Hall. **CP-HallD**

Gold—ah, that most beautiful of words. Poem On Gold. Malcolm Lowry. **CP-LowrM**

Gold and Frankincense. Robert Herrick. **CP-HerrR**

Gold and iron are good. Politics. Ralph Waldo Emerson. **CP-EmerR**

Gold and Malachite. Robert Ranke Graves. **CP-GravR**

Gold and Silver Fishes in a Vase. William Wordsworth. **CP-WorW2**

Gold beard combd down like chinese fire gold hair braided at skull-nape. G.S. Reading Poesy at Princeton. Allen Ginsberg. **CP-GinsA**

Gold, before Goodnesse. Robert Herrick. **CP-HerrR**

Gold buttons in the garden today. Flowers Tell Months. Carl Sandburg. **CP-SandC**

Gold Cloud. Robert Ranke Graves. **CP-GravR**

Gold dung and urinous straw from the horse garages. Derek Walcott. **CP-WalcD** *Fr.* Midsummer.

Gold fringe on the purpling hem, A. Sunset on the Bearcamp. John Greenleaf Whittier. **CP-WhitJ**

Gold Glade. Robert Penn Warren. **SP-WarrR**

Gold Hair. Robert Browning. **CP-BroR1**

Gold Hesperidee, The. Robert Frost. **CP-FrosR**

Gold I have none, but I present my need. To God, His Good Will. Robert Herrick. **CP-HerrR**

Gold is for the mistress—silver for the maid. Cold Iron. Rudyard Kipling. **CP-KiplR**

Gold is not autumn's privilege. The Wearing of the Green. Donald Davie. **CP-DavDo**

Gold I've none, for use or show. Lyric[k] for Legacies. Robert Herrick. **CP-HerrR**

Gold Key, The. Anne Sexton. **CP-SextA**

Gold Leaf. Muriel Rukeyser. **CP-RukeM**

Gold Man on the Beckler, The. Richard Hugo. **CP-HugoR**

Gold Mouths Cry. Sylvia Plath. **CP-PlatS**

Gold Mud. Carl Sandburg. **CP-SandC**

Gold of a ripe oat straw, gold of a southwest moon. Falltime. Carl Sandburg. **CP-SandC**

Gold of her promise, The. America. Maya Angelou. **SP-AngeM**

Gold of that Land is Good, The. Christina Georgina Rossetti. **CP-RosC2**

Gold onions rooted in the sky. Moscow. John Updike. *Fr.* Postcards from Soviet Cities. **CP-UpdiJ**

Gold or iv'ry's not intended. 2.18. Horace. **SP-SmarC**, *tr. by* Christopher Smart; *Fr.* Odes.

Gold Pocket Watch, A. Charles Bukowski. **SP-BukC1**

Gold serves for Tribute to the King. Gold and Frankincense. Robert Herrick. **CP-HerrR**

Gold Stone. Richard Hugo. **CP-HugoR**

Gold, with an innermost speck. Street Lamps. David Herbert Lawrence. **CP-LawrD**

Golden Age, The. Wystan Hugh Auden. **CP-AudeW** *Fr.* Man of La Mancha.

Golden air has come back. Maud Gonne Rode Out on a White Horse to Coolgreany. James Liddy. **CP-LiddJ**

Golden Anchor. Robert Ranke Graves. **CP-GravR**

Golden Apollo, that thro' heaven wide. An Imitation of Spen[s]er. William Blake. **CP-BlakW**

Golden blood of the sun, The. Blood of the Sun. Kenneth Patchen. **CP-PatcK**

Golden blossom on the banks. The Jade Elegy. John Gould Fletcher. **SP-FletJ**

Golden Boy, The. John Hewitt. **CP-HewiJ**

Golden Day, A. Paul Laurence Dunbar. **CP-DunbP**

Golden Demon, The. John Gould Fletcher. **SP-FletJ**

Golden eagle swooped out of the sky, The. Salmon Drowns Eagle. Malcolm Lowry. **CP-LowrM**

Golden flie one shew'd to me, A. Upon a Flie. Robert Herrick. **CP-HerrR**

Golden Flowers. Kathleen Jessie Raine. *Fr.* Bheinn Naomh. **SP-RainK**

Golden gates of Sleep unbar, The. *see also* Epithalamium *and* Another Version of the Same. Percy Bysshe Shelley. **CP-ShelP**

Golden girl / in a golden gown. College Formal: Renaissance Casino. Langston Hughes. **SP-HughL**

Golden Glories. Christina Georgina Rossetti. **CP-RosC2**

Golden guineas filter through the mist, The. Canto XI. Louis MacNeice. *Fr.* Autumn Sequel. **CP-MacNL**

Golden-haired Ally whose name is one with mine. To Alfred Tennyson, My Grandson. Tennyson. **CP-TennA**

Golden haired and golden hearted. The Irish Unionist's Farewell to Greta Hellstrom in 1922. Sir John Betjeman. **CP-BetjA**

Golden-hairèd Bacchus did espouse, The. Bacchus and Ariadne. Hesiod. **CP-BroEB,** *tr. by* Elizabeth Barrett Browning; *Fr.* Theogony.

Golden haired, lily white, / Will you pluck me lilies? As Cold Water to a Thirsty Soul, So Is Good News from a Far Country. Christina Georgina Rossetti. **CP-RosC2**

Golden haired, lily white / Will you pluck me lilies. Rivals. Christina Georgina Rossetti. **CP-RosC3**

Golden head by golden head. Laura and Lizzie Asleep. Christina Georgina Rossetti. **PeHV** *Fr.* Goblin Market. **CP-RosC1**

Golden Holly. Christina Georgina Rossetti. **CP-RosC3**

Golden Leaf, The. Kathleen Jessie Raine. **SP-RainK**

Golden Loom. "Bob Dylan." **CP-DylaB**

Golden maples had not yet begun their work, The. Leaves Apples. Grace Paley. **CP-PaleG**

Golden Net, The. William Blake. **CP-BlakW**

Golden one is gone from the banquets, The. Epigram. Hilda Doolittle. **CP-DoolH**

Golden photon white on granulated red. Sunshine on Sandstone. John Updike. **CP-UpdiJ**

Golden rose the house, in the portal I saw. Apparuit. Ezra Pound. **SP-PounE**

Golden sheep are feeding, and, The. To a Very Slow Air. Philip Larkin. **CP-LarkP**

Golden Silences. Christina Georgina Rossetti. **CP-RosC2**

Golden Slumbers. The Beatles. **CP-Beatl**

Golden Wedding of Longwood, The. John Greenleaf Whittier. **CP-WhitJ**

Golden Whales of California. Nicholas Vachel Lindsay. **CP-LindV**

    Chanting of the Whales, The.

    St. Francis of San Francisco.

    Short Walk along the Coast, A.

    Voice of the Earthquake, The.

Golden-winged Angel stood, A. Fragment: Satan Broken Loose. Percy Bysshe Shelley. **CP-ShelP**

Golden-winged, silver-winged. Paradise: in a Symbol. Christina Georgina Rossetti. **CP-RosC3**

Golden Woman in a Silver Mirror, A. Wallace Stevens. **CP-StevW**

Golden Year, The. Tennyson. **CP-TennA**

Goldeneye and Goldfish. Malcolm Lowry. **CP-LowrM**

Goldeneye whistles across the lake, A. Daybreak. Barton Sutter. **SP-SuttB**

Goldenrod. Mary Oliver. **SP-OlivM**

Goldfinch and hawk. Geoffrey Hill. *Fr.* The Pentecost Castle. **CP-HillG**

Goldfinch scatters thistle-flowers, The. An Episode. Wystan Hugh Auden. **CP-AudWJ**

Goldfinches. John Keats. *See* Sometimes goldfinches one by one will drop.

Goldfinches. Mary Oliver. **SP-OlivM**

Goldfish. Charles Bukowski. **SP-BukC2**

Goldfish. Howard Nemerov. **CP-NemeH**

Goldfish Floats to the Top of His Life, The. Ted Kooser. **SP-KoosT**

Golding from green, gorgeous the mountain. Vision under the October Mountain: A Love Poem. Robert Penn Warren. **SP-WarrR**

Goldoni. Robert Browning. **CP-BroR2**

Goldwing Moth. Carl Sandburg. **CP-SandC**

Goldwing moth is between the scissors and the ink bottle on the desk, A. Goldwing Moth. Carl Sandburg. **CP-SandC**

Golfers. John Updike. **CP-UpdiJ**

Goliath. Walter de la Mare. **CP-DeLaW**

Goliathus goliathus, the one banana. The Zoo. Gilbert Sorrentino. **SP-SorrG**

Golly, How Truth Will Out. Ogden Nash. **CP-NashO**

(Goma / Homa) / I have raised pure flames. To Fire. Gary Snyder. **CP-SnydG**

Gon is my joy while heere I mourne. Song. Mary Sidney, Countess of Montgomery Wroth. *Fr.* Part 1. *Fr.* Urania. **CP-WrotM**

—GON splashes-sink. Edward Estlin Cummings. **CP-CummE**

Gone. Carl Sandburg. **CP-SandC**

Gone. John Greenleaf Whittier. **CP-WhitJ**

Gone: and to an undisclosed region. Golden Anchor. Robert Ranke Graves. **CP-GravR**

Gone are the drab monosyllabic days. Tilth. Robert Ranke Graves. **CP-GravR**

Gone are the lovers under the bush. The Later Autumn. Thomas Hardy. **CP-HardT**

Gone Away. Phoebe Hesketh. **SP-HeskP**

Gone Away. Denise Levertov. **CP-LeveD**

Gone Away Blues. Thomas McGrath. **SP-McGrT**

Gone Before. Christina Georgina Rossetti. **CP-RosC3**

Gone before us, O our brother. Lines on the Death of S. Oliver Torrey. John Greenleaf Whittier. **CP-WhitJ**

Gone Boy. Langston Hughes. **SP-HughL**

Gone down / from the upper air. Roy Fisher. **SP-FishR** *Fr.* Glenthorne Poems.

Gone—faded out of the story, the sea-faring friend I remember? Pasa Thalassa Thalassa. Edwin Arlington Robinson. **CP-RobiE**

Gone for Ever. Christina Georgina Rossetti. **CP-RosC1**

Gone Gone / Another weaver of black dreams has gone. For Langston Hughes. Etheridge Knight. **SP-KnigE**

Gone, gone again is Summer the lovely. Song. Edna St. Vincent Millay. **CP-MillE**

Gone, gone,—sold and gone. Farewell, The. John Greenleaf Whittier. **CP-WhitJ**

Gone hath the Spring, with all its flowers. Autumn Thoughts. John Greenleaf Whittier. **CP-WhitJ**

Gone, I say and walk from church. The Truth the Dead Know. Anne Sexton. **CP-SextA**

Gone in good sooth you are: not even in dream. Edna St. Vincent Millay. **CP-MillE**

Gone is the wind. The Lost Secret. Wystan Hugh Auden. **CP-AudWJ**

Gone now the baby's nurse. Home after Three Months Away. Robert Lowell. **SP-LoweR**

Gone she is a long, long way. Upon a Maid. Robert Herrick. **CP-HerrR**

Gone silence down lowered sun. Lowellville Cemetery: Twilight. Kenneth Patchen. **CP-PatcK**

Gone the three ancient ladies. Frau Bauman, Frau Schmidt, and Frau Schwartze. Theodore Roethke. **CP-RoetT**

Gone to his rest / Bright little Bouby! Christina Georgina Rossetti. **CP-RosC3**

Gone to hunt; and my brothers. Birthday Greeting. Basil Bunting. **CP-BuntB**

Gone to thy Heavenly Father's rest! To the Memory of Thomas Shipley! John Greenleaf Whittier. **CP-WhitJ**

Gone-Tomorrow, The. Louis MacNeice. *Fr.* A Hand of Snapshots. **CP-MacNL**

Gone were but the Winter. Spring Quiet. Christina Georgina Rossetti. **ArNa; BoNaP; BoTP; CH; CP-RosC1; GTBS-6; GTBS-P; InPS; LoBV; MeMBP; PoE; PoEL-5; WPE** *Fr.* Spring Fancies. **CP-RosC3**

Gone with the wind. What remains of the charred. Late Night Movies II. John Yau. **SP-YauJo**

Gonfalon Raised Tonight, The. Charles Olson. **CP-OlsoC**

Gong of Time, The. Carl Sandburg. **CP-SandC**

Gonna Change My Way of Thinking. "Bob Dylan." **CP-DylaB**

Goo'-by, Jinks, I got to hump. The Delinquent. Paul Laurence Dunbar. **CP-DunbP**

Goo-dmore-ning(en / ter)nize-aday(most). Edward Estlin Cummings. **CP-CummE**

Goo Girl. Theodore Roethke. **CP-RoetT**

Good. Stephen Berg. **SP-BergS**

Good. William Matthews. **SP-MattW**

Good, and Bad. Robert Herrick. **CP-HerrR**

Good and Bad Children. Robert Louis Stevenson. **CP-StevR**

Good, and great God, can I not think[e] of thee. To Heaven. Ben Jonson. **CP-JonsB**

Good and great God! How should [*or* sho'd] I fear[e]. No Coming to God without Christ. Robert Herrick. **CP-HerrR**

Good are attracted by Mens perceptions, The. Motto to the Songs of Innocence & of Experience. William Blake. **CP-BlakW**

Good at maps and vistas, poor. The Arch. Charles Tomlinson. **CP-TomlC**

Good Boy, A. Robert Louis Stevenson. **CP-StevR**

Good brother Philip, I have borne you long. Sonnet 83. Sir Philip Sidney. **PBBP** *Fr.* Astrophil and Stella. **SP-SidnP**

Good-by and Keep Cold. Robert Frost. **CP-FrosR**

Good-by is a loose word, a yellow ribbon. Different Kinds of Good-by. Carl Sandburg. **CP-SandC**

Good-by now to the streets and the clash of wheels and locking hubs. A Teamster's Farewell. Carl Sandburg. **CP-SandC**

Good-By, Old Year, You Oaf or Why Don't They Pay the Bonus. Ogden Nash. **CP-NashO**

Good-by to you whom I shall see tomorrow. Stepping Backward. Adrienne Rich. **CP-RicAE; SP-RicA2**

Good-bye. Sir John Betjeman. **CP-BetjJ**

Good-bye. Walter de la Mare. **CP-DeLaW**

Good-bye. Ralph Waldo Emerson. **CP-EmerR**

"Good-bye," I said to my conscience. Conscience and Remorse. Paul Laurence Dunbar. **CP-DunbP**

Good-Bye, My Fancy! ("Good-bye, my Fancy! / Farewell dear mate, dear love!"). Walt Whitman. **CP-WhitW**

Good-Bye My Fancy ("Good-bye my fancy—(I had a word to say,)"). Walt Whitman. **CP-WhitW**

Good-bye, proud world! I'm going home. Good-bye. Ralph Waldo Emerson. **CP-EmerR**

"Good-bye," they always whisper, "oh God," clinging. Hayden Carruth. *Fr.* The Sleeping Beauty. **CP-CarHL**

Good-Bye to the Mezzogiorno. Wystan Hugh Auden. **CP-AudeW**

Good-bye Twilight. "Hugh MacDiarmid."
"Back to the great music, Scottish Gaels. Too long." **SP-MacDH**

Good-bye, Wendover; Good-bye, Mountain Home. Randall Jarrell. **CP-JarrR**

Good Carpenters. Erica Jong. **SP-JongE**

Good cause have I to sing and vapour. To Dean Swift. Jonathan Swift. **CP-SwifJ**

Good Charles the springs adorer. Ralph Waldo Emerson. **CP-EmerR**

Good Christians. Robert Herrick. **CP-HerrR**

Good Company. Walter de la Mare. **CP-DeLaW**

Good Company. William Matthews. **SP-MattW**

Good Comrade, The. Ludwig Uhland, *tr. fr. German by* George Meredith. **CP-MerG2**

Good Counsel to a Young Maid ("When you the sun-burnt pilgrim see"). Thomas Carew. **CP-CareT**

Good creatures, do you love your lives. Alfred Edward Housman. **CP-HousA**

Good Day for Seeing Your Limitations, A. Richard Hugo. **CP-HugoR**

[*Amin.*] Good day, *Mitrillo.* [*Mirt.*] And to you no lesse. A Pastorall Upon the Birth of Prince Charles. Robert Herrick. **CP-HerrR**

Good Day Sunshine. The Beatles. **CP-Beatl**

Good deal of superciliousness, A. Platitudinous Reflection. Ogden Nash. **CP-NashO**

Good Death, A. Robert Herrick. **CP-HerrR**

Good Dream. Louis MacNeice. **CP-MacNL**

Good enough: so I never returned. I no longer grieve. Star. Pablo Neruda, *tr. fr. Spanish by* Ben Belitt. **SP-NeruP**

Good evening. At the feet of the king, my Lord. Overseas Prayer. John Berryman. **CP-BerrJ**

Good evening, Charlie. Yes, I know. You rise. A Christmas Greeting. James Wright. **CP-WrigJ**

Good evening, daddy! / I know you've heard. Boogie: 1 A.M. Langston Hughes. **SP-HughL**

Good Evening Mr. Waldheim. "Lou Reed." **SP-ReedL**

Good Father!. . . It was eve in middle June. The Peasant's Confession. Thomas Hardy. **CP-HardT**

Good Father John O'Hart. The Ballad of Father O'Hart. William Butler Yeats. **CP-YeatW**

Good Fight, The. Leonard Cohen. **CP-CoheL**

"Good folk," said Lizzie. Christina Georgina Rossetti. **FaBoVe** *Fr.* Goblin Market. **CP-RosC1**

Good for You, Gavin. Philip Larkin. **CP-LarkP**

Good Fortune. Chuang Tzu, *tr. fr. Chinese by* Thomas Merton. **CP-MertT**

Good Friday. George Herbert. **CP-HerbG**

Good Friday. Christina Georgina Rossetti. **CP-RosC1**

Good Friday. Christina Georgina Rossetti. **CP-RosC2**

Good Friday. Charles Tomlinson. *Fr.* Three Wagnerian Lyrics. **CP-TomlC**

Good Friday Evening. Christina Georgina Rossetti. **CP-RosC2**

Good Friday Morning. Christina Georgina Rossetti. **CP-RosC2**

Good Friday, 1971. Driving Westward. Paul Muldoon. **SP-MuldP**

Good Friday: Rex Tragicus, or, Christ Going to His Cross[e]. Robert Herrick. **CP-HerrR**

Good Friday [*or* Goodfriday], 1613. Riding Westward. John Donne. **CP-DonnJ**

Good Friday was the day. The Martyr. Herman Melville. **SP-MelvH**

Good friend, / it is a long afternoon. Hunter's Moon—Eating the Bear. Mary Oliver. **SP-OlivM**

Good gray [*or* grey] guardians of art, The. Museum Piece. Richard Wilbur. **CP-WilbR**

Good Great Man, The. Samuel Taylor Coleridge. **CP-ColeS**

Good guys lost the city first, The. A Reading of History. Leonard Nathan. **SP-NathL**

Good Heart, that ownest all! Lover's Petition. Ralph Waldo Emerson. **CP-EmerR**

Good Hours. Robert Frost. **CP-FrosR**

Good house, and ground whereon, A. The Salt Garden. Howard Nemerov. **CP-NemeH**

Good hunting!—aye, good hunting. The Forest Greeting. Paul Laurence Dunbar. **CP-DunbP**

Good Husband, A. Robert Herrick. **CP-HerrR**

Good Husbandry. Geoffrey Hill. *Fr.* Locust Songs. **CP-HillG**

Good Husbands Make Unhappy Wives. David Herbert Lawrence. **CP-LawrD**

Good is what goes on the road of Nature. Hafiz, *tr. by* Ralph Waldo Emerson. **CP-EmerR** *Fr.* Odes.

Good Kosciusko, thy great name alone. To Kosciusko. John Keats. **CP-KeatJ**

Good Life, The. Charles Bukowski. **SP-BukC1**

Good Life, A. Stephen Dunn. **SP-DunnS**

Good Lord, thy bottom, lass. Question of Anatomy. David Markson. **CP-MarkD**

Good Lord, today / I scarce find breath to say. Christina Georgina Rossetti. **CP-RosC2**

Good Loser, The. Charles Bukowski. **SP-BukC1**

Good Luck. Malcolm Lowry. **CP-LowrM**

Good Luck Not Lasting. Robert Herrick. **CP-HerrR**

Good man, A. Likeness. Adrienne Rich. **CP-RicAE**

Good Man, The. Mona Van Duyn. **SP-VanDM**

Good Man Has No Shape, The. Wallace Stevens. **CP-StevW**

Good Man in a Bad Time, A. Archibald MacLeish. **CP-MacLA**

Good man ther[e] was of religioun [*or* religion], A. Geoffrey Chaucer. **ACP; NOCV** *Fr.* The General Prologue. **FHYEP; NAWM-1; OAEL-1; PoE** *Fr.* The Canterbury Tales. **CP-ChauG**

Good Manners at Meat. Robert Herrick. **CP-HerrR**

Good many times I've come down among you, A. Low Voice, Out Loud. James Dickey. **CP-DickJ**

Good Martha / you back into town like a tug. Martha as the Angel Gabriel. Marge Piercy. **SP-PierM**

Good meal can somewhat repair, A. After-Dinner Remarks. Philip Larkin. **CP-LarkP**

Good Men Afflicted Most. Robert Herrick. **CP-HerrR**

Good men, shew, if you can tell. Thomas Campion. **CP-CampT**

Good Mirrors are Not Cheap. Audre Lorde. **SP-LordA**

Good morning! / Good morning! Elegy. Al Young. **CP-YounA**

Good Morning. Langston Hughes. **SP-HughL** *Fr.* Lenox Avenue Mural.

Good Morning. James Schuyler. **CP-SchuJ**

Good morning! Address more inspections. Thomas Merton. *Fr.* Cables to the Ace. **CP-MertT**

Good Morning, America. Carl Sandburg. **CP-SandC**
"Now it's Uncle Sam sitting on top of the world." **OFD**

Good morning, daddy! Dream Boogie. Langston Hughes. **SP-HughL**

Good morning, daddy! Good Morning. Langston Hughes. **SP-HughL** *Fr.* Lenox Avenue Mural.

Good Morning Good Morning. The Beatles. **CP-Beatl**

Good Morning—Midnight. Emily Dickinson. **CP-DickE**

Good morning. The horses are ready. The trail. Topographical Map. Richard Hugo. **CP-HugoR**

Good Morning to Our Sweetest Harteebeeste! Malcolm Lowry. **CP-LowrM**

Good Morrow, The. John Donne. **CP-DonnJ**

Good morrow to the day so fair. The Mad Maid's Song. Robert Herrick. **CP-HerrR**

Good Mother: Out. Charles Kenneth Williams. **SP-WillC**

Good-nature is thy sterling name. Loveliness. Christopher Smart. **NOCV** *Fr.* Hymns for the Amusement of Children. **SP-SmarC**

Good-Nature to Animals. Christopher Smart. *Fr.* Hymns for the Amusement of Children. **SP-SmarC**

Good-Night. Paul Laurence Dunbar. **CP-DunbP**

Good-Night. Carl Sandburg. **CP-SandC**

Good-Night. Percy Bysshe Shelley. **CP-ShelP**

Good Night! Gilbert Sorrentino. **SP-SorrG**

Good Night, A. Barton Sutter. **SP-SuttB**

Good Night. William Carlos Williams. **CP-WilW1**

Good night, because we must. Emily Dickinson. **CP-DickE**

Good-night; ensured release. Parta Quies. Alfred Edward Housman. **CP-HousA**

Good night, good rest. Ah, neither be my share. *Various Authors.* **CP-ShaWS** *Fr.* The Passionate Pilgrim. **CP-ShaWS**

Good-night, my love, for I have dreamed of thee. Absence. Paul Laurence Dunbar. **CP-DunbP**

Good-Night, or Blessing, The. Robert Herrick. **CP-HerrR**

Good Night, Sweet Mind. Ogden Nash. *Fr.* All's Brillig in Tin Pan Alley. **CP-NashO**

Good night! the gossips cry; Good night! A Carol of Jack Frost. George Meredith. **CP-MerG2**

Good Night to the Old Gods. Robert Ranke Graves. **CP-GravR**

Good Night! Which put the Candle out? Emily Dickinson. **CP-DickE**

Good Night, Willie Lee, I'll See You in the Morning. Alice Walker. **CP-WalkA**

Good now bee still, and doe nott mee torment. Sonnet 45. Mary Sidney, Countess of Montgomery Wroth. *Fr.* Pamphilia to Amphilanthus. **CP-WrotM**

Good of the Chaplain to enter Lone Bay. Billy in the Darbies. Herman Melville. **SP-MelvH** *Fr.* Billy Budd, Foretopman.

Good old ale, mild or pale. Robert Louis Stevenson. **CP-StevR**

"Good old times"—all times when old are good, The. The Age of Bronze. Byron. **CP-Byron**

Good One, A. Charles Bukowski. **SP-BukC1**

Good Parent's Garden of Vision, A. Ogden Nash. **CP-NashO**

Good Parson, The, *mod. vers.* by H.C. Leonard. Geoffrey Chaucer. *See* A Good man ther[e] was of religioun [*or* religion].

Good Play, A. Robert Louis Stevenson. **CP-StevR**

Good Plays Are Scarce. Byron. **CP-Byron**

Good Precepts, or Counsell. Robert Herrick. **CP-HerrR**

Good Precepts we must firmly hold. Precepts. Robert Herrick. **CP-HerrR**

Good Princes must be pray'd for: for the bad. Duty to Tyrants. Robert Herrick. **CP-HerrR**

Good Resolution, The. Mona Van Duyn. **SP-VanDM**

Good Riddance, but Now What? Ogden Nash. **CP-NashO**

Good Servant, The. Richard Wilbur. **CP-WilbR**

Good Shepherd, The. Christina Georgina Rossetti. **CP-RosC2**

Good Ships. John Crowe Ransom. **SP-RansJ**

Good Silence, The. Robert Bly. **SP-BlyR**

Good snow the sky black, The. A Wolf. Paul Éluard, *tr. fr. French by* William Carlos Williams. **CP-WilW2**

Good soul, my mother holds my daughter. Three Views of a Mother. John Ciardi. **SP-CiarJ**

Good speed, for I this day. To the Lark. Robert Herrick. **CP-HerrR**

Good thing about the younger generations, The. The Young Are Not Mean in Material Things. David Herbert Lawrence. **CP-LawrD**

Good things, that come of course, far lesse doe please. Casualties. Robert Herrick. **CP-HerrR**

Good Time Girl. Charles Bukowski. **SP-BukC3**

Good times are always mutual. Emily Dickinson. **SP-DickE**

Good, to forgive. Robert Browning. **CP-BroR2**

Good to hide, and hear 'em hunt! Emily Dickinson. **CP-DickE**

Good, true enough stories, The. Temporarily. Stephen Dunn. **SP-DunnS**

Good View from Flagstaff, A. Richard Hugo. **CP-HugoR**

Good we must love, and must hate ill. Community. John Donne. **CP-DonnJ**

Good weather / is like / good women—. Cows in Art Class. Charles Bukowski. **SP-BukC2**

Good while after, on the upstairs east sleeping porch he used for a studio, A. After Joe Was at the Island. James Schuyler. **CP-SchuJ**

Good Will of a Flower, The. Emily Dickinson. **CP-DickE**

Good Woman Feeling Bad, A. Maya Angelou. **SP-AngeM**

Good Wyf [*or* Wif] was ther of bisyde [*or* biside] Bathe, A. Geoffrey Chaucer. **EBEV; InPS** *Fr.* The General Prologue. **FHYEP; NAWM-1; OAEL-1; PoE** *Fr.* The Canterbury Tales. **CP-ChauG**

(Seven Pilgrims: A Wyf of Bathe.) **TrGrPo**

(Seven Pilgrims: A Wyf of Bathe.) **TrGrPo**

Goodby Betty, don't remember me. Edward Estlin Cummings. **CP-CummE**

Goodbye. Charles Bukowski. **SP-BukC3**

Goodbye. Robert Creeley. **CP-CreeR**

Goodbye. Galway Kinnell. **SP-KinnG**

Goodbye. Bill Knott. **SP-KnotB**

Goodbye. Philip Levine. **SP-LeviP**

Goodbye. Alun Lewis. **CP-LewiA**

Goodbye, A. Mona Van Duyn. **SP-VanDM**

"Goodbye!" called the stockholders as the ship pulled out from. The Cruise. Muriel Rukeyser. **CP-RukeM**

Goodbye, Göteborg. John Updike. **CP-UpdiJ**

Goodbye Harry I must have you by me for a time. The Wedding Photograph. Stevie Smith. **CP-SmitS**

Goodbye, he waved, entering the apple. Fruits & Vegetables. Erica Jong. **SP-JongE**

Goodbye Hemingway goodbye Celine (you died on the same day). Goodbye. Charles Bukowski. **SP-BukC3**

Goodbye in fear, goodbye in sorrow. Christina Georgina Rossetti. **CP-RosC2**

Goodbye, Iowa. Richard Hugo. **CP-HugoR**

Goodbye, lady in Bangor, who sent me. The Correspondence School Instructor Says Goodbye to His Poetry Students. Galway Kinnell. **SP-KinnG**

Goodbye, mother / of my mother, old bone. Margaret Atwood. *Fr.* Five Poems for Grandmothers. **SP-AtwM2**

Goodbye, old venerable barn. Doggerel of a Diehard Who Sleeps in a Nest of Newspapers. Jean Garrigue. **SP-GarrJ**

Goodbye red moon. Moonset, Gloucester, December 1, 1957, 1:58 A.M. Charles Olson. **CP-OlsoC; SP-OlsoC**

Goodbye to London. Louis MacNeice. **CP-MacNL**

Goodbye to Serpents. James Dickey. **CP-DickJ**

Goodbye to the Poetry of Calcium. James Wright. **CP-WrigJ**

Goodbye, Winter, / The days are getting longer. Prognosis. Louis MacNeice. **CP-MacNL**

Goodheart I beat years of Sundays ago at golf. In Praise of an Understudy. Malcolm Lowry. **CP-LowrM**

Goodies are shaken / from the papa-tree. Stanley Jasspon Kunitz. *Fr.* Journal for My Daughter. **CP-KuniS**

Goodly friars feel it will not do, The. The Death of the Virgin. David Markson. **CP-MarkD**

Goodman sat beside his door, The. The Exiles. John Greenleaf Whittier. **CP-WhitJ**

Goodnesse of His God, The. Robert Herrick. **CP-HerrR**

Goodnight. John Ciardi. **SP-CiarJ**

Goodnight. David Herbert Lawrence. **CP-LawrD**

Goodnight. The Beatles. **CP-Beatl**

Goodnight. Stevie Smith. **CP-SmitS**

Goodnight, A. William Carlos Williams. **CP-WilW1**

Goods. Wendell Berry. **CP-BerrW**

Goody Blake and Harry Gill. William Wordsworth. **CP-WorW1**

"Oh! what's the matter? what's the matter?" **Par**

Goody for Our Side and Your Side Too. Ogden Nash. **CP-NashO**

Goodyere, I am [*or* I'm] glad and grateful to report. To Sir Henry Goodyere. Ben Jonson. **CP-JonsB**

Goofing Again. Gary Snyder. **CP-SnydG**

Googies Are Coming, The. Shel Silverstein. **SP-SilS2**

Goose. Ted Hughes. **SP-HughT**

Goose Fish, The. Howard Nemerov. **CP-NemeH**

Goose-Girl, The. Edna St. Vincent Millay. **CP-MillE**

Goose Pond. Stanley Jasspon Kunitz. **CP-KuniS**

Gooseberries. Stephen Berg. **SP-BergS**

Gooseflesh Abbey. Robert Ranke Graves. **CP-GravR**

Gooseprairie. Richard Hugo. **CP-HugoR**

Go(perpe)go / (tu)to(al). Edward Estlin Cummings. **CP-CummE**

Gordale. William Wordsworth. **CP-WorW2**

Gordon, Jim, / Life and Limb. George Meredith. **CP-MerG2**

Gordon of Khartoum. George Meredith. **CP-MerG1**

Gorge, The. Robert Ranke Graves. **CP-GravR**

Gorge, The. Frederick Morgan. **SP-MorgF**

"Noon is the hour of choice."

"River in the dream, The."

"What voice is it that speaks."

Gorge, The. Charles Tomlinson. **CP-TomlC**

Gorged on red, green, purple, tomatoes, peppers, aubergine. Louis MacNeice. *Fr.* The Island. **CP-MacNL**

Gorgon Mask. Robert Ranke Graves. **CP-GravR**

Goring, The. Sylvia Plath. **CP-PlatS**

Gorse is yellow on the heath, The. Charlotte Smith. **CP-SmitC**

(Swallow, The.) **CP-SmitC**

Goshawk, The. John Haines. **SP-HainJ**

Goshen Pass: Winter. Dabney Stuart. **SP-StuaD**

Gospel. Rita Dove. **SP-DoveR**

Gospel Noble Truths. Allen Ginsberg. **CP-GinsA**

Gospel of Beauty, A. Nicholas Vachel Lindsay. **CP-LindV**

Illinois Village, The.

On the Building of Springfield. **WHA**

Proud Farmer, The.

Gospel Singer. Dabney Stuart. **SP-StuaD**

Gossamer, The. Charlotte Smith. **CP-SmitC**

Gossamers, The. Charles Tomlinson. **CP-TomlC**

Gossips, The. William Carlos Williams. **CP-WilW2**

Gossips agreed all was wrong with poor Sally! The Falling of Sally. George Meredith. **CP-MerG2**

Got a date with a bottle of / gin. Malcolm Lowry. **CP-LowrM**

Got a good reason for taking the easy way out. Day Tripper. John Lennon *and* Paul McCartney. **CP-Beatl**

Got a two-handed woman, she loves me night and day. Blues. Edwin Rolfe. **CP-RolfE**

Got drunk once with another cowpuncher. He. Ron Koertge. **SP-KoerR**

Got it down so tight the hinges squeaked. Take It. Charles Bukowski. **SP-BukC3**

Got Me Home, the Light Snow Gives the Air, Falling. Charles Olson. **SP-OlsoC** *Fr.* The Maximus Poems.

Got to be there, so that she'll know. Tom Clark. *Fr.* Suite. **SP-ClarT**

Got to Get You into My Life. The Beatles. **CP-Beatl**

Got to the track early to study my figures and here's this. Charles Bukowski. *Fr.* Horsemeat. **SP-BukC3**

Got up with a cry. The Wild Duck. Ted Hughes. **SP-HughT**

Gothic Candor. William Carlos Williams. **CP-WilW2**

Gothic looks solemn, The. John Keats. **CP-KeatJ** (Lines Rhymed in a Letter Received (by J. H. R[eynolds]) from Oxford.) **CP-KeatJ**

Goths, Vandals, Huns, Isaurian mountaineers. The Cuirassiers of the Frontier. Robert Ranke Graves. **CP-GravR**

Gotta hold your nose. Metric Figure. William Carlos Williams. **CP-WilW2**

Gotta Serve Somebody. "Bob Dylan." **CP-DylaB**

Gottéron Landscape. Stephen Dobyns. **SP-DobyS**

Gourd, The. Paul Laurence Dunbar. **CP-DunbP**

Gourmet's roulette. Stalking the Wild Mushroom. Barton Sutter. **SP-SuttB**

Governess, The. Stevie Smith. **CP-SmitS**

Government. Carl Sandburg. **CP-SandC**

Government—I heard about the Government and I went out to find, The. Government. Carl Sandburg. **CP-SandC**

Government of your body, sweet, The. The United States. William Carlos Williams. **CP-WilW2**

Governor came to visit in the mountains, The. He Shot Arrows, but Not at Birds Perching. Gary Snyder. **CP-SnydG**

Governor it was proclaimed this time, A. The Generations of Men. Robert Frost. **CP-FrosR**

Governor your husband lived so long, The. John Berryman. **MoVE; NOBA; TwAmPo** *Fr.* Homage to Mistress Bradstreet. **CP-BerrJ**

Goya & the Sleep of Reason. Lawrence Ferlinghetti. **SP-FerlL**

Goya's "Two Old People Eating Soup." Mona Van Duyn. **SP-VanDM**

Gr, a / eyhaire / d(m). Edward Estlin Cummings. **CP-CummE**

Gr-r-r—there go, my heart's abhorrence! Soliloquy of the Spanish Cloister. Robert Browning. **CP-BroR1**

Grace. Wendell Berry. **CP-BerrW**

Grace. Ralph Waldo Emerson. **CP-EmerR**

Grace, A. Donald Hall. **CP-HallD**

Grace. George Herbert. **CP-HerbG**

Grace. Richard Wilbur. **CP-WilbR**

Grace after Dinner. Robert Burns. **FaBoEE** *Fr.* After Dinner. *Fr.* Graces——at the Globe Tavern. **CP-BurnR**

Grace after Meat. Robert Burns. **CP-BurnR**

Grace and Love. George Meredith. **CP-MerG1**

Grace and Providence. William Cowper. *Fr.* Olney Hymns. **CP-CowpW**

Grace, Beauty, and Caprice. Manners. Ralph Waldo Emerson. **CP-EmerR**

Grace before Dinner, Extempore, A. Robert Burns. **CP-BurnR**

Grace Darling. William Wordsworth. **CP-WorW2**

Grace-face: hot-pot. Readie Pome. William Carlos Williams. **CP-WilW1**

Grace in the Fore Street. Donald Davie. **CP-DavDo**

Grace is the focal point. Bar Giamaica, 1959-60. Charles Wright. **SP-WrigC**

Grace—Myself—might not obtain, The. Emily Dickinson. **CP-DickE**

Grace-Note, The. Denise Levertov. **CP-LeveD**

Grace Notes. Robert Ranke Graves. **CP-GravR**

Grace, thou source of each perfection. Epiphany. Christopher Smart. **NOCV** *Fr.* Hymns and Spiritual Songs for the Fasts and Festivals of the Church of England. **SP-SmarC**

Grace to be born and live as variously as possible. Ted Berrigan. **SP-BerrT** *Fr.* The Sonnets.

Grace to Be Said at the Supermarket. Howard Nemerov. **CP-NemeH**

Grace to Be Said before Committee Meetings. Howard Nemerov. **CP-NemeH**

Grace, triumphant in the throne. Not of Works. William Cowper. *Fr.* Olney Hymns. **CP-CowpW**

Graceful Bastion, The. William Carlos Williams. **CP-WilW2**

Graceful in name and in thyself, our river. To G. G. John Greenleaf Whittier. **CP-WhitJ**

Gracefullest leaper, the dappled fox-cub. Young Reynard. George Meredith. **CP-MerG1**

Graceland. Carl Sandburg. **CP-SandC**

Graces——at the Globe Tavern. Robert Burns. **CP-BurnR** After Dinner.
> Grace after Dinner. **FaBoEE**
> "L—d, we [thee] thank an' thee adore."
Before Dinner.

Graces for Children. Robert Herrick. *See* What God gives, and what we take.

Grace's House. Thomas Merton. **CP-MertT; SP-MertT**

Graces, yes—and the airs! To airs and graces, The. Yorkshire. Donald Davie. **CP-DavDo**

Gracie, thou art a man of worth. On Mr. James Gracie. Robert Burns. **CP-BurnR**

Gracious gods, The. To Empty the Mind. Charles Olson. **CP-OlsoC**

Gracious Goodness. Marge Piercy. **SP-PierM**

Gracious Lord, our children see. Prayer for Children. William Cowper. *Fr.* Olney Hymns. **CP-CowpW**

Gracious spirit o'er this earth presides, A. William Wordsworth. **OBRV** *Fr.* Books. *Fr.* The Prelude; Growth of a Poet's Mind [1805 vers.]. **CP-WorW3**

Gracious Spirit sings as it comes, A. Desolation. Wendell Berry. **CP-BerrW**

Grackle / flicks, A. Modality. Archie Randolph Ammons. **SP-AmmoA**

Grackle, The. Ogden Nash. **CP-NashO**

Grackles, The. Brendan Galvin. **SP-GalvB**

Grackles sing avant the spring, The. Snow and Stars. Wallace Stevens. **CP-StevW**

Gradations of Black. John Updike. **CP-UpdiJ**

Grade surmounted, we were riding high, The. The Figure in the Doorway. Robert Frost. **CP-FrosR**

Gradually in gardens. Journey of the Snowmen. Howard Nemerov. **CP-NemeH**

Gradually it is. At the Home for Unwed Mothers. James Dickey. **CP-DickJ**

Graduate, The. Robert Lowell. **SP-LoweR**

Graduation. Langston Hughes. **SP-HughL**

Gradus ad Parnassum. Muriel Rukeyser. **CP-RukeM**

Graecinus (well I wot) thou told'st me once. 2.10. Ovid, *tr. by* Christopher Marlowe. **CP-MarlC** *Fr.* Elegies.

Graffiti from the Gare Saint-Manqué. Marilyn Hacker. **SP-HackM**

Graffiti 12th Cubicle Men's Room Syracuse Airport. Allen Ginsberg. **CP-GinsA**

Graii, sive magis iuvat vetustum. *acc. by English translation.* Thomas Campion. **CP-CampT**

Grammar for Doctrine, A. Roy Fisher. **SP-FishR**

Grammar Lesson. Stanley Jasspon Kunitz. **CP-KuniS**

Grammar of cause, The. Kenneth Rexroth. **CP-RexKL** *Fr.* A Prolegomenon to a Theodicy.

Grammar-Rules. Sir Philip Sidney. *See* Sonnet 63: "O grammar rules, O now your virtues show."

Grammarian's Funeral, A. Robert Browning. **CP-BroR1**

Gran freddo è infuori, e dentro è freddo in poco. Christina Georgina Rossetti. **CP-RosC3**

Grand Canyon, The. Jean Garrigue. **SP-GarrJ**

Grand Central Station. Muriel Rukeyser. **CP-RukeM**

Grand Central, with Soldiers, in Early Morning. Howard Nemerov. **CP-NemeH**

Grand Duo. James Schuyler. **CP-SchuJ**

Grand Galop. John Ashbery. **SP-AshbJ**

Grand hotels, dancing girls, The. Hop o' My Thumb. John Ashbery. **SP-AshbJ**

Grand is the Seen. Walt Whitman. **CP-WhitW**

Grand Palace of Versailles, The. Kenneth Patchen. **CP-PatcK**

Grand Question Debated, The. Jonathan Swift. **CP-SwifJ**

Grand rough old Martin Luther. The Twins. Robert Browning. **CP-BroR1**

Grand time when the words, The. Diction. Robert Creeley. **CP-CreeR**

Granddaughter. Robinson Jeffers. **CP-JefR3**

Granddaughter. Adrienne Rich. *Fr.* Grandmothers. **SP-RicA2**

Grandeur. Robert Pack. **SP-PackR**

Grandfather. Ted Kooser. **SP-KoosT**

Grandfather. Derek Mahon. **SP-MahoD**

Grandfather and grandfather's uncle stand looking at the harbor. Destroyers. Carl Sandburg. **CP-SandC**

Grandfather Bridgeman. George Meredith. **CP-MerG1**

Grandfather Cap, The. Ted Kooser. **SP-KoosT**

Grandfather-Father Poem, The. Charles Olson. **CP-OlsoC**

Grandfather of mammoths. Juggernaut. Lewis Turco. **SP-TurcL**

Grandfather Poem, The. Stephen Dobyns. **SP-DobyS**

Grandfather Poem. Frederick Morgan. **SP-MorgF**

Grandfather Robinson Dies in 1898. John Hewitt. **CP-HewiJ**

Grandfather, sleepless in a room upstairs. John Berryman. **CP-BerrJ** *Fr.* The Black Book.

Grandfather stepped out from the clock. Grandfather Poem. Frederick Morgan. **SP-MorgF**

Grandfather, Your Wound. Anne Sexton. **CP-SextA**

Grandfathering. Richard Shelton. *Fr.* Three Poems For A Twenty-Fifth Anniversary. **SP-ShelR**

Grandfather's Grave. John Gould Fletcher. **SP-FletJ**

Grandior et primis fatis post terga relictis. *acc. by English translation.* Thomas Campion. **CP-CampT**

Grandma sleeps with / my sick. Medicine. Alice Walker. **CP-WalkA**

Grandmas are all coming down like f-101's like gulls, The. What Did the Man Do with the Clouds? Charles Kenneth Williams. **CP-WillC**

Grandmother, The. Wendell Berry. **CP-BerrW**

Grandmother. Siv Cedering Fox. **SP-CedeS**

Grandmother. Louise Glück. *Fr.* Dedication to Hunger. **SP-GlücL**

Grandmother in Heaven. Philip Levine. **SP-LeviP**

Grandmother in the Garden. Louise Glück. **SP-GlücL**

Grandmothers. Adrienne Rich. **SP-RicA2**

   Granddaughter.

   Hattie Rice Rich.

   Mary Gravely Jones. **MDDM**

Grandmothers who wring the necks. Classic Ballroom Dances. Charles Simic. **SP-SimiC**

Grandparents. Robert Lowell. **SP-LoweR**

Grandparents. Stephen Spender. **CP-SpenS**

Grange, The. Stevie Smith. **CP-SmitS**

Granite. John Updike. **CP-UpdiJ**

Granite and Cypress. Robinson Jeffers. **CP-JefR1**

Granite and Grass. Donald Hall. **CP-HallD**

Granite and Steel. Marianne Craig Moore. **CP-MoorM**

Granite Chip. Seamus Heaney. **SP-HeanS** *Fr.* Shelf Life.

Granny Saunders. Louise McNeill. **SP-McNeL**

Granny's gone a-visitin'. Opportunity. Paul Laurence Dunbar. **CP-DunbP**

Granny's Story. Louise McNeill. **SP-McNeL**

Grant. Patti Smith. **SP-SmitP**

Grant had a sledgehammer pounding and pounding and Lee had a sledge. Hammers Pounding. Carl Sandburg. **CP-SandC**

Grant me, indulgent Heaven, that I may live. Robert Burns. *Fr.* Annotations in Verse. **CP-BurnR**

Grant me the muse, ye Gods! whose humble flight. In a Letter to C.P. William Cowper. **CP-CowpW**

Grant Park: August 28, 1968. Allen Ginsberg. **CP-GinsA**

Grant, that by this unsparing hurricane. Reflections. William Wordsworth. *Fr.* Ecclesiastical Sonnets. **CP-WorW2**

Grant us, O Lord, that patience and that faith. Lord, It Is Good for Us to Be Here. Christina Georgina Rossetti. **CP-RosC2**

Grant us such grace that we may work Thy Will. Christina Georgina Rossetti. **CP-RosC2**

Granta—A Medley. Byron. **CP-Byron**

Granted that what we summon is absurd. President and Poet. Donald Hall. **CP-HallD**

Granted the all / saving our young kiss only. Edward Estlin Cummings. **CP-CummE**

Grant's Tomb Revisited. Karl Shapiro. **SP-ShapK**

Granular surface of the snow shines like parchment, The. The Body of Romulus. Stephen Dobyns. **SP-DobyS**

Grape conserve from the red Caco vine. A Gift of Light. Marge Piercy. **SP-PierM**

Grape-Hyacinth. Louis Zukofsky. **CP-ZukLS**

Grape is my mulatto mother. Wino. Ted Hughes. *Fr.* Boom. **SP-HughT**

Grape Sherbet. Rita Dove. **SP-DoveR**

Grapes. David Herbert Lawrence. **CP-LawrD**

Grapes were big and fresh, The. Emily Dickinson. **SP-DickE**

Grapevine, The. John Ashbery. **SP-AshbJ**

Graph, The. John Ciardi. **SP-CiarJ**

Graph. William Carlos Williams. **CP-WilW2**

Graph for Action. William Carlos Williams. **CP-WilW1**

Grass. Joseph Ceravolo. **SP-CeraJ**

Grass. James Merrill. **SP-MerrJ**

Grass. Carl Sandburg. **CP-SandC**

Grass. Walt Whitman. *See* A Child said *What is the grass?.*

Grass below the willow, The. Grandmother in the Garden. Louise Glück. **SP-GlücL**

Grass bends low, the pregnant trees, The. Singing in the Rain. Countee Cullen. **CP-CullC**

Grass-blade is not without, The. Ted Hughes. **SP-HughT** *Fr.* Gaudete.

Grass caught in willow tells the flood's height that has subsided. Basil Bunting. **FaBoMo** *Fr.* Briggflatts [An Autobiography]. **CP-BuntB**

"As the player's breath warms the fipple the tone clears." **PWE**

Grass clutches at the dark dirt with finger holds. Grassroots. Carl Sandburg. **CP-SandC**

Grass commence a-comin'. Spring Fever. Paul Laurence Dunbar. **CP-DunbP**

Grass from Two Years. Robert Bly. **SP-BlyR**

Grass-green and aspen-green. Variables of Green. Robert Ranke Graves. **CP-GravR**

Grass grows out of every sidewalk crack. A Summer Afternoon an Old Man Gives Some Thought to the Central Questions. Miller Williams. **SP-WillM**

Grass is green, The. Oh Grateful Colours, Bright Looks! Stevie Smith. **CP-SmitS**

Grass is half-covered with snow, The. Snowfall in the Afternoon. Robert Bly. **SP-BlyR**

Grass is in seed, The. The young birds are flying. Ghosts as Cocoons. Wallace Stevens. **CP-StevW**

Grass is very green, my friend, The. A Unison. William Carlos Williams. **CP-WilW2**

Grass lives, goes to sleep, lives again, The. Carl Sandburg. *Fr.* The People, Yes. **CP-SandC**

Grass people bow, The. To Turn Back. John Haines. **SP-HainJ**

Grass resurrects to mask, to strangle. The Distant Fury of Battle. Geoffrey Hill. **CP-HillG**

Grass shakes. / Smoke streaks, no, The. Growing Dark. James Schuyler. **CP-SchuJ**

Grass smooth on the prairies. Ernest Hemingway. **CP-HemiE**

Grass so green, the sky so blue, The. Miniature on a Book of Hours. Alun Lewis. **CP-LewiA**

Grass so little has to do, The. Emily Dickinson. **CP-DickE**

Grass yellow hill. Carmel Valley. Allen Ginsberg. **CP-GinsA**

Grasse-Hopper, The. Richard Lovelace. *See* O[h] thou that swing'st [*or* swingest] upon the waving hair[e] [*or* ear *or* eare].

Grasse: The Olive Trees. Richard Wilbur. **CP-WilbR**

Grasses. Thom Gunn. **CP-GunnT**

Grassflower. Louis Zukofsky. **CP-ZukLS**

Grasshopper, A. Richard Wilbur. **CP-WilbR**

Grasshopper and the Ant, The. Jean de La Fontaine, *tr. fr. French.* **CP-WilbR**

("Grasshopper, having sung her song.") **CP-WilbR**, *tr. by* Richard Wilbur.

Grasshopper, having sung her song. Jean de La Fontaine. *See* The Grasshopper and the Ant.

Grasshopper Is a Burden. David Herbert Lawrence. **CP-LawrD**

Grasshopper, the grasshopper, The. An Explanation of the Grasshopper. Nicholas Vachel Lindsay. **CP-LindV**

Grasshoppers. John Clare. **SP-ClarJ**

Grasshoppers Are Very Intelligent. Ogden Nash. **CP-NashO**

Grasshoppers go in many a thrumming spring. Grasshoppers. John Clare. **SP-ClarJ**

Grassroots. Carl Sandburg. **CP-SandC**

Grateful change! Favonius, and the spring, A. 1.4. Horace. **SP-SmarC**, *tr. by* Christopher Smart; *Fr.* Odes.

Grateful is Sleep, my life in stone bound fast. Michelangelo Buonarroti, *tr. fr. Italian by* William Wordsworth. **CP-WorW1**

Gratefulness. George Herbert. **CP-HerbG**

Gratiana Dancing [*or* Dauncing] and [*or* &] Singing. Richard Lovelace. **CP-LoveR**

Gratitude. Stephen Berg. **SP-BergS**

Gratitude. William Cowper. **CP-CowpW**

Gratitude. Louise Glück. **SP-GlücL**

Gratitude. Christopher Smart. **LAuP; NOEC** *Fr.* Hymns for the Amusement of Children. **SP-SmarC**

Gratitude and Love to God. Jeanne Marie Bouvier de la Motte-Guyon, *tr. fr. French by* William Cowper. **CP-CowpW**

Gratitude for a Nightmare. Robert Ranke Graves. **CP-GravR**

Gratitude—is not the mention. Emily Dickinson. **CP-DickE**

Gratitude is the timid wealth. Emily Dickinson. **SP-DickE**

Gratitude to Mother Earth, sailing through night and day. Prayer for the Great Family. Gary Snyder. **CP-SnydG**

Gratitude to the Unknown Instructors. William Butler Yeats. **CP-YeatW**

Graubelle Man, The. Seamus Heaney. **SP-HeanS**

Grave, A. Marianne Craig Moore. **CP-MoorM**

Grave, A. James Schuyler. **CP-SchuJ**

Grave by a Holm-Oak. Stevie Smith. **CP-SmitS**

Grave by the Lake, The. John Greenleaf Whittier. **CP-WhitJ**

Grave Creek Inscribed Stone, The. Louise McNeill. **SP-McNeL**

Grave Dean of St. Patrick's, how comes it to pass. The Dean to Himself on St. Cecilia's Day. Jonathan Swift. **CP-SwifJ**

Grave *Jonas Kindred*, Sibyl Kindred's sire. The Frank Courtship. George Crabbe. **SP-CrabG** *Fr.* Tales.

Grave my little cottage is, The. Emily Dickinson. **CP-DickE**

Grave Near Cairo, A. Rudyard Kipling. *Fr.* Epitaphs of the War [1914–1918]. **CP-KiplR**

Grave of Alexander Hamilton is in Trinity yard, The. Trinity Place. Carl Sandburg. **CP-SandC**

Grave of Keats, The. Percy Bysshe Shelley. *See* Go Thou to Rome.

Grave of the Hundred Dead, The. Rudyard Kipling. **CP-KiplR**

Grave Piece. Richard Eberhart. **CP-EberR**

Grave the Well, The. Donald Hall. **CP-HallD**

Grave-worm revels now, The. Death. Christina Georgina Rossetti. **CP-RosC3**

Gravel rattles against the fenders of the van. Once on a Night in the Delta: A Report From Hell. Etheridge Knight. **SP-KnigE**

Gravel road rides with a slow gallop, The. So This Is Nebraska. Ted Kooser. **SP-KoosT**

Gravepiece. Jean Garrigue. **SP-GarrJ**

Graves. Richard Hugo. **CP-HugoR**

Graves. Carl Sandburg. **CP-SandC**

Grave's a seed will get some monstrous bloom, The. Richard Eberhart. *Fr.* Suite in Prison. **CP-EberR**

Graves at Coupeville. Richard Hugo. **CP-HugoR**

Graves at Elkhorn. Richard Hugo. **CP-HugoR**

Graves at Mukilteo. Richard Hugo. **CP-HugoR**

Graves in Queens. Richard Hugo. **CP-HugoR**

Graves in Uig. Richard Hugo. **CP-HugoR**

Gravestone upon the Floor in the Cloisters of Worcester Cathedral, A. William Wordsworth. **CP-WorW2**

Graveyard, The. Jane Cooper. **NePoEA-2** *Fr.* Acceptances. **SP-CoopJ**

Graveyard by the Sea, The. Paul Valéry, *tr. fr. French by* C. Day Lewis. "This hushed surface where the doves parade." **SP-SchwD**

Graveyard of Dead Creeds, The. Thomas Hardy. **CP-HardT**

Gravity. Charles Simic. **SP-SimiC**

Gray. Alice Walker. **CP-WalkA**

Gray are the pages of record. Black Samson of Brandywine. Paul Laurence Dunbar. **CP-DunbP**

Gray Brother, The. Sir Walter Scott. **SP-ScotW**

Gray clouds blot sunglare, mountains float west, plane. Over Denver Again. Allen Ginsberg. **CP-GinsA**

Gray dawn on the mountain top, The. Day. Paul Laurence Dunbar. **CP-DunbP**

Gray dawn seeping through stone. Hayden Carruth. *Fr.* Michigan Water: a Few Riffs before Dawn. **CP-CarHL**

Gray Day. James Schuyler. **CP-SchuJ**

Gray earth peeping through snow. To P.L., 1916–1937. Philip Levine. **SP-LeviP**

Gray Eyes. Tess Gallagher. **SP-GallT**

Gray fox, female, nine pounds three ounces, A. *Hsiang-yen.* Gary Snyder. **CP-SnydG**

Gray Graeae, The. Classical Optical. John Updike. **CP-UpdiJ**

Gray Heron, The. Galway Kinnell. **SP-KinnG**

Gray, Intermittently Blue, Eyed Hero. James Schuyler. **CP-SchuJ**

Gray is the palace where she dwells. My Lady of Castle Grand. Paul Laurence Dunbar. **CP-DunbP**

Gray king died in his hour, The. Nicholas Vachel Lindsay. *Fr.* The Tale of the Tiger Tree. **CP-LindV**

Gray light, The. A Moment of Sleep (For Schnu). Chuck Miller. **SP-MillC**

Gray light awakening. Chuck Miller. **SP-MillC**

Gray maidservant lets me in, A. Matinees. James Merrill. **SP-MerrJ**

Gray miles that go off into the distance, The. Kattegat. Chuck Miller. **SP-MillC**

Gray night falls, The. The Battlefield. Kay Boyle. **CP-BoylK**

Gray of Dawn. A tremor slight, The. Empty Stirrups. Herman Melville. **SP-MelvH** *Fr.* Clarel: A Poem and Pilgrimage in the Holy Land.

Gray of the sea, and the gray of the sky, The. Her Thought and His. Paul Laurence Dunbar. **CP-DunbP**

Gray prinked with rose. The High-School Lawn. Thomas Hardy. **CP-HardT**

Gray searcher of the upper air. Mount Agiochook. John Greenleaf Whittier. **CP-WhitJ**

Gray sky smudges the tops of buildings, A. Sunday Afternoon. Stephen Berg. **SP-BergS**

Gray steel, cloud-shadow-stained. Watch the Lights Fade. Robinson Jeffers. **CP-JefR3**

Gray Stone. Richard Hugo. **CP-HugoR**

Gray Stones and Gray Pigeons. Wallace Stevens. **CP-StevW**

Gray Weather. Robinson Jeffers. **CP-JefR2**

Gray whales are going south: I see their fountains, The. Ocean. Robinson Jeffers. **CP-JefR3**

Gray's Apocrypha. Mona Van Duyn. **SP-VanDM**

Grazia Deledda, Young. Donald Davie. **CP-DavDo**

Grazing Locomotives. Archibald MacLeish. **CP-MacLA**

Great. Leonard Nathan. **SP-NathL**

Great, A / man / is / gone. Edward Estlin Cummings. **CP-CummE**

Great advantage of being alive, The. Edward Estlin Cummings. **CP-CummE; SP-CummE**

Great Alexander sailing was from his true course turned. The Speaking Tree. Muriel Rukeyser. **CP-RukeM**

Great American Novel, The. Daniel Gerard Hoffman. **SP-HoffD**

Great and bounteous Benefactor. The Nativity of St. John the Baptist. Christopher Smart. **ChIV-2** *Fr.* Hymns and Spiritual Songs for the Fasts and Festivals of the Church of England. **SP-SmarC**

Great & dramatic he is sprouting a truant. Some of the Things I See for You. Anne Waldman. **SP-WaldA**

Great and glorious thing it is, A. Arithmetic on the Frontier. Rudyard Kipling. **CP-KiplR**

Great and Small. Chuang Tzu, *tr. fr. Chinese by* Thomas Merton. **CP-MertT**

Great are the Hittites. Concerning My Neighbors, the Hittites. Charles Simic. **SP-SimiC**

Great Are the Myths. Walt Whitman. **CP-WhitW**

Great automobile turns slowly in, A. The Dazzling Burden. Kenneth Patchen. **CP-PatcK**

Great bed of the world, The. The Bed of the World. Erica Jong. **SP-JongE**

Great bird is swooping over our yard, A. Muse. Jenny Joseph. *Fr.* Fables. **SP-JoseJ**

Great bird landed here, A. Heptonstall Old Church. Ted Hughes. **SP-HughT**

Great Birds, The. Kenneth Patchen. **CP-PatcK**

Great Blue. Brendan Galvin. **SP-GalvB**

Great blue mountain! Ghost. Mount Kearsarge. Donald Hall. **CP-HallD**

Great Boast, Small Rost. Robert Herrick. **CP-HerrR**

Great, bright portal. The Cliff Temple. Hilda Doolittle. **CP-DoolH**

Great bulk, huge mass, thesaurus. Canto 5. Ezra Pound. *Fr.* Cantos. **CP-PoCan**

Great Caesar! Condescend. Emily Dickinson. **CP-DickE**

Great Carbuncle, The. Sylvia Plath. **CP-PlatS**

Great carnal mountains crouching in the cloud. Sunset. Edward Estlin Cummings. **CP-CummE**

Great Central Railway, Sheffield Victoria to Banbury. Sir John Betjeman. **CP-BetjJ**

Great Charles, among the holy gifts of grace. An Epigram. To K[ing] Charles for a[n] Hundred Pounds He Sent Me in My Sickness. 1629. Ben Jonson. **CP-JonsB**

Great citadels whereon the gold sun falls. John Berryman. *Fr.* Sonnets to Chris. **CP-BerrJ**

Great Cities seldom[e] rest: If there be none. Peace not Permanent. Robert Herrick. **CP-HerrR**

Great cold shoulders bared, The. McKane's Falls. James Merrill. **SP-MerrJ**

Great command will never be obsolete, The. Know Thyself. David Herbert Lawrence. **CP-LawrD**

Great Contemporary Discoveries. Archibald MacLeish. **CP-MacLA**

Great cracked shadow of the Sierra Nevada, The. Gambling in Stateline, Nevada. James Wright. **CP-WrigJ**

Great cry went up from the stockyards and, A. The Delicate, Plummeting Bodies. Stephen Dobyns. **SP-DobyS**

Great Dante stands in Florence, looking down. Edward Estlin Cummings. **CP-CummE**

Great dawn-color rose widening the petals around her gold eye, A. The Shears. Robinson Jeffers. **CP-JefR3**

Great Day, The. William Butler Yeats. **CP-YeatW**

Great Day in the Cows' House. Donald Hall. **CP-HallD**

Great Death, The. Hayden Carruth. *Fr.* Contra Mortem. **CP-CarHL**

Great Depression, The. Louise McNeill. **SP-McNeL**

Great Destiny the commissary of God. John Donne. **OxBoCh** *Fr.* The Progress[e] of the Soul[e]. **CP-DonnJ**

Great Doubters of History, The. Stephen Dobyns. **SP-DobyS**

Great dream stinks like a whale gone aground, The. Why the Soup Tastes Like the *Daily News*. Marge Piercy. **SP-PierM**

Great-enough both accepts and subdues; the great frame takes all creatures. Phenomena. Robinson Jeffers. **CP-JefR1**

Great Event, A. John Hewitt. **CP-HewiJ**

Great Explosion, The. Robinson Jeffers. **CP-JefR3**

Great Feast in Quebec, A. Leonard Cohen. **CP-CoheL**

Great Figure, The. William Carlos Williams. **CP-WilW1**

Great folks are of a finer mould. An Epigram on Scolding. Jonathan Swift. **CP-SwifJ**

Great geometrical winter constellations, The. Requiem for the Spanish Dead. Kenneth Rexroth. **SP-RexrK**

Great glimmering wagons rumble across this sky. Lenada. Kenneth Patchen. **CP-PatcK**

Great gold apples of night, The. People. David Herbert Lawrence. **CP-LawrD**

"Great, good and just" was once applied. To His Grace the Archbishop of Dublin. Jonathan Swift. **CP-SwifJ**

Great, good, just, kind and loving God. God. Edward Estlin Cummings. **CP-CummE**

Great-Grandmother, The. Robert Ranke Graves. **CP-GravR**

Great gray *gaviota*, The. Baja Beatitudes. Lawrence Ferlinghetti. **SP-FerlL**

Great green ships. Azores. John Updike. **CP-UpdiJ**

Great Grief, Great Glory. Robert Herrick. **CP-HerrR**

Great Gulf, The. Richard Shelton. **SP-ShelR**

Great Headmaster, A. John Hewitt. **CP-HewiJ**

Great-Heart. Rudyard Kipling. **CP-KiplR**

Great Hope fell, A. Emily Dickinson. **CP-DickE**

Great Horned Owl, The. Charles Simic. **SP-SimiC**

Great Horned Owls. Brendan Galvin. **SP-GalvB**

Great Horse Strode without a Rider, The. Daniel Gerard Hoffman. **SP-HoffD**

Great House, The. Paul Zimmer. **SP-ZimmP**

Great Hungers feed themselves. Emily Dickinson. **SP-DickE**

Great Hunt, The. Carl Sandburg. **CP-SandC**

Great Infirmities. Charles Simic. **SP-SimiC**

Great is Caesar: He has conquered Seven Kingdoms. Wystan Hugh Auden. **LiTM** *Fr.* The Summons. *Fr.* For the Time Being; a Christmas Oratorio. **CP-AudeW**

Great is the Lord, and greatly to be praised in the city of our God. Psalm 48. Bible, *O.T. Fr.* Psalms. **CP-Psal**

Great is the sun, and wide [*or* wise] he goes. Summer Sun. Robert Louis Stevenson. **CP-StevR**

Great Jove, to whose almighty throne. From the Prometheus Vinctus of Aeschylus. Byron. **CP-Byron**

Great King, there is no hatred in this heart for you. The People's Cry. Kay Boyle. **CP-BoylK**

Great Knowledge. Chuang Tzu, *tr. fr. Chinese by* Thomas Merton. **CP-MertT**

Great lady painter / what can she do now. Georgia O'Keeffe. Patti Smith. **SP-SmitP**

Great light cage has broken up in the air, The. Rain Towards Morning. Elizabeth Bishop. *Fr.* Four Poems. **CP-BishE**

Great Maladies, Long Medicines. Robert Herrick. **CP-HerrR**

Great Men. Robinson Jeffers. **CP-JefR3**

Great Men & Fools do often me Inspire. William Blake. **CP-BlakW**

Great men by small meanes oft are overthrown. Losse from the Heat. Robert Herrick. **CP-HerrR**

Great men have been among us; hands that penned. William Wordsworth. **CP-WorW1**

Great Men of Former Times, The. Thomas Merton. **CP-MertT**

Great moon, white-westering past our battlement. Moonlight Observed from Ruined Fortress. Robert Penn Warren. *Fr.* Man in Moonlight. **SP-WarrR**

Great Mullen. William Carlos Williams. **CP-WilW1**

Great Muse, that from this hall absent for long. Invocation to the Muses. Edna St. Vincent Millay. **CP-MillE**

Great Nebula of Andromeda, The. Kenneth Rexroth. **SP-RexrK** *Fr.* The Lights in the Sky are Stars.

Great Newspaper Editor to His Subordinate, The. David Herbert Lawrence. **CP-LawrD**

Great Night, The, *tr. fr. the German of* Rilke. Randall Jarrell. **CP-JarrR**

Great one, austere. Prayer before Work. May Sarton. **SP-SartM**

Great ones pass, The. Sky. Leonard Cohen. **CP-CoheL**

Great or small below, / Great or small above. Ye That Fear Him, Both Small and Great. Christina Georgina Rossetti. **CP-RosC2**

Great Overdog, The. Canis Major. Robert Frost. **CP-FrosR**

Great Owl. Daniel Gerard Hoffman. **SP-HoffD**

Great peace in Europe! Order reigns. The Peace of Europe. John Greenleaf Whittier. **CP-WhitJ**

Great Polish, The. The Translators' Party. Daniel Gerard Hoffman. **SP-HoffD**

Great Praises. Richard Eberhart. **CP-EberR**

Great Prayer. Alfonso Cortes, *tr. fr. Spanish by* Thomas Merton. **CP-MertT**

Great Principles Are Thrown Down by Time. Richard Eberhart. **CP-EberR**

Great Proud Wagon Wheels Go On, The. Carl Sandburg. **CP-SandC**

Great pulsation passed. Glass lay around me, The. Rejoice in the Abyss. Stephen Spender. **CP-SpenS**

Great ruin of the face of Paul Verlaine. Le Bateau d'Amour Descried on the Briny. Gilbert Sorrentino. *Fr.* Twelve Études for Voice and Kazoo. **SP-SorrG**

Great Sadnesses, The. Kenneth Patchen. **CP-PatcK**

Great Scarf of Birds, The. John Updike. **CP-UpdiJ**

Great screw-turner knows, The. Reflections. Phoebe Hesketh. **SP-HeskP**

Great-Sledmakers, The. Kenneth Patchen. **CP-PatcK**

Great snowy owl, A. Emblem. Richard Eberhart. **CP-EberR**

Great Society, Mark X, The. Howard Nemerov. **CP-NemeH**

Great Son of Mars! and of Minerva too! On the Truly Honourable Coll. Richard Lovelace, Occasioned by the Publication of His Posthume-Poems. Symon Ognell. *Fr.* Elegies, 1660. **CP-LoveR**

Great song ceased, The. A Moment in Eternity. "Hugh MacDiarmid." **SP-MacDH**

Great Sphinx and the Pyramids say, The. Carl Sandburg. *Fr.* The People, Yes. **CP-SandC**

Great Spirit whom the sea of boundless thought. Fragment. Percy Bysshe Shelley. **CP-ShelP**

Great Spirits Now on Earth. John Keats.
(Addressed to Haydon.) **CP-KeatJ**

Great Spirits Supervive. Robert Herrick. **CP-HerrR**

Great Statue of the General Du Puy, The. Wallace Stevens. **LiTA** *Fr.* It Must Change. *Fr.* Notes toward a Supreme Fiction. **CP-StevW**

Great stone / Above the river, The. George Oppen. *Fr.* Of Being Numerous. **CP-OppeG**

Great Streets of silence led away. Emily Dickinson. **CP-DickE**

Great Sunset, The. Robinson Jeffers. **CP-JefR2**

Great tarry wings splatter grayly up out of the blinding glare of. Family Portrait. Kenneth Patchen. **CP-PatcK**

Great Things [Are Done]. William Blake. **ArNa; OxBSP** *Fr.* Gnomic Verses. **CP-BlakW**

Great Things. Thomas Hardy. **CP-HardT**

Great things are done when Men and Mountains meet. Great Things [Are Done]. William Blake. **ArNa; OxBSP** *Fr.* Gnomic Verses. **CP-BlakW**

Great Toby is dead, The. Lament for Toby, a French Poodle. May Sarton. **SP-SartM**

Great toy-maker, light-bringer, patient, A. Edison. Robinson Jeffers. **CP-JefR2**

Great Unaffected Vampires and the Moon. Stevie Smith. **CP-SmitS**

Great Uncle Beefheart. Rita Dove. **SP-DoveR**

Great Vine left its glory to reign as Forest King, The. Maundy Thursday. Christina Georgina Rossetti. **CP-RosC2**

Great voice that calls us in the wind of dawn. Tree Ceremonies. Edna St. Vincent Millay. **CP-MillE**

Great wave of youth, ere you be spent. Sew the Flags Together. Nicholas Vachel Lindsay. **CP-LindV**

Great Western Plains, The. Hart Crane. **CP-CranH**

Great work laid upon his twoscore years. Thomas Starr King. John Greenleaf Whittier. **CP-WhitJ**

Great year and place, A. France, The 18th Year of These States. Walt Whitman. **CP-WhitW**

Greater Grand Rapids Lover, The. Marge Piercy. **SP-PierM**

Greater Grandeur. Robinson Jeffers. **CP-JefR3**

Greater light is set, my love; our fitful lamp, The. A World Whose Sun Retreats Before the Brave. Kenneth Patchen. **CP-PatcK**

Greater Love. Wilfred Owen. **CP-OwenW**

Greater than memory of Achilles or Ulysses. The Wallabout Martyrs. Walt Whitman. **CP-WhitW**

Greatest error ever erred, The. Oh, Shucks, Ma'am, I Mean Excuse Me. Ogden Nash. **CP-NashO**

Greatest in thy wars. Thomas Campion. *Fr.* Observations in the Art of English Poesie. **CP-CampT**

Greatest monarch may be stabbed by night, The. To a Friend Who Had Been Much Abused in Many Inveterate Libels. Jonathan Swift. **CP-SwifJ**

Greatest of These Is Charity, The. Christina Georgina Rossetti. **CP-RosC2**

Greatest poets undergo a kind of crisis in their art, The. "Hugh MacDiarmid." **SP-MacDH** *Fr. Further Passages from* The Kind of Poetry I Want.

Greatest Thing in North America, The. Delmore Schwartz. **SP-SchwD**

Greatness. Warmth, and human insight. Music. A Chromium-Plated Hat. Inlaid with Scenes from Siegfried. Howard Nemerov. **CP-NemeH**

Grecian Windflower. Louis Zukofsky. **CP-ZukLS**

Greece. Robert Browning. **OtMeF** *Fr. Cleon.* **CP-BroR1**

Greece. James Thomson. *Fr. Liberty.* **CP-ThomJ**

Greece is a good place. Days of Kindness. Leonard Cohen. **CP-CoheL**

Greece, sound thy Homer's, Rome, thy Virgil's name. To John Milton. *Unknown. Fr.* Complimentary Pieces to Milton. **CP-CowpW**

Greed. Charles Kenneth Williams. **SP-WillC**

Greedy Child, The. Stephen Dobyns. **SP-DobyS**

Greedy the people, The. Edward Estlin Cummings. **CP-CummE**

Greek, The. Charles Bukowski. **SP-BukC1**

Greek Architecture. Herman Melville. **SP-MelvH**

Greek Masonry. Herman Melville. **SP-MelvH**

Greek National Anthem, The. Rudyard Kipling. *See* We knew thee of old.

Greek Orthodox. Sir John Betjeman. **CP-BetjJ**

Greek Women, The. Thomas Merton. **CP-MertT; SP-MertT**

Greeks, The. Tom Clark. **SP-ClarT**

Greeks Are Coming!, The. David Herbert Lawrence. **CP-LawrD**

Greeks called the king of the gods Zeus and the Romans, The. Leda's Fortunate Gaffe. Ogden Nash. *Fr.* Fables Bullfinch Forgot. **CP-NashO**

Greeks were wrong who said our eyes have rays, The. Lamarck Elaborated. Richard Wilbur. **CP-WilbR**

Green. Charles Bukowski. **SP-BukC3**

Green. David Herbert Lawrence. **CP-LawrD**

Green air, children sat under trees with the old. Grant Park: August 28, 1968. Allen Ginsberg. **CP-GinsA**

Green and silent spot, amid the hills, A. Fears in Solitude. Samuel Taylor Coleridge. **CP-ColeS**

Green and White. Wendell Berry. **CP-BerrW**

Green Automobile, The. Allen Ginsberg. **CP-GinsA**

Green bearded Arthur with his men still blinking from underground wars. Fall '66. Thomas Merton. **CP-MertT**

Green Beer. James McAuley.
"I dream a flag snaps in a cold wind." **SP-McAuJ**
"On Saint Paddy's Day, the jukebox plays." **SP-McAuJ**

Green-blue ground, The. On Gay Wallpaper. William Carlos Williams. **CP-WilW1**

Green Buddhas / On the fruit stand. Watermelons. Charles Simic. **SP-SimiC**

Green bug sleeps in the white lily car, The. Small Homes. Carl Sandburg. **CP-SandC**

Green Bus, The. Jim Carroll. **SP-CarrJ**

Green Castle, The. Robert Ranke Graves. **CP-GravR**

Green catalpa tree has turned, The. April Inventory. William DeWitt Snodgrass. **SP-SnodW**

Green Cornfield, A. Christina Georgina Rossetti. **CP-RosC1**

Green Door, The. James Schuyler. **CP-SchuJ**

Green Evening, A. Brendan Galvin. **SP-GalvB**

Green Eyes. William Carlos Williams, *tr. fr. Spanish by* William Carlos Williams. **CP-WilW2**

Green eyes from under cornsheaf curls. A Garland for Ronsard. Donald Davie. **CP-DavDo**

Green ferns that lift from the forest's damp floor, The. Coal Fern. Louise McNeill. **SP-McNeL**

Green fingers / holding the hillside. Holding On. Philip Levine. **SP-LeviP**

Green Fires, The. Kenneth Patchen. **CP-PatcK**

Green from the apple orchard farther west. Before Even This. Leonard Nathan. **SP-NathL**

Green going through the jungle of those years. Poem. Muriel Rukeyser. **CP-RukeM**

Green Grass and Yellow Balloons. Etheridge Knight. **SP-KnigE**

Green grass is bowing, The. To Ellen, at the South. Ralph Waldo Emerson. **CP-EmerR**

Green Grow the Rashes [*or* Rushes] [A Fragment]. Robert Burns. **CP-BurnR**

Green Grow[s] the Rashes. Robert Burns.
(Fragment, A: "Green grow the rashes, O; / Green grow the rashes, O; / The lasses they hae wimble bores.") **CP-BurnR**

Green in light are the hills, and a calm wind flowing. The Reawakening. Walter de la Mare. **CP-DeLaW**

Green Is a Feeling, Not a Color. Al Young. **CP-YounA**

Green is the color of everything. One West Coast. Al Young. **CP-YounA**

Green is the night, green kindled and apparelled. The Candle a Saint. Wallace Stevens. **CP-StevW**

Green Lake Is Awake, The. Joseph Ceravolo. **SP-CeraJ**

Green lamp flares on the table, The. This Life. Rita Dove. **SP-DoveR**

Green lawn / a picket fence. Once. Alice Walker. **CP-WalkA**

Green leaf that will outlast the winter. Louis Zukofsky. **CP-ZukLS**

'Green Leinster never weep. 1977, Near Mullingar. Donald Davie. *Fr.* Two from Ireland. **CP-DavDo**

Green limb hangs in the crotch, A. Gary Snyder. **CP-SnydG** *Fr.* Logging. *Fr.* Myths and Texts.

Green Limits. Muriel Rukeyser. **CP-RukeM**

Green Linnet, The. William Wordsworth. **CP-WorW1**

Green Man, The. Charles Olson. **CP-OlsoC**

Green Memory. Langston Hughes. **SP-HughL**

Green men march along the ground, The. Frederick Morgan. *Fr.* Blue Hill Poems. **SP-MorgF**

Green Mistletoe! / Oh, I remember now. Winter. Walter de la Mare. **CP-DeLaW**

Green Mountain Idyl. Hayden Carruth. **CP-CarHS**

Green o'er the copses Spring's soft hues are spreading. April. Charlotte Smith. **CP-SmitC**

Green Plant, The. Wallace Stevens. **CP-StevW**

Green plant grows, The. Louis Zukofsky. **CP-ZukLS**

Green points on the shrub. An Elegy for D.H. Lawrence. William Carlos Williams. **CP-WilW1**

Green Quinces. Charles Tomlinson. **CP-TomlC**

Green River. Donald Davie. **CP-DavDo**

Green Rock, Winthrop Bay. Sylvia Plath. **CP-PlatS**

Green Room. Michael Hartnett. **SP-HarMi**

Green rustlings, more-than-regal charities. Royal Palm. Hart Crane. **CP-CranH**

Green-Sailed Vessel, The. Robert Ranke Graves. **CP-GravR**

Green-shadowed people sit, or walk in rings. Spring. Philip Larkin. **CP-LarkP**

Green Shelf, The. Donald Hall. **CP-HallD**

Green Shoot, The. John Hewitt. **CP-HewiJ**

Green Shutters, shut your shutters! Windyridge. Beside the Seaside. Sir John Betjeman. **CP-BetjJ**

Green shutters, shut your shutters! Windyridge. Sir John Betjeman. **OxBTC** *Fr.* Beside the Seaside. **CP-BetjJ**

Green silk, or a shot silk, blue. Green River. Donald Davie. **CP-DavDo**

Green skeletons of fish, they swim across the pale. Windowscape. Louis MacNeice. **CP-MacNL**

Green Slates. Thomas Hardy. **CP-HardT**

Green Sleeves [and Tartan Ties]. Robert Burns. **CP-BurnR**

Green sludge of a riverbank. One Volume Missing. Rita Dove. **SP-DoveR**

Green smoke and white ash. John Haines. *Fr.* Homestead. **SP-HainJ**

Green sprout the grasses. I Have a Message unto Thee. Christina Georgina Rossetti. **CP-RosC3**

Green star Sirius. Winter Dawn. David Herbert Lawrence. **CP-LawrD**

Green Stone. Richard Hugo. **CP-HugoR**

Green Symphony. John Gould Fletcher. **SP-FletJ**

Green upon the flooded Avon shone the after-storm-wet-sky. Bristol. Sir John Betjeman. **CP-BetjJ**

Green upright rope. Old-Fashioned Lightning Rod. John Updike. **CP-UpdiJ**

Green Valentine Blues. Allen Ginsberg. **CP-GinsA**

Green Ways. Stanley Jasspon Kunitz. **CP-KuniS**

Green Wolf, The. Ted Hughes. **SP-HughT**

Green Woods of Unrest, The. Robert Ranke Graves. **CP-GravR**

Green world thinks the sun, The. Sky. Tom Clark. **SP-ClarT**

Greenaway. Sir John Betjeman. **CP-BetjJ**

Greendoon's Song. Robert Creeley. **CP-CreeR**

Greenhouse is my summer seat, The. The Faithful Friend. William Cowper. **CP-CowpW**

Greenock. William Wordsworth. *Fr.* Poems Composed or Suggested During a Tour, in the Summer of 1833. **CP-WorW2**

GrEEn's d / an / cing on hollow was. Edward Estlin Cummings. **CP-CummE**

Greenwich Avenue. James Schuyler. **CP-SchuJ**

Greenwich 1930's, I. Frederick Morgan. **SP-MorgF**

Greenwich 1930's, II. Frederick Morgan. **SP-MorgF**

Greeting. May Sarton. **SP-SartM**

Greeting, The. Charles Tomlinson. **CP-TomlC**

Greeting, A. John Greenleaf Whittier. **CP-WhitJ**

Greeting. John Greenleaf Whittier. **CP-WhitJ**

Greeting for Old Age. William Carlos Williams. **CP-WilW2**

Greeting the dawn, / A shift of rubber workers presses down. Porphyro in Akron. Hart Crane. **CP-CranH**

Greeting to you both in hearty wise. Sir Thomas Wyatt. **CP-WyatT**

Greetings. Alun Lewis. **CP-LewiA**

Greetings from the Chateau. James Schuyler. **CP-SchuJ**

Gregory Corso's Story. Allen Ginsberg. **CP-GinsA**

Gregory Nazianzen. Frank Templeton Prince. **CP-PrinF**

Grenadier. Alfred Edward Housman. **CP-HousA**

Grendel. Lewis Turco. **SP-TurcL**

Grenoble Café. Jean Garrigue. **SP-GarrJ**

Greta, what fearful listening! when huge stones. To the River Greta, near Keswick. William Wordsworth. *Fr.* Poems Composed or Suggested During a Tour, in the Summer of 1833. **CP-WorW2**

Gretel. Ron Koertge. **SP-KoerR**

Gretel in Darkness. Louise Glück. **SP-GlücL**

Grew hair for fun. Ike. Rita Dove. **SP-DoveR**

Grey and White. John Hewitt. **CP-HewiJ**

Grey apparitions at verandah ends. Verandah. Derek Walcott. **CP-WalcD**

Grey brick upon brick. Dublin. Louis MacNeice. **CIP; FaBoPP; IIP; OBTV; OxBTC** *Fr.* The Closing Album. **CP-MacNL**

Grey day, but the heart is not grey? Villanelle, an Interview on Morale. Malcolm Lowry. **CP-LowrM**

Grey day for the Show, but cars jam the narrow lanes. Show Saturday. Philip Larkin. **CP-LarkP**

Grey day of high tempestuous seas, A. Reflection to Windward. Malcolm Lowry. **CP-LowrM**

Grey efficient masks rock home by bus, The. The Mask. John Hewitt. **CP-HewiJ**

Grey English road hissed emptily under the tires, The. Derek Walcott. **CP-WalcD** *Fr.* Midsummer.

Grey Evening. David Herbert Lawrence. **CP-LawrD**

Grey eyes watchful and a lightened hand, The. To Natty Bumppo. Thom Gunn. **CP-GunnT**

Grey gaunt days dividing us in twain, The. The Minute before Meeting. Thomas Hardy. **CP-HardT**

Grey girl who had not been singing stopped, The. New Year's Eve. John Berryman. **CP-BerrJ**

Grey haunted eyes, absent-mindedly glaring. The Face in the Mirror. Robert Ranke Graves. **CP-GravR**

Grey horse, Death, in profile bears the young Titus, The. The Polish Rider. Derek Walcott. **CP-WalcD**

Grey Monk, The. William Blake. **CP-BlakW**

Grey Nurse, The. David Herbert Lawrence. *Fr.* Bits. **CP-LawrD**

Grey Ones, The. Louis MacNeice. **CP-MacNL**

Grey Rock, The. William Butler Yeats. **CP-YeatW**

Grey [or Gray] sea and the long black land, The. Meeting at Night. Robert Browning. **CP-BroR1**

Grey sea, grey sky / two things are bright. Grey and White. John Hewitt. **CP-HewiJ**

Grey ship with yellow red lights, A. A Picture. Malcolm Lowry. **CP-LowrM**

Grey Sparrow Addresses the Mind's Ear. Denise Levertov. **CP-LeveD**

Grey Symphony. John Gould Fletcher. **SP-FletJ**

Grey water tanks in grey mist. Bayonne Turnpike to Tuscarora. Allen Ginsberg. **CP-GinsA**

Grey weather beating across the upland. Roy Fisher. **SP-FishR** *Fr.* Diversions.

Grey with all honours of age! but fresh-featured and ruddy. The Poetry of Chaucer. George Meredith. **CP-MerG1**

Greybeard, old wisdom, may boast of his treasures, The. Robert Burns. *Fr.* Lines *Written on the Windows of the Globe Tavern, Dumfries.* **CP-BurnR**

Greyday. Maya Angelou. **SP-AngeM**

Greyly tremendous the thunder. A Lincolnshire Church. Sir John Betjeman. **CP-BetjJ**

Greyness Is All. Louis MacNeice. **CP-MacNL**

Greystone Cottage. Richard Hugo. **CP-HugoR**

Grief. Wendell Berry. **CP-BerrW**

Grief. Elizabeth Barrett Browning. **CP-BroEB**

Grief. Catullus. *See* Carmen 65: "Although entangled in prolonged grief."

Grief. Stephen Dobyns. **SP-DobyS**

Grief. George Herbert. **CP-HerbG**

Grief ("I thought when the grave was sodded"). John Hewitt. **CP-HewiJ**

Grief ("When men lie down for ever / and names their tombstones take"). John Hewitt. **CP-HewiJ**

Grief. David Herbert Lawrence. **CP-LawrD**

Grief, *sl. diff. vers.* David Herbert Lawrence. *See* Firelight and Nightfall.

Grief Ago, A. Dylan Thomas. **CP-ThomD**

Grief comes to eat without a mouth. The Past. William Matthews. **SP-MattW**

Grief Engrossed. Thomas Carew. **CP-CareT**

Grief, find the words, for thou hast made my brain. Sonnet 94. Sir Philip Sidney. *Fr.* Astrophil and Stella. **SP-SidnP**

Grief, have I denied thee? A Lamentation. Denise Levertov. **CP-LeveD**

Grief is a Mouse. Emily Dickinson. **CP-DickE**

Grief may have thought it was grief. They Were Welcome to Their Belief. Robert Frost. **CP-FrosR**

Grief now hath pacified her face. The Widow. Walter de la Mare. **CP-DeLaW**

Grief of an Heir, The. William Cowper. **CP-CowpW**

Grief of Cafeterias, The. John Updike. **CP-UpdiJ**

Grief of wonder at her fate. Emily Dickinson. **SP-DickE**

Grief reached across the world to get me. Catullus. *See* Carmen 65: "Although entangled in prolonged grief."

Grief sate upon a rock and sighed one day. The Claim. Elizabeth Barrett Browning. **CP-BroEB**

Grief-tailed fish, / Sunday-eye in walking shorts. I Write This Upon the Last Drink's Hammer. Charles Bukowski. **SP-BukC2**

Grief that is grief and properly so hight. Edna St. Vincent Millay. **CP-MillE**

Grief Thief of Time. Dylan Thomas. **CP-ThomD**

Grief, thou hast lost an ever ready friend. William Wordsworth. **CP-WorW1**

Grief Was to Go Out, Away. Jean Garrigue. **SP-GarrJ**

Griefe ("Consider sorroowes, how they are aright"). Robert Herrick. **CP-HerrR**

Griefe ("Sorrowes divided amongst many, lesse"). Robert Herrick. **CP-HerrR**

Griefe, killing griefe: have nott my torments binn. Sonnet 28. Mary Sidney, Countess of Montgomery Wroth. **KTR** *Fr.* Pamphilia to Amphilanthus. **CP-WrotM**

Griefes. Robert Herrick. **CP-HerrR**

Griefs / Marking indelibly our later loves. Wedding Presents. Muriel Rukeyser. **CP-RukeM**

Grieg Being Dead. Carl Sandburg. **CP-SandC**

Grievance, A. Paul Laurence Dunbar. **CP-DunbP**

Grieve for the loveless, spiritless, faceless men. Dead Hand. Robert Ranke Graves. **CP-GravR**

Grieve for the Man who hither came bereft. At the Convent of Camaldoli. William Wordsworth. *Fr.* Memorials of a Tour in Italy, 1837. **CP-WorW2**

Grieve not for happy Claudius, he is dead. Epitaph. Edna St. Vincent Millay. **CP-MillE**

Grieve not, my Celia, but with haste. To His Mistress. Thomas Carew. **CP-CareT**

Grim Dean, who sleeps within his pulpit's shade. John Hewitt. *Fr.* Two Sonnets on the Free State of Censorship Bill. **CP-HewiJ**

Grim Grizzle. Robert Burns. **CP-BurnR**

Grim in my little black coat as the sleazy beetle. Tom, Tom, the Piper's Son. John Crowe Ransom. *Fr.* Sixteen Poems in Eight Pairings. **SP-RansJ**

Grim New Englanders stand around, The. Once More, O Ye. Richard Eberhart. **CP-EberR**

Grim Skeleton. Allen Ginsberg. **CP-GinsA**

Grim Skeleton come back & put me out of Action. Grim Skeleton. Allen Ginsberg. **CP-GinsA**

Grin and Bear Left. Ogden Nash. **CP-NashO**

Grin without a / face(a look), A. Edward Estlin Cummings. **CP-CummE**

Grindstone, The. Robert Frost. **CP-FrosR**

Grinning monster out side the system. Charles Olson. **CP-OlsoC**

Grip of the ice is gone now, The. The Wind Sings Welcome in Early Spring. Carl Sandburg. **CP-SandC**

Grip of winter tightening, its thinned, The. The Flock. Derek Walcott. **CP-WalcD**

Gripping Serial. Donald Davie. **CP-DavDo**

Gripping the mantel with thick fingers. The Greedy Child. Stephen Dobyns. **SP-DobyS**

Gripus. John Keats. **CP-KeatJ**

Griselda's dead, and so's her patience. *mod. vers. by* Edward Hodnett. Geoffrey Chaucer. **PoRA** *Fr.* The Clerk's Tale. *Fr.* The Canterbury Tales. **CP-ChauG**

Grisly Grit. Archie Randolph Ammons. **SP-AmmoA**

Gristly bare-bone fingers. The Song of the Sturdy Snails. Nicholas Vachel Lindsay. **CP-LindV**

Grit / of things, The. Song. Robert Creeley. **CP-CreeR**

Grizzled Athenian ordered to hemlock, The. Anecdote of Hemlock for Two Athenians. Carl Sandburg. **CP-SandC**

Grizzled doorman lets the doctors' wives, The. Marilyn Hacker. **SP-HackM** *Fr.* Taking Notice.

Grizzly Peak. Al Young. **CP-YounA**

Groan then, groan. Stoic. David Herbert Lawrence. **CP-LawrD**

Groans of nature in this nether world, The. William Cowper. **NoP** *Fr.* The Winter Walk at Noon. *Fr.* The Task. **CP-CowpW**

Grocery. Charles Simic. **SP-SimiC**

Grocery Bouquet, The. Isabella Gardner. **CP-GardI**

Groin, come of age, his [']state sold out of hand. On Groin. Ben Jonson. **CP-JonsB**

Groined by deep glens and walled along the west. The Glens. John Hewitt. **CP-HewiJ**

Groom's Still Waiting at the Altar, The. "Bob Dylan." **CP-DylaB**

Grooved disc, a sliver of diamond, and the music rises, A. Turntables. Dabney Stuart. **SP-StuaD**

Grooving clam shell. Wave. Gary Snyder. **CP-SnydG**

Groping back to bed after a piss. Sad Steps. Philip Larkin. **CP-LarkP**

Gross, Coarse, Hideous. David Herbert Lawrence. **CP-LawrD**

Grotesque. William Carlos Williams. **CP-WilW1**

Grotesques. Robert Ranke Graves. **CP-GravR**

Grottamare. Lawrence Ferlinghetti. **SP-FerlL**

Ground / under a maple-tree. Sigil. Hilda Doolittle. **CP-DoolH**

Ground-Mist, The. Denise Levertov. **CP-LeveD**

Ground swayed like a sea, The. A Dream. Howard Nemerov. *Fr.* Seven Macabre Songs. **CP-NemeH**

Groundhog, The. Richard Eberhart. **CP-EberR**

Groundhog on the mountain did not run, The. Incommunicado. Sylvia Plath. **CP-PlatS**

Groundhog Revisiting, The. Richard Eberhart. **CP-EberR**

Groundswell, The. John Gould Fletcher. *Fr.* Sand and Spray: A Sea-Symphony. **SP-FletJ**

Group Life: Letchworth. Sir John Betjeman. **CP-BetjJ**

Group of little children with their ways and chatter flow in, A. After the Argument. Walt Whitman. **CP-WhitW**

Groupie. Al Young. **CP-YounA**

Grove, The. Richard Eberhart. *Fr.* Burr Oaks. **CP-EberR**

Grove, The. Octavio Paz, *tr. fr. Spanish by* Elizabeth Bishop. **CP-BishE**

Grove is a stately place, calm and free, The. The Grove. Richard Eberhart. *Fr.* Burr Oaks. **CP-EberR**

Grove kept us dry, The. Mediation. Archie Randolph Ammons. **SP-AmmoA**

Groves are down, The. Gary Snyder. **CP-SnydG** *Fr.* Logging. *Fr.* Myths and Texts.

Groves of Eden, vanished now so long, The. Alexander Pope. **OAEL-1** *Fr.* Windsor-Forest [*or* Windsor Forest]. **CP-PopeA**

Grove's Way. Archie Randolph Ammons. **SP-AmmoA**

Grow. Joseph Ceravolo. **SP-CeraJ**

Grow angry, sweetheart, if you must, with me. The Ugly Secret. Robert Ranke Graves. **CP-GravR**

Grow for two ends, it matters not at all. The Rosemarie Branch. Robert Herrick. **CP-HerrR**

Grow not too high, grow not too far from home. Edna St. Vincent Millay. **CP-MillE**

Grow old along with me! Robert Browning. **FaBV; ImPo; LPA; PoToHe** *Fr.* Rabbi Ben Ezra. **CP-BroR1**

Grow old along with me! Rabbi Ben Ezra. Robert Browning. **CP-BroR1**

Grow plumpe, leane Death; hhis Holinesse a feast. Upon the Gunpowder Treason. Richard Crashaw. **CP-CrasR**

Grow thin by walking and go inland. Wystan Hugh Auden. **CP-AudWJ**

Grow up in Beauty, as thou do'st begin. On Tomasin Parsons. Robert Herrick. **CP-HerrR**

Grower of trees, the gardener, the man born to farming, The. The Man Born to Farming. Wendell Berry. **CP-BerrW**

Growin' Gray. Paul Laurence Dunbar. **CP-DunbP**

Growing a Ghost. Howard Nemerov. **CP-NemeH**

Growing Dark. James Schuyler. **CP-SchuJ**

Growing Deaf. Peter Meinke. **SP-MeinP**

Growing idleness of summer grass, The. A Lesson for This Sunday. Derek Walcott. **CP-WalcD**

Growing in the vale / By the uplands hilly. Christina Georgina Rossetti. **CP-RosC2**

Growing Old. Matthew Arnold. **SP-ArnoM**

Growing Old. Byron. **NOBE; SCV** *Fr.* Canto the First. **EnRP; NAEL-2; NoP; OAEL-2; PoE** *Fr.* Don Juan. **CP-Byron**

Growing Old Again. Allen Ginsberg. **CP-GinsA**

Growing old in shabby clothes. Rummage. Hayden Carruth. **CP-CarHS**

Growing Pains. Robert Ranke Graves. **CP-GravR**

Growing Up. Jim Carroll. **SP-CarrJ**

Growing Up Askew. Mona Van Duyn. **SP-VanDM**

Growing weather; enough rain. The Satisfactions of the Mad Farmer. Wendell Berry. **CP-BerrW**

Grown and Flown. Christina Georgina Rossetti. **CP-RosC1**

Grown Cold. Christina Georgina Rossetti. **CP-RosC3**

Grown old in courts, thou art not surely one. Translations from Metastasio. Pietro Metastasio, *tr. by* Samuel Johnson. **CP-JohnS** *Fr.* Adriano in Syria.

Grown old in Love from Seven till Seven times Seven. William Blake. **CP-BlakW**

Grown old in Rhyme, 'twere barbarous to discard. Prologue Design'd for Mr. Durfy's Last Play. Alexander Pope. **CP-PopeA**

Grown out of granite. Witch Tree. Barton Sutter. **SP-SuttB**

Grown Up. Hilda Doolittle. *Fr.* Child Poems. **CP-DoolH**

Grown-Up, The, *tr. fr. the German of* Rilke. Randall Jarrell. **CP-JarrR**

Grown-up. Edna St. Vincent Millay. **CP-MillE**

Grown-Ups, The. Donald Hall. **CP-HallD**

Grown used to New York weather. Thank You, Fog. Wystan Hugh Auden. **CP-AudeW**

Grows till it is not what but which. The Web One Weaves of Italy. Marianne Craig Moore. **CP-MoorM**

Growth (Harriet). Robert Lowell. **SP-LoweR**

Growth in May. Thomas Hardy. **CP-HardT**

Growth of "Lorraine," The. Edwin Arlington Robinson. **CP-RobiE**

Growth of Man—like Growth of Nature. Emily Dickinson. **CP-DickE**

Groynes, for his fleshly *Burglary* of late. Upon Groynes. Robert Herrick. **CP-HerrR**

Grub First, Then Ethics. Wystan Hugh Auden. *Fr.* Thanksgiving for a Habitat. **CP-AudeW**

(On Installing an American Kitchen in Lower Austria.) **NYBP**

Grub-white mulberries redden among leaves. Moonrise. Sylvia Plath. **CP-PlatS**

Grubs loves his Wife and Children, while that they. Upon Grubs. Robert Herrick. **CP-HerrR**

Grudge of the Old, The. David Herbert Lawrence. **CP-LawrD**

Grudge on who list, this is my lot. Sir Thomas Wyatt. **CP-WyatT**

Grudging Respect. Donald Davie. **CP-DavDo**

Grudgings turnes bread to stones, when to the Poore. Upon Grudgings. Robert Herrick. **CP-HerrR**

Gruffly growled the wind on Toller downland broad and bare. The Homecoming. Thomas Hardy. **CP-HardT**

Gryll eates, but ne're sayes grace; to speak the troth. Upon Gryll. Robert Herrick. **CP-HerrR**

G.S. Reading Poesy at Princeton. Allen Ginsberg. **CP-GinsA**

Guaranteed Antique. Carl Sandburg. **CP-SandC**

Guard, Civility, with guns. Wystan Hugh Auden. *Fr.* Shorts [1948–1957] ("At peace under this mandarin, sleep, Lucina"). **CP-AudeW**

Guard has a right to despair. He stands by God, The. In Galleries. Randall Jarrell. **CP-JarrR; SP-JarrR**

Guard the knowledge. The Desert as Garden of Paradise. Adrienne Rich. **SP-RicA1**

Guard yourself from the terrible empty light of space, the bottomless. Quia Absurdum. Robinson Jeffers. **CP-JefR3**

Guardian-Angel, The. Robert Browning. **CP-BroR1**

Guardian Angel, The. Stephen Dunn. **SP-DunnS**

Guardian Angels. Edmund Spenser. *See* And is there care in heauen [*or* heaven]? and is there loue [*or* love].

Guardian of Helicon, Urania's son. Catullus. *See* Carmen 61: "Hill (breeder) of Helicon."

Guardian Prince of Albion burns in his nightly tent, The. A Prophecy. William Blake. **FaBoEH** *Fr.* America; a Prophecy. **CP-BlakW**

Guardians, The. Geoffrey Hill. **CP-HillG**

Guardianship. Steve Griffiths. **SP-GrifS**

Guards. David Herbert Lawrence. **CP-LawrD**

Guatemala: 1964. Charles Kenneth Williams. **SP-WillC**

Gubbinal. Wallace Stevens. **CP-StevW**

Gubbs call's his children Kitlings: and wo'd bound. Upon Gubbs. Robert Herrick. **CP-HerrR**

Gude pity me, because I'm little. Adam A———'s Prayer. Robert Burns. **CP-BurnR**

Gude Wallace. Robert Burns. **CP-BurnR**

Gudeen to You Kimmer. Robert Burns. **CP-BurnR**

Guelder Roses. David Herbert Lawrence. **CP-LawrD**

Guerdon of new childhood is reose, The. Edwin Arlington Robinson. *Fr.* Octaves. **CP-RobiE**

Guerrillas, The. Edwin Rolfe. **CP-RolfE**

Guess I'm Doin' Fine. "Bob Dylan." **CP-DylaB**

Guess what smells so. . . You didn't guess. *after Henrikas Radauskas.* Randall Jarrell. **CP-JarrR**

Guesse cuts his shooes, and limping, goes about. Upon Guesse. Robert Herrick. **CP-HerrR**

Guesses. Christina Georgina Rossetti. **CP-RosC3**

Guest, The. Wendell Berry. **CP-BerrW**

Guest, A. May Sarton. **SP-SartM**

Guest am I to have. Emily Dickinson. **CP-DickE**

Guest is gold and crimson, The. Emily Dickinson. **CP-DickE**

Guest Room. George Oppen. **CP-OppeG**

Guest, still drunk, sprawls in my bed, The. After the Party. Meng Hao Jan, *tr. fr. Chinese by* William Carlos Williams *with* David Rafael Wang. **CP-WilW2**

Guesthouse, The. Steve Griffiths. **SP-GrifS**

Guests, The. Leonard Cohen. **CP-CoheL**

Guests, The. Louis Zukofsky. **CP-ZukLS**

Guests in their summer colors have fled, The. The Last Picnic. Stanley Jasspon Kunitz. **CP-KuniS**

Guevara. John Haines. **SP-HainJ**

Guid-mornin to your MAJESTY. A Dream. Robert Burns. **CP-BurnR**

Guid New-year I wish thee, Maggie!, A. The Auld Farmer's New-Year-Morning Salutation to His Auld Mare, Maggie, on Giving Her the Accustomed Ripp of Corn to Hansel in the New-Year. Robert Burns. **CP-BurnR**

Guid speed an' furder to you Johny. Third Epistle to J. Lapraik. Robert Burns. **CP-BurnR**

Guide to the Ruins. Howard Nemerov. **CP-NemeH**

Guidebooks play deception, The; oceans are. Itinerary. Adrienne Rich. **CP-RicAE**

Guided by / none the. Preexistence. Archie Randolph Ammons. **SP-AmmoA**

Guided Tour, The. Jim Morrison. **SP-MorrJ**

Guido / I would that you me & Lapo. Guido, i' vorrei che tu e Lapo ed io. Robert Creeley. **CP-CreeR**

Guido, i' vorrei che tu e Lapo ed io. Robert Creeley. **CP-CreeR**

Guido, I would that Lapo, thou, and I. Dante Alighieri, *tr. fr. Italian by* Shelley. **CP-ShelP**

　(Sonnet: [From the Italian of Dante.] Dante Alighieri to Guido Cavalcanti.) **CP-ShelP**

Guiffre's Nightmusic. Thomas McGrath. **SP-McGrT**

Guillaume de Machault (1300-1377) Ballade: Plourès, dames. Louis Zukofsky. **CP-ZukLS**

Guillermo tells everyone / Guillermo sold the field. El Santuario de Chimayó. Martin Edmunds. *Fr.* The High Road to Taos. **SP-EdmuM**

Guillermo's Wedding. Siv Cedering Fox. **SP-CedeS**

Guilt. Richard Shelton. **SP-ShelR**

Guilt and Sorrow; or Incidents upon Salisbury Plain. William Wordsworth. **CP-WorW1**

　Salisbury Plain and Stonehenge. **FaBoPP**

Guilt is the cause of more disauders. Edward Estlin Cummings. **CP-CummE**

Guilt of man does not defer the sun, The. 1935. Kenneth Patchen. **CP-PatcK**

Guilt said the bony man. A Song of Another Tribe. Muriel Rukeyser. **CP-RukeM**

Guiltless Inconstant, The. Sir John Suckling. **CP-CareT; CP-SuckJ**

Guiltlesse Lady Imprisoned; after Penanced, A. Richard Lovelace. **CP-LoveR**

Guilty, be wise; and though thou know'st the crimes. To Person Guilty. Ben Jonson. **CP-JonsB**

Guilty, because I bad you late be wise. To Person Guilty. Ben Jonson. **CP-JonsB**

Guilty Man, The. Stanley Jasspon Kunitz. **CP-KuniS**

Guilty undertaker sighs, The. I Want You. "Bob Dylan." **CP-DylaB**

Guinevere. Tennyson. *Fr.* Idylls of the King. **CP-TennA**

Guitar. David St. John. **SP-StJoD**

Guitar Lesson, The. Stephen Dobyns. **SP-DobyS**

Gulbeyaz. Byron. **PoEL-4** *Fr.* Canto the Fifth. *Fr.* Don Juan. **CP-Byron**

Gulelme gente Perciorum ab inclita. *acc. by English translation.* Thomas Campion. **CP-CampT**

Gulf, The. David Herbert Lawrence. **CP-LawrD**

Gulf, The. Derek Walcott. **CP-WalcD**

Gulf between us and the brutes, The. Louis MacNeice. **CP-MacNL** *Fr.* Jigsaws. **CP-MacNL**

Gulf of All Human Possessions, The. Jonathan Swift. *Fr.* Riddles. **CP-SwifJ**

Gulf of Maine, The. Charles Olson. **SP-OlsoC** *Fr.* The Maximus Poems.

Gulf of seven and fifty years, The. The Reunion. John Greenleaf Whittier. **CP-WhitJ**

Gulf Stream. John Gould Fletcher. **SP-FletJ**

Gull. Anne Sexton. **CP-SextA**

Gull. Charles Tomlinson. **CP-TomlC**

Gull Hardly Explained, The. Richard Hugo. **CP-HugoR**

Gull hundreds of miles below him, The. Louis MacNeice. *Fr.* Visitations. **CP-MacNL**

Gull rides on the ripples of a dream, A. A Walk in Late Summer. Theodore Roethke. **CP-RoetT**

Gull shall whistle in his wake, the blind wave break in fire, The. The Voortrekker. Rudyard Kipling. **CP-KiplR**

Gull, up close, A. Seagulls. John Updike. **CP-UpdiJ**

Gulled. Richard Eberhart. **CP-EberR**

Gullies as deep as halls held these surveyors. Muriel Rukeyser. **CP-RukeM**

Gulliver. Sylvia Plath. **CP-PlatS**

Gulls, The. John Gould Fletcher. *Fr.* Sand and Spray: A Sea-Symphony. **SP-FletJ**

Gulls. Robert Earl Hayden. **CP-HaydR**

Gulls / loudly insist on indefensible rights. Gulls. James Schuyler. **CP-SchuJ**

Gulls, The. Howard Nemerov. **CP-NemeH**

Gulls. James Schuyler. **CP-SchuJ**

Gulls. William Carlos Williams. **CP-WilW1**

Gulls are baaing in the creek, The. Fiesta. Malcolm Lowry. **CP-LowrM**

Gulls at Gloucester. Marsden Hartley. **CP-HartM**

Gulls at the plough's tail and rooks in the fallow, the. On a January Train Journey. John Hewitt. **CP-HewiJ**

Gulls began at daybreak in the mist, The. The Return. John Hewitt. **CP-HewiJ**

Gull's Cry. Robert Penn Warren. *Fr.* To a Little Girl, One Year Old, in a Ruined Fortress. **SP-WarrR**

Gulls flock in to feed from the waste. From the Motorway. Charles Tomlinson. **CP-TomlC**

Gull's image and the gull, The. Before March. Archibald MacLeish. **CP-MacLA**

Gulls Land and Cease to Be. John Ciardi. **SP-CiarJ**

Gulls on the grass / and the odor of live worms / and worms dead on the walk. Conqueror. Charles Olson. **CP-OlsoC**

Gulls over a rotting hull. Louis Zukofsky. **CP-ZukLS**

Gum-Gatherer, The. Robert Frost. **CP-FrosR**

Gun, The. Stephen Dobyns. **SP-DobyS**

Gun, The. "Lou Reed." **SP-ReedL**

Gunga Din. Rudyard Kipling. **CP-KiplR**

Gunmetal feathers, The. And the Falcon Came. Ted Hughes. **SP-HughT**

Gunmetal snow icecolored sky. Hayden Carruth. *Fr.* North Winter. **CP-CarHL**

Gunner. Randall Jarrell. **CP-JarrR**

Gunpowder Plot. William Wordsworth. *Fr.* Ecclesiastical Sonnets. **CP-WorW2**

Guns / Long, steel guns. Iron. Carl Sandburg. **CP-SandC**

Guns at Fort Flagler. Richard Hugo. **CP-HugoR**

Guns at the camp (I hear them suddenly). The Guns of Fort Knox. Thomas Merton. **CP-MertT; SP-MertT**

Guns from the sea open against us:. Dawn Bombardment. Robert Ranke Graves. **CP-GravR**

Guns of Fort Knox, The. Thomas Merton. **CP-MertT; SP-MertT**

Guns on the battle lines have pounded now a year between Brussels and. Salvage. Carl Sandburg. **CP-SandC**

Guns salute, and crowds and pigeons fly. The Village Improvement Parade. Nicholas Vachel Lindsay. **CP-LindV**

Guppy, The. Ogden Nash. **CP-NashO**

Gurney, Hampton, Cradock Newton, last. Cradock Newton: From an Epitaph. Charles Tomlinson. **CP-TomlC**

Guru. Charles Bukowski. **SP-BukC1**

Guru. Allen Ginsberg. **CP-GinsA**

Guru Om. Allen Ginsberg. **CP-GinsA**

Gus in the Streets. Paul Zimmer. **SP-ZimmP**

Gus Sees Wanda Drinking. Paul Zimmer. **SP-ZimmP**

Gut eats all day, and lechers all the night. On Gut. Ben Jonson. **CP-JonsB**

Guttersnipe and the albatross, The. Drifting Off. Seamus Heaney. **SP-HeanS** *Fr.* Sweeney Redivivus.

Guttural Muse, The. Seamus Heaney. **SP-HeanS**

Guy. Ralph Waldo Emerson. **CP-EmerR**

Guy in the front court can't, The. The Greek. Charles Bukowski. **SP-BukC1**

Guy sat there barefoot on an old wooden bench, The. Nicaraguan Journal. Chuck Miller. **SP-MillC**

Guyana. Derek Walcott. **CP-WalcD**

Guyon's Voyage to the Bower of Bliss. Edmund Spenser. **NoSic** *Fr.* The Faerie Queene. **CP-Spens**

"Two dayes now in that sea he sayled has." **OxBoS**

G'way an' quit dat noise, Miss Lucy. When Malindy Sings. Paul Laurence Dunbar. **CP-DunbP**

Gwin, King of Norway. William Blake. **CP-BlakW**

Gyges['] ring they bear[e] about them still, A. Lovers How They Come and Part. Robert Herrick. **CP-HerrR**

Gymnasts, The. Phoebe Hesketh. **SP-HeskP**

Gypsies. William Wordsworth. **CP-WorW1**

Gypsies Metamorphosed, The. Ben Jonson.

"Cocklorel would needs have the devil his guest." **CP-JonsB**

"Fairy [*or* Faery *or* Faiery] beam[e] upon you, The." **CP-JonsB**

"From the famous Peak of Derby." **CP-JonsB**

"To the old, long life and treasure." **CP-JonsB**

Gypsies Near Del Mar, The. Charles Bukowski. **SP-BukC2**

Gypsy. Paul Muldoon. *Fr.* 7, Middagh Street. **SP-MuldP**

Gypsy. Carl Sandburg. **CP-SandC**

Gypsy gal, the hands of Harlem. Spanish Harlem Incident. "Bob Dylan." **CP-DylaB**

Gypsy Lou. "Bob Dylan." **CP-DylaB**

Gypsy Melodies. Langston Hughes. **SP-HughL**

Gypsy Mother. Carl Sandburg. **CP-SandC**

Gypsy, new bawd, is turned physician. On Gypsy. Ben Jonson. **CP-JonsB**

Gypsy Wife, The. Leonard Cohen. **CP-CoheL**

Gyres, The. William Butler Yeats. **CP-YeatW**

Gyroscope. Howard Nemerov. **CP-NemeH**

Gyroscope, The. Muriel Rukeyser. **CP-RukeM**

H

H. Robert Ranke Graves. **CP-GravR**

H. D. Donald Davie. **CP-DavDo**

H may be N for those who speak. H. Robert Ranke Graves. **CP-GravR**

H. W. in Hibernia Belligeranti. John Donne. **CP-DonnJ**

H₂O. Al Young. **CP-YounA**

H.A. and A.S. Emily Brontë. **CP-BronE**

Ha, but the sun among us. Archibald MacLeish. *Fr.* Hamlet of A. Macleish. **CP-MacLA**

Ha ha ha! the sun is shining! Nothing but Nature. Ogden Nash. **CP-NashO**

Ha! Ha! Houdini! Patti Smith. **SP-SmitP**

Ha! Original Sin! Ogden Nash. **CP-NashO**

Ha' we lost the goodliest fere o' all. Ballad of the Goodly Fere. Ezra Pound. **CP-PounE**

Ha! whare ye gaun, ye crowlin' [*or* crowlan] ferlie! To a Louse [On Seeing One on a Lady's Bonnet at Church]. Robert Burns. **CP-BurnR**

Haakon Jarl. Leonard Nathan. **SP-NathL**

Habit of Mercy, The. John Hewitt. **CP-HewiJ**

Habit of Perfection, The. Gerard Manley Hopkins. **CP-HopkG**

Habitation. Margaret Atwood. **SP-AtwM1**

Habitation, The. Lewis Turco. **SP-TurcL**

Habitations. James McAuley.

"Fire's gone down: burnt pine, The." **SP-McAuJ**

"In this trance before sleep." **SP-McAuJ**

"Mother, sisters, brother." **SP-McAuJ**

Habits, The. Louis MacNeice. **CP-MacNL**

Hackney'd in business, wearied at that oar. Retirement. William Cowper. **CP-CowpW**

Had a bay stallion once that the Triple Bar C. He. Ron Koertge. **SP-KoerR**

Had died, but for now let us take some comfort. The Human Fabric. Robert Penn Warren. *Fr.* Fall Comes in Back-Country Vermont. **SP-WarrR**

Had everything including monogrammed sandwiches. Royce Newport Money. Ron Koertge. **SP-KoerR**

Had Fortune parted us / Fortune is blind. Christina Georgina Rossetti. **CP-RosC3**

Had God but made me a religious man. A Common Saw. Howard Nemerov. **CP-NemeH**

Had he and I but met. The Man He Killed. Thomas Hardy. **CP-HardT**

Had I a cave on some wild, distant shore. Song. Robert Burns. **CP-BurnR**

Had I a golden-broidered life? In Praise of Elizabeth. John Hewitt. **CP-HewiJ**

Had I a man's fair form, then might my sighs. To ———: "Had I a man's fair form, then might my sighs." John Keats. **CP-KeatJ**

Had I a pleasure you had not. Emily Dickinson. **SP-DickE**

Had I been at that scene. James McAuley. **SP-McAuJ** *Fr.* Witness.

Had I been the seventh son of a seventh son. The Cure for Warts. Paul Muldoon. **SP-MuldP**

Had I but lived a hundred years ago. At Lulworth Cove a Century Back. Thomas Hardy. **CP-HardT**

Had I but plenty of money, money enough and to spare. Up at a Villa— Down in the City. Robert Browning. **CP-BroR1**

Had I but the torrent's might. The Death of Hoel. Thomas Gray. **CP-GrayT**

Had I ever a young field. Alun Lewis. *Fr.* Pastorals. **CP-LewiA**

Had I known that the first was the last. Emily Dickinson. **CP-DickE**

Had I known that the heart. Prescience. Maya Angelou. **SP-AngeM**

Had I known that you were going. To One Who Might Have Borne a Message. Edna St. Vincent Millay. **CP-MillE**

Had I loved butt att that rate. William Herbert, Earl of Pembroke. *Fr.* Part 2. *Fr.* Urania. **CP-WrotM**

"Had I my will," the shrill wind sang. Che Farò Senza Euridice. Randall Jarrell. **CP-JarrR**

Had I not seen the Sun. Emily Dickinson. **CP-DickE**

Had I not This, or This, I said. Emily Dickinson. **CP-DickE**

Had I presumed to hope. Emily Dickinson. **CP-DickE**

Had I the Choice. Walt Whitman. **PP; Poetr; SoSe** *Fr.* Fancies at Navesink. **CP-WhitW**

Had I the heavens' embroidered cloths. He Wishes for the Cloths of Heaven. William Butler Yeats. **CP-YeatW**

Had I the power that have the will. Robert Louis Stevenson. **CP-StevR**

Had I the time I'd like to see. Aesthete's Renunciation. John Hewitt. **CP-HewiJ**

Had I the world for my enemy. Sadi, *tr. fr. Persian by* Ralph Waldo Emerson. **CP-EmerR**

Had I the Wyte She Bade Me. Robert Burns. **CP-BurnR**

Had I wist that now I wot. Sir Thomas Wyatt. **CP-WyatT**

Had it worked well even once? Can one point. The Community. Stephen Dobyns. **SP-DobyS**

Had Lucan hid the truth to please the time. To the Translator of Lucan [*or* Lucan's Pharsalia, 1614]. Sir Walter Ralegh. **CP-RaleW**

Had not / thought / of it. . . . Thinking. Robert Creeley. **CP-CreeR**

Had old Hippocrates, or Galen. Ben Jonson. **CP-JonsB** *Fr.* Volpone.

Had the gods loved me I had lain. Exile. Walter de la Mare. **CP-DeLaW**

Had there been falsehood in my breast. Emily Brontë. **CP-BronE**

Had these eyes never seen you. Adieu. Walter de la Mare. **CP-DeLaW**

Had this effulgence disappeared. Composed upon an Evening of Extraordinary Splendour and Beauty. William Wordsworth. **CP-WorW2**

Had this fair figure which this frame displays. On Seeing a Portrait of Mrs Montagu. Samuel Johnson. **CP-JohnS**

Had this one Day not been. Emily Dickinson. **CP-DickE**

Had those that dwell in error foul. Ben Jonson. **CP-JonsB** *Fr.* The Masque of Beauty.

Had we but world enough, and time. To His Coy Mistress. Andrew Marvell. **CP-MarvA**

Had we known the Ton she bore. Emily Dickinson. **CP-DickE**

Had we less to say to those we love. Emily Dickinson. **SP-DickE**

Had we our senses. Emily Dickinson. **CP-DickE**

Had you an Hour unengrossed. Emily Dickinson. **SP-DickE**

Had you died when we were together. The Fire. Louise Glück. **SP-GlücL**

Had you the eyes of a goat. The Disappointment. Robert Creeley. **CP-CreeR**

Had You Wept. Thomas Hardy. **CP-HardT**

Hada is light, Estela is harmony. The Three Sisters. Alfonso Cortes, *tr. fr. Spanish by* Thomas Merton. **CP-MertT**

Hadda be flashing like the Daily Double. Hadda Be Playing on the Jukebox. Allen Ginsberg. **CP-GinsA**

Hadda Be Playing on the Jukebox. Allen Ginsberg. **CP-GinsA**

Haddington Masque, The. Ben Jonson.

Epithalamion: "Up, youths and virgins, up, and praise." **CP-JonsB**

Hadn't heard of the atom bomb. The Seals in Penobscot Bay. Daniel Gerard Hoffman. **SP-HoffD**

Hadn't I been / aching, for you. Distance. Robert Creeley. **CP-CreeR**

Hadramauti. Rudyard Kipling. **CP-KiplR** *Fr.* Plain Tales from the Hills.

Hadrian's Address to His Soul When Dying. Emperor Hadrian, *tr. fr. Latin by* Byron.

"Ah! gentle, fleeting, wav'ring sprite." **CP-Byron**

(Adrian's Address to His Soul When Dying.) **CP-Byron**

Hadst thou lived in days of old. To [Mary Frogley]. John Keats. **CP-KeatJ**

'*H*advantageous' breathes Arrius heavily. Carmen 84. Catullus. *Fr.* Carmina. **CP-Catul**

Haec Fabula Docet. Robert Frost. **CP-FrosR**

Haec te jubent salvere, quod possunt, loca. Gerard Manley Hopkins. **CP-HopkG**

Haeredem (ut spes est) pariet nova nupta Scot Anglum. *accompanied by English translation.* Thomas Campion. *Fr.* Lord Hay's Mask.

Hafiz. Ralph Waldo Emerson. *Fr.* Quatrains. **CP-EmerR**

Hafiz since on the world. Hafiz, *tr.* by Ralph Waldo Emerson. **CP-EmerR** *Fr.* Odes.

Hafiz thou art from Eternity. Hafiz, *tr.* by Ralph Waldo Emerson. **CP-EmerR** *Fr.* Odes.

Hag is astride, The. Hag, The. Robert Herrick. **CP-HerrR**

Hag-Ridden. Robert Ranke Graves. **CP-GravR**

Hag, The ("Hag is astride, The"). Robert Herrick. **CP-HerrR**

Hag[g], The ("Staff[e] is now greased [*or* greas'd], The"). Robert Herrick. **CP-HerrR**

Haggard woman with a hacking cough and a deathless love whispers, The. Cups of Coffee. Carl Sandburg. **CP-SandC**

Hagia Sophia. Thomas Merton. **CP-MertT**

Dawn. The Hour of Lauds.

Early Morning. The Hour of Prime.

High Morning. The Hour of Tierce.

Sunset. The Hour of Compline. Salve Regina.

Haglets, The. Herman Melville. **SP-MelvH**

Hah! not what's wrote down, I reckon. I'm leaving. Hayden Carruth. *Fr.* The Sleeping Beauty. **CP-CarHL**

Haidee. Byron. **SeCePo** *Fr.* Canto the Fourth. *Fr.* Don Juan. **CP-Byron**

Haidée and Don Juan. Byron. **OBNC** *Fr.* Canto the Second. *Fr.* Don Juan. **CP-Byron**

Haidée and Juan carpeted their feet. Byron. **NOBRP** *Fr.* Canto the Third. *Fr.* Don Juan. **CP-Byron**

Haiku: "Eastern guard tower." Etheridge Knight. **SP-KnigE**

Haiku: "Two hours I've walked." Etheridge Knight. **SP-KnigE**

Haiku 1: "Slender Finger of Light, A." Etheridge Knight. **SP-KnigE**

Hail and beware the dead who will talk life until you are blue. A Newly Discovered "Homeric" Hymn. Charles Olson. **CP-OlsoC; SP-OlsoC**

Hail Bishop Valentine, whose day this is. Epithalamion, An, or Marriage Song on the Lady Elizabeth and Count Palatine Being Married on St. Valentine's Day. John Donne. **CP-DonnJ**

Hail! Childish slaves of social rules. Robert Louis Stevenson. **CP-StevR**

Hail, Common Sense! most rare of all! George Meredith. **CP-MerG2**

Hail, door, to husband and to father dear! Catullus. *See* Carmen 67: "Sweet entrance to a husband's pleasure."

Hail Energeia! hail, my native tongue. Christopher Smart. **SP-SmarC**

Hail, future friend, whose present I. Bathtub Thoughts. Wystan Hugh Auden. **CP-AudeW**

Hail, garden of confident hope! God's Acre. Christina Georgina Rossetti. **CP-RosC2**

Hail goes / dancing, The. Charles Kenneth Williams. **CP-WillC**

Hail, guest, and enter freely! All you see. Robert Louis Stevenson. **CP-StevR**

Hail, happy genius of this ancient pile! Lord Bacon's Birthday. Ben Jonson. **CP-JonsB**

Hail, heavenly gift! within the human breast. Benevolence. John Greenleaf Whittier. **CP-WhitJ**

Hail heav'nly harp, where Memnon's skill is shewn. Inscriptions on an Aeolian Harp. Christopher Smart. **SP-SmarC**

Hail, Holy Light[!]. John Milton. *See* Hail holy Light, ofspring [*or* offspring] of Heav'n [*or* Heaven] first-born.

Hail holy Light, ofspring [*or* offspring] of Heav'n [*or* Heaven] first-born. John Milton. **OAEL-1; SCV; TOF,** *ll.* 1–55; **NAEL-1,** *ll.* 1–587; **PeECV,** *ll.* 1–69; **FaBoEn; FiP; ImPo; LiTB; NOBE; NOSC; OBEV; OBS; PlP; WHA** *Fr.* Book III. *Fr.* Paradise Lost. **CP-MiltJ**

(Hail, Holy Light[!].) **FiP; ImPo; WHA,** *ll.* 1–55; **PlP,** *ll.* 1–55, *abr.;*

(Holy Light.) **NOBE,** *ll.* 1–55;

(Hymn to Light.) **FaBoEn,** *ll.* 1–50;

(Invocation to Light.) **NOSC,** *ll.* 1–55;

(Light.) **LiTB; OBEV; OBS,** *ll.* 1–55;

Hail holy Light, ofspring of Heav'n first-born. Book III. John Milton. *Fr.* Paradise Lost. **CP-MiltJ**

Hail, horrors, hail! ye ever gloomy bowers. Hymn to Ignorance. Thomas Gray. **CP-GrayT**

Hail is shot from heavy skies, The. A February Dawn. Wystan Hugh Auden. **CP-AudWJ**

Hail[!] lovely flower, first honour of the year! On a Daffodil, the First Flower the Author Had Seen That Year. Samuel Johnson. **CP-JohnS**

Hail Mary, full of grace, it once was said. An Epigram to the Queen, Then Lying In. 1630. Ben Jonson. **CP-JonsB**

Hail Mary—Mother of everything. Soldier on His Knees in the Snow. Marsden Hartley. **CP-HartM**

Hail, mildly pleasing solitude. Hymn on Solitude. James Thomson. **CP-ThomJ**

Hail, most high, most humble one! *ad. fr. the Medieval Latin* De Beata Virgine. Richard Crashaw. **CP-CrasR**

Hail, Muse! et caetera.--We left Juan sleeping. Byron. **OAEL-2** *Fr.* Canto the Third. *Fr.* Don Juan. **CP-Byron**

Hail, Muse! et caetera.--We left Juan sleeping. Canto the Third. Byron. *Fr.* Don Juan. **CP-Byron**

Hail native Language, that by sinews weak. At a Vacation Exercise [in the Col[l]e[d]ge [, Part Latin, Part English]]. John Milton. **CP-MiltJ**

Hail native language, that by sinews weak. John Milton. **JCP; OBS; PlP** *Fr.* At a Vacation Exercise [in the Col[l]e[d]ge [, Part Latin, Part English]. **CP-MiltJ**

Hail, noble face of noble friend! Christina Georgina Rossetti. **CP-RosC3**

Hail, orient Conqueror of Gloomy Night! Ode: The Morning of the Day Appointed for a General Thanksgiving. January 18, 1816. William Wordsworth. **CP-WorW2**

Hail, Poesie! thou nymph reserv'd! Sketch. Robert Burns. **CP-BurnR**

Hail! Power Divine, who by thy sole command. Hymn to God's Power. James Thomson. **CP-ThomJ**

Hail requiem of departed time. To the Clock. Ralph Waldo Emerson. **CP-EmerR**

Hail sacred spring, whose fruitful stream. *in imitation of* Cowley. Alexander Pope. **CP-PopeA**

Hail, sister springs! The Weeper. Richard Crashaw. **CP-CrasR**

Hail, Sympathy! thy soft idea brings. William Lisle Bowles. Byron. **OBNC** *Fr.* English Bards and Scotch Reviewers. **CP-Byron**

Hail, thairm-inspirin, rattlin Willie! Epistle to Captn Willm Logan at Park. Robert Burns. **CP-BurnR**

Hail the tree's meadow. A Madrigal for 3 Voices. Louis Zukofsky. **CP-ZukLS**

Hail to posterity! The Pennsylvania Pilgrim. John Greenleaf Whittier. **CP-WhitJ**

Hail to the Chief Who in Triumph Advances, *sels.* Sir Walter Scott. *Fr.* The Lady of the Lake.

(Boat Song.) **SP-ScotW**

Hail to the crown by Freedom shaped—to gird. The Churchyard among the Mountains. William Wordsworth. *Fr.* The Excursion. **CP-WorW2**

Hail to the fields—with Dwellings sprinkled o'er. Open Prospect. William Wordsworth. *Fr.* The River Duddon [A Series of Sonnets]. **CP-WorW2**

Hail to the man who upward strives. On Ignaz Moscheles. Robert Browning. **CP-BroR2**

Hail to the Sons of Roosevelt. Nicholas Vachel Lindsay. **CP-LindV**

Hail to thee, blithe Spirit! To a Skylark. Percy Bysshe Shelley. **CP-ShelP**

Hail to thee, Cambria; for the unfettered wind. On Leaving London for Wales. Percy Bysshe Shelley. **CP-ShelP**

Hail, Twilight, sovereign of one peaceful hour! William Wordsworth. **CP-WorW1**

Hail, venerable Night! Translation of a Greek Ode on Astronomy. Samuel Taylor Coleridge. **CP-ColeS**

Hail, Virgin Queen! o'er many an envious bar. Elizabeth. William Wordsworth. *Fr.* Ecclesiastical Sonnets. **CP-WorW2**

Hail[e] wedded love, mysterious law, true source. Their Wedded Love. John Milton. **NOSC; OBS; SeCePo** *Fr.* Book IV. **OAEL-1** *Fr.* Paradise Lost. **CP-MiltJ**

Hail, wond'rous Being, who in pow'r supreme. On the Eternity of the Supreme Being. Christopher Smart. **SP-SmarC**

Hail, ye hills and heaths of Ecclefechan! Terse Verse. Robert Browning. **CP-BroR2**

Hail, Zaragoza! If with unwet eye. William Wordsworth. **CP-WorW1**

Haile holy, and all-honour'd Tomb. To His Saviours Sepulcher: His Devotion. Robert Herrick. **CP-HerrR**

Hailstones. Seamus Heaney. **SP-HeanS**

Hain't you see my Mandy Lou. A Plantation Portrait. Paul Laurence Dunbar. **CP-DunbP**

Hair of her head could be a bed, The. Charles Henri Ford. *Fr.* Epigrams. **SP-FordC**

Hair, wax, rouge, honey, teeth, you buy. On a Battered Beauty. *Unknown, tr. fr. Greek by* William Cowper. **CP-CowpW**

Hair your a brook. Edward Estlin Cummings. **CP-CummE**

Haircut. Karl Shapiro. **SP-ShapK**

Hairdresser, Age 55, Dalston. Steve Griffiths. **SP-GrifS**

Hairless and worse than leathery, the skin. Corrib: An Emblem. Donald Davie. **CP-DavDo**

Hairnet with Stars, A. Ted Kooser. **SP-KoosT**

Hairs turn gold upon my thigh, The. The Value of Gold. Thom Gunn. **CP-GunnT**

Hairy full stern face, The. Attila. Kenneth Patchen. **CP-PatcK**

Hal o' the Draft. Rudyard Kipling. *Fr.* Puck of Pook's Hill.
Prophets at Home. **CP-KiplR**
Smuggler's Song, A. **CP-KiplR**

Halbert and Hob. Robert Browning. **CP-BroR2**

Halcyon. Hilda Doolittle. **CP-DoolH**

"I'm not here." **MoAmPo**

Halcyon Days. Walt Whitman. **CP-WhitW**

Half a league, half a league. The Charge of the Light Brigade. Tennyson. **CP-TennA**

Half a million dead wops. D'Annunzio. Ernest Hemingway. **CP-HemiE**

Half a moon is flaming in the south. Daybreak. William Carlos Williams. **CP-WilW1**

Half a year after war's end, Roosevelt and Hitler dead, Stalin tired. Greater Grandeur. Robinson Jeffers. **CP-JefR3**

Half a year, then a year and a half, then. Harriet. Robert Lowell. **SP-LoweR**

Half asleep on the cold grass. For a Stone Girl at Sanchi. Gary Snyder. **CP-SnydG**

Half awake in my Sunday nap. Three Green Windows. Anne Sexton. **CP-SextA**

Half-Ballad of Waterval. Rudyard Kipling. **CP-KiplR**

Half-bent Man. Richard Eberhart. **CP-EberR**

Half-Blind, The. David Herbert Lawrence. **CP-LawrD**

Half circle's come before we know. Italian Morning. Louise Bogan. **CP-BogaL**

Half close your eyelids, loosen your hair. He Thinks of Those Who Have Spoken Evil of His Beloved. William Butler Yeats. **CP-YeatW**

"Half-cracked" to Higginson, living. I Am in Danger—Sir—. Adrienne Rich. **CP-RicAE; SP-RicA1; SP-RicA2**

Half Dead. Christina Georgina Rossetti. **CP-RosC2**

Half-dollar in the hand of a gypsy, A. Fame If Not Fortune. Carl Sandburg. **CP-SandC**

Half drunk. Shit Time. Charles Bukowski. **SP-BukC1**

Half-Finished Letter, The. Robert Ranke Graves. **CP-GravR**

Half free / And half mad. George Oppen. *Fr.* Of Being Numerous. **CP-OppeG**

Half hearing, half in a veil, to lope. Roy Fisher. **SP-FishR** *Fr.* New Diversions.

Half hidden by trees, the sheer roof of the barn. The Barn. Stephen Spender. **CP-SpenS**

Half-hidden in a graveyard. The Stranger. Walter de la Mare. **CP-DeLaW**

Half-Moon, The. Richard Shelton. *Fr.* Five Lies About the Moon. **SP-ShelR**

Half Moon In a High Wind. Carl Sandburg. **CP-SandC**

Half Moon Shows a Face of Plaintive Sweetness, The. Christina Georgina Rossetti. **CP-RosC2**

Half-moon westers low, my love, The. Alfred Edward Housman. **CP-HousA**

Half my friends are dead. Sea Canes. Derek Walcott. **CP-WalcD**

Half of my life is gone, and I have let. Mezzo Cammin. Henry Wadsworth Longfellow. **SP-LongH**

Half of my youth I watched the soldiers. The Corporal. Thom Gunn. **CP-GunnT**

Half of the fellow father as he doubles. My World Is Pyramid. Dylan Thomas. **CP-ThomD**

Half of the harm that is done in this world. Malcolm Lowry. **CP-LowrM**

Half of what I say is meaningless. Julia. The Beatles. **CP-Beatl**

Half Past Home. Marge Piercy. **SP-PierM**

Half pear, cool, A. Fruit, for sculpture. Charles Tomlinson. **CP-TomlC**

Half reconciled, half healed: but. Roy Fisher. **SP-FishR** *Fr.* New Diversions.

Half squatter, half tenant (no rent). Manuelzinho. Elizabeth Bishop. **CP-BishE**

Half-starved goat followed the man, The. He Is Guarded by Crowds and Shackled with Formalities. Kenneth Patchen. **CP-PatcK**

Half-stripped trees, The. Approach of Winter. William Carlos Williams. **CP-WilW1**

Half Truth from Cape Town. Louis MacNeice. **CP-MacNL**

Half-turned, as if reluctant, the lady of water. Hayden Carruth. *Fr.* The Sleeping Beauty. **CP-CarHL**

"Half was not told me," said Sheba's Queen, The. She Came from The Uttermost Part of the Earth. Christina Georgina Rossetti. **CP-RosC2**

Half Way. Wystan Hugh Auden. **CP-AudeW**

Half Way. Carl Sandburg. **CP-SandC**

Half-way, for one commandment broken. Alfred Edward Housman. **CP-HousA**

Half-way House, The. Gerard Manley Hopkins. **CP-HopkG**

Half yet remains unsung, but narrower bound. John Milton. **FaBoPV** *Fr.* Book VII. *Fr.* Paradise Lost. **CP-MiltJ**

Halflives. Daniel Gerard Hoffman. **SP-HoffD**

Halfnaked children / met us singing for coins. Kodachromes of the Island. Robert Earl Hayden. **CP-HaydR**

Halfway. Adrienne Rich. **CP-RicAE; SP-RicA2**

Halfway between the rain and Washington. My Fifth Trip to Washington Ended in Northeast Delaware. Audre Lorde. **SP-LordA**

Halfway down Constitution Hill the report of a pistol. 1847. Brendan Galvin. **SP-GalvB**

Halfway to China. John Yau. **SP-YauJo**

Halfway up from the little harbor of sardine boats. The Net-Menders. Sylvia Plath. **CP-PlatS**

Halfworld, The. William Carlos Williams. **CP-WilW1**

Hall, a hall, A. Sir John Suckling. *Fr.* Brennoralt. **CP-SuckJ**

Hall Five. Hayden Carruth. **CP-CarHS** *Fr.* The Bloomingdale Papers.

Hallelujah. Leonard Cohen. **CP-CoheL**

Hallelujah! kneel and sing / Praises to the heav'nly king. Bible, *O.T. See* Psalm 148: "Praise ye the Lord. Praise ye the Lord from the heavens."

Hallelujah. Praise ye the Lord from the heavens. Bible, *O.T. See* Psalm 148: "Praise ye the Lord. Praise ye the Lord from the heavens."

Halley's Comet. Kenneth Rexroth. **SP-RexrK** *Fr.* The Lights in the Sky are Stars.

Hallow Eve with Spaces for Ghosts. Marge Piercy. **SP-PierM**

Halloween. Robert Burns. **CP-BurnR**

Halloween is black and orange. Broadway! Broadway! Gilbert Sorrentino. **SP-SorrG**

Halloween on Hennepin. Barton Sutter. **SP-SuttB**

Halloween Parade, The. "Lou Reed." **SP-ReedL**

Hallowee: A Glensman Speaks. John Hewitt. **CP-HewiJ**

Hallowing of Pain, The. Emily Dickinson. **CP-DickE**

Halls of Bedlam, The. Robert Ranke Graves. **CP-GravR**

Hallucinogenic Halleluuuu. Al Young. **CP-YounA**

Halsted Street Car. Carl Sandburg. **CP-SandC**

Halt, The. Kathleen Jessie Raine. **SP-RainK**

Halted against the shade of a last hill. Spring Offensive. Wilfred Owen. **CP-OwenW**

Halves. Stephen Dunn. **SP-DunnS**

Halves. Charles Kenneth Williams. **CP-WillC; SP-WillC**

Hamatreya. Ralph Waldo Emerson. **CP-EmerR**

Hamburg, 1929. Stephen Spender. **CP-SpenS**

Hamelin Town's in Brunswick. The Pied Piper of Hamelin. Robert Browning. **CP-BroR1**

Hamilton, if he rides you down, remember. On the Way. Edwin Arlington Robinson. **CP-RobiE**

Hamlen Brook. Richard Wilbur. **CP-WilbR**

Hamlet. Walter de la Mare. **CP-DeLaW**

Hamlet. Nicholas Vachel Lindsay. **CP-LindV**

Hamlet Father, The. Richard Eberhart. **CP-EberR**

Hamlet of A. Macleish. Archibald MacLeish. **CP-MacLA**
"Ay, sure, this is most brave."
"Bearing the long lance, their banners before them."
"But men have known."
"From these night fields and waters do men raise."
"Ha, but the sun among us."
"It is time we should accept."
"Let there be shelters built in the wild fern."
"MacLeish goes up the."
"Night after night I lie like this listening."
"Or play the strong boy, spit in the world's face, shout."
"Protect us help us forgive us help give."
"Where wilt thou lead me? Speak."
"Whether before have been."
"Why—what men were they that beneath the moon."

Hamlin Garland rose up from the Oklahoma powwow and declared with spirit. Money Musk. James Schuyler. **SP-SchuJ**

Hammer, The. Carl Sandburg. **CP-SandC**

Hammer, a bagful of staples, five strands of wire, A. Weathering. Martin Edmunds. **SP-EdmuM**

!Hammer and tongs! !The ducks are creating! With Sweetest Devotion from *All* the Little Animals to Their Most Beloved Harteebeeste. Malcolm Lowry. **CP-LowrM**

Hammerfest. Wystan Hugh Auden. **CP-AudeW**

Hammers pound there above. Along Galeana Street. Octavio Paz, *tr. fr. Spanish by* Elizabeth Bishop. **CP-BishE**

Hammers Pounding. Carl Sandburg. **CP-SandC**

Hammond Organ lubricates the air, The. The Widow. Miller Williams. **SP-WillM**

Hampshire. Donald Davie. **CP-DavDo**

Hampstead Highgate Finchley Hendon Muswell hill: rage loud. William Blake. **NOBRP** *Fr.* Jerusalem; The Emanation of the Giant Albion. **CP-BlakW**

Hampstead; the Horse Chestnut Trees. Thom Gunn. **CP-GunnT**

Hampton Beach. John Greenleaf Whittier. **CP-WhitJ**

Hampton Court. Alexander Pope. *See* Close by those meads, for ever crowned with flow'rs.

Hamster, The. Ogden Nash. *Fr.* The Astigmatic Naturalist. **CP-NashO**

Hanch, since he (lately) did interre his wife. Upon Hanch a Schoolmaster. Robert Herrick. **CP-HerrR**

Hand, The. Richard Eberhart. **CP-EberR**

Hand / holding on to this. Maintenant. Charles Tomlinson. **CP-TomlC**

Hand. Robinson Jeffers. **CP-JefR3**

Hand a shade of moonlight on the pillow, The. Non Ti Fidar. Louis Zukofsky. **CP-ZukLS**

Hand and the Shadow, The. Richard Eberhart. **CP-EberR**

Hand and Tongue, The. Robert Herrick. **CP-HerrR**

Hand as a Being, The. Wallace Stevens. **CP-StevW**

Hand at Callow Hill Farm, The. Charles Tomlinson. **CP-TomlC**

Hand between the candle and the wall, The. Poem with Rhythms. Wallace Stevens. **CP-StevW**

Hand by which no King but Serjeant dies, The. Pentadius, *tr. fr. Latin by* Richard Lovelace. **CP-LoveR**

Hand comforts held out to one who's sinking, A. Tashtego Believed Red. Malcolm Lowry. *Fr.* The Roar of the Sea and the Darkness. **CP-LowrM**

Hand Games. Marge Piercy. **SP-PierM**

Hand gripping the girl's thigh, pressed nearly upon. The Guitar Lesson. Stephen Dobyns. **SP-DobyS**

Hand is risen from the earth, The. The Familiar. Wendell Berry. **CP-BerrW**

Hand made a number, A. 2 8 3 2 5 6 7 4 5 4 9. Pablo Neruda, *tr. fr. Spanish by* Ben Belitt. **SP-NeruP**

Hand Me Down My Old School Sliding Pads, or, There's a Hint of Strawberry Leaves in the Air. Ogden Nash. **CP-NashO**

Hand-Mirror, A. Walt Whitman. **CP-WhitW**

Hand of Art here torpid lies, The. An Epitaph on William Hogarth. Samuel Johnson. **CP-JohnS**

Hand of man. The Stonecarver's Poem. Denise Levertov. **CP-LeveD**

Hand of sacred Cato bad to tear, The. Pentadius, *tr. fr. Latin by* Richard Lovelace. **CP-LoveR**

Hand of Snapshots, A. Louis MacNeice. **CP-MacNL**
   Back-Again, The.
   Gone-Tomorrow, The.
   Here-and-Never, The.
   Left-Behind, The. **FaBCIP**
   Once-in-Passing, The. **FaBCIP**

Hand over Hand. John Hewitt. **CP-HewiJ**

Hand penetrated an abyss of shadow, The. The Hand and the Shadow. Richard Eberhart. **CP-EberR**

Hand-Rolled Cigarettes. Stanley Jasspon Kunitz. **CP-KuniS**

Hand that aches for the pitchfork heft, The. Work. Robert Penn Warren. SaC *Fr.* Boy's Will, Joyful Labor without Pay, and Harvest Home (1918). **SP-WarrR**

Hand that rounded Peter's dome, The. Ralph Waldo Emerson. **EyDe** *Fr.* The Problem. **CP-EmerR**

Hand That Signed the Paper, The. Dylan Thomas. **CP-ThomD**

Handbook of Versification. Gilbert Sorrentino. **SP-SorrG**

Handclap. Muriel Rukeyser. **CP-RukeM**

Handfast Point. Frank Templeton Prince. **CP-PrinF**

Handfuls. Carl Sandburg. **CP-SandC**

Handing Down, The. Wendell Berry. **CP-BerrW**
   Conversation, The.
   Fern, The.
   Freedom of Loving, The.
   He Has Lived through Another Night.
   He Is in the Habit of the World.
   He Looks out the Window at the Town.
   He Takes His Time.
   Heaviness of His Wisdom, The.
   Light, The.
   New House, The.
   Old Man Is Older in History than in Time, The.
   Though He Can't Know Death, He Must Study Dying.
   Wilderness Starts towards Him, A.

Young Man, Thinking of the Old, The.

Handkerchiefs of Khaibar Khan, The. John Updike. **CP-UpdiJ**

Hands. Wystan Hugh Auden. **CP-AudeW**

Hands. Siv Cedering Fox. **SP-CedeS**

Hands, The. Robert Creeley. **CP-CreeR**

Hands. Robinson Jeffers. **CP-JefR2**

Hands. Archibald MacLeish. **CP-MacLA**

Hands and arms and legs and mouths. The Bitter Spring Again. Al Young. **CP-YounA**

Hands and Eyes. Louis MacNeice. **CP-MacNL**

Hands Are Paid. Robert Penn Warren. *Fr.* Boy's Will, Joyful Labor without Pay, and Harvest Home (1918). **SP-WarrR**

Hands, do what you're bid. The Balloon of the Mind. William Butler Yeats. **CP-YeatW**

Hands explore tentatively, The. The Feel of Hands. Thom Gunn. **CP-GunnT**

Hands, hard and veined all over. Orders for the Day. Theodore Roethke. **CP-RoetT**

Hands of God, The. David Herbert Lawrence. **CP-LawrD**

Hands of the Betrothed, The. David Herbert Lawrence. **CP-LawrD**

Hands of the Blindman, The. Tess Gallagher. **SP-GallT**

Hands off! thou tithe-fat plunderer! play. Elliott. John Greenleaf Whittier. **CP-WhitJ**

Handshake, the Entrance, The. John Berryman. **CP-BerrJ**

Handsome and clever and he went cruising. Edward Estlin Cummings. **CP-CummE**

Handsome and self-absorbed young man, The. True Love at Last. David Herbert Lawrence. **CP-LawrD**

Handsome Heart, The. Gerard Manley Hopkins. **CP-HopkG**

Handsome men wearing red ties walk past my window. Love. Grace Paley. **CP-PaleG**

Handsworth Liberties. Roy Fisher. **SP-FishR**
   "At the end of the familiar." **SP-FishR**
   "Falling away, A." **SP-FishR**
   "From here to there—." **SP-FishR**
   "Hit the bottom and spread out." **SP-FishR**
   "Lazily into the curve." **SP-FishR**
   "Mild blight, a sterility, A." **SP-FishR**
   "No dark in the body." **SP-FishR**
   "Open— / and away." **SP-FishR**
   "Riding out of the built-up." **SP-FishR**
   "Shines coldly away." **SP-FishR**
   "Something has to happen here." **SP-FishR**
   "Tall place, The." **SP-FishR**
   "Thin smoke, A." **SP-FishR**
   "This is where the game gets dirty." **SP-FishR**
   "Tranquility a manner." **SP-FishR**
   "Travesties of the world." **SP-FishR**

Handy Mole who plied no shovel, A. Christina Georgina Rossetti. **CP-RosC3**

Hang-Glider's Daughter, The. Marilyn Hacker. **SP-HackM**

Hang it all, Ezra Pound, there is only the one sestina. Sestina. Donald Hall. **CP-HallD**

Hang it all, Robert Browning. Canto 2. Ezra Pound. **AmPP; CoBMV; FaBoDD; HAP; MeMAP; MoAB; MoAmPo; NOBA; NePA; NoAM; OxBA; PoA; SP-PounE; TwAmPo** *Fr.* Cantos. **CP-PoCan**

Hang up Hooks, and shears[or Sheers] to scare. Another Charme for Stables. Robert Herrick. **CP-HerrR**

Hang up those dull, and envious fools. Another. In Defense of Their Inconstancy [or Inconstancie]. A Song. Ben Jonson. **CP-JonsB**

Hanged / if n / y in a real hot spell. Edward Estlin Cummings. **CP-CummE**

Hanged man on the gallows, The. Randall Jarrell. **CP-JarrR**

Hanging from fresh trees. Lemons, Lemons. Al Young. **CP-YounA**

Hanging from the beam. The Portent. Herman Melville. **SP-MelvH**

Hanging Man, The. Sylvia Plath. **CP-PlatS**

Hanging of the Mouse, The. Elizabeth Bishop. **CP-BishE**

Hangman, The. Anne Sexton. **CP-SextA**

Hangman at Home, The. Carl Sandburg. **CP-SandC**

Hangman's Great Hands, The. Kenneth Patchen. **CP-PatcK**

Hangman's Oak. Edna St. Vincent Millay. **CP-MillE**

Hangover. Al Young. **CP-YounA**

Hangover and Sick Leave. Charles Bukowski. **SP-BukC2**

Hangover—Reading Rilke, Schnitzler or Someone, A. Malcolm Lowry. **CP-LowrM**

Hangs by a thread. Two Riddles. Charles Simic. **SP-SimiC**

Hangs heavy / down into trees: dawn. Haze. James Schuyler. **CP-SchuJ**

Hank Fedder. Lewis Turco. *Fr.* Bordello. **SP-TurcL**

Hannibal. Robert Frost. **CP-FrosR**

Hanoverian silverware, this jug. On Generous Lines. Donald Davie. **CP-DavDo**

Hans Euler. Johann Gabriel Seidl, *tr. fr. German by* George Meredith. **CP-MerG2**

Hans-in-Kelder, Hans-in-Kelder. Wystan Hugh Auden. *Fr.* Shorts [1939–1947] ("Motionless, deep in his mind, lies the past the poet's forgotten"). **CP-AudeW**

Hans is killed / Now twilight begins at four. Breslau, November-December 1917. Jane Cooper. *Fr.* Threads: Rosa Luxemburg from Prison. **SP-CoopJ**

Hans, there are moments when the whole mind. Dedication. James Merrill. **SP-MerrJ**

Hansel and Gretel. Anne Sexton. **CP-SextA**

Hansome you are, and Proper you will be. To the Most Comely and Proper M. Elizabeth Finch. Robert Herrick. **CP-HerrR**

Hap. Thomas Hardy. **CP-HardT**

Hap happeth oft unlooked for. Sir Thomas Wyatt. **CP-WyatT**

Happenstance. Rita Dove. **SP-DoveR**

Happier, happier, now. Louis Zukofsky. *Fr.* 29 Songs. **CP-ZukLS**

Happiest Day, the Happiest Hour, The. Edgar Allan Poe. **CP-PoeEd**

Happiest February. Louis Zukofsky. *Fr.* Songs of Degrees. **CP-ZukLS**

Happiest of Hartebeeste Days and Devoted Love Eterne. Malcolm Lowry. **CP-LowrM**

Happily I had a sight. A Vow to Venus. Robert Herrick. **CP-HerrR**

Happiness. Stephen Dunn. **SP-DunnS**

Happiness. Louise Glück. **SP-GlücL**

Happiness. Malcolm Lowry. **CP-LowrM**

Happiness. Mary Oliver. **SP-OlivM**

Happiness. Wilfred Owen. **CP-OwenW**

Happiness. Carl Sandburg. **CP-SandC**

Happiness. Stevie Smith. **CP-SmitS**

Happiness in the Trees. Joseph Ceravolo. **SP-CeraJ**

Happiness Is a Warm Gun. The Beatles. **CP-Beatl**

Happiness Makes Up in Height for What It Lacks in Length. Robert Frost. **CP-FrosR**

"Happiness" without a cause, The. Emily Dickinson. **SP-DickE**

Happinesse. Robert Herrick. **CP-HerrR**

Happinesse to Hospitalitie, or a Hearty Wish to Good House-Keeping. Robert Herrick. **CP-HerrR**

Happy are men who yet before they are killed. Insensibility. Wilfred Owen. **CP-OwenW**

Happy are the mad for they are able. To the Mad Poets. Richard Eberhart. **CP-EberR**

Happy are those who have never tasted evil. Sophocles, *tr. by* Stephen Spender. **CP-SpenS** *Fr.* Antigone.

Happy birthday to you. Malcolm Lowry. **CP-LowrM**

Happy Boy, A. John Hewitt. **CP-HewiJ**

Happy Britannica. James Thomson. **OBEC; SeCePo** *Fr.* Summer. *Fr.* The Seasons. (Britannica.) **FaBoPP,** *ll.* 1–19;

Happy Cat, The. Randall Jarrell. **CP-JarrR**

Happy Change, The. William Cowper. *Fr.* Olney Hymns. **CP-CowpW**

Happy Childhood, A. William Matthews. **SP-MattW**

Happy Encounter, The. Walter de la Mare. **CP-DeLaW**

Happy End. Charles Simic. **SP-SimiC**

Happy Ending. Wystan Hugh Auden. **CP-AudeW**

Happy Ending of Mr. Train, The. Ogden Nash. **CP-NashO**

Happy Families. Louis MacNeice. **CP-MacNL**

Happy, happy glowing fire! Song of Four Faeries. John Keats. **CP-KeatJ**

Happy he whose eyes have view'd. Boethius, *tr. by* Samuel Johnson. **CP-JohnS; OBVE** *Fr.* Consolation of Philosophy, The ("De Consolacione Philosophie"). **CP-ChauG**

Happy Home, The. Samuel Taylor Coleridge. **CP-ColeS**

Happy Husband, The. Samuel Taylor Coleridge. **CP-ColeS**

Happy Is England! I Could Be Content. John Keats. **CP-KeatJ**

Happy [or Happie] is he, that from all business clear. The Praises of a Country Life. Horace, *tr. by* Ben Jonson. **CP-JonsB** *Fr.* Epodes.

Happy Is the Man. Bible, *O.T. See* Psalm 1: "Blessed is the man that walketh. . ."

Happy Isle. Edmund Spenser. **OBSC** *Fr.* The Faerie Queene. **CP-Spens**

Happy leave no clues. The frightened man, The. The Happy Man. John Hewitt. **CP-HewiJ**

Happy Life of a Country Parson, The, *in imitation of* Swift. Alexander Pope. **CP-PopeA**

Happy lip—breaks sudden, A. Emily Dickinson. **CP-DickE**

Happy love, this. Robert Creeley. **CP-CreeR**

Happy lover who has come, A. Tennyson. **EBVVPR; EnVR** *Fr.* In Memoriam A. H. H. **CP-TennA**

Happy Man, A. Carphyllides. **AWP** *Fr.* Variations of Greek Themes. **CP-RobiE**

Happy Man, The. Robert Creeley. **CP-CreeR**

Happy Man, The. John Hewitt. **CP-HewiJ**

Happy Man, The. James Thomson. **CP-ThomJ**

Happy Marriage, The. Archibald MacLeish.
  "And he had used love's dream of love before." **CP-MacLA**
  "Beauty is that Medusa's head." **CP-MacLA**
  "Beside her in the dark the chime." **CP-MacLA**
  "But she was both,—she was both loved and love." **CP-MacLA**
  "First I will tell you something of these two." **CP-MacLA**
  "He had used love or lust or what's between." **CP-MacLA**
  "He leans against the window-sill." **CP-MacLA**
  "Here, O wanderer, here is the hill and the harbor." **CP-MacLA**
  "Humid air precipitates, The." **CP-MacLA**
  "Love is the way that lovers never know." **CP-MacLA**
  "No doubt he'd once had eyes to see." **CP-MacLA**
  "O hide your eyes." **CP-MacLA**
  "Passing her in the day he had but dared." **CP-MacLA**
  "She was herself, not his, not anything." **CP-MacLA**
  "They say they are one flesh." **CP-MacLA**
  "Things he had loved because he knew them lost." **CP-MacLA**
  "This was not love but love's true negative." **CP-MacLA**
  "Throwing a careless pebble in the lake." **CP-MacLA**
  "Under an elm tree where the river reaches." **CP-MacLA**
  "Well, he was drunk. That much was clear." **CP-MacLA**
  "White of her Colonial, The." **CP-MacLA**
  "Whom do you see, she said, when you look out." **CP-MacLA**

Happy me! o happy sheepe!, *par. by* Richard Crashaw. Bible, *O.T. See* Psalm 23: "Lord is my shepherd, I shall not want, The."

Happy on Heimaey. "Hugh MacDiarmid." **SP-MacDH**

Happy people die whole, they are all dissolved in a moment, they have had what they wanted. Post Mortem. Robinson Jeffers. **CP-JefR1**

Happy Solitude—Unhappy Men. Jeanne Marie Bouvier de la Motte-Guyon, *tr. fr. French by* William Cowper. **CP-CowpW**

Happy songster! perch'd above. On the Grasshopper. *Unknown, tr. fr. Greek by* William Cowper. **CP-CowpW**

Happy that first white age! when wee. Boethius, *tr. by* Henry Vaughan. **NOSC; OBVE; PAI** *Fr.* Consolation of Philosophy, The ("De Consolacione Philosophie"). **CP-ChauG**

Happy the feeling from the bosom thrown. William Wordsworth. **CP-WorW2**

(To ———: "Happy the feeling from the bosom thrown.") **CP-WorW2**

Happy the Man. Joachim Du Bellay, *tr. fr. French by* Richard Wilbur. **CP-WilbR**

Happy the man who, journeying far and wide. Happy the Man. Joachim Du Bellay, *tr. fr. French by* Richard Wilbur. **CP-WilbR**

Happy the man who loves what / he has and worked for it also. The Puritan Ethos. Robert Creeley. **CP-CreeR**

Happy the man whose wish and care. Ode on Solitude. Alexander Pope. **CP-PopeA**

Happy the nations of the moral North! Donna Julia. Byron. **PoEL-4** *Fr.* Canto the First. **EnRP; NAEL-2; NoP; OAEL-2; PoE** *Fr.* Don Juan. **CP-Byron**

Happy? The very eye of the world. Charles Henri Ford. *Fr.* Epigrams. **SP-FordC**

Happy Thought. Robert Louis Stevenson. **CP-StevR**

Happy Three, The. Theodore Roethke. **CP-RoetT**

Happy time. Each walled town was a big family which fear kept together. At the Gates of Aerea. René Char, *tr. fr. French by* Thomas Merton. **CP-MertT**

Happy, too happy was the world. Boethius, *tr. fr. Latin.* **MLL,** *tr. by* Helen Waddell; *Fr.* Consolation of Philosophy, The ("De Consolacione Philosophie"). **CP-ChauG**

Happy Too Much. Boethius, *tr. by* Elizabeth I, Queen of England. **CTC** *Fr.* Consolation of Philosophy, The ("De Consolacione Philosophie"). **CP-ChauG**

Happy Townland, The. William Butler Yeats. **CP-YeatW**

Happy Tree, The. Wystan Hugh Auden. **CP-AudWJ**

Happy verses! that were prest. To Ethelinda. Christopher Smart. **SP-SmarC**

Happy young friends, sit by me. How the Robin Came. John Greenleaf Whittier. **CP-WhitJ**

Happy youth! that shalt possess[e]. To My Cousin (C.R.) Marrying My Lady (A.) Thomas Carew. **CP-CareT**

Happy's that man, to whom God gives. None Truly Happy Here. Robert Herrick. **CP-HerrR**

Harbinger to the Progress, The. John Donne. *Fr.* Of the Progres[se] of the Soule; the Second Anniversarie. **CP-DonnJ**

Harbingers are come. See, see their mark, The. The Forerunners. George Herbert. **CP-HerbG**

Harbor, The. Carl Sandburg. **CP-WilbR**

Harbor Dawn, The. Hart Crane. AP; AmPP; CMoP; CoBMV; CrMA; FaBV; GOA; LiTM; MoAB; MoAmPo; MoPo; NOBA; NYP; NePA; NoAM; OxBA; PrIm; SeCeV; TrGrPo; TwAmPo *Fr.* Powhatan's Daughter. *Fr.* The Bridge. **CP-CranH**

Harbour, The. Derek Walcott. **CP-WalcD**

Harbour Bridge, The. Thomas Hardy. **CP-HardT**

Hard & Noble Patience, A. David St. John. **SP-StJoD**

Hard are the two first staires unto a Crowne. Beginning, Difficult. Robert Herrick. **CP-HerrR**

Hard as hurdle arms, with a broth of goldish flue. Harry Ploughman. Gerard Manley Hopkins. **CP-HopkG**

Hard blood falls back in the manly fount. Shame. Karl Shapiro. *Fr.* Adam and Eve. **SP-ShapK**

Hard-Boiled Conservatives. David Herbert Lawrence. **CP-LawrD**

Hard by a rivers side a virgin faire. Joachim Du Bellay. *Fr.* The Visions of Bellay. **CP-Spens**

Hard, chilly colors. Conquest. William Carlos Williams. **CP-WilW1**

Hard climb. Worn flag steps, A. Baldungan Castle. James McAuley. **SP-McAuJ**

Hard cold fire of the northerner, The. Belfast. Louis MacNeice. **CP-MacNL**

Hard Core of Beauty, The. William Carlos Williams. **CP-WilW2**

Hard Daddy. Langston Hughes. **SP-HughL**

Hard Day's Night, A. The Beatles. **CP-Beatl**

Hard Death, A. May Sarton. **SP-SartM**

Hard. Hard. As she-cat whelped in desert mountains. Carmen 60. Catullus. *Fr.* Carmina. **CP-Catul**

Hard, hard to learn—. A Crystal Maze. William Carlos Williams. **CP-WilW1**

Hard is it to persuade the public mind of its plain duty & true interest. Ralph Waldo Emerson. **CP-EmerR**

Hard is my pillow. The Princess Recalls Her One Adventure. Edna St. Vincent Millay. **CP-MillE**

Hard is the doubt, and difficult to deeme. Edmund Spenser. **OAEL-1** *Fr.* The Faerie Queene. **CP-Spens**

Hard is the fate of him who loves. The Lover's Fate. James Thomson. **CP-ThomJ**

Hard journey—yes, A. Hayden Carruth. **CP-CarHS** *Fr.* The Clay Hill Anthology.

Hard Listener, The. William Carlos Williams. **CP-WilW1; CP-WilW2**

Hard Love Rock. Audre Lorde. **SP-LordA**

Hard Love Rock II. Audre Lorde. **SP-LordA**

Hard Part, The. Charles Kenneth Williams. **CP-WillC**

Hard Rain's A-Gonna Fall, A. "Bob Dylan." **CP-DylaB**

Hard Road, The. Louise McNeill. **SP-McNeL**

Hard Rock / was / "known not to take no shit." Hard Rock Returns to Prison from the Hospital for the Criminal Insane. Etheridge Knight. **SP-KnigE**

Hard Rock Returns to Prison from the Hospital for the Criminal Insane. Etheridge Knight. **SP-KnigE**

Hard sand breaks, The. Hermes of the Ways. Hilda Doolittle. **CP-DoolH**

Hard Sayings. John Gould Fletcher. **SP-FletJ** *Fr.* The Parables of Antichrist.

Hard seeds of hate I planted. Blight. Edna St. Vincent Millay. **CP-MillE**

Hard Structure of the World, The. Richard Eberhart. **CP-EberR**

Hard task! exclaim the undisciplined, to lean. At Bologna, in Remembrance of the Late Insurrections, 1837, Continued. William Wordsworth. **CP-WorW2**

Hard Times. William Carlos Williams. **CP-WilW2**

Hard Times in New York Town. "Bob Dylan." **CP-DylaB**

Hard water (water-). Afica. Charles Olson. **CP-OlsoC**

Hard Way, The. Robert Lowell. **SP-LoweR**

Hard Weather. George Meredith. **CP-MerG1**

Hard Work 1956. Stephen Dunn. **SP-DunnS**

Hardcastle Crags. Sylvia Plath. **CP-PlatS**

Harden now thy tyred hart, with more than flinty rage. Catullus. *See* Carmen 8: "Break off / fallen Catullus."

Hardening into Print. Richard Eberhart. **CP-EberR**

Harder lesson, to learn continence, A. Cymochles and Phaedria. Edmund Spenser. **OBSC** *Fr.* The Faerie Queene. **CP-Spens**

Harder perhaps than a newengland bed. Edward Estlin Cummings. **CP-CummE**

Hardest headlands / Gravel down, The. La Rose des Vents. Richard Wilbur. **CP-WilbR**

Hardly a day passes I don't think of him. Robert Schumann. Mary Oliver. **SP-OlivM**

Hardly a ghost left to talk with. The slavs moved on. The River Now. Richard Hugo. **CP-HugoR**

Hardly a one but here he is improved. After the Match. Donald Davie. **CP-DavDo**

Hardly ever, now, has a human face. The Human Face. David Herbert Lawrence. **CP-LawrD**

Hardness of Light, The. Donald Davie. **CP-DavDo**

Hardning of Hearts. Robert Herrick. **CP-HerrR**

Hardship of Accounting, The. Robert Frost. **FaBoCh; FaBoCo; FaFP; OBAL; WhC** *Fr.* Ten Mills. **CP-FrosR**

Hardship Put upon Ladies, The. Jonathan Swift. **CP-SwifJ**

Hardy Garden, The. Edna St. Vincent Millay. **CP-MillE**

Hardy Perennial. Richard Eberhart. **CP-EberR**

Hardy, thy brain is valiant, 'tis confessed. To Brain-Hardy. Ben Jonson. **CP-JonsB**

Hare, A. Walter de la Mare. **CP-DeLaW**

Hare: An Earlier Episode, The. William Everson. **SP-EverW**

Hare running for life in the sparse growth, The. The Hare: An Earlier Episode. William Everson. **SP-EverW**

Hare's Message. Thomas Merton. *Fr.* Two Moralities. *Fr.* South. *Fr.* The Geography of Lograire. **CP-MertT**

Hark, All You Ladies [That Do Sleep]. Thomas Campion. (Canto Primo.) **CP-CampT**

("Harke, al[l] you ladies that do sleep [*or* doo sleepe].") **CP-CampT**

Hark! Hark! / The dogs do bark! Hibiscus and Salvia Flowers. David Herbert Lawrence. **CP-LawrD**

Hark hark the lark, no it is not a lark, it is a robin singing like a lark. Who Called That Robin a Piccolo Player? Ogden Nash. **CP-NashO**

Hark, hearer, hear what I do; lend a thought now, make believe. Epithalamion. Gerard Manley Hopkins. **CP-HopkG**

Hark, how my Celia, with the choice. Celia Singing. Thomas Carew. **CP-CareT**

Hark, how the birds do sing. Man's Medley. George Herbert. **CP-HerbG**

Hark how the Mower Damon sung. Damon the Mower. Andrew Marvell. **CP-MarvA**

Hark, I hear the bells of Westgate. Westgate-on-Sea. Sir John Betjeman. **CP-BetjJ**

Hark in the Dusk! David Herbert Lawrence. **CP-LawrD**

Hark, Martha! some one knocks without; go, let him in, I pray! Hans Euler. Johann Gabriel Seidl, *tr. fr. German by* George Meredith. **CP-MerG2**

Hark, my soul! it is the Lord. Lovest Thou Me? William Cowper. **ChIV-2; HBV 1-2; OBEC** *Fr.* Olney Hymns. **CP-CowpW**

Hark news, O envy, thou shalt hear descried. Julia. John Donne. *Fr.* Elegies. **CP-DonnJ**

H[e]ark! O h[e]ark, you guilty trees. Orpheus to Woods. Richard Lovelace. **CP-LoveR**

Hark, plaintiff ghosts! Infernal furies, hark, *speech of Gynecia*. Sir Philip Sidney. **SP-SidnP** *Fr.* Arcadia.

Like Those Sick Folks. **OxBSP**

Hark, *said the dying man, and sighed*. The Valley of the Shadow of Death. "Lewis Carroll." **CP-CarrL**

Hark, some wild trumpeter, some strange musician. The Mystic Trumpeter. Walt Whitman. **CP-WhitW**

Hark! the Alleluias of the great salvation. Christina Georgina Rossetti. **CP-RosC2**

Hark! the cock proclaims the morning. St. Matthias. Christopher Smart. *Fr.* Hymns and Spiritual Songs for the Fasts and Festivals of the Church of England. **SP-SmarC**

Hark, the mavis' evening sang. Ca' the Yowes [to the Knowes]. Robert Burns. **CP-BurnR**

Hark! the owlet flaps her wing. Ghasta; or, The Avenging Demon!!! Percy Bysshe Shelley. *Fr.* Original Poetry by Victor and Cazire. **CP-ShelP**

Hark! the owlet flaps his wings. Fragment: Omens. Percy Bysshe Shelley. **CP-ShelP**

Hark! through the city, quiet, cool, and starred. Saturday Night: Horses Going to Pasture. John Gould Fletcher. **SP-FletJ**

Hark! 'Tis the Thrush, Undaunted, Undeprest. William Wordsworth. **CP-WorW2**

Hark! 'tis the twanging born o'er yonder bridge. The Winter Evening. William Cowper. *Fr.* The Task. **CP-CowpW**

Hark to the locusts in their shrill armadas. I Happen To Know. Ogden Nash. **CP-NashO**

Hark to the song of greeting! the tall trees. Summer. Christina Georgina Rossetti. **CP-RosC3**

Hark to the whimper of the sea-gull. The Sea-Gull. Ogden Nash. **CP-NashO**

Hark what, now loud, now low, the pining flute complains. The Flute. Jelaluddin Rumi, *sometimes at. to* Hilali, *tr. fr.* Persian by Ralph Waldo Emerson. **CP-EmerR**

Harke, al[l] you ladies that do sleep [*or* doo sleepe]. Thomas Campion. *See* Hark, All You Ladies [That Do Sleep].

Harke shee is called, the parting houre is come. Hymn in the Assumption. Richard Crashaw. **CP-CrasR**

Harkness light! Another hour spelled out, The. Quartermaster at the Wheel. Malcolm Lowry. *Fr.* The Roar of the Sea and the Darkness. **CP-LowrM**

Harlem. Langston Hughes. **SP-HughL** *Fr.* Lenox Avenue Mural.

Harlem. Etheridge Knight. *Fr.* Indiana Haiku—2. **SP-KnigE**

Harlem Hopscotch. Maya Angelou. **SP-AngeM**

Harlem Night Song. Langston Hughes. **SP-HughL**

Harlequin / is said to assimilate himself to a condition. Hayden Carruth. *Fr.* North Winter. **CP-CarHL**

Harley, the nation's great support. Horace, Epistle VII, Book I: Imitated and Addressed to the Earl of Oxford. Jonathan Swift. **CP-SwifJ**

Harlot squatted, The. Jesus Raises Up the Harlot. Anne Sexton. **CP-SextA**

Harm. Charles Kenneth Williams. **SP-WillC**

Harm of Years is on him, The. Emily Dickinson. **CP-DickE**

Harmless Streets. Tess Gallagher. **SP-GallT**

Harmonica Humdrums. Carl Sandburg. **CP-SandC**

Harmonies of Excess, The. Thomas Merton. *Fr.* Cables to the Ace. **CP-MertT**

Harmony of colours, features, grace, The. Epitaph on the Lady S.: Wife of Sir W.S. Thomas Carew. **CP-CareT**

Harold, are you asleep? Harold's Leap. Stevie Smith. **CP-SmitS**

Harold Fogel Could Be Anywhere. Gary Gildner. **SP-GildG**

Harold's Leap. Stevie Smith. **CP-SmitS**

Harold's Song. Sir Walter Scott. *See* Rosabelle.

Harp, The. Ralph Waldo Emerson. **CP-EmerR**

Harp at Nature's advent strung, The. The Worship of Nature. John Greenleaf Whittier. **CP-WhitJ**

Harp! couldst thou venture on thy boldest string. Afflictions of England. William Wordsworth. *Fr.* Ecclesiastical Sonnets. **CP-WorW2**

Harp of Aengus, The. William Butler Yeats. **CP-YeatW**

Harp of the North, Farewell! The Hills Grow Dark. Sir Walter Scott. *Fr.* The Lady of the Lake.
(Farewell.) **SP-ScotW**

Harp of the North! that mouldering long hast hung. The Chase. Sir Walter Scott. *Fr.* The Lady of the Lake.

Harp of wild and dream-like strain. Emily Brontë. **CP-BronE**

Harp Song of the Dane Women. Rudyard Kipling. **CP-KiplR** *Fr.* The Knights of the Joyous Venture. *Fr.* Puck of Pook's Hill.

Harp the Monarch Minstrel Swept, The. Byron. **CP-Byron**

Harpies. Malcolm Lowry. **CP-LowrM**

Harpist's Dream, The. Dabney Stuart. **SP-StuaD**

Harps in Heaven. Nicholas Vachel Lindsay. **CP-LindV**

Harried / earth is swept, The. The Wind Increases. William Carlos Williams. **CP-WilW1**

Harriet. Robert Lowell. **SP-LoweR**

Harriet. Robert Lowell. **SP-LoweR**

Harriet. Robert Lowell. **SP-LoweR**

Harriet Beecher Stowe. Paul Laurence Dunbar. **CP-DunbP**

Harriet! To see such Circumspection. To Harriet ("Harriet! To see such Circumspection"). Byron. **CP-Byron**

Harriet's Dream. Robert Lowell. **SP-LoweR**

Harrison loves my country too. A Case for Jefferson. Robert Frost. **CP-FrosR**

Harrison Street Court. Carl Sandburg. **CP-SandC**

Harrow, The. Donald Davie. **CP-DavDo**

Harrow-on-the-Hill. Sir John Betjeman. **CP-BetjJ**

Harrowed by These Apprehensions He Resolved to Commit Himself to the Mercy of the Storm. Kenneth Patchen. **CP-PatcK**

Harry. Robert Creeley. **CP-CreeR**

Harry has written / all he knows. Names. Robert Creeley. **CP-CreeR**

Harry of Hereford, Lancaster, and Derby. The School Play. James Merrill. **SP-MerrJ**

Harry Orchard. Richard Shelton. **SP-ShelR**

Harry, our King in England, from London town is gone. King Henry VII. And the Shipwrights. Rudyard Kipling. **CP-KiplR**

Harry Ploughman. Gerard Manley Hopkins. **CP-HopkG**

Harry Rouclere!!! / ever hear of him? Ha! Ha! Houdini! Patti Smith. **SP-SmitP**

Harry Semen. "Hugh MacDiarmid." **SP-MacDH**

Harry, whose tuneful[l] and well-measured [*or* well-measur'd] song. John Milton. **CP-MiltJ**
(Sonnet 13: "Harry, whose tunefull and well-measur'd song.") **CP-MiltJ**

Harsh Climate. Charles Simic. **SP-SimiC**

Harsh Country, The. Theodore Roethke. **CP-RoetT**

Harsh in the face. Self-Portraits and Their Mirrors. Roy Fisher. **SP-FishR**

Harsh Judgment, The. Stanley Jasspon Kunitz. **CP-KuniS**

Harsh World That Lashest Me. Countee Cullen. **CP-CullC**

Harsk, Harsk. Carl Sandburg. **CP-SandC**

Harsk, harsk, the wind blows tonight. Harsk, Harsk. Carl Sandburg. **CP-SandC**

Hart Crane. Robert Creeley. **CP-CreeR**

Hart Crane 2. Robert Creeley. **CP-CreeR**

Hart-Leap Well. William Wordsworth. **CP-WorW1**

Hartebeeste Both Grave and Gay, The. Malcolm Lowry. **CP-LowrM**

Harteebeeste Is Here Again, The. Malcolm Lowry. **CP-LowrM**

Harteebeeste is very good, The. The Hartebeeste Both Grave and Gay. Malcolm Lowry. **CP-LowrM**

Harteebeeste with flying hoof, The. Malcolm Lowry. **CP-LowrM**

Hartnett in Worcester. David Markson. **CP-MarkD**

Hart's-Horn Tree, near Penrith. William Wordsworth. **CP-WorW2**

Harum-scarum haze on the Pollock streets / The fleet drifts in on an angry tidal wave. Lines for Lauren Owen. Ted Berrigan. **SP-BerrT** *Fr.* The Sonnets.

Harum-scarum haze on the Pollock streets / Where Snow White sleeps among the silent dwarfs. Ted Berrigan. **SP-BerrT** *Fr.* The Sonnets.

Harun Omar and Master Hafiz. Puella Mea. Edward Estlin Cummings. **CP-CummE**

Harvard '61: Battle Fatigue. Robert Penn Warren. *Fr.* Two Studies in Idealism: Short Survey of American and Human History. **SP-WarrR**

Harvard Stadium. Richard Eberhart. **CP-EberR**

Harvest. John Haines. **SP-HainJ**

Harvest / of nail parings, A. Notes on the Death of Nels Paulssen, Farmer, at the Ripe Old Age of 93. Ted Kooser. **SP-KoosT**

Harvest. Carl Sandburg. **CP-SandC**

Harvest approaches with its bustling day. August. John Clare. **SP-ClarJ** *Fr.* The Shepherd's [*or* Shepheards] Calendar.

Harvest Bow, The. Seamus Heaney. **SP-HeanS**

Harvest Festival: at Ozleworth. Charles Tomlinson. **CP-TomlC**

Harvest Home. John Dryden. *Fr.* King Arthur.
(Song by Comus and Three Peasants, A.) **SP-DrydJ**

Harvest Home, A. Howard Nemerov. **CP-NemeH**

Harvest Hymn. Sir John Betjeman. **CP-BetjJ**

Harvest Hymn. John Greenleaf Whittier. **OHIP** *Fr.* For an Autumn Festival. **CP-WhitJ**

Harvest Moon, The. Ted Hughes. **SP-HughT**

Harvest of learning I have reaped. Kathleen Jessie Raine. **SP-RainK**

Harvest shall flourish in wintry weather, The. Merlins Prophecy. William Blake. **CP-BlakW**

Harvest Sunset. Carl Sandburg. **CP-SandC**

Harvest-Supper, The. Thomas Hardy. **CP-HardT**

Harvesters. Chuck Miller. **SP-MillC**

Harvey, the happy above happiest men. To the Right Worshipfull, My Singular Good Frend, Master Gabriell Harvey, Doctor of the Lawes. Edmund Spenser. **NoSic** *Fr.* Commendatory Sonnets. **CP-Spens**

Has a new double-knit suit with slightly flared. He. Ron Koertge. **SP-KoerR**

Has All. Emily Dickinson. **SP-DickE**

Has Any One Supposed It Lucky to Be Born? Walt Whitman. **NAs** *Fr.* Song of Myself.

Has Anybody Seen My Noumenon? Ogden Nash. **CP-NashO**

Has auld Kilmarnock [*or* K*********] seen the Deil? Tam Samson's Elegy. Robert Burns. **CP-BurnR**

Has bath and shave. Homecoming. Derek Mahon. **SP-MahoD**

Has-Been, The. Carl Sandburg. **CP-SandC**

Has conquered. He has surrendered everything. The Knight. Ted Hughes. **SP-HughT**

Has not led us into these waste seas. The Shadowy Waters. William Butler Yeats. **CP-YeatW**

Has he tempered the viol's wood, *subsel.* Ezra Pound. *See* Canto 81: "Zeus lies in Ceres' bosom."

Has never written me a letter himself. He. Ron Koertge. **SP-KoerR**

Has no one said those daring. Two Years Later. William Butler Yeats. **CP-YeatW**

Has no sense of honor. I challenged him. Death. Richard Shelton. **SP-ShelR**

Has not altered. Spenser's Ireland. Marianne Craig Moore. **CP-MoorM**

Has not yet been cut. The Stone. Ted Hughes. **SP-HughT**

Has packed the Supreme Court. Canto 100. Ezra Pound. *Fr.* Cantos. **CP-PoCan**

Has the sum. Louis Zukofsky. **CP-ZukLS**

Has thine enemy slandered thy house. Hafiz, *tr.* by Ralph Waldo Emerson. **CP-EmerR** *Fr.* Odes.

Has Your Soul Sipped? Wilfred Owen. **CP-OwenW**

Haschish, The. John Greenleaf Whittier. **CP-WhitJ**

Hasn't the sky? Returned from moving the other. Clepsydra. John Ashbery. **SP-AshbJ**

Hast Du Dich Verirrt? Stevie Smith. **CP-SmitS**

Hast ever seen a man. Epigramme. William Carlos Williams. **CP-WilW1**

Hast Never Come to Thee an Hour. Walt Whitman. **CP-WhitW**

Hast thou a charm to stay the morning-star. Hymn before Sunrise, in the Vale of Chamouni. Samuel Taylor Coleridge. **CP-ColeS**

Hast thou a friend? Thou hast indeed. On a True Friend. *Unknown, tr. fr. Greek by* William Cowper. **CP-CowpW**

Hast thou attempted greatnesse? then go on. Regression Spoiles Resolution. Robert Herrick. **CP-HerrR**

Hast thou begun an act? ne're then give o're. Perseverance. Robert Herrick. **CP-HerrR**

Hast thou determined to strangle me, O God? Man Hauling a Wagon. David Herbert Lawrence. *Fr.* Bits. **CP-LawrD**

Hast thou from the caves of Golconda a gem. On Receiving a Curious Shell, and a Copy of Verses, from the Same Ladies. John Keats. **CP-KeatJ**

Hast thou named all the birds without a gun? Forbearance. Ralph Waldo Emerson. **CP-EmerR**

Hast thou not seen, officious with delight. Pedro Calderón de la Barca, *tr. by* Shelley. **CP-ShelP** *Fr.* Cisma de Inglaterra.

Hast thou seen the down i' th' air. A Song to a Lute. Sir John Suckling. *Fr.* The Sad One. **CP-SuckJ**

Hast thou seen, with flash incessant. William Wordsworth. *Fr.* Inscriptions Supposed to Be Found in and near a Hermit's Cell; 1818. **CP-WorW2**

Hast thou then nought wiser to bring. The Catechism. Walter de la Mare. **CP-DeLaW**

Hast thou then survived. William Wordsworth. **EvOK; Par** *Fr.* Address to My Infant Daughter, Dora on Being Reminded That She Was a Month Old That Day, September 16. **CP-WorW1**

Hasta la Victoria Siempre. Chuck Miller. **SP-MillC**

Haste Hurtfull. Robert Herrick. **CP-HerrR**

Haste is unhappy: what we Rashly do. Haste Hurtfull. Robert Herrick. **CP-HerrR**

Haste thee harsh verse as fast as thy lame measure. To Mr. T. W. John Donne. **CP-DonnJ**

Haste thee, nymph, and bring with thee. John Milton. **FaBV; GN** *Fr.* L'Allegro. **CP-MiltJ**

(Mirth, with Thee I Mean to Live.) **FaBV**

Hasten to your own gun, to your own star, to your own tribe. But the Images of His Former Dreams Still Haunted Him. Kenneth Patchen. **CP-PatcK**

Hastily Adam our driver swallowed a curse in the darkness. *parody of* Arthur Clough. Rudyard Kipling. **CP-KiplR** *Fr.* The Muse among the Motors.

Hastings! I knew thee young, and of a mind. To Warren Hastings. William Cowper. **CP-CowpW**

Hat. Shel Silverstein. **SP-SilS2**

Hat, The. Stevie Smith. **CP-SmitS**

Hat on the table, The. Headdress. Rita Dove. **SP-DoveR**

Hat Salesman and a Capable Ruler, A. Chuang Tzu, *tr. fr. Chinese by* Thomas Merton. **CP-MertT**

Hatband, The. Thomas Hardy. **CP-HardT**

Hate. Charles Olson. **CP-OlsoC**

Hate. Carl Sandburg. **CP-SandC**

Hate blows a bubble of despair into. Edward Estlin Cummings. **CP-CummE; SP-CummE**

Hate is only one of many responses. Poem. Frank O'Hara. **SP-OharF**

Hate-Song, A. Percy Bysshe Shelley. **CP-ShelP**

Hate whom ye list for I care not. Sir Thomas Wyatt. **CP-WyatT**

Hateful are those false themes of speculation. Sonnet. George Meredith. **CP-MerG2**

Hateful cure with hate to heal, A, *speech of Dametas.* Sir Philip Sidney. **SP-SidnP** *Fr.* Arcadia.

Hater he came and sat by a ditch, A. A Hate-Song. Percy Bysshe Shelley. **CP-ShelP**

Hath aged winter, fleg'd with feathered raine. Elegy upon the Death of Mr. Stanninow Fellow of Queenes Colledge. Richard Crashaw. **CP-CrasR**

Hath onely Anger an Omnipotence. Upon the Asse That Bore Our Saviour. Richard Crashaw. **CP-CrasR**

Hatred. Frank O'Hara. **SP-OharF**

Hatred and vengeance, my eternal portion. Lines Written During a Period of Insanity. William Cowper. **CP-CowpW**

Hatred of Men with Black Hair. Robert Bly. **SP-BlyR**

("I hear spokesmen praising Tshombe, and the Portuguese.") **SP-BlyR**

Hatred of Sin. William Cowper. *Fr.* Olney Hymns. **CP-CowpW**

Hatred of the Old River. Richard Eberhart. **CP-EberR**

Hats. Carl Sandburg. **CP-SandC**

Hats. James Schuyler. **CP-SchuJ**

"Hats off," cried the midget. Thomas Merton. *Fr.* Cables to the Ace. **CP-MertT**

Hats, where do you belong? Hats. Carl Sandburg. **CP-SandC**

Hattie Bloom. Mary Oliver. **SP-OlivM**

Hattie Rice Rich. Adrienne Rich. *Fr.* Grandmothers. **SP-RicA2**

Hatton's "God of War." George Meredith. **CP-MerG2**

Haughty Snail-King, The. Nicholas Vachel Lindsay. **CP-LindV**

Haughty Spaniard, who, with hopeless eye, The. Prologue to William Godwin, *Antonio: or, The Soldier's Return.* Charlotte Smith. **CP-SmitC**

Haunched like a faun, he hooed. Faun. Sylvia Plath. **CP-PlatS**

Haunted. Walter de la Mare. **CP-DeLaW**

Haunted Country. Robinson Jeffers. **CP-JefR1**

Haunted House, The. Robert Ranke Graves. **CP-GravR**

Haunted Landscape. John Ashbery. **SP-AshbJ**

Haunted Oak, The. Paul Laurence Dunbar. **CP-DunbP**

Haunted of Beauty, like the marvelous youth. An Artist of the Beautiful. John Greenleaf Whittier. **CP-WhitJ**

Haunted Palace, The, From "The Fall of the House of Usher." Edgar Allan Poe. **CP-PoeEd**

Haunted Tree; To———, The. William Wordsworth. **CP-WorW2**

Haunter, The. Thomas Hardy. **CP-HardT**

Haunting, A. Ted Hughes. *Fr.* Scapegoats and Rabies. **SP-HughT**

Haunting Fingers. Thomas Hardy. **CP-HardT**

Haunting Poe's Baltimore. Allen Ginsberg. **CP-GinsA**

Haunts. Carl Sandburg. **CP-SandC**

Haunts me the lugubrious shape. Half-bent Man. Richard Eberhart. **CP-EberR**

Havana Dreams. Langston Hughes. **SP-HughL**

Havana 1953. Allen Ginsberg. **CP-GinsA**

Havana Rose. Hart Crane. **CP-CranH**

Have a Genuine American Horror-&-Mist on the Rocks. John Berryman. **CP-BerrJ**

Have a Good Time. Wystan Hugh Auden. **CP-AudeW**

Have a Seat behind the Potted Palm, Sir. Ogden Nash. **CP-NashO**

Have another helping of blue snow. Bleeding Gums. James Schuyler. **CP-SchuJ**

Have any like Myself. Emily Dickinson. **CP-DickE**

Have danced in ecstasy. Poem for the Liberation of Southern Africa. Etheridge Knight. **SP-KnigE**

Have dead men long to wait?— / There is a certain term. What Good Shall My Life Do Me? Christina Georgina Rossetti. **CP-RosC2**

Have Done With It. David Herbert Lawrence. **CP-LawrD**

Have ever you harked to the jackass wild. The Wild Jackass. Ogden Nash. **CP-NashO**

Have fáir fallen, O fáir, fáir have fállen, so déar. Henry Purcell. Gerard Manley Hopkins. **CP-HopkG**

Have, have ye no regard, all ye. His Saviour['s] Words, Going to the Cross[e]. Robert Herrick. **CP-HerrR**

Have I a hundred years since or. Jean Sans Terre Leads the Caravan. Iwan Goll, *tr. fr. French by* William Carlos Williams. **CP-WilW2**

Have I broken the smaller tabernacles, O Lord? Broken Tabernacles. Carl Sandburg. **CP-SandC**

Have I caught my heav'nly jewel. Second Song. Sir Philip Sidney. **NoSic** *Fr.* Astrophil and Stella. **SP-SidnP**

Have I lost my liberty. Mary Sidney, Countess of Montgomery Wroth. *Fr.* Part 1. *Fr.* Urania. **CP-WrotM**

Have I no weapon-word for thee—some message brief and fierce? To the Pending Year. Walt Whitman. **CP-WhitW**

Have I not blessed thee? Then go forth; nor fear. To His Book[e]. Robert Herrick. **CP-HerrR**

Have I not striven, my God, and watched and prayed? Christina Georgina Rossetti. **CP-RosC2**

Have I not voyaged, friend beloved, with thee. In Quest. John Greenleaf Whittier. **CP-WhitJ**

Have I not walked without an upward look. Bravado. Robert Frost. *Fr.* Five Nocturnes. **CP-FrosR**

Have I seen her? Portrait of a Young Man with a Bad Heart. William Carlos Williams. **CP-WilW1**

Have I told any man to be a liar for my sake? Questionnaire. Carl Sandburg. **CP-SandC**

Have Me. Carl Sandburg. **CP-SandC**

Have me in the blue and the sun. Have Me. Carl Sandburg. **CP-SandC**

Have men beheld the graces dance. Ben Jonson. **CP-JonsB** *Fr.* Love Restored.

Have mercy, Lord! Sinner. Langston Hughes. **SP-HughL**

Have mercy, Thou my God; mercy, my God. Out of the Deep. Christina Georgina Rossetti. **CP-RosC3**

Have mercy upon me, O God, according to thy lovingkindness. Psalm 51. Bible, *O.T.* *Fr.* Psalms. **CP-Psal**

Have Patience. Christina Georgina Rossetti. **CP-RosC3**

Have speciall care, that valiant povertie, *ad. fr. Latin of* Juvenal. Sir Walter Ralegh. **CP-RaleW**

"Have, then, thy wish!" He whistled shrill. The Ambuscade. Sir Walter Scott. **SP-ScotW** *Fr.* The Lady of the Lake.

Have they not, the lonely, understood those. The Lonely Return to the Lonely, the divine to the Divine—Proclus. Marsden Hartley. **CP-HartM**

Have we heard morning being broken. Some Moments with Locatelli. Marsden Hartley. **CP-HartM**

Have we managed to fade them out like God? The Concentration Camps. May Sarton. **BTR; SRLS** *Fr.* The Invocation to Kali. **SP-SartM**

Have we now not spent three years waiting. Three Years Waiting. Robert Ranke Graves. **CP-GravR**

Have ye beheld (with much delight). Upon the Nipples of Julia's Breast. Robert Herrick. **CP-HerrR**

Have ye heard of our hunting, o'er mountain and glen. The Hunters of Men. John Greenleaf Whittier. **CP-WhitJ**

Have ye seen the caterpillar. Ralph Waldo Emerson. **CP-EmerR**

Have ye seen the tusky boar. Caradoc. Thomas Gray. **CP-GrayT**

Have you any old clothes to sell? The Old Clothes Man. Stanley Jasspon Kunitz. **CP-KuniS**

Have you been to the land of carnivorous birds. Death Row. Richard Shelton. **SP-ShelR**

Have you been to The Land of Happy. The Land of Happy. Shel Silverstein. **SP-SilS2**

Have you bought a suit at Spand and Spitz? Consider the Lapel, Sir. Ogden Nash. **CP-NashO**

Have you built your ship of death, oh have you? *draft vers.* David Herbert Lawrence. **CP-LawrD**

Have you crouched with your rifle, in woods, in autumn. Arrogant Law. Robert Penn Warren. **SP-WarrR**

Have you ever been in a room. Insomnia. Charles Bukowski. **SP-BukC2**

Have you ever lost your early start on a six-hundred-mile trip and. I Want a Drink of Water, but Not from the Thermos. Ogden Nash. **CP-NashO**

Have you ever seen / anything / in your life. The Sun. Mary Oliver. **SP-OlivM**

Have you ever seen. Hayden Carruth. **CP-CarHS** *Fr.* The Clay Hill Anthology.

Have you ever seen the little piggies crawling in the dirt. Piggies. George Harrison. **CP-Beatl**

Have You Forgotten? Christina Georgina Rossetti. **CP-RosC3**

Have you forgotten what we were like then. Animals. Frank O'Hara. **SP-OharF**

Have you gone skiing down hill through snow. The Arctic Remembered. Edwin Rolfe. **CP-RolfE**

Have you got a Brook in your little heart. Emily Dickinson. **CP-DickE**

Have you heard about Mr. Bratuscha? Cannibal Bratuscha. Muriel Rukeyser. **CP-RukeM**

Have you heard of tiny Melinda Mae. Melinda Mae. Shel Silverstein. **SP-SilS2**

Have You Killed Your Man for Today? Kenneth Patchen. **CP-PatcK**

Have you learn'd lessons only of those who admired you, and were tender with you, and stood aside for you? Stronger Lessons. Walt Whitman. **CP-WhitW**

Have you news of my boy Jack? My Boy Jack. Rudyard Kipling. **CP-KiplR**

Have you no Bananas, simple townsmen all. A Song of Bananas. Rudyard Kipling. **CP-KiplR**

Have you not been paid servants in love's house. Cantico Per Lo Tuo Amore IV. James Liddy. **CP-LiddJ**

Have you not heard the song. The Song That Sounds like This. James Fenton. **SP-FentJ**

Have you not read. Despite and Still. Robert Ranke Graves. **CP-GravR**

Have you noticed? Ghosts. Mary Oliver. **SP-OlivM**

Have you read the biography of Mr. Schwellenbach? You can miss. The Strange Case of the Cautious Motorist. Ogden Nash. **CP-NashO**

Have you seen / dylan's dog. Dog Dream. Patti Smith. **SP-SmitP**

Have you seen men handed refusals. Carl Sandburg. **CP-SandC** *Fr.* The People, Yes. **CP-SandC**

Have You Seen This Movie? Allen Ginsberg. **CP-GinsA**

Have you time for a story. Charity Overcoming Envy. Marianne Craig Moore. **CP-MoorM**

Have You Tried Staying Awake? or, They'll Find a Way to Stop That, Too. Ogden Nash. **CP-NashO**

Haverhill. John Greenleaf Whittier. **CP-WhitJ**

Having a Coke with You. Frank O'Hara. **SP-OharF**

Having a wheel and four legs of its own. The Grindstone. Robert Frost. **CP-FrosR**

Having abdicated with comparative ease. Half Way. Wystan Hugh Auden. **CP-AudeW**

Having accepted the trust so many years back. Letter about Money, Love, or Other Comfort, If Any. Robert Penn Warren. **SP-WarrR**

Having already decided to salvage him. Frigg. Frederick Morgan. **SP-MorgF**

Having Arrived by Bike at Battery Park. Grace Paley. **CP-PaleG**

Having Been Asked "What is a Man?" I Answer. Philip Levine. **SP-LeviP**

Having Been Near. Kenneth Patchen. **CP-PatcK**

Having been shewn, with innocent pride. In the Lenin Library, Dushanbe. John Hewitt. **CP-HewiJ**

Having been tenant long to a rich Lord. Redemption. George Herbert. **CP-HerbG**

Having been whipped through Paradise. The Way We Live. John Haines. **SP-HainJ**

Having bitten on life like a sharp apple. Aubade. Louis MacNeice. **CP-MacNL**

Having come to this place. This Place in the Ways. Muriel Rukeyser. **CP-RukeM**

Having danced until nearly. Wendell Berry. *Fr.* Rising. **CP-BerrW**

Having descried the nation. Charles Olson. **SP-OlsoC** *Fr.* The Maximus Poems.

Having died / one is at great advantage. Spring Song. William Carlos Williams. **CP-WilW1**

Having disregarded exhortations to join the. Since Half the World is H_2O. "Lou Reed." **SP-ReedL**

Having done all I can for now. Listening by a Woodpile, Night of Moon after Snow. Brendan Galvin. **SP-GalvB**

Having eaten their mackerel, drunk their milk. The Sign. Randall Jarrell. **CP-JarrR**

Having Eaten Two Pillows. Alice Walker. **CP-WalkA**

Having fallen down the manhole. Rick De Travaille. Lewis Turco. **SM** *Fr.* Bordello. **SP-TurcL**

Having fed impalpably on the ineluctable. Seeing is Deceiving. Richard Eberhart. **CP-EberR**

Having finished the Blue-plate Special. In Schrafft's. Wystan Hugh Auden. **CP-AudeW**

Having forced the peace, the Eskimos. After the War With the Eskimos. Stephen Dobyns. **SP-DobyS**

Having gathered power and resonance. Regraduating the Lute. William DeWitt Snodgrass. **SP-SnodW**

Having given great offence by writing in Prose. Blakes apology for His Catalogue. William Blake. **CP-BlakW**

Having Grown Up in Shade of Church and State. Philip Larkin. **CP-LarkP**

Having heard the instruction. One Modern Poet. Carl Sandburg. **CP-SandC**

Having in the mind thought. The Goat. William Carlos Williams. **CP-WilW2**

Having inherited a vigorous mind. My Descendants. William Butler Yeats. **CP-YeatW; LiTB** *Fr.* Meditations in Time of Civil War. **CP-YeatW**

Having invented a new Holocaust. U. S. 1946 King's X. Robert Frost. **CP-FrosR**

Having lately taken up residence. Prism. James Merrill. **SP-MerrJ**

Having left the great mean city, I make. Goodbye to London. Louis MacNeice. **CP-MacNL**

Having looked long at two gardens rows. Corn and Beans. Carl Sandburg. **CP-SandC**

Having Lost All Capacity. Stephen Dunn. **SP-DunnS**

Having Lost My Sons, I Confront the Wreckage of the Moon: Christmas, 1960. James Wright. **CP-WrigJ**

Having lost the woman I loved. Ho-Hum Again. Hayden Carruth. **CP-CarHS**

Having mislaid it, and then. The Way of a World. Charles Tomlinson. **CP-TomlC**

Having misread the house, What. The Question. Charles Tomlinson. **CP-TomlC**

Having No Ear. Donald Davie. **CP-DavDo**

Having once put his hand into the ground. The Current. Wendell Berry. **CP-BerrW**

Having outlived self-offense. Louis Zukofsky. *Fr.* Sequence 1944-6. **CP-ZukLS**

Having passed over the world. The Last Frontier. John Gould Fletcher. **SP-FletJ**

Having planted our little Northern Spy at the wrong season. "I've Never Seen Such a Real Hard Time Before": Three-Part Invention. Hayden Carruth. **CP-CarHS**

Having reached perfection. Perfection. Alice Walker. **CP-WalkA**

Having read the promise of the hedgerow. A Sketch of the Great Dejection. Thom Gunn. **CP-GunnT**

Having said *no* more times than. Loki. Frederick Morgan. **SP-MorgF**

Having sat, and smouldered on himself. Brown Gulls. Marsden Hartley. **CP-HartM**

Having searched in every vain crevice of his hopeful imagination. Are You There, Rose Trumbull? Marsden Hartley. **CP-HartM**

Having this day my horse, my hand, my lance. Sonnet 41. Sir Philip Sidney. **EnRePo; HAP; NAEL-1; OAEP; OBSC; PoE; Son** *Fr.* Astrophil and Stella. **SP-SidnP**

Having thought all his life. Question Mark. Richard Eberhart. **CP-EberR**

Having to— / what do I think. Robert Creeley. **CP-CreeR**

Having used every subterfuge. A Renewal. James Merrill. **SP-MerrJ**

Having, with bold Horatius, stamped her feet. Bold Horatius. Wilfred Owen. **CP-OwenW**

Haw Lantern, The. Seamus Heaney. **SP-HeanS**

Hawaii Dantesca. Charles Wright. **SP-WrigC**

Hawarden. George Meredith. **CP-MerG1**

Hawk, The. Robert Bly. **SP-BlyR**

Hawk. Mary Oliver. **SP-OlivM**

Hawk, The. William Butler Yeats. **CP-YeatW**

Hawk in Uig. Richard Hugo. **CP-HugoR**

Hawk or shrike has done this deed. Whimper of Sympathy. George Meredith. **CP-MerG1**

Hawk Revisited, The. Al Young. **CP-YounA**

Hawk Roosting. Ted Hughes. **SP-HughT**

Hawk sweeps down from his aerie, The. The Hawk. Robert Bly. **SP-BlyR**

Hawks. Charles Tomlinson. **CP-TomlC**

Hawk's Shadow. Louise Glück. **SP-GlücL**

Hawkshead and Dachau in a Christmas Glass. Donald Davie. **CP-DavDo**

Hawkweed, The. Edna St. Vincent Millay. **CP-MillE**

Hawley's Leaving Town. Charles Bukowski. **SP-BukC1**

Haworth Churchyard. Matthew Arnold.
    "Turn we next to the dead." **SP-ArnoM**

Hawthorn Hath a Deathly Smell, The. Walter de la Mare. **CP-DeLaW**

Hawthorne. Henry Wadsworth Longfellow. **SP-LongH**

Hawthorne. Robert Lowell. **SP-LoweR**

Hay. John Hewitt. **CP-HewiJ**

Hay. Charles Tomlinson. **CP-TomlC**

Hay Fever. Leonard Nathan. **SP-NathL**

Hay for the Horses. Gary Snyder. **CP-SnydG**

Hay-time when the Boston forecast. New England Weather. Archibald MacLeish. **CP-MacLA**

Haydon! forgive me that I cannot speak. To B.R. Haydon, with a Sonnet Written on Seeing the Elgin Marbles. John Keats. **CP-KeatJ**

Haydon! let worthier judges praise the skill. To B.R. Haydon, On Seeing His Picture of Napoleon Buonaparte on the Island of St Helena. William Wordsworth. **CP-WorW2**

Hayfoot; strawfoot; the illiterate seasons. Wessex Guidebook. Louis MacNeice. **CP-MacNL**

Haying Before Storm. Muriel Rukeyser. **CP-RukeM**

Hayley, thy tenderness fraternal shown. To Hayley. William Cowper. **CP-CowpW**

Hayloft, The. Robert Louis Stevenson. **CP-StevR**

Haymaking. William Carlos Williams. **NoAM** *Fr.* Pictures from Brueghel. **CP-WilW2**

Haymaking in the Low Meadow. John Hewitt. **CP-HewiJ**

Hays Says Ray Lies. Sin City, D.C. John Updike. **CP-UpdiJ**

Haystack, The. Richard Eberhart. **CP-EberR**

Hazardous Occupations. Carl Sandburg. **CP-SandC**

Haze. Carl Sandburg. **CP-SandC**

Haze. James Schuyler. **CP-SchuJ**

Haze, char, and the weather of All Souls'. In the Elegy Season. Richard Wilbur. **CP-WilbR**

Haze Gold. Carl Sandburg. **CP-SandC**

Haze of noon wanned silver-grey, The. Sotto Voce. Walter de la Mare. **CP-DeLaW**

Hazel. "Bob Dylan." **CP-DylaB**

Hazel Blossoms. John Greenleaf Whittier. **CP-WhitJ**

Hazel Grove, The. Robert Ranke Graves. **CP-GravR**

Hazel Leaf, The. Robert Penn Warren. *Fr.* Dark Woods. **SP-WarrR**

Hazel Stick for Catherine Ann, A. Seamus Heaney. **SP-HeanS**

He. John Ashbery. **SP-AshbJ**

He / in the dark stall, no day now for him, to paw. Charles Olson. **CP-OlsoC**

He. Randall Jarrell. **CP-JarrR**

He ("Bought a three-bedroom house in 1948"). Ron Koertge. **SP-KoerR**

He ("Drove a school bus for the extra money"). Ron Koertge. **SP-KoerR**

He ("Gave me 50 dollars for Christmas one year"). Ron Koertge. **SP-KoerR**

He ("Gave me his car"). Ron Koertge. **SP-KoerR**

He ("Got drunk once with another cowpuncher"). Ron Koertge. **SP-KoerR**

He ("Had a bay stallion once that the Triple Bar C"). Ron Koertge. **SP-KoerR**

He ("Has a new double-knit suit with slightly flared"). Ron Koertge. **SP-KoerR**

He ("Has never written me a letter himself"). Ron Koertge. **SP-KoerR**

He ("Told me that I shouldn't have books like that"). Ron Koertge. **SP-KoerR**

He ("Used to climb trees that were"). Ron Koertge. **SP-KoerR**

He ("Used to do most everything himself"). Ron Koertge. **SP-KoerR**

He ("Walked in the basement all winter. For exercise"). Ron Koertge. **SP-KoerR**

He ("Was looking for work at forty-seven and the owner of a"). Ron Koertge. **SP-KoerR**

He ("Was never called Wild Bill"). Ron Koertge. **SP-KoerR**

He. Stanley Jasspon Kunitz. **CP-KuniS**

He. Howard Nemerov. **CP-NemeH**

He ("Was taken out of school after"). Ron Koertge. **SP-KoerR**

He, a grave poet, fell in love with her. Beatrice and Dante. Robert Ranke Graves. **CP-GravR**

He a recreant; in me a true knight thou dub'st, and. Rhyming Exercises. Robert Browning. **CP-BroR2**

He Abjures Love. Thomas Hardy. **CP-HardT**

He adored the desk, its brown-oak inlaid with ebony. Geoffrey Hill. **HAP; NoAM; NoP** *Fr.* Mercian Hymns. **CP-HillG**

He & I had a fight in the pub. But He Says I Misunderstood. Alice Notley. **SP-NotlA**

He and I sought together. Heliodora. Hilda Doolittle. **CP-DoolH**

He and She. Christina Georgina Rossetti. **CP-RosC2**

He and She. William Butler Yeats. **CP-YeatW**

He angled the bright shield. Baroque Image. May Sarton. **SP-SartM**

He arises. Oriane / the lurcher wants. Red Brick and Brown Stone. James Schuyler. **CP-SchuJ**

He arrives, and makes deliveries, after 3:00. Crystal. Thom Gunn. *Fr.* Transients and Residents. **CP-GunnT**

He as o, A / ld as who stag. Edward Estlin Cummings. **CP-CummE**

He ate and drank the precious Words. Emily Dickinson. **CP-DickE**

He avoided the empty millyards. Under the Viaduct, 1932. Rita Dove. **SP-DoveR**

He avoids the momentous rhythm. The Last Man. Thom Gunn. **OxAEP-2** *Fr.* Misanthropos. **CP-GunnT**

He bad / o he bad / He make a honky. The Pusher. Maya Angelou. **SP-AngeM**

He Bathes in the Morning. Frank Templeton Prince. *Fr.* Chaka. **CP-PrinF**

He becomes the terrain an enemy force. Sickness. Daniel Gerard Hoffman. **SP-HoffD**

He begged his ghost a vision of the sea. The Western Ocean. Malcolm Lowry. **CP-LowrM**

He begins the knowledge. He Has Lived through Another Night. Wendell Berry. *Fr.* The Handing Down. **CP-BerrW**

He being the big thing he is. Window Cleaner to Nude Manikin. Marsden Hartley. **CP-HartM**

He bends his travel-tarnished feet. The Supplanter. Thomas Hardy. **CP-HardT**

He bent his head upon his breast. Garibaldi. Elizabeth Barrett Browning. **CP-BroEB**

He Bids His Beloved Be at Peace. William Butler Yeats. *See* I hear the shadowy horses, their long manes a-shake.

He blinks he sighs. A King in Funeral Procession. Stevie Smith. **CP-SmitS**

He blurred the famous face in the first take. The Photographer's Model. James McAuley. **SP-McAuJ**

He boots a cat, ass over claws, and laughs. Maratea Porto: The Bitter Man. Richard Hugo. **CP-HugoR**

He bore an agony whereof the name / Hath turned his fellows pale. St. Bartholomew. Christina Georgina Rossetti. **CP-RosC2**

He bore himself, or the self he had was borne. Knight. Roy Fisher. **SP-FishR** *Fr.* Five Pilgrims in the Prologue to the Canterbury Tales.

He bought one pair of boots, then another. Toting It Up. Stephen Dobyns. **SP-DobyS**

He breaks as the river knots about their knees. His Dream of Flood: And Eden. Muriel Rukeyser. **CP-RukeM**

He brings me cast-off innertubes. It's a Smallworld. Kenneth Patchen. **CP-PatcK**

He brought me to the foot of the. The Pilgrimage, and the Game Warden. Marsden Hartley. **CP-HartM**

He brought our saviour to the western side. Rome. John Milton. **NOSC** *Fr.* Book IV. *Fr.* Paradise Regained [*or* Regain'd]. **CP-MiltJ**

He called eel grass. A Romance. Stephen Dunn. **SP-DunnS**

He came / in flowing robes. Armah: October 12, 1990. Alice Walker. **CP-WalkA**

He came across the ice. A Field Mouse at My Fishing Hole. Gary Gildner. **SP-GildG**

He came all this way. Jane Cooper. *Fr.* A Mission with the Night. **SP-CoopJ**

He came like a dream in the dawn of life. Percy Bysshe Shelley. *Fr.* Fragments of an Unfinished Drama. **CP-ShelP**

He came to him in the extasy of pray'r. Fragment. William Cowper. **CP-CowpW**

He came to the day that made him a hopeless husband. The Spouse. Gilbert Sorrentino. **SP-SorrG**

He came to the door one night wet thin beaten and. The History of a Tough Motherfucker. Charles Bukowski. **SP-BukC3**

He can say, I am / watching a boat tug. The Problem. Robert Creeley. **CP-CreeR**

He Cannot Deny Himself. Christina Georgina Rossetti. **CP-RosC2**

He cannot move the furniture. The Ear. Robert Creeley. **CP-CreeR**

He carried a ball of darkness with him, unrolled it. The Preacher. Louis MacNeice. *Fr.* Novelettes. **CP-MacNL**

He carries / His own strength. Young Sailor. Langston Hughes. **SP-HughL**

He cast off all his golden robes. In Memoriam: William Cannastra, 1922–1950. Allen Ginsberg. **CP-GinsA**

He catches my eye, my fancy. Anne Waldman. **SP-WaldA** *Fr.* Iovis Omnia Plena.

He ceased; and Satan stayed not to reply. Satan. John Milton. **SeCePo; WHA** *Fr.* Book II. **FHYEP; NAEL-1; OxAEP-1** *Fr.* Paradise Lost. **CP-MiltJ**

He chases his tail. Analysand. Stevie Smith. **CP-SmitS**

He clasps the crag with crooked hands. The Eagle. Tennyson. **CP-TennA**

He clench'd his pamphlets in his fist. Robert Burns. *Fr.* Extempore, in the Court of S———. **CP-BurnR**

He climbed to the top. Fergus Falling. Galway Kinnell. **SP-KinnG**

He climbs the eastern slope to stand. Gabriel MacElmain, Pioneer. Louise McNeill. **SP-McNeL**

He Climbs the Hill Where the Tree Grows. Nicholas Vachel Lindsay. *Fr.* The Tree of Laughing Bells or The Wings of the Morning. **CP-LindV**

He coils so close around his double-bass. Double Bass. Robert Ranke Graves. **CP-GravR**

He collected facts / as a pigeon picking up corn. Academic. Phoebe Hesketh. **SP-HeskP**

He comes along the street, singing. To Go By Singing. Wendell Berry. **CP-BerrW**

He comes,—he comes,—the Frost Spirit comes! You may trace his footsteps now. The Frost Spirit. John Greenleaf Whittier. **CP-WhitJ**

He comes toward me with lashless eyes. Upon Meeting Don L. Lee, in a Dream. Rita Dove. **SP-DoveR**

He comes with western winds, with evening's wandering airs. Emily Brontë. **ELP** *Fr.* The Prisoner. **CP-BronE**

He Compares Old Customs with Those of His Kingdom. Frank Templeton Prince. *Fr.* Chaka. **CP-PrinF**

He concentrated, as he ought. JVC. Thom Gunn. **CP-GunnT**

He continued to consult her for her beauty. Popular Songs. John Ashbery. **SP-AshbJ**

He could condense cerulean ether. Ralph Waldo Emerson. **CP-EmerR**

He could not die when trees were green. The Dying Child. John Clare. **SP-ClarJ**

He could remember that in the past, seven months ago. The Hole. Donald Hall. **CP-HallD**

He could see the blue mountain out his bedroom window. Country Life. James Liddy. *Fr.* Ossie Esmonde. *Fr.* His Resplendent Neighbours. **CP-LiddJ**

He could squint his eye up a white pine trunk. Sol Brady. Louise McNeill. **SP-McNeL**

He couldn't get the puck into the net. Hog. Charles Bukowski. **SP-BukC3**

He coveted her portrait. The Moon Is a Painter. Nicholas Vachel Lindsay. **CP-LindV**

He crawls to the edge of the foaming creek. Meeting the Mountains. Gary Snyder. **CP-SnydG**

He crossed the country like a wire. The Gull Hardly Explained. Richard Hugo. **CP-HugoR**

He Cut His Finger on Eternity. Charles Henri Ford. **SP-FordC**

He cuts down the lakes so they appear straight. He. John Ashbery. **SP-AshbJ**

He danced in feathers, with paint across his nose. Learning About the Indians. Mary Oliver. **SP-OlivM**

He dances to that music in the wood. The Andean Flute. Derek Mahon. **SP-MahoD**

He decided to live. Alone. One room. Quaking. Hayden Carruth. *Fr.* The Sleeping Beauty. **CP-CarHL**

He, did he love her? France was his weapon, shrewd. George Meredith. *Fr.* Napoléon. **CP-MerG1**

He Did Not Know Me. Thomas Hardy. **CP-HardT**

He did not pretend. Exile. Louise Glück. **SP-GlücL**

He didn't deny it. The Curly Blue Buppo. Kenneth Patchen. **CP-PatcK**

He didn't go away. The Way He Went. Daniel Gerard Hoffman. **SP-HoffD**

He didn't want to do it with skill. Lion & Honeycomb. Howard Nemerov. **CP-NemeH**

He died for me: what can I offer Him? Not Yours But You. Christina Georgina Rossetti. **CP-RosC3**

He died in December. He must descend. Epilogue. John Berryman. **CP-BerrJ**

He died in Rome, in all that sunlight. Death of a Romantic. Erica Jong. **SP-JongE**

He died in unknown tongues. Latin he'd heard. Epilogue: The Burial of the Last Elder. John Ciardi. **SP-CiarJ**

He "Digesteth Harde Yron." Marianne Craig Moore. **CP-MoorM**

He Digs, He Dug, He Has Dug. Ogden Nash. **CP-NashO**

He dines alone surrounded by reflections. Witch Doctor. Robert Earl Hayden. **CP-HaydR**

He dipped the host of his house in the wine of the street. Holden. James Liddy. **CP-LiddJ**

He disappeared in the dead of winter. In Memory of W. B. Yeats. Wystan Hugh Auden. **CP-AudeW**

He discovers himself on an old airfield. The Old Pilot. Donald Hall. **CP-HallD**

He does not have to feel because he thinks. Edward Estlin Cummings. **CP-CummE**

He does not think that I haunt here nightly. The Haunter. Thomas Hardy. **CP-HardT**

He doesn't touch / the microphone, but the way. Gospel Singer. Dabney Stuart. **SP-StuaD**

He drags his bare feet. Sakyamuni Coming Out from the Mountain. Allen Ginsberg. **CP-GinsA**

He drank enough. David Herbert Lawrence. **RR** *Fr.* Snake. **CP-LawrD**

He drank strong waters and his speech was coarse. Rudyard Kipling. **CP-KiplR** *Fr.* A Bank Fraud. *Fr.* Plain Tales from the Hills.

He drives, she mostly sleeps; when she's awake, they quarrel, and now, in a violet dusk. Travelers. Charles Kenneth Williams. **SP-WillC**

He dropped, [—]more sullenly than wearily. The Dead-Beat. Wilfred Owen. **CP-OwenW**

He drove at evening through the hushed Vosges. The. Geoffrey Hill. *Fr.* Mercian Hymns. **CP-HillG**

He drums the piano wood. Shakespeare Say. Rita Dove. **SP-DoveR**

He dwelt in himself. The Master. Seamus Heaney. **SP-HeanS** *Fr.* Sweeney Redivivus.

He eats (a moment's stoppage to his song). The Tramp. John Clare. **SP-ClarJ**

He ended and the kebars sheuk. Robert Burns. *Fr.* The Jolly Beggars.

He ended, and they both descend the hill. John Milton. **NAWM-1** *Fr.* Book XII. *Fr.* Paradise Lost. **CP-MiltJ**
(Adam Fallen ("He ended, and they both descend the hill").)

He ended; and thus *Adam* last reply'd. John Milton. **HeIP; PoEL-3** *Fr.* Book XII. *Fr.* Paradise Lost. **CP-MiltJ**
(Retreat from Paradise, The.) **PoEL-3**

He enters, and mute on the edge of a chair. In the Study. Thomas Hardy. *Fr.* Satires of Circumstance in Fifteen Glimpses. **CP-HardT**

He Fears His Good Fortune. Thomas Hardy. **CP-HardT**

He feeds me with HIs manna every day. A Soliloquy of One of the Spies Left in the Wilderness. Gerard Manley Hopkins. **CP-HopkG**

He feels a breeze rise from. The Conversation of Old Men. Thom Gunn. **CP-GunnT**

He feels small as he awakens. The Awakening. Robert Creeley. **CP-CreeR**

He felt the wild beast in him betweenwhiles. George Meredith. **EnVR; NOBVV** *Fr.* Modern Love. **CP-MerG1**

He ferreted first things to their first cause. Her Obedient Servant. Daniel Gerard Hoffman. **SP-HoffD**

He flies so high. Look, Look. Stevie Smith. **CP-SmitS**

He followed their lilting stanzas. A Local Poet. John Hewitt. **CP-HewiJ**

He Follows a Woman. Jim Morrison. **SP-MorrJ**

He Follows Himself. Thomas Hardy. **CP-HardT**

He forgo—and I—remembered. Emily Dickinson. **CP-DickE**

He fought like those Who've nought to lose. Emily Dickinson. **CP-DickE**

He found her by the ocean's moaning verge. George Meredith. **EnVR; HBV; NoP; OAEL-2; OAEP** *Fr.* Modern Love. **CP-MerG1**

He found my Being—set it up. Emily Dickinson. **CP-DickE**

He from the wind-bitten North with ship and companions descended. A Drifter off Tarentum. Rudyard Kipling. **FaBoEE; MMA; NSI; PeFWW; PoPle; PoWW** *Fr.* Epitaphs of the War [1914–1918]. **CP-KiplR**

He fumbles at your Soul. Emily Dickinson. **CP-DickE**

He gave away his Life. Emily Dickinson. **CP-DickE**

He gave the solid rail a hateful kick. The Egg and the Machine. Robert Frost. **CP-FrosR**

He gave up fine cordials and. Compendium. Rita Dove. **SP-DoveR**

He gazed and gazed and gazed and gazed. Rhyme for a Child Viewing a Naked Venus in a Painting of "The Judgement of Paris." Robert Browning. **CP-BroR2**

He Gives Her Botticelli's Birth of Venus as a Wedding Gift. Alun Lewis. *Fr.* War Wedding. **CP-LewiA**

He Gives His Beloved Certain Rhymes. William Butler Yeats. **CP-YeatW**

He Gives What He Won to the Indian Girl. Nicholas Vachel Lindsay. *Fr.* The Tree of Laughing Bells or The Wings of the Morning. **CP-LindV**

He Glimpses a Nobler Vision. Miller Williams. **SP-WillM**

He-Goat. David Herbert Lawrence. **CP-LawrD**

He goes free of the earth. Wendell Berry. *Fr.* Three Elegiac Poems. **CP-BerrW**

He goes out with his chainsaw into the cold bright. Hayden Carruth. *Fr.* The Sleeping Beauty. **CP-CarHL**

He grew up by the sea. Adam. William Carlos Williams. **CP-WilW1**

He grins, he plunges into orgy. It moves about. Thom Gunn. *Fr.* Tom-Dobbin. **CP-GunnT**

He Had a Quality of Growth. Muriel Rukeyser. **CP-RukeM**

He had asked for immortal life. Thetis. Hilda Doolittle. **CP-DoolH**

He had awaited me. A Meeting. Daniel Gerard Hoffman. **SP-HoffD**

He had been born in eighteen forty-one. Scottish Interlude. John Hewitt. **CP-HewiJ**

He had been stuttering, by the edge. Hart Crane. Robert Creeley. **CP-CreeR**

He had bowed down to drunkenness. The Disenthralled. John Greenleaf Whittier. **CP-WhitJ**

He had clowned it through. Being born. Louis MacNeice. *Fr.* As In Their Time. **CP-MacNL**

He had come nearly half a thousand miles. The Strayed Village. Adrienne Rich. **CP-RicAE**

He had come to the age. Uncle Adler. Ted Kooser. **SP-KoosT**

He had devirginated my friend Nan. Days of 1959. Marilyn Hacker. **SP-HackM**

He had done for her all that a man could. I Will Write. Robert Ranke Graves. **CP-GravR**

He had driven half the night. Hay for the Horses. Gary Snyder. **CP-SnydG**

He had had it told to him on the sward. Another Chain Letter. John Ashbery. **SP-AshbJ**

He Had His Dream. Paul Laurence Dunbar. **CP-DunbP**

He had not looked. During the Eichmann Trial. Denise Levertov. **CP-LeveD**

He had outlived his day, old Papworth said. The Last Call. John Hewitt. **CP-HewiJ**

He had used love or lust or what's between. Archibald MacLeish. **CP-MacLA** *Fr.* The Happy Marriage.

He halted in the wind, and—what was that. A Boundless Moment. Robert Frost. **CP-FrosR**

He hands / down the gift. The Gift. Robert Creeley. **CP-CreeR**

He hangs a crown over his filthy kitchen. *see also* This Marriage *and* Commentary—This Marriage. Leonard Cohen. **CP-CoheL**

He harried lions up the peaks. Nicholas Vachel Lindsay. *Fr.* A Rhyme for All Zionists. **CP-LindV**

He has a luminous. Charles Henri Ford. **SP-FordC** *Fr.* Secret Haiku.

He Has Beaten about the Bush Long Enough. William Carlos Williams. **CP-WilW2**

He has come back, as some expected, and may be heard. Revenant. John Hewitt. **CP-HewiJ**

He has done the work of a true man. George L. Stearns. John Greenleaf Whittier. **CP-WhitJ**

He has dust in his eyes and a fan for a wing. One Guess. Robert Frost. *Fr.* Ten Mills. **CP-FrosR**

He has gone over to new flowers in a garden. The Groundhog Revisiting. Richard Eberhart. **CP-EberR**

He has had his Future. Emily Dickinson. **SP-DickE**

He has hid his face, and he's gone! Dirge. George Meredith. **CP-MerG2**

He has just cornered and skewered. Why We Are Going Back to Paradise Island. Marilyn Hacker. **SP-HackM**

He has known a tunnel. Wendell Berry. *Fr.* Window Poems. **CP-BerrW**

He Has Lived through Another Night. Wendell Berry. *Fr.* The Handing Down. **CP-BerrW**

He has married me with a ring, a ring of bright water. The Ring. Kathleen Jessie Raine. *Fr.* The Marriage of Psyche. **SP-RainK**

He has observed the golden rule. William Blake. **TrGrPo** *Fr.* Gnomic Verses. **CP-BlakW**

He has on. Late for Summer Weather. William Carlos Williams. **CP-WilW1**

He has only to pass by a tree moodily walking head down. The Fiend. James Dickey. **CP-DickJ**

He has refused absolution and moved piece by piece. In the Hospital. Stephen Dobyns. **SP-DobyS**

He has stamped the clay with his hostile. Cup with a Jaguar for the Drinking of Health. Pablo Antonio Cuadra, *tr. fr. Spanish by* Thomas Merton. **CP-MertT**

He has this wound. A Marked Man. Daniel Gerard Hoffman. **SP-HoffD**

He has to put it somewhere, the violence. White Collar. Stephen Dunn. **SP-DunnS**

He has two antennae. Gnat on My Paper. Richard Eberhart. **CP-EberR**

He has woven rose-vines. C 33. Hart Crane. **CP-CranH**

He hasn't gone to work. The Poem Circling Hamtramck, Michigan, All Night in Search of You. Philip Levine. **SP-LeviP**

He hasn't taken his eyes off you since we walked in, although you seem not to notice particularly. The Silence. Charles Kenneth Williams. **SP-WillC**

He hath abolished the old drouth. Gerard Manley Hopkins. **CP-HopkG**

He hath wrong'd his queen, but still he is her lord. Sardanapalus. Byron. **CP-Byron**

He heard the centuries tick slowly. The Pivot. Stanley Jasspon Kunitz. **CP-KuniS**

He heard the coughing tiger in the night. Edna St. Vincent Millay. **CP-MillE** *Fr.* Epitaph for the Race of Man. **CP-MillE**

He hears lithe trees and last leaves swatting the glass—. TV Off. Ted Hughes. **SP-HughT**

He Hears That His Beloved Has Become Engaged. Philip Larkin. **CP-LarkP**

He Hears the Bugle at Killarney. Tennyson. *See* The Splendor falls on castle walls.

He Hears the Cry of the Sedge. William Butler Yeats. **CP-YeatW**

He hears with gladdened heart the thunder. Robert Louis Stevenson. **CP-StevR**

He hie fie finger / speak in simple sound. The Man. Robert Creeley. **CP-CreeR**

He holds a volume open in his hands. Boy with Book of Knowledge. Howard Nemerov. **CP-NemeH**

He holds him from desire, all but stops his breathing lest. What Magic Drum? William Butler Yeats. **CP-YeatW**

He hopes his arm is strong as the gods'. The Poet. Richard Eberhart. **CP-EberR**

He, hunger-stung, hard to slake. The Glutton. Sylvia Plath. **CP-PlatS**

He hungered for the fame of Bouguereau. Cézanne's Ambition. Stephen Dobyns. **SP-DobyS**

He Inadvertently Cures His Love-Pains. Thomas Hardy. **CP-HardT**

He is a Cock would. William Blake. **CP-BlakW**

He is a good workman. 2 Propositions and 3 Proof. Charles Olson. **CP-OlsoC**

He is a knowing fellow who devotes. Administration. John Hewitt. **CP-HewiJ**

He is a tower unleaning. But how he'll break. John Crowe Ransom. *See* Vaunting Oak.

He is alive, this morning. Emily Dickinson. **CP-DickE**

He Is an. Kenneth Patchen. **CP-PatcK**

He is breaking the nets in his wildness for the real. Muriel Rukeyser. **CP-RukeM**

He is busy destroying the landscape with lightning bolts. Fred and the Holy Grail. William Dickey. **SP-DickW**

He is earthed to his girl, one hand fastened. Aran. Derek Mahon. **SP-MahoD**

He is forever trapped. Audre Lorde. *See* Suffer the Children.

He is found with the homeless dogs. Kid. Robert Earl Hayden. **CAD; NCSH** *Fr.* An Inference of Mexico. **CP-HaydR**

He is going to the woman. Roy Fisher. **SP-FishR** *Fr.* The Six Deliberate Acts.

He is gone on the mountain. Coronach. Sir Walter Scott. **BSV; CH; EnRP; GTBS; GTBS-6; GTBS-P; HBV 1-2; NOBRP; OAEP; OBRV; OHIP; OxAEP-2; SCGP; SP-ScotW; TrGrPo; TreFS; WHA** *Fr.* The Lady of the Lake.

He Is Guarded by Crowds and Shackled with Formalities. Kenneth Patchen. **CP-PatcK**

He is here, come down to look for you. Eurydice. Margaret Atwood. **SP-AtwM2**

He is here, Urania's son. Epithalamium. Alfred Edward Housman. **CP-HousA**

He is Huitzilopochtli. Second Song of Huitzilopochtli. David Herbert Lawrence. **CP-LawrD**

He is ill. Richard Shelton. *Fr.* The Stone Garden. **SP-ShelR**

He is in his room sulked shut. The small. Boy. John Ciardi. **SP-CiarJ**

He Is in the Habit of the World. Wendell Berry. *Fr.* The Handing Down. **CP-BerrW**

He is just plain drunk. I Am a Sioux Brave, He Said in Minneapolis. James Wright. **CP-WrigJ**

He is leading his grandfather under the sun to market. Niño Leading an Old Man to Market. Leonard Nathan. **SP-NathL**

He is made one with Nature; there is heard. Percy Bysshe Shelley. **EPCY; WGRP** *Fr.* Adonais; An Elegy on the Death of John Keats. **CP-ShelP**

He is no fugitive—escaped, escaping. Escapist—Never. Robert Frost. **CP-FrosR**

He is no more dead than Finland herself is dead. Tapiola. William Carlos Williams. **CP-WilW2**

He is no one I really know. Piccola Commedia. Richard Wilbur. **CP-WilbR**

He is not de[a]d that sometime [*or* somtyme] hath a fall. Sir Thomas Wyatt. **CP-WyatT**

He is not here, the old sun. No Possum, No Sop, No Taters. Wallace Stevens. **CP-StevW**

He is not the last one. The Small Blue Heron. James Wright. **CP-WrigJ**

He is one of / The human machines. Solipsist. Stephen Spender. **CP-SpenS**

He is quick, thinking in clear images. In Broken Images. Robert Ranke Graves. **CP-GravR**

He is quite captive to the Lady of the Well-Spring. The Lady of the Well-Spring. Stevie Smith. **CP-SmitS**

He is said to have been the last Red Man. The Vanishing Red. Robert Frost. **CP-FrosR**

He is something he is falling into. The Grandfather Poem. Stephen Dobyns. **SP-DobyS**

He is stark mad, who ever says. The Broken Heart. John Donne. **CP-DonnJ**

He is that fallen lance that lies as hurled. A Soldier. Robert Frost. **CP-FrosR**

He is the Devil. He whores Nature. Love is a word in his Mouth. He has no Mouth. Charles Olson. **CP-OlsoC**

He is the final builder of the total building. Sketch of the Ultimate Politician. Wallace Stevens. **CP-StevW**

He is the Way. Wystan Hugh Auden. **EaLo** *Fr.* The Flight into Egypt. **CP-AudeW** *Fr.* For the Time Being; a Christmas Oratorio. **CP-AudeW**

He is there, somewhere. The Enemy. Thomas McGrath. **SP-McGrT**

He is thinking of us. The Prisoner. Charles Simic. **SP-SimiC**

He is thirty-seven. they cut off his leg. Rimbaud Dead. Patti Smith. **SP-SmitP**

He is to weet a melancholy carle. John Keats. **CP-KeatJ** (Character of Charles Brown.) **CP-KeatJ**

He is twice blessed, the old one buried here. With Ripley at the Grave of Albert Parenteau. Richard Hugo. **CP-HugoR**

He is wisest who has the most caution. Debris. Walt Whitman. **CP-WhitW**

He isn't looking at anything. Doveglion. Edward Estlin Cummings. **CP-CummE**

He journeyed through America. The Rover Come Home. Thomas Hardy. **CP-HardT**

He jumped out of a window. The Story of Richard Maxfield. Diane Wakoski. **SP-WakoD**

He kicked the world, and lunging long ago. The Horse. James Wright. **CP-WrigJ**

He knocked, and I beheld him at the door. Alma Mater. Edwin Arlington Robinson. **CP-RobiE**

He knows / the hunger, walking. Hunger. Robert Creeley. **CP-CreeR**

He knows he will be hurt. Night Piece. Louise Glück. **SP-GlücL**

He knows that when he has to go to sleep. The Man Who Stays Up Late. Miller Williams. **SP-WillM**

He knows the ship, its dizzy flight. The Cook in the Galley. Malcolm Lowry. **CP-LowrM**

He lay awake with a harassed air. A Conversation at Dawn. Thomas Hardy. **CP-HardT**

He leads me into much that is sorrow. The Poor Child with the Hooked Hands. Kenneth Patchen. **CP-PatcK**

He leads: we hear our Seaman's call. Trafalgar Day. George Meredith. **CP-MerG2**

He leans against the window-sill. Archibald MacLeish. **CP-MacLA** *Fr.* The Happy Marriage.

He leaped. With none to hinder. Empedocles. George Meredith. **CP-MerG1**

He learned, as a dissenter, he must be. A Mobile Mollusc. John Hewitt. **CP-HewiJ**

He learned the ways of life on some dull street. Requiem for a Twentieth-Century Outlaw. John Gould Fletcher. **SP-FletJ**

He learns to imagine. Umpire. Dabney Stuart. **SP-StuaD**

He learns what love can do and what it can't do. Fly Me to the Moon. Miller Williams. **SP-WillM**

He left himself on my doorstep. A Foundling. Margaret Atwood. **SP-AtwM1**

He left his pants upon a chair. The Mistake. Theodore Roethke. **OBCoV** *Fr.* Three Epigrams. **CP-RoetT**

He lets her pick the color. Nothing Down. Rita Dove. **SP-DoveR**

He licks the last chocolate ice cream. Sweet Things. Thom Gunn. **CP-GunnT**

He licks the tallest tree, and takes a bite. Sundown and Starlight. James Merrill. *Fr.* Five Old Favorites. **SP-MerrJ**

He: Life is an old / casino in the park. I. Hayden Carruth. **CP-CarHS** *Fr.* The Clay Hill Anthology.

He liked the whores in Guatemala. In South America on Business He Does Something He Is Ashamed of yet on the Way Home Dreams of It Again and Again. Ron Koertge. **SP-KoerR**

He liked to fight. I can remember how. The Twin. Robert Pack. **SP-PackR**

He liked to joke and all of his jokes were practical. Sunday Night at Grandfather's. Rita Dove. **SP-DoveR**

He liked to watch the big cats. Letting the Puma Go. Stephen Dunn. **SP-DunnS**

He lines the walls with mirrors. Vanity. Stephen Dobyns. **SP-DobyS**

He listened at the porch that day. A Year's Spinning. Elizabeth Barrett Browning. **CP-BroEB**

He lived / from his second year. A Garland for Thomas Eakins. Charles Tomlinson. **CP-TomlC**

He lived in a small farm-house. A Refusal to Mourn. Derek Mahon. **SP-MahoD**

He lived on the wings of storm. Memoir of a Proud Boy. Carl Sandburg. **CP-SandC**

He lived the Life of Ambush. Emily Dickinson. **CP-DickE**

He lives among a dog. The Child. Donald Hall. **CP-HallD**

He lives in a house with a swimming pool. About My Very Tortured Friend, Peter. Charles Bukowski. **SP-BukC2**

He lives not who can refuse me. Ralph Waldo Emerson. **CP-EmerR**

He lives who lives to God alone. On a Similar Occasion for the Year 1793. William Cowper. **CP-CowpW**

He looked / Just as your Sign-post lions do. Robert Burns. *Fr.* Versicles on Sign-Posts. **CP-BurnR**

He looked at me with eyes I thought. Alfred Edward Housman. **CP-HousA**

He looked in all His wisdom from His throne. Wystan Hugh Auden. *Fr.* Sonnets from China. **CP-AudeW**

He looked more like an Arab than a Jew. Remembering a Conversation: Itzik Manger at the PEN Conference, Edinburgh, 1950. John Hewitt. **CP-HewiJ**

He looks. Looks. Looks in rapture. Man in Majesty. Randall Jarrell. **CP-JarrR**

He Looks out the Window at the Town. Wendell Berry. *Fr.* The Handing Down. **CP-BerrW**

He look't [*or* looked] and saw what numbers numberless. The Parthians. John Milton. **NOSC; OBS** *Fr.* Book III. *Fr.* Paradise Regained [*or* Regain'd]. **CP-MiltJ**

He loved cloud covers. Weight. Archie Randolph Ammons. **SP-AmmoA**

He loved her and she loved him. Lovesong. Ted Hughes. **SP-HughT**

He loved her, and through many years. Then and Now. Paul Laurence Dunbar. **CP-DunbP**

He loved his cabin: there. Salt Water Story. Richard Hugo. **CP-HugoR**

He loved the way her fingers loved the ground. Midas and Wife. Mona Van Duyn. **SP-VanDM**

He loved to watch & wake. Ralph Waldo Emerson. **CP-EmerR**

He lurks and sidles away out of sight. But when you stand. Dogfish. Daniel Gerard Hoffman. **SP-HoffD**

He made, a thousand years ago, a-many songs. John Berryman. *Fr.* Sonnets to Chris. **CP-BerrJ**

He mailed that letter many years ago. The Letter. Frederick Morgan. **SP-MorgF**

He makes the Lame to walk we all agree. On the Venetian Painter. William Blake. **CP-BlakW**

He making speedy way through spersed ayre. Edmund Spenser. **NoSic** *Fr.* The Faerie Queene. **CP-Spens**

He marked the pattern of the sky. Hilda Doolittle. **CP-DoolH** *Fr.* Electra-Orestes.

He may be envied, who with tranquil breast. Charlotte Smith. **CP-SmitC**

He might be slow and something feckless first. Gerard Manley Hopkins. **CP-HopkG**

He motions me over with a question. Kidnap[p]er. Tess Gallagher. **SP-GallT**

He mounts the stand &. Your Basic Black Poet. Al Young. **CP-YounA**

He Mourns for the Change That Has Come upon Him and His Beloved, and Longs for the End of the World. William Butler Yeats. *See* Do you not hear me calling, white deer with no horns?

He must go down in the mine—. Overheard on a Bus (Miner's Wife). Louise McNeill. **SP-McNeL**

He must have / Droll fancies sometimes cross his quiet thoughts. Ralph Waldo Emerson. **CP-EmerR**

He must have been born with greased feet. Rootless. Stephen Dobyns. **SP-DobyS**

He must have been just as old in. Ballad of Mister Dutcher and the Last Lynching in Gupton. Robert Penn Warren. **SP-WarrR**

He must have come aboard at Tinos. To Piraeus. John Hewitt. **CP-HewiJ**

He Nears the Goal. Nicholas Vachel Lindsay. *Fr.* The Tree of Laughing Bells or The Wings of the Morning. **CP-LindV**

He needs the antiseptic of the sunlight: neither. The Stranger. Kenneth Patchen. **CP-PatcK**

He Never Expected Much. Thomas Hardy. **CP-HardT**

He never felt twice the same about the flecked river. This Solitude of Cataracts. Wallace Stevens. **CP-StevW**

He never listened while friends talked. Chicago English Afternoon. Ted Berrigan. **SP-BerrT**

He never made the dive—not while I watched. The Springboard. Louis MacNeice. **CP-MacNL**

He never spoke a word to me. Simon the Cyrenian Speaks. Countee Cullen. **CP-CullC**

He nothing common did or mean. King Charles on [*or* upon] the Scaffold. Andrew Marvell. **ChTr; FaBoRV** *Fr.* An Horatian Ode upon Cromwell's Return from Ireland. **CP-MarvA**

He numbed my heart, he stole away my truth. Purification. Robert Ranke Graves. **CP-GravR**

He, of his gentleness. In the Wilderness. Robert Ranke Graves. **CP-GravR**

He offered her his paucity. Ballad. Wystan Hugh Auden. **CP-AudWJ**

He offers, between planes. Conversation with a Fireman from Brooklyn. Tess Gallagher. **SP-GallT**

He often gazes on the air. An Agnostic. Stevie Smith. **CP-SmitS**

He often would ask us. The Choirmaster's Burial. Thomas Hardy. **CP-HardT**

He omits, Goya, not even the good news. John Updike. *Fr.* Spanish Sonnets. **CP-UpdiJ**

He, on whose natal hour you glance. 4.3. Horace. **SP-SmarC,** *tr. by* Christopher Smart; *Fr.* Odes.

He ought to be hung. At Don's Garage. Daniel Gerard Hoffman. **SP-HoffD**

He outstripped Time with but a Bout. Emily Dickinson. **CP-DickE**

He paces the blue rug. It is the end of summer. On Looking at *La Grande Jatte*, the Czar Wept Anew. Frank O'Hara. **SP-OharF**

He parried every question that they hurled. Wystan Hugh Auden. *Fr.* The Quest. **CP-AudeW**

He parts Himself—like Leaves. Emily Dickinson. **CP-DickE**

He passed her through the sermon's dull defile. George Meredith. *Fr.* The Sage Enamoured and the Honest Lady. **CP-MerG1**

He passed in the very battle-smoke. Lord Roberts. Rudyard Kipling. **CP-KiplR**

He passes down the churchyard track. The Sexton at Longpuddle. Thomas Hardy. **CP-HardT**

He past; a soul of nobler tone. Tennyson. *Fr.* In Memoriam A. H. H. **CP-TennA**

He paused on the sill of a door ajar. The Newcomer's Wife. Thomas Hardy. **CP-HardT**

He picks up what he thinks is. My Father: October 1942. William Stafford. **SP-StafW**

He planned his course on Orinoco charts. A Troubadour Removed. Richard Hugo. **CP-HugoR**

He play'd his wings as though for flight. Love Preparing to Fly. Gerard Manley Hopkins. **CP-HopkG**

He played jacks with me. The Rocker. Donald Hall. **CP-HallD**

He played with a toy they bought. Don't Break It. Joseph Ceravolo. **SP-CeraJ**

He plays the piano with a razor. Malcolm Lowry. *Fr.* Songs for Second Childhood. **CP-LowrM**

He prayed to his ghost for a vision of the sea. *sl. diff. vers. incl. in* Pijijiapan. Malcolm Lowry. *Fr.* The Roar of the Sea and the Darkness. **CP-LowrM**

He Prayeth Best. Samuel Taylor Coleridge. **FaPON** *Fr.* The Rime of the Ancient Mariner. **CP-ColeS**

He Prayeth Well. Samuel Taylor Coleridge. **BoTP** *Fr.* The Rime of the Ancient Mariner. **CP-ColeS**

He preached upon "Breadth" till it argued him narrow. Emily Dickinson. **CP-DickE**

He Prefers Her Earthly. Thomas Hardy. **CP-HardT**

He pushes behind the words. Waiting. Robert Creeley. **CP-CreeR**

He put the Belt around my life. Emily Dickinson. **CP-DickE**

He ran his hands thru her hair. Some Recent Fiction. Al Young. **CP-YounA**

He ran the course and as he ran he grew. Innocence. Thom Gunn. **CP-GunnT**

He reads: / "That is one of the great tragedies". Hayden Carruth. *Fr.* The Sleeping Beauty. **CP-CarHL**

He reads and finds the meaning plain. The Letter. Wystan Hugh Auden. **CP-AudWJ**

He reads and reads, this poet to be. Thoughts to Be Erased from My Destiny. Malcolm Lowry. **CP-LowrM**

He reads there, only a boy, fifteen, in the dingy. Hayden Carruth. *Fr.* The Sleeping Beauty. **CP-CarHL**

He Receives the Bells. Nicholas Vachel Lindsay. *Fr.* The Tree of Laughing Bells or The Wings of the Morning. **CP-LindV**

He remained silent on many things. My Father's Birthday. Kathleen Jessie Raine. **SP-RainK**

He Remembereth That We Are Dust. Adrienne Rich. **CP-RicAE**

He remembers: / There was this big house they called the Hatch. Hayden Carruth. *Fr.* The Sleeping Beauty. **CP-CarHL**

He Remembers Forgotten Beauty. William Butler Yeats. **CP-YeatW**

He replied to his own question, and with the unmannered. A Meditation on John Constable. Charles Tomlinson. **CP-TomlC**

He Reproves the Curlew. William Butler Yeats. **CP-YeatW**

He Resigns. John Berryman. **CP-BerrJ**

He Resolves to Say No More. Thomas Hardy. **CP-HardT**

He rested on the seventh day, and so. Sunday. Howard Nemerov. **CP-NemeH**

He rested through the winter, watched the rain. Death of a Gardener. Phoebe Hesketh. **SP-HeskP**

He resteth: weep not! Resurrection Eve. Christina Georgina Rossetti. **CP-RosC3**

He Revisits Cambridge. Tennyson. *See* I past [*or* passed] beside the reverend walls.

He Revisits His First School. Thomas Hardy. **CP-HardT**

He Revisits the Spot. Wystan Hugh Auden. **CP-AudWJ**

He rides at their head. The College Colonel. Herman Melville. **SP-MelvH**

He rises and begins to round. The Lark Ascending. George Meredith. **CP-MerG1**

He rises he stretches he liquefies he is hammered again. Squeal. Allen Ginsberg. **CP-GinsA**

He rode across like a cavalier, *see also* "From where she stood the air she craved." Two Who Crossed a Line. Countee Cullen. **CP-CullC**

He rode through the woods on a big blue ox. Paul Bunyan. Shel Silverstein. **SP-SilS2**

He rose up on his dying bed. Hope. Langston Hughes. **SP-HughL**

He runs before the wise men: He. He. Stanley Jasspon Kunitz. **CP-KuniS**

He runs his eyes out idly, sliding. The Tower. Randall Jarrell. **CP-JarrR**

He said: / All right then, I *was*, o.k.? Screwing. Hayden Carruth. *Fr.* The Sleeping Beauty. **CP-CarHL**

He Said:. Alice Walker. **CP-WalkA**

He said: "Awake my soul, and with the sun." Barthélémon at Vauxhall. Thomas Hardy. **CP-HardT**

He Said Come. Alice Walker. **CP-WalkA**

He said he would be back and we'd drink wine together. Waiting for Icarus. Muriel Rukeyser. **CP-RukeM**

He said: Here is my soul. Gift. Alice Walker. **CP-WalkA**

He said: "I do not know you." He Did Not Know Me. Thomas Hardy. **CP-HardT**

He said—(I only give the heads)—he said. Byron. **EPCY** *Fr.* The Vision of Judgment. **CP-Byron**

He said: I want you to be happy. He Said:. Alice Walker. **CP-WalkA**

He said, I'm just out of hospital. R.A.F. Hilda Doolittle. **CP-DoolH**

He said no word of her to us. Nor We of Her to Him. Stevie Smith. **CP-SmitS**

He said that he was God. The Fool. "Hugh MacDiarmid." **SP-MacDH**

He said to me: You don't trust me! The Emotional Friend. David Herbert Lawrence. **CP-LawrD**

He said to me: Your life will be so much the poorer. Refused Friendship. David Herbert Lawrence. **CP-LawrD**

He said, turning, unconscious of. Gangster. Robert Creeley. **CP-CreeR**

He said you should not give a shout. On Hearing a Traveller's Tale of the Alps. John Hewitt. **CP-HewiJ**

He sang / How the swan blanched forever. Owl's Song. Ted Hughes. **SP-HughT**

He sang of life, serenely sweet. The Poet. Paul Laurence Dunbar. **CP-DunbP**

He sat in a wheeled chair, waiting for dark. Disabled. Wilfred Owen. **CP-OwenW**

He sate, no stiller stands a rock. Arthur Hugh Clough. **SP-ClouA**

He Saved Others. . . . Phoebe Hesketh. **SP-HeskP**

He saw a fire dancer take two flambeaus. Impossible Iambics. Carl Sandburg. **CP-SandC**

He saw a laughing girl. Emily Dickinson. Richard Eberhart. **CP-EberR**

He saw her from the bottom of the stairs. Home Burial. Robert Frost. **CP-FrosR**

He saw her once, and in the glance. Three Sunsets. "Lewis Carroll." **CP-CarrL**

He saw her: that is, he labored. Gloss on the Sin of Ixion. Thomas Merton. **CP-MertT**

He saw the portrait of his enemy, offered. The Enemy's Portrait. Thomas Hardy. **CP-HardT**

He says he doesn't feel like working today. My Erotic Double. John Ashbery. **SP-AshbJ**

He says he is a perfect poet. The Perfect Poet. Erica Jong. **SP-JongE**

He says that old men fool themselves by claiming. On Reading Terence de Vere White on Landor. John Hewitt. **CP-HewiJ**

He says that religious thought and all our nerviness. A Religious Man. Stevie Smith. **CP-SmitS**

He says the waves in the ship's wake. Leaving Forever. Denise Levertov. **CP-LeveD**

He says when he comes in a bar. Meeting My Best Friend from the Eighth Grade. Gary Gildner. **SP-GildG**

He scanned it—staggered. Emily Dickinson. **CP-DickE**

He scarce had ceas't [or ceased] when the superior fiend. Satan and the Fallen Angels. John Milton. **LiTB; NOSC; OBS; SeCePo** *Fr.* Book I. **FHYEP; NAEL-1; OAEL-1; OxAEP-1** *Fr.* Paradise Lost. **CP-MiltJ**

He scribbles some in prose and verse. Dilettante, The: A Modern Type. Paul Laurence Dunbar. **CP-DunbP**

He sees the dawn expanding from a seashell. Alun Lewis. *Fr.* The Madman. **CP-LewiA**

He sees the world as a boisterous place. John and Jane. Thomas Hardy. **CP-HardT**

He Sees Through Stone. Etheridge Knight. **SP-KnigE**

He seized me by the waist and kissed my throat. Charleston in the Eighteen-Sixties. Adrienne Rich. **CP-RicAE; SP-RicA2**

He set his claim upon the bark. The Clearing. Louise McNeill. **SP-McNeL**

He set out and kept hunting. The Hunter. Frank O'Hara. **SP-OharF**

He shakes the dust from off his feet. Battle of Murfreesboro. Allen Tate. **CP-TateA**

He Shall Go No More Out. Christina Georgina Rossetti. **CP-RosC2**

He Shot Arrows, but Not at Birds Perching. Gary Snyder. **CP-SnydG**

He shouts amain, he shouts again. Madrigal. "Lewis Carroll." **CP-CarrL**

He shuffles, and his face is white and lazy. Clam Man. Mary Oliver. **SP-OlivM**

He sighed with relief. He had the job. He was safe. Schoolmaster. Philip Larkin. **CP-LarkP**

He sipped at a weak hock and seltzer. The Arrest of Oscar Wilde at the Cadogan Hotel. Sir John Betjeman. **CP-BetjJ**

He sits before me now, reptilian, cold. Old Man Drunk. James Wright. **CP-WrigJ**

He sits between the doctor and the law. The Poet Down. Michael Hartnett. *Fr.* Notes on My Contemporaries. **SP-HarMi**

He sits in blue trunks on the sand, and children sing. Mad Young Aristocrat on Beach. Robert Penn Warren. **SP-WarrR**

He sits in your room, his tomb, with a fist full of tacks. Can You Please Crawl Out Your Window? "Bob Dylan." **CP-DylaB**

He sits there. Not To Worry. Charles Bukowski. **SP-BukC3**

He sleeps on the top of a mast. The Unbeliever. Elizabeth Bishop. **CP-BishE**

He smiles in a mirror, shrinking the whole. Meeting. Ted Hughes. **SP-HughT**

He smiles to see His children, born to sin. The God of This World. Howard Nemerov. **CP-NemeH**

He spake no dream, for as his words had end. The Banquet. John Milton. **NOSC** *Fr.* Book II. *Fr.* Paradise Regained [or Regain'd]. **CP-MiltJ**

He speaks cautiously to the Tea phone when it invites. Thomas Merton. *Fr.* Cables to the Ace. **CP-MertT**

He speaks of eating three hot meals a day. Courtesies of the Interregnum. Thom Gunn. **CP-GunnT**

He Speaks to His Arguing Friends and to Himself. Miller Williams. **SP-WillM**

He, standing hushed, a pace or two apart. Alfred Edward Housman. **CP-HousA**

He stands before me. He must be. The Mathematics. Gilbert Sorrentino. **SP-SorrG**

He stands, filling the doorway. The Risen. Ted Hughes. **SP-HughT**

He stands with his forefeet on the drum. Two Performing Elephants. David Herbert Lawrence. **CP-LawrD**

He stares upward at a monstrous face. The Pietà, Rhenish, 14th C., the Cloisters. Mona Van Duyn. **SP-VanDM**

He starts awake in the city. Orion believing. Muriel Rukeyser. **CP-RukeM**

He Starts on the Return Journey. Nicholas Vachel Lindsay. *Fr.* The Tree of Laughing Bells or The Wings of the Morning. **CP-LindV**

He stayed, and was imprisoned in possession. Wystan Hugh Auden. **CMoP** *Fr.* Sonnets from China. **CP-AudeW**

He stepped out of bed at night. The Truncated Bird. Richard Eberhart. **CP-EberR**

He steps around a gate of bushes. Cold Water. Donald Hall. **CP-HallD**

He steps down from the dark train, blinking; stares. Ten Days Leave. William DeWitt Snodgrass. **SP-SnodW**

He steps out from the crowd. Stanley Jasspon Kunitz. *Fr.* The Lincoln Relics. **CP-KuniS**

He steps out singing in the blazing field. Pantoum Approaching the Speed of Light. Robert Pack. **SP-PackR**

He stept so lightly to the land. Lady Muriel's Song. "Lewis Carroll." **CP-CarrL** *Fr.* Sylvie and Bruno. **CP-CarrL**

He stirs, beginning to awake. A Field Hospital. Randall Jarrell. **CP-JarrR; SP-JarrR**

He stood—a bitter scolding man. New Jerusalem. John Hewitt. **CP-HewiJ**

He stood, a point / on a sheet of green paper. Progressive Insanities of a Pioneer. Margaret Atwood. **SP-AtwM1**

He stood against the stove. Mearl Blankenship. Muriel Rukeyser. **CP-RukeM**

He stood among a crowd at Drumahair [or Dromahair]. The Man Who Dreamed of Faeryland. William Butler Yeats. **CP-YeatW**

He stood and call'd / His legions, angel forms, who lay intranced. Satan's Legions and the Beech Leaves of the Casentino. John Milton. **FaBoPP,** *ll.* 300–304; **WHA** *Fr.* Book I. **FHYEP; NAEL-1; OAEL-1; OxAEP-1** *Fr.* Paradise Lost. **CP-MiltJ**

He stood, and heard the steeple. Eight O'Clock. Alfred Edward Housman. **CP-HousA**

He stood before her. Dreamjot: 1962. Al Young. **CP-YounA**

He stood beside the station rail. Goin' Back. Paul Laurence Dunbar. **CP-DunbP**

He stood naked at one of the two windows. An Essay on Liberation. David St. John. **SP-StJoD**

He stood on the brow of the well-known hill. The Fratricide. John Greenleaf Whittier. **CP-WhitJ**

He stood on the ground. Wendell Berry. *Fr.* Window Poems. **CP-BerrW**

He strained my faith. Emily Dickinson. **CP-DickE**

He Suggests a Solution. John Hewitt. *Fr.* Two Sonnets. **CP-HewiJ**

He summons Edith, which is Paul's own desire. Fait Accompli. John Crowe Ransom. *Fr.* Two Gentlemen in Bonds. **SP-RansJ**

He suspects that the seasons. A Set of Seasons. Donald Hall. **CP-HallD**

He Takes His Time. Wendell Berry. *Fr.* The Handing Down. **CP-BerrW**

He tasted love with half his mind. Tennyson. *Fr.* In Memoriam A. H. H. **CP-TennA**

He Tells a Valley Full of Lovers. William Butler Yeats. **CP-YeatW**

He tells it, who knew the law. George Meredith. *Fr.* The Day of the Daughter of Hades. **CP-MerG1**

He tells me in Bangkok he's robbed. Baby Villon. Philip Levine. **SP-LeviP**

He Tells of the Perfect Beauty. William Butler Yeats. **CP-YeatW**

He tells you when you've got on too much lipstick. The Perfect Husband. Ogden Nash. **CP-NashO**

He thanks God daily. Profile. Wystan Hugh Auden. **CP-AudeW**

He that ascended in a cloud, shall come. Clouds. Robert Herrick. **CP-HerrR**

He that cannot choose but love. Self Love. John Donne. **CP-DonnJ**

He that doth paint the beauties of your verse. To His Much Honoured Friend Mr. Richard Lovelace, on His Poems. Sir Benjamin Rudyerd. *Fr.* Commendatory Poems. **CP-LoveR**

He that dwelleth in the secret place of the most High. Psalm 91. Bible, *O.T.* **AWP; TrGrPo; WGRP** *Fr.* Psalms. **CP-Psal**

He that fears death, or mourns it, in the just. Of Death. Ben Jonson. **CP-JonsB**

He that has sail'd upon the dark blue sea. Byron. **MOS** *Fr.* Childe Harold's Pilgrimage. **CP-Byron**

He that has seen a great oak dry and dead. Joachim Du Bellay. **FaBoPP** *Fr.* Ruins of Rome. **CP-Spens**

He that hath a Gospel. The Disciple. Rudyard Kipling. **CP-KiplR**

He that hath set his headlong heart. Boethius, *tr. fr. Latin.* **MLL,** *tr. by* Helen Waddell; *Fr.* Consolation of Philosophy, The ("De Consolacione Philosophie"). **CP-ChauG**

He that his myrth hath lost. Dyer's Phancy Turned to a Sinner's Complainte. Robert Southwell. **CP-SoutR**

He that ingenious art did first descry. In the French Translation of Lucan by Monsieur De Brebeuf Are These Verses: Lib 3. Lucan, *tr. fr. Latin of* Andrew Marvell, *fr. the French of* de Brebeuf by Sir Philip Meadows. **CP-MarvA** *Fr.* Pharsalia.

He that is hurt seeks help: sin is the wound. The Eucharist. Robert Herrick. **CP-HerrR**

He that is one. Trinity Sunday. George Herbert. **CP-HerbG**

He that is robbed and smiles. Emily Dickinson. **SP-DickE**

He that is weary, let him sit. George Herbert. **CP-HerbG** (Employment (2).) **CP-HerbG**

He that loves a rosy cheek. Disdain Returned. Thomas Carew. **CP-CareT**

He that loves a rosy cheek. The True Beauty. Thomas Carew. **GTBS; GTBS-6; GTBS-P; PFP** *Fr.* Disdain Returned. **CP-CareT**

He that made the vow under the fig tree. Thirty Rings. Leonard Nathan. **SP-NathL**

He that may sin, sins least; Leave to transgresse. More Potent, Lesse Peccant. Robert Herrick. **CP-HerrR**

He that should search all glories of the gown. An Epigram on Sir Edward Coke, when He Was Lord Chief Justice of England. Ben Jonson. **CP-JonsB**

He that will live of all cares dispossest. Suspicion Makes Secure. Robert Herrick. **CP-HerrR**

He that will not love must be. Not To Love. Robert Herrick. **CP-HerrR**

He there now does enjoy eternal rest. Edmund Spenser. **ChTr; MOS** *Fr.* The Faerie Queene. **CP-Spens** (Sleep after Toil.) **ChTr**

He thinks / always things. Out of Sight. Robert Creeley. **CP-CreeR**

He thinks how, often when his semen spews. Hayden Carruth. *Fr.* The Sleeping Beauty. **CP-CarHL**

He thinks in wonder how love was all that was. Hayden Carruth. *Fr.* The Sleeping Beauty. **CP-CarHL**

He thinks of classical women. Hayden Carruth. *Fr.* The Sleeping Beauty. **CP-CarHL**

He Thinks of His Past Greatness When a Part of the Constellations of Heaven. William Butler Yeats. **CP-YeatW**

He Thinks of Those Who Have Spoken Evil of His Beloved. William Butler Yeats. **CP-YeatW**

He thought he kept the universe alone. The Most of It. Robert Frost. **CP-FrosR**

He thought he saw an elephant [*or* a banker's clerk *or* a buffalo]. The Mad Gardener's Song. "Lewis Carroll." **CP-CarrL** *Fr.* Sylvie and Bruno.

He Thought of Mad Ellen's Ravings and of the Wretched Skeleton on the Rock. Kenneth Patchen. **CP-PatcK**

He, through the eyes of the first marauder. To a Girl Who Knew What Side Her Bread Was Buttered On. Audre Lorde. **SP-LordA**

He tied it with a piece of string. Eskimo Tales. John Yau. **SP-YauJo**

He told a homely tale. Emily Dickinson. **CP-DickE**

He Told His Life Story to Mrs. Courtly. Stevie Smith. (Autumn.) **CP-SmitS**

He told me he had all the gas on. Suicide. Charles Bukowski. **SP-BukC2**

He told me he loved me. The Broken Heart. Stevie Smith. **CP-SmitS**

He told me to come around midnight, unobserved. Captain Blaze. Frederick Morgan. **SP-MorgF**

He told us we were free to choose. Friday's Child. Wystan Hugh Auden. **CP-AudeW**

He toned the sprightly beam of morning. The Marchioness of Brinvilliers. Herman Melville. **SP-MelvH**

He too has eaten well—. The Lizard. Theodore Roethke. **CP-RoetT**

He too has flitted from his secret nest. The Pang More Sharp Than All. Samuel Taylor Coleridge. **CP-ColeS**

He Too Wore a Butterfly. Marsden Hartley. **CP-HartM**

He took a frayed hat from his head. Peace on Earth. Edwin Arlington Robinson. **CP-RobiE**

He took every job now / brought to the door. Ecce Homo. John Hewitt. **CP-HewiJ**

He took his mountain fiddle up. Fiddler. Louise McNeill. **SP-McNeL**

He took the color of his vest. Forester. Ralph Waldo Emerson. *Fr.* Quatrains. **CP-EmerR**

He took us to the Christmas Pantomime. First Pantomime. John Hewitt. **CP-HewiJ**

He touched me, so I live to know. Emily Dickinson. **CP-DickE**

He travels three hundred miles to New York. Traveler. Grace Paley. **CP-PaleG**

He treads on edges of being where the drop. Charles Olson. **CP-OlsoC**

He tried to spit out the truth. Ultimately. Ernest Hemingway. **CP-HemiE**

He tried to tell them what he felt. Paint Box. Phoebe Hesketh. **SP-HeskP**

He trilled a carol fresh and free. The First Voice. "Lewis Carroll." *Fr.* The Three Voices. **CP-CarrL**

He trod in dream upon the brim. Death's Ostracism. Stevie Smith. **CP-SmitS**

He turned cruel. Absorbed in his own cruelty. Muriel Rukeyser. **CP-RukeM**

He turned his field into a meeting-place. Wystan Hugh Auden. **PoPl; SCV** *Fr.* Sonnets from China. **CP-AudeW**

He turns through the lucid stars of a lit city. Muriel Rukeyser. **CP-RukeM**

He, unto whom thou art so partial. Martial, Lib. I. Epig. I. Byron. **CP-Byron**

He used to pass, well-trimmed and brushed. The Passer-By. Thomas Hardy. **CP-HardT**

He used to think his escape was in lucidity. Hayden Carruth. *Fr.* The Sleeping Beauty. **CP-CarHL**

He waited in the sadness of the sun's intention. The Sun. Donald Hall. **CP-HallD**

He waits, and it is not without. The Lover. Frank O'Hara. **SP-OharF**

He waits by the door of his cave. Nicholas Vachel Lindsay. *Fr.* The Sea Serpent Chantey. **CP-LindV**

He walked in the world. Knew the lust of the eye. The Sound of That Wind. Robert Penn Warren. *Fr.* Audubon. **SP-WarrR**

He walked the streets of great New York. Ralph Waldo Emerson. **CP-EmerR**

He walks his fields, and every glance. Real Estate. John Hewitt. **CP-HewiJ**

He walks on the street, in. Gilbert Sorrentino. **SP-SorrG**

He walks out of the village. The road. A Village in East Anglia. Donald Hall. **CP-HallD**

He walks still upright from the root. The Hewel, or Woodpecker. Andrew Marvell. **ChTr** *Fr.* Upon Appleton House [To My Lord Fairfax]. **CP-MarvA**

He walks the high wire in his sleep. The Man Who Never Loses His Balance. Stephen Dunn. **SP-DunnS**

He walks up to my Volks. Fear. Charles Bukowski. **SP-BukC1**

He wandered down the mountain grade. *parody of* William Wordsworth. Rudyard Kipling. **CP-KiplR** *Fr.* The Muse among the Motors.

He wandering far along the lonely main. Orpheus and Eurydice. Virgil, *tr. by* William Wordsworth. **CP-WorW1** *Fr.* Georgics.

He wanders, like a day-appearing dream. Fragment: A Wanderer. Percy Bysshe Shelley. **CP-ShelP**

He wanted his potatoes carried through the streets. Translate into Latin for my Epitaph. James Liddy. **CP-LiddJ**

He wanted to have a theory, all. Wishing He Had a Theory in Key West. Peter Meinke. **SP-MeinP** *Fr.* Lines from Key West.

He wanted to look in the news. The New York Times: A Poem for the Ross Feld. Gilbert Sorrentino. **SP-SorrG**

He wanted to own his own past. Parable of the Fictionist. Stephen Dunn. **SP-DunnS**

He wanted to tamper. The Executive Discovers Poetry. Dabney Stuart. **SP-StuaD**

He wants to be an Indian. Yellow. Robert Creeley. **CP-CreeR**

He wants to dance in the grave. Spell. Dabney Stuart. **SP-StuaD**

He Was. Richard Wilbur. **CP-WilbR**

He was a big man, says the size of his shoes. Abandoned Farmhouse. Ted Kooser. **SP-KoosT**

He was a gash an' faithfu' tyke. Luath. Robert Burns. **GDP** *Fr.* The Twa Dogs. **CP-BurnR**

He was a hard painter to pose for. Hours stuck. Cézanne's Doubts. Stephen Dobyns. **SP-DobyS**

He was a king or a shah, an ahkoond or rajah. Carl Sandburg. *Fr.* The People, Yes. **CP-SandC**

He was a man made a bank. The Friend. Charles Olson. **CP-OlsoC**

He was a man of his time and of its distresses and he rode. August. Hayden Carruth. **CP-CarHS**

He was a might poet—and. Percy Bysshe Shelley. **EPCY** *Fr.* Peter Bell the Third. **CP-ShelP**

He was a poet who wrote clever verses. Confirmation. Paul Laurence Dunbar. **CP-DunbP**

He was a shepherd of the Arcadian mood. Richard. Gerard Manley Hopkins. **CP-HopkG**

He was a soaring pine-tree. Marriage. John Gould Fletcher. **SP-FletJ**

He was a soldier, he was a madman, he was a hermit. Hayden Carruth. *Fr.* The Sleeping Beauty. **CP-CarHL**

He was a soldier in the army. Casualty. Langston Hughes. **SP-HughL**

He was a two-bit Petrarchist who lounged. Ritratto. Erica Jong. **SP-JongE**

He was Alone (As in Reality) Upon His Humble Bed. Kenneth Patchen. **CP-PatcK**

He was at Naples writing letters home. Esthétique du Mal. Wallace Stevens. **CP-StevW**

He was at Naples writing letters home. Wallace Stevens. **CMoP; MeMAP; NOBA** *Fr.* Esthétique du Mal. **CP-StevW**

He was beautifully arrayed. To the Memory of Bernard Berenson. James Liddy. **CP-LiddJ**

He was boring often with his laborious talk. A Difficult Man. John Hewitt. **CP-HewiJ**

He was born in Alabama. Of De Witt Williams on His Way to Lincoln Cemetery. Gwendolyn Brooks. **NOBA; NoAM** *Fr.* A Street in Bronzeville. **SP-BrooG**

He was born in Deutschland, as you would suspect. The Progress of Faust. Karl Shapiro. **SP-ShapK**

He was born in Dublin, but two years later. A Biography of the Author: A Cento. Charles Tomlinson. **CP-TomlC**

He was born to wonder about numbers. Number Man. Carl Sandburg. **CP-SandC**

He was buried in a vacant property, for he was a stranger. The Burial Place of Ibn Abbad. Thomas Merton. *Fr.* Readings from Ibn Abbad. **CP-MertT**

He was content to speak of little things. The Lives of the Poets: Three Profiles. Erica Jong. **SP-JongE**

He was crude as a loon on land. His tongue. The Swimmer at Lake Edward. Richard Hugo. **CP-HugoR**

He was depressed so he made something. The Nihilist. Stephen Dobyns. **SP-DobyS**

He was farouche / with grey moustache. Fisherman Poet. Phoebe Hesketh. **SP-HeskP**

He Was Formidable. Robert Penn Warren. **LiSp** *Fr.* Ballad: Between the Boxcars. **SP-WarrR**

He was found by the Bureau of Statistics to be. The Unknown Citizen. Wystan Hugh Auden. **CP-AudeW**

He was in Cincinnati, she in Burlington. A Couple. Carl Sandburg. **CP-SandC**

He was just a. One for the Old Boy. Charles Bukowski. **SP-BukC3**

He was leaning by a face. Mismet. Thomas Hardy. **CP-HardT**

He was lying banged and battered, skewered. Dime Store Mystery. "Lou Reed." **SP-ReedL**

He was my host—he was my guest. Emily Dickinson. **CP-DickE**

He was my third roommate. We were together for twenty-four. The Telephone Call. John Yau. **SP-YauJo**

He was not able to read or write. The Gardener. Louis MacNeice. **FaBCIP; IIP** *Fr.* Novelettes. **CP-MacNL**

He was not bad, as emperors go, not really—. Apology for Domitian. Robert Penn Warren. **SP-WarrR**

He was not changed. His friends around the grave. Lazarus Not Raised. Thom Gunn. **CP-GunnT**

He was safe / behind the whitened face. Clown. Phoebe Hesketh. **SP-HeskP**

He was sitting in front of the fire, looking out. The Zenith and After. Ron Koertge. **SP-KoerR**

He was skin-and-bones, she was fat. Two. Frederick Morgan. *Fr.* Eight Triolets. **SP-MorgF**

He was the finest of our happy men. For a Dead Citizen. Allen Tate. **CP-TateA**

He was the first who had returned. Daniel Gerard Hoffman. **SP-HoffD**

He was the man—Pope Sixtus, that Fifth, that swineherd's son. The Bean-Feast. Robert Browning. **CP-BroR2**

He was the man you thought. Louis MacNeice. *Fr.* As In Their Time. **CP-MacNL**

He was the surveyor of his own ice-world. An Order of Service. Geoffrey Hill. **CP-HillG**

He was the youngest son of a strange brood. Otto. Theodore Roethke. **CP-RoetT**

He was their servant (some say he was blind). Wystan Hugh Auden. **CMoP** *Fr.* Sonnets from China. **CP-AudeW**

He was there as the yachts went by. A Maine Roustabout. Richard Eberhart. **CP-EberR**

He was there in my room. The Caged Bird. May Sarton. **SP-SartM**

He was thorn / pierced through my flesh. Cross. Phoebe Hesketh. **SP-HeskP**

He was to be found in directories. Louis MacNeice. *Fr.* As In Their Time. **CP-MacNL**

He was to weet a man of full ripe years. Edmund Spenser. **UV,** *sect.* 4, *canto* 3; *Fr.* The Faerie Queene. **CP-Spens**

He was too good, that's why he never got anywhere. The Burglar. Ron Koertge. **SP-KoerR**

He was very beautiful. The Master. Hilda Doolittle. **CP-DoolH**

He was very much the less attractive of the two: heavyset, part punk, part L.L. Bean. Love: Wrath. Charles Kenneth Williams. **SP-WillC**

He was weak, and I was strong—then. Emily Dickinson. **CP-DickE**

He was wise, / they said, / in being dead. The Message. Robert Creeley. **CP-CreeR**

He wastes time walking and telling the air, "I am superior even to the wind." Sketch of a Poet. Carl Sandburg. **CP-SandC**

He watched the stars and noted birds in flight. Wystan Hugh Auden. **CMoP** *Fr.* Sonnets from China. **CP-AudeW**

He watched with all his organs of concern. Wystan Hugh Auden. **PoA** *Fr.* The Quest. **CP-AudeW**

(Poem: "He watched with all his organs of concern.") **PoA**

He wears a rose of celluloid in water. Sweet Old Man. Marsden Hartley. **CP-HartM**

He went by sleep that drowsy route. Emily Dickinson. **CP-DickE**

He went to being called a Colored man. The Calling of Names. Maya Angelou. **SP-AngeM**

He went up under the gray leaves. *tr. fr. the German of* Rilke. Randall Jarrell. **CP-JarrR**

He went when I was four. Unmetalled Road. Steve Griffiths. **SP-GrifS**

He where the great sun looks his last. George Meredith. **CP-MerG2**

He who beneath thy shelt'ring wing resides. *ad. by* Alexander Pope. Bible, *O.T. See* Psalm 91: "He that dwelleth in the secret place. . . ."

He who binds to himself a joy. Eternity. William Blake. **AWP; ArNa; EBEV; EnlH; FaBoEE; ImPo; LAuP; LoBV; MeMBP; NOBE; NTP; NoP; OBNC; OxBSP; PFP; Poetr; RB; SCGP; SoSe; Spl; TrGrPo** *Fr.* Several Questions Answered. **CP-BlakW**

He who by peaceful inland water steers. Inland Waterway. Sir John Betjeman. **CP-BetjJ**

He-who-came-forth was. The Son. Denise Levertov. **CP-LeveD**

He who commends the vanquisht, speaks the Power. The Credit of the Conquerer. Robert Herrick. **CP-HerrR**

He who continually struck poses. Finale. Alun Lewis. **CP-LewiA**

He Who Excuses Himself Also Accuses Himself. Delmore Schwartz. **SP-SchwD**

He who, grown aged in this world of woe. Byron. **EPCY** *Fr.* Childe Harold's Pilgrimage. **CP-Byron**

He who had gone a beast. John Chrysostom. Richard Wilbur. **CP-WilbR**

He who has a thousand friends has not a friend to spare. Omar Khayyám, *tr. fr. Persian by* Ralph Waldo Emerson. **CP-EmerR**

He who has compared himself to the eye of a horse. Boris Pasternak. "Anna Akhmatova", *tr. fr. Russian by* Stanley Kunitz *with* Max Hayward. **CP-KuniS**

He who has looked upon Earth. The Day of the Daughter of Hades. George Meredith. **CP-MerG1**

He who has looked upon Earth. George Meredith. *Fr.* The Day of the Daughter of Hades. **CP-MerG1**

He who has made his reckoning with life. Boethius, *tr. fr. Latin.* **MLL,** *tr. by* Helen Waddell; *Fr.* Consolation of Philosophy, The ("De Consolacione Philosophie"). **CP-ChauG**

He who has no hands. Orator. Ralph Waldo Emerson. **OxBA** *Fr.* Quatrains. **CP-EmerR**

He, who has suffer'd Ship-wrack, feares to saile. Ship-Wrack. Robert Herrick. **CP-HerrR**

He who in Himself believes. Emily Dickinson. **CP-DickE**

He, Who, in His Abandnoned Infancy, Spoke of Jesus, Caesar, Those Who Beg, and Hell. Charles Olson. **CP-OlsoC**

He, who in his youth. William Wordsworth. **TOF** *Fr.* Books. *Fr.* The Prelude; Growth of a Poet's Mind [1850 vers.]. **CP-WorW3**

He who is ridden by a conscience. Reflection of the Fallibility of Nemesis. Ogden Nash. **CP-NashO**

He, who navigated with success. Death of a Young Son by Drowning. Margaret Atwood. **SP-AtwM1**

He who of Rankine [*or* R--k-n] sang, lies stiff and dead. Robert Burns. **CP-BurnR**

(Lines: "He who of R--k-n sang, lies stiff and dead.") **CP-BurnR**

He, who once was my brother, is dead by his own hand. Justice Is Reason Enough. Diane Wakoski. **SP-WakoD**

He who proposes. On a Proposed Celebration of Ezra Pound. Donald Davie. **CP-DavDo**

He who remains. Richard Shelton. **SP-ShelR**

He who rules men lives in confusion. The Empty Boat. Chuang Tzu, *tr. fr. Chinese by* Thomas Merton. **CP-MertT**

He who saw everything, of him learn, o my land, learn. Bigmans II. Charles Olson. **CP-OlsoC**

He who sits from day to day. On a Similar Occasion for the Year 1790. William Cowper. **CP-CowpW**

He who sublime in epic numbers roll'd. *Fr. the Latin of Domitius Marsus.* Byron. **CP-Byron**

He who taught man to vanquish whatsoever. Percy Bysshe Shelley. *Fr.* Ode to Liberty. **CP-ShelP**

He who wears Blacks, and mournes not for the Dead. False Mourning. Robert Herrick. **CP-HerrR**

He who will not work shall not eat. George Oppen. *Fr.* Of Being Numerous. **CP-OppeG**

He whom God had thus preferred. Ralph Waldo Emerson. **CP-EmerR**

He whom the dread of want ensnares. 3.24. Horace. **CP-JohnS**, *tr. by* Samuel Johnson; *Fr.* Odes.

He whom we anatomized. Basil Bunting. *Fr.* Villon. **CP-BuntB**

He whose law is within himself. The Inner Law. Chuang Tzu, *tr. fr. Chinese by* Thomas Merton. **CP-MertT**

He will bomb the final town. North. Richard Hugo. **CP-HugoR**

He will watch the hawk with an indifferent eye. Stephen Spender. **CP-SpenS**

(Airman.) **CP-SpenS**

He Wishes for the Cloths of Heaven. William Butler Yeats. **CP-YeatW**

He Wishes His Beloved Were Dead. William Butler Yeats. **CP-YeatW**

He with body waged a fight. The Four Ages of Man. William Butler Yeats. **CP-YeatW**

He with the Beating Wings. Lawrence Ferlinghetti. **SP-FerlL**

He woke in his usual room, decided. Good Dream. Louis MacNeice. **CP-MacNL**

He woke in terror to a sky more bright. Edna St. Vincent Millay. *Fr.* Epitaph for the Race of Man. **CP-MillE**

He won her Classic races, at the start. The Last Fistful. Robert Ranke Graves. **CP-GravR**

He Wonders about Himself. Thomas Hardy. **CP-HardT**

He wore a butterfly upon his flanks. He Too Wore a Butterfly. Marsden Hartley. **CP-HartM**

He wore his coffin for a hat. For a Pessimist. Countee Cullen. **CP-CullC**

He worried every morning about the bomb. He Glimpses a Nobler Vision. Miller Williams. **SP-WillM**

He would declare and could himself believe. Never Again Would Birds' Song Be the Same. Robert Frost. **CP-FrosR**

He would do as he had done in other states. Muriel Rukeyser. **CP-RukeM**

He would drink by himself. Casualty. Seamus Heaney. **SP-HeanS**

He would hoard this hill, this salal. Triangle for Green Men. Richard Hugo. **CP-HugoR**

He would like not to kill. He would like. The Robber Bridegroom. Margaret Atwood. **SP-AtwM2**

He would never say any of this. Barton Sutter. *Fr.* What the Country Man Knows By Heart. **SP-SuttB**

He would not stay for me; and who can wonder? Alfred Edward Housman. **CP-HousA**

He wounds with ecstasy. All. Geoffrey Hill. *Fr.* Tenebrae. **CP-HillG**

He writes: Let us bear. The Days: Spring. Adrienne Rich. **CP-RicAE**

He writes to the editors. An Old Buddy. Charles Bukowski. **SP-BukC3**

He wrote for the dead, but the ubiquitous dead. Malcolm Lowry. *Fr.* Songs for Second Childhood. **CP-LowrM**

He Wrote the History Book. Marianne Craig Moore. **CP-MoorM**

He wrote *The I and the It*. On the Death of a German Philosopher. Stevie Smith. **CP-SmitS**

He/She. Stephen Dunn. **SP-DunnS**

Head. Carl Sandburg. **CP-SandC**

Head, A. James Schuyler. **CP-SchuJ**

Head a ray helix good morning. Sprengeri. Louis Zukofsky. **CP-ZukLS**

Head above the Fog, The. Thomas Hardy. **CP-HardT**

Head against White. Margaret Atwood. **SP-AtwM1**

Head-Aim, The. James Dickey. **CP-DickJ**

Head-Ake, The. Robert Herrick. **CP-HerrR**

Head alone shows you in the prodigious act. Perseus. Sylvia Plath. **CP-PlatS**

Head Byzantine or from, The. Resting Figure. Denise Levertov. **CP-LeveD**

Head: egg of all, The. Right Thinking Man. Marge Piercy. **SP-PierM**

Head fast / in out as dead. Dread Nay. Samuel Beckett. **CP-BeckS**

Head first, face down, into Mercator's world. For a Boy Born in Wartime. Jane Cooper. **SP-CoopJ**

Head Hewn with an Axe. Charles Tomlinson. **CP-TomlC**

Head is launc'd to worke the bodie's cure, The. The Circumcision. Robert Southwell. **CP-SoutR**

Head Lines. Louis Zukofsky. **CP-ZukLS**

Head man did the right thing. He displayed, The. Late Night Movies III. John Yau. **SP-YauJo**

Head of. A. Robert Creeley. **CP-CreeR**

Head of a Woman. Al Young. **CP-YounA**

Head of Bran the Blest, The. George Meredith. **CP-MerG1**

Head of the District, The. Rudyard Kipling. *Fr.* Life's Handicap. "There's a convict more in the Central Jail." **CP-KiplR**

Head of Wisdom, The. Randall Jarrell. **CP-JarrR**

Head on the Table, The. John Haines. **SP-HainJ**

Head or Tail—which does he lack?, A. The Hippo. Theodore Roethke. **CP-RoetT**

Head pure, sinless quite of brain or soul, A. Robert Burns. **FaBoEE** *Fr.* Versicles on Sign-Posts. **CP-BurnR**

Head thrusts in as for the view, A. All Revelation. Robert Frost. **CP-FrosR**

Head to limp head, the sunk-eyed wounded scanned. Smile, Smile, Smile. Wilfred Owen. **CP-OwenW**

Headdress. Rita Dove. **SP-DoveR**

Heading for Nandi. John Updike. **CP-UpdiJ**

Heading North, straw hat. Jiving. Rita Dove. **SP-DoveR**

Headland towers over ocean, The. California. George Oppen. **CP-OppeG**

Headless, lacking foot and hand. Unknown Female Corpse. Rudyard Kipling. **PoWW** *Fr.* Epitaphs of the War [1914–1918]. **CP-KiplR**

Headless squirrel, some blood, A. A Day Begins. Denise Levertov. **CP-LeveD**

Headlights fading out at dawn, The. A New Day. Philip Levine. **SP-LeviP**

Heads. James Dickey. **CP-DickJ**

Heads, impenetrable / And the slow bulk, The. Oxen: Ploughing at Fiesole. Charles Tomlinson. **CP-TomlC**

Heads in the Women's Ward. Philip Larkin. **CP-LarkP**

Heads up to the sky. Juggler's Thought. Robert Creeley. **CP-CreeR**

Heagles how they fly in great circles!, The. Kraken, Eagles, in British Columbia. Malcolm Lowry. **CP-LowrM**

Heal the soul, O still-featured host. Progress to a View of Life. Kenneth Patchen. **CP-PatcK**

Heal us, Emmanuel, here we are. Jehovah-Rophi. William Cowper. *Fr.* Olney Hymns. **CP-CowpW**

Healall. William Carlos Williams. **CP-WilW1**

Healed Heart shows its shallow scar, The. Emily Dickinson. **CP-DickE**

Healer, The. Charles Simic. **SP-SimiC**

Healer, The. John Greenleaf Whittier. **CP-WhitJ**

Healing. David Herbert Lawrence. **CP-LawrD**

Health. Robert Herrick. **CP-HerrR**

Health-Food Diner, The. Maya Angelou. **SP-AngeM**

Health is everything, health is all. Bathing Resort. David Herbert Lawrence. **CP-LawrD**

Health is no other (as the learned hold). Health. Robert Herrick. **CP-HerrR**

Health is the first good lent to men. Four[e] Things Make Us Happy Here. Robert Herrick. **CP-HerrR**

Health Lantern. Patti Smith. **SP-SmitP**

Health to the Maxwels' veteran Chief! To Terraughty, on His Birth-Day. Robert Burns. **CP-BurnR**

Health to the nut-brown lass, A. Sir John Suckling. *Fr.* The Goblins. **CP-SuckJ**

Healthy human child will keep, The. The Absentees. Ogden Nash. *Fr.* Posies from a Second Childhood, or, Hark How Gaffer Do Chaffer. **CP-NashO**

Healthy Spot, A. Wystan Hugh Auden. **CP-AudeW**

Heaney, one can get word-perfect at. Summer Lightning. Donald Davie. **CP-DavDo**

Heap cassia, sandal-buds and stripes. Robert Browning. **OBEV** *Fr.* Paracelsus. **CP-BroR1**

Heap high the farmer's wintry hoard! The Corn-Song. John Greenleaf Whittier. **GN; OHIP** *Fr.* The Huskers. **CP-WhitJ**

Heap not on this mound. Epitaph. Edna St. Vincent Millay. **CP-MillE** *Fr.* Memorial to D. C. **CP-MillE**

Heap of Broken Images, A. Lawrence Ferlinghetti. **SP-FerlL**

Heap we these coppered hulls. Voyage. Archibald MacLeish. **CP-MacLA**

Heaped hemlock, The. Celestial Dealings. Archie Randolph Ammons. **SP-AmmoA**

Hear, Alfred, father of the state. To Alfred. James Thomson *and* David Mallet. **CP-ThomJ** *Fr.* Alfred: A Masque.

Hear her / (Clear mirror). With a Valentine (the 14 February). Louis Zukofsky. *Fr.* Songs of Degrees. **CP-ZukLS**

Hear, her. Songs of Degrees. Louis Zukofsky. **CP-ZukLS**

Hear, her. With a Valentine (the 12 February). Louis Zukofsky. *Fr.* Songs of Degrees. **CP-ZukLS**

Hear it tease question will. Crocus. Louis Zukofsky. **CP-ZukLS**

Hear, Jehovah! / May the eternal serpent's curse be on him! Byron. **NOBRP** *Fr.* Cain: A Mystery. **CP-Byron**

Hear, Land o' Cakes, and brither Scots. On the Late Captain Grose's Peregrinations thro' Scotland, Collecting the Antiquities of That King. Robert Burns. **CP-BurnR**

Hear, Lord, the song of praise and pray'r. Hymn for the Sunday School at Olney. William Cowper. **CP-CowpW**

Hear Me. Philip Levine. **SP-LeviP**

Hear me [*or* Heare mee], O God! A Hymn[e] to God the Father. Ben Jonson. **CP-JonsB**

Hear me when I call, O God of my righteousness. Psalm 4. Bible, *O.T.* *Fr.* Psalms. **CP-Psal**

Hear, my belovéd, an old Milesian story! Catullian Hendecasyllables. Samuel Taylor Coleridge. **CP-ColeS**

Hear my cry, O God; attend unto my prayer. Psalm 61. Bible, *O.T.* *Fr.* Psalms. **CP-Psal**

Hear my prayer my father. Charles Olson. **CP-OlsoC**

Hear my prayer, O Lord, and let my cry come unto thee. Psalm 102. Bible, *O.T.* **BiP** *Fr.* Psalms. **CP-Psal**

Hear my prayer, O Lord, give ear to my supplications. Psalm 143. Bible, *O.T.* *Fr.* Psalms. **CP-Psal**

Hear my prayer, O Lord, hear my request. Bible, *O.T.* *See* Psalm 143: "Hear my prayer, O Lord, give ear. . . ."

Hear my rigamarole. A Reflex. Robert Frost. **CP-FrosR**

Hear my voice, O God, in my prayer. Psalm 64. Bible, *O.T.* *Fr.* Psalms. **CP-Psal**

Hear now a curious dream I dreamed last night. My Dream. Christina Georgina Rossetti. **CP-RosC1**

Hear now the mission of good wine. George Meredith. **CP-MerG2**

Hear now the Song of the Dead—in the North by the torn berg-edges. The Song of the Dead. Rudyard Kipling. **CP-KiplR**

Hear, O Lord, my loud cry, *vv. 7–14 of diff. tr., by* McFadyen. Bible, *O.T.* *See* Psalm 27: "Lord is my light and my salvation, The. . . ."

Hear, sweet spirit, hear the spell. Invocation, An. Samuel Taylor Coleridge. **CP-ColeS** *Fr.* Remorse.

Hear the beautiful tinny voices of the trumpets. Hearing. Kenneth Koch. **SP-KochK**

Hear the right, O Lord, attend unto my cry. Psalm 17. Bible, *O.T.* *Fr.* Psalms. **CP-Psal**

Hear the sledges with the bells. The Bells. Edgar Allan Poe. **CP-PoeEd**

Hear the voice of the Bard! Introduction. William Blake. **CP-BlakW** *Fr.* Songs of Experience.

Hear then the pride & knowledge of a Sailor. William Blake. **CP-BlakW** *Fr.* An Island in the Moon.

Hear this, all ye people; give ear, all ye inhabitants of the world. Psalm 49. Bible, *O.T.* *Fr.* Psalms. **CP-Psal**

Hear this, and tremble, all. Upon My Lord Chief Justice's Election of My Lady Anne Wentworth [*or* A.W.] for His Mistress. Thomas Carew. **CP-CareT**

Hear[e] us, O hear[e] us Lord; to thee. John Donne. *Fr.* A Litany. **CP-DonnJ**

Hear what British Merlin sung. Motto to "Considerations by the Way." Ralph Waldo Emerson. **CP-EmerR**

Hear what God the Lord hath spoken. The Future Peace and Glory of the Church. William Cowper. **ChIV-1** *Fr.* Olney Hymns. **CP-CowpW**

Hear what the glass will tell thee. Hafiz, *tr. by* Ralph Waldo Emerson. **CP-EmerR** *Fr.* Odes.

Hear what the mournful linnets say. Christina Georgina Rossetti. **CP-RosC2**

Hear ye not the gloomy yelling. Madness. Robert Browning. **FL** *Fr.* The Dance of Death. **CP-BroR2**

Hear[e] ye Virgins, and I'll [*or* Ile] teach. To Virgins. Robert Herrick. **CP-HerrR**

Heard and Seen. Wystan Hugh Auden. **CP-AudeW**

Heard by a Girl. Louise Bogan. **CP-BogaL**

Heard in a Violent Ward. Theodore Roethke. **CP-RoetT**

Heard melodies are sweet, but those unheard. John Keats. *Fr.* Ode on a Grecian Urn. **CP-KeatJ**

Heard say that four times four is eight. A Footnote. Stephen Spender. **CP-SpenS**

Heard ye o' the tree o' France. The Tree of Liberty. Robert Burns. **CP-BurnR**

Heard ye the arrow hurtle in the sky? The Elections to the Hebdomadal Council. "Lewis Carroll." **CP-CarrL**

Heard'st thou yon universal cry. Destruction of the Bastile. Samuel Taylor Coleridge. **CP-ColeS**

Hearing. Kenneth Koch. **SP-KochK**

Hearing a car pass—. Sound. Robert Creeley. **CP-CreeR**

Hearing a white saint rave. On the Plethora of Dryads. Sylvia Plath. **CP-PlatS**

Hearing from some how the Sierra answers. Frontenac. Donald Davie. **CP-DavDo**

Hearing Irish Spoken. Brendan Galvin. **SP-GalvB**

Hearing of harvests rotting in the valleys. Wystan Hugh Auden. **CP-AudeW** (Paysage Moralisé.) **CP-AudeW**

Hearing of you, I never lost a brother. Stepping Outside. Tess Gallagher. **SP-GallT**

Hearing offstage the taps filling the bath. Schizophrene. Louis MacNeice. **CP-MacNL**

Hearing one saga, we enact the next. Remembering the 'Thirties. Donald Davie. **CP-DavDo**

Hearing Russian Spoken. Donald Davie. **CP-DavDo**

Hearing that you would come who by my love. Incantatory Poem. Jean Garrigue. **SP-GarrJ**

Hearing the hawk squeal in the high sky. The Rabbit. Edna St. Vincent Millay. **CP-MillE**

Hearing the thunder of the intransitive weirs. Arthur Rimbaud, *tr. by* Derek Mahon. **SP-MahoD** *Fr.* The Drunken Boat.

Hearing your words, and not a word among them. Edna St. Vincent Millay. **CP-MillE**

Heark Faile one how what e're here is / Doth laugh and sing at thy distresse. A Guiltlesse Lady Imprisoned; after Penanced. Richard Lovelace. **CP-LoveR**

Heark how she laughs aloud. Lucasta Laughing. Richard Lovelace. **CP-LoveR**

Hearke Reader! wilt be learn'd ith' warres? To My Truely Valiant, Learned Friend, Who in His Booke Resolv'd the Art Gladiatory into the Mathematick's. Richard Lovelace. **CP-LoveR**

Hearken, hearken! / Rapid river carrieth, The. Sounds. Elizabeth Barrett Browning. **CP-BroEB**

Hearken, landsmen, hearken, seamen. The Land of Biscay. Alfred Edward Housman. **CP-HousA**

Hearken!—now the hermit bee. The Quiet Enemy. Walter de la Mare. **CP-DeLaW**

Hearken, O dear, now strikes the hour we die. Life. Walter de la Mare. **CP-DeLaW**

Hearken, thou craggy ocean pyramid! To Ailsa Rock. John Keats. **CP-KeatJ**

Hearken! Tiny, clear, discrete. Clavichord. Walter de la Mare. **CP-DeLaW**

Hearken! 'Tis news I cry! News. Walter de la Mare. **CP-DeLaW**

Hears't thou, my soul, what serious things. Dies Irae. Thomas of Celano, *tr. fr. Latin by* Richard Crashaw. **CP-CrasR**

Hearst thou, sweet spirit, thou hast heard before. Ralph Waldo Emerson. **CP-EmerR**

Heart, The. Robert Herrick. **CP-HerrR**

Heart-affluence in discursive talk. Tennyson. *Fr.* In Memoriam A. H. H. **CP-TennA**

Heart and service to you proffered, The. Sir Thomas Wyatt. **CP-WyatT**

Heart asks Pleasure—first, The. Emily Dickinson. **CP-DickE**

Heart Attack. Gary Gildner. **SP-GildG**

Heart Beats. Donald Davie. **CP-DavDo**

Heart can think of no devotion, The. Devotion. Robert Frost. **CP-FrosR**

Heart, do not bruise the breast. Edna St. Vincent Millay. *Fr.* Theme and Variations. **CP-MillE**

Heart drops distilling like a new cut-vine. Mary Sidney, Countess of Montgomery Wroth. *Fr.* Urania. **CP-WrotM**

Heart Feels the Water. Joseph Ceravolo. **SP-CeraJ**

Heart has many Doors, The. Emily Dickinson. **CP-DickE**

Heart has narrow Banks, The. Emily Dickinson. **CP-DickE**

Heart has need of some deceit, The. Only the Polished Skeleton. Countee Cullen. **CP-CullC**

Heart, have no pity on this house of bone. Edna St. Vincent Millay. **CP-MillE**

Heart Healed and Changed by Mercy, The. William Cowper. *Fr.* Olney Hymns. **CP-CowpW**

Heart, heart, heart. . . yes, I know thee! The Meaning of Life. Kenneth Patchen. **CP-PatcK**

Heart, in the ardor of Whose holy day. The Transformation: For the Sacred Heart. Thomas Merton. **CP-MertT**

Heart is a clock, The. Charles Olson. **CP-OlsoC; SP-OlsoC**

Heart is the Capital of the Mind, The. Emily Dickinson. **CP-DickE**

Heart is the only workman, The. Emily Dickinson. **SP-DickE**

Heart Knoweth Its Own Bitterness, The. Christina Georgina Rossetti. **CP-RosC2**

Heart Knoweth Its Own Bitterness, The. Christina Georgina Rossetti. **CP-RosC3**

Heart may live a lifetime in an hour, The. Time. George Meredith. **CP-MerG2**

Heart, my heart, what will you do? Flight of the Heart. Louis MacNeice. **CP-MacNL**

Heart, not so heavy as mine. Emily Dickinson. **CP-DickE**

Heart of All the Scene, The. Ralph Waldo Emerson. **AA** *Fr.* Woodnotes I ("For this present, hard"). **CP-EmerR**

Heart of God. Nicholas Vachel Lindsay. **CP-LindV**

Heart of Herakles, The. Kenneth Rexroth. **NU** *Fr.* The Lights in the Sky are Stars. **SP-RexrK**

Heart of Joy, The. John Hewitt. **CP-HewiJ**

Heart of Man, The. David Herbert Lawrence. **CP-LawrD**

Heart of Mine. "Bob Dylan." **CP-DylaB**

Heart of my heart, the day is chill. A Misty Day. Paul Laurence Dunbar. **CP-DunbP**

Heart of the Southland, heed me pleading now. To the South. Paul Laurence Dunbar. **CP-DunbP**

Heart of the Woman, The. William Butler Yeats. **CP-YeatW**

Heart of Thomas Hardy, The. Sir John Betjeman. **CP-BetjJ**

Heart once broken is a heart no more, The. Edna St. Vincent Millay. **CP-MillE**

Heart oppressed [*or* oppress'd] with desperate thought. Sir Thomas Wyatt. **CP-WyatT**

Heart pounds / To be among them, the buildings, The. George Oppen. *Fr.* Tourist Eye. **CP-OppeG**

Heart-sick of his journey was the Wanderer. The Journey. Walter de la Mare. **CP-DeLaW**

Heart Test with an Echo Chamber. Margaret Atwood. **SP-AtwM2**

Heart too human. Louis Zukofsky. *Fr.* Sequence 1944-6. **CP-ZukLS**

Heart trapezing gaily about the ropes: hull. Baudelaire in Cythera. Basil Bunting, *after the French of* Baudelaire. **CP-BuntB**

Heart us invisbly thyme time. Louis Zukofsky. **CP-ZukLS**

Heart wants what it wants, The. Emily Dickinson. **SP-DickE**

Heart warm as Summer, fresh as Spring. Lady Isabella. Christina Georgina Rossetti. **CP-RosC3**

Heart! We [*or* Heart, we] will forget him! Emily Dickinson. **CP-DickE**

Heart, with what lonely fears you ached. Leda. Robert Ranke Graves. **CP-GravR**

Heartache. Stephen Berg. **SP-BergS**

Heartbeat trembling. Refusing Silence. Tess Gallagher. **SP-GallT**

Heartbreak October moon of sun. Where the Danube and Sava Rivers Meet. Al Young. **CP-YounA**

Heartfelt installations. / Beginnings are benevolent. Charles Henri Ford. **SP-FordC** *Fr.* Secret Haiku.

Hearth, The. Robert Ranke Graves. **CP-GravR**

Hearth Eternal, The. Nicholas Vachel Lindsay. **CP-LindV**

Heartily heartily / Nothing be false. Ralph Waldo Emerson. **CP-EmerR**

Heartily heartily sing. Ralph Waldo Emerson. **CP-EmerR**

Hearts' and Flowers'. Archibald MacLeish. **CP-MacLA**

Hearts and Flowers or What I Know about Bolivar Black. Ogden Nash. **CP-NashO**

Heart's Chill Between. Christina Georgina Rossetti. **CP-RosC3**

Heart's Ease. Louis Zukofsky. **CP-ZukLS**

Heart's Garden, the Garden's Heart, The. Kenneth Rexroth.

"Dust of man's trouble rises, The." **CP-RexKL**

"Eve of Ch'ing Ming—Clear Bright, The." **CP-RexKL; SP-RexrK**

"Gathering early morning / Mushrooms, the music of the." **CP-RexKL**

"Pausing in my sixth d-ecade." **CP-RexKL; SP-RexrK**

"Sound of gongs, the songs of birds, The." **CP-RexKL; SP-RexrK**

"Tea drinking, garden viewing." **CP-RexKL**

"Under the full moon strange birds." **CP-RexKL**

"Water in a bottle, The." **CP-RexKL**

"Water is always the same." **CP-RexKL**

"Young rice plants are just being." **CP-RexKL**

Hearts I lift out of snow, The. On Valentine's Day to Friends. Louis Zukofsky. **CP-ZukLS**

Hearts in Amherst ache tonight, The. Emily Dickinson. **SP-DickE**

Heart's Location, The. Peter Meinke. **SP-MeinP**

Heart's Music. Thomas Campion. **CP-CampT**

Heart's Needle. William DeWitt Snodgrass. **SP-SnodW**

Child of My Winter Born. **MoAmPo**

"Easter has come around." **CAPP; ConAP; NMP; NePoEA; VCAP**

"Here in the scuffled dust." **NCSH; NMP; NePoEA**

"I thumped on you the best I could." **NePoEA; NoAM**

"Late April and you are three; today." **NePoEA; VCAP**

"No one can tell you why." **ConAP; NePoEA**

"Vicious winter finally yields, The." **MoLi; NePoEA; SM**

Hearts-Of-Gold. Herman Melville. **SP-MelvH**

Hearts of Gold. Ogden Nash. **CP-NashO**

Hearts that never lean, must fall, The. Emily Dickinson. **SP-DickE**

Hearts Together. Sir John Betjeman. **CP-BetjJ**

Heartsease heart's ease love-in-idleness viola. Heart's Ease. Louis Zukofsky. **CP-ZukLS**

Heartsease I found, where Love-lies-bleeding / Empurpled all the ground. Balm in Gilead. Christina Georgina Rossetti. **CP-RosC2**

Heartsease in my garden bed, / With sweetwilliam white and red. Christina Georgina Rossetti. **CP-RosC2**

Heat. Allen Ginsberg. **CP-GinsA**

Heat-blaze, white dazzle: and white is the dust. Place and Time. Robert Penn Warren. **SP-WarrR**

Heat from the sky, and from the rubble of stones. The Geyser. Thom Gunn. *Fr.* The Geysers. **CP-GunnT**

Heat over all; not a lark can rise. Heat-Wave. Phoebe Hesketh. **SP-HeskP**

Heat-Wave. Phoebe Hesketh. **SP-HeskP**

Heat Wave. Malcolm Lowry. **CP-LowrM**

Heated Minutes, The. Louis MacNeice. **CP-MacNL**

Heath, The. Charlotte Smith. **CP-SmitC**

Heathen Are Come into Thine Inheritance, The. Bible, *O.T.* *See* Psalm 79: "O God, the heathen are come. . . ."

Heathen doth believe in Christ, The. Lines to Pope. Jonathan Swift. **CP-SwifJ**

Heather Ale: A Galloway Legend. Robert Louis Stevenson. **CP-StevR**

Heather and Calendulas. James Schuyler. **CP-SchuJ**

Heather and holly. Bites and Kisses. Robert Ranke Graves. **CP-GravR**

Heather was blooming, the meadows were mawn, The. Hunting Song. Robert Burns. **CP-BurnR**

Heave the anchor short! Sail Out for Good, Eidólon Yacht! Walt Whitman. **CP-WhitW**

Heaven. John Berryman. **CP-BerrJ**

Heaven. Robert Creeley. **CP-CreeR**

Heaven. Robert Ranke Graves. **CP-GravR**

Heaven. George Herbert. **CP-HerbG**

Heaven ("Heav'n is most fair"). Robert Herrick. **CP-HerrR**

Heaven ("Heaven is not given"). Robert Herrick. **CP-HerrR**

Heaven. Langston Hughes. **SP-HughL**

Heaven. Philip Levine. **SP-LeviP**

Heaven. John Milton. **OBS** *Fr.* Book III. *Fr.* Paradise Lost. **CP-MiltJ**

Heaven. Christina Georgina Rossetti. **CP-RosC3**

Heaven / was only half as far that night. Lawrence Ferlinghetti. **SP-FerlL**

Heaven and Earth. Elizabeth Barrett Browning. **CP-BroEB**

Heaven and Earth. Byron. **CP-Byron**

Heaven and Earth. Kenneth Patchen. **CP-PatcK**

Heaven and earth, and all that hear me plain. Sir Thomas Wyatt. **CP-WyatT**

Heaven and Earth one forme did beare, *ad. fr.* Greek *of* Euripides. Sir Walter Ralegh. **CP-RaleW**

"Heaven bless the babe!" they said. Humoresque. Edna St. Vincent Millay. **CP-MillE**

"Heaven" has different Signs—to me. Emily Dickinson. **CP-DickE**

Heaven-Haven. Gerard Manley Hopkins. **CP-HopkG**

Heaven is but a little way. Emily Dickinson. **SP-DickE**

Heaven is full of definite stars. Kenneth Rexroth. **CP-RexKL** *Fr.* The Homestead Called Damascus.

Heaven is full of definite stars. Kenneth Rexroth. **SP-RexrK** *Fr.* Heaven is full of definite stars. **CP-RexKL** *Fr.* The Homestead Called Damascus.

"Heaven is full of definite stars." **SP-RexrK**

Heaven Is Not Far. Christina Georgina Rossetti.

(Yet a Little While.) **CP-RosC2**

Heaven is not given for our good works here. Heaven. Robert Herrick. **CP-HerrR**

Heaven is so far of the Mind. Emily Dickinson. **CP-DickE**

"Heaven"—is what I cannot reach! Emily Dickinson. **CP-DickE**

Heaven now is not strives, alone, our breasts to fill. A Panegyre, on the Happy Entrance of James, Our Sovreign, to His First High Session of Parliament in This Kingdom, the 19 of March, 1603. Ben Jonson. **CP-JonsB**

Heaven of Animals, The. James Dickey. **CP-DickJ**

Heaven of the Poor, The. Richard Shelton. **SP-ShelR**

Heaven opened wide / Her ever during gates, harmonious sound. John Milton. **ChIV-1** *Fr.* Book VII. *Fr.* Paradise Lost. **CP-MiltJ**

Heaven or Hell. Jim Morrison. **SP-MorrJ**

Heaven overarches earth and sea. Christina Georgina Rossetti. **CP-RosC3**

Heaven, the earth, and all the liquid mayne, The. Virgil, *tr.* by Sir Walter Ralegh. **CP-RaleW** *Fr.* The Aeneid [*or* Eneados, *Aeneis*].

Heaven vests for Each, The. Emily Dickinson. **CP-DickE**

Heaven will not be as good as Earth. Emily Dickinson. **SP-DickE**

Heaven won't have to do with its multitudes. The Saints. Robert Creeley. **CP-CreeR**

Heavenly Archer, bend thy bow. Dust to Dust. Walter de la Mare. **CP-DeLaW**

Heavenly Circuit; Berenice's Hair, The. Veronica's Napkin. William Butler Yeats. **CP-YeatW**

Heavenly City, The. Thomas Merton. **SP-MertT** *Fr.* Figures for an Apocalypse. **CP-MertT**

Heavenly City, The. Stevie Smith. **CP-SmitS**

"Heavenly Father"—take to thee. Emily Dickinson. **CP-DickE**

Heavens, The. Bible, *O.T.* *See* Psalm 19: "Heavens declare the glory of God, The."

Heavens Above and the Law Within, The, *sl. diff. vers., fr.* Moulton, Modern Readers' Bible. Bible, *O.T.* *See* Psalm 19: "Heavens declare the glory of God, The."

Heavens are lying like wreaths, The. A Last Song. "Hugh MacDiarmid." **SP-MacDH**

Heaven's chimes are slow, but sure to strike at last. Christina Georgina Rossetti. **CP-RosC2**

Heavens declare God's glory, The, *par.* by Stephen Mitchell. Bible, *O.T.* *See* Psalm 19: "Heavens declare the glory of God, The."

Heavens declare the glory of God, The. Psalm 19. Bible, *O.T.* **AWP; BLRP; BiP; ChTr; FaPON; NAWM-1; OBVE; TRV; TrGrPo; TrJP; WBLP** *Fr.* Psalms. **CP-Psal**

Heavens doe declare, The / The majesty of God, *fr.* the Bay Psalm Book. Bible, *O.T.* *See* Psalm 19: "Heavens declare the glory of God, The."

Heaven's glory shone where he was laid. Emily Brontë. **CP-BronE**

Heavens rejoice in motion, why should I, The. Variety. John Donne. *Fr.* Elegies. **CP-DonnJ**

Heavens sway at his touch, The. There Is One Who Watches. Kenneth Patchen. **CP-PatcK**

Heavens! What a goodly prospect spreads around. Happy Britannica. James Thomson. **FaBoPP; OBEC; SeCePo** *Fr.* Summer. *Fr.* The Seasons. **CP-ThomJ**

Heaviest of Flowers, the Head. Philip Larkin. **CP-LarkP**

Heaviness May Endure for a Night, But Joy Cometh in the Morning. Christina Georgina Rossetti. **CP-RosC2**

Heaviness of His Wisdom, The. Wendell Berry. *Fr.* The Handing Down. **CP-BerrW**

Heavnly Frame sets forth the Fame, The, *sel. of par.* by Sir Philip Sidney. Bible, *O.T.* *See* Psalm 19: "Heavens declare the glory of God, The."

Heavy and Light. Carl Sandburg. **CP-SandC**

Heavy and yellow with the clay wrack from the flooded valley. Robinson Jeffers. **CP-JefR3**

Heavy blue chain, The. Ralph Waldo Emerson. **CP-EmerR**

Heavy crow, the jay and daw, The. Dawn in Threshing Time. Robert Bly. **SP-BlyR**

Heavy Date. Wystan Hugh Auden. **CP-AudeW**

Heavy gloves / or better. Hayden Carruth. *Fr.* North Winter. **CP-CarHL**

Heavy hangs the raindrop. A.E. Emily Brontë. **NBM** *Fr.* The Two Children. **CP-BronE**

Heavy hangs the raindrop. The Two Children. Emily Brontë. **CP-BronE**

Heavy heart, Belovèd, have I borne, A. Sonnet. Elizabeth Barrett Browning. *Fr.* Sonnets from the Portuguese. **CP-BroEB**

Heavy heart, if ever heart was heavy, A. Christina Georgina Rossetti. **CP-RosC2**

Heavy mahogany door with its wrought-iron screen, The. Devonshire Street W.1. Sir John Betjeman. **CP-BetjJ**

Heavy old man in his bed at night, The. The Call of the Wild. Gary Snyder. **CP-SnydG**

Heavy Sermon!, A—Sure the error's great. Impromptu on Hearing a Sermon by the Rev. T. R—Pronounced "Heavy." Robert Browning. **CP-BroR2**

Heavy Surf, A. Pablo Neruda, *tr. fr. Spanish* by Ben Belitt. **SP-NeruP**

Heavy umbrellas / aren't worth their weight, The. Crocus Night. James Schuyler. **CP-SchuJ**

Heavy white rooves. Stillness. William Carlos Williams. **CP-WilW1**

Heavy Women. Sylvia Plath. **CP-PlatS**

Heber. Stevie Smith. **CP-SmitS**

Hebrew Nation did not write it, The. William Blake. **CP-BlakW**

Hebrides. Archibald MacLeish. **CP-MacLA**

Hebrides, The. Louis MacNeice. **CP-MacNL**

Hecate. George Meredith. **CP-MerG2**

Hector and Andromache. Homer. **CP-BroEB,** *tr.* by Elizabeth Barrett Browning; *Fr.* The Iliad.

Hector (for example) is dead. So also. The Baron Baedeker Blew His Nose and, Sighing, Departed. Howard Nemerov. **CP-NemeH**

Hector in the Garden. Elizabeth Barrett Browning. **CP-BroEB**

Hector spake to them thus, & the Trojans cheered with applauses. Night Watch of the Trojans before Troy. Homer, *tr.* by George Meredith. **CP-MerG2** *Fr.* The Iliad.

Hector the Collector. Shel Silverstein. **SP-SilS2**

Hector, this heard without a moment's stay. Translation of Part of the Dialogue Between Hector and Andromach; from the Sixth Book of Homer's *Iliad* (VI 390–502). Homer, *tr.* by Samuel Johnson. **CP-JohnS** *Fr.* The Iliad.

Hecuba. Euripides, *tr. fr. Greek.* **CP-DoolH** Sea-Choros.

He'd be alive today if he wasn't pretty. James Liddy. *Fr.* A Munster Song of Love and War. **CP-LiddJ**

He'd been a clod, he knew, yes, always aiming toward his vision of the good life, always acting on it. Alzheimer's: The Husband. Charles Kenneth Williams. **SP-WillC**

He'd been fighting it for years. Frozen Food Section. Charles Bukowski. **SP-BukC3**

He'd had enough / Of the patterns of heroes. The Return. Dabney Stuart. **SP-StuaD**

Hedge has torn some blossom from the cart of May, The. A Visit. Wystan Hugh Auden. **CP-AudWJ**

Hedge-Hog Seen in a Frequented Path, The. Charlotte Smith. **CP-SmitC**

Hedge Life. James Dickey. **CP-DickJ**

Hedge of Hemlocks, The. Edna St. Vincent Millay. **CP-MillE**

Hedgehog, The. John Clare. **SeCeV** *Fr.* The Hedgehog. **SP-ClarJ**

Hedgehog, The. John Clare. **SP-ClarJ**

Hedgehog, The. **SeCeV**

Hedgehog. John Hewitt. **CP-HewiJ**

Hedgehog. Paul Muldoon. **SP-MuldP**

Hedgehog: For R., The. John Hewitt. **CP-HewiJ**

Hedgehog hides beneath the rotten hedge, The. The Hedgehog. John Clare. **SeCeV** *Fr.* The Hedgehog. **SP-ClarJ**

Hedgehog hides beneath the rotten hedge, The. The Hedgehog. John Clare. **SP-ClarJ**

Hedgerows. Charles Tomlinson. **CP-TomlC**

Hedges Freaked With Snow. Robert Ranke Graves. **OxBTC** *Fr.* Three Songs for the Lute. **CP-GravR**

Hee-balou, my sweet, wee Donald. The Highland Balou. Robert Burns. **CP-BurnR**

Hee may owr profitt, and out Tuter prove. Sonnet 6. Mary Sidney, Countess of Montgomery Wroth. *Fr.* A Crowne of Sonetts Dedicated to Love. *Fr.* Pamphilia to Amphilanthus. **CP-WrotM**

Hee that shunns love doth love him self the less. Sonnet 8. Mary Sidney, Countess of Montgomery Wroth. *Fr.* A Crowne of Sonetts Dedicated to Love. *Fr.* Pamphilia to Amphilanthus. **CP-WrotM**

Heed the old oracles. The Undersong. Ralph Waldo Emerson. **AA** *Fr.* Woodnotes II ("As sunbeams stream through liberal space"). **CP-EmerR**

Heed the story of the man. Beautiful Soup. Gilbert Sorrentino. **SP-SorrG**

Heel and toe, heel and toe. The Dance. Paul Laurence Dunbar. **CP-DunbP**

Heel & Toe to the End. William Carlos Williams. **CP-WilW2**

Hee's dead: Oh what harsh musicks there. Upon the Death of a Freind. Richard Crashaw. **CP-CrasR**

Heh! Walk her round. Heave, ah, heave her short again! Anchor Song. Rudyard Kipling. **CP-KiplR**

Heidelberg Landlady, The. Erica Jong. **SP-JongE**

Heifetz—On the Air, Bell Telephone Program. Marsden Hartley. **CP-HartM**

"Heigh, boys!" cried Grandfather Bridgeman, "it's time before dinner to-day." Grandfather Bridgeman. George Meredith. **CP-MerG1**

Heigh-ho on a Winter Afternoon. Donald Davie. **CP-DavDo**

Heigh me! brazen of front, thou glutton for plunder, now can one. The Invective of Achilles. Homer, *tr.* by George Meredith. **CP-MerG1** *Fr.* The Iliad.

Heigho! the lark and the owl! Percy Bysshe Shelley. **PBBP** *Fr.* Charles the First. **CP-ShelP**

"Heigho!" yawned one day King Francis. The Glove. Robert Browning. **CP-BroR1**

Height of Man, The. Richard Eberhart. **CP-EberR**

Heights, The. Louis Zukofsky. **CP-ZukLS**

Heights, I never climbed through windows. Crossroads. Stephen Dobyns. **SP-DobyS**

Heights of Macchu Picchu, III, The. Pablo Neruda, *tr. fr. Spanish* by James Wright. **CP-WrigJ**

Heimdall. Frederick Morgan. **SP-MorgF**

Heine, Too, Lived in Germany. Kenneth Patchen. **CP-PatcK**

HEINRICH•HIMMLER•REICHSFUEHRER•SS—8•APRIL•1945•. William DeWitt Snodgrass. **SP-SnodW**

HEINRICH•HIMMLER•FORMER•REICHSFUEHRER•SS—29•APRIL•1945•. William DeWitt Snodgrass. **SP-SnodW**

HEINRICH•HIMMLER, FORMER•REICHSFUEHRER•SS—1•MAY•1945•. William DeWitt Snodgrass. **SP-SnodW**

Heir being born, was in his tender age, The. To My Honoured Friend, Master Thomas May, Upon His Comedy *The Heir*. Thomas Carew. **CP-CareT**

Heir to the office of a man not dead. A Miltonic Sonnet for Mr. Johnson on His Refusal of Peter Hurd's Official Portrait. Richard Wilbur. **CP-WilbR**

Heiress and Architect. Thomas Hardy. **CP-HardT**

Heirloom. Leonard Cohen. **CP-CoheL**

Heirloom. Kathleen Jessie Raine. **SP-RainK**

Heisenberg, Schrodinger, and Dirac. Quanta. Richard Eberhart. **CP-EberR**

Hélas. Robert Creeley. **CP-CreeR**

Hélas! Or Christus fails. Hélas. Robert Creeley. **CP-CreeR**

Held between wars / my lifetime. Käthe Kollwitz. Muriel Rukeyser. **CP-RukeM**

Held Breath, A. James Schuyler. **CP-SchuJ**

Held on the slightest of bamboo poles. Ode to the Chinese Paper Snake. Richard Eberhart. **CP-EberR**

Helen. Wystan Hugh Auden. **CP-AudWJ**

Helen. Edward Estlin Cummings. **CP-CummE**

Helen. Hilda Doolittle. **CP-DoolH**

Helen. Christopher Marlowe. *See* Was This the Face.

Helen. Peter Meinke. **SP-MeinP**

Helen. Paul Valéry, *tr. fr. French* by Richard Wilbur. **CP-WilbR**

Helen. Charles Kenneth Williams. **SP-WillC**

Helen All Alone. Rudyard Kipling. **CP-KiplR**

Helen, did Homer never see. Ode, An. Ben Jonson. **CP-JonsB**

Helen Grey. Christina Georgina Rossetti. **CP-RosC3**

Helen, had I known yesterday. Release. David Herbert Lawrence. **CP-LawrD**

Helen of Troy. Christopher Marlowe. *See* Was This the Face.

Helen on the Skaian Gates. Homer, *tr.* by George Meredith. **CP-MerG2** *Fr.* The Iliad.

Helen, thy beauty is to me. To Helen. Edgar Allan Poe. **CP-PoeEd**

Helena brought me / hang their heads. Lilacs. James Schuyler. **CP-SchuJ**

Helena Morley. Donald Davie. **CP-DavDo**

Helena, Where Homes Go Mad. Richard Hugo. **CP-HugoR**

Helen's Rape. Thom Gunn. **CP-GunnT**

Helen's Tower. Robert Browning. **CP-BroR2**

Helga. Carl Sandburg. **CP-SandC**

Heliodora. Hilda Doolittle. **CP-DoolH**

Helios. Hilda Doolittle. **CP-DoolH**

Helios and Athene. Hilda Doolittle. **CP-DoolH**

Helios makes all things right. Helios. Hilda Doolittle. **CP-DoolH**

Hell. Wystan Hugh Auden. **CP-AudeW**

Hell. Robert Ranke Graves. **CP-GravR**

Hell ("Hell is no other, but a soundless pit"). Robert Herrick. **CP-HerrR**

Hell ("Hell is the place where whipping-cheer abounds"). Robert Herrick. **CP-HerrR**

Hell ("At once with him they rose"). John Milton. **OBS** *Fr.* Book II. **FHYEP; NAEL-1; OxAEP-1** *Fr.* Paradise Lost. **CP-MiltJ**

Hell Fire ("Fire of Hell this strange condition hath, The"). Robert Herrick. **CP-HerrR**

Hell Fire ("One onely fire has Hell; but yet it shall"). Robert Herrick. **CP-HerrR**

Hell Gate. Alfred Edward Housman. **CP-HousA**

He'll hie me, par *is* he? The God divide her. Catullus. *See* Carmen 51: "Godlike the man who."

Hell is a city much like London. Percy Bysshe Shelley. **OBD; OBSV** *Fr.* Peter Bell the Third. **CP-ShelP**

Hell is Graduated. Max Jacob, *tr. fr. French* by Elizabeth Bishop. **CP-BishE**

Hell is neither here nor there. Hell. Wystan Hugh Auden. **CP-AudeW**

Hell is no other, but a soundless pit. Hell. Robert Herrick. **CP-HerrR**

Hell is the place where whipping-cheer abounds. Hell. Robert Herrick. **CP-HerrR**

Hell on the Wabash. Carl Sandburg. **CP-SandC**

Hell Poem, The. John Berryman. **CP-BerrJ**

Hell, they'll never let him in. Let Me In! Kenneth Patchen. **CP-PatcK**

He'll to the Moors. Michael Hartnett. **SP-HarMi**

Hellas. Percy Bysshe Shelley. **CP-ShelP**

    "But Greece and her foundations are." **GrIP**

    "Darkness has dawned in the east." **EnRP**

    "Life may change, but it may fly not." **EnRP**

    "World's great age begins anew, The." **AWP; ChTr; EBEV; EnRP; FiP; HAP; HeIP; ImPo; MeMBP; NAEL-2; NOBE; NoP; OAEL-2; OBEV; PoE; PoEL-4; SeCePo; TEP; TrGrPo**

    (Chorus from "Hellas.") **AWP**

    (Chorus: "World's great age begins anew, The.") **EBEV; HAP; NOBE; NoP; OAEL-2; PoEL-4**

    (Final Chorus, The.) **SeCePo**

    (Hellas.) **ChTr; OBEV**

    (New World, A.) **TrGrPo**

    (World's Great Age, The.) **ImPo; MeMBP**

    "Worlds on worlds are rolling ever." **EnRP; HeIP; NAEL-2; NoP; TEP**

    (Chorus: "Worlds on worlds are rolling ever.") **NAEL-2**

    (Worlds on Worlds.) **HeIP**

Hellas. Percy Bysshe Shelley. *See* The World's great age begins anew.

Hellenistics. Robinson Jeffers. **CP-JefR2**

Hello. John Berryman. **CP-BerrJ**

Hello. Robert Creeley. **CP-CreeR**

Hello Again. Leonard Nathan. **SP-NathL**

Hello Goodbye. The Beatles. **CP-Beatl**

Hello is what a mirror says. Edward Estlin Cummings. **CP-CummE**

Hello It's Me. "Lou Reed." **SP-ReedL**

Hello, little bearded squirrel-eyed fellow. Aor Against the Philistine Who Destroyed Lovely Dublin Vistas With His Ugly Erections, Then Absconded to London. James McAuley. **SP-McAuJ**

Hello, ole man, you're a-gittin' gray. Growin' Gray. Paul Laurence Dunbar. **CP-DunbP**

Hello, sailor boy. Port Town. Langston Hughes. **SP-HughL**

He*llo* there, Biscuit! You're a better-looking broad. Hello. John Berryman. **CP-BerrJ**

Hello to you, lady / who will not stay with me. An Irishman's Lament on the Approaching Winter. Robert Creeley. **CP-CreeR**

Hello Up There. Marge Piercy. **SP-PierM**

Hello, Willie Shoemaker. Charles Bukowski. **SP-BukC2**

Hello young sailor. / You are betrayed and. Martial Choreograph. Maya Angelou. **SP-AngeM**

Hells and Heavens. Carl Sandburg. **CP-SandC**

Hellvellyn. Sir Walter Scott. **SP-ScotW**

Helmet, The. Philip Levine. **SP-LeviP**

Helmet of Goliath, The. Robert Duncan. **SP-DuncR**

Helms Bakery Man, The. Diane Wakoski. **SP-WakoD**

Helmsman, The. Hilda Doolittle. **CP-DoolH**

Helmsman came in a yellow truck, The. The Helms Bakery Man. Diane Wakoski. **SP-WakoD**

Helmut. Stephen Spender. **CP-SpenS**

Heloise. Ted Berrigan. **SP-BerrT**

Help! The Beatles. **CP-Beatl**

Help. John Greenleaf Whittier. **CP-WhitJ**

Help for a patriot distressed, a spotless spirit hurt. Cleared. Rudyard Kipling. **CP-KiplR**

Help for the Memory of the Grand Independent; A New Song, A. William Wordsworth. **CP-WorW2**

Help, help all tongues to celebrate this wonder. Ben Jonson. **CP-JonsB** *Fr.* The Masque of Queens.

Help! Help! they want to burn my pictures. Auto-Da-Fé. David Herbert Lawrence. **CP-LawrD**

Help, Lord; for the godly man ceaseth. Psalm 12. Bible, *O.T. Fr.* Psalms. **CP-Psal**

Help[e] me! help[e] me! now I call. To His Mistresses. Robert Herrick. **CP-HerrR**

Help me, Julia, for to pray. To Julia. Robert Herrick. **CP-HerrR**

Help[e] me to seek [*or* seke] for I lost it there. Sir Thomas Wyatt. **CP-WyatT**

Help Me, Venus, You Who Led Me On. Charles Olson. **CP-OlsoC**

Help Me with the Buttons. Siv Cedering Fox. **SP-CedeS**

Help Wanted. Charles Simic. **SP-SimiC**

Helping. Shel Silverstein. **SP-SilS2**

Helping the Dreamer. Anne Waldman. **SP-WaldA**

Helpless submarine is left aglow, The. Malcolm Lowry. *Fr.* The Canadian Turned Back at the Border. **CP-LowrM**

Helplessly besieging: it is dim. Snow Thickets. James Dickey. **CP-DickJ**

Helpmeet For Him, A. Christina Georgina Rossetti. **CP-RosC2**

Helter Skelter. The Beatles. **CP-Beatl**

Helter Skelter. Jonathan Swift. **CP-SwifJ**

Helves surling out of eakspeasies per(reel)hapsingly. Edward Estlin Cummings. **CP-CummE**

Hemingway. Archibald MacLeish. **CP-MacLA**

Hemlock and Cedar. Carl Sandburg. **CP-SandC**

Hemmed-in Males. William Carlos Williams. **CP-WilW1** *Fr.* A Folded Skyscraper.

Hemorrhage, The. Stanley Jasspon Kunitz. **CP-KuniS**

Hemp. . . / A stick. Gauge. Langston Hughes. **SP-HughL**

Hen and the Cock: A Glens Folk Rhyme, The. John Hewitt. **CP-HewiJ**

Hen Flower, The. Galway Kinnell. **SP-KinnG**

Henbane. Erica Jong. **SP-JongE**

Hence a blessed soule is fled. Upon a Maide. Robert Herrick. **CP-HerrR**

Hence, avaunt, ('tis holy ground). Ode for Music. Thomas Gray. **CP-GrayT**

Hence Burgundy, Claret, and Port. John Keats. **CP-KeatJ**

Hence, hence, profane; soft silence let us have. A Dirge upon the Death of the Right Valiant Lord, Bernard Stuart. Robert Herrick. **CP-HerrR**

Hence, hence prophane, and none appeare. Another New-Yeeres Gift, or Song for the Circumcision. Robert Herrick. **CP-HerrR**

Hence loathed Melancholy. L'Allegro. John Milton. **CP-MiltJ**

Hence my epistle—skim the deep—fly o'er. John Milton. *See* Elegy 4: To Thomas Young.

Hence sensual gross desires. Il Mystico. Gerard Manley Hopkins. **CP-HopkG**

Hence, soul-dissolving Harmony. Ode on the Ottery and Tiverton Church Music. Samuel Taylor Coleridge. **CP-ColeS**

Hence that fantastic wantonness of woe. Addressed to a Young Man of Fortune. Samuel Taylor Coleridge. **CP-ColeS**

Hence these arrears, this flinty cabinet crammed. Canto V. Louis MacNeice. *Fr.* Autumn Sequel. **CP-MacNL**

Hence they have born my Lord: Behold! the Stone. His Coming to the Sepulcher. Robert Herrick. **CP-HerrR**

Hence vain deluding joy[e]s. Il Penseroso. John Milton. **CP-MiltJ**

Hence, vain intruder, haste away! To My Rival. Thomas Carew. **CP-CareT**

Henceforth, from the Mind. Louise Bogan. **CP-BogaL**

Henceforth my slow skill I must only spend. Interim. John Hewitt. **CP-HewiJ**

Henceforth my slow wits I must only spend. Retreaded Rhymes. John Hewitt. **CP-HewiJ**

Henceforth of her the Gods are known. George Meredith. *Fr.* France. **CP-MerG1**

Henchman, The. John Greenleaf Whittier. **CP-WhitJ**

Hendecasyllabics. Algernon Charles Swinburne. **SP-SwinA**

Hendecasyllabics. Tennyson. **CP-TennA**

Hendecasyllables. Stevie Smith. **CP-SmitS**

Hendecasyllables, help! Come to my call. Catullus. *See* Carmen 42: "From the quarters of the compass."

Henley-on-Thames. Sir John Betjeman. **CP-BetjJ**

Henley Regatta. Thomas Hardy. **CP-HardT**

Henpeck'd Husband, The. Robert Burns. **CP-BurnR**

Henriette. David Herbert Lawrence. **CP-LawrD**

Henry Adams / Was mortally afraid of Madams. Wystan Hugh Auden. **OBAL** *Fr.* Academic Graffiti. **CP-AudeW**

Henry and Mary. Robert Ranke Graves. **CP-GravR**

Henry by Night. John Berryman. **CP-BerrJ**

Henry Hardiman. Christina Georgina Rossetti. **CP-RosC3**

Henry James. Robert Louis Stevenson. **CP-StevR**

Henry Purcell. Gerard Manley Hopkins. **CP-HopkG**

Henry was a young king. Henry and Mary. Robert Ranke Graves. **CP-GravR**

Henry's nocturnal habits were the terror of his women. Henry by Night. John Berryman. **CP-BerrJ**

Henyard Round, The. Donald Hall. **CP-HallD**

Heptonstall. Ted Hughes. **SP-HughT**

Heptonstall Cemetery. Ted Hughes. **SP-HughT**

Heptonstall Old Church. Ted Hughes. **SP-HughT**

Her / flesh / Came / at. Edward Estlin Cummings. **CP-CummE**

Her. Richard Shelton. **SP-ShelR**

Her advent was not hailed with shouts. Impromptu Lines to Greet Marie Bancroft. Robert Browning. **CP-BroR2**

Her & It. John Berryman. **CP-BerrJ**

Her Anxiety. William Butler Yeats. **CP-YeatW**

Her Apotheosis. Thomas Hardy. **CP-HardT**

Her arms around me—child—. From a Photograph. George Oppen. **CP-OppeG**

Her arms semaphore fat triangles. Momma Welfare Roll. Maya Angelou. **SP-AngeM**

Her arms two branches of the almond-tree that sway at morn in the. George Meredith. *Fr.* Arabic Poems. **CP-MerG2**

Her attachment may differ from yours in degree. Love and Friendship Opposite. Samuel Taylor Coleridge. **CP-ColeS**

Her back is bent beneath a million loads. Susan O'Kane. Louise McNeill. **SP-McNeL**

Her Beauty. Robert Ranke Graves. **CP-GravR**

Her Becoming. Theodore Roethke. *Fr.* Meditations of an Old Woman. **CP-RoetT**

Her Bed. Robert Herrick. **CP-HerrR**

Her big basket. Three Poems for Joanne. Gary Snyder. **CP-SnydG**

Her body is not so white as. Queen-Anne's-Lace. William Carlos Williams. **CP-WilW1**

Her breast big with rainbows. The Dove Came. Ted Hughes. **SP-HughT**

Her breast is cold; her hands how faint and wan! Virtue. Walter de la Mare. **CP-DeLaW**

Her breast is fit for pearls. Emily Dickinson. **CP-DickE**

Her breasts / Naked, the soft. The Zulu Girl. George Oppen. **CP-OppeG**

Her Brief Withdrawal. Robert Ranke Graves. **CP-GravR**

Her Broom, or the Ride of the Witch. Erica Jong. **SP-JongE**

Her brother is coming back tonight. Tennyson. *Fr.* Maud [A Monodrama]. **CP-TennA**

Her brown falcon perches above the sink. Exiles. Marilyn Hacker. **SP-HackM**

Her careful distinct sex whose sharp lips comb. Edward Estlin Cummings. **CP-CummE**

Her charms had struck a sturdy CAIRD. Robert Burns. *Fr.* The Jolly Beggars.

Her cheeks are as a crystal goblet held to the sun. George Meredith. *Fr.* Arabic Poems. **CP-MerG2**

Her Confession. Thomas Hardy. **CP-HardT**

Her conversation is interminable. In the Underground Station. Ron Koertge. **SP-KoerR**

Her counsel was accepted: the times are grave. Lady Luncheon Club. Maya Angelou. **SP-AngeM**

Her cunt lifts on a / velvet couch, red. Irish. Robert Creeley. **CP-CreeR**

Her Daddie forbad, her Minnie forbad. Jumpin John. Robert Burns. **CP-BurnR**

Her Daughter. Marsden Hartley. **CP-HartM**

Her Dead Brother. Robert Lowell. **SP-LoweR**

Her Death and After. Thomas Hardy. **CP-HardT**

Her Definition. Thomas Hardy. **CP-HardT**

Her Dilemma. Thomas Hardy. **CP-HardT**

Her Dream. Hayden Carruth. *Fr.* The Fifth Version. *Fr.* The Mythology of Dark and Light. **CP-CarHL**

Her Dream, *fr.* Words for Music Perhaps. William Butler Yeats. **CP-YeatW**

Her Dream, Half Remembered. Charles Olson. **CP-OlsoC**

Her dreameries had been raided. For Such a Bird He Had No Convenient Cage. Jean Garrigue. **SP-GarrJ**

Her dying feels to me. Emily Dickinson. **SP-DickE**

Her Eyes. John Crowe Ransom. **SP-RansJ**

Her Eyes. Edwin Arlington Robinson. **CP-RobiE**

Her eyes are homes of silent prayer. Tennyson. *Fr.* In Memoriam A. H. H. **CP-TennA**

Her eyes are like the putrid sores of infants. Mais L'Amour Infini Me Montera Dans L'Ame. Richard Eberhart. **CP-EberR**

Her Eyes Are Wild. William Wordsworth. **CP-WorW1**

Her eyes flood lickes his feets faire staine. Luke 7; She Began To Wash His Feet with Teares and Wipe Them with the Haires of Her Head. Bible, *N.T.* **CP-CrasR,** *tr. by* Richard Crashaw; *Fr.* St. Luke.

Her Eyes Had. . . . Hart Crane. **CP-CranH**

Her eyes the glow-worm[e] lend thee. The Night-Piece, to Julia. Robert Herrick. **CP-HerrR**

Her face is applewhite, just where the. Musicologist—Preference, Prokofieff. Marsden Hartley. *Fr.* City Vignettes. **CP-HartM**

Her face like a rain-beaten stone on the day she rolled off. Elegy. Theodore Roethke. **CP-RoetT**

Her face the Book of—Love Delights in—Praises. Louis Zukofsky. **CP-ZukLS**

Her face this moon a house. Cameo of a Chinese Woman on Mulberry Street. John Yau. **SP-YauJo**

Her face was in a bed of hair. Emily Dickinson. **CP-DickE**

Her face was like an opening rose. The Last Look. Christina Georgina Rossetti. **CP-RosC3**

Her fate seizes her and brings her. Her First Calf. Wendell Berry. **CP-BerrW**

Her Father. Thomas Hardy. **CP-HardT**

Her father. Spirit of '76. William Carlos Williams. **CP-WilW1**

Her father was a policeman who went fishing summer Sundays and. Two Women and Their Fathers. Carl Sandburg. **CP-SandC**

Her father's brother rapes her! The Fountain of Cyanë. Donald Davie. **CP-DavDo**

Her fayre inflaming eyes. Thomas Campion. **CP-CampT**

Her feet beneath her petticoat. The Bride. Sir John Suckling. **TrGrPo** *Fr.* A Ballad[e] [upon a Wedding]. **CP-SuckJ**

Her final Summer was it. Emily Dickinson. **CP-DickE**

Her fingers shame the ivory keys. John Greenleaf Whittier. **AnAmPo; BeLS** *Fr.* Amy Wentworth. **CP-WhitJ**

Her First Calf. Wendell Berry. **CP-BerrW**

Her flowing locks, the raven's wing. Fragment. Robert Burns. **CP-BurnR**

Her gentle limbs did she undress. Christabel and Geraldine. Samuel Taylor Coleridge. **PeHV** *Fr.* Christabel. **CP-ColeS**

Her Grace is all she has. Emily Dickinson. **CP-DickE**

Her grace is not of any part. The Unwithered Garland. Stanley Jasspon Kunitz. **CP-KuniS**

Her Grave. Mary Oliver. **SP-OlivM**

Her great adventure ended. S-sss-ss-sh! Langston Hughes. **SP-HughL**

Her hair burns but is never consumed. Her. Richard Shelton. **SP-ShelR**

Her hair is a brilliant red, and her voice like a bumblebee's hum. My Best Girl. Paul Laurence Dunbar. **CP-DunbP**

Her hair was tawny with gold, her eyes with purple were dark. A Court Lady. Elizabeth Barrett Browning. **CP-BroEB**

Her hands intend no harm. Portrait. Philip Larkin. **CP-LarkP**

Her hands, like albino frogs. Making a Sacher Torte. Diane Wakoski. **SP-WakoD**

Her Hat. Robert Penn Warren. **SP-WarrR**

Her Haunting-Ground. Thomas Hardy. **CP-HardT**

Her heart a bruise on the Christ-flesh suffered out of locked agonies of rebirth. The Rose of Solitude. William Everson. **SP-EverW** *Fr.* The Rose of Solitude.

Her heart that loved me once is rottenness. Two Thoughts of Death. Christina Georgina Rossetti. **CP-RosC3**

Her house loomed at the end of a Berkshire lane. Not at Home. Robert Ranke Graves. **CP-GravR**

Her house loooked cold from the foggy lea. In Her Precincts. Thomas Hardy. **CP-HardT**

Her Husband. Ted Hughes. **SP-HughT**

Her imaginary playmate was a grown-up. Cinderella. Randall Jarrell. **CP-JarrR; SP-JarrR**

Her Immortality. Thomas Hardy. **CP-HardT**

Her inevitable complaint or accusation. Semi-Detached. Robert Ranke Graves. **CP-GravR**

Her Initials. Thomas Hardy. **CP-HardT**

Her Irish maids could never spoon out mush. Mary Winslow. Robert Lowell. **SP-LoweR**

Her iron beats. Michael Hartnett. **SP-HarMi**

(Bread.) **SP-HarMi**

Her jaw wagging. His Daughter. William Carlos Williams. **CP-WilW2**

Her jealous Husband an Adultresse gave. Ausonius, *tr. fr. Latin by* Richard Lovelace. **CP-LoveR**

Her Kind. Anne Sexton. **CP-SextA**

Her—"last Poems." Emily Dickinson. **CP-DickE**

Her Late Husband. Thomas Hardy. **CP-HardT**

Her laugh was not in the middle of her face quite. A Countenance. Thomas Hardy. **CP-HardT**

Her laughter was infectious; so, some found. The Ecstasies of Dialectic. Howard Nemerov. **CP-NemeH**

Her Legs. Robert Herrick. **CP-HerrR**

Her little Parasol to lift. Emily Dickinson. **CP-DickE**

Her long with ardent look his Eye pursu'd. John Milton. **UnPo** *Fr.* Book IX. **FHYEP; NAEL-1; NAWM-1; NoP; OAEL-1** *Fr.* Paradise Lost. **CP-MiltJ**

Her Longing. Theodore Roethke. **CP-RoetT**

Her loss is as something beautiful in air. Loss. Richard Eberhart. **CP-EberR**

Her Losses make our Gains ashamed. Emily Dickinson. **CP-DickE**

Her Love-Birds. Thomas Hardy. **CP-HardT**

Her luchts o' yellow hair. The Huntress and Her Dogs. "Hugh MacDiarmid." *Fr.* Au Clair de la Lune. **SP-MacDH**

Her Majesty. The Beatles. **CP-Beatl**

Her Majesty / Showing the Library. Vivat. Frank Templeton Prince. **CP-PrinF**

Her Majesty never shall be my exalter. Epigram on the Hermitage at Richmond. Jonathan Swift. **CP-SwifJ**

Her Majesty's Servants. Rudyard Kipling. *Fr.* The Jungle Book. Parade-Song of the Camp Animals. **CP-KiplR**

Her mama said, "Don't eat with your fingers." Ridiculous Rose. Shel Silverstein. **SP-SilS2**

Her Man Described by Her Own[e] Dictamen. Ben Jonson. *Fr.* A Celebration of Charis in Ten Lyric[k] Pieces [*or* Peeces]. **CP-JonsB**

Her milk don't seem to. Detail. William Carlos Williams. **CP-WilW2**

Her ministration was to heal. Granny Saunders. Louise McNeill. **SP-McNeL**

Her Muffe. Richard Lovelace. **CP-LoveR**

Her name is as a word of old romance. Robert Louis Stevenson. **CP-StevR**

Her name was Ate, mother of debate. The House of Ate. Edmund Spenser. **OBSC** *Fr.* The Faerie Queene. **CP-Spens**

Her name was written somewhere in cobwebs. The Lady Who Sang. Diane Wakoski. *Fr.* Fifteen Poems for a Lunar Eclipse None of Us Saw. **SP-WakoD**

Her Obedient Servant. Daniel Gerard Hoffman. **SP-HoffD**

Her of your name, whose fair inheritance. To Mrs. Magdalen Herbert: of St. Mary Magdalen. John Donne. **CP-DonnJ**

Her Only Pilot the Soft Breeze, the Boat. William Wordsworth. **CP-WorW2**

Her parents and her dolls destroyed. Belsen, Day of Liberation. Robert Earl Hayden. **CP-HaydR**

Her passions the shy violet. Hafiz. Ralph Waldo Emerson. *Fr.* Quatrains. **CP-EmerR**

Her pen drops eloquence as sweet. On a Letter of Miss Fanshawe. William Cowper. **CP-CowpW**

Her Pet. Thom Gunn. **CP-GunnT**

Her planted eye to-day controls. Fate. Ralph Waldo Emerson. **APN-1** *Fr.* Quatrains. **CP-EmerR**

Her Praise. William Butler Yeats. **CP-YeatW**

Her pretty feet. Upon Her Feet. Robert Herrick. **CP-HerrR**

Her prime of life—cut down too soon. Gerard Manley Hopkins. **CP-HopkG**

Her red dress stretched across the remembered small. No More Access to Her Underpants. John Updike. *Fr.* Two Sonnets Whose Titles Came to Me Simultaneously. **CP-UpdiJ**

Her reluctances are sweeter. Emily Dickinson. **SP-DickE**

Her Reproach. Thomas Hardy. **CP-HardT**

Her Reserved Looks. Richard Lovelace. **CP-LoveR**

Her Reticence. Theodore Roethke. **CP-RoetT**

Her Room. Kathleen Jessie Raine. **SP-RainK**

"Her room,"you'd say—and wonder why you'd called it. Sketch for a Portrait of Mme. G———M———. Archibald MacLeish. **CP-MacLA**

Her roots bound. A Woman Is Not a Potted Plant. Alice Walker. **CP-WalkA**

Her rosie cheekes, her ever smiling eyes. Thomas Campion. **CP-CampT**

Her sacred body bear: the tenement. At the Funeral. George Meredith. **CP-MerG2**

Her Second Husband Hears Her Story. Thomas Hardy. **CP-HardT**

Her Secret. Thomas Hardy. **CP-HardT**

Her Seed; It Shall Bruise Thy Head. Christina Georgina Rossetti. **CP-RosC2**

Her shroud was made of walnut drab. Jane Renick MacElmain (2). Louise McNeill. **SP-McNeL**

Her situation seemed a piteous thing. John Hewitt. *Fr.* October Sonnets. **CP-HewiJ**

Her skin / covered me, illuminated. Charles Olson. **CP-OlsoC**

Her sleeping head with its great gelid mass. Perseus. Robert Earl Hayden. **CP-HaydR**

Her smile was shaped like other smiles. Emily Dickinson. **CP-DickE**

—"Her Soil's Birth." Louis Zukofsky. *Fr.* 29 Songs. **CP-ZukLS**

Her son, albeit the Muse's livery. An Orson of the Muse. George Meredith. **CP-MerG1**

Her Song. Thomas Hardy. **CP-HardT**

Her soul was bred by a throne, and fed. Nature's Remorses. Elizabeth Barrett Browning. **CP-BroEB**

Her sovereign People. Emily Dickinson. **CP-DickE**

Her spirit rose to such a height. Emily Dickinson. **CP-DickE**

Her strong enchantments failing. Alfred Edward Housman. **CP-HousA**

Her Sweet turn to leave the Homestead. Emily Dickinson. **CP-DickE**

Her sweet Weight on my Heart a Night. Emily Dickinson. **CP-DickE**

Her Talents. . . Of. Kenneth Patchen. **CP-PatcK**

Her tawny eyes are onyx of thoughtlessness. The Hands of the Betrothed. David Herbert Lawrence. **CP-LawrD**

Her teacher's certainty it must be Mabel. Maple. Robert Frost. **CP-FrosR**

Her Telepathic-Station transmits thought-waves. Circe. Wystan Hugh Auden. **CP-AudeW**

Her Temple. Thomas Hardy. **CP-HardT**

Her terrace was the sand. Infanta Marina. Wallace Stevens. **CP-StevW**

Her that I love, I hate! "How's that, do you know?" they wonder. Catullus. *See* Carmen 85: "I hate and I love. And if you ask me how."

Her thot's tho' they are older. Emily Dickinson. **SP-DickE**

Her Thought and His. Paul Laurence Dunbar. **CP-DunbP**

Her Thoughts. Samuel Taylor Coleridge. **CP-ColeS**

Her Time. Theodore Roethke. **CP-RoetT**

Her tiny heart / pierced on a thorn. Saint Theresa. Jim Carroll. **SP-CarrJ**

Her Triumph. Ben Jonson. **CBLP; CTC; EBEV; EIL; InvP; JCP; NOSC; OPOP; PoEL-2; PrIm; SeCV-1** *Fr.* A Celebration of Charis in Ten Lyric[k] Pieces [*or* Peeces]. **CP-JonsB**

  (Triumph of Charis, The.) **ELP; LiTB; NOBE; NoP; TFi**

Her Triumph, *fr.* A Woman Young and Old. William Butler Yeats. **CP-YeatW**

Her trousers are red; she wears a coatee. George Meredith. **CP-MerG2**

Her veil was artificial flowers and leaves. Christopher Marlowe. **HoPM** *Fr.* Hero and Leander. **CP-MarlC**

Her Vision in the Wood, *fr.* A Woman Young and Old. William Butler Yeats. **CP-YeatW**

Her voice did quiver as we parted. On Fanny Godwin. Percy Bysshe Shelley. **CP-ShelP**

Her voice is a magnet into which flows. Eyes of a Blind Man. Edwin Rolfe. **CP-CareT; CP-RolfE**

Her voice is heard, and then the child's. Tom Clark. *Fr.* Suite. **SP-ClarT**

Her voice, that scooped me out of the games of the others. Remedies, Maladies, Reasons. Mona Van Duyn. **SP-VanDM**

Her whole life is an Epigram smack smooth & neatly pend. William Blake. **CP-BlakW**

Her womanhood collected into a pale. James McAuley. *Fr.* Three Acts from a Play. **SP-McAuJ**

Her Words. Theodore Roethke. **CP-RoetT**

Her Wrath. Theodore Roethke. **CP-RoetT**

Her young employers, having got in late. A Summer Morning. Richard Wilbur. **CP-WilbR**

Her-zie. Stevie Smith. **CP-SmitS**

Heraclitus on Rivers. Derek Mahon. **SP-MahoD**

Herakles. Robert Browning. **CP-BroR2**

Herakles. Charles Kenneth Williams. **SP-WillC**

Herba Apollinaris / Circe's herb. Henbane. Erica Jong. **SP-JongE**

Herba Santa. Herman Melville. **CP-MelvH**

Herbalist's Rose, The. Pablo Neruda, *tr. fr. Spanish by* Ben Belitt. **SP-NeruP**

Herbs, garlic / cheese, please let me in! The Fury of Cooks. Anne Sexton. *Fr.* The Furies. **CP-SextA**

Herclots's preachings I'll no longer hear. On One Who Borrowed His Sermons. Gerard Manley Hopkins. *Fr.* Seven Epigrams. **CP-HopkG**

Hercules and Antaeus. Seamus Heaney. **SP-HeanS**

Hercules at Nemea. Robert Ranke Graves. **CP-GravR**

Hercules, Deianira, Nessus. Charles Kenneth Williams. **SP-WillC**

Hercules Furens. Seneca, *tr. fr. Latin by* Jasper Heywood.
  "Capricious fortune ever joys." **CP-JohnS**
  "O! save ye Gods, omnipotent and kind." **CP-JohnS**

Herd, The. Robert Creeley. **CP-CreeR**

Herd of Buffalo Crossing the Missouri on Ice. William Matthews. **SP-MattW**

Herda, herda, herda, sing my sisters. Lullaby. Louise McNeill. **SP-McNeL**

Here. Robert Creeley. **CP-CreeR**

Here. Robert Creeley. **CP-CreeR**

Here. Robert Creeley. **CP-CreeR**

Here. Robert Creeley. **CP-CreeR**

Here. Robert Creeley. **CP-CreeR**

Here / I am cutting you. For Kenneth & Miriam Patchen. Al Young. **CP-YounA**

Here, / in the room of my life. The Room of My Life. Anne Sexton. **CP-SextA**

Here / in the wombed room. A Zorro Man. Maya Angelou. **SP-AngeM**

Here. Philip Larkin. **CP-LarkP**

Here / walls are cool / and coolness is. Chaconne for Unaccompanied Violin. Charles Tomlinson. **CP-TomlC**

Here a little child I stand. Robert Herrick. **CP-HerrR**
  (Another Grace for a Child.) **CP-HerrR**

Here a pretty baby lies. Robert Herrick.
  ("Upon a Child.") **CP-HerrR**

Here a solemn[e] fast keep[e]. An Epitaph upon a Virgin. Robert Herrick. **CP-HerrR**

Here, a Sunday, when light. Proensa. Charles Olson. **CP-OlsoC**

Here, above, / cracks in the buildings are filled with battered moonlight. The Man-Moth. Elizabeth Bishop. **CP-BishE**

Here again. Robert Creeley. **CP-CreeR**

Here, again. A smell of dying in the milk-pale carton. Pouring Milk Away. Muriel Rukeyser. **CP-RukeM**

Here all alone in silence might I mourne. Mary Sidney, Countess of Montgomery Wroth. *Fr.* Part 1. *Fr.* Urania. **CP-WrotM**

Here all is sunny, and when the truant gull. Skerryvore: the Parallel. Robert Louis Stevenson. **CP-StevR**

Here alone by the logs in my chamber. The Flirt's Tragedy. Thomas Hardy. **CP-HardT**

Here am I yet, another twelvemonth spent. Arthur Hugh Clough. *Fr.* Blank Misgivings of a Creature Moving About in Worlds Not Realized. **SP-ClouA**

Here among long-discarded cassocks. Diary of a Church Mouse. Sir John Betjeman. **CP-BetjJ**

Here among tables lit with bottled tapers. The Kursaal at Interlaken. Adrienne Rich. **CP-RicAE**

Here among them the americans this baffling. American Journal. Robert Earl Hayden. **CP-HaydR**

Here-and-Never, The. Louis MacNeice. *Fr.* A Hand of Snapshots. **CP-MacNL**

Here and There. Stephen Dunn. **SP-DunnS**

Here and there / in the trees' understories. Whirl Is King. Brendan Galvin. **SP-GalvB**

Here and there in the searing beam. Deer among Cattle. James Dickey. **CP-DickJ**

Here are all the captivities, the cells are real. Schoolchildren. Wystan Hugh Auden. **CP-AudeW**

Here, are five letters in this blessed name. The Garland [*or* Ghyrlond] of the Blessèd Virgin Mary [*or* Marie]. Ben Jonson. **CP-JonsB**

Here are five simple facts no sub. POEM(or "the divine right of majorities, that illegitimate offspring of the divine right of kings" Homer Lea). Edward Estlin Cummings. **CP-CummE**

Here Are My Black Clothes. Louise Glück. **SP-GlücL**

Here are shapes form'd fit for heaven. The Second Song. Thomas Carew. **CP-CareT** *Fr.* Carew's Masque. **CP-CareT**

Here are sweet peas, on tiptoe for a flight. Sweet Peas. John Keats. **FHYEP; GN** *Fr.* I Stood Tip-Toe upon a Little Hill. **CP-KeatJ**

Here are the fireworks. The men who conspired and labored. Pearl Harbor. Robinson Jeffers. **CP-JefR3**

Here are the holy birds. Margaret Atwood. *Fr.* Circe / Mud Poems. **SP-AtwM1**

Here are the long fields inviolate of thought. Notes for a Poem. Muriel Rukeyser. **CP-RukeM**

Here are the perfect / fans of the scallops. Whelks. Mary Oliver. **SP-OlivM**

Here are the skies, the planets seven. Alfred Edward Housman. **CP-HousA**

Here are the tracks upon the sand. Four Footprints. Thomas Hardy. **CP-HardT**

Here are two pupils. On Looking into the Eyes of a Demon Lover. Sylvia Plath. **CP-PlatS**

Here at a distance, rocked by hopes and fears. An Ulsterman in England Remembers. John Hewitt. **CP-HewiJ**

Here at last is ending. Ocean on Monday. Richard Hugo. **CP-HugoR**

Here at right of the entrance this bronze head. A Bronze Head. William Butler Yeats. **CP-YeatW**

Here at the atomic Crack-end of Time XX Century. A Methedrine Vision in Hollywood. Allen Ginsberg. **CP-GinsA**

Here at the gate where understanding ends. Vision. Phoebe Hesketh. **SP-HeskP**

Here at the height of passion. As Lovers Do. "Hugh MacDiarmid." **SP-MacDH**

Here at the level of leaves supposedly for good. Sustainment. James Dickey. **CP-DickJ**

Here at the Super Duper, in a glass tank. Lobsters. Howard Nemerov. **CP-NemeH**

Here at the Tide's Turn. John Hewitt. **CP-HewiJ**

Here at the Vespasian-Carlton, it's just one. Boom! Howard Nemerov. **CP-NemeH**

Here at these verses' head I write your name. To Robert Telford Hewitt. John Hewitt. **CP-HewiJ**

Here Awa' There Awa ["Here awa', there awa' wandering, Willie"], *see also* Here Awa', There Awa': "Here awa', there awa, here awa' Willie." Robert Burns. **CP-BurnR**

Here brewer Gabriel's fire's extinct. On Gabriel Richardson. Robert Burns. **CP-BurnR**

Here, but Unable to Answer. Richard Hugo. **CP-HugoR**

Here by the baring bough. Autumn in King's Hintock Park. Thomas Hardy. **CP-HardT**

Here by the fire, in his favorite chair. The Poet's House Preserved as a Museum. Leonard Nathan. **SP-NathL**

Here by the moorway you returned. Your Last Drive. Thomas Hardy. **CP-HardT**

Here by the windy docks I stand alone. Edwin Arlington Robinson. *Fr.* Octaves. **CP-RobiE**

Here chimes no clock, no pedant calendar. Seashore. Ralph Waldo Emerson. **CP-EmerR**

Here closed the Tenant of that lonely vale. Despondency Corrected. William Wordsworth. *Fr.* The Excursion. **CP-WorW2**

Here come exploding waves. Bounty. Robert Pack. **SP-PackR**

Here come I, old April Fool. April Fool. Louis MacNeice. **CP-MacNL**

Here come I to my own again. The Prodigal Son. Rudyard Kipling. **CP-KiplR** *Fr.* Kim.

Here come old flat top. Come Together. John Lennon *and* Paul McCartney. **CP-Beatl**

Here come real stars to fill the upper skies. Fireflies in the Garden. Robert Frost. **CP-FrosR**

Here come the capybaras on their bikes. Wild Ones[, The]. James Fenton. **SP-FentJ** *Fr.* Wild Life Studies.

Here come the line-gang pioneering by. The Line-Gang. Robert Frost. **CP-FrosR**

Here Come the Saints. Thom Gunn. **CP-GunnT**

Here Comes. Erica Jong. **SP-JongE**

Here comes man the master. Man the Master. Thomas Merton. **CP-MertT**

Here comes the blind thread to sew it shut. The Needle's Eye, the Lens. William Matthews. **SP-MattW**

Here comes the fishhead singing. The Most. Charles Bukowski. **SP-BukC1**

Here comes the man! He's talking a lot. Wrong Train. Ted Berrigan. **SP-BerrT**

Here comes the Marshal. The Proclamation. Henry Wadsworth Longfellow. **PAH** *Fr.* Act II. *Fr.* John Endicott. **SP-LongH**

Here comes the modulation. Roy Fisher. **SP-FishR** *Fr.* Diversions.

Here comes the powdered milk I drank. Spring Snow. William Matthews. **SP-MattW**

Here Comes the Sun. The Beatles. **CP-Beatl**

Here comes the woman who wears the plastic prick. Bowlers Anonymous. Stephen Dobyns. **SP-DobyS**

Here cursing swearing Burton lies. Robert Burns. **CP-BurnR** (Epitaph on Mr. Burton.) **CP-BurnR**

Here dead lie we because we did not choose. Alfred Edward Housman. **CP-HousA**

Here dock and tare. In the Grave No Flower. Edna St. Vincent Millay. **CP-MillE**

Here down my wearyed limbs Ile lay. On Himselfe ("Here down my wearyed limbs Ile lay"). Robert Herrick. **CP-HerrR**

Here ended Hall, and our last light, that long. *conclusion to* Morte d'Arthur. Tennyson. **NAEL-2** *Fr.* Morte d'Arthur. **CP-TennA**

Here, every lost act. Jim Carroll. *Fr.* The Runners. **SP-CarrJ**

Here Everything Is Still Floating. John Ashbery. **SP-AshbJ**

Here first the duties of to-day, the lessons of the concrete. The United States to Old World Critics. Walt Whitman. **CP-WhitW**

Here Follow Certain Other Verses, as Charms to Unlock the Mystery of the Crudities. Ben Jonson. **CP-JonsB**

Here Follow[es] Some Verses upon the Burning of Our House [July 10th, 1966. Copied Out of a Loose Paper]. Anne Bradstreet. *See* In silent night, when rest I took.

Here, foremost in the dang'rous paths of fame. Epitaph on Sir William Williams. Thomas Gray. **CP-GrayT**

Here four of you got mischances to plague you. Upon Four Dismal Stories in the Doctor's Letter. Jonathan Swift. **CP-SwifJ**

Here *Francis Ch[artre]s* lies—Be civil! Epitaph on Chartres. Alexander Pope. **CP-PopeA**

Here, free from a riot's hated noise. Inscription for a Moss-House. William Cowper. **CP-CowpW**

Here, freed from pain, secure from misery, lies. Epitaph on a Child. Thomas Gray. **CP-GrayT**

Here from the corridor of an English train. The Wild Sky. Adrienne Rich. **CP-RicAE**

Here from the field's edge we survey. Highway: Michigan. Theodore Roethke. **CP-RoetT**

Here from the restless bed of lingering pain. Written at Bristol in the Summer of 1794. Charlotte Smith. **CP-SmitC**

Here further up the mountain slope. The Birthplace. Robert Frost. **CP-FrosR**

Here goes a man of seventy-four. Seventy-four and Twenty. Thomas Hardy. **CP-HardT**

Here green is king again. Vermont. John Updike. **CP-UpdiJ**

Here gunned he homeward in the birdy breast. The Young Hunter. Richard Eberhart. **CP-EberR**

Here hand was still on her sword-hilt, the spur was still on her heel. The Young Queen. Rudyard Kipling. **CP-KiplR**

Here has my salient faith annealed me. Key West. Hart Crane. **CP-CranH**

Here have I been these one and twenty years. Arthur Hugh Clough. **SP-ClouA**

Here he comes, big with statistics. Robert Louis Stevenson. **CP-StevR**

Here he is of course. It was his best. Rastignac at 45. Thom Gunn. **CP-GunnT**

Here he is whom you read and clamor for. Martial, *tr. by* William Matthews. **SP-MattW** *Fr.* Epigrams.

Here, here I live. His Almes. Robert Herrick. **CP-HerrR**

Here, here I live with what my board. His Content in the Country. Robert Herrick. **CP-HerrR**

Here, here, oh here Eurydice [*or* Euridice]. Orpheus to Beasts. Richard Lovelace. **CP-LoveR**

Here hills and vales, the woodland and the plain. Alexander Pope. **ECEV** *Fr.* Windsor-Forest [*or* Windsor Forest]. **CP-PopeA**

Here him play / That sinister melody. Malcolm Lowry. **CP-LowrM**

Here Hitler had his first success, disguised. Munich. John Updike. **CP-UpdiJ**

Here *Hobson* lies amongst his many betters. Hobsons Epitaph. John Milton. **CP-MiltJ**

Here I Am. Charles Bukowski. **SP-BukC3**

Here I am again. The Cloud. William Matthews. **SP-MattW**

Here I am, an old man in a dry month. Gerontion. Thomas Stearns Eliot. **CP-ElioT**

Here I am at 8:08 p.m. indefinable ample rhythmic frame. Red Shift. Ted Berrigan. **SP-BerrT**

Here I am at my desk. The. A Pleasant Thought from Whitehead. Frank O'Hara. **SP-OharF**

Here I am, digging worms behind the chickenhouse. Digging Worms. Robert Bly. **SP-BlyR**

Here i am, naked. Charles Olson. **CP-OlsoC**

Here I am, walking along your eyelid again. In There. Charles Kenneth Williams. **SP-WillC**

Here I am yours, and here, and here. Song. Jane Cooper. **SP-CoopJ**

Here I myself [*or* my selfe] might likewise die. Poetry Perpetuates the Poet. Robert Herrick. **CP-HerrR**

Here I sit. Bad Morning. Langston Hughes. **SP-HughL**

Here I sit with my paper, my pen and my ink. Percy Bysshe Shelley. *Fr.* Original Poetry by Victor and Cazire. **CP-ShelP**

Here I stand head in hand. You've Got to Hide Your Love Away. The Beatles. **CP-Beatl**

Here I walked with a memory of workers in midtown. Jim Carroll. **SP-CarrJ**

Here, if the road shall bring thee back. New Year's Eve. Boethius, *tr. fr.* Latin. **MLL,** *tr. by* Helen Waddell; *Fr.* Consolation of Philosophy, The ("De Consolacione Philosophie"). **CP-ChauG**

Here I'll be. Clean Old Man. Charles Bukowski. **SP-BukC1**

Here I'm gazing, wide awake. Inscription for a Sketch. Robert Browning. **CP-BroR2**

Here in a cage the dollars come down. Girl in a Cage. Carl Sandburg. **CP-SandC**

Here in a Rocky Cup. Edna St. Vincent Millay. **CP-MillE**

Here, in front of the summer hotel. The Kite. Anne Sexton. **CP-SextA**

Here in my head, the home that is left for you. Burning the Letters. Randall Jarrell. **CP-JarrR**

Here in my workroom, in its listlessness. For Robert Kennedy Nineteen Twenty-Five to Sixty-Eight. Robert Lowell. **SP-LoweR**

Here in Nantucket does the tiny soul. Phenomenal Survivals of Death in Nantucket. Louise Glück. **SP-GlücL**

Here in our aging district the wood pigeon lives with us. All Morning. Theodore Roethke. **CP-RoetT**

Here in the darkness of these dry, bird-sounding lofts. Seasoning Barn. William DeWitt Snodgrass. **SP-SnodW**

Here in the dim of the dusk with the wings of birds and. Homage to Karl Marx. Edwin Rolfe. **CP-RolfE**

Here in the great cemetery. Francisco, I'll Bring You Red Carnations. Philip Levine. **SP-LeviP**

Here in the hauf licht hoo I've grown! "Hugh MacDiarmid." **SP-MacDH** *Fr.* Frae Anither Window in Thrums.

Here in the hauf licht waitin' till the clock. "Hugh MacDiarmid." **SP-MacDH** *Fr.* Frae Anither Window in Thrums.

Here in the hill-rimmed house / where the angelus bell is heard. The Bell. John Hewitt. **CP-HewiJ**

Here in the olive grove. The Olive Grove. May Sarton. **SP-SartM**

Here in the quiet eve. Voluntary. Robert Louis Stevenson. **CP-StevR**

Here in the scuffled dust. William DeWitt Snodgrass. **NCSH; NMP; NePoEA** *Fr.* Heart's Needle. **SP-SnodW**

Here in the South of France cicadas rasp, rasp, needles. The Stones of a Seventeenth Century Village. Kay Boyle. **CP-BoylK**

Here, in the summer city. William Dickey. **SP-DickW** *Fr.* In The Dreaming. **SP-DickW**

Here in the thrust-green. Remnant Water. James Dickey. **CP-DickJ**

Here in the window beaming across. Love Watches a Window. Thomas Hardy. **CP-HardT**

Here, in the withered arbor, like the arrested wind. Statue and Birds. Louise Bogan. **CP-BogaL**

Here in the yellowing. Deserted Cabin. John Haines. **SP-HainJ**

Here in this Irish room / the man from Malabar. The Man from Malabar. John Hewitt. **CP-HewiJ**

Here in this picture on the mantelpiece. Knock Knock. Jenny Joseph. **SP-JoseJ**

Here in This Spring. Dylan Thomas. **CP-ThomD**

Here in this territory of state or mind, this precinct. On Taking up Residence in Virginia. Kay Boyle. **CP-BoylK**

Here in this valley of discreet acadamies. Above the Oxbow. Sylvia Plath. **CP-PlatS**

Here in Violet Light. Al Young. **CP-YounA**

Here interposing, as the Goddess paused. The Prospect. James Thomson. *Fr.* Liberty. **CP-ThomJ**

Here is a coast; here is a harbor. Arrival at Santos. Elizabeth Bishop. **CP-BishE**

Here is a curious picture. Cynical. Gilbert Sorrentino. **SP-SorrG**

Here is a dream. / It is my dream. My Dream. Ogden Nash. *Fr.* My My. **CP-NashO**

Here is a face that says half-past seven the same way whether a murder or. Clocks. Carl Sandburg. **CP-SandC**

Here is a fat animal, a bear. Self-Portrait as a Bear. Donald Hall. **CP-HallD**

Here is a glass of water from my well. A Glass of Water. May Sarton. **SP-SartM**

Here is a head with a blur of horizons. Head. Carl Sandburg. **CP-SandC**

Here is a horse to tame. Verses on Games. Rudyard Kipling. **CP-KiplR**

Here is a room with heavy-footed chairs. The Nature of an Action. Thom Gunn. **CP-GunnT**

Here is a story shall stir you! Stand up, Greeks dead and gone. Echetlos. Robert Browning. **CP-BroR2**

Here is a symbol in which. Rock and Hawk. Robinson Jeffers. **CP-JefR2**

Here is a thing that happened. Like wild beasts whelped, for den. Halbert and Hob. Robert Browning. **CP-BroR2**

Here is a wound that never will heal, I know. Edna St. Vincent Millay. **CP-MillE**

Here is dust remembers it was a rose. Dust. Carl Sandburg. **CP-SandC**

Here is fresh matter, poet. Church and State. William Butler Yeats. **CP-YeatW**

Here is his coat. Last Articles. Gary Gildner. **SP-GildG**

Here is how I sum it up. Perfect Joy. Chuang Tzu, *tr. fr. Chinese by* Thomas Merton. **CP-MertT**

Here is how it all began. Old Anut made him some man and woman. Cargo Catechism. Thomas Merton. *Fr.* East. *Fr.* The Geography of Lograire. **CP-MertT**

Here is its mark left, thumbnail of enigma. Death of a Voice. Donald Davie. **CP-DavDo**

Here is Joe Blow the poet. On Being Asked for a Peace Poem. Howard Nemerov. **CP-NemeH**

Here is little Effie's Head. Edward Estlin Cummings. **CP-CummE; SP-CummE**

Here is my room, smiling like a forest. Seltzer. Jim Carroll. **SP-CarrJ**

Here is no mined and cratered deep. Midnight in India. Alun Lewis. **CP-LewiA**

"Here is nothing new nor aught unproven," say the Trumpets. The Old Issue. Rudyard Kipling. **CP-KiplR**

Here is one leaf already gone from green. The First Leaf. Howard Nemerov. **CP-NemeH**

Here is ouzo (she said) to try you. Ouzo Unclouded. Robert Ranke Graves. **CP-GravR**

Here is poor Villon's final word. A Ballade to End With. François Villon, *tr. fr. French by* Richard Wilbur. **CP-WilbR**

Here is the ample place. Mediterranean. May Sarton. **SP-SartM**

Here is the ancient floor. The Self-Unseeing. Thomas Hardy. **CP-HardT**

Here is the doctor, an abstracted lover. Death By Aesthetics. Mona Van Duyn. **SP-VanDM**

Here is the endless / wet thick / cosmos, the center. Crossing the Swamp. Mary Oliver. **SP-OlivM**

Here is the fern's frond, unfurling a gesture. Fern. Ted Hughes. **SP-HughT**

Here is the first level, the high ground. Poem with Levels of Meaning. Gary Gildner. **SP-GildG**

Here is the girl's head like an exhumed gourd. Strange Fruit. Seamus Heaney. **SP-HeanS**

Here is the glen, and here the bower. Banks of Cree. Robert Burns. **CP-BurnR**

Here is the man of the islands. Poem. Thomas Merton. **CP-MertT**

Here is the man who fancies Arab ponies. The Man in the Wind. Thomas Merton. **CP-MertT; SP-MertT**

Here is the ocean,this is moonlight:say. Edward Estlin Cummings. **CP-CummE**

Here is the place I came to. John Haines. *Fr.* Homestead. **SP-HainJ**

Here is the place; right over the hill. Telling the Bees. John Greenleaf Whittier. **CP-WhitJ**

Here is the pond, here sky, and the long grasses. Composition. May Sarton. **SP-SartM**

Here is the shadow of truth, for only the shadow is true. A Way to Love God. Robert Penn Warren. **SP-WarrR**

Here is the ship then, with decks all holy white. No Kraken Shall Be Found Till Sought By Name. Malcolm Lowry. **CP-LowrM**

Here is the skull of a man: a man's thoughts and emotions. De Rerum Virtute. Robinson Jeffers. **CP-JefR3**

Here is the threshold of holiness in the dust of the road. Tomb Cover of Imam Riza. *Unknown, tr. fr. Persian by* Thomas Merton. **CP-MertT**

Here is the world's end. When our fathers forded the first river in Asia we crossed the world's end. The Torch-Bearers' Race. Robinson Jeffers. **CP-JefR1**

Here is your parents' dwelling with its curtained windows telling. The Dawn after the Dance. Thomas Hardy. **CP-HardT**

Here it begins: the worm of love breeding. The Hearth. Robert Ranke Graves. **CP-GravR**

Here it is hanging in the sun. A Gentleman's Second-Hand Suit. Thomas Hardy. **CP-HardT**

Here it is, near the house. Right in the Trail. Gary Snyder. **CP-SnydG**

Here it is spring again. The Late Singer. William Carlos Williams. **CP-WilW1**

Here It is: squamous, hooded. Snake Charming. Leonard Nathan. **SP-NathL**

Here it was here and now, but never. The Here-and-Never. Louis MacNeice. *Fr.* A Hand of Snapshots. **CP-MacNL**

Here Jack and Tom are paired with Moll and Meg. George Meredith. **EnVR; InvP; NBM; PoEL-5** *Fr.* Modern Love. **CP-MerG1**

Here Johnson lies—a sage by all allow'd. Epitaph on Dr. Johnson. William Cowper. **CP-CowpW**

Here let me rest, here nurse the uneasy qualm. The Cruel Mistress. Robert Louis Stevenson. **CP-StevR**

Here lie Ciardi's pearly bones. Elegy Just in Case. John Ciardi. **SP-CiarJ**

Here lie Willie Michie's [or M—he's] banes. Robert Burns. **CP-BurnR** (On a Schoolmaster in Cleish Parish, Fifeshire.) **CP-BurnR**

Here lies / A worthy matron of unspotted life. Epitaph on my Dear and Ever Honored Mother Mrs. Dorothy Dudley. Anne Bradstreet. **CP-BradA**

Here Lies a Lady, *"A" version.* John Crowe Ransom. **AWP; CMoP; CoBMV; EvOK; HAP; HBMV; InvP; LiTM; MeMAP; MoAB; MoAmPo; MoP; NAAL-2; NoAM; PoRA; RB; TAP; TwAmPo; VGW** *Fr.* Sixteen Poems in Eight Pairings. **SP-RansJ**

Here Lies a Lady, *"B" version.* John Crowe Ransom. *Fr.* Sixteen Poems in Eight Pairings. **SP-RansJ**

Here lies a lady. Day was her double pain. Billie Holiday. Hayden Carruth. **CP-CarHS**

Here lies a mock Marquis whose titles were shamm'd. Epitaph Extempore, on a Person Nicknamed the Marquis, Who Desired Burns to Write One on Him. Robert Burns. **CP-BurnR**

Here lies a most beautiful lady. Epitaph, An. Walter de la Mare. **CP-DeLaW**

Here lies a poet who would not write. Voice from the Tomb (1). Stevie Smith. **CP-SmitS**

Here lies a round Woman, who thought *mighty odd.* Epitaph (of By-Words). Alexander Pope. **CP-PopeA**

Here lies a Scots mile of a chiel. Epitaph for J. H. Writer in Ayr. Robert Burns. **CP-BurnR**

Here lies a Virgin, and as sweet. Upon his Kinswoman Mrs. M. S. Robert Herrick. **CP-HerrR**

Here lies, and none to mourn him but the sea. Edna St. Vincent Millay. **HeIP** *Fr.* Epitaph for the Race of Man. **CP-MillE**

Here lies Boghead among the dead. Robert Burns. **CP-BurnR**
  (On Jas. Grieve, Laird of Boghead, Tarbolton.) **CP-BurnR**

Here Lies Erotion. Robert Louis Stevenson. **CP-StevR**

Here lies Erotion, whom at six years old. Epitaphium Erotii. Robert Louis Stevenson. **CP-StevR**

Here lies George Edward Cook, a man. Epitaph on Our Gardener, Dead Near Liverpool. Malcolm Lowry. **CP-LowrM**

Here lies Hobinall, our Pastor while ere. Epitaph on the Earl of Salisbury. *Unknown, sometimes at. to* Sir Walter Ralegh. **CP-RaleW**

Here lies in earth a root of H-ll. Epitaph on D——— C———. Robert Burns. **CP-BurnR**

Here lies J-hn B-shby, *honest man!.* Epitaph on J-hn B-shby. Robert Burns. **CP-BurnR**

Here lies John Trot, the Friend of all mankind. Another [Epitaph]. William Blake. **CP-BlakW**

Here lies Johnny Pidgeon. Epitaph on John Dove [Innkeeper, Mauchline]. Robert Burns. **CP-BurnR**

Here lies Jonson [*or* lyes Johnson] with the rest. Upon Ben Jo[h]nson. Robert Herrick. **CP-HerrR**

Here lies 'mang ither useless matters. On an Innkeeper in Tarbolton. Robert Burns. **CP-BurnR**

Here lies nipped in this narrow cyst. Epitaph for G. K. Chesterton. Thomas Hardy. **CP-HardT**

Here lies old *Hobson*, Death hath broke his girt. On the University Carrier Who Sick'n'd [*or* Sickened] in the Time of His Vacancy [, Being Forbid to go to London, by Reason of the Plague]. John Milton. **CP-MiltJ**

Here lies one, who never drew. Epitaph, An. William Cowper. **CP-CowpW**

Here lies [*or* lyes] the noble warrior [*or* Warryor] that never blunted sword. Epitaph on the Earl of Leicester [*or* Leceister]. Sir Walter Ralegh. **CP-RaleW**

Here lies to each her parents' ruth. On My First Daughter. Ben Jonson. **CP-JonsB**

Here Lies Treasure: Here Be Monsters. Jenny Joseph. **SP-JoseJ**

Here lies, whom hound did ne'er pursue. Epitaph on a Hare. William Cowper. **CP-CowpW**

Here lieth one who did most truly prove. Another on the Same. John Milton. **CP-MiltJ**

Here lieth One whose name was writ on water. Fragment on Keats. Percy Bysshe Shelley. **CP-ShelP**

Here, like Arion, our Coriat doth draw. Here Follow Certain Other Verses, as Charms to Unlock the Mystery of the *Crudities*. Ben Jonson. **CP-JonsB**

Here, long ere kings to battle rode. English Downs. Walter de la Mare. **CP-DeLaW**

Here luxury's common lot. The light. Grasse: The Olive Trees. Richard Wilbur. **CP-WilbR**

Here lyes Squire Hugh———ye harlot crew. Epitaph for H——— L———, Esq., of L———. Robert Burns. **CP-BurnR**

Here Man more purely lives, less oft doth fall. Cistertian Monastery. William Wordsworth. *Fr.* Ecclesiastical Sonnets. **CP-WorW2**

Here, melting, mixed with air the ideal forms. Rome. James Thomson. *Fr.* Liberty. **CP-ThomJ**

Here might have been the thinking of mountains. Kenneth Patchen. **CP-PatcK**

Here, my dear friend, is a new book for you. *see also* Epipsychidion. Percy Bysshe Shelley. **CP-ShelP**

Here, no woman, nor man besides. Man in a Room. William Carlos Williams. **CP-WilW1**

Here not long enough after the hospital happened. The Closet. Bill Knott. **SP-KnotB**

Here now in this unlikely town. At Malcolm Lowry's Grave. David Markson. **CP-MarkD**

Here now is Winter. Winter, after all. Christina Georgina Rossetti. *Fr.* Later Life: A Double Sonnet of Sonnets. **CP-RosC2**

Here, O wanderer, here is the hill and the harbor. Archibald MacLeish. **CP-MacLA** *Fr.* The Happy Marriage.

Here, often, a man provoked has said his say. The Iron Circle. John Hewitt. **CP-HewiJ**

Here, on our native soil, we breathe once more. Composed in the Valley near Dover, on the Day of Landing. William Wordsworth. **CP-WorW1**

Here on the dark rocks. Lines Written at Taormina, Sicily. John Gould Fletcher. **SP-FletJ**

Here on the edge of hell. Puzzled. Langston Hughes. **SP-HughL**

Here on the poop each lousy night I stand. Bosun's Song. Malcolm Lowry. **CP-LowrM**

Here on the rim, cringing. A Place: Fragments. Margaret Atwood. **SP-AtwM1**

Here, on the rivershore, the edge of music. Brickyards at Beacon. Edwin Rolfe. **CP-RolfE**

Here on the vast edges drear. James McAuley. *Fr.* Aor Against the Ingrate Who Abused Our Hospitality. **SP-McAuJ**

Here on their knees men swore: the stones were black. The Black Stones of Iona. William Wordsworth. *Fr.* Poems Composed or Suggested During a Tour, in the Summer of 1833. **CP-WorW2**

Here on this headland sheer a thousand feet. Garron Top. John Hewitt. **CP-HewiJ**

Here once engaged the stragner's view. On Revisiting Harrow. Byron. **CP-Byron**

Here, our possessions are cut. Highest Altitude. Margaret Atwood. **SP-AtwM1**

Here pasture ends— / this girl and boy. Edward Estlin Cummings. **CP-CummE**

Here pause: the poet claims at least this praise. William Wordsworth. **CP-WorW1**
  (1811 ("Here pause: the poet claims at least this praise").) **CP-WorW1**

Here redbuds like momentary trees. Locus. Robert Earl Hayden. **CP-HaydR**

Here rests a Woman, good without pretence. Epitaph on Mrs. Corbet, Who Died of a Cancer in Her Breast. Alexander Pope. **CP-PopeA**

Here rests his head upon the lap of earth. *see also* Shelley's "Hic sinu fessum caput hospitali." Thomas Gray. **FHYEP; FaBoPV; SCGP** *Fr.* Elegy Written in a Country Churchyard. **CP-GrayT**

Here, Romans owned the need—to give. Harvest Festival: at Ozleworth. Charles Tomlinson. **CP-TomlC**

Here she beholds the chaos dark and deep. Alexander Pope. **FHYEP** *Fr.* To Dr. Jonathan Swift. **OxAEP-1**, *book* I, *ll.* 1–330; **CBNP** *Fr.* The Dunciad. **CP-PopeA**

Here she comes / the Queen of Moons! Pictures of Philippa. Donald Hall. **CP-HallD**

Here she lies, a pretty bud. Upon a Child That Died [*or* Dyed]. Robert Herrick. **CP-HerrR**

Here she lies [*or* lyes] (in Bed of Spice). Upon a Maid[e]. Robert Herrick. **CP-HerrR**

Here shift the scene, to represent. Jonathan Swift. **OBD** *Fr.* Verses on the Death of Dr. Swift, D.S.P.D. **CP-SwifJ**

Here Sleeps. Walter de la Mare. **CP-DeLaW**

Here something stubborn comes. Seed Leaves. Richard Wilbur. **CP-WilbR**

Here Sowter **** in Death does sleep. On a Celebrated Ruling Elder. Robert Burns. **CP-BurnR**

Here space, time, peace are given a habitation. These Pure Arches. May Sarton. **SP-SartM**

Here stand the mountains of this state. American Citizen. Kay Boyle. **CP-BoylK**

Here Stewarts once in triumph reign'd. Robert Burns. *Fr.* Lines on Stirling.
  On Seeing the Royal Palace at Stirling in Ruins. **DBV**

Here stood an Oak, that long had borne affixed. Hart's-Horn Tree, near Penrith. William Wordsworth. **CP-WorW2**

Here take my picture, though I bid farewell. His Picture. John Donne. **EnRePo; FaBoEn; MeLP; MePo; OBS; OXAEP-1** *Fr.* Elegies. **CP-DonnJ**

Here, take this gift. To a Certain Cantatrice. Walt Whitman. **CP-WhitW**

Here Tantalus in water seek[e]s for water, and doth miss[e]. Ovid. **CP-RaleW**, *tr. by* Sir Walter Ralegh; *Fr.* Amores.

Here the crow starves, here the patient stag. Rannoch, by Glencoe. Thomas Stearns Eliot. **FaBoPP; NAEL-2; PoSH** *Fr.* Landscapes. **CP-ElioT**

Here the fig lets down the leaf, the leaf. The Leaf. Robert Penn Warren. **SP-WarrR**

Here the Frailest Leaves of Me. Walt Whitman. **CP-WhitW**

Here the hangman stops his cart. The Carpenter's Son. Alfred Edward Housman. **CP-HousA**

Here the human past is dim and feeble and alien to us. Haunted Country. Robinson Jeffers. **CP-JefR1**

Here the jack-hammer jabs into the ocean. Colloquy in Black Rock. Robert Lowell. **SP-LoweR**

Here, the nuns are rumored cruel. Beat. Holy Family. Richard Hugo. **CP-HugoR**

Here the snake across your path. George Meredith. *Fr.* The Woods of Westermain. **CP-MerG1**

Here the weather remains the same. Constant. Letter Beginning with the First Line of Your Letter. Stephen Dobyns. **SP-DobyS**

Here then / She lies / Her hair a scroll along. One. Stephen Spender. **CP-SpenS**

Here, then, the equivocal catch of a long voyage. A Dedication. Edwin Rolfe. **CP-RolfE**

Here, There and Everywhere. The Beatles. **CP-Beatl**

Here There Are Three of Us Driving South in This Expensive Car. William Dickey. **SP-DickW**

Here there is death. But even here, they say. The Dead Village. Edwin Arlington Robinson. **CP-RobiE**

Here they all come to die. The Country of a Thousand Years of Peace. James Merrill. **SP-MerrJ**

Here they always drain the cup. Bicentennial Words for the Liberal Magistrates of 1798. James Liddy. **CP-LiddJ**

Here they are. The soft eyes open. The Heaven of Animals. James Dickey. **CP-DickJ**

Here they come / grey and beastly. The End. Charles Bukowski. **SP-BukC2**

Here they sit. Islands in Penobscot Bay. Marsden Hartley. **CP-HartM**

Here too are life's victims. In Nature. John Haines. **SP-HainJ**

Here too, as in my childhood, twilight. Louis MacNeice. Fr. Country Week-End. **CP-MacNL**

Here too, 'tis sung, of old Diana stray'd. Alexander Pope. **OXAEP-1** Fr. Windsor-Forest [or Windsor Forest]. **CP-PopeA**

Here too you came and sat a time once, drinking. John Berryman. Fr. Sonnets to Chris. **CP-BerrJ**

Here under the radiant rays of the sun. Facing the Chair. "Hugh MacDiarmid." **SP-MacDH**

Here upon the prairie. The Prairie Battlements. Nicholas Vachel Lindsay. **CP-LindV**

Here Usually Comes the Bride. Ogden Nash. **CP-NashO**

Here war is harmless like a monument. Wystan Hugh Auden. **OBWP** Fr. Sonnets from China. **CP-AudeW**

Here was I with my arm and heart. Too Late. Robert Browning. **CP-BroR1**

Here was my relation with the woman who lived all last autumn and winter day and night. Thirst. Charles Kenneth Williams. **SP-WillC**

Here we are all, by day; by night we are [or w'are] hurled. Dream[e]s. Robert Herrick. **CP-HerrR**

Here we are, I drink to you. Descartes—You There? Jenny Joseph. **SP-JoseJ**

Here we are, picking the first fern-shoots. Song of the Bowmen of Shu. Ezra Pound, after the Chinese. **SP-PounE**

Here we are: the Bowl, the thousands. A Nursery Rhyme. Randall Jarrell. **CP-JarrR**

Here we broached the Christmas barrel. The House of Hospitalities. Thomas Hardy. **CP-HardT**

Here we go in a flung festoon. Road Song of the Bandar-Log. Rudyard Kipling. **CP-KiplR** Fr. Kaa's Hunting. Fr. The Jungle Book.

Here We Go Quietly Nuts in May. Ogden Nash. **CP-NashO**

Here we have thirst. An Egyptian Pulled Glass Bottle in the Shape of a Fish. Marianne Craig Moore. **CP-MoorM**

Here we have watched ten thousand. View from Rosehill Cemetery: Vicksburg. Alice Walker. **CP-WalkA**

Here we securely live, and eate. An Ode to Sir Clipsebie Crew. Robert Herrick. **CP-HerrR**

Here: wear this spectacle bra. It is the fashion. An Issue of Life. Howard Nemerov. **CP-NemeH**

Here, where I dwell, I waste to skin and bone. By the Waters of Babylon. B.C. 570. Christina Georgina Rossetti. **CP-RosC1**

Here where I live. Two Twilights for William Carlos Williams. Kay Boyle. **CP-BoylK**

Here, where my fresh-turned furrows run. The Settler. Rudyard Kipling. **CP-KiplR**

Here, where, of havoc tired and rash undoing. At Furness Abbey. William Wordsworth. **CP-WorW2**

Here, where our Lord once laid his Head. Upon the Sepulchre of our Lord. Richard Crashaw. **CP-CrasR**

Here, where the Daisies fit my Head. Emily Dickinson. **CP-DickE**

Here, where the rose opens. Anacreon's Grave. Johann Wolfgang von Goethe, tr. fr. German by James Wright. **CP-WrigJ**

Here, where the Scotish Muse immortal lives. To Miss Graham of Fintray. Robert Burns. **CP-BurnR**

Here, where Vespasian's legions struck the sands. Embarcation. Thomas Hardy. **CP-HardT**

Here where we are, wrapped in the afternoon. Obligations. Jane Cooper. **SP-CoopJ**

Here where you left me alone. Letter from Slough Pond. Isabella Gardner. **CP-GardI**

Here, while the loom of Winter weaves. A Memory. John Greenleaf Whittier. **CP-WhitJ**

Here with approaching age / a stranger in the land. My Own and Not My Own. John Hewitt. **CP-HewiJ**

Here, with my knee upon thy stone. Emily Brontë. **CP-BronE**

Here, Withers, rest! thou bravest, gentlest mind. Epitaph on General Henry Withers, in Westminster-Abbey, 1729. Alexander Pope. **CP-PopeA**

Here without question is the bird-torn design. I Am with the Roots of Flowers. Charles Bukowski. **SP-BukC2**

Here women, frightened, bring their sex. Boston Lying-In. John Updike. Fr. Waiting Rooms. **CP-DickE**

Here you rest among the valleys, maiden known to but a few. Robert Louis Stevenson. **CP-StevR**

Here you stay / Night and day. To a Tree in London. Thomas Hardy. **CP-HardT**

Hereafter, I will pick no Rose. Emily Dickinson. **SP-DickE**

Heredity. Thomas Hardy. **CP-HardT**

Herefordshire. Donald Davie. **CP-DavDo**

Herefordshire Carol, The. Geoffrey Hill. Fr. An Apology for the Revival of Christian Architecture in England. **CP-HillG**

Herein a Blossom lies. Emily Dickinson. **CP-DickE**

Here's, a bottle and an honest friend. Robert Burns. **CP-BurnR**

Here's a fine bag of meat. Bags of Meat. Thomas Hardy. **CP-HardT**

Here's a good rule of thumb. Reflection on Ingenuity. Ogden Nash. **CP-NashO**

Here's a Happy New Year! But with Reason. Byron. **CP-Byron**

Here's a Health to Ane I Lo'e Dear. Robert Burns. **CP-BurnR**

Here's a Health to Them That's Awa'. Robert Burns. **CP-BurnR**

Here's a little mouse)and. Edward Estlin Cummings. **CP-CummE; SP-CummE**

Here's a question for us. Help me. From a Window. William Carlos Williams. **CP-WilW2**

Here's a verse about rabbits. The Rabbits. Ogden Nash. **CP-NashO**

Here's a Woman of the Town. An Extempore Elegy. Samuel Johnson. **CP-JohnS**

Here's all at an end between us, or I'll never taste sack again. parody of William Shakespeare. Rudyard Kipling. **CP-KiplR** Fr. The Muse among the Motors.

Here's first a gloveless hand warm from my pocket. To a Moth Seen in Winter. Robert Frost. **CP-FrosR**

Here's His Health in Water. Robert Burns. **CP-BurnR**

Here's Holy Willie's sair worn clay. Epitaph on Holy Willie. Robert Burns. **CP-BurnR**

Here's my case. Of old I used to love him. Fears and Scruples. Robert Browning. **CP-BroR2**

Here's no more news, than virtue, I may as well. To Sir Henry Wotton. John Donne. **CP-DonnJ**

Here's one in whom Nature feared—faint at such vying. Cardinal Bembo's Epitaph on Raphael. Thomas Hardy, after Pietro Bembo. **CP-HardT**

Here's one of those warm simple letters. The Coat. Stephen Berg. **SP-BergS**

Here's Room 506. Chelsea Girls. "Lou Reed." **SP-ReedL**

Here's s / omething round(& so). Edward Estlin Cummings. **CP-CummE**

Here's that old drunk, already mellow. Fall. Mona Van Duyn. **SP-VanDM**

Here's the cave where Sorrow dwells. The Stratagem. Walter de la Mare. **CP-DeLaW**

Here's the garden she walked across. The Flower's Name. Robert Browning. **CTC** Fr. Garden Fancies. **CP-BroR1**

Here's the mould of a musical bird long passed from light. In a Museum. Thomas Hardy. **CP-HardT**

Here's to Adhering. Maya Angelou. **SP-AngeM**

Here's to Her Who Long. Byron. **CP-Byron**

Here's to Johnny with his Jo and Micky's got a wife. Home of the Brave. "Lou Reed." **SP-ReedL**

Here's to opening and upward,to leaf and to sap. Edward Estlin Cummings. **CP-CummE; SP-CummE**

Here's to the Freshman of bashful eighteen! A Bachanalian Ode. "Lewis Carroll." **CP-CarrL**

Here's to the Spirit of Fire. Nicholas Vachel Lindsay. **CP-LindV**

Here's to thy health, my bonie lass. Robert Burns. **CP-BurnR**

Here's where I started / running from a little bee. Or. Charles Kenneth Williams. **CP-WillC**

Heresy. Walter de la Mare. **CP-DeLaW**

Heretic's Tragedy, The. Robert Browning. **CP-BroR1**

Hereto I come to view a voiceless ghost. After a Journey. Thomas Hardy. **CP-HardT**

Hereunder Jacob Schmidt who, man and bones. Immortal Helix. Archibald MacLeish. **CP-MacLA**

Heri, Cras, Hodie. Ralph Waldo Emerson. Fr. Quatrains. **CP-EmerR**

Heriot's Ford. Rudyard Kipling. **CP-KiplR** Fr. The Light That Failed.

Heritage. Countee Cullen. **CP-CullC**

Heritage, The. Rudyard Kipling. **CP-KiplR**

Herman Melville. Wystan Hugh Auden. **CP-AudeW**

Hermann Göring, Former Reichsmarschall. William DeWitt Snodgrass. **SP-SnodW**

Hermann Helmholtz said the problem facing. Hermann Ludwig Ferdinand Von Helmholtz. Peter Meinke. **SP-MeinP**

Hermann Ludwig Ferdinand Von Helmholtz. Peter Meinke. **SP-MeinP**

Hermaphrodite, The. Dabney Stuart. **SP-StuaD**

Hermaphroditic Telephones, The. William Carlos Williams. **CP-WilW1**

Hermes and Mr Shaw. Donald Davie. **CP-DavDo**

Hermes it was. Hermes with wingéd heels. Getting the Message. Miller Williams. **SP-WillM**

Hermes of the Ways. Hilda Doolittle. **CP-DoolH**

Hermes Trismegistus. Hilda Doolittle. **NALW** *Fr.* Tribute to the Angels. **CP-DoolH**

Hermes Trismegistus / is patron of alchemists. Tribute to the Angels. Hilda Doolittle. **CP-DoolH**

Hermetic Poem. Stanley Jasspon Kunitz. **CP-KuniS**

Hermione. Ralph Waldo Emerson. **CP-EmerR**

Hermit, The. Diane Wakoski. **SP-WakoD**

Hermit at Outermost House, The. Sylvia Plath. **CP-PlatS**

Hermit Crab, The. Mary Oliver. **SP-OlivM**

Hermit Hoar. Samuel Johnson.
 (Lines on Thomas Warton's Poems ("Hermit hoar, in solemn cell").) **CP-JohnS**

Hermit of Cape Rosier, The. Daniel Gerard Hoffman. **SP-HoffD**

Hermit of Hudson Pond, The. Mona Van Duyn. **SP-VanDM**

Hermit of the Thebaid, The. John Greenleaf Whittier. **CP-WhitJ**

Hermit (or if 'chance you hold), A. The Moralizer Corrected. William Cowper. **CP-CowpW**

Hermitage, The. John Haines. **SP-HainJ**

Hermitage at the Center, The. Wallace Stevens. **CP-StevW**

Hermocratia nam'd—save only me. On Hermocratia. *Unknown, tr. fr. Greek by* William Cowper. **CP-CowpW**

Hermonax. Hilda Doolittle. **CP-DoolH**

Hernani. George Meredith. **CP-MerG1**

Hero, The. Robert Creeley. **CP-CreeR**

Hero. Robert Creeley. **CP-CreeR**

Hero, The. Robert Ranke Graves. **CP-GravR**

Hero, The. Marianne Craig Moore. **CP-MoorM** *Fr.* Part of a Novel, Part of a Poem, Part of a Play.

Hero, The. John Greenleaf Whittier. **CP-WhitJ**

Hero. William Carlos Williams. **CP-WilW1**

Hero and Leander. John Donne. **CP-DonnJ**

Hero and Leander. Christopher Marlowe, First *and* Second Sestiads, *completed by* George Chapman. **CP-MarlC**
 "Amorous Leander, beautiful and young." **PeHV**
 Amorous Neptune. **NOBE**
 "And now the sun that through the horizon peeps." **OAEL-1**
 Bridal Song: "O come, soft rest of cares, come Night." **NOBE; OBEV**
 "By this, Leander, being near the land." **EBEV; ErPo**
 Epithalamion Teratos. **EiL; LoBV; NoSic**
 "Her veil was artificial flowers and leaves." **HoPM**
 Hero Feels the Shaft of Love. **GBL**
 "It lies not in our power to love, or hate." **BLPL; EBEvV; FaFP; ImPo; LiTB; TrGrPo; WHA**
  (Who Ever Loved, That Loved Not at First Sight?) **BLPL; FaFP; ImPo; LiTB**
 "Leander to the envious light." **OAEL-1**
 Leander's Return. **EBNV**
 Love at First Sight. **NOBE**
 "New light gives new directions, fortunes new." **NoSic; OAEL-1**
 "Now from Leander's place she rose, and found." **EBEV**
 "O none but gods have power their love to hide." **OXAEP-1**
 "On Hellespont, guilty of true love's blood." **LoBV; NoSic; OAEL-1; OAEP; PoE; PoEL-2; SeCePo; TEP**
 Repentance. **OBSC**
 "So on she goes, and in her idle flight." **PoE**
 Wedding of Alcmane and Mya, The. **OBSC**

Hero Blues. "Bob Dylan." **CP-DylaB**

Hero Comes Home in His Hamper, and Is Exhibited at the World's Fair, The. Howard Nemerov. **CP-NemeH**

Hero Feels the Shaft of Love. Christopher Marlowe. **GBL** *Fr.* Hero and Leander. **CP-MarlC**

Hero of moment is no bigger than a bean, The. Childhood of the Hero. Kenneth Patchen. **CP-PatcK**

Hero of phantasies and catcher of chills. Poetaster. Theodore Roethke. **CP-RoetT**

Hero Sandwiches. Charles Tomlinson. **CP-TomlC**

Hero Speech. Muriel Rukeyser. **CP-RukeM**

Hero with Girl and Gorgon. Howard Nemerov. **CP-NemeH**

Hero Worship at Key West on the 4th of July. Peter Meinke. **SP-MeinP** *Fr.* Lines from Key West.

Herodion, Apelles, Amplias. The Three Taverns. Edwin Arlington Robinson. **CP-RobiE**

Herod's Lament for Mariamne. Byron. **CP-Byron**

Heroes, The. John Berryman. **CP-BerrJ**

Heroes. Jim Carroll. **SP-CarrJ**

Heroes. Robert Creeley. **CP-CreeR**

Heroes. Walt Whitman. *See* I understand the large hearts of heroes.

Heroes, and Kings! your distance keep. *see also* Epitaph for One Who Would Not be Buried in Westminster Abbey ("Under this Marble, or under this Sill"). Alexander Pope. **CP-PopeA**

Heroes of Childhood, The. Thomas McGrath. **SP-McGrT**

Heroes of Our Times, The. Richard Shelton. **SP-ShelR**

Heroes paused upon the plain, The. The Byrnies. Thom Gunn. **CP-GunnT**

Heroic comedy, I suggest. Third Epistle. Donald Davie. *Fr.* Six Epistles to Eva Hesse. **CP-DavDo**

Heroic Sculpture. Frank O'Hara. **SP-OharF**

Heroic stars spending themselves, The. The Epic Stars. Robinson Jeffers. **CP-JefR3**

Heroic Vengeance. John Milton. **OBS** *Fr.* Samson Agonistes. **CP-MiltJ**

Heroides. Ovid, *tr. fr. Latin.*
 "Strong Ilion thou shalt see with walls and towers high." **CP-RaleW**
 "Succeeding years thy early frame destroy." **CP-JohnS**

Heroin. "Lou Reed." **SP-ReedL**

Heroine, The. William Dickey. **SP-DickW**

Heroine, The. "Lou Reed." **SP-ReedL**

Heroine stood up on the deck, The. The Heroine. "Lou Reed." **SP-ReedL**

Heroines. Adrienne Rich. **SP-RicA2**

Heroism. William Cowper. **CP-CowpW**

Heroism. Ralph Waldo Emerson. **CP-EmerR**

Heron, The. Wendell Berry. **CP-BerrW**

Heron, The. Theodore Roethke. **CP-RoetT**

Heron Ballads, 1795, The. Robert Burns.
 Buy Braw Troggin. An Excellent New Song. **CP-BurnR**
 Election: A New Song, The. **CP-BurnR**
 Johnie B———'s Lament. **CP-BurnR**
 "Wham will we send to London town." **CP-BurnR**

Heron-billed pale cattle-birds, The. At Algeciras—a Meditation upon Death. William Butler Yeats. **CP-YeatW**

Heron flies across the morning marsh and brakes, A. Derek Walcott. *Fr.* Two Poems on the Passing of an Empire. **CP-WalcD**

Heron warps its neck, a broken pick, The. The Mills of the Kavanaughs. Robert Lowell. **SP-LoweR**

Herr Lignitz knows Old Berlin. It is near the Post Office. Basil Bunting. *Fr.* Aus Dem Zweiten Reich. **CP-BuntB**

Herrick Hospital, Fifth Floor. Al Young. **CP-YounA**

Herring. Kenneth Rexroth. **HoPM; SP-RexrK** *Fr.* A Bestiary. **SP-RexrK**

Herring is prolific, the. Herring. Kenneth Rexroth. **HoPM; SP-RexrK** *Fr.* A Bestiary. **SP-RexrK**

Herrings. Jonathan Swift. **AnIV; NCEP; OnYI** *Fr.* Verses Made for the Women Who Cry Apples, etc. **CP-SwifJ**

Hers was the last authentic rape. Helen's Rape. Thom Gunn. **CP-GunnT**

Herself a Rose Who Bore the Rose. Christina Georgina Rossetti. **CP-RosC2**

Hertfordshire. Sir John Betjeman. **CP-BetjJ**

Hertfordshire. Donald Davie. **CP-DavDo**

Hervé Riel. Robert Browning. **CP-BroR2**

Hes a Blockhead who wants a proof of what he Cant Percieve. William Blake. **CP-BlakW**

He's a real nowhere man. Nowhere Man. The Beatles. **CP-Beatl**

He's all that bad, I know; a knave, a flat. On a Dunce Who Had Not a Word to Say for Himself. Gerard Manley Hopkins. *Fr.* Seven Epigrams. **CP-HopkG**

He's dead / the dog won't have to. Death. William Carlos Williams. **CP-WilW1**

He's in his grave and on his head. The Dancer. Alun Lewis. **CP-LewiA**

He's in the dark-room again. He Saved Others. . . . Phoebe Hesketh. **SP-HeskP**

He's lying in poor water, a yard or so depth of poor safety. An October Salmon. Ted Hughes. **SP-HughT**

He's not sure how to get the jack on—he must have recently bought the car, although it's ancient. Reading: Winter. Charles Kenneth Williams. **SP-WillC**

He's not the happy man, to whom is given. The Happy Man. James Thomson. **CP-ThomJ**

He's out on the loggia. Charles Henri Ford. **SP-FordC** *Fr.* Secret Haiku.

He's out stuck in a bird's craw. Maitreya the Future Buddha. Gary Snyder. **CP-SnydG** *Fr.* Burning. *Fr.* Myths and Texts.

He's peeled another skin. Truth Game. Phoebe Hesketh. **SP-HeskP**

He's still standing in. Narcissus Dreaming. Dabney Stuart. **SP-StuaD**

He's the infallible man. Kill the Umpire! Edwin Rolfe. **CP-RolfE**

He's tucked his feet into corduroy scuffs. Recovery. Rita Dove. **SP-DoveR**

He's wedded to his theory, they say. By Mrs. Hopley. Gerard Manley Hopkins. **CP-HopkG**

Hesiod attributes those Bette Davis peepers of the Moirai. Fate Spinners in Time-Editing Studio, Eternity Blvd., 2 A.M. Tom Clark. **SP-ClarT**

Hesitant Memorial. John Hewitt. **CP-HewiJ**

Hesitate to Call. Louise Glück. **SP-GlücL**

Hesitation, The. Charles Tomlinson. **CP-TomlC**

Hesitations Outside the Door. Margaret Atwood. **SP-AtwM1**

Hesperia the Gr[a]ecians call the place. Virgil, *tr.* by Sir Walter Ralegh. **CP-RaleW** *Fr.* The Aeneid [*or* Eneados, *Aeneis*].

Hesperian evenings certainly. James Liddy. *Fr.* Birds. **CP-LiddJ**

Hesperus the Bringer. Byron. *See* Evening.

Heu non maturo mihi fato, dulcis Huissi. *acc. by English translation.* Thomas Campion. **CP-CampT**

"Heu Quam Praeciph Mersa Profundo." Boethius. *See* Alas, his mind is sunk.

Heu Quam Precipiti. Boethius, *tr.* by John Walton. **OBMV** *Fr.* Consolation of Philosophy, The ("De Consolacione Philosophie"). **CP-ChauG**

Heu! Quam Remotus. William Cowper. **CP-CowpW**

Hewel, or Woodpecker, The. Andrew Marvell. **ChTr** *Fr.* Upon Appleton House [To My Lord Fairfax]. **CP-MarvA**

Hex, The. Anne Sexton. **CP-SextA**

Hexahedrons of wood and glass. Objects & Apparitions. Octavio Paz, *tr. fr. Spanish by* Elizabeth Bishop. **CP-BishE**

Hexameters. Samuel Taylor Coleridge. **CP-ColeS**

Hey! / Can I have some more. Detail. William Carlos Williams. **CP-WilW2**

Hey. Robert Creeley. **CP-CreeR**

Hey, Basho, you there! Hayden Carruth. **CP-CarHS** *Fr.* The Clay Hill Anthology.

Hey Bulldog. The Beatles. **CP-Beatl**

Hey Bungalow Bill what did you kill Bungalow Bill. The Continuing Story of Bungalow Bill. John Lennon *and* Paul McCartney. **CP-Beatl**

Hey Ca' thro'. Robert Burns. **CP-BurnR**

Hey, Ezra, Listen to This. Charles Bukowski. **SP-BukC3**

Hey Father Death, I'm flying home. Father Death Blues. Allen Ginsberg. **SM** *Fr.* Don't Grow Old. **CP-GinsA**

Hey for a Lass wi' a Tocher. Robert Burns. **CP-BurnR**

("Then hey, for a lass wi' a tocher, then hey, for a lass wi' a tocher.") **CP-BurnR**

Hey, hey, daddio. November Jeans Song. Hayden Carruth. **CP-CarHS**

Hey Jude. The Beatles. **CP-Beatl**

Hey man! Somebody yells down to me through my broken / window. Somebody Always Breaking My Dainty Solitude. . . . Charles Bukowski. **SP-BukC2**

Hey man, what's your style. Kicks. "Lou Reed." **SP-ReedL**

Hey man you want girls. Can We Resolve the Past. Jim Morrison. **SP-MorrJ**

Hey! Mister Tambourine Man, play a song for me. Mr. Tambourine Man. "Bob Dylan." **CP-DylaB**

Hey now bitch, now baby you'd better. Temporary Thing. "Lou Reed." **SP-ReedL**

Hey Red! William Carlos Williams. **CP-WilW2**

Hey, said my friend, I want you to meet. Twins. Charles Bukowski. **SP-BukC1**

Hey that cunt's not breathing, I think she's had too much. Street Hassle: Street Hassle. "Lou Reed." **SP-ReedL**

Hey, That's No Way to Say Goodbye. Leonard Cohen. **CP-CoheL**

Hey the dusty Miller. Dusty Miller. Robert Burns. **CP-BurnR**

Hey there, you in the macadam suit! Mr. U.S. Highway #1. Just outside Tombstone. Kenneth Patchen. **CP-PatcK**

Hey Tuti Tatey. Robert Burns. **CP-BurnR**

Hi, hi, I was running after you for a long time. Wave. Patti Smith. **SP-SmitP**

Hi-Ho the Ambulance-O. Ogden Nash. **CP-NashO**

Hi, Kuh, / those / gold'n bees / are I's. I's (Pronounced *Eyes*). Louis Zukofsky. **CP-ZukLS**

Hi, open up a dozen. At the Bar. William Carlos Williams. **CP-WilW1**

Hi, tent-boy, get that tent down. Basil Bunting, *after* Manuchehri. **CP-BuntB**

Hi! The creator too is blind. Negation. Wallace Stevens. **CP-StevW**

Hi There! Robert Creeley. **CP-CreeR**

Hiatus. Louis MacNeice. **CP-MacNL**

Hiawatha's Childhood. Henry Wadsworth Longfellow. **SP-LongH** *Fr.* The Song of Hiawatha.

"By the shores of Gitche[e] Gumee." **EBEvV; FaPON; FaPoB; OHFP; PFP; WBLP**

Hiawatha's Fasting. Henry Wadsworth Longfellow. **SP-LongH** *Fr.* The Song of Hiawatha.

Hiawatha's Photographing. "Lewis Carroll." **CP-CarrL**

Hibiscus and Salvia Flowers. David Herbert Lawrence. **CP-LawrD**

Hibiscus on the Sleeping Shores. Wallace Stevens. **CP-StevW**

Hic etiam jacet. *see also* Epitaph on a Hare. William Cowper. **CP-CowpW**

Hic Jacet. William Carlos Williams. **CP-WilW1**

Hic sinu fessum caput hospitali. *Latin vers. of epitaph in* Gray's Elegy Written in a Country Churchyard; *see also* "Here rests his head upon the lap of earth." Percy Bysshe Shelley. **CP-ShelP**

Hiccoughs of old ladies. Marsden Hartley. **CP-HartM**

Hid by the august foliage and fruit. To a Chameleon. Marianne Craig Moore. **CP-MoorM**

Hidden by old age awhile. *fr.* A Woman Young and Old. William Butler Yeats. **CP-YeatW**

Hidden Door. Lawrence Ferlinghetti. **SP-FerlL**

Hidden from the darkness of our mortal sight. Antipas. Christina Georgina Rossetti. **CP-RosC2**

Hidden Garden, The. Robert Ranke Graves. **CP-GravR**

Hidden harmony is better than the open, The. Thomas Merton. *Fr.* The Legacy of Herakleitos. **CP-MertT**

Hidden Ice. Louis MacNeice. **CP-MacNL**

Hidden in this heaven-harbor. Clairvaux. Thomas Merton. **CP-MertT**

Hidden Lane, The. Wystan Hugh Auden. **CP-AudWJ**

Hidden Law, The. Wystan Hugh Auden. **CP-AudeW**

Hidden Life, The. William Cowper. *Fr.* Olney Hymns. **CP-CowpW**

Hidden lovers in the soil. The Harmonies of Excess. Thomas Merton. *Fr.* Cables to the Ace. **CP-MertT**

Hidden Meanings. Dabney Stuart. **SP-StuaD**

Hidden, oh hidden. Song for the Rainy Season. Elizabeth Bishop. **CP-BishE**

Hidden Singer, The. Wendell Berry. **CP-BerrW**

Hidden strength, A. Chastity. John Milton. **OBS** *Fr.* Comus; a Masque Presented at Ludlow Castle.

Hidden Within the Sleeves of Those Dark Robes. Stephen Dobyns. **SP-DobyS**

Hide [*or* Hyd], Absalon, thy gilte tresses clere. Geoffrey Chaucer. **AWP; ChTr; EBEvV; EnVB; FiP; GBL; HAP; ImPo; LoBV; MeEL; NOBE; OAEL-1; OBEV; SCGP; SeCeV** *Fr.* The Legend of Good Women. **CP-ChauG**

(Lady without Paragon, A.) **MeEL**

Hide and Seek. Thom Gunn. **CP-GunnT**

Hide & Seek. Howard Nemerov. **CP-NemeH**

Hide in the hollow trunk. Oracle. Seamus Heaney. **SP-HeanS**

Hide not, sweetest Love, a sight so pleasing. Thomas Campion. **CP-CampT**

Hideous dragon, dreadfull to behold, A. Edmund Spenser. *Fr.* Visions of the World's Vanity [*or* Vanitie]. **CP-Spens**

Hideousness of the inland spine of Cornwall!, The. Short Run to Camborne. Donald Davie. **CP-DavDo**

Hideout. Richard Hugo. **CP-HugoR**

Hideyoshi. Frederick Morgan. **SP-MorgF**

Hiding in the church of an abandoned stone. Confession to J. Edgar Hoover. James Wright. **CP-WrigJ**

Hieroglyph. Leonard Nathan. **SP-NathL**

Hieroglyphic. Hart Crane. **CP-CranH**

Hieros Gamos. Kathleen Jessie Raine. **SP-RainK**

High above Plymouth, not so high. Among Artisans' Houses. Donald Davie. **CP-DavDo**

High above the world's pursuit. St. Peter. Christopher Smart. *Fr.* Hymns and Spiritual Songs for the Fasts and Festivals of the Church of England. **SP-SmarC**

High above themselves. Above everything, flux, ooze. Hayden Carruth. **Jaz** *Fr.* Paragraphs. **CP-CarHS**

High amid / gothic rocks the altar stands. Sub Specie Aeternitatis. Robert Earl Hayden. **AmPP** *Fr.* An Inference of Mexico. **CP-HaydR**

High and smaller goes the moon, she is small and very far from me. A Pang of Reminiscence. David Herbert Lawrence. **CP-LawrD**

High as my heart!—the quip be mine. Mother and Daughter. Robert Louis Stevenson. *Fr.* The Family. **CP-StevR**

High bliss is only for a higher state. Farewell Lines. William Wordsworth. **CP-WorW2**

High blue sky clicks into place, A. Vision of the City from a Window. Gilbert Sorrentino. **SP-SorrG**

High Bridge above the Tagus River at Toledo, The. William Carlos Williams. **CP-WilW2**

High, burnished sky, / the snow squall roars off south. A Bad Turn. John Clellon Holmes. **SP-HolmJ**

High ceilingd and the double mirrors, the. Bubbs Creek Haircut. Gary Snyder. **CP-SnydG**

High-Class Bananas, The. Gary Gildner. **SP-GildG**

High-class families, The. Dullness in February: Japan. Gary Snyder. **CP-SnydG**

High climbs June's wild rose. The Wild Rose. George Meredith. **CP-MerG2**

High Conspiratorial Persons. Carl Sandburg. **CP-SandC**

High deck. Blue skies overhead. White distance, A. Jane Cooper. *Fr.* The Flashboat. **SP-CoopJ**

High deeds, O Germans, are to come from you! A Prophecy February, 1807. William Wordsworth. **CP-WorW1**

High Devil, Deep Pit. Jenny Joseph. **SP-JoseJ**

High dormers are rising / So sharp and surprising. An Edwardian Sunday, Broomhill, Sheffield. Sir John Betjeman. **CP-BetjJ**

High Embrace, The. William Everson. **SP-EverW**

High Fidelity. Thom Gunn. **CP-GunnT**

High fog, white sky. Fennel. Thom Gunn. **CP-GunnT**

High Frequency. Marge Piercy. **SP-PierM**

High from the earth I heard a bird. Emily Dickinson. **CP-DickE**

High Grass Prairie. Richard Hugo. **CP-HugoR**

High heart, O Hafiz! though not thine. Hafiz, *tr. by* Ralph Waldo Emerson. **CP-EmerR** *Fr.* Odes.

High-Hearts, The. John Updike. **CP-UpdiJ**

"High heavenly priest of the White Lake" is now, The. Portrait of the Artist with Li Po. Charles Wright. **SP-WrigC**

High, high and still. The Loch. Kathleen Jessie Raine. *Fr.* Bheinn Naomh. **SP-RainK**

High horses of the sea broke their white riders. How Yesterday Looked. Carl Sandburg. **CP-SandC**

High in front advanced. John Milton. **EBEvV** *Fr.* Book XII. *Fr.* Paradise Lost. **CP-MiltJ**

High in the breathless Hall the Minstrel sate. Song at the Feast of Brougham Castle upon the Restoration of Lord Clifford, the Shepherd, to the Estates and Honours of His Ancestors. William Wordsworth. **CP-WorW1**

High in the dome, suspended, of Hell, sad triumph, behold us! Ixion. Robert Browning. **CP-BroR2**

High in the midst, surrounded by his peers. Thoughts Suggested by a College Examination. Byron. **CP-Byron**

High is our calling, Friend!—Creative Art. To B.R. Haydon. William Wordsworth. **CP-WorW2**

High is the dark clouds. Caught in the Swamp. Joseph Ceravolo. **SP-CeraJ**

High life. Jenny Joseph. *Fr.* Life and Turgid Times of A. Citizen. **SP-JoseJ**

High Moments. Carl Sandburg. **CP-SandC**

High Morning. The Hour of Tierce. Thomas Merton. *Fr.* Hagia Sophia. **CP-MertT**

High mounted on an Ant *Nanus* the tall. On Nanus Mounted on an Ant. Ausonius, *tr. fr. Latin by* Richard Crashaw. **CP-CrasR**

High nave, in a place of ships, The. At Saint Mary's Church. Charles Tomlinson. **CP-TomlC**

High noon has me pitchblack, so in hope out. Sext. John Berryman. **CP-BerrJ**

High noon. White sun flashes on the Michigan Avenue asphalt. Drum. In a Breath. Carl Sandburg. **CP-SandC**

High o'er the silver rocks I roved. Beauty and Moonlight. William Wordsworth. **CP-WorW1**

High on a broad unfertile tract of forest-skirted Down. The Norman Boy. William Wordsworth. **CP-WorW2**

High on a gorgeous seat, that far out-shone. Alexander Pope. *Fr.* The Dunciad. **CP-PopeA**

"This labour passed, by Bridewell all descend." **FHYEP**

"Three college sophs, and three pert templars came." **FHYEP**

High on a hill a goodly cedar grewe. Edmund Spenser. *Fr.* Visions of the World's Vanity [*or* Vanity]. **CP-Spens**

High on a mountain's highest ridge. William Wordsworth. **Par** *Fr.* The Thorn. **CP-WorW1**

High on a slope in New Guinea. The Man in the Dead Machine. Donald Hall. **CP-HallD**

High on a throne of royal state, which far. John Milton. **OAEL-1**, *ll.* 1–309; **NIP**, *ll.* 1–42; *Fr.* Book II. **FHYEP; NAEL-1; OxAEP-1** *Fr.* Paradise Lost. **CP-MiltJ**

High on a Throne of Royal State, which far. Book II. John Milton. **FHYEP; NAEL-1; OxAEP-1** *Fr.* Paradise Lost. **CP-MiltJ**

High on her speculative tower. The Eclipse of the Sun, 1820. William Wordsworth. *Fr.* Memorials of a Tour of the Continent; 1820. **CP-WorW2**

High on his figured couch beyond the waves. Theseus and Ariadne. Robert Ranke Graves. **CP-GravR**

High on his stockroom ladder like a dunce. Playboy. Richard Wilbur. **CP-WilbR**

High on Laughing Gas. Laughing Gas. Allen Ginsberg. **CP-GinsA**

High on our hill a vast cloud laps us round. Season's End. John Hewitt. **CP-HewiJ**

High on Rebellion. Patti Smith. **SP-SmitP**

High ones, Berryman said, die, die, die, The. March 4th. Anne Sexton. **CP-SextA**

High over the graves of our comrades, banked. Leaflet (Two). Kenneth Patchen. **CP-PatcK**

High over the October wood the Lion. The Lion. Thomas Merton. **CP-MertT**

High Pasture, The. Donald Hall. **CP-HallD**

High Priests of telescopes and cyclotrons, The. Ode to Terminus. Wystan Hugh Auden. **CP-AudeW**

High Quality Information. Gary Snyder. **CP-SnydG**

High-Rise of the New World, The. Charles Bukowski. **SP-BukC2**

High Road to Taos, The. Martin Edmunds. **SP-EdmuM**
   El Santuario de Chimayó.
   Hill Village, A.
   Morada La Muerte, The.
   Taos.

High rock face above Flathead Lake, A. The Eye in the Rock. John Haines. **SP-HainJ**

High-School Lawn, The. Thomas Hardy. **CP-HardT**

High Society. Daniel Gerard Hoffman. **SP-HoffD**

High-spirited friend, / I send not balms, nor corsives to your wound. Ode, An. Ben Jonson. **CP-JonsB**

High streaks of cottony-white cloud fill the sky. The Old South. John Gould Fletcher. **SP-FletJ**

High Summer. Kathleen Jessie Raine. **SP-RainK**

High Summer. Charles Tomlinson. **CP-TomlC**

High Talk. William Butler Yeats. **CP-YeatW**

High the vanes of Shrewsbury gleam. The Welsh Marches. Alfred Edward Housman. **CP-HousA**

High time now gan it wex for Una faire. Edmund Spenser. **FHYEP** *Fr.* The Faerie Queene. **CP-Spens**

High to Low. Langston Hughes. **SP-HughL**

High-Toned Old Christian Woman, A. Wallace Stevens. **CP-StevW**

High treachery sails / unveils. "Bob Dylan." *Fr.* Some Other Kinds of Songs. **CP-DylaB**

High up on the patio window, centered exactly. Impact. Karl Shapiro. **SP-ShapK**

High up the steep dark mountain. St Rosalie: Monte Pellegrino. John Hewitt. **CP-HewiJ**

High voices in domestic chapels; praise. Who Are These Coming to the Sacrifice? Geoffrey Hill. *Fr.* An Apology for the Revival of Christian Architecture in England. **CP-HillG**

High was her heart, and yet was well inclined. A.H. Ralph Waldo Emerson. *Fr.* Quatrains. **CP-EmerR**

High waving heather, 'neath stormy blasts bending. Emily Brontë. **CP-BronE**

High wind yesterday. Reorganization. Archie Randolph Ammons. **SP-AmmoA**

High Windows. Philip Larkin. **CP-LarkP**

High Wire. Dabney Stuart. **SP-StuaD**

High wisdom holds my wisdom less. Tennyson. *Fr.* In Memoriam A. H. H. **CP-TennA**

High wooded hill near Florence, an April, A. In Memory: Stuart Egnal. Wendell Berry. **CP-BerrW**

Higher Argument. John Milton. *See* No more of talk where God or Angel Guest.

Higher than gulls' nests, higher than children go. Rock Climbing. Jane Cooper. **SP-CoopJ**

Higher than the handsomest hotel. The Building. Philip Larkin. **CP-LarkP**

Highest Altitude. Margaret Atwood. **SP-AtwM1**

Highest Place in Town, The. John Ciardi. **SP-CiarJ**

Highland Balou, The. Robert Burns. **CP-BurnR**

Highland Broach, The. William Wordsworth. **CP-WorW2**

Highland Graveyard. Kathleen Jessie Raine. *Fr.* Eileann Chanaidh. **SP-RainK**

Highland Hut. William Wordsworth. **CP-WorW2**

Highland lad my Love was born, A. Robert Burns. *Fr.* The Jolly Beggars.

Highland Laddie. Robert Burns. **CP-BurnR**

Highland Lassie O. Robert Burns. **CP-BurnR**

Highland Mary. Robert Burns. **CP-BurnR**

Highland Widow's Lament, The. Robert Burns. **CP-BurnR**

Highlands 1966, The. Martin Edmunds. **SP-EdmuM**

Highmindedness, a jealousy for good. Addressed to Haydon. John Keats. **CP-KeatJ**

Highway, The. Leonard Nathan. **SP-NathL**

Highway, The. Sir Philip Sidney. *See* Sonet 84: "Highway, since you my chief Parnassus be."

Highway ended, The. 7 Years from Somewhere. Philip Levine. **SP-LeviP**

Highway is full of big cars, The. Come, And Be My Baby. Maya Angelou. **SP-AngeM**

Highway: Michigan. Theodore Roethke. **CP-RoetT**

Highway Report. Jim Carroll. **SP-CarrJ**

Highway, since you my chief Parnassus be. Sonnet 84. Sir Philip Sidney. **EIL; EnRePo; LiTB; OAEP; OBEV; OBSC; OXAEP-1; SCGP** *Fr.* Astrophil and Stella. **SP-SidnP**

Highway 61 Revisited. "Bob Dylan." **CP-DylaB**

Highway 61 Revisited (liner Notes). "Bob Dylan." **CP-DylaB**

Highway 30. Ted Kooser. **SP-KoosT**

Hike on the Downs, A. Sir John Betjeman. **CP-BetjJ**

Hiking the Miller Creek trail. The Blood Lake. John Haines. **SP-HainJ**

Hilarious God. Lawrence Ferlinghetti. **SP-FerlL**

Hilda. John Crowe Ransom. **SP-RansJ**

Hilda's Morning and Evening Dose of Rhyme. George Meredith. **CP-MerG2**

Hill, The. Robert Creeley. **CP-CreeR**

—Hill / Heaven and every field, are still. Gerard Manley Hopkins. **CP-HopkG**

Hill, The. Charles Tomlinson. **CP-TomlC**

Hill. Louis Zukofsky. **CP-ZukLS**

Hill behind the Town, The. Roy Fisher. *Fr.* City. **SP-FishR**

Hill blue among the leaves in summer. Cheap Blue. Carl Sandburg. **CP-SandC**

Hill (breeder) of Helicon. Carmen 61. Catullus. *Fr.* Carmina. **CP-Catul**

Hill Daughter. Louise McNeill. **SP-McNeL**

Hill Dream of Youth, Thirty Years Later. Richard Eberhart. **CP-EberR**

Hill-Farm, The. John Hewitt. **CP-HewiJ**

Hill Field, The. Donald Davie. **CP-DavDo**

Hill Has Something to Say, The. Rita Dove. **SP-DoveR**

Hill of Beans, A. Rita Dove. **SP-DoveR**

Hill of the Graces, The. Edmund Spenser. **NOBE** *Fr.* The Faerie Queene. **CP-Spens**

Hill of the white skull in the summer moon, The. Three Hills Look Different in the Moonshine. Carl Sandburg. **CP-SandC**

Hill of Truth, The, *shorter vers.* John Donne. *See* Satire 3: "Kind pity [*or* Kinde pitty] chokes my spleen[e]; brave scorn forbids."

Hill pasture, an open place among the trees, The. In This World. Wendell Berry. **CP-BerrW**

Hill-sides are dark. In the Woods. George Meredith. **CP-MerG2**

Hill Song. Louise McNeill. **SP-McNeL**

Hill-Top, The. John Greenleaf Whittier. **CP-WhitJ**

Hill-top schloss, The. Legend. Charles Tomlinson. **CP-TomlC**

Hill Village, A. Martin Edmunds. *Fr.* The High Road to Taos. **SP-EdmuM**

Hill Walk. Charles Tomlinson. **CP-TomlC**

Hill Wife, The. Robert Frost. **CP-FrosR**
  House Fear. **NTP; VGW; WSC**
  Impulse, The. **ArLo; HoPM; NePA; RaBo**
  Loneliness. **FaBoEn; VGW**
  Oft-Repeated Dream, The. **Poetr**
  Smile, The.

Hillcrest. Edwin Arlington Robinson. **CP-RobiE**

Hillocky *alpine rosy bells* name. Alpine Rosy Bells. Louis Zukofsky. **CP-ZukLS**

Hills, The. David Herbert Lawrence. **CP-LawrD**

Hills / like poets put on, The. Edward Estlin Cummings. **CP-CummE**

Hills, The. George Oppen. **CP-OppeG**

Hills and a cloud have hid away the sun. Autumn Evening. Wystan Hugh Auden. **CP-AudWJ**

Hills and the night and your love are last seclusion, The. Donna MacElmain. Louise McNeill. **SP-McNeL**

Hills are grey elephants. Sing, Mister, Sing. Charles Olson. **CP-OlsoC**

Hills are tipped with sunshine, while I walk / In shadows dim and cold. Christina Georgina Rossetti. **CP-RosC2**

Hills behind, The. One Year. Gary Snyder. **CP-SnydG**

Hills chime with thrush. Edward Estlin Cummings. **CP-CummE**

Hills erect their Purple Heads, The. Emily Dickinson. **CP-DickE**

Hills in Purple syllables, The. Emily Dickinson. **CP-DickE**

Hills in Their Recumbent Postures, The. Philip Larkin. **CP-LarkP**

Hills lie thick, The. Roy Fisher. **SP-FishR** *Fr.* Glenthorne Poems.

Hills of Annesley! bleak and barren. Fragment Written Shortly after the Marriage of Miss Chaworth. Byron. **CP-Byron**

Hills of May, The. Robert Ranke Graves. **CP-GravR**

Hills of this tractor, The. Bear Gulch Road. Al Young. **CP-YounA**

Hills step off into whiteness, The. Sheep in Fog. Sylvia Plath. **CP-PlatS**

Hills uncap their tops, The. Life and Death at Sunrise. Thomas Hardy. **CP-HardT**

Hillside Thaw, A. Robert Frost. **CP-FrosR**

Hilltop, The. Richard Hugo. **CP-HugoR**

Him loved she. Lo, now was he veiled. George Meredith. *Fr.* The Day of the Daughter of Hades. **CP-MerG1**

Him not the golden fang of furious heaven. Edna St. Vincent Millay. *Fr.* Epitaph for the Race of Man. **CP-MillE**

Him the Almighty Power. Satan Defiant. John Milton. **WHA,** *ll.* 44–109; **FaBoEn** *Fr.* Book I. **FHYEP; NAEL-1; OAEL-1; OxAEP-1** *Fr.* Paradise Lost. **CP-MiltJ**

Him with His Tail in His Mouth. David Herbert Lawrence. **CP-LawrD**

Himmaleh was known to stoop, The. Emily Dickinson. **CP-DickE**

Himself. Daniel Gerard Hoffman. **SP-HoffD**

Himself it was who wrote. Astræa. Ralph Waldo Emerson. **CP-EmerR**

"Himself let him unknown contain." Tom Clark. **SP-ClarT**

Hind and the Panther, The. John Dryden.
  "Swallow, privileged above the rest, The." **SP-DrydJ**

Hindu Babe / I love you. Malcolm Lowry. **CP-LowrM**

Hindu Sepoy in France. Rudyard Kipling. *Fr.* Epitaphs of the War [1914–1918]. **CP-KiplR**

Hint from the Mountains for Certain Political Pretenders. William Wordsworth. **CP-WorW2**

Hints for the Fancy. William Wordsworth. *Fr.* The River Duddon [A Series of Sonnets]. **CP-WorW2**

Hints from Horace. Byron. **CP-Byron**
  "Peace to Swift's faults! his wit hath made them pass." **EPCY**

Hippety hoppety down. Nathaniel Hawthorne. Robert Creeley. **CP-CreeR**

Hippo, The. Theodore Roethke. **CP-RoetT**

Hippo sandwich is easy to make, A. Recipe For A Hippopotamus Sandwich. Shel Silverstein. **SP-SilS2**

Hippolytus. Euripides, *tr. fr. Classical Greek by* Rex Warner.
  Chorus of Troizenian Women. **CP-DoolH**
  "Daemon initiate, spirit." **CP-DoolH**
  "Lift my head, help me up." **CP-DoolH**
  "Men you strike." **CP-DoolH**
  "No more, O my spirit." **CP-DoolH**
  "O for wings." **CP-DoolH**
  "O Spirit, / spark by spark." **CP-DoolH**

Hippolytus. Seneca, *tr. fr. Latin.*
  "Not faster in the summer's ray." **CP-JohnS**

Hippolytus Temporizes. Hilda Doolittle. **CP-DoolH**

Hippopotamus, The. Thomas Stearns Eliot. **CP-ElioT**

Hippopotamus, The. Ogden Nash. **CP-NashO**

Hippy-Mo. Stevie Smith. **CP-SmitS**

Hips lOOsest OOping shoulders blonde& pastoral hair,strong. Edward Estlin Cummings. **CP-CummE**

Hiram Powers' "Greek Slave." Elizabeth Barrett Browning. **CP-BroEB**

Hired Lad's Farewell, The. John Hewitt. **CP-HewiJ**

His Age, Dedicated to His Peculiar Friend, Master John Wickes, under the Name of Posthumus. Robert Herrick. **CP-HerrR**

His ageing nature is the same. Wystan Hugh Auden. *Fr.* Shorts [1939–1947] ("Motionless, deep in his mind, lies the past the poet's forgotten"). **CP-AudeW**

His Almes. Robert Herrick. **CP-HerrR**

His Answer to a Friend. Robert Herrick. **CP-HerrR**

His Answer to a Question. Robert Herrick. **CP-HerrR**

His Anthem, to Christ on the Crosse. Robert Herrick. **CP-HerrR**

His Apologies. Rudyard Kipling. **CP-KiplR**

His appearances are incalculable. Gratitude for a Nightmare. Robert Ranke Graves. **CP-GravR**

His are the generous days that balance. The Generous Days. Stephen Spender. **CP-SpenS**

His armour glittered in the [   ]. Fragments: Drafts, Mostly or All for a Poem on a Heroic Theme. William Wordsworth. **CP-WorW1**

His attitude towards woman is the basic point. "Hugh MacDiarmid." **SP-MacDH** *Fr.* Cornish Heroic Song for Valda Trevlyn.

His awful skin. Bat. Anne Sexton. **CP-SextA**

His Banner over Me Was Love. Christina Georgina Rossetti. **CP-RosC2**

His Bargain, *fr.* Words for Music Perhaps. William Butler Yeats. **CP-YeatW**

His bark/ The daring mariner shall urge far o'er. Prophecy. Luigi Pulci. **PAH** *Fr.* The Morgante Maggiore. **CP-Byron**

His beak could open a bottle. Little Owl Who Lives in the Orchard. Mary Oliver. **SP-OlivM**

His Bill an Auger is. Emily Dickinson. **CP-DickE**

His Bill is clasped—his Eye forsook. Emily Dickinson. **CP-DickE**

His blood on my arm is warm as a bird. Prayer for Messiah. Leonard Cohen. **CP-CoheL**

His body, caught there in the mirror, lean. Hayden Carruth. *Fr.* The Sleeping Beauty. **CP-CarHL**

His bought arms Mong' not liked; for his first day. On Mongrel Esquire. Ben Jonson. **CP-JonsB**

His brain simplified itself. My Father at 89. Grace Paley. **CP-PaleG**

His care-free swagger was a fine invention. Wystan Hugh Auden. **CMoP** *Fr.* Sonnets from China. **CP-AudeW**

His Cavalier. Robert Herrick. **CP-HerrR**

His Chance in Life. Rudyard Kipling. *Fr.* Plain Tales from the Hills. "Then a pile of heads he laid." **CP-KiplR**

His Change. Robert Herrick. **CP-HerrR**

His Charge to Julia at His Death. Robert Herrick. **CP-HerrR**

His Cheek is his Biographer. Emily Dickinson. **CP-DickE**

His chosen comrades thought at school. What Then? William Butler Yeats. **CP-YeatW**

His class released, he guided us with care. Art Room in a City School. John Hewitt. **CP-HewiJ**

His coat resembles the snow. The Polar Bear. William Carlos Williams. **CP-WilW2**

His comb was redder than the fine coral. Geoffrey Chaucer. **PBBP** *Fr.* The Nun's Priest's Tale. **FHYEP; NAEL-1; NAWM-1; NoP; OAEL-1; TrGrPo** *Fr.* The Canterbury Tales. **CP-ChauG**

His Comfort. Robert Herrick. **CP-HerrR**

His Coming to the Sepulcher. Robert Herrick. **CP-HerrR**

His Confession. Robert Herrick. **CP-HerrR**

His Confidence, *fr.* Words for Music Perhaps. William Butler Yeats. **CP-YeatW**

His Content in the Country. Robert Herrick. **CP-HerrR**

His corpse owre a' the city lies. The Dead Liebknecht. "Hugh MacDiarmid." **SP-MacDH**

His Country. Thomas Hardy. **CP-HardT**

His Covenant or Protestation to Julia. Robert Herrick. **CP-HerrR**

His Creed. Robert Herrick. **CP-HerrR**

His Daughter. William Carlos Williams. **CP-WilW2**

His Death from Cancer. William Dickey. **SP-DickW**

His Descendents. William Wordsworth. *Fr.* Ecclesiastical Sonnets. **CP-WorW2**

His Desire. Robert Herrick. **CP-HerrR**

His Discourse with Cupid. Ben Jonson. *Fr.* A Celebration of Charis in Ten Lyric[k] Pieces [*or* Peeces]. **CP-JonsB**

His Dog and Pilgrim. Frank Templeton Prince. **CP-PrinF**

His Dream. Hayden Carruth. *Fr.* The Fifth Version. The Mythology of Dark and Light. **CP-CarHL**

His dream: / He is dressed in a white sheet, riding. Hayden Carruth. *Fr.* The Sleeping Beauty. **CP-CarHL**

His Dream[e]. Robert Herrick. **CP-HerrR**

His Dream. Sir John Suckling. **CP-SuckJ**

His Dream. William Butler Yeats. **CP-YeatW**

His Dream of Flood: And Eden. Muriel Rukeyser. **CP-RukeM**

His Ejaculation to God. Robert Herrick. **CP-HerrR**

His Embalming to Julia. Robert Herrick. **CP-HerrR**

His enemy, the universe, surrounds him nightly with stars. The Bird Killer. Wendell Berry. **CP-BerrW**

His energy did him in, came flooding. Tony. Richard Hugo. **CP-HugoR**

His Excellency. Wystan Hugh Auden. **CP-AudeW**

His Excuse for Loving. Ben Jonson. **EnRePo; JCP; NOSC; PoEL-2; QFR; SeCV-1** *Fr.* A Celebration of Charis in Ten Lyric[k] Pieces [*or* Peeces]. **CP-JonsB**

His eyes are darker than he knows. Narcissus. May Sarton. **SP-SartM**

His eyes are quickened so with grief. Lost Love. Robert Ranke Graves. **CP-GravR**

His eyes he opened, shut, again unclosed. Juan and Haiidée. Byron. **EBNV** *Fr.* Canto the Second. *Fr.* Don Juan. **CP-Byron**

His face was charged with beauty as a cloud. Storm. Wilfred Owen. **CP-OwenW**

His face was like a snake's—wrinkled and loose. Fragment: A Serpent-Face. Percy Bysshe Shelley. **CP-ShelP**

His face with smile eternal drest. Robert Burns. *Fr.* Versicles on Sign-Posts. **CP-BurnR**

His faces crack. . . if mine could crack and breathe! Rembrandt. Robert Lowell. **SP-LoweR**

His fair large front and eye sublime declared. Paradise. John Milton. **PlP** *Fr.* Book IV. **OAEL-1** *Fr.* Paradise Lost. **CP-MiltJ**

His Farewell [*or* Fare-well] to Sack. Robert Herrick. **CP-HerrR**

His father gave him a box of truisms. The Truisms. Louis MacNeice. **CP-MacNL**

His father is lost and away. Muriel Rukeyser. **CP-RukeM**

His father's sense, his mother's grace. On the Birth of John William Rizzo Hoppner. Byron. **CP-Byron**

His Feet are shod with Gauze. Emily Dickinson. **CP-DickE**

His fingers tangled in his beard. The Monarch. John Hewitt. **CP-HewiJ**

His fingers wake, and flutter; up the bed. Conscious. Wilfred Owen. **CP-OwenW**

His first official act was to bless. 1949 (After Reading a News Item). Edwin Rolfe. **CP-RolfE**

His flaggy wings when forth he did display. The Dragon. Edmund Spenser. **SeCePo** *Fr.* The Faerie Queene. **CP-Spens**

His flames ar joyes, his bands true lovers might. Sonnet 3. Mary Sidney, Countess of Montgomery Wroth. *Fr.* A Crowne of Sonetts Dedicated to Love. *Fr.* Pamphilia to Amphilanthus. **CP-WrotM**

His Foreboding. Theodore Roethke. **CP-RoetT**

His foundation is in the holy mountains. Psalm 87. Bible, *O.T.* *Fr.* Psalms. **CP-Psal**

His gay words, words of delight. Muriel Rukeyser. **CP-RukeM**

His gilded rowels. Gerard Manley Hopkins. *Fr.* Fragments. **CP-HopkG**

His gloves were meant. Winter. Richard Shelton. **CP-ShelR**

His Grace! impossible! what, dead! A Satirical Elegy on the Death of a Late Famous General. Jonathan Swift. **CP-SwifJ**

His Grace's Answer to Jonathan. Jonathan Swift. **CP-SwifJ**

His Granddaughter Arrives. Dabney Stuart. **SP-StuaD**

His Grange. Robert Herrick. **CP-HerrR**

His Grange, or Private Wealth. Robert Herrick. **CP-HerrR**

. . . his hair an aureole, white. Mark Twain, 1909. Daniel Gerard Hoffman. **SP-HoffD**

His hand changed in the kitchen. In a Court. Hart Crane. **CP-CranH**

His Head is Full of Faces. Muriel Rukeyser. **CP-RukeM**

His Heart. Thomas Hardy. **CP-HardT**

His heart has a quicker beat. Shrew. Daniel Gerard Hoffman. **SP-HoffD**

His heart made a last fist. William Matthews. *Fr.* In Memory of W. H. Auden. **SP-MattW**

His Heart was darker then the starless night. Emily Dickinson. **CP-DickE**

His heatless room the watcher of the stars. Edna St. Vincent Millay. *Fr.* Epitaph for the Race of Man. **CP-MillE**

His Hope or Sheet-Anchor. Robert Herrick. **CP-HerrR**

His house / in the branches of. Charles Olson. **CP-OlsoC**

His Immortality. Thomas Hardy. **CP-HardT**

His innocence was to trust. Stanley Jasspon Kunitz. *Fr.* The Lincoln Relics. **CP-KuniS**

His instant thought the Poet spoke. Ralph Waldo Emerson. **CP-EmerR**

His intimate the green fern. The Fern. Wendell Berry. *Fr.* The Handing Down. **CP-BerrW**

His Lachrimae or Mirth, Turn'd to Mourning. Robert Herrick. **CP-HerrR**

His Lady queen of woods to meet. The Youthful Quest. George Meredith. **CP-MerG1**

His Lady's Cruelty. Sir Philip Sidney. *See* Sonnet 31: "With how sad steps, O Moon, thou climb'st the skies."

His land may burst the galling chain. Emily Brontë. **CP-BronE**

His Last Case. Frederick Morgan. **SP-MorgF**

His Last Request to Julia. Robert Herrick. **CP-HerrR**

His last train home is Purgatory in reverse. The Drunkard. Louis MacNeice. **CP-MacNL**

His late losse the Wireless *Higs* in order. Epigramme. Thomas Campion. *Fr.* Observations in the Art of English Poesie. **CP-CampT**

His laurels fresh from song and lay. Our Autocrat. John Greenleaf Whittier. **CP-WhitJ**

His learning truly lifted Hafiz to Heaven. Hafiz, *tr.* by Ralph Waldo Emerson. **CP-EmerR** *Fr.* Odes.

His Letanie, To the Holy Spirit. Robert Herrick. **CP-HerrR**

His library annoyed him with its look. Wystan Hugh Auden. *Fr.* The Quest. **CP-AudeW**

His life, at the end, seemed—even the anguish—simple. The Sign Whereby He Knew. Robert Penn Warren. *Fr.* Audubon. **SP-WarrR**

His life frightened him. The sun in the sky. Fear. Stephen Dobyns. **SP-DobyS**

His life is in the body of the living. The Soul and Body of John Brown. Muriel Rukeyser. **CP-RukeM**

His life started / as an anecdote. Light Years. Dabney Stuart. **SP-StuaD**

His Life was so shy and his tastes so unknown. Emily Dickinson. **SP-DickE**

His little Hearse like Figure. Emily Dickinson. **CP-DickE**

His Losse. Robert Herrick. **CP-HerrR**

His love returns / and walks among the trees. Wendell Berry. *Fr.* Window Poems. **CP-BerrW**

His lungs heaving all day in a sulphur mist. Black Money. Tess Gallagher. **SP-GallT**

His Majesty's Inspectors. John Hewitt. **CP-HewiJ**

His Mansion in the Pool. Emily Dickinson. **CP-DickE**

His Master taken from his head. On the Death of a Minister. William Cowper. *Fr.* Olney Hymns. **CP-CowpW**

His Meditation upon Death. Robert Herrick. **CP-HerrR**

His Memories. William Butler Yeats. *Fr.* A Man Young and Old. **CP-YeatW**

His memories lived in the place. A Praise. Wendell Berry. **CP-BerrW**

His memory was shaped by forgetting. The Snow Man. Louis MacNeice. **CP-MacNL**

His mind gone from the window. Wendell Berry. *Fr.* Window Poems. **CP-BerrW**

His mind is an inarticulated question. Alun Lewis. *Fr.* The Madman. **CP-LewiA**

His Mind like Fabrics of the East. Emily Dickinson. **CP-DickE**

His mind of man, a secret makes. Emily Dickinson. **CP-DickE**

His Misery in a Mistresse. Robert Herrick. **CP-HerrR**

His Mistris to Him at His Farwell. Robert Herrick. **CP-HerrR**

His most kind sister all his secrets knew. Repentance. George Chapman. **OBSC** *Fr.* Hero and Leander. **CP-MarlC**

His mother dear Cupid offended late. Sonnet 17. Sir Philip Sidney. *Fr.* Astrophil and Stella. **SP-SidnP**

His Music. Stephen Dunn. **SP-DunnS**

His name is Legion, and with a red eye. Armistice. Howard Nemerov. **CP-NemeH**

His number is zero, or twenty-one. The Fool. Charles Olson. **CP-OlsoC**

His Offering, with the Rest, at the Sepulcher. Robert Herrick. **CP-HerrR**

His old fame is dumb. Frank Templeton Prince. *Fr.* Yüan Chên Variations. **CP-PrinF**

His oriental heresies. Emily Dickinson. **CP-DickE**

His Own Epitaph. Robert Herrick. **CP-HerrR**

His Own Face Hidden. Carl Sandburg. **CP-SandC**

His own fair countenance, his kingly forehead. Inward Light. Samuel Taylor Coleridge. **CP-ColeS**

His pads furring the scarp's rime. The Snow-Leopard. Randall Jarrell. **CP-JarrR**

His paintings grew darker every year. The Artist. Stanley Jasspon Kunitz. **CP-KuniS**

His Parting from Her. John Donne. **EBEV** *Fr.* Elegies. **CP-DonnJ** (Elegie: His Parting from Her.) **OBS**

His Parting from Mistress Dorothy Keneday. Robert Herrick. **CP-HerrR**

His passion for the books. Critics Can Bleed. Roy Fisher. **SP-FishR**

His peasant parents killed themselves with toil. Wystan Hugh Auden. *Fr.* The Quest. **CP-AudeW**

His Petition. Robert Herrick. **CP-HerrR**

His Phoenix. William Butler Yeats. **CP-YeatW**

His Picture. John Donne. **EnRePo; FaBoEn; MePo** *Fr.* Elegies. **CP-DonnJ** (Elegie V: His Picture.) **MeLP; OBS; OXAEP-1**

His piercing pince-nez. Some dim frieze. Ted Berrigan. **SP-BerrT** *Fr.* The Sonnets.

His place, as he sat and as he thought, was not. A Quiet Normal Life. Wallace Stevens. **CP-StevW**

His plane exploded. Death of Fathers. James McAuley. **SP-McAuJ**

His plunge matched the waters poured aglow. George Meredith. *Fr.* Prestige. **CP-MerG2**

His Poetry His Pillar. Robert Herrick. **CP-HerrR**

His Power. Robert Herrick. **CP-HerrR**

His Prayer for Absolution. Robert Herrick. **CP-HerrR**

His Prayer to Ben[.] Jo[h]nson. Robert Herrick. **CP-HerrR**

His pride / Had cast him out from Heaven, with all his host. Satan. John Milton. **TrGrPo** *Fr.* Book I. **FHYEP; NAEL-1; OAEL-1; OxAEP-1** *Fr.* Paradise Lost. **CP-MiltJ**

His Protestation to Perilla. Robert Herrick. **CP-HerrR**

His Recantation. Robert Herrick. **CP-HerrR**

His Refugees. James Liddy. *Fr.* His Resplendent Neighbours. **CP-LiddJ**

His Request to Julia. Robert Herrick. **CP-HerrR**

His Resplendent Neighbours. James Liddy. **CP-LiddJ**
　His Refugees.
　Lady Fitzwilliam.
　Ossie Esmonde.
　　After Life.
　　City Life.
　　Country Life.

His Return to London. Robert Herrick. **CP-HerrR**

His Rooms in College. Thom Gunn. **CP-GunnT**

His Sailing from Julia. Robert Herrick. **CP-HerrR**

His Saviour[']s Words, Going to the Cross[e]. Robert Herrick. **CP-HerrR**

His Shield. Marianne Craig Moore. **CP-MoorM**

His Shining Helmet; Its Horsehair Crest. Tess Gallagher. **SP-GallT**

His Shirt. Rita Dove. **SP-DoveR**

His simple truths did Andrew glean. Oak and the Broom, The; A Pastoral. William Wordsworth. **CP-WorW1**

His sin was to speak first. Origen. Thomas Merton. **CP-MertT**

His Smile. Robert Penn Warren. **SP-WarrR**

His soul curdled /. John J. Maya Angelou. **SP-AngeM**

His soul stretched tight across the skies. Thomas Stearns Eliot. *Fr.* Preludes (I–IV). **CP-ElioT**

His spots are the joy of the Leopard: his horns are the Buffalo's pride. Rudyard Kipling. **CP-KiplR** *Fr.* Kaa's Hunting. *Fr.* The Jungle Book.

His stalk the dark delphinium. Edna St. Vincent Millay. **CP-MillE**

His Steps. Daniel Gerard Hoffman. **SP-HoffD**

His studio's bed and stove staked narrow space. Peter Peri (1899-1967). John Hewitt. **CP-HewiJ**

His suicide was simply not a puzzle. Purest of Occasions. Leonard Cohen. **CP-CoheL**

His sweet moist eye missed nothing—the vague guerilla. Alexander. Robert Lowell. **SP-LoweR**

His talk composed a crowded tapestry. Jenny Geddes. John Hewitt. **CP-HewiJ**

His tears fell from his veins. The Writer. Muriel Rukeyser. **CP-RukeM**

His Tears to Thamesis [or Thamasis]. Robert Herrick. **CP-HerrR**

His Themes. Donald Davie. **CP-DavDo**

His tongue was framed to music. Motto to "Power." Ralph Waldo Emerson. **CP-EmerR**

His Tuning of the Night. Erica Jong. **SP-JongE**

His Visitor. Thomas Hardy. **CP-HardT**

His voice decrepit was with Joy. Emily Dickinson. **CP-DickE**

His was a mind alive by a pure greed. William Matthews. *Fr.* In Memory of W. H. Auden. **SP-MattW**

His was the treasure of two thousand years. James Thomson. **EPCY** *Fr.* Summer. *Fr.* The Seasons. **CP-ThomJ**

His Weaknesse in Woes. Robert Herrick. **CP-HerrR**

His Wedded Wife. Rudyard Kipling. *Fr.* Plain Tales from the Hills. "Cry 'Murder' in the market-place, and each." **CP-KiplR**

His whole world revolves around light dark. Michael At Sixteen Months. Al Young. **CP-YounA**

His Wife at Bellevue. Marilyn Hacker. **SP-HackM** *Fr.* The Navigators.

His wife nods, and a secret smile. James Fenton. **SCBI** *Fr.* A German Requiem. **SP-FentJ**

His wife worked and bought his. Big John of Echo Park. Charles Bukowski. **SP-BukC3**

His Wildness. William Butler Yeats. *Fr.* A Man Young and Old. **CP-YeatW**

His Winding-Sheet. Robert Herrick. **CP-HerrR**

His Wish ("Fat be my Hinde"). Robert Herrick. **CP-HerrR**

His Wish. Robert Herrick. **CP-HerrR**

His Wish to God. Robert Herrick. **CP-HerrR**

His Wish to Privacie. Robert Herrick. **CP-HerrR**

His Words to Christ, Going to the Cross. Robert Herrick. **CP-HerrR**

His words were magic and his heart was true. Uncle Ananias. Edwin Arlington Robinson. **CP-RobiE**

Hissing Urn, The. William Cowper. *See* Reading the Newspaper.

Hist, but a word, fair and soft! Master Hugues of Saxe-Gotha. Robert Browning. **CP-BroR1**

Hist　whist / little ghostthings. Edward Estlin Cummings. **CP-CummE**

Historian, A. Daniel Gerard Hoffman. **SP-HoffD**

Historian came to the school and gave a, A. To the Liberal Magistrates. James Liddy. **CP-LiddJ**

Historians may scorn the close engagement. Tomorrow's Envy of Today. Robert Ranke Graves. **CP-GravR**

Historic be the survey of our kind. Society. George Meredith. **CP-MerG1**

Historic Pun. George Oppen. **CP-OppeG**

Historical Associations. Robert Louis Stevenson. **CP-StevR**

Historical Choice. Robinson Jeffers. **CP-JefR3**

Historical Epitaphs. Allen Tate. **CP-TateA**
  On the Father of Liberty.
  On the Founder of the Industrial System in the United States.
  On the Great Conciliator: Now Honored in the Old Dominion.
  On the Martyr of Harpers Ferry.

History. Wendell Berry. **CP-BerrW**

History. Wendell Berry. *Fr.* History. **CP-BerrW**
  "All the lives this place."
  History.
  "Since then I have arrived here."

History. Ralph Waldo Emerson.
  "I am owner of the sphere." **CP-EmerR**
  Mottoes to "History." **CP-EmerR**

History. David Herbert Lawrence. **CP-LawrD**

History. James Liddy. *Fr.* Love Songs of Corca Bascinn. **CP-LiddJ**

History. James Liddy. *See* Tell us, streaming lady.

History. Robert Lowell. **SP-LoweR**

History. Thomas McGrath. **SP-McGrT**

History. Frederick Morgan. **SP-MorgF**

History. Richard Shelton. **SP-ShelR**

History. Charles Simic. **SP-SimiC**

History. Charles Tomlinson. **CP-TomlC**

History. Robert Penn Warren. **SP-WarrR**

History. Charles Kenneth Williams. **SP-WillC**

History. William Carlos Williams. **CP-WilW1**

History among the Rocks. Robert Penn Warren. **CBCWP; GOA; MoAmPo; MoVE** *Fr.* Kentucky Mountain Farm. **SP-WarrR**

History & prophecy are alike. Ralph Waldo Emerson. **CP-EmerR**

History as Poetry. Geoffrey Hill. **CP-HillG**

History bless me. Relevant Is Different Points on the Circle. Audre Lorde. **SP-LordA**

History Book. Charles Simic. **SP-SimiC**

History falls like rain. For Shoshana Rihn—Pat Swinton. Marge Piercy. **SP-PierM**

History has to live with what was here. History. Robert Lowell. **SP-LoweR**

History has tongues / Has angels has guns. The Exiles. Stephen Spender. **CP-SpenS**

History in a Minor Key. Kenneth Patchen. **CP-PatcK**

History is a dialogue between. Tower of Babel. Thomas Merton. **CP-MertT**

History Is a Throne and a Gate. Kenneth Patchen. **CP-PatcK**

History is blood; or so history says. Love for the Dragon. David St. John. *Fr.* To Pasolini. **SP-StJoD**

History melts my houses. Love and its Doors and Windows. Muriel Rukeyser. **CP-RukeM**

History of a Literary Movement. Howard Nemerov. **CP-NemeH**

History of a Malady. Charles Tomlinson. **CP-TomlC**

History of a Tough Motherfucker, The. Charles Bukowski. **SP-BukC3**

History of an Hour, The. Thomas Hardy. **CP-HardT**

History of Bears, The. Paul Zimmer. **SP-ZimmP**

History of Hair from World War II to the Present. Howard Nemerov. **CP-NemeH**

History of Love, A. William Carlos Williams. **CP-WilW2**

History of melancholia, The. Melancholia. Charles Bukowski. **SP-BukC1**

History of Science, The. Wystan Hugh Auden. **CP-AudeW**

History of strangers in their dreams, The. Desire Is a World by Night. John Berryman. **CP-BerrJ**

History of the cosmos, The. God Is Born. David Herbert Lawrence. **CP-LawrD**

History of the Fall. Robert Ranke Graves. **CP-GravR**

History of the Moon, The. William Dickey. **SP-DickW**

History of the Sketch, A. Richard Hugo. **CP-HugoR**

History of the World: a TV Docu-Drama. Lawrence Ferlinghetti. **SP-FerlL**

History of Truth, The. Wystan Hugh Auden. **CP-AudeW**

History of Vanbrug's House, The. Jonathan Swift. **CP-SwifJ**

Hit Album, A. Gilbert Sorrentino. **SP-SorrG**

Hit me! Jab me! Third Degree. Langston Hughes. **SP-HughL**

Hit the bottom and spread out. Roy Fisher. **SP-FishR** *Fr.* Handsworth Liberties.

Hitch up honey for the / market race all. Folk Song, A. Robert Creeley. **CP-CreeR**

Hitch Your Wagon to a Star. Allen Tate. **CP-TateA**

Hitchhiker, The. Jim Morrison. **SP-MorrJ**

Hitching into Frisco. Thom Gunn. **CP-GunnT** *Fr.* Three Songs.

Hither, Blanche! 'Tis you and I. Montaigne and His Kitten. Herman Melville. **SP-MelvH**

Hither, come hither, my little foot-page. The Little Foot-Page. George Meredith. **CP-MerG2**

Hither, Hither, Love. John Keats. **CP-KeatJ**

Hither, in half blown garlands drest. To the Mulberry-Tree. Charlotte Smith. **CP-SmitC**

Hither, O captives, hither let you come. Boethius, *tr. fr. Latin.* **MLL,** *tr. by* Helen Waddell; *Fr.* Consolation of Philosophy, The ("De Consolacione Philosophie"). **CP-ChauG**

Hither the heroes and the nymphs resort. Alexander Pope. **ECEV** *Fr.* The Rape of the Lock[, an Heroi-Comical Poem]. **CP-PopeA**

Hither, where tangled thickets of the acacia. The Babiaantje. Frank Templeton Prince. **CP-PrinF**

Hither with hallowed steps as is the Ground. An Elegie. On the Death of Mrs. Cassandra Cotton. Richard Lovelace. **CP-LoveR**

Hitler. Leonard Cohen. **CP-CoheL**

Hitler had fingertips of apprehension. Attila, Hitler. Robert Lowell. **SP-LoweR**

Hits and Runs. Carl Sandburg. **CP-SandC**

Hit's been drizzlin' an' been sprinklin'. Drizzle. Paul Laurence Dunbar. **CP-DunbP**

Hive, The. Hart Crane. **CP-CranH**

Hive at Gettysburg, The. John Greenleaf Whittier. **CP-WhitJ**

Hiway Poesy: L.A.–Albuquerque–Texas–Witchita. Allen Ginsberg. **CP-GinsA**

Ho. Al Young. **CP-YounA**

Ho—all to the borders! Vermonters, come down. The Song of the Vermonters, 1779. John Greenleaf Whittier. **CP-WhitJ**

Ho, everyone that thirsteth. Alfred Edward Housman. **CP-HousA**

Ho, Giant! This is I! The Bean-Stalk. Edna St. Vincent Millay. **CP-MillE**

Ho Ho Ho Caribou. Joseph Ceravolo. **SP-CeraJ**

Ho-Hum Again. Hayden Carruth. **CP-CarHS**

Ho! in the dawn. Side by Side. Adrienne Rich. **CP-RicAE**

Ho. The horses can water. We are miles. Three Stops to Ten Sleep. Richard Hugo. **CP-HugoR**

Ho! thou who seekest late and long. The Sentence of John L. Brown. John Greenleaf Whittier. **CP-WhitJ**

Ho, Varlet! My Two Cents' Worth of Penny Postcard! Ogden Nash. **CP-NashO**

Ho! workers of the old time styled. The Shoemakers. John Greenleaf Whittier. **CP-WhitJ**

Hoar-frost crumbles in the sun, The. Endless Anxiety. David Herbert Lawrence. **CP-LawrD**

Hoarder, The. Anne Sexton. **CP-SextA**

Hoarfrost and Fog. Barton Sutter. **SP-SuttB**

Hobbes clearly proves that every creature. Jonathan Swift. **HAP; SCV; SeCePo** *Fr.* On Poetry: a Rhapsody. **CP-SwifJ** (Critics.) **SeCePo**

Hoboken Broken Down: A Hasty Recollection. Al Young. **CP-YounA**

Hobsons Epitaph. John Milton. **CP-MiltJ**

Hock and Soda Water. Byron. **FaBoDD** *Fr.* Canto the Second. *Fr.* Don Juan. **CP-Byron**

Hock-Cart, or Harvest Home, The. Robert Herrick. **CP-HerrR**

Hockey Poem, The. Robert Bly. **SP-BlyR**

Hodge Looks toward London. Wystan Hugh Auden. **CP-AudWJ**

Hoeing. John Updike. **CP-UpdiJ**

Hoeing the hataké, pull out all the clover bulb. November. Gary Snyder. *Fr.* Six Years. **CP-SnydG**

Hofer. William Wordsworth. **CP-WorW1**

Hog. Charles Bukowski. **SP-BukC3**

Hog. Anne Sexton. **CP-SextA**

Hog has a place i'th'Kitchen, and his share. Upon Hog. Robert Herrick. **CP-HerrR**

Hog Heaven. Charles Kenneth Williams. **CP-WillC; SP-WillC**

(Hogpen, deciduous growth, etc. The Rites. Robert Creeley. **CP-CreeR**

Hohensalzburg: Fantastic Variations on a Theme of Romantic Character. Randall Jarrell. **CP-JarrR**

Hohokam. Adrienne Rich. *Fr.* Turning the Wheel. **SP-RicA2**

Hoist sail, little bark of my wit! Distance Traveled. Anne Waldman. **SP-WaldA**

Hoist up and I could lean over, A. The Bull Moses. Ted Hughes. **SP-HughT**

Hoisting yourself. Climbing Katahdin. Daniel Gerard Hoffman. **SP-HoffD**

Hokku. Edward Estlin Cummings. **CP-CummE**

Hokum. "Hugh MacDiarmid." **SP-MacDH**

Hokusai on the Trent. Charles Tomlinson. **CP-TomlC**

Hokusai's portrait of himself. His Own Face Hidden. Carl Sandburg. **CP-SandC**

Holbein's More, my patron saint as a convert. Sir Thomas More. Robert Lowell. **SP-LoweR**

Hold a glass of pure water to the eye of the sun! The Glass of Pure Water. "Hugh MacDiarmid." **SP-MacDH**

Hold, are you mad? you damned [*or* damn'd] confounded dog. Epilogue to *Tyrannic[k] Love*. John Dryden. **SP-DrydJ** *Fr.* Tyrannic Love.

Hold Back! David Herbert Lawrence. **CP-LawrD**

Hold down the skylines now with your themes. Carl Sandburg. **CP-SandC** *Fr.* The People, Yes. **CP-SandC**

Hold Hard, These Ancient Minutes in the Cuckoo's Month. Dylan Thomas. **CP-ThomD**

Hold it in a high wind. The fender curving over the. Supplication to the Muses on a Trying Day. Hart Crane. **CP-CranH**

Hold it up sternly—see this it sends back, (who is it? is it you?). A Hand-Mirror. Walt Whitman. **CP-WhitW**

Hold Me. Philip Levine. **SP-LeviP**

Hold me / till only, these are my. White Fish in Reeds. Joseph Ceravolo. **SP-CeraJ**

Hold Me Tight. The Beatles. **CP-Beatl**

Hold my hand, Auntie, Auntie. The British Workman and the Government. David Herbert Lawrence. **CP-LawrD**

Hold not thy peace, O God of my praise. Psalm 109. Bible, *O.T. Fr.* Psalms. **CP-Psal**

Hold of the Maker, not the made. Ralph Waldo Emerson. **CP-EmerR**

Hold On. "Lou Reed." **SP-ReedL**

Hold thy tongue, death! Kenneth Patchen. **CP-PatcK**

Hold-up. Louis MacNeice. **CP-MacNL**

Holden. James Liddy. **CP-LiddJ**

Holden, a Thought From Abroad. James Liddy. **CP-LiddJ**

Holdfast, The. George Herbert. **CP-HerbG**

Holding / for one / instant this / moment—. Two. Robert Creeley. **CP-CreeR**

Holding habit-shaped memories in a leopard-skin apron. St.-John Perse. Charles Henri Ford. *Fr.* Four Elegies. **SP-FordC**

Holding in reserve. Marsden Hartley. **CP-HartM**

Holding its huge life open to the sky. To My Friends. Stephen Berg. **SP-BergS**

Holding my arms down. Margaret Atwood. *Fr.* Circe / Mud Poems. **SP-AtwM1**

Holding On. Archie Randolph Ammons. **SP-AmmoA**

Holding On. Philip Levine. **SP-LeviP**

Holding onto myself by the hand. The Other. James Dickey. **CP-DickJ**

Holding Out. Jane Cooper. **SP-CoopJ**

Holding Out. Adrienne Rich. **CP-RicAE; SP-RicA2**

Holding Pattern. Leonard Nathan. **SP-NathL**

Holding the Mirror Up to Nature. Howard Nemerov. **CP-NemeH**

Hole, The. Robert Creeley. **CP-CreeR**

Hole, The. Donald Hall. **CP-HallD**

Hole. Leonard Nathan. **SP-NathL**

Hole in the Clouds, A. Jim Morrison. **SP-MorrJ**

Hole in the Floor, A. Richard Wilbur. **CP-WilbR**

Hole in the Sky, A. Robert Pack. **SP-PackR**

Hole time burns in my breathing, The. Coral. Tom Clark. **SP-ClarT**

Holes, The. Stephen Berg. **SP-BergS**

Holi. Alun Lewis. **CP-LewiA**

Holiday: / every / yard or, A. Charles Kenneth Williams. **CP-WillC**

Holiday. Adrienne Rich. **CP-RicAE**

Holiday in Reality. Wallace Stevens. **CP-StevW**

Holidays. Ralph Waldo Emerson. **CP-EmerR**

Holidays. George Meredith. **CP-MerG2**

Holiness[e] on the head. Aaron. George Herbert. **CP-HerbG**

Holland, that scarce deserves the name of land. The Character of Holland. Andrew Marvell. **CP-MarvA**

Holland, that scarce deserves the name of land. Andrew Marvell. **ChTr** *Fr.* Holland, that scarce deserves the name of land. **OBSV** *Fr.* The Character of Holland. **CP-MarvA**

Holland, that scarce deserves the name of land. Andrew Marvell. **OBSV** *Fr.* The Character of Holland. **CP-MarvA**

"Holland, that scarce deserves the name of land." **ChTr**

Hollander's Animal Faith. Marsden Hartley. **CP-HartM**

Hollis Brown / He lived on the outside of town. Ballad of Hollis Brown. "Bob Dylan." **CP-DylaB**

Hollow Hill, The. Kathleen Jessie Raine. **SP-RainK**

"It is time, heart, to recall."

"One night in a dream."

"Outside, sun, frost, wind, rain."

"Rock is written with the sign, The."

"Tree of night is spangled with a thousand stars, The."

"Whiteness of moonlight builds a house that is not there."

Hollow Men, The. Thomas Stearns Eliot. **CP-ElioT**

Hollow rang the house when I knocked at the door. Turned Down. David Herbert Lawrence. **CP-LawrD**

Hollow-Sounding and Mysterious. Christina Georgina Rossetti. **CP-RosC2**

Hollow Tree, A. Robert Bly. **SP-BlyR**

Hollows. Archie Randolph Ammons. **SP-AmmoA**

Hollows round His eager Eyes, The. Emily Dickinson. **CP-DickE**

Holly. Seamus Heaney. **SP-HeanS** *Fr.* Sweeney Redivivus.

Holly and Hickory. Robert Penn Warren. **SP-WarrR**

Holly came from Miami F-L-A. Walk on the Wild Side. "Lou Reed." **SP-ReedL**

Hollyhocks against the Wall, The. John Hewitt. **CP-HewiJ**

Hollywood Everything, A. John Ashbery. **CBCK** *Fr.* Daffy Duck in Hollywood. **SP-AshbJ**

Holy and heavenly Spirits as they are. Same, The [Eminent Reformers]. William Wordsworth. *Fr.* Ecclesiastical Sonnets. **CP-WorW2**

Holy, & holy. The damned are said to say. John Berryman. *Fr.* Eleven Addresses to the Lord. **CP-BerrJ**

Holy, as I suppose I dare to call you. John Berryman. *Fr.* Eleven Addresses to the Lord. **CP-BerrJ**

Holy Baptism (1). George Herbert. **CP-HerbG**

Holy Baptism (2). George Herbert. **CP-HerbG**

Holy Child's Song, The. Thomas Merton. **CP-MertT**

Holy City, New Jerusalem, The. Christina Georgina Rossetti. **CP-RosC2**

H[oly] Communion, The. George Herbert. **CP-HerbG**

Holy Communion, The. George Herbert. **CP-HerbG**

Holy Communion: the City. Thomas Merton. **CP-MertT**

Holy-Cross Day. Robert Browning. **CP-BroR1**

Holy Fair, The. Robert Burns. **CP-BurnR**

Holy Family. Richard Hugo. **CP-HugoR**

Holy Family. Muriel Rukeyser. **CP-RukeM**

Holy Ghost, The. John Donne. **NOCV** *Fr.* A Litany. **CP-DonnJ**

Holy Ghost on the Nod over the Body of Bliss. Allen Ginsberg. **CP-GinsA**

Holy Grail, The. Tennyson. *Fr.* Idylls of the King. **CP-TennA**

Percivale's Quest. **OAEL-2**

"When the hermit made an end." **PeVV**

Holy haloes / Ring me round. Lord, in My Heart. Maya Angelou. **SP-AngeM**

Holy, heavenly chime / Rings fulness in of time, A. Christina Georgina Rossetti. *Fr.* Christmas Carols. **CP-RosC2**

Holy! Holy! Holy! Holy! Holy! Holy! Footnote to Howl. Allen Ginsberg. **CP-GinsA**

Holy Innocent gone home, A. Michael F. M. Rossetti. Christina Georgina Rossetti. **CP-RosC3**

Holy Innocents, The. Robert Lowell. **SP-LoweR**

Holy Innocents. Christina Georgina Rossetti. **CP-RosC2**

Holy Innocents. Christina Georgina Rossetti. **CP-RosC3**

Holy Innocents, The. Christopher Smart. *Fr.* Hymns and Spiritual Songs for the Fasts and Festivals of the Church of England. **SP-SmarC**

Holy Is Your Name. Leonard Cohen. **CP-CoheL**

Holy Isles, The. Kathleen Jessie Raine. **SP-RainK**

Iona.

Lindisfarne.

Holy Land, The, *ad. fr. the French of Lamartine*. John Greenleaf Whittier. **CP-WhitJ**

Holy Light. John Milton. *See* Hail holy Light, ofspring [*or* offspring] of Heav'n [*or* Heaven] first-born.

Holy Lord God! I love thy truth. Hatred of Sin. William Cowper. *Fr.* Olney Hymns. **CP-CowpW**

Holy man said to me, "Split the stick", A. Howard Nemerov. *Fr.* Runes. **CP-NemeH**

Holy Place, A. John Hewitt. **CP-HewiJ**

Holy-Rood come forth and shield. The Old Wives Prayer. Robert Herrick. **CP-HerrR**

Holy Sacrament of the Altar, The. Thomas Merton. **CP-MertT**

Holy Saturday night. Easter. Charles Olson. **CP-OlsoC**

Holy Satyr. Hilda Doolittle. **SP-DoolH**

Holy Scriptures (1), The. George Herbert. **CP-HerbG**

Holy Scriptures (2), The. George Herbert. **CP-HerbG**

Holy Sonnet. John Donne. *See* Death[,] be not proud, though some have called thee.

Holy Sonnets, Holy Sonnets *is the title often given to* Divine Meditations, *the collection of 19 sonnets comprising the second part of this longer work.* John Donne. **CP-DonnJ**

Divine Meditations. **CP-DonnJ**

(Holy Sonnets.) AnAnS-1; ESCV; MasP

"As due by many titles I resign[e]." JCP; MePo; OBS

"At the round earth's imagined corners, blow." BLPL; CABA; ChIV-2; ChTr; ClHu; EBCP; EBEV; EaLo; EnRePo; FHYEP; FaBoEn; FaBoRV; HAP; HeIL; HeIP; ImPo; InPS; JCP; LiTB; LoBV; MeLP; MePo; NAEL-1; NAWM-1; NOBE; NOSC; NoP; OAEL-1; OAEP; OBD; OBS; OxAEP-1; OxBoCh; PAI; PFP; PPP; PPoe; PeECV; PoE; PoEL-2; PoPle; QFR; SCGP; SeCP; SeCV-1; SeCeV; Son; TEP; TFi; TOF; TreFT

(Blow Your Trumpets.) ChTr; EBCP

"Batter my heart, three-personed [*or* three person'd] God; for you." BLPL; BiP; CABA; ClHu; EBEV; EBEvV; EaLo; EnRePo; FF; FHYEP; FaFP; GoBC; HAP; HeIP; HoPM; ImPo; InPK; InPS; JCP; LiTB; MeLP; MePo; NAEL-1; NIP; NOBE; NOSC; NoP; OAEL-1; OAEP; OBS; OxAEP-1; OxBoCh; PAI; PPP; PPoe; PeECV; PoE; PoEL-2; Poetr; PrIm; SeCP; SeCV-1; SeCePo; SeCeV; SoSe; Son; TEP; TFi; TOF; TrCP; TrGrPo; TrPWD; TreFT

"Death[,] be not proud, though some have called thee." BiP; CABA; ChTr; DL; EBEvV; EiL; EnRePo; FF; FHYEP; FPL; FaBV; FaBoEn; FaBoRV; FaFP; GoBC; HAP; HBV 1-2; HeIL; HeIP; ImPo; InPK; InPS; InvP; JCP; LiTB; LoBV; MeLP; MePo; NAEL-1; NAWM-1; NIP; NOBE; NOSC; NoP; OAEL-1; OAEP; OBD; OBS; OPOU; OxAEP-1; PAI; PBMP; PPP; PPoe; PoE; PoEL-2; PoRA; Poetr; PrIm; SCGP; SCV; SeCP; SeCV-1; SeCeV; SoSe; TEP; TRP; TRV; TrCP; TrGrPo; TreFS; WHA; WeW

(Holy Sonnet.) OPOU

"Father, part of his double interest." JCP; OBS

"I am a little world made cunningly." CABA; ChIV-1; EnRePo; NAEL-1; NIP; NoP; OBS; OxBoCh; PoE; SeCP; Son; TEP

"If faithful soul[e]s be alike glorified [*or* glorifi'd]." OBS

"If poisonous [*or* poysonous] mineral[l]s, and if that tree." BiP; CABA; EBEV; EnRePo; FaBoVe; ImPo; JCP; LiTB; MePo; NAEL-1; NoP; OAEL-1; OBS; OxAEP-1; PFP; PPP; PoEL-2; SCGP; SeCP; Son; UnPo; WHA

"O might those sigh[e]s and tear[e]s return[e] again[e]." BiP; OBS

"Oh my black[e] soul[e]! now thou art summoned." EBEV; JCP; OAEL-1; OBS; OxAEP-1; Poetr; Son; TEP; TOF

"Oh, to vex me, contraries [*or* conraryes] meet in one." NOSC; OAEL-1; PoEL-2; SeCePo; Son

(Devout Fits.) SeCePo

("Oh, to vex me, two contraries meet in one.") ChIV-2

"Show me dear[e] Christ, thy spouse, so bright and clear." MeLP; NAEL-1; NOSC; NoP; OAEP; OBS; PoE; Son

("Show me, dear Christ, Thy Spouse, so bright and clear.") PeECV

"Since she whom I loved [*or* lov'd] hath paid [*or* payd] her last debt." JCP; MePo; NAEL-1; NOSC; OAEP; Son

"Spit in my face ye [*or* you] Jew[e]s, and pierce my side." JCP; OBS; OxBoCh; Son; TOF

"This is my play's [*or* playes] last scene, here heavens appoint." EBEV; FaBoVe; JCP; LoBV; MeLP; MePo; NIP; OAEP; OBS; OxBoCh; PAI; SeCP; Son; TEP

"Thou hast made me, and shall thy work[e] decay?" AnAnS-1; EBEV; EnRePo; FaBoEn; MasP; MeLP; NAEL-1; NOBE; NOCV; NOSC; NoP; OAEP; OBS; OxAEP-1; OxBoCh; PoEL-2; SCGP; SeCP; Son; TEP

"What if this present were the world's last night?" EBEV; HeIP; ImPo; InPS; JCP; LiTB; MeLP; NAEL-1; NOCV; NOSC; OAEP; OBS; OxAEP-1; PeECV; PoE; SeCeV; Son; TEP

"Why are we[e] by all creatures waited on?" CABA; JCP; NOCV; OBS; PoE; PoEL-2; TrCP

"Wilt thou love God, as he thee? [*or* thee!] then digest." JCP; OBS; TrCP

La Corona. ChIV-2; ESCV; OBS; Son

Annunciation. TrCP

Ascension [*or* Ascention].

Crucifying.

"Deign[e] at my hands this crown[e] of prayer and praise." ChIV-2; ESCV; OBS; Son

(Crown, The.) ChIV-2

(La Corona.) ESCV; OBS; Son

Nativity [*or* Nativitie].

Resurrection. ESCV; OBS

("Moyst with one drop of thy blood, my dry soule.") ESCV; OBS

Temple.

Holy Sonnets. John Donne. *See* Divine Meditations.

Holy Spring. Dylan Thomas. **CP-ThomD**

Holy thorn of Glastonbury sprouted in this dark time, The. The Road from Glastonbury. Jenny Joseph. **SP-JoseJ**

Holy Thursday (" 'Twas on a Holy Thursday, their innocent faces clean"). William Blake. CH; EnRP; FHYEP; HBV; HoFi; InPS; LAuP; MeMBP; NAEL-2; NAWM-2; NOBE; NOBRP; NOEC; NoP; OAEL-2; OAEP; OBEC; OFD; PeECV; PoE; SCV; TEP; TFi; TrCP *Fr.* Songs of Innocence. **CP-BlakW**

Holy Thursday ("Is this a holy thing to see"). William Blake. **CP-BlakW** *Fr.* Songs of Experience.

Holy Thursday. Geoffrey Hill. **CP-HillG**

Holy Thursday. Paul Muldoon. **SP-MuldP**

Holy Thursday. Charles Wright. **SP-WrigC**

Holy Trinity, Sloane Street. Sir John Betjeman. **CP-BetjJ**

Holy Tulzie, The. Robert Burns. **CP-BurnR**

Holy War, The. Rudyard Kipling. **CP-KiplR**

Holy water come and bring. The Spell. Robert Herrick. **CP-HerrR**

Holy waters hither bring. To Julia. Robert Herrick. **CP-HerrR**

Holy Well, A. Brendan Galvin. **SP-GalvB**

Holy Willie's Prayer. Robert Burns. **CP-BurnR**

Holyhead. September 25, 1727. Jonathan Swift. **CP-SwifJ**

Homage. William Carlos Williams. **CP-WilW1**

Homage. Louis Zukofsky. **CP-ZukLS**

Homage to a Government. Philip Larkin. **CP-LarkP**

Homage to Arnaut. Gilbert Sorrentino. **SP-SorrG**

Homage to Austin Warren. Laurence Lieberman. **SP-LiebL**

Homage to Bly & Lorca. In London. Robert Creeley. **CP-CreeR**

Homage to Cesare Pavese. Charles Wright. **SP-WrigC**

Homage to Claude Lorrain. Charles Wright. **SP-WrigC**

Homage to Clichés. Louis MacNeice. **CP-MacNL**

Homage to Clio. Wystan Hugh Auden. **CP-AudeW**

Homage to Conor Cruise O'Brien. James Liddy. **CP-LiddJ**

Homage to Edward Thomas. Derek Walcott. **CP-WalcD**

Homage to George Whitefield. Donald Davie. **CP-DavDo**

Homage to Ghosts. Jean Garrigue. **SP-GarrJ**

Homage to John Cowper Powys. Stevie Smith. **CP-SmitS**

Homage to John L. Stephens. Donald Davie. **CP-DavDo**

Homage to John Lyly and Frankie Newton. Hayden Carruth. **CP-CarHS**

Homage to Karl Marx. Edwin Rolfe. **CP-RolfE**

Homage to Literature. Muriel Rukeyser. **CP-RukeM**

Homage to Malcolm Lowry. Derek Mahon. **SP-MahoD**

Homage to Mistress Bradstreet. John Berryman. **CP-BerrJ**

"Governor your husband lived so long, The." MoVE; NOBA; TwAmPo

"I trundle the bodies, on the iron bars." NOBA

"O all your ages at the mercy of my loves." NOBA

"So squeezed, wince you I scream? I love you & hate." FF

"Winters close, springs open, no child stirs, The." NAAL-2; NAs

Homage to Paul Cézanne. Charles Wright. **SP-WrigC**

"At night, in the fish-light of the moon, the dead wear our white shirts."

"Dead are a cadmium blue, The." HCAP

"Dead are waiting for us in our rooms, The."

"Dead are with us to stay, The."

"Dead fall around us like rain, The."

"Each year the dead grow less dead, and nudge."

"In steeps and sighs."

"We're out here, our feet in the soil, our heads craned up at the sky."

Homage to Paul Robeson. Robert Earl Hayden. **CP-HaydR**

Homage to Sextus Propertius. Ezra Pound. **SP-PounE**

Difference of Opinion with Lygdamus. MeMAP

"Me happy, night, night full of brightness." ErPo; InvP; MeMAP; VGW

(Elegy VII.) ErPo; InvP; VGW

"Midnight, and a letter comes to me from." MeMAP

"Now if ever it is time to cleanse Helicon." CrMA; VGW

"Persephone and Dis, Dis, have mercy upon her." MeMAP

"Shades of Callimachus, Coan ghosts of Philetas." CMoP; HAP; MoAB; MoVE; NOBA; OBVE; OxBA; PP

"Twisted rhombs ceased their clamour of accompaniment, The." MeMAP

"When, when, and whenever death closes our eyelids." MeMAP; MoAB; OBMV; PoA

"Who, who will be the next man to entrust his girl to a friend?" FaBoMo

Homage to the Afterlife. Stephen Berg. **SP-BergS**

Homage to the Divers. Stephen Dunn. **SP-DunnS**

Homage to the Empress of the Blues. Robert Earl Hayden. **CP-HaydR**

Homage to the North. Richard Eberhart. **CP-EberR**

Homage to Theodore Dreiser. Robert Penn Warren. **SP-WarrR**
  Moral Assessment.
  Psychological Profile.
  Vital Statistics.
Homage to William Cowper. Donald Davie. **CP-DavDo**
Homage to Wren. Louis MacNeice. **CP-MacNL**
Home. Robert Creeley. **CP-CreeR**
Home. George Herbert. **CP-HerbG**
Home. Robinson Jeffers. **CP-JefR1**
Home after Three Months Away. Robert Lowell. **SP-LoweR**
Home agin, an' home to stay. Bein' Back Home. Paul Laurence Dunbar. **CP-DunbP**
Home, and I've. Marilyn Hacker. **SP-HackM**
Home at Grasmere. William Wordsworth. **CP-WorW1** *Fr.* The Recluse; Home at Grasmere.
Home Ballad, The. John Berryman. **CP-BerrJ**
Home beyond this life? Or through it? If through, how? Louis MacNeice. *Fr.* Day of Returning. **CP-MacNL**
Home Burial. Robert Frost. **CP-FrosR**
  "With anyone to death, comes so far short." **OBF**
  (Temperament.) **OBF**
  "You could sit there with the stains on your shoes." **OBD**
Home by different ways. Yet all. The End Is Not Yet. Christina Georgina Rossetti. **CP-RosC2**
Home-Coming, The. Robert Ranke Graves. **CP-GravR**
Home-Coming of the Bride, The. John Greenleaf Whittier. **CP-WhitJ**
Home Fires. Carl Sandburg. **CP-SandC**
Home for Aged Bomb Throwers—U.S.S.R. Louis Zukofsky. *Fr.* 29 Songs. **CP-ZukLS**
Home for the aged opens its windows in May, The. Next Door. Richard Wilbur. **CP-WilbR**
Home for the Holidays. Howard Nemerov. **CP-NemeH**
Home for the night on my ten years' workbed. Sleepless. Robert Lowell. **SP-LoweR**
Home from Guatemala, back at the Waldorf. Arrival at the Waldorf. Wallace Stevens. **CP-StevW**
Home from his morning task the swain retreats. James Thomson. **FM** *Fr.* Summer. *Fr.* The Seasons. **CP-ThomJ**
Home from the daisied meadows, where you linger yet. Robert Louis Stevenson. **CP-StevR**
Home Front, The. Derek Mahon. **FaBCIP** *Fr.* Autobiographies. **SP-MahoD**
Home, home, / Wild birds home! Spell to Bring Lost Creatures Home. Kathleen Jessie Raine. **SP-RainK**
Home Home Home. Lawrence Ferlinghetti. **SP-FerlL**
Home. Home. I knew it entering. The Only Bar in Dixon. Richard Hugo. **CP-HugoR**
Home in Dark Grass, A. Robert Bly. **SP-BlyR**
Home is my Bethlehem. January 19th. Anne Sexton. **CP-SextA**
Home is so far from Home. Emily Dickinson. *See* Home itself is far from home.
Home Is So Sad. Philip Larkin. **CP-LarkP**
Home is the riddle of the wise. Emily Dickinson. **SP-DickE**
Home is the sailor, home from sea. R. L. S. Alfred Edward Housman. **CP-HousA**
Home itself is far from home. Emily Dickinson. **SP-DickE**
  ("Home is so far from Home.") **SP-DickE**
Home late, one lamp turned low. At Our House. William Stafford. **SP-StafW**
Home Longings. Paul Laurence Dunbar. **CP-DunbP**
Home means that / when the certainly. Edward Estlin Cummings. **CP-CummE**
Home Movies. John Updike. **CP-UpdiJ**
Home no more home to me, whither must I wander? Robert Louis Stevenson. **CP-StevR**
Home of the Brave. "Lou Reed." **SP-ReedL**
Home Olga. Samuel Beckett. **CP-BeckS**
Home Pianist's Companion, The. Roy Fisher. **SP-FishR**
Home-Sick. Samuel Taylor Coleridge. **CP-ColeS**
Home they brought her warrior dead. Tennyson. **OXAEP-2; TrGrPo** *Fr.* The Princess. **CP-TennA**
Home Thoughts. Carl Sandburg. **CP-SandC**
Home Thoughts. Lewis Turco. **SP-TurcL**
Home-Thoughts, from Abroad. Robert Browning. **CP-BroR1**
Home Thoughts from Abroad. Alun Lewis. **CP-LewiA**
Home thoughts from home; we read you every day. Muriel Rukeyser. *Fr.* Letter to the Front. **CP-RukeM**
Home-Thoughts, from the Sea. Robert Browning. **CP-BroR1**

Home Town. William DeWitt Snodgrass. **SP-SnodW**
Home town of moving lace curtains, A. Expectations. Steve Griffiths. **SP-GrifS**
Home when he came, he seemed not to be there. Leander's Return. Christopher Marlowe. **EBNV** *Fr.* Hero and Leander. **CP-MarlC**
Homecoming, A. Wendell Berry. **CP-BerrW**
Homecoming. Hayden Carruth. **CP-CarHS**
Homecoming, The. Thomas Hardy. **CP-HardT**
Homecoming. Langston Hughes. **SP-HughL**
Homecoming. Derek Mahon. **SP-MahoD**
Homecoming. Christian J. Van Geel, *tr. fr. Dutch by* Adrienne Rich. **CP-RicAE**
Homecoming: Anse La Raye. Derek Walcott. **CP-WalcD**
Homecoming (August 7, 1934). Edwin Rolfe. **CP-RolfE**
Homecomings. Pablo Neruda, *tr. fr. Spanish by* Ben Belitt. **SP-NeruP**
Homeless. Samuel Taylor Coleridge. **CP-ColeS**
Homely War, The. Marge Piercy. **SP-PierM**
  "For two years I broke from these cycles, simply."
  "I am sick, sick to desperation."
  "I lack a light touch."
  "Madeline, in your purity I find myself rebuked."
  "My old friend, how we sustain."
  "Seeking from women nurturance, feedback, idea."
  "Wrote two letters while rain."
Homemade Boat. Shel Silverstein. **SP-SilS2**
Homeowners unite. The Firebombing. James Dickey. **CP-DickJ**
Homer da Vinci. The Part. Denise Levertov. **CP-LeveD**
Homer was wrong in saying: "Would that conflict might perish from among gods and men." Thomas Merton. *Fr.* The Legacy of Herakleitos. **CP-MertT**
Homeric Hexameter, The. Samuel Taylor Coleridge. **CP-ColeS**
Homeric Hymns. *Unknown, tr. fr. Greek by* Shelley.
  Homer's Hymn to Minerva. **CP-ShelP**
  Homer's Hymn to the Sun. **CP-ShelP**
  Homer's Hymn to Venus. **CP-ShelP**
  Hymn to Castor and Pollux.
    (Homer's Hymn to Castor and Pollux.) **CP-ShelP**
  Hymn to Earth the Mother of All.
    (Homer's Hymn to the Earth: Mother of All.) **CP-ShelP**
  Hymn to Mercury. **CP-ShelP**
  Hymn to Selene.
    (Homer's Hymn to the Moon.) **CP-ShelP**
Homer's Argos hearing. Louis Zukofsky. *Fr.* Chloride of Lime and Charcoal. **CP-ZukLS**
Homer's Art. Alice Notley. **SP-NotlA**
Homer's Hymn to Castor and Pollux. *Unknown. See* Hymn to Castor and Pollux.
Homer's Hymn to Minerva. *Unknown.* **CP-ShelP** *Fr.* Homeric Hymns.
Homer's Hymn to the Earth: Mother of All. *Unknown. See* Hymn to Earth the Mother of All.
Homer's Hymn to the Moon. *Unknown. See* Hymn to Selene.
Homer's Hymn to the Sun. *Unknown.* **CP-ShelP** *Fr.* Homeric Hymns.
Homer's Hymn to Venus. *Unknown.* **CP-ShelP** *Fr.* Homeric Hymns.
Homer's Seeing-Eye Dog. William Matthews. **SP-MattW**
Homesick. Walter de la Mare. **CP-DeLaW**
Homesick. Marge Piercy. **SP-PierM**
Homestead. John Haines. **SP-HainJ**
  "From the spent dream behind me."
  "Green smoke and white ash."
  "Here is the place I came to."
  "It is nearly thirty years."
  "Old ladders shorten, pulled down."
  "One morning in my first winter."
  "What did I come for? To see."
Homestead. John Hewitt. **CP-HewiJ**
Homestead, The. Lewis Turco. **SP-TurcL**
Homestead, The. John Greenleaf Whittier. **CP-WhitJ**
Homestead Called Damascus, The, *sels.* Kenneth Rexroth.
  Autumn of Many Years, The. **CP-RexKL**
    "How short a time for a life to last." **SP-RexrK**
  Double Hellas, The. **CP-RexKL**
    "World is composed of a pair of, The." **SP-RexrK**
  "Heaven is full of definite stars." **CP-RexKL**
    "Heaven is full of definite stars." **SP-RexrK**
  Stigmata of Fact, The. **CP-RexKL**
    "Morphology repeats ontology." **SP-RexrK**

Hometown Piece for Messrs. Alston and Reese. Marianne Craig Moore. **CP-MoorM**

Homeward the / Shepherds moved. William Wordsworth. **EnRP** *Fr.* The Solitary. *Fr.* The Excursion. **CP-WorW2**

Homeward we turn. Isle of Columba's Cell. William Wordsworth. *Fr.* Poems Composed or Suggested During a Tour, in the Summer of 1833. **CP-WorW2**

Homework. Allen Ginsberg. **CP-GinsA**

Homework. Mona Van Duyn. **SP-VanDM**

Homewreck. Karl Shapiro. **SP-ShapK**

Homily. Allen Tate. **CP-TateA**

Homing. Barton Sutter. **SP-SuttB**

Homo Gratia Artis. Isabella Gardner. **CP-GardI**

Homo Sapiens. Jenny Joseph. **SP-JoseJ**

Homo Sum, Nihil Humani—. Arthur Hugh Clough. **SP-ClouA**

Homoeopathic Blues in J. Malcolm Lowry. **CP-LowrM**

Homunculus. Louise Bogan. **CP-BogaL**

Homunculus. Lewis Turco. **SP-TurcL**

Homunculus et la Belle Étoile. Wallace Stevens. **CP-StevW**

Hon. Sec., The. Sir John Betjeman. **CP-BetjJ**

Honest lover whosoever. Song. Sir John Suckling. **CP-SuckJ**

Honest man here lies at rest, An. Epitaph on My Own Friend, and My Father's Friend, Wm Muir in Tarbolton Miln. Robert Burns. **CP-BurnR**

Honest morning blesses the Sun's beauty. Blessed Sun. Robert Ranke Graves. **CP-GravR**

Honest Tear, An. Emily Dickinson. **CP-DickE**

Honesty. Stephen Dunn. **SP-DunnS**

Honesty. Christopher Smart. *Fr.* Hymns for the Amusement of Children. **SP-SmarC**

Honesty. Louis Zukofsky. **CP-ZukLS**

Honey and Salt. Carl Sandburg. **CP-SandC**

Honey, darling, baby. . . but no endearments. Sonnet. Hayden Carruth. **CP-CarHS** *Fr.* Sonnets.

Honey from silkworms who can gather. Lines to a Critic. Percy Bysshe Shelley. **CP-ShelP**

Honey I'd split your kindling. Green Mountain Idyl. Hayden Carruth. **CP-CarHS**

Honey, Just Allow Me One More Chance. "Bob Dylan." **CP-DylaB**

Honey of man is, The. Second Didactic Poem. Denise Levertov. **CP-LeveD**

Honey Pie. The Beatles. **CP-Beatl**

Honey Pie Honey Pie. Wild Honey Pie. The Beatles. **CP-Beatl**

Honey you went so far to seek, The. Emily Dickinson. **SP-DickE**

Honeyed, small and fair. He Receives the Bells. Nicholas Vachel Lindsay. *Fr.* The Tree of Laughing Bells or The Wings of the Morning. **CP-LindV**

Honeymoon, *sl. diff. vers.* David Herbert Lawrence. *See* Excursion Train.

Honeymoon Time at an Inn. Thomas Hardy. **CP-HardT**

Honeysuckle. Louis Zukofsky. **CP-ZukLS**

Honeysuckle hanging her fangs. Night Arrival of Sea-Trout. Ted Hughes. **SP-HughT**

Hong Kong. Wystan Hugh Auden. *Fr.* A Voyage. **CP-AudeW**

Honky Tonk in Cleveland, Ohio. Carl Sandburg. **CP-SandC**

Honor / of being human, The. For the Graduation. Robert Creeley. **CP-CreeR**

Honor Among Scamps. Nicholas Vachel Lindsay. **CP-LindV**

Honor and shame from no condition rise. Alexander Pope. **TrGrPo** *Fr.* An Essay on Man. **CP-PopeA**

Honor bright o muse. Ralph Waldo Emerson. **CP-EmerR**

Honor is saved by the national will. Peace in Our Time. Howard Nemerov. **CP-NemeH**

Honor now injoye the day. Mary Sidney, Countess of Montgomery Wroth. *Fr.* Part 2. *Fr.* Urania. **CP-WrotM**

Honorable Mention. Leonard Nathan. **SP-NathL**

Honour. Christopher Smart. *Fr.* Hymns for the Amusement of Children. **SP-SmarC**

Honour and hapiness unite. The Christian. William Cowper. *Fr.* Olney Hymns. **CP-CowpW**

Honour and magnify this man of men. Alfred the Great. Stevie Smith. **CP-SmitS**

Honour corruption villainy holiness. Edward Estlin Cummings. **CP-CummE**

Honour is so sublime perfection. To the Countess of Bedford. John Donne. **CP-DonnJ**

Honour thy parents; but good manners call. God to Be First Served. Robert Herrick. **CP-HerrR**

Honour to you who sit! An Hymne to the Muses. Robert Herrick. **CP-HerrR**

Honours Are Hindrances. Robert Herrick. **CP-HerrR**

Hony-Combe, The. Robert Herrick. **CP-HerrR**

"Ho[o]!" quod the Knyght, "good sir[e], namo[o]re of this!". The Prologue of the Nun's Priest's Tale. Geoffrey Chaucer. **FHYEP; OAEL-1** *Fr.* The Canterbury Tales. **CP-ChauG**

Hood. Charles Kenneth Williams. **CP-WillC; SP-WillC**

Hooded Flame. Robert Ranke Graves. **CP-GravR**

Hooded Night. Robinson Jeffers. **CP-JefR2**

Hoodlums. Carl Sandburg. **CP-SandC**

Hoof Dusk. Carl Sandburg. **CP-SandC**

Hook has let go, The. That Particular Air. Lewis Turco. **SP-TurcL**

Hook nosed angel with spring plumage, The. The Glaucous Winged Gull. Malcolm Lowry. **CP-LowrM**

Hook-nosed was I, loose-lipped; greed fixed its gaze. Isaac Meek. Walter de la Mare. **CP-DeLaW**

Hook of adrenaline shoves, The. Anger against Beasts. Wendell Berry. **CP-BerrW**

Hookah. Chuck Miller. **SP-MillC**

Hooked for two years now on wrinkle creams   creams. Aging. Erica Jong. **SP-JongE**

Hooks. Charles Kenneth Williams. **SP-WillC**

Hoop, the darling justly of the fair, The. On the Hoop. James Thomson. **CP-ThomJ**

Hooper was ninety. One September dawn. Squire Hooper. Thomas Hardy. **CP-HardT**

Hoopoe Tells Us How, The. Robert Ranke Graves. **CP-GravR**

Hoot!—daur ye shaw ye're face again. The Drunkard to His Bottle. John Greenleaf Whittier. **CP-WhitJ**

Hoot Owls. Richard Eberhart. **CP-EberR**

Hop hop, thump thump. The Dedicated Dancing Bull and the Water Maid. Stevie Smith. **CP-SmitS**

Hop hop, thump thump. Stevie Smith. **WPE** *Fr.* The Dedicated Dancing Bull and the Water Maid. **CP-SmitS**

Hop o' My Thumb. John Ashbery. **SP-AshbJ**

Hop-o'-my-thumb and little Jack Horner. Christina Georgina Rossetti. **CP-RosC2**

Hop, Skip, and Jump. Gary Snyder. **CP-SnydG**

Hop-Toad, The. Richard Eberhart. **CP-EberR**

Hop-toad jumped away, missing the blade, The. The Hop-Toad. Richard Eberhart. **CP-EberR**

Hope. Emily Brontë. **CP-BronE**

Hope. William Cowper. **CP-CowpW**

"Though clasp'd and cradled in his nurse's arms." **PoEL-3**

Hope. Paul Laurence Dunbar. **CP-DunbP**

!Hope / faith! / !life / love! Edward Estlin Cummings. **CP-CummE**

Hope. George Herbert. **CP-HerbG**

Hope. Langston Hughes. **SP-HughL**

Hope. Langston Hughes. **SP-HughL**

Hope. Randall Jarrell. **CP-JarrR**

Hope. Randall Jarrell. **CP-JarrR**

Hope. William Matthews. **SP-MattW**

Hope. Howard Nemerov. **CP-NemeH**

Hope. Christopher Smart. **ChIV-1** *Fr.* Hymns for the Amusement of Children. **SP-SmarC**

Hope. A Rondeau. Charlotte Smith. **CP-SmitC**

Hope & fear hopes & fears. Hopes & Fears. Anne Waldman. **SP-WaldA**

Hope and Time. Samuel Taylor Coleridge. **CP-ColeS**

Hope and Tranquillity. Samuel Taylor Coleridge. **CP-ColeS**

Hope, art thou true, or dost thou flatter me? Sonnet 67. Sir Philip Sidney. *Fr.* Astrophil and Stella. **SP-SidnP**

Hope Carol, A. Christina Georgina Rossetti. **CP-RosC2**

Hope. . . goosestep. Shorts / Excerpts. Bill Knott. **SP-KnotB**

Hope Heartens. Robert Herrick. **CP-HerrR**

Hope holds to Christ. Gerard Manley Hopkins. **CP-HopkG**

Hope humbly her; with trembling pinions soar. Alexander Pope. **EBEvV; TrGrPo** *Fr.* An Essay on Man. **CP-PopeA**

Hope I dreamed of was a dream, The. Mirage. Christina Georgina Rossetti. **CP-RosC1**

Hope in Grief. Christina Georgina Rossetti. **CP-RosC3**

Hope is a knave befools us evermore. Nicolas-Sébastien Roch Chamfort, *tr. fr. French by* Samuel Beckett. **CP-BeckS**

Hope is a strange invention. Emily Dickinson. **CP-DickE**

Hope is a subtle Glutton. Emily Dickinson. **CP-DickE**

Hope is a tattered flag and a dream out of time. Carl Sandburg. *Fr.* The People, Yes. **CP-SandC**

Hope Is Just. Jim Morrison. **SP-MorrJ**

Hope is like a harebell trembling from its birth. Christina Georgina Rossetti. **CP-RosC2**

Hope is Not for the Wise. Robinson Jeffers. **CP-JefR2**

Hope is the counterpoise of fear / While night enthralls us here. Christina Georgina Rossetti. **CP-RosC2**

"Hope" is the thing with feathers. Emily Dickinson. **CP-DickE**

Hope, like the short-liv'd ray that gleams awhile. William Cowper. **CP-CowpW**

Hope new born one pleasant morn. Dead Hope. Christina Georgina Rossetti. **CP-RosC1**

Hope, not Love, twangles her single string. Poor Others. Robert Ranke Graves. **CP-GravR**

Hope of the Resurrection, The. Nicholas Vachel Lindsay. *Fr.* Two Easter Stanzas. **CP-LindV**

Hope rules a land for ever green. The Wishing-Gate. William Wordsworth. **CP-WorW2**

Hope smiled when your nativity was cast. Flowers on the Top of the Pillars at the Entrance of the Cave. William Wordsworth. *Fr.* Poems Composed or Suggested During a Tour, in the Summer of 1833. **CP-WorW2**

Hope springs eternal in the human breast. The Pleasure of Hope. Alexander Pope. **ACP** *Fr.* An Essay on Man. **CP-PopeA**

Hope that you may understand! The Realists. William Butler Yeats. **CP-YeatW**

Hope was but a timid friend. Hope. Emily Brontë. **CP-BronE**

Hope Well and Have Well: or, Faire after Foule Weather. Robert Herrick. **CP-HerrR**

Hope, whose weak[e] being ruined [or ruin'd] is. Against Hope. Richard Crashaw. **CP-CrasR** *Fr.* The Mistress.

Hope, wreathed with roses. Euphrasy. Walter de la Mare. **CP-DeLaW**

Hope ye, my verses, that posterity. Joachim Du Bellay. **PoE** *Fr.* Ruins of Rome. **CP-Spens**

Hopeful each morning I arise. Song Before Breakfast. Ogden Nash. **CP-NashO**

Hopeless and Felons. Thomas Merton. **CP-MertT**

Hopeless Case, A. Christina Georgina Rossetti. **CP-RosC3**

Hopelessly wound round with the cords of streets. Hamburg, 1929. Stephen Spender. **CP-SpenS**

Hopes. Robert Louis Stevenson. **CP-StevR**

Hopes & Fears. Anne Waldman. **SP-WaldA**

Hopes, that swell in youthful breasts. Love's Rose. Percy Bysshe Shelley. **CP-ShelP**

Hopes what are they?—Beads of morning. William Wordsworth. *Fr.* Inscriptions Supposed to Be Found in and near a Hermit's Cell; 1818. **CP-WorW2**

Hopping frog, hop here and be seen. Christina Georgina Rossetti. **CP-RosC2**

Horace at Twenty. Alun Lewis. **CP-LewiA**

Horace, Book I, Ode XIV, *see also* William Ewart Gkladstone's "Oh ship! new billows sweep thee out." Jonathan Swift. **CP-SwifJ**

Horace, Epistle VII, Book I: Imitated and Addressed to the Earl of Oxford. Jonathan Swift. **CP-SwifJ**

Horace, Lib. 2, Sat. 6. Jonathan Swift. **CP-SwifJ**

Horace: Odi Profanum Volgus Et Arceo. Horace. *See* 3.1: "Tread back— and back, the lewd and lay!"

Horace of course is not. Wombwell on Strike. Donald Davie. **CP-DavDo**

Horace, of the Art of Poetry. Ben Jonson, *adapted from the Latin of Horace.* **CP-JonsB**

Horace: Persicos Odi, Puer, Apparatus. Horace. *See* 1.38: Simplicity.

Horace to Leuconoë. Edwin Arlington Robinson. **CP-RobiE**

Horae Canonicae. Wystan Hugh Auden. **CP-AudeW**

  Compline.

  Lauds. **TrCP**

  Nones.

  Prime. **CMoP; PoE**

  Sext.

  Terce. **CMoP; PoE**

  Vespers. **FaBoMo**

Horae Canonicae. Donald Davie. **CP-DavDo**

  Compline.

  Nones.

  Prime.

  Sext.

  Terce.

  Vespers.

Horatian Epode to the Duchess of Malfi. Allen Tate. **CP-TateA**

Horatian Ode upon Cromwell's Return from Ireland, An. Andrew Marvell. **CP-MarvA**

  King Charles on [or upon] the Scaffold. **ChTr; FaBoRV**

  "What field of all the civil wars." **FaBoEH**

"Where, twining subtile fears with hope." **OBD**

Horatians, The. Wystan Hugh Auden. **CP-AudeW**

Horatio took me to the cliff. Hamlet. Nicholas Vachel Lindsay. **CP-LindV**

Horizon. Robert Ranke Graves. **CP-GravR**

Horizon of islands shifting. The Outer Banks. Muriel Rukeyser. **CP-RukeM**

Horizon to horizon, lies outspread. The Flower. Walter de la Mare. **CP-DeLaW**

Horizons release skies. Rules and Ranges for Ian Tyson. Roy Fisher. **SP-FishR**

Horizons ring me like faggots, The. Wuthering Heights. Sylvia Plath. **CP-PlatS**

Horn has sounded, The. Praeludium. Charles Tomlinson. *Fr.* Antecedents. **CP-TomlC**

Horn of Egremont Castle, The. William Wordsworth. **CP-WorW1**

Horne sells to others teeth; but has not one. Upon Horne. Robert Herrick. **CP-HerrR**

Horned Purple. William Carlos Williams. **CP-WilW1**

Hornet. Donald Davie. **CP-DavDo**

Hornet. Anne Sexton. **CP-SextA**

Hornet, thou hast thy wife dressed, for the stall. To Hornet. Ben Jonson. **CP-JonsB**

Hornets by the Sill. Richard Eberhart. **CP-EberR**

Hornets nesting under the weatherboarding. Cousins. Archie Randolph Ammons. **SP-AmmoA**

Horns. John Haines. **SP-HainJ**

Horns crowding toward us. Dream 3: Night Bear Which Frightened Cattle. Margaret Atwood. **SP-AtwM1**

Horns of the Morning, The. Philip Larkin. **CP-LarkP**

Horologe of the Fields, The. Charlotte Smith. **CP-SmitC**

Horologikos. Hayden Carruth. **CP-CarHS**

Horoscope. Ralph Waldo Emerson. *Fr.* Quatrains. **CP-EmerR**

Horowitz. Marsden Hartley. **CP-HartM**

Horrible of hue, hideous to behold. Sir Thomas Wyatt. **CP-WyatT**

Horrible Religious Error, A. Ted Hughes. **SP-HughT**

Horror came / When I was in my mother's womb, The. After an Old Song. Kenneth Patchen. **CP-PatcK**

Horrors. "Lewis Carroll." **CP-CarrL**

Horrors of the personal, revealed, The. Rooms in Bloomsbury. Marilyn Hacker. **SP-HackM**

Hors crâne seul dedans, *Author's own French vers. of his* "Something there." Samuel Beckett. **CP-BeckS**

Horse. Louise Glück. **SP-GlücL**

Horse, The. Philip Levine. **SP-LeviP**

Horse. Kenneth Rexroth. **NNaP** *Fr.* A Bestiary. **SP-RexrK**

Horse. Anne Sexton. **CP-SextA**

Horse, The. William Carlos Williams. **CP-WilW2**

Horse, The. William Wordsworth. **CP-WorW1**

Horse, The. James Wright. **CP-WrigJ**

Horse beneath me seemed, The. The Ride. Richard Wilbur. **CP-WilbR**

Horse Chestnut Tree, The. Richard Eberhart. **CP-EberR**

Horse-Chestnut Trees and Roses. James Schuyler. **CP-SchuJ**

Horse could scarcely pluck its stumbling heel, The. Landscape. Wystan Hugh Auden. **CP-AudWJ**

Horse Fiddle. Carl Sandburg. **CP-SandC**

Horse from Hell, The. Erica Jong. **SP-JongE**

Horse, huge / On the hilltop / Leaning. Inviolable. Daniel Gerard Hoffman. **SP-HoffD**

Horse in the Drugstore, The. Tess Gallagher. **SP-GallT**

Horse is breathing on his hands, The. Heartache. Stephen Berg. **SP-BergS**

Horse is ridden—the jockey rides, The. MARCH (*Racing*). Rudyard Kipling. *Fr.* Verses on Games. **CP-KiplR**

Horse is white. Or it, The. Saving the Appearances. Charles Tomlinson. **CP-TomlC**

Horse Latitudes. Jim Morrison. **SP-MorrJ**

Horse moves, The. The Horse. William Carlos Williams. **CP-WilW2**

Horse moves / this weekend, A. Silver Mirrors. Jim Carroll. **SP-CarrJ**

Horse of Desire, The. Robert Bly. **SP-BlyR**

Horse on Fire. Charles Bukowski. **SP-BukC2**

Horse, our poor creature, we treat as if elemental. Equestrian Sestina. Donald Davie. **CP-DavDo**

Horse Show, The. William Carlos Williams. **CP-WilW2**

Horse With Greenblue Eyes, A. Charles Bukowski. **SP-BukC1**

Horseback on Sunday morning. The Wild Geese. Wendell Berry. **CP-BerrW**

Horseman high-alone as an eagle on the spur of the mountain over. The Coast-Road. Robinson Jeffers. **CP-JefR2**

Horsemeat. Charles Bukowski. **SP-BukC3**

"Being alone has always been very necessary to me. At one time I."
"Driving in for a wash and."
"Fat Mexican woman in front of me in line, A."
"Got to the track early to study my figures and here's this."
"I am at the track."
"I am sitting in the stands with a."
"I don't know where they come from."
"I had been up until 3 a.m. the night before."
"I have a saying, 'You will find the lowest of the breed at the'."
"I have my figures ready for the."
"I lost a dollar at the track today and I know that's."
"I park, get out, lock the car, it's a perfect day, warm and."
"I pay my way in, find a seat far from everybody, sit down."
"I was out there again today. There are some creatures out there."
"I've been going to the track for years."
"My women of the past keep trying to locate me." **NGP**
"Some fat son-of-a-bitch with."
"Ten minutes before post time."
"20 minutes later." **NGP**
"Two old guys behind me were talking, The."
Horsemen, The. Louise McNeill. **SP-McNeL**
Horses. Wendell Berry. **CP-BerrW**
Horses, The. Siv Cedering Fox. **SP-CedeS**
Horses, The. Jorge Guillén, *tr. fr. Spanish by* Richard Wilbur. **CP-WilbR**
Horses, The. Phoebe Hesketh. **SP-HeskP**
Horses, The. Ted Hughes. **SP-HughT**
Horses. Louis MacNeice. **VoGa** *Fr.* Circus. **CP-MacNL**
Horses Aboard. Thomas Hardy. **CP-HardT**
Horses and hummingbirds do not mate. Chirico—and There are Blue and White. Marsden Hartley. **CP-HartM**
Horses and Men in the Rain. Carl Sandburg. **CP-SandC**
Horses and Prisoners. James Dickey. **CP-DickJ**
Horses, black-lidded mouths peeled back. Florentines. Geoffrey Hill. **CP-HillG**
Horses face out over the world, The. Shadows and Spring Flowers. Kenneth Patchen. **CP-PatcK**
Horses in horsecloths stand in a row. Horses Aboard. Thomas Hardy. **CP-HardT**
Horse's Mouth, The. Steve Griffiths. **SP-GrifS**
Horse's name was Remorse, The. Remorse. Carl Sandburg. **CP-SandC**
Horses of Achilles, The. Homer, *tr. by* George Meredith. **CP-MerG1** *Fr.* The Iliad.
Horses of the Sea, The. Christina Georgina Rossetti. **CP-RosC2**
Horses of the sea, The. Christina Georgina Rossetti. **FaPON; GoJo; NTCP; SUS** *Fr.* Sing-Song. **CP-RosC2**
Horses of the sea; remember, The. On a Horse Carved in Wood. Donald Hall. **CP-HallD**
Horses running. Communion. Charles Bukowski. **SP-BukC1**
Horses that wake me, The. The Horses. Siv Cedering Fox. **SP-CedeS**
Hortatory Address to the Greeks. Saint Justin Martyr.
"Then marking this my sacred speech, but truly lend." **CP-RaleW**, *tr. by* Sir Walter Ralegh;
Hortus, *see also* The Garden. Andrew Marvell. **CP-MarvA**
Hosanna! God be prais'd. Bible, *O.T. See* Psalm 149: "Praise ye the Lord. Sing unto the Lord a new song."
Hosanna—musick is divine, *par. by* Christopher Smart. Bible, *O.T. See* Psalm 147: "Praise ye the Lord: for it is good. . . ."
Hosanna! praise the Lord, and bless. Bible, *O.T. See* Psalm 150: "Praise ye the Lord. Praise God in his sanctuary."
Hosanna! yet again, / Another glorious day. St. John the Evangelist. Christopher Smart. *Fr.* Hymns and Spiritual Songs for the Fasts and Festivals of the Church of England. **SP-SmarC**
Hospitable Irish / come out to see who passes, The. In the Rosses. John Hewitt. **CP-HewiJ**
Hospital. Walter de la Mare. **CP-DeLaW**
Hospital. Karl Shapiro. **SP-ShapK**
Hospital, and the father's room, where light. Daughter. James Dickey. **CP-DickJ**
Hospital barber, for instance, The. Whispers in the Next Room. Charles Simic. **SP-SimiC**
Hospital Barge at Cérisy. Wilfred Owen. **CP-OwenW**
Hospital in Winter, The. Roy Fisher. **SP-FishR**
Hospital of Lies, The. Dabney Stuart. **SP-StuaD**
Hospital racket, nurses' iron smiles. The Hell Poem. John Berryman. **CP-BerrJ**
Hospital, The: it wasn't her idea. Darlene's Hospital. John Ashbery. **SP-AshbJ**

Hospital Visits. Philip Larkin. **CP-LarkP**
Hospital Window, The. James Dickey. **CP-DickJ**
Hospital Window. Allen Ginsberg. **CP-GinsA**
Hospitality. Malcolm Lowry. **CP-LowrM**
Hospitality: For E.K. John Hewitt. **CP-HewiJ**
Host. John Hewitt. **CP-HewiJ**
Host, The. William Carlos Williams. **CP-WilW2**
Host, he says that all is well, The. Fear. Hart Crane. **CP-CranH**
Host is riding from Knocknarea, The. The Hosting of the Sidhe. William Butler Yeats. **CP-YeatW**
Host of the Air, The. William Butler Yeats. **CP-YeatW**
Host of things I take on trust: I take, A. Christina Georgina Rossetti. *Fr.* Later Life: A Double Sonnet of Sonnets. **CP-RosC2**
Hostage. Malcolm Lowry. **CP-LowrM**
Hostage, The. Stevie Smith. **CP-SmitS**
Hostess, in pink satin and blond hair, The. The Delicacies. William Carlos Williams. **CP-WilW1**
Hostile Sun, The. David Herbert Lawrence. **CP-LawrD**
Hosting of the Sidhe, The. William Butler Yeats. **CP-YeatW**
Hosts of the glittering fay return, The. The Kingdom of Jerusalem. Robert Duncan. **SP-DuncR**
Hot beautiful furless animals. Adultery. Thom Gunn. **CP-GunnT**
Hot chili peppers in the blistering sun. Romance in Durango. "Bob Dylan." **CP-DylaB**
Hot gold runs a winding stream on the inside of a green bowl. Crucible. Carl Sandburg. **CP-SandC**
Hot Hands. Donald Davie. **CP-DavDo**
Hot House. Al Young. **CP-YounA**
Hot in his mind, Tom watches Dobbin fuck. Thom Gunn. *Fr.* Tom-Dobbin. **CP-GunnT**
Hot mice feeding in red, The. Paul Klee. John Haines. **SP-HainJ**
Hot Night in Wheat Country, A. Ted Kooser. **SP-KoosT**
Hot night makes us keep our bedroom windows open, The. To Speak of Woe That Is in Marriage. Robert Lowell. **SP-LoweR**
Hot shallows and seas we bring our blood from, The. Fourth of July. Ted Hughes. **SP-HughT**
Hot Springs. Richard Hugo. **CP-HugoR**
Hot summer day / on the River Road. Connections: Vermont Vietnam (I). Grace Paley. **CP-PaleG**
Hot summer has exhausted her intent. Two Quatrains for First Frost. Richard Wilbur. **CP-WilbR**
Hot summer nights a space hum at my window. Romancing with Our Beasts. John Ciardi. **SP-CiarJ**
Hot Water. John Updike. **CP-UpdiJ**
Hotblood on Friday. Thom Gunn. **CP-GunnT**
Hotel Breakfast. Archibald MacLeish. **CP-MacLA**
Hôtel de la Truite. Peter Meinke. **SP-MeinP**
Hotel de l'Univers et Portugal. James Merrill. **SP-MerrJ**
Hotel François Ier. Gertrude Stein. **CP-SteiG**
Hôtel Lion d'Or. Peter Meinke. **SP-MeinP**
Hotel Normandie Pool, The. Derek Walcott. **CP-WalcD**
Hotel of Ash. David St. John. *Fr.* To Pasolini. **SP-StJoD**
Hotel room is tawdry, nondescript, The. Hotel of Ash. David St. John. *Fr.* To Pasolini. **SP-StJoD**
Hotel Sierra. David St. John. **SP-StJoD**
Hotel Steinplatz, Berlin, December 25 (1966). Charles Olson. **SP-OlsoC** *Fr.* The Maximus Poems.
Hôtel Transylvanie. Frank O'Hara. **SP-OharF**
Hototogisu—horobirete. Kenneth Rexroth. **SP-RexrK** *Fr.* The Silver Swan.
Hound of Ulster, The. Stevie Smith. **CP-SmitS**
Hound Voice. William Butler Yeats. **CP-YeatW**
Hounded Lovers, The. William Carlos Williams. **CP-WilW2**
Hounded slave that flags in the race, leans by the fence, The. The Wounded Person. Walt Whitman. **PoNe** *Fr.* Song of Myself. **CP-WhitW**
Hounding Mercy. Charles Kenneth Williams. **CP-WillC**
Hounds, The. Louise McNeill. **SP-McNeL**
Hounds can't / Come in, The. James Liddy. *Fr.* A Munster Song of Love and War. **CP-LiddJ**
Hounds of Spring, The. Algernon Charles Swinburne. **SP-SwinA** *Fr.* Atalanta in Calydon.
Hounds pass here? The. At Wynard's Gap. Thomas Hardy. **CP-HardT**
Houndsooth stone. Aberdeen of the mind. Granite Chip. Seamus Heaney. **SP-HeanS** *Fr.* Shelf Life.
Hour and the Ghost, The. Christina Georgina Rossetti. **CP-RosC1**
Hour before Dawn, The. William Butler Yeats. **CP-YeatW**
Hour before the dawn, An. Fetching Her. Thomas Hardy. **CP-HardT**
Hour-bell sounds, and I must go, The. William Wordsworth. **CP-WorW1**

Hour by hour the storm deepened. He read. The Mountain Cabin. Hayden Carruth. **CP-CarHS**

Hour for books, those enthralling friends, An. Emily Dickinson. **SP-DickE**

Hour-Glass, The. Walter de la Mare. **CP-DeLaW**

Hour-Glass [or Houre-Glasse], The. Ben Jonson. **CP-JonsB**

Hour-glass whispers to the lion's roar, The. Our Bias. Wystan Hugh Auden. **CP-AudeW**

Hour is a Sea, An. Emily Dickinson. **CP-DickE**

Hour of evening—supper hour, for my neighbors—quietness, The. Charles Olson. **SP-OlsoC** *Fr.* The Maximus Poems.

Hour of Peace, The. John Gould Fletcher. **SP-FletJ**

Hour of the Angel, The. Rudyard Kipling. **CP-KiplR** *Fr.* Land and Sea Tales.

Hour we fixed to leave for holiday, The. Leaving for Holiday. John Hewitt. **CP-HewiJ**

Hour When We Shall Meet Again, The. Samuel Taylor Coleridge. **CP-ColeS**

Hour with E.M.F. at Ninety, An. John Hewitt. **CP-HewiJ**

Hourglass. James Merrill. **SP-MerrJ**

Hours Continuing Long. Walt Whitman. **CP-WhitW**

Hours have tumbled their leaden, monotonous sands, The. Rondeau of a Conscientious Objector. David Herbert Lawrence. **CP-LawrD**

Hours have tumbled their lustreless, tarnished sands. *also stands as a sl. diff. separate poem,* Rondeau of a Conscientious Objector. David Herbert Lawrence. *Fr.* The Schoolmaster [A]. **CP-LawrD**

Hours have Wings. Emily Dickinson. **SP-DickE**

Hours in themselves are fiercely umbrageous. Gulls at Gloucester. Marsden Hartley. **CP-HartM**

Hours rise up putting off stars and it is, The. Edward Estlin Cummings. **CP-CummE**

House.———House, and / a dead man in it. House, and a Dead Man In It. Kenneth Patchen. **CP-PatcK**

House. Robert Browning. **CP-BroR2**

House, The. Robert Creeley. **CP-CreeR**

House, The. Walter de la Mare. **CP-DavDo**

House, The. Ralph Waldo Emerson. **CP-EmerR**

House, The. Peter Meinke. **SP-MeinP**

House, The. James Merrill. **SP-MerrJ**

House, The. Mary Oliver. **SP-OlivM**

House, The. Charles Olson. **CP-OlsoC**

House, The. Kathleen Jessie Raine. *Fr.* The Marriage of Psyche. **SP-RainK**

House. Carl Sandburg. **CP-SandC**

House, The. Anne Sexton. **CP-SextA**

House, The. Lewis Turco. **SP-TurcL**

House, The. William Carlos Williams. **CP-WilW1**

House, and a Dead Man In It. Kenneth Patchen. **CP-PatcK**

House and hollow; village and valley-side. Winter Encounters. Charles Tomlinson. **CP-TomlC**

House at Ballyholme, The. John Hewitt. **CP-HewiJ**

House at the Cascades, The. Adrienne Rich. **CP-RicAE; SP-RicA2**

House Beautiful, The. Robert Louis Stevenson. **CP-StevR**

House Burning Down. James McAuley. **SP-McAuJ**

House can be haunted by those who were never there, A. Selva Oscura. Louis MacNeice. **CP-MacNL**

House Demolished, A. John Hewitt. **CP-HewiJ**

House Dog's Grave, The. Robinson Jeffers. **CP-JefR3**

House-dust mite (*Dermatophagoides farinae*), A. Mites. John Updike. **CP-UpdiJ**

House Fear. Robert Frost. **NTP; VGW; WSC** *Fr.* The Hill Wife. **CP-FrosR**

House Fly, The. James Merrill. **SP-MerrJ**

House Growing, The. John Updike. **CP-UpdiJ**

House Guest. Elizabeth Bishop. **CP-BishE**

House had gone to bring again, The. The Need of Being Versed in Country Things. Robert Frost. **CP-FrosR**

House has rotten places: cellar walls, A. Rats. John Updike. **CP-UpdiJ**

House-Hunting in the Bicentennial Year. Erica Jong. **SP-JongE**

House in Taos, A. Langston Hughes. **SP-HughL**

House in the Tree. Phoebe Hesketh. **SP-HeskP**

House in the tree now tenanted by the wind, The. House In The Tree. Phoebe Hesketh. **SP-HeskP**

House in the Vacant Lot, The. Miller Williams. **SP-WillM**

House in the Wood, The. Randall Jarrell. **CP-JarrR**

House in Winter, The. May Sarton. **SP-SartM**

House is bleak and cold, The. Everything Comes. Thomas Hardy. **CP-HardT**

House is filled. The last heartthrob, The. Near the Ocean. Robert Lowell. **SP-LoweR**

House is named of night. Pale maidens sing, The. Two Poems. Howard Nemerov. **CP-NemeH**

House is silent, it is late at night, I am alone, The. Forsaken and Forlorn. David Herbert Lawrence. **CP-LawrD**

House is so quiet now, The. The Vacuum. Howard Nemerov. **CP-NemeH**

House is still that shook with glee, The. Napping in the Shadow of Day. Anne Waldman. **SP-WaldA**

House like a man all lean and coughing, A. Even Numbers. Carl Sandburg. **CP-SandC**

House-martin. Donald Davie. **CP-DavDo**

House of Ate, The. Edmund Spenser. **OBSC** *Fr.* The Faerie Queene. **CP-Spens**

House of Busyrane, The. Edmund Spenser. **NoSic** *Fr.* The Faerie Queene. **CP-Spens**

House of Caiphas, The. Thomas Merton. **CP-MertT; SP-MertT**

House of cards / Is neat and small, A. Christina Georgina Rossetti. **CP-RosC2**

House of Clouds, The. Elizabeth Barrett Browning. **CP-BroEB**

House of Fame, The. Geoffrey Chaucer. **CP-ChauG**

House of Friends, The. Walt Whitman. **CP-WhitW**

House of Hospitalities, The. Thomas Hardy. **CP-HardT**

House of Mercy, A. Stevie Smith. **CP-SmitS**

House of Mourning Written by Mr Scott, The. John Keats. **CP-KeatJ**

House of Music, A. Kathleen Jessie Raine. **SP-RainK**

House of Over-Dew, The. Stevie Smith. **CP-SmitS**

House of Prayer, The. William Cowper. **ChIV-2** *Fr.* Olney Hymns. **CP-CowpW**

House of Rest. Sir John Betjeman. **CP-BetjJ**

House of Rest. Sir John Betjeman. **OxAEP-2** *Fr.* House of Rest. **CP-BetjJ**

House of Rest. **OxAEP-2**

House of Richesse, The. Edmund Spenser. **CH** *Fr.* The Faerie Queene. **CP-Spens**

House of Silence, The. Thomas Hardy. **CP-HardT**

House of Splendour, The. Ezra Pound. **SP-PounE**

House of Tembinoka, The. Robert Louis Stevenson. **CP-StevR**

House of the body, The. Touch. Erica Jong. **SP-JongE**

House of the Injured, The. John Haines. **SP-HainJ**

House on a Cliff. Louis MacNeice. **CP-MacNL**

House on Bishop Street, The. Rita Dove. **SP-DoveR**

House on Buder Street, The. Gary Gildner. **SP-GildG**

House on 15th S.W., The. Richard Hugo. **CP-HugoR**

House on the Edge of the Serious Wood, The. Philip Larkin. **CP-LarkP**

House on the Hill, The. John Hewitt. **CP-HewiJ**

House on the Hill, The. Edwin Arlington Robinson. **CP-RobiE**

House out to sea. Hayden Carruth. *Fr.* The Sleeping Beauty. **CP-CarHL**

House Skin, The. Laurence Lieberman. **SP-LiebL**

House Slave, The. Rita Dove. **SP-DoveR**

House-snake dwells here still, The. The Closed World. Denise Levertov. **CP-LeveD**

House stands just as it has always stood, The. Motherhood. Wystan Hugh Auden. **CP-AudWJ**

House That Jack Built, The. Samuel Taylor Coleridge. *See* On a Ruined House in a Romantic Country.

House the Poet Built, The. William DeWitt Snodgrass. **SP-SnodW**

House-Top, The. Herman Melville. **SP-MelvH**

House upon the Height, A. Emily Dickinson. **CP-DickE**

House was Dutch, The. The Judge and the Bird. Louis Zukofsky. **CP-ZukLS**

House was dying when I saw it; gaunt, The. The Dying House. Wystan Hugh Auden. **CP-AudWJ**

House Was Quiet and the World Was Calm, The. Wallace Stevens. **CP-StevW**

House was shaken by a rising wind, The. Brainstorm. Howard Nemerov. **CP-NemeH**

House we built gradually, The. The Small Cabin. Margaret Atwood. **SP-AtwM1**

House with a History, A. Thomas Hardy. **CP-HardT**

House with 7 or 8 people, A. The Good Life. Charles Bukowski. **SP-BukC1**

House you're moving from is not this house, The. Houses. Richard Hugo. **CP-HugoR**

Houseboat Days. John Ashbery. **SP-AshbJ**

Houseboy, then cook's assistant, went to sea. R.K. John Hewitt. **CP-HewiJ**

Housecleaning. Richard Shelton. *Fr.* Three Poems For A Twenty-Fifth Anniversary. **SP-ShelR**

Housecooling. William Matthews. **SP-MattW**

Household, A. Wystan Hugh Auden. **CP-AudeW**

Household, The. Robert Duncan. **SP-DuncR** *Fr.* Dante Études.

Household to provide shelter, The. The Household. Robert Duncan. **SP-DuncR** *Fr.* Dante Études.

Householder, The. Robert Browning. **CP-BroR2**

Householder issuing to the street, The. Vulcan. George Oppen. **CP-OppeG**

Housekeeper, The. Robert Frost. **CP-FrosR**

Housekeeping. Donald Davie. **CP-DavDo**

Houseless Dead, The. David Herbert Lawrence. **CP-LawrD**

Houses— / the dark side silhouetted. Night. William Carlos Williams. **CP-WilW1**

Houses. Richard Hugo. **CP-HugoR**

Houses, The. Rudyard Kipling. **CP-KiplR**

Houses, an embassy, the hospital. Days of 1964. James Merrill. **SP-MerrJ**

Houses and rooms are full of perfumes. Walt Whitman. **EBEvV; TrGrPo; UnPo** *Fr.* Song of Myself. **CP-WhitW**

Houses are dark now. People asleep, The. People Asleep. Dabney Stuart. **SP-StuaD**

Houses are haunted, The. Disillusionment of Ten O'Clock. Wallace Stevens. **CP-StevW**

Houses at the Edge of Town. Ted Kooser. **SP-KoosT**

Houses begin to come down, The. It Must All Be Done Over. John Haines. **SP-HainJ**

Houses fade in a melt of mist, The. Parliament Hill in the Evening. David Herbert Lawrence. **CP-LawrD**

Houses haunt me. February 11th. Anne Sexton. **CP-SextA**

Houses in / the ring. The Circle. Robert Creeley. **CP-CreeR**

Houses Lie, Believe the Lying Sea. Richard Hugo. **CP-HugoR**

Houses of the city no longer hum and play, The. John Gould Fletcher. **SP-FletJ** *Fr.* Irradiations.

Houses rolled into the sun, The. Wystan Hugh Auden. **CP-AudWJ**

"Houses"—so the wise men tell me. Emily Dickinson. **CP-DickE**

Houses stand still, but the people are gone, The. Taconite Harbor. Barton Sutter. **SP-SuttB**

Housewife. Anne Sexton. **CP-SextA**

Housework. William Matthews. **SP-MattW**

Housework, the factory work, the work, The. Checklist. Stephen Dunn. **SP-DunnS**

Housing. Grace Paley. **CP-PaleG**

Housman came, savage recluse. Cambridgeshire. Donald Davie. **CP-DavDo**

Housman was perfectly right. A Shock. Wystan Hugh Auden. **CP-AudeW**

Houston in October. Al Young. **CP-YounA**

Hovenweep. Kenneth Patchen. **CP-PatcK**

How. Philip Larkin. **CP-LarkP**

How / ses humble. Edward Estlin Cummings. **CP-CummE**

How / tinily / of / squir(two be). Edward Estlin Cummings. **CP-CummE**

How a Little Girl Danced. Nicholas Vachel Lindsay. **CP-LindV**

How a Little Girl Sang. Nicholas Vachel Lindsay. **CP-LindV**

How about an oak leaf. Poem. James Schuyler. **CP-SchuJ**

How address you, greatest of givers. Kathleen Jessie Raine. *Fr.* To the Sun. **SP-RainK**

How all is one way wrought! Gerard Manley Hopkins. **CP-HopkG**

How am I bound to Two! God, who doth give. God, and the King. Robert Herrick. **CP-HerrR**

How am I ravisht! When I do but see. On Julia's Picture. Robert Herrick. **CP-HerrR**

How amiable are thy tabernacles, O Lord of hosts! Psalm 84. Bible, *O.T.* **TRV** *Fr.* Psalms. **CP-Psal**

How Annandale Went Out. Edwin Arlington Robinson. **CP-RobiE**

How are we off for awares? Correcting Manuscript. Malcolm Lowry. **CP-LowrM**

How are you harry the. The Drums. Robert Creeley. **CP-CreeR**

How art thou alter'd! since afar. To the Fire-Fly of Jamaica, Seen in a Collection. Charlotte Smith. **CP-SmitC**

How art thou named? In search of what strange land. To the Torrent at the Devil's Bridge, North Wales, 1824. William Wordsworth. **CP-WorW2**

How at the midnight of his age the Poet hurls himself on the. Kenneth Patchen. *Fr.* The Hunted City. **CP-PatcK**

How Bacchus Comforts Ariadne. Nonnus. **CP-BroEB** *Fr.* Dionysiaca.

How Bad It Is to Say. William Carlos Williams. **CP-WilW2**

How Ballad Writing Affects Our Seniors. Ernest Hemingway. **CP-HemiE**

How barren would this valley be. Pastoral 6. George Meredith. *Fr.* Pastorals. **CP-MerG1**

How Beastly the Bourgeois Is. David Herbert Lawrence. **CP-LawrD**

How beautiful are the young, walking. Robert Penn Warren. *Fr.* Saul at Gilboa. **SP-WarrR**

How beautiful it was, that one bright day. Hawthorne. Henry Wadsworth Longfellow. **SP-LongH**

How beautiful the Earth is still. Emily Brontë. **CP-BronE** (Anticipation.) **CP-BronE**

How Beautiful the Queen of Night, on High. William Wordsworth. **CP-WorW2**

How beautiful to think. Fellatio. John Updike. **CP-UpdiJ**

How beautiful when up a lofty height. The Widow on Windmere Side. William Wordsworth. **CP-WorW2**

How beautiful you are. Seventh April. Al Young. **CP-YounA**

How beautiful your presence, how benign. Primitive Saxon Clergy. William Wordsworth. *Fr.* Ecclesiastical Sonnets. **CP-WorW2**

"How beautifully it falls," you said. The Leaf. Kathleen Jessie Raine. **SP-RainK**

How, best of kings, dost thou a scepter bear[e]! To King James. Ben Jonson. **CP-JonsB**

How, beyond all foresight. Against Portraits. Charles Tomlinson. **CP-TomlC**

How big and white the night is! Rebuked. David Herbert Lawrence. **CP-LawrD**

How big of breast our Mother Gaea laughed. The Cageing of Ares. George Meredith. **CP-MerG1**

How bland and sweet the greeting of this breeze. Chalkley Hall. John Greenleaf Whittier. **CP-WhitJ**

How blessed is he, who for his country dies. To the Earl of Oxford, Late Lord Treasurer. Jonathan Swift. **CP-SwifJ**

How blessed is he who leads a country life. To My Honoured [*or* Honour'd] Kinsman, John Driden [of Chesterton in the County of Huntingdon, Esquire. John Dryden. **SP-DrydJ**

How blest art thou, canst love the country [*or* countrey], Wroth. To Sir Robert Wroth. Ben Jonson. **CP-JonsB**

How blest bee they then, who his favors prove. Sonnet 7. Mary Sidney, Countess of Montgomery Wroth. *Fr.* A Crowne of Sonetts Dedicated to Love. *Fr.* Pamphilia to Amphilanthus. **CP-WrotM**

How blest the Maid whose heart—yet free. The Three Cottage Girls. William Wordsworth. **HBV 1-2** *Fr.* Memorials of a Tour of the Continent; 1820. **CP-WorW2**

How blest the youth whom Fate ordains. William Cowper. **CP-CowpW**

How blest thy creature is, O God. The Happy Change. William Cowper. *Fr.* Olney Hymns. **CP-CowpW**

How Blind! Walter de la Mare. **CP-DeLaW**

How bright it would be, I'd been warned. Recovery Room. William Matthews. **SP-MattW**

How brittle are the Piers. Emily Dickinson. **CP-DickE**

How broad-minded were Nature and My Parents. A Contrast. Wystan Hugh Auden. **CP-AudeW**

How came pride in Man. William Blake. **CP-BlakW**

How came this ranger. The Chambermaid's First Song. William Butler Yeats. **CP-YeatW**

How came you in Hob's pound to cool. New Song to the Tune of "Whare Hae Ye Been a' Day, My Boy Tammy O? Courting O' a Young Thing, Just Come Frae Her Mammie O?" Byron. **CP-Byron**

How can a man by naming call to mind. April. John Hewitt. **CP-HewiJ**

How can a two-fingered poem catch a plover. Plovers. Peter Meinke. **SP-MeinP**

How Can He Possess. Delmore Schwartz. **SP-SchwD**

How can I care whether you sigh for me. Song: How Can I Care? Robert Ranke Graves. **CP-GravR**

How can I choose but love, and follow her. *see also* Upon Julia's Haire Fill'd with Dew. Robert Herrick. **CP-HerrR**

How can I help thy Husbands copying Me. To Nancy F[laxman]. William Blake. **CP-BlakW**

How can I teach you when your blue. David Herbert Lawrence. **CP-LawrD** *Fr.* The Schoolmaster [A]. **CP-LawrD**

How can I, that girl standing there. Politics. William Butler Yeats. **CP-YeatW**

How can I then return in happy plight. Sonnet 28. William Shakespeare. **OBSC** *Fr.* Sonnets. **CP-ShaWS**

How can I think what thoughts. Candle, Lamp & Firefly. Tess Gallagher. **SP-GallT**

How can it be done / Without delay. Thomas Merton. *Fr.* Cables to the Ace. **CP-MertT**

How can my muse want subject to invent. Sonnet 38. William Shakespeare. *Fr.* Sonnets. **CP-ShaWS**

How can my poor heart be glad. On the Seas and Far Away. Robert Burns. **CP-BurnR**

How can one man, how can all men, / How can we be like St. Paul. Every One That Is Perfect Shall Be as His Master. Christina Georgina Rossetti. **CP-RosC2**

How can there be a difference between twice once and twice twice once. With a Wife. Gertrude Stein. **CP-SteiG**

How can we endure? Dow Jones: Down. Charles Bukowski. **SP-BukC2**

How can we tell a paper bird. Paper Cranes. Thomas Merton. **CP-MertT**

How can we thank each other. Emily Dickinson. **SP-DickE**

How can you be quite so uncouth? After sharing. Ode to the Diencephalon. Wystan Hugh Auden. **CP-AudeW**

How can you forget me? Low to High. Langston Hughes. **SP-HughL**

How Careful Fire Can Be. William Matthews. **SP-MattW**

How careful was I, when I took my way. Sonnet 48. William Shakespeare. *Fr.* Sonnets. **CP-ShaWS**

How carefully, fastidiously. To a Dead Drunk. James Wright. **CP-WrigJ**

How cast changes is the mind that took to my Lesbia, culprit. Catullus. *See* Carmen 75: "Reason blinded by sin, Lesbia."

How changed is here each spot man makes or fills! Matthew Arnold. **FaBoPP** *Fr.* Thyrsis. **SP-ArnoM**

How changed is here each spot man makes or fills! Thyrsis. Matthew Arnold. **SP-ArnoM**

How clean these shallows. Labrador. William Carlos Williams. **CP-WilW2**

How clear, how keen, how marvellously bright. November 1. William Wordsworth. **CP-WorW2**

How clear, how lovely bright. Alfred Edward Housman. **CP-HousA**

How Clear She Shines! Emily Brontë. **CP-BronE**

How close the clouds press this October first. No Map. Stephen Dobyns. **SP-DobyS**

How close to becoming spirit something is. Juan Ramón Jiménez. *Fr.* Ten Short Poems. **CP-WrigJ**

How closely these long years have bound us. Love Charms. Robert Ranke Graves. **CP-GravR**

How co'd Luke Smeaton weare a shoe, or boot. Upon Smeaton. Robert Herrick. **CP-HerrR**

How cold is that bosom which folly once fired. Monody on Maria. Robert Burns. **CP-BurnR**

How come a thickish tree. A View. James Schuyler. **CP-SchuJ**

How Come He Got Canned at the Ribbon Factory. Allen Ginsberg. **CP-GinsA**

How come to town she was, tied bright and prim. On a Photograph of My Mother at Seventeen. Miller Williams. **SP-WillM**

How come when grandpa is teaching the little boy. Ashes Ashes We All Fall Down. Charles Kenneth Williams. **CP-WillC**

How Come You're Not Unlisted? Charles Bukowski. **SP-BukC1**

How comes it, Flora, that, whenever we. The Queen of Hearts. Christina Georgina Rossetti. **CP-RosC1**

How comes it that, at even-tide. To the Companions. Rudyard Kipling. **CP-KiplR** *Fr.* Debits and Credits.

How comforting it is, once or twice a year. James Fenton. **SCBI** *Fr.* A German Requiem. **SP-FentJ**

How could I be aware. At Mayfair Lodgings. Thomas Hardy. **CP-HardT**

How could I have come so far? Poem. Thomas McGrath. **SP-McGrT**

How could she come to us inviolate. Aphrodite. Daniel Gerard Hoffman. **SP-HoffD**

How could we sleep in that pension. Fontaine-les-Dijon Revisited. Daniel Gerard Hoffman. **SP-HoffD**

How could you be so happy, now some thousand years. Note to Wang Wei. John Berryman. **CP-BerrJ**

How could you dare stay constant to. Magda Goebbels ("How could you dare stay constant to"). William DeWitt Snodgrass. **SP-SnodW**

How Could You Ever Be Fine. Stephen Dobyns. **SP-DobyS**

How could you, Gay, disgrace the muses' train. To Mr. Gay. Jonathan Swift. **CP-SwifJ**

How countlessly they congregate. Stars. Robert Frost. **CP-FrosR**

How courteous is the Japanese. The Japanese. Ogden Nash. **CP-NashO**

How credible, the room which you evoke. Advice from the Muse. Richard Wilbur. **CP-WilbR**

How cruel are the Parents. Altered from an Old English Song. Robert Burns. **CP-BurnR**

How Cruel Is the Story of Eve. Stevie Smith. **CP-SmitS**

How dare one say it? The Unexpress'd. Walt Whitman. **CP-WhitW**

How dare the robins sing. Emily Dickinson. **CP-DickE**

How dark and single,where he ends,the earth. Edward Estlin Cummings. **CP-CummE**

How daur ye ca' me "Howlet-face." Robert Burns. **CP-BurnR** (Keekin' Glass, The.) **CP-BurnR**

How delightful to meet Mr. Hodgson! Lines to Ralph Hodgson Esqre. Thomas Stearns Eliot. **NBLV; OBAL; PeLV** *Fr.* Five-Finger Exercises. **CP-ElioT**

How destitute is he. Emily Dickinson. **CP-DickE**

How did a great Red-tailed Hawk. The Dead by the Side of the Road. Gary Snyder. **CP-SnydG**

How did all this begin, and why am I here. Malcolm Lowry. *Fr.* The Cantinas. **CP-LowrM**

How did I bear it—how could I possibly as a child. Edna St. Vincent Millay. **CP-MillE**

How did midsummer come so soon. Solstice. Louis MacNeice. **CP-MacNL**

How did she leave the world? with what contempt? Ben Jonson. **OBD** *Fr.* An Elegy [*or* Elegie] on the Lady Jane Pawlet [*or* Paulet], [Marchioness of Winton]. **CP-JonsB**

How did the Devil come? When first attack? Norfolk. Sir John Betjeman. **CP-BetjJ**

How did the stones vote. The Election. Leonard Nathan. **SP-NathL**

How did they fume, and stamp, and roar, and chafe. Atticus ("How did they fume, and stamp, and roar, and chafe"). Alexander Pope. **InPK; OBEC; TW; WHA** *Fr.* Epistle to Dr. Arbuthnot. **CP-PopeA**

How died Melissa none dares shape in words. Periander. George Meredith. **CP-MerG1**

How different, in the midst of snow, the great school rises red! School on the Outskirts. David Herbert Lawrence. **CP-LawrD**

How difficult it was to look at them. Careers. Stephen Dobyns. **SP-DobyS**

How difficult to be an angel. The Noise the Hairless Make. Stephen Dobyns. **SP-DobyS**

"How disappeared he?" Ask the newt and toad. The Brownie. William Wordsworth. **CP-WorW2**

How Distant. Philip Larkin. **CP-LarkP**

How do I feel today? I feel as unfit as an unfiddle. They Won't Believe, on New Year's Eve, that New Year's Day Will Come What May. Ogden Nash. **CP-NashO**

How do I get onto these trivial subjects? Only you are subject to. Postcards from Nebraska. John Yau. **SP-YauJo**

How do I know it was a fox? Blue Teal's Mother. James Wright. **CP-WrigJ**

How do I know what Order brings. Song of the Dynamo. Rudyard Kipling. **CP-KiplR**

How do I love on summer nights. Written in Aspin Castle. Emily Brontë. **CP-BronE**

How Do I Love Thee? Elizabeth Barrett Browning. *See* Sonnet: "How do I love thee? Let me count the ways."

How do I love thee? Let me count the ways. Sonnet. Elizabeth Barrett Browning. **ArLo; BWW; BoLoP; CTC; EBEvV; EBVV; EnVR; FF; FPL; FaBV; FaBoBe; FaFP; FaPoB; HBV; HeIP; HoPM; ImPo; InPK; LPA; LiTB; NAEL-2; NALW; NIP; NoP; OAEP; OHCV; OLR; OPOU; OXAEP-2; OxBM; PoE; PoLF; PoPl; PoRA; PoToHe; Poetr; Son; TEP; TFi; TRV; TrGrPo; TreF; UV; UnPo; WHA; WPE** *Fr.* Sonnets from the Portuguese. **CP-BroEB**

How do I sleep? Well, but. Report on August. Roy Fisher. **SP-FishR**

How do the birds do it? How to Do It. Phoebe Hesketh. **SP-HeskP**

How do the days press on, and lay. The Flight. Walter de la Mare. **CP-DeLaW**

How Do They Get Your Number? Charles Bukowski. **SP-BukC3**

How do they know. Each Summer's Swallows. John Updike. **CP-UpdiJ**

How do we know, by the bank-high river. The Last Lap. Rudyard Kipling. **CP-KiplR** *Fr.* Land and Sea Tales.

How do we know where we are going? The Perpetual Migration. Marge Piercy. **SP-PierM**

How do we tell if a window is open? Stone Telling. Shel Silverstein. **SP-SilS2**

How Do You Do, Dr Berryman, Sir? John Berryman. **CP-BerrJ**

How do you know that the pilgrim track. The Year's Awakening. Thomas Hardy. **CP-HardT**

How do you know what effigy of self. A Letter to the Inventors of a Tradition. Kenneth Patchen. **CP-PatcK**

How do you like the music of Adolph. Fantasy. Frank O'Hara. **SP-OharF**

How do you like to go up in a swing. The Swing. Robert Louis Stevenson. **CP-StevR**

How Do You Say Ha-Ha in French. Ogden Nash. **CP-NashO**

How Do You See? Stevie Smith. **CP-SmitS**

How do you spell change. Audre Lorde. *See* New York City 1970.

How Do You Tell a Story? Diane Wakoski. **SP-WakoD**

How Do You Think It Feels. "Lou Reed." **SP-ReedL**

How doe I find my soules extreamest anguish. Mary Sidney, Countess of Montgomery Wroth. *Fr.* Part 1. *Fr.* Urania. **CP-WrotM**

How Does a Madsong Know That's What It Is? Miller Williams. **SP-WillM**

How does a person get to be a capable liar? Golly, How Truth Will Out. Ogden Nash. **CP-NashO**

How does he come to be wearing that suit. Roy Fisher. **SP-FishR** *Fr.* Metamorphoses.

How does it feel to be one of the beautiful people. Baby You're a Rich Man. John Lennon *and* Paul McCartney. **CP-Beatl**

How does one stand. The American Sublime. Wallace Stevens. **CP-StevW**

How does the pot pray. Utensil. Archie Randolph Ammons. **SP-AmmoA**

How does the true man of Tao. Wholeness. Chuang Tzu, *tr. fr. Chinese by* Thomas Merton. **CP-MertT**

How doth the little crocodile. "Lewis Carroll." **CP-CarrL** *Fr.* Alice's Adventures in Wonderland.

How drearily in College hall. Ralph Waldo Emerson. **CP-EmerR**

How Dulcenia del Toboso Is Like the Left Wing of a Bird. Nicholas Vachel Lindsay. **CP-LindV**

How dull and dead are books, that cannot show. To the Right Honourable, Philip, Earle of Pembroke, and Montgomerie. Robert Herrick. **CP-HerrR**

How easily happiness begins by. Onions. William Matthews. **SP-MattW**

How eas'ly wert thou chained. Thomas Campion. **CP-CampT**

How eloquent are eyes! Eyes: A Fragment. Percy Bysshe Shelley. **CP-ShelP**

How emerald the chalky depths. Hearts Together. Sir John Betjeman. **CP-BetjJ**

How exactly good it is. The Cold. Wendell Berry. **CP-BerrW**

How faint the horn sounds in the mountain passes. May Sarton. **SP-SartM** *Fr.* To the Living.

How far / Must that star descend. Star of Bethlehem. Kathleen Jessie Raine. **SP-RainK**

How Far. Charles Tomlinson. **CP-TomlC**

How Far Can You Press a Poet? Stevie Smith. **CP-SmitS**

How far is it? Getting There. Sylvia Plath. **CP-PlatS**

How far is it to Heaven? Emily Dickinson. **CP-DickE**

How far is St. Helena from a little child at play? A St. Helena Lullaby. Rudyard Kipling. **CP-KiplR**

How far upon these songs with my strict wrist. John Berryman. *Fr.* Sonnets to Chris. **CP-BerrJ**

How far we had to go. The Machines. Richard Shelton. **SP-ShelR**

How fares it with the happy dead? Tennyson. *Fr.* In Memoriam A. H. H. **CP-TennA**

How fares it with you, Mrs. Cooper my bride? The Sea-Widow. Stevie Smith. **CP-SmitS**

How fast the Marian death-list is unrolled! Latimer and Ridley. William Wordsworth. *Fr.* Ecclesiastical Sonnets. **CP-WorW2**

How fast thou fliest, O Time, on loves swift wings. Sonnet 32. Mary Sidney, Countess of Montgomery Wroth. *Fr.* Pamphilia to Amphilanthus. **CP-WrotM**

How fast thou hast'st (O spring) with sweetest speed. Sonnet 44. Mary Sidney, Countess of Montgomery Wroth. *Fr.* Pamphilia to Amphilanthus. **CP-WrotM**

How Festivals Were Celebrated. Frank Templeton Prince. *Fr.* Chaka. **CP-PrinF**

How fever'd is the man who cannot look. John Keats. **CP-KeatJ** *Fr.* Two Sonnets on Fame.

(On Fame ("How fever'd is the man who cannot look").) **CP-KeatJ**

How few, of all the hearts that loved. E.W. to A.G.A. Emily Brontë. **CP-BronE**

How fierce was I, when I did see. Upon Julia['s] Washing Herself in the River. Robert Herrick. **CP-HerrR**

How fine / to have a long-legged house. Wendell Berry. *Fr.* Window Poems. **CP-BerrW**

How firm Eternity must look. Emily Dickinson. **CP-DickE**

How fit our well-rank'd Feasts doe follow. Upon the Powder Day. Richard Crashaw. **CP-CrasR**

How fits his Umber Coat. Emily Dickinson. **CP-DickE**

How fleet—how indiscreet an one. Emily Dickinson. **CP-DickE**

How fortunate the Grave. Emily Dickinson. **CP-DickE**

How fresh, O Lord, how sweet and clean. The Flower. George Herbert. **CP-HerbG**

How funny, she beat him, she. Grazia Deledda, Young. Donald Davie. **CP-DavDo**

How funny you are today New York. Steps. Frank O'Hara. **SP-OharF**

How generous is that himself the sun. Edward Estlin Cummings. **CP-CummE**

How glad I am that I was bound apprentice. For Patrick, Aetat: LXX. Sir John Betjeman. **CP-BetjJ**

How gleewoorme like the sunn doth now apeere. Sonnet 8. Mary Sidney, Countess of Montgomery Wroth. *Fr.* Pamphilia to Amphilanthus. **CP-WrotM**

How Glorious Is Thy Name. Bible, *O.T. See* Psalm 8: "O Lord our Lord, how excellent. . . ."

How God Was Made. Kenneth Patchen. **CP-PatcK**

How golden bright from earth and heaven. Emily Brontë. **CP-BronE**

How good his Lava Bed. Emily Dickinson. **CP-DickE**

How good of Mrs. Metz! The blur. Snapshots. John Updike. **CP-UpdiJ**

How gorgeous that shock of red lilies, and larkspur cleaving. Twofold. David Herbert Lawrence. **CP-LawrD**

How great is little man! / Sun, moon, and stars respond to him. Christina Georgina Rossetti. **CP-RosC2**

How Great My Grief. Thomas Hardy. **CP-HardT**

How happy are the new-born race. The Testimony of Divine Adoption. Jeanne Marie Bouvier de la Motte-Guyon, *tr. fr. French by* William Cowper. **CP-CowpW**

How happy I was if I could forget. Emily Dickinson. **CP-DickE**

How happy I was the day I told the young Blandina of three-legged giraffes. . . . Analysis of a Theme. Wallace Stevens. **CP-StevW**

How happy is the blameless vestal's lot! The Vestal. Alexander Pope. **ACP; ECEV** *Fr.* Eloisa to Abelard. **CP-PopeA**

How happy is the little Stone. Emily Dickinson. **CP-DickE**

How happy the lover. Song. John Dryden. **SP-DrydJ** *Fr.* King Arthur.

How happy were the subject if he knew. An Epigram. To our Great and Good K[ing] Charles on his Anniversary Day. 1629. Ben Jonson. **CP-JonsB**

How hard it is for me, who live. Marriage. Wendell Berry. **CP-BerrW**

How Hard It Is to Keep from Being King When It's in You and in the Situation. Robert Frost. **CP-FrosR**

How has New England's romance fled. Extract from "A New England Legend." John Greenleaf Whittier. **CP-WhitJ**

How Has the Way Been Found? William Carlos Williams. **CP-WilW1**

How hasten? hearten? O morning star and. A Letter on Liberty. Kenneth Patchen. **CP-PatcK**

How have I bin religious? / what strange good. To Fletcher Reviv'd. Richard Lovelace. **CP-LoveR**

How have I served you? I have let you waste. John Hewitt. **CP-HewiJ; PNI** *Fr.* Sonnets for Roberta (1954). **CP-HewiJ**

How have I wandered here to this vaulted room. Next Morning. David Herbert Lawrence. **CP-LawrD**

How He Saw Her. Ben Jonson. **EnRePo; OAEP; QFR; SeCV-1** *Fr.* A Celebration of Charis in Ten Lyric[k] Pieces [or Peeces]. **CP-JonsB**

How he sleepeth, having drunken. A Child Asleep. Elizabeth Barrett Browning. **CP-BroEB**

How he survived them they could never understand. Diaspora. Wystan Hugh Auden. **CP-AudeW**

How He Would Drinke His Wine. Robert Herrick. **CP-HerrR**

How healthily their feet upon the floor. Edna St. Vincent Millay. **CP-MillE**

How Heav'n in Scorn of human Arrogance. Samuel Johnson. **CP-JohnS** *Fr.* Irene.

How heavy do I journey on the way. Sonnet 50. William Shakespeare. **OXAEP-1** *Fr.* Sonnets. **CP-ShaWS**

How high they build hospitals! How. Philip Larkin. **CP-LarkP**

How high Thou art! our songs can own. The Mediator. Elizabeth Barrett Browning. **CP-BroEB**

How His Soule Came Ensnared. Robert Herrick. **CP-HerrR**

How hollow heart and full. Nicolas-Sébastien Roch Chamfort, *tr. fr. French by* Samuel Beckett. **CP-BeckS**

How horrible late Spring is, with the full death of the frozen tight bulbs. Wooden Spring. Muriel Rukeyser. **CP-RukeM**

"How, how," he said. "Friend Chang," I said. The Chinese Nightingale. Nicholas Vachel Lindsay. **CP-LindV**

How Human Nature dotes. Emily Dickinson. **CP-DickE**

How humble is thy Muse (Deare) that can daign. On the Poems. Norris Jephson. *Fr.* Commendatory Poems. **CP-LoveR**

How Humble We Were before This. Charles Kenneth Williams. **CP-WillC**

How I Can Lie to You. Maya Angelou. **SP-AngeM**

How I do[e] love thee, Beaumont, and thy Muse. To Francis Beaumont. Ben Jonson. **CP-JonsB**

How I Got Started. Charles Bukowski. **SP-BukC3**

How I grieve that I am well! To Ellinda. Upon His Late Recovery. Richard Lovelace. **CP-LoveR**

How I hate myself, this body which is me. Eloi, Eloi, Lama Sabachthani? David Herbert Lawrence. **CP-LawrD**

How I lived, ere my human life began. Rephan. Robert Browning. **CP-BroR2**

How I loved one like you when I was little! Slug. Theodore Roethke. **CP-RoetT**

How I loved that melody. Gilbert Sorrentino. **SP-SorrG**

How I miss my father. Poem at Thirty-nine. Alice Walker. **CP-WalkA**

How I remember cleaning that strange picture! The Collector Cleans His Picture. Thomas Hardy. **CP-HardT**

How I was caught. The Missed Train. Thomas Hardy. **CP-HardT**

How I wish I were able to say what I think. Gertrude Stein. **PBWP** *Fr.* Stanzas in Meditation. **CP-SteiG**

How I wish the Argo had never reached the land. Medea. Euripides. **CP-JefR3**, *tr.* by Robinson Jeffers;

How I woke to the color-tone. Remembering. Denise Levertov. **CP-LeveD**

How ill doth he deserve a lover's name. Eternity of Love Protested. Thomas Carew. **CP-CareT**

How in all wonder Columbus got over. Arthur Hugh Clough. **SP-ClouA**

How innocent of me and my dark pain. Edna St. Vincent Millay. **CP-MillE**

How innocent we lie among. Edna St. Vincent Millay. **CP-MillE**

How instant joy, how clang. Mediterranean Beach, Day after Storm. Robert Penn Warren. *Fr.* Love: Two Vignettes. **SP-WarrR**

How intelligent he looks! Changing Diapers. Gary Snyder. **CP-SnydG**

How is it, Gellius. Carmen 80. Catullus. *Fr.* Carmina. **CP-Catul**

How is it never the same. Woodsmoke at 70. Hayden Carruth. **CP-CarHS**

How is it some of us don't believe. The Kingdom of Stinking Wishes. Charles Kenneth Williams. **CP-WillC**

How is it, tell me, that this new self can be—. Sonnet. Hayden Carruth. **CP-CarHS** *Fr.* Sonnets.

How is it that my saints from Voraigne. Colloquy with a Polish Aunt. Wallace Stevens. **CP-StevW**

How Is My Sun. Sir Philip Sidney. **SP-SidnP** *Fr.* Arcadia.
   This Cave Is Dark. **SiPSBD**

How is my sun, whose beams are shining bright. How Is My Sun. Sir Philip Sidney. **SP-SidnP** *Fr.* Arcadia.

How is the word made flesh made steel made shit. Sewerplant Grows In Harlem Or I'm a Stranger Here Myself. . . . Audre Lorde. **SP-LordA**

How it came to an end! The Coming of the End. Thomas Hardy. **CP-HardT**

How it feels to be touching. We Become New. Marge Piercy. **SP-PierM**

How It Happened. Charles Tomlinson. *Fr.* Four Kantian Lyrics. **CP-TomlC**

How It Is. Richard Eberhart. **CP-EberR**

How It Is. William Stafford. **SP-StafW**

How it rained. We Field-Women. Thomas Hardy. **CP-HardT**

How it reminds me of that day! The Photograph. Stephen Spender. **CP-SpenS**

How It Started. Robert Ranke Graves. **CP-GravR**

How It Strikes a Contemporary. Robert Browning. **CP-BroR1**

How It Was at the End. Stephen Dobyns. **SP-DobyS**

How Jimsey O'Roon and Peter Stack, Coal Miners, Came to Be Put in the Ferbettville (Pa.) Jail Early One Saturday Night. Kenneth Patchen. **CP-PatcK**

How Johnny Appleseed Walked Alone in the Jungles of Heaven. Nicholas Vachel Lindsay. **CP-LindV**

How joyously the young sea-mew. The Sea-Mew. Elizabeth Barrett Browning. **CP-BroEB**

How kind, how secret[ly], [now] the sun. The Garden. Robert Penn Warren. **SP-WarrR**

How know I that it looms lovely that land I have never seen. That Where I Am, There Ye May Be Also. Christina Georgina Rossetti. **CP-RosC2**

How know it from a Summer's Day? Emily Dickinson. **CP-DickE**

How lang and dreary is the night. Robert Burns. **CP-BurnR**
   ("For Oh, her lanely nights are lang.") **CP-BurnR**

How Lewisburg, Pa., Escaped the Avenging Angel. Hayden Carruth. **CP-CarHS**

How Liberty, girl, can it be by thee nam'd? To the Beautiful Miss Eliza J———n, on Her Principles of Liberty and Equality. Robert Burns. **CP-BurnR**

How life and death in Thee. Richard Crashaw. **CP-CrasR**
   (Upon Our Saviour's Tomb[e] Wherein Never Man Was Laid.) **CP-CrasR**

How light the heavy world becomes, when with transparent waters. The Song of the Traveller. Thomas Merton. **CP-MertT**

How like a column, Radcliffe, left alone. To Sir John Radcliffe. Ben Jonson. **CP-JonsB**

How like a fire doth love increase in me[e]. Sonnet 48. Mary Sidney, Countess of Montgomery Wroth. **NOSC** *Fr.* Pamphilia to Amphilanthus. **CP-WrotM**

How like a golden dreame you met and parted. To the Most Illustrious and Mighty Fredericke the Fift, Count Palantine of the Rhein. Thomas Campion. **CP-CampT**

How like a man, is Man, who rises late. Eye-Opener. Malcolm Lowry. **CP-LowrM**

How like a winter hath my absence been[e]. Sonnet 97. William Shakespeare. **AWP; CABA; EIL; EnLoPo; EnRePo; EyDe; FaBoEn; GTBS; GTBS-6; GTBS-P; HeIP; NAEL-1; NOBE; NoSic; OAEL-1; OBEV; OBSC; OXAEP-1; PoRA; SCGP; Son; TEP; TFi; TrGrPo** *Fr.* Sonnets. **CP-ShaWS**

How like the sea / to be. Marsden Hartley. **CP-HartM**

How like to threads of flax, *par.* by Francis Quarles. Bible, *O.T. See* Psalm 119: "Blessed are the undefiled in the way."

How Lillies Came White. Robert Herrick. **CP-HerrR**

How little I know / about you finally. Margaret Atwood. **CrSp** *Fr.* Five Poems for Grandmothers. **SP-AtwM2**

How little seen, and little understood. Ambition. George Meredith. **CP-MerG2**

How lonesome the Wind must feel Nights. Emily Dickinson. **CP-DickE**

How lonesome to be an Article! Emily Dickinson. **SP-DickE**

How long / Is a song? / O Lord / How long? The Screen with the Face with the Voice. Ogden Nash. **CP-NashO**

How long ago was man promised? Death by Water. Patti Smith. **SP-SmitP**

How Long Has This Been Going On? Oh, Quite Long. Ogden Nash. **CP-NashO**

How Long Is the Night? Stanley Jasspon Kunitz. **CP-KuniS**

How long it takes to learn a simple thing. Endor. Howard Nemerov. **CP-NemeH**

How long, O lord, shall I forgotten be?, *par.* by Sir Philip Sidney. Bible, *O.T. See* Psalm 13: "How long wilt thou forget me, O Lord?"

How long, *Perenna*, wilt thou see. To Perenna. Robert Herrick. **CP-HerrR**

How long shall this like dying life endure. Edmund Spenser. **AAS; EnRePo** *Fr.* Amoretti. **CP-Spens**

How long was the peril, how breathless the day. St. Barnabas, Oxford. Sir John Betjeman. **CP-BetjJ**

How Long We Wait. Thomas Merton. **CP-MertT**

How long will these graves go on? Graves in Queens. Richard Hugo. **CP-HugoR**

How long will ye round me be roaring. Address to the Ocean. William Wordsworth. **CP-WorW1**

How long will ye round me be swelling. The Complaint of Ninathóma. Samuel Taylor Coleridge. *Fr.* Effusions. **CP-ColeS**

How long will you remain? The midnight hour. Emily Brontë. **CP-BronE**

How long wilt thou forget me, O Lord? Psalm 13. Bible, *O.T. Fr.* Psalms. **CP-Psal**

How long would a rhinoceros last. Pablo Neruda, *tr. fr. Spanish* by Ben Belitt. **SP-NeruP** *Fr.* Question Book.

How Looks the Night? Gerard Manley Hopkins. *See* How looks the night? There does not miss a star.

How looks the night? There does not miss a star. Gerard Manley Hopkins. **OxBSP** *Fr.* Fragments. **CP-HopkG**
   (How Looks the Night?) **OxBSP**

How loud the storm sounds round the Hall! Emily Brontë. **CP-BronE**

How Love came in, I do not know. Of Love. A Sonnet. Robert Herrick. **CP-HerrR**

How lovely all that glitters. Four Songs the Night Nurse Sang. Robert Duncan. **SP-DuncR**

par. by Milton. Bible, *O.T. See* Psalm 84: "How amiable are thy tabernacles, O Lord of hosts!"

How lovely are thy dwellings fair!, *par.* by Milton. Bible, *O.T. See* Psalm 84: "How amiable are thy tabernacles. . . ."

How lovely are thy tabernacles. Bible, *O.T.* **TrJP** *Fr.* Psalm 84: "How amiable are thy tabernacles, O Lord of hosts!" **CP-MiltJ; TRV; TrPWD** *Fr.* Psalms. **CP-Psal**

How lovely are thy tabernacles, *sel. of diff. vers., vv. 1–4.* Bible, *O.T. See* Psalm 84: "How amiable are thy tabernacles. . . ."

How lovely the elder brother's. Brothers. Gerard Manley Hopkins. **CP-HopkG**

How low when angels fall their black descent. The Promise in Disturbance. George Meredith. **CP-MerG1**

How Lucy Backslid. Paul Laurence Dunbar. **CP-DunbP**

How luscious is the dripping. Emily Dickinson. **SP-DickE**

How mad would he have to be to say, "He beheld." In a Bad Time. Wallace Stevens. **CP-StevW**

How many / Times round. Louis Zukofsky. *Fr.* 29 Poems. **CP-ZukLS**

How many a father have I seen. Tennyson. **EBVVPR; EnVR** *Fr.* In Memoriam A. H. H. **CP-TennA**

How many a thing which we cast to the ground. George Meredith. **HBV 1-2** *Fr.* Modern Love. **CP-MerG1**

How many a time have I. Swimming. Byron. **GN** *Fr.* The Two Foscari. **CP-Byron**

How many authors are my first! Christina Georgina Rossetti. **CP-RosC3**

How Many Bards Gild the Lapses of Time! John Keats. **CP-KeatJ**

How many between East and West. To Miss Creuzé. William Cowper. **CP-CowpW**

How many big events to shake the earth. The Future. Ralph Waldo Emerson. **CP-EmerR**

How many dawns, chill from his rippling rest. To Brooklyn Bridge. Hart Crane. **AP; AiP; AmFP; AmPP; BLPL; CABA; CMoP; ChIV-1; ClHu; CoBMV; CrMA; EyDe; FaBoEn; HAP; HeIP; HoFi; ImPo; InPS; LiTA; LiTM; MeMAP; MoAB; MoAmPo; MoPo; NOBA; NYP; NePA; NoAM; NoP; OxBA; PoE; PoPl₁ PrIm; SeCeV; TAP; TFi; TRP; WeW** *Fr.* The Bridge. **CP-CranH**

How many eyes poore Love hast thou to guard. Sonnet 33. Mary Sidney, Countess of Montgomery Wroth. *Fr.* Pamphilia to Amphilanthus. **CP-WrotM**

How many feet ran with sunlight, water, and air? Garden Wireless. Carl Sandburg. **CP-SandC**

How many Flowers fail in Wood. Emily Dickinson. **CP-DickE**

How many gifted pens have penned. Compliments of a Friend. Ogden Nash. **CP-NashO**

How many guys are sitting at their kitchen tables. Ray. Hayden Carruth. **CP-CarHS**

How many kisses, Lesbia, you ask. Catullus. *See* Carmen 7: "Curious to learn / how may kiss- / es of your lips."

How many lives were torn apart. Philip Levine. **SP-LeviP** *Fr.* A Poem with No Ending.

How many moments must(amazing each). Edward Estlin Cummings. **CP-CummE**

How many more this morning are there dead of. Morning Sun. Howard Nemerov. **CP-NemeH**

How many more times will I shake my bells. The Death of Artists. James Liddy. **CP-LiddJ**

How Many Nights. Galway Kinnell. **SP-KinnG**

How many nights have I with paine indur'd. Sonnet 5. Mary Sidney, Countess of Montgomery Wroth. *Fr.* Pamphilia to Amphilanthus. **CP-WrotM**

How many roads must a man walk down. Blowin' in the Wind. "Bob Dylan." **CP-DylaB**

How many schemes may die. Emily Dickinson. **CP-DickE**

How many Scientists have written. The Shark. Ogden Nash. **CP-NashO**

How Many Seconds in a Minute? Christina Georgina Rossetti. **CP-RosC2**

How many secret nooks in copse or glen. The Beds of Grainne and Diarmuid. Robert Ranke Graves. **CP-GravR**

How many sights / do I have that I'm. Soul in Migration. Joseph Ceravolo. **SP-CeraJ**

How many times, Death. O All Down within the Pretty Meadow. Kenneth Patchen. **CP-PatcK**

How many times have I come here. Looking at Pictures. Charles Wright. **SP-WrigC**

How many times have I come to you out of my head. Wendell Berry. *Fr.* The Country of Marriage. **CP-BerrW**

How many times have I counted my blessings in the baker's. This day our daily. . . . Jenny Joseph. *Fr.* Life and Turgid Times of A. Citizen. **SP-JoseJ**

How many times, like lotus lilies risen. Lotus and Frost. David Herbert Lawrence. **CP-LawrD**

How many times these low feet staggered. Emily Dickinson. **CP-DickE**

How many turn back toward dreams and magic, how many children. Thebaid. Robinson Jeffers. **CP-JefR2**

How many winds forget the sea! Divagation. Allen Tate. *Fr.* The Progress of Œnia. **CP-TateA**

How many years will I live? Two Little Songs. Stephen Berg. **SP-BergS**

How Marigolds Came Yellow. Robert Herrick. **CP-HerrR**

How Mary Grew. John Greenleaf Whittier. **CP-WhitJ**

How may a lover draw two bows at once. Circus Ring. Robert Ranke Graves. **CP-GravR**

How Meadows Trick You. Richard Hugo. **CP-HugoR**

How most unnatural-seeming, yet how proper. Sirocco at Deyá. Robert Ranke Graves. **CP-GravR**

How Much? Carl Sandburg. **CP-SandC**

How Much Can It Hurt? Philip Levine. **SP-LeviP**

How much death works. Eyes Fastened with Pins. Charles Simic. **SP-SimiC**

How much do you love me, a million bushels? How Much? Carl Sandburg. **CP-SandC**

How Much Earth. Philip Levine. **SP-LeviP**

How much, egregious *Moore*, are we. To Mr. John Moore, Author of the Celebrated Worm-Powder. Alexander Pope. **CP-PopeA**

How much havoc this woman spills. Mothers. Margaret Atwood. **SP-AtwM2**

How much I disapprove of it! Revolving Meditation. Stanley Jasspon Kunitz. **CP-KuniS**

How much I want to sit down. Silver. Diane Wakoski. **SP-WakoD**

How Much Longer Will I Be Able to Inhabit the Divine Sepulcher. John Ashbery. **SP-AshbJ**

How much money would erase him in a dream. Beggar in Sapri. Richard Hugo. **CP-HugoR**

How much of me is sandwiches radio beer? Lonesome in the Country. Al Young. **CP-YounA**

How much of Source escapes with thee. Emily Dickinson. **CP-DickE**

How much of the great poetry. Civilization and Its Discontents. William Matthews. **SP-MattW**

How much of you is in my verse. For R. John Hewitt. **CP-HewiJ**

How much, Preventing God! how much I owe. Grace. Ralph Waldo Emerson. **CP-EmerR**

How much shall I love her? The Echo-Elf Answers. Thomas Hardy. **CP-HardT**

How much the present moment means. Emily Dickinson. **CP-DickE**

How much there was had escaped him. The Thief's Journal. Charles Tomlinson. **CP-TomlC**

How my city has grown! Air. Louis Zukofsky. **CP-ZukLS**

How, my dear Mary,—are you critic-bitten. The Witch of Atlas. Percy Bysshe Shelley. **CP-ShelP**

How My Fever Left. James Wright. **CP-WrigJ**

How my own hills / and how Gloucester Harbor suddenly. Got Me Home, the Light Snow Gives the Air, Falling. Charles Olson. **SP-OlsoC** *Fr.* The Maximus Poems.

How Naked, How Without a Wall. Edna St. Vincent Millay. **CP-MillE**

How near this suffering Summer. Emily Dickinson. **SP-DickE**

How News must feel when travelling. Emily Dickinson. **CP-DickE**

How nice it is to be superior! To Be Superior. David Herbert Lawrence. **CP-LawrD**

How nice it is to slink the streets at night. Suburb. Stevie Smith. **CP-SmitS**

How noteless Men, and Pleiads, stand. Emily Dickinson. **CP-DickE**

How Now, Sirrah? Oh, Anyhow. Ogden Nash. **CP-NashO**

How of his fate, the Pilgrims' soldier-guide. A Camel-Driver. Robert Browning. **CP-BroR2**

How oft have I, my dear [*or* dere] and cruel[l] foe. Petrarch, *tr. fr. Italian by* Sir Thomas Wyatt. **CP-WyatT**

How oft, when thou, my music, music play'st. Sonnet 128. William Shakespeare. **EiL; NAEL-1; OXAEP-1; PoE** *Fr.* Sonnets. **CP-ShaWS**

How often does it happen. A Cloak for a Man Who Has No Heed for Winter. Kay Boyle. **CP-BoylK**

How often have I carried our family word. Quoof. Paul Muldoon. **SP-MuldP**

How often have I said before. Loving True, Flying Blind. Robert Ranke Graves. **CP-GravR**

How often have my tears. In Allusion to the French Song. Richard Lovelace. **CP-LoveR**

How often I have said. Life Encompassed. Donald Davie. **CP-DavDo**

How often must we. Reverses. Maya Angelou. **SP-AngeM**

How often sit I, poring o'er. Arthur Hugh Clough. *Fr.* Blank Misgivings of a Creature Moving About in Worlds Not Realized. **SP-ClouA**

How often the blues begin early morning. Blue Notes. William Matthews. **SP-MattW**

How often, these hours, have I heard the monotonous crool of a dove. The Dove. Walter de la Mare. **CP-DeLaW**

How often we forget all time, when lone. Stanzas. Edgar Allan Poe. **CP-PoeEd**

How Old the World Is! Kenneth Patchen. **CP-PatcK**

How One Chose. Christina Georgina Rossetti. **CP-RosC3**

How overjoyed I am to get your letter. Malcolm Lowry. **CP-LowrM**

How overwhelming / that Lester tune. Topsy: Part 2. Al Young. **CP-YounA**

How Pansies or Hearts-Ease Came First. Robert Herrick. **CP-HerrR**

How patient man is in his time! The day. The Clock in the Tower of the Church. Randall Jarrell. **CP-JarrR**

How pitiful is her sleep. In Memory of Kathleen. Kenneth Patchen. **CP-PatcK**

How pleasant the banks of the clear-winding Devon. The Banks of the Devon. Robert Burns. **CP-BurnR**

How pleasant to sit on the beach. Pretty Halcyon Days. Ogden Nash. **CP-NashO**

How Poems Are Made: A Discredited View. Alice Walker. **CP-WalkA**

How Poetry Comes to Me. Gary Snyder. **CP-SnydG**

How precious Thought and Speech are! Emily Dickinson. **SP-DickE**

How precise it seems, like a doll house. Housework. William Matthews. **SP-MattW**

How Primroses Came Green. Robert Herrick. **CP-HerrR**

How profitless the relics that we cull. Roman Antiquities. William Wordsworth. **CP-WorW2**

How pure at heart and sound in head. Tennyson. **MeMBP** *Fr.* In Memoriam A. H. H. **CP-TennA**

How pure the hearts of lovers as they walk. Prothalamion. May Sarton. **SP-SartM**

How quick the change from joy to woe. Written after Leaving Her at New Burns. William Cowper. **CP-CowpW**

How quickly morphology. Old Light. Al Young. **CP-YounA**

How quickly the postures shift. On Your Own. Tess Gallagher. **SP-GallT**

How quiet must be the road where. After New York—May Seventeenth. Kay Boyle. *Fr.* Two Poems for a Poet. **CP-BoylK**

How quiet the diversion stands. Plural of "Jack-in-the-Box,"The. John Ashbery. **SP-AshbJ**

How rare to be born a human being! Gary Snyder. **CP-SnydG** *Fr.* Hunting. *Fr.* Myths and Texts.

How red the rose that is the soldier's wound. Wallace Stevens. **CMoP; NOBA; WaP; WaaP** *Fr.* Esthétique du Mal. **CP-StevW** (Soldier's Wound, The.) **WaaP**

How Relaxed. Jim Carroll. **SP-CarrJ**

How rich a man is, all desire to know. Gold, before Goodnesse. Robert Herrick. **CP-HerrR**

How rich and pleasing thou, my Julia, art. To Julia. Robert Herrick. **CP-HerrR**

How Rich That Forehead's Calm Expanse! William Wordsworth. **CP-WorW2**

How richly glows the water's breast. Lines Written While Sailing in a Boat at Evening. William Wordsworth. **CP-WorW1**

How Roses Came Red ("Roses at first"). Robert Herrick. **CP-HerrR**

How Roses Came Red ("'Tis said"). Robert Herrick. **CP-HerrR**

How ruthless are the gentle. Emily Dickinson. **CP-DickE**

How sad a welcome! To each voyager. Iona. William Wordsworth. *Fr.* Poems Composed or Suggested During a Tour, in the Summer of 1833. **CP-WorW2**

How safe, methinks, and strong, behind. After Floods on the Wharfe. Andrew Marvell. **FaBoPP** *Fr.* Upon Appleton House [To My Lord Fairfax]. **CP-MarvA**

How Samson Bore Away the Gates of Gaza. Nicholas Vachel Lindsay. **CP-LindV**

How seldom, friend, a good, great man inherits. The Good Great Man. Samuel Taylor Coleridge. **CP-ColeS**

How shall I be a poet? Poeta Fit, Non Nascitur. "Lewis Carroll." **CP-CarrL**

How shall I behold the face. John Milton. **TOF** *Fr.* Book IX. **FHYEP; NAEL-1; NAWM-1; NoP; OAEL-1** *Fr.* Paradise Lost. **CP-MiltJ**

How shall I come to you with this to say to you. To America. Kay Boyle. **CP-BoylK**

How shall I do, to pass the weary time. John Berryman. *Fr.* Sonnets to Chris. **CP-BerrJ**

How shall I keep this violence in. Rover. Stanley Jasspon Kunitz. **CP-KuniS**

How shall I know, unless I go. To the Not Impossible Him. Edna St. Vincent Millay. **CP-MillE**

How shall I know when the end of things is coming? A Sign. Walter de la Mare. **CP-DeLaW**

How shall I paint thee?—Be this naked stone. William Wordsworth. *Fr.* The River Duddon [A Series of Sonnets]. **CP-WorW2**

How shall I sing, western & dry & thin. John Berryman. *Fr.* Sonnets to Chris. **CP-BerrJ**

How Shall I Woo Thee. Paul Laurence Dunbar. **CP-DunbP**

How Shall My Animal. Dylan Thomas. **CP-ThomD**

How shall she know the worship we would do her? The Song for the Women. Rudyard Kipling. **CP-KiplR**

How shall the wine be drunk, or the woman known? A Voice from under the Table. Richard Wilbur. **CP-WilbR**

How shall we apostrophise the vileness of women. A Curse. Malcolm Lowry. **CP-LowrM**

How shall we tell. The Chrysanthemum. William Carlos Williams. **CP-WilW2**

How she held up the horses' heads. A Woman Driving. Thomas Hardy. **CP-HardT**

How She Went to Ireland. Thomas Hardy. **CP-HardT**

How she would have loved. Lament. Thomas Hardy. **CP-HardT**

How she would welcome my hands. The Girl of My Dreams. Dabney Stuart. **SP-StuaD**

How short a time for a life to last. Kenneth Rexroth. **SP-RexrK** *Fr.* The Autumn of Many Years. **CP-RexKL** *Fr.* The Homestead Called Damascus.

How should I / Be so pleasant. Sir Thomas Wyatt. **CP-WyatT**

How should I not be glad to contemplate. Everything Is Going to Be All Right. Derek Mahon. **SP-MahoD**

How should I praise thee, Lord! how should my r[h]ymes. The Temper (1). George Herbert. **CP-HerbG**

How should the dreamer, on those slow. Clouds. Charles Tomlinson. **CP-TomlC**

How should the world be luckier if this house. Upon a House Shaken by the Land Agitation. William Butler Yeats. **CP-YeatW**

How sick I am! Marijuana Notation. Allen Ginsberg. **CP-GinsA**

How sick—to wait—in any place—but thine. Emily Dickinson. **CP-DickE**

How silent are the things of heaven. Kenneth Patchen. **CP-PatcK**

How silent comes the water round that bend. Minnows. John Keats. **GN** *Fr.* I Stood Tip-Toe upon a Little Hill. **CP-KeatJ**

How simple was the relationship between the sexes in the days. It's about Time. Ogden Nash. **CP-NashO**

How simply / for another. Song. Robert Creeley. **CP-CreeR**

How sits this city, late most populous. John Donne. **ChIV-1** *Fr.* Lamentations of Jeremy, for the Most Part According to Tremeullius. **CP-DonnJ**

How sits this city, late most populous. Lamentations of Jeremy, for the Most Part According to Tremeullius. John Donne. **CP-DonnJ**

How Sleep the Brave. Walter de la Mare. **CP-DeLaW**

How slow the Wind. Emily Dickinson. **CP-DickE**

How Slowly Time Lengthens. Stevie Smith. **CP-SmitS**

How small the furniture of bliss! Emily Dickinson. **SP-DickE**

How small the news was. Some Good News. Charles Olson. **SP-OlsoC** *Fr.* The Maximus Poems.

How smartly the quarters of the hour march by. Copying Architecture in an Old Minster. Thomas Hardy. **CP-HardT**

How smiled the land of France. To a Friend. John Greenleaf Whittier. **CP-WhitJ**

How smiles he at a generation ranked. The Spirit of Shakespeare: Continued. George Meredith. **CP-MerG1**

How soft a Caterpillar steps. Emily Dickinson. **CP-DickE**

How soft this Prison is. Emily Dickinson. **CP-DickE**

How Solemn as One by One. Walt Whitman. **CP-WhitW**

How solemn! sweeping this dense black tide! The Mississippi at Midnight. Walt Whitman. **CP-WhitW**

How soon—alas! did Man, created pure. William Wordsworth. *Fr.* Ecclesiastical Sonnets. **CP-WorW2**

How soon doth man decay! Mortification. George Herbert. **CP-HerbG**

How soon hath Time the suttle [or subtle] theef [or thief] of youth. John Milton. **CP-MiltJ** (Sonnet 7: "How soon hath Time the suttle theef of youth.") **CP-MiltJ**

How Soon the Servant Sun. Dylan Thomas. **CP-ThomD**

How spacious must be the Heart. Emily Dickinson. **SP-DickE**

How Spring Comes. Alice Notley. **SP-NotlA**

How Springs Came First. Robert Herrick. **CP-HerrR**

How Stars Start. Al Young. **CP-YounA**

How stern are the woes of the desolate mourner. Bereavement. Percy Bysshe Shelley. *Fr.* Poems from St. Irvyne, or, The Rosicrucian. **CP-ShelP**

How still, / How strangely still. Sea Calm. Langston Hughes. **SP-HughL**

How still, how happy! These [or Those] are words. Emily Brontë. **CP-BronE**

How still the Bells in Steeples stand. Emily Dickinson. **CP-DickE**

How Still the Hawk. Charles Tomlinson. **CP-TomlC**

How straight it flew, how long it flew. Seaside Golf. Sir John Betjeman. **CP-BetjJ**

How strange / That they arrange. Tardy Poet: 1978. David Markson. **CP-MarkD**

How strange!—but, first of all, the little fact. *with music.* Robert Browning. **CP-BroR2**

How strange it is to awake. Charles Wright. **SP-WrigC** *Fr.* Three Poems for the New Year. (Three Poems for the New Year [2].) **SP-WrigC**

How strange it seems! These Hebrews in their graves. The Jewish Cemetery at Newport. Henry Wadsworth Longfellow. **SP-LongH**

How strange it was to hear the furniture being moved around in the apartment upstairs! The Magic of Numbers. Kenneth Koch. **SP-KochK**

How strange it would be if some women came forward and said. Sun-Women. David Herbert Lawrence. **CP-LawrD**

How strange that Nature does not knock. Emily Dickinson. **SP-DickE**

How strange to be gone in a minute / Bearden is dead Gallup is dead Margie is dead. Ted Berrigan. **SP-BerrT** *Fr.* The Sonnets.

How strange to be gone in a minute! A man. A Final Sonnet. Ted Berrigan. **SP-BerrT** *Fr.* The Sonnets.

How strange to greet, this frosty morn. Flowers in Winter. John Greenleaf Whittier. **CP-WhitJ**

How strange to think of giving up all ambition! Watering the Horse. Robert Bly. **SP-BlyR**

How strangely crows the Gallic cock. The New Era the Army of the Future the Egg of an Army. George Meredith. **CP-MerG2**

How strong should the wine be? Vir II. James Liddy. *Fr.* Vir I–XII. **CP-LiddJ**

How struts my love my cavalier. Cock-a-Hoop. Isabella Gardner. **CP-GardI**

How sweet and dear it was of. My Beloved Harteebeeste. Malcolm Lowry. **CP-LowrM**

How sweet and lovely dost thou make the shame. Sonnet 95. William Shakespeare. **HeIP; MasP; SCGP; TrGrPo** *Fr.* Sonnets. **CP-ShaWS**

How sweet, how passing sweet, is solitude! William Cowper. **OBF** *Fr.* Retirement. **CP-CowpW**

How Sweet I Roamed [*or* roam'd] from Field to Field. William Blake. (Song: "How sweet I roamed [*or* roam'd] from field to field.") **CP-BlakW**

How sweet in sleep to pass the careless hours. Tibullus, *tr.* by Samuel Johnson. **CP-JohnS** *Fr.* Elegies.

How sweet is the shepherd's sweet life! The Masque of Plenty. Rudyard Kipling. **CP-KiplR**

How sweet is the shepherd's sweet lot! The Shepherd. William Blake. **BoTP; EnRP; FHYEP; HBV; LoBV; OBEC; PFP; TiPo** *Fr.* Songs of Innocence. **CP-BlakW**

How sweet is the sun, is the sun. Louis Zukofsky. *Fr.* There when the water was not potable. *Fr.* Chloride of Lime and Charcoal. **CP-ZukLS**

How sweet it is to sit and read the tales. Fragment: Music and Sweet Poetry. Percy Bysshe Shelley. **CP-ShelP**

How sweet it is, when mother Fancy rocks. William Wordsworth. **CP-WorW1**

How sweet on sunny afternoons. Pastoral 1. George Meredith. *Fr.* Pastorals. **CP-MerG1**

How sweet on sunny afternoons. Pastorals. George Meredith. **CP-MerG1**

How sweet that he rose in the morning. Emily Dickinson. **SP-DickE**

How sweet the birds of Avondale. Avondale. Stevie Smith. **CP-SmitS**

How sweet the "Life that now is." Emily Dickinson. **SP-DickE**

How sweet the music sounded. An Old Memory. Paul Laurence Dunbar. **CP-DunbP**

How sweet the silent backward tracings! Memories. Walt Whitman. **CP-WhitW**

How sweet the sound in the city an hour before sunrise. English Sparrows. Edna St. Vincent Millay. **CP-MillE**

How sweet the walk along the woody steep. At the Isle of Wight. 1793. William Wordsworth. **CP-WorW1**

How sweet, when crimson colours dart. Alcaeus to Sappho. William Wordsworth. **CP-WorW1**

How sweetly came the holy psalms. The Memory of Burns. John Greenleaf Whittier. **CP-WhitJ**

How sweetly doth *My Master* sound! *My Master!*. Odour, The. (2 Corinthians 2). George Herbert. **CP-HerbG**

How sweetly on the wood-girt town. Pentucket. John Greenleaf Whittier. **CP-WhitJ**

How sweetly shines through azure skies. Oscar of Alva. Byron. **CP-Byron**

How swiftly they cease to be. To the Nieuport Scout. Geoffrey Hill. **CP-HillG**

How swiftly through Heaven's wide expanse. St. Irvyne's Tower. Percy Bysshe Shelley. *Fr.* Poems from St. Irvyne, or, The Rosicrucian. **CP-ShelP**

How tall the buildings were as I began. Untilted. John Ashbery. **SP-AshbJ**

How that fact of. Robert Creeley. **CP-CreeR**

How the Camel Got His Hump. Rudyard Kipling. *Fr.* Just-So Stories. "Camel's hump is an ugly lump, The." **CP-KiplR**

How the children have changed! Rapt, we stare. Home Movies. John Updike. **CP-UpdiJ**

How the days went. Now That I Am Forever with Child. Audre Lorde. **SP-LordA**

How the Earth turns round under the Sun I know. The Ballad of the Enamord Image. Robert Duncan. **SP-DuncR**

How the elements solidify! Event. Sylvia Plath. **CP-PlatS**

How the Elephant Got His Hump. Miller Williams. **SP-WillM**

How the Fear Came. Rudyard Kipling. *Fr.* The Second Jungle Book. "Now this the Law of the Jungle—as old and as true as the sky." **CP-KiplR** (Law of the Jungle, The.) **CP-KiplR**

How the Leopard Got His Spots. Rudyard Kipling. *Fr.* Just-So Stories. "I am the Most Wise Baviaan, saying in most wise tones." **CP-KiplR**

How the old Mountains drip with Sunset. Emily Dickinson. **CP-DickE**

How the Rainbow Works. Al Young. **CP-YounA**

How the red bells rang. He Nears the Goal. Nicholas Vachel Lindsay. *Fr.* The Tree of Laughing Bells or The Wings of the Morning. **CP-LindV**

How the Rhinoceros Got His Skin. Rudyard Kipling. *Fr.* Just-So Stories. "This Uninhabited Island." **CP-KiplR**

How the River Ninfa Runs through the Ruined Town Beneath the Lime Quarry. Archibald MacLeish. **CP-MacLA**

How the Robin Came. John Greenleaf Whittier. **CP-WhitJ**

How the Sestina (Yawn) Works. Anne Waldman. **SP-WaldA**

How the Wall-Flower Came First, and Why So Called. Robert Herrick. **CP-HerrR**

How the Waters closed above Him. Emily Dickinson. **CP-DickE**

How the Whale Got his Throat. Rudyard Kipling. *Fr.* Just-So Stories. "When the cabin port-holes are dark and green." **CP-KiplR**

How the Wings Were Made. Nicholas Vachel Lindsay. *Fr.* The Tree of Laughing Bells or The Wings of the Morning. **CP-LindV**

How the Women Went from Dover. John Greenleaf Whittier. **CP-WhitJ**

How the young attempt / and are broken. Generation. Audre Lorde. **SP-LordA**

How These Words Happened. William Stafford. **SP-StafW**

How they are provided for upon the earth, (appearing at intervals). Beginners. Walt Whitman. **CP-WhitW**

How They Brought the Good News from Ghent to Aix. Robert Browning. **CP-BroR1** "Not a word to each other; we kept the great pace." **Poetr**

How thin and sharp is the moon tonight! Winter Moon. Langston Hughes. **SP-HughL**

How Things Change. Charles Olson. **CP-OlsoC**

How this morning. Chuck Miller. **SP-MillC**

How this tart fable instructs. Virgin in a Tree. Sylvia Plath. **CP-PlatS**

How this uncouth enchanted. Edward Estlin Cummings. **CP-CummE**

How times change, old friend. The Old Worshipper. William Carlos Williams. **CP-WilW1**

How Tit'rus you supine and careless laid. Translation of Virgil: Pastoral I. Virgil, *tr.* by Samuel Johnson. **CP-JohnS** *Fr.* Pastorals.

How To. Hayden Carruth. **CP-CarHS**

How to Amuse a Stone. Richard Shelton. **SP-ShelR**

How to Be a Great Writer. Charles Bukowski. **SP-BukC1**

How to Be Happy: Another Memo to Myself. Stephen Dunn. **SP-DunnS**

How to Be Married without a Spouse, or, Mr. Kipling, What Have You Done with Mr. Hauksbee? Ogden Nash. **CP-NashO**

How to Be Uncle Sam. John Updike. **CP-UpdiJ**

How to Do It. Phoebe Hesketh. **SP-HeskP**

How to do it from the beginning. Let Me Tell You. Miller Williams. **SP-WillM**

How to Enter a Big City. Thomas Merton. **CP-MertT**

How to fit. The Problem. William Carlos Williams. **CP-WilW2**

How to Foretell a Change in the Weather. Ted Kooser. **SP-KoosT**

How to Get On in Society. Sir John Betjeman. **CP-BetjJ**

How to Grow Cucumbers. William Cowper. **FaBoUs** *Fr.* The Garden. *Fr.* The Task. **CP-CowpW**

How to Harry a Husband, or, Is That Accessory Really Necessary? Ogden Nash. **CP-NashO**

How to keep—is there ány any, is there none such, nowhere known. The Leaden Echo and the Golden Echo. Gerard Manley Hopkins. **CP-HopkG**

How to Know Love from Deceit. William Blake. **CP-BlakW**

How To Like It. Stephen Dobyns. **SP-DobyS**

How to Live. What to Do. Wallace Stevens. **CP-StevW**

How to Make Rhubarb Wine. Ted Kooser. **SP-KoosT**

How to Name Your Familiar. Erica Jong. **SP-JongE**

How to Regain Your Soul. William Stafford. **SP-StafW**

How to remove oneself from oneself. Dying. Pablo Neruda, *tr. fr. Spanish by* Ben Belitt. **SP-NeruP**

How to repair my shattered ranks. Emily Dickinson. **SP-DickE**

How to Sleep. Philip Larkin. **CP-LarkP**

How to Speak Poetry, *see also* Commentary—How to Speak Poetry. Leonard Cohen. **CP-CoheL**

How to speak with the dead. In Memoriam Thomas Hardy. Charles Tomlinson. **CP-TomlC**

How to Stop Smoking. Miller Williams. **SP-WillM**

How To Tell One Country from Another. Margaret Atwood. **SP-AtwM2**

How to the invisible. Elementary Cosmogony. Charles Simic. **SP-SimiC**

How to Unbewitch a Backtracking Hound. Louise McNeill. **SP-McNeL**

How to Use a Storm. Richard Hugo. **CP-HugoR**

How unpleasant to meet Mr. Eliot! Lines for Cuscuscaraway and Mirza Murad Ali Beg. Thomas Stearns Eliot. **FiBHP; NBLV; NTP; OBAL; OBCoV; PeLV; PoPl; SpRo; UV; VoGa** *Fr.* Five-Finger Exercises. **CP-ElioT**

How uply screwed's the knot. On Being Denied for Being Already Took. David Markson. **CP-MarkD**

How vainly lovers marvel, all. A Lover's Garden. Allen Ginsberg. **CP-GinsA**

How vainly men themselves amaze. *see also* Hortus. Andrew Marvell. **CP-MarvA**

How vast is the chastisement of Beauty. Emily Dickinson. **SP-DickE**

How very hard it is to be. Easter-Day. Robert Browning. **CP-BroR1**

How Violets Came Blue. Robert Herrick. **CP-HerrR**

How Wallace fought for Scotland, left the name. Composed at Cora Linn in Sight of Wallace's Tower. William Wordsworth. **CP-WorW2**

How warm this woodland wild Recess! Recollections of Love. Samuel Taylor Coleridge. **CP-ColeS**

How was he first aware he would never walk again? Muriel Rukeyser. **CP-RukeM**

How was this I did not see. The Faded Face. Thomas Hardy. **CP-HardT**

How Water Began to Play. Ted Hughes. **SP-HughT**

How We Danced. Anne Sexton. **DIP** *Fr.* The Death of the Fathers. **CP-SextA**

How We Did It. Muriel Rukeyser. **CP-RukeM**

How we loved them. The Bicycles and the Apex. George Oppen. **CP-OppeG**

How we made them sleep and purified them. Chant to Be Used in Processions around a Site with Furnaces. Thomas Merton. **CP-MertT**; **SP-MertT**

How we marvel and must when most. Poem: How Marvelous Man's Kind Is. Delmore Schwartz. **SP-SchwD**

How welcome death would be. Welcome Death. David Herbert Lawrence. **CP-LawrD**

How well contented in this private Grange. His Grange. Robert Herrick. **CP-HerrR**

How well, fair crown of your fair sex, might he. To Mary, Lady Wroth. Ben Jonson. **CP-JonsB**

How well her name an *Army* doth present. Ana(Mary-Army)gram. George Herbert. **CP-HerbG**

How well I have repressed the dream of death I had after the war when I was nine in Newark. The Dream. Charles Kenneth Williams. **SP-WillC**

How well I knew Her not. Emily Dickinson. **CP-DickE**

How well I know what I mean to do. By the Fire-Side. Robert Browning. **CP-BroR1**

How well poore hart thou wittnes canst I love. Sonnet 36. Mary Sidney, Countess of Montgomery Wroth. *Fr.* Pamphilia to Amphilanthus. **CP-WrotM**

How well you served me above ground. Spirit's Song. Louise Bogan. **CP-BogaL**

How white how calm the hours are. This Man Was Your Brother. Kenneth Patchen. **CP-PatcK**

How will he hear the bell at school. Mutterings over the Crib of a Deaf Child. James Wright. **CP-WrigJ**

How will you catch these clues at the moment of waking. Clues. Muriel Rukeyser. **CP-RukeM**

How Wisdom and Folly meet, mix and unite. Sketch. Inscribed to the Rt. Hon. Ch. J. Fox Esq. Robert Burns. **CP-BurnR**

How wise age is—. Robert Creeley. **CP-CreeR**

How wise am I to have instructed the butler to instruct the first. I Do, I Will, I Have. Ogden Nash. **CP-NashO**

How wisely Nature did decree. Eyes and Tears. Andrew Marvell. **CP-MarvA**

How wonderful is Death. Daemon of the World, The; A Fragment. Percy Bysshe Shelley. **CP-ShelP**

How wonderful it is to say. A Word and Its Meaning. Marsden Hartley. **CP-HartM**

How wonderful, Tomasito! Celebration. Thomas McGrath. **SP-McGrT**

How wonderfully your songs begin. To Goethe: a Complaint. Wystan Hugh Auden. *Fr.* Shorts I ("Watch upon my wrist, The"). **CP-AudeW**

How would it be, then, if I showed you. Coyote's Song. William Dickey. **SP-DickW**

How would we know who we are. The Exile Takes Stock of His Surroundings. James McAuley. **SP-McAuJ**

How, yes how? In this mirrored maze—. Louis MacNeice. *Fr.* The Window. **CP-MacNL**

How, yes how! To achieve in a world of flux and bonfires. Louis MacNeice. *Fr.* The Window. **CP-MacNL**

How Yesterday Looked. Carl Sandburg. **CP-SandC**

How you murdered your family. Letter. Leonard Cohen. **CP-CoheL**

How you shine from the inside. In the Wet. Marge Piercy. **SP-PierM**

How young and fresh I am tonight. Ben Jonson. **CP-JonsB** *Fr.* Mercury Vindicated.

How young and unassuming. A Rogers Group. Robert Frost. **CP-FrosR**

Howard at Atlanta. John Greenleaf Whittier. **CP-WhitJ**

Howdy, Honey, Howdy! Paul Laurence Dunbar. **CP-DunbP**

Howe'er the brightness may amaze. Ben Jonson. **CP-JonsB** *Fr.* News from the New World.

However, / in all their games. Margaret Atwood. *Fr.* The Circle Game. **SP-AtwM1**

However artfully you transformed yourself. The Ample Garden. Robert Ranke Graves. **CP-GravR**

However it began, it began almost at once—. Life & Death in Skokie. Gary Gildner. **SP-GildG**

However just and anxious I have been. A Standing Ground. Wendell Berry. **CP-BerrW**

However legendary, / The stone is still a stone. The Diamond Cutters. Adrienne Rich. **CP-RicAE**; **SP-RicA1**; **SP-RicA2**

However that principle of reason. The Shapes and Intensities of This Man, This Confucius. Kenneth Patchen. **CP-PatcK**

However the image enters. Afterimages. Audre Lorde. **SP-LordA**

However you stem Nature. Emily Dickinson. **SP-DickE**

Howl. Allen Ginsberg. **CP-GinsA**

  "I saw the best minds of my generation destroyed by madness." **MoP**; **NaP**; **NoAM**; **NoP**; **PmAP**; **VCAP**

  "What sphinx of cement and aluminum bashed open their skulls." **NeAP**; **PoCh**; **SOTW**; **TAP**

Howle not you Ghosts & furies while I sing. Orpheus and Pluto. Robert Herrick. **CP-HerrR**

Howling of Wolves, The. Ted Hughes. **SP-HughT**

Howres for the Hours of Matines, The. Richard Crashaw. **CP-CrasR**

How's a man to write a sonnet, can you tell. The Poet and the Baby. Paul Laurence Dunbar. **CP-DunbP**

Hrishikesa, destroyer of Titans, ogres and canailles. Thomas Merton. **CP-MertT**

H.T. Louis Zukofsky. **CP-ZukLS**

Hub of the Universe, The. Walt Whitman. *See* I have said that the soul is not more than the body.

Hubbub of the Hall of Languages, our Babel, The. Sonnet. Hayden Carruth. **CP-CarHS** *Fr.* Sonnets.

Huc omnes pariter. Boethius, *tr. by* John Walton. **OBMV** *Fr.* Consolation of Philosophy, The ("De Consolacione Philosophie"). **CP-ChauG**

Huddle of Need, A. John Berryman. **CP-BerrJ**

Hudor / HUDOR et Pax. Canto 83. Ezra Pound. *Fr.* Cantos. **CP-PoCan**

Hudson Ferry. James Schuyler. **CP-SchuJ**

Hue and Cry, The. James Shirley. *See* In Love's name you are charged: oh, fly [*or* charged hereby].

Hue and Cry of John Lewars, The. Robert Burns. **CP-BurnR**

Hueless Love, The. George Meredith. **CP-MerG1**

Huff! Kitchen matches. Puff! Kitchen matches. Huge Man in Tight Pants. Gilbert Sorrentino. *Fr.* Twelve Études for Voice and Kazoo. **SP-SorrG**

Hug, The. Tess Gallagher. **SP-GallT**

Hug, The. Thom Gunn. **CP-GunnT**

Hug o' War. Shel Silverstein. **SP-SilS2**

Huge are the canna in the dreams of. Anecdote of Canna. Wallace Stevens. **CP-StevW**

Huge dog, Broderick, and, The. The Messengers. Robert Creeley. **CP-CreeR**

Huge Ear Rings. Charles Bukowski. **SP-BukC1**

Huge figure kneeling, The. The Strange, Moving Lights of People Handle Holinesses Unknown. Kenneth Patchen. **CP-PatcK**

Huge frostbank of the North, The. November: Indian Summer. Hayden Carruth. **CP-CarHS**

Huge head tosses on the roof of the village, A. How Old the World Is! Kenneth Patchen. **CP-PatcK**

Huge Leviathian, The. Edmund Spenser. *See* Toward the sea turning my troubled eye.

Huge Man in Tight Pants. Gilbert Sorrentino. *Fr.* Twelve Études for Voice and Kazoo. **SP-SorrG**

Huge old female on the drum, The. On the Drum. David Herbert Lawrence. **CP-LawrD**

Huge red-buttressed mesa over yonder, The. Rain in the Desert. John Gould Fletcher. *Fr.* Arizona Poems. **SP-FletJ**

Huge upon the hazy plain. Grazing Locomotives. Archibald MacLeish. **CP-MacLA**

Huge vapours brood above the clifted shore. Written near a Port on a Dark Evening. Charlotte Smith. **CP-SmitC**

Huge white poplar half fills the prison garden, A. Wronke, Spring 1917. Jane Cooper. *Fr.* Threads: Rosa Luxemburg from Prison. **SP-CoopJ**

Huge wound in my head began to heal, The. The Wound. Thom Gunn. **CP-GunnT**

Hugerl, for a decade now. Glad. Wystan Hugh Auden. *Fr.* Three Posthumous Poems. **CP-AudeW**

Hugest of engines, a much limited man. George Meredith. *Fr.* Napoléon. **CP-MerG1**

Hugh Selwyn Mauberley. Ezra Pound. *See* For three years, out of key with his time.

Hugh Selwyn Mauberley. (Life and Contacts). Ezra Pound. **SP-PounE**

"Age demanded an image, The." **HAP; MoAmPo; VGW**

"Beneath the sagging roof." **MoAmPo**

Brennbaum. **MoAmPo**

"Conservatrix of Milesien."

"Daphne with her thighs in bark."

Envoi (1919). **HAP; MoP; UnPo; VGW**

(Envoi: "Go, dumb-born book.") **MoAB; MoAmPo; OxBA**

"For three years, out of key with his time." **FaBoMo; HAP; MeMAP; MoAmPo; MoP; NAAL-2; NoAM; OxBA; UnPo; VGW**

(E. P. Ode Pour l'Election de Son Sepulchre.) **HAP; MoAmPo; MoP; NAAL-2; NoAM; VGW**

(Hugh Selwyn Mauberley.) **MeMAP**

(Pour l'Election de Son Sepulchre, I-V.) **FaBoMo**

Mauberly (1920).

Age Demanded, The.

"For three years, diabolus in the scale."

"Luini in porcelain!"

"Scattered Moluccas."

"Turned from the 'eau-forte'."

Mr. Nixon. **MoAmPo**

Siena Mi Fe'; Disfecemi Maremma. **MoAmPo**

"Tea-rose tea-gown, etc., The." **MoAmPo; NOBE**

"There died a myriad." **FF; FaBoEH; MoAmPo; NOBE; PoE; TRP; WaaP**

"These fought in any case." **FF; FaBoEH; HeIL; HeIP; MoAmPo; NOBE; OBWP; PoE; PoWW; TRP; VGW; WaaP**

Yeux Glauques. **MoAmPo**

Hugh Stuart Boyd [His Blindness]. Elizabeth Barrett Browning. **CP-BroEB**

Hugh Stuart Boyd [His Death, 1848]. Elizabeth Barrett Browning. **CP-BroEB**

Hugh Stuart Boyd [Legacies]. Elizabeth Barrett Browning. **CP-BroEB**

Hughie Graham. Robert Burns. **CP-BurnR**

Hughley Steeple. Alfred Edward Housman. **CP-HousA**

Hugy spider stooping through the door, The. Some Oddities. Donald Hall. **CP-HallD**

Hui Tzu said to Chang Tzu. The Useless. Chuang Tzu, *tr. fr. Chinese by* Thomas Merton. **CP-MertT**

Hui Tzu said to Chuang: / I have a big tree. The Useless Tree. Chuang Tzu, *tr. fr. Chinese by* Thomas Merton. **CP-MertT**

Hui Tzu was Prime Minister of Liang. Owl and Phoenix. Chuang Tzu, *tr. fr. Chinese by* Thomas Merton. **CP-MertT**

Huitzilopochtli Gives the Black Blade of Death. David Herbert Lawrence. **CP-LawrD**

Huitzilopochtli's Watch. David Herbert Lawrence. **CP-LawrD**

Hula-Hula. William Carlos Williams. **CP-WilW1**

Hulk, three masted once, three stubbed now, A. The Benefits of an Education. John Ciardi. **SP-CiarJ**

Hum and whisper of the class, like a little wind, The. Morning / Scripture Lesson. David Herbert Lawrence. *Fr.* The Schoolmaster [A]. **CP-LawrD**

Hūm Bom! Allen Ginsberg. **CP-GinsA**

Hum drum, sauce for a cony. Ben Jonson. **CP-JonsB** *Fr.* Christmas His Masque.

Hum of shaft-wheel, whirr and clamour. The Rhondda. Alun Lewis. **CP-LewiA**

Hum of the bees in the pear-tree bloom, The. She Was a Good Little Wife. David Herbert Lawrence. **CP-LawrD**

Human Abstract, The. William Blake. **CP-BlakW** *Fr.* Songs of Experience.

Human Affection. Stevie Smith. **CP-SmitS**

Human all key mog knee this pecks it loom in a moon the. Catullus. *See* Carmen 66: "Who scans the bright machinery of the skies."

Human Arrangement. Wallace Stevens. **CP-StevW**

Human Being is a Lonely Creature, The. Richard Eberhart. **CP-EberR**

Human Communion. Traces, The. Robert Duncan. **SP-DuncR**

Human Condition, The. Howard Nemerov. **CP-NemeH**

Human Dignity. William Butler Yeats. *Fr.* A Man Young and Old. **CP-YeatW**

Human Fabric, The. Robert Penn Warren. *Fr.* Fall Comes in Back-Country Vermont. **SP-WarrR**

Human Face, The. David Herbert Lawrence. **CP-LawrD**

Human face becoming locked insect face. Richard Hunt's "Arachne." Robert Earl Hayden. **CP-HaydR**

Human Folly. Alexander Pope. *See* Whate'er the passion--knowledge, fame, or pelf.

Human Frailty. William Cowper. **CP-CowpW**

Human Hymn. Vasil Sotirov, *tr. fr. Bulgarian by* William Matthews. **SP-MattW**

Human Image, The, *see also* The Human Abstract. William Blake. **CP-BlakW**

Human kites, fantastic. Charles Henri Ford. **SP-FordC** *Fr.* Emblems of Arachne.

Human Life. Tom Clark. **SP-ClarT**

Human Life; on the Denial of Immortality. Samuel Taylor Coleridge. **CP-ColeS**

Human Life's Mystery. Elizabeth Barrett Browning. **CP-BroEB**

Human Love is all electrical, a whirring. Jolt. Al Young. **CP-YounA**

Human Pile, The. Robert Pack. **SP-PackR**

Human Sacrifice, The. John Greenleaf Whittier. **CP-WhitJ**

Human Seasons, The. John Keats. **CP-KeatJ**

Human soul was threshed out like maize in the endless, The. The Heights of Macchu Picchu, III. Pablo Neruda, *tr. fr. Spanish by* James Wright. **CP-WrigJ**

Human spirits saw I on a day, The. Arthur Hugh Clough. **SP-ClouA**

Human Things. Howard Nemerov. **CP-NemeH**

Human will is free, ultimately, to choose one of two things, The. Free Will. David Herbert Lawrence. **CP-LawrD**

Humane Materialist at the Burning of a Heretic, A. Stevie Smith. **CP-SmitS**

Humanist, The. Richard Eberhart. **CP-EberR**

Humanist, The. Geoffrey Hill. **CP-HillG**

Humanist, The. Alun Lewis. **CP-LewiA**

Humanist's Tragedy, The. Robinson Jeffers. **CP-JefR1**

Humanities Building, The. Karl Shapiro. **SP-ShapK**

Humanities Course. John Updike. **CP-UpdiJ**

Humanity. Walter de la Mare. **CP-DeLaW**

Humanity. William Wordsworth. **CP-WorW2**

Humanity, delighting to behold. The French Army in Russia 1812–1813. William Wordsworth. **CP-WorW2**

Humanity i love you. Edward Estlin Cummings. **CP-CummE; SP-CummE**

Humanity Needs Pruning. David Herbert Lawrence. **CP-LawrD**

Humanly Speaking. Donald Davie. **CP-DavDo**

Humble-Bee, The. Ralph Waldo Emerson. **CP-EmerR**

Humble in victory, chivalrous in defeat. 1930's. Robert Lowell. **SP-LoweR**

Humble lichens dye with gold these grey stone walls, The. Skyreholme Mill. Wystan Hugh Auden. **CP-AudWJ**

Humble one(gifted with / illimitable joy). Edward Estlin Cummings. **CP-CummE**

Humble Petition of Bruar Water to the Noble Duke of Athole, The. Robert Burns. **CP-BurnR**

"Sober laverock, warbling wild, The." **PBBP**

Humble Petition of Poor Ben to the Best of Monarchs, Masters, Men, King Charles, The. Ben Jonson. **CP-JonsB**

Humble we must be, if to Heaven we go. Humility. Robert Herrick. **CP-HerrR**

Humbly—but without caution in unbridled vigor of faith: acceptful. Court of First Appeal. Kenneth Patchen. **CP-PatcK**

Humdrum. Carl Sandburg. **CP-SandC**

Humid air precipitates, The. Archibald MacLeish. **CP-MacLA** *Fr.* The Happy Marriage.

Humiliation. David Herbert Lawrence. **CP-LawrD**

Humility. Robert Browning. **CP-BroR2**

Humility. George Herbert. **CP-HerbG**

Humility. Robert Herrick. **CP-HerrR**

Humility. David Herbert Lawrence. **CP-LawrD**

Humility Mongers. David Herbert Lawrence. **CP-LawrD**

Humility the Mother of Charity. Samuel Taylor Coleridge. **CP-ColeS**

Hummer, The. William Matthews. **SP-MattW**

Humming a Tune for an Old Lady in West Virginia. James Wright. **CP-WrigJ**

Humming bee—a little tinkling rill, A. Despondency. William Wordsworth. *Fr.* The Excursion. **CP-WorW2**

Humming-Bird. David Herbert Lawrence. **CP-LawrD**

Humming bird darning the trumpet vine, A. 11:02 A.M. The Bird Disappeared. John Ciardi. **SP-CiarJ**

Humming Birds and Orioles. Emily Dickinson. **SP-DickE**

Humming like a hawk in motion. Poem for Omar Khayyam (1050?-1123? A.D.) Al Young. **CP-YounA**

Hummingbird make yr mark he said and then something about. Thank God for Alleys. Charles Bukowski. **SP-BukC2**

Hummingbird Pauses at the Trumpet Vine. Mary Oliver. **SP-OlivM**

Hummingbird, slow through the camera, A. For Robert Smithson. Jim Carroll. **SP-CarrJ**

Hummingbird Woman. Carl Sandburg. **CP-SandC**

Humoresque. Edna St. Vincent Millay. **CP-MillE**

Humpbacks. Mary Oliver. **SP-OlivM**

Humpty Dumpty. Wystan Hugh Auden. **CP-AudWJ**

Humpty Dumpty. May Sarton. **SP-SartM**

Humpty Dumpty's Recitation. "Lewis Carroll." *See* In winter, when the fields are white.

Hun turned sculptor spoke, A. Sculptures in Hungary. Donald Davie. **CP-DavDo**

Hunchback Girl: She Thinks of Heaven. Gwendolyn Brooks. *Fr.* A Street in Bronzeville. **SP-BrooG**

Hunchback in the Park, The. Dylan Thomas. **CP-ThomD**

Hunchback in the park with halo of pigeons, The. Emblems of Exile. Thomas McGrath. **SP-McGrT**

Hunchback on the corner, with gum and shoelaces, The. Pursuit. Robert Penn Warren. **SP-WarrR**

Hunched in the dark beneath his mother's heart. The Origin of Laughter. John Updike. **CP-UpdiJ**

Huncks ha's no money (he do's sweare, or say). Upon Huncks: Epigram. Robert Herrick. **CP-HerrR**

Hundred, a thousand to one; even so, A. In the Round Tower at Jhansi, June 8, 1857. Christina Georgina Rossetti. **CP-RosC1**

Hundred Collars, A. Robert Frost. **CP-FrosR**

Hundred mares, all white! their manes, A. The Mares of the Camargue. Frédéric Mistral, *tr.* by George Meredith. **CP-MerG1** *Fr.* Mirèio.

Hundred million cars running out of gasoline. Yes and It's Hopeless. Allen Ginsberg. **CP-GinsA**

Hundred thousand birds salute the day, A. Christina Georgina Rossetti. *Fr.* Later Life: A Double Sonnet of Sonnets. **CP-RosC2**

Hundred yards along the other side, A. The Prisoners on the Roof. John Hewitt. **CP-HewiJ**

Hundred years have passed, and he, The. October 21, 1905. George Meredith. **CP-MerG2**

Hundred years I slept beneath a thorn, A. The Traveller. Kathleen Jessie Raine. **SP-RainK**

Hundred Years Since, A. Thomas Hardy. **CP-HardT**

Hundreds of birds are singing in the square. Marché aux Oiseaux. Richard Wilbur. **CP-WilbR**

Hundreds of birds in the air. 14 November, 1973. Sir John Betjeman. **CP-BetjJ**

Hundreds of yards of woodland. The Forest Beyond the Glass. Lewis Turco. **SP-TurcL**

Hundreds upon hundreds of years of Lapiths. Prelude. Roy Fisher. **SP-FishR** *Fr.* On the Neglect of Figure Composition.

Hung from a foot, I walk upon my head. Eight Riddles from Symphosius. Richard Wilbur. **CP-WilbR**

Hung there in the thermal. Vultures. Margaret Atwood. **SP-AtwM2**

Hung up there in the sky. Looking at the Stars. Richard Eberhart. **CP-EberR**

Hung Wu Vase, The. Robert Ranke Graves. **CP-GravR**

Hungarian Air. George Meredith. **CP-MerG2**

Hungarian Horse-Herd, The. Karl Beck, *tr. fr.* German by George Meredith. **CP-MerG2**

Hunger. Robert Creeley. **CP-CreeR**

Hunger. Countee Cullen. **CP-CullC**

Hunger. John Haines. **SP-HainJ**

Hunger. Robert Herrick. **CP-HerrR**

Hunger. Malcolm Lowry. **CP-LowrM**

Hunger / of Mountains / spoke. Cries from Chiapas. Muriel Rukeyser. **CP-RukeM**

Hunger. Adrienne Rich. **SP-RicA2**

Hunger and Cold. Carl Sandburg. **CP-SandC**

Hunger and only hunger changes worlds? Carl Sandburg. *Fr.* The People, Yes. **CP-SandC**

Hunger, and sultry heat, and nipping blast. The French and the Spanish Guerrillas. William Wordsworth. **CP-WorW1**

Hunger long gone holds little heroic. Hunger and Cold. Carl Sandburg. **CP-SandC**

Hunger Moon. Jane Cooper. **CABA** *Fr.* March. **SP-CoopJ**

Hungerfield. Robinson Jeffers. **CP-JefR3**

Hungry and Laughing Men. Carl Sandburg. **CP-SandC**

Hungry cancer will not let him rest, A. A Thorn Forever in the Breast. Countee Cullen. **CP-CullC**

Hungry for music with a desperate hunger. Written for a Musician. Nicholas Vachel Lindsay. **CP-LindV**

Hungry Mungry. Shel Silverstein. **SP-SilS2**

Hungry winter, this winter. To Hell with It. Frank O'Hara. **SP-OharF**

Hunt. Kay Boyle. **CP-BoylK**

Hunt, The. Alexander Pope. **NIP** *Fr.* Windsor-Forest [*or* Windsor Forest]. **CP-PopeA**

Hunt by Night, The. Derek Mahon. **SP-MahoD**

Hunt ceases, The. St. Eustace. Derek Mahon. **SP-MahoD**

Hunt Goes By, The. Howard Nemerov. *Fr.* Epigrams: "Wasp, climbing the window pane." **CP-NemeH**

Hunt, hunt again. If you do not find it, you. Treasure Hunt. Robert Penn Warren. **SP-WarrR**

Hunt in the Black Forest, A. Randall Jarrell. **CP-JarrR**

Hunted by friends who think that life is play. In the Immaculate Conception Church. Nicholas Vachel Lindsay. **CP-LindV**

Hunted City, The. Kenneth Patchen. **CP-PatcK**

"Gatherers of wild seed and froststained fruit."

"How at the midnight of his age the Poet hurls himself on the."

"I compel you to question me about my motives."

"I despise these poets with their puerile little chalk-talks of the soul."

"I saw three hundred fat cattle putting their forlornly comic faces."

"Little hill climbs up to the village and puts its green hands, The." **NaP**

"That blue hole, Heaven, carry its tide over the wounded within."

Hunter, The. Walter de la Mare. **CP-DeLaW**

Hunter, The. Ogden Nash. **CP-NashO**

Hunter, The. Frank O'Hara. **SP-OharF**

Hunter, The. Kenneth Patchen. **CP-PatcK**

Hunter, The. William Carlos Williams. **CP-WilW1**

Hunter, Prey. Dabney Stuart. **SP-StuaD**

Hunter Trials. Sir John Betjeman. **CP-BetjJ**

Hunter Went Killing: A Fable, A. Edwin Rolfe. **CP-RolfE**

Hunters are back / from beating the winter's face, The. The Woman Thing. Audre Lorde. **SP-LordA**

Hunters in the Snow, The. William Carlos Williams. **LCAP** *Fr.* Pictures from Brueghel. **CP-WilW2**

Hunter's Moon—Eating the Bear. Mary Oliver. **SP-OlivM**

Hunters of Men, The. John Greenleaf Whittier. **CP-WhitJ**

Hunters' shack will do, The. Holding Out. Adrienne Rich. **CP-RicAE; SP-RicA2**

Hunting. Robert Pack. **SP-PackR**

Hunting. Gary Snyder. *Fr.* Myths and Texts.

First Shaman Song. **CP-SnydG**

"Flung from demonic wombs." **CP-SnydG**

"How rare to be born a human being!" **CP-SnydG**

"Now I'll also tell what food." **CP-SnydG**

"Sealion, salmon, offshore." **CP-SnydG**

This Poem Is for Bear. **CP-SnydG**

This Poem Is for Birds. **CP-SnydG**

This Poem Is for Deer. **CP-SnydG**

Hunting and Fishing. Alexander Pope. *See* See! from the brake the whirring Pheasant springs.

Hunting and gathering in sexual refuge theatre. Theatre. Tom Clark. **SP-ClarT**

Hunting Civil War Relics at Nimblewill Creek. James Dickey. **CP-DickJ**

Hunting for coppers of Alaskan braves. The Only Relic. Isabella Gardner. **CP-GardI**

Hunting for the truly human. The Humanist. Richard Eberhart. **CP-EberR**

Hunting Moon. Lewis Turco. **SP-TurcL**

Hunting of the Snark, The. "Lewis Carroll." **CP-CarrL**

Baker's Tale, The. **EBEV; NAEL-2; OXAEP-2**

"Bellman himself they all praised to the skies—, The." **OBCoV**

Dedication.

Fit the Fifth: The Beaver's Lesson.

Fit the Fourth: The Hunting.

Fit the Seventh: The Banker's Fate.

Fit the Sixth: The Barrister's Dream. **EBNV**

" 'Just the place for a Snark!' the Bellman cried." **EBEvV; FaPoB**

(Fit the First: The Landing.) **EBEvV**

Vanishing, The. **OXAEP-2**

Hunting Pheasants in a Cornfield. Robert Bly. **SP-BlyR**

Hunting Season. Wystan Hugh Auden. **CP-AudeW**

Hunting season: / Once every year, the Deer catch human beings. They. Long Hair. Gary Snyder. **CP-SnydG**

Hunting Song. Robert Burns. **CP-BurnR**

Hunting Song. Samuel Taylor Coleridge. *See* Up, up! ye dames, ye [*or* dames and ye] lasses gay!

Hunting Song. Paul Laurence Dunbar. **CP-DunbP**

Hunting Song. Sir Walter Scott. **SP-ScotW**

Hunting Song of the Seeonee Pack. Rudyard Kipling. **CP-KiplR** *Fr.* Mowgli's Brothers. *Fr.* The Jungle Book.

Huntingdonshire. Donald Davie. **CP-DavDo**

Huntington sleeps in a house six feet long. Southern Pacific. Carl Sandburg. **CP-SandC**

Huntress. Hilda Doolittle. **CP-DoolH**

Huntress and Her Dogs, The. "Hugh MacDiarmid." *Fr.* Au Clair de la Lune. **SP-MacDH**

Huntsman, What Quarry? Edna St. Vincent Millay. **CP-MillE**

Huon of Bordeaux. Robert Duncan. **SP-DuncR**

Hup! I come to a halt, facing the sea. Count. James McAuley. *Fr.* The Exile on His Failing Vision. **SP-McAuJ**

Hurdle of water, and O these waters are cold. Formal Elegy. John Berryman. **CP-BerrJ**

HURLUB / ERL UH. Thomas Merton. *Fr.* A Selection of Concrete Poems. **CP-MertT**

Hurrah for revolution and more cannon shot. The Great Day. William Butler Yeats. **CP-YeatW**

Hurrah for the next. On Hearing About the Death of Mitzi Mayfair. Miller Williams. **SP-WillM**

Hurrah! the seaward breezes. The Fishermen. John Greenleaf Whittier. **CP-WhitJ**

Hurrahing in Harvest. Gerard Manley Hopkins. **CP-HopkG**

Hurray! Hurry! / Come through the keyhole. Starvation. Maya Angelou. **SP-AngeM**

Hurree Chunder Mookerjee, pride of Bow Bazar. What Happened. Rudyard Kipling. **CP-KiplR**

Hurricane, The. Hart Crane. **CP-CranH**

Hurricane. "Bob Dylan" *and* Jacques Levy. **CP-DylaB**

Hurricane. Archibald MacLeish. **CP-MacLA**

Hurricane, The. William Carlos Williams. **CP-WilW2**

Hurricane and Eclipse. Jim Morrison. **SP-MorrJ**

Hurricane Season. Charles Simic. **SP-SimiC**

Hurried Meeting, A. Thomas Hardy. **CP-HardT**

Hurried meeting called for Law Reform, The. As You Like It. John Hewitt. **CP-HewiJ**

Hurry, Godfather death. Godfather Death. Anne Sexton. **CP-SextA**

Hurry of bell-notes, A. Station Island. Seamus Heaney. **SP-HeanS**

Hurry to bless the hands that play. The Players Ask for a Blessing on the Psalteries and on Themselves. William Butler Yeats. **CP-YeatW**

Hurry to Your Dinner, *see also* Commentary—Hurry to Your Dinner. Leonard Cohen. **CP-CoheL**

Hurry Up Please It's Time. Anne Sexton. **CP-SextA**

Hurry, worry, unwary. Old Amusement Park. Marianne Craig Moore. **CP-MoorM**

Hurrying to catch my Comet. Naturally the Foundation Will Bear Your Expenses. Philip Larkin. **CP-LarkP**

Hurt Hawks. Robinson Jeffers. **CP-JefR1**

Hurt No Living Thing. Christina Georgina Rossetti. **CP-RosC2**

Hurt No Living Thing. Christina Georgina Rossetti. **FM; FaPON; OTCP; PDV; RHPC; SiSoPo; SiSoSe; SoPo; TSS** *Fr.* Sing-Song. **CP-RosC2**

Hurt was the nation with a mighty wound. Lincoln. Paul Laurence Dunbar. **CP-DunbP**

Hurucan. Derek Walcott. **CP-WalcD**

Husband, / last night I dreamt. Where It Was at Back Then. Anne Sexton. **CP-SextA**

Husband. Miller Williams. **SP-WillM**

Husband and Wife. Christina Georgina Rossetti. **CP-RosC3**

Husband and wife had planned it for a long time, The. Trying. Miller Williams. **SP-WillM**

Husband has the nearest acres, The. Ralph Waldo Emerson. **CP-EmerR**

Husband, husband, cease your strife. English Song. Robert Burns. **CP-BurnR**

Husband is a man who two minutes after his head touches the, A. The Trouble with Women Is Men. Ogden Nash. **CP-NashO**

Husband of the widow care for her, The. Our Widowed Queen. Christina Georgina Rossetti. **CP-RosC3**

Husband stands at door of flat. How to Harry a Husband, or, Is That Accessory Really Necessary? Ogden Nash. **CP-NashO**

Husbandry. Barton Sutter. **SP-SuttB**

Husbands are things that wives have to get used to putting up with. What Almost Every Woman Knows Sooner or Later. Ogden Nash. **CP-NashO**

Husband's View, The. Thomas Hardy. **CP-HardT**

Hush! Ralph Waldo Emerson. *Fr.* Quatrains. **CP-EmerR**

Hush) / noones / are coming. Edward Estlin Cummings. **CP-CummE**

Hush. David St. John. **SP-StJoD**

Hush-a-by lady, in Alice's lap! The Red Queen's Lullaby. "Lewis Carroll." **CP-CarrL** *Fr.* Through the Looking-Glass.

Hush-ah-hush, hush-ah-hush, lullaby. Pioneer Lullaby. Rennie McOwan. **SP-McNeL**

Hush, Here They Come. Ogden Nash. **CP-NashO**

Hush, hush! tread softly! hush, hush my dear. Song. John Keats. **CP-KeatJ**

Hush is over all the teeming lists, A. Frederick Douglass. Paul Laurence Dunbar. **CP-DunbP**

Hush then / why do you cry? Why Does She Weep? David Herbert Lawrence. **CP-LawrD**

Hush, thrush! / Hush, missen-thrush, I listen. Elegy in April and September. Wilfred Owen. **CP-OwenW**

Hush! ye clamorous Cares! be mute! To the Rev. W. J. Hort. Samuel Taylor Coleridge. **CP-ColeS**

Hushaby baby, on a tree top. Broadcasting to the G.B.P. David Herbert Lawrence. **CP-LawrD**

Hushaby, hushaby, dark one at my knee. A Negro Mother's Lullaby. Countee Cullen. **CP-CullC**

Hush'd are the winds, and still the evening gloom. On the Death of a Young Lady. Byron. **CP-Byron**

Hush'd be the Camps To-day. Walt Whitman. **OHIP; SAmP** *Fr.* Memories of President Lincoln. **CP-WhitW**

Hushed now the sweet consoling tongue. On a Fly-Leaf of Longfellow's Poems. John Greenleaf Whittier. **CP-WhitJ**

Hushing of the Wye, The. Tennyson. *See* The Danube to the Severn gave.

Huskers, The. John Greenleaf Whittier. **CP-WhitJ**
  Corn-Song, The. **GN; OHIP**

Husks, rags and bones, waste paper, excrement. Hell. Robert Ranke Graves. **CP-GravR**

Hustings, The ("Future sucks, The"). Charles Olson. **CP-OlsoC**

Hustings, The ("Under the eyes"). Charles Olson. **CP-OlsoC**

Hustle, The. Charles Bukowski. **SP-BukC3**

Hut of the man alone, The. Donald Hall. **CP-HallD**

Hutch. Anne Sexton. **CP-SextA**

Huxley Hall. Sir John Betjeman. **CP-BetjJ**

Huzza! Hodgson, we are going. Lines to Mr Hodgson. Byron. **CP-Byron**

Hyacinth. Hilda Doolittle. **CP-DoolH**

Hyacinth. Louise Glück. **SP-GlücL**

Hyacinth. Edna St. Vincent Millay. **CP-MillE**

Hyacinth, The. Kathleen Jessie Raine. **SP-RainK**

Hyacinth. Louis Zukofsky. **CP-ZukLS**

Hyænas [*or* Hyenas], The. Rudyard Kipling. **CP-KiplR**

Hyde Park at Night, before the War. David Herbert Lawrence. **CP-LawrD**

Hyde Park was only like Avondale in that. Many Mansions. James Liddy. **CP-LiddJ**

Hydra 1960. Leonard Cohen. **CP-CoheL**

Hydrangea, The / pink cheeked nods its head. The Lesson. William Carlos Williams. **CP-WilW2**

Hyeah come Cæesar Higgins. Jealous. Paul Laurence Dunbar. **CP-DunbP**

Hyeah dat singin' in de medders. When Sam'l Sings. Paul Laurence Dunbar. **CP-DunbP**

Hygiene. David Markson. **CP-MarkD**

Hygienic bells, pale. The Bells: a Period Piece. Charles Tomlinson. *Fr.* Antecedents. **CP-TomlC**

Hyla Brook. Robert Frost. **CP-FrosR**

Hymen. Hilda Doolittle. **CP-DoolH**
  For Bryher and Perdita.
  "Never more will the wind." **CTC; TrGrPo**

Hymen, O Hymen king. Cassandra. Hilda Doolittle. **CP-DoolH**

Hymeneal. Catullus. **PeHV,** *tr. by* James Michie; *Fr.* Carmen 61: "Hill (breeder) of Helicon." **CP-ZukLS; OxBM** *Fr.* Carmina. **CP-Catul**

Hymeneal[l] Dialogue, An. Thomas Carew. **CP-CareT**

Hymmnn. Allen Ginsberg. **CP-GinsA**

Hymn: "At morn—at noon—at twilight dim." Edgar Allan Poe. **CP-PoeEd**

Hymn, The. Richard Crashaw. *See* In the Holy Nativity of Our Lord God.

Hymn: "I well remember / A time when." Alice Walker. **CP-WalkA**

Hymn: "Nativity of Our Lord and Saviour Jesus Christ, The." Christopher Smart. *See* The Nativity of Our Lord and Saviour Jesus Christ.

Hymn: "Noon in an English county." John Hewitt. **CP-HewiJ**

Hymn: "O Holy Father! just and true." John Greenleaf Whittier. **CP-WhitJ**

Hymn: "O li'l lamb out in de col' ". Paul Laurence Dunbar. **CP-DunbP**

Hymn: "O the bitter shame and sorrow." Christina Georgina Rossetti. **CP-RosC3**

Hymn: "O Thou, whose presence went before." John Greenleaf Whittier. **CP-WhitJ**

Hymn: "Room, room, make room for the bouncing belly." Ben Jonson. **CP-JonsB** *Fr.* Pleasure Reconciled to Virtue.

Hymn: "To the God Who reigns on high." Christina Georgina Rossetti. **CP-RosC3**

Hymn: "We hadn't eaten in two days. we were entirely intoxicated." Patti Smith. **SP-SmitP**

Hymn: "When storms arise." Paul Laurence Dunbar. **CP-DunbP**

Hymn, A: "Lead gently, Lord, and slow." Paul Laurence Dunbar. **CP-DunbP**

Hymn Among the Ruins. Octavio Paz, *tr. fr. Spanish by* William Carlos Williams. **CP-WilW2**

Hymn before Action. Rudyard Kipling. **CP-KiplR**

Hymn before Sunrise, in the Vale of Chamouni. Samuel Taylor Coleridge. **CP-ColeS**

Hymn for Christmas Day, A. Christina Georgina Rossetti. **CP-RosC3**

Hymn for New Year's Day. Richard Crashaw. **CP-CrasR**

Hymn for Saturday. Christopher Smart. *See* For Saturday.

Hymn for the Boatmen, as They Approach the Rapids under the Castle of Heidelberg. William Wordsworth. *Fr.* Memorials of a Tour of the Continent; 1820. **CP-WorW2**

Hymn for the Celebration of Emancipation at Newburyport. John Greenleaf Whittier. **CP-WhitJ**

Hymn for the Dead. Sir Walter Scott. **SP-ScotW** *Fr.* The Lay of the Last Minstrel.

Hymn for the Feast of Duns Scotus. Thomas Merton. **CP-MertT**

Hymn for the House of Worship at Georgetown. John Greenleaf Whittier. **CP-WhitJ**

Hymn for the Opening of Plymouth Church. John Greenleaf Whittier. **CP-WhitJ**

Hymn for the Opening of Thomas Starr King's House of Worship. John Greenleaf Whittier. **CP-WhitJ**

Hymn for the Sunday School at Olney. William Cowper. **CP-CowpW**

Hymn from a Watermelon Pavilion. Wallace Stevens. **CP-StevW**

Hymn in the Assumption. Richard Crashaw. **CP-CrasR**

Hymn in the Glorious Epiphanie. Richard Crashaw. *See* Bright Babe! whose awfull beautyes [*or* beauties] make.

Hymn of Breaking Strain. Rudyard Kipling. **CP-KiplR**

Hymn of Empedocles. Matthew Arnold. *See* It is so small a thing.

Hymn of Not Much Praise for New York City. Thomas Merton. **CP-MertT**

Hymn of Pan. Percy Bysshe Shelley. **CP-ShelP**

Hymn of the Children. John Greenleaf Whittier. **CP-WhitJ**

Hymn of the Dunkers. John Greenleaf Whittier. **CP-WhitJ**

Hymn of the Triumphant Airman. Rudyard Kipling. **CP-KiplR**

Hymn of the World Without. Bible, *O.T. See* Psalm 104: "Bless the Lord, O my soul. . . ."

Hymn on Solitude. James Thomson. **CP-ThomJ**

Hymn on the Morning of Christ's Nativity [*or* On the Morning of Christ's Nativity]. John Milton. **FiP; NAEL-1; NOBE; OBEV; OtMeF** *Fr.* On the Morning of Christs Nativity. **CP-MiltJ**

"But peaceful was the night." **FaBoCh**

"Oracles are dumm, The." **GrIP**

Hymn[e] on the Nativity [*or* Nativitie] of My Saviour, A. Ben Jonson. **CP-JonsB**

Hymn on the Seasons, A. James Thomson. **EnRP; LAuP; OxBoCh** *Fr.* The Seasons. **CP-ThomJ**

Hymn Sung at Christmas by the Scholars of St. Helena's Island, S.C. John Greenleaf Whittier. **CP-WhitJ**

Hymn[:] Sung at the Completion of the Concord Monument, April 19, 1836. Ralph Waldo Emerson. *See* By the rude bridge that arched the flood.

Hymn Sung at the Second Church, Boston, at the Ordination of Rev. Chandler Robbins. Ralph Waldo Emerson. **CP-EmerR**

Hymn 10. William Cowper. *See* The Future Peace and Glory of the Church.

Hymn to a Trench Gun. Kenneth Patchen. **CP-PatcK**

Hymn to Adversity. Thomas Gray. **CP-GrayT**

Hymn[e] to Bacchus, A ("Bacchus, let . . ."). Robert Herrick. **CP-HerrR**

Hymn to Castor and Pollux. *Unknown. Fr.* Homeric Hymns.

(Homer's Hymn to Castor and Pollux.) **CP-ShelP**

Hymn [*or* Hymne] to Christ, at the Author's Last Going into Germany, A. John Donne. **CP-DonnJ**

Dark Churches. **FaBoRV**

Hymn to Colour. George Meredith. **CP-MerG1**

Hymn to Commerce. Thomas Merton. **CP-MertT**

Hymn to Diana. Catullus. *See* Carmen 34: "Moving in her radiant care."

Hymn to Earth the Mother of All. *Unknown. Fr.* Homeric Hymns.

(Homer's Hymn to the Earth: Mother of All.) **CP-ShelP**

Hymn to Eros. Denise Levertov. **CP-LeveD**

Hymn[e] to God My God, In My Sicknesse[e]. John Donne. **CP-DonnJ**

Hymn to God the Father, A. John Donne. **CP-DonnJ**

Hymn[e] to God the Father, A. Ben Jonson. **CP-JonsB**

Hymn to God's Power. James Thomson. **CP-ThomJ**

Hymn to Ignorance. Thomas Gray. **CP-GrayT**

Hymn to Intellectual Beauty. Percy Bysshe Shelley. **CP-ShelP**

Hymn to Life. James Schuyler. **CP-SchuJ**

Hymn to Light. John Milton. *See* Hail holy Light, ofspring [*or* offspring] of Heav'n [*or* Heaven] first-born.

Hymn to Love and Life. Charlotte Smith. **CP-SmitC**

Hymn to Love Ended. William Carlos Williams. **CP-WilW1**

Hymn to Mercury. *Unknown.* **CP-ShelP** *Fr.* Homeric Hymns.

Hymn to Nothingness. David Herbert Lawrence. **CP-LawrD**

Hymn to Pan. John Keats. **ChER; MeMBP; OBRV; PoEL-4** *Fr.* Endymion: Poetic Romance. **CP-KeatJ**

Hymn to Physical Pain. Rudyard Kipling. **CP-KiplR**

Hymn to Priapus. David Herbert Lawrence. **CP-LawrD**

Hymn to Proserpine. Charles Olson. **CP-OlsoC**

Hymn to Saint Teresa. Richard Crashaw. *See* A Hymn to Sainte Teresa.

Hymn to Sainte Teresa, A. Richard Crashaw. **HAP; NOSC** *Fr.* A Hymn to the Name and Hono[u]r of the Admirable Saint[e] T[h]eresa. **CP-CrasR**

(Hymn to Saint Teresa.) **ACP; EBEV; ESCV; GeHe; MeLP; MePo; WGRP**

Hymn to Selene. *Unknown. Fr.* Homeric Hymns.

(Homer's Hymn to the Moon.) **CP-ShelP**

Hymn to the Earth, *ad. fr. the German of* Stolberg's "Hymne an die Erde." Samuel Taylor Coleridge. **CP-ColeS**

Hymn to the Name and Hono[u]r of the Admirable Saint[e] T[h]eresa, A. Richard Crashaw. **CP-CrasR**

Hymn to Sainte Teresa, A. **HAP; NOSC**

(Hymn to Saint Teresa.) **ACP; EBEV; ESCV; GeHe; MeLP; MePo; WGRP**

"Thou art love's victim; and must die." **OBD**

Hymn to the Saints, and to Marquis Hamilton[, An]. John Donne. **CP-DonnJ**

Hymn to the Seal. Stevie Smith. **CP-SmitS**

Hymn to the Spirit of Nature. Percy Bysshe Shelley. *See* Life of Life.

Hymn to the Supreme Being. Christopher Smart. **SP-SmarC**

"But, O immortals! What had I to plead." **NOEC**

Hymn to the Virgin. Elizabeth Bishop. **CP-BishE**

Hymn to the Word. Charles Olson. **CP-OlsoC**

Hymne in Honour of Beautie, An. Edmund Spenser. *Fr.* Fowre Hymnes. **CP-Spens**

Hymne in Honour of Love, An. Edmund Spenser. *Fr.* Fowre Hymnes. **CP-Spens**

Hymne in Praise of Neptune, A. Thomas Campion. *See* Of Neptune's empire [*or* Empyre] let us sing.

Hymne of Heavenly Beautie, An. Edmund Spenser. **PeECV** *Fr.* Fowre Hymnes. **CP-Spens**

"But whoso may, thrice happy man him hold." **WGRP**

Hymne of Heavenly Love, An, *sels.* Edmund Spenser. *Fr.* Fowre Hymnes. **CP-Spens**

Hymne of the Nativity, Sung by the Shepheards, A. Richard Crashaw. **CP-CrasR**

Hymne to Bacchus, A ("I sing . . ."). Robert Herrick. **CP-HerrR**

Hymne to Cupid, An. Robert Herrick. **CP-HerrR**

Hymne to Juno, An. Robert Herrick. **CP-HerrR**

Hymne to Love, An. Robert Herrick. **CP-HerrR**

Hymne to Sir Clipseby Crew, A. Robert Herrick. **CP-HerrR**

Hymne to the Graces, A. Robert Herrick. **CP-HerrR**

Hymne, to the Lares, A. Robert Herrick. **CP-HerrR**

Hymne to the Muses, An. Robert Herrick. **CP-HerrR**

Hymne to the Muses, A ("O! You the Virgins nine!"). Robert Herrick. **CP-HerrR**

Hymne to Venus, and Cupid, A. Robert Herrick. **CP-HerrR**

Hymneal Song, on the Nuptials of the Lady Ann Wentworth and the Lord Lovelace. Thomas Carew. **CP-CareT**

Hymnos Aymnos. Arthur Hugh Clough. **SP-ClouA**

Hymns and Backward Glances. Steve Griffiths. **SP-GrifS**

Hymns and Backward Glances. Steve Griffiths. **SP-GrifS**

At the Consecration.

Christmas Night.

"Returning I live with a huge space."

Hymns and Spiritual Songs for the Fasts and Festivals of the Church of England. Christopher Smart. **SP-SmarC**

Accession of King George III, The.

All Saints.

Annunciation of the Blessed Virgin.

Ascension of Our Lord Jesus Christ, The. **NOCV**

Ash Wednesday. First Day of Lent.

Circumcision.

Conversion of St. Paul.

Crucifixion of Our Blessed Lord. **ChIV-2**

Easter Day.

Epiphany. **NOCV**

Fifth of November, The.

Holy Innocents, The.

King Charles the Martyr.

King's Restoration, The.

Nativity of Our Lord and Saviour Jesus Christ, The. **NOCV; SBVL**
> (Hymn: "Nativity of Our Lord and Saviour Jesus Christ, The.") **NAs; NOEC**
> (Nativity of Our Lord, The.) **EBEV; HAP; LAuP; LoBV; NOBE; PoEL-3; SCGP; WeW**
> Christmas Day. **ChTr; OBCP**

Nativity of St. John the Baptist, The. **ChIV-2**

New Year.

Presentation of Christ in the Temple, The.

St. Andrew.

St. Barnabas.

St. Bartholomew.

St. James.

St. John the Evangelist.

St. Luke.

St. Mark.

St. Matthew.

St. Matthias.

St. Michael and All Angels.

St. Peter.

St. Philip and St. James. **LoBV; NOCV; NOEC**

St. Simon and St. Jude.

St. Stephen.

St. Thomas. **ChIV-2**

Trinity Sunday.

Whitsunday.

Hymns for the Amusement of Children. Christopher Smart. **SP-SmarC**

Against Despair.

At Dressing in the Morning.

At Undressing in the Evening.

Beauty.

Charity.

Conclusion of the Matter, The. **ChIV-1**

Elegance. **NOCV**

Faith. **ChIV-1**

For Saturday. **FaBoCh; LAuP; NOEC; OxBChV**
> (Hymn for Saturday.) **OxBChV**
> (Lark's Nest, A.) **FaBoCh**

For Sunday.

Fortitude. **ChIV-2**

Generosity.

Good-Nature to Animals.

Gratitude. **LAuP; NOEC**

Honesty.

Honour.

Hope. **ChIV-1**

Immortality.

Justice.

Learning.

Long-Suffering of God. **LAuP; NOCV**

Loveliness. **NOCV**

Melancholy.

Mercy.

Mirth. **LAuP; OxBChV**

Moderation. **NOCV**

Mutual Subjection. **NOCV**
> (Consideration for Others.) **OxBChV**

Patience.

Peace.

Plenteous Redemption.

Praise. **OxBChV**

Pray Remember the Poor. **NOEC**

Prayer.

Prudence.

Silence.

Taste. **ChIV-1; NOCV**

Temperance.

Truth.

Watching.

Hymns from the French of Lamartine. John Greenleaf Whittier. **CP-WhitJ**

Hymns of Lograire. Thomas Merton. *Fr.* South. *Fr.* The Geography of Lograire. **CP-MertT**

Hymns of the Brahmo Somaj. John Greenleaf Whittier. **CP-WhitJ**

Hymns to Our Lady of Chartres. Geoffrey Hill. **CP-HillG**
> "Eia ergo. For this is Sion's twin city."
> "Eia, with handbells, jews' harps, risible." **DiPo**
> "Redemptrice of all vows and fealties, Dame."

Hype. Archie Randolph Ammons. **SP-AmmoA**

Hyperion; a Fragment. John Keats. **CP-KeatJ**
> Bruised Titans, The. **OBNC; OBRV**
> "Deep in the shady sadness of a vale." **OXAEP-2,** *book* I–III; **ChER; FHYEP; FaBoEn; FiP; NOBRP; OAEP; OBNC; OBRV; PoEL-4; TrGrPo**
> (Saturn.) **OBNC; TrGrPo**

Hyperion and Saturn. **SeCePo**
> Recollection of the Stone Circle near Keswick, A. **FaBoPP**
> "So ended Saturn; and the God of the Sea." **FHYEP**
> "Thus in alternate uproar and sad peace." **FHYEP**

Hyperion and Saturn. John Keats. **SeCePo** *Fr.* Hyperion; a Fragment. **CP-KeatJ**

Hyphens. Donald Davie. **CP-DavDo**

Hyphens. Charles Tomlinson. **CP-TomlC**

Hypnos on Ida. Homer, *tr. by* George Meredith. **CP-MerG1** *Fr.* The Iliad.

Hypochondriac Logic. Donald Davie. **CP-DavDo**

Hypochondriacs / Spend the winter at the bottom of Florida and the summer on top of the Adirondriacs. Oh to Be Odd! Ogden Nash. **CP-NashO**

Hypocrite Auteur. Archibald MacLeish. **CP-MacLA**

Hypocrite! Oxford Grouper! Yahoo! Malcolm Lowry. **CP-LowrM**

Hypocrite Swift. Louise Bogan. **CP-BogaL**

Hypocrite Women. Denise Levertov. **CP-LeveD**

Hypocrites shed tears. On Watching Politicians Perform at Martin Luther King's Funeral. Etheridge Knight. **SP-KnigE**

Hypsithilla, ask me over. Catullus. *See* Carmen 32: "Call me to you / at siesta."

Hysteria. Thomas Stearns Eliot. **CP-ElioT**

I

I. . . / cemetery of other men's bastards let. Reading X's Collected Works. Basil Bunting. **CP-BuntB**

I / am / forced. Jackie McLean: Alto Saxophone. Al Young. **CP-YounA**

I. Robert Creeley. **CP-CreeR**

I? / I walk alone. Soliloquy of the Solipsist. Sylvia Plath. **CP-PlatS**

I: "Loving in truth, and fain[e] in verse my love to show." Sir Philip Sidney. **AWP; BLPL; CABA; EBEV; EPCY; FaBoEn; GBL; GGP; HAP; HBV; ImPo; InPS; LiTB; MasP; NAEL-1; NoP; NoSic; OAEL-1; OAEP; OBSC; OXAEP-1; PP; PoE; Poetr; SCGP; SeCePo; SeCeV; Son; TEP; TFi; TrGrPo; TreFT** *Fr.* Astrophil and Stella. **SP-SidnP**

I / (meet)t(touch). Edward Estlin Cummings. **CP-CummE**

I / never / guessed any / thing(even a). Edward Estlin Cummings. **CP-CummE**

I. Kenneth Rexroth. **SP-RexrK** *Fr.* A Bestiary. **SP-RexrK**

I a Dirge will pen for thee. To Perenna. Robert Herrick. **CP-HerrR**

I, a princess, king-descended, decked with jewels, gilded, drest. A Royal Princess. Christina Georgina Rossetti. **CP-RosC1**

I, a writer, at one time hipped on. Raindrops on a Briar. William Carlos Williams. **CP-WilW2**

I abdicate my daily self that bled. Vita Nuova. Stanley Jasspon Kunitz. **CP-KuniS**

I abhor the slimy [or slimie] kiss [or kisse]. Kisses Loathesome. Robert Herrick. **CP-HerrR**

I abide and abide and better abide. Sir Thomas Wyatt. **CP-WyatT**

I admire all the brave and robust people live on shoestrings. Civilization. Diane Wakoski. **SP-WakoD**

I admire my native city because. "Lewiston Is a Pleasant Place." Marsden Hartley. **CP-HartM**

I admire the Bishops of the Church of England. The Bishops of the Church of England. Stevie Smith. **CP-SmitS**

I admire the roughness and brutality of the sea. Recognition. Richard Eberhart. **CP-EberR**

I admit it: there was a moment of pity. Are You Now or Have You Ever Been. Edwin Rolfe. **CP-RolfE**

I admit the briar. *fr.* A Woman Young and Old. William Butler Yeats. **CP-YeatW**

I advocate a semi-revolution. A Semi-Revolution. Robert Frost. **CP-FrosR**

I ain't gonna work on Maggie's Farm no more. Maggie's Farm. "Bob Dylan." **CP-DylaB**

I ain't got nobody. Evolutionary Poem No. 1. Etheridge Knight. **SP-KnigE**

I ain't lookin' to compete with you. All I Really Want to Do. "Bob Dylan." **CP-DylaB**

I ain't no Christian or no born-again saint. Average Guy. "Lou Reed." **SP-ReedL**

I all-creation sing my song of praise. "All Thy Works Praise Thee, O Lord": A Processional of Creation. Christina Georgina Rossetti. **CP-RosC2**

I almost love you. I've wanted to be you. Gerda in the Aerie. Marilyn Hacker. **SP-HackM**

I almost never think about you, I don't care. In the Evening. Stephen Berg. **SP-BergS**

I Almost Remember. Maya Angelou. **SP-AngeM**

I almost step on. Trigger. Archie Randolph Ammons. **SP-AmmoA**

I almost strangled on an almond. Death Demonstrates His Presence to Zimmer. Paul Zimmer. **SP-ZimmP**

I almost trust myself to know. Amnesia. Adrienne Rich. **SP-RicA2**

I almost went to bed. Song. Leonard Cohen. **CP-CoheL**

I alone, solemn land. The Three. James Dickey. **CP-DickJ**

I, Alphonso, live and learn. Alphonso of Castile. Ralph Waldo Emerson. **CP-EmerR**

I always admire a beautiful woman. The Rehearsal. Stevie Smith. **CP-SmitS**

I always believed, he said, the examined life. Writing the Great American Poem in Key West. Peter Meinke. **SP-MeinP** *Fr.* Lines from Key West.

I always found my daughters' beaux. Daddy's Home, See You Tomorrow. Ogden Nash. *Fr.* Posies from a Second Childhood, or, Hark How Gaffer Do Chaffer. **CP-NashO**

I always have Speranza. Mothermas. James Liddy. *Fr.* Glass after Oblivion. **CP-LiddJ**

I always hope to find you circling here. Falstaff. Thom Gunn. *Fr.* Transients and Residents. **CP-GunnT**

I always ran Home to Awe when a child. Emily Dickinson. **SP-DickE**

I always remember your beautiful flowers. Pad, Pad. Stevie Smith. **CP-SmitS**

I always return to this place. Kenneth Patchen. **CP-PatcK**

I Always Say There's No Place Like New York in the Summer, or, That Cottage Small by a Waterfall Was Snapped Up Last February. Ogden Nash. **CP-NashO**

I always take my judgement from a Fool. Cromek Speaks. William Blake. **CP-BlakW**

I always wanted to ball. Dead Now. Charles Bukowski. **SP-BukC1**

I Am. John Clare. **SP-ClarJ**

I Am. Phoebe Hesketh. **SP-HeskP**

I Am. Stevie Smith. **CP-SmitS**

I am a barber, and I'd have you know. A Barber. Sir John Suckling. **CP-SuckJ**

I am a Bard of no regard. Robert Burns. **PoE** *Fr.* The Jolly Beggars.

I am a beggar always. Edward Estlin Cummings. **CP-CummE**

I am a black Pierrot. A Black Pierrot. Langston Hughes. **SP-HughL**

I am a cat with a tick. Tick. Lewis Turco. **SP-TurcL**

I am a chest of drawers. Jean Sans Terre The Chest of Drawers. Iwan Goll, *tr. fr. French by* Isabella Gardner. **CP-GardI**

I am a copper wire slung in the air. Under a Telephone Pole. Carl Sandburg. **CP-SandC**

I am a democrat in so far as I love the free sun in men. Democracy. David Herbert Lawrence. **CP-LawrD**

I am a displaced person. My Heart Has Reopened to You. Alice Walker. **CP-WalkA**

I am a fanatic lover of liberty, considering it. Hayden Carruth. *Fr.* Paragraphs. **CP-CarHS**

I am a fly if these are not stones. Mountains. Ted Hughes. **SP-HughT**

I am a frog. The Frog Prince. Stevie Smith. **CP-SmitS**

I am a gentleman in a dustcoat trying. Piazza Piece. John Crowe Ransom. **SP-RansJ**

I Am a Girl Who Loves to Shoot. Stevie Smith. **CP-SmitS**

I am a goddess of the ambrosial courts. Artemis Prologizes. Robert Browning. **CP-BroR1**

I am a gray man leaning in a corner. His Granddaughter Arrives. Dabney Stuart. **SP-StuaD**

I am a hoodlum, you are a hoodlum, we and all of us are a world of. Hoodlums. Carl Sandburg. **CP-SandC**

I am a hunchback, yellow faced. Robert Louis Stevenson. **CP-StevR**

I am a keeper of the law. Verses. Robert Burns. **CP-BurnR**

I am a kind of farthing dip. A Portrait. Robert Louis Stevenson. **CP-StevR**

I am a King, / Or an Emperor rather. Christina Georgina Rossetti. **CP-RosC2**

I Am A Light You Could Read By. Marge Piercy. **SP-PierM**

I am a little church(no great cathedral). Edward Estlin Cummings. **CP-CummE**

I am a little world made cunningly. John Donne. **CABA; ChIV-1; EnRePo; NAEL-1; NIP; NoP; OBS; OxBoCh; PoE; SeCP; Son; TEP** *Fr.* Divine Meditations. **CP-DonnJ** *Fr.* Holy Sonnets. **CP-DonnJ**

I am a lonely Troll after my gala night. Troll's Courtship. Louis MacNeice. **CP-MacNL**

I Am a Lonesome Hobo. "Bob Dylan." **CP-DylaB**

I am a man of war and might. A Soldier. Sir John Suckling. **CP-SuckJ**

I am a man with no ambitions. The Advantages of Learning. Martial, *tr. fr. Latin by* Kenneth Rexroth. **SP-RexrK**

I am a miner. The light burns blue. Nick and the Candlestick. Sylvia Plath. **CP-PlatS**

I am a monarch of all I survey. Alexander Selkirk. William Cowper. **CP-CowpW**

I am a moody woman. Moody. Alice Walker. **CP-WalkA**

I Am a Most Fleshly Man. Robert Duncan. **SP-DuncR**

I am a Negro. Negro. Langston Hughes. **SP-HughL**

I am a painter. A Jingle on the Times. Thomas Hardy. **CP-HardT**

I am a panther shut up and bellowing in. A Report Upon the Consumption of Myself. Charles Bukowski. **SP-BukC2**

I am a poet of the Hudson River and the heights above it. America, America! Delmore Schwartz. **SP-SchwD**

I am a profound man sitting in a park. Redemption. Richard Eberhart. **CP-EberR**

I am a shepherd of those sheep. Nuit Blanche. Edna St. Vincent Millay. **CP-MillE**

I Am a Sioux Brave, He Said in Minneapolis. James Wright. **CP-WrigJ**

I am a Son of Mars who have been in many wars. Robert Burns. *Fr.* The Jolly Beggars.

I am a star dwelling on high. The Song of the Star. Christina Georgina Rossetti. **CP-RosC3**

I am a trombone. By the chinaberry tree. New Orleans. Hayden Carruth. **CP-CarHS**

I Am a Victim of Telephone. Allen Ginsberg. **CP-GinsA**

I am a widow. could be charleville could be anywhere. Dream of Rimbaud. Patti Smith. **SP-SmitP**

I am a woman lying on a leaf. Deep Analysis. Philip Larkin. **CP-LarkP**

I am a writer. From a Play. William Carlos Williams. **CP-WilW2**

I am a young executive. No cuffs than mine are cleaner. Executive. Sir John Betjeman. **CP-BetjJ**

I am about to make my home. Thomas Merton. *Fr.* Cables to the Ace. **CP-MertT**

I am afraid. Wedding Day. Seamus Heaney. **SP-HeanS**

I am afraid for you a little, for your sense of shame; I feel you are accustomed to ordinary evil. Bishop Tutu's Visit to the White House: 1984. Charles Kenneth Williams. **SP-WillC**

I am afraid if I go there again. Fear of the Waldorf Cafeteria. Brendan Galvin. **SP-GalvB**

I am afraid of nature. Fear. Grace Paley. **CP-PaleG**

I am afraid these verses will not please you, but, *bracketed before line beginning* "If I esteemed. . . ." Percy Bysshe Shelley. *See* Sonnet to Byron.

I am afraid to own a Body. Emily Dickinson. **CP-DickE**

I am agog for foam. Tumultuous come. Basil Bunting. **CP-BuntB**

I am alive at night. Moon Song, Woman Song. Anne Sexton. **CP-SextA**

I am alive—I guess. Emily Dickinson. **CP-DickE**

I am all mouth, / must have it filled. Mouth. John Clellon Holmes. **SP-HolmJ**

I am almost 90. *see also* Commentary—Final Examination. Leonard Cohen. **CP-CoheL**

I am alone in my own mind. January 24th. Anne Sexton. **CP-SextA**

I am alone in my banishment. Song: "Forever." George Meredith. **CP-MerG2**

I am alone. Sad is my solitude. Ralph Waldo Emerson. **CP-EmerR**

I am alone tonight. Report of Health. John Updike. **CP-UpdiJ**

I am an ancient reluctant conscript. Old Timers. Carl Sandburg. **CP-SandC**

I Am an Atheist Who Says His Prayers. Karl Shapiro. **SP-ShapK**

I am an exhausted not-that-chrysanthemum Oh brother. Waltzing Matilda. Alice Notley. **SP-NotlA**

I am an exile from my home; heavily. Ralph Waldo Emerson. **CP-EmerR**

I am an inconvenient woman. The Nuisance. Marge Piercy. **SP-PierM**

I am an island— / My mother was a mountain once. Marsden Hartley. *Fr.* Ironies out of St. George's. **CP-HartM**

I am an old and solitary man. Aeschylus' Soliloquy. Robert Browning. **CP-BroR2**

I am approaching. Past dry. Loot. Thom Gunn. **CP-GunnT**

I am as a spirit who has dwelt. Fragment: Wedded Souls. Percy Bysshe Shelley. **CP-ShelP**

I am as brisk. John Keats. **CBNP** *Fr.* Three Undated Fragments. **CP-KeatJ**

I am as brisk. Three Undated Fragments. John Keats. **CP-KeatJ**

I am as I am and so will I be. Sir Thomas Wyatt. **CP-WyatT**

I am ashamed—I hide. Emily Dickinson. **CP-DickE**

I am asked why I do not. In the Glass of Fashion. Howard Nemerov. **CP-NemeH**

I am at the track. Charles Bukowski. *Fr.* Horsemeat. **SP-BukC3**

I am attracted by the dust. In the House. Stephen Dunn. **SP-DunnS**

I am becalmed in a deep sea. Look! Stevie Smith. **CP-SmitS**

I am become a stranger to my dreams. Dream. Kathleen Jessie Raine. **SP-RainK**

I am blind, you out there. That is a curse. *tr. from the German of* Rilke. Randall Jarrell. **CP-JarrR**

I am bone lonely. The Idea of the Good. James Wright. **CP-WrigJ**

I am bringing out a little Granite Book. Emily Dickinson. **SP-DickE**

"I am but clay," the sinner plead. Distinction. Paul Laurence Dunbar. **CP-DunbP**

I am buying presents for everyone. The Night before Christmas. Howard Nemerov. **CP-NemeH**

I Am Cassander Come Down From the Sky. Samuel Johnson. (Translation from a Pantomime Version of Benserade's *Ballet de Cassandre.*) **CP-JohnS**

I am causing a sensation here in the County Clerk's crummy. Getting the License. Ron Koertge. **SP-KoerR**

I am cold in my folded blanket. Kenneth Rexroth. **CP-RexKL** *Fr.* The Phoenix and the Tortoise.

I am cold in my folded blanket. Kenneth Rexroth. **SP-RexrK** *Fr.* I am cold in my folded blanket. **CP-RexKL** *Fr.* The Phoenix and the Tortoise.

"I am cold in my folded blanket." **SP-RexrK**

I am commited. A Commitment. Richard Eberhart. **CP-EberR**

I am confirm'd a woman can. Verses. Sir John Suckling. **CP-SuckJ**

I am dancing on the silver beach. Drunken Charlie. Robinson Jeffers. **CP-JefR3**

I am dead, to be sure. A Small Fig Tree. Donald Hall. **CP-HallD**

I am divorcing Daddy—Dybbuk! Dybbuk! Divorce, Thy Name Is Woman. Anne Sexton. **CP-SextA**

I am done with apologies. If contrariness is my. The Contrariness of the Mad Farmer. Wendell Berry. **CP-BerrW**

I am doubted, therefore I am. Thomas Merton. *Fr.* Cables to the Ace. **CP-MertT**

I Am Dreaming of a White Christmas: The Natural History of a Vision. Robert Penn Warren. **SP-WarrR**

I am dressed in my big shoes and wrinkled socks. The X-Ray Waiting Room in the Hospital. Randall Jarrell. **CP-JarrR**

I am driving down Wilton Avenue. Sex. Charles Bukowski. **SP-BukC1**

I am driving; it is dusk; Minnesota. Driving toward the Lac Qui Parle River. Robert Bly. **SP-BlyR**

I am drunk with the honey wine. Fragment: Wine of the Fairies. Percy Bysshe Shelley. **CP-ShelP**

I Am Dying. Leonard Cohen. **CP-CoheL**

I am dying Egypt dying. Death of Mr. Mounsel. Stevie Smith. **CP-SmitS**

I am Fake Saint. Blame the Thought, Cling to the Bummer. Allen Ginsberg. **CP-GinsA**

I am fond of the Swallow—I learn from her flight. The Swallow. Jeanne Marie Bouvier de la Motte-Guyon, *tr. fr. French by* William Cowper. **CP-CowpW**

I am for sleeping and forgetting. Requiescam. Countee Cullen. **CP-CullC**

I am forgetting Louie the buoyant. Louie. Thomas Hardy. **CP-HardT**

I am Freed. César Vallejo, *tr. fr. Spanish by* James Wright. **CP-WrigJ**

I am frightened by the sorrow. In the Face of Hatred. James Wright. **CP-WrigJ**

I am frightened Master, quivering with fear. Misericordia. William Carlos Williams. **CP-WilW1**

I Am Full of Previous Experience. Ogden Nash. **CP-NashO**

I am Gilgamesh. Tomorrow. Charles Olson. **CP-OlsoC**

I am glad God saw Death. The Junk Man. Carl Sandburg. **CP-SandC**

I am glad I am here: I have said. Witness at Leipzig. Edwin Rolfe. **CP-RolfE**

I am glad, I think, my happy mother died. Memory of England. Edna St. Vincent Millay. **CP-MillE**

I am glad you are in the open Air. Emily Dickinson. **SP-DickE**

I am going home by sea. Derek Mahon. **IIP** *Fr.* Afterlives. **SP-MahoD**

I am going on with my beautiful procession. In Your Body All Bodies Lie. Kenneth Patchen. **CP-PatcK**

I am going to rip myself down the middle into two pieces. Halves. Charles Kenneth Williams. **CP-WillC; SP-WillC**

I am going to try a comedy like that. A Comedy like That. Gertrude Stein. **CP-SteiG**

I am going to utter a tree,Noboby. Edward Estlin Cummings. **CP-CummE**

I am happiest. I Live in New York. Erica Jong. **SP-JongE**

I am hard to disgust. Mercifully. Marianne Craig Moore. **CP-MoorM**

I am he as you are he as you are me and we are all together. I Am the Walrus. John Lennon *and* Paul McCartney. **CP-Beatl**

I Am He That Aches with Love. Walt Whitman. **CP-WhitW**

I Am He That Walks with the Tender and Growing Night. Walt Whitman. **ChTr** *Fr.* I am the poet of the Body and I am the poet of the Soul. **BiP; SeCeV; WeW** *Fr.* Song of Myself. **CP-WhitW**

I am he who writes of the Prince of faded colors. Ultima Despedida del Principe Poniatowski de Su Familia. Gilbert Sorrentino. *Fr.* Twelve Études for Voice and Kazoo. **SP-SorrG**

I am heaping the bones of the old mother. To the House. Robinson Jeffers. **CP-JefR1**

I am hearing the shape of the rain. In the Mountain Tent. James Dickey. **CP-DickJ**

I am Hectate Queen of Hags. Hectate. George Meredith. **CP-MerG2**

I Am Held by My Fear of Death. Robert Creeley. **CP-CreeR**

I am here myself; as though this heave of effort. Rose of All the World. David Herbert Lawrence. **CP-LawrD**

I am here to time, you see. The Duel. Thomas Hardy. **CP-HardT**

I am here with my beautiful bountiful [downy] womanful child. At a Summer Hotel. Isabella Gardner. **CP-GardI**

I am hiding beside you to tell you. Reading *Genesis* to a Blind Child. James Dickey. **CP-DickJ**

I am holy, while I stand. To Silvia. Robert Herrick. **CP-HerrR**

I am Huitzilopochtli. First Song of Huitzilopochtli. David Herbert Lawrence. **CP-LawrD**

I am Humphrey Bogart. This Is No Dream, This Is My Life. Dabney Stuart. **SP-StuaD**

I am I, old Father Fisheye that begat the ocean, the worm. The End. Allen Ginsberg. **CP-GinsA**

I am in a cliff-hollow, surrounded by fossils and furry. Sitting on Some Rocks in Shaw Cove. Robert Bly. **SP-BlyR**

I Am in a Novel. David Herbert Lawrence. **CP-LawrD**

I am in a painting by Camille Pissarro. Returning to Paris with Pissarro. Lawrence Ferlinghetti. **SP-FerlL**

I am in a room. Dream and Reality. John Updike. **CP-UpdiJ**

I Am in Danger—Sir—. Adrienne Rich. **CP-RicAE; SP-RicA1; SP-RicA2**

I am in love, meantime, you think; no doubt you would think so. Claude to Eustace. Arthur Hugh Clough. **EnVR; FaBoVe** *Fr.* Amours de Voyage. **SP-ClouA**

I am in love with him to whom a hyacinth is dearer. Hyacinth. Edna St. Vincent Millay. **CP-MillE**

I am in love with my womb. Gardener. Erica Jong. **SP-JongE**

I am in mourning. Natural Star. Alice Walker. **CP-WalkA**

I am in need of music that would flow. Sonnet. Elizabeth Bishop. **CP-BishE**

I am in Rome, Vatican bells tolling. An Apartment with a View. John Ciardi. **SP-CiarJ**

I am indeed the personage you know. A Forgiveness. Robert Browning. **CP-BroR2**

I am interested alone in making ready. John Berryman. *Fr.* Sonnets to Chris. **CP-BerrJ**

I am invisible tonight. Invisible Tonight. Leonard Cohen. **CP-CoheL**

I am just another particle cloud gliding across the screen. Genghis Chan: Private Eye VI. John Yau. **SP-YauJo**

I am just going outside and may be some time. Antarctica. Derek Mahon. **SP-MahoD**

I am just two and two, I am warm, I am cold. Riddle. William Cowper. **CP-CowpW**

I am kneading my bread Winnie Mandela. The Evening News. Audre Lorde. **SP-LordA**

I am kneeling on my grave this lonely. Meditation Among the Tombs. Galway Kinnell. **SP-KinnG**

I am laughing by the brook with her. Dream Is—Which? The. Thomas Hardy. **CP-HardT**

I am leading a quiet life. *See also* Autobiography ("I am leading a quiet life") *by* Sonja [dA]kesson. Lawrence Ferlinghetti. **SP-FerlL**

I am learning to see. Choral Amphisbaena. John Yau. **SP-YauJo**

I Am like a Rose. David Herbert Lawrence. **CP-LawrD**

—I am like a slip of comet. Gerard Manley Hopkins. **CP-HopkG**

I am like one that for long days had sate. Robert Louis Stevenson. **CP-StevR**

I am like one that has sat alone. Robert Louis Stevenson. **CP-StevR**

I am listening here in Rome. A Song for the Ragged Schools of London. Elizabeth Barrett Browning. **CP-BroEB**

I am living more alone now than I did. The Last Chapter. Walter de la Mare. **CP-DeLaW**

I Am Long Weaned. William Everson. **SP-EverW**

I am lost. / I had swum before. May. Joseph Ceravolo. **SP-CeraJ**

I am made all things to all men. At His Execution. Rudyard Kipling. **CP-KiplR**

I am made to sow the thistle for wheat, the nettle for a nourishing dainty. The Price of Experience. William Blake. **EnRP; PoE; Prf** *Fr.* Vala; or The Four Zoas. **CP-BlakW**

I am making a Cartoon of a Woman. She is the People. She is the Great. Cartoon. Carl Sandburg. **CP-SandC**

I am making a cave. Waking. Jenny Joseph. *Fr.* Life and Turgid Times of A. Citizen. **SP-JoseJ**

I am Mantra. Charles Henri Ford. **SP-FordC** *Fr.* Emblems of Arachne.

I am married and would like to fuck someone else. Graffiti 12th Cubicle Men's Room Syracuse Airport. Allen Ginsberg. **CP-GinsA**

I am Miles, I did not die. The Last Turn of the Screw. Stevie Smith. **CP-SmitS**

I am mourning a murder; one I have done. In Mourning for Betrayal. Robert Bly. **SP-BlyR**

I am my father. White and the River. Siv Cedering Fox. **SP-CedeS**

I am my mammie's ae bairn. I'm Owre [*or* O'er] Young to Marry Yet. Robert Burns. **CP-BurnR**

I am myself at last; now I achieve. I Am like a Rose. David Herbert Lawrence. **CP-LawrD**

I am no Homers Hero You all know. William Blake. **CP-BlakW**

I am no priests of crooks nor creeds. Religion. Paul Laurence Dunbar. **CP-DunbP**

I am no tree. The Transcript. Gilbert Sorrentino. **SP-SorrG**

I am no trumpet, but a reed. A Reed. Elizabeth Barrett Browning. **CP-BroEB**

I Am Not a Camera. Wystan Hugh Auden. **CP-AudeW**

I am not a mechanism, an assembly of various sections. Healing. David Herbert Lawrence. **CP-LawrD**

I am not a painter, I am a poet. Why I Am Not a Painter. Frank O'Hara. **SP-OharF**

I am not an actress anymore. Micky. Jim Carroll. **SP-CarrJ**

I am not black in my mind. Ralph Waldo Emerson. **CP-EmerR**

I am not dead, I have only become inhuman. Inscription for a Gravestone. Robinson Jeffers. **CP-JefR2**

I am not fond of Oliver Montrose. Nevertheless. Ogden Nash. **CP-NashO**

I am not God's little lamb. Little Boy Sick. Stevie Smith. **CP-SmitS**

I am not going to talk to you about islands. Life and Turgid Times of A. Citizen. Jenny Joseph. **SP-JoseJ**

I am not going to talk to you about islands. PROEM: *Against metaphor—but how then?.* Jenny Joseph. *Fr.* Life and Turgid Times of A. Citizen. **SP-JoseJ**

I am not interested. Anti-Matter. Erica Jong. **SP-JongE**

I Am Not Kurt Schwitters. Jim Carroll. **SP-CarrJ**

I am not lazy. Frenzy. Anne Sexton. **CP-SextA**

I am not of those miserable males. George Meredith. *Fr.* Modern Love. **CP-MerG1**

I am not one who much or oft delight. Personal Talk. William Wordsworth. **CP-WorW1**

I Am Not Resigned. Phoebe Hesketh. **SP-HeskP**

I am not resigned to the shutting away of loving hearts in the hard ground. Dirge Without Music. Edna St. Vincent Millay. **CP-MillE**

I am not sure I would always fight for my life. What Would You Fight For? David Herbert Lawrence. **CP-LawrD**

I am not treacherous, callous, jealous, superstitious. A Face. Marianne Craig Moore. **CP-MoorM**

I am not well civilized, really alien here: trust me not. The Trap. Robinson Jeffers. **CP-JefR2**

I am not willing you should go. To S. M. Edna St. Vincent Millay. **CP-MillE**

I am not wiser for my age. Climacteric. Ralph Waldo Emerson. *Fr.* Quatrains. **CP-EmerR**

I am not yet born; O hear me. Prayer before Birth. Louis MacNeice. **CP-MacNL**

I am now about to make a remark that I suppose most parents will. Our Child Doesn't Know Anything. Ogden Nash. **CP-NashO**

I am of all bereft. The Plunder. Robert Herrick. **CP-HerrR**

I Am of Ireland, *fr.* Words for Music Perhaps. William Butler Yeats. **CP-YeatW**

I Am of Old and Young. Walt Whitman. **ImGa** *Fr.* Song of Myself. **CP-WhitW**

I am of old and young, of the foolish as much as the wise. I Am of Old and Young. Walt Whitman. **ImGa** *Fr.* Song of Myself. **CP-WhitW**

I am old. Fire Spirit. William Carlos Williams. **CP-WilW1**

I am old and in the ordinary course of nature shall die soon, but the. Birth and Death. Robinson Jeffers. **CP-JefR3**

I am old, I am alone. Kathleen Jessie Raine. *Fr.* Testimony. **SP-RainK**

I am old, stony-faced, and hard. Edgar Lee Masters. Richard Eberhart. **CP-EberR**

I am oppressed by all the room taken up by the dead. The Farmer among the Tombs. Wendell Berry. **CP-BerrW**

I am oppressed, I am oppressed, I am oppressed—. Eurydice. Robert Ranke Graves. **CP-GravR**

I am out alone on the road. On the Road. David Herbert Lawrence. **CP-LawrD**

I am owner of the sphere. Ralph Waldo Emerson. **CP-EmerR** *Fr.* History.

I am pale with sick desire. I Will Lift Up Mine Eyes unto the Hills. Christina Georgina Rossetti. **CP-RosC1**

I am part of these walls. The Caves. Jim Carroll. **SP-CarrJ**

"I am playing my oldest tunes," declared she. The Last Performance. Thomas Hardy. **CP-HardT**

I am poor brother Lippo, by your leave! Fra Lippo Lippi. Robert Browning. **CP-BroR1**

I Am Punished. Leonard Cohen. **CP-CoheL**

I am pure loneliness. The Unloved. Kathleen Jessie Raine. **SP-RainK**

I am put high over all others in the city today. Killers. Carl Sandburg. **CP-SandC**

I am putting makeup on empty space. Makeup on Empty Space. Anne Waldman. **SP-WaldA**

I am ready and ever will be. Sir Thomas Wyatt. **CP-WyatT**

I am reft to the innermost heart. Direadh III. "Hugh MacDiarmid." **SP-MacDH**

I am riding on a limited express, one of the crack trains of the nation. Limited. Carl Sandburg. **CP-SandC**

I am saying goodbye to the trees. Going Home. Derek Mahon. **SP-MahoD**

"I am self-evident," the mirror said. Critic. Howard Nemerov. **CP-NemeH**

I am sending back the key. Bluebeard. Sylvia Plath. **CP-PlatS**

I am seventy-four years old and suddenly all my strength. Robinson Jeffers. **CP-JefR3**

I am sick, because I have given myself away. Sick. David Herbert Lawrence. **CP-LawrD**

I am sick of people's cerebral emotions. Cerebral Emotions. David Herbert Lawrence. **CP-LawrD**

I am sick, sick to desperation. Marge Piercy. *Fr.* The Homely War. **SP-PierM**

I am silver and exact. I have no preconceptions. Mirror. Sylvia Plath. **CP-PlatS**

I am singing to you. Killers. Carl Sandburg. **CP-SandC**

I am sitting at a table in the mall drinking coffee while. The Skaters. Charles Bukowski. **SP-BukC3**

I am sitting in the clubhouse. Ginsberg? Charles Bukowski. **SP-BukC3**

I am sitting in the stands with a. Charles Bukowski. *Fr.* Horsemeat. **SP-BukC3**

I am sitting on a kitchen chair. Marge Piercy. *Fr.* Excursions, Incursions. **SP-PierM**

I am sitting on the / edge of the impartial. Margaret Atwood. **SP-AtwM1**

I am Sive-like, and can hold. Upon Himselfe. Robert Herrick. **CP-HerrR**

I am slow as the world. I am very patient. Three Women. Sylvia Plath. **CP-PlatS**

I Am Small and of No Reputation. Christina Georgina Rossetti. **CP-RosC2**

I am so delighted. Moon. James Wright. **CP-WrigJ**

I am so glad and very. Edward Estlin Cummings. **CP-CummE**

I am so glad to be moving. Moving Out Or the End of Cooperative Living. Audre Lorde. **SP-LordA**

I Am So Small You Can Hardly See Me. Charles Olson. **CP-OlsoC**

I am so thankful I have seen. On Sight. Alice Walker. **CP-WalkA**

I am so weak my enemies. A Celebration of Rust. Barton Sutter. **SP-SuttB**

I am sober and industrious. To a Poet. Frank O'Hara. **SP-OharF**

I am some man come out of some strange place. Configuration. Richard Eberhart. **CP-EberR**

I am someone who boots myself from bed. Rainy 4th. Marge Piercy. **SP-PierM**

I am sorry that the rich man must go. Disguises. Leonard Cohen. **CP-CoheL**

I am sorry you need Health. Emily Dickinson. **SP-DickE**

I am speechlessly grateful for a friend. Emily Dickinson. **SP-DickE**

I am speeding through the northern lights. Malcolm Lowry. **CP-LowrM**

I am spinning. The Fierceness of Female. Anne Sexton. **CP-SextA**

I am standing among the coal black. The Will. James Merrill. **SP-MerrJ**

I am standing on one foot. At the Battery. Grace Paley. **CP-PaleG**

I am stopped from hoping what I have hoped before. Concerning Agnes. Thomas Hardy. **CP-HardT**

I am stretched out under the lean-to. Promises, Promises. Paul Muldoon. **SP-MuldP**

I am stuck with a snarl. The Man with the Hot Nose. Charles Bukowski. **SP-BukC2**

I am studying music now with the jays. Emily Dickinson. **SP-DickE**

I am supposed to apologize. Mustered into the Avant-Garde. Donald Davie. **CP-DavDo**

I am supposed to say. And Don't Think I Won't Be Waiting. Audre Lorde. **SP-LordA**

I am sure I feel as Noah did. Emily Dickinson. **SP-DickE**

I am sure that if anybody into the condition of humanity cares to probe. Little Miss Muffet Sat on a Prophet—and Quite Right, Too! Ogden Nash. **CP-NashO**

I am surprised to see. Letter Written on a Ferry While Crossing Long Island Sound. Anne Sexton. **CP-SextA**

I am taking a walk about 2:30 p.m. Promenade. Charles Bukowski. **SP-BukC3**

I am telling you, kid. James Liddy. *Fr.* A Munster Song of Love and War. **CP-LiddJ**

I am that Adam who, with Snake for guest. The Exile. Walter de la Mare. **CP-DeLaW**

I am that Dido which thou here do'st see. Ausonius, *tr. fr. Latin by* Sir Walter Ralegh. **CP-RaleW**

I am that Persephone. Persephone. Stevie Smith. **CP-SmitS**

I am that star most dreaded by the wise. The Summons. Wystan Hugh Auden. *Fr.* For the Time Being; a Christmas Oratorio. **CP-AudeW**

I am that vile worm of Satan. The Assassin. Richard Eberhart. **CP-EberR**

I am the amber-eyed black. Short Journeys Before Daybreak. James McAuley. **SP-McAuJ**

I am the American heartbreak. American Heartbreak. Langston Hughes. **SP-HughL**

I Am the Bitter Name. Charles Kenneth Williams. **CP-WillC; SP-WillC**

I am the combination to a door. Howard Nemerov. *Fr.* Quaerendo Invenietis. **CP-NemeH**

I Am the Doore. Richard Crashaw. **CP-CrasR**

I am the falcon of the spirit world. The Soul. Jelaluddin Rumi, *tr. fr. Persian by* Ralph Waldo Emerson. **CP-EmerR**

I am the family face. Heredity. Thomas Hardy. **CP-HardT**

I am the father of no country. George Oppen. *Fr.* A Narrative. **CP-OppeG**

I am the ghost of Shadwell Stair. Shadwell Stair. Wilfred Owen. **CP-OwenW**

I am the ghost of the weed garden. The Weed Garden. Lewis Turco. **SP-TurcL**

I am the giver of gifts, the bringer of life. The Giver of Gifts. Stephen Dobyns. **SP-DobyS**

I am The Great White Way of the city. Poems Done on a Late Night Car. Carl Sandburg. **CP-SandC**

I am the Gutter Dream. Nicholas Vachel Lindsay. *Fr.* The Kallyope Yell. **CP-LindV**

I am the heart of a murdered woman. Owl Song. Margaret Atwood. *Fr.* Songs of the Transformed. **SP-AtwM1**

I am the hounds. The High Pasture. Donald Hall. **CP-HallD**

I am the Kallyope, Kallyope, Kallyope. Nicholas Vachel Lindsay. *Fr.* The Kallyope Yell. **CP-LindV**

I am the land of their fathers. The Recall. Rudyard Kipling. **CP-KiplR**

I am the lightness that I know. Love Poem, A. Richard Eberhart. **CP-EberR**

I am the Living Quetzalcoatl. The Living Quetzalcoatl. David Herbert Lawrence. **CP-LawrD**

I am the love killer. Killing the Love. Anne Sexton. **CP-SextA**

I am the magical mouse. The Magical Mouse. Kenneth Patchen. **CP-PatcK**

I am the man on the rack. Thom Gunn. *Fr.* Jack Straw's Castle. **CP-GunnT**

I am the mist, the impalpable mist. The Mist. Carl Sandburg. **CP-SandC**

I am the Most Wise Baviaan, saying in most wise tones. Rudyard Kipling. **CP-KiplR** *Fr.* How the Leopard Got His Spots. *Fr.* Just-So Stories.

I am the mother of sorrows. The Paradox. Paul Laurence Dunbar. **CP-DunbP**

I am the Muse who sung alway. Solution. Ralph Waldo Emerson. **CP-EmerR**

I am the music you were born to. Silence. Stephen Dobyns. **SP-DobyS**

I am the nigger. Nigger. Carl Sandburg. **CP-SandC**

I Am the One. Thomas Hardy. **CP-HardT**

I am the one. Snakebite. James Dickey. **CP-DickJ**

I am the one that drew. The Chosen. Daniel Gerard Hoffman. **SP-HoffD**

I am the one who gnawed the blanket through. Message from Outside. Gary Snyder. **CP-SnydG**

I am the only actor. The Play. Anne Sexton. **CP-SextA**

I am the only being whose doom. Emily Brontë. **CP-BronE**

I am the past time, am old, but. Robert Penn Warren. *Fr.* Saul at Gilboa. **SP-WarrR**

I Am the People, the Mob. Carl Sandburg. **CP-SandC**

I am the people—the mob—the crowd—the mass. I Am the People, the Mob. Carl Sandburg. **CP-SandC**

I am the poet of the Body and I am the poet of the Soul. Walt Whitman. **BiP; SeCeV; WeW** *Fr.* Song of Myself. **CP-WhitW**

I Am He That Walks with the Tender and Growing Night. **ChTr**

I am the same yes as you others, only—. The Pacifist's Song. John Berryman. **CP-BerrJ**

I am the self-appointed guardian of English literature. Souvenir de Monsieur Poop. Stevie Smith. **CP-SmitS**

I am the shadow you once blessed. Shadow. David St. John. **SP-StJoD**

I am the simplest of disguises. Anger. Stephen Dobyns. **SP-DobyS**

I am the Son of the Morning Star, and child of the deeps. Son of the Morning Star. David Herbert Lawrence. **CP-LawrD**

I am the son who steers his father's chair, his hawk. Passion Play. Gary Gildner. **SP-GildG**

I am the Sphinx. Egyptology. Erica Jong. **SP-JongE**

"I am the stream," I said. Kathleen Jessie Raine. *Fr.* Monessie Gorge. **SP-RainK**

I Am the Sun. Daniel Gerard Hoffman. **SP-HoffD**

I am the undertow. Under. Carl Sandburg. **CP-SandC**

I am the unicorn and bow my head. The Lady and the Unicorn. May Sarton. **SP-SartM**

I Am the Walrus. John Lennon *and* Paul McCartney. **CP-Beatl**

I am the woman / In the window. Woman in the Window. Jim Morrison. **SP-MorrJ**

I am the woman who sits by the river. Let Us Gather at the River. Marge Piercy. **SP-PierM**

I am the world-crier, and this is my dangerous career. Early in the Morning. Kenneth Patchen. **CP-PatcK**

I am thirty this November. The Double Image. Anne Sexton. **CP-SextA**

I am thy soul, Nikoptis. I have watched. The Tomb of Akr Caar. Ezra Pound. **SP-PounE**

I am tired of gadgets with cocktails. Isn't That a Dainty Dish? No! Ogden Nash. **CP-NashO**

I am tired of hearing the insane. Essay on Sanity. Stephen Dunn. **SP-DunnS**

I am to dine, friend, where I must be weighed. Epistle to Mr Arthur Squib. Ben Jonson. **CP-JonsB**

I am to follow her. There is much grace. George Meredith. **NAEL-2; NOBVV** *Fr.* Modern Love. **CP-MerG1**

I am too angry to sleep beside you. Love Letter Postmarked Van Beethoven. Diane Wakoski. **SP-WakoD**

I am too big, too big by far. Pity me. Giant Toad. Elizabeth Bishop. *Fr.* Rainy Season; Sub-Tropics. **CP-BishE**

I am too fucking innocent to be gay, he roared. Let there be born. Issues from the Hand of God. Charles Olson. **CP-OlsoC**

I am too young to grow a beard. Street Song. Thom Gunn. **CP-GunnT**

I am torn in two. The Civil War. Anne Sexton. **CP-SextA**

I am trajectory and flight—. Poet. Louise McNeill. **SP-McNeL**

I am trotting / Where I should. His Dog and Pilgrim. Frank Templeton Prince. **CP-PrinF**

I am trying to abide by the clues. Jim Carroll. **SP-CarrJ**

I am trying to decide to go swimming. The Wind Is Blowing West. Joseph Ceravolo. **SP-CeraJ**

I am trying to imagine. Re-forming the Crystal. Adrienne Rich. **SP-RicA1; SP-RicA2**

I am trying to write at a desk that is mine. This Room Is Full of Clocks. Isabella Gardner. **CP-GardI**

I am 20 years old and holding on. After "Les Fleurs." Anne Waldman. **SP-WaldA**

I am two days from death. Shame. Frederick Morgan. *Fr.* Enigmas. **SP-MorgF**

I am two fools, I know. The Triple Fool. John Donne. **CP-DonnJ**

I am unable, yonder beggar cries. A Lame Beggar. John Donne. **CP-DonnJ**

I am unjust, but I can strive for justice. Why I Voted the Socialist Ticket. Nicholas Vachel Lindsay. **CP-LindV**

I Am Vertical. Sylvia Plath. **CP-PlatS**

I am very happy to be here at the Villa Hügel. Image of the Buddha Preaching. Frank O'Hara. **SP-OharF**

I am very small. Malcolm Lowry. **CP-LowrM**

I Am Visited by an Editor and a Poet. Charles Bukowski. **SP-BukC2**

I am waiting for my case to come up. Lawrence Ferlinghetti. **SP-FerlL** *Fr.* Oral Messages.

I am walking rapidly through striations of light and dark thrown under an arcade. I Dream I'm the Death of Orpheus. Adrienne Rich. **CP-RicAE; SP-RicA1; SP-RicA2**

I Am Washed upon a Rock. Philip Larkin. **CP-LarkP**

I am watching the white gannets. Gannets. Mary Oliver. **SP-OlivM**

I am: what I am. Hafiz, *tr. by* Ralph Waldo Emerson. **CP-EmerR** *Fr.* Odes.

I am what is around me. Theory. Wallace Stevens. **CP-StevW**

I am where the blðebell dies. The Height of Man. Richard Eberhart. **CP-EberR**

I am who the trail took. Exploration. Daniel Gerard Hoffman. **SP-HoffD**

I Am with the Roots of Flowers. Charles Bukowski. **SP-BukC2**

I am working at a poem, pray excuse me. Work Drafts. Robert Ranke Graves. **CP-GravR**

I am worn out. The Effort of Love. David Herbert Lawrence. **CP-LawrD**

I am worn out with dreams. Men Improve with the Years. William Butler Yeats. **CP-YeatW**

I am writing these poems. It's Dark In Here. Shel Silverstein. **SP-SilS2**

I am writing to the / Chinese Association for the Study. Letter. Grace Paley. **CP-PaleG**

I am writing you. Epistles. Lewis Turco. **SP-TurcL**

I am—yet what I am none cares or knows. I Am. John Clare. **SP-ClarJ**

I am your garbage man. What you leave. Trash. Charles Kenneth Williams. **CP-WillC**

I am your son, white man! Mulatto. Langston Hughes. **SP-HughL**

I am zeellesse, prethee pray. To Julia. Robert Herrick. **CP-HerrR**

I am zero, naught, one ciper. Carl Sandburg. *Fr.* The People, Yes. **CP-SandC**

I, an ambassador of Otherwhere. From the Embassy. Robert Ranke Graves. **CP-GravR**

I and Clive were friends—and why not? Friends! I think you laugh, my lad. Clive. Robert Browning. **CP-BroR2**

I and I. "Bob Dylan." **CP-DylaB**

I And Your Eyes. Etheridge Knight. **SP-KnigE**

I approach the standards of the air. The Standards. Richard Eberhart. **CP-EberR**

I approach upon the headlands. Light, Time, Dark. Richard Eberhart. **CP-EberR**

I approach with such. Something. Robert Creeley. **CP-CreeR**

I arise from dreams of thee. The Indian Serenade. Percy Bysshe Shelley. **CP-ShelP**

I Arrive in Madrid. Al Young. **CP-YounA**

I ask and receive. The Dream Flood. James Dickey. **CP-DickJ**

I ask but right: let her that caught me late. 1.3. Ovid, *tr. by* Christopher Marlowe. **CP-MarlC** *Fr.* Elegies.

I ask dim questions of California Friends. Crool Time. Gilbert Sorrentino. **SP-SorrG**

I ask good things that I detest. Prayer. Robert Louis Stevenson. **CP-StevR**

I ask not now for gold to gild. The Wish of To-day. John Greenleaf Whittier. **CP-WhitJ**

I ask the unyielding Sentence that shows Itself forth in the language. Robert Duncan. **SP-DuncR** *Fr.* The Structure of Rime.

I ask you: Has the Singer sung. Non Omnis Moriar. Allen Tate. **CP-TateA**

I ask you this. Prayer. Langston Hughes. **SP-HughL**

I ask'd [or asked] my fair one happy day. *ad. fr. the German of* Gotthold Lessing. Samuel Taylor Coleridge. **CP-ColeS**

I asked a gypsy pal. Gypsy. Carl Sandburg. **CP-SandC**

I asked a thief to steal me a peach. William Blake. **CP-BlakW**

I asked a Whig the other night. Upon the Horrid Plot Discovered by Harlequin the Bishop of Rochester's French Dog. Jonathan Swift. **CP-SwifJ**

I asked her, "Is Aladdin's lamp." The Sorceress! Nicholas Vachel Lindsay. **CP-LindV**

I asked if I should pray. Mohini Chatterjee. William Butler Yeats. **CP-YeatW**

I asked my ailing mother if she beat me. Shoeshine. Stephen Berg. **SP-BergS**

I asked [or askd] my Dear Friend, Orator Prigg. William Blake. **CP-BlakW**

I asked no other thing. Emily Dickinson. **CP-DickE**

I asked no quarter and I gave none. An Old Fashioned American Business Man. Richard Eberhart. **CP-EberR**

I asked of your face. The God. Hilda Doolittle. **CP-DoolH**

I asked professors who teach the meaning of life to tell me what is happiness. Happiness. Carl Sandburg. **CP-SandC**

I asked the Lord: "Sire, is this true." A Dream Question. Thomas Hardy. **CP-HardT**

I asked the Mayor of Gary about the 12-hour day and the 7-day week. The Mayor of Gary. Carl Sandburg. **CP-SandC**

I asked [or ask't] thee oft what poets thou hast read. Upon the Same. Robert Herrick. **CP-HerrR**

I asked you, baby. Maybe. Langston Hughes. **SP-HughL**

I askt my Lucia but a kisse. Upon Lucia. Robert Herrick. **CP-HerrR**

I ate at the counter. A Hairnet with Stars. Ted Kooser. **SP-KoosT**

I ate my fill of a whale that died. Natural Theology. Rudyard Kipling. **CP-KiplR**

I Ate My Love Alive. David Markson. **CP-MarkD**

I ate pancakes one night in a Pancake House. The Player Piano. Randall Jarrell. **CP-JarrR; SP-JarrR**

I attempted to concentrate. Allen Ginsberg. **CP-GinsA**

I attended school and I liked the place. Values in Use. Marianne Craig Moore. **CP-MoorM**

I awoke happy, the house. The Revelation. William Carlos Williams. **CP-WilW1**

I awoke in profuse sweat, arms aching. Hag-Ridden. Robert Ranke Graves. **CP-GravR**

I awoke in the midsummer not-to-call night, in the white and the walk of the morning. Gerard Manley Hopkins. **CP-HopkG**

(Moonrise June 19 1876.) **CP-HopkG**

I awoke w/new strength. Robert Bresson. Patti Smith. **SP-SmitP**

I Awoke with the Room Cold. Marge Piercy. **SP-PierM**

I bade, because the wick and oil are spent. The Living Beauty. William Butler Yeats. **CP-YeatW**

I bade my Lady think what she might mean. George Meredith. *Fr.* Modern Love. **CP-MerG1**

I balance myself carefully. Wish: Metamorphosis to Heraldic Emblem. Margaret Atwood. **SP-AtwM1**

I banged it out. Stone and Flower Series. Charles Olson. **CP-OlsoC**

I batter the wheel of heaven. Hafiz, *tr. by* Ralph Waldo Emerson. **CP-EmerR** *Fr.* Odes.

I bear a basket lined with grass. *Shorter and diff. vers. of* Lines for a Picture of St. Dorothea; *see also* St. Dorothea. Gerard Manley Hopkins. **CP-HopkG**

I bear a basket lined with grass. *For shorter and diff. vers., see also* For a Picture of St. Dorothea *and* St. Dorothea. Gerard Manley Hopkins. **CP-HopkG**

I bear a basket lined with grass. *For shorter and diff. vers., see also* For a Picture of Saint Dorothea *and* Lines for a Picture of St. Dorothea. Gerard Manley Hopkins. **CP-HopkG**

I bear in youth the sad infirmities. Written in Sickness. Ralph Waldo Emerson. **CP-EmerR**

I became a single sinew. James McAuley. **SP-McAuJ** *Fr.* Cheiron.

I been t'inkin' 'bout de preachah; whut he said de othah night. Philosophy. Paul Laurence Dunbar. **CP-DunbP**

I Beg You Come Back & Be Cheerful. Allen Ginsberg. **CP-GinsA**

I began by loving women. Blood & Honey. Erica Jong. **SP-JongE**

I began in Ohio. Stages on a Journey Westward. James Wright. **CP-WrigJ**

I began to be followed by a voice saying. Song in a Year of Catastrophe. Wendell Berry. **CP-BerrW**

I begged my love to wait a bit. All I Tell You From My Heart. Robert Ranke Graves. **CP-GravR**

I begin to die. I have been. I Can't Live Without You. Dabney Stuart. **SP-StuaD**

I beginne to waine in sight. Upon His Eye-Sight Failing Him. Robert Herrick. **CP-HerrR**

I beheld her, on a day. How He Saw Her. Ben Jonson. **EnRePo; OAEP; QFR; SeCV-1** *Fr.* A Celebration of Charis in Ten Lyric[k] Pieces [or Peeces]. **CP-JonsB**

I, being born a woman and distressed. Edna St. Vincent Millay. **CP-MillE**

I believe a leaf of grass is no less than the journey-work of the stars. Walt Whitman. **EaPr; PDV; SAmP; SeCeV; TRV; TiPo** *Fr.* Song of Myself. **CP-WhitW**

I believe in Nothing. Credo. Phoebe Hesketh. **SP-HeskP**

I believe in the day hung between your hands. Comedy of Belief. Charles Henri Ford. **SP-FordC**

I believe in the flesh and the appetites. Walt Whitman. **Prf** *Fr.* Song of Myself. **CP-WhitW**

I Believe in You. "Bob Dylan." **CP-DylaB**

I Believe in You. Charles Olson. **CP-OlsoC**

I believe in you my soul. Walt Whitman. **Prf** *Fr.* Song of Myself. **CP-WhitW**

Swiftly Arose. **TrCP**

I believe it was out of the red one that George Washington. The Buddha Inherits 6 Cars on His Birthday. Diane Wakoski. **SP-WakoD**

I believe my apprenticeship. Pro Nobis. George Oppen. **CP-OppeG**

I believe my favorite country's German. Deutsch durch Freud. Randall Jarrell. **CP-JarrR; SP-JarrR**

I believe my old lady's. What? So Soon! Langston Hughes. **SP-HughL**

I believe that a young woman. Irkalla's White Caves. Kenneth Patchen. **CP-PatcK**

I believe that you heard your master sing. Master Song. Leonard Cohen. **CP-CoheL**

I believe you did not have a happy life. A Bitterness. Mary Oliver. **SP-OlivM**

I be'n down in ole Kentucky. After a Visit. Paul Laurence Dunbar. **CP-DunbP**

I bend over an old hollow cottonwood stump. A Hollow Tree. Robert Bly. **SP-BlyR**

I bend over her but she waves. Girl of My Dreams Is Dying. Dabney Stuart. **SP-StuaD**

I bend to the ground. Noon. Philip Levine. **SP-LeviP**

I bent in the deep of night. The Pedigree. Thomas Hardy. **CP-HardT**

I bet with every Wind that blew. Emily Dickinson. **CP-DickE**

I bet you don't know who I am. Malcolm Lowry. **CP-LowrM**

I bid Love come; but lo. The Coming of Love. Wystan Hugh Auden. **CP-AudWJ**

I bid you cast out pity. At a Deathbed in the Year Two Thousand. Adrienne Rich. **CP-RicAE**

"I bite into an apple & then get bored." Flying You Home. Erica Jong. **SP-JongE**

I bless thee, O Father of Heaven & Earth, that ever I saw Flaxman's face. To John Flaxman, 12 September 1800. William Blake. **CP-BlakW**

I bless[e] Thee, Lord, because I GROW. Paradise. George Herbert. **CP-HerbG**

I blink, but there he sits, unreal. The Man Selling Pencils Outside the B. Dalton Bookstore. Barton Sutter. **SP-SuttB**

I blow an arouse / Thro' the world's wide house. March. Christina Georgina Rossetti. *Fr.* The Months: A Pageant. **CP-RosC2**

I bore a daughter flower-fair. A Sunday Morning Tragedy. Thomas Hardy. **CP-HardT**

I bore with thee long weary days and nights. The Love of Christ Which Passeth Knowledge. Christina Georgina Rossetti. **CP-RosC1**

I bought a dishmop. Youth and Beauty. William Carlos Williams. **CP-WilW1**

I bought a new. William Carlos Williams. **CP-WilW1** *Fr.* Paterson.

I bought my wife a stane o' lint. The Weary Pund o' Tow. Robert Burns. **CP-BurnR**

I bought the river from an old man. Anna Karenina and the Love-sick River. Kenneth Patchen. **CP-PatcK**

I bow down to the great goiter of Verdun. Verdun. Robert Lowell. **SP-LoweR**

I braced the drum to my arm, a flat drum, and began to play. Dream-Drumming. Muriel Rukeyser. **CP-RukeM**

I brake thy Bracelet 'gainst my will. The Bracelet of Pearle: To Silvia. Robert Herrick. **CP-HerrR**

I break my pace now for a sonic boom. John Berryman. *Fr.* Sonnets to Chris. **CP-BerrJ**

I breathe, sweet Gib [or Ghib], the temperate air of Wrest. To my Friend G.N. from Wrest. Thomas Carew. **CP-CareT**

I breathe the air you have breathed. Kathleen Jessie Raine. **SP-RainK**

I breathed enough to take the Trick. Emily Dickinson. **CP-DickE**

I bring an unaccustomed wine. Emily Dickinson. **CP-DickE**

I bring fresh showers for the thirsting flowers. The Cloud. Percy Bysshe Shelley. **CP-ShelP**

I Bring These. Jim Morrison. **SP-MorrJ**

I bring to countryside my father's sense. Poem for My Father. Charles Tomlinson. **CP-TomlC**

I bring ye love. Quest. What will love do? Upon Love, by Way of Question and Answer. Robert Herrick. **CP-HerrR**

I bring you now these flowers. Elegy for Maria Alves. Joaquim Cardozo, *tr. fr. Portuguese by* Elizabeth Bishop. **CP-BishE**

I bring you with reverent hands. A Poet to His Beloved. William Butler Yeats. **CP-YeatW**

I broke a thorn from a leaning crab tree. Tillie Sage (2). Louise McNeill **SP-McNeL**

I broke my heart this mornin'. Cora. Langston Hughes. **SP-HughL**

I brought a book to make the time pass. On a Trailways Bus a Man Who Holds His Head Strangely Speaks to the Seat Behind Him. Miller Williams. **SP-WillM**

I brought a man his dinner. Morocco. Leonard Cohen. **CP-CoheL**

I built her a tower when I was young. For Una. Robinson Jeffers. **CP-JefR3**

I built my soul a lordly pleasurehouse. The Palace of Art. Tennyson. **CP-TennA**

I buried a skunk in the garden. Dead Skunk. Richard Eberhart. **CP-EberR**

I burn[e], and cruel[l] you, in vain[e]. To My Mistress [or Mistris], I Burning in Love. Thomas Carew. **CP-CareT**

I burn, I burn; and beg of you. To Dewes. A Song. Robert Herrick. **CP-HerrR**

I Burn Money. Ogden Nash. **CP-NashO**

I burned my life, that I might find. The Alchemist. Louise Bogan. **CP-BogaL**

I Bury My Girlfriend. Leonard Cohen. **CP-CoheL**

I busied myself to find a sure. Misconception. Thomas Hardy. **CP-HardT**

I Call and I Call. Robert Herrick. **CP-HerrR**

I call her beautiful;—she says. Ralph Waldo Emerson. **CP-EmerR**

I call no goddess to inspire my strains. To Mr. Graham of Fintry, On Being Appointed to My Excise Division. Robert Burns. **CP-BurnR**

I call on the dead, I call on the defeated, on the starved. The Judgment. Marge Piercy. *Fr.* Laying Down the Tower. **SP-PierM**

I call on those that call me son. Are You Content. William Butler Yeats. **CP-YeatW**

I call out a sceret name, the name. Making Light of It. Philip Levine. **SP-LeviP**

I call the old time back: I bring my lay. Mabel Martin. John Greenleaf Whittier. **CP-WhitJ**

I Call Your Name. The Beatles. **CP-Beatl**

I called her across the room. The Woman. Robert Creeley. **CP-CreeR**

I called him to come in. Evening. James Wright. **CP-WrigJ**

I came an errand one cloud-blowing evening. The Census-Taker. Robert Frost. **CP-FrosR**

I came back from Cape Cod. White. James Schuyler. **CP-SchuJ**

I came back from the depths of the sea. Another One. Pablo Neruda, *tr. fr. Spanish by* Ben Belitt. **SP-NeruP**

I came back into my own house. How Things Change. Charles Olson. **CP-OlsoC**

I came before the water. Mussel Hunter at Rock Harbor. Sylvia Plath. **CP-PlatS**

I came by myself to a very crowded place. Lady Midnight. Leonard Cohen. **CP-CoheL**

I came far. The Dancer. Hilda Doolittle. **CP-DoolH**

I came home and found a lion in my living room. The Lion for Real. Allen Ginsberg. **CP-GinsA**

I came home from the movies with nothing on my mind. 345 W. 15th St. Allen Ginsberg. **CP-GinsA**

I came out to the barn lot. The Adze. Wendell Berry. **CP-BerrW**

I came so far for beauty. Came So Far for Beauty. Leonard Cohen. **CP-CoheL**

I came to a great door. The Beast. Theodore Roethke. **CP-RoetT**

I came to a meadow. Pastoral. Charles Simic. **SP-SimiC**

I Came to buy a smile—today. Emily Dickinson. **CP-DickE**

I came to the house. It was dark. If We Are to Know Where We Live. Kenneth Patchen. **CP-PatcK**

I came to their white terror first. Release Time. Audre Lorde. **SP-LordA**

I came to this place. Poem of the Forgotten. John Haines. **SP-HainJ**

I came to this place one November day. Hayden Carruth. *Fr.* The Asylum. **CP-CarHL**

I came to this place one November day. Hayden Carruth. *Fr.* The Asylum. **CP-CarHL**

I came too late to the hills: they were swept bare. The Wilderness. Kathleen Jessie Raine. **SP-RainK**

I came upon it in a dream. Dream. Stevie Smith. **CP-SmitS**

I can almost see it. Elegy. Thom Gunn. **CP-GunnT**

I can barely speak. Endings. Stephen Berg. **SP-BergS**

I can be more solitary. Frank Templeton Prince. *Fr.* Yüan Chên Variations. **CP-PrinF**

I can but name thee, and methinks I call. To His Honoured Kinsman Sir William Soame. Robert Herrick. **CP-HerrR**

I can call up old ghosts, and they will come. Old Ghosts. Stevie Smith. **CP-SmitS**

I come to your bedroom door. My Debt. Jim Carroll. **SP-CarrJ**

I come up to a break. Beachhead. Derek Walcott. **CP-WalcD**

I come, ye little noisy Crew. Address to the Scholars of the Village School of—1798. William Wordsworth. **CP-WorW1**

I commend you to George Washington Hill. Instructions. Carl Sandburg. **CP-SandC**

I compel you to question me about my motives. Kenneth Patchen. *Fr.* The Hunted City. **CP-PatcK**

I complain like the flute. Banks. Max Jacob, *tr. fr. French by* Elizabeth Bishop. **CP-BishE**

I concentrate. / My books hypnotize each other. February 20th. Anne Sexton. **CP-SextA**

I confess all creatures I have killed. Confession, Curse and Prayer. Paul Zimmer. **SP-ZimmP**

I confess that I love him. Emily Dickinson. **SP-DickE**

I consign to the ship of the rose. The Herbalist's Rose. Pablo Neruda, *tr. fr. Spanish by* Ben Belitt. **SP-NeruP**

I cornered the thief in the garage at dusk. Frederick Morgan. *Fr.* Death Mother. **SP-MorgF**

I cough a lot (sinus?) so I. Getting Up Ahead of Someone (Sun). Frank O'Hara. **SP-OharF**

I could be kneeling in my garden on. Place. Robert Pack. **SP-PackR**

I could be well content, allow'd the use. The Four Ages. William Cowper. **CP-CowpW**

I could be worse employed. On Making Certain Anything Has Happened. Robert Frost. *Fr.* Five Nocturnes. **CP-FrosR**

I could begin with that grave form, "Here lies." To the Memory of That Most Honoured Lady Jane, Eldest Daughter to Cuthbert, Lord Ogle: and Countess of Shrewsbury. Ben Jonson. **CP-JonsB**

I Could Believe. Philip Levine. **SP-LeviP**

I could bring You Jewels—had I a mind to. Emily Dickinson. **CP-DickE**

I could climb a mountain / for a view. For Anybody. Robert Creeley. **CP-CreeR**

I could come to believe. I Could Believe. Philip Levine. **SP-LeviP**

I could cry for roses, thinking of you. They Met Young. Carl Sandburg. **CP-SandC**

I could die—to know. Emily Dickinson. **CP-DickE**

I could digest the white slick watery mash. Cafeteria in Boston. Thom Gunn. **CP-GunnT**

I could draw its map by heart. Amor Loci. Wystan Hugh Auden. **CP-AudeW**

I Could Give All to Time. Robert Frost. **CP-FrosR**

I could have been no more than three years old. The Faded Leaf: A Chapter of Family History. John Hewitt. **CP-HewiJ**

I could have painted pictures like that youth's. Pictor Ignotus. Robert Browning. **CP-BroR1**

I could have told much by the way. Kathleen Jessie Raine. **SP-RainK**

I could hear a gown-skirt rustling. On a Heath. Thomas Hardy. **CP-HardT**

I Could Let Tom Go—But What about the Children. Stevie Smith. **CP-SmitS**

I could look at. Joy. Robert Creeley. **CP-CreeR**

I could look at you a long time. Face. Adrienne Rich. **CP-RicAE**

I could love you. Offering and Rebuff. Carl Sandburg. **CP-SandC**

I could make you crawl. "Bob Dylan." *Fr.* Some Other Kinds of Songs. **CP-DylaB**

I could not bring this splendid world nor any trading beast. Lines Written in Recapitulation. Edna St. Vincent Millay. **CP-MillE**

I could not choose but gaze; a fascination. Percy Bysshe Shelley. **ChER** *Fr.* The Revolt of Islam. **CP-ShelP**

I could not dig: I dared not rob. A Dead Statesman. Rudyard Kipling. **FaBoEE; IHNG; NBLV; OPOU; PoWW** *Fr.* Epitaphs of the War [1914–1918]. **CP-KiplR**

I could not drink it, Sweet. Emily Dickinson. **CP-DickE**

I could not, ever and anon, forbear. William Wordsworth. **EnRP** *Fr.* The Solitary. *Fr.* The Excursion. **CP-WorW2**

I could not live here, though I must and do. Low Lands. Donald Davie. **CP-DavDo**

I could not look on Death, which being known. The Coward. Rudyard Kipling. **FaBoEE; FaBoTw; OAEP; PeFWW** *Fr.* Epitaphs of the War [1914–1918]. **CP-KiplR**

I could not prove the Years had feet. Emily Dickinson. **CP-DickE**

I could not speak for amazement at your beauty. A Russell Flint. Sir John Betjeman. **CP-BetjJ**

I could not tell. What Feeling Is This? Marge Piercy. *Fr.* Walking into Love. **SP-PierM**

I could not trade you for a nightingale. *see also* Commentary—The Change. Leonard Cohen. **CP-CoheL**

I could not wear that pink dress tonight. The Pink Dress. Diane Wakoski. **SP-WakoD**

I could not weigh myself, Myself. Emily Dickinson. **SP-DickE**

I could of / If I would of. My Conscience. Ogden Nash. *Fr.* My My. **CP-NashO**

I could replace. Earth Psalm. Denise Levertov. **CP-LeveD**

I could say, / red. Hilda Doolittle. **AnAn** *Fr.* Sigil. **CP-DoolH**

I could say it's the happiest period of my life. The Ongoing Story. John Ashbery. **SP-AshbJ**

I could say the day began / behind the Sierras. Wednesday. Philip Levine. **SP-LeviP**

I could see bruises or shadows. My Grandfather Dying. Ted Kooser. **SP-KoosT**

I could see God once when I believed telling. On Wet Iota. John Ciardi. **SP-CiarJ**

I could suffice for Him, I knew. Emily Dickinson. **CP-DickE**

I Could Take. Hayden Carruth. **CP-CarHS**

I could take the Harlem night. Juke Box Love Song. Langston Hughes. **SP-HughL**

I could wish you all, who love. To All Young Men That Love. Robert Herrick. **CP-HerrR**

I couldnt ever tell you. Paris. Al Young. **CP-YounA**

"I *couldn't leave* you" you confessed next day. John Berryman. *Fr.* Sonnets to Chris. **CP-BerrJ**

I couldn't take my eyes off. At an Intersection. Thom Gunn. **CP-GunnT**

I couldn't tell fact from fiction. Senses of Insecurity. Maya Angelou. **SP-AngeM**

I count the dismal time by months and years. The Prisoner. Elizabeth Barrett Browning. **CP-BroEB**

I cradle my four-year-old daughter. Mississippi Winter III. Alice Walker. **CP-WalkA**

I crawle, I creep; my *Christ*, I come. To Christ. Robert Herrick. **CP-HerrR**

I creature being mad. A Poem of Margery Kempe. Howard Nemerov. **CP-NemeH**

I cried at Pity—not at Pain. Emily Dickinson. **CP-DickE**

I cried out to the Lord. The Screed of the Flesh. William Everson. **SP-EverW**

I cried over beautiful things knowing no beautiful thing lasts. Autumn Movement. Carl Sandburg. **CP-SandC**

I cried unto God with my voice, even unto God with my voice. Psalm 77. Bible, *O.T.* **AWP** *Fr.* Psalms. **CP-Psal**

I cried unto the Lord with my voice. Psalm 142. Bible, *O.T.* *Fr.* Psalms. **CP-Psal**

I cried when the moon was murmuring to the birds. The Withering of the Boughs. William Butler Yeats. **CP-YeatW**

I cross a laboured plot of ground. Alien Harvest. John Hewitt. **CP-HewiJ**

I cross till I am weary. Emily Dickinson. **CP-DickE**

I crossed / the street. Variations on Corpse and Mirror (Second Set). John Yau. **SP-YauJo**

I crossed sand-hills. Chorus of the Women of Chalkis. Euripides, *tr. by* Hilda Doolittle ("H.D."). **CP-DoolH** *Fr.* Iphigenia [*or* Iphigeneia] in Aulis.

I crossed the dreary moor. Incipient Madness. William Wordsworth. **CP-WorW1**

I cry, / Echo answers faintly. From the Japanese, III. John Gould Fletcher. **SP-FletJ**

I cry. / Once of this world. William Everson. *Fr.* The Kiss of the Cross. **SP-EverW** *Fr.* The Rose of Solitude.

I cry. / Once of this world. The Kiss of the Cross. William Everson. **SP-EverW** *Fr.* The Rose of Solitude.

I cry I cry. No Categories! Stevie Smith. **CP-SmitS**

I Cry, Love! Love! Theodore Roethke. **CP-RoetT**

I cry out war to those who spend their utmost. Stormy Nights. Robert Louis Stevenson. **CP-StevR**

I Cry Your Mercy, Pity, Love—Ay, Love! John Keats. **CP-KeatJ**

I cuffed you into shape. I molded you. The Robber Woman. Marilyn Hacker. **SP-HackM**

I cursed thee oft, I pity now thy case. Sonnet 46. Sir Philip Sidney. *Fr.* Astrophil and Stella. **SP-SidnP**

I cut the middle fingernail of the middle. Like a Flower in the Rain. Charles Bukowski. **SP-BukC1**

I cut the sentence. Song of a Camera. Thom Gunn. **CP-GunnT**

I dance in circles holding. The Wedding Ring Dance. Anne Sexton. **CP-SextA**

I dance on all the mountains. This Poem Is for Deer. Gary Snyder. **CP-SnydG** *Fr.* Hunting. *Fr.* Myths and Texts.

I Dare Do All. David Herbert Lawrence. **CP-LawrD**

I dare interpret: Adonai of rescue. Unknowable? Perhaps Not Altogether. John Berryman. **CP-BerrJ**

I dare not ask a kiss[e]. To Electra. Robert Herrick. **CP-HerrR**

I, dark in light, exposed. John Milton. **TrGrPo** *Fr.* The Blindness of Samson. **ImPo; LiTB** *Fr.* Samson Agonistes. **CP-MiltJ**

I deal in wisdom, not in dry desire. Supper with Lindsay. Theodore Roethke. **CP-RoetT**

I deal with farmers, things like dips and feed. Philip Larkin. *Fr.* Livings. **CP-LarkP**

I deal with farmers, things like dips and feed. Livings. Philip Larkin. **CP-LarkP**

I deamt that people from the Land of Chimes. On the Belgian Expatriation. Thomas Hardy. **CP-HardT**

I Decided. Leonard Cohen. **CP-CoheL**

I dedicate, I consecrate this grove to thee. Carmen 18. Catullus. *Fr.* Carmina. **CP-Catul**

I despise these poets with their puerile little chalk-talks of the soul. Kenneth Patchen. *Fr.* The Hunted City. **CP-PatcK**

I determined to find out whose it was. The Rival. Thomas Hardy. **CP-HardT**

I Did believe I was in Heav'n. *see also* Song: "In mine one [*or* own] monument I lie [*or* lye]." Richard Lovelace. **CP-LoveR**

I did but dream. I never knew. The Clear Vision. John Greenleaf Whittier. **CP-WhitJ**

I did but prompt the age to quit their [*or* thir] clogs. John Milton. **CP-MiltJ**

(Sonnet 11: "I did but prompt the age to quit their [*or* thir] clogs.") **CP-MiltJ**

I did not chide him, tho' I knew. Heart's Chill Between. Christina Georgina Rossetti. **CP-RosC3**

I did not expect you. The Letter. Robert Creeley. **CP-CreeR**

I did not know / that the Mexicans. Brave Bull. Charles Bukowski. **SP-BukC2**

I did not know Love had settled down on me. Love Comes Late. David Herbert Lawrence. **CP-LawrD**

I did not know that life could be so sweet. The Awakening. Paul Laurence Dunbar. **CP-DunbP**

I did not know then and I do not know now. Card Island or Cod Island? Isabella Gardner. **CP-GardI**

I did not know you when you came in there. William Dickey. **SP-DickW** *Fr.* Part Song, With Concert of Recorders. **SP-DickW**

I did not lose my heart in summer's even. Alfred Edward Housman. **CP-HousA**

I did not meet him in the gleaming years. George Sterling. Robinson Jeffers. **CP-JefR1**

I did not plow her darkness. So She Said. James Wright. **CP-WrigJ**

I did not protest. I spoke nothing but the truth. Jane Cooper. *Fr.* The Flashboat. **SP-CoopJ**

I did not reach Thee. Emily Dickinson. **CP-DickE**

I did not sleep; 'twas noon of day. Lines by Claudia. Emily Brontë. **CP-BronE**

I did not think that I should find them there. The Clerks. Edwin Arlington Robinson. **CP-RobiE**

I did not think to see them once again. Hieros Gamos. Kathleen Jessie Raine. **SP-RainK**

I did not want to appear again in these pages. *see also* How to Speak Poetry. Leonard Cohen. **CP-CoheL**

I did not want to die. I wanted you. Sacco Writes to His Son. Alun Lewis. **CP-LewiA**

I did not want to suffer again. From the Last Dream of a Dying Woman Aged Eighty. Howard Nemerov. *Fr.* Seven Macabre Songs. **CP-NemeH**

I did the dragon's will until you came. *fr.* A Woman Young and Old. William Butler Yeats. **CP-YeatW**

I didn't / want / to hurt you. Pieces. Robert Creeley. **CP-CreeR**

I didn't feel good. The Unchosen. Daniel Gerard Hoffman. **SP-HoffD**

I didn't get much sleep last night. Underwear. Lawrence Ferlinghetti. **SP-FerlL**

I didn't know it would be like this—snow. With Akhmatova at the Black Gates. Stephen Berg. **SP-BergS**

I didn't know the burly old man who lived in a small house like ours down the block in Newark. Secrets. Charles Kenneth Williams. **SP-WillC**

I didn't like the way he went away. The Smile. Robert Frost. *Fr.* The Hill Wife. **CP-FrosR**

I didn't make you know how glad I was. A Servant to Servants. Robert Frost. **CP-FrosR**

I didn't mean to treat you so bad. One of Us Must Know (Sooner or Later). "Bob Dylan." **CP-DylaB**

I didn't mind dying—it wasn't that at all. Harvard '61: Battle Fatigue. Robert Penn Warren. *Fr.* Two Studies in Idealism: Short Survey of American and Human History. **SP-WarrR**

I didn't notice. Invention of Nothing. Charles Simic. **SP-SimiC**

I Didn't Say a Word, or, Who Called That Piccolo Player a Father? Ogden Nash. **CP-NashO**

I didn't see anyone else, I just saw Lies. John Berryman. *Fr.* Sonnets to Chris. **CP-BerrJ**

I didn't used to care much. Barton Sutter. *Fr.* Cedarhome. **SP-SuttB**

I didn't want it, you wanted it. Married Blues. Kenneth Rexroth. **SP-RexrK** *Fr.* Written to Music.

I die; but when the grave shall press. Emily Brontë. **CP-BronE** (Lines: "I die; but when the grave shall press.") **CP-BronE**

I die I die the Mother said. The Grey Monk. William Blake. **CP-BlakW**

I die, no matter what I do I die. Sestina. Richard Eberhart. **CP-EberR**

I died, a follower of Cade. The Rebel. John Hewitt. **CP-HewiJ**

I died for Beauty—but was scarce. Emily Dickinson. **CP-DickE**

I died for lack of company. Voice from the Tomb (4). Stevie Smith. **CP-SmitS**

I died so many times when drunk. Alcoholic. Malcolm Lowry. **CP-LowrM**

I dig my foot into the stubborn grass. His Death from Cancer. William Dickey. **SP-DickW**

I Digress. . . . Anne Waldman. **SP-WaldA**

I dined at Natorp's yester-eve. Last Poem. Robert Browning. **CP-BroR2**

I dislikt but know no reason. Upon Himself. Robert Herrick. **CP-HerrR**

I do. / Victim. / Sales. Study Nature. Gertrude Stein. **CP-SteiG**

I do believe, and yet, in grief. The Chapel of the Hermits. John Greenleaf Whittier. **CP-WhitJ**

I do believe that die I must. His Creed. Robert Herrick. **CP-HerrR**

I do but ask that you be always fair. Edna St. Vincent Millay. **CP-MillE**

I do[e] but name thee Pembroke, and I find. To William, Earl[e] of Pembroke. Ben Jonson. **CP-JonsB**

I do confess thou art sae fair. Robert Burns. **CP-BurnR**

I do crazy things when. Memo #5. Etheridge Knight. **SP-KnigE**

I Do, I Will, I Have. Ogden Nash. **CP-NashO**

I do, Lord, I do. Therefore I am. After You Die You Don't Give a Piddling Damn. Miller Williams. **SP-WillM**

I do not always understand what you say. Poem. James Schuyler. **CP-SchuJ**

I do not ask for mercy for understanding for peace. I Do Not Speak. Stevie Smith. **CP-SmitS**

I do not bother with rhymes. Fernando Pessoa. *Fr.* Twelve Poems from *The Keeper of the Flocks.* **CP-MertT**

I do not care for Bolivar Black. Hearts and Flowers or What I Know about Bolivar Black. Ogden Nash. **CP-NashO**

I do not claim to put an end to anything. Poetry Ends with Me. Nicanor Parra, *tr. fr. Spanish by* Thomas Merton. **CP-MertT**

I do not count the day. What the Grecian Earns. Kenneth Patchen. **CP-PatcK**

I do not count the hours I spend. Waldeinsamkeit. Ralph Waldo Emerson. **CP-EmerR**

I do not fear to own me kin. Robert Louis Stevenson. **CP-StevR**

I do not feel spring's windy ingress. The Scarf of June. Richard Eberhart. **CP-EberR**

I do not have a fiddle so. Gob Music. Theodore Roethke. **CP-RoetT**

I do not imagine anyone I know, including myself, would like to. John Yau. **SP-YauJo** *Fr.* Two Meditations on Guanajuato.

I do not know if the color of the day. A Poem of Attrition. Etheridge Knight. **SP-KnigE**

I do not know if the world has lied. What I'm Doing Here. Leonard Cohen. **CP-CoheL**

I do not know more than the sea tells me. Achilles' Song. Robert Duncan. **SP-DuncR**

I do not know much about gods; but I think that the river. The Dry Salvages. Thomas Stearns Eliot. **AiP; LiTB; NoP; OxBA; SeCePo** *Fr.* Four Quartets. **CP-EliotT**

I do not know what we say. I know that your poems. Epistle to Léon-Paul Fargue. Archibald MacLeish. **CP-MacLA**

I do not know whether it is possible to present. The Bowl of Blood. Robinson Jeffers. **CP-JefR3**

I do not know who is out in the snow. Ernesto Cardenal, *tr. by* Thomas Merton. **CP-MertT** *Fr.* Gethsemani, KY.

I do not like the winter wind. It's Never Fair Weather. Ogden Nash. **CP-NashO**

I do not look for holy saints to guide me on my way. A Pilgrim's Way. Rudyard Kipling. **CP-KiplR**

I Do Not Look for Love That Is a Dream. Christina Georgina Rossetti. (Lady Montrevor.) **CP-RosC3**

I do not love my Empire's foes. Piet. Rudyard Kipling. **CP-KiplR**

I do not love, nor can it be. Of Love. Robert Herrick. **CP-HerrR**

I do not love thee, Isabel, and yet thou art most fair! Isabel. John Greenleaf Whittier. **CP-WhitJ**

I do not love to wed. The Poet Loves a Mistress, but Not to Marry. Robert Herrick. **CP-HerrR**

I do not mean the symbol. The Woman Who Could Not Live With Her Faulty Heart. Margaret Atwood. **SP-AtwM2**

I do not much mind what happens to me when you have done. Old Man Going. Jenny Joseph. **SP-JoseJ**

I do not say that I will annoint against him that boy. Robert Penn Warren. *Fr.* Saul at Gilboa. **SP-WarrR**

I do not see the hills around. The Rambler. Thomas Hardy. **CP-HardT**

I Do Not Speak. Stevie Smith. **CP-SmitS**

I do not want a plain box, I want a sarcophagus. Last Words. Sylvia Plath. **CP-PlatS**

I do not want to be reflective any more. Wolves. Louis MacNeice. **CP-MacNL**

I do not want to be told any more of your facts! The Impossibility of Dying in Your Arms Does Not Sadden Me. Charles Henri Ford. **SP-FordC**

I do not weep, I would not weep. A.S. to G.S. Emily Brontë. **CP-BronE**

I do not wish to live. Malcolm Lowry. **CP-LowrM**

I do not wish to win your vow. A Maiden's Pledge. Thomas Hardy. **CP-HardT**

I do not wonder, stones. Chartres. Archibald MacLeish. **CP-MacLA**

I do put art before. Charles Henri Ford. **SP-FordC** *Fr.* Secret Haiku.

I Do Set My Bow in the Cloud. Christina Georgina Rossetti. **CP-RosC3**

I doe love I know not what. No Luck in Love. Robert Herrick. **CP-HerrR**

I done got 'uligion, honey, an' I's happy ez a king. Temptation. Paul Laurence Dunbar. **CP-DunbP**

I done shot dope, been to jail, swilled. Cop-Out Session. Etheridge Knight. **SP-KnigE**

I don't / want to. Quit That. Archie Randolph Ammons. **SP-AmmoA**

I don't ask the Foreign Legion. On Working White Liberals. Maya Angelou. **SP-AngeM**

I don't ask to be forgiven. How Stars Start. Al Young. **CP-YounA**

I don't beat the walls with my fists. Madness. Charles Bukowski. **SP-BukC1**

I don't believe in 'ristercrats. My Sort o' Man. Paul Laurence Dunbar. **CP-DunbP**

I don't believe the radio stations. Style. Leonard Cohen. **CP-CoheL**

I don't believe the sleepers in this house. A Cabin in the Clearing. Robert Frost. **CP-FrosR**

I Don't Believe You (She Acts Like We Never Have Met). "Bob Dylan." **CP-DylaB**

I don't blame the kettle drums—they are hungry. Blizzard Notes. Carl Sandburg. **CP-SandC**

I don't care whether I am beautiful to you. One Woman to All Women. David Herbert Lawrence. **CP-LawrD**

I don't come here after June when rattlesnakes. Taneum Creek. Richard Hugo. **CP-HugoR**

I don't dare start thinking in the morning. Blues at Dawn. Langston Hughes. **SP-HughL**

I don't give a damn / For Alabam'. Croon. Langston Hughes. **SP-HughL**

I don't hate you lately. Robert Creeley. **CP-CreeR**

I don't know. The Gonfalon Raised Tonight. Charles Olson. **CP-OlsoC**

I don't know / how late it is. I'm writing. Essential Resources. Adrienne Rich. **SP-RicA2**

I don't know as I get what D.H. Lawrence is driving at. Poem. Frank O'Hara. **SP-OharF**

I don't know exactly how long ago Hector was a pup. Nature Knows Best. Ogden Nash. **CP-NashO**

I don't know how he came. Osawatomie. Carl Sandburg. **CP-SandC**

I don't know how many bottles of beer. Beer. Charles Bukowski. **SP-BukC1**

I don't know how to kiss. The Burning Mystery of Anna in 1951. Kenneth Koch. **SP-KochK**

I don't know if I helped him up. The Transport or Slaves From Maryland to Mississippi. Rita Dove. **SP-DoveR**

I don't know if you doubt it. Poem V (F) W. Frank O'Hara. **SP-OharF**

I don't know, it was raining and I had fallen down. Parts of an Opera, Parts of a Guitar, Part of Nowhere. Charles Bukowski. **SP-BukC2**

I don't know just where I'm going. Heroin. "Lou Reed." **SP-ReedL**

I don't know what day or year of their secret cycle this blazing golden afternoon might be. Dominion: Depression. Charles Kenneth Williams. **SP-WillC**

I don't know what the hell happened all that summer. Recovery. John Berryman. **SP-BerrJ**

I don't know where my father's ashes should lie. Remembering and Forgetting. Stephen Berg. **SP-BergS**

I don't know where they come from. Charles Bukowski. *Fr.* Horsemeat. **SP-BukC3**

I don't know whether you know what's new in juvenile literature. Fee Fi Ho Hum, No Wonder Baby Sucks Her Thumb. Ogden Nash. **CP-NashO**

I don't know why or how. A Leaf from Mr. Dyer's Woods. Hayden Carruth. **CP-CarHS**

I don't know why they had to put him. The Dwarf and Doctor Freud. Robert Pack. **SP-PackR**

I don't like diamonds. Voracities and Verities Sometimes Are Interacting. Marianne Craig Moore. **CP-MoorM**

I don't like guilt be it stoned or stupid. New Sensations. "Lou Reed." **SP-ReedL**

I don't like the government where I live. *with music.* Allen Ginsberg. **CP-GinsA**

I don't mean, just like that, to put down. Maximus, to Gloucester. Charles Olson. **SP-OlsoC** *Fr.* The Maximus Poems.

I don't mind dying. As Befits a Man. Langston Hughes. **SP-HughL**

I don't mind eels. The Eel. Ogden Nash. **CP-NashO**

I Don't Need a Bedsheet with Slits for Eyes to Kill You In. Charles Bukowski. **SP-BukC2**

I don't need no sleepin' medecince. What, No Sheep? Ogden Nash. **CP-NashO**

I don't remember anything of then, down there around the magnolias. Ode to Michael Goldberg ('s Birth and Other Births). Frank O'Hara. **SP-OharF**

I don't remember what I was arguing. A Five-Year Step. John Ciardi. **SP-CiarJ**

I don't rememeber / where I was going. At Forty. Richard Shelton. **SP-ShelR**

I don't say you can't find him in New Hampshire. Hayden Carruth. *Fr.* Vermont. **CP-CarHL**

I don't see your head. To Frantz Fanon. Adrienne Rich. **CP-RicAE**

I don't show my work to anybody, I am quite alone. Monkhood. John Berryman. **CP-BerrJ**

I don't think / the rain will end. Grace Paley. **CP-PaleG**

I don't think we shall. The Centenarian. William Carlos Williams. **CP-WilW1**

I don't travel on planes. The Unwinged Ones. Ogden Nash. **CP-NashO**

"I don't want." Heaven. Robert Creeley. **CP-CreeR**

I don't want to be. Western Music. Diane Wakoski. *Fr.* Fifteen Poems for a Lunar Eclipse None of Us Saw. **SP-WakoD**

I don't want to be classed among the pedantics. Grin and Bear Left. Ogden Nash. **CP-NashO**

I don't want to criticize war. Malcolm Lowry. **CP-LowrM**

I don't want to hear any news of the radio. The Morning Roundup. Gilbert Sorrentino. **SP-SorrG**

I Don't Want to Spoil the Party. The Beatles. **CP-Beatl**

I Don't Want to Startle but They Are Going to Kill Most of Us. Kenneth Patchen. **CP-PatcK**

I doubt if ten men in all Tilbury Town. Edwin Arlington Robinson. **PoEL-5** *Fr.* Captain Craig. **CP-RobiE**

I doubt it not—then more, far more. Shakspeare-Bacon's Cipher. Walt Whitman. **CP-WhitW**

I doubt not God is good, well meaning, kind. Yet Do I Marvel. Countee Cullen. **CP-CullC**

I doubt that you remember her—except. Secrets. Robert Pack. **SP-PackR**

I drank at every vine. Feast. Edna St. Vincent Millay. **CP-MillE**

I drank cool water from the fountain. The Raisin. Donald Hall. **CP-HallD**

I drank cough syrup in alcoves. Jim Carroll. **SP-CarrJ**

I drank musty ale at the Illinois Athletic Club with the millionaire. Fellow Citizens. Carl Sandburg. **CP-SandC**

I draw a head. You ask. Tom Clark. *Fr.* Suite. **SP-ClarT**

I Draw Aside the Curtain. Leonard Cohen. **CP-CoheL**

I draw hats on rabbits, sew women back. The Prestidigitator 2. Al Young. **CP-YounA**

I dreaded that first Robin, so. Emily Dickinson. **CP-DickE**

I dream a flag snaps in a cold wind. James McAuley. **SP-McAuJ** *Fr.* Green Beer.

I dream about father every night. Emily Dickinson. **SP-DickE**

I dream an inescapable dream. The Dream. Wendell Berry. **CP-BerrW**

I Dream I'm the Death of Orpheus. Adrienne Rich. **CP-RicAE; SP-RicA1; SP-RicA2**

I dream of a red-rose tree. Women and Roses. Robert Browning. **CP-BroR1**

I dream of journeys repeatedly. The Far Field. Theodore Roethke. **NAAL-2; NoAM; NoP; PrIm; SeCeV** *Fr.* North American Sequence. **CP-RoetT**

I Dream of Leslie. Kenneth Rexroth. **SP-RexrK**

I dream of poems like the bread-knife. "Hugh MacDiarmid." **SP-MacDH** *Fr.* The Kind of Poetry I Want.

I dream of you to wake: would that I might. Christina Georgina Rossetti. *Fr.* Monna Innominata. **CP-RosC2**

I dream of you walking at night along the streams. Wendell Berry. *Fr.* The Country of Marriage. **CP-BerrW**

I dream that the dearest I ever knew. Bereft, She Thinks She Dreams. Thomas Hardy. **CP-HardT**

I dream'd I lay where flowers were springing. Robert Burns. **CP-BurnR**

I Dream'd in a Dream. Walt Whitman. **CP-WhitW**

I dreamed a dream: I dreamt that I espied. Arthur Hugh Clough. **SP-ClouA**

I dreamed a tiger. Continuity. Steve Griffiths. **SP-GrifS**

I dreamed and did not seek: today I seek. Yet A Little While. Christina Georgina Rossetti. **CP-RosC2**

I dreamed as in my bed I lay. *fr.* Words for Music Perhaps. William Butler Yeats. **CP-YeatW**

I dreamed I already loved you. Three Poems with Yevtushenko. James Dickey. **CP-DickJ**

I dreamed I called you on the telephone. For the Dead. Adrienne Rich. **SP-RicA1; SP-RicA2**

I dreamed I moved among the Elysian fields. Edna St. Vincent Millay. **CP-MillE**

I Dreamed I Saw St. Augstine. "Bob Dylan." **CP-DylaB**

I dreamed I was among the conquerors. Sonnet. Edward Estlin Cummings. **CP-CummE**

I dreamed I was president of these United States. The Day John Kennedy Died. "Lou Reed." **SP-ReedL**

I dreamed, Justine, we chanced on one another. The Apparition. Charles Tomlinson. **CP-TomlC**

I dreamed kind Jesus fouled the big-gun gears. Soldier's Dream. Wilfred Owen. **CP-OwenW**

I Dreamed My Genesis. Dylan Thomas. **CP-ThomD**

I dreamed of a tiger, wounded. Two Pendants: For the Ears. William Carlos Williams. **CP-WilW2**

I dreamed of an instrument of political torture. Another Dollar. Charles Kenneth Williams. **CP-WillC**

I Dreamed of an Out-Thrust Arm of Land. Philip Larkin. **CP-LarkP**

I dreamed of forest alleys fair. Robert Louis Stevenson. **CP-StevR**

I dreamed of horses in the night. South Wind. John Haines. **SP-HainJ**

I dreamed one man stood against a thousand. Graves. Carl Sandburg. **CP-SandC**

I dreamed [*or* dream'd] that, as I wandered [*or* wander'd] by the way. The Question. Percy Bysshe Shelley. **CP-ShelP**

I dreamed that dead, and meditating. The Weed. Elizabeth Bishop. **CP-BishE**

I dreamed that I married. Skagway. John Haines. **SP-HainJ**

I dreamed that I stood in a valley, and amid sighs. He Tells a Valley Full of Lovers. William Butler Yeats. **CP-YeatW**

I dreamed that I was dead, as all men do. But Only Mine. James Wright. **CP-WrigJ**

I Dreamed That I Was Old. Stanley Jasspon Kunitz. **CP-KuniS**

I dreamed that loving me he would love on. Zara. Christina Georgina Rossetti. **CP-RosC3**

I dreamed that Milton's spirit rose, and took. Fragment: Milton's Spirit. Percy Bysshe Shelley. **CP-ShelP**

I dreamed that one had died in a strange place. A Dream of Death. William Butler Yeats. **CP-YeatW**

I dreamed the play was real. Doll's "Arabian Nights," A. Nicholas Vachel Lindsay. **CP-LindV**

I dreamed there was once held a feast. Gerousios Oinos. Robert Browning. **CP-BroR2**

I dreamed there would be Spring no more. Tennyson. **NOBE** *Fr.* In Memoriam A. H. H. **CP-TennA**

I dreamed this coast before Croatia. Sailing Dalmatia. Richard Hugo. **CP-HugoR**

I dreamed [*or* dream'd] this mortal part of mine. The Vine. Robert Herrick. **CP-HerrR**

I dreamed [*or* dream'd] we both were in bed. The Vision to Electra. Robert Herrick. **CP-HerrR**

I Dreamt a Dream! what can it mean? The Angel. William Blake. **CP-BlakW** *Fr.* Songs of Experience.

I dreamt all night such glad painful exultant dreams. A Dream of What Is Missing. Robert Bly. **SP-BlyR**

I dreamt he drove me back to the asylum. John Berryman. *Fr.* Sonnets to Chris. **CP-BerrJ**

I dreamt her sensual proportions. The Death of Venus. Robert Creeley. **CP-CreeR**

I dreamt I caught a little owl. Christina Georgina Rossetti. **CP-RosC2**

I dreamt I dwelt in marble halls. Lays of Mystery, Imagination, and Humour, No. 1: The Palace of Humbug. "Lewis Carroll." **CP-CarrL**

I dreamt. I saw three ladies in a tree. The Three Ladies. Robert Creeley. **CP-CreeR**

I dreamt last night. For No Clear Reason. Robert Creeley. **CP-CreeR**

I dreamt last night I heard someone speak your name. How Could You Ever Be Fine. Stephen Dobyns. **SP-DobyS**

I Dreamt, last night, Thou didst transfuse. His Dream[e]. Robert Herrick. **CP-HerrR**

I Dreamt My Love A-Dying Lay. Daniel Gerard Hoffman. **SP-HoffD**

I dreamt of a seal. Seal. Anne Sexton. **CP-SextA**

I dreamt the roses one time went. The Parliament of Roses to Julia. Robert Herrick. **CP-HerrR**

I dreamt we slept in a moss in Donegal. Seamus Heaney. **NoP** *Fr.* Glanmore Sonnets. **SP-HeanS**

I drew solitude over me, on the lone shore. Prelude. Robinson Jeffers. **CP-JefR1**

I drew the letter out, while gleamed. The Sun on the Letter. Thomas Hardy. **CP-HardT**

I drip, drip here. The Sundial on a Wet Day. Thomas Hardy. **CP-HardT**

I drive my car / through a valley. Countryside. Charles Bukowski. **SP-BukC2**

I drive my car to supermarket. Superman. John Updike. **CP-UpdiJ**

I dropped my pen; and listened to the Wind. William Wordsworth. **CP-WorW1**

(Composed at the Same Time and on the Same Occasion.) **CP-WorW1**

I dropped to depth. Birth and Death. Richard Eberhart. **CP-EberR**

I drove up to the graveyard, which. The Soul Longs to Return Whence It Came. Richard Eberhart. **CP-EberR**

I dug and dug amongst the snow. Christina Georgina Rossetti. **CP-RosC2**

I dwell alone—I dwell alone, alone. Autumn. Christina Georgina Rossetti. **CP-RosC1**

I dwell amid the city ever. The Soul's Travelling. Elizabeth Barrett Browning. **CP-BroEB**

I dwell in a lonely house I know. Ghost House. Robert Frost. **CP-FrosR**

I dwell in Grace's court[e]. Content and Ri[t]ch[e]. Robert Southwell. **CP-SoutR**

I dwell in Possibility. Emily Dickinson. **CP-DickE**

I dwelled in Hell on earth to write this rhyme. Two Sonnets. Allen Ginsberg. **CP-GinsA**

I dwelt alone. Eulalie—A Song. Edgar Allan Poe. **CP-PoeEd**

I dwelt in the shade of a city. A Gentleman's Epitaph on Himself and a Lady, Who Were Buried Together. Thomas Hardy. **CP-HardT**

I Dye Alive. Robert Southwell. **CP-SoutR**

I Dye Without Desert. Robert Southwell. **CP-SoutR**

I employ the blind mandolin player. A Music. Wendell Berry. **CP-BerrW**

I end up then. "Bob Dylan." *Fr.* 11 Outlined Epitaphs. **CP-DylaB**

I end up then. 11 Outlined Epitaphs. "Bob Dylan." **CP-DylaB**

I enter a daisy-and-buttercup land. Growth in May. Thomas Hardy. **CP-HardT**

I enter thy garden of roses. Translation of the Romaic Song *Mpeno mes to periboli, Horaiotate Haide, k. t. l.* Byron. **CP-Byron**

I enter your night / like a darkened boat, a smuggler. Corpse Song. Margaret Atwood. *Fr.* Songs of the Transformed. **SP-AtwM1**

I entered the cave of the amethysts. Pablo Neruda, *tr. fr. Spanish by* Ben Belitt. **SP-NeruP** *Fr.* Skystones.

I entered weary of my woes. The Rose. John Crowe Ransom. **SP-RansJ**

I entrust my all to you, Aurelius. Catullus. *See* Carmen 15: "*My love & I are yours to command.*"

I Envy Not in Any Moods. Tennyson. **EBEvV; FHYEP; FaBoEn; HBV; ImPo; LiTB; MeMBP; OAEL-2; OBNC; PeHV** *Fr.* In Memoriam A. H. H. **CP-TennA**

"I hold it true, whate're befall." **UV**

I envy seas—whereon He rides. Emily Dickinson. **CP-DickE**

I envy you your chance of death. Fragment 68. Hilda Doolittle. **CP-DoolH**

I exhibit here the well-known failure of. The Hero Comes Home in His Hamper, and Is Exhibited at the World's Fair. Howard Nemerov. **CP-NemeH**

I expect you from the North. The path winds in. John Berryman. *Fr.* Sonnets to Chris. **CP-BerrJ**

I expected him to look dead in the casket. Elegy. Richard Hugo. **CP-HugoR**

I expected to be greeted by one of the figures. Pleasures of This Gentle Day. Kenneth Patchen. **CP-PatcK**

I face impossible feats at your command. Pride of Love. Robert Ranke Graves. **CP-GravR**

I fain would sing of Cadmus king. Transcriptions from the "Anacreontea." Robert Browning. **CP-BroR2**

I faint, I perish with my love! I grow. Fragment. Percy Bysshe Shelley. **CP-ShelP**

I fall asleep, and dream I am working in the fields. A Dream of a Brother. Robert Bly. **SP-BlyR**

I fall asleep these days too easily. Dozing on the Lawn. Archibald MacLeish. **CP-MacLA**

I fall into It Without Trying. Charles Bukowski. **SP-BukC3**

I fall out / crush the useless excess of god. Sea Battle. Jim Carroll. **SP-CarrJ**

I fancy the good fairies dressed in white. Christina Georgina Rossetti. **CP-RosC3**

I farm a pasture where the boulders lie. Of the Stones of the Place. Robert Frost. **CP-FrosR**

I fasted for some forty days on bread and buttermilk. The Pilgrim. William Butler Yeats. **CP-YeatW**

I fear a Man of frugal Speech. Emily Dickinson. **CP-DickE**

I fear it much as I fear death. The Dollarton Bus Stop. Malcolm Lowry. **CP-LowrM**

I fear my conscience because it makes me lie. Symptoms. Robert Lowell. **SP-LoweR**

I fear[e] no Earthly Powers. On Himselfe ("I fear no Earthly Powers"). Robert Herrick. **CP-HerrR**

I fear the ladies and. Rencontres Funestes. Stevie Smith. **CP-SmitS**

I fear thy kisses, gentle maiden. Percy Bysshe Shelley. **CP-ShelP**

(To ———: "I fear thy kisses, gentle maiden.") **CP-ShelP**

I fear to draw the wing of the sparrow. Written Next to a Blue Flower. Pablo Antonio Cuadra, *tr. fr. Spanish by* Thomas Merton. **CP-MertT**

I fear we think too lightly of. Emily Dickinson. **SP-DickE**

I fear you have much happiness. Emily Dickinson. **SP-DickE**

I feard the fury [*or* roughness] of my wind. William Blake. **CP-BlakW**

I feared these present years. On Being Twenty-Six. Philip Larkin. **CP-LarkP**

I feed a flame within, which so torments me. Song. John Dryden. **SP-DrydJ** *Fr.* Secret Love; or, The Maiden Queen.

I fee'd a man at Martinmass. *see also* The Plowman: "I paid a man at Martinmass." Robert Burns. **CP-BurnR**

I feel a mortal isolation. Every Lovely Limb's a Desolation. Stevie Smith. **CP-SmitS**

I feel absolute reverence to nobody and to nothing human. Absolute Reverence. David Herbert Lawrence. **CP-LawrD**

I feel all right. Now. White Rose. César Vallejo, *tr. fr. Spanish by* James Wright. **CP-WrigJ**

I feel an unvintageable contempt. From This Acceptance, Sir, We Might Proceed. Malcolm Lowry. **CP-LowrM**

I feel as if I am at a dead. Allen Ginsberg. **CP-GinsA**

I feel congruity, feel colleagueship. Relations. John Berryman. **CP-BerrJ**

I Feel Drunk All the Time. Kenneth Patchen. **CP-PatcK**

I Feel Fine. The Beatles. **CP-Beatl**

I feel funny today. A Picnic Cantata. James Schuyler. **CP-SchuJ**

I feel ill. What can the matter be? Come, Death (2). Stevie Smith. **CP-SmitS**

I feel illimitable essence. Undercliff Evening. Richard Eberhart. **CP-EberR**

I feel like / I feel like shit. Jeanne D'Arc. Patti Smith. **SP-SmitP**

I feel like dancin', baby. Sunday by the Combination. Langston Hughes. **SP-HughL**

I feel my face being bitten by the tides. The Knowledge That Comes through Experience. Jane Cooper. **SP-CoopJ**

I feel terribly strong today. The Beginning of April. Charles Kenneth Williams. **CP-WillC; SP-WillC**

I feel the caress of my own fingers. The Gentle Man. William Carlos Williams. **CP-WilW1**

I feel wonderful today after a long night. In Death I Know Well Enough All Things End in Emptiness. Stephen Berg. **SP-BergS**

I fell in love at my first evening party. A Dream of Frances Speedwell. Robert Ranke Graves. **CP-GravR**

I fell in love with a girl. John Berryman. **CP-BerrJ**

I fell in love with Major Spruce. Progression. Stevie Smith. **CP-SmitS**

I Fellowed Sleep. Dylan Thomas. **CP-ThomD**

I felt a Cleaving in my Mind. Emily Dickinson. **CP-DickE**

I felt a Funeral, in my Brain. Emily Dickinson. **CP-DickE**

I felt life coming on. Listing. Richard Eberhart. **CP-EberR**

I felt my forefinger. Charles Henri Ford. **SP-FordC** *Fr.* Secret Haiku.

I felt my life with both my hands. Emily Dickinson. **CP-DickE**

I felt the chill of the meadow underfoot. The Quest of the Purple-Fringed. Robert Frost. **CP-FrosR**

I felt the empty cabin wasn't abandoned. Living Alone. Richard Hugo. **CP-HugoR**

I felt the lurch and halt of her heart. Lightning. David Herbert Lawrence. **CP-LawrD**

I felt the universe with my fingers; and it was. Fever. Alun Lewis. **CP-LewiA**

I felt the wind soft from the land of souls. Olives and Mountains. Elizabeth Barrett Browning. **FaBoPP; OBTV** *Fr.* Aurora Leigh. **CP-BroEB**

I felt, under my old breasts, this April day. Kathleen Jessie Raine. **SP-RainK**

I fight and fight. / I wake up. Grow. Joseph Ceravolo. **SP-CeraJ**

I fight with the tools of the mind. Ways and Means. Richard Eberhart. **CP-EberR**

I figured you as nude between. The Apostrophe to Vincentine. Wallace Stevens. **CP-StevW**

I find among the poems of Schiller. The Caterpillar. Ogden Nash. *Fr.* The Astigmatic Naturalist. **CP-NashO**

I find it now, the schoolhouse by the tree. The Schoolhouse. Galway Kinnell. **SP-KinnG**

I find it very difficult to enthuse. Everybody Tells Me Everything. Ogden Nash. **CP-NashO**

I find it written of SIMONIDES. William Wordsworth. **CP-WorW1**

I find no peace and all my war[r] is done. Petrarch, *tr. by* Sir Thomas Wyatt. **CP-WyatT** *Fr.* Sonnets to Laura.

I find nothing to say. Inditing a Good Matter. Donald Davie. **CP-DavDo**

I finished my wine. Night on a Visa Card. Charles Bukowski. **SP-BukC3**

I first discovered what was killing these men. Absalom. Muriel Rukeyser. **CP-RukeM**

I first saw you in a trance. Erosong. Al Young. **CP-YounA**

I first tasted under Apollo's lips. Evadne. Hilda Doolittle. **CP-DoolH**

I first thought sex was creation—sweet-bitter joke. Eugene Connolly. James Liddy. **CP-LiddJ**

I fit for them. Emily Dickinson. **CP-DickE**

I fix[e] mine eye on thine, and there. Witchcraft by a Picture. John Donne. **CP-DonnJ**

I flash-glimpsed in the headlights—the high moment. Coming Down through Somerset. Ted Hughes. **SP-HughT**

I follow thought and what the world announces. Sonnet. Delmore Schwartz. **SP-SchwD**

I followed my Duke ere I was a lover. Sir Richard's Song. Rudyard Kipling. **CP-KiplR** *Fr.* Young Men at the Manor. *Fr.* Puck of Pook's Hill.

I followed the narrow cliffside trail half way up the mountain. The Deer Lay Down Their Bones. Robinson Jeffers. **CP-JefR3**

I followed Thee, my God, I followed Thee / To see the end. Christina Georgina Rossetti. **CP-RosC2**

I for whom the world is a clear stream. In San Marco, Venezia. William Carlos Williams. **CP-WilW1**

I forget the names of towns without rivers. The Towns We Know and Leave Behind, the Rivers We Carry with Us. Richard Hugo. **CP-HugoR**

I found a / weed. Reflective. Archie Randolph Ammons. **SP-AmmoA**

I found a dimpled spider, fat and white. Design. Robert Frost. **CP-FrosR**

I found a house in the forest. The House of the Injured. John Haines. **SP-HainJ**

I found a loose cement slab outside the icecream store. The Best Way to Get Famous Is to Run Away. Charles Bukowski. **SP-BukC2**

I found a pigeon's skull on the machair. Perfect. "Hugh MacDiarmid." **SP-MacDH**

I found a torrent falling in a glen. The Torrent. Edwin Arlington Robinson. **CP-RobiE**

I Found Her Out There. Thomas Hardy. **CP-HardT**

I found in dreams a place of wind and flowers. A Ballad of Life. Algernon Charles Swinburne. **SP-SwinA**

I found Love in a certain place. In a Certain Place. Christina Georgina Rossetti. **CP-RosC3**

I found me in a great surging space. The Masked Face. Thomas Hardy. **CP-HardT**

I found myself inside a massive concrete shell. The Trade. Gary Snyder. **CP-SnydG**

I found that ivory image there. *fr.* Words for Music Perhaps. William Butler Yeats. **CP-YeatW**

I found the words to every thought. Emily Dickinson. **CP-DickE**

I found them blind I taught how to see. On F[laxman] & S[tothard]. William Blake. **CP-BlakW**

I found them blind, I taught them how to see, *see also* On F[laxamn] & S[tothard]. William Blake. **CP-BlakW**

I found this jawbone at the sea's edge. Relic. Ted Hughes. **SP-HughT**

I found you and I lost you. A Golden Day. Paul Laurence Dunbar. **CP-DunbP**

I found you on a rainy morning. Nansen. Gary Snyder. **CP-SnydG**

I freeze, I freeze, and nothing dwels. The Frozen Heart. Robert Herrick. **CP-HerrR**

I Fucked the Dregs. Jim Morrison. **SP-MorrJ**

I fumbled with my oldish books last night. Doctor Trustus: Man of Good Will. John Clellon Holmes. **SP-HolmJ**

I gaed a waefu' gate, yestreen. The Blue-Eyed Lassie. Robert Burns. **CP-BurnR**

I gaed up to Dunne. Robin Shure in Hairst. Robert Burns. **CP-BurnR**

I gained it so. Emily Dickinson. **CP-DickE**

I gat your letter, winsome Willie. Robert Burns. **CP-BurnR** (To W. S*****n, Ochiltree.) **CP-BurnR**

I gather groups of freshmen. I distribute. "These Students Couldn't Write Their Way out of a Paper Bag"—Anonymous. Ron Koertge. **SP-KoerR**

I gather thyme upon the sunny hills. Immalee. Christina Georgina Rossetti. **CP-RosC3**

I gather up the giant holes. Post-Modernism. Jim Carroll. **SP-CarrJ**

I Gave a Sweet Smell. Christina Georgina Rossetti. **CP-RosC2**

I Gave Away That Kid. Grace Paley. **CP-PaleG**

I gave myself to Him. Emily Dickinson. **CP-DickE**

I gave this part away from me. Matriarchly. Anne Waldman. **SP-WaldA**

I gave to Hope a watch of mine: but he. Hope. George Herbert. **CP-HerbG**

I gaze at you. The Tattooed Man. Robert Earl Hayden. **CP-HaydR**

I gazed through the mist. From the Japanese, VI. John Gould Fletcher. **SP-FletJ**

I gazed upon the cloudless moon. Emily Brontë. **CP-BronE**

I gazed within thine earnest eyes. Emily Brontë. **CP-BronE**

I Genitori Perduti. Lawrence Ferlinghetti. **SP-FerlL**

I get closer to the dream, trying to remember. Increasing Night. Laurence Lieberman. **SP-LiebL**

I get high when I see you go by. It's Only Love. The Beatles. **CP-Beatl**

I get many phonecalls now. 462-0614. Charles Bukowski. **SP-BukC1**

I get more and more mimeo chapbooks in the mail. A Note to the Boys in the Back Room. Charles Bukowski. **SP-BukC3**

I get, surprisingly, a sense of space. To Londoners. Donald Davie. **CP-DavDo**

I get too many. A Good One. Charles Bukowski. **SP-BukC1**

I get up late and ask what has to be done today. Getting Up Late. Robert Bly. **SP-BlyR**

I Give Death to a Son. Phoebe Hesketh. **SP-HeskP**

I give her all my love. And I Love Her. John Lennon *and* Paul McCartney. **CP-Beatl**

I give the undertakers permission to haul my body. Testament. Carl Sandburg. **CP-SandC**

I give thee joy!—I know to thee. Naples. John Greenleaf Whittier. **CP-WhitJ**

I give you a Caribbean isle of seventy years ago. History. Frederick Morgan. **SP-MorgF**

I give you now Professor Twist. The Purist. Ogden Nash. **CP-NashO**

I give you the cosmos, freely the whole works. Scriptsmith. Carl Sandburg. **CP-SandC**

I give you the end of a golden string. William Blake. **CP-BlakW; NTP EnRP; OBNC; Spl; WGRP** *Fr.* Jerusalem; The Emanation of the Giant Albion. **CP-BlakW**

(Epigraph.) **OBNC**

(To the Christians.) **EnRP; WGRP**

I give you what is unbounded, passing from dark to dark. Wendell Berry. *Fr.* The Country of Marriage. **CP-BerrW**

I glimpsed a woman's muslined form. On Stinsford Hill at Midnight. Thomas Hardy. **CP-HardT**

I go a road / among the upturned. In the Underworld. Muriel Rukeyser. **CP-RukeM**

I go everywhere underground. It is a burden I have. To Impress the Girl Next Door. Ron Koertge. **SP-KoerR**

I go in under foliage. In Rain. Wendell Berry. **CP-BerrW**

I go into the men's room Springfield bus station. The Love Nut. Lawrence Ferlinghetti. **SP-FerlL**

I Go Out in the Long Nights. Paul Zimmer. **SP-ZimmP**

I go out like a ghost. Home Town. William DeWitt Snodgrass. **SP-SnodW**

I go out of the house for the first time. Miller Williams. **SP-WillM**

I Go Out of the House for the First Time. Miller Williams. **SP-WillM**

I go through hollyhocks. Las Trampas U. S. A. Charles Tomlinson. **CP-TomlC**

I go to concert, party, ball. My Rival. Rudyard Kipling. **CP-KiplR**

I go to my desk to write a letter. The Second Month It's Not Itemized. Ogden Nash. **CP-NashO**

I go to pick her up. Huge Ear Rings. Charles Bukowski. **SP-BukC1**

I Go to School. John Hewitt. **CP-HewiJ**

I go to seek the peace we could not save. Epitaph for a Conscript, 1940. John Hewitt. **CP-HewiJ**

I go to the door often. The Indigo Bunting. Robert Bly. **SP-BlyR**

I go to this window. Edward Estlin Cummings. **CP-CummE**

I got / a syringe. Sure. Jim Carroll. **SP-CarrJ**

I got a job now. Elevator Boy. Langston Hughes. **SP-HughL**

I got a seat down front and started. Bad Action. Charles Bukowski. **SP-BukC3**

I got his ashes, she said, and I took them. Ashes. Charles Bukowski. **SP-BukC1**

I got mixed up confusion. Mixed Up Confusion. "Bob Dylan." **CP-DylaB**

I got my hair cut. Poem. James Schuyler. **CP-SchuJ**

I got so I could take his name. Emily Dickinson. **CP-DickE**

I got something to say that might cause you pain. You Can't Do That. The Beatles. **CP-Beatl**

I Got the Fat Poet into a Corner. Kenneth Patchen. **CP-PatcK**

I got there by dusk. Opening the Door of a Barn I Thought Was Empty on New Year's Eve. Robert Bly. **SP-BlyR**

I got this graveyard woman, you know she keeps my kid. From a Buick 6. "Bob Dylan." **CP-DylaB**

I got three bulls and a native cutthroat, lover. Phoning from Sweathouse Creek. Richard Hugo. **CP-HugoR**

I got tired of writing the wrong stories. The Journalist Buys a Pig Farm. Miller Williams. **SP-WillM**

I got to know, Lord, when to pull back on the reins. Trouble in Mind. "Bob Dylan." **CP-DylaB**

I got up in the night. The Riverman. Elizabeth Bishop. **CP-BishE**

I gotta / buy me a new. Après le Bain. William Carlos Williams. **CP-WilW2**

I grant thou wert not married to my Muse. Sonnet 132. William Shakespeare. *Fr.* Sonnets. **CP-ShaWS**

I grant you friendship is a royal thing. Edwin Arlington Robinson. *Fr.* Octaves. **CP-RobiE**

I grant you: peace is desirable. Peace. William Carlos Williams. **CP-WilW1**

I grew a rose once more to please mine eyes. Fulfilment. Paul Laurence Dunbar. **CP-DunbP**

I grew a rose within a garden fair. Promise. Paul Laurence Dunbar. **CP-DunbP**

I grew to his exact same size. My Father at His Height. Barton Sutter. **SP-SuttB**

I grew up bent over. Prodigy. Charles Simic. **SP-SimiC**

I grieve and grieve for what I have done. At Shag's Heath. Thomas Hardy. **CP-HardT**

I grieve not, Courtling, thou art started up. To Courtling. Ben Jonson. **CP-JonsB**

I grieve that better souls than mine. Ralph Waldo Emerson. **CP-EmerR**

I grieved for Buonaparté, with a vain. 1801. William Wordsworth. **CP-WorW1**

I grizzle the embers of our onetime life. Randall Jarrell 2. Robert Lowell. **SP-LoweR**

I groped for him before I knew. Emily Dickinson. **CP-DickE**

I grow old under an intensity. Mirror. James Merrill. **SP-MerrJ**

I grow so weary: is it death. A Yawn. Christina Georgina Rossetti. **CP-RosC3**

I grumble over life. Discontent. John Gould Fletcher. **SP-FletJ**

—I guess all I'm trying to say is I saw Crazy Horse die for. You Can Start the Poetry Now, Or: News from Crazy Horse. Thomas McGrath. **SP-McGrT**

I guess because it was Key West. Meeting the Reincarnation Analyst. Gary Gildner. **SP-GildG**

I guess I am just an old fogey. I Remember Yule. Ogden Nash. **CP-NashO**

I guess I must address you. Your Dailiness. Alice Notley. **SP-NotlA**

I guess it is farewell to grammatical compunction. Oafishness Sells Good, Like an Advertisement Should. Ogden Nash. **CP-NashO**

I Guess You Ought to Know Who You Are. Robert Penn Warren. *Fr.* Ballad of a Sweet Dream of Peace. **SP-WarrR**

I guessed the letter. Thrush. Paul Muldoon. **SP-MuldP**

I ha' seen them 'mid the clouds on the heather. The White Stag. Ezra Pound. **SP-PounE**

I had a barrel organ and I cranked its distant tones. Organ. Alfonso Cortes, *tr. fr. Spanish by* Thomas Merton. **CP-MertT**

I had a bear that danced. Song in Sligo. Jean Garrigue. **SP-GarrJ**

I had a daily Bliss. Emily Dickinson. **CP-DickE**

I had a Donkey, that was all right. The Donkey. Theodore Roethke. **CP-RoetT**

I had a dove and the sweet dove died. Song. John Keats. **CP-KeatJ**

I had a dream / and I could see. Nightmare Boogie. Langston Hughes. **SP-HughL**

I Had a Dream. Stevie Smith. **CP-SmitS**

I had a dream. A wondrous thing. Spring and Death. Gerard Manley Hopkins. **CP-HopkG**

I had a dream I was a bird. Avondall. Stevie Smith. **CP-SmitS**

I had a dream of nourishment. A Dream of Nourishment. Stevie Smith. **CP-SmitS**

I had a dream three walls stood up wherein a raven bird. Anger's Freeing Power. Stevie Smith. **CP-SmitS**

I had a dream, which was not all a dream. Darkness. Byron. **CP-Byron**

I had a gardener. I had him until haying-time. The Gardener in Haying-Time. Edna St. Vincent Millay. **CP-MillE**

I had a guinea golden. Emily Dickinson. **CP-DickE**

"I had a holiday once," said the woman. Expectation and Experience. Thomas Hardy. **CP-HardT**

I had a little chamber in the house. Elizabeth Barrett Browning. **FaBoPP** *Fr.* Aurora Leigh. **CP-BroEB**

I had a little Sorrow. The Penitent. Edna St. Vincent Millay. **CP-MillE**

I had a love in soft south land. Love from The North. Christina Georgina Rossetti. **CP-RosC1**

I had a misfortune in September. Detail. William Carlos Williams. **CP-WilW2**

I had a nurse when I was very small. Betrayal. John Hewitt. **CP-HewiJ**

I had a picture by him—a print, I think—on my bedroom wall. Homage to Claude Lorrain. Charles Wright. **SP-WrigC**

I had a strange dream the other night after I had left you. Reported Missing. Jenny Joseph. **SP-JoseJ**

I had a sweet bird. Hippy-Mo. Stevie Smith. **CP-SmitS**

I had a terrible dream the other night. A Dream. "Lou Reed." **SP-ReedL**

I had a vision when the night was late. The Vision of Sin. Tennyson. **CP-TennA**

I had a wife and children. *see also* Commentary—A Working Man. Leonard Cohen. **CP-CoheL**

I had a wooden boat to float and sail. Lost *Argo*, Islandmagee, Summer 1919. John Hewitt. **CP-HewiJ**

I had already won. Camp Wakonda, 1940. Robert Pack. **SP-PackR**

I had an evil day when I. On Some Ghostly Companions at a Spa. Robert Louis Stevenson. **CP-StevR**

I had as lief be embraced by the porter at the hotel. Two Figures in Dense Violet Night. Wallace Stevens. **CP-StevW**

I had been his fool. Cuchulain. William Carlos Williams. **CP-WilW2**

I had been hungry, all the Years. Emily Dickinson. **CP-DickE**

I had been on the road before. The first time. Belt. Richard Hugo. **CP-HugoR**

I had been reading what you have written of your idleness. La Flor. William Carlos Williams. **CP-WilW1**

I had been thinking of Bosnians and Serbs. Wind in a Jar. Stephen Dunn. **SP-DunnS**

I had been thinking of Gabriel. Hilda Doolittle. **NALW** *Fr.* Tribute to the Angels. **CP-DoolH**

I had been up until 3 a.m. the night before. Charles Bukowski. *Fr.* Horsemeat. **SP-BukC3**

I had come all the way here from the sea. And Bees of Paradise. Hart Crane. **CP-CranH**

I had come to a strange city, without belongings. The Beginning. Louise Glück. *Fr.* Marathon. **SP-GlücL**

I had come to the edge of the water. Seamus Heaney. **FaBCIP; PBCIP** *Fr.* Station Island. **SP-HeanS**

I had come to the house, in a cave of trees. Medusa. Louise Bogan. **CP-BogaL**

I had eight birds hatcht [*or* hatched] in one nest. In Reference to Her Children, 23 June, 1659 [*or* 1656]. Anne Bradstreet. **CP-BradA**

I had finished my dinner. An Easy Decision. Kenneth Patchen. **CP-PatcK**

I had for my winter evening walk. Good Hours. Robert Frost. **CP-FrosR**

I had forgotten Hertfordshire. Hertfordshire. Sir John Betjeman. **CP-BetjJ**

I had forgotten how the frogs must sound. Assault. Edna St. Vincent Millay. **CP-MillE**

I had gone to a freightyard auction of sealed crates. A Crate of Sterling Loving Cups. John Ciardi. **SP-CiarJ**

I had grown invisible as a city sparrow. Some Collisions Bring Luck. Marge Piercy. **SP-PierM**

I had had / a beetle. Charles Olson. **CP-DoolH**

I had heard / before, of an / American who would have preferred. Mr. Brodsky. Charles Tomlinson. **CP-TomlC**

I had high hopes for this book. The Price of This Book. Leonard Cohen. **CP-CoheL**

I had hold of the comet's mane. The Comet of Prophecy. Nicholas Vachel Lindsay. **CP-LindV**

I Had Hope When Violence Was Ceas't. Geoffrey Hill. **CP-HillG**

I had hoped to express more. Emily Dickinson. **SP-DickE**

I Had It for a Moment. Leonard Cohen. **CP-CoheL**

I had just won $115 from the headshakers and. I Am Visited by an Editor and a Poet. Charles Bukowski. **SP-BukC2**

I had long known the diverse tastes of the wood. Gift of Sight. Robert Ranke Graves. **CP-GravR**

I had no Cause to be awake. Emily Dickinson. **CP-DickE**

I Had No Idea It Was So Late. Ogden Nash. **CP-NashO**

I had no thought to find. Dabney Stuart. **NGP** *Fr.* The Opposite Field. **SP-StuaD**

I had no time to Hate. Emily Dickinson. **CP-DickE**

I had not expected Imbellis here. Zimmer Finds Imbellis in the Ancient Graves. Paul Zimmer. **SP-ZimmP**

I had not known before. Forever. Paul Laurence Dunbar. **CP-DunbP**

I had not minded—Walls. Emily Dickinson. **CP-DickE**

I had not much thought of mercy. The Lasting Seasons. Kenneth Patchen. **CP-PatcK**

I had not thought so tame a thing. Edna St. Vincent Millay. *Fr.* Theme and Variations. **CP-MillE**

I had not thought to have unlockt my lips. Temperance and Virginity. John Milton. **OBS** *Fr.* Comus; a Masque Presented at Ludlow Castle.

I had nothing to do with it. I was not here. A Centenary Note: Inscribed to Little Crow, Leader of the Sioux Rebellion in Minnesota, 1862. James Wright. **CP-WrigJ**

I had once poured oil on his head. Robert Penn Warren. *Fr.* Saul at Gilboa. **SP-WarrR**

I had over-prepared the event. Villanelle: The Psychological Hour. Ezra Pound. **SP-PounE**

I had piano lessons once a week. Music Lessons. John Hewitt. **CP-HewiJ**

I had practiced for years. Whenever I had a chance. The Juggler. Siv Cedering Fox. **SP-CedeS**

I had read a long time. All afternoon. *tr. fr. the German of* Rilke. Randall Jarrell. **CP-JarrR**

I had said improbable. I. Names. Hayden Carruth. **CP-CarHS**

I had seen a tree before. The Tree. Charles Tomlinson. **CP-TomlC**

I had seen, as dawn was breaking. La Nuit Blanche. Rudyard Kipling. **CP-KiplR**

I had some cards printed. Madam's Calling Cards. Langston Hughes. **SP-HughL**

I had some friends—but I dreamed that they were dead. The Friends. Rudyard Kipling. **CP-KiplR**

I had some things that I called mine. Emily Dickinson. **CP-DickE**

I had the Glory—that will do. Emily Dickinson. **CP-DickE**

I had the most lovely journey through life and death. Orpheus as a Christian Scientist. James Liddy. *Fr.* Glass after Oblivion. **CP-LiddJ**

I had this room in front on DeLongpre. The Strangest Sight You Ever Did See—. Charles Bukowski. **SP-BukC1**

I had this thought a while ago. Words. William Butler Yeats. **CP-YeatW**

I had thought of the bear in his lair as fiercely free, feasting. Part of the Darkness. Isabella Gardner. **CP-GardI**

I had time and a shovel. I began to dig. In the Hole. John Ciardi. **SP-CiarJ**

I had to assure myself. Screech-Owl. Donald Davie. **CP-DavDo**

I had to drive to Palos Verdes to do some business at the. Sweater. Charles Bukowski. **SP-BukC3**

I had to kick their law into their teeth in order to save them. Negro Hero. Gwendolyn Brooks. **SP-BrooG**

I had to take a shit. A Lovely Couple. Charles Bukowski. **SP-BukC1**

I had to unship the mast or we would have been over, & in, to. The Mast. Charles Olson. **CP-OlsoC**

I had two husbands. Madam and Her Might-Have-Been. Langston Hughes. **SP-HughL**

I had walked since dawn and lay down to rest on a bare hillside. Vulture. Robinson Jeffers. **CP-JefR3**

I had wanted a quiet testament. Song, A. Robert Creeley. **CP-CreeR**

I had withdrawn in forest, and my song. A Dream Pang. Robert Frost. **CP-FrosR**

I had worked my charms on her. Problems About the Other Woman. Charles Bukowski. **SP-BukC1**

I had you for a servant, once, Dick Brome. To My Old Faithful Servant: And (by His Continued Virtue) My Loving Friend: The Author of this Work, M[r] Rich[ard] Brome. Ben Jonson. **CP-JonsB**

I hadn't noticed. Kind. Leonard Nathan. **SP-NathL**

I hadn't seen him in twelve years. The Friend. Miller Williams. **SP-WillM**

I Hae a Wife o' My Ain. Robert Burns. **CP-BurnR**

I hae been at Crookieden. Bonie Laddie, Highland Laddie. Robert Burns. **CP-BurnR**

I hang on by. Charles Olson. **CP-OlsoC**

I hang the cloth water bag from the door mirror. Driving across the American Desert and Thinking of the Sahara. John Ciardi. **SP-CiarJ**

I Happen To Know. Ogden Nash. **CP-NashO**

I hardly hear the curlew cry. Baile and Aillinn. William Butler Yeats. **CP-YeatW**

I hardly slept across the North Atlantic. London. John Berryman. **CP-BerrJ**

I hardly suppose I know anybody who wouldn't rather be a success than a failure. Kindly Unhitch That Star, Buddy. Ogden Nash. **CP-NashO**

I has hyeahd o' people dancin' an' I's hyeahd o' people singin'. with music. Paul Laurence Dunbar. **CP-DunbP**

I hate and love. And if you ask me how. Carmen 85. Catullus. Fr. Carmina. **CP-Catul**

I hate and love. / And if you ask me why. Catullus. See Carmen 85: "I hate and I love. And if you ask me how."

I hate and love. Why? You may ask but. Catullus. See Carmen 85: "I hate and I love. And if you ask me how."

I hate and love, wouldst thou the reason know? Catullus. See Carmen 85: "I hate and I love. And if you ask me how."

I hate, and yet I love thee too. Catullus. See Carmen 85: "I hate and I love. And if you ask me how."

I hate my verses, every line, every word. Love the Wild Swan. Robinson Jeffers. **CP-JefR2**

I hate myself for lovin' you and the weakness that it showed. Dirge. "Bob Dylan." **CP-DylaB**

I hate reading about dead men knowing. Saturday. Charles Kenneth Williams. **CP-WillC**

I hate that Andrew Jones: he'll breed. Andrew Jones. William Wordsworth. **CP-WorW1**

I hate the clamours of the smoky towns. On a Country Life. James Thomson. **CP-ThomJ**

I hate the dogs, the cats, the road, the weather, the shadows, everything that seems. The Slough of Despond: Or the House of Hope. Malcolm Lowry. **CP-LowrM**

I hate the dreadful hollow behind the little wood. Tennyson. **EBVVPR** Fr. Maud [A Monodrama]. **CP-TennA**

I hate the very noise of troublous man. Love and Solitude. John Clare. **SP-ClarJ**

I HATE THIS GIRL. Stevie Smith. **CP-SmitS**

I hate this yoke; for the world's sake here put it on. The Perfect Marriage. Nicholas Vachel Lindsay. **CP-LindV**

"I hate to lose something." / then she bent her head. No Loser, No Weeper. Maya Angelou. **SP-AngeM**

I hated thee, fallen tyrant! I did groan. Feelings of a Republican on the Fall of Bonaparte. Percy Bysshe Shelley. **CP-ShelP**

I hauled down lifeless mattresses to sidewalk refuse-piles. Rain-Wet Asphalt Heat, Garbage Curbed Cans Overflowing. Allen Ginsberg. **CP-GinsA**

I have a Band-Aid on my finger. Band-Aids. Shel Silverstein. **SP-SilS2**

I have a bird in my head and a pig in my stomach. Alive for an Instant. Kenneth Koch. **SP-KochK**

I have a Bird in spring. Emily Dickinson. **CP-DickE**

I have a bone to pick with Fate. Lines on Facing Forty. Ogden Nash. **CP-NashO**

I have a book, it has grown. Correspondence. Roy Fisher. **SP-FishR**

I have a boy of five years old. Anecdote for Fathers. William Wordsworth. **CP-WorW1**

I have a certain skill in phrase. Dedication. John Hewitt. **CP-HewiJ**

I have a country but no town. Talking Myself to Sleep at One More Hilton. John Ciardi. **SP-CiarJ**

I have a deep identity. Red Jacket's Grave. James Wright. **CP-WrigJ**

I have a dream—a dreadful dream. The Mother's Son. Rudyard Kipling. **CP-KiplR**

I have a dream of where (when I grow old. To France. Countee Cullen. **CP-CullC**

I have a fairy by my side. My Fairy. "Lewis Carroll." **CP-CarrL**

I have a fantasy that a small idea. Fantasy of a Small Idea. Richard Eberhart. **CP-EberR**

I have a foolishness here which is lamp-like. New Poem. Charles Olson. **CP-OlsoC**

I have a friend. Black March. Stevie Smith. **CP-SmitS**

I have a friend. Gray. Alice Walker. **CP-WalkA**

I have a friend; I have a story. Robert Louis Stevenson. **CP-StevR**

I have a friend in ghostland. A Coast-Nightmare. Christina Georgina Rossetti. **CP-RosC3**

I have a friend named Mr. Sherman who is far from dodderin'. Sic Semper Mr. Sherman's Temper, or Kindly Place Your Order in English. Ogden Nash. **CP-NashO**

I have a friend who is a giant. Me and My Giant. Shel Silverstein. **SP-SilS2**

I have a friend who would give a price for those long fingers all of one length. Snakes, Mongooses, Snake-Charmers, and the Like. Marianne Craig Moore. **CP-MoorM**

I have a funny daddy. My Daddy. Ogden Nash. **CP-NashO**

I have a grief. Agitato Ma Non Troppo. John Crowe Ransom. **OxBA** Fr. Sixteen Poems in Eight Pairings. **SP-RansJ**

I have a happy nature. Mother. Stevie Smith. **CP-SmitS**

I have a hoard of treasure in my breast. Robert Louis Stevenson. Fr. Sonnets. **CP-StevR**

I have a hope that's like a star. George Meredith. **CP-MerG2**

I have a horse—a ryghte goode horse. Ye Capete Knyghte. "Lewis Carroll." **CP-CarrL**

I have a house, the house of prayer. Honesty. Christopher Smart. Fr. Hymns for the Amusement of Children. **SP-SmarC**

I have a King, who does not speak. Emily Dickinson. **CP-DickE**

I have a leaden, thou a shaft of gold. To Cupid. Robert Herrick. **CP-HerrR**

I have a little book. Song. Wystan Hugh Auden. **CP-AudWJ**

I have a little dog. Please Pass the Biscuit. Ogden Nash. **CP-NashO**

I have a little husband / And he is gone to sea. Christina Georgina Rossetti. **CP-RosC2**

I have a little. . . not fame, call it reputation—for writing verses. The Old Wolf My Father. Robinson Jeffers. **CP-JefR3**

I have a little shadow that goes in and out with me. My Shadow. Robert Louis Stevenson. **CP-StevR**

I have a Love I love too well. The Sacrilege. Thomas Hardy. **CP-HardT**

I have a lover, but he's made of paper. Protean Lover. Phoebe Hesketh. **SP-HeskP**

I Have a Message unto Thee. Christina Georgina Rossetti. **CP-RosC3**

I have a name, a little name. The Pet-Name. Elizabeth Barrett Browning. **CP-BroEB**

I have a pack of letters. The Inventory of Goodbyes. Anne Sexton. **CP-SextA**

I have a photograph here. Father, the Cavalier. Donald Davie. **CP-DavDo**

I have a plant. Aloe. Siv Cedering Fox. **SP-CedeS**

I have a Poll parrot, / And Poll is my doll. Christina Georgina Rossetti. **CP-RosC2**

I have a rendezvous with Life. Countee Cullen. **CP-CullC**

I have a rendezvous with Life. Life's Rendezvous. Countee Cullen. **CP-CullC**

I have a room of my own. Mother and Jack and the Rain. Anne Sexton. **CP-SextA**

I have a saying, "the tough ones always come." One to the Breastplate. Charles Bukowski. **SP-BukC1**

I have a saying, "You will hold the lowest of the breed at the". Charles Bukowski. Fr. Horsemeat. **SP-BukC3**

I have a singular talent: the ability to make old women cry. The Monster. Richard Shelton. **SP-ShelR**

I have a smiling face, she said. The Mask. Elizabeth Barrett Browning. **CP-BroEB**

I have a terrible age and I part. Hatred. Frank O'Hara. **SP-OharF**

"I have a thousand men," said he. Rudyard Kipling. **CP-KiplR** Fr. The Light That Failed.

I have a tree in my arm. Maze. Richard Eberhart. **CP-EberR**

I have a wide, friendly face. Zimmer Envying Elephants. Paul Zimmer. **SP-ZimmP**

I have abhorred the wars and despised the liars, laughed at the frightened. We Are Those People. Robinson Jeffers. **CP-JefR3**

I have, alas, no taste. Taste. John Updike. **CP-UpdiJ**

I have already come to the verge of. An Unborn Child. Derek Mahon. **SP-MahoD**

I have always found that Angels have the vanity to speak of themselves as the only wise; this they do with a confident insolence sprouting from systematic reasoning. Opposition Is True Friendship. William Blake. Fr. The Marriage of Heaven and Hell. **CP-BlakW**

I have always loved the word guitar. Guitar. David St. John. **SP-StJoD**

I have an arrow that can find its mark. Ralph Waldo Emerson. **CP-EmerR**

I have become a gate. Lot's Wife. Howard Nemerov. **CP-NemeH**

I have been a lover. Sir Thomas Wyatt. **CP-WyatT**

I have been alone for two days, and still everything is cloudy. Falling Asleep. Robert Bly. **SP-BlyR**

I have been an ability—a machine—up to. Charles Olson. **SP-OlsoC** Fr. The Maximus Poems.

I have been becoming as I. Coda. Jim Carroll. **SP-CarrJ**

I have been defeated and dragged down by pain. Kissing and Horrid Strife. David Herbert Lawrence. **CP-LawrD**

I have been given my charge to keep. The Fairies' Siege. Rudyard Kipling. **CP-KiplR** Fr. Kim.

I have been heavy and had much selecting. I saw a star which. Lifting Belly. Gertrude Stein. **CP-SteiG**

I have been here before. Frederick Morgan. *Fr.* Eight Triolets. **SP-MorgF**

I have been here in the Moon-light. Fragment from Dove Cottage Manuscript 44 (I). William Wordsworth. **CP-WorW1**

I have been idly leafing through the Book of Proverbs and the book of Deuteronomy. Woman Pulls the Wires. Ogden Nash. **CP-NashO**

I have been in a place where. A Place Where Nothing Is. Robert Penn Warren. **SP-WarrR**

I have been in Pennsylvania. Pennsylvania. Carl Sandburg. **CP-SandC**

I have been in the meadows all the day. Irreparableness. Elizabeth Barrett Browning. **CP-BroEB**

I have been in this garden of unripe fruit. First Love. "Hugh MacDiarmid." **SP-MacDH**

I have been instructed by your sacred Majesty to examine the histories. What to Think When It Rains Blood. Thomas Merton. **CP-MertT; SP-MertT**

I have been lying here for a long time in stillness. Penicillin. Patti Smith. **SP-SmitP**

I have been one acquainted with the night. Acquainted with the Night. Robert Frost. **CP-FrosR**

I have been out looking for you. Looking for You, Barbara. Ted Kooser. **SP-KoosT**

I have been reading about Paul Eluard tonight. Paul Eluard. Anne Waldman. **SP-WaldA**

I have been reading, telling people I have not, knowing this. Branded for Slaughter. Kay Boyle. **CP-BoylK**

I have been saying what I have to say. Don't. Charles Kenneth Williams. **CP-WillC**

I have been silent a lifetime. After Dunkirk. Alun Lewis. **CP-LewiA**

I have been so innerly proud, and so long alone. Humiliation. David Herbert Lawrence. **CP-LawrD**

I have been spared another day. A Poem of Thanks. Wendell Berry. **CP-BerrW**

I have been stone, dust of space, sea and sphere. Michael Hartnett. **SP-HarMi** *Fr.* Thirteen Sonnets.

I have been thinking / about living. Lilies. Mary Oliver. **SP-OlivM**

I have been thinking of the victims bound. The Prisoners of Naples. John Greenleaf Whittier. **CP-WhitJ**

I have been treading on leaves all day until I am autumn-tired. A Leaf-Treader. Robert Frost. **CP-FrosR**

I have been urged by earnest violins. Music. Wilfred Owen. **CP-OwenW**

I have been wanton, and too bold I feare. His Last Request to Julia. Robert Herrick. **CP-HerrR**

I have been warned. It is more than thirty years since I wrote. Robinson Jeffers. **CP-JeffR3**

I have been watching the war map slammed up for advertising in front of the newspaper office. Buttons. Carl Sandburg. **CP-SandC**

I have been woven among meshes of long ropes. Carl Sandburg. *Fr.* Timesweep. **CP-SandC**

I have been young, and now am old. Saw I Never the Righteous Forsaken. Donald Davie. **CP-DavDo**

I have begun to count my dead. Written in a Year When Many of My People Died. Nicholas Vachel Lindsay. *Fr.* Alexander Campbell. **CP-LindV**

I have begun to die. The Sentry. Alun Lewis. **CP-LewiA**

I have behelde two louers in a night. Mr. Robert Hericke His Farwell unto Poetrie. Robert Herrick. **CP-HerrR**

I have boarded up the stations of waiting. The Gambit. Richard Shelton. **SP-ShelR**

I have brought back a good message from the land of 102°. Fever. John Updike. **CP-UpdiJ**

I have builded to my longing a great tower. The Tower. John Gould Fletcher. **SP-FletJ**

I have but one chance left,—and that is going to Florence. Claude to Eustace—*from Bellagio.* Arthur Hugh Clough. **FaBoVe** *Fr.* Amours de Voyage. **SP-ClouA**

I have but one rose in the world. Christina Georgina Rossetti. **CP-RosC2**

I Have Called You, *ad. fr.* Isaiah 43:1. Thomas Merton. **CP-MertT**

I have called you many times. No Reply at Christmas. Phoebe Hesketh. **SP-HeskP**

I have caught a glimpse of the seamless garment. In the Slums of Glasgow. "Hugh MacDiarmid." **SP-MacDH**

I have chosen this place. Richard Shelton. *Fr.* Dry Season. **SP-ShelR**

I have come all this way. Ways of Day. Robert Penn Warren. **SP-WarrR**

I have come back to ancient shores where it is always now. The Return. Kathleen Jessie Raine. **SP-RainK**

I have come by lonely Orra round the glen. Glenaan. John Hewitt. **CP-HewiJ**

I have come far enough. A Form of Women. Robert Creeley. **CP-CreeR**

I have come into the time of the ant. A Note to La Fontaine. Jean Garrigue. **SP-GarrJ**

I have come often to this forest. Children Are Game. Isabella Gardner. **CP-GardI**

I have come to explore. Merak. Siv Cedering Fox. *Fr.* Seven Letters to Zakarias. **SP-CedeS**

I have come to the church and chancel. She Revisits Alone the Church of Her Marriage. Thomas Hardy. **CP-HardT**

I have come to the end. Wendell Berry. *Fr.* The Strait. **CP-BerrW**

I have come to the house of God. Irreverent Thoughts. David Herbert Lawrence. **CP-LawrD**

I have come to the house of God. Maiden's Prayer. David Herbert Lawrence. *Fr.* Bits. **CP-LawrD**

I have committed many errors. The Visit. William Carlos Williams. **CP-WilW2**

I have compassion on the carpeting. Lines Given with a Penwiper. Christina Georgina Rossetti. **CP-RosC3**

I have considered [*or* consider'd] it, and find[e]. The Reprisal[l]. George Herbert. **CP-HerbG**

I have desired, and I have been desired. Soeur Louise De La Miséricorde. Christina Georgina Rossetti. **CP-RosC2**

I have desired to go. Heaven-Haven. Gerard Manley Hopkins. **CP-HopkG**

I have died many times. Journey. Phoebe Hesketh. **SP-HeskP**

I have discovered a country. Connais-Tu le Pays? Richard Shelton. **SP-ShelR**

I have done all I could. The Tree and the Lady. Thomas Hardy. **CP-HardT**

I have done I know not what,—what have I done? Christina Georgina Rossetti. *Fr.* If Thou Sayest, Behold, We Knew It Not. **CP-RosC2**

I have done it again. Lady Lazarus. Sylvia Plath. **CP-PlatS**

I have done mostly what most men do. Four-Feet. Rudyard Kipling. **CP-KiplR**

I have done one braver thing. The Undertaking. John Donne. **CP-DonnJ**

I have done with hope. Christina Georgina Rossetti. **CP-RosC3**

I have drawn my hands away. Meditation. Hart Crane. **CP-CranH**

I have dreamed of Death:—what will it be to die. Christina Georgina Rossetti. *Fr.* Later Life: A Double Sonnet of Sonnets. **CP-RosC2**

I have drunk ale from the Country of the Young. He Thinks of His Past Greatness When a Part of the Constellations of Heaven. William Butler Yeats. **CP-YeatW**

I have eaten. This Is Just to Say. William Carlos Williams. **CP-WilW1**

I have eaten your bread and salt. Prelude to "Departmental Ditties." Rudyard Kipling. **CP-KiplR**

I have escaped in the dream; I was in danger, at peril, at immediate, furious, frightening risk. History. Charles Kenneth Williams. **SP-WillC**

I have examined his death. *see also* Final Examination. Leonard Cohen. **CP-CoheL**

I Have Exhausted the Delighted Range. Michael Hartnett. **SP-HarMi**

I have experienc'd / The worst, the World can wreak on me; the worst. Despair. Samuel Taylor Coleridge. **CP-ColeS**

I have felt darkness lead me by the hand. Suicide. Allen Tate. **CP-TateA**

I have felt like a troubled Top. Emily Dickinson. **SP-DickE**

I have fetched the tears up out of the little wells. *also stands as sl. diff. separate poem.* David Herbert Lawrence. *Fr.* The Schoolmaster [A]. **CP-LawrD**

I have fetched the tears up out of the little wells. The Punisher. David Herbert Lawrence. **CP-LawrD**

"I have finished another year," said God. New Year's Eve. Thomas Hardy. **CP-HardT**

I have finished my combat with the sun. From the Misery of Don Joost. Wallace Stevens. **CP-StevW**

I have finished with saying I'm sorry and waiting. If you can't join them beat them. Jenny Joseph. *Fr.* Life and Turgid Times of A. Citizen. **SP-JoseJ**

I have followed you as far as I can. Brand. John Haines. **SP-HainJ**

I have food for my children in the cart. I Can't Understand! I Can't Understand! Kenneth Patchen. **CP-PatcK**

I Have Fought a Good Fight. Christina Georgina Rossetti. **CP-RosC3**

I have found a nobler love. Ralph Waldo Emerson. **CP-EmerR**

I have found a place of loneliness. Elysium. David Herbert Lawrence. **CP-LawrD**

I have found what pleases my friend's chubby, rosy, gloriously shining-eyed year-old daughter. The Gift. Charles Kenneth Williams. **CP-WillC; SP-WillC**

I have found what you are like. Edward Estlin Cummings. **CP-CummE**

I have gone out, a possessed witch. Her Kind. Anne Sexton. **CP-SextA**

I have gone past all those times when the poets. In Memory of Leopardi. James Wright. **CP-WrigJ**

I have got into the slow train. In the Stopping Train. Donald Davie. **CP-DavDo**

I have gret wonder, be this lyght. The Book of the Duchesse. Geoffrey Chaucer. **CP-ChauG**

I have had enough. Sheltered Garden. Hilda Doolittle. **CP-DoolH**

I have had enough of them, more than enough. A Poem about the Jews. Kay Boyle. **CP-BoylK**

I have had my dream—like others. Thursday. William Carlos Williams. **CP-WilW1**

I have had my time   dressed up as something else. False Youth: Two Seasons. James Dickey. **CP-DickJ**

I have had such privilege. Privilege. Stephen Dunn. **SP-DunnS**

I have had to learn the simplest things. Maximus, to Himself. Charles Olson. **SP-OlsoC** *Fr.* The Maximus Poems.

I Have Had to Learn to Live with My Face. Diane Wakoski. **SP-WakoD**

I have had to write this down. Love Poem to Be Read to an Illiterate Friend. Tess Gallagher. **SP-GallT**

I have heard all day the voices. Winds. Kathleen Jessie Raine. **SP-RainK**

I have heard it said. To the Muse. Denise Levertov. **CP-LeveD**

I have heard of fish. The Sun. Anne Sexton. **CP-SextA**

I have heard of reasons manifold. Reason for Love's Blindness. Samuel Taylor Coleridge. **CP-ColeS**

I have heard rumors all over town. Tell Me That It Isn't True. "Bob Dylan." **CP-DylaB**

I have heard that hysterical women say. Lapis Lazuli. William Butler Yeats. **CP-YeatW**

I have heard the dread song I had not heard. Tanto e Amara. Charles Olson. **CP-OlsoC**

I have heard the pigeons of the Seven Woods. In the Seven Woods. William Butler Yeats. **CP-YeatW**

I Have Increased Power. Allen Ginsberg. **CP-GinsA**

I have instructed you to follow me. Jesus to His Disciples. Edna St. Vincent Millay. **CP-MillE**

I have invented new worlds. I have dreamed. The Birth of the Sun. Pablo Antonio Cuadra, *tr. fr. Spanish by* Thomas Merton. **CP-MertT**

I Have It on Good Authority. Ogden Nash. **CP-NashO**

I have just come down from my father. The Hospital Window. James Dickey. **CP-DickJ**

I have just returned from a foreign tour. My Trip Daorba. Ogden Nash. **CP-NashO**

I have kept all, not one is thrown away, not one given to the ragman, not. Films. Carl Sandburg. **CP-SandC**

I have killed our lives together. Divorce. Anne Sexton. **CP-SextA**

I have known a city of dreadful night. Malcolm Lowry. *Fr.* The Cantinas. **CP-LowrM**

I have known all the storms that roll. Skald's Death. "Hugh MacDiarmid." **SP-MacDH**

I have known the imperial power of secretaries. Paper Cuts. Erica Jong. **SP-JongE**

I have known the inexorable sadness of pencils. Dolor. Theodore Roethke. **CP-RoetT**

I have lain in bed all day. Farewell, Foolish Objects. Charles Bukowski. **SP-BukC2**

I have learned not to worry about love. New Face. Alice Walker. **CP-WalkA**

I have learned this winter that, yes. 1971. Alice Walker. **CP-WalkA**

I have learned to sit quietly. Her Becoming. Theodore Roethke. *Fr.* Meditations of an Old Woman. **CP-RoetT**

I have learned what I wanted from the mermaid. Robert Lowell. *Fr.* Mermaid. **SP-LoweR**

I have led her home, my love, my only friend. Tennyson. **CBLP; ChER; EBVV; ELP; FiP; MeMBP; NAEL-2; NOBVV** *Fr.* Maud [A Monodrama]. **CP-TennA**

"There is none like her, none." **FaBoEn; OBNC**

I have left all upon the shameful field. The Vanquished Knight. Robert Louis Stevenson. **CP-StevR**

I have lighted the candles, Mary. Kenneth Patchen. **CP-PatcK**

I have lived and followed my fate without flinching, followed it gladly. Dido's Farewell to Aeneas. Stevie Smith. **CP-SmitS**

I have lived at Cold Mountain, *after* Han-shan. Gary Snyder. **CP-SnydG**

I have lived in a single landscape. Every tone. At Stoke. Charles Tomlinson. **CP-TomlC**

I Have Lived in England. Charles Bukowski. **SP-BukC2**

I Have Lived with Shades. Thomas Hardy. **CP-HardT**

I have lives in many half-worlds myself. . . and so I know you. Flying Fish. Carl Sandburg. **CP-SandC**

I have long been a Lunatic on Bulbs. Emily Dickinson. **SP-DickE**

I Have Longed to Move Away. Dylan Thomas. **CP-ThomD**

I have looked at them long. To the Romantic Traditionists. Allen Tate. **CP-TateA**

I have looked at this photograph. Rescue. Dabney Stuart. **SP-StuaD**

I have looked upon thee—and I have loved thee. Edward Estlin Cummings. **CP-CummE**

I have lost, and lately, these. Upon the Loss[e] of His Mistresses. Robert Herrick. **CP-HerrR**

I have lost the wood, the heath, *fr. the French of* Villiers de l'Isle Adam. The Avowal. Richard Wilbur. **CP-WilbR**

I have love / And a child. Losses. Carl Sandburg. **CP-SandC**

I have loved you for long long years Ellen. Song. Christina Georgina Rossetti. **CP-RosC3**

I have loved, let us see if that's all. Edward Estlin Cummings. **CP-CummE**

I have made for you a song. To Thomas Atkins. Rudyard Kipling. **CP-KiplR**

I have many playmates. Diabolo. Marsden Hartley. **CP-HartM**

I have many prayers to say. Ah, Muriel! David Herbert Lawrence. **CP-LawrD**

I have met them at close of day. Easter, 1916. William Butler Yeats. **CP-YeatW**

I have migrated to another place. This Neighborhood. Isabella Gardner. **CP-GardI**

I have my figures ready for the. Charles Bukowski. *Fr.* Horsemeat. **SP-BukC3**

I have my Laurel Chaplet on my head. To Sir George Parrie, Doctor of the Civill Law. Robert Herrick. **CP-HerrR**

I have my piety too, which could. An Epitaph on Master Vincent Corbet[t]. Ben Jonson. **CP-JonsB**

I have never / clearly given to you. The Woman. Robert Creeley. **CP-CreeR**

I have never been. Sconset. Charles Tomlinson. **CP-TomlC**

I have never beheld you, O pawky Scot. Who Taught Caddies to Count? or A Burnt Golfer Fears the Child. Ogden Nash. **CP-NashO**

I have never heard them. Memoria. Louise McNeill. **SP-McNeL**

I have never seen a. One Jay at a Time. John Ciardi. **SP-CiarJ**

I have never seen a cicada, but nothing so pollutes. Walking the Dog: A Diatribe. Mona Van Duyn. **SP-VanDM**

I have never seen "Volcanoes." Emily Dickinson. **CP-DickE**

I have never tried love. Adamson. Frederick Morgan. *Fr.* Eight Triolets. **SP-MorgF**

I have no answer, time or will, to answer those. The Mechanical Heart. Kenneth Patchen. **CP-PatcK**

I have no brothers & no peers. Ralph Waldo Emerson. **CP-EmerR**

I have no clock, yet I can hear. Louis MacNeice. *Fr.* Candles. **CP-MacNL**

I have no desire any more. Desire Goes Down into the Sea. David Herbert Lawrence. **CP-LawrD**

I have no doubt that it is very important and so are you. Very Very Important. Carl Sandburg. **CP-SandC**

I have no fancy for that ancient cant. The Right to Die. Paul Laurence Dunbar. **CP-DunbP**

I have no ghosts. / My dead are safely dead. Ghosts. John Hewitt. **CP-HewiJ**

I have no happiness in dreaming of Brycelinde. Under the Moon. William Butler Yeats. **CP-YeatW**

I have no hoarded treasure. Hafiz, *tr. by* Ralph Waldo Emerson. **CP-EmerR** *Fr.* Odes.

I have no Life but this. Emily Dickinson. **CP-DickE**

"I have no master," said the Blind Boy. The Blind Boy. Walter de la Mare. **CP-DeLaW**

I have no name. Infant Joy. William Blake. **FHYEP; FaPON; GoJo; HBV; HBVY; LAuP; LoBV; NAEL-2; NAs; NTP; OXAEP-2; OxBSP; PoLF; SiSoSe; TEP** *Fr.* Songs of Innocence. **CP-BlakW**

I Have No Place to Take Thee. Kenneth Patchen. **CP-PatcK**

I have no promises to keep. Collage of Echoes. Isabella Gardner. **CP-GardI**

I have no respect for you. No Respect. Stevie Smith. **CP-SmitS**

I have no time to worship. I must live. Sonnet. John Hewitt. **CP-HewiJ**

I have no wine of Gaza, nor Falerna wine, *ad. fr. Latin of* Sidonius. Sir Walter Ralegh. **CP-RaleW**

I Have No Wings. Richard Shelton. **SP-ShelR**

I have no wit, no words, no tears. A Better Resurrection. Christina Georgina Rossetti. **CP-RosC1**

I have not entered the raga. Dear Ravi Shankar. Al Young. **CP-YounA**

I have not ever seen my father's grave. Father Son and Holy Ghost. Audre Lorde. **SP-LordA**

I have not felt, o'er seas of sand. *ad. fr. the French of Lamartine.* John Greenleaf Whittier. **CP-WhitJ**

I have not lain with beauty all my life. Lawrence Ferlinghetti. **SP-FerlL**

I Have Not Lingered in European Monasteries. Leonard Cohen. **CP-CoheL**

I have not loved the world, nor the world me. The Poet and the World. Byron. **SeCePo** *Fr.* Childe Harold's Pilgrimage. **CP-Byron**

I have not loved you in the noblest way. Sonnet. Countee Cullen. **CP-CullC**

I have not seen God face to face. What Is God? Phoebe Hesketh. **SP-HeskP**

I have not so much emulated the birds that musically sing. To Soar in Freedom and in Fullness of Power. Walt Whitman. **CP-WhitW**

I have not sought Thee, I have not found Thee. Christina Georgina Rossetti. **CP-RosC2** ("Love Is Strong As Death.") **CP-RosC2**

I have not told my garden yet. Emily Dickinson. ("I haven't told my garden yet.") **CP-DickE**

I have nothing to give you but these days. Geographer. Marilyn Hacker. **SP-HackM**

I have nothing to put in my stew, you see. Me-Stew. Shel Silverstein. **SP-SilS2**

I have nothing to say about the way the sky tilts. Charles Wright. **SP-WrigC** *Fr.* Three Poems for the New Year. (Three Poems for the New Year [1].) **SP-WrigC**

I have noticed that people who talk a lot about loyalty. Talk of Loyalty. David Herbert Lawrence. **CP-LawrD**

I have nowhere / to go and. Stills. Archie Randolph Ammons. **SP-AmmoA**

I have old women's secrets now. The Secrets of the Old. William Butler Yeats. *Fr.* A Man Young and Old. **CP-YeatW**

I have opened the window to warm my hands on the sill. *sl. diff version of poems* Drams Old and Nascent: Old *and* Dreams Old and Nascent: Nascent. David Herbert Lawrence. **CP-LawrD**

I have opened the windows to warm my hands on the sill. Dreams Old and Nascent: Old. David Herbert Lawrence. **CP-LawrD**

I have perceiv'd that to be with those I like is enough. Walt Whitman. **SAmP** *Fr.* I sing the body electric. **CP-WhitW**

"I have" poem, The. Oak Openings. Donald Davie. **CP-DavDo**

I have pointed out the yelling pack. The Death of the Hare. William Butler Yeats. *Fr.* A Man Young and Old. **CP-YeatW**

I have ransacked the encyclopedia. Old-Fashioned Requited Love. Carl Sandburg. **CP-SandC**

I have reached a time when words no longer help. For a Birthday. Thom Gunn. **CP-GunnT**

I have reached, alas, the long shadow. *tr. of* / Dante's "Al poco giorno. . .". James Schuyler. **CP-SchuJ**

I have reached the stage when questioning myself. Conception. "Hugh MacDiarmid." **SP-MacDH**

I have read the Review; it is learned and wise. On a Review Condemning Thelyphthora. William Cowper. **CP-CowpW**

I have recently been pondering the life expectancy which the Bible. What I Know About Life. Ogden Nash. **CP-NashO**

I have refused the discipline. This. Charles Bukowski. **SP-BukC2**

I have risen again. The Moon Looks In. Thomas Hardy. **CP-HardT**

I have said that the soul is not more than the body. Walt Whitman. **EnlH; FaFP; ImPo** *Fr.* Song of Myself. **CP-WhitW** (Hub of the Universe, The.) **FaFP; ImPo**

I have said to the elephant and the flea, "Each of us makes his life." Carl Sandburg. *Fr.* Timesweep. **CP-SandC**

I Have Said, Ye Are Gods. Donald Davie. **CP-DavDo**

I have sat in the recreation ground. Reading in the Evening. David Herbert Lawrence. **CP-LawrD**

I have sat in this garden yearly. Big Rock. Richard Eberhart. **CP-EberR**

I have seen / The old gods go. The Hammer. Carl Sandburg. **CP-SandC**

I have seen a loneliness sit. Canadians and Pottawatomies. Carl Sandburg. **CP-SandC**

I have seen camels at the outer gate. The Twisted Heart. John Hewitt. **CP-HewiJ**

I have seen Eden. It is a light of place. Eden. Charles Tomlinson. **CP-TomlC**

I have seen enough: ugliness. Knowing All Ways, Including the Transposition of Continents. Charles Olson. **CP-OlsoC**

I have seen full many a sight. Dinah Kneading Dough. Paul Laurence Dunbar. **CP-DunbP**

I have seen God O Yes. Mystic. Dabney Stuart. **SP-StuaD**

I have seen her a stealthily frail. Edward Estlin Cummings. **CP-CummE**

I have seen her in gowns the brightest. The Old Gown. Thomas Hardy. **CP-HardT**

I have seen higher holier things than these. Arthur Hugh Clough. *Fr.* Blank Misgivings of a Creature Moving About in Worlds Not Realized. **SP-ClouA**

I have seen him dine. The Poet as Black Sheep. Michael Hartnett. *Fr.* Notes on My Contemporaries. **SP-HarMi**

I have seen many Maidens to have haire. Upon Blanch. Robert Herrick. **CP-HerrR**

I have seen my ghost broken. To Conquer Variety. Hart Crane. **CP-CranH**

I have seen one Bird and part of another. Emily Dickinson. **SP-DickE**

I have seen peoples come and go. Old. Paul Laurence Dunbar. **CP-DunbP**

I have seen the Baker's horse. Fragment: The Baker's Cart. William Wordsworth. **CP-WorW1**

I have seen the hills blue. Stroller. William Carlos Williams. **CP-WilW1**

I have seen the mob of late. The Uncle Speaks in the Drawing Room. Adrienne Rich. **CP-RicAE; SP-RicA1**

I have seen the sun / Spilling its copper petals on the Black Sea. From the Legend of St. Clement. Thomas Merton. **CP-MertT**

I have seen them asleep on the grass. The Infinite Horses. Silvina Ocampo, *tr. by* William Carlos Williams. **CP-WilW2**

I have seen this city in the day and the sun. Tangibles. Carl Sandburg. **CP-SandC**

I have seen 21 beautiful and naked. In the Graeco-Roman Room. Daniel Gerard Hoffman. **SP-HoffD**

I have sharpened my knives, I have. Farm Country. Mary Oliver. **SP-OlivM**

I Have Shit Stains in My Underwear Too. Charles Bukowski. **SP-BukC1**

I have slain none except my Mother. She. An Only Son. Rudyard Kipling. *Fr.* Epitaphs of the War [1914–1918]. **CP-KiplR**

I have slept shallow a long while. Roy Fisher. **SP-FishR** *Fr.* Glenthorne Poems.

I have so much that I am supposed to do. A Winter Poem for Tony Weinburger Written on the Occasion of Feeling Very Happy. Diane Wakoski. **SP-WakoD**

I have something for you to laugh at, Cato. Catullus. *See* Carmen 56: "Matter for mirth, Cato, & a smile, A."

I have sought for myself. Thomas Merton. *Fr.* The Legacy of Herakleitos. **CP-MertT**

I have sought long with steadfastness. Sir Thomas Wyatt. **CP-WyatT**

I have spent most of my life. The Great American Novel. Daniel Gerard Hoffman. **SP-HoffD**

I have spent the whole day, or is it twenty years. Avalanche. William Dickey. **SP-DickW**

I Have Started to Say. Philip Larkin. **CP-LarkP**

I have studied the tight curls. Movement Song. Audre Lorde. **SP-LordA**

I have supped with the gods tonight. Ralph Waldo Emerson. **CP-EmerR**

I have taken in the light. Prayer after Eating. Wendell Berry. **CP-BerrW**

I have taken scales from off. Fishmonger. Marsden Hartley. **CP-HartM**

I Have That Sure Enclitic. Hart Crane. **CP-CranH**

I have the friend who loves me. Emily Dickinson. **SP-DickE**

I have thought / Of thee, thy learning, gorgeous eloquence. Coleridge's Mind a Life Unto Itself. William Wordsworth. **EPCY** *Fr.* Cambridge and the Alps. *Fr.* The Prelude; Growth of a Poet's Mind [1850 vers.]. **CP-WorW3**

I have thought of beaches, fields. Bundles. Carl Sandburg. **CP-SandC**

I have thought of you stepping out of your doorway at dawn, your son in your tracks. Wendell Berry. *Fr.* To a Siberian Woodsman. **CP-BerrW**

I have three simple eyes. The Maimed Grasshopper Speaks Up. Jean Garrigue. **SP-GarrJ**

I have to believe it's a limited society. A Knothole in Spent Time. John Ciardi. **SP-CiarJ**

I have to weep when I see it, the grown boy fretting. Euryclea's Tale. Adrienne Rich. **CP-RicAE**

I have told you in another poem, whether you've read it or not. Robinson Jeffers. **CP-JefR3**

I have trailed you in several senses. Nearness. Steve Griffiths. **SP-GrifS**

I have travelled, and looked at the world, and loved it. Travel Is Over. David Herbert Lawrence. **CP-LawrD**

I have travelled so fast that I have come to the waterfall of Sgriol. Golden Flowers. Kathleen Jessie Raine. *Fr.* Bheinn Naomh. **SP-RainK**

I have tried and I have tried to find you. I Have Tried to Find You. Martin Edmunds. **SP-EdmuM**

I Have Tried to Find You. Martin Edmunds. **SP-EdmuM**

I have tried to show the atom as a source. Muriel Rukeyser. **CP-RukeM**

I have trod the upward and the downward slope. Robert Louis Stevenson. **CP-StevR**

I have trod this path a hundred times. The Miracle. Ralph Waldo Emerson. **CP-EmerR**

I have turned to the landscape because men disappoint me. The Ram's Horn. John Hewitt. **CP-HewiJ**

I Have Two Bars of Soap. Leonard Cohen. **CP-CoheL**

I hesitate which word to take. Emily Dickinson. **SP-DickE**

I hi hi hi hi hi hi / Dig a pony. Dig a Pony. John Lennon *and* Paul McCartney. **CP-Beatl**

I hide myself within my flower. Emily Dickinson. **CP-DickE**

I hired a carpenter. The Death King. Anne Sexton. **CP-SextA**

I hoed and trenched and weeded. Alfred Edward Housman. **CP-HousA**

I hold a key in my hand. The Key. Muriel Rukeyser. **CP-RukeM**

I hold it, Sir, my bounden duty. To Mr Gavin Hamilton, Mauchline. Robert Burns. **CP-BurnR**

I hold it true, whate're befall. Tennyson. **UV** *Fr.* I Envy Not in Any Moods. **EBEvV; FHYEP; FaBoEn; HBV; ImPo; LiTB; MeMBP; OAEL-2; OBNC; PeHV** *Fr.* In Memoriam A. H. H. **CP-TennA**

I hold my honey and I store my bread. My Dreams, My Works, Must Wait Till after Hell. Gwendolyn Brooks. **SP-BrooG**

I hold not with the fatalist creed. Ultimatum. Countee Cullen. **CP-CullC**

I hold this goblet under the running tap. Tripping down. Jenny Joseph. *Fr.* Life and Turgid Times of A. Citizen. **SP-JoseJ**

I hold your head tight between. Kenneth Rexroth. **SP-RexrK** *Fr.* Love Poems of Marichiko.

I honor you. Dancing Naked. Al Young. **CP-YounA**

I hook my fingers into the old tennis court fence. Of What Is Past. Charles Kenneth Williams. **CP-WillC; SP-WillC**

I hope I'm. The Mark. Archie Randolph Ammons. **SP-AmmoA**

I hope my child'll / Never love a man. Lament over Love. Langston Hughes. **SP-HughL**

I hope that George enjoys the gifts. Jim Carroll. *Fr.* Birthday Poem. **SP-CarrJ**

I hope that in my eldering age I'm not becoming noticeably querulous. Is This Seat Taken? Yes, or, My Neck Is Sticking In. Ogden Nash. **CP-NashO**

I hope that you are well. Emily Dickinson. **SP-DickE**

I hope you are joyful frequently. Emily Dickinson. **SP-DickE**

I hope you may not go. Emily Dickinson. **SP-DickE**

I hope you may sometime be. Emily Dickinson. **SP-DickE**

I hope your rambles have been sweet. Emily Dickinson. **SP-DickE**

I humm'd an air of sweet Mozart. George Meredith. **CP-MerG2**

I hung my verses in the wind. The Test. Ralph Waldo Emerson. **CP-EmerR**

I hurt. Hungrier flowers try my rank ground. Hayden Carruth. *Fr.* The Asylum. **CP-CarHL**

"I," I mused, "yes, I," and turned to the fenestrations of the night. Wonderful World. James Schuyler. **CP-SchuJ**

I idly cut a parsley stalk. On a Midsummer Eve. Thomas Hardy. **CP-HardT**

"I, if I perish, perish"—Esther spake. Christina Georgina Rossetti. *Fr.* Monna Innominata. **CP-RosC2**

I imagine, as I imagine us. Postures. Geoffrey Hill. *Fr.* The Songbook of Sebastian Arrurruz. **CP-HillG**

I imagine Druids timeless, so lacking. Druid Stones at Kensaleyre. Richard Hugo. **CP-HugoR**

I imagine him still with heavy brow. Beethoven's Death Mask. Stephen Spender. **CP-SpenS**

I imagine it is not God that judges us. Panhandle (For Annette). Chuck Miller. **SP-MillC**

I imagine this [*or*the] midnight moment's forest. The Thought-Fox. Ted Hughes. **SP-HughT**

I, in disgust with the living, having read. Edna St. Vincent Millay. **CP-MillE**

I, in My Intricate Image. Dylan Thomas. **CP-ThomD**

I innocently meant to go away. I mentioned digestion. I heard it. Painted Lace. Gertrude Stein. **CP-SteiG**

I, io, ich, yo. Alphabet Poem: To the Letter I. Erica Jong. **SP-JongE**

I is the total black. Audre Lorde. *See* Coal.

I John Frim—Volcano ancestor—Karaperamun. John the Volcano. Thomas Merton. *Fr.* East. *Fr.* The Geography of Lograire. **CP-MertT**

I John saw. I testify. Hilda Doolittle. **NALW** *Fr.* Tribute to the Angels. **CP-DoolH**

I journey not whence nor whither. Song for Ditherers. Ogden Nash. **CP-NashO**

I journeyed from my native spot. His Country. Thomas Hardy. **CP-HardT**

I journeyed to the suburbs, and there I was told, fr. sect. 1. Thomas Stearns Eliot. **UV** *Fr.* Choruses from "The Rock." **CP-ElioT**

I joy, dear[e] Mother, when I view. The British Church. George Herbert. **CP-HerbG**

I joy in grief, and do detest all joys, *dialogue of Strephon and Klaius.* Sir Philip Sidney. **SP-SidnP** *Fr.* Arcadia.

I jump with terror seeing him. Modes of Pleasure. Thom Gunn. **CP-GunnT**

I just came by the prison-door. Pray Remember the Poor. Christopher Smart. **NOEC** *Fr.* Hymns for the Amusement of Children. **SP-SmarC**

I just got here myself and I feel like hell. Rituals. Miller Williams. **SP-WillM**

I just had the old Dodge in the shop. Eternity Blues. Hayden Carruth. **CP-CarHS**

I just knew it when we swept above the old roofs of Dijon. Elizabeth Barrett Browning. **PeVV** *Fr.* Aurora Leigh. **CP-BroEB**

I just passed. Charles Olson. **CP-OlsoC**

I just saw two boys. Details for Paterson. William Carlos Williams. **CP-WilW2**

I keep a fire and tell a story. John Haines. *Fr.* The Turning. **SP-HainJ**

I keep a TV monitor on my chest. Shorts / Excerpts. Bill Knott. **SP-KnotB**

I keep him waiting, tuck in the curtains. Planning the Perfect Evening. Rita Dove. **MAYP** *Fr.* A Suite for Augustus. **SP-DoveR**

I keep my diamond necklace in a pond of sparkling water for invisibility. Fabergé. James Schuyler. **CP-SchuJ**

I keep my pledge. Emily Dickinson. **CP-DickE**

I keep on dying again. The Lesson. Maya Angelou. **SP-AngeM**

I keep practicing death. Practice. Charles Bukowski. **SP-BukC2**

I keep pushing this. The Prophets. Richard Shelton. **SP-ShelR**

I keep putting the empties out back but. Conversation in a Cheap Room. Charles Bukowski. **SP-BukC2**

I keep six honest serving-men. Rudyard Kipling. **CP-KiplR** *Fr.* The Elephant's Child. *Fr.* Just-So Stories.

I keep so many deaths in reserve. Coming Back. Pablo Neruda, *tr. fr. Spanish* by Ben Belitt. **SP-NeruP**

I keep thinking it will be outside. Stolen. Charles Bukowski. **SP-BukC1**

"I Keep to Myself Such Measures. . . ." Robert Creeley. **CP-CreeR**

I keep trying to figure out what it means. Notebook. Patti Smith. **SP-SmitP**

I keep your old snaps in my bottom drawer. The Old Snaps. Derek Mahon. **SP-MahoD**

I ken these islands each inhabited. Harry Semen. "Hugh MacDiarmid." **SP-MacDH**

I kind of like the playful porpoise. The Porpoise. Ogden Nash. **CP-NashO**

I kiss your lips / on a grain: the forest. Spring in This World of Poor Mutts. Joseph Ceravolo. **SP-CeraJ**

I kissed my father as he lay in bed. That Actor Kiss. Michael Hartnett. **SP-HarMi**

I kissed the rock near which. Recognition of Region. Marsden Hartley. **CP-HartM**

I kissed them in fancy as I came. Two Lips. Thomas Hardy. **CP-HardT**

I kissed you, bride and lost, and went. The Loser. Adrienne Rich. **CP-RicAE; SP-RicA2**

I kissed you in the dead of dark. The Accusation. James Wright. **CP-WrigJ**

I Kneel. Charles Bukowski. **SP-BukC2**

I kneel beside her. Love's Body. Dabney Stuart. **SP-StuaD**

I kneel down to peer into a culvert. Kneeling Down to Look [*or* Peer] into a Culvert. Robert Bly. **SP-BlyR**

I Knelt Beside a Stream. Leonard Cohen. **CP-CoheL**

I knelt down / at the edge of the water. Alligator Poem. Mary Oliver. **SP-OlivM**

I knew a Bird that would sing as firm. Emily Dickinson. **SP-DickE**

I Knew a Lady. Thomas Hardy. **CP-HardT**

I knew a man without a heart. Queer Poem. Malcolm Lowry. **CP-LowrM**

"I knew a real man once," says Agatha in the slendor of a shagbark. Plaster. Carl Sandburg. **CP-SandC**

I knew a silver head was bright beyond compare. In Memoriam, E.H. Robert Louis Stevenson. **CP-StevR**

I Knew a Woman. Theodore Roethke. **CP-RoetT**

I knew her for a little ghost. The Little Ghost. Edna St. Vincent Millay. **CP-MillE**

I knew him by a huge stomach laugh. Edward. Gary Gildner. **SP-GildG**

I knew him well, and yet I did not know. The Rank-and-Filer. John Hewitt. **CP-HewiJ**

I knew not 'twas so dire a crime. Song By J. Brenzaida To G.S. Emily Brontë. **CP-BronE**

I knew that I had gained. Emily Dickinson. **CP-DickE**

I knew the General only by name of course. I Don't Want to Startle You but They Are Going to Kill Most of Us. Kenneth Patchen. **CP-PatcK**

I knew the tune. I Was Born to Speak Your Name. Tom Clark. **SP-ClarT**

I knew thee strong and quiet like the hills. To ———. Robert Louis Stevenson. **CP-StevR**

I knew where they were. People. Robert Creeley. **CP-CreeR**

I knew you forever and you were always old. Some Foreign Letters. Anne Sexton. **CP-SextA**

I knew you once so well I know you still. Old Poems. Randall Jarrell. **CP-JarrR**

I knocked upon thy door ajar. In Vain. Walter de la Mare. **CP-DeLaW**

I Know. John Berryman. **CP-BerrJ**

I know / nothing anymore. Charles Kenneth Williams. **CP-WillC; SP-WillC**

I Know. David St. John. **SP-StJoD**

I know a baby, such a baby,— / Round blue eyes and cheeks of pink. Christina Georgina Rossetti. **CP-RosC2**

I know a girl who is in Paris, France. Absence Makes the Heart Grow Heart Trouble. Ogden Nash. **CP-NashO**

I know a guy, 63.5 years old. Tanck's Song About the Younger Generation. Hayden Carruth. **CP-CarHS** *Fr.* Songs About What Comes Down: The Complete Works of Mr. Septic Tank.

I know a Jew fish crier down on Maxwell Street. Fish Crier. Carl Sandburg. **CP-SandC**

I know a little restaurant. Try It Suns. and Hols.; It's Closed Then. Ogden Nash. **CP-NashO**

I know a lot of people who once seemed. Je Connai Gens de Toutes Sortes. Gilbert Sorrentino. **SP-SorrG**

I Know a Man. Robert Creeley. **CP-CreeR**

I know a man. The Sand-Man. Paul Laurence Dunbar. **CP-DunbP**

I know a man named Mr. Nagle. I Know Exactly Who Dropped the Overalls in Mrs. Murphy's Chowder. Ogden Nash. **CP-NashO**

I know a Mount, the gracious Sun perceives. Rudel to the Lady of Tripoli. Robert Browning. **CP-BroR1**

I Know a Noble Englishman, *sl. diff. vers.* David Herbert Lawrence. *See* The Noble Englishman.

I know a noble Englishman. The Noble Englishman. David Herbert Lawrence. **CP-LawrD**

I know a place where all is real. Interjection #3: I Know a Place Where All Is Real. Robert Penn Warren. **SP-WarrR**

I know a place where Summer strives. Emily Dickinson. **CP-DickE**

I know a pool where nightshade preens. Crazed. Walter de la Mare. **CP-DeLaW**

I know a quiet avenue. Aristocratic Area. John Hewitt. **CP-HewiJ**

I know a renegade hotel. Traveler's Rest. Ogden Nash. **CP-NashO**

I know a retired dentist who only paints mountains. Mountains. Wystan Hugh Auden. **FaBoPV** *Fr.* Bucolics. **CP-AudeW**

I know a seraph who has golden eyes. Alone in the Wind, on the Prairie. Nicholas Vachel Lindsay. **CP-LindV**

I know a very lonely lane. Bawbee. Wystan Hugh Auden. **CP-AudWJ**

I know a woman. One for Old Snaggle-Tooth. Charles Bukowski. **SP-BukC1**

I know all dreams grow to the size of a grapefruit. Dragon's Blood I. John Yau. **SP-YauJo**

I Know All This When Gipsy Fiddles Cry. Nicholas Vachel Lindsay. **CP-LindV**

I know, although when looks meet. *fr.* Words for Music Perhaps. William Butler Yeats. **CP-YeatW**

I Know an Aged Man Constrained to Dwell. William Wordsworth. **CP-WorW2**

I know an ice handler who wears a flannel shirt. Ice Handler. Carl Sandburg. **CP-SandC**

I know but little of Little Ones. Emily Dickinson. **SP-DickE**

I Know Exactly Who Dropped the Overalls in Mrs. Murphy's Chowder. Ogden Nash. **CP-NashO**

I know him, February's thrush. The Thrush in February. George Meredith. **CP-MerG1**

I know I am but summer to your heart. Edna St. Vincent Millay. **CP-MillE**

I know I am noble with the nobility of the sun. Noble. David Herbert Lawrence. **CP-LawrD**

I know I am nothing. Nullus. David Herbert Lawrence. **CP-LawrD**

I know I change / have changed. Daguerreotype Taken in Old Age. Margaret Atwood. **SP-AtwM1**

I know I have the best of time and space. Walt Whitman. Walt Whitman. **BiP; NoAM** *Fr.* Song of Myself. **CP-WhitW**

I know, I know—though the evidence. Blow, West Wind. Robert Penn Warren. **SP-WarrR**

I know I might have lived in such a way. Fontaine, Je Ne Boirai Pas De Ton Eau! Edna St. Vincent Millay. **CP-MillE**

I Know, I Remember, But How Can I Help You. Hayden Carruth. **CP-CarHS**

I know it is dark; and though I have lain. An Ode to the Rain. Samuel Taylor Coleridge. **CP-ColeS**

I know it is my sin[ne] which locks thine ear[e]s. Church-Lock and Key. George Herbert. **CP-HerbG**

I know lives, I could miss. Emily Dickinson. **CP-DickE**

I know lots of men who are in love and lots of men who are. I Never Even Suggested It. Ogden Nash. **CP-NashO**

I know monks masturbate at night. The Earnest Liberal's Lament. Ernest Hemingway. **CP-HemiE**

I know my love is true. Ballad. Paul Laurence Dunbar. **CP-DunbP**

I know my mind and I have made my choice. Edna St. Vincent Millay. **CP-MillE**

I know my time, which is obscure, silent and brief. Night-Flowering Cactus. Thomas Merton. **CP-MertT; SP-MertT**

I know no greater delight than the sheer delight of being alone. Delight of Being Alone. David Herbert Lawrence. **CP-LawrD**

I know no poet's use of words. Poem to be Placed at the Conclusion of a Long Obscure Passionate and Eloquent Book of Poems. Malcolm Lowry. **CP-LowrM**

I know not how, but as I count. Robert Louis Stevenson. **CP-StevR**

I know not how it falls on me. Emily Brontë. **CP-BronE**

I know not how it is with you. Robert Louis Stevenson. **CP-StevR**

I know not how it may be with others. Old Furniture. Thomas Hardy. **CP-HardT**

I know not how to thank you. Emily Dickinson. **SP-DickE**

I know not in Whose hands are laid. The Necessitarian. Rudyard Kipling. **CP-KiplR**

I know not, Time and Space so intervene. The Countess. John Greenleaf Whittier. **CP-WhitJ**

I know not what the future hath. John Greenleaf Whittier. **BLRP; NOCV** *Fr.* The Eternal Goodness. **CP-WhitJ**

I know not what to do. Fragment 36. Hilda Doolittle. **CP-DoolH**

I know not where my heavy sighs to hide. Sir Thomas Wyatt. **CP-WyatT**

I know nothing but this scene. James Liddy. **BiHa** *Fr.* Epithalamion I–IV: "Along a leafy lonely river God-shy-eyed fisher boys." **CP-LiddJ**

I know now how a man whose blood is hot. Sonnet. Countee Cullen. **CP-CullC**

I know of one without compare. Song for My Wife. Malcolm Lowry. **CP-LowrM**

I know of people in the Grave. Emily Dickinson. **CP-DickE**

I know only the bare rocks of today. Prelude, A. William Carlos Williams. **CP-WilW1**

I know, Sister, that solitude. To a Severe Nun. Thomas Merton. **CP-MertT; SP-MertT**

I know so much. Spleen. Frank O'Hara. **SP-OharF**

I know so well this turfy mile. Greenaway. Sir John Betjeman. **CP-BetjJ**

I know some lonely Houses off the Road. Emily Dickinson. **CP-DickE**

I know Suspense, it steps so terse. Emily Dickinson. **CP-DickE**

I know that a little verse is a versicle but I don't know if a little phrase is a phrasical. From a Manhattan Tomb. Ogden Nash. **CP-NashO**

I know that behind these walls is the city, over these rooftops. Foghorn in Horror. Muriel Rukeyser. **CP-RukeM**

I know that He exists. Emily Dickinson. **CP-DickE**

I know that I shall meet my fate. An Irish Airman Foresees His Death. William Butler Yeats. **CP-YeatW**

I know that some night. We Will Taste the Islands and the Sea. Charles Bukowski. **SP-BukC1**

I know that this was Life,—the track. Tennyson. *Fr.* In Memoriam A. H. H. **CP-TennA**

I know that tonight the wind is sighing. M.A. Written on the Dungeon Wall. Emily Brontë. **CP-BronE**

I know that what our neighbours call *longueurs*. Byron. **OBSV** *Fr.* Canto the Third. *Fr.* Don Juan. **CP-Byron**

I know that you will die / before I do. Keep. Margaret Atwood. **SP-AtwM2**

I know the appointed hour. Ralph Waldo Emerson. **CP-EmerR**

I know the bottom, she says. I know it with my great tap root. Elm. Sylvia Plath. **CP-PlatS**

I know the face of Falsehood and her tongue. Edna St. Vincent Millay. **CP-MillE**

I know the hair, tissue, skin. Kenneth Patchen. *Fr.* Eight Early Poems. **CP-PatcK**

I know the moon is troubling. I Know. David St. John. **SP-StJoD**

I know the [or a] thing that's most uncommon. On a Certain Lady at Court. Alexander Pope. **CP-PopeA**

I know the touch of things: the play of mind. The Touch of Things. John Hewitt. **CP-HewiJ**

I know the way[e]s of learning; both the head. George Herbert. **CP-HerbG** (Pearl. Matthew 13:45, The.) **CP-HerbG**

I know them at their worst, when by the shore. The Gulls. Howard Nemerov. **CP-NemeH**

I know there are some fools that care. The Deformed Mistress. Sir John Suckling. **CP-SuckJ**

I know there is a country where we go. Hayden Carruth. **CP-CarHS** *Fr.* The Bloomingdale Papers.

I know there is still time. The Still Time. Galway Kinnell. **SP-KinnG**

I know there shall dawn a day. Reverie. Robert Browning. **CP-BroR2**

I know there's no such thing. 1967. Leonard Cohen. **CP-CoheL**

I know this perilous love-lane. Hafiz, *tr. by* Ralph Waldo Emerson. **CP-EmerR** *Fr.* Odes.

I know three women that are you. John Haines. *Fr.* Daphne. **SP-HainJ**

I know 'tis but a Dream, yet feel more anguish. The Night-Mare Death in Life. Samuel Taylor Coleridge. **CP-ColeS**

I know to whom I write. Here, I am sure. An Epistle to Master John Selden. Ben Jonson. **CP-JonsB**

I know to whom I write. Here, I am sure. Ben Jonson. **OBF,** *ll.* 1–14; *Fr.* An Epistle to Master John Selden. **CP-JonsB**

I know two women / and the one. The Wife. Robert Creeley. **CP-CreeR**

I know very little. Hangover and Sick Leave. Charles Bukowski. **SP-BukC2**

I know very well, goddess, she is not beautiful. Calypso's Island. Archibald MacLeish. **CP-MacLA**

I know well / You are not infallible. Ted Hughes. **SP-HughT** *Fr.* Gaudete.

I know what my heart is like. Ebb. Edna St. Vincent Millay. **CP-MillE**

I know what the caged bird feels, alas! Sympathy. Paul Laurence Dunbar. **CP-DunbP**

I know what you're doing, you figures standing at gates. Modern witches 2: sentinels. Jenny Joseph. *Fr.* Life and Turgid Times of A. Citizen. **SP-JoseJ**

I know when you are at your happiest. For Roberta in the Garden. John Hewitt. **CP-HewiJ**

I know where lurk. Fear. Walter de la Mare. **CP-DeLaW**

I know where Wells grow—Droughtless Wells. Emily Dickinson. **CP-DickE**

I know why, getting up in the cold dawn. To a Daughter with Artistic Talent. Peter Meinke. **SP-MeinP**

I know why the yellow forsythia. Spring Song. Edna St. Vincent Millay. **CP-MillE**

I know: you are glycerine. Any Husband to Any Wife. Adrienne Rich. **CP-RicAE**

I know you hardly ever leave your room now. Dear . . . . John Yau. **SP-YauJo**

I Know You Not. Christina Georgina Rossetti. **CP-RosC3**

I Know You'll Like Them. Ogden Nash. **CP-NashO**

I lack a light touch. Marge Piercy. *Fr.* The Homely War. **SP-PierM**

I lafs und sings, und shumps aroundt. Lager Beer. Paul Laurence Dunbar. **CP-DunbP**

I laid beside thy gate, am Lazarus. Son, Remember. Christina Georgina Rossetti. **CP-RosC2**

I laid me down upon a bank. William Blake. **CP-BlakW**

I laid my inventory at the hand. Even In The Grave. Walter de la Mare. **CP-DeLaW**

I laid on a dune, I looked at the sky. Sara. "Bob Dylan." **CP-DylaB**

I lang hae thought, my youthfu' friend. Epistle to a Young Friend. Robert Burns. **CP-BurnR**

I late the Roman youth's loud prayse and pride. *ad. fr. the Latin* Uxoris Sancti Alexii Querimoniae. Richard Crashaw. **CP-CrasR**

I lately fri'd, but now behold. Upon Himselfe . Robert Herrick. **CP-HerrR**

I laugh and sing, but cannot tell. To Lucasta. Richard Lovelace. **CP-LoveR**

I laughed. Calvus. I laughed today. Carmen 53. Catullus. *Fr.* Carmina. **CP-Catul**

I lay at the edge of a well. The Underground Stream. James Dickey. **CP-DickJ**

I lay beside my sleeping son. *see also* Commentary—Beside My Son. Leonard Cohen. **CP-CoheL**

I lay down in my grave. Elegy. Maya Angelou. **SP-AngeM**

I lay in my bed and fiddled. In the Small Hours. Thomas Hardy. **CP-HardT**

I lay in sheets of softest linen. Song. Alun Lewis. **CP-LewiA**

I Lay Love on My Knee. Allen Ginsberg. **CP-GinsA**

I lay me down and slumber. Alfred Edward Housman. **CP-HousA**

I lay my branch of laurel down. To Lord Thurlow. Byron. **CP-Byron**

I lay on my back in Portugal. Autobiographies. Frederick Morgan. **SP-MorgF**

I lay six eggs, says the Hen. The Hen and the Cock: A Glens Folk Rhyme. John Hewitt. **CP-HewiJ**

I lay waiting. Bog Queen. Seamus Heaney. **SP-HeanS**

I lay your face along my palm and make. (Face) (Autumn) (En Face). Bill Knott. **SP-KnotB**

I lead a life unpleasant, nothing glad. Sir Thomas Wyatt. **CP-WyatT**

I leaned to hear your song. Poem for Kathleen Ferrier. James Wright. **CP-WrigJ**

I leant [*or* leaned] upon a coppice gate. The Darkling Thrush. Thomas Hardy. **CP-HardT**

I Learn About Art. John Hewitt. **CP-HewiJ**

I learn from the lake. Second Party. Archie Randolph Ammons. **SP-AmmoA**

I learn to count without pointing at my fingers. This is Pinocchio. John Yau. **SP-YauJo** *Fr.* Predella.

I learned a world from each. Allen Ginsberg. **CP-GinsA**

I learned—at least—what Home could be. Emily Dickinson. **CP-DickE**

I learned this from the old: odor of lake. A History of the Sketch. Richard Hugo. **CP-HugoR**

I learned to catch her quiet murmuring. On Choosing Some Verses for My Sister's Cremation. John Hewitt. **CP-HewiJ**

I learned to use the Public Library. Reading. John Hewitt. **CP-HewiJ**

I learnt the collects and the catechism. Elizabeth Barrett Browning. **EnVR; TEP** *Fr.* Aurora Leigh. **CP-BroEB**

I leave Don Juan for the present, safe. Byron. **NOBRP** *Fr.* Canto the Fourth. *Fr.* Don Juan. **CP-Byron**

I leave the book, I leave the wine. Ralph Waldo Emerson. **CP-EmerR**

I leave the number and a short. The Ubiquity of the Need for Love. Ron Koertge. **SP-KoerR**

I leave thy praises unexpressed. Tennyson. *Fr.* In Memoriam A. H. H. **CP-TennA**

I leave you in your garden. To Yvor Winters, 1955. Thom Gunn. **CP-GunnT**

I leave you on that downtown street of. Roland Navarro (1939-1961). Al Young. **CP-YounA**

I leave you these, good daughters and honest son. For Lucinda, Robert, and Karyn. Miller Williams. **SP-WillM**

I Left a Woman, *see also* I Left a Woman Waiting. Leonard Cohen. **CP-CoheL**

I Left a Woman Waiting, *see also* I Left a Woman. Leonard Cohen. **CP-CoheL**

I left my dreamy page & sallied forth. Ralph Waldo Emerson. **CP-EmerR**

I left my room at last, I walked. The Monster. Thom Gunn. **CP-GunnT**

I left the graveyard by a chosen path. John Haines. *Fr.* The Stone Bear. **SP-HainJ**

I left you in the morning. Flower-Gathering. Robert Frost. **CP-FrosR**

I let it go for the fact of it for as fast as it will. Reading the Newsapaper on Microfilm. Miller Williams. **SP-WillM**

I let my grandfather's canoe. Messages. Robert Pack. **SP-PackR**

I let myself in at the kitchen door. The Housekeeper. Robert Frost. **CP-FrosR**

I Lie Alone. John Hewitt. **CP-HewiJ**

I lie and imagine a first light gleam in the bay. Achill. Derek Mahon. **SP-MahoD**

I lie and live. The Stealer. Thom Gunn. **CP-GunnT**

I lie down and spread my legs and arms. O Sleepless Night. James Schuyler. **CP-SchuJ**

I lie for a long time on my left side and my right side. Dead Color. Charles Wright. **SP-WrigC**

I lie here thinking of you. Love Song. William Carlos Williams. **CP-WilW1**

I lie in my crib midday this is. Baby's Pantoum. Anne Waldman. **SP-WaldA**

I lie in the bath and contemplate the toilet-paper. From a Play: Publisher's Song. Muriel Rukeyser. **CP-RukeM**

I lie on my hospital bed. With the World in My Blood Stream. Thomas Merton. **CP-MertT**

I lift—lift you five States away your glass. John Berryman. **FaBoDD** *Fr.* Sonnets to Chris. **CP-BerrJ**

(At Six O'Clock.) **FaBoDD**

I lift mine eyes, and see / Thee, tender Lord, in pain upon the tree. Palm Sunday. Christina Georgina Rossetti. **CP-RosC2**

I lift mine eyes to see: earth vanisheth. Christina Georgina Rossetti. **CP-RosC2**

I lift my heavy heart up solemnly. Sonnet. Elizabeth Barrett Browning. **NALW** *Fr.* Sonnets from the Portuguese. **CP-BroEB**

I lift the lid to my box of Phantoms. Emily Dickinson. **SP-DickE**

I lift the small brown mouse. Encounter. Mary Oliver. **SP-OlivM**

I lift up mine eyes unto the hills. The Hills. David Herbert Lawrence. **CP-LawrD**

I like / to think that on. Edward Estlin Cummings. **CP-CummE**

I like a church; I like a cowl. The Problem. Ralph Waldo Emerson. **CP-EmerR**

I like a look of Agony. Emily Dickinson. **CP-DickE**

I like a man to know a lot more than I do, but I. My Kind of Man. Anne Waldman. **SP-WaldA**

I Like Americans. Ernest Hemingway. **CP-HemiE**

I like bars close to home and home run down. The Hilltop. Richard Hugo. **CP-HugoR**

I like being tired. After Working. Roy Fisher. **SP-FishR**

I Like Canadians. Ernest Hemingway. **CP-HemiE**

I like it back here. Ars Poetica. Charles Wright. **SP-WrigC**

I like it when. My Weariness of Epic Proportions. Charles Simic. **SP-SimiC**

I like it when it's spring. Lindsay Speaks. Anne Waldman. **SP-WaldA**

I like my body when it is with your. Edward Estlin Cummings. **CP-CummE; SP-CummE**

I like nonliterary. Camels. Archie Randolph Ammons. **SP-AmmoA**

I like not that dainty-cut raiment, those earrings of pearl. A Daughter Returns. Thomas Hardy. **CP-HardT**

I like people quite well. People. David Herbert Lawrence. **CP-LawrD**

I like relativity and quantum theories. Relativity. David Herbert Lawrence. **CP-LawrD**

I like the crush here. What Virginia Said. Charles Tomlinson. **CP-TomlC**

I like the duck-billed platypus. The Platypus. Ogden Nash. *Fr.* The Astigmatic Naturalist. **CP-NashO**

I like the rich—the way. The Rich. Charles Tomlinson. **CP-TomlC**

I like the sidewalks of an American city. Agave in the West. Donald Davie. **CP-DavDo**

I like the way, in winter, cars. The Short Days. John Updike. **CP-UpdiJ**

I like the way these old brick garden walls. On Leaving Wantage 1972. Sir John Betjeman. **CP-BetjJ**

I Like the Way You Opposed Me. Leonard Cohen. **CP-CoheL**

I like the wind. Wind Secrets. Diane Wakoski. **SP-WakoD**

I like things my way. Mon Semblable. Stephen Dunn. **SP-DunnS**

I Like to Collapse. Joseph Ceravolo. **SP-CeraJ**

I like to get off with people. Conviction (iv). Stevie Smith. **CP-SmitS**

I like to hear of wealth and gold. Common Things. Paul Laurence Dunbar. **CP-DunbP**

I Like to Play with Him. Stevie Smith. **CP-SmitS**

I like to see him drink the gash. God the Drinker. Stevie Smith. **CP-SmitS**

I like to see it lap the Miles. Emily Dickinson. **CP-DickE**

I like to see, when I am low. Mediterranean Song. Richard Eberhart. **CP-EberR**

I like to spend some time in Mozambique. Mozambique. "Bob Dylan" *and* Jacques Levy. **CP-DylaB**

I like to think about that great French critic and historian, Hippolyte Adolphe Taine. If He Scholars, Let Him Go. Ogden Nash. **CP-NashO**

I like to toss him up and down. My Cats. Stevie Smith. **CP-SmitS**

I like to watch the clouds roll by. The Cherub. Ogden Nash. **CP-NashO**

I like wallpaper that makes sense. Robert Herrick. John Yau. **SP-YauJo**

I like your muse because she's gay and witty. Wystan Hugh Auden. **NOBL** *Fr.* Letter to Lord Byron. **CP-AudeW**

I liked it coming out of that expensive. Some of My Readers. Charles Bukowski. **SP-BukC3**

I likes a woman. Preference. Langston Hughes. **SP-HughL**

I lingered through the night to break of day. Her Definition. Thomas Hardy. **CP-HardT**

I list you from the past with food. Szostak. Gary Gildner. **SP-GildG**

I 'listed at home for a lancer. Lancer. Alfred Edward Housman. **CP-HousA**

I listen—but no faculty of mine. On Hearing the "Ranz des Vaches" on the Top of the Pass of St Gothard. William Wordsworth. *Fr.* Memorials of a Tour of the Continent; 1820. **CP-WorW2**

I listen for the sounds of cannon, cries. On Lookout Mountain. Robert Earl Hayden. **CP-HaydR**

I listen for your footsteps coming up the drive. Don't Pass Me By. "Ringo Starr." **CP-Beatl**

I listen to the holy antheming. St. Andrew's Church. Christina Georgina Rossetti. **CP-RosC3**

I listen to the stillness of you. Listening. David Herbert Lawrence. **CP-LawrD**

I listened to the Phantom by Ontario's shore. The Poet. Walt Whitman. **MoAmPo** *Fr.* By Blue Ontario's Shore. **CP-WhitW**

I lit a stick of incense. Fragment from a Journal. Leonard Cohen. **CP-CoheL**

I lit a thin green candle. One of Us Cannot Be Wrong. Leonard Cohen. **CP-CoheL**

I lit upon the graveyard of dead creeds. The Graveyard of Dead Creeds. Thomas Hardy. **CP-HardT**

I live among ideal men. Ralph Waldo Emerson. **CP-EmerR**

I live at the top of old West Chop. Martha's Vineyard. Ogden Nash. **CP-NashO**

I live here: "Wessex" is my name. A Popular Personage at Home. Thomas Hardy. **CP-HardT**

I live in a middle class neighborhood of an unfashionable. A Sad Poem. Charles Bukowski. **SP-BukC3**

I live in an orchard. Confetti of bruised petals. Postcard from the Garden. Marge Piercy. **SP-PierM**

I live in my wooden legs and O. Where I Live in This Honorable House of the Laurel Tree. Anne Sexton. **CP-SextA**

I Live in New York. Erica Jong. **SP-JongE**

I live in these hills, made heavy. Cinco de Mayo. Jim Carroll. *Fr.* 3 Short Poems. **SP-CarrJ**

I live on the water. Winding Up. Derek Walcott. **CP-WalcD**

I live only here, between your eyes and you. To Be Written on the Mirror in Whitewash. Elizabeth Bishop. **CP-BishE**

I live underneath / the light of day. Charles Olson. **SP-OlsoC** *Fr.* The Maximus Poems.

I live where Frost lived. Hayden Carruth. **CP-CarHS** *Fr.* The Clay Hill Anthology.

I live with Him—I see His face. Emily Dickinson. **CP-DickE**

I lived in a dry well. Wells. Donald Hall. **CP-HallD**

I lived in the first century of world wars. Poem. Muriel Rukeyser. **CP-RukeM**

I lived no-color. In a gray room I talked. No Color Man. Donald Hall. **CP-HallD**

I lived on a back street where. The Ambassador. Pablo Neruda, *tr. fr. Spanish by* Ben Belitt. **SP-NeruP**

I lived on Dread. Emily Dickinson. **CP-DickE**

I lived with Mr. Punch, they said my name was Judy. Variations. Randall Jarrell. **CP-JarrR**

I lived with visions for my company. Sonnet. Elizabeth Barrett Browning. **BWW** *Fr.* Sonnets from the Portuguese. **CP-BroEB**

I loathe, O Lord, this life below. A Complaint on the Miseries of Life. James Thomson. **CP-ThomD**

I Long For a Horse. Ussin Kerim, *tr. fr. Bulgarian by* William Matthews. **SP-MattW**

I long for joy, O Lord, I long for gold / I long for all Thou profferest to me. The Gold of that Land is Good. Christina Georgina Rossetti. **CP-RosC2**

I long for the black ink. for Mary McCarthy. Robert Lowell. **SP-LoweR**

I long for the desolate valleys. Lot's Wife. Stevie Smith. **CP-SmitS**

I long not now, a little while at least. Protest. Countee Cullen. **CP-CullC**

I Long to Hold Some Lady. Leonard Cohen. **CP-CoheL**

I long to talk[e] with some old lover's ghost. Love's Deity [*or* Deitie]. John Donne. **CP-DonnJ**

I longed for companionship rather. In the Night. Stevie Smith. **CP-SmitS**

I longed to kill you once, when I was young. Devotions. James Wright. **CP-WrigJ**

I longed to love a full-boughed beech. The Ivy-Wife. Thomas Hardy. **CP-HardT**

I look a long way back. Stratford on Avon. Donald Davie. **CP-DavDo**

I look across the ocean. Robert Louis Stevenson. **CP-StevR**

I look at the bottle, when mournful I feel. The Bottle of Aspirins. Stevie Smith. **CP-SmitS**

I look at the Greek-derived design that nourished my infancy — this. Hellenistics. Robinson Jeffers. **CP-JefR2**

I look at the nephew. Thom Gunn. *See* Slow Waker.

I look at the pines on the hillside. Louis Zukofsky. *Fr.* Sequence 1944-6. **CP-ZukLS**

I look at the pins on the hillside. Sequence 1944-6. Louis Zukofsky. **CP-ZukLS**

I look at the rock and the house. Stories. Donald Hall. **CP-HallD**

I look at the swaling sunset. In Trouble and Shame. David Herbert Lawrence. **CP-LawrD**

I look at you all see the love there that's sleeping. While My Guitar Gently Weeps. George Harrison. **CP-Beatl**

I look back to you, and cherish what I wanted. Searching. Robert Lowell. **SP-LoweR**

I Look for the Lord. Christina Georgina Rossetti. **CP-RosC3**

I Look in Her Face. Thomas Hardy. **CP-HardT**

I look in the glass. The Repentance of Lady T. Stevie Smith. **CP-SmitS**

I look in the mirror. The Ghost of Ware. Stevie Smith. **CP-SmitS**

I Look into My Glass. Thomas Hardy. **CP-HardT**

I look on the specious electrical light. A Rhyme About an Electrical Advertising Sign. Nicholas Vachel Lindsay. **CP-LindV**

I look onto an alley here. A Day for Anne Frank. Charles Kenneth Williams. **CP-WillC; SP-WillC**

I look out over the sterile snow. World Breaking Apart. Louise Glück. **SP-GlücL**

I look round the cluttered. Selves. Thom Gunn. **CP-GunnT**

I Look to the North. Robert Burns. **CP-BurnR**

I look up at the cliffs. The Canyon Wren. Gary Snyder. **CP-SnydG**

I look up, you are standing. Margaret Atwood. **SP-AtwM1**

I look upon the map that hangs by me. The Place on the Map. Thomas Hardy. **CP-HardT**

I look'd for my poet—he came not! George Meredith. **CP-MerG2**

I looked and I saw. Who But the Lord? Langston Hughes. **SP-HughL**

I looked and thought, "All is too gray and cold." Aberdeen. Thomas Hardy. **CP-HardT**

I looked at the book. Good Carpenters. Erica Jong. **SP-JongE**

I Looked Back. Thomas Hardy. **CP-HardT**

I looked down. Genghis Chan: Private Eye II. John Yau. **SP-YauJo**

I looked for that which is not, nor can be. A Pause of Thought. Christina Georgina Rossetti. **CP-RosC1; CoGr; FaBoEn; NOBE; OBNC** *Fr.* Three Stages. **CP-RosC3**

I looked from the book of the story of men. George Meredith. **CP-MerG2**

I looked in my heart while the wild swans went over. Wild Swans. Edna St. Vincent Millay. **CP-MillE**

I looked into the eyes of Robert Frost. Worldly Failure. Richard Eberhart. **CP-EberR**

I looked long and long at my mother's miniature. Roma II. Charles Wright. **SP-WrigC**

I looked out of the window. Magritte Imitated Himself. Roy Fisher. **SP-FishR**

I looked toward the movie, the common dream. Metro-Goldwyn-Mayer. Delmore Schwartz. **SP-SchwD**

I looked up and saw. Charles Olson. **SP-OlsoC** *Fr.* The Maximus Poems.

I Looked Up from My Writing. Thomas Hardy. **CP-HardT**

I, Lord, Thy foolish sinner low and small. Christina Georgina Rossetti. **CP-RosC2**

I lost a dollar at the track today and I know that's. Charles Bukowski. *Fr.* Horsemeat. **SP-BukC3**

I lost a World—the other day! Emily Dickinson. **CP-DickE**

I Lost My Way. Leonard Cohen. **CP-CoheL**

I lounge on the warm step, watching the child. James McAuley. **SP-McAuJ** *Fr.* Sunflowers: An Ode.

I Love. Stevie Smith. **CP-SmitS**

I love a man who is not worth / my love. Did This Happen to Your Mother? Did Your Sister Throw Up a Lot? Alice Walker. **CP-WalkA**

I love and hate. Ah! never ask why so! Catullus. *See* Carmen 85: "I hate and I love. And if you ask me how."

I love, and he loves me again. A Nymph's Passion. Ben Jonson. **CP-JonsB**

I love and love not: Lord, it breaks my heart. Dost Thou Not Care? Christina Georgina Rossetti. **CP-RosC1**

I love being here, like this. In It. Stephen Berg. **SP-BergS**

I love breasts, hard. Breasts. Charles Simic. **SP-SimiC**

I love crystal fringe on a dance frock. Frock. James Schuyler. **CP-SchuJ**

I love him, I love him, ran the patter of her lips. Circle of Doors. Carl Sandburg. **CP-SandC**

I love I love I love and oh. Baldur Was Beautiful Too. Isabella Gardner. **CP-GardI**

I love life, I love life so dearly, I could almost die. Life and the Human Consciousness. David Herbert Lawrence. **CP-LawrD**

I love little Heber. Heber. Stevie Smith. **CP-SmitS**

I love, loved, and so doth she. Sir Thomas Wyatt. **CP-WyatT**

I love Meng-fu-tsu. To Meng Hao-Jan. Li Po, *tr. fr. Chinese by* William Carlos Williams *with* David Rafael Wang. **CP-WilW2**

I love my animal heart. Charles Henri Ford. *Fr.* Epigrams. **SP-FordC**

I love my beautiful hat more than anything. The Hat. Stevie Smith. **CP-SmitS**

I Love My Jean. Robert Burns. *See* Of A' the Airts [the Wind Can Blaw].

I love my little son, and yet when he was ill. The Two Parents. "Hugh MacDiarmid." **SP-MacDH**

I Love My Love in Secret. Robert Burns. **CP-BurnR**

I love my neighbour. Love Thy Neighbour. David Herbert Lawrence. **CP-LawrD**

I love my work and my children. God. Ovid in the Third Reich. Geoffrey Hill. **CP-HillG**

I love not me but what you see and for. Sonnet for My Acquaintances. Isabella Gardner. **CP-GardI**

I love Nowhere where the factories die of malnutrition. Nebraska. Karl Shapiro. **SP-ShapK**

I love one, and he loveth me. The Novice. Christina Georgina Rossetti. **CP-RosC3**

I love Russia; and Isadora in the dance. (Sergey) (Yesenin) Speaking (Isadora) (Duncan). Bill Knott. **SP-KnotB**

I love the accomplishments of trees. A Final Affection. Paul Zimmer. **SP-ZimmP**

I love the dear old ballads best. Songs. Paul Laurence Dunbar. **CP-DunbP**

I love the jocund dance. Song. William Blake. **CP-BlakW**

I love the Lord, because he hath heard my voice and my supplications. Psalm 116. Bible, *O.T.* *Fr.* Psalms. **CP-Psal**

"I love the Lord," is still the strain. Love Increased by Suffering. Jeanne Marie Bouvier de la Motte-Guyon, *tr. fr. French by* William Cowper. **CP-CowpW**

I love the old melodious lays. Proem. John Greenleaf Whittier. **CP-WhitJ**

I love the past, which doesn't exist. Loves. Stephen Dunn. **SP-DunnS**

I love the quiet, hard. Eternity. Al Young. **CP-YounA**

I love the sex, and sometimes would reverse. Byron. **CBLP** *Fr.* Canto the Sixth. *Fr.* Don Juan. **CP-Byron**

I love the stillness of the wood. Solitude. "Lewis Carroll." **CP-CarrL**

I love the thought of his anger. An Artist. Seamus Heaney. **SP-HeanS** *Fr.* Sweeney Redivivus.

I love the Turkana tribesman who gave me his cane. To Kenya Tribesmen, the Turkana. Richard Eberhart. **CP-EberR**

I love the way Janie Crawford. Janie Crawford. Alice Walker. **CP-WalkA**

I love the way the weave, when two or three or. Osip Emilevich Mandelstam. *Fr.* Octets. **CP-DavDo**

I love the way the weave, when two or three or. Osip Emilevich Mandelstam. *Fr.* Octets. **CP-DavDo**

I love thee, Baby! for thine own sweet sake. To Ianthe. Percy Bysshe Shelley. **CP-ShelP**

I love thee, love thee, Giulio. Parting Lovers. Elizabeth Barrett Browning. **CP-BroEB**

I love thee, mournful, sober-suited Night! To Night. Charlotte Smith. **CP-SmitC**

I Love Those Little Booths at Benvenuti's. Gwendolyn Brooks. **SP-BrooG** *Fr.* The Womanhood.

I love thy music, mellow bell. Ralph Waldo Emerson. **CP-EmerR**

I love to be warm by the red fireside. Robert Louis Stevenson. **CP-StevR**

I love to go out in late September. Blackberry Eating. Galway Kinnell. **SP-KinnG**

I love to go out on summer nights and watch the stones grow. The Stones. Richard Shelton. **SP-ShelR**

I love to hear the cock crow in. Cock-a-Doo. Stevie Smith. **CP-SmitS**

I love to lie down weary. Sleep. Wendell Berry. **CP-BerrW**

I love to rise in a summer morn. The School Boy. William Blake. **CP-BlakW** *Fr.* Songs of Experience.

I love to see boards lying on the ground in early spring. Old Boards. Robert Bly. **SP-BlyR**

I love to see the summer beaming forth. Sonnet. John Clare. **SP-ClarJ**

I love to stay in bed. Summer Morning. Charles Simic. **SP-SimiC**

I love to toy with the Platonic notion. Boeotian. Robert Frost. **CP-FrosR**

I love upon a stormy night. William Wordsworth. **CP-WorW1**

I love you / Cause you tell me things I want to know. Ask Me Why. The Beatles. **CP-Beatl**

I love you / for your little,startled,thoughtless ways. Edward Estlin Cummings. **CP-CummE**

I love you / I need you. Dancing in the Laundromat [or] Dust: an Ordinary Song. Al Young. **CP-YounA**

"I love you," / spoken in rhapsodic metre. Hilda Doolittle. **AnAn** *Fr.* Sigil. **CP-DoolH**

I love you and it makes me rather dull. Villanelle: Late Summer. Marilyn Hacker. **SP-HackM**

I love you and you know it—this at least. Christina Georgina Rossetti. **CP-RosC3**

I love you as a sheriff searches for a walnut. To You. Kenneth Koch. **SP-KochK**

I love you first because your face is fair. V-Letter. Karl Shapiro. **SP-ShapK**

I love you more than ever, more than time and more than love. Wedding Song. "Bob Dylan." **CP-DylaB**

I love you much(most beautiful darling). Edward Estlin Cummings. **CP-CummE**

I love you, rotten. Medlars and Sorb-Apples. David Herbert Lawrence. **CP-LawrD**

I love you so. . . .Gone? Who will swear you wouldn't. For Eugene McCarthy. Robert Lowell. **SP-LoweR**

I love you so much with this curiously alive and lonely body. The Cry Going Out over Pastures. Robert Bly. **SP-BlyR**

I Love Your Crazy Bones. Barton Sutter. **SP-SuttB**

I love your faces I saw the many years. The Red Son. Carl Sandburg. **CP-SandC**

I loved—alas! our life is love. *see also* Scene from "Tasso." Percy Bysshe Shelley. **CP-ShelP**

I loved bar room fights. My Friend. Charles Bukowski. **SP-BukC3**

I loved Miss Beech. Eeny, Meeny, Miney, Mo, Miss Beech. Gary Gildner. **SP-GildG**

I loved my love from green of Spring. Grown and Flown. Christina Georgina Rossetti. **CP-RosC1**

I loved the children. Yes, and I loved Tim. Jane Renick MacElmain (1). Louise McNeill. **SP-McNeL**

I loved the wood because I found in it. Praise Is Traditional and Appropriate. Delmore Schwartz. **SP-SchwD**

I loved Theotormon. Visions of the Daughters of Albion. William Blake. **CP-BlakW**

I loved to watch him shave, his splayed thumb pressed. A Holy Place. John Hewitt. **CP-HewiJ**

I loved you first: but afterwards your love. Christina Georgina Rossetti. **VBLP** *Fr.* Monna Innominata. **CP-RosC2**

I loved you for a long long time. I know this love is. Ain't No Cure for Love. Leonard Cohen. **CP-CoheL**

I loved you in the morning. Hey, That's No Way to Say Goodbye. Leonard Cohen. **CP-CoheL**

I loved you, too. There was no use. I had no time. Randall Jarrell. **CP-JarrR**

I loving only the word. First Poem to Mary in London. Ernest Hemingway. **CP-HemiE**

I made a fire; being tired. Burning the Letters. Sylvia Plath. **CP-PlatS**

I Made a Mistake. Charles Bukowski. **SP-BukC1**

I made a posy [*or* posie], while the day ran by. Life. George Herbert. **CP-HerbG**

I made an opening. Planting Crocuses. Wendell Berry. **CP-BerrW**

I made hay while the sun shone. The Last Laugh. Sir John Betjeman. **CP-BetjJ**

I made love to myself. Allen Ginsberg. **CP-GinsA**

I made Man with too many faults. Yet I love him. God Speaks. Stevie Smith. **CP-SmitS**

I made my song a coat. A Coat. William Butler Yeats. **CP-YeatW**

I made myself an expert in farewells. Tristia. Stanley Jasspon Kunitz. **CP-KuniS**

I made no choice / I decided nothing. Margaret Atwood. **NALW** *Fr.* Circe / Mud Poems. **SP-AtwM1**

I made slow Riches but my Gain. Emily Dickinson. **CP-DickE**

I make a pact with you, Walt Whitman. A Pact. Ezra Pound. **SP-PounE**

I make a trip to each clock in the apartment. Paris, 7 A.M. Elizabeth Bishop. **CP-BishE**

I make a Y. La Ultima Carta: A Young Wife Writes to Her Husband in the Mountains. Miller Williams. **SP-WillM**

I make His Crescent fill or lack. Emily Dickinson. **CP-DickE**

I make my children promises. Teacher. Audre Lorde. **SP-LordA**

I make my head, as I used to. A Paper Bag. Margaret Atwood. **SP-AtwM2**

I make no haste to have my Numbers read. Glorie. Robert Herrick. **CP-HerrR**

I make the old sign. Ad Castitatem. Louise Bogan. **CP-BogaL**

I Make This in a Warring Absence. Dylan Thomas. **CP-ThomD**

I many times thought Peace had come. Emily Dickinson. **CP-DickE**

I marched [*or* march'd] three miles through scorching sand. Verses Spoken Extempore by Dean Swift on His Curate's Complaint of Hard Duty. Jonathan Swift. **CP-SwifJ**

I mark not without. Before. Wystan Hugh Auden. **CP-AudWJ**

I mark the months in liveries dank and dry. A Sign-Seeker. Thomas Hardy. **CP-HardT**

I marked her ruined hues. Amabel. Thomas Hardy. **CP-HardT**

I marked when the weather changed. A Night in November. Thomas Hardy. **CP-HardT**

I marked where lovely Venus and her court. Venus's Looking-Glass. Christina Georgina Rossetti. **CP-RosC1**

I married Isis on the fifth day of May. Isis. "Bob Dylan" *and* Jacques Levy. **CP-DylaB**

I married the Earl of Egremont. The Castle. Stevie Smith. **CP-SmitS**

I marvel how Nature could ever find space. A Character. William Wordsworth. **CP-WorW1**

I maun hae a wife, whatsoe'er she be. Broom Besoms ["I maun hae a wife, whatsoe'er she be"]. Robert Burns. **CP-BurnR**

I may be oversusceptible to news. Roger Clay's Proposal. James Merrill. **SP-MerrJ**

I may be smelly and I may be old. The River God. Stevie Smith. **CP-SmitS**

I may even be. Power and Light. James Dickey. **CP-DickJ**

I May, I Might, I Must. Marianne Craig Moore. **CP-MoorM**

I may sing; but minstrel's singing. Stanzas. Elizabeth Barrett Browning. **CP-BroEB**

I Me Mine. The Beatles. **CP-Beatl**

I Mean, No. Charles Olson. **CP-OlsoC**

I mean not to defend the scapes of any. 2.4. Ovid. **CP-MarlC,** *tr. by* Christopher Marlowe; *Fr.* Elegies.

I mean that too, but yet a hidden strength. Chastity ("I Mean That Too, But Yet a Hidden Strength"). John Milton. **NOSC** *Fr.* Comus; a Masque Presented at Ludlow Castle.

I mean to build a hall anon. The Spell of the Rose. Thomas Hardy. **CP-HardT**

I meant to find Her when I came. Emily Dickinson. **CP-DickE**

I meant to have but modest needs. Emily Dickinson. **CP-DickE**

I meanwhile in the populous house apart. Robert Louis Stevenson. *Fr.* The Family. **CP-StevR**

I measure every Grief I meet. Emily Dickinson. **CP-DickE**

I meditate upon a swallow's flight. Coole Park, 1929. William Butler Yeats. **CP-YeatW**

I meet him in the spaces. Vows. Daniel Gerard Hoffman. **SP-HoffD**

I meet you in an evil time. An Eclogue for Christmas. Louis MacNeice. **CP-MacNL**

I, Mencius, Pupil of the Master. Charles Olson. **CP-OlsoC**

I mentioned my demon to a friend. Demon. Anne Sexton. **CP-SextA**

I mentioned trimming. Bulletin. Archie Randolph Ammons. **SP-AmmoA**

I met a fellow in whose hand. Tax-Free Encounter. John Updike. **CP-UpdiJ**

I met a girl from Derrygarve. A New Song. Seamus Heaney. **SP-HeanS**

I met a guy I used to know, who said. Ozymandias II. Howard Nemerov. **CP-NemeH**

I met a King this afternoon! Emily Dickinson. **CP-DickE**

I met a lady from the South who said. New Hampshire. Robert Frost. **CP-FrosR**

I met a Lady Poet. Impeccable Conception. Maya Angelou. **SP-AngeM**

I met a little cottage Girl. William Wordsworth. **UV** *Fr.* We Are Seven. **CP-WorW1**

I met a magician. In the Secret Room, East of the Sun, West of the Moon. Diane Wakoski. **SP-WakoD**

I Met a Man. Thomas Hardy. **CP-HardT**

I met a man in South Street, tall. Cutty Sark. Hart Crane. **FaBoMo** *Fr.* The Bridge. **CP-CranH**

I met a man under the moon. Edward Estlin Cummings. **CP-CummE**

I met a man who had got drunk with Christ. Malcolm Lowry. **CP-LowrM**

I met a man who suffered more than I. Malcolm Lowry. *Fr.* The Comedian. **CP-LowrM**

I met a ragged man. Song, The. Theodore Roethke. **CP-RoetT**

I met a seer. Eidólons. Walt Whitman. **CP-WhitW**

I met a traveler [*or* traveller] from an antique land. Ozymandias [of Egypt]. Percy Bysshe Shelley. **CP-ShelP**

I met a traveller from the holy desert. Prophet. Thomas Merton. **CP-MertT**

I met a woman long ago. Teachers. Leonard Cohen. **CP-CoheL**

I met an aged, aged man / Upon the lonely moor. Upon the Lonely Moor. "Lewis Carroll." **CP-CarrL**

I met at morn a girl of the tribes, bearing a milk-bowl. George Meredith. *Fr.* Arabic Poems. **CP-MerG2**

I met at noon the white-haired oldster, walking along easily. Encounter. Frederick Morgan. **SP-MorgF**

I met ayont the cairney. Empty Vessel. "Hugh MacDiarmid." **SP-MacDH**

I met Death—he was a sportsman—on Cole's. Cole's Island. Charles Olson. **SP-OlsoC** *Fr.* The Maximus Poems.

I met Einstein in a dream. Xmas Gift. Allen Ginsberg. **CP-ColeS; CP-GinsA**

I met her as a blossom on a stem. The Dream. Theodore Roethke. **CP-RoetT**

I met her, as we had privily planned. Her Father. Thomas Hardy. **CP-HardT**

I met her in the summertime. There were red flowers in the lanes. Not If He Has Any Sense, He Won't Be Back. Kenneth Patchen. **CP-PatcK**

I met him, as one meets a ghost or two. Old Trails. Edwin Arlington Robinson. **CP-RobiE**

I met him in the street. The Man in the Street. David Herbert Lawrence. **CP-LawrD**

I met him quite by accident. The Love-Letters. Thomas Hardy. **CP-HardT**

I met, in a close City square. The Linnet-Hawker. George Meredith. **CP-MerG2**

I met Ivan in a marvelous foxfur coat. Foxfur. Robert Lowell. **SP-LoweR**

I met Louisa in the shade. Louisa; After Accompanying Her on a Mountain Excursion. William Wordsworth. **CP-WorW1**

I met my Angel last night on Cinvat Bridge. Charles Olson. **CP-OlsoC**

I Met My Love. David Markson. **CP-MarkD**

I met my mates in the morning (and oh, but I am old!). Lukannon. Rudyard Kipling. **CP-KiplR** *Fr.* The White Seal. *Fr.* The Jungle Book.

I met the Bishop on the road. *fr.* Words for Music Perhaps. William Butler Yeats. **CP-YeatW**

I met the spirit of tragedy in the wood. Malcolm Lowry. **CP-LowrM**

I met you first—ah, when did I first meet you? Apostrophe to an Old Psalm Tune. Thomas Hardy. **CP-HardT**

I might by no means surmise. Sir Thomas Wyatt. **CP-WyatT**

I might have been a rabbi, Clayfeld thought. Clayfeld Prunes His Apple Trees. Robert Pack. **SP-PackR**

I might have writ of Belmarie. The Songs I Sing. John Hewitt. **CP-HewiJ**

I might, unhappy word, O me, I might. Sonnet 33. Sir Philip Sidney. **OAEL-1; OBSC** *Fr.* Astrophil and Stella. **SP-SidnP**

I mind as 'ow the night afore that show. The Chances. Wilfred Owen. **CP-OwenW**

I mind it weel in early date. Answer, The [To the Guidwife of Wauchope-House]. Robert Burns. **CP-BurnR**

I mind me how when first I looked at her. Medusa. Countee Cullen. **CP-CullC**

I mind me in the days departed. The Deserted Garden. Elizabeth Barrett Browning. **CP-BroEB**

I mind when [my] first wife died. "Hugh MacDiarmid." **SP-MacDH** *Fr.* Ode to All Rebels.

I miss my volley; walking back to serve. The Northern Snows. Randall Jarrell. **CP-JarrR**

I miss the long swing. The Long Swing. Richard Eberhart. **CP-EberR**

I miss the polished brass, the powerful black horses. On the Road to Woodlawn. Theodore Roethke. **CP-RoetT**

I miss you in the dawn, of gradual flowering lights. Longing. Edward Estlin Cummings. **CP-CummE**

I Missed His Book, but I Read His Name. John Updike. **CP-UpdiJ**

I missed one night, but the next I went. The Second Night. Thomas Hardy. **CP-HardT**

I mist my end, and lost my way. 1.24. Horace. **CP-JohnS,** *tr. by* Samuel Johnson; *Fr.* Odes.

I mock thee not, though I by thee am mocked. To F[laxman]. William Blake. **CP-BlakW**

I mourn Adonis dead—loveliest Adonis—. Fragment of the Elegy on the Death of Adonis. Bion, *tr. fr. Greek by* Shelley. **CP-ShelP**

I mourn for Adonis—the Loves are lamenting. Bion. *See* Lament for Adonis.

I mourn no more my vanished years. My Psalm. John Greenleaf Whittier. **CP-WhitJ**

I mourn upon this battle-field. In Memoriam. Ralph Waldo Emerson. **CP-EmerR**

I move my hand over. Poem of Night. Galway Kinnell. **SP-KinnG**

I Move that We Adjourn the Meeting. Nicanor Parra. *See* I Move the Meeting Be Adjourned.

I Move the Meeting Be Adjourned. Nicanor Parra, *tr. by* Miller Williams. *Fr.* Manifesto.

(I Move that We Adjourn the Meeting.) **CP-MertT,** *tr. by* Thomas Merton;

("Ladies and Gentlemen: / I am going to ask just one question.") **CP-MertT,** *tr. by* Thomas Merton;

I moved like a double agent among the big concepts. England's Difficulty. Seamus Heaney. **SP-HeanS**

I murder hate by field or flood. Song. Robert Burns. **NCEP** *Fr.* Lines Written on the Windows of the Globe Tavern, Dumfries. **CP-BurnR**

I Muriel stood at the altar-table. Don Baty, the Draft Resister. Muriel Rukeyser. **CP-RukeM**

I mused/ Up and down, up and down, the terraced streets. Elizabeth Barrett Browning. **OBTV** *Fr.* Aurora Leigh. **CP-BroEB**

I must / Not trust. Anacreontike. Robert Herrick. **CP-HerrR**

I must be flattered. The imperious. George Meredith. *Fr.* Modern Love. **CP-MerG1**

I must believe some miracles still be. To Mrs Phillip Sidney. Ben Jonson. **CP-JonsB**

I must complain, yet doe enjoy my Love. Thomas Campion. **CP-CampT**

I must confess, when I did part from you. To My Lady E.C. at Her Going Out of England. Sir John Suckling. **CP-SuckJ**

I must go walk[e] the woods so wild. Sir Thomas Wyatt. **CP-WyatT**

I must have been dozing in the tub. The Soap-Pig. Paul Muldoon. **SP-MuldP**

I must have misunderstood something. Overpopulation. Lawrence Ferlinghetti. **SP-FerlL**

I must have woken earlier. Stolen Clothes. Robert Pack. **SP-PackR**

I must hunt down the prize. Gerard Manley Hopkins. **CP-HopkG**

I must hurry, I must go somewhere. The World Is a Parable. Robert Penn Warren. **SP-WarrR**

I must love the questions. Reassurance. Alice Walker. **CP-WalkA**

I must not borrow light. Ralph Waldo Emerson. **CP-EmerR**

I must not die of pity; I must live. Edna St. Vincent Millay. **CP-MillE**

I Must Remember. Shel Silverstein. **SP-SilS2**

I must say / Yes, sir. Porter. Langston Hughes. **SP-HughL**

I must tell you. Young Sycamore. William Carlos Williams. **CP-WilW1**

I Must Tell You about My Novel. Ogden Nash. **CP-NashO**

I must undo my robes of the air. Transvestite. Laurence Lieberman. **SP-LiebL**

I must, Varus, tell you. Carmen 22. Catullus. *Fr.* Carmina. **CP-Catul**

I myself saw furious with blood. Aeneas at Washington. Allen Tate. **CP-TateA**

I name my comrades, though they may not know. Roll Call. John Hewitt. **CP-HewiJ**

I named a ballad round a sparking fire. The Ballad. John Hewitt. **CP-HewiJ**

I need a harem of men. Ballad of Isabelle Eberhardt. Patti Smith. **SP-SmitP**

I need a shot of love, I need a shot of love. Shot of Love. "Bob Dylan." **CP-DylaB**

I Need, I Need. Theodore Roethke. **CP-RoetT**

I need no assurances, I am a man who is pre-occupied of his own soul. Assurances. Walt Whitman. **CP-WhitW**

I need not ask thee, for my sake. Lines on a Fly-Leaf. John Greenleaf Whittier. **CP-WhitJ**

I Need Not Go. Thomas Hardy. **CP-HardT**

I need to be dancing over the birth. Face the Orient. Anne Waldman. **SP-WaldA**

I need to walk down a sidewalk. Truce. Charles Bukowski. **SP-BukC3**

I Need You. George Harrison. **CP-Beatl**

I never asked or heard enough to know. My Parents' Courtship. John Hewitt. **CP-HewiJ**

I never barked when out of season. On a Dog of Lord Eglinton's. Robert Burns. **CP-BurnR**

I never cared for Life: Life cared for me. Epitaph. Thomas Hardy. **CP-HardT**

I never dared be radical when young. Precaution. Robert Frost. *Fr.* Ten Mills. **CP-FrosR**

I never dared be radical when young. Ten Mills. Robert Frost. **CP-FrosR**

I never drank of Aganippe well. Sonnet 74. Sir Philip Sidney. **CABA; EnRePo; HeIP; NAEL-1; NoSic; OBSC; Son** *Fr.* Astrophil and Stella. **SP-SidnP**

I Never Even Suggested It. Ogden Nash. **CP-NashO**

I never felt at Home—Below. Emily Dickinson. **CP-DickE**

I never gave a lock of hair away. Sonnet. Elizabeth Barrett Browning. **EBVV; HAP; HBV** *Fr.* Sonnets from the Portuguese. **CP-BroEB**

I never got on good. Success Story. Archie Randolph Ammons. **SP-AmmoA**

I Never Had Any Other Desire So Strong. Kenneth Patchen. **CP-PatcK**

I never had the luck to keep a pet. The Pet Shop. John Hewitt. **CP-HewiJ**

I never happened to contrast. Two Leading Lights. Robert Frost. **CP-FrosR**

I never hear that one is dead. Emily Dickinson. **CP-DickE**

I never hear the word "escape." Emily Dickinson. **CP-DickE**

I never heard the birds until today. March Day. John Hewitt. **CP-HewiJ**

I never knew a broken Heart. Emily Dickinson. **SP-DickE**

I never knew but one. Ralph Waldo Emerson. **CP-EmerR**

I never knew the road. The Sirens. Richard Wilbur. **CP-WilbR**

I never know what people mean when they complain of loneliness. Loneliness. David Herbert Lawrence. **CP-LawrD**

I never learnt to attract, you see. The Sad Heart. Stevie Smith. **CP-SmitS**

I/ never liked/ white folks. Alice Walker. **PoBA** *Fr.* Once. **CP-WalkA**

I never lost as much but twice. Emily Dickinson. **CP-DickE**

I never loved a dear gazelle. Tèma con Variazioni. "Lewis Carroll." **CP-CarrL**

I never met a single. Prestige. David Herbert Lawrence. **CP-LawrD**

I never pass that inn "The Ring of Bells." The Whaler's Wife. Thomas Hardy. **CP-HardT**

I never picture an immedicable grief. Jokes Aloft. Malcolm Lowry. **CP-LowrM**

I never played for you. You'd have thrown. For the Death of Vince Lombardi. James Dickey. **CP-DickJ**

I never really like this cat though she is. V—Is for Victory as You Can Plainly See. Marsden Hartley. **CP-HartM**

I never really liked my mother's mother. My Grandmother's Garter. John Hewitt. **CP-HewiJ**

I never remember holding a full drink. Party Politics. Philip Larkin. **CP-LarkP**

I never said I loved you, John. No, Thank You, John. Christina Georgina Rossetti. **CP-RosC1**

I never saw a Moor. Emily Dickinson. **CP-DickE**

I never saw a wild thing. Self-Pity. David Herbert Lawrence. **CP-LawrD**

I never saw my father old. A Celebration for George Sarton. May Sarton. **SP-SartM**

I never saw that you did painting need. Sonnet 83. William Shakespeare. *Fr.* Sonnets. **CP-ShaWS**

I never saw the man whom you describe. The Foster-Mother's Tale. Samuel Taylor Coleridge. **CP-ColeS**

I never shall furgit that night when father hitched up Dobbin. The Spellin'-Bee. Paul Laurence Dunbar. **CP-DunbP**

I never stooped so low, as they. Negative Love. John Donne. **CP-DonnJ**

I never thought we'd end up. Rural Delivery. Charles Simic. **SP-SimiC**

I never told the buried gold. Emily Dickinson. **CP-DickE**

I never understood the girls. The Girls. Diane Wakoski. **SP-WakoD**

I never used to like eggs, that conspicuous. Eggs. Stephen Dunn. **SP-DunnS**

I never warmed to them. The Scribes. Seamus Heaney. **SP-HeanS** *Fr.* Sweeney Redivivus.

I never was attached to that great sect. The Longest Journey. Percy Bysshe Shelley. **OtMeF; OxBM** *Fr.* Epipsychidion. **CP-ShelP**

I never wear dark shades. Dark Shades. Charles Bukowski. **SP-BukC1**

I never went out of my country. Hafiz, *tr.* by Ralph Waldo Emerson. **CP-EmerR** *Fr.* Odes.

I—"Next Poet?" No, my hearties. At the "Mermaid." Robert Browning. **CP-BroR2**

I note the moods and feelings men betray. Sancti Dominici Pallium. Samuel Taylor Coleridge. **CP-ColeS**

I notice where Death has been introduced. Emily Dickinson. **SP-DickE**

I noticed People disappeared. Emily Dickinson. **CP-DickE**

I now mean to be serious;—it is time. Canto the Thirteenth. Byron. **MeMBP; PoEL-4** *Fr.* Don Juan. **CP-Byron**

I, now, O friend, whom noiselessly the snows. Robert Louis Stevenson. **CP-StevR**

I now think[e], Love is rather deaf[e], than blind. My Picture Left in Scotland. Ben Jonson. **CP-JonsB**

I nurs'd love where he lay. I Lay Love on My Knee. Allen Ginsberg. **CP-GinsA**

I nursed it in my bosom while it lived. Memory. Christina Georgina Rossetti. **CP-RosC1**

I objurgate the centipede. The Centipede. Ogden Nash. **CP-NashO**

I observe, as I hold my lonely course. The Very Unclubbable Man. Ogden Nash. **CP-NashO**

I observe: "Our sentimental friend the moon!" Conversation Galante. Thomas Stearns Eliot. **CP-ElioT**

I offer you a heart of red eisinglass outlined in tinsel. A Valentine for Harry Crosby. Kay Boyle. **CP-BoylK**

I often passed the village. Emily Dickinson. **CP-DickE**

I often see flowers from a passing car. A Passing Glimpse. Robert Frost. **CP-FrosR**

I often wish I was a grass. Emily Dickinson. **SP-DickE**

I often wished that I had clear. Horace, Lib. 2, Sat. 6. Jonathan Swift. **CP-SwifJ**

I often wonder how. Emily Dickinson. **SP-DickE**

I on my horse, and Love on me doth try. Sonnet 49. Sir Philip Sidney. **NAEL-1; NoP; OAEL-1; PoE** *Fr.* Astrophil and Stella. **SP-SidnP**

I once believed a single line. For E. J. P. Leonard Cohen. **CP-CoheL**

I once bought a toy rabbit. The Look:. Charles Bukowski. **SP-BukC2**

I once gave my daughters, separately, two conch shells. Derek Walcott. **CP-WalcD** *Fr.* Midsummer.

I once had a cow that jumped over the moon. Lines Written in Dejection on the Eve of Great Success. Robert Frost. **CP-FrosR**

I once had a girl. Norwegian Wood. The Beatles. **CP-Beatl**

I once held her in my arms. I Threw It All Away. "Bob Dylan." **CP-DylaB**

I once loved a girl, her skin it was bronze. Ballad in Plain D. "Bob Dylan." **CP-DylaB**

I once played truant, mitching round the rocks. I Still Had a Friend. John Hewitt. **CP-HewiJ**

I Once Was a Maid. Robert Burns. **NBLV; OxBoLi** *Fr.* The Jolly Beggars.

I once was happy, when, while yet a child. Charlotte Smith. **WPE** *Fr.* Beachy Head. **CP-SmitC**

I once wrote a letter as follows. The Invoice. Robert Creeley. **CP-CreeR**

I, one thing, as relation to one thing. Canto 111, Notes for. Ezra Pound. **CP-PoCan** *Fr.* Cantos. **CP-PoCan**

I Only Am Escaped Alone to Tell Thee. Howard Nemerov. **CP-NemeH**

I only dreamed that high cliff we were on. With Kathy in Wisdom. Richard Hugo. **CP-HugoR**

I only knew one poet in my life. How It Strikes a Contemporary. Robert Browning. **CP-BroR1**

I only live in the light. From the Japanese, I. John Gould Fletcher. **SP-FletJ**

I only mark. Precisely, Not Violets. Diane Wakoski. **SP-WakoD**

I only regret the days wasted in no pain. Penance. Charles Kenneth Williams. **CP-WillC**

I open my journal, write a few. Words Rising. Robert Bly. **SP-BlyR**

I open the door, return to the familiar mercy. Widower's Monologue. Alí Chumacero, *tr. fr. Spanish by* William Carlos Williams. **CP-WilW2**

I opened my eyes. Rain. Shel Silverstein. **SP-SilS2**

I opened my shutter at sunrise. The Death of Regret. Thomas Hardy. **CP-HardT**

I opened the door so my last look. One More Brevity. Robert Frost. **CP-FrosR**

I opened this poem with a yawn. How the Sestina (Yawn) Works. Anne Waldman. **SP-WaldA**

I order you to operate. I was not made to suffer. So Going Around Cities. Ted Berrigan. **SP-BerrT**

I ordered this, this clean wood box. The Arrival of the Bee Box. Sylvia Plath. **CP-PlatS**

I ought to be glad. Louis MacNeice. **OBCoV** *Fr.* Which things being so, as we said when we studied. *Fr.* Autumn Journal. **CP-MacNL**

I, Ovid, poet of my wantonness. 2.1. Ovid, *tr.* by Christopher Marlowe. **CP-MarlC** *Fr.* Elegies.

I owe a lot to someone. The Tenth Try. Jim Carroll. **SP-CarrJ**

I owe much thanks to players everywhere. Dedication. John Hewitt. **CP-HewiJ**

I owe you, do I not, a roofer: though. John Berryman. *Fr.* Sonnets to Chris. **CP-BerrJ**

I owe you this picture. Total Incandescence. Al Young. **CP-YounA**

I own I am shock'd at the purchase of slaves. Pity for Poor Africans. William Cowper. **CP-CowpW**

I own the ticks on a horse. Seahorse. Charles Bukowski. **SP-BukC2**

I own 'tis not my bread and butter. Mad Mullinix and Timothy. Jonathan Swift. **CP-SwifJ**

I owned a slope full of stones. The Stones. Wendell Berry. **CP-BerrW**

I pace along, the rain-shafts riddling me. A Wet Night. Thomas Hardy. **CP-HardT**

I pace these lanes where progress and decay. Palimpsest. John Hewitt. **CP-HewiJ**

I paid fifteen million dollars, twelve hundred and seventy-two cents. Sitting on a Barbed-Wire Fence. "Bob Dylan." **CP-DylaB**

I paid the woman what she asked and followed her down to the water-side. Come Little Birds. Robinson Jeffers. **CP-JefR3**

I paid this one's fare all the way from Houston. Waving and Waving Goodbye. Charles Bukowski. **SP-BukC1**

I paid you off. / Now I want you to steal me. Ocean. Joseph Ceravolo. **SP-CeraJ**

I Paint so ill, my peece had need to bee. With a Picture Sent to a Friend. Richard Crashaw. **CP-CrasR**

I painted her a gushing thing. "Lewis Carroll." **CP-CarrL** (My Fancy.) **CP-CarrL**

I painted on the roof of a skyscraper. People Who Must. Carl Sandburg. **CP-SandC**

I pant for the music which is divine. Music. Percy Bysshe Shelley. **CP-ShelP**

I panted in the grassy wood. He Gives What He Won to the Indian Girl. Nicholas Vachel Lindsay. *Fr.* The Tree of Laughing Bells or The Wings of the Morning. **CP-LindV**

I park, get out, lock the car, it's a perfect day, warm and. Charles Bukowski. *Fr.* Horsemeat. **SP-BukC3**

I park the car half in the ditch and switch off and sit. Ted Hughes. **SP-HughT** (Stealing Trout on a May Morning.) **SP-HughT**

I part the out thrusting branches. Woods. Wendell Berry. **CP-BerrW**

I pass enough savages on the street. Daemons. John Ciardi. **SP-CiarJ**

I pass the cruet and I see the lake. Lake District. Sir John Betjeman. **CP-BetjJ**

I passed a Poet in a dismal street. Note on Intellectuals. John Hewitt. **CP-HewiJ**

I passed along the water's edge below the humid trees. Indian upon God, The [*or* An]. William Butler Yeats. **CP-YeatW**

I passed the lodge and avenue. The Widow Betrothed. Thomas Hardy. **CP-HardT**

I passed you many times as I went down the cliff walk. Mediterranean. Thomas McGrath. **SP-McGrT**

I past [or passed] beside the reverend walls. Tennyson. **EBVV; FaBoPP** Fr. In Memoriam A. H. H. **CP-TennA**
(He Revisits Cambridge.) **FaBoPP**

I paused by the fence / and looked up. A Green Evening. Brendan Galvin. **SP-GalvB**

I paused on the threshold, I turned to the sky. Emily Brontë. **CP-BronE**

I paused to read a letter of hers. Read by Moonlight. Thomas Hardy. **CP-HardT**

I pay—in Satin Cash. Emily Dickinson. **CP-DickE**

I pay my way in, find a seat far from everybody, sit down. Charles Bukowski. Fr. Horsemeat. **SP-BukC3**

I peeled bits o strews and I got switches too. John Clare. See Song: "I peeled bits of straw and I got switches too."

I peered within, and saw a world of sin. Escape to the Mountain. Christina Georgina Rossetti. **CP-RosC2**

I Perceived the Outline of Your Breasts. Leonard Cohen. **CP-CoheL**

I perch upon a humbler promontory. Byron. **EPCY** Fr. Canto the Fifteenth. Fr. Don Juan. **CP-Byron**

I pick up a loaded pen and twiddle it. Pastime. James Schuyler. **CP-SchuJ**

I pick up my life. One-Way Ticket. Langston Hughes. **SP-HughL**

I picked up a leaf. Les Étiquettes Jaunes. Frank O'Hara. **SP-OharF**

I pitched my day's leazings in Crimmercrock Lane. The Dark-Eyed Gentleman. Thomas Hardy. **CP-HardT**

I Pity the Poor Immigrant. "Bob Dylan." **CP-DylaB**

I place a dead butterfly on the page. Instead of You. Stephen Dunn. **SP-DunnS**

I place an off'ring at thy shrine. The Perfect Sacrifice. Jeanne Marie Bouvier de la Motte-Guyon, tr. fr. French by William Cowper. **CP-CowpW**

I place my hand before my beard with awe. Waking in New York. Allen Ginsberg. **CP-GinsA**

I placed a jar in Tennessee. Anecdote of the Jar. Wallace Stevens. **CP-StevW**

I plaid with Love, as with the fire. Upon Love. Robert Herrick. **CP-HerrR**

I plan it all and I take my place. Odds and Ends. "Bob Dylan." **CP-DylaB**

I planned a little fountain. James McAuley. **SP-McAuJ** Fr. Sunflowers: An Ode.

I plant a tree whose leaf. The Romaunt of Margret. Elizabeth Barrett Browning. **CP-BroEB**

I planted a hand / And there came up a palm. Christina Georgina Rossetti. **CP-RosC2**

I planted a young tree when I was young. A Dumb Friend. Christina Georgina Rossetti. **CP-RosC3**

I play at Riches—to appease. Emily Dickinson. **CP-DickE**

I play for Seasons; not Eternities! George Meredith. **FaBoEn; OBNC; SCGP** Fr. Modern Love. **CP-MerG1**

I play it cool. Motto. Langston Hughes. **SP-HughL**

I play my old sweet airs. Lost Love. Thomas Hardy. **CP-HardT**

I play your furies back to me at night. High Fidelity. Thom Gunn. **CP-GunnT**

I pledge my allegiance. Carl Sandburg. Fr. The People, Yes. **CP-SandC**

I plodded to Fairmile Hill-top, where. The Dear. Thomas Hardy. **CP-HardT**

I pluck words out of speech of countrymen. On the Use of Dialect Words. John Hewitt. **CP-HewiJ**

I plucked pink blossoms from mine apple tree. An Apple Gathering. Christina Georgina Rossetti. **CP-RosC1**

I pointed to the picture of Collins on the wall. Note. James Liddy. Fr. A Munster Song of Love and War. **CP-LiddJ**

I pounded on a farmhouse. Motorpsycho Nightmare. "Bob Dylan." **CP-DylaB**

I pour water slowly. The Desert Casino. Jim Carroll. **SP-CarrJ**

I praise the Frenchman, his remark was shrewd. William Cowper. **BLPA** Fr. Retirement. **CP-CowpW**

I praised the myrtle and the rose. Charity. Christina Georgina Rossetti. **CP-RosC3**

I pray for my uncle. Kneeling in the Snow. Gary Gildner. **SP-GildG**

I pray! My little body and whole span. Supplication of the Black Aberdeen. Rudyard Kipling. **CP-KiplR**

I pray that I may form a prayer, oh Lord. Prayer. Malcolm Lowry. **CP-LowrM**

I pray that the great world's flowering stay as it is. The Gardener to His God. Mona Van Duyn. **SP-VanDM**

I pray you are always above me. Artemis. Anne Waldman. **SP-WaldA**

I pray you if you love me, bear my joy. Edna St. Vincent Millay. **CP-MillE**

I pray you not, Leuconoë, to pore. Horace to Leuconoë. Edwin Arlington Robinson. **CP-RobiE**

I prayed, at first, a little Girl. Emily Dickinson. **CP-DickE**

I prayed to say a word as simple. Blepharipappus Glandulosus or White Tidy-Tips. Malcolm Lowry. Fr. The Moon in Scandinavia. **CP-LowrM**

I precede you in emergencies. I betray you. Six Poems on Moving. Stephen Dobyns. **SP-DobyS**

I press[e] not to the choir [or quire], nor dare I greet. To My Worthy Friend Master George Sands [or Sandys], on His Translation of the Psalms. Thomas Carew. **CP-CareT**

I prest my Julia's lips, and in the kisse. Love Palpable. Robert Herrick. **CP-HerrR**

I prithee send me back my heart. Song. Sir John Suckling. **CP-SuckJ**

I prithee spare me, gentle boy. Song. Sir John Suckling. **CP-SuckJ**

I, proclaiming that there is. fr. Words for Music Perhaps. William Butler Yeats. **CP-YeatW**

I promise nothing: friends will part. Alfred Edward Housman. **CP-HousA**

I promise you these days and an understanding. Tourist Death. Archibald MacLeish. **CP-MacLA**

I promised myself. Joyce Carol Oates Plays the Saturn Piano. Diane Wakoski. **SP-WakoD**

I promised once if I got hold of. Written in a Copy of Swift's Poems, for Wayne Burns. James Wright. **CP-WrigJ**

I prop up my face and go out, avoiding the sunlight. Aging Female Poet on Laundry Day. Margaret Atwood. **SP-AtwM2**

I propose to you. The Statue. Robert Creeley. **CP-CreeR**

I protest against the manner of these ruins. O Howling Cells. Kenneth Patchen. **CP-PatcK**

I prove a theorem and the house expands. Geometry. Rita Dove. **SP-DoveR**

I pull dead shafts. Spring Clearing. Archie Randolph Ammons. **SP-AmmoA**

I pull it down while glancing through. Venetian Blind. Thom Gunn. **CP-GunnT**

I pulled him back. Another Day. Paul in the Mountains of Fantasy. Paul Tells His Adventure. Muriel Rukeyser. **CP-RukeM**

I pulled out for San Anton'. Lo and Behold! "Bob Dylan." **CP-DylaB**

I pulled the street up as you suggested. Something for Easter. Robert Creeley. **CP-CreeR**

I put down / the splintered ax. Stoning Stone. Archie Randolph Ammons. **SP-AmmoA**

I put my book down and open it. The Kiss. Stephen Berg. **SP-BergS**

I put my book face down. August 14, 1961. Hayden Carruth. **CP-CarHS**

I put my hat upon my head. Samuel Johnson. **CP-JohnS**
(Parodies of Bishop Percy's Hermit of Warkworth.) **CP-JohnS**

I put my hat upon my head. A Second Stanza. Donald Hall. **CP-HallD**

I Put My Mouth. Philip Larkin. **CP-LarkP**

I put my nickel. Midnight Raffle. Langston Hughes. **SP-HughL**

I put on my poetry suit. The Poetry Suit. Erica Jong. **SP-JongE**

I put on my travelling clothes. Travelling to the Capital. Gary Snyder. **CP-SnydG**

I put those things there.—See them burn. The Song of the Demented Priest. John Berryman. **CP-BerrJ**

I quitted and betook myself to France. William Wordsworth. **OxAEP-2** Fr. Residence in France ("As oftentimes a river, it might seem"). Fr. The Prelude; Growth of a Poet's Mind [1805 vers.]. **CP-WorW3**

I, Rainey Betha, 22. Charles Henri Ford. **CP-FordC**

I raise only robins on my farm. Emily Dickinson. **SP-DickE**

I raised my gun. Es War Einmal. Stevie Smith. **CP-SmitS**

I rake no coffined clay, nor publish wide. Ralph Waldo Emerson. **CP-EmerR**

I rake the hotbed straw. Thread. Stephen Berg. **SP-BergS**

I ran / my neck broken I ran. Galway Kinnell. Fr. The Dead Shall Be Raised Incorruptible. **SP-KinnG**

I ran through the snow like a young Czarevitch! Poem. Frank O'Hara. **SP-OharF**

I ransack'd, for a theme of song. Annus Memorabilis, 1789. William Cowper. **CP-CowpW**

I ranted to the knave and fool. Remorse for Intemperate Speech. William Butler Yeats. **CP-YeatW**

I reach for you. You smile and I am male. For a Northern Woman. Richard Hugo. **CP-HugoR**

I reach the marble-streeted town. The Marble-Streeted Town. Thomas Hardy. **CP-HardT**

I reached up into the top of the closet. I Made a Mistake. Charles Bukowski. **SP-BukC1**

I read a novel by a friend of mine. I Am in a Novel. David Herbert Lawrence. **CP-LawrD**

I read, before my eyelids dropt their shade. A Dream of Fair Women. Tennyson. **CP-TennA**

I read, dear friend, in your dear face. To F.J.S. Robert Louis Stevenson. **CP-StevR**

I read how Quixote in his random ride. Parable. Richard Wilbur. **CP-WilbR**

I read in the papers about the / Freedom Train. Freedom Train. Langston Hughes. **SP-HughL**

I read it quickly: all the old clichés. Time and the Thing-in-Itself in a Textbook. Randall Jarrell. **CP-JarrR**

I read last Saturday in the. My Groupie. Charles Bukowski. **SP-BukC1**

I read my sentence—steadily. Emily Dickinson. **CP-DickE**

I read on the porch of a palace bold. Ibn-i-Yamin, *tr. fr. Persian by* Ralph Waldo Emerson. **CP-EmerR**

I Read the "Christabel." Byron. **CP-Byron**

I read the news today oh boy. A Day in the Life. John Lennon *and* Paul McCartney. **CP-Beatl**

I read your name when you were strange to me. To an Actress. Thomas Hardy. **CP-HardT**

I realized early they were dying like a wall. Bone Hunting. Richard Hugo. **CP-HugoR**

I really believe He's here all over this room. The Facts & Issues. John Berryman. **CP-BerrJ**

I really care a lot although I look like I do not. Nobody But You. "Lou Reed." **SP-ReedL**

I reason, Earth is short. Emily Dickinson. **CP-DickE**

I received in mail offer beautiful certificate National Conference Synagogue Youth. Junk Mail. Allen Ginsberg. **CP-GinsA**

I recheck the map and count the stones. Dragon's Blood II. John Yau. **SP-YauJo**

I reckon—when I count at all. Emily Dickinson. **CP-DickE**

I recognize the quiet and the charm. Dutch Interior. May Sarton. **SP-SartM**

I reenter a day in a late summer. Philip Levine. **SP-LeviP** *Fr.* A Poem with No Ending.

I refuse to name the gods, because they have no name. Name the Gods! David Herbert Lawrence. **CP-LawrD**

I regret that before people can be reformed they have to be sinners. Piano Tuner, Untune Me That Tune. Ogden Nash. **CP-NashO**

I remark that this beach has been used too.   much Too.   originally. Edward Estlin Cummings. **CP-CummE**

I Remember. John Hewitt. **CP-HewiJ**

I Remember. Anne Sexton. **CP-SextA**

I Remember. Stevie Smith. **CP-SmitS**

I remember a fight / In a snow fall. Larry. James Wright. **CP-WrigJ**

I remember a house where all were good. In the Valley of the Elwy. Gerard Manley Hopkins. **CP-HopkG**

I remember a past. Those Mythical Silver Pears. Diane Wakoski. **SP-WakoD**

I remember a square of New York's Hudson River glinting. Time of the Missile. George Oppen. **CP-OppeG**

I remember asking / where does my shadow go at night? Driving Alongside the Housatonic River Alone on a Rainy April Night. William Matthews. **SP-MattW**

I remember black winter waters. New Hampshire Again. Carl Sandburg. **CP-SandC**

I remember hearing a story of a whole family. There are more accidents in the home than on the roads. Jenny Joseph. *Fr.* Life and Turgid Times of A. Citizen. **SP-JoseJ**

I remember here by the fire. Fire Dreams. Carl Sandburg. **CP-SandC**

I remember how it used to be. Desire. Stephen Dunn. **SP-DunnS**

I remember how, long ago, I found. Crystals like Blood. "Hugh MacDiarmid." **SP-MacDH**

I Remember, I Remember. Philip Larkin. **CP-LarkP**

I remember I was 9 or 10 so the year I guess. Chapter Forever. David St. John. **SP-StJoD**

I remember, long ago. The Fair Bedfellow. George Meredith. **CP-MerG2**

I remember, my littlest one in a field. One Morning. John Ciardi. **SP-CiarJ**

I remember once I ran after you and tagged the fluttering shirt of you in. Shirt. Carl Sandburg. **CP-SandC**

I remember one death in my boyhood. Of John Davidson. "Hugh MacDiarmid." **SP-MacDH**

I remember one evening—we were small—. The Mouse. William DeWitt Snodgrass. **SP-SnodW**

I remember sitting together in parks. Love's Advocate. Phoebe Hesketh. **SP-HeskP**

I remember that Garden Party / in June of the Festival Year. The "Lass of Richmond Hill", or The Royal Garden Party. John Hewitt. **CP-HewiJ**

I remember that wooden wheel on the kitchen shelf. The Wheel. John Hewitt. **CP-HewiJ**

I remember the Chillicothe ball players grappling the Rock. Hits and Runs. Carl Sandburg. **CP-SandC**

I remember the crossing tender's geranium border. The Reminder. Theodore Roethke. **CP-RoetT**

I remember the dread with which I at a quarter past four. False Security. Sir John Betjeman. **CP-BetjJ**

I remember the forehead born. Uncle. Philip Levine. **SP-LeviP**

I remember the leaves were falling. Emily Dickinson. **SP-DickE**

I remember the neckcurls, limp and damp as tendrils. Elegy for Jane. Theodore Roethke. **CP-RoetT**

I remember the new-dropped colts in the time when I was a boy. Used Up. Thomas McGrath. **SP-McGrT**

I remember the Roman Emperor, one of the cruellest of them. Exeat. Stevie Smith. **CP-SmitS**

I remember the scarlet setts. In Chopin's Garden. Donald Davie. **CP-DavD**

I remember the sea when I was six. Frederick Morgan. **SP-MorgF**

I remember the synagogue at Amsterdam. Sometimes. James Schuyler. **CP-SchuJ**

I remember the United States of America. A Box Comes Home. John Ciardi. **SP-CiarJ**

I remember this tree. The Apple Tree. Galway Kinnell. **SP-KinnG**

I remember watching / from the porch of a cottage. The Sea. Donald Hall. **CP-HallD**

I remember when freezing. Recording. Archie Randolph Ammons. **SP-AmmoA**

I remember when I wrote The Circus. The Circus. Kenneth Koch. **SP-KochK**

I remember you bowed. A Gesture. Dabney Stuart. **SP-StuaD**

I remember you well in the Chelsea Hotel. Chelsea Hotel. Leonard Cohen. **CP-CoheL**

I remember your coming as serious sweetness. Emily Dickinson. **SP-DickE**

I Remember Yule. Ogden Nash. **CP-NashO**

I remind myself at that time of Plato's uterus. Two Organs. John Berryman. **CP-BerrJ**

I renounce the blindness of the magazines. A Prayer to Escape from the Market Place. James Wright. **CP-WrigJ**

I reserve the triangle. Drawing the Triangle. Charles Simic. **SP-SimiC**

I resolved it, I. Some Place. Robert Creeley. **CP-CreeR**

I rest with the dogs across the feathers of birds. Jim Carroll. **SP-CarrJ**

I return late / on a wintry road: the beam. Or Traveller's Joy. Charles Tomlinson. **CP-TomlC**

I returned to a long strand. North. Seamus Heaney. **SP-HeanS**

I rise, gentlemen, it is the pleasant hour. The Meaning of Death. Allen Tate. **CP-TateA**

I rise in the dawn, and I kneel and blow. The Song of the Old Mother. William Butler Yeats. **CP-YeatW**

I rise out of my depths with my language. Jabberers. Carl Sandburg. **CP-SandC**

I Rob My Breast. Hart Crane. **CP-CranH**

I robbed the Woods. Emily Dickinson. **CP-DickE**

I rock Thee to sleep now, My King and My Baby. Mary's Lullaby. John Hewitt. **CP-HewiJ**

I rode one evening with Count Maddalo. Julian and Maddalo; A Conversation. Percy Bysshe Shelley. **CP-ShelP**

I Rode with My Darling. Stevie Smith. **CP-SmitS**

I Rose and Went to Rou'tor Town. Thomas Hardy. **CP-HardT**

I rose at night, and visited. The Unborn. Thomas Hardy. **CP-HardT**

I rose at the dead of night. A Chilly Night. Christina Georgina Rossetti. **CP-RosC3**

I rose—because He sank. Emily Dickinson. **CP-DickE**

I Rose Up as My Custom Is. Thomas Hardy. **CP-HardT**

I rose up at the dawn of day. William Blake. **CP-BlakW**

I rose up in the world, Ooray! A Rise in the World. David Herbert Lawrence. **CP-LawrD**

I rose while yet the cattle, heat-opprest. Journey Renewed. William Wordsworth. *Fr.* The River Duddon [A Series of Sonnets]. **CP-WorW2**

I rose with my own human might. Mortesto. George Meredith. **CP-MerG2**

I rowed: the dimpled tide was at the turn. Singing Lovers. Thomas Hardy. **CP-HardT**

I rub my head and find a turtle shell. The Neo-Classical Urn. Robert Lowell. **SP-LoweR**

I Rubens am a Statesman & a Saint. William Blake. **CP-BlakW** ("Rubens had been a Statesman or a Saint.") **CP-BlakW**

I run up the stairs too fast every morning. Maratea Porto: The Dear Postmistress There. Richard Hugo. **CP-HugoR**

I sacrifice to God the Beefe, which you adore, *ad. fr. Latin of* Anaxandrides. Sir Walter Ralegh. **CP-RaleW**

I Said. Hilda Doolittle. **CP-DoolH**

I said: / Now will the poets sing. Scottsboro, Too, Is Worth Its Song. Countee Cullen. **CP-CullC**

I said, / "the town bird." In the Rain. Hilda Doolittle. **CP-DoolH**

I said "All's over"—& I make my. Christina Georgina Rossetti. **CP-RosC3**

I Said and Sang Her Excellence. Thomas Hardy. **CP-HardT**

I said, Because it is so horrible between us. *see also* Commentary—This Marriage *and* Commentary Two—This Marriage. Leonard Cohen. **CP-CoheL**

I said: dark voyage, I am deeply wounded. Photograph of a Lighthouse Through Fog. Tess Gallagher. **SP-GallT**

I said,—for Love was laggard, oh, Love was slow to come. Indifference. Edna St. Vincent Millay. **CP-MillE**

I said: I cannot tell you. The Instant of Our Parting. Alice Walker. **CP-WalkA**

I said I stood upon thy grave. Arisen at Last. John Greenleaf Whittier. **CP-WhitJ**

I said, I will take heed to my ways. Psalm 39. Bible, *O.T.* **TrJP** *Fr.* Psalms. **CP-Psal**

I said in the beginning, did I not? Edna St. Vincent Millay. **CP-MillE**

I said: Mighty men have encamped against me. Defensio in Extremis. John Berryman. **CP-BerrJ**

I said: "O let me sing the praise." He Inadvertently Cures His Love-Pains. Thomas Hardy. **CP-HardT**

I said of laughter: it is vain. A Testimony. Christina Georgina Rossetti. **CP-RosC1**

I said our lives are improvisation and it sounded. Improvisation. Thom Gunn. **CP-GunnT**

I said out of sleeping. Second Song. Louise Bogan. **CP-BogaL**

I said, seeing how the winter gale increased. Edna St. Vincent Millay. **CP-MillE**

I said that you should stint your wit. To My Sister. Frank Templeton Prince. **CP-PrinF**

I said the glint was thistle. It turned out tin. How Meadows Trick You. Richard Hugo. **CP-HugoR**

I said—Then, dearest, since 'tis so. The Last Ride Together. Robert Browning. **CP-BroR1**

I said: This is a beautiful fresh rose. Once for All. (Margaret). Christina Georgina Rossetti. **CP-RosC1**

I said to Alvin. Life Is Like a Game of Cards, Or Another One of Those Metaphysical Statements from a Distant Reader. Diane Wakoski. **SP-WakoD**

I said to heaven that glowed above. From Hafiz. Hafiz. **CP-EmerR** *Fr.* I said to heaven that glowed above. *Fr.* Odes.

I said to heaven that glowed above. Hafiz, *tr. by* Ralph Waldo Emerson. *Fr.* Odes.

From Hafiz. **CP-EmerR**

"If my darling should depart." **CP-EmerR**

I said to It: "We grasp not what you meant." An Inquiry. Thomas Hardy. **CP-HardT**

I Said to Love. Thomas Hardy. **CP-HardT**

I said to my baby. Same in Blues. Langston Hughes. **SP-HughL** *Fr.* Lenox Avenue Mural.

I said to myself almost in prayer. A Trial Run. Robert Frost. **CP-FrosR**

I said to myself: "That's enough." The Thirty-Ninth Psalm, Adapted. Donald Davie. **CP-DavDo**

I Said to Poetry. Alice Walker. **CP-WalkA**

I said to Poetry: "I'm finished." I Said to Poetry. Alice Walker. **CP-WalkA**

I said to the East wind. Hafiz, *tr. by* Ralph Waldo Emerson. **CP-EmerR** *Fr.* Odes.

I said to the stone, "Am I standing all right?" The Poet as Eagle Scout. Howard Nemerov. **CP-NemeH**

I said to the watcher at the gate. The Signal from the House. Stanley Jasspon Kunitz. **CP-KuniS**

I said within myself: I am a fool. Christina Georgina Rossetti. **CP-RosC3**

I sailed a little shallop. The Path in the Sky. Nicholas Vachel Lindsay. **CP-LindV**

I sailed too long over that monstered ocean. Sinbad. Allen Tate. **CP-TateA**

I salute the section of our lordly Sunday journals which is entitled. One Man's Meed Is Another Man's Overemphasis. Ogden Nash. **CP-NashO**

I saluted a nobody. Chicago Poet. Carl Sandburg. **CP-SandC**

I Sang. Carl Sandburg. **CP-SandC**

I sang a canto in a canton. Country Words. Wallace Stevens. **CP-StevW**

I sang that song on Sunday. Her Song. Thomas Hardy. **CP-HardT**

I sang the song slowly. Eternal Circle. "Bob Dylan." **CP-DylaB**

I sang to you and the moon. I Sang. Carl Sandburg. **CP-SandC**

I sank past bitten leaves. John Haines. *Fr.* Cicada. **SP-HainJ**

I sat all morning in the college sick bay. Mid-Term Break. Seamus Heaney. **SP-HeanS**

I sat at dinner in my prime. At the Dinner-Table. Thomas Hardy. **CP-HardT**

I sat beneath a willow tree, / Where water falls and calls. In the Willow Shade. Christina Georgina Rossetti. **CP-RosC2**

I sat by the window and trod my loom. Cassandra. Louise McNeill. **SP-McNeL**

I sat down, my requirement. Renouncing an Epigram. Frank Templeton Prince. **CP-PrinF**

I sat in the Muses' hall at the mid of the day. Rome: The Vatican: Sala delle Muse. Thomas Hardy. **CP-HardT**

I sat. It was all past. Just the Same. Thomas Hardy. **CP-HardT**

I sat on cushioned otter-skin. The Madness of King Goll. William Butler Yeats. **CP-YeatW**

I sat on the Dogana's steps. Canto 3. Ezra Pound. **MeMAP; SP-PounE; TAP** *Fr.* Cantos. **CP-PoCan**

I sat on the eve-lit weir. Before My Friend Arrived. Thomas Hardy. **CP-HardT**

I sat on the long form / and sponged my slate. Middle Infant. John Hewitt. **CP-HewiJ**

I sat one sprinkling day upon the lea. Childhood among the Ferns. Thomas Hardy. **CP-HardT**

I sat only two tables off from the one I was sacked at. Caprice. Sir John Betjeman. **CP-BetjJ**

I sat upon the ground. Ralph Waldo Emerson. **CP-EmerR**

I sat with a dynamiter at supper in a German saloon eating steak and. Dynamiter. Carl Sandburg. **CP-SandC**

I sat with Morgan Forster for a while. An Hour with E.M.F. at Ninety. John Hewitt. **CP-HewiJ**

I Save Your Coat, But You Lose It Later. Tess Gallagher. **SP-GallT**

I saved a chipmunk from a cat. The Vastness and Indifference of the World. Richard Eberhart. **CP-EberR**

I saw a bird alone, / In its nest it sat alone. Let Patience Have Her Perfect Work. Christina Georgina Rossetti. **CP-RosC3**

I saw a chapel all of gold. William Blake. **CP-BlakW**

I saw a Cherry weep, and why? The Weeping Cherry. Robert Herrick. **CP-HerrR**

I saw a cottage in the sky. Friends. John Ashbery. **SP-AshbJ**

I saw a dead man's finer part. His Immortality. Thomas Hardy. **CP-HardT**

I saw a famous man eating soup. Soup. Carl Sandburg. **CP-SandC**

I saw a fly [*or* Flie] within a Bead[e]. The Amber Bead. Robert Herrick. **CP-HerrR**

I saw a high window struck blind. Note Slipped Under a Door. Charles Simic. **SP-SimiC**

I saw a little Diety, / *Minerva* in Epitomy. Princesse Löysa drawing. Richard Lovelace. **CP-LoveR**

I saw a little dog locked in a car. Timetable for a Town. Jenny Joseph. **SP-JoseJ**

I saw a Monk of Charlemaine. The Monk. William Blake. **CP-BlakW; EnRP; OBRV** *Fr.* Jerusalem; The Emanation of the Giant Albion. **CP-BlakW**

I saw a Mother's eye intensely bent. Confirmation Continued. William Wordsworth. *Fr.* Ecclesiastical Sonnets. **CP-WorW2**

I saw a mouth jeering. Gargoyle. Carl Sandburg. **CP-SandC**

I saw a phoenix in the wood alone. Petrarch. **ChTr** *Fr.* The Visions of Petrarch. **CP-Spens**

I saw a picture of Rilke. Portrait of Rilke. Richard Eberhart. **CP-EberR**

I saw a proud, mysterious cat. The Mysterious Cat. Nicholas Vachel Lindsay. **CP-LindV**

I saw a querulous old man, the tobacconist of Eighth Street. The Tobacconist of Eighth Street. Richard Eberhart. **CP-EberR**

I saw a regiment of soldiers shuffling and stumbling. Robinson Jeffers. **CP-JefR3**

I saw a river swift, whose fomy billowes. Joachim Du Bellay. *Fr.* The Visions of Bellay. **CP-Spens**

I saw a rose, in bloom, but sad. The Fading Rose. Thomas Hardy. **CP-HardT**

I saw a Saint.—How canst thou tell that he. Embertide. Christina Georgina Rossetti. **CP-RosC2**

I saw a shadow on a jut of stone. Hollander's Animal Faith. Marsden Hartley. **CP-HartM**

I saw a ship of martial build. The Berg. Herman Melville. **SP-MelvH**

I saw a slowly-stepping train. God's Funeral. Thomas Hardy. **CP-HardT**

I saw a spring out of a rocke forth rayle. *Fr.* The Visions of Bellay. **CP-Spens**

I saw a staring virgin stand. Two Songs from a Play. William Butler Yeats. **CP-YeatW**, *sect.* 1-2; *Fr.* The Resurrection.

I saw a telegram handed a two hundred pound man at a desk. And the. Telegram. Carl Sandburg. **CP-SandC**

I saw a wolfe under a rockie cave. Joachim Du Bellay. *Fr.* The Visions of Bellay. **CP-Spens**

I saw a woman getting out of a car. Memphis, 2 P.M. Miller Williams. **SP-WillM**

I saw a young snake glide. Snake. Theodore Roethke. **CP-RoetT**

I saw about her spotless wrist. Upon a Black Twist, Rounding the Arm of the Countess of Carlisle. Robert Herrick. **CP-HerrR**

I saw again in a dream the other night. Two Girls. Howard Nemerov. **CP-NemeH**

I saw again the spirits on a day. Bethesda: A Sequel. Arthur Hugh Clough. **CP-ClouA**

I saw an aged Beggar in my walk. The Old Cumberland Beggar. William Wordsworth. **CP-WorW1**

I saw, as in a dream sublime. The Occultation of Orion. Henry Wadsworth Longfellow. **SP-LongH**

I saw at a table of the bombed café. Naples. John Ciardi. **SP-CiarJ**

I saw brown Corib lean upon his urn. On Sutton Strand. Donald Davie. **CP-DavDo**

I saw by looking in his eyes. The Wandering Jew. Edwin Arlington Robinson. **CP-RobiE**

I Saw Eternity. Louise Bogan. **CP-BogaL**

I Saw Euterpe Kissing Santa Claus. Ogden Nash. *Fr.* All's Brillig in Tin Pan Alley. **CP-NashO**

I saw far off, the dark top of a Pine. The Pine of Monte Mario at Rome. William Wordsworth. *Fr.* Memorials of a Tour in Italy, 1837. **CP-WorW2**

I saw four silver ponies. Ballad of the Rest Home. Louise McNeill. **SP-McNeL**

I saw from the bus. George Oppen. *Fr.* A Narrative. **CP-OppeG**

I saw from the gliding train. Autumn Journey. Frank Templeton Prince. **CP-PrinF**

I saw, from under Him, the beginning. Charles Olson. **CP-OlsoC**

I saw her as something in my inner eye. Statue of Liberty. Richard Eberhart. **CP-EberR**

I saw her; she was lovely. Song. Christina Georgina Rossetti. **CP-RosC3**

I Saw Her Standing There. The Beatles. **CP-Beatl**

I saw her when I was in the left lane. The Girl on the Bus Stop Bench. Charles Bukowski. **SP-BukC1**

I saw him / in a dry place / on a hot day. Water Snake. Mary Oliver. **SP-OlivM**

I saw him dead, a leaden slumber lyes [*or* lies]. Andrew Marvell. **ChTr; FaBoEH; JCP; OBS** *Fr.* A Poem upon the Death of Oliver Cromwell. (Cromwell Dead.) **ChTr**

I saw him in the Café Royal. On Seeing an Old Poet in the Café Royal. Sir John Betjeman. **CP-BetjJ**

I saw him on the street. Street Meeting. Lewis Turco. **SP-TurcL**

I saw him once. Cummings. David Markson. **CP-MarkD**

I saw him pass as the new day dawned. The Youth Who Carried a Light. Thomas Hardy. **CP-HardT**

I saw him steal the light away. God's Education. Thomas Hardy. **CP-HardT**

I saw his round mouth's crimson deepen as it fell. Fragment. Wilfred Owen. **CP-OwenW**

I Saw in Louisiana a Live-Oak Growing. Walt Whitman. **CP-WhitW**

I saw in that glittering distance. John Haines. *Fr.* The Dream of the Police. **SP-HainJ**

I saw it advertised one day. Talking Bear Mountain Picnic Massacre Blues. "Bob Dylan." **CP-DylaB**

I saw it—pink and white—revealed. A Thought in Two Moods. Thomas Hardy. **CP-HardT**

I saw it, the mystical beast in the shadows. The Mystical Beast in the Shadows. Richard Eberhart. **CP-EberR**

I saw King George in open carriage drive. The King Concerned. John Hewitt. **CP-HewiJ**

I saw Lord Buddha towering by my gate. With a Bouquet of Twelve Roses. Nicholas Vachel Lindsay. *Fr.* Poems Speaking of Buddha, Prince Siddartha. **CP-LindV**

I saw magic on a green country road. Michael Hartnett. **SP-HarMi** *Fr.* Thirteen Sonnets.

I saw man, the man-hunter. Man, the Man-Hunter. Carl Sandburg. **CP-SandC**

I saw my father die. For two long years. John Hewitt. *Fr.* October Sonnets. **CP-HewiJ**

I saw my toes the other day. In Extremis. John Updike. **CP-UpdiJ**

I saw no Way. The Heavens were stitched. Emily Dickinson. **CP-DickE**

I Saw Old Dylan. David Markson. **CP-MarkD**

I Saw Old General at Bay. Walt Whitman. **CP-WhitW**

I saw old Idleness, fat, with great cheeks. Idleness. Walter de la Mare. **CP-DeLaW**

"I saw, on awakening," "what I had not" "seen before:" "at the." From *The Descent of Alette*, Book 3. Alice Notley. **SP-NotlA**

I saw on the slant hill a putrid lamb. For a Lamb. Richard Eberhart. **CP-EberR**

I saw one standing aside, alone. Wendell Berry. *Fr.* Elegy: "To be at home on its native ground." **CP-BerrW**

I saw past the door, today. Mictlantecuhtli. Charles Tomlinson. **CP-TomlC**

I saw raysde up on yvorie pillours tall. Joachim Du Bellay. *Fr.* The Visions of Bellay. **CP-Spens**

I saw red evening through the rain. Robert Louis Stevenson. **CP-StevR**

I saw Roshi early this morning. *see also* Roshi. Leonard Cohen. **CP-CoheL**

I saw St. Francis by a stream. The Voice of St. Francis of Assisi. Nicholas Vachel Lindsay. **CP-LindV**

I saw sweet Poetry turn troubled eyes. The Happy Encounter. Walter de la Mare. **CP-DeLaW**

I saw that the Flake was on it. Emily Dickinson. **CP-DickE**

I saw that the shanty town had grown over the graves and that the crowd lived among the memorials. Lines for Translation into Any Language. James Fenton. **SP-FentJ**

I saw the baby possum stray too far. Turning Fifty. Stephen Dunn. **SP-DunnS**

I saw the best minds of my generation destroyed by madness. Allen Ginsberg. **MoP; NaP; NoAM; NoP; PmAP; VCAP** *Fr.* Howl. **CP-GinsA**

I saw the bird that can the sun endure. Joachim Du Bellay. **Son** *Fr.* The Visions of Bellay. **CP-Spens**

I saw the busy street you crossed the last time I saw you. Momentum. Tom Clark. **SP-ClarT**

I saw the dove come down. The Dove. Leonard Cohen. **CP-CoheL**

I saw the figure of a lovely Maid. William Wordsworth. *Fr.* Ecclesiastical Sonnets. **CP-WorW2**

I saw the first pear. Orchard. Hilda Doolittle. **CP-DoolH**

I saw the garden where my aunt had died. The Entertainment of War. Roy Fisher. *Fr.* City. **SP-FishR**

I saw the ghostly lady fleeting. The Story I Have Told. Stevie Smith. **CP-SmitS**

I saw the Jays this Morning. Emily Dickinson. **SP-DickE**

I saw the laboratory animals: throat-bandaged dogs cowering in cages, still. Memoir. Robinson Jeffers. **CP-JefR2**

I saw the midlands. Kisses in the Train. David Herbert Lawrence. **CP-LawrD**

I saw the mountains in a rose-fire light. Poem. Jean Garrigue. **SP-GarrJ**

I saw the old Chinese men standing. Some Painful Butterflies Pass Through. Tess Gallagher. **SP-GallT**

I saw the sailor dead at sea. Virgin and Martyr. Howard Nemerov. **CP-NemeH**

I saw the sky descending, black and white. Where the Rainbow Ends. Robert Lowell. **SP-LoweR**

I saw the sky was lit. Moon New-Risen. David Herbert Lawrence. **CP-LawrD**

I saw the Sphinx on the sands of Egypt. Sphinx. Richard Eberhart. **CP-EberR**

I saw the spiders marching through the air. Mr. Edwards and the Spider. Robert Lowell. **SP-LoweR**

I saw the spring's first daffodil today. Season's Return. John Hewitt. **CP-HewiJ**

I saw the tall bush burn. Fall in Massachusetts. Isabella Gardner. **CP-GardI**

I saw the two starlings. The Maneuver [*or* Manoeuvre]. William Carlos Williams. **CP-WilW2**

I saw the valley, patch by coloured patch. Glendun. John Hewitt. **CP-HewiJ**

I saw the virtues sitting hand in hand. Humility. George Herbert. **CP-HerbG**

I saw the wind within her. Emily Dickinson. **CP-DickE**

I saw thee, child, one summer's day. Emily Brontë. **CP-BronE**

I saw thee on thy bridal day. To ———. Edgar Allan Poe. **CP-PoeEd**

I saw thee once—once only—years ago. To Helen. Edgar Allan Poe. **CP-PoeEd**

I Saw Thee Weep. Byron. **CP-Byron**

I saw three hundred fat cattle putting their forlornly comic faces. Kenneth Patchen. *Fr.* The Hunted City. **CP-PatcK**

I saw three ships go sailing by. The North Ship. Philip Larkin. **CP-LarkP**

I saw trees walking upside down across. Jonathan Lazarus Wright, 1702–1729. Martin Edmunds. **SP-EdmuM**

I saw what there was to write and I wrote it. Roy Fisher. *Fr.* Diversions.

I saw wild domes and bowers. The Angel and the Clown. Nicholas Vachel Lindsay. **CP-LindV**

I saw you once, Medusa; we were alone. The Muse as Medusa. May Sarton. **SP-SartM**

I saw you toss the kites on high. The Wind. Robert Louis Stevenson. **CP-StevR**

I saw young Spring leap over the hills. George Meredith. **CP-MerG2**

I saw your hands. Audre Lorde. *See* Pirouette.

I saw your shoulder swell and pitch. Erinna to Sappho. James Wright. **CP-WrigJ**

I say at once there's a light on the slope. At Once. Roy Fisher. **SP-FishR**

I say farewell to English verse. Michael Hartnett. **SP-HarMi** *Fr.* A Farewell to English.

I say, I am quite done. Let Zeus Record. Hilda Doolittle. **CP-DoolH**

I say *I laid siege—you enchanted me.* John Berryman. *Fr.* Sonnets to Chris. **CP-BerrJ**

I Say, "I'll Seek Her." Thomas Hardy. **CP-HardT**

I say no more for Clavering. Clavering. Edwin Arlington Robinson. **CP-RobiE**

I say no world. Edward Estlin Cummings. **CP-CummE; SP-CummE**

I say now, Fernando, that on that day. Hibiscus on the Sleeping Shores. Wallace Stevens. **CP-StevW**

I say, "She was as good as fair!" The Inconsistent. Thomas Hardy. **CP-HardT**

I say, that but for black Foakes'-day. George Meredith. **CP-MerG2**

I say that Roger Casement. Roger Casement. William Butler Yeats. **CP-YeatW**

I say this evening [*we'd*] we'll all get drunk. William Blake. **CP-BlakW** *Fr.* An Island in the Moon.

"I say this evening we'll all get drunk." **CBNP**

I say to the lead. Poem without a Title. Charles Simic. **SP-SimiC**

I, says the buzzard. From Virgil. George Oppen. **NNaP** *Fr.* Five Poems about Poetry. **CP-OppeG**

I scanned her picture, dreaming. Song from Heine. Thomas Hardy. **CP-HardT**

I scarce believe [*or* beleeve] my love to be so pure. Love's Growth. John Donne. **CP-DonnJ**

I scoop a bucket. Cup of Cold Water. Siv Cedering Fox. **SP-CedeS**

I search in vain your childlike face to see. A Young Girl. Walter de la Mare. **CP-DeLaW**

I see / a bunch of old Jews sitting around, mumbling. On the Steps. Stephen Berg. **SP-BergS**

I see a fair young couple in a wood. Time and Sentiment. George Meredith. **CP-MerG1**

I see a fresh-cheeked figure. She Would Welcome Old Tribulations. Thomas Hardy. **CP-HardT**

I See a Girl Dragged by the Wrists. Philip Larkin. **CP-LarkP**

I see all, am all, all. Childhood. Kathleen Jessie Raine. **SP-RainK**

I see all human wits. Shakspeare. Ralph Waldo Emerson. *Fr.* Quatrains. **CP-EmerR**

I see around me here. The Wanderer Recalls the Past. William Wordsworth. **OBNC** *Fr.* The Wanderer. **EnRP** *Fr.* The Excursion. **CP-WorW2**

I see around me tombstones grey. Emily Brontë. **CP-BronE**

I see before me now a traveling army halting. Bivouac on a Mountain Side. Walt Whitman. **CP-WhitW**

I see before me the gladiator lie. The Dying Gladiator. Byron. **NOBE** *Fr.* Childe Harold's Pilgrimage. **CP-Byron**

I see birds below me with massive shoulders. The Woman Bewildered. Robert Bly. **SP-BlyR**

I see everything / through a window that shines. The Kitchen. John Haines. **SP-HainJ**

I see from the paper that Florrie Forde is dead. Death of an Actress. Louis MacNeice. **CP-MacNL**

I see her in my sleep, my red, terrible girl. Sylvia Plath. **TV** *Fr.* Three Women. **CP-PlatS**

"I see herrin'."—I hear the glad cry. With the Herring Fishers. "Hugh MacDiarmid." **SP-MacDH**

I see him moving, in his legendary fleece. The Buffalo Coat. Thomas McGrath. **SP-McGrT**

I see him old, trapped in a burly house. A Pauper. Allen Tate. **CP-TateA**

I see in you the estuary that enlarges and spreads itself grandly as it pours in the great sea. To Old Age. Walt Whitman. **CP-WhitW**

I see it passing. Jim Carroll. *Fr.* The New Death. **SP-CarrJ**

I see it zooming down. New Orleans Intermission. Al Young. **CP-YounA**

I see men in a barley field. September. Wystan Hugh Auden. **CP-AudWJ**

I see my plaint with open ears. Sir Thomas Wyatt. **CP-WyatT**

I see my Scotland now, a puzzle. A Vision of Scotland. "Hugh MacDiarmid." **SP-MacDH**

I see myself, sad now, as in a mirror. Love Poem. Jim Carroll. **SP-CarrJ**

I see now I see. Resurrection. Margaret Atwood. **SP-AtwM1**

I See Phantoms of Hatred and of the Heart's Fullness and of the Coming Emptiness. William Butler Yeats. **CP-YeatW; LiTB** *Fr.* Meditations in Time of Civil War. **CP-YeatW**

I see so clearly now my similar years. Edna St. Vincent Millay. **CP-MillE**

I See That All Things Come to an End. Christina Georgina Rossetti. **CP-RosC2**

I see that chance hath chosen me. Sir Thomas Wyatt. **CP-WyatT**

I see the blue, the green, the golden and the red. Angelus. Kathleen Jessie Raine. **SP-RainK**

I See the Boys of Summer. Dylan Thomas. **CP-ThomD**

I see the change from that that was. Sir Thomas Wyatt. **CP-WyatT**

I see the country where the lemon blossoms. Die Gold Orangen. Robert Lowell. *Fr.* Eight Months Later. **SP-LoweR**

I see the crack in the world. Crack in the World. Anne Waldman. **SP-WaldA**

I see the dawn creep round the world. Song at Dawn. Robert Louis Stevenson. **CP-StevR**

I see the Four-fold Man. The Humanity in deadly sleep. William Blake. **NOBRP** *Fr.* Jerusalem; The Emanation of the Giant Albion. **CP-BlakW**

I see the ghost of a perished day. A Procession of Dead Days. Thomas Hardy. **CP-HardT**

I see the grass shake in the sun for leagues on either hand. The Prairie. Rudyard Kipling. **CP-KiplR**

I see the horses and the sad streets. The Eye. Allen Tate. **CP-TateA**

I see the house; my heart thyself contain. Sonnet 85. Sir Philip Sidney. *Fr.* Astrophil and Stella. **SP-SidnP**

I see the low black wherry. House-martin. Donald Davie. **CP-DavDo**

I see the oak's bride in the oak's grasp. Ted Hughes. **SP-HughT** *Fr.* Gaudete.

I see the sleeping babe nestling the breast of its mother. Mother and Babe. Walt Whitman. **CP-WhitW**

I see the tree think it will turn. Autumn. James Dickey. **CP-DickJ**

I see the urn against the yew. Church of England Thoughts Occasioned by Hearing the Bells of Magdalen Tower from the Botanic Garden, Oxford on St. Mary Magdalen's Day. Sir John Betjeman. **CP-BetjJ**

I see the winding water make. Henley-on-Thames. Sir John Betjeman. **CP-BetjJ**

I see thee better—in the Dark. Emily Dickinson. **CP-DickE**

I see thee clearer for the Grave. Emily Dickinson. **CP-DickE**

I see these winds, these are the tops of trees. These Winds. Robert Lowell. **SP-LoweR**

I see thine image through my tears tonight. Sonnet. Elizabeth Barrett Browning. *Fr.* Sonnets from the Portuguese. **CP-BroEB**

I see You / Brown-skinned, / Neat Afro. Thank You, Lord. Maya Angelou. **SP-AngeM**

I see you as a baby killer whale. Robert Lowell. *Fr.* Mermaid. **SP-LoweR**

I see you, child, standing above the river. Leaving Water Hyacinths. Jane Cooper. **SP-CoopJ**

I see you drinking at a fountain with tiny. An Almost Made Up Poem. Charles Bukowski. **SP-BukC1**

I see you fugitive, stumbling across the prarie. Margaret Atwood. **SP-AtwM1**

I See You on a Greek Mattress. Leonard Cohen. **CP-CoheL**

I see you strangling. In Memory of a Spanish Poet. James Wright. **CP-WrigJ**

I seek among the living & I seek. Christina Georgina Rossetti. **CP-RosC3**

I seek my father—that minister. The Recurring Dream. Lewis Turco. **SP-TurcL**

I seek not what his soul desires. Two Races. Rudyard Kipling. **CP-KiplR**

I seek you in the hospital where you work. Thomas Merton. *Fr.* Cables to the Ace. **CP-MertT**

I seem to hear winches and peaveys. Daily Library Visitor. Marsden Hartley. **CP-HartM**

I seemed to see you some Sebastian. The Puppet Show. Jenny Joseph. **SP-JoseJ**

I seize in a central knot. George Meredith. **CP-MerG2**

I send, I send here my supremest kiss. His Tears to Thamesis [*or* Thamasis]. Robert Herrick. **CP-HerrR**

I send my heart up to thee, all my heart. In a Gondola. Robert Browning. **CP-BroR1**

I send to you, commissioners. To the Commissioners of Northern Lights. Robert Louis Stevenson. **CP-StevR**

I send Two Sunsets. Emily Dickinson. **CP-DickE**

I send you a Christmas present, sweet. Alun Lewis. *Fr.* Letter From the Cape. **CP-LewiA**

I send you a decrepit flower. Emily Dickinson. **CP-DickE**

I send you here a sort of allegory. *preface to* The Palace of Art. Tennyson. **CP-TennA**

I Sent a Mental to My Love. Kenneth Patchen. **CP-PatcK**

I sent a message to my dear. The Miracles. Rudyard Kipling. **CP-KiplR**

I sent my mother copies of my poems in print. Poems. Gary Gildner. **SP-GildG**

I Sent Thee Late. Louis Zukofsky. **CP-ZukLS**

I serve you not, if you I follow. Etienne de la Boéce. Ralph Waldo Emerson. **CP-EmerR**

I set forth one misted white day of June. On the Great Atlantic Rainway. Kenneth Koch. **SP-KochK**

I set out from the Port of Acapulco on the twenty-third of March. Drake in the Southern Sea. Ernesto Cardenal, *tr. fr. Spanish by* Thomas Merton. **CP-MertT**

I set this down as humble prayer. Malcolm Lowry. **CP-LowrM**

I settled at Cold Mountain long ago, *after* Han-shan. Gary Snyder. **CP-SnydG**

I shake an absolute around the world. What Gives. Richard Eberhart. **CP-EberR**

I Shall Be Free. "Bob Dylan." **CP-DylaB**

I Shall Be Free No. 10. "Bob Dylan." **CP-DylaB**

I shall be glad to be silent, Mother, and hear you speak. The White Thought. Stevie Smith. **CP-SmitS**

I shall be in the Shenandoah some day. Shenandoah Journey. Carl Sandburg. **CP-SandC**

I Shall Be Released. "Bob Dylan." **CP-DylaB**

I shall be still stronger. I Want to Sleep. Jorge Guillén, *tr. fr. Spanish by* James Wright. **CP-WrigJ**

I shall be with you when hollow faces. Loyalty Is the Life You Are. Kenneth Patchen. **CP-PatcK**

I shall begin with a rose for courage. The Poem of Flight. Philip Levine. **SP-LeviP**

I shall cry God to give me a broken foot. Flash Crimson. Carl Sandburg. **CP-SandC**

I shall die, but that is all that I shall do for Death. Conscientious Objector. Edna St. Vincent Millay. **CP-MillE**

I shall die in Paris, in a rainstorm. Black Stone on Top of a White Stone. César Vallejo, *tr. fr. Spanish by* Thomas Merton. **CP-MertT**

I shall expect / you in to dine. Carmen 13. Catullus. *Fr.* Carmina. **CP-Catul**

I shall foot it. The Road and the End. Carl Sandburg. **CP-SandC**

I shall forget you presently, my dear. Edna St. Vincent Millay. **CP-MillE**

I shall go back again to the bleak shore. Edna St. Vincent Millay. **CP-MillE**

I shall go down. Geoffrey Hill. **HAP** *Fr.* The Pentecost Castle. **CP-HillG**

I shall go from my sickbed to heaven. Hafiz, *tr. by* Ralph Waldo Emerson. **CP-EmerR** *Fr.* Odes.

I shall grieve, I grieve, I am grieving. Lament on the Eve of Parting. Ogden Nash. **CP-NashO**

I shall imagine life. Edward Estlin Cummings. **CP-CummE**

I shall keep singing! Emily Dickinson. **CP-DickE**

I shall know why—when Time is over. Emily Dickinson. **CP-DickE**

I Shall Laugh Purely. Robinson Jeffers. **CP-JefR3**

I shall never forget the wind. North Wind: Portrush. Derek Mahon. **SP-MahoD**

I shall never forget you, Broadway. Broadway. Carl Sandburg. **CP-SandC**

I shall never get out of this! There are two of me now. In Plaster. Sylvia Plath. **CP-PlatS**

I shall never get you put together entirely. The Colossus. Sylvia Plath. **CP-PlatS**

I shall never, in the years remaining. Robert Browning. **EPCY** *Fr.* One Word More. **CP-BroR1**

I shall not ask Jean Jacques Rousseau. Pairing Time Anticipated. William Cowper. **CP-CowpW**

I shall not die for you. Alfred Edward Housman. **CP-HousA**

I shall not murmur if at last. Emily Dickinson. **CP-DickE**

I shall not see the end of this unweaving. May Sarton. **SP-SartM** *Fr.* A Divorce of Lovers.

I shall not see thee. Dare I say. Tennyson. *Fr.* In Memoriam A. H. H. **CP-TennA**

I shall not see your face for so long now. A Night Letter. Kay Boyle. **CP-BoylK**

I shall not sing a May song. The Crazy Woman. Gwendolyn Brooks. **SP-BrooG**

I shall not soon forget. Still Life. Thom Gunn. **CP-GunnT**

I shall not soon forget that sight. Raphael. John Greenleaf Whittier. **CP-WhitJ**

I shall paint/ God in the midst. Robert Browning. **Prf** *Fr.* Fra Lippo Lippi. **CP-BroR1**

I shall rot here, with those whom in their day. In Death Divided. Thomas Hardy. **CP-HardT**

I shall sit here through the evening. Narcissus. Wystan Hugh Auden. **CP-AudWJ**

I shall watch your passage from Crutch to Cane. Emily Dickinson. **SP-DickE**

I shall write of the old men I knew. In These Dissenting Times. Alice Walker. **CP-WalkA**

I shiver, Spirit fierce and bold. At the Grave of Burns (1803, Seven Years After His Death). William Wordsworth. **CP-WorW1**

I shot my eyes through the drawers of your empty coffins. Wheels, Fireclouds. Leonard Cohen. **CP-CoheL**

I shot my friend to save my country's life. The Body Politic. Donald Hall. **CP-HallD**

I should always have known; those who sang from the river. Hohensalzburg: Fantastic Variations on a Theme of Romantic Character. Randall Jarrell. **CP-JarrR**

I should have been a plumber fixing drains. Albert Einstein to Archibald MacLeish. Delmore Schwartz. **SP-SchwD**

I should have been delighted there to hear. The Cold Divinities. James Wright. **CP-WrigJ**

I should have been too glad, I see. Emily Dickinson. **CP-DickE**

I should have deem'd it once an effort vain. On Receiving Heyne's Virgil. William Cowper. **CP-CowpW**

I Should Have Known Better. The Beatles. **CP-Beatl**

I should have known if you gave me flowers. Then Came Flowers. Rita Dove. **SP-DoveR**

I should have thought. At Baia. Hilda Doolittle. **CP-DoolH**

I should have to be. The Flowers Alone. William Carlos Williams. **CP-WilW1**

I should like to come upon. Hula-Hula. William Carlos Williams. **CP-WilW1**

I should like to rise and go. Travel. Robert Louis Stevenson. **CP-StevR**

I should like to see that country's tiles, bedrooms. Keeping Their World Large. Marianne Craig Moore. **CP-MoorM**

I should not dare to be so sad. Emily Dickinson. **CP-DickE**

I should not dare to leave my friend. Emily Dickinson. **CP-DickE**

I should not have shown in the flesh. He Revisits His First School. Thomas Hardy. **CP-HardT**

I should sleep now. A Debt for Tomorrow. Roy Fisher. **SP-FishR**

I should walk maniacal. Old Question. Richard Eberhart. **CP-EberR**

I shouldered a kind of manhood. Funeral Rites. Seamus Heaney. **SP-HeanS**

I showed her Heights she never saw. Emily Dickinson. **CP-DickE**

I shuffle through the leaves of the worn out woods. The Small White Flower that Contains the Sun. Barton Sutter. **SP-SuttB**

I shut the door on the racket. Shoe Shop. Barton Sutter. **SP-SuttB**

I sieze the sphery harp. I strike the strings. Enitharmon Revives with Los. William Blake. **ChTr; OBNC** *Fr.* Vala; or The Four Zoas. **CP-BlakW**

I sifted the coarse yellow sand. Glory. James McAuley. *Fr.* Requiem. **SP-McAuJ**

I sigh at day-dawn, and I sigh. Sappho. Christina Georgina Rossetti. **CP-RosC3**

I sigh, fair injur'd stranger! for thy fate. On a Late Connubial Rupture in High Life. Samuel Taylor Coleridge. **CP-ColeS**

I sigh for the heavenly country. The Heavenly City. Stevie Smith. **CP-SmitS**

I sing a place of wherein agree. Double Acrostic: I sing a place wherein agree. "Lewis Carroll." **CP-CarrL**

I sing no harm good sooth to any wight. A Tale of a Citizen and His Wife. John Donne. *Fr.* Elegies. **CP-DonnJ**

I sing not of the Drapier's [*or* draper's] praise, nor yet of William Wood. An Excellent New Song upon His Grace Our Good Lord Archbishop of Dublin. Jonathan Swift. **CP-SwifJ**

I sing of a journey to Clifton. The Distressed Travellers. William Cowper. **CP-CowpW**

I sing of a Whistle, a Whistle of worth. The Whistle. A Ballad. Robert Burns. **CP-BurnR**

I sing of autumn and the falling fruit. *draft vers.* David Herbert Lawrence. **CP-LawrD**

I sing of brooks, of blossom[e]s, birds, and bowers. The Argument of His Book. Robert Herrick. **CP-HerrR**

I sing of Cornwall. "Hugh MacDiarmid." **SP-MacDH** *Fr.* Cornish Heroic Song for Valda Trevlyn.

I sing of deadly dolorous debate. Muiopotmos: or The Fate of the Butterflie. Edmund Spenser. **CP-Spens**

I sing of Morrisville. Song of the Two Crows. Hayden Carruth. **CP-CarHS**

I sing of Olaf glad and big. Edward Estlin Cummings. **CP-CummE; SP-CummE**

I sing of Pedro de Cieza de Leon, one. William Matthews. *Fr.* This Spud's for You. **SP-MattW**

I sing the birth, was born[e] tonight. A Hymn[e] on the Nativity [*or* Nativitie] of My Saviour. Ben Jonson. **CP-JonsB**

I sing the body electric. Walt Whitman. **CP-WhitW**

I sing the body electric. Walt Whitman. **SAmP** *Fr.* I sing the body electric. **CP-WhitW**

"I have perceiv'd that to be with those I like is enough." **SAmP**

"I sing the body electric." **SAmP**

"Man's body at auction, A." **SAmP**

"O my body! I dare not desert the likes of you in other men and women, nor the likes of the parts of you." **ErPo**

"This is the female form." **ErPo**

I sing the canny potato, already buried. William Matthews. *Fr.* This Spud's for You. **SP-MattW**

I sing the glorious Power with azure eyes. Homer's Hymn to Minerva. *Unknown.* **CP-ShelP** *Fr.* Homeric Hymns.

I sing the joy of poverty, not such. Malcolm Lowry. **CP-LowrM**

I sing the Name which none can say. To the Name above Every Name, the Name of Jesus, a Hymn. Richard Crashaw. **CP-CrasR**

I sing the Sofa. I, who lately sang. The Sofa. William Cowper. *Fr.* The Task. **CP-CowpW**

I sing the song of the sleeping wife. Sing Song. Robert Creeley. **CP-CreeR**

I sing the tree is a heron. Merce of Egypt. Charles Olson. **CP-OlsoC; SP-OlsoC**

I sing thy praise Iacchus. A Hymne to Bacchus. Robert Herrick. **CP-HerrR**

I sing to him that rests below. Tennyson. **OAEL-2** *Fr.* In Memoriam A. H. H. **CP-TennA**

I sing to use the Waiting. Emily Dickinson. **CP-DickE**

I sing what was lost and dread what was won. What Was Lost. William Butler Yeats. **CP-YeatW**

I sit a queen, and am no widow, and shall see no sorrow. Christina Georgina Rossetti. **CP-RosC3**

I sit a throne upon the times. Let's Majeste. Maya Angelou. **SP-AngeM**

I sit all day outside a bank. He. Randall Jarrell. **CP-JarrR**

I Sit Alone. Walter de la Mare. **CP-DeLaW**

I sit among the green shady valleys oft. Christina Georgina Rossetti. **CP-RosC3**

I Sit and Look Out. Walt Whitman. **CP-WhitW**

I sit and wait a pair of oars. To H.F. Brown. Robert Louis Stevenson. **CP-StevR**

I sit at a gold table with my girl. At the Altar. Robert Lowell. **InPK** *Fr.* Between the Porch and the Altar. **SP-LoweR**

I Sit at My Desk Alone. Erica Jong. **SP-JongE**

I Sit Down to Type. James Schuyler. **CP-SchuJ**

I sit for hours staring at my own right hand. January 10, 1973. Alice Walker. **CP-WalkA**

I sit here, doing nothing, alone, worn out by long winter. Mary Bly. James Wright. **CP-WrigJ**

I sit here eating milk-toast in my lap-robe. Money. Randall Jarrell. **CP-JarrR**

I sit here gazing at the tranquil bay. Ocean, 1940. John Hewitt. **CP-HewiJ**

I sit here in these stocks. In Weatherbury Stocks. Thomas Hardy. **CP-HardT**

I sit here on a Sunday. A Plantation a Beginning. Charles Olson. **SP-OlsoC** *Fr.* The Maximus Poems.

I sit high on this bridge in Laventille. The Spoiler's Return. Derek Walcott. **CP-WalcD**

I sit in a chair and read the newspapers. Smoke. Carl Sandburg. **CP-SandC**

I sit in an office at 244 Madison Avenue. Spring Comes to Murray Hill. Ogden Nash. **CP-NashO**

I sit in my room. Charles Kenneth Williams. **CP-WillC; SP-WillC**

I sit in my window with a tommy gun across my knees. I Never Had Any Other Desire So Strong. Kenneth Patchen. **CP-PatcK**

I sit in the black leather chair. Aura. Erica Jong. **SP-JongE**

I sit in the dusk. I am all alone. Tableau at Twilight. Ogden Nash. **CP-NashO**

I sit in the marsh-. River and Light. Siv Cedering Fox. **SP-CedeS**

I sit in the shade of the trees of the land I was born in. Wendell Berry. *Fr.* To a Siberian Woodsman. **CP-BerrW**

I sit in the top of the wood, my eyes closed. Hawk Roosting. Ted Hughes. **SP-HughT**

I sit looking at my features. Looking Head On. Richard Eberhart. **CP-EberR**

I sit looking dumbly at this stuffed red devil on my desk. I am in. A Valentine Gift. Charles Bukowski. **SP-BukC3**

I sit musing, ten minutes from the Jap. A Letter for Marian. Thomas McGrath. **SP-McGrT**

I sit not here the noble horse to see. 3.2. Ovid. **CP-MarlC**, *tr. by* Christopher Marlowe; *Fr.* Elegies.

I sit on a stone by a pond. On the Other Side of Uji Bridge. Siv Cedering Fox. **SP-CedeS**

I sit on the bank and mourn. Persephone Returns. Jenny Joseph. **SP-JoseJ**

I sit, sit listening; my lashes droop. The Bad Music. Randall Jarrell. **CP-JarrR**

I sit under Rand MacNally's. Westering. Seamus Heaney. **SP-HeanS**

I sit up here at midnight. Robert Louis Stevenson. **CP-StevR**

I sit upon the old sea wall. On the Sea Wall. Paul Laurence Dunbar. **CP-DunbP**

I sit with Joseph Conrad in Monet's garden. Zimmer Imagines Heaven. Paul Zimmer. **SP-ZimmP**

I sleep in it. The Writing Machine. Dabney Stuart. **SP-StuaD**

I sleep on a tar roof. Fragment: Little N.Y. Ode. Jim Carroll. **SP-CarrJ**

I sleep so you will be alive. The Dream of Mourning. Louise Glück. **SP-GlücL**

I slept a few minutes ago. In the Cold House. James Wright. **CP-WrigJ**

I slept across the front of the clock. A Watcher's Regret. Thomas Hardy. **CP-HardT**

I slept under rhododendron. Siwashing It Out Once in Siuslaw Forest. Gary Snyder. *Fr.* Four Poems for Robin. **CP-SnydG**

I slept, when Venus enter'd: to my bed. By Moschus. Moschus, *tr. fr. Greek by* William Cowper. **CP-CowpW**

I slide my face along to the mirror. Looking-glass. Denise Levertov. **CP-LeveD**

I slouch in bed. James Wright. *Fr.* Two Hangovers. **CP-WrigJ**

I slumbered with your poems on my breast. To E.T. Robert Frost. **CP-FrosR**

I smell a smell of death. July, 1964. Donald Davie. **CP-DavDo**

I smell it on the wind—a stranger's scent! Hunting. Robert Pack. **SP-PackR**

I snap on the light. In the Kitchen, at Midnight. Ted Kooser. **SP-KoosT**

I snatch a grape from her breast. Poem. Jim Carroll. **SP-CarrJ**

I snuggle down under the electric blanket. Christmas Morning. Howard Nemerov. **CP-NemeH**

I so admired you then. Ending. Alice Walker. **CP-WalkA**

I sometimes drop it, for a Quick. Emily Dickinson. **CP-DickE**

I sometimes fear that I shall never view. John Updike. *See* Déjà, Indeed.

I sometimes fear the younger generation will be deprived. Hoeing. John Updike. **CP-UpdiJ**

I sometimes hold it half a sin. Tennyson. **EPCY; EnVR; IMW; OAEL-2; PeECV; TOF** *Fr.* In Memoriam A. H. H. **CP-TennA**

I Sometimes Think. Thomas Hardy. **CP-HardT**

I sometimes think of those pale, perfect faces. The One Remains. Wilfred Owen. **CP-OwenW**

I sometimes think that I shall never view. Déjà, Indeed. John Updike. **CP-UpdiJ**

I sometimes write about the 30's because. John Dillinger Marches On. Charles Bukowski. **SP-BukC3**

I sought a theme and sought for it in vain. The Circus Animals' Desertion. William Butler Yeats. **CP-YeatW**

I sought to put the sunshine in a song. Limitations. John Hewitt. **CP-HewiJ**

I speak not, I trace not, I breathe not thy name. Stanzas for Music. Byron. **CP-Byron**

I speak now, tell you a bright truth. The Poet Tires of Those Who Disparage His City. Gilbert Sorrentino. **SP-SorrG**

I speak of it as a thing with a future. In Defense of Homosexuality. Kay Boyle. **CP-BoylK**

I speak of love that comes to mind. An Eastern Ballad. Allen Ginsberg. **CP-GinsA**

I speak this poem now with grave and level voice. Immortal Autumn. Archibald MacLeish. **CP-MacLA**

I speak to the unbeautiful of this bird. The Peacock. James Merrill. **SP-MerrJ**

I speak to you as a friend speaks. Conversations in Crisis. Audre Lorde. **SP-LordA**

I spent a night turning in bed. The Whip. Robert Creeley. **CP-CreeR**

I spent a wonderful day. Leaving N.Y.C. Jim Carroll. **SP-CarrJ**

I spent last night in the nursery of a house in Pennsylvania. Ontario. Paul Muldoon. **SP-MuldP**

I spent the night after my mother died. Autumn 1980. Marilyn Hacker. **SP-HackM**

I spin like a solitary star, I swoon. Thom Gunn. *Fr.* Jack Straw's Castle. **CP-GunnT**

I spoke to thee. Edward Estlin Cummings. **CP-CummE**

I spot the hills. Theme in Yellow. Carl Sandburg. **CP-SandC**

I sprang to the stirrup, and Joris, and he. How They Brought the Good News from Ghent to Aix. Robert Browning. **CP-BroR1**

I spread a scanty board too late. Greeting. John Greenleaf Whittier. **CP-WhitJ**

I spread my gorgeous sail. Ralph Waldo Emerson. **CP-EmerR**

I spring joy out of my rib cage. Incidence of Flight. Richard Eberhart. **CP-EberR**

I Spy, or, The Depravity of Privacy. Ogden Nash. **CP-NashO**

I squeezed up the last stair to the room in the roof. Unfinished Poem. Philip Larkin. **CP-LarkP**

I stand above the city's rush and din. From the Porch at Runnymede. Paul Laurence Dunbar. **CP-DunbP**

I stand again on the shore. Abstract Study—Circles. Jenny Joseph. **SP-JoseJ**

I stand alone, nor tho' my Heart should break. Loss. Samuel Taylor Coleridge. **CP-ColeS**

I stand amid the roar. Edgar Allan Poe. **ChTr** *Fr.* A Dream within a Dream. **CP-PoeEd**

I stand and watch for minutes by the pond. This, That, & the Other. Howard Nemerov. **CP-NemeH**

I stand as on some mighty eagle's beak. From Montauk Point. Walt Whitman. **CP-WhitW**

I stand at the cistern in front of the old barn. Wendell Berry. *Fr.* Three Elegiac Poems. **CP-BerrW**

I stand before the sea. The Consecrating Mother. Anne Sexton. **CP-SextA**

I stand beside the window here. The Old Story. Paul Laurence Dunbar. **CP-DunbP**

I stand by the river where both of us stood. That Day. Elizabeth Barrett Browning. **CP-BroEB**

I stand here in the sight of everyone a man full of sense. The Pretty Redhead. Guillaume Apollinaire, *tr. fr. French by* James Wright. **CP-WrigJ**

I stand I fall. Does No Love Last? Stevie Smith. **CP-SmitS**

I stand in the center of a twilight field. Sixty Five. William Everson. **SP-EverW**

I stand in the ring. The Red Shoes. Anne Sexton. **CP-SextA**

I stand near Soberanes Creek, on the knoll over the sea, west of the road. I. Theory of Truth. Robinson Jeffers. **CP-JefR2**

I stand on gritty Goonamarris. Lines for Jack Clemo. Daniel Gerard Hoffman. **SP-HoffD**

I stand on slenderness all fresh and fair. A Cut Flower. Karl Shapiro. **SP-ShapK**

I stand on the first step under the torn mouths of hours. Patience Is When You Stop Waiting. Charles Kenneth Williams. **CP-WillC**

I stand on the mark beside the shore. The Runaway Slave at Pilgrim's Point. Elizabeth Barrett Browning. **CP-BroEB**

I stand upon a hill and see. A Map of the City. Thom Gunn. **CP-GunnT**

I stand upon dry leaves. Autumn at Whitewell. Phoebe Hesketh. **SP-HeskP**

I stand with standing stones. All the Earth, All the Air. Theodore Roethke. **CP-RoetT**

I stare at the day as though I had suckled it. First Winter. Pablo Neruda, *tr. fr. Spanish by* Ben Belitt. **SP-NeruP**

I stared, but not to seize. On a Theme of Pasternak. Charles Tomlinson. *Fr.* Four Kantian Lyrics. **CP-TomlC**

I start out for a walk at last after weeks at the desk. After Long Busyness. Robert Bly. **SP-BlyR**

I started Early—Took my Dog. Emily Dickinson. **CP-DickE**

I stay; / But it isn't as if. An Empty Threat. Robert Frost. **CP-FrosR**

I stayed [*or* staid] the night for shelter at a farm. The Witch of Coös. Robert Frost. **InPS; LiTM; MeMAP; MoAB; MoP; NOBA; NoAM; PoE** *Fr.* Two Witches. **CP-FrosR**

I steal your mailbox, leave. Spite. Stephen Dobyns. **SP-DobyS**

I stepped from a bank with sea pink and long tufts. Lost Hold. Jenny Joseph. **SP-JoseJ**

I stepped from Plank to Plank. Emily Dickinson. **CP-DickE**

I stepped into an avalanche. Avalanche. Leonard Cohen. **CP-CoheL**

I still balk at my preference for rhyme. Marilyn Hacker. **SP-HackM** *Fr.* Separations.

I Still Had a Friend. John Hewitt. **CP-HewiJ**

I still have some money. In Terror of Hospital Bills. James Wright. **CP-WrigJ**

I still hear those azure carillons. 1939 World's Fair. Gilbert Sorrentino. **SP-SorrG**

I still remember Ed and Clyde. After Thirty Years. Richard Shelton. **SP-ShelR**

I stole forth dimly in the dripping pause. Moon Compasses. Robert Frost. **CP-FrosR**

I stole them from a Bee. Emily Dickinson. **CP-DickE**

I stood above the sown and generous sea. The Morality of Poetry. James Wright. **CP-WrigJ**

I stood amid the new-mown hay. To a Field-mouse. Wystan Hugh Auden. **CP-AudWJ**

I stood among my sheep. The Skaters. Randall Jarrell. **CP-JarrR**

I stood and gazed. The hills were hid in mist. Morning Moment. John Hewitt. **CP-HewiJ**

I stood and heard the steps of the city. Song (3). Wendell Berry. **CP-BerrW**

I stood at 6 a.m. on the wharf. Someone's Blood. Rita Dove. **SP-DoveR**

I stood at the back of the shop, my dear. At the Draper's. Thomas Hardy. **MoAB; MoBrPo; OBD; OxBM** *Fr.* Satires of Circumstance in Fifteen Glimpses. **CP-HardT**

I stood at the gate of the cot. Change in Recurrence. George Meredith. **CP-MerG1**

I stood at twilight on a mound. Apparition. John Hewitt. **CP-HewiJ**

I stood behind a white gate in a still orchard. Decision. Steve Griffiths. **SP-GrifS**

I stood beside the grave of him who blazed. Churchill's Grave. Byron. **CP-Byron**

I stood between them. Making Strange. Seamus Heaney. **SP-HeanS**

I stood by the shore at the death of day. The Wind and the Sea. Paul Laurence Dunbar. **CP-DunbP**

I stood by weeping. Only Believe. Christina Georgina Rossetti. **CP-RosC3**

I stood in Venice on the Bridge of Sighs. Byron. **EnRP; FaBoPP; OBTV** *Fr.* Childe Harold's Pilgrimage. **CP-Byron**
(On the Bridge of Sighs.) **FaBoPP**

I stood in Venice on the Bridge of Sighs. Canto the Fourth. Byron. *Fr.* Childe Harold's Pilgrimage. **CP-Byron**

I stood knee-deep in the sea. Venus When Young Choosing Death. Stevie Smith. **CP-SmitS**

I stood on Brocken's sovran [*or* sovereign] height, and saw. Lines Written in the Album at Elbingerode, in the Har[t]z Forest. Samuel Taylor Coleridge. **CP-ColeS**

I stood on the reed bank. Fishing for Eel Totems. Margaret Atwood. **SP-AtwM1**

I stood once more in that garden. Dream 1: the Bush Garden. Margaret Atwood. **SP-AtwM1**

I stood still and was a tree amid the wood. The Tree. Ezra Pound. **SP-PounE**

I Stood Tip-Toe upon a Little Hill. John Keats. **CP-KeatJ**
Minnows. **GN**

"Sometimes goldfinches one by one will drop." **GN; PBBP** (Goldfinches.) **GN**

Sweet Peas. **FHYEP; GN**

I stood upon a heaven-cleaving turret. Fragment. Percy Bysshe Shelley. **CP-ShelP**

I stood within the City disinterred. At Pompeii. Percy Bysshe Shelley. **FaBoPP** *Fr.* Ode to Naples. **CP-ShelP**

I stood within the City disinterred. Ode to Naples. Percy Bysshe Shelley. **CP-ShelP**

I stood within the gate / Of a great temple, 'mid the living stream. After Three Days. "Lewis Carroll." **CP-CarrL**

I stop my car at the signal. The Beautiful Young Girl Walking Past the Graveyard—. Charles Bukowski. **SP-BukC1**

I stopped the car. Blueflags. William Carlos Williams. **CP-WilW1**

I Stopped to Listen. Leonard Cohen. **CP-CoheL**

I stored daylight in secret attics. Jim Carroll. **SP-CarrJ**

I strolled across. The Waking. Theodore Roethke. **CP-RoetT**

I struck the board, and cried [*or* cry'd], "No more!" The Collar. George Herbert. **CP-HerbG**

I stuck out my palm. On the Rush. Jim Carroll. **SP-CarrJ**

I studied it and it taught me nothing. Wisdom. Thomas Merton. **CP-MertT; SP-MertT**

I study out a dark similitude. The Swan. Theodore Roethke. **CP-RoetT**

I study the lives on a leaf: the little. The Minimal. Theodore Roethke. **CP-RoetT**

I stumbled out of bed. I Can't Forget. Leonard Cohen. **CP-CoheL**

I Suddenly Became Conscious That This Thing Was Looking at Me Intently. Kenneth Patchen. **CP-PatcK**

I sued the News—yet feared—the News. Emily Dickinson. **CP-DickE**

I suffer fruitless anguish day by day. The Vicissitudes Experienced in the Christian Life. Jeanne Marie Bouvier de la Motte-Guyon, *tr. fr. French by* William Cowper. **CP-CowpW**

I suggest that this day be made holy. Kenneth Patchen. **CP-PatcK**

I summon to the winding ancient stair. A Dialogue of Self and Soul. William Butler Yeats. **CP-YeatW**

I summoned Christopher Columbus. Navigator. Charles Simic. **SP-SimiC**

I suppose it's raining in some Spanish town. Weather Report. Charles Bukowski. **SP-BukC1**

I suppose like any other boy. The Bee. Charles Bukowski. **SP-BukC1**

I suppose tarts are called tarts because they're tart. Tarts. David Herbert Lawrence. **CP-LawrD**

I suppose that plumbers' children know more about plumbing than. There's Nothing Like Instinct, Fortunately. Ogden Nash. **CP-NashO**

I suppose the time will come. Emily Dickinson. **CP-DickE**

I suppose they would've shot the moon down. In Memory of God. Jenny Joseph. **SP-JoseJ**

I suppose you just gape and let your gaspings. Ted Hughes. **HAP** *Fr.* Skylarks. **SP-HughT**

I suppose you never heard of Ben's first meeting with Shady Rovers. Ben's Last Fight. Thomas Merton. **CP-MertT**

I swayed upon the gaudy stern. His Dream. William Butler Yeats. **CP-YeatW**

I swept underneath and got him. Dagwood and Blondie. Charles Bukowski. **SP-BukC3**

I take a jewel from a junk-shop tray. Nothing. James Fenton. **SP-FentJ**

I take advantage of breakfast time. Soda Fountains. Nicanor Parra, *tr. fr. Spanish by* Thomas Merton. **CP-MertT**

I take my stand by the Ulster names. Ulster Names. John Hewitt. **CP-HewiJ**

I take my women any way they come. Jasper Olson. Lewis Turco. *Fr.* Bordello. **SP-TurcL**

I take no virtue of this as I finger the hand gun. Suicide Note. Richard Eberhart. **CP-EberR**

I take the taxi to Newport and study the wrinkles in the. Very. Charles Bukowski. **SP-BukC2**

I take the unity my senses offer. The Child, the Chair, the Leaf. John Hewitt. **CP-HewiJ**

I take your hand. I want to touch your eyes. Blind Girl. Jane Cooper. **SP-CoopJ**

I Talked and Raged and Planned. John Hewitt. **CP-HewiJ**

I tarry in days shaped like the high staired street. A Birthday Memorial to Seventh Street. Audre Lorde. **SP-LordA**

I taste a liquor never brewed. Emily Dickinson. **CP-DickE**

I teach in a high school. The Wrong Kind of Insurance. John Ashbery. **SP-AshbJ**

I tell Beauty, at Her most loving, to shut up. One for Beauty. Leonard Nathan. **SP-NathL**

I tell my love in rhyme. Song. Wendell Berry. **CP-BerrW**

I tell my secret? No indeed, not I. Winter: My Secret. Christina Georgina Rossetti. **CP-RosC1**

I tell thee, Dick, where I have been. A Ballad[e] [upon a Wedding]. Sir John Suckling. **CP-SuckJ**

I tell thee, fellow, whoe'er thou be. Sir John Suckling's Answer. Sir John Suckling. **CP-SuckJ**

I tell them where the wind comes from. People with Proud Chins. Carl Sandburg. **CP-SandC**

I tell this tale, which is strictly true. The Truthful Song. Rudyard Kipling. **CP-KiplR**

I tell you, Chickadee. S M. Alice Walker. **CP-WalkA**

I Tell You For Several Years of My Madness I Heard the Voice of Lilith Singing in the Trees of Chicago. Hayden Carruth. **CP-CarHS**

I tell you, hopeless grief is passionless. Grief. Elizabeth Barrett Browning. **CP-BroEB**

"I tell you it couldn't have been." Dream. Hilda Doolittle. *Fr.* Child Poems. **CP-DoolH**

I tell you, Lesbia, life is love. Catullus. *See* Carmen 5: "Lesbia / live with me."

I tell you that I see her still. I Only Am Escaped Alone to Tell Thee. Howard Nemerov. **CP-NemeH**

I tell you what I dreamed last night. Christina Georgina Rossetti. **PeVV** *Fr.* The Convent Threshold. **CP-RosC1**

I tend my flowers for thee. Emily Dickinson. **CP-DickE**

I tend to suppose the part I know least. Cumberland. Donald Davie. **CP-DavDo**

I test my bath before I sit. Samson Agonistes. Ogden Nash. **CP-NashO**

I thank all who have loved me in their hearts. Sonnet. Elizabeth Barrett Browning. *Fr.* Sonnets from the Portuguese. **CP-BroEB**

I thank You God for most this amazing. Edward Estlin Cummings. **CP-CummE; SP-CummE**

I, that ame of all most crost. Song. Mary Sidney, Countess of Montgomery Wroth. **KTR** *Fr.* Pamphilia to Amphilanthus. **CP-WrotM**

I that have been a lover, and could show it. A Sonnet to the Noble Lady, the Lady Mary Wroth. Ben Jonson. **CP-JonsB**

I that indulgently. In Memory of Lemuel Ayers, Scene Designer, Dead of Cancer in His Fortieth Year. Isabella Gardner. **CP-GardI**

I, the city mouse, have traveled from a long ways away. Something Similar. John Ashbery. **SP-AshbJ**

I' the how-dumb-deid o' the cauld hairst nicht. The Eemis-Stane. "Hugh MacDiarmid." **SP-MacDH**

I, the man with the red scarf. Gipsy. David Herbert Lawrence. **CP-LawrD**

I, the performer / in the tense arena, glittered. Speeches for Dr Frankenstein. Margaret Atwood. **SP-AtwM1**

I the poet Gary Snyder. Poem Left in Sourdough Mountain Lookout. Gary Snyder. **CP-SnydG**

I, the poet William Yeats. To Be Carved on a Stone at Thoor Ballylee. William Butler Yeats. **CP-YeatW**

I therefore pray thee, Renny dear. Samuel Johnson. **CP-JohnS** (Parodies of Bishop Percy's *Hermit of Warkworth*.) **CP-JohnS**

I, therefore, will begin. Soul of the age! Ben Jonson. **FaBoEH; NOBE** *Fr.* To the Memory of My Beloved, the Author Mr [*or* Master] William Shakespeare[: And What He Hath Left Us]. **CP-JonsB**

I Think. James Schuyler. **CP-SchuJ**

I think a lot about. The Three-Penny Opera. Frank O'Hara. **SP-OharF**

I think a lot about you, Ed. To Ed Sissman. John Updike. **CP-UpdiJ**

I think an impulse stronger than my mind. Mood. Countee Cullen. **CP-CullC**

I think and think; yet still I fail. The Veil. Walter de la Mare. **CP-DeLaW**

I think continually of the differences. Sonnet. Hayden Carruth. **CP-CarHS** *Fr.* Sonnets.

I Think Continually of Those Who Were Truly Great. Stephen Spender. (The Truly Great.) **CP-SpenS**

I think he was a shipbuilder. Oil Terminal. Steve Griffiths. **SP-GrifS**

I think I could turn and live awhile with animals. Walt Whitman. **EaPr; FaFP; HAP; ImPo; NU; PDV; PFP; SAmP; TrGrPo; WGRP; WeW** *Fr.* Song of Myself. **CP-WhitW** (Animals.) **FaFP; ImPo**

I think I grow tensions. The Flower. Robert Creeley. **CP-CreeR**

I think I have never been so exalted. Aux Imagistes. William Carlos Williams. **CP-WilW1**

I think I know why in death's unrelenting moment you thought of the water. The Water. Hayden Carruth. *Fr.* Mother. **CP-CarHL**

I think I learned much about writing when. Hey, Ezra, Listen to This. Charles Bukowski. **SP-BukC3**

I think I loved the palomino best. In a Dream of Horses. Stephen Dunn. **SP-DunnS**

I think I must have lived. The Fox. Philip Levine. **SP-LeviP**

I think I see my father's sister stand. Elizabeth Barrett Browning. **NALW** *Fr.* Aurora Leigh. **CP-BroEB**

I think I should have loved you presently. Edna St. Vincent Millay. **CP-MillE**

I think I was enchanted. Emily Dickinson. **CP-DickE**

I think I will learn some beautiful language, useless for commercial. Intention to Escape from Him. Edna St. Vincent Millay. **CP-MillE**

I think I'm gonna be sad I think it's today. Ticket to Ride. The Beatles. **CP-BeatI**

I think I'm in love & yet complain. Sidney's Complaynt. Anne Waldman. **SP-WaldA**

I think, in connection with this weeping elm. The Camperdown Elm. Marianne Craig Moore. **CP-MoorM**

I think it better that in times like these. On Being Asked for a War Poem. William Butler Yeats. **CP-YeatW**

I think it must be lonely to be God. The Preacher: Ruminates Behind the Sermon. Gwendolyn Brooks. **PBMP** *Fr.* A Street in Bronzeville. **SP-BrooG**

I think it sad to have a friend. Emily Dickinson. **SP-DickE**

I think it was on the sabbath. Grant. Patti Smith. **SP-SmitP**

I think just how my shape will rise. Emily Dickinson. **CP-DickE**

I think most people are relieved the first time they actually know someone who goes crazy. The Cave. Charles Kenneth Williams. **CP-WillC; SP-WillC**

I think now and then of the old family button. Buttons for Swallows. Marsden Hartley. **CP-HartM**

I think now it is better to love no one. Here Are My Black Clothes. Louise Glück. **SP-GlücL**

I think of a coffin's quiet. Audre Lorde. *See* A Poem for a Poet.

I think of a man on foot. Thomas Bewick. Thom Gunn. **CP-GunnT**

I think of all the toughs through history. Lines for a Book. Thom Gunn. **CP-GunnT**

I think of Amundsen, enormously bit. On the Eyes of an SS Officer. Richard Wilbur. **CP-WilbR**

I think of automobiles parked in a. When I Think of Myself Dead. Charles Bukowski. **SP-BukC1**

I think of corner shots, the ball. Day and Night Handball. Stephen Dunn. **SP-DunnS**

I think of Glasgow, where reluctantly. Sonnet. John Hewitt. **CP-HewiJ**

I think of how the gulls hang. Always in Late Summer Now, in the City. Gary Gildner. **SP-GildG**

I think of Issa, a man of few words. Night Journal. Charles Wright. **SP-WrigC**

I think of that grave woman in the dark. For J. Jean Garrigue. **SP-GarrJ**

I think of that old woman in the song. A Ghost, a Real Ghost. Randall Jarrell. **CP-JarrR**

I think of the Celts as rather a whining lady. The Celts. Stevie Smith. **CP-SmitS**

I think of the saints I have known, and lift up mine eyes. So Great a Cloud of Witnesses. Christina Georgina Rossetti. **CP-RosC2**

I think of the slope where the rabbits fed. The Background and the Figure. Thomas Hardy. **CP-HardT**

I think of thee! My thoughts do twine and bud. Sonnet. Elizabeth Barrett Browning. *Fr.* Sonnets from the Portuguese. **CP-BroEB**

I think of us lying asleep. The Thief. Wendell Berry. **CP-BerrW**

I think of waking / In the country inn. Frank Templeton Prince. *Fr.* Yüan Chēn Variations. **CP-PrinF**

I think of you. Now That I Am in Madrid and Can Think. Frank O'Hara. **SP-OharF**

I think of you as a great king, cold and austere. To Death. Robinson Jeffers. **CP-JefR3**

I think poetry must / I think it must. Thomas Merton. *Fr.* Cables to the Ace. **CP-MertT**

I think she sleeps: it must be sleep, when low. George Meredith. **NAEL-2** *Fr.* Modern Love. **CP-MerG1**

I think sometimes. Blue Waves. David St. John. **SP-StJoD**

I think that I have never trod. Ernest Hemingway. **CP-HemiE**

I think that I shall never see / A billboard. Song of the Open Road. Ogden Nash. **CP-NashO**

I think that I shall never see. Malcolm Lowry. **CP-LowrM**

I think that look of Christ might seem to say. The Meaning of the Look. Elizabeth Barrett Browning. **CP-BroEB**

I think that the Root of the Wind is Water. Emily Dickinson. **CP-DickE**

I think that though the clouds be dark. After While. Paul Laurence Dunbar. **CP-DunbP**

I think that we should never freeze / Such lively assets as our cheese. Chee$e. Thomas Merton. **CP-MertT**

I think the dead are tender. Shall we kiss?—. She. Theodore Roethke. **CP-RoetT**

I think the deaths of domestic animals. Animals. Miller Williams. **SP-WillM**

I think the deed was richer than the dying. The Last Full Measure of Devotion. Kenneth Patchen. **CP-PatcK**

I think the Hemlock likes to stand. Emily Dickinson. **CP-DickE**

I think the longest Hour of all. Emily Dickinson. **CP-DickE**

I think the soul. Hieroglyph. Leonard Nathan. **SP-NathL**

I think these empty pews are not deserted. St. Philip's Church in Antigua. Archibald MacLeish. **CP-MacLA**

I think they came. Two Beggars: A Reminiscence. Frank Templeton Prince. **CP-PrinF**

I think this qualifies as great religious poetry. *see also* Change, The. Leonard Cohen. **CP-CoheL**

I think this was a dream, and yet we saw. The Swans. May Sarton. **SP-SartM**

I think, though I don't believe it, you were my airhole. To Daddy. Robert Lowell. **SP-LoweR**

I think to compose a sonnet. The Apology. Robert Creeley. **CP-CreeR**

I think to Live—may be a Bliss. Emily Dickinson. **CP-DickE**

I think we are too ready with complaint. Cheerfulness Taught by Reason. Elizabeth Barrett Browning. **CP-BroEB**

I think we better talk this over. We Better Talk This Over. "Bob Dylan." **CP-DylaB**

I think when Judas' mother heard. Judas Iscariot. Countee Cullen. **CP-CullC**

I think you are fools to speak French. French and English. Leonard Cohen. **CP-CoheL**

"I think you like." Edward Estlin Cummings. **CP-CummE**

I think you would understand. Moon. Martin Edmunds. **SP-EdmuM**

I thirst, but not as once I did. My Soul Thirsteth for God. William Cowper. *TrCP Fr.* Olney Hymns. **CP-CowpW**

I thirst for / the Kool-Aid. Black Queen for More Than a Day. Al Young. **CP-YounA**

I thought a germ of Consciousness. The Aerolite. Thomas Hardy. **CP-HardT**

I thought about you a lot. To a Fellow Student. Leonard Cohen. **CP-CoheL**

I thought and thought of thy crass clanging town. From Her in the Country. Thomas Hardy. **CP-HardT**

I thought as I lay on my bed one night, I am only a passing cloud. The Passing Cloud. Stevie Smith. **CP-SmitS**

I thought, as I wiped my eyes on the corner of my apron. An Ancient Gesture. Edna St. Vincent Millay. **CP-MillE**

I thought because I had looked into your eyes. The Star. Kathleen Jessie Raine. **SP-RainK**

I thought he was dumb. Tortoise Shout. David Herbert Lawrence. **CP-LawrD**

I thought I could leave my habitation for the summer. Stealth and Subtleties of Growth. Richard Eberhart. **CP-EberR**

I thought I heard Indra's. Charles Henri Ford. **SP-FordC** *Fr.* Secret Haiku.

I thought I saw my late wife (a very respectable woman). Basil Bunting. *Fr.* Attis: Or, Something Missing. **CP-BuntB**

I thought I was going to the poets, but I am going to the. Flying to Hanoi. Muriel Rukeyser. **CP-RukeM**

I thought I was so tough. Tamer and Hawk. Thom Gunn. **CP-GunnT**

I thought I would / sit down at one of those park department tables. Having Arrived by Bike at Battery Park. Grace Paley. **CP-PaleG**

I thought I'd say a thing to please myself. Damn You, Jim D., You Woke Me Up. John Berryman. **CP-BerrJ**

I thought in the sweet stink of the funeral parlor. It Looks As If It Were Just Sleeping. Leonard Nathan. **SP-NathL**

I thought it would last my time. Going, Going. Philip Larkin. **CP-LarkP**

I thought, my dear, you might have known. *Sans.* David Markson. **CP-MarkD**

I Thought, My Heart. Thomas Hardy. **CP-HardT**

I thought no more was needed. Song, A. William Butler Yeats. **CP-YeatW**

I thought of a house where the stones seemed suddenly changed. Lo! A Child Is Born. "Hugh MacDiarmid." **SP-MacDH**

I thought of Alun Lewis. Dylan Thomas, and Now Matthew Mead—as He Himself, "To Edward Thomas." Charles Olson. **CP-OlsoC**

I thought of Chatterton, the marvellous Boy. We Poets in Our Youth. William Wordsworth. **FaBoRV** *Fr.* Resolution and Independence. **CP-WorW1**

I thought of happiness, how it is woven. The Work of Happiness. May Sarton. **SP-SartM**

I thought of her as the wishing tree that died. The Wishing Tree. Seamus Heaney. **SP-HeanS**

I thought of killing myself because I am only a bricklayer and you a. Bricklayer Love. Carl Sandburg. **CP-SandC**

I thought of offering you apothegms. Put Off the Wedding Five Times and Nobody Comes to It. Carl Sandburg. **CP-SandC**

I thought of the flowers I picked for her. A Senorita's Bouquet. Gilbert Sorrentino. **SP-SorrG**

I thought of Thee, my partner and my guide. William Wordsworth. **EnRP; FaBoPP; FaBoRV; NOBE; OBEV; OBNC; SeCePo** *Fr.* The River Duddon [A Series of Sonnets]. **CP-WorW2**

(After-Thought.) **EnRP; OBNC; SeCePo**

(To the River Duddon: After-Thought.) **FaBoPP**

(Valediction to the River Duddon.) **NOBE**

(Valedictory Sonnet to the River Duddon.) **OBEV**

I thought of walking round and round a space. Seamus Heaney. *Fr.* Clearances. **SP-HeanS**

I thought of your beauty, and this arrow. The Arrow. William Butler Yeats. **CP-YeatW**

I thought once how Theocritus had sung. Sonnet. Elizabeth Barrett Browning. **BWW; EBVV; EnVR; GBL; HBV; NOBE; NoP; OAEP;**

OBEV; OBNC; OXAEP-2; TreFT; WPE *Fr.* Sonnets from the Portuguese. **CP-BroEB**

I thought once, that your hillshapes swam and swayed. Van Gogh. Charles Tomlinson. **CP-TomlC**

I thought that being a Poem one's self. Emily Dickinson. **SP-DickE**

I thought that I would like to see. Next! Ogden Nash. **CP-NashO**

I thought that if I were broken enough. The Revelation. Robert Creeley. **CP-CreeR**

I Thought That Knowledge Alone Would Suffice. Walt Whitman. **CP-WhitW**

I thought that nature was enough. Emily Dickinson. **CP-DickE**

I thought that the north. In April. Charles Tomlinson. **CP-TomlC**

I thought that you would have written: my birthday came and went. A Complaint. Gerard Manley Hopkins. **CP-HopkG**

I thought the / woods afire. Enough. Archie Randolph Ammons. **SP-AmmoA**

I thought the earth / remembered me, she. Sleeping in the Forest. Mary Oliver. **SP-OlivM**

I thought the Greek root would tell me something I didn't know. Oblivion. Stephen Berg. **SP-BergS**

I thought the Train would never come. Emily Dickinson. **CP-DickE**

I thought they'd be strangers aroun' me. The Curate's Kindness. Thomas Hardy. **CP-HardT**

I thought to deal the death-stroke at a blow. Christina Georgina Rossetti. *Fr.* Three Stages. **CP-RosC3**

I thought to hear him speak. Nossis. Hilda Doolittle. **CP-DoolH**

I thought to shun the Loneliness. Emily Dickinson. **SP-DickE**

I thought tonight of all the lovers gone. Sonnet. John Hewitt. **CP-HewiJ**

I thought when the grave was sodded. Grief. John Hewitt. **CP-HewiJ**

I thought you a fire. At Moonrise and Onwards. Thomas Hardy. **CP-HardT**

I thought your approbation Fame. Emily Dickinson. **SP-DickE**

I thought your face as lovely. Demonstration. Kenneth Patchen. **CP-PatcK**

"I thought your search was over,"—"So I thought." A Discovery. Christina Georgina Rossetti. **CP-RosC3**

I threat'ned to observe the strict decree. The Holdfast. George Herbert. **CP-HerbG**

I threw a stick. The dog. Between. John Ciardi. **SP-CiarJ**

I Threw It All Away. "Bob Dylan." **CP-DylaB**

I threw the inside of my gizzard out, splashing. Zimmer Drunk and Alone, Dreaming of Old Football Games. Paul Zimmer. **SP-ZimmP**

I thumped on you the best I could. William DeWitt Snodgrass. **NePoEA; NoAM** *Fr.* Heart's Needle. **SP-SnodW**

I tie a second necktie over the first;. Double Vision. Robert Lowell. **SP-LoweR**

I tie my Hat—I crease my Shawl. Emily Dickinson. **CP-DickE**

I tipped my head. North Street. Archie Randolph Ammons. **SP-AmmoA**

I tiptoed into her sleep. Mirru. Kenneth Patchen. **CP-PatcK**

I to my garden went. Ralph Waldo Emerson. **CP-EmerR**

I to my perils. Alfred Edward Housman. **CP-HousA**

I to the hills lift up mine eyes. Bible, *O.T.* See Psalm 121: "I will lift up mine eyes unto the hills."

I toiled on, but thou. Christina Georgina Rossetti. **CP-RosC3**

I told a lie once in a verse. I said. To Bhain Campbell. John Berryman. **CP-BerrJ**

I told her that my mother would make. Kibali-Ituri. Kenneth Patchen. **CP-PatcK**

I told her then in bed. All the Casualties. . . . Charles Bukowski. **SP-BukC3**

I told her when I left one day. In the Night She Came. Thomas Hardy. **CP-HardT**

I told him: The time has come, I must be gone. The Animal Trainer. John Berryman. **CP-BerrJ**

I Told My Heart to Rest. John Hewitt. **CP-HewiJ**

I told my love I told my love, *see also* "Never seek to tell thy love." William Blake. **CP-BlakW**

I told you about strawberry fields. Glass Onion. The Beatles. **CP-Beatl**

I, Too. Langston Hughes. **SP-HughL**

I too / once lived / in the country. Pachuta, Mississippi/a Memoir. Al Young. **CP-YounA**

I too a sister had! too cruel Death! On Seeing a Youth Affectionately Welcomed by a Sister. Samuel Taylor Coleridge. **CP-ColeS**

I, too, dislike it. / Reading it, however, with a perfect contempt for it, one discovers in. Marianne Craig Moore. *See* Poetry.

I too have a garret of old playthings. Upstairs. Carl Sandburg. **CP-SandC**

I, too, have been a Wanderer; but, alas! William Wordsworth. **OxAEP-2** *Fr.* Cambridge and the Alps. *Fr.* The Prelude; Growth of a Poet's Mind [1805 vers.]. **CP-WorW3**

I too have taken the god into my mouth. Eating Snake. Margaret Atwood. **SP-AtwM2**

I, too, have trailed my father's spirit. Immrama. Paul Muldoon. **SP-MuldP**

I too limped into Merrion Square. The City of Dreadful Knight. James Liddy. *Fr.* Glass after Oblivion. **CP-LiddJ**

I, too, once hoped to have a hoopoe. Pooem. John Updike. **CP-UpdiJ**

I, too, saw God through mud. Apologia Pro Poemate Meo. Wilfred Owen. **CP-OwenW**

I too volunteered to monitor. The Charred Voice of Max Ernst. John Yau. **SP-YauJo**

I took a tree for a guide—I mean. Tree. Charles Tomlinson. **CP-TomlC**

I took away three pictures. Sandhill People. Carl Sandburg. **CP-SandC**

I took down *Pictures from Brueghel*. In Touch. Roy Fisher. **SP-FishR**

I took my heart in my hand. Twice. Christina Georgina Rossetti. **CP-RosC1**

I took my life and threw it on the skip. The Skip. James Fenton. **SP-FentJ**

I took my Power in my Hand. Emily Dickinson. **CP-DickE**

I took one Draught of Life. Emily Dickinson. **CP-DickE**

I took the blue pill this morning. The Blue Pill. Jim Carroll. **SP-CarrJ**

I tore it open, by one end, & found. My Special Fate. John Berryman. **CP-BerrJ**

I tore your letter into strips. The Torn Letter. Thomas Hardy. **CP-HardT**

I touch you in the night, whose gift was you. The Science of the Night. Stanley Jasspon Kunitz. **CP-KuniS**

I towered far, and lo! I stood within. God-Forgotten. Thomas Hardy. **CP-HardT**

I traced the Circus whose grey stones incline. In the Old Theatre, Fiesole. Thomas Hardy. **CP-HardT**

I Travel as a Phantom Now. Thomas Hardy. **CP-HardT**

I travel on by barren farms. The Wind's Prophecy. Thomas Hardy. **CP-HardT**

I traveled [*or* travell'd] among unknown men. William Wordsworth. **AWP; FaBV; GTBS; GTBS-6; GTBS-P; OAEP; OBRV** *Fr.* Lucy. **CP-WorW1**

I travelled on, seeing the hill, where lay. The Pilgrimage. George Herbert. **CP-HerbG**

I travelled [*or* traveld] thro' a land of men. The Mental Traveller. William Blake. **CP-BlakW**

I travelled to where in her lifetime. They Would Not Come. Thomas Hardy. **CP-HardT**

I traversed a dominion. Mute Opinion. Thomas Hardy. **CP-HardT**

I tried all night to sleep. Fragile! Charles Bukowski. **SP-BukC2**

I tried each thing, only some were immortal and free. As One Put Drunk into the Packet-Boat. John Ashbery. **SP-AshbJ**

I tried it standing up. The End of a Short Affair. Charles Bukowski. **SP-BukC1**

I tried to help. Suffering catfish, I tried! Tanck's Song About Pride. Hayden Carruth. **CP-CarHS** *Fr.* Songs About What Comes Down: The Complete Works of Mr. Septic Tank.

I Tried to Leave You. Leonard Cohen. **CP-CoheL**

I tried to move. The Dream. Louise McNeill. **SP-McNeL**

I tried to put a bird in a cage. The Fool's Song. William Carlos Williams. **CP-WilW1**

I tried to think a lonelier Thing. Emily Dickinson. **CP-DickE**

I tried to think of something good, *sl. diff. vers. incl. in* Pijijiapan. Malcolm Lowry. **CP-LowrM**

I tried to tip my hat to Miss McGaffry. Tight Hat. Shel Silverstein. **SP-SilS2**

I trod a foreign path, dears. Voice from the Tomb (2). Stevie Smith. **CP-SmitS**

I trundle the bodies, on the iron bars. John Berryman. **NOBA** *Fr.* Homage to Mistress Bradstreet. **CP-BerrJ**

I trust I am not a spoil sport, but there is one thing I deplore. The Party Next Door. Ogden Nash. **CP-NashO**

I trust I have not wasted breath. Tennyson. **EnVR; FHYEP; ImOP; OAEL-2; SeCePo** *Fr.* In Memoriam A. H. H. **CP-TennA**

I trust none of them. Only my existence. For a Sister. Adrienne Rich. **SP-RicA2**

I trust this sweet May Morning. Emily Dickinson. **SP-DickE**

I trust you may have the dearest summer. Emily Dickinson. **SP-DickE**

I Try to Keep in Touch. Leonard Cohen. **CP-CoheL**

I Try to Waken and Greet the World Once Again. James Wright. *Fr.* Two Hangovers. **CP-WrigJ**

I turn myself into a sack. Travelling. Charles Simic. **SP-SimiC**

I turn round. The Lady's First Song. William Butler Yeats. **CP-YeatW**

I turn the market corner, then peer down. The Banana Dwarf. Laurence Lieberman. **SP-LiebL**

I Turn to Trees. John Hewitt. **CP-HewiJ**

I turned from side to side, from image to image, to put you down. Poem in Prose. Louise Bogan. **CP-BogaL**

I turned—heaven knows we women turn too much. *parody of* E.B. Browning. Rudyard Kipling. **CP-KiplR** *Fr.* The Muse among the Motors.

I turned my eyes from the drifting body. Warning from False Cape Horn. Malcolm Lowry. **CP-LowrM**

I Turned My Touch to Campion. John Hewitt. **CP-HewiJ**

I turned out the light to see the snow. Ernesto Cardenal, *tr. by* Thomas Merton. **CP-MertT** *Fr.* Gethsemani, KY.

I turned: quivering yellow stars in blackness. Philosophia Perennis. Anne Waldman. **CP-WaldA**

I turned to speak to God. Not All There. Robert Frost. **FaBoCo** *Fr.* Ten Mills. **CP-FrosR**

I turned where the sun came up and he held my hand. Richard Eberhart. *Fr.* Suite in Prison. **CP-EberR**

I twined a net; I drove a stake; laid a glittering bait. The Captive. Walter de la Mare. **CP-DeLaW**

I type at a window that faces the street. The New Place. Charles Bukowski. **SP-BukC2**

I understand the large hearts of heroes. Walt Whitman. **AA; SAmP** *Fr.* Song of Myself. **CP-WhitW** (Heroes.) **AA**

I undress and lie down next to you in bed. On This Side of the River. Stephen Berg. **SP-BergS**

I unearthed / what seemed like the jawbone of an ass. Bone. Charles Tomlinson. **CP-TomlC**

I upon the first creation. Gratitude. Christopher Smart. **LAuP; NOEC** *Fr.* Hymns for the Amusement of Children. **SP-SmarC**

I use the knife. Ralph Waldo Emerson. **CP-EmerR**

I used t' hate enzo. "Bob Dylan." *Fr.* Some Other Kinds of Songs. **CP-DylaB**

I used to get up, in the tent. The Place of the Skull. James Dickey. **CP-DickJ**

I used to have a fear of tools, largely because of my father. When. Electric Drills. John Yau. **SP-YauJo**

I used to have tricks, dodges, a whole sackful. Porcupine Meditation. Margaret Atwood. **SP-AtwM2**

I used to imagine him. Stanley Kunitz. Mary Oliver. **SP-OlivM**

I used to imagine we were a fine two-headed. Alive. Hayden Carruth. **CP-CarHS**

I used to know a breadwinner named Mr. Purefoy. There'll Always Be a War between the Sexes, or, A Woman Can Be Sometimes Pleased, but Never Satisfied. Ogden Nash. **CP-NashO**

I used to press tools in the Texas oil fields. Muriel Rukeyser. **CP-RukeM**

I used to see her in the door. Paul. James Wright. **CP-WrigJ**

I used to spend 3 days a week. Girls. Charles Bukowski. **SP-BukC3**

I used to take the back off. I'm Getting Back to Where I Was. Charles Bukowski. **SP-BukC1**

I used to think that life wouldn't always be wounded. A Man Lives Here. Kenneth Patchen. **CP-PatcK**

I used to think that obstacles to love. During an Absence. Thom Gunn. **CP-GunnT**

I used to think, when the corn was blowing. Life Transcendent. Nicholas Vachel Lindsay. **CP-LindV**

I used to walk quickly. On Walking Slowly after an Accident. Stevie Smith. **CP-SmitS**

I used to watch it on the ledge. The Crippling. Marge Piercy. **SP-PierM**

I used to watch you, sleeping. Kathleen Jessie Raine. **NAs** *Fr.* My Mother's Birthday. **SP-RainK**

I used to wonder. Border Line. Langston Hughes. **SP-HughL**

I used to write in the café sometimes. Marsyas. James Merrill. **SP-MerrJ**

I vex my heart with fancies dim. Tennyson. *Fr.* In Memoriam A. H. H. **CP-TennA**

I view, in the flying time. Faces of Girls Looking at Themselves in the River. Pablo Antonio Cuadra, *tr. fr. Spanish by* Thomas Merton. **CP-MertT**

I violinize peace. Al Young. **CP-YounA** *Fr.* The Song Turning Back into Itself.

I visited Père Lachaise to look for the remains of Apollinaire. At Apollinaire's Grave. Allen Ginsberg. **CP-GinsA**

I wage no warr, yet peace I none enjoy. What Joy to Live. Robert Southwell. **CP-SoutR**

I wage not any feud with Death. Tennyson. **ImPo; LiTB; OBF; PPON** *Fr.* In Memoriam A. H. H. **CP-TennA**

I wait and watch: before my eyes. The Waiting. John Greenleaf Whittier. **CP-WhitJ**

I wait for a meaning in the coming words. Vigil. John Hewitt. **CP-HewiJ**

I wait. I deepen in the room. Twilight. Stanley Jasspon Kunitz. **CP-KuniS**

I Wait in the White Rain. Charles Bukowski. **SP-BukC2**

I Waited. Theodore Roethke. **CP-RoetT**

I waited at home all the while they were boating together. The Two Wives. Thomas Hardy. **CP-HardT**

I waited patiently for the Lord. Psalm 40. Bible, *O.T. Fr.* Psalms. **CP-Psal**

I waited today for a freight train to pass. 'Boes. Carl Sandburg. **CP-SandC**

I waited too long. In a Boat Shed. Robert Creeley. **CP-CreeR**

I wake and feel the fell of dark, not day. Gerard Manley Hopkins. **CP-HopkG**

I wake and find myself in the woods, far from the castle. Night Frogs. Robert Bly. **SP-BlyR**

I wake, birds flashing on my lids. The dead. A Good Day for Seeing Your Limitations. Richard Hugo. **CP-HugoR**

I wake, but before I know it it is done. Aging. Randall Jarrell. **CP-JarrR; SP-JarrR**

I wake earlier, now that the birds have come. No Voyage. Mary Oliver. **SP-OlivM**

I wake early. Two Fragments. Stephen Berg. **SP-BergS**

I wake from dreams and turning. Alfred Edward Housman. **CP-HousA**

I wake in a dark flat. Derek Mahon. *Fr.* Afterlives. **SP-MahoD**

I wake in the early dawn and my hand has fallen asleep. Praises IV. Thomas McGrath. **SP-McGrT**

I wake in the night. Middle of the Way. Galway Kinnell. **SP-KinnG**

I wake late and leave. A Cardinal. William DeWitt Snodgrass. **SP-SnodW**

I wake now to find myself this long alone. Sick. Robert Lowell. **SP-LoweR**

I wake to a glittering world. Stanley Jasspon Kunitz. *Fr.* Journal for My Daughter. **CP-KuniS**

I wake to move easy. In This Room Particularly. Jim Carroll. **SP-CarrJ**

I wake to sleep, and take my waking slow. The Waking. Theodore Roethke. **CP-RoetT**

I wake to the sound of a soft, low patter. Night Rain. Countee Cullen. **CP-CullC**

I wake up cold, I who. The Man With Night Sweats. Thom Gunn. **CP-GunnT**

I wake up from / a nap. Self. Archie Randolph Ammons. **SP-AmmoA**

I wake up in your bed. I know I have been dreaming. Adrienne Rich. **NAAL-2; NoAM; TRP; UnAS; VBLP** *Fr.* Twenty-one Love Poems. **SP-RicA1; SP-RicA2**

I waked, and sat out the watch, the night. The Night. Charles Olson. **CP-OlsoC**

I waked at midmost in the night. A Dream. Allen Ginsberg. **CP-GinsA**

I, wakeful for the skylark voice in men. To Cardinal Manning. George Meredith. **CP-MerG1**

I waken and / lean and look out. Stepping Backward. Hayden Carruth. **CP-CarHS**

I walk / on human stilts. Rigor Vitus. Bill Knott. **SP-KnotB**

I walk / Unwind with activity of legs. Ted Hughes. **SP-HughT** *Fr.* Seven Dungeon Songs.

I walk before no man, a hawk in his fist. Jonathan Swift. **CP-SwifJ** (I Walk before No Man (Composed While Asleep).) **CP-SwifJ**

I Walk before No Man (Composed While Asleep). Jonathan Swift. *See* I walk before no man, a hawk in his fist.

I walk [*or* walked] beside the prisoners to the road. A Camp in the Prussian Forest. Randall Jarrell. **CP-JarrR; SP-JarrR**

I walk in the old street. Louis Zukofsky. **CP-ZukLS**

I walk into your house, a friend. A Friend. William DeWitt Snodgrass. **SP-SnodW**

I walk on my cliff above the Pacific Ocean and feel the tides. Robinson Jeffers. **CP-JefR3**

I walk six blocks to the park. Hoarfrost and Fog. Barton Sutter. **SP-SuttB**

I walk the floor, read, watch a cop-show, drink. Her Pet. Thom Gunn. **CP-GunnT**

I walk the forest by the Daniel Boone trail. Nicholas Vachel Lindsay. *Fr.* A Rhymed Address to All Renegade Campbellites, Exhorting Them to Return. *Fr.* Alexander Campbell. **CP-LindV**

I walk the purple carpet into your eye. Inside Out. Diane Wakoski. **SP-WakoD**

I walk the streets. This Late in the Century. Stephen Dunn. **SP-DunnS**

I walk through the high-ceilinged. Don't Look Back. Dabney Stuart. **SP-StuaD**

I walk through the long schoolroom questioning. Among School Children. William Butler Yeats. **CP-YeatW**

I walk uphill through the snow. Carrying Food Home in Winter. Margaret Atwood. **SP-AtwM1**

I walked abroad in [*or* on] a snowy day. Soft Snow. William Blake. **CP-BlakW**

I walked abroad in Easter Park. Conviction (ii). Stevie Smith. **CP-SmitS**

I walked alone and thinking. Sinner's Rue. Alfred Edward Housman. **CP-HousA**

I walked among the seven woods of Coole. William Butler Yeats. **CP-YeatW**

I walked among the streets of an old city and the streets were as lean as the. Streets Too Old. Carl Sandburg. **CP-SandC**

I walked at night and. For Doyle Fosso. Archie Randolph Ammons. **SP-AmmoA**

I walked down alone Sunday after church. Pea Brush. Robert Frost. **CP-FrosR**

I walked in loamy Wessex lanes, afar. The Pity of It. Thomas Hardy. **CP-HardT**

I walked into a loge in the Teatro Melisso. Pound at Spoleto. Lawrence Ferlinghetti. **SP-FerlL**

I walked into the cocktail party. In Society. Allen Ginsberg. **CP-GinsA**

I walked on the banks of the tincan banana dock. Sunflower Sutra. Allen Ginsberg. **CP-GinsA**

I walked out, before. Che Di Lor Suona Su Nella Tua Vita. Louis Zukofsky. **CP-ZukLS**

I walked out on the lamp shadowed concrete at midnight May Day passing. Manhattan May Day Midnight. Allen Ginsberg. **CP-GinsA**

I Walked Out to the Graveyard to See the Dead. Richard Eberhart. **CP-EberR**

I Walked over the Grave of Henry James. Richard Eberhart. **CP-EberR**

I walked the boulevard. Edward Estlin Cummings. **CP-CummE**

I walked the streets of a market town. The Son's Portrait. Thomas Hardy. **CP-HardT**

I walked the unwalked garden of rose-beds. Fable of the Rhododendron Stealers. Sylvia Plath. **CP-PlatS**

I Walked Thru. Jim Morrison. **SP-MorrJ**

I walked to the edge of you, looked over. History Is a Throne and a Gate. Kenneth Patchen. **CP-PatcK**

I walked, when love was gone. A Breath of Air. James Wright. **CP-WrigJ**

I wander all night in my vision. The Sleepers. Walt Whitman. **CP-WhitW**

I wander by the edge. He Hears the Cry of the Sedge. William Butler Yeats. **CP-YeatW**

I wander down on Clinton street south of Polk. Clinton South of Polk. Carl Sandburg. **CP-SandC**

I wander [thro] each dirty street. William Blake. *See* London ("I wander through each chartered street").

I wander through [or thro'] each chartered [or charter'd] street. London. William Blake. **CP-BlakW** *Fr.* Songs of Experience.

I wandered in the garden of my dreams. In the Garden of Dreams. John Gould Fletcher. **SP-FletJ**

I wandered [or wander'd] lonely as a Cloud. William Wordsworth. **CP-WorW1**

I wandered lonely where the pinetrees made. The Trailing Arbutus. John Greenleaf Whittier. **CP-WhitJ**

I wandered to a crude coast. The Discovery. Thomas Hardy. **CP-HardT**

I wandered to the surfy marge. Sea Knell. John Updike. **CP-UpdiJ**

I wandering went / Among the haunts and dwellings of mankind. Percy Bysshe Shelley. **FiP** *Fr.* Prometheus Unbound. **CP-ShelP**

I Wanna Be Black. "Lou Reed." **SP-ReedL**

I Wanna Be Your Lover. "Bob Dylan." **CP-DylaB**

I wanna be your lover baby. I Wanna Be Your Man. The Beatles. **CP-Beatl**

I Wanna Be Your Man. The Beatles. **CP-Beatl**

I want a bedroom near the sky, an astrologer's cave. Landscape (After Baudelaire). John Ashbery. **SP-AshbJ**

I Want a Drink of Water, but Not from the Thermos. Ogden Nash. **CP-NashO**

I want a hero: an uncommon want. Canto the First. Byron. **EnRP; NAEL-2; NoP; OAEL-2; PoE** *Fr.* Don Juan. **CP-Byron**

I want a love that's right. Old Brown Shoe. George Harrison. **CP-Beatl**

"I want," he says again, through his tears, in this unfamiliar voice, again, "I want, I want." Good Mother: Out. Charles Kenneth Williams. **SP-WillC**

I Want, I Want. Sylvia Plath. **CP-PlatS**

"I want"—it pleaded—All its life. Emily Dickinson. **CP-DickE**

I want, like a little boat, to be isolate. Laguna Dantesca. Charles Wright. **SP-WrigC**

I want live things in their pride to remain. In Which Many Autos Pass Westward. Nicholas Vachel Lindsay. *Fr.* The Santa-Fé Trail (A Humoresque). **CP-LindV**

I want mother's milk. Food. Anne Sexton. **CP-SextA**

I want no easy light to lift my eyes. There's a Train Leaving Soon. Kenneth Patchen. **CP-PatcK**

I want no tricks in speaking of this man. Adolf Eichmann. Hayden Carruth. **CP-CarHS**

I want no willow cabin at your gate. Convalescence in Summer 1949. Isabella Gardner. **CP-GardI**

I want no wonder's cloud or church to wake me. Note for a Diary. Kenneth Patchen. **CP-PatcK**

I want that height and prospect such as music. Movements. Charles Tomlinson. **CP-TomlC**

I want the cries of my geese. A Prelude. Charles Tomlinson. **CP-TomlC**

I want the jailed / light to awaken: I want. Pablo Neruda, *tr. fr. Spanish by* Ben Belitt. **SP-NeruP** *Fr.* Skystones.

I want to be. The Last of the Fire Kings. Derek Mahon. **SP-MahoD**

I want to be known as the most brilliant man in America. Ego Confession. Allen Ginsberg. **CP-GinsA**

I want to be sick, I want to meet everyone again. Nothingness. Stephen Berg. **SP-BergS**

I want to be where Fordie is. Incognito. William Carlos Williams. **CP-WilW2**

I want to be with you. Telling. Alice Walker. **CP-WalkA**

I want to be your pinkie. Le Désert de l'Amour. Stevie Smith. **CP-SmitS**

I want to do a complaint now. Which is to say. Sonnet. Hayden Carruth. **CP-CarHS** *Fr.* Sonnets.

I want to fuck you. Robert Creeley. **CP-CreeR**

I Want to Go Wandering. Nicholas Vachel Lindsay. **CP-LindV**

I want to help you. The Friends. Robert Creeley. **CP-CreeR**

I Want to Hold Your Hand. The Beatles. **CP-Beatl**

I Want to Sleep. Jorge Guillén, *tr. fr. Spanish by* James Wright. **CP-WrigJ**

I want to speak in my voice! Suicide Blues. Muriel Rukeyser. **CP-RukeM**

I Want to Tell You. George Harrison. **CP-Beatl**

I want to Tell You. Jim Morrison. **SP-MorrJ**

I Want You. "Bob Dylan." **CP-DylaB**

I Want You. The Beatles. **CP-Beatl**

I want you to be healthy. Health Lantern. Patti Smith. **SP-SmitP**

I wanted a house. There Are No Such Trees in Alpine, California. John Haines. **SP-HainJ**

I wanted a man's face looking into the jaws and throat of life. Aztec Mask. Carl Sandburg. **CP-SandC**

I wanted it depressed, one dusty road. Fairfield. Richard Hugo. **CP-HugoR**

I Wanted My Name on the Side of a Building I Wanted to Be as Feared as the Word Biopsy. Ron Koertge. **SP-KoerR**

I wanted so ably. The World. Robert Creeley. **CP-CreeR**

I wanted to be a cauliflower. The Cauliflower. John Haines. **SP-HainJ**

I Wanted to Be a Doctor. Leonard Cohen. **CP-CoheL**

I wanted to be more human. Forms of the Human. Richard Eberhart. **CP-EberR**

I wanted to be sure to reach you. To the Harbormaster. Frank O'Hara. **SP-OharF**

I wanted to give him some gift. To Evan. Richard Eberhart. **CP-EberR**

I wanted to marry, but father said, "No." The Orphaned Old Maid. Thomas Hardy. **CP-HardT**

I wanted to take a walk. Walking Past Paul Blackburn's Apt. on 7th St. Diane Wakoski. **SP-WakoD**

I wanted to take up room. What a strange dream! I wanted to take up as much room as I could. Room. Charles Kenneth Williams. **SP-WillC**

I wanted wisdom, yet the indifferent glance. False Solomon's Seal. Howard Nemerov. **CP-NemeH**

I wanted you / without virtue—. Again. Robert Creeley. **CP-CreeR**

I wanted you, nameless Woman of the South. Southern Cross. Hart Crane. *Fr.* Three Songs. **NAAL-2** *Fr.* The Bridge. **CP-CranH**

I was / the girl of the chain letter. Love Song. Anne Sexton. **CP-SextA**

I was a beautiful plant. The Stroke. Stevie Smith. **CP-SmitS**

I was a boy when I heard three red words a thousand Frenchmen. Threes. Carl Sandburg. **CP-SandC**

I was a cottage maiden. Cousin Kate. Christina Georgina Rossetti. **CP-RosC1**

I was a frenetic wretch of a man. Making It. Charles Bukowski. **SP-BukC3**

I was a good child. Katy Did. James Wright. **CP-WrigJ**

I was a groveling creature once. Lively Hope, and Gracious Fear. William Cowper. **CP-CowpW** *Fr.* Olney Hymns. **CP-CowpW**

I was a lookout posted and forgotten. In the Beech. Seamus Heaney. **SP-HeanS** *Fr.* Sweeney Redivivus.

I was a Phoebe—nothing more. Emily Dickinson. **CP-DickE**

I was a pretty baby. Amoebaean for Daddy. Maya Angelou. **SP-AngeM**

I was a shepherd to fools. Convoy Escort. Rudyard Kipling. *Fr.* Epitaphs of the War [1914–1918]. **CP-KiplR**

I was a slow developer. Too Late. Charles Bukowski. **SP-BukC3**

"I Was a Stranger and Ye Took Me in." John Greenleaf Whittier. **CP-WhitJ**

I was a stricken deer, that left the herd. William Cowper. **EnRP; FaBoRV; FiP; LoBV; NAEL-1; OAEP; OxBoCh; PAI; PoE** *Fr.* The Garden. *Fr.* The Task. **CP-CowpW**

("Morning finds the self-sequestr'd man, The.") **PoE**

(Stricken Deer, The.) **FiP; LoBV**

I was a weapon. I brandished myself, I was used in the air. The Knight of Swords. Marge Piercy. *Fr.* Laying Down the Tower. **SP-PierM**

I was a young guy in Los Angeles. Training for Kid Aztec. Charles Bukowski. **SP-BukC3**

I was a young pilot in World War I, remember? Traffic. Jim Carroll. **SP-CarrJ**

I Was Afraid of Dying. James Wright. **CP-WrigJ**

I was alone, I took a ride. Got to Get You into My Life. The Beatles. **CP-Beatl**

I was alone once, waiting. For the Marsh's Birthday. James Wright. **CP-WrigJ**

I was always a thoughtful youngster. Northumberland House. Stevie Smith. **CP-SmitS**

I was always away from myself. Return. Phoebe Hesketh. **SP-HeskP**

I was always called in early for dinner. Don't Forget. Stephen Berg. **SP-BergS**

I was always one for being alone. Fourth Meditation. Theodore Roethke. *Fr.* Meditations of an Old Woman. **CP-RoetT**

I was an ice baby. The Death Baby. Anne Sexton. **CP-SextA**

I was angry with my friend. William Blake. **OBF** *Fr.* A Poison Tree. **CP-BlakW** *Fr.* Songs of Experience.

I was angry with my friend. A Poison Tree. William Blake. **CP-BlakW** *Fr.* Songs of Experience.

I was asking for something specific and perfect for my city. Mannahatta. Walt Whitman. **CP-WhitW**

I was at peace until you came. The Remonstrance. Walter de la Mare. **CP-DeLaW**

I was awakened from a dream. Daughter. John Updike. **CP-UpdiJ**

I was better with the sounds of the sea. "Hugh MacDiarmid." **SP-MacDH** *Fr.* The War with England.

I was blinded by the devil. Saved. "Bob Dylan." **CP-DylaB**

I was born during the night sea-journey. December 23, 1926. Robert Bly. **SP-BlyR**

I was born here. New Yorkers. Langston Hughes. **SP-HughL**

I was born in a beauty salon. Don't Go Home with Your Hard-on. Leonard Cohen. **CP-CoheL**

I was born in Belfast between the mountain and the gantries. Carrickfergus. Louis MacNeice. **CP-MacNL**

I was born in Illinois. My Fathers Came from Kentucky. Nicholas Vachel Lindsay. **AmFN; HBMV** *Fr.* Alexander Campbell. **CP-LindV**

I Was Born in Lucerne. Philip Levine. **SP-LeviP**

I was born in Mississippi. A Poem for Myself (or Blues for a Mississippi Black Boy). Etheridge Knight. **SP-KnigE**

I was born in the month of the bull. Brooding Likeness. Louise Glück. **SP-GlücL**

I was born in the morning of the world. Carl Sandburg. *Fr.* Timesweep. **CP-SandC**

I was born in Wyoming, Cody is my home town. Stool Pigeon Blues. Allen Ginsberg. **CP-GinsA**

I was born on the banks of the green Gulf Stream. Gulf Stream. John Gould Fletcher. **SP-FletJ**

I was born on the island of New England. World-Passport Visa. Marsden Hartley. **CP-HartM**

I was born on the prairie and the milk of its wheat, the red of its clover. Prairie. Carl Sandburg. **CP-SandC**

I Was Born to Hustle Roses Down the Avenues of the Dead. Charles Bukowski. **SP-BukC2**

I Was Born to Speak Your Name. Tom Clark. **SP-ClarT**

I was born to this crowded waste. Hunger. John Haines. **SP-HainJ**

I was born when she was thirty-eight. Mother. Marilyn Hacker. **SP-HackM**

I was buried near this dyke [*or* Dike]. William Blake. **CP-BlakW**

(Another [Epitaph]: "I was buried near this Dike.") **CP-BlakW**

I was but a half-grown boy. Genesis. Nicholas Vachel Lindsay. **CP-LindV**

I was calling airspeed. Where We Crashed. Richard Hugo. **CP-HugoR**

I was coming off an affair that had gone badly. Numb Your Ass and Your Brain and Your Heart—. Charles Bukowski. **SP-BukC1**

I was conceived in the summer of Nineteen Eighteen. *See also* Mock Confessional. Lawrence Ferlinghetti. **SP-FerlL**

I was considering how. Edward Estlin Cummings. **CP-CummE**

I was consumed by so much hate. A Man I Am. Stevie Smith. **CP-SmitS**

I was down by the mill at last. The Ants. Charles Bukowski. **SP-BukC2**

I was drunk and they. The Star. Charles Bukowski. **SP-BukC3**

I was eating a chicken sandwich with mayonnaise. Frenchie. Stephen Dobyns. **SP-DobyS**

I was fairly and squarely behind the eight. Immram. Paul Muldoon. **SP-MuldP**

I was fishing in the abandoned reservoir. Quinnapoxet. Stanley Jasspon Kunitz. **CP-KuniS**

I was floating through a cross section. John Yau. **SP-YauJo**

(Genghis Chan: Private Eye I.) **SP-YauJo**

I was flying. Belonging. Steve Griffiths. **SP-GrifS**

I was foolish about windows. Foolish About Windows. Carl Sandburg. **CP-SandC**

I was foretold, your rebel[l] sex. A Deposition from Love. Thomas Carew. **CP-CareT**

I was fortunate enough to have. Lives of the Poets. Mona Van Duyn. **SP-VanDM**

I was full of sadness, and I was sitting silent with no companion. Elegy 3. John Milton, *tr. fr. Latin by* John T. Shawcross. **CP-MiltJ**

I was given my bedding, and a bunk. A Meaningless Institution. Allen Ginsberg. **CP-GinsA**

I was glad when they said unto me, Let us go into the house of the Lord. Psalm 122. Bible, *O.T.* **TRV** *Fr.* Psalms. **CP-Psal**

I was going to make something of it. Testimony. Richard Eberhart. **CP-EberR**

I was happy you were born. Stanley Jasspon Kunitz. *Fr.* Journal for My Daughter. **CP-KuniS**

I was having dinner with my friends Howie and Francine. Somewhere It Still Moves. Stephen Dobyns. **SP-DobyS**

I was helpless, my breasts were freezing. Last Meeting. Stephen Berg. **SP-BergS**

I was here alone. Seraph. William Carlos Williams. **CP-WilW1**

I was high on tea in my fo'c'sle near the forepeak hatch listening to the stars. Battleship Newsreel. Allen Ginsberg. **CP-GinsA**

I was hungry, and Thou feddest me. Because He First Loved Us. Christina Georgina Rossetti. **CP-RosC2**

I was ill, lying on my bed of old papers. The Secret Garden. Rita Dove. **SP-DoveR**

I was in a printing house in Hell & I saw the method in. Memorable Fancy, A. William Blake. *Fr.* The Marriage of Heaven and Hell. **CP-BlakW**

I was in Mannheim when my agent phoned me. Krutz. Charles Bukowski. **SP-BukC3**

I was in the days of peace. An Airman Considers His Power. Richard Eberhart. **CP-EberR**

I was in your presence for an hour or so. In the Summertime. "Bob Dylan." **CP-DylaB**

I was invested in mother-earth, the crypt of roots. Geoffrey Hill. **NoAM** *Fr.* Mercian Hymns. **CP-HillG**

I was kissed once. The Kiss. Alice Walker. **CP-WalkA**

I was led into a miniature amphitheater of white porcelain. After/Words. Patti Smith. **SP-SmitP**

I was living in San Francisco. A Phonecall from Frank O'Hara. Anne Waldman. **SP-WaldA**

I Was Looking a Long While. Walt Whitman. **CP-WhitW**

I was looking for a way out of a lifetime's consolations. Adrienne Rich. **SP-RicA2** *Fr.* Shooting Script. **CP-RicAE**

I was Lord of Cities very sumptuously builded. The Song of Seven Cities. Rudyard Kipling. **CP-KiplR**

I was lost. The Road to Larissa. Leonard Cohen. **CP-CoheL**

I was making my way home late one night. Aisling. Paul Muldoon. **SP-MuldP**

I was micro-tagging Chinook salmon. Chinook. Paul Muldoon. **SP-MuldP**

I was never bothered by the rose. The Rose. Leonard Cohen. **CP-CoheL**

I was never so upset. Robert Creeley. **CP-CreeR**

I was not dead when you left me. Letter to Peter Wilkins. Siv Cedering Fox. **SP-CedeS**

I Was Not He. Thomas Hardy. **CP-HardT**

I was not meant to hear. Marathon. Louise Glück. *Fr.* Marathon. **SP-GlücL**

I was not; now I am—a few days hence. The Mystery. Paul Laurence Dunbar. **CP-DunbP**

I was not pure. A Dead Priestess Speaks. Hilda Doolittle. **CP-DoolH**

I was of delicate mind. I stepped aside for my needs. The Refined Man. Rudyard Kipling. **FaBoEE; FaBoTw; MMA; PeFWW** *Fr.* Epitaphs of the War [1914–1918]. **CP-KiplR**

I was of late a barren plant. On the Reed. *Unknown, tr. fr. Greek by* William Cowper. **CP-CowpW**

I was once a part. Three Songs. Louise Bogan. **CP-BogaL**

I was once the snake woman. Snake Woman. Margaret Atwood. **SP-AtwM2**

I was only the girl under the stairs. The Big House. Paul Muldoon. **SP-MuldP**

I was out last night. The Miser. Mona Van Duyn. **SP-VanDM**

I was out of your Church for 43 years, my Dear. Back. John Berryman. **CP-BerrJ**

I was out there again today. There are some creatures out there. Charles Bukowski. *Fr.* Horsemeat. **SP-BukC3**

I was playing records on Sunday. Records. Robert Lowell. **SP-LoweR**

I was prepared for places. Back. Jane Cooper. *Fr.* March. **SP-CoopJ**

I was promoted to the school upstairs. The School Upstairs. John Hewitt. **CP-HewiJ**

I was promoted when Grandfather died. I Lie Alone. John Hewitt. **CP-HewiJ**

I was raised in a state of mind. Outcast. Richard Shelton. **SP-ShelR**

I was reading the novel. His Shining Helmet; Its Horsehair Crest. Tess Gallagher. **SP-GallT**

I was riding on the Mayflower. Bob Dylan's 115th Dream. "Bob Dylan." **CP-DylaB**

I was seduced by innocence. Odysseus on Hermes. Thom Gunn. **CP-GunnT**

I was shacked with a. Who in the Hell is Tom Jones? Charles Bukowski. **SP-BukC1**

I was sick of being a woman. Beast, Book, Body. Erica Jong. **SP-JongE**

I was sittin' home on the West End. The Original Wrapper. "Lou Reed." **SP-ReedL**

I was sittin' on a stump. Bob Dylan's New Orleans Rag. "Bob Dylan." **CP-DylaB**

I was sitting, / She was knitting. She, I, and They. Thomas Hardy. **CP-HardT**

I was sitting in mcsorley's.   outside it was New York and beauti- / fully snowing. Edward Estlin Cummings. **CP-CummE**

I was sleeping gently napping when I heard the phone. N.Y. Telephone Conversation. "Lou Reed." **SP-ReedL**

I was sleeping in Madison, Anthony Bradbury's spare room. Milkers Broken Up. Donald Hall. **CP-HallD**

I Was So Full. Stevie Smith. **CP-SmitS**

I was so sick last night I. Morning After. Langston Hughes. **SP-HughL**

I was spading a flower bed while the old dog. Knowing Bitches. John Ciardi. **SP-CiarJ**

I was stranger on earth. Stanley Jasspon Kunitz. *Fr.* The Flight of Apollo. **CP-KuniS**

I was stretched out on the earth   so that a wild geranium. Charles Olson. **CP-OlsoC**

I was strolling sorrowfully. The Trees' Counselling. Christina Georgina Rossetti. **CP-RosC3**

I was talking one day. Angel of Grace. Stevie Smith. **CP-SmitS**

I was talking to "The Eliminators." Waiting with Two Members of a Motorcycle Gang for My Child to Be Born. Stephen Dunn. **SP-DunnS**

I was the first of fools. Dreaming Fool. Carl Sandburg. **CP-SandC**

I Was the Midmost. Thomas Hardy. **CP-HardT**

I was the slightest in the House. Emily Dickinson. **CP-DickE**

I was the staunchest of our fleet. The Derelict. Rudyard Kipling. **CP-KiplR**

I was the wing. Wing. Patti Smith. **SP-SmitP**

I was the witch in the window at Ballykilty, at. Dorcas. James Liddy. **CP-LiddJ**

I was there—by the curtains. Peeping Tom. Walter de la Mare. **CP-DeLaW**

I was thinking, Mother, of that poor old horse. Reserved. Walter de la Mare. **CP-DeLaW**

I was thinking of. One Side of the Story. Stephen Dunn. **SP-DunnS**

I was thinking of a son. Menstruation at Forty. Anne Sexton. **CP-SextA**

I was three-ish. The Right Arm. Paul Muldoon. **SP-MuldP**

I was thy Neighbour once, thou rugged Pile! Elegiac Stanzas Suggested by a Picture of Peele Castle, in a Storm [Painted by Sir George Beaumont]. William Wordsworth. **CP-WorW1**

I was tired of being a woman. Consorting with Angels. Anne Sexton. **CP-SextA**

I was too old to be married. The Widow Lester. Ted Kooser. **SP-KoosT**

I was trying to write the perfect poem. For Judy. Gary Gildner. **SP-GildG**

I was twelve when my father gave me this .22. Merle Bascom's .22. Donald Hall. **CP-HallD**

I was up in the morning with the TV blarin'. Sick of You. "Lou Reed." **SP-ReedL**

I was very well pleased with what I knowed. Brookland Road. Rudyard Kipling. **CP-KiplR**

I was walking a mile. Tennyson. **EBVV** *Fr.* Maud [A Monodrama]. **CP-TennA**

I was walking in a dark valley. Returning. Wendell Berry. **CP-BerrW**

I was walking my garden. Silent Visit. Robert Ranke Graves. **CP-GravR**

I was watching the great God dance. Ellora. Leonard Nathan. **SP-NathL**

I was watching the telly not serious you know just looking. Hayden Carruth. *Fr.* Paragraphs. **CP-CarHS**

I was with you in all the loneliness. Emily Dickinson. **SP-DickE**

I was wondering about the gods. The Gods of Washington, D.C. Richard Eberhart. **CP-EberR**

I was working real hard. Work Song. Patti Smith. **SP-SmitP**

I was wrapped in black. Us. Anne Sexton. **CP-SextA**

I washd them out & washd them in. The Washer Womans Song. William Blake. **CP-BlakW**

I washed lobster and stale gin. Love Song for K. Owyne. Anne Sexton. **CP-SextA**

I Watch, and Long Have Watched [with Calm Regret]. William Wordsworth. **CP-WorW2**

I watch him, dying an old. A Going Man. Marsden Hartley. **CP-HartM**

I watch the filthy light seep through. Hear Me. Philip Levine. **SP-LeviP**

I watch the Indians dancing to help the young corn at Taos pueblo. The old men squat in a ring. New Mexican Mountain. Robinson Jeffers. **CP-JefR2**

I watch the stack tilt on the garth fulfilled. October's Child. John Hewitt. **CP-HewiJ**

I watch'd thee when the foe was at our side. Love and Death. Byron. **CP-Byron**

I Watched a Blackbird. Thomas Hardy. **CP-HardT**

I watched a rosebud very long. Symbols. Christina Georgina Rossetti. **CP-RosC1**

I watched a street gang heading. Jim Carroll. **SP-CarrJ**

I watched an armory combing its bronze bricks. Poem. Frank O'Hara. **SP-OharF**

I watched her face to see which way. Emily Dickinson. **CP-DickE**

I watched my father's friends. Makings. Gary Snyder. **CP-SnydG**

I watched the Moon around the House. Emily Dickinson. **CP-DickE**

I watched the old barn lean. The Farm. Gary Gildner. **SP-GildG**

I watched the prairie repeat itself. Round Trip. Stephen Dunn. **SP-DunnS**

I watched the secret. For Ezra Pound. Jim Carroll. **SP-CarrJ**

I watched the seeds come down this afternoon. At a Country Hotel. Howard Nemerov. **CP-NemeH**

I watched them from the window, thy children at their play. Arthur Hugh Clough. **SP-ClouA**

I watched, upon a vase's rim. The Round. Walter de la Mare. **CP-DeLaW**

I watched your houseboat, young patrician. The Island. Alun Lewis. **CP-LewiA**

I watches me climb. First Flight. Daniel Gerard Hoffman. **SP-HoffD**

I wayfared at the nadir of the sun. Murmurs in the Gloom. Thomas Hardy. **CP-HardT**

I wear no badge; no tinsel star. Ralph Waldo Emerson. **CP-EmerR**

I wear them. They help me. But I. Glasses. John Updike. **CP-UpdiJ**

I weary of my life / Thro' the long sultry day. Of My Life. Christina Georgina Rossetti. **CP-RosC3**

I weave for the Lamp of Evening. Emily Dickinson. **SP-DickE**

I weep for Adonais—he is dead! Adonais; An Elegy on the Death of John Keats. Percy Bysshe Shelley. **CP-ShelP**

I Weep, Fountain of Jazer. Charles Olson. **CP-OlsoC**

I well remember / A time when. Hymn. Alice Walker. **CP-WalkA**

I well remember Elias Gove, or at least I think I do. Elias Gove—or, The Second Coming. Marsden Hartley. **CP-HartM**

I went / into / his. Tom's Attempt to Seduce Big Brother Steve. James Schuyler. **CP-SchuJ**

I Went. Pablo Neruda, *tr. fr. Spanish by* Ben Belitt. **SP-NeruP**

I went and stood outside myself. At a Seaside Town in 1869. Thomas Hardy. **CP-HardT**

I Went Back. Archie Randolph Ammons. **SP-AmmoA**

I went back in the alley. Homecoming. Langston Hughes. **SP-HughL**

I went by footpath and by stile. Paying calls. Thomas Hardy. **CP-HardT**

I went by star and planet shine. The Well-Beloved. Thomas Hardy. **CP-HardT**

I went by the Druid stone. The Shadow on the Stone. Thomas Hardy. **CP-HardT**

I went disguised in it. Incertus. Seamus Heaney. **SP-HeanS**

I went down / Into the cavern. All the Way Down. Thomas Merton. **CP-MertT**

I Went Down into the Desert. Nicholas Vachel Lindsay. *See* I Went Down into the Desert to Meet Elijah.

I Went Down into the Desert to Meet Elijah. Nicholas Vachel Lindsay.

(I Went Down into the Desert.) **CP-LindV**

I went down not long ago. Tecumseh. Mary Oliver. **SP-OlivM**

I went down to the place where I knew she lay waiting. The Night Comes On. Leonard Cohen. **CP-CoheL**

I went down to the port with my wife. The Unclean Start. Leonard Cohen. **CP-CoheL**

I went down to the river. Life Is Fine. Langston Hughes. **SP-HughL**

I went farther and deeper. John Haines. *Fr.* The Mirror. **SP-HainJ**

I went in Bangor to the Sunday School. Our Sunday School Teacher. John Hewitt. **CP-HewiJ**

I went in the forest to look for a sign. Green Valentine Blues. Allen Ginsberg. **CP-GinsA**

I went into a public-'ouse to get a pint o' beer. Tommy. Rudyard Kipling. **CP-KiplR**

I went into my parlor. The Irate Songster. Kenneth Patchen. **CP-PatcK**

I went into the deserts of dim sleep—. Fragment: The Deserts of Dim Sleep. Percy Bysshe Shelley. **CP-ShelP**

I Went into the Maverick Bar. Gary Snyder. **CP-SnydG**

I went into the wood one day. Fairy Story. Stevie Smith. **CP-SmitS**

I went out / from the news of your illness. Three Poems for James Wright. Mary Oliver. **SP-OlivM**

I went out alone. *fr.* Words for Music Perhaps. William Butler Yeats. **CP-YeatW**

I went out early. Geoffrey Hill. *Fr.* The Pentecost Castle. **CP-HillG**

I went out in the naked light. Kathleen Jessie Raine. **SP-RainK**

I went out to the hazel wood. The Song of Wandering Aengus. William Butler Yeats. **CP-YeatW**

I went out walking. On Mother's Day. Grace Paley. **CP-PaleG**

I went timid to that town. The Carnival Inside. Richard Hugo. **CP-HugoR**

I went to a party / out in Hollywood. Here's to Adhering. Maya Angelou. **SP-AngeM**

I went to Egypt to escape. The Cuban Doctor. Wallace Stevens. **CP-StevW**

I went to find the pot of gold. The Search. Shel Silverstein. **SP-SilS2**

I went to Heaven. Emily Dickinson. **CP-DickE**

I went to his fortieth birthday. Wystan Auden. James Schuyler. **CP-SchuJ**

I went to look for Joy. Joy. Langston Hughes. **SP-HughL**

I went to ma daddy. Hard Daddy. Langston Hughes. **SP-HughL**

I went to school when I was four or five. I Go to School. John Hewitt. **CP-HewiJ**

I Went to See Irving Babbitt. Richard Eberhart. **CP-EberR**

I went to thank Her. Emily Dickinson. **CP-DickE**

I went to the bird. What the Bird with the Human Head Knew. Anne Sexton. **CP-SextA**

I went to the cupboard, I opened the door. Song: Not There. Randall Jarrell. **CP-JarrR**

I went to the edge of the wood. Horns. John Haines. **SP-HainJ**

I went to the field to break. Unsteady Yellow. Tess Gallagher. **SP-GallT**

I went to the Garden of Love. The Garden of Love. William Blake. **CP-BlakW** *Fr.* Songs of Experience.

I went to the Gypsy's. Ballad of the Gypsy. Langston Hughes. **SP-HughL**

I went to the opera and God was not there. Faustus and I. Anne Sexton. **CP-SextA**

I went to the physician to complain. Bursting Rapture. Robert Frost. **CP-FrosR**

I went to turn the grass once after one. The Tuft of Flowers. Robert Frost. **CP-FrosR**

I went under cover of night. Nicodemus. Howard Nemerov. **CP-NemeH**

I went up the hill / At moonrise. The Despairing Man Draws a Serpent. Pablo Antonio Cuadra, *tr. fr. Spanish* by Thomas Merton. **CP-MertT**

I went walkin'. Blue Bayou. Langston Hughes. **SP-HughL**

I went walking (said the girl). Septentrion. René Char, *tr. fr. French* by Thomas Merton. **CP-MertT**

I went way back and asked the old. Origin. Howard Nemerov. **CP-NemeH**

I went with General Logans men and we. Gary Gildner. *Fr.* Letters from Vicksburg. **SP-GildG**

I went with two ladies. A 56 Year Old Poem. Charles Bukowski. **SP-BukC1**

I, which that am the sorwefulleste man. Complaynt d'Amours. Geoffrey Chaucer. **CP-ChauG**

I whispered, "I am too young." Brown Penny. William Butler Yeats. **CP-YeatW**

I, who accompanied with faithful pace. Introduction. William Wordsworth. *Fr.* Ecclesiastical Sonnets. **CP-WorW2**

I who all the winter through. Robert Louis Stevenson. **CP-StevR**

I, who doe feele the highest part of griefe. Mary Sidney, Countess of Montgomery Wroth. *Fr.* Part 1. *Fr.* Urania. **CP-WrotM**

I who e're while the happy Garden sung. Book I. John Milton. *Fr.* Paradise Regained [*or* Regain'd]. **CP-MiltJ**

I who erewhile the happy Garden sung. John Milton. **PeECV** *Fr.* Book I. *Fr.* Paradise Regained [*or* Regain'd]. **CP-MiltJ**

I, who had been erased. Departure from the Bush. Margaret Atwood. **SP-AtwM1**

I who have favour'd many, come to be. To the Most Learned, Wise, and Arch-Antiquary, M. John Selden. Robert Herrick. **CP-HerrR**

I, who have the gift of almost seeing. *Country Gentleman, The.* Alun Lewis. *Fr.* Poems from the Chinese. **CP-LewiA**

I who picked up the neat. Eleanor's Letters. Donald Hall. **CP-HallD**

I who was promised. Richard Shelton. *Fr.* Dry Season. **SP-ShelR**

I who was young so long. On His Pitiable Transformation. Robert Louis Stevenson. **CP-StevR**

I who witnessed the nail's desire. Valediction. Richard Shelton. **SP-ShelR**

I whom Apollo sometime visited. Robert Louis Stevenson. **CP-StevR**

I Will. The Beatles. **CP-Beatl**

I will accept thy will to do and be. A Bruised Reed Shall He Not Break. Christina Georgina Rossetti. **CP-RosC1**

I will and yet I may not. The Ballad of Will. Sir Thomas Wyatt. **CP-WyatT**

I Will Arise. Christina Georgina Rossetti. **CP-RosC2**

I Will Arise and Go Now. Ogden Nash. **CP-NashO**

I will arise and go now, and go to Innisfree. The Lake Isle of Innisfree. William Butler Yeats. **CP-YeatW**

I will be / M o ving in the Street of her. Edward Estlin Cummings. **CP-CummE**

I will be drunk and down with wine. Hafiz, *tr.* by Ralph Waldo Emerson. **CP-EmerR** *Fr.* Odes.

I will be faithful to thee; aye, I will! Thomas Hardy. *Fr.* She, to Him. **CP-HardT**

I will be happy if but for once. Dubiety. Robert Browning. **CP-BroR2**

I will be lonely at half past dead. Knowing. Isabella Gardner. **CP-GardI**

I will be short, and having quickly hurl'd. To M. Leonard Willan His Peculiar Friend. Robert Herrick. **CP-HerrR**

I will be silent, Mother earth. Earth's Praises. Wystan Hugh Auden. **CP-AudWJ**

I will be the gladdest thing. Afternoon on a Hill. Edna St. Vincent Millay. **CP-MillE**

I will become smaller. As I Grow Older. Richard Shelton. **SP-ShelR**

I will bless the Lord at all times. Psalm 34. Bible, *O.T. Fr.* Psalms. **CP-Psal**

I will bring you great harps in Heaven. Harps in Heaven. Nicholas Vachel Lindsay. **CP-LindV**

I will build you a house. Tou Wan Speaks to Her Husband Liu Sheng. Rita Dove. **SP-DoveR**

I will climb thirty steps to my room. Ugly Sister. Philip Larkin. **CP-LarkP**

I Will Come and Heal Him. Christina Georgina Rossetti. **CP-RosC2**

I will commit. Words. Daniel Gerard Hoffman. **SP-HoffD**

I will confess. An Hymne to Love. Robert Herrick. **CP-HerrR**

I will consider the outnumbering dead. Merlin. Geoffrey Hill. **CP-HillG**

I will cultivate within. Edward Estlin Cummings. **CP-CummE**

I will enjoy thee now, my Celia, come. A Rapture. Thomas Carew. **CP-CareT**

I will extol thee, my God, O king. Psalm 145. Bible, *O.T. Fr.* Psalms. **CP-Psal**

I will extol thee, O Lord; for thou hast lifted me up. Psalm 30. Bible, *O.T. Fr.* Psalms. **CP-Psal**

I will forgive you everything. Nature and Free Animals. Stevie Smith. **CP-SmitS**

I will get a new string for my fiddle. A Merrymaking in Question. Thomas Hardy. **CP-HardT**

I will get up and go to Marble country. Thomas Merton. *Fr.* Cables to the Ace. **CP-MertT**

I will give you all my keys. Tease. David Herbert Lawrence. **CP-LawrD**

I will go to my mother's house. The Blue Dress. Siv Cedering Fox. **SP-CedeS**

I will grieve alone. In Response to a Rumor that the Oldest Whorehouse in Wheeling, West Virginia, Has Been Condemned. James Wright. **CP-WrigJ**

I will haunt these States. A Vow. Allen Ginsberg. **CP-GinsA**

I will have to accept women. This Form of Life Needs Sex. Allen Ginsberg. **CP-GinsA**

I will keep you and bring hands to hold you against a great hunger. Mascots. Carl Sandburg. **CP-SandC**

I will let loose against you the fleet-footed vines. Mowgli's Song against People. Rudyard Kipling. **CP-KiplR** *Fr.* Letting in the Jungle. *Fr.* The Second Jungle Book.

I will lift up mine eyes unto the hills. Psalm 121. Bible, *O.T.* **AWP; FaPON; TrGrPo; WGRP** *Fr.* Psalms. **CP-Psal**

I Will Lift Up Mine Eyes unto the Hills ("I am pale with such desire"). Christina Georgina Rossetti. **CP-RosC1**

I Will Lift Up Mine Eyes unto the Hills ("When sick of life and all the world"). Christina Georgina Rossetti. **CP-RosC2**

(Chiefest among Ten Thousand, The.) **CP-RosC3**

I will love thee, O Lord, my strength. Psalm 18. Bible, *O.T. Fr.* Psalms. **CP-Psal**

I will make an homage. Sexual Disappointments. Dabney Stuart. **SP-StuaD**

I will make you brooches and toys for your delight. Robert Louis Stevenson. **CP-StevR**

I will marry this clump of flowers. The Kadava Kumbis Devise a Way to Marry for Love. Rita Dove. **SP-DoveR**

I will never be only a Lesbian. Marilyn Hacker. **SP-HackM** *Fr.* Taking Notice.

I will never leave you darling. The Starling. Stevie Smith. **CP-SmitS**

I will no longer kiss. On Himselfe. Robert Herrick. **CP-HerrR**

I Will Not Be Your Sickness. Marge Piercy. **SP-PierM**

I will not build on yonder mount. The Dean's Reasons for Not Building at Drapier's Hill. Jonathan Swift. **CP-SwifJ**

I WILL NOT CARE FOR TIME. FORBIDDING ME. Time Hinder Not Me; His Arms Reach Here and There. Muriel Rukeyser. **CP-RukeM**

I Will Not Dare to Ask One Question. Richard Eberhart. **CP-EberR**

I will not faint, but trust in God. In Patience. Christina Georgina Rossetti. **CP-RosC3**

I will not go down under the ground. Let Me Die in My Footsteps. "Bob Dylan." **CP-DylaB**

I will not go with you where dark spears scatter. Wife. Louise McNeill. **SP-McNeL**

I will not grace you with a name. . . Even "you," however modest the convention: not here. One of the Muses. Charles Kenneth Williams. **CP-WillC**

I will not hesitate to speak the word. Ralph Waldo Emerson. **CP-EmerR**

I will not live out of me. Ralph Waldo Emerson. **CP-EmerR**

I will not look in it again. Fear of *Gray's Anatomy*. Brendan Galvin. **SP-GalvB**

I will not love one minute more, I swear. Love Turned to Hatred. Sir John Suckling. **CP-SuckJ**

I will not play at tug o' war. Hug o' War. Shel Silverstein. **SP-SilS2**

I will not shut me from my kind. Tennyson. **EnVR; FHYEP** *Fr.* In Memoriam A. H. H. **CP-TennA**

I will not think of her in her coffin. The Virgin. Richard Eberhart. **CP-EberR**

I will not walk on that road again. The Goshawk. John Haines. **SP-HainJ**

I will now sing a song for you, Miss Lorence. Another Day (I will now sing). Muriel Rukeyser. **CP-RukeM**

I will paint her as I see her. A Portrait. Elizabeth Barrett Browning. **CP-BroEB**

I Will Praise the Lord at All Times. William Cowper. *Fr.* Olney Hymns. **CP-CowpW**

I will praise thee ev'ry day. O Lord I Will Praise Thee. William Cowper. *Fr.* Olney Hymns. **CP-CowpW**

I will praise thee, O Lord, with my whole heart. Psalm 9. Bible, *O.T.* **FaPON** *Fr.* Psalms. **CP-Psal**

I will praise thee with my whole heart. Psalm 138. Bible, *O.T. Fr.* Psalms. **CP-Psal**

I will put Chaos into fourteen lines. Edna St. Vincent Millay. **CP-MillE**

I will put Truth in a box because. Colney Hatch. John Hewitt. **CP-HewiJ**

I will read ashes for you, if you ask me. Fire Pages. Carl Sandburg. **CP-SandC**

I will remember well. To the Dead Owner of a Gym. Thom Gunn. **CP-GunnT**

I will remember what I was. I am sick of rope and chain. Rudyard Kipling. **CP-KiplR** *Fr.* Toomai of the Elephants. *Fr.* The Jungle Book.

I will rise / from my troth. Wine Bowl. Hilda Doolittle. **CP-DoolH**

I will scrawl on the walls of the night. Sharaku Dreams. John Gould Fletcher. **SP-FletJ**

I Will Sing a Joyous Song. William Carlos Williams. **CP-WilW1**

I will sing of mercy and judgment. Psalm 101. Bible, *O.T. Fr.* Psalms. **CP-Psal**

I will sing of the mercies of the Lord for ever. Psalm 89. Bible, *O.T. Fr.* Psalms. **CP-Psal**

I Will Sing Praise, *sel., vv. 1–2*. Bible, *O.T. See* Psalm 9: "I will praise thee, O Lord. . . ."

I will sing you a song of Los. the Eternal Prophet. The Song of Los. William Blake. **CP-BlakW**

I Will Sing You One-O. Robert Frost. **CP-FrosR**

I will take your heart. To Artina. Langston Hughes. **SP-HughL**

I will teach you my townspeople. Tract. William Carlos Williams. **CP-WilW1**

I will tell you what Joseph of Arimathea. William Blake. **CP-BlakW**

I will tell you when they met. One Day. Christina Georgina Rossetti. **CP-RosC1**

I will wade out. Edward Estlin Cummings. **CP-CummE**

I will wait here in the fields. Stay Home. Wendell Berry. **CP-BerrW**

I will walk out today. Blessing. James McAuley. *Fr.* Requiem. **SP-McAuJ**

I Will Write. Robert Ranke Graves. **CP-GravR**

I will write you a letter. I Think. James Schuyler. **CP-SchuJ**

I, William Lyon Mackenzie King. The Visions of Mackenzie King. John Updike. **CP-UpdiJ**

I Wish. Stevie Smith. **CP-SmitS**

I wish a storm would. Hurricane and Eclipse. Jim Morrison. **SP-MorrJ**

I wish de day was neah at han'. Goin' Home. Paul Laurence Dunbar. **CP-DunbP**

I wish for you that when you wake. Aubade. Donald Davie. **CP-DavDo**

I wish I could remember the [*or* that] first day. Christina Georgina Rossetti. **BLPL; BoLoP; FaBoBe; GBL; LPA; Son** *Fr.* Monna Innominata. **CP-RosC2**

(First Day, The.) **BLPL; BoLoP; FaBoBe; GBL; LPA**

(Sonnet: "I wish I could remember the first day.")

I wish I could teach you how ugly. On Flunking a Nice Boy out of School. John Ciardi. **SP-CiarJ**

I wish I had been at Rodmell. Virginia Woolf. James Schuyler. **CP-SchuJ**

I Wish I Knew a Woman. David Herbert Lawrence. **CP-LawrD**

I wish I might say one liquid word. Emily Dickinson. **SP-DickE**

I wish I was a gentleman. True Democracy. David Herbert Lawrence. **CP-LawrD**

I wish I were a little bird. Christina Georgina Rossetti. **CP-RosC3**

I wish I were a Thibetan monk. Away from It All. Ogden Nash. **CP-NashO**

I wish it were over the terrible pain. Introspective. Christina Georgina Rossetti. **CP-RosC3**

I wish it were spring in the world. Craving for Spring. David Herbert Lawrence. **CP-LawrD**

I wish it were the nineteen-fifties. Nostalgia for Edith Sitwell. Richard Eberhart. **CP-EberR**

I wish my mother could see me now, with a fence-post under my arm. M. I. Rudyard Kipling. **CP-KiplR**

I wish my past had been. Driving Gloves. Diane Wakoski. **SP-WakoD**

I wish not to lie here. Iona: the Graves of the Kings. Robinson Jeffers. **CP-JefR2**

I wish one could be sure the suffering. Emily Dickinson. **SP-DickE**

I wish people, when you sit near them. Talk. David Herbert Lawrence. **CP-LawrD**

I wish that when you died last May. May and Death. Robert Browning. **CP-BroR1**

I wish the long ship Argo had never passed that perilous channel between the Symplegades. Medea. Robinson Jeffers. **CP-JefR3**

I wish the rent. Little Lyric (of Great Importance). Langston Hughes. **SP-HughL**

I wish thy lot, now bad, still worse my friend. To a Friend in Distress. William Cowper, *tr. fr. the Latin of Owen.* **CP-CowpW**

I wish to God I never saw you, Mag. Mag. Carl Sandburg. **CP-SandC**

I wish to own only the warmth. Thief. Alice Walker. **CP-WalkA**

I wish to see it never. Concerning His Old Home. Thomas Hardy. **CP-HardT**

I wish to tune my quivering lyre. *Fr. the Greek of Anacreon.* Byron. **CP-Byron**

I wish we once were wedded,—then I must be true. Look on This Picture and on This. Christina Georgina Rossetti. **CP-RosC3**

I wish you triumphs that are yours already. For Marianne Moore's Birthday. Kay Boyle. **CP-BoylK**

I wish you were a pleasant wren. Child's Talk in April. Christina Georgina Rossetti. **CP-RosC1**

I wish your body were in the grave. A Song of Sour Grapes. Countee Cullen. **CP-CullC**

I wish'd the world a blindness. George Meredith. **CP-MerG2**

I wished, all the mild days of middle March. John Berryman. *Fr.* Sonnets to Chris. **CP-BerrJ**

I wist not that I had the pow'r to sing. A Question. Paul Laurence Dunbar. **CP-DunbP**

I wist not what to wish, yet sure thought I. Anne Bradstreet. **PBWP** *Fr.* Contemplations. **CP-BradA**

I with foolish mind and heedless zeal formerly. John Milton, *tr. fr. Latin by* John T. Shawcross. **CP-MiltJ**

("Such were the trophies, that, in earlier days.") CP-CowpW, *tr. by* William Cowper;

I, with legs crossed along the daylight, watch. Prelude. Derek Walcott. **CP-WalcD**

I within me holding. Alun Lewis. *Fr.* The Soldier. **CP-LewiA**

I woke / Just about daybreak, and fell back. Poems to a Brown Cricket. James Wright. **CP-WrigJ**

I woke and found a fire in my desk. The Fire. Martin Edmunds. **SP-EdmuM**

I woke at six. Birds cried from the roofs. What I Wanted to Say. Stephen Berg. **SP-BergS**

I woke before the morning, I was happy all the day. A Good Boy. Robert Louis Stevenson. **CP-StevR**

I woke from a first-day-of-snow dream. A Dream on the Night of First Snow. Robert Bly. **SP-BlyR**

I woke in the mornin', wand'rin'. Black Crow Blues. "Bob Dylan." **CP-DylaB**

I woke in the night and heard the wind, and it blowing half a gale. Edna St. Vincent Millay. **CP-MillE**

I woke to a shout: "I am Alpha and Omega." Gog. Ted Hughes. **SP-HughT**

I woke to the sound of rain, and lay there. Urgencies. Stephen Dunn. **SP-DunnS**

I woke up. From A Go to B, If You Can Find It. Diane Wakoski. **SP-WakoD**

I woke up (merely) and found. Glass Globe. Archie Randolph Ammons. **SP-AmmoA**

I woke up this mornin'. George Jackson. "Bob Dylan." **CP-DylaB**

I woke up this mornin'. Sylvester's Dying Bed. Langston Hughes. **SP-HughL**

I woke up tousled, one strap falling. Little Poems. John Updike. **CP-UpdiJ**

I wol biwaille in manere of tragedie. The Monk's Tale. Geoffrey Chaucer. *Fr.* The Canterbury Tales. **CP-ChauG**

I wonder / as I am driving to the Market Basket. Cobra Lilies in the Supermarket. Diane Wakoski. **SP-WakoD**

I Wonder. Charles Henri Ford. **SP-FordC**

I wonder about the trees. The Sound of Trees. Robert Frost. **CP-FrosR**

I wonder by my troth, what thou, and I. The Good Morrow. John Donne. **CP-DonnJ**

I wonder, can the night go by. Excursion Train. David Herbert Lawrence. **CP-LawrD**

I wonder do you feel today. Two in the Campagna. Robert Browning. **CP-BroR1**

I wonder how long it has been. The Calendar in the Attic. John Gould Fletcher. **SP-FletJ** *Fr.* The Ghosts of an Old House.

I wonder how many old men last winter. The Minneapolis Poem. James Wright. **CP-WrigJ**

I Wonder How Many People in This City. Leonard Cohen. **CP-CoheL**

I wonder if his appetite was good? Byron. **OAEL-2** *Fr.* Canto the Fifth. *Fr.* Don Juan. **CP-Byron**

I wonder if the sap is stirring yet. The First Spring Day. Christina Georgina Rossetti. **CP-RosC1**

I wonder if with you, as it is with me. After Many Days. David Herbert Lawrence. **CP-LawrD**

I wonder what they called. Spray. Carl Sandburg. **CP-SandC**

I wonder whether the Girls are mad. William Bond. William Blake. **CP-BlakW**

I wonder whether writing poems. The Bear on the Unicycle. Robert Pack. **SP-PackR**

I wonder whether you would make. Camberley. Sir John Betjeman. **CP-BetjJ**

I wonder why Proust should have thought. Phèdre. Stevie Smith. **CP-SmitS**

I wondered about their things. Were they large or small? A Huddle of Need. John Berryman. **CP-BerrJ**

I wondered ever too what my fate would be. The Search. John Berryman. **CP-BerrJ**

I wondered if the others felt. The Search Party. William Matthews. **SP-MattW**

I wondered what had. They. Robert Creeley. **CP-CreeR**

I won't be at this boring poetry reading / again! Ann Arbor Song. Ted Berrigan. **SP-BerrT**

I won't go with you. I want to stay with Grandpa! My Last Afternoon with Uncle Devereux Winslow. Robert Lowell. **SP-LoweR**

I Won't Hatch. Shel Silverstein. **SP-SilS2**

I won't take a lot of shit. George Washington Writes Home About Harvesting His Hemp. Diane Wakoski. **SP-WakoD**

I wore a garland of the briar that put me now in awe. Scallop Song. Anne Waldman. **SP-WaldA**

I work all day, and get half-drunk at night. Aubade. Philip Larkin. **CP-LarkP**

I work in my garden. Roy Fisher. **SP-FishR** *Fr.* New Diversions.

I work to drive the awe away. Emily Dickinson. **SP-DickE**

I worked by will then, he. Wendell Berry. *Fr.* Rising. **CP-BerrW**

I worked for a woman. Madam and Her Madam. Langston Hughes. **SP-HughL**

I worked for chaff and earning Wheat. Emily Dickinson. **CP-DickE**

I Worked No Wile to Meet You. Thomas Hardy. **CP-HardT**

I worship the greatest first. Hippolytus Temporizes. Hilda Doolittle. **CP-DoolH**

I worshiped there, and named it only love. Loss. David Markson. **CP-MarkD**

I woudn't / embarrass you. Song. Robert Creeley. **CP-CreeR**

I would at this late hour little as may be. Compline. John Berryman. **CP-BerrJ**

I would be ignorant as the dawn. The Dawn. William Butler Yeats. **CP-YeatW**

I would be married, but I'd[e] have no wife. On Marriage. Richard Crashaw. **CP-CrasR**

I would be one with the dark, dark earth. The Traveller-Heart. Nicholas Vachel Lindsay. **CP-LindV**

I would be the bounding deer. Song. George Meredith. **CP-MerG2**

I would beat out your face in brass. Face. Carl Sandburg. **CP-SandC**

I would begin by explaining. Poem for D. H. Lawrence. Robert Creeley. **CP-CreeR**

I would build a cloudy House. The House of Clouds. Elizabeth Barrett Browning. **CP-BroEB**

I would build my house of crystal. In the Long Night. Robert Frost. *Fr.* Five Nocturnes. **CP-FrosR**

I would call Attila on his little horse. Attila. David Herbert Lawrence. **CP-LawrD**

I would distil a cup. Emily Dickinson. **CP-DickE**

I would have each couple turn. The Dance. Wendell Berry. **CP-BerrW**

I would have gone; God bade me stay. Weary in Well-Doing. Christina Georgina Rossetti. **CP-RosC1**

I would have her go to school. For Deirdre. John Hewitt. **CP-HewiJ**

I would have left the me that was then. Shell. Daniel Gerard Hoffman. **SP-HoffD**

I would have taken this road on sight. The Braes. Richard Hugo. **CP-HugoR**

I would have touched the heavenly key. Emily Brontë. **CP-BronE**

I Would I Were a Careless Child. Byron. **CP-Byron**

I would I were the drop of rain. Song. George Meredith. **CP-MerG1**

I would I were with Jean. George Meredith. **CP-MerG2**

I would like a few men to be at peace with. Compari. David Herbert Lawrence. **CP-LawrD**

I would like my last poem thus. My Last Poem. Manuel Bandeira, *tr. fr. Portuguese by* Elizabeth Bishop. **CP-BishE**

I would like my love to die, *Author's own English vers. of his* "Je voudrais que mon amour meure." Samuel Beckett. **CP-BeckS**

I would like to bury. The Fury of Hating Eyes. Anne Sexton. *Fr.* The Furies. **CP-SextA**

I would like to lose my faith in this poet. *see also* It's Probably Spring. Leonard Cohen. **CP-CoheL**

I would like to remind / the management. The Music Crept by Us. Leonard Cohen. **CP-CoheL**

I would like to sleep with deer. A Moral Poem Freely Accepted from Sappho. James Wright. **CP-WrigJ**

I would like to watch you sleeping. Variation on the Word *Sleep*. Margaret Atwood. **SP-AtwM2**

I would liken you. Ardella. Langston Hughes. **SP-HughL**

I would live all my life in nonchalance and insouciance. Introspective Reflection. Ogden Nash. **CP-NashO**

I would live happy. Sweeney Astray. Seamus Heaney. **SP-HeanS**

I would make all as single as a song. To William Carlos Williams. Richard Eberhart. **CP-EberR**

I would never have sold. Youth and Age. Frank Templeton Prince. **CP-PrinF**

I would not be a king—enough. Fragment. Percy Bysshe Shelley. **CP-ShelP**

"I Would Not Change For Thine." William Carlos Williams. **CP-WilW2**

I would not despoil this page. Flow of Thought. Richard Eberhart. **CP-EberR**

I would not give the winter for a rose. In Wintertime. Allen Tate. *Fr.* The Progress of Œnia. **CP-TateA**

I would not if I could undo my past. They Desire a Better Country. Christina Georgina Rossetti. **CP-RosC1**

I would not paint—a picture. Emily Dickinson. **CP-DickE**

I would not run from the holocaust. Fly into the Sun. "Lou Reed." **SP-ReedL**

I would not sin, in this half-playful strain. The Tent on the Beach. John Greenleaf Whittier. **CP-WhitJ**

I would not wish to sit. Between Two Prisoners. James Dickey. **CP-DickJ**

I would rather look down. From a Book. William Carlos Williams. **CP-WilW1**

I would rather sit still in a state of peace on a stone. Choice. David Herbert Lawrence. **CP-LawrD**

I would that folk forgot me quite. Tess's Lament. Thomas Hardy. **CP-HardT**

I would that we were, my beloved, white birds on the foam of the sea! The White Birds. William Butler Yeats. **CP-YeatW**

I would the gift I offer here. Dedication. John Greenleaf Whittier. **CP-WhitJ**

I would the saints could hear our prayers! Divine and Human Pleading. Christina Georgina Rossetti. **CP-RosC3**

I would to God I were quenched and fed. The Anguish. Edna St. Vincent Millay. **CP-MillE**

I would to God, that mine old age might have. His Wish to God. Robert Herrick. **CP-HerrR**

I would to heaven that I were so much clay. Fragment. Byron. **CTC; FiP; NAEL-2; NOBL; NoP; OAEL-2; OxBSP; PrIm** *Fr.* Don Juan. **CP-Byron**

I wouldn't know how rare they come these days. A Recognition. May Sarton. **SP-SartM**

I wouldn't much object, if I were black. A Negro Cemetery Next to a White One. Howard Nemerov. **CP-NemeH**

I wouldn't say it was a particularly low time, it was. Overhead Mirrors. Charles Bukowski. **SP-BukC3**

I wound myself in a white cocoon of singing. The Dragonfly. Edna St. Vincent Millay. **CP-MillE**

I wrastle not with rage. Robert Southwell. **OBF** *Fr.* Content and Ri[t]ch[e]. **CP-SoutR**

I wrestled with my father in my dream. Jacob and the Angel. John Hewitt. **CP-HewiJ**

I Write For. John Hewitt. **CP-HewiJ**

I write for antiquity. Enemy Number One. Carl Sandburg. **CP-SandC**

I write in the midst of Sweet-Peas. Emily Dickinson. **SP-DickE**

I write my name as one. An Autograph. John Greenleaf Whittier. **CP-WhitJ**

I write now in English and now in Scots. The Caledonian Antisyzygy. "Hugh MacDiarmid." **SP-MacDH**

I write the lips of the moon upon her shoulders. In a temple of. Not Many Kingdoms Left. Kenneth Patchen. **CP-PatcK**

I write the Rascal thanks till he & I. On H[ayley] the Pick Thank. William Blake. **CP-BlakW**

I write these lines to cripple the dead. Shorts / Excerpts. Bill Knott. **SP-KnotB**

I write this for your eyes and ears and heart. Things About You. Tom Clark. **SP-ClarT**

I Write This Upon the Last Drink's Hammer. Charles Bukowski. **SP-BukC2**

I write to avenge my mother's death. Declaration of Dependence. Barton Sutter. **SP-SuttB**

I write what I know on one side of the paper. Paper II. Carl Sandburg. **CP-SandC**

I write you out of fear. Leonard Nathan. **SP-NathL** *Fr.* To Be Read to Yourself in a Public Place, July 4, 1976.

I write you this out of another province. Letter from the Land of Sinners. Adrienne Rich. **CP-RicAE; SP-RicA2**

I wrote a poem on the mist. Last Answers. Carl Sandburg. **CP-SandC**

I wrote: In the dark cavern of our birth. Malcolm Lowry. **CP-LowrM**

I wrote it over forty years ago. The Bloody Brae. John Hewitt. **CP-HewiJ**

I wrote stubbornly into the evening. Nexus. Rita Dove. **SP-DoveR**

I wrote under a pen-name. Poem (How I Lost My Pen-Name). Bill Knott. **SP-KnotB**

I Years had been from Home. Emily Dickinson. **CP-DickE**

I Yield to My Learned Brother or Is There a Candlestick Maker in the House? Ogden Nash. **CP-NashO**

"I yield you my whole heart, Countess," said he. A Question of Marriage. Thomas Hardy. **CP-HardT**

Iago. Walter de la Mare. **CP-DeLaW**

Iago. Robert Ranke Graves. **CP-GravR**

Iago learned from that old witch, his mother. Iago. Robert Ranke Graves. **CP-GravR**

Iam si rite sequor prisci vestigia facti. Gerard Manley Hopkins. *Fr.* Fragments on St. Winefred. **CP-HopkG**

Iamb; / Ergo sum. Preference of Metre. David Markson. **CP-MarkD**

Ian. Al Young. **CP-YounA**

Ianists and Zoggists Resting between Engagements, in Rocky Terrain. Sketch for the First Exhibition of the New Heroic Art. Roy Fisher. **SP-FishR** *Fr.* On the Neglect of Figure Composition.

Ibn Abbad Described by a Friend (Ibn Qunfud). Thomas Merton. *Fr.* Readings from Ibn Abbad. **CP-MertT**

Ibycus of Samos. Robert Ranke Graves. **CP-GravR**

Icarium Mare. Richard Wilbur. **CP-WilbR**

Icarus. James Liddy. **CP-LiddJ**

Ice. Siv Cedering Fox. **SP-CedeS**

Ice. Robert Lowell. **SP-LoweR**

Ice. Mary Oliver. **SP-OlivM**

Ice. Stephen Spender. **CP-SpenS**

Ice age is here, The. Attention. Adrienne Rich. **CP-RicAE; SP-RicA2**

Ice Cream. Robert Creeley. **CP-CreeR**

Ice Cream at Blauenberg. Charles Tomlinson. **CP-TomlC**

Ice-Cream Wars, The. John Ashbery. **SP-AshbJ**

Ice Eagle, The. Diane Wakoski. **SP-WakoD**

Ice Fishing. Siv Cedering Fox. **SP-CedeS**

Ice from the wings, a rattle against metal. All right, come down. Muriel Rukeyser. **CP-RukeM**

Ice-gate over the land, a shock of closure. Muriel Rukeyser. **CP-RukeM**

Ice Handler. Carl Sandburg. **CP-SandC**

Ice House, The. Lewis Turco. **SP-TurcL**

Ice not / wet not. Blue. Robert Creeley. **CP-CreeR**

Ice on the Highway. Thomas Hardy. **CP-HardT**

Ice Shanties. Gary Gildner. **SP-GildG**

Ice Skin, The. James Dickey. **CP-DickJ**

Ice Storm. Robert Earl Hayden. **CP-HaydR**

Iceberg, The. Randall Jarrell. **CP-JarrR**

Icebergs. Louis MacNeice. **CP-MacNL**

Icebergs italicize the Sea. Emily Dickinson. **SP-DickE**

Iced over soon; it's nothing; we're used to sickness. Ice. Robert Lowell. **SP-LoweR**

Iced with a vanilla. A Meeting of Cultures. Donald Davie. **CP-DavDo**

Icehouse. Barton Sutter. **SP-SuttB**

Icehouse in Summer, The. Howard Nemerov. **CP-NemeH**

Icehouse, Pointe au Baril, Ontario, The. William Matthews. **SP-MattW**

Icehouses lie scattered, The. Icehouse. Barton Sutter. **SP-SuttB**

Iceland. Louis MacNeice. **CP-MacNL**

Iceland Revisited. Wystan Hugh Auden. **CP-AudeW**

Iceman, Again, The. Gilbert Sorrentino. **SP-SorrG**

Ich Dien. Byron. **CP-Byron**

Ichabod[!]. John Greenleaf Whittier. **CP-WhitJ**

Ichetucknee. Richard Eberhart. **CP-EberR**

Ichneumon. Marsden Hartley. **CP-HartM**

Ichneumons are fond of little ichneumons. Some of My Best Friends Are Children. Ogden Nash. **CP-NashO**

Icicles crack and drop. Indianapolis Winter, 1973. Etheridge Knight. *Fr.* Indiana Haiku. **SP-KnigE**

Ickle Me, Pickle Me, Tickle Me Too. Shel Silverstein. **SP-SilS2**

Icon. Leonard Nathan. **SP-NathL**

Icon. Marge Piercy. **SP-PierM**

Iconia. George Meredith. **CP-MerG2**

Icos. Charles Tomlinson. **CP-TomlC**

Icosasphere, The. Marianne Craig Moore. **CP-MoorM**

Icta fenestra Euri flatu stridebat, avarus. Avarus et Plutus. John Gay, *tr. fr.* *English by* William Cowper. **CP-CowpW**

Icy evil that struck his father down, The. El-Hajj Malik El-Shabazz. Robert Earl Hayden. **CP-HaydR**

I'd almost know, the nights I snuck in late. Fifteen to Eighteen. Marilyn Hacker. **SP-HackM**

I'd Die for You. Robert Ranke Graves. **CP-GravR**

I'd forgotten and / how could I ever. Charles Kenneth Williams. **CP-WillC**

I'd give bushels of blooms. Gardening. Archie Randolph Ammons. **SP-AmmoA**

I'd gone for walks upon that land. The Hidden Lane. Wystan Hugh Auden. **CP-AudWJ**

I'd Hate to Be You on That Dreadful Day. "Bob Dylan." **CP-DylaB**

I'd have the silence like a heavy chock. Zip! Donald Davie. **CP-DavDo**

I'd Have You Any Time. "Bob Dylan" *and* George Harrison. **CP-DylaB**

I'd like every girl in the world to have a poem of her own. Yours. Charles Kenneth Williams. **CP-WillC; SP-WillC**

I'd like to / Pull. The Intelligent Sheepman and the New Cars. William Carlos Williams. **CP-WilW2**

I'd like to be able to say a good word for parsley, but I can't. Parsley for Vice-President! Ogden Nash. **CP-NashO**

I'd like to be under the sea. Octopus's Garden. "Ringo Starr." **CP-Beatl**

I'd like to die like this. Crossing on Staten Island Ferry. Kenneth Patchen. **CP-PatcK**

I'd like to linger. Charles Henri Ford. **SP-FordC** *Fr.* Secret Haiku.

I'd like to live on Tulip Street. Passaic, N.J. William Carlos Williams. **CP-WilW2**

I'd Like to Read. Leonard Cohen. **CP-CoheL**

I'd like to see it once. Gravity. Charles Simic. **SP-SimiC**

I'd like to talk about you, Fanny, as a jewel. Fanny's Cold Blue Eyes. Diane Wakoski. **SP-WakoD**

I'd never seen pain so bland. Bud Powell, Paris, 1959. William Matthews. **SP-MattW**

I'd rather / be / suckled by. Swoggled. Archie Randolph Ammons. **SP-AmmoA**

I'd rather be Muriel. Not to Be Printed, Not to Be Said, Not to Be Thought. Muriel Rukeyser. **CP-RukeM**

I'd rather read an account. Song. William Carlos Williams. **CP-WilW2**

I'd rather recollect a setting. Emily Dickinson. **CP-DickE**

I'd ride a cock horse to Banbury Cross. The Absentees. Ogden Nash. **CP-NashO**

I'd seen / their hoofprints in the deep. Five A.M. in the Pinewoods. Mary Oliver. **SP-OlivM**

I'd seen wallpaper—I had buckaroos all over my. Good. William Matthews. **SP-MattW**

I'd tell them to have an unhappy love. Now, If You Were Teaching Creative Writing, He Asked, What Would You Tell Them? Charles Bukowski. **SP-BukC1**

I'd think "wonder / if" if. Edward Estlin Cummings. **CP-CummE**

I'd up / up up. Likely Story. Archie Randolph Ammons. **SP-AmmoA**

I'd want her eyes to fill with wonder. Kenneth Patchen. **CP-PatcK**

Iddio C'illumini! Christina Georgina Rossetti. *Fr.* Il Rosseggiar Dell'Oriente Canzoniere. **CP-RosC3**

Idea. Howard Nemerov. **CP-NemeH**

Idea blazes in darkness, a lonely star. Idea. Howard Nemerov. **CP-NemeH**

Idea of Ancestry, The. Etheridge Knight. **SP-KnigE**

Idea of defence, The. Roy Fisher. **SP-FishR** *Fr.* New Diversions.

Idea of Flying, The. Donald Hall. **CP-HallD**

Idea of justice may be precious, An. Ode. Frank O'Hara. **SP-OharF**

Idea of Order at Key West, The. Wallace Stevens. **CP-StevW**

Idea of the Good, The. James Wright. **CP-WrigJ**

Idea of Trust, The. Thom Gunn. **CP-GunnT**

Idea ran about the world, An. The Return. Muriel Rukeyser. **CP-RukeM**

Ideal and the Real, The. Richard Eberhart. **CP-EberR**

Ideal Landscape. Adrienne Rich. **CP-RicAE; SP-RicA2**

Idealism. Ralph Waldo Emerson. **CP-EmerR**

Ideals are the Fairy Oil. Emily Dickinson. **CP-DickE**

Ideals of Satire, The. Alexander Pope. **FiP** *Fr.* The First Epistle of the Second Book of Horace Imitated. **CP-PopeA**

Ideas go / through most. Course Work. Archie Randolph Ammons. **SP-AmmoA**

Ideas hit life like / planks hitting water. Some skim. Hayden Carruth. **CP-CarHS** *Fr.* The Clay Hill Anthology.

Identities. Paul Muldoon. **SP-MuldP**

Identities. Al Young. **CP-YounA**

Identity of opposites had linked us, The. The Pact. Robert Ranke Graves. **CP-GravR**

Ides of March, The. Richard Eberhart. **CP-EberR**

Idiom of the Hero. Wallace Stevens. **CP-StevW**

Idiot, The. Hart Crane. **CP-CranH**

Idiot. Allen Tate. **CP-TateA**

Idiot bird leaps out and drunken leans, The. Doomsday. Sylvia Plath. **CP-PlatS**

Idiot Boy, The, *parody of* William Wordsworth. Rudyard Kipling. **CP-KiplR** *Fr.* The Muse among the Motors.

Idiot Boy, The. William Wordsworth. **CP-WorW1**

Idiot greens the meadows with his eyes, The. Idiot. Allen Tate. **CP-TateA**

Idiot Joe Prays in Pershing Square and Gets Hauled in for Vagrancy. Edwin Rolfe. **CP-RolfE**

Idiot, last night, I prayed thee but forbear. To Groom Idiot. Ben Jonson. **CP-JonsB**

Idiot Wind. "Bob Dylan." **CP-DylaB**

Idle boys the Sunday never heed, The. Young Rabbits. John Clare. **SP-ClarJ**

Idle dayseye, the laborious wheel, The. 1. Richard Wilbur. **CP-WilbR**

Idle I sat—my book upon my knee. A Dream. Walter de la Mare. **CP-DeLaW**

Idle Pursuits. Alexander Pope. *See* Next, bidding all draw near on bended knees.

Idle Shepherd-Boys, The; or, Dungeon-Ghyll Force. A Pastoral. William Wordsworth. **CP-WorW1**

Idle Talk. Louis MacNeice. **CP-MacNL**

Idleness. Walter de la Mare. **CP-DeLaW**

Idleness gilds an encompassing giantess. The Giantess. Richard Eberhart. **CP-EberR**

Idol. Robert Earl Hayden. *Fr.* An Inference of Mexico. **CP-HaydR**

Idol of Sarapis, The. Clement of Alexandria, *tr. by* Thomas Merton. **CP-MertT** *Fr.* Diatribe Against the Old Gods.

Idrigill. Charles Tomlinson. **CP-TomlC**

Idris—Ilyas: two names / One star, one prophet. Lubnan. Thomas Merton. **CP-MertT**

Idyl: "In a valley late bees with whining gold." Allen Tate. **CP-TateA**

Idyl: "They say to me, 'There is.'" William Carlos Williams. **CP-WilW1**

Idyl: "Wine of the grey sky." William Carlos Williams. **CP-WilW1**

Idyl, An: "Come down, O maid, from yonder mountain height." Tennyson. *See* Come down, O maid, from yonder mountain height.

Idyll: "As a horn of the high moon veers in clear skies over Main Street." Donald Davie. **CP-DavDo**

Idyll: "Door: / PER L'UNIVERSO / is what it says, A." Charles Tomlinson. **CP-TomlC**

Idyll: "Now as from maple to elm the flittermice skitter and twirl." Theodore Roethke. **CP-RoetT**

Idylls of the King. Geoffrey Hill. **FaBoRV; NoAM; PoE** *Fr.* An Apology for the Revival of Christian Architecture in England. **CP-HillG**

Idylls of the King. Tennyson. **CP-TennA**

  Balin and Balan.

    Vivien's Song. **OAEL-2**

  Coming of Arthur, The.

    Merlin's Riddling. **FaBoRV**

  Dedication: "These to His Memory—since he held them dear."

  Gareth and Lynette.

  Geraint and Enid.

    Enid's Song. **FaBoRV**

  Guinevere.

  Holy Grail, The.

    Percivale's Quest. **OAEL-2**

    "When the hermit made an end." **PeVV**

  Lancelot and Elaine.

    Song of Love and Death, The. **OBNC**

  Last Tournament, The.

    Lincolnshire Shores. **FaBoPP**

    Tristram's Song. **FaBoRV**

  Marriage of Geraint, The.

  Merlin and Vivien.

    In Love, If Love Be Love. **CABA; PoEL-5; TrGrPo**

    (All in All.) **ImPo; LiTB; TRV**

    (Vivien's Song.) **FaBoEn; OBNC**

    "There lay she all her length and kiss'd his feet." **EBVVPR**

  Passing of Arthur, The. **FHYEP; NAEL-2; OBNC**

    "And answer made King Arthur, breathing hard." **PeECV,** *ll.* 330–440;

    "And slowly answered Arthur from the barge." **FaBoEH**

    "But now farewell. I am going a long way." **FaBoRV**

    Prayer: "Pray for my soul. More things are wrought by prayer." **WGRP**

    "So all day long the noise of battle rolled." **FaBoRV**

    "Then rose the King and moved his host by night." **PeVV**

  Pelleas and Ettarre. **NAEL-2**

    "Rose, but one, none other rose had I, A." **PoEL-5**

  To the Queen.

Iernë's eyes were glazed and dim. Emily Brontë. **CP-BronE**

If. Edward Estlin Cummings. **CP-CummE**

If. Paul Laurence Dunbar. **CP-DunbP**

If. Rudyard Kipling. **CP-KiplR**

If / one night / I write. The Sickness. Charles Bukowski. **SP-BukC3**

If. Christina Georgina Rossetti. *See* If he would come to-day, to-day, to-day.

If a bush were to speak with a tongue of fire. Burning Bush. Daniel Gerard Hoffman. **SP-HoffD**

If a cheerfulest Elephantangelchild should sit. Edward Estlin Cummings. **CP-CummE; SP-CummE**

If a city / takes its rhythms. St. Louis Out of Time. Audre Lorde. **SP-LordA**

If a clear delight visits you. To C———. Marsden Hartley. **CP-HartM**

If a clear [*or* cleere] fountain[e] still keeping a sad course. Mary Sidney, Countess of Montgomery Wroth. **WPE** *Fr.* Part 1. *Fr.* Urania. **CP-WrotM**

  (Duke's Song, The.) **WPE**

If a cuckoo comes into the village. The Way It Is. Charles Simic. **SP-SimiC**

If a little bit of useless stone. King Amenemhat III. Marsden Hartley. **CP-HartM**

If a man calls himself a poet. Steely Silence. Diane Wakoski. **SP-WakoD**

If a man can find rich consolation, remembering his good deeds and. Catullus. *See* Carmen 76: "If evocations of past kindness shed."

If a man can say of his life or. The Mind's Games. William Carlos Williams. **CP-WilW2**

If a man finds it necessary to eat garbage, he should resist the. Wendell Berry. *Fr.* Prayers and Sayings of the Mad Farmer. **CP-BerrW**

If a man steps on a stranger's foot. Apologies. Chuang Tzu, *tr. fr. Chinese by* Thomas Merton. **CP-MertT**

If a moment out of voiceless history. Same Fragment—Second Look. Marsden Hartley. **CP-HartM**

If a mouse could fly, / Or if a crow could swim. Christina Georgina Rossetti. **CP-RosC2**

If a mouse makes a nest. Salutations to a Mouse. Marsden Hartley. **CP-HartM**

If a Phoenician born I am, what then?, *ad. fr. Greek of* Diogenes. Sir Walter Ralegh. **CP-RaleW**

If a pig wore a wig, / What could we say? Christina Georgina Rossetti. **CP-RosC2**

If a Poem Can Be Headed into Its Proper Current. Kenneth Patchen. **CP-PatcK**

If a stranger passed the tent of Hóseyn, he cried "A churl's!" Muléykeh. Robert Browning. **CP-BroR2**

If a woman wants to be a poet. The Commandments. Erica Jong. **SP-JongE**

If Accusation onely can draw blood. Accusation. Robert Herrick. **CP-HerrR**

If, after attaining Buddhahood, anyone in my land. Amitabha's Vow. Gary Snyder. **CP-SnydG** *Fr.* Burning. *Fr.* Myths and Texts.

If after rude and boisterous seas. The Plaudite, or End of Life. Robert Herrick. **CP-HerrR**

If all a top physicist knows. After Reading a Child's Guide to Modern Physics. Wystan Hugh Auden. **CP-AudeW**

If all rivers are sweet. Pablo Neruda, *tr. fr. Spanish by* Ben Belitt. **SP-NeruP** *Fr.* Question Book.

If all the gentlest-hearted friends I know. An Apprehension. Elizabeth Barrett Browning. **CP-BroEB**

If all the grief and woe and bitterness. *From the Provençal of Bertrans de Born.* Ezra Pound. **SP-PounE**

If all the griefs I am to have. Emily Dickinson. **CP-DickE**

If all the world. Resources. John Milton. **FaBoDD** *Fr.* Comus; a Masque Presented at Ludlow Castle.

If all the world and love [*or* loue] were young. The Nimphs [*or* Nymph's] Reply to the Sheepheard [*or* Shepherd]. Sir Walter Ralegh. **CP-MarlC; CP-RaleW**

If all these Cupids now were blind. Ben Jonson. **CP-JonsB** *Fr.* The Masque of Beauty.

If all this world had no original[l]. Lucretius. **CP-RaleW**, *tr. by* Sir Walter Ralegh; *Fr.* De Rerum Natura (On the Nature of Things).

If all those females who so passionately loved. Film Passion. David Herbert Lawrence. **CP-LawrD**

If all transgressions here should have their pay. Gods Providence. Robert Herrick. **CP-HerrR**

If all were rain and never sun. Christina Georgina Rossetti. **CP-RosC2**

If all you boast of your great art be true. To Alchemists. Ben Jonson. **CP-JonsB**

If amorous faith in heart unfeigned. Sir Thomas Wyatt. **CP-WyatT**

If an expert does not have some problem to vex him, he is unhappy! Active Life. Chuang Tzu, *tr. fr. Chinese by* Thomas Merton. **CP-MertT**

If, antique hateful bird. The Raven. Adrienne Rich. **CP-RicAE**

If any day a promised play. At a Rehearsal of One of J.M.B.'s Plays. Thomas Hardy. **CP-HardT**

If any duck in any brook. Sonatina to Hans Christian. Wallace Stevens. **CP-StevW**

If any God should say. Rebirth. Rudyard Kipling. **CP-KiplR**

If any hath the heart to kill. Thomas Campion. **CP-CampT**

If any man drew near. A Woman Homer Sung. William Butler Yeats. **CP-YeatW**

If any mourn us in the workshop, say. Batteries Out of Ammunition. Rudyard Kipling. **MMA** *Fr.* Epitaphs of the War [1914–1918]. **CP-KiplR**

If any question why we died. Common Form. Rudyard Kipling. **FaBoEE; FaBoTw; PV; PeFWW** *Fr.* Epitaphs of the War [1914–1918]. **CP-KiplR**

If any sink, assure that this, now standing. Emily Dickinson. **CP-DickE**

If any thing delight me for to print. To God. Robert Herrick. **CP-HerrR**

If any vague desire should rise. Tennyson. *Fr.* In Memoriam A. H. H. **CP-TennA**

If any vision should reveal. Tennyson. *Fr.* In Memoriam A. H. H. **CP-TennA**

If anybody says conversation in our day is as good as it was in. Let's Not Play Lotto, Let's Just Talk. Ogden Nash. **CP-NashO**

If anybody's friend be dead. Emily Dickinson. **CP-DickE**

If anything should put an end to This. The Planners. Robert Frost. **CP-FrosR**

If as a flower [*or* flowre] doth spread and die. Employment (1). George Herbert. **CP-HerbG**

If, as mine is, thy life a slumber be. To Mr. R. W. John Donne. **CP-DonnJ**

If as the wind[e]s and waters here below. The Storm. George Herbert. **CP-HerbG**

If, as their ends, their fruits were so, the same. On Bawds and Usurers. Ben Jonson. **CP-JonsB**

If, as they say, some dust thrown in my eyes. Dust in the Eyes. Robert Frost. **CP-FrosR**

If at your coming princes disappear. Samuel Johnson. **CP-JohnS** (Translation of a Distich on the Duke of Modena.) **CP-JohnS**

If Auntie doesn't love me. The Working Man. David Herbert Lawrence. **CP-LawrD**

If being mortised with a dream. Edward Estlin Cummings. **CP-CummE**

If black were truly black not grey. Greyness Is All. Louis MacNeice. **CP-MacNL**

If Blame be my side—forfeit Me. Emily Dickinson. **CP-DickE**

If Blood Were Not as Powerful as It Is. Tess Gallagher. **SP-GallT**

If bright the sun, he tarries. Ralph Waldo Emerson. **CP-EmerR**

If but some vengeful god would call to me. Hap. Thomas Hardy. **CP-HardT**

If by Dull Rhymes Our English Must Be Chained. John Keats. **CP-KeatJ**

If, by general consent, it should be decided. Carmen 108. Catullus. *Fr.* Carmina. **CP-Catul**

If by his torturing, savage foes untraced. The Captive Escaped in the Wilds of America. Addressed to the Hon. Mrs. O'Neill. Charlotte Smith. **CP-SmitC**

If calendars are square holes, something. January 1. John Ciardi. **SP-CiarJ**

If, Calvus, effects of grief. Carmen 96. Catullus. *Fr.* Carmina. **CP-Catul**

If chance assigned [*or* assign'd]. Sir Thomas Wyatt. **CP-WyatT**

If "compression is the first grace of style." To a Snail. Marianne Craig Moore. **CP-MoorM**

If, Cornelius, we entrust our secrets. Carmen 102. Catullus. *Fr.* Carmina. **CP-Catul**

If Croesus over Halys goe, *ad. fr. Latin of* Cicero. Sir Walter Ralegh. **CP-RaleW**

If curses be the wage of love. Ralph Waldo Emerson. **CP-EmerR**

If Cynthia Be a Queen. Sir Walter Ralegh. (If Synthia Be a Queene, a Princes, and Supreame.) **CP-RaleW**

If dead, we cease to be; if total gloom. Human Life; on the Denial of Immortality. Samuel Taylor Coleridge. **CP-ColeS**

If, deare Anthea, my hard fate it be. To Anthea. Robert Herrick. **CP-HerrR**

If, dearest "Dismal," you for once can dine. Toland's Invitation to Dismal to Dine with the Calves' Head Club. Jonathan Swift. **CP-SwifJ**

If Death should claim me for her own to-day. Love-Song. Paul Laurence Dunbar. **CP-DunbP**

If distance lends enchantment to the view. Eight Years After. Donald Davie. **CP-DavDo**

If Dogs Run Free. "Bob Dylan." **CP-DylaB**

If dogs run free, then why not we. If Dogs Run Free. "Bob Dylan." **CP-DylaB**

If down here I chance to die. A Ballade of Burial. Rudyard Kipling. **CP-KiplR**

If dragonflies can mate atop the surface tension. Herd of Buffalo Crossing the Missouri on Ice. William Matthews. **SP-MattW**

If ever against this easy blue and silver. Interruption. Robert Ranke Graves. **CP-GravR**

If ever anyone / was deservedly plagued by a goat under his armpits. Carmen 71. Catullus. *Fr.* Carmina. **CP-Catul**

If ever anyone anywhere, Lesbia, is looking. Carmen 107. Catullus. *Fr.* Carmina. **CP-Catul**

If ever happiness hath lodg'd with man. Consummate Happiness. William Wordsworth. **OBNC** *Fr.* Summer Vacation. *Fr.* The Prelude; Growth of a Poet's Mind [1805 vers.]. **CP-WorW3**

If ever I am old, and all alone. On the Night of a Friend's Wedding. Edwin Arlington Robinson. **CP-RobiE**

If ever I had dreamed of my dead name. To My Friend. Wilfred Owen. **CP-OwenW**

If ever I render back your heart. Song for a Slight Voice. Louise Bogan. **CP-BogaL**

If ever I should condescend to prose. Poetical Commandments. Byron. **FiP; OBRV; OxBoLi; PeLV,** *canto* 1, *stanzas* 204–206; **SeCePo** *Fr.* Canto the First. **EnRP; NAEL-2; NoP; OAEL-2; PoE** *Fr.* Don Juan. **CP-Byron**

If ever I walk to church to wed. The Satin Shoes. Thomas Hardy. **CP-HardT**

If ever joy leave. The Face at the Casement. Thomas Hardy. **CP-HardT**

If ever love had force in huma[i]ne brest? Sonnet 42. Mary Sidney, Countess of Montgomery Wroth. **BWW** *Fr.* Pamphilia to Amphilanthus. **CP-WrotM**

If ever man might him avaunt. Sir Thomas Wyatt. **CP-WyatT**

If ever Pitty were acquainted. Another on [Mr. Herrys]. Richard Crashaw. **CP-CrasR**

If ever the lid gets off my head. Emily Dickinson. **CP-DickE**

If ever there was a beginning. Let There Be Light! David Herbert Lawrence. **CP-LawrD**

If ever two were one, then surely we. To My Dear and Loving Husband. Anne Bradstreet. **CP-BradA**

If ever you meet a rhinoceros. Replies to Challenges to Rhyme. Robert Browning. **CP-BroR2**

If everything happens that can't be done. Edward Estlin Cummings. **CP-CummE; SP-CummE**

If evocations of past kindness shed. Carmen 76. Catullus. *Fr.* Carmina. **CP-Catul**

If external action is effete. The Past Is the Present. Marianne Craig Moore. **CP-MoorM**

If faithful soul[e]s be alike glorified [*or* glorifi'd]. John Donne. **OBS** *Fr.* Divine Meditations. **CP-DonnJ** *Fr.* Holy Sonnets. **CP-DonnJ**

If, fallen in evil days on evil tongue. Byron. **EPCY** *Fr.* Dedication: "Bob Southey! You're a poet--poet-laureate." **CTC; EnRP; OAEL-2; OBSV** *Fr.* Don Juan. **CP-Byron**

If fancy can not erre which vertue guides. Epigramme. Thomas Campion. *Fr.* Observations in the Art of English Poesie. **CP-CampT**

If fancy [*or* fansy] would favour. Sir Thomas Wyatt. **CP-WyatT**

If fate should seal my Death to-morrow. Egotism. A Letter to J.T. Becker. Byron. **CP-Byron**

If feels alright now. Hold Me Tight. The Beatles. **CP-Beatl**

If felt and heard, (unseen) thou dost me please. Upon Deb. Robert Herrick. **CP-HerrR**

If fictive music fails your lyre, confess. What's Good for the Soul is Good for Sales. Richard Wilbur. **NBLV** *Fr.* Flippancies. **CP-WilbR**

If for Silver, or for Gold. Byron. **CP-Byron**

If forgiveness comes / it will be gradual. William Dickey. **SP-DickW** *Fr.* In The Dreaming. **SP-DickW**

If freckles were lovely, and day was night. If. Edward Estlin Cummings. **CP-CummE**

If from the earth we came, it was an earth. Anatomy of Monotony. Wallace Stevens. **CP-StevW**

If from the public way you turn your steps. Michael [A Pastoral Poem]. William Wordsworth. **CP-WorW1**

If Fun Is Fun, Isn't That Enough? Ogden Nash. **CP-NashO**

If gibbets, axes, confiscations, chains. Fragment of a Satire on Satire. Percy Bysshe Shelley. **CP-ShelP**

If Gideon's fleece, which drench'd with dew he found. To a Young Friend. William Cowper. **CP-CowpW**

If God compel thee to this destiny. A Thought for a Lonely Death-Bed. Elizabeth Barrett Browning. **CP-BroEB**

If God has any voice it is the wind. Wind. John Updike. **CP-UpdiJ**

If God has been good enough to give you a poet. Let Them Alone. Robinson Jeffers. **CP-JefR3**

If God is a Dog. Erica Jong. **SP-JongE**

If grief come early. First or Last. Thomas Hardy. **CP-HardT**

If Grief Could Burn Out. Philip Larkin. **CP-LarkP**

If grief dismiss me not to them that rest. Sonnet. Petrarch, *tr. fr. Italian by* William Wordsworth. **CP-WorW1**

If grief for grief can touch thee. Emily Brontë. **CP-BronE**

If groves are choirs and sanctuaried fanes. Children of Darkness. Richard Wilbur. **CP-WilbR**

If Hands Could Free You, Heart. Philip Larkin. **CP-LarkP**

If Hanson Baldwin got a bullet in his brain, outrage. Chicago to Salt Lake by Air. Allen Ginsberg. **CP-GinsA**

If hap it must, that I must see thee lye. To His Book[e]. Robert Herrick. **CP-HerrR**

If he asks, "Is now the time?", it is not the time. Is Now the Time? Robert Ranke Graves. **CP-GravR**

If he could solve the riddle. Sphinx. Robert Earl Hayden. **CP-HaydR**

If He dissolve—then—there is nothing—more. Emily Dickinson. **CP-DickE**

If he go apart. Ralph Waldo Emerson. **CP-EmerR**

If He Had Not Had Two Hands Tattooed on His Chest. Siv Cedering Fox. **SP-CedeS**

If He play, being young and unskilful, for shekhels of silver and gold. Maxim. Rudyard Kipling. **OtMeF** *Fr.* Certain Maxims of Hafiz. **CP-KiplR**

If He Scholars, Let Him Go. Ogden Nash. **CP-NashO**

If he should live a thousand years. A Woman's Trust. Thomas Hardy. **CP-HardT**

If He were living—dare I ask. Emily Dickinson. **CP-DickE**

If he will be heaven after death. Prelude to Objects. Wallace Stevens. **CP-StevW**

If he would come to-day, to-day, to-day. Christina Georgina Rossetti. **CP-RosC3**

(If.) **CP-RosC3**

If heaven were to do again. The Peaceful Shepherd. Robert Frost. **CP-FrosR**

If hell is hot, this must be heaven. Lost in *Antarctica*. Barton Sutter. **SP-SuttB**

If help there is not, but the Muse. Arthur Hugh Clough. **SP-ClouA**

If hope grew on a bush, / And joy grew on a tree. Christina Georgina Rossetti. **CP-RosC2**

If hours be years the twain are blest. At a Hasty Wedding. Thomas Hardy. **CP-HardT**

If I / could count the silence. Song. William Carlos Williams. **CP-WilW2**

If i / or anybody don't. Edward Estlin Cummings. **CP-CummE; SP-CummE**

If I address it to you I have not, have I. Sweetheart. Alice Notley. **SP-NotlA**

If I am really walking with ordinary habit. The Waiting Head. Anne Sexton. **CP-SextA**

If i believe / in death be sure. Edward Estlin Cummings. **CP-CummE**

. . . If I can / remember anything, it. For Helen. Robert Creeley. **CP-CreeR**

If I can stop one Heart from breaking. Emily Dickinson. **CP-DickE**

If I cannot love myself, can you? Flight. Robert Lowell. **SP-LoweR**

If I can't be buried / in one of these passage graves. Carrowkeel. Brendan Galvin. **SP-GalvB**

If I can't hope then to hell with it. Entre Nous. Robert Creeley. **CP-CreeR**

If I choose remorse. Kathleen Jessie Raine. **SP-RainK**

If I could arise and travel away. Robert Louis Stevenson. **CP-StevR**

If I could be anything in the world that flew. Andy's Chest. "Lou Reed." **SP-ReedL**

If I Could Be Like Wallace Stevens. William Stafford. **SP-StafW**

If I could begin anything. Words Written Near a Candle. Tess Gallagher. **SP-GallT**

If I could blame it all on the weather. The Earth Falls Down. Anne Sexton. **CP-SextA**

If I could bribe them by a Rose. Emily Dickinson. **CP-DickE**

If I could but abide. A Wish for Unconsciousness. Thomas Hardy. **CP-HardT**

If I Could But Forget. Paul Laurence Dunbar. **CP-DunbP**

If I could go on kissing your honeyed eyes. Catullus. *See* Carmen 48: "Iuventius, / were I allowed."

If I could have. Moriturus. Edna St. Vincent Millay. **CP-MillE**

If I could have put you in my heart. The End. David Herbert Lawrence. **CP-LawrD**

If I could I would sing you to sleep. *tr. fr. the German of* Rilke. Randall Jarrell. **CP-JarrR**

If I could keep her. Another Old Woman. William Carlos Williams. **CP-WilW2**

If I could let you go as trees let go. May Sarton. **SP-SartM** *Fr.* The Autumn Sonnets.

If I Could Only Live at the Pitch That Is near Madness. Richard Eberhart. **CP-EberR**

If I could put my woods in song. My Garden. Ralph Waldo Emerson. **CP-EmerR**

If I could send him only. Her Reticence. Theodore Roethke. **CP-RoetT**

If I could set the moon upon. The Encyclopædia. Nicholas Vachel Lindsay. **CP-LindV**

If I could slide my hands over your thighs. ALLEGORY: *Old Man's Fancy* (Poussin). Jenny Joseph. *Fr.* Altarpiece (A Meditation on Lust, Desire and Love). **SP-JoseJ**

If I could tell how glad I was. Emily Dickinson. **CP-DickE**

If I Could Tell You. Wystan Hugh Auden. **CP-AudeW**

If I Could Trust Mine Own Self. Christina Georgina Rossetti. **EBCP** *Fr.* Monna Innominata. **CP-RosC2**

If I could write : Summer waits your coming. Letter, Unposted. Muriel Rukeyser. **CP-RukeM**

If I could write a poem without meaning. Meaningless Poem. Richard Eberhart. **CP-EberR**

If I cried out in anger against music. Death by Drums. Robert Ranke Graves. **CP-GravR**

If I dare write to You, my Lord, who are. To the Right Honourable Edward Earle of Dorset. Robert Herrick. **CP-HerrR**

If I declare *Peace*. Roy Fisher. **SP-FishR**   *Fr.* New Diversions.

If I Didn't. Roy Fisher. **SP-FishR**

If I die solvent—die, that is to say. Edna St. Vincent Millay. **CP-MillE**

If I die today, which statistically speaking. Sonnet. Hayden Carruth. **CP-CarHS**   *Fr.* Sonnets.

If I do not know where He is. Circulations of the Song. Robert Duncan. **SP-DuncR**

If I do not sin, she said, you shall not. Venus Over the Desert. William Carlos Williams. **CP-WilW2**

If I Don't Be There by Morning. "Bob Dylan" *and* Helena Springs. **CP-DylaB**

If I don't love you I. Scorpio. Ted Berrigan. **SP-BerrT**

If I eer Grow to a Mans Estate. William Blake. **CP-BlakW**

If I embraced a horse, baby. A Modest Boast at Meridian. Robert Pack. **SP-PackR**

If I envy anyone it must be. Answers. Mary Oliver. **SP-OlivM**

If I esteemed you less, Envy would kill. Sonnet to Byron. Percy Bysshe Shelley. **CP-ShelP**

If I ever hit for a dollar. Numbers. Langston Hughes. **SP-HughL**

If I Fell. The Beatles. **CP-Beatl**

If I freely may discover. Ben Jonson. **CP-JonsB**   *Fr.* The Poetaster.

If I grow bitterly. Scrub. Edna St. Vincent Millay. **CP-MillE**

If I Had A Brontosaurus. Shel Silverstein. **SP-SilS2**

If I had a Green Automobile. The Green Automobile. Allen Ginsberg. **CP-GinsA**

If I had a million lives to live. Humdrum. Carl Sandburg. **CP-SandC**

If I had a shining head. These Heroics. Leonard Cohen. **CP-CoheL**

If I had been, in the beginning, God. Big Bang. Robert Pack. **SP-PackR**

If I Had but Two Little Wings, *after the German folk song* Wenn ich ein Vöglein wär. Samuel Taylor Coleridge. (Something Childish, but Very Natural.) **CP-ColeS**

If I had clamoured at Thy Gate. The Rebel. Rudyard Kipling. *Fr.* Epitaphs of the War [1914–1918]. **CP-KiplR**

If I had erased my life there. Mississippi Winter I. Alice Walker. **CP-WalkA**

If I had given you that love and care. John Hewitt. **PNI**   *Fr.* Sonnets for Roberta (1954). **CP-HewiJ**

If I had said out passions as they were. Cadenza on Garnette. John Berryman. **CP-BerrJ**

If I had, uncut, the fingernails. The Pruned Roses. William Dickey. **SP-DickW**

If I had wings, my lady, like a dove. Robert Louis Stevenson. **CP-StevR**

If I Had Words. Christina Georgina Rossetti. **CP-RosC3**

If I have been born. Dwarf in the Woods. Mona Van Duyn. **SP-VanDM**

If I have faltered more or less. The Celestial Surgeon. Robert Louis Stevenson. **CP-StevR**

If I have given you delight. The Appeal. Rudyard Kipling. **CP-KiplR**

If i have made, my lady, intricate. Edward Estlin Cummings. **CP-CummE; SP-CummE**

If I have plaid the Truant, or have here. To God. Robert Herrick. **CP-HerrR**

If I have seemed more prompt to censure wrong. To Charles Sumner. John Greenleaf Whittier. **CP-WhitJ**

If I have taken the common clay. Rudyard Kipling. **CP-KiplR**   *Fr.* The Light That Failed.

If I have to choose between the bourgeois and the bolshevist. Choice of Evils. David Herbert Lawrence. **CP-LawrD**

If I hope, I pine; if I feare, I faint and die. *At.* to Thomas Campion *and to* Philip Rosseter. **CP-CampT**

If I just had a piano. Testimonial. Langston Hughes. **SP-HughL**

If I kiss[e] Anthea's bre[a]st. Love Perfumes All Parts. Robert Herrick. **CP-HerrR**

If I lay on that beach with you. Adrienne Rich. *Fr.* Twenty-one Love Poems. **SP-RicA1; SP-RicA2**

If I leaped. Blue Skies. Archie Randolph Ammons. **SP-AmmoA**

If I leave all for thee, wilt thou exchange. Sonnet. Elizabeth Barrett Browning. **Son**   *Fr.* Sonnets from the Portuguese. **CP-BroEB**

If I Lie Down. Stevie Smith. **CP-SmitS**

If I, like Solomon. O to Be a Dragon. Marianne Craig Moore. **CP-MoorM**

If I lived in sight of the lake. A Matter of Locality. Paul Laurence Dunbar. **CP-DunbP**

If i love You. Edward Estlin Cummings. **CP-CummE; SP-CummE**

If I lye unburied Sir. To the Passenger. Robert Herrick. **CP-HerrR**

If I make the lashes dark. *fr.* A Woman Young and Old. William Butler Yeats. **CP-YeatW**

If I may have it, when it's dead. Emily Dickinson. **CP-DickE**

If I might have at mine own will. Sir Thomas Wyatt. **CP-WyatT**

If I might only love my God and die! If Only. Christina Georgina Rossetti. **CP-RosC1**

If I might see another Spring. Another Spring. Christina Georgina Rossetti. **CP-RosC1**

If I might take a weight of bronze. Red Roses for Bronze. Hilda Doolittle. **CP-DoolH**

If I must of my Senses lose. Prayer. Theodore Roethke. **CP-RoetT**

If I Needed Someone. George Harrison. **CP-Beatl**

If I painted, I'd paint landscapes[. In museums]. Landscapes. Richard Hugo. **CP-HugoR**

If I rest for a moment near The Equestrian. Music. Frank O'Hara. **SP-OharF**

If I saw you liked that dull unhappy boy. The Road Map. Thom Gunn. **CP-GunnT**

If I say I have heard voices. Pastoral. William Carlos Williams. **CP-WilW1**

If I say Thy name, art Thou there ? It may be so. John Berryman. *Fr.* Eleven Addresses to the Lord. **CP-BerrJ**

If I should cease to bring a Rose. Emily Dickinson. **CP-DickE**

If I should die. Emily Dickinson. **CP-DickE**

If I should ever say "my heart is in my home." Christina Georgina Rossetti. **CP-RosC2**

If I should go away. Post-Script: for Gweno. Alun Lewis. **CP-LewiA**

If I should learn, in some quite casual way. Edna St. Vincent Millay. **CP-MillE**

If I should need to name, O Western World, your powerfulest scene and show. Election Day, November, 1884. Walt Whitman. **CP-WhitW**

If I should pamphleteer twenty years against royalists. To the Ghost of John Milton. Carl Sandburg. **CP-SandC**

If I should pass the tomb of Jonah. Losers. Carl Sandburg. **CP-SandC**

If i should sleep with a lady called death. Edward Estlin Cummings. **CP-CummE**

If I shouldn't be alive. Emily Dickinson. **CP-DickE**

If I sometimes say that flowers smile. Fernando Pessoa. *Fr.* Twelve Poems from *The Keeper of the Flocks*. **CP-MertT**

If I stink / while I'm smoking, I'll be good. The Cabbage in History. Dabney Stuart. **SP-StuaD**

If I suffer at this. The Meek Have Inherited. Charles Bukowski. **SP-BukC1**

If I Take the Wings of the Morning. Donald Davie. **CP-DavDo**

If I talk to things. Pastoral 2. William Carlos Williams. **CP-WilW1**

If I think of a horse wandering about sleeplessly. Night. Robert Bly. **SP-BlyR**

If I told you I used to know the circular truth. Eagles. James Dickey. **CP-DickJ**

If I told you that the old woman. These Streets. Philip Levine. **SP-LeviP**

If I told you the trees spoke, there being no wind. April Thirtieth 1960. Kay Boyle. *Fr.* Two Poems for a Poet. **CP-BoylK**

If I urge my kinde desires. *At.* to Thomas Campion *and to* Philip Rosseter. **CP-CampT**

If I use my imagination. Dear Life. Richard Shelton. **SP-ShelR**

If I walk in Autumn's even. Stanza. Percy Bysshe Shelley. **CP-ShelP**

If I was a member of the Church of Rome. The Church. David Herbert Lawrence. **CP-LawrD**

If I were a foreigner, as you say. Margaret Atwood. *Fr.* Two-Headed Poems. **SP-AtwM2**

If I were a jeweler. Emerald Ice. Diane Wakoski. **SP-WakoD**

If I were a king and did not know it. Tauler. James Fenton. **SP-FentJ**

If I Were a Queen. Christina Georgina Rossetti. **CP-RosC2**

If I were called in. Water. Philip Larkin. **CP-LarkP**

If I were doing my Laundry I'd wash my dirty Iran. Homework. Allen Ginsberg. **CP-GinsA**

If I were hanged on the highest hill. Mother o' Mine. Rudyard Kipling. **CP-KiplR**   *Fr.* The Light That Failed.

If I were in the middle of the Atlantic. Drowning (I). Grace Paley. **CP-PaleG**

If I were Sophocles, brave with truth. Kaire. Richard Eberhart. **CP-EberR**

If I were thou, O butterfly. Wisdom Unapplied. Elizabeth Barrett Browning. **CP-BroEB**

If I Were Tickled by the Rub of Love. Dylan Thomas. **CP-ThomD**

If I were to walk this way. The Wood Road. Edna St. Vincent Millay. **CP-MillE**

If I were well-to-do. Birthday. David Herbert Lawrence. **CP-LawrD**

If I were you. Kate's. Robert Creeley. **CP-CreeR**

If I were you, I wouldn't listen. Conceit. Lewis Turco. **SP-TurcL**

If I would wish, for truth, and not for show. To the Same [Benjamin Rudyerd]. Ben Jonson. **CP-JonsB**

If I write any more, it will make my poor muse sick. To Dr. Sheridan. Jonathan Swift. **CP-SwifJ**

If I write not to you. Letter in Verse. William Cowper. **CP-CowpW**

If icebergs were warm below the water. Icebergs. Louis MacNeice. **CP-MacNL**

If I'm dead and don't know it. Pablo Neruda, *tr. fr. Spanish by* Ben Belitt. **SP-NeruP** *Fr.* Question Book.

If I'm lost—now. Emily Dickinson. **CP-DickE**

If, in a fisherman's hut, you poke. Hand-Rolled Cigarettes. Stanley Jasspon Kunitz. **CP-KuniS**

If, in an odd angle of the hutment. Eighth Air Force. Randall Jarrell. **CP-JarrR; SP-JarrR**

If in beginning twilight of winter will stand. Edward Estlin Cummings. **CP-CummE**

If in his study he hath so much care. Antiquary. John Donne. **CP-DonnJ**

If in me Anger, or disdaine / In you, or both, made me refraine. To Ellinda, That Lately I Have Not Written. Richard Lovelace. **CP-LoveR**

If, in search of a given honesty. Concert. Marsden Hartley. **CP-HartM**

If in that Syrian garden, ages slain. Easter Hymn. Alfred Edward Housman. **CP-HousA**

If, in the Foggy Aleutians. Edna St. Vincent Millay. **CP-MillE**

If in the future. Sitting Alone at Sunrise: Problems in the Space-Time Continuum. Miller Williams. **SP-WillM**

If in the latter. Epitaph for Liberal Poets. Louis MacNeice. **CP-MacNL**

If, in the light of things, you fade. Star. Derek Walcott. **CP-WalcD**

If, in the month of dark December. Written after Swimming from Sestos to Abydos. Byron. **CP-Byron**

If, in the silent mind of One all-pure. In Utrumque Paratus. Matthew Arnold. **SP-ArnoM**

If in the world there be more woe. Sir Thomas Wyatt. **CP-WyatT**

If in the years to come you should recall. Edna St. Vincent Millay. **CP-MillE**

If in thy second state sublime. Tennyson. *Fr.* In Memoriam A. H. H. **CP-TennA**

If, into this evening as the grass receives the dew. Kathleen Jessie Raine. **SP-RainK**

If it be pleasant to look on, stalled in the packed *serai*. Rudyard Kipling. *Fr.* Certain Maxims of Hafiz. **CP-KiplR**

If it be so that I forsake thee. Sir Thomas Wyatt. **CP-WyatT**

If it be very strange and sorrowful. Sonnet Autumnal. Wilfred Owen. **CP-OwenW**

If It Be Your Will. Leonard Cohen. **CP-CoheL**

If it chance your eye offend you. Alfred Edward Housman. **CP-HousA**

If it ever is. The Invitation. Robert Creeley. **CP-CreeR**

If it falls flat / I'm used to it. Yet. The Kid. Robert Creeley. **CP-CreeR**

If it form the one landscape that we, the inconstant ones. In Praise of Limestone. Wystan Hugh Auden. **CP-AudeW**

If it had no pencil. Emily Dickinson. **CP-DickE**

If it had not been the Lord who was on our side, now may Israel say. Psalm 124. Bible, *O.T. Fr.* Psalms. **CP-Psal**

If it is a question of him or me. My Enemy. David Herbert Lawrence. **CP-LawrD**

If it is a world without a genius. In the Element of Antagonisms. Wallace Stevens. **CP-StevW**

If it is thou whose casual hand withdraws. Arthur Hugh Clough. *Fr.* Seven Sonnets. **SP-ClouA**

If it is true that. Dedication, A. Lewis Turco. **SP-TurcL**

If it is True What the Prophets write. William Blake. **CP-BlakW**

If it is unpermissible, in fact fatal. To a Giraffe. Marianne Craig Moore. **CP-MoorM**

If it should rain—(the sneezy moon). Edna St. Vincent Millay. **CP-MillE**

If it was treason it was so well handled that it. The Absence of a Noble Presence. John Ashbery. **SP-AshbJ**

If it were done, 'twere well it were done quickly. Artist's Model. Robert Lowell. **SP-LoweR**

(If it were evening on a dead man's watch. Blues for Jimmy. Thomas McGrath. **SP-McGrT**

If it were not for the charm of. Metaphysic. Marsden Hartley. **CP-HartM**

If It Were Not for You. Hayden Carruth. **CP-CarHS**

If it were only still! Pastoral. Edna St. Vincent Millay. **CP-MillE**

If It Were the Eye. Marsden Hartley. **CP-HartM**

If it weren't for you Mr Jukebox with yr aluminum belly roaring & thirty teeth eating dirty drx. Seabattle of Salamis Took Place off Perama. Allen Ginsberg. **CP-GinsA**

If It's Ever Spring Again. Thomas Hardy. **CP-HardT**

If It's No Problem. Jim Morrison. **SP-MorrJ**

If it's raining and you're sitting behind a shade with. I Don't Need a Bedsheet with Slits for Eyes to Kill You In. Charles Bukowski. **SP-BukC2**

If it's weary work to live. Christina Georgina Rossetti. *Fr.* Spring Fancies. **CP-RosC3**

If James the King of wit. Théophile De Viau, *tr. fr. French by* Richard Lovelace. **CP-LoveR**

If Jesus be reveal'd. Trinity Sunday. Christopher Smart. *Fr.* Hymns and Spiritual Songs for the Fasts and Festivals of the Church of England. **SP-SmarC**

If, jetting, I committed the noble fault. My Heat. Frank O'Hara. **SP-OharF**

If John marries Mary, and Mary alone. Impromptu ["If John marries Mary, and Mary alone"]. William Cowper. **CP-CowpW**

If Jupiter and Saturn meet. Conjunctions. William Butler Yeats. **CP-YeatW**

If Kings and kingdomes, once dsitracted be. Warre. Robert Herrick. **CP-HerrR**

If kissing them would quiet them. Sexist Stanza. David Markson. **CP-MarkD**

If learned darkness from our searched world. Edward Estlin Cummings. **CP-CummE**

If life were but a dream, my love. If. Paul Laurence Dunbar. **CP-DunbP**

If Life were slumber on a bed of down. Stanzas Suggested in a Steamboat off Saint Bees' Head, on the Coast of Cumberland. William Wordsworth. *Fr.* Poems Composed or Suggested During a Tour, in the Summer of 1833. **CP-WorW2**

If little labour, little are our gaines. No Paines, No Gaines. Robert Herrick. **CP-HerrR**

If long enough I sit here, she, she'll pass. John Berryman. *Fr.* Sonnets to Chris. **CP-BerrJ**

If Love be dead. Love's Burial-Place. Samuel Taylor Coleridge. **CP-ColeS**

If love is not worth loving, then life is not worth living. Christina Georgina Rossetti. **CP-RosC2**

If Love loves truth, then women doe not love. Thomas Campion. **CP-CampT**

If love make me forsworn, how shall I swear to love? *Various Authors.* **CP-ShaWS** *Fr.* The Passionate Pilgrim. **CP-ShaWS**

If Luther's day expand to Darwin's year. Epilogue. Herman Melville. **SP-MelvH** *Fr.* Clarel: A Poem and Pilgrimage in the Holy Land.

If man might know. Ei Men Een Mathein. Sir John Suckling. **CP-SuckJ**

If man only looks to man, and no-one sees beyond. False Democracy and Real. David Herbert Lawrence. **CP-LawrD**

If Mary came would Mary. A Penitent Considers Another Coming of Mary. Gwendolyn Brooks. **SP-BrooG**

If Maudie doesn't love us. Clydesider. David Herbert Lawrence. **CP-LawrD**

If meat the gods give, I the steam. Steam in Sacrifice. Robert Herrick. **CP-HerrR**

If men, and times were now. Ode. Ben Jonson. **CP-JonsB**

If Men can say that beauty dyes. Upon a Comely, and Curious Maide. Robert Herrick. **CP-HerrR**

If men get name, for some one virtue: then. To Sir Edward Herbert. Ben Jonson. **CP-JonsB**

If men only fought outwards into the world. Female Coercion. David Herbert Lawrence. **CP-LawrD**

If Men will act like a maid smiling over a Churn. William Blake. **CP-BlakW**

If Michael, leader of God's host. The Rose of Peace. William Butler Yeats. **CP-YeatW**

If Michelangelo had not painted God reaching his hand. If He Had Not Had Two Hands Tattooed on His Chest. Siv Cedering Fox. **SP-CedeS**

If mine eyes can speak to do hearty errand, *speech of Cleophila*. Sir Philip Sidney. **SP-SidnP** *Fr.* Arcadia.

If Mr. Bright retiring does not please. Counterblast on Penny Trumpet. Christina Georgina Rossetti. **CP-RosC3**

If modest Youth, with cool Reflection crown'd. Epitaph on Edmund Duke of Buckingham, Who Died in the Nineteenth Year of His Age, 1735. Alexander Pope. **CP-PopeA**

If money I lack. Placard for a Poll Bearing an Old Shirt. William Wordsworth. **CP-WorW2**

If money made the mind more sane. Stanzas: Written at Night in Radio City. Allen Ginsberg. **CP-GinsA**

If 'mongst my many Poems, I can see. To Cedars. Robert Herrick. **CP-HerrR**

If more than once, as annals tell. Timoleon. Herman Melville. **SP-MelvH**

If, Mother and Daddy, you were to visit us. Returning. Robert Lowell. **SP-LoweR**

If mouth could open its cliff. Ted Hughes. **SP-HughT** *Fr.* Seven Dungeon Songs.

If music and sweet poetry agree. Richard Barnfield. **CP-ShaWS** *Fr.* The Passionate Pilgrim. **CP-ShaWS**

If music be the muses' paragon. Heart Beats. Donald Davie. **CP-DavDo**

If my Bark sink. Emily Dickinson. **CP-DickE**

If My Darling. Philip Larkin. **CP-LarkP**

If my darling should depart. Hafiz. **CP-EmerR** *Fr.* I said to heaven that glowed above. *Fr.* Odes.

If my dear love were but the child of state. Sonnet 124. William Shakespeare. **NoSic** *Fr.* Sonnets. **CP-ShaWS**

If My Head Hurt a Hair's Foot. Dylan Thomas. **CP-ThomD**

If, my irrepressible Calvus, I didn't. Carmen 14. Catullus. *Fr.* Carmina. **CP-Catul**

If my pen hand were snapped by a Broadway truck. After Whitman & Reznikoff. Allen Ginsberg. **CP-GinsA**

If, my religion safe, I durst embrace. To Sir Henry [or Henrie] Savile [upon His Translation of Tacitus]. Ben Jonson. **CP-JonsB**

If my Valentine you won't be. Ernest Hemingway. **CP-HemiE**

If Nature do deny. Painting Sometimes Permitted. Robert Herrick. **CP-HerrR**

If Nature, for a favourite child. Matthew. William Wordsworth. **CP-WorW1**

If nature is life, nature is death. Phoenix Lyrics. Delmore Schwartz. **SP-SchwD**

If nature is life, nature is death. Delmore Schwartz. *Fr.* Phoenix Lyrics. **SP-SchwD**

If Nature smiles—the Mother must. Emily Dickinson. **CP-DickE**

If neither brass, nor marble, can withstand. The Power of Time. Jonathan Swift. **CP-SwifJ**

If night is staining the window. Farewell to Melancholy. Lewis Turco. **SP-TurcL**

If night's mostness(and whom did merely day / close). Edward Estlin Cummings. **CP-CummE**

If nine times you your bridegroom[e] kiss[e]. The Tithe [or Tythe]: To the Bride. Robert Herrick. **CP-HerrR**

If No Cuckoo Sings. Robert Ranke Graves. **CP-GravR**

If no love is, O God, what fele I so. Geoffrey Chaucer. **AWP; FF; OAEL-1** *Fr.* Troilus and Criseyde [or Criseide]. **CP-ChauG**

(Song of Troylus, The.) **AWP**

If no one moved on order, she would kill—. My Mother Was a Soldier. William Stafford. **SP-StafW**

If noisy Tom should in the senate prate. On Noisy Tom. Jonathan Swift. **CP-SwifJ**

If not by all that his friends boast. Carmen 54. Catullus. *Fr.* Carmina. **CP-Catul**

If Not for You. "Bob Dylan." **CP-DylaB**

If not white shorts—then in a princess gown. John Berryman. *Fr.* Sonnets to Chris. **CP-BerrJ**

If not, why should the willow bend? It bends. Willow. James Merrill. **SP-MerrJ**

If not with hope of life, / Begin with fear of death. Christina Georgina Rossetti. **CP-RosC2**

If now, having dismissed your hired impersonators with verdicts. Caliban to the Audience. Wystan Hugh Auden. *Fr.* The Sea and the Mirror. **CP-AudeW**

If objects are of two kinds—those. Prose Poem. Charles Tomlinson. **CP-TomlC**

If, of meaner happiness. Passage from Mary Barker's *Lines Addressed to a Noble Lord* (His Lordship Will Know Why). William Wordsworth. **CP-WorW2**

If old Bacchus were the speaker. Wine of Cyprus. Elizabeth Barrett Browning. **CP-BroEB**

If, on account of the political situation. Wystan Hugh Auden. **LiTA; WaP** *Fr.* Advent. *Fr.* For the Time Being; a Christmas Oratorio. **CP-AudeW**

If on any warm day when you ramble around. The Lizard. Thomas Hardy. **CP-HardT**

If on the Book itself we cast our view. The Scriptures. John Dryden. **OBS** *Fr.* Religio Laici. **SP-DrydJ**

If once a year / the house of the dead. De Sole. Charles Tomlinson. **CP-TomlC**

If one could have that little head of hers. A Face. Robert Browning. **CP-BroR1**

If one sets aside the standard schlock. The Next Step. Dabney Stuart. **SP-StuaD**

If one should bring me this report. Tennyson. **EBVV; EnVR; FHYEP; ImPo; MeMBP** *Fr.* In Memoriam A. H. H. **CP-TennA**

(Of One Dead.) **ImPo**

If one should tell them what's clearly seen. Crumbs or the Loaf. Robinson Jeffers. **CP-JefR2**

If Only. Christina Georgina Rossetti. **CP-RosC1**

If only daffodils had caught the light. It Would Have Been Enough. Robert Pack. **SP-PackR**

If Only I. Jim Morrison. **SP-MorrJ**

If only she'd call me Mister again. The Good Fight. Leonard Cohen. **CP-CoheL**

If only something would happen! Dialogue *En Route*. Sylvia Plath. **CP-PlatS**

If only the phantom would stop reappearing! Faust. John Ashbery. **SP-AshbJ**

If only they hadn't shown that cruel mercy. A Girl Who Has Drowned Herself Speaks. Stephen Spender. **CP-SpenS**

If only we weren't so small next to the stars. Cellophane. Charles Kenneth Williams. **CP-WillC**

If orphane childe, enwrapt in swathing bands. I Dye Without Desert. Robert Southwell. **CP-SoutR**

If Orpheus' voice had force to breathe such music's love. Third Song. Sir Philip Sidney. **PoEL-1** *Fr.* Astrophil and Stella. **SP-SidnP**

If Other Students. Ron Koertge. **SP-KoerR**

If out of a dire suspicion. Wet Hair: If Now His Mother Should Come. Robert Penn Warren. **NoAM** *Fr.* Penological Study: Southern Exposure. **SP-WarrR**

If pain for peace prepares. Emily Dickinson. **CP-DickE**

If, passenger, thou canst but read. An Epitaph, on Henry L[ord] La-ware. To the Passer-By. Ben Jonson. **CP-JonsB**

If passion and grief and pain and hurt. The East. Alun Lewis. **CP-LewiA**

If Pegasus will let *thee* ride him. A Mathematical Problem. Samuel Taylor Coleridge. **CP-ColeS**

If people insist on my having. Fernando Pessoa. *Fr.* Twelve Poems from *The Keeper of the Flocks*. **CP-MertT**

If Pliny, Lord High Treasurer of all. Painture [or Peinture]. Richard Lovelace. **CP-LoveR**

If Poetry Were Not a Morality. Tess Gallagher. **SP-GallT**

If poisonous [or poysonous] mineral[l]s, and if that tree. John Donne. **BiP; CABA; EBEV; EnRePo; FaBoVe; ImPo; JCP; LiTB; MePo; NAEL-1; NoP; OAEL-1; OBS; OxAEP-1; PFP; PPP; PoEL-2; SCGP; SeCP; Son; UnPo; WHA** *Fr.* Divine Meditations. **CP-DonnJ** *Fr.* Holy Sonnets. **CP-DonnJ**

If poor (you say) she drains her husband's purse. Geoffrey Chaucer. **OBSV** *Fr.* The Wife of Bath. **CP-PopeA** *Fr.* The Canterbury Tales. **CP-ChauG**

If reading verse be your delight. To the Rev. William Bull. William Cowper. **CP-CowpW**

If recollecting were forgetting. Emily Dickinson. **CP-DickE**

If Rome so great, and in her wisest age. To Edward Alleyn. Ben Jonson. **CP-JonsB**

If roses had not faded. Emily Dickinson. **SP-DickE**

If rustic Phidyle her prayer renews. 3.23. Horace. **CP-JohnS**, *tr. by* Samuel Johnson. *Fr.* Odes.

If Sackville, all that have the power to do[e]. An Epistle to Sir Edward Sackville, now Earl of Dorset. Ben Jonson. **CP-JonsB**

If seasons all were summers. The Farm-Woman's Winter. Thomas Hardy. **CP-HardT**

If seventy were young / and death uncommon. Edward Estlin Cummings. **CP-CummE**

If shame can on a soldier's vein-swollen front. King Stephen. A Fragment of a Tragedy. John Keats. **CP-KeatJ**

If shame can on a soldier's vein-swoll'n front. John Keats. **FaBoEH** *Fr.* King Stephen. A Fragment of a Tragedy. **CP-KeatJ**

If she appears, hands ringed with rings. Apparition. Adrienne Rich. *Fr.* Turning the Wheel. **SP-RicA2**

If she forsake me, I must die. At. to Thomas Campion *and to* Philip Rosseter. **CP-CampT**

If She grow suddenly gracious—reflect. Is it all for thee? Rudyard Kipling. *Fr.* Certain Maxims of Hafiz. **CP-KiplR**

If she had been the Mistletoe. Emily Dickinson. **CP-DickE**

If She have spoken a word, remember thy lips are sealed. Rudyard Kipling. *Fr.* Certain Maxims of Hafiz. **CP-KiplR**

If she waits late at night. A Persuasion. Hart Crane. **CP-CranH**

If she would come to me here. Dog-Tired. David Herbert Lawrence. **CP-LawrD**

If shepherd to nymph were the whole story. Louis MacNeice. *Fr.* Suite for Recorders. **CP-MacNL**

If sinne be captive, grace must finde release. The Assumption of Our Lady. Robert Southwell. **CP-SoutR**

If sixteen shadows flapping on the line. The Times Worsen. Randall Jarrell. **CP-JarrR**

If Sleep and Death Be Truly One. Tennyson. **MeMBP; OBNC; PeECV** *Fr.* In Memoriam A. H. H. **CP-TennA**

If so be a toad be laid. A Charme, or an Allay for Love. Robert Herrick. **CP-HerrR**

If So Hap May Be. Carl Sandburg. **CP-SandC**

If some confectioner were willing. Assorted Chocolates. Ogden Nash. **CP-NashO**

If someone asked you to be happy. Charles Henri Ford. *Fr.* Epigrams. **SP-FordC**

If someone is pleased to boast. The Outlaw of the Lowest Planet. Kenneth Patchen. **CP-PatcK**

If something is too. Immoderation. Archie Randolph Ammons. **SP-AmmoA**

If Sometimes in the Haunts of Men. Byron. **CP-Byron**

If stars dropped out of heaven, / And if flowers took their place. Christina Georgina Rossetti. **CP-RosC2**

If Still Your Orchards Bear. Edna St. Vincent Millay. **CP-MillE**

If strange things happen where she is. On Portents. Robert Ranke Graves. **CP-GravR**

If such a thing had been my thought. Misunderstandings. "Lewis Carroll." **CP-CarrL**

If Synthia Be a Queene, a Princes, and Supreame. Sir Walter Ralegh. *See* If Cynthia Be a Queen.

If Teares could wash the Ill away. To His Deare Brother Colonel F.L. Richard Lovelace. **CP-LoveR**

If That High World. Byron. **CP-Byron**

If that my Fate has now fulfill'd my yeere. On Himselfe. Robert Herrick. **CP-HerrR**

If that the sicke may grone. Saint Peter's Afflicted Mynde. Robert Southwell. **CP-SoutR**

If that thou hast the gift of strength, then know. The Burden of Strength. George Meredith. **CP-MerG1**

If that we thus are guilty doth appear. Thesis and Antithesis. Arthur Hugh Clough. **SP-ClouA**

If that's water you wash your hands in. Cannot Sweeten. Christina Georgina Rossetti. **CP-RosC3**

If the / green / opens. Edward Estlin Cummings. **CP-CummE**

If the anguish of others helped one with one's own. Emily Dickinson. **SP-DickE**

If the autumn would. Winter Is Another Country. Archibald MacLeish. **CP-MacLA**

If the Birds Knew. John Ashbery. **SP-AshbJ**

If the blue channel through the ice ahead. Haakon Jarl. Leonard Nathan. **SP-NathL**

If the blues would let me. Miss Blues'es Child. Langston Hughes. **SP-HughL**

If the Christmas tree at Rockefeller Center were. Multiplication Table. Robert Penn Warren. **SP-WarrR**

If the city has roots, they are in filth. The Source. George Oppen. **CP-OppeG**

If the clock had stopped in 1936. Mother and Father 1. Robert Lowell. **SP-LoweR**

If the desire of Glory speak a mind. To Colonel Richard Lovelace, on the Publishing of His Ingenious Poems. Joseph Hall. *Fr.* Commendatory Poems. **CP-LoveR**

If the dull substance of my flesh were thought. Sonnet 44. William Shakespeare. **Son** *Fr.* Sonnets. **CP-ShaWS**

If the firefly and the glowworm. Of Fitness to Survive. Louise McNeill. **SP-McNeL**

If the foolish, call them "flowers." Emily Dickinson. **CP-DickE**

If the future is mighty as the past. Emily Dickinson. **SP-DickE**

If the great outside system—species and stars—proceeds. Across Space and Time. Charles Olson. **CP-OlsoC**

If the hill overlooking our city has always been known as Adam's Grave. Vespers. Wystan Hugh Auden. **FaBoMo** *Fr.* Horae Canonicae. **CP-AudeW**

If the horse you ride. Some Things I Wanted to Say to You. Stephen Dunn. **SP-DunnS**

If the houses in Wyeth's Christina's dream. My Grandfather's Wake. Paul Muldoon. **SP-MuldP**

If the Led Striker call it a strike. An American. Rudyard Kipling. **CP-KiplR**

If the lost word is lost, if the spent word is spent. Thomas Stearns Eliot. **UV** *Fr.* Ash Wednesday [*or* Ash-Wednesday]. **CP-ElioT**

If the Lovestar grows most big. Edward Estlin Cummings. **CP-CummE**

If the Man who Turneps cries. Samuel Johnson. *See* The Turnip Vendor.

If the moon came from heaven, / Talking all the way. Christina Georgina Rossetti. **CP-RosC2**

If the moon smiled, she would resemble you. The Rival. Sylvia Plath. **CP-PlatS**

If the muse were mine to tempt it. The Colored Soldiers. Paul Laurence Dunbar. **CP-DunbP**

If the night is dark. Geoffrey Hill. *Fr.* The Pentecost Castle. **CP-HillG**

If the night were not so dark. Seven Attempted Moves. Roy Fisher. **SP-FishR**

If the oriole calls like last year. The South Wind Says So. Carl Sandburg. **CP-SandC**

If the Owl Calls Again. John Haines. **SP-HainJ**

If the poem is a trajectory. The Poem as Trajectory. Richard Eberhart. **CP-EberR**

If the poetry of X was music. The Creations of Sound. Wallace Stevens. **CP-StevW**

If the pool were still. Peace of Mind. Kathleen Jessie Raine. **SP-RainK**

If the quick spirits in your eye. Persuasions to Enjoy. Thomas Carew. **CP-CareT**

If the rain comes they run and hide their heads. Rain. The Beatles. **CP-Beatl**

If the red slayer think he slays. Brahma. Ralph Waldo Emerson. **CP-EmerR**

If the robot can recognise the clean flame of life. Real Democracy. David Herbert Lawrence. **CP-LawrD**

If the sky were green instead of blue its green. The Leaves. Hayden Carruth. *Fr.* Contra Mortem. **CP-CarHL**

If the sun could tell us half / That he hears and sees. Christina Georgina Rossetti. **CP-RosC2**

If the universe is like this gaol where now. Richard Coeur-de-Lion. Louis Aragon, *tr. fr.* French by Louis MacNeice. **CP-MacNL**

If the water forms. Poem, A. Robert Creeley. **CP-CreeR**

If the water were clear enough. King of the River. Stanley Jasspon Kunitz. **CP-KuniS**

If the weather breaks. Jane Cooper. *Fr.* The Weather of Six Mornings. **SP-CoopJ**

If the whole weight of what we think and feel. Retirement. William Wordsworth. **CP-WorW2**

If the work be not direct. Bible, *O.T. See* Psalm 127: "Except the Lord build the house."

If the World Was Crazy. Shel Silverstein. **SP-SilS2**

If there are any heavens my mother will(all by herself)have. Edward Estlin Cummings. **CP-CummE; SP-CummE**

If there are any wives present who wish to irritate their husbands. Don't Wait, Hit Me Now! Ogden Nash. **CP-NashO**

If there be a power of sweetness, let it lie. *see also* Blackberry Winter ("If the lady hath any loveliness, let it die"). John Crowe Ransom. **SP-RansJ**

If there be any one can take my place. Christina Georgina Rossetti. *Fr.* Monna Innominata. **CP-RosC2**

If there be nothing new, but that which is. Sonnet 59. William Shakespeare. *Fr.* Sonnets. **CP-ShaWS**

If there be prophets on whose spirits rest. Conjectures. William Wordsworth. *Fr.* Ecclesiastical Sonnets. **CP-WorW2**

If there be truth in what you sing. On Reading Dr. Young's Satires. Jonathan Swift. **CP-SwifJ**

If there had been only. A Buddha in the Woodpile. Lawrence Ferlinghetti. **SP-FerlL**

If there has been no spiritual change of kind. Mutations. Louis MacNeice. **CP-MacNL**

If there is a man white as marble. Metaphor as Degeneration. Wallace Stevens. **CP-StevW**

If there is anything of which American industry has a superfluity. First Chime. Ogden Nash. *Fr.* Ring out the Old, Ring in the New, but Don't Get Caught in Between. **CP-NashO**

If there must be a god in the house, must be. Less and Less Human, O Savage Spirit. Wallace Stevens. **CP-StevW**

If there was a broken whispering by night. Parting at Dawn. John Crowe Ransom. **SP-RansJ**

If There Was Any Justice. Alice Walker. **CP-WalkA**

If there were balm in Gilead, I would go. Czecho-Slovakia. Edna St. Vincent Millay. **CP-MillE**

If there were in my kalendar. Conjecture. Thomas Hardy. **CP-HardT**

If there were no authority on earth. Geoffrey Chaucer. **OxBM** *Fr.* The Wife of Bath's Prologue. **FHYEP; NAEL-1; OAEL-1,** *ll.* 1–862 *complete; Fr.* The Canterbury Tales. **CP-ChauG**

If there were not an utter and absolute dark. The End, The Beginning. David Herbert Lawrence. **CP-LawrD**

If there's any thing you want. From Me to You. The Beatles. **CP-Beatl**

If these are letters, they will have to be misread. 8/4/68. Adrienne Rich. **CP-RicAE** *Fr.* Ghazals: Homage to Ghalib. **SP-RicA2**

If these brief lays, of Sorrow born. Tennyson. *Fr.* In Memoriam A. H. H. **CP-TennA**

If these brief Records, by the Muses' art. To ————. William Wordsworth. **CP-WorW2**

If these lines that I. Absence. Stephen Dobyns. **SP-DobyS**

If Thetis and the Morn their sons did wail. 3.8. Ovid. **CP-MarlC**, *tr. by* Christopher Marlowe; *Fr.* Elegies.

If They Come in the Night. Marge Piercy. **SP-PierM**

If they had shape, how beautiful might be that shape. Hidden Within the Sleeves of Those Dark Robes. Stephen Dobyns. **SP-DobyS**

If this comes creased and creased again and soiled. Pocket Poem. Ted Kooser. **SP-KoosT**

If this country is a bastard. Request. Maya Angelou. **SP-AngeM**

If This Great World of Joy and Pain. William Wordsworth. **CP-WorW2**

If this importunate heart trouble your peace. Lover Asks Forgiveness because of His Many Moods. William Butler Yeats. **CP-YeatW**

If this is death, it is not hard to bear. Vittoria Concluding the Opera of "Camilla." George Meredith. **CP-MerG2**

If this is "fading." Emily Dickinson. **CP-DickE**

If this is showbiz, then am I. Ian. Al Young. **CP-YounA**

If this is the word, how did you know it? Eskimo Villanelle. John Yau. **SP-YauJo**

If this looks like a poem. The Cuckold's Song. Leonard Cohen. **CP-CoheL**

If this uncertain age in which we dwell. The Lesson for Today. Robert Frost. **CP-FrosR**

If this uncertain living, these days that mount. To Thine Own Self. Edwin Rolfe. **CP-RolfE**

If This Were Faith. Robert Louis Stevenson. **CP-StevR**

If those I loved were lost. Emily Dickinson. **CP-DickE**

If "Those People" Like You. Alice Walker. **CP-WalkA**

If those who live in shepherd's bower. Contentment. James Thomson *and* David Mallet. **CP-ThomJ** *Fr.* Alfred: A Masque.

If thou art balked, O Freedom. The House of Friends. Walt Whitman. **CP-WhitW**

If thou art sorrowful, hide thy face! George Meredith. **CP-MerG2**

If thou art sweet as they are sad. Thule. Walter de la Mare. **CP-DeLaW**

If thou aske me (Deare) wherefore. To Mistresse Dorothy Parsons. Robert Herrick. **CP-HerrR**

If thou be dead, forgive and thou shalt live. Christina Georgina Rossetti. **CP-RosC2**

If thou beest he; but O how fall'n! how chang'd. John Milton. **SCV** *Fr.* Book I. **FHYEP; NAEL-1; OAEL-1; OxAEP-1** *Fr.* Paradise Lost. **CP-MiltJ**

If Thou beest taken, God forbid. Another, to His Saviour. Robert Herrick. **CP-HerrR**

If thou be'st ice, I do admire. The Miracle. Sir John Suckling. **CP-SuckJ**

If thou canst bear. Γνωθι Σεαυτον. Ralph Waldo Emerson. **CP-EmerR**

If thou chance for to find. To My Successor. George Herbert. **CP-HerbG**

If thou dislik'st the piece thou light'st on first. To the Sour[e] Reader. Robert Herrick. **CP-HerrR**

If thou hast found an honie-combe. The Hony-Combe. Robert Herrick. **CP-HerrR**

If thou in the dear love of some one Friend. For the Spot Where the Hermitage Stood on St Herbert's Island, Derwent-Water. William Wordsworth. **CP-WorW1**

If thou indeed derive thy light from Heaven. William Wordsworth. **CP-WorW1**

If thou longst so much to learne (sweet boy) what 'tis to love. Thomas Campion. **CP-CampT**

If thou must love me, let it be for nought. Sonnet. Elizabeth Barrett Browning. **BWW; CTC; FaFP; HBV; HeIP; InPS; LiTB; OBEV; OBNC; OBVV; OHCV; OXAEP-2; PFP; PoToHe; SoSe; TrGrPo; TreFS; WHA** *Fr.* Sonnets from the Portuguese. **CP-BroEB**

If Thou Sayest, Behold, We Knew It Not. Christina Georgina Rossetti. **CP-RosC2**

"Each soul I might have succoured, may have slain."

"I have done I know not what,—what have I done?"

"Thou Who hast borne all burdens, bear our load."

If thou survive my well-contented day. Sonnet 32. William Shakespeare. **EIL; GTBS; GTBS-6; GTBS-P; HBV; OBSC; PP** *Fr.* Sonnets. **CP-ShaWS**

If thou wert here, these tears were tears of light! Day-Dream, The ("If thou wert here, these tears were tears of light"). Samuel Taylor Coleridge. **CP-ColeS**

If thou wilt mighty be, flee from the rage. Sir Thomas Wyatt. **CP-WyatT**

If thou wouldst know the virtues of mankind. An Epigram on William, Lord Burl[eigh], Lo[rd] High Treasurer of England. Ben Jonson. **CP-JonsB**

If thou wouldst view the Belfry aright. The New Belfry of Christ Church, Oxford. "Lewis Carroll." **CP-CarrL**

If thought can reach to Heaven. The Rabbi's Song. Rudyard Kipling. **CP-KiplR**

If thro' the sea of night which here surrounds me. Anchored. Paul Laurence Dunbar. **CP-DunbP**

If thy body pine. Ralph Waldo Emerson. **CP-EmerR**

If thy darling favor thee. Hafiz, *tr. by* Ralph Waldo Emerson. **CP-EmerR** *Fr.* Odes.

If thy soul check thee that I come so near. Sonnet 136. William Shakespeare. *Fr.* Sonnets. **CP-ShaWS**

If time is only another dimension, then all that dies. Hungerfield. Robinson Jeffers. **CP-JefR3**

If tired of trees I seek again mankind. The Vantage Point. Robert Frost. **CP-FrosR**

If to a woman's head a painter would. Horace, of the Art of Poetry. Ben Jonson, *adapted from the Latin of Horace.* **CP-JonsB**

If to admire were to commend, my praise. To Mr Joshua Sylvester. Ben Jonson. **CP-JonsB**

If to be absent were to be. To Lucasta, [on] Going beyond the Seas. Richard Lovelace. **CP-LoveR**

If to be left were to be left alone. Edna St. Vincent Millay. **CP-MillE**

If to be sprong of high and princely blood. To the Right Noble and Vertuous Theophilus Howard, Lorde of Walden, Sonne and Heire to the Right Honorable the Earle of Suffolke. Thomas Campion. *Fr.* Lord Hay's Mask.

If to dance the hotel ballroom. 1975. Thom Gunn. **CP-GunnT**

If to my mind, great lord, I had a state. To the Right Honourable, the Lord Treasurer of England. An Epigram. Ben Jonson. **CP-JonsB**

If to that place. Place of grass. Insomnia. Robert Penn Warren. *Fr.* Tale of Time. **SP-WarrR**

If to Tradition faith be due. The Highland Broach. William Wordsworth. **CP-WorW2**

If to write, rewrite, and write again. Arthur Hugh Clough. **SP-ClouA**

If today, I follow death. Mourning Grace. Maya Angelou. **SP-AngeM**

If today was not an endless highway. Tomorrow Is a Long Time. "Bob Dylan." **CP-DylaB**

If(touched by love's own secret)we, like homing. Edward Estlin Cummings. **CP-CummE; SP-CummE**

If trees remain and carrion crows. The New Corbies. Louise McNeill. **SP-McNeL**

If truth in hearts that perish. Alfred Edward Housman. **CP-HousA**

If 'twere fair to suppose. Suppose. Paul Laurence Dunbar. **CP-DunbP**

If two may read aright. To Willie and Henrietta. Robert Louis Stevenson. **CP-StevR**

If underneath the water. Peter Grump. Christina Georgina Rossetti. **CP-RosC3**

If underwater and glowing, a red stone. Red Stone. Richard Hugo. **CP-HugoR**

If up's the word;and a world grows greener. Edward Estlin Cummings. **CP-CummE**

If vampires do suck blood, if space is time. How Does a Madsong Know That's What It Is? Miller Williams. **SP-WillM**

If Vertue be thy guide. To the Christian Reader of "Short Rules of Good Life." Robert Southwell. **CP-SoutR**

If waker care, if sudden [*or* sodayne] pale colo[u]r. Sir Thomas Wyatt. **CP-WyatT**

If warre, or want shall make me grow so poore. His Petition. Robert Herrick. **CP-HerrR**

If wars were won by feasting. The Dutch in the Medway. Rudyard Kipling. **CP-KiplR**

If we are to exist. Dying. Robert Creeley. **CP-CreeR**

If We Are to Know Where We Live. Kenneth Patchen. **CP-PatcK**

If we ask you to gladden through the tears. Kisses, Can You Come Back Like Ghosts? Carl Sandburg. **CP-SandC**

If We Could. Marsden Hartley. **CP-HartM**

If we could get the hang of it entirely. Entirely. Louis MacNeice. **CP-MacNL**

If we could reverse the world to what it changed. Outlivers (Harriet and Elizabeth). Robert Lowell. **SP-LoweR**

If we could see below. The Foil. George Herbert. **CP-HerbG**

If we fall in the race, though we win, the hoof-slide is scarred on the course. Rudyard Kipling. *Fr.* Certain Maxims of Hafiz. **CP-KiplR**

If we go back to where. But. Robert Creeley. **CP-CreeR**

If we had been given names to love. Bird-Window-Flying. Tess Gallagher. **SP-GallT**

If we happen to choke up on history, none too soon. A Serious Case. Mona Van Duyn. **SP-VanDM**

If we meet a gorilla. We Must Be Polite. Carl Sandburg. **CP-SandC**

If we must live again, not us; we might. Seals. Robert Lowell. **SP-LoweR**

If we rally at all, today, instead of keeping stark asunder. Rallying-Point. David Herbert Lawrence. **CP-LawrD**

If we shall live, we live. Meeting. Christina Georgina Rossetti. **CP-RosC3**

If we spend our life remembering what we love. Remember Graham. Richard Hugo. **CP-HugoR**

If We Take All Gold. Louise Bogan. **CP-BogaL**

If we talk, we're too tired to make love; if we. Marilyn Hacker. **SP-HackM** *Fr.* Taking Notice.

If we were such and so, the same as these. Purple Martins. Carl Sandburg. **CP-SandC**

If we will have the wisdom to survive. A Vision. Wendell Berry. *Fr.* Work Song. **CP-BerrW**

If well the Dice runne, lets applaud the cast. Good Luck Not Lasting. Robert Herrick. **CP-HerrR**

If well thou hast begun, goe on fore-right. The End. Robert Herrick. **CP-HerrR**

If What we could—were what we would. Emily Dickinson. **CP-DickE**

If what we remember is what we are. Pine Creek Parish Hall. Barton Sutter. **SP-SuttB**

If when Don Cupid's dart. Sir John Suckling. **CP-SuckJ**

If when my wife is sleeping. Danse Russe. William Carlos Williams. **CP-WilW1**

If when the sun at noon displays. Thomas Carew. **CP-CareT** (Song: Beautiful Mistress, A.) **CP-CareT**

If when these Lyricks (Cesar) You shall heare. To the King. Robert Herrick. **CP-HerrR**

If, when tomorrow's Sun with upward ray. Lines Composed in Passing through a Forest in Germany. Charlotte Smith. **CP-SmitC**

If, while my passion I impart. Imitated from the Welch. Samuel Taylor Coleridge. *Fr.* Effusions. **CP-ColeS**

If wholsome Diet can re-cure a man. Diet. Robert Herrick. **CP-HerrR**

If wishes would carry me over the land. Ralph Waldo Emerson. **CP-EmerR**

If with complaint the pain might be expressed. Sir Thomas Wyatt. **CP-WyatT**

If with old love of you, dear Hills! I share. Composed at Rydal on May Morning, 1838. William Wordsworth. *Fr.* Memorials of a Tour in Italy, 1837. **CP-WorW2**

If within tonight's erect. Edward Estlin Cummings. **CP-CummE**

If wounds in clothes, Cuts calls his rags, 'tis cleere. Upon Cuts. Robert Herrick. **CP-HerrR**

If wrecked upon the Shoal of Thought. Emily Dickinson. **CP-DickE**

If ye fear[e] to be affrighted. Robert Herrick. **CP-HerrR** (Another ("If ye fear to be affrighted").) **CP-HerrR**

If ye gae up to yon hill-tap. The Tarbolton Lasses. Robert Burns. **CP-BurnR**

If ye will with Mab find grace. The Fairies. Robert Herrick. **CP-HerrR**

If yellow betokens infidelity. Injudicious Gardening. Marianne Craig Moore. **CP-MoorM**

If yet I have not all thy love. Lovers' Infiniteness[e]. John Donne. **CP-DonnJ**

If You. Robert Creeley. **CP-CreeR**

If you and i awakening. Edward Estlin Cummings. **CP-CummE**

If you and I could change to beasts, what beast should either be? White Witchcraft. Robert Browning. **CP-BroR2**

If you are a dreamer, come in. Invitation. Shel Silverstein. **SP-SilS2**

If you are a man. How to Stop Smoking. Miller Williams. **SP-WillM**

If You Are a Man. David Herbert Lawrence. **CP-LawrD**

If you are become an eternal idea. To Giacomo Leopardi in the Sky. Charles Wright. **SP-WrigC**

If you are Black and for me. To a Suitor. Maya Angelou. **SP-AngeM**

If you are merry sing away. Mirth. Christopher Smart. **LAuP; OxBChV** *Fr.* Hymns for the Amusement of Children. **SP-SmarC**

If you are Phœbus Sister Delia, pray. Porcius Licinus, *tr. fr. Latin by* Richard Lovelace. **CP-LoveR**

If you are still alive when you read this. Goodbye. Bill Knott. **SP-KnotB**

If you ask him he will talk for hours. The Artist as an Old Man. Erica Jong. **SP-JongE**

If you asked. John Yau. **SP-YauJo**

If you believe nothing is always what's left. Welcome. Stephen Dunn. **SP-DunnS**

If you can come to no conclusion about death whatever. New Entrepreneurial Plan. Nelle Richmond Eberhart. **CP-EberR**

If you can imagine love letters written back and forth between Mary. Carl Sandburg. *Fr.* The People, Yes. **CP-SandC**

If you can keep your head when all about you. If. Rudyard Kipling. **CP-KiplR**

If you can't eat you got to. Edward Estlin Cummings. **CP-CummE**

If you can't finance it undercover. Romance Without Finance. Al Young. **CP-YounA**

If you can't join them beat them. Jenny Joseph. *Fr.* Life and Turgid Times of A. Citizen. **SP-JoseJ**

If you can't make a joke. Chuck Miller. **SP-MillC**

If you close the door, the night could last forever. Afterhours. "Lou Reed." **SP-ReedL**

If you come as softly. Memorial I. Audre Lorde. **SP-LordA**

If You Come Back. Erica Jong. **SP-JongE**

If you could shape in stone the thing you seek. Poem for a Painter Who Drinks Wine. Kay Boyle. **CP-BoylK**

If you could sit with me beside the sea to-day. Longing. Paul Laurence Dunbar. **CP-DunbP**

If you danced from midnight. The Twelve Dancing Princesses. Anne Sexton. **CP-SextA**

If you don't go you don't go. Ceremonial. Richard Eberhart. **CP-EberR**

If you don't know the kind of person I am. A Ritual to Read to Each Other. William Stafford. **SP-StafW**

If You find it in Your heart, can I be forgiven? Saving Grace. "Bob Dylan." **CP-DylaB**

If you from spoil of th' old world's farthest end. Cales and Guiana. John Donne. **CP-DonnJ**

If you get enough money. Sayings of Henry Stephens. Carl Sandburg. **CP-SandC**

If you getcha one girl, better get two. Gypsy Lou. "Bob Dylan." **CP-DylaB**

If You Gotta Go, Go Now. "Bob Dylan." **CP-DylaB**

If you had come away with me. April. William Carlos Williams. **CP-WilW1**

If You Had Known. Thomas Hardy. **CP-HardT**

If you had sat with Eilshemius. Eilshemius. Marsden Hartley. **CP-HartM**

If you happen upon my love. Love Message. David Herbert Lawrence. **CP-LawrD**

If you have acquired a taste for happiness. Grace Paley. **CP-PaleG**

If you have ceased. Kathleen Jessie Raine. **SP-RainK**

If you have formed [*or* formd] a Circle to go into. To God. William Blake. **CP-BlakW**

If you have revisited the town, thin Shade. To a Shade. William Butler Yeats. **CP-YeatW**

If you have taken this rubble for my past. Delta. Adrienne Rich. **SP-RicA1**

If you ignore the possibilities of art. For a Low Voice. William Carlos Williams. **CP-WilW1**

If you keep command of yourself. Nightpiece. Robinson Jeffers. **CP-JefR3**

If you knew where suffering comes from. Talking. Stephen Berg. **SP-BergS**

If you let me take your heart. Tell Me What You See. The Beatles. **CP-Beatl**

If you like my poems let them. Edward Estlin Cummings. **CP-CummE**

If you live with all the other people. Worm Either Way. David Herbert Lawrence. **CP-LawrD**

If you live where I come from. Excerpts from the Notebook of the Poet of Santo Tomas. Richard Shelton. **SP-ShelR**

If you look at the sky. Mission to Linz. Richard Hugo. **CP-HugoR**

If you look at your succession of desires. Muriel Rukeyser. **CP-RukeM**

If you make a revolution, make it for fun. A Sane Revolution. David Herbert Lawrence. **CP-LawrD**

If you mean to Please Every body you will. English Encouragement of Art Cromeks Opinions Put Into Rhyme. William Blake. **CP-BlakW**

If you meet my young man. Message to Perfidious Soldier. David Herbert Lawrence. *Fr.* Bits. **CP-LawrD**

If you never came with a pigeon rainbow purple. Sumach and Birds. Carl Sandburg. **CP-SandC**

If you never do anything for anyone else. The Immoral Proposition. Robert Creeley. **CP-CreeR**

If you open the door some evening. The Visitor. Siv Cedering Fox. **SP-CedeS**

If you play a Game of Chance know before you begin. William Blake. **CP-BlakW**

If you put in enough hours in bars, sooner or later you get to hear every imaginable kind of bullshit. Bob. Charles Kenneth Williams. **CP-WillC; SP-WillC**

If you rattle along like your mistress's tongue. Robert Burns. **CP-BurnR** (Pinned to Mrs R————'s Carriage.) **CP-BurnR**

If you refuse me once and think again. Song. Sir John Suckling. **CP-SuckJ**

If you see a child that shivers when it hears. Sonnet. Hayden Carruth. **CP-CarHS** *Fr.* Sonnets.

If You See Her, Say Hello. "Bob Dylan." **CP-DylaB**

If you see this song, my dear. Apologetic Postscript of a Year Later. Robert Louis Stevenson. **CP-StevR**

If you seek a heavenly light. Song: If You Seek. Thomas Merton. **CP-MertT**

If you should ever choose. Instructions. Shel Silverstein. **SP-SilS2**

If You Should Go. Countee Cullen. **CP-CullC**

If you should go there on such a day. The Park. Roy Fisher. *Fr.* City. **SP-FishR**

If you should look for this place after a handful of lifetimes. Tor House. Robinson Jeffers. **CP-JefR1**

If you should rise from Nowhere up to Somewhere. The Fear of God. Robert Frost. **CP-FrosR**

If you speak to me, some night, *fr. the French of* Villiers de l'Isle Adam. The Gifts. Richard Wilbur. **CP-WilbR**

If you stare out over the waters. The Waters. William Matthews. *Fr.* Flood. **SP-MattW**

If you start in loneliness. Leonard Nathan. **SP-NathL** *Fr.* To Be Read to Yourself in a Public Place, July 4, 1976.

If you stop to find out what your wages will be. Mary's Son. Rudyard Kipling. **CP-KiplR**

If you stopped there it was only to refuel. After a Train Trip, One Town Remains. Richard Hugo. **CP-HugoR**

If you take a poem. Sets. Roy Fisher. **SP-FishR**

If you take the moon in your hands. Hilda Doolittle. **AnAn; BoWoP; FaBoWP; NYBP** *Fr.* Sigil. **CP-DoolH**

(Moon in Your Hands, The.) **BoWoP; NYBP**

If you taste tears too often, inquisitive tongue. The Reprimand. Elizabeth Bishop. **CP-BishE**

If you tell me the wild boar. Wild Boar. Shel Silverstein. **SP-SilS2**

If you, that have grown old, were the first dead. The New Faces. William Butler Yeats. **CP-YeatW**

If you trap the moment before its ripe. William Blake. **CP-BlakW**

If you travel alone, hitchhiking. Traveling. Stephen Dunn. **SP-DunnS** *Fr.* Sympathetic Magic.

If you wake at midnight, and hear a horse's feet. A Smuggler's Song. Rudyard Kipling. **CP-KiplR** *Fr.* Hal o' the Draft. *Fr.* Puck of Pook's Hill.

If you walk back. Equilibrations. Archie Randolph Ammons. **SP-AmmoA**

If you wander far enough. Oh No. Robert Creeley. **CP-CreeR**

If you want a lover. I'm Your Man. Leonard Cohen. **CP-CoheL**

If you want justice. Demon Justice. David Herbert Lawrence. **CP-LawrD**

If you want my apartment, sleep in it. Rent. Jane Cooper. **SP-CoopJ**

If you want to get a glimpse of future possibilities. Signs of the Times. David Herbert Lawrence. **CP-LawrD**

If you want to have sex, you've got to trust. Sex and Trust. David Herbert Lawrence. **CP-LawrD**

If you want to know yourself. Know Thyself, and That Thou Art Mortal. David Herbert Lawrence. **CP-LawrD**

If you want to marry me, here's what you'll have to do. My Rules. Shel Silverstein. **SP-SilS2**

If you want to mumble roses and sheet steel. Cruel Experiments Continue! Gilbert Sorrentino. **SP-SorrG**

If you want to say no say. The Lighthouses. George Oppen. **CP-OppeG**

If you wear red tonight. Yes It Is. The Beatles. **CP-Beatl**

If you were bred on fairy tales. Still Reading Fairy Stories. Jenny Joseph. **SP-JoseJ**

If you were coming in the Fall. Emily Dickinson. **CP-DickE**

If you were exchanged in the cradle and. A Story That Could Be True. William Stafford. **SP-StafW**

If you were only one inch tall, you'd ride a worm to school. One Inch Tall. Shel Silverstein. **SP-SilS2**

If you were running, now you are. Sloth. Stephen Dobyns. **SP-DobyS**

If you were to stop and ask me. The Conductor of Nothing. Philip Levine. **SP-LeviP**

If you were to try to say. William Everson. **SP-EverW** *Fr.* The Blowing of the Seed.

If you were twenty-seven. Heaven. Philip Levine. **SP-LeviP**

If you will go down into yourself, under your surface personality. The Primal Passions. David Herbert Lawrence. **CP-LawrD**

If You Will Let Me Sing. Hilda Doolittle. **CP-DoolH**

If you will sit in the chair of the flower it will bear you, *one-line poem.* Inadequate Orderly Simplification, The. But the Three Natural Units. And Only Arbitrary Constants. Charles Olson. **CP-OlsoC**

If you will tell me why the fen. I May, I Might, I Must. Marianne Craig Moore. **CP-MoorM**

If you would go down into the dead. La Chute II. Charles Olson. **CP-OlsoC**

If you would guess, fond man, the secret. Help Me, Venus, You Who Led Me On. Charles Olson. **CP-OlsoC**

If you would happy company win. Titmouse. Walter de la Mare. **CP-DeLaW**

If you would have my heart love on. To Madame du Châtelet. Voltaire, *tr. fr. French by* Richard Wilbur. **CP-WilbR**

If you would poison your mind. Bitter Herb. Erica Jong. **SP-JongE**

If you would run. For the Running of the New York City Marathon. James Dickey. **CP-DickJ**

If you'll busk you as a bride. Boy Johnny. Christina Georgina Rossetti. **CP-RosC2**

If Your Eyes Had Been Blue. Hilda Doolittle. *Fr.* Child Poems. **CP-DoolH**

If your hound dog runs the backtrack. How to Unbewitch a Backtracking Hound. Louise McNeill. **SP-McNeL**

If your mem'ry serves you well. This Wheel's on Fire. "Bob Dylan." **CP-DylaB**

If your neighbour disappears. Warning. Leonard Cohen. **CP-CoheL**

If your Nerve, deny you. Emily Dickinson. **CP-DickE**

If your tired unspeaking head. Homily. Allen Tate. **CP-TateA**

If you're / not in. Market Adviser. Archie Randolph Ammons. **SP-AmmoA**

If you're great enough. Shame on You. Langston Hughes. **SP-HughL**

If you're list'ning to this song. Only a Northern Song. George Harrison. **CP-Beatl**

If you're off to Philadelphia in the morning. Philadelphia. Rudyard Kipling. **CP-KiplR**

If you've ever been in a car. Stun. James Schuyler. **CP-SchuJ**

If you've ever stole a pheasant-egg be'ind the keeper's back. Loot. Rudyard Kipling. **CP-KiplR**

If you've just once been happy. The Summit. Frederick Morgan. **SP-MorgF**

If Zeus chose us a King of the flowers in his mirth. Song of the Rose. Sappho, *tr. fr. Greek by* Elizabeth Barrett Browning. **CP-BroEB**

If(among / silent skies). Edward Estlin Cummings. **CP-CummE**

Iff I were giv'n to mirthe 't'wowld be more cross. Sonnet 39. Mary Sidney, Countess of Montgomery Wroth. *Fr.* Pamphilia to Amphilanthus. **CP-WrotM**

If(you are i why certainly). Edward Estlin Cummings. **CP-CummE**

Iglits and His Wife. Carl Sandburg. **CP-SandC**

Iglits' wife spoke of her own novel, of a Norwegian's novel and came. Iglits and His Wife. Carl Sandburg. **CP-SandC**

Ignis. Hayden Carruth. *Fr.* Journey to a Known Place. **CP-CarHL**

Ignoble Procession, The. David Herbert Lawrence. **CP-LawrD**

Ignominy to receive, The. Emily Dickinson. **SP-DickE**

Ignorance. Philippe Jaccottet. *Fr.* Three Poems by Phillipe Jaccottet. **SP-MahoD**

Ignorance. Philip Larkin. **CP-LarkP**

Ignorance a Sunset, An. Emily Dickinson. **CP-DickE**

Ignorance came in stones of gold. Medley. Carl Sandburg. **CP-SandC**

Ignorance, error, cupidity, and sin. To the Reader. Charles Baudelaire, *tr. fr. French by* Stanley Kunitz. **CP-KuniS**

Ignorant, in the sense. Death of an Irishwoman. Michael Hartnett. **SP-HarMi**

Ignorant sun / Shone, shone in winter, The. February. Daniel Gerard Hoffman. **SP-HoffD**

Ignorant two, we glide. On Minding One's Own Business. James Wright. **CP-WrigJ**

Ignotum spatiari horto, dicumbere mensis. Ad Reverendum Patrem Fratrem Thomam Burke O.P. Collegium S. Beunonis Invisentem. Gerard Manley Hopkins. **CP-HopkG**

Ignu. Allen Ginsberg. **CP-GinsA**

Igor Stravinsky. Charles Olson. **CP-OlsoC**

Ike. Rita Dove. **SP-DoveR**

IKEY(GOLDBERG)'S WORTH I'M. Edward Estlin Cummings. **CP-CummE**

Il etait une petite fille de dix ans. Si Peu Séduisante. Stevie Smith. **CP-SmitS**

Il Mystico. Gerard Manley Hopkins. **CP-HopkG**

Il Penseroso. John Milton. **CP-MiltJ**

Poetry and the Melancholy Man. **EPCY**

"Sweet bird that shunn'st the noise of folly." **CH**

Il Piccolo Rifiuto. Louis MacNeice. **CP-MacNL**

Il Rosseggiar Dell'Oriente Canzoniere. Christina Georgina Rossetti. **CP-RosC3**

Amicizia: Sirocchia Son D'Amor.

Amico e Più Che Amico Mio.

Amor Dormente?

Amor Si Sveglia?

"Blumine" Risponde.

Eppure Allora Venivi.

Finestra Mia Orientale.

Iddio C'illumini!

Lassù Fia Caro Il Rivederci.

Lassuso Il Caro Fiore.

Luscious and Sorrowful.

Non Son Io La Rosa Ma Vi Stetti Appresso.

Nostre Voluntà Quieti Virtù di Carità.

Oggi.

Oh Forza Irresistibile Dell'umile Preghiera.

Per Preferenza.

Ripetizione.

Sapessi Pure!

Se Cossi Fosse.

Se Fossi Andata a Hastings.

Si Rimanda La Tocca-Caldaja.

Il y a Cent Ans. George Meredith. **CP-MerG2**

Il y avait cinq vierges. *see also* The Five Virgins, *tr. by* William Davis. Thomas Merton. **CP-MertT**

I'le come, I'le creep, (though Thou dost threat). To God. Robert Herrick. **CP-HerrR**

Ile doe my nothing too; and try / To dabble to thy memory. To My Deare Brother, Colonel Richard Lovelace. Dudley Posthume Lovelace. *Fr.* Commendatory Poems. **CP-LoveR**

Ile dote noe more, nor shall mine eyes. Sonnet, A. Robert Herrick. **CP-HerrR**

Ile get me hence. Of Love. Robert Herrick. **CP-HerrR**

I'le hope no more. To His Deere God. Robert Herrick. **CP-HerrR**

Ile sing no more, nor will I longer write. On Himselfe. Robert Herrick. **CP-HerrR**

I'le to thee a Simnell bring. To Dianeme; a Ceremonie in Glocester. Robert Herrick. **CP-HerrR**

Ilford Rose Book. James Schuyler. **CP-SchuJ**

Iliad, The. Homer, *tr. fr. Greek.*

  Achilles over the Trench. **CP-MerG2**

  Agamemnon in the Fight. **CP-MerG1**

  Assembly of the Achaians. **CP-MerG2**

  "Bibber besotted, with scowl of a cur, having heart of a deer, thou!" **CP-MerG1**

  Clash in Arms of the Achaians and Trojans. **CP-MerG1**

  Episode of Sarpedon, The. **CP-PopeA**

  "Thus *Hector*, great in Arms, contends in vain."

  "Frail as the leaves that quiver on the sprays." **CP-JohnS**

  Hector and Andromache. **CP-BroEB**, *tr. by* Elizabeth Barrett Browning;

  Helen on the Skaian Gates. **CP-MerG2**

  Horses of Achilles, The. **CP-MerG1**

  Hypnos on Ida. **CP-MerG1**

  Invective of Achilles, The. **CP-MerG1**

  Marshalling of the Achaians. **CP-MerG1**

  Night Watch of the Trojans before Troy. **CP-MerG2**

  Nourishment before Battle. **CP-MerG2**

  Odysseus Encircled. **CP-MerG2**

  Paris and Diomedes. **CP-MerG1**

  Shield of Achilles, The. **CP-MerG2**

  Translation of Part of the Dialogue Between Hector and Andromach; from the Sixth Book of Homer's *Iliad* (VI 390–502). **CP-JohnS**

  Vengeance of Apollo, The. **CP-MerG2**

  "Work'd into sudden rage by wintry show'rs." **CP-JohnS**

I'll Ay[e] Ca' in by Yon Town. Robert Burns. **CP-BurnR**

I'll Be Back. The Beatles. **CP-Beatl**

I'll be in my own room, upstairs. A Nightmare of the Suburbs. Jane Cooper. **SP-CoopJ**

I'll Be Your Baby Tonight. "Bob Dylan." **CP-DylaB**

I'll Be Your Mirror. "Lou Reed." **SP-ReedL**

I'll bet that Hubble made. The Red Shift. Robert Pack. **SP-PackR**

I'll call you Bedford, Ed. That's what you called me. Last Words to James Wright. Richard Hugo. **CP-HugoR**

I'll carry you off. Fragment of an Agon. Thomas Stearns Eliot. **LiTB** *Fr.* Sweeney Agonistes. **CP-ElioT**

I'll clutch—and clutch. Emily Dickinson. **CP-DickE**

I'll [*or* Ile] come to thee in all those shapes. To Electra. Robert Herrick. **CP-HerrR**

I'll come when thou art saddest. Emily Brontë. **CP-BronE**

I'll crush you, said sea. Flatfish. Dabney Stuart. **SP-StuaD**

I'll Cry Instead. The Beatles. **CP-Beatl**

I'll dabble in specifics in my bath. Marilyn Hacker. **SP-HackM** *Fr.* Separations.

I'll do what the raids suggest. A Boy. John Ashbery. **SP-AshbJ**

I'll [*or* I'le] do [*or* doe] my best to win, when'ere I wooe. Zeal Required in Love. Robert Herrick. **CP-HerrR**

I'll drink if I can find it. A Holy Well. Brendan Galvin. **SP-GalvB**

I'll drink to thee only with my eyes. Salute Valentine. Delmore Schwartz. *Fr.* Occasional Poems. **SP-SchwD**

I'll Eat My Split-Level Turkey in the Breezeway. Ogden Nash. **CP-NashO**

Ill fared it now with my poor wife, I ween. Fragment: A Somersetshire Tragedy. William Wordsworth. **CP-WorW1**

Ill-fated Genius! Heaven-taught Fergusson. Robert Burns. **CP-BurnR**

Ill-fated Heart! and can it be. On a Cornelian Heart Which Was Broken. Byron. **CP-Byron**

I'll Follow the Sun. The Beatles. **CP-Beatl**

I'll gaze no more on her bewitching face. Thomas Carew. **CP-CareT** (Song: Murdering Beauty.) **CP-CareT**

I'll get along he said with blue champagne. Strambotto. Gilbert Sorrentino. **SP-SorrG**

I'll Get One Tomorrow. Ogden Nash. **CP-NashO**

I'll Get You. The Beatles. **CP-Beatl**

I'll go and sit down a few minutes with my soul. Hello. Of the United States. Charles Olson. **CP-OlsoC**

I'll go into the bedroom silently and lie down between the bridegroom and the bride. Love Poem on Theme by Whitman. Allen Ginsberg. **CP-GinsA**

Ill Government. Robert Herrick. **CP-HerrR**

I'll haunt this town, though gone the maids and men. The Dream of All the Springfield Writers. Nicholas Vachel Lindsay. **CP-LindV**

I'll have you by the short and curly hair. Catullus. *See* Carmen 16: "Pedicabo et irrumabo."

I'll Have Your Heart. Stevie Smith. **CP-SmitS**

I'll keep a little tavern. Tavern. Edna St. Vincent Millay. **CP-MillE**

I'll Keep It with Mine. "Bob Dylan." **CP-DylaB**

I'll know no more;—the heart is torn. Sir Eustace Grey. George Crabbe. **SP-CrabG**

I'll Mak You Be Fain to Follow Me. Robert Burns. **CP-BurnR**

I'll make it; but it may take me. O, Thou Opening, O. Theodore Roethke. **CP-RoetT**

I'll miss the small birds that come. The Birds. Robert Creeley. **CP-CreeR**

I'll never get to where I'm going! Everything in Order. Thomas McGrath. **SP-McGrT**

I'll not discuss death with you by any name, however gently, soberly, you ask. A Poem for Samuel Beckett. Kay Boyle. **CP-BoylK**

I'll not mis-spend in praise the narrow room. To My Worthy Friend, Master Davenant Upon His Excellent Play, *The Just Italian*. Thomas Carew. **CP-CareT**

I'll not offend thee with a vain tear more. To the Same [Sir John Roe]. Ben Jonson. **CP-JonsB**

I'll not weep that thou art going to leave me. Emily Brontë. **CP-BronE** (Stanzas: "I'll not weep that thou art going to leave me.") **CP-BronE**

Ill-omen'd bird! whose cries portentous float. Supposed To Have Been Written in America. Charlotte Smith. **CP-SmitC**

I'll put this in my diary. Turkey in the Straw. William Carlos Williams. **CP-WilW2**

I'll Remember You. "Bob Dylan." **CP-DylaB**

I'll restore this old church for our marriage. The Church and the Wedding. Thomas Hardy. **CP-HardT**

I'll say goodbye to the hope of fame. Frederick Morgan. *Fr.* Eight Triolets. **SP-MorgF**

I'll say she's handsome, by all laws. Faithful Wilson. Thomas Hardy. **CP-HardT**

I'll send the feather from my Hat! Emily Dickinson. **CP-DickE**

I'll shake the bees. The Shepherd. Hilda Doolittle. **CP-DoolH**

I'll sing you a poem of a silly young king. Peanut-Butter Sandwich. Shel Silverstein. **SP-SilS2**

I'll sing you a song, ain't very long. Man on the Street. "Bob Dylan." **CP-DylaB**

I'll swing / By my ankles. The Acrobats. Shel Silverstein. **SP-SilS2**

I'll Take the High Road Commission. Ogden Nash. **CP-NashO**

I'll tell—being past all praying for. On the Death-Bed. Thomas Hardy. *Fr.* Satires of Circumstance in Fifteen Glimpses. **CP-HardT**

I'll tell my deaf mother on you! Fall on the floor. Punk Rock Your My Big Crybaby. Allen Ginsberg. **CP-GinsA**

I'll tell everything I can. "Lewis Carroll." **CP-CarrL** *Fr.* Through the Looking-Glass.

(White Knight's Ballad, The.) **CP-CarrL**

I'll tell thee now (dear love) what thou shalt do. Valediction, A: Of the Book. John Donne. **CP-DonnJ**

I'll tell you a dream i had once i was away up in the sky Blue,everything. Edward Estlin Cummings. **CP-CummE**

I'll tell you a tale of a Wife. Song. Robert Burns. **CP-BurnR**

I'll tell you how the Sun rose. Emily Dickinson. **CP-DickE**

I'll tell you the story of Jimmy Jet. Jimmy Jet and His TV Set. Shel Silverstein. **SP-SilS2**

I'll tell you what I don't want: an affair. Marilyn Hacker. **SP-HackM** *Fr.* Taking Notice.

I'll tell you what it was. I thought about those. In Nashville, Standing in the Wooden Circle Sawed Out from the Old Ryman Stage, the Picker has a vision. Miller Williams. **SP-WillM**

I'll tell you what to do. Defense. William Carlos Williams. **CP-WilW2**

Ill wind is stalking, An. Temper of Time. Sylvia Plath. **CP-PlatS**

I'll [*or* Ile] write, because I'll [*or* Ile] give. To Critic[k]s. Robert Herrick. **CP-HerrR**

I'll [*or* Il'e] write no more of Love; but now repent. On Himselfe. Robert Herrick. **CP-HerrR**

I'll Write Their Number Down When We Get Home. Ogden Nash. **CP-NashO**

Ille Terrarum. Robert Louis Stevenson. **CP-StevR**

Illegal Aliens. Grace Paley. **CP-PaleG**

Illegal Heart, The. Malcolm Lowry. **CP-LowrM**

Illegitimate Things. William Carlos Williams. **CP-WilW2**

Illic Jacet. Alfred Edward Housman. **CP-HousA**

Illinois Farmer. Carl Sandburg. **CP-SandC**

Illinois Village, The. Nicholas Vachel Lindsay. *Fr.* A Gospel of Beauty. **CP-LindV**

Illness, An. Robert Creeley. **CP-CreeR**

Illness, The. Charles Henri Ford. **SP-FordC**

Illness had wanted to kill her, The. The Smoke Shop Owner's Daughter. Jean Garrigue. **SP-GarrJ**

Ills I sorrow at, The. Any Human to Another. Countee Cullen. **CP-CullC**

Illumination, The. Stanley Jasspon Kunitz. **CP-KuniS**

Illuminations. Louise Glück. **SP-GlücL**

Illusion of Eternity, The. Richard Eberhart. **CP-EberR**

Illusion works impenetrable. Maia. Ralph Waldo Emerson. **CP-EmerR**

Illusionist, The. Stanley Jasspon Kunitz. **CP-KuniS**

Illusions like the tints of pearl. Ralph Waldo Emerson. **CP-EmerR**

Illustrated Books and Newspapers. William Wordsworth. **CP-WorW2**

Illustration [—a Footnote], The. Denise Levertov. **CP-LeveD**

Illustration. John Ashbery. **SP-AshbJ**

Illustration. Donald Hall. **CP-HallD**

Illustration, The / is nothing to you without the application. To a Steam Roller. Marianne Craig Moore. **CP-MoorM**

Illustration; the Jung-Frau and the Fall of the Rhine near Schaffhausen. William Wordsworth. *Fr.* Ecclesiastical Sonnets. **CP-WorW2**

Illustrative Lines. Robert Duncan. **SP-DuncR**

Illustrious Holland! hard would be his lot. Byron. **OBRV; OBSV** *Fr.* English Bards and Scotch Reviewers. **CP-Byron**

Illustrissimo, Potentissimoque Principi, *Frederico* Quinto, Rheni Comiti Palatino, Duci Bavariae, &c. Thomas Campion. **CP-CampT**

Illustrissimo Viro Domino Lanceloto Josepho de Maniban Grammatomanti [To That Renowned Man Lord Lancelot Joseph de Maniban Graphologist]. Andrew Marvell, *tr. fr. Latin by* William A. McQueen *and* Kiffin A. Rockwell. **CP-MarvA**

Illyrian woodlands, echoing falls. To E.L., on His Travels in Greece. Tennyson. **CP-TennA**

Ils ont vus les Pays-Bas, ils rentrent à Terre Haute. Lune de Miel. Thomas Stearns Eliot. **CP-ElioT**

Ilu, the Talking Drum. Etheridge Knight. **SP-KnigE**

I'm / asking / you dear to. Edward Estlin Cummings. **CP-CummE**

I'm a bow, my dual kiss, Ipsithilla. Catullus. *See* Carmen 32: "Call me to you / at siesta."

I'm a lofty lovely woman. The Lady in the Furs. Thomas Hardy. **CP-HardT**

I'm a long way from that place. What Is and Is Not. Charles Kenneth Williams. **CP-WillC**

I'm a Loser. The Beatles. **CP-Beatl**

I'm a Pleasure to Shop for. Ogden Nash. **CP-NashO**

I'm a riddle in nine syllables. Metaphors. Sylvia Plath. **CP-PlatS**

I'm about to go shopping. Song. James Schuyler. **CP-SchuJ**

I'm afraid of needles. Old. Anne Sexton. **CP-SextA**

I'm afraid the fellows in Putney rather wish they had. The 'Varsity Students' Rag. Sir John Betjeman. **CP-BetjJ**

I'm afraid there's many a spectacled sod. Wystan Hugh Auden. *Fr.* Shorts [1927–1932] ("Pick a quarrel, go to war"). **CP-AudeW**

I'm all alone in this world, she said. 50–50. Langston Hughes. **SP-HughL**

I'm almost / done, the hour. Echo. Robert Creeley. **CP-CreeR**

I'm at a table with Canadians. First Night at Sea. John Berryman. **CP-BerrJ**

I'm attached, and he's. Charles Henri Ford. **SP-FordC** *Fr.* Secret Haiku.

I'm beginning to lose patience. Wystan Hugh Auden. *Fr.* Shorts [1927–1932] ("Pick a quarrel, go to war"). **CP-AudeW**

I'm being punished this time for crying. Jetsam. Charles Kenneth Williams. **CP-WillC**

I'm big. The 6 Foot Goddess. Charles Bukowski. **SP-BukC1**

I'm Big Barney Zang of the railroad gang. Bang-Klang. Shel Silverstein. **SP-SilS2**

I'm call'd Will Whistle by a throng. Will Whistle. George Meredith. **CP-MerG2**

I'm ceded—I've stopped being Theirs. Emily Dickinson. **CP-DickE**

I'm cruising fast on a motorcycle. Bottoming Out. "Lou Reed." **SP-ReedL**

I'm crying all the time now. Tears. Allen Ginsberg. **CP-GinsA**

I'm delighted to see you. The Constellation Orion. Ted Kooser. **SP-KoosT**

I'm Down. The Beatles. **CP-Beatl**

I'm dyed, not dead. Animals' Last Words. Phoebe Hesketh. **SP-HeskP**

"I'm EMInent in RHYME!" she said. Rhyme? and Reason? "Lewis Carroll." **CP-CarrL**

I'm 'ere in a ticky ulster an' a broken billycock 'at. Back to the Army Again. Rudyard Kipling. **CP-KiplR**

I'm fixing a hole where the rain gets in and stops my mind from wandering where it will go. Fixing a Hole. The Beatles. **CP-Beatl**

I'm free from thee; and thou no more shalt heare. To Love. Robert Herrick. **CP-HerrR**

I'm from Connecticut. But please, not Stamford. Hayden Carruth. *Fr.* Vermont. **CP-CarHL**

I'm fucking the dead people now. This Wretch. Leonard Cohen. **CP-CoheL**

I.M. George Fitzpatrick. James Liddy. *Fr.* Love Songs of Corca Bascinn. **CP-LiddJ**

I'm Getting Back to Where I Was. Charles Bukowski. **SP-BukC1**

I'm getting better but Mendelssohn was right. Schumann Adds Trombones to His Second Symphony After Mendelssohn Conducts the First Performance. Miller Williams. **SP-WillM**

I'm getting tired of not wearing underwear. F. (Missive & Walk) I. #53. Frank O'Hara. **SP-OharF**

I'm getting weary looking in my baby's eyes. True Love Tends to Forget. "Bob Dylan." **CP-DylaB**

I'm glad it didn't offend me. Otherwise. John Ashbery. **SP-AshbJ**

I'm glad when they arrive. Scarlet. Charles Bukowski. **SP-BukC1**

I'm goin' down south. California. "Bob Dylan." **CP-DylaB**

I'm going down to Rose Marie's. Goin' to Acapulco. "Bob Dylan." **CP-DylaB**

I'm going on with this affair. Second Epistle. Donald Davie. *Fr.* Six Epistles to Eva Hesse. **CP-DavDo**

I'm going out to clean the pasture spring. The Pasture. Robert Frost. **CP-FrosR**

I'm going to be just like you, Ma. A Dance for Ma Rainey. Al Young. **CP-YounA**

I'm going to get. Winter Solstice. Charles Olson. **CP-OlsoC**

I'm going to lie down next to you. Chorus for One Voice. Charles Simic. **SP-SimiC**

I'm going to live without you. For My Father. Louise Glück. **MoLi** *Fr.* Metamorphosis. **SP-GlücL**

I'm going to roll up. Jack's Blues. Robert Creeley. **CP-CreeR**

I'm going to swim for my life. All Havens Astern. Charles Olson. **CP-OlsoC**

I'm going to write a novel, hey. Ode, An. John Updike. **CP-UpdiJ**

I'm gonna walk to the graveyard. Young Gal's Blues. Langston Hughes. **SP-HughL**

I'm growing much fonder of Barlow. Barlow. Stevie Smith. **CP-SmitS**

I'm half awake. Why Are We Here? Stephen Berg. **SP-BergS**

I'm happiest when most away. Emily Brontë. **CP-BronE**

I'm Happy Just to Dance with You. The Beatles. **CP-Beatl**

I'm happy, Kerouac, your madman Allen's. Malest Cornifici Tuo Catullo. Allen Ginsberg. **CP-GinsA**

I'm having a real day of it. Anxiety. Frank O'Hara. **SP-OharF**

I'm Here. Theodore Roethke. **CoAP; NYBP** *Fr.* Meditations of an Old Woman. **CP-RoetT**

I'm here; it's here. Memory. Stephen Berg. **SP-BergS**

I'm just an untutored traveling man. Have a Seat behind the Potted Palm, Sir. Ogden Nash. **CP-NashO**

I'm just average, common too. I Shall Be Free No. 10. "Bob Dylan." **CP-DylaB**

I'm just happy to be being. New Moon Over Grove Street. Al Young. **CP-YounA**

I'm just in love with all these three. A Three-Part Song. Rudyard Kipling. **CP-KiplR** *Fr.* Dymchurch Flit. *Fr.* Puck of Pook's Hill.

"Endlessly, endlessly, / The definition of mortality."

"Likely as not a ruined head gasket."

"On that water / Grey with morning."

"What ends / Is that."

Image of the poet's in the breeze, The. My House. "Lou Reed." **SP-ReedL**

Image of True Lovers' Death, The. Thomas Merton. **CP-MertT**

Image the images the great games therefore the locked. The Book of Job and a Draft of a Poem to Praise the Paths of the Living. George Oppen. **CP-OppeG**

Images. Kathleen Jessie Raine. **SP-RainK**

Images for Godard. Adrienne Rich. **CP-RicAE**

Images (holiness more / than image) extend like. At a Czech Tomb in Tuam. James Liddy. **CP-LiddJ**

Images of death arise. Richard Eberhart. *Fr.* The Lyric Absolute. **CP-EberR**

Images of Elspeth. John Berryman. **CP-BerrJ**

Images of Perfection. Charles Tomlinson. **CP-TomlC**

Imaginable Conference, An. John Updike. **CP-UpdiJ**

Imaginary Happening, London, An. Lawrence Ferlinghetti. **SP-FerlL**

Imaginary Iceberg, The. Elizabeth Bishop. **CP-BishE**

Imaginary Landscapes. Erica Jong. **CP-JongE**

Imaginary Number. Archie Randolph Ammons. **SP-AmmoA**

Imaginary Rose in a Book, An. Allen Ginsberg. **CP-GinsA**

Imaginary Universes. Allen Ginsberg. **CP-GinsA**

Imagination. Phoebe Hesketh. **SP-HeskP**

Imagination. William Wordsworth. **FiP** *Fr.* Cambridge and the Alps. *Fr.* The Prelude; Growth of a Poet's Mind [1850 vers.]. **CP-WorW3**

Imagination and Reality. Charles Bukowski. **SP-BukC1**

Imagination and Taste, How Impaired and Restored. William Wordsworth. **EnRP** *Fr.* The Prelude; Growth of a Poet's Mind [1850 vers.]. **CP-WorW3**

"In such strange passion, if I may once more." **OAEL-2**

"Oh! mystery of man, from what a depth." **FiP**

"There are in our existence spots of time." **PoEL-4; TOF**, *book* 12, *ll.* 208–335; **PoE**

(Spots of Time.) **PoE**, *book* 12, *ll.* 208–282;

Imagination—here the Power so called. Imagination. William Wordsworth. **FiP** *Fr.* Cambridge and the Alps. *Fr.* The Prelude; Growth of a Poet's Mind [1850 vers.]. **CP-WorW3**

Imagination, How Impaired and Restored. William Wordsworth. *Fr.* The Prelude; Growth of a Poet's Mind [1805 vers.]. **CP-WorW3**

"One Christmas-time, / The day before the holidays began." **RB**

"Ye motions of delight, that through the fields." **OBNC**

Imagination—ne'er before content. Ode: 1815. William Wordsworth. **CP-WorW2**

Imagination's Pride, The. Walter de la Mare. **CP-DeLaW**

Imaginative Life, The. Geoffrey Hill. **CP-HillG**

Imaginative Regrets. William Wordsworth. *Fr.* Ecclesiastical Sonnets. **CP-WorW2**

Imagine a black lake. Man as Image (MASSIF; CHEMISTRY). Jenny Joseph. *Fr.* Man as Matter. **SP-JoseJ**

Imagine a crowded war-time street. White Feather. John Berryman. **CP-BerrJ**

Imagine an empty house—a mansion, vast. Hot Water. John Updike. **CP-UpdiJ**

Imagine bird bones. Hayden Carruth. **CP-CarHS** *Fr.* The Clay Hill Anthology.

Imagine or remember how the road at last led us. Nocturne Militaire. Thomas McGrath. **SP-McGrT**

Imagine si ceci. Samuel Beckett. **CP-BeckS**

Imagine that any mind ever *thought* a red geranium! Red Geranium and Godly Mignonette. David Herbert Lawrence. **CP-LawrD**

Imagine what it must have been to have existence. Think—! David Herbert Lawrence. **CP-LawrD**

Imagining a Father. The Tale-Teller. Daniel Gerard Hoffman. **SP-HoffD**

Imagining Delaware. Richard Hugo. **CP-HugoR**

Imagining How It Would Be to Be Dead. Richard Eberhart. **CP-EberR**

Imagining in Writing. Robert Duncan. **SP-DuncR**

Imaginings. Thomas Hardy. **CP-HardT**

Imago. Wallace Stevens. **CP-StevW**

Imbecile. Wilfred Owen. **CP-OwenW**

Imbecile Night. Charles Bukowski. **SP-BukC2**

Imbellis, the bully, catches me in the dark. The Sweet Night Bleeds From Zimmer. Paul Zimmer. **SP-ZimmP**

Imber Nocturnus. Elizabeth Bishop. **CP-BishE**

Imberbi, si cui, Laurentia nubere vovit. *acc. by English translation.* Thomas Campion. **CP-CampT**

Imbued / with the light. Charles Olson. **SP-OlsoC** *Fr.* The Maximus Poems.

(Im)c-a-t(mo). Edward Estlin Cummings. **CP-CummE**

Imerro. Ezra Pound. *See* Thy soul / Grown delicate with satieties.

Imitated from Ossian. Samuel Taylor Coleridge. *Fr.* Effusions. **CP-ColeS**

Imitated From the Arpa Evangelica: Page 121. Christina Georgina Rossetti. **CP-RosC3**

Imitated from the Japanese. William Butler Yeats. **CP-YeatW**

Imitated from the Welch. Samuel Taylor Coleridge. *Fr.* Effusions. **CP-ColeS**

Imitation. Louis Zukofsky. *Fr.* 29 Songs. **CP-ZukLS**

Imitation Dance, The. Al Young. **CP-YounA**

Imitation of Juvenal — Satire VIII. William Wordsworth. **CP-WorW1**

Imitation of Pope A Compliment to the Ladies. William Blake. *See* Wondrous the Gods, more wondrous are the Men.

Imitation of Spen[s]er, An. William Blake. **CP-BlakW**

Imitation of Spenser. John Keats. **CP-KeatJ**

Imitation of Tibullus. Byron. **CP-Byron**

Imitations of Drowning. Anne Sexton. **CP-SextA**

Imitative Fragment. David Markson. **CP-MarkD**

Immaculate / December garden, An. Last Days of the Miser. Charles Tomlinson. **CP-TomlC**

Immalee. Christina Georgina Rossetti. **CP-RosC3**

Immature Pebbles. Louis Zukofsky. *Fr.* 29 Songs. **CP-ZukLS**

Immeasurable height, The. Types and Symbols of Eternity. William Wordsworth. **CBCK** *Fr.* Cambridge and the Alps. *Fr.* The Prelude; Growth of a Poet's Mind [1850 vers.]. **CP-WorW3**

Immediacy. Archie Randolph Ammons. **SP-AmmoA**

Immediacy's stone / has. Digging Wonder. Archie Randolph Ammons. **SP-AmmoA**

"Immediate Aim, The." Louis Zukofsky. *Fr.* 29 Songs. **CP-ZukLS**

Immediately on emerging from the dark tunnel. Orpheus. Stephen Dobyns. **SP-DobyS**

Immemorial, / And after us. Memory of V. I. Ulianov. Louis Zukofsky. *Fr.* 29 Poems. **CP-ZukLS**

Immense hope, and forbearance, The. Spring Day. John Ashbery. **SP-AshbJ**

Immense sadness / of approaching winter, The. Poem. John Haines. **SP-HainJ**

Immensity cloistered [or Immensitie cloysterd] in thy dear womb [or deare wombe]. Nativity [or Nativitie]. John Donne. *Fr.* La Corona. **ChIV-2; ESCV; OBS; Son** *Fr.* Holy Sonnets. **CP-DonnJ**

Immigrants, The. Margaret Atwood. **SP-AtwM1**

Immigrants. Robert Frost. **CP-FrosR**

Imminent Seventies, The. Robert Ranke Graves. **CP-GravR**

Immoderation. Archie Randolph Ammons. **SP-AmmoA**

Immolated. Herman Melville. **SP-MelvH**

Immoral Man. David Herbert Lawrence. **CP-LawrD**

Immoral Proposition, The. Robert Creeley. **CP-CreeR**

Immorality. David Herbert Lawrence. **CP-LawrD**

Immorality, The. David Herbert Lawrence. **CP-LawrD**

Immortal, The. William Blake. **LiTB; LoBV; MeMBP** *Fr.* The Book of Los. **CP-BlakW**

Immortal. William Carlos Williams. **CP-WilW1**

Immortal Autumn. Archibald MacLeish. **CP-MacLA**

Immortal[l] clothing I put on. The Transfiguration. Robert Herrick. **CP-HerrR**

Immortal Face. Marsden Hartley. **CP-HartM**

Immortal Hate. John Milton. **NOBE** *Fr.* Book I. **FHYEP; NAEL-1; OAEL-1; OxAEP-1** *Fr.* Paradise Lost. **CP-MiltJ**

Immortal Heat, O let thy greater flame. Love (2). George Herbert. **CP-HerbG**

Immortal Helix. Archibald MacLeish. **CP-MacLA**

Immortal is an ample word. Emily Dickinson. **CP-DickE**

Immortal Love, author of this great frame. Love (1). George Herbert. **CP-HerbG**

Immortal Love, forever full. Our Master. John Greenleaf Whittier. **CP-WhitJ**

Immortal Part, The. Alfred Edward Housman. **CP-HousA**

Immortal spheres, O luscious pair. To a Lady, a Part of Her. David Markson. **CP-MarkD**

Immortal stood frozen amidst, The. The Immortal. William Blake. **LiTB; LoBV; MeMBP** *Fr.* The Book of Los. **CP-BlakW**

Immortality. John Hewitt. **CP-HewiJ**

Immortality. Christopher Smart. *Fr.* Hymns for the Amusement of Children. **SP-SmarC**

Immortality of Flowers, The. Emily Dickinson. **SP-DickE**

Immortality of the soul, The. Animula. Robinson Jeffers. **CP-JefR3**

Immortality she gave, The. Emily Dickinson. **CP-DickE**

Immortals. James Dickey. **CP-DickJ**

Immram. Paul Muldoon. **SP-MuldP**

Immrama. Paul Muldoon. **SP-MuldP**

"Immurata" Sister, An. Christina Georgina Rossetti. **CP-RosC2**

Immured in Bothwell's towers, at times the Brave. Bothwell Castle. William Wordsworth. **CP-WorW2**

Immured in Heaven! Emily Dickinson. **CP-DickE**

Imogen. Walter de la Mare. **CP-DeLaW**

Imp Within, The. Walter de la Mare. **CP-DeLaW**

Impact. Karl Shapiro. **SP-ShapK**

Impalpabilities, The. Charles Tomlinson. **CP-TomlC**

Imparitie doth ever discord bring. Meane, The. Robert Herrick. **CP-HerrR**

Impartial Law enrolled a name, The. My Name and I. Robert Ranke Graves. **CP-GravR**

Impasse. Carl Sandburg. **CP-SandC**

Impasto of what is past, The. Travels. Denise Levertov. **CP-LeveD**

Impatiens. Louis Zukofsky. **CP-ZukLS**

Impatient all the foggy day for night. Fever. Thom Gunn. **CP-GunnT**

Impatient as we were for all of them to join us. The Bungalows. John Ashbery. **SP-AshbJ**

Impatient with cripples, foreigners, children. Il Piccolo Rifiuto. Louis MacNeice. **CP-MacNL**

Impeccable Conception. Maya Angelou. **SP-AngeM**

Impeccable is possible, The. Selectric II. Al Young. **CP-YounA**

Imperante Augusto Natus Est. Robert Browning. **CP-BroR2**

Imperator Victus. Hart Crane. **CP-CranH**

Impercipient, The. Thomas Hardy. **CP-HardT**

Imperfect Lover, The. Nicanor Parra, *tr. fr. Spanish by* Thomas Merton. **CP-MertT**

Imperial bird, who wont to soar. On an Eagle Confined in a College-Court. Christopher Smart. **SP-SmarC**

Imperial by the People's will. Ode to H.I.M. Napoleon 3d. George Meredith. **CP-MerG2**

Imperial consort of the Fairy-king, The. The Wild Duck's Nest. William Wordsworth. **CP-WorW2**

Imperial Rescript, An. Rudyard Kipling. **CP-KiplR**

Imperial Stature, the colossal stride, The. Recollection of the Portrait of King Henry Eighth, Trinity Lodge, Cambridge. William Wordsworth. **CP-WorW2**

Imperiously ringing, "Νὰ τὰ ποῦμε." Chimes for Yahya. James Merrill. **SP-MerrJ**

Imperturbable miller's man, The. The Miller's Man. Robert Ranke Graves. **CP-GravR**

Impetus, awesome!, The. Sixth Epistle. Donald Davie. *Fr.* Six Epistles to Eva Hesse. **CP-DavDo**

Implications. Carl Sandburg. **CP-SandC**

Implies that some therefore. All Do Not All Things Well. Thom Gunn. **CP-GunnT**

Imploring Mecca / to achieve. Be-Bop Boys. Langston Hughes. **SP-HughL**

Implosions. Adrienne Rich. **CP-RicAE; SP-RicA1; SP-RicA2**

Impomptu, on Mrs. W. Riddell's Birthday, 4th Novr. 1793. Robert Burns. **CP-BurnR**

Imponderable the dinosaur. Cape Hatteras. Hart Crane. **InPS; MoAB; MoAmPo** *Fr.* The Bridge. **CP-CranH**

Import, of body a hostess at lunch to my friend a representative, The. A Woman's Nipples Is the Rose of the World. Charles Olson. **CP-OlsoC**

Importance of Being Toothless, The. Chuang Tzu, *tr. fr. Chinese by* Thomas Merton. **CP-MertT**

Importance of Elsewhere, The. Philip Larkin. **CP-LarkP**

Importance of its hat to a form becomes, The. The Pastor Caballero. Wallace Stevens. **CP-StevW**

Importer, An. Robert Frost. **CP-FrosR**

Importunate for attention. Bowing the Head. Donald Davie. **CP-DavDo**

Importunately / inopportune, / blessed is he that cometh in. Benedictus. Donald Davie. **CP-DavDo**

Importuned through the mails, accosted over the telephone. Cave Canem. Edna St. Vincent Millay. **CP-MillE**

Impossibilities to His Friend. Robert Herrick. **CP-HerrR**

Impossibility, like Wine. Emily Dickinson. **CP-DickE**

Impossibility of Dying in Your Arms Does not Sadden Me, The. Charles Henri Ford. **SP-FordC**

Impossible, The. Robert Ranke Graves. **CP-GravR**

Impossible Day, The. Robert Ranke Graves. **CP-GravR**

Impossible Iambics. Carl Sandburg. **CP-SandC**

Impossible, I'd have bet. Bulwark. Laurence Lieberman. **SP-LiebL**

Impossible Indispensability of the Ars Poetica, The. Hayden Carruth. **CP-CarHS**

Impossible Marriage, The. Donald Hall. **CP-HallD**

Impossible Poem, The. George Oppen. **NNaP** *Fr.* Some San Francisco Poems. **CP-OppeG**

Impossible, rightly, to define these / conditions of. For Rainer Gerhardt. Robert Creeley. **CP-CreeR**

Impossible to doubt the world: it can be seen. Parousia. George Oppen. *Fr.* Five Poems about Poetry. **CP-OppeG**

Impossible to speak to her, and worse. John Berryman. *Fr.* Sonnets to Chris. **CP-BerrJ**

Impossibly / motivated by midnight. Edward Estlin Cummings. **CP-CummE**

Impoverished Irish Peer, An. Sir John Betjeman. **CP-BetjJ**

Impresario of neediness. Carmen 21. Catullus. *Fr.* Carmina. **CP-Catul**

Impression: Fog Off the Coast of Dorset. Edna St. Vincent Millay. **CP-MillE**

Impressionists, The. Erica Jong. **SP-JongE**

Imprimis he was "broke." Thereafter left. Giffen's Debt. Rudyard Kipling. **CP-KiplR**

Imprint. Phoebe Hesketh. **SP-HeskP**

Imprisoned in a Liverpool of self. Malcolm Lowry. **CP-LowrM**

Imprisoned in these wires of rain, I watch. Return to D'Ennery; Rain. Derek Walcott. **CP-WalcD**

Impromptu ["If John marries Mary, and Mary alone"]. William Cowper. **CP-CowpW**

Impromptu ["So I have seen the maids in vain"]. William Cowper. **CP-CowpW**

Impromptu. Byron. **CP-Byron**

Impromptu. Thomas Gray. **CP-GrayT**

Impromptu, in Reply to a Friend. Byron. **CP-Byron**

Impromptu Lines to Greet Marie Bancroft. Robert Browning. **CP-BroR2**

Impromptu on Hearing a Sermon by the Rev. T. R—Pronounced "Heavy." Robert Browning. **CP-BroR2**

Impromptu on Richard Wagner. Robert Browning. **CP-BroR2**

Impromptu on Winter. John Clare. **SP-ClarJ**

Impromptu Solo on a Balcony. Gilbert Sorrentino. *Fr.* Twelve Études for Voice and Kazoo. **SP-SorrG**

Impromptu: The Suckers. William Carlos Williams. **CP-WilW1**

Impromptu to Lady Winchelsea. Alexander Pope. **CP-PopeA**

Improved Farm Land. Carl Sandburg. **CP-SandC**

Improvisation. Thom Gunn. **CP-GunnT**

Improvisation. Al Young. **CP-YounA**

Improvisation upon the Theme of the Lady and the Unicorn, An. Jean Garrigue. **SP-GarrJ**

Improvisatore, The. Samuel Taylor Coleridge. **CP-ColeS**

Impulse, The. Robert Frost. **ArLo; HoPM; NePA; RaBo** *Fr.* The Hill Wife. **CP-FrosR**

Impulse. David Herbert Lawrence. **CP-LawrD**

In / s p i r e d/the aspirate. For a Muse Meant. Robert Duncan. **SP-DuncR**

In / Spring comes(no- / one). Edward Estlin Cummings. **CP-CummE**

In a Back Alley. Carl Sandburg. **CP-SandC**

In a Bad Time. Wallace Stevens. **CP-StevW**

In a Balcony. Robert Browning. **CP-BroR1**

In a Bath Teashop. Sir John Betjeman. **CP-BetjJ**

In a between world, a world of amber. Spring Sunshine. Louis MacNeice. **CP-MacNL**

In a Bird Sanctuary. Richard Wilbur. **CP-WilbR**

In a blue bar at the crossroads, before you turn. The Liberator. Derek Walcott. **CP-WalcD**

In a Blue Smoke. James Liddy. **CP-LiddJ**

In a Boat. David Herbert Lawrence. **CP-LawrD**

In a Boat Shed. Robert Creeley. **CP-CreeR**

In a bookshelf at the dark living room's end. Illustration. Donald Hall. **CP-HallD**

In a bookstore on the East Side. Burning Oneself In. Adrienne Rich. **SP-RicA2**

In a borrowed field they dig in their feet. Women's Tug of War at Lough Arrow. Tess Gallagher. **SP-GallT**

In a Breath. Carl Sandburg. **CP-SandC**

In a broken / mirror you might. The Point. Hayden Carruth. **CP-CarHS**

In a Brooklyn Park. Charles Tomlinson. **CP-TomlC**

In a brown field stood a tree. Lines to a Yorkshire Terrier. Thomas Stearns Eliot. *Fr.* Five-Finger Exercises. **CP-ElioT**

In a Bye-Canal. Herman Melville. **SP-MelvH**

In a car Gray smoke over Elmira. Flash Back. Allen Ginsberg. **CP-GinsA**

In a Carriage, upon the Banks of the Rhine. William Wordsworth. *Fr.* Memorials of a Tour of the Continent; 1820. **CP-WorW2**

In a Cathedral City. Thomas Hardy. **CP-HardT**

In a cave at the mouth of Dead Man's Holler. Moonshiner. Louise McNeill. **SP-McNeL**

In a Certain Place. Christina Georgina Rossetti. **CP-RosC3**

In a chain reaction. Atomic Pantoum. Peter Meinke. **SP-MeinP**

In a Church of Padua. Herman Melville. **SP-MelvH**

In a Churchyard. James Schuyler. **CP-SchuJ**

In a Churchyard. Richard Wilbur. **CP-WilbR**

In a cleft that's christened Alt. Man and the Echo. William Butler Yeats. **CP-YeatW**

In a coffee house at 3 a.m. My Son and I. Philip Levine. **SP-LeviP**

In a cold night. Blood. James Dickey. **CP-DickJ**

In a corner are the young women. Distance Between Us. Chuck Miller. **SP-MillC**

In a corner of a parlor-car. En Route to Southampton. James Schuyler. **CP-SchuJ**

In a Country Cemetery in Iowa. Ted Kooser. **SP-KoosT**

In a Country Churchyard. Wystan Hugh Auden. **CP-AudWJ**

In a country without saints or shrines. The Springs. Wendell Berry. **CP-BerrW**

In a Court. Hart Crane. **CP-CranH**

In a cove reaching back between ridges. The Persimmons. Gary Snyder. **CP-SnydG**

In a covered way along the outside of the building. Continuity. Roy Fisher. **SP-FishR**

In a Crumbling. Kenneth Patchen. **CP-PatcK**

In a Dark House. Muriel Rukeyser. **CP-RukeM**

In a day we pass from the Northern Lights. Flounder. Robert Lowell. **SP-LoweR**

In a deep thought of you and concentration. The Terraced Valley. Robert Ranke Graves. **CP-GravR**

In a dense wood, a drear wood. Bitter Waters. Walter de la Mare. **CP-DeLaW**

In a disingenuous letter. The Oranges Returned. Gilbert Sorrentino. **SP-SorrG**

In a Disused Graveyard. Robert Frost. **CP-FrosR**

In a dream I meet. A Meeting. Wendell Berry. **CP-BerrW**

In a dream I was in a tunnel struggling. The Dream. Richard Eberhart. **CP-EberR**

In a Dream of Horses. Stephen Dunn. **SP-DunnS**

In a dream one sees it. The Charm. Gilbert Sorrentino. **SP-SorrG**

In a dream within a dream I dreamt a dream. Rough Song of Animals Dying. Lawrence Ferlinghetti. **SP-FerlL**

In a dream you had. Charles Henri Ford. **SP-FordC** *Fr.* Emblems of Arachne.

In a Dreame, Love bad me go. Upon Love. Robert Herrick. **CP-HerrR**

In a dull hour thinking of the swan. Roy Fisher. **SP-FishR** *Fr.* New Diversions.

In a dusty square hemmed by pink stucco. A Married Walk in a Hot Place. Marge Piercy. **SP-PierM**

In a English Garden. Paul Laurence Dunbar. **CP-DunbP**

In a Eweleaze near Weatherbury. Thomas Hardy. **CP-HardT**

In a fantastic light. Gilbert Sorrentino. **SP-SorrG**

In a far-away northern county in the placid pastoral region. The Ox-Tamer. Walt Whitman. **CP-WhitW**

In a far-distant land they dwell. The Lotus-Eaters: Ulysses to Penelope. Christina Georgina Rossetti. **CP-RosC3**

In a far far land where men are men. The Snow King. Rita Dove. **SP-DoveR**

In a fashionable suburb of Santa Barbara. In Montecito. Randall Jarrell. **CP-JarrR**

In a ferny byway. The Alarm. Thomas Hardy. **CP-HardT**

In a fine country, in a sunny country. Short Story. Edna St. Vincent Millay. **CP-MillE**

In a five-minute stillness in September. Frederick Morgan. **SP-MorgF**

In a Former Resort after Many Years. Thomas Hardy. **CP-HardT**

In a fourfold silence the music. Two Deliberate Exercises. William Carlos Williams. **CP-WilW2**

In a fright-wig / that is his own hair. Performances. William Dickey. **SP-DickW**

In a garden shady this holy lady. Wystan Hugh Auden. **FaBoTw; MP; TwCP** *Fr.* Anthem for St. Cecilia's Day. **CP-AudeW**

In a Garret. Herman Melville. **SP-MelvH**

In a gigantic pot du chambre, scrolled. Rustication. Adrienne Rich. **CP-RicAE**

In a Glass of Cider. Robert Frost. **CP-FrosR**

In a Gondola. Robert Browning. **CP-BroR1**

"Moth's kiss, first, The!" **BoLoP; GBL; OBEV; TrGrPo**
(Song: "Moth's kiss, first, The!") **TrGrPo**

In a Gradually Moving Car Somewhere in Calcutta. Miller Williams. **SP-WillM**

In a Green Night. Derek Walcott. **CP-WalcD**

In a grove most rich of shade. Eighth Song. Sir Philip Sidney. **NoSic; OAEP; OBSC** *Fr.* Astrophil and Stella. **SP-SidnP**

In a hand like a bowl. The Restored. Theodore Roethke. **CP-RoetT**

In a Hard Intellectual Light. Richard Eberhart. **CP-EberR**

In a hard intellectual light / I will kill all delight. In a Hard Intellectual Light. Richard Eberhart. **CP-EberR**

In a heavy time I dogged myself. He Follows Himself. Thomas Hardy. **CP-HardT**

In a high wind. Hands and Eyes. Louis MacNeice. **CP-MacNL**

In a high wind the. Poem. Archie Randolph Ammons. **SP-AmmoA**

In a hole-in-a-wall on Halsted Street sits a gypsy woman. Gypsy Mother. Carl Sandburg. **CP-SandC**

In a Hospital Garden, *after Henrikas Radauskas*. Randall Jarrell. **CP-JarrR**

In a house he remembers in the Howlong valley. Old Hokusai Print. Carl Sandburg. **CP-SandC**

In a house like that. Croydon. Sir John Betjeman. **CP-BetjJ**

In a hundred places in North Dakota. Something Is Dying Here. Thomas McGrath. **SP-McGrT**

In a hut of mud and fire. Gautama in the Deer Park at Benares. Kenneth Patchen. **CP-PatcK**

In a jeweler's shop I saw a man beating. Thin Strips. Carl Sandburg. **CP-SandC**

In a land that the sand overlays—the ways to her gates are untrod. The City of Brass. Rudyard Kipling. **CP-KiplR**

In a late Impressionist dream I am riding in an open touring-car with a. Late Impressionist Dream. Lawrence Ferlinghetti. **SP-FerlL**

In a Letter to C.P. William Cowper. **CP-CowpW**

In a Letter to the Same [C. P.]. William Cowper. **CP-CowpW**

In a Library. Walter de la Mare. **CP-DeLaW**

In a limpidity of silences. Limpidity of Silences. Kenneth Patchen. **CP-PatcK**

In a little, half-built street, where red and white villas. After School. David Herbert Lawrence. **CP-LawrD**

In a little house keep I pictures suspended, it is not a fix'd house. My Picture-Gallery. Walt Whitman. **CP-WhitW**

In a little house pictures I keep, many pictures hanging suspended—It is not a fixed house. Pictures. Walt Whitman. **CP-WhitW**

In a little room, a little plot, a little lifetime. Louis MacNeice. *Fr.* Suite for Recorders. **CP-MacNL**

In a little side street. The Living Theatre. Lawrence Ferlinghetti. **SP-FerlL**

In a living hold / of legs and table-spars. The Guesthouse. Steve Griffiths. **SP-GrifS**

In a London Flat. Thomas Hardy. **CP-HardT**

In a Lurgan Pub. John Hewitt. **CP-HewiJ**

In a magazine. Ernest Hemingway. **CP-HemiE**

In a manmade lake at first light. Jungle Clearance Ceylon. Louis MacNeice. **CP-MacNL**

In a middle of a room. Edward Estlin Cummings. **CP-CummE**

In a minute the doctor will find out what is wrong. A Utopian Journey. Randall Jarrell. **CP-JarrR**

In a minute, two inches of rain stream through my dry. Bosworth Field. Robert Lowell. **SP-LoweR**

In a moment exaggeration. Portrait by Holbein. May Sarton. **SP-SartM**

In a Moonlit Hermit's Cabin. Allen Ginsberg. **CP-GinsA**

In a Museum. Thomas Hardy. **CP-HardT**

In a Myrtle [or Mirtle] Shade. William Blake. **CP-BlakW**
("To a lovely mirtle shade.") **CP-BlakW**

In a nation of one hundred fine, mob-hearted, lynching, relenting, repenting millions. Nicholas Vachel Lindsay. *Fr.* Bryan, Bryan, Bryan, Bryan. **CP-LindV**

In a national magazine of repute. 10 Lions and the End of the World. Charles Bukowski. **SP-BukC2**

In a Neighborhood of Murder. Charles Bukowski. **SP-BukC1**

In a Notebook. James Fenton *and* John Fuller. **SP-FentJ**

In a pine tree, / A few yards from my window sill. I Try to Waken and Greet the World Once Again. James Wright. *Fr.* Two Hangovers. **CP-WrigJ**

In a Poem. Robert Frost. **CP-FrosR**

In a poem made by Cummings, long since, his. John Berryman. *Fr.* Sonnets to Chris. **CP-BerrJ**

In a Province. Frank Templeton Prince. **CP-PrinF**

In a public darkness. Shrinking Horizon. Steve Griffiths. **SP-GrifS**

In a pyloned desert where the scorpion reigns.　Red Stains.　Allen Tate. **CP-TateA**

In a red winter hat blue.　Self-Portrait.　William Carlos Williams.　**LCAP** *Fr.* Pictures from Brueghel.　**CP-WilW2**

In a refrigerator car at Empress.　Deserter.　Malcolm Lowry.　**CP-LowrM**

In a robot-democracy, nobody is willing to serve.　Robot-Democracy.　David Herbert Lawrence.　**CP-LawrD**

In a Roman tram, where the famous Roman mob.　The Thief.　Stanley Jasspon Kunitz.　**CP-KuniS**

In a room on West Tenth Street in June.　Fate.　Kenneth Koch.　**SP-KochK**

In a Room with Picassos.　Jane Cooper.　**SP-CoopJ**

In a Row.　Stephen Dobyns.　**SP-DobyS**

In a ruddy light, in a craggy.　The Autumn of Many Years.　Kenneth Rexroth.　**CP-RexKL** *Fr.* The Homestead Called Damascus.

In a rundown tenement.　The Healer.　Charles Simic.　**SP-SimiC**

In a season of deaths.　The Exam Dream.　Erica Jong.　**SP-JongE**

In a shoe box stuffed in an old nylon stocking.　The Meadow Mouse. Theodore Roethke.　**CP-RoetT**

In a short time we shall have cleared the gazebo.　A Vacant Possession. James Fenton.　**SP-FentJ**

In a shower of tears I sped my fears.　And the Clouds Return after the Rain.　Stevie Smith.　**CP-SmitS**

In a small and lonely cabin out of noisy traffic's way.　The Voice of the Banjo.　Paul Laurence Dunbar.　**CP-DunbP**

In a small town in the mountains they tell of a man.　The Story.　Miller Williams.　**SP-WillM**

In a small underground machine the brain of a.　Late Night Movies I. John Yau.　**SP-YauJo**

In a solitude of the sea.　The Convergence of the Twain.　Thomas Hardy. **CP-HardT**

In a Spanish Tram-Car.　David Herbert Lawrence.　**CP-LawrD**

In a stable of boats I lie still.　The Lifeguard.　James Dickey.　**CP-DickJ**

In a Station of the Metro.　Ezra Pound.　**SP-PounE**

In a storm of voices, a voice.　In the Red Corner.　James McAuley.　**SP-McAuJ**

In a Strange House.　Stanley Jasspon Kunitz.　**CP-KuniS**

In a Suburban Avenue.　John Hewitt.　**CP-HewiJ**

In a summer forest, when the profuse season.　Muriel Rukeyser.　**CP-RukeM**

In a tangle of cliffs I chose a place, *after* Han-shan.　Gary Snyder.　**CP-SnydG**

In a temporary room.　Painting by Flashlight.　Jim Carroll.　**SP-CarrJ**

In a thousand years, if there's History.　Ecologue.　Allen Ginsberg.　**CP-GinsA**

In a throng, / A festal company of Maids and Youths.　William Wordsworth.　**EBEV; OBRV** *Fr.* Summer Vacation. *Fr.* The Prelude; Growth of a Poet's Mind [1805 vers.].　**CP-WorW3**

In a Time.　Maya Angelou.　**SP-AngeM**

In a time that breaks.　To Think of the Life of a Man.　Wendell Berry. **CP-BerrW**

In a tissue-thin monotone of blue-grey buds.　Spring Strains.　William Carlos Williams.　**CP-WilW1**

In a tobacco trance.　Life at the Back of the Plane.　Al Young.　**CP-YounA**

In a Train.　Wystan Hugh Auden.　**CP-AudWJ**

In a Twinkling, the green.　Al Young.　**CP-YounA**

In a Vale.　Robert Frost.　**CP-FrosR**

In a valley late bees with whining gold.　Idyl.　Allen Tate.　**CP-TateA**

In a Vermont bedroom closet.　A Record Stride.　Robert Frost.　**CP-FrosR**

In a vicious world—to love virtue.　Marianne Moore.　Edward Estlin Cummings.　**CP-CummE**

In a Victorian mansion.　A Sentence.　Siv Cedering Fox.　*Fr.* Onna-E, Pictures of Women.　**SP-CedeS**

In a Viennese Cemetery.　James Wright.　**CP-WrigJ**

In a Waiting-Room.　Thomas Hardy.　**CP-HardT**

In a war where every second counts.　Making Love in Poetry.　Lawrence Ferlinghetti.　**SP-FerlL**

In a Washington of poetry readings.　The Nail of the Index Finger.　Siv Cedering Fox.　**SP-CedeS**

In a wet season, when the tractor's bogged.　Resource.　John Hewitt.　**CP-HewiJ**

In a while they rose and went out aimlessly riding.　Merlin Enthralled. Richard Wilbur.　**CP-WilbR**

In a Whispering Gallery.　Thomas Hardy.　**CP-HardT**

In a wife I would desire.　William Blake.　**CP-BlakW**

In a winter sunset near Springfield, Illinois.　Carl Sandburg.　*Fr.* The People, Yes.　**CP-SandC**

In a Wood.　Thomas Hardy.　**CP-HardT** ("Pale beech and pine so blue.")　**CP-HardT**

In a World too full of Beauty for Peace.　Emily Dickinson.　**SP-DickE**

In a Year.　Robert Browning.　**CP-BroR1**

In a Yiddish eating place on Rivington Street. . . faces. . . coffee.　Home Fires.　Carl Sandburg.　**CP-SandC**

In a yoke of steel laughs.　The Prospects of Nostradamus.　Thomas Merton. *Fr.* Cables to the Ace.　**CP-MertT**

In Abeyance.　Denise Levertov.　**CP-LeveD**

In Abraham Lincoln's city.　Knucks.　Carl Sandburg.　**CP-SandC**

In Adriatick waves when Neptune saw.　Sanazar's Hexaflick.　*Unknown, tr. fr. Latin by* Richard Lovelace.　**CP-LoveR**

In aerobatics, white, red, speckled & spectacular.　Chickens in San Francisco.　William Dickey.　**SP-DickW**

In aeternum I was once determed.　Sir Thomas Wyatt.　**CP-WyatT**

In Africa the wine is cheap, and it is.　A Certain Slant of Sunlight.　Ted Berrigan.　**SP-BerrT**

In Africa, when river beds.　The Lung Fish.　John Ciardi.　**SP-CiarJ**

In after Time.　Richard Eberhart.　**CP-EberR**

In After-Time, a Sage of Mickle Lore.　John Keats.　**CP-KeatJ**

In ages past ere wisdom's height.　God Reigns.　Paul Laurence Dunbar. **CP-DunbP**

In agony saying: "The last night of his life".　Double Dialogue: *Homage to Robert Frost*.　Muriel Rukeyser.　**CP-RukeM**

In Aix.　Grace Paley.　**CP-PaleG**

In Alicante they bowl the barrels.　Alicante Lullaby.　Sylvia Plath.　**CP-PlatS**

In all creation, only man cowers and is afraid of life.　Cowards.　David Herbert Lawrence.　**CP-LawrD**

In all of Greater Grand Rapids you.　The Greater Grand Rapids Lover. Marge Piercy.　**SP-PierM**

In all our daily war of words.　George Meredith.　**CP-MerG2**

In all our high designments, 'twill appeare.　The First Marrs or Makes. Robert Herrick.　**CP-HerrR**

In all story before hero come.　Ode to Good Men Fallen Before Hero Come.　Peter Meinke.　**SP-MeinP**

In all the cities of this year.　King's Mountain.　Muriel Rukeyser.　**CP-RukeM**

In all the good Greek of Plato.　Survey of Literature.　John Crowe Ransom. **SP-RansJ**

In all the grove, nor stream nor bird.　The Woodman.　Robert Louis Stevenson.　**CP-StevR**

In all the land of the tribe was neither fish nor fruit.　The Feast of Famine: Marquesan Manners.　Robert Louis Stevenson.　**CP-StevR**

In all the ways of going who can tell.　Alun Lewis.　*Fr.* On Embarkation. **CP-LewiA**

In All These Acts.　William Everson.　**SP-EverW**

In all those stories the hero.　Heroes.　Robert Creeley.　**CP-CreeR**

IN) all those who got.　Edward Estlin Cummings.　**CP-CummE**

In all thy need, be thou possest.　Good Precepts, or Counsell.　Robert Herrick.　**CP-HerrR**

In Allusion to the French Song.　Richard Lovelace.　**CP-LoveR**

In Allusion to Various Recent Histories and Notices of the French Revolution.　William Wordsworth.　**CP-WorW2**

In Allusion to Various Recent Histories and Notices of the French Revolution, Concluded.　William Wordsworth.　**CP-WorW2**

In Allusion to Various Recent Histories and Notices of the French Revolution, Continued.　William Wordsworth.　**CP-WorW2**

In Alsace, during the war.　George Oppen.　**APSN** *Fr.* Route.　**CP-OppeG**

In Amaze / Lost, I gaze.　To Quinbus Flestrin the Man-Mountain, a Lilliputian Ode.　Alexander Pope.　**CP-PopeA**

"In America," began / the lecturer, "everyone must have a."　The Student. Marianne Craig Moore.　**CP-MoorM**

In among the silver birches winding ways of tarmac wander.　Indoor Games near Newbury.　Sir John Betjeman.　**CP-BetjJ**

In Amorem Divinum, *ad. fr. the Latin*.　Richard Crashaw.　**CP-CrasR**

In an Act of Pity.　Robert Creeley.　**CP-CreeR**

In an afternoon bright with / September, on an old dissension.　This Song.　Hayden Carruth.　**CP-CarHS**

In an Age of Fops and Toys.　Ralph Waldo Emerson.　**FPL; LiTA; PoLF** *Fr.* Voluntaries.　**CP-EmerR**

Duty.　**FaFP; GN; HBV 1-2; HBVY; TRV; TreF; TreFS; YaD**

In an Artist's Studio.　Christina Georgina Rossetti.　**CP-RosC3**

In an asylum, "obsessed with sexual fantasies."　Mother Is.　Siv Cedering Fox.　**SP-CedeS**

In an Automotive Store.　Charles Olson.　**CP-OlsoC**

In an envelope marked.　Personal.　Langston Hughes.　**SP-HughL**

In an Old Apple Orchard.　Ted Kooser.　**SP-KoosT**

In an olive dress / The amoreuse.　Come Dance in Baronies.　René Char, *tr. fr. French by* Thomas Merton.　**CP-MertT**

In an upper room at midnight.　The Love Feast.　Wystan Hugh Auden.　**CP-AudeW**

In ancient shadows and twilights. The Lost Girls. Derek Mahon. **FaBCIP** *Fr.* Autobiographies. **SP-MahoD**

In ancient tales, O friend, thy spirit dwelt. Et Tu In Arcadia Vixisti. Robert Louis Stevenson. **CP-StevR**

In ancient times. Music. Frederick Morgan. **SP-MorgF**

In ancient times, as story tells. *ad. fr.* Ovid, Metamorphoses, 8.626–724. Jonathan Swift. **CP-SwifJ**

In ancient times the wise were able. An Answer to Dr. Delany's Fable of the Pheasant and the Lark. Jonathan Swift. **CP-SwifJ**

In and Come In. Archibald MacLeish. **CP-MacLA**

In & Out. John Berryman. **CP-BerrJ**

In and out the bushes, up the ivy. The Chipmunk's Day. Randall Jarrell. **CP-JarrR**

In anguish of my heart replete with woes. Upon Some Distemper of Body. Anne Bradstreet. **CP-BradA**

In another country, black poplars shake themselves over a pond. The North Country. David Herbert Lawrence. **CP-LawrD**

In Another Town. Miller Williams. **SP-WillM**

In Anselm Hollo's Poems. Ted Berrigan. **SP-BerrT**

In Answer of an Elegiacal[l] Letter, Upon the Death of the King of Sweden [from Aurelian Townsend, Inviting Me to Write on That Subject]. Thomas Carew. **CP-CareT**

In Answer to One Who Affirmed of a Well Known Character Here, Dr B—— ——, That There Was Falsehood in His Very Looks. Robert Burns. *See* That there is falsehood in his looks.

In Answer to Your Silly Question. Alice Walker. **CP-WalkA**

In antient Time, as Story tells. Jonathan Swift. *See* Baucis and Philemon.

In April / the ponds / open / like black blossoms. Blossom. Mary Oliver. **SP-OlivM**

In April. Charles Tomlinson. **CP-TomlC**

In April summer arrives. Survival. Richard Shelton. **SP-ShelR**

In April the lake water is clear. Late Spring. Meng Hao Jan, *tr. fr. Chinese by* William Carlos Williams *with* David Rafael Wang. **CP-WilW2**

In April the Morgan was bred. I was chased away. Spring. Mary Oliver. **SP-OlivM**

In April the spring of the year / it was the spring of the world. Spring of the Year. John Hewitt. **CP-HewiJ**

In April, thirteen centuries ago. Gnomons. Richard Wilbur. **CP-WilbR**

In April, when our land last died. A Mysterious Song in the Spring of the Year. Thomas Merton. **CP-MertT**

In April, when the yellow whin. The Ballad of Chaldon Down. Edna St. Vincent Millay. **CP-MillE**

In Arden. Charles Tomlinson. **CP-TomlC**

In Arizona / (how many years in the mountains). Louis Zukofsky. **TRP** *Fr.* 29 Songs. **CP-ZukLS**

(In Arizona.) **TRP**

In Arizona. Louis Zukofsky. *See* In Arizona / (how many years in the mountains).

In Armorik, that is called Britayne [*or* Britaine]. The Franklin's Tale. Geoffrey Chaucer. **NAEL-1; OAEL-1** *Fr.* The Canterbury Tales. **CP-ChauG**

In Attica. Stephen Spender. **CP-SpenS**

In audible dreams I'm forever going back. My Spanish Heart. Al Young. **CP-YounA**

In August. Paul Laurence Dunbar. **CP-DunbP**

In August nineteen hundred thirty-two it must have been. The Turtle. Frederick Morgan. **SP-MorgF**

In Authorem. Ben Jonson. **CP-JonsB**

In autumn-time he often stood to mark. The Village Minstrel. John Clare. **SP-ClarT**

In autumn when the woods are red. Robert Louis Stevenson. **CP-StevR**

In back deep the jewel. From a Phrase of Simone Weil's and Some Words of Hegel's. George Oppen. **CP-OppeG**

In Back of the Real. Allen Ginsberg. **CP-GinsA**

In balmy / iconic / prague. The Smell of Lebanon. Alice Walker. **CP-WalkA**

In Bangor, brother John the bachelor. My Uncle Johnny. John Hewitt. **CP-HewiJ**

In Bangor for some months I went to school. Bangor, Spring 1916. John Hewitt. **CP-HewiJ**

In Bangor's eastward suburb, Ballyholme. Ellendene. John Hewitt. **CP-HewiJ**

In Barnum, *acc. by English translation*. Thomas Campion. **CP-CampT**

In Barnum, *acc. by English translation*. Thomas Campion. **CP-CampT**

In Battailes what disasters fall. Blame. Robert Herrick. **CP-HerrR**

In battles of no renown. The Defeated. Alfred Edward Housman. **CP-HousA**

In Bayreuth once. Mary Desti's Ass. Frank O'Hara. **SP-OharF**

In Bed. Kenneth Koch. **SP-KochK**

In bed, dull man[?]. Upon My Lord Brohall's Wedding. Sir John Suckling. **CP-SuckJ**

In bed I muse on Tenier's [*or* Teniers'] boors. The Bench of Boors. Herman Melville. **SP-MelvH**

In Bed Not Dead. John Crowe Ransom. *Fr.* Two Gentlemen in Bonds. **SP-RansJ**

In bed on my green purple pink. Journal Night Thoughts. Allen Ginsberg. **CP-GinsA**

In bed we laugh, in bed we cry. Samuel Johnson, *after the French of* Isaac Benserade. **CP-JohnS**

(Translation of Benserade's Verses *À Son Lit.*) **CP-JohnS**

In Benidorm there are melons. Fiesta Melons. Sylvia Plath. **CP-PlatS**

In Bethlehem / On Christmas morn. Christus Natus Est. Countee Cullen. **CP-CullC**

In between the route marks. I'll Take the High Road Commission. Ogden Nash. **CP-NashO**

In Blackwater Woods. Mary Oliver. **SP-OlivM**

In blazing driftwood / the green keeps showing at the same place. The Plumet Basilisk. Marianne Craig Moore. **CP-MoorM**

In Blood's Domaine. Robert Duncan. **SP-DuncR** *Fr.* Passages.

In Blue Light. Stephen Berg. **SP-BergS**

In books the various scenes of life he drew. 2.1. Horace, *tr. by* Samuel Johnson. **CP-JohnS** *Fr.* Satires.

In bounding youth the night & train. Hafiz, *tr. by* Ralph Waldo Emerson. **CP-EmerR** *Fr.* Odes.

In bower and field he sought, where any tuft. John Milton. **TEP**, *ll.* 417–792; **OBS** *Fr.* Book IX. **FHYEP; NAEL-1; NAWM-1; NoP; OAEL-1** *Fr.* Paradise Lost. **CP-MiltJ**

(Eve.) **OBS**, *ll.* 417–466;

In Bretonem, *acc. by English translation*. Thomas Campion. **CP-CampT**

In bright morning sunlight, the horse appears pink. The Triangular Field. Stephen Dobyns. **SP-DobyS**

In brilliant gas light. Good Night. William Carlos Williams. **CP-WilW1**

In Britain's Isle, no matter where. A Long Story. Thomas Gray. **CP-GrayT**

In Broken Images. Robert Ranke Graves. **CP-GravR**

In Brueghel's great picture, The Kermess. The Dance. William Carlos Williams. **CP-WilW2**

In Bruges town is many a street. Incident at Bruges. William Wordsworth. **OBTV** *Fr.* Memorials of a Tour of the Continent; 1820. **CP-WorW2**

In Buckinghamshire hedgerows. The Icosasphere. Marianne Craig Moore. **CP-MoorM**

In burning summer I saw a season of betrayal. Sixth Elegy. River Elegy. Muriel Rukeyser. **CP-RukeM**

In Cabin'd Ships at Sea. Walt Whitman. **CP-WhitW**

In California. Donald Davie. **CP-DavDo**

In calm and cool and silence, once again. First-Day Thoughts. John Greenleaf Whittier. **CP-WhitJ**

In Cambrum, *acc. by English translation*. Thomas Campion. **CP-CampT**

In Camp. William Stafford. **SP-StafW**

In Canaan's Happy Land. Stevie Smith. **CP-SmitS**

In Candiac by Nimes in Languedoc. Montcalm. Donald Davie. **CP-DavDo**

In Cape Cod with Conrad Aiken. Malcolm Lowry. **CP-LowrM**

In Carrowdore Churchyard. Derek Mahon. **SP-MahoD**

In case of this. Subject-Cases: The Background of a Detective Story. Gertrude Stein. **CP-SteiG**

In Casterbridge there stood a noble pile. A Man. Thomas Hardy. **CP-HardT**

In caves emptied of their workers, turning. The Angels at Hamburg. Randall Jarrell. **CP-JarrR**

In celebration of Mitos. Charles Olson. **CP-OlsoC**

In Celebration of My Uterus. Anne Sexton. **CP-SextA**

In Celebration of Surviving. Chuck Miller. **SP-MillC**

In Celia's face a question did arise. Lips and Eyes. Giovanni Battista Marino, *tr. fr. Italian by* Thomas Carew. **CP-CareT**

In Central Park we talked of our own cowardice. 7/14/68: i. Adrienne Rich. **CP-RicAE** *Fr.* Ghazals: Homage to Ghalib. **SP-RicA2**

In Chains. William Carlos Williams. **CP-WilW2**

In Charidemum. Robert Louis Stevenson. **CP-StevR**

In Childbed. Thomas Hardy. **CP-HardT**

In Chopin's Garden. Donald Davie. **CP-DavDo**

In Church. Thomas Hardy. **IHNG; InPK; MoAB; MoBrPo; SCV** *Fr.* Satires of Circumstance in Fifteen Glimpses. **CP-HardT**

In Church. David Herbert Lawrence. **CP-LawrD**

"In churches," said the Pardoner, "when I preach." Geoffrey Chaucer. *See* The Pardoner's Prologue.

In churches, when the infirmity [*or* the'infirmitie]. John Donne. *Fr.* A Litany. **CP-DonnJ**

In Cicatrices Domini Jesu. Richard Crashaw. **CP-CrasR**

In cities is always the expectation. *Civil Servant, The.* Alun Lewis. *Fr.* Poems from the Chinese. **CP-LewiA**

In Claremont woods we wandered once. George Meredith. **CP-MerG2**

In Clarke County, the story goes, the family name. Virginia Reel. Charles Wright. **SP-WrigC**

In climes beyond the solar road. Thomas Gray. **OXAEP-1** *Fr.* The Progress of Poesy. **CP-GrayT**

In cloudy quiet of the day. The Spectre. Walter de la Mare. **CP-DeLaW**

In Cnidus born, the consort I became. By Heraclides. *Unknown, tr. fr. Greek* by William Cowper. **CP-CowpW**

In cock-wattle sunset or grey. Nostalgia. Louis MacNeice. **CP-MacNL**

In Colcha embroidery, I learn. Self-hatred. Adrienne Rich. *Fr.* Turning the Wheel. **CP-RicA2**

In cold / the snow. Hayden Carruth. *Fr.* North Winter. **CP-CarHL**

In cold blood, I cannot feel goddesses in the summer evening. Cold Blood. David Herbert Lawrence. **CP-LawrD**

In Cold Hell, in Thicket. Charles Olson. **CP-OlsoC; SP-OlsoC**

In comin by the brig o' Dye. Theniel Menzies' Bony Mary. Robert Burns. **CP-BurnR**

In Connecticut. Charles Tomlinson. **CP-TomlC**

In constancy content with one man, there. Carmen 111. Catullus. *Fr.* Carmina. **CP-Catul**

In controversial foul impureness. Arthur Hugh Clough. **SP-ClouA**

In cooking *petits pois,* or lesser peas. Reflections on the Vernacular. Ogden Nash. **CP-NashO**

In Copeman's ear this truth let Echo tell. Thanks for a Gift of Pheasants. William Cowper. **CP-CowpW**

In Copley Square, the derelicts sit side by side. The Invisibles. Stephen Dobyns. **SP-DobyS**

In countless upward-striving waves. Ralph Waldo Emerson. **CP-EmerR** (Motto to "Nominalist and Realist.") **CP-EmerR**

In Country Sleep. Dylan Thomas. **CP-ThomD**

In court to serve, decked with fresh array. Sir Thomas Wyatt. **CP-WyatT**

In crisp italic, meticulous and signed. The Man Who Wrote Yeats, the Man Who Wrote Mozart. Michael Hartnett. **SP-HarMi**

In Crispinum, *acc. by English translation.* Thomas Campion. **CP-CampT**

In-curve scooped out and necklaced with light. Bridge Through My Window. Audre Lorde. **SP-LordA**

In Dante, no, in Shakespeare, no. The Search. Malcolm Lowry. **CP-LowrM**

In darkroom of your eye the moonly mind. Sonnet to Satan. Sylvia Plath. **CP-PlatS**

In days of yore how fortunately fared. The Solitary. William Wordsworth. *Fr.* The Excursion. **CP-WorW2**

In days when men found joy in war. The Sick Battle-God. Thomas Hardy. **CP-HardT**

In de dead of night I sometimes. The Old Cabin. Paul Laurence Dunbar. **CP-DunbP**

In dead of winter. Approximations. Robert Earl Hayden. **CP-HaydR**

In Deadly Fear. William Blake. **SeCePo** *Fr.* Jerusalem; The Emanation of the Giant Albion. **CP-BlakW**

In death alone is what consoles; and life. Death to the Poor. Charles Baudelaire, *tr. fr. French* by Countee Cullen. **CP-CullC**

In Death, Cannot Reach What Is Most Near. Allen Ginsberg. **CP-GinsA**

In Death Divided. Thomas Hardy. **CP-HardT**

In Death I Know Well Enough All Things End in Emptiness. Stephen Berg. **SP-BergS**

In death, you face life with a child and a wife. No Time to Think. "Bob Dylan." **CP-DylaB**

In December. Charles Tomlinson. **CP-TomlC**

In December. Charles Tomlinson. **CP-TomlC**

In deep winter the sea roams. Hayden Carruth. **CP-CarHS** *Fr.* The Bloomingdale Papers.

In deepest summer / the milkweed flower. Grace Paley. **CP-PaleG**

In Defence of Metaphysics. Charles Tomlinson. **CP-TomlC**

In Defense of Homosexuality. Kay Boyle. **CP-BoylK**

In Defense of the English Portrait School. Erica Jong. **SP-JongE**

In Den'-shire Kerzie Lusk (when he was dead). Upon Luske. Robert Herrick. **CP-HerrR**

In desp'rate cases, all, or most are known. Most Words, Lesse Workes. Robert Herrick. **CP-HerrR**

In desultory walk through orchard grounds. Prelude, Prefixed to the Volume Entitled "Poems Chiefly of Early and Late Years." William Wordsworth. **CP-WorW2**

In Dickens, sure, philosophy was lacking. Reflections on Reading a Life of Dickens. Robert Browning. **CP-BroR2**

In Disgrace. Walter de la Mare. **CP-DeLaW**

In Disguise. Robert Ranke Graves. **CP-GravR**

In distant countries have I been. The Last of the Flock. William Wordsworth. **CP-WorW1**

In Distrust of Merits. Marianne Craig Moore. **CP-MoorM**

In Divés' Dive. Robert Frost. **VGW** *Fr.* Ten Mills. **CP-FrosR**

In doggerel and stout let me honour this country. Western Landscape. Louis MacNeice. **CP-MacNL**

In doing justice, God shall then be known. The Judgement Day. Robert Herrick. **CP-HerrR**

In-doors, warm by the wide mouthed fireplace, idly the farmer. Henry Wadsworth Longfellow. **APN-1** *Fr.* Now had the seasons returned, when the nights grow colder and longer. *Fr.* Part the First. *Fr.* Evangeline, a Tale of Acadie. **SP-LongH**

In doubtful breast whilst motherly Pity. Sir Thomas Wyatt. **CP-WyatT**

In Dream Time. Thomas McGrath. **SP-McGrT**

In dreams / the same bad dream goes on. The House. Anne Sexton. **CP-SextA**

In dreams a dark château. The Dark Château. Walter de la Mare. **CP-DeLaW**

In dreams I crossed a barren land. Ballade of Broken Flutes. Edwin Arlington Robinson. **CP-RobiE**

In dreams I descend. Without Parachutes. Erica Jong. **SP-JongE**

In dreams I was a ship, and sail'd the boundless seas. Ship Ahoy! Walt Whitman. **CP-WhitW**

In dreams, unhappy, I behold you stand. Unforgotten I, The. Robert Louis Stevenson. **CP-StevR**

In Dream's Wake. Ts'un Hsu Li, *tr. fr. Chinese* by William Carlos Williams *with* David Rafael Wang. **CP-WilW2**

In dreamy woods, what forms abound. Ralph Waldo Emerson. **CP-EmerR**

In Drear-nighted December. John Keats. **CP-KeatJ**

In Duc Ninh a village of 1,654 households. Two Villages. Grace Paley. **CP-PaleG**

In due observance of an ancient rite. William Wordsworth. **CP-WorW1**

In Due Season. Wystan Hugh Auden. **CP-AudeW**

In Due Season. Wystan Hugh Auden. **CP-AudWJ**

In due season the amphibious crocodile. John Crowe Ransom. **SP-RansJ** (Crocodile.) **SP-RansJ**

In dungeons dark I cannot sing. Emily Brontë. **CP-BronE**

In each man's heart that doth begin. Love's World. Sir John Suckling. **CP-SuckJ**

In Eandem Reginae Sueciae Transmissam [To Christina, Queen of Sweden]. Andrew Marvell, *tr. fr. Latin* by William A. McQueen *and* Kiffin A. Rockwell. **CP-MarvA**

In Earliest Morning. James Schuyler. **CP-SchuJ**

In early April the trees. Lesson. Carl Sandburg. **CP-SandC**

In early August among the spruce. 8/12/70. James Schuyler. **CP-SchuJ**

In Early Autumn. Thomas McGrath. **SP-McGrT**

In early autumn, there's a concerto. The Music One Looks Back On. Stephen Dobyns. **SP-DobyS**

In early hymns cries came faint. Repairing the House, the Church, Restoring the Music. Richard Hugo. **CP-HugoR**

In early spring, so much like a late autumn. Mud Season. May Sarton. **SP-SartM**

In early twilight I can hear. The Manor House, Hale, Near Liverpool. Sir John Betjeman. **CP-BetjJ**

In early youth's unclouded scene. Thirty-Eight (Addressed to Mrs. H----Y). Charlotte Smith. **CP-SmitC**

In Eastern climes was once a cock, whose fame. George Meredith. *Fr.* Prestige. **CP-MerG2**

In easy days I joined my voice with them. New Jerusalem 1. John Hewitt. **CP-HewiJ**

In eaves sole sparrow[e] sit[t]s not more alone. David's Peccavi. Robert Southwell. **CP-SoutR**

In Ebon Box, when years have flown. Emily Dickinson. **CP-DickE**

In Eden palm and open-handed pine. A Problem from Milton. Richard Wilbur. **CP-WilbR**

In Edinburgh town they've made a law. Act Sederunt of the Session—A Scots Ballad. Robert Burns. **CP-BurnR**

In Effigiem Oliveri Cromwell [On a Portrait of Oliver Cromwell]. Andrew Marvell, *tr. fr. Latin* by William A. McQueen *and* Kiffin A. Rockwell. **CP-MarvA**

In Egg Time. Brendan Galvin. **SP-GalvB**

In eighteen fifty-nine, that Year of Grace. Year of Grace and My Great-Grandfather. John Hewitt. **CP-HewiJ**

In either hand the hast'ning angel caught. The Expulsion from Eden. John Milton. **OPOU** *Fr.* Book XII. *Fr.* Paradise Lost. **CP-MiltJ**

In Emanuel's Nightmare: Another Coming of Christ. Gwendolyn Brooks. **SP-BrooG**

In English the poetics became meubles—furniture. A Later Note on Letter #15. Charles Olson. **SP-OlsoC** *Fr.* The Maximus Poems.

In eosdem, *acc. by English translation.* Thomas Campion. **CP-CampT**

In Error. Rudyard Kipling. *Fr.* Plain Tales from the Hills. "They burnt a corpse upon the sand." **CP-KiplR**

In Evening Air. Theodore Roethke. **CP-RoetT**

In every classroom, hotel lobby. Prague, or Novotny, If You Remember Him. John Hewitt. **CP-HewiJ**

In every farmhouse through the thorn-white Glens. May Alter. John Hewitt. **CP-HewiJ**

In every greeting a final goodbye is said. Hello Again. Leonard Nathan. **SP-NathL**

In every heart there is a coward and a procrastinator. The Kookaburras. Mary Oliver. **SP-OlivM**

In every language studied up to now. The Long and the Short of What's Good and What's Bad. Robert Pack. **SP-PackR**

In every room, encircled by a name. Thanksgiving. Louise Glück. **SP-GlücL**

In every town and village. Where We Belong, A Duet. Maya Angelou. **SP-AngeM**

In ev'ry town, where Thamis rolls his tyde. *in imitation of* Spenser. Alexander Pope. **CP-PopeA**

In Excelsis. Anne Sexton. **CP-SextA**

In Explanation of Our Times. Langston Hughes. **SP-HughL**

In exposition getting heated. At the Maison Lyons. Wystan Hugh Auden. **CP-AudWJ**

In extended observation of the ways and works of man. Et Dona Ferentes. Rudyard Kipling. **CP-KiplR**

In Extremis. John Updike. **CP-UpdiJ**

In Extremis in Hardy, Arkansas. Miller Williams. **SP-WillM**

In fable all things hold discourse. Aye and No: A Fable. Jonathan Swift. **CP-SwifJ**

In fairyland the little boys. The Dangerous Little Boy Fairies. Nicholas Vachel Lindsay. **CP-LindV**

In faith, I do[e] not love thee with mine eyes. Sonnet 141. William Shakespeare. **HeIP; OXAEP-1; PoEL-2; TrGrPo** *Fr.* Sonnets. **CP-ShaWS**

In faith I not [well] what to say. Sir Thomas Wyatt. **CP-WyatT**

In faith, Squier, thou hast thee wel yquit. Introduction to the Franklin's Prologue and Tale. Geoffrey Chaucer. **NAEL-1** *Fr.* The Canterbury Tales. **CP-ChauG**

In Faiths and Food and Books and Friends. The Glories. Rudyard Kipling. **CP-KiplR**

In falling the dream was broken. Wrested from Mirrors. Nicolas Calas, *tr. fr. French by* William Carlos Williams. **CP-WilW2**

In falling Timbers buried. Emily Dickinson. **CP-DickE**

In far Esthonian solitudes. A Forest Thought. Robert Browning. **CP-BroR2**

In far Tibet / There live a lama. I Will Arise and Go Now. Ogden Nash. **CP-NashO**

In Fargo, North Dakota, a man. To Flood Stage Again. James Wright. **CP-WrigJ**

In Farsistan the violet spreads. The Exile. Khvaju of Kerman, *tr. fr. Persian by* Ralph Waldo Emerson. **CP-EmerR**

In Favor of One's Time. Frank O'Hara. **SP-OharF**

In Fear of Harvests. James Wright. **CP-WrigJ**

In fear of the rich mouth. The Frightened Man. Louise Bogan. **CP-BogaL**

In festum pentecostes, anno domini 1580, 21 maii. Robert Southwell. **CP-SoutR**

In 15 minutes. California Peninsula: El Camino Real. Al Young. **CP-YounA**

In filthy Puerto Rico lives a bird with no. Hayden Carruth. *Fr.* Paragraphs. **CP-CarHS**

In fits and starts around. Squirrels Mating. John Updike. **CP-UpdiJ**

In five-score summers! All new eyes. 1967. Thomas Hardy. **CP-HardT**

In flat America, in Chicago. Visiting a Dead Man on a Summer Day. Marge Piercy. **SP-PierM**

In Flaundres whilom was a compaignye. The Three Rioters. Geoffrey Chaucer. **EBNV** *Fr.* The Pardoner's Tale. **FHYEP; NAEL-1; NAWM-1; NoP; OAEL-1; PoE** *Fr.* The Canterbury Tales. **CP-ChauG**

In Fla[u]ndres whylom [*or* whilom] was a companye [*or* compaignye]. The Pardoner's Tale. Geoffrey Chaucer. **FHYEP; NAEL-1; NoP; OAEL-1; PoE** *Fr.* The Canterbury Tales. **CP-ChauG**

In flowed [*or* flow'd] at once a gay embroidered [*or* embroider'd] race. A Young Traveller Is Presented to the Goddess Dulness. Alexander Pope. **NOEC** *Fr.* Yet, yet a moment, one dim ray of light. **NAEL-1; OAEL-1; PoEL-3** *Fr.* The Dunciad. **CP-PopeA**

In Former Songs. Walt Whitman. **CP-WhitW**

In Four Seasons. Jim Carroll. **SP-CarrJ**

In fourteen hundred and ninety-two. Look What You Did, Christopher! Ogden Nash. **CP-NashO**

In frames as large as rooms that face all ways. Essential Beauty. Philip Larkin. **CP-LarkP**

In France. Grace Paley. **CP-PaleG**

In France, the Men who for their desperate ends. William Wordsworth. **OBRV** *Fr.* Residence in France and French Revolution. *Fr.* The Prelude; Growth of a Poet's Mind [1805 vers.]. **CP-WorW3**

In France, through archways, the archaic stonework. Hayden Carruth. *Fr.* The Sleeping Beauty. **CP-CarHL**

In freshfallen snow. Hayden Carruth. *Fr.* North Winter. **CP-CarHL**

In front of. Christopher Marlowe. *See* Doctor Faustus.

In front of me, the palings of a fence. For Signs. Thom Gunn. **CP-GunnT**

In front of the cathedral hovered a mumbling nobody:its greenish fumbling. After Seeing French Funeral. Edward Estlin Cummings. **CP-CummE**

In Front of the Landscape. Thomas Hardy. **CP-HardT**

In front of the mighty washing machine. The Small Lady. Stevie Smith. **CP-SmitS**

In front of the sombre mountains. On the Balcony. David Herbert Lawrence. **CP-LawrD**

In front of you, long tables leading down to the sun. The Vegetarians. John Ashbery. **SP-AshbJ**

In front of your house i. Edward Estlin Cummings. **CP-CummE**

In front the awful Alpine track. Stanzas in Memory of the Author of "Obermann." Matthew Arnold. **SP-ArnoM**

In Fur. William Stafford. **SP-StafW**

In futurity / I prophetic see. The Little Girl Lost. William Blake. **CP-BlakW** *Fr.* Songs of Experience.

In futurity / I prophetic see. The Little Girl Lost. William Blake. **CP-BlakW; FHYEP; NOBRP** *Fr.* Songs of Innocence. **CP-BlakW**

In Galleries. Randall Jarrell. **CP-JarrR; SP-JarrR**

In Gentler Times. Peter Meinke. **SP-MeinP**

In glassy, incandescent glory. The Indiana Gig. Al Young. **CP-YounA**

In God there's nothing, but 'tis known to be. God. Robert Herrick. **CP-HerrR**

In Gods Commands, ne're ask the reason why. Gods Commands. Robert Herrick. **CP-HerrR**

In going from room to room in the dark. The Door in the Dark. Robert Frost. **CP-FrosR**

In gold light here a small guard. Galileo's Chair. Richard Hugo. **CP-HugoR**

In Golden Gate Park that day. Lawrence Ferlinghetti. **SP-FerlL**

In gorgeous robes befitting the occasion. The Council. Wystan Hugh Auden. **CP-AudeW**

In Goya's greatest scenes we seem to see. Lawrence Ferlinghetti. **SP-FerlL**

In grade school I wondered. Zimmer in Grade School. Paul Zimmer. **SP-ZimmP**

In gray, battle-scarred Leningrad. The Enemy. Alice Walker. **CP-WalkA**

In greenwoods once these relics must have known. Driftwood. Richard Wilbur. **CP-WilbR**

In grimy winter dusk / We slowed for a concrete platform. Stop. Richard Wilbur. **CP-WilbR**

In guest-house lounges / elderly ladies shrivel away. Yew Tree Guest House. Phoebe Hesketh. **SP-HeskP**

In Hades, Orpheus. Muriel Rukeyser. **CP-RukeM**

In hammamet did camping queers et al). Edward Estlin Cummings. **CP-CummE**

In Hanoi 1969. Grace Paley. **CP-PaleG**

In happier hours, ere yet so keenly blew. To Dr. Parry of Bath, with Some Botanic Drawings Which Had Been Made Some Years. Charlotte Smith. **CP-SmitC**

In Harbor. William Carlos Williams. **CP-WilW1**

In Hardwood Groves. Robert Frost. **CP-FrosR**

In Harmony with Nature. Matthew Arnold. **SP-ArnoM**

In harmony would you excel. A Cantata. Jonathan Swift. **CP-SwifJ**

In Havana in 1948 I ate fried dog. Salts and Oils. Philip Levine. **SP-LeviP**

In Havenpool Harbour the ebb was strong. The Mongrel. Thomas Hardy. **CP-HardT**

In Healey's Palace I was sitting. Edward Estlin Cummings. **CP-CummE**

In hearts like thine ne'er may I hold a place. Answer to ——'s Professions of Affection. Byron. **CP-Byron**

In Heaven a spirit doth dwell. Israfel. Edgar Allan Poe. **CP-PoeEd**

In heaven-high musings and many. Euripides, *tr. by* A. E. Housman. **CP-HousA** *Fr.* Alcestis.

In Heaven, if not on earth. The Celestial Circus. Nicholas Vachel Lindsay. **CP-LindV**

In heaven, too. Heard in a Violent Ward. Theodore Roethke. **CP-RoetT**

In heavenly realms of hellas dwelt. Edward Estlin Cummings. **CP-CummE**

In Her Burning. Muriel Rukeyser. **CP-RukeM**

In her cheeks that dwell. Gerard Manley Hopkins. *Fr.* Fragments. **CP-HopkG**

In her eyes is the living light. Beatrice. "Lewis Carroll." **CP-CarrL**

In her first passion woman loves her lover. Byron. **ErPo** *Fr.* Don Juan. **CP-Byron**

In her gnarled sleep it. The Cherry Tree. Thom Gunn. **CP-GunnT**

In Her Only Way. Robert Ranke Graves. **OxBSP** *Fr.* Three Songs for the Lute. **CP-GravR**

In Her Praise. Robert Ranke Graves. **CP-GravR**

In Her Precincts. Thomas Hardy. **CP-HardT**

In her room at the prow of the house. The Writer. Richard Wilbur. **CP-WilbR**

In here, caught by the storm. How the rain beats. Missing the Bo in the Henhouse. Hayden Carruth. **CP-CarHS**

In highest way of heav'n the sun did ride. Sonnet 22. Sir Philip Sidney. **OBSC; Son** *Fr.* Astrophil and Stella. **SP-SidnP**

In him inexplicably mixed appeared. Byron. **NOBRP; OAEL-2** *Fr.* The Serfs are glad through Lara's wide domain. *Fr.* Lara. **CP-Byron**

In hintertime Praxiteles. Lawrence Ferlinghetti. **SP-FerlL**

In his black armour. The Fly. Leonard Cohen. **CP-CoheL**

In his dream zealous. A Bad Night. Wystan Hugh Auden. **CP-AudeW**

In his early days he was quite surprised. The Sweet Hussy. Thomas Hardy. **CP-HardT**

In his fur the animal rode, and in his fur he strove. It Filled My Heart with Love. Stevie Smith. **CP-SmitS**

In his last phase when hardly bothering. Autolycus. Louis MacNeice. **CP-MacNL**

In his packet Anacharsis found the lines. From the Packet of Anacharsis. Wallace Stevens. **CP-StevW**

In his perpetual cycle Time, rolling back. Elegy 5: On the Coming of Spring. John Milton, *tr. fr. Latin by* John T. Shawcross. **CP-MiltJ**

In his poem the poet. Address to the National Council on the Arts. Gilbert Sorrentino. **SP-SorrG**

In his school of "The Fiddle and Bow". Preface to "Bob Taylor's Birthday." Nicholas Vachel Lindsay. **CP-LindV**

In his tenth July some instinct. For Johnny Pole on the Forgotten Beach. Anne Sexton. **CP-SextA**

In hollows of the land. The Ground-Mist. Denise Levertov. **CP-LeveD**

In holy meetings, there a man may be. The Crowd and Company. Robert Herrick. **CP-HerrR**

In homes all green, but cold in death. Our Martyred Soldiers. Paul Laurence Dunbar. **CP-DunbP**

In honest Bacon's ingle-neuk. To William Stewart. Robert Burns. **CP-BurnR**

In Honor of David Anderson Brooks, My Father. Gwendolyn Brooks. **SP-BrooG**

In Honor of Du Bartas, 1641. Anne Bradstreet. **CP-BradA**

In Honour of St. Alphonsus Rodriguez. Gerard Manley Hopkins. **CP-HopkG**

In Honour of That High and Mighty Princess Queen Elizabeth of Happy Memory. Anne Bradstreet. **CP-BradA**

In Honour of the Author by *Tho: Campion* Doctor in Physicke. To the Reader. Thomas Campion. **CP-CampT**

In honour of the dumb the blind the deaf. Paul Éluard. **RHTwFP** *Fr.* Second Nature. **CP-BeckS**

In Horologium. Percy Bysshe Shelley. **CP-ShelP**

In horror the God-thrown lie. Kenneth Patchen. **CP-PatcK**

In hose and doublet and great ruff you stand. The Photograph of a Boy in Costume. Wystan Hugh Auden. **CP-AudWJ**

In Hospital: Poona (1). Alun Lewis. **CP-LewiA**

In Hospital: Poona (2). Alun Lewis. **CP-LewiA**

In how many of the miserable little life dramas I play out in my mind am I unforgivable. Conscience. Charles Kenneth Williams. **SP-WillC**

In Hydaspia, by Howzen. Oak Leaves Are Hands. Wallace Stevens. **CP-StevW**

In idle August, while the sea soft. The *Schooner* Flight. Derek Walcott. **CP-WalcD**

In ignorance of the source, our want. Song (1). Wendell Berry. **CP-BerrW**

In Illo Tempore. Seamus Heaney. **SP-HeanS** *Fr.* Sweeney Redivivus.

In Ilopongo Prison. The Women's Prison: El Salvador / The Ballad of Visiting Day. Grace Paley. **CP-PaleG**

In Ireland I Remembered the Foxes of Truro, Massachusetts. Brendan Galvin. **SP-GalvB**

In Isfahan the fair / Surrounded by orchards. Isfahan. Thomas Merton. *Fr.* East with Ibn Battuta. *Fr.* East. *Fr.* The Geography of Lograire. **CP-MertT**

In It. Stephen Berg. **SP-BergS**

In itself, this old, three-storey brownstone. Carson. Paul Muldoon. *Fr.* 7, Middagh Street. **SP-MuldP**

In Jakarta, / among the vendors. Acid. Mary Oliver. **SP-OlivM**

In January. James Schuyler. **CP-SchuJ**

In January everything freezes. One Third of a Calendar. Ogden Nash. **CP-NashO**

In Jinoteca women greeted us. The Dance in Jinoteca. Grace Paley. **CP-PaleG**

In Joe Brainard's collage its white arrow. Ted Berrigan. **SP-BerrT** *Fr.* The Sonnets.

In Judah is God known: his name is great in Israel. Psalm 76. Bible, *O.T. Fr.* Psalms. **CP-Psal**

In Judgment of the Leaf. Kenneth Patchen. **CP-PatcK**

In July / No goodbye. Christina Georgina Rossetti. **CP-RosC3**

In June, amid the golden fields. The Groundhog. Richard Eberhart. **CP-EberR**

In June the bush we call. The Victors. Denise Levertov. **CP-LeveD**

In June two oaks fell. Ethnobotany. Gary Snyder. **CP-SnydG**

In June, when the star jasmine. Lancaster Street. Martin Edmunds. **SP-EdmuM**

In junior high school. Big Max. Charles Bukowski. **SP-BukC1**

In Just- / spring when the world is mud-. Edward Estlin Cummings. **CP-CummE; SP-CummE**

In Kansas a shadow is moving. After Midnight. Brendan Galvin. **SP-GalvB**

In Kofukuji museum stands a phalanx. The Kofukuji Arsonists. Laurence Lieberman. **SP-LiebL**

In Köhln [Köln], a town of monks and bones. Cologne. Samuel Taylor Coleridge. **CP-ColeS**

In La Mancha he mopeth. The Rusty Man. Herman Melville. **SP-MelvH**

In land that obviously northern, no record ever. George Stubbs at Yale. Richard Hugo. **CP-HugoR**

In lands I never saw—they say. Emily Dickinson. **CP-DickE**

In language warm as could be breath'd or penn'd. On Receiving Hayley's Picture. William Cowper. **CP-CowpW**

In last night's dream who put into my hand. Dream-flowers. Kathleen Jessie Raine. **SP-RainK**

In late April, cherry blossoms engulf the front of the house. Cherries. Stephen Berg. **SP-BergS**

In late winter. The Bear. Galway Kinnell. **SP-KinnG**

In late winter cold nights. Hayden Carruth. *Fr.* North Winter. **CP-CarHL**

In latter days, remembering this I shall certainly go mad. Returning to the Country for a Brief Visit. Allen Ginsberg. **CP-GinsA**

In Laurentiam, *acc. by English translation.* Thomas Campion. **CP-CampT**

In law an infant and in years a boy. Damaetas. Byron. **CP-Byron**

In Legationem Domini Oliveri St John ad Provincias Foederatas [On the Embassy of Lord Oliver St John to the United Provinces]. Andrew Marvell, *tr. fr. Latin by* William A. McQueen *and* Kiffin A. Rockwell. **CP-MarvA**

In less than half-light. The Fourth Version. Hayden Carruth. *Fr.* The Mythology of Dark and Light. **CP-CarHL**

In Lieu. Louis MacNeice. **CP-MacNL**

In Lieu of the Lyre. Marianne Craig Moore. **CP-MoorM**

In life our absent friend is far away. Christina Georgina Rossetti. *Fr.* Later Life: A Double Sonnet of Sonnets. **CP-RosC2**

In life we could seldom meet. Visit. Tu Fu, *tr. fr. Chinese by* William Carlos Williams *with* David Rafael Wang. **CP-WilW2**

In Life's Red Sea with faith I plant my feet. Mare Rubrum. Paul Laurence Dunbar. **CP-DunbP**

In Ligonem, *acc. by English translation.* Thomas Campion. **CP-CampT**

In lilac trained on the colonnade's archway, what. Hornet. Donald Davie. **CP-DavDo**

In Limbo. Richard Wilbur. **CP-WilbR**

In line at lunch I cross my fork and spoon. Objector. William Stafford. **SP-StafW**

In Little Rock the people bear. The Chicago Defender Sends a Man to Little Rock. Gwendolyn Brooks. **SP-BrooG**

In Lombardy. William Wordsworth. *Fr.* Memorials of a Tour in Italy, 1837. **CP-WorW2**

In London. Robert Creeley. **CP-CreeR**

In long shapes over the channel's. Roy Fisher. **SP-FishR** *Fr.* Matrix.

In Longfellow's Library. Charles Tomlinson. **CP-TomlC**

In Love, If Love Be Love. Tennyson. **CABA; PoEL-5; TrGrPo** *Fr.* Merlin and Vivien. *Fr.* Idylls of the King. **CP-TennA**

(All in All.) **ImPo; LiTB; TRV**

(Vivien's Song.) **FaBoEn; OBNC**

In Love, if Love be Love, if Love be ours. In Love, If Love Be Love. Tennyson. **CABA; FaBoEn; ImPo; LiTB; OBNC; PoEL-5; TRV; TrGrPo** *Fr.* Merlin and Vivien. *Fr.* Idylls of the King. **CP-TennA**

In Love with You. Kenneth Koch. **SP-KochK**

In Love's name you are charged: oh, fly [*or* charged hereby]. James Shirley. **CP-CareT**

(Hue and Cry, The.) **CP-CareT**

In loving thee thou know'st I am forsworn. Sonnet 152. William Shakespeare. **HeIP** *Fr.* Sonnets. **CP-ShaWS**

In Lowestoft a boat was laid. The Lowestoft Boat. Rudyard Kipling. **CP-KiplR**

In lowly dale, fast by a river's side. James Thomson. **EnRP; NOEC; SeCePo** *Fr.* The Castle of Indolence. **CP-ThomJ**

(Land of Indolence, The.) **SeCePo**

In Lupum. Robert Louis Stevenson. **CP-StevR**

In Lycium et Clytham, *acc. by English translation.* Thomas Campion. **CP-CampT**

In Maceio. Tess Gallagher. **SP-GallT**

In making Marjorie god hurried. Edward Estlin Cummings. **CP-CummE**

In man, ambition is the common'st thing. Ambition. Robert Herrick. **CP-HerrR**

In man it is the truth affirm'd. Honour. Christopher Smart. *Fr.* Hymns for the Amusement of Children. **SP-SmarC**

In Manhattan, I learned a public kindness. Kindness. Stephen Dunn. **SP-DunnS**

In Mantua-territory half is slough. Robert Browning. **EBVVPR** *Fr.* Sordello. **CP-BroR1**

In many and reportless places. Emily Dickinson. **CP-DickE**

In many forms we try. The Bohemian Hymn. Ralph Waldo Emerson. **CP-EmerR**

In many tongues, hawkers scream our fingers. Pike Place Market. Richard Hugo. **CP-HugoR**

In many ways does the full heart reveal. Eros aei lalethros hetairos. Samuel Taylor Coleridge. **CP-ColeS**

In March. Charles Tomlinson. **CP-TomlC**

In March the dust of Tartary has swept over the capital. The Knight. Li Po, *tr. fr. Chinese by* William Carlos Williams *with* David Rafael Wang. **CP-WilW2**

In March's black boat. St. Francis Einstein of the Daffodils. William Carlos Williams. **CP-WilW1**

In Marin Again. Al Young. **CP-YounA**

In Marion, the honey locust trees are falling. Two Poems about President Harding. James Wright. **CP-WrigJ**

In martial sports I had my cunning tried. Sonnet 53. Sir Philip Sidney. **NAEL-1; NoSic** *Fr.* Astrophil and Stella. **SP-SidnP**

In Mauchline there dwells six proper young Belles. Song. Robert Burns. **CP-BurnR**

In Maximum. Robert Louis Stevenson. **CP-StevR**

In May. Paul Laurence Dunbar. **CP-DunbP**

In May, approaching the city, I. The Ritualists. William Carlos Williams. **CP-WilW2**

In May, late, under an open sky. On Colinward: The Scattering. John Hewitt. **CP-HewiJ**

In May of nineteen-hundred forty-two. Fathering the Map. Robert Pack. **SP-PackR**

In May, that moder is of monthes glade. Geoffrey Chaucer. **EnVB** *Fr.* Troilus and Criseyde [*or* Criseide]. **CP-ChauG**

In May, was it, Ophelia drowned? Tanck's Song About His Unicameral Mind. Hayden Carruth. **CP-CarHS** *Fr.* Songs About What Comes Down: The Complete Works of Mr. Septic Tank.

In May, when sea-winds pierced our solitudes. Rhodora, The [On Being Asked Whence Is the Flower]. Ralph Waldo Emerson. **CP-EmerR**

In me there is a rage to defy. Rage. Alice Walker. **CP-WalkA**

In meadow ribbed with secret bog. Corncrake. John Hewitt. **CP-HewiJ**

In medieval churches those stained glass windows I love best. Belief. Alun Lewis. **CP-LewiA**

In Melleam, *acc. by English translation.* Thomas Campion. **CP-CampT**

In Melleam, *acc. by English translation.* Thomas Campion. **CP-CampT**

In Memoriam. Hayden Carruth. **CP-CarHS**

In Memoriam. Ralph Waldo Emerson. **CP-EmerR**

In Memoriam. John Updike. **CP-UpdiJ**

In Memoriam: A. C., R. J. O., K. S. Sir John Betjeman. **CP-BetjJ** *Fr.* Old Friends. **CP-BetjJ**

In Memoriam A. H. H. Tennyson. **CP-TennA**

"Again at Christmas did we weave." **EBVV; IMW; OAEL-2; PeECV**

"And all is well, though [*or* tho'] faith and form." **EBVVPR; OAEL-2**

And buds and blossoms like the rest. **EBVV; FHYEP; FaBoEn; FaBoRV; GTBS-6; GTBS-P; NOBE; OBNC; SeCeV**

"And was the day of my delight." **OAEL-2**

"As sometimes in a dead man's face." **ImPo; LiTB**

Baby New to Earth and Sky, The. **MeMBP**

"Be near me when my light is low." **EBVV; EBVVPR; ELP; EnVR;**

HAP; HeIP; LiTB; MeMBP; NOCV; NoP; OAEL-2; PeECV; PoEL-5; SCGP; SCV

"By night we lingered [*or* linger'd] on the lawn." **EBVV; EnVR; FHYEP; HAP; LoBV; NoP; OAEL-2; OBNC; PeECV; PoEL-5; TOF**

"Till now the doubtful dusk reveal'd." **GTBS-6; GTBS-P**

"Calm is the morn without a sound." **ChTr; EBEV; EBVV; ELP; EnVR; FHYEP; FaBoEn; FaBoPP; FaBoRV; FiP; HeIP; LiTB; NOBE; NoP; OBNC; PeECV; PlP; PoEL-5; SeCeV; TrGrPo**

(Lincolnshire Wolds and Lincolnshire Sea.) **FaBoPP**

"Churl in spirit, up or down, Thou."

"Contemplate all this work of Time." **EBVV; EnVR; FF; OAEL-2; SBVL; SeCeV**

"Could I have said while he was here."

"Could we forget the widowed hour."

"Danube to the Severn gave, The." **EBVV; EBVVPR; EnVR; FF; FaBoPP; GTBS-6; GTBS-P; LoBV; NoP**

(Hushing of the Wye, The.) **FaBoPP**

"Dark house, by which once more I stand." **EBEV; EBVV; EBVVPR; EnVR; FHYEP; FaBoEn; GTBS-6; GTBS-P; HAP; HeIP; ImPo; InPK; LiTB; MeMBP; NOBE; NoP; OAEL-2; OBD; OBNC; PPoe; PeHV; PoEL-5; SCGP; SCV; SeCeV; SoSe; UnPo**

(Dark House.) **ImPo; LiTB; SCGP**

"Dear friend, far off, my lost desire." **EBVVPR; FHYEP; OAEL-2**

"Dip down upon the northern shore." **EBVV**

"Do we indeed desire the dead." **EBVVPR; EnVR; OAEL-2; OBD**

"Doors, where my heart was used to beat." **EnVR; FHYEP; NoP; OBNC; PoEL-5; SCV**

"Dost thou look back on what hath been."

"Fair ship, that from the Italian shore." **EBVV; EBVVPR; EnVR; OAEL-2; PeHV**

"From art, from nature, from the schools." **OAEL-2**

"Happy lover who has come, A." **EBVVPR; EnVR**

"He past; a soul of nobler tone."

"He tasted love with half his mind."

"Heart-affluence in discursive talk."

"Her eyes are homes of silent prayer."

"High wisdom holds my wisdom less."

"How fares it with the happy dead?"

"How many a father have I seen." **EBVVPR; EnVR**

"How pure at heart and sound in head." **MeMBP**

"I cannot love thee as I ought." **EBVVPR; EnVR**

"I cannot see the features right." **ImPo; LiTB; MeMBP; PoEL-5**

"I climb the hill: from end to end." **EBVV; FHYEP; PoEL-5**

"I dreamed there would be Spring no more." **NOBE**

I Envy Not in Any Moods. **EBEvV; FHYEP; FaBoEn; HBV; ImPo; LiTB; MeMBP; OAEL-2; OBNC; PeHV**

"I hold it true, whate're befall." **UV**

"I hear the noise about thy keel." **EBVV; EnVR**

I Held It Truth (with Him Who Sings). **EBVV; EBVVPR; EnVR; HeIP; LiTB; MeMBP; NoP; OAEL-2; OBNC**

"I know that this was Life,—the track."

"I leave thy praises unexpressed."

"I past [*or* passed] beside the reverend walls." **EBVV; FaBoPP**

(He Revisits Cambridge.) **FaBoPP**

"I shall not see thee. Dare I say."

"I sing to him that rests below." **OAEL-2**

"I sometimes hold it half a sin." **EPCY; EnVR; IMW; OAEL-2; PeECV; TOF**

"I trust I have not wasted breath." **EnVR; FHYEP; ImOP; OAEL-2; SeCePo**

"I vex my heart with fancies dim."

"I wage not any feud with Death." **ImPo; LiTB; OBF; PPON**

"I will not shut me from my kind." **EnVR; FHYEP**

"If any vague desire should rise."

"If any vision should reveal."

"If, in thy second state sublime."

"If one should bring me this report." **EBVV; EnVR; FHYEP; ImPo; MeMBP**

(Of One Dead.) **ImPo**

If Sleep and Death Be Truly One. **MeMBP; OBNC; PeECV**

"If these brief lays, of Sorrow born."

"In those sad words I took farewell." **EnVR**

"Is it, then, regret for buried time." **FHYEP**

"It is the day when he was born." **EBVV; FHYEP**

"Lesser griefs that may be said, The."

"Lo, as a dove when up she springs." **LoBV**

"Love is and was my Lord and King." **ChTr; EBVVPR; HBV; NOBE;**

NOCV; OBEV; OBNC; PeECV; SeCeV
　(My Lord and King.) **ChTr**
"Love that rose on stronger wings, The." **EBVVPR**
"More than my brothers are to me." **OAEL-2**
"My love has talked with rocks and trees."
"My own dim life should teach me this." **EnVR; FHYEP; OAEL-2; SeCePo**
"Now, sometimes in my sorrow shut."
"O days and hours, your work is this." **HBV 1-2; PeECV**
"O living will that shalt endure." **EBVV; EBVVPR; FaBoBe; MeMBP; OAEL-2; WGRP**
　(Prayer, The: "O living will that shalt endure.") **WGRP**
"O Sorrow, cruel fellowship." **EBVVPR; EnVR; HAP; OAEL-2**
"O Sorrow, wilt thou live with me."
"O thou that after toil and storm." **PeECV**
"O true and tried, so well and long." **OAEL-2**
　"And, star and system rolling past." **ImOP**
　"O happy hour, and happier hours." **EnVR**
"O, wast thou with me, dearest, then." **MeMBP**
Oh Yet We Trust. **EBVV; EBVVPR; EaLo; EnVR; FHYEP; ImPo; LiTB; MeMBP; NoP; OAEL-2; OBNC; PeECV; TrGrPo**
　(Larger Hope, The.) **WGRP**
"Old warder of these buried bones." **PeECV; PoEL-5**
"Old yew, which graspest at the stones." **EBVV; EBVVPR; ELP; EnVR; GTBS-6; GTBS-P; NOBE; NoP; OAEL-2; OBNC; PAI; PoEL-5; SeCeV; UnPo**
"On that last night before we went." **OAEL-2; PoEL-5**
"One writes, that 'Other friends remain'." **EnVR; PoEL-5**
"Path by which we twain did go, The." **EBVV; PeECV; SCV**
"Peace; come away: the song of woe." **EBVV; EBVVPR; EnVR; FHYEP; IMW**
"Ring out, wild bells, to the wild sky." **FaPON,** *sect.* 106, *ll.* 1–8; **BLPL; EBEvV; EBVV; FHYEP; FaF; FaPoR; FiP; HBV; ImPo; LiTB; MeMBP; OAEL-2; OFD; OXAEP-2; PGD; PeECV; PIP; SBVL; SeCeV; TRV; TrGrPo; WBLP**
　(Ring Out the Old, Ring In the New.) **WBLP**
"Risest thou thus, dim dawn, again." **EBVV**
"Risest thou thus, dim dawn, again." **OBNC; PeECV; PoEL-5**
"Sad Hesper o'er the buried sun." **EBVV; EnVR; NoP**
"Sleep, kinsman thou to death and trance."
" 'So careful of the type?' but no." **EBVV; EBVVPR; EnVR; FF; FHYEP; HAP; HBV; LoBV; NoP; OAEL-2; OBNC; TOF**
"So many worlds, so much to do." **HBV 1-2**
"Still onward winds the dreary way."
"Strong Son of God, immortal Love." **EBVV; EBVVPR; EaLo; EnVR; HAP; HBV; LiTB; MeMBP; NAWM-2; OAEL-2; SeCeV; TRV; TrCP; TrGrPo; TrPWD; TreF; WGRP; WHA**
"Sweet after showers, ambrosial air." **EBVV**
"Sweet soul, do you with me as thou wilt."
"Take wings of fancy, and ascend."
"Tears of the widower, when he sees." **PeHV**
"That each, who seems a separate whole."
"That which we dare invoke to bless." **EBVV; FHYEP; NOCV; OAEL-2; TOF; WGRP**
"There rolls the deep where grew the tree." **FaBoRV; HAP; NOBE; OAEL-2; SeCePo; SeCeV**
"This truth came borne with bier and pall."
"Thou comest, much wept for: such a breeze." **EBVV; PeECV**
"Though if an eye that's downward cast."
"Though truths in manhood darkly join." **OAEL-2**
"Thy converse drew us with delight."
"Thy spirit ere our fatal loss."
"Thy voice is on the rolling air." **EBVV; EBVVPR; FHYEP; HeIP; NoP; OAEL-2; PeHV**
"Time draws near the birth of Christ, The." **EBVV; EBVVPR; FHYEP; FaBoRV; NOCV; OAEL-2; SoSe**
"Time draws near the birth of Christ, The." **EBVV; OAEL-2; SBVL**
" 'Tis held that sorrow makes us wise."
" 'Tis well, 'tis something; we may stand." **EBVV**
"To Sleep I give my powers away." **EnVR**
To-night the Winds Begin. **BiP; EBVV; FaBoEn; GTBS-6; GTBS-P; ImPo; LiTB; NOBE; OAEL-2; OBNC; PeECV; PoEL-5**
"Tonight ungathered let us leave." **EBVV; FHYEP; OAEL-2**
"Unwatched [*or* unwatch'd], the garden bough shall sway." **EBVV; ELP; FHYEP; FaBoPP; GTBS-6; GTBS-P; OBNC; PeECV; PoEL-5; PoPle; SCV; SeCeV**
　(Somersby, Lincolnshire; after Leaving the Refectory.) **FaBoPP**
"Urania speaks with darkened brow." **OAEL-2**

"We leave the well-beloved place." **EBVV; FHYEP; PoEL-5**
"We ranging down this lower track."
"What hope is here for modern rhyme." **EnVR; MeMBP; PP**
"What words are these have fallen from me?" **EBEV**
"Whatever I have said or sung."
"When I contemplate all alone."
"When in the down I sink my head."
"When Lazarus left his charnel-cave." **EBVV; FHYEP; OAEL-2; PeECV; TOF**
When on My Bed the Moonlight Falls. **LoBV; MeMBP; NoP; OAEL-2; PeECV; SCGP; SeCePo; SeCeV**
"When rosy plumelets tuft the larch." **FHYEP; FaBoEn; OBNC**
"Who loves not Knowledge? Who shall rail."
"Wild bird, whose warble, liquid sweet." **NoP; PBBP**
"Wish, that of the living whole, The." **EBVV; EBVVPR; EnVR; FHYEP; HAP; NoP; OAEL-2; OBNC; TOF**
"Witch-elms that counterchange the floor." **EBVV; OBNC**
"With such compelling cause to grieve." **EBVV**
"With trembling fingers did we weave." **EBVV; FHYEP; OAEL-2**
"With weary steps I loiter on."
"Yet if some voice that man could trust." **OAEL-2**
"Yet pity for a horse o'er-driven."
"You leave us: you will see the Rhine."
"You say, but with no touch of scorn." **NOCV; WGRP**
　(Doubt.) **WGRP**
"You thought my heart too far diseased."
In Memoriam, E.H. Robert Louis Stevenson. **CP-StevR**
In Memoriam F. A. S. Robert Louis Stevenson. **CP-StevR**
In Memoriam Felis Felis. John Updike. **CP-UpdiJ**
In Memoriam Francis Ledwidge. Seamus Heaney. **SP-HeanS**
In Memoriam; Ingvald Bjorndal and His Comrade. Malcolm Lowry. **CP-LowrM**
In Memoriam James Joyce. "Hugh MacDiarmid."
　"All dreams of 'imperialism' must be exorcised." **SP-MacDH**
　"And all this here, everything I write, of course." **SP-MacDH**
　"So, like him, we cry *'l'honneur des hommes: Saint Langage'.*" **SP-MacDH**
In Memoriam L. K.-A. 1950–1952. Wystan Hugh Auden. *Fr.* Shorts [1948–1957] ("At peace under this mandarin, sleep, Lucina"). **CP-AudeW**
In Memoriam (1914–1953). John Berryman. **CP-BerrJ**
In Memoriam P.B. Gilbert Sorrentino. **SP-SorrG**
In Memoriam: Robert Fitzgerald. Martin Edmunds. **SP-EdmuM**
In Memoriam Thomas Hardy. Charles Tomlinson. **CP-TomlC**
In Memoriam: William Cannastra, 1922–1950. Allen Ginsberg. **CP-GinsA**
In Memorium: D.H. Lawrence. John Hewitt. **CP-HewiJ**
In Memory. Jean Garrigue. **SP-GarrJ**
In Memory. John Greenleaf Whittier. **CP-WhitJ**
In memory I see a youth. The Haystack. Richard Eberhart. **CP-EberR**
In Memory of a Child. Nicholas Vachel Lindsay. **CP-LindV**
In Memory of a Spanish Poet. James Wright. **CP-WrigJ**
In Memory of Alfred Pollexfen. William Butler Yeats. **CP-YeatW**
In Memory of Arthur Winslow. Robert Lowell.
　Death from Cancer. **SP-LoweR**
In Memory of Basil, Marquess of Dufferin and Ava. Sir John Betjeman. **CP-BetjJ**
In Memory of Boris Pasternak. Denise Levertov. **CP-LeveD**
In Memory of Ernst Toller. Wystan Hugh Auden. **CP-AudeW**
In Memory of Eva Gore-Booth and Con Markievicz. William Butler Yeats. **CP-YeatW**
In Memory of George Whitby, Architect. Sir John Betjeman. **CP-BetjJ**
In Memory of God. Jenny Joseph. **SP-JoseJ**
In Memory of Jane Fraser [*or* Frazer]. Geoffrey Hill. **CP-HillG**
In Memory of John Thorton. William Cowper. **CP-CowpW**
In Memory of Kathleen. Kenneth Patchen. **CP-PatcK**
In Memory of Lemuel Ayers, Scene Designer, Dead of Cancer in His Fortieth Year. Isabella Gardner. **CP-GardI**
In Memory of Leopardi. James Wright. **CP-WrigJ**
In Memory of Major Robert Gregory. William Butler Yeats. **CP-YeatW**
In Memory of My Dear Grandchild Anne Bradstreet. Anne Bradstreet. **CP-BradA**
In Memory of My Dear Grandchild Elizabeth Bradstreet Who Deceased August, 1665, Being a Year and a Half Old. Anne Bradstreet. **CP-BradA**
In Memory of My Feelings. Frank O'Hara. **SP-OharF**
In Memory of My Friend, Joyce Kilmer, Poet and Soldier. Nicholas Vachel Lindsay. **CP-LindV**
In Memory of Sigmund Freud. Wystan Hugh Auden. **CP-AudeW**

In Memory of the Horse David, Who Ate One of my Poems. James Wright. **CP-WrigJ**

In Memory of the Spanish Poet Federico Garcia Lorca. Thomas Merton. **CP-MertT; SP-MertT**

In Memory of the Utah Stars. William Matthews. **SP-MattW**

In Memory of W. B. Yeats. Wystan Hugh Auden. **CP-AudeW**
    "Earth, receive an honoured guest." **ChMP; ChTr; FaBoRV; FaBoTw; Mes**

In Memory of W. H. Auden. William Matthews. **SP-MattW**
    "His heart made a last fist."
    "His was a mind alive by a pure greed."
    "My friend said Auden died."
    "They were not painting about suffering."

In Memory: Stuart Egnal. Wendell Berry. **CP-BerrW**

In Memphis—in Tennessee. On the Birth of a Black / Baby / Boy. Etheridge Knight. **SP-KnigE**

In Mexico. Frederick Morgan. **SP-MorgF**

In Mexico the little mixed herds come home in the evening. Recovery. Mona Van Duyn. **SP-VanDM**

In Michoacán. Charles Tomlinson. **CP-TomlC**

In mid-August, in the second year. Wolf Knife. Donald Hall. **CP-HallD**

In Midas' Country. Sylvia Plath. **CP-PlatS**

In middle age an evil thing. Archduchess Anne. George Meredith. **CP-MerG1**

In midmost Ind, beside Hydaspes cool. The Cap and Bells; or, The Jealousies. John Keats. **CP-KeatJ**

In midnight sleep of many a face of anguish. Old War-Dreams. Walt Whitman. **CP-WhitW**

In midnights of November. Alfred Edward Housman. **CP-HousA**

In Midsummer Quiet. Charles Simic. **SP-SimiC**

In midtown again the way you stop. Jim Carroll. **SP-CarrJ**

In Mind. Denise Levertov. **CP-LeveD**

In mine one [or own] monument I lie [or lye]. Song. Richard Lovelace. **CP-LoveR**

In minute gestures / that jet wetly slight. Song. Jim Carroll. **SP-CarrJ**

In mole-blue indolence the sun. The Jungle. Alun Lewis. **CP-LewiA**

In Montecito. Randall Jarrell. **CP-JarrR**

In mony a foreign pairt I've been. The Scotsman's Return from Abroad. Robert Louis Stevenson. **CP-StevR**

In Moonlight, Somewhere, They Are Singing. Robert Penn Warren. **SP-WarrR**

In Morachum, *acc. by English translation*. Thomas Campion. **CP-CampT**

In more precision now of light and dark. Gerard Manley Hopkins. *Fr.* Dawn. **CP-HopkG**

In Moscow, wakening long past midnight. Moscow Moment. John Hewitt. **CP-HewiJ**

In Mourning for Betrayal. Robert Bly. **SP-BlyR**

In mourning wise since daily I increase. Sir Thomas Wyatt. **CP-WyatT**

In movies I prefer something unpretentious, like "Marty." What's in a Name? Here's What's in a Name, or, I Wonder What Became of John and Mary. Ogden Nash. **CP-NashO**

In moving-slow he has no Peer. The Sloth. Theodore Roethke. **CP-RoetT**

In Mrs Shelley's story, Frankenstein. Fables for Stormont. John Hewitt. **CP-HewiJ**

In Murray, Kentucky, I lay once. Self-Portrait. Charles Wright. **SP-WrigC**

In my Autumn garden I was fain. An October Garden. Christina Georgina Rossetti. **CP-RosC2**

In my bachelor days, no parent I. A Good Parent's Garden of Vision. Ogden Nash. **CP-NashO**

In my beginning is my end. In succession. East Coker. Thomas Stearns Eliot. **HAP; PPP; VGW** *Fr.* Four Quartets. **CP-ElioT**

In my beginning was the memory, somehow. After Jonah. Hart Crane. **CP-CranH**

In my best dream I have crossed the border. The Anacortes-Sydney Run. Richard Hugo. **CP-HugoR**

In My Cauldron under the Full Moon. Erica Jong. **SP-JongE**

In my cellar the poisoned mice, thirsty to death. Mouse Sex. John Updike. **CP-UpdiJ**

In my childhood trees were green. Autobiography. Louis MacNeice. **CP-MacNL**

In my childhood when I first. The Reflecting Trees of Being and Not Being. Kenneth Rexroth. **SP-RexrK** *Fr.* Seven Poems for Marthe, My Wife.

In my cottage near the Styx. Charon. Christina Georgina Rossetti. **CP-RosC3**

In My Craft or Sullen Art. Dylan Thomas. **CP-ThomD**

In My Crib. Joseph Ceravolo. **SP-CeraJ**

In my distress I cried unto the Lord, and he heard me. Psalm 120. Bible, *O.T. Fr.* Psalms. **CP-Psal**

In my distress I sought the Lord. From Another Sore Fit. Anne Bradstreet. **CP-BradA**

In my dream. The Author of the Jesus Papers Speaks. Anne Sexton. **CP-SextA**

In my dream. 45 Mercy Street. Anne Sexton. **CP-SextA**

In my dream, children. Jerusalem. Adrienne Rich. **CP-RicAE; SP-RicA2**

In my dream, methought I trod. My Dream. John Greenleaf Whittier. **CP-WhitJ**

In my dream, my belly is yellow, panels. The Serpent. Robert Lowell. **SP-LoweR**

In my dream there is light. Minotaur. Lewis Turco. **SP-TurcL**

In my dreams. Sex and/or Love. Charles Bukowski. **SP-BukC3**

In My Dreams. Stevie Smith. **CP-SmitS**

In My End Is My Beginning. Chuang Tzu, *tr. fr. Chinese by* Thomas Merton. **CP-MertT**

In my ending is my meaning. The Night of Destiny. Thomas Merton. **CP-MertT**

In my family. People in My Family. Grace Paley. **CP-PaleG**

In my Father's bedroom. Father's Bedroom. Robert Lowell. **SP-LoweR**

In my first thirty years of life, *after* Han-shan. Gary Snyder. **CP-SnydG**

In my garden three ways meet. Ralph Waldo Emerson. **CP-EmerR**

In my gay room, bare as a barn. Eine Kleine Nachtmusik. Randall Jarrell. **CP-JarrR**

In my hair he's put. Charles Henri Ford. **SP-FordC** *Fr.* Secret Haiku.

In my hand I hold. The Stone Crock. William Carlos Williams. **CP-WilW2**

In my harsh city, when a Catholic priest. The Green Shoot. John Hewitt. **CP-HewiJ**

In my head I am. Walking. Robert Creeley. **CP-CreeR**

In my head the juxtapositions. Vision of Labor, A: 1931. William Carlos Williams. **CP-WilW2**

In my heart a phoenix flame. Song: A Phoenix Flame. Robert Ranke Graves. **CP-GravR**

In my imagination I was the pivot of a fresh beginning. Adrienne Rich. **SP-RicA2** *Fr.* Shooting Script. **CP-RicAE**

In my imaginings I wish to drop. Zimmer Remembering Wanda. Paul Zimmer. **SP-ZimmP**

In My Life. The Beatles. **CP-Beatl**

In my line of paperwork. An Autumn Burning. Wendell Berry. **CP-BerrW**

In my loamy nook. The Milestone by the Rabbit-Burrow. Thomas Hardy. **CP-HardT**

In my love's house. The House. Kathleen Jessie Raine. *Fr.* The Marriage of Psyche. **SP-RainK**

In My Mind's Eye a Temple, Like a Cloud. William Wordsworth. **CP-WorW2**

In my most spectacular, technicolored dream. Zimmer's Love Poem After A Hard Dream. Paul Zimmer. **SP-ZimmP**

In my native province when I was young. From the Tibetan. John Hewitt. **CP-HewiJ**

In my own shire, if I was sad. Alfred Edward Housman. **CP-HousA**

In my own time I watch the light of nature falling. Personal Angel Glimpsed. Tom Clark. **SP-ClarT**

In my paintings for they are present. Ted Berrigan. **SP-BerrT** *Fr.* The Sonnets.

In my poems there's seldom. Of the Empirical Self and for Me. Roy Fisher. **SP-FishR**

In my room at the Hotel Continentàl. Buenos Aires. Robert Lowell. **SP-LoweR**

In my room, the world is beyond my understanding. Of the Surface of Things. Wallace Stevens. **CP-StevW**

In my sage moments I can say. Come Not; Yet Come! Thomas Hardy. **CP-HardT**

In my serpentine researches. Olympus. John Berryman. **CP-BerrJ**

In My Solitary Hours in My Dear Husband His Absence. Anne Bradstreet. **CP-BradA**

In my stone eyes I see. What Riddle Asked the Sphinx. Archibald MacLeish. **CP-MacLA**

In my street. Dancing Day to Day. Al Young. **CP-YounA**

In my town the old sea-captain. Vigil. James McAuley. *Fr.* Requiem. **SP-McAuJ**

In my unlikeliest dream, my dead are with me again, companions again, in an ordinary way. The Covenant. Charles Kenneth Williams. **SP-WillC**

In my youngest years I used t' kneel. Joan Baez in Concert, Part 2. "Bob Dylan." **CP-DylaB**

In my youth's summer I did sing of One. Byron. **NOBRP** *Fr.* Is thy face like thy mother's, my fair child. *Fr.* Childe Harold's Pilgrimage. **CP-Byron**

In my youth's summer I did sing of one. The Wandering Outlaw. Byron. **FiP** *Fr.* Childe Harold's Pilgrimage. **CP-Byron**

In narrow room nature's whole wealth, yea more. Paradise. John Milton. **NOSC** *Fr.* Book IV. **OAEL-1** *Fr.* Paradise Lost. **CP-MiltJ**

In Nashville, Standing in the Wooden Circle Sawed Out from the Old Ryman Stage, the Picker has a vision. Miller Williams. **SP-WillM**

In Nature. John Haines. **SP-HainJ**

In nature apt to like when I did see. Sonnet 16. Sir Philip Sidney. **NAEL-1** *Fr.* Astrophil and Stella. **SP-SidnP**

In Nature is no rearward step allowed. George Meredith. *Fr.* Alsace-Lorraine. **CP-MerG1**

In Nature There Is Neither Right nor Left nor Wrong. Randall Jarrell. **CP-JarrR**

In Nature's pieces still I see. A Divine Mistress. Thomas Carew. **CP-CareT**

In Neglect. Robert Frost. **CP-FrosR**

In Nervam, *acc. by English translation.* Thomas Campion. **CP-CampT**

In Nervam, *acc. by English translation.* Thomas Campion. **CP-CampT**

In New York beautiful girls can become more beautiful by going. A Brief Guide to New York. Ogden Nash. **CP-NashO**

In New York, it is said. A Place (Any Place) to Transcend All Places. William Carlos Williams. **CP-WilW2**

In night yett may wee see some kind of light. Sonnet 1. Mary Sidney, Countess of Montgomery Wroth. *Fr.* Pamphilia to Amphilanthus. **CP-WrotM**

In Nine Sleep Valley. James Merrill. **SP-MerrJ**

In 1945, when the keepers cried kaput. The Gift. John Ciardi. **SP-CiarJ**

In 1943 the Germans sent me postcards. Crossed Wires. Jim Carroll. **SP-CarrJ**

In nineteen hundred / *Jeunes filles* wondered. Reflection on the Passage of Time, Its Inevitability and Its Quirks. Ogden Nash. **CP-NashO**

In nineteen-nine a fire swept our coast hills. Cawdor. Robinson Jeffers. **CP-JefR1**

In 1935, the year I was born. Chinese Journal. Charles Wright. **SP-WrigC**

In nineteen-thirty-four we [I] spent July. 1934. Donald Hall. **CP-HallD**

In 1929. Stephen Spender. **CP-SpenS**

In Nishapur did Khaibar Khan. The Handkerchiefs of Khaibar Khan. John Updike. **CP-UpdiJ**

In No Direction. Robert Ranke Graves. **CP-GravR**

In North Africa, Delacroix had seen a Jewish wedding which he. The Sleepness Night of Eugene Delacroix. John Yau. **SP-YauJo**

In Northern seas there roams a fish called K'un. The P'eng That Was a K'un. Chuang Tzu, *tr. fr. Chinese by* Robert Graves. **CP-GravR**

In northwest Worcestershire / in eighteen-sixty. Witley Court. James Schuyler. **CP-SchuJ**

In Nottingham. David Herbert Lawrence. **CP-LawrD**

In Nottingham county there lives at Swan Green. Epigram on an Old Lady Who Had Some Curious Notions Respecting the Soul. Byron. **CP-Byron**

In Nottingham, that dismal town. Nottingham's New University. David Herbert Lawrence. **CP-LawrD**

In November, in the days to remember the dead. St. Malachy. Thomas Merton. **CP-MertT; SP-MertT**

In November they pollarded the plane trees. Dijon. Daniel Gerard Hoffman. **SP-HoffD**

In numbers, and but these few. An Ode on the Birth of Our Saviour. Robert Herrick. **CP-HerrR**

In nuova primavera / Rinasce il genio antico. Amor Si Sveglia? Christina Georgina Rossetti. *Fr.* Il Rosseggiar Dell'Oriente Canzoniere. **CP-RosC3**

In Oberlin the university park. John Haines. *Fr.* In the Middle of America. **SP-HainJ**

In obitum Gual. Devoreux fratris clariss. Comitus Essexiae, *acc. by English translation.* Thomas Campion. **CP-CampT**

In Obitum Hen. Mag. Brit. Principis, *acc. by English translation.* Thomas Campion. **CP-CampT**

acc. by English translation. Christopher Marlowe. **CP-MarlC**

In obitum Iacobi Huissii, *acc. by English translation.* Thomas Campion. **CP-CampT**

In October. Charles Tomlinson. **CP-TomlC**

In October of the year. Ox Cart Man. Donald Hall. **CP-HallD**

In, of all places, Tashkent. Two Widows in Tashkent. Donald Davie. **CP-DavDo**

In Ohio. James Wright. **CP-WrigJ**

In Ohio we did not have boats, we had horses. Bailing the Boat. Mary Oliver. **SP-OlivM**

In Oklahoma, / Bonnie and Josie. Life Is Motion. Wallace Stevens. **CP-StevW**

In old days / driving through soft waters. Carmen 64. Catullus. *Fr.* Carmina. **CP-Catul**

In old King George's June. Sports without Blood—a Letter to Dylan Thomas (1948). Thomas Merton. **CP-MertT**

In old-world nursery vacant now of children. Juliet's Nurse. Walter de la Mare. **CP-DeLaW**

In one age or other, if not in this. Charles Olson. **CP-OlsoC**

In one dread night our city saw, and sigh'd. Address. Byron. **CP-Byron**

In one of the Assyrian wars. Wading at Wellfleet. Elizabeth Bishop. **CP-BishE**

In one of these excursions, travelling then. Conclusion. William Wordsworth. *Fr.* The Prelude; Growth of a Poet's Mind [1805 vers.]. **CP-WorW3**

In one of these excursions, travelling then. William Wordsworth. **OxAEP-2**, book 13, *ll.* 1–65; **FaBoPP; FaBoRV** *Fr.* Conclusion: "In one of these excursions, travelling then." *Fr.* The Prelude; Growth of a Poet's Mind [1805 vers.]. **CP-WorW3**

(Climb to Snowdon, The.) **FaBoRV,** book 13;

(Snowdon Sunrise, The.) **FaBoPP,** book 13, *ll.* 1–65;

In one of those excursions (may they ne'er). Conclusion. William Wordsworth. **OAEL-2; OBNC** *Fr.* The Prelude; Growth of a Poet's Mind [1850 vers.]. **CP-WorW3**

In one of those excursions (may they ne'er). William Wordsworth. **EBEV,** book 14, *ll.* 1–119; *Fr.* Conclusion: "In one of those excursions (may they ne'er)." **OAEL-2; OBNC** *Fr.* The Prelude; Growth of a Poet's Mind [1850 vers.]. **CP-WorW3**

In one who felt as once he felt. On Finding a Fan. Byron. **CP-Byron**

In Order to. Kenneth Patchen. **CP-PatcK**

In our bed you offer me your maid. Les Italiennes. John Clellon Holmes. **SP-HolmJ**

In our beginning. Eulogy. Wystan Hugh Auden. *Fr.* Eleven Occasional Poems. **CP-AudeW**

In our houses, the snow keeps us. Snowheart. Tess Gallagher. **SP-GallT**

In our old shipwrecked days there was an hour. George Meredith. **BoLoP; EnVR; HBV; NOBVV; SeCePo; WHA** *Fr.* Modern Love. **CP-MerG1**

(Love Dies.) **SeCePo**

In our period, they say there is free speech. In Our Time. Muriel Rukeyser. **CP-RukeM**

In Our Time. Muriel Rukeyser. **CP-RukeM**

In Our Town. Hilda Doolittle. **CP-DoolH**

In packing boxes of spiders and amber. Elizabeth and the Golden Oranges. Diane Wakoski. **SP-WakoD**

In pain I hung. Odin's Song. Frederick Morgan. **SP-MorgF**

In painted plumes superbly drest. The Parrot. Vincent Bourne, *tr. fr. Latin by* William Cowper. **CP-CowpW**

In Pandarum, *acc. by English translation.* Thomas Campion. **CP-CampT**

In paper sacks the customers carry away millions of tons of goods daily. Carl Sandburg. **CP-SandC** *Fr.* The People, Yes. **CP-SandC**

In paradise I poised my foot above the boat and said. Father. James Wright. **CP-WrigJ**

In Paris, at the Louvre, there have I seen. George Meredith. *Fr.* Modern Love. **CP-MerG1**

In Paris in a loud dark winter. Lawrence Ferlinghetti. **SP-FerlL**

In Paris where the rue de la Nuit. Annie from Miami. Gilbert Sorrentino. **SP-SorrG**

In Part from Moschus's Lament for Bion, *see also translations by* Chapman ("Ye mountain valleys. . .") *and* Shelley ("Ye Dorian woods and waves. . ."). William Wordsworth. **CP-WorW1**

In particular one man. The Drum World. Charles Olson. **CP-OlsoC**

In paschall feast, the end of a[u]ncient rite. Of the Blessed Sacrament of the Altar [*or* Aulter]. Robert Southwell. **CP-SoutR**

In passage along an endless, eventless pavement. Endless Pavement. Robert Ranke Graves. **CP-GravR**

In passing with my mind. The Right of Way. William Carlos Williams. **CP-WilW1**

In pasture where the leaf and wood. The Quest. James Wright. **CP-WrigJ**

in pathos, seemingly numb. After the Fire—The Woman. Tom Clark. **SP-ClarT**

In Paths Untrodden. Walt Whitman. **CP-WhitW**

In Patience. Christina Georgina Rossetti. **CP-RosC3**

In Patterdale. William Wordsworth. **FaBoRV** *Fr.* Introduction—Childhood and School-Time. *Fr.* The Prelude; Growth of a Poet's Mind [1805 vers.]. **CP-WorW3**

In Peace. John Greenleaf Whittier. **CP-WhitJ**

In peace tomorrow, when your slack hands weigh. 1945: The Death of the Gods. Randall Jarrell. **CP-JarrR**

In people, nothing is clear. They knot together. The History of the Moon. William Dickey. **SP-DickW**

In perfect printed breath. Leaving Rochester. Al Young. **CP-YounA**

In Perspective. Robert Ranke Graves. **CP-GravR**

In Piam Memoriam. Geoffrey Hill. **CP-HillG**

In picture, they which truly understand. To the Author. Ben Jonson. **CP-JonsB**

In pious times ere priest-craft did begin. Absalom and Achitophel, Pt. I. John Dryden. **SP-DrydJ**

In pious times ere [*or* e'r] priest-craft did begin. John Dryden. **EBEvV; FHYEP; FaBoPV; HAP; NOSC; NoP; OAEL-1; PoE; SeCV-2** *Fr.* Absalom and Achitophel, Pt. I. **SP-DrydJ**

In Piranezi's rarer prints. Prelusive. Herman Melville. **SP-MelvH** *Fr.* Clarel: A Poem and Pilgrimage in the Holy Land.

In Piso's suite / are empty pockets. Carmen 28. Catullus. *Fr.* Carmina. **CP-Catul**

In pity to the emptying town. Jonathan Swift. **CP-SwifJ**

In Place of a Curse. John Ciardi. **SP-CiarJ**

In place of scutcheons, that should deck thy hearse. On Sir John Roe. Ben Jonson. **CP-JonsB**

In place with you, as I come and go. Wendell Berry. *Fr.* Letter. **CP-BerrW**

In placid hours well-pleased we dream. Art. Herman Melville. **SP-MelvH**

In Plaster. Sylvia Plath. **CP-PlatS**

In Pliny, *Phoenice*. Phoenicians. What Day Is. Robert Penn Warren. **SP-WarrR**

In politics if thou would'st mix. Robert Burns. *Fr.* Lines *Written on the Windows of the Globe Tavern, Dumfries.* **CP-BurnR**

In Portsmouth, New Hampshire, plugged with morphia. The Messiah. Louis MacNeice. **CP-MacNL**

In Praise Of. Edwin Rolfe. **CP-RolfE**

In Praise of an Understudy. Malcolm Lowry. **CP-LowrM**

In Praise of $(C_{10}H_9O_5)x$. John Updike. **CP-UpdiJ**

In Praise of Cities. Thom Gunn. **CP-GunnT**

In Praise of Elizabeth. John Hewitt. **CP-HewiJ**

In Praise of Gloriana's Remarkable Golden Hair. Nicholas Vachel Lindsay. *Fr.* This Section Is a Christmas Tree. **CP-LindV**

In Praise of His Mistress. Thomas Carew. **CP-CareT**

In Praise of Johnny Appleseed. Nicholas Vachel Lindsay. **CP-LindV**
Indians Worship Him, but He Hurries On, The.
Johnny Appleseed's Old Age.
Over the Appalachian Barricade.

In Praise of Limestone. Wystan Hugh Auden. **CP-AudeW**

In Praise of Necessity. Thomas McGrath. **SP-McGrT**

In Praise of Prairie. Theodore Roethke. **CP-RoetT**

In Praise of Songs That Die. Nicholas Vachel Lindsay. **CP-LindV**

In Praise of the Author, Mistress Anne Bradstreet, Virtue's True and Lively Pattern. *Unknown, poem signed* "N. H." **CP-BradA**

In Praise of Women. Robert Herrick. **CP-HerrR**

In Prayer the Lips ne're act the winning part. The Heart. Robert Herrick. **CP-HerrR**

In Prisons of Established Craze. Richard Eberhart. **CP-EberR**

In Procession. Robert Ranke Graves. **CP-GravR**

In Progress. Christina Georgina Rossetti. **CP-RosC3**

In Progress you have little faith, say you. Progress. George Meredith. **CP-MerG1**

In Protocreation. Stevie Smith. **CP-SmitS**

In Provence. Daniel Gerard Hoffman. **SP-HoffD**

In public Her face turneth to thee, and pleasant Her smile when ye meet. Rudyard Kipling. *Fr.* Certain Maxims of Hafiz. **CP-KiplR**

In purest song one plays the constant fool. Infirmity. Theodore Roethke. **CP-RoetT**

In Quest. John Greenleaf Whittier. **CP-WhitJ**

In rags mysterious as these. Emily Dickinson. **CP-DickE**

In Railway Halls. Stephen Spender. **CP-SpenS**

In Rain. Wendell Berry. **CP-BerrW**

In rain like this what you want is an open barn door. It Is Teeming. Charles Kenneth Williams. **CP-WillC**

In Rainy September. Robert Bly. **SP-BlyR**

In Recollection of Drumcliffe, September 1948. John Hewitt. **CP-HewiJ**

In Reference to Her Children, 23 June, 1659 [*or* 1656]. Anne Bradstreet. **CP-BradA**

In Remembrance of Joseph Sturge. John Greenleaf Whittier. **CP-WhitJ**

In renovationem votorum, festis natalis domini. Robert Southwell. **CP-SoutR**

In Response to a Rumor that the Oldest Whorehouse in Wheeling, West Virginia, Has Been Condemned. James Wright. **CP-WrigJ**

In restaurants we argue. They Eat Out. Margaret Atwood. **SP-AtwM1**

In resurrection is it awfuller. Christina Georgina Rossetti. **CP-RosC3**

In Retrospect. Maya Angelou. **SP-AngeM**

In right field I am so far out. Thurman Dreaming in Right Field. Paul Zimmer. **SP-ZimmP**

In rigorous hours, when down the iron lane. Winter. Robert Louis Stevenson. **CP-StevR**

In Rivum a Mola Stoana Lichfeldiæ Diffluentem. Samuel Johnson. **CP-JohnS**

In Robin Hood Cove. Marsden Hartley. **CP-HartM**

In ruck and quibble of courtfolk. The Queen's Complaint. Sylvia Plath. **CP-PlatS**

In Russia. Hayden Carruth. **CP-CarHS**

In S. Winefridam. Gerard Manley Hopkins. **CP-HopkG**

In Sabbath quiet, a street. The Grace-Note. Denise Levertov. **CP-LeveD**

In Saginaw, in Saginaw. The Saginaw Song. Theodore Roethke. **CP-RoetT**

In St. Josaphat's the priest was explaining that the. Richard, Oremus. James Liddy. **CP-LiddJ**

In St. Paul's a While Ago. Thomas Hardy. **CP-HardT**

In San Marco, Venezia. William Carlos Williams. **CP-WilW1**

In San Salvador (I). Grace Paley. **CP-PaleG**

In San Salvador (II). Grace Paley. **CP-PaleG**

In Sannium, *acc. by English translation*. Thomas Campion. **CP-CampT**

In Santa Maria del Popolo. Thom Gunn. **CP-GunnT**

In scarecrow patches and tatters, face. The Rag Man. Robert Earl Hayden. **CP-HaydR**

In scenery I like flat country. Passing Remark. William Stafford. **SP-StafW**

In *Schnee der Alpen*—so it runs. To Mrs. MacMarland. Robert Louis Stevenson. **CP-StevR**

In School-Days. John Greenleaf Whittier. **CP-WhitJ**

In Schrafft's. Wystan Hugh Auden. **CP-AudeW**

In Scotland's realm, where trees are few. Tale, A. William Cowper. **CP-CowpW**

In se, *acc. by English translation*. Thomas Campion. **CP-CampT**

In sea-cold Lyonesse. Sunk Lyonesse. Walter de la Mare. **CP-DeLaW**

In Search of a Love Poem. Siv Cedering Fox. **SP-CedeS**
"And night comes."
"And the lovers meet again."
"In the factory where dolls are made."
"In the taxidermist's shop." **AMV-81**
"Modern woman in search of a soul."
"There was, perhaps, a time."

In search of the desert witch, the shamaness. Particularity. Adrienne Rich. *Fr.* Turning the Wheel. **SP-RicA2**

In secret / the out's in—. Robert Creeley. **CP-CreeR**

In secret place where once I stood. The Flesh and the Spirit. Anne Bradstreet. **CP-BradA**

In Seditionem Horrendum. William Cowper. **CP-CowpW**

In Seed Time Learn. William Blake. **FF** *Fr.* Proverbs of Hell. **MeMBP** *Fr.* The Marriage of Heaven and Hell. **CP-BlakW**

In seed time learn, in harvest teach, in winter enjoy. Proverbs of Hell. William Blake. **MeMBP** *Fr.* The Marriage of Heaven and Hell. **CP-BlakW**

In seed time spill, in harvest be platonic, in winter new feelings. Proverbs of Corca Bascinn. James Liddy. *Fr.* Love Songs of Corca Bascinn. **CP-LiddJ**

In se'enteen hunder'n [*or* hunder an'] forty-nine. On Andrew Turner. Robert Burns. **CP-BurnR**

In Senahar, my first born sleeps. Sadi, *tr. fr. Persian by* Ralph Waldo Emerson. **CP-EmerR**

In September greasebands are put on standard apple. James Fenton. *Fr.* Exempla. **SP-FentJ**

In settling the property question between them. The Property Question. David Herbert Lawrence. **CP-LawrD**

In shade of death's sad TREE. *ad. fr. the Medieval* Stabat Mater Dolorosa. Richard Crashaw. **CP-CrasR**

In shadings of an obscure punishment. Kenneth Patchen. **CP-PatcK**

In Shadow. Hart Crane. **CP-CranH**

In Shame and Humiliation. James Wright. **CP-WrigJ**

In shapes that grow organic and bizarre. Air Show. John Updike. **CP-UpdiJ**

In shards the sylvan vases lie. The Ravaged Villa. Herman Melville. **SP-MelvH**

In Sherborne Abbey. Thomas Hardy. **CP-HardT**

In short, convince you that however wise. Fragment of the "Castle Builder." John Keats. **CP-KeatJ**

In Shylock's bargain for the flesh was found. "Lewis Carroll." *Fr.* Solutions. *Fr.* Puzzles from Wonderland. **CP-CarrL**

In Sickness. Jonathan Swift. **CP-SwifJ**

In Sickness and in Health. Wystan Hugh Auden. **CP-AudeW**

In Sickness Like Sleep. Thomas McGrath. **SP-McGrT**

In Sight of the Town of Cockermouth. William Wordsworth. *Fr.* Poems Composed or Suggested During a Tour, in the Summer of 1833. **CP-WorW2**

In Silence. Thomas Merton. **CP-MertT**

In Silence. Frederick Morgan. **SP-MorgF**

In Silence Where We Breathe. Jane Cooper. *Fr.* March. **SP-CoopJ**

In silent barren Synod met. Stanzas on Some Skulls in Beauly Abbey, Near Inverness. John Keats. **CP-KeatJ**

In silent gaze the tuneful choir among. Thomas Gray. **CP-GrayT** (Stanzas to Mr Richard Bentley.) **CP-GrayT**

In silent night, when rest I took. Anne Bradstreet. **CP-BradA** (Here Follow[es] Some Verses upon the Burning of Our House [July 10th, 1966. Copied Out of a Loose Paper].) **CP-BradA**

In simmer when the hay was mawn. Country Lassie. Robert Burns. **CP-BurnR**

In simple location. Simple Location. Roy Fisher. **SP-FishR**

In Singapore, in the airport. Singapore. Mary Oliver. **SP-OlivM**

In Sisterly Fashion. William Carlos Williams. **CP-WilW2**

In six-inch scale, the Mayo baronies. James McAuley. **SP-McAuJ**, *sect.* 1; *Fr.* Map.

In skilful gathering ruffled hairs in order. 1.11. Ovid. **CP-MarlC**, *tr. by* Christopher Marlowe; *Fr.* Elegies.

In sky and wave the white clouds swam. The Maids of Attitash. John Greenleaf Whittier. **CP-WhitJ**

In sleep I am not, I am gone. Sleep and Waking. David Herbert Lawrence. **CP-LawrD**

In sleep where all that's past goes on. Alba (1952). Louis Zukofsky. **CP-ZukLS**

In Sligo the country was soft; there were turkeys. Sligo and Mayo. Louis MacNeice. **FaBoPP** *Fr.* The Closing Album. **CP-MacNL**

In smug delight we swaggered through the park. The Searchlight. Isabella Gardner. **CP-GardI**

In snow thou comest. Emily Dickinson. **CP-DickE**

In sober mornings, doe [*or* do] not thou reherse [*or* rehearse]. When He Would Have His Verses Read. Robert Herrick. **CP-HerrR**

In Society. Allen Ginsberg. **CP-GinsA**

In softness, languor, bloom and growth. Then Shall Perceive. Walt Whitman. **CP-WhitW**

In some small flatland town. Encounter. Richard Shelton. **SP-ShelR**

In some strange replica or congruence. Old Tale. Gilbert Sorrentino. **SP-SorrG**

In some suburban cellar. A Rat Rises. Charles Bukowski. **SP-BukC2**

In some, the man they made. Dreams About Clothes. James Merrill. **SP-MerrJ**

In some unused lagoon, some nameless bay. The Dismantled Ship. Walt Whitman. **CP-WhitW**

In South America on Business He Does Something He Is Ashamed of yet on the Way Home Dreams of It Again and Again. Ron Koertge. **SP-KoerR**

In Spite of Death. Countee Cullen. **CP-CullC**

In spite of everything. Edward Estlin Cummings. **CP-CummE; SP-CummE**

In spite of her sniffle. The Sniffle. Ogden Nash. **CP-NashO**

In spite of Pope, in spite of Gay. A Pastoral Dialogue between Richmond Lodge and Marble Hill. Jonathan Swift. **CP-SwifJ**

In spring / a bluster. Resurrections. Archie Randolph Ammons. **SP-AmmoA**

In spring from the black branches of the flowering plum tree. Flowering Plum. Louise Glück. **SP-GlücL**

In spring looking at a. The Art. William Carlos Williams. **CP-WilW2**

In spring of youth it was my lot. The Lake: To———. Edgar Allan Poe. **CP-PoeEd**

In spring the blue azures bow down. Spring Azures. Mary Oliver. **SP-OlivM**

In spring this mountain was a fish. Hayden Carruth. *Fr.* North Winter. **CP-CarHL**

In Spring we waited. Princes felt. In Due Season. Wystan Hugh Auden. **CP-AudWJ**

In spring you sleep and never know when the morn comes. Meng Hao Jan, *tr. fr. Chinese by* William Carlos Williams *with* David Rafael Wang. **CP-WilW2**

In Springtime. Rudyard Kipling. **CP-KiplR**

In springtime when the leaves are young. Seasons. Christina Georgina Rossetti. **CP-RosC3**

In St. Peter's Basilica in the City of Rome. Notes from the Agent on Earth: How to be Human. Miller Williams. **SP-WillM**

In Stafford Country. Richard Hugo. **CP-HugoR**

In stature the Manlet was dwarfish. The Little Man That Had a Little Gun. "Lewis Carroll." **CP-CarrL** *Fr.* Sylvie and Bruno Concluded.

In steeps and sighs. Charles Wright. *Fr.* Homage to Paul Cézanne. **SP-WrigC**

In still grey dawn a delicate tendril. Louis MacNeice. *Fr.* Flowers in the Interval. **CP-MacNL**

In Stratis Viarum I. Arthur Hugh Clough. *See* Each for himself is still the rule.

In Stratis Viarum II. Arthur Hugh Clough. **SP-ClouA**

In Stratis Viarum III. Arthur Hugh Clough. **SP-ClouA**

In Stratis Viarum IV. Arthur Hugh Clough. *See* Put forth thy leaf, thou lofty plane.

In struggling to get. Charles Henri Ford. **SP-FordC** *Fr.* Emblems of Arachne.

In such a tremendous window. For Richard Wilbur. James Dickey. **CP-DickJ**

In such an armor he may rise and raid. Bronzeville Man with a Belt in the Back. Gwendolyn Brooks. **SP-BrooG**

In such luxurious plentie of all pleasure. Edmund Spenser. **OAEL-1** *Fr.* The Faerie Queene. **CP-Spens**

In such strange passion, if I may once more. William Wordsworth. **OAEL-2** *Fr.* Imagination and Taste, How Impaired and Restored. **EnRP** *Fr.* The Prelude; Growth of a Poet's Mind [1850 vers.]. **CP-WorW3**

In Suffolk they are no longer there. Hedgerows. Charles Tomlinson. **CP-TomlC**

In Summer. Paul Laurence Dunbar. **CP-DunbP**

In Summer Time. Paul Laurence Dunbar. **CP-DunbP**

In summers day, when Phœbus fairly shone. Edmund Spenser. *Fr.* Visions of the World's Vanity [*or* Vanitie]. **CP-Spens**

In summer's heat, and mid-time of the day. 1.5. Ovid, *tr. by* Christopher Marlowe. **CP-MarlC** *Fr.* Elegies.

In summer's mellow midnight. The Night Wind. Emily Brontë. **CP-BronE**

In summertime on Bredon. Bredon Hill. Alfred Edward Housman. **CP-HousA**

In sun-whetted / morning. Gulls. Robert Earl Hayden. **CP-HaydR**

In sunless air, under pines. Child's Park Stones. Sylvia Plath. **CP-PlatS**

In sunlight now, after the weeks it rained. Flooded Meadows. Thom Gunn. **CP-GunnT**

In sunlight on the Avenue. Galway Kinnell. **LiTM** *Fr.* The Avenue Bearing the Initial of Christ into the New World. **SP-KinnG**

In Surrye whilom dwelte a compaignye. The Man of Law's Tale. Geoffrey Chaucer. *Fr.* The Canterbury Tales. **CP-ChauG**

In Sylvia Plath Country. Erica Jong. **SP-JongE**

In "taking charge of your possessions when you saw them" you became a golden jay. To the Peacock of France. Marianne Craig Moore. **CP-MoorM**

In Tall Grass. Carl Sandburg. **CP-SandC**

In tapestries, in dreams, they gathered, as it was enacted. Geoffrey Hill. *Fr.* Mercian Hymns. **CP-HillG**

In Tara's Halls. William Butler Yeats. **CP-YeatW**

In Tarbolton, ye ken, there are proper young men. The Ronalds of the Bennals. Robert Burns. **CP-BurnR**

In tema e in pena addio. Christina Georgina Rossetti. **CP-RosC3**

In tempest and storm blackness of darkness for ever. Where Their Worm Dieth Not, and the Fire Is Not Quenched. Christina Georgina Rossetti. **CP-RosC2**

In Tenebris. Thomas Hardy. **CP-HardT**

"There have been times when I well might have passed and the ending have come." **OAEL-2**

"When the clouds' swoln bosoms echo back the shouts of the many and strong." **BrPo; CMoP; ChIV-1; LiTM; NoAM; OxBTC; VLP**

"Wintertime nighs." **NoAM; OAEL-2; SCGP**

In Terror of Hospital Bills. James Wright. **CP-WrigJ**

In terror of my typewriter's greed for profit. Song of the Thrush. Laurence Lieberman. **SP-LiebL**

In Thankful Acknowledgement for the Letters I Received from My Husband Out Of England. Anne Bradstreet. **CP-BradA**

In Thankful[l] Remembrance for My Dear Husband[']s Safe Arrival[l]. Anne Bradstreet. **CP-BradA**

In that ago when being was believing. The History of Truth. Wystan Hugh Auden. **CP-AudeW**

In that bad year and city of your birth. To the New World. Randall Jarrell. **CP-JarrR**

In that bad year, in a city to have now no name. Answer to Prayer. Robert Penn Warren. **SP-WarrR**

In that black forest, where, when day is done. The Cry of a Lost Soul. John Greenleaf Whittier. **CP-WhitJ**

In that building, long and low. The Ropewalk. Henry Wadsworth Longfellow. **SP-LongH**

In that 'corridor of garments'. Byzantium. Charles Tomlinson. **CP-TomlC**

In that country the animals. The Animals in That Country. Margaret Atwood. **SP-AtwM1**

In that dark year an angry rain came down. The Rain of Blood. Adrienne Rich. **CP-RicAE**

In that dawn it was girl to be alive the country. Katherine Young. James Liddy. **CP-LiddJ**

In that delightful land which is washed by the Delaware's waters. Henry Wadsworth Longfellow. *Fr.* Part the Second. *Fr.* Evangeline, a Tale of Acadie. **SP-LongH**

    Finding of Gabriel, The. **AA**

In That Fair and Pleasant Land. John Hewitt. **CP-HewiJ**

In that first spring. At the Edge of the Suburbs. Siv Cedering Fox. **SP-CedeS**

In That High House. Daniel Gerard Hoffman. **SP-HoffD**

In that hotel my life. The Illumination. Stanley Jasspon Kunitz. **CP-KuniS**

In that I loved you, Love, I worshipped you. To Eros. Wilfred Owen. **CP-OwenW**

In that instant. An Image from Beckett. Derek Mahon. **SP-MahoD**

In that November off Tehuantepec. Sea Surface Full of Clouds. Wallace Stevens. **CP-StevW**

In that oblivious, concentrated, fiercely fetal decontraction peculiar to the lost. The Park. Charles Kenneth Williams. **SP-WillC**

In that old house of many generations. First Travels of Max. John Crowe Ransom. **SP-RansJ**

In that part of the book of my memory. *See also* La Vita Nuova *tr. by* Dante Gabriel Rossetti. Dante Alighieri, *tr. fr. Italian by* Ralph Waldo Emerson. **CP-EmerR**

In that place, shepherd, all the men are dead. Eclogue of the Liberal and the Poet. Allen Tate. **CP-TateA**

In that Poussin the clouds are like golden tea. Poussin. Louis MacNeice. **CP-MacNL**

In that same gardin all the goodly flowres. Edmund Spenser. **NOBE** *Fr.* The Garden of Adonis. **NOBE; PoEL-1** *Fr.* The Faerie Queene. **CP-Spens**

In that situation, all the signs were right: scars. The Sorcerer's Daughter. Louise Bogan. **CP-BogaL**

In that soft season, when descending show'rs. *see also Chaucer's* House of Fame. Alexander Pope. **CP-PopeA**

In that stage of psychosexual development called latency, when not that much, at least supposedly. Child Psychology. Charles Kenneth Williams. **SP-WillC**

In that this happening. Louis Zukofsky. **CP-BuntB** *Fr.* 29 Songs. **CP-ZukLS**

(incl. *Latin tr. by* Basil Bunting.) **CP-BuntB**

In that town, the Golden Highway ended. The Highway. Leonard Nathan. **SP-NathL**

In that world we weary to attain, / Love's furled banner floats at large unfurled. His Banner over Me Was Love. Christina Georgina Rossetti. **CP-RosC2**

In That Year. Jim Morrison. **SP-MorrJ**

In the / mouth—a. Robert Creeley. **CP-CreeR**

In the Acadian land, on the shores of the Basin of Minas. Henry Wadsworth Longfellow. *Fr.* Part the First. *Fr.* Evangeline, a Tale of Acadie. **SP-LongH**

    Evangeline in Acadie. **AA**

In the Acadian land, on the shores of the Basin of Minas. Part the First. Henry Wadsworth Longfellow. *Fr.* Evangeline, a Tale of Acadie. **SP-LongH**

In the afternoon / When no one is in the house. The Back Stairs. John Gould Fletcher. **SP-FletJ** *Fr.* The Ghosts of an Old House.

In the afternoon I watched. Happiness. Mary Oliver. **SP-OlivM**

In the April rain I climbed up to drink. Meditation in the Spring Rain. Wendell Berry. **CP-BerrW**

In the Arden Apartments. The Night before the Night before Christmas. Randall Jarrell. **CP-JarrR**

In the arid sun, over the field. Crow Song. Margaret Atwood. *Fr.* Songs of the Transformed. **SP-AtwM1**

In the autumn brilliance. Air of November. Denise Levertov. **CP-LeveD**

In the Aztec design God crowds. Ultimate Problems. William Stafford. **SP-StafW**

In the back gardens at Lake Balaton. Conversations in Hungary, August 1969. John Hewitt. **CP-HewiJ**

In the back of a garbage truck parked on a side street. Santiago: Five Men in the Street: Number Two. Stephen Dobyns. **SP-DobyS**

In the bad old days a bewigged country Squire. Wigs and Beards. Robert Ranke Graves. **CP-GravR**

In the bad old days it was not so bad. The Managers. Wystan Hugh Auden. **CP-AudeW**

In the Baggage Room at Greyhound. Allen Ginsberg. **CP-GinsA**

In the Balance. Charles Tomlinson. **CP-TomlC**

In the bare trees old husks make new designs. Aigeltinger. William Carlos Williams. **CP-WilW2**

In the barn you know the large soft cows. The Barn. Richard Eberhart. *Fr.* Burr Oaks. **CP-EberR**

In the basement it is cool. The Church. Lewis Turco. **SP-TurcL**

In the basement of the waxworks the old guard puts on his. *after* Henrikas Radauskas. Randall Jarrell. **CP-JarrR**

In the Bay of Fundy the clams. The Clams. Daniel Gerard Hoffman. **SP-HoffD**

In the Beach House. Anne Sexton. **CP-SextA**

In the Beck. Kathleen Jessie Raine. **SP-RainK**

In the bedchamber window, near the glass. The Flower's Tragedy. Thomas Hardy. **CP-HardT**

In the Beech. Seamus Heaney. **SP-HeanS** *Fr.* Sweeney Redivivus.

In the Beginning. Gary Gildner. **SP-GildG**

In the Beginning. Daniel Gerard Hoffman. **SP-HoffD**

In the Beginning. Nicholas Vachel Lindsay. *Fr.* An Indian Summer Day on the Prairie. **CP-LindV**

In the Beginning. Dylan Thomas. **CP-ThomD**

In the beginning and in the end the only decent. Plain Speaking. Louis MacNeice. **CP-MacNL**

In the beginning, at every step, he turned. The Sickness of Adam. Karl Shapiro. **AP; CRP; CoBMV; MoAB** *Fr.* Adam and Eve. **SP-ShapK**

In the beginning I couldn't speak to you. Love in the Cathedral. Miller Williams. **SP-WillM**

In the beginning life was good to me. *tr. fr. the German of* Rilke. Randall Jarrell. **CP-JarrR**

In the Beginning of Beginnings was Void of Void, the Nameless. In My End Is My Beginning. Chuang Tzu, *tr. fr. Chinese by* Thomas Merton. **CP-MertT**

In the beginning Was the Word. Richard Shelton. **SP-ShelR**

In the beginning was the Word next God. The Morgante Maggiore. Luigi Pulci, *tr. fr. Italian by* Byron. **CP-Byron**

In the belovèd hour that ushers day. To Dr. Hake. Robert Louis Stevenson. **CP-StevR**

In the big maple / behind the willow. Scarlet Tanager. James Schuyler. **CP-SchuJ**

In the Black Country. Roy Fisher. **SP-FishR**

In the Black Museum. Howard Nemerov. **CP-NemeH**

In the black winter morning. Bereft. Thomas Hardy. **CP-HardT**

In the bleak mid-winter. Christmas Carol, A. Christina Georgina Rossetti. **CP-RosC1**

In the blizzard night. Blizzard. Louise McNeill. **SP-McNeL**

In the blue hour. The Citizen Dreaming. Thomas McGrath. **SP-McGrT**

In the blue hubbub of the same-through-wealth sky. Geography. Kenneth Koch. **SP-KochK**

In the blue night. Pine Tree Tops. Gary Snyder. **CP-SnydG**

In the blue, singa. Gilbert Sorrentino. **SP-SorrG**

In the blue winter of 1812. Johann Gaertner (1793–1887). Gary Gildner. **SP-GildG**

"In the Bond Scandals. . . ." Tom Clark. **SP-ClarT**

In the Boston Public Library on Boylston Street, where all the bums come in stinking from the cold. The Critic. Charles Kenneth Williams. **SP-WillC**

In the *Boston Sunday Herald* just three lines. To an American Poet Just Dead. Richard Wilbur. **CP-WilbR**

In the bowers of the rising moon. To a Nightingale. George Meredith. **CP-MerG2**

In the Bowling Alley. James Liddy. **CP-LiddJ**

In the bran-new pulpit the bishop stands. Whispered at the Church-Opening. Thomas Hardy. **CP-HardT**

In the branches of / the great plane tree. A Cardinal. James Schuyler. **CP-SchuJ**

In the branches of your nerves. Green Is a Feeling, Not a Color. Al Young. **CP-YounA**

In the Breach. William Everson. **SP-EverW**

In the British Museum. Thomas Hardy. **CP-HardT**

In the Bulrush. Rita Dove. **SP-DoveR**

In the burlesque fantasy of Seneca. The Moirai. Tom Clark. **SP-ClarT**

In the burned- / out highway. Beer Bottle. Ted Kooser. **SP-KoosT**

In the Bus. Grace Paley. **CP-PaleG**

In the cab there was a song. Open Fire Near a Shed. Tess Gallagher. **SP-GallT**

In the Cage. Robert Lowell. **SP-LoweR**

In the cage no word is spoken. Hayden Carruth. *Fr.* Michigan Water: a Few Riffs before Dawn. **CP-CarHL**

In the Camp There Was One Alive. Randall Jarrell. **CP-JarrR**

In the Carolinas. Wallace Stevens. **CP-StevW**

In the Cathedral at Cologne. William Wordsworth. *Fr.* Memorials of a Tour of the Continent; 1820. **CP-WorW2**

In the cave which wild weeds cover. Fragment: A Roman's Chamber. Percy Bysshe Shelley. **CP-ShelP**

In the cave with a long-ago flare. Painters. Muriel Rukeyser. **CP-RukeM**

In the caverns, where the light. The Cave. Louise McNeill. **SP-McNeL**

In the Cemetery. Thomas Hardy. **InPK; Son** *Fr.* Satires of Circumstance in Fifteen Glimpses. **CP-HardT**

In the cemetery of Childhood. Cemetery of Childhood. Joaquim Cardozo, *tr. fr. Portuguese by* Elizabeth Bishop. **CP-BishE**

In the center of a peach. Research, Again. Gilbert Sorrentino. **SP-SorrG**

In the center of the bloodvein. My Uncle is My Honor and a Guest in My House. Etheridge Knight. **SP-KnigE**

In the Central Park Zoo, just past the ants. Zoo Bats. John Updike. **CP-UpdiJ**

In the chain store or the independent it is the people meeting the people. Carl Sandburg. *Fr.* The People, Yes. **CP-SandC**

In the Channel, between the Coast of Cumberland and the Isle of Man. William Wordsworth. *Fr.* Poems Composed or Suggested During a Tour, in the Summer of 1833. **CP-WorW2**

In the chapel where I could praise. Icon. Marge Piercy. **SP-PierM**

In the Children's Hospital. "Hugh MacDiarmid." **SP-MacDH**

In the children's story of Ferdinand the Bull. Querencia. Stephen Dobyns. **SP-DobyS**

In the Child's Night. James Dickey. **CP-DickJ**

In the Chill— / what is nameless but the Source, the Cause. The Radiance in a Dark Wood. Kenneth Patchen. **CP-PatcK**

In the chill rains of the early winter I hear something—. All the Dead Soldiers. Thomas McGrath. **SP-McGrT**

In the choir the boys are singing the hymn. In Church. David Herbert Lawrence. **CP-LawrD**

In the churchyard of Bromham the yews intertwine. Ireland's Own; or the Burial of Thomas Moore. Sir John Betjeman. **CP-BetjJ**

In the circus tent of a hurricane. Circus in Three Rings. Sylvia Plath. **CP-PlatS**

In the Cities. David Herbert Lawrence. **CP-LawrD**

In the city got a little exercise. Fisherman's Return. Malcolm Lowry. **CP-LowrM**

In the city that ruled me. The Street Has Changed. Randall Jarrell. **CP-JarrR**

In the city, under the saw-toothed leaves of an oak. Straw Hat. Rita Dove. **SP-DoveR**

In the clean, anodyne. Nostalgia for India. May Sarton. **SP-SartM**

In the clear atmosphere. The Wild Birds. Randall Jarrell. **CP-JarrR**

In the clear dark lake a lady dived. George Meredith. **CP-MerG2**

In the clear night the hills. The House Skin. Laurence Lieberman. **SP-LiebL**

In the Clear Season of Grapes. Wallace Stevens. **CP-StevW**

In the cockpit they found his rotted tunic. More than Grass. Phoebe Hesketh. **SP-HeskP**

In the cold, cold parlor. First Death in Nova Scotia. Elizabeth Bishop. **CP-BishE**

In the Cold House. James Wright. **CP-WrigJ**

In the Cold Kingdom. Mona Van Duyn. **SP-VanDM**

In the cold light of morning she was looking rather queer. Gnädiges Fräulein. Stevie Smith. **CP-SmitS**

In the cold morning the rested street stands up. Perimeters. Allen Tate. **CP-TateA**

In the cold shed sharpening saws. Sixth-Month Song in the Foothills. Gary Snyder. **CP-SnydG**

In the cold spring night. Smelt Fishing. Robert Earl Hayden. **CP-HaydR**

In the Colonial Luncheonette on Sixth Street they know everything there is to know, the shits. The Regulars. Charles Kenneth Williams. **CP-WillC; SP-WillC**

In the Commercial Gardens. Howard Nemerov. **CP-NemeH**

In the common mind a corked bottle. Lines on Receiving *The Dial's* Award: 1927. William Carlos Williams. **CP-WilW1**

In the concrete cells of the hatchery. Winter Trout. James Dickey. **CP-DickJ**

In the concrete shed among the calves. Dungannon Cattle Market. John Hewitt. **CP-HewiJ**

In the converted stable where I work. The Resurrection. Stephen Dunn. **SP-DunnS**

In the cool of the night time. Interior. Carl Sandburg. **CP-SandC**

In the corncrib you remember. For Mickey. Chuck Miller. **SP-MillC**

In the Corners of Fields. Ted Kooser. **SP-KoosT**

In the court- / yard at midnight, at. La Noche. Robert Creeley. **CP-CreeR**

In the Courtyard of Secret Life. Kenneth Patchen. **CP-PatcK**

In the cream gilded cabin of his steam yacht. Mr. Nixon. Ezra Pound. **MoAmPo** *Fr.* Hugh Selwyn Mauberley. (Life and Contacts). **SP-PounE**

In the damp park, no larger than a stamp. The Banyan Tree, Old Year's Night. Derek Walcott. **CP-WalcD**

In the Dark. David Herbert Lawrence. **CP-LawrD**

In the dark a boxcar grinds. Argo. Richard Hugo. **CP-HugoR**

In the Dark Mountains, Brilliant. Tom Clark. **SP-ClarT**

In the Dark None Dainty. Robert Herrick. **CP-HerrR**

In the dark of the moon, in flying snow, in the dead of winter. February 2, 1968. Wendell Berry. **CP-BerrW**

In the dark silence of an ancient room. The Path of Roses. "Lewis Carroll." **CP-CarrL**

In the dark tie-up seven huge Holsteins. Great Day in the Cows' House. Donald Hall. **CP-HallD**

In the dark with an old song. Trappers. Charles Kenneth Williams. **CP-WillC**

In the darkness of the first world. Song of the Hogan. Richard Shelton. **SP-ShelR**

In the dawn-dirty light, in the biggest snow of the year. Roe-Deer. Ted Hughes. **SP-HughT**

In the dawn freshness, when the mists are slowly rising from the. Irvington. Frederick Morgan. **SP-MorgF**

In the dawn of a sumptuous November. November. Stevie Smith. **CP-SmitS**

In the Day of His Espousals. Christina Georgina Rossetti. **CP-RosC2**

In the day of the mustering of thine army. Church Militant. Donald Davie. **CP-DavDo**

In the Days of Crinoline. Thomas Hardy. **CP-HardT**

In the days of lace-ruffles, perukes and brocade. Brown Bess. Rudyard Kipling. **CP-KiplR**

In the days of my youth. Typical Optical. John Updike. **CP-UpdiJ**

In the days of President Washington. Over the Appalachian Barricade. Nicholas Vachel Lindsay. *Fr.* In Praise of Johnny Appleseed. **CP-LindV**

In the Days of Prismatic Color. Marianne Craig Moore. **CP-MoorM**

In the Days of Rin-Tin-Tin. Daniel Gerard Hoffman. **SP-HoffD**

In the days of the cockade and the brass pistol. Carl Sandburg. **CP-SandC** *Fr.* The People, Yes. **CP-SandC**

In the days that were early the music came easy. Louis MacNeice. *Fr.* Autumn Journal. **CP-MacNL**

In the days when twenty fellows. The Effusions of a School-Patriarch. Arthur Hugh Clough. **SP-ClouA**

In the daytime, when she moved about me. Rudyard Kipling. **CP-KiplR** *Fr.* The Bronkhorst Divorce Case. *Fr.* Plain Tales from the Hills.

In the dead man's dream I stood. Blackburn's Dream. Gilbert Sorrentino. **SP-SorrG**

In the deep afternoon. Frederick Morgan. *Fr.* Blue Hill Poems. **SP-MorgF**

In the Deep Channel. William Stafford. **SP-StafW**

In the deep fall, terror increases. A Home in Dark Grass. Robert Bly. **SP-BlyR**

In the Deep Green Vase. Jim Carroll. **SP-CarrJ**

In the deep heart of man a poet dwells. Ralph Waldo Emerson. **CP-EmerR**

In the Deep Museum. Anne Sexton. **CP-SextA**

In the denouement of the beautiful storm. The Pigeons. Karl Shapiro. **SP-ShapK**

In the depths of the Greyhound Terminal. In the Baggage Room at Greyhound. Allen Ginsberg. **CP-GinsA**

In the desert. The Kingdom of the Moon. Richard Shelton. **SP-ShelR**

In the Desert. Herman Melville. **SP-MelvH**

In the desert of Itabira. Travelling in the Family. Carlos Drummond de Andrade, *tr. fr. Portuguese by* Elizabeth Bishop. **CP-BishE**

In the deserted, moon-blanched [*or* moon-blanch'd] street. A Summer Night. Matthew Arnold. **SP-ArnoM**

In the dining room against the wall. Aunt Mary. Peter Meinke. **SP-MeinP**

In the distant past I can see. After Pasternak. Derek Mahon. **SP-MahoD**

In the ditch. Galway Kinnell. *Fr.* The Dead Shall Be Raised Incorruptible. **SP-KinnG**

In the ditch by the dirt back road. A Drive in the Country. Ted Kooser. **SP-KoosT**

In the Dock. Walter de la Mare. **CP-DeLaW**

In the dome of my sires as the clear moonbeam falls. Newstead Abbey. Byron. **CP-Byron**

In the door, / Long legged, tall. George Oppen. *Fr.* Blood from the Stone. **CP-OppeG**

In the Doorway. Robert Browning. **SCGP** *Fr.* James Lee's Wife. **CP-BroR1**

In the doorway of the bar. Le Seul Malheur Est que Je ne sais pas Lire. Archibald MacLeish. **CP-MacLA**

In the dour ages. A Lesson in Vengeance. Sylvia Plath. **CP-PlatS**
In the dream. The Stand-Ins. Anne Sexton. **CP-SextA**
In the dream I enter the house. Bone-Flower Elegy. Robert Earl Hayden. **CP-HaydR**
In the dream of death where I listen, the voices of the dream keep diminishing, fading away. To Listen. Charles Kenneth Williams. **SP-WillC**
In the dream, the message. Don't Ask. Roy Fisher. **SP-FishR**
In The Dreaming. William Dickey. **SP-DickW**
  "At Maganosc / in the stone bedroom." **SP-DickW**
  "Here, in the summer city." **SP-DickW**
  "If forgiveness comes / it will be gradual." **SP-DickW**
  "In the dreaming / we walk throug the streets of Oxford." **SP-DickW**
  "Thinking of me / think of what was." **SP-DickW**
  "We meet, eating, smoking." **SP-DickW**
In the dreaming / we walk throug the streets of Oxford. William Dickey. **SP-DickW** *Fr.* In The Dreaming. **SP-DickW**
In the Dry. George Meredith. **CP-MerG2**
In the dumbest movie they can play it on us with a sunrise and a passage of adagio Vivaldi. Nostalgia. Charles Kenneth Williams. **SP-WillC**
In the dungeon-crypts, idly did I stray. *see also* Julian M. and A.G. Rochelle *and* The Visionary. Emily Brontë. **CP-BronE**
In the dusk of the evening. Old Mountain Road. Charles Simic. **SP-SimiC**
In the dusk of the river, the wind. The Porch over the River. Wendell Berry. **CP-BerrW**
In the dust are my father's beautiful hands. At Night. Richard Eberhart. **CP-EberR**
In the early evening, as now, a man is bending. Poem. Louise Glück. **SP-GlücL**
In the early morning dark. Wendell Berry. *Fr.* Window Poems. **CP-BerrW**
In the earth, the earth, thou shalt be laid. Emily Brontë. **CP-BronE**
  (Warning and Reply.) **CP-BronE**
In the east the morning comes. Dirge for a Soldier. Paul Laurence Dunbar. **CP-DunbP**
In the eaves of the barn. The Knowledge of Old Towns. Kenneth Patchen. **CP-PatcK**
In the eerie phosphorous. Bathed. Tom Clark. **SP-ClarT**
In the Elegy Season. Richard Wilbur. **CP-WilbR**
In the Element of Antagonisms. Wallace Stevens. **CP-StevW**
In the emplacements of the wood. The Automaton. Randall Jarrell. **CP-JarrR**
In the emptied stadium he leans. Commencement. Dabney Stuart. **SP-StuaD**
In the empty lot—a place. The Wild. Wendell Berry. **CP-BerrW**
In the empty stadium he stood. Pocoangelini 26. Lewis Turco. **SP-TurcL**
In the end you are weary of this ancient world. Zone. Guillaume Apollinaire, *tr. fr. French.* **CP-BeckS,** *tr. by* Samuel Beckett;
In the Estuary. Charles Tomlinson. **CP-TomlC**
In the eternal dream-time. Sueño Real. Lawrence Ferlinghetti. **SP-FerlL**
In the evening. Another Night in the Ruins. Galway Kinnell. **SP-KinnG**
In the Evening. Stephen Berg. **SP-BergS**
In the Evening. Thomas Hardy. **CP-HardT**
In the Evening. Adrienne Rich. **CP-RicAE; SP-RicA2**
In the evening of a brightly. Greenwich Avenue. James Schuyler. **CP-SchuJ**
In the evening the dusk. The Poet Is Dead. William Everson. **SP-EverW**
In the evening the smoke blows far away. Roy Fisher. **SP-FishR** *Fr.* New Diversions.
In the evening there is a sunset sonata comes to the cities. Good Morning, America. Carl Sandburg. **CP-SandC**
In the evening there were flocks of nighthawks. September 2, 1969. Wendell Berry. **CP-BerrW**
In the evening we came back. A Light Left On. May Sarton. **SP-SartM**
In the evening, when the world knew he was dead. In the Evening. Thomas Hardy. **CP-HardT**
In the Evil Days. John Greenleaf Whittier. **CP-WhitJ**
In the exigencies of consciousness. Hayden Carruth. *Fr.* The Sleeping Beauty. **CP-CarHL**
In the Eyes of Men. Leonard Cohen. **CP-CoheL**
In the Face of Hatred. James Wright. **CP-WrigJ**
In the factory where dolls are made. Siv Cedering Fox. *Fr.* In Search of a Love Poem. **SP-CedeS**
In the fair land o'erwatched by Ischia's mountains. In Remembrance of Joseph Sturge. John Greenleaf Whittier. **CP-WhitJ**
In the Fall. Robert Creeley. **CP-CreeR**
In the far South the sun of autumn is passing. Like Decorations in a Nigger Cemetery. Wallace Stevens. **CP-StevW**

In the farmyard the white moon of autumn shines. The Rats. Georg Trakl, *tr. fr. German by* James Wright. **CP-WrigJ**
In the featherbeds of grander times. Not Quite So Soon. Charles Bukowski. **SP-BukC2**
In the Fictive Wish. William Everson. **SP-EverW**
  "But masked of the self."
  "But now having seen."
  "So him in dream."
  "Wader, / Watcher by water."
In the Field. Richard Wilbur. **CP-WilbR**
In the field the air writhes, a heat-pocket. Halfway. Adrienne Rich. **CP-RicAE; SP-RicA2**
In the field, two horses. Winter. Philip Larkin. **CP-LarkP**
In the fields / we let them have. Goldfinches. Mary Oliver. **SP-OlivM**
In the fifth grade. Birthday on the Acropolis. May Sarton. **SP-SartM**
In the 51st State. Ted Berrigan. **SP-BerrT**
In the fine rain small birds made merry din. Ophelia. John Hewitt. **CP-HewiJ**
In the First Age the frogs dwelt. Moralities. Wystan Hugh Auden. *Fr.* Six Commissioned Texts. **CP-AudeW**
In the first canto of the final canticle. The Hand as a Being. Wallace Stevens. **CP-StevW**
In the First Page of an Album by One Whose Handwriting Is Wretchedly Bad. William Wordsworth. **CP-WorW2**
In the first rank of these did Zimri stand. John Dryden. **HAP; SeCePo** *Fr.* Absalom and Achitophel, Pt. I. **SP-DrydJ**
  (Zimri: "In the first rank of These did Zimri stand.") **SeCePo**
In the first ruder age, when love was wild. Love's Force. Thomas Carew. **CP-CareT**
In the first taxi he was alone tra-la. The Taxis. Louis MacNeice. **CP-MacNL**
In the first world we know there is only the present. Sir. Miller Williams. **SP-WillM**
In the first year of freedom's second dawn. George III. Byron. **TW** *Fr.* The Vision of Judgment. **CP-Byron**
In the first year of the first war called the *World*. The Soldier. Randall Jarrell. **CP-JarrR**
In the first years, when your hair. Early Pompeian. Derek Walcott. **CP-WalcD**
In the Firth of Clyde, Ailsa Crag. William Wordsworth. *Fr.* Poems Composed or Suggested During a Tour, in the Summer of 1833. **CP-WorW2**
In the flame of the flickering fire. My Soul. Stevie Smith. **CP-SmitS**
In the flashes and black shadows. The Hunter. William Carlos Williams. **CP-WilW1**
In the folded and quiet yesterdays. Carl Sandburg. *Fr.* The People, Yes. **CP-SandC**
In the footsteps of the walking air. Kenneth Patchen. **CP-PatcK**
In the Ford plant. The Foundations of American Industry. Donald Hall. **CP-HallD**
In the foreground we see time and life. Cézanne's Ports. Allen Ginsberg. **CP-GinsA**
In the Forenoon I rose up. Noon Apocrypha. James McAuley. **SP-McAuJ**
In the forenoon's restful quiet. When the Old Man Smokes. Paul Laurence Dunbar. **CP-DunbP**
In the forest below the stairs. The Hermitage. John Haines. **SP-HainJ**
In the Frail Wood. Marsden Hartley. **CP-HartM**
In the French Translation of Monsieur De Brebeuf Are These Verses: Lib 3. Lucan, *tr. fr. Latin of* Andrew Marvell, *fr. the French of* de Brebeuf by Sir Philip Meadows. **CP-MarvA** *Fr.* Pharsalia.
In the French Translation of Monsieur De Brebeuf Are These Verses: Lib 3. Lucan, *tr. fr. Latin of* Andrew Marvell, *fr. the French of* de Brebeuf by William A. McQueen *and* Kiffin A. Rockwell. **CP-MarvA** *Fr.* Pharsalia.
In the full sun. In the fruitfall season. The Children's Orchard. Muriel Rukeyser. **CP-RukeM**
In the Fullness of Time. Charles Tomlinson. **CP-TomlC**
In the Garden. Walter de la Mare. **CP-DeLaW**
In the Garden. "Bob Dylan." **CP-DylaB**
In the Garden. Richard Eberhart. **CP-EberR**
In the Garden. Thomas Hardy. **CP-HardT**
In the Garden at Swainston. Tennyson. **CP-TennA**
In the Garden City Café with its murals on the wall. Huxley Hall. Sir John Betjeman. **CP-BetjJ**
In the Garden of Dreams. John Gould Fletcher. **SP-FletJ**
In the garden. Sun / on the river. We Walk. James Schuyler. **CP-SchuJ**
In the garden that seems an abyss. Butterfly. Nicanor Parra, *tr. fr. Spanish by* Thomas Merton. **CP-MertT**
In the Gears. Jim Carroll. **SP-CarrJ**

In the geological rock garden. Glacials. Archie Randolph Ammons. **SP-AmmoA**

In the Glass-Bottomed Boat. Erica Jong. **SP-JongE**

In the Glass of Fashion. Howard Nemerov. **CP-NemeH**

In the glittering collection of paste diamonds one in particular ranks very high. Oh, Stop Being Thankful All over the Place. Ogden Nash. **CP-NashO**

In the gold mouth of a flower. Another Spring. Denise Levertov. **CP-LeveD**

In the Grace of Wit, of Tongue and Face. Sir Walter Ralegh. **CP-RaleW**

In the Graeco-Roman Room. Daniel Gerard Hoffman. **SP-HoffD**

In the Grave No Flower. Edna St. Vincent Millay. **CP-MillE**

In the graveyard, in the graveyard. The English Visitor. Stevie Smith. **CP-SmitS**

In the great circle, dancing in. Our Children, Coming of Age. Wendell Berry. **CP-BerrW**

In the great City rear'd, my fancy rude. Hope and Time. Samuel Taylor Coleridge. **CP-ColeS**

In the Great Hall of the Library. Stanley Jasspon Kunitz. *Fr.* The Lincoln Relics. **CP-KuniS**

In the Great Hall where Lady Ann by firelight after dining alone. The Revolution. Donald Hall. **CP-HallD**

In the great place the great house is gone from   in the sun. Slave Quarters. James Dickey. **CP-DickJ**

In the great world—which, being interpreted. Byron. **OxBoLi; PeLV** *Fr.* Canto the Eleventh. **NOBRP** *Fr.* Don Juan. **CP-Byron**

In the green and gallant Spring. Robert Louis Stevenson. **CP-StevR**

In the greenest growth of the Maytime. An Interlude. Algernon Charles Swinburne. **SP-SwinA**

In the greenest of our valleys. From "The Fall of the House of Usher." Edgar Allan Poe. **CP-PoeEd**

In the gutter / boys who try. Up-Beat. Langston Hughes. **SP-HughL**

In the Hall of Mirrors. James Merrill. **SP-MerrJ**

In the hall of the Hofbräuhaus. At the German Writers Conference in Munich. Rita Dove. **SP-DoveR**

In the hard brightness of that winter day. Page from a Tale. Wallace Stevens. **CP-StevW**

In the Heart of the Beast. Charles Kenneth Williams. **CP-WillC**

In the heart of the night. The Two Houses. Thomas Hardy. **CP-HardT**

In the heave of the queen anne's lace, a knot of blood. The Knot. Adrienne Rich. **CP-RicAE; SP-RicA2**

In the heat of a sentence I stopped. You waited. The Dandelion Sermon. James Merrill. *Fr.* Five Old Favorites. **SP-MerrJ**

In the heave of the hankering sea. Carl Sandburg. *Fr.* Timesweep. **CP-SandC**

In the heavy earth the miner. The Gourd. Paul Laurence Dunbar. **CP-DunbP**

In the heroic days when Ferdinand. The Theologian's Tale: Torquemada. Henry Wadsworth Longfellow. **SP-LongH** *Fr.* Tales of a Wayside Inn.

In the heron's eye. Wendell Berry. *Fr.* Window Poems. **CP-BerrW**

In the hexameter rises the fountain's silvery column. The Ovidian Elegiac Metre. Samuel Taylor Coleridge. **CP-ColeS**

In the heydays of 'forty-five. For George Santayana. Robert Lowell. **SP-LoweR**

In the high seat, before-dawn dark. Why Log Truck Drivers Rise Earlier than Students of Zen. Gary Snyder. **CP-SnydG**

In the highlands, in the country places. Robert Louis Stevenson. **CP-StevR**

In the Hill at Newgrange. Robinson Jeffers. **CP-JefR2**

In the Hills South of Capernaum, Port. Charles Olson. **CP-OlsoC**

In the Hole. John Ciardi. **SP-CiarJ**

In the Holy Nativity of Our Lord God. Richard Crashaw.

  (Hymn, The.) **CP-CrasR**

Shepherd's Hymn, The ("We saw Thee in Thy balmy nest"). **ACP; TrGrPo**

  (Verses from the Shepherd's Hymn.) **OBEV**

Shepherds' Hymn, The. **NOBE**

In the Home Stretch. Robert Frost. **CP-FrosR**

In the hope of ease to come. Sufferance. Robert Herrick. **CP-HerrR**

In the Hospital. Stephen Dobyns. **SP-DobyS**

In the Hospital for Tests. Mona Van Duyn. **SP-VanDM**

In the hospitals and jails. The Worst and the Best. Charles Bukowski. **SP-BukC1**

In the hospitals I've been in. Bedpans. Charles Bukowski. **SP-BukC1**

In the hot high summer I came. Hayden Carruth. **CP-CarHS** *Fr.* The Bloomingdale Papers.

In the houre of my distresse. His Letanie, To the Holy Spirit. Robert Herrick. **CP-HerrR**

In the House. Stephen Dunn. **SP-DunnS**

In the house / of the vine-grower. Rhenish Winter. Charles Tomlinson. **CP-TomlC**

In the house of. Robert Creeley. **CP-CreeR**

In the house of power grown old but unyielding. The Emperor. Marge Piercy. *Fr.* Laying Down the Tower. **SP-PierM**

In the House of Suddhoo. Rudyard Kipling. *Fr.* Plain Tales from the Hills. "Stone's throw out on either hand, A." **CP-KiplR**

In the House of the Dying. Jane Cooper. **SP-CoopJ**

In the House of the Rising Sun. Gary Snyder. **CP-SnydG**

In the house on the cliff. Margaret Atwood. *Fr.* Five Poems for Grandmothers. **SP-AtwM2**

In the human cities, never again to. Despisals. Muriel Rukeyser. **CP-RukeM**

In the Hungry Thirties. Economics. Wystan Hugh Auden. *Fr.* Shorts I ("Watch upon my wrist, The"). **CP-AudeW**

In the imitation of Gothic. Imitation. Louis Zukofsky. *Fr.* 29 Songs. **CP-ZukLS**

In the Immaculate Conception Church. Nicholas Vachel Lindsay. **CP-LindV**

In the "immaculately neat" cabin it is calm and warm. The Hermit of Hudson Pond. Mona Van Duyn. **SP-VanDM**

In the Intensity of Final Light. Charles Tomlinson. **CP-TomlC**

In the Japanese. Grey Sparrow Addresses the Mind's Ear. Denise Levertov. **CP-LeveD**

In the Keyfood Market on Broadway. Keyfoods. Audre Lorde. **SP-LordA**

In the kingdom of Poesy Hafiz waves like a banner. Hafiz, *tr. by* Ralph Waldo Emerson. **CP-EmerR** *Fr.* Odes.

In the Kitchen, at Midnight. Ted Kooser. **SP-KoosT**

In the Kitchen of the Old House. Donald Hall. *See* In the kitchen of the old house, late.

In the kitchen of the old house, late. Donald Hall. **CP-HallD**

  (In the Kitchen of the Old House.) **CP-HallD**

In the kitchen the dishwasher is eating the dishes. The Kitchen. Lewis Turco. **SP-TurcL**

In the Land of Shinar. Siv Cedering Fox. **SP-CedeS**

In the land of turkeys in turkey weather. Dance of the Macabre Mice. Wallace Stevens. **CP-StevW**

In the Lane. Christina Georgina Rossetti. **CP-RosC3**

In the last Battle that Arthur fought, the most Beautiful was one. Verse from the Advertisement to Blake's Exhibition of Paintings, 1809. William Blake. **CP-BlakW**

In the last bus last night that dead musician. Exile of Music. Muriel Rukeyser. **CP-RukeM**

In the Last Few Moments Came the Old German Cleaning Woman. Jane Cooper. **SP-CoopJ**

In the last hour of night, a zebra racing dawn. Muriel Rukeyser. **CP-RukeM**

In the last light of a late. Sundowner. Phoebe Hesketh. **SP-HeskP**

In the last minutes he said more to her. Seamus Heaney. **PNI** *Fr.* Clearances. **SP-HeanS**

In the last sad watches of night. Between Moon and Moon. Robert Ranke Graves. **CP-GravR**

In the last village before the frontier. The Republic 1939. James Liddy. **CP-LiddJ**

In the late night listening from bed. Thinking for Berky. William Stafford. **SP-StafW**

In the Lenin Library, Dushanbe. John Hewitt. **CP-HewiJ**

In the light of the cold glimmer of what everybody knows, why should the. Carl Sandburg. *Fr.* The People, Yes. **CP-SandC**

In the *lines* that you sent, are the *Muses* and *Graces.* Alexander Pope. *Fr.* Epigrams Occasion'd by an Invitation to Court. **CP-PopeA**

In the list of one thousand false addresses. Poem. Thomas McGrath. **SP-McGrT**

In the little movie. Calder's Hands. John Updike. **CP-UpdiJ**

In the little tired spring. The Topaz of the Sixties. Marsden Hartley. **CP-HartM**

In the livingroom you are someplace else like a cat. Concerning the Mathematician. Marge Piercy. **SP-PierM**

In the loam we sleep. Loam. Carl Sandburg. **CP-SandC**

In the lodges of the perishable souls. Shakspere. Gerard Manley Hopkins. **CP-HopkG**

In the long flat panhandle of Texas. Carl Sandburg. *Fr.* The People, Yes. **CP-SandC**

In the long journey out of the self. Journey to the Interior. Theodore Roethke. **DiPo; PFL** *Fr.* North American Sequence. **CP-RoetT**

In the Long Night. Robert Frost. *Fr.* Five Nocturnes. **CP-FrosR**

In the long, sleepless watches of the night. The Cross of Snow. Henry Wadsworth Longfellow. **SP-LongH**

In the lower left-hand corner. An Imaginary Happening, London. Lawrence Ferlinghetti. **SP-FerlL**

In the lowlands lie his reaches. Grendel. Lewis Turco. **SP-TurcL**

In the Lupanar at Pompeii. James Dickey. **CP-DickJ**

In the Luxembourg Gardens. John Hewitt. **CP-HewiJ**

In the magic the Homer dusk. Dortmunder. Samuel Beckett. **CP-BeckS**

In the Mail. Robert Lowell. **SP-LoweR**

In the main[e] sea the i[s]le of Cre[e]te doth lie. Virgil, *tr.* by Sir Walter Ralegh. **CP-RaleW** *Fr.* The Aeneid [*or* Eneados, *Aeneis*].

In the maple grove wind moves. The Maple Works. Lewis Turco. **SP-TurcL**

In the Marble Quarry. James Dickey. **CP-DickJ**

In the Marquee. Thomas Hardy. **CP-HardT**

In the mating of trees. Planting Trees. Wendell Berry. **CP-BerrW**

In the Matter of One Compass. Rudyard Kipling. **CP-KiplR**

In the maze of the. Charles Henri Ford. **SP-FordC** *Fr.* Emblems of Arachne.

In the meadow—what in the meadow? Christina Georgina Rossetti. **CP-RosC2**

In the Men's Room(s). Marge Piercy. **SP-PierM**

In the metropolis of hooligans. The Stare of the Man from the Provinces. Howard Nemerov. **CP-NemeH**

In the middle / of a bite of. Charles Kenneth Williams. **CP-WillC; SP-WillC**

In the middle distance. The Tree and the Cloud. Donald Hall. **CP-HallD**

In the Middle of America. John Haines. **SP-HainJ**

In the middle of America. John Haines. *Fr.* In the Middle of America. **SP-HainJ**

   "In Oberlin the university park."

   "In the middle of America."

   "Thereafter on that cold."

In the middle of Ivy Day, no ivy on the trees. A Letter to Eamonn Wall. James Liddy. **CP-LiddJ**

In the middle of the night. In Childbed. Thomas Hardy. **CP-HardT**

In the Middle of the Road. Carlos Drummond de Andrade, *tr. fr. Portuguese* by Elizabeth Bishop. **CP-BishE**

In the middle of the winter. Midwinter Blues. Langston Hughes. **SP-HughL**

In the midst of the battle I turned. On Reading Omar Khayyam. Nicholas Vachel Lindsay. **CP-LindV**

In the midst of the deepest. Sea Fogs at the Chequammitt Inn. Brendan Galvin. **SP-GalvB**

In the midst of things. Louis Zukofsky. **CP-ZukLS**

In the Midwest of Willa Cather. For Julia in Nebraska. Adrienne Rich. **SP-RicA2**

In the mind of the kiss occurs a thought so rich. Sonnet. Hayden Carruth. **CP-CarHS** *Fr.* Sonnets.

In the Mind's Eye. Thomas Hardy. **CP-HardT**

In the mind's eye. On the Bank Street Pier. Grace Paley. **CP-PaleG**

In the mind's house of heaven the great night never. Hayden Carruth. *Fr.* The Sleeping Beauty. **CP-CarHL**

In the minister's morning sermon. The Minister's Daughter. John Greenleaf Whittier. **CP-WhitJ**

In the Missouri Ozarks. Mona Van Duyn. **SP-VanDM**

In the misty night humming to themselves like morons. Louis MacNeice. *Fr.* The Trolls. **CP-MacNL**

In the moment of looking back. Orpheus in the Underground. Phoebe Hesketh. **SP-HeskP**

In the Month of May. Robert Bly. **SP-BlyR**

In the month of the long decline of roses. Hendecasyllabics. Algernon Charles Swinburne. **SP-SwinA**

In the month when the Kamchatka bugbane. Going. James Schuyler. **CP-SchuJ**

In the moon as Phebus stood over his oriental Gardening. William Blake. **CP-BlakW** *Fr.* An Island in the Moon.

In the Moonlight. Thomas Hardy. **NoAM** *Fr.* Satires of Circumstance in Fifteen Glimpses. **CP-HardT**

In the moonlight / I met Berserk. Anecdote of the Prince of Peacocks. Wallace Stevens. **CP-StevW**

In the moonlight under a shag-bark hickory tree. Shag-Bark Hickory. Carl Sandburg. **CP-SandC**

In the Morning. Paul Laurence Dunbar. **CP-DunbP**

In the morning / it shuffles, unhurried. A Certain Sharpness in the Morning Air. Mary Oliver. **SP-OlivM**

In the Morning. Kenneth Koch. **SP-KochK**

In the morning, / The jack-rabbit sang to the Arkansaw. The Jack-Rabbit. Wallace Stevens. **CP-StevW**

In the morning, a Sunday morning, shadows of sea and adumbrants of. Chords. Carl Sandburg. **CP-SandC**

In the morning did the passengers. The Ship Translated Being La Paquebot. Ernest Hemingway. **CP-HemiE**

In the morning eyes of the brown-eyed Susans. Field People. Carl Sandburg. **CP-SandC**

In the morning his mood failed, for gray buffalo-clouds were going. Thunderstorm in the Ozarks. John Gould Fletcher. **SP-FletJ**

In the morning I saw three great ships. The Calm. John Gould Fletcher. *Fr.* Sand and Spray: A Sea-Symphony. **SP-FletJ**

In the morning, in December. Azaleas. Peter Meinke. **SP-MeinP**

In the morning, in the morning. Alfred Edward Housman. **CP-HousA**

In the morning the rivers will blaze up blue like sulphur. Tomorrow Morning. Robert Penn Warren. *Fr.* Penological Study: Southern Exposure. **SP-WarrR**

In the morning there is the east wind. The Homestead. Lewis Turco. **SP-TurcL**

In the morning, when it was raining. Poem. Delmore Schwartz. **SP-SchwD**

In the morning when ye rise. Another. Robert Herrick. **CP-HerrR**

In the Mountain Tent. James Dickey. **CP-DickJ**

In the mountains. The Guests. Louis Zukofsky. **CP-ZukLS**

In the mountains behind the chateau where no one could live. Boar. Daniel Gerard Hoffman. **SP-HoffD**

In the mountains it's cold, *after* Han-shan. Gary Snyder. **CP-SnydG**

In the Museum. Isabella Gardner. **CP-GardI**

In the mustardseed sun. Poem on His Birthday. Dylan Thomas. **CP-ThomD**

In the Name of the Empress of India, make way. The Overland Mail. Rudyard Kipling. **CP-KiplR**

In the name of the Lord put I my trust. Psalm 11. Bible, *O.T. Fr.* Psalms. **CP-Psal**

In the Name of Virtue. Alfred Percival Graves. **CP-GravR**

In the nap there are numerous doors, boudoirs, a talking hall. Six Naps in One Day. Donald Hall. **CP-HallD**

In the narcotic and act / of omniscience. For Martin. Robert Creeley. **CP-CreeR**

In the nativity of time. Love Made in the First Age[: To Chloris]. Richard Lovelace. **CP-LoveR**

In the natural year come two thanksgivings. The Sabbath of Mutual Respect. Marge Piercy. **SP-PierM**

In the Neolithic Age. Rudyard Kipling. **CP-KiplR**

Wide, Wide World, The. **OtMeF**

In the never, still arriving, I find you. Dwingelo. Gerrit Achterberg, *tr. fr. Dutch* by Adrienne Rich. **CP-RicAE**

In the New Garden. Walt Whitman. **CP-WhitW**

In the newspaper office—who are the spooks? Palladiums. Carl Sandburg. **CP-SandC**

In the next life. Charles Kenneth Williams. **CP-WillC; SP-WillC**

In the night / in the day. Cool Breeze. Joseph Ceravolo. **SP-CeraJ**

In the Night. Stevie Smith. **CP-SmitS**

In the Night Desert. William Stafford. **SP-StafW**

In the night fouled the nets. Shark Meat. Gary Snyder. **CP-SnydG**

In the Night She Came. Thomas Hardy. **CP-HardT**

In the Night the Sound Woke Us. Muriel Rukeyser. **CP-RukeM**

In the night the white skin. Boil. John Updike. **CP-UpdiJ**

In the night, when the sea-winds take the city in their arms. Night Movement—New York. Carl Sandburg. **CP-SandC**

In the North. Adrienne Rich. **CP-RicAE**

In the northern hemisphere. Kangaroo. David Herbert Lawrence. **CP-LawrD**

In the nowhere between dark and dawn. At Four A.M. Phoebe Hesketh. **SP-HeskP**

In the Nuptial Chamber. Thomas Hardy. **InPK** *Fr.* Satires of Circumstance in Fifteen Glimpses. **CP-HardT**

In the Nursery. Wystan Hugh Auden. **CP-AudWJ**

In the Oaxaca Train, *sl. diff. st. order.* Malcolm Lowry. *See* April 1937 In the Oaxaca Train.

In the old age black was not counted fair. Sonnet 127. William Shakespeare. **OXAEP-1** *Fr.* Sonnets. **CP-ShaWS**

In the old brownstone on W. 35th. A Reading of Rex Stout. Mona Van Duyn. **SP-VanDM**

In the Old Colony days, in Plymouth the land of the Pilgrims. Henry Wadsworth Longfellow. **AiP; TreFS** *Fr.* Miles Standish. *Fr.* The Courtship of Miles Standish. **SP-LongH**

In the Old Colony days, in Plymouth the land of the Pilgrims. Miles Standish. Henry Wadsworth Longfellow. *Fr.* The Courtship of Miles Standish. **SP-LongH**

In the Old Country, then, two ladies and two boys. Mona Van Duyn. **SP-VanDM**

In the old days (a custom laid aside). Abraham Davenport. John Greenleaf Whittier. **CP-WhitJ**

In the old days with married women's stockings. The Libertine. Louis MacNeice. **CP-MacNL**

In the old deep sing-song of the sea. Old Deep Sing-Song. Carl Sandburg. **CP-SandC**

In the old forever-never days. The Beaverhouse Downriver. Barton Sutter. **SP-SuttB**

In the old Hebrew myth the lion's frame. The Hive at Gettysburg. John Greenleaf Whittier. **CP-WhitJ**

In the Old Neighborhood. Rita Dove. **SP-DoveR**

In the old neighborhood, each funeral parlor. Teach Us to Number Our Days. Rita Dove. **SP-DoveR**

In the old, scratched, cheap wood of the typing stand. Dreamwood. Adrienne Rich. **SP-RicA1**

In the old Scripture I have often read. Lip Labour. Robert Herrick. **CP-HerrR**

In the "Old South." John Greenleaf Whittier. **CP-WhitJ**

In the Old Theatre, Fiesole. Thomas Hardy. **CP-HardT**

In the old wars drum of hoofs and the beat of shod feet. Wars. Carl Sandburg. **CP-SandC**

In the one state of ours that is a shire. To the Right Person. Robert Frost. **CP-FrosR**

In the Orchard. Algernon Charles Swinburne. **SP-SwinA**

In the Oregon Country. William Stafford. **SP-StafW**

In the other 'eighties, a hundred midsummers gone. Derek Walcott. **CP-WalcD** *Fr.* Midsummer.

In the other gardens. Autumn Fires. Robert Louis Stevenson. **CP-StevR**

In the outskirts of the village. The Sycamores. John Greenleaf Whittier. **CP-WhitJ**

In the pantry the dear dense cheeses, Cheddars and harsh. O Cheese. Donald Hall. **CP-HallD**

In the Paralelo a one-legged. Barcelona in Wartime. Louis MacNeice. *Fr.* Entered in the Minutes. **CP-MacNL**

In the Park. Stevie Smith. **CP-SmitS**

In the Parking Lot of the Supermarket. Chuck Miller. **SP-MillC**

In the Person of a Lady To Her Inconstant Servant. Thomas Carew. **CP-CareT**

In the Person of Womankind [A Song Apologetic]. Ben Jonson. **CP-JonsB**

In the pit of the night our bodies merge. Marge Piercy. *Fr.* Doing It Differently. **SP-PierM**

In the Pitch of Night. Daniel Gerard Hoffman. **SP-HoffD**

In the place of the west. The Coming of Quetzalcoatl. David Herbert Lawrence. **CP-LawrD**

In the place that is my own place, whose earth. The Sycamore. Wendell Berry. **CP-BerrW**

In the Planetarium. Siv Cedering Fox. **SP-CedeS**

In the play Amy didn't want to be. First Grade. William Stafford. **SP-StafW**

In the playpen of. Charles Henri Ford. **SP-FordC** *Fr.* Emblems of Arachne.

In the pleasant orchard-closes. The Lost Bower. Elizabeth Barrett Browning. **CP-BroEB**

In the Pocket. James Dickey. **CP-DickJ**

In the poplars' lengthening shadows on this hill. Eveningsong at Bellosguardo. Erica Jong. **SP-JongE**

In the pounding white is a man to kill. Ballad of the Upper Bumping. Richard Hugo. **CP-HugoR**

In the prebirth of the evening. Cherry Blossoms at Evening. William Carlos Williams. **CP-WilW2**

In the predicament of other lives. Wendell Berry. *Fr.* The Clearing. **CP-BerrW**

In the preposterous sunlight. Zei Gesund. Isabella Gardner. **CP-GardI**

In the Pride of His Youth. Rudyard Kipling. *Fr.* Plain Tales from the Hills. "'Stopped in the straight when the race was his own." **CP-KiplR**

In the Public Garden. Marianne Craig Moore. **CP-MoorM**

In the Public Gardens. Sir John Betjeman. **CP-BetjJ**

In the purple light, heavy with redwood, the slopes drop seaward. Apology for Bad Dreams. Robinson Jeffers. **CP-JefR1**

In the push of time, it's all too easy. Why a Hush Should Not Be Rushed. Al Young. **CP-YounA**

In the pushcart market, on Sunday. Galway Kinnell. **NaP** *Fr.* The Avenue Bearing the Initial of Christ into the New World. **SP-KinnG**

In the quiet, chill blue night. The Blessing of the Worms. John Gould Fletcher. **SP-FletJ** *Fr.* The Parables of Antichrist.

In the quiet house. Listening in October. John Haines. **SP-HainJ**

In the quiet house, on a morning of snow. The Christmas Tree. Frederick Morgan. **SP-MorgF**

In the quiet, in the snow. Year's End. John Clellon Holmes. **SP-HolmJ**

In the quiet spaces between equinoctial gales. Just before Fall. James Schuyler. **CP-SchuJ**

In the quiet waters. Fafnir and the Knights. Stevie Smith. **CP-SmitS**

In the Railway Hotel at Cordoba. Steve Griffiths. **SP-GrifS**

In the rain- / darkness, the sunset. Edward Estlin Cummings. **CP-CummE**

In the Rain. Hilda Doolittle. **CP-DoolH**

In the Rain and the Sun. Thomas Merton. **CP-MertT; SP-MertT**

In the rain in the rain in the rain in the rain in Spain. Ernest Hemingway. **CP-HemiE** *Fr.* The Soul of Spain with McAlmon and Bird the Publishers.

In the rain, the lonesome. The Banner Bearer. William Carlos Williams. **CP-WilW2**

In the rain, the naked old father is dancing, he will get wet. Natural History. Robert Penn Warren. **SP-WarrR**

In the ranks of the Austrian you found him. The Forced Recruit. Elizabeth Barrett Browning. **CP-BroEB**

In the reading room in the New York Public Library. Reading Room, The New York Public Library. Richard Eberhart. **CP-EberR**

In the rectory garden on his evening walk. Dialogue between Ghost and Priest. Sylvia Plath. **CP-PlatS**

In the recurring dream. Stanley Jasspon Kunitz. *Fr.* The Testing-Tree. **CP-KuniS**

In the Red Corner. James McAuley. **SP-McAuJ**

In the redwood house sailing off. Sailing Home. Erica Jong. **SP-JongE**

In the reeds, the search for food by grebes. Hideout. Richard Hugo. **CP-HugoR**

In the region of daffodils. The Planet over Eastern Parkway. Thomas Merton. *Fr.* Cables to the Ace. **CP-MertT**

In the Restaurant. Thomas Hardy. **MoAB; MoBrPo** *Fr.* Satires of Circumstance in Fifteen Glimpses. **CP-HardT**

In the Ripeness of the Weed. William Everson. **SP-EverW** *Fr.* The Falling of the Grain.

In the riprap, / in the cool caves. Mussels. Mary Oliver. **SP-OlivM**

In the Room of the Bride-Elect. Thomas Hardy. **InPK** *Fr.* Satires of Circumstance in Fifteen Glimpses. **CP-HardT**

In the room, our old room, barred with moonlight. A Summer Night. Randall Jarrell. **CP-JarrR**

In the rose garden in the park. Another Year. William Carlos Williams. **CP-WilW2**

In the Rosses. John Hewitt. **CP-HewiJ**

In the Round. James Schuyler. **CP-SchuJ**

In the Round Tower at Jhansi, June 8, 1857. Christina Georgina Rossetti. **CP-RosC1**

In the Rue Monsieur le Prince. Song for "Buvez les Vins du Postillion"—Advt. Jean Garrigue. **SP-GarrJ**

In the Ruins of New York. Thomas Merton. *Fr.* Figures for an Apocalypse. **CP-MertT**

In the, same in (when qualm?) thick wee poetry, putrid Victi. Catullus. *See* Carmen 98: "Same can be said of you, Victius, The."

In the same place, when Nature wore. H.A. and A.S. Emily Brontë. **CP-BronE**

In the Sap. George Meredith. **CP-MerG2**

In the 'Sconset Bus. William Carlos Williams. **CP-WilW1**

In the sea, Biscayne, there prinks. Homunculus et la Belle Étoile. Wallace Stevens. **CP-StevW**

In the sea rocks, / in the stone pockets. Starfish. Mary Oliver. **SP-OlivM**

In the secret heart all men are free. The Secret Heart. Richard Eberhart. **CP-EberR**

In the Secret Room, East of the Sun, West of the Moon. Diane Wakoski. **SP-WakoD**

In the Servants' Quarters. Thomas Hardy. **CP-HardT**

In the Seven Woods. William Butler Yeats. **CP-YeatW**

In the Seventies. Thomas Hardy. **CP-HardT**

In the shabby train no seat is vacant. The Refugees. Randall Jarrell. **CP-JarrR**

In the Shadow of the Palace. Carl Sandburg. **CP-SandC**

In the shadow of the second world. Legend for a Little Child. Kenneth Patchen. **CP-PatcK**

In the shaft graves, butterflies. Mycenae. Donald Hall. **CP-HallD**

In the shape of this night, in the still fall. At the New Year. Kenneth Patchen. **LiTM** *Fr.* Eight Early Poems. **CP-PatcK**

In the Shenandoah Valley, one rider gray and one rider blue, and the sun. Shenandoah. Carl Sandburg. **CP-SandC**

In the shows of the round Ox. Song: In the Shows of the Round Ox. Thomas Merton. **CP-MertT; SP-MertT**

In the Shreve High football stadium. Autumn Begins in Martins Ferry, Ohio. James Wright. **CP-WrigJ**

In the shut drawer, even now, they rave and grieve. Packet of Letters. Louise Bogan. **CP-BogaL**

In the silence of flowers is found a sacred love. The Flower of the Fruit. Alfonso Cortes, *tr. fr. Spanish by* Thomas Merton. **CP-MertT**

In the silence of my heart. Communion. Paul Laurence Dunbar. **CP-DunbP**

In the silence that prolongs the span. Black Jackets. Thom Gunn. **CP-GunnT**

In the silent hour of even. The Water Spirit's Song. Christina Georgina Rossetti. **CP-RosC3**

In the sky of men the bread of stars seemed to me shadowy and hardened. Fighters. René Char, *tr. fr. French by* Thomas Merton. **CP-MertT**

In the Sleep of Reason. Thomas McGrath. **SP-McGrT**

In the slow world of dream. Memory. Theodore Roethke. **CP-RoetT**

In the Slums of Glasgow. "Hugh MacDiarmid." **SP-MacDH**

In the small beauty of the forest. Psalm. George Oppen. **CP-OppeG**

In the small classroom / next to the girls' yard. Miss Murdoch. John Hewitt. **CP-HewiJ**

In the small coffin of his house, the pensioner. Derek Walcott. *Fr.* Two Poems on the Passing of an Empire. **CP-WalcD**

In the Small Hours. Thomas Hardy. **CP-HardT**

In the small territory and time. Sandpipers. Howard Nemerov. **CP-NemeH**

In the Smoking-Car. Richard Wilbur. **CP-WilbR**

In the snarl-up you generate cursory images. Shamanism, Dalston. Steve Griffiths. **SP-GrifS**

In the snow light. The Snow Light. May Sarton. **SP-SartM**

In the snowy woods of morning. Hayden Carruth. *Fr.* North Winter. **CP-CarHL**

In the Social Security Office. Gary Gildner. **SP-GildG**

In the solemn days of old, The. Calef in Boston. John Greenleaf Whittier. **CP-WhitJ**

In the Sound of Mull. William Wordsworth. **CP-WorW2**

In the Spanish kingdom. Breakfast. Diane Wakoski. **SP-WakoD**

In the spread kingdom of Acacia. Hay Fever. Leonard Nathan. **SP-NathL**

In the Spring. Tennyson. **BoNaP** *Fr.* Locksley Hall. **CP-TennA**

In the spring of the year, in the spring of the year. The Spring and the Fall. Edna St. Vincent Millay. **CP-MillE**

In the spring thaw. Winter Roads. Thomas McGrath. **SP-McGrT**

In the square room. The Hands of the Blindman. Tess Gallagher. **SP-GallT**

In the stands, one old man tries to remember. O-Mok-See at Nine Mile. Richard Hugo. **CP-HugoR**

In the staring darkness. Gerard Manley Hopkins. **CP-HopkG**

In the States. Robert Louis Stevenson. **CP-StevR**

In the still evening of the sixth long day. John Gould Fletcher. **SP-FletJ** *Fr.* Branches of Adam.

In the still of night / Have we wept. Mothers. Kay Boyle. **CP-BoylK**

In the stilled place that once was a road going down. Sowing. Wendell Berry. **CP-BerrW**

In the Stopping Train. Donald Davie. **CP-DavDo**

In the story of Patroclus. The Triumph of Achilles. Louise Glück. **SP-GlücL**

In the Street. Thomas Hardy. **CP-HardT**

In the street outside a school. The Bees. Audre Lorde. **SP-LordA**

In the streets of the city: there is my love. Allegiance. René Char, *tr. fr. French by* Thomas Merton. **CP-MertT**

In the Studio. Charles Tomlinson. **CP-TomlC**

In the Study. Thomas Hardy. *Fr.* Satires of Circumstance in Fifteen Glimpses. **CP-HardT**

In the suburbs, in the town. Motto to "New England Reformers." Ralph Waldo Emerson. **CP-EmerR**

In the suburbs of the ganglia. The Provocation of the Dream. Marge Piercy. **SP-PierM**

In the sudden white silence, where are you? Requiem. Jean Garrigue. **SP-GarrJ**

In the Sultan's apartments / I saw a *Júgí*. Delhi. Thomas Merton. *Fr.* East with Ibn Battuta. *Fr.* East. *Fr.* The Geography of Lograire. **CP-MertT**

In the summer, when the Archduke dies. Sarajevo. Howard Nemerov. **CP-NemeH**

In the Summertime. "Bob Dylan." **CP-DylaB**

In the sun of a late summer I return. Bleasdale: The Wooden Circle. Phoebe Hesketh. **SP-HeskP**

In the swamp in secluded recesses. Walt Whitman. **RFM** *Fr.* When Lilacs Last in the Dooryard Bloom'd. **OFD**, *sect.* 1, 2, and 6; **AP; APN-1; AWP; AmPP; BiP; CABA; CBCWP; FPL; FaBoEn; HAP; HBV; LiTA; LoBV; MasP; MeMAP; MoAmPo; NAAL-1; NAAL-3; NIP; NOBA; NoP; OxBA; PAI; PAL; PPP; PPoe; PoEL-5; PoRA; SAmP; SeCeV; TAP; TFi; TrGrPo; TreF** *Fr.* Memories of President Lincoln. **CP-WhitW**

In the swamplands long ago. The Yipiyuk. Shel Silverstein. **SP-SilS2**

In the sweet shire of Cardigan. Simon Lee [the Old Huntsman]. William Wordsworth. **CP-WorW1**

In the sweet solitude of this calm place. Pedro Calderón de la Barca, *tr. by* Shelley. **CP-ShelP** *Fr.* Magico Prodigioso.

In the Tank. Thom Gunn. **CP-GunnT**

In the taxidermist's shop. Siv Cedering Fox. **AMV-81** *Fr.* In Search of a Love Poem. **SP-CedeS**

In the taxidermist's shop. In Search of a Love Poem. Siv Cedering Fox. **SP-CedeS**

In the technician's thicket. The Laboratory. Randall Jarrell. **CP-JarrR**

In the Tender Woodland. Al Young. **CP-YounA**

In the tentacles. Charles Henri Ford. **SP-FordC** *Fr.* Emblems of Arachne.

In the Tents of Akbar. Paul Laurence Dunbar. **CP-DunbP**

In the theatre / The actors play the rituals of their parts. The Furies. Stephen Spender. **CP-SpenS**

In the theosophy of light. Suchness. Kenneth Rexroth. **SP-RexrK**

In the thick of a teeming snowfall. Afterflakes. Robert Frost. **CP-FrosR**

In the thin classroom, where your face. Elegy in the Classroom. Anne Sexton. **CP-SextA**

In the third-class seat sat the journeying boy. Midnight on the Great Western. Thomas Hardy. **CP-HardT**

In the thought of you I imagine myself free of the weapons and the official hates that I have borne on my back like a hump. Wendell Berry. *Fr.* To a Siberian Woodsman. **CP-BerrW**

In the time of early love. George Meredith. **CP-MerG2**

In the Time of Hesitation. Edwin Rolfe. **CP-RolfE**

In the time of my confession, in the hour of my deepest need. Every Grain of Sand. "Bob Dylan." **CP-DylaB**

In the tired face of the mirror. Old Nursery. John Gould Fletcher. **SP-FletJ** *Fr.* The Ghosts of an Old House.

In the top and front of a bus, eager to meet his fate. Figure of Eight. Louis MacNeice. **CP-MacNL**

In the Touch of This Bosom There Worketh a Spell. Samuel Taylor Coleridge. **RB** *Fr.* Christabel and Geraldine. **PeHV** *Fr.* Christabel. **CP-ColeS**

In the town where I was born. Eagle Rock. Alice Walker. **CP-WalkA**

In the town where I was born. Yellow Submarine. The Beatles. **CP-Beatl**

In the town's graveyard the oldest plot now frees itself. The Meadow. Wendell Berry. **CP-BerrW**

In the Tree House at Night. James Dickey. **CP-DickJ**

In the Tub. John Updike. *Fr.* Living with a Wife. **CP-UpdiJ**

In the turbulent beauty. South Wind. Ralph Waldo Emerson. **CP-EmerR**

In the Turpitude of Time: N.D. Robert Penn Warren. *Fr.* Mortmain. **SP-WarrR**

In the Turret. Herman Melville. **SP-MelvH**

In the turret's great glass dome, the apparition, death. Siegfried. Randall Jarrell. **CP-JarrR**

In the 20th Century. Stephen Dunn. **SP-DunnS**

In the Twentieth Century of my trespass on earth. Galway Kinnell. **TW** *Fr.* The Dead Shall Be Raised Incorruptible. **SP-KinnG**

In the twenty-sixth year of my age. Birthday Poem. Jenny Joseph. **SP-JoseJ**

In the typewriter shop. Chuck Miller. **SP-MillC**

In the umber icon of a kitchen window. Icon. Leonard Nathan. **SP-NathL**

In the Underground Station. Ron Koertge. **SP-KoerR**

In the undergrowth / There dwells a Bloath. The Bloath. Shel Silverstein. **SP-SilS2**

In the Underworld. Muriel Rukeyser. **CP-RukeM**

In the ungreased field they cling. The Conviviality of Cows. Stephen Dobyns. **SP-DobyS**

In the unreason of a rainy midnight. The Night Train. Thomas Merton. **CP-MertT; SP-MertT**

In the vacant lot. Burn-Out. Gary Gildner. **SP-GildG**

In the Valley. Jim Carroll. **SP-CarrJ**

In the Valley of Cauteretz. Tennyson. **CP-TennA**

In the Valley of the Elwy. Gerard Manley Hopkins. **CP-HopkG**

In the Valley of Waters. Byron. **CP-Byron**

In the Vanities. Theatrical Reflection. Ogden Nash. **CP-NashO**

In the Vaulted Way. Thomas Hardy. **CP-HardT**

In the Vestry. Robert Ranke Graves. **CP-GravR**

In the victim's room. The Fatigue of Objects. Thomas McGrath. **SP-McGrT**

In the village of the dead. First Shaman Song. Gary Snyder. **CP-SnydG** *Fr.* Hunting. *Fr.* Myths and Texts.

In the Waiting Room. Elizabeth Bishop. **CP-BishE**

In the Wake of Home. Adrienne Rich. **SP-RicA1; SP-RicA2**

In the Wall. Roy Fisher. **SP-FishR**

In the walled off swimming-pool the water is perfectly flat. Pleasure Seas. Elizabeth Bishop. **CP-BishE**

In the wan sun of a December day. The Threshing. John Hewitt. **CP-HewiJ**

In the war where many men fell. Horses and Prisoners. James Dickey. **CP-DickJ**

In the Ward. Charles Tomlinson. **CP-TomlC**

In the Ward: The Sacred Wood. Randall Jarrell. **CP-JarrR**

In the warm mud of alcoholic gloom. Old Woman. Al Young. **CP-YounA**

In the way that most of the wind. Wind and Tree. Paul Muldoon. **SP-MuldP**

In the way you went you were important. A Memorial: Son Bret. William Stafford. **SP-StafW**

In the weed of summer comes this green sprout why. Questions Are Remarks. Wallace Stevens. **CP-StevW**

In the well-fed cage-sound of diesels. Them, Crying. James Dickey. **CP-DickJ**

In the west day is drawn into the smelter of sunset. For Judy. Chuck Miller. **SP-MillC**

In the West of the country where I was. Ballad of the Sixties. May Sarton. **SP-SartM**

In the Wet. Marge Piercy. **SP-PierM**

In the White Giant's Thigh. Dylan Thomas. **CP-ThomD**

In the white morning, where is the enchanted room of the night before? Married in June. David Herbert Lawrence. **CP-LawrD**

In the White Sky. William Stafford. **SP-StafW**

In the whole world coal. The Whole World Coal. Gilbert Sorrentino. **SP-SorrG**

In the wild October night-time, when the wind raved round the land. The Night of Trafalgar. Thomas Hardy. **CP-HardT** *Fr.* The Dynasts.

In the Wilderness. Robert Ranke Graves. **CP-GravR**

In the Willow Shade. Christina Georgina Rossetti. **CP-RosC2**

In the Wineshop of Chinling. Li Po, *tr. fr. Chinese* by William Carlos Williams *with* David Rafael Wang. **CP-WilW2**

In the winter walking on my. Trapped. Charles Bukowski. **SP-BukC1**

In the Wood. Frank Templeton Prince. **CP-PrinF**

In the wood of Wallow. The Ass. Stevie Smith. **CP-SmitS**

In the Woods. George Meredith. **CP-MerG2**

In the Woods. Adrienne Rich. **CP-RicAE; SP-RicA1; SP-RicA2**

In the woods as I did walk. The Stranger. Walter de la Mare. **CP-DeLaW**

In the Woods of Rydal. William Wordsworth. **CP-WorW2**

In the world are millions and millions of men, and each man. Angel and Stone. Howard Nemerov. **CP-NemeH**

In the world of mules. The Mules. Ogden Nash. **CP-NashO**

In the world of purple light. The World of Purple Light. Frederick Morgan. **SP-MorgF**

In the world today / there is. Note from St. Francis. Joseph Ceravolo. **SP-CeraJ**

In the world which He has created according to his will Blessed Praised. Hymmnn. Allen Ginsberg. **CP-GinsA**

In the worst room, with mat half-hung. The Duke of Buckingham. Alexander Pope. **FaBoDD; FiP; NOBE; OBEC** *Fr.* Epistle III, to Allen Lord Bathurst. **CP-PopeA**

In the yard, by the house of boxes. Stalag Luft. Randall Jarrell. **CP-JarrR**

In the year 1945 an Original Child was born. Original Child Bomb. Thomas Merton. **CP-MertT**

In The Year of Pompey's First Consulate, Cinna. Carmen 113. Catullus. *Fr.* Carmina. **CP-Catul**

In the year since Jesus died for men. The Siege of Corinth. Byron. **CP-Byron**

In the years since I saw you on Sunday. A Separate Time. Stephen Dobyns. **SP-DobyS**

In the years that pass through. Waking at Dusk from a Nap. William Matthews. **SP-MattW**

In the yellow light, an old man. "Between the Clock and the Bed." Donald Hall. **CP-HallD**

In the zero of the night, in the lipping hour. The Approach to Thebes. Stanley Jasspon Kunitz. **CP-KuniS**

In thee, I fondly hoped to clasp. To D———. Byron. **CP-Byron**

In thee, O Lord, do I put my trust; let me never be ashamed. Psalm 31. Bible, *O.T. Fr.* Psalms. **CP-Psal**

In thee, O Lord, do I put my trust: let me never be put to confusion. Psalm 71. Bible, *O.T. Fr.* Psalms. **CP-Psal**

In their congealed light. Through Binoculars. Charles Tomlinson. **CP-TomlC**

In their conventicles. The Elect. Donald Davie. **CP-DavDo**

In their deepest caverns of limestone. The Threshold. Rudyard Kipling. **CP-KiplR**

In their faint photographs. Jean Rhys. Derek Walcott. **CP-WalcD**

In their own way, by their own lights. Meditations for a Savage Child. Adrienne Rich. **SP-RicA2**

In Themclam Virginem. Gerard Manley Hopkins. **CP-HopkG**

In There. Charles Kenneth Williams. **CP-WillC**

In these days when we are living on the rim of a crater. Listen to the Linotype. Ogden Nash. **CP-NashO**

In these deep solitudes and awful cells. Eloisa to Abelard. Alexander Pope. **CP-PopeA**

"In these degenerate days," we oft hear said. "Lewis Carroll." *Fr.* Solutions. *Fr.* Puzzles from Wonderland. **CP-CarrL**

In These Dissenting Times. Alice Walker. **CP-WalkA**

Women. **GOA; WPOW**

In these explanations it is presumed. George Oppen. *Fr.* Of Being Numerous. **CP-OppeG**

In These Fair Vales Hath Many a Tree. William Wordsworth. **CP-WorW2**

In these gay thoughts the Loves and Graces shine. Epistle to Miss Blount, with the Works of Voiture. Alexander Pope. **CP-PopeA**

In these hands, the cities; in my weather, the armies. Have You Killed Your Man for Today? Kenneth Patchen. **CP-PatcK**

In these mountains there was coal. Best House They Was Ever In (Retired Coal Operator). Louise McNeill. **SP-McNeL**

In these sad hours, a prey to ceaseless pain. R.S.S. Written in a Fit of Illness. William Cowper. **CP-CowpW**

In these stern times of ours, when crimson strife. Prologue. Thomas Hardy. **CP-HardT** *Fr.* The Dynasts.

In these two seperate rooms we sit. June. Thom Gunn. **CP-GunnT**

In these vast bodies of the stupendous. Giant and Saint. Marsden Hartley. **CP-HartM**

In things a moderation keep[e]. Moderation. Robert Herrick. **CP-HerrR**

In This Age of Hard Trying, Nonchalance Is Good and. Marianne Craig Moore. **CP-MoorM**

In this beloved marble view. Byron. **CP-Byron**

(In This Beloved Marble View.) **CP-Byron**

In This Beloved Marble View. Byron. *See* In this beloved marble view.

In this café Durruti. The Midget. Philip Levine. **SP-LeviP**

In this camera shot. Blue Bug. Marianne Craig Moore. **CP-MoorM**

In this city / of the generous. From a Paris Window—High. Marsden Hartley. **CP-HartM**

In this country of grapes. The Mediterranean. Charles Tomlinson. **CP-TomlC**

In this country there is neither measure nor balance. Two Campers in Cloud Country. Sylvia Plath. **CP-PlatS**

In this dark-grained news photograph, whose glare. Che. Derek Walcott. **CP-WalcD**

In this dark place I am still with God. Simon Judson. Lewis Turco. **SM** *Fr.* Bordello. **SP-TurcL**

In this day and age Lord. Loss. Charles Kenneth Williams. **CP-WillC; SP-WillC**

In this dehydrated time of digests, pills. Howard Nemerov. *Fr.* Runes. **CP-NemeH**

In This Dim Cave. Jim Morrison. **SP-MorrJ**

In this dream that dogs me I am part. Traumerai. Philip Larkin. **CP-LarkP**

In this evening room there is no stir, no fuss. Evening Indoors. Louis MacNeice. **CP-MacNL**

In this fair niche above the unslumbering sea. A Singer Asleep. Thomas Hardy. **CP-HardT**

In this fairly temperate clime. Man Bites Dog-Days. Ogden Nash. **CP-NashO**

In this field / Where the small animals ran from a brush fire. Brush Fire. James Wright. **CP-WrigJ**

In this foolish world, there is nothing more numerous. Very Funny, Very Funny. Ogden Nash. **CP-NashO**

In this great city now the haunt. A True Story. Christina Georgina Rossetti. **CP-RosC3**

In this high pasturage, the Blunden time. The Archaeological Picnic. Sir John Betjeman. **CP-BetjJ**

In this hopeless & wasting love of mine. Carmen 91. Catullus. *Fr.* Carmina. **CP-Catul**

In this house I am not ugly—nowhere. Lafe Grat. Lewis Turco. *Fr.* Bordello. **SP-TurcL**

In this house (in a dying orchard. Margaret Atwood. **CrSp** *Fr.* Solstice Poem. **SP-AtwM2**

In this house of the chemical error. With Anne at the Peabody. Brendan Galvin. **SP-GalvB**

In this house there are swallows. Back Road Country. Marsden Hartley. **CP-HartM**

In this land, Rilke's country if you will. At Muzot. May Sarton. **SP-SartM**

In this little Urn[e] is laid. Upon Prue [or Prew], His Maid. Robert Herrick. **CP-HerrR**

In this little vault she lyes. Upon a Wife That Dyed Mad with Jealousie. Robert Herrick. **CP-HerrR**

In this long room, upon each western pane. Colophon. Adrienne Rich. **CP-RicAE**

In this mimic form of a matron in years. Denner's Old Woman. Vincent Bourne, tr. fr. Latin by William Cowper. **CP-CowpW**

In this misfortune Kings doe most excell. Bad Wages for Good Service. Robert Herrick. **CP-HerrR**

In this moist season. Mushrooms. Margaret Atwood. **SP-AtwM2**

In this month arks. Your Daughter. Jim Carroll. **SP-CarrJ**

In this motel where I was told to wait. The Human Condition. Howard Nemerov. **CP-NemeH**

In this my green world. What There Is. Kenneth Patchen. **CP-PatcK**

In this, my last poem about my father. Cherish the Ladies. Paul Muldoon. **SP-MuldP**

In this my valley how should I revolt. The Belfastman. John Hewitt. **CP-HewiJ**

In this nation. George Oppen. **GOA** Fr. Of Being Numerous. **CP-OppeG**

In this old garden, fair, I walk to-day. In a English Garden. Paul Laurence Dunbar. **CP-DunbP**

In this photo, circa 1934. A Snapshot of the Auxiliary. Richard Hugo. **CP-HugoR**

In this place of helmets and tar. On Being Asked to Leave a Place of Honor for One of Comfort, Preferably in the Northern Suburbs. Alice Walker. **CP-WalkA**

In this place of shafts, I hope. Emily Dickinson. **SP-DickE**

In this pond of placid water. The Pond. Edna St. Vincent Millay. **CP-MillE**

"In This River. . . ." Tom Clark. **SP-ClarT**

In This Room Particularly. Jim Carroll. **SP-CarrJ**

In this short Life. Emily Dickinson. **CP-DickE**

In this silence. This Silence. Daniel Gerard Hoffman. **SP-HoffD**

In this single world. Fellow Soul, Sound Hunting to Thy Immeasurable Heart. Kenneth Patchen. **CP-PatcK**

In this sleep an old Chinese. The Scroll. Leonard Nathan. **SP-NathL**

In this sombre garden close. The Monk's Walk. Paul Laurence Dunbar. **CP-DunbP**

In this sour world, o summerwind. Ralph Waldo Emerson. **CP-EmerR**

In this squalid, dirty dooryard. The Pear Tree. Edna St. Vincent Millay. **CP-MillE**

In this still place, remote from men. Glen-Almain; Or, the Narrow Glen. William Wordsworth. **CP-WorW1**

In this strang labourinth how shall I turne? Sonnet 1. Mary Sidney, Countess of Montgomery Wroth. Fr. A Crowne of Sonetts Dedicated to Love. Fr. Pamphilia to Amphilanthus. **CP-WrotM**

In this strange land, this uncouth clime. Epistle to Hugh Parker. Robert Burns. **CP-BurnR**

In this stucco house there is nothing but air. Night Watch. Rita Dove. **SP-DoveR**

In this suspense of ours before the fall. Annunciation. May Sarton. **SP-SartM**

In this, the City of my Discontent. Springfield Magical. Nicholas Vachel Lindsay. **CP-LindV**

In this town the shops are all the same. The Trouble with the Times. Thomas McGrath. **SP-McGrT**

In this trance before sleep. James McAuley. **SP-McAuJ** Fr. Habitations.

In this tumultuous sphere, for thee unfit. To Tranquillity. Charlotte Smith. **CP-SmitC**

In this unyielding, even. Stone Walls: at Chew Magna. Charles Tomlinson. **CP-TomlC**

In this woman the earth speaks. Earth and Fire. Wendell Berry. **CP-BerrW**

In This World. Wendell Berry. **CP-BerrW**

In this world of. Spouts. William Carlos Williams. **CP-WilW1**

In this world, (the Isle of Dreames). The White Island: or Place of the Blest. Robert Herrick. **CP-HerrR**

In this yard, barnyard / I dig with a shovel. Digging. Margaret Atwood. **SP-AtwM1**

In This Year of Grace. John Hewitt. **CP-HewiJ**

In tholde [or th'olde] dayes of the king Arthour. See also Wife of Bath, The mod. vers. by Alexander Pope. Geoffrey Chaucer. **FHYEP; NAEL-1; OAEL-1** Fr. The Canterbury Tales. **CP-ChauG**

In those days / In a pool of noise. Kenneth Rexroth. **CP-RexKL** Fr. A Prolegomenon to a Theodicy.

In those days / In a pool of noise. Kenneth Rexroth. Fr. In those days / In a pool of noise. **CP-RexKL** Fr. A Prolegomenon to a Theodicy.

"In those days / In a pool of noise."

"Light / Light / The sliver in the firmament." **SP-RexrK**

In Those Days. Randall Jarrell. **CP-JarrR; SP-JarrR**

In those days always the School Manager. Methodists. John Hewitt. **CP-HewiJ**

In those days, you know, we had a house with a big garden. An Animal Story. Jenny Joseph. **SP-JoseJ**

In Those Exquisite Areas. Marsden Hartley. **CP-HartM**

In those sad words I took farewell. Tennyson. **EnVR** Fr. In Memoriam A. H. H. **CP-TennA**

In Three Days. Robert Browning. **CP-BroR1**

In Throne of Blood, when they come to kill. Sympathetic. William Matthews. **SP-MattW**

In through the window a sea-mustang brought me. Being a Seven-Year-Old Boy's Elaborate Memory of the Day of His Birth. Nicholas Vachel Lindsay. Fr. Doctor Mohawk. **CP-LindV**

In thy holiday of life. Hafiz, tr. by Ralph Waldo Emerson. **CP-EmerR** Fr. Odes.

In thy long Paradise of Light. Emily Dickinson. **CP-DickE**

In thy western halls of gold. Ode to Apollo. John Keats. **CP-KeatJ**

In Tilbury Town did Old King Cole. Old King Cole. Edwin Arlington Robinson. **CP-RobiE**

In Time. Robert Ranke Graves. **CP-GravR**

In Time, AIDS. Jim Carroll. **SP-CarrJ**

In time all undertakings are made good. In Time. Robert Ranke Graves. **CP-GravR**

In time and measure perfect moves. Dupont's Round Fight. Herman Melville. **CP-MelvH**

In Time Like Air. May Sarton. **SP-SartM**

In Time of Absence. Robert Ranke Graves. **CP-GravR**

In Time of Carnival. Adrienne Rich. **CP-RicAE**

In Time of Cloudburst. Robert Frost. **CP-FrosR**

In time of daffodils(who know. Edward Estlin Cummings. **CP-CummE**

In time of life, I grac't ye with my Verse. To Flowers. Robert Herrick. **CP-HerrR**

In Time of Plague. Thom Gunn. **CP-GunnT**

In Time of Silver Rain. Langston Hughes. **SP-HughL**

In Time of "The Breaking of Nations." Thomas Hardy. **CP-HardT**

In Time of Wars and Tumults. Thomas Hardy. **CP-HardT**

In time, these people all will know each other. Reflexion of a Novelist. Howard Nemerov. **CP-NemeH**

In time's a noble mercy of proportion. Edward Estlin Cummings. **CP-CummE**

In times behind, I too. "Bob Dylan." Fr. 11 Outlined Epitaphs. **CP-DylaB**

In Time's concatenation and. After Night Flight Son Reaches Bedside of Already Unconscious Father, Whose Right Hand Lifts in a Spasmodic Gesture, as Though Trying to Make Contact: 1955. Robert Penn Warren. **DiL; NOBA; Prf** Fr. Mortmain. **SP-WarrR**

In times o'ergrown with rust and ignorance. Priestcraft and Private Judgement. John Dryden. **OBS** Fr. Religio Laici. **SP-DrydJ**

In times of old, when time was young. Vanbrug's House. Jonathan Swift. **CP-SwifJ**

In times of stormy weather. Strange Hurt. Langston Hughes. **SP-HughL**

In Times When Nothing Stood. Philip Larkin. **SP-LarkP**

In Tobey Woods. Hayden Carruth. **CP-CarHS**

In today's mail a poem. Sparks. Denise Levertov. **CP-LeveD**

In tombs of gold and lapis lazuli. Oil and Blood. William Butler Yeats. **CP-YeatW**

In Touch. Roy Fisher. **SP-FishR**

In town, your friends play hide-and-seek. September. William DeWitt Snodgrass. **SP-SnodW**

In trance and dream of old, God's prophet saw. Garibaldi. John Greenleaf Whittier. **CP-WhitJ**

In Trance At A Distance. Robert Ranke Graves. **CP-GravR**

In Transit. Wystan Hugh Auden. **CP-AudeW**

In trees still dripping night some nameless birds. Morning in a New Land. Mary Oliver. **SP-OlivM**

In trellised shed with clustering roses gay. William Wordsworth. **EPCY** Fr. White Doe of Rylstone, The; or, The Fate of the Nortons. **CP-WorW1**

In troth, I do myself persuade [or perswade]. Richard Lovelace. **CP-LoveR** (Love Inthron'd.) **CP-LoveR**

In Trouble and Shame. David Herbert Lawrence. **CP-LawrD**

In Truth and Honour's name—AMEN. Libel Summons. Robert Burns. **CP-BurnR**

In truth, O Love, with what a boyish kind. Sonnet 11. Sir Philip Sidney. **CBLP; EIL; InvP; PoE** Fr. Astrophil and Stella. **SP-SidnP**

In truth your fair eyes, my lady. Sonnet 5. John Milton, tr. fr. Italian by John T. Shawcross. **CP-MiltJ**

In twos and threes, they have not far to roam. Six o'clock in Princes Street. Wilfred Owen. **CP-OwenW**

In Uganda an Early King. Alice Walker. **CP-WalkA**

In unplowed Maine he sought the lumberers' gang. Ralph Waldo Emerson. **MeMAP; TAP** *Fr.* Woodnotes I ("For this present, hard"). **CP-EmerR**

In Upperville, the upper crust. Upon Learning That a Town Exists in Virginia Called Upperville. John Updike. **CP-UpdiJ**

In using there are always two. Song of the Fucked Duck. Marge Piercy. **SP-PierM**

In Utrumque Paratus. Matthew Arnold. **SP-ArnoM**

In Vain. Walter de la Mare. **CP-DeLaW**

In vain did Time and Nature toil to throw. Fragment: "In vain did Time and Nature. . . ." William Wordsworth. **CP-WorW1**

In vain, in vain—the all-composing Hour. The Reign of Chaos. Alexander Pope. **EBEV; FaBoPV; FiP; LoBV; NOBE; NoP; SCV** *Fr.* Yet, yet a moment, one dim ray of light. **NAEL-1; OAEL-1; PoEL-3** *Fr.* The Dunciad. **CP-PopeA**

In Vain, Mine Eyes. Sir Philip Sidney. **SP-SidnP** *Fr.* Arcadia.

In vain, mine eyes, you labour to amend. In Vain, Mine Eyes. Sir Philip Sidney. **SP-SidnP** *Fr.* Arcadia.

In vain our labours are, whatsoe're they be. Gods Blessing. Robert Herrick. **CP-HerrR**

In vain to live from age to age. Lines Written for Miss Patty More. William Cowper. **CP-CowpW**

In vain to me the smiling [*or* smileing] Mornings shine. Sonnet [on the Death of Mr. Richard West]. Thomas Gray. **CP-GrayT**

In vain would Prudence, with decorous sneer. Passion's Cry. Robert Burns. **CP-BurnR**

In vain ye woo me to your harmless joys. Love Faithful in the Absence of the Beloved. Jeanne Marie Bouvier de la Motte-Guyon, *tr. fr. French by* William Cowper. **CP-CowpW**

In vain you boast poetic names of yore. Impromptu to Lady Winchelsea. Alexander Pope. **CP-PopeA**

In valleys green and still. Alfred Edward Housman. **CP-HousA**

In vaulted place where shadows flit. In a Church of Padua. Herman Melville. **SP-MelvH**

In vayne mine eyes in vaine you wast your teares. Anaphora, or the Figure of Report. Sir Walter Ralegh. *Fr.* The Arte of English Poesie. **CP-RaleW**

In Verdi Square. Charles Tomlinson. **CP-TomlC**

In vestibules the doormen. Lament for Doormen. Charles Tomlinson. **CP-TomlC**

In view of the fading animals. They Are Hostile Nations. Margaret Atwood. **SP-AtwM1**

In Villa Acuña where the luna bright. Jaime Valerosa y Borracho Consults His Journal. Gilbert Sorrentino. *Fr.* Twelve Études for Voice and Kazoo. **SP-SorrG**

In villages from which their childhoods came. Wystan Hugh Auden. *Fr.* The Quest. **CP-AudeW**

In vinum solui cupis Aufilena quod haurit. *acc. by English translation.* Thomas Campion. **CP-CampT**

In Vision I Roamed. Thomas Hardy. **CP-HardT**

In visions of the dark night. A Dream. Edgar Allan Poe. **CP-PoeEd**

In Waking. Robert Duncan. **SP-DuncR**

In Walden wood the chickadee. Ralph Waldo Emerson. **CP-EmerR**

In Wales at Laugharne at last I stand beside. Belated Palinode for Dylan Thomas. Lawrence Ferlinghetti. **SP-FerlL**

In Washington Square. Stephen Berg. **SP-BergS**

In water-heavy nights behind grandmother's porch. Adolescence—I. Rita Dove. **SP-DoveR**

In wavering shadow and silted with soot, her face. Hayden Carruth. *Fr.* The Sleeping Beauty. **CP-CarHL**

In wayes to greatnesse, think on this. Ambition. Robert Herrick. **CP-HerrR**

In weariness and painfulness St. Paul. Christina Georgina Rossetti. **CP-RosC2**

In Weatherbury Stocks. Thomas Hardy. **CP-HardT**

In Webster and the town of Slatersville. On the Founder of the Industrial System in the United States. Allen Tate. *Fr.* Historical Epitaphs. **CP-TateA**

In western fields of corn and northern timber lands. Jungheimer's. Carl Sandburg. **CP-SandC**

In westerns the man who saddles up at night. Pity and Fear. Miller Williams. **SP-WillM**

In Westminster Abbey. Sir John Betjeman. **CP-BetjJ**

In Westminster's royal halls. The Curse of the Charter-Breakers. John Greenleaf Whittier. **CP-WhitJ**

In wet green midspring, midnight and the wind. Mrs. Walpurga. Muriel Rukeyser. **CP-RukeM**

In what at least. 18 West 11th Street. James Merrill. **SP-MerrJ**

In what esteem did the gods hold. Feminine Honour. Thomas Carew. *Fr.* Four Songs, by Way of Chorus To a Play. **CP-CareT**

In what torn ship soever I embark. A Hymn [*or* Hymne] to Christ, at the Author's Last Going into Germany. John Donne. **CP-DonnJ**

In Which a Racing Auto Comes from the East. Nicholas Vachel Lindsay. *Fr.* The Santa-Fé Trail (A Humoresque). **CP-LindV**

In which case a minister here from Congress wd / be useful. Canto 69. Ezra Pound. *Fr.* Cantos. **CP-PoCan**

In Which Many Autos Pass Westward. Nicholas Vachel Lindsay. *Fr.* The Santa-Fé Trail (A Humoresque). **CP-LindV**

In Which Roosevelt Is Compared to Saul. Nicholas Vachel Lindsay. **CP-LindV**

In which the audience doesn't warn him. Unwritten Chapters. Steve Griffiths. **SP-GrifS**

In Which the Poet Is Ashamed but Pleased. Ogden Nash. **CP-NashO**

In Which There is Nothing Up the Sleeve. Gilbert Sorrentino. *Fr.* Twelve Études for Voice and Kazoo. **SP-SorrG**

In whose heart it / burns. Epigon. Charles Olson. **CP-OlsoC**

In wild October when the low hills lie. Two States of Prayer. Thomas Merton. **CP-MertT**

In wilful riches I have found poverty. Sir Thomas Wyatt. **CP-WyatT**

In Willesden Churchyard. Sir John Betjeman. **CP-BetjJ**

In winter, Germans gone, the sea insane. Maratea Porto. Richard Hugo. **CP-HugoR**

In winter I get up at night. Bed in Summer. Robert Louis Stevenson. **CP-StevR**

In winter in Diamantina. Helena Morley. Donald Davie. **CP-DavDo**

In Winter in my Room. Emily Dickinson. **CP-DickE**

In winter, in the dark hours, when others. How These Words Happened. William Stafford. **SP-StafW**

In winter in the woods alone. Robert Frost. **CP-FrosR**

In winter the beach is empty. Georgia Beach. Margaret Atwood. **SP-AtwM2**

In winter when each day is harvested. The Fourteenth Anniversary. Richard Shelton. **SP-ShelR**

In winter, when the fields are white. "Lewis Carroll." **CP-CarrL** *Fr.* Through the Looking-Glass.

(Humpty Dumpty's Recitation.) **CP-CarrL**

In Winter Woods. Charles Tomlinson. **CP-TomlC**

Focus.

Meeting, The.

Nocturnal.

Snow Sequence.

In winter you have. Where Buildings Congregate. Edwin Rolfe. **CP-RolfE**

In Wintertime. Allen Tate. *Fr.* The Progress of Œina. **CP-TateA**

In Wiro language. Charles Olson. **CP-OlsoC**

In Wiry Winter. James Schuyler. **CP-SchuJ**

In wit, as nature, what affects our hearts. Alexander Pope. **HAP** *Fr.* An Essay on Criticism. **CP-PopeA**

In wood and wild, ye warbling throng. On the Death of Echo, a Lap-Dog. Robert Burns. **CP-BurnR**

In woods where many rivers run. Lawrence Ferlinghetti. **SP-FerlL**

In Worcester, Massachusetts. In the Waiting Room. Elizabeth Bishop. **CP-BishE**

In world, world / of terror. The Whisper. Denise Levertov. **CP-LeveD**

In worldly merymentes lurketh much misery. Fortune's Falsehoode. Robert Southwell. **CP-SoutR**

In Xanadu did Kubla Khan. Kubla Khan; or, A Vision in a Dream. Samuel Taylor Coleridge. **CP-ColeS**

In Xannadù did Cubla Khan, *sl. diff. vers., fr. the Crewe Manuscript.* Samuel Taylor Coleridge. *See* Kubla Khan; or, A Vision in a Dream.

In years defaced and lost. A Spot. Thomas Hardy. **CP-HardT**

In your time, there have been those who spoke clearly. Muriel Rukeyser. **CP-RukeM**

In yonder grave a Druid lies. William Collins. **CP-ThomJ**

(Ode on the Death of [Mr.] Thomson.) **CP-ThomJ**

In Your Bad Dream. Richard Hugo. **CP-HugoR**

In Your Big Dream. Richard Hugo. **CP-HugoR**

In Your Blue Dream. Richard Hugo. **CP-HugoR**

In Your Body All Bodies Lie. Kenneth Patchen. **CP-PatcK**

In your drawings / my face is one-celled. The Field of Inheritance. Brendan Galvin. **SP-GalvB**

In Your Dream after Falling in Love. Richard Hugo. **CP-HugoR**

In Your Dream on the Eve of Success. Richard Hugo. **CP-HugoR**

In Your Fugitive Dream. Richard Hugo. **CP-HugoR**

In Your Good Dream. Richard Hugo. **CP-HugoR**

In your green anorak. I Cannot Look into the Sun. Phoebe Hesketh. **SP-HeskP**

In Your Hot Dream. Richard Hugo. **CP-HugoR**

In your indignation what mercy appears. Epigram, An. Jonathan Swift. **CP-SwifJ**

In your minds you jump from doors. Writer's Prologue to a Play in Verse. William Carlos Williams. **CP-WilW2**

In your next letter I wish you'd say. Letter to N. Y. Elizabeth Bishop. **CP-BishE**

In Your Own Words Without Lying Tell Something of Your Background With Particular Attention to Anything Relating to the Position For Which You Are Applying. Press Down. Miller Williams. **SP-WillM**

In Your Racing Dream. Richard Hugo. **CP-HugoR**

In Your Small Dream. Richard Hugo. **CP-HugoR**

In Your War Dream. Richard Hugo. **CP-HugoR**

In Your Wild Dream. Richard Hugo. **CP-HugoR**

In Your Young Dream. Richard Hugo. **CP-HugoR**

In youth exalted high in air. Jonathan Swift. *Fr.* Riddles. **CP-SwifJ**

In youth from rock to rock I went. To the Daisy. William Wordsworth. **CP-WorW1**

In youth I thought I could live without pleasure as the stones live their. Pleasures. Robinson Jeffers. **CP-JefR3**

In youth we dream of death. Hardy Perennial. Richard Eberhart. **CP-EberR**

In Zululand the huts are round. Zulus Live in Land without a Square. John Updike. **CP-UpdiJ**

Inadequate illumination / In the Museum of Tomb Paintings. Baby Book Fate Dream. Tom Clark. **SP-ClarT**

Inadequate Orderly Simplification, The. But the Three Natural Units. And Only Arbitrary Constants. Charles Olson. **CP-OlsoC**

Inamoratas, with an approbation. The Sundays of Satin-Legs Smith. Gwendolyn Brooks. **SP-BrooG**

Inapprehensiveness. Robert Browning. **CP-BroR2**

Inappropriate Gestures. Stephen Dobyns. **SP-DobyS**

Inaudible consonant inaudible vowel. Silent Journal. Charles Wright. **SP-WrigC**

Inauguration Day. Jim Carroll. **SP-CarrJ**

Inauguration Day: January 1953. Robert Lowell. **SP-LoweR**

Incalculably old. The Crystal. Robert Ranke Graves. **CP-GravR**

Incantate the Cockatrice. Isabella Gardner. **CP-GardI**

Incantation. Walter de la Mare. **CP-DeLaW**

Incantation. Anne Waldman. **SP-WaldA**

Incantatory Poem. Jean Garrigue. **SP-GarrJ**

Incarcerate me in yourself. Emily Dickinson. **SP-DickE**

Incarcerating sunlight, world damnation. Richard Eberhart. *Fr.* Suite in Prison. **CP-EberR**

Incarnate Devil. Dylan Thomas. **CP-ThomD**

Inca's Daughter, The. Walt Whitman. **CP-WhitW**

Incense. Nicholas Vachel Lindsay. **CP-LindV**

Incense and splendor haunt me as I go. Johnny Appleseed Speaks of Great Cities in the Future. Nicholas Vachel Lindsay. **CP-LindV**

Incense and Splendor haunt me as I go. The Rhymer's Reply: Incense and Splendor. Nicholas Vachel Lindsay. *Fr.* An Argument. **CP-LindV**

Incense of the Lucky Virgin. Robert Earl Hayden. **CP-HaydR**

Incense under Horse Heaven Hills. Northwest Passage. Allen Ginsberg. **CP-GinsA**

Incertus. Seamus Heaney. **SP-HeanS**

Inches. Charles Kenneth Williams. **CP-WillC**

Inchicore Haiku. Michael Hartnett. **SP-HarMi**

Inchiquin Lake, Penobscot Bay. Richard Eberhart. **CP-EberR**

Incidence of Flight. Richard Eberhart. **CP-EberR**

Incident, An. Arthur Hugh Clough. **SP-ClouA**

Incident. Countee Cullen. **CP-CullC**

Incident, An. John Hewitt. **CP-HewiJ**

Incident, An. Louis Zukofsky. **CP-ZukLS**

Incident at Bruges. William Wordsworth. **OBTV** *Fr.* Memorials of a Tour of the Continent; 1820. **CP-WorW2**

Incident Characteristic of a Favourite Dog. William Wordsworth. **CP-WorW1**

Incident here and there, An. Hilda Doolittle. **OBWP** *Fr.* The Walls Do Not Fall. **CP-DoolH**

Incident here and there, An. The Walls Do Not Fall. Hilda Doolittle. **CP-DoolH**

Incident in the Early Life of Ebenezer Jones, Poet, 1828, An. Sir John Betjeman. **CP-BetjJ**

Incident in the Life of a Prophet, An. Thomas McGrath. **SP-McGrT**

Incident of Cherries and Peaches. Diane Wakoski. **SP-WakoD**

Incident of May. Hayden Carruth. **CP-CarHS**

Incident of the French Camp. Robert Browning. **CP-BroR1**

Incident on a Journey. Thom Gunn. **CP-GunnT**

Incidents of love, The. Emily Dickinson. **CP-DickE**

Incipience. Adrienne Rich. **SP-RicA2**

Incipient Madness. William Wordsworth. **CP-WorW1**

Incipient summer, scorch of the sun. Steelhead. William Everson. **SP-EverW**

Incipit Thomas Campianus Medicinae Doctor. In Peragrantissimi, Itinerosissimi, *Montiscandentissimique Peditis, Thomae Coryati,* viginti-hebdomadarium *Diarium, sex pedibus gradiens,* partim vero claudicans, Encomiasticon, Accompanied by English translation. Thomas Campion. **CP-CampT**

Incognito. William Carlos Williams. **CP-WilW2**

Incoherent rushing of the train, The. Way-Station. Archibald MacLeish. **CP-MacLA**

Incommunicability of Love. Thomas Carew. *Fr.* Four Songs, by Way of Chorus To a Play. **CP-CareT**

Incommunicado. Sylvia Plath. **CP-PlatS**

Incomparable Light, The. Richard Eberhart. **CP-EberR**

Incomparable Soporific Doctor, The. James Thomson. **CP-ThomJ**

Incomplete Latin Version of "In all things beautiful" by Robert Bridges. Robert Bridges, *tr. fr. English by* Gerard Manley Hopkins. **CP-HopkG**

Inconceivably solemn! Emily Dickinson. **CP-DickE**

Inconsistent, The. Thomas Hardy. **CP-HardT**

Incorrigible, brash, / They brightened the cinder path of my childhood. Dandelions. Louis MacNeice. *Fr.* Nature Notes. **CP-MacNL**

Incorrigible Dirigible, The. Hayden Carruth. **CP-CarHS**

Incorrigible, ruthless, / It rattled the shingly beach of my childhood. The Sea. Louis MacNeice. *Fr.* Nature Notes. **CP-MacNL**

Incorrigible, uncommitted, / They leavened the long flathours of my childhood. Cats. Louis MacNeice. *Fr.* Nature Notes. **CP-MacNL**

Incorrigible, unmusical, / They bridged the surrounding hedge of my childhood. Corncrakes. Louis MacNeice. *Fr.* Nature Notes. **CP-MacNL**

Increasing Night. Laurence Lieberman. **SP-LiebL**

Incredible happens, he knows, The. The Heaviness of His Wisdom. Wendell Berry. *Fr.* The Handing Down. **CP-BerrW**

Incredible never surprises us, The. Emily Dickinson. **SP-DickE**

Incredible the Lodging. Emily Dickinson. **SP-DickE**

Incredulous, he stared at the amused. Wystan Hugh Auden. *Fr.* The Quest. **CP-AudeW**

Increment. Archie Randolph Ammons. **SP-AmmoA**

Incubus. Daniel Gerard Hoffman. **SP-HoffD**

Incunabula, 1958. Charles Olson. **CP-OlsoC**

Incurable Home, The. John Haines. **SP-HainJ**

Indeed I feel as if I came too soon. June. Christina Georgina Rossetti. *Fr.* The Months: A Pageant. **CP-RosC2**

Indeed this very love which is my boast. Sonnet. Elizabeth Barrett Browning. **HBV 1-2** *Fr.* Sonnets from the Portuguese. **CP-BroEB**

Indefensible impulse of my blood, The. Robert Louis Stevenson. **CP-StevR**

Indelicate is he who loathes. Epidermal Macabre. Theodore Roethke. **CP-RoetT**

Independence Day. Wendell Berry. **CP-BerrW**

Independence Day. Allen Ginsberg. **CP-GinsA**

Independent Man, The. Gwendolyn Brooks. *Fr.* A Street in Bronzeville. **SP-BrooG**

Index. Richard Hugo. **CP-HugoR**

India ink, ink of India. Ensenada. Jim Morrison. **SP-MorrJ**

Indian, The. Randall Jarrell. **CP-JarrR**

Indian Arm. Malcolm Lowry. **CP-LowrM**

Indian Caves in the Dry Country. William Stafford. **SP-StafW**

Indian Day. Alun Lewis. **CP-LewiA**

"Dawn's cold imperative compels."

"Night bibles India in her wilderness."

"Sun the thunder and the hunher grow, The."

"Yellow ramtilla stiffens in the noon."

Indian Emperor, The. John Dryden.

"Ah fading joy, how quickly art thou past!" **SP-DrydJ**

(Song: "Ah fading joy, how quickly art thou past!") **SP-DrydJ**

Indian Girl. Richard Hugo. **CP-HugoR**

Indian Girl Tells the Hero Where to Go to Get the Laughing Bell, The. Nicholas Vachel Lindsay. *Fr.* The Tree of Laughing Bells or The Wings of the Morning. **CP-LindV**

Indian Girl Who Made Them, The. Nicholas Vachel Lindsay. *Fr.* The Tree of Laughing Bells or The Wings of the Morning. **CP-LindV**

Indian Graves at Jocko. Richard Hugo. **CP-HugoR**

Indian Market in Mexico, An. Randall Jarrell. **CP-JarrR**

Indian Pipe. Richard Eberhart. **CP-EberR**

Indian Point. Marsden Hartley. **CP-HartM**

Indian River. Wallace Stevens. **CP-StevW**

Indian saw the butterfly, The. Cahokia. Carl Sandburg. **CP-SandC**

Indian Serenade, The. Percy Bysshe Shelley. **CP-ShelP**

Indian Suffering. Joseph Ceravolo. **SP-CeraJ**

Indian Summer at Land's End. Stanley Jasspon Kunitz. **CP-KuniS**

Indian Summer Day on the Prairie, An. Nicholas Vachel Lindsay. **CP-LindV**
  In the Beginning.
  Mid-Morning.
  Noon.
  Sunset.

Indian-summer-sun / With crimson feathers whips away the mists. October-November. Hart Crane. **CP-CranH**

Indian to His Love, The. William Butler Yeats. **CP-YeatW**

Indian trinity and my son an Etchimin. Charles Olson. **CP-OlsoC**

Indian upon God, The [or An]. William Butler Yeats. **CP-YeatW**

Indian Village. Louis MacNeice. **CP-MacNL**

Indiana. Hart Crane. *Fr.* Powhatan's Daughter. *Fr.* The Bridge. **CP-CranH**

Indiana Avenue, 1949. Etheridge Knight. *Fr.* Indiana Haiku. **SP-KnigE**

Indiana Gig, The. Al Young. **CP-YounA**

Indiana Haiku. Etheridge Knight. **SP-KnigE**
  Indiana Avenue, 1949.
  Indianapolis Winter, 1973.
  Riverside Park.

Indiana Haiku—2. Etheridge Knight. **SP-KnigE**
  Crown Hill Cemetary, Indianapolis.
  Harlem.
  Indianapolis War Memorial.
  Penal Farm, The.
  Vigo County.

Indianapolis. John Updike. **CP-UpdiJ**

Indianapolis War Memorial. Etheridge Knight. *Fr.* Indiana Haiku—2. **SP-KnigE**

Indianapolis Winter, 1973. Etheridge Knight. *Fr.* Indiana Haiku. **SP-KnigE**

Indians. Robert Creeley. **CP-CreeR**

Indians Worship Him, but He Hurries On, The. Nicholas Vachel Lindsay. *Fr.* In Praise of Johnny Appleseed. **CP-LindV**

Indifference. Edna St. Vincent Millay. **CP-MillE**

Indifference of the Heavens, The. Samuel Taylor Coleridge. **CP-ColeS**

Indifferent, The. John Donne. **CP-DonnJ**
  I Can Love Both Fair and Brown. **CBCK**

Indifferent to the indifference that conceived her. In Praise of Cities. Thom Gunn. **CP-GunnT**

Indignant at the fumbling wits, the obscure spite. Paudeen. William Butler Yeats. **CP-YeatW**

Indignant Bard composed this furious ode, The. A Devonshire Road. Samuel Taylor Coleridge. **CP-ColeS**

Indignation of a High-Minded Spaniard 1810. William Wordsworth. **CP-WorW1**

Indigo Bunting, The. Robert Bly. **SP-BlyR**

Indigo Buntings. Peter Meinke. **SP-MeinP**

Indigo, mottle of purple and amber, ink. Littoral. Louis MacNeice. **CP-MacNL**

Inditing a Good Matter. Donald Davie. **CP-DavDo**

Individualist, The. Ogden Nash. **CP-NashO**

Individualist Speaks, The. Louis MacNeice. **CP-MacNL**

Indo-European root *pha*, suggesting light and clarity, surfaces in *phenomenon*, The. The Mother. Hayden Carruth. *Fr.* Mother. **CP-CarHL**

Indo-European vision said clouds, The. When One Age Goes with It Suddenly Its Errors Evaporate. Charles Olson. **CP-OlsoC**

Indolence. Alun Lewis. **CP-LewiA**

Indolent youth, / Drawn by everything in turn. From the French (1). Stevie Smith. **CP-SmitS**

Indonesia. Mary Oliver. **SP-OlivM**

Indoor Games near Newbury. Sir John Betjeman. **CP-BetjJ**

Indoor Sports. Louis MacNeice. **CP-MacNL**
  Crossword Puzzles.
  Darts.
  Shove Halfpenny.
  Vingt-et-un.

Indoor winter white begonia fibril. White Begonia. Louis Zukofsky. **CP-ZukLS**

Indoors the tang of a tiny oil lamp. Outdoors. House on a Cliff. Louis MacNeice. **CP-MacNL**

Indra; my house; the. Charles Henri Ford. **SP-FordC** *Fr.* Emblems of Arachne.

Indra needs a haircut. Charles Henri Ford. **SP-FordC** *Fr.* Secret Haiku.

Induction, The. John Milton. *See* Of Man's First Disobedience, and the Fruit.

Indulge no more may we. The End of the Episode. Thomas Hardy. **CP-HardT**

Indulgent, or candid, or uncommon reader. A Conversation with the Devil. Randall Jarrell. **CP-JarrR**

Industrial Archaeology. James Schuyler. **CP-SchuJ**

Ineffable, The. Richard Eberhart. **CP-EberR**

Inert and in the twilight. . . Peace is not hers. Bored to Choresis. Allen Tate. **CP-TateA**

Inert in his chair. Drugged. Walter de la Mare. **CP-DeLaW**

Inert Perfection. Edna St. Vincent Millay. **CP-MillE**

Inevitable. Sir John Betjeman. **CP-BetjJ**

Inexorable Rembrant rays, which stab. Thomas Epilogizes. Wystan Hugh Auden. **CP-AudWJ**

Inexpensive Progress. Sir John Betjeman. **CP-BetjJ**

Inexpressible, The. Ernest Hemingway. **CP-HemiE**

Infallible symbolist!—Tanker driven ashore. John Berryman. *Fr.* Sonnets to Chris. **CP-BerrJ**

Infamous poetry, abject love. Basil Bunting. *Fr.* The Well of Lycopolis. **CP-BuntB**

Infancy. Carlos Drummond de Andrade, *tr. fr. Portuguese by* Elizabeth Bishop. **CP-BishE**

Infancy and Age. George Meredith. **CP-MerG2**

Infancy! fearless, lustful, happy, nestling for delight. William Blake. **OXAEP-2** *Fr.* Visions of the Daughters of Albion. **CP-BlakW**

Infant. Stevie Smith. **CP-SmitS**

Infant Boy at Midcentury. Robert Penn Warren. **SP-WarrR**
  Brightness of Distance.
  Modification of Landscape.
  When the Century Dragged. **MoAmPo**

Infant Joy. William Blake. **FHYEP; FaPON; GoJo; HBV; HBVY; LAuP; LoBV; NAEL-2; NAs; NTP; OXAEP-2; OxBSP; PoLF; SiSoSe; TEP** *Fr.* Songs of Innocence. **CP-BlakW**

Infant M— M—, The. William Wordsworth. **CP-WorW2**

Infant Sorrow. William Blake. **CP-BlakW** *Fr.* Songs of Experience.

Infanta Marina. Wallace Stevens. **CP-StevW**

Infantry. Alun Lewis. **CP-LewiA**

Infatuate Britons, will you still proclaim. Lines Written on 29 May / The Anniversary of the Restoration of Charles the 2nd. John Keats. **CP-KeatJ**

Infelice. Stevie Smith. **CP-SmitS**

Inference of Mexico, An. Robert Earl Hayden. **CP-HaydR**
  Day of the Dead (Tehuantepec).
  Idol.
  Kid. **CAD; NCSH**
  La Corrida.
  Market.
  Mountains.
  Sub Specie Aeternitatis. **AmPP**
  Veracruz. **AmNP**

Inferential. Edwin Arlington Robinson. **CP-RobiE**

Inferential Knowledge, The. Emily Dickinson. **SP-DickE**

Infernall Spirits listen to my moanes. Mary Sidney, Countess of Montgomery Wroth. *Fr.* Part 1. *Fr.* Urania. **CP-WrotM**

Inferno. Dante Alighieri. *Fr.* Divina Commedia.
  Francesca di Rimini. **CP-Byron**
  Ugolino. **CP-ShelP**

Infinite a sudden Guest, The. Emily Dickinson. **CP-DickE**

"Infinite Beauty"—of which you speak, The. Emily Dickinson. **SP-DickE**

Infinite consanguinity it bears. Hart Crane. **MoPo; MoVE; OxBA** *Fr.* Voyages. **CP-CranH**

Infinite Horses, The. Silvina Ocampo, *tr. by* William Carlos Williams. **CP-WilW2**

Infinite jukethrob smoke & swallow to dis. Edward Estlin Cummings. **CP-CummE**

Infinite Reason, The. Archibald MacLeish. **CP-MacLA**

Infinite shining heavens, The. Robert Louis Stevenson. **CP-StevR**

Infinite's being so wide, The. Triple Bronze. Robert Frost. **CP-FrosR**

Infinity. Walt Whitman. **AA** *Fr.* Song of Myself. **CP-WhitW**

Infirmity. Theodore Roethke. **CP-RoetT**

Inflections of joy. The inflections of, The. Bonfire. Tess Gallagher. **SP-GallT**

Influence Abused. William Wordsworth. *Fr.* Ecclesiastical Sonnets. **CP-WorW2**

Influence of Natural Objects [in Calling Forth and Strengthening the Imagination in Boyhood and Early Youth]. William Wordsworth. **AWP; CP-WorW1; OBRV** *Fr.* Introduction—Childhood and School-Time. **EnRP; FHYEP** *Fr.* The Prelude; Growth of a Poet's Mind [1850 vers.]. **CP-WorW3**

"Informal" (dancing on the zebra floor). *sl. diff. vers. incl. in Pijijiapan.* Malcolm Lowry. *Fr.* Songs for Second Childhood. **CP-LowrM**

Informative Object, An. William Carlos Williams. **CP-WilW2**

Infrequently but massively I hear. A Word From the Piazza del Limbo. Isabella Gardner. **CP-GardI**

Infrequently, dreams ar heavenly. David Dancing. Donald Davie. **CP-DavDo**

Ingenuities of Debt, The. Robert Frost. **CP-FrosR**

Ingrateful[l] Beauty Threatened. Thomas Carew. **CP-CareT**

Inhabitants of heavenly land, *par.* by Countess of Pembroke, Mary Sidney Herbert. Bible, *O.T. See* Psalm 148: "Praise ye the Lord. Praise ye the Lord from the heavens."

Inhabitants of Old Jerusalem, The. The Popish Plot. John Dryden. **ACP** *Fr.* Absalom and Achitophel, Pt. I. **SP-DrydJ**

Inheritance, The. David Herbert Lawrence. **CP-LawrD**

Inheritance, The. Thomas McGrath. **SP-McGrT**

Inheritance. Robert Pack. **SP-PackR**

Inheritance. Charles Simic. **SP-SimiC**

Inheritances. Jane Cooper. *Fr.* Dispossessions. **SP-CoopJ**

Inheritances. Marilyn Hacker. **SP-HackM**

Inherited Estate, The. Thom Gunn. **CP-GunnT**

Inhuman man! curse on thy barb'rous art. On Seeing a Wounded Hare Limp by Me, Which a Fellow Had Just Shot At. Robert Burns. **CP-BurnR**

Inhumanist, The. Robinson Jeffers. *Fr.* The Double Axe. **CP-JefR3**

Iniquity of the Fathers upon the Children, The. Christina Georgina Rossetti. **CP-RosC1**

Initial. Pablo Neruda, *tr. fr. Spanish by* Ben Belitt. **SP-NeruP**

Initial, Dæmonic, and Celestial Love. Ralph Waldo Emerson. **CP-EmerR** Dæmonic and the Celestial Love, The. **APN-1**

Initiation Degrees. David Herbert Lawrence. **CP-LawrD**

Injian Ocean sets an' smiles, The. For to Admire. Rudyard Kipling. **CP-KiplR**

Injudicious Gardening. Marianne Craig Moore. **CP-MoorM**

Injure yourself, you injure me. Injuries. Robert Ranke Graves. **CP-GravR**

Injured Choriant or Paeonic. Malcolm Lowry. **CP-LowrM**

Injured Sire. John Crowe Ransom. *Fr.* Two Gentlemen in Bonds. **SP-RansJ**

Injured Stuart line is gone, The. On Seeing the Royal Palace at Stirling in Ruins. Robert Burns. **DBV** *Fr.* Here Stewarts once in triumph reign'd. *Fr.* Lines on Stirling. **CP-BurnR**

Injuries. Robert Ranke Graves. **CP-GravR**

Injury, The. William Carlos Williams. **CP-WilW2**

Ink-Sack. Robinson Jeffers. **CP-JefR3**

Inkidoo and the Queen of Babel. Robert Ranke Graves. **CP-GravR**

Inkling only, whisper in the bones, An. The Dowser. Louis MacNeice. **CP-MacNL**

Inland. Edna St. Vincent Millay. **CP-MillE**

Inland Sea, The. Jenny Joseph. **SP-JoseJ**

Inland Waterway. Sir John Betjeman. **CP-BetjJ**

Inland, within a hollow Vale, I stood. William Wordsworth. **CP-WorW1** (September, 1802. Near Dover.) **CP-WorW1**

Inlet, The. Louise Glück. **SP-GlücL**

Inlet. George Oppen. **CP-OppeG**

Inmate of a mountain-dwelling. To—, on Her First Ascent to the Summit of Helvellyn. William Wordsworth. **CP-WorW2**

Inn, The. Frank Templeton Prince. **CP-PrinF**

Inn Album, The. Robert Browning. **CP-BroR2**

Inn Song. Wystan Hugh Auden. **CP-AudWJ**

Innate Helium. Robert Frost. **CP-FrosR**

Inner Distance. Marsden Hartley. **CP-HartM**

Inner Law, The. Chuang Tzu, *tr. fr. Chinese by* Thomas Merton. **CP-MertT**

Inner Light, The. George Harrison. **CP-Beatl**

Inner Man, The. Charles Simic. **SP-SimiC**

Inner not outer, without gnash of teeth. A Martyr. Christina Georgina Rossetti. **CP-RosC2**

Inner Vision, The. William Wordsworth. *See* Most Sweet It Is with Unuplifted Eyes.

Innerly / UningstrolL / (stamens & pistil). Edward Estlin Cummings. **CP-CummE**

Innings. Charles Kenneth Williams. **CP-WillC**

Innocence, The. Robert Creeley. **CP-CreeR**

Innocence. Thom Gunn. **CP-GunnT**

Innocence? / In a sense. A Life. Howard Nemerov. **CP-NemeH**

Innocence! Innocence is the condition of heaven. The Woodpecker. William Carlos Williams. **CP-WilW2**

Innocence is the children's country, these. Giant in the Garden. May Sarton. **SP-SartM**

Innocent England. David Herbert Lawrence. **CP-LawrD**

Innocent eyes not ours / Are made to look on flowers. Christina Georgina Rossetti. **CP-RosC2** (These All Wait upon Thee.) **CP-RosC2**

Innocent locomotive, The. East Coocoo. William Carlos Williams. **CP-WilW2**

Innocent soul / ghosting for its lost. Geoffrey Hill. *Fr.* Churchill's Funeral. **CP-HillG**

Innocent Thief, The. Vincent Bourne, *tr. fr. Latin by* William Cowper. **CP-CowpW**

Innocents, The. Adrienne Rich. **CP-RicAE**

Innocents tug blindly at the yielding, The. An Essay on the Human Will. Randall Jarrell. **CP-JarrR**

Innocents were condemned to death in the Hall of Justice, The. After Tu Fu (A.D. 713-770). Edwin Rolfe. **CP-RolfE**

Innumerable and unnameable, foreign flowers. Hill Walk. Charles Tomlinson. **CP-TomlC**

Innumerable Christ, The. "Hugh MacDiarmid." **SP-MacDH**

Inquest. William DeWitt Snodgrass. **SP-SnodW**

Inquiry, An. Thomas Hardy. **CP-HardT**

Inquiry, The. Thomas Hardy. *Fr.* At Casterbridge Fair. **CP-HardT**

Inquisitors, The. Robinson Jeffers. **CP-JefR3**

In's Tusc'lanes, Tullie doth confesse. Foolishnesse. Robert Herrick. **CP-HerrR**

Insane Always Loved Me, The. Charles Bukowski. **SP-BukC1**

Insane Waiters, The. Gilbert Sorrentino. **SP-SorrG**

Inscribed on the Flyleaf of Richard Shay's Copy of Rimbaud's *Illuminations.* James Liddy. **CP-LiddJ**

Inscribed upon a Rock. William Wordsworth. **SyP** *Fr.* Inscriptions Supposed to Be Found in and near a Hermit's Cell; 1818. **CP-WorW2**

Inscribenda Luparae [To Be Written on the Louvre]. Andrew Marvell, *tr. fr. Latin by* William A. McQueen *and* Kiffin A. Rockwell. **CP-MarvA**

Inscription: "Eagle, stooping from yon snow-blown peaks, The." John Greenleaf Whittier. **CP-WhitJ**

Inscription, The. Thomas Hardy. **CP-HardT**

Inscription: "To them who crossed the flood." Herman Melville. **SP-MelvH**

Inscription by the Sea, An. Glaukos. **AWP; ChTr; ELU; FaBoEE** *Fr.* Variations of Greek Themes. **CP-RobiE**

Inscription for a Bust of Homer. William Cowper. **CP-CowpW**

Inscription for a Fountain on a Heath. Samuel Taylor Coleridge. **CP-ColeS**

Inscription for a Gravestone. Robinson Jeffers. **CP-JefR2**

Inscription for a Monument in Crossthwaite Curch, in the Vale of Keswick. William Wordsworth. **CP-WorW2**

Inscription for a Moss-House. William Cowper. **CP-CowpW**

Inscription for a Seat by a Roadside, Half Way up a Steep Hill, Facing the South. William Wordsworth. **CP-WorW1**

Inscription for a Seat by the Pathway Side Ascending to Windy Brow. William Wordsworth. **CP-WorW1**

Inscription for a Sketch. Robert Browning. **CP-BroR2**

Inscription for a Stone. William Cowper. **CP-CowpW**

Inscription for an Hermitage. William Cowper. **CP-CowpW**

Inscription for the Tank. James Wright. **CP-WrigJ**

Inscription for the Tomb of Hamilton. William Cowper. **CP-CowpW**

Inscription in a Garden of the Same, *see also* Inscription in the Grounds of Coleorton, the Seat of Sir George Beaumont, BART., Leicestershire *and* Written at the Request of Sir George Beaumont, BART., and in His Name, for an Urn, Placed by Him at the Termination of a Newly-Planted Avenue, in the Same Grounds. William Wordsworth. **CP-WorW1**

Inscription in the Grounds of Coleorton, the Seat of Sir George Beaumont, BART., Leicestershire, *see also* Written at the Request of Sir George Beaumont, BART., and in His Name, for an Urn, Placed by Him at the Termination of a Newly-Planted Avenue, in the Same Grounds *and* Inscription in a Garden of the Same. William Wordsworth. **CP-WorW1**

Inscription on a Goblet. Robert Burns. **CP-BurnR**

Inscription on a Rock at Rydal Mount. William Wordsworth. **CP-WorW2**

Inscription on a Stone, in the Church-Yard at Boreham. Charlotte Smith. **CP-SmitC**

Inscription on a Well in Memory of the Martyrs of the War. Ralph Waldo Emerson. **CP-EmerR**

Inscription on the Monument of a Newfoundland Dog. Byron. **CP-Byron**

Inscription, The: "While yet Rolfe's foot in stirrup stood." Herman Melville. **SP-MelvH** *Fr.* Clarel: A Poem and Pilgrimage in the Holy Land.

Inscriptions. John Greenleaf Whittier. **CP-WhitJ**

Inscriptions for a Peal of Eight Bells. Thomas Hardy. **CP-HardT**

Inscriptions for Bluebeard's Castle. Roy Fisher.
 Armoury, The. **SP-FishR**
 Castle, The. **SP-FishR**
 Garden, The. **SP-FishR**
 Instruments of Torture, The. **SP-FishR**
 Lake of Tears, The. **SP-FishR**
 Land, The. **SP-FishR**
 Last Door, The. **SP-FishR**
 Portcullis, The. **SP-FishR**
 Treasure House, The. **SP-FishR**

Inscriptions on an Aeolian Harp. Christopher Smart. **SP-SmarC**
 ("Salve, quae fingis proprio modulamine carmen.") **SP-SmarC**

Inscriptions Supposed to Be Found in and near a Hermit's Cell; 1818.
 William Wordsworth. **CP-WorW2**
 "Hast thou seen, with flash incessant."
 "Hopes what are they?—Beads of morning."
 Inscribed upon a Rock. **SyP**
 Near the Spring of the Hermitage.
 "Not seldom, clad in radiant vest."

Insect world appealed to Fabre, The. Creeps and Crawls. Ogden Nash.
 CP-NashO

Insects, The. John Haines. **SP-HainJ**

Insensibility. Wilfred Owen. **CP-OwenW**

Inside. Pablo Neruda, *tr. fr. Spanish by* Ben Belitt. **SP-NeruP**

Inside / that mud-hive, that gas-sponge. The Lilies Break Open Over the
 Dark Water. Mary Oliver. **SP-OlivM**

Inside a cave in a narrow canyon near Tassajara. Hands. Robinson Jeffers.
 CP-JefR2

Inside, a hundred doors by which to leave. The Harsh Judgment. Stanley
 Jasspon Kunitz. **CP-KuniS**

Inside a lung somewhere. Cortege. Richard Shelton. **SP-ShelR**

Inside and Outside. Allen Tate. **CP-TateA**

Inside Chance, The. Marge Piercy. **SP-PierM**

Inside each of us. No Word. Stephen Berg. **SP-BergS**

Inside everybody's nose / There lives a sharp-toothed snail. Warning. Shel
 Silverstein. **SP-SilS2**

Inside many of us. Rumpelstiltskin. Anne Sexton. **CP-SextA**

Inside, my darling wife. The Happy Three. Theodore Roethke. **CP-RoetT**

Inside of King's College Chapel, Cambridge. William Wordsworth. **EnRP;
 OBNC** *Fr.* Ecclesiastical Sonnets. **CP-WorW2**
 (Within King's College Chapel, Cambridge.) **GTBS; GTBS-6; GTBS-P**

Inside or out, the key is pain. It holds. Hospital. Karl Shapiro. **SP-ShapK**

Inside Out. Diane Wakoski. **SP-WakoD**

Inside-Outside Game, The. Thom Gunn. **CP-GunnT**

Inside the Gyroscope. Laurence Lieberman. **SP-LiebL**

Inside the River. James Dickey. **CP-DickJ**

Inside the shell of our skulls. John Haines. *Fr.* The Fossil. **SP-HainJ**

Inside the veins there are navies setting forth. Waking from Sleep. Robert
 Bly. **SP-BlyR**

Inside these bottles / Rows of tenements are burning. The Ad Man's
 Daughter. Jim Carroll. **SP-CarrJ**

Inside this music there is someone. Listening to Bach. Robert Bly. *Fr.* Six
 Winter Privacy Poems. **SP-BlyR**

Inside us there is a listener who listens for what we say. The Watcher.
 Robert Bly. **SP-BlyR**

Insight. Mona Van Duyn. **SP-VanDM**

Insignificant Elephants. Wystan Hugh Auden. **CP-AudeW**

Insistence being of its nature. Wind. Charles Tomlinson. **CP-TomlC**

Insistence of Things, The. Charles Tomlinson. **CP-TomlC**

Insistent / this yearning / toward. Robert Creeley. **CP-CreeR**

Insistent resolution like, The. When the Berry Bush Dies I'll Swim Down
 the Green River with My Hair on Fire. Charles Bukowski. **SP-BukC2**

Insistently through sleep—a tide of voices. The Harbor Dawn. Hart Crane.
 **AP; AmPP; CMoP; CoBMV; CrMA; FaBV; GOA; LiTM; MoAB;
 MoAmPo; MoPo; NOBA; NYP; NePA; NoAM; OxBA; PrIm;
 SeCeV; TrGrPo; TwAmPo** *Fr.* Powhatan's Daughter. *Fr.* The Bridge.
 CP-CranH

Insolent Storm Strikes at the Skull. Sylvia Plath. **CP-PlatS**

Insomnia. Elizabeth Bishop. **CP-BishE**

Insomnia. Charles Bukowski. **SP-BukC2**

Insomnia. Stephen Dunn. **SP-DunnS**

Insomnia. Robert Penn Warren. *Fr.* Tale of Time. **SP-WarrR**

Insomnia & Poetry. Erica Jong. **SP-JongE**

Insomnia, old tree, when will you shed me? Dawn. William Matthews.
 SP-MattW

Insomnia the Gem of the Ocean. John Updike. **CP-UpdiJ**

Insomniac. Maya Angelou. **SP-AngeM**

Insomniac. Sylvia Plath. **CP-PlatS**

Insomniac since four, hearing this narrow. Nearing Forty. Derek Walcott.
 CP-WalcD

Insomniac Sleeps Well for Once and, The. Hayden Carruth. **CP-CarHS**

Insomniacs, The. Adrienne Rich. **CP-RicAE**

Inspecting eye / shows cold, The. Crow. Charles Tomlinson. **CP-TomlC**

Inspection. Wilfred Owen. **CP-OwenW**

Inspectors called at anxious intervals. His Majesty's Inspectors. John
 Hewitt. **CP-HewiJ**

Inspectors here crunched bags on injured locks. Malcolm Lowry. *Fr.* The
 Canadian Turned Back at the Border. **CP-LowrM**

Inspiration. Paul Laurence Dunbar. **CP-DunbP**

Inspiration caught from dubious hues, An. A Later Alexandrian. George
 Meredith. **CP-MerG1**

Inspiration of the Great West Wind, The. George Meredith. *Fr.* Wandering
 Willie. **CP-MerG2**

Inspired we must forget our books. Ralph Waldo Emerson. **CP-EmerR**

Inspiring music's thrilling sound, The. Emily Brontë. **CP-BronE**

Instance, The. Charles Tomlinson. **CP-TomlC**

Instans Tyrannus. Robert Browning. **CP-BroR1**

Instant coffeee with slightly sour cream. Poem. Frank O'Hara. **SP-OharF**

Instant of Our Parting, The. Alice Walker. **CP-WalkA**

Instant on the Viaduct, An. Jenny Joseph. **SP-JoseJ**

Instantly they are about me, presences. Descent Into Hades. Kathleen Jessie
 Raine. **SP-RainK**

Instead of / the flower of the hawthorn. Franklin Square. William Carlos
 Williams. **CP-WilW2**

Instead of a song, boys, I'll give you a toast. A Toast. Robert Burns. **CP-
 BurnR**

Instead of an Elegy. John Hewitt. **CP-HewiJ**

Instead of an Essay. Charles Tomlinson. **CP-TomlC**

Instead of gazing at the sea. Going to the Bakery. Elizabeth Bishop. **CP-
 BishE**

Instead of Orient pearls, of Jet. The Carkanet. Robert Herrick. **CP-HerrR**

Instead of pearls—a wrought clasp. The Gift. Hilda Doolittle. **CP-DoolH**

Instead of throwing them away. An Old Pair of Shoes. Kenneth Patchen.
 CP-PatcK

Instead of You. Stephen Dunn. **SP-DunnS**

Instigator of the ruin— / Whichsoever thou mayst be. Cry of the Homeless.
 Thomas Hardy. **CP-HardT**

Instinct. Charles Kenneth Williams. **SP-WillC**

Institit acris hiemps: glacies simul imbrices ad imas. Unfinished Rendering
 of "When Icicles Hang by the Wall." Gerard Manley Hopkins. *Fr.*
 Songs from Shakespeare, in Latin and Greek. **CP-HopkG**

Institutions of society, The. Mermaid Emerging. Robert Lowell. **SP-
 LoweR**

Instruct me now, what love will do. Of Love. Robert Herrick. **CP-HerrR**

Instructed by my mother, father, friends. The Fool's Cap. John Hewitt.
 CP-HewiJ

Instruction booklet on a certain effect, An. Light. Louis Zukofsky. **CP-
 ZukLS**

Instruction Manual, The. John Ashbery. **SP-AshbJ**

Instructions. Carl Sandburg. **CP-SandC**

Instructions. Shel Silverstein. **SP-SilS2**

Instructions for Angels. Kenneth Patchen. **CP-PatcK**

Instructions for the World Librarian. John Clellon Holmes. **SP-HolmJ**

Instructions for Use of This Toy. Howard Nemerov. **CP-NemeH**

Instructions to a Medium, to be Transmitted to the Shade of W.B. Yeats, the
 Latter Having Responded in a Séance Held on 13 June 1965, Its
 Hundredth Birthday. Daniel Gerard Hoffman. **SP-HoffD**

Instructions to a Sentry. John Haines. **SP-HainJ**

Instructions to the Double. Tess Gallagher. **SP-GallT**

Instructions to the Orphic Adept. Robert Ranke Graves. **CP-GravR**

Instructor, The. Rudyard Kipling. **CP-KiplR**

Instructor said, The. Theme for English B. Langston Hughes. **SP-HughL**

Instrument, The. Kathleen Jessie Raine. *Fr.* Three Poems on Illusion. **SP-
 RainK**

Instruments. Richard Eberhart. *Fr.* Aesthetics after War. **CP-EberR**

Instruments of Torture, The. Roy Fisher. **SP-FishR** *Fr.* Inscriptions for
 Bluebeard's Castle.

Insu nli gh t / o / verand. Edward Estlin Cummings. **CP-CummE**

Insufficiency. Elizabeth Barrett Browning. **CP-BroEB**

Insufficiency of Earth, An. Charles Tomlinson. *Fr.* Four Kantian Lyrics.
 CP-TomlC

Insult, The. Charles Kenneth Williams. **SP-WillC**

Insulting chance ne'er call'd with louder voice. Seneca, *tr. by* Samuel Johnson. **CP-JohnS** *Fr.* Troades.

Insusceptibles, The. Adrienne Rich. **CP-RicAE**

Integration. Phoebe Hesketh. **SP-HeskP**

Integrity. Adrienne Rich. **SP-RicA1; SP-RicA2**

Intellect. Ralph Waldo Emerson.

Intellect / Gravely broods apart on joy. Ralph Waldo Emerson. **CP-EmerR**

Intellect of man is forced to choose, The. The Choice. William Butler Yeats. **CP-YeatW**

Intellectual, The. Karl Shapiro. **SP-ShapK**

Intellectual Detachment. Allen Tate. **CP-TateA**

Intellectual Englishman shrank away from the bedside, The. Oh, If Only. Stevie Smith. **CP-SmitS**

Intellectuals. Robinson Jeffers. **CP-JefR2**

Intellectuals at the feast, The. The Supper Before Last. Stanley Jasspon Kunitz. **CP-KuniS**

Intelligence does help, sometimes. Bindweed. John Updike. **CP-UpdiJ**

Intelligent companion, / Talented—yes, and blind—but can. The Door. Jane Cooper. **SP-CoopJ**

Intelligent Sheepman and the New Cars, The. William Carlos Williams. **CP-WilW2**

Intended Angle of Vision Is from My Kitchen, The. Charles Olson. **CP-OlsoC**

Intense and terrible beauty, how has our race with the frail naked nerves. Gale in April. Robinson Jeffers. **CP-JefR1**

Intense and terrible, I think, must be the loneliness. Edna St. Vincent Millay. **CP-MillE**

Intensification of compassion; extraordinary; incalculable. The Unanswering Correspondences. Kenneth Patchen. **CP-PatcK**

Intensity, when greatest, may. Auricle's Oracle. Daniel Gerard Hoffman. **SP-HoffD**

Intent gets blocked by noise. Hand Games. Marge Piercy. **SP-PierM**

Intent in the / night in the. The Cowshed Blues. Hayden Carruth. **CP-CarHS**

Intent on Gathering Wool from Hedge and Brake. William Wordsworth. **CP-WorW2**

Intention, The. Frank Templeton Prince. **CP-PrinF**

Intention to Escape from Him. Edna St. Vincent Millay. **CP-MillE**

Inter marmoreas Leonorae pendula colles. In Horologium. Percy Bysshe Shelley. **CP-ShelP**

Inter-Office Memorandum. Ogden Nash. **CP-NashO**

Interalienation of their hearts. Perfectionists. Robert Ranke Graves. **CP-GravR**

Interdict, An. William Wordsworth. *Fr.* Ecclesiastical Sonnets. **CP-WorW2**

Interest grows not knowing dahlia. Dahlia. Louis Zukofsky. **CP-ZukLS**

"Interesting, but futile," said his diary. A Writer. Philip Larkin. **CP-LarkP**

Interesting Glass, The. Gilbert Sorrentino. **SP-SorrG**

Interests of a black man in a cellar, The. Black Tambourine. Hart Crane. **CP-CranH**

Interests of 1926. William Carlos Williams. **CP-WilW1**

Interference. Archie Randolph Ammons. **SP-AmmoA**

Interim. John Hewitt. **CP-HewiJ**

Interim. Edna St. Vincent Millay. **CP-MillE**

Interim, The. Robert Penn Warren. *Fr.* Tale of Time. **SP-WarrR**

Interior. Hart Crane. **CP-CranH**

Interior. Carl Sandburg. **CP-SandC**

Interior: *The Man Turns the Sheet for the Musician* (Dutch). Jenny Joseph. *Fr.* Altarpiece (A Meditation on Lust, Desire and Love). **SP-JoseJ**

Interior (With Jane). Frank O'Hara. **SP-OharF**

Interiorly. Frederick Morgan. **SP-MorgF**

Interiors. Howard Nemerov. **CP-NemeH**

Interiors with Various Figures. Roy Fisher.

    Arrival, The. **SP-FishR**

    Billiard Table, The. **SP-FishR**

    Experimenting. **SP-FishR**

    Foyer, The. **SP-FishR**

    Lampshade, The. **SP-FishR**

    Small Room, The. **SP-FishR**

    Steam Crane, The. **SP-FishR**

    Truants. **SP-FishR**

    Wrestler, The. **SP-FishR**

    Wrong Time, The. **SP-FishR**

Interjection #8: Or, Sometimes, Night. Robert Penn Warren. **SP-WarrR**

Interjection #5: Solipsism and Theology. Robert Penn Warren. **SP-WarrR**

Interjection #4: Bad Year, Bad War: A New Year's Card, 1969. Robert Penn Warren. **SP-WarrR**

Interjection #1: The Need For Re-evaluation. Robert Penn Warren. **SP-WarrR**

Interjection #7: Remarks of Soul to Body. Robert Penn Warren. *See* You've toughed it out pretty well, old Body, done.

Interjection #6: What You Sometimes Feel on Your Face at Night. Robert Penn Warren. **SP-WarrR**

Interjection #3: I Know a Place Where All Is Real. Robert Penn Warren. **SP-WarrR**

Interjection #2: Caveat. Robert Penn Warren. **SP-WarrR**

Interloper, The. Thomas Hardy. **CP-HardT**

Interlude, An. Walter de la Mare. **CP-DeLaW**

Interlude. Theodore Roethke. **CP-RoetT**

Interlude, The. Karl Shapiro. **SP-ShapK**

Interlude. Charles Simic. **SP-SimiC**

Interlude, An. Algernon Charles Swinburne. **SP-SwinA**

Interlude at the Grand Hotel, An. Dabney Stuart. **SP-StuaD**

Interlude: Hephaestion's Prayer. David St. John. **SP-StJoD**

Interlude, with Alter Ego. James McAuley. **SP-McAuJ** *Fr.* Meditations of Afternoon.

Interludium. Hart Crane. **CP-CranH**

Interlunar. Margaret Atwood. **SP-AtwM2**

"Internal and External Forms." Donald Hall. **CP-HallD**

Internal Harmony. George Meredith. **CP-MerG1**

Interne at Provident. Langston Hughes. **SP-HughL**

Interpolation. Robert Burns. **CP-BurnR**

Interpolation Sounds. Walt Whitman. **CP-WhitW**

Interpretation of Dreams, The. William Matthews. **SP-MattW**

"Interpretation! that's the act of mind". Delmore Schwartz. **SP-SchwD** *Fr.* Genesis.

Interrogate the Stones. Archibald MacLeish. **CP-MacLA**

Interrogation of the Man of Many Hearts, The. Anne Sexton. **CP-SextA**

Interrogation II. Charles Kenneth Williams. **SP-WillC**

Interruption. Robert Ranke Graves. **CP-GravR**

Interruption. Thom Gunn. *Fr.* Transients and Residents. **CP-GunnT**

Interstitial Office. John Berryman. **CP-BerrJ**

Interval. John Hewitt. **CP-HewiJ**

Interval, An: the view across the fields. A View of Merton College. Adrienne Rich. **CP-RicAE**

Intervals. Robert Creeley. **CP-CreeR**

Intervals in a Busy Life. Donald Davie. **CP-DavDo**

Interview, The. Robert Creeley. **CP-CreeR**

Interview, An. Howard Nemerov. **CP-NemeH**

Interview is acres. Emily Dickinson. **SP-DickE**

Interviewed by a Guggenheim Recipient. Charles Bukowski. **SP-BukC2**

Inthe,exquisite; / morning sure lyHer eye s exactly sit,ata little roundtable. Edward Estlin Cummings. **CP-CummE**

Intimacy. Al Young. **CP-YounA**

Intimate Guest, The. Kenneth Patchen. **CP-PatcK**

Intimates. David Herbert Lawrence. **CP-LawrD**

Intimation of Immortality. Stevie Smith. **CP-SmitS**

Intimations of Immortality. William Wordsworth. *See* Our birth is but a sleep and a forgetting.

Intimations of Mortality. Louis MacNeice. **CP-MacNL**

Intimations of Sublimity. William Wordsworth. **OBNC** *Fr.* School-Time. *Fr.* The Prelude; Growth of a Poet's Mind [1805 vers.]. **CP-WorW3**

Into a gentle wildness and confusion. Sea Side. Robert Ranke Graves. **CP-GravR**

Into a swamp this heart is flying. Jim Carroll. *Fr.* Living at the Movies. **SP-CarrJ**

Into a truly / curving form. Edward Estlin Cummings. **CP-CummE**

Into another mission / Circling my exposed continent. Kenneth Patchen. **CP-PatcK**

Into any little room. Sleep Song. Carl Sandburg. **CP-SandC**

Into Broad Daylight. Robert Penn Warren. **SP-WarrR**

Into Distance. Charles Tomlinson. **CP-TomlC**

Into exile with only a few shirts. The Cloak. Robert Ranke Graves. **CP-GravR**

Into Her Lying Down Head. Dylan Thomas. **CP-ThomD**

Into her mother's bedroom to wash the ballooning body. Jessie Mitchell's Mother. Gwendolyn Brooks. **SP-BrooG**

Into his kit when sent to the front he had tucked. Favorite Iraqi Soldier. Stephen Dobyns. **SP-DobyS**

Into Mexico. Mona Van Duyn. **SP-VanDM**

Into my heart an air that kills. Alfred Edward Housman. **CP-HousA**

Into My Own. Robert Frost. **CP-FrosR**

Into the acres of the newborn state. The Proud Farmer. Nicholas Vachel Lindsay. *Fr.* A Gospel of Beauty. **CP-LindV**

Into the blue river hills. Sunset from Omaha Hotel Window. Carl Sandburg. **CP-SandC**

Into the closed air of the slow. Ted Berrigan. **SP-BerrT** *Fr.* The Sonnets.

Into the Dusk-Charged Air. John Ashbery. **SP-AshbJ**

Into the flame Godmother put her hand. David's Night in Veliès. James Merrill. **SP-MerrJ**

Into the Flats, thru Cleveland's. Cleveland, the Flats. Allen Ginsberg. **CP-GinsA**

Into the forest again. The Traveller. Robert Creeley. **CP-CreeR**

Into the Glacier. John Haines. **SP-HainJ**

Into the golden vessel of great song. Edna St. Vincent Millay. **CP-MillE**

Into the Grand Canyon of the Colorado. An Enthusiast Is a Devotee Is a Rooter, or, Mr. Hemingway, Meet Mr. Stengel. Ogden Nash. **CP-NashO**

Into the gulf and the pit of the dark night, the cold night, there is a man. John Ericsson Day Memorial, 1918. Carl Sandburg. **CP-SandC**

Into the inmost temple thus I came. The Temple of Venus. Edmund Spenser. **EIL; WHA** *Fr.* The Faerie Queene. **CP-Spens**

Into the Interior. Denise Levertov. **CP-LeveD**

Into the Known. Tess Gallagher. **SP-GallT**

Into the laps / of black celebrities. Mellow. Langston Hughes. **SP-HughL**

Into the lower right / Square of the window frame. A Sketch. Richard Wilbur. **CP-WilbR**

Into the night, into the blanket of night. Slabs of the Sunburnt West. Carl Sandburg. **CP-SandC**

Into the open air John Alden, perplexed and bewildered. John Alden. Henry Wadsworth Longfellow. *Fr.* The Courtship of Miles Standish. **SP-LongH**

Into the open air John Alden, perplexed and bewildered. Henry Wadsworth Longfellow. **TreFS** *Fr.* John Alden. *Fr.* The Courtship of Miles Standish. **SP-LongH**

Into the pool at 5 AM to freshen. Ferrini—I. Charles Olson. **CP-OlsoC**

Into the purpose: or out. Timelessness of Desire. Roy Fisher. **SP-FishR**

Into the sacred precincts come the savage sages. A Relation of Art and Life. Howard Nemerov. **CP-NemeH**

Into the shadow-white chamber silts the white. Two Wives. David Herbert Lawrence. **CP-LawrD**

Into the slain tons of needles. By Canoe through the Fir Forest. James Dickey. **NYBP** *Fr.* On the Coosawattee. **CP-DickJ**

Into the slain tons of needles. On the Coosawattee. James Dickey. **CP-DickJ**

Into the smiting / sky tense. Edward Estlin Cummings. **CP-CummE**

Into the Stone. James Dickey. **CP-DickJ**

Into the street the Piper stept. Robert Browning. **BoTP; OXAEP-2** *Fr.* The Pied Piper of Hamelin. **CP-BroR1**

Into the strenuous briefness. Edward Estlin Cummings. **CP-CummE**

Into the the air far. Into the opposites. Muriel Rukeyser. **CP-RukeM**

Into the Twilight. William Butler Yeats. **CP-YeatW**

Into thir inmost bower. John Milton. **FF**, *ll.* 738–757; **TOF**, *ll.* 738–775; *Fr.* Book IV. **OAEL-1** *Fr.* Paradise Lost. **CP-MiltJ**

Into this narrow vault I came when young. Sanders Theater. Richard Eberhart. **CP-EberR**

Into this place whereas the elfin knight. The Nymphs and Graces Dancing. Edmund Spenser. **DIP** *Fr.* The Faerie Queene. **CP-Spens**

Into this pleasant Shadow all the weak & weary. William Blake. **NOBRP** *Fr.* Milton. **CP-BlakW**

Into this wild abyss. Satan's Journey. John Milton. **NOSC** *Fr.* Book II. **FHYEP; NAEL-1; OxAEP-1** *Fr.* Paradise Lost. **CP-MiltJ**

Into what fictive worlds can imagination. The Horatians. Wystan Hugh Auden. **CP-AudeW**

Into what pattern, into what music have the spheres whirled us. Kathleen Jessie Raine. **SP-RainK**

Into your outstretched hands come pouring. Song: Come, Enjoy Your Sunday! Robert Ranke Graves. **CP-GravR**

Intolerably sad, profound. Before the Anæsthetic; or, A Real Fright. Sir John Betjeman. **CP-BetjJ**

Intra Sepulchrum. Thomas Hardy. **CP-HardT**

Intrepid sons of Albion! not by you. Occasioned by the Battle of Waterloo (the Last Six Lines Intended for an Inscription) February, 1816. William Wordsworth. **CP-WorW2**

Intricacies of a devious mind. Princess Di. James Schuyler. **CP-SchuJ**

Intricacy of engines, / Delicacy of darkness. Trapezists. Louis MacNeice. **VoGa** *Fr.* Circus. **CP-MacNL**

Intricate ship / Thing well / in my heart. Alice Ordered Me to be Made. Alice Notley. **SP-NotlA**

Introduction: "Hear the voice of the Bard!" William Blake. **CP-BlakW** *Fr.* Songs of Experience.

Introduction: "I, who accompanied with faithful pace." William Wordsworth. *Fr.* Ecclesiastical Sonnets. **CP-WorW2**

Introduction, The. Louis MacNeice. **CP-MacNL**

Introduction, The. Ogden Nash. **CP-NashO**

Introduction: "Of nothing but me, me." John Updike. *Fr.* Midpoint. **CP-UpdiJ**

Introduction: "Piping down the valleys wild." William Blake. *See* Piping Down the Valleys Wild.

Introduction—Childhood and School-Time. William Wordsworth. **EnRP; FHYEP** *Fr.* The Prelude; Growth of a Poet's Mind [1850 vers.]. **CP-WorW3**

Introduction—Childhood and School-Time. William Wordsworth. *Fr.* The Prelude; Growth of a Poet's Mind [1805 vers.]. **CP-WorW3**

"And in the frosty season, when the sun." **FaBoCh; PIP**

(On the Frozen Lake.) **FaBoCh**

"Dust as we are, the immortal spirit grows." **SCV**

"Ere I had told / Ten birthdays when among the mountain-slopes." **TOF**

"Fair seed time had my soul, and I grew up." **NoP**, *book* 1, *ll.* 301–646;

"Fair seed-time had my soul, and I grew up." **OBNC; OxAEP-2**, *book* 1, *ll.* 305–489; **FaBoPP**

(On the Solitary Fells around Hawkshead.) **FaBoPP**, *book* 1, *ll.* 305–350;

Fishing. **SD**

In Patterdale. **FaBoRV**

Influence of Natural Objects [in Calling Forth and Strengthening the Imagination in Boyhood and Early Youth]. **AWP; CP-WorW1; OBRV**

"O there is blessing in this gentle breeze." **OAEL-2**

"One evening (surely I was led by her)." **FaBoPP; OBRV; RB**

(Boat Stealing.) **RB**

(On Ullswater.) **FaBoPP**

"One summer evening (led by her) I found." **FiP; NU**

(Lines: "One summer evening (led by her) I found.") **NU**

Skating. **CH; SD**

"Was it for this." **RB**

"Wisdom and Spirit of the universe!" **NOBE**

Wordsworth Skates on Esthwaite Water. **FaBoPP**

Introduction to the Franklin's Prologue and Tale. Geoffrey Chaucer. **NAEL-1** *Fr.* The Canterbury Tales. **CP-ChauG**

Introduction to the Hoh. Richard Hugo. **CP-HugoR**

Introduction to the Man of Law's Tale. Geoffrey Chaucer. **FiP** *Fr.* The Canterbury Tales. **CP-ChauG**

Introduction to the Nun's Priest's Tale, The, *see* Prologue of the Nun's Priest's Tale, The. Geoffrey Chaucer. *See* The Prologue of the Nun's Priest's Tale.

Introduction to the Pardoner's Prologue and Tale. Geoffrey Chaucer. *See* Introduction to the Pardoner's Tale.

Introduction to the Pardoner's Tale. Geoffrey Chaucer. *Fr.* The Canterbury Tales. **CP-ChauG**

(Introduction to the Pardoner's Prologue and Tale.) **FHYEP; NAEL-1; NoP; PoE**

(Introduction to the Pardoner's Prologue and Tale.) **FHYEP; NAEL-1; NoP; PoE**

Introduction to the Parson's Tale, The. Geoffrey Chaucer. **NAEL-1** *Fr.* The Canterbury Tales. **CP-ChauG**

Introduction to the Squire's Tale. Geoffrey Chaucer. *Fr.* The Canterbury Tales. **CP-ChauG**

Introduction to the 20th Century. Stephen Dunn. **SP-DunnS**

Introspectional. Hayden Carruth. *Fr.* Poetical Abstracts. **CP-CarHS**

Introspective. Christina Georgina Rossetti. **CP-RosC3**

Introspective Reflection. Ogden Nash. **CP-NashO**

Intruder, The. Roy Fisher. **SP-FishR**

Intruder, An. May Sarton. **SP-SartM**

Intruding. Marge Piercy. **SP-PierM**

Intrusiveness of flowers. Emily Dickinson. **SP-DickE**

Intuition. Robert Penn Warren. *Fr.* Two Poems about Suddenly and a Rose. **SP-WarrR**

Inundatio Oxoniana. Gerard Manley Hopkins. **CP-HopkG**

Inundation of the Spring, The. Emily Dickinson. **CP-DickE**

Inundation, says the fable, An. On the Words "Brother Protestants and Fellow Christians." Jonathan Swift. **CP-SwifJ**

Invaders, The. John Haines. **SP-HainJ**

Invading nightmare, spinning up through sleep. Three Black Women. Muriel Rukeyser. **CP-RukeM**

Invariably when wine redeems the sight. The Wine Menagerie. Hart Crane. **CP-CranH**

Invasion. Robinson Jeffers. **CP-JefR3**

Invasion Exercise on the Poultry Farm. Sir John Betjeman. **CP-BetjJ**

Invasion North. Richard Hugo. **CP-HugoR**

Invasion of Sleep Walkers, The. John Ciardi. **SP-CiarJ**

Invective against Swans. Wallace Stevens. **CP-StevW**

Invective of Achilles, The. Homer, *tr. by* George Meredith. **CP-MerG1** *Fr.* The Iliad.

Inventing a story with grass. A Birth. James Dickey. **CP-DickJ**

Inventing Ballygalvin. Brendan Galvin. **SP-GalvB**

Invention. Shel Silverstein. **SP-SilS2**

Invention of Nothing. Charles Simic. **SP-SimiC**

Invention of Poetry, The. Kenneth Koch. *Fr.* Days and Nights. **SP-KochK**

Invention sleeps within a skull. Death Piece. Theodore Roethke. **CP-RoetT**

Inventor, The, *parody of* Ralph Waldo Emerson. Rudyard Kipling. **CP-KiplR** *Fr.* The Muse among the Motors.

Inventory, The. Robert Burns. **CP-BurnR**

Inventory of Goodbyes, The. Anne Sexton. **CP-SextA**

Inversely, As the Square of Their Distances Apart. Kenneth Rexroth. **SP-RexrK**

Inversnaid. Gerard Manley Hopkins. **CP-HopkG** Wildness. **EaPr; OtMeF**

Inverts. Jenny Joseph. *Fr.* Life and Turgid Times of A. Citizen. **SP-JoseJ**

Investigation of Certain Interesting Questions. Kenneth Patchen. **CP-PatcK**

Investigator is here, The. Margaret Atwood. *Fr.* Two-Headed Poems. **SP-AtwM2**

Investment, The. Robert Frost. **CP-FrosR**

Invideat quamvis sua verba Latina Britannis. *acc. by English translation.* Thomas Campion. **CP-CampT**

Invincibility. Frank O'Hara. **SP-OharF**

Invincible Summer. Chuck Miller. **SP-MillC**

Inviolable. Daniel Gerard Hoffman. **SP-HoffD**

Invisible Boy. Shel Silverstein. **SP-SilS2**

Invisible chariots, The. Isle of Patmos. Carl Sandburg. **CP-SandC**

Invisible envelopes, / A standstill afternoon. Charles Henri Ford. **SP-FordC** *Fr.* Emblems of Arachne.

Invisible gulls with human voices cry in the sea-cloud. Fog. Robinson Jeffers. **CP-JefR1**

Invisible Hand, The. Robert Pack. **SP-PackR**

Invisible, indivisible Spirit. Hilda Doolittle. **BoWoP** *Fr.* Tribute to the Angels. **CP-DoolH**

Invisible Sleep. Jim Carroll. **SP-CarrJ**

Invisible Tonight. Leonard Cohen. **CP-CoheL**

Invisible Trouble, The. Leonard Cohen. **CP-CoheL**

Invisibles, The. Stephen Dobyns. **SP-DobyS**

Invitation, The. Robert Creeley. **CP-CreeR**

Invitation, An. Thom Gunn. **CP-GunnT**

Invitation. Marsden Hartley. **CP-HartM**

Invitation, The. George Herbert. **CP-HerbG**

Invitation, The. Robert Herrick. **CP-HerrR**

Invitation. Phoebe Hesketh. **SP-HeskP**

Invitation. Shel Silverstein. **SP-SilS2**

Invitation. William Carlos Williams. **CP-WilW1**

Invitation. William Carlos Williams. **CP-WilW1**

Invitation. Al Young. **CP-YounA**

Invitation to a Hay. Jean Garrigue. **SP-GarrJ**

Invitation to an Invitation, An. Catullus. *See* Carmen 32: "Call me to you / at siesta."

Invitation to Bristol. Robert Ranke Graves. **CP-GravR**

Invitation to Love. Paul Laurence Dunbar. **CP-DunbP**

Invitation to Miss Marianne Moore. Elizabeth Bishop. **CP-BishE**

Invitation to the Bee. Charlotte Smith. **CP-SmitC**

Invitation to the Country. George Meredith. **CP-MerG1**

Invitation to the Redbreast. Vincent Bourne, *tr. fr. Latin by* William Cowper. **CP-CowpW**

Inviting a Friend to Supper. Ben Jonson, *after* Martial. **CP-JonsB**

Invocation: "Burning fire shakes in the night, The." Walter de la Mare. **CP-DeLaW**

Invocation: "Come out of the dark earth." May Sarton. **SP-SartM**

Invocation: "Dolphin plunge, fountain play." Louis MacNeice. **CP-MacNL**

Invocation: "Earth, ocean, air, belovèd brotherhood!" Percy Bysshe Shelley. **FiP; NAEL-2** *Fr.* Alastor; or, The Spirit of Solitude. **CP-ShelP**

Invocation: "Harp of the North! that mouldering long hast hung." Sir Walter Scott. **SP-ScotW** *Fr.* The Chase. *Fr.* The Lady of the Lake.

Invocation. John Milton. *See* Of Man's First Disobedience, and the Fruit.

Invocation: "Senator Smoot (Republican, Ut.)" Ogden Nash. **CP-NashO**

Invocation: "Soul of my soul, in the ancestral wood." Stanley Jasspon Kunitz. **CP-KuniS**

Invocation: "Through Thy clear spaces, Lord, of old." John Greenleaf Whittier. **CP-WhitJ**

Invocation: "Wasp, climbing the window pane." Howard Nemerov. *Fr.* Epigrams: "Wasp, climbing the window pane." **CP-NemeH**

Invocation, An: "Hear, sweet spirit, hear the spell." Samuel Taylor Coleridge. **CP-ColeS** *Fr.* Remorse.

Invocation and Conclusion. William Carlos Williams. **CP-WilW1**

Invocation for "The Map of the Universe." Nicholas Vachel Lindsay. **CP-LindV**

Invocation of Comus, The. John Milton. *See* The Star That Bids the Shepherd Fold.

Invocation of Death. Kathleen Jessie Raine. *See* Death, I repent.

Invocation, The: "Ye juster Powers of Love and Fate." Sir John Suckling. **CP-SuckJ**

Invocation to Evening. John Gould Fletcher. **SP-FletJ**

Invocation to Kali, The. May Sarton. **SP-SartM**
Concentration Camps, The. **BTR; SRLS**
Kingdom of Kali, The. **SRLS**
"There are times when." **SRLS,** *sect.* 1;
Time of Burning, The. **SRLS**

Invocation to Light. John Milton. *See* Hail holy Light, ofspring [*or* offspring] of Heav'n [*or* Heaven] first-born.

Invocation to Misery. Percy Bysshe Shelley. **CP-ShelP**

Invocation to Old Windylocks. Jean Garrigue. **SP-GarrJ**

Invocation to St. Lucy, An. Thomas Merton. **CP-MertT**

Invocation to the Earth; February, 1816. William Wordsworth. **CP-WorW2**

Invocation to the Faerie Queene. Edmund Spenser. *See* The Legend of the Knight of the Red Crosse, or of Holinesse.

Invocation to the Moon. David Herbert Lawrence. **CP-LawrD**

Invocation to the Muses. Edna St. Vincent Millay. **CP-MillE**

Invocation to the Social Muse. Archibald MacLeish. **CP-MacLA**

Invocation to Urania. John Milton. *See* Descend from Heaven [*or* Heav'n], Urania, by that name.

Invoice, The. Robert Creeley. **CP-CreeR**

Involved (The Spider). Louise McNeill. **SP-McNeL**

Inward coky assertiveness of the Spaniard seems to say, The. Spanish Privilege. David Herbert Lawrence. **CP-LawrD**

Inward Light. Samuel Taylor Coleridge. **CP-ColeS**

Inward parcels / Outward parcels. Kandy Express. Thomas Merton. **CP-MertT**

Io. Gerard Manley Hopkins. **CP-HopkG**

Io Baccho! William Carlos Williams. **CP-WilW2**

Io piùa ti amai che non mi amasti tu. Se Cossi Fosse. Christina Georgina Rossetti. *Fr.* Il Rosseggiar Dell'Oriente Canzoniere. **CP-RosC3**

Io venni luogo d'ogni luce muto. Canto 14. Ezra Pound. *Fr.* Cantos. **CP-PoCan**

Ion. Euripides.
"Birds from Parnassus, / swift." **CP-DoolH**

Iona. Kathleen Jessie Raine. *Fr.* The Holy Isles. **SP-RainK**

Iona ("How sad a welcome! To each voyager"). William Wordsworth. *Fr.* Poems Composed or Suggested During a Tour, in the Summer of 1833. **CP-WorW2**

Iona ("On to Iona!—What can she afford"). William Wordsworth. *Fr.* Poems Composed or Suggested During a Tour, in the Summer of 1833. **CP-WorW2**

Iona: the Graves of the Kings. Robinson Jeffers. **CP-JefR2**

Ione. Paul Laurence Dunbar. **CP-DunbP**

Iopas's Song. Sir Thomas Wyatt. **CP-WyatT**

Iota Subscript. Robert Frost. **CP-FrosR**

Iovis Omnia Plena. Anne Waldman.
"He catches my eye, my fancy." **SP-WaldA**
"Mature love you say but my wounds come out through inner temple." **SP-WaldA**

Iowa. Stephen Berg. **SP-BergS**

Iowa. Donald Davie. **CP-DavDo**

Iowa. John Updike. **CP-UpdiJ**

Iowa City Zoo. Jean Garrigue. **SP-GarrJ**

Iowa Déjà Vu. Richard Hugo. **CP-HugoR**

Iphigenia [*or* Iphigeneia] in Aulis. Euripides, *tr. fr. Greek.*
"And Pergamos, / City of the Phrygians." **CP-DoolH**
"Burnished-head / By burnished-head." **CP-DoolH**
Chorus of the Women of Chalkis. **CP-DoolH**
"Crowd of the Greek force, The." **CP-DoolH**
"It is not for me, the day." **CP-DoolH**
"Now sing, O slight girls." **CP-DoolH**
"Paris came to Ida." **CP-DoolH**

Iphigenia in Aulis. Agamemnon Speaks. Malcolm Lowry. **CP-LowrM**

Iphigenia: Politics. Thomas Merton. **CP-MertT**

Irate Songster, The. Kenneth Patchen. **CP-PatcK**

Ireland. John Hewitt. **CP-HewiJ**

Ireland. George Meredith. **CP-MerG2**

Ireland. Jonathan Swift. **CP-SwifJ**

Ireland is now our royal care. Apollo's Edict. Jonathan Swift. **CP-SwifJ**

Ireland with Emily. Sir John Betjeman. **CP-BetjJ**

Ireland's Own; or the Burial of Thomas Moore. Sir John Betjeman. **CP-BetjJ**

Irene. Samuel Johnson.
    "Aginst the Head which Innocence secures." **CP-JohnS**
    "Ambition is the Stamp impress'd by Heav'n." **CP-JohnS**
    "Aspasia, yet pursue the sacred Theme." **CP-JohnS**
    "At my Command yon' Iron Gates unfold." **CP-JohnS**
    "How Heav'n in Scorn of human Arrogance." **CP-JohnS**
    "Sons of *Greece*, The." **CP-JohnS**
    "Unhappy Lot of all that shine in Courts." **CP-JohnS**
    "What Plagues, what Tortures are in store for thee." **CP-JohnS**
    "Ye glitt'ring Train! whom Lace and Velvet bless." **CP-JohnS**

Irene ducks and runs amuck, The. George Meredith. **CP-MerG2**

Irene Gogle. Paul Zimmer. **SP-ZimmP**

Iride swordblade road *dutch purple*. Dutch White Iris. Louis Zukofsky. **CP-ZukLS**

Iris. Muriel Rukeyser. **CP-RukeM**

Iris. David St. John. **SP-StJoD**

Iris by Night. Robert Frost. **CP-FrosR**

Iris-Eaters, The. Muriel Rukeyser. **CP-RukeM**

Iris leaves / threes-in-one. Triplet. Archie Randolph Ammons. **SP-AmmoA**

Irish. Robert Creeley. **CP-CreeR**

Irish Airman Foresees His Death, An. William Butler Yeats. **CP-YeatW**

Irish and the Italians own the place, The. The Enemies of the Angels. John Berryman. **CP-BerrJ**

Irish Avatar, The. Byron. **CP-Byron**

Irish Bull, An. James McAuley. **SP-McAuJ**

Irish Catholic. Richard Eberhart. *Fr.* Attitudes. **CP-EberR**

Irish cheekbones and close-set eyes. Roy Fisher. **SP-FishR** *Fr.* Mystery Poems.

Irish Cliffs of Moher, The. Wallace Stevens. **CP-StevW**

Irish Dimension, The. John Hewitt. **CP-HewiJ**

Irish Glass. John Hewitt. **CP-HewiJ**

Irish Guards, The. Rudyard Kipling. **CP-KiplR**

Irish Headland, An. Robinson Jeffers. **CP-JefR2**

Irish Masque, The. Ben Jonson.
    "Bow both your heads at once, and hearts." **CP-JonsB**
    "So breaks the sun earth's rugged chains." **CP-JonsB**

Irish poets, learn your trade. William Butler Yeats. **OXAEP-2** *Fr.* Under Ben Bulben. **CP-YeatW**

Irish sea with the one ship on it. Your Pleasure in my Cemetery. James Liddy. *Fr.* Glass after Oblivion. **CP-LiddJ**

Irish Unionist's Farewell to Greta Hellstrom in 1922, The. Sir John Betjeman. **CP-BetjJ**

Irishman in Coventry, An. John Hewitt. **CP-HewiJ**

Irishman's Lament on the Approaching Winter, An. Robert Creeley. **CP-CreeR**

Irishman's Song, The. Percy Bysshe Shelley. *Fr.* Original Poetry by Victor and Cazire. **CP-ShelP**

Irkalla's White Caves. Kenneth Patchen. **CP-PatcK**

Iron. Carl Sandburg. **CP-SandC**

Iron and Stone. John Hewitt. **CP-HewiJ**

Iron Characters, The. Howard Nemerov. **CP-NemeH**

Iron Circle, The. John Hewitt. **CP-HewiJ**

Iron doors we shut on ammo rooms, The. Fort Casey, without Guns. Richard Hugo. **CP-HugoR**

Iron growing in the dark. Fist. Philip Levine. **SP-LeviP**

Iron hand it ain't no match for the iron rod, The. When He Returns. "Bob Dylan." **CP-DylaB**

Iron Hans. Anne Sexton. **CP-SextA**

Iron Horse. Allen Ginsberg. **CP-GinsA**

Iron Horse is rusting, The. The End of the Line. Thomas McGrath. **SP-McGrT**

Iron Landscapes (and the Statue of Liberty). Thom Gunn. **CP-GunnT**

Iron Mike. Charles Bukowski. **SP-BukC1**

Iron Palace. Robert Ranke Graves. **CP-GravR**

Iron Pot, The. John Hewitt. **CP-HewiJ**

Iron rails run into the sun, The. Slow Program. Carl Sandburg. **CP-SandC**

Iron rusts, and bronze has its green sickness; while flint, the hard stones. The Stone Axe. Robinson Jeffers. **CP-JefR2**

Iron Thoughts Sail Out at Evening. Malcolm Lowry. *Fr.* The Roar of the Sea and the Darkness. **CP-LowrM**

Iron thoughts sail out at evening on iron ships. Iron Thoughts Sail Out at Evening. Malcolm Lowry. *Fr.* The Roar of the Sea and the Darkness. **CP-LowrM**

Iron wheel hangs, The. The Old Colliery. Wystan Hugh Auden. **CP-AudWJ**

Ironies out of St. George's. Marsden Hartley. **CP-HartM**
    "Blandly she lies."
    "I am an island— / My mother was a mountain once."
    "Just one more / at the breast, she said—."
    "Like ice his blood."
    "Red targets blowing."
    "She had a way of doing."
    "Shepherd of the morning."
    "We are knitting now."
    "Where should we go."

Ironist, The. Donald Davie. **CP-DavDo**

Irony here, The. Tithonus. Derek Mahon. **SP-MahoD**

Irradiations. John Gould Fletcher.
    "As I wandered over the city through the night." **SP-FletJ**
    "Flickering of incessant rain." **SP-FletJ**
    "Houses of the city no longer hum and play, The." **SP-FletJ**
    "Morning is clean and blue and the wind blows up the clouds, The." **SP-FletJ**
    "My stiff-spread arms / Break into sudden gesture." **SP-FletJ**
    "Over the roof-tops race the shadows of clouds." **SP-FletJ**
    "Spattering of the rain upon pale terraces, The." **SP-FletJ**
    "Trees, like great jade elephants, The." **SP-FletJ**

Irrefutable, beautifully smug. Heavy Women. Sylvia Plath. **CP-PlatS**

Irregular rattle (shutters) and, An. The Master of the Golden Glow. James Schuyler. **CP-SchuJ**

Irrelevance characterizes the behavior of our puppy. A Kind of Music. Mona Van Duyn. **SP-VanDM**

Irreparableness. Elizabeth Barrett Browning. **CP-BroEB**

Irreproachable ladies firmly lewd. Edward Estlin Cummings. **CP-CummE**

Irresponsive silence of the land, The. Christina Georgina Rossetti. **NOBE; OBEV; OBNC; TrGrPo** *Fr.* The Thread of Life. **CP-RosC2**
    (Aloof.) **OBEV; TrGrPo**

Irreverent Thoughts. David Herbert Lawrence. **CP-LawrD**

Irreversible. Roy Fisher. **SP-FishR**

Irrevocable, The. Walter de la Mare. **CP-DeLaW**

Irritability unnatural. Arthur Hugh Clough. **SP-ClouA**

Irritations of comfort—, The. Provision. Roy Fisher. **SP-FishR**

Irvington. Frederick Morgan. **SP-MorgF**

Is / it / because there struts a distinct silver lady. Edward Estlin Cummings. **CP-CummE**

Is / Not. Margaret Atwood. **SP-AtwM1**

Is a condition. New England. William Carlos Williams. **CP-WilW1**

I's a-gittin' weary of de way dat people do. Faith. Paul Laurence Dunbar. **CP-DunbP**

Is a monstrance, / the blue dogs bay. The Moon Is the Number 18. Charles Olson. **CP-OlsoC; SP-OlsoC**

Is a nice month to be / born, don't you agree. November. James Schuyler. **CP-SchuJ**

Is all our Life, then, but a dream. Acrostic: Is all our Life, then, but a dream. "Lewis Carroll." **CP-CarrL** *Fr.* Sylvie and Bruno.

Is all peace a dove's peace? Pablo Neruda, *tr. fr. Spanish by* Ben Belitt. **SP-NeruP** *Fr.* Question Book.

Is an enchanted thing. The Mind Is an Enchanting Thing. Marianne Craig Moore. **CP-MoorM**

Is any grieved or tired? Yea, by God's Will. Mid-Lent. Christina Georgina Rossetti. **CP-RosC2**

Is Bliss then, such Abyss. Emily Dickinson. **CP-DickE**

I's boun' to see my gal to-night. On the Road. Paul Laurence Dunbar. **CP-DunbP**

Is *Death*, when evil against good has fought. William Wordsworth. *Fr.* Sonnets upon the Punishment of Death. **CP-WorW2**

Is even more fun than going to San Sebastian, Irún, Hendaye, Biarritz, Bayonne. Having a Coke with You. Frank O'Hara. **SP-OharF**

Is far out, umbilically extravagant. Key West. Richard Eberhart. **CP-EberR**

I's feelin kin' o' lonesome in my little room to-night. To the Eastern Shore. Paul Laurence Dunbar. **CP-DunbP**

Is 4 always 4 for everybody? Pablo Neruda, *tr. fr. Spanish by* Ben Belitt. **SP-NeruP** *Fr.* Question Book.

Is Germany's bestiality, in detail. The Mirrors. William Carlos Williams. **CP-WilW2**

Is he a blood relation of yours. Charles Henri Ford. **SP-FordC** *Fr.* Seven Poems.

Is Heaven a Physician? Emily Dickinson. **CP-DickE**

Is Helena's birthday: / she isn't getting any. Tomorrow. James Schuyler. **CP-SchuJ**

Is his sweet wife too faint to remember. Emily Dickinson. **SP-DickE**

Is Immortality a bane. Emily Dickinson. **CP-DickE**

Is is too late to touch you, Dear? Emily Dickinson. **CP-DickE**

Is is true, dear Sue? Emily Dickinson. **CP-DickE**

Is it a joyous expanse of Year. Emily Dickinson. **SP-DickE**

Is it a reed that's shaken by the wind. Calais, August, 1802. William Wordsworth. **CP-WorW1**

Is it any better in Heaven, my friend Ford. To Ford Madox Ford in Heaven. William Carlos Williams. **CP-WilW2**

Is it bad to have come here. Gallant Château. Wallace Stevens. **CP-StevW**

Is it dirty. Song. Frank O'Hara. **SP-OharF**

Is it enough? I'm Here. Theodore Roethke. **CoAP; NYBP** *Fr.* Meditations of an Old Woman. **CP-RoetT**

Is it for fear to wet a widow's eye. Sonnet 9. William Shakespeare. **MasP** *Fr.* Sonnets. **CP-ShaWS**

Is it for naught that where the tired crowds see. The Town of American Visions. Nicholas Vachel Lindsay. **CP-LindV**

Is it for Satan's, God's, or Nature's uses. New Weapons in the Old War. Howard Nemerov. **CP-NemeH**

Is it good in broad day to reflect on death? De Mortuis. James McAuley. **SP-McAuJ** *Fr.* Meditations of Afternoon.

Is It Happy? Stevie Smith. **CP-SmitS**

Is it illusion? or does there a spirit from perfecter ages. Arthur Hugh Clough. **EBEV; OBNC; OXAEP-2** *Fr.* Amours de Voyage. **SP-ClouA**

(Spirit from Perfecter Ages.) **OBNC**

Is it indeed so? If I lay here dead. Sonnet. Elizabeth Barrett Browning. *Fr.* Sonnets from the Portuguese. **CP-BroEB**

Is it Intellect that the Patriot means. Emily Dickinson. **SP-DickE**

Is it less than your brilliance, Ishtar. To Ishtar. Richard Wilbur. **CP-WilbR**

Is it my clothes, my way of walking. Disembarking at Quebec. Margaret Atwood. **SP-AtwM1**

Is it not by his high superfluousness we know. The Excesses of God. Robinson Jeffers. **CP-JefR1**

Is it not interesting to see. Thoughts about the Christian Doctrine of Eternal Hell. Stevie Smith. **CP-SmitS**

Is It Now Or For Always. Philip Larkin. **CP-LarkP**

Is it possible. George Washington. Louis Zukofsky. **CP-ZukLS**

Is it possible. The Maiden without Hands. Anne Sexton. **CP-SextA**

Is it possible. Sir Thomas Wyatt. **CP-WyatT**

Is it possible, poor kids, you must not come out? John Berryman. *Fr.* Sonnets to Chris. **CP-BerrJ**

Is it really a revolution, though? Lunch with Pancho Villa. Paul Muldoon. **SP-MuldP**

Is it so hard for men to stand by themselves. Intellectuals. Robinson Jeffers. **CP-JefR2**

Is it that in some brighter sphere. Fragment. Percy Bysshe Shelley. **CP-ShelP**

Is it that you feel not our dying? Hymn to a Trench Gun. Kenneth Patchen. **CP-PatcK**

Is it the Eternal Triune, is it He. The Wandering Jew's Soliloquy. Percy Bysshe Shelley. **CP-ShelP**

Is it the palm, the cocoa-palm. The Palm-Tree. John Greenleaf Whittier. **CP-WhitJ**

Is it, then, regret for buried time. Tennyson. **FHYEP** *Fr.* In Memoriam A. H. H. **CP-TennA**

Is it, then, your opinion. The Poet Ridiculed by Hysterical Academics. William DeWitt Snodgrass. **SP-SnodW**

Is it thy will thy image should keep open. Sonnet 61. William Shakespeare. **PoEL-2** *Fr.* Sonnets. **CP-ShaWS**

Is it tommorrow yet? To the Jewish People. Kenneth Patchen. **CP-PatcK**

Is It True? Anne Sexton. **CP-SextA**

Is it true that amber contains. Pablo Neruda, *tr. fr. Spanish by* Ben Belitt. **SP-NeruP** *Fr.* Question Book.

Is it true the ribs can tell. A Kind of Love, Some Say. Maya Angelou. **SP-AngeM**

Is it Ulysses that approaches from the east. The World as Meditation. Wallace Stevens. **CP-StevW**

Is it useful to have a mythology of death. Frederick Morgan. *Fr.* Death Mother. **SP-MorgF**

Is It Well with The Child? Christina Georgina Rossetti. **CP-RosC2**

Is It Wise? Stevie Smith. **CP-SmitS**

Is it worth while, dear, now. Long Plighted. Thomas Hardy. **CP-HardT**

Is Jove immortal / So is Cerberus at his portal. Ralph Waldo Emerson. **CP-EmerR**

Is life strife, is it the long combat? Battle of Life. David Herbert Lawrence. **CP-LawrD**

Is love so prone to change and rot. A Bed of Forget-Me-Nots. Christina Georgina Rossetti. **CP-RosC3**

Is made up of reservoirs. The Hard Structure of the World. Richard Eberhart. **CP-EberR**

Is melting an old frost moon. Dawn's Rose. Ted Hughes. **SP-HughT** *Fr.* Crow.

Is merry glory. Langston Hughes. Gwendolyn Brooks. **SP-BrooG**

Is much as before. Night. Afterward. James Schuyler. **CP-SchuJ**

Is murther no sin? or a sin so cheape. To Pontius Washing His Blood-Stained Hands. Richard Crashaw. **CP-CrasR**

Is my concern. That's this moment. The Overthrow of One o'Clock at Night. Muriel Rukeyser. **CP-RukeM**

Is my dress appropriate? American Glamour. Al Young. **CP-YounA**

Is My Heart Really Big As My Fist? Gary Gildner. **SP-GildG**

Is my team ploughing. Alfred Edward Housman. **CP-HousA**

Is not an absent friend as mysterious. Emily Dickinson. **SP-DickE**

Is not based upon ability. Courage. Richard Shelton. **SP-ShelR**

Is not for fire to tell. How Careful Fire Can Be. William Matthews. **SP-MattW**

Is not the distinction of Affection. Emily Dickinson. **SP-DickE**

Is not the messenger return'd? Marino Faliero, Doge of Venice. Byron. **CP-Byron**

Is not the wondrous sense of being flung. David Herbert Lawrence. *Fr.* Two Fragments on Sleep. **CP-LawrD**

Is not this house a harp whose living chords. Poem, Spoken Before the ΦBK Society, August, 1834. Ralph Waldo Emerson. **CP-EmerR**

Is not thy sacred hunger of science. To Mr. B. B. John Donne. **CP-DonnJ**

Is not to-day enough? Why do I peer. Fragment: Sufficient Unto the Day. Percy Bysshe Shelley. **CP-ShelP**

Is now a church parking lot, the church. Where the House Was. Richard Hugo. **CP-HugoR**

Is Now the Time? Robert Ranke Graves. **CP-GravR**

Is one game that no-one quits while he or she's ahead. The. Writing Poetry. Isabella Gardner. **CP-GardI**

Is Paris Burning? Inscribed on the Flyleaf of Richard Shay's Copy of Rimbaud's *Illuminations*. James Liddy. **CP-LiddJ**

Is pink and many-petalled: / it rests on the rim. The Rose of Marion. James Schuyler. **CP-SchuJ**

I's (Pronounced *Eyes*). Louis Zukofsky. **CP-ZukLS**

Is reform needed? is it through you? To a Pupil. Walt Whitman. **CP-WhitW**

Is she the star of one that is away? Fireside Reverie. George Meredith. **CP-MerG2**

Is shut / 22 hours a day and all day Sunday. The Pitt-Rivers Museum, Oxford. James Fenton. **FaBoMo** *Fr.* Exempla. **SP-FentJ**

Is small and stamped, / MADE IN ITALY. This Notebook. James Schuyler. **CP-SchuJ**

Is some such word / as the chord. Propriety. Marianne Craig Moore. **CP-MoorM**

Is such a touching child. Nature. John Updike. **CP-UpdiJ**

. . . is superficially / The same as a hotel, grand and de luxe. Fragment from Correspondence. Howard Nemerov. **CP-NemeH**

Is that an attitude for a flower, to stand. Hyacinth. Louise Glück. **SP-GlücL**

Is that dance slowing in the mind of man. The Dance. Theodore Roethke. **DIP** *Fr.* Four for Sir John Davies. **CP-RoetT**

Is that dance slowing in the mind of man. Four for Sir John Davies. Theodore Roethke. **CP-RoetT**

Is that despotism. Canto 33. Ezra Pound. *Fr.* Cantos. **CP-PoCan**

Is that the moon. Dream-Confused. David Herbert Lawrence. **CP-LawrD**

Is the basketball coach a homosexual lemon manufacturer? It is suspected by O'Ryan in his submarine. Aus Einer Kindheit. Kenneth Koch. **SP-KochK**

Is the color of our times. The Color of Stepped on Gum. Tom Clark. **SP-ClarT**

Is the confession of the leaf. Rapture. Marsden Hartley. *Fr.* Boston Portrait Projections. **CP-HartM**

Is the dilatory lightningbug more free. Prison Life. Charles Henri Ford. **SP-FordC**

Is the governor falling. The Brassiere Factory. Kenneth Koch. **SP-KochK**

Is the grandson / of Thomas L. Creeley, who acquired. I. Robert Creeley. **CP-CreeR**

Is the house not homely yet? The New House. Robert Louis Stevenson. **CP-StevR**

Is the man here, they said. Beauharnois. Margaret Atwood. *Fr.* Four Small Elegies. **SP-AtwM2**

Is the Moon Tired? Christina Georgina Rossetti. **CP-RosC2**

Is the pace of nature slow? Ralph Waldo Emerson. **CP-EmerR**

Is the rose the same after it is seen? Propositions. Richard Eberhart. *Fr.* Aesthetics after War. **CP-EberR**

Is the slim tall. Sandra. Charles Bukowski. **SP-BukC1**

Is the soul solid, like iron? Some Questions You Might Ask. Mary Oliver. **SP-OlivM**

Is the spider a monster in miniature? Spiders. Delmore Schwartz. **SP-SchwD**

Is the stair here? The Abyss. Theodore Roethke. **CP-RoetT**

Is then no nook of English ground secure. On the Projected Kendal and Windermere Railway. William Wordsworth. **CP-WorW2**

Is then the final page before me spread. Desultory Stanzas, upon Receiving the Preceding Sheets from the Press. William Wordsworth. *Fr.* Memorials of a Tour of the Continent; 1820. **CP-WorW2**

Is there a flower(whom). Edward Estlin Cummings. **CP-CummE**

Is there a hope, that man would thankful be. To Esmé, Lord Aubigny. Ben Jonson. **CP-JonsB**

Is there a modern reader that can measure up. *see also* Beetle, The. Leonard Cohen. **CP-CoheL**

Is there a moment when the moon explodes in autumn. The Moon Explodes in Autumn as a Milkweed Pod. Diane Wakoski. **SP-WakoD**

Is there a power that can sustain and cheer. William Wordsworth. **CP-WorW1**

Is there a solitary wretch who hies. On Being Cautioned against Walking on an Headland Overlooking the Sea, because It Was Frequented by a Lunatic. Charlotte Smith. **CP-SmitC**

Is there a spot on earth, / Where time is not? On Mesa Verde. John Gould Fletcher. **SP-FletJ**

Is there a story? Where. Of Time & the Body. David St. John. *Fr.* Study for the World's Body. **SP-StJoD**

Is there a whim-inspir'd fool. A Bard's Epitaph. Robert Burns. **CP-BurnR**

Is there an imagination that sits enthroned. Wallace Stevens. **HCAP** *Fr.* The Auroras of Autumn. **CP-StevW**

Is There Any Easy Road to Freedom? Carl Sandburg. **CP-SandC**

Is there anybody going to listen to my story. Girl. The Beatles. **CP-Beatl**

"Is there anybody there?" said the Traveller. The Listeners. Walter de la Mare. **CP-DeLaW**

Is there anything crazier in this life. Pablo Neruda, *tr. fr. Spanish by* Ben Belitt. **SP-NeruP** *Fr.* Question Book.

Is there anything emptier. The Drawer's Condition on November 28, 1961. Leonard Cohen. **CP-CoheL**

Is there, for honest poverty. Robert Burns. **CP-BurnR**

(Song—For A' That and A' That.) **CP-BurnR**

Is there no song that I can sing. Malcolm Lowry. **CP-LowrM**

Is this a fast, to keep. To Keep a True Lent. Robert Herrick. **CP-HerrR**

Is this a holy thing to see. Holy Thursday. William Blake. **CP-BlakW** *Fr.* Songs of Experience.

Is this a life, to break thy sleep? Paranæticall, or Advisive Verse, to His Friend, M. John Wicks. Robert Herrick. **CP-HerrR**

Is this a sentence passed upon us both. The Sentence. Robert Ranke Graves. **CP-GravR**

Is this all we know of the dark. The Cairn in Loch An Duin. Richard Hugo. **CP-HugoR**

Is this an airplane roaring in my room? Prelude to Another Drink. Malcolm Lowry. **CP-LowrM**

Is this man turning angel as he stares. The Messenger. Thom Gunn. **CP-GunnT**

Is this really me? Of course not, for Time. Interjection #1: The Need For Re-evaluation. Robert Penn Warren. **SP-WarrR**

Is This Seat Taken? Yes, or, My Neck Is Sticking In. Ogden Nash. **CP-NashO**

Is this Sir Philip Sidney, this loud clown. The Knight in Disguise. Nicholas Vachel Lindsay. **CP-LindV**

Is this that Name as ointment poured forth. King of Kings and Lord of Lords. Christina Georgina Rossetti. **CP-RosC2**

Is this the bliss for which you've tried to live? At the End of the Rainbow. John Updike. **CP-UpdiJ**

Is this the end? is there no end but this? / Yea, none beside. Standing Afar Off for the Fear of Her Torment. Christina Georgina Rossetti. **CP-RosC2**

Is this the Face that thrills with awe. The Descent from the Cross. Christina Georgina Rossetti. **CP-RosC2**

Is this the God of Gods, the one I heard about. Holy Ghost on the Nod over the Body of Bliss. Allen Ginsberg. **CP-GinsA**

Is this the Hope that opens and shuts. Emily Dickinson. **SP-DickE**

("This is the World that opens and shuts.") **SP-DickE**

Is this the land our fathers loved. Stanzas for the Times. John Greenleaf Whittier. **CP-WhitJ**

Is this the moment? / No, not yet. Linen. James Schuyler. **CP-SchuJ**

Is this the mouth of truth. The Mouth of truth. Lawrence Ferlinghetti. **SP-FerlL**

Is this the night the world must burn like Troy? Like Ilium. Thomas Merton. **CP-MertT**

Is this the region, this the soil, the clime. John Milton. **FF**, *ll.* 242–255; **TreFS**, *ll.* 242–263; **TEP**, *ll.* 242–270; **FiP** *Fr.* Book I. **FHYEP**; **NAEL-1**; **OAEL-1**; **OxAEP-1** *Fr.* Paradise Lost. **CP-MiltJ**

(Fall of the Angels, The.) **FiP**, *ll.* 242–263;

Is this the sir, who, some waste wife to win. To Sir Luckless Woo-All. Ben Jonson. **CP-JonsB**

Is this thy plighted, fond regard. Can You Leave Me Thus, My Katy. Robert Burns. **CP-BurnR**

Is this thy voice whose treble notes of fear. To a Southern Statesman. John Greenleaf Whittier. **CP-WhitJ**

Is this what we wanted. Margaret Atwood. *Fr.* Two-Headed Poems. **SP-AtwM2**

Is This What You Wanted. Leonard Cohen. **CP-CoheL**

Is this, ye Gods, the Capitolian Hill? At Rome. William Wordsworth. *Fr.* Memorials of a Tour in Italy, 1837. **CP-WorW2**

Is thy face like thy mother's, my fair child! Byron. **ChER; EnRP; OAEL-2** *Fr.* Childe Harold's Pilgrimage. **CP-Byron**

Is thy face like thy mother's, my fair child. Byron. *Fr.* Childe Harold's Pilgrimage. **CP-Byron**

"In my youth's summer I did sing of One." **NOBRP**

"Lake Leman woos me with its crystal face." **NOBRP**

"Sky is changed!—and such a change! Oh night, The." **NOBRP**

"There is a very life in our despair." **NOBRP**

Is Time on my hands? Yes it is, it is on my hands and my face and. Thoughts Thought While Waiting for a Pronouncement from a Doctor, an Editor, a Big Executive, the Department of Internal Revenue or Any Other Momentous Pronouncer. Ogden Nash. **CP-NashO**

Is to have an old but firmly painted name. To Die in Milltown. Richard Hugo. **CP-HugoR**

Is to leave all, and take the thread of love. Sonnet 2. Mary Sidney, Countess of Montgomery Wroth. *Fr.* A Crowne of Sonetts Dedicated to Love. *Fr.* Pamphilia to Amphilanthus. **CP-WrotM**

Is trying to sell cattle. He is like a man. The Formal Auctioneer. Ted Hughes. **SP-HughT**

Is what I wanted to write. A Little Uncomplicated Hymn. Anne Sexton. **CP-SextA**

Is where you find it. Maestria. Howard Nemerov. **CP-NemeH**

Is Wisdom a Lot of Language? Carl Sandburg. **CP-SandC**

Is without world. The Howling of Wolves. Ted Hughes. **SP-HughT**

. . . is worked this way. Release the striking arm. Instructions for Use of This Toy. Howard Nemerov. **CP-NemeH**

Is Your Love in Vain? "Bob Dylan." **CP-DylaB**

Is Zelot pure? he is: ye see he weares. Upon Zelot. Robert Herrick. **CP-HerrR**

Isaac and Archibald. Edwin Arlington Robinson. **CP-RobiE**

Isaac McKeown. John Hewitt. **CP-HewiJ**

Isaac Meek. Walter de la Mare. **CP-DeLaW**

Isabel. John Greenleaf Whittier. **CP-WhitJ**

Isabella of Austria. John Greenleaf Whittier. **CP-WhitJ**

Isabella; or, The Pot of Basil. John Keats. **CP-KeatJ**

Isaiah. Leonard Cohen. **CP-CoheL**

Isaiah, the country-boy, marched against the jazz. Babylon, Babylon, Babylon the Great. Nicholas Vachel Lindsay. **CP-LindV**

Ischia. Wystan Hugh Auden. **CP-AudeW**

Iseult of Brittany. Matthew Arnold. **SP-ArnoM** *Fr.* Tristram and Iseult.

Isfahan. Thomas Merton. *Fr.* East with Ibn Battuta. *Fr.* East. *Fr.* The Geography of Lograire. **CP-MertT**

Isidora. Christina Georgina Rossetti. **CP-RosC3**

Isis. "Bob Dylan" *and* Jacques Levy. **CP-DylaB**

Isis is dead: her fame is hid. Ashes in the Wind. John Hewitt. **CP-HewiJ**

Island, An. Elizabeth Barrett Browning. **CP-BroEB**

Island, The. Byron. **CP-Byron**

Island, The. James Dickey. **CP-DickJ**

Island. Langston Hughes. **SP-HughL**

Island. Langston Hughes. **SP-HughL** *Fr.* Lenox Avenue Mural.

Island, The. Randall Jarrell. **CP-JarrR**

Island, The. Alun Lewis. **CP-LewiA**

Island, The. Louis MacNeice. **CP-MacNL**

"First the distant cocks. A hairfine."

"Gorged on red, green, purple, tomatoes, peppers, aubergine."

"Our shadows now grow long in the sun."

"Which still is much. Here in this mountain village."

Island / Of the hungry bishop, The. James Liddy. *Fr.* Cliffs. **CP-LiddJ**

Island, An. Edwin Arlington Robinson. **CP-RobiE**

Island cast, An. After the Calamitous Convoy (July 1942). Donald Davie. **CP-DavDo**

Island Cemetery, An. Wystan Hugh Auden. **CP-AudeW**

Island Cross, The. Kathleen Jessie Raine. *Fr.* Eileann Chanaidh. **SP-RainK**

Island dreams under the dawn, The. The Indian to His Love. William Butler Yeats. **CP-YeatW**

Island (VIII), The. Pablo Neruda, *tr. fr. Spanish by* Ben Belitt. **SP-NeruP** *Fr.* The Separate Rose.

Island Folk Tale, An. John Hewitt. **CP-HewiJ**

Island Funeral. "Hugh MacDiarmid." **SP-MacDH**

Island Galaxy, An. John Ciardi. **SP-CiarJ**

Island in the Moon, An, *sels.* William Blake.

  Chapter Six.

  "Ah said Sipsop, I only wish Jack [*Hunter*] Tearguts had." **CP-BlakW**

  "Crowned king, A." **CP-BlakW**

  "Hear then the pride & knowledge of a Sailor." **CP-BlakW**

  "I say this evening [*we'd*] we'll all get drunk." **CP-BlakW**

  "I say this evening we'll all get drunk." **CBNP**

  "In the moon as Phebus stood over his oriental Gardening." **CP-BlakW**

  "O I say you Joe." **CP-BlakW**

  "Phebe drest like beauties Queen." **CP-BlakW**

  "Then the Cynic sung." **CP-BlakW**

  "Upon a holy thursday their innocent faces clean." **CP-BlakW**

Island in the Works. James Merrill. **SP-MerrJ**

Island of Catholic statues and Protestant writers. Cracks in the Pavement. James Liddy. **CP-LiddJ**

Island people first were mainland people, The. The Mainland. John Hewitt. **CP-HewiJ**

Island Quarry. Hart Crane. **CP-CranH**

Island (VII), The. Pablo Neruda, *tr. fr. Spanish by* Ben Belitt. **SP-NeruP** *Fr.* The Separate Rose.

Island (XVII), The. Pablo Neruda, *tr. fr. Spanish by* Ben Belitt. **SP-NeruP** *Fr.* The Separate Rose.

Island Sun. John Updike. **CP-UpdiJ**

"Island! That mark, South Bay; look—" "Yes", The. Not a Rootless Lily. Jenny Joseph. **SP-JoseJ**

Island Trashfires. Laurence Lieberman. **SP-LiebL**

Island (XII), The. Pablo Neruda, *tr. fr. Spanish by* Ben Belitt. **SP-NeruP** *Fr.* The Separate Rose.

Island (XX), The. Pablo Neruda, *tr. fr. Spanish by* Ben Belitt. **SP-NeruP** *Fr.* The Separate Rose.

Island with Army, Pines and Wind. Steve Griffiths. **SP-GrifS**

Islanded, my wife turned on the radio for news of home. On an Island. John Updike. **CP-UpdiJ**

Islander, The. Louise Glück. **SP-GlücL**

Islanders. Siv Cedering Fox. **SP-CedeS**

Islanders, The. Rudyard Kipling. **CP-KiplR**

Islands. Wystan Hugh Auden. *Fr.* Bucolics. **CP-AudeW**

Islands, The. Hilda Doolittle. **CP-DoolH**

Islands, The. Robert Earl Hayden. **CP-HaydR**

Islands, The. Randall Jarrell. **CP-JarrR**

Islands. Muriel Rukeyser. **CP-RukeM**

Islands. Derek Walcott. **CP-WalcD**

Islands and the mountains in the day, The. Percy Bysshe Shelley. **ChER** *Fr.* The Revolt of Islam. **CP-ShelP**

Islands dry out enlarging. Close Relations. Archie Randolph Ammons. **SP-AmmoA**

Islands in Penobscot Bay. Marsden Hartley. **CP-HartM**

Isle, The. Percy Bysshe Shelley. **CP-ShelP**

Isle Iranim. John Gould Fletcher. **SP-FletJ**

Isle of Man ("Youth too certain of his power to wade, A"). William Wordsworth. *Fr.* Poems Composed or Suggested During a Tour, in the Summer of 1833. **CP-WorW2**

Isle of Man ("Youth too certain of his power to wade, A"). William Wordsworth. *Fr.* Poems Composed or Suggested During a Tour, in the Summer of 1833. **CP-WorW2**

Isle of Man Wildflowers. Malcolm Lowry. **CP-LowrM**

Isle of Patmos. Carl Sandburg. **CP-SandC**

Isle of Portland, The. Alfred Edward Housman. **CP-HousA**

Isled in the midnight air. The Moth. Walter de la Mare. **CP-DeLaW**

Isle's Enchantress, The. Robert Browning. **CP-BroR2**

Isles of Greece, the isles of Greece!, The. Byron. **AWP; ChTr; FaBoEn; FaPoB; FaPoR; FiP; HBV; LiTB; NOBE; OBEV; OBRV; OBTV;**

OXAEP-2; RoGo; SeCeV; TreFS; WHA *Fr.* Canto the Third. *Fr.* Don Juan. **CP-Byron**

Isles of Greece, the isles of Greece!, The. Byron. **GrIP** *Fr.* The Isles of Greece, the isles of Greece! **AWP; ChTr; FaBoEn; FaPoB; FaPoR; FiP; HBV; LiTB; NOBE; OBEV; OBRV; OBTV; OXAEP-2; RoGo; SeCeV; TreFS; WHA** *Fr.* Canto the Third. *Fr.* Don Juan. **CP-Byron**

"Fill high the bowl with Samian wine!" **GrIP**

"Isles of Greece, the isles of Greece!, The." **GrIP**

Islet the Dachs. George Meredith. **CP-MerG1**

Isn't it nice (Diane Keaton). Snowdrops 1987. John Updike. **CP-UpdiJ**

Isn't it plain the sheets of moss, except that. Landscape. Mary Oliver. **SP-OlivM**

Isn't it poetical, a chap's mind in the dumps? Basil Bunting, *after the Persian of* Hafiz. **CP-BuntB**

Isn't she lovely, "the Mistress"? Lenten Thoughts of a High Anglican. Sir John Betjeman. **CP-BetjJ**

Isn't That a Dainty Dish? No! Ogden Nash. **CP-NashO**

Isobel's Child. Elizabeth Barrett Browning. **CP-BroEB**

Isolate city spread alongside water. Bridge for the Living. Philip Larkin. **CP-LarkP**

Isolation: To Marguerite. Matthew Arnold. **SP-ArnoM** *Fr.* Switzerland.

Israael in ancient days. Old-Testament Gospel. William Cowper. **ChIV-2; TrCP** *Fr.* Olney Hymns. **CP-CowpW**

Israel. Leonard Cohen. **CP-CoheL**

Israel. Karl Shapiro. **SP-ShapK**

Israel á la Begin, begins: "We." A Poem on the Middle East "Peace Process." Etheridge Knight. **SP-KnigE**

Israel, and you who call yourself Israel. Israel. Leonard Cohen. **CP-CoheL**

Israel's Lament. Samuel Taylor Coleridge. **CP-ColeS**

Israfel. Edgar Allan Poe. **CP-PoeEd**

Issue, Mood. Charles Olson. **CP-OlsoC**

Issue of Life, An. Howard Nemerov. **CP-NemeH**

Issues from the Hand of God. Charles Olson. **CP-OlsoC**

Issues from the Hand of God, the simple soul. Animula. Thomas Stearns Eliot. **CP-ElioT**

Istanbul. 21 March. I woke today. The Thousand and Second Night. James Merrill. **SP-MerrJ**

It. Gary Snyder. **CP-SnydG**

It ain't a woman. Da Boyg. Charles Olson. **CP-OlsoC**

It Ain't Me, Babe. "Bob Dylan." **CP-DylaB**

It ain't no use to sit and wonder why, babe. Don't Think Twice, It's All Right. "Bob Dylan." **CP-DylaB**

It ain't there. Come off it, Rousseau. Teaching Poetry at a Country School in Florida. Peter Meinke. **SP-MeinP**

It all began so easy. Christina. Louis MacNeice. *Fr.* Novelettes. **CP-MacNL**

It all begins with fear of *mana*. Comp. Religion. John Updike. **CP-UpdiJ**

It always felt to me—a wrong. Emily Dickinson. **CP-DickE**

It appears that each bare branch of this. The Bare Tree. Gilbert Sorrentino. **SP-SorrG**

It arose with him as a joke. Joke Gold. Carl Sandburg. **CP-SandC**

It baffles the foreigner like an idiom. Drug Store. Karl Shapiro. **SP-ShapK**

It beats love because there aren't any. Sweet Music. Charles Bukowski. **SP-BukC1**

It began with A—years before in a room. Robert Schumann, Or: Musical Genius Begins with Affliction. Rita Dove. **SP-DoveR**

It began with begging. The Fire Thief. Anne Sexton. **CP-SextA**

It begins quietly. The Deviation. Louise Glück. *Fr.* Dedication to Hunger. **SP-GlücL**

It begins when you smell a funny smell. Seaside Serenade. Ogden Nash. **CP-NashO**

It begins with one or two soldiers. Truce. Paul Muldoon. **SP-MuldP**

It beguiles— / This little Odyssey. Battle-Scene. Sylvia Plath. **CP-PlatS**

It being in this life forbidden to move. The Death-Wish. Louis MacNeice. **CP-MacNL**

It bends far over Yell'ham Plain. The Comet at Yell'ham. Thomas Hardy. **CP-HardT**

It Bids Pretty Fair. Robert Frost. **CP-FrosR**

It bloomed and dropt, a Single Noon. Emily Dickinson. **CP-DickE**

It blows a snowing gale in the winter of the year. Robert Louis Stevenson. **CP-StevR**

It Breaks. Marge Piercy. **SP-PierM**

It breaks my heart to sell this fruit. The Mad Applegrower. John Hewitt. **CP-HewiJ**

It burneth yet, alas, my heart's desire. Sir Thomas Wyatt. **CP-WyatT**

It burns in the void. The World. Kathleen Jessie Raine. **SP-RainK**

It came about that there was no way of passing. The Pursuit of Happiness. John Ashbery. **SP-AshbJ**

It came at last, a letter of true love. The Love Letter. Robert Ranke Graves. **CP-GravR**

It came at last but prompter Death. Emily Dickinson. **CP-DickE**

It came down to this: that merely naming the creatures. Channel 13. James Merrill. **SP-MerrJ**

It came his turn to beg. Emily Dickinson. **CP-DickE**

It came into her mind, seeing how the snow. Edna St. Vincent Millay. *Fr.* Sonnets from an Ungrafted Tree. **CP-MillE**

It came to me on the Nile my passport lied. Beni Hasan. Louis MacNeice. **CP-MacNL**

It came to me that all this time. Days and Nights. Kenneth Koch. **SP-KochK**

It came to me that all this time. The Invention of Poetry. Kenneth Koch. *Fr.* Days and Nights. **SP-KochK**

IT CAN BE beautiful this sitting by oneself all alone except for. Moon Watching by Lake Chapala. Al Young. **CP-YounA**

It can be done. The seal of frost. Working Outdoors in Winter. John Updike. **CP-UpdiJ**

It can be practically nothing, the nearly invisible. A Dread. Daniel Gerard Hoffman. **SP-HoffD**

It cannot be. Where is that mighty joy. The Temper (2). George Herbert. **CP-HerbG**

It cannot come because desired. Daniel Gerard Hoffman. **SP-HoffD**

It can't be "Summer"! Emily Dickinson. **CP-DickE**

It can't be the passing of time that casts. RIP. James Wright. **CP-WrigJ**

It ceased to hurt me, though so slow. Emily Dickinson. **CP-DickE**

It chanced his lips did meet her forehead cool. George Meredith. **CBLP; EnVR; NOBVV** *Fr.* Modern Love. **CP-MerG1**

It chanced that while the pious troops of France. The Dream of Pio Nono. John Greenleaf Whittier. **CP-WhitJ**

It chaunced me on day beside the shore. The Ruines of Time. Edmund Spenser. **CP-Spens**

It comes about that the drifting of these curtains. The Curtains in the House of the Metaphysician. Wallace Stevens. **CP-StevW**

It comes blundering over the. How Poetry Comes to Me. Gary Snyder. **CP-SnydG**

It comes in black. The Telephone. Maya Angelou. **SP-AngeM**

It comes oozing. The Evil Eye. Anne Sexton. **CP-SextA**

It Comes to This. Robert Pack. **SP-PackR**

It comes to you tonight. For Juan Rulfo. Chuck Miller. **SP-MillC**

It comes up out of the darkness, and it returns. Beyond the Pleasure Principle. Howard Nemerov. **CP-NemeH**

It comforts the Criminal little to know. Emily Dickinson. **SP-DickE**

It commonly sings. Xmas. Robert Creeley. **CP-CreeR**

It consoles the happy Sorrow of Autumn. Emily Dickinson. **SP-DickE**

It corners the sun and caroms one. Prism. Howard Nemerov. **CP-NemeH**

It could be a jaw-bone. Viking Dublin: Trial Pieces. Seamus Heaney. **SP-HeanS**

It could be, Christopher, from your leafed-in house. To Isherwood Dying. Thom Gunn. **CP-GunnT**

It could be like one of those dreams. Slipping Away. Stephen Dobyns. **SP-DobyS**

It could be that you are driving by. The Gap. Charles Tomlinson. **CP-TomlC**

It crossed my mind. Kathleen Jessie Raine. *Fr.* Monessie Gorge. **SP-RainK**

It darkened; I was cold. The Princess Wakes in the Wood. Randall Jarrell. **CP-JarrR**

It darted across the pond. The Catch. Stanley Jasspon Kunitz. **CP-KuniS**

It Depends on Whose Science. Kenneth Patchen. **CP-PatcK**

It depends who's talking if you're a 'Sabine'. Carmen 44. Catullus. *Fr.* Carmina. **CP-Catul**

It Did. Robert Lowell. **SP-LoweR**

It did not surprise me. Emily Dickinson. **CP-DickE**

It discovers by night. Poem, The. Donald Hall. **CP-HallD**

It does amaze me, when the clicking hour. Fragments. Gerard Manley Hopkins. **CP-HopkG**

It does for the time of man to walk here. S.P.Q.R. A Letter from Rome. John Ciardi. **SP-CiarJ**

It does no good to speak of the big, blue bush. Study of Images I. Wallace Stevens. **CP-StevW**

It does not come round in hundreds of thousands of years. Déjà Vu. Louis MacNeice. **CP-MacNL**

It does not impress me that I have. Will. Alice Walker. **CP-WalkA**

It does not know / its name. It sits. The Corner. Donald Hall. **CP-HallD**

It doesn't / matter. Substantial Planes. Archie Randolph Ammons. **SP-AmmoA**

"It doesn't get much light," the real. Change of Address. William Matthews. **SP-MattW**

It Doesn't Matter. Jim Carroll. **SP-CarrJ**

It doesn't show / how the cold edge of starlight. Old Map of Barnstable County. Brendan Galvin. **SP-GalvB**

It Don't Mean a Thing if it Ain't Got That Swing. William Matthews. **SP-MattW**

It don't sound so terrible—quite—as it did. Emily Dickinson. **CP-DickE**

It dreams in the deepest sleep, it remembers the storm last month or it feels the far storm. Ocean. Robinson Jeffers. **CP-JefR1**

It drifts out like / the essence of a tree. Woodsmoke. Brendan Galvin. **SP-GalvB**

It dropped so low—in my Regard. Emily Dickinson. **CP-DickE**

It ended, and the morrow brought the task. George Meredith. **EnVR** *Fr.* Modern Love. **CP-MerG1**

It ends with the painter. 16 Lines. Gilbert Sorrentino. **SP-SorrG**

It faces west, and round the back and sides. Domicilium. Thomas Hardy. **CP-HardT**

It falles me here to write of Chastity. The Legend of Britomartis, or of Chastitie. Edmund Spenser. **NAEL-1** *Fr.* The Faerie Queene. **CP-Spens**

It falleth like a stick. My Love. Robert Creeley. **CP-CreeR**

It falls onto my page like rain. Poem. Charles Tomlinson. **CP-TomlC**

It feels a shame to be Alive. Emily Dickinson. **CP-DickE**

It feels good as it is without the giant. Wallace Stevens. **MoPo; NOBA** *Fr.* It Must Be Abstract. *Fr.* Notes toward a Supreme Fiction. **CP-StevW**

It fell in the ancient periods. Uriel. Ralph Waldo Emerson. **CP-EmerR**

It fell in the days of old, as the men of Taiárapu tell. The Song of Rahéro: A Legend of Tahiti. Robert Louis Stevenson. **CP-StevR**

It Fell on a Summer's [or Sommers] Day [or Daie]. Thomas Campion. **CampT**

It Fell upon a Holy [or Holly] Eve. Edmund Spenser. **CBLP; InvP** *Fr.* August. *Fr.* The Shepheardes [or Shepeards or Shepherd's] Calender. **CP-Spens**

(Roundelay, A: "It fell upon a holy eve.") **EIL**

It Figures. Ogden Nash. *See* A Lady from near Rising Sun.

It Filled My Heart with Love. Stevie Smith. **CP-SmitS**

It fills me with elation. We Would Refer You to Our Service Department, If We Had One. Ogden Nash. **CP-NashO**

It finds the park first, and the trees. The Flood. Elizabeth Bishop. **CP-BishE**

It fits not only him that makes a book. To the Worthy Author on *The Husband*. Ben Jonson. **CP-JonsB**

It flatters and deceives thy view. To Demosthenis. *Unknown, tr. fr. Greek by* William Cowper. **CP-CowpW**

It flows out of mystery into mystery: there is no beginning—. Robinson Jeffers. **CP-JefR3**

It follows now you are to prove. Ben Jonson. **CP-JonsB** *Fr.* Pleasure Reconciled to Virtue.

It fortifies my soul to know. Arthur Hugh Clough. **SP-ClouA**

It fortuned (as faire it then befell). Edmund Spenser. **OAEL-1** *Fr.* The Faerie Queene. **CP-Spens**

It gets dark at four o'clock now. Dark at Four O'Clock. Leonard Cohen. **CP-CoheL**

It goes, all inside itself. It keeps touching. Machine. John Ciardi. **SP-CiarJ**

It goes, it / Goes. Song. Jim Carroll. **SP-CarrJ**

It got beyond all orders an' it got beyond all 'ope. That Day. Rudyard Kipling. **CP-KiplR**

It got to cost $1,000,000 to kill an Indian. The Nerves Are Staves, and When the Tears Come There Is Voice. Charles Olson. **CP-OlsoC**

It grew in the black mud. Rice. Mary Oliver. **SP-OlivM**

It grows cold in the forest. Choosing a Stone. John Haines. **SP-HainJ**

It had been easier, not loving. Ways. Alun Lewis. **CP-LewiA**

It had no name and we docked at midnight. / Its darkness spoke indecision and menace. On Reading R.L.S. Malcolm Lowry. *Fr.* The Roar of the Sea and the Darkness. **CP-LowrM**

It had no name and we docked at midnight. *sl. diff. fr.* On Reading R.L.S. Malcolm Lowry. **CP-LowrM**

It had to be, of course, a rock. The Rock-Old Dogma. William Carlos Williams. **CP-WilW2**

It hangs from heaven to earth. Tapestry. Charles Simic. **SP-SimiC**

It happened like this: I heard. How It Happened. Charles Tomlinson. *Fr.* Four Kantian Lyrics. **CP-TomlC**

It happened once, before the duller. Green Slates. Thomas Hardy. **CP-HardT**

It happened slowly / as a cygnet turns from grey to white. Changing Colour. Phoebe Hesketh. **SP-HeskP**

It happened this month, in this country. Cherries. Pablo Neruda, *tr. fr. Spanish by* Ben Belitt. **SP-NeruP**

It happened thus: my slab, though new. Bad Dreams IV. Robert Browning. **CP-BroR2**

It happened when they came to find our brother. The Image of True Lovers' Death. Thomas Merton. **CP-MertT**

It happening in that country that the King. Bad News. John Crowe Ransom. *Fr.* Two Gentlemen in Bonds. **SP-RansJ**

It happens. Will it go on? Paralytic. Sylvia Plath. **CP-PlatS**

It has a black throat. The Observation Tower. Lewis Turco. **SP-TurcL**

It has an edge, or many edges. Berlin in Ruins. Thom Gunn. **CP-GunnT**

It has been / a long flight. Like flak. The Pilot. Lewis Turco. **SP-TurcL**

It has been a long journey. The Edge of the River. Thomas McGrath. **SP-McGrT**

It has been a long time. The Orphan. Thomas McGrath. **SP-McGrT**

It has been raining now since. Rain Downriver. Philip Levine. **SP-LeviP**

It Has Been Said. Jim Morrison. **SP-MorrJ**

It has been snowing. Past nidnight, drunk on purple wine, you leave. A Winter Night. Georg Trakl, *tr. fr. German by* James Wright. **CP-WrigJ**

It has been well said that quietness. A Dog's Best Friend Is His Illiteracy. Ogden Nash. **CP-NashO**

It has disintegrated. At No Distance. Roy Fisher. **SP-FishR**

It has happened. In Fear of Harvests. James Wright. **CP-WrigJ**

It has happened suddenly. Je Suis une Table. Donald Hall. **CP-HallD**

It has rained like showers of arrows. Last Light in Clare's Mind. James Liddy. **CP-LiddJ**

It has taken me decades to realize. How I Got Started. Charles Bukowski. **SP-BukC3**

It has to be a hill. The Person as Dreamer: We Talk about the Future. Michael Hartnett. **PBCIP** *Fr.* Notes on My Contemporaries. **SP-HarMi**

It has turned cold. I have been gathering wood. Memoirs of the World. Thom Gunn. *Fr.* Misanthropos. **CP-GunnT**

It hath been questioned, Michael, if I be. The Vision of Ben Jonson, on the Muses of His Friend M. Drayton. Ben Jonson. **CP-JonsB**

It hath been said of old that plays are feasts. To the Reader of Master William Davenant's Play [*The Wits*]. Thomas Carew. **CP-CareT**

It hath been told. William Wordsworth. **EnRP** *Fr.* France (Concluded). *Fr.* The Prelude; Growth of a Poet's Mind [1850 vers.]. **CP-WorW3**

It held its head still. The Gray Heron. Galway Kinnell. **SP-KinnG**

It huddled there. Laventille. Derek Walcott. **CP-WalcD**

It interferes very little. On Going by Train to White River Junction, Vt. Jean Garrigue. **SP-GarrJ**

It Is. Stephen Berg. **SP-BergS**

It is a beauteous Evening, calm and free. William Wordsworth. **CP-WorW1**

It is a beauteous morning but the air turns sick. Tornado Warning. Karl Shapiro. **SP-ShapK**

It is a broken country. Wild Orchard. William Carlos Williams. **CP-WilW1**

It is a certain satisfaction to overlook a cemetary. On First Opening the Lyric Year. William Carlos Williams. **CP-WilW1**

It is a chilly god, a god of shades. Ouija. Sylvia Plath. **CP-PlatS**

It is a classic picture. Classic Picture. William Carlos Williams. **CP-WilW2**

It is a clearing deep in a forest: overhanging boughs. Johnson's Cabinet Watched by Ants. Robert Bly. **SP-BlyR**

It is a common fancy that trees are somehow conscious and. The Thought of Trees. Howard Nemerov. **CP-NemeH**

It is a cramped little state with no foreign policy. Shame. Richard Wilbur. **CP-WilbR**

It is a dawn quick as swallows. Awaken, Bells Falling. Lewis Turco. **SP-TurcL**

It is a day of the earth's renewing without any man's doing or help. Rain. Wendell Berry. **CP-BerrW**

It is a decade now since he and she. Provence. Louis MacNeice. *Fr.* Novelettes. **CP-MacNL**

It is a dim April. The Swan at Sheffield Park. David St. John. **SP-StJoD**

It is a dry word in a dry book. The Old Professor and the Sphinx. Lewis Turco. **SP-TurcL**

It is a fearful thing to fall into the hands of the living God. The Hands of God. David Herbert Lawrence. **CP-LawrD**

"It is a foolish thing," said I. Tolerance. Thomas Hardy. **CP-HardT**

It is a footprint / In sand or snow. Imprint. Phoebe Hesketh. **SP-HeskP**

It is a formal and deserted garden. Out of Time. Stevie Smith. **CP-SmitS**

It is a God-damned lie to say that these. *see also* Housman, "Epitaph on an Army of Mercenaries." "Hugh MacDiarmid." **SP-MacDH**

It is a good thing. Baskets. Louise Glück. **SP-GlücL**

It is a good thing to give thanks unto the Lord. Psalm 92. Bible, *O.T.* *Fr.* Psalms. **CP-Psal**

It is a hard thing to say that when I first saw. For Zadkine. Louis Zukofsky. **CP-ZukLS**

It is a hollow garden, under the cloud. Winter Swan. Louise Bogan. **CP-BogaL**

It is a human universe: & I. Ted Berrigan. **SP-BerrT** *Fr.* The Sonnets.

It is a hundred years since Parnell died from love. Notes towards an Ivy Leaf Video. James Liddy. **CP-LiddJ**

It is a hundred years since your shy feet. La Salette. Thomas Merton. **CP-MertT; SP-MertT**

It is a kind of chalky russet. Sandstone Keepsake. Seamus Heaney. **SP-HeanS**

It is a land with neither night nor day. Cobwebs. Christina Georgina Rossetti. **CP-RosC3**

It is a lie—their Priests, their Pope. The Confessional. Robert Browning. **CP-BroR1**

It Is a Living Coral. William Carlos Williams. **CP-WilW1**

It is a lonely walk into the mind's retreat. Kenneth Patchen. *Fr.* Eight Early Poems. **CP-PatcK**

It is a lonesome Glee. Emily Dickinson. **CP-DickE**

It is a lost road into the air. An Airstrip in Essex, 1960. Donald Hall. **CP-HallD**

It is a lovely sight and good. Woods in Rain. Wystan Hugh Auden. **CP-AudWJ**

It is a matter for the human will. Will. John Hewitt. **CP-HewiJ**

It is a maxim of much weight. William Cowper. **CP-CowpW**

It is a multiple million eyed monster. Lysergic Acid. Allen Ginsberg. **CP-GinsA**

It is a nation of nothing but poetry. Charles Olson. **CP-OlsoC**

It is a normal day. Poem Found Emptying Out My Pockets. Al Young. **CP-YounA**

It is a Pilgrim village; heavy rain is falling. Pilgrim Fish Heads. Robert Bly. **SP-BlyR**

It is a pity the shock-waves. Robinson Jeffers. **CP-JefR3**

It is a place. George Oppen. *Fr.* A Narrative. **CP-OppeG**

It is a place where poets crowned may feel the heart's decaying. Cowper's Grave. Elizabeth Barrett Browning. **CP-BroEB**

It is a poet's privilege and fate. Darien. Robert Ranke Graves. **CP-GravR**

It is a posture for two multiplied. Butterandeggs. William Carlos Williams. **CP-WilW1**

It is a quality of air, a temperate sharpness. At Holwell Farm. Charles Tomlinson. **CP-TomlC**

It is a real one—no more symbolic. The Castle. Charles Tomlinson. **CP-TomlC**

It is a satisfaction. Portrait of a Woman at Her Bath. William Carlos Williams. **CP-WilW2**

It Is a Small Plant. William Carlos Williams. **CP-WilW1**

It is a spiral way that trues my arc. Howard Nemerov. *Fr.* Quaerendo Invenietis. **CP-NemeH**

It is a Spring Afternooon. Anne Sexton. **CP-SextA**

It is a squad car idling. Lust. William Matthews. **SP-MattW**

It is a storm strid night, winds footing swift. Night-Time in Mid-Fall. Thomas Hardy. **CP-HardT**

It is a stubble field, where a black rain is falling. De Profundis. Georg Trakl, *tr. fr. German by* James Wright. **CP-WrigJ**

It is a Suffering, to have a sea. Emily Dickinson. **SP-DickE**

It is a summer evening. Lullaby. Anne Sexton. **CP-SextA**

It is a theatre floating through the clouds. Wallace Stevens. **HCAP** *Fr.* The Auroras of Autumn. **CP-StevW**

It is a waste of time to hate a mirror. Good Mirrors are Not Cheap. Audre Lorde. **SP-LordA**

It is a willow when summer is over. Willow Poem. William Carlos Williams. **CP-WilW1**

It is a winter's tale. A Winter's Tale. Dylan Thomas. **CP-ThomD**

It is a wonder foam is so beautiful. Spray. David Herbert Lawrence. **CP-LawrD**

It is a year of strategy. Clairvaux Prison. Thomas Merton. **CP-MertT**

It is accomplishèd. Eva B Hitler, geb. Braun. William DeWitt Snodgrass. **SP-SnodW**

It is afternoon   a sailor is crying above the waterfall. Jim Carroll. *Fr.* Living at the Movies. **SP-CarrJ**

It is all / Happening to the sun. West Laithe. Ted Hughes. **SP-HughT**

It is all a rhythm. The Rhythm. Robert Creeley. **CP-CreeR**

It Is All Around Me. Leonard Cohen. **CP-CoheL**

It is all here. The Shad-Blow Tree. Louise Glück. **SP-GlücL**

It is all much worse than I dreamed. Child in the Great Wood. Muriel Rukeyser. **CP-RukeM**

It is all right. All they do. To the Muse. James Wright. **CP-WrigJ**

It is all to clear that order wasn't our invention. Pot-au-feu. Mona Van Duyn. **SP-VanDM**

It Is Almost the Year Two Thousand. Robert Frost. **CP-FrosR**

It is almost unbearably harmonious. The Good Man. Mona Van Duyn. **SP-VanDM**

It is already late, my sister. Dreams. Randall Jarrell. **CP-JarrR**

It is already six. From the steeple. The Mausoleum. Charles Tomlinson. **CP-TomlC**

It is always a temptation to an armed and agile nation. Dane-Geld. Rudyard Kipling. **CP-KiplR**

It is always best, of course. Object Lesson. Charles Bukowski. **SP-BukC2**

It is always there. Food. John Updike. **CP-UpdiJ**

It is an accurate nose. Nose. Donald Hall. **CP-HallD**

It is an age. Giving It Up. Charles Kenneth Williams. **CP-WillC; SP-WillC**

It is an ancient mariner. The Rime of the Ancient Mariner. Samuel Taylor Coleridge.

It is an ancyent Marinere, *sl. diff. 1798 vers.* Samuel Taylor Coleridge. *See* The Rime of the Ancient Mariner.

It is an honorable Thought. Emily Dickinson. **CP-DickE**

It is an illusion that we were ever alive. The Rock. Wallace Stevens. **CP-StevW**

It is an orange / animal. The High-Rise of the New World. Charles Bukowski. **SP-BukC2**

It is Anguish I long conceal from you. Emily Dickinson. **SP-DickE**

It is as if a silver chord. To a Dead Friend. Paul Laurence Dunbar. **CP-DunbP**

It is as if at times. Marsden Hartley. **CP-HartM**

It is as one imagined it: an English garden. An English Garden in Austria. Randall Jarrell. **CP-JarrR**

It is as simple as it can be. What I Want to Say. Mona Van Duyn. **SP-VanDM**

It is as still as falling. Stone and Shadow. Lewis Turco. **SP-TurcL**

It is as though the thought of angels fell. Snow. Daniel Gerard Hoffman. **SP-HoffD**

It is as though three forms move on a road. To Whom It May Concern. Kenneth Patchen. **CP-PatcK**

It is as true as Caesar's name was Kaiser. An Equalizer. Robert Frost. **CP-FrosR**

It is at moments after i have dreamed. Edward Estlin Cummings. **CP-CummE**

It Is at Times. Robert Creeley. **CP-CreeR**

It is August moonlight in the tall plantation. A Hurried Meeting. Thomas Hardy. **CP-HardT**

It is August. Your father is walking you. 1940. William Stafford. **SP-StafW**

It is autumn and there are no flowers in this desert garden. The Near and the Far. Charles Tomlinson. **CP-TomlC**

It is autumn but early. No crow cries from the dry woods. Woodcut. Thomas McGrath. **SP-McGrT**

It is autumn still, but at three in the morning. October Week-End. Robinson Jeffers. **CP-JefR2**

It is bad enough crying for children. Charles Kenneth Williams. *See* Ten Below.

It is because of the savage mystery. Matador. Richard Eberhart. **CP-EberR**

It is beginning oh. Robert Earl Hayden. **CP-HaydR** *Fr.* The Snow Lamp.

It is best to begin in the morning with. Zimmer at the Diggings. Paul Zimmer. **SP-ZimmP**

It is better in the long run to possess an abscess or a tumor. Don't Grin, or You'll Have to Bear It. Ogden Nash. **CP-NashO**

It is better this year. If the Birds Knew. John Ashbery. **SP-AshbJ**

It Is Better To Go into Heaven with One Eye. Richard Crashaw. **CP-CrasR**

It Is Big Inside a Man. Kenneth Patchen. **CP-PatcK**

It is black night, spades. Cards. Gilbert Sorrentino. **SP-SorrG**

It is blue-butterfly day here in spring. Blue-Butterfly Day. Robert Frost. **CP-FrosR**

It is borne in upon me that pain. The Human Being is a Lonely Creature. Richard Eberhart. **CP-EberR**

It is certain that who his mind. Hafiz, *tr. by* Ralph Waldo Emerson. **CP-EmerR** *Fr.* Odes.

It is certainly the mystical hour of day. Solace. Richard Eberhart. **CP-EberR**

It is charged he's been known to warble. The Charges Against Cock Robin. William DeWitt Snodgrass. **SP-SnodW**

It is clear that the letters were whacked. From the Journal of Immutable Truths. Gilbert Sorrentino. **SP-SorrG**

It is cold. / The bitter of the winter. Winter Weather. Carl Sandburg. **CP-SandC**

It is cold in my refrigerator. A Lean and Hungry Look. Howard Nemerov. **CP-NemeH**

It is cold. The white moon. The Cold Night. William Carlos Williams. **CP-WilW1**

It is colder now. Epistle to Be Left in the Earth. Archibald MacLeish. **CP-MacLA**

It is common knowledge to every schoolboy and even every Bachelor of Arts. Portrait of the Artist as a Prematurely Old Man. Ogden Nash. **CP-NashO**

It is conceit that kills us. Conceit. David Herbert Lawrence. **CP-LawrD**

It is contagious as a dance. Franz, a Goose. May Sarton. **SP-SartM**

It is cool at night on the roofs of the city. Flat Roofs. Ernest Hemingway. **CP-HemiE**

It is curious I cannot feel it yet. The Beautiful Captive. Robinson Jeffers. **CP-JefR3**

It is curious, too, that though the modern man in the street. Robot Feelings. David Herbert Lawrence. **CP-LawrD**

It Is Dangerous to Read Newspapers. Margaret Atwood. **SP-AtwM1**

It is dark, *pencil version.* David Herbert Lawrence. *See* Glory of Darkness.

It is dark as a cave. The Clock-Winder. Thomas Hardy. **CP-HardT**

It is dark in the sky. Looking Across. Thomas Hardy. **CP-HardT**

It is dead. Find it. Emily Dickinson. **CP-DickE**

It is Death that consoles us and keeps us alive. Death of the Poor. James Liddy. **CP-LiddJ**

It is delicate that each Mind is itself. Emily Dickinson. **SP-DickE**

It is difficult now to speak of poetry. George Oppen. **NNaP** *Fr.* Of Being Numerous. **CP-OppeG**

It is difficult to read. The page is dark. Phosphor Reading by His Own Light. Wallace Stevens. **CP-StevW**

It is difficult to separate the tapestry. Tapestry. John Ashbery. **SP-AshbJ**

It is done! Laus Deo! John Greenleaf Whittier. **CP-WhitJ**

It is early afternoon. Your Face on the Dog's Neck. Anne Sexton. **CP-SextA**

It is easier to forgive an enemy than to forgive a friend. William Blake. **OAEL-2** *Fr.* Jerusalem; The Emanation of the Giant Albion. **CP-BlakW**

It is easier to look behind at a pain. Emily Dickinson. **SP-DickE**

It is easy, often, and natural even. In Trance At A Distance. Robert Ranke Graves. **CP-GravR**

It is easy to work when the soul is at play. Emily Dickinson. **CP-DickE**

"It is enough, enough", one said. Books In the Running Brooks. Christina Georgina Rossetti. **CP-RosC3**

It is equal to living in a tragic land. Dry Loaf. Wallace Stevens. **CP-StevW**

It is evening. One bat dances. A Soul. Randall Jarrell. **CP-JarrR**

It is fifty years now. The Pumping Engine, Cashwell. Wystan Hugh Auden. **CP-AudWJ**

It Is Finished. Christina Georgina Rossetti. **CP-RosC2**

It Is for Us the Living. Kenneth Patchen. **CP-PatcK**

It is forbidden to go further. Howard Nemerov. *Fr.* Seven Macabre Songs. **CP-NemeH**

It is Friday, a usual day. Gift for a Believer. Philip Levine. **SP-LeviP**

It is fun to ride the horse. Horse. Kenneth Rexroth. **NNaP** *Fr.* A Bestiary. **SP-RexrK**

It is funny—strange—to see the young. Robert Creeley. **CP-CreeR**

It is funny,you will be dead some day. Edward Estlin Cummings. **CP-CummE**

It is getting dark and time he drew to a house. Willful Homing. Robert Frost. **CP-FrosR**

It is globed. The Lampshade. Roy Fisher. **SP-FishR** *Fr.* Interiors with Various Figures.

It Is God that Moves in Your Heart. Al Young. **CP-YounA**

It is good for strangers. Flying Home. Galway Kinnell. **SP-KinnG**

It is good for strength not to be merciful. To a Young Artist. Robinson Jeffers. **CP-JefR1**

It is good to attend to the flesh and groom the pelt. LANDSCAPE: *Jungle Days* (Dutch). Jenny Joseph. *Fr.* Altarpiece (A Meditation on Lust, Desire and Love). **SP-JoseJ**

It is good to be last not first, / Pending the present distress. Lent. Christina Georgina Rossetti. **CP-RosC2**

It is good, when leaving a place. Seeking the Chosen. James Dickey. **CP-DickJ**

It is green, it is made of willow. The Day-Bed. Richard Eberhart. **CP-EberR**

It is half winter, half spring. In Excelsis. Anne Sexton. **CP-SextA**

It is hard going to the door. The Door. Robert Creeley. **CP-CreeR**

It is hard to be a man. The Falcon Woman. Robert Ranke Graves. **CP-GravR**

It is hard to fight / against one's heart's desire. Thomas Merton. *Fr.* The Legacy of Herakleitos. **CP-MertT**

It is here, the long Awaited bleap-blast light that Speaks one red toungue like. Television Was a Baby Crawling toward That Deathchamber. Allen Ginsberg. **CP-GinsA**

It is I, O Azure, come from the caves below. Helen. Paul Valéry, *tr. fr. French by* Richard Wilbur. **CP-WilbR**

It is I, Odysseus—Elpenor. Elpenor. Archibald MacLeish. **CP-MacLA**

It is *ignorant* money I declare. Wendell Berry. *Fr.* The Mad Farmer Manifesto: the First Amendment. **CP-BerrW**

It is impossible to know by your letter whether the wine is to be. From Dr. Swift to Dr. Sheridan. Jonathan Swift. **CP-SwifJ**

It is impossible to see anything. Inversely, As the Square of Their Distances Apart. Kenneth Rexroth. **CP-RexrK**

It is in captivity. The Bull. William Carlos Williams. **CP-WilW1**

It is in her eyes—the odd light. Dybbuk. Lewis Turco. **SP-TurcL**

It is in its way like bumping into. Scene Twelve: Take Seven. John Ciardi. **SP-CiarJ**

It is in the jungle one finds the secret springs. The Jungle. Richard Eberhart. *MoAB Fr.* Burr Oaks. **CP-EberR**

It is in the minds. Light Shall Not Enter. William Carlos Williams. **CP-WilW2**

It is in the orchard where a symbol flourishes. The Orchard. Richard Eberhart. *Fr.* Burr Oaks. **CP-EberR**

It is in the small things we see it. Courage. Anne Sexton. **CP-SextA**

It is in us they burn. Kathleen Jessie Raine. **SP-RainK**

It is Isis the mystery. Don Juan. David Herbert Lawrence. **CP-LawrD**

It is June, it is June. Andraitx—Pomegranate Flowers. David Herbert Lawrence. **CP-LawrD**

It is just what they would do eventually. Prudence Caution and Foresight: A Story of Avignon. Gertrude Stein. **CP-SteiG**

It is late at night and still I am losing. In Divés' Dive. Robert Frost. **VGW** *Fr.* Ten Mills. **CP-FrosR**

It is late December; I walk through the pasture. Out Picking up Corn. Robert Bly. **SP-BlyR**

It is like a monster come to dinner. Saturday Afternoon. Robert Creeley. **CP-CreeR**

It is like tanks come through Hungary and. Spain Sits Like a Hidden Flower in My Coffeepot. Charles Bukowski. **SP-BukC2**

It is like this perhaps. In Sickness Like Sleep. Thomas McGrath. **SP-McGrT**

It is likely enough that lions and scorpions. Ante Mortem. Robinson Jeffers. **CP-JefR1**

It is long now I met a man. Boston Common—Long Time Ago. Marsden Hartley. **CP-HartM**

It is low tide. Fog. I have climbed down the cliffs from Pierce Ranch to the tide pools. The Starfish. Robert Bly. **SP-BlyR**

It is made up of (in our latitude). Risk. Joseph Ceravolo. **SP-CeraJ**

It is May: 'A bad winter'. Providence. Charles Tomlinson. **CP-TomlC**

It is May on every hand. Bird Song. William Carlos Williams. **CP-WilW2**

It is midnight now, it is very still. Kilroy's Carnival; A Poetic Prologue for TV. Delmore Schwartz. **SP-SchwD**

It Is Morning. Joseph Ceravolo. **SP-CeraJ**

It is morning again in the west. John Haines. *Fr.* Roadways. **SP-HainJ**

It is most true that eyes are formed to serve. Sonnet 5. Sir Philip Sidney. **NAEL-2; NoSic; OAEL-1; OBSC; Son** *Fr.* Astrophil and Stella. **SP-SidnP**

It is most true that God to Israel, *par. by* Countess of Pembroke, Mary Sidney Herbert. Bible, *O.T. See* Psalm 73: "Truly God is good to Israel."

It Is Much. Carl Sandburg. **CP-SandC**

It is much like ocean the way it opens. Open Country. Richard Hugo. **CP-HugoR**

It is myself. To a Dog Injured in the Street. William Carlos Williams. **CP-WilW2**

It is na, Jean, thy bonie face. Robert Burns. **CP-BurnR**

It is nearly thirty years. John Haines. *Fr.* Homestead. **SP-HainJ**

It is never enough to know what you want. The Wish to Be Believed. Mona Van Duyn. **SP-VanDM**

It is night for the last time. The Letters. Louise Glück. **SP-GlücL**

It is night. You are asleep. And beautiful tears. Ted Berrigan. **SP-BerrT** *Fr.* The Sonnets.

It is no answer. Derivations. Jenny Joseph. **SP-JoseJ**

It is no answer. Translation. Jenny Joseph. *Fr.* Derivations. **SP-JoseJ**

It is no gift I tender. Alfred Edward Housman. **CP-HousA**

It is no longer necessary for sunlight. "E Pluribus Unum." John Yau. **SP-YauJo**

It is no longer necessary to sleep. A Man Walking and Singing. Wendell Berry. **CP-BerrW**

It is no longer night. But there is a sameness. A Tone Poem. John Ashbery. **SP-AshbJ**

It is no madness to say. Hilda Doolittle. **FaBoMo** *Fr.* The Flowering of the Rod. **CP-DoolH**

It is no night to drown in. Lorelei. Sylvia Plath. **CP-PlatS**

It is no spirit who from heaven hath flown. William Wordsworth. **CP-WorW1**

It is no vulgar nature I have wived. George Meredith. **NAEL-2** *Fr.* Modern Love. **CP-MerG1**

It is not a turtle. The Dead Heart. Anne Sexton. **CP-SextA**

It is not bad. Let them play. The Bloody Sire. Robinson Jeffers. **CP-JefR3**

It is not because we are going—. When We Say Goodbye. Thomas McGrath. **SP-McGrT**

It is not blasphemy to hope that Heaven. To Harriet ("It is not blasphemy to hope that Heaven"). Percy Bysshe Shelley. **CP-ShelP**

It is not death, O Christ, to die for Thee: / Nor is that silence of a silent land. Christina Georgina Rossetti. **CP-RosC2**

"It is not death that harrows us," they lipped. Spectres That Grieve. Thomas Hardy. **CP-HardT**

It is not difficult to come here. Thinking Rock. Kenneth Patchen. **CP-PatcK**

It is not difficult to kill. From My Notes for a Series of Lectures on Murder. Stevie Smith. **CP-SmitS**

It is not easy to die, O it is not easy. Difficult Death. David Herbert Lawrence. **CP-LawrD**

It is not easy to fall out of the hands of the livng God. Abysmal Immortality. David Herbert Lawrence. **CP-LawrD**

It is not enough. Finale. Louis MacNeice. *Fr.* Out of the Picture. **CP-MacNL**

It is not far from here to. The Desert of Melancholy. Lewis Turco. **SP-TurcL**

It is not for earthly bread, Annie. Annie. Christina Georgina Rossetti. **CP-RosC3**

It is not for her even brow. Song. Christina Georgina Rossetti. **CP-RosC3**

It is not for me, the day. Euripides, *tr. by* Hilda Doolittle ("H.D."). **CP-DoolH** *Fr.* Iphigenia [*or* Iphigeneia] in Aulis.

It is not four years ago. Proffered Love Rejected. Sir John Suckling. **CP-SuckJ**

It is not good to be poor. On the Road. John Haines. **SP-HainJ**

It Is Not Growing Like a Tree. Ben Jonson. **ChTr; HelP; ImPo; LiTB** *Fr.* To the Immortal[l] Memory [*or* Memorie] and Friendship of That Noble Pair[e], Sir Lucius Cary and Sir H. [*or* Henry] Morison. **CP-JonsB**

(Noble Nature, The.) **ArNa; GN; GTBS; GTBS-6; GTBS-P; PFP**

(Oak and Lily.) **TrGrPo**

(Part of an Ode, A.) **OBEV**

It is not in the books. The Three Movements. Donald Hall. **CP-HallD**

It is not life being short. A Winter Landscape Near Ely. Donald Davie. **CP-DavDo**

It is not long since, here among all these folk. Frost Flowers. David Herbert Lawrence. **CP-LawrD**

It is not music, though one has tried music. Words in a Certain Appropriate Mode. Hayden Carruth. **CP-CarHS**

It is not now I learn. Song. Louise Bogan. **CP-BogaL**

It is not only the ant that walks on the carpenter's board alone. "Out of the Rolling Ocean, the Crowd . . . ." Robert Bly. **SP-BlyR**

It is not only the present that is at stake. Statement by Willkie after Returning from England. Muriel Rukeyser. **CP-RukeM**

It is not pride, it is not shame. Emily Brontë. **CP-BronE**

It is not sleep itself but dreams we miss. The Dawn Chorus. Derek Mahon. **SP-MahoD**

It is not so much trying to keep alive. Prisoner at a Desk. May Sarton. **SP-SartM**

It Is Not So with Me. William Blake. **SeCePo** *Fr.* Vala; or The Four Zoas. **CP-BlakW**

It is not spring. The furnace. It's SPRing AgAIN! Charles Olson. **CP-OlsoC**

It is not the moon, I tell you. Mock Orange. Louise Glück. **SP-GlücL**

It is not the still weight. The Jungle. William Carlos Williams. **CP-WilW1**

It is not the things themselves. Margaret Atwood. *Fr.* Five Poems for Grandmothers. **SP-AtwM2**

It is not to be thought of that the Flood. William Wordsworth. **CP-WorW1**

It is not to tell you anything. My Greed. Leonard Cohen. **CP-CoheL**

It is not too soon to provide by every. Wendell Berry. *Fr.* The Mad Farmer Manifesto: the First Amendment. **CP-BerrW**

It is not vertue, wisdom, valour, wit. Woman. John Milton. **OBS** *Fr.* Samson Agonistes. **CP-MiltJ**

It is not what they built. It is what they knocked down. James Fenton. **SCBI** *Fr.* A German Requiem. **SP-FentJ**

It is not what they intend. The Fear of Angels. May Sarton. **SP-SartM**

It is not, y' are deceav'd, it is not blisse. Pentadius, *tr. fr. Latin by* Richard Lovelace. **CP-LoveR**

It is not yet the grey and frosty time. After the Night Office—Gethsemani Abbey. Thomas Merton. **CP-MertT; SP-MertT**

It is not yours, O mother, to complain. Robert Louis Stevenson. **CP-StevR**

It is nothing that you think it is. Little Bird Alone. Marsden Hartley. *Fr.* Word Arrangements for Pictures by Morris Graves. **CP-HartM**

It is November nineteen ninety-two. Matisse at the Modern, Magritte at the Met. Lawrence Ferlinghetti. **SP-FerlL**

It is now a decline. Kenneth Rexroth. **CP-RexKL** *Fr.* A Prolegomenon to a Theodicy.

It is now time for me to build a house. Homestead. John Hewitt. **CP-HewiJ**

It is odd, again, about the young. The Young Want to Be Just. David Herbert Lawrence. **CP-LawrD**

It is odd that the English. Encomium Balnei. Wystan Hugh Auden. *Fr.* Thanksgiving for a Habitat. **CP-AudeW**

It is of Realms unratified. Emily Dickinson. **SP-DickE**

It is one / thing. One Thing and Another. Archie Randolph Ammons. **SP-AmmoA**

It is one man alone, what. Gilbert Sorrentino. **SP-SorrG**

It is only immoral. Immorality. David Herbert Lawrence. **CP-LawrD**

It is only mourning for the lost. Antiquarian. Tom Clark. **SP-ClarT**

It is only that this warmth and movement are like. The Woman in Sunshine. Wallace Stevens. **CP-StevW**

It is over now, with no more need. In the Vestry. Robert Ranke Graves. **CP-GravR**

It is over the horrible pain. A Martyr. Christina Georgina Rossetti. **CP-RosC3**

It is over. What is over? Amen. Christina Georgina Rossetti. **CP-RosC1**

It is patent to the eye that cannot face the sun. Plurality. Louis MacNeice. **CP-MacNL**

It is people at the edge who say. Sayings from the Northern Ice. William Stafford. **SP-StafW**

It is portentous, and a thing of state. Abraham Lincoln Walks at Midnight. Nicholas Vachel Lindsay. **CP-LindV**

It is posed and it is posed. Add This to Rhetoric. Wallace Stevens. **CP-StevW**

It is possible, in words, to speak. Enough. Robert Creeley. **CP-CreeR**

It is possible that a change may come. "Hugh MacDiarmid." **SP-MacDH** *Fr.* England Is Our Enemy.

It is possible that most individual and international social and economic collisions. Are You a Snodgrass? Ogden Nash. **CP-NashO**

It is possible that to seem—it is to be. Description without Place. Wallace Stevens. **CP-StevW**

It is possible to rest here. Poetry. Al Young. **CP-YounA**

It is presumptuous and irresponsible to pray for other people. A. Wendell Berry. *Fr.* Prayers and Sayings of the Mad Farmer. **CP-BerrW**

It is quick it is far it is over it is. New Ribbon. Thomas Merton. **CP-MertT**

It is quite easy to appear modern. A Word on the Quick and Modern Poem-Makers. Charles Bukowski. **SP-BukC2**

It is raining. Self-Portrait 2. William Carlos Williams. **CP-WilW1**

It is really the most miniscule thing. Shaving. Stephen Dobyns. **SP-DobyS**

It is remarkable but it is no less painful for that, how rarely. O What a Revolution! Kenneth Patchen. **CP-PatcK**

It is right / to be exactly the way it is. For Your Birthday. Jim Carroll. **SP-CarrJ**

It is right in there. Peril of Hope. Robert Frost. **CP-FrosR**

It is sad that so many of worth. While Drawing in a Churchyard. Thomas Hardy. **CP-HardT**

It is said that he laughs at himself. Alzheimer's Disease. Donald Davie. **CP-DavDo**

It is said that man is gulled but I. Gulled. Richard Eberhart. **CP-EberR**

It is said the palace was modeled on a dream, but even what the. Two Kinds of Song. John Yau. **SP-YauJo**

It is seven years now that we first loved. The Scared Child. Robert Ranke Graves. **CP-GravR**

It is she alone that matters. Bouquet of Belle Scavoir. Wallace Stevens. **CP-StevW**

It is snowing and death bugs me. Oh. Anne Sexton. **CP-SextA**

It is snowing heavily across. Between Us. Stephen Berg. **SP-BergS**

It is so hard to be victorious. Biography. Edwin Rolfe. **CP-RolfE**

It is so long since my heart has been with yours. Edward Estlin Cummings. **CP-CummE**

It is so peaceful on the ceiling! Sleeping on the Ceiling. Elizabeth Bishop. **CP-BishE**

It is so rare and new a thing to see. To His Much Honoured the Lord Lepington upon His Translation of Malvezzi, His "Romulus" and "Tarquin." Sir John Suckling. **CP-SuckJ**

It is so small a thing. Matthew Arnold. **OBEV; OBVV** *Fr.* Empedocles on Etna. **SP-ArnoM**

(Hymn of Empedocles.) **OBEV**

It is solemn to remember. Emily Dickinson. **SP-DickE**

It is some school, brick, green, a sleepy hill. An Officers' Prison Camp Seen from a Troop-Train. Randall Jarrell. **CP-JarrR**

It is some time since I have been. The Hill. Robert Creeley. **CP-CreeR**

It is something to face the sun and know you are free. Clean Hands. Carl Sandburg. **CP-SandC**

It is sometimes refreshing. *see also* News You Really Hate, The. Leonard Cohen. **CP-CoheL**

It is spring. Interests of 1926. William Carlos Williams. **CP-WilW1**

It is Spring in the Common. Resistance Meeting: Boston Common. Jean Garrigue. **SP-GarrJ**

It is still as distinct as Paradise. Emily Dickinson. **SP-DickE**

It is stormy, and raindrops cling like silver bees to the panes. Discipline. David Herbert Lawrence. **CP-LawrD**

It is strange that I should want. Prisoners. Hilda Doolittle. **CP-DoolH**

It is strange to think of the Annas, the Vronskys, the Pierres, all the Tolstoyan lot wiped out. Fate and the Younger Generation. David Herbert Lawrence. **CP-LawrD**

It is such a beautiful day I had to write you a letter. Thoughts of a Young Girl. John Ashbery. **SP-AshbJ**

It is sufficient if we pray. His Wish. Robert Herrick. **CP-HerrR**

It is summer, it is warm in the city square. Winter's Ghost Plagues Them. Edwin Rolfe. **CP-RolfE**

It is summer, winter, any. Birds and Flowers. William Carlos Williams. **CP-WilW1**

It is summertime. L'Homme et La Bête. Philip Levine. **SP-LeviP**

It is Sunday afternoon. At the End of the Weekend. Ted Kooser. **SP-KoosT**

It is Sunday, day of roughhousing. We are let out in the woods. Kentucky, 1833. Rita Dove. **SP-DoveR**

It is supernal what a youth can take. Down & Back. John Berryman. **CP-BerrJ**

It Is Teeming. Charles Kenneth Williams. **CP-WillC**

It is ten years, now, since we rowed to Children's Island. The Babysitters. Sylvia Plath. **SP-PlatS**

It is *that* light. George Oppen. *Fr.* Of Being Numerous. **CP-OppeG**

It is the air of atrocity. George Oppen. *Fr.* Of Being Numerous. **CP-OppeG**

It is the bird of burial. Oh Stubborn Race of Cadmus' Seed. Stevie Smith. **CP-SmitS**

It is the cause the cause, still, it is (and she, still). The Cause, the Cause. Charles Olson. **CP-OlsoC**

It is the continuous welling up from the earth. Ichetucknee. Richard Eberhart. **CP-EberR**

It is the daily love, grass high. Healall. William Carlos Williams. **CP-WilW1**

It is the day when all the sons of God. Hellas. Percy Bysshe Shelley. **CP-ShelP**

It is the day when he was born. Tennyson. **EBVV; FHYEP** *Fr.* In Memoriam A. H. H. **CP-TennA**

It is the end of the grape. A Song at the Winepresses. Kenneth Rexroth. **CP-RexKL**

It is the evening. Nativity Poem. Louise Glück. **SP-GlücL**

It is the fashion now to wave aside. Edna St. Vincent Millay. **CP-MillE**

It is the first day of the world. The Venetian Blind. Randall Jarrell. **CP-JarrR**

It is the first mild day of March. To My Sister. William Wordsworth. **CP-WorW1**

It is the greatness of Thy love, dear Lord, that we would celebrate. Passiontide. Christina Georgina Rossetti. **CP-RosC2**

It is the hour of indecision. From a Record of Disappointment. Howard Nemerov. **CP-NemeH**

It is the hour when all is dark and still. The Hour of Peace. John Gould Fletcher. **SP-FletJ**

It is the hour when from the boughs. Parisina. Byron. **CP-Byron**

It Is the Hush of Night. Byron. **LiTB; MeMBP** *Fr.* Childe Harold's Pilgrimage. **CP-Byron**

Lake Leman ("Clear, placid Leman! thy contrasted lake"). **OBNC**

It is the hush of night, and all between. It Is the Hush of Night. Byron. **LiTB; MeMBP** *Fr.* Childe Harold's Pilgrimage. **CP-Byron**

It is the lawyer's daughter. The Lyceum. "Lewis Carroll." **CP-CarrL**

It is the Meek that Valor wear. Emily Dickinson. **SP-DickE**

It is the moon that disappears. Guru. Allen Ginsberg. **CP-GinsA**

It is the Old Man through the sleeping town. The Fall Again. Howard Nemerov. **CP-NemeH**

It is the opposite or so of the friendly gossip from upstairs who stops by every other evening. End of Drought. Charles Kenneth Williams. **SP-WillC**

It is the poem, yes. Work, for the Day Is Coming. Muriel Rukeyser. **CP-RukeM**

It is the responsibility of society to let the poet be a poet. Responsibility. Grace Paley. **CP-PaleG**

It is the sea, in the earth. Rosebushes. Juan Ramón Jiménez. *Fr.* Ten Short Poems. **CP-WrigJ**

It is the season now to go. Robert Louis Stevenson. **CP-StevR**

It is the season of the sweet wild rose. George Meredith. **GBL; NBM; PoEL-5** *Fr.* Modern Love. **CP-MerG1**

It is the sense / of things that we must include. The Impalpabilities. Charles Tomlinson. **CP-TomlC**

It is the shoes that show the breaking point. Receivers of the World's Attention. Stephen Dobyns. **SP-DobyS**

It is the sink of the afternoon. Sowing. Audre Lorde. **SP-LordA**

It is the sinking of things. Rain. James Wright. **CP-WrigJ**

It Is the Sinner's Dust-Tongued Bell. Dylan Thomas. **CP-ThomD**

It is the sixth year of the war in China. Muriel Rukeyser. **CP-RukeM**

It is the unregarded congruence. History. Charles Tomlinson. **CP-TomlC**

It is the very bewitching hour of eight. Hendecasyllables. Stevie Smith. **CP-SmitS**

It is the whales that drive. Fish. William Carlos Williams. **CP-WilW1**

It is the word *pejorative* that hurts. Sailing after Lunch. Wallace Stevens. **CP-StevW**

It is the young fresh rainy leaf. George Meredith. **CP-MerG2**

It Is There. Muriel Rukeyser. **CP-RukeM**

It is there, above him, beyond, behind. The Being. James Dickey. **CP-DickJ**

It is there where the worm has egress. Gravepiece. Jean Garrigue. **SP-GarrJ**

It is this that you get for being so far-sighted. Not so many years. The Road to the Past. Edna St. Vincent Millay. **CP-MillE**

It Is This Way with Men. Charles Kenneth Williams. **CP-WillC; SP-WillC**

It is time for all the heroes to go home. Allegiances. William Stafford. **SP-StafW**

It is time for applause. My hands rest. My Hands. William Stafford. **SP-StafW**

It is time for grandfathering. Grandfathering. Richard Shelton. *Fr.* Three Poems For A Twenty-Fifth Anniversary. **SP-ShelR**

It is time for the others to come. The Magus. James Dickey. **CP-DickJ**

It is time, heart, to recall. Kathleen Jessie Raine. *Fr.* The Hollow Hill. **SP-RainK**

It is time I came back to my real life. Return. May Sarton. **SP-SartM**

It is time men took their thoughts off women. Love as an Escape. David Herbert Lawrence. **CP-LawrD**

It is time that beats in the breast and it is time. The Pure Good of Theory. Wallace Stevens. **CP-StevW**

It is time the big bird with the angry neck. The Phoenix. May Sarton. **SP-SartM**

It is time to be old. Terminus. Ralph Waldo Emerson. **CP-EmerR**

It is time to break a house. Divorced, Husband Demolishes Home. John Ciardi. **SP-CiarJ**

It is time to drive in the hills. A Day in Late October. Mona Van Duyn. **SP-VanDM**

It is time to write a poem. Poem. Lewis Turco. **SP-TurcL**

It is time we should accept. Archibald MacLeish. *Fr.* Hamlet of A. Macleish. **CP-MacLA**

It is to make a fill, not find a land. Toward a Definition of Marriage. Mona Van Duyn. **SP-VanDM**

It Is to You I Turn. Leonard Cohen. **CP-CoheL**

It is too easy not to like. J, My Good Friend (Another Foolish Innocent). Alice Walker. **CP-WalkA**

It Is Too Late. Henry Wadsworth Longfellow. **BLPL; PoLF** *Fr.* Morituri Salutamus. **SP-LongH**

(Too Late?) **WBLP**

It is too late for the ambiguous thrush. Ultimate Song. Richard Eberhart. **CP-EberR**

It is too late to call thee now. Emily Brontë. **CP-BronE**

It is true--/ I've always loved. Alice Walker. **NMM; PoBA** *Fr.* Once. **CP-WalkA**

It is true, that even in the best-run state. The Murder of William Remington. Howard Nemerov. **CP-NemeH**

It is true that half the glory is gone. Salvage. Robinson Jeffers. **CP-JefR3**

It is true that, older than man and ages to outlast him, the Pacific surf. Gray Weather. Robinson Jeffers. **CP-JefR2**

It is true that rivers went nosing like swine. Frogs Eat Butterflies. Snakes Eat Frogs. Hogs Eat Snakes. Men Eat Hogs. Wallace Stevens. **CP-StevW**

It is true that you have been cast adrift because of me. The Servants of the Emperor. Siv Cedering Fox. **SP-CedeS**

It is 12:10 in New York and I am wondering. Adieu to Norman, Bon Jour to Joan and Jean-Paul. Frank O'Hara. **SP-OharF**

It is 12:20 in New York a Friday. The Day Lady Died. Frank O'Hara. **SP-OharF**

It is two hundred years since he got in his stride. The Newest Bath Guide. Sir John Betjeman. **CP-BetjJ**

It is unwise. The Photograph. Lewis Turco. **SP-TurcL**

It is useless, good woman, useless: the spark fails me. Death of Franco of Cologne, The: His Prophecy of Beethoven. William Carlos Williams. **CP-WilW1**

It is very meritorious to work very hard in a garden. What Does She See When She Shuts Her Eyes. Gertrude Stein. **CP-SteiG**

It is very nice to think. A Thought. Robert Louis Stevenson. **CP-StevR**

It is very wrong that you were ill. Emily Dickinson. **SP-DickE**

It is war. They put us on a train and. How It Is. William Stafford. **SP-StafW**

It is well the widow is gone, for here winter's. The Bear and the Last Person to Remember. Robert Penn Warren. *Fr.* Fall Comes in Back-Country Vermont. **SP-WarrR**

It is well to be disciplined in all the social usages. Behaviour. David Herbert Lawrence. **CP-LawrD**

It is what he does not know. On a Squirrel Crossing the Road in Autumn, in New England. Richard Eberhart. **CP-EberR**

It is what I never quite understood. A Testament. Richard Eberhart. **CP-EberR**

It is winter a moon in the afternoon. Edward Estlin Cummings. **CP-CummE**

It is winter, ending on earth. For Elizabeth. Jim Carroll. **SP-CarrJ**

It is winter. We have ransacked. Winter. Charles Tomlinson. **CP-TomlC**

It is with a strange malice. The Weeping Burgher. Wallace Stevens. **CP-StevW**

It is with terror that the jeweled bat. The Jeweled Bat. Charles Henri Ford. *Fr.* For Djuna Barnes. **SP-FordC**

It is with the poet as with a guinea worm. To a Friend and Fellow Poet. "Hugh MacDiarmid." **SP-MacDH**

It is worth it to get. Drifting. James Dickey. **CP-DickJ**

It Is Writing. Roy Fisher. **SP-FishR**

It is written in the Book of Usable Minutes. Train Rising Out of the Sea. John Ashbery. **SP-AshbJ**

It is You have borne the shame and sorrow. Last Words to Muriel. David Herbert Lawrence. **CP-LawrD**

It is you who have made light crawl. Lazarus to the Assembled. James Dickey. **CP-DickJ**

It is yourself you seek. Man Alone. Louise Bogan. **CP-BogaL**

It isna fair to my wife and weans. Hokum. "Hugh MacDiarmid." **SP-MacDH**

It isn't easy running through the halls. A Nice Place. Charles Bukowski. **SP-BukC2**

It isn't even interesting. My Children Going. Dabney Stuart. **SP-StuaD**

It isn't my word but my mother's. Charles Olson. **CP-OlsoC**

It isn't supposed to happen. Snow in May. Marge Piercy. **SP-PierM**

It isn't the body. The Inner Man. Charles Simic. **SP-SimiC**

It isn't very far as highways lie. Going to Walden. Mary Oliver. **SP-OlivM**

It! It! / That's what the unknown bird said. Forest Birds. Charles Simic. **SP-SimiC**

It just says 'church' on the map. Trumpan. Richard Hugo. **CP-HugoR**

It keeps eternal whisperings around. On the Sea. John Keats. **CP-KeatJ**

It keeps out everything! It goes. The Umbrella. Donald Hall. **CP-HallD**

It kept treading air, as if it were a ghost with claims on us. Visitant. Seamus Heaney. **SP-HeanS**

It kissed us, soft, to cut our throats, this coast. Not to Live. John Berryman. **CP-BerrJ**

It knew no lapse, nor Diminution. Emily Dickinson. **CP-DickE**

It knew no Medicine. Emily Dickinson. **CP-DickE**

It lies not in our power to love, or hate. Christopher Marlowe. **BLPL; EBEvV; FaFP; ImPo; LiTB; TrGrPo; WHA** *Fr.* Hero and Leander. **CP-MarlC**

(Who Ever Loved, That Loved Not at First Sight?) **BLPL; FaFP; ImPo; LiTB**

It lies on its side in the grassy Mall. Vietnam Memorial. Karl Shapiro. **SP-ShapK**

It lieth, gazing on the midnight sky. On the Medusa of Leonardo da Vinci in the Florentine Gallery. Percy Bysshe Shelley. **CP-ShelP**

It little profits that an idle king. Ulysses. Tennyson. **CP-TennA**

It Looks As If It Were Just Sleeping. Leonard Nathan. **SP-NathL**

It looks like to me. Little Green Tree. Langston Hughes. **SP-HughL**

It looks like we are the Last Unmarried. Country & Western II. Marilyn Hacker. **SP-HackM**

It makes no difference abroad. Emily Dickinson. **CP-DickE**

It makes so little difference, at so much more. Long and Sluggish Lines. Wallace Stevens. **CP-StevW**

It matters not that we shall cease to be. Sonnet II. Wystan Hugh Auden. **CP-AudWJ**

It may be good, like it who list. Sir Thomas Wyatt. **CP-WyatT**

It may be grubs / and worms and. Roads. Robert Creeley. **CP-CreeR**

It may be misery not to sing at all. Life's Tragedy. Paul Laurence Dunbar. **CP-DunbP**

It may be the sea-moving moon. Near Darien. James Dickey. **CP-DickJ**

It may happen again—this much. The Flight. John Haines. **SP-HainJ**

It may have been she came to show you. Emily Dickinson. **SP-DickE**

It may have been the pride in me for aught. The Corridor. Edwin Arlington Robinson. **CP-RobiE**

It may indeed be phantasy, when I. To Nature. Samuel Taylor Coleridge. **CP-ColeS**

It may not always be so; and i say. Edward Estlin Cummings. **CP-CummE; SP-CummE**

It may not cover all theodicy. Zander on God. Howard Nemerov. **CP-NemeH**

It might be anywhere. A Lighthouse in Maine. Derek Mahon. **SP-MahoD**

It might be fun to have a kid that I could kick around. Beginning of a Great Adventure. "Lou Reed." **SP-ReedL**

It might be lonelier. Emily Dickinson. **CP-DickE**

It might be that horses would be useful. Fence Posts. Gary Snyder. **CP-SnydG**

It might have been white paint. The Ambassador. Gilbert Sorrentino. **SP-SorrG**

It mounts at sea, a concave wall. From the Wave. Thom Gunn. **CP-GunnT**

It Must All Be Done Over. John Haines. **SP-HainJ**

It Must Be Abstract. Wallace Stevens. *Fr.* Notes toward a Supreme Fiction. **CP-StevW**

   "Begin, ephebe, by perceiving the idea." **NOBA**

   "First idea was not our own, The. Adam." **NOBA**

   "It feels good as it is without the giant." **MoPo; NOBA**

   "Major abstraction is the idea of man, The." **NOBA**

It Must Be the Milk. Ogden Nash. **CP-NashO**

It Must Change. Wallace Stevens. *Fr.* Notes toward a Supreme Fiction. **CP-StevW**

   "Bethou me, said sparrow, to the crackled blade." **LiTM; MoPo**

   Great Statue of the General Du Puy, The. **LiTA**

   President Ordains the Bee to Be, The. **LiTA**

   Two Things of Opposite Natures Seem to Depend. **MeMAP**

It Must Give Pleasure. Wallace Stevens. *Fr.* Notes toward a Supreme Fiction. **CP-StevW**

   Whistle Aloud, Too Weedy Wren. **LiTA**

It must have been a profound and a serene communion. The Parker River. Richard Eberhart. **CP-EberR**

It must have been as if he had come. Emily Dickinson. **SP-DickE**

It must have recesses. There is a great charm in a room broken up. The Architecture. Robert Duncan. **SP-DuncR** *Fr.* Passages.

It must hop, having but one leg. Nasnas. Lewis Turco. **SP-TurcL**

It must make a great difference, having friends. Catullus on Friendship. Donald Davie. **CP-DavDo**

It nearly cancels my fear of death, my dearest said. Robinson Jeffers. **CP-JefR3**

It needs there to be no one. Looking Out from Ferrara. Donald Davie. **CP-DavDo**

It Never Looks Like Summer. Thomas Hardy. **CP-HardT**

It never was known that circular letters. To Mr. Sheridan, upon His Verse, Written in Circles. Jonathan Swift. **CP-SwifJ**

It nods and curtseys and recovers. Alfred Edward Housman. **CP-HousA**

It occurs to me now. The Lesson. Charles Simic. **SP-SimiC**

It often falls (as here it erst befell). Edmund Spenser. **OBF** *Fr.* The Faerie Queene. **CP-Spens**

It once might have been, once only. Youth and Art. Robert Browning. **CP-BroR1**

It ought to be lovely to be old. Beautiful Old Age. David Herbert Lawrence. **CP-LawrD**

It perished with beautiful reluctance. Emily Dickinson. **SP-DickE**

It pleased her to step in front and sit. The Figure in the Scene. Thomas Hardy. **CP-HardT**

It pleased me more. William Wordsworth. **OAEL-2** *Fr.* Residence in France and French Revolution. *Fr.* The Prelude; Growth of a Poet's Mind [1850 vers.]. **CP-WorW3**

It Pleases. Gary Snyder. **CP-SnydG**

It pleasures her to gather. Katchie Verner's Harvest. Louise McNeill. **SP-McNeL**

It promises quiet here. A green Plymouth. 2433, First Home, Last House in Missoula. Richard Hugo. **CP-HugoR**

It pusheth us out before it, out, and to the side. The Dry Ode. Charles Olson. **CP-OlsoC**

It quickened [or quickned] next a toyful[l] ape, and so. John Donne. **PoEL-2** *Fr.* The Progress[e] of the Soul[e]. **CP-DonnJ**

It rained dark and cold on the Day of St. Theresa of the Heart. Thomas Merton. *Fr.* Cables to the Ace. **CP-MertT**

It Rained Last Night. Isabella Gardner. **CP-GardI**

It rained toward day. The morning came sad and white. Colder Fire. Robert Penn Warren. **LiTM** *Fr.* To a Little Girl, One Year Old, in a Ruined Fortress. **SP-WarrR**

It rained when it should have snowed. Holly. Seamus Heaney. **SP-HeanS** *Fr.* Sweeney Redivivus.

It really must / be Nice, never to. Edward Estlin Cummings. **CP-CummE**

It remained silent. The Closed House. Frederick Morgan. **SP-MorgF**

It requires great love of it deeply to read. Scotland. "Hugh MacDiarmid." **SP-MacDH**

It rests me to be among beautiful women. Tame Cat. Ezra Pound. **SP-PounE**

It rises—passes—on our South. Emily Dickinson. **CP-DickE**

It rules out use. Porcelain Bowl. Louise Glück. **SP-GlücL**

It runs ahead. And now. The Barometer. Charles Tomlinson. **CP-TomlC**

It said "Come home, here is an end, a goal." Woodrow Wilson. Robinson Jeffers. **CP-JefR1**

It sat between my husband and my children. Seele im Raum. Randall Jarrell. **CP-JarrR; SP-JarrR**

It seemed / the sky was a harbor, into which rode. Casualty. Edwin Rolfe. **CP-RolfE**

It seemed a curious place to rest one's body and take one's ease. Road Up. Stevie Smith. **CP-SmitS**

It seemed a fine day for a canter. When in Rome. . . . Isabella Gardner. **CP-GardI**

It seemed at the time like a slow road and a late afternoon. Tree. Muriel Rukeyser. **CP-RukeM**

It seemed I was a mite of sediment. In a Glass of Cider. Robert Frost. **CP-FrosR**

It seemed that out of battle I escaped. Strange Meeting. Wilfred Owen. **CP-OwenW**

It seemed the very garments that I wore. William Wordsworth. **OAEL-2** *Fr.* Summer Vacation. *Fr.* The Prelude; Growth of a Poet's Mind [1850 vers.]. **CP-WorW3**

It seemed to be a monk, plausibly disguised. The Demonstration. Frederick Morgan. **SP-MorgF**

It seems a day. Nutting. William Wordsworth. **CP-WorW1**

It seems absurd I should avert. Variations on a Theme. John Hewitt. **CP-HewiJ**

It seems an easy thing / Mayhap one day to sing. Then Shall Ye Shout. Christina Georgina Rossetti. **CP-RosC2**

It seems as if. . . or did the actual chance. With Christopher Smart. Robert Browning. **CP-BroR2**

It seems I have misplaced the directions for childhood. Jim Carroll. **SP-CarrJ**

It seems like the world's most useless profession. Cuidadores de Autos. Stephen Dobyns. **SP-DobyS**

It seems now far off and foolish, a memory. Lot Later. Howard Nemerov. **CP-NemeH**

It seems so long ago, Nancy was alone. Seems So Long Ago, Nancy. Leonard Cohen. **CP-CoheL**

It seems to be DARK all the time. Despair. John Berryman. **CP-BerrJ**

It seems to be the trouble, everyone. Sonnet. Howard Nemerov. **CP-NemeH**

It seems to me that for five thousand years at least. Triumph. David Herbert Lawrence. **CP-LawrD**

It seems to me that if you must be sociable it is better to go and see. Suppose I Darken Your Door. Ogden Nash. **CP-NashO**

It Seems You Never Were. Charles Henri Ford. **SP-FordC**

It seems you've been misled through. Helping the Dreamer. Anne Waldman. **SP-WaldA**

It sheds a shy solemnity. Interior. Hart Crane. **CP-CranH**

It should not matter how I shaped my lines. On the Preservation of Work Sheets. John Hewitt. **CP-HewiJ**

It sifts from Leaden Sieves. Emily Dickinson. **CP-DickE**

It sits on top of an old shadeless gooseneck in his tailorshop window. Lightbulb. Stephen Berg. **SP-BergS**

It snowed / last night. Settlement. Archie Randolph Ammons. **SP-AmmoA**

It snowed in spring on earth so dry and warm. Our Singing Strength. Robert Frost. **CP-FrosR**

It snows in my soul. After Verlaine. Phoebe Hesketh. **SP-HeskP**

It sounded as if the Streets were running. Emily Dickinson. **CP-DickE**

It Sounds It. Anne Waldman. **SP-WaldA**

It speaks, it moves. La Belle Dame de Tous les Jours. William Carlos Williams. **CP-WilW1**

It sprang up out of him in the dark. A Poet's Thoughts. Thomas Hardy. **CP-HardT**

It spreads, the campaign—carried on. Carnegie Hall: Rescued. Marianne Craig Moore. **CP-MoorM**

It started just now with a hummingbird. Migration of Birds. Gary Snyder. **CP-SnydG**

It started, unexpectedly of course. How It Started. Robert Ranke Graves. **CP-GravR**

It started when Bill's chip let on to. Edward Estlin Cummings. **CP-CummE**

It still makes sense. Song, The. Robert Creeley. **CP-CreeR**

It stills, incites, infatuates. Emily Dickinson. **SP-DickE**

It stinks. It stinks and it stinks and it stinks and it stinks. Hog Heaven. Charles Kenneth Williams. **CP-WillC; SP-WillC**

It stole along so stealthy. Emily Dickinson. **CP-DickE**

It struck me—every Day. Emily Dickinson. **CP-DickE**

It takes a fast car. Lost Parents. Lawrence Ferlinghetti. **SP-FerlL**

It takes a heap o' pluggin' t' make a classic sell. Publius Vergilius Maro, the Madison Avenue Hick. John Updike. **CP-UpdiJ**

It Takes a Lot to Laugh, It Takes a Train to Cry. "Bob Dylan." **CP-DylaB**

It takes a philosopher or fool. Ralph Waldo Emerson. **CP-EmerR**

It takes all sorts of in- and outdoor schooling. Robert Frost. **CP-FrosR**

It Takes Few Kinds. Kenneth Patchen. **CP-PatcK**

It takes me aback at times. Frederick Morgan. *Fr.* Meditations for Autumn. **SP-MorgF**

It takes so long to look down. Two Times. Robert Creeley. **CP-CreeR**

It Took Four Flowerboats to Convoy My Father's Black. John Ciardi. **SP-CiarJ**

It took that pause to make him realize. Time Out. Robert Frost. **CP-FrosR**

It took us two days in heat to mow. The Games in the Field. Paul Zimmer. **SP-ZimmP**

It tossed—and tossed. Emily Dickinson. **CP-DickE**

It troubled me as once I was. Emily Dickinson. **CP-DickE**

It turns on its axis. Dialogue. Charles Tomlinson. **CP-TomlC**

It used to be, farms. Garden State. Allen Ginsberg. **CP-GinsA**

It used to be hard. The Deaths of the Goddesses. Erica Jong. **SP-JongE**

It used to be only Sunday afternoons. Watching Football on TV. Howard Nemerov. **CP-NemeH**

It Uses Us! Leonard Cohen. **CP-CoheL**

It was a beautiful and silent day. Residence in France and French Revolution. William Wordsworth. *Fr.* The Prelude; Growth of a Poet's Mind [1805 vers.]. **CP-WorW3**

It was a beautiful and silent day. Residence in France and French Revolution. William Wordsworth. *Fr.* The Prelude; Growth of a Poet's Mind [1850 vers.]. **CP-WorW3**

It was a beautiful and silent day. William Wordsworth. **OxAEP-2**, *book* 10, *ll.* 1–736, *abr.*; *Fr.* Residence in France and French Revolution. *Fr.* The Prelude; Growth of a Poet's Mind [1805 vers.]. **CP-WorW3**

It was a beauty that I saw. Ben Jonson. **CP-JonsB** *Fr.* The New Inn.

It was a big house, bleak. Order to View. Louis MacNeice. **CP-MacNL**

It Was a Bomby Evening. Kenneth Patchen. **CP-PatcK**

It was a bright and cheerful afternoon. Summer and Winter. Percy Bysshe Shelley. **CP-ShelP**

It was a close, warm, breezeless summer night. William Wordsworth. **PoEL-4** *Fr.* Conclusion: "In one of those excursions (may they ne'er)." **OAEL-2; OBNC** *Fr.* The Prelude; Growth of a Poet's Mind [1850 vers.]. **CP-WorW3**

It was a coat worth keeping even with. I Save Your Coat, But You Lose It Later. Tess Gallagher. **SP-GallT**

It was a cool season, full of reserve. Common Ground. Dabney Stuart. **SP-StuaD**

It was a cynical babe. Infant. Stevie Smith. **CP-SmitS**

It was a dream and shouldn't I bother about a dream? Songe d'Athalie. Stevie Smith. **CP-SmitS**

It was a dream delivered the epilogue. Epilogue, The. Charles Tomlinson. **CP-TomlC**

It was a dreary morning when the chaise. Residence at Cambridge. William Wordsworth. *Fr.* The Prelude; Growth of a Poet's Mind [1805 vers.]. **CP-WorW3**

It was a dreary morning when the chaise. William Wordsworth. **FaBoPP; OxAEP-2** *Fr.* Residence at Cambridge. *Fr.* The Prelude; Growth of a Poet's Mind [1805 vers.]. **CP-WorW3**

It was a dreary morning when the wheels. Residence at Cambridge. William Wordsworth. *Fr.* The Prelude; Growth of a Poet's Mind [1850 vers.]. **CP-WorW3**

It was a face which darkness could kill. Lawrence Ferlinghetti. **SP-FerlL**

It was a' for our rightfu' king. Robert Burns. **CP-BurnR**

It Was a Funky Deal. Etheridge Knight. **SP-KnigE**

It was a goodly co. Edward Estlin Cummings. **CP-CummE**

It was a Grave, yet bore no Stone. Emily Dickinson. **CP-DickE**

It was a graveyard scene. The crescent moon. Great Unaffected Vampires and the Moon. Stevie Smith. **CP-SmitS**

It was a hard thing to undo this knot. Gerard Manley Hopkins. **CP-HopkG**

It was a house of female habitation. A House of Mercy. Stevie Smith. **CP-SmitS**

It was a human face in my oblivion. Oblivion. Stevie Smith. **CP-SmitS**

It was a kind and northern face. Praise for an Urn. Hart Crane. **CP-CranH**

It was a language of water, light and air. The Marl Pits. Charles Tomlinson. **CP-TomlC**

It was a little captive cat. The Singing Cat. Stevie Smith. **CP-SmitS**

It was a long time ago. As I Grew Older. Langston Hughes. **SP-HughL**

It was a long time ago—but everyone says. Immortal Face. Marsden Hartley. **CP-HartM**

It Was a Lording's Daughter. William Shakespeare. *See* It was a lording's daughter, the fairest one of three.

It was a lording's daughter, the fairest one of three. William Shakespeare. **CP-ShaWS; EIL** *Fr.* The Passionate Pilgrim. **CP-ShaWS**

(It Was a Lording's Daughter.) **EIL**

It was a lovely day. After the Storm. Wystan Hugh Auden. **CP-AudWJ**

It was a Maine lobster town. Water. Robert Lowell. **SP-LoweR**

It was a mile of greenest grass. The Occasional Yarrow. Stevie Smith. **CP-SmitS**

It was a *moral* end for which they fought. On the Final Submission of the Tyrolese. William Wordsworth. **CP-WorW1**

It was a most unfriendly part. The Journal of a Modern Lady. Jonathan Swift. **CP-SwifJ**

It was a place. A Story. Charles Olson. **CP-OlsoC**

It was a place of force. The Rabbit Catcher. Sylvia Plath. **CP-PlatS**

It was a quiet seeming Day. Emily Dickinson. **CP-DickE**

It was a quiet way. Emily Dickinson. **CP-DickE**

It was a sad, ay, 'twas a sad farewell. An Elegy on Parting. James Thomson. **CP-ThomJ**

It was a slender British bird. A British Song. Stevie Smith. **CP-SmitS**

It was a smart caprice. John Donne in His Shroud. Marsden Hartley. **CP-HartM**

It was a stew of a night. The power failed. A Conversation with Leonardo. John Ciardi. **SP-CiarJ**

It was a Summer's night, a close warm night. William Wordsworth. **OBNC** *Fr.* Conclusion: "In one of these excursions, travelling then." *Fr.* The Prelude; Growth of a Poet's Mind [1805 vers.]. **CP-WorW3**

It was a terrible rebellion. The Rebellion. Leonard Cohen. **CP-CoheL**

It was a time to find a new world: who was sent forth? Columbus, that is. Real and Half Real. Robinson Jeffers. **CP-JefR3**

It was a very little while and they had gone in. Hotel François Ier. Gertrude Stein. **CP-SteiG**

It was a violent time. Wheels, racks, and fires. A Mirror for Poets. Thom Gunn. **CP-GunnT**

It was a waning crescent. July Dawn. Louise Bogan. **CP-BogaL**

It was a wet wan hour in spring. The King's Experiment. Thomas Hardy. **CP-HardT**

It was a woman's voice, Russian or Czech. The Day Before Thanksgiving, a Call Comes to Me Concerning Insulation. Gary Gildner. **SP-GildG**

It was about the deep of night. A Ballad of Christmas. Walter de la Mare. **CP-DeLaW**

It was agreed we would not mount by those. Jacob's Ladder. Donald Davie. **CP-DavDo**

It was all a dream. Munich. Patti Smith. **SP-SmitP**

It was all an appropriate if nervous afternoon. Joy. William Dickey. **SP-DickW**

It was all different; that, at least, seemed sure. Mutability. William DeWitt Snodgrass. **SP-SnodW**

It was all the clods at once become. Earth Dweller. William Stafford. **SP-StafW**

It Was All Very Tidy. Robert Ranke Graves. **CP-GravR**

It was almost easy to say goodby. The Soldiers Returning. Richard Shelton. **SP-ShelR**

It was almost post time, the horses were. The Day Alvero Pineda Was Killed. Ron Koertge. **SP-KoerR**

It was already raining. They discovered all the bags were empty. Thomas Merton. *Fr.* Cables to the Ace. **CP-MertT**

It was also my violent heart that broke. The Break. Anne Sexton. **CP-SextA**

It was always fiercer, brighter, gentler than could be told. The Yet Unsayable. Robert Ranke Graves. **CP-GravR**

It was always November there. The farms. The Chateau Hardware. John Ashbery. **SP-AshbJ**

It was among ferns I learned about eternity. Ferns. Robert Bly. **SP-BlyR**

It was amusing on that antique grass. Recorders in Italy. Adrienne Rich. **CP-RicAE**

It was *Amyntor's* Grove, that *Chloris*. Amyntor's Grove. Richard Lovelace. **CP-LoveR**

It was an April morning: fresh and clear. William Wordsworth. **CP-WorW1**

It was an artless *Bandar* and he danced upon a pine. Divided Destinies. Rudyard Kipling. **CP-KiplR**

It was an August evening and, in snowy garments clad. Municipal. Rudyard Kipling. **CP-KiplR**

It was an English ladye bright. Song of Albert Graeme. Sir Walter Scott. **SP-ScotW** *Fr.* The Lay of the Last Minstrel.

It was an epoch of heroes. A Parable. Louise Glück. **SP-GlücL**

It was an hill placed in an open plain. The Dance of the Graces. Edmund Spenser. **OBSC; TrGrPo** *Fr.* The Faerie Queene. **CP-Spens**

It was an icy day. Complete Destruction. William Carlos Williams. **CP-WilW1**

It was, and still my care is. A Hymne, to the Lares. Robert Herrick. **CP-HerrR**

It was as if a pterodactyl had landed. Smiles. Stephen Dunn. **SP-DunnS**

It was as if I woke. Looking in a Mirror. Margaret Atwood. **SP-AtwM1**

It was, as if the Heaven. Moonlight Night. Joseph, Freiherr von Eichendorff, *tr. fr. German by* George Meredith. **CP-MerG2**

It was as if thunder took form upon. Woman Looking at a Vase of Flowers. Wallace Stevens. **CP-StevW**

It was as though it had begun to rain lightly. The Day the Perfect Speakers Left. Leonard Nathan. **SP-NathL**

It was as though we met at McDonald's. For Janet Kafka, Dead at 30. Al Young. **CP-YounA**

It was as though you struggled against. Letter. Robert Earl Hayden. **CP-HaydR**

It was as though you were a man in a wheelchair. Seated Figure. Louise Glück. **SP-GlücL**

It was at first your great. Bone. Thom Gunn. **CP-GunnT**

It was at the town convention. "Chronic Kicker," The. Paul Laurence Dunbar. **CP-DunbP**

It was at the very date to which we have come. An Anniversary. Thomas Hardy. **CP-HardT**

It was because you trusted gods and men. Tyr. Frederick Morgan. **SP-MorgF**

It Was Beginning Winter. Theodore Roethke. **NAAL-2** *Fr.* The Lost Son. **CP-RoetT**

It Was Being. Kenneth Patchen. **CP-PatcK**

It was better when we were. For My Mother. Louise Glück. **SP-GlücL**

It was blowing a storm in the red light district. Danish Sailor's Song. Malcolm Lowry. **CP-LowrM**

It was born in perhaps the Holland Tunnel. Love in a Bus. Thomas McGrath. **SP-McGrT**

It was but a little thing. The Peace-Offering. Thomas Hardy. **CP-HardT**

It was Catlett driving, de Paris blowing strong. Hayden Carruth. *Fr.* The Sleeping Beauty. **CP-CarHL**

It was Chrismus Eve, I mind hit fu' a mighty gloomy day. Chrismus on the Plantation. Paul Laurence Dunbar. **CP-DunbP**

It was cold and windy, scarcely the day. The End of March. Elizabeth Bishop. **CP-BishE**

It was Easter as I walked in the public gardens. 1929. Wystan Hugh Auden. **CP-AudeW**

It was easy enough. Circe. Hilda Doolittle. **CP-DoolH**

It was everything to me to think well of one man. Euripides. *Fr.* Medea. **CP-JefR3,** *tr. by* Robinson Jeffers;

It was far in the sameness of the wood. The Demiurge's Laugh. Robert Frost. **CP-FrosR**

It was given to me by the Gods. Emily Dickinson. **CP-DickE**

It was going to rain. The Smile. James Merrill. **SP-MerrJ**

It was Gold's junkhouse, the one the clacking. Galway Kinnell. *Fr.* The Avenue Bearing the Initial of Christ into the New World. **SP-KinnG**

It was good going along with the sun. Good Friday, 1971. Driving Westward. Paul Muldoon. **SP-MuldP**

It was good of my father, whom I hated at times. Robinson Jeffers. **CP-JefR3**

It was gray. Goya's "Two Old People Eating Soup." Mona Van Duyn. **SP-VanDM**

It was Hackensack, no, Hoboken, the town. Hoboken Broken Down: A Hasty Recollection. Al Young. **CP-YounA**

It was held in God's great temple. The Concert. Paul Laurence Dunbar. **CP-DunbP**

It was in North Dakota. Woman on the Road. John Haines. **SP-HainJ**

It was in October, a favorite season. Elegy for a Nature Poet. Howard Nemerov. **CP-NemeH**

It was in sweet Senegal that my foes did me enthrall. The Slave's Lament. Robert Burns. **CP-BurnR**

It was in the earth only. Yellow Afternoon. Wallace Stevens. **CP-StevW**

It was in the fields. The trees grew still. Jeanne d'Arc. Louise Glück. **SP-GlücL**

It was in the old days. Los Angeles, 1954. David St. John. **SP-StJoD**

It was in winter. Steeples, spires. The Fortunate Traveller. Derek Walcott. **CP-WalcD**

It was John the Baptist, son to Zechariah. Birth of a Goddess. Robert Ranke Graves. **CP-GravR**

It was late in mild October, and the long autumnal rain. The Huskers. John Greenleaf Whittier. **CP-WhitJ**

It was late in September when you took me. The Metaphysical Garden. May Sarton. **SP-SartM**

It was late in the afternoon when I returned with the paper bag. Nantucket. John Yau. **SP-YauJo**

It was late summer. John Haines. *Fr.* Cicada. **SP-HainJ**

It was late when they came in. The Moon of Melancholy. Lewis Turco. **SP-TurcL**

It was like a cave of snow, no. Merlin. David St. John. **SP-StJoD**

It was like everything else, like everything. The Iris-Eaters. Muriel Rukeyser. **CP-RukeM**

It was like listening to the record of a symphony before you knew anything at all about the music. First Desires. Charles Kenneth Williams. **SP-WillC**

It was like passing a boundary to dive. A Lot of People Bathing in a Stream. Wallace Stevens. **CP-StevW**

It was like the approach of flame. What It Was Like. Charles Tomlinson. *Fr.* Four Kantian Lyrics. **CP-TomlC**

It was long before the national performance. For Fun. Muriel Rukeyser. **CP-RukeM**

It was long I lay. I Will Sing You One-O. Robert Frost. **CP-FrosR**

It was Mabbie without the grammar school gates. The Ballad of Chocolate Mabbie. Gwendolyn Brooks. **CAPP** *Fr.* A Street in Bronzeville. **SP-BrooG**

It was many and many a year ago. Annabel Lee. Edgar Allan Poe. **CP-PoeEd**

It was me here. Though. And whether this. At the Inn. John Ashbery. **SP-AshbJ**

It was midnight and cold. From the inn. Metamorphosis. Frederick Morgan. **SP-MorgF**

It was more sleepwalk than spasm. The First Flight. Seamus Heaney. **SP-HeanS** *Fr.* Sweeney Redivivus.

It was more than could have been hoped for. A Poem in One Sentence. Kay Boyle. **CP-BoylK**

It was much easier to be a genius in the twenties, there were. The Last Generation. Charles Bukowski. **SP-BukC3**

It was much later in his life he rose. Gibbs. Muriel Rukeyser. **CP-RukeM**

It was much later in his life he rose. Muriel Rukeyser. **ImOP** *Fr.* Gibbs. **CP-RukeM**

It was much stronger than they said. Noisier. F.O.M. Muriel Rukeyser. **CP-RukeM**

It was much—that far and ill. Emily Dickinson. **SP-DickE**

It was my bridal night I remember. I Remember. Stevie Smith. **CP-SmitS**

It was my choice, it was no chance. Sir Thomas Wyatt. **CP-WyatT**

It was my thirtieth year to heaven. Poem in October. Dylan Thomas. **CP-ThomD**

It was near evening, the room was cold. The Oath. Allen Tate. **CP-TateA**

It was near last century's ending. In the Marquee. Thomas Hardy. **CP-HardT**

It was nearly morning when the giant. The Reason for Skylarks. Kenneth Patchen. **CP-PatcK**

It was never meant to be sensible. To a Friend in Love with the Wrong Man Again. Stephen Dunn. **SP-DunnS**

It was new about eighteen-sixty. Dates: Penkhull New Road. Charles Tomlinson. **CP-TomlC**

It was night, and on the mountains. Emily Brontë. **CP-BronE**

It was night, and the mist. The Ghost. Frederick Morgan. **SP-MorgF**

It was nine o'clock at midnight at a quarter after three. The Bagpipe Who Didn't Say No. Shel Silverstein. **SP-SilS2**

It was no costume jewellery I sent. With a Gift of Rings. Robert Ranke Graves. **CP-GravR**

It was no place for the faithless. Walking the Marshland. Stephen Dunn. **SP-DunnS**

It was no vast dynastic fate. A Father's Death. John Hewitt. **CP-HewiJ**

It was not a heart, beating. Night Shift. Sylvia Plath. **CP-PlatS**

It was not a part of their blood. The Beginnings. Rudyard Kipling. **CP-KiplR**

It was not as if he didn't try. Great Uncle Beefheart. Rita Dove. **SP-DoveR**

It was not Death, for I stood up. Emily Dickinson. **CP-DickE**

It was not dying: everybody died. Losses. Randall Jarrell. **CP-JarrR; SP-JarrR**

It was not God that told us. We knew. Le Secret Humain. Archibald MacLeish. **CP-MacLA**

It was not he who broke their compact. Broken Compact. Robert Ranke Graves. **CP-GravR**

It Was Not I. Phoebe Hesketh. **SP-HeskP**

It was not in the open fight. Rudyard Kipling. **CP-KiplR** *Fr.* The Rout of the White Hussars. *Fr.* Plain Tales from the Hills.

It was not my fault, these animals. Margaret Atwood. *Fr.* Circe / Mud Poems. **SP-AtwM1**

It was not my mother or my daughter. Coda. Marilyn Hacker. *Fr.* The Regent's Park Sonnets. **SP-HackM**

It was not Saint—it was too large. Emily Dickinson. **CP-DickE**

It was not the words, nor the melody. Grace Notes. Robert Ranke Graves. **CP-GravR**

It was not warning that our fathers lacked. Changing Chimes. Christina Georgina Rossetti. **CP-RosC2**

It was not what you bore with you, Woman. Without, Not within Her. Thomas Hardy. **CP-HardT**

It was not you I came to please. The Dissemblers. Thomas Hardy. **CP-HardT**

It was October. It was the Depression. Money. What Happened. Robert Penn Warren. *Fr.* Tale of Time. **SP-WarrR**

It was on a winter's day, as cold, as clear. Sunderland. Howard Nemerov. **CP-NemeH**

It was on evenings like this. A Good Life. Stephen Dunn. **SP-DunnS**

It was on the old Paterson and. Period Piece: 1834. William Carlos Williams. **CP-WilW2**

It was one of those clear,sharp,mistless days. The Eagle. Edward Estlin Cummings. **CP-CummE**

It was only a bird call at evening, unidentified. Ornithology in a World of Flux. Robert Penn Warren. **SP-WarrR**

It was only important. The Moss of His Skin. Anne Sexton. **CP-SextA**

It was our city too. Chrome and glass. Hayden Carruth. *Fr.* The Asylum. **CP-CarHL**

It was our war-ship *Clampherdown*. The Ballad of the *Clampherdown*. Rudyard Kipling. **CP-KiplR**

It was outside a place. The Fight. William Carlos Williams. **CP-WilW2**

It was patience / protecting the soul as clothing the body. Expedient, An—Leonardo da Vinci's—and a Query. Marianne Craig Moore. **CP-MoorM**

It was quiet in there after the crushing. The Engine House. Wystan Hugh Auden. **CP-AudWJ**

It Was Raining in the capital. John Ashbery. **SP-AshbJ**

It was roses, roses, all the way. Patriot, The [An Old Story]. Robert Browning. **CP-BroR1**

It was rumored on the block. The Figure Motioned with Its Mangled Hand Toward the Wall Behind It. Kenneth Patchen. **CP-PatcK**

It was Saturday the 1st day of April, toward noon. Canto 88. Ezra Pound. *Fr.* Cantos. **CP-PoCan**

It was 7 or 8 years ago. The Lady Poet. Charles Bukowski. **SP-BukC3**

It was so delicious to see you. Emily Dickinson. **SP-DickE**

It was so hot although I didn't have much time I went to the. True Story of Being at the Pool. Anne Waldman. **SP-WaldA**

It was so pleasurable. Attempting to Persuade You to Go for a Walk in the Public Gardens. Jean Garrigue. **SP-GarrJ**

It was so windy. The Scour. Archie Randolph Ammons. **SP-AmmoA**

It was some Spirit, Sheridan! that breath'd. To Richard Brinsley Sheridan, Esq. Samuel Taylor Coleridge. *Fr.* Effusions. **CP-ColeS**

It was something I'd overheard. Lucifer in Starlight. David St. John. **SP-StJoD**

It was something to see that their white was different. Holiday in Reality. Wallace Stevens. **CP-StevW**

It was such a pretty little donkey. The Donkey. Stevie Smith. **CP-SmitS**

It was summer then. Jet Fizzle. Jim Carroll. **SP-CarrJ**

It was summer. We were there. And THERE WAS NO. Ted Berrigan. **SP-BerrT** *Fr.* The Sonnets.

It was supposed to be Arts & Crafts for a week. At the Smithville Methodist Church. Stephen Dunn. **SP-DunnS**

It was taken some time ago. This Is a Photograph of Me. Margaret Atwood. **SP-AtwM1**

It was ten days after the event. The Place Where the Boy Pointed. Robert Penn Warren. **SP-WarrR**

It was that lonely day, folks. Crossing. Langston Hughes. **SP-HughL**

It was the charming month of May. Robert Burns. **CP-BurnR**

(Song, Altered from an Old English One.) **CP-BurnR**

It was the cooling hour, just when the rounded. Haidée and Don Juan. Byron. **OBNC** *Fr.* Canto the Second. *Fr.* Don Juan. **CP-Byron**

It was the country I loved. The Invaders. John Haines. **SP-HainJ**

It was the custom of my tribe to be silent. Hayden Carruth. *Fr.* Paragraphs. **CP-CarHS**

It was the dingiest bird. Robin Redbreast. Stanley Jasspon Kunitz. **CP-KuniS**

It was the end of the harvest season. Sweeney Praises the Trees. Seamus Heaney. **SP-HeanS**

It was the Great Alexander. Alexander. Walter de la Mare. **CP-DeLaW**

It was the hour of night, when thus the Son. John Milton. **EBEV; PeECV** *Fr.* Book II. *Fr.* Paradise Regained [*or* Regain'd]. **CP-MiltJ**

It was the hour when night makes the mountains lament. Rainbow. Max Jacob, *tr. fr. French by* Elizabeth Bishop. **CP-BishE**

It was the mighty Engine Drain, the Engine Drain, the Engine Drain. The Engine Drain. Stevie Smith. **CP-SmitS**

It was the month in which the righteous Maide. Prosopopoia: or Mother Hubberds Tale. Edmund Spenser. **CP-Spens**

It was the month of May. Far down the Beautiful River. Henry Wadsworth Longfellow. *Fr.* Part the Second. *Fr.* Evangeline, a Tale of Acadie. **SP-LongH**

Lakes of the Atchafalaya, The. **PoEL-5**

On the Atchafalaya. **AA**

"Softly the evening came. The sun from the western horizon." **APN-1**

It was the night of the flood first took away. The Flood. Charles Tomlinson. **CP-TomlC**

It was the place to go in nineteen-thirty. Gladstone Street. Charles Tomlinson. **CP-TomlC**

It was the schooner *Hesperus*. The Wreck of the *Hesperus*. Henry Wadsworth Longfellow. **SP-LongH**

It was the season, when through all the land. Birds of Killingworth, The (The Poet's Tale). Henry Wadsworth Longfellow. **SP-LongH** *Fr.* Tales of a Wayside Inn.

It was the sky all day I grew to and saw. John Berryman. *Fr.* Sonnets to Chris. **CP-BerrJ**

It was the smoke, blue. Invitation. Phoebe Hesketh. **SP-HeskP**

It was the time, when rest, soft sliding downe. Joachim Du Bellay. **AWP; Son** *Fr.* The Visions of Bellay. **CP-Spens**

It was the twilight of the iguana. Some Beasts. Pablo Neruda, *tr. fr. Spanish by* James Wright. **CP-WrigJ**

It was the War. A Soldier Dear to Us. Stevie Smith. **CP-SmitS**

It was the west wind caught her up, as. The Ring of. Charles Olson. **CP-OlsoC; SP-OlsoC**

It was the winter wild[e]. Hymn on the Morning of Christ's Nativity [*or* On the Morning of Christ's Nativity]. John Milton. **FiP; NAEL-1; NOBE; OBEV; OtMeF** *Fr.* On the Morning of Christs Nativity. **CP-MiltJ**

It was the work of fortune. Now She Dwells Here. Tom Clark. **SP-ClarT**

It was the year. Jesus Awake. Anne Sexton. **CP-SextA**

It was there, in that little town. Francesco and Clare. David St. John. **SP-StJoD**

It was to learn that grief is a major. Marsden Hartley. **CP-HartM**

It was to our interest to be quiet. Though I Had Much More To Say. Kenneth Patchen. **CP-PatcK**

It was too late for Man. Emily Dickinson. **CP-DickE**

It was too lonely for her there. The Impulse. Robert Frost. **ArLo; HoPM; NePA; RaBo** *Fr.* The Hill Wife. **CP-FrosR**

It was too simple and too right. Four Dancers at an Irish Wedding. Tess Gallagher. **SP-GallT**

It was 20 years ago I saw the fox. The Fox. Phoebe Hesketh. **SP-HeskP**

It was twenty years ago today Sergeant Pepper taught the band to play. Sgt. Pepper's Lonely Hearts Club Band. The Beatles. **CP-Beatl**

It was upon a Lammas night. Robert Burns. **CP-BurnR**

(Song: "It was upon a Lammas night.") **CP-BurnR**

It was when / Whirls of thick waters laved me. The Something that Saved Him. Thomas Hardy. **CP-HardT**

It was when he began to see fields. Comedy. Charles Tomlinson. **CP-TomlC**

It was when I said. On the Road Home. Wallace Stevens. **CP-StevW**

It was when I was walking I came upon. Beaucaire. Jean Garrigue. **SP-GarrJ**

It was with resolution that she gave up the. The Ice Eagle. Diane Wakoski. **SP-WakoD**

It was yesterday morning. Little Old Letter. Langston Hughes. **SP-HughL**

It was your birthday, we had drunk and dined. The Hug. Thom Gunn. **CP-GunnT**

It was your smell that, for a day after, I carried with me. The Anniversary. William Dickey. **SP-DickW**

It was your vision of the pilot. Adrienne Rich. *Fr.* Twenty-one Love Poems. **SP-RicA1; SP-RicA2**

It was your way, my dear. Without Ceremony. Thomas Hardy. **CP-HardT**

It wasn't Ernest; it wasn't Scott—. Song for the Squeeze-Box. Theodore Roethke. **CP-RoetT**

It Wasn't Me. "Lou Reed." **SP-ReedL**

It wasn't ringworm he. New York. Thom Gunn. **CP-GunnT**

It wasn't safe to stay in Saint-Brieuc. Days of 1944: Three Friends. Marilyn Hacker. **SP-HackM**

It wasn't that he liked being miserable. His Music. Stephen Dunn. **SP-DunnS**

It wasn't your crippled rhythm. The Woman Makes Peace with Her Faulty Heart. Margaret Atwood. **SP-AtwM2**

It went many years. The Lockless Door. Robert Frost. **CP-FrosR**

It will be February there. The Afterlife. Ted Kooser. **SP-KoosT**

It will be honorable to pity. The Lost, Alone. Marsden Hartley. **CP-HartM**

It will be looked for, book[e], when some but see. To My Book. Ben Jonson. **CP-JonsB**

It will be much better when. When Dead. Thomas Hardy. **CP-HardT**

It will be Summer—eventually. Emily Dickinson. **CP-DickE**

It will come to be, but only when the myth. The Final Version. Hayden Carruth. *Fr.* The Mythology of Dark and Light. **CP-CarHL**

It will not be questioned that some men. Cellaphon–a Favorite Word with Picabia. Marsden Hartley. **CP-HartM**

It will not be simple, it will not be long. Final Notations. Adrienne Rich. **SP-RicA1**

It will not shine again. Emily Brontë. **CP-BronE**

It will seem strange, no more this range on range. John Berryman. *Fr.* Sonnets to Chris. **CP-BerrJ**

It Won't Be Long. The Beatles. **CP-Beatl**

It won't stand up to the light. The Zodiac. Donald Davie. **CP-DavDo**

It Would. Alice Notley. **SP-NotlA**

It would be at the end. The End of the Street. John Haines. **SP-HainJ**

It would be bound to be like this. Eagle of the Inner Eye. Marsden Hartley. *Fr.* Word Arrangements for Pictures by Morris Graves. **CP-HartM**

It would be nice to die at the typer instead of with my. Suggestion for an Arrangement. Charles Bukowski. **SP-BukC3**

It would be nice to explain some things except that. The Interesting Glass. Gilbert Sorrentino. **SP-SorrG**

It would be pretty to have roses. Living Off Other People—Welfare. Jenny Joseph. **SP-JoseJ**

It would be so easy. Any Inner City Blues. Al Young. **CP-YounA**

It would be that / but only if I knew how. It Would. Alice Notley. **SP-NotlA**

It would be wonderful to be quiet now. Inches. Charles Kenneth Williams. **CP-WillC**

It would be wrong to let one man. Thomas Merton. **CP-MertT**

It Would Have Been Enough. Robert Pack. **SP-PackR**

It Would Have Been Quicker to Walk, or, Don't Tell Me We're There Already. Ogden Nash. **CP-NashO**

It would have delighted Bishop Berkeley by. TV. Howard Nemerov. **CP-NemeH**

It would have starved a Gnat. Emily Dickinson. **CP-DickE**

It would never be Common—more—I said. Emily Dickinson. **CP-DickE**

It would not know if it were spurned. Emily Dickinson. **CP-DickE**

It would take more than that to banish. A Bus along St Clair: December. Margaret Atwood. **SP-AtwM1**

It wounded well—one time and. The War Wound. James Dickey. **CP-DickJ**

It yawns at me the cavernous gulf. Litany. Thomas Merton. **CP-MertT**

Italia, Io Ti Saluto! Christina Georgina Rossetti. **CP-RosC2**

Italian Days. Charles Wright. **SP-WrigC**

Italian Garden. May Sarton. **SP-SartM**

Italian Garden, The. William Carlos Williams. **CP-WilW2**

Italian in England, The. Robert Browning. **CP-BroR1**

Italian Itinerant, and the Swiss Goatherd, The. William Wordsworth. *Fr.* Memorials of a Tour of the Continent; 1820. **CP-WorW2**

Italian Morning. Louise Bogan. **CP-BogaL**

Italian Music in Dakota. Walt Whitman. **CP-WhitW**

Italian prisoners of war still haunted. Huntingdonshire. Donald Davie. **CP-DavDo**

Italian Town Abandoned. Richard Hugo. **CP-HugoR**

Italy. Byron. **OBRV; PIP; SeCePo** *Fr.* Beppo; a Venetian Story. **CP-Byron**

   (Italy versus England.) **NOBE**

Italy. George Meredith. **CP-MerG2**

Italy. Patti Smith. **SP-SmitP**

Italy. John Greenleaf Whittier. **CP-WhitJ**

Italy and the World. Elizabeth Barrett Browning. **CP-BroEB**

Italy breaking her bones for bread. How the River Ninfa Runs through the Ruined Town Beneath the Lime Quarry. Archibald MacLeish. **CP-MacLA**

Italy, my Italy? Robert Browning. **PIP** *Fr.* De Gustibus. **CP-BroR1**

Italy of the South. Robert Browning. *See* What I love best in all the world.

Italy versus England. Byron. *See* Italy.

Itch, Come and Gone. Charles Bukowski. **SP-BukC2**

Itching Heels. Paul Laurence Dunbar. **CP-DunbP**

It'd been twenty minutes at least. Waiting. Ron Koertge. **SP-KoerR**

Ité. Ezra Pound. **SP-PounE**

Ite procul tetrici, moneo, procul ite severi. *acc. by English translation.* Thomas Campion. **CP-CampT**

Item. Edward Estlin Cummings. **CP-CummE**

Item. William Carlos Williams. **CP-WilW1**

Item:is / Clumsily with of. Edward Estlin Cummings. **CP-CummE**

I'th' Autumn of a Summers day. Lucasta at the Bath. Richard Lovelace. **CP-LoveR**

Ithers seek they kenna what. Jockey Fou and Jenny Fain. Robert Burns. **CP-BurnR**

Ithiel Falls, below the Nazarene campground. A name. Hayden Carruth. *Fr.* Paragraphs. **CP-CarHS**

Itinerant through numerous domains, of his lord's. Geoffrey Hill. *Fr.* Mercian Hymns. **CP-HillG**

Itinerary. Adrienne Rich. **CP-RicAE**

It)It will it. Edward Estlin Cummings. **CP-CummE**

It's / snowing defective. James Schuyler. *See* Self-Pity Is a Kind of Lying, Too.

It's / so damn sweet when Anybody. Edward Estlin Cummings. **CP-CummE**

It's a bad Good Friday, snow and mud. St. Ignatius Where the Salish Wail. Richard Hugo. **CP-HugoR**

It's a brand new morning. Leonard Nathan. **SP-NathL** *Fr.* To Be Read to Yourself in a Public Place, July 4, 1976.

It's a dark drama, this; and yet I know the house, and date. The Mock Wife. Thomas Hardy. **CP-HardT**

It's a fact / that before his death. To the National Endowment for the Arts. Jim Carroll. **SP-CarrJ**

It's a Gay Li-ife. Louis Zukofsky. *Fr.* 29 Songs. **CP-ZukLS**

It's a Grand Parade It Will Be, Modern Design. Ogden Nash. **CP-NashO**

It's a great pleasure to. Many Happy Returns. Ted Berrigan. **SP-BerrT**

It's a hot day: / not so hot. Overcast, Hot. James Schuyler. **CP-SchuJ**

It's a jazz affair, drum crashes and cornet razzes. Honky Tonk in Cleveland, Ohio. Carl Sandburg. **CP-SandC**

It's a lean car. . . a long-legged dog of a car. . . a gray-ghost eagle. Portrait of a Motorcar. Carl Sandburg. **CP-SandC**

It's a little thing. Good. Stephen Berg. **SP-BergS**

It's a little Walden. You All Know the Story of the Other Woman. Anne Sexton. **CP-SextA**

It's a plain table. And Finally. Leonard Nathan. **SP-NathL**

It's a problem, why I'm here with amplified rock. Changes at Meridian. Richard Hugo. **CP-HugoR**

It's a rare Brueghel without people. Brueghel in the Doria. Richard Hugo. **CP-HugoR**

It's a room I dream about. February 4th. Anne Sexton. **CP-SextA**

It's a sleepwalker's fate to dream with his eyes. The Door Gunner to the Moment, (A Shau Valley 1968). Tom Clark. **SP-ClarT**

It's a Smallworld. Kenneth Patchen. **CP-PatcK**

It's a strange courage. El Hombre. William Carlos Williams. **CP-WilW1**

It's a Sunday kind / of Sunday, the first. Up. James Schuyler. **CP-SchuJ**

It's a weary life, it is; she said. From the Antique. Christina Georgina Rossetti. **CP-RosC3**

It's a year almost that I have not seen her. A Bird Song. Christina Georgina Rossetti. **CP-RosC1.**

It's about Time. Ogden Nash. **CP-NashO.**

It's about to be too late. Long. William Matthews. **SP-MattW**

It's abstract nouns, among the myths of mind. The Metaphysical Automobile. Howard Nemerov. **CP-NemeH**

It's all a farce,—these tales they tell. Merry Autumn. Paul Laurence Dunbar. **CP-DunbP**

It's all I have to bring today. Emily Dickinson. **CP-DickE**

It's all in / the sound. A song. Poem, The. William Carlos Williams. **CP-WilW2**

It's All Over Now, Baby Blue. "Bob Dylan." **CP-DylaB**

It's all right for them to make a stinking mess of everything. Don't Wash Your Hair in the Streetcar, Nora Dear. Kenneth Patchen. **CP-PatcK**

It's All Too Much. George Harrison. **CP-Beatl**

It's almost a month since we touched, or wanted to. Both. Stephen Berg. **SP-BergS**

It's Alright, Ma (I'm Only Bleeding). "Bob Dylan." **CP-DylaB**

It's always been a mystery. The Battle of Copenhagen. Ernest Hemingway. **CP-HemiE**

It's always been like this with me. The Hawk Revisited. Al Young. **CP-YounA**

It's always there. My back's. The Cell. Louise Glück. **SP-GlücL**

It's always too early. Elegies for Walker Dabney Stuart, Jr. Dabney Stuart. **SP-StuaD**

It's amazing all / this motion going. Spaceship. Archie Randolph Ammons. **SP-AmmoA**

It's an overcome sooth for age an' youth. Robert Louis Stevenson. **CP-StevR**

It's around / the corner. For Arthur Okamura. Robert Creeley. **CP-CreeR**

It's as if the wife. Widowhood. Leonard Nathan. **SP-NathL**

It's awf'lly bad luck on Diana. Hunter Trials. Sir John Betjeman. **CP-BetjJ**

It's awful, Amos. Hayden Carruth. *Fr.* The Sleeping Beauty. **CP-CarHL**

It's bad enough crying for children. Ten Below. Charles Kenneth Williams. **SP-WillC**

Its balmy lips the infant blest. Epitaph on an Infant. Samuel Taylor Coleridge. **CP-ColeS**

It's Because Your Heart Is Pure, Honey. Kenneth Patchen. **CP-PatcK**

It's been A Hard Day's Night. A Hard Day's Night. The Beatles. **CP-Beatl**

It's been a long long long time. Long Long Long. George Harrison. **CP-Beatl**

It's been a long time. Wait. The Beatles. **CP-Beatl**

It's been a long time since I've spoken to you. Dirt. "Lou Reed." **SP-ReedL**

It's been going on a long time. A Way of Life. Howard Nemerov. **CP-NemeH**

It's been hard since I left The Garden. Not Going Back. Leonard Cohen. **CP-CoheL**

It's been raining in the trenches all day long, dripping down to my clothes. Need a Woman. "Bob Dylan." **CP-DylaB**

It's best to work before dawn. School Figures. William Matthews. **SP-MattW**

Its body is like that. Xoanon. Lewis Turco. **SP-TurcL**

It's Christmas Eve and I run in the sun. Gift of Tongue. Tom Clark. **SP-ClarT**

It's coming—the postponeless Creature. Emily Dickinson. **CP-DickE**

It's coming through a hole in the air. Democracy. Leonard Cohen. **CP-CoheL**

Its crisp sheets, unfolded. Letter from Costa Brava. Charles Tomlinson. **CP-TomlC**

It's cutting into me on its bareback with talons lifted. Savoy. Frank O'Hara. **SP-OharF**

It's Dark In Here. Shel Silverstein. **SP-SilS2**

It's dark in this wood, soft mocker. Praise to the End! Theodore Roethke. **CP-RoetT**

It's dark when they scuff off to school. Schoolboys with Dog, Winter. William Matthews. **SP-MattW**

Its days are over now; no farmyard airs. The Traction Engine. Wystan Hugh Auden. **CP-AudWJ**

Its dialectic difficulty lends. Contradiction. David Markson. **CP-MarkD**

It's easy to invent a Life. Emily Dickinson. **CP-DickE**

It's easy to write when you've nothing to write about. Good for You, Gavin. Philip Larkin. **CP-LarkP**

It's 8:54 a.m. in Brooklyn it's the 28th [*or* 26th] of July [and]. Ted Berrigan. **SP-BerrT** *Fr.* The Sonnets.

It's Either You Fight or You Die. David Herbert Lawrence. **CP-LawrD**

It's enough to make one think they knew. Folk Tale. Daniel Gerard Hoffman. **SP-HoffD**

It's evening and the orchestra of winds. Emily Dickinson. **SP-DickE**

It's everybody's fault but me. "Drive All Blames into One." Allen Ginsberg. **CP-GinsA**

It's farewell to the drawing-room's mannerly cry. Danse Macabre. Wystan Hugh Auden. **CP-AudeW**

It's fine to wake up and hug your knees. Afternoons. Tom Clark. **SP-ClarT**

It's for Regency now I'm enthusing. Winthrop Mackworth Redivivus. Sir John Betjeman. **CP-BetjJ**

Its former green is blue and thin. The Garden Seat. Thomas Hardy. **CP-HardT**

It's forth across the roaring foam, and on towards the west. Robert Louis Stevenson. **CP-StevR**

It's forty in the shade to-day, the spouting eaves declare. Pan in Vermont. Rudyard Kipling. **CP-KiplR**

It's four in the morning, the end of December. Famous Blue Raincoat. Leonard Cohen. **CP-CoheL**

It's 4:30 in Cambridge. James Schuyler. *Fr.* Four Poems. **CP-SchuJ**

It's fragrant news, to know they pine. Emily Dickinson. **SP-DickE**

It's French, of course—our name. And I must think. Hayden Carruth. *Fr.* Vermont. **CP-CarHL**

It's funny early spring weather, mild and washy. 3/23/66. James Schuyler. **CP-SchuJ**

It's funny, Howard, I never thought I'd be. Eros to Howard Nemerov. Mona Van Duyn. **SP-VanDM**

It's getting better all the time. Getting Better. The Beatles. **CP-Beatl**

It's going to be the sunny side. Walking to Work. Frank O'Hara. **SP-OharF**

It's going to come out all right—do you know? Caboose Thoughts. Carl Sandburg. **CP-SandC**

It's Got to This. Charles Olson. **CP-OlsoC**

It's great to be miserable and know it. Great. Leonard Nathan. **SP-NathL**

It's Halloween going on midnight. Boo. Halloween on Hennepin. Barton Sutter. **SP-SuttB**

It's hard / to live. The Upshot. Archie Randolph Ammons. **SP-AmmoA**

It's hard to see but think of a sea. Louis Zukofsky. **CP-ZukLS**

It's here again, it moves, its tin-white scythe. 1914. Stephen Berg. **SP-BergS**

It's here in whatever shoots come up. Contrast. Joseph Ceravolo. **SP-CeraJ**

It's horrible, being run over by a bus. Shells. Charles Kenneth Williams. **CP-WillC**

It's hot to-day. The bees is buzzin'. A Summer Pastoral. Paul Laurence Dunbar. **CP-DunbP**

Its Hour with itself. Emily Dickinson. **CP-DickE**

Its huge red prow / Uplifted in a tragic attitude. The Wreck. John Gould Fletcher. *Fr.* Sand and Spray: A Sea-Symphony. **SP-FletJ**

It's Important. Ted Berrigan. **SP-BerrT**

It's in the heart of the grape. Baby Picture. Anne Sexton. **CP-SextA**

It's India. Al Young. **CP-YounA**

It's jolly / odd what pops into. Edward Estlin Cummings. **CP-CummE**

It's July. He always dies in July. The Funeral. Dabney Stuart. **SP-StuaD**

It's June and summer's height. 6/21. Adrienne Rich. **SP-RicA1**

It's just like a coffin's. Edward Estlin Cummings. **CP-CummE**

Its leading characters are wise and witty. Hong Kong. Wystan Hugh Auden. *Fr.* A Voyage. **CP-AudeW**

It's like the Light. Emily Dickinson. **CP-DickE**

It's like the riddle Tolstoy. Slow Dance. David St. John. **SP-StJoD**

It's Like This. Stephen Dobyns. **SP-DobyS**

Its little Ether Hood. Emily Dickinson. **CP-DickE**

It's little I care what path I take. Departure. Edna St. Vincent Millay. **CP-MillE**

It's made of everything, slow. Sandy's Sunday Best. Ted Berrigan. **SP-BerrT**

It's many a penny you'll pay to go. George Meredith. **CP-MerG2**

It's me or a book report and they are taking. Reading at the Local High School. Ron Koertge. **SP-KoerR**

Its metal top refused my father's twisting. The Soup Jar. Dabney Stuart. **SP-StuaD**

It's mid-December in Rome, yet the sun's. Winter Sun. David St. John. *Fr.* To Pasolini. **SP-StJoD**

It's more than a hundred years now. He Thought of Mad Ellen's Ravings and of the Wretched Skeleton on the Rock. Kenneth Patchen. **CP-PatcK**

It's moughty tiahsome layin' 'roun'. W'en I Gits Home. Paul Laurence Dunbar. **CP-DunbP**

It's my lunch hour, so I go. A Step Away from Them. Frank O'Hara. **SP-OharF**

It's My Town! Kenneth Patchen. **CP-PatcK**

It's mystery, not wind, the men. Plunking the Skagit. Richard Hugo. **CP-HugoR**

Its narrow head that gnaws the breast. The Separation. Stanley Jasspon Kunitz. **CP-KuniS**

It's natural the Boys should whoop it up for. Moon Landing. Wystan Hugh Auden. **CP-AudeW**

It's Never Fair Weather. Ogden Nash. **CP-NashO**

It's nice / after dinner. Reading. Archie Randolph Ammons. **SP-AmmoA**

It's night and Tom / comes in and says. Suddenly. James Schuyler. **CP-SchuJ**

It's no coincidence / this is a used. Tricks With Mirrors. Margaret Atwood. **SP-AtwM1**

It's no go the merry-go-round, [or merrygoround], it's no go the rickshaw. Bagpipe Music. Louis MacNeice. **CP-MacNL**

It's No Good! David Herbert Lawrence. **CP-LawrD**

It's no good my dear. So There! David Herbert Lawrence. **CP-LawrD**

It's Not / the Erotic. Charles Olson. **CP-OlsoC**

It's not a fancy restaurant, nor is it. Tenderly. Stephen Dobyns. **SP-DobyS**

It's not enough / That doom shall find us whole of hate. A Letter to the Liberals. Kenneth Patchen. **CP-PatcK**

It's not my office, after all; it's yours. The Senator Explains a Vote. Miller Williams. **SP-WillM**

It's not that I'm out of touch. Suicide Note. Jane Cooper. **SP-CoopJ**

It's not the case, though some might wish it so. Orchard Trees, January. Richard Wilbur. **CP-WilbR**

It's Not Who Lived Here. Charles Bukowski. **SP-BukC2**

It's not you, this dead long moan from the past. Museum of Cruel Days. Richard Hugo. **CP-HugoR**

It's nothing more than last. Percussion. Dabney Stuart. **SP-StuaD**

It's Nothing to Laugh About. Charles Bukowski. **SP-BukC2**

"It's nothing," whatever. Martial, tr. by William Matthews. **SP-MattW** Fr. Epigrams.

It's odd enough to be alive with others. Brother. Robert Ranke Graves. **CP-GravR**

It's of three rioters I have to tell. Geoffrey Chaucer. **SCV** Fr. The Pardoner's Tale. **FHYEP; NAEL-1; NAWM-1; NoP; OAEL-1; PoE** Fr. The Canterbury Tales. **CP-ChauG**

It's oh in Paradise that I fain would be. Saints and Angels. Christina Georgina Rossetti. **CP-RosC1**

It's on ordinary days, isn't it. All That We Have. Stephen Dunn. **SP-DunnS**

It's Only Love. The Beatles. **CP-Beatl**

It's over a(see just). Edward Estlin Cummings. **CP-CummE**

It's over now. I watch. Charles Kenneth Williams. **CP-WillC**

It's over now; I've known it all. Emily Brontë. **CP-BronE**

Its piers less black for sunny smiles above. The Good Servant. Richard Wilbur. **CP-WilbR**

Its power to deceive. Jim Carroll. Fr. The New Death. **SP-CarrJ**

It's Probably Spring, see also Leonard Cohen. **CP-CoheL**

Its quick soft silver bell beating, beating. Auto Wreck. Karl Shapiro. **SP-ShapK**

It's quite true we live / in a kind of rural twilight. Concerning Necessity. Hayden Carruth. **CP-CarHS**

It's rainin'. Weet's the gairden sod. The Blast—1875. Robert Louis Stevenson. **CP-StevR**

It's rather sad we can only meet people. Posthumous Letter to Gilbert White. Wystan Hugh Auden. **CP-AudeW**

Its roots are bristling in the air. The Tree. Thomas Hardy. **CP-HardT**

It's sad this vision required. Poem. Jim Carroll. **SP-CarrJ**

It's said by the thoughtful masters that to know death. Sonnet. Hayden Carruth. **CP-CarHS** Fr. Sonnets.

It's Saturday afternoon at the edge of the world. Laguna Blues. Charles Wright. **SP-WrigC**

It's simple but I find it hard to explain. A Terminal Moraine. James Fenton. **SCBI** Fr. Exempla. **SP-FentJ**

Its skin tough and unpliable as scar, the pulp out of focus, weak, granular, powdery, blank. The Modern. Charles Kenneth Williams. **SP-WillC**

It's snowing on the unpedimented lions. On ventilator hoods. April and Its Forsythia. James Schuyler. **CP-SchuJ**

It's Snug to Be Smug. Ogden Nash. **CP-NashO**

It's so beautiful, life, goddamn death. The Thing Was Moving. Charles Olson. **CP-OlsoC; SP-OlsoC**

It's so cold. Grisly Grit. Archie Randolph Ammons. **SP-AmmoA**

It's so cold my cock is furled. Pissing off the Back of the Boat into the Nivernais Canal. William Matthews. **SP-MattW**

It's so pure in the cemetery. Not like That. Adrienne Rich. **CP-RicAE**

It's so still / today that a. Spruce Woods. Archie Randolph Ammons. **SP-AmmoA**

It's some kind of little gray-leafed. Honorable Mention. Leonard Nathan. **SP-NathL**

It's something like the Merode altarpiece by Campin. I Digress. . . . Anne Waldman. **SP-WaldA**

It's somewhere, somewhere, thought beats stupidly. Cicero, the Sacrificial Killing. Robert Lowell. **SP-LoweR**

It's SPRing AgAIN! Charles Olson. **CP-OlsoC**

It's spring again. Providence, Rhode Island. Al Young. **CP-YounA**

It's Spring, Lover. Gary Gildner. **SP-GildG**

It's still gray and wet almost pink. Jim Carroll. Fr. Birthday Poem. **SP-CarrJ**

It's strange that God should fash to frame. The Counterblast Ironical. Robert Louis Stevenson. **CP-StevR**

It's strange what the past brings back. Driving through Tennessee. Charles Wright. **SP-WrigC**

It's such a / Bore. Ennui. Langston Hughes. **SP-HughL**

It's such a little thing to weep. Emily Dickinson. **CP-DickE**

It's taken years to stop the voices. The Return. Stephen Dunn. **SP-DunnS**

It's that delicate time / when things could spill. Fog Township. Brendan Galvin. **SP-GalvB**

It's the anarchy of poverty. The Poor. William Carlos Williams. **CP-WilW1**

It's the fact. Trees Eat Sunshine. John Updike. **CP-UpdiJ**

It's the greyness said greendoon. Greendoon's Song. Robert Creeley. **CP-CreeR**

It's the immemorial feelings. Goods. Wendell Berry. **CP-BerrW**

It's the incompetence. Giving Them What For. Steve Griffiths. **SP-GrifS**

It's the ocean of western steel. West Wind. Kenneth Koch. **SP-KochK**

It's the opposite of boorishness. The Sound of a Moment at Scariff. James Liddy. **CP-LiddJ**

It's the same as before. This Then—. Charles Bukowski. **SP-BukC1**

It's the story that counts. Margaret Atwood. **NALW** Fr. Circe / Mud Poems. **SP-AtwM1**

It's the very end of summer. Moonlight in Vermont. William Matthews. **SP-MattW**

It's the Way You Play the Game. Charles Bukowski. **SP-BukC1**

It's the wrong time; that makes it the wrong room. The Wrong Time. Roy Fisher. **SP-FishR** Fr. Interiors with Various Figures.

It's this crazy weather we've been having. Crazy Weather. John Ashbery. **SP-AshbJ**

It's thoughts—and just One Heart. Emily Dickinson. **CP-DickE**

It's time again. / Tear up the violets. Earth's Holocaust. James Schuyler. **CP-SchuJ**

It's time the clock got thrown out the window. April Blue. Al Young. **CP-YounA**

It's time to put fertilizer on the grass again. Notes from a Suburban Heart. Mona Van Duyn. **SP-VanDM**

It's time we went out to finish the dam. Damming Stream. Wystan Hugh Auden. **CP-AudWJ**

It's time you learned something. Roses. Rita Dove. **SP-DoveR**

It's too much: this hard work—. Night Work. Thomas McGrath. **SP-McGrT**

It's too obscure, it's as it were. Dominoes. Gilbert Sorrentino. **SP-SorrG**

It's too wrestling at the beach the sand. Colloque Sentimental. Frank O'Hara. **SP-OharF**

It's true Mattie Lee. Unidentified Flying Object. Robert Earl Hayden. **CP-HaydR**

It's true that all the men you knew were dealers who said they. The Stranger Song. Leonard Cohen. **CP-CoheL**

It's true then that you still overeat, fat friend. Two Photographs. Basil Bunting. **CP-BuntB**

It's true. When a crazy woman. Unnatural Unselection. Hayden Carruth. **CP-CarHS**

Its up wi' the Sutors o Selkirk. Sutors o' Selkirk. Robert Burns. **CP-BurnR**

It's Venice, late August, outside after lunch, and Hart. Portrait of the Artist with Hart Crane. Charles Wright. **SP-WrigC**

It's very cold, Catherine is bundled in a coat, a poncho on the top of that, high boots, gloves. Snow: II. Charles Kenneth Williams. **SP-WillC**

Its voice / Is the blade of the desert, a fighting of light. And the Phoenix Has Come. Ted Hughes. **SP-HughT**

It's what I planned. The barbershop alone. Cattails. Richard Hugo. **CP-HugoR**

Its windows flashing to the sky. The Preacher. John Greenleaf Whittier. **CP-WhitJ**

It's wonderful how I jog. Animals Are Passing from Our Lives. Philip Levine. **SP-LeviP**

It's you and me again, Duststroke. Taking the Wheel. Dabney Stuart. **SP-StuaD**

Itself a lightning-flash ripping the dark. John Berryman. *Fr.* Sonnets to Chris. **CP-BerrJ**

Itt is nott love which you poore fooles do deeme. Sonnet 40. Mary Sidney, Countess of Montgomery Wroth. *Fr.* Pamphilia to Amphilanthus. **CP-WrotM**

Itylus. Algernon Charles Swinburne. **SP-SwinA**

Iuventius, / were I allowed. Carmen 48. Catullus. *Fr.* Carmina. **CP-Catul**

Iva asks me for stories of her father's. Inheritances. Marilyn Hacker. **SP-HackM**

Ivàn Ivànovitch. Robert Browning. **CP-BroR2**

Ivana. Robert Lowell. **SP-LoweR**

Ivanhoe. Sir Walter Scott.
Rebecca's Hymn. **SP-ScotW**

Iva's Birthday Poem. Marilyn Hacker. **SP-HackM**

Iva's Pantoum. Marilyn Hacker. **SP-HackM**

I've a Friend, over the sea. Time's Revenges. Robert Browning. **CP-BroR1**

I've a head like a concertina, I've a tongue like a buttonstock. Cells. Rudyard Kipling. **CP-KiplR**

I've a humble little motto. Keep A-Pluggin' Away. Paul Laurence Dunbar. **CP-DunbP**

Ive already told you about the dance. Backtracking. Al Young. **CP-YounA**

I've always been a faithful man. After Many Days. Paul Laurence Dunbar. **CP-DunbP**

I've always had trouble with. $$$$$$. Charles Bukowski. **SP-BukC1**

I've always wanted a gig. Prevalent At One Time. Marianne Craig Moore. **CP-MoorM**

I've been drunk in front of cracked bathroom mirrors. Green. Charles Bukowski. **SP-BukC3**

I've been going right on, page by page. The Errand. Anne Sexton. **CP-SextA**

I've been going to the track for years. Charles Bukowski. *Fr.* Horsemeat. **SP-BukC3**

I've been here fur many days. Home Longings. Paul Laurence Dunbar. **CP-DunbP**

I've been list'nin' to them lawyers. The Lawyers' Ways. Paul Laurence Dunbar. **CP-DunbP**

I've been married. Milepost. Archie Randolph Ammons. **SP-AmmoA**

I've been scarred and battered. Still Here. Langston Hughes. **SP-HughL**

I've been thinking it through, as I play here to-night, to play never again. The Chapel-Organist. Thomas Hardy. **CP-HardT**

I've been thinking—mean, cogitating. Avec Ardeur. Marianne Craig Moore. **CP-MoorM**

I've been to Palestine. John Brown. Nicholas Vachel Lindsay. **MoAmPo** *Fr.* The Booker Washington Trilogy. **CP-LindV**

I've been trying for hours to figure out who I was reminded of by the welterweight fighter. Combat. Charles Kenneth Williams. **CP-WillC; SP-WillC**

I've been wandering in the greenwoods. Emily Brontë. **CP-BronE**

I've been watchin' of 'em, parson. Deacon Jones' Grievance. Paul Laurence Dunbar. **CP-DunbP**

I've changed my ways a little; I cannot now. The House Dog's Grave. Robinson Jeffers. **CP-JefR3**

I've come by, she says, to tell you. Eat Your Heart Out. Charles Bukowski. **SP-BukC1**

I've come clean. Peace. Leonard Cohen. **CP-CoheL**

I've come to ask you if there isn't a. Edward Estlin Cummings. **CP-CummE**

I've come to give you fruit from out my orchard. The Crossed Apple. Louise Bogan. **CP-BogaL**

I've died, but you are still living! Feathers. Jane Cooper. *Fr.* March. **SP-CoopJ**

I've done it, I've done it! Invention. Shel Silverstein. **SP-SilS2**

I've drawn this landscape now for thirty years. The Glens of Atrim. John Hewitt. **CP-HewiJ**

I've dreamed so much of you. The Last Poem (after Robert Desnos). Tom Clark. **SP-ClarT**

I've dropped my Brain—My Soul is numb. Emily Dickinson. **CP-DickE**

I've fond anticipation of a day. The Uses of Poetry. William Carlos Williams. **CP-WilW1**

I've found out why, that day, that suicide. John Berryman. **PoE** *Fr.* Sonnets to Chris. **CP-BerrJ**

Ive found peace & it's good sleeping late today—head full of. Sunday Illumination. Al Young. **CP-YounA**

I've found the dainty malice out. Ralph Waldo Emerson. **CP-EmerR**

I've found three people now who claim they've seen. *with music.* Robert Pack. **SP-PackR**

I've Got a Feeling. The Beatles. **CP-Beatl**

I've got a stubborn goose whose gut's. Rhyme. Sylvia Plath. **CP-PlatS**

I've got a word or two. Think For Yourself. George Harrison. **CP-Beatl**

I've got an arrow here. Emily Dickinson. **CP-DickE**

I've got Ev'ry reason on earth to be mad. I'll Cry Instead. The Beatles. **CP-Beatl**

I've got nothing about gay guys. The Slide. "Lou Reed." **SP-ReedL**

I've got the children to tend. Woman Work. Maya Angelou. **SP-AngeM**

I've got to get out of the sun. Vulture Peak: Gridhakuta Hill. Allen Ginsberg. **CP-GinsA**

I've got two / hundred / dollars. Ballad of the Brown Girl. Alice Walker. **CP-WalkA**

Ive had dreams of Paradise where all you do is open your heart. Dreams of Paradise. Al Young. **CP-YounA**

I've had it here craving for New York City every day. Paris Day. Anne Waldman. **SP-WaldA**

I've had my eye on me. San Francisco Streets. Thom Gunn. **CP-GunnT**

I've heard an Organ talk, sometimes. Emily Dickinson. **CP-DickE**

I've heard there was a secret chord. Hallelujah. Leonard Cohen. **CP-CoheL**

I've heard yogis talk of a divine / emptiness. Emptiness. Stephen Dunn. **SP-DunnS**

I've journeyed 'roun' consid'able. Possum Trot. Paul Laurence Dunbar. **CP-DunbP**

I've just reached a place. Going, Going, Gone. "Bob Dylan." **CP-DylaB**

I've Just Seen a Face. The Beatles. **CP-Beatl**

I've known a Heaven, like a Tent. Emily Dickinson. **CP-DickE**

I've known an edginess, come evening. Night Truths. Stephen Dunn. **SP-DunnS**

I've known ere now an interfering branch. The Axe-Helve. Robert Frost. **CP-FrosR**

I've Known Her Turn from Bitter Phrase. John Hewitt. **CP-HewiJ**

I've known rivers. The Negro Speaks of Rivers. Langston Hughes. **SP-HughL**

I've lived at Cold Mountain—how many autumns, *after* Han-shan. Gary Snyder. **CP-SnydG**

I've lived in two countries. The Old Man Is Older in History than in Time. Wendell Berry. *Fr.* The Handing Down. **CP-BerrW**

I've looked out from being president. Allende at the End. Miller Williams. **SP-WillM**

I've lost place, / coming here. Berlin: First Night & Early Morning. Robert Creeley. **CP-CreeR**

"I've made it," she said, "I've come". Chicago. Charles Bukowski. **SP-BukC1**

I've met your friend at last, your violent friend. John Berryman. *Fr.* Sonnets to Chris. **CP-BerrJ**

I've multiplied, I'm 2. Number Song. Anne Waldman. **SP-WaldA**

I've never bet on a so-called horse. Turns in a Worm's Lane. Ogden Nash. **CP-NashO**

I've never gone to Donaghadee. Donaghadee. Thomas Hardy. **CP-HardT**

I've never had much trouble finding chaos. The Invisible Hand. Robert Pack. **SP-PackR**

I've never sailed the Amazon. Rudyard Kipling. **CP-KiplR** *Fr.* The Beginning of the Armadilloes. *Fr.* Just-So Stories.

I've never seen an abominable snowman. The Abominable Snowman. Ogden Nash. *Fr.* Nature-Walks, or, Not to Mention a Dopping of Sheldrakes. **CP-NashO**

"I've Never Seen Such a Real Hard Time Before": Three-Part Invention. Hayden Carruth. **CP-CarHS**

I've never wanted to be Number One—. The Wolf Pack. Robert Pack. **SP-PackR**

I've never washed my shadow out. Shadow Wash. Shel Silverstein. **SP-SilS2**

I've none to tell me but Thee. Emily Dickinson. **CP-DickE**

I've nothing else—to bring, You know. Emily Dickinson. **CP-DickE**

I've nothing to say. A Fixture. Gilbert Sorrentino. **SP-SorrG**

I've often wish'd that I had clear. The Sixth Satire of the Second Book of Horace Imitated. Alexander Pope. **CP-PopeA**

I've often wondered why she laughed. Edges. Allen Tate. **CP-TateA**

I've paid for your sickest fancies; I've humoured your crackedest whim. The Mary Gloster. Rudyard Kipling. **CP-KiplR**

I've paid thee what I promised; that's not all:. To His Peculiar Friend Master Thomas Shapcott, Lawyer. Robert Herrick. **CP-HerrR**

I've put Miss Hopper upon the train. Polterguest, My Polterguest. Ogden Nash. **CP-NashO**

I've read all the books but one. Kathleen Jessie Raine. **SP-RainK**

I've read that Luther said (it's come to me). The Author to the Reader. Randall Jarrell. **CP-JarrR**

I've read your poem, lady, and admire. Another to Mrs. Anne Bradstreet, Author of this Poem. *Unknown, poem signed* "H. S." **CP-BradA**

I've Said Goodbye to Shanghai. Malcolm Lowry. **CP-LowrM**

I've said: I wouldn't ever. Apology. Adrienne Rich. **CP-RicAE**

I've seen a Dying Eye. Emily Dickinson. **CP-DickE**

I've seen bees, in the spell of a queen. Workers. Stephen Dunn. **SP-DunnS**

I've seen love go by my door. You're Gonna Make Me Lonesome When You Go. "Bob Dylan." **CP-DylaB**

I've seen no more than three loved persons die. John Hewitt. *Fr.* October Sonnets. **CP-HewiJ**

I've seen one in a fairground. The Bearded Woman, by Ribera. Paul Muldoon. **SP-MuldP**

". . . I've seen people in front of." After the Reading. Charles Bukowski. **SP-BukC1**

I've seen them: the fixers. Little Devils. Pablo Neruda, *tr. fr. Spanish by* Ben Belitt. **SP-NeruP**

I've seen this dell in July's shine. A Farewell To Alexandria. Emily Brontë. **CP-BronE**

I've seen thousands, millions by now, and still they amaze me. Why Birch Trees Are White. Barton Sutter. **SP-SuttB**

I've Seen Too Many Glazed-Eyed Bums Sitting under a Bridge Drinking Cheap Wine. Charles Bukowski. **SP-BukC1**

I've sought out corner bars, lived in corner houses. Corners. Stephen Dunn. **SP-DunnS**

I've stayed in the front yard all my life. A Song in the Front Yard. Gwendolyn Brooks. **IDB; NAAL-2; NOBA; NoAM; PoBA** *Fr.* A Street in Bronzeville. **SP-BrooG**

I've taken my fun where I've found it. The Ladies. Rudyard Kipling. **CP-KiplR**

I've thought upon't; and cannot tell which way. Prologue. Sir John Suckling. *Fr.* Aglaura. **CP-SuckJ**

I've tried the new moon tilted in the air. The Freedom of the Moon. Robert Frost. **CP-FrosR**

I've tried to seal it in. The Knot. Stanley Jasspon Kunitz. **CP-KuniS**

I've walked this street in far too many towns. Walking Praed Street. Richard Hugo. **CP-HugoR**

I've watched them mother, and I know. Fiammetta Breaks Her Peace. Rita Dove. **SP-DoveR**

I've watched you now a full half-hour. William Wordsworth. **CP-WorW1** *Fr.* To a Butterfly.

I've zeroed an altimeter on the floor. Measurements. John Ciardi. **SP-CiarJ**

Ives. Richard Eberhart. **CP-EberR**

Ives. Muriel Rukeyser. **CP-RukeM**

Ivory Corner was only a wooden section of wall painted white, The. The Ship's Orchestra. Roy Fisher. **SP-FishR**

Ivory performing rose, The. Edward Estlin Cummings. **CP-CummE**

Ivory Tower, The. John Ashbery. **SP-AshbJ**

Ivory Tower, The. Allen Tate. **CP-TateA**

Ivy, The. Robert Penn Warren. **SP-WarrR**

Ivy Crown, The. William Carlos Williams. **CP-WilW2**

Ivy is trembling in the hammock, The. Poem. Frank O'Hara. **SP-OharF**

Ivy-Wife, The. Thomas Hardy. **CP-HardT**

Ixion. Robert Browning. **CP-BroR2**

J

J. C. M. George Meredith. **CP-MerG1**

J Car, The. Thom Gunn. **CP-GunnT**

J might be made sit up for a jade of hope (and exile, don't you know). Home Olga. Samuel Beckett. **CP-BeckS**

J, My Good Friend (Another Foolish Innocent). Alice Walker. **CP-WalkA**

Ja, we had it hard. Mona Van Duyn. **SP-VanDM**

Jabberers. Carl Sandburg. **CP-SandC**

Jabberwocky. "Lewis Carroll." **CP-CarrL** *Fr.* Through the Looking-Glass.

Jabón. Gary Gildner. **SP-GildG**

Jabowsky's place is on a side street and only the rain washes the dusty three balls. Three Balls. Carl Sandburg. **CP-SandC**

Jack. Randall Jarrell. **CP-JarrR**

Jack. Carl Sandburg. **CP-SandC**

Jack & Harry. George Meredith. **CP-MerG2**

Jack and Jill. Robert Herrick. **CP-HerrR**

Jack and Joan they think no ill. Thomas Campion.
("*Jacke* and *Jone*, they thinke no ill.") **CP-CampT**

Jack and the Beanstalk. Jenny Joseph. *Fr.* Fables. **SP-JoseJ**

Jack Baker / rises when / the steeple. Valley of Morning. Donald Hall. **CP-HallD**

Jack Barrett went to Quetta. The Story of Uriah. Rudyard Kipling. **CP-KiplR**

Jack Frost at Bedtime. Paul Laurence Dunbar. **CP-DunbP**

Jack, if you got to be a rounder. Street Song. Langston Hughes. **SP-HughL**

Jack-Knife. Charles Bukowski. **SP-BukC3**

Jack London and O. Henry. Carl Sandburg. **CP-SandC**

Jack o' diamonds / jack o' diamonds. "Bob Dylan." *Fr.* Some Other Kinds of Songs. **CP-DylaB**

Jack of Hearts, The. Lawrence Ferlinghetti. **SP-FerlL**

Jack, oh big Jack. The Surgeon. Anne Sexton. **CP-SextA**

Jack-Rabbit, The. Wallace Stevens. **CP-StevW**

Jack Roy. Herman Melville. **SP-MelvH**

Jack Straw sits. Thom Gunn. *Fr.* Jack Straw's Castle. **CP-GunnT**

Jack Straw's Castle. Thom Gunn. **CP-GunnT**
"Door opens, The."
"Down in the cellars, nothing is visible."
"Down panic, down. The castle is still here."
"Dream sponsors: / Charles Manson, tongue."
"I am the man on the rack."
"I spin like a solitary star, I swoon."
"Jack Straw sits."
"Might it not have been."
"My coldness wakes me."
"Pig Pig she cries."
"Rain stops. I look round: a square of floor, The."

Jack was a swarthy, swaggering son-of-a-gun. Jack. Carl Sandburg. **CP-SandC**

Jack with the Sun, is twenty-one. Atlas. George Meredith. **CP-MerG2**

Jack Would Speak through the Imperfect Medium of Alice. Alice Notley. **SP-NotlA**

Jackdaw, The. Vincent Bourne, *tr. fr. Latin by* William Cowper. **CP-CowpW**

Jacke and *Jone*, they thinke no ill. Thomas Campion. *See* Jack and Joan they think no ill.

Jacket, The. Rudyard Kipling. **CP-KiplR**

Jackie McLean: Alto Saxophone. Al Young. **CP-YounA**

Jackknife swandive gainer twist. Elegy for a Diver. Peter Meinke. **SP-MeinP**

Jack's Blues. Robert Creeley. **CP-CreeR**

Jack's Letter. John Crowe Ransom. **SP-RansJ**

Jack's white horse(up). Edward Estlin Cummings. **CP-CummE**

Jacob and the Angel. John Hewitt. **CP-HewiJ**

Jacob Gods Beggar was; and so we wait. Beggars. Robert Herrick. **CP-HerrR**

Jacob's Ladder. Donald Davie. **CP-DavDo**

Jacob's Ladder, The. Denise Levertov. **CP-LeveD**

Jade— / Stone of the side. Purdah. Sylvia Plath. **CP-PlatS**

Jade. Louis Zukofsky. **CP-ZukLS**

Jade Elegy, The. John Gould Fletcher. **SP-FletJ**

Jagg'd mountain peaks and skies ice-green. Breughel's Winter. Walter de la Mare. **CP-DeLaW**

Jaguar, The. Ted Hughes. **SP-HughT**

Jaguar king sent to my eyes, The. The Eye Is a Dog Howling in the Distance. Pablo Antonio Cuadra, *tr. fr. Spanish by* Thomas Merton. **CP-MertT**

Jaguar Myth, The. Pablo Antonio Cuadra, *tr. fr. Spanish by* Thomas Merton. **CP-MertT**

Jailer, The. Sylvia Plath. **CP-PlatS**

Jaime Valerosa y Borracho Consults His Journal. Gilbert Sorrentino. *Fr.* Twelve Études for Voice and Kazoo. **SP-SorrG**

Jair son of Manasseh went and seized the encampments. Place Names. Thomas Merton. **ChIV-1** *Fr.* East. *Fr.* The Geography of Lograire. **CP-MertT**

Jake Balokowsky, my biographer. Posterity. Philip Larkin. **CP-LarkP**

Jake hates / all the girls(the). Edward Estlin Cummings. **CP-CummE**

Jam Lucis Orto Sidere. *Unknown. Fr.* Four Medieval Latin Poems. **CP-MacNL**

Jam Session. Langston Hughes. **SP-HughL**

Jam Trap, The. Charles Tomlinson. **CP-TomlC**

James A. Wright, my difficult older brother. Elevens. Marilyn Hacker. **SP-HackM**

James Brydges and the Dean had long been friends. The Dean and the Duke. Jonathan Swift. **CP-SwifJ**

James Cotton Band at Keystone, The. Al Young. **CP-YounA**

James derided the Purgatorial fire of the soul. On the Same ["James derided the Purgatorial fire of the soul"]. John Milton, *tr. fr. Latin by* John T. Shawcross. **CP-MiltJ**

James Honeyman. Wystan Hugh Auden. **CP-AudeW**

James, it is snowing here. It is November. A Letter to James Stephens. May Sarton. **SP-SartM**

James Lee's Wife. Robert Browning. **CP-BroR1**
   Among the Rocks. **OxBSP**
   In the Doorway. **SCGP**

James Russell Lowell. Ralph Waldo Emerson. **CP-EmerR**

James Russell Lowell. John Greenleaf Whittier. **CP-WhitJ**

James I. Rudyard Kipling. **CP-KiplR**

James Watt / Was the hard-boiled kind of Scot. Wystan Hugh Auden. **InPK** *Fr.* Academic Graffiti. **CP-AudeW**

James Whitcomb Riley. Paul Laurence Dunbar. **CP-DunbP**

Jamesian. Thom Gunn. **CP-GunnT**

Jamestown. Randall Jarrell. **CP-JarrR**

Jamie Come Try Me. Robert Burns. **CP-BurnR**

Jan Kubelik. Carl Sandburg. **CP-SandC**

Jan, the Son of Thomas. Carl Sandburg. **CP-SandC**

Jan van Hogspeuw staggers to the door. The Card-Players. Philip Larkin. **CP-LarkP**

Jane Austen Beecher Stowe De Rouse. The Mare's Nest. Rudyard Kipling. **CP-KiplR**

Jane Awake. Frank O'Hara. **SP-OharF**

Jane awoke Ralph so gently on one morning. Morning. John Crowe Ransom. **SP-RansJ**

Jane Renick MacElmain (1). Louise McNeill. **SP-McNeL**

Jane Renick MacElmain (2). Louise McNeill. **SP-McNeL**

Jane Seagrim's Party. Leonard Nathan. **SP-NathL**

JANE SNEED BEGAN IT: My poor John, alas. Eclogue. John Crowe Ransom. **SP-RansJ**

Jane went to Paradise. Jane's Marriage. Rudyard Kipling. **CP-KiplR** *Fr.* Debits and Credits.

Jane's Marriage. Rudyard Kipling. **CP-KiplR** *Fr.* Debits and Credits.

Janet Waking. John Crowe Ransom. **SP-RansJ**

Jangle Bells. Ogden Nash. **CP-NashO**

Jangle of the jeering crows, The. Black Humor. Archibald MacLeish. **CP-MacLA**

Janie Crawford. Alice Walker. **CP-WalkA**

Janis Joplin's Dead: Long Live Pearl. James Schuyler. **CP-SchuJ**

Januaries, Nature greets our eyes. Brazil, January 1, 1502. Elizabeth Bishop. **CP-BishE**

January. Donald Davie. **CP-DavDo**

January. Alice Notley. **SP-NotlA**

January. Christina Georgina Rossetti. *Fr.* The Months: A Pageant. **CP-RosC2**

January. Gary Snyder. *Fr.* Six Years. **CP-SnydG**

January! / The beginning of all things! Invocation and Conclusion. William Carlos Williams. **CP-WilW1**

January, / the dragon maple sunk in its bones. A Journal of the Year of the Ox. Charles Wright. **SP-WrigC**

January? / The month is dumb. The Sermon of the Twelve Acknowledgements. Anne Sexton. **CP-SextA**

January. William Carlos Williams. **CP-WilW1**

January. Al Young. **CP-YounA**

January: A Winters Day. John Clare. **SP-ClarJ** *Fr.* The Shepherd's [*or* Shepheards] Calendar.

January and May, or the Merchant's Tale, *see also* Merchant's Tale, The. Geoffrey Chaucer. **CP-PopeA** *Fr.* The Canterbury Tales. **CP-ChauG**

January cold desolate; / February all dripping wet. Christina Georgina Rossetti. **CP-RosC2**

January Eclogue. Edmund Spenser. **FiP** *Fr.* The Shepheardes [*or* Shepeards *or* Shepherd's] Calender. **CP-Spens**

January 18, 1979. John Yau. **SP-YauJo**

January First. Octavio Paz, *tr. fr. Spanish by* Elizabeth Bishop. **CP-BishE**

January 1st. Anne Sexton. **CP-SextA**

JANUARY (*Hunting*). Rudyard Kipling. *Fr.* Verses on Games. **CP-KiplR**

January in New York. Erica Jong. **SP-JongE**

January Night, A. Thomas Hardy. **CP-HardT**

January 1938. Randall Jarrell. **CP-JarrR**

January 19th. Anne Sexton. **CP-SextA**

January 1. John Ciardi. **SP-CiarJ**

January 10, 1973. Alice Walker. **CP-WalkA**

January! The beginning! Moon and Stars. William Carlos Williams. **CP-WilW2**

January 24th. Anne Sexton. **CP-SextA**

January 22, 1982. Miles III. James Liddy. **CP-LiddJ**

Japan invades. Far Eastern vines. Kudzu. James Dickey. **CP-DickJ**

Japanese, The. Ogden Nash. **CP-NashO**

Japanese girl thinks she will die today, The. Japanese Girl with Red Table. Stephen Dobyns. **SP-DobyS**

Japanese Girl with Red Table. Stephen Dobyns. **SP-DobyS**

Japanese Prints. May Sarton. **SP-SartM**

Japanese Wife, The. Charles Bukowski. **SP-BukC2**

Japonica. Louise Glück. **SP-GlücL**

Jas Jargon. Charles Olson. **CP-OlsoC**

Jasmine's Beautiful Thoughts Underneath the Willow. Wallace Stevens. **CP-StevW**

Jason and Medea. Alun Lewis. **CP-LewiA**

Jason Potter. Lewis Turco. *Fr.* Bordello. **SP-TurcL**

Jason, the valiant prince of Greece. Mr. Jason Hassard, a Woolen Draper in Dublin. Jonathan Swift. **CP-SwifJ**

Jasper Olson. Lewis Turco. *Fr.* Bordello. **SP-TurcL**

Jaunt. Louis Zukofsky. **CP-ZukLS**

Jaunty style of Arnold Bennett's "Card." Staffordshire. Donald Davie. **CP-DavDo**

Jaweh and Allah Battle. Allen Ginsberg. **CP-GinsA**

Jaweh with Atom Bomb. Jaweh and Allah Battle. Allen Ginsberg. **CP-GinsA**

Jaws. Carl Sandburg. **CP-SandC**

Jay his Castanet has struck, The. Emily Dickinson. **CP-DickE**

Jay in Masquerade, The. Charlotte Smith. **CP-SmitC**

Jays shrieking in the fir clump, a world enraged. Hayden Carruth. *Fr.* The Sleeping Beauty. **CP-CarHL**

Jazz as Was. Al Young. **CP-YounA**

Jazz Fantasia. Carl Sandburg. **CP-SandC**

Jazz notes and Brahms intermittently. To My Contemporaries. Edwin Rolfe. **CP-RolfE**

J.B. Shelton (1876–1958), The Coventry Antiquarian. John Hewitt. **CP-HewiJ**

Je Connai Gens de Toutes Sortes. Gilbert Sorrentino. **SP-SorrG**

Je Crois En L'Amour. Thomas Merton. **CP-MertT**

Je suis ce cours de sable qui glisse, *Author's own French vers. of his* "My way is in the sand flowing." Samuel Beckett. **CP-BeckS**

Je Suis une Table. Donald Hall. **CP-HallD**

Je Vois dans le Hasard Tous les Biens Que J'espere. Robert Creeley. **CP-CreeR**

Je voudrais que mon amour meure, *Author's own French vers. of his* "I would like my love to die." Samuel Beckett. **CP-BeckS**

Je vous lis les sonnets d'un capitaine aveugle, *incl. English tr. by* William Davis. Thomas Merton. *Fr.* Cables to the Ace. **CP-MertT**

Jealosie. John Donne. *See* Jealousy.

Jealous. Paul Laurence Dunbar. **CP-DunbP**

Jealous, and with Love o'erflowing. Love Pure and Fervent. Jeanne Marie Bouvier de la Motte-Guyon, *tr. fr. French by* William Cowper. **CP-CowpW**

Jealous girls these sometimes were. How Marigolds Came Yellow. Robert Herrick. **CP-HerrR**

Jealous Lovers, The. Donald Hall. **CP-HallD**

Jealous Man, A. Robert Ranke Graves. **CP-GravR**

Jealousy. John Donne. **FF** *Fr.* Elegies. **CP-DonnJ**
   (Jealosie.) **CBLP; ESCV**

Jealousy. David Herbert Lawrence. **CP-LawrD**

Jealousy. Whispered weather reports. Errors. John Ashbery. **SP-AshbJ**

Jean, death comes close to us all. The Child Bearers. Anne Sexton. **CP-SextA**

Jean Rhys. Derek Walcott. **CP-WalcD**

Jean Sans Terre at the Final Port. Iwan Goll, *tr. fr. French by* William Carlos Williams. **CP-WilW2**

Jean Sans Terre Circles the Earth Seven Times. Iwan Goll, *tr. fr. French by* William Carlos Williams. **CP-WilW2**

Jean Sans Terre Discovers the West Pole. Iwan Goll, *tr. fr. French by* William Carlos Williams. **CP-WilW2**

Jean Sans Terre Leads the Caravan. Iwan Goll, *tr. fr. French by* William Carlos Williams. **CP-WilW2**

Jean Sans Terre Reviews the Fathers. Iwan Goll, *tr. fr. French by* William Carlos Williams. **CP-WilW2**

Jean Sans Terre The Chest of Drawers. Iwan Goll, *tr. fr. French by* Isabella Gardner. **CP-GardI**

Jean Sans Terre Wraps Himself in a Red Coat. Iwan Goll, *tr. fr. French by* Isabella Gardner. **CP-GardI**

Jeanne d'Arc. Louise Glück. **SP-GlücL**

Jeanne D'Arc. Patti Smith. **SP-SmitP**

Jed is breathlessly, deliriously happy because he's just been deftly ambushed and gunned down. War. Charles Kenneth Williams. **SP-WillC**

Jed Kane. Louise McNeill. **SP-McNeL**

Jed says: How come I'm afraid to climb on the jungle game when even the littler kids aren't? The Body. Charles Kenneth Williams. **SP-WillC**

Jefferson had many charms. On the Father of Liberty. Allen Tate. *Fr.* Historical Epitaphs. **CP-TateA**

Jefferson spoke of freedom but he held slaves. Secrets of American Civilization. Muriel Rukeyser. **CP-RukeM**

JEHOVAH. Robert Herrick. **CP-HerrR**

Jehovah buried, Satan dead. Edward Estlin Cummings. **CP-CummE; SP-CummE**

Jehovah-Jesus. William Cowper. *Fr.* Olney Hymns. **CP-CowpW**

Jehovah-Jireh. William Cowper. *Fr.* Olney Hymns. **CP-CowpW**

Jehovah-Nissi. William Cowper. *Fr.* Olney Hymns. **CP-CowpW**

Jehovah Our Righteousness. William Cowper. **NOCV** *Fr.* Olney Hymns. **CP-CowpW**

Jehovah-Rophi. William Cowper. *Fr.* Olney Hymns. **CP-CowpW**

Jehovah-Shalom. William Cowper. *Fr.* Olney Hymns. **CP-CowpW**

Jehovah-Shammah. William Cowper. *Fr.* Olney Hymns. **CP-CowpW**

Jehovah to my words give ear, *par.* by Milton. Bible, *O.T. See* Psalm 5: "Give ear to my words, O Lord, consider my meditation."

Jehovah's Immovable Throne, *sl. diff. vers.* Bible, *O.T. See* Psalm 93: "Lord reigneth, The. . . ."

Jehu. Louis MacNeice. **CP-MacNL**

Jelaludin Muhammed Akbar, Guardian of Mankind. Akbar's Bridge. Rudyard Kipling. **CP-KiplR**

Jelly Jelly. James Schuyler. **CP-SchuJ**

Jellyfish, A. Marianne Craig Moore. **CP-MoorM**

Jellyfish, The. Ogden Nash. **CP-NashO**

Jellyfish washed up. Nova Scotia. Stephen Dunn. **SP-DunnS**

Jemez. Charles Tomlinson. **CP-TomlC**

Jengiz to Chang Chun: China. Basil Bunting. *Fr.* Vestiges. **CP-BuntB**

Jennie—my Jennie Humphrey. Emily Dickinson. **SP-DickE**

Jenny and Me were engaged, you see. Pink Dominoes. Rudyard Kipling. **CP-KiplR**

Jenny Geddes. John Hewitt. **CP-HewiJ**

Jenny said when she was just five years old. Rock 'N' Roll. "Lou Reed." **SP-ReedL**

Jenny sits up i' the laft. Brose and Butter. Robert Burns. **CP-BurnR**

Jenny Wren. Walter de la Mare. **CP-DeLaW**

Jephson, thou man of men, to whose loved name. To Sir William Jephson. Ben Jonson. **CP-JonsB**

Jephtha's Daughter. Byron. **CP-Byron**

Jerboa, The. Marianne Craig Moore. **CP-MoorM**

    Too Much. **CMoP**

Jeremiah 15th Ch. 10 V. Robert Burns. **CP-BurnR**

Jericho. Louis MacNeice. **CP-MacNL**

Jerome. Randall Jarrell. **CP-JarrR**

Jerome had lived alone for thirty years. The Hut of the man alone. Donald Hall. **CP-HallD**

Jerónimo's House. Elizabeth Bishop. **CP-BishE**

Jersey hills / to grandfather's house, The. Over the Hills. James Schuyler. **CP-SchuJ**

Jersey Lyric. William Carlos Williams. **CP-WilW2**

Jerusalem. William Blake. *See* And Did Those Feet in Ancient Time.

Jerusalem. Adrienne Rich. **CP-RicAE; SP-RicA2**

Jerusalem is built of gold, / Of crystal, pearl, and gem. The Holy City, New Jerusalem. Christina Georgina Rossetti. **CP-RosC2**

Jerusalem of fire / And gold and pearl and gem. Christina Georgina Rossetti. **CP-RosC2**

Jerusalem; The Emanation of the Giant Albion. William Blake. **CP-BlakW**

  "But still the thunder of Los peals loud and thus the thunder's cry." **OAEL-2**

  "England! awake! awake! awake!" **EnRP; FHYEP; NoP; OBNC; OBRV** (Prelude: "England! awake! awake! awake!") **OBNC**

  "Fearing that Albion should turn his back against the Divine Vision." **OAEL-2**

  Fields from Islington to Marybone, The. **ChTr; FaBoPV; OBNV; OBRV** (Prelude: "Fields from Islington to Marybone, The.") **OBNC**

  "Hampstead Highgate Finchley Hendon Muswell hill: rage loud." **NOBRP**

  "I give you the end of a golden string." **EnRP; OBNC; Spl; WGRP** (Epigraph.) **OBNC**

  (To the Christians.) **EnRP; WGRP**

  "I give you the end of a golden string." **CP-BlakW; NTP**

  "I see the Four-fold Man. The Humanity in deadly sleep." **NOBRP**

  In Deadly Fear. **SeCePo**

  "It is easier to forgive an enemy than to forgive a friend." **OAEL-2**

  Male & Female Loves in Beulah. **OBNC**

Monk, The. **CP-BlakW; EnRP; OBRV**

"Shuddring the Spectre howls, his howlings terrify the night." **OAEL-2**

Jes' lak toddy wahms you thoo'. Dely. Paul Laurence Dunbar. **CP-DunbP**

Jess and Jill are pretty girls. A Ring Posy. Christina Georgina Rossetti. **CP-RosC1**

Jessamine shows like a star, The. Queen Rose. Christina Georgina Rossetti. **CP-RosC3**

Jessie—A New Scots Song. Robert Burns. **CP-BurnR**

Jessie Cameron. Christina Georgina Rossetti. **CP-RosC1**

Jessie, Jessie Cameron. Jessie Cameron. Christina Georgina Rossetti. **CP-RosC1**

Jessie Mitchell's Mother. Gwendolyn Brooks. **SP-BrooG**

Jester, The. Rudyard Kipling. **CP-KiplR**

Jester walked in the garden, The. The Cap and Bells. William Butler Yeats. **CP-YeatW**

Jesu. George Herbert. **CP-HerbG**

Jesu! bless our slender Boat. Hymn for the Boatmen, as They Approach the Rapids under the Castle of Heidelberg. William Wordsworth. *Fr.* Memorials of a Tour of the Continent; 1820. **CP-WorW2**

Jesu Dulcis Memoria. Gerard Manley Hopkins. **CP-HopkG**

JESU is in my heart, his sacred name. Jesu. George Herbert. **CP-HerbG**

Jesu, no more! It is full tide. Richard Crashaw. **TrGrPo** *Fr.* On the Bleeding Wounds of Our Crucified Lord. **CP-CrasR**

Jesu, no more, it is full tide. On the Bleeding Wounds of Our Crucified Lord. Richard Crashaw. **CP-CrasR**

Jesu that dost in Mary dwell. Oratio Patris Condren: O Jesu Vivens in Maria. Gerard Manley Hopkins. **CP-HopkG**

Jesuits in North America, The. Donald Davie. **CP-DavDo**

Jesus alone:—if thus it were to me. Christina Georgina Rossetti. **CP-RosC3**

Jesus and His Mother. Thom Gunn. **CP-GunnT**

Jesus Asleep. Anne Sexton. **CP-SextA**

Jesus Awake. Anne Sexton. **CP-SextA**

Jesus Cooks. Anne Sexton. **CP-SextA**

Jesus died for somebody's sins. Oath. Patti Smith. **SP-SmitP**

Jesus, do I love Thee? Ash Wednesday. Christina Georgina Rossetti. **CP-RosC3**

Jesus emptied the devils of one man into forty hogs and the hogs took. Always the Mob. Carl Sandburg. **CP-SandC**

Jesús, Estrella, Esperanza, Mercy. Middle Passage. Robert Earl Hayden. **CP-HaydR**

Jesus-faced man walking crowned with flies, The. Martyrium. Geoffrey Hill. *Fr.* Lachrimae; or Seven Tears Figured in Seven Passionate Pavans. **CP-HillG**

Jesus' Farewell. David Herbert Lawrence. **CP-LawrD**

Jesus had gone far up the dark slope, when he looked back. Quetzalcoatl Looks Down on Mexico. David Herbert Lawrence. **CP-LawrD**

Jesus Hasting to Suffer. William Cowper. *Fr.* Olney Hymns. **CP-CowpW**

Jesus here has got something to answer for. What the Irish Soldier Said. Malcolm Lowry. **CP-LowrM**

Jesus it's beautiful! I Feel Drunk All the Time. Kenneth Patchen. **CP-PatcK**

Jesus, Lord God from all eternity, / Whom love of us brought down to shame. The Name of Jesus. Christina Georgina Rossetti. **CP-RosC2**

Jesus loved the sunsets on Galilee. Epistle. Carl Sandburg. **CP-SandC**

Jesus. Marye. Robert Southwell. **CP-SoutR**

Jesus Raises Up the Harlot. Anne Sexton. **CP-SextA**

Jesus saw Lazarus. Jesus Summons Forth. Anne Sexton. **CP-SextA**

Jesus saw the multitudes were hungry. Jesus Cooks. Anne Sexton. **CP-SextA**

Jesus slept as still as a toy. Jesus Asleep. Anne Sexton. **CP-SextA**

Jesus Suckles. Anne Sexton. **CP-SextA**

Jesus Summons Forth. Anne Sexton. **CP-SextA**

Jesus, the Actor, Plays the Holy ghost. Anne Sexton. **CP-SextA**

Jesus! thy Crucifix. Emily Dickinson. **CP-DickE**

Jesus to cast one thought upon. Jesu Dulcis Memoria. Gerard Manley Hopkins. **CP-HopkG**

Jesus to His Disciples. Edna St. Vincent Millay. **CP-MillE**

Jesus Unborn. Anne Sexton. **CP-SextA**

Jesus Walking. Anne Sexton. **CP-SextA**

Jesus, where'er thy people meet. On Opening a Place for Social Prayer. William Cowper. *Fr.* Olney Hymns. **CP-CowpW**

Jesus, whose blood so freely stream'd. Jehovah-Shalom. William Cowper. *Fr.* Olney Hymns. **CP-CowpW**

Jesus will take care of it. Mr. Boyd. Frederick Morgan. **SP-MorgF**

Jet Fizzle. Jim Carroll. **SP-CarrJ**

Jet Flakes. Patti Smith. **SP-SmitP**

Jet Must Be Hunting for Something, The. Robert Penn Warren. **SP-WarrR**

Jet Ring Sent, A. John Donne. **CP-DonnJ**

J'étais confus à cet instant. Sincèrement. Robert Ranke Graves. **CP-GravR**

Jetsam. Charles Kenneth Williams. **CP-WillC**

Jetty. Dover, The. Muriel Rukeyser. **CP-RukeM**

Jeune Fille, The. David Herbert Lawrence. **CP-LawrD**

Jew did not go to his synagogue, The. Winter Bells. Wallace Stevens. **CP-StevW**

Jew Is Angry with His Friend Who Does Not Believe in Circumcision, A. Stevie Smith. **CP-SmitS**

Jewel, The. James Dickey. **CP-DickJ**

Jewel, The. James Wright. **CP-WrigJ**

Jewel of the almost islands and the isles. Catullus. *See* Carmen 31: "Apple of islands, Sirmio, & bright peninsulas, set."

Jewel Stairs' Grievance, The, *fr. the Chinese of* Li Po (701-62). Ezra Pound. **SP-PounE**

Jeweled Bat, The. Charles Henri Ford. *Fr.* For Djuna Barnes. **SP-FordC**

Jewelled steps are already quite white with dew, The. *fr. the Chinese of* Li Po (701-62). Ezra Pound. **SP-PounE**

Jewels here lie heaped for you. Song: Basket of Blossom. Robert Ranke Graves. **CP-GravR**

Jewes their beds, and offices of ease, The. North and South. Robert Herrick. **CP-HerrR**

Jewes, when they built Houses (I have read), The. Observation. Robert Herrick. **CP-HerrR**

Jewess and the V.C., The. David Herbert Lawrence. *Fr.* Bits. **CP-LawrD**

Jewess was happy, The. The Resemblance. William Carlos Williams. **CP-WilW2**

Jewish atheist stubborn as Freud, A. A Memory of My Friend. Howard Nemerov. **CP-NemeH**

Jewish Cemetery at Newport, The. Henry Wadsworth Longfellow. **SP-LongH**

Jewish Family (in a Small Valley Opposite St Goar, upon the Rhine), A. William Wordsworth. **CP-WorW2**

Jewish Graveyards, Italy. Philip Levine. **SP-LeviP**

Jews: / Groceries / Suits, The. Likewise. Langston Hughes. **SP-HughL**

Jews, The. George Herbert. **CP-HerbG**

Jews among the Nations, The. Kay Boyle. **CP-BoylK**

Jews at Haifa. Randall Jarrell. **CP-JarrR; SP-JarrR**

Jews of my childhood were / resident strangers and neighbors, The. Strangers and Neighbors. John Hewitt. **CP-HewiJ**

Jezreel. Thomas Hardy. **CP-HardT**

Jig for Harmonica. Isabella Gardner. *Fr.* Saloon Suite. **CP-GardI**

Jig, like Noah's donkey in the Ark, The. Malcolm Lowry. *Fr.* Peter Gaunt and the Canals. **CP-LowrM**

Jigsaws. Louis MacNeice. **CP-MacNL**

"Although we say we disbelieve." **CP-MacNL**

"Fresh from the knife and coming to." **CP-MacNL**

"Gulf between us and the brutes, The." **CP-MacNL**

"Property! Property! Let us extend." **IHNG**

(On Property.) **IHNG**

"What ghosts of cuckoo-spit and dew." **CP-MacNL**

Jilted. Paul Laurence Dunbar. **CP-DunbP**

Jilted. Sylvia Plath. **CP-PlatS**

Jim Jim / where is our party? "Bob Dylan." *Fr.* 11 Outlined Epitaphs. **CP-DylaB**

Jim Wright, who was a good poet and my friend, died two or three years ago. Not Transhistorical Death, or at Least Not Quite. Hayden Carruth. **CP-CarHS**

Jimmall Ring, or True-Love-Knot, The. Robert Herrick. **CP-HerrR**

Jimmie's got a goil. Edward Estlin Cummings. **CP-CummE**

Jimmy Jet and His TV Set. Shel Silverstein. **SP-SilS2**

Jimmy Wimbledon listened a first week in June. Young Bullfrogs. Carl Sandburg. **CP-SandC**

Jingle. William Carlos Williams. **CP-WilW2**

Jingle on the Times, A. Thomas Hardy. **CP-HardT**

Jingles of the Morning, The. Louis MacNeice. *Fr.* Out of the Picture. **CP-MacNL**

Jingo and the Minstrel, The. Nicholas Vachel Lindsay. **CP-LindV**

Jittery, missing their cues. The Plot Against Hitler. Stanley Jasspon Kunitz. *Fr.* Around Pastor Bonhoeffer. **CP-KuniS**

Jittoku, Buddhist Mystic—15th Century. Jane Cooper. **SP-CoopJ**

Jiving. Rita Dove. **SP-DoveR**

Joan and Darby. Robert Ranke Graves. **CP-GravR**

Joan Baez in Concert, Part 2. "Bob Dylan." **CP-DylaB**

Joan, Joan, can you be. To the Maid of Orleans. Edna St. Vincent Millay. **CP-MillE**

Joan of Arc. Leonard Cohen. **CP-CoheL**

Joan was quizical studied metaphysical. Maxwell's Silver Hammer. The Beatles. **CP-Beatl**

Joannes jacet hic Mirandula—cætera norunt. *see also* Epitaph on Chartres. Alexander Pope. **CP-PopeA**

Job. Wystan Hugh Auden. **CP-AudWJ**

Job of hunting of shooting in hunting season of, The. Grace Paley. *Fr.* Stanzas: Old Age and the Conventions of Retirement Have Driven My Friends from the Work They Love. **CP-PaleG**

Job the Father. Richard Shelton. **CP-ShelR**

Job the Rejected. Edwin Arlington Robinson. **CP-RobiE**

Jobson's Amen. Rudyard Kipling. **CP-KiplR**

Jochanan Hakkadosh. Robert Browning. **CP-BroR2**

Jock of Hazeldean. Sir Walter Scott. **SP-ScotW**

Jockey, A. Ron Koertge. **SP-KoerR**

Jockey Fou and Jenny Fain. Robert Burns. **CP-BurnR**

Jockey's Ta'en the Parting Kiss. Robert Burns. **CP-BurnR**

Joe, / the other day I tried to get my class. Letter About Myself to You. Stephen Dunn. **SP-DunnS**

Joe Bittner, he was a mountain lad. Ballad of Joe Bittner. Louise McNeill. **SP-McNeL**

Joe Blow has decided. The Archetype Poem. Allen Ginsberg. **CP-GinsA**

Joe Hill Listens to the Praying. Kenneth Patchen. **CP-PatcK**

Joe Louis. Langston Hughes. **SP-HughL**

JOE WILLIAMS is. Memo #32. Etheridge Knight. **SP-KnigE**

Joe's Jacket. Frank O'Hara. **SP-OharF**

Joey. "Bob Dylan" *and* Jacques Levy. **CP-DylaB**

Joey. Shel Silverstein. **SP-SilS2**

Jog-Trot Pair, A. Thomas Hardy. **CP-HardT**

Jogger. Daniel Gerard Hoffman. **SP-HoffD**

Joggin' Erlong. Paul Laurence Dunbar. **CP-DunbP**

Joggle i think will do it although the glad. Gert. Edward Estlin Cummings. *Fr.* Five Americans. **CP-CummE**

Johann. Alice Walker. **CP-WalkA**

Johann Gaertner (1793–1887). Gary Gildner. **SP-GildG**

Johanna. David Markson. **CP-MarkD**

Johannes Agricola in Meditation. Robert Browning. **CP-BroR1**

Johannes Kepler (1571–1630). Siv Cedering Fox. *Fr.* Letters from the Astronomers. **SP-CedeS**

John 3; But Men Loved Darknesse Rather than Light. Bible, *N.T.* **CP-CrasR**, *tr.* by Richard Crashaw; *Fr.* St. John.

John 15; Upon Our Lords Last Comfortable Discourse with His Disciples. Bible, *N.T.* **CP-CrasR**, *tr.* by Richard Crashaw; *Fr.* St. John.

John 16; Verily I Say unto You, Yee Shall Weep and Lament. Bible, *N.T.* **CP-CrasR**, *tr.* by Richard Crashaw; *Fr.* St. John.

John Adams lies here, of the parish of Southwell. Epitaph on John Adams, of Southwell. Byron. **CP-Byron**

John Alden. Henry Wadsworth Longfellow. *Fr.* The Courtship of Miles Standish. **SP-LongH**

"Into the open air John Alden, perplexed and bewildered." **TreFS** War-Token, The. **PAH**

John and I have decided. The Menu. Robert Creeley. **CP-CreeR**

John and Jane. Thomas Hardy. **CP-HardT**

John Anderson my jo, John / When we were first acquent. Robert Burns. **CP-BurnR**

John Barleycorn [a Ballad]. Robert Burns. **CP-BurnR**

John Boyle O'Reilly. Paul Laurence Dunbar. **CP-DunbP**

John Brown. "Bob Dylan." **CP-DylaB**

John Brown. Robert Earl Hayden. **CP-HaydR**

John Brown. Nicholas Vachel Lindsay. **MoAmPo** *Fr.* The Booker Washington Trilogy. **CP-LindV**

John Brown. Edwin Arlington Robinson. **CP-RobiE**

John Brown of Ossawatomie spake on his dying day. Brown of Ossawatomie. John Greenleaf Whittier. **CP-WhitJ**

John Brown of Ossawattamie. On the Martyr of Harpers Ferry. Allen Tate. *Fr.* Historical Epitaphs. **CP-TateA**

John Brown went off to war to fight on a foreign shore. John Brown. "Bob Dylan." **CP-DylaB**

John Brown's body under the morning stars. Old Osawatomie. Carl Sandburg. **CP-SandC**

John Burke. Charles Olson. **SP-OlsoC** *Fr.* The Maximus Poems.

John Button Birthday. Frank O'Hara. **SP-OharF**

John Chapman. Richard Wilbur. **CP-WilbR**

John Chrysostom. Richard Wilbur. **CP-WilbR**

John Coltrane Dance, The. Al Young. **CP-YounA**

John Come Kiss Me Now. Robert Burns. **CP-BurnR**

John Dillinger Marches On. Charles Bukowski. **SP-BukC3**

John Donne in His Shroud. Marsden Hartley. **CP-HartM**

John Dryden. Hayden Carruth. **CP-CarHS**

John Endicott. Henry Wadsworth Longfellow. **SP-LongH**

  Act II.

    Proclamation, The. **PAH**

  Prologue: "To-night we strive to read, as we may best."

John Ericsson Day Memorial, 1918. Carl Sandburg. **CP-SandC**

John Evereldown. Edwin Arlington Robinson. **CP-RobiE**

John Finley. Richard Eberhart. **CP-EberR**

John Fleming walked in the house his cousin left him. Beau of the Dead. Donald Hall. **CP-HallD**

John Fowles's book, *The French Lieutenant's Woman.* Dorset. Donald Davie. **CP-DavDo**

John gave his brother James a box. "Lewis Carroll." *Fr.* Puzzles. *Fr.* Puzzles from Wonderland. **CP-CarrL**

John Gilpin. William Cowper. **CP-CowpW**

John Gorham. Edwin Arlington Robinson. **CP-RobiE**

John J. Maya Angelou. **SP-AngeM**

John, John of Ottenhaw! George Meredith. **CP-MerG2**

John Jordan said there are two kinds of dead. Miles. James Liddy. **CP-LiddJ**

John Kinsella's Lament for Mrs. Mary Moore. William Butler Yeats. **CP-YeatW**

John L. Sullivan, the Strong Boy of Boston. Nicholas Vachel Lindsay. **CP-LindV**

John Lackland. George Meredith. **CP-MerG1**

John Landless leads his landless folk. Jean Sans Terre Discovers the West Pole. Iwan Goll, *tr. fr. French by* William Carlos Williams. **CP-WilW2**

John Landless sailing on a helmless boat. Jean Sans Terre at the Final Port. Iwan Goll, *tr. fr. French by* William Carlos Williams. **CP-WilW2**

John Ledyard. Richard Eberhart. **CP-EberR**

John Lennon in the Porto Santo Stefano. Lawrence Ferlinghetti. **SP-FerlL**

John Littlehouse the redhead was a large ruddy man. The Blacksmith's Serenade. Nicholas Vachel Lindsay. **CP-LindV**

John Maclean (1879-1923). "Hugh MacDiarmid." **SP-MacDH**

John Marr. Herman Melville. **SP-MelvH**

  "Since as in night's deck-watch ye show." **APN-2; SP-MelvH**

John Maydew or The Allotment. Charles Tomlinson. **CP-TomlC**

John Milton. Allen Tate. **CP-TateA**

John Muir on Mt. Ritter. Gary Snyder. **CP-SnydG** *Fr.* Burning. *Fr.* Myths and Texts.

John, oh John. St John. David Herbert Lawrence. **CP-LawrD**

John the tailor had gone racing up the stairs in back of his store and because he was so frightened. Crime. Charles Kenneth Williams. **SP-WillC**

John the Volcano. Thomas Merton. *Fr.* East. *Fr.* The Geography of Lograire. **CP-MertT**

John Underhill. John Greenleaf Whittier. **CP-WhitJ**

John Wesley Harding. "Bob Dylan." **CP-DylaB**

John Wesley Harding (Liner Notes). "Bob Dylan." **CP-DylaB**

John Wilmot's dead three hundred years this year. Tricentennial: 1980. David Markson. **CP-MarkD**

Johnie B———'s Lament. Robert Burns. **CP-BurnR** *Fr.* The Heron Ballads, 1795.

Johnie Blunt. Robert Burns. **CP-BurnR**

Johnie Cope. Robert Burns. **CP-BurnR**

Johnny. Wystan Hugh Auden. *See* O the valley in the summer where I and my John.

Johnny. Christina Georgina Rossetti. **CP-RosC2**

Johnny Appleseed Speaks of Great Cities in the Future. Nicholas Vachel Lindsay. **CP-LindV**

Johnny Appleseed Speaks of the Appleblossom Amaranth That Will Come to This City. Nicholas Vachel Lindsay. **CP-LindV**

Johnny Appleseed's Hymn to the Sun. Nicholas Vachel Lindsay. **CP-LindV**

Johnny Appleseed's Old Age. Nicholas Vachel Lindsay. *Fr.* In Praise of Johnny Appleseed. **CP-LindV**

Johnny Appleseed's Ship Comes In. Nicholas Vachel Lindsay. **CP-LindV**

Johnny Appleseed's Wife from the Palace of Eve. Nicholas Vachel Lindsay. **CP-LindV**

Johnny Appleseed's Wife of the Mind. Nicholas Vachel Lindsay. **CP-LindV**

  "Come let us pray to the Lord of the sky."

  "Slender maiden found me sleeping, The."

Johnny had a golden head / Like a golden mop in blow. Johnny. Christina Georgina Rossetti. **CP-RosC2**

Johnny (little johnny) / with his father's hammer. "Bob Dylan." *Fr.* Some Other Kinds of Songs. **CP-DylaB**

Johnny, since to-day is. Many Happy Returns. Wystan Hugh Auden. **CP-AudeW**

Johnny Spain's White Heifer. Hayden Carruth. **CP-CarHS**

Johnny Speaks. Paul Laurence Dunbar. **CP-DunbP**

Johnny's in the basement. Subterranean Homesick Blues. "Bob Dylan." **CP-DylaB**

Johnson's Cabinet Watched by Ants. Robert Bly. **SP-BlyR**

Johnson's pentameters, nailed by the solid *ictus.* Northumberland. Donald Davie. **CP-DavDo**

Joint. James Schuyler. **CP-SchuJ**

Joints were none that mortar sealed. Greek Masonry. Herman Melville. **SP-MelvH**

Joinville and Louis IX. Robert Lowell. **SP-LoweR**

Joinville and Louis the Ninth. Joinville and Louis IX. Robert Lowell. **SP-LoweR**

Jojo was a man who thought he was a loner. Get Back. The Beatles. **CP-Beatl**

Joke, The. Robert Creeley. **CP-CreeR**

Joke, The. Phoebe Hesketh. **SP-HeskP**

Joke county, smallest in England. Rutland. Donald Davie. **CP-DavDo**

Joke Gold. Carl Sandburg. **CP-SandC**

Joke: once, if I remember well, I sat judy on my knees and. Notice 2. Patti Smith. **SP-SmitP**

Jokerman. "Bob Dylan." **CP-DylaB**

Jokes Aloft. Malcolm Lowry. **CP-LowrM**

Jokes Amidships. Malcolm Lowry. **CP-LowrM**

Jokes in the Galley. Malcolm Lowry. **CP-LowrM**

Jokes on the Poop. Malcolm Lowry. **CP-LowrM**

Jokes, the feuds, the puns, the punishments, The. A Louis Sonnet. Muriel Rukeyser. **CP-RukeM**

Joliet. Carl Sandburg. **CP-SandC**

Jolly and Jillie, bite and scratch all day. Upon Jolly and Jilly. Robert Herrick. **CP-HerrR**

Jolly Beggars, The. Robert Burns.

  (Love and Libery—A Cantata.) **CP-BurnR**

  "Caird prevail'd—th' unblushing fair, The."

  "He ended and the kebars sheuk."

  "Her charms had struck a sturdy CAIRD."

  "Highland lad my Love was born, A."

  "I am a Bard of no regard." **PoE**

  "I am a Son of Mars who have been in many wars."

  I Once Was a Maid. **NBLV; OxBoLi**

  "Let me ryke up to dight that tear."

  "My bonie lass I work in brass."

  "Pigmy Scraper wi' his Fiddle, A."

  "Poor Merry-andrew, in the [*or* a] neuk." **OBCoV**

  "See the smoking bowl before us." **GoTS; PoE**

    (Drinking Song.) **TrGrPo**

    ("Fig for those by law protected!, A.") **TrGrPo**

  "Sir Wisdom's a fool when he's fou." **OBCoV**

  "So sung the BARD—and Nansie's waws." **PoE**

  "Then niest outspak a raucle carlin."

  "When lyart leaves bestrow the yird."

Jolly boys of St. Kevin's, St. Patrick's, Donore. The Yahoo's Overthrow. Jonathan Swift. **CP-SwifJ**

Jolly Gauger, The. Robert Burns. **CP-BurnR**

Jolly Good Fellow, A. Phoebe Hesketh. **SP-HeskP**

Jolly Greene Giant, The. John Updike. **CP-UpdiJ**

Jolly Young Carpenter, The. George Meredith. **CP-MerG2**

Jolt. Al Young. **CP-YounA**

Jonah. Randall Jarrell. **CP-JarrR**

Jonah. May Sarton. **SP-SartM**

Jonah made his living. Making a Living. Anne Sexton. **CP-SextA**

Jonathan Aging. Miller Williams. **SP-WillM**

Jonathan Edwards in Western Massachusetts. Robert Lowell. **SP-LoweR**

Jonathan feels like a character out of Dickens. Jonathan Aging. Miller Williams. **SP-WillM**

Jonathan Hawkins. Lewis Turco. *Fr.* Bordello. **SP-TurcL**

Jonathan Jukes is full of health. Tell It to the Eskimos or Tell it to the Esquimaux. Ogden Nash. **CP-NashO**

Jonathan Lazarus Wright, 1702–1729. Martin Edmunds. **SP-EdmuM**

Jonathan Swift / Had the gift. Lines on a Drawing of a Monument to Swift's Grandfather. Alexander Pope. **CP-PopeA**

Jonathan Swift, that scorpion. A Prayer. Dabney Stuart. **SP-StuaD**

Jonathan, the last of the giant tortoises. Stanley Jasspon Kunitz. *Fr.* Signs and Portents. **CP-KuniS**

Jone is a wench that's painted. Upon Jone and Jane. Robert Herrick. **CP-HerrR**

Jone wo'd go tel her haires; and well she might. On Jone. Robert Herrick. **CP-HerrR**

Jones! as from Calais southward you and I. Composed Near Calais on the Road Leading to Ardres, August 7, 1802. William Wordsworth. **CP-WorW1**

Jones took the little daily dose. Homoeopathic Blues in J. Malcolm Lowry. **CP-LowrM**

Jordan (1). George Herbert. *See* Who say[e]s that fictions onl[e]y and false hair.

Jordan (2). George Herbert. **CP-HerbG**

Jormungand. Frederick Morgan. **SP-MorgF**

Josef Weinheber. Wystan Hugh Auden. *Fr.* Eleven Occasional Poems. **CP-AudeW**

Joseph and Mary. Robert Ranke Graves. **CP-GravR**

Joseph Conrad. Malcolm Lowry. **CP-LowrM**

Josepha. George Meredith. **CP-MerG2**

Josephe's Amazement. Robert Southwell. **CP-SoutR**

Joseph's Coat. George Herbert. **CP-HerbG**

Joshua on Eighth Avenue. John Ciardi. **SP-CiarJ**

Josie. James Liddy. **CP-LiddJ**

Jouga. Wallace Stevens. **CP-StevW**

Journal. Edna St. Vincent Millay. **CP-MillE**

Journal for My Daughter. Stanley Jasspon Kunitz. **CP-KuniS**

"Demonstrations in the streets."

"Goodies are shaken / from the papa-tree."

"I wake to a glittering world."

"I was happy you were born."

"Night when Coleridge, The."

"There was a big blond uncle-bear."

"You cried. You cried."

"Your first dog was a Pekinese."

"Your turn, Grass of confusion."

Journal in Cephalonia. Byron. **CP-Byron**

Journal Night Thoughts. Allen Ginsberg. **CP-GinsA**

Journal of a Modern Lady, The. Jonathan Swift. **CP-SwifJ**

Journal of English Days, A. Charles Wright. **SP-WrigC**

Journal of One Significant Landscape, A. Charles Wright. **SP-WrigC**

Journal of Southern Rivers, A. Charles Wright. **SP-WrigC**

Journal of the Year of the Ox, A. Charles Wright. **SP-WrigC**

Journal of Three Questions, A. Charles Wright. **SP-WrigC**

Journal of True Confessions, A. Charles Wright. **SP-WrigC**

Journalist Buys a Pig Farm, The. Miller Williams. **SP-WillM**

Journalists. Rudyard Kipling. *Fr.* Epitaphs of the War [1914–1918]. **CP-KiplR**

Journey, The. Walter de la Mare. **CP-DeLaW**

Journey. Phoebe Hesketh. **SP-HeskP**

Journey, The. Alun Lewis. **CP-LewiA**

Journey. Edna St. Vincent Millay. **CP-MillE**

Journey, The. Mary Oliver. **SP-OlivM**

Journey, The. Kathleen Jessie Raine. **SP-RainK**

Journey, The. Charles Tomlinson. **CP-TomlC**

Journey Day. John Gould Fletcher. **SP-FletJ**

Journey Home. Archibald MacLeish. **CP-MacLA**

Journey in darkness hs a trivial jargon, The. Dark Continent. Tom Clark. **SP-ClarT**

Journey is always return, The. The Crossing. Richard Shelton. **SP-ShelR**

Journey of a Poem Compared to All the Sad Variety of Travel, The. Delmore Schwartz. **SP-SchwD**

Journey of the Magi. Thomas Stearns Eliot. **CP-ElioT**

Journey of the Snowmen. Howard Nemerov. **CP-NemeH**

Journey Renewed. William Wordsworth. *Fr.* The River Duddon [A Series of Sonnets]. **CP-WorW2**

Journey Starts Swiftly, The. Nicholas Vachel Lindsay. *Fr.* The Tree of Laughing Bells or The Wings of the Morning. **CP-LindV**

Journey to a Known Place. Hayden Carruth. **CP-CarHL**

Aer.

Aqua.

Ignis.

Terra.

Journey to Iceland. Wystan Hugh Auden. **CP-AudeW**

Journey to the Interior. Margaret Atwood. **SP-AtwM1**

Journey to the Interior. Theodore Roethke. **DiPo; PFL** *Fr.* North American Sequence. **CP-RoetT**

Journey toward Poetry. May Sarton. **SP-SartM**

Journey With a Conjuror. James McAuley. **SP-McAuJ** *Fr.* The Exile's Recurring Nightmare.

Journeying over many seas and through many countries. Carmen 101. Catullus. *Fr.* Carmina. **CP-Catul**

Jours-Fixes. James Liddy. *Fr.* Glass after Oblivion. **CP-LiddJ**

Jove call'd before him t'other Day. Verses Occasioned by an &c. at the End of Mr. D'Urfy's Name in the Title to One of His Plays. Alexander Pope. **CP-PopeA**

Jove may afford us thousands of reliefs. Griefes. Robert Herrick. **CP-HerrR**

Joy. Wystan Hugh Auden. **CP-AudWJ**

Joy. Robert Creeley. **CP-CreeR**

Joy. William Dickey. **SP-DickW**

Joy. John Gould Fletcher. **SP-FletJ**

Joy. Langston Hughes. **SP-HughL**

Joy. Robinson Jeffers. **CP-JefR1**

Joy. Denise Levertov. **CP-LeveD**

Joy. Carl Sandburg. **CP-SandC**

Joy and Agony of Improvisation, The. Hayden Carruth. **CP-CarHS**

Joy and Peace in Believing. William Cowper. **NOCV; TRV** *Fr.* Olney Hymns. **CP-CowpW**

Joy comes / Not to the sound of beaten drums. Joy. Wystan Hugh Auden. **CP-AudWJ**

Joy, did I [*or* I did] lock thee up; but some bad man. The Bunch of Grapes. George Herbert. **CP-HerbG**

Joy in Martyrdom. Jeanne Marie Bouvier de la Motte-Guyon, *tr. fr. French by* William Cowper. **CP-CowpW**

Joy is a trick in the air. Birth-Dues. Robinson Jeffers. **CP-JefR1**

Joy is but sorrow, / While we know. Christina Georgina Rossetti. **CP-RosC2**

Joy is fleet, / Sorrow slow. George Meredith. **CP-MerG1**

Joy of Fishes, The. Chuang Tzu, *tr. fr. Chinese by* Thomas Merton. **CP-MertT**

Joy of man, the pride of brutes, The. Jonathan Swift. *Fr.* Riddles. **CP-SwifJ**

Joy of my life! you tell me this. Carmen 109. Catullus. *Fr.* Carmina. **CP-Catul**

Joy of Saints, like incense turned to fire, The. Christina Georgina Rossetti. **CP-RosC2**

Joy of the Cross, The. Jeanne Marie Bouvier de la Motte-Guyon, *tr. fr. French by* William Cowper. **CP-CowpW**

Joy of wax teeth, The. Hallow Eve with Spaces for Ghosts. Marge Piercy. **SP-PierM**

Joy, Shipmate, Joy! Walt Whitman. **CP-WhitW**

Joy so short alas, the pain so near, The. Sir Thomas Wyatt. **CP-WyatT**

Joy that has no stem nor core, The. Emily Dickinson. **CP-DickE**

Joy, the, "well. . . joyfulness of." Joy. Denise Levertov. **CP-LeveD**

Joy to have merited the Pain. Emily Dickinson. **CP-DickE**

Joy we most revere, The. Emily Dickinson. **SP-DickE**

Joy. . . weaving two violet petals for a coat lapel. Brass Keys. Carl Sandburg. **CP-SandC**

Joy you say the Heavens in motion trie, The. Mary Sidney, Countess of Montgomery Wroth. *Fr.* Part 1. *Fr.* Urania. **CP-WrotM**

Joy/Spring. Al Young. **CP-YounA**

Joyce Carol Oates Plays the Saturn Piano. Diane Wakoski. **SP-WakoD**

Joyce was afraid of thunder. Volcano. Derek Walcott. **CP-WalcD**

Joycentenary Ode. Derek Mahon. **SP-MahoD**

Joye in the risinge of our orient starr. Our Ladie's Nativitye. Robert Southwell. **CP-SoutR**

Joyful / And woful. Song. Johann Wolfgang von Goethe, *tr. fr. German by* George Meredith. **CP-MerG2**

Joyful lady, sing! / And I will lurk here listening. To a Lady Playing and Singing in the Morning. Thomas Hardy. **CP-HardT**

Joyful your complete fearless and pure love. Edward Estlin Cummings. **CP-CummE**

Joyfull pleasant spring. Mary Sidney, Countess of Montgomery Wroth. *Fr.* Love's Victorie. **CP-WrotM**

Joyfull Spring did ever last, The. Ovid, *tr. by* Sir Walter Ralegh. **CP-RaleW** *Fr.* Metamorphoses.

Joys faces friends / feet terrors fate. Edward Estlin Cummings. **CP-CummE**

Joys of Memory. Thomas Hardy. **CP-HardT**

J.S. Bach. Wystan Hugh Auden. **CP-AudWJ**

Juan and Haidée. Byron. **EBNV** *Fr.* Canto the Second. *Fr.* Don Juan. **CP-Byron**

Juan embark'd--the ship got under way. Byron. **MOS** *Fr.* Canto the Second. *Fr.* Don Juan. **CP-Byron**

Juan in England. Byron. **FaBoVe**, *canto* 11, *stanza* 8–20; *Fr.* Canto the Eleventh. **NOBRP** *Fr.* Don Juan. **CP-Byron**

Juan knew several languages—as well. Byron. **OAEL-2** *Fr.* Canto the Eleventh. **NOBRP** *Fr.* Don Juan. **CP-Byron**

Juanita Tinsley. Muriel Rukeyser. **CP-RukeM**

Juan's Song. Louise Bogan. **CP-BogaL**

Juan's Twilight Dance. Marge Piercy. **SP-PierM**

Jubal and Tubal Cain. Rudyard Kipling. **CP-KiplR**

Jubal sang of the Wrath of God. Jubal and Tubal Cain. Rudyard Kipling. **CP-KiplR**

Jubilate. Thomas Hardy. **CP-HardT**

Jubilate Agno. Christopher Smart. **SP-SmarC**

  Fragment A.

  "Let Anaiah bless with the Dragon-fly, who sails over the pond by the wood-side and feedeth on the cresses." FaBoVe, *ll.* 100–113;

  "Rejoice in God, O ye Tongues; give the glory to the Lord, and the Lamb." FaBoVe, *ll.* 1–22;

  "Rejoice in God, O ye Tongues; give the glory to the Lord, and the Lamb." PoE, *ll.* 1–11;

  Fragment B.

  "For I bless the PRINCE of PEACE and pray that all the guns may be nail'd up, save such as are for the rejoicing days." **InPS**

  "For I will consider my Cat Jeoffry." **CTC; ChTr; FM; FaBoCh; HAP; HeIP; InPK; LAuP; LiTB; NAEL-1; NOEC; NTP; NU; NoP; OBF; OBWVE; OFC; OxAEP-1; PAI; PCat; PPP; PoE; PoEL-3; PrIm; Prf; RB; SCV; SeCePo; SeCeV; SoCa; TRP; TTTS; WeW; WiR**

  (My Cat Jeoffry.) **ChTr; FaBoCh; LiTB; PoE; RB; SeCePo; SoCa; WiR**

  (Of Jeoffry, His Cat.) **NU; PrIm**

  "For I will consider my Cat Jeoffry." **UV**

  "For man is between the pinchers while his soul is shaping and purifying." **ChIV-1**

  "For the Air is purified by prayer which is made aloud and with all our might." **Prf**

  "For the doubling of flowers is the improvement of the gard'ner's talent." **ChIV-2; LAuP; NOEC**

  "For the spiritual musick is as follows." **NOEC**

  Let Elizur Rejoice with the Partridge. **PoEL-3**

  God Hath Sent Me to Sea for Pearls. **CBCK**

  "Let Elizur[e] rejoice with the Partridge." **OAEL-1**

  "Let Ephah rejoice with Buprestis, the Lord endue us with temperance and humanity, till every cow have her mate!" **NOEC**

  "Let Peter rejoice with the Moon Fish who keeps up the life in the waters by night." **ChIV-2**

  "Let Shobi rejoice with the Kastrel—blessed be the name JESUS in falconry and in the MALL." **NOEC**

  Fragment C.

  "For I prophesy that they will understand the blessing and virtue of the rain." **ECEV**

  "For I prophesy that we shall have our horns again." **ChIV-1**

  Fragment D.

    Mineral Rejoicings. **CBCK**

Jubilate Canis. Erica Jong. **SP-JongE**

Jubilee. Leonard Nathan. **SP-NathL**

Jubilee of a Magazine, The. Thomas Hardy. **CP-HardT**

Jubilee Singers, The. John Greenleaf Whittier. **CP-WhitJ**

Jubilemus omnes una Deo nostro qui creavit omnia, *see also* Thomas Merton *tr.* Prose in Advent Time. *Unknown.* **CP-MertT**

Jubilo. Allen Tate. **CP-TateA**

Judas. James Dickey. **CP-DickJ**

Judas. Jonathan Swift. **CP-SwifJ**

Judas Iscariot. Countee Cullen. **CP-CullC**

Judas Iscariot. First Version. Countee Cullen. **CP-CullC**

Judge and the Bird, The. Louis Zukofsky. **CP-ZukLS**

Judge Every One with Perfect Calm. Alice Walker. **CP-WalkA**

Judge his favour timely then extends, The. Another to Him. Ben Jonson. **CP-JonsB**

Judge is like the Owl, The. Emily Dickinson. **CP-DickE**

Judge me, O God, and plead my cause against an ungodly nation. Psalm 43. Bible, *O.T. Fr.* Psalms. **CP-Psal**

Judge me, O Lord; for I have walked in mine integrity. Psalm 26. Bible, *O.T. Fr.* Psalms. **CP-Psal**

Judge mildly the tasked world; and disincline. The World's Advance. George Meredith. **CP-MerG1**

Judge Not. Theodore Roethke. **CP-RoetT**

Judge Not According to the Appearance. Christina Georgina Rossetti. **CP-RosC2**

Judge Nothing before the Time. Christina Georgina Rossetti. **CP-RosC2**

Judge removed, though he's no more My Lord, The. Prologue to *Don Sebastian.* John Dryden. **SP-DrydJ** *Fr.* Don Sebastian.

Judgement. George Herbert. **CP-HerbG**

Judgement Day, The. Robert Herrick. **CP-HerrR**

Judgement of Paris. Robert Ranke Graves. **CP-GravR**

Judges, The. Robert Ranke Graves. **CP-GravR**

Judging the Pageant. Jim Carroll. **SP-CarrJ**

Judgment, The. Marge Piercy. *Fr.* Laying Down the Tower. **SP-PierM**

Judgment-Day, The. Robert Herrick. **CP-HerrR**

Judgment Day. Langston Hughes. **SP-HughL**

Judgment Day. Ogden Nash. **CP-NashO**

Judgment is justest. Emily Dickinson. **CP-DickE**

Judgment occurs, but is not. Three Beyond. Donald Davie. **CP-DavDo**

Judgment of the Poets, The. William Cowper. **CP-CowpW**

Judith. Muriel Rukeyser. **CP-RukeM**

Judith at the Tent of Holofernes. John Greenleaf Whittier. **CP-WhitJ**

Judith has cast her old-skin, and got new. Upon Judith. Robert Herrick. **CP-HerrR**

Judith of Bethulia. John Crowe Ransom. **SP-RansJ**

Judith Revisited. Patti Smith. **SP-SmitP**

Judy Sugden! Judy, I made you caper. Barnsley and District. Donald Davie. **CP-DavDo**

Jug. Carl Sandburg. **CP-SandC**

Juggernaut. Lewis Turco. **SP-TurcL**

Juggernaut chanting. Charles Henri Ford. **SP-FordC** *Fr.* Emblems of Arachne.

Juggler, The. Siv Cedering Fox. **SP-CedeS**

Juggler. Richard Wilbur. **CP-WilbR**

Juggler to His Audience, The. Bill Knott. **SP-KnotB**

Juggler's Hat her Country is, The. Emily Dickinson. **CP-DickE**

Jugglers keep six bottles in the air. Hazardous Occupations. Carl Sandburg. **CP-SandC**

Juggler's Song, The. Rudyard Kipling. **CP-KiplR** *Fr.* Kim.

Juggler's Thought. Robert Creeley. **CP-CreeR**

Juggling Jerry. George Meredith. **CP-MerG1**

Jugum Improbum. Robert Ranke Graves. **CP-GravR**

Juice. Archie Randolph Ammons. **SP-AmmoA**

Juke Box Love Song. Langston Hughes. **SP-HughL**

Julia. John Donne. *Fr.* Elegies. **CP-DonnJ**

Julia. The Beatles. **CP-Beatl**

Julia and I did lately sit. Cherry-Pit. Robert Herrick. **CP-HerrR**

Julia, I bring. A Ring Presented to Julia. Robert Herrick. **CP-HerrR**

Julia, if I chance to die. His Request to Julia. Robert Herrick. **CP-HerrR**

Julia Now. David Markson. **CP-MarkD**

Julia was carelesse, and withall. Upon Julia's Fall. Robert Herrick. **CP-HerrR**

Julia, when thy Herrick dies. To Julia. Robert Herrick. **CP-HerrR**

Julian [A Fragment]. Byron. **CP-Byron**

Julian and Maddalo; A Conversation. Percy Bysshe Shelley. **CP-ShelP**

Julian Barely Misses Zimmer's Brains. Paul Zimmer. **SP-ZimmP**

Julian M. and A.G. Rochelle, *see also* The Visionary *and* The Prisoner. Emily Brontë. **CP-BronE**

Julian the Apostate. Thom Gunn. **CP-GunnT**

Julia's Churching, or Purification. Robert Herrick. **CP-HerrR**

Julia's Petticoat. Robert Herrick. **CP-HerrR**

Julie-Jane. Thomas Hardy. **CP-HardT**

Juliet. Langston Hughes. **SP-HughL**

Juliet's Garden. Charles Tomlinson. **CP-TomlC**

Juliet's Nurse. Walter de la Mare. **CP-DeLaW**

July. John Hewitt. **CP-HewiJ**

July. George Meredith. **CP-MerG1**

July. Christina Georgina Rossetti. *Fr.* The Months: A Pageant. **CP-RosC2**

July. Gary Snyder. *Fr.* Six Years. **CP-SnydG**

July. John Updike. **CP-UpdiJ**

JULY (Archery). Rudyard Kipling. *Fr.* Verses on Games. **CP-KiplR**

July, August, suspense. / Wall Street lost to sense. Nicholas Vachel Lindsay. *Fr.* Bryan, Bryan, Bryan, Bryan. **CP-LindV**

July Dawn. Louise Bogan. **CP-BogaL**

July Fourth by the Ocean. Robinson Jeffers. **CP-JefR1**

July in Washington. Robert Lowell. **SP-LoweR**

July Is Over and There's Very Little Trace. Frank O'Hara. **SP-OharF**

July Morning. Robert Bly. **SP-BlyR**

July's Farewell. Arthur Hugh Clough. **SP-ClouA**

July. The conspiracy of colors. Augustus Observes the Sunset. Rita Dove. *Fr.* A Suite for Augustus. **SP-DoveR**

July, 1773. Wendell Berry. **CP-BerrW**

July, 1964. Donald Davie. **CP-DavDo**

July 2nd, 1916. Phoebe Hesketh. **SP-HeskP**

July 8 or July 9 the eighth surely, certainly / 1976 that I know. The Morning of the Poem. James Schuyler. **CP-SchuJ**

7/12/68. Adrienne Rich. **CP-RicAE** *Fr.* Ghazals: Homage to Ghalib. **SP-RicA2**

7/13/68. Adrienne Rich. **CP-RicAE** *Fr.* Ghazals: Homage to Ghalib. **SP-RicA2**

7/14/68: i. Adrienne Rich. **CP-RicAE** *Fr.* Ghazals: Homage to Ghalib. **SP-RicA2**

7/16/68: i. Adrienne Rich. **CP-RicAE** *Fr.* Ghazals: Homage to Ghalib. **SP-RicA2**

7/16/68: ii. Adrienne Rich. **CP-RicAE** *Fr.* Ghazals: Homage to Ghalib. **SP-RicA2**

7/17/68. Adrienne Rich. **CP-RicAE** *Fr.* Ghazals: Homage to Ghalib. **SP-RicA2**

7/26/68: i. Adrienne Rich. **CP-RicAE** *Fr.* Ghazals: Homage to Ghalib. **SP-RicA2**

Jumbled in one common box. Domesday Song. Wystan Hugh Auden. *Fr.* Ten Songs. **CP-AudeW**

Jumbo. Stevie Smith. **CP-SmitS**

Jumbo. Wallace Stevens. **CP-StevW**

Jump stone hand leaf shadow sun. The Fire. Robert Duncan. **SP-DuncR** *Fr.* Passages.

Jump-to-Glory Jane. George Meredith. **CP-MerG1**

Jumpin John. Robert Burns. **CP-BurnR**

Jumping from the certain earth, the river so. The Transfer. Richard Eberhart. **CP-EberR**

Jumping out of the straw. The Supposed Dancer. Roy Fisher. **SP-FishR**

Jumping Rope. Shel Silverstein. **SP-SilS2**

Junction, A. Louis Zukofsky. *Fr.* 29 Songs. **CP-ZukLS**

Junction, on a Warm Afternoon, The. Howard Nemerov. **CP-NemeH**

June. Thom Gunn. **CP-GunnT**

June. Christina Georgina Rossetti. *Fr.* The Months: A Pageant. **CP-RosC2**

June. Carl Sandburg. **CP-SandC**

June. James Schuyler. **CP-SchuJ**

June. Gary Snyder. *Fr.* Six Years. **CP-SnydG**

June Bracken and Heather. Tennyson. **CP-TennA**

June Bug. Anne Sexton. **CP-SextA**

JUNE (*Cricket*). Rudyard Kipling. *Fr.* Verses on Games. **CP-KiplR**

June day dawns, the joy-winds rush, The. Clover. Herman Melville. **SP-MelvH**

June, 1820. William Wordsworth. **CP-WorW2**

June is the floodtide of green. Cod Summer. Marge Piercy. **SP-PierM**

June Leaves and Autumn. Thomas Hardy. **CP-HardT**

June Light. Richard Wilbur. **CP-WilbR**

June means weddings in everyone's lexicon. Here Usually Comes the Bride. Ogden Nash. **CP-NashO**

June 9. William Carlos Williams. **CP-WilW2**

June, 1981. You are forty. Dabney Stuart. *Fr.* The Opposite Field. **SP-StuaD**

June 19, 1953. Edwin Rolfe. **CP-RolfE**

June on the Merrimac. John Greenleaf Whittier. **CP-WhitJ**

June 6, 1970. Robert Creeley. **CP-CreeR**

June 16, 1992. James Liddy. **CP-LiddJ**

June 30, 1974. James Schuyler. **CP-SchuJ**

June Thunder. Louis MacNeice. **CP-MacNL**

June was not over. Another Way of Love. Robert Browning. **CP-BroR1**

June's edge. The sun. Solstice. Louise Glück. **SP-GlücL**

Junes were free and full, driving through tiny, The. June Thunder. Louis MacNeice. **CP-MacNL**

Jungheimer's. Carl Sandburg. **CP-SandC**

Jungle, The. Richard Eberhart. **MoAB** *Fr.* Burr Oaks. **CP-EberR**

Jungle, The. Alun Lewis. **CP-LewiA**

Jungle, The. William Carlos Williams. **CP-WilW1**

Jungle Book, The, *sels.* Rudyard Kipling. **CP-KiplR**

　Her Majesty's Servants.

　Parade-Song of the Camp Animals.

　Kaa's Hunting.

　"His spots are the joy of the Leopard: his horns are the Buffalo's pride."

　Road Song of the *Bandar-Log.*

　Mowgli's Brothers.

　Hunting Song of the Seeonee Pack.

　"Now Chil the Kite brings home the night."

　Rikki-Tikki-Tavi.

　"At the hole where he went in."

　Darzee's Chaunt.

　Toomai of the Elephants.

　"I will remember what I was. I am sick of rope and chain."

　Shiv and the Grasshopper.

　White Seal, The.

　Lukannon.

　"Oh! hush thee, my baby, the night is behind us."

　"You mustn't swim till you're six weeks old."

Jungle Clearance, Ceylon. Louis MacNeice. **CP-MacNL**

Jungle Husband, The. Stevie Smith. **CP-SmitS**

Jungle Strut. Al Young. **CP-YounA**

Junior High School Concert: Salle Rossini. Charles Kenneth Williams. **SP-WillC**

Juniper and cedar in the sand. The Feast. Galway Kinnell. **SP-KinnG**

Junk. Richard Wilbur. **CP-WilbR**

Junk and the Dhow, The. Rudyard Kipling. **CP-KiplR** *Fr.* Land and Sea Tales.

Junk-Heap at Murano. Muriel Rukeyser. **CP-RukeM**

Junk Mail. Allen Ginsberg. **CP-GinsA**

Junk Man, The. Carl Sandburg. **CP-SandC**

Junked hypodermics made it hard to walk. Bella Roma. Martin Edmunds. **SP-EdmuM**

Junkie Monkey Reel. Maya Angelou. **SP-AngeM**

Junkies. Charles Bukowski. **SP-BukC1**

Juno still jealouse of her husband Jove. Sonnet 3. Mary Sidney, Countess of Montgomery Wroth. *Fr.* Pamphilia to Amphilanthus. **CP-WrotM**

Jurors refuse to take oath. Canto 65. Ezra Pound. *Fr.* Cantos. **CP-PoCan**

Jury's the *mot juste* under our ground rules. On Being a Member of the Jury for a Poetry Prize. Howard Nemerov. **CP-NemeH**

Jus Primae Noctis. Robert Ranke Graves. **CP-GravR**

Jusque dans la caverne ciel et sol. Samuel Beckett. **CP-BeckS**

Just a few of the roses we gathered from the Isar, *also stands as sl. diff. and separate poem* Roses on the Breakfast Table. David Herbert Lawrence. *Fr.* All of Roses. **CP-LawrD**

Just a few of the roses we gathered from the Isar. Roses on the Breakfast Table. David Herbert Lawrence. **CP-LawrD**

Just a herd of Negroes. Share-Croppers. Langston Hughes. **SP-HughL**

Just a Merry Little Ditty of Welcome for the Most Beloved Harteebeeste on Easter Sunday. Malcolm Lowry. **CP-LowrM**

Just a minute before you leave, girl. Don't Fall Apart on Me Tonight. "Bob Dylan." **CP-DylaB**

Just a rainy day or two. Souvenir. Edna St. Vincent Millay. **CP-MillE**

Just a short time ago I sat with him. At The Canoe Club. Richard Eberhart. **CP-EberR**

Just a snack for lunch. Jenny Joseph. *Fr.* Life and Turgid Times of A. Citizen. **SP-JoseJ**

Just after sunset. *see also* Commentary—She Has Given Me the Bullet. Leonard Cohen. **CP-CoheL**

Just after the sun. The Vegetable King. James Dickey. **CP-DickJ**

Just and fit actions, Ptolemy (he saith). Lucan, *tr.* by Ben Jonson. **CP-JonsB** *Fr.* Pharsalia.

　(Speech out of Lucan, A.) **CP-JonsB**

Just Anger, A. Marge Piercy. **SP-PierM**

Just are the ways of God. The Transcendence of God. John Milton. **OBS** *Fr.* Samson Agonistes. **CP-MiltJ**

Just as He spoke it from his hands. Emily Dickinson. **CP-DickE**

Just as his dream foretold, he met them all. A Misunderstanding. Wystan Hugh Auden. **CP-AudeW**

Just as I used to say. Lawrence Ferlinghetti. **SP-FerlL**

Just as I wonder at the twofold screen. Edwin Arlington Robinson. *Fr.* Two Sonnets. **CP-RobiE**

Just as my fingers on these keys. Peter Quince at the Clavier. Wallace Stevens. **CP-StevW**

Just as the world was ending. Hurricane Season. Charles Simic. **SP-SimiC**

Just as those final words were penned, the sun broke out in power. *sequel to* The Norman Boy. William Wordsworth. **CP-WorW2**

Just as those who gaze get higher than those who climb. The Glacier. Louis MacNeice. **CP-MacNL**

Just as we were amazed to learn. The Psychopathology of Everyday Life. William Matthews. **SP-MattW**

Just at the corner of the wall. The Two Soldiers. Thomas Hardy. **CP-HardT**

Just at the self-same beat of Time's wide wings. The Bruised Titans. John Keats. **OBNC; OBRV** *Fr.* Hyperion; a Fragment. **CP-KeatJ**

Just because I can't understand you. To the Secret Poets of Kansas. Jim Carroll. **SP-CarrJ**

Just because there is music. Maybe I'm Amazed. Jim Carroll. **SP-CarrJ**

Just because you wear a natural baby. Dancing in the Street. Al Young. **CP-YounA**

Just Before April Came. Carl Sandburg. **CP-SandC**

Just before Fall. James Schuyler. **CP-SchuJ**

Just before the high time of autumn. Proud Torsos. Carl Sandburg. **CP-SandC**

Just beguiler, / Kindest love, yet only chastest. Thomas Campion. *Fr.* Observations in the Art of English Poesie. **CP-CampT**

Just beside my track through the dark. Roy Fisher. **SP-FishR** *Fr.* Diversions.

Just Beyond my reaching. Slave Coffle. Maya Angelou. **SP-AngeM**

Just down the slope from my own deck. Wild Turkeys in Paradise. Robert Pack. **SP-PackR**

Just for a handful of silver he left us. The Lost Leader. Robert Browning. **CP-BroR1**

Just for a Time. Maya Angelou. **SP-AngeM**

Just friend, you are my only friend. Song: Just Friends. Robert Ranke Graves. **CP-GravR**

Just Friends. Robert Creeley. **CP-CreeR**

Just full of springs the world was in Illinois. Mona Van Duyn. **SP-VanDM**

Just God! and these are they. Clerical Oppressors. John Greenleaf Whittier. **CP-WhitJ**

Just hope that when you lie down your toes are a firing-squad. Beddybye. Bill Knott. **SP-KnotB**

"Just how much are you worth?" Xerxes asks Pythius, reputedly the richest man in Lydia. Allies: According to Herodotus. Charles Kenneth Williams. **SP-WillC**

Just imagine yourself seated on a shadowy terrace. That Reminds Me. Ogden Nash. **CP-NashO**

Just in the gray of the dawn, as the mists uprose from the meadows. The Expedition to Wessagusset. Henry Wadsworth Longfellow. **PAH** *Fr.* The Sailing of the Mayflower. *Fr.* The Courtship of Miles Standish. **SP-LongH**

Just in the gray of the dawn, as the mists uprose from the meadows. The Sailing of the Mayflower. Henry Wadsworth Longfellow. *Fr.* The Courtship of Miles Standish. **SP-LongH**

Just Inside the Vigil of Christmas. Charles Olson. **CP-OlsoC**

Just junk / is what it amounts to. The Moral. William Carlos Williams. **CP-WilW2**

Just Keep Quiet and Nobody Will Notice. Ogden Nash. **CP-NashO**

Just learning to talk, I watched. Barton Sutter. *Fr.* Cedarhome. **SP-SuttB**

Just lift me to the window while the British boys march by. The Loyal Soldier. George Meredith. **CP-MerG2**

Just like a shadow in an empty room. The Songs We Know Best. John Ashbery. **SP-AshbJ**

Just Like a Woman. "Bob Dylan." **CP-DylaB**

Just like Hope is yonder bow. Hope. A Rondeau. Charlotte Smith. **CP-SmitC**

Just like Job. Maya Angelou. **SP-AngeM**

Just like old Saxophone Joe. Country Pie. "Bob Dylan." **CP-DylaB**

Just Like Tom Thumb's Blues. "Bob Dylan." **CP-DylaB**

Just Looking, Thank You. Leonard Nathan. **SP-NathL**

Just lost, when I was saved! Emily Dickinson. **CP-DickE**

Just Man, A. Robert Herrick. **CP-HerrR**

Just man followed then his angel guide, The. Lot's Wife. "Anna Akhmatova," *tr. fr. Russian* by Richard Wilbur. **CP-WilbR**

Just man's like a Rock that turnes the wroth, A. A Just Man. Robert Herrick. **CP-HerrR**

Just Me, Just Me. Shel Silverstein. **SP-SilS2**

Just north of the Yaak River, one man sits bolt upright. Mount Caribou at Night. Charles Wright. **SP-WrigC**

Just now I had a funny sensation. Galway Kinnell. *Fr.* Ruins under the Stars. **SP-KinnG**

Just off the highway to Rochester, Minnesota. A Blessing. James Wright. **CP-WrigJ**

Just-on-the-brink-of-snow feel, A. Snow Sequence. Charles Tomlinson. *Fr.* In Winter Woods. **CP-TomlC**

Just Once. Anne Sexton. **CP-SextA**

Just Once! Oh least Request! Emily Dickinson. **CP-DickE**

Just one more / at the breast, she said—. Marsden Hartley. *Fr.* Ironies out of St. George's. **CP-HartM**

Just outside Tombstone. Kenneth Patchen. **CP-PatcK**

Just Right. Charles Kenneth Williams. **CP-WillC**

Just so it goes: the day, the night. An Ordinary Evening in Cleveland. Lewis Turco. **SP-TurcL**

Just so—Jesus—raps. Emily Dickinson. **CP-DickE**

Just-So Stories, *sels.* Rudyard Kipling.

   Beginning of the Armadilloes, The.

   "I've never sailed the Amazon." **CP-KiplR**

   Butterfly That Stamped, The.

   "There was never a queen like Balkis." **CP-KiplR**

   Cat That Walked by Himself, The.

   "Pussy can sit by the fire and sing." **CP-KiplR**

   Crab That Played with the Sea, The.

   "China-going P. & O.'s." **CP-KiplR**

   Elephant's Child, The.

   "I keep six honest serving-men." **CP-KiplR**

   How the Camel Got His Hump.

   "Camel's hump is an ugly lump, The." **CP-KiplR**

   How the Leopard Got His Spots.

   "I am the Most Wise Baviaan, saying in most wise tones." **CP-KiplR**

   How the Rhinoceros Got His Skin.

   "This Uninhabited Island." **CP-KiplR**

   How the Whale Got his Throat.

   "When the cabin port-holes are dark and green." **CP-KiplR**

   Merrow Down. **CP-KiplR**

   Sing-Song of Old Man Kangaroo, The.

   "This is the mouth-filling song of the race that was run by a Boomer." **CP-KiplR**

Just so that each stark. Crows. Charles Simic. **SP-SimiC**

Just so you shouldn't have to ask again. What Kind of a Guy Was He? Howard Nemerov. **CP-NemeH**

Just some love and kisses. Malcolm Lowry. **CP-LowrM**

Just take a look at the servants of the idols. The Priests of the Old Gods. Clement of Alexandria, *tr.* by Thomas Merton. **CP-MertT** *Fr.* Diatribe Against the Old Gods.

Just tell me straight: did you go to bed with him? The Passive Partner. Roy Fisher. **SP-FishR**

Just the kind of a guy who. Key West. Charles Olson. **CP-OlsoC**

"Just the place for a Snark!" the Bellman cried. "Lewis Carroll." **EBEvV;** **FaPoB** *Fr.* The Hunting of the Snark. **CP-CarrL**

   (Fit the First: The Landing.) **EBEvV**

Just the Same. Thomas Hardy. **CP-HardT**

Just the thought of them makes your jawbone ache. Relatives. John Updike. **CP-UpdiJ**

Just there, in a corner of the whin-field. Our Lady of Ardboe. Paul Muldoon. **SP-MuldP**

Just trees and the smell. I Went. Pablo Neruda, *tr. fr. Spanish* by Ben Belitt. **SP-NeruP**

Just Vengeance Claims Thy Soul for Rights Invaded? William Wordsworth. **CP-WorW2**

Just Walking Around. John Ashbery. **SP-AshbJ**

Just when I imagined I had conquered nostalgia so odious. Letter to Maxine Sullivan. Hayden Carruth. **CP-CarHS**

Just when it has seemed I couldn't bear / one more friend. Sweetness. Stephen Dunn. **SP-DunnS**

Just when our drawing-rooms begin to blaze. William Cowper. **NOEC** *Fr.* The Winter Evening. *Fr.* The Task. **CP-CowpW**

Just Whistle a Bit. Paul Laurence Dunbar. **CP-DunbP**

Just who was so powerful and clever? Silence. Stanley Jasspon Kunitz. **CP-KuniS**

Just why should it invariably happen. The Awakening. Robert Ranke Graves. **CP-GravR**

Just Wrap It Up, and I'll Throw It Away Later. Ogden Nash. **CP-NashO**

Just yesterday afternoon I heard a man. The Way of the Conventicle of the Trees. Hayden Carruth. **CP-CarHS**

Just You Wait! Donald Davie. **CP-DavDo**

Justice. Paul Laurence Dunbar. **CP-DunbP**

Justice. Rudyard Kipling. **CP-KiplR**

Justice. Christopher Smart. *Fr.* Hymns for the Amusement of Children. **SP-SmarC**

Justice Denied in Massachusetts. Edna St. Vincent Millay. **CP-MillE**

Justice hath heaved a sword to plunge in Albion's breast. Prologue to King John. William Blake. **CP-BlakW**

Justice is done in the end. Lines for a Dead Alderman. John Hewitt. **CP-HewiJ**

Justice Is Reason Enough. Diane Wakoski. **SP-WakoD**

Justice of bells persistent in ringing, The. The Ways of Keys. Stephen Dobyns. **SP-DobyS**

Justice (1). George Herbert. **CP-HerbG**

Justice (2). George Herbert. **CP-HerbG**

Justice we ask / From grey-clad, clean-lined figures. Love and Justice. Jenny Joseph. **SP-JoseJ**

Justice's Tale, The, *parody of* Geoffrey Chaucer. Rudyard Kipling. **CP-KiplR** *Fr.* The Muse among the Motors.

Justification of blood and rock is. Freedom: The Unmolested Eagle of Myself. Charles Bukowski. **SP-BukC2**

Justin. Thom Gunn. **CP-GunnT**

Justly our dearest Saviour may abhorre us. Christs Suffering. Robert Herrick. **CP-HerrR**

Justus Quidem Tu Es, Domine. Gerard Manley Hopkins. *See* Thou Art Indeed Just, Lord, If I Contend.

Juvencius, thy fair sweet Eyes. Catullus. *See* Carmen 48: "Iuventius, / were I allowed."

Juvenilia. Adrienne Rich. **CP-RicAE; SP-RicA2**

Juventius, could you not find in this great crowd of men. Catullus. *See* Carmen 81: "Surely, Iuventius, one of this throng in Rome."

Juventius, my honey, while you played. Catullus. *See* Carmen 99: "Purloining while you played in honeyed youth."

Juxtaposition. Arthur Hugh Clough. **OBNC** *Fr.* Amours de Voyage. **SP-ClouA**

(Claude to Eustace.) **CBLP**

Juxtaposition is great,—but, you tell me, affinity greater. Claude to Eustace. Arthur Hugh Clough. **CBLP** *Fr.* Amours de Voyage. **SP-ClouA**

JVC. Thom Gunn. **CP-GunnT**

K

K, The. Charles Olson. **CP-OlsoC**

K. McB. William Carlos Williams. **CP-WilW1**

K. von F.—1914—Arras-Bouquoi. Marsden Hartley. **CP-HartM**

K with quick laughter, honey skin and hair. Brise Marine. Derek Walcott. **CP-WalcD**

Kaa's Hunting. Rudyard Kipling. *Fr.* The Jungle Book. "His spots are the joy of the Leopard: his horns are the Buffalo's pride." **CP-KiplR**

Road Song of the *Bandar-Log.* **CP-KiplR**

Kabul town's by Kabul river. Ford o' Kabul River. Rudyard Kipling. **CP-KiplR**

Kadava Kumbis Devise a Way to Marry for Love, The. Rita Dove. **SP-DoveR**

Kaddish. Allen Ginsberg. **CP-GinsA**

Kafka. Ted Hughes. *Fr.* Boom. **SP-HughT**

Kai, Today. Gary Snyder. **CP-SnydG**

Kai twists / rubs "bellybutton." The Egg. Gary Snyder. **CP-SnydG**

Kaire. Richard Eberhart. **CP-EberR**

Kairos and Logos. Wystan Hugh Auden. **CP-AudeW**

Kalamazoo. Nicholas Vachel Lindsay. **CP-LindV**

Kale Soup. Brendan Galvin. **SP-GalvB**

Kali Ma tottering up steps to shelter tin roof, feeling her way to curb, around. Describe: The Rain on Dasaswamedh Ghat. Allen Ginsberg. **CP-GinsA**

Kallundborg Church. John Greenleaf Whittier. **CP-WhitJ**

Kallyope Yell, The. Nicholas Vachel Lindsay. **CP-LindV**

"Born of mobs, born of steam."

"Every soul / Resident / In the earth's one circus tent!"

"I am the Gutter Dream."

"I am the Kallyope, Kallyope, Kallyope."

"Proud men / Eternally / Go about."

Kandy Express. Thomas Merton. **CP-MertT**

Kane Relief Expedition, sels. Thomas Merton. *Fr.* North. *Fr.* The Geography of Lograire. **CP-MertT**

Kangaroo. David Herbert Lawrence. **CP-LawrD**

Kangaroo, The. Ogden Nash. **CP-NashO**

Kansas. Nicholas Vachel Lindsay. **CP-LindV**

Kansas City to Saint Louis. Allen Ginsberg. **CP-GinsA**

Kansas Emigrants, The. John Greenleaf Whittier. **CP-WhitJ**

Kansas Lessons. Carl Sandburg. **CP-SandC**

Kapowsin. Richard Hugo. **CP-HugoR**

Kapuzinerberg (Salzburg). Pierre Jean Jouve, *tr. fr. French by* Louise Bogan. **CP-BogaL**

Karamojongs. Alice Walker. **CP-WalkA**

Karanje Village. Alun Lewis. **CP-LewiA**

Karenge Ya Marenge. Countee Cullen. **CP-CullC**

Karl Onyx. George Meredith. **CP-MerG2**

Karma. Walter de la Mare. **CP-DeLaW**

Karshish, the picker-up of learning's crumbs. An Epistle Containing the Strange Medical Experience of Karshish, the Arab Physician. Robert Browning. **CP-BroR1**

Katahdin. Frederick Morgan. *Fr.* Eight Triolets. **SP-MorgF**

Katchie Verner's Harvest. Louise McNeill. **SP-McNeL**

Kate can fancy only berdles husbands. Epigramme. Thomas Campion. *Fr.* Observations in the Art of English Poesie. **CP-CampT**

Kate's. Robert Creeley. **CP-CreeR**

Katharine. Robert Louis Stevenson. **CP-StevR**

Käthe Kollwitz. Muriel Rukeyser. **CP-RukeM**

Katherine Young. James Liddy. **CP-LiddJ**

Kathleen. John Greenleaf Whittier. **CP-WhitJ**

Kathleen ni Houlihan. The Celtic Fringe. Stevie Smith. **CP-SmitS**

Katia Reading. Stephen Dobyns. **SP-DobyS**

Katie at the Pool. Derek Mahon. **SP-MahoD**

Katie is making / velvet roses: next. Velvet Roses. James Schuyler. **CP-SchuJ**

Kattegat. Chuck Miller. **SP-MillC**

Katy Did. James Wright. **CP-WrigJ**

Kayser! to whom, as to a second self. To the Young Artist. Samuel Taylor Coleridge. **CP-ColeS**

KE 6-8018. Anne Sexton. **CP-SextA**

Keats at Highgate. Thom Gunn. **CP-GunnT**

Keekin' Glass, The. Robert Burns. *See* How daur ye ca' me "Howlet-face."

Keen. Edna St. Vincent Millay. **CP-MillE**

Keen as an eagle whose flight towards the dim empyréan. The Poetry of Southey. George Meredith. **CP-MerG1**

Keen, Fitful Gusts Are Whispering Here and There. John Keats. **CP-KeatJ**

Keen stars were twinkling, The. Percy Bysshe Shelley. **CP-ShelP**

(To Jane: The Keen Stars Were Twinkling.) **CP-ShelP**

Keen to Leaky Flowers. Richard Hugo. **CP-HugoR**

Keener tempests come, The: and fuming dun. James Thomson. **EBEV; EnRP; NoP** *Fr.* Winter. *Fr.* The Seasons. **CP-ThomJ**

Keep. Margaret Atwood. **SP-AtwM2**

Keep A-Pluggin' Away. Paul Laurence Dunbar. **CP-DunbP**

Keep a red heart of memories. Haze. Carl Sandburg. **CP-SandC**

Keep a Song Up on de Way. Paul Laurence Dunbar. **CP-DunbP**

Keep away, son, these lakes are salt. These flowers. Advice to a Young Prophet. Thomas Merton. **CP-MertT; SP-MertT**

Keep ever on your eagle flight. To the High-Flyers. Johann Gabriel Seidl, *tr. fr. German by* George Meredith. **CP-MerG2**

"Keep faith: you know he is with you." Press Conference: King James Version. James McAuley. **SP-McAuJ**

Keep for the Young the impassioned smile. To Enterprise. William Wordsworth. **CP-WorW2**

Keep fresh the grass upon his grave. Wordsworth's Grave. Matthew Arnold. **FaBoPP** *Fr.* Memorial Verses. **SP-ArnoM**

Keep going. *There's nothing else to do.* Past. Hayden Carruth. *Fr.* Paragraphs. **CP-CarHS**

Keep Innocency. Walter de la Mare. **CP-DeLaW**

Keep It. Charles Kenneth Williams. **CP-WillC**

Keep It Up. David Herbert Lawrence. **CP-LawrD**

Keep love and he wings. Fragment 40. Hilda Doolittle. **CP-DoolH**

Keep love for youth, and violets for the spring. Autumn Violets. Christina Georgina Rossetti. **CP-RosC1**

Keep me from Thelma's sister Pearl! Agricultural Caress. Sir John Betjeman. **CP-BetjJ**

Keep Not Thou Silence. Bible, *O.T. See* Psalm 83: "Keep not thou silence, O God."

Keep not thou silence, O God. Psalm 83. Bible, *O.T. Fr.* Psalms. **CP-Psal**

Keep That Morphine Moving, Cap. Robert Penn Warren. *Fr.* Penological Study: Southern Exposure. **SP-WarrR**

Keep the dream alive and growing always. Song. Edwin Rolfe. **CP-RolfE**

"Keep the peace, Borso!" Where are we? Canto 21. Ezra Pound. *Fr.* Cantos. **CP-PoCan**

Keep this flower to remember me by. High Moments. Carl Sandburg. **CP-SandC**

Keep Troth. Basil Bunting. **CP-BuntB**

Keep your eyes open when you kiss: do: when. John Berryman. *Fr.* Sonnets to Chris. **CP-BerrJ**

Keep your laughter to yourself, Dixieland band. Leaving the Bar and Low Life at Closing, I Unsuccessfully Pursue Sainthood. Stephen Dobyns. **SP-DobyS**

Keep your toys and small possessions. Covetousness. Stephen Dobyns. **SP-DobyS**

Keeper, / Is silent is living in the air not, The. Two Poems of Going Home. James Dickey. **CP-DickJ**

Keeper, The. Bill Knott. **SP-KnotB**

Keeper's Wood. Frank Templeton Prince. **CP-PrinF**

Keeping. John Ciardi. **SP-CiarJ**

Keeping Clear. Dabney Stuart. **SP-StuaD**

Keeping Informed in D.C. Howard Nemerov. **CP-NemeH**

Keeping of a Promise, The. Etheridge Knight. **SP-KnigE**

Keeping the City. Anne Sexton. **CP-SextA**

Keeping the Faith. Leonard Nathan. **SP-NathL**

Keeping Their World Large. Marianne Craig Moore. **CP-MoorM**

Keepsake, The. Samuel Taylor Coleridge. **CP-ColeS**

Keepsake Boxes. Carl Sandburg. **CP-SandC**

Keepsake Mill. Robert Louis Stevenson. **CP-StevR**

Keepsakes. Robert Penn Warren. *Fr.* Ballad of a Sweet Dream of Peace. **SP-WarrR**

Keller Gegen Dom. William Carlos Williams. **CP-WilW1**

Kellyburnbraes. Robert Burns. **CP-BurnR**

Kemble, thou cur'st my unbelief. On Seeing Mrs. Kemble in Yarico. Robert Burns. **CP-BurnR**

Ken ye ought o' Captain Grose? Robert Burns. **CP-BurnR**

Ken Ye What Meg o' the Mill Has Gotten. Robert Burns. **CP-BurnR**

Kendal. . . Shap Fell! Is that in Westmorland? Westmorland. Donald Davie. **CP-DavDo**

Keng Sang Chu. Chuang Tzu, *tr. fr. Chinese by* Thomas Merton. **CP-MertT**

Keng's Disciple. Chuang Tzu, *tr. fr. Chinese by* Thomas Merton. **CP-MertT**

Kennedy *Ucciso.* Richard Hugo. **CP-HugoR**

Kennedy's Inauguration. Robert Bly. **SP-BlyR**

Kenneths. John Updike. **CP-UpdiJ**

Kenoza Lake. John Greenleaf Whittier. **CP-WhitJ**

Kensington Church Walk, St. Mary Abbots. A Journal of English Days. Charles Wright. **SP-WrigC**

Kensington Notebook, A. Derek Mahon. **SP-MahoD**

Kent. Donald Davie. **CP-DavDo**

Kent. Thom Gunn. *Fr.* Breaking Ground. **CP-GunnT**

Kentucky. Edwin Rolfe. **CP-RolfE**

Kentucky Derby Day, Belfast, Maine. Stephen Dobyns. **SP-DobyS**

Kentucky, 1833. Rita Dove. **SP-DoveR**

Kentucky Mountain Farm. Robert Penn Warren. **SP-WarrR**
   At the Hour of the Breaking of the Rocks.
   History among the Rocks. **CBCWP; GOA; MoAmPo; MoVE**
   Rebuke of the Rocks.
   Return, The.

Kentucky River Junction. Wendell Berry. **CP-BerrW**

Kentucky water, clear springs: a boy fleeing. The Swimmers. Allen Tate. **CP-TateA**

Keokuk. Richard Hugo. **CP-HugoR**

Keppel, returning from afar. The Trail of Admiral Keppel. William Cowper. **CP-CowpW**

Kept. Louise Bogan. **CP-BogaL**

Kept up by relays of generations young. Jack Roy. Herman Melville. **SP-MelvH**

Kernel escaped from the nut uncracked, The. The Miracle. George Meredith. **CP-MerG2**

Kerouac's Ronsard Dance. James Liddy. **CP-LiddJ**

Kettle changes its note, The. The Unknown. Denise Levertov. **CP-LeveD**

Kettle descants in a cosy drone, The. At Tea. Thomas Hardy. *Fr.* Satires of Circumstance in Fifteen Glimpses. **CP-HardT**

Kettle descants in a cosy drone, The. Satires of Circumstance in Fifteen Glimpses. Thomas Hardy. **CP-HardT**

Kevin, Kevin Rooney, is it you? Re-Acquaintance. Hayden Carruth. **CP-CarHS**

Key, The. Adrienne Rich. **CP-RicAE**

Key, The. Muriel Rukeyser. **CP-RukeM**

Key and bar, key and bar. Love's Castle. Paul Laurence Dunbar. **CP-DunbP**

Key-Note, The. Christina Georgina Rossetti. **CP-RosC2**

Key of Water, The. Octavio Paz, *tr. fr. Spanish by* Elizabeth Bishop. **CP-BishE**

Key-reist, I am fed and sick unto death with this. Sonnet. Hayden Carruth. **CP-CarHS** *Fr.* Sonnets.

Key. The door. Open, A. Tom. James Schuyler. **CP-SchuJ**

Key West. Hart Crane. **CP-CranH**

Key West. Richard Eberhart. **CP-EberR**

Key West. Charles Olson. **CP-OlsoC**

Keyfoods. Audre Lorde. **SP-LordA**

Keys. Daniel Gerard Hoffman. **SP-HoffD**

Keys, The. Erica Jong. **SP-JongE**

Keys of Morning, The. Walter de la Mare. **CP-DeLaW**

Khan came from Bokhara town, The. The Khan's Devil. John Greenleaf Whittier. **CP-WhitJ**

Khan's Devil, The. John Greenleaf Whittier. **CP-WhitJ**

Khing, the master carver, made a bell stand. The Woodcarver. Chuang Tzu, *tr. fr. Chinese by* Thomas Merton. **CP-MertT**

Khrushchev is coming on the right day! Poem. Frank O'Hara. **SP-OharF**

Kibali-Ituri. Kenneth Patchen. **CP-PatcK**

Kick / of the foot against. . . , The. Robert Creeley. **CP-CreeR**

Kick at the rock, Sam Johnson, break your bones. Epistemology. Richard Wilbur. **CP-WilbR**

Kick the blanket away. Aubade, 1925. Louis Zukofsky. *Fr.* 29 Poems. **CP-ZukLS**

Kick Up the Fire, and Let the Flames Break Loose. Philip Larkin. **CP-LarkP**

Kicking. Al Young. **CP-YounA**

Kicking a ragged ball from lamp to lamp. Encounter Nineteen Twenty. John Hewitt. **CP-HewiJ**

Kicking his mother until she let go of his soul. Mundus et Infans. Wystan Hugh Auden. **CP-AudeW**

Kicking the Leaves. Donald Hall. **CP-HallD**

Kicking through sasa / bear grass bamboo. July. Gary Snyder. *Fr.* Six Years. **CP-SnydG**

Kicks. Howard Nemerov. **CP-NemeH**

Kicks. "Lou Reed." **SP-ReedL**

Kid, The. William Blake. **CP-BlakW**

Kid, The. Robert Creeley. **CP-CreeR**

Kid. Robert Creeley. **CP-CreeR**

Kid. Robert Earl Hayden. **CAD; NCSH** *Fr.* An Inference of Mexico. **CP-HaydR**

Kid found its loose pages, A. History Book. Charles Simic. **SP-SimiC**

Kid in the Park. Langston Hughes. **SP-HughL**

Kid Sleepy. Langston Hughes. **SP-HughL**

Kidnaped. Paul Laurence Dunbar. **CP-DunbP**

Kidnap[p]er. Tess Gallagher. **SP-GallT**

Kidnapped. Rudyard Kipling. *Fr.* Plain Tales from the Hills. "There is a tide in the affairs of men." **CP-KiplR**

Kids, The. "Lou Reed." **SP-ReedL**

Kids walking beach. Robert Creeley. **CP-CreeR**

Kids went off to school, The. An Oddly Lovely Day Alone. John Updike. **CP-UpdiJ**

Kierkegaard, a / cripple and a Dane. Die Neuen Heiligen. John Updike. **CP-UpdiJ**

Kiev. John Updike. *Fr.* Postcards from Soviet Cities. **CP-UpdiJ**

Kike is the most dangerous, A. Edward Estlin Cummings. **CP-CummE**

Kiki. Robert Creeley. **CP-CreeR**

Kill, The. Donald Hall. **CP-HallD**

Kill me not every [*or* ev'ry] day. George Herbert. **CP-HerbG** (Affliction (2).) **CP-HerbG**

Kill Money. David Herbert Lawrence. **CP-LawrD**

Kill of loose-voiced reason, The. The Continual Ministry of Thy Anger. Kenneth Patchen. **CP-PatcK**

Kill the bright cobra. The Passage of Time. Louise McNeill. **SP-McNeL**

Kill the Umpire! Edwin Rolfe. **CP-RolfE**

Kill your Balm—and its Odors bless you. Emily Dickinson. **CP-DickE**

Kill Your Sons. "Lou Reed." **SP-ReedL**

Killala. Donald Davie. **CP-DavDo**

Killdeer. Dabney Stuart. *See* One, and then another, they settled before me like flakes of air.

Killed Piave—July 8—1918. Ernest Hemingway. **CP-HemiE**

Killer, A. Charles Bukowski. **SP-BukC1**

Killer, The. Richard Eberhart. **CP-EberR**

Killer Snails, The. James Fenton. **SP-FentJ**

Killers, The. Leonard Cohen. **CP-CoheL**

Killers. [("I am put high. . .").] Carl Sandburg. **CP-SandC**

Killers. [("I am singing. . .").] Carl Sandburg. **CP-SandC**

Killers. Alice Walker. **CP-WalkA**

Killiecrankie. Robert Burns. **CP-BurnR**

Killing is not evil. Murder. David Herbert Lawrence. **CP-LawrD**

Killing summer heat wraps up the city, A. A Poem for Women in Rage. Audre Lorde. **SP-LordA**

Killing the Calves. Robert Earl Hayden. **CP-HaydR**

Killing the Love. Anne Sexton. **CP-SextA**

Killing the Spring. Anne Sexton. **CP-SextA**

Killings continue, each second, The. City Psalm. Denise Levertov. **CP-LeveD**

K********* Wabsters, fidge an' claw. The Ordination. Robert Burns. **CP-BurnR**

Kilmuir Cemetery: Stone with Two Skulls and No Name. Richard Hugo. **CP-HugoR**

Kilmuir Cemetery: The Knight in Blue-Green Relief. Richard Hugo. **CP-HugoR**

Kilroy's Carnival; A Poetic Prologue for TV. Delmore Schwartz. **SP-SchwD**

Kim. Rudyard Kipling.
   Fairies' Siege, The. **CP-KiplR**
   Juggler's Song, The. **CP-KiplR**
   Prayer, The: "My brother kneels, so saith Kabir." **CP-KiplR**

Prodigal Son, The. **CP-KiplR**

Two-Sided Man, The. **CP-KiplR**

"Unto whose use the pregnant suns are poised." **CP-KiplR**

Wishing-Caps, The. **CP-KiplR**

Kimono. Laurence Lieberman. **SP-LiebL**

Kimono, The. James Merrill. **SP-MerrJ**

Kin. Maya Angelou. **SP-AngeM**

Kin. Charles Olson. **CP-OlsoC**

Kin. Carl Sandburg. **CP-SandC**

Kin. Charles Kenneth Williams. **SP-WillC**

Kin: quiet grasses. Above. Deborah as Scion. James Dickey. **CP-DickJ**

Kin to Sorrow. Edna St. Vincent Millay. **CP-MillE**

Kinaesthesia. Richard Eberhart. **CP-EberR**

Kind. Leonard Nathan. **SP-NathL**

Kind) / YM&WC / (of sort of). Edward Estlin Cummings. **CP-CummE; SP-CummE**

Kind & holy were the words. Ralph Waldo Emerson. **CP-EmerR**

Kind Are Her Answers. Thomas Campion. **CP-CampT** ("Kinde are her answeres.") **CP-CampT**

Kind Ghosts, The. Wilfred Owen. **CP-OwenW**

Kind in every kinde. Thomas Campion. *Fr.* Observations in the Art of English Poesie. **CP-CampT**

Kind is his mouth and smiling are his eyes. Chaucer. Edward Estlin Cummings. **CP-CummE**

Kind kinderpark. Bears and Waterfalls. May Sarton. **SP-SartM**

Kind o'er the kinderbank leans my Myfanwy. Myfanwy. Sir John Betjeman. **CP-BetjJ**

Kind of Act Of, The. Robert Creeley. **CP-CreeR**

Kind of an Ode to Duty. Ogden Nash. **CP-NashO**

Kind of change came in my fate, A. Byron. **NOBE** *Fr.* The Prisoner of Chillon. **CP-Byron**

Kind of empty in the way it sees everything, the earth gets to its feet. For John Clare. John Ashbery. **SP-AshbJ**

Kind of Ethics, A. Thom Gunn. **CP-GunnT**

Kind of Garden: A Poem for my Sister, A. George Oppen. **CP-OppeG**

Kind of Glory, A. Richard Shelton. **SP-ShelR**

Kind of Lecture on a Dull Day When There Isn't Even a Fly Around to Kill, A. Charles Bukowski. **SP-BukC2**

Kind of Love, Some Say, A. Maya Angelou. **SP-AngeM**

Kind of monkey or pine-lemur, A. The Monkey Puzzle. Marianne Craig Moore. **CP-MoorM**

Kind of Music, A. Mona Van Duyn. **SP-VanDM**

Kind of Poetry I Want, The, *see also* Further Passages from The Kind of Poetry I Want. "Hugh MacDiarmid."

"Ah, sweetheart, what a pool! Broad, deep, strong, silent, and sedate!" **SP-MacDH**

"And a poetry in which as in a film." **SP-MacDH**

"And thus a poetry which fully understands." **SP-MacDH**

"I dream of poems like the bread-knife." **SP-MacDH**

"Poetry full of *cynghanedd*, and hair-trigger relationships, A." **SP-MacDH**

"Poetry in which all connections will constantly render such services, A." **SP-MacDH**

"Poetry like the character of Indian culture, A." **SP-MacDH**

"Poetry like the hope of achieving ere very long." **SP-MacDH**

"Poetry of such an integration as cannot be effected." **SP-MacDH**

"Poetry that goes all the way, A." **SP-MacDH**

"Poetry that never for a moment forgets, A." **SP-MacDH**

"Poetry the quality of which, A." **SP-MacDH**

Kind of poetry I want to write is, The. Learning from MacDiarmid. James Wright. *Fr.* Many of Our Waters: Variations on a Poem by a Black Child. **CP-WrigJ**

Kind of rain we knew is a thing of the past, The. Kinsale. Derek Mahon. **SP-MahoD**

Kind of Scorn, A. Nicholas Vachel Lindsay. **CP-LindV**

Kind of wooden Boston, crowding toward, A. Charleston. John Updike. **CP-UpdiJ**

Kind of you, sunshine, to come out just now. Against the Personality Cult. Jenny Joseph. **SP-JoseJ**

Kind old face, the egg-shaped head, The. On a Portrait of a Deaf Man. Sir John Betjeman. **CP-BetjJ**

Kind pity [*or* Kinde pitty] chokes my spleen[e]; brave scorn forbids. Satire 3. John Donne. **EBEV; ESCV; FHYEP; JCP; MeLP; MePo; NAEL-1; NoP; NoSic; OAEL-1; OBS; OXAEP-1; PoE; PoEL-2; SeCP; SeCV-1** *Fr.* Satires. **CP-DonnJ**

Kind Reader! take your choice to cry or laugh. Substitute for an Epitaph. Byron. **CP-Byron**

Kind Sir, I've read your paper through. To a Gentleman Who Had Sent Him a News-Paper, and Offered to Continue It Free of Expense. Robert Burns. **CP-BurnR**

Kind Sir: These Woods. Anne Sexton. **CP-SextA**

Kind Sir: This is an old game. Kind Sir: These Woods. Anne Sexton. **CP-SextA**

Kind solace in a dying hour! Tamerlane. Edgar Allan Poe. **CP-PoeEd**

Kinde are her answeres. Thomas Campion. *See* Kind Are Her Answers.

Kinde in unkindnesse, when will you relent. *At. to* Thomas Campion *and to* Philip Rosseter. **CP-CampT**

Kindergarten children first come forth, The. The May Day Dancing. Howard Nemerov. **CP-NemeH**

Kindest and gentlest here are the, The. Carl Sandburg. *Fr.* The People, Yes. **CP-SandC**

Kindest of traps, The. A Day Marked with a Small White Stone. Charles Simic. **SP-SimiC**

Kindle the Christmas Brand, and then. The Ceremonies for Candlemasse Day. Robert Herrick. **CP-HerrR**

Kindly I envy thy song's [*or* songs] perfection. To Mr. R. W. John Donne. **CP-DonnJ**

Kindly Unhitch That Star, Buddy. Ogden Nash. **CP-NashO**

Kindly Widow Lady, who lived upon a hill, A. Ballad of the Clairvoyant Widow. Theodore Roethke. **CP-RoetT**

Kindness, A. William Dickey. **SP-DickW**

Kindness. Stephen Dunn. **SP-DunnS**

Kindness. Sylvia Plath. **CP-PlatS**

Kindness glides about my house. Kindness. Sylvia Plath. **CP-PlatS**

Kindred forgets Thee. Love. George Meredith. **CP-MerG2**

Kinds of Trees to Plant. Edmund Spenser. **OHIP** *Fr.* The Faerie Queene. **CP-Spens**

King, The. Rudyard Kipling. **CP-KiplR**

King!, The. William Carlos Williams. **CP-WilW2**

King Amenemhat III. Marsden Hartley. **CP-HartM**

King and No King, A. Robert Herrick. **CP-HerrR**

King and No King. William Butler Yeats. **CP-YeatW**

"King and Queen." Donald Hall. **CP-HallD**

King and queen will stand to the child, The. Royal Sponsors. Thomas Hardy. **CP-HardT**

King and Queenie in their imaginary. The River Video. James Liddy. **CP-LiddJ**

King and the Sea, The. Rudyard Kipling. **CP-KiplR**

King Arthur. John Dryden.

Harvest Home.

(Song by Comus and Three Peasants, A.) **SP-DrydJ**

Song: "How happy the lover." **SP-DrydJ**

Song of Venus.

(Song: "Fairest isle, all isles excelling.") **SP-DrydJ**

King Arthur made new knights to fill the gap. Pelleas and Ettarre. Tennyson. **NAEL-2** *Fr.* Idylls of the King. **CP-TennA**

King Arthur rode in another world. The Blue from Heaven. Stevie Smith. **CP-SmitS**

King Arthur's Men Have Come Again. Nicholas Vachel Lindsay. **CP-LindV**

King Charles on [*or* upon] the Scaffold. Andrew Marvell. **ChTr; FaBoRV** *Fr.* An Horatian Ode upon Cromwell's Return from Ireland. **CP-MarvA**

King Charles the Martyr. Christopher Smart. *Fr.* Hymns and Spiritual Songs for the Fasts and Festivals of the Church of England. **SP-SmarC**

King Concerned, The. John Hewitt. **CP-HewiJ**

King David Dances. John Berryman. **CP-BerrJ**

King Edward the Third. William Blake. **CP-BlakW**

King Eochaid came at sundown to a wood. The Two Kings. William Butler Yeats. **CP-YeatW**

King Fisher courted Lady Bird. The King-Fisher [*or* King-Fisher's] Song. "Lewis Carroll." **CP-CarrL** *Fr.* Sylvie and Bruno Concluded.

King-Fisher [*or* King-Fisher's] Song, The. "Lewis Carroll." **CP-CarrL** *Fr.* Sylvie and Bruno Concluded.

King Hamlet's Ghost. Stevie Smith. **CP-SmitS**

King Harald's Trance. George Meredith. **CP-MerG1**

King has called for priest and cup, The. The Last Rhyme of True Thomas. Rudyard Kipling. **CP-KiplR**

King Henry VII. And the Shipwrights. Rudyard Kipling. **CP-KiplR**

King. If farmers make my land secure. Ralph Waldo Emerson. **CP-EmerR**

King in Funeral Procession, A. Stevie Smith. **CP-SmitS**

King is Dead, The. Paul Laurence Dunbar. **CP-DunbP**

King Julius left the south country. Song. Emily Brontë. **CP-BronE**

King Lear blinded Oedipus in a dream. Only God Knows How. Malcolm Lowry. *Fr.* The Moon in Scandinavia. **CP-LowrM**

King Leer. Ogden Nash. **CP-NashO**

King Mark who / Unwilling prognosticator. The Potion. Charles Tomlinson. *Fr.* Three Wagnerian Lyrics. **CP-TomlC**

King Marsilius of Saragossa. Death of Count Roland. Robert Lowell. **SP-LoweR**

King of Beasts, The. Robinson Jeffers. **CP-JefR3**

King of Glory, King of Peace. Praise (2). George Herbert. **CP-HerbG**

King of glory [or glorie], king of peace, / With the one make war[re] to cease. L'Envoy. George Herbert. **CP-HerbG**

King of Hearts a broadsword bears, The. Song: Sword and Rose. Robert Ranke Graves. **CP-GravR**

King of Kings, A King among the Kings, A. Delmore Schwartz. "Come, let us rejoice in James Joyce, in the greatness of this poet." **SP-SchwD**

King of Kings and Lord of Lords. Christina Georgina Rossetti. **CP-RosC2**

King of rock 'n' roll, The. Painkillers. Thom Gunn. **CP-GunnT**

King of sempiternal sway. Whitsunday. Christopher Smart. *Fr.* Hymns and Spiritual Songs for the Fasts and Festivals of the Church of England. **SP-SmarC**

King of Sweden, The. William Wordsworth. **CP-WorW1**

King of the dark tower is a lug, The. Gilbert Sorrentino. **SP-SorrG**

King of the Ditchbacks, The. Seamus Heaney. **SP-HeanS**

King of the Monkeys tried to marry her, The. Candy Darling. Charles Henri Ford. *Fr.* Four Elegies. **SP-FordC**

King of the perennial holly-groves, the riven sandstone. Geoffrey Hill. **HAP; NoAM** *Fr.* Mercian Hymns. **CP-HillG**

King of the River. Stanley Jasspon Kunitz. **CP-KuniS**

King of the Wood / King of the Dead. Charles Olson. **CP-OlsoC**

King of us all, we cried to thee, cried to thee. King Victor Emanuel Entering Florence, April, 1860. Elizabeth Barrett Browning. **CP-BroEB**

King of Yellow Butterflies, The. Nicholas Vachel Lindsay. **CP-LindV**

King Prajadhipok his cataract. The Rape of the Cataract. Richard Eberhart. **CP-EberR**

King said to his son, The: "Enough of this!" How Hard It Is to Keep from Being King When It's in You and in the Situation. Robert Frost. **CP-FrosR**

King shall rejoice in thy strength, O Lord, The. Psalm 21. Bible, *O.T.* *Fr.* Psalms. **CP-Psal**

King Solomon and the Ants. John Greenleaf Whittier. **CP-WhitJ**

King Solomon and the Queen of Shiba. Nicholas Vachel Lindsay. *Fr.* The Booker Washington Trilogy. **CP-LindV**

King Solomon drew merchantmen. The Merchantmen. Rudyard Kipling. **CP-KiplR**

King Solomon: my master and the imbeciles. Thomas Merton. **CP-MertT**

King Stephen. A Fragment of a Tragedy. John Keats. **CP-KeatJ**
"Another sword! And what if I could seize." **FaBoEH**
"If shame can on a soldier's vein-swoll'n front." **FaBoEH**

King, the story oft was told, A. The Golden Boy. John Hewitt. **CP-HewiJ**

King, to a backward scholar of common laws, The. Primer for Statesmen. John Crowe Ransom. *Fr.* Two Gentlemen in Bonds. **SP-RansJ**

King Victor Emanuel Entering Florence, April, 1860. Elizabeth Barrett Browning. **CP-BroEB**

King Volmer and Elsie. John Greenleaf Whittier. **CP-WhitJ**

King was on his throne, The. The Vision of Belshazzar. Byron. **CP-Byron**

King watches at Night, The. Frank Templeton Prince. *Fr.* Chaka. **CP-PrinF**

Kingdom, The. Rudyard Kipling. **CP-KiplR** *Fr.* The Naulahka.

Kingdom, The. Louis MacNeice. **CP-MacNL**
"All is well, said the voice from the tiny pulpit."
" 'Drunk again! Where do you think you are?'." **CP-MacNL**
"Little dapper man but with shiny elbows, A."
"Over the roofs and cranes, blistered cupola and hungry smokestack." **LiTM**
"Take this old man with the soldierly straight back."
"Too large in feature for a world of cuties."
"Under the surface of flux and of fear there is an underground movement." **LiTM**
"When she had her stroke the china dogs." **CP-MacNL**

Kingdom Come. John Crowe Ransom. *Fr.* Two Gentlemen in Bonds. **SP-RansJ**

Kingdom of air, of lightly looming air, The. Attention Makes Infinity. Richard Wilbur. **CP-WilbR**

Kingdom of Jerusalem, The. Robert Duncan. **SP-DuncR**

Kingdom of Kali, The. May Sarton. **SRLS** *Fr.* The Invocation to Kali. **SP-SartM**

Kingdom of Number is all boundaries, The. Numbers and Faces. Wystan Hugh Auden. **CP-AudeW**

Kingdom of Stinking Wishes, The. Charles Kenneth Williams. **CP-WillC**

Kingdom of the Moon, The. Richard Shelton. **SP-ShelR**

Kingdoms of Heaven. Denise Levertov. **CP-LeveD**

Kingfisher, The. Andrew Marvell. **ChTr; PB** *Fr.* Upon Appleton House [To My Lord Fairfax]. **CP-MarvA**

Kingfisher Flat. William Everson. **SP-EverW**

Kingfishers, The. Charles Olson. **CP-OlsoC; SP-OlsoC**

Kingfisher's Boxing Gloves, The. James Fenton. **SP-FentJ**

Kingfishers in British Columbia. Malcolm Lowry. **CP-LowrM**

Kingly bird, that beares Joves thunder-clap, The. Edmund Spenser. *Fr.* Visions of the World's Vanity [or Vanitie]. **CP-Spens**

Kingly Man, The. Chuang Tzu, *tr. fr. Chinese by* Thomas Merton. **CP-MertT**

Kingpin. Archie Randolph Ammons. **SP-AmmoA**

Kings. Robert Herrick. **CP-HerrR**

Kings and Bishops murder law. Moult sont Prud'hommes les Templiers. Frank Templeton Prince. **CP-PrinF**

Kings and Tyrants. Robert Herrick. **CP-HerrR**

King's Ankus, The. Rudyard Kipling. *Fr.* The Second Jungle Book. Song of the Little Hunter, The. **CP-KiplR**
"These are the four that are never content, that have never been filled since the Dews began." **CP-KiplR**

Kings Are Gone, The. Charles Bukowski. **SP-BukC2**

King's Cliffe, in the evening: that Northampton stone. Northamptonshire. Donald Davie. **CP-DavDo**

King's Daughter is all glorious within, The. She Shall Be Brought unto the King. Christina Georgina Rossetti. **CP-RosC2**

King's Experiment, The. Thomas Hardy. **CP-HardT**

King's Gift, The. Elizabeth Barrett Browning. **CP-BroEB**

Kings Good-night, The. Thomas Campion. *Fr.* The Ayres that Were Sung and Played, at *Brougham Castle* in *Westmerland*, in the Kings Entertainment. **CP-CampT**

King's Horses, The. John Hewitt. **CP-HewiJ**

King's Job, The. Rudyard Kipling. **CP-KiplR**

King's Missive, The. John Greenleaf Whittier. **CP-WhitJ**

King's most humble servant, I, The. Answer to an Invitation. Robert Burns. **CP-BurnR**

King's Mountain. Charles Olson. **CP-OlsoC**

King's Mountain. Muriel Rukeyser. **CP-RukeM**

Kings must be dauntlese: Subjects will contemne. Upon Kings. Robert Herrick. **CP-HerrR**

Kings must not oft be seen by publike eyes. Distance Betters Dignities. Robert Herrick. **CP-HerrR**

Kings must not only cherish up the good. Clemency in Kings. Robert Herrick. **CP-HerrR**

Kings must not use the Axe for each offence. Patience in Princes. Robert Herrick. **CP-HerrR**

King's Pilgrimage, The. Rudyard Kipling. **CP-KiplR**

King's Restoration, The. Christopher Smart. *Fr.* Hymns and Spiritual Songs for the Fasts and Festivals of the Church of England. **SP-SmarC**

Kings River Canyon. Kenneth Rexroth. **NaP** *Fr.* Andrée Rexroth. **SP-RexrK**

King's Soliloquy, A. Thomas Hardy. **CP-HardT**

King's Task, The. Rudyard Kipling. **CP-KiplR**

Kings who slept in the caves are awake and out, The. The National Gallery. Louis MacNeice. **CP-MacNL**

Kingship. Donald Davie. **CP-DavDo**

Kinsale. Derek Mahon. **SP-MahoD**

Kinsman. John Greenleaf Whittier. **CP-WhitJ**

Kinsman belov'd, and as a son, by me! To John Johnson. William Cowper. **CP-CowpW**

Kipling. Ernest Hemingway. **CP-HemiE**

Kipling's Vermont. Ogden Nash. **CP-NashO**

Kirilov on a Skyscraper. Randall Jarrell. **CP-JarrR**

Kirk of Scotland's Garland—a New Song, The, *incl. additional verses.* Robert Burns. *See* Orthodox, Orthodox, wha [or who] believe in John Knox.

Kirk of Ulpha to the pilgrim's eye, The. William Wordsworth. *Fr.* The River Duddon [A Series of Sonnets]. **CP-WorW2**

Kirkby with Muckby-cum-Sparrowby-cum-Spinx. A Lincolnshire Tale. Sir John Betjeman. **CP-BetjJ**

Kisiabaton. Gary Snyder. **CP-SnydG**

Kiss, The. Stephen Berg. **SP-BergS**

Kiss, The. Samuel Taylor Coleridge. *Fr.* Effusions. **CP-ColeS**

"Kiss, The." Donald Hall. **CP-HallD**

Kiss, A. Thomas Hardy. **CP-HardT**

Kiss[e], A. Robert Herrick. **CP-HerrR**

Kiss, A. David Herbert Lawrence. **CP-LawrD**

Kiss, The. Robert Pack. **SP-PackR**

Kiss, The. Anne Sexton. **CP-SextA**

Kiss, The. Karl Shapiro. *Fr.* Adam and Eve. **SP-ShapK**

Kiss, The. Alice Walker. **CP-WalkA**

Kiss. Al Young. **CP-YounA**

Kiss, and a clasp, and an eye to eye, A. George Meredith. **CP-MerG2**

Kiss Ass. Allen Ginsberg. **CP-GinsA**

Kiss at Bayreuth, The. Thom Gunn. **CP-GunnT**

Kiss, dear maid! thy lip has left, The. On Parting. Byron. **CP-Byron**

Kiss-Fest, The. Catullus. *See* Carmen 5: "Lesbia / live with me."

Kiss had been given and taken, The. The Last Time. Thomas Hardy. **CP-HardT**

Kiss, lovely Celia, and be kind. Love's Courtship. Thomas Carew. **CP-CareT**

Kiss me and comfort my heart. The Beggar's Valentine. Nicholas Vachel Lindsay. **CP-LindV**

Kiss me, Miami, thou most constant one. To the Miami. Paul Laurence Dunbar. **CP-DunbP**

Kiss[e] me, sweet: the wary [*or* warie] Lover, *after* Catullus, Carmina 5 and 7, *passim.* To the Same [Celia]. Ben Jonson. **CP-JonsB** *Fr.* Volpone.

"—Kiss me there where pride is glittering [*or* glistening]". Aria. Delmore Schwartz. **ErPo** *Fr.* Two Lyrics from Kilroy's Carnival: A Masque. **SP-SchwD**

Kiss of the Cross, The. William Everson. **SP-EverW** *Fr.* The Rose of Solitude.

"I cry. / Once of this world."

Kiss to the Bride, A. Walt Whitman. **CP-WhitW**

Kissass is the Part of Peace. Kiss Ass. Allen Ginsberg. **CP-GinsA**

Kisse, The. Robert Herrick. **CP-HerrR**

Kisses. Samuel Taylor Coleridge. *Fr.* Effusions. **CP-ColeS**

Kisses. Robert Herrick. **CP-HerrR**

Kisses, Can You Come Back Like Ghosts? Carl Sandburg. **CP-SandC**

Kisses Forgotten. Carl Sandburg. **CP-SandC**

Kisses in the Train. David Herbert Lawrence. **CP-LawrD**

Kisses Loathesome. Robert Herrick. **CP-HerrR**

Kissing and Bussing. Robert Herrick. **CP-HerrR**

Kissing and Horrid Strife. David Herbert Lawrence. **CP-LawrD**

Kissing Helena. Plato, *tr. fr. Greek by* Shelley. **CP-ShelP**

Kissing Her Hair. Algernon Charles Swinburne.
(Rondel: "Kissing her hair.") **SP-SwinA**

Kissing Usurie. Robert Herrick. **CP-HerrR**

Kitchen. Robert Creeley. **CP-CreeR**

Kitchen, The. John Haines. **SP-HainJ**

Kitchen, The. Lewis Turco. **SP-TurcL**

Kitchen chair speaks to the bread knife, The. Love Letter to Hans Christian Andersen. Carl Sandburg. **CP-SandC**

Kitchen Chimney, The. Robert Frost. **CP-FrosR**

Kitchen is its readiness, The. This Winter Day. Maya Angelou. **SP-AngeM**

Kitchener's School. Rudyard Kipling. **CP-KiplR**

Kitchenette Building. Gwendolyn Brooks. **BPo; FF; FaBoWP; NAAL-2; NoP; PoE; PoNe; Poetr; UnPo** *Fr.* A Street in Bronzeville. **SP-BrooG**

Kite, The. Anne Sexton. **CP-SextA**

Kite for Michael and Christopher, A. Seamus Heaney. **SP-HeanS**

Kite Is a Victim, A. Leonard Cohen. **CP-CoheL**

Kites are the best sort of gods, The. Roy Fisher. **SP-FishR** *Fr.* Diversions.

Kitten, The. Ogden Nash. **CP-NashO**

Kitten and [the] Falling Leaves, The. William Wordsworth. **CP-WorW1**
Kitten at Play, The. **FaPON; PCat**
"Where is he, that giddy sprite." **PBBP**

Kitten at Play, The. William Wordsworth. **FaPON; PCat** *Fr.* The Kitten and [the] Falling Leaves. **CP-WorW1**

Kitten can, A. Where Knock Is Open Wide. Theodore Roethke. **CP-RoetT**

Kitten! Kitten! grown woman! Mama. William Carlos Williams. **CP-WilW2**

Kitty-Cat Bird, The. Theodore Roethke. **CP-RoetT**

Kitty Hawk. Robert Frost. **CP-FrosR**
But God's Own Descent. **EaLo**

Kitty Hawk is a Caesar among monuments. The Structure of the Plane. Muriel Rukeyser. **CP-RukeM**

"Kitty."sixteen,5'1",white,prostitute. Edward Estlin Cummings. **CP-CummE**

Kitville. Frank O'Hara. **SP-OharF**

Kiver up yo' haid, my little lady. Lullaby. Paul Laurence Dunbar. **CP-DunbP**

Klimt and Schiele Confront the Cunt. John Updike. **CP-UpdiJ**

Klockius. John Donne. **CP-DonnJ**

Klockius so deeply hath sworn[e], ne'er more to come. Klockius. John Donne. **CP-DonnJ**

Klondike, The. Edwin Arlington Robinson. **CP-RobiE**

Klonk! The smoker's trick. Roy Fisher. **SP-FishR** *Fr.* New Diversions.

Knave of darkness, limber in the leaves, The. Death for the Dark Stranger. Thomas McGrath. **SP-McGrT**

Knave who scampered through the needle's eye, A. The Favorite. Theodore Roethke. **CP-RoetT**

Knee Song. Anne Sexton. **CP-SextA**

Kneel down, fair Love, and fill thyself with tears. A Ballad of Death. Algernon Charles Swinburne. **SP-SwinA**

Kneeling at the Pipes. Marge Piercy. **SP-PierM**

Kneeling Down to Look [*or* Peer] into a Culvert. Robert Bly. **SP-BlyR**

Kneeling in the Snow. Gary Gildner. **SP-GildG**

Kneeling like the White Rock Girl. Narcissism. Tom Clark. **SP-ClarT**

Knees, The / Of this proud woman / are bone. Cadenza. Carl Sandburg. **CP-SandC**

Knell, The. George Herbert. **CP-HerbG**

Kneller, by Heav'n and not a Master taught. Epitaph on Sir Godfrey Kneller, in Westminster-Abbey, 1723. Alexander Pope. **CP-PopeA**

Knew'st thou, one moneth wo'd take thy life away. Teares, and Laughter. Robert Herrick. **CP-HerrR**

Knife, The. John Hewitt. **CP-HewiJ**

Knife. Charles Simic. **SP-SimiC**

Knife blade of cold air keeps prying, A. Upstate. Derek Walcott. **CP-WalcD**

Knife that makes long scars, The. Victims. John Haines. **SP-HainJ**

Knife, the priest, the heifer, The. Fragment of a *Bas Relief*. John Ciardi. **SP-CiarJ**

Knight, The. Paul Laurence Dunbar. **CP-DunbP**

Knight, The. Roy Fisher. **SP-FishR** *Fr.* Five Pilgrims in the Prologue to the Canterbury Tales.

Knight, The. Ted Hughes. **SP-HughT**

Knight, The. Li Po, *tr. fr. Chinese by* William Carlos Williams *with* David Rafael Wang. **CP-WilW2**

Knight, The. Adrienne Rich. **CP-RicAE; SP-RicA1; SP-RicA2**

Knight, a true sister-love. After Schiller. Thomas Hardy. **CP-HardT**

Knight came home from the quest, The. The Quest. Rudyard Kipling. **CP-KiplR**

Knight, Death, and the Devil, The. Randall Jarrell. **CP-JarrR**

Knight had ridden down from Wensley Moor, The. Hart-Leap Well. William Wordsworth. **CP-WorW1**

Knight in Disguise, The. Nicholas Vachel Lindsay. **CP-LindV**

Knight of gallant deeds, A. The Romaunt of the Page. Elizabeth Barrett Browning. **CP-BroEB**

Knight of St. John, The. John Greenleaf Whittier. **CP-WhitJ**

Knight of Swords, The. Marge Piercy. *Fr.* Laying Down the Tower. **SP-PierM**

Knight rides into the noon, A. The Knight. Adrienne Rich. **CP-RicAE; SP-RicA1; SP-RicA2**

Knight [*or* Knyght] ther[e] was, and that a worthy man, A. Geoffrey Chaucer. **UV,** *ll.* 43–72; **InPS,** *ll.* 43–78; **FaBoEH; TrGrPo** *Fr.* The General Prologue. **FHYEP; NAWM-1; OAEL-1; PoE** *Fr.* The Canterbury Tales. **CP-ChauG**
(Knighthood, The.) **FaBoEH**
(Seven Pilgrims: A Knight.) **TrGrPo**

Knighthood, The. Geoffrey Chaucer. *See* A Knight [*or* Knyght] ther[e] was, and that a worthy man.

Knight's Interruption of the Monk's Tale, The, *see* Nun's Priest's Prologue, The. Geoffrey Chaucer. *See* The Prologue of the Nun's Priest's Tale.

Knights mine, all that be in hall. The Masque of Queen Bersabe. Algernon Charles Swinburne. **SP-SwinA**

Knights of the Joyous Venture, The. Rudyard Kipling. *Fr.* Puck of Pook's Hill.
Harp Song of the Dane Women. **CP-KiplR**
Thorkild's Song. **CP-KiplR**

Knight's Tale, The. Geoffrey Chaucer. *Fr.* The Canterbury Tales. **CP-ChauG**
"But in the dome of mighty Mars the red." **OBWP**
"This Palamon gan knytte his browes tweye." **OBF**

Knight's Tomb, The. Samuel Taylor Coleridge. **CP-ColeS**

Knobs and Levers. Robert Ranke Graves. **CP-GravR**

Knock. James Dickey. **CP-DickJ**

Knock is at her door, but she is weak, A. Dead. Paul Laurence Dunbar. **CP-DunbP**

Knock Knock. Jenny Joseph. **SP-JoseJ**

Knock off that hincty blowing, you Megarians. A Little Old Funky Homeric Blues for Herm. Hayden Carruth. **CP-CarHS**

Knock or none, that woman hears a knocking. The Way a Ghost Behaves. Richard Hugo. **CP-HugoR**

Knock with tremor. Emily Dickinson. **CP-DickE**

Knockin' on Heavin's Door. "Bob Dylan." **CP-DylaB**

Knokke. Robert Creeley. **CP-CreeR**

Knot, The. Stanley Jasspon Kunitz. **CP-KuniS**

Knot, The. Adrienne Rich. **CP-RicAE; SP-RicA2**

Knot, The. Charles Kenneth Williams. **SP-WillC**

Knot Hole Gang, The. Brendan Galvin. **SP-GalvB**

Knot which first my heart did strain, The. Sir Thomas Wyatt. **CP-WyatT**

Knothole in Spent Time, A. John Ciardi. **SP-CiarJ**

Know-All. David Herbert Lawrence. **CP-LawrD**

Know all men by these presents, Death the tamer. An Elegy on the Much Lamented Death of Mr. Demar, the Famous Rich Userer. Jonathan Swift. **CP-SwifJ**

Know, Celia, since thou art so proud. Ingrateful[l] Beauty Threatened. Thomas Carew. **CP-CareT**

Know Deeply, Know Thyself More Deeply. David Herbert Lawrence. **CP-LawrD**

Know he who tills this lonely field. Ralph Waldo Emerson. **CP-EmerR**

Know, that I would accounted be. To Ireland in the Coming Times. William Butler Yeats. **CP-YeatW**

Know the pinetrees. Know the orange dryness of sickness. The Runes. Denise Levertov. **CP-LeveD**

Know the world by heart. Theory of Poetry. Archibald MacLeish. **CP-MacLA**

Know Then Thyself. Alexander Pope. *See* Know then thyself, presume not God to scan.

Know then thyself, presume not God to scan. Alexander Pope. **BLPL; ECEV; NOEC; OAEL-1; SeCePo; TrGrPo,** *ll.* 1–18; **TFi,** *ll.* 1–42; **ACP; EBEvV; FHYEP; FaFP; FiP; GoBC; ImPo; LiTB; NAEL-1; NOBE; NoP; OBEC; PAI; PPoe; PoEL-3; PrIm; TRV** *Fr.* An Essay on Man. **CP-PopeA**

(Know Then Thyself.) **ImPo,** *ll.* 1–66;

(Know Thyself.) **NOBE,** *ll.* 1–18;

(Man.) **PrIm,** *ll.* 1–18;

(Paragon of Animals, The.) **ACP,** *ll.* 1–30;

(Proper Study of Mankind, The.) **FiP,** *ll.* 1–30;

(Riddle of the World.) **FaFP,** *ll.* 1–18;

Know this, my brethren, Heaven is clear. The Song of the Old Guard. Rudyard Kipling. **CP-KiplR**

Know this, O King! that if thou shalt destroy. The Philosopher and the King. William Cowper. **CP-CowpW**

Know thou, O stranger to the fame. For R. A. Esq. Robert Burns. **CP-BurnR**

Know Thyself. David Herbert Lawrence. **CP-LawrD**

Know Thyself. Alexander Pope. *See* Know then thyself, presume not God to scan.

Know Thyself, and That Thou Art Mortal. David Herbert Lawrence. **CP-LawrD**

Know when to speake; for many times it brings. Caution in Councell. Robert Herrick. **CP-HerrR**

Know ye the land where the cypress and myrtle. The Bride of Abydos. Byron. **CP-Byron**

Know you fair[e], on what you look[e]? On Mr. G. Herberts Booke, The Temple. Richard Crashaw. **CP-CrasR**

Know you the low pervading breeze. Twilight Music. George Meredith. **CP-MerG1**

Know you the river near to Grez. Robert Louis Stevenson. **CP-StevR**

Know you, winds that blow your course. Alice. Paul Laurence Dunbar. **CP-DunbP**

Knowing. Isabella Gardner. **CP-GardI**

Knowing again / that nothing / has been spoken. The War Comes into my Room. Muriel Rukeyser. **CP-RukeM**

Knowing All Ways, Including the Transposition of Continents. Charles Olson. **CP-OlsoC**

Knowing (as John did) nothing of the way. Asbestos. Edwin Rolfe. **CP-RolfE**

Knowing Bitches. John Ciardi. **SP-CiarJ**

Knowing he must learn to die. Though He Can't Know Death, He Must Study Dying. Wendell Berry. *Fr.* The Handing Down. **CP-BerrW**

Knowing I leave tomorrow, I look. Recruit. Edwin Rolfe. **CP-RolfE**

Knowing that nothing is in it. The Sprinter at Forty. James Dickey. **CP-DickJ**

Knowing the dead, and how some are disposed. Two Formal Elegies. Geoffrey Hill. **CP-HillG**

Knowing the shape of the country. Knowing the midway to. Fifth Elegy. A Turning Wind. Muriel Rukeyser. **CP-RukeM**

Knowing the voices of the country, gathering. Ives. Muriel Rukeyser. **CP-RukeM**

Knowing this man, who calls himself comrade. Definition. Edwin Rolfe. **CP-RolfE**

Knowing what it bore. A Leaving. Thomas Hardy. **CP-HardT**

Knowledge. Louise Bogan. **CP-BogaL**

Knowledge. Robert Herrick. *See* Science in God.

Knowledge. Howard Nemerov. **CP-NemeH**

Knowledge. John Greenleaf Whittier. *See* The Book Our Mothers Read.

"Knowledge deposed, then!"—groaned whom that most grieved. A Pillar at Sebzevar. Robert Browning. **CP-BroR2**

Knowledge my nakedness. Muriel Rukeyser. **CP-RukeM**

Knowledge not of sorrow, you were, The. George Oppen. **CP-OppeG**

Knowledge of history fetches, A. Love and the Times. Donald Davie. **CP-DavDo**

Knowledge of Old Towns, The. Kenneth Patchen. **CP-PatcK**

Knowledge That Comes through Experience, The. Jane Cooper. **SP-CoopJ**

Knowledge wandered north. When Knowledge Went North. Chuang Tzu, *tr. fr. Chinese* by Thomas Merton. **CP-MertT**

Known color gown mountain laurel. Mountain Laurel. Louis Zukofsky. **CP-ZukLS**

Known Had I. Thomas Hardy. **CP-HardT**

Known Soldier, The. Kenneth Patchen. **CP-PatcK**

Knows he who tills this lonely field. Dirge. Ralph Waldo Emerson. **CP-EmerR**

Knows how to forget! Emily Dickinson. **CP-DickE**

Know'st thou, O slave-cursed land! Mithridates at Chios. John Greenleaf Whittier. **CP-WhitJ**

Know'st thou the land where the pale citrons grow. Mignon's Song. Johann Wolfgang von Goethe, *tr. fr. German* by Samuel Taylor Coleridge. **CP-ColeS**

Knowst thou the luck the friends face to see. Hafiz, *tr.* by Ralph Waldo Emerson. **CP-EmerR** *Fr.* Odes.

Know'st thou this, Souldier? 'tis a much chang'd plant, which yet. Upon the Thornes Taken Downe from Our Lords Head Bloody. Richard Crashaw. **CP-CrasR**

Knucks. Carl Sandburg. **CP-SandC**

Knut Hamsun in Old Age. Derek Mahon. **SP-MahoD**

Kodachromes of the Island. Robert Earl Hayden. **CP-HaydR**

K.O.D.A.K. Patti Smith. **SP-SmitP**

Koenig of the River. Derek Walcott. **CP-WalcD**

Kofukuji Arsonists, The. Laurence Lieberman. **SP-LiebL**

Komboloi. James Merrill. **SP-MerrJ**

Komë Berenikes floating. Frederick Morgan. *Fr.* Poems of the Two Worlds. **SP-MorgF**

Komm Schöpfer Geist I bellow as Herr Beer. Whitsunday in Kirchstetten. Wystan Hugh Auden. **CP-AudeW**

Kookaburras, The. Mary Oliver. **SP-OlivM**

"Kookoorookoo! kookoorookoo!" / Crows the cock before the morn. Christina Georgina Rossetti. **CP-RosC2**

Kore. Robert Creeley. **CP-CreeR**

Kore. Kathleen Jessie Raine. **SP-RainK**

Korean / Lady mime, / you suspend yourself beside the stunned. Psychodrama: Tokyo Mime Film. Laurence Lieberman. **SP-LiebL**

Korean Mums. James Schuyler. **CP-SchuJ**

Koskiusko. Samuel Taylor Coleridge. **EnRP** *Fr.* Effusions. **CP-ColeS**

Kosmos. Walt Whitman. **CP-WhitW**

Kossuth. John Greenleaf Whittier. **CP-WhitJ**

Kostas Tympakianákis. James Merrill. **SP-MerrJ**

Koto Music/Singing. Al Young. **CP-YounA**

Kraken, The. Tennyson. **CP-TennA**

Kraken, Eagles, in British Columbia. Malcolm Lowry. **CP-LowrM**

Kral Majales. Allen Ginsberg. **CP-GinsA**

Kredemon . . . / kredemon . . . / and the wave concealed her. Canto 96. Ezra Pound. *Fr.* Cantos. **CP-PoCan**

Kreisler. Carl Sandburg. **CP-SandC**

Kreutzer Sonata. Ted Hughes. **SP-HughT**

Krishna climbs up there. Charles Henri Ford. **SP-FordC** *Fr.* Emblems of Arachne.

Krutz. Charles Bukowski. **SP-BukC3**

Ku Klux. Langston Hughes. **SP-HughL**

Kubla Khan; or, A Vision in a Dream. Samuel Taylor Coleridge. **CP-ColeS**

Kudzu. James Dickey. **CP-DickJ**

Kumrads die because they're told). Edward Estlin Cummings. **CP-CummE;** **SP-CummE**

Kung walked / by the dynastic temple. Canto 13. Ezra Pound. **CMoP;** **FaBoMo; PoE; SP-PounE** *Fr.* Cantos. **CP-PoCan**

Kung Wen Hsien saw a maimed official. The Man with One Foot and the Marsh Pheasant. Chuang Tzu, *tr. fr.* Chinese by Thomas Merton. **CP-MertT**

Kursaal at Interlaken, The. Adrienne Rich. **CP-RicAE**

Kušiwoqqóbī. Gary Snyder. **CP-SnydG**

Kusta ben Luka is my name, I write. The Gift of Harun Al-Rashid. William Butler Yeats. **CP-YeatW**

Kuzan—First Avenue. Marsden Hartley. **CP-HartM**

Kuzan swings a wicked thurifer. Kuzan—First Avenue. Marsden Hartley. **CP-HartM**

Kyoto Born in Spring Song. Gary Snyder. **CP-SnydG**

Kyoto: March. Gary Snyder. **CP-SnydG**

Kyrie Eleison, O wild lynx! The Godhead as Lynx. May Sarton. **SP-SartM**

1. Richard Wilbur. **CP-WilbR**

L

L. A. Rams in those days had, The. The Gentleman and the Bastard. Charles Bukowski. **SP-BukC3**

L. E. L. Christina Georgina Rossetti. **CP-RosC1**

L. E. L.'s Last Question. Elizabeth Barrett Browning. **CP-BroEB**

L M F B R. Gary Snyder. **CP-SnydG**

L of G. Walt Whitman. **CP-WhitW**

L. of G.'s Purport. Walt Whitman. **CP-WhitW**

L the simple shape. Gilbert Sorrentino. **SP-SorrG**

L(a / le / af / fa / ll / s). Edward Estlin Cummings. **CP-CummE**

L.A. John Updike. **CP-UpdiJ**

La Bella Bona Roba. Richard Lovelace. **CP-LoveR**

La Belle au Bois Dormant. Randall Jarrell. **CP-JarrR**

La Belle Dame de Tous les Jours. William Carlos Williams. **CP-WilW1**

La Belle Dame Sans Merci. John Keats. **CP-KeatJ**

La Belle, La Douce, La Grande. Countee Cullen. **CP-CullC**

La Brea. John Yau. **SP-YauJo**

La Chute. Charles Olson. **CP-OlsoC; SP-OlsoC**

La Chute III. Charles Olson. **CP-OlsoC**

La Chute II. Charles Olson. **CP-OlsoC**

La Clemenza di Tito. Pietro Metastasio.

   Translations from Metastasio ("Would you hope to gain my heart"). **CP-JohnS**

La colline du mystère. Solitary here. The stone. Hayden Carruth. *Fr.* The Sleeping Beauty. **CP-CarHL**

La Comparsa en Oriente. Thomas Merton. **CP-MertT**

La Corona, La Corona *is a title also given sometimes to the first sonnet in this collection of seven sonnets.* John Donne. **ChIV-2; ESCV; OBS; Son** *Fr.* Holy Sonnets. **CP-DonnJ**

   Annunciation. **TrCP**

   Ascension [*or* Ascention].

   Crucifying.

   "Deign[e] at my hands this crown[e] of prayer and praise." **ChIV-2; ESCV; OBS; Son**

    (Crown, The.) **ChIV-2**

    (La Corona.) **ESCV; OBS; Son**

   Nativity [*or* Nativitie].

   Resurrection. **ESCV; OBS**

    ("Moyst with one drop of thy blood, my dry soule.") **ESCV; OBS**

   Temple.

La Corona. John Donne. *See* Deign[e] at my hands this crown[e] of prayer and praise.

La Corrida. Robert Earl Hayden. *Fr.* An Inference of Mexico. **CP-HaydR**

La Crosse at Ninety Miles an Hour. Richard Eberhart. **CP-EberR**

La Fayette. Samuel Taylor Coleridge. *Fr.* Effusions. **CP-ColeS**

   (LaFayette.) **EnRP**

La Figlia Che Piange. Thomas Stearns Eliot. **CP-ElioT**

La Flor. William Carlos Williams. **CP-WilW1**

La Foce. Archibald MacLeish. **CP-MacLA**

La Fontaine de Vaucluse. Marilyn Hacker.

   "Azure striation swirls beyond the stones." **SP-HackM**

La Force. Louise Glück. **SP-GlücL**

La Gretchen de Nos Jours (I). Stevie Smith. **CP-SmitS**

La Gretchen de Nos Jours (II). Stevie Smith. **CP-SmitS**

La Mejicana. Robert Ranke Graves. **CP-GravR**

La Mouche. Samuel Beckett. **CP-BeckS**

La Muerte de Joselito. James Liddy. **CP-LiddJ**

La Noche. Robert Creeley. **CP-CreeR**

La Nuit Blanche. Rudyard Kipling. **CP-KiplR**

   ("Much—discerning Public hold, A.") **CP-KiplR**

La nuit venue où l'âme allait. Samuel Beckett. **CP-BeckS**

La petite vie, a young man called it later, it had been the. Historic Pun. George Oppen. **CP-OppeG**

La Préface. Charles Olson. **CP-OlsoC**

La Prisonnière. Thom Gunn. **CP-GunnT**

La Promenade de Protée. Charles Tomlinson. *Fr.* Two Poems on titles proposed by Octavio and Marie José Paz. **CP-TomlC**

La Push. Richard Hugo. **CP-HugoR**

La Revanche. Byron. **CP-Byron**

La rosa china il volto rosseggiato. Christina Georgina Rossetti. **CP-RosC3**

La Rose des Vents. Richard Wilbur. **CP-WilbR**

La Saisiaz. Robert Browning. **CP-BroR2**

La Salette. Thomas Merton. **CP-MertT; SP-MertT**

La Speakerine de Putney. Stevie Smith. **CP-SmitS**

La Torre. Charles Olson. **CP-OlsoC**

La Ultima Carta: A Young Wife Writes to Her Husband in the Mountains. Miller Williams. **SP-WillM**

La Vie En Rose. Kenneth Rexroth. **SP-RexrK**

La vie est difficile, monsieur. Café du Pont. Peter Meinke. **SP-MeinP**

La Vita Nuova, *See also* Dante's Vita Nuova, *tr.* by Ralph Waldo Emerson. Dante Alighieri, *tr. fr.* Italian.

   "What Mary is when she a little smiles." **CP-ShelP,** *tr.* by Percy Bysshe Shelley;

L.A. Woman. Jim Morrison. **SP-MorrJ**

Labor and Tribulation. James McAuley. *Fr.* Requiem. **SP-McAuJ**

Labor Day. Louise Glück. **SP-GlücL**

Labor Day. James Schuyler. **CP-SchuJ**

Labor might fatigue. Emily Dickinson. **SP-DickE**

Labor to breathe that younger, rawer air:, The. Bobby Delano. Robert Lowell. **SP-LoweR**

Laboratory, The. Randall Jarrell. **CP-JarrR**

Laboratory, The [Ancien Régime]. Robert Browning. **CP-BroR1**

Laborie, Choiseul, Vieuxfort, Dennery. Sainte Lucie. Derek Walcott. **CP-WalcD**

Labors of Hercules, The. Marianne Craig Moore. **CP-MoorM**

Labour. Robert Herrick. **CP-HerrR**

Labour Battalion. David Herbert Lawrence. **CP-LawrD**

Labour them, these drenched heights. Richard Eberhart. *Fr.* Four Lakes' Days. **CP-EberR**

Labour Victory, A. John Hewitt. **CP-HewiJ**

Labourer, The. George Meredith. **CP-MerG2**

Labourer's Noon-Day Hymn, The. William Wordsworth. **CP-WorW2**

Labouring at sixteen, / Austin Healey Sprite at eighteen. Out of a Descended Generation. Steve Griffiths. **SP-GrifS**

Labrador. William Carlos Williams. **CP-WilW2**

Labyrinthine forest's spoor, The. The Minotaur. Isabella Gardner. **CP-GardI**

Lace cushions were considered by a tall. Le Travail Rajeunit. Marilyn Hacker. **SP-HackM**

Lacedaemonian Instruction. William Blake. **CP-BlakW**

Lachesis. Kathleen Jessie Raine. **SP-RainK**

Lachin y Gair. Byron. **CP-Byron**

Lachrimae Amantis. Geoffrey Hill. **GTBS-6; NOCV** *Fr.* Lachrimae; or Seven Tears Figured in Seven Passionate Pavans. **CP-HillG**

Lachrimae Antiquae Novae. Geoffrey Hill. *Fr.* Lachrimae; or Seven Tears Figured in Seven Passionate Pavans. **CP-HillG**

Lachrimae Coactae. Geoffrey Hill. *Fr.* Lachrimae; or Seven Tears Figured in Seven Passionate Pavans. **CP-HillG**

Lachrimae; or Seven Tears Figured in Seven Passionate Pavans. Geoffrey Hill. **CP-HillG**

   Lachrimae Amantis. **GTBS-6; NOCV**

   Lachrimae Antiquae Novae.

   Lachrimae Coactae.

   Lachrimae Verae. **NAEL-2; NoAM; NoP**

   Martyrium.

   Masque of Blackness, The. **NoAM**

   Pavana Dolorosa.

Lachrimae Verae. Geoffrey Hill. **NAEL-2; NoAM; NoP** *Fr.* Lachrimae; or Seven Tears Figured in Seven Passionate Pavans. **CP-HillG**

Lachrymae Christi. Hart Crane. **CP-CranH**

Lack. Robert Ranke Graves. **CP-GravR**

Lack Love. Allen Ginsberg. **CP-GinsA**

Lack of Repose, The. Wallace Stevens. **CP-StevW**

Lackawanna Twilight. Carl Sandburg. **CP-SandC**

Lacking my love, I go from place to place. Edmund Spenser. **EIL; NoSic** Fr. Amoretti. **CP-Spens**

Lacking Sense, The. Thomas Hardy. **CP-HardT**

Lacoste. Charles Tomlinson. **CP-TomlC**

Lacrimae of the body, for whom do you weep? Sweat. Stephen Dobyns. **SP-DobyS**

Lacunae. Charles Tomlinson. Fr. Antecedents. **CP-TomlC**

Lad came to the door at night, The. The True Lover. Alfred Edward Housman. **CP-HousA**

Lad of Athens, faithful be. Emily Dickinson. **CP-DickE**

Ladakh Buddhess Biker. Lawrence Ferlinghetti. **SP-FerlL**

Ladder, The. Malcolm Lowry. **CP-LowrM**

Ladder, The. Kenneth Patchen. **CP-PatcK**

Ladder, flag, and amplifier. Corner Meeting. Langston Hughes. **SP-HughL**

Ladder horned against moonlight. Days of 1935. James Merrill. **SP-MerrJ**

Laddies by the banks o' Nith, The. Robert Burns. **CP-BurnR**

Laden senses cram my mind, The. Bleeze. John Hewitt. **CP-HewiJ**

Ladie [or Lady], that in the prime of earliest youth. Sonnet 9. John Milton. **CP-MiltJ**

Ladies, The. Rudyard Kipling. **CP-KiplR**

Ladies and Gentlemen: / I am going to ask just one question. Nicanor Parra. See I Move the Meeting Be Adjourned.

Ladies and gentlemen: / I have only one question. I Move the Meeting Be Adjourned. Nicanor Parra, tr. by Miller Williams. Fr. Manifesto.

"Ladies and Gentlemen" seems stiff and cold. Prologue. "Lewis Carroll." **CP-CarrL**

Ladies and gentlemen this little girl. Edward Estlin Cummings. **CP-CummE**

Ladies and gentlemen, you have made most remarkable. Wystan Hugh Auden. See The Progress you have made is very remarkable.

Ladies and the Pigeons, The. Marsden Hartley. **CP-HartM**

Ladies at the Troy Laundry pressed, The. One for the Ladies at the Troy Laundry Who Cooled Themselves for Zimmer. Paul Zimmer. **SP-ZimmP**

Ladies, fly from love's smooth tale. Conquest by Flight. Thomas Carew. **CP-CareT**

Ladies, I crave your indulgence for. The Young Laundryman. William Carlos Williams. **CP-WilW1**

Ladies in red capes and golden bracelets, The. The Greek Women. Thomas Merton. **CP-MertT; SP-MertT**

Ladies, ladies! what you offer. Conventional Ballad. William Carlos Williams. **CP-WilW2**

Ladies of the garden club, The. Correction: Eve Delved and Adam Span. Ogden Nash. **CP-NashO**

Ladies of Tlatilco, The. Thomas Merton. Fr. South. Fr. The Geography of Lograire. **CP-MertT**

Ladies who in chains of wedlock. A Preaching from a Spanish Ballad. George Meredith. **CP-MerG1**

Lads in their hundreds to Ludlow come in for the fair, The. Alfred Edward Housman. **CP-HousA**

Lads of the Village, The. Stevie Smith. **CP-SmitS**

Lady. Ted Berrigan. **SP-BerrT**

Lady. Hayden Carruth. **CP-CarHS**

Lady / i pray to what is unimaginable. Edward Estlin Cummings. **CP-CummE**

Lady. Jenny Joseph. Fr. Derivations. **SP-JoseJ**

Lady A. L., My Asylum [in a Great Extremity], The. Richard Lovelace. **CP-LoveR**

Lady! a Pen (perhaps with thy regard). Lines Written in the Album of the Countess of Lonsdale. William Wordsworth. **CP-WorW2**

Lady, accept a birth-day thought—haply an idle gift and token. For Queen Victoria's Birthday. Walt Whitman. **SP-WhitW**

Lady, accept the box a hero wore. Napoleon's Snuff-Box. Byron. **CP-Byron**

Lady Acheson Weary of the Dean. Jonathan Swift. **CP-SwifJ**

Lady Adeline Amundeville. Byron. See Canto the Thirteenth.

Lady and the Bear, The. Theodore Roethke. **CP-RoetT**

Lady and the Earthenware Head, The. Sylvia Plath. **CP-PlatS**

Lady and the Painter, The. Robert Browning. **CP-BroR2**

Lady and the Unicorn, The. May Sarton. **SP-SartM**

Lady asks me, A. Lady Bird. Robert Creeley. **CP-CreeR**

Lady asks me, A / I speak in season, tr. fr. Italian of Guido Cavalcanti. Canto 36. Ezra Pound. **CTC; OBVE** Fr. Cantos. **CP-PoCan**

Lady Barbara; or, The. Ghost. George Crabbe. **SP-CrabG** Fr. Tales of the Hall.

Lady Bates. Randall Jarrell. **CP-JarrR; SP-JarrR**

Lady Bird. Robert Creeley. **CP-CreeR**

Lady C. M., The. George Meredith. **CP-MerG1**

Lady came to a Bear by a Stream, A. The Lady and the Bear. Theodore Roethke. **CP-RoetT**

Lady Clara Vere de Vere / Was eight years old, she said. Echoes. "Lewis Carroll." **CP-CarrL**

Lady Cochrane. Donald Davie. **CP-DavDo**

Lady dear, if Fairies may. Christmas Greetings. "Lewis Carroll." **CP-CarrL** Fr. Alice's Adventures in Wonderland.

Lady dying of diabetes, A. A Thought Revolved. Wallace Stevens. **CP-StevW**

Lady, farewell, whom[e] I in silence serve. Sir Walter Ralegh. **CP-RaleW** (Poem Put into My Lady Laiton's Pocket by Sr W. Rawleigh, A.) **CP-RaleW**

Lady feeds Her little Bird, The. Emily Dickinson. **CP-DickE**

Lady Fitzwilliam. James Liddy. Fr. His Resplendent Neighbours. **CP-LiddJ**

Lady, for Samuel Johnson's sake. The Youthful Poet's Unspoke Response to a Woman Talking Too Loudly in His Favorite Bookstore. David Markson. **CP-MarkD**

Lady from near Rising Sun, A. Ogden Nash. **CP-NashO** (It Figures.) **CP-NashO**

Lady gave me a gift she had not, A. Sir Thomas Wyatt. **CP-WyatT**

Lady Geraldine's Courtship. Elizabeth Barrett Browning. **CP-BroEB**

Lady Geraldine's Hardship, parody of E.B. Browning. Rudyard Kipling. **CP-KiplR** Fr. The Muse among the Motors.

Lady Godiva here dressed so demurely. Lady Godiva's Operation. "Lou Reed." **SP-ReedL**

Lady Godiva's Operation. "Lou Reed." **SP-ReedL**

Lady Hope should look ridiculous, and she does, The. Hope. Howard Nemerov. **CP-NemeH**

Lady, I cannot act, though I admire. The Tramp's Refusal. Nicholas Vachel Lindsay. **CP-LindV**

Lady I intreate yow weare. Upon a Cherrystone Sent to the Tip of the Lady Jemmonia Walgraves Eare. Robert Herrick. **CP-HerrR**

Lady I know disapproves of the vulgarization of Christmas, A. I'll Eat My Split-Level Turkey in the Breezeway. Ogden Nash. **CP-NashO**

Lady! I rifled a Parnassian Cave. To the Lady Mary Lowther. William Wordsworth. **CP-WorW2**

Lady! if for the cold and cloudy clime. The Prophecy of Dante. Byron. **CP-Byron**

Lady in Black. Robert Creeley. **CP-CreeR**

Lady in black. Alun Lewis. **CP-LewiA**

Lady in black. Alun Lewis. **CP-LewiA**

Lady in her silver, The. Caravan. John Berryman. **CP-BerrJ**

Lady in Kicking Horse Reservoir, The. Richard Hugo. **CP-HugoR**

Lady in pink sits on her porch, A. Mother and Son. Charles Bukowski. **SP-BukC2**

Lady in red, she in the chile con carne red, The. Dancer. Carl Sandburg. **CP-SandC**

Lady in the Furs, The. Thomas Hardy. **CP-HardT**

Lady in the Single, The. Louise Glück. **SP-GlücL**

Lady! in whose heroic port. Ode to a Lady Whose Lover Was Killed by a Ball, Which at the Same Time Shivered a Portrait next His Heart. Byron. **CP-Byron**

Lady, in your Palace Hall. Emily Brontë. **CP-BronE**

Lady Isabella. Christina Georgina Rossetti. **CP-RosC3**

Lady Isabella. Christina Georgina Rossetti. **CP-RosC3**

Lady! It cannot be, but that thine eyes. John Milton. See Sonnet 5: "In truth your fair eyes, my lady."

Lady Lazarus. Sylvia Plath. **CP-PlatS**

Lady Lost. John Crowe Ransom. **SP-RansJ** ("This morning, flew up the lane.") **SP-RansJ**

Lady Love. Paul Éluard, tr. fr. French. **CP-BeckS,** tr. by Samuel Beckett; Lady, lovely lady. Vain and Careless. Robert Ranke Graves. **CP-GravR**

Lady Luncheon Club. Maya Angelou. **SP-AngeM**

Lady Madonna. The Beatles. **CP-Beatl**

Lady Mary Villiers lies, The. Epitaph on the Lady Mary Villiers. Thomas Carew. **CP-CareT**

Lady Midnight. Leonard Cohen. **CP-CoheL**

Lady Montrevor. Christina Georgina Rossetti. See I Do Not Look for Love That Is a Dream.

Lady Muriel's Song. "Lewis Carroll." **CP-CarrL** Fr. Sylvie and Bruno.

Lady of dusk-wood fastnesses. First Praise. William Carlos Williams. **CP-WilW1**

Lady of Forebodings, The. Thomas Hardy. **CP-HardT**

Lady of Heaven, Queen of nature. Ballade. François Villon, tr. fr. French by Isabella Gardner. **CP-GardI**

Lady of Light, and our best woman, and queen. Speak Now for Peace. Nicholas Vachel Lindsay. *Fr.* To Jane Addams at the Hague. **CP-LindV**

Lady of light, I would admit a dream. The Buried Lake. Allen Tate. **CP-TateA**

Lady of May, The. Sir Philip Sidney.
   "Come, *Espilus*, come now declare thy skill." **SP-SidnP**
   "*Silvanus* long in love, and long in vain." **SP-SidnP**
   "To one whose state is raised over all." **SP-SidnP**

Lady of Shalott, The. Tennyson. **CP-TennA**

Lady of Shalott, Her Mirror Broken, The. William Dickey. **SP-DickW**

Lady of Silence. Edward Estlin Cummings. **CP-CummE**

Lady of the Ladle, The. "Lewis Carroll." **CP-CarrL**

Lady of the Lake, The. Sir Walter Scott.
   Allan-Bane's Lament. **SP-ScotW**
   Ambuscade, The. **SP-ScotW**
   Chase, The.
     Invocation: "Harp of the North! that mouldering long hast hung." **SP-ScotW**
   Coronach. BSV; CH; EnRP; GTBS; GTBS-6; GTBS-P; HBV 1-2; NOBRP; OAEP; OBRV; OHIP; OxAEP-2; SCGP; SP-ScotW; TrGrPo; TreFS; WHA
   Ellen's Song. **SP-ScotW**
   Fiery Cross, The. **SP-ScotW**
   Hail to the Chief Who in Triumph Advances.
     (Boat Song.) **SP-ScotW**
   Harp of the North, Farewell! The Hills Grow Dark.
     (Farewell.) **SP-ScotW**
   Lay of the Imprisoned Huntsman. **SP-ScotW**
   Ride to Stirling, The. **SP-ScotW**
   Trossachs, The. **SP-ScotW**

Lady of the Pearls, The. Alexandre Dumas, *tr. fr. French by* Gerard Manley Hopkins.
   Trossachs, The. **SP-ScotW**

Lady of the Well-Spring, The. Stevie Smith. **CP-SmitS**

Lady on a Balcony, A, *tr. fr. the German of* Rilke. Randall Jarrell. **CP-JarrR**

Lady on the corner is out in the woodlot, The. Coign of Vantage. Ron Koertge. **SP-KoerR**

Lady Onlie. Robert Burns. **CP-BurnR**

Lady Poet, The. Charles Bukowski. **SP-BukC3**

Lady Poets With Foot Notes, The. Ernest Hemingway. **CP-HemiE**

Lady red—amid the Hill, A. Emily Dickinson.
   ("Lady red amid the Hill, A.") **CP-DickE**

Lady red amid the Hill, A. Emily Dickinson. *See* A Lady red—amid the Hill.

Lady, Rescued from Death by a Knight, Who in the Instant Leaves Her, Complains Thus, A. Thomas Carew. **CP-CareT**

Lady, reserved by the heav'ns to do pastors' company honour, *dialogue of Dorus and Cleophila.* Sir Philip Sidney. **SP-SidnP** *Fr.* Arcadia.

Lady "Rogue" Singleton. Stevie Smith. **CP-SmitS**

Lady Sings, The. John Milton. *See* Echo.

Lady speaks, The. William Carlos Williams. **CP-WilW2**

Lady, the night is falling and the dark. To the Immaculate Virgin, on a Winter Night. Thomas Merton. **CP-MertT**

Lady! the songs of Spring were in the grove. To Lady Beaumont. William Wordsworth. **CP-WorW1**

Lady, the strange malignancy. Frederick Morgan. *Fr.* Two Poems to a Dead Woman. **SP-MorgF**

Lady thus calls me, Lady, and they always has. Lady. Hayden Carruth. **CP-CarHS**

Lady Thinks She Is Thirty, A. Ogden Nash. **CP-NashO**

Lady thus address'd her spouse, The. Mutual Forbearance. William Cowper. **CP-CowpW**

Lady, to Death we're doom'd, our crime the same! Alla Sua Amica. Samuel Taylor Coleridge. **CP-ColeS**

Lady to Her Guitar, The, *sl. diff.* Emily Brontë. *See* For him who struck thy foreign string.

Lady Venetia Digby, The. Ben Jonson. *See* Elegy on My Muse.

Lady Vi. Thomas Hardy. **CP-HardT**

Lady was sitting at a table at dinner, The. The Hand. Richard Eberhart. **CP-EberR**

Lady[,] Weeping at the Crossroads. Wystan Hugh Auden. **CP-AudeW**

Lady, what are you laughing at? Is it the joke. The Grown-Ups. Donald Hall. **CP-HallD**

Lady, when you were born. Frederick Morgan. *Fr.* Death Mother. **SP-MorgF**

Lady Who Sang, The. Diane Wakoski. *Fr.* Fifteen Poems for a Lunar Eclipse None of Us Saw. **SP-WakoD**

Lady Whom You here Behold, The. William Wordsworth. **CP-WorW2**

Lady Wife. David Herbert Lawrence. **CP-LawrD**

Lady will you come with me into. Edward Estlin Cummings. **CP-CummE**

Lady, wise as well as fair, A. An Apology to the Lady Carteret. Jonathan Swift. **CP-SwifJ**

Lady with a Falcon. May Sarton. **SP-SartM**

Lady with a Falcon on Her Fist, A. Richard Lovelace. **CP-LoveR**

Lady without Paragon, A. Geoffrey Chaucer. *See* Hide [*or* Hyd], Absalon, thy gilte tresses clere.

Lady you have written me a letter. Edward Estlin Cummings. **CP-CummE**

Lady, your room is lousy with flowers. Leaving Early. Sylvia Plath. **CP-PlatS**

Lady/Lord in Doorway. James Liddy. **CP-LiddJ**

Ladye she stood at her lattice high, The. The Lang Coortin'. "Lewis Carroll." **CP-CarrL**

Lady,i will touch you with my mind. Edward Estlin Cummings. **CP-CummE**

Lady's Boogie. Langston Hughes. **SP-HughL**

Lady's Dressing Room, The. Jonathan Swift. **CP-SwifJ**

Lady's First Song, The. William Butler Yeats. **CP-YeatW**

Lady's in return may grasp as much, The. Nicholas Vachel Lindsay. **DIP** *Fr.* The Booker Washington Trilogy. **CP-LindV**

Lady's Second Song, The. William Butler Yeats. **CP-YeatW**

Lady's Song, The. John Dryden. **SP-DrydJ**

Lady's Song. John Milton. *See* Echo.

Lady's Third Song, The. William Butler Yeats. **CP-YeatW**

Lady's "Yes," The. Elizabeth Barrett Browning. **CP-BroEB**

Lady,since your footstep. Edward Estlin Cummings. **CP-CummE**

Læstrygonians, The. William Dickey. **SP-DickW**

LaFayette. Samuel Taylor Coleridge. *See* La Fayette.

Lafe Grat. Lewis Turco. *Fr.* Bordello. **SP-TurcL**

Lag, The. Adrienne Rich. **CP-RicAE**

Lagan in October, The. John Hewitt. **CP-HewiJ**

Lager Beer. Paul Laurence Dunbar. **CP-DunbP**

Laguna Blues. Charles Wright. **SP-WrigC**

Laguna Dantesca. Charles Wright. **SP-WrigC**

Laid out for dead, let thy last kindness be. To Robin Redbreast. Robert Herrick. **CP-HerrR**

Lain in Nature—so suffice us. Emily Dickinson. **CP-DickE**

Lais. Hilda Doolittle. **CP-DoolH**

Lais to Aphrodite. Plato. **FaBoEE** *Fr.* Variations of Greek Themes. **CP-RobiE**

Lak of Stedfastnesse. Geoffrey Chaucer. **CP-ChauG**

Lake, The. Matthew Arnold. *Fr.* Switzerland.
   (Meeting.) **SP-ArnoM**

Lake, The. Tom Clark. **SP-ClarT**

Lake, The. Raissa Maritain, *tr. fr. French by* Thomas Merton. **CP-MertT**

Lake, a sea itself, whose gentle crash, A. Malcolm Lowry. *Fr.* Peter Gaunt and the Canals. **CP-LowrM**

Lake allows an average father, walking slowly, A. Lakes. Wystan Hugh Auden. **NePA; NePoAm** *Fr.* Bucolics. **CP-AudeW**

Lake at Bled. Trees thick to water's edge, The. Lake Bled, Slovenia. John Hewitt. **CP-HewiJ**

Lake Bled, Slovenia. John Hewitt. **CP-HewiJ**

Lake Byron, Maybe Gordon Lord. Richard Hugo. **CP-HugoR**

Lake District. Sir John Betjeman. **CP-BetjJ**

Lake full of glass houses, The. The Lake. Raissa Maritain, *tr. fr. French by* Thomas Merton. **CP-MertT**

Lake in the head, A. The Dream. Robert Creeley. **CP-CreeR**

Lake in the Park, The. Louis MacNeice. **CP-MacNL**

Lake in the Sky, The. John Haines. **SP-HainJ**

Lake is known as West Branch Pond, The. The Ballad of Blossom. Mona Van Duyn. **SP-VanDM**

Lake is thine, The. To the Evening Star over Grasmere Water. William Wordsworth. **CP-WorW1**

Lake Isle, The. Ezra Pound. **SP-PounE**

Lake Isle of Innisfree, The. William Butler Yeats. **CP-YeatW**

Lake Leman ("Clear, placid Leman! thy contrasted lake"). Byron. **OBNC** *Fr.* It Is the Hush of Night. **LiTB; MeMBP** *Fr.* Childe Harold's Pilgrimage. **CP-Byron**

Lake Leman. Byron. *See* Lake Leman woos me with its crystal face.

Lake Leman woos me with its crystal face. Byron. **InPS; PoEL-4** *Fr.* Childe Harold's Pilgrimage. **CP-Byron**
   (Lake Leman.) **PoEL-4**

Lake Leman woos me with its crystal face. Byron. **NOBRP** *Fr.* Is thy face like thy mother's, my fair child. *Fr.* Childe Harold's Pilgrimage. **CP-Byron**

Lake Michigan Morning. Carl Sandburg. **CP-SandC**

Lake of green. Canadaigua. Frederick Morgan. **SP-MorgF**

Lake of Tears, The. Roy Fisher. **SP-FishR** *Fr.* Inscriptions for Bluebeard's Castle.

Lake Shore at Night. John Gould Fletcher. **SP-FletJ**

Lake sunken among, A. Woman Skating. Margaret Atwood. **SP-AtwM1**

Lake that looks like a sea, The. The Stockyard. Lewis Turco. **SP-TurcL**

Lake: To——, The. Edgar Allan Poe. **CP-PoeEd**

Lakes. Wystan Hugh Auden. **NePA; NePoAm** *Fr.* Bucolics. **CP-AudeW**

Lake's dark breast, The. The Rising of the Storm. Paul Laurence Dunbar. **CP-DunbP**

Lakes of the Atchafalaya, The. Henry Wadsworth Longfellow. **PoEL-5** *Fr.* It was the month of May. Far down the Beautiful River. *Fr.* Part the Second. *Fr.* Evangeline, a Tale of Acadie. **SP-LongH**

Lakes of Värmland. James Dickey. **CP-DickJ**

Lakes where the sunsheen is mystic with splendour and softness. The Poetry of Spenser. George Meredith. **CP-MerG1**

Lakeside, The. John Greenleaf Whittier. **CP-WhitJ**

Lalage! Charles Olson. **CP-OlsoC**

Lalage's coming: / Where is she now, O? Timing Her. Thomas Hardy. **CP-HardT**

L'Allegro. John Milton. **CP-MiltJ**

"Haste thee, nymph, and bring with thee." **FaBV; GN**

(Mirth, with Thee I Mean to Live.) **FaBV**

Mirth and Poetry. **EPCY**

Lama, The. Ogden Nash. **CP-NashO**

Lamarck Elaborated. Richard Wilbur. **CP-WilbR**

Lamb, The. William Blake. **BLPL; BoTP; CABA; CH; ChIV-2; EBCP; EBEvV; EaLo; EnRP; FHYEP; FaBoBe; FaBoCh; FaPON; GoJo; HBV; HeIL; HelP; ImPo; InPS; LAuP; LiTB; LoBV; MeMBP; NAEL-2; NAWM-2; NIP; NOBRP; NOEC; NoP; OAEL-2; OAEP; OBEC; OXAEP-2; OxBChV; OxBoCh; PAI; PoE; PoPl; Poetr; SBVL; SUS; SeCeV; SoSe; TEP; TFi; TRP; TRV; TrCP; TrGrPo; TreF; UnPo; WGRP; WHA** *Fr.* Songs of Innocence. **CP-BlakW**

Lamb, The. John Ciardi. **SP-CiarJ**

Lamb, The. Theodore Roethke. **CP-RoetT**

Lamb could not get born. Ice wind, A. February 17th. Ted Hughes. **SP-HughT**

Lamb dead, dead lamb. Death Bereaves Our Common Mother Nature Grieves for My Dead Brother. Stevie Smith. **CP-SmitS**

Lamb just says, I AM!, The. The Lamb. Theodore Roethke. **CP-RoetT**

Lambs of Grasmere, 1860, The. Christina Georgina Rossetti. **CP-RosC1**

Lambs that learn to walk in snow. First Sight. Philip Larkin. **CP-LarkP**

Lame Beggar, A. John Donne. **CP-DonnJ**

Lame boy / Met a fairy, A. The Lame Boy and the Fairy. Nicholas Vachel Lindsay. **CP-LindV**

Lame Boy and the Fairy, The. Nicholas Vachel Lindsay. **CP-LindV**

Lament: "All is far", tr. fr. the German of Rilke. Randall Jarrell. **CP-JarrR**

Lament: "How she would have loved." Thomas Hardy. **CP-HardT**

Lament: "Listen, children: / Your father is dead." Edna St. Vincent Millay. **CP-MillE**

Lament: "My love is gone." David Markson. **CP-MarkD**

Lament: "My mother wants to be burned, she told me." Stephen Berg. **SP-BergS**

Lament: "Nashe's old queens who bartered young and fair." Richard Wilbur. **CP-WilbR**

Lament: "Now let all lovely things embark." Countee Cullen. **CP-CullC**

Lament: "Oh Absalom, beloved, what can I say?" Alun Lewis. **CP-LewiA**

Lament: "Someone is dead." Anne Sexton. **CP-SextA**

Lament: "What face, in the water." William Carlos Williams. **CP-WilW2**

Lament: "When I was a windy boy and a bit." Dylan Thomas. **CP-ThomD**

Lament: "Your dying was a difficult enterprise." Thom Gunn. **CP-GunnT**

Lament, A: "Circle is broken, one seat is forsaken, The." John Greenleaf Whittier. **CP-WhitJ**

Lament, A: "O world! O life! O time!" Percy Bysshe Shelley. **CP-ShelP**

Lament for Adonis. Bion, *tr. fr. Greek by* John Addington Symonds. **CP-BroEB**

("I mourn for Adonis—the Loves are lamenting.") **CP-BroEB**, *tr. by* Elizabeth Barrett Browning;

Lament, for Cocoa. John Updike. **CP-UpdiJ**

Lament! for Diocletian's fiery sword. Persecution. William Wordsworth. *Fr.* Ecclesiastical Sonnets. **CP-WorW2**

Lament for Doormen. Charles Tomlinson. **CP-TomlC**

Lament for James, Earl of Glencairn. Robert Burns. **CP-BurnR**

Lament for Javier Heraud. Thomas Merton. **CP-MertT**

Lament for Moira McCavendish, A. Sir John Betjeman. **CP-BetjJ**

Lament for My Brother on a Hayrake. James Wright. **CP-WrigJ**

Lament for my cock. Lament for the Death of My Cock. Jim Morrison. **SP-MorrJ**

Lament for Pablo Neruda. Thomas McGrath. **SP-McGrT**

Lament for Pasiphaë. Robert Ranke Graves. **CP-GravR**

Lament for Tadhg Cronin's Children. Michael Hartnett. **SP-HarMi**

Lament for the Death of My Cock. Jim Morrison. **SP-MorrJ**

Lament for the Makers. Monday comes; at noon. Canto XVIII. Louis MacNeice. *Fr.* Autumn Sequel. **CP-MacNL**

Lament for the Makers of Songs. Kenneth Patchen. **CP-PatcK**

Lament for Toby, a French Poodle. May Sarton. **SP-SartM**

Lament 'im Mauchline husbands a'. Epitaph on a Wag in Mauchline. Robert Burns. **CP-BurnR**

Lament in rhyme, lament in prose. Poor Mailie's Elegy. Robert Burns. **CP-BurnR**

Lament in the Pacific Northwest. Malcolm Lowry. **CP-LowrM**

Lament—June 1944. Malcolm Lowry. **CP-LowrM**

Lament my loss[e], my labo[u]r, and my pain [*or* payne]. Sir Thomas Wyatt. **CP-WyatT**

Lament not, o Hafiz, the distribution. Hafiz, *tr. by* Ralph Waldo Emerson. **CP-EmerR** *Fr.* Odes.

Lament, o graces of Venus, and Cupids. Catullus. *See* Carmen 3: "Who loves beauty / vel her statues."

Lament. Occasioned by the Unfortunate Issue of a Friend's Amour, The. Robert Burns. **CP-BurnR**

Lament of a Graying Woman. Wen Chun Cho, *tr. fr. Chinese by* William Carlos Williams *with* David Rafael Wang. **CP-WilW2**

Lament of a Maiden for the Warrior's Death. Pablo Antonio Cuadra, *tr. fr. Spanish by* Thomas Merton. **CP-MertT**

Lament of a New England Mother, The. Richard Eberhart. **CP-EberR**

Lament of a Slug-a-Bed's Wife. Stevie Smith. **CP-SmitS**

Lament of Mary Queen of Scots on the Approach of Spring. Robert Burns. **CP-BurnR**

Lament of Mary Queen of Scots on the Eve of a New Year. William Wordsworth. **CP-WorW2**

Lament of Tasso, The. Byron. **CP-Byron**

Lament of the Border Cattle Thief, The. Rudyard Kipling. **CP-KiplR**

Lament of the Children of Israel in Rome, *after* Ferdinand Gregorovius. Randall Jarrell. **CP-JarrR**

fr. the Chinese of Li Po (701-62). Ezra Pound. **SP-PounE**

Lament of the Looking-Glass, The. Thomas Hardy. **CP-HardT**

Lament on the Eve of Parting. Ogden Nash. **CP-NashO**

Lament over Love. Langston Hughes. **SP-HughL**

Lament upon the Waters, The. John Ashbery. **SP-AshbJ**

Lamentation, A. Thomas Campion. **CP-CampT**

Lamentation, A. Denise Levertov. **CP-LeveD**

Lamentation of Enion, The. William Blake. **OBNC** *Fr.* Vala; or The Four Zoas. **CP-BlakW**

Lamentation of Glumdalclitch for the Loss of Grildrig, The. Alexander Pope. **CP-PopeA**

Lamentation of the Old Pensioner, The. William Butler Yeats. **CP-YeatW**

Lamentations. Louise Glück. **SP-GlücL**

Lamentations of Jeremy, for the Most Part According to Tremeullius. John Donne. **CP-DonnJ**

"How sits this city, late most populous." **ChIV-1**

Laments for a Noble Lady. Robert Southwell. **CP-SoutR**

L'America. Jim Morrison. **SP-MorrJ**

Lamia. John Keats. **CP-KeatJ**

Banquet, The. **SeCePo**

"Upon a time, before the faery broods." **NOBRP**

Lamia in Love. Robert Ranke Graves. **CP-GravR**

L'Amitié Est L'Amour Sans Ailes. Byron. **CP-Byron**

Lamoille River Valley otherwise known, The. Hayden Carruth. *Fr.* Paragraphs. **CP-CarHS**

Lamp, The. Robert Herrick. **CP-HerrR**

Lamp, The. Charles Olson. **CP-OlsoC; SP-OlsoC**

Lamp burns sure—within, The. Emily Dickinson. **CP-DickE**

Lamp full of shadows burned, A. John Haines. *Fr.* The Traveler. **SP-HainJ**

Lamp must be replenish'd, but even then, The. Manfred: A Dramatic Poem. Byron. **CP-Byron**

Lamp of day, with ill-presaging glare, The. On the Death of Sir J. Hunter Blair. Robert Burns. **CP-BurnR**

Lamped in a postered arch, her settecento name. Dorabella's Naples Watercolor. James Schuyler. **CP-SchuJ**

Lampfall. Derek Walcott. **CP-WalcD**

Lamplight. John Updike. **CP-UpdiJ**

Lamplighter, The. Robert Louis Stevenson. **CP-StevR**

Lamps, The. Mary Oliver. **SP-OlivM**

Lamps are on: terrestrial galaxies, The. Night Ride. Charles Tomlinson. **CP-TomlC**

Lamps now glitter down the street, The. Armies in the Fire. Robert Louis Stevenson. **CP-StevR**

Lampshade, The. Roy Fisher. **SP-FishR** *Fr.* Interiors with Various Figures.

L'An Trentiesme de Mon Eage. Archibald MacLeish. **CP-MacLA**

Lana. Hayden Carruth. **CP-CarHS**

Lancashire. Donald Davie. **CP-DavDo**

Lancaster bore him—such a little town. A Hundred Collars. Robert Frost. **CP-FrosR**

Lancaster Street. Martin Edmunds. **SP-EdmuM**

Lance, shield, and sword relinquished—at his side. Seclusion. William Wordsworth. *Fr.* Ecclesiastical Sonnets. **CP-WorW2**

Lancelot. Edwin Arlington Robinson. **CP-RobiE**

Lancelot and Elaine. Tennyson. *Fr.* Idylls of the King. **CP-TennA**

Song of Love and Death, The. **OBNC**

Lancer. Alfred Edward Housman. **CP-HousA**

Land, The. Roy Fisher. **SP-FishR** *Fr.* Inscriptions for Bluebeard's Castle.

Land, The. Rudyard Kipling. **CP-KiplR**

Land. Patti Smith. **SP-SmitP**

Land and Sea Tales. Rudyard Kipling.

Counting-Out Song, A. **CP-KiplR**

Departure, A. **CP-KiplR**

Hour of the Angel, The. **CP-KiplR**

Junk and the Dhow, The. **CP-KiplR**

Last Lap, The. **CP-KiplR**

Master-Cook, The. **CP-KiplR**

Nurses, The. **CP-KiplR**

Preface, A: "To all to whom this little book may come." **CP-KiplR**

Land breaks yellow south below, pale squares. A View from Cortona. Richard Hugo. **CP-HugoR**

Land is an ark, full of things waiting, The. A Wet Time. Wendell Berry. **CP-BerrW**

Land is dry enough to make the rivers, The. John Updike. *Fr.* Spanish Sonnets. **CP-UpdiJ**

Land is rich where'er we go, The. Brotherhood. George Meredith. **CP-MerG2**

Land lies in water; it is shadowed green. The Map. Elizabeth Bishop. **CP-BishE**

Land o' Used to Be, The. Paul Laurence Dunbar. **CP-DunbP**

Land of Biscay, The. Alfred Edward Housman. **CP-HousA**

Land of Cotton. Gilbert Sorrentino. **SP-SorrG**

Land of Counterpane, The. Robert Louis Stevenson. **CP-StevR**

Land of Dreams, The. William Blake. **CP-BlakW**

Land of Fuck, The. Erica Jong. **SP-JongE**

Land of Happy, The. Shel Silverstein. **SP-SilS2**

Land of Indolence, The. James Thomson. *See* In lowly dale, fast by a river's side.

Land of leaning ice, A. North Labrador. Hart Crane. **CP-CranH**

Land of my fathers and blood, oh my fathers, whatever. Hill Daughter. Louise McNeill. **SP-McNeL**

Land of Nod, The. Robert Louis Stevenson. **CP-StevR**

Land of Our Birth. Rudyard Kipling. *Fr.* Puck of Pook's Hill.

Land of Story-Books, The. Robert Louis Stevenson. **CP-StevR**

Land of Whipperginny, The. Robert Ranke Graves. **CP-GravR**

Land O'Lakes, Wisc. Allen Ginsberg. **CP-GinsA**

Land O'Lakes, Wisconsin: Vajrayana Seminary. Allen Ginsberg. **CP-GinsA**

Land outside, and the night is the enemy's, The. The House. Charles Olson. **CP-OlsoC**

Land runs in a flat strip of jungle along the coast, The. Coastal Strip. George Oppen. **CP-OppeG**

Land, that, from the rule of kings, The. The Bartholdi Statue. John Greenleaf Whittier. **CP-WhitJ**

Land that has no song, The. Trimountain. Ralph Waldo Emerson. **CP-EmerR**

Land was all electric, The. Ralph Waldo Emerson. **CP-EmerR**

Land was ours before we were the land's, The. The Gift Outright. Robert Frost. **CP-FrosR**

Land was overmuch like scenery, The. Beowulf. Richard Wilbur. **CP-WilbR**

Land was pale with famine, The. The Dole of Jarl Thorkell. John Greenleaf Whittier. **CP-WhitJ**

Land We Did Not Know, The. Jean Garrigue. **SP-GarrJ**

Land we from our fathers had in trust, The. Feelings of the Tyrolese. William Wordsworth. **CP-WorW1**

Land where I was born sits by the seas, The. Francesca of Rimini. Dante Alighieri, *tr.* by Byron. **CP-Byron** *Fr.* Inferno. *Fr.* Divina Commedia.

Land-Worker. David Herbert Lawrence. *Fr.* Bits. **CP-LawrD**

Landau, The, *parody of* W.M. Praed. Rudyard Kipling. **CP-KiplR** *Fr.* The Muse among the Motors.

Landcrab I. Margaret Atwood. **SP-AtwM2**

Landcrab II. Margaret Atwood. **SP-AtwM2**

Landed Fish. Marge Piercy. **SP-PierM**

Landfall, The. Thomas Merton. **CP-MertT; SP-MertT**

Landfall, Grenada. Derek Walcott. **CP-WalcD**

Landing / At four o'clock in the morning. The Approach—Calcutta. May Sarton. **SP-SartM**

Landing, The. Charles Tomlinson. **CP-TomlC**

Landing in Cairo. Martin Edmunds. **SP-EdmuM**

Landing in the Rain at La Guardia. John Updike. **CP-UpdiJ**

Landlady, The. Margaret Atwood. **SP-AtwM1**

Landlady count the lawin. Hey Tuti Tatey. Robert Burns. **CP-BurnR**

Landlady's Daughter, The, *see also* "From the German of Uhland," tr. James Weldon Johnson. Ludwig Uhland, *tr. fr. German by* George Meredith. **CP-MerG2**

Landlord, landlord. Ballad of the Landlord. Langston Hughes. **SP-HughL**

Landlord walks up and down the hall, The. Breakout. Charles Bukowski. **SP-BukC2**

Landlord's hammer in the yard. Passing On. Adrienne Rich. **CP-RicAE**

Landlord's Tale: Paul Revere's Ride, The. Henry Wadsworth Longfellow. *See* Paul Revere's Ride (The Landlord's Tale).

Landmarks, The. John Greenleaf Whittier. **CP-WhitJ**

Landor, not that I doubt your word. Unnatural Love. Allen Tate. **CP-TateA**

Landowners. Sylvia Plath. **CP-PlatS**

Land's End. Archibald MacLeish. **CP-MacLA**

Land's end. And sound and river come. The Point. Robert Earl Hayden. **CP-HaydR**

Landscape. Wystan Hugh Auden. **CP-AudWJ**

Landscape, The. Stephen Dunn. **SP-DunnS**

Landscape. John Hewitt. **CP-HewiJ**

Landscape. Thomas Merton. **CP-MertT; SP-MertT**

Landscape. Mary Oliver. **SP-OlivM**

Landscape. Octavio Paz, *tr. fr. Spanish by* Charles Tomlinson. **CP-TomlC**

Landscape. Carl Sandburg. **CP-SandC**

Landscape. Carl Sandburg. **CP-SandC**

Landscape (After Baudelaire). John Ashbery. **SP-AshbJ**

Landscape as a Nude. Archibald MacLeish. **CP-MacLA**

Landscape at the End of the Century. Stephen Dunn. **SP-DunnS**

Landscape: Beast. Thomas Merton. **SP-MertT** *Fr.* Figures for an Apocalypse. **CP-MertT**

Landscape for Wyn Henderson, A. Kay Boyle. **CP-BoylK**

Landscape Goat. Robert Pack. **SP-PackR**

Landscape Including Three States of the Union. Carl Sandburg. **CP-SandC**

Landscape is the same wherever we go, The. Islanders. Siv Cedering Fox. **SP-CedeS**

LANDSCAPE: *Jungle Days* (Dutch). Jenny Joseph. *Fr.* Altarpiece (A Meditation on Lust, Desire and Love). **SP-JoseJ**

Landscape near an Aerodrome, The. Stephen Spender. **CP-SpenS**

Landscape of love, The. Erotic Epigrams. John Updike. **CP-UpdiJ**

Landscape of the Star. Adrienne Rich. **CP-RicAE**

Landscape, Prophet and Wild-dog. Thomas Merton. **SP-MertT** *Fr.* Figures for an Apocalypse. **CP-MertT**

Landscape (the landscape!) again: Gloucester, The. The Librarian. Charles Olson. **CP-OlsoC; SP-OlsoC**

Landscape: Wheatfields. Thomas Merton. **CP-MertT**

Landscape where I lie, The. Song for a Lyre. Louise Bogan. **CP-BogaL**

Landscape Winter. Anne Sexton. **CP-SextA**

Landscape With A Woman. Richard Shelton. **SP-ShelR**

Landscape with Boat. Wallace Stevens. **CP-StevW**

Landscape with Crutches, A. Charles Simic. **SP-SimiC**

Landscape with Figures. Howard Nemerov. **CP-NemeH**

Landscape with Seated Figure and Olive Trees. Charles Wright. **SP-WrigC**

Landscape with the Fall of Icarus. William Carlos Williams. **LCAP; NAAL-2; NoAM; PPP** *Fr.* Pictures from Brueghel. **CP-WilW2**

Landscape with Wave Approaching. Muriel Rukeyser. **CP-RukeM**

Landscape, Without Color. Charles Olson. **CP-OlsoC**

Landscapes. Thomas Stearns Eliot. **CP-ElioT**

Cape Ann. **GoJo; NAEL-2; NoAM**

New Hampshire. **FaBoCh; GTBS-6; GTBS-P; NoAM; WeW**

Rannoch, by Glencoe. **FaBoPP; NAEL-2; PoSH**

Usk. **FaBoCh; NOCV; PeECV**

Virginia. **InPK**

Landscapes. Richard Hugo. **CP-HugoR**

Landscapes reverence the Frost. Emily Dickinson. **SP-DickE**

Landscape's upper frame was bounded by, The. Below the Mournes in May. John Hewitt. **CP-HewiJ**

Lane of Yellow led the eye, A. Emily Dickinson. **CP-DickE**

Lane painted true color, and drew. An "Enthusiasm." Charles Olson. **CP-OlsoC**

Lanes of Death and Birth. Edwin Rolfe. **CP-RolfE**

Lang Coortin', The. "Lewis Carroll." **CP-CarrL**

Lang hae we parted been. Lassie Lie near Me. Robert Burns. **CP-BurnR**

Langaig. Richard Hugo. **CP-HugoR**

Langston Hughes. Gwendolyn Brooks. **SP-BrooG**

Language, The. Robert Creeley. **CP-CreeR**

Language as city: Wittgenstein. Images for Godard. Adrienne Rich. **CP-RicAE**

Language Barrier, The. Gilbert Sorrentino. **SP-SorrG**

Language doesn't inhere / in anything. A label. Coming To. Dabney Stuart. **SP-StuaD**

Language Journal. Charles Wright. **SP-WrigC**

Language of Flowers, Etc., The. Hayden Carruth. **CP-CarHS**

Language of life is green, The. Evergreen. Phoebe Hesketh. **SP-HeskP**

Language of New York, A. George Oppen. **CP-OppeG**

"City of the corporations, A."

"I cannot even now / Altogether disengage myself."

"Possible / To use."

"Strange that the youngest people I know."

"There can be a brick."

"Unable to begin / At the beginning, the fortunate."

"Which act is / Violence."

"Whitman: 'April 19, 1864'."

Language of Postcards, The. Richard Shelton. **SP-ShelR**

Language of the Seasons. Robert Ranke Graves. **CP-GravR**

Language Teaching: Naming. Jenny Joseph. **SP-JoseJ**

Language thou art too narrow, and too weak. An Elegy upon the Death of Mistress Boulstred. John Donne. **CP-DonnJ**

Languages. Carl Sandburg. **CP-SandC**

Langue d'Oc. Ezra Pound, *after the Provençal of* Arnaut Daniel. Alba ("When the nightingale to his mate"). **SP-PounE**

Languedocienne. Marilyn Hacker. **SP-HackM**

Languid the songs I wish [willed . . .I] I try. John Berryman. *Fr.* Sonnets to Chris. **CP-BerrJ**

Languidly month by month. Change of Life. David Herbert Lawrence. **CP-LawrD**

Languishing Moon, The. Sir Philip Sidney. *See* Sonnet 31: "With how sad steps, O Moon, thou climb'st the skies."

Languor, uselessness & general swamp I'd be or. 8/9. Anne Waldman. **SP-WaldA**

Lank potato, darkening. Kent. Thom Gunn. *Fr.* Breaking Ground. **CP-GunnT**

Lansing Bad Penny Come Again Blues, The. Marge Piercy. **SP-PierM**

Lantern-light from deeper in the barn, A. The Fear. Robert Frost. **CP-FrosR**

Lantern Out of Doors, The. Gerard Manley Hopkins. **CP-HopkG**

Lanterns dangle at the end of long wires, The. From the Chinese. John Gould Fletcher. **SP-FletJ**

Lanternslides grinding out B-flat minor, The. Lunch. Kenneth Koch. **SP-KochK**

Lao Tan lay dead / Chin Shih attended the wake. Lao Tzu's Wake. Chuang Tzu, *tr. fr. Chinese by* Thomas Merton. **CP-MertT**

Lao Tsze. Kenneth Patchen. **CP-PatcK**

Lao Tzu's Wake. Chuang Tzu, *tr. fr. Chinese by* Thomas Merton. **CP-MertT**

Laocoön. Richard Eberhart. **CP-EberR**

Laocoön is the Name of the Figure. Marge Piercy. **SP-PierM**

Laodamia. William Wordsworth. **CP-WorW2**

Lapis dawn is gleaming, A. Malcolm Lowry. **CP-LowrM**

Lapis Lazuli. William Butler Yeats. **CP-YeatW**

Lapis sky. No moon. The evening stars, A. Egypt. Martin Edmunds. **SP-EdmuM**

Laplander, The. Charlotte Smith. **CP-SmitC**

Lapping of waters / thick, upon razorblade. Marsden Hartley. **CP-HartM**

Lapse, The. Paul Laurence Dunbar. **CP-DunbP**

Lapse of time and rivers is the same, The. A Comparison. William Cowper. **CP-CowpW**

Lapwing's wavering flight, The. Kathleen Jessie Raine. *Fr.* By the River Eden. **SP-RainK**

Lara. Byron. **CP-Byron**

"Serfs are glad through Lara's wide domain, The."

"In him inexplicably mixed appeared." **NOBRP; OAEL-2**

L'ara sul rostro / 20 years of the dream. Ezra Pound. *See* Canto 76: "And the sun high over horizon hidden in cloud bank."

Large Bad Picture. Elizabeth Bishop. **CP-BishE**

Large bead on the. Charles Henri Ford. **SP-FordC** *Fr.* Emblems of Arachne.

Large Bounds Doe but Bury Us. Robert Herrick. **CP-HerrR**

Large Cool Store, The. Philip Larkin. **CP-LarkP**

Large-leaved day grows rapidly, The. The Red Fern. Wallace Stevens. **CP-StevW**

Large rains had long since passed in thunder, The. The Diagrams. Frederick Morgan. **SP-MorgF**

Large Red Man Reading. Wallace Stevens. **CP-StevW**

Larger Hope, The. Tennyson. *See* Oh Yet We Trust.

Larger than the sky. A Woe. Daniel Gerard Hoffman. **SP-HoffD**

Largess, The. Richard Eberhart. **CP-EberR**

Largest Fire ever known, The. Emily Dickinson. **CP-DickE**

Lark Ascending, The. George Meredith. **CP-MerG1**

Lark begins to go up, The. Ted Hughes. **HAP** *Fr.* Skylarks. **SP-HughT**

Lark-bright the air; the light / from leafing hedge and willow. April Awake. John Hewitt. **CP-HewiJ**

Lark did all louden, The. Feminine Ending or, Abandoned, She Died. Isabella Gardner. **CP-GardI**

Lark has no tree, The. He with the Beating Wings. Lawrence Ferlinghetti. **SP-FerlL**

Lark is silent in his nest, The. Good-Night. Paul Laurence Dunbar. **CP-DunbP**

Lark will make her hymn to God, The. Rudyard Kipling. **CP-KiplR** *Fr.* The Light That Failed.

Larks, The. Daniel Gerard Hoffman. **SP-HoffD**

Lark's Nest, A. Christopher Smart. *See* For Saturday.

Lark's Nest, The. Charlotte Smith. **CP-SmitC**

Lark's Song, The. William Blake. *See* Thou hearest the nightingale begin the song of spring.

Larks, this year, The. The Lesson. Charles Tomlinson. **CP-TomlC**

Larkspur; windy July. On the Verandah. John Gould Fletcher. **SP-FletJ**

Larr's Portion, and the Poets Part. Robert Herrick. **CP-HerrR**

Larry. James Wright. **CP-WrigJ**

Las Trampas U. S. A. Charles Tomlinson. **CP-TomlC**

Las Vegas: Verses Improvised for El Dorado H.S. Newspaper. Allen Ginsberg. **CP-GinsA**

Lasalle. Donald Davie. **CP-DavDo**

Lasciviousnesse. Robert Herrick. **CP-HerrR**

Lashes of white light. Peace. Adrienne Rich. **CP-RicAE**

Lass of Ecclefechan, The. Robert Burns. **CP-BurnR**

"Lass of Richmond Hill", or The Royal Garden Party, The. John Hewitt. **CP-HewiJ**

Lassie, lend me your braw hemp-heckle. The Bob o' Dumblane. Robert Burns. **CP-BurnR**

Lassie Lie near Me. Robert Burns. **CP-BurnR**

Lassie wi' the Lintwhite Locks. Robert Burns. **CP-BurnR**

Lassitudes of Contemplation, The. Emily Dickinson. **CP-DickE**

Lassù Fia Caro Il Rivederci. Christina Georgina Rossetti. *Fr.* Il Rosseggiar Dell'Oriente Canzoniere. **CP-RosC3**

Lassuso Il Caro Fiore. Christina Georgina Rossetti. *Fr.* Il Rosseggiar Dell'Oriente Canzoniere. **CP-RosC3**

Last, The. Charles Kenneth Williams. **CP-WillC**

Last Answer, The. Christina Georgina Rossetti. **CP-RosC3**

Last Answers. Carl Sandburg. **CP-SandC**

Last Arrival, The. Daniel Gerard Hoffman. **SP-HoffD**

Last Arrow, The. Walter de la Mare. **CP-DeLaW**

Last as first the question rings. Last Chorus. Thomas Hardy. **CP-HardT** *Fr.* The Dynasts.

Last Attachment, A. Frank Templeton Prince. **CP-PrinF**

Last before America. Louis MacNeice. **CP-MacNL**

Last Bus, Saturday Night. Wystan Hugh Auden. **CP-AudWJ**

Last Call, The. John Hewitt. **CP-HewiJ**

Last Came, and Last Did Go. John Milton. **TW** *Fr.* Lycidas. **CP-MiltJ**

Last Chantey, The. Rudyard Kipling. **CP-KiplR**

Last Chapter, The. Walter de la Mare. **CP-DeLaW**

Last Chorus. Thomas Hardy. **CP-HardT** *Fr.* The Dynasts.

Last Chrysanthemum, The. Thomas Hardy. **CP-HardT**

Last cigarette / a companion, A. Louis Zukofsky. **CP-ZukLS**

Last cloud to pass, The. Art Is Not for Grown-ups. James Liddy. **CP-LiddJ**

Last Coachload, The. Walter de la Mare. **CP-DeLaW**

Last *Complaint*, The. Christina Georgina Rossetti. **CP-RosC3**

Last Confession, A, *fr.* A Woman Young and Old. William Butler Yeats. **CP-YeatW**

Last Conservative, The. Robinson Jeffers. **CP-JefR3**

Last Contention, The. George Meredith. **CP-MerG1**

Last Crusade, The. John Hewitt. **CP-HewiJ**

Last Day. Margaret Atwood. **SP-AtwM2**

Last Day There. Richard Hugo. **CP-HugoR**

Last Days. Mary Oliver. **SP-OlivM**

Last Days at Teddington. Thom Gunn. **CP-GunnT**

Last Days of Alice. Allen Tate. **CP-TateA**

Last Days of the Miser. Charles Tomlinson. **CP-TomlC**

Last Deaths, The. Charles Kenneth Williams. **CP-WillC; SP-WillC**

Last Decision, The. Maya Angelou. **SP-AngeM**

Last Department, The. Rudyard Kipling. **CP-KiplR**

Last Door, The. Roy Fisher. **SP-FishR** *Fr.* Inscriptions for Bluebeard's Castle.

Last Droplets. Walt Whitman. **CP-WhitW**

Last Drowning, The. Robert Pack. **CP-PackR**

Last Elegy. Stephen Berg. **SP-BergS**

Last Eve of Summer, The. John Greenleaf Whittier. **CP-WhitJ**

Last evening a city man. Fernando Pessoa. *Fr.* Twelve Poems from *The Keeper of the Flocks*. **CP-MertT**

Last evening I entered a pool. To My Father. John Haines. **SP-HainJ**

Last evening the moon rose above this rock. How to Live. What to Do. Wallace Stevens. **CP-StevW**

Last Farewell, The. Edward Bliss Emerson. **CP-EmerR**

Last Fistful, The. Robert Ranke Graves. **CP-GravR**

Last flame / sole leaf, A. Elemental. Charles Tomlinson. **CP-TomlC**

Last Frontier, The. John Gould Fletcher. **SP-FletJ**

Last Full Measure of Devotion, The. Kenneth Patchen. **CP-PatcK**

Last full moon of February, The. Hunger Moon. Jane Cooper. **CABA** *Fr.* March. **SP-CoopJ**

Last Generation, The. Charles Bukowski. **SP-BukC3**

Last Great American Whale. "Lou Reed." **SP-ReedL**

Last Hill in a Vista. Louise Bogan. **CP-BogaL**

Last Hours. David Herbert Lawrence. **CP-LawrD**

Last Instructions to a Painter, The. Andrew Marvell. **CP-MarvA**

"After two sittings, now our Lady State." **APAS; OBSV**

Dutch in the Medway, The. **FaBoEH; OBS**

"Paint Castlemaine in colours that will hold." **OBSV**

"Paint last the King, and a dead shade of night." **OBS; OBSV**

(Charles II.) **OBS**

Last Invocation, The. Walt Whitman. **CP-WhitW**

Last Journal. Charles Wright. **SP-WrigC**

Last Journey, A. Thomas Hardy. **CP-HardT**

Last Judgement. Charles Tomlinson. **CP-TomlC**

Last Judgment, The. John Gould Fletcher. **SP-FletJ** *Fr.* The Parables of Christ.

Last Lap, The. Rudyard Kipling. **CP-KiplR** *Fr.* Land and Sea Tales.

Last Laugh, The. Sir John Betjeman. **CP-BetjJ**

Last Laugh, The. Wilfred Owen. **CP-OwenW**

Last Leaf, The. Thomas Hardy. **CP-HardT**

Last leaves fell like notes from a piano, The. Forest of Europe. Derek Walcott. **CP-WalcD**

Last Lesson of the Afternoon. David Herbert Lawrence. **CP-LawrD**

Last Letter. Louise Glück. *Fr.* Marathon. **SP-GlücL**

Last Letter to the Scholar. Jean Garrigue. **SP-GarrJ**

Last Light in Clare's Mind. James Liddy. **CP-LiddJ**

Last light purples the mirrors of paddy, the tracks, The. Louis MacNeice. *Fr.* Didymus. **CP-MacNL**

Last Look, The. Christina Georgina Rossetti. **CP-RosC3**

Last Look round St. Martin's Fair. Thomas Hardy. **CP-HardT**

Last Looks at the Lilacs. Wallace Stevens. **CP-StevW**

Last love, / proper in conclusion, A. Recovery. Maya Angelou. **SP-AngeM**

Last Love-Word. Thomas Hardy. **CP-HardT**

Last Lynx. Daniel Gerard Hoffman. **SP-HoffD**

Last Man, The. Thom Gunn. **OxAEP-2** *Fr.* Misanthropos. **CP-GunnT**

Last Man in the Dôme, The. Malcolm Lowry. *Fr.* The Cantinas. **CP-LowrM**

Last Man in the Quabbin, The. Brendan Galvin. **SP-GalvB**

Last May a braw wooer cam down the lang glen. Scotish Ballad. Robert Burns. **CP-BurnR**

Last Meeting. Stephen Berg. **SP-BergS**

Last Minute, The. David Herbert Lawrence. *Fr.* Bits. **CP-LawrD**

Last-Minute Change of Plans. Ron Koertge. **SP-KoerR**

Last Monarch of the Season, The. Gary Gildner. **SP-GildG**

Last Month. John Ashbery. **SP-AshbJ**

Last month, two years to a day since Dave Shaw's. Prayer against the Curse Bomb. Laurence Lieberman. **SP-LiebL**

Last Mornings in California. James Merrill. **SP-MerrJ**

Last Mowing, The. Robert Frost. **CP-FrosR**

Last night / in the fields. White Flowers. Mary Oliver. **SP-OlivM**

Last Night. Christina Georgina Rossetti. **CP-RosC3**

Last night / the daughters of ignorance. November 1st. Richard Shelton. **SP-ShelR**

Last night a January wind was ripping at the shingles over our house and. Manitoba Childe Roland. Carl Sandburg. **CP-SandC**

Last night a star followed. My Grandmother Steals Her Last Trout. Brendan Galvin. **SP-GalvB**

Last night a thief came to me. Thief in the Night. David Herbert Lawrence. **CP-LawrD**

Last night as I crossed. Print from a Lucite Block. Kay Boyle. **CP-BoylK**

Last night as I lay cold with hear. Aubade to Fear (Heavy with Child). Louise McNeill. **SP-McNeL**

Last night at black midnight I woke with a cry. Nicholas Vachel Lindsay. **CP-LindV**

(Ghost of the Buffaloes, The.) **CP-LindV**

Last night at dinner at *Vecchia Roma*. 1984. David St. John. *Fr.* To Pasolini. **SP-StJoD**

Last night, before I came to bear. The Angel. James Wright. **CP-WrigJ**

Last night during a thunderstorm. Letter Home. Stephen Dunn. **SP-DunnS**

Last night from Troy's high battlements. Omens and Auguries. John Hewitt. **CP-HewiJ**

"Last night," he said, "I slept well." The Dream. Sylvia Plath. **CP-PlatS**

Last night he walked out on himself. Walking Away. Phoebe Hesketh. **SP-HeskP**

Last night I did not fight for sleep. In Hospital: Poona (1). Alun Lewis. **CP-LewiA**

Last night, I don't know if from habit or intent. Sonnet. Hayden Carruth. **CP-CarHS** *Fr.* Sonnets.

Last night I dreamed. The NIght-Apple. Allen Ginsberg. **CP-GinsA**

Last night I dreamed we were in Venice. Song of Invisible Boundaries. Louise Glück. **SP-GlücL** *Fr.* Marathon. **SP-GlücL**

Last night I dreamt. Dream. Langston Hughes. **SP-HughL**

Last night I drew up mine Account. The Summe, and the Satisfaction. Robert Herrick. **CP-HerrR**

Last night I dropped in at the Con- / cord—out on Erie? You. Lana. Hayden Carruth. **CP-CarHS**

Last night I fled until I came. Light. Allen Tate. **CP-TateA**

Last night I heard wolves howling. Wolves. John Haines. **SP-HainJ**

Last night I lay upon my bed and would have slept. After a Visit. Countee Cullen. **CP-CullC**

Last night I met you in my sister's house. The Stelae. Adrienne Rich. **CP-RicAE; SP-RicA2**

Last night I murdered a thousand cells. Barney Hung Over. Paul Zimmer. **SP-ZimmP**

Last night I said these words to my girl. Please Please Me. The Beatles. **CP-Beatl**

Last night I saw you in my sleep. Bad Dreams I. Robert Browning. **CP-BroR2**

Last night I seemed in your embrace. Kathleen Jessie Raine. **SP-RainK**

Last night I stood beside a woman's bed. The Doctor Muses. John Hewitt. **CP-HewiJ**

Last night I thought of Torri del Benaco again. Lost Bodies. Charles Wright. **SP-WrigC**

Last night I woke in fright: you were not there. Without a Counterpart. Thom Gunn. **CP-GunnT**

Last Night in Calcutta. Allen Ginsberg. **CP-GinsA**

Last night Joan Sutherland was nuancing. Something Like Happiness. Stephen Dunn. **SP-DunnS**

Last night, just as the tints of autumn's sky. The Fruit-Gift. John Greenleaf Whittier. **CP-WhitJ**

Last night returning from my twilight walk. A Ballad of Past Meridian. George Meredith. **CP-MerG1**

Last Night that She lived, The. Emily Dickinson. **CP-DickE**

Last night the / fluffiest inhabitant. Snow Roost. Archie Randolph Ammons. **SP-AmmoA**

Last night the cold wind and the rain blew. Sunday at the End of Summer. Howard Nemerov. **CP-NemeH**

Last night the geese came back. Two Kinds of Deliverance. Mary Oliver. **SP-OlivM**

Last night there was / a lunar eclipse: the. Moon. James Schuyler. **CP-SchuJ**

Last night thou didst invite me home to eat[e]. Upon Showbread [*or* Shewbread]: Epigram. Robert Herrick. **CP-HerrR**

Last night watching the Pleiades. An Autumn Morning in Shokoku-ji. Gary Snyder. **HAP; VGW; WeW** *Fr.* Four Poems for Robin. **CP-SnydG**

Last night we had a thunderstorm in style. Robert Louis Stevenson. **CP-StevR**

Last night we sat with the stereopticon. Readings of History. Adrienne Rich. **CP-RicAE**

Last Night with Rafaella. David St. John. **SP-StJoD**

Last night, without a voice, that Vision spake. Patriotic Sympathies. William Wordsworth. *Fr.* Ecclesiastical Sonnets. **CP-WorW2**

Last night without sight of you my brain was ablaze. Basil Bunting, *after the Persian of* Sadi. **CP-BuntB**

Last night you wrote on the wall: Revolution is poetry. 7/26/68: i. Adrienne Rich. **CP-RicAE** *Fr.* Ghazals: Homage to Ghalib. **SP-RicA2**

Last night your watchdog barked all night. An Unstamped Letter in Our Rural Letter Box. Robert Frost. **CP-FrosR**

Last night's / drizzle's. Deaf Zone. Archie Randolph Ammons. **SP-AmmoA**

Last Ode, The, *after* Horace, Book 5, Ode 31. Rudyard Kipling. **CP-KiplR** *Fr.* Debits and Credits.

Last of last words spoken is, Good-bye, The. Good-bye. Walter de la Mare. **CP-DeLaW**

Last of Night, The. Charles Tomlinson. **CP-TomlC**

Last of Summer is Delight, The. Emily Dickinson. **CP-DickE**

Last of the Fire Kings, The. Derek Mahon. **SP-MahoD**

Last of the Flock, The. William Wordsworth. **CP-WorW1**

Last of the Light Brigade, The. Rudyard Kipling. **CP-KiplR**

Last of the Old Year, The. Wystan Hugh Auden. **CP-AudWJ**

Last one / died and she, The. Late Look. Archie Randolph Ammons. **SP-AmmoA**

Last Open-Air Concert, The. Brendan Galvin. **SP-GalvB**

Last party before I left was in an old, run-down apartment house, The. Flight. Charles Kenneth Williams. **CP-WillC**

Last Performance, The. Thomas Hardy. **CP-HardT**

Last Picnic, The. Stanley Jasspon Kunitz. **CP-KuniS**

Last Poem. Ted Berrigan. **SP-BerrT**

Last Poem. Robert Browning. **CP-BroR2**

Last Poem, A. Robert Ranke Graves. **CP-GravR**

Last Poem. Frank Templeton Prince. **CP-PrinF**

Last Poem (after Robert Desnos), The. Tom Clark. **SP-ClarT**

Last Post sounded. After the War. Thomas Hardy. **CP-HardT**

Last Quatrain of the Ballad of Emmett Till, The. Gwendolyn Brooks. **SP-BrooG**

Last Question, The. Stanley Jasspon Kunitz. **CP-KuniS**

Last Resort, The. Derek Mahon. *Fr.* Autobiographies. **SP-MahoD**

Last Rhyme of True Thomas, The. Rudyard Kipling. **CP-KiplR**

Last Ride Together, The. Robert Browning. **CP-BroR1**

Last River, The. Galway Kinnell. **SP-KinnG**

Last Shot, The. "Lou Reed." **SP-ReedL**

Last Sight, The. Robert Louis Stevenson. **CP-StevR**

Last Signal, The. Thomas Hardy. **CP-HardT**

Last silk-floating thought has gone from the dandelion stem, The. Repulsed. David Herbert Lawrence. **CP-LawrD**

Last Song, A. "Hugh MacDiarmid." **SP-MacDH**

Last Song. Adrienne Rich. **CP-RicAE**

Last Song of Lucifer, The. Nicholas Vachel Lindsay. **CP-LindV**

Last Songs. Galway Kinnell. **SP-KinnG**

Last spring you said. The Dead Tree. Peter Meinke. **SP-MeinP**

Last Step, The. Philip Levine. **SP-LeviP**

Last step taken found your heft, The. To a Thinker. Robert Frost. **CP-FrosR**

Last, Stone, a little yet. Epitaph, An. Walter de la Mare. **CP-DeLaW**

Last Stroke Strike Sure, The. Robert Herrick. **CP-HerrR**

Last Summer, For Roberta (1975), The. John Hewitt. **CP-HewiJ**

Last sunbeam, The. Dirge for Two Veterans. Walt Whitman. **CP-WhitW**

Last Sunday afternoon I went. Any Rich Suburban Church. John Hewitt. **CP-HewiJ**

Last Supper, by Leonardo da Vinci, in the Refectory of the Convent of Maria della Grazia—Milan, The. William Wordsworth. *Fr.* Memorials of a Tour of the Continent; 1820. **CP-WorW2**

Last Suttee, The. Rudyard Kipling. **CP-KiplR**

Last sweet night, The. Robert Creeley. **CP-CreeR**

Last tall son of Lot and Bellicent, The. Gareth and Lynette. Tennyson. *Fr.* Idylls of the King. **CP-TennA**

Last Thoughts on Woody Guthrie. "Bob Dylan." **CP-DylaB**

Last Time, The. Wystan Hugh Auden. **CP-AudWJ**

Last Time, The. Marilyn Hacker. **SP-HackM**

Last Time, The. Thomas Hardy. **CP-HardT**

Last Time, The. William DeWitt Snodgrass. **SP-SnodW**

Last Time, The. Alice Walker. **CP-WalkA**

Last time I saw Donald Armstrong, The. The Performance. James Dickey. **CP-DickJ**

Last time I talked to you in my head, The. Separate Lives. Marilyn Hacker. **SP-HackM**

Last time I visited, I saw despair's. Back Home. Martin Edmunds. **SP-EdmuM**

Last time we met. The Last Time. Wystan Hugh Auden. **CP-AudWJ**

Last Tournament, The. Tennyson. *Fr.* Idylls of the King. **CP-TennA** Lincolnshire Shores. **FaBoPP** Tristram's Song. **FaBoRV**

Last Translation, The, *ad.fr.*Heine. Elizabeth Barrett Browning. **CP-BroEB**

Last Trump, The. Isabella Gardner. **CP-GardI**

Last Turn, The. William Carlos Williams. **CP-WilW2**

Last Turn of the Screw, The. Stevie Smith. **CP-SmitS**

Last Vision of Eoghan Rua Ó Súilleabháin, The. Michael Hartnett. **SP-HarMi**

Last Walk in Autumn, The. John Greenleaf Whittier. **CP-WhitJ**

Last Wandering of Poor Willie, The. George Meredith. *Fr.* Wandering Willie. **CP-MerG2**

Last week a doctor told me. Beauty I Would Suffer For. Marge Piercy. **SP-PierM**

Last week I saw a child. As It Moves. Stephen Dunn. **SP-DunnS**

Last week I saw myself with green ivy sprouting from the centre. Passion Week Monday after Palm Sunday. Martin Edmunds. **SP-EdmuM**

Last Week in October. Thomas Hardy. **CP-HardT**

Last week on my way to the shrink between connections. Visiting the Stone. Stephen Berg. **SP-BergS**

Last week—the Lord be praised for all His mercies. Letter from a Missionary of the Methodist Episcopal Church South, in Kansas, to a Distiguished Politician. John Greenleaf Whittier. **CP-WhitJ**

Last white sawdust on the floor was grown, The. Edna St. Vincent Millay. *Fr.* Sonnets from an Ungrafted Tree. **CP-MillE**

Last Will and Testament. Philip Larkin. **CP-LarkP**

Last Word of a Bluebird, The. Robert Frost. **CP-FrosR**

Last Words, *sl. diff.* Emily Brontë. *See* Song By J. Brenzaida To G.S.

Last Words. Stanley Jasspon Kunitz. **CP-KuniS**

Last Words. James Merrill. **SP-MerrJ**

Last Words. Sylvia Plath. **CP-PlatS**

Last Words. Theodore Roethke. **CP-RoetT**

Last Words. Dabney Stuart. **SP-StuaD**

Last Words By "Slick." Etheridge Knight. **SP-KnigE**

Last Words from Maratea. Richard Hugo. **CP-HugoR**

Last Words of My English Grandmother, The. William Carlos Williams. **CP-WilW1**

Last Words of My Grandmother. William Carlos Williams. **CP-WilW1**

Last Words of St. Telemachus, The. Christina Georgina Rossetti. **CP-RosC3**

Last Words on Greece. Byron. **CP-Byron**

Last Words to a Dumb Friend. Thomas Hardy. **CP-HardT**

Last Words to James Wright. Richard Hugo. **CP-HugoR**

Last Words to Miriam. David Herbert Lawrence. **CP-LawrD**

Last Words to Muriel. David Herbert Lawrence. **CP-LawrD**

Last World, A. John Ashbery. **SP-AshbJ**

Last year changed its seasons. In Retrospect. Maya Angelou. **SP-AngeM**

Last year I abstained / this year I devour. Margaret Atwood. *Fr.* Circe / Mud Poems. **SP-AtwM1**

Last year I called this world of gaingivings. At the War Office, London. Thomas Hardy. **CP-HardT**

Last year I used to ride theJ CHURCH Line. The J Car. Thom Gunn. **CP-GunnT**

Last year of youth, The. Hayden Carruth. **CP-CarHS** *Fr.* The Clay Hill Anthology.

Last year's leaves are on the beech, The. Loneliness. Sir John Betjeman. **CP-BetjJ**

Lasting Seasons, The. Kenneth Patchen. **CP-PatcK**

Lastly came Winter cloathèd all in frize. Winter. Edmund Spenser. **GN** *Fr.* The Faerie Queene. **CP-Spens**

Lastness. Galway Kinnell. **SP-KinnG**

Lat take a cat, and fostre him wel[l] with milk. Geoffrey Chaucer. **OFC,** *ll.* 71–78; **ChTr** *Fr.* The Manciple's Tale. *Fr.* The Canterbury Tales. **CP-ChauG**

...at. 10 Degrees North, Long. 45 Degrees West. Muriel Rukeyser. **CP-RukeM**

...ate. Louise Bogan. **CP-BogaL**

...ate Abed. Archibald MacLeish. **CP-MacLA**

...ate afternoon light between peach trees. View from an Empty Chair. Tess Gallagher. **SP-GallT**

...ate afternoon light slices through the dormer window. The Gun. Stephen Dobyns. **SP-DobyS**

...ate Afternoon, Running: Close Reasoning, Listening Closely. James McAuley. **SP-McAuJ**

...ate Air. Elizabeth Bishop. **CP-BishE**

...ate Annie in her bower lay. The Ballad of the Late Annie. Gwendolyn Brooks. *Fr.* Notes from the Childhood and the Girlhood. **SP-BrooG**

...ate Anniversary, A. Donald Davie. **CP-DavDo**

...ate Answer, A. Philip Levine. **SP-LeviP**

...ate April and you are three; today. William DeWitt Snodgrass. **NePoEA; VCAP** *Fr.* Heart's Needle. **SP-SnodW**

...ate at Night. David Herbert Lawrence. **CP-LawrD**

...ate Aubade, A. Richard Wilbur. **CP-WilbR**

...ate August. Margaret Atwood. **SP-AtwM1**

...ate August. Marilyn Hacker. **SP-HackM**

...ate August, given heavy rain and sun. Blackberry-Picking. Seamus Heaney. **SP-HeanS**

...ate August Letter. Marilyn Hacker. **SP-HackM**

...ate Autumn in Venice. Rainer Maria Rilke, *tr. fr. German by* Delmore Schwartz. **SP-SchwD**

...ate Butterflies. Howard Nemerov. **CP-NemeH**

...ate Came the God. Rudyard Kipling. **CP-KiplR** *Fr.* Debits and Credits.

...ate Comer, The. Robert Creeley. **CP-CreeR**

...ate crippled of an arm, and now a leg. To R***** G***** of F*****, Esq. Robert Burns. **CP-BurnR**

...ate Echo. John Ashbery. **SP-AshbJ**

...ate February. Ted Kooser. **SP-KoosT**

...ate February, five o'clock: the cantaloupe-colored light. Language Journal. Charles Wright. **SP-WrigC**

...ate-flowering Lust. Sir John Betjeman. **CP-BetjJ**

...ate for Summer Weather. William Carlos Williams. **CP-WilW1**

...ate Gracie Allen was a very lucid comedienne, The. Sonnet. Alice Notley. **SP-NotlA**

...ate Hymn from the Myrrh-Mountain. Wallace Stevens. **CP-StevW**

...ate I fell in the ecstasy. Gerard Manley Hopkins. **CP-HopkG**

...ate Impressionist Dream. Lawrence Ferlinghetti. **SP-FerlL**

...ate in November, on a single night. The Consent. Howard Nemerov. **CP-NemeH**

...ate in the aftrenon. Letter From an Inland Province. Richard Shelton. **SP-ShelR**

...ate in the day when light is sandwiched. New Autumn, New York. Al Young. **CP-YounA**

...ate in the Forest I did Cupid see. Sonnet 2. Mary Sidney, Countess of Montgomery Wroth. **KTR** *Fr.* Pamphilia to Amphilanthus. **CP-WrotM**

...ate in the nicht in bed I lay. Robert Louis Stevenson. **CP-StevR**

...ate in the night I pay. Awake at Night. Wendell Berry. **CP-BerrW**

...ate in the winter came one day. Blossom Themes. Carl Sandburg. **CP-SandC**

...ate January / Snow is on everything. Waiting for the Paper to be Delivered. Miller Williams. **SP-WillM**

...ate January. John Updike. **CP-UpdiJ**

...ate Last Night. Langston Hughes. **SP-HughL**

...ate Late Show. Howard Nemerov. **CP-NemeH**

...ate lies the wintry sun a-bed. Winter Time [*or* Winter-Time]. Robert Louis Stevenson. **CP-StevR**

...ate Lights in Minnesota. Ted Kooser. **SP-KoosT**

...ate Look. Archie Randolph Ammons. **SP-AmmoA**

...ate Moon. Robert Bly. **SP-BlyR**

...ate Moon. Philip Levine. **SP-LeviP**

...ate Morning Talk. James McAuley. **SP-McAuJ**

...ate, my grandson! half the morning have I paced these sandy tracts. Locksley Hall Sixty Years After. Tennyson. **CP-TennA**

...ate Night Movies I. John Yau. **SP-YauJo**

...ate Night Movies II. John Yau. **SP-YauJo**

...ate Night Movies III. John Yau. **SP-YauJo**

...ate Night Movies IV. John Yau. **SP-YauJo**

...ate night on the porch, thinking. *see also* Essay on Marriage. Hayden Carruth. **CP-CarHS**

...ate November. Archie Randolph Ammons. **SP-AmmoA**

...ate November, driving to Wichita. For a Friend. Ted Kooser. **SP-KoosT**

...ate November in a Field. James Wright. **CP-WrigJ**

Late, O miller. Robert Louis Stevenson. **CP-StevR**

Late October. Maya Angelou. **SP-AngeM**

Late October Camping in the Sawtooths. Gary Snyder. **CP-SnydG**

Late on a breezy vernal eve. Sometimes att. to Wordsworth. Samuel Taylor Coleridge. **CP-ColeS; CP-WorW1**

Late on Christams Eve, in the street alone. Two Serenades. Thomas Hardy. **CP-HardT**

Late on Saturday morning I sat reading Hardy again. The Gift of Prophecy Lost. Miller Williams. **SP-WillM**

Late one night—one of those mild, hazy nights. Three Voices. Stephen Berg. **SP-BergS**

Late one night she told me. Edward's Anecdote. Donald Hall. **CP-HallD**

Late peach yields a subtle musk, The. The Coming of the Cold. Theodore Roethke. **CP-RoetT**

Late September. Ted Kooser. **SP-KoosT**

Late September. Chuck Miller. **SP-MillC**

Late Show. Miller Williams. **SP-WillM**

Late Singer, The. William Carlos Williams. **CP-WilW1**

Late Snow. Louise Glück. **SP-GlücL**

Late Snow & Lumber Strike of the Summer of Fifty-four, The. Gary Snyder. **CP-SnydG**

Late snow fell this early morning of spring. Love Is Like Sounds. Donald Hall. **CP-HallD**

Late Spring. Hilda Doolittle. **CP-DoolH**

Late Spring. John Hewitt. **CP-HewiJ**

Late Spring. Meng Hao Jan, *tr. fr. Chinese by* William Carlos Williams *with* David Rafael Wang. **CP-WilW2**

Late Spring, 1912. John Hewitt. **CP-HewiJ**

Late spring this year had its grave tragedies. Late Spring, 1912. John Hewitt. **CP-HewiJ**

Late Stravinsky Listening to Late Beethoven. Stephen Spender. **CP-SpenS**

Late Subterfuge. Robert Penn Warren. **SP-WarrR**

Late Summer. Howard Nemerov. **CP-NemeH**

Late Summer. Edwin Arlington Robinson. **CP-RobiE**

Late summer, and at midnight. The Guttural Muse. Seamus Heaney. **SP-HeanS**

Late Summer at *Milgate*. Robert Lowell. **SP-LoweR**

Late Summer, Drummond. Richard Hugo. **CP-HugoR**

Late sun opening the book. And Return to the States. Allen Ginsberg. **CP-GinsA**

Late. The back road "slicker than owl shit." Snow. Hayden Carruth. *Fr.* The Sleeping Beauty. **CP-CarHL**

Late tired with woe, e'en ready for to pine. Sonnet 62. Sir Philip Sidney. *Fr.* Astrophil and Stella. **SP-SidnP**

Late Walk, A. Robert Frost. **CP-FrosR**

Late War, The. David Herbert Lawrence. **CP-LawrD**

Late wind failed; high on the hill, The. The Fleeting. Walter de la Mare. **CP-DeLaW**

Late-winter afternoons. Blanc de Blanc. Siv Cedering Fox. *Fr.* Onna-E, Pictures of Women. **SP-CedeS**

Lately having escaped three-kinded death. A Birth. Muriel Rukeyser. **CP-RukeM**

Lately I saw a sight most quaint. Gross, Coarse, Hideous. David Herbert Lawrence. **CP-LawrD**

Latent Desire, The. David Herbert Lawrence. **CP-LawrD**

Later Alexandrian, A. George Meredith. **CP-MerG1**

Later Autumn, The. Thomas Hardy. **CP-HardT**

Later he'll say Death stepped right up. The Stroke. Rita Dove. **SP-DoveR**

Later I'd understand how it put. Hearing Irish Spoken. Brendan Galvin. **SP-GalvB**

Later I'll pull down the shade. Pictures of the People in the War. Louise Glück. **SP-GlücL**

Later in Belleville: Career. Margaret Atwood. **SP-AtwM1**

Later Life: A Double Sonnet of Sonnets. Christina Georgina Rossetti. **CP-RosC2**

  "Before the mountains were brought forth, before." **Son**

  "Beyond the seas we know, stretch seas unknown."

  "Dream there is wherein we are fain to scream, A."

  "Here now is Winter. Winter, after all."

  "Host of things I take on trust: I take, A."

  "Hundred thousand birds salute the day, A."

  "I have dreamed of Death:—what will it be to die."

  "In life our absent friend is far away."

  "Let woman fear to teach and bear to learn."

  "Lifelong our stumbles, lifelong our regret."

  "Lord, Thou Thyself art Love and only Thou."

  "Mountains in their overwhelming might, The."

  "Our teachers teach that one and one make two."

"Rend hearts and rend not garments for our sins."

"Shame is a shadow cast by sin: yet shame."

"So late in Autumn half the world's asleep."

"So tired am I, so weary of today."

"Something this foggy day, a something which." **NAEL-2**

"Star Sirius and the Pole Star dwell afar."

This Life Is Full of Numbness. **Son**

"Thou Who didst make and knowest whereof we are / made."

To Love and to Remember. **Son**

"Tread softly! all the earth is holy ground."

"We feel and see with different hearts and eyes."

"We lack, yet cannot fix upon the lack."

"When Adam and when Eve left Paradise."

"When we consider what this life we lead."

"Wise do send their hearts before them to, The."

Later, more mother's help than mine alone. No Second Troy. John Hewitt. **CP-HewiJ**

Later Note on Letter #15, A. Charles Olson. **SP-OlsoC** *Fr.* The Maximus Poems.

Later or Sooner. Richard Eberhart. **CP-EberR**

Later Still. Philip Levine. **SP-LeviP**

Later when the gloated water. The Thin Edge of Your Pride. Kenneth Rexroth. **SP-RexrK**

Later you will touch on everything. Trying to Flatter Twelve Mile River. Brendan Galvin. **SP-GalvB**

Latest creed that has to be believed, The. A Concept Self-Conceived. Robert Frost. **CP-FrosR**

Latest Decalogue, The. Arthur Hugh Clough. **SP-ClouA**

Latest Face. Philip Larkin. **CP-LarkP**

Latest Freed Man, The. Wallace Stevens. **CP-StevW**

Latest sleeping on my pillow catches, The. One Night Stand. Charles Bukowski. **SP-BukC2**

Latesummer Blues. Kenneth Patchen. **CP-PatcK**

Lather as You Go. Ogden Nash. **CP-NashO**

Latimer and Ridley. William Wordsworth. *Fr.* Ecclesiastical Sonnets. **CP-WorW2**

Latitude, Longitude. George Oppen. **CP-OppeG**

Latitudinarianism. William Wordsworth. *Fr.* Ecclesiastical Sonnets. **CP-WorW2**

Latter-Day Sinners. David Herbert Lawrence. **CP-LawrD**

Lattice of his back grows, the dolphin-arching, till. Ringling. Muriel Rukeyser. **CP-RukeM**

Laud. William Wordsworth. *Fr.* Ecclesiastical Sonnets. **CP-WorW2**

Lauda Sion Salvatorem, *ad. fr. the Medieval* De Venerabili Sacramento. Richard Crashaw. **CP-CrasR**

Laudate Dominum, *par. by* Countess of Pembroke, Mary Sidney Herbert. Bible, *O.T. See* Psalm 148: "Praise ye the Lord. Praise ye the Lord from the heavens."

Laudate Dominum. Bible, *O.T. See* Psalm 150: "Praise ye the Lord. Praise God in his sanctuary."

Lauds. Wystan Hugh Auden. **TrCP** *Fr.* Horae Canonicae. **CP-AudeW**

Lauds. John Berryman. **CP-BerrJ**

Laugh, The. Robert Ranke Graves. **CP-GravR**

Laugh and Lie Downe. Robert Herrick. **CP-HerrR**

Laugh still, write always lovingly, for still. Heaven. Robert Ranke Graves. **CP-GravR**

Laughed every goblin. Christina Georgina Rossetti. **BrRo** *Fr.* Goblin Market. **CP-RosC1**

Laughing. Robert Creeley. **CP-CreeR**

Laughing bearded man / genial, witty, fond of jazz, The. Fontanel. John Hewitt. **CP-HewiJ**

Laughing Blue Steel. Carl Sandburg. **CP-SandC**

Laughing Corn. Carl Sandburg. **CP-SandC**

Laughing Gas. Allen Ginsberg. **CP-GinsA**

Laughing Life cries at the feast. Christina Georgina Rossetti. **CP-RosC2**

Laughing Ones, The. Charles Olson. **CP-OlsoC**

Laughing Song. William Blake. *See* When the Green Woods Laugh.

Laughing through clouds, his milk-teeth still unshed. R.A.F. (Aged Eighteen). Rudyard Kipling. **PoWW** *Fr.* Epitaphs of the War [1914–1918]. **CP-KiplR**

Laughing to find / Anyone's blind. Edward Estlin Cummings. **CP-CummE**

Laughing with ice. Midwinter. William Carlos Williams. **CP-WilW2**

Laughter. David Herbert Lawrence. **CP-LawrD**

Laughter not time destroyed my voice. The Friends of his Youth. William Butler Yeats. *Fr.* A Man Young and Old. **CP-YeatW**

Laughter of sisters, mingling. The Girls Next Door. Thom Gunn. **CP-GunnT**

Laughter of Steel 1. Marsden Hartley. **CP-HartM**

Laughter of Steel 2. Marsden Hartley. **CP-HartM**

"Launch out into the deep," Christ spake of old. St. Peter. Christina Georgina Rossetti. **CP-RosC2**

Launched into an opposing wind, hangs. The Atlantic. Charles Tomlinson. **CP-TomlC**

Launching themselves / beating silver. The Running of the Grunion. Muriel Rukeyser. **CP-RukeM**

Laura. Thomas Campion. *See* Rose-cheeked Laura[, Come].

Laura and Lizzie Asleep. Christina Georgina Rossetti. **PeHV** *Fr.* Goblin Market. **CP-RosC1**

LAURA, farewell my LAURA! Cantata, from Metastasio. William Wordsworth. **CP-WorW1**

Laureate, The. Robert Ranke Graves. **CP-GravR**

Laurel and eucalyptus, dry sharp smells. Grasses. Thom Gunn. **CP-GunnT**

Laurel Axe, The. Geoffrey Hill. **NAEL-2; NoAM; NoP; PoE** *Fr.* An Apology for the Revival of Christian Architecture in England. **CP-HillG**

Laurelled soldier he; yet who could find, A. A.H., 1855–1912. Thomas Hardy. **CP-HardT**

Laurels, The. John Greenleaf Whittier. **CP-WhitJ**

Laurels may flourish round the conqu'ror's tomb. Epitaph on Mrs. Higgins. William Cowper. **CP-CowpW**

Laus Deo! John Greenleaf Whittier. **CP-WhitJ**

Laus Veneris. Algernon Charles Swinburne. **SP-SwinA**

Lausanne: In Gibbon's Old Garden: 11–12 p.m. Thomas Hardy. **CP-HardT**

Lava Bed. William Everson. **SP-EverW**

Lavender blue for love, lavender green for youth. Louis MacNeice. *Fr.* Notes for a Biography. **CP-MacNL**

Lavender Cotton. Louis Zukofsky. **CP-ZukLS**

Lavender Lilies. Carl Sandburg. **CP-SandC**

Lavender lilies in Garfield Park lay lazy in the morning sun, The. Lavender Lilies. Carl Sandburg. **CP-SandC**

Lavender Sweep is drowned in Wandsworth. South London Sketch, 1844. Sir John Betjeman. **CP-BetjJ**

Lavender, vanilla, anything. In Memoriam P.B. Gilbert Sorrentino. **SP-SorrG**

Laventille. Derek Walcott. **CP-WalcD**

Law. Charles Olson. **CP-OlsoC**

Law and Order. Leonard Nathan. **SP-NathL**

Law like Love. Wystan Hugh Auden. **CP-AudeW**

Law of Jehovah is perfect, resting the soul, The, *vv.* 7–9 *of sl. diff. vers.* Bible, *O.T. See* Psalm 19: "Heavens declare the glory of God, The."

Law of the Jungle, The. Rudyard Kipling. *See* Now this the Law of the Jungle—as old and as true as the sky.

Law, say the gardeners, is the sun. Law like Love. Wystan Hugh Auden. **CP-AudeW**

Law says you and I belong to each other, George, The. Two Strangers Breakfast. Carl Sandburg. **CP-SandC**

Law That Marries All Things, The. Wendell Berry. **CP-BerrW**

Law whereby my lady moves, The. My Lady's Law. Rudyard Kipling. **CP-KiplR** *Fr.* The Naulahka.

Lawes ("When Lawes full power have to sway, we see"). Robert Herrick. **CP-HerrR**

Lawes ("Who violates the Customes, hurts the Health"). Robert Herrick. **CP-HerrR**

Lawne, The. Robert Herrick. **CP-HerrR**

Lawrence in Taos. John Clellon Holmes. **SP-HolmJ**

Lawrence of virtuous [*or* vertuous] Father virtuous [*or* vertuous] Son. John Milton. **CP-MiltJ**

(Sonnet 20: "Lawrence of vertuous Father vertuous Son.") **CP-MiltJ**

Laws Can Say, The. Louis Zukofsky. **CP-ZukLS**

Laws for Creations. Walt Whitman. **CP-WhitW**

Laws of God, the laws of man, The. Alfred Edward Housman. **CP-HousA**

Laws of the bronze gods, The. Cheap Rent. Carl Sandburg. **CP-SandC**

Lawsamassy, for heaven's sake! Lucy Lake. Ogden Nash. **CP-NashO**

Lawyer. Carl Sandburg. **CP-SandC**

"Lawyer," hiccuped a disbarred member of the bar, "is a man who", A. Carl Sandburg. *Fr.* The People, Yes. **CP-SandC**

Lawyers and salesmen muscled around. Pool at the Y. James McAuley. **SP-McAuJ**

Lawyers, Bob, know too much, The. The Lawyers Know Too Much. Carl Sandburg. **CP-SandC**

Lawyers Know Too Much, The. Carl Sandburg. **CP-SandC**

Lawyers' Ways, The. Paul Laurence Dunbar. **CP-DunbP**

Laxare Fibulam. Robert Herrick. **CP-HerrR**

Lay by the good a while; a resting field. Rest Refreshes. Robert Herrick. **CP-HerrR**

Lay down Lay down yr mountain Lay down God. Rolling Thunder Stones. Allen Ginsberg. **CP-GinsA**

Lay down these words. Riprap. Gary Snyder. **CP-SnydG**

Lay Down Your Weary Tune. "Bob Dylan." **CP-DylaB**

Lay in the house mostly living. Madness. James Dickey. **CP-DickJ**

Lay, Lady, Lay. "Bob Dylan." **CP-DylaB**

Lay me down beneaf de willers in de grass. Death Song[, A]. Paul Laurence Dunbar. **CP-DunbP**

"Lay me in a cushioned chair." The Ballad of the Foxhunter. William Butler Yeats. **CP-YeatW**

Lay me on an anvil, O God. Prayers of Steel. Carl Sandburg. **CP-SandC**

Lay not thine hand upon me; let me go. Phaedra. Algernon Charles Swinburne. **SP-SwinA**

Lay of Old Time, A. John Greenleaf Whittier. **CP-WhitJ**

Lay of the Brown Rosary, The. Elizabeth Barrett Browning. **CP-BroEB**

Lay of the Early Rose, A. Elizabeth Barrett Browning. **CP-BroEB**

Lay of the Imprisoned Huntsman. Sir Walter Scott. **SP-ScotW** *Fr.* The Lady of the Lake.

Lay of the Last Minstrel, The, *sels.* Sir Walter Scott.
  Bale-Fire, The. **SP-ScotW**
  Branksome Hall. **SP-ScotW**
  "Breathes there the [*or* a] Man [with Soul So Dead]." **SP-ScotW**
  (Caledonia.) **SP-ScotW**
    O Caledonia! **FaBoPP**
  Hymn for the Dead. **SP-ScotW**
  Melrose by Moonlight. **SP-ScotW**
  Rosabelle.
    (Harold's Song.) **SP-ScotW**
  Song of Albert Graeme. **SP-ScotW**

Lay the little bud i' the mould. Willie's Dirge on Little Marian. George Meredith. *Fr.* Wandering Willie. **CP-MerG2**

Lay this Laurel on the One. Emily Dickinson. **CP-DickE**

Lay to Eliza, The. Edmund Spenser. *See* Elisa ("Ye dainty nymphs, that in this blessed brook").

Lay Up for Yourselves Treasures in Heaven. Christina Georgina Rossetti. **CP-RosC2**

Lay warm gentle hand upon me. Marsden Hartley. **CP-HartM**

Lay your sleeping head, my love. Lullaby. Wystan Hugh Auden. **CP-AudeW**

Layabout. Archie Randolph Ammons. **SP-AmmoA**

Layer upon layer / late winter snow. Hayden Carruth. *Fr.* North Winter. **CP-CarHL**

Layers, The. Stanley Jasspon Kunitz. **CP-KuniS**

Laying Down the Tower. Marge Piercy. **SP-PierM**
  Eight of Swords, The.
  Emperor, The.
  Judgment, The.
  Knight of Swords, The.
  Magician, The.
  Nine of Cups, The.
  Queen of Pentacles, The.
  Seven of Pentacles, The. **CrSp**
  Sun, The. **WPOW**
    (Total Influence of Outcome of the Matter: The Sun, The.) **WPOW**
  Three of Cups, The.
  Tower Struck by Lightning Reversed; the Overturning of the Tower, The.

Layover. Charles Bukowski. **SP-BukC2**

Lays of Mystery, Imagination, and Humour, No. 1: The Palace of Humbug. "Lewis Carroll." **CP-CarrL**

Lays of Sorrow, No. 1. "Lewis Carroll." **CP-CarrL**

Lays of Sorrow, No. 2. "Lewis Carroll." **CP-CarrL**

Lazarus. Jenny Joseph. **SP-JoseJ**

Lazarus. Edwin Arlington Robinson. **CP-RobiE**

Lazarus lay to see the body turn. Come Forth. James Wright. **CP-WrigJ**

Lazarus Not Raised. Thom Gunn. **CP-GunnT**

Lazarus to the Assembled. James Dickey. **CP-DickJ**

Lazily into the curve. Roy Fisher. **SP-FishR** *Fr.* Handsworth Liberties.

Lazy / Lazy / Lazy / Lazy. Lazy Jane. Shel Silverstein. **SP-SilS2**

Lazy Day, A. Paul Laurence Dunbar. **CP-DunbP**

Lazy Jane. Shel Silverstein. **SP-SilS2**

Lazy, laughing South, The. The South. Langston Hughes. **SP-HughL**

Lazy Mist, The. Robert Burns. **CP-BurnR**

Lazy petals of magnolia-bloom float down the sluggish river. Elegy on a Nordic White Protestant. John Gould Fletcher. **SP-FletJ**

Lazy stadium night / Catfish on the mound. Catfish. "Bob Dylan" *and* Jacques Levy. **CP-DylaB**

Le Bateau d'Amour Descried on the Briny. Gilbert Sorrentino. *Fr.* Twelve Études for Voice and Kazoo. **SP-SorrG**

Le Christianisme. Wilfred Owen. **CP-OwenW**

Le conte de Beaumont carrying my daughter. White-Haired Girl. Archibald MacLeish. **CP-MacLA**

Le Désert de l'Amour. Stevie Smith. **CP-SmitS**

Le Directeur. Thomas Stearns Eliot. **CP-ElioT**

Le Fou. Robert Creeley. **CP-CreeR**

Le garçon délabré qui n'a rien à faire. Dans le Restauramt. Thomas Stearns Eliot. **CP-ElioT**

Le Livre Est sur la Table. John Ashbery. **SP-AshbJ**

Le Majeur Ydow. Stevie Smith. **CP-SmitS**

Le Marais du Cygne. John Greenleaf Whittier. **CP-WhitJ**

Le Médecin Malgré Lui. William Carlos Williams. **CP-WilW1**

Le Monde regrets it must report. Exposé. John Updike. **CP-UpdiJ**

Le Monocle de Mon Oncle. Wallace Stevens. **CP-StevW**

Le Musée Imaginaire. Charles Tomlinson. **CP-TomlC**

Le Petit Salvié. Charles Kenneth Williams. **SP-WillC**

Le Poète Contumace, *tr. fr. the French of* Tristan Corbière. Randall Jarrell. **CP-JarrR**

Le Rendez-Vous des Paysages. Charles Tomlinson. *Fr.* Two Poems on titles proposed by Octavio and Marie José Paz. **CP-TomlC**

Le Revenant. Stevie Smith. **CP-SmitS**

Le Secret, *see also English tr.* The Secret: "Since I am / Somebody's dream." Thomas Merton. **CP-MertT**

Le Secret Humain. Archibald MacLeish. **CP-MacLA**

Le Seul Malheur Est que Je ne Sais pas Lire. Archibald MacLeish. **CP-MacLA**

Le Singe qui swing. Stevie Smith. **CP-SmitS**

Le Travail Rajeunit. Marilyn Hacker. **SP-HackM**

Lea-Rig, The. Robert Burns. **CP-BurnR**

Lead gently, Lord, and slow. Hymn, A. Paul Laurence Dunbar. **CP-DunbP**

Lead in the Water. Jean Garrigue. **SP-GarrJ**

Lead Soldiers and Regimental Uniforms. John Hewitt. **CP-HewiJ**

Lead the black bull to slaughter, with the boar. Thomas Carew. **CP-CareT**
  (Upon Master W. Montague, His Return from Travel.) **CP-CareT**

Lead were their feet, and lead their heart and bone. Malcolm Lowry. *Fr.* Songs for Second Childhood. **CP-LowrM**

Leadbelly Song, The. Al Young. **CP-YounA**

Leaden August with the life gone out of it. Roy Fisher. **SP-FishR** *Fr.* Diversions.

Leaden Echo and the Golden Echo, The. Gerard Manley Hopkins. **CP-HopkG**

Leaden-Eyed, The. Nicholas Vachel Lindsay. **CP-LindV**

Leader, The. Charles Olson. **CP-OlsoC**

Leader, The. Stevie Smith. **CP-SmitS**

Leader and teacher, we whom you have taught. To William F. Bradbury. Edward Estlin Cummings. **CP-CummE**

Leader of Fashion, A. Thomas Hardy. **CP-HardT**

Leaders of the Crowd, The. William Butler Yeats. **CP-YeatW**

Lead's the Best. Wystan Hugh Auden. **CP-AudWJ**

Leaf. John Hewitt. **CP-HewiJ**
  ("O fall of the leaf I am tired.") **CP-HewiJ**

Leaf, The. Kathleen Jessie Raine. **SP-RainK**

Leaf, The. Robert Penn Warren. **SP-WarrR**

Leaf and the Tree, The. Edna St. Vincent Millay. **CP-MillE**

Leaf, catching the sun, transmits it, A. Frondes Agrestes. Charles Tomlinson. **CP-TomlC**

Leaf Eater, The. Dabney Stuart. **SP-StuaD**

Leaf for Hand in Hand, A. Walt Whitman. **CP-WhitW**

Leaf from leaf Christ knows; / Himself the Lily and the Rose. Christina Georgina Rossetti. **CP-RosC2**

Leaf from Mr. Dyer's Woods, A. Hayden Carruth. **CP-CarHS**

Leaf-lace, a simple intricate design. Leaf-Lace Dress. Robert Lowell. **SP-LoweR**

Leaf-Lace Dress. Robert Lowell. **SP-LoweR**

Leaf-Treader, A. Robert Frost. **CP-FrosR**

Leaf-veined fire, The. Feuer-Nacht. Louise Bogan. **CP-BogaL**

Leafbud straggles forth, The. Upper Broadway. Adrienne Rich. **SP-RicA2**

Leafing through a book on Oriental art. Sunset. John Hewitt. **CP-HewiJ**

Leafless Dodder, Rabbit's Silk. Revolution of the Children. Archibald MacLeish. **CP-MacLA**

Leaflet (One). Kenneth Patchen. **CP-PatcK**

Leaflet (Two). Kenneth Patchen. **CP-PatcK**

Leaflets. Adrienne Rich. **CP-RicAE; SP-RicA2**

Leaflets. Walt Whitman. **CP-WhitW**

Leaf's otherness, A. Egg-Head. Ted Hughes. **SP-HughT**

Leafshade stirring on lichened bark. Culture and Anarchy. Adrienne Rich. **SP-RicA2**

League gust strum ovally folium. Privet. Louis Zukofsky. **CP-ZukLS**

Leagues north, as fly the gull and auk. The Palatine. John Greenleaf Whittier. **CP-WhitJ**

Leaky Faucet, The. Ted Kooser. **SP-KoosT**

Lean and Hungry Look, A. Howard Nemerov. **CP-NemeH**

Lean candles hunger in. Edward Estlin Cummings. **CP-CummE**

Lean hands of wagon men, The. The Windy City. Carl Sandburg. **CP-SandC**

Leander to the envious light. George Chapman. **OAEL-1** *Fr.* Hero and Leander. **CP-MarlC**

Leanders Obsequies. Robert Herrick. **CP-HerrR**

Leander's Return. Christopher Marlowe. **EBNV** *Fr.* Hero and Leander. **CP-MarlC**

Leaning forward, I watch how the. On the Grand Dublin Canal: Musing on the "Two Nations" Theory. John Hewitt. **CP-HewiJ**

Leaning her head upon my breast. Love's Representation. Sir John Suckling. **CP-SuckJ**

Leaning on / the parapet stone. The Well. Charles Tomlinson. **CP-TomlC**

Leaning on my left hand. An Incident. Louis Zukofsky. **CP-ZukLS**

Leaning Up. Archie Randolph Ammons. **SP-AmmoA**

Leans now the fair willow, dreaming. The Willow. Walter de la Mare. **CP-DeLaW**

Leap, The. James Dickey. **CP-DickJ**

Leap, The. Robert Ranke Graves. **CP-GravR**

Leap Before You Look. Wystan Hugh Auden. **CP-AudeW**

Leap of Faith. David St. John. **SP-StJoD**

Leaped at the caribou. Ho Ho Ho Caribou. Joseph Ceravolo. **SP-CeraJ**

Leaping forth from their steep battlemented nest on the hillside. Sea-Sounding Bells. John Gould Fletcher. **SP-FletJ**

Leaping, leaping, leaping. The Angel Food Dogs. Anne Sexton. **CP-SextA**

Leaping leptons, gluons, and quarks—. Neanderthal Poem, "Ah," Number One. Robert Pack. **SP-PackR**

Lear. William Carlos Williams. **CP-WilW2**

Lear Is Gay. Robert Earl Hayden. **CP-HaydR**

Learn this of me, where e'r thy Lot doth fall. Lots to Be Liked. Robert Herrick. **CP-HerrR**

Learn to submit to the laws of destiny. On the Death of the Vice-Chancellor, a Physician. John Milton, *tr. fr. Latin by* John T. Shawcross. **CP-MiltJ**

Learn, ye nations of the earth. John Milton. *See* On the Death of the Vice-Chancellor, a Physician.

Learned King fought, The. "O Flodden Field." Donald Hall. **CP-HallD**

Learned Men, The. Archibald MacLeish. **CP-MacLA**

Learners, The. Randall Jarrell. **CP-JarrR**

Learners, The. Mona Van Duyn. **SP-VanDM**

Learning. Christopher Smart. *Fr.* Hymns for the Amusement of Children. **SP-SmarC**

Learning About the Indians. Mary Oliver. **SP-OlivM**

Learning by Doing. Howard Nemerov. **CP-NemeH**

Learning Experience. Leonard Nathan. **SP-NathL**

Learning Experience. Marge Piercy. **SP-PierM**

Learning From Barbara Deming. Grace Paley. **CP-PaleG**

Learning from MacDiarmid. James Wright. *Fr.* Many of Our Waters: Variations on a Poem by a Black Child. **CP-WrigJ**

Learning from Nature. Richard Eberhart. **CP-EberR**

Learning of many things does not teach understanding, or else it would have taught Hesiod and Pythagoras, The. Thomas Merton. *Fr.* The Legacy of Herakleitos. **CP-MertT**

Learning the Trees. Howard Nemerov. **CP-NemeH**

Learning to manage the process. Marge Piercy. *Fr.* Excursions, Incursions. **SP-PierM**

Leasing of September, The. John Ashbery. **SP-AshbJ**

Least, The. Roy Fisher. **SP-FishR**

Least Bee that brew. Emily Dickinson. **CP-DickE**

Least, if so I am; / If so, less than the least, The. I Am Small and of No Reputation. Christina Georgina Rossetti. **CP-RosC2**

Least Rivers—docile to some sea. Emily Dickinson. **CP-DickE**

Least, the meanest, The. The Least. Roy Fisher. **SP-FishR**

Leastlessly / out / of this. Edward Estlin Cummings. **CP-CummE**

Leather fringes, The. Alabaster. Gary Snyder. **CP-SnydG**

Leather Leggings. Carl Sandburg. **CP-SandC**

Leatherette relic smelling of musk and camphor falls, A. Homage to Austin Warren. Laurence Lieberman. **SP-LiebL**

Leave. Randall Jarrell. **CP-JarrR**

Leave April now, and autumn having. Reconciliation. Walter de la Mare. **CP-DeLaW**

Leave Cod, tobacco-like, burnt gums to take. To Sir Cod. Ben Jonson. **CP-JonsB**

"Leave colouring thy tresses", I did cry. 1.14. Ovid. **CP-MarlC**, *tr. by* Christopher Marlowe; *Fr.* Elegies.

Leave go my hands, let me catch breath and see. In the Orchard. Algernon Charles Swinburne. **SP-SwinA**

Leave me, Fear! thy throbs are base. Ralph Waldo Emerson. **CP-EmerR**

Leave me, O Love which reachest but to dust, *Wr. considered Sonnet CX of* Astrophil and Stella. Sir Philip Sidney. **SP-SidnP**

Leave me vain Hope, too long thou hast posses[s]t. Sonnet 5. Mary Sidney, Countess of Montgomery Wroth. **BWW** *Fr.* Lindamira's Complaint. *Fr.* Part 1. *Fr.* Urania. **CP-WrotM**

Leave me vaine Hope, too long thou hast possesst. Mary Sidney, Countess of Montgomery Wroth. *See* Sonnet: "O Memory [or Memorie], could I but loose thee now."

Leave now our streets, and in you plain behold. The Alms-House and Trustees. George Crabbe. **SP-CrabG** *Fr.* The Borough.

Leave now the beach, and even that perfect friendship. End of Season. Robert Penn Warren. **SP-WarrR**

Leave now the crest of thought's high secrecy. Anti-Promethean Ode. John Hewitt. **CP-HewiJ**

Leave off! Leave off! Leave off! The Sunset Verse. David Herbert Lawrence. **CP-LawrD**

Leave off my sheep: it is no time to feed, *speech of Philisides.* Sir Philip Sidney. **SP-SidnP** *Fr.* Arcadia.

Leave prolonging thy distresse. Thomas Campion. **CP-CampT**

Leave Sex Alone. David Herbert Lawrence. **CP-LawrD**

Leave Taking. John Milton. **FaBoEn** *Fr.* Book XII. *Fr.* Paradise Lost. **CP-MiltJ**

Leave-taking, A. Algernon Charles Swinburne. **SP-SwinA**

Leave the hair white, uncombed. James McAuley. **SP-McAuJ** *Fr.* Studies for a Self-Portrait at Forty.

Leave the Informed Sense. Jim Morrison. **SP-MorrJ**

Leave the uproar: at a leap. Nature and Life. George Meredith. **CP-MerG1**

Leave Train, The. Phoebe Hesketh. **SP-HeskP**

Leave your home behind, lad. The Recruit. Alfred Edward Housman. **CP-HousA**

Leaves. Stephen Berg. **SP-BergS**

Leaves, The. Hayden Carruth. *Fr.* Contra Mortem. **CP-CarHL**

Leaves. Derek Mahon. **SP-MahoD**

Leaves / Murmuring by myriads in the shimmering trees. From My Diary, July 1914. Wilfred Owen. **CP-OwenW**

Leaves and Ashes. John Haines. **SP-HainJ**

Leaves Apples. Grace Paley. **CP-PaleG**

Leaves are greygreen. Lines. William Carlos Williams. **CP-WilW1**

Leaves are piled thickly on the green tree, The. A Pastoral Dialogue. Frank O'Hara. **SP-OharF**

Leaves are struck and dance, the bird is blown, The. To the New World. Randall Jarrell. **CP-JarrR**

Leaves Compared with Flowers. Robert Frost. **CP-FrosR**

Leaves embrace, The. The Avenue of Poplars. William Carlos Williams. **CP-WilW1**

Leaves espaliered jade on our barn's loft window. Our Twentieth Wedding Anniversary (Elizabeth). Robert Lowell. **SP-LoweR**

Leaves fall from my fingers, The. October. Charles Wright. **SP-WrigC**

Leaves of Grass, VI *and* XX. Walt Whitman. *See* A Child said *What is the grass?.*

Leaves of Grass, Flowers of Grass. David Herbert Lawrence. **CP-LawrD**

Leaves of poplars pick Japanese prints against the west. Moonset. Carl Sandburg. **CP-SandC**

Leaves of Zimmer. Paul Zimmer. **SP-ZimmP**

Leaves on the macadam make a noise—, The. The Hermitage at the Center. Wallace Stevens. **CP-StevW**

Leaves on the trees, The. By Heart. Al Young. **CP-YounA**

Leaves pour blackly across. A Wind Flashes the Grass. Ted Hughes. **SP-HughT**

Leaves That Rustled on This Oak-Crowned Hill, The. William Wordsworth. **CP-WorW2**

Leaves that shifted overhead all summer, The. Autumn Equinox. Adrienne Rich. **CP-RicAE**

Leaves That Talk. Anne Sexton. **CP-SextA**

Leaves, though little time they have to live, The. October Maples, Portland. Richard Wilbur. **CP-WilbR**

Leaves throng thick above, The. The Last Leaf. Thomas Hardy. **CP-HardT**

Leaves were already on the trees, the fruit blossoms, The. With Janice. Kenneth Koch. **SP-KochK**

Leaves were fading when to Esthwaite's banks, The. Cambridge and the Alps. William Wordsworth. *Fr.* The Prelude; Growth of a Poet's Mind [1850 vers.]. **CP-WorW3**

Leaves were yellow when to Furness Fells, The. Cambridge and the Alps. William Wordsworth. *Fr.* The Prelude; Growth of a Poet's Mind [1805 vers.]. **CP-WorW3**

Leaves will fall again sometime and fill, The. Sunday Morning Apples. Hart Crane. **CP-CranH**

Leavetaking. Dabney Stuart. **SP-StuaD**

Leaving, A. Thomas Hardy. **CP-HardT**

Leaving. Richard Wilbur. **CP-WilbR**

Leaving Barra. Louis MacNeice. **CP-MacNL**

Leaving Church Early. John Updike. **CP-UpdiJ**

Leaving Early. Sylvia Plath. **CP-PlatS**

Leaving for Holiday. John Hewitt. **CP-HewiJ**

Leaving Forever. Denise Levertov. **CP-LeveD**

Leaving Home for Home. Al Young. **CP-YounA**

Leaving July. Roy Fisher. **SP-FishR**

Leaving K.C. Mo. past Independence past Liberty. Kansas City to Saint Louis. Allen Ginsberg. **CP-GinsA**

Leaving New York, I looked back fourteen times. Muriel Rukeyser. **CP-RukeM**

Leaving N.Y.C. Jim Carroll. **SP-CarrJ**

Leaving our hearth at midnight for his own. Company. John Hewitt. **CP-HewiJ**

Leaving Rochester. Al Young. **CP-YounA**

Leaving Syracuse. Al Young. **CP-YounA**

Leaving the Bar and Low Life at Closing, I Unsuccessfully Pursue Sainthood. Stephen Dobyns. **SP-DobyS**

Leaving the colleges and their half-remembered. Canto XIII. Louis MacNeice. *Fr.* Autumn Sequel. **CP-MacNL**

Leaving the Dream. Richard Hugo. **CP-HugoR**

Leaving the house each dawn I see the hawk. Workman. George Oppen. **CP-OppeG**

Leaving the Motel. William DeWitt Snodgrass. **SP-SnodW**

Leaving the Rest Unsaid. Robert Ranke Graves. **CP-GravR**

Leaving the splendid plaza and the esplanade—. Ah. . . to the Villages! Thomas McGrath. **SP-McGrT**

Leaving the white glow of filling stations. The Strand at Lough Beg. Seamus Heaney. **SP-HeanS**

Leaving Water Hyacinths. Jane Cooper. **SP-CoopJ**

Lebensweisheitspielerei. Wallace Stevens. **CP-StevW**

Lecture. Richard Hugo. **CP-HugoR**

Lecture. James McAuley. **SP-McAuJ**

Lecture on Time and Space, The. Gilbert Sorrentino. **SP-SorrG**

Lecture upon the Shadow, A. John Donne. **CP-DonnJ**

Lecturer in Bookstore. Ogden Nash. **CP-NashO**

Led by the light of an unusual star. Wystan Hugh Auden. **PChr** *Fr.* At the Manger. *Fr.* For the Time Being; a Christmas Oratorio. **CP-AudeW**

Led by the powre of griefe, to waylings brought. Sonnet 8. Mary Sidney, Countess of Montgomery Wroth. *Fr.* Pamphilia to Amphilanthus. **CP-WrotM**

Leda. Hilda Doolittle. **CP-DoolH**

Leda. Robert Ranke Graves. **CP-GravR**

Leda. David Herbert Lawrence. **CP-LawrD**

Leda. Mona Van Duyn. **SP-VanDM**

Leda and the Swan. William Butler Yeats. **CP-YeatW**

Leda Reconsidered. Mona Van Duyn. **SP-VanDM**

Leda's Fortunate Gaffe. Ogden Nash. *Fr.* Fables Bullfinch Forgot. **CP-NashO**

Leech boasts, he has a Pill, that can alone. Upon Leech. Robert Herrick. **CP-HerrR**

Leering across Pearl Street. Trouble. James Wright. **CP-WrigJ**

Lee's Lunch / Spaghetti. Brilliant Sad Sun. William Carlos Williams. **CP-WilW1**

Leezie Lindsay. Robert Burns. **CP-BurnR**

Leffingwell. Edwin Arlington Robinson. **CP-RobiE**

Left-Behind, The. Louis MacNeice. **FaBCIP** *Fr.* A Hand of Snapshots. **CP-MacNL**

Left by his friend to breakfast alone on the white. Edward Lear. Wystan Hugh Auden. **CP-AudeW**

Left by that father, who was known to few. Richard's Youth. George Crabbe. **SP-CrabG** *Fr.* Tales of the Hall.

Left by the ebbing tide of battle. Come On, Come Back. Stevie Smith. **CP-SmitS**

Left Hand Canyon. William Matthews. **SP-MattW**

Left hand holding distaff and wool retained on it (ah mixture). Catullus. *See* Carmen 64: "In old days / driving through soft waters."

Left-Handed Cellist, The. Rita Dove. **SP-DoveR**

Left-Handed Letter to Dr. Sheridan, A. Jonathan Swift. **CP-SwifJ**

Left in immortal Youth. Emily Dickinson. **CP-DickE**

Left leg flung out, head cocked to the right. Poet. Karl Shapiro. **SP-ShapK**

Left lying in the grass. A Bicycle Chain. John Updike. **CP-UpdiJ**

Left out of vacation. Robert Lowell. **SP-LoweR**

Left to himself and his invitations. Ballad of the Three Birds. Dabney Stuart. **SP-StuaD**

Left-wing poetry represents a rise in the price of bread. "Hugh MacDiarmid." **SP-MacDH** *Fr.* England's Double Knavery.

Leg, The. Karl Shapiro. **SP-ShapK**

Leg in a Plaster Cast, A. Muriel Rukeyser. **CP-RukeM**

Legacy [or Legacie], The. John Donne. **CP-DonnJ**

Legacy. Stephen Dunn. **SP-DunnS**

Legacy, A. John Greenleaf Whittier. **CP-WhitJ**

Legacy of Herakleitos, The. Thomas Merton. **CP-MertT**

　"All things are fire."

　"All things change. / The sun is new everyday."

　"Dogs bark at everyone they do not know."

　"God is day and night, winter and summer, conflict and peace."

　"Hidden harmony is better than the open, The."

　"Homer was wrong in saying: 'Would that conflict might perish from among gods and men'."

　"I have sought for myself."

　"It is hard to fight / against one's heart's desire."

　"Learning of many things does not teach understanding, or else it would have taught Hesiod and Pythagoras, The."

　"Lord whose is the oracle at Delphi neither utters nor hides his meaning, The."

　"Mysteries practiced among men are unholy mysteries, The."

　"Nature loves to hide."

　"Of all those discourses I have heard."

　"Souls smell in hades."

　"There await men when they die."

　"Those who speak with understanding must hold fast to what is common."

　"Time is a child playing draughts."

　"Way of man has no wisdom, but the way of God has, The."

　"Wisdom is one thing: it is to know the thought by which all things are steered through all things."

　"Wisest man is an ape compared to God."

Legal arm has reached up from the sea, The. The Courthouse. Lewis Turco. **SP-TurcL**

Legal children of a literary man, The. Relationships. Mona Van Duyn. **SP-VanDM**

Legal Reflection. Ogden Nash. **CP-NashO**

Legal Reform. Thom Gunn. **CP-GunnT**

Legate, I had the news last night—my cohort ordered home. The Roman Centurion's Song. Rudyard Kipling. **CP-KiplR**

Legend. Wystan Hugh Auden. **CP-AudeW**

Legend. Hart Crane. **CP-CranH**

Legend. Louise Glück. **SP-GlücL**

Legend. Charles Tomlinson. **CP-TomlC**

Legend. Charles Tomlinson. **CP-TomlC**

Legend for a Little Child. Kenneth Patchen. **CP-PatcK**

Legend in His Own Lifetime. John Hewitt. **CP-HewiJ**

Legend of Britomartis, or of Chastitie, The. Edmund Spenser. **NAEL-1** *Fr.* The Faerie Queene. **CP-Spens**

　Britomart in the House of Busirane. **FiP**

Legend of Good Women, The. Geoffrey Chaucer. **CP-ChauG**

　"Alas, that I ne had English, rhyme or prose." **EPCY**

　　CH; HeIP; ViBoPo

　"And as for me, though that I konne [or can] but [or my wit be] lyte." **AWP; ChTr; EBEV; EnVB; FiP; GBL; HAP; ImPo; LoBV; MeEL; NOBE; OAEL-1; OBEV; SCGP; SeCeV**

　"Hide [or Hyd], Absalon, thy gilte tresses clere."

　(Lady without Paragon, A.) **MeEL**

　This Fresshe Flour. **SeCePo**

Legend of Mirth, The. Rudyard Kipling. **CP-KiplR**

Legend of Paper Plates, The. John Haines. **SP-HainJ**

Legend of St. Mark, The. John Greenleaf Whittier. **CP-WhitJ**

Legend of the Dead Soldier, The. Bertolt Brecht, *tr. fr. German by* Louis MacNeice. **CP-MacNL**

Legend of the Foreign Office, A. Rudyard Kipling. **CP-KiplR**

　("This is the reason why Rustum Beg.") **CP-KiplR**

Legend of the Knight of the Red Crosse, or of Holinesse, The. Edmund Spenser. **EPCY; FHYEP; NAEL-1; OAEL-1** *Fr.* The Faerie Queene. **CP-Spens**

(Invocation to the Faerie Queene.) **FiP**

Legend of the Lake, A. John Greenleaf Whittier. **CP-WhitJ**

Legend of the One-Eyed Man, The. Anne Sexton. **CP-SextA**

Legend of the Tower, The. Thomas Merton. *Fr.* The Tower of Babel—A Morality. **CP-MertT**

Legend of Truth, A. Rudyard Kipling. **CP-KiplR** *Fr.* Debits and Credits.

Legend of Viable Women, A. Richard Eberhart. **CP-EberR**

Legendary Hearts. "Lou Reed." **SP-ReedL**

Legendary Progress. Thomas McGrath. **SP-McGrT**

Legende. Hart Crane. **CP-CranH**

Legends. Carl Sandburg. **CP-SandC**

Legends of Evil, The. Rudyard Kipling. **CP-KiplR**

Legetai Ti Khainon. Gerard Manley Hopkins. *Fr.* A Trio of Triolets. **CP-HopkG**

Leggett's Monument. John Greenleaf Whittier. **CP-WhitJ**

Legi operosum iamdudum, Camdene, volumen. *acc. by English translation.* Thomas Campion. **CP-CampT**

Legionnaire's Disease. "Bob Dylan." **CP-DylaB**

Legree's big house was white and green. Simon Legree—A Negro Sermon. Nicholas Vachel Lindsay. **HBMV; InMe; LiTA; MeMAP; MoAmPo; MoVE; NePA; TAP** *Fr.* The Booker Washington Trilogy. **CP-LindV**

Legs, The. Robert Ranke Graves. **CP-GravR**

Legs are gone and the hopes—the lava of outpouring, The. An Empire of Coins. Charles Bukowski. **SP-BukC2**

Legs hold a torso away from the earth. The Walking Man of Rodin. Carl Sandburg. **CP-SandC**

Legs of Lalage toss, and toss, and toss, The. Lalage! Charles Olson. **CP-OlsoC**

Legs of the elk punctured the snow's crust, The. To Christ Our Lord. Galway Kinnell. **SP-KinnG**

Leicestershire. Donald Davie. **CP-DavDo**

Leipzig. Thomas Hardy. **CP-HardT**

Lemme kiss your face, lick your neck. Sweet Boy, Gimme Yr Ass. Allen Ginsberg. **CP-GinsA**

Lemmings, The. John Haines. **SP-HainJ**

Lemonade Panel, The. Gilbert Sorrentino. **SP-SorrG**

Lemons, The. David St. John. **SP-StJoD**

Lemons, Lemons. Al Young. **CP-YounA**

Lemons, Limes. Siv Cedering Fox. **SP-CedeS**

Lenada. Kenneth Patchen. **CP-PatcK**

Lend me an ear. To a Sea-Cliff. Thomas Hardy. **CP-HardT**

Lend me your song, ye nightingales! oh, pour. James Thomson. **PBBP** *Fr.* Spring. *Fr.* The Seasons. **CP-ThomJ**

Leningrad. John Updike. *Fr.* Postcards from Soviet Cities. **CP-UpdiJ**

Lenitie. Robert Herrick. **CP-HerrR**

Lenny Bruce. "Bob Dylan." **CP-DylaB**

Lenore. Edgar Allan Poe. **CP-PoeEd**

Lenox Avenue / by daylight. Dive. Langston Hughes. **SP-HughL**

Lenox Avenue Mural. Langston Hughes.

Comment on Curb. **SP-HughL**

Good Morning. **SP-HughL**

Harlem. **SP-HughL**

Island. **SP-HughL**

Letter. **SP-HughL**

Same in Blues. **SP-HughL**

Lent. George Herbert. **CP-HerbG**

Lent. Thomas Merton. **CP-MertT**

Lent. Christina Georgina Rossetti. **CP-RosC2**

Lent in a Year of War. Thomas Merton. **CP-MertT; SP-MertT**

Lent Lily, The. Alfred Edward Housman. **CP-HousA**

Lenten Thoughts of a High Anglican. Sir John Betjeman. **CP-BetjJ**

L'Envoi. Edwin Arlington Robinson. **CP-RobiE**

L'Envoi; Departmental Ditties. Rudyard Kipling. **CP-KiplR**

L'Envoy. George Herbert. **CP-HerbG**

Lenvoy de Chaucer a Bukton. Geoffrey Chaucer. **CP-ChauG**

Lenvoy de Chaucer a Scogan. Geoffrey Chaucer. **CP-ChauG**

Leodogran, the King of Cameliard. The Coming of Arthur. Tennyson. *Fr.* Idylls of the King. **CP-TennA**

Leonardo. Anne Waldman. **SP-WaldA**

Leonardo Da Vinci's. Marianne Craig Moore. **CP-MoorM**

Leonora. Edwin Arlington Robinson. **CP-RobiE**

Leopard no more secret, A. Death In Moonlight. Stanley Jasspon Kunitz. **CP-KuniS**

Leopard-Skin Pill-Box Hat. "Bob Dylan." **CP-DylaB**

Leper, The. Algernon Charles Swinburne. **SP-SwinA**

Leper is a Lazar or a Meazel, A. Rites for the Extrusion of a Leper. Thomas Merton. **CP-MertT**

L'Epreuve. Thom Gunn. **CP-GunnT**

Leprosie in Cloathes. Robert Herrick. **CP-HerrR**

Leprosie in Houses. Robert Herrick. **CP-HerrR**

Lepus Multis Amicus. John Gay, *tr. fr. English by* William Cowper. **CP-CowpW**

Lerici. Thom Gunn. **CP-GunnT**

Les Baux. Marsden Hartley. **CP-HartM**

Les Cinq Vierges, *see also* The Five Virgins, *tr. by* William Davis. Thomas Merton. **CP-MertT**

Les Congés du Lépreux. Frank Templeton Prince. **CP-PrinF**

Les Étiquettes Jaunes. Frank O'Hara. **SP-OharF**

Les Italiennes. John Clellon Holmes. **SP-HolmJ**

Les Luths. Frank O'Hara. **SP-OharF**

Les Millwin. Ezra Pound. **SP-PounE**

Les Neiges d'Antan. Louis MacNeice. *Fr.* Out of the Picture. **CP-MacNL**

Les Noyades. Algernon Charles Swinburne. **SP-SwinA**

Les Plus Belles Pages. Wallace Stevens. **CP-StevW**

Les Saints Nouveaux. John Updike. **CP-UpdiJ**

Les Sylphides. Louis MacNeice. **BoLoP; CoBMV** *Fr.* Novelettes. **CP-MacNL**

Lesbia. Catullus. See Carmen 5: "Lesbia / live with me."

Lesbia. Catullus. See Carmen 92: "Lesbia loads me night & day with her curses."

Lesbia / live with me. *see also sts. 1-3,* Stomping with Catullus (*by* Robert Creeley *in his* Collected Poems 1945-1975. Catullus. *Fr.* Carmina. **CP-Catul**

Lesbia forever on me rails. Catullus. See Carmen 92: "Lesbia loads me night & day with her curses."

Lesbia is extraordinarily vindictive. Carmen 83. Catullus. *Fr.* Carmina. **CP-Catul**

Lesbia loads me night & day with her curses. Carmen 92. Catullus. **BoLoP** *Fr.* Carmina. **CP-Catul**

Lesbia may dicker simper maul or nag talk at whom, come. Catullus. See Carmen 92: "Lesbia loads me night & day with her curses."

Lesbia, my love, let's be gay and enjoy ourselves. Catullus. See Carmen 5: "Lesbia / live with me."

Lesbia (my price scent t'her hero) mauls and deplores me, 'dig it'. Catullus. See Carmen 83: "Lesbia is extraordinarily vindictive."

Lesbia, our Lesbia, the same old Lesbia. Carmen 058. Catullus. *Fr.* Carmina. **CP-Catul**

Lesbia Railing. Catullus. See Carmen 92: "Lesbia loads me night & day with her curses."

Lesbia says she'ld rather marry me. *see also sts. 1-3,* Stomping with Catullus (*by* Robert Creeley). Catullus. *Fr.* Carmina. **CP-Catul**

Lesbia! since far from you I've ranged. To Lesbia. Byron. **CP-Byron**

Lesbia speaks evil of me with her husband near and he (damned. Catullus. See Carmen 83: "Lesbia is extraordinarily vindictive."

Lesbia's sparrow! / Lesbia's plaything. Carmen 2. Catullus. *Fr.* Carmina. **CP-Catul**

Lesbius has pooled her: kidney? whom Lesbia my—lit. Catullus. See Carmen 79: "They nickname Lesbia's brother 'pulcher.' "

Lesbos. James Liddy. **CP-LiddJ**

Lesbos. Sylvia Plath. **CP-PlatS**

Lese-Wiat, from Caul Gate. Louis Zukofsky. *Fr.* Michtam. **CP-ZukLS**

Less and Less Human, O Savage Spirit. Wallace Stevens. **CP-StevW**

Less than a score, the dregs of the last day. End of Camp Alamoosook. Robert Lowell. **SP-LoweR**

'Less you want your toes trod off you'd better get back at once. Rudyard Kipling. **CP-KiplR**

Lesse our sorrowes here and suffrings cease, The. Great Grief, Great Glory. Robert Herrick. **CP-HerrR**

Lesser griefs that may be said, The. Tennyson. *Fr.* In Memoriam A. H. H. **CP-TennA**

Lesser proof than old Voltaire's, yet greater, A. Orange Buds by Mail from Florida. Walt Whitman. **CP-WhitW**

Lesson, The. Maya Angelou. **SP-AngeM**

Lesson, The. Wystan Hugh Auden. **CP-AudeW**

Lesson, The. Paul Laurence Dunbar. **CP-DunbP**

Lesson, The. Rudyard Kipling. **CP-KiplR**

Lesson. Bill Knott. **SP-KnotB**

Lesson. Carl Sandburg. **CP-SandC**

Lesson, The. Charles Simic. **SP-SimiC**

Lesson, The. Charles Tomlinson. **CP-TomlC**

Lesson, The. William Carlos Williams. **CP-WilW2**

Lesson. Al Young. **CP-YounA**

Lesson for This Sunday, A. Derek Walcott. **CP-WalcD**

Lesson for Today, The. Robert Frost. **CP-FrosR**

Lesson in Anatomy, A. Kay Boyle. **CP-BoylK**

Lesson in Composition, The. Roy Fisher. **SP-FishR**

Lesson in Geography, A. Kenneth Rexroth. **SP-RexrK**

Lesson in Latin, A. "Lewis Carroll." **CP-CarrL**

Lesson in Vengeance, A. Sylvia Plath. **CP-PlatS**

Lesson of Grief, The. George Meredith. **CP-MerG1**

Lessons. Walt Whitman. **CP-WhitW**

Lessons from the Gorse. Elizabeth Barrett Browning. **CP-BroEB**

Lessons in Hunger. Anne Sexton. **CP-SextA**

Lessons on Becoming. Jim Morrison. **SP-MorrJ**

Lessons we learned here, The. At the Museum of Natural History. Erica Jong. **SP-JongE**

Lest any doubt that we are glad that they were born Today. Emily Dickinson. **CP-DickE**

Lest it may more quarrels breed. Twelve Articles. Jonathan Swift. **CP-SwifJ**

Lest men suspect your tale to be untrue. The Devil's Advice to Story-Tellers. Robert Ranke Graves. **CP-GravR**

Lest the fair cheeks begin their shrivelling. Homework. Mona Van Duyn. **SP-VanDM**

Lest the hoar frost grip the iridescent tent of your marriage. James Liddy. *Fr.* Epithalamion I–IV: "Along a leafy lonely river God-shy-eyed fisher boys." **CP-LiddJ**

Lest they should come—is all my fear. Emily Dickinson. **CP-DickE**

Lest this be Heaven indeed. Emily Dickinson. **CP-DickE**

Lest you should think that verse shall die. Part of the Ninth Ode of Horace Imitated. Alexander Pope. **CP-PopeA**

Lest you should think this story true. Rudyard Kipling. *See* A Code of Morals.

Lester. Shel Silverstein. **SP-SilS2**

Lester Leaps In. Al Young. **CP-YounA**

Lester Tells of the End of the Summer. Paul Zimmer. **SP-ZimmP**

Lester Tells of Wanda and the Big Snow. Paul Zimmer. **SP-ZimmP**

Lester thrashes in his blankets. Zimmer with Lester Under the Moon. Paul Zimmer. **SP-ZimmP**

Lester was given a magic wish. Lester. Shel Silverstein. **SP-SilS2**

Let a florid music praise. Wystan Hugh Auden. *Fr.* Twelve Songs. **CP-AudeW**

Let a fool throw a stone into a well. Uncle Joe. Peter Meinke. **SP-MeinP**

Let a joy keep you. Joy. Carl Sandburg. **CP-SandC**

Let a man alone in a cabin. Lament for Javier Heraud. Thomas Merton. **CP-MertT**

Let all chaste matrons, when they chance to see. Upon a Young Mother of Many Children. Robert Herrick. **CP-HerrR**

Let all rejoice with a boa whose twenty feet loosen the tree. Seventh Psalm. Anne Sexton. *Fr.* O Ye Tongues. **CP-SextA**

Let all the little poets be gathered together in classes. To School! Stevie Smith. **CP-SmitS**

Let all the world in ev'ry corner sing / My God and King. Antiphon. George Herbert. **CP-HerbG**

Let Anaiah bless with the Dragon-fly, who sails over the pond by the wood-side and feedeth on the cresses. Christopher Smart. **FaBoVe,** *ll.* 100–113; *Fr.* Fragment A. *Fr.* Jubilate Agno. **SP-SmarC**

Let Banister now lend his aid. William Cowper. **CP-CowpW**

Let Beauty awake in the morn from beautiful dreams. Robert Louis Stevenson. **CP-StevR**

Let both our Common Rooms combine to cheer. Wystan Hugh Auden. *Fr.* Three Occasional Poems. **CP-AudeW**

Let but a thrush begin. Lyric. John Hewitt. **CP-HewiJ**

Let but the rational prevail. George Meredith. *Fr.* Alsace-Lorraine. **CP-MerG1**

Let but thy voice engender with the string. Upon Her Voice. Robert Herrick. **CP-HerrR**

Let *Caesar* spread his conquests far, *fr.* Carmen Seculare. Horace, *tr. fr.* Latin by Samuel Johnson. **CP-JohnS**

Let chaos storm! Pertinax. Robert Frost. *Fr.* Ten Mills. **CP-FrosR**

Let choirs of educated men compose. Thomas Merton. *Fr.* Cables to the Ace. **CP-MertT**

Let Christopher and Anne come forth with a pig as bold as an. Fifth Psalm. Anne Sexton. *Fr.* O Ye Tongues. **CP-SextA**

Let confusion be the design. Design for November. William Carlos Williams. **CP-WilW2**

Let craft, ambition, spite, / Be quenched in Reason's night. The Warden's Charm. "Lewis Carroll." **CP-CarrL** *Fr.* Sylvie and Bruno.

Let dainty wits cry on the sisters nine. Sonnet 3. Sir Philip Sidney. **NoSic; OAEL-1; OBSC; Son** *Fr.* Astrophil and Stella. **SP-SidnP**

Let Dew, house of Dew rejoice with Xanthenes a precious stone of an amber colour. Fragment D. Christopher Smart. *Fr.* Jubilate Agno. **SP-SmarC**

Let Dew, house of Dew rejoice with Xanthenes a precious stone of an amber colour. Mineral Rejoicings. Christopher Smart. **CBCK** *Fr.* Fragment D. *Fr.* Jubilate Agno. **SP-SmarC**

Let down the Bars, Oh Death. Emily Dickinson. **CP-DickE**

Let down your braids of hair, lady. Glimmer. Carl Sandburg. **CP-SandC**

Let Eagle bid the Tortoise sunward soar. The Eagle and the Tortoise. Samuel Taylor Coleridge. **CP-ColeS**

Let Elizur Rejoice with the Partridge. Christopher Smart. **PoEL-3** *Fr.* Fragment B. *Fr.* Jubilate Agno. **SP-SmarC**

God Hath Sent Me to Sea for Pearls. **CBCK**

"Let Elizur[e] rejoice with the Partridge." **OAEL-1**

Let Elizur[e] rejoice with the Partridge. Christopher Smart. **OAEL-1** *Fr.* Let Elizur Rejoice with the Partridge. **PoEL-3** *Fr.* Fragment B. *Fr.* Jubilate Agno. **SP-SmarC**

Let Elizur[e] rejoice with the Partridge, who is a prisoner of state and is proud of his keepers. Fragment B. Christopher Smart. *Fr.* Jubilate Agno. **SP-SmarC**

Let Elizur[e] rejoice with the Partridge, who is a prisoner of state and is proud of his keepers. Let Elizur Rejoice with the Partridge. Christopher Smart. **PoEL-3** *Fr.* Fragment B. *Fr.* Jubilate Agno. **SP-SmarC**

Let Ephah rejoice with Buprestis, the Lord endue us with temperance and humanity, till every cow have her mate! Christopher Smart. **NOEC** *Fr.* Fragment B. *Fr.* Jubilate Agno. **SP-SmarC**

Let Esau not enriched by Jacob's bounty be. Of Mercy. Isabella Gardner. **CP-GardI**

Let Everything That Hath Breath Praise the Lord. Christina Georgina Rossetti. **CP-RosC2**

Let faire or foule my Mistresse be. Light Lightly Pleased. Robert Herrick. **CP-HerrR**

Let Fate or Insufficiency provide. To J.M. George Meredith. **CP-MerG1**

Let[t] folly praise that fancy [*or* phancy] loves, I praise and love that Child[e]. A Child[e] My Choice [*or* Choyse]. Robert Southwell. **CP-SoutR**

Let Folly smile, to view the names. To E———. Byron. **CP-Byron**

Let fools great Cupid's yoke disdain. Thomas Carew. **CP-CareT**

(Willing Prisoner to His Mistress, The.) **CP-CareT**

Let foreign [*or* forrain] nations of their language boast. The Son[ne]. George Herbert. **CP-HerbG**

Let God arise, let his enemies be scattered. Psalm 68. Bible, *O.T.* *Fr.* Psalms. **CP-Psal**

Let her be seen, a voice on a platform, heard. Ann Burlak. Muriel Rukeyser. **CP-RukeM**

Let her who walks in Paphos. Lais. Hilda Doolittle. **CP-DoolH**

Let him answer as he will. The Companion. Edwin Arlington Robinson. **CP-RobiE**

Let him be safe in sleep. Spell of Sleep. Kathleen Jessie Raine. **SP-RainK**

Let him escape hospital and doctor. Wendell Berry. *Fr.* Three Elegiac Poems. **CP-BerrW**

Let him pan. His sluice will rot and flake. The Gold Man on the Beckler. Richard Hugo. **CP-HugoR**

Let him rehearse the gifts reserved for age. Artifex in Extremis. Donald Davie. **CP-DavDo**

Let him that will be free and keep his hart from care. At. to Thomas Campion *and to* Philip Rosseter. **CP-CampT**

Let him, who from his tyrant mistress did. An Elegy on the La: Pen: Sent to My Mistress Out of France. Thomas Carew. **CP-CareT**

Let him who may. To Be Recited to Flossie on Her Birthday. William Carlos Williams. **CP-WilW2**

Let his days be few and let. Basil Bunting. *Fr.* Villon. **CP-BuntB**

Let History Be My Judge. Wystan Hugh Auden. **CP-AudeW**

Let hoary TIME's vast Bowels be the Grave. On the Frontispiece of Isaacsons Chronologie Explained. Richard Crashaw. **CP-CrasR**

Let It Be. The Beatles. **CP-Beatl**

Let it be alleys. Let it be a hall. A Lovely Love. Gwendolyn Brooks. **SP-BrooG**

Let it be Rome's great Pope, adored. Ballade in Old French. François Villon, *tr. fr.* French by Richard Wilbur. **CP-WilbR**

Let it go on; let the love of this hour be poured out till all the answers. Let Love Go On. Carl Sandburg. **CP-SandC**

Let it go—the. Edward Estlin Cummings. **CP-CummE; SP-CummE**

Let it no longer be a forlorn[e] hope. Richard Crashaw. **CP-CrasR**

(Acts 8; On the Baptized Æthiopian.) **CP-CrasR,** *tr. by* Richard Crashaw;

Let it not your wonder move. His Excuse for Loving. Ben Jonson. **EnRePo; JCP; NOSC; PoEL-2; QFR; SeCV-1** *Fr.* A Celebration of Charis in Ten Lyric[k] Pieces [*or* Peeces]. **CP-JonsB**

Let it stand / A stone guest. Aqueduct. Charles Tomlinson. **CP-TomlC**

Let Kings and Rulers, learn[e] this line from me. Strength to Support Soveraignty. Robert Herrick. **CP-HerrR**

Let kings command, and do[e] the best they may. The Power in the People. Robert Herrick. **CP-HerrR**

Let klumps of Earth however glorified. *after* J. P. F. Richter. Samuel Taylor Coleridge. **CP-ColeS**

Let Love go, if go she will. Robert Louis Stevenson. **CP-StevR**

Let Love Go On. Carl Sandburg. **CP-SandC**

Let man's soul [*or* Soule] be a sphere [*or* Spheare], and then, in this. Good Friday [*or* Goodfriday], 1613. Riding Westward. John Donne. **CP-DonnJ**

Let me be / a splinter in your side. Hilda Doolittle. **AnAn** *Fr.* Sigil. **CP-DoolH**

Let Me Be. Philip Levine. **SP-LeviP**

Let me be at the place of the castle. Psalm Concerning the Castle. Denise Levertov. **CP-LeveD**

Let me be monosyllabic today, O Lord. Monosyllabic. Carl Sandburg. **CP-SandC**

Let me be my own fool. A Counterpoint. Robert Creeley. **CP-CreeR**

Let me be prodigal as sun in praising you. Geography of Music. Kenneth Patchen. **UnAS** *Fr.* Eight Early Poems. **CP-PatcK**

Let me be to Thee as the circling bird. Gerard Manley Hopkins. **CP-HopkG**

Let me be warme; let me be fully fed. Love Kill'd by Lack. Robert Herrick. **CP-HerrR**

Let me be what I am, as Virgil cold. Elegy [*or* Elegie], An. Ben Jonson. **CP-JonsB**

Let me be your baby, south wind. Baby Song of the Four Winds. Carl Sandburg. **CP-SandC**

Let Me Begin Again. Philip Levine. **SP-LeviP**

Let Me Believe. Thomas Hardy. **CP-HardT**

Let me celebrate you. I. A Dialogue of Watching. Kenneth Rexroth. **SP-RexrK** *Fr.* Seven Poems for Marthe, My Wife.

Let me close the eyes of my soul. Despair. Paul Laurence Dunbar. **CP-DunbP**

Let me confess that we two must be twain. Sonnet 36. William Shakespeare. **HeIP; OAEP; PeHV** *Fr.* Sonnets. **CP-ShaWS**

Let Me Die in My Footsteps. "Bob Dylan." **CP-DylaB**

Let Me Enjoy. Thomas Hardy. **CP-HardT**

Let me gaze, gaze forever. Camera. John Updike. **CP-UpdiJ**

Let me go where'er I will. Music. Ralph Waldo Emerson. **CP-EmerR**

Let me hip you to the streets. Letter to an Aspiring Junkie. Maya Angelou. **SP-AngeM**

Let Me In! Kenneth Patchen. **CP-PatcK**

Let me in here, I know I've been here. I'd Have You Any Time. "Bob Dylan" *and* George Harrison. **CP-DylaB**

Let Me in This Ae Night. Robert Burns. **CP-BurnR**

Let me know. Appetite. Stevie Smith. **CP-SmitS**

Let me look at what I was, before I die. Jamestown. Randall Jarrell. **CP-JarrR**

Let me my properties explain. To Quilca. Jonathan Swift. **CP-SwifJ**

Let me no more, my love, be what I've seemed to you. Sulpicia to Cerinthus. Tibullus, *tr. fr. Latin by* Allen Tate. **CP-TateA**

Let me not, ever, to the marriage in Cana. Sonnet Suggested by Homer, Chaucer, Shakespeare, Edgar Allan Poe, Paul Valéry, James Joyce, et al. Delmore Schwartz. **SP-SchwD**

Let me not forget at least. Aginst the Sky. William Carlos Williams. **CP-WilW2**

Let me not live, if I not love. On Himselfe. Robert Herrick. **CP-HerrR**

Let me not mar that perfect Dream. Emily Dickinson. **CP-DickE**

Let me not say it, let me not reveal. Green Ways. Stanley Jasspon Kunitz. **CP-KuniS**

Let me not thirst with this Hock at my Lip. Emily Dickinson. **CP-DickE**

Let me not to the marriage of true minds. Sonnet 116. William Shakespeare. **AWP; ArLo; ClHu; EBEvV; EIL; EnLoPo; EnRePo; FPL; FaBV; FaFP; FaPoB; GBL; GGP; GTBS; GTBS-6; GTBS-P; HAP; HeIL; HeIP; ImPo; InPS; InvP; LiTB; NAEL-1; NIP; NOBE; NoP; NoSic; OAEL-1; OBEV; OBSC; OXAEP-1; OxBM; PBMP; PPP; PeHV; PlP; PoE; PoEL-2; PoRA; Poetr; PrIm; SCGP; SCV; SeCePo; SoSe; Son; TEP; TFi; TRP; TrGrPo; UnPo; WeW** *Fr.* Sonnets. **CP-ShaWS**

Let me obtain forgiveness of thee, Samson. John Milton. **EBEV** *Fr.* Samson Agonistes. **CP-MiltJ**

Let me play to you tunes without measure or end. Bagpipe Music. "Hugh MacDiarmid." **SP-MacDH**

Let me pour [*or* powre] forth. Valediction, A: Of Weeping. John Donne. **CP-DonnJ**

Let me put on record for posterity. Her Beauty. Robert Ranke Graves. **CP-GravR**

Let me ryke up to dight that tear. Robert Burns. *Fr.* The Jolly Beggars.

Let me say beginning I don't believe in Soul. Manifesto. Allen Ginsberg. **CP-GinsA**

Let me say (in anger) that since the day we were married. The Crisis. Robert Creeley. **CP-CreeR**

Let me sleep this night away. Upon Himselfe Being Buried. Robert Herrick. **CP-HerrR**

Let me take this other glove off. In Westminster Abbey. Sir John Betjeman. **CP-BetjJ**

Let me take you down. Strawberry Fields Forever. The Beatles. **CP-Beatl**

Let me tell you. June 30, 1974. James Schuyler. **CP-SchuJ**

Let Me Tell You. Miller Williams. **SP-WillM**

Let me tell you a little story. Miss Gee. Wystan Hugh Auden. **CP-AudeW**

Let me tell you how it will be. Taxman. George Harrison. **CP-Beatl**

Let me tell you, Mac, it's sure great. New Hartford. Hayden Carruth. **CP-CarHS**

Let me tell you of Aloysius Buck. The Outcome of Mr. Buck's Superstition. Ogden Nash. **CP-NashO**

Let me tell you the story of how I began. Song: Lift-Boy. Robert Ranke Graves. **CP-GravR**

Let me try again. I look. Bound upon a Wheel. Jenny Joseph. **SP-JoseJ**

Let me wake in the night. Wendell Berry. *Fr.* Prayers and Sayings of the Mad Farmer. **CP-BerrW**

Let me walk through the fields of paper. A Walk through the Notebooks. Denise Levertov. **CP-LeveD**

Let me walk to you. Out. Robert Creeley. **CP-CreeR**

Let mind be more precious than soul; it will not. Geoffrey Hill. *Fr.* Funeral Music. **CP-HillG**

Let moderation on thy passions waite. Moderation. Robert Herrick. **CP-HerrR**

Let More Ambitious Poets Take the Heart. William Wordsworth. **CP-WorW2**

Let mother Earth now deck herself in flowers. Sir Philip Sidney. **SP-SidnP** *Fr.* Arcadia.

Let my first Knowing be of thee. Emily Dickinson. **CP-DickE**

Let my marriage be brought to the ground. Wendell Berry. *Fr.* Prayers and Sayings of the Mad Farmer. **CP-BerrW**

Let my snow-tracks lead. Hayden Carruth. **CP-CarHS** *Fr.* The Clay Hill Anthology.

Let Noah build an ark out of the old lady's shoe and. Third Psalm. Anne Sexton. **NALW** *Fr.* O Ye Tongues. **CP-SextA**

Let not conceited sages laugh aloud. Ralph Waldo Emerson. **CP-EmerR**

Let not in—difference. Fence Between. Marsden Hartley. **CP-HartM**

Let not my love be call'd idolatry. Sonnet 105. William Shakespeare. *Fr.* Sonnets. **CP-ShaWS**

Let not old age disgrace my high desire. Sir Philip Sidney. **SP-SidnP** *Fr.* Arcadia.

Let not our town be large, remembering. On the Building of Springfield. Nicholas Vachel Lindsay. **WHA** *Fr.* A Gospel of Beauty. **CP-LindV**

Let not that Day Gods Friends and Servants scare. Doomes-Day. Robert Herrick. **CP-HerrR**

Let not the proud of heart condemn. Little Sonnet to Little Friends. Countee Cullen. **CP-CullC**

Let not the sad perplexity. Love Letter. Allen Ginsberg. **CP-GinsA**

Let not this praising of thine ass. Unfinished. David Markson. **CP-MarkD**

Let not thy Tomb-stone er'e be laid by me. To Electra. Robert Herrick. **CP-HerrR**

Let not Woman e'er complain. Song. Robert Burns. **CP-BurnR**

Let not young souls be smothered out before. The Leaden-eyed. Nicholas Vachel Lindsay. **CP-LindV**

Let now your soul in this substantial world. An End of Travel. Robert Louis Stevenson. **CP-StevR**

Let Observation with extensive View. Samuel Johnson. **UV** *Fr.* The Vanity of Human Wishes [The Tenth Satire of Juvenal Imitated]. **CP-JohnS**

Let Observation with extensive View. The Vanity of Human Wishes [The Tenth Satire of Juvenal Imitated]. Samuel Johnson. **CP-JohnS**

Let other bards of angels sing. To ———. William Wordsworth. **CP-WorW2**

Let other heroes boast their scars. Nature's Law. Robert Burns. **CP-BurnR**

Let other poets raise a fracas. Scotch Drink. Robert Burns. **CP-BurnR**

Let others creep by timid steps, and slow. A Certain Type of Scientist Speaks. Alexander Pope. **ECEV** *Fr.* Yet, yet a moment, one dim ray of light. **NAEL-1; OAEL-1; PoEL-3** *Fr.* The Dunciad. **CP-PopeA**

Let others look for Pearle and Gold. The New-Yeeres Gift. Robert Herrick. **CP-HerrR**

Let others pray for the passenger pigeon. Elegy for the Giant Tortoises. Margaret Atwood. **SP-AtwM1**

Let others probe the mystery if they can. The Right Thing. Theodore Roethke. **CP-RoetT**

Let others quarrel alone about my grief. [*similar to* Thoughts While Drowning: But Try to Eliminate the Argument. Malcolm Lowry. **CP-LowrM** *Fr.* The Lighthouse Invites the Storm. **CP-LowrM**

Let others quarrel alone about my grief. Thoughts While Drowning: But Try to Eliminate the Argument. Malcolm Lowry. **CP-LowrM**

Let others to the Printing Press[e] run fast. Posting to Printing. Robert Herrick. **CP-HerrR**

Let others with Parnassus swell their theme. A Description of Mother Ludwell's Cave. Jonathan Swift. **CP-SwifJ**

Let out where two fears intersect, a point selected. In Transit. Wystan Hugh Auden. **CP-AudeW**

Let Paris read Joyce! Those Coke to Newcastle Blues. Malcolm Lowry. **CP-LowrM**

Let Patience Have Her Perfect Work. Christina Georgina Rossetti. **CP-RosC2**

Let Peter rejoice with the Moon Fish who keeps up the life in the waters by night. Christopher Smart. **ChIV-2** *Fr.* Fragment B. *Fr.* Jubilate Agno. **SP-SmarC**

Let pride grow big, my rose, and let the clear[e]. On a Damask[e] Rose, Sticking upon a Lady's Breast. Thomas Carew. **CP-CareT**

Let Ramah rejoice with Cochineal. Fragment C. Christopher Smart. *Fr.* Jubilate Agno. **SP-SmarC**

Let Shobi rejoice with the Kastrel—blessed be the name JESUS in falconry and in the MALL. Christopher Smart. **NOEC** *Fr.* Fragment B. *Fr.* Jubilate Agno. **SP-SmarC**

Let sin be preordained. Howard Nemerov. *Fr.* Dialectical Songs. **CP-NemeH**

Let some sad trumpeter stand. Back on Times Square, Dreaming of Times Square. Allen Ginsberg. **CP-GinsA**

Let something else be / the question—. Robert Creeley. **CP-CreeR**

Let something in through the open window. Faces No Longer White. Edwin Rolfe. **CP-RolfE**

Let Sporus tremble--"What? That thing of silk." Alexander Pope. **AWP; ChTr; NOBE; OBSV; SCV** *Fr.* Epistle to Dr. Arbuthnot. **CP-PopeA** (Sporus.) **AWP; ChTr; NOBE; OBSV**

Let that which stood in front go behind. Reversals. Walt Whitman. **CP-WhitW**

Let the bird of loudest [*or* lowdest] lay. The Phoenix and the Turtle. William Shakespeare. **CP-ShaWS**

Let the Blurb be strong. The Making of the Book. Roy Fisher. **SP-FishR**

Let the boy try along this bayonet-blade. Arms and the Boy. Wilfred Owen. **CP-OwenW**

Let the Brothels of Paris be opened. William Blake. **CP-BlakW**

Let the chipmunk praise the Lord as he bounds up Jacob's Ladder. Ninth Psalm. Anne Sexton. *Fr.* O Ye Tongues. **CP-SextA**

Let the clods fall, then silence and cold dew. Epitaph in the Imperative Mode. Louise McNeill. **SP-McNeL**

Let the crows go by hawking their caw and caw. River Roads. Carl Sandburg. **CP-SandC**

Let the day glare: O memory, your tread. Ode to Fear. Allen Tate. **CP-TateA**

Let the Dead Bury Their Dead. David Herbert Lawrence. **CP-LawrD**

Let the downpour roil and toil! In Time of Cloudburst. Robert Frost. **CP-FrosR**

Let the engines roar. Let the engines roar. Chant for the Five-Year Plan. John Hewitt. **CP-HewiJ**

Let the flowers make a journey. The Fury of Flowers and Worms. Anne Sexton. *Fr.* The Furies. **CP-SextA**

Let the flute. Chirico. Roy Fisher. **SP-FishR**

Let the foul Scene proceed. The Marionettes. Walter de la Mare. **CP-DeLaW**

Let the great song come. Wendell Berry. *Fr.* From the Crest. **CP-BerrW**

Let the inhuman, drab machines. John Haines. *Fr.* The End of the Summer. **SP-HainJ**

Let the loud men grow louder, weak weaker. We Hold These Truths to Be Self-Evident. Kenneth Patchen. **CP-PatcK**

Let the love-lorn lover cure insomnia. Sedative Reflection. Ogden Nash. **CP-NashO**

Let the Nations Be Glad, *sel., vv. 1–5.* Bible, *O.T. See* Psalm 67: "God be merciful unto us, and bless us."

Let the nickels and dimes explain. Carl Sandburg. **CP-SandC** *Fr.* The People, Yes. **CP-SandC**

Let the oboe and the flute. Song for a Birth Day in Exile. Edwin Rolfe. **CP-RolfE**

Let the old broken hag die on the street. Nuthin but Brass. Edwin Rolfe. **CP-RolfE**

Let the old geezers jig on Penn. Stanley Jasspon Kunitz. *Fr.* The Mound Builders. **CP-KuniS**

Let the phantom love that enrolls the sparrow. Emily Dickinson. **SP-DickE**

Let the place of the solitaires. The Place of the Solitaires. Wallace Stevens. **CP-StevW**

Let the Priests of the Raven of dawn, no longer in deadly black. Chorus. William Blake. *Fr.* The Marriage of Heaven and Hell. **CP-BlakW**

Let the Railsplitter Awake! *Ad. fr.* Allen Ginsberg. **CP-GinsA**

Let the reformers descend from the stands where they are forever brawling—let an idiot or insane person appear on each of the stands. Transpositions. Walt Whitman. **CP-WhitW**

Let the snake wait under. A Sort of a Song. William Carlos Williams. **CP-WilW2**

Let the superstitious wife. Another. Robert Herrick. **CP-HerrR**

Let the tale's sailor from a Christian voyage. Dylan Thomas. **CMoP; FaBoMo; OAEL-2** *Fr.* Altarwise by Owl-Light. **CP-ThomD**

Let the Tight Lizard on the Wall. Richard Eberhart. **CP-EberR**

Let the weeks end as well they must. The Green Woods of Unrest. Robert Ranke Graves. **CP-GravR**

Let the world's sharpness, like a clasping knife. Sonnet. Elizabeth Barrett Browning. **NOBVV** *Fr.* Sonnets from the Portuguese. **CP-BroEB**

Let Them Alone. Robinson Jeffers. **CP-JefR3**

Let Them Ask Your Pardon. Carl Sandburg. **CP-SandC**

Let them bury your big eyes. Elegy. Edna St. Vincent Millay. **CMoP; MoAB; MoAmPo; OxBA; PoRA** *Fr.* Memorial to D. C. **CP-MillE**

Let them fight it out, friend! things have gone too far. Before. Robert Browning. **CP-BroR1**

Let them give up the ghost, then there is nothing but dust. Put Not Your Trust in Princes. Donald Davie. **CP-DavD0**

Let them not war in me. Triplex. Hilda Doolittle. **CP-DoolH**

Let Them Rejoice in Their Beds. Christina Georgina Rossetti. **CP-RosC2**

Let Them Rejoice in Their Beds. Christina Georgina Rossetti. **CP-RosC3**

Let them remember Samangan, the bridge and tower. Basil Bunting. **CP-BuntB**

Let them return, saying you blush again for the great. The Mango Tree. Hart Crane. **CP-CranH**

Let them stand still for the bullet, and stare the shooter in the eye. For the Hog Killing. Wendell Berry. **CP-BerrW**

Let there be a God as large as a sunlamp to laugh his heat at you. First Psalm. Anne Sexton. *Fr.* O Ye Tongues. **CP-SextA**

Let There Be Colored Light. Robert Pack. **SP-PackR**

Let There Be Light! David Herbert Lawrence. **CP-LawrD**

"Let there be light!" God spake of old. The Library. John Greenleaf Whittier. **CP-WhitJ**

"Let there be light!" said God, and there was light! Byron. **OBWP** *Fr.* Canto the Seventh. *Fr.* Don Juan. **CP-Byron**

Let there be Patrons; Patrons like to thee. To the Patron of Poets, M. End: Porter. Robert Herrick. **CP-HerrR**

Let there be shelters built in the wild fern. Archibald MacLeish. *Fr.* Hamlet of A. Macleish. **CP-MacLA**

Let there be treaties, bridges. Against Extremity. Charles Tomlinson. **CP-TomlC**

Let there stem (Gellius). Carmen 90. Catullus. *Fr.* Carmina. **CP-Catul**

Let these memorials of built stone—music's. Defense of the Islands. Thomas Stearns Eliot. **CP-ElioT**

Let this be scattered far and wide, laid low. Counter Mood. Countee Cullen. **CP-CullC**

Let this book as it ends. The Calendar. John Haines. **SP-HainJ**

Let this last lyric of a passing day. Lyric. John Hewitt. **CP-HewiJ**

Let those who are in favour with their stars. Sonnet 25. William Shakespeare. **OBSC; OXAEP-1; PAW; SCGP** *Fr.* Sonnets. **CP-ShaWS**

Let those who pine in pride or in revenge. Marenghi. Percy Bysshe Shelley. **CP-ShelP**

Let those who will stride on their barren roads. A Roadway. Paul Laurence Dunbar. **CP-DunbP**

Let those whom folly prompts to sneer. Phaedrus, *tr. by* Samuel Johnson. **CP-JohnS** *Fr.* Fabulae.

Let those whose low delights to Earth are given. Faith, Hope, and Charity. Samuel Taylor Coleridge. **CP-ColeS**

Let thy wheel-barrow alone. To a Sexton. William Wordsworth. **CP-WorW1**

Let us abandon then our gardens and go home. Justice Denied in Massachusetts. Edna St. Vincent Millay. **CP-MillE**

Let us admit into our land the winds. Winds of Another Sphere. Edwin Rolfe. **CP-RolfE**

Let us admit it fairly, as a business people should. The Lesson. Rudyard Kipling. **CP-KiplR**

Let us be aware of the true dark gods. Love and Marilyn Monroe. Delmore Schwartz. **SP-SchwD**

Let us be circumspect, surrounded as we are. Two Voices. Edna St. Vincent Millay. **CP-MillE**

Let us be honest; the lady was not a harlot until she married a corporation. Soiled Dove. Carl Sandburg. **CP-SandC**

Let Us Be Men. David Herbert Lawrence. **CP-LawrD**

Let us be quiet today. The earth is still. Thy Love Is One Thou'st Not Yet Known. Jean Garrigue. **SP-GarrJ**

Let us become the overhanging day. Percy Bysshe Shelley. **OAEL-2** *Fr.* Epipsychidion. **CP-ShelP**

Let us begin and carry up this corpse. A Grammarian's Funeral. Robert Browning. **CP-BroR1**

Let us begin to understand the argument. The Ivory Tower. Allen Tate. **CP-TateA**

Let us call her Mrs. Mipping, but her name is legion. It Would Have Been Quicker to Walk, or, Don't Tell Me We're There Already. Ogden Nash. **CP-NashO**

Let us call Yorkshire pudding. Yorkshire Pudding. Ogden Nash. *Fr.* Table Talk. **CP-NashO**

Let us come upon him first as if in a dream. Chorus of Furies. Basil Bunting. **CP-BuntB**

Let us cool your bitter sweet charm with incense and verse. Thomas Merton. *Fr.* Cables to the Ace. **CP-MertT**

Let us do justice to the skink. The Skink. Ogden Nash. **CP-NashO**

Let us explain it. Consider if it is. Poetry, Then. . . . John Hewitt. **CP-HewiJ**

Let us forget that it is spring and celebrate the riderless will of five victims. An Elegy for Five Old Ladies. Thomas Merton. **CP-MertT; SP-MertT**

Let Us Gather at the River. Marge Piercy. **SP-PierM**

Let us give him the benefit of some doubts. Malcolm Lowry. *Fr.* Peter Gaunt and the Canals. **CP-LowrM**

Let us go hence, my songs; she will not hear. A Leave-taking. Algernon Charles Swinburne. **SP-SwinA**

Let us go out into the daylight. Vesper Hymn for Tuesday and June, after the Visit of Henry Wells. Marsden Hartley. **CP-HartM**

Let us go out of the fog, John, out of the filmy persistent drizzle on the. In the Shadow of the Palace. Carl Sandburg. **CP-SandC**

Let us go then, you and I. Thomas Stearns Eliot. **UV** *Fr.* The Love Song of J. Alfred Prufrock. **CP-ElioT**

Let us go then, you and I. The Love Song of J. Alfred Prufrock. Thomas Stearns Eliot. **CP-ElioT**

Let us go to the Animal Ball, disguised as bipeds! The Animal Ball. Edna St. Vincent Millay. **CP-MillE**

Let us grow old with modesty. A Poem about Black Power. Kay Boyle. **CP-BoylK**

Let Us Have Madness Openly. Kenneth Patchen. **CP-PatcK**

Let us honour if we can. Wystan Hugh Auden. **PeLV** *Fr.* Shorts [1927–1932] ("Pick a quarrel, go to war"). **CP-AudeW**

   (Dedication: "Let us honour if we can.") **PeLV**

Let us know each other by this. Danse Manhattanique. Stephen Dunn. **SP-DunnS**

Let us lie here in the disturbing grass. Edward Estlin Cummings. **CP-CummE**

Let us live in a lull of the long winter-winds. For C.W.B. Elizabeth Bishop. **CP-BishE**

Let us look into the matter of debt. First Payment Deferred. Ogden Nash. **CP-NashO**

Let us make a circle here—. Fox and Geese. Louise McNeill. **SP-McNeL**

Let us make of day a delirium. Charles Henri Ford. *Fr.* Epigrams. **SP-FordC**

Let us never name that royal certitude. The Unnamed Spell. Robert Ranke Graves. **CP-GravR**

Let us not sit upon the ground. An Elegy to Dispel Gloom. Lawrence Ferlinghetti. **SP-FerlL**

Let us not speak, for the love we bear one another. In a Bath Teashop. Sir John Betjeman. **CP-BetjJ**

Let us not turn for this aside to die. At a Parting. Countee Cullen. **CP-CullC**

Let us now consider the ocean. A Beginner's Guide to the Ocean. Ogden Nash. **CP-NashO**

Let us now praise famous men. A School Song. Rudyard Kipling. **CP-KiplR**

Let us now sing of Loves delight. Thomas Campion. *Fr.* Description of a Maske: Presented in the Banqueting Roome at *Whitehall*, on Saint Stephens Night Last, at the Marriage of the Right Honourable the Earle of *Somerset:* and the Right Noble the Lady FRANCES *Howard.* **CP-CampT**

Let us now take time, and play. To Sappho. Robert Herrick. **CP-HerrR**

Let us off and search, and find a place. The Recalcitrants. Thomas Hardy. **CP-HardT**

Let us play, and dance, and sing. The Vision of Delight. Ben Jonson.

Let Us play Yesterday. Emily Dickinson. **CP-DickE**

Let us praise, / while time to praise remains. Idiot Joe Prays in Pershing Square and Gets Hauled in for Vagrancy. Edwin Rolfe. **CP-RolfE**

Let us praise death that turns pink cheeks to ashes. Praise for Death. Donald Hall. **CP-HallD**

Let us praise our Maker, with true passion extol Him. Anthem. Wystan Hugh Auden. **CP-AudeW**

Let us quit the leafy arbour. The Longest Day; Addressed to My Daughter. William Wordsworth. **CP-WorW2**

Let us rejoice on our cots, for His nocturnal miracles. Lauds. John Berryman. **CP-BerrJ**

Let us remember, here recall. Wire Brier. Louise McNeill. **SP-McNeL**

Let us say there is an ideal realm. The House. Peter Meinke. **SP-MeinP**

Let us sing of our beloved, let us sing of that which is sweetest. George Meredith. *Fr.* Arabic Poems. **CP-MerG2**

Let us sing together to our God, Who made all things. *tr. from* "Jubilemus omnes una Deo nostro qui creavit omnia." *Unknown, tr. fr. Latin by* Thomas Merton. **CP-MertT**

Let us sit by the hissing steam radiator a winter's day, grey wind pattering. Horses and Men in the Rain. Carl Sandburg. **CP-SandC**

Let us strip the desk for action—now we have a horse. Havana Rose. Hart Crane. **CP-CranH**

Let us suspect,chérie,this not very big. Edward Estlin Cummings. **CP-CummE**

Let Us Talk, Let Us Laugh. David Herbert Lawrence. **CP-LawrD**

Let us think of these. March. Archibald MacLeish. **CP-MacLA**

Let us (though late) at last (my Silvia) wed. To Silvia to Wed. Robert Herrick. **CP-HerrR**

(Let us tremble)a personal radiance sits. Edward Estlin Cummings. **CP-CummE**

Let us twain walk aside from the rest. To You. Walt Whitman. **CP-WhitW**

Let us walk where reeds are growing. A Walk by the Water. Charlotte Smith. **CP-SmitC**

Let us, who part like brothers, part like bards. The House of Tembinoka. Robert Louis Stevenson. **CP-StevR**

Let us with a gladsome mind, *par. by* Milton. Bible, *O.T. See* Psalm 136: "O give thanks unto the Lord. . . ."

Let us with a gladsom[e] mind. Psalm 136. John Milton. **CP-MiltJ**

Let who will think of what they will. The Lion and the Dog. Robert Creeley. **CP-CreeR**

Let wits contest. The Posy [*or* Posie]. George Herbert. **CP-HerbG**

Let woman fear to teach and bear to learn. Christina Georgina Rossetti. *Fr.* Later Life: A Double Sonnet of Sonnets. **CP-RosC2**

Let wonder leave us for another place. Aquarium. John Hewitt. **CP-HewiJ**

Let Y stand for you who says. You. Kenneth Rexroth. **HoPM** *Fr.* A Bestiary. **SP-RexrK**

Let you not say of me when I am old. Edna St. Vincent Millay. **CP-MillE**

Let Zeus Record. Hilda Doolittle. **CP-DoolH**

   "Stars wheel in purple, yours is not so rare." **MoAmPo; NOBA; TAP**

L'etat C'est Moi. John Crowe Ransom. *Fr.* Two Gentlemen in Bonds. **SP-RansJ**

Letcher was Carted first about the streets. Upon Letcher: Epigram. Robert Herrick. **CP-HerrR**

Lethargic vs violence as alternatives of each other for los americanos, The. Anecdotes of the Late War. Charles Olson. **CP-OlsoC**

Lethe. Hilda Doolittle. **CP-DoolH**

Lethe. Edna St. Vincent Millay. **CP-MillE**

"Lethe" in my flower. Emily Dickinson. **CP-DickE**

L'Etoile. Richard Wilbur. **CP-WilbR**

Let's all get up and dance. Your Mother Should Know. The Beatles. **CP-Beatl**

Let's All Hear It for Mildred Bailey! James Schuyler. **CP-SchuJ**

Let's be jocund while we amy. An End Decreed. Robert Herrick. **CP-HerrR**

Let's Be Merry. Christina Georgina Rossetti. **FaPON; TLR; TiPo** *Fr.* Sing-Song. **CP-RosC2**

Lets call for Hymen if agreed thou art. To Anthea. Robert Herrick. **CP-HerrR**

Let's Call This. Gilbert Sorrentino. **SP-SorrG**

Let's contend no more, Love. A Woman's Last Word. Robert Browning. **CP-BroR1**

Let's count the bodies over again. Counting Small-boned Bodies. Robert Bly. **SP-BlyR**

Let's give it the Kamjian-Boyadjian Post. Assembling a Street. Brendan Galvin. **SP-GalvB**

Let's go over to Lily's. The Queen Is in the Parlor. Ogden Nash. **CP-NashO**

Let's Keep It Between Us. "Bob Dylan." **CP-DylaB**

Let's live in hast; use pleasures while we may. To Live Freely. Robert Herrick. **CP-HerrR**

Let's live, my Lesbia, and love. Catullus. *See* Carmen 5: "Lesbia / live with me."

Let's live, my Lesbia, and make love. Catullus. *See* Carmen 5: "Lesbia / live with me."

Let's live suddenly without thinking. Edward Estlin Cummings. **CP-CummE**

Let's live with that smal pittance that we have. The Covetous Still Captives. Robert Herrick. **CP-HerrR**

Let's love each other for what we are. Randall Jarrell. **CP-JarrR**

Let's Majeste. Maya Angelou. **SP-AngeM**

Let's Not Climb the Washington Monument Tonight. Ogden Nash. **CP-NashO**

Let's Not Play Lotto, Let's Just Talk. Ogden Nash. **CP-NashO**

Lets now take our time. To Be Merry. Robert Herrick. **CP-HerrR**

Let's skip a few short years of hollow peace. George the Third. Byron. **FiP; TW** *Fr.* The Vision of Judgment. **CP-Byron**

Let's spin the bottle. The Game. Stanley Jasspon Kunitz. **CP-KuniS**

Let's start a magazine. Edward Estlin Cummings. **CP-CummE**

Let's strive to be the best; the Gods, we know it. Parcell-gil't-Poetry. Robert Herrick. **CP-HerrR**

Let's swim to the moon. Moonlight Drive. Jim Morrison. **SP-MorrJ**

Let's take a walk. Spring. Kenneth Koch. **SP-KochK**

Let's take a walk, you. Poem. Frank O'Hara. **SP-OharF**

Let's take it as it is: acres flowing. A Good View from Flagstaff. Richard Hugo. **CP-HugoR**

Let's talk of Judas for a while. Judas Iscariot. Countee Cullen. **CP-CullC**

Let's throw it. Let's throw ice at her face. Another Day. For a Moment Slipping Back, Again the Unreal King. Muriel Rukeyser. **CP-RukeM**

Let's Wait. Pablo Neruda, *tr. fr. Spanish by* Ben Belitt. **SP-NeruP**

Let's,from some loud unworld's most rightful wrong. Edward Estlin Cummings. **CP-CummE**

Letsuzstayawayfromparades. O'Ryan 11-15. Charles Olson. **CP-OlsoC**

Lett fickle Fortune runn her blyndest race. From Fortune's Reach. Robert Southwell. **CP-SoutR**

Lett griefe as farr bee from your deerest brest. Sonnet. Mary Sidney, Countess of Montgomery Wroth. *Fr.* Pamphilia to Amphilanthus. **CP-WrotM**

Letter, The. Wystan Hugh Auden. **CP-AudeW**

Letter, The. Wystan Hugh Auden. **CP-AudWJ**

Letter. Wendell Berry. **CP-BerrW**
"In place with you, as I come and go."
"To search for what belongs where it is."
"Turning always in my mind toward you."

Letter. Leonard Cohen. **CP-CoheL**

Letter, The. Robert Creeley. **CP-CreeR**

Letter, A. James Dickey. **CP-DickJ**

Letter, A. Paul Laurence Dunbar. **CP-DunbP**

Letter. Robert Earl Hayden. **CP-HaydR**

Letter. Langston Hughes. **SP-HughL** *Fr.* Lenox Avenue Mural.

Letter, A. Li Po, *tr. fr. Chinese by* William Carlos Williams *with* David Rafael Wang. **CP-WilW2**

Letter, The. Frederick Morgan. **SP-MorgF**

Letter. Leonard Nathan. **SP-NathL**

Letter. Leonard Nathan. **SP-NathL**

"Letter / once in a while," he said, A. Write. Diane Wakoski. *Fr.* Fifteen Poems for a Lunar Eclipse None of Us Saw. **SP-WakoD**

Letter, The. Wilfred Owen. **CP-OwenW**

Letter. Grace Paley. **CP-PaleG**

Letter. Frank Templeton Prince. **CP-PrinF**

Letter. Edwin Rolfe. **CP-RolfE**

Letter, A. John Greenleaf Whittier. **CP-WhitJ**

Letter about Money, Love, or Other Comfort, If Any. Robert Penn Warren. **SP-WarrR**

Letter About Myself to You. Stephen Dunn. **SP-DunnS**

Letter always seemed to me, A. Emily Dickinson. **SP-DickE**

Letter Beginning with the First Line of Your Letter. Stephen Dobyns. **SP-DobyS**

Letter for Marian, A. Thomas McGrath. **SP-McGrT**

Letter for Melville 1951. Charles Olson. **CP-OlsoC**

Letter from a Coward to a Hero. Robert Penn Warren. **SP-WarrR**

Letter from a Missionary of the Methodist Episcopal Church South, in Kansas, to a Distiguished Politician. John Greenleaf Whittier. **CP-WhitJ**

Letter From an Inland Province. Richard Shelton. **SP-ShelR**

Letter from Armenia, A. Geoffrey Hill. *Fr.* The Songbook of Sebastian Arrurruz. **CP-HillG**

Letter From Aunt Belle, A. Ted Kooser. **SP-KoosT**

Letter from Brooklyn, A. Derek Walcott. **CP-WalcD**

Letter from Chicago. May Sarton. **SP-SartM**

Letter from Costa Brava. Charles Tomlinson. **CP-TomlC**

Letter from Dean Swift to Dean Smedley, A. Jonathan Swift. **CP-SwifJ**

Letter from Goose Creek: April. Marilyn Hacker. **SP-HackM**

Letter from Home, A. Mary Oliver. **SP-OlivM**

Letter from India. Louis MacNeice. **CP-MacNL**

Letter From My Good Hand, A. Gary Gildner. **SP-GildG**

Letter from Oaxaca to North Africa 1936. Malcolm Lowry. **CP-LowrM**

Letter from our Man in Blossomtime. Louise Glück. **SP-GlücL**

Letter from Persephone. Margaret Atwood. **SP-AtwM2**

Letter from Phillis Wheatley, A. Robert Earl Hayden. **CP-HaydR**

Letter from Provence. Louise Glück. **SP-GlücL**

Letter from Slough Pond. Isabella Gardner. **CP-GardI**

Letter From the Cape. Alun Lewis. **CP-LewiA**
"Across seven thousand miles of sea and time."
"And now we seek once more the burning breeze."
"And still the heart breaks, wakeful all the night?"
"I send you a Christmas present, sweet."
"Yet we are safely at this port of call."

Letter from the Land of Sinners. Adrienne Rich. **CP-RicAE; SP-RicA2**

Letter from the North. Charles Bukowski. **SP-BukC2**

Letter from the Snake Woman. Siv Cedering Fox. **SP-CedeS**

Letter from Town: On a Grey Morning in March. David Herbert Lawrence. **CP-LawrD**

Letter from Town: The Almond-Tree. David Herbert Lawrence. **CP-LawrD**

Letter Home. Stephen Dunn. **SP-DunnS**

Letter in my mailbox says you've made it, A. To the Girl Who Lives In a Tree. Audre Lorde. **SP-LordA**

Letter in November. Sylvia Plath. **CP-PlatS**

Letter in Verse. William Cowper. **CP-CowpW**

Letter is a joy of Earth, A. Emily Dickinson. **CP-DickE**

Letter of Poor Birds, The. Louis Zukofsky. **CP-ZukLS**

Letter on Liberty, A. Kenneth Patchen. **CP-PatcK**

Letter on the Use of Machine Guns at Weddings, A. Kenneth Patchen. **CP-PatcK**

Letter Poem #3. James Schuyler. **CP-SchuJ**

Letter Poem #2. James Schuyler. **CP-SchuJ**

Letter S. Carl Sandburg. **CP-SandC**

Letter to a Dead Father. Richard Shelton. **SP-ShelR**

Letter to a Friend about Girls. Philip Larkin. **CP-LarkP**

Letter to a Friend: Who Is Nancy Daum? James Schuyler. **CP-SchuJ**

Letter to a Lost Friend. Richard Shelton. **SP-ShelR**

Letter to a Policemen in Kansas City, A. Kenneth Patchen. **CP-PatcK**

Letter to a Purist. Sylvia Plath. **CP-PlatS**

Letter to a Substitute Teacher. Gary Gildner. **SP-GildG**

Letter to a Sufi Who Has Abandoned Sufism to Study Law. Thomas Merton. *Fr.* Readings from Ibn Abbad. **CP-MertT**

Letter to America, A. Thomas Merton. **CP-MertT**

Letter to Ammons from Maratea. Richard Hugo. **CP-HugoR**

Letter to an Aspiring Junkie. Maya Angelou. **SP-AngeM**

Letter to an English Poet. Donald Hall. **CP-HallD**

Letter to Annick from Boulder. Richard Hugo. **CP-HugoR**

Letter to Archibald Craig, A. Kay Boyle. **CP-BoylK**

Letter to be Disguised as a Gas Bill. Marge Piercy. **SP-PierM**

Letter to Bell from Missoula. Richard Hugo. **CP-HugoR**

Letter to Birch from Deer Lodge. Richard Hugo. **CP-HugoR**

Letter to Blessing from Missoula. Richard Hugo. **CP-HugoR**

Letter to Bly from La Push. Richard Hugo. **CP-HugoR**

Letter to comfort a friend. Jenny Joseph. *Fr.* Life and Turgid Times of A. Citizen. **SP-JoseJ**

Letter to Curtis Bradford, A. Donald Davie. **CP-DavDo**

Letter to Doctor Ingelo, A. Andrew Marvell, *tr. fr. Latin by* William A. McQueen *and* Kiffin A. Rockwell. **CP-MarvA**

Letter to Eamonn Wall, A. James Liddy. **CP-LiddJ**

Letter to Francis Picabia, A. Kay Boyle. **CP-BoylK**

Letter to Gale from Ovando. Richard Hugo. **CP-HugoR**

Letter to Garber from Skye. Richard Hugo. **CP-HugoR**

Letter to Gildner from Wallace. Richard Hugo. **CP-HugoR**

Letter to Goldbarth from Big Fork. Richard Hugo. **CP-HugoR**

Letter to Graham and Anna. Louis MacNeice. **CP-MacNL**

Letter to Haislip from Hot Springs. Richard Hugo. **CP-HugoR**

Letter to Hanson from Miami. Richard Hugo. **CP-HugoR**

Letter to Her. Robert Bly. **SP-BlyR**

Letter to Her Husband, Absent upon Public[k] Employment, A. Anne Bradstreet. **CP-BradA**

Letter to Hill from St. Ignatius. Richard Hugo. **CP-HugoR**

Letter to His Brother. John Berryman. **CP-BerrJ**

Letter to James Stephens, A. May Sarton. **SP-SartM**

Letter to J——s T——t, Gl—nc——r. Robert Burns. **CP-BurnR**

Letter to Jeffrey Gustavson. Martin Edmunds. **SP-EdmuM**

Letter to John Fuller. James Fenton. **SP-FentJ**

Letter to Kathy from Wisdom. Richard Hugo. **CP-HugoR**

Letter to Kizer from Seattle. Richard Hugo. **CP-HugoR**

Letter to Levertov from Butte. Richard Hugo. **CP-HugoR**

Letter to Libbey from St. Regis. Richard Hugo. **CP-HugoR**

Letter to Logan from Milltown. Richard Hugo. **CP-HugoR**

Letter to Lord Byron. Wystan Hugh Auden. **CP-AudeW**

  "England, my England--you have been my tutrix." **OBSV**

  "I like your muse because she's gay and witty." **NOBL**

  "Now for the spirit of the people. Here." **FaBoPV**

  "Ottava Rima would, I know, be proper." **NOBL**

  "Thought of writing came to me today, The." **NOBL**

  "You lived and moved among the best society." **OBSV**

Letter to Lucy Larcom. John Greenleaf Whittier. **CP-WhitJ**

Letter to Mantsch from Havre. Richard Hugo. **CP-HugoR**

Letter to Maria Gisborne. Percy Bysshe Shelley. **CP-ShelP**

  To Maria Gisborne in England, from Italy. **NOBE**

  "You are now / In London, that great sea." **ChER; EBEV; OBRV**

  "You will see Coleridge, he who sits obscure." **EPCY**

Letter to Matthews from Barton Street Flats. Richard Hugo. **CP-HugoR**

Letter to Maxine Sullivan. Hayden Carruth. **CP-CarHS**

Letter to Mayo from Missoula. Richard Hugo. **CP-HugoR**

Letter to Mr. Clapcott sir you sonofabitch you notice we have now cut down your coconut trees. Dialog with Mister Clapcott. Thomas Merton. *Fr.* East. *Fr.* The Geography of Lograire. **CP-MertT**

Letter to My Friends, A. Thomas Merton. **CP-MertT**

Letter to My Lover after Seven Years. Erica Jong. **SP-JongE**

Letter to My Widow. Robert Pack. **SP-PackR**

Letter to N. Y. Elizabeth Bishop. **CP-BishE**

Letter to Oberg from Pony. Richard Hugo. **CP-HugoR**

Letter to One Who Has Abandoned The Way. Thomas Merton. *Fr.* Readings from Ibn Abbad. **CP-MertT**

Letter to Pablo Antonio Cuadra Concerning Giants, A. Thomas Merton. **CP-MertT**

Letter to Peter Wilkins. Siv Cedering Fox. **SP-CedeS**

Letter to Peterson from the Pike Place Market. Richard Hugo. **CP-HugoR**

Letter to Pierre Emmanuel. Kathleen Jessie Raine. **SP-RainK**

Letter to Reed from Lolo. Richard Hugo. **CP-HugoR**

Letter to Richard Hugo From Drumcliff. James McAuley. **SP-McAuJ**

Letter to Sainte-Beuve. James Liddy. **CP-LiddJ**

Letter to Sara Hutchinson. Samuel Taylor Coleridge. **CP-ColeS**

Letter to Scanlon from Whitehall. Richard Hugo. **CP-HugoR**

Letter to Simic from Boulder. Richard Hugo. **CP-HugoR**

Letter to Sister Madeline from Iowa City. Richard Hugo. **CP-HugoR**

Letter to Snyder from Montana. Richard Hugo. **CP-HugoR**

Letter to Stafford from Polson. Richard Hugo. **CP-HugoR**

Letter to the Countess of Denbigh. Richard Crashaw. *See* What heaven-entreated [or heaven-besiegèd or heav'n-beseiged] heart is this?

Letter to the Denouncers, A. Edwin Rolfe. **CP-RolfE**

Letter to the Front. Muriel Rukeyser. **CP-RukeM**

  "Among all the waste there are the intense stories."

  "Even during war, moments of delicate peace." **TrJP**

  "Evening, bringing me out of the government building."

  "Home thoughts from home; we read you every day."

  "Much later, I lie in a white seaport night."

  Sestina: "Coming to Spain on the first day of the fighting."

  "Surely it is time for the true grace of women."

  "They called us to a change of heart."

  "To be a Jew in the twentieth century." **NALW; TrJP**

  "Women and poets see the truth arrive."

Letter to the Inventors of a Tradition, A. Kenneth Patchen. **CP-PatcK**

Letter to the Lady Carey, and Mistress Essex Rich, from Amiens, A. John Donne. **CP-DonnJ**

Letter to the Liberals, A. Kenneth Patchen. **CP-PatcK**

Letter to the Old Men. Kenneth Patchen. **CP-PatcK**

Letter to the Patrol Twenty Years After. Leonard Nathan. **SP-NathL**

Letter to the Reverend Dr. Sheridan, A. Jonathan Swift. **SP-SwifJ**

Letter to the Young Men, A. Kenneth Patchen. **CP-PatcK**

Letter to Those Who Are About to Die. Kenneth Patchen. **CP-PatcK**

Letter to Vincent. Phoebe Hesketh. **SP-HeskP**

Letter to Wagoner from Port Townsend. Richard Hugo. **CP-HugoR**

Letter to Welch from Browning. Richard Hugo. **CP-HugoR**

Letter to W.H. Auden, A. Daniel Gerard Hoffman. **SP-HoffD**

Letter to William Carlos Williams, A. Kenneth Rexroth. **SP-RexrK**

Letter to William Frohock. Daniel Gerard Hoffman. **SP-HoffD**

Letter to William Kinter of Muhlenberg, A. Denise Levertov. **CP-LeveD**

Letter to Wright from Gooseprairie. Richard Hugo. **CP-HugoR**

Letter, Unposted. Muriel Rukeyser. **CP-RukeM**

Letter Written by Sir H. G. and J. D. alternis vicibus, A. John Donne. **CP-DonnJ**

Letter Written During a January Northeaster. Anne Sexton. **CP-SextA**

Letter Written on a Ferry While Crossing Long Island Sound. Anne Sexton. **CP-SextA**

Lettered Snow, The. John Hewitt. **CP-HewiJ**

Letters. Jane Cooper. **SP-CoopJ**

Letters ("My tongue is prone to lose the way"). Ralph Waldo Emerson. **CP-EmerR**

Letters. ("Every day brings. . ."). Ralph Waldo Emerson. **CP-EmerR**

Letters, The. Louise Glück. **SP-GlücL**

Letters always just evade the hand, The. Mail Call. Randall Jarrell. **CP-JarrR**

Letters ask, The. Notes from India. May Sarton. **SP-SartM**

Letters come, the phone rings, you sit by your window. Holding Out. Jane Cooper. **SP-CoopJ**

Letters for the Dead. Philip Levine. **SP-LeviP**

Letters from a Father. Mona Van Duyn. **SP-VanDM**

Letters from Amherst. Charles Tomlinson. **CP-TomlC**

Letters from the Astronomers. Siv Cedering Fox. **SP-CedeS**

  Albert Einstein (1879–1955).

  Caroline Herschel (1750–1848).

  Galileo Galilei (1564–1642).

  Johannes Kepler (1571–1630).

  Nicholas Copernicus (1473–1543).

Letters from the Island. Siv Cedering Fox. **SP-CedeS**

Letters from Vicksburg. Gary Gildner. **SP-GildG**

  "Dear and most Loved wife it is with pleasure."

  "Dear and Mutch Loved One with pleasure I take."

  "Dear Cecelia we hav hat some warm times."

  "Dear Cecelia well its shel and shel and."

  "Dear loved one did I mention General Grants."

  "Dear loved one well the last 2 days I spent."

  "Dear wife and bosom friend I hat seen had."

  "Dear wife and friend I dozed but now will try."

  "Dear wife and friend I hav not mutch to write."

  "Dear wife I feal prety rested now."

  "Dear woman I again take pen in hand."

  "Dear woman I am sor a littel bit."

  "Dear woman I am well and hope you ar."

  "Dear woman I was glat to hear from you."

  "I went with General Logans men and we."

  "Mrs. Blood. Dear Madam. Yours of Sept. 13."

  "Some boys ar playing cards but I dont feal."

  "We left the River seven days ago."

Letters: March 1969. Adrienne Rich. **CP-RicAE; SP-RicA2**

Letters of the Jews as strict as flames, The. The Alphabet. Karl Shapiro. **SP-ShapK**

Letters she left to clutter up the desk. A Gesture by a Lady with an Assumed Name. James Wright. **CP-WrigJ**

Letters to a corridor: "Put the whole family out into the hall." Thomas Merton. *Fr.* Cables to the Ace. **CP-MertT**

Letters to Che: Canto Bilingue. Thomas Merton. **CP-MertT**

Letters to Dead Imagists. Carl Sandburg. **CP-SandC**

Letters to Dr. Y. Anne Sexton. **CP-SextA**

Letters to the Vatican. "Lou Reed." **SP-ReedL**

Letter's Triumph, The. Thomas Hardy. **CP-HardT**

Letting go / in order to hold on. How Poems Are Made: A Discredited View. Alice Walker. **CP-WalkA**

Letting Go. Richard Shelton. **SP-ShelR**

Letting his wisdom be the whole of love. The World and the Child. James Merrill. **SP-MerrJ**

Letting in the Jungle. Rudyard Kipling. *Fr.* The Second Jungle Book.
  Morning Song in the Jungle. **CP-KiplR**
  Mowgli's Song against People. **CP-KiplR**
  "Veil them, cover them, wall them round." **CP-KiplR**
Letting midnight / out on bail. Jam Session. Langston Hughes. **SP-HughL**
Letting the eye descend from reeking stack. A Glance from the Bridge.
  Richard Wilbur. **CP-WilbR**
Letting the mind go. Zen & the Art of Poetry. Erica Jong. **SP-JongE**
Letting the Puma Go. Stephen Dunn. **SP-DunnS**
Lettuce long bolted to exotic, The. Fall Squashes. Brendan Galvin. **SP-GalvB**
Level mind in crooked times, A. Aequam Memento. Horace. *Fr.* Three
  Odes of Horace. **CP-MacNL**
Leveling of the water, its increase, The. The Winter Rain. Wendell Berry.
  CP-BerrW
Levelled Churchyard, The. Thomas Hardy. **CP-HardT**
Leven. Robert Herrick. **CP-HerrR**
Leviathan. John Milton. **AmMo** *Fr.* Book VII. *Fr.* Paradise Lost. **CP-MiltJ**
Leviathan. Frederick Morgan. *Fr.* Eight Triolets. **SP-MorgF**
Leviathan. George Oppen. **CP-OppeG**
Leviathan. Robert Pack. **SP-PackR**
Leviathan. Lewis Turco. **SP-TurcL**
Leviathan swam on the brimming deep. Leviathan. Frederick Morgan. *Fr.*
  Eight Triolets. **SP-MorgF**
Levite and the Samaritan, The. John Gould Fletcher. **SP-FletJ** *Fr.* The
  Parables of Antichrist.
Levity. Donald Davie. **CP-DavDo**
Lew Welch just turned up one day. For/From Lew. Gary Snyder. **CP-SnydG**
Lewd Love Is Loss[e]. Robert Southwell. **CP-SoutR**
"Lewiston Is a Pleasant Place." Marsden Hartley. **CP-HartM**
Lewti. Samuel Taylor Coleridge. **CP-ColeS**
Lexicon ad finem longo luctamine tandem. Gnothi Seauton (Post Lexicon
  Anglicanum Auctum et Emendatum). Samuel Johnson. **CP-JohnS**
Lexington. John Greenleaf Whittier. **CP-WhitJ**
L'Homme et La Bête. Philip Levine. **SP-LeviP**
Li Po. Charles Olson. **CP-OlsoC**
Liadan and Curithir. Robert Ranke Graves. **CP-GravR**
Liaison. David Herbert Lawrence. **CP-LawrD**
Liar, The. John Donne. **CP-DonnJ**
Liar goes in fine clothes, A. The Liars. Carl Sandburg. **CP-SandC**
Liars, The. Carl Sandburg. **CP-SandC**
'Lias! 'Lias! Bless de Lawd! In the Morning. Paul Laurence Dunbar. **CP-DunbP**
Libel on the Reverend Dr. Delany and His Excellency John, Lord Carteret.
  Jonathan Swift. **CP-SwifJ**
Libel Summons. Robert Burns. **CP-BurnR**
Liber, of all thy friends, thou sweetest care. Epigramma Martialis. Lib. VIII.
  lxxvii. The Same Translated. Ben Jonson, *tr. fr. the Latin of* Martial.
  CP-JonsB
Liberation. Louise Glück. **SP-GlücL**
Liberator, The. Derek Walcott. **CP-WalcD**
Liberator Explodes, The. James Dickey. **CP-DickJ**
Libertad! Igualdad! Fraternidad! William Carlos Williams. **CP-WilW1**
Libertas & natale solum. Whitshed's Motto on His Coach. Jonathan Swift.
  CP-SwifJ
Libertine, The. Louis MacNeice. **CP-MacNL**
Liberty. Charles Bukowski. **SP-BukC1**
Liberty. Robert Herrick. **CP-HerrR**
Liberty. Archibald MacLeish. **CP-MacLA**
Liberty. Percy Bysshe Shelley. **CP-ShelP**
Liberty. James Thomson. **CP-ThomJ**
  Ancient and Modern Italy Compared.
  Britain.
  Greece.
  Prospect, The.
  Rome.
Liberty. William Wordsworth. **CP-WorW2**
  "Beetle loves his unpretending track, The." **FaBoCo; FiBHP; Par**
Liberty's Old Old Story. David Herbert Lawrence. **CP-LawrD**
Librarian, The. Charles Olson. **CP-OlsoC; SP-OlsoC**
Libraries are bulged and ballasted, The. Survival. John Hewitt. **CP-HewiJ**
Library, The. John Greenleaf Whittier. **CP-WhitJ**
License plate was another state and year, The. Mecanic on Duty at All
  Times. Miller Williams. **SP-WillM**
License to Kill. "Bob Dylan." **CP-DylaB**

Licentious Person, A. John Donne. **CP-DonnJ**
Lichen and liverwort. Hayden Carruth. *Fr.* North Winter. **CP-CarHL**
Lichen is a hardy plant. Hayden Carruth. *Fr.* North Winter. **CP-CarHL**
Lichtenberg. Rudyard Kipling. **CP-KiplR**
Licorice Fields at Pontefract, The. Sir John Betjeman. **CP-BetjJ**
Lictor or heavy slave would wear it best. Julian the Apostate. Thom
  Gunn. **CP-GunnT**
Lictors bundl'd up their rods: beside, The. Cunctation in Correction. Robert
  Herrick. **CP-HerrR**
Lid, The. John Gould Fletcher. **SP-FletJ**
Liddell and Scott. Thomas Hardy. **CP-HardT**
Liddell, the Oxford lexicographer. The Fourth of July. Richard Wilbur.
  CP-WilbR
Lie, The. Maya Angelou. **SP-AngeM**
Lie, The. Sir Walter Ralegh. **CP-RaleW**
Lie, The. Anne Waldman. **SP-WaldA**
Lie a-bed, / Sleepy head, / Shut up eyes, bo-peep. Christina Georgina
  Rossetti. **CP-RosC2**
Lie down and rest—the fight is done. Rodric Lesley. 1830. Emily Brontë.
  CP-BronE
Lie here, without a record of thy worth. Tribute to the Memory of the Same
  Dog. William Wordsworth. **CP-WorW1**
Lie in bed and watch the night. At Darragh's I. James Schuyler. **CP-SchuJ**
Lie of 10, or the Concept of Zero, The. Charles Olson. **CP-OlsoC**
Lie shone in her face before she spoke it, The. Nike. James Merrill. **SP-MerrJ**
Lie still, be still, love, be thou not shaken. Song, the Brain-Coral. Muriel
  Rukeyser. **CP-RukeM**
Lie still, my restive heart, lie still. What Is That to Thee? Follow Thou
  Me. Christina Georgina Rossetti. **CP-RosC2**
Lie Still, Sleep Becalmed. Dylan Thomas. **CP-ThomD**
Lie, that we come from water, A. Landcrab I. Margaret Atwood. **SP-AtwM2**
Lie there, in sweat and dream, I do, and "there." What I See. Muriel
  Rukeyser. **CP-RukeM**
Liebe Frau Emma. Elegy. Wystan Hugh Auden. *Fr.* Eleven Occasional
  Poems. **CP-AudeW**
Liebe, meine liebe, I had not hoped. If It Were Not for You. Hayden
  Carruth. **CP-CarHS**
Liebestod. Charles Tomlinson. *Fr.* Three Wagnerian Lyrics. **CP-TomlC**
Lied von Castelli. George Meredith. **CP-MerG2**
Lief Ericson crossed the sea. Lief the Lucky. Carl Sandburg. **CP-SandC**
Lief the Lucky. Carl Sandburg. **CP-SandC**
Lies. David Herbert Lawrence. **CP-LawrD**
Lies About Love. David Herbert Lawrence. **CP-LawrD**
Lies on the same couch that he used to. My Father. Ron Koertge. **SP-KoerR**
Lieutenant ordered me to ask Abdhul, The. The Sorrow of Obedience. John
  Ciardi. **SP-CiarJ**
Life. Elizabeth Barrett Browning. **CP-BroEB**
Life. Samuel Taylor Coleridge. **CP-ColeS**
Life. Walter de la Mare. **CP-DeLaW**
Life. Paul Laurence Dunbar. **CP-DunbP**
Life. Ralph Waldo Emerson. **CP-EmerR**
Life. John Gould Fletcher. **SP-FletJ**
Life. George Herbert. **CP-HerbG**
Life. Juan Ramón Jiménez. *Fr.* Ten Short Poems. **CP-WrigJ**
"Life? / Listen"the feline she with radishred. Marj. Edward Estlin
  Cummings. *Fr.* Five Americans. **CP-CummE**
Life. Henry Wadsworth Longfellow. **GN** *Fr.* A Psalm of Life. **SP-LongH**
Life, A. Howard Nemerov. **CP-NemeH**
Life. Grace Paley. **CP-PaleG**
Life, A. Sylvia Plath. **CP-PlatS**
Life / shuts &)opens the world. Edward Estlin Cummings. **CP-CummE**
Life. Walt Whitman. **CP-WhitW**
Life, The. James Wright. **CP-WrigJ**
Life Again. John Keats. **SeCePo** *Fr.* Endymion: Poetic Romance. **CP-KeatJ**
Life ahead, life behind—. Marsden Hartley. **CP-HartM**
Life and Death. Richard Eberhart. **CP-EberR**
Life and Death. Christina Georgina Rossetti. **CP-RosC1**
Life and Death. Walt Whitman. **CP-WhitW**
Life, and Death, and Giants. Emily Dickinson. **CP-DickE**
Life and Death at Sunrise. Thomas Hardy. **CP-HardT**
Life & Death in Skokie. Gary Gildner. **SP-GildG**
Life and Genuine Character of Dr Swift, The. Jonathan Swift. **CP-SwifJ**

From The Life and Character of Dean Swift. **NOBL**

Life and Letters. Adrienne Rich. **CP-RicAE**

Life and Love. Elizabeth Barrett Browning. **CP-BroEB**

Life and the Human Consciousness. David Herbert Lawrence. **CP-LawrD**

Life and Thought. Matthew Arnold. **FiP** *Fr.* Empedocles on Etna. **SP-ArnoM**

Life and Turgid Times of A. Citizen. Jenny Joseph. **SP-JoseJ**

　But they could *do* something about that.

　Butcher's.

　Chorale.

　Chrysanth.

　Going to Sylvie's.

　High life.

　If you can't join them beat them.

　Inverts.

　Just a snack for lunch.

　Letter to comfort a friend.

　Little dots.

　Modern witches 1: crouching.

　Modern witches 2: sentinels.

　Moon in the morning.

　Not able to resist the spring.

　Patient old cripple, A.

　PROEM: *Against metaphor—but how then?.*

　Subscription.

　Sunripe.

　There are more accidents in the home than on the roads.

　This day our daily. . . .

　Tripping down.

　Visiting.

　Waking.

Life as Visionary Spirit. Richard Eberhart. **CP-EberR**

Life at the Back of the Plane. Al Young. **CP-YounA**

Life at War. Denise Levertov. **CP-LeveD**

Life boosts herself rapidly at me. Edward Estlin Cummings. **CP-CummE**

Life contracts and death is expected. The Death of a Soldier. Wallace Stevens. **CP-StevW**

Life Cycle of Common Man. Howard Nemerov. **CP-NemeH**

Life deflowers itself / petal by petal. Deflowering. Lawrence Ferlinghetti. **SP-FerlL**

Life Doesn't Frighten Me. Maya Angelou. **SP-AngeM**

Life Encompassed. Donald Davie. **CP-DavDo**

Life flows down to death; we cannot bind. An "Immurata" Sister. Christina Georgina Rossetti. **CP-RosC2**

Life for My Child is Simple, and Is Good. Gwendolyn Brooks. **SP-BrooG** *Fr.* The Womanhood.

Life-Force. Louise McNeill. **SP-McNeL**

Life from the Lifeless. Robinson Jeffers. **CP-JefR2**

Life goes on. The Truth of the Matter. John Gould Fletcher. **SP-FletJ**

Life Hidden. Christina Georgina Rossetti. **CP-RosC3**

Life hurl my. Edward Estlin Cummings. **CP-CummE**

Life I have led, The. In the 51st State. Ted Berrigan. **SP-BerrT**

Life in a day: he took his girl to the ballet. Les Sylphides. Louis MacNeice. **BoLoP; CoBMV** *Fr.* Novelettes. **CP-MacNL**

Life in a Love. Robert Browning. **CP-BroR1**

Life in Death. Samuel Taylor Coleridge. **CP-ColeS**

Life in its brief episodes. Austere Poem. Richard Eberhart. **CP-EberR**

Life is a bitter aspic. We are not. Wallace Stevens. **CMoP** *Fr.* Esthétique du Mal. **CP-StevW**

Life is a flame (he said). Maitreya. Frederick Morgan. **SP-MorgF**

Life is But Losse. Robert Southwell. **CP-SoutR**

Life is death we're lengthy at. Emily Dickinson. **SP-DickE**

Life Is Fine. Langston Hughes. **SP-HughL**

Life is fleeting, joy is fleeting. The Time of Waiting. Christina Georgina Rossetti. **CP-RosC3**

Life is forever turning toward a man an infinitely vacant. Unfinished Double Sonnet. Stephen Berg. **SP-BergS**

Life is funny. Peograms. Charles Olson. **CP-OlsoC**

Life is great / Men are small. Ralph Waldo Emerson. **CP-EmerR**

Life is just a bowl of cherries. Guaranteed Antique. Carl Sandburg. **CP-SandC**

Life Is Like a Game of Cards, Or Another One of Those Metaphysical Statements from a Distant Reader. Diane Wakoski. **SP-WakoD**

Life is more true than reason will deceive. Edward Estlin Cummings. **CP-CummE**

Life Is Motion. Wallace Stevens. **CP-StevW**

Life is not at all what you might think it to be. Some Words. John Ashbery. **SP-AshbJ**

Life is not sweet. One day it will be sweet. Life and Death. Christina Georgina Rossetti. **CP-RosC1**

Life is nothing without religion. Religion. David Herbert Lawrence. **CP-LawrD**

'Life is over and you are its. They, to Me. Donald Davie. **CP-DavDo**

Life is so strong a vision. Emily Dickinson. **SP-DickE**

Life Is the Body's [*or* Bodies] Light. Robert Herrick. **CP-HerrR**

Life is the finest secret. Emily Dickinson. **SP-DickE**

Life is the story of a body, you say. Dialectic. Charles Tomlinson. **CP-TomlC**

Life Is Trying to Be Life. Ted Hughes. **SP-HughT**

Life—is what we make it. Emily Dickinson. **CP-DickE**

Life is your privilege, not your belonging. Forty Years. Wendell Berry. **CP-BerrW**

Life itself like championship chess. Deep Chess. Lawrence Ferlinghetti. **SP-FerlL**

Life Laughs Onward. Thomas Hardy. **CP-HardT**

Life limited his scope to this small plot. Epitaph for a Gardener. John Hewitt. **CP-HewiJ**

Life longs to a perfection it never achieves. The Supreme Authority of the Imagination. Richard Eberhart. **CP-EberR**

Life may change, but it may fly not. Percy Bysshe Shelley. **EnRP** *Fr.* Hellas. **CP-ShelP**

Life Moving More Rapidly Than Hands Can Manage. William Dickey. **SP-DickW**

Life ne'er exulted in so rich a prize. A Fragment, Which Was Meant for the Beginning of an Elegy on the Late Miss Burnet of Monboddo. Robert Burns. **CP-BurnR**

Life Notes. Tom Clark. **SP-ClarT**

Life of a Nun. Alexander Pope. *See* The Vestal.

Life of hope deferred too often is, A. Redeeming the Time. Christina Georgina Rossetti. **CP-RosC2**

Life of Life. Percy Bysshe Shelley. **CH; FiP; MeMBP; NOBE; PoE; PoEL-4** *Fr.* Prometheus Unbound. **CP-ShelP**

　(Hymn to the Spirit of Nature.) **GTBS; GTBS-6; GTBS-P**

Life of my life, take not so soon thy flight. To His Dying Brother, Master William Herrick. Robert Herrick. **CP-HerrR**

Life of plants, The. To-night at Seven-thirty. Wystan Hugh Auden. *Fr.* Thanksgiving for a Habitat. **CP-AudeW**

Life of Service, The. Donald Davie. **CP-DavDo**

Life of the Otter, The. Thom Gunn. **CP-GunnT**

Life of the Party, The. Ogden Nash. **CP-NashO**

Life of the Wolf, The. Gary Gildner. **SP-GildG**

Life of the world depends on that he is. The. Wild Ducks, People and Distances. Wallace Stevens. **CP-StevW**

Life on the Edge of the Continent. Ron Koertge. **SP-KoerR**

Life Out of Death. Christina Georgina Rossetti. **CP-RosC3**

Life relinquishing, by life relinquished. The Burial. Archibald MacLeish. **CP-MacLA**

Life spent seeking it, A. High Quality Information. Gary Snyder. **CP-SnydG**

Life stood on the top stair a moment. Resurgam. Allen Tate. **CP-TateA**

Life that tied too tight escapes, The. Emily Dickinson. **CP-DickE**

Life that was born today / Must make no stay. Christina Georgina Rossetti. **CP-RosC2**

Life there was is, The. In Waking. Robert Duncan. **SP-DuncR**

Life Transcendent. Nicholas Vachel Lindsay. **CP-LindV**

Life wakeful over all knew no gradation. Unity with Nature. Samuel Taylor Coleridge. **CP-ColeS**

Life was Greek before Greeks came. The swamp. Paestum. Richard Hugo. **CP-HugoR**

Life was mine full of the close concern, A. Love. Paul Laurence Dunbar. **CP-DunbP**

Life we have is very great, The. Emily Dickinson. **CP-DickE**

Life, were thy pains as are the pains of hell. Edna St. Vincent Millay. **CP-MillE**

Life with a Hole in It, The. Philip Larkin. **CP-LarkP**

Life with yon Lambs, like day, is just begun. Composed on a May Morning. William Wordsworth. **CP-WorW2**

Life without location—, A. Without Location. Roy Fisher. **SP-FishR**

Life without Passion, The. William Shakespeare. *See* Sonnet 94: "They that have power to hurt[e], and will do[e] none."

Lifeguard, The. James Dickey. **CP-DickJ**

Lifeguard's whistle organized our swimming, The. The River. Dabney Stuart. **SP-StuaD**

Lifelong ago such days. Kathleen Jessie Raine. **SP-RainK**

Lifelong our stumbles, lifelong our regret. Christina Georgina Rossetti. *Fr.* Later Life: A Double Sonnet of Sonnets. **CP-RosC2**

Lifelong the way—. Binah. Kathleen Jessie Raine. **SP-RainK**

Lifelong to be / Seemed the fair colour of the time. The Musical Box. Thomas Hardy. **CP-HardT**

Lifers file into the hall, The. In the Cage. Robert Lowell. **SP-LoweR**

Life's a jail where men have common lot. The Gamblers. Nicholas Vachel Lindsay. **CP-LindV**

Life's all getting and giving. The Wishing-Caps. Rudyard Kipling. **CP-KiplR** *Fr.* Kim.

Life's buried treasure's buried deeper still. Elderly Sex. John Updike. **CP-UpdiJ**

Life's Death, Love's Life. Robert Southwell. **CP-SoutR**

Life's Handicap, *sels.* Rudyard Kipling.
  At the End of the Passage.
    "Sky is lead, and our faces are red, The." **CP-KiplR**
  Courting of Dinah Shadd, The.
    Private Ortheris's Song. **CP-KiplR**
  Head of the District, The.
    "There's a convict more in the Central Jail." **CP-KiplR**
  Man Who Was, The.
    "Earth gave up her dead that tide, The." **CP-KiplR**
  My New-Cut Ashlar. **CP-KiplR**
  Return of Imray, The.
    "Doors were wide, the story saith, The." **CP-KiplR**
  Without Benefit of Clergy.
    "Before my Spring I garnered Autumn's gain." **CP-KiplR**

Life's Last Scene. Samuel Johnson. **OBEC; SeCePo** *Fr.* The Vanity of Human Wishes [The Tenth Satire of Juvenal Imitated]. **CP-JohnS**

Life's norm is lost: no doubt it is put away with Plato's. What of It? Robinson Jeffers. **CP-JefR3**

Life's Parallels, A. Christina Georgina Rossetti. **CP-RosC2**

Life's Poor Play. Alexander Pope. **OBEC; SeCePo** *Fr.* An Essay on Man. **CP-PopeA**

Life's Rendezvous. Countee Cullen. **CP-CullC**

Life's Tragedy. Paul Laurence Dunbar. **CP-DunbP**

Lifetime is for two. Emily Dickinson. **SP-DickE**

Lift again the stately emblem on the Bay State's rusted shield. The Pine-Tree. John Greenleaf Whittier. **CP-WhitJ**

Lift it—with the Feathers. Emily Dickinson. **CP-DickE**

Lift me, God, from the Self's diurnal fussing. Late Afternoon, Running: Close Reasoning, Listening Closely. James McAuley. **SP-McAuJ**

Lift my head, help me up. Euripides, *tr. by* Hilda Doolittle ("H.D."). **CP-DoolH** *Fr.* Hippolytus.

Lift not the painted veil which those who live. Sonnet. Percy Bysshe Shelley. **CP-ShelP**

Lift through the Breaking Day. Philip Larkin. **CP-LarkP**

Lift to the spirit, when everything fell into place!, A. Cheshire. Donald Davie. **CP-DavDo**

Lift up thine eyes to seek the invisible. Christina Georgina Rossetti. **CP-RosC2**

Lift up Thy little lips. The Nameless Speaks. Marsden Hartley. **CP-HartM**

Lift up to heav'n, sad wretch, thy heavy spright. Thomas Campion. **CP-CampT**

Lift up your eyes on high. Erige Cor Tuum ad Me in Caelum. Hilda Doolittle. **CP-DoolH**

Lift Up Your Heads. Bible, *O.T. See* Psalm 24: "Earth is the Lord's and the fulness thereof, The."

"Lift up your hearts." "We lift them up."Ah me! Sursum Corda. Christina Georgina Rossetti. **CP-RosC2**

Lift your flowers. Chicory and Daisies. William Carlos Williams. **CP-WilW1**

Lifting, The. John Hewitt. **CP-HewiJ**

Lifting Belly. Gertrude Stein. **CP-SteiG**

Lifting his arms, the man half swims. Night Swimmer. Stephen Dobyns. **SP-DobyS**

Lifting Illegal Nets by Flashlight. James Wright. **CP-WrigJ**

Lifting my coffee cup, I notice a caterpillar crawling. A Caterpillar. Robert Bly. **SP-BlyR**

Lifting the thunder of their acclamation. Percy Bysshe Shelley. **ChER** *Fr.* The Revolt of Islam. **CP-ShelP**

Lifts heavily / and cloud and sea. The Sun. William Carlos Williams. **CP-WilW1**

Light, The. Wendell Berry. *Fr.* The Handing Down. **CP-BerrW**

Light, The. Paul Laurence Dunbar. **CP-DunbP**

Light, The. Lawrence Ferlinghetti. **SP-FerlL**

Light / Light / The sliver in the firmament. Kenneth Rexroth. **SP-RexrK** *Fr.* In those days / In a pool of noise. **CP-RexKL** *Fr.* A Prolegomenon to a Theodicy.

Light. Louise McNeill. **SP-McNeL**

Light. John Milton. *See* Hail holy Light, ofspring [*or* offspring] of Heav'n [*or* Heaven] first-born.

Light / Of the closed pages, tightly closed, packed against each other, The. George Oppen. *Fr.* Of Being Numerous. **CP-OppeG**

Light. Allen Tate. **CP-TateA**

Light. Diane Wakoski. *Fr.* Fifteen Poems for a Lunar Eclipse None of Us Saw. **SP-WakoD**

Light. Louis Zukofsky. **CP-ZukLS**

Light, a form, a / shadow at the edge of the window, a. Medallion. Robert Creeley. **CP-CreeR**

Light, a winged, & a holy thing, A. The Poet at Forty. Howard Nemerov. **CP-NemeH**

Light and diplomatic bird, A. Gwendolyn Brooks. **SP-BrooG** *Fr.* The Womanhood.

Light and Glory of the World, The. William Cowper. *Fr.* Olney Hymns. **CP-CowpW**

Light and Moonbells. Carl Sandburg. **CP-SandC**

Light and shade, E green, I blue, U purple and yellow, O red, A. The Vowels. John Gould Fletcher. **SP-FletJ**

Light and Shadow. "Hugh MacDiarmid." **SP-MacDH**

Light & Shadow. Anne Waldman. **SP-WaldA**

Light as a skiff, manoeuvrable. Wolfe Tone. Seamus Heaney. **SP-HeanS**

Light as motion, people flit lightly along. Incantation. Anne Waldman. **SP-WaldA**

Light as my heart was long ago. Robert Louis Stevenson. **CP-StevR**

Light as the Breeze. Leonard Cohen. **CP-CoheL**

Light as the linnet on my way I start. Robert Louis Stevenson. **CP-StevR**

Light as thin-winged swallows pirouetting and gyrating. Sailboats. John Gould Fletcher. **SP-FletJ** *Fr.* Sand and Spray: A Sea-Symphony. **SP-FletJ**

Light at a window. Someone up. White Night. Adrienne Rich. **SP-RicA2**

Light Baggage. Alice Walker. **CP-WalkA**

Light bangs empty barracks where. At Cronkhite. Richard Hugo. **CP-HugoR**

Light beats upon me, The. Mid-day. Hilda Doolittle. **CP-DoolH**

Light Becomes Darkness. William Carlos Williams. **CP-WilW1**

Light beyond compare is the light I saw, The. The Incomparable Light. Richard Eberhart. **CP-EberR**

Light Blue Above. James Schuyler. **CP-SchuJ**

LIght blue above, darker below, lightly roughened by the stirring air. Light Blue Above. James Schuyler. **CP-SchuJ**

Light Breaks Where No Sun Shines. Dylan Thomas. **CP-ThomD**

Light Breather, A. Theodore Roethke. **CP-RoetT**

Light Brown. Charles Bukowski. **SP-BukC1**

Light burns through blood. Through Closed Eyes. Charles Tomlinson. **CP-TomlC**

Light by the Barn, The. William Stafford. **SP-StafW**

Light catches the sudden metal of the streams. Couplet. Charles Tomlinson. **CP-TomlC**

Light   clarity   avocado salad in the morning. Poem. Frank O'Hara. **SP-OharF**

Light-Colonel Trinkett, you there. Citation on Retirement. John Ciardi. **SP-CiarJ**

Light colourless doth colour all things else. Truly the Light Is Sweet. Christina Georgina Rossetti. **CP-RosC2**

Light come from my head, A. The Island. James Dickey. **CP-DickJ**

Light comes back with Columbine,; she brings, The. Edna St. Vincent Millay. **CP-MillE**

Light Comes Brighter, The. Theodore Roethke. **CP-RoetT**

Light crawls timid over fields. Dixon. Richard Hugo. **CP-HugoR**

Light cursed falling in a singular block. Edward Estlin Cummings. **CP-CummE**

Light exists in Spring, A. Emily Dickinson. **CP-DickE**

Light eyes would have been more fortunate. The Interview. Robert Creeley. **CP-CreeR**

Light fails, in crossing a river. Awaiting the Swimmer. James Dickey. **CP-DickJ**

Light falling on that filled will drives. Muriel Rukeyser. **CP-RukeM**

Light Fantastic Round, A. John Milton. *See* The Star That Bids the Shepherd Fold.

Light flares from the tombstones. . . . Poem. Thomas McGrath. **SP-McGrT**

Light flower leaves its little core, The. The Changed Woman. Louise Bogan. **CP-BogaL**

Light flows our war of mocking words, and yet. The Buried Life. Matthew Arnold. **SP-ArnoM**

Light foot and tight foot. Song. Robert Louis Stevenson. **CP-StevR**

Light foot hears you and the brightness begins, The. A Poem Beginning with a Line by Pindar. Robert Duncan. **SP-DuncR**

Light From Above. Richard Eberhart. **CP-EberR**

Light from Canada. James Schuyler. **CP-SchuJ**

Light from Fundy. Brendan Galvin. **SP-GalvB**

Light from the planet Venus, soon to set. Evening-Star. Louise Bogan. **CP-BogaL**

Light from the river brightens your old room. Beaverbank. Richard Hugo. **CP-HugoR**

Light goes: that once powerful sun, The. The Dusk. William Everson. **SP-EverW**

Light going out in the forehead, A. Swimming by Night. James Merrill. **SP-MerrJ**

Light Hearted William. William Carlos Williams. **CP-WilW1**

Light-Heavy at Prayer. Marsden Hartley. **CP-HartM**

Light human nature is too lightly lost. Discontent. Elizabeth Barrett Browning. **CP-BroEB**

Light in the Locust Tree. Hayden Carruth. **CP-CarHS**

Light in the morning, The. Kitchen. Robert Creeley. **CP-CreeR**

Light in the window seemed perpetual, The. The Room above the Square. Stephen Spender. **CP-SpenS**

Light into the olive entered. After Greece. James Merrill. **SP-MerrJ**

Light is a vehicle for shadows. Wonders of the World. Richard Shelton. **SP-ShelR**

Light is in the pupil. Thom Gunn. *Fr.* Tom-Dobbin. **CP-GunnT**

Light is like a spider, The. Tattoo. Wallace Stevens. **CP-StevW**

Light is our sorrow for it ends tomorrow. Whither the Tribes Go Up, Even the Tribes of the Lord. Christina Georgina Rossetti. **CP-RosC2**

Light is Speech. Marianne Craig Moore. **CP-MoorM**

Light is sufficient to itself. Emily Dickinson. **CP-DickE**

Light Journal. Charles Wright. **SP-WrigC**

Light-Keeper, The. Robert Louis Stevenson. **CP-StevR**

Light lay the earth on Billy's breast. On Capt. W——— R-dd-ck of C-rb—ton. Robert Burns. **CP-BurnR**

Light Left On, A. May Sarton. **SP-SartM**

Light lies layered in the leaves, The. Song. James Schuyler. **CP-SchuJ**

Light lifts from the water. Basil Bunting. **OAEL-2; PoPo** *Fr.* Drip-icicle's gone. *Fr.* Briggflatts [An Autobiography]. **CP-BuntB**

Light Lightly Pleased. Robert Herrick. **CP-HerrR**

Light Listened. Theodore Roethke. **CP-RoetT**

Light Love. Christina Georgina Rossetti. **CP-RosC1**

Light may be had for nothing. Little Candle. Carl Sandburg. **CP-SandC**

Light Music. Derek Mahon. **SP-MahoD**

Light, my light, let me never be again. Gilbert Sorrentino. *Fr.* Elegiacs of Sulpicia. **SP-SorrG**

Light of egg faces, lights of monkey skulls. Smoke Shapes. Carl Sandburg. **CP-SandC**

Light of evening, Lissadell, The. In Memory of Eva Gore-Booth and Con Markievicz. William Butler Yeats. **CP-YeatW**

Light of Life, The. Stevie Smith. **CP-SmitS**

Light of Light. Christina Georgina Rossetti. **CP-RosC2**

Light of my eyes, there *is* something to be said. Hafiz, *tr.* by Basil Bunting. **CP-BuntB**

Light of Night. Marsden Hartley. **CP-HartM**

Light of the mind is poorer, The. Of Beginning Light. Charles Tomlinson. **CP-TomlC**

Light of the yellow flowers, The. Butter Colors. Carl Sandburg. **CP-SandC**

Light on the leaves, The. Never Two Songs the Same. Carl Sandburg. **CP-SandC**

Light Out), A. Edward Estlin Cummings. **CP-CummE; SP-CummE**

Light passes, The. Evening. Hilda Doolittle. **CP-DoolH**

Light plays like a radio in the iron tree. Poem. Thomas Merton. **CP-MertT**

Light Poem. Theodore Roethke. **CP-RoetT**

Light pulses through underground chambers. Noon. Adrienne Rich. **CP-RicAE**

Light rain stands / in little pools, A. Sparks. James Schuyler. **CP-SchuJ**

Light rising into her features where. Jim Carroll. *Fr.* Living at the Movies. **SP-CarrJ**

Light Shall Not Enter. William Carlos Williams. **CP-WilW2**

Light Shining out of Darkness. William Cowper. **EBEV; EBEvV; ECEV; ELP; EaLo; EnRP; FHYEP; FPL; FaBoCh; FiP; HBV 1-2; HeIP; ImPo; LiTB; NOBE; NOCV; NOEC; NoP; OBEC; PWR; PoEL-3;** SCGP; SeCePo; TFi; TOF; TRV; TrGrPo; WGRP *Fr.* Olney Hymns. **CP-CowpW**

Light Snow-Fall after Frost, A. Thomas Hardy. **CP-HardT**

Light spray over a daisy chain of days. One. Tom Clark. **SP-ClarT**

Light spreads darkly downwards from the high. Friday Night in the Royal Station. Philip Larkin. **CP-LarkP**

Light strives with darkness, right with wrong. Wystan Hugh Auden. **CP-AudWJ**

Light Switches. John Updike. **CP-UpdiJ**

Light takes new attribute. Projector. Hilda Doolittle. **CP-DoolH**

Light That Failed, The. Rudyard Kipling.
   "And you may lead a thousand men." **CP-KiplR**
   Blue Roses. **CP-KiplR**
   Heriot's Ford. **CP-KiplR**
   " 'I have a thousand men,' said he." **CP-KiplR**
   "If I have taken the common clay." **CP-KiplR**
   "Lark will make her hymn to God, The." **CP-KiplR**
   Mother o' Mine. **CP-KiplR**
   "So we settled it all when the storm was done." **CP-KiplR**
   "Then we brought the lances down—then the trumpets blew." **CP-KiplR**
   "There were three friends that buried the fourth." **CP-KiplR**
   "Wolf-cub at even lay hid in the corn, The." **CP-KiplR**
   "Yet at the last, ere our spearmen had found him." **CP-KiplR**

Light That Is Felt, The. John Greenleaf Whittier. **CP-WhitJ**

Light that rises on Jehosophat, The. Two Desert Fathers. Thomas Merton. **CP-MertT**

Light the first light of evening, as in a room. Final Soliloquy of the Interior Paramour. Wallace Stevens. **CP-StevW**

Light. The rain. The eye. The rainbow—, The. The Land. Roy Fisher. **SP-FishR** *Fr.* Inscriptions for Bluebeard's Castle.

Light the sun withdraws the leaves replace, The. November. John Updike. **CP-UpdiJ**

Light, Time, Dark. Richard Eberhart. **CP-EberR**

Light up thy halls! 'Tis closing day. F. de Samara to A. G. A. Emily Brontë. **CP-BronE**

Light, warmth, and sprouting greenness, and o'er all. Pictures. John Greenleaf Whittier. **CP-WhitJ**

Light was calloused in the leaded panes of the college chapel. Cloistered. Seamus Heaney. **SP-HeanS**

Light was eerie, unreal. In our rush, The. The Event at Konna. Kenneth Patchen. **CP-PatcK**

Light was faint, and soft the air, The. Stolen Waters. "Lewis Carroll." **CP-CarrL**

Light was gaunt and crawly, The. You May All Go Home Now. Kenneth Patchen. **CP-PatcK**

Light was no doubt the same, the ecology different, The. On the Four Masters. Louis MacNeice. *Fr.* Dark Age Glosses. **CP-MacNL**

Light was on the golden sands, The. Paul Laurence Dunbar. **CP-DunbP**

Light weighs / light, to the hand. Two. Robert Creeley. **CP-CreeR**

Light wheels and comes in, The. Sunburst. Donald Davie. **CP-DavDo**

Light wind at Grand Prairie, drifting snow. Weather Report. William Stafford. **SP-StafW**

Light wind beyond the window, A. Lost and Found. Philip Levine. **SP-LeviP**

Light Within, The. James Schuyler. **CP-SchuJ**

Light Woman, A. Robert Browning. **CP-BroR1**

Light words forsook them. When Men Got to the Summit. Ted Hughes. **SP-HughT**

Light words they were, and lightly, falsely said. Arthur Hugh Clough. **SP-ClouA**

Light Years. Dabney Stuart. **SP-StuaD**

Lightbulb. Stephen Berg. **SP-BergS**

Lighted Windows (For Judy). Chuck Miller. **SP-MillC**

Lighten, heavy hart, thy spright. Thomas Campion. **CP-CampT**

Lighthouse. Joseph Ceravolo. **SP-CeraJ**

Lighthouse, The. Charles Tomlinson. **CP-TomlC**

Lighthouse and a graveyard and gaunt pines, A. Point Pinos and Point Lobos. Robinson Jeffers. **CP-JefR1**

Lighthouse in Maine, A. Derek Mahon. **SP-MahoD**

Lighthouse Invites the Storm, The. Malcolm Lowry. **CP-LowrM**
   April 1937 In the Oaxaca Train.
   November, 1937.
   Of the Francia.
   Perhaps for Eridanus.
   Pijijiapan.
   Thought While Drowning (Acapulco). **CP-LowrM**

Lighthouse Invites the Storm, The. Malcolm Lowry. *See* The Lighthouse invites the storm and lights it.

Lighthouse invites the storm and lights it, The. Malcolm Lowry. **NOBC** Fr. The Roar of the Sea and the Darkness. **CP-LowrM**

(Lighthouse Invites the Storm, The.) **NOBC**

Lighthouse keeper's world is round, The. Round and Round. Thom Gunn. **CP-GunnT**

Lighthouses, The. George Oppen. **CP-OppeG**

Lighting a spill late in the afternoon. A Winter Talent. Donald Davie. **CP-DavDo**

Lightly Bound. Stevie Smith. **CP-SmitS**

Lightly, in the April mountains. Straight-Creek—Great Burn. Gary Snyder. **CP-SnydG**

Lightly, lightly, so lightly. Fernando Pessoa. Fr. Twelve Poems from The Keeper of the Flocks. **CP-MertT**

Lightly stepped a yellow star. Emily Dickinson. **CP-DickE**

Lightness. Richard Wilbur. **CP-WilbR**

Lightnin' Blues. Rita Dove. **SP-DoveR**

Lightning, The. John Berryman. **CP-BerrJ**

Lightning. David Herbert Lawrence. **CP-LawrD**

Lightning. Mary Oliver. **SP-OlivM**

Lightning, Divine Lightning. Al Young. **CP-YounA**

Lightning enclosed by a vast ring of mirrors. Blackening Sky. Robert Ranke Graves. **CP-GravR**

Lightning ignited the treetops. Once as a Child I Had Bad Dreams. Paul Zimmer. **SP-ZimmP**

Lightning is a yellow Fork, The. Emily Dickinson. **CP-DickE**

Lightning! Lightning! Lightning! Without thunder! Flushing Meadows, 1939. Daniel Gerard Hoffman. **SP-HoffD**

Lightning of a summer, The. Lady Bates. Randall Jarrell. **CP-JarrR; SP-JarrR**

Lightning playeth—all the while, The. Emily Dickinson. **CP-DickE**

Lightning Storm on Fuji. Howard Nemerov. **CP-NemeH**

Lights / Shine, the fire, The. George Oppen. Fr. A Narrative. **CP-OppeG**

Lights among Redwood. Thom Gunn. **CP-GunnT**

Lights are beginning to go out in the barracks, The. Absent with Official Leave. Randall Jarrell. **CP-JarrR; SP-JarrR**

Lights are on; / flesh is next to the body, The. Fly. Joseph Ceravolo. **SP-CeraJ**

Lights from the parlour and kitchen shone out, The. Escape at Bedtime. Robert Louis Stevenson. **CP-StevR**

Lights I Have Seen Before. Philip Levine. **SP-LeviP**

Lights in the Hallway, The. James Wright. **CP-WrigJ**

Lights in the Sky are Stars, The. Kenneth Rexroth.

Lights in the Sky are Stars, The. Kenneth Rexroth. **SP-RexrK**

Great Nebula of Andromeda, The. **SP-RexrK**

Halley's Comet. **SP-RexrK**

Heart of Herakles, The. **NU**

Sword in a Cloud of Light, A. **SP-RexrK**

Light's lives lurch / a once world quickly from rises. Edward Estlin Cummings. **CP-CummE**

Lights or no lights. Books Men Die For. Carl Sandburg. **CP-SandC**

Lights out. Shades up. Girl in a Nightgown. Wallace Stevens. **CP-StevW**

Lights that blaze and promise, The. George Oppen. Fr. Tourist Eye. **CP-OppeG**

Lights that travel on her spectacles, The. The Fernery. Hart Crane. **CP-CranH**

Lights up on the living. A Bulletin from the Stadium. Thom Gunn. **CP-GunnT**

Lights were red, refused to change, The. Hold-up. Louis MacNeice. **CP-MacNL**

Lightweight poets are happier, The. Poetry and Games. Richard Eberhart. **CP-EberR**

Like a, A / grey / rock wanderin. Edward Estlin Cummings. **CP-CummE**

Like a big tired buffalo. Life Notes. Tom Clark. **SP-ClarT**

Like a bird on the wire. Bird on the Wire. Leonard Cohen. **CP-CoheL**

Like a blind child is the loving heart. George Meredith. **CP-MerG2**

Like a bucket. Thought I Was Dying. Daniel Gerard Hoffman. **SP-HoffD**

Like a Bulwark. Marianne Craig Moore. **CP-MoorM**

Like a cat haunting the familiar porch. The Same Kiss After Many Years. Tess Gallagher. **SP-GallT**

Like a child. Arthur Hugh Clough. Fr. Blank Misgivings of a Creature Moving About in Worlds Not Realized. **SP-ClouA**

"Like a child," Mary Cassatt said, describing. Cézanne's Outrageousness. Stephen Dobyns. **SP-DobyS**

Like a compass needle. Trying to Dream Up an Answer. Barton Sutter. **SP-SuttB**

Like a convalescent, I took the hand. Seamus Heaney. **FaBoPV; NAEL-2; NoAM; TOF** Fr. Station Island. **SP-HeanS**

Like a coy maiden, ease, when courted most. Ease. William Cowper. **TEP** Fr. The Sofa. Fr. The Task. **CP-CowpW**

Like a cross between a hinge. Backtalk. Brendan Galvin. **SP-GalvB**

Like a cylindrical tank fresh silvered. To All Gentleness. William Carlos Williams. **CP-WilW2**

Like a dream, which when one. Pastel Dresses. Stephen Dobyns. **SP-DobyS**

Like a dry fish flung inland far from shore. Lost Anchors. Edwin Arlington Robinson. **CP-RobiE**

Like a fawn you dodge me, Molly. Basil Bunting, after the Latin of Horace. **CP-BuntB**

Like a first coat of whitewash when it's wet. Twelfth Morning; or What You Will. Elizabeth Bishop. **CP-BishE**

Like a flat sea. Population. George Oppen. **CP-OppeG**

Like a flood river whirled at rocky banks. The Test of Manhood. George Meredith. **CP-MerG1**

Like a Flower in the Rain. Charles Bukowski. **SP-BukC1**

Like a foldout. Charles Olson. **CP-OlsoC**

Like a frozen lake the sky in the bitterest. Hayden Carruth. Fr. North Winter. **CP-CarHL**

Like a gaunt, scraggly pine. Lincoln. John Gould Fletcher. **SP-FletJ**

Like a girl holding, spread, / Stiff skirts, a ruffled dancer. Dogwood. John Gould Fletcher. **SP-FletJ**

Like A Green Branch. Martin Edmunds. **SP-EdmuM**

Like a huntsman. Edmund Spenser. **EnRePo; GBL; HeIP; NAEL-1; NoP; OAEP; PoE; PoEL-1; SeCePo; Son; TrGrPo** Fr. Amoretti. **CP-Spens**

Like a huntsman after weary chase. Like a huntsman. Edmund Spenser. **EnRePo; GBL; HeIP; NAEL-1; NoP; OAEP; PoE; PoEL-1; SeCePo; Son; TrGrPo** Fr. Amoretti. **CP-Spens**

Like a jeweled peacock he stirs all over. The Moslems' Angel of Death. Thomas Merton. **CP-MertT; SP-MertT**

Like a little bear twilight. Edward Estlin Cummings. **CP-CummE**

Like a lizard in the sun, though not scuttling. The Laureate. Robert Ranke Graves. **CP-GravR**

Like a lone Arab, old and blind. Love's Apparition and Evanishment. Samuel Taylor Coleridge. **CP-ColeS**

Like a lustrous bird threading the maze. Marsden Hartley. Fr. Several Pieces for Jose Garcia Villa. **CP-HartM**

Like a man committed to searching. Robert Creeley. **CP-CreeR**

Like a man on a stick on a sidewalk being peddled by a low pitchman. Jas Jargon. Charles Olson. **CP-OlsoC**

Like a Memoir of the Sun. Emily Dickinson. **SP-DickE**

Like a Mourningless Child. Kenneth Patchen. **CP-PatcK**

Like a pile of gold that his breath. Saint. Frank O'Hara. **SP-OharF**

Like a poor ghost the night I seek. Verses, on the death of [Henrietta O'Neill], written in September, 1794. Charlotte Smith. **CP-SmitC**

Like a propped skull. Tutorial. Ted Hughes. Fr. Boom. **SP-HughT**

Like a rabid goat, this obsession. Jim Carroll. **SP-CarrJ**

Like a rainstorm, he said, the braided colors. Worsening Situation. John Ashbery. **SP-AshbJ**

Like a ringdove fat with sun. Indolence. Alun Lewis. **CP-LewiA**

Like a river she was. The Memory. Robert Creeley. **CP-CreeR**

Like a Roling Stone. Dig It. The Beatles. **CP-Beatl**

Like a Rolling Stone. "Bob Dylan." **CP-DylaB**

Like a room / high up. (Poem). Bill Knott. **SP-KnotB**

Like a room, the clear stanza. An Architecture. Wendell Berry. **CP-BerrW**

Like a rotten old ladder, sl. diff. vers. begins Perhaps for Eridanus. The Ladder. Malcolm Lowry. **CP-LowrM**

Like a rotten old ladder. Perhaps for Eridanus. Malcolm Lowry. Fr. The Lighthouse Invites the Storm. **CP-LowrM**

Like a shiprecked Sailor tost. To — Upon the Birth of Her First-Born Child, March, 1833. William Wordsworth. **CP-WorW2**

Like a skein of loose silk blown against a wall. The Garden. Ezra Pound. **SP-PounE**

Like a spear afterwards / cut out. Autumn-Time, Wind and the Planet Pluto. Joseph Ceravolo. **SP-CeraJ**

Like a steel drum. Coming To. Archie Randolph Ammons. **SP-AmmoA**

Like a surgeon at the drugged decisive. Marianne Moore. Marsden Hartley. **CP-HartM**

Like a tide it comes in. The Arrival. Wendell Berry. **CP-BerrW**

Like a vein of hard coal, it was the strike. Gate City Breakdown. Charles Wright. **SP-WrigC**

Like a Vocation. Wystan Hugh Auden. **CP-AudeW**

Like a white wall whereon forever breaks. Edwin Arlington Robinson. Fr. Octaves. **CP-RobiE**

Like a wild bird he. Charles Henri Ford. **SP-FordC** Fr. Secret Haiku.

Like a Woman in the Kitchen. Siv Cedering Fox. **SP-CedeS**

Like Aesop's fellow-slaves, O Mercury. Mercurius Gallo-Belgicus. John Donne. **CP-DonnJ**

Like all his people he felt at home in the forest. The Bearer. Hayden Carruth. **CP-CarHS**

Like an art-lover looking at the Mona Lisa in the Louvre. Political Reflection. Ogden Nash. **CP-NashO**

Like an awl-tip breaking ice. Ode to Growth. John Updike. *Fr.* Seven Odes to Seven Natural Processes. **CP-UpdiJ**

Like an oarless boat through midnight's watery. Moon Clock. Donald Hall. **CP-HallD**

Like an old battle, youth is wild. Keep Innocency. Walter de la Mare. **CP-DeLaW**

Like any wandering pervert. History. James Liddy. *Fr.* Love Songs of Corca Bascinn. **CP-LiddJ**

Like as a ship, that through the ocean wyde. Edmund Spenser. **EtS; MOS** *Fr.* The Faerie Queene. **CP-Spens**

Like as a terrible fire feeds fast on a forest enormous. Marshalling of the Achaians. Homer, *tr.* by George Meredith. **CP-MerG1** *Fr.* The Iliad.

Like as the bird in the cage enclosed. Sir Thomas Wyatt. **CP-WyatT**

Like as the dove which seeled-up doth fly. Sir Philip Sidney. **SP-SidnP**

Like As the Hart Desireth the Water Brooks. Christina Georgina Rossetti. **CP-RosC2**

Like as the Oak whose roots descend. Samuel Pepys. Rudyard Kipling. **CP-KiplR**

Like as the swan towards her death. Sir Thomas Wyatt. **CP-WyatT**

Like as the tide that comes from th' Ocean main. Edmund Spenser. **HoPM** *Fr.* The Faerie Queene. **CP-Spens**

Like as the Waves. William Shakespeare. *See* Sonnet 60: "Like as the waves make towards the pebbled shore."

Like as the waves make towards the pebbled shore. Sonnet 60. William Shakespeare. **ChTr; EBEV; EIL; EnRePo; FPL; FaBoEn; FaFP; FaPoB; GTBS; GTBS-6; GTBS-P; HBV; ImPo; LiTB; LoBV; NIP; NOBE; NoSic; OBSC; OXAEP-1; PeHV; PoRA; SCGP; SeCeV; Son; TEP; TFi; UnPo** *Fr.* Sonnets. **CP-ShaWS**

Like as the wind with raging blast. Sir Thomas Wyatt. **CP-WyatT**

Like as, to make our appetites more keen. Sonnet 118. William Shakespeare. **CABA; SCGP** *Fr.* Sonnets. **CP-ShaWS**

Like battered old millhands, they stand in the orchard—. Old Apple Trees. William DeWitt Snodgrass. **CP-SnodW**

Like black plunging dolphins with red bellies. Steamers. John Gould Fletcher. *Fr.* Sand and Spray: A Sea-Symphony. **SP-FletJ**

Like Brooms of Steel. Emily Dickinson. **CP-DickE**

Like Decorations in a Nigger Cemetery. Wallace Stevens. **CP-StevW**

Like divers, we ourselves must make the jump. The Springboard. Adrienne Rich. **CP-RicAE**

Like diverse flowers, whose diverse beauties serve, *speech of Pamela.* Sir Philip Sidney. **SP-SidnP** *Fr.* Arcadia.

Like dogs in Mexico. As It Happens. Denise Levertov. **CP-LeveD**

Like early snow they come. Christmas Blackmail. Phoebe Hesketh. **SP-HeskP**

Like Egypt and the Sphinx, you have been part of my fantasy life for. Preface. Diane Wakoski. **SP-WakoD**

Like empty beer cans, like cigarette butts. Ernesto Cardenal, *tr.* by Thomas Merton. **CP-MertT** *Fr.* Gethsemani, KY.

Like Eyes that looked on Wastes. Emily Dickinson. **CP-DickE**

Like flowers sequestered from the sun. The Lowest Room. Christina Georgina Rossetti. **CP-RosC1**

Like Flowers, that heard the news of Dews. Emily Dickinson. **CP-DickE**

Like ghosts / much talked about. Love (after La Rochefoucauld). Tom Clark. **SP-ClarT**

Like gossamer / On the swift breath of morn, the vessel flew. Ever as We Sailed. Percy Bysshe Shelley. **SeCePo** *Fr.* The Revolt of Islam. **CP-ShelP**

Like Henry the Eighth, Mohammed got religion. Like Henry VIII, Mohammed got religion. Robert Lowell. **SP-LoweR**

Like Henry VIII, Mohammed got religion. Robert Lowell. **SP-LoweR**

(Like, *Her Cardboard Lover*). Thinness. James Schuyler. **CP-SchuJ**

Like her the Saints retire. Emily Dickinson. **CP-DickE**

Like ice his blood. Marsden Hartley. *Fr.* Ironies out of St. George's. **CP-HartM**

Like Ilium. Thomas Merton. **CP-MertT**

Like large dark / lazy / butterflies they sweep over. Vultures. Mary Oliver. **SP-OlivM**

Like Leonardo's idea. A Map of Europe. Derek Walcott. **CP-WalcD**

Like lines of verse REDBURN. The Collected Poems of. Charles Olson. **CP-OlsoC**

Like liquid shadows. The ice is thin. Reflections. Charles Tomlinson. **CP-TomlC**

Like Little Birds. Charles Kenneth Williams. **CP-WillC**

Like little blackbirds in the street. A Norther—Key West. Elizabeth Bishop. **CP-BishE**

Like long terraces the evening clouds. The Evening Clouds. John Gould Fletcher. **SP-FletJ**

Like Lorraine Ellison. James Schuyler. **CP-SchuJ**

Like Loves His Like. Robert Herrick. **CP-HerrR**

Like Magellan, let us find our islands. Magellan. Mary Oliver. **SP-OlivM**

Like mail order brides. Seedlings in the Mail. Marge Piercy. **SP-PierM**

Like many a one, when you had gold. The Old Story. Argentarius. **AWP** *Fr.* Variations of Greek Themes. **CP-RobiE**

Like Men and Women Shadows walk. Emily Dickinson. **CP-DickE**

Like Mighty Foot Lights—burned the Red. Emily Dickinson. **CP-DickE**

Like mine, the veins of these that slumber. Alfred Edward Housman. **CP-HousA**

Like most godhouses this particular house. Edward Estlin Cummings. **CP-CummE**

Like mourning women veiled to the feet. Distant Rainfall. Robinson Jeffers. **CP-JefR2**

"Like Musical Instruments. . . ." Tom Clark. **SP-ClarT**

Like Oedipus I am losing my sight. The Legend of the One-Eyed Man. Anne Sexton. **CP-SextA**

Like one that in a dream would fain arise. Arthur Hugh Clough. **SP-ClouA**

Like one who in [*or* who'in] her third widowhood [*or*widdowhood] doth profess[e]. To Mr. Roland Woodward. John Donne. **CP-DonnJ**

Like other men, when I go past. Wystan Hugh Auden. **CP-AudWJ**

Like Owls. Robert Ranke Graves. **CP-GravR**

Like Pattern, Like People. Robert Herrick. **CP-HerrR**

Like pendant flakes of vegetating snow. To the Snow-Drop. Charlotte Smith. **CP-SmitC**

Like porches they trust their attachments. Rhododendrons. Tess Gallagher. **SP-GallT**

Like Princes crowned they bore them. A Pageant of Elizabeth. Rudyard Kipling. **CP-KiplR**

Like Rain it sounded till it curved. Emily Dickinson. **CP-DickE**

Like right now it's the summertime. The Old O.O. Blues. Al Young. **CP-YounA**

Like rock-and-roll with headlights. Night Ways. Brendan Galvin. **SP-GalvB**

Like sea-washed sand upon the shore. On a Clean Book. Paul Laurence Dunbar. **CP-DunbP**

Like Shuttles Fleet the Clouds. Gerard Manley Hopkins. *See* Like shuttles fleet the clouds, and after.

Like shuttles fleet the clouds, and after. Gerard Manley Hopkins. **CP-HopkG**

(Like Shuttles Fleet the Clouds.) **CP-HopkG**

Like skyscrapers with high windows staring down from the sun. Louis MacNeice. Stephen Spender. **CP-SpenS**

Like Snow. Robert Ranke Graves. **CP-GravR**

Like snows the camps on Southern hills. The Armies of the Wilderness. Herman Melville. **SP-MelvH**

Like Some Old fashioned Miracle. Emily Dickinson. **CP-DickE**

Like some weak lords, neighboured by mighty kings. Sonnet 29. Sir Philip Sidney. *Fr.* Astrophil and Stella. **SP-SidnP**

Like somebody's ass in a Friday Nite Video. Flirt. Al Young. **CP-YounA**

Like something washed up by the sea, something naked, invincible. The Men (XVIII). Pablo Neruda, *tr. fr. Spanish* by Ben Belitt. **SP-NeruP** *Fr.* The Separate Rose.

Like souls that balance joy and pain. Sir Launcelot and Queen Guinevere. Tennyson. **CP-TennA**

Like talk overheard across water, they seem to have come. Men in Dark Suits. William Matthews. **SP-MattW**

Like that ancestral judge who bore his name. Samuel E. Sewall. John Greenleaf Whittier. **CP-WhitJ**

Like the black iron steps. Malcolm Lowry. **CP-LowrM**

Like the blush upon the rose. Love's Pictures. Paul Laurence Dunbar. **CP-DunbP**

Like the clear sound of crushed snow underfoot. Christmas Night. Steve Griffiths. *Fr.* Hymns and Backward Glances. **SP-GrifS**

Like the clear sound of crushed snow underfoot. Hymns and Backward Glances. Steve Griffiths. **SP-GrifS**

Like the flights of ducks. Ernesto Cardenal, *tr.* by Thomas Merton. **CP-MertT** *Fr.* Gethsemani, KY.

Like the ghost of a dear friend dead. Time Long Past. Percy Bysshe Shelley. **CP-ShelP**

Like the Green Candles of Malintzi. David Herbert Lawrence. **CP-LawrD**

Like the magnificent stationary animal it is. Sonnet. Hayden Carruth. **CP-CarHS** *Fr.* Sonnets.

Like the moon her kindness is. Human Dignity. William Butler Yeats. *Fr.* A Man Young and Old. **CP-YeatW**

Like the oceans, or the leaves of fine Southern. Louis Zukofsky. *Fr.* 29 Poems. **CP-ZukLS**

Like the shark who feels low but. Sleepy Day at Half Moon Bay. Al Young. **CP-YounA**

Like the shore's alternation of door wave. Crows. Tom Clark. **SP-ClarT**

Like the soldier, like the sailor, like the bib and tuck. A Letter on the Use of Machine Guns at Weddings. Kenneth Patchen. **CP-PatcK**

Like the stars in commons blue. Field Asters. Herman Melville. **SP-MelvH**

Like the sun on February ice dazzling. Snow, Snow. Marge Piercy. **SP-PierM**

Like the Train's Beat. Philip Larkin. **CP-LarkP**

Like the unicorn, Uncle. Uncle Sam. Kenneth Rexroth. **SP-RexrK** *Fr.* A Bestiary. **SP-RexrK**

Like the vain curlings of the watery maze. The First Anniversary of the Government under His Highness the Lord Protector, 1655. Andrew Marvell. **CP-MarvA**

Like the wind in the trees and the bells. George Oppen. *Fr.* Of Being Numerous. **CP-OppeG**

Like the woods of old Kentucky. Nicholas Vachel Lindsay. *Fr.* A Rhymed Address to All Renegade Campbellites, Exhorting Them to Return. *Fr.* Alexander Campbell. **CP-LindV**

Like They Say. Robert Creeley. **CP-CreeR**

Like This Together. Adrienne Rich. **CP-RicAE; SP-RicA1; SP-RicA2**

Like thosae infernall Deities which eate. Bad Princes Pill Their People. Robert Herrick. **CP-HerrR**

Like those flailing flames. Ted Hughes. **HAP,** *sect.* 7; *Fr.* Skylarks. **SP-HughT**

Like Those Sick Folks. Sir Philip Sidney. **OxBSP** *Fr.* Hark, plaintful ghosts! Infernal furies, hark. **SP-SidnP** *Fr.* Arcadia.

Like thousands, I took just pride and more than just. Reading Myself. Robert Lowell. **SP-LoweR**

Like Time's insidious wrinkle. Emily Dickinson. **CP-DickE**

Like to a Bride, come forth my Book, at last. To His Booke. Robert Herrick. **CP-HerrR**

Like to a fading flower in May. To the Memory of the Unfortunate Miss Burns 1791. Robert Burns. **CP-BurnR**

Like to a god he seems to me. Catullus. *See* Carmen 51: "Godlike the man who."

Like to a Hermit[e] Poor[e]. Sir Walter Ralegh. **CP-RaleW**

Like to a hermit[e] poor[e][,] in place obscure. Like to a Hermit[e] Poor[e]. Sir Walter Ralegh. **CP-RaleW**

Like to huge clowds of smoke which well may hide. Sonnet 5. Mary Sidney, Countess of Montgomery Wroth. *Fr.* Pamphilia to Amphilanthus. **CP-WrotM**

Like to some deep-chested organ whose grand inspiration. The Poetry of Milton. George Meredith. **CP-MerG1**

Like to the hand, that hath been used to play. Mr. Carew to His Friend. Thomas Carew. **CP-CareT**

Like to the Income must be our expence. Reverence to Riches. Robert Herrick. **CP-HerrR**

Like to the Indians, scorched with the sun[ne]. Sonnet 22. Mary Sidney, Countess of Montgomery Wroth. **NOSC** *Fr.* Pamphilia to Amphilanthus. **CP-WrotM**

Like to the sentinel stars, I watch all night. To Lucasta. Richard Lovelace. **CP-LoveR**

Like to these unme[a]surable montains [*or* mountayns]. Jacopo Sannazaro, *tr. fr. Italian by* Sir Thomas Wyatt. **CP-WyatT**

Like Trains of Cars on Tracks of Plush. Emily Dickinson. **CP-DickE**

Like truthles[s] dream[e]s, so are my joys expired. Farewell to the Court. Sir Walter Ralegh. **CP-RaleW**

Like unto Them That Dream. Bible, *O.T. See* Psalm 126: "When the Lord turned again the captivity of Zion. . . ."

Like Us, Maybe. Leonard Nathan. **SP-NathL**

Like vaulters in the circus round. Ralph Waldo Emerson. **CP-EmerR**

Like watching rings extended in water. For You. Robert Creeley. **CP-CreeR**

Like well diggers. The Inheritance. Thomas McGrath. **SP-McGrT**

Like white giraffes the fishing craft. After Labour Day. Malcolm Lowry. **CP-LowrM**

Like will to like, each Creature loves his kinde. Like Loves His Like. Robert Herrick. **CP-HerrR**

Likely as not a ruined head gasket. George Oppen. *Fr.* Image of the Engine. **CP-OppeG**

Likely last nostalgic warmth of autumn, The. Mountain Ash Without Cedar Waxwings. Robert Pack. **SP-PackR**

Likely Story. Archie Randolph Ammons. **SP-AmmoA**

Likeness, A. Robert Browning. **CP-BroR1**
    Spoils of Youth, The. **CBCK**

Likeness, The. Leonard Nathan. **SP-NathL**

Likeness. Adrienne Rich. **CP-RicAE**

Likeness has made them animal and shy. The Twins. Karl Shapiro. **SP-ShapK**

Likewise. Langston Hughes. **SP-HughL**

Li'l' Gal. Paul Laurence Dunbar. **CP-DunbP**

Lilac. Louis Zukofsky. **CP-ZukLS**

Lilac is an ancient shrub, The. Emily Dickinson. **CP-DickE**

Lilac moon of the earth's backyard, The. May 31, 1961. Charles Olson. **CP-OlsoC; SP-OlsoC**

Lilac speaks without a voice: pure blue. Transformation. Richard Eberhart. **CP-EberR**

Lilacs. James Schuyler. **CP-SchuJ**

Lilacs, The. Richard Wilbur. **CP-WilbR**

Lilacs and the Roses, The. Louis Aragon, *tr. fr. French by* Louis MacNeice. **CP-MacNL**

Lilacs wither in the Carolinas, The. In the Carolinas. Wallace Stevens. **CP-StevW**

Lilibulero. John Hewitt. **CP-HewiJ**

Lilienthal said : I heard him saying words like these. Muriel Rukeyser. **CP-RukeM**

Lilies, The. Wendell Berry. **CP-BerrW**

Lilies. Mary Oliver. **SP-OlivM**

Lilies. Louis Zukofsky. **CP-ZukLS**

Lilies Break Open Over the Dark Water, The. Mary Oliver. **SP-OlivM**

Lilies in the Fire. David Herbert Lawrence. **CP-LawrD**

Lilies will languish; violets look ill. The Sadness of Things for Sappho's Sickness. Robert Herrick. **CP-HerrR**

Lilly in a Christal, The. Robert Herrick. **CP-HerrR**

Lilt and a swing, A. At the Tavern. Paul Laurence Dunbar. **CP-DunbP**

Lily, The. William Blake. **CP-BlakW** *Fr.* Songs of Experience.

Lily, The. William Carlos Williams. **CP-WilW1**

Lily and the Rose, The. William Cowper. **CP-CowpW**

Lily at Noon, A. Donald Davie. **CP-DavDo**

Lily, being white not red, The. Epilogue. Countee Cullen. **CP-CullC**

Lily has a rose. Edward Estlin Cummings. **CP-CummE**

Lily has a smooth stalk, / Will never hurt your hand, The. Christina Georgina Rossetti. **CP-RosC2**

Lily has an air, / And the snowdrop a grace, The. Christina Georgina Rossetti. **CP-RosC2**

Lily of the Valley, The. Paul Laurence Dunbar. **CP-DunbP**

Lily-of-the-Valley. Louis Zukofsky. **CP-ZukLS**

Lily-of-the-Valley Fortunei. Louis Zukofsky. **CP-ZukLS**

Lily, Rosemary, and the Jack of Hearts. "Bob Dylan." **CP-DylaB**

Lily, there isn't a thing you lack. The Life of the Party. Ogden Nash. **CP-NashO**

Limb to limb, mouth to mouth. Winter Quiet. William Carlos Williams. **CP-WilW1**

Limbo. Samuel Taylor Coleridge. **CP-ColeS**

Limbo. Seamus Heaney. **SP-HeanS**

Limbo. Phoebe Hesketh. **SP-HeskP**

Limbo Culture. Wystan Hugh Auden. **CP-AudeW**

Limbs are caught in each other, The. Clearing. Tess Gallagher. **SP-GallT**

Limerick, A. "Lewis Carroll." **CP-CarrL**

Limerick: "As the poets have mournfully sung." Wystan Hugh Auden. *See* As the poets have mournfully sung.

Limestone, faulted with marble; the lengthening swell. Geneva Restored. Charles Tomlinson. **CP-TomlC**

Limitations. Paul Laurence Dunbar. **CP-DunbP**

Limitations. John Hewitt. **CP-HewiJ**

Limited. Carl Sandburg. **CP-SandC**

Limited Achievement. Donald Davie. **CP-DavDo**

Limited air drafts. The Occurrences. George Oppen. **CP-OppeG**

Limits. Howard Nemerov. **CP-NemeH**

Limpidity of Silences. Kenneth Patchen. **CP-PatcK**

Lin Hui of Kia took to flight. The Flight of Lin Hui. Chuang Tzu, *tr. fr. Chinese by* Thomas Merton. **CP-MertT**

L'Incognita. Christina Georgina Rossetti. **CP-RosC3**

Lincoln. Paul Laurence Dunbar. **CP-DunbP**

Lincoln. John Gould Fletcher. **SP-FletJ**

LINCOLN? / He was a mystery in smoke and flags. Carl Sandburg. *Fr.* The People, Yes. **CP-SandC**

Lincoln. Nicholas Vachel Lindsay. **OHIP** *Fr.* Litany of the Heroes. **CP-LindV**

Lincoln Relics, The. Stanley Jasspon Kunitz. **CP-KuniS**
    "Cold-eyed, in Naples once."
    "He steps out from the crowd."
    "His innocence was to trust."

"In the Great Hall of the Library."

"To be old and to be young."

Lincolnshire. Donald Davie. **CP-DavDo**

Lincolnshire Church, A. Sir John Betjeman. **CP-BetjJ**

Lincolnshire Shores ("A still salt pool locked in with bars of sand"). Tennyson. **FaBoPP** *Fr.* The Palace of Art. **CP-TennA**

Lincolnshire Shores ("As the crest of some slow. . ."). Tennyson. **FaBoPP** *Fr.* The Last Tournament. *Fr.* Idylls of the King. **CP-TennA**

Lincolnshire Tale, A. Sir John Betjeman. **CP-BetjJ**

Lincolnshire Wolds and Lincolnshire Sea. Tennyson. *See* Calm is the morn without a sound.

Linda, you are leaving. Mother and Daughter. Anne Sexton. **CP-SextA**

Linda, your birthday was the worst one. 16 February. Patti Smith. **SP-SmitP**

Lindamira's Complaint. Mary Sidney, Countess of Montgomery Wroth. *Fr.* Part 1. *Fr.* Urania. **CP-WrotM**

Sonnet: "O Memory [*or* Memorie], could I but loose thee now." **BWW; WPE**

("Leave me vaine Hope, too long thou hast possesst.") **BWW**

Sonnet 1: "Deare eyes farewell, my Sunne once, now my end."

Sonnet 2: "O deadly rancour to a constant heart."

Sonnet 3: "Surgeon I would aske, but 'tis too late."

Sonnet 5: "Leave me vain Hope, too long hath posses[s]t." **BWW**

Sonnet 6: "Though you forsake me, yet alas permit."

Sonnet 7: "Some doe, perhaps, both wrong my love, and care."

Linden Branch, The. Archibald MacLeish. **CP-MacLA**

Linden Trees, The. Archibald MacLeish. **CP-MacLA**

Lindisfarne. Kathleen Jessie Raine. *Fr.* The Holy Isles. **SP-RainK**

Lindsay mistakes the matter quite. Answer to "Paulus," The. Jonathan Swift. **CP-SwifJ**

Lindsay Speaks. Anne Waldman. **SP-WaldA**

Line, The. Hayden Carruth. **CP-CarHS**

Line-Gang, The. Robert Frost. **CP-FrosR**

Line in long array where they wind betwixt green islands, A. Cavalry Crossing a Ford. Walt Whitman. **CP-WhitW**

Line of eve o'er the moorland, A. George Meredith. **CP-MerG2**

Line of Verse of Yeats, A. Richard Eberhart. **CP-EberR**

Line-storm clouds fly tattered and swift, The. A Line-Storm Song. Robert Frost. **CP-FrosR**

Line-Storm Song, A. Robert Frost. **CP-FrosR**

Lineage, A. Wendell Berry. *Fr.* Work Song. **CP-BerrW**

Linear. Roy Fisher. **SP-FishR**

Lined up / like chocolates in their perfect paper jackets. Overnight Projects with Woods. Diane Wakoski. **SP-WakoD**

Linen. James Schuyler. **CP-SchuJ**

Liner She's a Lady, The. Rudyard Kipling. **CP-KiplR**

Lines: "Before we part to alien thoughts and aims." Thomas Hardy. **CP-HardT**

Lines: "Cold earth slept below, The." Percy Bysshe Shelley. **CP-ShelP**

Lines: "Dear Becher, you tell me to mix with mankind." Byron. **CP-Byron**

Lines: "Far away is the land of rest." Emily Brontë. **CP-BronE**

Lines: "Far, far away, O ye." Percy Bysshe Shelley. **CP-ShelP**

Lines: "He who of R--k-n sang, lies stiff and dead." Robert Burns. *See* He who of Rankine [*or* R--k-n] sang, lies stiff and dead.

Lines: "I die; but when the grave shall press." Emily Brontë. *See* I die; but when the grave shall press.

Lines, The. Randall Jarrell. **CP-JarrR**

Lines: "Leaves are greygreen." William Carlos Williams. **CP-WilW1**

Lines: "Loud is the Vale! the Voice is up." William Wordsworth. **CP-WorW1**

Lines: "Nay, Traveller! rest. This lonely Yew-tree stands." William Wordsworth. **CP-WorW1**

Lines: "One summer evening (led by her) I found." William Wordsworth. *See* One summer evening (led by her) I found.

Lines: "Soft unclouded blue of air, The." Emily Brontë. **CP-BronE**

Lines. Dabney Stuart. **SP-StuaD**

Lines. Tennyson. *See* For I Dipped [*or* Dipt] into the Future.

Lines: "That time is dead for ever, child!" Percy Bysshe Shelley. **CP-ShelP**

Lines. Charles Tomlinson. **CP-TomlC**

Lines: "Unfelt, unheard, unseen." John Keats. **CP-KeatJ**

Lines: "We meet not as we parted." Percy Bysshe Shelley. **CP-ShelP**

Lines: "When the lamp is shattered." Percy Bysshe Shelley. **CP-ShelP**

Lines Addressed to a Young Lady. Byron. **CP-Byron**

Lines Addressed to Mr. John Ranken. Robert Burns. **CP-BurnR**

Lines after the Manner of Homer. William Cowper. **CP-CowpW**

Lines & Circularities. Howard Nemerov. **CP-NemeH**

Lines are keen against today's bad sky, The. The Church on Comiaken Hill. Richard Hugo. **CP-HugoR**

Lines are straight and swift between the stars, The. Stars at Tallapoosa. Wallace Stevens. **CP-StevW**

Lines by Claudia. Emily Brontë. **CP-BronE**

Lines Composed a Few Miles above Tintern Abbey on Revisiting the Banks of the Wye during a Tour, July 13, 1798. William Wordsworth. **CP-WorW1**

"For I have learned." **NU**

"For thou art with me here upon the banks." **Prf**

"Sounding cataract, The/ Haunted me like a passion." **FaBoEn; WGRP**

Lines Composed in a Concert-Room. Samuel Taylor Coleridge. **CP-ColeS**

Lines Composed in Passing through a Forest in Germany. Charlotte Smith. **CP-SmitC**

Lines Composed While Climbing the Left Ascent of Brockley Coomb, in the County of Somerset, May, 1795. Samuel Taylor Coleridge. *Fr.* Effusions. **CP-ColeS**

Lines Declining a Transatlantic Dinner Invitation. Marilyn Hacker. **SP-HackM**

Lines for a Book. Thom Gunn. **CP-GunnT**

Lines for a Dead Alderman. John Hewitt. **CP-HewiJ**

Lines for a Gift. Robert Browning. **CP-BroR2**

Lines for a Grave-Stone. Edna St. Vincent Millay. **CP-MillE**

Lines for a Hospital. Countee Cullen. **CP-CullC**

Lines for a Memorial of Ashley Cowper. William Cowper. **CP-CowpW**

Lines for a Painting by Leighton. Robert Browning. **CP-BroR2**

Lines for a Picture of St. Dorothea, *For shorter and diff. vers., see also* For a Picture of St. Dorothea *and* St. Dorothea. Gerard Manley Hopkins. **CP-HopkG**

Lines for a Prologue. Archibald MacLeish. **CP-MacLA**

Lines for an Interment. Archibald MacLeish. **CP-MacLA**

Lines for an Old Man. Thomas Stearns Eliot. **CP-ElioT**

Lines for Cuscuscaraway and Mirza Murad Ali Beg. Thomas Stearns Eliot. **FiBHP; NBLV; NTP; OBAL; OBCoV; PeLV; PoPl; SpRo; UV; VoGa** *Fr.* Five-Finger Exercises. **CP-ElioT**

Lines for Elizabeth Mayer. Wystan Hugh Auden. *Fr.* Eleven Occasional Poems. **CP-AudeW**

Lines for Jack Clemo. Daniel Gerard Hoffman. **SP-HoffD**

Lines for Lauren Owen. Ted Berrigan. **SP-BerrT** *Fr.* The Sonnets.

Lines for My 55th Birthday. Thom Gunn. **CP-GunnT**

Lines for Scott Nearing. Daniel Gerard Hoffman. **SP-HoffD**

Lines for the Jubilee Window. Robert Browning. **CP-BroR2**

Lines for the Tomb of Levi Lincoln Thaxter. Robert Browning. **CP-BroR2**

Lines for Translation into Any Language. James Fenton. **SP-FentJ**

Lines from a Letter to a Young Clerical Friend. John Greenleaf Whittier. **CP-WhitJ**

Lines from Cadenus to Vanessa. Jonathan Swift. **CP-SwifJ**

Lines from Catullus. Catullus. *See* The Sunne may set and rise.

Lines from Key West. Peter Meinke.

Hero Worship at Key West on the 4th of July. **SP-MeinP**

Playing Shuffleboard, Drunk, in Key West, Fla. **SP-MeinP**

Wishing He Had a Theory in Key West. **SP-MeinP**

Writing the Great American Poem in Key West. **SP-MeinP**

Lines Given with a Penwiper. Christina Georgina Rossetti. **CP-RosC3**

Lines Have Their Linings, and Bookes Their Buckram. Robert Herrick. **CP-HerrR**

Lines in the Manner of Spenser. Samuel Taylor Coleridge. *Fr.* Effusions. **CP-ColeS**

Lines Indited with All the Depravity of Poverty. Ogden Nash. **CP-NashO**

Lines Inscribed in a Copy of His Poems Sent to the Queen for the Royal Library at Windsor. William Wordsworth. **CP-WorW2**

Lines Inscribed upon a Cup Formed from a Skull. Byron. **CP-Byron**

Lines Muttered in Sleep. Rita Dove. **SP-DoveR**

Lines of this new song are nothing, The. Louis Zukofsky. **CP-ZukLS**

Lines on a Carp. Gary Snyder. **CP-SnydG**

Lines on a Drawing of a Monument to Swift's Grandfather. Alexander Pope. **CP-PopeA**

Lines on a Fly-Leaf. John Greenleaf Whittier. **CP-WhitJ**

Lines on a Friend. Samuel Taylor Coleridge. **CP-ColeS**

Lines on a Portrait of a Lady. Samuel Taylor Coleridge. **CP-ColeS**

Lines on a Tudor Mansion. Alun Lewis. **CP-LewiA**

Lines on a Young Girl. Alun Lewis. **CP-LewiA**

Lines on a Young Lady's Photograph Album. Philip Larkin. **CP-LarkP**

Lines on Facing Forty. Ogden Nash. **CP-NashO**

Lines on Hearing That Lady Byron Was Ill. Byron. **CP-Byron**

Lines on Leaving Appledore. John Greenleaf Whittier. **CP-WhitJ**

Lines on Marlefield. James Thomson. **CP-ThomJ**

Lines on Receiving His Mother's Picture. William Cowper. **CH; OHIP** *Fr.* On the Receipt of My Mother's Picture out of Norfolk [the Gift of My Cousin Ann Bodham]. **CP-CowpW; FiP**

Lines on Receiving *The Dial's* Award: 1927. William Carlos Williams. **CP-WilW1**

Lines on Stirling. Robert Burns. **CP-BurnR**
  "Here Stewarts once in triumph reign'd."
    On Seeing the Royal Palace at Stirling in Ruins. **DBV**
  "Rash mortal, and slanderous Poet, thy name."
  "With Esop's lion, Burns says, sore I feel."

Lines on Swinburne. Robert Browning. **CP-BroR2**

Lines on the Death of Miss M. B. Farnham. Ralph Waldo Emerson. **CP-EmerR**

Lines on the Death of S. Oliver Torrey. John Greenleaf Whittier. **CP-WhitJ**

Lines on the Expected Invasion 1803. William Wordsworth. **CP-WorW1**

Lines on the Mermaid Tavern. John Keats. **CP-KeatJ**

Lines on the Opening of the Belgrade Theatre. John Hewitt. **CP-HewiJ**

Lines on the Poet Being Informed That His Epic About the Philistines Etc. Needed Cutting. Malcolm Lowry. **CP-LowrM**

Lines on the Portrait of a Celebrated Publisher. John Greenleaf Whittier. **CP-WhitJ**

Lines on Thomas Warton's Poems ("Wheresoe'er I turn my view"). Samuel Johnson. **CP-JohnS**

Lines on Thomas Warton's Poems ("Hermit hoar, in solemn cell"). Samuel Johnson. *See* Hermit Hoar.

Lines Prefixed to John Davies' Translation of Voiture's Letters, 1657. Richard Lovelace. **CP-LoveR**

Lines Rhymed in a Letter Received by (J. H. R[eynolds]) from Oxford. John Keats. *See* The Gothic looks solemn.

Lines Sent to Sir John Whiteford, of Whiteford, Bart. with the Foregoing Poem. Robert Burns. **CP-BurnR**

Lines Suggested By a Portrait from the Pencil of F. Stone. William Wordsworth. **CP-WorW2**

Lines Suggested by the Last Words of Berengarius. Samuel Taylor Coleridge. **CP-ColeS**

Lines to a Beautiful Spring in a Village. Samuel Taylor Coleridge. **CP-ColeS**

Lines to a Comic Author, on an Abusive Review. Samuel Taylor Coleridge. **CP-ColeS**

Lines to a Critic. Percy Bysshe Shelley. **CP-ShelP**

Lines to a Duck in a Park. Thomas Stearns Eliot. *Fr.* Five-Finger Exercises. **CP-ElioT**

Lines to a Friend Visiting America. George Meredith. **CP-MerG1**

Lines to a Girl 5 Days After Her 21st Birthday. Ernest Hemingway. **CP-HemiE**

Lines to a Lady Weeping. Byron. **CP-Byron**

Lines to a Movement in Mozart's E-Flat Symphony. Thomas Hardy. **CP-HardT**

Lines to a Persian Cat. Thomas Stearns Eliot. *Fr.* Five-Finger Exercises. **CP-ElioT**

Lines to a Reviewer. Percy Bysshe Shelley. **CP-ShelP**

Lines to a Seagreen Lover. Isabella Gardner. **CP-GardI**

Lines to a Three-Name Lady. Ogden Nash. **CP-NashO**

Lines to a World-famous Poet Who Failed to Complete a World-famous Poem; or, Come Clean, Mr. Guest! Ogden Nash. **CP-NashO**

Lines to a Yorkshire Terrier. Thomas Stearns Eliot. *Fr.* Five-Finger Exercises. **CP-ElioT**

Lines to a Young Lady on Her Having Very Nearly Won a Vögel. Ernest Hemingway. **CP-HemiE**

Lines to Be Embroidered on a Bib, or, The Child Is Father of the Man, but Not for Quite a While. Ogden Nash. **CP-NashO**

Lines To Be Mumbled At Ovington's. Ogden Nash. **CP-NashO**

Lines to Be Read at the Casting of Scott FitzGerald's Balls into the Sea from Eden Roc (Antibes, Alpes Maritimes). Ernest Hemingway. **CP-HemiE**

Lines to Be Scribbled on Somebody Else's Thirtieth Milestone. Ogden Nash. **CP-NashO**

Lines to Dr Walter Birk On His Retiring from General Practice. Wystan Hugh Auden. *Fr.* Eleven Occasional Poems. **CP-AudeW**

Lines to Mr Frost. John Berryman. **CP-BerrJ**

Lines to Mr Hodgson. Byron. **CP-Byron**

Lines to My Father. Countee Cullen. **CP-CullC**

Lines to My Grandfather. Christina Georgina Rossetti. **CP-RosC3**

Lines to Pope. Jonathan Swift. **CP-SwifJ**

Lines to Ralph Hodgson Esqre. Thomas Stearns Eliot. **NBLV; OBAL; PeLV** *Fr.* Five-Finger Exercises. **CP-ElioT**

Lines to the Memory of James Dow. Robert Browning. **CP-BroR2**

Lines to Thomas Poole. Samuel Taylor Coleridge. **CP-ColeS**

Lines upon Leaving a Sanitarium. Theodore Roethke. **CP-RoetT**

Lines with a Pocket Book. Christopher Smart. **SP-SmarC**

Lines with Two Cockscombs. William Cowper. **CP-CowpW**

Lines Written among the Euganean Hills. Percy Bysshe Shelley. **CP-ShelP**

Lines Written as a School Exercise at Hawkshead, Anno Aetatis 14. William Wordsworth. **CP-WorW1**

Lines Written at Taormina, Sicily. John Gould Fletcher. **SP-FletJ**

Lines Written at the King's Arms, Ross, Formerly the House of the "Man of Ross." Samuel Taylor Coleridge. **CP-ColeS**

Lines Written beneath a Picture. Byron. **CP-Byron**

Lines Written beneath an Elm in the Churchyard of Harrow. Byron. **CP-Byron**

Lines Written During a Period of Insanity. William Cowper. **CP-CowpW**

Lines Written During the Castlereagh Administration. Percy Bysshe Shelley. **CP-ShelP**

Lines Written for Gene Kelly to Dance To. Carl Sandburg. **CP-SandC**

Lines Written for Miss Patty More. William Cowper. **CP-CowpW**

Lines Written in an Album. John Greenleaf Whittier. **CP-WhitJ**

Lines Written in an Album, at Malta. Byron. **CP-Byron**

Lines Written in an Asylum. Hayden Carruth. **CP-CarHS**

Lines Written in Dejection. William Butler Yeats. **CP-YeatW**

Lines Written in Dejection on the Eve of Great Success. Robert Frost. **CP-FrosR**

Lines Written in Early Spring. William Wordsworth. **CP-WorW1**

Lines Written in Recapitulation. Edna St. Vincent Millay. **CP-MillE**

Lines Written in the Album at Elbingerode, in the Har[t]z Forest. Samuel Taylor Coleridge. **CP-ColeS**

Lines Written in the Album of the Countess of Lonsdale. William Wordsworth. **CP-WorW2**

Lines Written in the Bay of Lerici. Percy Bysshe Shelley. **CP-ShelP**

Lines Written in the Euganean Hills. Charles Tomlinson. **CP-TomlC**

Lines Written in the Fannie Farmer Cookbook. Elizabeth Bishop. **CP-BishE**

Lines Written in the Highlands after a Visit to Burns's Country. John Keats. **CP-KeatJ**

Lines Written in the Kirk of Lamington. Robert Burns. **CP-BurnR**

Lines Written in the Monthly Review. William Cowper. **CP-CowpW**

Lines Written in the Travellers' Book at Orchomenus. Byron. **CP-Byron**

Lines Written on a Bank-Note. Robert Burns. **CP-BurnR**

Lines Written on a Blank Leaf in a Copy of the Author's Poem "The Excursion", upon Hearing of the Death of the Late Vicar of Kendal. William Wordsworth. **CP-WorW2**

Lines Written on a Blank Leaf of the "Pleasures of Memory." Byron. **CP-Byron**

Lines *Written on a Window, at the King's Arms Tavern, Dumfries.* Robert Burns. **CP-BurnR**

Lines Written on Hearing the News of the Death of Napoleon. Percy Bysshe Shelley. **CP-ShelP**

Lines Written on Reading Dostoievski. Malcolm Lowry. *Fr.* The Roar of the Sea and the Darkness. **CP-LowrM**

Lines *Written on the Windows of the Globe Tavern, Dumfries.* Robert Burns. **CP-BurnR**
  "Greybeard, old wisdom, may boast of his treasures, The."
  "In politics if thou would'st mix."
  "My bottle is a holy pool."
  Song: "I murder hate by field or flood." **NCEP**

Lines Written on 29 May / The Anniversary of the Restoration of Charles the 2nd. John Keats. **CP-KeatJ**

Lines Written to Martyn Skinner Before His Departure from Oxfordshire in Search of Quiet—1961. Sir John Betjeman. **CP-BetjJ**

Lines Written upon a Window-Shutter at Weston. William Cowper. **CP-CowpW**

Lines Written While Sailing in a Boat at Evening. William Wordsworth. **CP-WorW1**

LING / Our dynasty came in because of a great sensibility. Canto 85. Ezra Pound. *Fr.* Cantos. **CP-PoCan**

Lingard and the Stars. Edwin Arlington Robinson. **CP-RobiE**

Linger not in my library. *Mine Host.* Alun Lewis. *Fr.* Poems from the Chinese. **CP-LewiA**

Lingering Last Drops. Walt Whitman. **CP-WhitW**

Link between Barnum and Calas, The. The Phoenix and the Tortoise. William Carlos Williams. **CP-WilW2**

Link your arm in mine, my lad. Robert Louis Stevenson. **CP-StevR**

Linnet, The. Walter de la Mare. **CP-DeLaW**

Linnet-Hawker, The. George Meredith. **CP-MerG2**

Linnet in a gilded cage,— / A linnet on a bough, A. Christina Georgina Rossetti. **CP-RosC2**

Linnet in the rocky dells, The. Song. Emily Brontë. **CP-BronE**

Linnet's warble, sinking toward a close, The. By the Side of Rydal Mere. William Wordsworth. **CP-WorW2**

Linnit playes rarely on the Lute, we know. Upon Linnit. Robert Herrick. **CP-HerrR**

Linoleum. Tess Gallagher. **SP-GallT**

Lint Pulling, The. John Hewitt. **CP-HewiJ**

L'Invitation au Voyage. Charles Baudelaire, *tr. fr. French by* Richard Wilbur. **CP-WilbR**

Lion, The. Nicholas Vachel Lindsay. **CP-LindV**

Lion, The. Thomas Merton. **CP-MertT**

Lion, The. Ogden Nash. **CP-NashO**

Lion. Kenneth Rexroth. **HoPM; SP-RexrK** *Fr.* A Bestiary. **SP-RexrK**

Lion, The. William Carlos Williams. **CP-WilW2**

Lion & Honeycomb. Howard Nemerov. **CP-NemeH**

Lion and lioness, the mild. The Assisi Fragments. Geoffrey Hill. **CP-HillG**

Lion and the Dog, The. Robert Creeley. **CP-CreeR**

Lion and the Rose, The. May Sarton. **SP-SartM**

Lion dishonoured bids death come, The. Reversionary. Stevie Smith. **CP-SmitS**

Lion Farm, The. Leonard Nathan. **SP-NathL**

Lion for Real, The. Allen Ginsberg. **CP-GinsA**

Lion-Gentle. Robert Ranke Graves. **CP-GravR**

Lion-girl of the Rue Payenne. Serenade to Leonor. Charles Henri Ford. **SP-FordC**

Lion-heart, you prowl alone. *Song:* Crown of Stars. Robert Ranke Graves. **CP-GravR**

Lion In Love, The. Marianne Craig Moore. **CP-MoorM** *Fr.* Fables of La Fontaine.

Lion in the path, a lion, A. Song: Dream Warning. Robert Ranke Graves. **CP-GravR**

Lion is a kingly beast, The. The Lion. Nicholas Vachel Lindsay. **CP-LindV**

Lion is called the king, The. Lion. Kenneth Rexroth. **HoPM; SP-RexrK** *Fr.* A Bestiary. **SP-RexrK**

Lion Lover. Robert Ranke Graves. **CP-GravR**

Lion of St. Mark's upon the glass, The. Her Dead Brother. Robert Lowell. **SP-LoweR**

Lion sits within his cage, The. The Zoo. Stevie Smith. **CP-SmitS**

Lion upon the Floor, A. Charles Olson. **CP-OlsoC**

Lions, The. Robert Earl Hayden. **CP-HaydR**

Lions Copulating. Richard Eberhart. **CP-EberR**

Lions in Sweden. Wallace Stevens. **CP-StevW**

Lions in the street & roaming. Celebration of the Lizard. Jim Morrison. **SP-MorrJ**

Lions of fire, The. Kenneth Patchen. **CP-PatcK**

Lions who ate the Christians on the sands of the arena, The. Sunt Leones. Stevie Smith. **CP-SmitS**

Lip Labour. Robert Herrick. **CP-HerrR**

Lips and Eyes. Giovanni Battista Marino, *tr. fr. Italian by* Thomas Carew. **CP-CareT**

Lips half-willing in a doorway. Village in Late Summer. Carl Sandburg. **CP-SandC**

Lips so apt for deeds of passion, The. Portrait. Wystan Hugh Auden. **CP-AudWJ**

Lips Tongueless[e]. Robert Herrick. **CP-HerrR**

Liquid Paper. Peter Meinke. **SP-MeinP**

Liquor and love. The World Narrowed to a Point. William Carlos Williams. **CP-WilW2**

Lis / -ten / you know what i mean when. Edward Estlin Cummings. **CP-CummE**

Lisetta all' Amante. Christina Georgina Rossetti. **CP-RosC3**

Lisette and Eileen. Edwin Arlington Robinson. **CP-RobiE**

Lispeth. Rudyard Kipling. *Fr.* Plain Tales from the Hills.

"Look, you have cast out Love! What Gods are these." **CP-KiplR**

List! the bell-Sprite stuns my ears. Dirge Sung by a Minstrel. William Wordsworth. **CP-WorW1**

List the harp in window wailing. The Æolian Harp. Herman Melville. **SP-MelvH**

List, the winds of March are blowing. Warning, The. William Wordsworth. **CP-WorW2**

List—'twas the Cuckoo.—O with what delight. Cuckoo at Laverna May 25, 1837, The. William Wordsworth. *Fr.* Memorials of a Tour in Italy, 1837. **CP-WorW2**

List, ye, who pass by Lyulph's Tower. The Somnambulist. William Wordsworth. *Fr.* Poems Composed or Suggested During a Tour, in the Summer of 1833. **CP-WorW2**

Listen / beloved / i dreamed. Edward Estlin Cummings. **CP-CummE**

Listen. Hayden Carruth. **CP-CarHS**

Listen! / Dear dream of utter aliveness. Demand. Langston Hughes. **SP-HughL**

Listen, / if I came to you, out of the wind. Michael Hartnett. *Fr.* Anatomy of a Cliché. **SP-HarMi**

Listen. / It is by this / shore. On This Shore. Siv Cedering Fox. **SP-CedeS**

Listen / Listen / O what is that sound. Kenneth Patchen. *Fr.* Wanderers of the Pale Wood. **CP-PatcK**

Listen. Ogden Nash. **CP-NashO**

Listen, / stop tanning yourself. Without Commercials. Alice Walker. **CP-WalkA**

(Listen) / this a dog barks and. Edward Estlin Cummings. **CP-CummE**

Listen. Alice Walker. **CP-WalkA**

Listen a while, the moon is a lovely woman, a lonely woman, lost in a. Night Stuff. Carl Sandburg. **CP-SandC**

Listen, all of you, listen, all of you. To Dean Inge Lecturing on Origen. Stevie Smith. **CP-SmitS**

Listen, and I will tell you of a face. Christina Georgina Rossetti. **CP-RosC3**

Listen, and you shall hear above the storm. Overture for an Ulster Literature. John Hewitt. **CP-HewiJ**

Listen brother love you. Hard Love Rock II. Audre Lorde. **SP-LordA**

Listen, buds, it's March twenty-first. Spring Song. Ogden Nash. **CP-NashO**

Listen but once to the words written out by my hand. Short Summary. Louise Bogan. **CP-BogaL**

Listen carefully. / I'm meditating. Charles Kenneth Williams. **CP-WillC; SP-WillC**

Listen, children: / Your father is dead. Lament. Edna St. Vincent Millay. **CP-MillE**

Listen, children, if you'll only stop throwing peanuts and bananas. Let's Not Climb the Washington Monument Tonight. Ogden Nash. **CP-NashO**

Listen: from sleep's long pillow I arise. Last Words. Stanley Jasspon Kunitz. **CP-KuniS**

Listen, good people, and you shall hear. The Ballad of Barnaby. Wystan Hugh Auden. **OBNV** *Fr.* Six Commissioned Texts. **CP-AudeW**

Listen here. I've never played it safe. August 8th. Anne Sexton. **SP-SextA**

Listen here, sistren and brethren, I am goddamn tired. The Sociology of Toyotas and Jade Chrysanthemums. Hayden Carruth. **CP-CarHS**

Listen how the river berates me: all one. In Memoriam: Robert Fitzgerald. Martin Edmunds. **SP-EdmuM**

Listen, I went to get a haircut, it was a perfectly good day. Big Bastard with a Sword. Charles Bukowski. **SP-BukC2**

Listen, in night's last tender hour. Hayden Carruth. *Fr.* Michigan Water: a Few Riffs before Dawn. **CP-CarHL**

Listen! It's never sung like that! Listen! Fever. Hendrick De Vries, *tr. fr. Dutch by* Adrienne Rich. **CP-RicAE**

Listen, Kid Sleepy. Kid Sleepy. Langston Hughes. **SP-HughL**

Listen, listen, Mary mine. Passage of the Apennines. Percy Bysshe Shelley. **CP-ShelP**

Listen motorists, and learn. The Strange Case of Mr. Niobob's Transmogrification. Ogden Nash. **CP-NashO**

Listen my children and you. Edward Estlin Cummings. **CP-CummE**

Listen, my children, and you shall hear. Paul Revere's Ride (The Landlord's Tale). Henry Wadsworth Longfellow. **SP-LongH** *Fr.* Tales of a Wayside Inn.

Listen, Ripley. Richard Hugo. **CP-HugoR**

Listen, Saints. Thomas Merton. **CP-MertT**

Listen—she's coming now. Jubilee. Leonard Nathan. **SP-NathL**

Listen sweet Dove unto my song. Whitsunday. George Herbert. **CP-HerbG**

Listen, the dark lark chants once more. He Who Excuses Himself Also Accuses Himself. Delmore Schwartz. **SP-SchwD**

Listen, the hay-bells tinkle as the cart. The Holy Innocents. Robert Lowell. **SP-LoweR**

Listen, the last stroke of death's noon has struck. The Plague. Christina Georgina Rossetti. **CP-RosC3**

Listen! the sky! Vast conflagration! Midsummer Dawn. Archibald MacLeish. **CP-MacLA**

Listen to me, angel tot. Thunder over the Nursery. Ogden Nash. **CP-NashO**

Listen to me, baby. If You Gotta Go, Go Now. "Bob Dylan." **CP-DylaB**

Listen to people laughing. Laughter. David Herbert Lawrence. **CP-LawrD**

Listen to the Band! David Herbert Lawrence. **CP-LawrD**

Listen to the Linotype. Ogden Nash. **CP-NashO**

Listen To The Mustn'ts. Shel Silverstein. **SP-SilS2**

Listen to the stories. On Hearing a Name Long Unspoken. Leonard Cohen. **CP-CoheL**

Listen to the tale of the sensitive car. Wrote This Last Night. Allen Ginsberg. **CP-GinsA**

Listen to the ticking of the old Great Clock. Altgeld. Carl Sandburg. **CP-SandC**

Listen to yo' prophets. Shout. Langston Hughes. **SP-HughL**

Listen! when your hair, like mine. From a Dungeon Wall in the Southern College. Emily Brontë. **CP-BronE**

Listen. Wind hangs in the pine branches. Audit. Leonard Nathan. **SP-NathL**

Listen with a tremor to the aero-captain. Thomas Merton. *Fr.* Cables to the Ace. **CP-MertT**

Listener, The. Stephen Dunn. **SP-DunnS**

Listener, The. John Hewitt. **CP-HewiJ**

Listener, The. Stevie Smith. **CP-SmitS**

Listeners, The. Walter de la Mare. **CP-DeLaW**

Listening. David Herbert Lawrence. **CP-LawrD**

Listening. Christina Georgina Rossetti. **CP-RosC3**

Listening. William Stafford. **SP-StafW**

Listening by a Woodpile, Night of Moon after Snow. Brendan Galvin. **SP-GalvB**

Listening for reality. Creed. Leonard Nathan. **SP-NathL**

Listening in October. John Haines. **SP-HainJ**

Listening, listening; it is never still. The Märchen. Randall Jarrell. **CP-JarrR; SP-JarrR**

Listening one day on the radio. The Listener. Stevie Smith. **CP-SmitS**

Listening to Bach. Robert Bly. *Fr.* Six Winter Privacy Poems. **SP-BlyR**

Listening to Bruckner on the radio. Defeat. Charles Bukowski. **SP-BukC1**

Listening to Foxhounds. James Dickey. **CP-DickJ**

Listening to hard bop. Zimmer's Last Gig. Paul Zimmer. **SP-ZimmP**

Listening to Jefferson Airplane. Thom Gunn. **CP-GunnT**

Listening to the Köln Concert. Robert Bly. **SP-BlyR**

Listening to the Mourners. James Wright. **CP-WrigJ**

Listening to the Music. Marsden Hartley. **CP-HartM**

Listen,you morons great and small. Ballad of an Intellectual. Edward Estlin Cummings. **CP-CummE**

Listeth, lordes, in good entent. Sir Thopas. Geoffrey Chaucer. **BXAP; NAEL-1; Par** *Fr.* The Canterbury Tales. **CP-ChauG**

Listing. Richard Eberhart. **CP-EberR**

Listless, / the heat rises—. Robert Creeley. **CP-CreeR**

Listless beauty of the hour, The. History. David Herbert Lawrence. **CP-LawrD**

Lists, The. Leonard Cohen. **CP-CoheL**

Lisy's Parting with Her Cat. James Thomson. **CP-ThomJ**

Lit clouds diffuse tree. Shading Flight In. Archie Randolph Ammons. **SP-AmmoA**

Lit the fire last night. X marks the spot. A postcard from home. Jenny Joseph. *Fr.* Derivations. **SP-JoseJ**

Litany: "All holy souls / pray for us fellows." Thomas Merton. **CP-MertT**

Litany. John Ashbery. **SP-AshbJ**

"Some certified nut." **SP-AshbJ**

Litany, A. John Donne. **CP-DonnJ**

"And through that bitter agony [*or* agonie]."

"And whilst [*or* whil'st] this universal choir [*or* universall Quire]."

Angels, The.

Apostles, The.

Confessors, The.

"Deliver us for thy descent."

Doctors, The.

Father, The. **NOCV**

"From being anxious, or secure."

"From needing danger, to be[e] good."

"From tempting Satan to tempt us."

"Hear[e] us, O hear[e] us Lord; to thee."

Holy Ghost, The. **NOCV**

"In churches, when the infirmity [*or* the'infirmitie]."

Martyrs, The.

Patriarchs, The.

Prophets, The.

Son, The. **NOCV**

"Son[ne] of God hear[e] us, and since thou."

"That learning, thine ambassador."

"That living law, the magistrate."

"That our ears' sickness we [*or* eares sicknesse wee] may cure."

"That we[e] may change to evenness[e]."

"Through thy submitting all, to blow[e]s."

Virgin Mary, The.

Virgins, The.

"When senses, which thy so[u]ldiers are."

Litany: "Gather up / In the arms of your pity." Langston Hughes. **SP-HughL**

Litany: "It yawns at me the cavernous gulf." Thomas Merton. **CP-MertT**

Litany: "Sing miserere / For the men who must die." Thomas Merton. **CP-MertT**

Litany of Grey Nurses. David Herbert Lawrence. *Fr.* Bits. **CP-LawrD**

Litany of Satan, The. James Liddy. **CP-LiddJ**

Litany of the Dark People, The. Countee Cullen. **CP-CullC**

Litany of the Heroes. Nicholas Vachel Lindsay. **CP-LindV**

Lincoln. **OHIP**

Literary Discovery, A. Sir John Betjeman. **CP-BetjJ**

Literary Dublin. John Updike. **CP-UpdiJ**

Literary Life, The. Charles Bukowski. **SP-BukC2**

Literary Reflection. Ogden Nash. **CP-NashO**

Literary Scene, The. Ogden Nash. **CP-NashO**

Literary World, The. Philip Larkin. **CP-LarkP**

Literate Farmer and the Planet Venus, The. Robert Frost. **CP-FrosR**

Literature is a phase of life. If one is afraid of it. Picking and Choosing. Marianne Craig Moore. **CP-MoorM**

Lithuanian lithographer, A. A Song of Paternal Care. John Updike. **CP-UpdiJ**

Litter under the tree, The. Bone Poem. Mary Oliver. **SP-OlivM**

Little / house with, A. A Picture. Robert Creeley. **CP-CreeR**

Little / water, A. For Marisol. Robert Creeley. **CP-CreeR**

Little after 5:00 the curb in front of, A. Panty Hose. Ron Koertge. **SP-KoerR**

Little airplanes of the heart, The. Sandinista Avioncitos. Lawrence Ferlinghetti. **SP-FerlL**

Little and Loud. Robert Herrick. **CP-HerrR**

Little Apocalypse; Hölderlin: 1770–1843. Geoffrey Hill. **CP-HillG**

Little ash, a painted rose, a name, A. After a Death. Charles Tomlinson. **CP-TomlC**

Little Ballad for Americans—1954. Edwin Rolfe. **CP-RolfE**

Little biplane that has the river-meadow for landing-field, The. The Machine. Robinson Jeffers. **CP-JefR1**

Little Bird Alone. Marsden Hartley. *Fr.* Word Arrangements for Pictures by Morris Graves. **CP-HartM**

Little bird has told me that today will appear, A. A Song in July. Nicholas Vachel Lindsay. **CP-LindV**

Little bird sits in the nest and sings, The. Preparation. Paul Laurence Dunbar. **CP-DunbP**

Little bird, with plumage brown, A. The Sparrow. Paul Laurence Dunbar. **CP-DunbP**

Little Birds, *sels.* "Lewis Carroll." *Fr.* Sylvie and Bruno Concluded.

"Little Birds are dining." **CP-CarrL**

Little Birds Are Playing. **OxBoLi; PeLV**

Little Birds are dining. "Lewis Carroll." **CP-CarrL** *Fr.* Little Birds. *Fr.* Sylvie and Bruno Concluded.

Little Birds Are Playing. **OxBoLi; PeLV**

Little Birds are dining. Little Birds. "Lewis Carroll." *Fr.* Sylvie and Bruno Concluded.

Little Birds Are Playing. "Lewis Carroll." **OxBoLi; PeLV** *Fr.* Little Birds are dining. **CP-CarrL** *Fr.* Little Birds. *Fr.* Sylvie and Bruno Concluded.

Little Birds are playing. Little Birds Are Playing. "Lewis Carroll." **OxBoLi; PeLV** *Fr.* Little Birds are dining. **CP-CarrL** *Fr.* Little Birds. *Fr.* Sylvie and Bruno Concluded.

Little birds sit on your shoulders. For Miriam. Kenneth Patchen. **CP-PatcK**

Little Black Boy, The. William Blake. **AWP; BiP; CABA; CH; EnRP; FHYEP; HBV; HeIP; HoFi; InPK; LauP; NAEL-2; NAWM-2; NOBRP; NOEC; NoP; OAEL-2; OAEP; OBEC; OBEV; OBNC; OxBChV; OxBoCh; PeECV; PoE; PoEL-4; PoNe; SCGP; SeCeV; TFi; TrGrPo; TreFS** *Fr.* Songs of Innocence. **CP-BlakW**

Little black thing among the snow, A. Chimney Sweeper, The. William Blake. **CP-BlakW** *Fr.* Songs of Experience.

Little Black Train, The. Kenneth Patchen. **CP-PatcK**

Little Blind Fish, thou art marvellous wise! Rudyard Kipling. **CP-KiplR** *Fr.* The Bisara of Pooree. *Fr.* Plain Tales from the Hills.

Little Blue Engine, The. Shel Silverstein. **SP-SilS2**

Little Blue Nude. William Matthews. **SP-MattW**

Little boat at anchor, The. Fourth of July Night. Carl Sandburg. **CP-SandC**

Little bonus / of my hand on your breast, The. Love Poem (Later). Jim Carroll. **SP-CarrJ**

Little Bourgeois is Upset, The. John Hewitt. *Fr.* Two Sonnets. **CP-HewiJ**

Little boy / Will you stop. The Hound of Ulster. Stevie Smith. **CP-SmitS**

Little Boy and Lost Shoe. Robert Penn Warren. **SP-WarrR**

Little-Boy Brilliant. David Herbert Lawrence. **CP-LawrD**

Little Boy Found, The. William Blake. **EnRP; FHYEP; LAuP; NoP** Fr. Songs of Innocence. **CP-BlakW**

Little boy legged on through the dark. No Bell-Ringing. Thomas Hardy. **CP-HardT**

Little Boy Lost, A ("Nought loves another as itself"). William Blake. **CP-BlakW** Fr. Songs of Experience.

Little Boy Lost, The ("Father, father, where are you going?"). William Blake. **EnRP; FHYEP; LAuP; NoP; TiPo** Fr. Songs of Innocence. **CP-BlakW**

Little Boy Lost. Stevie Smith. **CP-SmitS**

Little boy lost in the lonely fen, The. The Little Boy Found. William Blake. **EnRP; FHYEP; LAuP; NoP** Fr. Songs of Innocence. **CP-BlakW**

Little-boy lover, The. For All Who Ever Sent Lace Valentines. Nicholas Vachel Lindsay. **CP-LindV**

Little Boy Sick. Stevie Smith. **CP-SmitS**

Little Boy, to show his might and power, The. The Metamorphosis. Sir John Suckling. **CP-SuckJ**

Little boy wears my mistakes, A. As I Grew Up Again. Audre Lorde. **SP-LordA**

Little boys, faces smeared. Charles Henri Ford. **SP-FordC** Fr. Secret Haiku.

Little bread, a crust, a crumb, A. Emily Dickinson. **CP-DickE**

Little Brown Baby. Paul Laurence Dunbar. **CP-DunbP**

Little brown face full of smiles. Liza May. Paul Laurence Dunbar. **CP-DunbP**

Little calls as they pass. Surrounded by Wild Turkeys. Gary Snyder. **CP-SnydG**

Little Candle. Carl Sandburg. **CP-SandC**

Little Cannibal's Bedtimesong. Kenneth Patchen. **CP-PatcK**

Little child, A. The Eternal Child. Kathleen Jessie Raine. **SP-RainK**

Little Child. The Beatles. **CP-Beatl**

Little Child of Brightest Face. Stevie Smith. **CP-SmitS**

Little children have been fighting, The. I Am the Bitter Name. Charles Kenneth Williams. **CP-WillC; SP-WillC**

Little Christmas Basket, A. Paul Laurence Dunbar. **CP-DunbP**

Little cirque, horizon-wide, The. Evening. Walter de la Mare. **CP-DeLaW**

Little city looks as if it had been, The. The Outcast City on the Kennebec. Marsden Hartley. **CP-HartM**

Little Coat, The. Stephen Spender. **CP-SpenS**

Little colt—broncho, loaned to the farm, A. The Broncho That Would Not Be Broken. Nicholas Vachel Lindsay. **CP-LindV**

Little cousin is dead, by foul subtraction, The. Dead Boy. John Crowe Ransom. **SP-RansJ**

Little cullud boys / with fears. Tag. Langston Hughes. **SP-HughL**

Little cullud boys with beards. Flatted Fifths. Langston Hughes. **SP-HughL**

Little dapper man but with shiny elbows, A. Louis MacNeice. Fr. The Kingdom. **CP-MacNL**

Little Daughters of America, The. Stevie Smith. **CP-SmitS**

Little Death, The. Hayden Carruth. Fr. Contra Mortem. **CP-CarHL**

Little Death, The. John Hewitt. **CP-HewiJ**

Little Devils. Pablo Neruda, tr. fr. Spanish by Ben Belitt. **SP-NeruP**

Little Ditty for This Day to the Beloved Harteebeeste, A. Malcolm Lowry. **CP-LowrM**

Little Dog that wags his tail, A. Emily Dickinson. **CP-DickE**

Little dots. Jenny Joseph. Fr. Life and Turgid Times of A. Citizen. **SP-JoseJ**

Little dreaming by the way, A. The Sum. Paul Laurence Dunbar. **CP-DunbP**

Little drops of grain alcohol. Ernest Hemingway. **CP-HemiE**

Little drunk, / a little high, / about to go off, A. Saturday Night. James Schuyler. **CP-SchuJ**

Little earth, water / walking on, sun. Here. Robert Creeley. **CP-CreeR**

Little East of Jordan, A. Emily Dickinson. **CP-DickE**

Little egg, little nub. The Birth of the Water Baby. Erica Jong. **SP-JongE**

Little Ellie sits alone. The Romance of the Swan's Nest. Elizabeth Barrett Browning. **CP-BroEB**

Little emissary to tomorrow. Noses. Stephen Dobyns. **SP-DobyS**

Little Exercise. Elizabeth Bishop. **CP-BishE**

Little Fanfare for Felix Magowan. James Merrill. **SP-MerrJ**

Little farm, motherland, made. Wendell Berry. Fr. From the Crest. **CP-BerrW**

Little Feet. Ogden Nash. **CP-NashO**

Little fellow, you're amusing. Song of the Ogres. Wystan Hugh Auden. **RHPC** Fr. Two Songs. **CP-AudeW**

Little figures in the architect's drawing, The. Artists, Providers, Places to Go. Roy Fisher. **SP-FishR**

Little Fire in the Woods, The. Hayden Carruth. **CP-CarHS**

Little Fish. David Herbert Lawrence. **CP-LawrD**

Little fish eats the tiny fish, The. Fish? Shel Silverstein. **SP-SilS2**

Little Flower grew in a lonely Vale, A. To Mrs Ann Flaxman. William Blake. **CP-BlakW**

Little Fly. William Blake. **CP-BlakW** Fr. Songs of Experience.

(Fly, The.) **CP-BlakW**

("Woe alas my guilty hand.") **CP-BlakW**

Little fogs were gathered in every hollow. The Country Wedding. Thomas Hardy. **CP-HardT**

Little Foot-Page, The. George Meredith. **CP-MerG2**

Little Friend, The. Elizabeth Barrett Browning. **CP-BroEB**

Little Fugue. Sylvia Plath. **CP-PlatS**

Little further, O my father, yet a little further, A. The Wanderings of Cain. Samuel Taylor Coleridge. **CP-ColeS**

Little garden within, The. Emily Dickinson. **SP-DickE**

Little gay bonnets! so many. Watching Neighbors' Children. Kenneth Patchen. **CP-PatcK**

Little Ghost, The. Edna St. Vincent Millay. **CP-MillE**

Little Gidding. Thomas Stearns Eliot. **FaBoMo; FaBoPV; FaBoTw; GTBS-6; GTBS-P; MoP; NAEL-2; NAWM-2; NOBA; NOBE; NoAM; OAEL-2; OXAEP-2; OxBTC; PeECV; PrIm; TAP; TFi** Fr. Four Quartets. **CP-ElioT**

"Ash on an old man's sleeve." **FaBoTw**

"We shall not cease from exploration." **ImOP**

Little girl / Dreaming of a baby grand piano. To Be Somebody. Langston Hughes. **SP-HughL**

Little Girl, Be Careful What You Say. Carl Sandburg. **CP-SandC**

Little Girl Found, The. William Blake. **CP-BlakW** Fr. Songs of Experience.

Little Girl Found, The. William Blake. **CP-BlakW; FHYEP; NOBRP** Fr. Songs of Innocence. **CP-BlakW**

Little Girl Lost, A. William Blake. **CP-BlakW** Fr. Songs of Experience.

Little Girl Lost, The. William Blake. **CP-BlakW** Fr. Songs of Experience.

Little Girl Lost, The. William Blake. **CP-BlakW; FHYEP; NOBRP** Fr. Songs of Innocence. **CP-BlakW**

Little Girl, My String Bean, My Lovely Woman. Anne Sexton. **CP-SextA**

Little Girl on Her Way to School, A. James Wright. **CP-WrigJ**

Little Girl Speakings. Maya Angelou. **SP-AngeM**

Little girl was given a new toy, A. Death Will Amuse Them. Kenneth Patchen. **CP-PatcK**

Little girl won't eat her sandwich, The. Blasting from Heaven. Philip Levine. **SP-LeviP**

Little Girls, The. Charles Bukowski. **SP-BukC1**

Little Glen, The. John Hewitt. **CP-HewiJ**

Little Good Fellows, The. Herman Melville. **SP-MelvH**

Little Green Snake. Marsden Hartley. **CP-HartM**

Little Green Tree. Langston Hughes. **SP-HughL**

Little guts, self drama and it's done, A. The Prado: Number 2671, Anonimo Español. Richard Hugo. **CP-HugoR**

Little has changed. Six dark mornings a week. Last Words from Maratea. Richard Hugo. **CP-HugoR**

Little head against my shoulder. The Sigh. Thomas Hardy. **CP-HardT**

Little hedgerow birds, The. William Wordsworth. **CP-WorW1**

(Animal Tranquility and Decay.) **CP-WorW1**

Little Hill, The. Edna St. Vincent Millay. **CP-MillE**

Little hill climbs up to the village and puts its green hands, The. Kenneth Patchen. **NaP** Fr. The Hunted City. **CP-PatcK**

Little Hole, The. George Oppen. Fr. Five Poems about Poetry. **CP-OppeG**

Little horse is newlY, The. Edward Estlin Cummings. **CP-CummE**

Little House, The. John Hewitt. **CP-HewiJ**

Little Indian, Sioux, or Crow. Foreign Children. Robert Louis Stevenson. **CP-StevR**

Little inmate, full of mirth. The Cricket. Vincent Bourne, tr. fr. Latin by William Cowper. **CP-CowpW**

Little islands out at sea, on the horizon. The Greeks Are Coming! David Herbert Lawrence. **CP-LawrD**

Little Jack Horner. Nursery Rhyme No. 2. Isabella Gardner. **CP-GardI**

Little joe gould has lost his teeth and doesn't know where. Edward Estlin Cummings. **CP-CummE; SP-CummE**

Little Julie / Has grown quite tall. Delinquent. Langston Hughes. **SP-HughL**

Little Known Bird of the Inner Eye. Marsden Hartley. Fr. Word Arrangements for Pictures by Morris Graves. **CP-HartM**

Little ladies more / than dead exactly dance. Edward Estlin Cummings. **CP-CummE**

Little lady at de do'. The Visitor. Paul Laurence Dunbar. **CP-DunbP**

Little Lamb, who lost thee?— / I myself, none other. Rejoice with Me. Christina Georgina Rossetti. **CP-RosC2**

Little Lamb, who made thee? / Dost thou know who made thee. The Lamb. William Blake. **BLPL; BoTP; CABA; CH; ChIV-2; EBCP; EBEvV; EaLo; EnRP; FHYEP; FaBoBe; FaBoCh; FaPON; GoJo; HBV; HeIL; HeIP; ImPo; InPS; LauP; LiTB; LoBV; MeMBP; NAEL-2; NAWM-2; NIP; NOBRP; NOEC; NoP; OAEL-2; OAEP; OBEC; OXAEP-2; OxBChV; OxBoCh; PAI; PoE; PoPl; Poetr; SBVL; SUS; SeCeV; SoSe; TEP; TFi; TRP; TRV; TrCP; TrGrPo; TreF; UnPo; WGRP; WHA** *Fr.* Songs of Innocence. **CP-BlakW**

Little lamb who made thee? / Ho but the egg is growing hair. Charles Henri Ford. *Fr.* Epigrams. **SP-FordC**

Little Land, The. Robert Louis Stevenson. **CP-StevR**

Little Learning, A. Alexander Pope. *See* A Little learning is a dangerous [*or* dang'rous] thing.

Little learning is a dangerous [*or* dang'rous] thing, A. Alexander Pope. **EBEvV; FPL; HAP; HoPM; PoLF; TrGrPo,** *ll.* 215–232; **ChTr; FaFP; ImPo; LiTB; NOBE; SeCePo** *Fr.* An Essay on Criticism. **CP-PopeA**

(Alps on Alps.) **FaFP,** *ll.* 215–232;

(Little Learning, A.) **ChTr; NOBE; SeCePo,** *ll.* 215–232; **ImPo; LiTB,** *ll.* 215–252;

Little less returned for him each spring, A. Anglais Mort à Florence. Wallace Stevens. **CP-StevW**

Little Litany for Moving Day, A. Barton Sutter. **SP-SuttB**

Little Lives of Earth and Form, The. Philip Larkin. **CP-LarkP**

Little Lough, The. John Hewitt. **CP-HewiJ**

Little love-god lying once asleep, The. Sonnet 154. William Shakespeare. *Fr.* Sonnets. **CP-ShaWS**

Little Lucy Landman. Paul Laurence Dunbar. **CP-DunbP**

Little Lyric (of Great Importance). Langston Hughes. **SP-HughL**

Little Madness in the Spring, A. Emily Dickinson. **CP-DickE**

Little maidens, when you look. Acrostic: Little maidens, when you look. "Lewis Carroll." **CP-CarrL**

Little man / (in a hurry). Edward Estlin Cummings. **CP-CummE**

Little Man That Had a Little Gun, The. "Lewis Carroll." **CP-CarrL** *Fr.* Sylvie and Bruno Concluded.

Little marsh-plant, yellow green, A. The Sundew. Algernon Charles Swinburne. **SP-SwinA**

Little Mary Bell had a fairy in a nut. Long John Brown & Little Mary Bell. William Blake. **CP-BlakW**

Little Master Home-from-School. A Father for a Fool. Stevie Smith. **CP-SmitS**

Little Mattie. Elizabeth Barrett Browning. **CP-BroEB**

Little Millwins attend the Russian Ballet, The. Les Millwin. Ezra Pound. **SP-PounE**

Little Miss Muffet Sat on a Prophet—and Quite Right, Too! Ogden Nash. **CP-NashO**

Little Mr. Wilson / Wrote a little book. Ernest Hemingway. **CP-HemiE**

Little moon rode up a high corner, The. Clefs. Carl Sandburg. **CP-SandC**

Little More, The. James Dickey. **CP-DickJ**

Little More Traveling Music, A. Al Young. **CP-YounA**

Little morsels of smoothed gray energy. Mole. Marsden Hartley. **CP-HartM**

Little Night Music, A. Charles Tomlinson. **CP-TomlC**

Little note we were going to write you last night, A. Good Morning to Our Sweetest Harteebeeste! Malcolm Lowry. **CP-LowrM**

Little Novel, A. Gertrude Stein. **CP-SteiG**

Little Ode on St. Anne's Day. Jim Carroll. **SP-CarrJ**

Little Odyssey of Jason Quint, of Science, Doctor, The. Thomas McGrath. **SP-McGrT**

Little oily fuzzbear. Sheep. Anne Sexton. **CP-SextA**

Little Old Funky Homeric Blues for Herm, A. Hayden Carruth. **CP-CarHS**

Little old house was out with a little new shed, The. A Roadside Stand. Robert Frost. **CP-FrosR**

Little Old Letter. Langston Hughes. **SP-HughL**

Little Old Table, The. Thomas Hardy. **CP-HardT**

Little one-room schoolhouse among the redwoods, The. The Loving Shepherdess. Robinson Jeffers. **CP-JefR2**

Little one sleeps in its cradle, The. Walt Whitman. **SAmP; TrGrPo** *Fr.* Song of Myself. **CP-WhitW**

Little one, you have been buzzing in the books. On the Way. Carl Sandburg. **CP-SandC**

Little onward lend thy guiding hand, A. John Milton. **FaBoPV; OXAEP-1** *Fr.* Samson Agonistes. **CP-MiltJ**

(Samson before the Prison in Gaza.) **FaBoPV**

Little Onward Lend Thy Guiding Hand, A. William Wordsworth. **CP-WorW2**

Little overflowing word, A. Emily Dickinson. **CP-DickE**

Little owl flew through the night, The. On the Adequacy of Landscape. Wallace Stevens. **CP-StevW**

Little Owl Who Lives in the Orchard. Mary Oliver. **SP-OlivM**

Little package of Ceylon, The. Emily Dickinson. **SP-DickE**

Little pansies by the road have turned, The. Meeting among the Mountains. David Herbert Lawrence. **CP-LawrD**

Little Peasant, The. Anne Sexton. **CP-SextA**

Little People, A. John Hewitt. **CP-HewiJ**

Little pig goes to market, The. Nursery Rhyme. Charles Simic. **SP-SimiC**

Little Pin: Fragment, The. George Oppen. **CP-OppeG**

Little places as / size of. Dimensions. Robert Creeley. **CP-CreeR**

Little plum / said the mother to her son. Hansel and Gretel. Anne Sexton. **CP-SextA**

Little Poem, A. Randall Jarrell. **CP-JarrR**

Little Poem, A. Miller Williams. **SP-WillM**

Little Poem About Jazz, A. Al Young. **CP-YounA**

Little poem we will write unto our Cousin John, A. Emily Dickinson. **SP-DickE**

Little Poems. John Updike. **CP-UpdiJ**

Little poppies, little hell flames. Poppies in July. Sylvia Plath. **CP-PlatS**

Little questions of eyestripe. Lying to Fall Warblers. Brendan Galvin. **SP-GalvB**

Little ragged girl, our ball-boy, A. A Game at Salzburg. Randall Jarrell. **CP-JarrR; SP-JarrR**

Little river twittering in the twilight, The. Bei Hennef. David Herbert Lawrence. **CP-LawrD**

Little Road—not made of Man, A. Emily Dickinson. **CP-DickE**

Little Robber Girl Considers the Wide World, The. Marilyn Hacker. **SP-HackM**

Little Robber Girl Gets On in the Wide World, The. Marilyn Hacker. **SP-HackM**

Little Rock Arkansas 1957. Isabella Gardner. **CP-GardI**

Little Saint best fits a little Shrine, A. A Ternarie of Littles, upon a Pipkin of Jellie [*or* Jelly] Sent to a Lady. Robert Herrick. **CP-HerrR**

Little Salamander, The. Walter de la Mare. **CP-DeLaW**

Little Scandal, A. Marge Piercy. *Fr.* Walking into Love. **SP-PierM**

Little scavenger away. Flute Song. Hilda Doolittle. **CP-DoolH**

Little Scraping, A. Robinson Jeffers. **CP-JefR2**

Little sentences I began, The. Emily Dickinson. **SP-DickE**

Little Ships. John Hewitt. **CP-HewiJ**

Little Shirt, The. Charles Kenneth Williams. **CP-WillC**

Little Shrub Growing By, A. Ben Jonson. **CP-JonsB**

Little silver rain-children were laughing in the street, The. Stayed No Longer in the Place Than to Hire a Guide for the Next Stage. Kenneth Patchen. **CP-PatcK**

Little Sister. "Lou Reed." **SP-ReedL**

Little sister, not all Black. For My Singing Sister. Audre Lorde. **SP-LordA**

Little Sketch. Carl Sandburg. **CP-SandC**

Little Sleep's-Head Sprouting Hair in the Moonlight. Galway Kinnell. **SP-KinnG**

Little slender lad, toad-headed. The Ambrosia of Dionysus and Semele. Robert Ranke Graves. **CP-GravR**

Little snail, / Dreaming you go. Snail. Langston Hughes. **SP-HughL**

Little Snow was here and there, A. Emily Dickinson. **CP-DickE**

Little soldiers thread the hills, The. Small Soldiers with Drum in Large Landscape. Robert Penn Warren. *Fr.* Mexico Is a Foreign Country: Four Studies in Naturalism. **SP-WarrR**

Little Song about Charity, A. Thomas McGrath. **SP-McGrT**

Little Song for Ivy Day, 1991. James Liddy. **CP-LiddJ**

Little Songs for Gaia. Gary Snyder. **CP-SnydG**

Little Sonnet to Little Friends. Countee Cullen. **CP-CullC**

Little soul so sleek and smiling. Animula, Vagula, Blandula. Stevie Smith. **CP-SmitS**

Little sparrows, The. Pastoral. William Carlos Williams. **CP-WilW1**

Little Stone in the Middle of the Road, in Florida, A. Muriel Rukeyser. **CP-RukeM**

Little sulfa, A. On Death, after Lying Wounded in the Thigh for Twenty-Six Days, of the Author of "Astrophel and Stella." David Markson. **CP-MarkD**

Little Tear Gland That Says, The. Charles Simic. **SP-SimiC**

Little thinks, in the field, yon red-cloaked clown. Each and All. Ralph Waldo Emerson. **CP-EmerR**

Little think'st thou, poor [*or* poore] flower. The Blossom [*or* Blossome]. John Donne. **CP-DonnJ**

Little Tigers Everywhere. Charles Bukowski. **SP-BukC1**

Little Time—and Place. Robert Creeley. **CP-CreeR**

Little to do on a HOT night but swat at. Naked at 92 Degrees. Charles Bukowski. **SP-BukC3**

Little too abstract, a little too wise, A. Return. Robinson Jeffers. **CP-JefR2**

Little Town at Evening, The. David Herbert Lawrence. **CP-LawrD**

Little tree / little silent Christmas tree. Edward Estlin Cummings. **CP-CummE; SP-CummE**

Little Turtle, The. Nicholas Vachel Lindsay. **CP-LindV**

Little Uncomplicated Hymn, A. Anne Sexton. **CP-SextA**

Little Vagabond, The. William Blake. **CP-BlakW** *Fr.* Songs of Experience.

Little Vesper, A. Jane Cooper. **SP-CoopJ**

Little voices of prairie dogs, The. The Great Western Plains. Hart Crane. **CP-CranH**

Little while, a little while, A. Emily Brontë. **CP-BronE**

Little white gibbon, with arms like palm branches, A. Third Universe. Diane Wakoski. *Fr.* The Universes. **SP-WakoD**

Little White Rose, The. "Hugh MacDiarmid." **SP-MacDH**

Little Will comes naked to its world, The. The Head of Wisdom. Randall Jarrell. **CP-JarrR**

Little woman when I knew her, stout, A. My Mother. John Hewitt. **CP-HewiJ**

Little Word, Little White Bird. Carl Sandburg. **CP-SandC**

Little Wowser, The. David Herbert Lawrence. **CP-LawrD**

Little wrists. So That Even a Lover. Louis Zukofsky. **CP-ZukLS**

Little you are; for Womans sake be proud. Little and Loud. Robert Herrick. **CP-HerrR**

Littleblood. Ted Hughes. **SP-HughT** *Fr.* Crow.

Littlenesse No Cause of Leanesse. Robert Herrick. **CP-HerrR**

Littleton, N.H. Robert Creeley. **CP-CreeR**

Littleton Whale, The. Charles Tomlinson. **CP-TomlC**

Littoral. Louis MacNeice. **CP-MacNL**

Liturgical / eighth day, The. Charles Olson. **CP-OlsoC**

Liturgy, The. William Wordsworth. *Fr.* Ecclesiastical Sonnets. **CP-WorW2**

Lityerses. Allen Tate. **CP-TateA**

Live. Anne Sexton. **CP-SextA**

Live all thy sweet life thro'. A Summer Wish. Christina Georgina Rossetti. **CP-RosC1**

Live and clean forget from day to day. Nicolas-Sébastien Roch Chamfort, *tr. fr. French by* Samuel Beckett. **CP-BeckS**

Live and Let Live. Langston Hughes. **SP-HughL**

Live by thy Muse thou shalt; when others die. On Himselfe. Robert Herrick. **CP-HerrR**

Live here, great heart; and love and dy and kill. Richard Crashaw. **OBS** *Fr.* The Flaming Heart. **CP-CrasR**

"Live-in-ease", and then to wash. Livingshayes. Donald Davie. **CP-DavDo**

Live in these conquering leaves; live all the same. Richard Crashaw. **OXAEP-1** *Fr.* The Flaming Heart. **CP-CrasR**

Live Jesus, Live, and let it bee. The Authors Motto. Richard Crashaw. **CP-CrasR**

"Live like the wind," he said, "unfettered." The Wind Bloweth Where It Listeth. Countee Cullen. **CP-CullC**

Live, live with me, and thou shalt see. To Phyllis to Love and Live with Him. Robert Herrick. **CP-HerrR**

Live on in me, remembered ones. Kathleen Jessie Raine. *Fr.* Monessie Gorge. **SP-RainK**

Live sparks rain from the central anvil. The Red Shower. Robert Ranke Graves. **CP-GravR**

Live thou gladly if so thou may. Sir Thomas Wyatt. **CP-WyatT**

Live with a thrifty, not a needy Fate. Expenses Exhaust. Robert Herrick. **CP-HerrR**

Live with me, and be my love. *Various Authors.* **CP-ShaWS** *Fr.* The Passionate Pilgrim. **CP-ShaWS**

Lived a woman wonderful. South Africa. Rudyard Kipling. **CP-KiplR**

Lived to see you throwing. Hesitate to Call. Louise Glück. **SP-GlücL**

Liveforever. Louis Zukofsky. **CP-ZukLS**

Lively and loathesome moe's respectably dead. Edward Estlin Cummings. **CP-CummE**

Lively Hope, and Gracious Fear. William Cowper. **CP-CowpW** *Fr.* Olney Hymns. **CP-CowpW**

Lively sparks that issue from those eyes, The. Sir Thomas Wyatt. **CP-WyatT**

Liverpool Epistle, A. Donald Davie. **CP-DavDo**

Liverpool to Manchester via Runcorn. Malcolm Lowry. *Fr.* Peter Gaunt and the Canals. **CP-LowrM**

Lives. Derek Mahon. **SP-MahoD**

Lives he in any other world. Emily Dickinson. **CP-DickE**

Lives of football men remind us. Dedicated to F. W. Ernest Hemingway. **CP-HemiE**

Lives of great men all remind us. Life. Henry Wadsworth Longfellow. **GN** *Fr.* A Psalm of Life. **SP-LongH**

Lives of Greeks in the old days were deep, The. Theseus Within the Labyrinth. Stephen Dobyns. **SP-DobyS**

Lives of Gulls and Children, The. Howard Nemerov. **CP-NemeH**

Lives of the Poets. Mona Van Duyn. **SP-VanDM**

Lives of the Poets: Three Profiles, The. Erica Jong. **SP-JongE**

Lives of the Swan. Kenneth Patchen. **CP-PatcK**

Live's on it. Dramatis Personae. Charles Olson. **CP-OlsoC**

Lives there a man with such base mettle. George Meredith. **CP-MerG2**

Living, A. David Herbert Lawrence. **CP-LawrD**

Living. Denise Levertov. **CP-LeveD**

Living a life. A Man. Denise Levertov. **CP-LeveD**

Living Alone. Hayden Carruth. **CP-CarHS**

Living Alone. Richard Hugo. **CP-HugoR**

Living among orchards, we are ruled. Language of the Seasons. Robert Ranke Graves. **CP-GravR**

Living among the Dead. William Matthews. **SP-MattW**

Living and a Dead Faith, A. William Cowper. *Fr.* Olney Hymns. **CP-CowpW**

Living at the Movies. Jim Carroll. **SP-CarrJ**

"Into a swamp this heart is flying."

"It is afternoon   a sailor is crying above the waterfall."

"Light rising into her features where."

"So months of cool flowers close in these arms."

"There is a stadium beside my window."

Living backwards means only. Precognition. Margaret Atwood. **SP-AtwM2**

Living Beauty, The. William Butler Yeats. **CP-YeatW**

Living by the Red River. James Wright. **CP-WrigJ**

Living come with grassy tread, The. In a Disused Graveyard. Robert Frost. **CP-FrosR**

Living frame which sustains my soul, The. *see also* Ode to Heaven. Percy Bysshe Shelley. **CP-ShelP**

Living friends live / in the past so they bore us. Poem. Gilbert Sorrentino. **SP-SorrG**

Living Happily Ever After. Erica Jong. **SP-JongE**

Living Heaven thy prayers respect, The. Spiritual Laws. Ralph Waldo Emerson. **CP-EmerR**

Living in a house. Near the Black Forest. Erica Jong. **SP-JongE**

Living in an apartment with a gelded cat. A Typical Affair. Allen Ginsberg. **CP-GinsA**

Living in Sin. Adrienne Rich. **SP-RicA1**

Living in the earth-deposits of our history. Power. Adrienne Rich. **SP-RicA1; SP-RicA2**

Living in the Moment. Marilyn Hacker. **SP-HackM**

Living in the Open. Marge Piercy. **SP-PierM**

"People ask questions."

"We are all hustling and dealing."

Living in the present is / surviving. Moving Staircase. Phoebe Hesketh. **SP-HeskP**

Living Landscape, The. John Hewitt. **CP-HewiJ**

Living Memory. Adrienne Rich. **SP-RicA1**

Living mother-of-pearl of a salmon, The. A Hazel Stick for Catherine Ann. Seamus Heaney. **SP-HeanS**

Living Near the Rehabilitation Home. Ted Kooser. **SP-KoosT**

Living Off Other People—Welfare. Jenny Joseph. **SP-JoseJ**

Living on the Plains. William Stafford. **SP-StafW**

Living on the Surface. Miller Williams. **SP-WillM**

Living Pearl, A. Kenneth Rexroth. **SP-RexrK**

Living quality of, The. Haymaking. William Carlos Williams. **NoAM** *Fr.* Pictures from Brueghel. **CP-WilW2**

Living Quetzalcoatl, The. David Herbert Lawrence. **CP-LawrD**

Living Room, The. Stephen Dobyns. **SP-DobyS**

Living-room, the catholic area you, A. The Common Life. Wystan Hugh Auden. *Fr.* Thanksgiving for a Habitat. **CP-AudeW**

Living someplace else is wrong. The Spring Offensive of the Snail. Marge Piercy. **SP-PierM**

Living the Blues. "Bob Dylan." **CP-DylaB**

Living Theatre, The. Lawrence Ferlinghetti. **SP-FerlL**

Living Water. Jeanne Marie Bouvier de la Motte-Guyon, *tr. fr. French by* William Cowper. **CP-CowpW**

Living While It May. Denise Levertov. **CP-LeveD**

Living with a Wife. John Updike. **CP-UpdiJ**

All the While.

At the Piano.

During Menstruation.

In the Tub.

Under the Sunlamp.

Livings. Philip Larkin. **CP-LarkP**

Livings. Philip Larkin. **CP-LarkP**

"I deal with farmers, things like dips and feed."

Seventy Feet Down. **RB**

"Tonight we dine without the Master." **FaBoDD**

Livingshayes. Donald Davie. **CP-DavDo**

Liz. Edward Estlin Cummings. *Fr.* Five Americans. **CP-CummE**

Liza May. Paul Laurence Dunbar. **CP-DunbP**

Lizard, The. Thomas Hardy. **CP-HardT**

Lizard. David Herbert Lawrence. **CP-LawrD**

Lizard, The. Theodore Roethke. **CP-RoetT**

Lizard, The. Theodore Roethke. **CP-RoetT**

Lizard, lover of heat, of high. The Old Man to the Lizard. Archibald MacLeish. **CP-MacLA**

Lizard ran out on a rock and looked up, listening, A. Lizard. David Herbert Lawrence. **CP-LawrD**

Lizard rusty as a leaf rubbed rough. Robert Lowell. **SP-LoweR** *Fr.* Mexico.

Lizard's iridescence, / the conch winged with mother-of-pearl, The. Earth. Pablo Neruda, *tr. fr. Spanish by Ben Belitt.* **SP-NeruP**

Llangefni Market. Steve Griffiths. **SP-GrifS**

Llantysilio, Overgrown. Steve Griffiths. **SP-GrifS**

Llewellyn and the Tree. Edwin Arlington Robinson. **CP-RobiE**

Lo! A Child Is Born. "Hugh MacDiarmid." **SP-MacDH**

Lo and Behold! "Bob Dylan." **CP-DylaB**

Lo! as a careful housewife runs to catch. Sonnet 143. William Shakespeare. **BiP; InPK; OAEP; SCGP** *Fr.* Sonnets. **CP-ShaWS**

Lo, as a dove when up she springs. Tennyson. **LoBV** *Fr.* In Memoriam A. H. H. **CP-TennA**

Lo, as a tree, whose wintry twigs. Pastoral 4. George Meredith. *Fr.* Pastorals. **CP-MerG1**

Lo, at its center one can find oneself. L.A. John Updike. **CP-UpdiJ**

Lo! Death has reared himself a throne. The City in the Sea. Edgar Allan Poe. **CP-PoeEd**

Lo[e] here a little volume, but great [*or* large] book[e]. Ode on a Prayer-Book. Richard Crashaw. **CP-CrasR**

Lo here I sit at Holyhead. Holyhead. September 25, 1727. Jonathan Swift. **CP-SwifJ**

Lo, here is God, and there is God. When Israel Came Out of Egypt. Arthur Hugh Clough. **SP-ClouA**

Lo here the faire *Chariclia!* in whom strove. Upon the Faire Ethiopian Sent to a Gentlewoman. Richard Crashaw. **CP-CrasR**

Lo, how I seek and sue to have. Sir Thomas Wyatt. **CP-WyatT**

Lo! I must tell a tale of chivalry. Specimen of an Induction to a Poem. John Keats. **CP-KeatJ**

Lo I the man, whose Muse whilome [*or* whylome] did maske. The Legend of the Knight of the Red Crosse, or of Holinesse. Edmund Spenser. **EPCY; FHYEP; FiP; NAEL-1; OAEL-1** *Fr.* The Faerie Queene. **CP-Spens**

Lo! in the burning west, the craggy nape. Sky-Prospect—From the Plain of France. William Wordsworth. *Fr.* Memorials of a Tour of the Continent; 1820. **CP-WorW2**

Lo, in the green enclosure here. To Priapus. Robert Louis Stevenson. **CP-StevR**

Lo! in the orient when the gracious light. Sonnet 7. William Shakespeare. *Fr.* Sonnets. **CP-ShaWS**

Lo! in thine honest eyes I read. Robert Louis Stevenson. **CP-StevR**

Lo, Lord, Thou ridest! The Hurricane. Hart Crane. **CP-CranH**

Lo! newborn Jesus / Soft and weak and small. Christina Georgina Rossetti. *Fr.* Christmas Carols. **CP-RosC2**

Lo now four other act upon the stage. Of the Four Ages of Man. Anne Bradstreet. **CP-BradA**

Lo, now, my guest, if aught amiss were said. Robert Louis Stevenson. **CP-StevR**

Lo the blessed assembly of virgins! Corona Virginum. Sigebert of Liege. *Fr.* Four Medieval Latin Poems. **CP-MacNL**

Lo the leaves. To Be Closely Written on a Small Piece of Paper Which Folded into a Tight Lozenge Will Fit Any Girl's Locket. William Carlos Williams. **CP-WilW1**

Lo, the moon's self! Phases of the Moon. Robert Browning. **ChTr** *Fr.* One Word More. **CP-BroR1**

Lo, the poor Indian! whose untutor'd mind. Alexander Pope. **NU** *Fr.* An Essay on Man. **CP-PopeA**

Lo, the unbounded sea. The Ship Starting. Walt Whitman. **CP-WhitW**

Lo! the Wild Cow of the Desert, her yeanling estrayed from her. Azrael's Count. Rudyard Kipling. **CP-KiplR**

Lo! thro' the dusky silence of the groves. A Wish. Samuel Taylor Coleridge. **CP-ColeS**

Lo! 'tis a gala night. The Conqueror Worm. Edgar Allan Poe. **CP-PoeEd**

Lo, Victress on the Peaks. Walt Whitman. **CP-WhitW**

"Lo, we descend like light. Light. Light". Delmore Schwartz. **SP-SchwD** *Fr.* Genesis.

Lo! what is this that I make—sudden, supreme, unrehearsed. *parody of* Robert Browning. Rudyard Kipling. **CP-KiplR** *Fr.* The Muse among the Motors.

Lo, what it is to love! Sir Thomas Wyatt. **CP-WyatT**

Lo, what my country should have done (have raised). To William, Lord Mounteagle. Ben Jonson. **CP-JonsB**

Lo! where from Heaven's high roof. Hafiz, *tr. by* Ralph Waldo Emerson. **CP-EmerR** *Fr.* Odes.

Lo, where hurricane flocks of the North-wind rattle their thunder. George Meredith. *Fr.* The Revolution. **CP-MerG1**

Lo! Where She Stands Fixed in a Saint-like Trance. William Wordsworth. **CP-WorW2**

Lo! where the Moon along the sky. A Night Thought. William Wordsworth. **CP-WorW2**

Lo! where the rosy-bosomed [*or* bosom'd] Hours. Ode on the Spring. Thomas Gray. **CP-GrayT**

Lo! where the silent marble weeps. Epitaph on Mrs Jane Clarke. Thomas Gray. **CP-GrayT**

Lo worms enjoy the seat of bliss. Robert Burns. **CP-BurnR**

(Epitaph: "Lo worms enjoy the seat of bliss.") **CP-BurnR**

Load. John Hewitt. **CP-HewiJ**

Load of brushes and baskets and cradles and chairs, A. No Buyers [*or* No Buyers: A Street Scene]. Thomas Hardy. **CP-HardT**

Load of Sugar-Cane, The. Wallace Stevens. **CP-StevW**

Loaded with mail of linked lies. Basil Bunting. **FaBoEH** *Fr.* Poet appointed dare not decline. *Fr.* Briggflatts [An Autobiography]. **CP-BuntB**

Loading and Unloading. Robert Herrick. **CP-HerrR**

Loam. Carl Sandburg. **CP-SandC**

Loan, The. Muriel Rukeyser. **CP-RukeM**

Loan that built the barn, The. Tom Ball's Barn. Ted Kooser. **SP-KoosT**

Loathing is as beautiful as the scourge. Malcolm Lowry. *Fr.* Songs for Second Childhood. **CP-LowrM**

Lobbed ball plops, then dribbles to the cup, The. Ford Madox Ford. Robert Lowell. **SP-LoweR**

Lobster. Anne Sexton. **CP-SextA**

Lobster-car, boat, or fishbasket. Ralph Waldo Emerson. **CP-EmerR**

Lobsters. Howard Nemerov. **CP-NemeH**

Lobsters in the Brain Coral. Laurence Lieberman. **SP-LiebL**

Lobsters in the Window. William DeWitt Snodgrass. **SP-SnodW**

Local Boys and Girls Small Town Stuff. Marsden Hartley. **CP-HartM**

Local Journal. Charles Wright. **SP-WrigC**

Local Knowledge. Richard Shelton. **SP-ShelR**

Local Legend. Robinson Jeffers. **CP-JefR3**

Local Poet, A. John Hewitt. **CP-HewiJ**

Local Snivels through the Field, The. Philip Larkin. **CP-LarkP**

Local Time. Stephen Dunn. **SP-DunnS**

Localities. Carl Sandburg. **CP-SandC**

Locate I / love you some-. The Language. Robert Creeley. **CP-CreeR**

Location. Adrienne Rich. *Fr.* Turning the Wheel. **SP-RicA2**

Locations and Times. Walt Whitman. **CP-WhitW**

L'Occupation Obsédée. Lawrence Ferlinghetti. **SP-FerlL**

Loch, The. Kathleen Jessie Raine. *Fr.* Bheinn Naomh. **SP-RainK**

Loch Coruisk. Sir Walter Scott. **SP-ScotW** *Fr.* The Lord of the Isles.

Lochinvar. Sir Walter Scott. **SP-ScotW** *Fr.* Marmion.

Lock up, fair lids, the treasure of my heart, *speech of Musidorus.* Sir Philip Sidney. **SP-SidnP** *Fr.* Arcadia.

Locke sank into a swoon. Fragments. William Butler Yeats. **CP-YeatW**

Locked arm in arm they cross the way. Tableau. Countee Cullen. **CP-CullC**

Locked Doors. Anne Sexton. **CP-SextA**

Locked House, A. William DeWitt Snodgrass. **SP-SnodW**

Locked in the dictionary on the table. Exasperations of a Novelist. Howard Nemerov. **CP-NemeH**

Locked Out. Robert Frost. **CP-FrosR**

Lockless Door, The. Robert Frost. **CP-FrosR**

Lockly spits apace, the rhewme he cals it. Epigramme. Thomas Campion. *Fr.* Observations in the Art of English Poesie. **CP-CampT**

Lockout. The seventh week. Men in the Square. Thanksgiving: Detroit. John Berryman. **CP-BerrJ**

Locks. Kenneth Koch. **SP-KochK**

Locks between her chamber and his will, The. Midnight. William Shakespeare. **OBSC** *Fr.* The Rape of Lucrece. **CP-ShaWS**

Locksley Hall. Tennyson. **CP-TennA**

For I Dipped [*or* Dipt] into the Future. **PGD; PoLF; TRV** (Lines.) **PAW**

(Prophecy.) **TreF; WBLP**

"In the Spring." **BoNaP**

"Make me feel the wild pulsation that I felt before the strife." **SaC**

"Not in vain the distance beacons. Foreward, forward let us range." **FaBoEH**

Locksley Hall Sixty Years After. Tennyson. **CP-TennA**

"Chaos! Cosmos! Cosmos, Chaos! who can tell how all will end?" **FaBoEH**

Locus. Robert Earl Hayden. **CP-HaydR**

Locust-Lovers, Attention! Ogden Nash. **CP-NashO**

Locust Songs. Geoffrey Hill. **CP-HillG**

Emblem, The.

Good Husbandry.

Shiloh Church, 1862: Twenty–Three Thousand.

Locust Tree in Flower, The. William Carlos Williams. **CP-WilW1**

("Among / the leaves.") **CP-WilW1**

Lodged. Robert Frost. **CP-FrosR**

Lodgepole / cone/seed waits for fire. Gary Snyder. **CP-SnydG** *Fr.* Logging. *Fr.* Myths and Texts.

Lodgepole Pine: the wonderful reproductive. Gary Snyder. **CP-SnydG** *Fr.* Logging. *Fr.* Myths and Texts.

Lodging-House Fuchsias, The. Thomas Hardy. **CP-HardT**

Loe, when backe mine eye. Thomas Campion. **CP-CampT**

Loft, The. Jim Carroll. **SP-CarrJ**

Lofty. Archie Randolph Ammons. **SP-AmmoA**

Lofty in the Palais de Danse. Thom Gunn. **CP-GunnT**

Lofty pine, from high Mount Pelion raught, The. 2.11. Ovid. **CP-MarlC,** *tr. by* Christopher Marlowe; *Fr.* Elegies.

Log. James Merrill. **SP-MerrJ**

Log Drive. Louise McNeill. **SP-McNeL**

Log shifting in the grate, A. Great Horned Owls. Brendan Galvin. **SP-GalvB**

Log train bellowed through the dark, The. The Spark. Louise McNeill. **SP-McNeL**

Logeorge / lo / wellifitisn't eddy how's the boy. Edward Estlin Cummings. **CP-CummE**

Loggerheads. David Herbert Lawrence. **CP-LawrD**

Logging. Gary Snyder. *Fr.* Myths and Texts.

"Ancient forests of China logged, The." **CP-SnydG**

("But ye shall destroy their altars.") **CP-SnydG**

"Each dawn is clear." **CP-SnydG**

"Felix Baran / Hugo Gerlot." **CP-SnydG**

"Green limb hangs in the crotch, A." **CP-SnydG**

"Groves are down, The." **CP-SnydG**

"Lodgepole / cone/seed waits for fire." **CP-SnydG**

"Lodgepole Pine: the wonderful reproductive." **CP-SnydG**

"Morning star is not a star, The." **CP-SnydG**

"Pines, under pines." **CP-SnydG**

"Ray Wells, a big Nisqually, and I." **CP-SnydG**

Logic. Robert Ranke Graves. **CP-GravR**

Logic. Marsden Hartley. **CP-HartM**

Logic. Charles Tomlinson. **CP-TomlC**

Logic and The Magic Flute. Marianne Craig Moore. **CP-MoorM**

Logical pleasure of expectant mercy, The. Retrospective Forelook. Richard Eberhart. **CP-EberR**

Logos. Miller Williams. **SP-WillM**

Logos is an engine. Natives. Archie Randolph Ammons. **SP-AmmoA**

Logos Our Teacher, The. Clement of Alexandria, *tr. fr. Greek by* Thomas Merton. **CP-MertT**

Logs give back, in burning, solar fire, The. Energy: A Villanelle. John Updike. **CP-UpdiJ**

Logs on the Hearth. Thomas Hardy. **CP-HardT**

Loin Cloth. Carl Sandburg. **CP-SandC**

Loin de l'Être. Stevie Smith. **CP-SmitS**

Loitering with a vacant eye. Alfred Edward Housman. **CP-HousA**

Loki. Frederick Morgan. **SP-MorgF**

Loki's Song. Frederick Morgan. **SP-MorgF**

Lollipops of the Pomeranian Baroque. James Fenton. **SP-FentJ**

("Skies remind you of those mounds of custard, The.") **SP-FentJ**

Lollius, *after* Horace, Book 5, Ode 13. Rudyard Kipling. **CP-KiplR**

Lollocks. Robert Ranke Graves. **CP-GravR**

London. John Berryman. **CP-BerrJ**

London ("I wander through each chartered street"). William Blake. **CP-BlakW** *Fr.* Songs of Experience.

("I wander ("thro") each dirty street.") **CP-BlakW**

London / crossfigured / creeping with trams. Lawrence Ferlinghetti. **SP-FerlL**

London. Randall Jarrell. **CP-JarrR**

London / Used to wear her lights splendidly. Town in 1917. David Herbert Lawrence. **CP-LawrD**

London: A Poem. Samuel Johnson. **CP-JohnS**

London air dims. Kathleen Jessie Raine. **SP-RainK**

London Bridge. Edwin Arlington Robinson. **CP-RobiE**

London by Lamplight. George Meredith. **CP-MerG1**

London, 1802. William Wordsworth. **CP-WorW1**

London, from Hampstead Heath. William Wordsworth. **FaBoPP** *Fr.* Extempore Effusion upon the Death of James Hogg. **CP-WorW2**

London Mercury. David Herbert Lawrence. **CP-LawrD**

London Rain. Louis MacNeice. **CP-MacNL**

London returned to after twelve years, A. Thom Gunn. *Fr.* Talbot Road. **CP-GunnT**

London Stone. Rudyard Kipling. **CP-KiplR**

London Street, A. John Donne. *See* Satire 1: "Away thou fondling motley humourist."

London Suburbs. William Cowper. **FaBoPP** *Fr.* Retirement. **CP-CowpW**

London *Times* tells me that "Mr. Humphrey", The. Second Universe. Diane Wakoski. *Fr.* The Universes. **SP-WakoD**

Lone Cheer from the Stands for a Bitter Crane. Richard Hugo. **CP-HugoR**

Lone Flower, hemmed in with snows and white as they. To a Snow-Drop. William Wordsworth. **CP-WorW2**

Lone Founts. Herman Melville. **SP-MelvH**

Lone gray bird, A. From the Shore. Carl Sandburg. **CP-SandC**

Lone Lake, Whidbey. Richard Hugo. **CP-HugoR**

Lone on the bleaky hills, the straying flocks. On the Death of the Late Lord President Dundas. Robert Burns. **CP-BurnR**

Lone Ranger, The. Donald Hall. **CP-HallD**

Lone streets inanimate, repetitive machine Crash cookie-cutting. Manhattan Thirties Flash. Allen Ginsberg. **CP-GinsA**

Lone Striker, A. Robert Frost. **CP-FrosR**

Lone train alarms the summer silence with a contralto trident, A. Thomas Merton. *Fr.* Cables to the Ace. **CP-MertT**

Lonedale Operator, The. John Ashbery. **SP-AshbJ**

Loneliness. Wystan Hugh Auden. **CP-AudeW**

Loneliness. Sir John Betjeman. **CP-BetjJ**

Loneliness[: An Outburst of Hexasyllables]. Hayden Carruth. **CP-CarHS**

Loneliness. Stephen Dunn. **SP-DunnS**

Loneliness. Robert Frost. **FaBoEn; VGW** *Fr.* The Hill Wife. **CP-FrosR**

Loneliness / Is a luxury beyond the reach. The Negative Virtues. Richard Shelton. **SP-ShelR**

Loneliness. David Herbert Lawrence. **CP-LawrD**

Loneliness. Al Young. **CP-YounA**

Loneliness in Jersey City. Wallace Stevens. **CP-StevW**

Loneliness One dare not sound, The. Emily Dickinson. **CP-DickE**

Lonely / As the wind. One. Langston Hughes. **SP-HughL**

Lonely as a dry and used orchard. The Blackbirds Are Rough Today. Charles Bukowski. **SP-BukC2**

Lonely at her window sitting. Emily Brontë. **CP-BronE**

Lonely Days. Thomas Hardy. **CP-HardT**

Lonely evening crouches, darkens as the hour, The. Pastoral. Edwin Rolfe. **CP-RolfE**

Lonely he sat, the men were strange. The Discontented Poet: A Masque. Ralph Waldo Emerson. **CP-EmerR**

Lonely heart, The. Ecce Sponsus. Hilda Doolittle. **CP-DoolH**

Lonely Heart, The. John Hewitt. *Fr.* Freehold. **CP-HewiJ**

Lonely her fate was. Lonely Days. Thomas Hardy. **CP-HardT**

Lonely in Ireland, since it was not home. The Importance of Elsewhere. Philip Larkin. **CP-LarkP**

Lonely in the Regent Palace. The Flight from Bootle. Sir John Betjeman. **CP-BetjJ**

Lonely little question mark. Kid in the Park. Langston Hughes. **SP-HughL**

Lonely, Lonesome, Loney—O! David Herbert Lawrence. **CP-LawrD**

Lonely Man, The. Randall Jarrell. **CP-JarrR**

Lonely Particular. Alice Walker. **CP-WalkA**

Lonely people are marching, The. Keep It. Charles Kenneth Williams. **CP-WillC**

Lonely Return to the Lonely, the divine to the Divine—Proclus, The. Marsden Hartley. **CP-HartM**

Lonely skyscrapers, deserted tombs of business risen. Gasman Invites the Skyscrapers to Dance. Marge Piercy. **SP-PierM**

Lonely Street, The. William Carlos Williams. **CP-WilW1**

Lonely, White Fields. Mary Oliver. **SP-OlivM**

Lonesome. Paul Laurence Dunbar. **CP-DunbP**

Lonesome Boy Blues. Kenneth Patchen. **CP-PatcK**

Lonesome Death of Hattie Carroll, The. "Bob Dylan." **CP-DylaB**

Lonesome for they know not What, The. Emily Dickinson. **CP-DickE**

Lonesome in the Country. Al Young. **CP-YounA**

Lonesome Pine Special. Charles Wright. **SP-WrigC**

Long. William Matthews. **SP-MattW**

Long after Chamfort. Nicolas-Sébastien Roch Chamfort, *tr. fr. French by* Samuel Beckett. **CP-BeckS**

Long after our departure. May Evening. Richard Eberhart. **CP-EberR**

Long after there were none of them alive. Recalled. Edwin Arlington Robinson. **CP-RobiE**

Long after you beat down the powerful hand. Girl at the Play. Muriel Rukeyser. **CP-RukeM**

Long after you have swung back. Losing Track. Denise Levertov. **CP-LeveD**

Long afterward, Oedipus, old and blinded. Myth. Muriel Rukeyser. **CP-RukeM**

Long Ages Past. Wilfred Owen. **CP-OwenW**

Long Ago. Paul Laurence Dunbar. **CP-DunbP**

Long ago and long ago. Maiden-Song. Christina Georgina Rossetti. **CP-RosC1**

Long Ago, Far Away. "Bob Dylan." **CP-DylaB**

Long ago from radiant palace. Mourn'st Thou Now? Walter de la Mare. **CP-DeLaW**

Long ago I found a seed. The Tree. Adrienne Rich. **CP-RicAE**

Long ago I learned how to sleep. Wind Song. Carl Sandburg. **CP-SandC**

Long ago I thought you young, bright daimon. Kathleen Jessie Raine. **SP-RainK**

Long ago, in Kentucky, I, a boy stood. Tell Me a Story. Robert Penn Warren. **MT** *Fr.* Audubon. **SP-WarrR**

Long ago on a night of danger and vigil. If They Come in the Night. Marge Piercy. **SP-PierM**

Long ago was the then beginning to seem like now. Blue Sonata. John Ashbery. **SP-AshbJ**

Long ago,between a dream and a dream. Edward Estlin Cummings. **CP-CummE**

Long Alley, The. Theodore Roethke. **CP-RoetT**

Long and dark the nights, dim and short the days. Vigil of the Presentation. Christina Georgina Rossetti. **CP-RosC2**

Long and Lazy [*or* Lazie]. Robert Herrick. **CP-HerrR**

Long and Sluggish Lines. Wallace Stevens. **CP-StevW**

Long and smelling good, the cemetery grass. The Other Grave. Richard Hugo. **CP-HugoR**

Long and the Short of What's Good and What's Bad, The. Robert Pack. **SP-PackR**

Long and Winding Road, The. The Beatles. **CP-Beatl**

Long Banister Lane. Li Po, *tr. fr. Chinese by* William Carlos Williams *with* David Rafael Wang. **CP-WilW2**

Long Barren. Christina Georgina Rossetti. **CP-RosC1**

Long before dawn has silvered the last star. Out of Sleep Awakened. Archibald MacLeish. **CP-MacLA**

Long before dawn your light. Chinese Nightingale. William Carlos Williams. **CP-WilW1**

Long before I hear it, Naples bright. Napoli Again. Richard Hugo. **CP-HugoR**

Long Bells, The. Charles Kenneth Williams. **CP-WillC**

Long Bridge, The. John Hewitt. **CP-HewiJ**

Long buried, ancient men-at-arms. Two British Airmen. Thomas Merton. **CP-MertT**

Long cloud edged with streaming grey, The. Autumn Even-Song. George Meredith. **CP-MerG1**

Long day on the road, R. H., and three trips now. Note to R. H. from Strongsville. Richard Hugo. **CP-HugoR**

Long days and changing weather. Division. Louise Bogan. **CP-BogaL**

Long Death, The. Marge Piercy. **SP-PierM**

Long deep Lane / So overshadow'd, it might seem one bower, A. Samuel Taylor Coleridge. *Fr.* Some Fragments, Mainly from Manuscripts of 1797–8. **CP-ColeS**

Long Distance. Charles Olson. **CP-OlsoC**

Long Distance. William Stafford. **SP-StafW**

Long-Distance Operator. "Bob Dylan." **CP-DylaB**

Long-drawn bray of the ass, The. The Ass. David Herbert Lawrence. **CP-LawrD**

Long-eared beast, and a field-house for cattle, A. Probatur Aliter. Jonathan Swift. **CP-SwifJ**

Long Enough. Thomas Merton. **CP-MertT**

Long Enough. Long Enough. Muriel Rukeyser. **CP-RukeM**

Long enough to remember the girl. An Atypical Affair. Allen Ginsberg. **CP-GinsA**

Long-expected one and twenty. A Short Song of Congratulation [*or* To a Young Heir]. Samuel Johnson. **CP-JohnS**

Long-favoured England! be thou not misled. In Allusion to Various Recent Histories and Notices of the French Revolution, Concluded. William Wordsworth. **CP-WorW2**

Long Fingers. Allen Tate. **CP-TateA**

Long freight swims upwind. Each 4 P.M., the river, A. Late Summer, Drummond. Richard Hugo. **CP-HugoR**

Long freight train / Wakes me in my cell, The. Ernesto Cardenal, *tr. by* Thomas Merton. **CP-MertT** *Fr.* Gethsemani, KY.

Long-gathering Old-end, I did fear thee wise. To Old-End Gatherer. Ben Jonson. **CP-JonsB**

Long Gone Blues. Gilbert Sorrentino. **SP-SorrG**

Long Goodbye. Thomas McGrath. **SP-McGrT**

Long Goodbye, The. Gilbert Sorrentino. **SP-SorrG**

Long Goodbye, The. Dabney Stuart. **SP-StuaD**

Long Guns. Carl Sandburg. **CP-SandC**

Long had I grieved at what I deemed abuse. Resignation. Paul Laurence Dunbar. **CP-DunbP**

Long Hair. Gary Snyder. **CP-SnydG**

Long-haired and black as shadow. The Cat. Lewis Turco. **SP-TurcL**

Long-Haired Boy, The. Shel Silverstein. **SP-SilS2**

Long has the dew been dried on tree and lawn. Near Rome, in Sight of St Peter's. William Wordsworth. *Fr.* Memorials of a Tour in Italy, 1837. **CP-WorW2**

Long have I borne much, mad thy faults me make. 3.10. Ovid. **CP-MarlC**, *tr. by* Christopher Marlowe; *Fr.* Elegies.

Long have I framed weak phantasies of Thee. Agnosto Theo [To an Unknown God]. Thomas Hardy. **CP-HardT**

Long have I longed, till I am tired. Till Tomorrow. Christina Georgina Rossetti. **CP-RosC2**

Long have I sighed for a calm; God grant I may find it at last! Tennyson. **EBVPR** *Fr.* Maud [A Monodrama]. **CP-TennA**

Long have mine eies gaz'd with delight. At. to Thomas Campion *and to* Philip Rosseter. **CP-CampT**

Long having deeply gron'd these visions sad. Joachim Du Bellay. *Fr.* The Visions of Bellay. **CP-Spens**

Long Home, The. John Berryman. **CP-BerrJ**

Long Hot Summer. Archibald MacLeish. **CP-MacLA**

Long house— / the fox gallery you called, A. The Fox Gallery. Charles Tomlinson. **CP-TomlC**

Long Hunter, The. Wendell Berry. **CP-BerrW**

Long I followed [*or* follow'd] happy guides. Forerunners. Ralph Waldo Emerson. **CP-EmerR**

Long in thy shackles [*or* shackels], liberty / I ask not from these walls, but thee. To Lucasta, from Prison. Richard Lovelace. **CP-LoveR**

Long Island Sound's. Meridian. Louise Glück. **SP-GlücL**

Long John Brown & Little Mary Bell. William Blake. **CP-BlakW**

Long lakes, flanked, The. Southwest of Buffalo. Donald Hall. **CP-HallD**

Long Last. Philip Larkin. **CP-LarkP**

Long-legged Fly. William Butler Yeats. **CP-YeatW**

Long Life. Robert Herrick. **CP-HerrR**

Long life, My lord, an' health be yours. Address of Beelzebub. Robert Burns. **CP-BurnR**

Long-lifes-day I've taken paines, A. Paines without Profit. Robert Herrick. **CP-HerrR**

Long light shakes across the lake, The. Lines to a Duck in a Park. Thomas Stearns Eliot. *Fr.* Five-Finger Exercises. **CP-ElioT**

Long lines of cliff breaking have left a chasm. Enoch Arden. Tennyson. **CP-TennA**

Long Lion Days. Philip Larkin. **CP-LarkP**

Long Live the Spiderweb. Allen Ginsberg. **CP-GinsA**

Long Live the Weeds. Theodore Roethke. **CP-RoetT**

Long locks of late our Zelot Peason weares. Upon Peason. Robert Herrick. **CP-HerrR**

Long, long after / When settlers put up beam and rafter. Johnny Appleseed's Old Age. Nicholas Vachel Lindsay. *Fr.* In Praise of Johnny Appleseed. **CP-LindV**

Long, Long Hence. Walt Whitman. **CP-WhitW**

Long long I lay in the sands. A Vast Confusion. Lawrence Ferlinghetti. **SP-FerlL**

Long, long legs, The. From the Country to the City. Elizabeth Bishop. **CP-BishE**

Long Long Long. George Harrison. **CP-Beatl**

Long—long Sleep—a famous—Sleep, A. Emily Dickinson. **CP-DickE**

Long long with wonder I thought you human. Ecce Homo. John Berryman. **CP-BerrJ**

Long Looked For. Christina Georgina Rossetti. **CP-RosC3**

Long Lookt for Comes at Last. Robert Herrick. **CP-HerrR**

Long[e] love that in my thought do[e]th [*or* I] harbour [*or* harber *or* harbar], The. Petrarch, *tr.* by Sir Thomas Wyatt. **CP-WyatT** *Fr.* Sonnets to Laura.

Long may live my lovely Hetty! Translation of Lines in Baretti's *Easy Phraseology.* Samuel Johnson. **CP-JohnS**

Long-mile street you trudge to school, The. The Mile-Long Street. John Hewitt. **CP-HewiJ**

Long must elapse ere you behold again. To My Wife. Robert Louis Stevenson. **CP-StevR**

Long Naked Walk of the Dead, The. Charles Kenneth Williams. **CP-WillC**

Long neglect has worn away. Emily Brontë. **CP-BronE**

Long note one wood thrush hear him low in waste pine places. Prologue: The Endless Inscription. Thomas Merton. *Fr.* The Geography of Lograire. **CP-MertT**

Long Novel, A. John Ashbery. **SP-AshbJ**

Long Past Moncada. Muriel Rukeyser. **CP-RukeM**

Long path sap sludges up, The. New. William Matthews. **SP-MattW**

Long Plighted. Thomas Hardy. **CP-HardT**

Long plung'd in sorrow, I resign. The Joy of the Cross. Jeanne Marie Bouvier de la Motte-Guyon, *tr. fr. French* by William Cowper. **CP-CowpW**

Long Pond Summer. Brendan Galvin. **SP-GalvB**

Long Race, The. Edwin Arlington Robinson. **CP-RobiE**

Long River, The. Donald Hall. **CP-HallD**

Long road and a village, A. Holy Family. Muriel Rukeyser. **CP-RukeM**

Long Roots Moor Summer to Our Side of Earth. Philip Larkin. **CP-LarkP**

Long rope of gray smoke was, A. William Stafford. *Fr.* Stories to Live in the World With. **SP-StafW**

Long Shadow. John Updike. **CP-UpdiJ**

Long Shadow of Lincoln: A Litany, The. Carl Sandburg. **CP-SandC**

Long sigh of the Frog, The. Emily Dickinson. **CP-DickE**

Long Sight in Age. Philip Larkin. **CP-LarkP**

Long since, a dream of heaven I had. Divine Compassion. John Greenleaf Whittier. **CP-WhitJ**

Long since, in sore distress, I heard one pray. The Warrior's Prayer. Paul Laurence Dunbar. **CP-DunbP**

Long since, the flicker brushed with shameless wing. Sonnet. Edward Estlin Cummings. **CP-CummE**

Long since the time their wives had set for them to come. How Jimsey O'Roon and Peter Stack, Coal Miners, Came to Be Put in the Ferbettville (Pa.) Jail Early One Saturday Night. Kenneth Patchen. **CP-PatcK**

Long since the years. Message II. Allen Ginsberg. **CP-GinsA**

Long Story. Stephen Dobyns. **SP-DobyS**

Long Story, A. Thomas Gray. **CP-GrayT**

Long-Suffering of God. Christopher Smart. **LAuP; NOCV** *Fr.* Hymns for the Amusement of Children. **SP-SmarC**

Long Summer. Robert Lowell. **SP-LoweR**

Long Summers. Robert Lowell. **SP-LoweR**

Long Summers. Robert Lowell. **SP-LoweR**

Long Summers. Robert Lowell. **SP-LoweR**

Long sweep / of prairie to the mountains, A. Song: The Famous Vision of America. Hayden Carruth. **CP-CarHS**

Long Swing, The. Richard Eberhart. **CP-EberR**

Long-tailed ponies go nosing the pine-lands. Parochial Theme. Wallace Stevens. **CP-StevW**

Long Term. Stephen Dunn. **SP-DunnS**

Long Term Suffering. Richard Eberhart. **CP-EberR**

Long time ago, we two set out. Vagrants. Paul Laurence Dunbar. **CP-DunbP**

Long time ago, when I was a child, A. The Snow Globe. Howard Nemerov. **CP-NemeH**

Long time ago, when the earth was green, A. The Unicorn. Shel Silverstein. **SP-SilS2**

Long Time Gone. "Bob Dylan." **CP-DylaB**

Long time hath Man's unhappiness and guilt. Imagination, How Impaired and Restored. William Wordsworth. *Fr.* The Prelude; Growth of a Poet's Mind [1805 vers.]. **CP-WorW3**

Long time have human ignorance and guilt. Imagination and Taste, How Impaired and Restored. William Wordsworth. **EnRP** *Fr.* The Prelude; Growth of a Poet's Mind [1850 vers.]. **CP-WorW3**

Long time I lay in little ease. Robert Louis Stevenson. **CP-StevR**

Long time, many years, we've had these wars, A. On a Certain Engagement South of Seoul. Hayden Carruth. **CP-CarHS**

Long time no see. The Stylist. William Carlos Williams. **CP-WilW2**

Long time since it seems to-day, A. Wystan Hugh Auden. **GOA** *Fr.* New Year Letter. **CP-AudeW**

Long time since the last scream cut short. Rathlin. Derek Mahon. **SP-MahoD**

Long time you have been making the trip, A. Of Hartford in a Purple Light. Wallace Stevens. **CP-StevW**

'Long To'ds Night. Paul Laurence Dunbar. **CP-DunbP**

Long, Too Long America. Walt Whitman. **CP-WhitW**

Long Trail, The. Rudyard Kipling. *See* There's a whisper down the field where the year has shot her yield.

Long Trip. Langston Hughes. **SP-HughL**

Long Tunnel of Wanting You, The. Erica Jong. **SP-JongE**

Long View from the Suburbs. Jane Cooper. **SP-CoopJ**

Long warned of many terrors more severe. Siege Perilous. Edwin Arlington Robinson. **CP-RobiE**

Long was the conflict, but now 'tis done. George Meredith. **CP-MerG2**

Long Waters, The. Theodore Roethke. **NYBP** *Fr.* North American Sequence. **CP-RoetT**

Long Way Outside Yellowstone, A. Thomas McGrath. **SP-McGrT**

Long whip lingers, The. Horses. Louis MacNeice. **VoGa** *Fr.* Circus. **CP-MacNL**

Long, white, summer cloud, like a cleared linen table, A. Derek Walcott. **CP-WalcD** *Fr.* Midsummer.

Long winter from home the gulls blew, A. To Lucasta, About That War. John Ciardi. **SP-CiarJ**

Long wintry months are past; the Moon that now. Charlotte Smith. *Fr.* The Emigrants. **CP-SmitC**

Disillusion with the French Revolution. **ECWP**

Long with us, now she leaves us; she has rest. Angela Burdett-Coutts. George Meredith. **CP-MerG2**

Long wound of the summer—, The. Poem. Thomas McGrath. **SP-McGrT**

Long year I squeezed out a tiny book, The. Martial, *tr.* by William Matthews. **SP-MattW** *Fr.* Epigrams.

Long years ago, ere R—lls or R—ce. The Curé. Rudyard Kipling. **CP-KiplR**

Long years ago, within a distant clime. Dream Song I. Paul Laurence Dunbar. **CP-DunbP**

Long Years apart can make no. Emily Dickinson. **CP-DickE**

Long years!—It tries the thrilling frame to bear. The Lament of Tasso. Byron. **CP-Byron**

Longa victa die, cum multo pulvere rerum. In Themclam Virginem. Gerard Manley Hopkins. **CP-HopkG**

Longe nightes, whan every creature, The. A Complaint unto His Lady. Geoffrey Chaucer. **CP-ChauG**

Longer ago than I had lived till then. . . . Anne Dick 2. 1936. Robert Lowell. **SP-LoweR**

Longer thred of life we spin, The. Long Life. Robert Herrick. **CP-HerrR**

Longer to muse. Sir Thomas Wyatt. **CP-WyatT**

Longer to trow ye. Sir Thomas Wyatt. **CP-WyatT**

Longer we are together, The. Ripening. Wendell Berry. **CP-BerrW**

Longer we stay here the harder, The. A Soul, Geologically. Margaret Atwood. **SP-AtwM1**

Longest Day, The. George Meredith. **CP-MerG1**

Longest Day; Addressed to My Daughter, The. William Wordsworth. **CP-WorW2**

Longest day that God appoints, The. Emily Dickinson. **CP-DickE**

Longest Journey, The. Percy Bysshe Shelley. **OtMeF; OxBM** *Fr.* Epipsychidion. **CP-ShelP**

Longest Night, The. Marge Piercy. **SP-PierM**

Longest night is past, The. Wendell Berry. *Fr.* Window Poems. **CP-BerrW**

Longest Nose, The. Shel Silverstein. **SP-SilS2**

Longfellow's Visit to Venice. Sir John Betjeman. **CP-BetjJ**

Longing. Edward Estlin Cummings. **CP-CummE**

Longing. Paul Laurence Dunbar. **CP-DunbP**

Longing. George Herbert. **CP-HerbG**

Longing, The. Theodore Roethke. *Fr.* North American Sequence. **CP-RoetT**

Longing for Death because of Feebleness. Stevie Smith. **CP-SmitS**

Longing is like the Seed. Emily Dickinson. **CP-DickE**

Longing To Be with Christ. William Cowper. **CP-CowpW**

Longitude 170° West, Latitude 35° North. Gary Snyder. **CP-SnydG**

Longships got this far. Then, The. For Billy Holt. Ted Hughes. **SP-HughT**

Longshot. Charles Bukowski. **SP-BukC1**

Lonsdale! it were unworthy of a Guest. To the Earl of Lonsdale. William Wordsworth. *Fr.* Poems Composed or Suggested During a Tour, in the Summer of 1833.

Lonsdale Street. John Hewitt. **CP-HewiJ**

Loo! loo! Lulu! lulu! Loo! loo! Loot! loot! Rudyard Kipling. **UV** *Fr.* Loot. **CP-KiplR**

Look, The. Elizabeth Barrett Browning. **CP-BroEB**

Look:, The. Charles Bukowski. **SP-BukC2**

Look. Robert Creeley. **CP-CreeR**

Look. Philip Levine. **SP-LeviP**

Look / my fingers,which. Edward Estlin Cummings. **CP-CummE**

Look! Stevie Smith. **CP-SmitS**

Look, a cypress tree. Hayden Carruth. **CP-CarHS** *Fr.* The Clay Hill Anthology.

Look, a naked runner / A messenger. A Messenger from the Horizon. Thomas Merton. **CP-MertT; SP-MertT**

Look, ah, dry / streets, still. Indian Suffering. Joseph Ceravolo. **SP-CeraJ**

Look and remember. Look upon this sky. Travelogue for Exiles. Karl Shapiro. **SP-ShapK**

Look at every white flower of winter. Cantico Per Lo Tuo Amore III. James Liddy. **CP-LiddJ**

Look at him / a withered man. The Millionaire. Charles Bukowski. **SP-BukC2**

Look at it / It's all blank. Praying Mantis. Jim Carroll. **SP-CarrJ**

Look at it hale, A. Pussy Willow. Louis Zukofsky. **CP-ZukLS**

Look at itsy-bitsy Mitzi! The Pizza. Ogden Nash. *Fr.* Table Talk. **CP-NashO**

Look at Jonah embarking from Joppa, deterred by. Tom Fool at Jamaica. Marianne Craig Moore. **CP-MoorM**

Look at my face. Mirror Meditation. Anne Waldman. **SP-WaldA**

Look at the fate of summer flowers. To ———. William Wordsworth. **CP-WorW2**

Look at the hands, kept out. Aor Against the Warmonger. James McAuley. **SP-McAuJ**

Look at the little darlings in the corn! Fireflies in the Corn. David Herbert Lawrence. **CP-LawrD**

"Look at the pigeons," you say. Night and Day. Siv Cedering Fox. **SP-CedeS**

Look at the stars! look, look up at the skies! The Starlight Night. Gerard Manley Hopkins. **CP-HopkG**

Look at the steady rifles, Joe. Joe Hill Listens to the Praying. Kenneth Patchen. **CP-PatcK**

Look at the wall, she said. Beyond Descartes. Jenny Joseph. **SP-JoseJ**

Look at them standing there in authority. The Revolutionary. David Herbert Lawrence. **CP-LawrD**

Look at this) a 75 done. Edward Estlin Cummings. **CP-CummE**

Look at this man in the room before you. Room with Revolutionists. Edwin Rolfe. **CP-RolfE**

Look Back. Gary Snyder. **CP-SnydG**

Look back, old Janus, and survey. A New Year's Gift. To the King. Thomas Carew. **CP-CareT**

Look back on Time, with kindly eyes. Emily Dickinson. **CP-DickE**

Look, beloved child, into my eyes, see there. Message. Kathleen Jessie Raine. **SP-RainK**

Look: between life and death hovers. Bal Masqué. Edwin Rolfe. **CP-RolfE**

Look closely: from nowhere he leaps into the screen. The Melancholy Comus. Edwin Rolfe. **CP-RolfE**

Look danger in the eye it vanishes. Ralph Waldo Emerson. **CP-EmerR**

Look down ever-intimate one. Marsden Hartley. **CP-HartM**

Look Down Fair Moon. Walt Whitman. **CP-WhitW**

Look down out how pretty. Pretty. Louis Zukofsky. **CP-ZukLS**

Look down the long valley and there stands a mountain. Too Anxious for Rivers. Robert Frost. **CP-FrosR**

Look down. There is snow. On a Landscape by Li Ch'eng. Charles Tomlinson. **CP-TomlC**

[*Look Flaxman & Stothard do*] old acquaintance well. William Blake. **CP-BlakW**

Look for the Silver Lining. Ogden Nash. **CP-NashO**

Look for us among those. Mandrakes. Thom Gunn. **CP-GunnT**

Look forward, truant, to your second childhood. The Death Room. Robert Ranke Graves. **CP-GravR**

Look, friend, you don't know the half. Me. Sam and Poll Go Back to the City. Hayden Carruth. **CP-CarHS**

Look, friend, you got troubles? Like it's. Marge. Hayden Carruth. **CP-CarHS**

Look from your stillness as the light resumes. The Request. Charles Tomlinson. **CP-TomlC**

Look Good, Smell Good, Feel. Al Young. **CP-YounA**

Look, he's let the kitchen fire go out. That Morning. Daniel Gerard Hoffman. **SP-HoffD**

Look[e] Home. Robert Southwell. **CP-SoutR**

Look how our foule Dayes do exceed our faire. His Confession. Robert Herrick. **CP-HerrR**

Look how the bittersweet with lazy muscle moves aside. Edna St. Vincent Millay. **CP-MillE**

Look, how the Rainbow doth appeare. The Rainbow. Robert Herrick. **CP-HerrR**

Look, how we curl into sleep after love. Coming & Going. James McAuley. **SP-McAuJ**

Look hyeah, Molly, ain't it jolly. To Mary Church Terrell. Paul Laurence Dunbar. **CP-DunbP**

Look, I strew beans. A Bean-Stripe: also, Apple-Eating. Robert Browning. **CP-BroR2**

Look in / and see him looking out. Wendell Berry. *Fr.* Window Poems. **CP-BerrW**

Look, in the attic, the unentered room. Before the Carnival. Thom Gunn. **CP-GunnT**

Look in the flower deep in the tulip cup. The Nothing I. Hayden Carruth. *Fr.* Contra Mortem. **CP-CarHL**

Look! In the lilac bush! Critics on the Lawn. Archibald MacLeish. **CP-MacLA**

Look in the night, look, look in the night. Thomas Merton. *Fr.* Figures for an Apocalypse. **CP-MertT**

Look in this mirror, tell me what you see. Glass Dialectic. Howard Nemerov. **CP-NemeH**

Look in thy glass, and tell the face thou viewest. Sonnet 3. William Shakespeare. **CABA; EnRePo; ImPo; LiTB; MasP; NAEL-1; OBSC; SCGP** *Fr.* Sonnets. **CP-ShaWS**

Look, Look. Stevie Smith. **CP-SmitS**

Look, love / springs. Hi There! Robert Creeley. **CP-CreeR**

Look, man, look. Fish, Fish. Stevie Smith. **CP-SmitS**

Look, Mitterrand baby, your telegram. Simone Signoret. James Schuyler. **CP-SchuJ**

Look not for spreading boughs. George Meredith. *Fr.* France. **CP-MerG1**

Look not in my eyes, for fear. Alfred Edward Housman. **CP-HousA**

Look now on that Adventurer who hath paid. William Wordsworth. **CP-WorW1**

Look of Death is both severe and mild, The. Robert Louis Stevenson. **CP-StevR**

Look of love alarms, The. William Blake. *Fr.* Several Questions Answered. **CP-BlakW**

Look of thee, what is it like, The. Emily Dickinson. **CP-DickE**

Look on her face in a dream, The. Roses. Mary Oliver. **SP-OlivM**

Look on him! through his dungeon grate. The Prisoner for Debt. John Greenleaf Whittier. **CP-WhitJ**

Look on myself, and thou shalt own at once. On the Engraver of His Pourtrait. William Cowper. **CP-CowpW**

Look on This Picture and on This. Christina Georgina Rossetti. **CP-RosC3**

Look once more ere we leave this specular Mount. John Milton. **PeECV,** *ll.* 236–271; **OBTV,** *ll.* 236–284; **NOSC; OBS** *Fr.* Book IV. *Fr.* Paradise Regained [*or* Regain'd]. **CP-MiltJ**

(Athens.) **NOSC; OBS,** *ll.* 236–364;

Look one way and the sun is going down. The Mockingbird. Randall Jarrell. **CP-JarrR; SP-JarrR**

Look, our farmer friend is finally. It's Spring, Lover. Gary Gildner. **SP-GildG**

Look-out, The. Hilda Doolittle. **CP-DoolH**

Look out across the fields, see me returning. When the Night Comes Falling from the Sky. "Bob Dylan." **CP-DylaB**

Look out how you use proud words. Primer Lesson. Carl Sandburg. **CP-SandC**

Look Out! The Bloody Bosun. Malcolm Lowry. **CP-LowrM**

Look out! there's that damned ape again. A Word with You. Elizabeth Bishop. **CP-BishE**

Look out your window, baby, there's a scene you'd like to catch. Man of Peace. "Bob Dylan." **CP-DylaB**

Look round, brown moon, brown bird, as you rise to fly. God is Good. It Is a Beautiful Night. Wallace Stevens. **CP-StevW**

Look round our world; behold the chain of love. Alexander Pope. **FHYEP; OBD** *Fr.* An Essay on Man. **CP-PopeA**

Look round: You see a little supper room. De Coenatione Micae. Martial, *tr. fr. Latin by* Robert Louis Stevenson. **CP-StevR**

"Look!" she cried. The Girl Who Died #1. Alice Walker. **CP-WalkA**

Look, stranger, on this island now. On This Island. Wystan Hugh Auden. **CP-AudeW**

Look the blue oxen / Come down from the altars. Thonga Lament. Thomas Merton. *Fr.* Two Moralities. *Fr.* South. *Fr.* The Geography of Lograire. **CP-MertT**

Look! The Engineer! He thinks he has caught something! Thomas Merton. *Fr.* Cables to the Ace. **CP-MertT**

Look, the raft, a signal flying. Far Off-Shore. Herman Melville. **SP-MelvH**

Look, the trees / are turning / their own bodies. In Blackwater Woods. Mary Oliver. **SP-OlivM**

Look, there are two curves in the air: the air. Diagram. Robinson Jeffers. **CP-JefR3**

Look, there goes the young lady across the street. William Carlos Williams, *with* David Rafael Wang, *at. to* Wang Wei, *tr. fr. Chinese.* **CP-WilW2**

Look, there it is—I'm sure that is the oak. Robert Pack. **SP-PackR**

Look there! The sunk road winding. The Bonfires. Wystan Hugh Auden. **CP-AudeW**

Look there! What a wheaten. The Hill Field. Donald Davie. **CP-DavDo**

Look to me faith, and look to my faith, God. Elegy upon the Untimely Death of the Incomparable Prince Henry. John Donne. **CP-DonnJ**

Look to the star that warns the morning in. Watching Morning In. John Clellon Holmes. **SP-HolmJ**

Look up into the dome. Altitudes. Richard Wilbur. **CP-WilbR**

Look up into the light of the lantern. Night Song. Louise Glück. *Fr.* Marathon. **SP-GlücL**

Look up, languishing Soul! Lo where the fair. *Ad. from the Medieval* Hymnus de Passione Domini. Richard Crashaw. **CP-CrasR**

Look up my dear at the dark. My Dear Love. Robinson Jeffers. **CP-JefR3**

Look up now at what's going on aloft—. Late Summer. Howard Nemerov. **CP-NemeH**

Look up, thou seed of envy, and still bring. On the Right Honourable and Virtuous Lord Weston, L[ord] High Treasurer of England, upon the Day He Was Made Earl of Portland, 17. Febr. 1632. To the Envious. Ben Jonson. **CP-JonsB**

Look upon Sapho's lip, and you will swear. Upon Sapho. Robert Herrick. **CP-HerrR**

Look What You Did, Christopher! Ogden Nash. **CP-NashO**

Look What You're Doing I'm feeling blue and lonely would it. What You're Doing. The Beatles. **CP-Beatl**

Look with the ears, said Orazio Vecchi. Words for the Madrigalist. Charles Tomlinson. **CP-TomlC**

Look, you have cast out Love! What Gods are these. Rudyard Kipling. **CP-KiplR** *Fr.* Lispeth. *Fr.* Plain Tales from the Hills.

Look You, I'll Go Pray. Nicholas Vachel Lindsay. **CP-LindV**

Look you, my simple friend, 'tis one of those. Arthur Hugh Clough. **SP-ClouA**

Looke how the woods, where enterlaced trees, *par. by* Countess of Pembroke, Mary Sidney Herbert. Bible, *O.T. See* Psalm 72: "Give the king thy judgments, O God."

Looke in my Book, and herein see. To a Friend. Robert Herrick. **CP-HerrR**

"Look!"he said, "all green!" but she. In Hades, Orpheus. Muriel Rukeyser. **CP-RukeM**

Looking. Gwendolyn Brooks. **SP-BrooG**

Looking. Muriel Rukeyser. **CP-RukeM**

Looking. William DeWitt Snodgrass. **SP-SnodW**

Looking Across. Thomas Hardy. **CP-HardT**

Looking across the Fields and Watching the Birds Fly. Wallace Stevens. **CP-StevW**

Looking across the River. William Stafford. **SP-StafW**

Looking as I've looked before, straight down the heart. The Stranger. Adrienne Rich. **SP-RicA1**

Looking at a Mountain Range While Listening to a Mozart Piano Concerto. Robert Pack. **SP-PackR**

Looking at a Picture on an Anniversary. Thomas Hardy. **CP-HardT**

Looking at Each Other. Muriel Rukeyser. **CP-RukeM**

Looking at Pictures. Charles Wright. **SP-WrigC**

Looking at Quilts. Marge Piercy. **SP-PierM**

Looking at the model of a pishkun. Pishkun. Richard Hugo. **CP-HugoR**

Looking at the Stars. Richard Eberhart. **CP-EberR**

Looking At The Stars. Richard Eberhart. **CP-EberR**

Looking at the stars we find. The Lyre. Siv Cedering Fox. **SP-CedeS**

Looking Back. Thomas Hardy. **CP-HardT**

Looking back along life's trodden way. Christina Georgina Rossetti. **CP-RosC2**

Looking back in my mind I can see. The Elementary Scene. Randall Jarrell. **CP-JarrR**

Looking back trying to decipher. Education of a Novelist. Adrienne Rich. **SP-RicA2**

Looking back 25 years I / imagine it simple. Simple. Hayden Carruth. **CP-CarHS**

Looking back, we cannot see. Traveling through Fog. Robert Earl Hayden. **CP-HaydR**

Looking by chance in at the open window. The Foreboding. Robert Ranke Graves. **CP-GravR**

Looking down at her. The Paradox. Robert Creeley. **CP-CreeR**

Looking down at the water. A Wish. Louis Zukofsky. *Fr.* Songs of Degrees. **CP-ZukLS**

Looking down into my father's / dead face. Good Night, Willie Lee, I'll See You in the Morning. Alice Walker. **CP-WalkA**

Looking Down on Nether Stowey. Samuel Taylor Coleridge. **FaBoPP** *Fr.* Fears in Solitude. **CP-ColeS**

Looking down on the stage. Monterey. Thom Gunn. *Fr.* Breaking Ground. **CP-GunnT**

Looking eastward through my picture window. Looking at a Mountain Range While Listening to a Mozart Piano Concerto. Robert Pack. **SP-PackR**

Looking far foorth into the ocean wide. Edmund Spenser. *Fr.* Visions of the World's Vanity [*or Vanitie*]. **CP-Spens**

Looking for a home, America. House-Hunting in the Bicentennial Year. Erica Jong. **SP-JongE**

Looking for a place. This Element. Erica Jong. **SP-JongE**

Looking for a Sunset Bird in Winter. Robert Frost. **CP-FrosR**

Looking for a way. Robert Creeley. **CP-CreeR**

Looking for life, I lost my mind. Roy Fisher. *Fr.* Five Morning Poems from a Picture by Manet. **SP-FishR**

Looking for You, Barbara. Ted Kooser. **SP-KoosT**

Looking Forward. Christina Georgina Rossetti. **CP-RosC3**

Looking Forward. Robert Louis Stevenson. *See* When I am grown to man's estate.

Looking Forward to See Jane Real Soon. James Schuyler. **CP-SchuJ**

Looking forward to the spring. Before and after Summer. Thomas Hardy. **CP-HardT**

Looking-Glass, A. Thomas Carew. **CP-CareT**

Looking Glass, The. Walter de la Mare. **CP-DeLaW**

Looking Glass, The. Paul Laurence Dunbar. **CP-DunbP**

Looking Glass. Thom Gunn. **CP-GunnT**

Looking Glass, The. Rudyard Kipling. **CP-KiplR**

Looking-glass. Denise Levertov. **CP-LeveD**

Looking-Glass River. Robert Louis Stevenson. **CP-StevR**

Looking Head On. Richard Eberhart. **CP-EberR**

Looking in a Mirror. Margaret Atwood. **SP-AtwM1**

Looking in my poem, I see myself. Billy McCoy. Gilbert Sorrentino. **SP-SorrG**

Looking in the mirrors at Macy's. Director of Alienation. Lawrence Ferlinghetti. **SP-FerlL**

Looking into History. Richard Wilbur. **CP-WilbR**

Looking into your eyes. Ndebele. Alice Walker. **CP-WalkA**

Looking Out. Robert Creeley. **CP-CreeR**

Looking Out from Ferrara. Donald Davie. **CP-DavDo**

Looking out of the dark of the town. A Letter. James Dickey. **CP-DickJ**

Looking over my shoulder. Four Haiku. Allen Ginsberg. **CP-GinsA**

Looking over my shoulder at you this morning, I'm listening to. Sarajevo Moonlight. Al Young. **CP-YounA**

Looking Seaward. Samuel Taylor Coleridge. **CP-ColeS**

Looking through boxes. The Toy Bone. Donald Hall. **CP-HallD**

Looking to the sea, it is a line. The Innocence. Robert Creeley. **CP-CreeR**

Looking up at the stars, I know quite well. The More Loving One. Wystan Hugh Auden. **CP-AudeW**

Looking up, of a sudden. Poem. William Carlos Williams. **CP-WilW2**

Looking Upwards in a Storm. William Cowper. *Fr.* Olney Hymns. **CP-CowpW**

Looks. Thom Gunn. **CP-GunnT**

Looks like what drives me crazy. Evil. Langston Hughes. **SP-HughL**

Looming and phosphorescent against the dark. Cryopexy. Charles Wright. **SP-WrigC**

Loon Call, A. Richard Eberhart. **CP-EberR**

Loon on Forrester's Pond, The. Hayden Carruth. **CP-CarHS**

Loon's Cry, The. Robert Bly. **SP-BlyR**

Loon's Cry, The. Howard Nemerov. **CP-NemeH**

Loon's cry is a chortle from another world, A. A Dream. Richard Eberhart. **CP-EberR**

Loop, A. Robert Creeley. **CP-CreeR**

Loophole, The. Leonard Nathan. **SP-NathL**

Looping off feline through the leisured air. The Waterfall at Powerscourt. Donald Davie. **CP-DavDo**

Loose lips now. Against Confidences. Donald Davie. **CP-DavDo**

Loose Mountain, A. Robert Frost. **CP-FrosR**

Loose no time nor youth but be. Song, A. Robert Herrick. **CP-HerrR**

Loose Saraband, A: ("Ah me! the little Tyrant Theefe!"). Richard Lovelace. **CP-LoveR**

Loose Saraband, A: ("Nay, prethee [*or* prithee] dear, draw nigher"). Richard Lovelace. **CP-LoveR**

Loose the baleful lion, snap / The frosty bars down from his cage. Request for Offering. Richard Eberhart. **CP-EberR**

Loose the knots of the heart; never think on thy fate. Hafiz, *tr. by* Ralph Waldo Emerson. **CP-EmerR** *Fr.* Odes.

Loose to the wind her golden tresses stream'd. Petrarch. *See* She used to let her golden hair fly free.

Loot. Thom Gunn. **CP-GunnT**

Loot. Rudyard Kipling. **CP-KiplR**

"Loo! loo! Lulu! lulu! Loo! loo! Loot! loot!" **UV**

Loppèd tree in time may grow again [*or* againe *or* agayne], The. Robert Southwell. **CP-SoutR**

(Times [*or* Tymes] Go[e] By Turn[e]s.) **CP-SoutR**

Lorca. Richard Eberhart. **CP-EberR**

Lord and Master, to thine altar. Bible, *O.T. See* Psalm 25: "Unto thee, O Lord, do I lift up my soul."

Lord Apollo, who has never died, The. Many Are Called. Edwin Arlington Robinson. **CP-RobiE**

Lord Archer, Death, whom sent you in your stead? Edna St. Vincent Millay. **CP-MillE**

Lord Babe, if Thou art He / We sought for patiently. Epiphany. Christina Georgina Rossetti. **CP-RosC2**

Lord Bacon's Birthday. Ben Jonson. **CP-JonsB**

Lord Barrenstock. Stevie Smith. **CP-SmitS**

"Lord, being dark," I said, "I cannot bear." The Shroud of Color. Countee Cullen. **CP-CullC**

Lord, but one wearies of flipping them. Light Switches. John Updike. **CP-UpdiJ**

Lord by thy sweet and saving sign. Compline. Richard Crashaw. **CP-CrasR**

Lord, by thy sweet and saving sign. Evensong. Richard Crashaw. **CP-CrasR**

Lord, by thy sweet and saving sign. For the Hour of Prime. Richard Crashaw. **CP-CrasR**

Lord, by thy sweet and saving sign. The Howres for the Hours of Matines. Richard Crashaw. **CP-CrasR**

Lord, by what inconceivable dim road / Thou leadest man on footsore pilgrimage! Christina Georgina Rossetti. **CP-RosC2**

Lord, carry me.—Nay, but I grant thee strength. Christina Georgina Rossetti. **CP-RosC2**

Lord, comest Thou to me? Christina Georgina Rossetti. **CP-RosC3**

Lord Cozens Hardy. Sir John Betjeman. **CP-BetjJ**

Lord, do not beat me. Another, to God. Robert Herrick. **CP-HerrR**

Lord, dost Thou look on me, and will not I. Christina Georgina Rossetti. **CP-RosC2**

Lord Dusiote sprang from priest and squire. George Meredith. *Fr.* The Young Princess. **CP-MerG1**

Lord Galloway. Robert Burns. **DBV; OxBoLi** *Fr.* Epigrams on Lord Galloway. **CP-BurnR**

Lord, give me blessed fear, / And much more blessed love. Perfect Love Casteth Out Fear. Christina Georgina Rossetti. **CP-RosC2**

Lord, give me grace / To take the lowest place. Sit Down in the Lowest Room. Christina Georgina Rossetti. **CP-RosC2**

Lord, give me love that I may love Thee much. Christina Georgina Rossetti. **CP-RosC2**

Lord God, bigger than the whole world, The. Ezekiel's Rabbit. William Dickey. **SP-DickW**

Lord God of Hosts, most Holy and most High. Christina Georgina Rossetti. **CP-RosC2**

Lord God that dost me save and keep, *par. by* Milton. Bible, *O.T. See* Psalm 88: "O God of my salvation."

Lord, grant me grace to love Thee in my pain. Christina Georgina Rossetti. **CP-RosC2**

Lord, Grant Us Calm. Christina Georgina Rossetti. **CP-RosC2**

Lord, grant us eyes to see and ears to hear, / And souls to love and minds to understand. Christina Georgina Rossetti. **CP-RosC2**

Lord, grant us grace to mount by steps of grace. And Now Why Tarriest Thou? Christina Georgina Rossetti. **CP-RosC2**

Lord, grant us grace to rest upon Thy word. Christina Georgina Rossetti. **CP-RosC2**

Lord, grant us wills to trust Thee with such aim. As the Sparks Fly Upwards. Christina Georgina Rossetti. **CP-RosC2**

Lord Gregory. Robert Burns. **CP-BurnR**

Lord had a job for me, but I had so much to do, The. Paul Laurence Dunbar. **CP-DunbP**

(Too Busy.) **CP-DunbP**

Lord, hast Thou so loved us, and will not we. Christina Georgina Rossetti. **CP-RosC2**

Lord, have mercy on my son: for he is lunatick. Opus Dei. John Berryman. **CP-BerrJ**

Lord Hay's Mask. Thomas Campion.

(Discription of a Maske, Presented before the Kinges Majestie *at Whitehall, on Twelfth Night* Last, in Honour of the Lord HAYES, and His Bride, Daughter and Heire to the *Honourable the Lord* Dnnye, *their* Marriage Having Been the Same Day at Court Solemnized, The.) **CP-CampT**

Ad Invictissimum Serenissimumque Iacobvm *Magnae Britanniae Regem.*

Epigram, An: "Merlin, the great King Arthur being slaine."

Epigramma: "Haeredem (ut spes est) pariet nova nupta Scot Anglum."

Epigramma: "Quid tu te numeris immisces? anne medentem."

"Neither buskin now, nor bayes."

"Shewes and nightly revels, signes of joy and peace."

Song: "Now hath Flora rob'd [*orrobbed*] her bowers."

(Roses.) **OBSC**

"Tell me, gentle howre of night."

"Time, that leads the fatall round."

To the Most Puisant and Gratious James King of Great Britaine.

To the Right Noble and Vertuous Theophilus Howard, Lorde of Walden, Sonne and Heire to the Right Honorable the Earle of Suffolke.

To the Right Vertuous, and Honorable, the Lord and Lady Hayes.

"Triumph now with Joy and mirth."

"With spotles mindes now mount we to the tree."

Lord hear [*or* here] my prayer [*or* prayre] and let my cry[e] pass[e]. Bible, *O.T. See* Psalm 102: "Hear my prayer, O Lord, and let my cry. . . " [*"Domine exaudi orationem meam"*].

Lord hear thee in the day of trouble, The. Psalm 20. Bible, *O.T. Fr.* Psalms. **CP-Psal**

Lord Heart, heal my right temple bang'd soft pain the bookshelf. On Illness. Allen Ginsberg. **CP-GinsA**

Lord, help, it is high time for me to call. Bible, *O.T. See* Psalm 12: "Help, Lord; for the godly man ceaseth."

Lord Himsel' in former days, The. Embro Hie Kirk. Robert Louis Stevenson. **CP-StevR**

Lord, how are they increased that trouble me! Psalm 3. Bible, *O.T. Fr.* Psalms. **CP-Psal**

Lord, how can man preach thy eternal[l] word? The Windows. George Herbert. **CP-HerbG**

Lord, how couldst thou so much appease. Faith. George Herbert. **CP-HerbG**

Lord, how I am all ague, when I seek. The Sinner. George Herbert. **CP-HerbG**

Lord, how is gamester changed! His hair close cut! On Reformed Gamester. Ben Jonson. **CP-JonsB**

Lord how many are my foes, *par. by* Milton. Bible, *O.T. See* Psalm 3: "Lord, how are the increased. . . ."

Lord, how mine eyes throw gazes to the east! *Various Authors.* **CP-ShaWS** *Fr.* The Passionate Pilgrim. **CP-ShaWS**

Lord, I am feeble and of mean account. Christina Georgina Rossetti. **CP-RosC2**

Lord, I am here.—But, child, I look for thee. Christina Georgina Rossetti. **CP-RosC2**

Lord, I am like to mistletoe. To God. Robert Herrick. **CP-HerrR**

Lord, I am waiting, weeping, watching for Thee. Of Him That Was Ready to Perish. Christina Georgina Rossetti. **CP-RosC2**

Lord, I believe, help Thou mine unbelief: / Lord, I repent, help mine impenitence. Cried Out with Tears. Christina Georgina Rossetti. **CP-RosC2**

Lord, I confess, that Thou alone art able. To His Saviour. Robert Herrick. **CP-HerrR**

Lord, I confess[e] my sin is great. Repentance. George Herbert. **CP-HerbG**

Lord, I cry unto thee: make haste unto me. Psalm 141. Bible, *O.T. Fr.* Psalms. **CP-Psal**

Lord, I have loved Your sky. Astrometaphysical. Robert Frost. **CP-FrosR**

Lord, I love the habitation. A Song of Mercy and Judgment. William Cowper. **CP-CowpW**

Lord, I will mean and speak thy praise. Praise (3). George Herbert. **CP-HerbG**

Lord, I'd rehearsed and rehearsed your loss. St. Clement's: Harris. Richard Hugo. **CP-HugoR**

Lord, if I love Thee and Thou lovest me. Why? Christina Georgina Rossetti. **CP-RosC2**

Lord, if Thy word had been "Worship Me not." Worship God. Christina Georgina Rossetti. **CP-RosC2**

Lord, in My Heart. Maya Angelou. **SP-AngeM**

Lord, in my silence how do I despise. Frailty. George Herbert. **CP-HerbG**

Lord in the Air, the. James Dickey. **CP-DickJ**

Lord in thine anger do not reprehend me, *par.* by Milton. Bible, *O.T. See* Psalm 6: "O Lord, rebuke me not in thine anger."

Lord Is Good, The, *ad. fr.* Psalm 71. Thomas Merton. **CP-MertT**

Lord is King, be the people, The. Curtains! Donald Davie. **CP-DavDo**

Lord is my herd, nae want sal fa' me, The, *par.* by P. Hately Waddell. Bible, *O.T. See* Psalm 23: "Lord is my shepherd, I shall not want, The."

Lord is my light and my salvation, The; whom shall I fear? Psalm 27. Bible, *O.T.* **WGRP** *Fr.* Psalms. **CP-Psal**

Lord is my shepherd, I shall not, The. Neothomist Poem. Ernest Hemingway. **CP-HemiE**

Lord is my shepherd, I shall not want, The. Psalm 23. Bible, *O.T.* **AMV-81; AWP; BLPL; BiP; FPL; FaBoBe; FaPON; FaPoB; NAWM-1; NIP; OHIP; PoLF; PoPl; TFi; TRP; TRV; TrGrPo; TrJP; WBLP; WGRP** *Fr.* Psalms. **CP-Psal**

Lord is my shepherd, The / and keeps me from wanting, *par.* by David Rosenberg. Bible, *O.T. See* Psalm 23: "Lord is my shepherd, I shall not want, The."

Lord is my shepherd, The; / I have everything I need. Bible, *O.T. See* Psalm 23: "Lord is my shepherd, I shall not want, The."

Lord, It Is Good for Us to Be Here. Christina Georgina Rossetti. **CP-RosC2**

Lord, it is my chief complaint. William Cowper. **TrPWD** *Fr.* Lovest Thou Me? **ChIV-2; HBV 1-2; OBEC** *Fr.* Olney Hymns. **CP-CowpW**

Lord, it is time. Summer was very great. Ted Berrigan. **SP-BerrT** *Fr.* The Sonnets.

Lord, it is time. The summer was so great. Rainer Maria Rilke. *See* Autumn Day.

Lord, it took no more than the wave of a glove. The Clearances. Richard Hugo. **CP-HugoR**

Lord Jesu, Thou art sweetness to my soul. Christina Georgina Rossetti. **CP-RosC2**

Lord Jesus Christ, grown faint upon the Cross. Good Friday. Christina Georgina Rossetti. **CP-RosC2**

Lord Jesus Christ, our Wisdom and our Rest. Whitsun Tuesday. Christina Georgina Rossetti. **CP-RosC2**

Lord Jesus, who would think that I am Thine? Christina Georgina Rossetti. **CP-RosC2**

Lord John Unalive(having a fortune of fifteengrand). Edward Estlin Cummings. **CP-CummE**

Lord, let the angels praise thy name. Misery [*or* Miserie]. George Herbert. **CP-HerbG**

Lord Lord I got the sickness blues, I must've done something wrong. Sickness Blues. Allen Ginsberg. **CP-GinsA**

Lord, make me coy and tender to offend. Unkindness. George Herbert. **CP-HerbG**

Lord, make me one with Thine own faithful ones. Christina Georgina Rossetti. **CP-RosC2**

Lord, make me pure: / Only the pure shall see Thee as Thou art. Christina Georgina Rossetti. **CP-RosC2**

Lord, Make Me to Know Mine End. Bible, *O.T. See* Psalm 39: "I said, I will take heed to my ways."

Lord, make us all love all: that when we meet / Even myriads of earth's myriads at Thy Bar. Christina Georgina Rossetti. **CP-RosC2**

Lord might have spared us the harsh joke, The. On a Text: Jonah IV, xi. Howard Nemerov. **CP-NemeH**

Lord Mope. Stevie Smith. **CP-SmitS**

Lord, my first fruits present themselves to thee. Dedication, The. George Herbert. **CP-HerbG**

Lord my God to thee I flie / Save me and secure me under, *par.* by Milton. Bible, *O.T. See* Psalm 7: "O Lord my God, in thee do I put my trust."

Lord, my heart is not haughty, nor mine eyes lofty. Psalm 131. Bible, *O.T. Fr.* Psalms. **CP-Psal**

Lord, my mind is not noisy with desires, *par.* by Stephen Mitchell. Bible, *O.T. See* Psalm 131: "Lord, my heart is not haughty, nor mine eyes lofty."

Lord my shepherd, me His sheep, The, *par.* by George Sandys. Bible, *O.T. See* Psalm 23: "Lord is my shepherd, I shall not want, The."

Lord, my soul with pleasure springs. True Pleasures. William Cowper. **CP-CowpW** *Fr.* Olney Hymns. **CP-CowpW**

Lord, of all, himself through all diffused, The. William Cowper. **OAEL-1** *Fr.* The Winter Walk at Noon. *Fr.* The Task. **CP-CowpW**

Lord of Elbë, on Elbë hill. A.G.A. to A.E. Emily Brontë. **CP-BronE**

Lord of my love, to whom in vassalage. Sonnet 26. William Shakespeare. **HeIP** *Fr.* Sonnets. **CP-ShaWS**

Lord of old has dealt in blood, The. George Meredith. **CP-MerG2**

Lord of the Isles, The. Sir Walter Scott.
    Autumn on Tweedside. **SP-ScotW**
    Brooch of Lorn, The. **SP-ScotW**

Death of Argentine, The. **SP-ScotW**
Loch Coruisk. **SP-ScotW**
Voyage to Arran, The. **SP-ScotW**

Lord of the Morning Star. David Herbert Lawrence. **CP-LawrD**

Lord Pam in the church (could [*or* cou'd] you think it) kneeled [*or* kneel'd] down. Epigram. Jonathan Swift. **CP-SwifJ**

Lord proclaims his grace abroad!, The. The Covenant. William Cowper. *Fr.* Olney Hymns. **CP-CowpW**

Lord, purge our eyes to see / Within the seed a tree. Judge Not According to the Appearance. Christina Georgina Rossetti. **CP-RosC2**

Lord, receive my prayer / Sweet as incense smoke. *ad. fr.* Psalm 140, 141. Thomas Merton. **CP-MertT**

Lord receives his highest praise, The. A Living and a Dead Faith. William Cowper. *Fr.* Olney Hymns. **CP-CowpW**

Lord reigneth, he is clothed [*or* apparelled] with majest, The. Psalm 93. Bible, *O.T.* **WGRP** *Fr.* Psalms. **CP-Psal**

Lord reigneth, The; let the earth rejoice. Psalm 97. Bible, *O.T. Fr.* Psalms. **CP-Psal**

Lord reigneth; let the people tremble, The. Psalm 98. Bible, *O.T. Fr.* Psalms. **CP-Psal**

Lord, remember David, and all his afflictions. Psalm 132. Bible, *O.T. Fr.* Psalms. **CP-Psal**

Lord Roberts. Rudyard Kipling. **CP-KiplR**

Lord Ronald My Son. Robert Burns. **CP-BurnR**

Lord said unto my Lord, The. Psalm 110. Bible, *O.T. Fr.* Psalms. **CP-Psal**

Lord, Save Us, We Perish. Christina Georgina Rossetti. **CP-RosC2**

Lord Say-and-Seal. Stevie Smith. **CP-SmitS**

Lord she's gone done left me done packed / up and split. Feeling Fucked Up. Etheridge Knight. **SP-KnigE**

Lord, stabilise me. My legs. Richard Eberhart. *Fr.* Suite in Prison. **CP-EberR**

Lord Tennyson and Lord Melchett. David Herbert Lawrence. **CP-LawrD**

Lord, the Lord my shepherd is, The. Bible, *O.T. See* Psalm 23: "Lord is my shepherd, I shall not want, The."

Lord, the Roman hyacinths are blooming in bowls and. A Song for Simeon. Thomas Stearns Eliot. **CP-ElioT**

Lord Thomas and Fair Margaret. Christina Georgina Rossetti. **CP-RosC3**

Lord, Thou art fulness, I am emptiness. Christina Georgina Rossetti. **CP-RosC3**

Lord, Thou art mine, and I am Thine. Clasping of Hands. George Herbert. **CP-HerbG**

Lord, thou hast been favourable unto thy land. Psalm 85. Bible, *O.T. Fr.* Psalms. **CP-Psal**

Lord, thou hast been our dwelling place in all generations. Psalm 90. Bible, *O.T.* **AWP; DL; EaLo** *Fr.* Psalms. **CP-Psal**

Lord, Thou hast given me a cell. A Thanksgiving to God for His House. Robert Herrick. **CP-HerrR**

Lord, Thou hast made this world below the shadow of a dream. McAndrew's Hymn. Rudyard Kipling. **CP-KiplR**

Lord, Thou Thyself art Love and only Thou. Christina Georgina Rossetti. *Fr.* Later Life: A Double Sonnet of Sonnets. **CP-RosC2**

Lord, to account who dares Thee call. On Commissary Goldie's Brains. Robert Burns. **CP-BurnR**

Lord to me a shepherd is, The, *fr.* Bay Psalm Book. Bible, *O.T. See* Psalm 23: "Lord is my shepherd, I shall not want, The."

Lord, to Thine own grant watchful hearts and eyes. Vigil of St. Bartholomew. Christina Georgina Rossetti. **CP-RosC2**

Lord Walter's Wife. Elizabeth Barrett Browning. **CP-BroEB**

Lord, we are rivers running to Thy sea. Christina Georgina Rossetti. **CP-RosC2**

Lord, we look to once for all, The. The Heretic's Tragedy. Robert Browning. **CP-BroR1**

L—d, let [thee] thank an' thee adore. Robert Burns. *Fr.* After Dinner. *Fr.* Graces——at the Globe Tavern. **CP-BurnR**

Lord, what have I that I may offer Thee? Christina Georgina Rossetti. **CP-RosC2**

Lord, what have I to offer? sickening fear. Christina Georgina Rossetti. **CP-RosC2**

Lord what is man, that he should find, *sts. 3–8 of par.* by Christopher Smart. Bible, *O.T. See* Psalm 8: "O Lord our Lord, how excellent. . . ."

Lord, what is man? why should he cost[e] thee [*or* you]. C[h]aritas Nimia; or, The Dear[e] Bargain. Richard Crashaw. **CP-CrasR**

Lord, when my heart was whole I kept it back. Afterward He Repented, and Went. Christina Georgina Rossetti. **CP-RosC2**

Lord, when the clock strikes. The Reader. Thomas Merton. **CP-MertT; SP-MertT**

Lord, when the sense of Thy sweet grace. Song. Richard Crashaw. **CP-CrasR**

Lord, when there is no escape, be my Defender. *ad. fr.* Psalm 4. Thomas Merton. **CP-MertT**

Lord, who createdst man in wealth and store. Easter Wings. George Herbert. **CP-HerbG**

Lord, who hast formed me out of mud. Trinity Sunday. George Herbert. **CP-HerbG**

Lord, who hast suffer'd all for me. Prayer for Patience. William Cowper. *Fr.* Olney Hymns. **CP-CowpW**

Lord, who shall abide in thy tabernacle? Psalm 15. Bible, *O.T. Fr.* Psalms. **CP-Psal**

Lord, whomsoever Thou shalt send to me, / Let that same be. Are They Not All Ministering Spirits? Christina Georgina Rossetti. **CP-RosC2**

Lord whose is the oracle at Delphi neither utters nor hides his meaning, The. Thomas Merton. *Fr.* The Legacy of Herakleitos. **CP-MertT**

Lord Will Happiness Divine, The. William Cowper. **NOCV** *Fr.* Olney Hymns. **CP-CowpW**

(Contrite Heart, The.) **CP-CowpW**

Lord, with what bounty and rare clemency. Ungratefulness. George Herbert. **CP-HerbG**

Lord, with what care hast thou begirt us round! Sin (1). George Herbert. **CP-HerbG**

Lord, with what glory [*or* glorie] wast thou served [*or* serv'd] of old. Sion. George Herbert. **CP-HerbG**

Lord, You may not recognize me. The Gift. Louise Glück. **SP-GlücL**

Lord, you've sent both. The Cancer Match. James Dickey. **CP-DickJ**

Lorde is my shepherde, The; therefore can I lack nothing, *par. by* Miles Coverdale. Bible, *O.T. See* Psalm 23: "Lord is my shepherd, I shall not want, The."

"Lording[e]s,"[*or* Lordynges] quod he, "in chirches whan I preche." The Pardoner's Prologue. Geoffrey Chaucer. **FHYEP; NAEL-1; NoP; OAEL-1; PoE** *Fr.* The Canterbury Tales. **CP-ChauG**

Lordly and Isolate Satyrs, The. Charles Olson. **CP-OlsoC**

Lordly and mighty language—eagle of time and space. The Power and Glory of Language. Delmore Schwartz. **SP-SchwD**

Lords are lordliest in their wine. As Lords. John Milton. **FaBoDD** *Fr.* Samson Agonistes. **CP-MiltJ**

Lords debate, the Commons brawl, The. George Meredith. **CP-MerG2**

Lord's lost Him His mockingbird. Mourning Poem for the Queen of Sunday. Robert Earl Hayden. **CP-HaydR**

Lords Mask[e], The. Thomas Campion.

(Description, Speeches, and Songs, of the Lords Maske, Presented in the Banquetting-House on the Marriage Night of the High and Mightie Count Palatine, *and the Royally Descended the Ladie* ELISABETH.) **CP-CampT**

"Breath you now, while Io Hymen."

"Dance, dance, and visit now the shadowes of our joy."

"Debetur alto iure Principium Iovi."

Full Song, A.

Song, A: "Come away; bring thy golden theft."

Song, The: "Wooe her, and win her, he that can."

Stars Dance, The. **OBSC**

Lord's my shepherd, I'll not want, The. Bible, *O.T. See* Psalm 23: "Lord is my shepherd, I shall not want, The."

Lords of Life Are the Masters of Death, The. David Herbert Lawrence. **CP-LawrD**

Lords of life, the lords of life, The. Experience. Ralph Waldo Emerson. **CP-EmerR**

Lords of the Court they sighed heart-sick, The. George Meredith. *Fr.* The Young Princess. **CP-MerG1**

Lord's Prayer. David Herbert Lawrence. **CP-LawrD**

Lords Strand of Northumberland, The. Sir Walter Scott. **SP-ScotW** *Fr.* Marmion.

Lords Welcome, sung before the Kings Good-night, The. Thomas Campion. *Fr.* The Ayres that Were Sung and Played, at *Brougham Castle* in *Westmerland,* in the Kings Entertainment. **CP-CampT**

Lordynges, ther is in Yorkshire, as I gesse. The Summoner's Tale. Geoffrey Chaucer. *Fr.* The Canterbury Tales. **CP-ChauG**

Lore. Howard Nemerov. **CP-NemeH**

Lorelei. James Merrill. **SP-MerrJ**

Lorelei. Sylvia Plath. **CP-PlatS**

Lorelei with wet hair riverine. Sedge. Tom Clark. **SP-ClarT**

Lorene—we thought she'd come home. But. Saint Matthew and All. William Stafford. **SP-StafW**

Lorna the Second. Thomas Hardy. **CP-HardT**

Lorna! Yes, you are so sweet. Lorna the Second. Thomas Hardy. **CP-HardT**

Lorrie. Lewis Turco. **SP-TurcL**

Los Angeles back-yarding in its blue-eyed waters. The Olympian. James Dickey. **CP-DickJ**

Los Angeles, 1954. David St. John. **SP-StJoD**

Los Guitaristas. Robert Creeley. **CP-CreeR**

Los Pobrecitos. Charles Tomlinson. **CP-TomlC**

Loser, The. Charles Bukowski. **SP-BukC2**

Loser, The. Adrienne Rich. **CP-RicAE; SP-RicA2**

Loser, The. Shel Silverstein. **SP-SilS2**

Losers. Carl Sandburg. **CP-SandC**

Losing Track. Denise Levertov. **CP-LeveD**

Loss. Samuel Taylor Coleridge. **CP-ColeS**

Loss. Hilda Doolittle. **CP-DoolH**

Loss. Richard Eberhart. **CP-EberR**

Loss. Randall Jarrell. **CP-JarrR**

Loss. David Herbert Lawrence. **CP-LawrD**

Loss. David Markson. **CP-MarkD**

Loss. Charles Kenneth Williams. **CP-WillC; SP-WillC**

Loss and Gain. Ralph Waldo Emerson. **CP-EmerR**

Loss and Gain. Geoffrey Hill. *Fr.* An Apology for the Revival of Christian Architecture in England. **CP-HillG**

Loss[e] in Delay[e]. Robert Southwell. **CP-SoutR**

Loss is also clearance. All Clear. Marge Piercy. **SP-PierM**

Loss is small to lose such one, The. Sir Thomas Wyatt. **CP-WyatT**

Loss, of Perhaps Love, in Our World of Contingency. Robert Penn Warren. **SP-WarrR**

Loss of something ever felt I, A. Emily Dickinson. **CP-DickE**

Loss of the Eurydice, The. Gerard Manley Hopkins. **CP-HopkG**

Losse from the Heat. Robert Herrick. **CP-HerrR**

Losses. Randall Jarrell. **CP-JarrR; SP-JarrR**

Losses. Carl Sandburg. **CP-SandC**

Loss[e] my molester at last patient be. Mary Sidney, Countess of Montgomery Wroth. **WPE** *Fr.* Part 1. *Fr.* Urania. **CP-WrotM**

(Pamphilia's Sonnet.) **WPE**

Lost. Wystan Hugh Auden. **FaBoEE** *Fr.* Shorts I ("Watch upon my wrist, The"). **CP-AudeW**

Lost. Hayden Carruth. **CP-CarHS**

Lost, The. Richard Eberhart. **CP-EberR**

Lost. Carl Sandburg. **CP-SandC**

Lost Acres. Robert Ranke Graves. **CP-GravR**

Lost, Alone, The. Marsden Hartley. **CP-HartM**

Lost Anchors. Edwin Arlington Robinson. **CP-RobiE**

Lost and Found. Archie Randolph Ammons. **SP-AmmoA**

Lost and Found. Philip Levine. **SP-LeviP**

Lost *Argo,* Islandmagee, Summer 1919. John Hewitt. **CP-HewiJ**

Lost Bodies. Charles Wright. **SP-WrigC**

Lost Bower, The. Elizabeth Barrett Browning. **CP-BroEB**

Lost Children, The. Richard Eberhart. **CP-EberR**

Lost Children, The. Randall Jarrell. **CP-JarrR; SP-JarrR**

Lost Continent, The. Jenny Joseph. **SP-JoseJ**

Lost Days. Stephen Spender. **CP-SpenS**

Chalk Blue.

Drowned under Grass.

Mosquito in Florence.

Lost Dogs of Phnom Penh, The. Kay Boyle. **CP-BoylK**

Lost Dream, A. Paul Laurence Dunbar. **CP-DunbP**

Lost Fish. Robert Lowell. **SP-LoweR**

Lost Follower, The. Robert Frost. **CP-FrosR**

Lost Girls, The. Derek Mahon. **FaBCIP** *Fr.* Autobiographies. **SP-MahoD**

Lost Hold. Jenny Joseph. **SP-JoseJ**

Lost in *Antarctica.* Barton Sutter. **SP-SuttB**

Lost in Heaven. Robert Frost. **CP-FrosR**

Lost in Ladispoli. Miller Williams. **SP-WillM**

Lost in Orbit. Louise McNeill. **SP-McNeL**

Lost in the brush, bound by the other path. The Quail. James Wright. **CP-WrigJ**

Lost in the Stars. Gilbert Sorrentino. **SP-SorrG**

Lost in Translation. James Merrill. **SP-MerrJ** *Fr.* The Book of Ephraim.

Lost Ingredient, The. Anne Sexton. **CP-SextA**

Lost Jewel, A. Robert Ranke Graves. **CP-GravR**

Lost Leader, The. Robert Browning. **CP-BroR1**

Lost Legion, The. Rudyard Kipling. **CP-KiplR**

Lost Lie, The. Anne Sexton. **CP-SextA**

Lost Love. Robert Ranke Graves. **CP-GravR**

Lost Love. Thomas Hardy. **CP-HardT**

Lost Love. Randall Jarrell. **CP-JarrR**

Lost Love, The. William Wordsworth. *See* She dwelt among the untrodden ways.

Lost manor where I walk continually. The Pier-Glass. Robert Ranke Graves. **CP-GravR**

Lost Mistress, The. Robert Browning. **CP-BroR1**

Lost My Voice? Of Course. Alice Walker. **CP-WalkA**

Lost Occasion, The. Robert Louis Stevenson. **CP-StevR**

Lost Occasion, The. John Greenleaf Whittier. **CP-WhitJ**

Lost on a fog-bound spit of sand. Lost. Wystan Hugh Auden. **FaBoEE** *Fr.* Shorts I ("Watch upon my wrist, The"). **CP-AudeW**

Lost Parents. Lawrence Ferlinghetti. **SP-FerlL**

Lost Pearl, The. Chuang Tzu, *tr. fr. Chinese by* Thomas Merton. **CP-MertT**

Lost Poem, A. Kenneth Patchen. **CP-PatcK**

Lost poems live a better. Courage for Lost Poems. Marsden Hartley. **CP-HartM**

Lost Pyx, The. Thomas Hardy. **CP-HardT**

Lost Romans, The. Muriel Rukeyser. **CP-RukeM**

Lost Sea, The. Jenny Joseph. **SP-JoseJ**

Lost Secret, The. Wystan Hugh Auden. **CP-AudWJ**

Lost Son, The. Theodore Roethke. **CP-RoetT**

　Flight, The. **NAAL-2; RB; TRP; TrGrPo**

　Gibber, The. **NAAL-2**

　It Was Beginning Winter. **NAAL-2**

　Pit, The. **NAAL-2**

　Return, The. **NAAL-2**

Lost Souls. Charles Wright. **SP-WrigC**

Lost Speakers, The. Archibald MacLeish. **CP-MacLA**

Lost Statesman, The. John Greenleaf Whittier. **CP-WhitJ**

Lost storm in this temperate place, A. Cowan Bridge; At the Site of 'Lowood School'. Geoffrey Hill. **CP-HillG**

Lost, sweetheart, how our memories creep. Lines Written in an Asylum. Hayden Carruth. **CP-CarHS**

Lost to the world; lost to my selfe; alone. On Himselfe . Robert Herrick. **CP-HerrR**

Lost Tune, The. Robert Lowell. **SP-LoweR**

Lost World, A. Robert Ranke Graves. **CP-GravR**

Lost World, The. Randall Jarrell. **CP-JarrR; SP-JarrR**

　Children's Arms.

　Night with Lions, A.

　Street off Sunset, A.

Lot is vacant still, The. Randall Jarrell. **CP-JarrR**

Lot Later. Howard Nemerov. **CP-NemeH**

Lot of love is chosen, The. I learnt that much. *fr.* A Woman Young and Old. William Butler Yeats. **CP-YeatW**

Lot of men and armies stand to take, A. A Letter to a Policemen in Kansas City. Kenneth Patchen. **CP-PatcK**

Lot of mouths and cocks, A. Under the World There's a Lot of Ass, a Lot of Cunt. Allen Ginsberg. **CP-GinsA**

Lot of People Bathing in a Stream, A. Wallace Stevens. **CP-StevW**

Loth to depart, but yet at last, each one. The Parting Verse, the Feast There Ended. Robert Herrick. **CP-HerrR**

Lotos-Eaters, The. Tennyson. *See* The Lotus-Eaters.

Lots of people are richer than me. Confession to Be Traced on a Birthday Cake. Ogden Nash. **CP-NashO**

Lots of swimming made Sam a sober man. Vir XII. James Liddy. *Fr.* Vir I–XII. **CP-LiddJ**

Lots to be Liked. Robert Herrick. **CP-HerrR**

Lot's Wife. "Anna Akhmatova", *tr. fr. Russian by* Richard Wilbur. **CP-WilbR**

Lot's wife, / married to chance. Epigraph. Robert Creeley. **CP-CreeR**

Lot's Wife. Howard Nemerov. **CP-NemeH**

Lot's Wife. Stevie Smith. **CP-SmitS**

Lotus and Frost. David Herbert Lawrence. **CP-LawrD**

Lotus-Eaters, The. Tennyson.

　(Lotos-Eaters, The.) **CP-TennA**

　"There is sweet music here that softer falls." **FaBV; FaFP; GGP; HeIP; ImPo; NOBE; OBEV; OBNC**

　(Choric Song: "There is sweet music here that softer falls.") **HeIP; OBNC**

　(Choric Song of the Lotos-Eaters.) **ImPo**

　(Choric Song of the Lotos-Eaters.) **FaFP**

　(Song of the Lotos-Eaters.) **GGP; NOBE; OBEV**

Lotus-Eaters: Ulysses to Penelope, The. Christina Georgina Rossetti. **CP-RosC3**

Lotus of toy china bells. Deutzia. Louis Zukofsky. **CP-ZukLS**

Loud and low in the chimney. Robert Louis Stevenson. **CP-StevR**

Loud blaw the frosty breezes. The Young Highland Rover. Robert Burns. **CP-BurnR**

Loud deep calls me home even now to feed it, The. Percy Bysshe Shelley. **ChER** *Fr.* Prometheus Unbound. **CP-ShelP**

Loud he sang the psalm of David! The Slave Singing at Midnight. Henry Wadsworth Longfellow. **SP-LongH**

Loud intolerant bells (the shrinking nightflower closes). Basil Bunting. **CP-BuntB**

Loud is the Vale! the Voice is up. Lines. William Wordsworth. **CP-WorW1**

Loud on the bright-necked grass. Two for History. Kenneth Patchen. **CP-PatcK**

Loud Song, Mother, A. Isabella Gardner. **CP-GardI**

Loud talk in the overlighted house. Ends. Robert Frost. **CP-FrosR**

Loud without the wind roaring. Emily Brontë. **CP-BronE**

Louder than gulls the little children scream. The Beach. Robert Ranke Graves. **CP-GravR**

Loudest sound [*or* thing] in our car, The. Vacation Trip. William Stafford. **SP-StafW**

Loue in thy youth fayre Mayde bee wise. Advice to a Maid. Robert Herrick. **CP-HerrR**

Lough Beg a sungleam, little Coney Island. By Air to Birmingham on a Mid-June Evening. John Hewitt. **CP-HewiJ**

Lough waters, The. Relic of Memory. Seamus Heaney. **SP-HeanS**

Louie. Thomas Hardy. **CP-HardT**

Louie the Barber. Lewis Turco. **SP-TurcL**

Louis. Paul Muldoon. *Fr.* 7, Middagh Street. **SP-MuldP**

Louis MacNeice. Stephen Spender. **CP-SpenS**

Louis Sonnet, A. Muriel Rukeyser. **CP-RukeM**

Louis, What Reck I by Thee. Robert Burns. **CP-BurnR**

Louis XVI. William Blake. **ChER** *Fr.* The French Revolution. **CP-BlakW**

Louisa; After Accompanying Her on a Mountain Excursion. William Wordsworth. **CP-WorW1**

Louisa to Strephon. Jonathan Swift. *Fr.* Riddles. **CP-SwifJ**

Louise. Stevie Smith. **CP-SmitS**

Loulachios pollaplasios philos estin emeia. Peri Tou Autou. John Harmarus. *Fr.* Commendatory Poems. **CP-LoveR**

Lourd on My Hert. "Hugh MacDiarmid." **SP-MacDH**

Lourd on my hert as winter lies. Lourd on My Hert. "Hugh MacDiarmid." **SP-MacDH**

Lout, The: "For Sunday's play he never makes excuse." John Clare. **SP-ClarJ**

Lout, The: "No sort of learning ever hurts his head." John Clare. **SP-ClarJ**

Lovable Babblers. Carl Sandburg. **CP-SandC**

Love— / let it / Out, / open up. Robert Creeley. **CP-CreeR**

Love / Asks nought his brother cannot give. Ralph Waldo Emerson. **CP-EmerR**

Love. Elizabeth Barrett Browning. **CP-BroEB**

Love. Robert Browning. **ArLo; EnLoPo** *Fr.* Earth's Immortalities. **CP-BroR1**

Love. Charles Bukowski. **SP-BukC3**

Love. Samuel Taylor Coleridge. **CP-ColeS**

Love. Paul Laurence Dunbar. **CP-DunbP**

Love. Ralph Waldo Emerson. *Fr.* Quatrains. **CP-EmerR**

Love ("Thou art too hard for me in Love"). George Herbert. **CP-HerbG**

Love. George Herbert. **CP-HerbG**

Love. Robert Herrick. **CP-HerrR**

Love. Langston Hughes. **SP-HughL**

Love / In whose rich honor. Song: Love in Whose Rich Honor. Muriel Rukeyser. **CP-RukeM**

Love / it takes so long. For Lois. Richard Shelton. **SP-ShelR**

Love. Philip Larkin. **CP-LarkP**

Love. David Herbert Lawrence. **CP-LawrD**

Love. George Meredith. **CP-MerG2**

Love. Howard Nemerov. *Fr.* Gnomes. **CP-NemeH**

Love. Alice Notley. **SP-NotlA**

Love. Charles Olson. **CP-OlsoC**

Love. Grace Paley. **CP-PaleG**

Love. Percy Bysshe Shelley. **CP-ShelP**

Love. Shel Silverstein. **SP-SilS2**

Love. Gary Snyder. **CP-SnydG**

Love. Edmund Spenser. *See* The Rugged forhead that with grave foresight.

Love / they say. *Barely* and *widely*. Louis Zukofsky. **CP-ZukLS**

Love. William Carlos Williams. **CP-WilW1**

Love a child is ever criing [*or* crying]. Song. Mary Sidney, Countess of Montgomery Wroth. **KTR; NOSC** *Fr.* Pamphilia to Amphilanthus. **CP-WrotM**

Love a Life can show Below, The. Emily Dickinson. **CP-DickE**

Love Abused. William Cowper. **CP-CowpW**

Love (after La Rochefoucauld). Tom Clark. **SP-ClarT**

Love after Love. Derek Walcott. **CP-WalcD**

Love Again. Philip Larkin. **CP-LarkP**

Love, all day there has been at the edge of my mind. Envoy. Wendell Berry. **CP-BerrW**

Love among the clouds did hover. Mary Sidney, Countess of Montgomery Wroth. *Fr.* Part 1. *Fr.* Urania. **CP-WrotM**

Love among the Manichees. William Dickey. **SP-DickW**

Love among the Roses. "Lewis Carroll." **CP-CarrL**

Love among the Ruins. Robert Browning. **CP-BroR1**

Love among The Ruins. Richard Eberhart. **CP-EberR**

Love and a Question. Robert Frost. **CP-FrosR**

Love and Death. Byron. **CP-Byron**

Love and Death. Catullus. *See* Carmen 96: "If, Calvus, effects of grief."

Love and Death. Christina Georgina Rossetti. **CP-RosC3**

Love and Death once ceased their strife. The Explanation. Rudyard Kipling. **CP-KiplR**

Love and Debt Alike Troublesome. Sir John Suckling. **CP-SuckJ**

Love and Folly. Jean de La Fontaine, *tr. fr. French by* Charlotte Smith. **CP-SmitC**

Love and forgetting might have carried them. Two Look at Two. Robert Frost. **CP-FrosR**

Love and Fortune and my mind, rememb'rer. Sir Thomas Wyatt. **CP-WyatT**

Love and Friendship. Emily Brontë. **CP-BronE**

Love and Friendship. Henry Wadsworth Longfellow. *TreFS Fr.* The Courtship of Miles Standish. **SP-LongH**

Love and Friendship Opposite. Samuel Taylor Coleridge. **CP-ColeS**

Love and Gold. Byron. **CP-Byron**

Love and Grief. Paul Laurence Dunbar. **CP-DunbP**

Love and harmony combine. Song. William Blake. · **CP-BlakW**

Love and Hope. Christina Georgina Rossetti. **CP-RosC3**

Love and How It Becomes Important in Our Day to Day Lives. Miller Williams. **SP-WillM**

Love and its Doors and Windows. Muriel Rukeyser. **CP-RukeM**

Love and Justice. Jenny Joseph. **SP-JoseJ**

Love and Knowledge. Robert Penn Warren. *Fr.* Audubon. **SP-WarrR**

Love and Law. Nicholas Vachel Lindsay. **CP-LindV**

Love and Libery—A Cantata. Robert Burns. *See* The Jolly Beggars.

Love and Marilyn Monroe. Delmore Schwartz. **SP-SchwD**

Love and my selfe (beleeve me) on a day. Love's Play at Push-Pin. Robert Herrick. **CP-HerrR**

Love and Night. Robert Ranke Graves. **CP-GravR**

Love and pity are ally'd. The Holy Innocents. Christopher Smart. *Fr.* Hymns and Spiritual Songs for the Fasts and Festivals of the Church of England. **SP-SmarC**

Love, and Reason once att warr. Mary Sidney, Countess of Montgomery Wroth. *Fr.* Love's Victorie. **CP-WrotM**

Love and Solitude. John Clare. **SP-ClarJ**

Love and Suspicion. John Gould Fletcher. **SP-FletJ**

Love and the Graces evermore do wait. Potentates. Robert Herrick. **CP-HerrR**

Love and the Hate, The. Robinson Jeffers. *Fr.* The Double Axe. **CP-JefR3**

Love and the Times. Donald Davie. **CP-DavDo**

Love and Thought. Ralph Waldo Emerson. **CP-EmerR**

Love and wisdom have no home. Malcolm Lowry. **CP-LowrM**

Love, any devil else but you. Love's Exchange. John Donne. **CP-DonnJ**

Love as an Escape. David Herbert Lawrence. **CP-LawrD**

Love as Lovelessness. Robert Ranke Graves. **CP-GravR**

Love as well can make abiding. Song. Mary Sidney, Countess of Montgomery Wroth. *Fr.* Pamphilia to Amphilanthus. **CP-WrotM**

Love at First Sight. Christopher Marlowe. **NOBE** *Fr.* Hero and Leander. **CP-MarlC**

"Love at first sight," some say, misnaming. At First Sight. Robert Ranke Graves. **CP-GravR**

Love at the lips was touch. To Earthward. Robert Frost. **CP-FrosR**

Love Attacked. Christina Georgina Rossetti. **CP-RosC3**

Love bade me aske a gift. On Love. Robert Herrick. **CP-HerrR**

Love bade me welcome; yet my soul drew back. Love. George Herbert. **CP-HerbG**

Love: Beginnnings. Charles Kenneth Williams. **SP-WillC**

Love Beyond Keeping. Carl Sandburg. **CP-SandC**

Love, born in Greece, of late fled from his native place. Sonnet 8. Sir Philip Sidney. *Fr.* Astrophil and Stella. **SP-SidnP**

Love, brave vertue's younger brother. Love's Horoscope. Richard Crashaw. **CP-CrasR**

Love brought Me down: and cannot love make thee / Carol for joy to Me? A Candlemas Dialogue. Christina Georgina Rossetti. **CP-RosC2**

Love brought me to a silent Grove. Upon Love ("Love brought me to a silent Grove"). Robert Herrick. **CP-HerrR**

Love builds a nest on earth and waits for rest. Christina Georgina Rossetti. **CP-RosC3**

Love built a stately house; where *Fortune* came. The World. George Herbert. **CP-HerbG**

Love butt a phantesie light, and vaine. Mary Sidney, Countess of Montgomery Wroth. *Fr.* Part 2. *Fr.* Urania. **CP-WrotM**

Love by ambition. Too Dear, Too Vague. Wystan Hugh Auden. **CP-AudeW**

Love, by sure proof I may call thee unkind. Sonnet 65. Sir Philip Sidney. **Son** *Fr.* Astrophil and Stella. **SP-SidnP**

Love Calls Us to the Things of This World. Richard Wilbur. **CP-WilbR**

Love came down at Christmas, / Love all lovely, Love Divine. Christmastide. Christina Georgina Rossetti. **CP-RosC2**

Love came up to me. Love Replied. Allen Ginsberg. **CP-GinsA**

Love can do all but raise the Dead. Emily Dickinson. **CP-DickE**

Love Charm, The. William Carlos Williams. **CP-WilW2**

Love Charms. Robert Ranke Graves. **CP-GravR**

Love-Children. Robinson Jeffers. **CP-JefR1**

Love Comes Late. David Herbert Lawrence. **CP-LawrD**

Love Comes Quietly. Robert Creeley. **CP-CreeR**

Love Conquer'd. Richard Lovelace. **CP-LoveR**

Love Constraining to Obedience. William Cowper. **NOCV** *Fr.* Olney Hymns. **CP-CowpW**

Love, death, sleeping. On Reading a Vast Anthology. Erica Jong. **SP-JongE**

Love Defended. Christina Georgina Rossetti. **CP-RosC3**

Love Despoiled. Paul Laurence Dunbar. **CP-DunbP**

Love Dies. George Meredith. *See* In our old shipwrecked days there was an hour.

Love Dislikes Nothing. Robert Herrick. **CP-HerrR**

Love doth so grace and dignify / That beggars treat as king with king. As a King, ...Unto the King. Christina Georgina Rossetti. **CP-RosC2**

Love Ephemeral. Christina Georgina Rossetti. **CP-RosC3**

Love ere he bleeds, an eagle in high skies. George Meredith. **HBV 1-2** *Fr.* Modern Love. **CP-MerG1**

Love Faithful in the Absence of the Beloved. Jeanne Marie Bouvier de la Motte-Guyon, *tr. fr. French by* William Cowper. **CP-CowpW**

Love farewell I now discover. Mary Sidney, Countess of Montgomery Wroth. *Fr.* Part 1. *Fr.* Urania. **CP-WrotM**

Love Feast, The. Wystan Hugh Auden. **CP-AudeW**

Love floods the tree of. Physics. Pablo Neruda, *tr. fr. Spanish by* Ben Belitt. **SP-NeruP**

Love, flute my veins. Fright among the Runes. Isabella Gardner. **CP-GardI**

Love for a Hand. Karl Shapiro. **SP-ShapK**

Love for One Orange, The. Randall Jarrell. **CP-JarrR**

Love for the Dragon. David St. John. *Fr.* To Pasolini. **SP-StJoD**

Love Forgiven, *with music*. Allen Ginsberg. **CP-GinsA**

Love Freed from Ignorance and Folly. Ben Jonson.
  "Crown, a crown for Love's bright head, A." **CP-JonsB**
  "Gentle Love, be not dismayed." **CP-JonsB**
  "What just excuse had agèd Time." **CP-JonsB**

Love from The North. Christina Georgina Rossetti. **CP-RosC1**

Love Gifts. Robert Ranke Graves. **CP-GravR**

Love God, we rather may, than. From Pico & the Women: A Life. Robert Creeley. **CP-CreeR**

LOVE, gone as lightning. Canto 95. Ezra Pound. *Fr.* Cantos. **CP-PoCan**

Love growne proud with victory. Mary Sidney, Countess of Montgomery Wroth. *Fr.* Part 1. *Fr.* Urania. **CP-WrotM**

Love had him fast but though he fought for breath. Meiosis. Wystan Hugh Auden. **CP-AudeW**

Love has crept out of her sealéd heart. Flapper. David Herbert Lawrence. **CP-LawrD**

Love has earth to which she clings. Bond and Free. Robert Frost. **CP-FrosR**

Love has gone and left me and the days are all alike. Ashes of Life. Edna St. Vincent Millay. **CP-MillE**

Love hath a name of Death. Christina Georgina Rossetti. **CP-RosC3**

Love hath again. Sir Thomas Wyatt. **CP-WyatT**

Love hath the wings of the butterfly. Love's Phases. Paul Laurence Dunbar. **CP-DunbP**

Love he that will; it best likes me. *see also* Upon Himself ("I dislikt but even now"). Robert Herrick. **CP-HerrR**

Love hid everywhere, including. Finding One of the Ghosts. Dabney Stuart. **SP-StuaD**

Love, Hope, and Patience in Education. Samuel Taylor Coleridge. **CP-ColeS**

Love, Hope, Desire and Fear. Percy Bysshe Shelley. **CP-ShelP**

Love I. Charles Olson. **CP-OlsoC**

Love, I have broke. Upon Love. Robert Herrick. **CP-HerrR**

Love, I recant. His Recantation. Robert Herrick. **CP-HerrR**

Love, I shall perfect for you the child. Poem. Seamus Heaney. **SP-HeanS**

Love I was shewn upon the mountain-side. The Half-way House. Gerard Manley Hopkins. **CP-HopkG**

Love, if I weep it will not matter. The Dream. Edna St. Vincent Millay. **CP-MillE**

Love! if Thy destined sacrifice am I. The Acquiescence of Pure Love. Jeanne Marie Bouvier de la Motte-Guyon, tr. fr. French by William Cowper. **CP-CowpW**

Love in a Bus. Thomas McGrath. **SP-McGrT**

Love in a Life. Robert Browning. **CP-BroR1**

Love in a showre of Blossomes came. The Showre of Blossomes. Robert Herrick. **CP-HerrR**

Love in a Valley. Sir John Betjeman. **CP-BetjJ**

Love in America. Marianne Craig Moore. **CP-MoorM**

Love in Barrenness. Robert Ranke Graves. **CP-GravR**

Love, in its separate being. Randall Jarrell. **CP-JarrR**

Love in Labrador. Carl Sandburg. **CP-SandC**

Love in the Asylum. Dylan Thomas. **CP-ThomD**

Love in the Cathedral. Miller Williams. **SP-WillM**

Love in the Museum. Adrienne Rich. **CP-RicAE**

Love in the Valley. George Meredith. **CP-MerG1**

Love in the Valley. Derek Walcott. **CP-WalcD**

Love Increased by Suffering. Jeanne Marie Bouvier de la Motte-Guyon, tr. fr. French by William Cowper. **CP-CowpW**

Love Inthron'd. Richard Lovelace. See In troth, I do myself persuade [or perswade].

Love is a circle, and an Endlesse Sphere. Upon Love. Robert Herrick. **CP-HerrR**

Love is a circle that doth restless[e] move. Love What It Is. Robert Herrick. **CP-HerrR**

Love Is a Deep and a Dark and a Lonely. Carl Sandburg. **CP-SandC**

Love Is a Dog from Hell. Charles Bukowski. **SP-BukC1**

Love is a door we shall open together. Moon Rondeau. Carl Sandburg. **CP-SandC**

Love Is a Fire. Leonard Cohen. **CP-CoheL**

Love is a game for only two to play at. Jus Primae Noctis. Robert Ranke Graves. **CP-GravR**

Love is a guess / that deepens. Edward Estlin Cummings. **CP-CummE**

Love is a kind of warre; Hence those who feare. On Love. Robert Herrick. **CP-HerrR**

Love is a Leven, and a loving kisse. Leven. Robert Herrick. **CP-HerrR**

Love Is a Parallax. Sylvia Plath. **CP-PlatS**

Love Is a Piece of Paper Torn to Bits. Charles Bukowski. **SP-BukC2**

Love is a place. Edward Estlin Cummings. **CP-CummE**

Love Is a Sirrup. Robert Herrick. **CP-HerrR**

Love is a spring at which. Edward Estlin Cummings. **CP-CummE**

Love Is a Star. Paul Laurence Dunbar. **CP-DunbP**

Love is a universal migraine. Symptoms of Love. Robert Ranke Graves. **CP-GravR**

Love is a vampire. the dead facts. energy undead. Doctor Love. Patti Smith. **SP-SmitP**

Love is all happiness, love is all beauty. Christina Georgina Rossetti. **CP-RosC3**

"Love is all/ Unsatisfied ." fr. Words for Music Perhaps. William Butler Yeats. **CP-YeatW**

Love is alone the worthy law of love: / All other laws have presupposed a taint. Quinquagesima. Christina Georgina Rossetti. **CP-RosC2**

Love is and was my Lord and King. Tennyson. **ChTr; EBVVPR; HBV; NOBE; NOCV; OBEV; OBNC; PeECV; SeCeV** Fr. In Memoriam A. H. H. **CP-TennA**

(My Lord and King.) **ChTr**

Love—is anterior to Life. Emily Dickinson. **CP-DickE**

Love is blind, and a wanton. Ben Jonson. **CP-JonsB** Fr. The Poetaster.

Love is done when Love's begun. Emily Dickinson. **CP-DickE**

"Love is enough," I read somewhere. To an Unknown Poet. Countee Cullen. **CP-CullC**

Love is feathered like a bird. Elizabeth Bishop. Fr. Three Valentines. **CP-BishE**

Love, is it a cat with claws and wild mate screams. Little Word, Little White Bird. Carl Sandburg. **CP-SandC**

Love Is Just a Four-Letter Word. "Bob Dylan." **CP-DylaB**

Love Is Like Sounds. Donald Hall. **CP-HallD**

Love is like the wild rose-briar. Love and Friendship. Emily Brontë. **CP-BronE**

Love is like water or the air. Riposte. William Carlos Williams. **CP-WilW1**

Love is lost, nor can his Mother. Out of the Greeke Cupid's Cryer. Moschus, tr. fr. Classical Greek by Richard Crashaw. **CP-CrasR**

Love is maintain'd by wealth; when all is spent. Adversity. Robert Herrick. **CP-HerrR**

Love is more thicker than forget. Edward Estlin Cummings. **CP-CummE; SP-CummE**

Love is my sin and thy dear virtue hate. Sonnet 142. William Shakespeare. Fr. Sonnets. **CP-ShaWS**

Love is not a profession. Is / Not. Margaret Atwood. **SP-AtwM1**

Love is not all: it is not meat nor drink. Edna St. Vincent Millay. **CP-MillE**

Love is not blind. I see with single eye. Edna St. Vincent Millay. **CP-MillE**

Love Is Not Concerned. Alice Walker. **CP-WalkA**

Love is not love demanding all, itself. Love's Way. Countee Cullen. **CP-CullC**

Love is not present now. Troilus. Charles Olson. **CP-OlsoC**

Love is still Love, and doeth all things well. He Cannot Deny Himself. Christina Georgina Rossetti. **CP-RosC2**

Love Is Strong as Death ("As flames that consume. . ."). Christina Georgina Rossetti. **CP-RosC2**

Love Is Strong As Death ("I have sought Thee. . ."). Christina Georgina Rossetti. See I have not sought Thee, I have not found Thee.

Love is sweet, and so are flowers. Love Ephemeral. Christina Georgina Rossetti. **CP-RosC3**

Love—is that later Thing than Death. Emily Dickinson. **CP-DickE**

Love is that one perfect labor. Emily Dickinson. **SP-DickE**

Love is the every only god. Edward Estlin Cummings. **CP-CummE; SP-CummE**

Love is the key of life and death, / Of hidden heavenly mystery. A Song for the Least of All Saints. Christina Georgina Rossetti. **CP-RosC2**

Love is the light of the world, my dear. Paul Laurence Dunbar. **CP-DunbP**

Love is the Lord whom I obey. Divine Love Endures No Rival. Jeanne Marie Bouvier de la Motte-Guyon, tr. fr. French by William Cowper. **CP-CowpW**

Love is the talk. Charles Olson. **CP-OlsoC**

Love is the very heart of spring. Robert Louis Stevenson. **CP-StevR**

Love is the way that lovers never know. Archibald MacLeish. **CP-MacLA** Fr. The Happy Marriage.

Love is too young to know what conscience is. Sonnet 151. William Shakespeare. **EBEV; HeIP; NoSic; OXAEP-1; PoE; PoEL-2** Fr. Sonnets. **CP-ShaWS**

Love is twain, it is not single. Love. William Carlos Williams. **CP-WilW1**

Love is winged for two. George Meredith. **CP-MerG1**

Love-Joy. George Herbert. **CP-HerbG**

Love Kill'd by Lack. Robert Herrick. **CP-HerrR**

Love kindle, / Death slay. Quenching the Red. Kathleen Jessie Raine. **SP-RainK**

Love knocked again at my door. Again! Again! Stanley Jasspon Kunitz. **CP-KuniS**

Love, leave me like the light. If You Should Go. Countee Cullen. **CP-CullC**

Love leave to urge, thou know'st thou hast the hand. Sonnet 7. Mary Sidney, Countess of Montgomery Wroth. Fr. Pamphilia to Amphilanthus. **CP-WrotM**

Love lett mee live, ore lett mee dye. Mary Sidney, Countess of Montgomery Wroth. Fr. Part 2. Fr. Urania. **CP-WrotM**

Love Letter, A. Paul Laurence Dunbar. **CP-DunbP**

Love Letter. Allen Ginsberg. **CP-GinsA**

Love Letter, The. Robert Ranke Graves. **CP-GravR**

Love Letter. Sylvia Plath. **CP-PlatS**

Love Letter Postmarked Van Beethoven. Diane Wakoski. **SP-WakoD**

Love Letter to Hans Christian Andersen. Carl Sandburg. **CP-SandC**

Love Letter Written in a Burning Building. Anne Sexton. **CP-SextA**

Love-Letters, The. Thomas Hardy. **CP-HardT**

Love Lies Bleeding. Christina Georgina Rossetti. **CP-RosC1**

Love Lies Bleeding. William Wordsworth. **CP-WorW2**

Love Lies Sleeping. Elizabeth Bishop. **CP-BishE**

Love, lift me up upon thy golden wings. An Hymne of Heavenly Love. Edmund Spenser. Fr. Fowre Hymnes. **CP-Spens**

Love-lighted eyes, that will not start. Acrostic: Love-lighted eyes, that will not start. "Lewis Carroll." **CP-CarrL**

Love, like a Beggar, came to me. Upon Cupid. Robert Herrick. **CP-HerrR**

Love, like a Gypsie, lately came. Upon Cupid. Robert Herrick. **CP-HerrR**

Love like a jugler, comes to play his prise. Sonnet 2. Mary Sidney, Countess of Montgomery Wroth. *Fr.* Pamphilia to Amphilanthus. **CP-WrotM**

Love long dormant showing itself. Palais des Arts. Louise Glück. **SP-GlücL**

Love-lorn Maid, at some far distant time, A. Tradition. William Wordsworth. *Fr.* The River Duddon [A Series of Sonnets]. **CP-WorW2**

Love, love, a lily's my care. Words for the Wind. Theodore Roethke. **CP-RoetT**

Love love begets, then never be. To Electra. Love Looks for Love. Robert Herrick. **CP-HerrR**

Love love love. All You Need Is Love. John Lennon *and* Paul McCartney. **CP-Beatl**

Love Love me do. Love Me Do. The Beatles. **CP-Beatl**

Love, love me now, because I place. To his Friend, Master J. Jincks. Robert Herrick. **CP-HerrR**

Love, Love, that having found a heart. What Sappho Would Have Said Had Her Leap Cured Instead of Killing Her. Christina Georgina Rossetti. **CP-RosC3**

Love, Love, who once didst pass the Dardan portals. Aurora and Tithonus. Euripides. **CP-BroEB**, *tr. by* Elizabeth Barrett Browning; *Fr.* Troades.

Love loveth Thee, and wisdom loveth Thee. Christina Georgina Rossetti. **CP-RosC2**

Love Made in the First Age[: To Chloris]. Richard Lovelace. **CP-LoveR**

Love Magick. Erica Jong. **SP-JongE**

Love, Maybe. Audre Lorde. **SP-LordA**

Love Me! Stevie Smith. **CP-SmitS**

Love me as I love thee. O double sweet! Gerard Manley Hopkins. **CP-HopkG**

Love Me but Leave My Dog Alone. Ogden Nash. **CP-NashO**

Love Me Do. The Beatles. **CP-Beatl**

"Love me, for I love you"—and answer me. Christina Georgina Rossetti. **Son** *Fr.* Monna Innominata. **CP-RosC2**

Love me. I care not what the circling years. Love's Apotheosis. Paul Laurence Dunbar. **CP-DunbP**

Love me,—I love you / Love me, my baby. Christina Georgina Rossetti. **CP-RosC2**

Love Me Little, Love Me Long. Robert Herrick. **CP-HerrR**

Love me, Love me, I cried to the rocks and the trees. Love Me! Stevie Smith. **CP-SmitS**

Love me no more, now let the god depart. Edna St. Vincent Millay. **CP-MillE**

Love Me or Not. Thomas Campion. **CP-CampT**

Love me or not, love her I must or die [*or* dye]. Love Me or Not. Thomas Campion. **CP-CampT**

Love me, Sweet, with all thou art. A Man's Requirements. Elizabeth Barrett Browning. **CP-BroEB**

Love Message. David Herbert Lawrence. **CP-LawrD**

Love Minus Zero/No Limit. "Bob Dylan." **CP-DylaB**

Love mistres is of many myndes. Love's Servile Lot[t]. Robert Southwell. **CP-SoutR**

Love must intend realities. —Goodbye! Exit Line. John Ciardi. **SP-CiarJ**

Love never count your labour lost. Song: Sullen Moods. Robert Ranke Graves. **CP-GravR**

Love, never disavow our vow. Lion-Gentle. Robert Ranke Graves. **CP-GravR**

Love ("Not enough. The question: what is"). Robert Creeley. **CP-CreeR**

Love Note I: Surely. Gwendolyn Brooks. **SP-BrooG**

Love Note II: Flags. Gwendolyn Brooks. *See* Still, it is dear defiance now to carry.

Love now no fire hath left him. Out of the Italain. Giovanni Battista Marino, *tr. fr. Italian by* Richard Crashaw. **CP-CrasR**

Love Nut, The. Lawrence Ferlinghetti. **SP-FerlL**

Love of a mother for her child, The. A Mother's Hearse. Stevie Smith. **CP-SmitS**

Love of a Seagull. Malcolm Lowry. **CP-LowrM**

Love of a woman, The. Air: "The Love of a Woman." Robert Creeley. **CP-CreeR**

Love of Christ Which Passeth Knowledge, The. Christina Georgina Rossetti. **CP-RosC1**

Love of God may be taught, The. Emily Dickinson. **SP-DickE**

Love of God the End of Life, The. Jeanne Marie Bouvier de la Motte-Guyon, *tr. fr. French by* William Cowper. **CP-CowpW**

Love of Lettuce, The. Marge Piercy. **SP-PierM**

Love of old men is not worth a lot, The. Lines for My 55th Birthday. Thom Gunn. **CP-GunnT**

Love of the bone, The. Reunion. Charles Bukowski. **SP-BukC2**

Love of the Woods. Johann N. Vogl, *tr. fr. German by* George Meredith. **CP-MerG2**

Love of the World Reproved, The. William Cowper. **CP-CowpW**

Love, oh my love, it will come. Geoffrey Hill. *Fr.* The Songbook of Sebastian Arrurruz. **CP-HillG**

Love on a day (wise poets tell). How Violets Came Blue. Robert Herrick. **CP-HerrR**

Love on his errand bound to go. Love. Ralph Waldo Emerson. *Fr.* Quatrains. **CP-EmerR**

Love on the Farm. David Herbert Lawrence. **CP-LawrD**

Love (1). George Herbert. **CP-HerbG**

Love our so right. Edward Estlin Cummings. **CP-CummE; SP-CummE**

Love Palpable. Robert Herrick. **CP-HerrR**

Love-Passage, A. David Herbert Lawrence. **CP-LawrD**

Love Passes Beyond the Incredible Hawk of Innocence. Diane Wakoski. **SP-WakoD**

Love Perfumes All Parts. Robert Herrick. **CP-HerrR**

Love peruse me, seeke, and finde. Mary Sidney, Countess of Montgomery Wroth. *Fr.* Part 1. *Fr.* Urania. **CP-WrotM**

Love Plant, The. Anne Sexton. **CP-SextA**

Love Poem, A. John Ashbery. **SP-AshbJ**

Love Poem, A. Charles Bukowski. **SP-BukC3**

Love Poem. Louise Glück. **SP-GlücL**

Love Poem: "I see myself, sad now, as in a mirror." Jim Carroll. **SP-CarrJ**

Love Poem. Audre Lorde. **SP-LordA**

Love Poem. Barton Sutter. **SP-SuttB**

Love Poem. Miller Williams. **SP-WillM**

Love Poem, A: "I am the lightness that I know." Richard Eberhart. **CP-EberR**

Love Poem, A:"Basic hatred / Sometimes has a flower." William Carlos Williams. **CP-WilW2**

Love poem at the bottom, A. Homage to the Divers. Stephen Dunn. **SP-DunnS**

Love Poem in Twos and Threes. Robert Bly. **SP-BlyR**

Love Poem (Later). Jim Carroll. **SP-CarrJ**

Love Poem 1990. Peter Meinke. **SP-MeinP**

Love Poem on Theme by Whitman. Allen Ginsberg. **CP-GinsA**

Love Poem to Be Read to an Illiterate Friend. Tess Gallagher. **SP-GallT**

Love Poems. Dabney Stuart. **SP-StuaD**

Love-Poems: for Mairi MacInnes. Donald Davie. **CP-DavDo**

Love Poems of Marichiko. Kenneth Rexroth.

　"As I came from the." **SP-RexrK**

　"I cannot forget." **SP-RexrK**

　"I hold your head tight between." **SP-RexrK**

　"Making love with you." **SP-RexrK**

　"Some day in six inches of." **SP-RexrK**

　"You wake me." **SP-RexrK**

　"Your tongue thrums and moves." **SP-RexrK**

Love Preparing to Fly. Gerard Manley Hopkins. **CP-HopkG**

Love Pure and Fervent. Jeanne Marie Bouvier de la Motte-Guyon, *tr. fr. French by* William Cowper. **CP-CowpW**

Love, Reason, Hate, did once bespeak. Sir John Suckling. **CP-SuckJ**

Love reckons by itself—alone. Emily Dickinson. **CP-DickE**

Love Replied. Allen Ginsberg. **CP-GinsA**

Love requires / talk of itself. The Alba. Charles Olson. **CP-OlsoC**

Love Restored. Ben Jonson.

　"Give end unto thy pastimes, Love." **CP-JonsB**

　"Have men beheld the graces dance." **CP-JonsB**

　"O how came Love, that is himself a fire." **CP-JonsB**

　"This motion was of love begot." **CP-JonsB**

Love Returned. Allen Ginsberg. **CP-GinsA**

Love returned with smiles. Love Returned. Allen Ginsberg. **CP-GinsA**

Love Rockets. Jim Carroll. **SP-CarrJ**

Love rose up between us. The Two Palm Trees. Miguel Hernández, *tr. fr. Spanish by* Thomas Merton. **CP-MertT**

Love said nay, while Hope kept saying / All his sweetest say. Now They Desire a Better Country. Christina Georgina Rossetti. **CP-RosC2**

Love, says the poet, has no reasons. The Old Gray Couple (2). Archibald MacLeish. **CP-MacLA**

Love scorch'd my finger, but did spare. Upon Love. Robert Herrick. **CP-HerrR**

Love seeketh not itself to please. The Clod and [*or* &] the Pebble. William Blake. **CP-BlakW** *Fr.* Songs of Experience.

Love set you going like a fat gold watch. Morning Song. Sylvia Plath. **CP-PlatS**

Love-sick I am, and must endure. On Himselfe. Robert Herrick. **CP-HerrR**

Love-sick Lass, The. "Hugh MacDiarmid." **SP-MacDH**

Love Song: "Daisies are broken." William Carlos Williams. **CP-WilW1**

Love Song: "For what as easy." Wystan Hugh Auden. *See* For what as easy.

Love Song: "I lie here thinking of you." William Carlos Williams. **CP-WilW1**

Love Song: "I was / the girl of the chain letter." Anne Sexton. **CP-SextA**

Love-Song: "If Death should claim me for her own to-day." Paul Laurence Dunbar. **CP-DunbP**

Love Song. Denise Levertov. **CP-LeveD**

Love Song: "One with eyes the fairest." Euripides. **AWP** *Fr.* The Cyclops. **CP-ShelP**

Love Song. Dabney Stuart. **SP-StuaD**

Love Song; "Sweep the house clean." William Carlos Williams. **CP-WilW1**

Love Song: "You have come between me and the terrifying presence." William Carlos Williams. **CP-WilW1**

Love Song, A: "Ah, love, my love is like a cry in the night." Paul Laurence Dunbar. **CP-DunbP**

Love Song, A: "Reject me not if I should say to you." David Herbert Lawrence. **CP-LawrD**

Love Song: First Version, 1915, A. William Carlos Williams. **CP-WilW1**

Love Song for K. Owyne. Anne Sexton. **CP-SextA**

Love Song in the Modern Taste, A. Jonathan Swift. **CP-SwifJ**

Love Song of Har Dyal, The. Rudyard Kipling. **CP-KiplR** *Fr.* Beyond the Pale. *Fr.* Plain Tales from the Hills.

Love Song of J. Alfred Prufrock, The. Thomas Stearns Eliot. **CP-ElioT**
    And Would It Have Been Worth It? **LPA**
    "Let us go then, you and I." **UV**

Love Song to a Morning. Jorge Guillén, *tr. fr. Spanish by* James Wright. **CP-WrigJ**

Love Songs in Age. Philip Larkin. **CP-LarkP**

Love Songs of Corca Bascinn. James Liddy. **CP-LiddJ**
    Anglos Have Gone, The.
    History.
    I.M. George Fitzpatrick.
    Proverbs of Corca Bascinn.
    "Tell us, streaming lady." **CIP**
    (History.) **CIP**

Love Spell: against Endings. Erica Jong. **SP-JongE**

Love still a boy, and oft a wanton is. Sonnet 74. Sir Philip Sidney. **HBV; OAEP; Son** *Fr.* Astrophil and Stella. **SP-SidnP**

Love Storm. David Herbert Lawrence. **CP-LawrD**

Love Story. Jim Carroll. **SP-CarrJ**

Love Story, A. Robert Ranke Graves. **CP-GravR**

Love, strong as Death, is dead. An End. Christina Georgina Rossetti. **CP-RosC1**

Love that drained her drained him she'd loved, though each. The Turtle Dove. Geoffrey Hill. **CP-HillG**

Love, that drained her, drained him she'd loved, though each. The Turtle Dove. Geoffrey Hill. **CP-HillG**

Love that is dead and buried, yesterday. Love Lies Bleeding. Christina Georgina Rossetti. **CP-RosC1**

Love That Is Hereafter, The. Walt Whitman. **CP-WhitW**

Love, that long since hast to thy mighty powre. An Hymne in Honour of Love. Edmund Spenser. *Fr.* Fowre Hymnes. **CP-Spens**

Love that rose on stronger wings, The. Tennyson. **EBVVPR** *Fr.* In Memoriam A. H. H. **CP-TennA**

Love that's pure hopes all things. Watered-Down Love. "Bob Dylan." **CP-DylaB**

Love, the Barber. Laurence Lieberman. **SP-LiebL**

Love the Monopolist. Thomas Hardy. **CP-HardT**

Love the quick profit, the annual raise. Manifesto: the Mad Farmer Liberation Front. Wendell Berry. **CP-BerrW**

Love, the sole Goddess fit for swearing by. Friday Night. Robert Ranke Graves. **CP-GravR**

Love, the sun lies warm along the wall. The Unlooked-For Season. Jenny Joseph. **SP-JoseJ**

Love, the Wild Swan. Robinson Jeffers. **CP-JefR2**

Love, the world. Letter in November. Sylvia Plath. **CP-PlatS**

Love, there have neccessarily been others. True Magic. Robert Ranke Graves. **CP-GravR**

Love they alone the joyful heart. George Meredith. **CP-MerG2**

Love ("Thing comes / of itself, The"). Robert Creeley. **CP-CreeR**

Love, this is not the way. Prison Walls. Robert Ranke Graves. **CP-GravR**

Love, thou art Absolute sole lord. A Hymn to Sainte Teresa. Richard Crashaw. **ACP; EBEV; ESCV; GeHe; HAP; MeLP; MePo; NOSC; WGRP** *Fr.* A Hymn to the Name and Hono[u]r of the Admirable Saint[e] T[h]eresa. **CP-CrasR**

Love—thou art high. Emily Dickinson. **CP-DickE**

Love, thou hast all, for now thou hast mee made. Sonnet 46. Mary Sidney, Countess of Montgomery Wroth. *Fr.* Pamphilia to Amphilanthus. **CP-WrotM**

Love thou saist. John Milton. **TOF** *Fr.* Book VIII. *Fr.* Paradise Lost. **CP-MiltJ**

Love, though for this you riddle me with darts. Edna St. Vincent Millay. **CP-MillE**

Love, though I sorrow, I shall never grieve. Hooded Flame. Robert Ranke Graves. **CP-GravR**

Love Thy Neighbour. David Herbert Lawrence. **CP-LawrD**

Love thy powerfull hand withdraw. Mary Sidney, Countess of Montgomery Wroth. *Fr.* Love's Victorie. **CP-WrotM**

Love, to be love, must walk Thy way / And work Thy Will. Christina Georgina Rossetti. **CP-RosC2**

Love to faults is always blind. How to Know Love from Deceit. William Blake. **CP-BlakW**

Love, to give law unto his subject hearts. Prologue. Sir Thomas Wyatt. **CP-WyatT** *Fr.* Penitential Psalms.

Love to keep? There is no love to keep. Hungry and Laughing Men. Carl Sandburg. **CP-SandC**

Love ("Tracking through this"). Robert Creeley. **CP-CreeR**

Love Tree, The. Countee Cullen. **CP-CullC**

Love Turned to Hatred. Sir John Suckling. **CP-SuckJ**

Love (2). George Herbert. **CP-HerbG**

Love: Two Vignettes. Robert Penn Warren. **SP-WarrR**
    Deciduous Spring. **ArNa**
    Mediterranean Beach, Day after Storm.

Love understands the mystery, whereof. Judge Nothing before the Time. Christina Georgina Rossetti. **CP-RosC2**

Love Unfeigned. Geoffrey Chaucer. **LO; NOBE; OBEV; OxBM** *Fr.* Troilus and Criseyde [*or* Criseide]. **CP-ChauG**

Love Unknown. George Herbert. **CP-HerbG**

Love used to carry a bow, you know. The Change. Paul Laurence Dunbar. **CP-DunbP**

Love was—entire excellently steep. Edward Estlin Cummings. **CP-CummE**

Love was in a constant state of liquid grace. Thermos. Patti Smith. **SP-SmitP**

Love Watches a Window. Thomas Hardy. **CP-HardT**

Love, We Must Part Now. Philip Larkin. **CP-LarkP**

Love wears down to bare truth. Lack Love. Allen Ginsberg. **CP-GinsA**

Love what art thou? A vaine thought. Song. Mary Sidney, Countess of Montgomery Wroth. *Fr.* Part 1. *Fr.* Urania. **CP-WrotM**

Love—what is love? A great and aching heart. Robert Louis Stevenson. **CP-StevR**

Love What It Is. Robert Herrick. **CP-HerrR**

Love, when you lost your keepsake. St Antony of Padua. Robert Ranke Graves. **CP-GravR**

Love whets the dullest wittes, his plagues be such. Canto Quarto. Thomas Campion. **CP-CampT**

Love which comes too late is like that black storm, *incl. in* Pijijiapan. Malcolm Lowry. *Fr.* The Comedian. **CP-LowrM**

Love which comes without aspect, The. Emily Dickinson. **SP-DickE**

Love which is imprinted in my soul, The, *speech of Philoclea.* Sir Philip Sidney. **SP-SidnP** *Fr.* Arcadia.

Love which is the most difficult mystery. Psyche with the Candle. Archibald MacLeish. **CP-MacLA**

Love, while you were away there came to me. The Wistful Lady. Thomas Hardy. **CP-HardT**

Love, who now deals to human hearts. Love and Folly. Jean de La Fontaine, *tr. fr. French by* Charlotte Smith. **CP-SmitC**

Love, whom I have loved too well. Isidora. Christina Georgina Rossetti. **CP-RosC3**

Love whom ye list and spare not. Sir Thomas Wyatt. **CP-WyatT**

Love, why have you led me here. The Young Cordwainer. Robert Ranke Graves. **CP-GravR**

Love Winter When the Plant Says Nothing. Thomas Merton. **CP-MertT; SP-MertT**

Love with his gilded bow and crystal arrows. Elizabeth Bishop. *Fr.* Three Valentines. **CP-BishE**

Love within the lover's breast. Song. George Meredith. **CP-MerG1**

Love without Frontiers. Phoebe Hesketh. **SP-HeskP**

Love without Hope. Robert Ranke Graves. **CP-GravR**

Love: Wrath. Charles Kenneth Williams. **SP-WillC**

Love you seek for, presupposes. Question and Answer. Elizabeth Barrett Browning. **CP-BroEB**

Love You To. George Harrison. **CP-Beatl**

Love You Too Much. "Bob Dylan" *and* Greg Lake. **CP-DylaB**

Love: Youth. Charles Kenneth Williams. **SP-WillC**

Loved feared hated. John Brown. Robert Earl Hayden. **CP-HaydR**

Loved I am, and yet complain[e] of Love, *speech of Cleophila.* Sir Philip Sidney. **SP-SidnP** *Fr. Arcadia.*

Loved in the black weather. . . The. Cruelties of the Sportive Power. Kenneth Patchen. **CP-PatcK**

Loved Once. Elizabeth Barrett Browning. **CP-BroEB**

Lovelace is dead! then let the World return. On My Brother. Dudley Posthume Lovelace. *Fr.* Elegies, 1660. **CP-LoveR**

Lovelier than the river in the spring. Manuela. Edwin Rolfe. **CP-RolfE**

Loveliest flowers, though crooked in their border. Gardener. Robert Ranke Graves. **CP-GravR**

Loveliest of trees, the cherry now. Alfred Edward Housman. **CP-HousA**

Loveliness. Stephen Dunn. **SP-DunnS**

Loveliness. Christopher Smart. **NOCV** *Fr.* Hymns for the Amusement of Children. **SP-SmarC**

Lovely Ad. William Carlos Williams. **CP-WilW1**

Lovely! all the essential parts. These Purists. William Carlos Williams. **CP-WilW2**

Lovely body gracefully is nodding, A. Something Amazing Just Happened. Ted Berrigan. **SP-BerrT**

Lovely city in a lovely land, / Whose citizens are lovely, and whose King, A. Beautiful For Situation. Christina Georgina Rossetti. **CP-RosC2**

Lovely Couple, A. Charles Bukowski. **SP-BukC1**

Lovely courier of the sky. Samuel Johnson. **CP-JohnS** (Translation of Anacreon's *Dove* (Ode ix).) **CP-JohnS**

Lovely Davies. Robert Burns. **CP-BurnR**

Lovely Face to sit by, A. Emily Dickinson. **SP-DickE**

Lovely flowers embarrass me, The. Emily Dickinson. **SP-DickE**

Lovely form there sate beside my bed, A. Phantom or Fact? Samuel Taylor Coleridge. **CP-ColeS**

Lovely house it was. We all thought so, A. The Fat Lady. Hayden Carruth. **CP-CarHS**

Lovely Lass o' Inverness, The. Robert Burns. **CP-BurnR** ("Luvely Lass o' Inverness, The.") **CP-BurnR**

Lovely Love, A. Gwendolyn Brooks. **SP-BrooG**

Lovely nun (submissive, but more meek), The. Same Subject, The [Dissolution of the Monasteries]. William Wordsworth. *Fr.* Ecclesiastical Sonnets. **CP-WorW2**

Lovely Polly Stewart. Robert Burns. **CP-BurnR**

Lovely Rita. The Beatles. **CP-Beatl**

Lovely, sleeping, lay in bed, The. The Sleeper. Walter de la Mare. **CP-DeLaW**

Lovely Spring, / A brief sweet thing. Tempus Fugit. Christina Georgina Rossetti. **CP-RosC2**

Lovely was the death. Samuel Taylor Coleridge. **EnRP** *Fr.* Religious Musings. **CP-ColeS**

Lovely was the night of May. The Postillion. Nikolaus Lenau, *tr. fr. German by* George Meredith. **CP-MerG2**

Lovely were the fruit trees in the evening. Richard Eberhart. *Fr.* Orchard. **CP-EberR**

Lovepet, The. Ted Hughes. **SP-HughT**

Lover, The. Robert Creeley. **CP-CreeR**

Lover, The. Frank O'Hara. **SP-OharF**

Lover & child, a little sing. John Berryman. **CP-BerrJ** *Fr.* The Black Book.

Lover and the Moon, The. Paul Laurence Dunbar. **CP-DunbP**

Lover as Fox. Muriel Rukeyser. **CP-RukeM**

Lover Asks Forgiveness because of His Many Moods. William Butler Yeats. **CP-YeatW**

Lover divine and perfect Comrade. Gods. Walt Whitman. **CP-WhitW**

Lover, in melodious verses, The. No Sorrow Peculiar to the Sufferer. Vincent Bourne, *tr. fr. Latin by* William Cowper. **CP-CowpW**

Lover, in the Disguise of an Amazon, Is Dearly Beloved of His Mistress, A. Thomas Carew. **CP-CareT**

Lover Mourns for the Loss of Love, The. William Butler Yeats. **CP-YeatW**

Lover of balsam lover of white pine. Hayden Carruth. *Fr.* North Winter. **CP-CarHL**

Lover of the moorland bare, A. To K. de M. Robert Louis Stevenson. **CP-StevR**

Lover Pleads with His Friend for Old Friends, The. William Butler Yeats. **CP-YeatW**

Lover Speaks to the Hearers of His Songs in Coming Days, The. William Butler Yeats. **CP-YeatW**

Lover Tells of the Rose in His Heart, The. William Butler Yeats. **CP-YeatW**

Lover to Mistress. Thomas Hardy. **CP-HardT**

Lover, upon an Accident Necessitating His Departure, Consults with Reason, A. Thomas Carew. **CP-CareT**

Lover whom duty called over the wave, A. The Lover and the Moon. Paul Laurence Dunbar. **CP-DunbP**

Lovers. Leonard Cohen. **CP-CoheL**

Lovers. Stephen Dunn. **SP-DunnS** *Fr.* Sympathetic Magic.

Lovers. Lewis Turco. **SP-TurcL**

Lovers are always walking through the streets of their city. In a Blue Smoke. James Liddy. **CP-LiddJ**

Lovers are happy. Secrecy. Robert Ranke Graves. **CP-GravR**

Lovers Are like Children. Adrienne Rich. **CP-RicAE**

Lover's Clock, The. Sir John Suckling. *See* That none beguiled be by time's quick flowing.

Lover's Complaint, A. William Shakespeare. **CP-ShaWS**

Lover's Complaint to His Mistress, A. Samuel Taylor Coleridge. **CP-ColeS**

Lover's death, how regular, The. Stark Major. Hart Crane. **CP-CranH**

Lover's Errand, The. Henry Wadsworth Longfellow. **TreFS** *Fr.* The Courtship of Miles Standish. **SP-LongH**

Lovers everywhere are bringing babies into the world. Make Love Not War. Howard Nemerov. **CP-NemeH**

Lover's Fate, The. James Thomson. **CP-ThomJ**

Lovers, forget your love. Wind and Window Flower. Robert Frost. **CP-FrosR**

Lover's Garden, A. Allen Ginsberg. **CP-GinsA**

Lovers Go Fly a Kite, The. William DeWitt Snodgrass. **SP-SnodW**

Lovers How They Come and Part. Robert Herrick. **CP-HerrR**

Lovers in the act dispense. The Thieves. Robert Ranke Graves. **CP-GravR**

Lovers in time of absence need not signal. In Time of Absence. Robert Ranke Graves. **CP-GravR**

Lovers in Winter. Robert Ranke Graves. **CP-GravR**

Lovers' Infiniteness[e]. John Donne. **CP-DonnJ**

Lovers' Lane. Wystan Hugh Auden. **CP-AudWJ**

Lover's Lane. Paul Laurence Dunbar. **CP-DunbP**

Lovers learne to speake butt truthe. Song 4. Mary Sidney, Countess of Montgomery Wroth. *Fr.* Pamphilia to Amphilanthus. **CP-WrotM**

Lovers' Litany, The. Rudyard Kipling. **CP-KiplR**

Lovers looked over the parapet-stone, The. Plena Timoris. Thomas Hardy. **CP-HardT**

Lovers may come and go. Hilda Doolittle. **CP-DoolH** *Fr.* Electra-Orestes.

Lover's Morning Salute to His Mistress, The. Robert Burns. **CP-BurnR**

Lovers, O lovers, listen to my call. Epilogue to the Adventures While Preaching the Gospel of Beauty. Nicholas Vachel Lindsay. **CP-LindV**

Lovers of the Poor, The. Gwendolyn Brooks. **SP-BrooG**

Lover's Petition. Ralph Waldo Emerson. **CP-EmerR**

Lovers' Quarrel, A. Robert Browning. **CP-BroR1**

Lovers Relentlessly. Stanley Jasspon Kunitz. **CP-KuniS**

Lover's Return. Langston Hughes. **SP-HughL**

Lover's Song, The. William Butler Yeats. **CP-YeatW**

Lover's Stars, The. Gerard Manley Hopkins. **CP-HopkG**

Lovers that burn and learnéd scholars cold. *See also* Lovers, Scholars—the fervent, the austere. Charles Baudelaire, *tr. fr. French by* Countee Cullen. **CP-CullC**

Lovers took within this ancient grove, The. Fancy and Tradition. William Wordsworth. **CP-WorW2**

Lovers tremble in the lost night, The. Night World. Edwin Rolfe. **CP-RolfE**

Lovers who among the grasses. Alun Lewis. *Fr.* Threnody for a Starry Night. **CP-LewiA**

Loversgrove lay / off to the lighthearted south. Scots Poem. John Berryman. **CP-BerrJ**

Loves. Stephen Dunn. **SP-DunnS**

Love's a thing, (as I do heare). Upon Love. Robert Herrick. **CP-HerrR**

Love's absence is illusion,alias time. Edward Estlin Cummings. **CP-CummE**

Love's Advocate. Phoebe Hesketh. **SP-HeskP**

Love's Alchemy [or Alchemie]. John Donne. **CP-DonnJ**

Love's Apotheosis. Paul Laurence Dunbar. **CP-DunbP**

Love's Apparition and Evanishment. Samuel Taylor Coleridge. **CP-ColeS**

Loves are the summer's. Summer like a bee. John Berryman. *Fr.* Sonnets to Chris. **CP-BerrJ**

Love's Body. Dabney Stuart. **SP-StuaD**

Love's Burial-Place. Samuel Taylor Coleridge. **CP-ColeS**

Love's Burning-Glass. Sir John Suckling. **CP-SuckJ**

Love's Castle. Paul Laurence Dunbar. **CP-DunbP**

Love's Chastening. Paul Laurence Dunbar. **CP-DunbP**

Love's Courtship. Thomas Carew. **CP-CareT**

Love's Deity [*or* Deitie]. John Donne. **CP-DonnJ**

Love's Diet. John Donne. **CP-DonnJ**

Love's Draft. Paul Laurence Dunbar. **CP-DunbP**

Love's Exchange. John Donne. **CP-DonnJ**

Love's faint trace. . . . Robert Creeley. **CP-CreeR**

Love's fiery chariot, Delia, take. *parody of* Ben Jonson. Rudyard Kipling. **CP-KiplR** *Fr.* The Muse among the Motors.

Love's Force. Thomas Carew. **CP-CareT**

Love's function is to fabricate unknownness. Edward Estlin Cummings. **CP-CummE; SP-CummE**

Love's Gardyne Greife. Robert Southwell. **CP-SoutR**

Love's Grave. George Meredith. *See* Mark where the pressing wind shoots javelin-like.

Love's Growth. John Donne. **CP-DonnJ**

Love's Horoscope. Richard Crashaw. **CP-CrasR**

Love's Humility. Paul Laurence Dunbar. **CP-DunbP**

Loves I allow and passions I aprove. Pavana Dolorosa. Geoffrey Hill. *Fr.* Lachrimae; or Seven Tears Figured in Seven Passionate Pavans. **CP-HillG**

Love's Last Adieu. Byron. **CP-Byron**

Love's Loneliness, *fr.* Words for Music Perhaps. William Butler Yeats. **CP-YeatW**

Loves of Anat, I, The. Charles Olson. **CP-OlsoC**

Love's of it self, too sweet; the best of all. Another on Love ("Love's of it self, too sweet"). Robert Herrick. **CP-HerrR**

Loves of the Peacocks. Laurence Lieberman. **SP-LiebL**

Loves of the Puppets. Richard Wilbur. **CP-WilbR**

Love's Parable. Robert Penn Warren. **SP-WarrR**

Love's Phases. Paul Laurence Dunbar. **CP-DunbP**

Love's Philosophy. Percy Bysshe Shelley. **CP-ShelP**

Love's Pictures. Paul Laurence Dunbar. **CP-DunbP**

Love's Play at Push-Pin. Robert Herrick. **CP-HerrR**

Love's Progress. John Donne. **LiTB; OAEL-1** *Fr.* Elegies. **CP-DonnJ**

Love's Progress. Theodore Roethke. **CP-RoetT**

Love's records, written on a heart like mine. Robert Burns. *Fr.* Annotations in Verse. **CP-BurnR**

Love's Representation. Sir John Suckling. **CP-SuckJ**

Love's Rose. Percy Bysshe Shelley. **CP-ShelP**

Love's Sanctuary. Samuel Taylor Coleridge. **CP-ColeS**

Love's Seasons. Paul Laurence Dunbar. **CP-DunbP**

Love's Servile Lot[t]. Robert Southwell. **CP-SoutR**

Love's specious information. Pride. Wystan Hugh Auden. **CP-AudWJ**

Love's stricken "why." Emily Dickinson. **CP-DickE**

Love's the boy stood on the burning deck. Casabianca. Elizabeth Bishop. **CP-BishE**

Love's the i guess most only verb that lives. Edward Estlin Cummings. **CP-CummE**

Love's Triumph through Callipolis. Ben Jonson.
Euclia's Hymn. **CP-JonsB**

Love's Usury. John Donne. **CP-DonnJ**

Love's Vicissitudes. Robert Louis Stevenson. **CP-StevR**

Love's Victorie. Mary Sidney, Countess of Montgomery Wroth. **CP-WrotM**

  "By a pleasant rivers side."

  "Cupid blessed bee thy might."

  "Joyfull pleasant spring."

  "Love, and Reason once att warr."

  "Love thy powerfull hand withdraw."

  "O my eyes how do you lead."

  "Silent woods with desarts shade."

  "When I doe see."

  "You pleasant floury meade."

Love's War. John Donne. *Fr.* Elegies. **CP-DonnJ**

Love's Way. Countee Cullen. **CP-CullC**

Love's World. Sir John Suckling. **CP-SuckJ**

Lovesong: "He loved her and she loved him." Ted Hughes. **SP-HughT**

Lovesong of O. O. Gabugah. Al Young. **CP-YounA**

Lovest Thou Me? William Cowper. **ChIV-2; HBV 1-2; OBEC** *Fr.* Olney Hymns. **CP-CowpW**

  "Lord, it is my chief complaint." **TrPWD**

Loving and Beloved. Sir John Suckling. **CP-SuckJ**

Loving Dexterity, The. William Carlos Williams. **CP-WilW2**

Loving feels lonely in a violent world. Community. Marge Piercy. **SP-PierM**

Loving friend, the gift of one. To Flush, My Dog. Elizabeth Barrett Browning. **CP-BroEB**

Loving in truth, and fain in verse to show. *often wr. titled* Astrophel and Stella. Sir Philip Sidney. **SP-SidnP**

Loving in truth, and fain[e] in verse my love to show. Sonnet 1. Sir Philip Sidney. **AWP; BLPL; CABA; EBEV; EPCY; FaBoEn; GBL; GGP; HAP; HBV; ImPo; InPS; LiTB; MasP; NAEL-1; NoP; NoSic; OAEL-1; OAEP; OBSC; OXAEP-1; PP; PoE; Poetr; SCGP; SeCePo; SeCeV; Son; TEP; TFi; TrGrPo; TreFT** *Fr.* Astrophil and Stella. **SP-SidnP**

Loving me with my shoes off. Barefoot. Anne Sexton. **CP-SextA**

Loving mind in this death-haunted body, The. Sonnet. Hayden Carruth. **CP-CarHS** *Fr.* Sonnets.

Loving she is, and tractable, though wild. Characteristics of a Child Three Years Old. William Wordsworth. **CP-WorW1**

Loving Shepherdess, The. Robinson Jeffers. **CP-JefR2**

Loving the Blest without Abode. Emily Dickinson. **SP-DickE**

Loving the Killer. Anne Sexton. **CP-SextA**

Loving True, Flying Blind. Robert Ranke Graves. **CP-GravR**

Loving Ugly. Ron Koertge. **SP-KoerR**

Loving you, flesh to flesh, I often thought. Travel. Leonard Cohen. **CP-CoheL**

Loving you less than life, a little less. Edna St. Vincent Millay. **CP-MillE**

Loving you Love loving you. Tango for Zither. Isabella Gardner. *Fr.* Saloon Suite. **CP-GardI**

Low and mournful be the strain. Voluntaries. Ralph Waldo Emerson. **CP-EmerR**

Low arch, its marble overlip. The Toy. Roy Fisher. **SP-FishR**

Low at my problem bending. Emily Dickinson. **CP-DickE**

Low at the knee that bore her once. Emily Dickinson. **SP-DickE**

Low beating of the tom-toms, The. Danse Africaine. Langston Hughes. **SP-HughL**

Low-built houses of the poor, The. Look. Philip Levine. **SP-LeviP**

Low-burning moon of moons, The. Grizzly Peak. Al Young. **CP-YounA**

Low-cloudly it whistles, changing heads. Pine. James Dickey. **CP-DickJ**

Low crippled clouds drag on a naked sky. Leaving July. Roy Fisher. **SP-FishR**

Low dead Thunder muttered thro' the Night, A. A Wish for Dreamful Sleep. Samuel Taylor Coleridge. **CP-ColeS**

Low December vault in June be up-lifted high. Ralph Waldo Emerson. **CP-EmerR**

Low-fi scrapes the phrases from the strings, The. Two Hours. John Ciardi. **SP-CiarJ**

Low in the east, against a white, cold dawn. The Christmas of 1888. John Greenleaf Whittier. **CP-WhitJ**

Low Lands. Donald Davie. **CP-DavDo**

Low murmurs creep along the woody vale. Written at Bignor Park in Sussex, in August, 1799. Charlotte Smith. **CP-SmitC**

Low note over the water, a moaning, A. I Hear the Wife of the Governor of Wisconsin Singing. James Liddy. **CP-LiddJ**

Low on my father's shelves there lay this book. I Learn About Art. John Hewitt. **CP-HewiJ**

Low-shot light of a sharp December. Beaumaris, December 21, 1963. Sir John Betjeman. **CP-BetjJ**

Low Sky, The. Robinson Jeffers. **CP-JefR2**

Low-Tide. Edna St. Vincent Millay. **CP-MillE**

Low to High. Langston Hughes. **SP-HughL**

Low Voice, Out Loud. James Dickey. **CP-DickJ**

Low was our pretty Cot: our tallest Rose. Reflections on Having Left a Place of Retirement. Samuel Taylor Coleridge. **CP-ColeS**

Lowden Sabbath Morn, A. Robert Louis Stevenson. **CP-StevR**

Lowell: Self-Portrait. Stephen Berg. **SP-BergS**

Lowellville Cemetery: Twilight. Kenneth Patchen. **CP-PatcK**

Lower Field—Enniscorthy. Charles Olson. **CP-OlsoC**

Lower your eyelids. Song to Make Me Still. Leonard Cohen. **CP-CoheL**

Lowest Place, The. Christina Georgina Rossetti. **CP-RosC1**

Lowest place. Ah, Lord, how steep and high, The. Called To Be Saints. Christina Georgina Rossetti. **CP-RosC2**

Lowest Room, The. Christina Georgina Rossetti. **CP-RosC1**

Lowestoft Boat, The. Rudyard Kipling. **CP-KiplR**

Lowlands of Holland, The, *sels.* Geoffrey Hill. *Fr.* Of Commerce and Society: Variations on a Theme. **CP-HillG**

Lowliest born of all the land, The. Wilson. John Greenleaf Whittier. **CP-WhitJ**

Lowly hill which overlooks a flat, A. Birchington Churchyard. Christina Georgina Rossetti. **CP-RosC2**

Lowry. David Markson. **CP-MarkD**

owther. William Wordsworth. *Fr.* Poems Composed or Suggested During a Tour, in the Summer of 1833. **CP-WorW2**

owther! in thy majestic Pile are seen. Lowther. William Wordsworth. *Fr.* Poems Composed or Suggested During a Tour, in the Summer of 1833. **CP-WorW2**

oyal. William Matthews. **SP-MattW**

oyal Scot, The. Andrew Marvell. **CP-MarvA**

oyal Soldier, The. George Meredith. **CP-MerG2**

oyalty Is the Life You Are. Kenneth Patchen. **CP-PatcK**

uath. Robert Burns. **GDP** *Fr.* The Twa Dogs. **CP-BurnR**

ubnan. Thomas Merton. **CP-MertT**

ucas at the Bath. Richard Lovelace. **CP-LoveR**

ucasta fair, but hapless Maid! Dedication To the Right Honorable John Lovelace. The. Richard Lovelace. **CP-LoveR**

ucasta frown and let me die. Her Reserved Looks. Richard Lovelace. **CP-LoveR**

ucasta Laughing. Richard Lovelace. **CP-LoveR**

ucasta Paying Her Obsequies. Richard Lovelace. **CP-LoveR**

ucasta, Taking the Waters at Tunbridge. Richard Lovelace. **CP-LoveR**

ucasta Weeping. Richard Lovelace. **CP-LoveR**

ucasta wept, and still the bright / Inamour'd God of Day. Lucasta Weeping. Richard Lovelace. **CP-LoveR**

ucasta's Fan[ne], with a Looking-Glass[e] in It. Richard Lovelace. **CP-LoveR**

ucasta's World. Richard Lovelace. **CP-LoveR**

ucid at dusk the city lies revealed. Night Flight : New York. Muriel Rukeyser. **CP-RukeM**

ucidity of the unredeemed. From the Terrace. Frederick Morgan. **SP-MorgF**

ucietta. A Fragment. Byron. **CP-Byron**

ucifer. David Herbert Lawrence. **CP-LawrD**

ucifer. Howard Nemerov. *Fr.* Dialectical Songs. **CP-NemeH**

ucifer blazing in superb effigies. The Bibliographers. Geoffrey Hill. **CP-HillG**

ucifer in Starlight. George Meredith. **CP-MerG1**

ucifer in Starlight. David St. John. **SP-StJoD**

ucifer in the Train. Adrienne Rich. **CP-RicAE**

ucilius. Howard Nemerov. *Fr.* Epigrams: "Wasp, climbing the window pane." **CP-NemeH**

ucilius the poet has informed me. Lucilius. Howard Nemerov. *Fr.* Epigrams: "Wasp, climbing the window pane." **CP-NemeH**

ucius Calpurnius Piso Caesoninus. Carmen 47. Catullus. *Fr.* Carmina. **CP-Catul**

uck. Charles Bukowski. **SP-BukC1**

uck. Langston Hughes. **SP-HughL**

uck is a star. The Fireborn Are at Home in Fire. Carl Sandburg. **CP-SandC**

uck is not chance. Emily Dickinson. **CP-DickE**

uck to the craft that bears this name of mine. To a Cape Ann Schooner. John Greenleaf Whittier. **CP-WhitJ**

uck, we've had it; our character the public's. It Did. Robert Lowell. **SP-LoweR**

ucks, my fair falcon, and your fellows all. Sir Thomas Wyatt. **CP-WyatT**

ucky black man in my dream. Frederick Morgan. **SP-MorgF**

ucky Little Britisher. David Herbert Lawrence. **CP-LawrD**

ucky means finding / Holes where. Edward Estlin Cummings. **CP-CummE**

ucrece's Death. William Shakespeare. **NoSic** *Fr.* The Rape of Lucrece. **CP-ShaWS**

ucretius felt the change of the world in his time, the great republic. Prescription of Painful Ends. Robinson Jeffers. **CP-JefR3**

ucretius versus the Lake Poets. Robert Frost. **CP-FrosR**

ucubration. Richard Eberhart. **CP-EberR**

ucy. Walter de la Mare. **CP-DeLaW**

ucy. William Wordsworth. **CP-WorW1**

"I traveled [*or* travell'd] among unknown men." **AWP; FaBV; GTBS; GTBS-6; GTBS-P; OAEP; OBRV;**

"She dwelt among the untrodden ways." **AWP; BLPA; BoLoP; CABA; EBEvV; ELP; EnLoPo; EnRP; FF; FPL; FaBV; FaBoEn; GTBS; GTBS-6; GTBS-P; HAP; HBVY; HeIL; HeIP; IMW; ImPo; LiTB; LoBV; MeMBP; NIP; NOBRP; NoP; OAEP; OBRV; OXAEP-2; OxBSP; PAI; PBMP; PPP; PWR; Poetr; PrIm; SpRo; TEP; TreF; UV; UnPo; WHA; WeW**

(Lost Love, The.) **GTBS; GTBS-6; GTBS-P**

(Song: "She dwelt among the untrodden ways.") **NOBRP**

"Slumber did my spirit seal, A." **AWP; BLPL; BiP; CABA; EBEvV; ELP; EnLoPo; FaBoCh; GGP; GTBS; GTBS-6; GTBS-P; HAP; HeIP; ImPo; InPK; InPS; InvP; MeMBP; NIP; NOBRP; NoP; PBMP; PPP; PoEL-4; PoRA; PrIm; SCV; TEP; TreFS; UnPo; WeW**

"Strange fits of passion have I known." **EBEV; EnRP; FiP; GBL; LO; LiTB; NAEL-2; NOBE; NOBRP; OAEL-2; OAEP; OBEV; OBNC; OBRV; PPP; PoE; TEP; TrGrPo**

"Three years she grew in sun and shower." **FiP; GN; GTBS; GTBS-6; GTBS-P; HAP; HBVY; LoBV; NoP; OAEP; OBRV; PoEL-4; SeCeV; TreFS**

(Education of Nature, The.) **GTBS; GTBS-6; GTBS-P**

Lucy done gone back on me. Jilted. Paul Laurence Dunbar. **CP-DunbP**

Lucy Gray; or, Solitude. William Wordsworth. **CP-WorW1**

Lucy Hooper. John Greenleaf Whittier. **CP-WhitJ**

Lucy in the Sky with Diamonds. The Beatles. **CP-Beatl**

Lucy Lake. Ogden Nash. **CP-NashO**

Lucy, whose day is in our darkest season. An Invocation to St. Lucy. Thomas Merton. **CP-MertT**

Lucy, you brightness[e] of our sphere [*or* spheare], who are. To Lucy, Countess[e] of Bedford, with Mr. Donnes Satire's [*or* Satyres]. Ben Jonson. **CP-JonsB**

Lueurs lisières. Samuel Beckett. **CP-BeckS**

Luftmenschen dream, the men who live on air. John Berryman. **CP-BerrJ** *Fr.* The Black Book.

Luftpost (For Levy). Chuck Miller. **SP-MillC**

Luggs, by the Condemnation of the Bench. Upon Luggs. Robert Herrick. **CP-HerrR**

Lugubre e vagabondo in terra e in mare. Christina Georgina Rossetti. **CP-RosC3**

Lugubrious, Salubrious Seaside, The. Louis MacNeice. **CP-MacNL**

Lui et Elle. David Herbert Lawrence. **CP-LawrD**

Luini in porcelain! Ezra Pound. *Fr.* Mauberly (1920). *Fr.* Hugh Selwyn Mauberley. (Life and Contacts). **SP-PounE**

Lukannon. Rudyard Kipling. **CP-KiplR** *Fr.* The White Seal. *Fr.* The Jungle Book.

Luke 10; And a Certaine Priest Comming that Way Looked on Him and Passed by. Bible, *N.T.* **CP-CrasR**, *tr.* by Richard Crashaw; *Fr.* St. Luke.

Luke 11; Blessed Be the Paps Which Thou Hast Sucked. Bible, *N.T. See* Blessed be the Paps which Thou hast Sucked.

Luke 11; Upon the Dumbe Devill Cast Out, and the Slanderous Jewes Put to Silence. Bible, *N.T.* **CP-CrasR**, *tr.* by Richard Crashaw; *Fr.* St. Luke.

Luke 15; On the Prodigall. Bible, *N.T.* **CP-CrasR**, *tr.* by Richard Crashaw; *Fr.* St. Luke.

Luke 16; Dives *Asking a Drop.* Bible, *N.T.* **CP-CrasR**, *tr.* by Richard Crashaw; *Fr.* St. Luke.

Luke 2; Quærit Jesum Suum Maria. Bible, *N.T.* **CP-CrasR**, *tr.* by Richard Crashaw; *Fr.* St. Luke.

Luke 7; She Began To Wash His Feet with Teares and Wipe Them with the Haires of Her Head. Bible, *N.T.* **CP-CrasR**, *tr.* by Richard Crashaw; *Fr.* St. Luke.

Luke Havergal. Edwin Arlington Robinson. **CP-RobiE**

Luke, physician of the wound. St. Luke. Christopher Smart. *Fr.* Hymns and Spiritual Songs for the Fasts and Festivals of the Church of England. **SP-SmarC**

Lull. Malcolm Lowry. *Fr.* The Moon in Scandinavia. **CP-LowrM**

Lull. Theodore Roethke. **CP-RoetT**

Lullaby. / Adult and child. Elizabeth Bishop. *Fr.* Songs for a Colored Singer. **CP-BishE**

Lullaby: "Bedtime's come fu' little boys." Paul Laurence Dunbar. **CP-DunbP**

Lullaby: "Din of work is subdued, The." Wystan Hugh Auden. **CP-AudeW**

Lullaby: "It is a summer evening." Anne Sexton. **CP-SextA**

Lullaby: "Kiver up yo' haid, my little lady." Paul Laurence Dunbar. **CP-DunbP**

Lullaby: "Lay your sleeping head, my love." Wystan Hugh Auden. **CP-AudeW**

Lullaby: "Sweet and low, sweet and low." Tennyson. *See* Sweet and low, sweet and low.

Lullaby: "Beloved, may your sleep be sound", *fr.* Words for Music Perhaps. William Butler Yeats. **CP-YeatW**

Lullaby, A: "For wars his life and half a world away." Randall Jarrell. **CP-JarrR**

Lullaby: A Motion Like Sleep. Robert Penn Warren. **SP-WarrR**

Lullaby and Exhortation for the Unwilling Hero. Roy Fisher. *Fr.* City. **SP-FishR**

Lullaby for a Summer Recess. James Fenton. **SP-FentJ**

Lullaby for the Cat. Elizabeth Bishop. **CP-BishE**

Lullaby: *"Herda, herda, herda, sing my sisters".* Louise McNeill. **SP-McNeL**

Lullaby: Moonlight Lingers. Robert Penn Warren. *Fr.* Man in Moonlight. **SP-WarrR**

Lullaby, oh lullaby! / Flowers are closed and lambs are sleeping. Christina Georgina Rossetti. **CP-RosC2**

Lullaby: Smile in Sleep. Robert Penn Warren. **SP-WarrR**

Lullaby: The Comforting of Cock Robin. William DeWitt Snodgrass. **SP-SnodW**

Lullabye for a Dybbuk. Erica Jong. **SP-JongE**

Lulled by the sound of pastoral bells. Elegiac Stanzas. William Wordsworth. *Fr.* Memorials of a Tour of the Continent; 1820. **CP-WorW2**

Lulls swears he is all heart, but you'l suppose. Upon Lulls. Robert Herrick. **CP-HerrR**

Lumber of a London-going dray, The. An Incident in the Early Life of Ebenezer Jones, Poet, 1828. Sir John Betjeman. **CP-BetjJ**

Lumber Yard Pools at Sunset. Carl Sandburg. **CP-SandC**

Lumbering down / in the early morning clatter. The Saturday Market. Erica Jong. **SP-JongE**

Lumbering logging lonesome. Baby Breakdown. Anne Waldman. **SP-WaldA**

Lumbermen, The. John Greenleaf Whittier. **CP-WhitJ**

Lumen / Ad revelationem gentium. The Candlemas Procession. Thomas Merton. **CP-MertT; SP-MertT**

Luminous tendril of celestial wish. Edward Estlin Cummings. **CP-CummE; SP-CummE**

Lunar Entrancement. Samuel Taylor Coleridge. **CP-ColeS**

Lunar Paraphrase. Wallace Stevens. **CP-StevW**

Lunatic Witch-fires! Ghosts of Light and Motion! *ad. fr. the German of* Stolberg. Samuel Taylor Coleridge. **CP-ColeS**

Lunch. Kenneth Koch. **SP-KochK**

Lunch in a Jim Crow Car. Langston Hughes. **SP-HughL**

Lunch Wagon on Highway 57. Kenneth Patchen. **CP-PatcK**

Lunch with Pancho Villa. Paul Muldoon. **SP-MuldP**

Lune de Miel. Thomas Stearns Eliot. **CP-ElioT**

Lunes. Martin Edmunds. **SP-EdmuM**

Lung Fish, The. John Ciardi. **SP-CiarJ**

Lungi da me il pensiere. Si Rimanda La Tocca-Caldaja. Christina Georgina Rossetti. *Fr.* Il Rosseggiar Dell'Oriente Canzoniere. **CP-RosC3**

Lungs (as some say) ne'r sets him down to eate. Upon Lungs. Robert Herrick. **CP-HerrR**

Lupes for the outside of his suit[e] has paid[e]. Upon Lupes. Robert Herrick. **CP-HerrR**

Lure. Jenny Joseph. **SP-JoseJ**

Lure of Murder. Robert Ranke Graves. **CP-GravR**

Lured by the wall, and drawn. A Poem about George Doty in the Death House. James Wright. **CP-WrigJ**

Lurking man in that half light, A. Seeing. Archibald MacLeish. **CP-MacLA**

Luscious and Sorrowful. Christina Georgina Rossetti. **CP-RosC2**

Luscious and Sorrowful. Christina Georgina Rossetti. *Fr.* Il Rosseggiar Dell'Oriente Canzoniere. **CP-RosC3**

Lush summer lit the trees to green. June Leaves and Autumn. Thomas Hardy. **CP-HardT**

Lust. William Matthews. **SP-MattW**

Lust Acts. William Matthews. **SP-MattW**

Lust in Action. William Shakespeare. *See* Sonnet 129: "Expense of spirit in a waste of shame, The [*or* Th']."

Lustra. Ezra Pound.

  "O helpless few in my country." **SP-PounE**

  (Rest, the.) **SP-PounE**

Lustral sweat in its fine slow beads, The. Grave Piece. Richard Eberhart. **CP-EberR**

Lustrum for You, E.P., A. Charles Olson. **CP-OlsoC**

Lustspiel. William Carlos Williams. **CP-WilW2**

Lusty Advice of a Fortune-Teller. Malcolm Lowry. **CP-LowrM**

Lusus amicitia est, uni nisi dedita, ceu fit. Lepus Multis Amicus. John Gay, *tr. fr. English by* William Cowper. **CP-CowpW**

Lute in the Attic, The. Kenneth Patchen. **CP-PatcK**

Lute Music. Kenneth Rexroth. **SP-RexrK**

Lutea Allison. Sir John Suckling. **CP-SuckJ**

Luther. Wystan Hugh Auden. **CP-AudeW**

Luther, they say, was unwise; he didn't see how things were going. Arthur Hugh Clough. **FaBoVe** *Fr.* Amours de Voyage. **SP-ClouA**

Luvely Lass o' Inverness, The. Robert Burns. *See* The Lovely Lass o' Inverness.

Luxurious man, to bring his vice in use. The Mower against Gardens. Andrew Marvell. **CP-MarvA**

Luxury. Denise Levertov. **CP-LeveD**

Luxury to apprehend, The. Emily Dickinson. **CP-DickE**

Luxury travel is something for which I pant. Change Here for Wichita Falls, or, Has Anybody Seen My Wanderlust? Ogden Nash. **CP-NashO**

LXIV. "Coming [*or* Comming] to kiss [*or* kisse] her lips [*or* lyps], (such grace I found)." Edmund Spenser. **EBEV; LoBV; NAEL-1; OAEL-1; Son** *Fr.* Amoretti. **CP-Spens**

Lycambes Talks to John. Allen Tate. **CP-TateA**

Lyceia. Robert Ranke Graves. **CP-GravR**

Lyceum, The. "Lewis Carroll." **CP-CarrL**

Lycidas. John Milton. **CP-MiltJ**

  "Ay me! whilst thee the shores and sounding seas." **Prf**

  "But now my oat proceeds." **OxBoS**

  Last Came, and Last Did Go. **TW**

  "Return Alpheus, the dread voice is past." **PeECV**

  "Weep no more, woful shepherds weep no more." **FaBoRV**

Lydia. Charlotte Smith. **CP-SmitC**

Lydia H. Sigourney. John Greenleaf Whittier. **CP-WhitJ**

Lydia Verner. Louise McNeill. **SP-McNeL**

Lydians, lords of Hermus river. Atys. Alfred Edward Housman. **CP-HousA**

Lyell's Hypothesis Again. Kenneth Rexroth. **SP-RexrK**

Lying, *with music*. Richard Wilbur. **CP-WilbR**

Lying a-dying. / Have done with vain sighing. Is It Well with The Child? Christina Georgina Rossetti. **CP-RosC2**

Lying adying— / Such sweet things untasted. Young Death. Christina Georgina Rossetti. **CP-RosC3**

Lying at a Reverend Friend's House One Night, the Author Left the Following *Verses* in the Room Where He Slept. Robert Burns. **CP-BurnR**

Lying at home. Dust. James Dickey. **CP-DickJ**

Lying Awake. Thomas Hardy. **CP-HardT**

Lying Awake. William DeWitt Snodgrass. **SP-SnodW**

Lying awake beside a sleeping girl. Malcolm Lowry. *Fr.* The Roar of the Sea and the Darkness. **CP-LowrM**

Lying between your sheets, I challenge. The Death Grapple. Robert Ranke Graves. **CP-GravR**

Lying disembodied under the trees. Deliverance. Robert Ranke Graves. **CP-GravR**

Lying full length. A Morality Play: Preface. George Oppen. **APSN; NNaP** *Fr.* Some San Francisco Poems. **CP-OppeG**

Lying here among grass, am I dead am I sleeping. Among Grass. Muriel Rukeyser. **CP-RukeM**

Lying here, everything in me. Margaret Atwood. **SP-AtwM1**

Lying in a Hammock at William Duffy's Farm in Pine Island, Minnesota. James Wright. **CP-WrigJ**

Lying in daylight, in the strong. Song: Lying in Daylight. Muriel Rukeyser. **CP-RukeM**

Lying in the hospital he often thought. Alun Lewis. *Fr.* Burma Casualty. **CP-LewiA**

Lying in the moment, she climbs white snows. The Wards. Muriel Rukeyser. **CP-RukeM**

Lying in the sun. Breathing Landscape. Muriel Rukeyser. **CP-RukeM**

Lying on the bed in the afternoon. Unlike Joubert. James Schuyler. **CP-SchuJ**

Lying on the hilltop. Involved (The Spider). Louise McNeill. **SP-McNeL**

Lying, thinking / Last night. Alone. Maya Angelou. **SP-AngeM**

Lying to Fall Warblers. Brendan Galvin. **SP-GalvB**

Lying under the stars. The Heart of Herakles. Kenneth Rexroth. **NU** *Fr.* The Lights in the Sky are Stars. **SP-RexrK**

Lying upon the beach. Mary Sidney, Countess of Montgomery Wroth. *Fr.* Part 2. *Fr.* Urania. **CP-WrotM**

Lyke-Wake Song, A. Algernon Charles Swinburne. **SP-SwinA**

Lynchings of Jesus, The. Muriel Rukeyser. **CP-RukeM**

Lynx-eyed Asia, you looked into my soul. 1945. Stephen Berg. **SP-BergS**

Lyonnesse. Sylvia Plath. **CP-PlatS**

Lyre, The. Siv Cedering Fox. **SP-CedeS**

Lyre at rest: / you fingered it awake, A. The Archer. Charles Tomlinson. **CP-TomlC**

Lyre! Though Such Power Do in Thy Magic Live. William Wordsworth. **CP-WorW2**

Lyric: "Chestnut and beech / sycamore and willow." John Hewitt. **CP-HewiJ**

Lyric: "Let but a thrush begin." John Hewitt. **CP-HewiJ**

Lyric: "Let this last lyric of a passing day." John Hewitt. **CP-HewiJ**

Lyric, A: "My lady love lives far away." Paul Laurence Dunbar. **CP-DunbP**

Lyric Absolute, The. Richard Eberhart. **CP-EberR**

  "Art, the holy care of life."

  "Images of death arise."

Lyric Evening. Phoebe Hesketh. **SP-HeskP**

Lyric[k] for Legacies. Robert Herrick. **CP-HerrR**

Lyric Meditation on Sour Locker Rooms, A. Dabney Stuart. **NGP** *Fr.* The Opposite Field. **SP-StuaD**

Lyric Sonorously Rhymed, The. John Hewitt. **CP-HewiJ**

Lyric, The: "Suffering / lament, sorrow and wild." Tom Clark. **SP-ClarT**

Lyric to Mirth, A. Robert Herrick. **CP-HerrR**

Lyrical Morning Poem. Malcolm Lowry. **CP-LowrM**

Lysergic Acid. Allen Ginsberg. **CP-GinsA**

M

M-Day's Child is Fair of Face. Muriel Rukeyser. **CP-RukeM**

M. Douglas to E.R. Gleneden. Emily Brontë. **CP-BronE**

M. I. Rudyard Kipling. **CP-KiplR**

M. le professeur in prominent senility. My Neighbor in the Mirror. Louise Glück. **SP-GlücL**

M. M. George Meredith. **CP-MerG1**

M. quarrels with N., for M. wrote a book. On Madan's Answer to Newton. William Cowper. **CP-CowpW**

M., Singing. Louise Bogan. **CP-BogaL**

M. Verdoux, The Wife Killer. Jim Carroll. **SP-CarrJ**

Ma. Paul Muldoon. **SP-MuldP**

Ma and God. Shel Silverstein. **SP-SilS2**

Ma Provence. Kenneth Koch. **SP-KochK**

"Ma questo," / said the Boss, "è divertente." Canto 41. Ezra Pound. *Fr.* Cantos. **CP-PoCan**

Ma, What's a Banker? or, Hush, My Child. Ogden Nash. **CP-NashO**

M.A. Written on the Dungeon Wall. Emily Brontë. **CP-BronE**

Ma'am, you should see your house! The Renovated Temple. Archibald MacLeish. **CP-MacLA**

Ma'arra and Sarmín: towns / Of abominable Shi'ites. Syria. Thomas Merton. *Fr.* East with Ibn Battuta. *Fr.* East. *Fr.* The Geography of Lograire. **CP-MertT**

Mabel Martin. John Greenleaf Whittier. **CP-WhitJ**

Mabel was married last week. Emily Writes Such a Good Letter. Stevie Smith. **CP-SmitS**

Mac Flecknoe. John Dryden. See MacFlecknoe; or, A Satire [or Satyr] upon the True-Blue [or -Blew] Protestant Poet T. S.

Macabre and golden the moon opened a slant of light. Feather Lights. Carl Sandburg. **CP-SandC**

Macabre simplicity of the white church, The. Reflex. Marsden Hartley. **CP-HartM**

Macadam, gun-grey as the tunny's belt. Van Winkle. Hart Crane. **AmPP; FaBV; MoAB; MoAmPo** *Fr.* Powhatan's Daughter. *Fr.* The Bridge. **CP-CranH**

Macao. Wystan Hugh Auden. **MeMAP** *Fr.* A Voyage. **CP-AudeW**

Macarius and the Pony. Thomas Merton. **CP-MertT**

Macarius the Younger. Thomas Merton. **CP-MertT**

Macbeth. Walter de la Mare. **CP-DeLaW**

MacDonnell's Question. John Hewitt. **CP-HewiJ**

MacDonough's Song. Rudyard Kipling. **CP-KiplR**

Macdougal Street. Edna St. Vincent Millay. **CP-MillE**

Macduff. Charles Tomlinson. **CP-TomlC**

Macer: A Character. Alexander Pope. **CP-PopeA**

MacFlecknoe; or, A Satire [or Satyr] upon the True-Blue [or -Blew] Protestant Poet T. S. John Dryden.

(Mac Flecknoe.) **SP-DrydJ**

"All human[e] things are subject to decay." **FiP; NOBE; OBCoV; OBS; SCV; TrGrPo**

(Crown Prince of Dullness, The.) **NOBE**

(Poet Shadwell, The.) **FiP**

(Primacy of Dullness, The.) **OBS**

"This is thy province, this thy wonderous way." **EPCY**

Machiavelli in Exile. Charles Tomlinson. **CP-TomlC**

Machine. John Ciardi. **SP-CiarJ**

Machine, The. Robinson Jeffers. **CP-JefR1**

Machine-Gun, The. Randall Jarrell. **CP-JarrR**

Machine. Gun. Nest. Margaret Atwood. **SP-AtwM2**

Machine will run on and on and on, The. On and On and On. David Herbert Lawrence. **CP-LawrD**

Machineries of Shame. Donald Davie. **CP-DavDo**

Machinery Doesn't Answer, Either, but You Aren't Married to It. Ogden Nash. **CP-NashO**

Machines, The. Richard Shelton. **SP-ShelR**

Macho Man. Charles Bukowski. **SP-BukC3**

Mackerel are in. Came on the in tide, The. Cleggan. Richard Hugo. **CP-HugoR**

Mackerel riffs iron-filing toward the west. November Dusk. Chuck Miller. **SP-MillC**

Mackerel shouldn't take, A. Malcolm Lowry. **CP-LowrM**

Mackinnon's Boat. Charles Tomlinson. **CP-TomlC**

MacLeish goes up the. Archibald MacLeish. *Fr.* Hamlet of A. Macleish. **CP-MacLA**

Mad Applegrower, The. John Hewitt. **CP-HewiJ**

Mad are mad for cigarretes, The. Mass. Mental Health. John Updike. *Fr.* Waiting Rooms. **CP-DickE**

Mad are predators. Too often lately they harbour, The. Geoffrey Hill. **NoP** *Fr.* Mercian Hymns. **CP-HillG**

Mad as the Mist and Snow, *fr.* Words for Music Perhaps. William Butler Yeats. **CP-YeatW**

Mad Druggest, The. Robert Penn Warren. *Fr.* Tale of Time. **SP-WarrR**

Mad Farmer in the City, The. Wendell Berry. **CP-BerrW**

Mad Farmer Manifesto: the First Amendment, The. Wendell Berry. **CP-BerrW**

"And I declare myself free."

"It is *ignorant* money I declare."

". . . it is not too soon to provide by every."

"To be sane in a mad time."

Mad Farmer Revolution, The. Wendell Berry. **CP-BerrW**

Mad farmer, the thirsty one, The. The Mad Farmer Revolution. Wendell Berry. **CP-BerrW**

Mad Farmer's Love Song, The. Wendell Berry. **CP-BerrW**

Mad Fight Song for William S. Carpenter, 1966, A. James Wright. **CP-WrigJ**

Mad Gardener's Song, The. "Lewis Carroll." **CP-CarrL** *Fr.* Sylvie and Bruno.

Mad girl with the staring eyes and long white fingers, The. Cassandra. Robinson Jeffers. **CP-JefR3**

Mad Gleam, A. Allen Ginsberg. **CP-GinsA**

Mad Hatter's Song, The. "Lewis Carroll." *See* Twinkle, twinkle, little bat!

Mad Judy. Thomas Hardy. **CP-HardT**

Mad kingfisher / Rocketing about in the, A. Kingfishers in British Columbia. Malcolm Lowry. **CP-LowrM**

Mad Maid's Song, The. Robert Herrick. **CP-HerrR**

Mad Monk, The. Samuel Taylor Coleridge, Sometimes att. to William Wordsworth. **CP-ColeS**

Mad Mullinix and Timothy. Jonathan Swift. **CP-SwifJ**

Mad Negro Soldier Confined at Munich, A. Robert Lowell. **SP-LoweR**

Mad paper stay, and grudge not here to burn. To Mrs. M. H. John Donne. **CP-DonnJ**

Mad Poem: Wind Blowing Through the Shack. Malcolm Lowry. **CP-LowrM**

Mad Scene, The. James Merrill. **SP-MerrJ**

Mad sculptor in our park, A. Helen. Peter Meinke. **SP-MeinP**

Mad Song. William Blake. **CP-BlakW**

Mad Young Aristocrat on Beach. Robert Penn Warren. **SP-WarrR**

Madam, / I know your heart cannot so guilty be. Upon the Black Spots Worn, by My Lady D.E. Sir John Suckling. **CP-SuckJ**

Madam, / Man to God's image, Eve, to man's was made. To the Countess of Huntingdon. John Donne. **CP-DonnJ**

Madam, / Reason is our soul's left hand, Faith her right. To the Countess of Bedford. John Donne. **CP-DonnJ**

Madam, / That I might make your cabinet my tomb. Epitaph on Himself. John Donne. **CP-DonnJ**

Madam, / Wi' braw new branks in mickle pride. On Willie Chalmers. Robert Burns. **CP-BurnR**

Madam, / You have refined me, and to worthiest things. To the Countess of Bedford. John Donne. **CP-DonnJ**

Madam, a stranger's purpose in these lays. An Epistle to a Protestant Lady in France. William Cowper. **CP-CowpW**

Madam and Her Madam. Langston Hughes. **SP-HughL**

Madam and Her Might-Have-Been. Langston Hughes. **SP-HughL**

Madam and the Census Man. Langston Hughes. **SP-HughL**

Madam and the Charity Child. Langston Hughes. **SP-HughL**

Madam and the Fortune Teller. Langston Hughes. **SP-HughL**

Madam and the Minister. Langston Hughes. **SP-HughL**

Madam and the Number Writer. Langston Hughes. **SP-HughL**

Madam and the Phone Bill. Langston Hughes. **SP-HughL**

Madam and the Rent Man. Langston Hughes. **SP-HughL**

Madam and the Wrong Visitor. Langston Hughes. **SP-HughL**

Madam could look in your hand. Ballad of the Fortune Teller. Langston Hughes. **SP-HughL**

Madam[e], had all antiquity [or antiquitie] been lost. To Mary, Lady Wroth. Ben Jonson. **CP-JonsB**

Madam, I told you late how I repented. To Lucy, Countess of Bedford. Ben Jonson. **CP-JonsB**

Madam, I you require. Sir Thomas Wyatt. **CP-WyatT**

Madam, men say you keep with dropping eyes. To the Countess of Anglesey. Thomas Carew. **CP-CareT**

Madam my action. Conversations. Thomas Merton. **CP-MertT**

Madam, the flower that I received from you. Verses on Receiving a Flower from his Mistress. James Thomson. **CP-ThomJ**

Madam, twice through the Muses' Grove I walked. Upon Mrs. Anne Bradstreet, Her Poems, Etc. John Rogers. **CP-BradA**

Madam, withouten many words. Sir Thomas Wyatt. **CP-WyatT**

Madam would speak with me. So, now it comes. George Meredith. **NOBVV** *Fr.* Modern Love. **CP-MerG1**

Madame, / Here, where by all, all saints invoked are. A Letter to the Lady Carey, and Mistress Essex Rich, from Amiens. John Donne. **CP-DonnJ**

Madame, / Whilst that, for which, all virtue now is sold. Epistle to Elizabeth, Countess of Rutland. Ben Jonson. **CP-JonsB**

Madame Arrives in the Mail. Anne Sexton. **CP-SextA**

Madame Eglantine. Geoffrey Chaucer. *See* Ther[e] was also a Nonne [or nun], a Prioress[e].

Madame, for your[e] newefangelnesse. Against Women Unconstant [or A Ballade against Woman Inconstant]. Geoffrey Chaucer. **CP-ChauG**

Madame, I have a confusion. Madame Arrives in the Mail. Anne Sexton. **CP-SextA**

Madame La Fleurie. Wallace Stevens. **CP-StevW**

Madame, ye be[e]n of al[le] beaute[e] shryne *or* shryne [or shrine]. To Rosamounde. Geoffrey Chaucer. **CP-ChauG**

Madam's Calling Cards. Langston Hughes. **SP-HughL**

Madam's Past History. Langston Hughes. **SP-HughL**

Madboy's Song. Muriel Rukeyser. **CP-RukeM**

Maddened by Earth's wrong and evil. What the Voice Said. John Greenleaf Whittier. **CP-WhitJ**

Madder. Charles Kenneth Williams. **CP-WillC**

Made me what I am. La Force. Louise Glück. **SP-GlücL**

Made of old rags of tongues. Snake. Anne Sexton. **CP-SextA**

Made to Order Smile, The. Paul Laurence Dunbar. **CP-DunbP**

Made worthy by excess of Love. Separation from Asra. Samuel Taylor Coleridge. **CP-ColeS**

Madeline, in your purity I find myself rebuked. Marge Piercy. *Fr.* The Homely War. **SP-PierM**

Mademoiselle—goddess instead. The Lion In Love. Marianne Craig Moore. **CP-MoorM** *Fr.* Fables of La Fontaine.

Mademoiselle Printemps, my sometimes instructress. À l'École Berlitz. John Updike. **CP-UpdiJ**

Madison and 42nd. Carl Sandburg. **CP-SandC**

Madison, Wis., Remembering the Bloom of Monticello (1931). Louis Zukofsky. *Fr.* 29 Songs. **CP-ZukLS**

Madly she came, and stood upon the lintel. Salem. Richard Eberhart. **CP-EberR**

Madman, The. Alun Lewis. **CP-LewiA**

"Exultantly he drives his screaming pinnace."

"He sees the dawn expanding from a seashell."

"His mind is an inarticulated question."

"Sensual mind in the wreaths of wine, The."

"Shattered crystal of his mind, The."

Madman I have been calld Fool they call thee. William Blake. **CP-BlakW**

Madness. Robert Browning. **FL** *Fr.* The Dance of Death. **CP-BroR2**

Madness. Charles Bukowski. **SP-BukC1**

Madness. James Dickey. **CP-DickJ**

Madness. Allen Tate. **CP-TateA**

Madness. Al Young. **CP-YounA**

Madness, madness, / Madness from the gods! The Skeptic. Ralph Waldo Emerson. **CP-EmerR**

Madness of King Goll, The. William Butler Yeats. **CP-YeatW**

Madonna, wherefore hast thou sent to me. To Emilia Viviani. Percy Bysshe Shelley. **CP-ShelP**

Madonnas Touched Up with a Goatee. Charles Simic. **SP-SimiC**

Madrid Madrid Madrid Madrid. Elegia. Edwin Rolfe. **CP-RolfE**

Madrid, Madrid, Madrid, Madrid / Invoco tu nombre de continuo, saboreándolo como un amante. Elegia. Edwin Rolfe, *tr. fr. Spanish by* Jose Rubia Barcia. **CP-RolfE**

Madrid, May, 1977. Mona Van Duyn. **SP-VanDM**

Madrid, 1974. Mona Van Duyn. **SP-VanDM**

Madrid 1963: Some Changes. Al Young. **CP-YounA**

Madrigal: "He shouts amain, he shouts again." "Lewis Carroll." **CP-CarrL**

Madrigal: "She is the darkness where I wander." Howard Nemerov. **CP-NemeH**

Madrigal: "Since Tuck is faithless found, no more." George Meredith. **CP-MerG2**

Madrigal, A: "Crabbed age and youth." William Shakespeare. *See* Crabbed age and youth cannot live together.

Madrigal, A: "Dream days of fond delight and hours." Paul Laurence Dunbar. **CP-DunbP**

Madrigal for 3 Voices, A. Louis Zukofsky. **CP-ZukLS**

Madrigale: "Seed in your heart, warm dust transmuted." Allen Tate. *Fr.* The Progress of Œnia. **CP-TateA**

Mae Marsh, Motion Picture Actress. Nicholas Vachel Lindsay. **CP-LindV**

"Arts are old, old as the stones, The."

"She is madonna in an art."

Maecenas, of a race renown'd. 1.1. Horace. **SP-SmarC**, *tr. by* Christopher Smart; *Fr.* Odes.

Maedoc of the floating stone. St. Maedoc. Thomas Merton. **CP-MertT**

Maerchen. Walter de la Mare. **CP-DeLaW**

Maestria. Howard Nemerov. **CP-NemeH**

Mag. Carl Sandburg. **CP-SandC**

Magda Goebbels ("How could you dare stay constant to"). William DeWitt Snodgrass. **SP-SnodW**

Magda Goebbels ("This is the needle that we give"). William DeWitt Snodgrass. **SP-SnodW**

Magellan. Mary Oliver. **SP-OlivM**

Magellanic Clouds, The. Diane Wakoski. **SP-WakoD**

Maggie a Lady. Christina Georgina Rossetti. **CP-RosC1**

Maggie and milly and molly and may. Edward Estlin Cummings. **CP-CummE**

Maggie B——. "Lewis Carroll." **CP-CarrL**

Maggie Mae. *Unknown.* **CP-Beatl**

Maggie's Farm. "Bob Dylan." **CP-DylaB**

Maggie's Visit to Oxford. "Lewis Carroll." **CP-CarrL**

Maggots, wrinkled white men. The Insects. John Haines. **SP-HainJ**

Magi, The. Louise Glück. **SP-GlücL**

Magi, The. John Milton. **ChTr** *Fr.* On the Morning of Christs Nativity. **CP-MiltJ**

Magi. Sylvia Plath. **CP-PlatS**

Magi, The. William Butler Yeats. **CP-YeatW**

Magic. Rita Dove. **SP-DoveR**

Magic. Shel Silverstein. **SP-SilS2**

Magic Arrival No. 7. Tom Clark. **SP-ClarT**

Magic, as it electrifies. Emily Dickinson. **SP-DickE**

Magic Car, The. Kenneth Patchen. **CP-PatcK**

Magic Car Moved On, The. Percy Bysshe Shelley. **GN** *Fr.* Queen Mab. **CP-ShelP**

Magic Casements. John Keats. **FaBV** *Fr.* Ode to a Nightingale. **CP-KeatJ**

Magic Castle, The. Sir Walter Scott. **SP-ScotW** *Fr.* The Bridal of Trierman.

Magic Curtain, The. Stanley Jasspon Kunitz. **CP-KuniS**

"At breakfast mother sipped her buttermilk."

"Downtown at the Front St. Bi-jo (spelt Bijou)."

"Five. . . four. . . three. . . two. . . one."

Magic factory chimneys stand in rows, The. The Magic World. Malcolm Lowry. **CP-LowrM**

Magic Is Alive. Leonard Cohen. **CP-CoheL**

Magic is tangled in a woman's hair. The Snap-Comb Wilderness. Robert Ranke Graves. **CP-GravR**

Magic Kingdom, The. Peter Meinke. **SP-MeinP**

Magic Morning, The. Stevie Smith. **CP-SmitS**

Magic of Numbers, The. Kenneth Koch. **SP-KochK**

Magic Psalm. Allen Ginsberg. **CP-GinsA**

Magic World, The. Malcolm Lowry. **CP-LowrM**

Magical Eraser. Shel Silverstein. **SP-SilS2**

Magical Mouse, The. Kenneth Patchen. **CP-PatcK**

Magical Mystery Tour. The Beatles. **CP-Beatl**

Magical Nature. Robert Browning. **CP-BroR2**

Magician [Master]. Hilda Doolittle. **CP-DoolH**

Magician, The. John Hewitt. **CP-HewiJ**

Magician, The. Marge Piercy. *Fr.* Laying Down the Tower. **SP-PierM**

Magician's Retreat, The. Marianne Craig Moore. **CP-MoorM**

Magicized in amethyst. Guillermo's Wedding. Siv Cedering Fox. **SP-CedeS**

Magico Prodigioso. Pedro Calderón de la Barca, *tr. fr. Spanish.*

"In the sweet solitude of this calm place." **CP-ShelP**

Magistrate spoke / Said the future was going to be for the public, The. Public Affairs. Thomas Merton. **CP-MertT**

Magna Est Veritas. Stevie Smith. **CP-SmitS**

Magnetic Lady to Her Patient, The. Percy Bysshe Shelley. **CP-ShelP**

Magnets. Countee Cullen. **CP-CullC**

Magnificent Democracy. David Herbert Lawrence. **CP-LawrD**

Magnificent Words. Stevie Smith. **CP-SmitS**

Magnolia Flowers. Langston Hughes. **SP-HughL**

Magnolia Shoals. Sylvia Plath. **CP-PlatS**

Magot frequents those houses of good-cheere. Upon Magot a Frequenter of Ordinaries. Robert Herrick. **CP-HerrR**

Magpie's Song. Gary Snyder. **CP-SnydG**

Magritte Imitated Himself. Roy Fisher. **SP-FishR**

Magus, A. John Ciardi. **SP-CiarJ**

Magus, The. James Dickey. **CP-DickJ**

Mahabalipuram. Louis MacNeice. **CP-MacNL**

Mahavveray. Louis MacNeice. **CP-MacNL**

Mahomet. Samuel Taylor Coleridge. **CP-ColeS**

Mahratta Ghats, The. Alun Lewis. **CP-LewiA**

Maia. Ralph Waldo Emerson. **CP-EmerR**

Maia. Howard Nemerov. **CP-NemeH**

Maia was one, all gold, fire, and sapphire. A Legend of Viable Women. Richard Eberhart. **CP-EberR**

Maid, The. *Unknown, tr. fr. Chinese by* William Carlos Williams *with David Rafael Wang.* **CP-WilW2**

Maid is blest that will not hear, The. *see also* Psalm 1. Alexander Pope. **CP-PopeA**

Maid of Athens, Ere We Part. Byron. **CP-Byron**

Maid of Keinton Mandeville, The. Thomas Hardy. **CP-HardT**

Maid of my love, sweet Genevieve! Genevieve. Samuel Taylor Coleridge. *Fr.* Effusions. **CP-ColeS**

Maid Quiet. William Butler Yeats. **CP-YeatW**

Maid whom now you court in vain, The. 2.5. Horace. **CP-JohnS,** *tr. by* Samuel Johnson; *Fr.* Odes.

Maiden, The. Robert Duncan. **SP-DuncR**

Maiden, The. Audre Lorde. **SP-LordA**

Maiden-Blush, The. Robert Herrick. **CP-HerrR**

Maiden caught me in the wild, The. The Crystal Cabinet. William Blake. **CP-BlakW**

Maiden May. Christina Georgina Rossetti. **CP-RosC2**

Maiden May sat in her bower, / In her blush rose bower in flower. Maiden May. Christina Georgina Rossetti. **CP-RosC2**

Maiden Name. Philip Larkin. **CP-LarkP**

Maiden, quench the glare of sorrow. To Mary, Who Died in This Opinion. Percy Bysshe Shelley. **CP-ShelP**

Maiden-Song. Christina Georgina Rossetti. **CP-RosC1**

Maiden Speech of the Æolian Harp. Ralph Waldo Emerson. **CP-EmerR**

Maiden, that with sullen brow. To an Unfortunate Woman at the Theatre. Samuel Taylor Coleridge. **CP-ColeS**

Maiden, though thy heart may quail. Acrostic: Maiden, though thy heart may quail. "Lewis Carroll." **CP-CarrL**

Maiden wept and, as a comforter, A. Passion and Love. Paul Laurence Dunbar. **CP-DunbP**

Maiden with Orb and Planets. Howard Nemerov. **CP-NemeH**

Maiden! with the fair brown tresses. To ———. John Greenleaf Whittier. **CP-WhitJ**

Maiden without Hands, The. Anne Sexton. **CP-SextA**

Maidens! if you love the tale. Acrostic: Maidens! if you love the tale. "Lewis Carroll." **CP-CarrL**

Maiden's Pledge, A. Thomas Hardy. **CP-HardT**

Maiden's Prayer. David Herbert Lawrence. *Fr.* Bits. **CP-LawrD**

Maidens shall weep at merry morn. The Summer Malison. Gerard Manley Hopkins. **CP-HopkG**

Maidens tell me I am old. Age Unfit for Love. Robert Herrick. **CP-HerrR**

Maids Are Bickering. Jim Morrison. **SP-MorrJ**

Maids Nay's Are Nothing. Robert Herrick. **CP-HerrR**

Maids of Attitash, The. John Greenleaf Whittier. **CP-WhitJ**

Maid's Thought, The. Robinson Jeffers. **CP-JefR1**

Mail box, the roadway, and the dump truck, The. The Project. Richard Eberhart. **CP-EberR**

Mail Call. Randall Jarrell. **CP-JarrR**

Mail is slow here. If I died, I wouldn't find out about it for, The. The Bus to Veracruz. Richard Shelton. **SP-ShelR**

Mail-train, Crewe, The. Wystan Hugh Auden. **CP-AudWJ**

Maillol. Charles Tomlinson. **CP-TomlC**

Mailman handing me a letter, The. In a Row. Stephen Dobyns. **SP-DobyS**

Maimed, beggared, grey; seeking an alms; with nod. Bellerophon. George Meredith. **CP-MerG1**

Maimed Grasshopper Speaks Up, The. Jean Garrigue. **SP-GarrJ**

Maimed Man, The. Allen Tate. **CP-TateA**

Main Regret, The. George Meredith. **CP-MerG1**

Main Street / is deserted, the hills. Charles Olson. **SP-OlsoC** *Fr.* The Maximus Poems.

Main Street. Miller Williams. **SP-WillM**

Maine Roustabout, A. Richard Eberhart. **CP-EberR**

Maine Winter. Charles Tomlinson. **CP-TomlC**

Mainland, The. John Hewitt. **CP-HewiJ**

Maintenant. Charles Tomlinson. **CP-TomlC**

Mais L'Amour Infini Me Montera Dans L'Ame. Richard Eberhart. **CP-EberR**

Maisie. James Merrill. **SP-MerrJ**

Maitreya. Frederick Morgan. **SP-MorgF**

Maitreya the Future Buddha. Gary Snyder. **CP-SnydG** *Fr.* Burning. *Fr.* Myths and Texts.

Majesty of horns sweeps in the stagtide. In a Crumbling. Kenneth Patchen. **CP-PatcK**

Majesty of Justice, The. "Lewis Carroll." **CP-CarrL**

Major abstraction is the idea of man, The. Wallace Stevens. **NOBA** *Fr.* It Must Be Abstract. *Fr.* Notes toward a Supreme Fiction. **CP-StevW**

Major faults in granite. Trio of Love Songs. Sylvia Plath. **CP-PlatS**

Major Hawkaby Cole Macroo. Major Macroo. Stevie Smith. **CP-SmitS**

Major is a fine cat. My Cat Major. Stevie Smith. **CP-SmitS**

Major Macroo. Stevie Smith. **CP-SmitS**

Major Patrick Ferguson. King's Mountain. Charles Olson. **CP-OlsoC**

Major Port, A. Wystan Hugh Auden. *Fr.* A Voyage. **CP-AudeW**

Major Road Ahead. "Hugh MacDiarmid." **SP-MacDH** *Fr.* The Battle Continues.

Major Work. Dabney Stuart. **SP-StuaD**

Make a joyful noise unto God, all ye lands. Psalm 66. Bible, *O.T.* Psalms. **CP-Psal**

Make a joyful noise unto the Lord, all ye lands. Psalm 100. Bible, *O.T.* **FaPON; OFD; OHIP; OtMeF; SUS; TRV; WGRP** *Fr.* Psalms. **CP-Psal**

Make and be eaten, the poet says. Muriel Rukeyser. **CP-RukeM**

Make Big Money at Home! Write Poems in Spare Time! Howard Nemerov. **CP-NemeH**

Make, for he loved thee well, our Merrimac. R. S. S., at Deer Island on the Merrimac. John Greenleaf Whittier. **CP-WhitJ**

Make haste away, and let one be. To His Book[e]. Robert Herrick. **CP-HerrR**

Make haste, O God, to deliver me. Psalm 70. Bible, *O.T. Fr.* Psalms. **CP-Psal**

Make Love Not War. Howard Nemerov. **CP-NemeH**

Make, make me Thine, my gracious God. To God. Robert Herrick. **CP-HerrR**

Make me a heaven, and make me there. The Eye. Robert Herrick. **CP-HerrR**

Make me a picture of the sun. Emily Dickinson. **CP-DickE**

Make me feel the wild pulsation that I felt before the strife. Tennyson. **SaC** *Fr.* Locksley Hall. **CP-TennA**

Make me well, I said.—And the delighted touch. Panacea. Muriel Rukeyser. **CP-RukeM**

Make miniatures of the once-monstrous theme. A Short History of British India (I). Geoffrey Hill. *Fr.* An Apology for the Revival of Christian Architecture in England. **CP-HillG**

Make my mortal dreams come true. John Greenleaf Whittier. *Fr.* Andrew Rykman's Prayer. **CP-WhitJ**

Make no mistake: if He rose at all. Seven Stanzas at Easter. John Updike. **CP-UpdiJ**

Make no mistake. The cedar. Barton Sutter. *Fr.* Cedarhome. **SP-SuttB**

"Make of yourself a light," / said the Buddha. The Buddha's Last Instruction. Mary Oliver. **SP-OlivM**

Make Rundle bishop; fie, for shame! On Dr. Rundle. Jonathan Swift. **CP-SwifJ**

Make there my tomb, beneath the lime-tree's shade. By the Same. Charlotte Smith. **CP-SmitC**

Make this night loveable. Wystan Hugh Auden. **TW** *Fr.* Five Songs ("Deftly, admiral, cast your fly"). **CP-AudeW**

(Song: "Make this night loveable.") **TW**

Make Up Mind. "Lou Reed." **SP-ReedL**

Make war songs out of these. The Four Brothers. Carl Sandburg. **CP-SandC**

Make way, make way, give leave to rove. The Little Good Fellows. Herman Melville. **SP-MelvH**

Maker, The. Wystan Hugh Auden. **CP-AudeW**

Maker of many mouths. Edward Estlin Cummings. **CP-CummE**

Maker to Posterity, The. Robert Louis Stevenson. **CP-StevR**

Makers of History. Wystan Hugh Auden. **CP-AudeW**

Makeup on Empty Space. Anne Waldman. **SP-WaldA**

Making a fire. Walter de la Mare. **CP-DeLaW**

Making a form for you. Re C—. Robert Creeley. **CP-CreeR**

Making a Living. Anne Sexton. **CP-SextA**

Making a Sacher Torte. Diane Wakoski. **SP-WakoD**

Making and unmaking. Optimism. Steve Griffiths. **SP-GrifS**

Making Certain It Goes On. Richard Hugo. **CP-HugoR**

Making his advances. Tortoise Gallantry. David Herbert Lawrence. **CP-LawrD**

Making It. Charles Bukowski. **SP-BukC3**

Making it, making it. Thirst Song. Denise Levertov. **CP-LeveD**

Making It New. Philip Levine. **SP-LeviP**

Making Light of It. Philip Levine. **SP-LeviP**

Making Love. William Dickey. **SP-DickW**

Making Love After Hours. Al Young. **CP-YounA**

Making Love in Poetry. Lawrence Ferlinghetti. **SP-FerlL**

Making love in the cabin, not to himself. Hayden Carruth. *Fr.* The Sleeping Beauty. **CP-CarHL**

Making love in the sun, in the morning sun. Layover. Charles Bukowski. **SP-BukC2**

Making love with you. Kenneth Rexroth. **SP-RexrK** *Fr.* Love Poems of Marichiko.

Making of the Book, The. Roy Fisher. **SP-FishR**

Making Repairs. James McAuley. **SP-McAuJ**

Making Strange. Seamus Heaney. **SP-HeanS**

Making the best and most of a visitation. Reflections on Deafness. Donald Davie. **CP-DavDo**

Making the Move. Paul Muldoon. **SP-MuldP**

Makings. Gary Snyder. **CP-SnydG**

Malachy stamped the diving decks. Superiorities. Richard Wilbur. **CP-WilbR**

Malacoda. Samuel Beckett. **CP-BeckS**

Malade. David Herbert Lawrence. **CP-LawrD**

Malady smote the earth one year, A. The Animals Sick of the Plague. Marianne Craig Moore. **CP-MoorM** *Fr.* Fables of La Fontaine.

Malagueña Salerosa. Al Young. **CP-YounA**

Malay took the Pearl, The. Emily Dickinson. **CP-DickE**

Malcolm. Alice Walker. **CP-WalkA**

Malcolm and Frere, Colebrooke and Elphinstone. A Short History of British India (III). Geoffrey Hill. *Fr.* An Apology for the Revival of Christian Architecture in England. **CP-HillG**

Malcolm, I love thee more than women love. From Frodmer's Drama "The Friends." Ralph Waldo Emerson. **CP-EmerR**

Malcolm's Messasge. Al Young. **CP-YounA**

Malcontents, The. John Dryden. **OBS** *Fr.* Absalom and Achitophel, Pt. I. **SP-DrydJ**

Maldive Shark, The. Herman Melville. **SP-MelvH**

Male? / Female? / God doesn't care. On the Avenue. Erica Jong. **SP-JongE**

Male & Female Loves in Beulah. William Blake. **OBNC** *Fr.* Jerusalem; The Emanation of the Giant Albion. **CP-BlakW**

Male-throated under the shallow sea-fog. October Evening. Robinson Jeffers. **CP-JefR1**

Malest Cornifici Tuo Catullo. Allen Ginsberg. **CP-GinsA**

Malham Cove. William Wordsworth. **CP-WorW2**

Malheur à la malheureuse Tamise. Le Directeur. Thomas Stearns Eliot. **CP-ElioT**

Malice Domestic. Ogden Nash. **CP-NashO**

Malicious Envy rode. Envy. Edmund Spenser. **TW** *Fr.* The Faerie Queene. **CP-Spens**

Mallard, The. Phoebe Hesketh. **SP-HeskP**

Mallarmé, / with this equestrian cliff clutching. Perusing Mallarmé in Maine. Marsden Hartley. **CP-HartM**

Mallarmé siren upside down,—rootedly! John Berryman. *Fr.* Sonnets to Chris. **CP-BerrJ**

Malleability / a precision, A. Portobello Carnival 1973. Charles Tomlinson. **CP-TomlC**

Malte Laurids, peevish: *And one has.* Inheritances. Jane Cooper. *Fr.* Dispossessions. **SP-CoopJ**

Malvern Hill. Herman Melville. **SP-MelvH**

Mama. William Carlos Williams. **CP-WilW2**

Mama and Daughter. Langston Hughes. **SP-HughL**

Mama never forgets her birds. Emily Dickinson. **CP-DickE**

Mama, please brush off my coat. Mama and Daughter. Langston Hughes. **SP-HughL**

Mama said I'd lose my head. The Loser. Shel Silverstein. **SP-SilS2**

Mama, take this badge off of me. Knockin' on Heavin's Door. "Bob Dylan." **CP-DylaB**

Mama, You Been on My Mind. "Bob Dylan." **CP-DylaB**

Mama, you tell me how's the family. Families. "Lou Reed." **SP-ReedL**

Mama's Got a Lover. "Lou Reed." **SP-ReedL**

Mame. Edward Estlin Cummings. *Fr.* Five Americans. **CP-CummE**

Mamertinus on Rhetoric, A.D. 291. Donald Davie. **CP-DavDo**

Mamie. Carl Sandburg. **CP-SandC**

Mamie beat her head against the bars of a little Indiana town and. Mamie. Carl Sandburg. **CP-SandC**

Mammal is with her young. She is unique, The. Thom Gunn. *Fr.* Tom-Dobbin. **CP-GunnT**

Mamma's got rings / Mamma's got things. Consolation. Malcolm Lowry. **CP-LowrM**

Mammy Hums. Carl Sandburg. **CP-SandC**

Mammy's in de kitchen, an' de do' is shet. Curiosity. Paul Laurence Dunbar. **CP-DunbP**

Man, The. Robert Creeley. **CP-CreeR**

Man, A. Thomas Hardy. **CP-HardT**

Man. George Herbert. **CP-HerbG**

Man. Randall Jarrell. **CP-JarrR**

Man, A. David Herbert Lawrence. **CP-LawrD**

Man, A. Denise Levertov. **CP-LeveD**

Man! Archibald MacLeish. **CP-MacLA**

Man. Alexander Pope. *See* Know then thyself, presume not God to scan.

Man. Kathleen Jessie Raine. *Fr.* Bheinn Naomh. **SP-RainK**

Man. Kenneth Rexroth. **SP-RexrK** *Fr.* A Bestiary. **SP-RexrK**

Man, The. Charles Simic. **SP-SimiC**

Man, a changeling, journeys across the radiant waste, The. Scream of the Butterfly. Patti Smith. **SP-SmitP**

Man: a flutter of pages. Plant and Phantom. Louis MacNeice. **CP-MacNL**

Man against the Sky, The. Edwin Arlington Robinson. **CP-RobiE**

Man alive, that mournst thy lot. Lines for a Grave-Stone. Edna St. Vincent Millay. **CP-MillE**

Man Alone. Louise Bogan. **CP-BogaL**

Man alone is immoral. Morality. David Herbert Lawrence. **CP-LawrD**

Man, am I sick. Seven New Ways of Looking at the Moon. John Updike. **CP-UpdiJ**

Man and a Woman Sit Near Each Other. Robert Bly. **SP-BlyR**

Man and Bat. David Herbert Lawrence. **CP-LawrD**

Man and Bird. Derek Mahon. *Fr.* Four Walks in the Country Near Saint-Brieuc. **SP-MahoD**

Man and Bottle. Wallace Stevens. **CP-StevW**

Man and Dog on an Early Winter Morning. Carl Sandburg. **CP-SandC**

Man and Machine. David Herbert Lawrence. **CP-LawrD**

Man and Nature. Elizabeth Barrett Browning. **CP-BroEB**

Man and Nature. Richard Eberhart. **CP-EberR**

Man and Nature. William Carlos Williams. **CP-WilW1**

Man and the Echo. William Butler Yeats. **CP-YeatW**

Man and the Goshawk, The. Gary Gildner. **SP-GildG**

Man and the maid go side by side, The. Sunday Afternoon in Italy. David Herbert Lawrence. **CP-LawrD**

Man and Wife. Robert Lowell. **SP-LoweR**

Man and Wife. Anne Sexton. **CP-SextA**

Man and Wife. Gilbert Sorrentino. **SP-SorrG**

Man and Woman. Robert Lowell. **SP-LoweR**

Man and woman lie on a white bed, A. Happiness. Louise Glück. **SP-GlücL**

Man approaching his chair: / from that horizon, tonight as before. All Seated. Pablo Neruda, *tr. fr. Spanish by* Ben Belitt. **SP-NeruP**

Man as Cannibal (PLAIN; BIOLOGY). Jenny Joseph. *Fr.* Man as Matter. **SP-JoseJ**

Man as Image (MASSIF; CHEMISTRY). Jenny Joseph. *Fr.* Man as Matter. **SP-JoseJ**

Man as Matter. Jenny Joseph. **SP-JoseJ**
  Man as Cannibal (PLAIN; BIOLOGY).
  Man as Image (MASSIF; CHEMISTRY).
  Man as Matter (ISLAND; PHYSICS).
  Man as Real (CITY; HUMAN).

Man as Matter (ISLAND; PHYSICS). Jenny Joseph. *Fr.* Man as Matter. **SP-JoseJ**

Man as Real (CITY; HUMAN). Jenny Joseph. *Fr.* Man as Matter. **SP-JoseJ**

Man at Play on the River, A. David Herbert Lawrence. **CP-LawrD**

Man beats his wife on the mountainside, A. The Mines in Sepia Tint. Steve Griffiths. **SP-GrifS**

Man begins in zoology / He is the saddest animal. First Lesson about Man. Thomas Merton. **CP-MertT**

Man behind the book may not be man, The. The Intellectual. Karl Shapiro. **SP-ShapK**

Man bent over his guitar, The. Wallace Stevens. **CMoP; NoAM; RaBo; VoGa** *Fr.* The Man with the Blue Guitar. **CP-StevW**

Man beside me in the country bus, The. The Beastie. John Hewitt. **CP-HewiJ**

Man Bites Dog-Days. Ogden Nash. **CP-NashO**

Man Born to Farming, The. Wendell Berry. **CP-BerrW**

Man-brained and man-handed ground-ape, physically, The. Original Sin. Robinson Jeffers. **CP-JefR3**

Man came slowly from the setting sun, A. William Butler Yeats. **CP-YeatW**

Man came to the pool of Bethesda, A. Pool of Bethesda. Carl Sandburg. **CP-SandC**

Man can lie to himself, A. Marge Piercy. *Fr.* A Shadow Play For Guilt. **SP-PierM**

Man can survive anything except not caring, A. Joshua on Eighth Avenue. John Ciardi. **SP-CiarJ**

Man can't fully live unless he dies and ceases to care, A. Full Life. David Herbert Lawrence. **CP-LawrD**

Man Carrying Thing. Wallace Stevens. **CP-StevW**

Man, child or woman, none from her. The Daughter, Teuila, Native Name for Adorner. Robert Louis Stevenson. *Fr.* The Family. **CP-StevR**

Man conceived us, men made us. We work. The Instruments of Torture. Roy Fisher. **SP-FishR** *Fr.* Inscriptions for Bluebeard's Castle.

Man could be a god, A. Walking on the River Ice. Wendell Berry. **CP-BerrW**

Man could be granted to live a dozen lives, A. I Didn't Say a Word, or, Who Called That Piccolo Player a Father? Ogden Nash. **CP-NashO**

Man decided once to go steal truth, A. Refuge, Serpent-Riders. Charles Kenneth Williams. **CP-WillC**

Man decides to exercise regularly and build up his body, A. Urban Renewal. Ron Koertge. **SP-KoerR**

Man dies too soon, beside his works half-planned. Doctors. Rudyard Kipling. **CP-KiplR**

Man-dirt and stomachs that the sea unloads; rockets. Eve of St. Agony, or the Middle Class Was Sitting on Its Fat. Kenneth Patchen. **CP-PatcK**

Man does not live by bread alone. The Shooting Incident. Stevie Smith. **CP-SmitS**

Man Does, Woman Is. Robert Ranke Graves. **CP-GravR**

Man eats a chicken every day for lunch, A. Spiritual Chickens. Stephen Dobyns. **SP-DobyS**

Man existed for seventeen spidery years, A. Divorce. Miller Williams. **SP-WillM**

Man finds himself no more omnipotent. Dethroned. Wystan Hugh Auden. **CP-AudWJ**

Man Fish and Bird. John Hewitt. **CP-HewiJ**

Man Flammonde, from God knows where, The. Flammonde. Edwin Arlington Robinson. **CP-RobiE**

Man fought against beasts, and won. Gripping Serial. Donald Davie. **CP-DavDo**

Man from Bethnal Green, that, The. Refugees. Steve Griffiths. **SP-GrifS**

Man from Ecuador beneath the Eiffel Tower, A. Jorge Carrera Andrade, *tr. fr. Spanish* by Thomas Merton. **CP-MertT**

Man from Malabar, The. John Hewitt. **CP-HewiJ**

Man from the Mountains, The. John Hewitt. **CP-HewiJ**

Man Gave Names to All the Animals. "Bob Dylan." **CP-DylaB**

Man goes to Man! Cry the challenge though the Jungle! Rudyard Kipling. **CP-KiplR** *Fr.* The Spring Running. *Fr.* The Second Jungle Book.

Man growing old is going, A. Shalom. Denise Levertov. **CP-LeveD**

Man hammers viciously / viciously like fucking, A. The Nut. Charles Kenneth Williams. **CP-WillC**

Man has a gun, The. The Gun. "Lou Reed." **SP-ReedL**

Man Hauling a Wagon. David Herbert Lawrence. *Fr.* Bits. **CP-LawrD**

Man He Killed, The. Thomas Hardy. **CP-HardT**

Man I Am, A. Stevie Smith. **CP-SmitS**

Man I once met / where I was a foreigner, A. The Man from the Mountains. John Hewitt. **CP-HewiJ**

Man I praise that once in Tara's Halls, A. In Tara's Halls. William Butler Yeats. **CP-YeatW**

Man I saw in the forest, The. Dream 2: Brian the Still-Hunter. Margaret Atwood. **SP-AtwM1**

Man, I suck me tooth when I hear. Parang. Derek Walcott. **CP-WalcD**

Man, if I said once, "I know." The Islands. Randall Jarrell. **CP-JarrR**

Man I'm telling you about brought himself back alive, The. The Zodiac. James Dickey. **CP-DickJ**

Man in a Bar. Jenny Joseph. **SP-JoseJ**

Man in a plane looks at the surface of land, A. Muriel Rukeyser. **CP-RukeM**

Man in a Room. William Carlos Williams. **CP-WilW1**

Man in a window? / When dead men sing. Songs. Thomas Merton. **CP-MertT**

Man in Black. Sylvia Plath. **CP-PlatS**

Man in Blue, A. James Schuyler. **CP-SchuJ**

Man in four blank walls will wither away, A. Man as Cannibal (PLAIN; BIOLOGY). Jenny Joseph. *Fr.* Man as Matter. **SP-JoseJ**

Man, in life where-ever plac'd, The. The First Psalm. Robert Burns. **CP-BurnR**

Man in Majesty. Randall Jarrell. **CP-JarrR**

Man in Me, The. "Bob Dylan." **CP-DylaB**

Man in Moonlight. Robert Penn Warren. **SP-WarrR**

    Lullaby: Moonlight Lingers.

    Moonlight Observed from Ruined Fortress.

    Walk by Moonlight in Small Town.

Man in Old Blue Suit at the Plaza. Gilbert Sorrentino. *Fr.* Twelve Études for Voice and Kazoo. **SP-SorrG**

Man in order to be erotic. The Price. James Liddy. **CP-LiddJ**

Man in perfect bloom. K. von F.—1914—Arras-Bouquoi. Marsden Hartley. **CP-HartM**

Man in terror of impotence, A. The Ninth Symphony of Beethoven Understood at Last as a Sexual Message. Adrienne Rich. **SP-RicA2**

Man in the Dead Machine, The. Donald Hall. **CP-HallD**

Man in the Moon, The. "Hugh MacDiarmid." **NeBP** *Fr.* Au Clair de la Lune. **SP-MacDH**

Man in the Moon, The. Gilbert Sorrentino. **SP-SorrG**

Man in the moon was better not a man, The. The Art of Poetry. Richard Hugo. **CP-HugoR**

Man in the next bed died just after eating lunch. You were star- / ing. We Are All Vultures. John Yau. **SP-YauJo**

Man in the Street, The. David Herbert Lawrence. **CP-LawrD**

Man in the Street. Robert Penn Warren. **SP-WarrR**

Man in the street is fed, The. Carl Sandburg. *Fr.* The People, Yes. **CP-SandC**

Man in the West. The Two Priests. Archibald MacLeish. **CP-MacLA**

Man in the Wind, The. Thomas Merton. **CP-MertT; SP-MertT**

Man in the Yellow Gloves, The. David St. John. **SP-StJoD**

Man in whom Tao, The. The Man of Tao. Chuang Tzu, *tr. fr. Chinese* by Thomas Merton. **CP-MertT**

Man inside the mandolin, The. Refrain. Rita Dove. **SP-DoveR**

Man, introverted man, having crossed. Science. Robinson Jeffers. **CP-JefR1**

Man invented the machine. Man and Machine. David Herbert Lawrence. **CP-LawrD**

Man is a glutton. Quick, Hammacher, My Stomacher! Ogden Nash. **CP-NashO**

Man is a lump[e], where all beasts kneaded be[e]. To Sir Edward Herbert[,] at Juliers [or Julyers]. John Donne. **CP-DonnJ**

Man Is a Spirit. Stevie Smith. **CP-SmitS**

Man is a Watch, wound up at first, but never. The Watch. Robert Herrick. **CP-HerrR**

Man is an animal who thinks himself important. The Moment of Truth. Thomas Merton. **CP-MertT**

Man Is Born in Tao. Chuang Tzu, *tr. fr. Chinese* by Thomas Merton. **CP-MertT**

Man is clothed, The. And When the Green Man Comes. John Haines. **SP-HainJ**

Man is coming out of the mountains. Touch and Go. Stevie Smith. **CP-SmitS**

Man is compos'd here of a two-fold part. Upon Man. Robert Herrick. **CP-HerrR**

Man is immoral because he has got a mind. Immoral Man. David Herbert Lawrence. **CP-LawrD**

Man is killing time—there's nothing else, The. The Drinker. Robert Lowell. **SP-LoweR**

Man is leaning on a cold iron rail, A. The Man Who Loved Islands. Derek Walcott. **CP-WalcD**

Man Is More Than *Homo Sapiens*. David Herbert Lawrence. **CP-LawrD**

Man is my darling, my love and my pain. God and Man. Stevie Smith. **CP-SmitS**

Man is not quite a man. Man Is More Than *Homo Sapiens*. David Herbert Lawrence. **CP-LawrD**

Man is old and, The. The Seated Man. George Oppen. **CP-OppeG**

Man is said to want but little here below. Jangle Bells. Ogden Nash. **CP-NashO**

Man is singing on the bus, A. An Ordinary Morning. Philip Levine. **SP-LeviP**

Man is the leaky bung. What the Vine Said to Eve. Archibald MacLeish. *Fr.* Songs for Eve. **CP-MacLA**

Man is the world, and death the ocean. Elegy on the Lady Markham. John Donne. **CP-DonnJ**

Man is the writing instrument. Man and Nature. Richard Eberhart. **CP-EberR**

Man Is to Man a Beast. Kenneth Patchen. **CP-PatcK**

Man is watching down the sun. All day, A. Machiavelli in Exile. Charles Tomlinson. **CP-TomlC**

Man knocked three times, A. Madam and the Wrong Visitor. Langston Hughes. **SP-HughL**

Man knows his day, it has. The Seven Songs. Charles Olson. **CP-OlsoC**

Man knows nothing. Know-All. David Herbert Lawrence. **CP-LawrD**

Man know[e]s where first he ships himself[e], but he. Man's Dying-Place Uncertain. Robert Herrick. **CP-HerrR**

Man like a Curtain, A. Ron Koertge. **SP-KoerR**

Man, like any creature. What the Wind Said to the Water: What the Water Replied. Archibald MacLeish. *Fr.* Songs for Eve. **CP-MacLA**

Man Lives Here, A. Kenneth Patchen. **CP-PatcK**

Man Locked Inside the Oak, The. Robert Bly. **SP-BlyR**

Man looking into the sea. A Grave. Marianne Craig Moore. **CP-MoorM**

Man-Made World, A. Stephen Spender. **CP-SpenS**

Man may at first transgress, but next do well. Bad May Be Better. Robert Herrick. **CP-HerrR**

Man may make a Remark, A. Emily Dickinson. **CP-DickE**

Man may objectively inherit / a role in history, A. Mosaic. John Hewitt. **CP-HewiJ**

Man may want land to live in; but for all. Buriall. Robert Herrick. **CP-HerrR**

Man Meets a Woman in the Street, A. Randall Jarrell. **CP-JarrR; SP-JarrR**

Man-Moth, The. Elizabeth Bishop. **CP-BishE**

Man must do well out of a good intent. Feare. Robert Herrick. **CP-HerrR**

Man, my friend, whose conscious heart, The. *see also* To Aristius Fuscus. Horace. **CP-JohnS,** *tr.* by Samuel Johnson; *Fr.* Odes.

Man named Philander S. Goo, A. Philander. Theodore Roethke. **CP-RoetT**

Man naturally loves delay. Punctuality. "Lewis Carroll." **CP-CarrL**

Man of Autumn, The. Richard Eberhart. *Fr.* The Seasons. **CP-EberR**

Man of Evil. Robert Ranke Graves. **CP-GravR**

Man of Faith, The. Isabella Gardner. **CP-GardI**

Man of firm and noble soul, The. *Fr. the Latin of Horace.* Byron. **CP-Byron**

Man of God. Tall man, man of oath. Mad man of ignorant causes. William Everson. Tendril in the Mesh. **SP-EverW**

Man of La Mancha. Wystan Hugh Auden.

  Golden Age, The. **CP-AudeW**

  "Progress you have made is very remarkable, The."

  ("Ladies and gentlemen, you have made most remarkable.") **CP-AudeW** (Recitative by Death.) **CP-AudeW**

Man of Law's Tale, The. Geoffrey Chaucer. *Fr.* The Canterbury Tales. **CP-ChauG**

Man of Life Upright, The. Thomas Campion. **CP-CampT**

Man of low degree was sore oppressed, A. The Crisis. Paul Laurence Dunbar. **CP-DunbP**

Man of massive meditation, A. Analogue of Unity in Multeity. Richard Eberhart. **CP-EberR**

Man of Mercy (says the Seer), The. Good-Nature to Animals. Christopher Smart. *Fr.* Hymns for the Amusement of Children. **SP-SmarC**

Man of Peace. "Bob Dylan." **CP-DylaB**

Man of Prayer, The. Christopher Smart. *See* Strong is the horse upon his speed.

Man of Summer, The. Richard Eberhart. *Fr.* The Seasons. **CP-EberR**

Man of Sung did business, A. A Hat Salesman and a Capable Ruler. Chuang Tzu, *tr. fr. Chinese by* Thomas Merton. **CP-MertT**

Man of Tao, The. Chuang Tzu. *tr. fr. Chinese by* Thomas Merton. **CP-MertT**

Man of the Middle Class, A. Gwendolyn Brooks. **SP-BrooG**

Man of Tyre, The. David Herbert Lawrence. **CP-LawrD**

Man of words and not of deeds, A. Voyage Autour de Mes Cartes Postales. James Schuyler. **CP-SchuJ**

Man on his own in a car, A. Meditation on the A30. Sir John Betjeman. **CP-BetjJ**

Man on the city corner, The. Defending the Provinces. Brendan Galvin. **SP-GalvB**

Man on the dubious waves of error toss'd. William Cowper. **NOCV** *Fr.* Truth. **CP-CowpW**

Man, on the dubious waves of error toss'd. Truth. William Cowper. **CP-CowpW**

Man on the Dump, The. Wallace Stevens. **CP-StevW**

Man on the mountain listens to star and stone. Man. Kathleen Jessie Raine. *Fr.* Bheinn Naomh. **SP-RainK**

Man on the radio mourns, The. The Frontier. James Wright. **CP-WrigJ**

Man on the radio talked of soft tissue, A. Elegy for John Tripp. Steve Griffiths. **SP-GrifS**

Man on the Street. "Bob Dylan." **CP-DylaB**

Man out of the fire rises, A. To the Tune of an Ancient Song. Kenneth Patchen. **CP-PatcK**

Man out walking alone in the snow, A. Winter Exercise. Howard Nemerov. **CP-NemeH**

Man owes me two hundred and fifty dollars, A. To a Friendly Dun. James Wright. **CP-WrigJ**

Man paid 110,000 guineas for Van Gogh's mother, A. Cutting Off One's Ears for Someone Else Is Wrong. Jenny Joseph. *Fr.* Fables. **SP-JoseJ**

Man passes through a gate, A. Torn Canvas. Jim Carroll. **SP-CarrJ**

Man peeing / by the woodpile. South Window. Grace Paley. **CP-PaleG**

Man prepar'd against all ills to come, A. Christian Militant. Robert Herrick. **CP-HerrR**

Man Reaches a Point. David Herbert Lawrence. **CP-LawrD**

Man remembers from the tales the rocket, The. The Romance of Science. Randall Jarrell. **CP-JarrR**

Man riding on the meaning of rivers, A. Are You Born? / I. Muriel Rukeyser. **CP-RukeM**

Man rising to the doom that shall not err. Christina Georgina Rossetti. *Fr.* Behold a Shaking. **CP-RosC2**

Man sails the deep a while. Robert Louis Stevenson. **CP-StevR**

Man sat in the felon's tank, alone, A. In the Tank. Thom Gunn. **CP-GunnT**

Man Saul, The. Stevie Smith. **CP-SmitS**

Man saw the whole world as a grinning skull and cross-bones. The, A. Bath. Carl Sandburg. **CP-SandC**

Man Seeking Experience Enquires His Way of a Drop of Water, The. Ted Hughes. **SP-HughT**

Man Selling Pencils Outside the B. Dalton Bookstore, The. Barton Sutter. **SP-SuttB**

Man she wanted all her life, The. Death of a Lady's Man. Leonard Cohen. **CP-CoheL**

Man shot through back while. The Simplicity of Everything in Viet Nam. Charles Bukowski. **SP-BukC2**

Man should never earn his living, A. A Living. David Herbert Lawrence. **CP-LawrD**

Man sick with whirling, A. 1789–1939. Randall Jarrell. **CP-JarrR**

Man sits fishing on the sultry bank, A. River Rising in India. Jenny Joseph. **SP-JoseJ**

Man sits in a timelessness, The. The Rescue. Robert Creeley. **CP-CreeR**

Man sits in the rocking bedroom, claws, The. Muriel Rukeyser. **CP-RukeM**

Man Speaks: / Though you move with a quiet grace, like a cloud, The. A Drama. David Herbert Lawrence. **CP-LawrD**

Man standing there, who is he?, The. Three Stanzas From Goethe. James Wright. **CP-WrigJ**

Man staring into the fire, A. The Miracle. Philip Levine. **SP-LeviP**

Man stomping over my bed in boots. The Neighbor. Marge Piercy. **SP-PierM**

Man stopped me in a lane, A. Fair Game. John Hewitt. **CP-HewiJ**

Man takes out his hearing aid, A. The Man with the Hearing Aid. Ted Kooser. **SP-KoosT**

Man, tamed by wine, by dress, by talk. Wild Life and Tamed Life. Richard Eberhart. **CP-EberR**

Man tears a chunk of bread off the brown loaf, A. Where We Are. Stephen Dobyns. **SP-DobyS**

Man that had six mortal wounds, a man, A. Cuchulain Comforted. William Butler Yeats. **CP-YeatW**

Man that is man is more than a man. Third Song of Huitzilopochtli. David Herbert Lawrence. **CP-LawrD**

Man that is open of heart to his neighbor, The. Neighbours. Rudyard Kipling. **CP-KiplR**

Man the Father, The. Marsden Hartley. **CP-HartM**

Man, the illogical animal. The others go wrong by anachronistic. To the Story-Tellers. Robinson Jeffers. **CP-JefR3**

Man, the imperial shape, then multiplied. Percy Bysshe Shelley. *Fr.* Ode to Liberty. **CP-ShelP**

Man, the Man-Hunter. Carl Sandburg. **CP-SandC**

Man the Master. Thomas Merton. **CP-MertT**

Man the Moon Shooter. Carl Sandburg. **CP-SandC**

Man thinks 'cause he rules the earth he can do with it as he please. License to Kill. "Bob Dylan." **CP-DylaB**

Man to a Woman, A. William Carlos Williams. **CP-WilW1**

Man to the Wound in Christ's Side. Robert Southwell. **CP-SoutR**

Man under the Bed, The. Erica Jong. **SP-JongE**

Man Upstairs, The. Stanley Jasspon Kunitz. **CP-KuniS**

Man Walking and Singing, A. Wendell Berry. **CP-BerrW**

Man walks, I learn, in fear of woman. Lore. Howard Nemerov. **CP-NemeH**

Man walks on the southern beach, The. A Conversation. Margaret Atwood. **SP-AtwM2**

Man was crucified. He came to the city a stranger, was accused, and, The. Silver Nails. Carl Sandburg. **CP-SandC**

Man Was Drawing Near to Me, A. Thomas Hardy. **CP-HardT**

Man was made of social earth. The Dæmonic and the Celestial Love. Ralph Waldo Emerson. **APN-1** *Fr.* Initial, Dæmonic, and Celestial Love. **CP-EmerR**

Man Was Made to Mourn, a Dirge. Robert Burns. **CP-BurnR**

  Man's Inhumanity to Man. **BLPA; FaFP**

Man watched / and though he was accustomed, The. Bringing It Down. Stephen Dunn. **SP-DunnS**

Man who ate mushrooms, The. Mistaken Identity. Richard Eberhart. **CP-EberR**

Man who cloaked his bitterness within, The. Thomas Hood. Edwin Arlington Robinson. **CP-RobiE**

Man Who Closed Shop, The. Stephen Dunn. **SP-DunnS**

Man Who Could Write, The. Rudyard Kipling. **CP-KiplR**

  ("Shun—shun the Bowl! That fatal, facile drink.") **CP-KiplR**

Man who died, The. Funeral. David Markson. **CP-MarkD**

Man Who Died, A. David Herbert Lawrence. **CP-LawrD**

Man who does not ask too much, A. Wendell Berry. *Fr.* The Clearing. **CP-BerrW**

Man who, doing violence, is saved, The. Of Conscience. Isabella Gardner. **CP-GardI**

Man Who Dreamed of Faeryland, The. William Butler Yeats. **CP-YeatW**

Man who fiercest charged in fight, The. Stonewall Jackson. Herman Melville. **SP-MelvH**

Man Who Forgot, The. Thomas Hardy. **CP-HardT**

Man who found the aardvark, The. Aardvark. Kenneth Rexroth. **SP-RexrK** *Fr.* A Bestiary. **SP-RexrK**

Man who had fallen among thieves, A. Edward Estlin Cummings. **CP-CummE; SP-CummE**

Man Who Loved Islands, The. Derek Walcott. **CP-WalcD**

Man who made her let me climb the derrick, The. John Berryman. *Fr.* Sonnets to Chris. **CP-BerrJ**

Man Who Never Loses His Balance, The. Stephen Dunn. **SP-DunnS**

Man Who Owns Sleep, The. Charles Kenneth Williams. **CP-WillC**

Man who pants for ample Sway, The. Boethius, *tr.* by Samuel Johnson. **CP-JohnS** *Fr.* Consolation of Philosophy, The ("De Consolacione Philosophie"). **CP-ChauG**

Man Who Rode Away, The. Lawrence Ferlinghetti. **SP-FerlL**

Man who sold his business to a business is looking for a business, The. Sad Invective. Stephen Berg. **SP-BergS**

Man who sold his lawn to standard oil, The. The War against the Trees. Stanley Jasspon Kunitz. **CP-KuniS**

Man Who Stays Up Late, The. Miller Williams. **SP-WillM**

Man who stood beside me, The. Sweet Will. Philip Levine. **SP-LeviP**

Man who tells you which is the whiter wash, The. Love and How It Becomes Important in Our Day to Day Lives. Miller Williams. **SP-WillM**

Man Who Was, The. Rudyard Kipling. *Fr.* Life's Handicap.

  "Earth gave up her dead that tide, The." **CP-KiplR**

Man who was about to hang himself, A. Circumstance. *Unknown, tr. fr. Greek by* Shelley. **CP-ShelP**

Man Who Was Blown Down by the Wind, A. Richard Eberhart. **CP-EberR**

Man Who Wrote Yeats, the Man Who Wrote Mozart, The. Michael Hartnett. **SP-HarMi**

Man who's married an attractive, somewhat younger woman conceives a painful jealousy of her, A. The Cautionary. Charles Kenneth Williams. **SP-WillC**

Man whose muscles I once admired, The. The Visitor. Barton Sutter. **SP-SuttB**

Man Whose Pharynx Was Bad, The. Wallace Stevens. **CP-StevW**

Man will surely fail who dares delay, The. Ovid, *tr. by* Samuel Johnson. **CP-JohnS** *Fr.* Remediae Amoris.

Man with a leaf in his head, A. The Mulch. Stanley Jasspon Kunitz. **CP-KuniS**

Man with a Past, The. Thomas Hardy. **CP-HardT**

Man with a scythe: the torrent of his swing. Gardens No Emblems. Donald Davie. **CP-DavDo**

Man with a tail heads eastward for the Fair. World-Telegram. John Berryman. **CP-BerrJ**

Man with his lion under the shed of wars, The. The Song of the Borderguard. Robert Duncan. **SP-DuncR**

Man With Night Sweats, The. Thom Gunn. **CP-GunnT**

Man with One Foot and the Marsh Pheasant, The. Chuang Tzu, *tr. fr. Chinese by* Thomas Merton. **CP-MertT**

Man with the axe stands profound and termless, The. Randall Jarrell. **CP-JarrR**

Man with the Blue Guitar, The. Wallace Stevens. **CP-StevW**

  "I cannot bring a world quite round." **CMoP; RaBo; VoGa**

  "Man bent over his guitar, The." **CMoP; NoAM; RaBo; VoGa**

  "Tom-tom, c'est moi. The blue guitar." **CMoP**

  "Tune beyond us as we are, A." **CMoP**

Man with the Broken Fingers, The. Carl Sandburg. **CP-SandC**

Man with the Broken Fingers throws a shadow, The. The Man with the Broken Fingers. Carl Sandburg. **CP-SandC**

Man with the Golden Adam's Apple, The. Kenneth Patchen. **CP-PatcK**

Man with the Hearing Aid, The. Ted Kooser. **SP-KoosT**

Man with the Hot Nose, The. Charles Bukowski. **SP-BukC2**

Man with the red hat, The. Glazunoviana. John Ashbery. **SP-AshbJ**

Man With Two New Suits, The. Ogden Nash. **CP-NashO**

Man without Sense of Direction. John Crowe Ransom. **SP-RansJ**

Man woman and child. Louis MacNeice. *Fr.* Visitations. **CP-MacNL**

Man Writes to a Part of Himself, A. Robert Bly. **SP-BlyR**

Man wrote to me: We missed it, you and I, A. Correspondence in After Years. David Herbert Lawrence. **CP-LawrD**

Man, you too, aren't you, one of these rough followers of the criminal? In the Servants' Quarters. Thomas Hardy. **CP-HardT**

Man Young and Old, A. William Butler Yeats. **CP-YeatW**

  Death of the Hare, The.

  Empty Cup, The.

  First Love.

  Friends of his Youth, The.

  From "Oedipus at Colonus."

  His Memories.

  His Wildness.

  Human Dignity.

  Mermaid, The.

  Secrets of the Old, The.

  Summer and Spring.

"Mana Man" / He gets them into the dark hour. Promises. Jim Morrison. **SP-MorrJ**

Mana of the Sea. David Herbert Lawrence. **CP-LawrD**

Manacled with blood. Ted Hughes. *Fr.* Skylarks. **SP-HughT**

Management Area of Cherokee, The. The Trout Map. Allen Tate. **CP-TateA**

Managers, The. Wystan Hugh Auden. **CP-AudeW**

Manatee, The. Ogden Nash. *Fr.* Nature-Walks, or, Not to Mention a Dopping of Sheldrakes. **CP-NashO**

Manatee is harmless, The. The Manatee. Ogden Nash. *Fr.* Nature-Walks, or, Not to Mention a Dopping of Sheldrakes. **CP-NashO**

Manciple there was, one of a Temple, A. *mod. vers. by* William Wordsworth *incl. description of the Manciple, fr* The General Prologue. Geoffrey Chaucer. **CP-WorW1** *Fr.* The Canterbury Tales. **CP-ChauG**

Manciple's Prologue, The. Geoffrey Chaucer. *Fr.* The Canterbury Tales. **CP-ChauG**

Manciple's Tale, The. Geoffrey Chaucer. *Fr.* The Canterbury Tales. **CP-ChauG**

  Controlling the Tongue. **OxBChV**

  "Lat take a cat, and fostre him wel[l] with milk." **OFC, *ll.* 71–78; ChTr**

Manciple's Tale—A Modernization, The. *mod. vers. by* William Wordsworth *incl. description of the Manciple, fr* The General Prologue. Geoffrey Chaucer. **CP-WorW1** *Fr.* The Canterbury Tales. **CP-ChauG**

Mandalay. Rudyard Kipling. **CP-KiplR**

Mandando una lettera. Nota in una Bottiglia. Erica Jong. **SP-JongE**

Mandelstam, on Dante. Donald Davie. **CP-DavDo**

Mandelstam's Hope for the Best. Donald Davie. **CP-DavDo**

Mandrake. Erica Jong. **SP-JongE**

Mandrakes. Thom Gunn. **CP-GunnT**

Manet: "The Execution of the Emperor Maximilian." William DeWitt Snodgrass. **SP-SnodW**

Maneuver [*or* Manoeuvre], The. William Carlos Williams. **CP-WilW2**

Manfred. George Meredith. **CP-MerG1**

Manfred: A Dramatic Poem. Byron. **CP-Byron**

  "Stars are forth, the moon above the tops, The." **OAEL-2**

Mangham. James Dickey. **CP-DickJ**

Mango on the Mango Tree, The. Robert Penn Warren. **MoP; NoAM** *Fr.* Mexico Is a Foreign Country: Four Studies in Naturalism. **SP-WarrR**

Mango Tree, The. Hart Crane. **CP-CranH**

Manhattan March, The 1970s. Al Young. **CP-YounA**

Manhattan May Day Midnight. Allen Ginsberg. **CP-GinsA**

Manhattan Miniature. John Yau. **SP-YauJo**

Manhattan Thirties Flash. Allen Ginsberg. **CP-GinsA**

Manhattan's streets I saunter'd pondering. Song of Prudence. Walt Whitman. **CP-WhitW**

Manhole Covers. Karl Shapiro. **SP-ShapK**

Manichaeans, The. Gary Snyder. **CP-SnydG**

Manifest reason glared at you and me. What Will Be, Is. Robert Ranke Graves. **CP-GravR**

Manifestation, The. Theodore Roethke. **CP-RoetT**

Manifesto. Allen Ginsberg. **CP-GinsA**

Manifesto. David Herbert Lawrence. **CP-LawrD**

Manifesto. Nicanor Parra, *tr. fr. Spanish.*
    I Move the Meeting Be Adjourned.
    (I Move that We Adjourn the Meeting.) **CP-MertT,** *tr. by* Thomas Merton;
    ("Ladies and Gentlemen: / I am going to ask just one question.") **CP-MertT,** *tr. by* Thomas Merton;

Manifesto: the Mad Farmer Liberation Front. Wendell Berry. **CP-BerrW**

Manifold Fusions, The. Kenneth Patchen. **CP-PatcK**

Manitoba Childe Roland. Carl Sandburg. **CP-SandC**

Mankind and Ocean. Robert Ranke Graves. **CP-GravR**

Mankind, you dismay me. Thoughts at Midnight. Thomas Hardy. **CP-HardT**

Manliness. John Donne. **CP-DonnJ**

Manna. Robert Herrick. **CP-HerrR**

Mannahatta: ("I was asking for something specific and perfect for my city"). Walt Whitman. **CP-WhitW**

Mannahatta: ("My city's fit and noble name resumed"). Walt Whitman. **CP-WhitW**

Manner of its Death, The. Emily Dickinson. **CP-DickE**

Manners. Elizabeth Bishop. **CP-BishE**

Manners. Ralph Waldo Emerson. **CP-EmerR**

Mannikins, we command you. Caligari. Carl Sandburg. **CP-SandC**

Manor Garden, The. Sylvia Plath. **CP-PlatS**

Manor House, Hale, Near Liverpool, The. Sir John Betjeman. **CP-BetjJ**

Manos Karastefanís. James Merrill. **SP-MerrJ**

Man's a bag of wind, the critics sneer, The. B.O.W. John Hewitt. **CP-HewiJ**

Man's and woman's bodies lay without souls. A Childish Prank. Ted Hughes. **SP-HughT**

Man's body at auction, A. Walt Whitman. **SAmP** *Fr.* I sing the body electric. **CP-WhitW**

Man's Civil[l] War[re]. Robert Southwell. **CP-SoutR**

Man's destination is his own village, A. To the Indians Who Died in Africa. Thomas Stearns Eliot. **CP-ElioT**

Mans disposition is for to requite. Revenge. Robert Herrick. **CP-HerrR**

Man's Dying-Place Uncertain. Robert Herrick. **CP-HerrR**

Man's earliest pastime, I suppose. And How Keen Was the Vision of Sir Launfal? Ogden Nash. **CP-NashO**

Man's Glory. Allen Ginsberg. **CP-GinsA**

Man's Greed and Envy Are So Great. Richard Eberhart. **CP-EberR**

Man's harvest is past, his summer is ended. For All. Christina Georgina Rossetti. **CP-RosC2**

Man's Image. David Herbert Lawrence. **CP-LawrD**

Man's Inhumanity to Man. Robert Burns. **BLPA; FaFP** *Fr.* Man Was Made to Mourn, a Dirge. **CP-BurnR**

Man's life is but a working day / Whose tasks are set aright. Christina Georgina Rossetti. **CP-RosC2**

Man's life is death. Yet Christ endured to live. Wednesday in Holy Week. Christina Georgina Rossetti. **CP-RosC2**

Man's life is like a Sparrow, mighty King! Persuasion. William Wordsworth. *Fr.* Ecclesiastical Sonnets. **CP-WorW2**

Man's life is threescore years and ten. The Imminent Seventies. Robert Ranke Graves. **CP-GravR**

Man's life so little worth. Basil Bunting. *Fr.* The Spoils. **CP-BuntB**

Man's Medley. George Herbert. **CP-HerbG**

Man's paradise is his good nature, A. Canto 93. Ezra Pound. *Fr.* Cantos. **CP-PoCan**

Man's Requirements, A. Elizabeth Barrett Browning. **CP-BroEB**

Mans transgressions God do's then remit, A. Penitencie. Robert Herrick. **CP-HerrR**

Man's Type. Richard Eberhart. **CP-EberR**

Man's Work, A. Archibald MacLeish. **CP-MacLA**

Mansion burned. Maids, The. Hayden Carruth. **CP-CarHS** *Fr.* The Clay Hill Anthology.

Mansion, string of cottages, a farm, A. The Inherited Estate. Thom Gunn. **CP-GunnT**

Manso. John Milton, *tr. fr. Latin by* John T. Shawcross. **CP-MiltJ**
    ("These verses also to thy praise the Nine.") **CP-CowpW,** *tr. by* William Cowper;
    (To Manso.) **CP-CowpW**

Mantegna on all the walls. Mantova. Charles Wright. **SP-WrigC**

"Mantis." Louis Zukofsky. **CP-ZukLS**

"Mantis," An Interpretation. Louis Zukofsky. **CP-ZukLS**

Mantis! praying mantis! since your wings' leaves. "Mantis." Louis Zukofsky. **CP-ZukLS**

Mantle of St. John de Matha, The. John Greenleaf Whittier. **CP-WhitJ**

Mantled in grey, the dusk steals slowly in. Winter Nocturne. Philip Larkin. **CP-LarkP**

Mantova. Charles Wright. **SP-WrigC**

Manual, A. Vincent Bourne, *tr. fr. Latin by* William Cowper. **CP-CowpW**

Manual System. Carl Sandburg. **CP-SandC**

Manuela. Edwin Rolfe. **CP-RolfE**

Manuelzinho. Elizabeth Bishop. **CP-BishE**

Manufactured Gods. Carl Sandburg. **CP-SandC**

Many a flower hath perfume for its dower. Exultate Deo. Christina Georgina Rossetti. **CP-RosC2**

Many a green isle needs must be. Lines Written among the Euganean Hills. Percy Bysshe Shelley. **CP-ShelP**

Many a miner has gone. The Fury of Jewels and Coal. Anne Sexton. *Fr.* The Furies. **CP-SextA**

Many a phrase has the English language. Emily Dickinson. **CP-DickE**

Many a time have they afflicted me from my youth, may Israel now say. Psalm 129. Bible, *O.T. Fr.* Psalms. **CP-Psal**

Many a weary year had passed since the burning of Grand-Pré, *sels.* Henry Wadsworth Longfellow. *Fr.* Part the Second. *Fr.* Evangeline, a Tale of Acadie. **SP-LongH**

Many a weary year had passed since the burning of Grand-Pré. Part the Second. Henry Wadsworth Longfellow. *Fr.* Evangeline, a Tale of Acadie. **SP-LongH**

Many a year is in its grave. *from the German of* J. L. Uhland. Paul Laurence Dunbar. **CP-DunbP**

Many an angel, with its needle. Emily Dickinson. **SP-DickE**

Many an infant that screams like a calliope. Pediatric Reflection. Ogden Nash. **CP-NashO**

Many an Outcast. Edwin Rolfe. **CP-RolfE**

Many and many a time I thought. The Dead Bastard. Thomas Hardy. **CP-HardT**

Many and sharp the num'rous Ills. Man's Inhumanity to Man. Robert Burns. **BLPA; FaFP** *Fr.* Man Was Made to Mourn, a Dirge. **CP-BurnR**

Many animals that our fathers killed in America. Fear Is What Quickens Me. James Wright. **CP-WrigJ**

Many Are Called. Edwin Arlington Robinson. **CP-RobiE**

Many are the deceivers. Red-Riding Hood. Anne Sexton. **CP-SextA**

Many are the joys. Intimations of Sublimity. William Wordsworth. **OBNC** *Fr.* School-Time. *Fr.* The Prelude; Growth of a Poet's Mind [1805 vers.]. **CP-WorW3**

Many are the sayings of the wise. The Ways of God to Men. John Milton. **OBS** *Fr.* Samson Agonistes. **CP-MiltJ**

Many are the thoughts that come to me. My Thoughts. Ralph Waldo Emerson. **CP-EmerR**

Many arrivals make us live: the tree becoming. The Manifestation. Theodore Roethke. **CP-RoetT**

Many birds and the beating of wings. Margaret. Carl Sandburg. **CP-SandC**

Many by valour have deserved renown. 4.9. Horace. **CP-RaleW,** *tr. by* Sir Walter Ralegh; *Fr.* Odes.

Many can boast a hollyhock. Emily Dickinson. **SP-DickE**

Many children in only one bed. Una Vita Violenta (1955). David St. John. *Fr.* To Pasolini. **SP-StJoD**

Many compacted summers. Sounds of a Devon Village. Donald Davie. **CP-DavDo**

Many cross the Rhine. Emily Dickinson. **CP-DickE**

Many desire, but few or none deserve. The Advice. Sir Walter Ralegh. **CP-RaleW**

Many Famous Feet Have Trod. Philip Larkin. **CP-LarkP**

Many Handles. Carl Sandburg. **CP-SandC**

Many Happy Returns. Wystan Hugh Auden. **CP-AudeW**

Many Happy Returns. Ted Berrigan. **SP-BerrT**

Many Hats. Carl Sandburg. **CP-SandC**

Many have died here, but few. Natural History I. Robert Penn Warren. **SP-WarrR**

Many have sung of love a root of bane. At Last. Christina Georgina Rossetti. **CP-RosC2**

Many in aftertimes will say of you. Christina Georgina Rossetti. **OBNC** *Fr.* Monna Innominata. **CP-RosC2**

Many ingenious lovely things are gone. William Butler Yeats. **BIrV;** **LiTB; MoAB; PoE** *Fr.* Nineteen Hundred and Nineteen. **CP-YeatW**

Many ingenius lovely things are gone. Nineteen Hundred and Nineteen. William Butler Yeats. **CP-YeatW**

Many Loves. Allen Ginsberg. **CP-GinsA**

Many male and female names. All Saints. Christopher Smart. *Fr.* Hymns and Spiritual Songs for the Fasts and Festivals of the Church of England. **SP-SmarC**

Many-maned scud-thumper, tub. Winter Ocean. John Updike. **CP-UpdiJ**

Many Mansions. David Herbert Lawrence. **CP-LawrD**

Many Mansions. James Liddy. **CP-LiddJ**

Many men have loved the bells. Take this Longing. Leonard Cohen. **CP-CoheL**

Many more happy Valentines. Happiest February. Louis Zukofsky. *Fr.* Songs of Degrees. **CP-ZukLS**

Many of legal age circled the bar of Reflection. Narcissus and the Young Men. James Liddy. **CP-LiddJ**

Many of Our Waters: Variations on a Poem by a Black Child. James Wright. **CP-WrigJ**

Gemela.

Learning from MacDiarmid.

Message from the Mountain Pool Where the Deer Come Down, A.

On the Way to the Planetarium.

"This morning / My beloved rose, before I did."

To the Ohio.

"You know / if a blind boy."

Many of the English. The English. Stevie Smith. **CP-SmitS**

Many of the three hundred and sixty-five days of the year are followed. Good-By, Old Year, You Oaf or Why Don't They Pay the Bonus. Ogden Nash. **CP-NashO**

Many our needs, yet we spare prayers. Hafiz, *tr.* by Ralph Waldo Emerson. **CP-EmerR** *Fr.* Odes.

Many paths in the woods have chos- / en me, many a time. Lost. Hayden Carruth. **CP-CarHS**

Many people have a thing they want to protect. Marge Piercy. *Fr.* A Shadow Play For Guilt. **SP-PierM**

Many people have asked me what was the most beautiful sight I. Pipe Dreams. Ogden Nash. **CP-NashO**

Many poems may be composed upon the same theme. Praising the Poets of That Country. Howard Nemerov. **CP-NemeH**

Many prophets have failed, their voices silent. Ode to Failure. Allen Ginsberg. **CP-GinsA**

Many roses in the wind. Love Storm. David Herbert Lawrence. **CP-LawrD**

Many seek and never see. The Eye Altering Alters All. Allen Ginsberg. **CP-GinsA**

Many sow, but only the chosen reap, The. Lines to My Father. Countee Cullen. **CP-CullC**

Many talents, oh hers was greatest, The. Her Talents. . . Of. Kenneth Patchen. **CP-PatcK**

Many thanks for deserting the tongue. *see also* Hurry to Your Dinner. Leonard Cohen. **CP-CoheL**

Many the wonders I this day have seen. To My Brother George. John Keats. **CP-KeatJ**

Many things I might have said today. Aprons of Silence. Carl Sandburg. **CP-SandC**

Many things in the world have. In the White Sky. William Stafford. **SP-StafW**

Many things to absorb I teach to help you become eleve of mine. To a Western Boy. Walt Whitman. **CP-WhitW**

Many times a last time I will look. Harmless Streets. Tess Gallagher. **SP-GallT**

Many times bound outward. John Haines. *Fr.* Roadways. **SP-HainJ**

Many trees can stand unshaded. Trees and Cattle. James Dickey. **CP-DickJ**

Many-volumned authoresses. Agatha Christie and Beatrix Potter. John Updike. **CP-UpdiJ**

Many Wagons Ago. John Ashbery. **SP-AshbJ**

Many waters cannot quench love. An Old Saying. Algernon Charles Swinburne. **SP-SwinA**

Many ways to spell good night. Good Night. Carl Sandburg. **CP-SandC**

Many we are, and yet but few possess. Few Fortunate. Robert Herrick. **CP-HerrR**

Many well-known people have been packed away in cemeteries. Basil Bunting, *after the Persian of* Sadi. **CP-BuntB**

Many years ago in China. Autumn Air. Charles Simic. **SP-SimiC**

Many years have I still to burn, detained. At a Loose End. David Herbert Lawrence. **CP-LawrD**

Manzanita. Gary Snyder. **CP-SnydG**

Map, The. Elizabeth Bishop. **CP-BishE**

Map. James McAuley.
"In six-inch scale, the Mayo baronies." **SP-McAuJ**, *sect.* 1.
"Papers everywhere—piled onto tables and shelves—." **SP-McAuJ**
"Rage swept them across the Vistula, Danube, Elbe." **SP-McAuJ**
"Was it greed for possession of these salty crags." **SP-McAuJ**

Map of Europe, A. Derek Walcott. **CP-WalcD**

Map of Montana in Italy, A. Richard Hugo. **CP-HugoR**

Map of Skye, A. Richard Hugo. **CP-HugoR**

Map of the City, A. Thom Gunn. **CP-GunnT**

Map of the New World. Derek Walcott. **CP-WalcD**

Map of the Peninsula, A. Richard Hugo. **CP-HugoR**

Map of the Western Part of the County of Essex in England, A. Denise Levertov. **CP-LeveD**

Maple. Robert Frost. **CP-FrosR**

"Maple leaf forever" / "in 1867—", The. Canada. Robert Creeley. **CP-CreeR**

Maple Syrup. Donald Hall. **CP-HallD**

Maple Works, The. Lewis Turco. **SP-TurcL**

Maples in a Spruce Forest. John Updike. **CP-UpdiJ**

Mapmaker on His Art, The. Howard Nemerov. **CP-NemeH**

Mara. Robinson Jeffers. **CP-JefR3**

Marat Dead. Charles Tomlinson. **CP-TomlC**

Maratea Antica. Richard Hugo. **CP-HugoR**

Maratea Porto. Richard Hugo. **CP-HugoR**

Maratea Porto: Saying Good-bye to the Vitolos. Richard Hugo. **CP-HugoR**

Maratea Porto: The Bitter Man. Richard Hugo. **CP-HugoR**

Maratea Porto: The Dear Postmistress There. Richard Hugo. **CP-HugoR**

Marathon. Louise Glück. **SP-GlücL**

Marathon. Louise Glück. *Fr.* Marathon. **SP-GlücL**
Beginning, The.
Encounter, The.
First Goodbye.
Last Letter.
Marathon.
Night Song.
Song of Invisible Boundaries.
Song of Obstacles.
Song of the River.
Summer.

Marathon of gulls / a chiming of chickadees, A. Malcolm Lowry. **CP-LowrM**

"Marat's Death." Donald Hall. **CP-HallD**

Marble nor monuments where of then we spoke. John Berryman. *Fr.* Sonnets to Chris. **CP-BerrJ**

Marble-Streeted Town, The. Thomas Hardy. **CP-HardT**

Marble Tablet, The. Thomas Hardy. **CP-HardT**

Marble, weep [*or* weepe], for thou dost cover. On Margaret Ratcliffe. Ben Jonson. **CP-JonsB**

March . . . Someone has walked across the snow. Vacancy in the Park. Wallace Stevens. **CP-StevW**

March. Wystan Hugh Auden. **CP-AudWJ**

March. Jane Cooper. **SP-CoopJ**
Back.
Coda.
El Sueño de la Razón. **FaBoWP**
Feathers.
Hunger Moon. **CABA**
In Silence Where We Breathe.
Middle Age.
No More Elegies.

March. Hart Crane. **CP-CranH**

March. Alfred Edward Housman. **CP-HousA**

March, A. Denise Levertov. **CP-LeveD**

March, The. Li Po, *tr. fr. Chinese by* William Carlos Williams *with* David Rafael Wang. **CP-WilW2**

March. Archibald MacLeish. **CP-MacLA**

March. Christina Georgina Rossetti. *Fr.* The Months: A Pageant. **CP-RosC2**

March. Gary Snyder. *Fr.* Six Years. **CP-SnydG**

March. Richard Wilbur. **CP-WilbR**

March. William Carlos Williams. **CP-WilW1**

March. James Wright. **CP-WrigJ**

March 1, The. Robert Lowell. **SP-LoweR**

March 2, The. Robert Lowell. **SP-LoweR**

March: A Birthday Poem. John Updike. **CP-UpdiJ**

March Calf, A. Ted Hughes. **SP-HughT**

March Day. John Hewitt. **CP-HewiJ**

March First. Louis Zukofsky. *Fr.* Songs of Degrees. **CP-ZukLS**

March 4th. Anne Sexton. **CP-SextA**

March gave clear days. Louis MacNeice. *Fr.* Trilogy for X. **CP-MacNL**

March has come to the bridge head. *fr. the Chinese of* Li Po (701-62). Ezra Pound. **SP-PounE**

March has flooded meadows. Mortimer. Frank Templeton Prince. **CP-PrinF**

March Heat. William Matthews. **SP-MattW**

March Here. James Schuyler. **CP-SchuJ**

March in the Ranks Hard-Prest, and the Road Unknown, A. Walt Whitman. **CP-WhitW**

March interrupted the light afternoon, The. The March Past. Philip Larkin. **CP-LarkP**

March into Virginia, The. Herman Melville. **SP-MelvH**

March Is a Light. William Carlos Williams. **CP-WilW1**

March is the Month of Expectation. Emily Dickinson. **CP-DickE**

March Journal. Charles Wright. **SP-WrigC**

March-Mad. May Sarton. **SP-SartM**

March Moon. Langston Hughes. **SP-HughL**

March of Miles Standish, The. Henry Wadsworth Longfellow. *Fr.* The Courtship of Miles Standish. **SP-LongH**

  "Meanwhile the stalwart Miles Standish was marching steadily northward." **TreFS**

March of the Hungry Mountains. Carl Sandburg. **CP-SandC**

March Past, The. Philip Larkin. **CP-LarkP**

MARCH (*Racing*). Rudyard Kipling. *Fr.* Verses on Games. **CP-KiplR**

March 7th. Anne Sexton. **CP-SextA**

March Snow. Wendell Berry. **CP-BerrW**

March Song. Wystan Hugh Auden. **CP-AudWJ**

March, the fierce! like a wind of garters. Poem In January. Frank O'Hara. **SP-OharF**

March! The mud is cakin' good about our trousies. "Birds of Prey" March. Rudyard Kipling. **CP-KiplR**

March to the Sea, The. Herman Melville. **SP-MelvH**

March 22, 1968. Wendell Berry. **CP-BerrW**

March Twilight. Louise Bogan. **CP-BogaL**

March wind on the ocean turns everything solemn. A Heavy Surf. Pablo Neruda, *tr. fr. Spanish by* Ben Belitt. **SP-NeruP**

March Winds. Wystan Hugh Auden. **CP-AudWJ**

Marchant was ther with a forked berd, A. Geoffrey Chaucer. **CTC** *Fr.* The General Prologue. **FHYEP; NAWM-1; OAEL-1; PoE** *Fr.* The Canterbury Tales. **CP-ChauG**

Marchant whilom dwelled at Seint-Denys, A. The Shipman's Tale. Geoffrey Chaucer. *Fr.* The Canterbury Tales. **CP-ChauG**

Marché aux Oiseaux. Richard Wilbur. **CP-WilbR**

Märchen, The. Randall Jarrell. **CP-JarrR; SP-JarrR**

Märchenbilder. John Ashbery. **SP-AshbJ**

Marching. Charles Simic. **SP-SimiC**

Marching, a dream of wind in our chests. Curse of the Earth Magician on a Metal Land. Marge Piercy. **SP-PierM**

Marching down the road to China. Malcolm Lowry. **CP-LowrM**

Marching Song. Robert Louis Stevenson. **CP-StevR**

Marching Song of the Children of Darkness. Edwin Rolfe. **CP-RolfE**

Marching through a Novel. John Updike. **CP-UpdiJ**

Marchioness of Brinvilliers, The. Herman Melville. **SP-MelvH**

Marco Polo. John Yau. **SP-YauJo**

Marco, thou disloyal sot. To a Mexican Poet Who Has Forsaken Drink. David Markson. **CP-MarkD**

Marcus Cato 234–149 B.C. Robert Lowell. **SP-LoweR**

Marcus Cato 95–42 B.C. Robert Lowell. **SP-LoweR**

Mare Alix breaks the world's trotting record in one day. I see her heels, The. Alix. Carl Sandburg. **CP-SandC**

Mare Rubrum. Paul Laurence Dunbar. **CP-DunbP**

Marenghi. Percy Bysshe Shelley. **CP-ShelP**

Marengo. Mary Oliver. **SP-OlivM**

Mare's Nest, The. Rudyard Kipling. **CP-KiplR**

Mares of the Camargue, The. Frédéric Mistral, *tr. by* George Meredith. **CP-MerG1** *Fr.* Mirèio.

Mare's skeleton in the clearing: another sign of life, The. Adrienne Rich. **FaBoWP; SP-RicA2** *Fr.* Shooting Script. **CP-RicAE**

Margaret. Carl Sandburg. **CP-SandC**

Margaret & Dusty. Alice Notley. **SP-NotlA**

Margaret, are you grieving. Spring and Fall. Gerard Manley Hopkins. **CP-HopkG**

Margaret Clitheroe. Gerard Manley Hopkins. **CP-HopkG**

Margaret Fuller Drowned. Robert Lowell. **SP-LoweR**

Margaret has a milking-pail, / And she rises early. Christina Georgina Rossetti. **CP-RosC2**

Margaret wrote a letter. Margaret & Dusty. Alice Notley. **SP-NotlA**

Margaret's Bridal-Eve. George Meredith. **CP-MerG1**

Margate, 1940. Sir John Betjeman. **CP-BetjJ**

Marge. Hayden Carruth. **CP-CarHS**

Margeries and the malcolms did, The. Malcolm Lowry. **CP-LowrM**

Margery. Christina Georgina Rossetti. **CP-RosC3**

Margery Tracy Barrow Dibb Thummell Sterling Carruth, you used to rattle out. The Ship. Hayden Carruth. *Fr.* Mother. **CP-CarHL**

Marginalia. Wystan Hugh Auden. **CP-AudeW**

  "Dead man, A/ who never caused others to die." **OAEL-2**

Marginalia. Richard Wilbur. **CP-WilbR**

Margrave. Robinson Jeffers. **CP-JefR2**

Margrave's Birthnight, The. Herman Melville. **SP-MelvH**

Marguerite. John Greenleaf Whittier. **CP-WhitJ**

Marguerite-chain all color not royal-or-blue. Chrysanthemum. Louis Zukofsky. **CP-ZukLS**

Mari Magno. Arthur Hugh Clough.

  Clergyman's Second Tale, The. **SP-ClouA**

  Currente Calamo. **SP-ClouA**

Mari Magno I. Arthur Hugh Clough. **SP-ClouA**

Mari Magno II. Arthur Hugh Clough. *See* Where lies the land to which the ship would go?

Maria, could Horace have guess'd. To Mrs. Throckmorton. William Cowper. **CP-CowpW**

Maria Hat Geholfen. Wystan Hugh Auden. **CP-AudWJ**

Maria Holt / Was not the dolt. Bereavement. Stevie Smith. **CP-SmitS**

Maria! I have ev'ry good. The Poet's New-Year's Gift. William Cowper. **CP-CowpW**

Maria Wentworth. Thomas Carew. **CP-CareT**

Marian: ("Clouds fly fast across the moon, The"). George Meredith. **CP-MerG2**

Marian: ("She can be as wise as we"). George Meredith. **CP-MerG1**

Mariana. Christina Georgina Rossetti. **CP-RosC2**

Mariana. Tennyson. **CP-TennA**

Mariana in the South. Tennyson. **CP-TennA**

Marianne Moore. Edward Estlin Cummings. **CP-CummE**

Marianne Moore. Marsden Hartley. **CP-HartM**

Marianne Moore. William Carlos Williams. **CP-WilW1**

Marianne Moore loved baseball. Are Poets Ball Players? Isabella Gardner. **CP-GardI**

Marianne's Dream. Percy Bysshe Shelley. **CP-ShelP**

Marie Laurencin!—. In the Frail Wood. Marsden Hartley. **CP-HartM**

Marigold. Louis Zukofsky. **CP-ZukLS**

Marijuana Notation. Allen Ginsberg. **CP-GinsA**

Marin-An. Gary Snyder. **CP-SnydG**

Marina. Thomas Stearns Eliot. **CP-ElioT**

Marina—. Malcolm Lowry. **CP-LowrM**

Marine. Charles Tomlinson. **CP-TomlC**

Mariner that on smooth waves doth glide, The. Anne Bradstreet. **WPOW** *Fr.* Contemplations. **CP-BradA**

Mariner unpracticed. Unsounded. Adrienne Rich. **CP-RicAE**

Marino Faliero, Doge of Venice. Byron. **CP-Byron**

Marion, why that pensive brow? To Marion. Byron. **CP-Byron**

Marionettes, The. Walter de la Mare. **CP-DeLaW**

Mariposa. Edna St. Vincent Millay. **CP-MillE**

Marita. Leonard Cohen. **CP-CoheL**

Marj. Edward Estlin Cummings. *Fr.* Five Americans. **CP-CummE**

Marjorie. Gilbert Sorrentino. **SP-SorrG**

Mark, The. Archie Randolph Ammons. **SP-AmmoA**

Mark, The. Louise Bogan. **CP-BogaL**

Mark. James Schuyler. **CP-SchuJ**

Mark 4; Why are Yee Afraid, O Yee of Little Faith? Bible, *N.T.* **CP-CrasR**, *tr. by* Richard Crashaw; *Fr.* St. Mark.

Mark 7; The Dumbe Healed, and the People Enjoyed Silence. Bible, *N.T.* **CP-CrasR**, *tr. by* Richard Crashaw; *Fr.* St. Mark.

Mark 10; The Blind Cured by the Word of Our Saviour. Bible, *N.T.* **CP-CrasR**, *tr. by* Richard Crashaw; *Fr.* St. Mark.

Mark 12; (Give to Cæsar———) (And to God———). Bible, *N.T.* **CP-CrasR**, *tr. by* Richard Crashaw; *Fr.* St. Mark.

Mark by what wretched steps Great [Marlborough] grows. *extended vers.* Alexander Pope. **CP-PopeA** *Fr.* An Essay on Man. **CP-PopeA**

Mark. Hair, one strand of it, can curl. Judas. James Dickey. **CP-DickJ**

Mark how the bashful morn in vain. Boldness[e] in Love. Thomas Carew. **CP-CareT**

Mark how the feathered tenants of the flood. Water Fowl. William Wordsworth. **CP-WorW1**

Mark how this polished [*or* polish'd] Eastern sheet. A Fancy. Thomas Carew. **CP-CareT**

Mark, how yond eddy steals away. To My Mistress Sitting by a River's Side; an Eddy. Thomas Carew. **CP-CareT**

Mark Only One Circle. Gary Gildner. **SP-GildG**

Mark the concentrated hazels that enclose. William Wordsworth. **CP-WorW1**

Mark this holy chapel well! *ad. fr. the German of* Stolberg. Samuel Taylor Coleridge. **CP-ColeS**

Mark Twain and Joan of Arc. Nicholas Vachel Lindsay. *Fr.* Three Poems About Mark Twain. **CP-LindV**

Mark Twain Centenary. Gertrude Stein. **CP-SteiG**

Mark Twain, 1909. Daniel Gerard Hoffman. **SP-HoffD**

Mark Twain's opinion was, he was entitled. Authors' Residences. John Updike. **CP-UpdiJ**

Mark Van Doren and the Brook. Archibald MacLeish. **CP-MacLA**

Mark where a credible ghost pulls bridle to view that bare. George Meredith. *Fr.* Alsace-Lorraine. **CP-MerG1**

Mark where the pressing wind shoots javelin-like. George Meredith. **EnLoPo; EnVR; FaBoEn; GBL; HBV; NBM; NOBE; OBEV; OBNC; PoEL-5; SCGP; SeCeV; TEP** *Fr.* Modern Love. **CP-MerG1** (Love's Grave.) **OBEV**

Mark yonder pomp of costly fashion. Song. Robert Burns. **CP-BurnR**

Mark you how the peacock's eye. The Peacock's Eye. Gerard Manley Hopkins. **CP-HopkG**

Mark you the floor[e]? that square and speckled stone. The Church-Floor[e]. George Herbert. **CP-HerbG**

Mark[e] but this flea, and mark[e] in this. The Flea. John Donne. **CP-DonnJ**

Marked by a more distant sky, I hold. Jim Carroll. **SP-CarrJ**

Marked Man, A. Daniel Gerard Hoffman. **SP-HoffD**

Markes that did limit *Lands* in former times. Of this Ensuing Discourse. Thomas Campion. **CP-CampT**

Market. Robert Earl Hayden. *Fr.* An Inference of Mexico. **CP-HaydR**

Market Adviser. Archie Randolph Ammons. **SP-AmmoA**

Market at Turk. Thom Gunn. **CP-GunnT**

Market Economy, The. Marge Piercy. **SP-PierM**

Market-Girl, The. Thomas Hardy. *Fr.* At Casterbridge Fair. **CP-HardT**

Market-Place, The. Walter de la Mare. **CP-DeLaW**

Market-Place, The. Howard Nemerov. **CP-NemeH**

Market this morning where dazzling rows. Morning in Padova. Richard Hugo. **CP-HugoR**

Marks / of the mother are. The Stretching of the Belly. Etheridge Knight. **SP-KnigE**

Marks and numbers / Cut in skin. Thomas Merton. **CP-MertT**

Mark's Sheep. Archibald MacLeish. **CP-MacLA**

Mark's sheep, I said, but they were only. Mark's Sheep. Archibald MacLeish. **CP-MacLA**

Marl Pits, The. Charles Tomlinson. **CP-TomlC**

Marl white road, the Dorée rushing cool, The. Tales of the Islands. Derek Walcott. **CP-WalcD**

Marlene Dietrich is singing a lament. The Blue Angel. Allen Ginsberg. **CP-GinsA**

Marlowe. Robert Lowell. **SP-LoweR**

Marmion. Sir Walter Scott.
    Battle, The ("Not far advanc'd was morning day").
       (Douglas and Marmion.) **SP-ScotW**
    Death of Marmion, The. **SP-ScotW**
    Edinburgh from the Pentland Hills.
       (Edinburgh From Blackford Hill.) **SP-ScotW**
    English Advance at Flodden, The. **SP-ScotW**
    Fitz-Eustace's Song. **SP-ScotW**
    Lochinvar. **SP-ScotW**
    Lords Strand of Northumberland, The. **SP-ScotW**
    Norham Castle. **SP-ScotW**
    Saint of Holy Island, The. **SP-ScotW**

Maroon with Silver Frost. Carl Sandburg. **CP-SandC**

Marooned by night in a canvas cathedral under bare bulbs. Flower Show. Louis MacNeice. **CP-MacNL**

Marostica, Val di Ser. Bassano del Grappa. Self-Portrait. Charles Wright. **SP-WrigC**

Marquis de Sade / Wasn't always mad, The. The Literary Scene. Ogden Nash. **CP-NashO**

Marquita had blossom fists. Portrait of a Child Settling Down for an Afternoon Nap. Carl Sandburg. **CP-SandC**

Marrakech. Richard Eberhart. **CP-EberR**

Marrèd Drives of Windsor, The, *parody of* William Shakespeare. Rudyard Kipling. **CP-KiplR** *Fr.* The Muse among the Motors.

Marriage. Wendell Berry. **CP-BerrW**

Marriage, A. Robert Creeley. **CP-CreeR**

Marriage. John Gould Fletcher. **SP-FletJ**

Marriage, A. Daniel Gerard Hoffman. **SP-HoffD**

Marriage. Marianne Craig Moore. **CP-MoorM**

Marriage. William Carlos Williams. **CP-WilW1**

Marriage aged one, A. The Anniversary. Ogden Nash. **CP-NashO**

Marriage, an Elegy, A. Wendell Berry. **CP-BerrW**

Marriage Bed, The. Alun Lewis. *Fr.* War Wedding. **CP-LewiA**

Marriage Ceremony, The. William Wordsworth. *Fr.* Ecclesiastical Sonnets. **CP-WorW2**

Marriage Counsel. John Updike. **CP-UpdiJ**

Marriage in the 'Sixties, A. Adrienne Rich. **CP-RicAE; SP-RicA1; SP-RicA2**

Marriage is not / a house or even a tent. Habitation. Margaret Atwood. **SP-AtwM1**

Marriage of Geraint, The. Tennyson. *Fr.* Idylls of the King. **CP-TennA**

Marriage of Heaven and Hell, The. William Blake. **CP-BlakW**
    Argument, The.
    Chorus: "Let the Priests of the Raven of dawn, no longer in deadly black."
    Memorable Fancy, A ("Angel came to me and said"). **NU**
    Memorable Fancy, A ("As I was walking among the fires of hell"). **NU**
    Memorable Fancy, A ("I was in a printing house in Hell & I saw the method in").
    Memorable Fancy, A ("Once I saw a Devil in a flame of fire").
    Memorable Fancy, A ("Prophets Isaiah and Ezekiel dined with me, and, The").
    Opposition Is True Friendship.
       (Plate 21.)
    Proverbs of Hell. **MeMBP**
       In Seed Time Learn. **FF**
       Pride of the Peacock, The. **FF; RaBo**
    Song of Liberty, A.
    Voice of the Devil, The. **NU**
       ("All Bibles or sacred codes have been the causes of the following Errors:.")

Marriage of Psyche, The. Kathleen Jessie Raine. **SP-RainK**
    House, The.
    Ring, The.

Marriage of Psyche and Cupid, *verse tr.fr.* Metamorphoses *by* Apuleius. Elizabeth Barrett Browning. **CP-BroEB**

Marriage of Souls, The. William Carlos Williams. **CP-WilW2**

Marriage of True Minds, The. William Shakespeare. *See* Sonnet 116: "Let me not to the marriage of true minds."

Marriage Portion, The. Adrienne Rich. **CP-RicAE**

Marriage Ritual, A. William Carlos Williams. **CP-WilW1**

Marriage Song for Florence and Harry, A. Louis Zukofsky. **CP-ZukLS**

Marriage, with Beasts. Mona Van Duyn. **SP-VanDM**

Marriages. Philip Larkin. **CP-LarkP**

Married and not for love. Geoffrey Hill. *Fr.* The Pentecost Castle. **CP-HillG**

Married Blues. Kenneth Rexroth. **SP-RexrK** *Fr.* Written to Music.

Married in June. David Herbert Lawrence. **CP-LawrD**

Married Man, The. Rudyard Kipling. **CP-KiplR**

Married People Going to Work. Jenny Joseph. **SP-JoseJ**

Married Walk in a Hot Place, A. Marge Piercy. **SP-PierM**

Married Woman, A. Thomas Carew. **CP-CareT**

Marrow, The. Theodore Roethke. **CP-RoetT**

Marrow unvisited, / And then, visited. Marry the Marrow. Charles Olson. **CP-OlsoC**

Marrucinus Asinius, that sinister. Catullus. *See* Carmen 12: "While everyone else is laughing & drinking."

Marry, and love thy Flavia, for, she. The Anagram. John Donne. *Fr.* Elegies. **CP-DonnJ**

Marry Nettie. Gertrude Stein. **CP-SteiG**

Marry the Marrow. Charles Olson. **CP-OlsoC**

Marrying left your maiden name disused. Maiden Name. Philip Larkin. **CP-LarkP**

Marrying the Hangman. Margaret Atwood. **SP-AtwM2**

Mars. Howard Nemerov. **CP-NemeH**

Mars is braw in crammasy. The Bonnie Broukit Bairn. "Hugh MacDiarmid." **SP-MacDH**

Marsh, The. William DeWitt Snodgrass. **SP-SnodW**

Marsh flat where they graze, The. Buffalo in Compound: Alberta. Margaret Atwood. **SP-AtwM1**

Marsh, Hawk. Margaret Atwood. **SP-AtwM2**

Marsh hummocks that were a sabbath hill. Sea Marshes in Winter. John Ciardi. **SP-CiarJ**

Marshal the quaint barren fogbeats in harbors. Prayer Not To Go to Paradise with the Asses. Kenneth Patchen. **CP-PatcK**

Marshall Field the First was spick and span while alive. Carl Sandburg. *Fr.* The People, Yes. **CP-SandC**

Marshall Washer. Hayden Carruth. **CP-CarHS**

Marshalling of the Achaians. Homer, *tr. by* George Meredith. **CP-MerG1** *Fr.* The Iliad.

Marston. Stephen Spender. **CP-SpenS**

Marsyas. James Merrill. **SP-MerrJ**

Marsyas, Midas and the Barber. Stephen Dobyns. **SP-DobyS**

Marten. John Clare. **SP-ClarJ**

Marten cat, long-shagged, of courage good, The. Marten. John Clare. **SP-ClarJ**

Martha. Walter de la Mare. **CP-DeLaW**

Martha. Audre Lorde. **SP-LordA**

Martha as the Angel Gabriel. Marge Piercy. **SP-PierM**

Martha MacElmain. Louise McNeill. **SP-McNeL**

Martha, Martha. Robert Herrick. **CP-HerrR**

Martha My Dear. John Lennon *and* Paul McCartney. **CP-Beatl**

Martha this is a catalog of days. Martha. Audre Lorde. **SP-LordA**

Martha was a girl after my own heart. She slept. Diaries. Anne Waldman. **SP-WaldA**

Martha's Vineyard. Ogden Nash. **CP-NashO**

Marthe Away (She is Away). Kenneth Rexroth. **SP-RexrK** *Fr.* Seven Poems for Marthe, My Wife.

Martial Cadenza. Wallace Stevens. **CP-StevW**

Martial Choreograph. Maya Angelou. **SP-AngeM**

Martial courage of a day is vain, The. William Wordsworth. **CP-WorW1**

Martial. Epigram XLVII, Book X, *See also Sir Richard Fanshawe's* "Things that make a life to please, The." Ben Jonson, *ad. fr. the Latin of Martial.* **CP-JonsB**

Martial, Lib. I. Epig. I. Byron. **CP-Byron**

Martial, thou gav'st far [*or* farre] nobler epigrams [*or* epigrammes]. To the Ghost of Martial. Ben Jonson. **CP-JonsB**

Martin and Katherine. William Carlos Williams. **CP-WilW1**

Martin I cannot say to you, old friend. Letter from Oaxaca to North Africa 1936. Malcolm Lowry. **CP-LowrM**

Martin Luther King, Malcolm X. Muriel Rukeyser. **CP-RukeM**

Martin Relph. Robert Browning. **CP-BroR2**

Martin said "every sane man" would hesitate to believe what we were now about to see. Martin's Predicament or Atlas Watches Every Evening. Thomas Merton. **CP-MertT**

Martin sat young upon his bed. St. Martin and the Beggar. Thom Gunn. **CP-GunnT**

Martin, Stevie, and Joe, and I. Snow Angels. Louise McNeill. **SP-McNeL**

Martini-time: time to draw the curtains and. The Garrison. Wystan Hugh Auden. **CP-AudeW**

Martin's Predicament or Atlas Watches Every Evening. Thomas Merton. **CP-MertT**

Martin's Puzzle. George Meredith. **CP-MerG1**

Martins: September. Walter de la Mare. **CP-DeLaW**

Martyr, The. Herman Melville. **SP-MelvH**

Martyr, A. Christina Georgina Rossetti. **CP-RosC2**

Martyr, A. Christina Georgina Rossetti. **CP-RosC3**

Martyr, The. Christina Georgina Rossetti. **CP-RosC3**

Martyr à la Mode. David Herbert Lawrence. **CP-LawrD**

Martyr Poets—did not tell, The. Emily Dickinson. **CP-DickE**

Martyrdom of Bishop Farrar, The. Ted Hughes. **SP-HughT**

Martyrdom of Saint Sebastian. Geoffrey Hill. *Fr.* Of Commerce and Society: Variations on a Theme. **CP-HillG**

Martyrium. Geoffrey Hill. *Fr.* Lachrimae; or Seven Tears Figured in Seven Passionate Pavans. **CP-HillG**

Martyrs, The. John Donne. *Fr.* A Litany. **CP-DonnJ**

Martyrs' Song. Christina Georgina Rossetti. **CP-RosC1**

Marvel [*or* Marvaill] no more although [*or* all tho]. Sir Thomas Wyatt. **CP-WyatT**

Marvel of Marvels. Christina Georgina Rossetti. **CP-RosC2**

Marvellous. Gilbert Sorrentino. **SP-SorrG**

Marvellous night, A. A Marvellous Woman. Leonard Cohen. **CP-CoheL**

Marvellous Woman, A. Leonard Cohen. **CP-CoheL**

Marvin McCabe. Hayden Carruth. **CP-CarHS**

Mary. William Blake. **CP-BlakW**

Mary. Phoebe Hesketh. **SP-HeskP**

Mary. Frederick Morgan. **SP-MorgF**

Mary and the Seasons. Kenneth Rexroth. **SP-RexrK** Spring Rain. **SP-RexrK**

Mary Bly. James Wright. **CP-WrigJ**

Mary called them buttonflowers. I called them by the name of. Donna Diane Wakoski. *Fr.* Fifteen Poems for a Lunar Eclipse None of Us Saw. **SP-WakoD**

Mary Desti's Ass. Frank O'Hara. **SP-OharF**

Mary Garvin. John Greenleaf Whittier. **CP-WhitJ**

Mary Gloster, The. Rudyard Kipling. **CP-KiplR**

Mary Gravely Jones. Adrienne Rich. **MDDM** *Fr.* Grandmothers. **SP-RicA2**

Mary green / cheerful & generous. Edward Estlin Cummings. **CP-CummE**

Mary Gulliver to Capt. Lemuel Gulliver. John Gay *and* Alexander Pope. **CP-PopeA**

Mary Hagan, Islandmagee, 1919. John Hewitt. **CP-HewiJ**

Mary has a thingamajig clamped on her ears. Manual System. Carl Sandburg. **CP-SandC**

Mary! I want a lyre with other strings. William Cowper. **CP-CowpW** (Sonnet to Mrs. Unwin.) **CP-CowpW**

Mary in the noisy seascape. Inlet. George Oppen. **CP-OppeG**

Mary Jane Colter, 1904. Adrienne Rich. *Fr.* Turning the Wheel. **SP-RicA2**

Mary Jane, she's after me. Black Hoyden. Donald Davie. **CP-DavDo**

Mary [*or Marie*] Magdalene. George Herbert. **CP-HerbG**

Mary Magdalene and the Other Mary. Christina Georgina Rossetti. **CP-RosC2**

Mary Magdalen's Blushe. Robert Southwell. **CP-SoutR**

Mary Magdalen's Complaint at Christ's Death. Robert Southwell. **CP-SoutR**

Mary McDonald. Allen Tate. **CP-TateA**

Mary Moody Emerson, R.I.P. Lewis Turco. **SP-TurcL**

Mary Morison. Robert Burns. **CP-BurnR**

Mary, Pity Women! Rudyard Kipling. **CP-KiplR**

Mary Queen of Scots. William Wordsworth. *Fr.* Poems Composed or Suggested During a Tour, in the Summer of 1833. **CP-WorW2**

Mary sat musing on the lamp-flame at the table. The Death of the Hired Man. Robert Frost. **CP-FrosR**

Mary Sheffield. James Dickey. **CP-DickJ**

Mary Sleeth. Muriel Rukeyser. **CP-RukeM**

Mary Stuart. Robert Lowell. **SP-LoweR**

Mary the Cook-Maid's Letter to Dr. Sheridan. Jonathan Swift. **CP-SwifJ**

Mary Trevellyn to Miss Roper. Arthur Hugh Clough. **FaBoVe** *Fr.* Amours de Voyage. **SP-ClouA**

Mary under the hawthorn / sat waiting. Mary. Phoebe Hesketh. **SP-HeskP**

Mary Winslow. Robert Lowell. **SP-LoweR**

Mary Wollstonecraft and Fuseli. Robert Browning. **CP-BroR2**

Mary, your great. Jesus Suckles. Anne Sexton. **CP-SextA**

Maryland, Virginia, Caroline. Emblems. Allen Tate. **CP-TateA**

Mary's Fancy. Robert Creeley. **CP-CreeR**

Mary's Lullaby. John Hewitt. **CP-HewiJ**

Mary's Son. Rudyard Kipling. **CP-KiplR**

Mary's Song. Sylvia Plath. **CP-PlatS**

Mary's Song. Anne Sexton. **CP-SextA**

Mascot, The. Ted Hughes. *Fr.* Scapegoats and Rabies. **SP-HughT**

Mascots. Carl Sandburg. **CP-SandC**

Mask, The. Elizabeth Barrett Browning. **CP-BroEB**

Mask, The. John Hewitt. **CP-HewiJ**

Mask, A. John Milton. **OxAEP-1** *Fr.* Comus; a Masque Presented at Ludlow Castle.

"Nay, lady, sit; if I but wave this wand." **OxAEP-1**

Mask, A. John Milton. *See* Comus; a Masque Presented at Ludlow Castle.

Mask, A. John Milton. *See* The Star That Bids the Shepherd Fold.

Mask. Carl Sandburg. **CP-SandC**

Mask. Carl Sandburg. **CP-SandC**

Mask, The. William Butler Yeats. **CP-YeatW**

Mask, a perpetual natural disguiser of herself, A. Visor'd. Walt Whitman. **CP-WhitW**

Mask and Knife, The. Jean Garrigue. **SP-GarrJ**

Mask [*or* Masque] of Anarchy, The. Percy Bysshe Shelley. **CP-ShelP** Cancelled Stanza of the Mask of Anarchy.

Mask of Cupid, The. Edmund Spenser. **OBSC** *Fr.* The Faerie Queene. **CP-Spens** (Masque of Cupid, The.)

"First was Fancy, like a lovely boy, The." **NOBE**

"Noble Mayde, still standing, all this vewd, The." **PoEL-1**

Mask of Mutability, The. Edmund Spenser. **OBSC** *Fr.* The Faerie Queene. **CP-Spens**

(Pageant of the Seasons and the Months, The.) **OXAEP-1**

(Seasons, The.) **GN**

Mask stares down at me, The. How Do You Tell a Story? Diane Wakoski. **SP-WakoD**

Mask thy wisdom with delight. Ralph Waldo Emerson. **CP-EmerR**

Masked Face, The. Thomas Hardy. **CP-HardT**

Masked Shrew, The. Isabella Gardner. **CP-GardI**

Masks without faces. Charles Henri Ford. **SP-FordC** *Fr.* Emblems of Arachne.

Masque of Augurs, The. Ben Jonson.
  Ballad: "Though it may seem rude." **CP-JonsB**
  "Which way and whence the lightning flew." **CP-JonsB**

Masque of Beauty, The. Ben Jonson.
  "Had those that dwell in error foul." **CP-JonsB**
  "If all these Cupids now were blind." **CP-JonsB**
  "So beauty on the waters stood." **CP-JonsB**
  "Still turn, and imitate the heaven." **CP-JonsB**
  "When Love at first did move." **CP-JonsB**

Masque of Blackness, The. Geoffrey Hill. **NoAM** *Fr.* Lachrimae; or Seven Tears Figured in Seven Passionate Pavans. **CP-HillG**

Masque of Blackness, The. Ben Jonson.
  "Daughters of the subtle flood." **CP-JonsB**
  "Now Dian, with her burning face." **CP-JonsB**
  "Sound, sound aloud / The welcome of the orient flood." **CP-JonsB**

Masque of Cupid, The. Edmund Spenser. *See* The Mask of Cupid.

Masque of Hymen. Ben Jonson.
  "Bid all profane away." **CP-JonsB**
  Epithalamion: "Glad time is at his point arrived." **CP-JonsB**
  "Now, now begin to set." **CP-JonsB**
  "O know to end, as to begin." **CP-JonsB**
  "These, these are they." **CP-JonsB**
  "Think yet how night doth waste." **CP-JonsB**

Masque of Mercy, A. Robert Frost. **CP-FrosR**

Masque of Plenty, The. Rudyard Kipling. **CP-KiplR**

Masque of Queen Bersabe, The. Algernon Charles Swinburne. **SP-SwinA**

Masque of Queens, The, *sels.* Ben Jonson.
  "Help, help all tongues to celebrate this wonder." **CP-JonsB**
  "Who, Virtue, can thy power forget." **CP-JonsB**

Witches' Charms, The.
  Charm[e]. **CP-JonsB**

Masque of Reason, A. Robert Frost. **CP-FrosR**

Mass. John Hewitt. **CP-HewiJ**

Mass Ave., Cambridge, Mass. James Schuyler. *Fr.* Four Poems. **CP-SchuJ**

Mass hysteria, wave after breaking wave. Willoware Cup. James Merrill. **SP-MerrJ**

Mass Man. Derek Walcott. **CP-WalcD**

Massachusetts. Robert Creeley. **CP-CreeR**

Massachusetts. John Greenleaf Whittier. **CP-WhitJ**

Mass. Mental Health. John Updike. *Fr.* Waiting Rooms. **CP-DickE**

Massachusetts to Virginia. John Greenleaf Whittier. **CP-WhitJ**

Massacre, The. Walter de la Mare. **CP-DeLaW**

Massacre of Perugia, The. Christina Georgina Rossetti. **CP-RosC3**

Massacre of the Innocents, The, *sels.* Wystan Hugh Auden. *Fr.* For the Time Being; a Christmas Oratorio. **CP-AudeW**

Massed in her creaseless black. The Fat Woman. Walter de la Mare. **CP-DeLaW**

Masses. Carl Sandburg. **CP-SandC**

Masses and Classes. David Herbert Lawrence. **CP-LawrD**

Massive engines lift beautifully from the deck. The Teeth Mother Naked at Last. Robert Bly. **SP-BlyR**

Massy Ways Carried across These Heights, The. William Wordsworth. **CP-WorW2**

Mast, The. Charles Olson. **CP-OlsoC**

Mastah drink his ol' Made'a. A Preference. Paul Laurence Dunbar. **CP-DunbP**

Master, The. Hilda Doolittle. **CP-DoolH**

Master, The. Seamus Heaney. **SP-HeanS** *Fr.* Sweeney Redivivus.

Master, The. Frederick Morgan. **SP-MorgF**

Master, The. Edwin Arlington Robinson. **CP-RobiE**

Master & Man. Donald Davie. **CP-DavDo**

Master and Mistress. Stanley Jasspon Kunitz. **CP-KuniS**

Master and the Leaves, The. Thomas Hardy. **CP-HardT**

Master and the slave go hand in hand, The. Sonnet. Edwin Arlington Robinson. **CP-RobiE**

Master at a Mediterranean Port, The. Howard Nemerov. **CP-NemeH**

Master closed the door. The unmodern words, The. Canto IX. Louis MacNeice. *Fr.* Autumn Sequel. **CP-MacNL**

Master-Cook, The, *parody of* Chaucer. Rudyard Kipling. **CP-KiplR** *Fr.* Land and Sea Tales.

Master Cotton Spinner. Phoebe Hesketh. **SP-HeskP**

Master deep-eyed, A. Nicholas Vachel Lindsay. *Fr.* The Master of the Dance. **CP-LindV**

Master, Grieved with Age, The. Hayden Carruth. **CP-CarHS**

Master Hugues of Saxe-Gotha. Robert Browning. **CP-BroR1**

Master Is Come, and Calleth for Thee, The. Christina Georgina Rossetti. **CP-RosC1**

Master Keng Sang Chu, a disciple of Lao Tzu. Keng Sang Chu. Chuang Tzu, *tr. fr. Chinese by* Thomas Merton. **CP-MertT**

Master Ki had eight sons. Good Fortune. Chuang Tzu, *tr. fr. Chinese by* Thomas Merton. **CP-MertT**

Master Meng said: There was once a fine forest on the Ox Mountain. The Ox Mountain Parable. Mencius, *tr. fr. Chinese by* Thomas Merton. **CP-MertT**

Master of a house (as I have read), A. A Good Husband. Robert Herrick. **CP-HerrR**

Master of All. Robert Creeley. **CP-CreeR**

Master of beauty, craftsman of the snowflake. John Berryman. **PAI; UnPo** *Fr.* Eleven Addresses to the Lord. **CP-BerrJ**

Master of eloquence and Rome's potent line. Catullus. *See* Carmen 49: "Silver-tongued among the sons of Rome."

Master of Rime told me, You must learn to lose heart, The. Robert Duncan. **SP-DuncR** *Fr.* The Structure of Rime.

Master of the Dance, The. Nicholas Vachel Lindsay. **CP-LindV**
  "Master deep-eyed, A."
  "Now soldiers we seem."
  "We thought to be proud."

Master of the Golden Glow, The. James Schuyler. **CP-SchuJ**

Master of the GREEK and ROMAN page, The. Epitaph on Henry Fielding, Esq. Christopher Smart. **SP-SmarC**

Master of the Winter Landscape, The. Leonard Nathan. **SP-NathL**

Master played the bishop's pawn, The. Atherton's Gambit. Edwin Arlington Robinson. **CP-RobiE**

Master-Player, The. Paul Laurence Dunbar. **CP-DunbP**

Master Song. Leonard Cohen. **CP-CoheL**

Master Speed, The. Robert Frost. **CP-FrosR**

Master Surveyor, you that first began. An Expostulation with Inigo Jones. Ben Jonson. **CP-JonsB**

Master, this is Thy Servant. He is rising eight weeks old. His Apologies. Rudyard Kipling. **CP-KiplR**

Master Tung Kwo asked Chuang. Where Is Tao? Chuang Tzu, *tr. fr. Chinese by* Thomas Merton. **CP-MertT**

Masterful. William Matthews. **SP-MattW**

Masterly lens-polisher, A. The Spectacle of Truth. John Hewitt. **CP-HewiJ**

Masterpieces in my sleep. A suppressed. Roy Fisher. **SP-FishR** *Fr.* New Diversions.

Masters, The. Hart Crane. **CP-CranH**

Masters, The. Paul Laurence Dunbar. **CP-DunbP**

Master's in the Garden Again. John Crowe Ransom. *Fr.* Sixteen Poems in Eight Pairings. **SP-RansJ**

Masters of War. "Bob Dylan." **CP-DylaB**

Masters, the mock orange is blooming in Syracuse without scent, having been bred. Of Distress Being Humiliated by the Classical Chinese Poets. Hayden Carruth. **CP-CarHS**

Masts at Dawn. Robert Penn Warren. **SP-WarrR**

Matachines, The. Charles Tomlinson. **CP-TomlC**

Matador. Richard Eberhart. **CP-EberR**

Match. Donald Hall. **CP-HallD**

Match, The. Andrew Marvell. **CP-MarvA**

Matchstick-Viewed-without-Regard-to-Its-Outer-Surface, A. Kenneth Patchen. **CP-PatcK**

Mater Jesu mei. Ad Matrem Virginem. Gerard Manley Hopkins. **CP-HopkG**

Mater Triumphans. Robert Louis Stevenson. **CP-StevR**

Material. Donald Hall. **CP-HallD**

Maternal Grief. William Wordsworth. **CP-WorW1**

Math. James Dickey. **CP-DickJ**

Mathematical Problem, A. Samuel Taylor Coleridge. **CP-ColeS**

Mathematical Secret, and the Apron, The. Charles Olson. **CP-OlsoC**

Mathematicians and physics men, The. Robinson Jeffers. **CP-JefR3**

Mathematics. John Hewitt. **CP-HewiJ**

Mathematics, The. Gilbert Sorrentino. **SP-SorrG**

Mathematics of Encounter. Isabella Gardner. **CP-GardI**

Mather, mother, let me go. The Queen and the Young Princess. Stevie Smith. **CP-SmitS**

Mathilde in Normandy. Adrienne Rich. **CP-RicAE**

Matilda Gathering Flowers. Dante Alighieri, *tr. by* Shelley. **CP-ShelP** *Fr.* Purgatorio. *Fr. Divina Commedia.*

Matilda! I have heard a sweet tune played. To Matilda Betham from a Stranger. Samuel Taylor Coleridge. **CP-ColeS**

Matilda Jane. "Lewis Carroll." **CP-CarrL** *Fr.* Sylvie and Bruno Concluded.

Matilde, sleeping / that feverish sleep, a day or a year. Final. Pablo Neruda, *tr. fr. Spanish by* Ben Belitt. **SP-NeruP**

Matin Pour Matta. Charles Henri Ford. **SP-FordC**

Matin sur le Port. Albert Samain, *tr. fr. French by* John Hewitt. **CP-HewiJ**

Matinees. James Merrill. **SP-MerrJ**

Matins. John Berryman. **CP-BerrJ**

Matins. George Herbert. *See* I cannot ope mine eyes.

Matins. Denise Levertov. **CP-LeveD**

Matins [*or* Mattens], or Morning Prayer. Robert Herrick. **CP-HerrR**

Matisse at the Modern, Magritte at the Met. Lawrence Ferlinghetti. **SP-FerlL**

Matisse: "The Red Studio." William DeWitt Snodgrass. **SP-SnodW**

Matlock Bath. Sir John Betjeman. **CP-BetjJ**

Matriarchly. Anne Waldman. **SP-WaldA**

Matris pennigerum alites Amorum. *acc. by English translation.* Thomas Campion. **CP-CampT**

Matrix. Roy Fisher.
"Blood-red and blue glass." **SP-FishR**
"Doctor Meinière—." **SP-FishR**
"Eight or nine yards." **SP-FishR**
"In long shapes over the channel's." **SP-FishR**
"Ocean-lights go flashing." **SP-FishR**
"Religious garden." **SP-FishR**
"So, the water gate." **SP-FishR**
"Sugar flowers." **SP-FishR**
"There is a place of cypress fingers." **SP-FishR**
"There's a time, finally." **SP-FishR**

Matrix of your legs. Sleep. Robert Creeley. **CP-CreeR**

Matron of Jedborough and Her Husband, The. William Wordsworth. **CP-WorW1**

Matter, The. Charles Kenneth Williams. **CP-WillC**

Matter for mirth, Cato, & a smile, A. Carmen 56. Catullus. *Fr.* Carmina. **CP-Catul**

Matter of Locality, A. Paul Laurence Dunbar. **CP-DunbP**

Matthew. William Wordsworth. **CP-WorW1**

Matthew 8; I Am Not Worthy that Thou Should'st Come Under my Roofe. Bible, *N.T.* **CP-CrasR,** *tr. by* Richard Crashaw; *Fr.* St. Matthew.

Matthew 16:25; Whosoever Shall Loose His Life. Bible, *N.T.* **CP-CrasR,** *tr. by* Richard Crashaw; *Fr.* St. Matthew.

Matthew 22; Neither Durst Any Man from that Day Aske Him Any More Questions. Bible, *N.T.* **CP-CrasR,** *tr. by* Richard Crashaw; *Fr.* St. Matthew.

Matthew 23; Yee Build the Sepulchres of the Prophets. Bible, *N.T.* **CP-CrasR,** *tr. by* Richard Crashaw; *Fr.* St. Matthew.

Matthew 27; And He Answered Them Nothing. Bible, *N.T.* **CP-CrasR,** *tr. by* Richard Crashaw; *Fr.* St. Matthew.

Matthew 28; Come See the Place where the Lord Lay. Bible, *N.T.* **CP-CrasR,** *tr. by* Richard Crashaw; *Fr.* St. Matthew.

Matthew and Mark and Luke and holy John. Epi-Strauss-ium. Arthur Hugh Clough. **SP-ClouA**

Matthew VIII, 28 ff. Richard Wilbur. **CP-WilbR**

Mature love you say but my wounds come out through inner temple. Anne Waldman. **SP-WaldA** *Fr.* Iovis Omnia Plena.

Maturity. Philip Larkin. **CP-LarkP**

Maturity only enhances mystery. Emily Dickinson. **SP-DickE**

Mauberly (1920). Ezra Pound. *Fr.* Hugh Selwyn Mauberley. (Life and Contacts). **SP-PounE**
Age Demanded, The.
"For three years, diabolus in the scale."
"Luini in porcelain!"
"Scattered Moluccas."
"Turned from the 'eau-forte'."

Mauberly's Son: A Summary. John Hewitt. **CP-HewiJ**

Mauchline Wedding, The. Robert Burns. **CP-BurnR**

Maud [A Monodrama]. Tennyson. **CP-TennA**
"Birds in the high Hall-garden." **EBVVPR; NAEL-2; PeVV**
"Cold and clear-cut face, why come you so cruelly meek." **EBVVPR**

"Come into the garden, Maud." **AWP; EBEvV; EBVV; EBVVPR; EnVR; FHYEP; FaBV; FiP; NOBE; NOBVV; OAEL-2; OXAEP-2; PlP; PoE; UV; VPP**
(Come into the Garden, Maud.) **PlP**
(Song: "Come into the garden, Maud.") **AWP**

"Courage, poor heart of stone!"

"Dead, long dead." **EBVVPR**

"Did I hear it half in a doze."

"Fault was mine, the fault was mine, The."

"Go not, happy day." **EBVV**

"Her brother is coming back tonight."

"I hate the dreadful hollow behind the little wood." **EBVVPR**

"I have led her home, my love, my only friend." **CBLP; ChER; EBVV; ELP; FiP; MeMBP; NAEL-2; NOBVV**
"There is none like her, none." **FaBoEn; OBNC**

"I was walking a mile." **EBVV**

"Long have I sighed for a calm; God grant I may find it at last!" **EBVVPR**

"Maud has a garden of roses." **FHYEP**
Sleeping House, The. **FaBoEn; OBNC**

"Million emeralds break from the ruby-budded lime, A."

"Morning arises stormy and pale." **EBVVPR**
"Ah, what shall I be at fifty." **NAEL-2**

My Day. **NAEL-2; NOBVV**

"My life has crept so long on a broken wing."

"O[h] that 'twere possible." **BoLoP; HBV; IMW; NAEL-2; NOBE; NOBVV; OAEL-2; OBEV; OBVV; PoE**

"Rivulet crossing my ground."

"Scorned, to be scorned by one that I scorn."

"See what a lovely shell." **GN**
(Shell, The.) **GN**

"She came to the village church." **EBVV; NAEL-2**

"Sick, am I sick of a jealous dread?"

"So dark a mind within me dwells."

"Strange, that I felt so gay."

"This lump of earth has left his estate."
"Catch not my breath, O clamorous heart." **NAEL-2**

"Voice by the cedar tree, A."

Maud Gonne Rode Out on a White Horse to Coolgreany. James Liddy. **CP-LiddJ**

Maud has a garden of roses. Tennyson. **FHYEP** *Fr.* Maud [A Monodrama]. **CP-TennA**
Sleeping House, The. **FaBoEn; OBNC**

Maud Muller. John Greenleaf Whittier. **CP-WhitJ**
Saddest Words, The. **ImPo**

Maud went to college. Sadie and Maud. Gwendolyn Brooks. **InPK; MoP; NOBA; NoAM; TAP** *Fr.* A Street in Bronzeville. **SP-BrooG**

Maude Clare. Christina Georgina Rossetti. **CP-RosC1**

Maudgalyâyana Saw Hell. Gary Snyder. **CP-SnydG** *Fr.* Burning. *Fr.* Myths and Texts.

Maudlin. Sylvia Plath. **CP-PlatS**

Maundy Thursday. Wilfred Owen. **CP-OwenW**

Maundy Thursday. Christina Georgina Rossetti. **CP-RosC2**

Maundy Thursday's Candles. Donald Hall. **CP-HallD**

Maureen in England, Joseph in Guelph. The Wishbone. Paul Muldoon. **SP-MuldP**

Mauriac, Green (Julian). Homage to Conor Cruise O'Brien. James Liddy. **CP-LiddJ**

Mausoleum, The. Charles Tomlinson. **CP-TomlC**

Mauve into purple, bent on foam-green stems. For Jean Migrenne. Marilyn Hacker. **SP-HackM**

Max Ernst. Charles Henri Ford. *Fr.* Four Elegies. **SP-FordC**

Max Schling, Max Schling, Lend Me Your Green Thumb. Ogden Nash. **CP-NashO**

Maxim. Rudyard Kipling. **OtMeF** *Fr.* Certain Maxims of Hafiz. **CP-KiplR**

Maximilian Esterhazy. Stevie Smith. **CP-SmitS**

Maxims of Sisyphus, The. Delmore Schwartz. **SP-SchwD**

Maximus. David Herbert Lawrence. **CP-LawrD**

Maximus, at the Harbor. Charles Olson. **SP-OlsoC** *Fr.* The Maximus Poems.

Maximus, from Dogtown-1. Charles Olson. **SP-OlsoC** *Fr.* The Maximus Poems.

Maximus, in Gloucester Sunday, LXV. Charles Olson. **SP-OlsoC** *Fr.* The Maximus Poems.

Maximus Letter # Whatever. Charles Olson. **SP-OlsoC** *Fr.* The Maximus Poems.

May we live, my Lesbia, love while we may. Catullus. *See* Carmen 5: "Lesbia / live with me."

May Weather. Philip Larkin. **CP-LarkP**

May well befall the common weal. Malcolm Lowry. **CP-LowrM**

May with its light behaving. May. Wystan Hugh Auden. **CP-AudeW**

May you bless the union of your mother and father. *see also* Beside My Son. Leonard Cohen. **CP-CoheL**

Maya. Al Young. **CP-YounA**

Maya Against Itzas. Charles Olson. **CP-OlsoC**

Maya-Quechua Indians plodding to market on feet as flat and tough as toads were semi-starving, The. Guatemala: 1964. Charles Kenneth Williams. **SP-WillC**

Mayakovsky / has it! Over Brooklyn Bridge. Charles Tomlinson. **CP-TomlC**

Mayakovsky. Frank O'Hara. **SP-OharF**

Mayakovsky was right. Kiss. Al Young. **CP-YounA**

Mayan Ground, The. George Oppen. **CP-OppeG**

Mayapple Hill. Louise McNeill. **SP-McNeL**

Maybe. Langston Hughes. **SP-HughL**

Maybe. David Herbert Lawrence. **CP-LawrD**

Maybe. Mary Oliver. **SP-OlivM**

Maybe. Carl Sandburg. **CP-SandC**

Maybe because they're so damn frigging rich. Hayden Carruth. *Fr.* The Sleeping Beauty. **CP-CarHL**

Maybe god / is a child. Edward Estlin Cummings. **CP-CummE**

Maybe he believes me, maybe not. Maybe. Carl Sandburg. **CP-SandC**

Maybe I should go back to the white leather. Desnos Reading the Palms of Men on Their Way to the Gas Chambers. Stephen Berg. **SP-BergS**

Maybe I shouldn't but I must tell you. A Brand New Morning Love Song. Al Young. **CP-YounA**

Maybe I shouldn't tell you this—you are. Trillium. Robert Pack. **SP-PackR**

Maybe I'll win the Irish Sweepstakes. Eaten by Butterflies. Charles Bukowski. **SP-BukC2**

Maybe I'm Amazed. Jim Carroll. **SP-CarrJ**

Maybe I'm seven in the open field—. Sudden Journey. Tess Gallagher. **SP-GallT**

Maybe I'm still hurting. Coming Back to You. Leonard Cohen. **CP-CoheL**

Maybe it ain't right. Live and Let Live. Langston Hughes. **SP-HughL**

Maybe it's his wife. Exercise. William Carlos Williams. **CP-WilW2**

Maybe it's not as bad as we like to think: no melodramatic rendings, sackcloths, nothing so acute. Failure. Charles Kenneth Williams. **SP-WillC**

Maybe Love. Allen Ginsberg. **CP-GinsA**

Maybe love will come. Maybe Love. Allen Ginsberg. **CP-GinsA**

Maybe morning lightens over. For My Grandmother, Bridget Halpin. Michael Hartnett. **SP-HarMi**

Maybe the martyrology until today. Elegy for a Trappist. Thomas Merton. **CP-MertT**

Maybe they believed anything that solid. Clachard. Richard Hugo. **CP-HugoR**

Maybe this summer I shall revisit Palermo. Vucceria. James Fenton. **SP-FentJ**

Maybe twenty of us in the late afternoon. 3rd November 1976. Roy Fisher. **SP-FishR**

Maybe we knew each other better. Coda. Louis MacNeice. **CP-MacNL**

Maybe You Can't Take It with You, but Look What Happens When You Leave It Behind. Ogden Nash. **CP-NashO**

Maybe you ranted in the grove. Ezry. Archibald MacLeish. **CP-MacLA**

Maybe you spoke to someone. City. Gerrit Achterberg, *tr. fr. Dutch by* Adrienne Rich. **CP-RicAE**

Mayday on Holderness. Ted Hughes. **SP-HughT**

Mayday: two came to field in such wise. Bucolics. Sylvia Plath. **CP-PlatS**

Maydes are simple, some men say. Thomas Campion. **CP-CampT**

Mayflies. Brendan Galvin. **SP-GalvB**

Mayflower. Sylvia Plath. **CP-PlatS**

Mayflower Cafè, the Vets' Club on, The. Kale Soup. Brendan Galvin. **SP-GalvB**

Mayflowers, The. John Greenleaf Whittier. **CP-WhitJ**

Mayfly. Louis MacNeice. **CP-MacNL**

Mayor of Gary, The. Carl Sandburg. **CP-SandC**

May's Love. Elizabeth Barrett Browning. **CP-BroEB**

May's, whose mouth was. A Death in the West. Donald Davie. **CP-DavDo**

Maytime. Gilbert Sorrentino. **SP-SorrG**

Mazdaism / has overcome. Charles Olson. **CP-OlsoC**

Maze, The. Wystan Hugh Auden. **CP-AudeW**

Maze, The. Vincent Bourne, *tr. fr. Latin by* William Cowper. **CP-CowpW**

Maze. Richard Eberhart. **CP-EberR**

Maze under the loess, The. The Dead. Randall Jarrell. **CP-JarrR**

Mazed in a splay of lonely corridors. Corridor. John Hewitt. **CP-HewiJ**

Mazeppa. Byron. **CP-Byron**

Mazuma, the jack, the shekels, the kale, The. Carl Sandburg. *Fr.* The People, Yes. **CP-SandC**

M.B. William Carlos Williams. **CP-WilW1**

McAndrew's Hymn. Rudyard Kipling. **CP-KiplR**

McKane's Falls. James Merrill. **SP-MerrJ**

McPherson's Farewell. Robert Burns. *See* Farewell, ye dungeons dark and strong.

Me. Charles Bukowski. **SP-BukC1**

Me and him / Him and me. Us. Shel Silverstein. **SP-SilS2**

Me and My Giant. Shel Silverstein. **SP-SilS2**

Me and my gift: kind Lord, behold. Christina Georgina Rossetti. **CP-RosC2**

Me and the Mule. Langston Hughes. **SP-HughL**

Me and the Rock. Stanley Jasspon Kunitz. **CP-KuniS**

Me, change! Me, alter! Emily Dickinson. **CP-DickE**

Me—come! My dazzled face. Emily Dickinson. **CP-DickE**

Me from Myself—to banish. Emily Dickinson. **CP-DickE**

Me, go to Florida! This Is Pioneer Weather. William Carlos Williams. **CP-WilW2**

Me happy, night, night full of brightness. Ezra Pound. **ErPo; InvP; MeMAP; VGW** *Fr.* Homage to Sextus Propertius. **SP-PounE** (Elegy VII.) **ErPo; InvP; VGW**

Me! he says, hand on his chest. Myself I Sing. George Oppen. **CP-OppeG**

Me Imperturbe. Walt Whitman. **CP-WhitW**

Me list no more to sing. Sir Thomas Wyatt. **CP-WyatT**

Me miserable! which way shall I fly. John Milton. **PoE** *Fr.* Book IV. **OAEL-1** *Fr.* Paradise Lost. **CP-MiltJ**

Me n' Asræ perferre jubes oblivia? et Asrae. *with tr. of the Latin.* Samuel Taylor Coleridge. **CP-ColeS**

Me on my back, you on your front. Love Poem. Barton Sutter. **SP-SuttB**

Me prove it now—Whoever doubt. Emily Dickinson. **CP-DickE**

Me-Stew. Shel Silverstein. **SP-SilS2**

Me that 'ave been what I've been. Chant-Pagan. Rudyard Kipling. **CP-KiplR**

Me thinks when Kings, Prophets, and Poets dye. Elegie, An. Samuel Holland. *Fr.* Elegies, 1660. **CP-LoveR**

Me thought, (last night) love in an anger came. The Dream. Robert Herrick. **CP-HerrR**

Me thoughte thus: that [h]it was May. The Dream. Geoffrey Chaucer. **FiP; PBBP** *Fr.* The Book of the Duchess. **CP-ChauG**

Me Time has Crook'd. no good Workman. From Cratetos. William Blake. **CP-BlakW**

Me to whatever state the Gods assign. To Delia. William Cowper. **CP-CowpW**

Me too, perchance, in future days. Stanzas on Milton's Remains. William Cowper. **CP-CowpW**

Me up at does. Edward Estlin Cummings. **CP-CummE**

Me you often meet / In London's crowded street. Christina Georgina Rossetti. **CP-RosC3**

Mea Culpa. Isabella Gardner. **CP-GardI**

Meadow, The. Wendell Berry. **CP-BerrW**

Meadow Bridge. James Dickey. **CP-DickJ**

Meadow Foam. Leonard Nathan. **SP-NathL**

Meadow House. Hayden Carruth. **CP-CarHS**

Meadow in Summer. Carl Sandburg. **CP-SandC**

Meadow Lark, The. Paul Laurence Dunbar. **CP-DunbP**

Meadow Mouse, The. Theodore Roethke. **CP-RoetT**

Meadow surrounds us on three sides, The. Charles Wright. *Fr.* Three Poems of Departure. **SP-WrigC**

Meadows of golden dust. The silver. In Midas' Country. Sylvia Plath. **CP-PlatS**

Meadowsweet centuries friends allowably carol. Spirea. Louis Zukofsky. **CP-ZukLS**

,Mean- / hum / a)now / (nit. Edward Estlin Cummings. **CP-CummE**

Mean deaths of the spirit in this age, The. Dying Lawrence. John Clellon Holmes. **SP-HolmJ**

Mean fate surrounds our life with fear, A. The World Is a Round Earthenware Plate. Pablo Antonio Cuadra, *tr. fr. Spanish by* Thomas Merton. **CP-MertT**

Mean grimy houses, shades drawn. May I Ask You a Question, Mr. Youngstown Sheet & Tube? Kenneth Patchen. **CP-PatcK**

Mean Mr. Mustard. The Beatles. **CP-Beatl**

Mean old murderous Leadbelly. The Midnight Special Revisited. Al Young. **CP-YounA**

Mean while the new-baptiz'd, who yet remain'd. Book II. John Milton. *Fr.* Paradise Regained [*or* Regain'd]. **CP-MiltJ**

Meane in Our Meanes, A. Robert Herrick. **CP-HerrR**

Meane, The ("Imparitie doth ever discord bring"). Robert Herrick. **CP-HerrR**

Meane, The ("'Tis much among the filthy to be clean"). Robert Herrick. **CP-HerrR**

Meane Things Overcome Mighty. Robert Herrick. **CP-HerrR**

Meaning by possession total possession. My Hypertrophic Devotion. Tom Clark. **SP-ClarT**

Meaning of Death, The. Allen Tate. **CP-TateA**

Meaning of Life, The. Kenneth Patchen. **CP-PatcK**

Meaning of Life, The. Allen Tate. **CP-TateA**

Meaning of the Look, The. Elizabeth Barrett Browning. **CP-BroEB**

Meaningless Institution, A. Allen Ginsberg. **CP-GinsA**

Meaningless Poem. Richard Eberhart. **CP-EberR**

Means there is something to hold. The Fact of a Doorframe. Adrienne Rich. **SP-RicA1**

Meantime a bird in a tree. The Bird in the Tree. Malcolm Lowry. **CP-LowrM**

Meantool amuck with her. Muck with her mean tool ah? Geared I. Catullus. *See* Carmen 94: "Stuffing, O'Toole naturally stuffs with his tool."

Meantool inhabits in style three times ten hewed acres, forty. Catullus. *See* Carmen 115: "O'Toole is the proud master of."

Meantool reconnoiters Pipléa scanning Their mountain. Catullus. *See* Carmen 105: "O'Toole / attempting an entry of the *mons Parnassus*."

Meanwhile [*or* Mean while] the Adversary of God and Man. John Milton. **EBEV,** *ll.* 629–734; **DL,** *ll.* 629–841; **OBNV** *Fr.* Book II. **FHYEP; NAEL-1; OxAEP-1** *Fr.* Paradise Lost. **CP-MiltJ**

(Sin and Death.) **OBNV,** *ll.* 629–889;

Meanwhile the choleric Captain strode wrathful away to the council. The War-Token. Henry Wadsworth Longfellow. **PAH** *Fr.* John Alden. *Fr.* The Courtship of Miles Standish. **SP-LongH**

Meanwhile the heinous [*or* hainous] and despiteful [*or* despightfull] act. Book X. John Milton. **FHYEP** *Fr.* Paradise Lost. **CP-MiltJ**

Meanwhile, the last of the human faculties. Happy on Heimaey. "Hugh MacDiarmid." **SP-MacDH**

Meanwhile the stalwart Miles Standish was marching steadily northward. Henry Wadsworth Longfellow. **TreFS** *Fr.* The March of Miles Standish. *Fr.* The Courtship of Miles Standish. **SP-LongH**

Meanwhile the stalwart Miles Standish was marching steadily northward. The March of Miles Standish. Henry Wadsworth Longfellow. *Fr.* The Courtship of Miles Standish. **SP-LongH**

Meanwhile the tepid caves and fens and shores. John Milton. **PBBP** *Fr.* Book VII. *Fr.* Paradise Lost. **CP-MiltJ**

Mearl Blankenship. Muriel Rukeyser. **CP-RukeM**

Mease brags of Pullets which he eats; but Mease. Upon Mease. Robert Herrick. **CP-HerrR**

Measure, The. Elizabeth Barrett Browning. **CP-BroEB**

Measure, The. Robert Creeley. **CP-CreeR**

Measure. Charles Olson. **CP-OlsoC**

Measure by your footsteps, sd the voice, the days. Kin. Charles Olson. **CP-OlsoC**

Measure of Casualness, A. Robert Ranke Graves. **CP-GravR**

Measure of Poetry, The. Howard Nemerov. **CP-NemeH**

Measured blood beats out the year's delay, The. Simple Autumnal. Louise Bogan. **CP-BogaL**

Measured Tread, A. Donald Davie. **CP-DavDo**

Measurements. John Ciardi. **SP-CiarJ**

Meat. Thom Gunn. **CP-GunnT**

Meat without Mirth. Robert Herrick. **CP-HerrR**

Meathooks, notebooks, / the whole city sky palely flaming. Depression in Early Spring. Erica Jong. **SP-JongE**

Meben. Kenneth Patchen. **CP-PatcK**

Mecanic on Duty at All Times. Miller Williams. **SP-WillM**

Mecca. Thomas Merton. *Fr.* East with Ibn Battuta. *Fr.* East. *Fr.* The Geography of Lograire. **CP-MertT**

Meccans are very elegant and clean in their dress, The. Mecca. Thomas Merton. *Fr.* East with Ibn Battuta. *Fr.* East. *Fr.* The Geography of Lograire. **CP-MertT**

Mechanic, The. Robert Creeley. **CP-CreeR**

Mechanic, The. Diane Wakoski. **SP-WakoD**

Mechanical Heart, The. Kenneth Patchen. **CP-PatcK**

Mechanics have always been the same. Politics As History. Al Young. **CP-YounA**

Mechanist, The. Richard Wilbur. **CP-WilbR**

Medal [*or* Medall], The. John Dryden. "Almighty crowd, thou shorten'st all dispute." **SP-DrydJ**

Medallion. Robert Creeley. **CP-CreeR**

Medallion. Sylvia Plath. **CP-PlatS**

Medallion. Carl Sandburg. **CP-SandC**

Meddow Verse; or, Aniversary to Mistris Bridget Lowman, The. Robert Herrick. **CP-HerrR**

Medea. Euripides. **CP-JefR3,** *tr.* by Robinson Jeffers; "It was everything to me to think well of one man." "Of all things which are living and can form a judgment." **GrIP** "This is the chief felicity of life." **CP-JohnS** Translations from the *Medea* of Euripedes ("Err shall they not, who resolute explore"). **CP-JohnS** Translations from the *Medea* of Euripedes ("The rites deriv'd from ancient days"). **CP-JohnS**

Medea. Robinson Jeffers. **CP-JefR3**

Medea. Kathleen Jessie Raine. **SP-RainK**

Mediaeval young made Sunday pilgrimages, The. Under Mynydd-y-Twr. Steve Griffiths. **SP-GrifS**

Mediation. Archie Randolph Ammons. **SP-AmmoA**

Mediator, The. Elizabeth Barrett Browning. **CP-BroEB**

Medicine. Alice Walker. **CP-WalkA**

Medicine Bow. Richard Hugo. **CP-HugoR**

Medieval town, with frieze, The. What Is Poetry. John Ashbery. **SP-AshbJ**

Mediocrity in Love Rejected. Thomas Carew. **CP-CareT**

Meditatio. Ezra Pound. **SP-PounE**

Meditation. John Berryman. **CP-BerrJ**

Meditation. Hart Crane. **CP-CranH**

Meditation, A. Richard Eberhart. **CP-EberR**

Meditation. David St. John. **SP-StJoD**

Meditation. William Stafford. **SP-StafW**

Meditation Among the Tombs. Galway Kinnell. **SP-KinnG**

Meditation at Oyster River. Theodore Roethke. **CAPP; CMoP; MoAmPo; NYBP** *Fr.* North American Sequence. **CP-RoetT**

Meditation before an Ancient Poem. Pablo Antonio Cuadra, *tr. fr.* Spanish by Thomas Merton. **CP-MertT**

Meditation Celestial & Terrestrial. Wallace Stevens. **CP-StevW**

Meditation for His Mistress[e], A. Robert Herrick. **CP-HerrR**

Meditation in Hydrotherapy. Theodore Roethke. **CP-RoetT**

Meditation in My Favorite Position. Marge Piercy. *Fr.* Walking into Love. **SP-PierM**

Meditation in the Presence of "Ostrich Walk." Hayden Carruth. **CP-CarHS**

Meditation in the Spring Rain. Wendell Berry. **CP-BerrW**

Meditation in Time of War, A. William Butler Yeats. **CP-YeatW**

Meditation of My Lady of Sorrows. Kenneth Patchen. **CP-PatcK**

Meditation of Simeon, The. Wystan Hugh Auden. *Fr.* For the Time Being; a Christmas Oratorio. **CP-AudeW**

Meditation of the Old Fisherman, The. William Butler Yeats. **CP-YeatW**

Meditation on a Constable Picture. Sir John Betjeman. **CP-BetjJ**

Meditation on a Holiday. Thomas Hardy. **CP-HardT**

Meditation on a News Item. John Updike. **CP-UpdiJ**

Meditation on John Constable, A. Charles Tomlinson. **CP-TomlC**

Meditation on Philosophy, A. Robert Bly. **SP-BlyR**

Meditation on Saviors. Robinson Jeffers. **CP-JefR1**

Meditation on the A30. Sir John Betjeman. **CP-BetjJ**

Meditation on Two Themes. Stephen Dunn. **SP-DunnS**

Meditation Two. Richard Eberhart. **CP-EberR**

Meditation under Stars. George Meredith. **CP-MerG1**

Meditations for a Savage Child. Adrienne Rich. **SP-RicA2**

Meditations for Autumn. Frederick Morgan. **SP-MorgF** "Before the great resumption." "From the being born to the dying." "It takes me aback at times." "People dressed in the styles." "You bear the mark of what you are."

Meditations in an Emergency. Frank O'Hara. **SP-OharF**

Meditations in Time of Civil War. William Butler Yeats. **CP-YeatW** Ancestral Houses. **CP-YeatW; LiTB; OAEL-2** I See Phantoms of Hatred and of the Heart's Fullness and of the Coming Emptiness. **CP-YeatW; LiTB** My Descendants. **CP-YeatW; LiTB** My House. **CP-YeatW; LiTB** My Table. **CP-YeatW; LiTB** Road at My Door, The. **BIrV; CP-YeatW; LiTB; NOBE; PoE** Stare's Nest by My Window, The. **BIrV; CP-YeatW; FaBoPV; GTBS-6; GTBS-P; InPS; LiTB; NOBE**

("Bees in the crevices, The.") **FaBoPV**

Meditations of Afternoon. James McAuley.

  Catnap, with Nightmare. **SP-McAuJ**

  De Mortuis. **SP-McAuJ**

  Interlude, with Alter Ego. **SP-McAuJ**

Meditations of an Old Woman. Theodore Roethke. **CP-RoetT**

  First Meditation. **LCAP; NOBA**

  Fourth Meditation.

  Her Becoming.

  I'm Here. **CoAP; NYBP**

  What Can I Tell My Bones? **AmPP; NOBA**

Meditations on an Old Shoe. Chuck Miller. **SP-MillC**

Meditations on Death. Stanley Jasspon Kunitz. **CP-KuniS**

  "Clouds took me by the hand."

  "Etcher of the secret wrinkles."

  "O beautiful prey, / night-voice."

  "O sister of the shadow."

  "Probing the deepest selves."

  "You have closed your eyes."

Mediterranean. Thomas McGrath. **SP-McGrT**

Mediterranean. Muriel Rukeyser. **CP-RukeM**

Mediterranean. May Sarton. **SP-SartM**

Mediterranean, The. Allen Tate. **CP-TateA**

Mediterranean, The. Charles Tomlinson. **CP-TomlC**

Mediterranean Beach, Day after Storm. Robert Penn Warren. *Fr.* Love: Two Vignettes. **SP-WarrR**

Mediterranean in January. David Herbert Lawrence. **CP-LawrD**

Mediterranean Song. Richard Eberhart. **CP-EberR**

Mediums. Walt Whitman. **CP-WhitW**

Medlars and Sorb-Apples. David Herbert Lawrence. **CP-LawrD**

Medley. Carl Sandburg. **CP-SandC**

Medusa. Louise Bogan. **CP-BogaL**

Medusa. Hart Crane. `CP-CranH`

Medusa. Countee Cullen. **CP-CullC**

Medusa. Sylvia Plath. **CP-PlatS**

Medusa. Charles Kenneth Williams. **SP-WillC**

Medusa. John Yau. **SP-YauJo**

Medusa and the Mot Juste. Ogden Nash. *Fr.* Fables Bullfinch Forgot. **CP-NashO**

Meek Have Inherited, The. Charles Bukowski. **SP-BukC1**

Meek Virgin Mother, more benign. Our Lady of the Snow. William Wordsworth. *Fr.* Memorials of a Tour of the Continent; 1820. **CP-WorW2**

Meet me again as at that time. To Louisa in the Lane. Thomas Hardy. **CP-HardT**

Meet Me in the Morning. "Bob Dylan." **CP-DylaB**

Meet me in the morning, 56th and Wabasha. Meet Me in the Morning. "Bob Dylan." **CP-DylaB**

Meet mr universe(who clean). Edward Estlin Cummings. **CP-CummE**

Meeting. Matthew Arnold. *See* The Lake.

Meeting, A. Wendell Berry. **CP-BerrW**

Meeting. John Berryman. **CP-BerrJ**

Meeting, The. Louise Bogan. **CP-BogaL**

Meeting, The. Tess Gallagher. **SP-GallT**

Meeting, The. Robert Ranke Graves. **CP-GravR**

Meeting, A. Daniel Gerard Hoffman. **SP-HoffD**

Meeting. Ted Hughes. **SP-HughT**

Meeting, The. George Meredith. **CP-MerG1**

Meeting. George Meredith. **CP-MerG2**

Meeting, A. Mary Oliver. **SP-OlivM**

Meeting. Christina Georgina Rossetti. **CP-RosC3**

Meeting, The. Muriel Rukeyser. **CP-RukeM**

Meeting, The. Gilbert Sorrentino. **SP-SorrG**

Meeting, The. Charles Tomlinson. *Fr.* In Winter Woods. **CP-TomlC**

Meeting, The. John Greenleaf Whittier. **CP-WhitJ**

Meeting, *fr.* A Woman Young and Old. William Butler Yeats. **CP-YeatW**

Meeting among the Mountains. David Herbert Lawrence. **CP-LawrD**

Meeting and Passing. Robert Frost. **CP-FrosR**

Meeting at Night. Robert Browning. **CP-BroR1**

Meeting by Accident. Emily Dickinson. **CP-DickE**

Meeting his mother makes him lose ten years. Between the Porch and the Altar. Robert Lowell. **SP-LoweR**

Meeting is well worth parting. Emily Dickinson. **CP-DickE**

Meeting My Best Friend from the Eighth Grade. Gary Gildner. **SP-GildG**

Meeting of Cultures, A. Donald Davie. **CP-DavDo**

Meeting Point. Louis MacNeice. **CP-MacNL**

Meeting the British. Paul Muldoon. **SP-MuldP**

Meeting the Mountains. Gary Snyder. **CP-SnydG**

Meeting the Opposition. Archie Randolph Ammons. **SP-AmmoA**

Meeting the Reincarnation Analyst. Gary Gildner. **SP-GildG**

Meeting Up. Jenny Joseph. **SP-JoseJ**

'Meeting' was what / I had intended. Misprint. Charles Tomlinson. **CP-TomlC**

Meeting when all the world was in the bud. Loves of the Puppets. Richard Wilbur. **CP-WilbR**

Meeting with Despair, A. Thomas Hardy. **CP-HardT**

Meeting with Time, slack thing, said I. Time. George Herbert. **CP-HerbG**

Meeting you at your parent's gate. The Crossroads. Jim Morrison. **SP-MorrJ**

Meetinghouse, The. Lewis Turco. **SP-TurcL**

Meetings Like Hungry Beaks. Marge Piercy. **SP-PierM**

Megalopsych, The. Wystan Hugh Auden. **CP-AudWJ**

Megg yesterday was troubled with a Pose. Upon Megg. Robert Herrick. **CP-HerrR**

Megrez. Siv Cedering Fox. *Fr.* Seven Letters to Zakarias. **SP-CedeS**

Meiosis. Wystan Hugh Auden. **CP-AudeW**

Melampus. George Meredith. **CP-MerG1**

Melancholetta. "Lewis Carroll." **CP-CarrL**

  "My dismal sister! Couldst thou know." **FiBHP**

Melancholia. Charles Bukowski. **SP-BukC1**

Melancholia. Paul Laurence Dunbar. **CP-DunbP**

Melancholy. Samuel Taylor Coleridge. **CP-ColeS**

Melancholy. Christopher Smart. *Fr.* Hymns for the Amusement of Children. **SP-SmarC**

Melancholy Comus, The. Edwin Rolfe. **CP-RolfE**

Melancholy face Charles Carville had, A. Charles Carville's Eyes. Edwin Arlington Robinson. **CP-RobiE**

Melancholy of Storm Windows, The. John Updike. **CP-UpdiJ**

Melancholy Pig, The. "Lewis Carroll." **FaPON** *Fr.* The Pig-Tale. **CP-CarrL** *Fr.* Sylvie and Bruno Concluded.

Melancholy slackening that ensued. William Wordsworth. **PoEL-4** *Fr.* Cambridge and the Alps. *Fr.* The Prelude; Growth of a Poet's Mind [1850 vers.]. **CP-WorW3**

Mélange Adultère de Tout. Thomas Stearns Eliot. **CP-ElioT**

Melchior Vulpius. Marianne Craig Moore. **CP-MoorM**

Meles and Mincio, both your urns depress. Epigram, An. *Unknown. Fr.* Complimentary Pieces to Milton. **CP-CowpW**

Melik & Edward struck coins-with-a-sword. Canto 97. Ezra Pound. *Fr.* Cantos. **CP-PoCan**

Melinda Mae. Shel Silverstein. **SP-SilS2**

Mélisande. Charles Tomlinson. **CP-TomlC**

Mellea mi si abeam promittit basia septem. *acc. by English translation.* Thomas Campion. **CP-CampT**

Mellow. Langston Hughes. **SP-HughL**

Mellow touch of musick most doth wound, The. Soft Musick. Robert Herrick. **CP-HerrR**

Mellowed *those*, I call *those* eyes, Juventius. Catullus. *See* Carmen 48: "Iuventius, / were I allowed."

Melodies. "Lewis Carroll." **CP-CarrL**

Melodious Arethusa, o'er my verse. From Vergil's Tenth Eclogue. Virgil, *tr. by* Shelley. **CP-ShelP** *Fr.* Eclogues.

Melodious skeletons, for all of last night's music. A Fish-Scale Sunrise. Wallace Stevens. **CP-StevW**

Melody / moving / downstream. A Music. Denise Levertov. **CP-LeveD**

Melody. Charles Tomlinson. **CP-TomlC**

Melody Grundy. Denise Levertov. **CP-LeveD**

Melody to a Scene of Former Times. Percy Bysshe Shelley. *Fr.* Posthumous Fragments of Margaret Nicholson. **CP-ShelP**

Melon-Seller, The. Robert Browning. **CP-BroR2**

Melongène. Richard Wilbur. **CP-WilbR**

Melpomene among her livid people. The Two Masks. George Meredith. **CP-MerG1**

Melrose by Moonlight. Sir Walter Scott. **SP-ScotW** *Fr.* The Lay of the Last Minstrel.

Melt earth to sea, sea flow to air. Ben Jonson. **CP-JonsB** *Fr.* Oberon, the Fairy Prince.

Melted snow the verdure now restores, The. Horace. *See* 4.7: "Snow dissolvd no more is seen, The" ("Diffugere nives").

Melting. John Updike. **CP-UpdiJ**

Memento Creatoris Tui. Wystan·Hugh Auden. **CP-AudWJ**

Memento Mori. Christina Georgina Rossetti. **CP-RosC2**

Mementos, 1. William DeWitt Snodgrass. **SP-SnodW**

Memo from the Cave. Louise Glück. **SP-GlücL**

Memo #5. Etheridge Knight. **SP-KnigE**

Memo #43. Etheridge Knight. **SP-KnigE**

Memo #9. Etheridge Knight. **SP-KnigE**

Memo #32. Etheridge Knight. **SP-KnigE**

Memo #2. Etheridge Knight. **SP-KnigE**

Memo: Preliminary Draft of a Prayer to God the Father. John Ciardi. **SP-CiarJ**

Memo to His Lady's Therapist. David Markson. **CP-MarkD**

Memoir. / A green harp, A. June 16, 1992. James Liddy. **CP-LiddJ**

Memoir. Robinson Jeffers. **CP-JefR2**

Memoir. Carl Sandburg. **CP-SandC**

Memoir of a Proud Boy. Carl Sandburg. **CP-SandC**

Memoirs. Richard Hugo. **CP-HugoR**

Memoirs in Oxford. Frank Templeton Prince. **CP-PrinF**

   "Being *incontentabile* / Like Foscolo, in making verse."

   "Fretted discoloured towers and domes."

   "Plato says that in Heaven there is."

   "Somewhere in Mauriac a girl." **PeSAV**

   "Sun shines on the gliding river, The."

Memoirs of a Son of Erin. James McAuley. **SP-McAuJ** *Fr.* The Exile's Recurring Nightmare.

Memoirs of a Spinach-Picker. Sylvia Plath. **CP-PlatS**

Memoirs of an Imaginary Man, The. John Clellon Holmes. **SP-HolmJ**

Memoirs of Glückel of Hameln, The. Randall Jarrell. **CP-JarrR**

Memoirs of the World. Thom Gunn. *Fr.* Misanthropos. **CP-GunnT**

   "Serving man. Curled my hair, A." **OxBC**

Memorabilia. Robert Browning. **CP-BroR1**

Memorabilia. Edward Estlin Cummings. **CP-CummE; SP-CummE**

Memorable Fancy, A ("Angel came to me and said"). William Blake. **NU** *Fr.* The Marriage of Heaven and Hell. **CP-BlakW**

Memorable Fancy, A ("As I was walking among the fires of hell"). William Blake. **NU** *Fr.* The Marriage of Heaven and Hell. **CP-BlakW**

Memorable Fancy, A ("I was in a printing house in Hell & I saw the method in"). William Blake. *Fr.* The Marriage of Heaven and Hell. **CP-BlakW**

Memorable Fancy, A ("Once I saw a Devil in a flame of fire"). William Blake. *Fr.* The Marriage of Heaven and Hell. **CP-BlakW**

Memorable Fancy, A ("Prophets Isaiah and Ezekiel dined with me, and, The"). William Blake. *Fr.* The Marriage of Heaven and Hell. **CP-BlakW**

Memoranda. William Dickey. **SP-DickW**

Memoranda. Carl Sandburg. **CP-SandC**

Memoranda to Horace. Louis MacNeice. **CP-MacNL**

   Aera perennius? Dissolving dialects.

   "Flaccus, there are creatures for you over-Gothic."

   " 'Or with the tangles' as one of our own said."

   "Returned from my far-near country, my erstwhile."

   "Though elderly poets profess to be inveterate."

Memorandum for the Moderates. John Hewitt. **CP-HewiJ**

Memoria. Louise McNeill. **SP-McNeL**

Memorial. Thomas McGrath. **SP-McGrT**

Memorial, A. John Greenleaf Whittier. **CP-WhitJ**

Memorial Brass, The: 186–. Thomas Hardy. **CP-HardT**

Memorial Day. Paul Laurence Dunbar. **CP-DunbP**

Memorial Day. Charles Olson. **CP-OlsoC**

Memorial Day 1950. Frank O'Hara. **SP-OharF**

Memorial for the City. Wystan Hugh Auden. **CP-AudeW**

Memorial Fountain, The. Roy Fisher. **SP-FishR**

Memorial near the Outlet of the Lake of Thun. William Wordsworth. *Fr.* Memorials of a Tour of the Continent; 1820. **CP-WorW2**

Memorial I. Audre Lorde. **SP-LordA**

Memorial Rain. Archibald MacLeish. **CP-MacLA**

Memorial Service. John Hewitt. **CP-HewiJ**

Memorial: Son Bret, A. William Stafford. **SP-StafW**

Memorial II. Audre Lorde. **SP-LordA**

Memorial III—from a Phone Booth on Broadway. Audre Lorde. **SP-LordA**

Memorial to D. C. Edna St. Vincent Millay. **CP-MillE**

   Chorus: "Give away her gowns."

   Dirge: "Boys and girls that held her dear."

   Elegy: "Let them bury your big eyes." **CMoP; MoAB; MoAmPo; OxBA; PoRA**

   Epitaph: "Heap not on this mound."

   "O, loveliest throat of all sweet throats." **OxBA**

   Prayer to Persphone.

Memorial Verses. Matthew Arnold. **SP-ArnoM**

   "And Wordsworth! Ah, pale ghosts, rejoice!" **EPCY**

   "When Byron's eyes were shut in death." **EPCY**

Wordsworth's Grave. **FaBoPP**

Memorials of a Tour in Italy, 1837. William Wordsworth. **CP-WorW2**

   After Leaving Italy.

   After Leaving Italy, Continued.

   Among the Ruins of a Convent in the Apennines.

   At Albano.

   At Florence. **VLP**

   At Florence—from Michaelangelo.

   At Rome ("Is this, ye Gods, the Capitolian Hill?").

   At Rome ("They—who have seen the noble Roman's scorn").

   At Rome.—Regrets.—In Allusion to Niebuhr and Other Modern Historians.

   At Rome.—Regrets.—In Allusion to Niebuhr and Other Modern Historians, Continued.

   At the Convent of Camaldoli.

   At the Convent of Camaldoli, Continued.

   At the Eremite or Upper Convent of Camaldoli.

   At Vallombrosa.

   Before the Picture of the Baptist, by Raphael, in the Gallery at Florence.

   Composed at Rydal on May Morning, 1838.

   Cuckoo at Laverna May 25, 1837 The.

   Eternal Lord! Eased from a Cumbrous Load. **TrPWD**

     (At Florence.—From Michelangelo: "Eternal Lord! eased from a cumbrous load.")

   From the Alban Hills, Looking towards Rome.

   In Lombardy.

   Musings near Aquapendente April, 1837.

   "Near Anio's stream, I spied a gentle Dove."

   Near Rome, in Sight of St Peter's.

   Near the Lake of Thrasymene.

   Near the Same Lake [Thrasymene].

   Pillar of Trajan, The.

   Pine of Monte Mario at Rome, The.

   Plea for the Historian.

   To Henry Crabbe Robinson.

Memorials of a Tour of the Continent; 1820. William Wordsworth. **CP-WorW2**

   After Landing—The Valley of Dover, Nover, 1820.

   After-Thought ("Oh Life! without thy chequered scene").

   After Visiting the Field of Waterloo.

   Aix-la-Chapelle.

   At Dover.

   Between Namur and Liege.

   Brugès ("Bruges I saw attired with golden light").

   Brugès ("Spirit of Antiquity—enshrined, The").

   Church of San Salvador Seen from the Lake of Lugano.

   Column Intended by Buonaparte for a Triumphal Edifice in Milan, Now Lying by the Way-Side in the Simplon Pass, The.

   Composed in One of the Catholic Cantons.

   Dedication (Sent with These Poems, in Ms., To —).

   Desultory Stanzas, upon Receiving the Preceding Sheets from the Press.

   Echo, upon the Gemmi.

   Eclipse of the Sun, 1820, The.

   Effusion in the Presence of the Painted Tower of Tell, at Altorf.

   Elegiac Stanzas.

   Engelberg, the Hill of Angels.

   Fall of the Aar—Handec, The.

   Fish-Women.—On Landing at Calais.

   Fort Fuentes.

   Hymn for the Boatmen, as They Approach the Rapids under the Castle of Heidelberg.

   In a Carriage, upon the Banks of the Rhine.

   In the Cathedral at Cologne.

   Incident at Brugès. **OBTV**

   Italian Itinerant, and the Swiss Goatherd, THe.

   Last Supper, by Leonardo da Vinci, in the Refectory of the Convent of Maria della Grazia—Milan, The.

   Memorial near the Outlet of the Lake of Thun.

   On Approaching the Staub-Bach, Lauterbrunnen.

   On Being Stranded near the Harbour of Boulogne.

   On Hearing the "Ranz des Vaches" on the Top of the Pass of St Gothard.

   Our Lady of the Snow.

   Processions Suggested on a Sabbath Morning in the Vale of Chamouny.

   Scene on the Lake of Brientz.

   Sky-Prospect—From the Plain of France.

   Source of the Danube, The.

   Stanzas Composed in the Simplon Pass.

   Three Cottage Girls, The. **HBV 1-2**

Town of Schwytz, The.

Memories. Leonard Cohen. **CP-CoheL**

Memories. Rudyard Kipling. **CP-KiplR**

Memories. Frederick Morgan. **SP-MorgF**

Memories. Walt Whitman. **CP-WhitW**

Memories. John Greenleaf Whittier. **CP-WhitJ**

Memories few and deep-grained. The Island Cross. Kathleen Jessie Raine. *Fr.* Eileann Chanaidh. **SP-RainK**

Memories of President Lincoln. Walt Whitman. **CP-WhitW**

    Hush'd be the Camps To-day. **OHIP; SAmP**

    O Captain! My Captain! **AA; APN-1; CBCWP; EBEvV; FPL; FaBV; FaBoBe; FaBoCh; FaFP; FaPON; FaPoR; GN; GOA; ImPo; InPK; LiTA; MOS; MeMAP; MoAmPo; OBCA; OHFP; OHIP; PAH; PBMP; PiP; PoLF; SAmP; TAP; TFi; TrGrPo**

    This Dust Was Once the Man.

    When Lilacs Last in the Dooryard Bloom'd. **OFD,** *sect.* 1, 2, and 6; **AP; APN-1; AWP; AmPP; BiP; CABA; CBCWP; FPL; FaBoEn; HAP; HBV; LiTA; LoBV; MasP; MeMAP; MoAmPo; NAAL-1; NAAL-3; NIP; NOBA; NoP; OxBA; PAI; PAL; PPP; PPoe; PoEL-5; PoRA; SAmP; SeCeV; TAP; TFi; TrGrPo; TreF**

    "Come lovely and soothing death." **DL; SCV**

    (Carol of Death, The.) **DL**

    "In the swamp in secluded recesses." **RFM**

Memories of the Ancient World. Carlos Drummond de Andrade, *tr. fr. Portuguese by* Thomas Merton. **CP-MertT**

Memories of West Street and Lepke. Robert Lowell. **SP-LoweR**

Memory, The. Maya Angelou. **SP-AngeM**

Memory. Stephen Berg. **SP-BergS**

Memory. Louise Bogan. **CP-BogaL**

Memory, The. Robert Creeley. **CP-CreeR**

Memory ("Ah Memory"). Walter de la Mare. **CP-DeLaW**

Memory ("When Summer"). Walter de la Mare. **CP-DeLaW**

Memory. Richard Eberhart. **CP-EberR**

Memory. Richard Eberhart. **CP-EberR**

Memory. Ralph Waldo Emerson. **APN-1** *Fr.* Quatrains. **CP-EmerR**

Memory, A. Gary Gildner. **SP-GildG**

Memory. Theodore Roethke. **CP-RoetT**

Memory. Christina Georgina Rossetti. **CP-RosC1**

Memory, The. Gilbert Sorrentino. **SP-SorrG**

Memory, A. John Greenleaf Whittier. **CP-WhitJ**

Memory. William Wordsworth. **CP-WorW2**

Memory. William Butler Yeats. **CP-YeatW**

Memory, A / carved of. Two Egyptian Portrait Masks. Robert Earl Hayden. **CP-HaydR**

Memory and Hope. Elizabeth Barrett Browning. **CP-BroEB**

Memory and I. Thomas Hardy. **CP-HardT**

Memory believes / fragrance of a town(whose). Edward Estlin Cummings. **CP-CummE**

Memory Gardens. Allen Ginsberg. **CP-GinsA**

Memory Green. Archibald MacLeish. **CP-MacLA**

Memory, hither come. Song. William Blake. **CP-BlakW**

Memory: I can take my head and strike it on a wall   on Cumberland Island. The Shark's Parlor. James Dickey. **CP-DickJ**

Memory is a strange Bell. Emily Dickinson. **SP-DickE**

Memory is a watery flower, when watered. In the Garden. Richard Eberhart. **CP-EberR**

Memory is not good. There is something loose, The. Amnesty. Howard Nemerov. **CP-NemeH**

Memory is the Sherry Flower. Emily Dickinson. **SP-DickE**

Memory is when you look back. Scroll. Carl Sandburg. **CP-SandC**

Memory, Mind, and Will. Charles Olson. **CP-OlsoC**

Memory of April. William Carlos Williams. **CP-WilW1**

Memory of Burns, The. John Greenleaf Whittier. **CP-WhitJ**

Memory of Cape Cod. Edna St. Vincent Millay. **CP-MillE**

Memory of Cassis. Edna St. Vincent Millay. **CP-MillE**

Memory of Edwin Muir is green, The. Edwin Muir. Archibald MacLeish. **CP-MacLA**

Memory of England. Edna St. Vincent Millay. **CP-MillE**

Memory of Martha, The. Paul Laurence Dunbar. **CP-DunbP**

Memory of My Friend, A. Howard Nemerov. **CP-NemeH**

Memory of rain falling slowly, The. Philip Levine. **SP-LeviP** *Fr.* A Poem with No Ending.

Memory of Swans. May Sarton. **SP-SartM**

Memory of the Hospitality of American Barmen. Malcolm Lowry. *Fr.* The Cantinas. **CP-LowrM**

Memory of the Sad Chair, A. John Ciardi. **SP-CiarJ**

Memory of the War, A. Howard Nemerov. **CP-NemeH**

Memory of time is here imprisoned, The. In a Strange House. Stanley Jasspon Kunitz. **CP-KuniS**

Memory of V. I. Ulianov. Louis Zukofsky. *Fr.* 29 Poems. **CP-ZukLS**

Memory of Wilmington. Galway Kinnell. **SP-KinnG**

Memory of you is. . . a blue spear of flower. Two. Carl Sandburg. **CP-SandC**

Memory of Youth, A. William Butler Yeats. **CP-YeatW**

Memory relies on emotion. Virtuoso Literature for Two and Four Hands. Diane Wakoski. **SP-WakoD**

Memory says: Want to do right? Don't count on me. Adrienne Rich. **SP-RicA1** *Fr.* Eastern War Time.

Memory: The Walk on the Beach. John Gould Fletcher. **SP-FletJ**

Memory Unsettled. Thom Gunn. **CP-GunnT**

Memory worsening — let it go as rain. Sorrel. Geoffrey Hill. **CP-HillG**

Memphis, 2 P.M. Miller Williams. **SP-WillM**

Men. Maya Angelou. **SP-AngeM**

Men. Archibald MacLeish. **CP-MacLA**

Men. Gertrude Stein. **CP-SteiG**

Men. Charles Kenneth Williams. **SP-WillC**

Men, The. William Carlos Williams. **CP-WilW1**

Men Against the Sky. John Haines. **SP-HainJ**

Men all, and birds, and creeping beasts. Sleep. Walter de la Mare. **CP-DeLaW**

Men always praise an honest whore, keen. Carmen 110. Catullus. *Fr.* Carmina. **CP-Catul**

Men and Man. George Meredith. **CP-MerG1**

Men and Women. David Herbert Lawrence. **CP-LawrD**

Men & women sang & played, The. World's Bliss. Alice Notley. **SP-NotlA**

Men and Women (the Boltzmann Distribution). Chuck Miller. **SP-MillC**

Men Are a Mockery of Angels. Geoffrey Hill. *Fr.* Four Poems Regarding the Endurance of Poets. **CP-HillG**

Men are dead that used to walk these dales, The. Rookhope (Weardale, Summer 1922). Wystan Hugh Auden. **CP-AudWJ**

Men are Heaven's piers; they evermore. Robert Louis Stevenson. **CP-StevR**

Men are laughing as I approach, The. Marge Piercy. *Fr.* Excursions, Incursions. **SP-PierM**

Men are not alike in the sight of God. The Sight of God. David Herbert Lawrence. **CP-LawrD**

Men Are Not Bad. David Herbert Lawrence. **CP-LawrD**

Men are not born Kings, but are men renown'd. Kings. Robert Herrick. **CP-HerrR**

Men are only known in memory. Charles Olson. *Fr.* Two Poems. *Fr.* West. **CP-OlsoC**

Men are suspicious; prone to discontent. Present Government Grievous. Robert Herrick. **CP-HerrR**

Men are what they do, women are what they are. In Nature There Is Neither Right nor Left nor Wrong. Randall Jarrell. **CP-JarrR**

Men ask the way to Cold Mountain, *after* Han-shan. Gary Snyder. **CP-SnydG**

Men asleep in their underwear. Tōji. Gary Snyder. **CP-SnydG**

Men, brother men, that after us yet live. The Epitaph in Form of a Ballad. François Villon, *tr. fr. French by* Algernon Charles Swinburne. **SP-SwinA**

Men can look at the ocean, but no one. From This Distance: The Last Poem of the Clare Bards in Praise of the MacDonnells of Kilkee. James Liddy. **CP-LiddJ**

Men dying in battle speak after speech has failed. War Guilt. Edwin Rolfe. **CP-RolfE**

Men (XVIII), The. Pablo Neruda, *tr. fr. Spanish by* Ben Belitt. **SP-NeruP** *Fr.* The Separate Rose.

Men fear the hollow man at the top of the tree. The Leader. Stevie Smith. **CP-SmitS**

Men fight for liberty, and win it with hard knocks. Liberty's Old Old Story. David Herbert Lawrence. **CP-LawrD**

Men, fires, feasts. Demeter. Hilda Doolittle. **CP-DoolH**

Men have these kinds. Spiritual. Tom Clark. **SP-ClarT**

Men! if manhood still ye claim. To Faneuil Hall. John Greenleaf Whittier. **CP-WhitJ**

Men, if you love us, play no more. In the Person of Womankind [A Song Apologetic]. Ben Jonson. **CP-JonsB**

Men Improve with the Years. William Butler Yeats. **CP-YeatW**

Men in Arab robes. Two. James Schuyler. **CP-SchuJ**

Men in Dark Suits. William Matthews. **SP-MattW**

Men in my life were, The. Robert Creeley. **CP-CreeR**

Men in New Mexico. David Herbert Lawrence. **CP-LawrD**

Men in the kitchens, The. Louis Zukofsky. **CP-ZukLS**

Men know but little more than we. The Caged Thrush Freed and Home Again. Thomas Hardy. **CP-HardT**

Men Like Gods. David Herbert Lawrence. **CP-LawrD**

Men Like Gods. David Herbert Lawrence. **CP-LawrD**

Men Loved Wholly beyond Wisdom. Louise Bogan. **CP-BogaL**

Men Made Out of Words. Wallace Stevens. **CP-StevW**

Men make them fires on the hearth. The Fires. Rudyard Kipling. **CP-KiplR**

Men Marry What They Need. John Ciardi. **SP-CiarJ**

Men marvel at the works of man. Robert Louis Stevenson. **CP-StevR**

Men may sing of their Havanas, elevating to the stars. My Corn-Cob Pipe. Paul Laurence Dunbar. **CP-DunbP**

Men Mind No State in Sicknesse. Robert Herrick. **CP-HerrR**

Men must have Bounds how far[re] to walk[e]; for we. Rules for Our Reach. Robert Herrick. **CP-HerrR**

Men (IX), The. Pablo Neruda, *tr. fr. Spanish by* Ben Belitt. **SP-NeruP** *Fr.* The Separate Rose.

Men (XIX), The. Pablo Neruda, *tr. fr. Spanish by* Ben Belitt. **SP-NeruP** *Fr.* The Separate Rose.

Men of business, of pleasure. Felicity's Fourth Order. Donald Davie. **CP-DavDo**

Men of careful turns, haters of forks in the road. Gwendolyn Brooks. **SP-BrooG** *Fr.* The Womanhood.

Men of Eleusis, ye that with long staves. At Eleusis. Algernon Charles Swinburne. **SP-SwinA**

Men of England, wherefore plough. Song to the Men of England. Percy Bysshe Shelley. **CP-ShelP**

Men of Good Fortune. "Lou Reed." **SP-ReedL**

Men of My Century Loved Mozart. Archibald MacLeish. **CP-MacLA**

Men of Old, The. John Greenleaf Whittier. **CP-WhitJ**

Men of our race, we send you one. Voyage of the "Ophir," The. George Meredith. **CP-MerG2**

Men of Sheepshead, The. George Oppen. **CP-OppeG**

Men of the North-land! where's the manly spirit. A Summons. John Greenleaf Whittier. **CP-WhitJ**

Men of the Western World! In Fate's Dark Book. William Wordsworth. **CP-WorW2**

Men phone and ask me that, The. How Come You're Not Unlisted? Charles Bukowski. **SP-BukC1**

Men, ropes, horses, strain. The Wheel King. Howard Nemerov. **CP-NemeH**

Men said at vespers: "All is well!" Chicago. John Greenleaf Whittier. **CP-WhitJ**

Men say y'are faire; and faire ye are, 'tis true. Upon a Painted Gentlewoman. Robert Herrick. **CP-HerrR**

Men should group themselves into a new order. Sun-Men. David Herbert Lawrence. **CP-LawrD**

Men, some to bus'ness, some to pleasure take. The Ghosts of Beauty. Alexander Pope. **OBSV** *Fr.* Epistle [II,] to a Lady[: Of the Characters of Women]. **CP-PopeA**

Men talking / Near the room's center. They have said, The. Eclogue. George Oppen. **CP-OppeG**

Men That Are Falling, The. Wallace Stevens. **CP-StevW**

Men that are safe, and sure, in all they do[e]. An Epistle Answering to One That Asked to Be Sealed of the Tribe of Ben. Ben Jonson. **CP-JonsB**

Men that cut their graves in the grey rocks, The. The Widow of Naim. Thomas Merton. **CP-MertT**

Men That Fought at Minden, The. Rudyard Kipling. **CP-KiplR**

Men the Angels eyed. Men and Man. George Meredith. **CP-MerG1**

Men think that men have more sense than women and women. Just Wrap It Up, and I'll Throw It Away Later. Ogden Nash. **CP-NashO**

Men took the skyscraper. Crucifixion of the Skyscraper. John Gould Fletcher. **SP-FletJ**

Men (II), The. Pablo Neruda, *tr. fr. Spanish by* Ben Belitt. **SP-NeruP** *Fr.* The Separate Rose.

Men (IV), The. Pablo Neruda, *tr. fr. Spanish by* Ben Belitt. **SP-NeruP** *Fr.* The Separate Rose.

Men wanted to be like gods. Men Like Gods. David Herbert Lawrence. **CP-LawrD**

Men went happily to death. Shock Troops. Ernest Hemingway. **CP-HemiE**

Men, who have ceased to reverence, soon defy. Distractions. William Wordsworth. *Fr.* Ecclesiastical Sonnets. **CP-WorW2**

Men who here in harness died, The. On the Home Guards. Herman Melville. **SP-MelvH**

Men who imagine themselves covered with fur and sprouting. Werewolf Movies. Margaret Atwood. **SP-AtwM2**

Men Who March Away. Thomas Hardy. **CP-HardT**

Men With Coats Thrashing. Malcolm Lowry. **CP-LowrM**

Men with Long Faces, The. Stephen Dobyns. **SP-DobyS**

Men with long faces have come after my knives, The. The Men with Long Faces. Stephen Dobyns. **SP-DobyS**

Men with picked voices chant the names. Overture to a Dance of Locomotives. William Carlos Williams. **CP-WilW1**

Men with the heads of eagles. Margaret Atwood. **NoAM** *Fr.* Circe / Mud Poems. **SP-AtwM1**

Men Working. Edna St. Vincent Millay. **CP-MillE**

Men working on the building going up here have got these great, The. The Sanctity. Charles Kenneth Williams. **CP-WillC; SP-WillC**

Men would never have come to need an attic. Up There. Wystan Hugh Auden. **OxBTC** *Fr.* Thanksgiving for a Habitat. **CP-AudeW**

Men you strike. Euripides, *tr. by* Hilda Doolittle ("H.D."). **CP-DoolH** *Fr.* Hippolytus.

Menace. The. Thom Gunn. **CP-GunnT**

Ménage à trois, like Tristan's,—difficult. John Berryman. *Fr.* Sonnets to Chris. **CP-BerrJ**

Menagerie at Versailles in 1775, The. John Updike. **CP-UpdiJ**

Mendel's Laws. Peter Meinke. **SP-MeinP**

"Double helix and the triple star, The."

"Monk can do his work on bended knees, A."

"When Eve was cloned from Adam's rib, and stood."

Mending Wall. Robert Frost. **CP-FrosR**

Mending, with books and papers and a fan. Alun Lewis. *Fr.* Burma Casualty. **CP-LewiA**

Mendings. Muriel Rukeyser. **CP-RukeM**

Mendocino, Like You Said. Richard Hugo. **CP-HugoR**

Menenius' wife, / a red-headed cat from Bologna. Carmen 59. Catullus. *Fr.* Carmina. **CP-Catul**

Men's can at Café Society Uptown, The. Let's All Hear It for Mildred Bailey! James Schuyler. **CP-SchuJ**

Mens Creatrix. Stanley Jasspon Kunitz. **CP-KuniS**

Mens Sana in Corpore Sano. Donald Davie. **CP-DavDo**

Menses. Edna St. Vincent Millay. **CP-MillE**

Menstruation at Forty. Anne Sexton. **CP-SextA**

Mental Cases. Wilfred Owen. **CP-OwenW**

Mental picture which the, The. Lady in Black. Robert Creeley. **CP-CreeR**

Mental Traveller, The. William Blake. **CP-BlakW**

Mentor. Audre Lorde. **SP-LordA**

Mentor and Pupils. George Meredith. **CP-MerG2**

Mentors. Gwendolyn Brooks. **SP-BrooG**

Menu, The. Robert Creeley. **CP-CreeR**

Menu of Melancholy, The. Lewis Turco. **SP-TurcL**

Merak. Siv Cedering Fox. *Fr.* Seven Letters to Zakarias. **SP-CedeS**

Merax & Mullin. Wystan Hugh Auden. **CP-AudeW**

Mercator, vigiles oculos ut fallere possit. Translation of Prior's Chloe and Euphelia. Matthew Prior, *tr. fr. English by* William Cowper. **CP-CowpW**

Merce of Egypt. Charles Olson. **CP-OlsoC; SP-OlsoC**

Mercenary Muse. David St. John. **SP-StJoD**

Merchandise. Archie Randolph Ammons. **SP-AmmoA**

Merchant, as crafty a man is he, The. Do You Plan to Speak Bantu? or Abbreviation is the Thief of Sanity. Ogden Nash. **CP-NashO**

speech of Dorus. Sir Philip Sidney. **SP-SidnP** *Fr.* Arcadia.

Merchant man, whom many seas have taught, The, *speech of Cleophila.* Sir Philip Sidney. **SP-SidnP** *Fr.* Arcadia.

Merchant of the Picturesque, The. Emily Dickinson. **CP-DickE**

Merchantmen, The. Rudyard Kipling. **CP-KiplR**

Merchants have multiplied more than the stars of heaven. The Executive's Death. Robert Bly. **SP-BlyR**

Merchants. of the sea and of finance. Move Over. Charles Olson. **CP-OlsoC; SP-OlsoC**

Merchant's Prologue, The. Geoffrey Chaucer. *Fr.* The Canterbury Tales. **CP-ChauG**

Merchant's Tale, The, *see also* January and May, or the Merchant's Tale, *mod. vers. by* Alexander Pope. Geoffrey Chaucer. *Fr.* The Canterbury Tales. **CP-ChauG**

"Fresh-hearted May on hearing what he said." **OxBM**

Merchants Wife, The. Alun Lewis. *Fr.* Poems from the Chinese. **CP-LewiA**

Mercian Hymns. Geoffrey Hill. **CP-HillG**

"And it seemed, while we waited, he began to walk towards us." **NoAM; NoP**

"At Pavia, a visitation of some sorrow. Boethius'."

"Behind the thorn-trees thin smoke, scutch-grass or."

"Brooding on the eightieth letter of *Fors ClaviGera*." **HAP; PoE**

"Clash of salutation. As keels thrust into shingle." **NoAM; NoP**

"Cohorts of charabancs fanfared Offa's province and."

"Coins handsome as Nero's; of good substance and." **FaBoMo; HAP; NoAM**

"Dismissing reports and men, he put pressure on the." **HAP**

"Fortified in their front parlours, at Yuletide men."

"Gasholders, russet among fields. Mildams, marpools." **HAP; NoAM; NoP**

"He adored the desk, its brown-oak inlaid with ebony." **HAP; NoAM; NoP**

"He drove at evening through the hushed Vosges. The."

"I was invested in mother-earth, the crypt of roots." **NoAM**

"In tapestries, in dreams, they gathered, as it was enacted."

"Itinerant through numerous domains, of his lord's."

"King of the perennial holly-groves, the riven sandstone." **HAP; NoAM**

"Mad are predators. Too often lately they harbour, The." **NoP**

"Not strangeness, but strange likeness. Obstinate." **HAP; NoAM**

" 'Now when King Offa was alive and dead', they were."

"On the morning of the crowning we chorused our." **HAP**

"Pet-name, a common name. Best-selling brand, curt, A." **NoAM**

"Primeval heathland spattered with the bones of mice."

"Princes of Mercia were badger and raven, The." **HAP; NAEL-2; NoAM; NoP; PoE**

"Processes of generation; deeds of settlement. The." **NoP**

"So much for the elves' wergild, the true governance." **NoAM**

"Strange church smelled a bit 'high,' of censers, The." **PoE**

"Their spades grafted through the variably-resistant." **PoE**

"Trim the lamp; polish the lens; draw, one by one, rare." **FaBoMo**

"Tutting, he wrenched at a snarled root of dead crab-apple."

"We ran across the meadow scabbed with cow-dung, past." **HAP**

Merciful Hand, The. Nicholas Vachel Lindsay. **CP-LindV**

Mercifully. Marianne Craig Moore. **CP-MoorM**

Mercies[s] Beaute [or Beautée or Beauty]. Geoffrey Chaucer. **CP-ChauG**

Merciless Beauty. **ACP; BoLoP; EnVB; NAEL-1; SCGP**

(Rondel of Merciles Beaute, A.) **TrGrPo**

Merciless Beauty, mod. vers. Geoffrey Chaucer. **ACP; BoLoP; EnVB; NAEL-1; SCGP** Fr. Merciles[s] Beaute [or Beautée or Beauty]. **CP-ChauG**

(Rondel of Merciles Beaute, A.) **TrGrPo**

(Rondel of Merciles Beaute, A.) **TrGrPo**

Mercurius Gallo-Belgicus. John Donne. **CP-DonnJ**

Mercury Carries Psyche to Olympus, verse tr.fr. Metamorphoses by Apuleius. Elizabeth Barrett Browning. **CP-BroEB**

Mercury Clouds. Jim Carroll. **SP-CarrJ**

Mercury, god of larceny. The Accomplice. Robert Ranke Graves. **CP-GravR**

Mercury shew'd Apollo, Bartas Book. Nathaniel Ward.
("Mercury showed Apollo Bartas' book.") **CP-BradA**

Mercury showed Apollo Bartas' book. Nathaniel Ward. See Mercury shew'd Apollo, Bartas Book.

Mercury Vindicated. Ben Jonson.

"How young and fresh I am tonight." **CP-JonsB**

"Soft, subtle fire, thou soul of art." **CP-JonsB**

Mercutio. Walter de la Mare. **CP-DeLaW**

Mercy. James Dickey. **CP-DickJ**

Mercy. Robert Herrick. **CP-HerrR**

Mercy. Christopher Smart. Fr. Hymns for the Amusement of Children. **SP-SmarC**

Mercy and Love. Robert Herrick. **CP-HerrR**

Mercy and Love have met thee on thy road. Druidical Excommunication. William Wordsworth. Fr. Ecclesiastical Sonnets. **CP-WorW2**

Mercy Jesus Mercy. Somersby. Richard Hugo. **CP-HugoR**

Mercy, O Eternal One!, The. Hymns of the Brahmo Somaj. John Greenleaf Whittier. **CP-WhitJ**

Mercy on us for our many birthdays. Sestina for Warm Seasons. Mona Van Duyn. **SP-VanDM**

Mercy, the wise Athenians held to be. Mercy. Robert Herrick. **CP-HerrR**

Mercy, Wherever You Are, Come Running in to Me and Grab Me in Your Good Arms—. Charles Bukowski. **SP-BukC2**

Mercy's so slight it's like. Precious Weak Fields. Archie Randolph Ammons. **SP-AmmoA**

Mere trees cast no coolness where you go, The. A Girl Walking into a Shadow. James Wright. **CP-WrigJ**

Merely the landscape of a vanished whim. Versailles. Adrienne Rich. **CP-RicAE**

Merely to Know. Adrienne Rich. **CP-RicAE; SP-RicA2**

Merely to name them is the prose. Islands. Derek Walcott. **CP-WalcD**

Merest nub of a notion, nothing more, The. Playing the Inventions. Howard Nemerov. **CP-NemeH**

Meridian. Louise Glück. **SP-GlücL**

Meridian. Richard Hugo. **CP-HugoR**

Meridian. David St. John. **SP-StJoD**

Meridians are a net. Objects. Richard Wilbur. **CP-WilbR**

Merits Make the Man. Robert Herrick. **CP-HerrR**

Merle Bascom's .22. Donald Hall. **CP-HallD**

Merlin. Ralph Waldo Emerson. **CP-EmerR**

"Rhyme of the poet, The." **PoEL-4**

"Thy trivial harp will never please." **AA; OxBA**

Merlin. Geoffrey Hill. **CP-HillG**

Merlin. Edwin Arlington Robinson. **CP-RobiE**

Merlin. David St. John. **SP-StJoD**

Merlin and the Deer. Thomas Merton. **CP-MertT**

Merlin and Vivien. Tennyson. Fr. Idylls of the King. **CP-TennA**

In Love, If Love Be Love. **CABA; PoEL-5; TrGrPo**

(All in All.) **ImPo; LiTB; TRV**

(Vivien's Song.) **FaBoEn; OBNC**

"There lay she all her length and kiss'd his feet." **EBVVPR**

Merlin Enthralled. Richard Wilbur. **CP-WilbR**

Merlin in the Cave: He Speculates without a Book. Thom Gunn. **CP-GunnT**

Merlin, the great King Arthur being slaine. Epigram, An. Thomas Campion. Fr. Lord Hay's Mask.

Merlins Prophecy. William Blake. **CP-BlakW**

Merlin's Riddling. Tennyson. **FaBoRV** Fr. The Coming of Arthur. Fr. Idylls of the King. **CP-TennA**

Merlin's Song. Ralph Waldo Emerson. **CP-EmerR**

Mermaid. Stephen Dobyns. **SP-DobyS**

Mermaid. Robert Lowell. **SP-LoweR**

"I have learned what I wanted from the mermaid."

"I see you as a baby killer whale."

"One wondered who would see and date you next."

"Our meetings are no longer like a screening."

Mermaid, The. Frederick Morgan. **SP-MorgF**

Mermaid, The. Ogden Nash. **CP-NashO**

Mermaid, The. William Butler Yeats. Fr. A Man Young and Old. **CP-YeatW**

Mermaid Emerging. Robert Lowell. **SP-LoweR**

Mermaid found a swimming lad, A. The Mermaid. William Butler Yeats. Fr. A Man Young and Old. **CP-YeatW**

Mermaid there, floating, A. The Mermaid. Frederick Morgan. **SP-MorgF**

Mermaids, The. Walter de la Mare. **CP-DeLaW**

Mermaids, The. Edmund Spenser. **ChTr** Fr. The Faerie Queene. **CP-Spens**

Merman under the Plough, The. Louis MacNeice. Fr. Visitations. **CP-MacNL**

Mermen, The. Hart Crane. **CP-CranH**

Merops. Ralph Waldo Emerson. **CP-EmerR**

Merriest cuckoo / Which haunted us in May, The. Song. Wystan Hugh Auden. **CP-AudWJ**

Merrily, merrily goes the bark. The Voyage to Arran. Sir Walter Scott. **SP-ScotW** Fr. The Lord of the Isles.

Merrily 'mid the faded leaves. To Robin Redbreast. George Meredith. **CP-MerG1**

Merrimac, The. John Greenleaf Whittier. **CP-WhitJ**

Merrow Down. Rudyard Kipling. **CP-KiplR** Fr. Just-So Stories.

Merry. Shel Silverstein. **SP-SilS2**

Merry Autumn. Paul Laurence Dunbar. **CP-DunbP**

Merry clerks of Oxenford they stretch themselves at ease, The. The Clerks and the Bells. Rudyard Kipling. **CP-KiplR**

Merry-Go-Round. Langston Hughes. **SP-HughL**

Merry Guide, The. Alfred Edward Housman. **CP-HousA**

Merry Hae I Been Teethin a Heckle. Robert Burns. **CP-BurnR**

Merry heart is a continual feast, A. Then I Commended Mirth. Christina Georgina Rossetti. **CP-RosC2**

Merry, La Belle / antichi, tilling. 4 Other Countries. Louis Zukofsky. **CP-ZukLS**

Merry Maid. John Clare. **SP-ClarJ**

Merry Maid, The. Edna St. Vincent Millay. **CP-MillE**

Merry, Merry Sparrow! The Blossom. William Blake. **FHYEP; GoJo; PB; PBBP** Fr. Songs of Innocence. **CP-BlakW**

Merry [or Merrie] World did on a day, The. The Quip. George Herbert. **CP-HerbG**

Merrymaking in Question, A. Thomas Hardy. **CP-HardT**

Meru. William Butler Yeats. **CP-YeatW**

Mescaline. Allen Ginsberg. **CP-GinsA**

Meseemeth I heard cry and groan. The Complaint of the Fair Armoress [*or* Armouress]. François Villon, *tr. fr. French by* Algernon Charles Swinburne. **SP-SwinA**

Mesh cast for mackerel. Basil Bunting. **CP-BuntB**

Mesmerism. Robert Browning. **CP-BroR1**

Mesopotamia. Rudyard Kipling. **CP-KiplR**

Mesopotamia. David Herbert Lawrence. *Fr.* Bits. **CP-LawrD**

Mess of Love, The. David Herbert Lawrence. **CP-LawrD**

Message. John Berryman. **CP-BerrJ**

Message, The. Robert Creeley. **CP-CreeR**

Message, The. John Donne. **CP-DonnJ**

Message. Allen Ginsberg. **CP-GinsA**

Message, The. Denise Levertov. **CP-LeveD**

Message. Denise Levertov. **CP-LeveD**

Message. Kathleen Jessie Raine. **SP-RainK**

Message II. Allen Ginsberg. **CP-GinsA**

Message for Rimbaud. Charles Henri Ford. **SP-FordC**

Message for the Sinecurist. Tess Gallagher. **SP-GallT**

Message from Abroad. Allen Tate. **CP-TateA**

Message from her set his brain aflame, A. George Meredith. **EnVR; NOBVV** *Fr.* Modern Love. **CP-MerG1**

Message from Home. Kathleen Jessie Raine. **SP-RainK**

Message from Outside. Gary Snyder. **CP-SnydG**

Message from the Assistant Chief of the Fly People, A. Kenneth Patchen. **CP-PatcK**

Message from the Mountain Pool Where the Deer Come Down, A. James Wright. *Fr.* Many of Our Waters: Variations on a Poem by a Black Child. **CP-WrigJ**

Message Hidden in an Empty Wine Bottle that I Threw into a Gully of Maple Trees One Night at an Indecent Hour, A. James Wright. **CP-WrigJ**

Message of Peace, A. Henry Wadsworth Longfellow. **WBLP** *Fr.* The Arsenal at Springfield. **SP-LongH**

Message to Be Inscribed on Mark Van Doren's Hamilton Medal. Thomas Merton. **CP-MertT**

Message to Perfidious Soldier. David Herbert Lawrence. *Fr.* Bits. **CP-LawrD**

Messages. Jane Cooper. **SP-CoopJ**

"Approaching my life I am terrified."

"Ragged and thrashing."

Messages. James Dickey. **CP-DickJ**

Messages. Robert Pack. **SP-PackR**

Messages spelled out in stars. Impromptu Solo on a Balcony. Gilbert Sorrentino. *Fr.* Twelve Études for Voice and Kazoo. **SP-SorrG**

Messenger, The. Thom Gunn. **CP-GunnT**

Messenger, The. Thomas Merton. **CP-MertT; SP-MertT**

Messenger from the Horizon, A. Thomas Merton. **CP-MertT; SP-MertT**

Messengers, The. Robert Creeley. **CP-CreeR**

Messengers. Louise Glück. **SP-GlückL**

Messengers much like ourselves? Explain it. By Disposition of Angels. Marianne Craig Moore. **CP-MoorM**

Messiah [a Sacred Eclogue, in Imitation of Virgil's Pollio]. Alexander Pope. **CP-PopeA**

"Rise, crowned with light, imperial Salem, rise!" **GoBC; WGRP**

Messiah, The. Louis MacNeice. **CP-MacNL**

Messiah, The ("So they in Heav'n their odes and vigils tun'd"). John Milton. *See* So they in Heav'n their odes and vigils tun'd.

Messias. Thomas Merton. **CP-MertT**

Messias. Karl Shapiro. **SP-ShapK**

Metacom. John Greenleaf Whittier. **CP-WhitJ**

Metal for Resistance. David Herbert Lawrence. **CP-LawrD**

Metal smokestack, The. Exercise No. 2. William Carlos Williams. **CP-WilW2**

Metallic sheath / derelict, that resounds. Roy Fisher. **SP-FishR** *Fr.* Three Ceremonial Poems.

Metalogue to The Magic Flute. Wystan Hugh Auden. *Fr.* Three Occasional Poems. **CP-AudeW**

Metals. Donald Davie. **CP-DavDo**

Metamorphoses. Roy Fisher.

"Cat's glinting face as it stared, The." **SP-FishR**

"Crumpled clothes come slowly off." **SP-FishR**

"How does he come to be wearing that suit." **SP-FishR**

"Red beans in to soak." **SP-FishR**

"She sleeps, in the day, in the silence." **SP-FishR**

Metamorphoses. Geoffrey Hill. **CP-HillG**

"Doubtless he saw some path clear, having found."

Drake's Drum.

Fear, The.

Re-birth of Venus, The. **NePoEA**

"Through scant pride to be so put out!"

Metamorphoses, The. Randall Jarrell. **CP-JarrR**

Metamorphoses. Howard Nemerov. **CP-NemeH**

Metamorphoses. Ovid, *tr. fr. Latin.*

"Bura and Helice on Achaian ground." **CP-RaleW**

"East winde with Aurora hath abiding, The." **CP-RaleW**

Fable of Dryope, The. **CP-PopeA**

"From thence our kinde hard-hearted is, enduring paine and care." **CP-RaleW**

"Joyfull Spring did ever last, The." **CP-RaleW**

"More holy than the rest, and understanding more." **CP-RaleW**

"No man was better, nor more just than hee." **CP-RaleW**

"Nought from my birth or ancestors I claim." **CP-JohnS**

"Various ills ordain'd to man by fate, The." **CP-JohnS**

Vertumnus and Pomona. **CP-PopeA**

"World discernes it selfe, while I the world behold, The." **CP-RaleW**

Metamorphoses of the Moon. Sylvia Plath. **CP-PlatS**

Metamorphosis. Chuang Tzu, *tr. fr. Chinese by* Thomas Merton. **CP-MertT**

Metamorphosis. Edward Estlin Cummings. **CP-CummE**

Metamorphosis. Louise Glück. **SP-GlückL**

For My Father. **MoLi**

"My father has forgotten me." **MoLi**

Night. **MoLi**

Metamorphosis. Robinson Jeffers. **CP-JefR3**

Metamorphosis. Frederick Morgan. **SP-MorgF**

Metamorphosis. Carl Sandburg. **CP-SandC**

Metamorphosis. May Sarton. **SP-SartM**

Metamorphosis. Wallace Stevens. **CP-StevW**

Metamorphosis, The. Sir John Suckling. **CP-SuckJ**

Metamorphosis, The. Charles Tomlinson. **CP-TomlC**

Metaphor. Wystan Hugh Auden. *Fr.* Shorts I ("Watch upon my wrist, The"). **CP-AudeW**

Metaphor, The. Robert Ranke Graves. **CP-GravR**

Metaphor as Degeneration. Wallace Stevens. **CP-StevW**

Metaphor to Action. Muriel Rukeyser. **CP-RukeM**

Metaphors. Sylvia Plath. **CP-PlatS**

Metaphors of a Magnifico. Wallace Stevens. **CP-StevW**

Metaphysic. Marsden Hartley. **CP-HartM**

Metaphysical. Hayden Carruth. *Fr.* Poetical Abstracts. **CP-CarHS**

Metaphysical Automobile, The. Howard Nemerov. **CP-NemeH**

Metaphysical Garden, The. May Sarton. **SP-SartM**

Metaphysics. Allen Ginsberg. **CP-GinsA**

Metempsychosis. Margaret Atwood. **SP-AtwM2**

Meteorite, The. Randall Jarrell. **CP-JarrR; SP-JarrR**

Meteorologist, September. Donald Davie. **CP-DavDo**

Meteorology, A. Jenny Joseph. **SP-JoseJ**

Meteors. Jane Cooper. **SP-CoopJ**

Meteor's arc of quiet; a voiceless rain, The. Faint Music. Walter de la Mare. **CP-DeLaW**

Methedrine Vision in Hollywood, A. Allen Ginsberg. **CP-GinsA**

Methinks that I could trip o'er heaviest soil. Eminent Reformers. William Wordsworth. *Fr.* Ecclesiastical Sonnets. **CP-WorW2**

Methinks that to some vacant hermitage. Continued [Seclusion]. William Wordsworth. *Fr.* Ecclesiastical Sonnets. **CP-WorW2**

Methinks the ills of life I fain would shun. Christina Georgina Rossetti. **CP-RosC3**

Methinks this heart should rest awhile. Emily Brontë. **CP-BronE**

Methinks 'twere no unprecedented feat. William Wordsworth. *Fr.* The River Duddon [A Series of Sonnets]. **CP-WorW2**

Methinks we do as fretful children do. The Prospect. Elizabeth Barrett Browning. **CP-BroEB**

Methinks I see thee decently array'd. William Cowper. **CP-CowpW**

Method, A. Robert Creeley. **CP-CreeR**

Method, The. George Herbert. **CP-HerbG**

Method. For Ronald Gaskell. Donald Davie. **CP-DavDo**

Method must be purest meat, The. On Burroughs, Work. Allen Ginsberg. **CP-GinsA**

Method of Actuality, The. Robert Creeley. **CP-CreeR**

Methodists. John Hewitt. **CP-HewiJ**

Methodus Amandi. Thomas Cary. **CP-CareT**

Methought I saw (as I did dream[e] in bed). The Vision. Robert Herrick. **CP-HerrR**

Methought [*or* Mee thought] I saw my late espoused saint. John Milton. **CP-MiltJ**

(Sonnet 23: "Mee thought I saw my late espoused saint.") **CP-MiltJ**

Methought I saw the footsteps of a throne. William Wordsworth. **CP-WorW1**

Methought I saw the grave where Laura lay. A Vision upon This Concei[p]t of the Faerie [or Faery] Queen[e]. Sir Walter Ralegh. **CP-RaleW** *Fr.* Commendatory Verses to Edmund Spenser's Fairy Queen.

Methought I stood where trees of every clime. A Dream. John Keats. **OBNC** *Fr.* The Fall of Hyperion. **CP-KeatJ**

Methought I stood where trees of every clime. John Keats. **OBRV** *Fr.* A Dream. **OBNC** *Fr.* The Fall of Hyperion. **CP-KeatJ**

Methought I walked a dismal place. Horrors. "Lewis Carroll." **CP-CarrL**

Methought I was a billow in the crowd. Fragment. Percy Bysshe Shelley. **CP-ShelP**

Meths Men, The. Phoebe Hesketh. **SP-HeskP**

Methusaleh Saw Many Repeaters. Carl Sandburg. **CP-SandC**

Methusaleh was a witness to many cabbages and kings. Methusaleh Saw Many Repeaters. Carl Sandburg. **CP-SandC**

Methusaleh was a witness to many cabbages and kings. Three Fragments for Fishers of Destiny. Carl Sandburg. **CP-SandC**

Meticulous, past midnight in clear rime. Hart Crane. **NAAL-2; PoE** *Fr.* Voyages. **CP-CranH**

Metric Figure. William Carlos Williams. **CP-WilW1**

Metric Figure. William Carlos Williams. **CP-WilW1**

Metric Figure. William Carlos Williams. **CP-WilW2**

Metrical Feet. Samuel Taylor Coleridge. **CP-ColeS**

Metro-Goldwyn-Mayer. Delmore Schwartz. **SP-SchwD**

Metropolitan / Museum of Art, The. Miss Pimberton Of. Siv Cedering Fox. **SP-CedeS**

Metropolitan Railway, The. Sir John Betjeman. **CP-BetjJ**

Metropolitan Sunday. Howard Nemerov. **CP-NemeH**

Mettle and Metal. Robert Browning. **CP-BroR2**

Meum Est Propositum. Archipoeta. *Fr.* Four Medieval Latin Poems. **CP-MacNL**

Mexcity drugstore table, giant. Violence. Allen Ginsberg. **CP-GinsA**

Mexican dancer shook her fans at, The. Yellow Cab. Charles Bukowski. **SP-BukC1**

Mexican Girls, The. Charles Bukowski. **SP-BukC2**

Mexican Guitar, A. Frank O'Hara. **SP-OharF**

Mexican Market Woman. Langston Hughes. **SP-HughL**

Mexican Quarter. John Gould Fletcher. **BPAW** *Fr.* Arizona Poems. **SP-FletJ**

Mexican Valley. James Dickey. **CP-DickJ**

Mexico. Robert Lowell.

"As if we chewed dry twigs and salt grasses." **SP-LoweR**

"Difficulties, the impossibilities, The." **SP-LoweR**

"Lizard rusty as a leaf rubbed rough." **SP-LoweR**

"Midwinter in Cuernavaca, tall red flowers." **SP-LoweR**

"No artist perhaps, you go beyond their phrases." **SP-LoweR**

"Poor child, you were kissed so much you thought you were walked on." **SP-LoweR**

"South of Boston, south of Washington." **SP-LoweR**

"Three pillows, end on end, rolled on a daybed." **SP-LoweR**

Mexico. Richard Shelton. **SP-ShelR**

Mexico City Lover. Al Young. **CP-YounA**

(Mexico)   could not. This. Charles Olson. **CP-OlsoC**

Mexico Is a Foreign Country: Four Studies in Naturalism. Robert Penn Warren. **SP-WarrR**

Butterflies over the Map.

Mango on the Mango Tree, The. **MoP; NoAM**

Small Soldiers with Drum in Large Landscape.

World Comes Galloping: A True Story, The.

Mezzo Cammin. Henry Wadsworth Longfellow. **SP-LongH**

Mezzo Forte. William Carlos Williams. **CP-WilW1**

M.G. For The U.S. Emily Brontë. **CP-BronE**

Mi-Carême. Daniel Gerard Hoffman. **SP-HoffD**

Miami. John Updike. **CP-UpdiJ**

Miami You Are About to Be Surprised, *sels.* Thomas Merton. *Fr.* South. *Fr.* The Geography of Lograire. **CP-MertT**

Mice rot in their tunnels in the field, The. Crop-Dusting. Daniel Gerard Hoffman. **SP-HoffD**

Michael [A Pastoral Poem]. William Wordsworth. **CP-WorW1**

Michael Angelo. David Herbert Lawrence. **CP-LawrD**

Michael At Sixteen Months. Al Young. **CP-YounA**

Michael F. M. Rossetti. Christina Georgina Rossetti. **CP-RosC3**

Michael Robartes and the Dancer. William Butler Yeats. **CP-YeatW**

Michelangelo would've wept. "Bob Dylan." *Fr.* Some Other Kinds of Songs. **CP-DylaB**

Michelle. The Beatles. **CP-Beatl**

Michigan Water: a Few Riffs before Dawn. Hayden Carruth. **CP-CarHL**

"Define. So the drum commands."

"Gray dawn seeping through stone."

"In the cage no word is spoken."

"Listen, in night's last tender hour."

"My brother and I, without hope."

"My Chicago, city of all."

"This hour is best, darkening."

Miching Mallecho. Robinson Jeffers. **CP-JefR3**

Michtam. Louis Zukofsky. **CP-ZukLS**

Lese-Wiat, from Caul Gate.

Romantic Portrait.

With a Capital P.

Micky. Jim Carroll. **SP-CarrJ**

Microscopic monster. Euglena. Miller Williams. **SP-WillM**

Mictlantecuhtli. Charles Tomlinson. **CP-TomlC**

Mid-April. John Hewitt. **CP-HewiJ**

Mid-August at Sourdough Mountain Lookout. Gary Snyder. **CP-SnydG**

Mid-Country Blow. Theodore Roethke. **CP-RoetT**

'Mid crowded obelisks and urns. To the Sons of Burns, after Visiting the Grave of Their Father. William Wordsworth. **CP-WorW1**

Mid-day. Hilda Doolittle. **CP-DoolH**

Mid-Day Verse, The. David Herbert Lawrence. **CP-LawrD**

Mid-December but still the ground's unfrozen, taking. Mild Winter. Hayden Carruth. **CP-CarHS**

'Mid Himalayan snow, / Where a mere step sufficed. Buddha and Christ. John Gould Fletcher. **SP-FletJ**

Mid-January, and still no snow. A Dry Winter Letter to Friends. Ted Kooser. **SP-KoosT**

Mid-Lent. Christina Georgina Rossetti. **CP-RosC2**

Mid-Life Crises: A Critical Review. Al Young. **CP-YounA**

Mid-Morning. Nicholas Vachel Lindsay. *Fr.* An Indian Summer Day on the Prairie. **CP-LindV**

Mid-morning / the light, what light. This Soft October. James Schuyler. **CP-SchuJ**

Mid-noon is past;—upon the sultry mead. The Resting-Place. William Wordsworth. *Fr.* The River Duddon [A Series of Sonnets]. **CP-WorW2**

Mid-September, and I miss my daughter. Towards Autumn. Marilyn Hacker. **SP-HackM**

Mid-Term Break. Seamus Heaney. **SP-HeanS**

Mid-Winter. Alun Lewis. **CP-LewiA**

Mid-Winter Waking. Robert Ranke Graves. **CP-GravR**

Midas and Wife. Mona Van Duyn. **SP-VanDM**

Midas eyes the seasonable glints. Legend. Charles Tomlinson. **CP-TomlC**

Midas, we are in story told. The Fable of Midas. Jonathan Swift. **CP-SwifJ**

Midday Construction. Pablo Neruda, *tr. fr.* Spanish by Ben Belitt. **SP-NeruP**

Middle, The. Ogden Nash. **CP-NashO**

Middle. William Carlos Williams. **CP-WilW1**

Middle Age. Jane Cooper. *Fr.* March. **SP-CoopJ**

Middle Age. Robert Lowell. **SP-LoweR**

Middle-Age Enthusiasms. Thomas Hardy. **CP-HardT**

Middle Age Poem. Grace Paley. **CP-PaleG**

Middle-aged, The. Adrienne Rich. **CP-RicAE; SP-RicA2**

Middle-aged life is merry, and I love to lead it. Peekaboo, I Almost See You. Ogden Nash. **CP-NashO**

Middle Aged Lovers, I. Erica Jong. **SP-JongE**

Middle Aged Lovers, II. Erica Jong. **SP-JongE**

Middle Ages, The. John Haines. **SP-HainJ**

Middle-Class Children. David Herbert Lawrence. **CP-LawrD**

Middle Classes, The. David Herbert Lawrence. **CP-LawrD**

Middle Infant. John Hewitt. **CP-HewiJ**

Middle-northern March, now as always, A. A Celebration. William Carlos Williams. **CP-WilW1**

Middle of May, when the iris blows. Iris. Muriel Rukeyser. **CP-RukeM**

Middle of the Month, The. Ogden Nash. **CP-NashO**

Middle of the night, she's wide awake, carefully lying as far away as she can from him, The. The Question. Charles Kenneth Williams. **SP-WillC**

Middle of the Way. Galway Kinnell. **SP-KinnG**

Middle of the World. David Herbert Lawrence. **CP-LawrD**

Middle Passage. Robert Earl Hayden. **CP-HaydR**

Middleness of the Road, The. Robert Frost. **CP-FrosR**

Middlesex. Sir John Betjeman. **CP-BetjJ**

Middlesex. Donald Davie. **CP-DavDo**

Midget, The. Philip Levine. **SP-LeviP**

Midget, The. Dabney Stuart. **SP-StuaD**

Midget in Sloppy Joe's, The. Hero Worship at Key West on the 4th of July. Peter Meinke. **SP-MeinP** *Fr.* Lines from Key West.

Midlands. Charles Tomlinson. **CP-TomlC**

Midlands' *a* is mostly an *i*, The. Stratford-on-Avon. Louis Zukofsky. **CP-ZukLS**

Midnight. Jim Carroll. **SP-CarrJ**

Midnight. Robert Creeley. **CP-CreeR**

Midnight. Stephen Dunn. **SP-DunnS**

Midnight. William Shakespeare. OBSC *Fr.* The Rape of Lucrece. **CP-ShaWS**

Midnight, and a letter comes to me from. Ezra Pound. MeMAP *Fr.* Homage to Sextus Propertius. **SP-PounE**

Midnight Dancer. Langston Hughes. **SP-HughL**

Midnight denies poursuivant of the dawn. Malcolm Lowry. **CP-LowrM**

Midnight in India. Alun Lewis. **CP-LewiA**

Midnight—in no midsummer tune. Prefatory Poem to My Brother's Sonnets. Tennyson. **CP-TennA**

Midnight in some midnight place. Midnight. Stephen Dunn. **SP-DunnS**

Midnight in the mid-Atlantic. On deck. On Deck. Sylvia Plath. **CP-PlatS**

Midnight, moonlight, most ancient of all seas. Exodus 1947. Edwin Rolfe. **CP-RolfE**

Midnight Moscow Airport / sucks me in from Siberia. Moscow in the Wilderness, Segovia in the Snow. Lawrence Ferlinghetti. **SP-FerlL**

Midnight Oil. John Clellon Holmes. **SP-HolmJ**

Midnight Oil. Edna St. Vincent Millay. **CP-MillE**

Midnight on Beechen, 187–. Thomas Hardy. **CP-HardT**

Midnight on the Great Western. Thomas Hardy. **CP-HardT**

Midnight Outcry. Robert Penn Warren. **SP-WarrR**

Midnight Raffle. Langston Hughes. **SP-HughL**

Midnight shadow has drooped and drooped, The. At Midnight. David Herbert Lawrence. **CP-LawrD**

Midnight shadow sinking down has slung, The. Mother's Son in Salonika. David Herbert Lawrence. *Fr.* Bits. **CP-LawrD**

Midnight shadows have come over what was the green of Spring. Sympathy. David Herbert Lawrence. **CP-LawrD**

Midnight Snack, The. James Merrill. *Fr.* Five Old Favorites. **SP-MerrJ**

Midnight Special. Kenneth Patchen. **CP-PatcK**

Midnight Special. Gilbert Sorrentino. **SP-SorrG**

Midnight Special Revisited, The. Al Young. **CP-YounA**

Midnight—the City. Marsden Hartley. **CP-HartM**

Midnight wooed the Morning-Star, The. The Barrier. Paul Laurence Dunbar. **CP-DunbP**

Midpoint. Charles Simic. **SP-SimiC**

Midpoint. John Updike. **CP-UpdiJ**

    Conclusion: "Easy Humanism plagues the land, An."

    Dance of the Solids, The.

    Introduction: "Of nothing but me, me."

    Play of Memory, The.

Mi(dreamlike)st / makes / big each dim. Edward Estlin Cummings. **CP-CummE**

Midst all the darke and knotty Snares. Matthew 22; Neither Durst Any Man from that Day Aske Him Any More Questions. Bible, *N.T.* **CP-CrasR**, *tr.* by Richard Crashaw; *Fr.* St. Matthew.

'Midst the men and things which will. Abram Morrison. John Greenleaf Whittier. **CP-WhitJ**

'Midst the palace bowers of Hungary, imperial Presburg's pride. Isabella of Austria. John Greenleaf Whittier. **CP-WhitJ**

Midsummer. Derek Mahon. **SP-MahoD**

Midsummer. Derek Walcott.

    "At the Queen's Park Hotel, with its white, high-ceilinged rooms." **CP-WalcD**

    "Before that thundercloud breaks from its hawsers." **CP-WalcD**

    "Camps hold [*or* held] their distance— [of] brown chestnuts and grey smoke, The." **CP-WalcD**

    "Certain things here are quietly American." **CP-WalcD**

    "Chicago's avenues, as white as Poland." **CP-WalcD**

    "Companion in Rome, whom Rome makes as old as Rome." **CP-WalcD**

    "Gold dung and urinous straw from the horse garages." **CP-WalcD**

    "Grey English road hissed emptily under the tires, The." **CP-WalcD**

    "I can sense it coming from far, too, Maman, the tide." **CP-WalcD**

    "I heard them marching the leaf-wet roads of my head." **CP-WalcD**

    "I once gave my daughters, separately, two conch shells." **CP-WalcD**

    "In the other 'eighties, a hundred midsummers gone." **CP-WalcD**

    "Long, white, summer cloud, like a cleared linen table, A." **CP-WalcD**

    "Midsummer sea, the hot pitch road, this grass, these shacks that made me, The." **CP-WalcD**

    "Midsummer stretches beside me with its cat's yawn." **CP-WalcD**

    "Mud. Clods. The sucking heel of the rain-flinger." **CP-WalcD**

    "My double, tired of morning, closes the door." **CP-WalcD**

    "Oak inns creak in their joints as light declines, The." **CP-WalcD**

    "Our houses are one step from the gutter. Plastic curtains." **CP-WalcD**

    "Since all of your work was really an effort to appease." **CP-WalcD**

    "Something primal in our spine makes the child swing." **CP-WalcD**

    "Sun has fired my face to terra-cotta, The." **CP-WalcD**

    "There was one Syrian, with his bicycle, in our town." **CP-WalcD**

    "Those grooves in that forehead of sand-coloured flesh." **CP-WalcD**

    Tropic Zone. **CP-WalcD**

    Watteau. **CP-WalcD**

    "Wind-scraped headland, a sludgy, dishwater sea, A." **CP-WalcD**

    "With the frenzy of an old snake shedding its skin." **CP-WalcD**

    "With the stampeding hiss and scurry of green lemmings." **CP-WalcD**

Midsummer Dawn. Archibald MacLeish. **CP-MacLA**

Midsummer Dawn at Sea. John Gould Fletcher. **SP-FletJ**

Midsummer Mobile. Sylvia Plath. **CP-PlatS**

Midsummer Night, 1940. Philip Larkin. **CP-LarkP**

Midsummer sea, the hot pitch road, this grass, these shacks that made me, The. Derek Walcott. **CP-WalcD** *Fr.* Midsummer.

Midsummer stretches beside me with its cat's yawn. Derek Walcott. **CP-WalcD** *Fr.* Midsummer.

Midsummer, Tobago. Derek Walcott. **CP-WalcD**

Midsummer, was it, when They died. Emily Dickinson. **CP-DickE**

Midsummer's Day. Howard Nemerov. **CP-NemeH**

Midsummer's Daymare. Ogden Nash. **CP-NashO**

Midtown pyromaniac, sunset, The. Dream of the Departing Soldier. Malcolm Lowry. **CP-LowrM**

Midway in our life's journey, I went astray. Inferno. Dante Alighieri. *Fr.* Divina Commedia.

Midwestern in the heat, this river's. Duwamish. Richard Hugo. **CP-HugoR**

Midwinter. William Carlos Williams. **CP-WilW2**

Midwinter Blues. Langston Hughes. **SP-HughL**

Midwinter in Cuernavaca, tall red flowers. Robert Lowell. **SP-LoweR** *Fr.* Mexico.

Midwinter night. An Open Window on Chicago. Allen Ginsberg. **CP-GinsA**

Midwinter, Presolstice. Margaret Atwood. **SP-AtwM1**

Midwinter spring is its own season. Little Gidding. Thomas Stearns Eliot. FaBoMo; FaBoPV; FaBoTw; GTBS-6; GTBS-P; MoP; NAEL-2; NAWM-2; NOBA; NOBE; NoAM; OAEL-2; OXAEP-2; OxBTC; PeECV; PrIm; TAP; TFi *Fr.* Four Quartets. **CP-ElioT**

Midwinter Sunset. John Gould Fletcher. **SP-FletJ**

Midwinter Waking. Philip Larkin. **CP-LarkP**

Mien to move a Queen, A. Emily Dickinson. **CP-DickE**

Might have been. Certainly these ashes might have been pleasures. This Place Rumord to Have Been Sodom. Robert Duncan. **SP-DuncR**

Might he [Cro-Magnon] have drawn bi- / son to induct a mys-. Cave Painting. Hayden Carruth. **CP-CarHS**

Might I as well within my song belay. Sir Thomas Wyatt. **CP-WyatT**

Might I, if you can find it, be given. Saint Nicholas. Marianne Craig Moore. **CP-MoorM**

Might I lie where leans her lute. Song. George Meredith. **CP-MerG2**

Might it not have been. Thom Gunn. *Fr.* Jack Straw's Castle. **CP-GunnT**

Might these be thrushes climbing through almost(do they). Edward Estlin Cummings. **CP-CummE**

Mightiest moments pass uncalendared, The. V.R. 1819–1901. Thomas Hardy. **CP-HardT**

Mighty creature is the germ, A. The Germ. Ogden Nash. **CP-NashO**

Mighty dog with three colossal necks, A. *verse tr. fr.* Metamorphoses *by* Apuleius. Elizabeth Barrett Browning. **CP-BroEB**

Mighty dome is rear'd in solemn state, A. The Congress of Nations. George Meredith. **CP-MerG2**

Mighty dying of my Father, The. Emily Dickinson. **SP-DickE**

Mighty Eagle. Percy Bysshe Shelley. **CP-ShelP**

Mighty Fortress, A. Bible, *O.T. See* Psalm 91: "He that dwelleth in the secret place. . . ."

Mighty Fountain, A. Samuel Taylor Coleridge. **CP-ColeS**

Mighty God, even the Lord, hath spoken, The. Psalm 50. Bible, *O.T.* BrRo *Fr.* Psalms. **CP-Psal**

Mighty guest of merely me. Edward Estlin Cummings. **CP-CummE**

Mighty Heart, The. Ralph Waldo Emerson. AA *Fr.* Woodnotes II ("As sunbeams stream through liberal space"). **CP-EmerR**

Mighty lyon, lord of all the wood, A. Edmund Spenser. *Fr.* Visions of the World's Vanity [*or* Vanitie]. **CP-Spens**

Mighty man and the mother-egg, The. From the Inca. Charles Olson. **CP-OlsoC**

Mighty Mother, and her son who brings, The. To Dr. Jonathan Swift. Alexander Pope. **OxAEP-1,** *book* I, *ll.* 1–330; *Fr.* The Dunciad. **CP-PopeA**

Mighty Neptune, may it please. Another to Neptune. Robert Herrick. **CP-HerrR**

Mighty Runner, A. Nicarchus of Alexandria. **MeMAP; OBAL; SD** *Fr.* Variations of Greek Themes. **CP-RobiE**

Mignon. Johann Wolfgang von Goethe, *tr.* by Edgar A. Bowring. **CP-ColeS**

Mignon's Song. Johann Wolfgang von Goethe, *tr. fr. German by* Samuel Taylor Coleridge. **CP-ColeS**

Migrant. Langston Hughes. **SP-HughL**

Migration: C.P.R. Margaret Atwood. **SP-AtwM1**

Migration of Birds. Gary Snyder. **CP-SnydG**

Migration of Cities, The. Thomas McGrath. **SP-McGrT**

Migratory Noon. Joseph Ceravolo. **SP-CeraJ**

Mihrab Shah. Robert Browning. **CP-BroR2**

Mike. James Schuyler. **CP-SchuJ**

Milady Reflects. John Updike. **CP-UpdiJ**

Milan Cathedral. Herman Melville. **CP-MelvH**

Milarepa Taste. Allen Ginsberg. **CP-GinsA**

Mild blight, a sterility, A. Roy Fisher. **SP-FishR** *Fr.* Handsworth Liberties.

Mild noon air of Spring again, The. A Riddle. Walter de la Mare. **CP-DeLaW**

Mild parochial talk was ours, A. In the Garden. Walter de la Mare. **CP-DeLaW**

Mild Splendor of the various-vested Night! To the Autumnal Moon. Samuel Taylor Coleridge. *Fr.* Effusions. **CP-ColeS**

Mild the mist upon the hill. Emily Brontë. **CP-BronE**

Mild Winter. Hayden Carruth. **CP-CarHS**

Mildred Klinghofer whirled through youth in bloom. Carl Sandburg. *Fr.* The People, Yes. **CP-SandC**

Mile an' a Bittock, A. Robert Louis Stevenson. **CP-StevR**

Mile-Long Street, The. John Hewitt. **CP-HewiJ**

Mile out in the marshes, under a sky, A. The Town Dump. Howard Nemerov. **CP-NemeH**

Milepost. Archie Randolph Ammons. **SP-AmmoA**

Miles. James Liddy. **CP-LiddJ**

Miles across the turbulent kingdoms. The Wise. William Everson. **SP-EverW** *Fr.* Triptych for the Living.

Miles of pram in the wind and Pam in the gorse track. Potpourri from a Surrey Garden. Sir John Betjeman. **CP-BetjJ**

Miles Standish. Henry Wadsworth Longfellow. *Fr.* The Courtship of Miles Standish. **SP-LongH**

"In the Old Colony days, in Plymouth the land of the Pilgrims." **AiP; TreFS**

Miles III. James Liddy. **CP-LiddJ**

Miles II. James Liddy. **CP-LiddJ**

Milestone by the Rabbit-Burrow, The. Thomas Hardy. **CP-HardT**

Milestones. My own; small things lost in a vast. Louis MacNeice. **NAs** *Fr.* Day of Renewal. **CP-MacNL**

Milford Dupree, though he knew it was rude. With His Mouth Full of Food. Shel Silverstein. **SP-SilS2**

Milgate kept standing for four centuries. Robert Lowell. *Fr.* Fall Weekend at *Milgate*. **SP-LoweR**

Milieux. Charles Tomlinson. *Fr.* Antecedents. **CP-TomlC**

Military Appointment, A. Thomas Hardy. **CP-HardT**

Milk. Stephen Berg. **SP-BergS**

Milk. James Schuyler. **CP-SchuJ**

Milk Bottle, The. Galway Kinnell. **SP-KinnG**

Milk-drops on your chin, Helga, The. Winter Milk. Carl Sandburg. **CP-SandC**

Milk Factory, The. Seamus Heaney. **SP-HeanS**

Milk flounces upward in the tea like smoke. Tea-time in November. Wystan Hugh Auden. **CP-AudWJ**

Milk-glass bowl hanging by three chains, A. The Corpse-Plant. Adrienne Rich. **CP-RicAE; SP-RicA2**

Milk stil your Fountains, and your Springs, for why? Draw, and Drinke. Robert Herrick. **CP-HerrR**

Milk used to come in tall glass, heavy and uncrystalline as frozen melted. Milk. James Schuyler. **CP-SchuJ**

Milk-White Moon, Put the Cows to Sleep. Carl Sandburg. **CP-SandC**

Milk-Wort and Bog Cotton. "Hugh MacDiarmid." **SP-MacDH**

Milkers Broken Up. Donald Hall. **CP-HallD**

Milkmaid, The. Thomas Hardy. **CP-HardT**

Milkman, The. Isabella Gardner. **CP-GardI**

Milkman came in the moonlight and the moonlight, The. Les Plus Belles Pages. Wallace Stevens. **CP-StevW**

Milkweed. Philip Levine. **SP-LeviP**

Milkweed. James Wright. **CP-WrigJ**

Milky love of this bland child, The. The Governess. Stevie Smith. **CP-SmitS**

Milky Turqoise Cloud. Tom Clark. **SP-ClarT**

Milky Way, / River of Heaven. Names and Travelers of the Milky Way. Siv Cedering Fox. **SP-CedeS**

Milky Way Is a Cowpath, The. Robert Frost. **CP-FrosR**

Mill, The. Wystan Hugh Auden. **CP-AudWJ**

Mill, The. Edwin Arlington Robinson. **CP-RobiE**

Mill, The. Lewis Turco. **SP-TurcL**

Mill, The. Richard Wilbur. **CP-WilbR**

Mill at Romesdal. Richard Hugo. **CP-HugoR**

Mill Clock, The. Phoebe Hesketh. **SP-HeskP**

Mill-Doors. Carl Sandburg. **CP-SandC**

Mill grinds the night, The. The Mill. Lewis Turco. **SP-TurcL**

Mill (Hempstead), The. Wystan Hugh Auden. **CP-AudWJ**

Mill-House, The. Robert Louis Stevenson. **CP-StevR**

Mill-stream, now that noises cease, The. Alfred Edward Housman. **CP-HousA**

Mill-wheel never seems to tire, The. Skyreholme Mill. Wystan Hugh Auden. **CP-AudWJ**

Mill-wheel reflections of sun on water. Indian Arm. Malcolm Lowry. **CP-LowrM**

Millennial Icon. Tom Clark. **SP-ClarT**

Millennium of sun—. Louis Zukofsky. *Fr.* 29 Poems. **CP-ZukLS**

"Millennium," yes; "pandemonium"! Hometown Piece for Messrs. Alston and Reese. Marianne Craig Moore. **CP-MoorM**

Miller, The. Randall Jarrell. **CP-JarrR**

Miller, stout and sturdy as the stone, The, *mod. vers. by* Louis Untermeyer. Geoffrey Chaucer. *See* Seven Pilgrims: A Miller.

Miller was a stout carl, for the nones, The. Seven Pilgrims: A Miller. Geoffrey Chaucer. **TrGrPo** *Fr.* The General Prologue. **FHYEP; NAWM-1; OAEL-1; PoE** *Fr.* The Canterbury Tales. **CP-ChauG**

Miller's Man, The. Robert Ranke Graves. **CP-GravR**

Miller's Prologue, The. Geoffrey Chaucer. **NAEL-1; NAWM-1; OAEL-1** *Fr.* The Canterbury Tales. **CP-ChauG**

("When the knight had finished, no one, young or old.") **NAWM-1**

Miller's [*or* Milleres] Tale, The. Geoffrey Chaucer. **FaBoBl; NAEL-1; NAWM-1; OAEL-1; OxBoLi; PeLV; TEP** *Fr.* The Canterbury Tales. **CP-ChauG**

("There used to be a rich old oaf.") **NAWM-1**

"Fair was this yonge wyf, and therwithal." **EBEV**

Miller's wife had waited long, The. The Mill. Edwin Arlington Robinson. **CP-RobiE**

Million buds are born that never blow, A. Buds and Babies. Christina Georgina Rossetti. **CP-RosC2**

Million Dollar Bash. "Bob Dylan." **CP-DylaB**

Million emeralds break from the ruby-budded lime, A. Tennyson. *Fr.* Maud [A Monodrama]. **CP-TennA**

Million simmering kettles: in the Destroyer's shrine, A. Louis MacNeice. *Fr.* Didymus. **CP-MacNL**

Million souls wandered out at midnight, A. The Promise. Frederick Morgan. **SP-MorgF**

Million whirling spinning-wheels of flowing gossamer, A. Genesis. Louis MacNeice. **CP-MacNL**

Million Young Workmen, 1915, A. Carl Sandburg. **CP-SandC**

Millionaire, The. Charles Bukowski. **SP-BukC2**

Millions of babies watching the skies. *with music.* Allen Ginsberg. **CP-GinsA**

Millipede, The. John Updike. **CP-UpdiJ**

Millpond. Lewis Turco. **SP-TurcL**

Mill's black finger, The. Master Cotton Spinner. Phoebe Hesketh. **SP-HeskP**

Mills of God, The. David Herbert Lawrence. **CP-LawrD**

Mills of the gods grind slowly. Mitrailliatrice. Ernest Hemingway. **CP-HemiE**

Mills of the Kavanaughs, The. Robert Lowell. **SP-LoweR**

Milltown Union Bar, The. Richard Hugo. **CP-HugoR**

Miltiades! thy valour best. On Miltiades. *Unknown, tr. fr. Greek by* William Cowper. **CP-CowpW**

Milton. William Blake. **CP-BlakW**

And Did Those Feet in Ancient Time. **AWP; CABA; ClHu; EBEvV; EnRP; FaBV; FaBoCh; FaBoPV; HAP; HeIP; InPS; LoBV; MAT; MeMBP; NAEL-2; NAWM-2; NOBRP; NoP; OAEL-2; OAEP;**

OBRV; PAI; PeECV; PlP; PoE; PoEL-4; PoRA; PrIm; SCGP; SeCeV; TFi; WGRP

(And Did Those Feet.) **ChIV-1**

(Jerusalem.) **BoTP; EaLo; EvOK; FHYEP; FaPoR; NOBE; NOCV; OBEV; OXAEP-2; OtMeF; RB; UV; WaaP**

(New Jerusalem, A.) **CoGr; FSW; FaBoEn; LiTB; SWP; TrGrPo**

(New Jerusalem, The.) **ImPo**

(Prelude: "And did those feet in ancient time.") **OBNC**

"And in the midst of the Great Assembly Palamabron pray'd." **OBF**

"But the Wine-press of Los is eastward of Golgonooza, before the Seat." **NOBRP**

"But turning toward Ololon in terrible majesty Milton." **OXAEP-2**

"Daughters of Beulah! Muses who inspire the Poets Song." **PeECV**

"Into this pleasant Shadow all the weak & weary." **NOBRP**

Reason and Imagination. **EnRP**

"Then Milton rose up from the heaven of Albion ardorous!" **OAEL-2**

"There is a place where Contrarities are equally True." **NOBRP**

"This wine-press is call'd war on earth." **EBEV; EnRP**

(Wine-Press of Los, The.) **EnRP**

"Thou hearest the nightingale begin the song of spring." **EnRP; NOBE; OBNC; PBBP; WiR**

(Choir of Day, The.) **EnRP**

(Lark's Song, The.) **WiR**

(Vision of Beulah, The ("Thou hearest the nightingale begin the song of spring").) **NOBE**

(Vision of the Lamentation of Beulah, A.) **OBNC**

Vision of Beulah, The ("There is a place where contrarieties are equally true"). **OAEL-2**

Wild Thyme, The. **WiR**

Milton. John Dryden, *tr. fr. English by* Gerard Manley Hopkins. **CP-HopkG**

Milton. George Meredith. **CP-MerG2**

Milton. John Greenleaf Whittier. **CP-WhitJ**

Milton by Firelight. Gary Snyder. **CP-SnydG**

Milton! thou should'st be living at this hour. London, 1802. William Wordsworth. **CP-WorW1**

Milton unlocked hell for us. Our Hells. Carl Sandburg. **CP-SandC**

Milton, we like thee not, forgive us, please. The Schoolboy's Complaint. Malcolm Lowry. **CP-LowrM**

Miltonic Sonnet for Mr. Johnson on His Refusal of Peter Hurd's Official Portrait, A. Richard Wilbur. **CP-WilbR**

Milton's fiends—Republican, bituminous—begin their scenarios. Thomas Merton. *Fr.* Cables to the Ace. **CP-MertT**

Milton's strong pinion now not heaven can bound. Alexander Pope. **EPCY** *Fr.* The First Epistle of the Second Book of Horace Imitated. **CP-PopeA**

Milton's the prince of poets—so we say. Byron. **NOBL** *Fr.* Canto the Third. *Fr.* Don Juan. **CP-Byron**

Mime. John Updike. **CP-UpdiJ**

Mime the loud wind in pain. To the Loud Wind. Donald Hall. **CP-HallD**

Min Schleppner. William Carlos Williams. **CP-WilW1**

Mind, The. Ben Jonson. *Fr.* Eupheme. **CP-JonsB**

(Picture of Her Mind, The.) **GoBC**

Mind. Richard Wilbur. **CP-WilbR**

Mind, an irremediable virgin, The. For the Deserted. Frank Templeton Prince. **CP-PrinF**

Mind and Nature. Richard Eberhart. **CP-EberR**

Mind Breathes. Allen Ginsberg. **CP-GinsA**

Mind has shown itself at times, The. Hart Crane. *Fr.* For the Marriage of Faustus and Helen. **CP-CranH**

Mind Hesitant, The. William Carlos Williams. **CP-WilW2**

Mind in its [or the] purest play is like some bat. Mind. Richard Wilbur. **CP-WilbR**

Mind, Intractable Thing, The. Marianne Craig Moore. **CP-MoorM**

Mind is a city like London, The. Overture. Delmore Schwartz. **SP-SchwD**

Mind is a most delicate evidence. On the Fragility of Mind. Richard Eberhart. **CP-EberR**

Mind Is an Enchanting Thing, The. Marianne Craig Moore. **CP-MoorM**

Mind is its own beautiful prisoner, The. Edward Estlin Cummings. **CP-CummE**

Mind is so near itself, The. Emily Dickinson. **SP-DickE**

Mind is the continuity, The. The Light. Wendell Berry. *Fr.* The Handing Down. **CP-BerrW**

Mind is the great poem of winter, the man, The. Man and Bottle. Wallace Stevens. **CP-StevW**

Mind is the terriblest force in the world, father, The. Saint John and the Back-Ache. Wallace Stevens. **CP-StevW**

Mind lives on the Heart, The. Emily Dickinson. **CP-DickE**

Mind may not mind death. It means, The. The Body's Strength. Stephen Dobyns. **SP-DobyS**

Mind of man is fram'd even like the breath, The. In Patterdale. William Wordsworth. **FaBoRV** *Fr.* Introduction—Childhood and School-Time. *Fr.* The Prelude; Growth of a Poet's Mind [1805 vers.]. **CP-WorW3**

Mind of mortals, in perverseness strong, The. Juvenal, *tr. by* Samuel Johnson. **CP-JohnS** *Fr.* Satires.

Mind of Professor Primrose, The. Ogden Nash. **CP-NashO**

Mind of the Frontispiece to a Book, The. Ben Jonson. **CP-JonsB**

Mind-Reader, The. Richard Wilbur. **CP-WilbR**

"What should I tell them?" **CRP**

Mind (the soul) is not, The. Attar of Roses. Donald Davie. **CP-DavDo**

Mind to body spoke the whole night through, The. Wystan Hugh Auden. **CP-AudWJ**

Mind went forth with naked eye, The. Druidic Rimes. Howard Nemerov. **CP-NemeH**

Mindes of men are ever so affected, The. Homer. **CP-RaleW**, *tr. by* Sir Walter Ralegh; *Fr.* Odyssey.

Mindful of you the sodden earth in spring. Edna St. Vincent Millay. **CP-MillE**

Mindless, meaning no harm. Amoeba. John Updike. **CP-UpdiJ**

Mind's(/ I never you never), The. Edward Estlin Cummings. **CP-CummE**

Mind's a queer sponge, the. May 1st Tomorrow. William Carlos Williams. **CP-WilW2**

Mind's eye sees as the heart mirrors:, The. To Sleep. Robert Ranke Graves. **CP-GravR**

Mind's Games, The. William Carlos Williams. **CP-WilW2**

Mind's Heart. Robert Creeley. **CP-CreeR**

Mind's heart, it must / be that some. Mind's Heart. Robert Creeley. **CP-CreeR**

Mind's Journey to Diss, A. Sir John Betjeman. **CP-BetjJ**

Mind's Notice, The. Charles Olson. **CP-OlsoC**

Mindseye is flitting like a moth among summer firs, The. The Being as Prevision. Hayden Carruth. *Fr.* Contra Mortem. **CP-CarHL**

Mine are the night and morning. Song of Nature. Ralph Waldo Emerson. **CP-EmerR**

Mine—by the Right of the White Election! Emily Dickinson. **CP-DickE**

Mine ear has rung, my spirit sunk subdued. Continued [Church to Be Erected]. William Wordsworth. *Fr.* Ecclesiastical Sonnets. **CP-WorW2**

Mine Enemy is growing old. Emily Dickinson. **CP-DickE**

Mine eye and heart are at a mortal war. Sonnet 46. William Shakespeare. **EyDe; HeIP** *Fr.* Sonnets. **CP-ShaWS**

Mine eye hath play'd the painter, and hath stell'd. Sonnet 24. William Shakespeare. **EyDe** *Fr.* Sonnets. **CP-ShaWS**

Mine eyes, like clouds, were drizzling rain. The Rainbow; or Curious Covenant. Robert Herrick. **CP-HerrR**

Mine eyes were dim with tears unshed. To Mary Wollstonecraft Godwin. Percy Bysshe Shelley. **CP-ShelP**

Mine eyes were swift to know thee, and my heart. Robert Louis Stevenson. **CP-StevR**

Mine Host. Alun Lewis. *Fr.* Poems from the Chinese. **CP-LewiA**

Mine is a body that should die at sea! Burial. Edna St. Vincent Millay. **CP-MillE**

Mine is a dauntless spirit, meaning a spirit that is hard to daunt. I'm a Pleasure to Shop for. Ogden Nash. **CP-NashO**

Mine old dear enemy. Frank Templeton Prince. *Fr.* Walks in Rome. **CP-PrinF**

Mine old dear enemy [or en'my] , my froward master. Petrarch, *tr. fr. Italian by* Sir Thomas Wyatt. **CP-WyatT**

Mine [or Myne] own[e] John Poyntz, since [or sins] ye delight to know. Sir Thomas Wyatt. **CP-WyatT** *Fr.* Satires.

Mine Sweepers. Rudyard Kipling. **CP-KiplR**

Mine there is no Man would own, A. Emily Dickinson. **CP-DickE**

Mine to watch the sun at work. Thermometer. Ralph Waldo Emerson. **CP-EmerR**

Mine was a midwest home—you can keep your world. One Home. William Stafford. **SP-StafW**

Mine was the woman to me, darkling I found her. The First Chantey. Rudyard Kipling. **CP-KiplR**

Mine will last though others fall to dust. The Enigma. Richard Eberhart. **CP-EberR**

Mined Country. Richard Wilbur. **CP-WilbR**

Mineral Rejoicings. Christopher Smart. **CBCK** *Fr.* Fragment D. *Fr.* Jubilate Agno. **SP-SmarC**

Miners. Wilfred Owen. **CP-OwenW**

Miners. James Wright. **CP-WrigJ**

Miner's Wife, The. Wystan Hugh Auden. **CP-AudWJ**

Minerva has vowed since the bishops do slight her. On Wisdom's Defeat in a Learned Debate. Jonathan Swift. **CP-SwifJ**

Mines in Sepia Tint, The. Steve Griffiths. **SP-GrifS**

Mingle with the genial bowl. Translation from Anacreon. Byron. **CP-Byron**

Mingled / breath and smell. Subway Rush Hour. Langston Hughes. **SP-HughL**

Mingled the moonlight with daylight—the last in the narrowing west. Thomas Hardy. Walter de la Mare. **CP-DeLaW**

Mingled, windows stuffed with grainsacks, "Lots". Hayden Carruth. *Fr.* The Sleeping Beauty. **CP-CarHL**

Miniature on a Book of Hours. Alun Lewis. **CP-LewiA**

Minim. Howard Nemerov. *Fr.* Gnomes. **CP-NemeH**

Minimal, The. Theodore Roethke. **CP-RoetT**

Minister. John Hewitt. **CP-HewiJ**

Minister of birds, / Keeper of islands and pools. Jean Garrigue. *See* Cortège for Colette.

Minister wet to lee, pour the Falernian. Catullus. *See* Carmen 27: "Falernian, / old Falernian!"

Ministers / Don't like bar sinisters. Birth Comes to the Archbishop. Ogden Nash. **CP-NashO**

Minister's Daughter, The. John Greenleaf Whittier. **CP-WhitJ**

Ministre and the norice unto vices, The. The Second Nun's Prologue. Geoffrey Chaucer. *Fr.* The Canterbury Tales. **CP-ChauG**

Miniver Cheevy. Edwin Arlington Robinson. **CP-RobiE**

Mink. Paul Muldoon. **SP-MuldP**

Minneapolis Poem, The. James Wright. **CP-WrigJ**

Minnelied. Wystan Hugh Auden. *Fr.* Three Posthumous Poems. **CP-AudeW**

Minnesota Thanksgiving. John Berryman. **CP-BerrJ**

("For that free Grace bringing us past great risks.") **CP-BerrJ**

Minnie and Mattie. Christina Georgina Rossetti. **CP-RosC2**

Minnie and Mattie. Christina Georgina Rossetti. **GoJo; InvP** *Fr.* Sing-Song. **CP-RosC2**

Minnie bakes oaten cakes, / Minnie brews ale. Christina Georgina Rossetti. **CP-RosC2**

Minnow, go to sleep and dream. Lullaby for the Cat. Elizabeth Bishop. **CP-BishE**

Minnow Minnie. Shel Silverstein. **SP-SilS2**

Minnows. John Keats. **GN** *Fr.* I Stood Tip-Toe upon a Little Hill. **CP-KeatJ**

Minnows leap like silver coins, The. The River Temple: Wai. Alun Lewis. **CP-LewiA**

Minoan Snake Goddess is flanked by a Chardin still-life, somber, The. The Postcards: A Triptych. Denise Levertov. **CP-LeveD**

Minor Bird, A. Robert Frost. **CP-FrosR**

Minor Impulse to Complain, A. Charles Bukowski. **SP-BukC2**

Minor Poet's Dilemma, 1940. John Hewitt. **CP-HewiJ**

Minor stupidities, The. Education a Failure. William Carlos Williams. **CP-WilW2**

Minor Toys of the Year are alike, The. Emily Dickinson. **SP-DickE**

Minor Victorian Painter, A. John Hewitt. **CP-HewiJ**

Minorities in Danger. David Herbert Lawrence. **CP-LawrD**

Minority Report. John Updike. **CP-UpdiJ**

Minotaur, The. Isabella Gardner. **CP-GardI**

Minotaur. John Hewitt. **CP-HewiJ**

Minotaur, The. Muriel Rukeyser. **CP-RukeM**

Minotaur. Lewis Turco. **SP-TurcL**

Minott, Lee, Willard, Hosmer, Meriam, Flint. Hamatreya. Ralph Waldo Emerson. **CP-EmerR**

Minstrel Boy. "Bob Dylan." **CP-DylaB**

Minstrel came singing in the way, A. Unheard Melodies. Walter de la Mare. **CP-DeLaW**

Minstrel in Labrador, A. Malcolm Lowry. **CP-LowrM**

Minstrel, what have you to do. To a Poet that Died Young. Edna St. Vincent Millay. **CP-MillE**

Minstrels played their Christmas tune, The. To the Rev. Dr Wordsworth (with the Sonnets to the River Duddon, and Other Poems in This Collection, 1820). William Wordsworth. *Fr.* The River Duddon [A Series of Sonnets]. **CP-WorW2**

Mint a spiked attar hot. Spearmint. Louis Zukofsky. **CP-ZukLS**

Mint bed is in / bloom: lavender haze, The. Sunday. James Schuyler. **CP-SchuJ**

Minuet in G. Peter Meinke. **SP-MeinP**

Minus One. John Ciardi. **SP-CiarJ**

Minuscule Things. William Matthews. **SP-MattW**

Minute before Meeting, The. Thomas Hardy. **CP-HardT**

Minute garden / you must not enter, A. In Verdi Square. Charles Tomlinson. **CP-TomlC**

Minutely Hurt. Countee Cullen. **CP-CullC**

Minutes are flying swiftly, and as yet. On Receiving a Laurel Crown from Leigh Hunt. John Keats. **CP-KeatJ**

Mips and ma the mooly moo. Theodore Roethke. **CBNP; NBLV; RB** *Fr.* Praise to the End! **CP-RoetT**

Mirabeau Bridge. Guillaume Apollinaire, *tr. fr. French by* Richard Wilbur. **CP-WilbR**

Miracle, The. Walter de la Mare. **CP-DeLaW**

Miracle, The. Ralph Waldo Emerson. **CP-EmerR**

Miracle, The. Thom Gunn. **CP-GunnT**

Miracle, The. Philip Levine. **SP-LeviP**

Miracle, The. George Meredith. **CP-MerG2**

Miracle, The. Sir John Suckling. **CP-SuckJ**

Miracle Cary, and His Twelve Loaves—Twelve Fishes. Marsden Hartley. **CP-HartM**

Miracle for Breakfast, A. Elizabeth Bishop. **CP-BishE**

Miracle is the Shortest Time, The. Charles Bukowski. **SP-BukC3**

Miracle of our land's speech—so known, The. The Birthright. Rudyard Kipling. **CP-KiplR** *Fr.* Debits and Credits.

Miracle of Purun Bhagat, The. Rudyard Kipling. *Fr.* The Second Jungle Book.

"Night we felt the earth would move, The." **CP-KiplR**

Song of Kabir, A. **CP-KiplR**

Miracle of the children the brilliant. Exodus. George Oppen. **CP-OppeG**

Miracles, The. Rudyard Kipling. **CP-KiplR**

Miracles. Walt Whitman. **CP-WhitW**

Mirage. Walter de la Mare. **CP-DeLaW**

Mirage, The. Kathleen Jessie Raine. *Fr.* Three Poems on Illusion. **SP-RainK**

Mirage. Christina Georgina Rossetti. **CP-RosC1**

Mirages, The. Robert Earl Hayden. **CP-HaydR**

Mirages. Walt Whitman. **CP-WhitW**

Miranda! mark where shrinking from the gale. To an Amiable Girl. Charlotte Smith. **CP-SmitC**

Mired in it! Stuck in the various. Zion. Donald Davie. **CP-DavDo**

Mirèio. Frédéric Mistral, *tr. fr. Provençal.*

Mares of the Camargue, The. **CP-MerG2**

Miriam. John Greenleaf Whittier. **CP-WhitJ**

Book Our Mothers Read, The. **BLRP**

(Knowledge.) **PoToHe**

Miriam and Horlick spend a great deal of time putting off going to bed. Goodnight. Stevie Smith. **CP-SmitS**

Miriam Tazewell. John Crowe Ransom. **SP-RansJ**

Miriam's Lucky Day. Ogden Nash. **CP-NashO**

Miror surgentem per puram Oriona noctem. Gerard Manley Hopkins. **CP-HopkG**

Mirror, The. Robert Creeley. **CP-CreeR**

Mirror, The. Robert Duncan. **SP-DuncR**

Mirror, The. Louise Glück. **SP-GlücL**

Mirror, The. John Haines. **SP-HainJ**

"Door turned its white face, A."

"Down the turning stairway."

"From the bed where I lay."

"I went farther and deeper."

"Tarpaper and wind / a street rolling stones."

Mirror. John Hewitt. **CP-HewiJ**

Mirror. James Merrill. **SP-MerrJ**

Mirror. Frederick Morgan. *Fr.* Enigmas. **SP-MorgF**

Mirror, The. Howard Nemerov. **CP-NemeH**

Mirror. Sylvia Plath. **CP-PlatS**

Mirror, The. Charles Kenneth Williams. **SP-WillC**

Mirror above my fireplace reflects the reflected, The. Reflections. Louis MacNeice. **CP-MacNL**

Mirror for Poets, A. Thom Gunn. **CP-GunnT**

Mirror from the twenties. What the Owl Sees. Marge Piercy. **SP-PierM**

Mirror hangs on the wall of the draughty cupola, A. The Cupola. Louise Bogan. **CP-BogaL**

Mirror in the Roadway, The. Charles Tomlinson. **CP-TomlC**

Mirror in Which Two Are Seen as One, The. Adrienne Rich. **SP-RicA2**

Mirror Lake, The. Summer Song. Li Po, *tr. fr. Chinese by* William Carlos Williams *with* David Rafael Wang. **CP-WilW2**

Mirror, let us through the glass. The Flight into Egypt. Wystan Hugh Auden. **CP-AudeW** *Fr.* For the Time Being; a Christmas Oratorio. **CP-AudeW**

Mirror Meditation. Anne Waldman. **SP-WaldA**

Mirror, Mirror. Jenny Joseph. **SP-JoseJ**

Mirror, mirror on the wall. Conduct and Work. Donald Hall. **CP-HallD**

Mirror mirror on the wall. STUDY: *A Lady in her Bedroom* (Bonnard). Jenny Joseph. *Fr.* Altarpiece (A Meditation on Lust, Desire and Love). **SP-JoseJ**

Mirror oval sabres playing, The. Louis Zukofsky. *Fr.* 29 Songs. **CP-ZukLS**

Mirror Speaks, The. Robert Louis Stevenson. **CP-StevR**

Mirror, turns black, The. Mirror. Frederick Morgan. *Fr.* Enigmas. **SP-MorgF**

Mirrored / the rear window. Carscape. Charles Tomlinson. **CP-TomlC**

Mirrorment. Archie Randolph Ammons. **SP-AmmoA**

Mirrors, The. William Carlos Williams. **CP-WilW2**

Mirrors are passive observers. Susanna. Siv Cedering Fox. *Fr.* Onna-E, Pictures of Women. **SP-CedeS**

Mirror's Mission, The. Jorge Carrera Andrade, *tr. fr. Spanish by* Thomas Merton. **CP-MertT**

Mirrors of Life and Death. Christina Georgina Rossetti. **CP-RosC2**

Mirru. Kenneth Patchen. **CP-PatcK**

Mirth. Robert Herrick. **CP-HerrR**

Mirth. Christopher Smart. LAuP; OxBChV *Fr.* Hymns for the Amusement of Children. **SP-SmarC**

Mirth and Poetry. John Milton. EPCY *Fr.* L'Allegro. **CP-MiltJ**

Mirth, with Thee I Mean to Live. John Milton. *See* Haste thee, nymph, and bring with thee.

Mis-shapen Time, copesmate of ugly Night. William Shakespeare. OAEL-1 *Fr.* The Rape of Lucrece. **CP-ShaWS**

Misael, civil servant in the Ministry of Labor, 63 years old. Brazilian Tragedy. Manuel Bandeira, *tr. fr. Portuguese by* Elizabeth Bishop. **CP-BishE**

Misanthrope. John Crowe Ransom. *Fr.* Two Gentlemen in Bonds. **SP-RansJ**

Misanthropos. Thom Gunn. **CP-GunnT**

Elegy on the Dust. NoAM

First Man, The.

Last Man, The. OxAEP-2

Memoirs of the World.

"Serving man. Curled my hair, A." OxBC

Misapprehension. Paul Laurence Dunbar. **CP-DunbP**

Miscellaneous weed / strands, stems, debris—. The Cod Head. William Carlos Williams. **CP-WilW1**

Misconception. Thomas Hardy. **CP-HardT**

Misconceptions. Robert Browning. **CP-BroR1**

Misdeeming eye! that stoopest to the lure. Lewd Love Is Loss[e]. Robert Southwell. **CP-SoutR**

Miser, The. Mona Van Duyn. **SP-VanDM**

Miser and the Mouse, The. Lucilius. *See* Asclepiades the Miser was horrified.

Miser, traversing his house, A. *see also* Treasure. *Unknown, tr. fr. Greek by* William Cowper. **CP-CowpW**

Miserable Catullus, stop being foolish. Catullus viii. Louis Zukofsky. **CP-ZukLS**

Miserable little woman. Divertimiento. William Carlos Williams. **CP-WilW1**

Misericordia. William Carlos Williams. **CP-WilW1**

Miseries. Robert Herrick. **CP-HerrR**

Miserly, is the best description of that poor fool. Con Brio. William Carlos Williams. **CP-WilW1**

"Miserrimus!" and neither name nor date. A Gravestone upon the Floor in the Cloisters of Worcester Cathedral. William Wordsworth. **CP-WorW2**

Misery [*or* Miserie]. George Herbert. **CP-HerbG**

Misery. Langston Hughes. **SP-HughL**

Misery. David Herbert Lawrence. **CP-LawrD**

Misery. The Beatles. **CP-Beatl**

Misery etcetera. The Day of the Sentry. David St. John. **SP-StJoD**

Misery is greater, as I live!, The. George Meredith. *Fr.* Modern Love. **CP-MerG1**

Misery may be folded. Jim Carroll. *Fr.* Things That Fly. **SP-CarrJ**

Misgiving. Robert Frost. **CP-FrosR**

Misgivings. Herman Melville. **SP-MelvH**

Mishima. Charles Henri Ford. *Fr.* Four Elegies. **SP-FordC**

Mismet. Thomas Hardy. **CP-HardT**

Misprint. Charles Tomlinson. **CP-TomlC**

Misrule, Towyn, 1990. Steve Griffiths. **SP-GrifS**

Miss. Archie Randolph Ammons. **SP-AmmoA**

Miss and Hit. Gilbert Sorrentino. **SP-SorrG**

Miss Blues'es Child. Langston Hughes. **SP-HughL**

Miss Drake Proceeds to Supper. Sylvia Plath. **CP-PlatS**

Miss Gardner's in her garden. Southern Mammy Sings. Langston Hughes. **SP-HughL**

Miss Gee. Wystan Hugh Auden. **CP-AudeW**

Miss Helen Slingsby was my maiden aunt. Aunt Helen. Thomas Stearns Eliot. **CP-ElioT**

Miss her, Catullus? don't be so inept to rail. Catullus. *See* Carmen 8: "Break off / fallen Catullus."

Miss J. Hunter Dunn, Miss J. Hunter Dunn. A Subaltern's Love-Song. Sir John Betjeman. **CP-BetjJ**

Miss Jones. "Lewis Carroll." **CP-CarrL**

Miss Loo. Walter de la Mare. **CP-DeLaW**

Miss Lorence, until I get to be somebody else—big me. Another Day. In a Field of Peace the Child, Playing. The Child Preparing for Daytime Sleep. Muriel Rukeyser. **CP-RukeM**

Miss Lorence, we are new to each other. Another Day (Miss Lorence). Muriel Rukeyser. **CP-RukeM**

Miss Lorence, you are a tree with leaves on. Muriel Rukeyser. **CP-RukeM**

Miss Marfy sco'n young Issac so. The Suitor. Paul Laurence Dunbar. **CP-DunbP**

Miss Millicent Maxse was fond of her Ma. George Meredith. **CP-MerG2**

Miss Moore at Assembly. John Updike. **CP-UpdiJ**

Miss M.'s a nightingale. 'Tis well. On a Poetess. Gerard Manley Hopkins. PP *Fr.* Seven Epigrams. **CP-HopkG**

Miss Murdoch. John Hewitt. **CP-HewiJ**

Miss Nancy Ellicott. Cousin Nancy. Thomas Stearns Eliot. **CP-ElioT**

Miss Pauncefort sang at the top of her voice. The Songster. Stevie Smith. **CP-SmitS**

Miss Pimberton Of. Siv Cedering Fox. **SP-CedeS**

Miss Rafferty wore taffeta. The Private Dining Room. Ogden Nash. **CP-NashO**

Miss Sally lay on her cornshuck bed. Ballad of Miss Sally. Louise McNeill. **SP-McNeL**

Miss Scarlet, Mr. Rhett and other Latter-Day Saints. Maya Angelou. **SP-AngeM**

Miss Story's character! too much you ask. Gerard Manley Hopkins. **CP-HopkG**

Missed Train, The. Thomas Hardy. **CP-HardT**

Missile to launch a missile, The. Venus and the Ark. Anne Sexton. **CP-SextA**

Missing. Wystan Hugh Auden. **CP-AudeW**

Missing, The. Thom Gunn. **CP-GunnT**

Missing All—prevented Me, The. Emily Dickinson. **CP-DickE**

Missing is a pain. Never-Never. Marge Piercy. **SP-PierM**

Missing Pages. John Yau. **SP-YauJo**

Missing Persons. Miller Williams. **SP-WillM**

Missing the Bo in the Henhouse. Hayden Carruth. **CP-CarHS**

Missing the Point. Adrienne Rich. **CP-RicAE**

Missing the Sea. Derek Walcott. **CP-WalcD**

Mission in Carmel. Richard Hugo. **CP-HugoR**

Mission to Linz. Richard Hugo. **CP-HugoR**

Mission with the Night, A. Jane Cooper. **SP-CoopJ**

"He came all this way."

"She is like that man."

Missionary, The. John Greenleaf Whittier. **CP-WhitJ**

Missionary from the Mau Mau told me, A. A Magus. John Ciardi. **SP-CiarJ**

Missions and Travels. William Wordsworth. *Fr.* Ecclesiastical Sonnets. **CP-WorW2**

Mississippi at Midnight, The. Walt Whitman. **CP-WhitW**

Mississippi Winter I. Alice Walker. **CP-WalkA**

Mississippi Winter II. Alice Walker. **CP-WalkA**

Mississippi Winter III. Alice Walker. **CP-WalkA**

Mississippi Winter IV. Alice Walker. **CP-WalkA**

Missive Missile, A. Robert Frost. **CP-FrosR**

Missoula in a Dusty Light. John Haines. **SP-HainJ**

Missoula Softball Tournament. Richard Hugo. **CP-HugoR**

Missouri Haiku. Etheridge Knight. **SP-KnigE**

Boone County.

Clay County.

Mizzu.

Outside St. Louis.

Mist. Edward Estlin Cummings. **CP-CummE**

Mist. Walter de la Mare. **CP-DeLaW**

Mist. Robert Ranke Graves. **CP-GravR**

Mist. John Hewitt. **CP-HewiJ**

Mist, The. Carl Sandburg. **CP-SandC**

Mist after frost. The woodlands. The Last of Night. Charles Tomlinson. **CP-TomlC**

Mist came up as a man's hand. New Weather. Carl Sandburg. **CP-SandC**

Mist clears and the cavities, The. Derry Morning. Derek Mahon. **SP-MahoD**

Mist Forms. Carl Sandburg. **CP-SandC**

Mist has left the greening plain, The. Morning. Paul Laurence Dunbar. **CP-DunbP**

Mist in the trees, and soiled water and grass cuttings splotch. Yard Journal. Charles Wright. **SP-WrigC**

Mist in the Valley. Edna St. Vincent Millay. **CP-MillE**

Mist Marches Across the Valley. Carl Sandburg. **CP-SandC**

Mist Sleeve Flight. Tom Clark. **SP-ClarT**

Mist that from the moor arose, A. Tregardock. Sir John Betjeman. **CP-BetjJ**

Mistake, The. Thomas Carew. **CP-CareT**

Mistake, The. Theodore Roethke. **OBCoV** *Fr.* Three Epigrams. **CP-RoetT**

Mistaken Identity. Richard Eberhart. **CP-EberR**

Mr. America last seen crossing the road. Gilbert Sorrentino. **SP-SorrG**

Mr. and Mrs. Billings. Donald Hall. **CP-HallD**

Mr. and Mrs. F.X. Pleasants. Lines To Be Mumbled At Ovington's. Ogden Nash. **CP-NashO**

Mr. and Mrs. Scott, and I. Christina Georgina Rossetti. **CP-RosC3**

Mr. Apollinax. Thomas Stearns Eliot. **CP-ElioT**

Mr. Artesian's Conscientiousness. Ogden Nash. **CP-NashO**

Mr. Attila. Carl Sandburg. **CP-SandC**

Mr. Barcalow's Breakdown. Ogden Nash. **CP-NashO**

Mr. Berryman's songs and sonnets say. Thank-You Note. Elizabeth Bishop. **CP-BishE**

Mr. Betts's Mind a Kingdom Is. Ogden Nash. **CP-NashO**

Mr. Boyd. Frederick Morgan. **SP-MorgF**

Mr. Brodsky. Charles Tomlinson. **CP-TomlC**

Mr. Burgess, Meet Mr. Barmecide. Ogden Nash. **CP-NashO**

Mr. Carew to His Friend. Thomas Carew. **CP-CareT**

Mr Cromek to Mr Stothard. William Blake. **CP-BlakW**

Mr Dean, Canons and Students of Christ Church, Ladies and Gentlemen. A Reminder. Wystan Hugh Auden. *Fr.* Six Commissioned Texts. **CP-AudeW**

Mr. Edwards and the Spider. Robert Lowell. **SP-LoweR**

Mister Faintheart Middleclass. John Hewitt. **CP-HewiJ**

Mr. Flood's Party. Edwin Arlington Robinson. **CP-RobiE**

Mr. Hericke his Daughter's Dowrye. Robert Herrick. **CP-HerrR**

[Mr. Herrys,] His Epitaph. Richard Crashaw. **CP-CrasR**

Mr. High-Mind. John Updike. **CP-UpdiJ**

Mr. Jason Hassard, a Woolen Draper in Dublin. Jonathan Swift. **CP-SwifJ**

Mr. Longfellow and His Boy. Carl Sandburg. **CP-SandC**

Mr. Longfellow, Henry Wadsworth Longfellow. Mr. Longfellow and His Boy. Carl Sandburg. **CP-SandC**

Mr. Longfellow spoke only part of the truth. A Boy's Will is the Wind's Will? Ogden Nash. *Fr.* Posies from a Second Childhood, or, Hark How Gaffer Do Chaffer. **CP-NashO**

Mr. Lowry's Good Friday under a Real Cactus. Malcolm Lowry. **CP-LowrM**

Mister Minister, I found. Why I Turned Vegetarian. Rita Dove. **SP-DoveR**

Mr. or Mrs. Nobody. William Stafford. **SP-StafW**

Mr. Osmosis / Is all right in small doses. Mistress Osmosis. Stevie Smith. **CP-SmitS**

Mr. Peachey's Predicament or No Mot Parades. Ogden Nash. **CP-NashO**

Mr. Pope. Allen Tate. **CP-TateA**

Mr. Robert Hericke His Farwell unto Poetrie. Robert Herrick. **CP-HerrR**

Mr Sharp in Florence. Donald Davie. **CP-DavDo**

Mr Sludge, "The Medium." Robert Browning. **CP-BroR1**

Mr. smith / is reading / his letter. Edward Estlin Cummings. **CP-CummE**

Mr Stothard to Mr Cromek. William Blake. **CP-BlakW**

Mr T. / bareheaded. The Artist. William Carlos Williams. **CP-WilW2**

Mr. Tambourine Man. "Bob Dylan." **CP-DylaB**

Mr u will not be missed. Edward Estlin Cummings. **CP-CummE**

Mr. Wakeville on Interstate 90. Donald Hall. **CP-HallD**

Mr youse needn't be so spry. Edward Estlin Cummings. **CP-CummE; SP-CummE**

Mistlines. Charles Tomlinson. **CP-TomlC**

Mistral Over the Graves. Archibald MacLeish. **CP-MacLA**

Mrs / and mr across the way are kind of. Edward Estlin Cummings. **CP-CummE**

Mistress, The. Abraham Cowley.
    Against Hope.

(On Hope.) **CP-CrasR**

Mrs. Alfred Uruguay. Wallace Stevens. **CP-StevW**

Mrs. Arbuthnot. Stevie Smith. **CP-SmitS**

Mrs. Blood. Dear Madam. Yours of Sept. 13. Gary Gildner. *Fr.* Letters from Vicksburg. **SP-GildG**

Mrs. Blow and her Animals. Stevie Smith. **CP-SmitS**

Mrs. Choate's House-Warming. John Greenleaf Whittier. **CP-WhitJ**

Mrs. Coley's three-flat brick. The Vacant Lot. Gwendolyn Brooks. **NAAL-2; NOBA; NoAM** *Fr.* A Street in Bronzeville. **SP-BrooG**

Mistress Dampgress, the Mother Joel—Don't, oh don't go barefoot. Down in Ol' Dontcaradama. Kenneth Patchen. **CP-PatcK**

Mrs. Eliz. Wheeler, Under the Name of the Lost Shepardesse. Robert Herrick. **CP-HerrR**

Mistress Fell. Walter de la Mare. **CP-DeLaW**

Mrs. Gabrielle Giovanitti comes along Peoria Street every morning. Onion Days. Carl Sandburg. **CP-SandC**

Mrs. Grundy. Walter de la Mare. **CP-DeLaW**

Mrs. Harris's Petition. Jonathan Swift. **CP-SwifJ**

Mrs. Hattie Boomer Spink. Lines to a Three-Name Lady. Ogden Nash. **CP-NashO**

Mrs. Mandrill. Howard Nemerov. **CP-NemeH**

Mrs. Marmaduke Moore, at the age of ten. The Seven Spiritual Ages of Mrs. Marmaduke Moore. Ogden Nash. **CP-NashO**

Mrs Masters's fuchsias hung. The Lodging-House Fuchsias. Thomas Hardy. **CP-HardT**

Mrs. Mouse / Come out of your house. Cat Asks Mouse Out. Stevie Smith. **CP-SmitS**

Mistress on her white horse at, The. James Liddy. *Fr.* Cliffs. **CP-LiddJ**

Mistress Osmosis. Stevie Smith. **CP-SmitS**

Mrs. Purvis Dreads Room Service. Ogden Nash. **CP-NashO**

Mrs. Sexton went out looking for the gods. Gods. Anne Sexton. **CP-SextA**

Mrs. Shepherd of Danbury, Conn., A. Malice Domestic. Ogden Nash. **CP-NashO**

Mrs. Siddons, *sometimes at. to* Charles Lamb. Samuel Taylor Coleridge. *Fr.* Effusions. **CP-ColeS**

Mistress [*or* Mistris], since you so much desire. Mistris [*or* Mistress] Since You So Much Desire. Thomas Campion. **CP-CampT**

Mrs. Someone's been to Asia. An Importer. Robert Frost. **CP-FrosR**

Mrs. Throckmorton's bull-finch sang a song. Homage to William Cowper. Donald Davie. **CP-DavDo**

Mrs. Wilmot sate scribbling a play. Another Simple Ballat. Byron. **CP-Byron**

Mistris [*or* Mistress] Since You So Much Desire. Thomas Campion. **CP-CampT**

Mistrust of the Beloved. William Carlos Williams. **CP-WilW2**

Mistrustful minds be moved. Sir Thomas Wyatt. **CP-WyatT**

Mists of fortune, The. Fortune's Mist. Richard Eberhart. **CP-EberR**

Mists over the River. William Carlos Williams. **CP-WilW2**

Misty Day, A. Paul Laurence Dunbar. **CP-DunbP**

Misty heat, now that the spring has gone, A. Midsummer's Day. Howard Nemerov. **CP-NemeH**

Misunderstanding, A. Wystan Hugh Auden. **CP-AudeW**

Misunderstandings. "Lewis Carroll." **CP-CarrL**

Mites. John Updike. **CP-UpdiJ**

Mithras, God of the morning, our trumpets waken the Wall! A Song to Mithras. Rudyard Kipling. **CP-KiplR** *Fr.* On the Great Wall. *Fr.* Puck of Pook's Hill.

Mithridates. Ralph Waldo Emerson. **CP-EmerR**

Mithridates at Chios. John Greenleaf Whittier. **CP-WhitJ**

Mitrailliatrice. Ernest Hemingway. **CP-HemiE**

Mitts and Gloves. Bill Knott. **SP-KnotB**

Mix a Pancake. Christina Georgina Rossetti. **CP-RosC2**

Mix a Pancake. Christina Georgina Rossetti. **NTCP** *Fr.* Sing-Song. **CP-RosC2**

(Pancake, The.) **BoTP**

Mix the Ingredients. Hayden Carruth. **CP-CarHS**

Mixed crop. I dig a clump, A. Parsnips. Charles Tomlinson. **CP-TomlC**

Mixed Feelings. John Ashbery. **SP-AshbJ**

Mixed Marriage, The. Paul Muldoon. **SP-MuldP**

Mixed pastries and new dresses. The Iceman, Again. Gilbert Sorrentino. **SP-SorrG**

Mixed Signals. Chuck Miller. **SP-MillC**

Mixed Up Confusion. "Bob Dylan." **CP-DylaB**

Mixer, The. Louis MacNeice. **CP-MacNL**

Mixup of kinkhead and high yaller. Prelude in Boricua. Luis Palés Matos, *tr. fr. Spanish by* William Carlos Williams. **CP-WilW2**

Mizzu. Etheridge Knight. *Fr.* Missouri Haiku. **SP-KnigE**

M'Liss and Louie. Carl Sandburg. **CP-SandC**

Mm, tell mama, / Where'd ya sleep last night? Poor Boy Blues. "Bob Dylan." **CP-DylaB**

Mnemosyne: The Empty Room. James McAuley. **SP-McAuJ**

Mo Ghrá Thú. Michael Hartnett. **PeIV** *Fr.* Anatomy of a Cliché. **SP-HarMi**

Moan / (is) / ing / the she of the. Edward Estlin Cummings. **CP-CummE**

Moan the loss, another. A *Scream* to the Editor. Charles Olson. **CP-OlsoC**

Moaning and Groaning. Charles Bukowski. **SP-BukC1**

Mob within the heart, The. Emily Dickinson. **CP-DickE**

Mobile Homes. Robert Creeley. **CP-CreeR**

Mobile, immaculate and austere. Geoffrey Hill. **CP-HillG**

Mobile Mollusc, A. John Hewitt. **CP-HewiJ**

Mobile of Birds. John Updike. **CP-UpdiJ**

Mobiles: / that the wind can catch at. Still Life Or. Robert Creeley. **CP-CreeR**

Mobs are like the Gulf Stream. The Would-Be Merman. Nicholas Vachel Lindsay. **CP-LindV**

Moccasin Flowers. Mary Oliver. **SP-OlivM**

Mock Charon, A. Richard Lovelace. **CP-LoveR**

Mock Confessional, *see also* True Confessional. Lawrence Ferlinghetti. **SP-FerlL**

Mock On, Mock On, Voltaire, Rousseau. William Blake. **CP-BlakW**

Mock Orange. Louise Glück. **SP-GlücL**

Mock Song, A. Richard Lovelace. **CP-LoveR**

Mock Turtle's Song, The. "Lewis Carroll." *See* "Will you walk a little faster?" said a [*or* the] whiting to a [*or* the] snail.

Mock Turtle's Song, The: "Beneath the waters of the sea." "Lewis Carroll." **CP-CarrL**

Mock Wife, The. Thomas Hardy. **CP-HardT**

Mockers Go to Kansas in Spring. Carl Sandburg. **CP-SandC**

Mocking Bird Song. Leonard Nathan. **SP-NathL**

Mocking hooligan laughing down your hooligan days. Albina. Chuck Miller. **SP-MillC**

Mockingbird, The. Brendan Galvin. **SP-GalvB**

Mockingbird, The. Randall Jarrell. **CP-JarrR; SP-JarrR**

Modality. Archie Randolph Ammons. **SP-AmmoA**

Model, The. Wystan Hugh Auden. **CP-AudeW**

Model for the Laureate, A. William Butler Yeats. **CP-YeatW**

Modelled Head, The. John Hewitt. **CP-HewiJ**

Models were changing, The. Paris Models. Leonard Cohen. **CP-CoheL**

Moderate, The. John Updike. **CP-UpdiJ**

Moderation. Robert Herrick. **CP-HerrR**

Moderation. Robert Herrick. **CP-HerrR**

Moderation. Christopher Smart. **NOCV** *Fr.* Hymns for the Amusement of Children. **SP-SmarC**

Modern, The. Charles Kenneth Williams. **SP-WillC**

Modern Athens, The. William Wordsworth. **CP-WorW2**

Modern Craft. Hart Crane. **CP-CranH**

Modern Declaration. Edna St. Vincent Millay. **CP-MillE**

Modern life is a tale told by an idiot. A Tale Told by an Idiot. David Herbert Lawrence. **CP-LawrD**

Modern Love. George Meredith. **CP-MerG1**

"All other joys of life he strove to warm." **EnVR**

"Along the garden terrace, under which." **NOBVV**

"Am I failing? For no longer can I cast." **CABA; EnVR; GBL; OAEP; SCGP**

"At dinner, she is hostess, I am host." **EnVR; HeIP; NOBVV; NoP; OHCV; PoE; Son**

(At Dinner, She Is Hostess.) **Son**

"At last we parley: we so strangely dumb."

"But where began the change; and what's my crime?" **NBM; PoEL-5**

"By this he knew she wept with waking eyes." **EnLoPo; EnVR; HBV; HeIP; HoPM; NAEL-2; NBM; NOBVV; NoP; OAEL-2; OAEP; OHCV; OxBM; PBMP; PoE; PoEL-5; Son**

(End of Love, The.) **HoPM**

"Distraction is the panacea, Sir!"

"Full faith I have she holds that rarest gift."

"Give to imagination some pure light."

"He felt the wild beast in him betweenwhiles." **EnVR; NOBVV**

"He found her by the ocean's moaning verge." **EnVR; HBV; NoP; OAEL-2; OAEP**

"Here Jack and Tom are paired with Moll and Meg." **EnVR; InvP; NBM; PoEL-5**

"How many a thing which we cast to the ground." **HBV 1-2**

"I am not of those miserable males."

"I am to follow her. There is much grace." **NAEL-2; NOBVV**

"I bade my Lady think what she might mean."

"I must be flattered. The imperious."

"I play for Seasons; not Eternities!" **FaBoEn; OBNC; SCGP**

"I think she sleeps: it must be sleep, when low." **NAEL-2**

"In our old shipwrecked days there was an hour." **BoLoP; EnVR; HBV; NOBVV; SeCePo; WHA**

(Love Dies.) **SeCePo**

"In Paris, at the Louvre, there have I seen."

"It chanced his lips did meet her forehead cool." **CBLP; EnVR; NOBVV**

"It ended, and the morrow brought the task." **EnVR**

"It is no vulgar nature I have wived." **NAEL-2**

"It is the season of the sweet wild rose." **GBL; NBM; PoEL-5**

"Love ere he bleeds, an eagle in high skies." **HBV 1-2**

"Madam would speak with me. So, now it comes." **NOBVV**

"Mark where the pressing wind shoots javelin-like." **EnLoPo; EnVR; FaBoEn; GBL; HBV; NBM; NOBE; OBEV; OBNC; PoEL-5; SCGP; SeCeV; TEP**

(Love's Grave.) **OBEV**

"Message from her set his brain aflame, A." **EnVR; NOBVV**

"Misery is greater, as I live!, The."

"My lady unto Madam makes her bow." **NOBVV**

"No state is enviable. To the luck alone."

"Not solely that the Future she destroys." **GBL; TEP**

"Out in the yellow meadows, where the bee." **GBL**

"She issues radiant from her dressing-room." **EnVR; NOBVV**

"She yields: my Lady in her noblest mood."

"Their sense is with their senses all mixed in." **NAEL-2; NoP; OAEL-2; OAEP; SCGP**

"They say, that Pity in Love's service dwells."

"This golden head has wit in it. I live." **NOBVV**

"This was the woman; what now of the man?" **EnVR; OHCV; Son**

"Thus piteously Love closed what he begat." **EBEV; EnLoPo; EnVR; FaBoEn; GTBS-6; GTBS-P; HAP; HBV; LoBV; NBM; NOBE; NOBVV; NoP; OAEL-2; OAEP; OBNC; OHCV; OXAEP-2; PoE; PoEL-5; SCGP; SeCePo; SeCeV; Son; TFi; TrGrPo; TreFT; WHA**

(Dusty Answer, A.) **SeCePo**

"'Tis Christmas weather, and a country house." **NAEL-2; NOBVV**

"We saw the swallows gathering in the sky." **ELP; EnLoPo; FaBoEn; GTBS-6; GTBS-P; Mes; NOBE; NOBVV; OAEL-2; OBNC; SeCeV; WHA**

(We Saw the Swallows.) **ELP**

"We three are on the cedar-shadowed lawn." **NOBVV**

"What are we first? First, animals; and next." **GBL; HAP; NBM; NoP; OAEP; PoEL-5**

"What may the woman labour to confess?"

"What soul would bargain for a cure that brings." **HBV 1-2**

"Yet it was plain she struggled, and that salt." **EnVR**

"You like not that French novel? Tell me why." **EnVR; NOBVV**

Modern Love. John Yau. **SP-YauJo**

Modern Patriot, The. William Cowper. **CP-CowpW**

Modern Poet, A. Howard Nemerov. **CP-NemeH**

Modern Poets. Gerard Manley Hopkins. *Fr.* Seven Epigrams. **CP-HopkG**

Modern Prayer. David Herbert Lawrence. **CP-LawrD**

Modern Problems. David Herbert Lawrence. **CP-LawrD**

Modern society is a mill. Give Us the Thebaïd. David Herbert Lawrence. **CP-LawrD**

Modern Version of Polonius' Advice, A. Ernest Hemingway. **CP-HemiE**

Modern Witches 1: Crouching. Jenny Joseph. *Fr.* Life and Turgid Times of A. Citizen. **SP-JoseJ**

Modern Witches 2: Sentinels. Jenny Joseph. *Fr.* Life and Turgid Times of A. Citizen. **SP-JoseJ**

Modern woman in search of a soul. Siv Cedering Fox. *Fr.* In Search of a Love Poem. **SP-CedeS**

Modernities. Edwin Arlington Robinson. **CP-RobiE**

Modes of Pleasure. Thom Gunn. **CP-GunnT**

Modes of Pleasure. Thom Gunn. **CP-GunnT**

Modest Achievement, The. William Carlos Williams. **CP-WilW2**

Modest, and fair, for fair and good are near. Ben Jonson. **CP-JonsB** *Fr.* Epicoene; or, The Silent Woman.

Modest bard, like many a bard unknown, The. Lines Written in the Travellers' Book at Orchomenus. Byron. **CP-Byron**

Modest Boast at Meridian, A. Robert Pack. **SP-PackR**

Modest front of this small floore, The. An Epitaph upon Mr. Ashton, a Conformable Citizen. Richard Crashaw. **CP-CrasR**

Modest Mound of Bones, A. John Updike. **CP-UpdiJ**

Modest rose puts forth a thorn, The. The Lily. William Blake. **CP-BlakW** *Fr.* Songs of Experience.

Modesties. Philip Larkin. **CP-LarkP**

Modesty, chastity. Charles Henri Ford. **SP-FordC** *Fr.* Secret Haiku.

Modification of Landscape. Robert Penn Warren. *Fr.* Infant Boy at Midcentury. **SP-WarrR**

Modigliani's Death Mask. Marsden Hartley. **CP-HartM**

Modigliani's Death Mask. John Updike. **CP-UpdiJ**

Moebius Strip, The. Charles Olson. **CP-OlsoC**

Mogg Megone. John Greenleaf Whittier. **CP-WhitJ**

Moguer. Juan Ramón Jiménez. *Fr.* Ten Short Poems. **CP-WrigJ**

Mohammed. Kenneth Patchen. **CP-PatcK**

Mohammed Bek Hadjetlache. Carl Sandburg. **CP-SandC**

Mohammedans say that the sound of bells, The. Bells. David Herbert Lawrence. **CP-LawrD**

Mohini Chatterjee. William Butler Yeats. **CP-YeatW**

Moira. Tom Clark. **SP-ClarT**

Moirai, The. Tom Clark. **SP-ClarT**

Moira's Messages. Tom Clark. **SP-ClarT**

Moist, moist, / the heat leaking through the hinges. The Fury of Sundays. Anne Sexton. *Fr.* The Furies. **CP-SextA**

Moist Moon People. Carl Sandburg. **CP-SandC**

Moist with one drop of thy blood, my dry soul. Resurrection. John Donne. *Fr.* La Corona. **ChIV-2; ESCV; OBS; Son** *Fr.* Holy Sonnets. **CP-DonnJ**

Moist[e]ned Osyer [or osier] of the hoarie Willow, The. Lucan, *tr.* by Sir Walter Ralegh. **CP-RaleW** *Fr.* Pharsalia.

Mole, The. John Haines. **SP-HainJ**

Mole. Marsden Hartley. **CP-HartM**

Mole, angel-dog of the pit. Star-Nosed Mole. Anne Sexton. **CP-SextA**

Mole-Catcher, The. John Clare. **SP-ClarJ**

Mole who knows. Back to Base. Jenny Joseph. **SP-JoseJ**

Moles. Ted Kooser. **SP-KoosT**

Mollis abuti, / Has an acuti. Anglo-Latin Verses. Jonathan Swift. **CP-SwifJ**

Molly Gone. Thomas Hardy. **CP-HardT**

Moloch in State Street. John Greenleaf Whittier. **CP-WhitJ**

Molten gold flows away from the sun, A. Evening Sea Wind. Carl Sandburg. **CP-SandC**

Molten pool, incandescent spilth of. Basil Bunting. **CP-BuntB**

Moly. Thom Gunn. **CP-GunnT**

Moment, A. Wystan Hugh Auden. **CP-AudWJ**

Moment. Robert Creeley. **CP-CreeR**

Moment, The. Walter de la Mare. **CP-DeLaW**

Moment. Howard Nemerov. **CP-NemeH**

Moment, The. Kathleen Jessie Raine. **SP-RainK**

Moment, The. Kathleen Jessie Raine. **SP-RainK**

Moment, The. Theodore Roethke. **CP-RoetT**

Moment, The. Charles Tomlinson. **CP-TomlC**

Moment and / over and with, A. Rachmaninoff's Third. James Schuyler. **CP-SchuJ**

Moment comes when my sound senses, The. A Time of Waiting. Robert Ranke Graves. **CP-GravR**

Moment Fugue. Hart Crane. **CP-CranH**

Moment hangs from Heaven like a webbed, The. Spiderweb. Malcolm Lowry. **CP-LowrM**

Moment in Eternity, A. "Hugh MacDiarmid." **SP-MacDH**

Moment of Equilibrium among the Islands. Richard Eberhart. **CP-EberR**

Moment of silence, first, then there it is, A. The Dial Tone. Howard Nemerov. **CP-NemeH**

Moment of Sleep (For Schnu), A. Chuck Miller. **SP-MillC**

Moment of Truth, The. Thomas Merton. **CP-MertT**

Moment of Vision, The. Richard Eberhart. **CP-EberR**

Moment to / moment the / body seems. Time. Robert Creeley. **CP-CreeR**

Moment tries to come in, A. Approaching Prayer. James Dickey. **CP-DickJ**

Moments. Frederick Morgan. **SP-MorgF**

"At sunset the hills turn purple."

"Whisper echoes, A."

"White clouds, red leaves flying."

Moments / when I care about nothing. Apologies. Marge Piercy. **SP-PierM**

Moments of Dawn Riders. Carl Sandburg. **CP-SandC**

Moments of Glory. Robinson Jeffers. **CP-JefR3**

Moments of Minnie. John Crowe Ransom. **SP-RansJ**

Moments of Vision. Thomas Hardy. **CP-HardT**

Moments passed as at a play, The. A Memory of Youth. William Butler Yeats. **CP-YeatW**

Moment's patience, gentle Mistris Anne, A. William Shakespeare to Mrs Anne, Regular Servant to the Rev. Mr Precentor of York. Thomas Gray. **CP-GrayT**

Moments Return, The. Allen Ginsberg. **CP-GinsA**

Momentum. Tom Clark. **SP-ClarT**

Momma Welfare Roll. Maya Angelou. **SP-AngeM**

Mommy mommy come and see. Ballad from Childhood. Audre Lorde. **SP-LordA**

Mommy what's this fork doing? January. Alice Notley. **SP-NotlA**

Momus. Edwin Arlington Robinson. **CP-RobiE**

Momus. Carl Sandburg. **CP-SandC**

Momus' Song to Mars. John Dryden. **OxBSP** *Fr.* The Secular Masque. **SP-DrydJ**

Mon Semblable. Stephen Dunn. **SP-DunnS**

Monadnoc. Ralph Waldo Emerson. **CP-EmerR**

"Every morn I lift my head." **APN-1**

Monadnock through the Trees. Edwin Arlington Robinson. **CP-RobiE**

Monarch, The. John Hewitt. **CP-HewiJ**

Monarch of Gods and Dæmons, and all Spirits. Prometheus Unbound. Percy Bysshe Shelley. **CP-ShelP**

Monarch of Gods and Dæmons, and all Spirits. Percy Bysshe Shelley. **FiP; NAEL-2; OAEL-2** *Fr.* Prometheus Unbound. **CP-ShelP**

Monastary, Tourliani, Mykonos. John Hewitt. **CP-HewiJ**

Monastery at Vršac, The. Charles Wright. **SP-WrigC**

Monastery of Old Bangor. William Wordsworth. *Fr.* Ecclesiastical Sonnets. **CP-WorW2**

Monastic Domes! following my downward way. Old Abbeys. William Wordsworth. *Fr.* Ecclesiastical Sonnets. **CP-WorW2**

Monastic Voluptuousness. William Wordsworth. *Fr.* Ecclesiastical Sonnets. **CP-WorW2**

Monday / Dearest, / It is snowing, grotesquely snowing. Letter Written During a January Northeaster. Anne Sexton. **CP-SextA**

Monday. Martin Edmunds. **SP-EdmuM**

Monday Beach, Cold Day. James Bukowski. **SP-BukC2**

Monday in Holy Week. Christina Georgina Rossetti. **CP-RosC2**

Monday is the day that everything starts all over again. Every Day Is Monday. Ogden Nash. **CP-NashO**

Monday's child in Boston looked like soot. Cal Coolidge and the Co. John Ciardi. **SP-CiarJ**

Moneses Uniflora. James Schuyler. *Fr.* The Cenotaph. **CP-SchuJ**

Monessie Gorge. Kathleen Jessie Raine. **SP-RainK**

" 'I am the stream,' I said."

"It crossed my mind."

"Live on in me, remembered ones."

"Seen from the train."

Monet: "Les Nymphéas." William DeWitt Snodgrass. **SP-SnodW**

Monet's "Waterlilies." Robert Earl Hayden. **CP-HaydR**

Money. Randall Jarrell. **CP-JarrR**

Money. Philip Larkin. **CP-LarkP**

Money. David Herbert Lawrence. **CP-LawrD**

Money. Jim Morrison. **SP-MorrJ**

Money. Howard Nemerov. **CP-NemeH**

Money and fame break in the room. The Strife between the Poet and Ambition. Thomas Merton. **CP-MertT**

Money Blues. "Bob Dylan" and Jacques Levy. **CP-DylaB**

Money Gets the Mastery [or Masterie]. Robert Herrick. **CP-HerrR**

Money is cheap / in the fall, The. In the Fall. Robert Creeley. **CP-CreeR**

Money is nothing now, even if I had it. Half Moon In a High Wind. Carl Sandburg. **CP-SandC**

Money-Madness. David Herbert Lawrence. **CP-LawrD**

Money Makes the Mirth. Robert Herrick. **CP-HerrR**

Money Musk. James Schuyler. **CP-SchuJ**

Money, Politics, Love, and Glory. Carl Sandburg. **CP-SandC**

Money Swing, The. Anne Sexton. **CP-SextA**

Money, the beauty of. Money. Jim Morrison. **SP-MorrJ**

Money, thou bane of bliss and source of woe. Avarice. George Herbert. **CP-HerbG**

Money thou ow'st me; prithee fix a day. Upon Bunce: Epigram. Robert Herrick. **CP-HerrR**

Mongolian Idiot. Karl Shapiro. **SP-ShapK**

Mongrel, The. Thomas Hardy. **CP-HardT**

Mongrel image for all summer, our scene for breakfast:, A. Wildrose. Robert Lowell. **SP-LoweR**

Mongst all the Palaces in Hells command. Giovanni Battista Marino. *Fr.* Sospetto d'Herode. **CP-CrasR** *Fr.* Strage degli innocenti, La.

'Mongst the worlds wonders, there doth yet remain. Female Glory. Richard Lovelace. **CP-LoveR**

'Mongst those long rowes of crownes that guild your race. To the Queen's Majesty. Richard Crashaw. **CP-CrasR**

Monk, The. William Blake. **CP-BlakW; EnRP; OBRV** *Fr.* Jerusalem; The Emanation of the Giant Albion. **CP-BlakW**

Monk can do his work on bended knees, A. Peter Meinke. *Fr.* Mendel's Laws. **SP-MeinP**

Monk sat in his den, The. The Weak Monk. Stevie Smith. **CP-SmitS**

Monk ther was, a fair for the maistrie, A. Geoffrey Chaucer. **CTC** *Fr.* A Monk ther was, a fair for the maistrye [or maistrie]. **OBCoV; TrGrPo** *Fr.* The General Prologue. **FHYEP; NAWM-1; OAEL-1; PoE** *Fr.* The Canterbury Tales. **CP-ChauG**

Monk ther was, a fair for the maistrie [or maistrie], A. Geoffrey Chaucer. **OBCoV; TrGrPo** *Fr.* The General Prologue. **FHYEP; NAWM-1; OAEL-1; PoE** *Fr.* The Canterbury Tales. **CP-ChauG**

("Monk there was, a monk of mastery, A.") **TrGrPo**

(Seven Pilgrims: A Monk.) **TrGrPo**

"Monk ther was, a fair for the maistrie, A." **CTC**

Monk there was, a monk of mastery, A. Geoffrey Chaucer. *See* A Monk ther was, a fair for the maistrye [or maistrie].

Monkey of Stars. Carl Sandburg. **CP-SandC**

Monkey Puzzle, The. Marianne Craig Moore. **CP-MoorM**

Monkeyman. Audre Lorde. **SP-LordA**

Monkeys, The. Marianne Craig Moore. **CP-MoorM**

Monkey's Paw, The. Peter Meinke. **SP-MeinP**

Monkhood. John Berryman. **CP-BerrJ**

Monks and Schoolmen. William Wordsworth. *Fr.* Ecclesiastical Sonnets. **CP-WorW2**

Monk's Tale, The. Geoffrey Chaucer. *Fr.* The Canterbury Tales. **CP-ChauG**

Monk's Walk, The. Paul Laurence Dunbar. **CP-DunbP**

Monkshood. Erica Jong. **SP-JongE**

Monmouth. George Meredith. **CP-MerG2**

Monmouthshire. Donald Davie. **CP-DavDo**

Monna Innominata. Christina Georgina Rossetti. **CP-RosC2**

"Come back to me, who wait and watch for you."

"I dream of you to wake: would that I might."

" 'I, if I perish, perish'—Esther spake."

"I loved you first: but afterwards your love." **VBLP**

"I wish I could remember the [or that] first day." **BLPL; BoLoP; FaBoBe; GBL; LPA; Son**

(First Day, The.) **BLPL; BoLoP; FaBoBe; GBL; LPA**

(Sonnet: "I wish I could remember the first day.")

If I Could Trust Mine Own Self. **EBCP**

"If there be any one can take my place."

" 'Love me, for I love you'—and answer me." **Son**

"Many in aftertimes will say of you." **OBNC**

"O my heart's heart, and you who are to me."

"Thinking of you, and all that was, and all."

"Time flies, hope flags, life plies a wearied wing."

"Trust me, I have not earned your dear rebuke."

"Youth gone, and beauty gone if ever there." **GBL; OBNC; Son**

Monody. David Markson. **CP-MarkD**

Monody. Herman Melville. **SP-MelvH**

Monody on Maria. Robert Burns. **CP-BurnR**

Monody on the Death of a Platonist Bank Clerk. Sir John Betjeman. **CP-BetjJ**

Monody on the Death of Aldersgate Street Station. Sir John Betjeman. **CP-BetjJ**

Monody on the Death of Chatterton, *1796 vers.* Samuel Taylor Coleridge. **CP-ColeS**

"Elate of heart and confidence of fame." **EPCY**

"O Spirit blest! / Whether th' eternal Throne around."

Monody on the Death of the Right Hon. R. B. Sheridan. Byron. **CP-Byron**

Monolith of a double flight, The. An Informative Object. William Carlos Williams. **CP-WilW2**

Monologue, The. Walter de la Mare. **CP-DeLaW**

Monologue. Alun Lewis. **CP-LewiA**

Monologue at Midnight. Robert Penn Warren. **SP-WarrR**

Monologue at 3 A.M. Sylvia Plath. **CP-PlatS**

Monologue of a Mother. David Herbert Lawrence. **CP-LawrD**

Monongah (December 6, 1907, Marion County, West Virginia, on the Monongahela River). Louise McNeill. **SP-McNeL**

Monosyllabic. Carl Sandburg. **CP-SandC**

Monotone. Carl Sandburg. **CP-SandC**

Monotone of the rain is beautiful, The. Monotone. Carl Sandburg. **CP-SandC**

Monotony Song, The. Theodore Roethke. **CP-RoetT**

Monroe's Blues. Langston Hughes. **SP-HughL**

Monsieur Étienne de Silhouette. Some Frenchmen. John Updike. **CP-UpdiJ**

Monsieur Pussy-Cat, Blackmailer. Stevie Smith. **CP-SmitS**

Monster, The. Thom Gunn. **CP-GunnT**

Monster, The. Richard Shelton. **SP-ShelR**

Monstering horror swallows, A. Thanksgiving (1956). Edward Estlin Cummings. **CP-CummE**

Monstrous and three-headed cur, The. Dream Recalled on Waking. Robert Ranke Graves. **CP-GravR**

Monstrous Marriage, The. William Carlos Williams. **CP-WilW2**

Mont Blanc. Percy Bysshe Shelley. **CP-ShelP**

Montage. Charles Tomlinson. **CP-TomlC**

Montaigne. Wystan Hugh Auden. **CP-AudeW**

Montaigne and His Kitten. Herman Melville. **SP-MelvH**

Montalbert. Charlotte Smith.

  On Passing Over a Dreary Tract of Country, and Near the Ruins of a Deserted Chapel, During a Tempest. **CP-SmitC**

  Written in a Tempestuous Night, on the Coast of Sussex. **CP-SmitC**

Montana Ranch Abandoned. Richard Hugo. **CP-HugoR**

Montcalm. Donald Davie. **CP-DavDo**

Montelepre. John Hewitt. **CP-HewiJ**

Monterey. Thom Gunn. *Fr.* Breaking Ground. **CP-GunnT**

Montes Scripturarum, the Mounts of the Scriptures. Robert Herrick. **CP-HerrR**

Montesano Unvisited. Richard Hugo. **CP-HugoR**

Montgomery Hollow. Richard Hugo. **CP-HugoR**

Montgomery! true, the common lot. Answer to a Beautiful Poem, Entitled "The Common Lot." Byron. **CP-Byron**

Month after month passed away, and in autumn the ships of the merchants. Henry Wadsworth Longfellow. **TreFS** *Fr.* The Spinning-Wheel. *Fr.* The Courtship of Miles Standish. **SP-LongH**

Month after month passed away, and in autumn the ships of the merchants. The Spinning-Wheel. Henry Wadsworth Longfellow. *Fr.* The Courtship of Miles Standish. **SP-LongH**

Month after month the gathered rains descend. To the Nile. Percy Bysshe Shelley. **CP-ShelP**

Month after month, year after year. Emily Brontë. **CP-BronE**

Month ago in fields, A. May Weather. Philip Larkin. **CP-LarkP**

Month before Easter, A. The Lamb. John Ciardi. **SP-CiarJ**

Month of flowering's finished, The. The fruit's in. Poem for a Birthday. Sylvia Plath. **CP-PlatS**

Month of the drowned dog. After long rain the land, The. November. Ted Hughes. **SP-HughT**

Month of vigilance draws to its close, A. Nothing Now Astonishes. Robert Ranke Graves. **CP-GravR**

Month or twain to live on honeycomb, A. Before Parting. Algernon Charles Swinburne. **SP-SwinA**

Months: A Pageant, The. Christina Georgina Rossetti. **CP-RosC2**

  April.

  August.

  December.

  February.

  January.

  July.

  June.

  March.

  May.

  November.

  October.

  September.

Months after the Muse. The Illustration [—a Footnote]. Denise Levertov. **CP-LeveD**

Month's Calendar, The. Thomas Hardy. **CP-HardT**

Month's eye blurs, The. After a Sentence in "Malte Laurids Brigge." Adrienne Rich. **CP-RicAE**

Months have ends—the Years—a knot, The. Emily Dickinson. **CP-DickE**

Months of it, and the inarticulate mist so thick. Long Summers. Robert Lowell. **SP-LoweR**

Months on, you hold me still. Two Songs. Derek Mahon. **SP-MahoD**

Months past the demolition. Women's House of Detention. David Markson. **CP-MarkD**

Monticello. May Sarton. **SP-SartM**

Montparnasse. Ernest Hemingway. **CP-HemiE**

Montrachet-le-Jardin. Wallace Stevens. **CP-StevW**

Montreal. Leonard Cohen. **CP-CoheL**

Monument, The. Elizabeth Bishop. **CP-BishE**

Monument. Robinson Jeffers. **CP-JefR3**

Monument. George Oppen. **CP-OppeG**

Monument Commonly Called Long Meg and Her Daughters, near the River Eden, The. William Wordsworth. *Fr.* Poems Composed or Suggested During a Tour, in the Summer of 1833. **CP-WorW2**

Monument-Maker, The. Thomas Hardy. **CP-HardT**

Monument of Mrs Howard. William Wordsworth. *Fr.* Poems Composed or Suggested During a Tour, in the Summer of 1833. **CP-WorW2**

Mood. Countee Cullen. **CP-CullC**

Mood Apart, A. Robert Frost. **CP-FrosR**

Mood Indigo. William Matthews. **SP-MattW**

Mood Indigo. James Schuyler. **CP-SchuJ**

Moods, The. William Butler Yeats. **CP-YeatW**

Moodsville. Tom Clark. **SP-ClarT**

Moody. Alice Walker. **CP-WalkA**

Moody child and wildly wise. Motto to "The Poet." Ralph Waldo Emerson. **CP-EmerR**

Mool 'tis homos,' Naso 'n' queer take 'im mool 'tis ho most *he*. Catullus. *See* Carmen 112: "Naso! an elevated personage."

Moon / and clouds, will. The Eye. Robert Creeley. **CP-CreeR**

Moon, The. Hayden Carruth. *Fr.* Contra Mortem. **CP-CarHL**

Moon, The. Robert Creeley. **CP-CreeR**

Moon. Martin Edmunds. **SP-EdmuM**

Moon, The. Donald Hall. **CP-HallD**

Moon, The. John Hewitt. **CP-HewiJ**

Moon. Jenny Joseph. *Fr.* Derivations. **SP-JoseJ**

Moon. James Schuyler. **CP-SchuJ**

Moon, The. Robert Louis Stevenson. **CP-StevR**

Moon, The. William Carlos Williams. **CP-WilW1**

Moon. James Wright. **CP-WrigJ**

Moon and Five Planets. Robinson Jeffers. **CP-JefR3**

Moon and Stars. William Carlos Williams. **CP-WilW2**

Moon and the Night and the Men, The. John Berryman. **CP-BerrJ**

Moon and the Nightingale, The. John Milton. *See* Now came still Ev'ning [*or* evening *or* Eevning] on, and Twilight gray [*or* grey].

Moon and the Waves, The. Samuel Taylor Coleridge. **CP-ColeS**

Moon and the Yew Tree, The. Sylvia Plath. **CP-PlatS**

Moon, aye, / I suck on green fruit, The. Lemons, Limes. Siv Cedering Fox. **SP-CedeS**

Moon begins her stately ride, The. Evening. Paul Laurence Dunbar. **CP-DunbP**

Moon came out full, you could see the white breathing of the. Kenneth Patchen. **CP-PatcK**

Moon Clock. Donald Hall. **CP-HallD**

Moon, cloud, tower, a patch of the battistero all of a whiteness. Canto 79. Ezra Pound. *Fr.* Cantos. **CP-PoCan**

Moon Compasses. Robert Frost. **CP-FrosR**

Moon "Continued." Kenneth Patchen. **CP-PatcK**

Moon drops one or two feathers into the field, The. Beginning. James Wright. **CP-WrigJ**

Moon empties its cigarettes over a row of clouds. Shanghai Shenanigans. John Yau. **SP-YauJo**

Moon Explodes in Autumn as a Milkweed Pod, The. Diane Wakoski. **SP-WakoD**

Moon falls through the autumn   Behind prisons she grins, The. Edward Estlin Cummings. **CP-CummE**

Moon Flock. James Dickey. **CP-DickJ**

Moon golden towards the full. Kathleen Jessie Raine. **SP-RainK**

Moon Hammock. Carl Sandburg. **CP-SandC**

Moon has a face like the clock in the hall, The. The Moon. Robert Louis Stevenson. **CP-StevR**

Moon has a swollen cheek, The. Ezra Pound. *See* Canto 79: "Moon, cloud, tower, a patch of the battistero all of a whiteness."

Moon has left the sky, love, The. Night of Love. Paul Laurence Dunbar. **CP-DunbP**

Moon has passed to the panes of the south-aisle wall, The. In Sherborne Abbey. Thomas Hardy. **CP-HardT**

Moon has set: while yet the dawn, The. Moloch in State Street. John Greenleaf Whittier. **CP-WhitJ**

Moon—how definite its orb!, The. Lunar Entrancement. Samuel Taylor Coleridge. **CP-ColeS**

Moon, How Do I Measure Up? Al Young. **CP-YounA**

Moon impoverished amid stars curtailed, A. The Greatest of These Is Charity. Christina Georgina Rossetti. **CP-RosC2**

Moon in Scandinavia, The. Malcolm Lowry. **CP-LowrM**

Blepharipappus Glandulosus or White Tidy-Tips.

"Exile is the luckiest of men, The."

"Fig for 6-par-T-pak ginger ale!, A."

"For Christ's sake and for mine and last for a child's god gone."

"God help those and others who."

Lull.

On Reading Edmund Wilson's Remarks about Rimbaud.

On Reading Redburn.

Only God Knows How.

Only God Knows How III.

Prayer: "Give way, you fiends, and give that man some happiness."

"Ukelele once in pawn I saw, A."

"Walls of remorse are steep, there is no belay, The."

"Wolf, wolf, cried the boy in the fable."

Moon in the bureau mirror, The. Insomnia. Elizabeth Bishop. **CP-BishE**

Moon in the morning. Jenny Joseph. *Fr.* Life and Turgid Times of A. Citizen. **SP-JoseJ**

Moon in the river, mother, is a red, red moon tonight, The. River Moon. Carl Sandburg. **CP-SandC**

Moon-in-the-Trees, / The old canoe awaits you. Edward Estlin Cummings. **CP-CummE**

Moon in Your Hands, The. Hilda Doolittle. *See* If you take the moon in your hands.

Moon Is a Painter, The. Nicholas Vachel Lindsay. **CP-LindV**

Moon is a sow, The. Song for Ishtar. Denise Levertov. **CP-LeveD**

Moon is able to command the valley tonight, The. Moist Moon People. Carl Sandburg. **CP-SandC**

Moon is alone in the sky, The. Song. George Meredith. **CP-MerG1**

Moon is broken in twain, and half a moon, The. Troth with the Dead. David Herbert Lawrence. **CP-LawrD**

Moon is but a candle-glow, The. What the Forester Said. Nicholas Vachel Lindsay. **CP-LindV**

Moon is but a censer swung, The. The Censer-Moon. Nicholas Vachel Lindsay. **CP-LindV**

Moon is but a golden skull, The. What the Hyena Said. Nicholas Vachel Lindsay. **CP-LindV**

Moon is dark. We have our drinks on a terrace, The. Aesthetic Distance. Miller Williams. **SP-WillM**

Moon is dead, you lovers!, The. Selene Afterwards. Archibald MacLeish. **CP-MacLA**

Moon is distant from the Sea, The. Emily Dickinson. **CP-DickE**

Moon is full this winter night, The. M. Douglas to E.R. Gleneden. Emily Brontë. **CP-BronE**

Moon Is Full Tonight, The. Philip Larkin. **CP-LarkP**

Moon is hiding in, The. Edward Estlin Cummings. **CP-CummE**

Moon is naked, The. March Moon. Langston Hughes. **SP-HughL**

Moon is now an opening flower, The. The Rose of Midnight. Nicholas Vachel Lindsay. **CP-LindV**

Moon is paler than an actress, The. In the Ruins of New York. Thomas Merton. *Fr.* Figures for an Apocalypse. **CP-MertT**

Moon is partly hidden, The. The Wrong Side. Frederick Morgan. **SP-MorgF**

Moon is sinking—the tempestuous weather, The. Robert Louis Stevenson. **CP-StevR**

Moon is the mother of pathos and pity, The. Lunar Paraphrase. Wallace Stevens. **CP-StevW**

Moon Is the Number 18, The. Charles Olson. **CP-OlsoC; SP-OlsoC**

Moon? It is a griffin's egg, The. Yet Gentle Will the Griffin Be. Nicholas Vachel Lindsay. **CP-LindV** *Fr.* Poems about the Moon.

Moon Landing. Wystan Hugh Auden. **CP-AudeW**

Moon-lit snow is falling like strange candy into the big eyes of the, The. Edward Estlin Cummings. **CP-CummE**

Moon looked into my window, The. Edward Estlin Cummings. **CP-CummE**

Moon Looks In, The. Thomas Hardy. **CP-HardT**

Moon Memory. David Herbert Lawrence. **CP-LawrD**

Moon-minded the sun goes. Gemini. Audre Lorde. **SP-LordA**

Moon, moon, me go now but. Pidgin Moon. Al Young. **CP-YounA**

Moon must be in Perigee the sea, The. May 20, 1959. Charles Olson. **CP-OlsoC**

Moon never makes use of the Sun's palette, The. The Colours of Night. Robert Ranke Graves. **CP-GravR**

Moon New-Risen. David Herbert Lawrence. **CP-LawrD**

Moon of Melancholy, The. Lewis Turco. **SP-TurcL**

Moon of moon & quintessential moonness. Coastal Moon. Al Young. **CP-YounA**

Moon of No Return. Al Young. **CP-YounA**

Moon of Other Days, The. Rudyard Kipling. **CP-KiplR**

Moon over gai. Edward Estlin Cummings. **CP-CummE**

Moon Over Matter. Al Young. **CP-YounA**

MOOn Over tOwns mOOn. Edward Estlin Cummings. **CP-CummE**

Moon Path. Carl Sandburg. **CP-SandC**

Moon profaned by, A. Wystan Hugh Auden. *Fr.* Shorts I ("Watch upon my wrist, The"). **CP-AudeW**

Moon revolves around outside; possibly, black air, The. Study in a Late Subway. Muriel Rukeyser. **CP-RukeM**

Moon Riders. Carl Sandburg. **CP-SandC**

Moon rises. The red cubs rolling, The. The Breath of Night. Randall Jarrell. **CP-JarrR; SP-JarrR**

Moon Rondeau. Carl Sandburg. **CP-SandC**

Moon: royal crown of an enormous head. A Divine Falling of Leaves. César Vallejo, *tr. fr. Spanish by* James Wright. **CP-WrigJ**

Moon shrinks behind a row of shriveled trees, The. A Different Cereal. John Yau. **SP-YauJo**

Moon smiles like a queen, The. Thomas Merton. **CP-MertT**

Moon Song, Woman Song. Anne Sexton. **CP-SextA**

Moon, that against the lintel of the west. Edna St. Vincent Millay. **CP-MillE**

Moon, The / ovoid. View. William Carlos Williams. **CP-WilW1**

Moon, the Whole Moon, and Nothing but the Moon, The. Al Young. **CP-YounA**

Moon turns round the earth, The. Shadows. Alun Lewis. **CP-LewiA**

Moon Up Close in Winter by the Telescope, The. Al Young. **CP-YounA**

Moon upon her fluent Route, The. Emily Dickinson. **CP-DickE**

Moon was but a Chin of Gold, The. Emily Dickinson. **CP-DickE**

Moon was in the Cambridge sky, The. A Ballad of the Investiture 1969. Sir John Betjeman. **CP-BetjJ**

Moon was like a full cup tonight, The. The Cows at Night. Hayden Carruth. **CP-CarHS**

Moon Watching by Lake Chapala. Al Young. **CP-YounA**

Moon-white dunes and the water like violets. The Beach. Robinson Jeffers. **CP-JefR1**

Moon will run all consciences to cover, The. Ditty. Allen Tate. **CP-TateA**

Moon with Roman numerals, there, A. A Clock With No Hands. Howard Nemerov. **CP-NemeH**

Moonbeam, leave the shadowy vale. To the Moonbeam. Percy Bysshe Shelley. **CP-ShelP**

Moonbeams kelter i' the lift, The. The Man in the Moon. "Hugh MacDiarmid." **NeBP** *Fr.* Au Clair de la Lune. **SP-MacDH**

Moondial. Jean Garrigue. **SP-GarrJ**

Moonflower, The. Frank Templeton Prince. **CP-PrinF**

Moonless darkness stumbles between. Gerard Manley Hopkins. **CP-HopkG**

Moonlessness. Al Young. **CP-YounA**

Moonlight. Walter de la Mare. **CP-DeLaW**

Moonlight and Maggots. Carl Sandburg. **CP-SandC**

Moonlight Drive. Jim Morrison. **SP-MorrJ**

Moonlight filters on the prairie, The. Moonlight and Maggots. Carl Sandburg. **CP-SandC**

Moonlight has touched them all, The. Ryder. John Haines. **SP-HainJ**

Moonlight in Vermont. William Matthews. **SP-MattW**

Moonlight landscape, sheep. Thoughts on Looking at a Samuel Palmer Etching at the Tate. Gary Snyder. **CP-SnydG**

Moonlight lingers down the air. Lullaby: Moonlight Lingers. Robert Penn Warren. *Fr.* Man in Moonlight. **SP-WarrR**

Moonlight Night. Joseph, Freiherr von Eichendorff, *tr. fr. German by* George Meredith. **CP-MerG2**

Moonlight Night: Carmel. Langston Hughes. **SP-HughL**

Moonlight Observed from Ruined Fortress. Robert Penn Warren. *Fr.* Man in Moonlight. **SP-WarrR**

Moonlight severing his ancient mariner's. Albert Ryder—Moonlightist. Marsden Hartley. **CP-HartM**

Moonlight the dead image of the day—. The Last Door. Roy Fisher. **SP-FishR** *Fr.* Inscriptions for Bluebeard's Castle.

Moonlighters. Laurence Lieberman. **SP-LiebL**

Moonlit river way out there in old Shanghai. I've Said Goodbye to Shanghai. Malcolm Lowry. **CP-LowrM**

Moonmouth and grasshopper that flee our page. A Name for All. Hart Crane. **CP-CranH**

Moonrise. Hilda Doolittle. **CP-DoolH**

Moonrise. David Herbert Lawrence. **CP-LawrD**

Moonrise. Sylvia Plath. **CP-PlatS**

Moonrise June 19 1876. Gerard Manley Hopkins. *See* I awoke in the midsummer not-to-call night, in the white and the walk of the morning.

Moon's a brass-hooped water-keg, The. What the Miner in the Desert Said. Nicholas Vachel Lindsay. **CP-LindV**

Moon's a cottage with a door, The. Drying Their Wings. Nicholas Vachel Lindsay. **CP-LindV**

Moon's a gong, hung in the wild, The. What the Gray-Winged Fairy Said. Nicholas Vachel Lindsay. **CP-LindV**

Moon's a holy owl-queen, The. What Grandpa Mouse Said. Nicholas Vachel Lindsay. **CP-LindV**

Moon's a little arch, The. A Classic Case. Gilbert Sorrentino. **SP-SorrG**

Moon's a little prairie-dog, The. What the Rattlesnake Said. Nicholas Vachel Lindsay. **CP-LindV**

Moon's a monk, unmated, The. The Strength of the Lonely. Nicholas Vachel Lindsay. **CP-LindV**

Moon's a paper jumping hoop, The. What the Clown Said. Nicholas Vachel Lindsay. **CP-LindV**

Moon's a peck of corn. It lies, The. The Old Horse in the City. Nicholas Vachel Lindsay. **CP-LindV**

Moon's a snowball. See the drifts, The. What the Snow Man Said. Nicholas Vachel Lindsay. **CP-LindV**

Moon's a steaming chalice, The. What Semiramis Said. Nicholas Vachel Lindsay. **CP-LindV**

Moon's an open furnace door, The. What the Coal-Heaver Said. Nicholas Vachel Lindsay. **CP-LindV**

Moons I have lost and suns unwept and gone. Don't, Have One for the Road. Malcolm Lowry. **CP-LowrM**

Moon's Last Quarter, The. Robert Ranke Graves. **CP-GravR**

Moon's man stands in his shell, The. The Everlasting Monday. Sylvia Plath. **CP-PlatS**

Moons of Jupiter, The. John Updike. **CP-UpdiJ**

Moon's Tear, The. Robert Ranke Graves. **CP-GravR**

Moon's the North Wind's Cooky, The. Nicholas Vachel Lindsay. **CP-LindV**

Moonset. Hayden Carruth. **CP-CarHS**

Moonset. Carl Sandburg. **CP-SandC**

Moonset, Gloucester, December 1, 1957, 1:58 A.M. Charles Olson. **CP-OlsoC; SP-OlsoC**

Moonshine. Howard Nemerov. **CP-NemeH**

Moonshine. Christina Georgina Rossetti. **CP-RosC3**

Moonshiner. Louise McNeill. **SP-McNeL**

Moonsong at Morning. Sylvia Plath. **CP-PlatS**

Moonstruck. "Hugh MacDiarmid." *Fr.* Au Clair de la Lune. **SP-MacDH** (Munestruck.) **NeBP**

Moony breadth of virgin face, A. Lines on the Portrait of a Celebrated Publisher. John Greenleaf Whittier. **CP-WhitJ**

Moorish King rides up and down, The. A Very Mournful Ballad. Byron. **CP-Byron**

Moose, The. Elizabeth Bishop. **CP-BishE**

Moose. Anne Sexton. **CP-SextA**

Moose Calling, A. John Haines. **SP-HainJ**

Moose in the Morning, Northern Maine. Mona Van Duyn. **SP-VanDM**

Moose Wallow, The. Robert Earl Hayden. **CP-HaydR**

Moosehead, The. John Haines. **SP-HainJ**

Mop-eyed I am, as some have said. Upon Himself. Robert Herrick. **CP-HerrR**

Mora Sponsi, the Stay of the Bridegroome. Robert Herrick. **CP-HerrR**

Morada La Muerte, The. Martin Edmunds. *Fr.* The High Road to Taos. **SP-EdmuM**

Moral, The, *parody.* Rudyard Kipling. **CP-KiplR** *Fr.* The Muse among the Motors.

Moral, The. William Carlos Williams. **CP-WilW2**

Moral Assessment. Robert Penn Warren. *Fr.* Homage to Theodore Dreiser. **SP-WarrR**

Moral Clothing. David Herbert Lawrence. **CP-LawrD**

Moral Poem Freely Accepted from Sappho, A. James Wright. **CP-WrigJ**

Moral Warfare, The. John Greenleaf Whittier. **CP-WhitJ**

Moralists. Stephen Dunn. **SP-DunnS**

Moralists tell us that Loving is Sinning, The. Queries to Casuists. Byron. **CP-Byron**

Moralities. Wystan Hugh Auden. *Fr.* Six Commissioned Texts. **CP-AudeW**

Morality. David Herbert Lawrence. **CP-LawrD**

Morality, *sl. diff. vers.* David Herbert Lawrence. *See* Man's Image.

Morality, A. Howard Nemerov. **CP-NemeH**

Morality of Poetry, The. James Wright. **CP-WrigJ**

Morality Play: Preface, A. George Oppen. **APSN; NNaP** *Fr.* Some San Francisco Poems. **CP-OppeG**

Morality, thou deadly bane. Robert Burns. **OBSV** *Fr.* A Dedication to G**** H******* Esq. **CP-BurnR**

Moralizer Corrected, the. William Cowper. **CP-CowpW**

Moralizing. Marsden Hartley. **CP-HartM**

Moralizing Overheard in a Forest. Jean Garrigue. **SP-GarrJ**

Moray eel lies wound amongst the stone, A. The Seabed. Thom Gunn. *Fr.* Three for Children. **CP-GunnT**

Mordanto fills the trump of fame. To the Earl of Peterborough. Jonathan Swift. **CP-SwifJ**

More a Man Has the More a Man Wants, The. Paul Muldoon. **SP-MuldP**

More About People. Ogden Nash. **CP-NashO**

More and More. Margaret Atwood. **SP-AtwM1**

More and more lately, as, not even minding the slippages yet, the aches and sad softenings. Repression. Charles Kenneth Williams. **SP-WillC**

More and more often as the years accumulate. Leaves. Stephen Berg. **SP-BergS**

More beautiful and soft than any moth. The Landscape near an Aerodrome. Stephen Spender. **CP-SpenS**

More beautiful than any gift you gave. The Token. Frank Templeton Prince. **CP-PrinF**

More circumspect good friend, if by "deceive." Marilyn Hacker. **SP-HackM** *Fr.* Separations.

More Clues. Muriel Rukeyser. **CP-RukeM**

More Clues to the Blues. Al Young. **CP-YounA**

More Country People. Carl Sandburg. **CP-SandC**

More discontents I never had. Discontents in Devon. Robert Herrick. **CP-HerrR**

More do I love cold. Old. Louis Zukofsky. **CP-ZukLS**

More experiences and sights, stranger, than you'd think for. Mirages. Walt Whitman. **CP-WhitW**

More Foreign Cities. Charles Tomlinson. **CP-TomlC**

More gaily, dance. Quick-Step. Robert Creeley. **CP-CreeR**

More Grammar for a Sentence. Gertrude Stein. **CP-SteiG**

More had she spoke, but yawn'd—All nature nods. Alexander Pope. **FHYEP** *Fr.* Yet, yet a moment, one dim ray of light. **NAEL-1; OAEL-1; PoEL-3** *Fr.* The Dunciad. **CP-PopeA**

More holy than the rest, and understanding more. Ovid, *tr.* by Sir Walter Ralegh. **CP-RaleW** *Fr.* Metamorphoses.

More I leaf through the dictionary in my physician's waiting, The. What the Well-Read Patient Is Talking About, or, Look, Ma, What I Got! Ogden Nash. **CP-NashO**

More Impatience. Malcolm Lowry. **CP-LowrM**

More Life—went out—when He went. Emily Dickinson. **CP-DickE**

More Love to His Life. Alice Walker. **CP-WalkA**

More Loving One, The. Wystan Hugh Auden. **CP-AudeW**

More May not Be by Human Art Exprest. William Wordsworth. **CP-WorW2**

More Mighty, the More Merciful, The. Robert Herrick. **CP-HerrR**

More Modest, More Manly. Robert Herrick. **CP-HerrR**

More money's lost, old gamblers understand. Two Pair. Howard Nemerov. **CP-NemeH**

More of a Corpse than a Woman. Muriel Rukeyser. **CP-RukeM**

More of the fathers are dying each day. Robert Bly. *Fr.* Six Winter Privacy Poems. **SP-BlyR**

More Pleasant Adventures. John Ashbery. **SP-AshbJ**

More pleasurable to look than feed upon. The Walgh-Vogel. Richard Wilbur. **CP-WilbR**

More Potent, Lesse Peccant. Robert Herrick. **CP-HerrR**

More safely truth to urge her claim presumes. Juvenal, *tr.* by Samuel Johnson. **CP-JohnS** *Fr.* Satires.

More shower than shine. Christina Georgina Rossetti. **CP-RosC3** (1880.) **CP-RosC3**

More Sonnets at Christmas. Allen Tate. **CP-TateA**
  "Again the native hour lets down the locks."
  "Day's at end and there's nowhere to go."
  "Gay citizen, myself, and thoughtful friend."
    ("Citizen, myself, or personal friend.") **WaP**
  "Give me this day a faith not personal."

More sweet than my refrain. Ralph Waldo Emerson. **CP-EmerR**

More Than a Fool's Song. Countee Cullen. **CP-CullC**

More than fifty millions. More. Adolf Hitler ("More than fifty millions. More"). William DeWitt Snodgrass. **SP-SnodW**

More than Flesh to Fathom. Edwin Rolfe. **CP-RolfE**

More than Grass. Phoebe Hesketh. **SP-HeskP**

More than half my life long. The Obliterate Tomb. Thomas Hardy. **CP-HardT**

More than halfway up the pass. The Times Table. Robert Frost. **CP-FrosR**

More than my brothers are to me. Tennyson. **OAEL-2** *Fr.* In Memoriam A. H. H. **CP-TennA**

More than once taking both roads one night. Mother, 1972. Robert Lowell. **SP-LoweR**

More than one cuckoo? Boys Then and Now. Thomas Hardy. **CP-HardT**

More than other song. Humming a Tune for an Old Lady in West Virginia. James Wright. **CP-WrigJ**

More than the Grave is closed to me. Emily Dickinson. **CP-DickE**

More than the sennet of the solstice pipe. Song, The. Charles Olson. **CP-OlsoC; SP-OlsoC**

More than this flecked thing. . . ? Under a Tree. Kenneth Patchen. **CP-PatcK**

More that— / who? the world. 1959 Valentine. Louis Zukofsky. **CP-ZukLS**

More things are wrought by prayer. Prayer. Tennyson. **BLRP** *Fr.* Morte d'Arthur. **DL; EBNV; EBVVPR; FaBoBe; FiP; NIP; NOBVV; OAEL-2; OBNV; OXAEP-2; PoEL-5** *Fr.* Morte d'Arthur. **CP-TennA**

More things come to them. Beautiful Women. Stephen Dunn. **SP-DunnS**

More Under Saturn. William Dickey. **SP-DickW**

More voice was in her cough tonight: its first harsh, stripping sound would weaken abruptly. Helen. Charles Kenneth Williams. **SP-WillC**

More white then whitest lilies far. To Electra. Robert Herrick. **CP-HerrR**

More you tackle the property dragon, The. St George and the Dragon. David Herbert Lawrence. **CP-LawrD**

Morea's Sonnet. Mary Sidney, Countess of Montgomery Wroth. *See* Beare part with me most straight and pleasant Tree.

Morgan the lonely. An Elegy for the Poet Morgan Blum. James Wright. **CP-WrigJ**

Morgante Maggiore, The. Luigi Pulci, *tr. fr. Italian* by Byron. **CP-Byron** Prophecy. **PAH**

Mortiuri Salutamus. Henry Wadsworth Longfellow. **SP-LongH**
  "For age is opportunity no less." **PoToHe**
  It Is Too Late. **BLPL; PoLF**
  (Too Late?) **WBLP**

Moriturus. Edna St. Vincent Millay. **CP-MillE**

Morlaix: Into the Future with Neil Young. Lawrence Ferlinghetti. **SP-FerlL**

Morn was bright, the steeds were light, The. The Willow-Tree. "Lewis Carroll." **CP-CarrL**

Morn when first it thunders in March, The. Old Pictures in Florence. Robert Browning. **CP-BroR1**

Morning, A. Margaret Atwood. **SP-AtwM1**

Morning. William Blake. **CP-BlakW**

Morning. Louise Bogan. **CP-BogaL**

Morning. Jim Carroll. **SP-CarrJ**
  "Proper authorities served us with precautions."
  "Today the room is filled with tomorrows."

Morning. Donald Davie. **CP-DavDo**

Morning, A. James Dickey. **CP-DickJ**

Morning. Paul Laurence Dunbar. **CP-DunbP**

Morning. Allen Ginsberg. **CP-GinsA**

Morning. Louise Glück. **SP-GlücL**

Morning. Derek Mahon. *Fr.* Four Walks in the Country Near Saint-Brieuc. **SP-MahoD**

Morning. Mary Oliver. **SP-OlivM**

Morning. John Crowe Ransom. **SP-RansJ**

Morning, The. James Schuyler. **CP-SchuJ**

Morning / Scripture Lesson. David Herbert Lawrence. *Fr.* The Schoolmaster [A]. **CP-LawrD**

Morning / The chatter of meats. Thomas Merton. *Fr.* Cables to the Ace. **CP-MertT**

Morning. Robert Penn Warren. *Fr.* Boy's Will, Joyful Labor without Pay, and Harvest Home (1918). **SP-WarrR**

Morning. William Carlos Williams. **CP-WilW1**

Morning, a glass door, flashes. Arrival. Philip Larkin. **CP-LarkP**

Morning. A river view. Frederick Morgan. *Fr.* The River. **SP-MorgF**

Morning Address of Love to the Beloved Harteebeeste. Malcolm Lowry. **CP-LowrM**

Morning After. Langston Hughes. **SP-HughL**

Morning after the seminar, The. Executives Third Tier. John Hewitt. **CP-HewiJ**

Morning after Woe, The. Emily Dickinson. **CP-DickE**

Morning and evening. Goblin Market. Christina Georgina Rossetti. **CP-RosC1**

Morning and evening. Christina Georgina Rossetti. **BoTP; CBCK; EBEvV** *Fr.* Goblin Market. **CP-RosC1**
  (Worrying Fruit.) **CBCK**

Morning arises stormy and pale. Tennyson. **EBVVPR** *Fr.* Maud [A Monodrama]. **CP-TennA**
  "Ah, what shall I be at fifty." **NAEL-2**

Morning at Last: There in the Snow. Philip Larkin. **CP-LarkP**

Morning at nine, seven ultra-masculine men. In Your Bad Dream. Richard Hugo. **CP-HugoR**

Morning at the Window. Thomas Stearns Eliot. **CP-ElioT**

Morning Athletes. Marge Piercy. **SP-PierM**

Morning bird is bathing, The. Malcolm Lowry. **CP-LowrM**

Morning bird is eating, The. Lyrical Morning Poem. Malcolm Lowry. **CP-LowrM**

Morning bird is honing, The. Spark Poetry. Malcolm Lowry. **CP-LowrM**

Morning bird is shrilling, The. Morning Address of Love to the Beloved Harteebeeste. Malcolm Lowry. **CP-LowrM**

Morning bird is singing, The. Billetin. Malcolm Lowry. **CP-LowrM**

Morning bird is singing, The. Fragments from the Duck Anthology to Greet Our Beloved Harteebeeste in the Morning Watch. Malcolm Lowry. **CP-LowrM**

Morning bird is singing, The. Malcolm Lowry. **CP-LowrM**

Morning bird is singing, The. Reveille. Malcolm Lowry. **CP-LowrM**

Morning bird is singing, The. With Sweetest Morning Love to Their Beloved Harteebeeste. Malcolm Lowry. **CP-LowrM**

Morning bird is throstling, The. Morning Song for the Harteebeeste. Malcolm Lowry. **CP-LowrM**

Morning bird is warbling, The. Happiest of Harteebeeste Days and Devoted Love Eterne. Malcolm Lowry. **CP-LowrM**

Morning bird sits mutely, The. Malcolm Lowry. **CP-LowrM**

Morning breaks like a pomegranate, The. Wedding Morn. David Herbert Lawrence. **CP-LawrD**

Morning bright as summer. The job on hand, A. Canto XXVI. Louis MacNeice. *Fr.* Autumn Sequel. **CP-MacNL**

Morning by tree of blood is moistened. Adam. Stephen Spender. **CP-SpenS**

Morning came at last / The storm over we sighted. Kane Relief Expedition. Thomas Merton. *Fr.* North. *Fr.* The Geography of Lograire. **CP-MertT**

Morning, clear morning. Love Song to a Morning. Jorge Guillén, *tr. fr. Spanish by* James Wright. **CP-WrigJ**

Morning coat is walking, A. Malcolm Lowry. **CP-LowrM**

Morning comes, the night decays, the watchmen leave their stations, The. Empire Is No More. William Blake. **EnRP** *Fr.* America; a Prophecy. **CP-BlakW**

Morning comes. The old woman, a spot, The. Grief. Wendell Berry. **CP-BerrW**

Morning comes to consciousness, The. Thomas Stearns Eliot. *Fr.* Preludes (I–IV). **CP-ElioT**

Morning comes to life. Taos. Martin Edmunds. *Fr.* The High Road to Taos. **SP-EdmuM**

Morning cried by the bed. Thousands of Days. Muriel Rukeyser. **CP-RukeM**

Morning day is hazy, The. Report on Conditions. Malcolm Lowry. **CP-LowrM**

Morning Dream, The. William Cowper. **CP-CowpW**

Morning drum-call on my eager ear, The. Robert Louis Stevenson. **CP-StevR**

Morning. Eleven. The billiard table has been slept on. The Billiard Table. Roy Fisher. **SP-FishR** *Fr.* Interiors with Various Figures.

Morning, evening, noon and night. The Boy and the Angel. Robert Browning. **CP-BroR1**

Morning Exercise, A. William Wordsworth. **CP-WorW2**

Morning fair: A noontide dubious, A. New Year's Day, 1848. Walt Whitman. **CP-WhitW**

Morning finch is chirping, The. Morning song of El Leon. Malcolm Lowry. **CP-LowrM**

Morning finds the self-sequestr'd man, The. William Cowper. *See* I was a stricken deer, that left the herd.

Morning fog is bracing, The. As from All the Little Animals. Malcolm Lowry. **CP-LowrM**

Morning glories, pale as a mist drying. Bees and Morning Glories. John Ciardi. **SP-CiarJ**

Morning Glory Blue. Carl Sandburg. **CP-SandC**

Morning glory, climbing the morning long, The. Indiana. Hart Crane. *Fr.* Powhatan's Daughter. *Fr.* The Bridge. **CP-CranH**

Morning. Good for foliage to resist the faithful wind. Thomas Merton. *Fr.* Cables to the Ace. **CP-MertT**

Morning Half-Life Blues, The. Marge Piercy. **SP-PierM**

Morning has gone / before the day begins. Focus. Charles Tomlinson. *Fr.* In Winter Woods. **CP-TomlC**

Morning Has Spread Again. Philip Larkin. **CP-LarkP**

Morning Hymn. John Hewitt. **CP-HewiJ**

Morning Hymn of Adam. John Milton. **TrPWD,** *ll.* 153–208, *abr.; Fr.* Book V. *Fr.* Paradise Lost. **CP-MiltJ**
(Adam's Morning Hymn.) **WGRP,** *ll.* 153–210.

Morning Hymn to a Dark Girl. James Wright. **CP-WrigJ**

Morning: I Know Perfectly How in a Minute You Will Stretch and Smile. John Ciardi. **SP-CiarJ**

Morning ice on the window. Hayden Carruth. *Fr.* North Winter. **CP-CarHL**

Morning in a New Land. Mary Oliver. **SP-OlivM**

Morning in Padova. Richard Hugo. **CP-HugoR**

Morning in the Country, The. James Thomson. **CP-ThomJ**

Morning in the Hospital Solarium. Sylvia Plath. **CP-PlatS**

Morning in the windows smells blue, The. The Stable. Lewis Turco. **SP-TurcL**

Morning is clean and blue and the wind blows up the clouds, The. John Gould Fletcher. **SP-FletJ** *Fr.* Irradiations.

Morning is due to all. Emily Dickinson. **CP-DickE**

Morning is maturing, The. With Dearest Morning Love and Kisses. Malcolm Lowry. **CP-LowrM**

Morning is so gray that the grass is gray and the side of the white horse grazing, The. On Learning of a Friend's Illness. Charles Kenneth Williams. **CP-WillC; SP-WillC**

Morning—is the place for Dew. Emily Dickinson. **CP-DickE**

Morning lights / whiteness that has touched the world, The. March Snow. Wendell Berry. **CP-BerrW**

"Morning"—means "Milking"—to the Farmer. Emily Dickinson. **CP-DickE**

Morning, Midday, and Evening Sacrifice. Gerard Manley Hopkins. **CP-HopkG**

Morning Moment. John Hewitt. **CP-HewiJ**

Morning Moon, The. Derek Walcott. **CP-WalcD**

Morning, My Prince—the Eye That Walks. Kenneth Patchen. **CP-PatcK**

Morning News, The. Charles Olson. **CP-OlsoC**

Morning newspaper is useful, The. The Press is Peculiar. Carl Sandburg. **CP-SandC**

Morning of sleeplessness up to heckle wife as jokes. Day Kennedy Died. Al Young. **CP-YounA**

Morning of the Poem, The. James Schuyler. **CP-SchuJ**

Morning on the St. John's. Jane Cooper. **SP-CoopJ**

Morning, or heartache. In / the night it rained. Good Morning. James Schuyler. **CP-SchuJ**

Morning Poem. Mary Oliver. **SP-OlivM**

Morning Poem for Michael, A. Al Young. **CP-YounA**

Morning quivers in the thorns; above the budded snowdrops. To Autumn. Louise Glück. **SP-GlücL**

Morning Radio. Derek Mahon. **SP-MahoD**

Morning rain is rained, The. Malcolm Lowry. **CP-LowrM**

Morning rain is raining / A morning pain is paining, The. Malcolm Lowry. **CP-LowrM**

Morning rain is raining / The morning leg is paining, The. Malcolm Lowry. **CP-LowrM**

Morning rain is sleeting, The. Malcolm Lowry. **CP-LowrM**

Morning rain is weeping, The. Malcolm Lowry. **CP-LowrM**

Morning rattles the tall spike fence. Half Past Home. Marge Piercy. **SP-PierM**

Morning Roundup, The. Gilbert Sorrentino. **SP-SorrG**

Morning sleet is sleeting, The. Malcolm Lowry. **CP-LowrM**

Morning sneat is snewing, The. Malcolm Lowry. **CP-LowrM**

Morning Song. Leonard Cohen. **CP-CoheL**

Morning Song. Stephen Dobyns. **SP-DobyS**

Morning Song. Leonard Nathan. **SP-NathL**

Morning Song. Sylvia Plath. **CP-PlatS**

Morning Song for the Harteebeeste. Malcolm Lowry. **CP-LowrM**

Morning Song in the Jungle. Rudyard Kipling. **CP-KiplR** *Fr.* Letting in the Jungle. *Fr.* The Second Jungle Book.

Morning song of El Leon. Malcolm Lowry. **CP-LowrM**

Morning song of Love. Paul Laurence Dunbar. **CP-DunbP**

Morning star is not a star, The. Gary Snyder. **CP-SnydG** *Fr.* Logging. *Fr.* Myths and Texts.

Morning stove is wheezing, The. Malcolm Lowry. **CP-LowrM**

Morning Sun. Louis MacNeice. **CP-MacNL**

Morning Sun. Howard Nemerov. **CP-NemeH**

Morning tanker gleameth, The. Malcolm Lowry. **CP-LowrM**

Morning tea is boiling, The. For Our Sweetharteebeeste on Harteebeeste Day. Malcolm Lowry. **CP-LowrM**

Morning that comes but once. Emily Dickinson. **CP-DickE**

Morning that I first loved you, The. The New Clouds. William Carlos Williams. **CP-WilW2**

Morning: the phone jangles me from words: you. Marilyn Hacker. **SP-HackM** *Fr.* Taking Notice.

Morning touches the waves and breaks. Leviathan. Lewis Turco. **SP-TurcL**

Morning up the eastern stair. God's Acre. Alfred Edward Housman. **CP-HousA**

Morning watch was come; the vessel lay, The. The Island. Byron. **CP-Byron**

Morning without you is a dwindled Dawn. Emily Dickinson. **SP-DickE**

Morning Work. David Herbert Lawrence. **CP-LawrD**

Mornings / of an impossible love. Alice Walker. **CP-WalkA**

Morning's breast was speckled like a thrush's. April. Wystan Hugh Auden. **CP-AudWJ**

Mornings: Catherine. Charles Kenneth Williams. **SP-WillC**

Mornings in a New House. James Merrill. **SP-MerrJ**

Mornings in bed / Are energetic mornings. In Bed. Kenneth Koch. **SP-KochK**

Morning's News, The. Wendell Berry. **CP-BerrW**

Morns are meeker than they were, The. Emily Dickinson. **CP-DickE**

Morns like these—we parted. Emily Dickinson. **CP-DickE**

Morocco. Leonard Cohen. **CP-CoheL**

Morpheus, the lively son of deadly sleep. Sonnet 32. Sir Philip Sidney. *Fr.* Astrophil and Stella. **SP-SidnP**

Morphology repeats ontology. Kenneth Rexroth. **SP-RexrK** *Fr.* The Stigmata of Fact. **CP-RexKL** *Fr.* The Homestead Called Damascus.

Morro Bay. Robinson Jeffers. **CP-JefR3**

Mors nox perpetua est; mori proinde. *acc. by English translation.* Thomas Campion. **CP-CampT**

Morsel miraculous and meaningless. Edward Estlin Cummings. **CP-CummE**

Mort de A.D. Samuel Beckett. **CP-BeckS**

Mortal Flesh, Is Not Your Place in the Ground? Edna St. Vincent Millay. **CP-MillE**

Mortal Girl. Muriel Rukeyser. **CP-RukeM**

Mortal mixed of middle clay. Guy. Ralph Waldo Emerson. **CP-EmerR**

Mortal my mate, bearing my rock-a-heart. To His Watch. Gerard Manley Hopkins. **CP-HopkG**

Mortal Place, The. John Hewitt. **CP-HewiJ**

Mortal Prudence, handmaid of divine Providence. The Testament of Perpetual Change. William Carlos Williams. **CP-WilW2**

Mortales decem tela inter Gallica caesos. *acc. by English translation.* Thomas Campion. **CP-CampT**

Mortales tua forma quod misellos. *acc. by English translation.* Thomas Campion. **CP-CampT**

Mortality. Sir John Betjeman. **CP-BetjJ**

Mortality. Paul Laurence Dunbar. **CP-DunbP**

Mortals) / climbi / ng i / nto eachness begi. Edward Estlin Cummings. **CP-CummE**

Mortals around your destin'd heads. William Cowper. **CP-CowpW**

Morte d'Arthur, *incorporated in* Idylls of the King *with changes, as* The Passing of Arthur. Tennyson. **DL; EBNV; EBVVPR; FaBoBe; FiP; NIP; NOBVV; OAEL-2; OBNV; OXAEP-2; PoEL-5** *Fr.* Morte d'Arthur. **CP-TennA**

Morte d'Arthur. Tennyson. **CP-TennA**

Epic, The [Morte d'Arthur]. **NAEL-2**

Epic, The [Morte d'Arthur]. **NAEL-2**

Morte d'Arthur. **DL; EBNV; EBVVPR; FaBoBe; FiP; NIP; NOBVV; OAEL-2; OBNV; OXAEP-2; PoEL-5**

Prayer: "More things are wrought by prayer." **BLRP**

"Then loudly cried the bold Sir Bedivere." **TOF**

"Then saw they how there hove a dusky barge." **FaPoB**

Prayer: "More things are wrought by prayer." **BLRP**

"Then loudly cried the bold Sir Bedivere." **TOF**

"Then saw they how there hove a dusky barge." **FaPoB**

Morte parmi. Samuel Beckett. **CP-BeckS**

Mortesto. George Meredith. **CP-MerG2**

Mortification. George Herbert. **CP-HerbG**

Mortimer. Frank Templeton Prince. **CP-PrinF**

Mortmain. Robert Penn Warren. **SP-WarrR**

After Night Flight Son Reaches Bedside of Already Unconscious Father, Whose Right Hand Lifts in a Spasmodic Gesture, as Though Trying to Make Contact: 1955. **NOBA; Prf**

(After Night Flight.) **DiL**

Dead Language: Circa 1885, A.

Fox-Fire: 1956.

In the Turpitude of Time: N.D.

Vision: Circa 1880, A.

Mortmain Reappears. Herman Melville. **SP-MelvH** *Fr.* Clarel: A Poem and Pilgrimage in the Holy Land.

Morwenna's Cliff. Charles Tomlinson. **CP-TomlC**

Mosaic. John Hewitt. **CP-HewiJ**

Mosaic for Marianne Moore, A. Wystan Hugh Auden. *Fr.* Eleven Occasional Poems. **CP-AudeW**

Mosaic: St. Praxed's. Raissa Maritain, *tr. fr. French by* Thomas Merton. **CP-MertT**

Mosaicist of minute, A. On Eleventh Street. Charles Tomlinson. **CP-TomlC**

Moscow. John Updike. *Fr.* Postcards from Soviet Cities. **CP-UpdiJ**

Moscow in the Wilderness, Segovia in the Snow. Lawrence Ferlinghetti. **SP-FerlL**

Moscow Moment. John Hewitt. **CP-HewiJ**

Moses. Howard Nemerov. **CP-NemeH**

"Moses" of Michael Angelo, The. Robert Browning. **CP-BroR2**

Moslems' Angel of Death, The. Thomas Merton. **CP-MertT; SP-MertT**

Mosquito. The. David Herbert Lawrence. **CP-LawrD**

Mosquito. John Updike. **CP-UpdiJ**

Mosquito in Florence. Stephen Spender. *Fr.* Lost Days. **CP-SpenS**

Mosquito Knows, The. David Herbert Lawrence. **CP-LawrD**

Mosquitoes in New Jersey. Gilbert Sorrentino. **SP-SorrG**

Moss. Al Young. **CP-YounA**

Moss-Gathering. Theodore Roethke. **CP-RoetT**

Moss of His Skin, The. Anne Sexton. **CP-SextA**

Moss on the milk is white, The. Why I Didn't Notice It. William Matthews. **SP-MattW**

Moss under your fingernails it feeds, The. Jim Carroll. **SP-CarrJ**

Mossbawn. Seamus Heaney. **SP-HeanS**

Mossbawn Sunlight. **BIrV**

(Sunlight.) **FaBCIP; NoP**

Seed Cutters, The. **FaBCIP; PNI**

Mossbawn Sunlight. Seamus Heaney. **BIrV** *Fr.* Mossbawn. **SP-HeanS**

(Sunlight.) **FaBCIP; NoP**

Most, The. Charles Bukowski. **SP-BukC1**

Most Alluring Clouds That Mount the Sky, The. William Wordsworth. **CP-WorW2**

Most ancient Metaphysics, (poor Metaphysics!). Madonnas Touched Up with a Goatee. Charles Simic. **SP-SimiC**

Most astonishing thing, A. Imitated from the Japanese. William Butler Yeats. **CP-YeatW**

Most beautiful of poisons. Monkshood. Erica Jong. **SP-JongE**

Most beautiful! the red-flowering eucalyptus. The Torso. Robert Duncan. **SP-DuncR** *Fr.* Passages.

Most binding labor / is, The. 86'd. Charles Bukowski. **SP-BukC2**

Most blessed Night, the happy time for love. Sonnet 3. Mary Sidney, Countess of Montgomery Wroth. *Fr.* Pamphilia to Amphilanthus. **CP-WrotM**

Most brainy woman, the sexuality of your thought. Sonnet. Hayden Carruth. **CP-CarHS** *Fr.* Sonnets.

Most candid critic, what if I. To a Critic. Samuel Taylor Coleridge. **CP-ColeS**

Most dear, and dearest at this moment most. Dakar Doldrums. Allen Ginsberg. **CP-GinsA**

Most deere, more hapy soverainsing harts. Mary Sidney, Countess of Montgomery Wroth. *Fr.* Part 2. *Fr.* Urania. **CP-WrotM**

Most excruciating / thing, The. Charles Kenneth Williams. **CP-WillC**

Most Expensive Picture in the World, The. Howard Nemerov. **CP-NemeH**

Most glorious lord of life that on this day. Edmund Spenser. **CABA; ChIV-2; EBCP; EiL; EnRePo; HAP; HBV; InPS; LiTB; NAEL-1; NOBE; NOCV; NoP; NoSic; OBEV; OHIP; OxBoCh; PoE; SeCeV; Son; TRV; TrPWD** *Fr.* Amoretti. **CP-Spens**

(Easter.) **NOBE; OBEV; PeECV**

(Easter Morning.) **OHIP; TRV**

("Most Glorious Lord of lyfe, that on this day.") **PeECV**

Most Glorious Lord of lyfe, that on this day. Edmund Spenser. *See* Most glorious lord of life that on this day.

Most graceful of misunderstandings, The. The Reef. David St. John. **SP-StJoD**

Most hapy memory bee ever blest. Mary Sidney, Countess of Montgomery Wroth. *Fr.* Part 2. *Fr.* Urania. **CP-WrotM**

Most holy Satyr. Holy Satyr. Hilda Doolittle. **CP-DoolH**

Most important happening / in the world today, The. Berryman's Dead. John Clellon Holmes. **SP-HolmJ**

Most important population, The. Emily Dickinson. **CP-DickE**

Most intimate, most far, most ethereally near. The Lost. Richard Eberhart. **CP-EberR**

Most Like an Arch This Marriage. John Ciardi. **SP-CiarJ**

Most Likely You Go Your Way (and I'll Go Mine). "Bob Dylan." **CP-DylaB**

Most marvelous is not, The. The Hard Core of Beauty. William Carlos Williams. **CP-WilW2**

Most men are rodents clothed. After fun. The Prado: Bosch: S. Antonio. Richard Hugo. **CP-HugoR**

Most men harry the world for fun. FEBRUARY (*Coursing*). Rudyard Kipling. *Fr.* Verses on Games. **CP-KiplR**

Most men use / their eyes. The Mechanic. Diane Wakoski. **SP-WakoD**

Most miraculous photograph, The. The Water's Fine, I'm Fine. Dabney Stuart. **SP-StuaD**

Most mornings I get away, slip out. Run before Dawn. William Stafford. **SP-StafW**

Most mornings we go running side by side. Morning Athletes. Marge Piercy. **SP-PierM**

Most musical of mourners, weep again! Percy Bysshe Shelley. **EPCY** *Fr.* Adonais; An Elegy on the Death of John Keats. **CP-ShelP**

Most nauseous of all drinks, what is your spell? Malcolm Lowry. *Fr.* The Cantinas. **CP-LowrM**

Most neglect this road, the concrete torn. Back of Gino's Place. Richard Hugo. **CP-HugoR**

Most of his friends, as expected. As Expected. Thom Gunn. **CP-GunnT**

Most of It, The. Robert Frost. **CP-FrosR**

Most of our Moments. Emily Dickinson. **SP-DickE**

Most of the houses were brick. The Red and the Black. Roy Fisher. **SP-FishR**

Most of the time he wrote, a sort of sleep. Homer's Seeing-Eye Dog. William Matthews. **SP-MattW**

Most of your life we have kept our separate places. Discovering My Daughter. Dabney Stuart. **SP-StuaD**

Most pathetic thing I do, The. Emily Dickinson. **CP-DickE**

Most patients believe. The Art of Healing. Wystan Hugh Auden. **CP-AudeW**

Most people don't do very well and I get discouraged with. 60 Yard Pass. Charles Bukowski. **SP-BukC3**

Most people know more as they get older. The Winter Palace. Philip Larkin. **CP-LarkP**

Most people, today, are chimaera. Chimaera. David Herbert Lawrence. **CP-LawrD**

Most people's downy couches have a footboard and a headboard. Have You Tried Staying Awake? or, They'll Find a Way to Stop That, Too. Ogden Nash. **CP-NashO**

Most recent in the long race that descends. The Doodler. James Merrill. **SP-MerrJ**

Most Saturday afternoons. The Weepies. Paul Muldoon. **SP-MuldP**

Most she touched me by her muteness. Emily Dickinson. **CP-DickE**

Most souls, 'tis true, but peep out once an age. Alexander Pope. **CH; FaBoRV** *Fr.* Elegy to the Memory of an Unfortunate Lady. **CP-PopeA**

(Dull, Sullen Prisoners.) **FaBoRV**

Most strange, my change, this nervous interim—. John Berryman. *Fr.* Sonnets to Chris. **CP-BerrJ**

Most sweet and pleasing are thy wayes, O God. Thomas Campion. **CP-CampT**

Most Sweet It Is with Unuplifted Eyes. William Wordsworth. **EnRP** *Fr.* Poems Composed or Suggested During a Tour, in the Summer of 1833. **CP-WorW2**

(Inner Vision, The.) **GTBS; GTBS-6; GTBS-P**

Most travelers eavesdrop / As unintentionally as autumn leaves drop. Everybody Wants to Get into the Baedeker. Ogden Nash. **CP-NashO**

Most triumphant Bird I ever knew or met, The. Emily Dickinson. **CP-DickE**

Most truly hono[u]red, and as truly dear. To Her Father, with Some Verses. Anne Bradstreet. **CP-BradA**

Most what I know of war is what I learned. A Memory of the War. Howard Nemerov. **CP-NemeH**

Most wicked words!-forbear to speak them out. Edna St. Vincent Millay. **CP-MillE**

Most Words, Lesse Workes. Robert Herrick. **CP-HerrR**

Most wounds can Time repair. At Ease. Walter de la Mare. **CP-DeLaW**

Most wretched heart, most miserable. Sir Thomas Wyatt. **CP-WyatT**

Mostly the animals dream. Dreams of the Animals. Margaret Atwood. **SP-AtwM1**

Mostly we occupy ocular zones, clinging. How the Rainbow Works. Al Young. **CP-YounA**

Mostly you don't see the ocean. The Road Behind the Last Dune. Marge Piercy. **SP-PierM** *Fr.* Sand Roads.

Most(people / simply / can't). Edward Estlin Cummings. **CP-CummE**

Motes that still disturbed her lidded calm, The. Night. Adrienne Rich. **CP-RicAE; SP-RicA2**

Motet. Louis Zukofsky. **CP-ZukLS**

Moth, The. Walter de la Mare. **CP-DeLaW**

Moth, The. Charlotte Smith. **CP-SmitC**

Moth and Rust. David Herbert Lawrence. **CP-LawrD**

Moth-force a small town always has. The Strength of Fields. James Dickey. **CP-DickJ**

Moth Happened, The. Isabella Gardner. **CP-GardI**

Moth Hour. Adrienne Rich. **CP-RicAE; SP-RicA2**

Moth in the Schoolroom. May Sarton. **SP-SartM**

Moth-Signal, The. Thomas Hardy. **CP-HardT**

Moth That Made God Blind, The. Hart Crane. **CP-CranH**

Moth the hue of this, A. Emily Dickinson. **CP-DickE**

Moth under the eaves, The. Prelude to Winter. William Carlos Williams. **CP-WilW2**

Mothball Fleet: Benicia, California. John Haines. **SP-HainJ**

Mother, The. Gwendolyn Brooks. **CrDW; CrSp; MDDM; NALW** *Fr.* A Street in Bronzeville. **SP-BrooG**

Mother, The. Hayden Carruth. *Fr.* Mother. **CP-CarHL**

Mother. Hayden Carruth. **CP-CarHL**

Death, The.

Event, The.

Mother, The.

Phantasmagoria, The.

Ship, The.

Son, The.

Water, The.

Mother, The. George Crabbe. **SP-CrabG** *Fr.* Tales.

Mother. Donald Davie. **CP-DavDo**

Mother, / each time I talk to God. Praying on a 707. Anne Sexton. **CP-SextA**

Mother. Marilyn Hacker. **SP-HackM**

Mother. Daniel Gerard Hoffman. **SP-HoffD**

Mother. Erica Jong. **SP-JongE**

Mother. Ussin Kerim, *tr. fr.* Bulgarian by William Matthews. **SP-MattW**

Mother, The. Stevie Smith. **CP-SmitS**

Mother, The. William DeWitt Snodgrass. **SP-SnodW**

Mother, / strange goddess face. Dreaming the Breasts. Anne Sexton. **CP-SextA**

Mother. John Greenleaf Whittier. **AA; OHIP** *Fr.* Snow-Bound [or Snow-Bound; a Winter Idyl]. **CP-WhitJ**

Mother, among the Dustbins. Stevie Smith. **CP-SmitS**

Mother and Babe. Walt Whitman. **CP-WhitW**

Mother and Child. Christina Georgina Rossetti. **CP-RosC3**

Mother & Child. Anne Waldman. **SP-WaldA**

Mother and Daughter. Anne Sexton. **CP-SextA**

Mother and Daughter. Robert Louis Stevenson. *Fr.* The Family. **CP-StevR**

Mother and Father 1. Robert Lowell. **SP-LoweR**

Mother and Father 2. Robert Lowell. **SP-LoweR**

Mother and Jack and the Rain. Anne Sexton. **CP-SextA**

Mother and listener she is, but she does not listen. The Question. Muriel Rukeyser. **CP-RukeM**

Mother and Poet. Elizabeth Barrett Browning. **CP-BroEB**

Mother and sire, to you do I commend. Here Lies Erotion. Robert Louis Stevenson. **CP-StevR**

Mother and Son. Charles Bukowski. **SP-BukC2**

Mother and Son. John Hewitt. **CP-HewiJ**

Mother and Son. Allen Tate. **CP-TateA**

Mother, because you never spoke to me. More Clues. Muriel Rukeyser. **CP-RukeM**

Mother Country. Christina Georgina Rossetti. **CP-RosC1**

Mother Country. Anne Waldman. **SP-WaldA**

Mother Earth: Her Whales. Gary Snyder. **CP-SnydG**

Mother, Father. The Money Swing. Anne Sexton. **CP-SextA**

Mother Garden's Round. Muriel Rukeyser. **CP-RukeM**

Mother Goose's Garland. Archibald MacLeish. **CP-MacLA**

Mother has come to the clean end. Book Club. Ted Kooser. **SP-KoosT**

Mother, I love you so. Human Affection. Stevie Smith. **CP-SmitS**

Mother-in-Law. Adrienne Rich. **SP-RicA2**

Mother Is. Siv Cedering Fox. **SP-CedeS**

Mother, it's such a lonely house. The House. Walter de la Mare. **CP-DavDo**

Mother-Lodge, The. Rudyard Kipling. **CP-KiplR**

Mother Marie Therese. Robert Lowell. **SP-LoweR**

Mother Mask. Alice Notley. **SP-NotlA**

Mother mine / Whom every year. 1879. Christina Georgina Rossetti. **CP-RosC3**

Mother (mother) unbent to give to / anyone, The. The Method of Actuality. Robert Creeley. **CP-CreeR**

Mother, mother, what illbred aunt. The Disquieting Muses. Sylvia Plath. **CP-PlatS**

Mother Mourns, The. Thomas Hardy. **CP-HardT**

Mother, my Mary Gray. The Division of Parts. Anne Sexton. **CP-SextA**

Mother Nature's Son. The Beatles. **CP-Beatl**

Mother, 1972. Robert Lowell. **SP-LoweR**

Mother, now at last I must speak to you. The hour, so late but even so, has come. The Event. Hayden Carruth. *Fr.* Mother. **CP-CarHL**

Mother o' Mine. Rudyard Kipling. **CP-KiplR** *Fr.* The Light That Failed.

Mother of flames. Crude Lament. William Carlos Williams. **CP-WilW1**

Mother of God, The. William Butler Yeats. **CP-YeatW**

Mother of God! Our Lady! For Eleanor and Bill Monahan. William Carlos Williams. **CP-WilW2**

Mother of heaven, regina of the clouds. Le Monocle de Mon Oncle. Wallace Stevens. **CP-StevW**

Mother of Hermes! and still youthful Maia! John Keats. **CP-KeatJ** (Ode to May. Fragment.) **CP-KeatJ**

Mother of Latin fun and Greek sexiness. Lesbos. James Liddy. **CP-LiddJ**

Mother of roots, you have not seeded. Goodbye to the Poetry of Calcium. James Wright. **CP-WrigJ**

Mother of the Buddhas, Queen of Heaven, Mother of the Sun; Marici, Goddess of the Dawn. Gary Snyder. **CP-SnydG**

Mother Political. Stephen Berg. **SP-BergS**

Mother procure for me a golden crown. The Crown of Gold. Stevie Smith. **CP-SmitS**

Mother-Right. Adrienne Rich. **SP-RicA2**

Mother said if I wore this hat. My Hat. Stevie Smith. **CP-SmitS**

Mother, Said the Child. Randall Jarrell. **CP-JarrR**

Mother says he looked like an Englishman. City Life. James Liddy. *Fr.* Ossie Esmonde. *Fr.* His Resplendent Neighbours. **CP-LiddJ**

Mother shake the cherry-tree. Let's Be Merry. Christina Georgina Rossetti. **FaPON; TLR; TiPo** *Fr.* Sing-Song. **CP-RosC2**

Mother shake the cherry-tree. Christina Georgina Rossetti. **CP-RosC2**

Mother, sisters, brother. James McAuley. **SP-McAuJ** *Fr.* Habitations.

Mother sits, the white of her eyes tinted, The. A Dream of Old Vienna. James Merrill. *Fr.* Five Old Favorites. **SP-MerrJ**

Mother slew her unborn babe, A. But Murderous. Stevie Smith. **CP-SmitS**

Mother, Summer, I. Philip Larkin. **CP-LarkP**

Mother, the pleasure. To return is, The. La Chute III. Charles Olson. **CP-OlsoC**

Mother, the sweet peas have gushed out of. 108 East 19th. William Stafford. **SP-StafW**

Mother, this is a ball of color. Gilbert Sorrentino. **SP-SorrG**

Mother ties the hair-ribbons of the child, The. Extraordinary References. Wallace Stevens. **CP-StevW**

Mother to Babe. George Meredith. **CP-MerG1**

"Mother," to me, is so sacred a Name. Emily Dickinson. **SP-DickE**

Mother to Son. Langston Hughes. **SP-HughL**

Mother II. Marilyn Hacker. **SP-HackM**

Mother Was a crack of light. Three Floors. Stanley Jasspon Kunitz. **CP-KuniS**

Mother Was a Good. Siv Cedering Fox. **SP-CedeS**

Mother who gave birth to Jeanne, The. George Meredith. *Fr.* Alsace-Lorraine. **CP-MerG1**

Mother whose breasts were our green mountains. Mother. Daniel Gerard Hoffman. **SP-HoffD**

Mother! whose virgin bosom was uncrost. The Virgin. William Wordsworth. **GoBC; ISi** *Fr.* Ecclesiastical Sonnets. **CP-WorW2**

Mother, will you come. Monologue. Alun Lewis. **CP-LewiA**

Motherhood. Wystan Hugh Auden. **CP-AudWJ**

Motherhood. Rita Dove. **SP-DoveR**

Mothering Blackness, The. Maya Angelou. **SP-AngeM**

Mothering void, ripe emptiness. Number. Robert Pack. **SP-PackR**

Motherless baby and babyless mother. Christina Georgina Rossetti. **CP-RosC2**

Motherless soft lambkin / Alone upon a hill. Christina Georgina Rossetti. **CP-RosC2**

Mothermas. James Liddy. *Fr.* Glass after Oblivion. **CP-LiddJ**

Mothers. Margaret Atwood. **SP-AtwM2**

Mothers. Kay Boyle. **CP-BoylK**

Mothers. Anne Sexton. **CP-SextA**

Mothers & daughters. Dear Marys, Dear Mother, Dear Daughter. Erica Jong. **SP-JongE**

Mothers are doubtless happier for their babes. Gerard Manley Hopkins. **CP-HopkG**

Mother's breast: / Safe refuge from her childish fears, A. A Nursery Darling. "Lewis Carroll." **CP-CarrL**

Mother's Curse. Anne Waldman. **SP-WaldA**

Mother's Day. William Stafford. **SP-StafW**

Mother's Day is a very fine day. Please Leave Father Alone. Ogden Nash. **CP-NashO**

Mother's dying almost stunned my spirit. Emily Dickinson. **SP-DickE**

Mother's gone a-visitin' to spend a month er two. Lonesome. Paul Laurence Dunbar. **CP-DunbP**

Mothers have come back, The. Ted Hughes. *Fr.* Sheep. **SP-HughT**

Mother's Hearse, A. Stevie Smith. **CP-SmitS**

Mother's Lament for the Loss of Her Only Son, A. Robert Burns. *See* Fate gave the word, the arrow sped.

Mothers! Mothers! It was visions of mothers that had been relentlessly haunting me. Epilogue to Mother's Day, Which Is To Be Published on Any Day But Mother's Day. Ogden Nash. **CP-NashO**

Mothers of America. Ave Maria. Frank O'Hara. **SP-OharF**

Mothers pass, / Sweet watermelon in a baby carriage. Summer Evening (Calumet Avenue). Langston Hughes. **SP-HughL**

Mother's Son, The. Rudyard Kipling. **CP-KiplR**

Mother's Son in Salonika. David Herbert Lawrence. *Fr.* Bits. **CP-LawrD**

Mothers you have met before still need you. Thomas Merton. **CP-MertT**

Moths, The. Mary Oliver. **SP-OlivM**

Moth's kiss, first, The! Robert Browning. **BoLoP; GBL; OBEV; TrGrPo** *Fr.* In a Gondola. **CP-BroR1**

(Song: "Moth's kiss, first, The!") **TrGrPo**

Moths white as ghosts among these hundreds cling. John Berryman. *Fr.* Sonnets to Chris. **CP-BerrJ**

Motifs. Alun Lewis. **CP-LewiA**

Motifs from the Dark Wood. Jean Garrigue. **SP-GarrJ**

Motion, The. Charles Olson. **CP-OlsoC**

Motion, The. Theodore Roethke. **CP-RoetT**

Motion, motion. / Within the body cells. To Fragmentation. John Updike. *Fr.* Seven Odes to Seven Natural Processes. **CP-UpdiJ**

Motion, 1953. Tom Clark. **SP-ClarT**

Motion: not things / moving where the harp's. Music's Trinity. Charles Tomlinson. **CP-TomlC**

Motion of Wish. Stanley Jasspon Kunitz. **CP-KuniS**

Motionless, deep in his mind, lies the past the poet's forgotten. Wystan Hugh Auden. *Fr.* Shorts [1939–1947] ("Motionless, deep in his mind, lies the past the poet's forgotten"). **CP-AudeW**

Motionless morning / no quiver or tremor. Autumn: Early Morning. Isabella Gardner. **CP-GardI**

Motions and Means, on land and sea at war. Steamboats, Viaducts and Railways. William Wordsworth. **NAEL-2; VLP** *Fr.* Poems Composed or Suggested During a Tour, in the Summer of 1833. **CP-WorW2**

Motions and means, on land and sea at war. Steamboats, Viaducts, and Railways. William Wordsworth. **CP-WorW2**

Motions of waking trouble winter air. Fare Well. John Berryman. **CP-BerrJ**

Motive for Metaphor, The. Wallace Stevens. **CP-StevW**

Motive of All of It, The. Muriel Rukeyser. **CP-RukeM**

Motives. John Hewitt. **CP-HewiJ**

Motley. Walter de la Mare. **CP-DeLaW**

Motley. George Meredith. **CP-MerG2**

Motor-Barge, The. William Carlos Williams. **CP-WilW2**

Motor idling, we warble our greetings to nine roadside. Stubby Carrot. Laurence Lieberman. **SP-LiebL**

Motorbike, A. Ted Hughes. **SP-HughT**

Motorcycle strums the empty streets. The Bed in the Sky. Gary Snyder. **CP-SnydG**

Motorcycle was saved when the driver's head, The. Paradise. John Yau. **SP-YauJo**

Motorpsycho Nightmare. "Bob Dylan." **CP-DylaB**

Mots survivants. Samuel Beckett. **CP-BeckS**

Motto. Langston Hughes. **SP-HughL**

Motto above my table says, The. Barton Sutter. *Fr.* Tools. **SP-SuttB**

Motto Intended for Poems on the Naming of Places. William Wordsworth. **CP-WorW1**

Motto on the King's Clock. William Cowper. **CP-CowpW**

Motto to "Circles." Ralph Waldo Emerson. *See* Nature centres into balls.

Motto to "Considerations by the Way." Ralph Waldo Emerson. **CP-EmerR**

Motto to "Fate." Ralph Waldo Emerson. **CP-EmerR**

Motto to "Gifts." Ralph Waldo Emerson. **CP-EmerR**

Motto to "Illusions." Ralph Waldo Emerson. *See* Flow, flow the waves hated.

Motto to "Intellect." Ralph Waldo Emerson. *See* Go, speed the stars of thought.

Motto to "Nature" ("Rounded world is fair to see, The"). Ralph Waldo Emerson. *See* The Rounded world is fair to see.

Motto to "Nature" ("Subtle chain of countless rings, A"). Ralph Waldo Emerson. *See* A Subtle chain of countless rings.

Motto to "New England Reformers." Ralph Waldo Emerson. **CP-EmerR**

Motto to "Nominalist and Realist." Ralph Waldo Emerson. *See* In countless upward-striving waves.

Motto to "Power." Ralph Waldo Emerson. **CP-EmerR**

Motto to "Prudence." Ralph Waldo Emerson. *See* Prudence.

Motto to "The Poet." Ralph Waldo Emerson. **CP-EmerR**

Motto to the Songs of Innocence & of Experience. William Blake. **CP-BlakW**

Mottoes to "History." Ralph Waldo Emerson. **CP-EmerR** *Fr.* History.

Moult sont Prud'hommes les Templiers. Frank Templeton Prince. **CP-PrinF**

Mound, The. Thomas Hardy. **CP-HardT**

Mound Builders, The. Stanley Jasspon Kunitz. **CP-KuniS**
"Let the old geezers jig on Penn."
"Mounds rise up on every side, The."
"Musician of the lost tribes."

Mounds rise up on every side, The. Stanley Jasspon Kunitz. *Fr.* The Mound Builders. **CP-KuniS**

Mount Agiochook. John Greenleaf Whittier. **CP-WhitJ**

Mount Aso uplands. A Volcano in Kyushu. Gary Snyder. **CP-SnydG**

Mount Caribou at Night. Charles Wright. **SP-WrigC**

Mt. Gabriel. Derek Mahon. **SP-MahoD**

Mount Kearsarge. Donald Hall. **CP-HallD**

Mount, not wearisome and bare and steep, A. To a Young Friend. Samuel Taylor Coleridge. **CP-ColeS**

Mount of Olives was thy seat, The. Peace. Christopher Smart. *Fr.* Hymns for the Amusement of Children. **SP-SmarC**

Mount of the Muses, The. Robert Herrick. **CP-HerrR**

Mount Stavros sits on. Charles Henri Ford. **SP-FordC** *Fr.* Emblems of Arachne.

Mount Zion. Ted Hughes. **SP-HughT**

Mountain, The. Elizabeth Bishop. **CP-BishE**

Mountain, The. Hayden Carruth. **CP-CarHS**

Mountain, The. Stephen Dobyns. **SP-DobyS**

Mountain, The. Robert Frost. **CP-FrosR**

Mountain, The. Louise Glück. **SP-GlücL**

Mountain / Mesquite. Flint and Steel. Thomas McGrath. **SP-McGrT**

Mountain above them rose, The. Retreat. Phoebe Hesketh. **SP-HeskP**

Mountain and the squirrel, The. Fable. Ralph Waldo Emerson. **CP-EmerR**

Mountain Ash Without Cedar Waxwings. Robert Pack. **SP-PackR**

Mountain Cabin, The. Hayden Carruth. **CP-CarHS**

Mountain Corn Song. Louise McNeill. **SP-McNeL**

Mountain Fastness, The. Hayden Carruth. *Fr.* Contra Mortem. **CP-CarHL**

Mountain gorses, ever-golden. Lessons from the Gorse. Elizabeth Barrett Browning. **CP-BroEB**

Mountain Impasse. John Updike. **CP-UpdiJ**

Mountain is old. They say she is a female mountain, The. A Poem for the Teesto Diné of Arizona. Kay Boyle. **CP-BoylK**

Mountain Laurel. Louis Zukofsky. **CP-ZukLS**

Mountain laurel in bloom, The. Adrienne Rich. *Fr.* The Spirit of Place. **SP-RicA2**

Mountain Lion. David Herbert Lawrence. **CP-LawrD**

Mountain Lovers. Robert Ranke Graves. **CP-GravR**

Mountain, mountain, mountain. Into the Interior. Denise Levertov. **CP-LeveD**

Mountain: One from Bryant. Muriel Rukeyser. **CP-RukeM**

Mountain over Aberdare, The. Alun Lewis. **CP-LewiA**

Mountain Pictures. John Greenleaf Whittier. **CP-WhitJ**

Mountain road ends here, The. Lyell's Hypothesis Again. Kenneth Rexroth. **SP-RexrK**

Mountain sat upon the Plain, The. Emily Dickinson. **CP-DickE**

Mountain stream its channel deep, A. The Truant Dove from Pilpay. Charlotte Smith. **CP-SmitC**

Mountain Tomb, The. William Butler Yeats. **CP-YeatW**

Mountaineer and Poet. Elizabeth Barrett Browning. **CP-BroEB**

Mountains. Wystan Hugh Auden. **FaBoPV** *Fr.* Bucolics. **CP-AudeW**

Mountains, The. Walter de la Mare. **CP-DeLaW**

Mountains. Robert Earl Hayden. *Fr.* An Inference of Mexico. **CP-HaydR**

Mountains. Ted Hughes. **SP-HughT**

Mountains, a moment's earth-waves rising and hollowing; the earth too's an ephemerid; the stars. The Treasure. Robinson Jeffers. **CP-JefR1**

Mountains and mountains and mountains. Autumn Leaves. James Schuyler. **CP-SchuJ**

Mountains and the shadows move away, The. Silence of Volcanoes. Muriel Rukeyser. **CP-RukeM**

Mountains between our lands and the sea—, The. In the Clear Season of Grapes. Wallace Stevens. **CP-StevW**

Mountains blanket-wrapped. Men in New Mexico. David Herbert Lawrence. **CP-LawrD**

Mountains blue now, The. The Mountains in the Desert. Robert Creeley. **CP-CreeR**

Mountains, cities, all so. Nanao Knows. Gary Snyder. **CP-SnydG**

Mountains cover me like rain. For an Atheist. Countee Cullen. **CP-CullC**

Mountains Covered with Cats. Wallace Stevens. **CP-StevW**

Mountains, Fall on Us. Michael Hartnett. **SP-HarMi**

Mountains, from this downward turn in the road, The. At a Glance. Charles Tomlinson. **CP-TomlC**

Mountains grow—unnoticed, The. Emily Dickinson. **CP-DickE**

Mountains in the Desert, The. Robert Creeley. **CP-CreeR**

Mountains in their overwhelming might, The. Christina Georgina Rossetti. *Fr.* Later Life: A Double Sonnet of Sonnets. **CP-RosC2**

Mountains, monuments, all forms. Elegiac Stanzas: On a Visit to Dove Cottage. Geoffrey Hill. **CP-HillG**

Mountains of California: Part 1, The. Al Young. **CP-YounA**

Mountains of California: Part 2, The. Al Young. **CP-YounA**

Mountains of twine and. Ted Berrigan. **SP-BerrT** *Fr.* The Sonnets.

Mountains stand up around the main street in Harper's Ferry. Landscape Including Three States of the Union. Carl Sandburg. **CP-SandC**

Mountains stood in Haze, The. Emily Dickinson. **CP-DickE**

Mountains stood on their bottom ends, The. Smoke Blue. Carl Sandburg. **CP-SandC**

Mountaintop stands in silence a minute after the murder, The. Orpheus. Muriel Rukeyser. **CP-RukeM**

Mounted as an Amazon. William Carlos Williams. **CP-WilW2**

Mounted on all four walls, the neat. Roy Fisher. **SP-FishR** *Fr.* New Diversions.

Mourn for Polly Botsford, aged thirty-nine. Sacred to the Memory. Stanley Jasspon Kunitz. *Fr.* Words for the Unknown Makers: A Garland of Commemorative Verses. **CP-KuniS**

Mourn, Israel! Sons of Israel, mourn! Israel's Lament. Samuel Taylor Coleridge. **CP-ColeS**

Mourn Not for Adonais. Percy Bysshe Shelley. *See* Peace, peace! he is not dead, he doth not sleep.

Mourn, ye wee songsters o' the wood. Robert Burns. **PBBP** *Fr.* Elegy on Captain Matthew Henderson [*or* Capt. M——— H———] [A *Gentleman* Who Held the Patent for His Honours Immediately from Almighty God!]. **CP-BurnR**

Mourne Mountains. John Hewitt. **CP-HewiJ**

Mourne Mountains like a team of bears, The. From the Chinese of Wang Li Shi. John Hewitt. **CP-HewiJ**

Mourners. James McAuley. *Fr.* Requiem. **SP-McAuJ**

Mournful Young Man. David Herbert Lawrence. **CP-LawrD**

Mournfully to and fro, to and fro the trees are waving. A Passing-Bell. David Herbert Lawrence. **CP-LawrD**

Mourning, A. Jean Garrigue. **SP-GarrJ**

Mourning. David Herbert Lawrence. *Fr.* Bits. **CP-LawrD**

Mourning. Andrew Marvell. **CP-MarvA**

Mourning and Longing. William Cowper. *Fr.* Olney Hymns. **CP-CowpW**

Mourning Grace. Maya Angelou. **SP-AngeM**

Mourning Mother, The. Elizabeth Barrett Browning. **CP-BroEB**

Mourning Muse of Thestylis, The. Edmund Spenser. *Fr.* Astrophel. **CP-Spens**

Mourning my heart doth sore oppress. Sir Thomas Wyatt. **CP-WyatT**

Mourning Picture. Adrienne Rich. **CP-RicAE; SP-RicA2**

Mourning Poem for the Queen of Sunday. Robert Earl Hayden. **CP-HaydR**

Mourning the broken balance, the hopeless prostration of the earth. Robinson Jeffers. *Fr.* The Broken Balance. **CP-JefR1**

Mourn'st Thou Now? Walter de la Mare. **CP-DeLaW**

Mouse, The. Hayden Carruth. **CP-CarHS**

Mouse, The. Jean Garrigue. **SP-GarrJ**

Mouse, The. William DeWitt Snodgrass. **SP-SnodW**

Mouse crawled through it, The. Hole. Leonard Nathan. **SP-NathL**

Mouse fell from a screech-owl's beak, A—a thing that I can not pretend. The Mouse Metamorphosed Into a Maid. Marianne Craig Moore. **CP-MoorM** *Fr.* Fables of La Fontaine.

Mouse Metamorphosed Into a Maid, The. Marianne Craig Moore. **CP-MoorM** *Fr.* Fables of La Fontaine.

Mouse Sex. John Updike. **CP-UpdiJ**

Mouse sharpens his teeth, The. The Mouse. Hayden Carruth. **CP-CarHS**

Mouse That Gnawed the Oak-Tree Down, The. Nicholas Vachel Lindsay. **CP-LindV**

Mouse was startled by its own unimpearled shadow, The. On the South-West Coast of Erehwemos Stands a Romantic Little Village. Kenneth Patchen. **CP-PatcK**

Mousemeal. Howard Nemerov. **CP-NemeH**

Mouse's Tale, The. "Lewis Carroll." *See* Fury said to a / mouse, That he.

Mouse's Tale, The: "We lived beneath the mat." "Lewis Carroll." **CP-CarrL**

Mouse)Won / derfully is. Edward Estlin Cummings. **CP-CummE**

Mouth. John Clellon Holmes. **SP-HolmJ**

Mouth of artifice. Mouth-Talk. Roy Fisher. **SP-FishR**

Mouth of the Hudson, The. Robert Lowell. **SP-LoweR**

Mouth of this man is a gaunt strong mouth, The. A Tall Man. Carl Sandburg. **CP-SandC**

Mouth of truth, The. Lawrence Ferlinghetti. **SP-FerlL**

Mouth-Talk. Roy Fisher. **SP-FishR**

Mouthings of water at the end of a world. Rubh An' Dunain. Charles Tomlinson. **CP-TomlC**

Mouths Nuzz. Robert Creeley. **CP-CreeR**

Move / deeply,rain / (dream hugely)wish. Edward Estlin Cummings. **CP-CummE**

Move Continuing, The. Al Young. **CP-YounA**

Move Eastward, Happy Earth, and Leave. Tennyson. **CP-TennA**

Move him into the sun. Futility. Wilfred Owen. **CP-OwenW**

Move Over. Charles Olson. **CP-OlsoC; SP-OlsoC**

Move that system. Vital Imperatives for Chester. Thomas Merton. *Fr.* Cables to the Ace. **CP-MertT**

Moved to the blessing of colour. Colour. John Hewitt. **CP-HewiJ**

Movement of Fish, The. James Dickey. **CP-DickJ**

Movement Song. Audre Lorde. **SP-LordA**

Movements. Charles Tomlinson. **CP-TomlC**

Movie. Muriel Rukeyser. **CP-RukeM**

Movie Actors Scribbling Letters Very Fast in Crucial Scenes. Jean Garrigue. **SP-GarrJ**

Movie House. John Updike. **CP-UpdiJ**

Movies. Langston Hughes. **SP-HughL**

Movies, the Old Law. TV is the New. Late Late Show. Howard Nemerov. **CP-NemeH**

Moving. Randall Jarrell. **CP-JarrR; SP-JarrR**

Moving. William Matthews. **SP-MattW**

Moving, A. Jim Morrison. **SP-MorrJ**

Moving / or movement, A. A Moving. Jim Morrison. **SP-MorrJ**

Moving Again. William Matthews. **SP-MattW**

Moving among the Creatures. Daniel Gerard Hoffman. **SP-HoffD**

Moving at evening across the viaduct. An Instant on the Viaduct. Jenny Joseph. **SP-JoseJ**

Moving Day. Ron Koertge. **SP-KoerR**

Moving from Cheer to Joy, from Joy to All. Next Day. Randall Jarrell. **CP-JarrR; SP-JarrR**

Moving from left to left, the light. View of the Capitol from the Library of Congress. Elizabeth Bishop. **CP-BishE**

Moving in a restless exhaustion. The Field of the Caribou. John Haines. **SP-HainJ**

Moving in her radiant care. Carmen 34. Catullus. *Fr.* Carmina. **CP-Catul**

Moving in Winter. Adrienne Rich. **CP-RicAE; SP-RicA2**

Moving, Merging, Fading, Standing Still. Al Young. **CP-YounA**

Moving must be in our nature. Premises. Karl Shapiro. **SP-ShapK**

Moving Out Or the End of Cooperative Living. Audre Lorde. **SP-LordA**

Moving over the hills, crossing the irrigation. George Oppen. **APSN; NNaP** *Fr.* Some San Francisco Poems. **CP-OppeG**

Moving slowly sweating a lot. Post the Lake Poets Ballad. Frank O'Hara. **SP-OharF**

Moving Staircase. Phoebe Hesketh. **SP-HeskP**

Moving sun-shapes on the spray, The. Going and Staying. Thomas Hardy. **CP-HardT**

Moving through the silent crowd. Unemployed. Stephen Spender. **CP-SpenS**

Mow the grass in the cemetery, darkies. Two at Norfolk. Wallace Stevens. **CP-StevW**

Mower, The. Philip Larkin. **CP-LarkP**

Mower against Gardens, The. Andrew Marvell. **CP-MarvA**

Mower stalled, twice, The; kneeling, I found. The Mower. Philip Larkin. **CP-LarkP**

Mower to the Glow-Worms [*or* Glowworms *or* Glo-Worms], The. Andrew Marvell. **CP-MarvA**

Mowers, The. David Herbert Lawrence. **CP-LawrD**

Mower's Song, The. Andrew Marvell. **CP-MarvA**

Mowgli's Brothers. Rudyard Kipling. *Fr.* The Jungle Book.
Hunting Song of the Seeonee Pack. **CP-KiplR**
"Now Chil the Kite brings home the night." **CP-KiplR**

Mowgli's Song against People. Rudyard Kipling. **CP-KiplR** *Fr.* Letting in the Jungle. *Fr.* The Second Jungle Book.

Mowing. Robert Frost. **CP-FrosR**

Mowing the east field under the ridge. Cutting the Firebreak. William Everson. **SP-EverW**

Moyst with one drop of thy blood, my dry soule. John Donne. *See* Resurrection.

Mozambique. "Bob Dylan" *and* Jacques Levy. **CP-DylaB**

Mozart Chemisier. Frank O'Hara. **SP-OharF**

Mozart, Goethe, and the Duke of Wellington. The Augsburg Adoration. Randall Jarrell. **CP-JarrR**

Mozart, 1935. Wallace Stevens. **CP-StevW**

Mr. Big. Ron Koertge. **SP-KoerR**

Mr. Bleaney. Philip Larkin. **CP-LarkP**

Mr. Eliot's Sunday Morning Service. Thomas Stearns Eliot. **CP-ElioT**

Mr Gladstone was a very good man. Daddy-Do-Nothing. David Herbert Lawrence. **CP-LawrD**

Mr. Mine. Anne Sexton. **CP-SextA**

Mr. Nixon. Ezra Pound. **MoAmPo** *Fr.* Hugh Selwyn Mauberley. (Life and Contacts). **SP-PounE**

Mr. Over. Stevie Smith. **CP-SmitS**

Mr Smith, Mr Smith. The Great Newspaper Editor to His Subordinate. David Herbert Lawrence. **CP-LawrD**

Mr Squire. David Herbert Lawrence. **CP-LawrD**

Mrs. Barton Sutter. **SP-SuttB**

Mrs Simpkins. Stevie Smith. **CP-SmitS**

Mrs. Small. Gwendolyn Brooks. **SP-BrooG**

Mrs. Walpurga. Muriel Rukeyser. **CP-RukeM**

Ms. Found in a Quagmire. Ogden Nash. **CP-NashO**

Ms. Found under a Serviette in a Lovely Home. Ogden Nash. **CP-NashO**

Ms. Lot. Muriel Rukeyser. **CP-RukeM**

M.T.—a Relative in Certain Aspects of Metaphysical Divination. Marsden Hartley. **CP-HartM**

Much ado about trees lichen. Gamut. Louis Zukofsky. **CP-ZukLS**

Much as I own I owe. Closed for Good. Robert Frost. **CP-FrosR**

Much-beaten-upon-looking, bedraggled blackbird, not a starling, with a mangled or tumourous claw, A. Greed. Charles Kenneth Williams. **SP-WillC**

Much did I rage when young. Youth and Age. William Butler Yeats. **CP-YeatW**

Much—discerning Public hold, A. Rudyard Kipling. *See* La Nuit Blanche.

Much have I travell'd [*or* travelled *or* traveled] in the realms of gold. On First Looking into Chapman's Homer. John Keats. **CP-KeatJ**

Much i cannot) / tear up the world:& toss. Edward Estlin Cummings. **CP-CummE**

Much I owe to the Lands that grew. The Two-Sided Man. Rudyard Kipling. **CP-KiplR** *Fr.* Kim.

Much later, I lie in a white seaport night. Muriel Rukeyser. *Fr.* Letter to the Front. **CP-RukeM**

Much madness is divinest sense. Emily Dickinson. **CP-DickE**

Much-more, provides, and hoords up like an Ant. Upon Much-More. Robert Herrick. **CP-HerrR**

Much of transfiguration that we hear. The Interlude. Karl Shapiro. **SP-ShapK**

Much of what I had thought mine. Wind is the Wall of the Year. Marge Piercy. **SP-PierM**

Much on my early youth I love to dwell. To a Young Lady. Samuel Taylor Coleridge. **CP-ColeS**

Much richer then that vessell seem'd to bee. Joachim Du Bellay. *Fr.* The Visions of Bellay. **CP-Spens**

Much wonder I—here long low-laid. The Bedridden Peasant. Thomas Hardy. **CP-HardT**

Muckers. Carl Sandburg. **CP-SandC**

Muckle-Mouth Meg. Robert Browning. **CP-BroR2**

Mud. Clods. The sucking heel of the rain-flinger. Derek Walcott. **CP-WalcD** *Fr.* Midsummer.

Mud is very deep, The. Emily Dickinson. **SP-DickE**

Mud Master. Wallace Stevens. **CP-StevW**

Mud-mattressed under the sign of the hag. Maudlin. Sylvia Plath. **CP-PlatS**

Mud put / upon mud. The House. Robert Creeley. **CP-CreeR**

Mud Season. May Sarton. **SP-SartM**

Mud Turtle, The. Howard Nemerov. **CP-NemeH**

Mud Vision, The. Seamus Heaney. **SP-HeanS**

Muddy rivers of spring, The. Mud Master. Wallace Stevens. **CP-StevW**

Muddy shallow waters, tired and old, The. Torcello. John Hewitt. **CP-HewiJ**

Mudge every morning to the Postern comes. Upon Mudge. Robert Herrick. **CP-HerrR**

Mudhens, cormorants and teals take. Duwamish No. 2. Richard Hugo. **CP-HugoR**

Mugging. Allen Ginsberg. **CP-GinsA**
"Tonite I walked out of my red apartment door on East tenth street's dusk." **HCAP**

Muiopotmos: or The Fate of the Butterflie. Edmund Spenser. **CP-Spens**

Muirland Meg. Robert Burns. **CP-BurnR**

Mujer. William Carlos Williams. **CP-WilW1**

Mulatto. Langston Hughes. **SP-HughL**

Mulberry Street ends in good works. Grace Paley. **CP-PaleG**

Mulch, The. Stanley Jasspon Kunitz. **CP-KuniS**

Mulciber. John Milton. **NOSC** *Fr.* Book I. **FHYEP; NAEL-1; OAEL-1; OxAEP-1** *Fr.* Paradise Lost. **CP-MiltJ**

Mule of water, The. Kenneth Patchen. **CP-PatcK**

Mules. Paul Muldoon. **SP-MuldP**

Mules, The. Ogden Nash. **CP-NashO**

Mules, I think, will not be here this hour, The. Empedocles on Etna. Matthew Arnold. **SP-ArnoM**

Muléykeh. Robert Browning. **CP-BroR2**

Mulford. John Greenleaf Whittier. **CP-WhitJ**

Mulholland's Contract. Rudyard Kipling. **CP-KiplR**

Mulish, unregenerate. In the North. Adrienne Rich. **CP-RicAE**

Mulled hosts their countries yet mulled there by a core of wake tossed. Catullus. *See* Carmen 101: "Journeying over many seas and through many countries."

Multiplication Table. Robert Penn Warren. **SP-WarrR**

Multitude. Robert Herrick. **CP-HerrR**

Multitudes. David Herbert Lawrence. **CP-LawrD**

Mumbe-jumble drones on, the hangman waits; the shabby surviving, The. War-Guilt Trials. Robinson Jeffers. **CP-JefR3**

Mumbo jumbo, what have we here? Midsummer's Daymare. Ogden Nash. **CP-NashO**

Mummies. Nicanor Parra, *tr. fr. Spanish by* Thomas Merton. **CP-MertT**

Mummified spider hung in its own web in the rafters striped legs coiled tightly, The. Spider Psyche. Charles Kenneth Williams. **SP-WillC**

Mummy. Carl Sandburg. **CP-SandC**

Munching a plum on. To a Poor Old Woman. William Carlos Williams. **CP-WilW1**

Municipal center / the morning of anger, The. Grace Paley. *Fr.* Stanzas: Old Age and the Conventions of Retirement Have Driven My Friends from the Work They Love. **CP-PaleG**

Mundus et Infans. Wystan Hugh Auden. **CP-AudeW**

Munestruck. "Hugh MacDiarmid." *See* Moonstruck.

Munich. Edwin Rolfe. **CP-RolfE**

Munich. Patti Smith. **SP-SmitP**

Munich. John Updike. **CP-UpdiJ**

Munich Agreement, The. Louis MacNeice. **FaBoEH** *Fr.* Sun shines easy, sun shines gay. *Fr.* Autumn Journal. **CP-MacNL**

Munich Mannequins, The. Sylvia Plath. **CP-PlatS**

Municipal. Rudyard Kipling. **CP-KiplR** (" 'Why is my District death-rate low?'.") **CP-KiplR**

Municipal Gallery Revisited, The. William Butler Yeats. **CP-YeatW**

Municipal Gallery Revisited, October 1954. John Hewitt. **CP-HewiJ**

Munificence and Modesty. Christopher Smart. **SP-SmarC**

Munitions. David Herbert Lawrence. *Fr.* Bits. **CP-LawrD**

Munster Song of Love and War, A. James Liddy. **CP-LiddJ**

"All the journeys / To be made for instance, over the seas."

"For all who trod / Golden North American streets."

"He'd be alive today if he wasn't pretty."

"Hounds can't / Come in, The."

"I am telling you, kid."

"New O'Dwyer's dim lights. 'You hate, The'."

Note.

"Talking to Clare as."

"We saw the star of knowledge."

"You are going to fall in love."

Mural of Wakeful Sleep, The. Laurence Lieberman. **SP-LiebL**

Murder. Steve Griffiths. **SP-GrifS**

Murder. David Herbert Lawrence. **CP-LawrD**

Murder, The. Frederick Morgan. **SP-MorgF**

Murder. Stevie Smith. **CP-SmitS**

Murder Mystery, The. "Lou Reed." **SP-ReedL**

Murder of Two Men by a Young Kid Wearing Lemon-colored Gloves, The. Kenneth Patchen. **CP-PatcK**

Murder of William Remington, The. Howard Nemerov. **CP-NemeH**

Murdered, well risen, the Life. James Wright. **CP-WrigJ**

Murdered Lover, The. Paul Laurence Dunbar. **CP-DunbP**

Murderer, The. Stevie Smith. **CP-SmitS**

Murderer's House, The. Mary Oliver. **SP-OlivM**

Murderer's little daughter, The. Sympathetic Portrait of a Child. William Carlos Williams. **CP-WilW1**

Murderess, The. Louise Glück. **SP-GlücL**

Murderfully in midmost o.can. Edward Estlin Cummings. **CP-CummE**

Murderous Weapons. David Herbert Lawrence. **CP-LawrD**

Muriel, Muriel, marry me Muriel. The Sorrowful Girl. Stevie Smith. **CP-SmitS**

Murmur in the Trees—to note, A. Emily Dickinson. **CP-DickE**

Murmur of a Bee, The. Emily Dickinson. **CP-DickE**

Murmuration of the shallow, Crane, A. John Berryman. *Fr.* Sonnets to Chris. **CP-BerrJ**

Murmuring of Bees, has ceased, The. Emily Dickinson. **CP-DickE**

Murmurings in a Field Hospital. Carl Sandburg. **CP-SandC**

Murmurs in the Gloom. Thomas Hardy. **CP-HardT**

Murphy and company jig with Cohen. Jig for Harmonica. Isabella Gardner. *Fr.* Saloon Suite. **CP-GardI**

Murray, you bid my plastic pen. Preface to "High and Low." Sir John Betjeman. **CP-BetjJ**

Murrays have moved to a house, The. You Have More Freedom in a House. Ogden Nash. **CP-NashO**

Muscat Pruning. William Everson. **SP-EverW**

Muscles which move the eyeballs, The. Poem. Charles Tomlinson. **CP-TomlC**

Musculatures and skulls. Later some throng. John Berryman. *Fr.* Sonnets to Chris. **CP-BerrJ**

Muse / Can at pleasure use, The. Ralph Waldo Emerson. **CP-EmerR**

Muse / is the "fate" of the poem, The. Charles Olson. **CP-OlsoC**

Muse. Jenny Joseph. *Fr.* Fables. **SP-JoseJ**

Muse, / tell me of this man of wit. Homer, *tr. by* Hilda Doolittle ("H.D."). **CP-DoolH** *Fr.* Odyssey.

Muse, The. Miller Williams. **SP-WillM**

Muse among the Motors, The. Rudyard Kipling.
Advertisement, The. **CP-KiplR**
Arterial. **CP-KiplR**
Ballad of the Cars, The. **CP-KiplR**
Beginner, The. **CP-KiplR**
Bother, The. **CP-KiplR**
Braggart, The. **CP-KiplR**
Carmen Circulare. **CP-KiplR**
Child's Garden, A. **CP-KiplR**
Consolations of Memory, The. **CP-KiplR**
Contradictions. **CP-KiplR**
Dying Chauffer, The. **CP-KiplR**
Fastness. **CP-KiplR**
Four Points, The. **CP-KiplR**
Idiot Boy, The. **CP-KiplR**
Inventor, The. **CP-KiplR**
Justice's Tale, The. **CP-KiplR**
Lady Geraldine's Hardship. **CP-KiplR**
Landau, The. **CP-KiplR**
Marrèd Drives of Windsor, The. **CP-KiplR**
Moral, The. **CP-KiplR**
Progress of the Spark, The. **CP-KiplR**
Sepulchral. **CP-KiplR**
To a Lady, Peruading Her to a Car. **CP-KiplR**
To Motorists. **CP-KiplR**
Tour, The. **CP-KiplR**
When the Journey Was Intended to the City. **CP-KiplR**

Muse as Medusa, The. May Sarton. **SP-SartM**

Muse Considered As a Demon Lover, The. Frank O'Hara. **SP-OharF**

Muse—Hide his name of whom I sing. Cock-Fighters Garland. William Cowper. **CP-CowpW**

Muse in the New World, The. Walt Whitman. **MoAmPo** *Fr.* Song of the Exposition. **CP-WhitW**

Muse not that by thy mind thy body is led. To Mr. R. W. John Donne. **CP-DonnJ**

Muse of native land! loftiest Muse! John Keats. **EnRP** *Fr.* Endymion: Poetic Romance. **CP-KeatJ**

Muse of the many-twinkling feet! whose charms. Byron. **DIP** *Fr.* Muse of the many-twinkling feet! whose charms. **OBSV** *Fr.* The Waltz. **CP-Byron**

Muse of the many-twinkling feet! whose charms. Byron. **OBSV** *Fr.* The Waltz. **CP-Byron**

"Muse of the many-twinkling feet! whose charms." **DIP**

Muse of the many-twinkling feet! whose charms. The Waltz. Byron. **CP-Byron**

Muse, sing the deeds of golden Aphrodite. Homer's Hymn to Venus. *Unknown.* **CP-ShelP** *Fr.* Homeric Hymns.

Muse that makes no pretensions to discourse, The. The Owl Minerva. Donald Davie. **CP-DavDo**

Muse, The / in her dark habit. The Well. Denise Levertov. **CP-LeveD**

Muse this one Verse to learn'd Pigot addresses, The. Presentation Verses to Nathaniel Pigott. Alexander Pope. **CP-PopeA**

Muse, 'tis enough: at length thy labour ends. Occasioned by Some Verses of his Grace the Duke of Buckingham. Alexander Pope. **CP-PopeA**

Muse Who Came to Stay, The. Erica Jong. **SP-JongE**

Muse Wooing: A Song. John Clellon Holmes. **SP-HolmJ**

Muse, you have bitten through my fool's-finger. Hercules at Nemea. Robert Ranke Graves. **CP-GravR**

Musée des Beaux Arts. Wystan Hugh Auden. **CP-AudeW**

Muses' garden, with pedantic weeds, The. On the Death of Donne. Thomas Carew. **NOBE** *Fr.* An Elegy upon the Death of the Dean of [St.] Paul's, Dr. John Donne.

Muses, I oft invoked your holy aid. Sonnet 55. Sir Philip Sidney. *Fr.* Astrophil and Stella. **SP-SidnP**

Museum! loveliest building of the plain. The Deserted Parks. "Lewis Carroll." **CP-CarrL**

Museum of Cruel Days. Richard Hugo. **CP-HugoR**

Museum Piece. Hayden Carruth. **CP-CarHS**

Museum Piece. Richard Wilbur. **CP-WilbR**

Museums. Louis MacNeice. **CP-MacNL**

Museums offer us, running from among the buses. Museums. Louis MacNeice. **CP-MacNL**

Mushroom Gatherers, The. Donald Davie. **CP-DavDo**

Mushroom is the Elf of Plants, The. Emily Dickinson. **CP-DickE**

Mushrooms. Margaret Atwood. **SP-AtwM2**

Mushrooms. Mary Oliver. **SP-OlivM**

Mushrooms. Sylvia Plath. **CP-PlatS**

Mushrooms. Charles Tomlinson. **CP-TomlC**

Music. Stephen Berg. **SP-BergS**

Music, A. Wendell Berry. **SP-BerrW**

Music. Edward Estlin Cummings. **CP-CummE**

Music ("O restless"). Walter de la Mare. **CP-DeLaW**

Music ("When music"). Walter de la Mare. **CP-DeLaW**

Music. Ralph Waldo Emerson. **CP-EmerR**

Music, A. Denise Levertov. **CP-LeveD**

Music. Frederick Morgan. **SP-MorgF**

Music. Frank O'Hara. **SP-OharF**

Music. Wilfred Owen. **CP-OwenW**

Music. Percy Bysshe Shelley. **CP-ShelP**

Music: a pattern etched into time. Billie. Al Young. **CP-YounA**

Music and Drum. Archibald MacLeish. **CP-MacLA**

Music and painting and all that. All the Fancy Things. William Carlos Williams. **CP-WilW1**

Music at the Villa Marina. Robert Louis Stevenson. **CP-StevR**

Music comes and goes on the wind, The. Listening to Jefferson Airplane. Thom Gunn. **CP-GunnT**

Music Crept by Us, The. Leonard Cohen. **CP-CoheL**

Music in a Snowy Street. Thomas Hardy. **CP-HardT**

Music is a dance, The. Los Guitaristas. Robert Creeley. **CP-CreeR**

Music Is International. Wystan Hugh Auden. **CP-AudeW**

Music is sweet from the thrush's throat! Music. Edward Estlin Cummings. **CP-CummE**

Music Lessons. John Hewitt. **CP-HewiJ**

Music of music is stillness, The, *sl. diff. and longer vers.* David Herbert Lawrence. *See* Corot.

Music of October, The. All Things. Hayden Carruth. **CP-CarHS**

Music of the spheres, The—that ends in Silence. Funny Death. Allen Ginsberg. **CP-GinsA**

Music of violins and of guitars / Rises up straight from the night. From Portofino Point. John Gould Fletcher. **SP-FletJ**

Music of words, The. Pieces. Adrienne Rich. **CP-RicAE; SP-RicA2**

Music One Looks Back On, The. Stephen Dobyns. **SP-DobyS**

Music Room, The. Isabella Gardner. **CP-GardI**

Music survives, composing her own sphere. Geoffrey Hill. *Fr.* Tenebrae. **CP-HillG**

Music Swims Back to Me. Anne Sexton. **CP-SextA**

Music Television. Jim Carroll. **SP-CarrJ**

Music[k], thou queen of heaven, care-charming spell. To Music: A Song. Robert Herrick. **CP-HerrR**

Music Unheard. Walter de la Mare. **CP-DeLaW**

Music was going on, The. At the Fillmore. Philip Levine. **SP-LeviP**

Music, when soft voices die. To ———. Percy Bysshe Shelley. **CP-ShelP**

Musical, A. Paul Laurence Dunbar. **CP-DunbP**

Musical Box, The. Thomas Hardy. **CP-HardT**

Musical Garden. Anne Waldman. **SP-WaldA**

Musical Incident, A. Thomas Hardy. **CP-HardT**

Musical Instrument, A. Elizabeth Barrett Browning. **CP-BroEB**

Musical Offering, A. Leonard Nathan. **SP-NathL**

Musical Strife; in a Pastoral Dialogue, The. Ben Jonson. **CP-JonsB**

Musician. Louise Bogan. **CP-BogaL**

Musician late at night in his little house, The. Æolian. Hayden Carruth. **CP-CarHS**

Musician of the lost tribes. Stanley Jasspon Kunitz. *Fr.* The Mound Builders. **CP-KuniS**

Musicians wrestle everywhere. Emily Dickinson. **CP-DickE**

Musick strides through these poems. Ted Berrigan. **SP-BerrT** *Fr.* The Sonnets.

Musicks maister, and the offspring. To the Worthy Author. Thomas Campion. **CP-CampT**

Musicologist—Preference, Prokofieff. Marsden Hartley. *Fr.* City Vignettes. **CP-HartM**

Music[k]'s Duel[l], *ad. fr. the Latin of* Strada. Richard Crashaw. **CP-CrasR**

Music's Empire. Andrew Marvell. **CP-MarvA**

Music's Trinity. Charles Tomlinson. **CP-TomlC**

Music[k] to hear[e], why hear'st thou music[k]. Sonnet 8. William Shakespeare. **PoEL-2** *Fr.* Sonnets. **CP-ShaWS**

Musing Maiden, The. Thomas Hardy. **CP-HardT**

Musing on the fate of Daphne. Daphne. George Meredith. **CP-MerG1**

Musing on the roaring ocean. Robert Burns. **CP-BurnR**

Musingly she mouths the end of her ballpoint pen as she stares down at the sheet of paper. Fast Food. Charles Kenneth Williams. **SP-WillC**

Musings near Aquapendente April, 1837. William Wordsworth. *Fr.* Memorials of a Tour in Italy, 1837. **CP-WorW2**

Musique de l'indifférence. Samuel Beckett. **CP-BeckS**

Musk-ox smells, The. The Long River. Donald Hall. **CP-HallD**

Musketaquid. Ralph Waldo Emerson. **CP-EmerR**

Mussel Hunter at Rock Harbor. Sylvia Plath. **CP-PlatS**

Mussels. Mary Oliver. **SP-OlivM**

Must be a Woe. Emily Dickinson. **CP-DickE**

Must be almost four. Night in NYC. Robert Creeley. **CP-CreeR**

Must be the Black Maria. Black Maria. Langston Hughes. **SP-HughL**

Must be thousands of sweet gourmets rustling through. Voznesensky's "Silent Tingling." Allen Ginsberg. **CP-GinsA**

Must being shall. Edward Estlin Cummings. **CP-CummE**

Must genius always struggle, always exaggerate. Sonnet. Hayden Carruth. **CP-CarHS** *Fr.* Sonnets.

Must I lose the Friend that saved my Life. Emily Dickinson. **SP-DickE**

Must I tell again. The Daemon. Louise Bogan. **CP-BogaL**

Must now accomplish the division of remains. The Accomplices. Isabella Gardner. **CP-GardI**

Must she then languish, and we sorrow thus. Upon the Sickness of E.S. Thomas Carew. **CP-CareT**

Must then all human love. The Diamond. Frank Templeton Prince. **CP-PrinF**

Must thou go, my glorious Chief. From the French. Byron. **CP-Byron**

Must we for ever eye through space? and make. The Separation. Thom Gunn. **CP-GunnT**

Must we part, Von Hügel, though much alike. William Butler Yeats. **OBMV** *Fr.* Vacillation. **CP-YeatW**

Must you leave, John Holmes, with the prayers and psalms. Somewhere in Africa. Anne Sexton. **CP-SextA**

Muster, The. Herman Melville. **SP-MelvH**

Mustered into the Avant-Garde. Donald Davie. **CP-DavDo**

Mutability. Percy Bysshe Shelley. **CP-ShelP**

Mutability. Percy Bysshe Shelley. **CP-ShelP**

Mutability. William DeWitt Snodgrass. **SP-SnodW**

Mutability. Edmund Spenser. **PoEL-1** *Fr.* The Faerie Queene. **CP-Spens**

Mutability. William Wordsworth. **EBEV; EnRP; HeIP; InPK; LiTB; MeMBP; NOBE; NoP; OAEL-2; OBEV; PoEL-4; PrIm** *Fr.* Ecclesiastical Sonnets. **CP-WorW2**

Mutability Claims to Rule the World. Edmund Spenser. **NoSic** *Fr.* The Faerie Queene. **CP-Spens**

Mutations. Louis MacNeice. **CP-MacNL**

Mutchmore and Not-So. Stevie Smith. **CP-SmitS**

Mute is thy wild harp, now, O Bard sublime! To the Shade of Burns. Charlotte Smith. **CP-SmitC**

Mute Opinion. Thomas Hardy. **CP-HardT**

Mute Phenomena, The. Derek Mahon. **SP-MahoD**

Mute thy Coronation. Emily Dickinson. **CP-DickE**

Mutely the mole toils on. Quiet. Walter de la Mare. **CP-DeLaW**

Mutes, The. Denise Levertov. **CP-LeveD**

Mutilation. David Herbert Lawrence. **CP-LawrD**

Mutinous & free I drifted off. The Form. John Berryman. **CP-BerrJ**

Mutinous in the half-light, & malignant, grind. John Berryman. *Fr.* Sonnets to Chris. **CP-BerrJ**

Muttering "fine upland staple," "prime Sea Island finer." What State Street Said to South Carolina, and What South Carolina Said to State Street. John Greenleaf Whittier. **CP-WhitJ**

Mutterings over the Crib of a Deaf Child. James Wright. **CP-WrigJ**

Mutual Forbearance. William Cowper. **CP-CowpW**

Mutual forgiveness of each vice. The Gates of Paradise. William Blake. **CP-BlakW**

Mutual Subjection. Christopher Smart. **NOCV** *Fr.* Hymns for the Amusement of Children. **SP-SmarC**

(Consideration for Others.) **OxBChV**

Muzzle and jowl and beastly brow. Basil Bunting. **CP-BuntB**

My adult unemployed son and I. Back Bay. John Updike. **CP-UpdiJ**

My age fallen away like white swaddling. Age. Philip Larkin. **CP-LarkP**

My Alba. Allen Ginsberg. **CP-GinsA**

My apple branch dressed. Charles Olson. **CP-OlsoC**

My architects, forsaking me. This Day This World. Stanley Jasspon Kunitz. **CP-KuniS**

My ardours for emprize nigh lost. On an Invitation to the United States. Thomas Hardy. **CP-HardT**

My Arkansas. Maya Angelou. **SP-AngeM**

My aspens dear, whose airy cages quelled. Binsey Poplars (Felled 1879). Gerard Manley Hopkins. **CP-HopkG**

My astonishment almost felicity. Giovanni Diodati. Charles Tomlinson. **CP-TomlC**

My attention has been recently focussed. Locust-Lovers, Attention! Ogden Nash. **CP-NashO**

My Aunt Ella Meets the Buddha on His Birthday. Diane Wakoski. **SP-WakoD**

My aunt kept turnips in a flock. Randall Jarrell. **CP-JarrR**

My Aunt Sarah and Uncle Joe. John Hewitt. **CP-HewiJ**

My author and disposer, what thou biddest. Thus Eve to Adam. John Milton. **FaBV** *Fr.* Book IV. **OAEL-1** *Fr.* Paradise Lost. **CP-MiltJ**

My baby has a father and a mother. Christina Georgina Rossetti. **CP-RosC1**

My baby has a mottled fist. Christina Georgina Rossetti. **CP-RosC2**

My baby says she's trav'ling on the One After Nine O Nine. One after 909. The Beatles. **CP-Beatl**

My baby's harelip's darned brilliantly. Courage. Steve Griffiths. **SP-GrifS**

My Back Pages. "Bob Dylan." **CP-DylaB**

My back toward the circle, I skate. Figure Eights. Siv Cedering Fox. **SP-CedeS**

My Baptismal Birthday [*or* Birth-Day]. Samuel Taylor Coleridge. **CP-ColeS**

My bean-pod boat you see here. Carmen 4. Catullus. *Fr.* Carmina. **CP-Catul**

My Beard. Shel Silverstein. **SP-SilS2**

My beautiful wife. Two A.M. Al Young. **CP-YounA**

My beautiful wooden leader. Margaret Atwood. **SP-AtwM1**

My bed grows narrower as I grow old. The Bed. Archibald MacLeish. **CP-MacLA**

My Bed Is a Boat. Robert Louis Stevenson. **CP-StevR**

My bed is like a little boat. My Bed Is a Boat. Robert Louis Stevenson. **CP-StevR**

My belly / sounds like an owl. Charles Olson. **CP-OlsoC**

My belly full of this domestic life. Canned Goods. Dabney Stuart. **SP-StuaD**

My Beloved Harteebeeste. Malcolm Lowry. **CP-LowrM**

My beloved land. Minority Report. John Updike. **CP-UpdiJ**

My best Acquaintances are those. Emily Dickinson. **CP-DickE**

My Best Girl. Paul Laurence Dunbar. **CP-DunbP**

My big round yew. Night Chill. Archie Randolph Ammons. **SP-AmmoA**

My Birthday. John Greenleaf Whittier. **CP-WhitJ**

My birthday was in March, when the weather was furious. Thomas Merton. *Fr.* The Early Legend. **CP-MertT**

My black sun, my. Song for a Dark Voice. Denise Levertov. **CP-LeveD**

My blessed mother dozing in her chair. Christina Georgina Rossetti. **CP-RosC3**

(Valentine, 1882, A.) **CP-RosC3**

My blessings on ye, honest wife. At Roslin Inn. Robert Burns. **CP-BurnR**

My blond niece speaks in riddles. Jim Carroll. *Fr.* Things That Fly. **SP-CarrJ**

My boat is on the shore. Byron. **CP-Byron**

(My Boat Is on the Shore.) **CP-Byron**

My Boat Is on the Shore. Byron. *See* My boat is on the shore.

My body & my self. Tiny Self-Portrait. Al Young. **CP-YounA**

My body has been perforated. Jim Carroll. **SP-CarrJ**

My Body in the Walls Captived. Sir Walter Ralegh. **CP-RaleW**

My body knows it will never bear children. Waiting. Jane Cooper. **SP-CoopJ**

My body opens over San Francisco like the day-. Splittings. Adrienne Rich. **SP-RicA1; SP-RicA2**

My body trots semblably. L'Epreuve. Thom Gunn. **CP-GunnT**

My body which my dungeon is. Robert Louis Stevenson. **CP-StevR**

My Bones Flew Apart. Richard Eberhart. **CP-EberR**

My Bonie Laddie's Young but He's Growin Yet. Robert Burns. **CP-BurnR**

My bonie lass I work in brass. Robert Burns. *Fr.* The Jolly Beggars.

My Bonnie [*or* Bony] Mary. Robert Burns. *See* Go fetch to me a pint o'wine.

My bonny man, the warld, it's true. The Counterblast—1886. Robert Louis Stevenson. **CP-StevR**

My Book, My Book. Charles Kenneth Williams. **SP-WillC**

My bottle is a holy pool. Robert Burns. *Fr.* Lines *Written on the Windows of the Globe Tavern, Dumfries.* **CP-BurnR**

My Boy Jack. Rudyard Kipling. **CP-KiplR**

My brain dried like spread turf, my stomach. Seamus Heaney. **CIP** *Fr.* Station Island. **SP-HeanS**

My brain swims empty and light. Robert Louis Stevenson. **CP-StevR**

My Brains Are Slipping in the Fields of Eros. Richard Eberhart. **CP-EberR**

My breast waited. The Wedlock. Anne Sexton. **CP-SextA**

"My brethren. . . " And a bland, elastic smile. The Evangelist. Donald Davie. **CP-DavDo**

"My bride is not coming, alas!" says the groom. At the Altar-Rail. Thomas Hardy. **MoAB; MoBrPo** *Fr.* Satires of Circumstance in Fifteen Glimpses. **CP-HardT**

My Brooklyn Uncle. John Hewitt. **CP-HewiJ**

My broom / with its tuft of roses. Her Broom, or the Ride of the Witch. Erica Jong. **SP-JongE**

My Brother. Hendrick De Vries, *tr. fr. Dutch by* Adrienne Rich. **CP-RicAE**

My brother and I planned to meet. The Black Hole. Robert Pack. **SP-PackR**

My brother and I, without hope. Hayden Carruth. *Fr.* Michigan Water: a Few Riffs before Dawn. **CP-CarHL**

My brother comes home from work. You Can Have It. Philip Levine. **SP-LeviP**

My brother kneels, so saith Kabir. Prayer, The. Rudyard Kipling. **CP-KiplR** *Fr.* Kim.

My Brother Luis. Stephen Spender. **CP-SpenS**

My brother saw a pig root in a field. Meat. Thom Gunn. **CP-GunnT**

My brother sighs in his sleep. A Good Night. Barton Sutter. **SP-SuttB**

My brother who knows. My Brother's Work. Stephen Dunn. **SP-DunnS**

My Brother's Work. Stephen Dunn. **SP-DunnS**

My Buddy. Richard Hugo. **CP-HugoR**

My business is words. Words are like labels. Said the Poet to the Analyst. Anne Sexton. **CP-SextA**

My Butterfly. Robert Frost. **CP-FrosR**

My Canary Bird. Walt Whitman. **CP-WhitW**

My candle burned alone in an immense valley. Valley Candle. Wallace Stevens. **CP-StevW**

My candle burns at both ends. First Fig. Edna St. Vincent Millay. **CP-MillE**

My carrier pigeon is a "fancy" pigeon. 4th May Morning. Christina Georgina Rossetti. **CP-RosC3**

My cat in a patch of sun. Cleanliness. Stephen Dunn. **SP-DunnS**

My cat is asleep on his haunches. Sleeping Cat. Ted Kooser. **SP-KoosT**

My Cat Jeoffry. Christopher Smart. *See* For I will consider my Cat Jeoffry.

My Cat Major. Stevie Smith. **CP-SmitS**

My Cats. Stevie Smith. **CP-SmitS**

My cheap toy lamp. Child's Song. Robert Lowell. **SP-LoweR**

My cheek was hit and hit. Hailstones. Seamus Heaney. **SP-HeanS**

My chest gapes open sometimes. Bereavement. David Herbert Lawrence. **CP-LawrD**

My chest hurts every breath I draw. Bronchitis at the Chelsea—or Salud Raul. Isabella Gardner. **CP-GardI**

My Chicago, city of. Hayden Carruth. *Fr.* Michigan Water: a Few Riffs before Dawn. **CP-CarHL**

My child and I hold hands on the way to school. September, the First Day of School. Howard Nemerov. **CP-NemeH**

My child as yet unborn, the doctors nod. March: A Birthday Poem. John Updike. **CP-UpdiJ**

My child is like a bird's wing, a bird's wing, a bird's wing. How Dulcenia del Toboso Is Like the Left Wing of a Bird. Nicholas Vachel Lindsay. **CP-LindV**

"My Child Is Phlegmatic. . . "—Anxious Parent. Ogden Nash. **CP-NashO**

My child, my child, watch how he goes. Hast Du Dich Verirrt? Stevie Smith. **CP-SmitS**

My child, my sister. L'Invitation au Voyage. Charles Baudelaire, *tr. fr.* French by Richard Wilbur. **CP-WilbR**

My child wants dolls, a tutu, that girls' world made. Marilyn Hacker. **SP-HackM** *Fr.* Taking Notice.

My children are, to me, / what is uncommon: they are dumb. The Charm. Robert Creeley. **CP-CreeR**

My Children at the Dump. John Updike. **CP-UpdiJ**

My Children Going. Dabney Stuart. **SP-StuaD**

My children make their way home. Sunset. James McAuley. **SP-McAuJ**

My Chinese uncle, gouty, deaf, half-blinded. Grotesques. Robert Ranke Graves. **CP-GravR**

My chosen bride shall bless the plough. Song. George Meredith. **CP-MerG2**

My Cicely. Thomas Hardy. **CP-HardT**

My city's fit and noble name resumed. Mannahatta. Walt Whitman. **CP-WhitW**

My client is a scoundrel and a thief. *In Extremis* in Hardy, Arkansas. Miller Williams. **SP-WillM**

My clothes leaped up when I came in. Courtesy Call. John Updike. **CP-UpdiJ**

My Coat Is Dirty. Kenneth Patchen. **CP-PatcK**

My Cocoon tightens—Colors tease. Emily Dickinson. **CP-DickE**

My Coed Wife. Gary Gildner. **SP-GildG**

My coldness wakes me. Thom Gunn. *Fr.* Jack Straw's Castle. **CP-GunnT**

My Collier Laddie. Robert Burns. **CP-BurnR**

My comfortable river / whose wide bends used to wind. Leavetaking. Dabney Stuart. **SP-StuaD**

My Comforter. Emily Brontë. **CP-BronE**

My comforts drop and melt away like snow. The Answer. George Herbert. **CP-HerbG**

My companion kept exclaiming. The Cypress Avenue. Donald Davie. **CP-DavDo**

My Comrades. Charles Bukowski. **SP-BukC1**

My Conscience. Ogden Nash. *Fr.* My My. **CP-NashO**

My Conscience! Robert Louis Stevenson. **CP-StevR**

My Corn-Cob Pipe. Paul Laurence Dunbar. **CP-DunbP**

My cot was down by a cypress grove. The Lesson. Paul Laurence Dunbar. **CP-DunbP**

My country need not change her gown. Emily Dickinson. **CP-DickE**

My country, O my land, my friends. Purgatorio. Hart Crane. **CP-CranH**

My Country, 'tis of thee. Emily Dickinson. **SP-DickE**

My Country Wife. Lewis Turco. **SP-TurcL**

My cousin, four years taller than myself. Portstewart, 1914. John Hewitt. **CP-HewiJ**

My Cousin in April. Louise Glück. **SP-GlücL**

My curse on your envenom'd stang. Address to the Tooth-Ache. Robert Burns. **CP-BurnR**

My dad gave me one dollar bill. Smart. Shel Silverstein. **SP-SilS2**

My Daddy. Ogden Nash. **CP-NashO**

My daddy played the market. January 1st. Anne Sexton. **CP-SextA**

My dad's old man was a carpenter. Barton Sutter. *Fr.* Tools. **SP-SuttB**

My dancing roses, dancing in November. One for the Roses. Jean Garrigue. **SP-GarrJ**

My dark companion photographs me among the daisies. The Photograph. Leonard Cohen. **SP-CoheL**

My darling since / you and. Edward Estlin Cummings. **CP-CummE**

My darling we are trolling Lake Fontal. Sweet Piece from Fontal. Richard Hugo. **CP-HugoR**

My darling's love shall close me up. Song. George Meredith. **CP-MerG2**

My daughter and I lie in the snow. Poem. Gary Gildner. **SP-GildG**

My daughter, at eleven. Little Girl, My String Bean, My Lovely Woman. Anne Sexton. **CP-SextA**

My daughter baby Clio lies on her back. Faces. Stephen Dobyns. **SP-DobyS**

My daughter crackles paper, blows. Margaret Atwood. *Fr.* Solstice Poem. **SP-AtwM2**

My Daughter Is Coming! Alice Walker. **CP-WalkA**

My daughter is most. Sitting in a Sandwich Joint. Charles Bukowski. **SP-BukC1**

My daughter marks the day that spring begins. Equinox. Audre Lorde. **SP-LordA**

My daughter, my daughter, what can I say. George Oppen. *Fr.* Of Being Numerous. **CP-OppeG**

My daughter needing half a dollar takes. Johanna. David Markson. **CP-MarkD**

My Daughter Says. Erica Jong. **SP-JongE**

My daughter wants to know. Is My Heart Really Big As My Fist? Gary Gildner. **SP-GildG**

My Day. Tennyson. **NAEL-2; NOBVV** *Fr.* Maud [A Monodrama]. **CP-TennA**

My dayes delight, my spring tyme joyes foredun. Conjectural First Draft of the Petition to Queen Anne. Sir Walter Ralegh. **CP-RaleW**

My days are burning. The Counter. William Carlos Williams. **CP-WilW2**

My day's delights, my spring[e]time joy[e]s for[e]done. The End of the Boo[c]k[e]s, of the Ocean's Love to Cynthia [or Scinthia], and the Beginning[e] of the 12 [or 22] Boo[c]k, Entreating of Sorrow. Sir Walter Ralegh. **CP-RaleW** *Fr.* The Ocean's Love to Cynthia.

My Days of Love Are Over. Byron. **OBNC** *Fr.* Canto the First. **EnRP; NAEL-2; NoP; OAEL-2; PoE** *Fr.* Don Juan. **CP-Byron**

My day's plan to write. Kathleen Jessie Raine. **SP-RainK**

My days roll by me like a train of dreams. Ralph Waldo Emerson. **CP-EmerR**

My dear —: / I do thank you, that we hear from you, but the. Letter for Melville 1951. Charles Olson. **CP-OlsoC**

My dear and I, we disagreed. Overtures. John Crowe Ransom. *Fr.* Sixteen Poems in Eight Pairings. **SP-RansJ**

My dear, darkened in sleep turned from the moon. To Judith Asleep. John Ciardi. **SP-CiarJ**

My Dear, How Ever Did You Think Up This Delicious Salad? Ogden Nash. **CP-NashO**

My dear, I wonder if before the end. To D———, Dead by Her Own Hand. Howard Nemerov. **CP-NemeH**

"My dear, indulgent, older (by five minutes) brother." *with music.* Robert Pack. **SP-PackR**

My dear, it was a moment. The Expatriates. Anne Sexton. **CP-SextA**

My dear Kafka. The Literary World. Philip Larkin. **CP-LarkP**

My Dear Love. Robinson Jeffers. **CP-JefR3**

My dear love died last night. Paul Laurence Dunbar. **CP-DunbP**

My dear Mrs. Bloomer. Part of a True Story. Marilyn Hacker. **SP-HackM**

My dear Mother and Sister:. Mary Jane Colter, 1904. Adrienne Rich. *Fr.* Turning the Wheel. **SP-RicA2**

My Dear Mr. Murray. Byron. **CP-Byron**

My dear, my dear, I know. To a Young Girl. William Butler Yeats. **CP-YeatW**

My Dear One is mine as mirrors are lonely. Wystan Hugh Auden. **NoAM** *Fr.* The Supporting Cast, Sotto Voce. *Fr.* The Sea and the Mirror. **CP-AudeW**

My dear spouse died—a tumour on the brain. John Hewitt. *Fr.* October Sonnets. **CP-HewiJ**

My dearest Anne. Dear Anne Sexton, II. Erica Jong. **SP-JongE**

My dearest Kathy: When I heard your tears and those of your. Letter to Kathy from Wisdom. Richard Hugo. **CP-HugoR**

My dearest Love, since thou wilt go. A Dialogue Betwixt Himselfe and Mistresse Eliza: Wheeler, Under the Name of Amarillis. Robert Herrick. **CP-HerrR**

My dearest Mary, wherefore hast thou gone. To Mary Shelley ("My dearest Mary, wherefore hast thou gone"). Percy Bysshe Shelley. **CP-ShelP**

My Dearest Mistress. William Corkine. **CP-CampT**

("My deerest mistrisse, let us live and love.") **CP-CampT**

My dearest rival, lest [or least] our love. Sir John Suckling. **CP-SuckJ**

My dears, don't I know? I esteem you more than you think. To Certain English Poets. Donald Davie. **CP-DavDo**

My dears, don't look at me, I am merely terrified of you. Don't Look at Me. David Herbert Lawrence. **CP-LawrD**

My death. Erica Jong. **SP-JongE**

My death was arranged by special plans in Heaven. A New England Bachelor. Richard Eberhart. **CP-EberR**

My death with a nail in his foot. Howard Nemerov. *Fr.* Seven Macabre Songs. **CP-NemeH**

My deathly body's deadly lady. Edward Estlin Cummings. **CP-CummE**

My Debt. Jim Carroll. **SP-CarrJ**

My deep-dyed husband trusts me. On Martock Moor. Thomas Hardy. **CP-HardT**

My deerest mistrisse, let us live and love. William Corkine. *See* My Dearest Mistress.

My Departure, *earlier vers. of* The Death of the Nature-Lover. Walt Whitman. **CP-WhitW**

My Descendants. William Butler Yeats. **CP-YeatW; LiTB** *Fr.* Meditations in Time of Civil War. **CP-YeatW**

My Dim-Wit Cousin. Theodore Roethke. **CP-RoetT**

My disappointments, large as capsized tugs. The Return of Odysseus. Richard Eberhart. **CP-EberR**

My dismal sister! Couldst thou know. "Lewis Carroll." **FiBHP** *Fr.* Melancholetta. **CP-CarrL**

My dissent is cheer. Definition. Grace Paley. **CP-PaleG**

My doctor has just come into his office. A Stethoscope Case. Charles Bukowski. **SP-BukC1**

My doctor, the comedian. Cripples and Other Stories. Anne Sexton. **CP-SextA**

My dog lay dead five days without a grave. The Pardon. Richard Wilbur. **CP-WilbR**

My dog woman. For Schnu. Chuck Miller. **SP-MillC**

My dog's dead. / I buried him in the garden near the wreck. Dead Dog. Pablo Neruda, tr. fr. Spanish by Ben Belitt. **SP-NeruP**

My Dolphin, you only guide me by surprise. Dolphin. Robert Lowell. **SP-LoweR**

My double, tired of morning, closes the door. Derek Walcott. **CP-WalcD** Fr. Midsummer.

My dove, my doe. Aubade. Stevie Smith. **CP-SmitS**

My Doves. Elizabeth Barrett Browning. **CP-BroEB**

My Dream. Ogden Nash. Fr. My My. **CP-NashO**

My Dream. Christina Georgina Rossetti. **CP-RosC1**

My Dream. John Greenleaf Whittier. **CP-WhitJ**

My dream a drink with Lonnie Johnson we discuss the code. Ted Berrigan. **SP-BerrT** Fr. The Sonnets.

My dream is of an island-place. An Island. Elizabeth Barrett Browning. **CP-BroEB**

My dreams are of a field afar. Alfred Edward Housman. **CP-HousA**

My Dreams, My Works, Must Wait Till after Hell. Gwendolyn Brooks. **SP-BrooG**

My driver's license is lapsing and so I appear. The Vision Test. Mona Van Duyn. **SP-VanDM**

My drum, hollowed out thru the thin slit. La Chute. Charles Olson. **CP-OlsoC; SP-OlsoC**

My ear is full of summer sounds. The Summons. John Greenleaf Whittier. **CP-WhitJ**

My earliest love, that stabbed and lacerated. Growing Pains. Robert Ranke Graves. **CP-GravR**

My earliest memory? why, the lassitude! James McAuley. Fr. The Autobiography of the Impotent Man. **SP-McAuJ**

My earnestness, which might at first offend. Edna St. Vincent Millay. **CP-MillE**

My eldest sister arrived home that morning. Cuba. Paul Muldoon. **SP-MuldP**

My embarrassment at his nakedness. The Pool. Robert Creeley. **CP-CreeR**

My enemies came to get me. A Form of Adaptation. Robert Creeley. **CP-CreeR**

My Enemy. David Herbert Lawrence. **CP-LawrD**

My English dam bursts. Inchicore Haiku. Michael Hartnett. **SP-HarMi**

My Eppie. Robert Burns. **CP-BurnR**

My Erotic Double. John Ashbery. **SP-AshbJ**

My errand brought me once again. The Hill-Farm. John Hewitt. **CP-HewiJ**

My Eye is fuller than my vase. Emily Dickinson. **CP-DickE**

My eyes are closing, my eyes are opening. Anemone. Muriel Rukeyser. **CP-RukeM**

My eyes are fond of the east side. Edward Estlin Cummings. **CP-CummE**

My eyes being downcast. Assuming the Burden. David Herbert Lawrence. **CP-LawrD**

My eyes catch and stick. The Consumer. Marge Piercy. **SP-PierM**

My eyes in your pledge, Quintius. Carmen 82. Catullus. Fr. Carmina. **CP-Catul**

My eyes make pictures, when they are shut. Day-Dream, A ("My eyes make pictures, when they are shut"). Samuel Taylor Coleridge. **CP-ColeS**

My face ends inside you. Portions of Manslayer. Charles Kenneth Williams. **CP-WillC**

My face, my other faces. Margaret Atwood. Fr. Circe / Mud Poems. **SP-AtwM1**

My faint spirit was sitting in the light. From the Arabic: An Imitation. Percy Bysshe Shelley. **CP-ShelP**

My fair says, she no spouse but me. Catullus. See Carmen 70: "Lesbia says she'ld rather marry me."

My Fairy. "Lewis Carroll." **CP-CarrL**

My faith / is a great weight. Small Wire. Anne Sexton. **CP-SextA**

My faith is in my native land. Britain. George Meredith. **CP-MerG2**

My Faith is larger than the Hills. Emily Dickinson. **CP-DickE**

My faithful friend, if you can see. Impossibilities to His Friend. Robert Herrick. **CP-HerrR**

My Faithful Lover. Phoebe Hesketh. **SP-HeskP**

My falcon to my wrist. On Thought in Harness. Edna St. Vincent Millay. **CP-MillE**

My family of Apparitions. Emily Dickinson. **SP-DickE**

My Fancy. "Lewis Carroll." See I painted her a gushing thing.

My father / (back blistered). Democratic Order, The: Such Things in Twenty Years I Understood. Alice Walker. **CP-WalkA**

My Father. John Hewitt. **CP-HewiJ**

My Father ("Lies on the same couch that he used to"). Ron Koertge. **SP-KoerR**

My Father ("Once owned a blind horse, a big gray who"). Ron Koertge. **SP-KoerR**

My Father ("Said, 'What the devil!' when he dropped"). Ron Koertge. **SP-KoerR**

My Father after Work. Gary Gildner. **SP-GildG**

My father almost every Easter went. Going up to Dublin. John Hewitt. **CP-HewiJ**

My father and I are catching spricklies. The Waking Father. Paul Muldoon. **SP-MuldP**

My father and mother both. Mississippi Winter IV. Alice Walker. **CP-WalkA**

My father and mother, my brother and sister. The Sightseers. Paul Muldoon. **SP-MuldP**

My Father at 85. Grace Paley. **CP-PaleG**

My Father at 89. Grace Paley. **CP-PaleG**

My Father at His Height. Barton Sutter. **SP-SuttB**

My father could hear a little animal step. Listening. William Stafford. **SP-StafW**

My father dead, the prince among my dead. My Father's Ghost. John Hewitt. **CP-HewiJ**

My father didn't really belong in history. Parentage. William Stafford. **SP-StafW**

My father died. The Rain the Stones the Darkness. Richard Shelton. **SP-ShelR**

My father died again in dreams, a twin. For Elektra. Marilyn Hacker. **SP-HackM**

My Father Dreams of Baseball. Laurence Lieberman. **SP-LiebL**

My father, Eating Small Boat. Autobiographical Note. Kenneth Patchen. **CP-PatcK**

My father entered the kingdom of roots. 1933. Philip Levine. **SP-LeviP**

My father, for example. A Visitor. Mary Oliver. **SP-OlivM**

My father found it after the war—. The House on Buder Street. Gary Gildner. **SP-GildG**

My father got on his horse and went to the field. Infancy. Carlos Drummond de Andrade, tr. fr. Portuguese by Elizabeth Bishop. **CP-BishE**

My father groaned; my mother wept. Rite. Muriel Rukeyser. **CP-RukeM**

My father had the contract for supplying shoes. Miles II. James Liddy. **CP-LiddJ**

My father has forgotten me. Louise Glück. **MoLi** Fr. Metamorphosis. **SP-GlücL**

My father, his mouth full of nails. Nails. Gary Gildner. **SP-GildG**

My father is a quiet man. Fruit of the Flower. Countee Cullen. **CP-CullC**

My father is in Captain Starns. Legacy. Stephen Dunn. **SP-DunnS**

My father is standing on a railroad platform. Departure. Louise Glück. **SP-GlücL**

My Father, it is surely a blue place. Hunchback Girl: She Thinks of Heaven. Gwendolyn Brooks. Fr. A Street in Bronzeville. **SP-BrooG**

My father joined the Masons later on. Free Mason. John Hewitt. **CP-HewiJ**

My father kept a vaulted conch. On the Decline of Oracles. Sylvia Plath. **CP-PlatS**

My father knew. How to Be Uncle Sam. John Updike. **CP-UpdiJ**

My father lay fifty years in St. Michael's bed. Epithalamium at St. Michael's Cemetary. John Ciardi. **SP-CiarJ**

My father liked Edgar Allan. Dear Pa and Ma. Charles Bukowski. **SP-BukC3**

My father moved through dooms of love. Edward Estlin Cummings. **CP-CummE; SP-CummE**

My father never finished. The Rafters. James Dickey. **CP-DickJ**

My Father: October 1942. William Stafford. **SP-StafW**

My Father Paints the Summer. Richard Wilbur. **CP-WilbR**

My father said / how will they get out of it. My Father at 85. Grace Paley. **CP-PaleG**

My father sat in his chair recovering. The Dream Time. Ted Hughes. Fr. Out. **SP-HughT**

My father sent me on an errand to the house of his friend Averroës. Song for the Death of Averroës. Thomas Merton. **CP-MertT**

My father spent his last winter. Ice. Mary Oliver. **SP-OlivM**

My father stands in the warm evening. Starlight. Philip Levine. **SP-LeviP**

My father used to say. Silence. Marianne Craig Moore. **CP-MoorM**

My father was a city schoolmaster. The Lonely Heart. John Hewitt. Fr. Freehold. **CP-HewiJ**

My father was a farmer upon the Carrick border O. Song. Robert Burns. **CP-BurnR**

My Father was a scholar and knew Greek. Development. Robert Browning. **CP-BroR2**

My father was a servant-boy. The Mixed Marriage. Paul Muldoon. **SP-MuldP**

My father was a working man. Red-Herring. David Herbert Lawrence. **CP-LawrD**

My father was an English Yankee who emigrated. Family Album in Red Plush. Marsden Hartley. **CP-HartM**

My father was born in Horton. Lancashire. Donald Davie. **CP-DavDo**

My father was born with a spade in his hand and traded it. Elegy. John Ciardi. **SP-CiarJ**

My father was brillant embarrassed funny handsome. Family. Grace Paley. **CP-PaleG**

My father was ribald / about religion: when. Mark. James Schuyler. **CP-SchuJ**

My father was the whipper-in. The Whipper-In. Thomas Hardy. **CP-HardT**

My father who found the English landscape tame. Woods. Louis MacNeice. **CP-MacNL**

My father, who since his death. Our Family. Leo Vroman, *tr. fr. Dutch by* Adrienne Rich. **CP-RicAE**

My father worked with a horse-plough. Follower. Seamus Heaney. **SP-HeanS**

My father writes all day, all night. Poem. Charles Simic. **SP-SimiC**

My father wrote his articles, reviews. A Domimie's Log. John Hewitt. **CP-HewiJ**

My Father's Birthday. Kathleen Jessie Raine. **SP-RainK**

My Fathers Came from Kentucky. Nicholas Vachel Lindsay. **AmFN; HBMV** *Fr.* Alexander Campbell. **CP-LindV**

My Father's Chair. Rudyard Kipling. **CP-KiplR**

My father's closest brother of his three. The Volunteer. John Hewitt. **CP-HewiJ**

My father's corn is knee-high for the Fourth. A Memory. Gary Gildner. **SP-GildG**

My Father's Death. May Sarton. **SP-SartM**

My Father's Death in Hospital. John Hewitt. **CP-HewiJ**

My father's eyes rolled upward in Paul's Diner. Father. Peter Meinke. **SP-MeinP**

My Father's Face. Hayden Carruth. **CP-CarHL**

My Father's Face. Siv Cedering Fox. **SP-CedeS**

My father's father breasted his four score. My Grandfather Dies, 1923. John Hewitt. **CP-HewiJ**

My father's father came. Legend. Louise Glück. **SP-GlückL**

My father's father saw it not. A British-Roman Song. Rudyard Kipling. **CP-KiplR** *Fr.* A Centurion of the Thirtieth. *Fr.* Puck of Pook's Hill.

My Father's Ghost. John Hewitt. **CP-HewiJ**

My Father's Honour. Donald Davie. **CP-DavDo**

My Father's Mother. John Hewitt. **CP-HewiJ**

My Father's Oldest Sister. Siv Cedering Fox. **SP-CedeS**

My Fathers sit on benches. Song for the Old Ones. Maya Angelou. **SP-AngeM**

My Father's Telescope. Rita Dove. **SP-DoveR**

My Father's Voice. John Hewitt. **CP-HewiJ**

My Father's Wedding. Robert Bly. **SP-BlyR**

My father's youngest brother stayed at home. Lonsdale Street. John Hewitt. **CP-HewiJ**

My feet in the ever-moving sea. Kathleen Jessie Raine. **SP-RainK**

My feet strike an apex of the apices of the stairs. Infinity. Walt Whitman. **AA** *Fr.* Song of Myself. **CP-WhitW**

My fellow man I do not care for. A Bas Ben Adhem. Ogden Nash. **CP-NashO**

My female friends, whose tender hearts. Jonathan Swift. **NOBL; SeCePo** *Fr.* Verses on the Death of Dr. Swift, D.S.P.D. **CP-SwifJ**

My fifth housebonde, god his soule blesse! Geoffrey Chaucer. **FiP** *Fr.* The Wife of Bath's Prologue. **FHYEP; NAEL-1; OAEL-1**, *ll.* 1–862 *complete*; *Fr.* The Canterbury Tales. **CP-ChauG**

My Fifth Trip to Washington Ended in Northeast Delaware. Audre Lorde. **SP-LordA**

My fiftieth year had come and gone. William Butler Yeats. **RaBo** *Fr.* Vacillation. **CP-YeatW**

My first and only wife. About Pain. Charles Bukowski. **SP-BukC3**

"My First—but don't suppose," he said. Canto II: Hys Fyve Rules. "Lewis Carroll." *Fr.* Phantasmagoria. **CP-CarrL**

My first gift and my last, to you. Dedication. Robert Louis Stevenson. **CP-StevR**

My *first* is no proof of my *second*. Charades. Christina Georgina Rossetti. **CP-RosC3**

My First is singular at best. "Lewis Carroll." *Fr.* Four Riddles. **CP-CarrL**

My first lends his aid when I plunge into trade. A Riddle. "Lewis Carroll." **CP-CarrL**

My first love, whom all beauties did adorn. The Guiltless Inconstant. Sir John Suckling. **CP-CareT; CP-SuckJ**

My first may be the firstborn. Charade. Christina Georgina Rossetti. **CP-RosC3**

My first remembrance: the yard of our earliest. The Blood of the Poet. William Everson. **SP-EverW**

My First Reported Words. John Hewitt. **CP-HewiJ**

My first shuts out Thieves from your house or your Room. Charade on Dr Thomas Barnard. Samuel Johnson. **CP-JohnS**

My first thought was, he lied in every word. Childe Roland to the Dark Tower Came. Robert Browning. **CP-BroR1**

My first well Day—since many ill. Emily Dickinson. **CP-DickE**

My flocks feed nor. Richard Barnfield. **CP-ShaWS** *Fr.* The Passionate Pilgrim. **CP-ShaWS**

My flowers are near and foreign. Emily Dickinson. **SP-DickE**

My Fly. Charles Kenneth Williams. **SP-WillC**

My fool walks on wobbling roads. The Spirit of Noplace. Kenneth Patchen. **CP-PatcK**

My footsteps in the shallow. Poem. Jim Carroll. **SP-CarrJ**

My former hopes are fled. William Cowper. **CP-CowpW; OxBoCh** *Fr.* Olney Hymns. **CP-CowpW**

(Shining Light, The.) **CP-CowpW**

My forty-year-old father learned to fly. The Hang-Glider's Daughter. Marilyn Hacker. **SP-HackM**

My four-year-old daughter. Katie at the Pool. Derek Mahon. **SP-MahoD**

My frame hath often trembled with delight. Tributary Stream. William Wordsworth. *Fr.* The River Duddon [A Series of Sonnets]. **CP-WorW2**

My Frantic Heart. Jean Garrigue. **SP-GarrJ**

My Friend. Charles Bukowski. **SP-BukC3**

My Friend. Christina Georgina Rossetti. **CP-RosC1**

My Friend. David St. John. **SP-StJoD**

My friend, a man I love as wholly. My Friend. David St. John. **SP-StJoD**

My friend Ann, the reference librarian. The Third Use of the Penis. Barton Sutter. **SP-SuttB**

My friend attacks my friend! Emily Dickinson. **CP-DickE**

My friend Dave knew a famous writer who used to have screwdrivers for breakfast. Friends. Charles Kenneth Williams. **CP-WillC**

My Friend Felix. Donald Hall. **CP-HallD**

My friend from Asia has powers and magic, he plucks a blue leaf from the young blue-gum. Credo. Robinson Jeffers. **CP-JefR1**

My Friend George. "Lou Reed." **SP-ReedL**

My friend hands me a coin of ancient stamp. Cleopatra. George Meredith. **CP-MerG2**

My friend is worried about dying. Doom and Siesta Time. Charles Bukowski. **SP-BukC1**

My friend keeps kissing me goodbye, the kisses. Devotion: That It Flow; That There Be Concentration. Tess Gallagher. **SP-GallT**

My friend must be a Bird. Emily Dickinson. **CP-DickE**

My friend, on the deck we sit. Marge Piercy. *Fr.* Women's Laughter. **SP-PierM**

My friend said Auden died. William Matthews. *Fr.* In Memory of W. H. Auden. **SP-MattW**

My friend the sculptor modelled the large head. The Modelled Head. John Hewitt. **CP-HewiJ**

My friend, this body is made of bone. The Origin of the Praise of God. Robert Bly. **SP-BlyR**

My friend, this body is made of energy compacted and whirling. We Love This Body. Robert Bly. **SP-BlyR**

My friend, this body offers to carry us for nothing. Finding the Father. Robert Bly. **SP-BlyR**

My friend, who was a heroin addict. Certain Choices. Richard Shelton. **SP-ShelR**

My friend writes of rejection and editors. Letter from the North. Charles Bukowski. **SP-BukC2**

My friends all know that I am shy. The Chipmunk. Ogden Nash. **CP-NashO**

My friends are gone and my hair is grey. The Tower of Song. Leonard Cohen. **CP-CoheL**

My friends are those who find agreement with me. Joan and Darby. Robert Ranke Graves. **CP-GravR**

My friends: If thirty people gather in a room. Open Letter, Personal. Mona Van Duyn. **SP-VanDM**

My friend's wife has a lover; I come to this conclusion—not suspicion, mind, conclusion. Signs. Charles Kenneth Williams. **SP-WillC**

My Future Wife. John Hewitt. **CP-HewiJ**

My future will not copy fair my past. Past and Future. Elizabeth Barrett Browning. **CP-BroEB**

My future will not copy fair my past. Sonnet. Elizabeth Barrett Browning. **EnVR** *Fr.* Sonnets from the Portuguese. **CP-BroEB**

My galley [*or* galy] charged with forgetfulness. Petrarch, *tr. by* Sir Thomas Wyatt. **CP-WyatT** *Fr.* Sonnets to Laura.

My Garden. Ralph Waldo Emerson. **CP-EmerR**

My garden blazes brightly with the rose-bush and the peach. In Springtime. Rudyard Kipling. **CP-KiplR**

My Garden—like the Beach. Emily Dickinson. **CP-DickE**

My garden roses long ago. Winter Roses. John Greenleaf Whittier. **CP-WhitJ**

My gate is swinging by one hinge. The Storm. John Hewitt. **CP-HewiJ**

My gaze is clear as a sunflower. Fernando Pessoa. *Fr.* Twelve Poems from *The Keeper of the Flocks*. **CP-MertT**

My Generation Reading the Newspapers. Kenneth Patchen. **CP-PatcK**

My gentle Anne, whom heretofore. To Anne Bodham. William Cowper. **CP-CowpW**

My gentle hill, I rest. Song (2). Wendell Berry. **CP-BerrW**

My Ghost. Robert Ranke Graves. **CP-GravR**

My Gift. Christina Georgina Rossetti. **FaPON; PChr; SiSoSe** *Fr.* Christmas Carol, A: "In the bleak mid-winter." **CP-RosC1**

My girl says she'll take no one else as a lover. Catullus. *See* Carmen 70: "Lesbia says she'ld rather marry me."

My girl she give me the go onest. Private Ortheris's Song. Rudyard Kipling. **CP-KiplR** *Fr.* The Courting of Dinah Shadd. *Fr.* Life's Handicap.

My girl she's airy, she's buxom and gay. Song. Robert Burns. **CP-BurnR**

My girlfriend, you know, she. Reggie's Version. Al Young. **CP-YounA**

My girl's tall with hard long eyes. Edward Estlin Cummings. **CP-CummE**

My glass shall not persuade me I am old. Sonnet 22. William Shakespeare. **OBSC; Son** *Fr.* Sonnets. **CP-ShaWS**

My God, a verse is not a crown. The Quidditie [*or* Quiddity]. George Herbert. **CP-HerbG**

My God, Bill, what have you done? Fragment. William Carlos Williams. **CP-WilW2**

My God—He sees thee. Emily Dickinson. **CP-DickE**

My God! How I deplore. Writer's Lament. David Markson. **CP-MarkD**

My God, how perfect are thy ways! Jehovah Our Righteousness. William Cowper. **NOCV** *Fr.* Olney Hymns. **CP-CowpW**

My God, I am weeping for the life that I live. The Eternal Dice. César Vallejo, *tr. fr. Spanish by* James Wright. **CP-WrigJ**

My God, I heard this day. Man. George Herbert. **CP-HerbG**

My God, I read this day. Afflction (5). George Herbert. **CP-HerbG**

My God, if writings may. Obedience. George Herbert. **CP-HerbG**

My God, I'm wounded by my sin. To God: an Anthem, Sung in the Chapel at White-Hall, Before the King. Robert Herrick. **CP-HerrR**

My God! looke on me with thine eye. His Ejaculation to God. Robert Herrick. **CP-HerrR**

My God most glad to look, most prone to hear [*or* heere], *par. by* Countess of Pembroke, Mary Sidney Herbert. Bible, *O.T. See* Psalm 55: "Give ear to my prayer, O God."

My God, my God, have mercy on my sin. Ash Wednesday. Christina Georgina Rossetti. **CP-RosC2**

My God, my God, let me for once look on thee. Robert Browning. **TrPWD** *Fr.* Pauline [*or* Pauline; A Fragment of a Confession]. **CP-BroR1**

My God, my God, what queer corner am I in? In the Deep Museum. Anne Sexton. **CP-SextA**

My God, my God, why hast thou forsaken me? Psalm 22. Bible, *O.T.* **TrGrPo** *Fr.* Psalms. **CP-Psal**

My God, my Lord, my help, my health, *par. by* Countess of Pembroke, Mary Sidney Herbert. Bible, *O.T. See* Psalm 88: "O God of my salvation."

My God, the poor expressions of my Love. Perseverance. George Herbert. **CP-HerbG**

My God, Thyself being Love Thy Heart is love. Trinity Sunday. Christina Georgina Rossetti. **CP-RosC2**

My God! till I receiv'd thy stroke. Ephraim Repenting. William Cowper. **ChIV-1** *Fr.* Olney Hymns. **CP-CowpW**

My God, to live: how didst Thou bear to live. None With Him. Christina Georgina Rossetti. **CP-RosC3**

My God, where is that ancient heat towards Thee. Sonnet. George Herbert. **CP-HerbG**

My God, wilt Thou accept, and will not we / Give aught to Thee? Christina Georgina Rossetti. **CP-RosC2**

My godlike Friend—nay do not stare. To Alexander Cunningham. Robert Burns. **CP-BurnR**

My Golden and My Fierce Assays. Richard Eberhart. **CP-EberR**

My goldfish stares with watery eyes. Goldfish. Charles Bukowski. **SP-BukC2**

My good blade carves the casques of men. Sir Galahad [*or* The Purple Heart]. Tennyson. **CP-TennA**

My Grandfather Dies, 1923. John Hewitt. **CP-HewiJ**

My Grandfather Dying. Ted Kooser. **SP-KoosT**

My Grandfather found / his grandchild's fogbound solitudes. Dunbarton. Robert Lowell. **SP-LoweR**

My grandfather had ploughed his master's land. Prelude and Fugue. Alun Lewis. **CP-LewiA**

My grandfather has been lying. The Hospital of Lies. Dabney Stuart. **SP-StuaD**

My grandfather said to me. Manners. Elizabeth Bishop. **CP-BishE**

My grandfather says he remembers he saw, when a youngster long ago. Martin Relph. Robert Browning. **CP-BroR2**

My grandfather was a tall German. A Gold Pocket Watch. Charles Bukowski. **SP-BukC1**

My grandfather, who blessed me as a child. Age Gap. Robert Ranke Graves. **CP-GravR**

My grandfather's name was Augusto. Carlotta's Confession. Donald Hall. **CP-HallD**

My Grandfather's Wake. Paul Muldoon. **SP-MuldP**

My Grandmother. Ron Koertge. **SP-KoerR**

My Grandmother. Karl Shapiro. **SP-ShapK**

My grandmother adored the great Miss Boyd. The Wedding Present. John Hewitt. **CP-HewiJ**

My grandmother moves to my mind in context of sorrow. My Grandmother. Karl Shapiro. **SP-ShapK**

My Grandmother Robinson. John Hewitt. **CP-HewiJ**

My grandmother said I was an atheist. God and Man. Richard Eberhart. **CP-EberR**

My Grandmother Steals Her Last Trout. Brendan Galvin. **SP-GalvB**

My grandmother used it, Dutch Cleanser. Dutch Cleanser. John Updike. **CP-UpdiJ**

My Grandmother's Garter. John Hewitt. **CP-HewiJ**

My Grandmother's Ghost. James Wright. **CP-WrigJ**

My Grandmother's Love Letters. Hart Crane. **CP-CranH**

My Grandmother's Restlessness. John Hewitt. **CP-HewiJ**

My grandpa wasn't salty. I Must Tell You about My Novel. Ogden Nash. **CP-NashO**

My great-aunt Elizabeth Fortune. Strawberry Moon. Mary Oliver. **SP-OlivM**

My great-aunt had a story she often repeated. Dead Baby. Stephen Dobyns. **SP-DobyS**

My great brother. A Psalm Praising the Hair of Man's Body. Denise Levertov. **CP-LeveD**

My great-grandfather spoke to Edmund Burke. The Seven Sages. William Butler Yeats. **CP-YeatW**

My Great-Grandfather's Refusal. John Hewitt. **CP-HewiJ**

My Great-Grandfather's Slaves. Wendell Berry. **CP-BerrW**

My great great grandpa Jethro walked. Stories at Evening (A Suburban Mother Tells Stories to Her Son). Louise McNeill. **SP-McNeL**

My Greed. Leonard Cohen. **CP-CoheL**

My greetings to you, sir, whose memory. The Apparition. William Carlos Williams. **CP-WilW2**

My Groupie. Charles Bukowski. **SP-BukC1**

My grown-ups told me when I started out. To the Bleeding Hearts Association of American Novelists. Howard Nemerov. **CP-NemeH**

My Guilt. Maya Angelou. **SP-AngeM**

My halting Muse, that dragg'st by choice along. John Milton. *See* To Salzilli, a Roman Poet, Being Ill.

My hand by chance. The Web. Robert Earl Hayden. **CP-HaydR**

My Hands. William Stafford. **SP-StafW**

My Hands Are My Enemies. Richard Shelton. **SP-ShelR**

My hands have not touched pleasure since your hands. Hart Crane. *See* Carrier Letter.

My hands that were not born completely. From Time. James Dickey. **CP-DickJ**

My happy happy dream is finished with. Christina Georgina Rossetti. *Fr.* Three Stages. **CP-RosC3**

My Harry was a gallant gay. Robert Burns. **CP-BurnR**

My hart is lost, what can I now expect. Sonnet 1. Mary Sidney, Countess of Montgomery Wroth. *Fr.* Pamphilia to Amphilanthus. **CP-WrotM**

My harvest is done, its promise is ended. For Each. Christina Georgina Rossetti. **CP-RosC2**

My Hat. Stevie Smith. **CP-SmitS**

My hat leaps up when I behold. W. D., Don't Fear That Animal. William DeWitt Snodgrass. **SP-SnodW**

My hate is as a wind that buffets me. Malcolm Lowry. **CP-LowrM**

My hated birthday looms. In the rude and wretched country. Gilbert Sorrentino. *Fr.* Elegiacs of Sulpicia. **SP-SorrG**

My hawk is tir'd of perch and hood. Lay of the Imprisoned Huntsman. Sir Walter Scott. **SP-ScotW** *Fr.* The Lady of the Lake.

My head and shoulders, and my book. The Signature of All Things. Kenneth Rexroth. **SP-RexrK**

My head doth ake. The Head-Ake. Robert Herrick. **CP-HerrR**

My head hurts like hell! Comfort. William Carlos Williams. **CP-WilW2**

My head is bald, my breath is bad. Late-flowering Lust. Sir John Betjeman. **CP-BetjJ**

My head is heavy, my limbs are weary. Fragment: Death in Life. Percy Bysshe Shelley. **CP-ShelP**

My head is open. Chromo. Martin Edmunds. **SP-EdmuM**

My head is wild with weeping for a grief. Fragment. Percy Bysshe Shelley. **CP-ShelP**

My head knocks against the stars. Who Am I? Carl Sandburg. **CP-SandC**

My head made wilderness, crowned of weed. The Cuckoo King. Howard Nemerov. **CP-NemeH**

My head, my heart, mine eyes, my life,—nay, more. A Letter to Her Husband, Absent upon Public[k] Employment. Anne Bradstreet. **CP-BradA**

My head, this wrinkled planet. Astronomy. James McAuley. **SP-McAuJ**

My Heart. Heinrich Heine, *tr. fr. German by* George Meredith. **CP-MerG2**

My Heart. Frank O'Hara. **SP-OharF**

My heart aches a drowsy numbness pains. Ode to a Nightingale. John Keats. **CP-KeatJ**

My Heart and I. Elizabeth Barrett Browning. **CP-BroEB**

My Heart, Being Hungry. Edna St. Vincent Millay. **CP-MillE**

My heart did heave, and there came forth, O God! Affliction (3). George Herbert. **CP-HerbG**

My heart faints in me for the distant sea. Sea-Magic. Walter de la Mare. **CP-DeLaW**

My heart felt need to die. The Scourge. Stanley Jasspon Kunitz. **CP-KuniS**

My Heart Goes Out. Stevie Smith. **CP-SmitS**

My Heart Has Reopened to You. Alice Walker. **CP-WalkA**

My heart has thank'd thee, Bowles! for those soft strains. To the Rev. [or Reverend] W. L. Bowles. Samuel Taylor Coleridge. **EnRP; Son** *Fr.* Effusions. **CP-ColeS**

My heart hath uttered. The Word—a Responsory. Thomas Merton. **CP-MertT**

My heart I gave thee not to do it pain. Sir Thomas Wyatt. **CP-WyatT**

"My heart in pieces. . . ." Tom Clark. *See* Climbing.

My heart in pieces like the bits. Tom Clark. *See* Climbing.

My heart is a-breaking, dear Tittie. Tam Glen. Robert Burns. **CP-BurnR**

My heart is aching. Relief. Langston Hughes. **SP-HughL**

My heart is easy, and my burthen light. Happy Solitude—Unhappy Men. Jeanne Marie Bouvier de la Motte-Guyon, *tr. fr. French by* William Cowper. **CP-CowpW**

My heart is fallen in despair. The Broken Friendship. Stevie Smith. **CP-SmitS**

My heart is inditing a good matter. Psalm 45. Bible, *O.T. Fr.* Psalms. **CP-Psal**

My heart is like a singing bird. A Birthday. Christina Georgina Rossetti. **CP-RosC1**

My heart is sair—I dare na tell. Robert Burns. **CP-BurnR**

(For the Sake o' Somebody.) **CP-BurnR**

My heart is wae and unco wae. Scots Ballad. Robert Burns. **CP-BurnR**

My heart is what it was before. Alms. Edna St. Vincent Millay. **CP-MillE**

My heart is yearnig: / Behold my yearning heart. Like As the Hart Desireth the Water Brooks. Christina Georgina Rossetti. **CP-RosC2**

My heart leaps up when I behold. Song to Be Sung by the Father of Infant Female Children. Ogden Nash. **CP-NashO**

My heart leaps up when I behold. William Wordsworth. **CP-WorW1**

My heart leaps up with streams of joy. The Word. Stevie Smith. **CP-SmitS**

My heart lies wrapped in red under your pillow. Arrears of Moonlight. Robert Ranke Graves. **CP-GravR**

My heart ran so to thee. Emily Dickinson. **CP-DickE**

My heart sank with our Claret-flask. Nationality in Drinks. Robert Browning. **CP-BroR1**

My heart says, puzzled, "Why do men kill each other?" And He Had Wilder Moments. Kenneth Patchen. **CP-PatcK**

My heart, so rarely rent. Dream Journey of the Head and Heart. Richard Eberhart. **CP-EberR**

My heart to thy heart. Song. Paul Laurence Dunbar. **CP-DunbP**

My Heart upon a little Plate. Emily Dickinson. **CP-DickE**

My heart was alive a bird's. A Voyage to Cytherea. James Liddy. **CP-LiddJ**

My heart was ance as blythe and free. To the Weaver's Gin Ye Go. Robert Burns. **CP-BurnR**

My Heart Was Full. Stevie Smith. **CP-SmitS**

My heart was heavy, for its trust had been. Forgiveness. John Greenleaf Whittier. **CP-WhitJ**

My heart, when first the blackbird sings. Robert Louis Stevenson. **CP-StevR**

My heart's aflutter! Mayakovsky. Frank O'Hara. **SP-OharF**

My heart's felt no wounds big or small. Ballade. Anne Waldman. **SP-WaldA**

My Heart's in the Highlands. Robert Burns. **CP-BurnR**

My Heat. Frank O'Hara. **SP-OharF**

My Heavenly Shiner (Elizabeth). Robert Lowell. **SP-LoweR**

My heavy step is treacherous in the shallows. Lost Fish. Robert Lowell. **SP-LoweR**

My Hero Bares His Nerves. Dylan Thomas. **CP-ThomD**

My hips are a desk. The Secretary Chant. Marge Piercy. **SP-PierM**

My history extends / Where moved my tourist hands. Abroad Thoughts from Home. Donald Hall. **CP-HallD**

My Hobby. Shel Silverstein. **SP-SilS2**

My home was at Cold Mountain from the start. Gary Snyder. **CP-SnydG**

My honored colonel, deep I feel. Poem on Life. Robert Burns. **CP-BurnR**

My Honour. Leonard Cohen. **CP-CoheL**

My hope, alas, hath me abused. Sir Thomas Wyatt. **CP-WyatT**

My horsemen wheel in a great circle shutting out the sun. The Old Lean Over the Tombstones. Kenneth Patchen. **CP-PatcK**

My horse's feet beside the lake. Farewell, A. Matthew Arnold. **SP-ArnoM** *Fr.* Switzerland.

My Hostess at the Renovated Inn. Dabney Stuart. **SP-StuaD**

My House. "Lou Reed." Robert Lowell. **SP-ReedL**

My House. William Butler Yeats. **CP-YeatW; LiTB** *Fr.* Meditations in Time of Civil War. **CP-YeatW**

My house, I say. But hark to the sunny doves. Robert Louis Stevenson. **CP-StevR**

My house is on fire red. During Menstruation. John Updike. *Fr.* Living with a Wife. **CP-UpdiJ**

My house, my fairy / palace. Jerónimo's House. Elizabeth Bishop. **CP-BishE**

My hovering[e] thought[e]s would fly to heaven. Man's Civil[l] War[re]. Robert Southwell. **CP-SoutR**

My humorous ghost precisely will. Edward Estlin Cummings. **CP-CummE**

My husband Bluebeard has a blue beard. Bluebeard's Wife. Howard Nemerov. *Fr.* Seven Macabre Songs. **CP-NemeH**

My Husband Says. Alice Walker. **CP-WalkA**

My husband and left—gone away. Overheard on a Bus (Woman with a Cleft Palate). Louise McNeill. **SP-McNeL**

My husband walks in the frosted field. The Wereman. Margaret Atwood. **SP-AtwM1**

My Hut. Hayden Carruth. **CP-CarHS**

My Hypertrophic Devotion. Tom Clark. **SP-ClarT**

My ideas are a curse. February 3rd. Anne Sexton. **CP-SextA**

My idleness curdles. Ted Hughes. **HAP,** *sect.* 5; *Fr.* Skylarks. **SP-HughT**

My intense friend was tall & strongly made. Freshman Blues. John Berryman. **CP-BerrJ**

My jolly friar, / Now lift thy cowl. George Meredith. **CP-MerG2**

My Kate. Elizabeth Barrett Browning. **CP-BroEB**

My Kind of Man. Anne Waldman. **SP-WaldA**

My Kingdom. Robert Louis Stevenson. **CP-StevR**

My Knees Go Before the Firing Squad at Dawn. Diane Wakoski. **SP-WakoD**

My Knight is over the sea, cried Kate. Squireless Kate. George Meredith. **CP-MerG2**

My lady / fair with / soft. A Token. Robert Creeley. **CP-CreeR**

My Lady Can Sleep. Leonard Cohen. **CP-CoheL**

My Lady has Diana's brows. George Meredith. **CP-MerG2**

My Lady in Her White Silk Shawl. Nicholas Vachel Lindsay. **CP-LindV**

My lady is an ivory garden. Edward Estlin Cummings. **CP-CummE**

My Lady Is Compared to a Young Tree. Nicholas Vachel Lindsay. **CP-LindV**

My lady love lives far away. Lyric, A. Paul Laurence Dunbar. **CP-DunbP**

My Lady of Castle Grand. Paul Laurence Dunbar. **CP-DunbP**

My Lady of the Rocks. Memoirs of a Son of Erin. James McAuley. **SP-McAuJ** *Fr.* The Exile's Recurring Nightmare.

My Lady of the Wood. Wystan Hugh Auden. **CP-AudWJ**

My lady unto Madam makes her bow. George Meredith. **NOBVV** *Fr.* Modern Love. **CP-MerG1**

My lady walks her morning round. The Henchman. John Greenleaf Whittier. **CP-WhitJ**

My Lady's Gown There's Gairs upon't. Robert Burns. **CP-BurnR**

My Lady's Lamentation and Complaint against the Dean. Jonathan Swift. **CP-SwifJ**

My Lady's Law. Rudyard Kipling. **CP-KiplR** *Fr.* The Naulahka.

My large back tooth, without a mate for years. Back Tooth. Muriel Rukeyser. **CP-RukeM**

My Last Afternoon with Uncle Devereux Winslow. Robert Lowell. **SP-LoweR**

My last—Cornificius—your Catullus'. Catullus. *See* Carmen 38: "Angst, / ennui & angst."

My last defense. Old Mary. Gwendolyn Brooks. **SP-BrooG**

My Last Duchess [Ferrara]. Robert Browning. **CP-BroR1**

My last fringed gentians. The Language of Flowers, Etc. Hayden Carruth. **CP-CarHS**

My last morning and so, here. Frank Templeton Prince. *Fr.* Walks in Rome. **CP-PrinF**

My Last Poem. Manuel Bandeira, *tr. fr. Portuguese by* Elizabeth Bishop. **CP-BishE**

My latest love appeared to me. The Last of the Old Year. Wystan Hugh Auden. **CP-AudWJ**

My latest tribute here I send. Verses on I Know Not What. Jonathan Swift. **CP-SwifJ**

My Legacy. Walt Whitman. **CP-WhitW**

My legs hinge on my foreshortened bathtub. 1930's. Robert Lowell. **SP-LoweR**

My Lesbia let us love and live. Catullus. *See* Carmen 5: "Lesbia / live with me."

My letters! all dead paper, mute and white. Sonnet. Elizabeth Barrett Browning. **HAP; HBV; OXAEP-2** *Fr.* Sonnets from the Portuguese. **CP-BroEB**

My letters I acquired from bottles, tins. First Letters. John Hewitt. **CP-HewiJ**

My lids with grief were tumid yet. John Milton. *See* On the Death of the Bishop of Ely.

My life / has appeared unclothed in court. Talking to Sheep. Anne Sexton. **CP-SextA**

My Life Before Dawn. Louise Glück. **SP-GlücL**

My life began. What Adam Said. Archibald MacLeish. *Fr.* Songs for Eve. **CP-MacLA**

My life closed twice before its close. Emily Dickinson. **CP-DickE**

My Life had stood—a Loaded Gun. Emily Dickinson. **CP-DickE**

My life has been. To My Brother Poet, Seeking Peace. Erica Jong. **SP-JongE**

My life has been too simple and stern. Emily Dickinson. **SP-DickE**

My life has crept so long on a broken wing. Tennyson. *Fr.* Maud [A Monodrama]. **CP-TennA**

My Life Has Turned to Blue. Maya Angelou. **SP-AngeM**

My Life in a Stolen Moment. "Bob Dylan." **CP-DylaB**

My life is a one-billionth part. Power. Daniel Gerard Hoffman. **SP-HoffD**

My life is bitter with thy love; thine eyes. Anactoria. Algernon Charles Swinburne. **SP-SwinA**

My life is too full of faces. The Edges. Gilbert Sorrentino. **SP-SorrG**

My life is vile. The Reason. Stevie Smith. **CP-SmitS**

My life, now, you say our love will last forever. Catullus. *See* Carmen 109: "Joy of my life! you tell me this."

My Life, the Quality of Which. Etheridge Knight. **SP-KnigE**

My life was never so precious. Inscription for the Tank. James Wright. **CP-WrigJ**

My life, your light green eyes. Last Words. James Merrill. **SP-MerrJ**

My Life's Delight. Thomas Campion. **CP-CampT**

My life's wave is at its crest. Wendell Berry. *Fr.* From the Crest. **CP-BerrW**

My limits crowd around me. Green Limits. Muriel Rukeyser. **CP-RukeM**

My little Balm might be o'erlooked. Emily Dickinson. **SP-DickE**

My little 'Bout-Town Gal Has Gone. Gwendolyn Brooks. **SP-BrooG**

My little boy's sick tonight. Untitled. Alice Notley. **SP-NotlA**

My Little Critics. David Herbert Lawrence. **CP-LawrD**

My little dog ten years ago. For a Good Dog. Ogden Nash. **CP-NashO**

My little doves have left a nest. My Doves. Elizabeth Barrett Browning. **CP-BroEB**

My little girl keeps talking to me. Conversation. John Updike. **CP-UpdiJ**

My little happiness. A Self-Glamourer. Thomas Hardy. **CP-HardT**

My little heart is so wonderfully sorry. Edward Estlin Cummings. **CP-CummE**

My little island girl. Snow and Swarts as before. Thomas Stearns Eliot. *Fr.* Two Songs from *Sweeny Agonistes.* **UnPo** *Fr.* Sweeney Agonistes. **CP-ElioT**

My little love, my darling. The Virgin Mother. David Herbert Lawrence. **CP-LawrD**

My Little March Girl. Paul Laurence Dunbar. **CP-DunbP**

My little son comes running with open arms! Poem. Thomas McGrath. **SP-McGrT**

My little son, laughing, singing. . . . Poem. Thomas McGrath. **SP-McGrT**

My little son, my Florentine. A Tale of Villafranca. Elizabeth Barrett Browning. **CP-BroEB**

My little son, when you could command marvels. Geoffrey Hill. **NoAM** *Fr.* Funeral Music. **CP-HillG**

My live telephone swings crippled into solitude. Marcus Cato 234–149 B.C. Robert Lowell. **SP-LoweR**

My lizard, my lively writher. Wish for a Young Wife. Theodore Roethke. **CP-RoetT**

My lonely chamber next the sea. A Flower in a Letter. Elizabeth Barrett Browning. **CP-BroEB**

My long two-pointed ladder's sticking through a tree. After Apple-picking. Robert Frost. **CP-FrosR**

My lord; / Poor wretched states, pressed by extremities. To the Right Honourable, the Lord High Treasurer of England. An Epistle Mendicant. 1631. Ben Jonson. **CP-JonsB**

My Lord, a diamond to me you sent. To the Right Hon. the Lord Chancellor (Bacon). George Herbert. **CP-HerbG**

My Lord a hunting he is gane. My Lady's Gown There's Gairs upon't. Robert Burns. **CP-BurnR**

My Lord and King. Tennyson. *See* Love is and was my Lord and King.

My Lord and Lady Darlington. Written in the Strangers' Book at "The Station," Opposite Bowness. William Wordsworth. **CP-WorW2**

My Lord came to me in the deep of night. The Encounter. William Everson. **SP-EverW**

My Lord complains, that Pope, stark mad with gardens. Epigram. Alexander Pope. **CP-PopeA**

My lord, hearing lately of your opulence in promises and your house. An Epistle to a Patron. Frank Templeton Prince. **CP-PrinF**

My Lord, I know, your noble ear. The Humble Petition of Bruar Water to the Noble Duke of Athole. Robert Burns. **CP-BurnR**

My Lord, in every trivial work, 'tis known. To My Much Honoured Friend, Henry, Lord Carey of Leppington, Upon His Translation of Malvezzi. Thomas Carew. **CP-CareT**

My Lord, My Lord. Just Like Job. Maya Angelou. **SP-AngeM**

My Lord, my Love! in pleasant pain. Imitated From the Arpa Evangelica: Page 121. Christina Georgina Rossetti. **CP-RosC3**

My Lord to find out who must deal. A Ballad on the Game of Traffic. Jonathan Swift. **CP-SwifJ**

My lost William, thou in whom. To William Shelley ("My lost William, thou in whom"). Percy Bysshe Shelley. **CP-ShelP**

My Lost Youth. Henry Wadsworth Longfellow. **SP-LongH**

My lov'd [*or* loved], my honor'd [*or* honored], much respected friend. The Cotter's Saturday Night [Inscribed to Robert Aiken [*or* R. A****], Esq.]. Robert Burns. **CP-BurnR**

My Love. Robert Creeley. **CP-CreeR**

My Love. Richard Shelton. **SP-ShelR**

My love / thy hair is one kingdom. Edward Estlin Cummings. **CP-CummE**

My love, / When you were here there was. A Letter. Li Po, *tr. fr. Chinese by* William Carlos Williams *with* David Rafael Wang. **CP-WilW2**

My love & I are yours to command. Carmen 15. Catullus. *Fr.* Carmina. **CP-Catul**

My love and I went swimming naked one afternoon. A Message from the Mountain Pool Where the Deer Come Down. James Wright. *Fr.* Many of Our Waters: Variations on a Poem by a Black Child. **CP-WrigJ**

My love, be calmer! Werner; or, The Inheritance. Byron. **CP-Byron**

My Love bound me with a kiss[e]. Thomas Campion. **CP-CampT** (Canto Tertio.) **CP-CampT**

My love don't give me presents. She's a Woman. The Beatles. **CP-Beatl**

My love for you, though true, wears the. Compact. Robert Ranke Graves. **CP-GravR**

My Love Has Been. Martin Edmunds. **SP-EdmuM**

My love has come to ride me home. Do We Understand Each Other? Allen Ginsberg. **CP-GinsA**

My love has talked with rocks and trees. Tennyson. *Fr.* In Memoriam A. H. H. **CP-TennA**

My Love Hath Vowd. Thomas Campion. *See* My love hath vow[e]d he[e] will forsake me[e].

My love hath vow[e]d he[e] will forsake me[e]. Thomas Campion. **CP-CampT** (My Love Hath Vowd.) **CP-CampT**

My Love Irene. Paul Laurence Dunbar. **CP-DunbP**

My Love Is Also / Like. Charles Olson. **CP-OlsoC**

My love is as a fever [*or* feaver],k longing still. Sonnet 147. William Shakespeare. **EBEV; HoPM; NAEL-1; OXAEP-1; PoEL-2; TEP** *Fr.* Sonnets. **CP-ShaWS**

My love is building a building. Edward Estlin Cummings. **CP-CummE**

My love is gone. Lament. David Markson. **CP-MarkD**

My love is lessened and must soon be past. The Beginning of the End. Gerard Manley Hopkins. **CP-HopkG**

My love is like Mies van der Rohe's. Dea ex Machina. John Updike. **CP-UpdiJ**

My Love Is Like to Ice. Edmund Spenser. **ErPo; FF; FPL; ImPo; LiTB; PAI; TrGrPo** *Fr.* Amoretti. **CP-Spens**

My love is like th'eternal fire. Sir Thomas Wyatt. **CP-WyatT**

My love is of a birth as rare. The Definition of Love. Andrew Marvell. **CP-MarvA**

My love is strengthen'd, though more weak in seeming. Sonnet 102. William Shakespeare. **AWP; EIL; OAEP; OBEV; OBSC** *Fr.* Sonnets. **CP-ShaWS**

My Love Is to the Light of Lights. "Hugh MacDiarmid." **SP-MacDH**

My Love Is Too Much. Erica Jong. **SP-JongE**

My love lies underground. Hymn to Priapus. David Herbert Lawrence. **CP-LawrD**

My love looks like a girl to-night. The Bride. David Herbert Lawrence. **CP-LawrD**

My love—my love says / she loves me. Stomping with Catullus. Robert Creeley. **CP-CreeR**

My love now lies upon his rump. Malcolm Lowry. **CP-LowrM**

My love she speaks like silence. Love Minus Zero/No Limit. "Bob Dylan." **CP-DylaB**

My love she turned so harsh, so cruel. Occupation. David Markson. **CP-MarkD**

My Love She's But a Lassie Yet. Robert Burns. **CP-BurnR**

My love, this is the bitterest, that thou. Any Wife to Any Husband. Robert Browning. **CP-BroR1**

My love took scorn my service to retain. Sir Thomas Wyatt. **CP-WyatT**

My love was born in Aberdeen. The White Cockade. Robert Burns. **CP-BurnR**

My love was stolen from me. Motifs from the Dark Wood. Jean Garrigue. **SP-GarrJ**

My love was warm; for that I crossed. Robert Louis Stevenson. **CP-StevR**

My love whose heart is tender said to me. Doeth Well. . . Doeth Better. Christina Georgina Rossetti. **CP-RosC2**

My lovely lady stood in the wind. Incident of May. Hayden Carruth. **CP-CarHS**

My lover never danced with me. Lines to a Seagreen Lover. Isabella Gardner. **CP-GardI**

My Love's Gone a-Fighting. Thomas Hardy. **CP-HardT** *Fr.* The Dynasts.

My love's manners in bed. The Way. Robert Creeley. **CP-CreeR**

My Lucia in the deaw did go. Upon Lucia Dabled in the Deaw. Robert Herrick. **CP-HerrR**

My lute, awake! Perform [the] last. Sir Thomas Wyatt. **CP-WyatT**

My lute, within thyself thy tunes enclose, *speech of Gynecia.* Sir Philip Sidney. **SP-SidnP** *Fr.* Arcadia.

My Luv. William Carlos Williams. **CP-WilW1**

My maister Bukton, whan of Crist oure kyng. Lenvoy de Chaucer a Bukton. Geoffrey Chaucer. **CP-ChauG**

My Maker—let me be. Emily Dickinson. **CP-DickE**

My many cares and much distress. His Change. Robert Herrick. **CP-HerrR**

My Martial owns a garden, famed to please. De Hortis Julii Martialis. Robert Louis Stevenson. **CP-StevR**

My Mary. John Clare. **CP-MacNL**

My Master said: / That which acts on all and meddles in none—is heaven. The Kingly Man. Chuang Tzu, *tr. fr. Chinese by* Thomas Merton. **CP-MertT**

My masters and friends, and good people draw near. Ben Jonson. **CP-JonsB** *Fr.* Bartholomew Fair.

My Meadow. Hayden Carruth. **CP-CarHS**

My meaning will be best unravelled. Tim and the Fables. Jonathan Swift. **CP-SwifJ**

My Memory's no worth a preen. Postscript [To W. S*****n, Ochiltree]. Robert Burns. **CP-BurnR**

My Merry men all, that drink with glee. Drinking versus Thinking. Samuel Taylor Coleridge. **CP-ColeS**

My midnight lamp is weary as my soul. The Student. Elizabeth Barrett Browning. **CP-BroEB**

My mind drifts back to those far days that bred. First Honey. John Hewitt. **CP-HewiJ**

My mind is. Edward Estlin Cummings. **CP-CummE**

My mind is clouded. Liberation. Louise Glück. **SP-GlücL**

My mind is intact, but the shapes. Riddle in the Garden. Robert Penn Warren. **SP-WarrR**

My mind is like a clamorous market-place. The Market-Place. Walter de la Mare. **CP-DeLaW**

My mind was heavy and my luck was dark. Richard Eberhart. *Fr.* Brotherhood of Men. **CP-EberR**

My mind was once the true survey. The Mower's Song. Andrew Marvell. **CP-MarvA**

My mind was overborne with questions. Wendell Berry. *Fr.* Elegy: "To be at home on its native ground." **CP-BerrW**

My Mistress Commanding Me to Return Her Letters. Thomas Carew. **CP-CareT**

My mistress' eyes are nothing like the sun. Sonnet 130. William Shakespeare. **AWP; BiP; BoLoP; CABA; EBEV; FF; HAP; HBV; HeIP; HoPM; ImPo; InPK; InPS; InvP; LiTB; NAEL-1; NIP; NoP; NoSic; OAEL-1; OAEP; OXAEP-1; OtMeF; PAI; PBMP; PP; PPP; PlP; PoE; PoPle; Poetr; PrIm; SeCeV; SoSe; Son; TEP; TFi; WeW** *Fr.* Sonnets. **CP-ShaWS**

My Mistresse sayes she'll marry none but me. Catullus. *See* Carmen 70: "Lesbia says she'ld rather marry me."

My Mistris blush'de, and therewithall. The Showre of Roses. Robert Herrick. **CP-HerrR**

My misunderstandings: for years I thought "muso bello" meant "Bell Muse," I thought it was a kind of. Taking a Walk with You. Kenneth Koch. **SP-KochK**

My momma told me you were bad new, honey. Love You Too Much. "Bob Dylan" *and* Greg Lake. **CP-DylaB**

My most distinguished guest and learnèd friend. Edna St. Vincent Millay. **CP-MillE**

My Mother. John Hewitt. **CP-HewiJ**

My mother acted like a god, crazy, because grown-ups are crazy. Bandage. Stephen Berg. **SP-BergS**

My mother and I debate. The Black Walnut Tree. Mary Oliver. **SP-OlivM**

My mother bids me bind my hair. Those Horrid Hurdy-Gurdies! "Lewis Carroll." **CP-CarrL**

My mother bore me in the southern wild. The Little Black Boy. William Blake. **AWP; BiP; CABA; CH; EnRP; FHYEP; HBV; HeIP; HoFi; InPK; LAuP; NAEL-2; NAWM-2; NOBRP; NOEC; NoP; OAEL-2; OAEP; OBEC; OBEV; OBNC; OxBChV; OxBoCh; PeECV; PoE; PoEL-4; PoNe; SCGP; SeCeV; TFi; TrGrPo; TreFS** *Fr.* Songs of Innocence. **CP-BlakW**

My mother dandled me and sang. Song from "The Player Queen,"A. William Butler Yeats. **CP-YeatW**

"My mother did it. She had to," she said. She took. Hayden Carruth. *Fr.* The Sleeping Beauty. **CP-CarHL**

My mother died as though. Closure. Leonard Nathan. **SP-NathL**

My mother groaned! [*or* groan'd!, *or* groaned!] my father wept. Infant Sorrow. William Blake. **CP-BlakW** *Fr.* Songs of Experience.

My mother had slapped a month-long news embargo. Profumo. Paul Muldoon. **SP-MuldP**

My mother had three brothers, each one died. The Unnecessary Dread. John Hewitt. **CP-HewiJ**

My mother! if thou love me, name no more. On Pedigree. *Unknown, tr. fr. Greek by* William Cowper. **CP-CowpW**

My mother knocked on my roominghouse door. On Being 20. Charles Bukowski. **SP-BukC3**

My mother never forgave my father. The Portrait. Stanley Jasspon Kunitz. **CP-KuniS**

My mother opens the scullery door. Trance. Paul Muldoon. **SP-MuldP**

My mother phoning from far off. Breathing Exercises. Leonard Nathan. **SP-NathL**

My mother played no games. She trimmed her hats. An Eye for Color. John Hewitt. **CP-HewiJ**

My mother, poor woman, lies tonight. Goodbye. Galway Kinnell. **SP-KinnG**

My Mother Remembers That She Was Beautiful. Tess Gallagher. **SP-GallT**

My Mother said: The child is changed. Seeking Rest. Christina Georgina Rossetti. **CP-RosC3**

My mother speaks from the dark—why. With Stars. Tess Gallagher. **SP-GallT**

My mother stands at the screen door, laughing. A Happy Childhood. William Matthews. **SP-MattW**

My Mother: 33 Years Later. Grace Paley. **CP-PaleG**

My mother. . . (thy uneasy rust). The Nervousness of Memory. Kenneth Patchen. **CP-PatcK**

My mother wants to be burned, she told me. Lament. Stephen Berg. **SP-BergS**

My mother was a Florentine. Elizabeth Barrett Browning. **NALW** *Fr.* Aurora Leigh. **CP-BroEB**

My mother was a giant squaw, my father. Tanck's Brag. Hayden Carruth. **CP-CarHS** *Fr.* Songs About What Comes Down: The Complete Works of Mr. Septic Tanck.

My mother was a romantic girl. Papa Love Baby. Stevie Smith. **CP-SmitS**

My Mother Was a Soldier. William Stafford. **SP-StafW**

My mother was Dutch. Portrait (II). Stevie Smith. **CP-SmitS**

My mother, who hates thunderstorms. Mother, Summer, I. Philip Larkin. **CP-LarkP**

My mother works here. Toy Factory. Charles Simic. **SP-SimiC**

My Mother Would Be a Falconress. Robert Duncan. **SP-DuncR**

My Mother Writes. . . . Gary Gildner. **SP-GildG**

My Mother's Birthday. Kathleen Jessie Raine. **SP-RainK**
  "I used to watch you, sleeping." **NAs**
  "November rain with thin fingers tapping."

My mother's elder sister married Tom. Aunt Cis and Uncle Tom. John Hewitt. **CP-HewiJ**

My mother's father, when he came to die. Eager Journey. John Hewitt. **CP-HewiJ**

My mother's friend cooked for the drunk-and-disorderlies. In the Hospital for Tests. Mona Van Duyn. **SP-VanDM**

My mother's lamp once out. Scenes of Childhood. James Merrill. **SP-MerrJ**

My Mother's Lips. Charles Kenneth Williams. **CP-WillC; SP-WillC**

My Mother's List of Names. Bill Knott. **SP-KnotB**

My mother's maids [or maydes] when they did sew [or sowe] and spin [or spynne]. Sir Thomas Wyatt. **CP-WyatT** *Fr.* Satires.

My mother's mother, born in forty-two. My Grandmother Robinson. John Hewitt. **CP-HewiJ**

My Mouse. Christina Georgina Rossetti. **CP-RosC3**

My mouth blooms like a cut. The Kiss. Anne Sexton. **CP-SextA**

My mouth doth water, and my breast doth swell. Sonnet 37. Sir Philip Sidney. **NAEL-1; Son** *Fr.* Astrophil and Stella. **SP-SidnP**

My mouth hovers across your breasts. Adrienne Rich. **SP-RicA1** *Fr.* Contradictions: Tracking Poems.

My Muse. Stevie Smith. **CP-SmitS**

My muse in meads has spent her many hours. To Mistress Katherine Bradshaw, the Lovely, That Crowned Him with Laurel. Robert Herrick. **CP-HerrR**

My Muse may well grudge at my heav'nly joy. Sonnet 70. Sir Philip Sidney. *Fr.* Astrophil and Stella. **SP-SidnP**

My muse now hapy, lay thy self to rest. Sonnet 9. Mary Sidney, Countess of Montgomery Wroth. *Fr.* Pamphilia to Amphilanthus. **CP-WrotM**

My Muse what ails this ardour. Sir Philip Sidney. **SP-SidnP** *Fr.* Arcadia.

My muvver's ist the nicest one. Appreciation. Paul Laurence Dunbar. **CP-DunbP**

My My. Ogden Nash. **CP-NashO**

My Conscience.

My Dream.

My Naked Aunt. Archibald MacLeish. **CP-MacLA**

My naked lady framed. Edward Estlin Cummings. **CP-CummE**

My Name and I. Robert Ranke Graves. **CP-GravR**

My name engraved herein. Valediction, A: Of My Name in the Window. John Donne. **CP-DonnJ**

My name is / Black Golden Amber / Changing. To a Man. Maya Angelou. **SP-AngeM**

My name is Donald White, you see. Ballad of Donald White. "Bob Dylan." **CP-DylaB**

My name is Edgar Poe and I was born. On the Edge. Philip Levine. **SP-LeviP**

My name is James A. Wright, and I was born. At the Executed Murderer's Grave. James Wright. **CP-WrigJ**

My Name Is Jesus. David Herbert Lawrence. *See* My name is Jesus, I am Mary's son.

My name is Jesus, I am Mary's son. David Herbert Lawrence. **CP-LawrD**
  (My Name Is Jesus.) **CP-LawrD**

My name is Johnson. Madam's Past History. Langston Hughes. **SP-HughL**

My name is not my own. The Meeting. Tess Gallagher. **SP-GallT**

My name is O'Kelly, I've heard the Revelly. Shillin' a Day. Rudyard Kipling. **CP-KiplR**

My name is Oriane, / the lurcher. Oriane. James Schuyler. **CP-SchuJ**

My name is Revolution—let me speak. Poem. John Hewitt. **CP-HewiJ**

My name is sand: I make. The Illusionist. Stanley Jasspon Kunitz. **CP-KuniS**

My name is Severino. The Death and Life of a Severino. João Cabral de Melo Neto, *tr. fr. Portuguese* by Elizabeth Bishop.

My name is Severino. João Cabral de Melo Neto. **CP-BishE** *Fr.* The Death and Life of a Severino.

My name is Solomon Levi. An Old Cracked Tune. Stanley Jasspon Kunitz. **CP-KuniS**

My name is Timmy Torin. Muriel Rukeyser. **CP-RukeM**

My name—my country—what are they to thee? Paulus Silentiarius, *tr. fr. Greek* by William Cowper. **CP-CowpW**

(Epitaph, An: "My name—my country—what are they to thee.") **CP-CowpW**

My name, my speech, my self I had forgot. Shock. Rudyard Kipling. *Fr.* Epitaphs of the War [1914–1918]. **CP-KiplR**

My Namesake. John Greenleaf Whittier. **CP-WhitJ**

My Naming. John Hewitt. **CP-HewiJ**

My Nannie's Awa'. Robert Burns. **CP-BurnR**

My Native Land. David Herbert Lawrence. *Fr.* Songs I Learnt at School. **CP-LawrD**

My Naughty Book. David Herbert Lawrence. **CP-LawrD**

My needs were few and pure. Jim Carroll. **SP-CarrJ**

My neighbor, a scientist and art-collector, telephones me in a. The Burning of Paper instead of Children. Adrienne Rich. **SP-RicA1; SP-RicA2**

My Neighbor in the Mirror. Louise Glück. **SP-GlücL**

My neighbor is a nice guy but he utterly. The Puzzle. Charles Bukowski. **SP-BukC3**

My neighbor lives on the hill. Differences. Paul Laurence Dunbar. **CP-DunbP**

My neighbor was a biker, a pusher, a dog. The Sudden Light and the Trees. Stephen Dunn. **SP-DunnS**

My neighbour moves less and less, attempts less. The Green Wolf. Ted Hughes. **SP-HughT**

My Neighbours Two Brothers. James Liddy. **CP-LiddJ**

My nephew / And my new. Louis Zukofsky. **CP-ZukLS**

My New-Cut Ashlar. Rudyard Kipling. **CP-KiplR** *Fr.* Life's Handicap.

My New Year's drink is mulled to-night. Ancestors. Robert Ranke Graves. **CP-GravR**

My night sweats grease his breakfast plate. The Jailer. Sylvia Plath. **CP-PlatS**

My northern pines are good enough for me. Boston. Edwin Arlington Robinson. **CP-RobiE**

My nose angles the air. From Waterloo Bridge, Ensuing Dark. Steve Griffiths. **SP-GrifS**

My nosegays are for Captives. Emily Dickinson. **CP-DickE**

My nostrils tell me: somewhere *mare nostro*. Road Ends at Tahola. Richard Hugo. **CP-HugoR**

My November Guest. Robert Frost. **CP-FrosR**

My offended contempt for the mental & stylistic workings of. Crisis. John Berryman. **CP-BerrJ**

My old admiration before I was twenty. Christina Georgina Rossetti. **CP-RosC3**

My old flame, my wife! The Old Flame. Robert Lowell. **SP-LoweR**

My old friend, how we sustain. Marge Piercy. *Fr.* The Homely War. **SP-PierM**

My old friend, the owner. The Plan. Wendell Berry. **CP-BerrW**

My Old Friends. Christina Georgina Rossetti. **CP-RosC3**

My Old Man. Charles Bukowski. **SP-BukC1**

My Old Man. "Lou Reed." **SP-ReedL**

My old man's a white old man. Cross. Langston Hughes. **SP-HughL**

My old mule. Me and the Mule. Langston Hughes. **SP-HughL**

My old time daddy. Lover's Return. Langston Hughes. **SP-HughL**

My old Welsh neighbor over the way. The Robin. John Greenleaf Whittier. **CP-WhitJ**

My oldest son comes to visit me. Having Been Asked "What is a Man?" I Answer. Philip Levine. **SP-LeviP**

My only love reads big books, behemoth works. Sometimes. Ron Koertge. **SP-KoerR**

My only sister, Eileen, always was. My Sister. John Hewitt. **CP-HewiJ**

My only son, more God's than mine. Jesus and His Mother. Thom Gunn. **CP-GunnT**

My only triumph is the challenge cup. What Sigbjørn Said. Malcolm Lowry. **CP-LowrM**

My other favorite cat seemed to be dying and. Terminology. Charles Bukowski. **SP-BukC3**

My Own and Not My Own. John Hewitt. **CP-HewiJ**

My own Beloved, who hast lifted me. Sonnet. Elizabeth Barrett Browning. *Fr.* Sonnets from the Portuguese. **CP-BroEB**

My own dim life should teach me this. Tennyson. **EnVR; FHYEP; OAEL-2; SeCePo** *Fr.* In Memoriam A. H. H. **CP-TennA**

My Own Heart. Gerard Manley Hopkins. *See* My Own Heart Let Me More Have Pity On.

My Own Heart Let Me More Have Pity On. Gerard Manley Hopkins.
  (My Own Heart.) **CP-HopkG**

My pain[e], still smothered [or smother'd] in my grievèd bre[a]st. Sonnet 6. Mary Sidney, Countess of Montgomery Wroth. **NOSC** *Fr.* Pamphilia to Amphilanthus. **CP-WrotM**

My Paistin Finn is my sole desire. Two Songs Rewritten for the Tune's Sake. William Butler Yeats. **CP-YeatW**

My Papa's Waltz. Theodore Roethke. **CP-RoetT**

My Parents. Stephen Spender. **CP-SpenS**

My Parents' Courtship. John Hewitt. **CP-HewiJ**

My parents raised me tenderly. Long Time Gone. "Bob Dylan." **CP-DylaB**

My parrot is emerald green. A Parrot. May Sarton. **SP-SartM**

My Peggy's Face. Robert Burns. **CP-BurnR**

My pen, take pain a little space. Sir Thomas Wyatt. **CP-WyatT**

My pens are all spilt, and my ink-glass is dry. William Cowper. **CP-CowpW**

My pensive Sara! thy soft cheek reclin'd. The Eolian Harp. Samuel Taylor Coleridge. **EnRP; FHYEP; NAEL-2; NOBRP; NoP; OAEL-2** *Fr.* Effusions. **CP-ColeS**

My peonies have lovely leaves. What Ails My Fern? James Schuyler. **CP-SchuJ**

My People. Langston Hughes. *See* The Night is beautiful.

My People. Carl Sandburg. **CP-SandC**

My people are gray. My People. Carl Sandburg. **CP-SandC**

My people grew potatoes. The Duchess Potatoes. Diane Wakoski. **SP-WakoD**

My period had come for Prayer. Emily Dickinson. **CP-DickE**

My pet creations fly away. Chop Chop. Jim Carroll. **SP-CarrJ**

My phoenix long ago secured. The Phoenix. Hafiz, *tr. by* Ralph Waldo Emerson. **CP-EmerR** *Fr.* Odes.

My Picture-Gallery. Walt Whitman. **CP-WhitW**

My Picture Left in Scotland. Ben Jonson. **CP-JonsB**

My pillow won't tell me. The Apparition. Theodore Roethke. **CP-RoetT**

My "place of clear water." Anahorish. Seamus Heaney. **SP-HeanS**

My Playmate. John Greenleaf Whittier. **CP-WhitJ**

My poems are never tired. A White Thought in a White Shade. James Liddy. **CP-LiddJ**

My poet, thou canst touch on all the notes. Sonnet. Elizabeth Barrett Browning. **BrRo; HBV; VLP; WHA** *Fr.* Sonnets from the Portuguese. **CP-BroEB**

My Poets. Philip Levine. **SP-LeviP**

My poor dumb body. Charles Olson. **CP-OlsoC**

My Portion is Defeat—today. Emily Dickinson. **CP-DickE**

My Prayer. Edward Estlin Cummings. **CP-CummE**

My prayers must meet a brazen heaven. Gerard Manley Hopkins. **CP-HopkG**

My Pretty Animals. Kenneth Patchen. **CP-PatcK**

My Pretty Rose Tree. William Blake. **CP-BlakW** *Fr.* Songs of Experience.

My proper prudence toward his proper probe. Riders to the Blood-Red Wrath. Gwendolyn Brooks. **SP-BrooG**

My Psalm. John Greenleaf Whittier. **CP-WhitJ**

My quality is such as common things. Having Been Near. Kenneth Patchen. **CP-PatcK**

My quietness has a man in it, he is transparent. In Memory of My Feelings. Frank O'Hara. **SP-OharF**

My race began as the sea began. Names. Derek Walcott. **CP-WalcD**

My remarkable body has. Song for Champagne Saturday. Dabney Stuart. **SP-StuaD**

My Reward for Being, was This. Emily Dickinson. **CP-DickE**

My right hand has suffered an amputation. The Good Resolution. Mona Van Duyn. **SP-VanDM**

My Rival. Rudyard Kipling. **CP-KiplR**

My River runs to thee. Emily Dickinson. **CP-DickE**

My Room. Leonard Cohen. **CP-CoheL**

My room is whitewashed. The Silence. Anne Sexton. **CP-SextA**

My Rose, Gravina, blooms anew. To Gravina. William Cowper. **CP-CowpW**

My Rules. Shel Silverstein. **SP-SilS2**

My sad-bad rain that falls. Rain Song. Jean Garrigue. **SP-GarrJ**

My Sad Captains. Thom Gunn. **CP-GunnT**

My Sad Self. Allen Ginsberg. **CP-GinsA**

My Sandy gied to me a ring. I Love My Love in Secret. Robert Burns. **CP-BurnR**

My science-friend, my noblest woman-friend. Going Somewhere. Walt Whitman. **CP-WhitW**

My Season's furthest flower. Emily Dickinson. **CP-DickE**

My second thoughts condemn. Wystan Hugh Auden. *Fr.* Ten Songs. **CP-AudeW**

My secrets cry aloud. Open House. Theodore Roethke. **CP-RoetT**

My seven aunts never left Brooklyn. Aunt Gertrud. Peter Meinke. **SP-MeinP**

My 71st Year. Walt Whitman. **CP-WhitW**

My shack has two rooms; I use one. Robert Bly. *Fr.* Six Winter Privacy Poems. **SP-BlyR**

My Shadow. Robert Louis Stevenson. **CP-StevR**

My shared bedroom's window. Elegies for Paradise Valley. Robert Earl Hayden. **CP-HaydR**

My sheep are thoughts, which I both guide and serve, *speech of Dorus.* Sir Philip Sidney. **CP-SidnP** *Fr.* Arcadia.

My Ship and I. Robert Louis Stevenson. **CP-StevR**

My ship departs next Saturday. Ruth knows. Remains. Robert Pack. **SP-PackR**

My shirt is a token and symbol. Shirt. Carl Sandburg. **CP-SandC**

My Shoes. Charles Simic. **SP-SimiC**

My shoes as I lean. The Nightingales. William Carlos Williams. **CP-WilW1**

My shoes were shined, my pants were cleaned and pressed. The Temptation of St. Joseph. Wystan Hugh Auden. *Fr.* For the Time Being; a Christmas Oratorio. **CP-AudeW**

My Shy Hand. Wilfred Owen. **CP-OwenW**

My sight with the clouds'. Kathleen Jessie Raine. **SP-RainK**

My signs are a rain-proof coat, good shoes, a staff cut from the woods. Walt Whitman. **Prf** *Fr.* Song of Myself. **CP-WhitW**

My silks and fine array. Song. William Blake. **CP-BlakW**

My silver stag is fallen—on the grass. The Silver Stag. Kathleen Jessie Raine. **SP-RainK**

My Sister. John Hewitt. **CP-HewiJ**

My sister and I are sewing. A Red Shirt. Margaret Atwood. **SP-AtwM2**

My sister, by the chiming kinks. Silverpoint. Louise Glück. **SP-GlücL**

My sister has my hair my mouth my eyes. A Family Resemblance. Audre Lorde. **SP-LordA**

My sister in her well-tailored silk blouse hands me. The Photos. Diane Wakoski. **SP-WakoD**

My sister! my sweet sister! if a name. Epistle to Augusta. Byron. **CP-Byron**

My sister walked me every day to school. The Way to School. John Hewitt. **CP-HewiJ**

My sisters, / do you remember the fiddlers. The Wonderful Musician. Anne Sexton. **CP-SextA**

My Sisters. Stanley Jasspon Kunitz. **CP-KuniS**

My Sisters, O My Sisters. May Sarton. **SP-SartM**

My situation almost the only one in the world. Canto 70. Ezra Pound. *Fr.* Cantos. **CP-PoCan**

My skin is kind of sort of brownish. Colors. Shel Silverstein. **SP-SilS2**

My smallheaded pearshaped. Edward Estlin Cummings. **CP-CummE**

My son / I promised you a world and see. Why I Never Went into Politics. Richard Shelton. **SP-ShelR**

My Son and I. Philip Levine. **SP-LeviP**

My son and I gao walking in the garden. New Season. Philip Levine. **SP-LeviP**

My son and I went for a walk. A Father Explains. John Hewitt. **CP-HewiJ**

My son as a child saying. A Little Stone in the Middle of the Road, in Florida. Muriel Rukeyser. **CP-RukeM**

My son enters the classroom. For Danny. Grace Paley. **CP-PaleG**

My Son, if a maiden deny thee and scuffingly bid thee give o'er. Rudyard Kipling. *Fr.* Certain Maxims of Hafiz. **CP-KiplR**

My son if I, Hafiz, thy father, take hold of thy knees in my pain. Rudyard Kipling. *Fr.* Certain Maxims of Hafiz. **CP-KiplR**

My son invites me to witness with him. Mousemeal. Howard Nemerov. **CP-NemeH**

My son is five years old and tonight he sang this song to me. A Loud Song, Mother. Isabella Gardner. **CP-GardI**

My son, keep well thy tongue, and keep thy friend. Controlling the Tongue. Geoffrey Chaucer. **OxBChV** *Fr.* The Manciple's Tale. *Fr.* The Canterbury Tales. **CP-ChauG**

My Son, My Executioner. Donald Hall. **CP-HallD**

"My son," said the Norman Baron, "I am dying, and you will be heir." Norman and Saxon. Rudyard Kipling. **CP-KiplR**

My son squats in the snow in his blue snowsuit. Illuminations. Louise Glück. **SP-GlücL**

My son was killed while laughing at some jest. I would I knew. A Son. Rudyard Kipling. **ChMP; FaBoEE; PeFWW** *Fr.* Epitaphs of the War [1914–1918]. **CP-KiplR**

My son who is stranger. A Variation. Robert Creeley. **CP-CreeR**

My son would not have been born. *Merchants Wife, The.* Alun Lewis. *Fr.* Poems from the Chinese. **CP-LewiA**

My Song, I fear that thou wilt find but few. *see also* Fragments Connected with Epipsychidion. Percy Bysshe Shelley. **CP-ShelP**

My song! It is time! Rendezvous. William Carlos Williams. **CP-WilW1**

My song shall bless the Lord of all. Jehovah-Jesus. William Cowper. *Fr.* Olney Hymns. **CP-CowpW**

My Songs Are Kandym in the Waste Land. "Hugh MacDiarmid." **SP-MacDH**

My sonnet is A light goes on in. Edward Estlin Cummings. **CP-CummE**

My sorrow is so wide. Kings River Canyon. Kenneth Rexroth. **NaP** *Fr.* Andrée Rexroth. **SP-RexrK**

My sorrow, when she's here with me. My November Guest. Robert Frost. **CP-FrosR**

My Sort o' Man. Paul Laurence Dunbar. **CP-DunbP**

My Soul. Stevie Smith. **CP-SmitS**

My Soul—accused me—And I quailed. Emily Dickinson. **CP-DickE**

My Soul and I. John Greenleaf Whittier. **CP-WhitJ**

My soul and I last night. Night Thought. Kathleen Jessie Raine. **SP-RainK**

My soul has had a long, hard day. Fatigue. David Herbert Lawrence. **CP-LawrD**

My Soul Is Dark. Byron. **CP-Byron**

My soul is enchanted boat. Percy Bysshe Shelley. **FHYEP** *Fr.* Prometheus Unbound. **CP-ShelP**

My soul is out back eating your soul. For Gail, When I Was Five. Charles Kenneth Williams. **CP-WillC; SP-WillC**

My soul is sad and much dismay'd. The Valley of the Shadow of Death. William Cowper. *Fr.* Olney Hymns. **CP-CowpW**

My soul looked down from a vague height, with Death. The Show. Wilfred Owen. **CP-OwenW**

My soul, lost in the music's mist. Song, The. Paul Laurence Dunbar. **CP-DunbP**

My soul, rejoice thou in thy God. Anne Bradstreet. **CP-BradA**

My Soul Thirsteth for God. Bible, *O.T. See* Psalm 42: "As the hart panteth after the water brooks."

My Soul Thirsteth for God. William Cowper. **TrCP** *Fr.* Olney Hymns. **CP-CowpW**

My soul within the shades of night. The Recluse. Stevie Smith. **CP-SmitS**

My soule would one day goe and seeke. How His Soule Came Ensnared. Robert Herrick. **CP-HerrR**

My Spanish Heart. Al Young. **CP-YounA**

My Special Fate. John Berryman. **CP-BerrJ**

My specialty is living said. Edward Estlin Cummings. **CP-CummE; SP-CummE**

My Spectre around Me Night and Day. William Blake. **CP-BlakW**

My spirit is too weak—mortality. On Seeing the Elgin Marbles. John Keats. **CP-KeatJ**

My spirit like a charmèd bark doth swim. Fragment: To One Singing. Percy Bysshe Shelley. **CP-ShelP**

My Spirit, Sore from Marching. Edna St. Vincent Millay. **CP-MillE**

My spirit to yours dear brother. To Him That Was Crucified. Walt Whitman. **CP-WhitW**

My Spirit Will Not Haunt the Mound. Thomas Hardy. **CP-HardT**

My Spouse! in whose presence I live. Aspirations of the Soul after God. Jeanne Marie Bouvier de la Motte-Guyon, *tr. fr.* French by William Cowper. **CP-CowpW**

My Star. Robert Browning. **CP-BroR1**

My stick fingers click with a snicker. Player Piano. John Updike. **CP-UpdiJ**

"My stick!" he says, and turns in the lane. Outside the Window. Thomas Hardy. *Fr.* Satires of Circumstance in Fifteen Glimpses. **CP-HardT**

My stiff-spread arms / Break into sudden gesture. John Gould Fletcher. **SP-FletJ** *Fr.* Irradiations.

My stock has gone down and my tailor has sent. A Companion's Progress. Paul Laurence Dunbar. **CP-DunbP**

My stock lies dead, and no increase. Grace. George Herbert. **CP-HerbG**

My stomach is the sky. Gluttony. Stephen Dobyns. **SP-DobyS**

My story begins in the town of Cambridge, Mass. The Mind of Professor Primrose. Ogden Nash. **CP-NashO**

My strength becoming wistful in a glib. Edward Estlin Cummings. **CP-CummE**

My students look at me expectantly. The Mountain. Louise Glück. **SP-GlücL**

My stutter, my cough, my unfinished sentences. The Second-Fated. Robert Ranke Graves. **CP-GravR**

My sudden daughter, grays are latent in that sea. With Melissa on the Shore. Richard Hugo. **CP-HugoR**

My suite is just, just lord to my suite hark, *par. by* Sir Philip Sidney. Bible, *O.T. See* Psalm 17: "Hear the right, O Lord. . . ."

My sun has set, I dwell. Despised and Rejected. Christina Georgina Rossetti. **CP-RosC1**

My supermarket is bigger than your supermarket. That's. Supermarket. Peter Meinke. **SP-MeinP**

My Surgeons. Stanley Jasspon Kunitz. **CP-KuniS**

My Sweeney, Mr. Eliot. Sweeney. Anne Sexton. **CP-SextA**

My sweet ache / is gone. Ache's End. Marge Piercy. **SP-PierM**

My sweet, alas, forget me not. Sir Thomas Wyatt. **CP-WyatT**

My Sweet Brown Gal. Paul Laurence Dunbar. **CP-DunbP**

My sweet-faced, tattle-tale brother was born blind. The Twins. Mona Van Duyn. **SP-VanDM**

My sweet old etcetera. Edward Estlin Cummings. **CP-CummE; SP-CummE**

"My sweet," you sang, and, "Sweet," I sang. Spring Reminiscence. Countee Cullen. **CP-CullC**

My Sweetest Lesbia [Let Us Live and Love]. Catullus. *See* Carmen 5: "Lesbia / live with me."

My sweetest Lesbia, let us live and love. Catullus. *See* Carmen 5: "Lesbia / live with me."

My Sweetheart is the TRUTH BEYOND THE MOON. Beyond the Moon. Nicholas Vachel Lindsay. **CP-LindV**

My swirling wants. Your frozen lips. A Valediction Forbidding Mourning. Adrienne Rich. **CP-RicAE; SP-RicA1; SP-RicA2**

My Table. William Butler Yeats. **CP-YeatW; LiTB** *Fr.* Meditations in Time of Civil War. **CP-YeatW**

My tea is nearly ready and the sun has left the sky. The Lamplighter. Robert Louis Stevenson. **CP-StevR**

My Tea with Madame Descartes. David St. John. **SP-StJoD**

My Teacher. Leonard Cohen. **CP-CoheL**

My Teachers. John Hewitt. **CP-HewiJ**

My thankful heart with glorying tongue. Anne Bradstreet. **CP-BradA**

My Thanks. John Greenleaf Whittier. **CP-WhitJ**

My Theme. George Meredith. **CP-MerG1**

My Theme: Continued. George Meredith. **CP-MerG1**

My Thoughts. Ralph Waldo Emerson. **CP-EmerR**

My thoughts are all in yonder town. The Friend's Burial. John Greenleaf Whittier. **CP-WhitJ**

My thoughts are crabbed and sallow. Jilted. Sylvia Plath. **CP-PlatS**

My thoughts are crowded with death. In Time of Plague. Thom Gunn. **CP-GunnT**

My thoughts arise and fade in solitude. Fragment: Thoughts Come and Go in Solitude. Percy Bysshe Shelley. **CP-ShelP**

My thoughts thou hast supported without rest. Mary Sidney, Countess of Montgomery Wroth. *Fr.* Part 1. *Fr.* Urania. **CP-WrotM**

My thoughts through yours refracted into speech. Sonnet. Muriel Rukeyser. **CP-RukeM**

My thoughts turn south. A White City. James Schuyler. **CP-SchuJ**

My thousand-thousand-leaved. Elm. John Updike. **CP-UpdiJ**

My three sisters are sitting. Women. Adrienne Rich. **CP-RicAE; SP-RicA2**

My tie is made of terylene. In Praise of $(C_{10}H_9O_5)x$. John Updike. **CP-UpdiJ**

My titillations have no foot-notes. Jasmine's Beautiful Thoughts Underneath the Willow. Wallace Stevens. **CP-StevW**

My title as an Genius thus is provd. William Blake. **CP-BlakW**

My Tocher's the Jewel. Robert Burns. **CP-BurnR**

My toes feel like nothing they are so cold. Muriel Rukeyser. **CP-RukeM**

My tongue is prone to lose the way. Letters. Ralph Waldo Emerson. **CP-EmerR**

My tongue moved, a swung relaxing hinge. Sibyl. Seamus Heaney. *Fr.* Triptych. **SP-HeanS**

My tongue-tied Muse in manners holds her still. Sonnet 85. William Shakespeare. **Son** *Fr.* Sonnets. **CP-ShaWS**

My townspeople, beyond in the great world. Gulls. William Carlos Williams. **CP-WilW1**

My trade takes me frequently into decaying houses. From a Museum Man's Album. John Hewitt. **CP-HewiJ**

My Treasures. Robert Louis Stevenson. **CP-StevR**

My trembling muse your honour does address. Poetical Epistle to Sir William Bennet, Bart. of Grubbat. James Thomson. **CP-ThomJ**

My Tribe. John Ciardi. **SP-CiarJ**

My Trip Daorba. Ogden Nash. **CP-NashO**

My Triumph. John Greenleaf Whittier. **CP-WhitJ**

My Triumph lasted till the Drums. Emily Dickinson. **CP-DickE**

My trouble / is that I have the spirit of Gertrude Stein. My Trouble. Diane Wakoski. **SP-WakoD**

My Trouble. Diane Wakoski. **SP-WakoD**

My true friend's poems about aging and death held my mind as in a sea-surge. No Supervening Thought of Grace. Hayden Carruth. **CP-CarHS**

My true love breathed her latest breath. The Murderer. Stevie Smith. **CP-SmitS**

My two-fold book! single in show. John Milton. *See* To John Rouse.

My two hands broke in two: and they broke me! Malcolm Lowry. **CP-LowrM**

My uncle / Daniel fought in the civil. Edward Estlin Cummings. **CP-CummE**

My Uncle. John Hewitt. **CP-HewiJ**

My uncle, a craftsman of hammers and wood. Willy Lyons. James Wright. **CP-WrigJ**

My Uncle Alec's friend, Dominic Cataldo. Feasts. John Ciardi. **SP-CiarJ**

My uncle Dick, my mother's youngest brother. First Ride. John Hewitt. **CP-HewiJ**

My Uncle from the realms of Death. Le Revenant. Stevie Smith. **CP-SmitS**

My Uncle is My Honor and a Guest in My House. Etheridge Knight. **SP-KnigE**

My Uncle Johnny. John Hewitt. **CP-HewiJ**

My uncle went down to the Dail to get the flag lowered. After Life. James Liddy. *Fr.* Ossie Esmonde. *Fr.* His Resplendent Neighbours. **CP-LiddJ**

My Uncle William was made principal. The Teacher's Residence. John Hewitt. **CP-HewiJ**

My Uncle Willy. John Hewitt. **CP-HewiJ**

My undergraduate eyes beholding. Cricket Master. Sir John Betjeman. **CP-BetjJ**

My unexpected knocking at the door. The Literate Farmer and the Planet Venus. Robert Frost. **CP-FrosR**

My verdict has been passed. M. Verdoux, The Wife Killer. Jim Carroll. **SP-CarrJ**

My very good lord, 'tis a very hard task. Verses Left in a Window of Dublin Castle. Jonathan Swift. **CP-SwifJ**

My vineyard that is mine I have to keep. Yea, I Have a Goodly Heritage. Christina Georgina Rossetti. **CP-RosC3**

My voice is a minor one, but I must raise it. I Spy, or, The Depravity of Privacy. Ogden Nash. **CP-NashO**

My Voice Not Being Proud. Louise Bogan. **CP-BogaL**

My Wars are laid away in Books. Emily Dickinson. **CP-DickE**

My way is in the sand flowing, *Author's own English vers. of his* "Je suis ce cours de sable qui glisse." Samuel Beckett. **CP-BeckS**

My Way Is Not Thy Way. David Herbert Lawrence. **CP-LawrD**

My wearied bark, O let it now be crowned! To Crown[e] It. Robert Herrick. **CP-HerrR**

My Weariness of Epic Proportions. Charles Simic. **SP-SimiC**

My wheel is in the dark! Emily Dickinson. **CP-DickE**

My whining lover, what needs all. Against Absence. Sir John Suckling. **CP-SuckJ**

My whiskey is / a tough way of life. Drink. William Carlos Williams. **CP-WilW1**

My whole eye was sunset red. Eye and Tooth. Robert Lowell. **SP-LoweR**

My whole life has led me here. Woolworth's. Donald Hall. **CP-HallD**

My Widowed Mother. John Hewitt. **CP-HewiJ**

My Wife. Robert Louis Stevenson. **CP-StevR**

My wife a-rattling. Addenda Quaedam. Jonathan Swift. **CP-SwifJ**

My Wife and I, *see also* Commentary—My Wife and I. Leonard Cohen. **CP-CoheL**

My wife and I, in one romantic cot. Robert Louis Stevenson. **CP-StevR**

My wife and I lived all alone. Ballad of the Despairing Husband. Robert Creeley. **CP-CreeR**

My wife gives me a pumpkin. Letters from the Island. Siv Cedering Fox. **SP-CedeS**

My wife hung it there, on the wall on the way to our bedroom. Self-Portrait at Six. Stephen Berg. **SP-BergS**

My Wife Reads the Paper at Breakfast on the Birthday of the Scottish Poet. Miller Williams. **SP-WillM**

My wife sleeps. Portrait of Mary. Etheridge Knight. **SP-KnigE**

My wife went out of town. Quietude. David Markson. **CP-MarkD**

My Wife's a Wanton Wee Thing. Robert Burns. **CP-BurnR**

My Wife's a Winsome Wee Thing. Robert Burns. **CP-BurnR**

My wife's new pink slippers. The Thinker. William Carlos Williams. **CP-WilW1**

My wife's slick needles click and slide. Pangur Ban. John Hewitt. **CP-HewiJ**

My wind is turned to bitter north. Arthur Hugh Clough. **SP-ClouA**

My window looks on the red brick wall. Breslau, Spring 1918. Jane Cooper. *Fr.* Threads: Rosa Luxemburg from Prison. **SP-CoopJ**

My window shews the travelling clouds. The Alchemist in the City. Gerard Manley Hopkins. **CP-HopkG**

My Woman. Catullus. *See* Carmen 70: "Lesbia says she'ld rather marry me."

My woman says she wants no other lover. Catullus. *See* Carmen 70: "Lesbia says she'ld rather marry me."

My woman says that she would rather wear the wedding-veil for me. Catullus. *See* Carmen 70: "Lesbia says she'ld rather marry me."

My women of the past keep trying to locate me. Charles Bukowski. **NGP** *Fr.* Horsemeat. **SP-BukC3**

My woods belong to woodcock and to deer. A Guest. May Sarton. **SP-SartM**

My wooing's ended: now my wedding's neere. To Rosemary and Baies. Robert Herrick. **CP-HerrR**

My words and thoughts do both express this notion. George Herbert. **CP-HerbG**

(Colossians 3:3.) **CP-HerbG**

My words I know do well set forth my mind. Sonnet 44. Sir Philip Sidney. *Fr.* Astrophil and Stella. **SP-SidnP**

My words, in hope to blaze my steadfast mind. Sir Philip Sidney. **SP-SidnP** *Fr.* Arcadia.

My words that once were virtuous and expressed. Edna St. Vincent Millay. **CP-MillE**

My World Is Pyramid. Dylan Thomas. **CP-ThomD**

My worship from this hour the Sparrow-Drawn. Edna St. Vincent Millay. **CP-MillE**

My Worthiness is all my Doubt. Emily Dickinson. **CP-DickE**

My wrath, where's the edge. Song. Theodore Roethke. **CP-RoetT**

My writing hand moves washed in the same light now. The Conspiracy. Charles Tomlinson. **CP-TomlC**

My Young Mother. Jane Cooper. **SP-CoopJ**

My youth came to me. Surprise Package. Marsden Hartley. **CP-HartM**

My youth is. Yacht for Sale. Archibald MacLeish. **CP-MacLA**

My youthful lady will have other lovers. Edward Estlin Cummings. **CP-CummE**

Mycenae. Donald Hall. **CP-HallD**

Mycenae and Epidaurus. John Hewitt. **CP-HewiJ**

Mycilla dyes her locks, 'tis said. On an Old Woman. Lucilius, *tr. fr. Greek by* William Cowper. **CP-CowpW**

Myfanwy. Sir John Betjeman. **CP-BetjJ**

Myfanwy at Oxford. Sir John Betjeman. **CP-BetjJ**

My(his from daughter's mother's zero mind). Edward Estlin Cummings. **CP-CummE**

Mykonos. John Hewitt. **CP-HewiJ**

Myopia: a Night. Robert Lowell. **SP-LoweR**

Myriad choices of his fate, The. Black Angel's Death Song. "Lou Reed." **SP-ReedL**

Myrrhina. Robert Ranke Graves. **CP-GravR**

Myrtle. Theodore Roethke. **CP-RoetT**

Myrtle Bough. Hilda Doolittle. **CP-DoolH**

Myrtle-leaf that, ill besped. To an Unfortunate Woman Whom the Author Had Known in the Days of Her Innocence. Samuel Taylor Coleridge. **CP-ColeS**

Myrtle the Turtle. Peter Meinke. **SP-MeinP**

Myrtle's Cousin. Theodore Roethke. **CP-RoetT**

Myself. Walter de la Mare. **CP-DeLaW**

Myself. Walt Whitman. *See* I celebrate myself, and sing myself.

Myself and Mine. Walt Whitman. **CP-WhitW**

Myself and my salmon friend were in the dusty river-road. The Reply of the Friend. James Liddy. **CP-LiddJ**

Myself can read the Telegrams. Emily Dickinson. **CP-DickE**

Myself, I rather like the bat. The Bat. Ogden Nash. **CP-NashO**

Myself I Sing. George Oppen. **CP-OppeG**

Myself to Me. May Sarton. **SP-SartM**

Myself unholy, from myself unholy. Gerard Manley Hopkins. **CP-HopkG**

Myself was formed—a Carpenter. Emily Dickinson. **CP-DickE**

Myself When I Am Real. Al Young. **CP-YounA**

Myself,walking in Dragon st. Edward Estlin Cummings. **CP-CummE**

Myselves / the grievers. Ceremony after a Fire Raid. Dylan Thomas. **CP-ThomD**

Mysteries, The. John Berryman. **CP-BerrJ**

Mysteries, The. Hilda Doolittle. **CP-DoolH**

Mysteries. Alice Walker. **CP-WalkA**

Mysteries of human nature, The. Emily Dickinson. **SP-DickE**

Mysteries practiced among men are unholy mysteries, The. Thomas Merton. *Fr.* The Legacy of Herakleitos. **CP-MertT**

Mysteries Sacred and Profane. Gilbert Sorrentino. **SP-SorrG**

Mysterious Biography. Carl Sandburg. **CP-SandC**

Mysterious Cat, The. Nicholas Vachel Lindsay. **CP-LindV**

Mysterious didactic urgency informs the compelling bedtime stories he is obsessively recounted, A. Herakles. Charles Kenneth Williams. **SP-WillC**

Mysterious Hint, A. Malcolm Lowry. **CP-LowrM**

Mysterious Song in the Spring of the Year, A. Thomas Merton. **CP-MertT**

Mystery, The. Paul Laurence Dunbar. **CP-DunbP**

Mystery. Langston Hughes. **SP-HughL**

Mystery. David Herbert Lawrence. **CP-LawrD**

Mystery. Edwin Rolfe. **CP-RolfE**

Mystery, A. John Greenleaf Whittier. **CP-WhitJ**

"Mystery Boy" Looks for Kin in Nashville. Robert Earl Hayden. **CP-HaydR**

Mystery here in this paperweight world, The. People of Letters. Al Young. **CP-YounA**

Mystery of creation is the divine urge of creation, The. The Work of Creation. David Herbert Lawrence. **CP-LawrD**

Mystery of Life, the Mystery, The. Mirrors of Life and Death. Christina Georgina Rossetti. **CP-RosC2**

Mystery of mysteries, the crude and hurried ceaseless flame, spontaneous, bearing on itself, The. A Thought of Columbus. Walt Whitman. **CP-WhitW**

Mystery of the Abstract. Richard Eberhart. **CP-EberR**

Mystery of the Charity of Charles Péguy, The. Geoffrey Hill. **CP-HillG**

　"Among the beetroots, where we are constrained."

　"Crack of a starting pistol. Jean Jaurès."

　"Dear lords of life, stump-toothed, with ragged breath." **DiPo**

　"Down in the river-garden a grey-gold."

　"Rage and regret are tireless to explain."

　"Salute us all, Christus with your iron."

　"There is an ancient landscape of green branches."

　"This world is different, belongs to them."

　"To dispense, with justice; or, to dispense."

　"Vistas of richness and reward. The cedar."

Mystery of the Dream. Jim Morrison. **SP-MorrJ**

"Mystery of things"—where is it found?, The. Fernando Pessoa. *Fr.* Twelve Poems from *The Keeper of the Flocks*. **CP-MertT**

Mystery Poems. Roy Fisher.

　"Irish cheekbones and close-set eyes." **SP-FishR**

　"Sloping and tapering away." **SP-FishR**

　"Upper corner—probably, The." **SP-FishR**

Mystery. Seed of every motion. Living Alone. Hayden Carruth. **CP-CarHS**

Mystery Story. Howard Nemerov. **CP-NemeH**

Mystery II. Edwin Rolfe. **CP-RolfE**

Mystic. David Herbert Lawrence. **CP-LawrD**

Mystic. Sylvia Plath. **CP-PlatS**

Mystic. Dabney Stuart. **SP-StuaD**

Mystic finishes in time, The. The Insomniacs. Adrienne Rich. **CP-RicAE**

Mystic, kneeling / in the forests of Malines, The. Marsden Hartley. **CP-HartM**

Mystic Sea, The. Paul Laurence Dunbar. **CP-DunbP**

Mystic Trumpeter, The. Walt Whitman. **CP-WhitW**

Mystical Beast in the Shadows, The. Richard Eberhart. **CP-EberR**

Mystical Forest, The. Marsden Hartley. **CP-HartM**

Mysticism Has Not the Patience To Wait for God's Revelation. Richard Eberhart. **CP-EberR**

Mystic's Christmas, The. John Greenleaf Whittier. **CP-WhitJ**

Myth. Peter Meinke. **SP-MeinP**

Myth. Muriel Rukeyser. **CP-RukeM**

Myth. May Sarton. **SP-SartM**

Myth & Ritual. Howard Nemerov. **CP-NemeH**

Myth of the Blaze. George Oppen. **CP-OppeG**

Myth on Mediterranean Beach: Aphrodite as Logos. Robert Penn Warren. **SP-WarrR**

Myth Science of Our Time, The. Al Young. **CP-YounA**

Myth tells us amber is the concretion. Fly in Amber. Isabella Gardner. **CP-GardI**

Mythic Fragment. Louise Glück. **SP-GlücL**

Mythological Beast. Howard Nemerov. *Fr.* Epigrams: "Wasp, climbing the window pane." **CP-NemeH**

Mythological Introduction. Philip Larkin. **CP-LarkP**

Mythology in an Age of Reason. Johann Christoph Friedrich von Schiller. **CP-ColeS** *Fr.* The Piccolomini.

Mythology of Dark and Light, The. Hayden Carruth. **CP-CarHL**

　Fifth Version, The.

　Her Dream.

　His Dream.

　Final Version, The.

　First Version, The.

　Fourth Version, The.

　Second Version, The.

　Third Version, The.

Myths and Texts, *sels.* Gary Snyder.

　Burning.

　　Amitabha's Vow. **CP-SnydG**

　　"Face in the crook of her neck." **CP-SnydG**

　　John Muir on Mt. Ritter. **CP-SnydG**

　　Maitreya the Future Buddha. **CP-SnydG**

　　Maudgalyâyana Saw Hell. **CP-SnydG**

　　Second Shaman Song. **CP-SnydG**

　　"Spikes of new smell driven up nostrils." **CP-SnydG**

　　"Stone-flake and salmon." **CP-SnydG**

　　Text, The. **CP-SnydG**

　　"Wash me on home, mama." **CP-SnydG**

　Hunting.

　　First Shaman Song. **CP-SnydG**

　　"Flung from demonic wombs." **CP-SnydG**

　　"How rare to be born a human being!" **CP-SnydG**

　　"Now I'll also tell what food." **CP-SnydG**

　　"Sealion, salmon, offshore." **CP-SnydG**

　　This Poem Is for Bear. **CP-SnydG**

　　This Poem Is for Birds. **CP-SnydG**

　　This Poem Is for Deer. **CP-SnydG**

　Logging.

　　"Ancient forests of China logged, The." **CP-SnydG**

　　("But ye shall destroy their altars.") **CP-SnydG**

　　"Each dawn is clear." **CP-SnydG**

　　"Felix Baran / Hugo Gerlot." **CP-SnydG**

　　"Green limb hangs in the crotch, A." **CP-SnydG**

　　"Groves are down, The." **CP-SnydG**

　　"Lodgepole / cone/seed waits for fire." **CP-SnydG**

　　"Lodgepole Pine: the wonderful reproductive." **CP-SnydG**

　　"Morning star is not a star, The." **CP-SnydG**

　　"Pines, under pines." **CP-SnydG**

　　"Ray Wells, a big Nisqually, and I." **CP-SnydG**

Myxomatosis. Philip Larkin. **CP-LarkP**

N / ot eth / eold almos. Edward Estlin Cummings. **CP-CummE**

N / OthI / n / g can / s / urPas / s. Edward Estlin Cummings. **CP-CummE**

N / Umb a / stree / t's wintr. Edward Estlin Cummings. **CP-CummE**

Na Audiart. Ezra Pound. **SP-PounE**

Na Khi talk made out of wind noise. Canto 104. Ezra Pound. *Fr.* Cantos. **CP-PoCan**

Naaman's Song. Rudyard Kipling. **CP-KiplR**

Nabokov's Blues. William Matthews. **SP-MattW**

Nabokov's Death. William Matthews. **SP-MattW**

Nachtmusik. David Markson. **CP-MarkD**

Nae gentle dames tho' ne'er sae fair. Highland Lassie O. Robert Burns. **CP-BurnR**

Nae Heathen Name shall I prefix. To Miss Ferrier. Robert Burns. **CP-BurnR**

Nagasaki Days. Allen Ginsberg. **CP-GinsA**

Nagging at myself something awful. Malcolm Lowry. **CP-LowrM**

Nahoa Urn, for a Woman. Pablo Antonio Cuadra, *tr. fr. Spanish by* Thomas Merton. **CP-MertT**

Nail his neck to the cross nail it with a nail. William Blake. **CP-BlakW**

Nail of the Index Finger, The. Siv Cedering Fox. **SP-CedeS**

Nail-paring moon in winter sky. Fayetteville Dawn (2). John Clellon Holmes. **SP-HolmJ**

Nails. Gary Gildner. **SP-GildG**

Naked. Alvaro Figueredo, *tr. by* William Carlos Williams. **CP-WilW2**

Naked / unarmored / before the open window. 6 A.M. Charles Bukowski. **SP-BukC2**

Naked. William Carlos Williams. **CP-WilW1**

Naked and grey the Cotswolds stand. Edgehill Fight. Rudyard Kipling. **CP-KiplR**

Naked and the Nude, The. Robert Ranke Graves. **CP-GravR**

Naked Ape, The. John Updike. **CP-UpdiJ**

Naked, as if for swimming, the martyr. Martyrdom of Saint Sebastian. Geoffrey Hill. *Fr.* Of Commerce and Society: Variations on a Theme. **CP-HillG**

Naked at 92 Degrees. Charles Bukowski. **SP-BukC3**

Naked before the glass she said. Young Woman. Howard Nemerov. **CP-NemeH**

Naked, but with my boots on / my son. Incunabula, 1958. Charles Olson. **CP-OlsoC**

Naked cornucopia of autumn fields, The. Cornucopia. Carl Sandburg. **CP-SandC**

Naked, he climbed to the wolf's lair. Holy Thursday. Geoffrey Hill. **CP-HillG**

Naked he found her? Two Women Talking. Archibald MacLeish. **CP-MacLA**

Naked, he lies in the blinded room. Soledad. Robert Earl Hayden. **CP-HaydR**

Naked house, a naked moor, A. The House Beautiful. Robert Louis Stevenson. **CP-StevR**

Naked Land, The. Kenneth Patchen. **CP-PatcK**

Naked Ostrich. Phoebe Hesketh. **SP-HeskP**

Naked spike chocolaty men white. Pachysandra. Louis Zukofsky. **CP-ZukLS**

Naked Surgeon, The. Michael Hartnett. **SP-HarMi**

Naked traveller, The. Ash Wednesday. Thomas Merton. **CP-MertT; SP-MertT**

Naked you saw the soul endure those blows. The Soul. Malcolm Lowry. **CP-LowrM**

Nakedly muscular, the beech no longer regrets. The Beech. Charles Tomlinson. **CP-TomlC**

Name, The. Robert Creeley. **CP-CreeR**

Name. Robert Ranke Graves. **CP-GravR**

Name, A. John Greenleaf Whittier. **CP-WhitJ**

Name and Number. John Hewitt. **CP-HewiJ**

Name any gentleman you spy. New Enigmas. Christina Georgina Rossetti. **CP-RosC3**

Name-Burning. Stephen Dobyns. **SP-DobyS**

Name Day. Robert Ranke Graves. **CP-GravR**

Name Day, A. James Schuyler. **CP-SchuJ**

Name-Day Night. Charles Olson. **CP-OlsoC**

Name for All, A. Hart Crane. **CP-CranH**

Name in a footnote. Faceless name. Crispus Attucks. Robert Earl Hayden. **CP-HaydR**

Name Is Too Familiar, The. Ogden Nash. **CP-NashO**

Name names, Paul Goodman. Black Mt. College Has a Few Words for a Visitor. Charles Olson. **CP-OlsoC**

Name of a fact: at home in that leafy world, A. Thoughts on Looking into a Thicket. John Ciardi. **SP-CiarJ**

Name—of it—is "Autumn", The. Emily Dickinson. **CP-DickE**

Name of Jesus, The. Christina Georgina Rossetti. **CP-RosC2**

Name the Gallic exile bore, The. A Name. John Greenleaf Whittier. **CP-WhitJ**

Name the Gods! David Herbert Lawrence. **CP-LawrD**

Name the Mystery Fin and Win a Doll. Richard Hugo. **CP-HugoR**

Name Us a King. Carl Sandburg. **CP-SandC**

Named Kovacs went down. A Jockey. Ron Koertge. **SP-KoerR**

Named she was a Smith, born Smith, but how related. Hayden Carruth. *Fr.* The Sleeping Beauty. **CP-CarHL**

Named them / and they danced. Orpheus. Donald Davie. **CP-DavDo**

Nameless. James Dickey. **CP-DickJ**

Nameless Islets. Kathleen Jessie Raine. *Fr.* Eileann Chanaidh. **SP-RainK**

Nameless Speaks, The. Marsden Hartley. **CP-HartM**

Names, The. Robert Browning. **CP-BroR2**

Names. Hayden Carruth. **CP-CarHS**

Names, *ad. fr. the German of* Gotthold Lessing. Samuel Taylor Coleridge. **CP-ColeS**

Names, The. Robert Creeley. **CP-CreeR**

Names. Robert Creeley. **CP-CreeR**

Names, The. Allen Ginsberg. **CP-GinsA**

Names. Robert Earl Hayden. **CP-HaydR**

Names. Derek Walcott. **CP-WalcD**

Names and things named don't match. Essex. Donald Davie. **CP-DavDo**

Names and Travelers of the Milky Way. Siv Cedering Fox. **SP-CedeS**

Names of Horses. Donald Hall. **CP-HallD**

Names of Mexican rivers I forgot, The. Malcolm Lowry. **CP-LowrM**

Names We Used, The. John Hewitt. **CP-HewiJ**

Naming for Love. Hayden Carruth. **CP-CarHS**

Naming the tree. Aromatic. Captain Marvell. Gilbert Sorrentino. **SP-SorrG**

Nana whispers her prayers. Fever. Martin Edmunds. **SP-EdmuM**

Nanao Knows. Gary Snyder. **CP-SnydG**

Nancy Hanks dreams by the fire. Fire-Logs. Carl Sandburg. **CP-SandC**

Nancy, Jimmy, Larry, Frank, & Berdie. Lady. Ted Berrigan. **SP-BerrT**

Nancy where art thou? Ezra Pound. *See* Canto 80: "Ain' committed no federal crime."

Nansen. Gary Snyder. **CP-SnydG**

Nantucket. William Carlos Williams. **CP-WilW1**

Nantucket. John Yau. **SP-YauJo**

Nap. Mona Van Duyn. **SP-VanDM**

Naphtha. Frank O'Hara. **SP-OharF**

Naples. John Ciardi. **SP-CiarJ**

Naples. John Greenleaf Whittier. **CP-WhitJ**

Naples, too credulous, ah! boast no more. John Milton. *See* To the Same ["Why, credulous Naples, do you vaunt your clear-voiced Siren"].

Napoleon. Walter de la Mare. **CP-DeLaW**

Napoleon. Robert Lowell. **SP-LoweR**

Napoléon. George Meredith. **CP-MerG1**
     "Behind the Northern curtain-folds he passed."
     "Bright from the shell of that much limited man."
     "But whom those errant moans accused."
     "Cannon his name."
     "Desire and terror then had each of each."
     "Flood that swept her to be slave, The."
     "He, did he love her? France was his weapon, shrewd."
     "Hugest of engines, a much limited man."
     "On him the long enchained, released."
     "Persistent through the brazen chorus round."
     "Poured streams of Europe's veins the flood."
     "Soon felt she in her shivered frame."
     "To weld the nation in a name of dread."

Napoleon shifted / Restless in the old sarcophagus. Statistics. Carl Sandburg. **CP-SandC**

Napoleon III in Italy. Elizabeth Barrett Browning. **CP-BroEB**

Napoleon!—years ago, and that great word. Crowned and Buried. Elizabeth Barrett Browning. **CP-BroEB**

Napoleon's Farewell. Byron. **CP-Byron**

Napoleon's Snuff-Box. Byron. **CP-Byron**

Napoli Again. Richard Hugo. **CP-HugoR**

Napping in the Shadow of Day. Anne Waldman. **SP-WaldA**

Nara Park: Twilight Deer Feeding. Laurence Lieberman. **SP-LiebL**

Narciss, my numerous cancellations prefer. Basil Bunting. **CP-BuntB**

Narcissism. Tom Clark. **SP-ClarT**

Narcissus. Wystan Hugh Auden. **CP-AudWJ**

Narcissus. Sir John Betjeman. **CP-BetjJ**

Narcissus. David Herbert Lawrence. **CP-LawrD**

Narcissus. May Sarton. **SP-SartM**

Narcissus. Louis Zukofsky. **CP-ZukLS**

Narcissus and the Young Men. James Liddy. **CP-LiddJ**

Narcissus Blues. William Matthews. **SP-MattW**

Narcissus Dreaming. Dabney Stuart. **SP-StuaD**

Narcissus in the Desert. Nicolas Calas, *tr. fr. French by* William Carlos Williams. **CP-WilW1**

Narcissus Moving. John Berryman. **CP-BerrJ**

Narcissus, speaking in the first person. Prologue. Delmore Schwartz. **SP-SchwD**

Narcissus Unbound. William Dickey. **SP-DickW**

Narrative, A. George Oppen. **CP-OppeG**
     "And truth? O, / Truth!"
     "But at night the park."
     "Constant singing / Of the radios, and the art, The."
     "Enclave / Filled with their own, An."
     "I am the father of no country."
     "I saw from the bus."
     "It is a place."
     "Lights / Shine, the fire, The."
     "River of our substance."
     "Serpent, Ouroboros / Whose tail is in his mouth: he is the root."
     "Some of the young men."

Narrator. Wystan Hugh Auden. *See* Well, so that is that. Now we must dismantle the tree.

Narrow backyard garden, The. Hermes and Mr Shaw. Donald Davie. **CP-DavDo**

Narrow Escape, A. James Merrill. **SP-MerrJ**

Narrow Fellow in the Grass, A. Emily Dickinson. **CP-DickE**

Narrow girdle of rough stones and crags, A. William Wordsworth. **CP-WorW1**

Narrow lanes are vacant and wet, The. Storm. Robert Louis Stevenson. **CP-StevR**

Narrow Sea, The. Robert Ranke Graves. **CP-GravR**

Narrow Way, The. William Cowper. *Fr.* Olney Hymns. **CP-CowpW**

Narrowing life because of the fears. For My Sister, against Narrowness. Erica Jong. **SP-JongE**

Narrowing line. / Walking on the burning ground, The. What Is the Beautiful? Kenneth Patchen. **CP-PatcK**

Narrows, The. Jim Carroll. **SP-CarrJ**

Narrows of Birth, The. William Everson. **SP-EverW**

Nasal whine of power whips a new universe. Hart Crane. **MoAB; MoAmPo** *Fr.* Cape Hatteras. **InPS; MoAB; MoAmPo** *Fr.* The Bridge. **CP-CranH**

(Power.) **MoAmPo**

Nashe's old queens who bartered young and fair. Lament. Richard Wilbur. **CP-WilbR**

Nashville Mornings. Donald Davie. **CP-DavDo**

Nasnas. Lewis Turco. **SP-TurcL**

Naso! an elevated personage. Carmen 112. Catullus. *Fr.* Carmina. **CP-Catul**

Naso, you are many men's man; and yet. Catullus. *See* Carmen 112: "Naso! an elevated personage."

Nasturtium. Thom Gunn. **CP-GunnT**

Nasty surprise in a sandwich, A. God, A Poem. James Fenton. **SP-FentJ**

Nat Bacon's Bones. Archibald MacLeish. **CP-MacLA**

Natcha. Langston Hughes. **SP-HughL**

Nathaniel Hawthorne. Robert Creeley. **CP-CreeR**

Nation, The. Roy Fisher. **SP-FishR**

Nation spoke to a Nation, A. Our Lady of the Snows. Rudyard Kipling. **CP-KiplR**

National day, The. The Nation. Roy Fisher. **SP-FishR**

National Gallery, The. Louis MacNeice. **CP-MacNL**

National Security. Archibald MacLeish. **CP-MacLA**

National Winter Garden. Hart Crane. **ErPo; InPS; LiTM; NAAL-2; OxBA** *Fr.* Three Songs. **NAAL-2** *Fr.* The Bridge. **CP-CranH**

Nationality in Drinks. Robert Browning. **CP-BroR1**

Nations have used up their desire, The. Madder. Charles Kenneth Williams. **CP-WillC**

Nations ten thousand years before these States, and many times ten thousand years before these States. Unnamed Lands. Walt Whitman. **CP-WhitW**

Native-Born, The. Rudyard Kipling. **CP-KiplR**

Native Moments. Walt Whitman. **CP-WhitW**

Native of Afric's arid lands. To a Geranium Which Flowered during the Winter. Charlotte Smith. **CP-SmitC**

Native Water-Carrier (M.E.F.) Rudyard Kipling. *Fr.* Epitaphs of the War [1914–1918]. **CP-KiplR**

Natives. Archie Randolph Ammons. **SP-AmmoA**

Natives here have given up their backyards, The. Champagne. Rita Dove. **SP-DoveR**

Nativity [*or* Nativitie]. John Donne. *Fr.* La Corona. **ChIV-2; ESCV; OBS; Son** *Fr.* Holy Sonnets. **CP-DonnJ**

Nativity, The. Jeanne Marie Bouvier de la Motte-Guyon, *tr. fr. French by* William Cowper. **CP-CowpW**

Nativity, A. Rudyard Kipling. **CP-KiplR**

Nativity. May Sarton. **SP-SartM**

Nativity, A. William Butler Yeats. **CP-YeatW**

Nativity of Christ[e], The. Robert Southwell. **CP-SoutR**

Nativity of Our Lord, The. Christopher Smart. *See* The Nativity of Our Lord and Saviour Jesus Christ.

Nativity of Our Lord and Saviour Jesus Christ, The. Christopher Smart. **NOCV; SBVL** *Fr.* Hymns and Spiritual Songs for the Fasts and Festivals of the Church of England. **SP-SmarC**

(Hymn: "Nativity of Our Lord and Saviour Jesus Christ, The.") **NAs; NOEC**

(Nativity of Our Lord, The.) **EBEV; HAP; LAuP; LoBV; NOBE; PoEL-3; SCGP; WeW**

Christmas Day. **ChTr; OBCP**

Nativity of St. John the Baptist, The. Christopher Smart. **ChIV-2** *Fr.* Hymns and Spiritual Songs for the Fasts and Festivals of the Church of England. **SP-SmarC**

Nativity Poem. Louise Glück. **SP-GlücL**

Natur / aabho / rrret / vacuu / uuuum. Thomas Merton. *Fr.* A Selection of Concrete Poems. **CP-MertT**

Natura Naturans. Arthur Hugh Clough. **SP-ClouA**

Natura Naturans. Kathleen Jessie Raine. **SP-RainK**

Natural Complexion. David Herbert Lawrence. **CP-LawrD**

Natural History. Thomas Merton. **CP-MertT**

Natural History. Sylvia Plath. **CP-PlatS**

Natural History. Robert Penn Warren. **SP-WarrR**

Natural History I. Robert Penn Warren. **SP-WarrR**

Natural Linguistics. Wystan Hugh Auden. **CP-AudeW**

Natural Magic. Robert Browning. **CP-BroR2**

Natural Music. Robinson Jeffers. **CP-JefR1**

Natural Philosopher, A. Daniel Gerard Hoffman. **SP-HoffD**

Natural Question. John Updike. **CP-UpdiJ**

Natural Resources. Adrienne Rich. **SP-RicA2**

Natural Star. Alice Walker. **CP-WalkA**

Natural strange beatitudes. Cycle. Geoffrey Hill. **CP-HillG**

Natural Theology. Rudyard Kipling. **CP-KiplR**

Naturally. Stephen Dunn. **SP-DunnS**

Naturally tender, flesh and such. Under the Skin of It. Gary Snyder. **CP-SnydG**

Naturally the Foundation Will Bear Your Expenses. Philip Larkin. **CP-LarkP**

Nature ("Day by day for her darlings to her much she added more"). Ralph Waldo Emerson. **CP-EmerR**

Nature. Ralph Waldo Emerson. *Fr.* Quatrains. **CP-EmerR**

Nature. Marsden Hartley. **CP-HartM**

Nature. George Herbert. **CP-HerbG**

Nature. Henry Wadsworth Longfellow. **SP-LongH**

Nature. Mary Oliver. **SP-OlivM**

Nature. John Updike. **CP-UpdiJ**

Nature 1 ("Winters know / Easily to shed the snow"). Ralph Waldo Emerson. **CP-EmerR**

Nature 2 ("She is gamesome and good"). Ralph Waldo Emerson. **CP-EmerR**

Nature affects to be sedate. Emily Dickinson. **CP-DickE**

Nature Alive. Jorge Guillén, *tr. fr. Spanish by* James Wright. **CP-WrigJ**

Nature and Art. Paul Laurence Dunbar. **CP-DunbP**

Nature & Art in this together Suit. A Pretty Epigram for [Those] the Entertainment of Those Who [Pay] Have Paid Great Sums in the Venetian & Flemish Ooze. William Blake. **CP-BlakW**

Nature and Free Animals. Stevie Smith. **CP-SmitS**

Nature and God—I neither knew. Emily Dickinson. **CP-DickE**

Nature and Life. George Meredith. **CP-MerG1**

Nature and Man. George Meredith. **CP-MerG2**

Nature and Nature's Laws lay hid in Night. Alexander Pope. **CP-PopeA** (Epitaph Intended for Sir Isaac Newton, in Westminster Abbey.) **CP-PopeA**

Nature assigns the Sun. Emily Dickinson. **CP-DickE**

Nature, by nature, has no answers. Saturday Morning Journal. Charles Wright. **SP-WrigC**

Nature can do no more. Emily Dickinson. **CP-DickE**

Nature centres into balls. Ralph Waldo Emerson. **CP-EmerR** (Motto to "Circles.") **CP-EmerR**

Nature Does Not Suffer Decay. John Milton, *tr. fr. Latin by* John T. Shawcross. **CP-MiltJ** ("Ah, how the human mind wearies her self.") **CP-CowpW**, *tr. by* William Cowper; (Nature Unimpaired by Time.) **CP-CowpW**, *tr. by* William Cowper;

Nature from life by piece and piece. Of Experience. Howard Nemerov. **CP-NemeH**

Nature gives her love. Emily Dickinson. **SP-DickE**

Nature had long a treasure made. The Match. Andrew Marvell. **CP-MarvA**

Nature had made them hide in crevices. New Hampshire, February. Richard Eberhart. **CP-EberR**

Nature has bought the steeple. In a Country Churchyard. Wystan Hugh Auden. **CP-AudWJ**

Nature here / is the multiplicity of luck. The Mirror in the Roadway. Charles Tomlinson. **CP-TomlC**

Nature in Leasts. Ralph Waldo Emerson. *Fr.* Quatrains. **CP-EmerR**

Nature invades: old rooks in each college garden. Oxford. Wystan Hugh Auden. **CP-AudeW**

Nature is a church where the pillars. Correspondences. James Liddy. **CP-LiddJ**

Nature is a Haunted House. Emily Dickinson. **SP-DickE**

Nature is full of teeth. The Wall. Anne Sexton. **CP-SextA**

Nature is our eldest mother. Emily Dickinson. **SP-DickE**

Nature is out there as. A Theory of the Universe. Tom Clark. **SP-ClarT**

"Nature" is what we see. Emily Dickinson. **CP-DickE**

Nature Knows Best. Ogden Nash. **CP-NashO**

Nature loves to hide. Thomas Merton. *Fr.* The Legacy of Herakleitos. **CP-MertT**

Nature Morte. Louis MacNeice. **CP-MacNL**

Nature Morte. Howard Nemerov. **CP-NemeH**

Nature must be too young to feel. Emily Dickinson. **SP-DickE**

Nature Note, A. Robert Frost. **CP-FrosR**

Nature Notes. Louis MacNeice. **CP-MacNL**
Cats.
Corncrakes.
Dandelions.
Sea, The.

Nature of a Mirror, The. Robert Penn Warren. **SP-WarrR**

Nature of an Action, The. Thom Gunn. **CP-GunnT**

Nature of This City, The. Grace Paley. **CP-PaleG**

Nature of This Flower Is to Bloom, The. Alice Walker. **CP-WalkA**

Nature Poem. Charles Tomlinson. **CP-TomlC**

Nature rarer uses Yellow. Emily Dickinson. **CP-DickE**

Nature responds so beautifully. Roses. David Herbert Lawrence. **CP-LawrD**

Nature saith / I am not infinite. Ralph Waldo Emerson. **CP-EmerR**

Nature says, / These craggy hills that front the dawn. Ralph Waldo Emerson. **CP-EmerR**

Nature seemed monstrous to his thirteen years. Orient and Immortal Wheat. Derek Walcott. **CP-WalcD**

Nature, seems in to myself. Emily Dickinson. **SP-DickE**

Nature, so far as in her lies. On a Mourner. Tennyson. **CP-TennA**

Nature—sometimes sears a Sapling. Emily Dickinson. **CP-DickE**

Nature that gave the bee so feat a grace. Sir Thomas Wyatt. **CP-WyatT**

Nature that washt her hands in milke. A Poem of Sir Walter Rawleighs. Sir Walter Ralegh. **CP-RaleW**

Nature—the Gentlest Mother is. Emily Dickinson. **CP-DickE**

Nature, through these generations. Genitrix Laesa. Thomas Hardy. **CP-HardT**

Nature Unimpaired by Time. John Milton. *See* Nature Does Not Suffer Decay.

Nature-Walks, or, Not to Mention a Dopping of Sheldrakes. Ogden Nash. **CP-NashO**

    Abominable Snowman, The.

    Manatee, The.

    Ostrich, The.

    Praying Mantis, The.

    Squab, The.

    Squid, The.

Nature will not lose. Ralph Waldo Emerson. **CP-EmerR**

Nature withheld Cassandra in the skies. Pierre de Ronsard, *tr. fr. French by* Keats. **CP-KeatJ**

(Translated from Ronsard.) **CP-KeatJ**

Nature within her inmost self divides. From Iron. Robert Frost. **CP-FrosR**

Nature's decorations glisten. Christmas Day. Christopher Smart. **ChTr; OBCP** *Fr.* The Nativity of Our Lord and Saviour Jesus Christ. **NOCV; SBVL** *Fr.* Hymns and Spiritual Songs for the Fasts and Festivals of the Church of England. **SP-SmarC**

Nature's faithful Blossoms. Emily Dickinson. **SP-DickE**

Nature's first green is gold. Nothing Gold Can Stay. Robert Frost. **CP-FrosR**

Nature's Law. Robert Burns. **CP-BurnR**

Nature's lay idiot [or Ideot], I taught thee to love. John Donne. **CBLP; NoP; OXAEP-1; PeLV; SeCP** *Fr.* Elegies. **CP-DonnJ**

(Elegie: "Nature's lay ideot, I taught thee to love.") **OXAEP-1; SeCP**

Nature's Lineaments. Robert Ranke Graves. **CP-GravR**

Nature's Questioning. Thomas Hardy. **CP-HardT**

Nature's Remorses. Elizabeth Barrett Browning. **CP-BroEB**

Nature's Reply to Mutability. Edmund Spenser. **NOBE** *Fr.* The Faerie Queene. **CP-Spens**

Nature's undoings / let. Scarecrow. Archie Randolph Ammons. **SP-AmmoA**

Natures web star broidered. Ralph Waldo Emerson. **CP-EmerR**

Naught are all Women: I say no. A Defence for Women. Robert Herrick. **CP-HerrR**

Naughty Boy. Robert Creeley. **CP-CreeR**

Nauhaught, the Deacon. John Greenleaf Whittier. **CP-WhitJ**

Naulahka, The. Rudyard Kipling.

    "Beat off in our last fight were we?" **CP-KiplR**

    "Because I sought it far from men." **CP-KiplR**

    "Beware the man who's crossed in love." **CP-KiplR**

    Kingdom, The. **CP-KiplR**

    My Lady's Law. **CP-KiplR**

    "Now it is not good for the Christian's health to hustle the Aryan brown." **CP-KiplR**

    Nursing Sister, The. **CP-KiplR**

    Sack of the Gods, The. **CP-KiplR**

    "There is pleasure in the wet, wet clay." **CP-KiplR**

    "There was a strife 'twixt man and maid." **CP-KiplR**

    "This I saw when the rites were done." **CP-KiplR**

    "We be the Gods of the East." **CP-KiplR**

    "We meet in an evil land." **CP-KiplR**

    "When a lover hies abroad." **CP-KiplR**

    "Will they gape for the husks that ye proffer." **CP-KiplR**

    "Your patience, Sirs. The Devil took me up." **CP-KiplR**

Nauset Billerica — to get the fid in. The Encounter. Charles Olson. **CP-OlsoC**

Nautilus Island's hermit. Skunk Hour. Robert Lowell. **SP-LoweR**

Navajo. William Carlos Williams. **CP-WilW2**

Navajo Setting the Record Straight. John Berryman. **CP-BerrJ**

Navajo Song. Richard Shelton. **SP-ShelR**

Navigator. Charles Simic. **SP-SimiC**

Navigators, The. Marilyn Hacker.

    "Across the mud flats and the wide roads, over rivers and borders." **SP-HackM**

    "Between us on our wide bed we cuddle an incubus." **SP-HackM**

    His Wife at Bellevue. **SP-HackM**

    "Orpheus and animus, / drawing back to journeys now." **SP-HackM**

    "When you told me that he was in jail." **SP-HackM**

    "You made algebra: his tastes in food." **SP-HackM**

Nay, but I fancy somehow, year by year. Robert Louis Stevenson. **CP-StevR**

Nay but you, who do not love her. Song. Robert Browning. **CP-BroR1**

Nay, cheer up sister. Life is not quite over. October. Christina Georgina Rossetti. *Fr.* The Months: A Pageant. **CP-RosC2**

Nay Cousin, Dearest. Elixir. David Herbert Lawrence. **CP-LawrD**

Nay, dearest Anna! why so grave? To a Lady. Samuel Taylor Coleridge. **CP-ColeS**

Nay, do not dream, designer dark. Death's Valley. Walt Whitman. **CP-WhitW**

Nay draw not yet the cork, my friend. Arthur Hugh Clough. **SP-ClouA**

Nay, if I had come back so. Where's Agnes? Elizabeth Barrett Browning. **CP-BroEB**

Nay, lady, sit; if I but wave this wand. John Milton. **OxAEP-1** *Fr.* A Mask. **OxAEP-1** *Fr.* Comus; a Masque Presented at Ludlow Castle.

Nay, learnèd doctor, these fine leeches fresh. Edna St. Vincent Millay. **CP-MillE**

Nay, nay, / You must not stay. Ben Jonson. **CP-JonsB** *Fr.* Oberon, the Fairy Prince.

Nay, no closed doors for me. December. Christina Georgina Rossetti. *Fr.* The Months: A Pageant. **CP-RosC2**

Nay, prethee [*or* prithee] dear, draw nigher. Loose Saraband, A. Richard Lovelace. **CP-LoveR**

Nay, read & spare not, Passenger. Epitaph on a Man who Had a Scold to His Wife. Robert Herrick. **CP-HerrR**

Nay, Tell Me Not To-day the Publish'd Shame. Walt Whitman. **CP-WhitW**

Nay, that, Furini, never I at least. With Francis Furini. Robert Browning. **CP-BroR2**

Nay, Traveller! rest. This lonely Yew-tree stands. Lines. William Wordsworth. **CP-WorW1**

Nazi Amphitheatre, The. Erica Jong. **SP-JongE**

Nazi within me thinks it's time to take charge, The. Confession. Stephen Dobyns. **SP-DobyS**

Ndebele. Alice Walker. **CP-WalkA**

Ne manquez pas à Stuttgart. Samuel Beckett. **CP-BeckS**

Ne manquez pas à Tanger. Samuel Beckett. **CP-BeckS**

Ne Plus Ultra. Samuel Taylor Coleridge. **CP-ColeS**

Ne Sit Ancillae Tibi Amor Pudori. Robert Louis Stevenson. **CP-StevR**

Ne' sogni ti veggo. Christina Georgina Rossetti. **CP-RosC3**

Ne thence the Irishe Rivers absent were. The Rivers of Ireland. Edmund Spenser. **CBCK** *Fr.* The Faerie Queene. **CP-Spens**

Ne tu me crudelis ames, nec basia labris. *acc. by English translation.* Thomas Campion. **CP-CampT**

Neal Cassady was my animal: he brought me to my knees. Many Loves. Allen Ginsberg. **CP-GinsA**

Neanderthal Poem, "Ah," Number One. Robert Pack. **SP-PackR**

Neapolitan John Baptist Manso, The. *Unknown. Fr.* Complimentary Pieces to Milton. **CP-CowpW**

Near. William Stafford. **SP-StafW**

Near Addison now. Hayden Carruth. *Fr.* The Sleeping Beauty. **CP-CarHL**

Near and the Far, The. Charles Tomlinson. **CP-TomlC**

Near Anio's stream, I spied a gentle Dove. William Wordsworth. *Fr.* Memorials of a Tour in Italy, 1837. **CP-WorW2**

Near Ceibwr. Charles Tomlinson. **CP-TomlC**

Near Corinium. Charles Tomlinson. **CP-TomlC**

Near Darien. James Dickey. **CP-DickJ**

Near dusk: approaching. Catch. Archie Randolph Ammons. **SP-AmmoA**

Near Eclipse, The. Robert Ranke Graves. **CP-GravR**

Near, far, unearthly, break the birds. Dawn. Walter de la Mare. **CP-DeLaW**

Near Garmsley Camp. Roy Fisher. **SP-FishR**

Near Hartland. Charles Tomlinson. **CP-TomlC**

Near Kalalock. Richard Hugo. **CP-HugoR**

Near Keokuk. Carl Sandburg. **CP-SandC**

Near Lanivet, 1872. Thomas Hardy. **CP-HardT**

Near Mexico, near April, in the morning. Target Practice. Muriel Rukeyser. **CP-RukeM**

Near Old Fort Pike on the Des Moines River. Chuck Miller. **SP-MillC**

Near Pah-Gotzin-Kay. Thomas McGrath. **SP-McGrT**

Near Perigord. Ezra Pound. **SP-PounE**

Near Rome, in Sight of St Peter's. William Wordsworth. *Fr.* Memorials of a Tour in Italy, 1837. **Fr.**

Near the Black Forest. Erica Jong. **SP-JongE**

Near the celebrated Lido where the breeze is fresh and free. Longfellow's Visit to Venice. Sir John Betjeman. **CP-BetjJ**

Near the dry river's water-mark we found. A Note Left in Jimmy Leonard's Shack. James Wright. **CP-WrigJ**

Near the Finish. James McAuley. *Fr.* Ten-Mile Run. **SP-McAuJ**

Near the Giant's House. Robert Bly. **SP-BlyR**

Near the Haunted Castle. Charles Kenneth Williams. **CP-WillC; SP-WillC**

Near the Lake of Thrasymene. William Wordsworth. *Fr.* Memorials of a Tour in Italy, 1837. **CP-WorW2**

Near the lone pile with ivy overspread. Elegy Imitated from One of Akenside's Blank-Verse Inscriptions. Samuel Taylor Coleridge. **CP-ColeS**

Near the Ocean. Robert Lowell. **SP-LoweR**

Near the Old People's Home. Howard Nemerov. **CP-NemeH**

Near the Same Lake [Thrasymene]. William Wordsworth. *Fr.* Memorials of a Tour in Italy, 1837. **CP-WorW2**

Near the Spring of the Hermitage. William Wordsworth. *Fr.* Inscriptions Supposed to Be Found in and near a Hermit's Cell; 1818. **CP-WorW2**

Near the top a bad turn some dare. Well. Whether There Is Sorrow in the Demons. John Berryman. **CP-BerrJ**

Near the waterfront / Mouth of a wide shed open. Burnishing, Oakland. Muriel Rukeyser. **CP-RukeM**

Near Things. Leonard Nathan. **SP-NathL**

Near to me as my flesh, my flesh and blood. Allen Tate. *See* Near to me as perfection in the blood.

Near to me as perfection in the blood. Allen Tate. *Fr.* Sonnets of the Blood. **CP-TateA**

("Near to me as my flesh, my flesh and blood.") **PoA**

Near to the bank of the river, o'ershadowed by oaks, from whose branches, *sels.* Henry Wadsworth Longfellow. *Fr.* Part the Second. *Fr.* Evangeline, a Tale of Acadie. **SP-LongH**

Near York. Charles Tomlinson. **CP-TomlC**

Nearer my God to rock of eyes. Hymns of Lograire. Thomas Merton. *Fr.* South. *Fr.* The Geography of Lograire. **CP-MertT**

Nearer:breath of my breath:take not thy tingling. Edward Estlin Cummings. **CP-CummE**

Nearest Dream recedes—unrealized, The. Emily Dickinson. **CP-DickE**

Nearing Equinox. Archie Randolph Ammons. **SP-AmmoA**

Nearing Forty. Derek Walcott. **CP-WalcD**

Nearing land, we heard the cry of gulls and. Death by Water. Edwin Rolfe. **CP-RolfE**

Nearly all the rivers color like the sky. Introduction to the Hoh. Richard Hugo. **CP-HugoR**

Nearly friendless, with only a few years to live. Cézanne's Love of Poetry. Stephen Dobyns. **SP-DobyS**

Nearly right, The. To the Tune of the Coventry Carol. Stevie Smith. **CP-SmitS**

Nearness. Steve Griffiths. **SP-GrifS**

Nearness of remoteness like a lion's eye, The. The Revenant. Louis MacNeice. **CP-MacNL**

Nearness to Tremendousness, A. Emily Dickinson. **CP-DickE**

Neat person. Shang Dynasty Oracle Bone 2 Say. Charles Olson. **CP-OlsoC**

Neath blue-bell or streamer. Song. Edgar Allan Poe. **AmPP; AnAmPo; OxBA** *Fr.* Song: "Young flowers were whispering in melody." **NOBA** *Fr.* Al Aaraaf. **CP-PoeEd**

'Neath my moon what doest thou. Night and the Merry Man. Elizabeth Barrett Browning. **CP-BroEB**

'Neath skies that winter never knew. "I Was a Stranger and Ye Took Me in." John Greenleaf Whittier. **CP-WhitJ**

Nebraska. Karl Shapiro. **SP-ShapK**

Nebuchadnezzar, Solus. Howard Nemerov. **CP-NemeH**

Nebuchadnezzar's Dream. John Keats. **CP-KeatJ**

Nebula. John Hewitt. **CP-HewiJ**

Nebulous, freezingly moist. Winter's Talents. Donald Davie. **CP-DavDo**

Necessaries. Roy Fisher. **SP-FishR**

Necessarily, we must think of the. Interjection #2: Caveat. Robert Penn Warren. **SP-WarrR**

Necessary Dirge, A. Ogden Nash. **CP-NashO**

Necessitarian, The. Rudyard Kipling. **CP-KiplR**

Necessitarian's Epitaph, A. Thomas Hardy. **CP-HardT**

Necessities of Life. Adrienne Rich. **CP-RicAE; SP-RicA1; SP-RicA2**

Necessity. Richard Eberhart. **CP-EberR**

Necessity. Langston Hughes. **SP-HughL**

Necessity, The. Denise Levertov. **CP-LeveD**

Necessity knows no Speech. Not even. A Short Ode to a Philologist. Wystan Hugh Auden. *Fr.* Eleven Occasional Poems. **CP-AudeW**

Necessity of Faith, The. Wendell Berry. **CP-BerrW**

Necessity of Self-Abasement. Jeanne Marie Bouvier de la Motte-Guyon, *tr. fr. French by* William Cowper. **CP-CowpW**

Necessity of Writing in This Tongue, The. James Liddy. **CP-LiddJ**

Necessity of writing in this tongue, The. The Slovak Tongue. James Liddy. **CP-LiddJ**

Neck of, The. The Real. Charles Olson. **CP-OlsoC**

Neck of an hour-glass on its side—. Louis MacNeice. *Fr.* The Window. **CP-MacNL**

Necklace, The. Robert Ranke Graves. **CP-GravR**

Necrological. John Crowe Ransom. **SP-RansJ**

Necropolis. Karl Shapiro. **SP-ShapK**

Ned Bratts. Robert Browning. **CP-BroR2**

Ned Skinner. Paul Muldoon. **SP-MuldP**

Need. Robert Herrick. **CP-HerrR**

Need: A Chorale for Black Woman Voices. Audre Lorde. **SP-LordA**

Need a Woman. "Bob Dylan." **CP-DylaB**

Need for Dictionaries II, The. Thomas McGrath. **SP-McGrT**

Need for Stoicism in the Stoa of Attalus, The. Thomas McGrath. **SP-McGrT**

Need is no vice at all; though here it be. Want. Robert Herrick. **CP-HerrR**

Need it be so niggardly of meaning too? Malcolm Lowry. **CP-LowrM**

Need of Being Versed in Country Things, The. Robert Frost. **CP-FrosR**

Need of this man was her ignoble secret:. Lamia in Love. Robert Ranke Graves. **CP-GravR**

Need to Win, The. Chuang Tzu, *tr. fr. Chinese by* Thomas Merton. **CP-MertT**

Needing one, I invented her. Aunt Leaf. Mary Oliver. **SP-OlivM**

Needle-point's swaying reminder, The. The Way In. Charles Tomlinson. **CP-TomlC**

Needle small, as small can be, A. An Ænigma. Vincent Bourne, *tr. fr. Latin by* William Cowper. **CP-CowpW**

Needle's Eye, A. William Butler Yeats. **CP-YeatW**

Needle's Eye, the Lens, The. William Matthews. **SP-MattW**

Needless Alarm, The. William Cowper. **CP-CowpW**

Needless Worry. Ralph Waldo Emerson. *See* Borrowing from the French.

Needs most / happily mutual. Night. Robert Creeley. **CP-CreeR**

Needsong. Brendan Galvin. **SP-GalvB**

Negation. Wallace Stevens. **CP-StevW**

Negation is the spectre, the reasoning power in man, The. Reason and Imagination. William Blake. **EnRP** *Fr.* Milton. **CP-BlakW**

Negative Hands. Pablo Neruda, *tr. fr. Spanish by* Ben Belitt. **SP-NeruP**

Negative Indicative. Philip Larkin. **CP-LarkP**

Negative Love. John Donne. **CP-DonnJ**

Negative Virtues, The. Richard Shelton. **SP-ShelR**

Negatives. Derek Walcott. **CP-WalcD**

Neglect. Robert Herrick. **CP-HerrR**

Neglect. Charles Kenneth Williams. **SP-WillC**

Neglected Lane, The. John Hewitt. **CP-HewiJ**

Negligence These Days. Archie Randolph Ammons. **SP-AmmoA**

Negress serene though underground. Eurydice. John Updike. **CP-UpdiJ**

Negro. Langston Hughes. **SP-HughL**

Negro, / With the trumpet at his lips, The. Trumpet Player. Langston Hughes. **SP-HughL**

Negro Cemetery Next to a White One, A. Howard Nemerov. **CP-NemeH**

Negro Hero. Gwendolyn Brooks. **SP-BrooG**

Negro holds firmly the reins of his four horses, The. The Drayman. Walt Whitman. **PoNe** *Fr.* Song of Myself. **CP-WhitW**

Negro Love Song, A. Paul Laurence Dunbar. **CP-DunbP**

Negro Mother, The. Langston Hughes. **SP-HughL**

Negro Mother's Lullaby, A. Countee Cullen. **CP-CullC**

Negro rich are nigger rich, The. The Road to Avallon. Ernest Hemingway. **CP-HemiE**

Negro Sermon—Simon Legree, A. Nicholas Vachel Lindsay. *See* Simon Legree—A Negro Sermon.

Negro Speaks of Rivers, The. Langston Hughes. **SP-HughL**

Negro Woman, A. William Carlos Williams. **CP-WilW2**

Negroes, / Sweet and docile. Roland Hayes Beaten (Georgia: 1942). Langston Hughes. **SP-HughL**

Negro's Complaint, The. William Cowper. **CP-CowpW**

Neighbor. Langston Hughes. **SP-HughL**

Neighbor. Richard Hugo. **CP-HugoR**

Neighbor, The. Marge Piercy. **SP-PierM**

Neighbor of mine in the village, A. A Girl's Garden. Robert Frost. **CP-FrosR**

Neighborhood Bully. "Bob Dylan." **CP-DylaB**

Neighbors. Audre Lorde. **SP-LordA**

Neighbors. Edwin Arlington Robinson. **CP-RobiE**

Neighbors. Carl Sandburg. **CP-SandC**

Neighbor's Funeral, A. John Hewitt. **CP-HewiJ**

Neighbours. Rudyard Kipling. **CP-KiplR**

Neighbours gathered to pull the lint, The. The Lint Pulling. John Hewitt. **CP-HewiJ**

Neither an Elegy Nor a Manifesto. John Hewitt. **CP-HewiJ**

Neither awake / (there's your general). Edward Estlin Cummings. **CP-CummE**

Neither buskin now, nor bayes. Thomas Campion. *Fr.* Lord Hay's Mask.

Neither childhood / nor future. Confession. George Oppen. **CP-OppeG**

Neither could say / (it comes so slow). Edward Estlin Cummings. **CP-CummE**

Neither dead nor alive, neither asleep nor awake. Revenge for Love. Donald Davie. **CP-DavDo**

Neither fearing Extinction. Emily Dickinson. **SP-DickE**

Neither her voice, her name. The Night Dream. Archibald MacLeish. **CP-MacLA**

Neither in Heaven nor Earth. Emily Dickinson. **SP-DickE**

Neither Moth Nor Rust. David Herbert Lawrence. *Fr.* Bits. **CP-LawrD**

Neither of them was better than the other. From Plane to Plane. Robert Frost. **CP-FrosR**

Neither our vices nor our virtues. Poetry, a Natural Thing. Robert Duncan. **SP-DuncR**

Neither Out Far nor In Deep. Robert Frost. **CP-FrosR**

Neither rose leaves gathered in a jar—respectably in Boston—these—nor. Whirls. Carl Sandburg. **CP-SandC**

Neither sadness nor desire. Robert Creeley. **CP-CreeR**

Neither the harps nor the crowns amused, nor the cherubs' dove-winged races. The Return of the Children. Rudyard Kipling. **CP-KiplR**

Neither wife nor child had Mr. Eastman and the manner of his death. Carl Sandburg. *Fr.* The People, Yes. **CP-SandC**

Nel Mezzo del Cammin di Nostra Vita. Robert Duncan. **SP-DuncR**

Nel verno accanto al fuoco. Christina Georgina Rossetti. **CP-RosC3**

Nell and the other maids danced their best. The Harvest-Supper. Thomas Hardy. **CP-HardT**

Nell Gwyn, / It says in the dictionary. The King! William Carlos Williams. **CP-WilW2**

Nell scolded in so loud a din. A Quiet Life and a Good Name. Jonathan Swift. **CP-SwifJ**

Nelson stands on a black pillar. Louis MacNeice. *Fr.* Autumn Journal. **CP-MacNL**

Week to Christmas, A. **TIRV**

Nemesis. Ralph Waldo Emerson. **CP-EmerR**

Nemesis. David Herbert Lawrence. **CP-LawrD**

Nempe ea formosa est: adeo omne quod aut facit aut fit. Incomplete Latin Version of "In all things beautiful" by Robert Bridges. Robert Bridges, *tr. fr. English by* Gerard Manley Hopkins. **CP-HopkG**

Nempe sic innumero succrescunt agmine libri. *see also* To His Worthy Friend Doctor Witty upon His Translation of the "Popular Errors." Andrew Marvell. **CP-MarvA**

Neo Boy. Patti Smith. **SP-SmitP**

Neo-Classical Urn, The. Robert Lowell. **SP-LoweR**

Neon Signs. Langston Hughes. **CP-HughL**

Neons flash red and green. Indiana Avenue, 1949. Etheridge Knight. *Fr.* Indiana Haiku. **SP-KnigE**

Neothomist Poem. Ernest Hemingway. **CP-HemiE**

Neotony. John Updike. **CP-UpdiJ**

Nepenthe. Charlotte Smith. **CP-SmitC**

Neptune's Little Affair with Freedom. David Herbert Lawrence. *Fr.* Songs I Learnt at School. **CP-LawrD**

Neptune's Triumph. Ben Jonson.

"Come, noble nymphs, and do not hide." **CP-JonsB**

Nero commanded; but withdrew his eyes. Cruelties. Robert Herrick. **CP-HerrR**

Neruda, the Wine. Muriel Rukeyser. **CP-RukeM**

Neruda's "Que dispierte el leñador", Ad. fr. Allen Ginsberg. **CP-GinsA**

Nerve us with patience, Lord, to toil or rest. Where Neither Rust Nor Moth Doth Corrupt. Christina Georgina Rossetti. **CP-RosC2**

Nerves. Robinson Jeffers. **CP-JefR3**

Nerves Are Staves, and When the Tears Come There Is Voice, The. Charles Olson. **CP-OlsoC**

Nervous face of my dear wife, The. The Devil-My-Wife. Stevie Smith. **CP-SmitS**

Nervous smile as gaze meets, A. Face to Face. Denise Levertov. **CP-LeveD**

Nervousness of Memory, The. Kenneth Patchen. **CP-PatcK**

Nervy with neons, the main drag. At Barstow. Charles Tomlinson. **CP-TomlC**

Ness. Richard Hugo. **CP-HugoR**

N'est-ce pas assez de ne me point haïr? Stevie Smith. **CP-SmitS**

Nest Eggs. Robert Louis Stevenson. **CP-StevR**

Nest of Vampires. James Fenton. **SP-FentJ**

Nesting-Ground. Seamus Heaney. **SP-HeanS**

Nestor's Bathtub. Rita Dove. **SP-DoveR**

Nestus Gurley. Randall Jarrell. **CP-JarrR; SP-JarrR**

Net-Menders, The. Sylvia Plath. **CP-PlatS**

Net to Snare the Moonlight, A. Nicholas Vachel Lindsay. **CP-LindV**

Netherlands, The. Samuel Taylor Coleridge. **CP-ColeS**

Nettles, The. Thomas Hardy. **CP-HardT**

Nettles of Offence. John Hewitt. **CP-HewiJ**

Network that emerges. At the ocean, A. Muriel Rukeyser. **CP-RukeM**

Neumático punturado—we stopped. John Updike. *Fr.* Spanish Sonnets. **CP-UpdiJ**

Neurotic demon, / Trying to convince himself. Charles Henri Ford. **SP-FordC** *Fr.* Emblems of Arachne.

Neurotics. Philip Larkin. **CP-LarkP**

Neuter your hair tugged back. Under the Sunlamp. John Updike. *Fr.* Living with a Wife. **CP-UpdiJ**

Neutral island facing the Atlantic, The. Neutrality. Louis MacNeice. **CP-MacNL**

Neutral Tones. Thomas Hardy. **CP-HardT**

Neutrality. Louis MacNeice. **CP-MacNL**

Neutrality Loathsome. Robert Herrick. **CP-HerrR**

Neutrals, The. Robinson Jeffers. **CP-JefR3**

Neutrinos. Robert Pack. **SP-PackR**

Neutrinos, they are very small. Cosmic Gall. John Updike. **CP-UpdiJ**

Never a careworn wife but shows. Wives in the Sere. Thomas Hardy. **CP-HardT**

Never Again. Stevie Smith. **CP-SmitS**

Never again / When the heat overwhelms us. Long Hot Summer. Archibald MacLeish. **CP-MacLA**

Never again remind me of it. Bank Account. Robert Ranke Graves. **CP-GravR**

Never Again Would Birds' Song Be the Same. Robert Frost. **CP-FrosR**

Never alone / While over unending sky. Cloud. Kathleen Jessie Raine. **SP-RainK**

Never and never, my girl riding far and near. In Country Sleep. Dylan Thomas. **CP-ThomD**

Never any more. In a Year. Robert Browning. **CP-BroR1**

Never ask of money spent. The Hardship of Accounting. Robert Frost. **FaBoCh; FaBoCo; FaFP; OBAL; WhC** *Fr.* Ten Mills. **CP-FrosR**

Never be disenchanted of. Through Nightmare. Robert Ranke Graves. **CP-GravR**

Never be happy until the golden hour. Formative Mastership. Richard Eberhart. **CP-EberR**

Never Being. Stephen Spender. **CP-SpenS**

Never believe all you hear. Wolf. Kenneth Rexroth. **NNaP; SP-RexrK** *Fr.* A Bestiary. **SP-RexrK**

Never, believe me, / Appear the Immortals. *ad. fr. the German of* Schiller. Samuel Taylor Coleridge. **CP-ColeS**

Never believe me, if I love. The Careless Lover. Sir John Suckling. **CP-SuckJ**

Never Born. Carl Sandburg. **CP-SandC**

Never Call a Babysitter in a Thunderstorm. Thomas Merton. **CP-MertT**

Never could anyone / who simply lives to die. Edward Estlin Cummings. **CP-CummE**

Never did sculptor's dream unfold. Sonnet of Michel Angelo Buonaroti. Michelangelo Buonarroti, *tr. fr. Italian by* Ralph Waldo Emerson. **CP-EmerR**

Never do sea birds sing. The Lost Speakers. Archibald MacLeish. **CP-MacLA**

Never enlivened with the liveliest ray. Companion to the Foregoing [Love Lies Bleeding]. William Wordsworth. **CP-WorW2**

Never for ever, for ever never, oh. Intimation of Immortality. Stevie Smith. **CP-SmitS**

Never for Society. Emily Dickinson. **CP-DickE**

Never forget who brings the rain. Turn of the Moon. Robert Ranke Graves. **CP-GravR**

Never Give All the Heart. William Butler Yeats. **CP-YeatW**

Never Gonna Be the Same Again. "Bob Dylan." **CP-DylaB**

Never has she known. A Leader of Fashion. Thomas Hardy. **CP-HardT**

Never have I been sad or glad. Quandary. Robert Frost. **CP-FrosR**

Never in a comedian's life have I laughed till then! Malcolm Lowry. **CP-LowrM**

Never in any circumstances think you can tell the men from the boys. (Or the sheep from the goats). The Incorrigible Dirigible. Hayden Carruth. **CP-CarHS**

Never let it be said. Hilda Doolittle. *Fr.* Electra-Orestes. **CP-DoolH**

Never love unless you can. Thomas Campion. **CP-CampT**

Never love with all your heart. Song in Spite of Myself. Countee Cullen. **CP-CullC**

Never married. Her bed filled. My Father's Oldest Sister. Siv Cedering Fox. **SP-CedeS**

Never mind the day we left, or the day the women clung to us. The Klondike. Edwin Arlington Robinson. **CP-RobiE**

Never Mind the Overcoat, Button Up That Lip. Ogden Nash. **CP-NashO**

Never More, Sailor. Walter de la Mare. **CP-DeLaW**

Never more will the wind. Hilda Doolittle. **CTC; TrGrPo** *Fr.* Hymen. **CP-DoolH**

Never my Book's perfection did appear. To the High and Noble Prince, George, Duke, Marquesse, and Earle of Buckingham. Robert Herrick. **CP-HerrR**

Never, my young men. No Joy in Life. David Herbert Lawrence. **CP-LawrD**

Never Naught Song, A. Robert Frost. **CP-FrosR**

Never-Never. Marge Piercy. **SP-PierM**

Never, never again / This moment, never. The Moment. Kathleen Jessie Raine. **SP-RainK**

Never, never may the fruit be plucked from the bough. Edna St. Vincent Millay. **CP-MillE**

Never, no never, listen too long. The Fool's Song. Walter de la Mare. **CP-DeLaW**

Never, O never, / Since dewy sweet Flora. The Rape of Aurora. George Meredith. **CP-MerG1**

Never offer your heart. Never Offer Your Heart to Someone Who Eats Hearts. Alice Walker. **CP-WalkA**

Never Offer Your Heart to Someone Who Eats Hearts. Alice Walker. **CP-WalkA**

Never on one single pore Eternity. Being Alone. Charles Kenneth Williams. **CP-WillC; SP-WillC**

Never on this side of the grave again. A Life's Parallels. Christina Georgina Rossetti. **CP-RosC2**

Never Pharaoh's Night. In the Desert. Herman Melville. **SP-MelvH**

Never put anything, they tell you'. W. D. Attempts to Swallow the Symbol ' ˙ ˙ ˙ ˙ ˙ ˙ ˙ ˙ ˙ ˙ ˙ ˙ ˙ '. William DeWitt Snodgrass. **SP-SnodW**

Never Say Goodbye. "Bob Dylan." **CP-DylaB**

Never seek [*or* pain] to tell thy love, *see also* "I told my love I told my love." William Blake. **CP-BlakW**

Never seek to tell thy stove. Malcolm Lowry. **CP-LowrM**

Never shall a young man. For Anne Gregory. William Butler Yeats. **CP-YeatW**

Never so lithe in the green dingle. Louis MacNeice. *Fr.* Visitations. **CP-MacNL**

Never Stronger. Wystan Hugh Auden. **CP-AudeW**

Never Such Love. Robert Ranke Graves. **CP-GravR**

Never take her away. Song. Vinícius de Moraes, *tr. fr.* Portuguese by Richard Wilbur. **CP-WilbR**

Never tell me that not one star of all. A Star in a Stoneboat. Robert Frost. **CP-FrosR**

Never the Time and the Place. Robert Browning. **CP-BroR2**

Never the tramp of foot or horse. Farewell to Anactoria. Sappho, *tr. fr. Greek by* Allen Tate. **CP-TateA**

Never-To-Be. Walter de la Mare. **CP-DeLaW**

Never to be lonely like that. Face to Face. Adrienne Rich. **CP-RicA1; SP-RicA2**

Never to fight unless from a pure motive. Bottleneck. Louis MacNeice. **CP-MacNL**

Never to hear, I know in myself complete. A Certain Music. Muriel Rukeyser. **CP-RukeM**

Never to say no to the algae suddenly. To the Algae. Charles Olson. **CP-OlsoC**

Never to walk from the station's lamps and laurels. Negative Indicative. Philip Larkin. **CP-LarkP**

Never Too Late to Dye. Robert Herrick. **CP-HerrR**

Never trust a white man. Advice to a Son. Ernest Hemingway. **CP-HemiE**

Never Try to Trick Me with a Kiss. Sylvia Plath. **CP-PlatS**

Never twice that river. Kathleen Jessie Raine. *Fr.* By the River Eden. **SP-RainK**

Never Two Songs the Same. Carl Sandburg. **CP-SandC**

Never until our souls are strong enough. Edwin Arlington Robinson. *Fr.* Two Sonnets. **CP-RobiE**

Never until the mankind making. A Refusal to Mourn the Death, by Fire, of a Child in London. Dylan Thomas. **CP-ThomD**

Never until this night have I been stirred. An Image from a Past Life. William Butler Yeats. **CP-YeatW**

Never was Day so over-sick with showres. Upon the Bishop of Lincolne's Imprisonment. Robert Herrick. **CP-HerrR**

Never was so profound a shadow thrown. Birth of Angels. Robert Ranke Graves. **CP-GravR**

Never was there a man much uglier. Vain Gratuities. Edwin Arlington Robinson. **CP-RobiE**

Never weather-beaten sail[e] more willing bent to shore. Thomas Campion. **CP-CampT**

Nevertheless. Marianne Craig Moore. **CP-MoorM**

Nevertheless. Ogden Nash. **CP-NashO**

Nevertheless, sleep / And as your eyes close. William Dickey. **SP-DickW** *Fr.* At Your Old House. **SP-DickW**

Nevertheless the Moon. Muriel Rukeyser. **CP-RukeM**

New. William Matthews. **SP-MattW**

New. Gertrude Stein. **CP-SteiG**

New Age, The. Stevie Smith. **CP-SmitS**

New Animals. Donald Hall. **CP-HallD**

New Autumn, New York. Al Young. **CP-YounA**

New Beatitudes, The. John Gould Fletcher. **SP-FletJ** *Fr.* The Parables of Antichrist.

New Being, The. Kenneth Patchen. **CP-PatcK**

New Belfry of Christ Church, Oxford, The. "Lewis Carroll." **CP-CarrL**

New Birth, A. Daniel Gerard Hoffman. **SP-HoffD**

New books of poetry will be written. A Coronal. William Carlos Williams. **CP-WilW1**

New Boots, The. Thomas Hardy. **CP-HardT**

New-born child of gospel-grace, The. The New Convert. William Cowper. *Fr.* Olney Hymns. **CP-CowpW**

New Brooms. David Herbert Lawrence. **CP-LawrD**

New Car. Charles Kenneth Williams. **SP-WillC**

New Cathedral Overlooking the Park, The. William Carlos Williams. **CP-WilW1**

New Charon, The. Robert Herrick. **CP-HerrR**

New Church-Yard. William Wordsworth. *Fr.* Ecclesiastical Sonnets. **CP-WorW2**

New Churches. William Wordsworth. *Fr.* Ecclesiastical Sonnets. **CP-WorW2**

New Clouds, The. William Carlos Williams. **CP-WilW2**

New coated / a winter white. The White Van. Charles Tomlinson. **CP-TomlC**

New commandment, said the smiling Muse, A. 'ΑΔΑΚΡΥΝ ΝΕΜΟΝΤΑΙ ΑΙΩΝΑ. Ralph Waldo Emerson. *Fr.* Quatrains. **CP-EmerR**

New Convert, The. William Cowper. *Fr.* Olney Hymns. **CP-CowpW**

New Corbies, The. Louise McNeill. **SP-McNeL**

New creatures; the Creator still the Same. Christina Georgina Rossetti. **CP-RosC2**

New Cry, The. Ben Jonson. **CP-JonsB**

New-dated from the terms that reappear. To Oxford. Gerard Manley Hopkins. **CP-HopkG**

New Dawn's Business, The. Thomas Hardy. **CP-HardT**

New Day, A. Philip Levine. **SP-LeviP**

New Death, The. Jim Carroll. **SP-CarrJ**
  "Found it once more in the ocean's rush."
  "I see it passing."
  "Its power to deceive."

New desire to understand, A. R. G. E. Richard Eberhart. **CP-EberR**

New Diversions. Roy Fisher.
  "Burnt year. Trick riders blunder about the concrete, A." **SP-FishR**
  "Counterfeit bucolic scene, A." **SP-FishR**
  "Dawn birds at noon." **SP-FishR**
  "Downpour that subdued everybody and, The." **SP-FishR**
  "Duchamp and Man Ray." **SP-FishR**
  "Eye ascending / is gone up, The." **SP-FishR**
  "Half hearing, half in a veil, to hear." **SP-FishR**
  "Half reconciled, half healed: but." **SP-FishR**
  "I work in my garden." **SP-FishR**

"Idea of defence, The." **SP-FishR**

"If I declare *Peace*." **SP-FishR**

"In a dull hour thinking of the swan." **SP-FishR**

"In the evening the smoke blows far away." **SP-FishR**

"Klonk! The smoker's trick." **SP-FishR**

"Masterpieces in my sleep. A suppressed." **SP-FishR**

"Mounted on all four walls, the neat." **SP-FishR**

"Out in the early morning, by empty roads." **SP-FishR**

"Rust. Limewash. The iron tyres." **SP-FishR**

"There's a belief to fix. It feels strong." **SP-FishR**

"Vigil / taking over hours and losing them." **SP-FishR**

"Wanting to get away." **SP-FishR**

New Emigration, The. Kay Boyle. **CP-BoylK**

New England. Anne Bradstreet. **KTR** *Fr.* A Dialogue between Old England and New. **CP-BradA**

New England. William Carlos Williams. **CP-WilW1**

New England Bachelor, A. Richard Eberhart. **CP-EberR**

New England Capitalist. Ralph Waldo Emerson. **CP-EmerR**

New England doesn't kid around. Granite. John Updike. **CP-UpdiJ**

New England is a region of the heart. The First Version. Hayden Carruth. *Fr.* The Mythology of Dark and Light. **CP-CarHL**

New England March. Charles Olson. **CP-OlsoC**

New England Protestant. Richard Eberhart. *Fr.* Attitudes. **CP-EberR**

New England Spring, 1942. Edna St. Vincent Millay. **CP-MillE**

New England Verses. Wallace Stevens. **CP-StevW**

Statue against a Clear Sky. **EyDe**

New England Weather. Archibald MacLeish. **CP-MacLA**

New England Winter. Erica Jong. **SP-JongE**

New Enigmas. Christina Georgina Rossetti. **CP-RosC3**

New Entrepreneurial Plan. Nelle Richmond Eberhart. **CP-EberR**

New Era the Army of the Future the Egg of an Army, The. George Meredith. **CP-MerG2**

New Eternity, The. Robert Ranke Graves. **CP-GravR**

New every morning is the love. Prime. Donald Davie. *Fr.* Horae Canonicae. **CP-DavDo**

New every morning is the power. Terce. Donald Davie. *Fr.* Horae Canonicae. **CP-DavDo**

New Exodus, The. John Greenleaf Whittier. **CP-WhitJ**

New Eyes Each Year. Philip Larkin. **CP-LarkP**

New Face. Alice Walker. **CP-WalkA**

New face, strange face, for my unrest. Modes of Pleasure. Thom Gunn. **CP-GunnT**

New Faces, The. William Butler Yeats. **CP-YeatW**

New Farm Tractor. Carl Sandburg. **CP-SandC**

New Feet. Carl Sandburg. **CP-SandC**

New feet within my garden go. Emily Dickinson. **CP-DickE**

New Georgia. Randall Jarrell. **CP-JarrR**

New Guinea Gardener Bird, The. Malcolm Lowry. **CP-LowrM**

New Hampshire. Thomas Stearns Eliot. **FaBoCh; GTBS-6; GTBS-P; NoAM; WeW** *Fr.* Landscapes. **CP-ElioT**

New Hampshire. Robert Frost. **CP-FrosR**

New Hampshire. Donald Hall. **CP-HallD**

New Hampshire. John Greenleaf Whittier. **CP-WhitJ**

New Hampshire Again. Carl Sandburg. **CP-SandC**

New Hampshire, February. Richard Eberhart. **CP-EberR**

New Hartford. Hayden Carruth. **CP-CarHS**

New Heaven and Earth. David Herbert Lawrence. **CP-LawrD**

New Heaven, New War[re]. Robert Southwell. **CP-SoutR**

New House, The. Wendell Berry. *Fr.* The Handing Down. **CP-BerrW**

New House, The. Robert Louis Stevenson. **CP-StevR**

New Houses, New Clothes. David Herbert Lawrence. **CP-LawrD**

New Inn, The. Ben Jonson.

"It was a beauty that I saw." **CP-JonsB**

New Jerusalem, The. William Blake. *See* And Did Those Feet in Ancient Time.

New Jerusalem. John Hewitt. **CP-HewiJ**

New Jerusalem. Louis MacNeice. **CP-MacNL**

New Jerusalem 1. John Hewitt. **CP-HewiJ**

New Jerusalem 2. John Hewitt. **CP-HewiJ**

New Knighthood, The. Rudyard Kipling. **CP-KiplR**

New Land. Mona Van Duyn. **SP-VanDM**

New Legends. Robert Ranke Graves. **CP-GravR**

New light gives new directions, fortunes new. George Chapman. **NoSic; OAEL-1** *Fr.* Hero and Leander. **CP-MarlC**

New Mexican Mountain. Robinson Jeffers. **CP-JefR2**

New Mexico. William Carlos Williams. **CP-WilW2**

New Mistress, The. Alfred Edward Housman. **CP-HousA**

New Mode of Production, The. Al Young. **CP-YounA**

New Moon. David Herbert Lawrence. **CP-LawrD**

New Moon in January. Ted Hughes. **SP-HughT**

New moon looks down on our sick sweet planet, A. Death on All Fronts. Allen Ginsberg. **CP-GinsA**

New Moon Over Grove Street. Al Young. **CP-YounA**

New Morning. "Bob Dylan." **CP-DylaB**

New Morning—and the Years Are Ours. Marsden Hartley. **CP-HartM**

New-mown hay smell and wind of the plain made her a woman whose. Population Drifts. Carl Sandburg. **CP-SandC**

New Mystic, The. Al Young. **CP-YounA**

New National Anthem, A. Percy Bysshe Shelley. **CP-ShelP**

New neighbors came to the corner house at Congress and Green Streets. Clean Curtains. Carl Sandburg. **CP-SandC**

New occasion like a star has risen, A. Sonnet (Aboard a Troopship) to Gweno. Alun Lewis. **CP-LewiA**

New O'Dwyer's dim lights. "You hate, The". James Liddy. *Fr.* A Munster Song of Love and War. **CP-LiddJ**

New Orleans. Hayden Carruth. **CP-CarHS**

New Orleans Intermission. Al Young. **CP-YounA**

New Personal Poem. Ted Berrigan. **SP-BerrT**

New Place, The. Charles Bukowski. **SP-BukC2**

New Place, The. William Dickey. **SP-DickW**

New Poem. Charles Olson. **CP-OlsoC**

New Pony. "Bob Dylan." **CP-DylaB**

New Prince, New Pomp[e]. Robert Southwell. **CP-SoutR**

New Prologue Spoken at the Representation of *Comus*, A. Samuel Johnson. **CP-JohnS**

New Psalm for the Chapel of Kilmarnock, on the Thanksgiving-Day for His Majesty's Recovery, A. Robert Burns. **CP-BurnR**

New Rains. Marsden Hartley. **CP-HartM**

New rains wash down. New Rains. Marsden Hartley. **CP-HartM**

New Readings. Gerard Manley Hopkins. **CP-HopkG**

New Realism, The. John Ashbery.

"There was calm rapture in the way she spoke." **SP-AshbJ**

New red houses spring like plants, The. Flat Suburbs, S.W., in the Morning. David Herbert Lawrence. **CP-LawrD**

New Ribbon. Thomas Merton. **CP-MertT**

New Ring, The. Karl Shapiro. **SP-ShapK**

New ring oppresses the finger, The. The New Ring. Karl Shapiro. **SP-ShapK**

New Road, The. Richard Shelton. **SP-ShelR**

New Roof, The. Wendell Berry. **CP-BerrW**

New Season. Philip Levine. **SP-LeviP**

New Sensations. "Lou Reed." **SP-ReedL**

New Song, The. Clement of Alexandria, *tr. fr. Greek by* Thomas Merton. **CP-MertT**

New Song, A. Seamus Heaney. **SP-HeanS**

New Song for Indiana Ophelias. Carl Sandburg. **CP-SandC**

New Song to the Tune of "Whare Hae Ye Been a' Day, My Boy Tammy O? Courting O' a Young Thing, Just Come Frae Her Mammie O?" Byron. **CP-Byron**

New Tenants, The. Edwin Arlington Robinson. **CP-RobiE**

New Toy, The. Thomas Hardy. **CP-HardT**

New-vamped Abbey shaped apace, The. The Abbey Mason. Thomas Hardy. **CP-HardT**

New Vicar of Bray, The. Byron. **CP-Byron**

New volcano has erupted, A. Crusoe in England. Elizabeth Bishop. **CP-BishE**

New Weapons in the Old War. Howard Nemerov. **CP-NemeH**

New Weather. Carl Sandburg. **CP-SandC**

New Wife and the Old, The. John Greenleaf Whittier. **CP-WhitJ**

New wood as old as carpentry, The. Carpenter's Boat. George Oppen. **CP-OppeG**

New Word, The. David Herbert Lawrence. **CP-LawrD**

New World, A. Percy Bysshe Shelley. *See* The World's great age begins anew.

New World. Derek Walcott. **CP-WalcD**

New world honors him whose lofty plea, The. Milton. John Greenleaf Whittier. **CP-WhitJ**

New Worlds. John Milton. *Fr.* Book III. *Fr.* Paradise Lost. **CP-MiltJ**

New Year. Philip Larkin. **CP-LarkP**

New Year. Christopher Smart. *Fr.* Hymns and Spiritual Songs for the Fasts and Festivals of the Church of England. **SP-SmarC**

New Year, The. John Greenleaf Whittier. **CP-WhitJ**

New year, forth looking out of Janus' gate. Edmund Spenser. **NoSic** *Fr.* Amoretti. **CP-Spens**

New Year Greeting, A. Wystan Hugh Auden. **CP-AudeW**

New Year Letter. Wystan Hugh Auden. **CP-AudeW**

  "Long time since it seems to-day, A." **GOA**

  "Our news is seldom good: the heart." **FaBoRV**

  "Self-educated WILLIAM BLAKE." **EPCY**

New Year met me somewhat sad. Christina Georgina Rossetti. *Fr.* Old and New Year Ditties. **CP-RosC1**

New Year Morning. Adrienne Rich. **CP-RicAE**

New Year! New Year! come over the snow. New Year's Eve. George Meredith. **CP-MerG2**

New Year 1970. Jim Carroll. **SP-CarrJ**

New Year on Dartmoor. Sylvia Plath. **CP-PlatS**

New Year Wishes for the English. Donald Davie. **CP-DavDo**

New Year's. Stephen Berg. **SP-BergS**

New Year's. Robert Creeley. **CP-CreeR**

New Year's Dawn, 1947. Robinson Jeffers. **CP-JefR3**

New Year's Day. Ted Kooser. **SP-KoosT**

New Year's Day. Audre Lorde. **SP-LordA**

New Year's Day, 1848. Walt Whitman. **CP-WhitW**

New Year's Eve. John Berryman. **CP-BerrJ**

New Year's Eve. Boethius, *tr. fr. Latin.* **MLL**, *tr. by* Helen Waddell; *Fr.* Consolation of Philosophy, The ("De Consolacione Philosophiae"). **CP-ChauG**

New Year's Eve. Thomas Hardy. **CP-HardT**

New Year's Eve. Alfred Edward Housman. **CP-HousA**

New Year's Eve. Robinson Jeffers. **CP-JefR2**

New Year's Eve. David Herbert Lawrence. **CP-LawrD**

New Year's Eve. George Meredith. **CP-MerG2**

New Year's Eve. Richard Shelton. **SP-ShelR**

New Year's Eve, and all through. Driving through Oregon (Dec. 1973). John Haines. **SP-HainJ**

New Year's Eve in War Time, A. Thomas Hardy. **CP-HardT**

New Year's Eve, 1979. Charles Wright. **SP-WrigC**

New years [*or* yeares], expect new gifts: sister, your harp[e]. Ben Jonson. **CP-JonsB**

New Year's Gift for Bec, A. Jonathan Swift. **CP-SwifJ**

New-Year's [*or* New-Yeares] Gift Sent to Sir Simeon Steward, A. Robert Herrick. **CP-HerrR**

New Year's Gift Sung to King Charles. 1635, A. Ben Jonson. **CP-JonsB**

New Year's Gift. To the King, A. Thomas Carew. **CP-CareT**

New Years Gift. To the Queen, A. Thomas Carew. **CP-CareT**

New Year's Night. David Herbert Lawrence. **CP-LawrD**

New Year's Sacrifice: To Lucinda, A. Thomas Carew. **CP-CareT**

New-Yeeres Gift, The. Robert Herrick. **CP-HerrR**

New-Yeeres Gift, or Circumcisions Song, Sung to the King in the Presence at White Hall, The. Robert Herrick. **CP-HerrR**

New York. Thom Gunn. **CP-GunnT**

New York. Marianne Craig Moore. **CP-MoorM**

N.Y. Louis Zukofsky. *Fr.* 29 Songs. **CP-ZukLS**

New York a grey haze with flights of. Kenneth Rexroth. **CP-RexKL** *Fr.* The Dragon and the Unicorn.

  "I come back to the cottage in." **SP-RexrK**

New York—Albany. Lawrence Ferlinghetti. **SP-FerlL**

New York City. Audre Lorde. *See* New York City 1970.

New York City 1970. Audre Lorde.

  ("How do you spell change.") **SP-LordA**

  (New York City.) **SP-LordA**

New York in August. Donald Davie. **CP-DavDo**

New York is a city of many cats. Three Slants at New York. Carl Sandburg. **CP-SandC**

New York 1962: Fragment. Robert Lowell. **SP-LoweR**

N.Y. Telephone Conversation. "Lou Reed." **SP-ReedL**

New York Times: A Poem for the Ross Feld, The. Gilbert Sorrentino. **SP-SorrG**

New Yorker, A. James Schuyler. **CP-SchuJ**

New Yorkers. Langston Hughes. **SP-HughL**

New York's lovely weather / hurts my forehead. Bean Spasms. Ted Berrigan. **SP-BerrT**

New York's lovely weather hurts my forehead. For You. Ted Berrigan. **SP-BerrT**

Newcomer's Wife, The. Thomas Hardy. **CP-HardT**

Newer garden of creation, no primal solitude, A. The Prairie States. Walt Whitman. **CP-WhitW**

Newer photograph shows you, A. Dabney Stuart. *Fr.* The Opposite Field. **SP-StuaD**

Newest Bath Guide, The. Sir John Betjeman. **CP-BetjJ**

Newly / cued / motif smites truly to beautifully, *See also* Surely / Cued. . . . Edward Estlin Cummings. **CP-CummE**

Newly Discovered "Homeric" Hymn, A. Charles Olson. **CP-OlsoC; SP-OlsoC**

Newly say dickered my love air my own would marry me all. Catullus. *See* Carmen 70: "Lesbia says she'ld rather marry me."

Newly, The / cued / motif smites truly to beautifully. Edward Estlin Cummings. *See* The Surely / Cued / motif smites truly to Beautifully.

Newlys of silence. Edward Estlin Cummings. **CP-CummE**

Newlyweds, The. John Updike. **CP-UpdiJ**

Newlywed's Cuisine, The. Wang Chien, *tr. fr. Chinese by* William Carlos Williams *with* David Rafael Wang. **CP-WilW2**

News, The. Robert Creeley. **CP-CreeR**

News. Walter de la Mare. **CP-DeLaW**

News, The. Paul Laurence Dunbar. **CP-DunbP**

News. Richard Eberhart. **CP-EberR**

News. Randall Jarrell. **CP-JarrR**

News! / What is the word that they tell now—now—now! The Runners. Rudyard Kipling. **CP-KiplR**

News and the Weather, The. Thomas McGrath. **SP-McGrT**

News and the Weather, The. Wallace Stevens. **CP-StevW**

News Bulletin. Allen Ginsberg. **CP-GinsA**

News clip; the invasion of Biafra, A. Negatives. Derek Walcott. **CP-WalcD**

News for Her Mother. Thomas Hardy. **CP-HardT**

News for the Delphic Oracle. William Butler Yeats. **CP-YeatW**

News for the Ear. Roy Fisher. **SP-FishR**

News from the Glacier. John Haines. **SP-HainJ**

  "After the twenty thousand year."

  "East from Glacier Park."

  "Nine thousand feet in the Rockies."

  "On a bend in the road near St. Mary."

  "Sunlight struck before us."

  "That mid-fall morning, driving north."

  "Toward Many Glaciers."

  "We climbed all afternoon."

  "West of Logan Pass, where."

News from the Low Country. Leonard Nathan. **SP-NathL**

News from the New World. Ben Jonson.

  "Howe'er the brightness may amaze." **CP-JonsB**

  "Now look and see in yonder throne." **CP-JonsB**

News from the School at Chartres. Thomas Merton. **CP-MertT**

News goes from the Underworld. John Updike. **CP-UpdiJ**

News goes desk to desk, The. A Death at the Office. Ted Kooser. **SP-KoosT**

NEWS (o the latest). A B Cs (3—for Rimbaud). Charles Olson. **CP-OlsoC**

News of a Marriage. Steve Griffiths. **SP-GrifS**

News of the Gold World of May. Delmore Schwartz. **SP-SchwD**

News-Reel, The. Louis MacNeice. **CP-MacNL**

News You Really Hate, The, *see also* Commentary—The News You Really Hate. Leonard Cohen. **CP-CoheL**

Newscast. Thomas Merton. *Fr.* Cables to the Ace. **CP-MertT**

Newspaper comes. It, The. The Sky Eats Up the Trees. James Schuyler. **CP-SchuJ**

Newspaper Picture of Spectators at a Hotel Fire, A. Miller Williams. **SP-WillM**

Newspaper, the coffee cup, the dog's, The. The Coffee Cup. Donald Hall. **CP-HallD**

Newspapermen say that of all work, newspaper work is the infernalist. I Am Full of Previous Experience. Ogden Nash. **CP-NashO**

Newspapers cover the floor. Metropolitan Sunday. Howard Nemerov. **CP-NemeH**

Newspapers rise high in the air over Maryland. At a March against the Vietnam War. Robert Bly. **SP-BlyR**

Newsreel. Adrienne Rich. **FaBoWP; HCAP; SP-RicA2** *Fr.* Shooting Script. **CP-RicAE**

Newsreel: Man and Firing Squad. Margaret Atwood. **SP-AtwM1**

Newstead Abbey. Byron. **CP-Byron**

Newstead! fast-falling, once-resplendent dome! Elegy on Newstead Abbey. Byron. **CP-Byron**

Newstime! Rise! Shine! Shake a leg! Daybreak. James McAuley. **SP-McAuJ**

Newton. William Wordsworth. **ImOP** *Fr.* Residence at Cambridge. *Fr.* The Prelude; Growth of a Poet's Mind [1850 vers.]. **CP-WorW3**

Newton watched a lot of balls. On the Nature of Scientific Law. Jenny Joseph. **SP-JoseJ**

Newton's Statue. William Wordsworth. *See* The Evangelist St John my patron was.

Next! Ogden Nash. **CP-NashO**

Next, bidding all draw near on bended knees. Alexander Pope. **ECEV; OBSV** *Fr.* Yet, yet a moment, one dim ray of light. **NAEL-1; OAEL-1; PoEL-3** *Fr.* The Dunciad. **CP-PopeA**

(Idle Pursuits.) **ECEV**, *book* IV, *ll.* 565–604;

Next came one / Who mourn'd in earnest, when the Captive Ark. John Milton. **EBEV** *Fr.* Book I. **FHYEP; NAEL-1; OAEL-1; OxAEP-1** *Fr.* Paradise Lost. **CP-MiltJ**

Next comes the dull disciple of thy school. Byron. **EPCY** *Fr.* English Bards and Scotch Reviewers. **CP-Byron**

Next Day. Randall Jarrell. **CP-JarrR; SP-JarrR**

Next day I drove by night, The. Louis MacNeice. *Fr.* Autumn Journal. **CP-MacNL**

Next Door. Jim Carroll. **SP-CarrJ**

Next Door. Richard Wilbur. **CP-WilbR**

Next door, outside the pink-fronted Bodega Hispano. Galway Kinnell. *Fr.* The Avenue Bearing the Initial of Christ into the New World. **SP-KinnG**

Next door they've finally brought home the new baby. For Every Last Batch When the Next One Comes Along. William Dickey. **SP-DickW**

Next is your lot, fair, to be numbered one. To His Kinswoman, Mrs. Penelope Wheeler. Robert Herrick. **CP-HerrR**

Next Morning. David Herbert Lawrence. **CP-LawrD**

Next morning Troilus began to clear. Troilus and Cresida. William Wordsworth. **CP-WorW1**

Next of Kin. Christina Georgina Rossetti. **CP-RosC3**

Next One, The. Leonard Cohen. **CP-CoheL**

Next, Please. Philip Larkin. **CP-LarkP**

Next Step, The. Dabney Stuart. **SP-StuaD**

Next! The Guards hitch up their belts and look around. Thomas Merton. *Fr.* Cables to the Ace. **CP-MertT**

Next Time, The. Robert Ranke Graves. **CP-GravR**

Next time we meet. Some Constantly Besieged Castle. Diane Wakoski. **SP-WakoD**

Next to Last Things. Stanley Jasspon Kunitz. *Fr.* Around Pastor Bonhoeffer. **CP-KuniS**

Next to me on the riverbank. Red Weed. Stephen Berg. **SP-BergS** *Fr.* For My Father.

Next to of course god america i. Edward Estlin Cummings. **CP-CummE; SP-CummE**

Next to the Last Poem about God, The. Charles Kenneth Williams. **CP-WillC**

Next to these ladies, but in nought allied. The Contented Peasant. George Crabbe. **SP-CrabG** *Fr.* The Parish Register.

Next War, The. Wilfred Owen. **CP-OwenW**

Next week, alas, BOULANGERIE. Farewell to the Shopping District of Antibes. John Updike. **CP-UpdiJ**

Next year the grave grass will cover us. Street Corner College. Kenneth Patchen. **CP-PatcK**

Next year we are to bring the soldiers home. Homage to a Government. Philip Larkin. **CP-LarkP**

Nexus. Rita Dove. **SP-DoveR**

Nexus. Richard Eberhart. **CP-EberR**

Niagara. Nicholas Vachel Lindsay. **CP-LindV**

"What marching men of Buffalo."

"Within the town of Buffalo."

Nicaraguan Journal. Chuck Miller. **SP-MillC**

Nice Day for a Lynching. Kenneth Patchen. **CP-PatcK**

Nice Place, A. Charles Bukowski. **SP-BukC2**

Nice spring day off big white cloud. Sounding Chinese at Inspiration Point. Tom Clark. **SP-ClarT**

Nice Try. Charles Bukowski. **SP-BukC3**

Niceties of symbolism & identification. In & Out. John Berryman. **CP-BerrJ**

Nicholas Copernicus (1473–1543). Siv Cedering Fox. *Fr.* Letters from the Astronomers. **SP-CedeS**

Nick and the Candlestick. Sylvia Plath. **CP-PlatS**

Nicked a gin-ace seeing hour. Four-o'clock. Louis Zukofsky. **CP-ZukLS**

Nickels click off fares in the slot machines of the subway, the elevated, The. Carl Sandburg. *Fr.* The People, Yes. **CP-SandC**

Nickname of Hell, The. Charles Kenneth Williams. **CP-WillC; SP-WillC**

Nicodemus. Howard Nemerov. **CP-NemeH**

Nicolai, Courier in Belgrade. John Hewitt. **CP-HewiJ**

Nid, am i Ti fy ngwared i. Ochenaid Sant Francis Xavier, Apostol Yr Indiaid. Gerard Manley Hopkins. **CP-HopkG**

Niece. George Oppen. **CP-OppeG**

Nieh Ch'ueh, who had no teeth. The Importance of Being Toothless. Chuang Tzu, *tr. fr. Chinese* by Thomas Merton. **CP-MertT**

Nigger. Carl Sandburg. **CP-SandC**

Nigger. Karl Shapiro. **SP-ShapK**

Nigger: as if it were not. Robert Penn Warren. **SP-WarrR** (Event, The.) **SP-WarrR**

Nigger Song: An Odyssey. Rita Dove. **SP-DoveR**

Nigh where the river flows. Bible, *O.T. See* Psalm 137: "By the rivers of Babylon. . . ."

Night - sky bird's world. Myth of the Blaze. George Oppen. **CP-OppeG**

Night / and in the warm blackness. Upon Your Leaving. Etheridge Knight. **SP-KnigE**

Night. William Blake. **BLPL; BoNaP; BoTP; CH; EnRP; FHYEP; FaBoBe; FaPON; HBV; HBVY; HoFi; MeMBP; OBEC; OBEV; OxBChV; OxBoCh; PoLF; TreFT; WiR** *Fr.* Songs of Innocence. **CP-BlakW**

Night. Robert Bly. **SP-BlyR**

Night. Louise Bogan. **CP-BogaL**

Night. Robert Creeley. **CP-CreeR**

Night. Edward Estlin Cummings. **CP-CummE**

Night ("All from the light"). Walter de la Mare. **CP-DeLaW**

Night ("That shining moon"). Walter de la Mare. **CP-DeLaW**

Night. Hilda Doolittle. **CP-DoolH**

Night. Paul Laurence Dunbar. **CP-DunbP**

Night. Louise Glück. **MoLi** *Fr.* Metamorphosis. **SP-GlücL**

Night / heat / the hot bath, barely endurable. The Bath House. Thom Gunn. *Fr.* The Geysers. **CP-GunnT**

Night. Robinson Jeffers. **CP-JefR1**

Night. David Herbert Lawrence. **CP-LawrD**

Night. Richard Lovelace. **CP-LoveR**

Night, The. Charles Olson. **CP-OlsoC**

Night. Adrienne Rich. **CP-RicAE; SP-RicA2**

Night, The. James Schuyler. **CP-SchuJ**

Night. Gary Snyder. **CP-SnydG**

Night / We went running to the garden. James Liddy. *Fr.* Birds. **CP-LiddJ**

Night. William Carlos Williams. **CP-WilW1**

Night. A dream so drowned my mind. The Scream. Charles Tomlinson. **CP-TomlC**

Night after night I lie like this listening. Archibald MacLeish. *Fr.* Hamlet of A. Macleish. **CP-MacLA**

Night after night the dead moon lit. The Difficult Resolution. Randall Jarrell. **CP-JarrR**

Night after wakeful night, Woman, nightmares are real. Fixing the Clock. Isabella Gardner. **CP-GardI**

Night and Day. Siv Cedering Fox. **SP-CedeS**

Night and Day. Robert Louis Stevenson. **CP-StevR**

Night and day arrive, and day after day goes by. For My Son Noah, Ten Years Old. Robert Bly. **SP-BlyR**

Night and Death. Christina Georgina Rossetti. **CP-RosC3**

Night and full moon. The Dreams of Wild Horses. Thomas McGrath. **SP-McGrT**

Night, and one single ridge of narrow path. Robert Browning. **EBVVPR** *Fr.* Pauline [*or* Pauline; A Fragment of a Confession]. **CP-BroR1**

Night and the City. John Berryman. **CP-BerrJ**

Night and the Merry Man. Elizabeth Barrett Browning. **CP-BroEB**

Night and the Merry Man. Elizabeth Barrett Browning. **CP-BroEB**

Night appeared to authorise it, The. Jason and Medea. Alun Lewis. **CP-LewiA**

Night-Apple, The. Allen Ginsberg. **CP-GinsA**

Night Arrival of Sea-Trout. Ted Hughes. **SP-HughT**

Night as well as brightest day hath her delight. Thomas Campion. *Fr.* A Relation of the Late Royall Entertainment Given by the Right Honourable the Lord *Knowles*, at *Cawsome*-House neere *Redding*: to Our Most *Gracious Queene, Queene* ANNE, *in her* Progresse toward the *Bathe*, upon *the Seven and Eight and Twentie Dayes of Aprill*. **CP-CampT**

Night at the Napi in Browning, A. Richard Hugo. **CP-HugoR**

Night at the Opera, A. Charles Tomlinson. **CP-TomlC**

Night attendant, a B.U. sophomore, The. Waking in the Blue. Robert Lowell. **SP-LoweR**

Night Before, The. The Beatles. **CP-Beatl**

Night before Christmas, The. Howard Nemerov. **CP-NemeH**

Night before Michael Was Born, The. Al Young. **CP-YounA**

Night before the Battle of Waterloo, The. Byron. *See* There was a sound of revelry by night.

Night before the Night before Christmas, The. Randall Jarrell. **CP-JarrR**

Night before Waterloo, The. Byron. *See* There was a sound of revelry by night.

Night Bells. Carl Sandburg. **CP-SandC**

Night bibles India in her wilderness. Alun Lewis. *Fr.* Indian Day. **CP-LewiA**

Night Bird. James Dickey. **CP-DickJ**

Night-Blooming Cereus, The. Robert Earl Hayden. **CP-HaydR**

Night-bound fire, A. Black Nude. Charles Tomlinson. **CP-TomlC**

Night café one 4 A.M., The. Havana 1953. Allen Ginsberg. **CP-GinsA**

Night calls many witnesses. Tall Timber. Carl Sandburg. **CP-SandC**

Night came on the Waters—all was rest, The. Julian [A Fragment]. Byron. **CP-Byron**

Night Chill. Archie Randolph Ammons. **SP-AmmoA**

Night City. Elizabeth Bishop. **CP-BishE**

Night closed my windows and. The Plough of Time. Lawrence Ferlinghetti. **SP-FerlL**

Night, clouds, I know where you are going. Sleepwalker's fate's. Night Patrol. Tom Clark. **SP-ClarT**

Night Club. Louis MacNeice. **FaBoDD; OxBSP** *Fr.* Entered in the Minutes. **CP-MacNL**

Night comes, an angel stands. Nocturn. Kathleen Jessie Raine. **SP-RainK**

Night Comes On, The. Leonard Cohen. **CP-CoheL**

Night comes with soft and drowsy plumes. Ernest Hemingway. **CP-HemiE**

Night covers the pond with its wing. The Pond. Louise Glück. **SP-GlücL**

Night creep down erlong de lan, De. The Tryst. Paul Laurence Dunbar. **CP-DunbP**

Night creeps onward, sad and slow, The. Faces in the Fire. "Lewis Carroll." **CP-CarrL**

Night Crow. Theodore Roethke. **CP-RoetT**

Night Dances, The. Sylvia Plath. **CP-PlatS**

Night, Death, Mississippi. Robert Earl Hayden. **CP-HaydR**

Night, Dim Night. Paul Laurence Dunbar. **CP-DunbP**

Night Dream, The. Archibald MacLeish. **CP-MacLA**

Night-dreams trace on Memory's wall. Memory. Ralph Waldo Emerson. **APN-1** *Fr.* Quatrains. **CP-EmerR**

Night Drive. Seamus Heaney. **SP-HeanS**

Night Drive. Derek Mahon. **SP-MahoD**

Night Feeding. Muriel Rukeyser. **CP-RukeM**

Night first settles in the corners of your mouth. Poeme en Forme de la Bouche. Anne Waldman. **SP-WaldA**

Night Fishers. Charles Tomlinson. **CP-TomlC**

Night Fishing. Daniel Gerard Hoffman. **SP-HoffD**

Night Flight : New York. Muriel Rukeyser. **CP-RukeM**

Night Flight. Mary Oliver. **SP-OlivM**

Night Flight. Marge Piercy. **SP-PierM**

Night Flight, over Ocean. John Updike. **CP-UpdiJ**

Night-flood rakes upon the stony shore, The. Written in a Tempestuous Night, on the Coast of Sussex. Charlotte Smith. **CP-SmitC** *Fr.* Montalbert.

Night-Flowering Cactus. Thomas Merton. **CP-MertT; SP-MertT**

Night: Four Songs. Langston Hughes. **SP-HughL**

Night Frogs. Robert Bly. **SP-BlyR**

Night from a railroad car window. Window. Carl Sandburg. **CP-SandC**

Night Funeral in Harlem. Langston Hughes. **SP-HughL**

Night Games. Ron Koertge. **SP-KoerR**

Night Gleam. Allen Ginsberg. **CP-GinsA**

Night has a sea which quenches the machine. Nocturne. Thomas Merton. **CP-MertT**

Night Has Been as Beautiful as Virginia. Kenneth Patchen. **CP-PatcK**

Night has come like something crawling. 22,000 Dollars in 3 Months. Charles Bukowski. **SP-BukC2**

Night has cut, The. Night. Hilda Doolittle. **CP-DoolH**

Night hath no wings, to him that cannot sleep. To His Sweet Saviour. Robert Herrick. **CP-HerrR**

Night her father asked her what, The. The Third Wish. Leonard Nathan. **SP-NathL**

Night Herons. Gary Snyder. **CP-SnydG**

Night herons nest in the cypress. Night Herons. Gary Snyder. **CP-SnydG**

Night hides our thefts; all faults then pardoned be. In the Dark None Dainty. Robert Herrick. **CP-HerrR**

Night! how I love thy silent shades. *see also* Watching unto God in the Night-Season. Jeanne Marie Bouvier de la Motte-Guyon, *tr. fr. French by* William Cowper. **CP-CowpW**

Night I Fucked My Alarm Clock, The. Charles Bukowski. **SP-BukC1**

Night II (Enion's Lament). William Blake. *See* The Price of Experience.

Night in Martindale. Kathleen Jessie Raine. **SP-RainK**

Night in NYC. Robert Creeley. **CP-CreeR**

Night in November, A. Thomas Hardy. **CP-HardT**

Night in the Kitchen. Adrienne Rich. **CP-RicAE**

Night in the Old Home. Thomas Hardy. **CP-HardT**

Night, in whose death did your ennui take refuge? Shorts / Excerpts. Bill Knott. **SP-KnotB**

Night is a cauldron. Hayden Carruth. *Fr.* North Winter. **CP-CarHL**

Night is beautiful, The. Langston Hughes. **SP-HughL** (My People.) **SP-HughL**

Night is covered with signs. The body and face of man, The. Akiba. Muriel Rukeyser. **CP-RukeM**

Night is darkening round me, The. Emily Brontë. **CP-BronE**

Night is dewy as a maiden's mouth, The. A Summer's Night. Paul Laurence Dunbar. **CP-DunbP**

Night is far spent, the day is at hand, The. Awake, Thou That Sleepest. Christina Georgina Rossetti. **CP-RosC2**

Night is filled with indecisions, The. The Night. James Schuyler. **CP-SchuJ**

Night is for sorrow and dawn is for joy. With the Lark. Paul Laurence Dunbar. **CP-DunbP**

Night is freezing fast, The. Alfred Edward Housman. **CP-HousA**

Night is hard by. I am vexed and bothered by sleep. Basil Bunting, *after* Manuchehri. **CP-BuntB**

Night is my favorite Day. Emily Dickinson. **SP-DickE**

Night is my sister, and how deep in love. Edna St. Vincent Millay. **CP-MillE**

Night is o'er England, and the winds are still. Peace. Walter de la Mare. **CP-DeLaW**

Night is on these hills, and some can sleep, The. Letter to His Brother. John Berryman. **CP-BerrJ**

Night is Personal. Robert Penn Warren. *Fr.* Penological Study: Southern Exposure. **SP-WarrR**

Night is quiet, The. Letter Poem #3. James Schuyler. **CP-SchuJ**

Night is uneasy, armed between streetlamps, The. Evening Stroll in the Suburbs. Mona Van Duyn. **SP-VanDM**

Night it was a holy [or haly] night, The. Godly Girzie. Robert Burns. **CP-BurnR**

Night Journal. Charles Wright. **SP-WrigC**

Night Journal II. Charles Wright. **SP-WrigC**

Night Journey. Theodore Roethke. **CP-RoetT**

Night knows nothing of the chants of night, The. Re-statement of Romance. Wallace Stevens. **CP-StevW**

Night lay upon the ocean like a sword. John Gould Fletcher. **SP-FletJ** *Fr.* Branches of Adam.

Night Letter, A. Kay Boyle. **CP-BoylK**

Night Letter. Stanley Jasspon Kunitz. **CP-KuniS**

Night Letter. Marge Piercy. **SP-PierM**

Night Light, The. Robert Frost. *Fr.* Five Nocturnes. **CP-FrosR**

Night, like a dying mother. By Morning Twilight. George Meredith. **CP-MerG1**

Night! loathed [or loathèd] jailor of the locked-up [or lock'd up] sun. Night. Richard Lovelace. **CP-LoveR**

Night Mail, The. Wystan Hugh Auden. **CP-AudeW**

Night makes no difference 'twixt the Priest and Clerk. No Difference in the Dark [or i'th'dark]. Robert Herrick. **CP-HerrR**

Night-March, The. Herman Melville. **CP-MelvH**

Night-Mare Death in Life, The. Samuel Taylor Coleridge. **CP-ColeS**

Night Movement—New York. Carl Sandburg. **CP-SandC**

Night Music. John Clellon Holmes. **SP-HolmJ**

Night-Music. Philip Larkin. **CP-LarkP**

Night-Music. Muriel Rukeyser. **CP-RukeM**

Night-Music. Muriel Rukeyser. **CP-RukeM**
  Adventures, Midnight.
  Child Asleep, The.
  "Flattered by grief, the changeable spirit."
  Time Exposures. **PoA**
  "When those who can never again forgive themselves."

Night music slanted. Cell Song. Etheridge Knight. **SP-KnigE**

Night my father got me, The. The Culprit. Alfred Edward Housman. **CP-HousA**

Night of Destiny, The. Thomas Merton. **CP-MertT**

Night of First Snow. Robert Bly. **SP-BlyR**

Night of Frost in May. George Meredith. **CP-MerG1**

Night of Love. Paul Laurence Dunbar. **CP-DunbP**

Night of my cousin's wedding, The. How We Danced. Anne Sexton. **DIP** *Fr.* The Death of the Fathers. **CP-SextA**

Night of Questionings, A. Thomas Hardy. **CP-HardT**

Night of Stars. John Gould Fletcher. *Fr.* Sand and Spray: A Sea-Symphony. **SP-FletJ**

Night of storms has passed, The. Emily Brontë. **CP-BronE**

Night of the comet, The. The Recompense. Charles Tomlinson. **CP-TomlC**

Night of the Dance, The. Thomas Hardy. **CP-HardT**

Night of the two moons. Night: Four Songs. Langston Hughes. **SP-HughL**

Night of Trafalgar, The. Thomas Hardy. **CP-HardT** *Fr.* The Dynasts.

Night of wonder! piled afar, A. Evening in Burmah. John Greenleaf Whittier. **CP-WhitJ**

Night on a Visa Card. Charles Bukowski. **SP-BukC3**

Night on Hatchet Cove. Denise Levertov. **CP-LeveD**

Night on the Chesapeake. Paul Laurence Dunbar. **CP-DunbP**

Night on the city of the Moor! Derne. John Greenleaf Whittier. **CP-WhitJ**

Night on the Prairies. Walt Whitman. **CP-WhitW**

Night opens the pillow book, The. Shunga. Siv Cedering Fox. **SP-CedeS**

Night, our [or the] black summer, simplifies her smells. Nights in the Gardens of Port of Spain. Derek Walcott. **CP-WalcD**

Night Out. Barton Sutter. **SP-SuttB**

Night Outing, A. Jim Carroll. **SP-CarrJ**

Night over England's interrupted pastoral. Foxes' Moon. Charles Tomlinson. **CP-TomlC**

Night passd and Enitharmon eer the dawn returnd in bliss. Song of Enitharmon. William Blake. **OAEL-2** *Fr.* Vala; or The Four Zoas. **CP-BlakW**

Night passes fast for me now, The. "Bob Dylan." *Fr.* 11 Outlined Epitaphs. **CP-DylaB**

Night Patrol. Tom Clark. **SP-ClarT**

Night Piece. Louise Glück. **SP-GlücL**

Night Piece, The. Thom Gunn. **CP-GunnT**

Night-Piece. Stanley Jasspon Kunitz. **CP-KuniS**

Night-Piece, A. William Wordsworth. **CP-WorW1**

Night-Piece: The Near and the Far. Charles Tomlinson. **CP-TomlC**

Night-Piece, to Julia, The. Robert Herrick. **CP-HerrR**

Night-Pieces: For a Child. Adrienne Rich. **CP-RicAE; SP-RicA2**

Night Poem. Margaret Atwood. **SP-AtwM2**

Night Pool, The. James Dickey. **CP-DickJ**

Night Post. Archie Randolph Ammons. **SP-AmmoA**

Night Rain. Countee Cullen. **CP-CullC**

Night rain, dripping unseen, The. Embankment at Night, before the War: Outcasts. David Herbert Lawrence. **CP-LawrD**

Night Ride. Charles Tomlinson. **CP-TomlC**

Night Rider, The. William Carlos Williams. **CP-WilW2**

Night Rides of My Neighbor, Lorca, That Prevent Sleep, The. Diane Wakoski. **SP-WakoD**

Night-Scene, The. Samuel Taylor Coleridge. **CP-ColeS**

Night Scene. George Oppen. **CP-OppeG**

Night shall eat these girls and boys. Edward Estlin Cummings. **CP-CummE**

Night Shift. Sylvia Plath. **CP-PlatS**

Night Shift: the Composing Room. Barton Sutter. **SP-SuttB**

Night Skater, The. Frederick Morgan. **SP-MorgF**

Night Sky, A. Robert Creeley. **CP-CreeR**

Night Sky. Kathleen Jessie Raine. **SP-RainK**

Night sky is only a sort of carbon paper, The. Insomniac. Sylvia Plath. **CP-PlatS**

Night-sky red, crackle and roar of flame, The. In This Year of Grace. John Hewitt. **CP-HewiJ**

Night slowly stretches o'er the changing skies. Original—"Apropos." Ralph Waldo Emerson. **CP-EmerR**

Night Song. John Gould Fletcher. **SP-FletJ**

Night Song. Louise Glück. *Fr.* Marathon. **SP-GlücL**

Night Songs. David Herbert Lawrence. **CP-LawrD**
　Tomorrow Night.
　Yesternight.

Night Stuff. Carl Sandburg. **CP-SandC**

Night swallowed the sun as. Basil Bunting, *after the Persian of Sadi.* **CP-BuntB**

Night Sweat. Robert Lowell. **SP-LoweR**

Night Swimmer. Stephen Dobyns. **SP-DobyS**

Night Taxi. Thom Gunn. **CP-GunnT**

Night the cold the solitude, The. From the Outside. Paul Éluard, *tr. fr. French by* William Carlos Williams. **CP-WilW2**

Night the half-moon was like a dancing-girl, A. Tamar. Robinson Jeffers. **CP-JefR1**

Night: The Motel down the Road from the Pen. Robert Penn Warren. *Fr.* Penological Study: Southern Exposure. **SP-WarrR**

Night—there lay the Days between, A. Emily Dickinson. **CP-DickE**

Night They Took Whitey, The. Charles Bukowski. **SP-BukC2**

Night Thought. Kathleen Jessie Raine. **SP-RainK**

Night Thought, A. William Wordsworth. **CP-WorW2**

Night Thoughts. Stevie Smith. **CP-SmitS**

Night-Time in Mid-Fall. Thomas Hardy. **CP-HardT**

Night-Time in the Cemetery. Stevie Smith. **CP-SmitS**

Night town of lights. August. Gary Snyder. *Fr.* Six Years. **CP-SnydG**

Night Train, The. Thomas Merton. **CP-MertT; SP-MertT**

Night-Train, The. Charles Tomlinson. **CP-TomlC**

Night Transfigured. Charles Tomlinson. **CP-TomlC**

Night Traveler, The. Mary Oliver. **SP-OlivM**

Night Truths. Stephen Dunn. **SP-DunnS**

Night turns slowly round, The. Going Back. David Herbert Lawrence. **CP-LawrD**

Night VIII (The Eternal Man). William Blake. **PoE** *Fr.* Vala; or The Four Zoas. **CP-BlakW**

Night-Walk, The. George Meredith. **CP-MerG1**

Night walks the earth with silver feet. George Meredith. **CP-MerG2**

Night was a failure, The. First Morning. David Herbert Lawrence. **CP-LawrD**

Night was cloyed with flowers, The. The Outskirts. Walter de la Mare. **CP-DeLaW**

Night was dark, yet winter breathed, The. Emily Brontë. **CP-BronE**

Night was down among the mountains. Judith at the Tent of Holofernes. John Greenleaf Whittier. **CP-WhitJ**

Night was near, a day was near, A. A Hope Carol. Christina Georgina Rossetti. **CP-RosC2**

Night was still, and o'er the hill, The. Robert Burns. **CP-BurnR**

Night was wide, and furnished scant, The. Emily Dickinson. **CP-DickE**

Night was winter in his roughest mood, The. William Cowper. **EnRP; FHYEP; TEP** *Fr.* The Winter Walk at Noon. *Fr.* The Task. **CP-CowpW**

"No noise is here, or none that hinders thought." **PBBP**

Night Watch. Rita Dove. **SP-DoveR**

Night Watch. Adrienne Rich. **CP-RicAE; SP-RicA2**

Night Watch. May Sarton. **SP-SartM**

Night Watch in the City of Boston. Archibald MacLeish. **CP-MacLA**

Night Watch of the Trojans before Troy. Homer, *tr. by* George Meredith. **CP-MerG2** *Fr.* The Iliad.

Night Watch on the Chesapeake. Peter Meinke. **SP-MeinP**

Night Ways. Brendan Galvin. **SP-GalvB**

Night we felt the earth would move, The. Rudyard Kipling. **CP-KiplR** *Fr.* The Miracle of Purun Bhagat. *Fr.* The Second Jungle Book.

Night, welcome art thou to my mind destrest. Sonnet 37. Mary Sidney, Countess of Montgomery Wroth. *Fr.* Pamphilia to Amphilanthus. **CP-WrotM**

Night when Coleridge, The. Stanley Jasspon Kunitz. *Fr.* Journal for My Daughter. **CP-KuniS**

Night whitened in the bubbling light that poured, The. A Barn Burnt in Ohio. Daniel Gerard Hoffman. **SP-HoffD**

Night Wind, The. Emily Brontë. **CP-BronE**

Night Wind, The. John Gould Fletcher. *Fr.* Sand and Spray: A Sea-Symphony. **SP-FletJ**

Night! with all thine eyes look down! *see also* Bridal Song, A *and* Epithalamium. Percy Bysshe Shelley. **CP-ShelP**

Night, with all thine eyes look down! *see also* Bridal Song, A *and* Another Version of the Same. Percy Bysshe Shelley. **CP-ShelP**

Night with Cindy at Heitman's, A. Richard Hugo. **CP-HugoR**

Night with Lions, A. Randall Jarrell. *Fr.* The Lost World. **CP-JarrR; SP-JarrR**

Night Without Sleep. Robinson Jeffers. **CP-JefR2**

Night Work. Thomas McGrath. **SP-McGrT**

Night World. Edwin Rolfe. **CP-RolfE**

Night World. Edwin Rolfe. **CP-RolfE**

Night you got away, I dreamed you rose, The. To a Fugitive. James Wright. **CP-WrigJ; SP-SchwD**

Nightbreak. Adrienne Rich. **CP-RicAE; SP-RicA1; SP-RicA2**

Nightclubbing. Jim Carroll. **SP-CarrJ**

Nightfall. Wystan Hugh Auden. **CP-AudWJ**

Nightfall. Wystan Hugh Auden. **CP-AudWJ**

Nightfall, cold eye—neither disheartens. The Beggars. Sylvia Plath. **CP-PlatS**

Nightfall, that saw the morning-glories float. On the Skeleton of a Hound. James Wright. **CP-WrigJ**

Nightgown. James Merrill. **SP-MerrJ**

Nightingale, The. Richard Barnfield. *See* As it fell upon a day.

Nightingale, The. Samuel Taylor Coleridge. **CP-ColeS**
　Nightingales. **ChTr**
　"No cloud, no relique of the sunken day." **PBBP,** *ll.* 1–69;

Nightingale, The. Gerard Manley Hopkins. **CP-HopkG**

Nightingale and Glow-Worm, The. William Cowper. **CP-CowpW**

"Nightingale, that all day long, A." **OnMSP**

Nightingale, that all day long, A. William Cowper. **OnMSP** *Fr.* The Nightingale and Glow-Worm. **CP-CowpW**

Nightingale, that all day long, A. The Nightingale and Glow-Worm. William Cowper. **CP-CowpW**

Nightingales. Samuel Taylor Coleridge. **ChTr** *Fr.* The Nightingale. **CP-ColeS**

Nightingales, The. William Carlos Williams. **CP-WilW1**

Nightingales sing, Lalage, The. Horace at Twenty. Alun Lewis. **CP-LewiA**

Nightingales warbled without. In the Garden at Swainston. Tennyson. **CP-TennA**

Nightmare. Rita Dove. **SP-DoveR**

Nightmare. Isabella Gardner. **CP-GardI**

Nightmare. Howard Nemerov. **CP-NemeH**

Nightmare, and the Next Thing, A. Thomas Hardy. **CP-HardT**

Nightmare Boogie. Langston Hughes. **SP-HughL**

Nightmare leaves fatigue. Louis MacNeice. **AnIL; BIrV; CIP; FaBCIP; PNI** *Fr.* Autumn Journal. **CP-MacNL**

Nightmare of beasthood, snorting, how to wake. Moly. Thom Gunn. **CP-GunnT**

Nightmare of Senility. Robert Ranke Graves. **CP-GravR**

Nightmare of the Suburbs, A. Jane Cooper. **SP-CoopJ**

Nightmare shower room. My tormentor leers, The. Days of 1941 and '44. James Merrill. **SP-MerrJ**

Nightpiece. Robinson Jeffers. **CP-JefR3**

Nightpiece. Gilbert Sorrentino. **SP-SorrG**

Nights belong to / What hurts. Rafael Alberti, *tr. by* Thomas Merton. **CP-MertT** *Fr.* Roman Nocturnes.

Night's black mirror is broken. Upon Reflection. Lawrence Ferlinghetti. **SP-FerlL**

Night's capacity varies. Emily Dickinson. **SP-DickE**

Night's eye / he could say / blandly, The. So Big. Robert Creeley. **CP-CreeR**

Nights in the Gardens of Port of Spain. Derek Walcott. **CP-WalcD**

Night's lantern / Pointed with piercèd lights, and breaks of rays. Gerard Manley Hopkins. *Fr.* Fragments. **CP-HopkG**

Night's Nothings Again. Carl Sandburg. **CP-SandC**

Nights of 1964-1966: The Old Reliable. Marilyn Hacker. *See* White decorators interested in Art.

Nights of 1962: The River Merchant's Wife. Marilyn Hacker. **SP-HackM**

Nights rolled upon the river's face. "Nikolai Nikolaevich Morshen." *Fr.* Two Poems. **CP-WilbR**

Nights, the railway-arches, the bad sky, The. Rimbaud. Wystan Hugh Auden. **CP-AudeW**

Nightshade. Siv Cedering Fox. **SP-CedeS**

Nightshade on the Way to School. Margaret Atwood. **SP-AtwM2**

Nightsong. Carl Sandburg. **CP-SandC**

Nihilist, The. Stephen Dobyns. **SP-DobyS**

Nihilist as Hero, The. Robert Lowell. **SP-LoweR**

Nike. James Merrill. **SP-MerrJ**

Nil, not my aim to study you, Caesar, to be—well, a placater. Catullus. *See* Carmen 93: "Utter indifference to your welfare, Caesar."

Nil Ptolomaeus agit, caelique volumina nescit. *acc. by English translation.* Thomas Campion. **CP-CampT**

Nimble as dolphins to. Isabella Gardner. **CP-GardI**

Nimble Rays of Day Bring Oxygen to Her Blood. Tom Clark. **SP-ClarT**

Nimmo. Edwin Arlington Robinson. **CP-RobiE**

Nimphs [*or* Nymph's] Reply to the Sheepheard [*or* Shepherd], The. Sir Walter Ralegh. **CP-MarlC; CP-RaleW**

Nine, The. Edwin Rolfe. **CP-RolfE**

Nine birds(rising / through a gold moment)climb. Edward Estlin Cummings. **CP-CummE**

Nine drops of water bead the jessamine. A Wet August. Thomas Hardy. **CP-HardT**

Nine egg sister better weeps little flower. French Pronunciation Simplified for Julian Trevelyan. Malcolm Lowry. **CP-LowrM**

Nine furlongs strecht lies Tityus, who for his wicked deedes, *ad. fr. Latin of* Tibullus. Sir Walter Ralegh. **CP-RaleW**

Nine harvests & nine winters since its inception. Carmen 95. Catullus. *Fr.* Carmina. **CP-Catul**

Nine, he thinks, and every one a failure. Hayden Carruth. *Fr.* The Sleeping Beauty. **CP-CarHL**

Nine leaves a minute. The Best She Could. Thomas Hardy. **CP-HardT**

Nine-light windows that never saw the sun. Windows from a Machine Shop. Malcolm Lowry. **CP-LowrM**

Nine Miles to the Railroad. Ogden Nash. **CP-NashO**

Nine Nectarines. Marianne Craig Moore. **CP-MoorM**

Nine of Cups, The. Marge Piercy. *Fr.* Laying Down the Tower. **SP-PierM**

Nine Poems for the Unborn Child. Muriel Rukeyser. **CP-RukeM** They Came to Me and Said, "There Is a Child." **Son**

Nine posts, five doors, up the Clivus. Carmen 37. Catullus. *Fr.* Carmina. **CP-Catul**

9 Rings. Charles Bukowski. **SP-BukC2**

Nine stories high Second Avenue. 44th Birthday Evening, at Harris's. Ted Berrigan. **SP-BerrT**

Nine thousand feet in the Rockies. John Haines. *Fr.* News from the Glacier. **SP-HainJ**

Nine truckloads of jewels. Figueras Castle. William Carlos Williams. **CP-WilW2**

Nine Variations in a Chinese Winter Setting. Charles Tomlinson. **CP-TomlC**

Nine white chickens come. A Black November Turkey. Richard Wilbur. **CP-WilbR**

Nine years old! The first of any. Hector in the Garden. Elizabeth Barrett Browning. **CP-BroEB**

Ninefold table of Heaven, The. Hafiz, *tr. by* Ralph Waldo Emerson. **CP-EmerR** *Fr.* Odes.

1984. David St. John. *Fr.* To Pasolini. **SP-StJoD**

1911. Stephen Berg. **SP-BergS**

1959 Valentine. Louis Zukofsky. **CP-ZukLS**

1951. Frank O'Hara. **SP-OharF**

1957-1972. John Hewitt. **CP-HewiJ**

1956. Daniel Gerard Hoffman. **SP-HoffD**

1940. William Stafford. **SP-StafW**

1945. Stephen Berg. **SP-BergS**

1945. Donald Davie. **CP-DavDo**

1945—1985: Poem for the Anniversary. Mary Oliver. **SP-OlivM**

1945: The Death of the Gods. Randall Jarrell. **CP-JarrR**

1949: Child Redmond to Dark Wexford Came. James Liddy. **CP-LiddJ**

1946 suddenly / to remember how it. Ancestors. Tom Clark. **SP-ClarT**

1914. Stephen Berg. **SP-BergS**

1914. Randall Jarrell. **CP-JarrR**

MCMXIV. Philip Larkin. **CP-LarkP**

1914. Wilfred Owen. **CP-OwenW**

Nineteen Hundred and Nineteen. William Butler Yeats. **CP-YeatW** Come Let Us Mock at the Great. **IHNG** "Many ingenious lovely things are gone." **BIrV; LiTB; MoAB; PoE** "Some moralist or mythological poet." **PoE** "When Loie Fuller's Chinese dancers enwound." **DIP**

1949. Frederick Morgan. **SP-MorgF**

1949 (After Reading a News Item). Edwin Rolfe. **CP-RolfE**

1904. Frederick Morgan. **SP-MorgF**

1935. Kenneth Patchen. **CP-PatcK**

1928. Frederick Morgan. *Fr.* Eight Triolets. **SP-MorgF**

XIX. "Merry cuckoo, messenger of spring, The." Edmund Spenser. **OBSC** *Fr.* Amoretti. **CP-Spens**

1909. Stephen Berg. **SP-BergS**

Nineteen-Seventeen. Donald Davie. **CP-DavDo**

1975. Thom Gunn. **CP-GunnT**

1971. Robert Creeley. **CP-CreeR**

1971. Alice Walker. **CP-WalkA**

1977, Near Mullingar. Donald Davie. *Fr.* Two from Ireland. **CP-DavDo**

1976. Marilyn Hacker. **SP-HackM**

1973. Marilyn Hacker. **SP-HackM**

Nineteen Sixteen, or the Terrible Beauty. John Hewitt. **CP-HewiJ**

1968. Tom Clark. **SP-ClarT**

1969, Ireland of the Bombers. Donald Davie. *Fr.* Two from Ireland. **CP-DavDo**

1967. Leonard Cohen. **CP-CoheL**

1967. Thomas Hardy. **CP-HardT**

1963. Rita Dove. *Fr.* A Suite for Augustus. **SP-DoveR**

1930's. Robert Lowell. **SP-LoweR**

1930's. Robert Lowell. **SP-LoweR**

1930's. Robert Lowell. **SP-LoweR**

1930's. Robert Lowell. **SP-LoweR**

1930's. Robert Lowell. **SP-LoweR**

1930's. Robert Lowell. **SP-LoweR**

1930's. Robert Lowell. **SP-LoweR**

Nineteen Thirty-Eight. John Berryman. **CP-BerrJ**

1938: at 5 in the morning I vomited on the grass in front of my house. Diaries of Death. Charles Olson. **CP-OlsoC**

1938: Tales from the Vienna Woods. Randall Jarrell. **CP-JarrR**

1938: The Spring Dances. Randall Jarrell. **CP-JarrR**
1934. Richard Eberhart. **CP-EberR**
1934. Donald Hall. **CP-HallD**
1939 World's Fair. Gilbert Sorrentino. **SP-SorrG**
Nineteen-thirty, our window had for view. Etruria Vale. Charles Tomlinson. **CP-TomlC**
1933. Philip Levine. **SP-LeviP**
1929. Wystan Hugh Auden. **CP-AudeW**
1921. John Gould Fletcher. **SP-FletJ** *Fr.* The Parables of Christ.
1922. Stephen Berg. **SP-BergS**
XIX, The. Pablo Neruda, *tr. fr. Spanish by* Ben Belitt. **SP-NeruP**
Nineteenth Century and After, The. William Butler Yeats. **CP-YeatW**
Nineteenth century foundations. Craig-y-Don. Steve Griffiths. **SP-GrifS**
Ninety-nine down: a one-letter word meaning something indefinite. Crossword Puzzles. Louis MacNeice. *Fr.* Indoor Sports. **CP-MacNL**
99 to One. Charles Bukowski. **SP-BukC1**
90 North. Randall Jarrell. **CP-JarrR**; **SP-JarrR**
Ninety percent of the mass of the Universe. Certainty Before Lunch. John Berryman. **CP-BerrJ**
96 Clifton Park Avenue and the Robinsons. John Hewitt. **CP-HewiJ**
Ninna nanna, ninna nanna! Christina Georgina Rossetti. **CP-RosC3**
Niño Leading an Old Man to Market. Leonard Nathan. **SP-NathL**
Ninth Book, The. Archibald MacLeish. *Fr.* Conquistador. **CP-MacLA**
Ninth Elegy. The Antagonists. Muriel Rukeyser. **CP-RukeM**
Ninth Mile. James McAuley. *Fr.* Ten-Mile Run. **SP-McAuJ**
Ninth Psalm. Anne Sexton. *Fr.* O Ye Tongues. **CP-SextA**
Ninth Song. Sir Philip Sidney. **NoSic** *Fr.* Astrophil and Stella. **SP-SidnP**
Ninth Symphony of Beethoven Understood at Last as a Sexual Message, The. Adrienne Rich. **SP-RicA2**
Niobe. John Donne. **CP-DonnJ**
Niobe. Kenneth Patchen. **CP-PatcK**
Niobe Now. Muriel Rukeyser. **CP-RukeM**
Niobe, your tears. Hayden Carruth. **CP-CarHS** *Fr.* The Clay Hill Anthology.
Nipping Pussy's Feet in Fun. Stevie Smith. **CP-SmitS**
Nis, he makes Verses; but the Lines he writes. Upon Nis. Robert Herrick. **CP-HerrR**
Nisus, the guardian of the portal, stood. The Episode of Nisus and Euryalus. Byron. **CP-Byron**
Nite) / thatthis / crou / ched. Edward Estlin Cummings. **CP-CummE**
Nithsdale's Welcome Hame. Robert Burns. **CP-BurnR**
Nitrate. Philip Levine. **SP-LeviP**
Njord. Frederick Morgan. **SP-MorgF**
No. John Berryman. **CP-BerrJ**
No. Robert Creeley. **CP-CreeR**
No. Hilda Doolittle. *Fr.* Child Poems. **CP-DoolH**
No / one / thing. A Loop. Robert Creeley. **CP-CreeR**
No / the two legg'd beasts. No No No No. Maya Angelou. **SP-AngeM**
No access to the Duke! You have not said. *see also* Song for "Tasso." Percy Bysshe Shelley. **CP-ShelP**
No ache, love, 's the way to start the New Year. Celia's Birthday Poem. Louis Zukofsky. **CP-ZukLS**
No Action Hard to Affection. Robert Herrick. **CP-HerrR**
No actor with cupboard full of masks. Mirror. John Hewitt. **CP-HewiJ**
No aimless wanderers, by the fiend Unrest. The Christian Tourists. John Greenleaf Whittier. **CP-WhitJ**
No and I don't know where. Chuck Miller. **SP-MillC**
No argument, no anger, no remorse. Hedges Freaked with Snow. Robert Ranke Graves. **OxBTC** *Fr.* Three Songs for the Lute. **CP-GravR**
No artist perhaps, you go beyond their phrases;. Robert Lowell. **SP-LoweR** *Fr.* Mexico.
No Autumn's intercepting Chill. Emily Dickinson. **CP-DickE**
No Avail. Michael Hartnett. **SP-HarMi**
No barometer but yellow. The One. James Dickey. **CP-DickJ**
No bars are set too close, no mesh too fine. Political Reflexion [*or* Reflection]. Howard Nemerov. **ELU; MoP; NIP** *Fr.* Epigrams: "Wasp, climbing the window pane." **CP-NemeH**
No Bashfulnesse in Begging. Robert Herrick. **CP-HerrR**
No beings but. Charles Henri Ford. **SP-FordC** *Fr.* Emblems of Arachne.
No Bell-Ringing. Thomas Hardy. **CP-HardT**
No Bells to Believe. Richard Hugo. **CP-HugoR**
No Berserk thirst of blood had they. Lexington. John Greenleaf Whittier. **CP-WhitJ**
No better lost than any other woman. Marilyn Hacker. **SP-HackM** *Fr.* Taking Notice.
No Better Than a "Withered Daffodil." Marianne Craig Moore. **CP-MoorM**
No Bird. Theodore Roethke. **CP-RoetT**

No bird-song floated down the hill. The River Path. John Greenleaf Whittier. **CP-WhitJ**
No bitterness: our ancestors did it. Ave Caesar. Robinson Jeffers. **CP-JefR2**
No blanch witloof handboud dry. Dandelion. Louis Zukofsky. **CP-ZukLS**
No boats oar slow, no barges pass. George Meredith. **CP-MerG2**
No Bobolink—reverse His Singing. Emily Dickinson. **CP-DickE**
No books, no songs. Old Man at Valdez. Charles Tomlinson. **CP-TomlC**
No, boy, we must not—so began. Filippo Baldinucci on the Privilege of Burial. Robert Browning. **CP-BroR2**
No breath of air to break the wave. The Giaour. Byron. **CP-Byron**
No Brigadier throughout the Year. Emily Dickinson. **CP-DickE**
No Buyers [*or* No Buyers: A Street Scene]. Thomas Hardy. **CP-HardT**
No cars go by. Dry Places. Thomas Merton. **CP-MertT; SP-MertT**
No castle time had I, no cattle shouts. Imitative Fragment. David Markson. **CP-MarkD**
No Categories! Stevie Smith. **CP-SmitS**
No cause, nor client fat, will Cheveril leese. On Cheveril the Lawyer. Ben Jonson. **CP-JonsB**
No Change of Place. Wystan Hugh Auden. *See* Who Will Endure.
No changes of support—only. Last Month. John Ashbery. **SP-AshbJ**
No Cherub's heart or hand for us might ache. Good Friday Evening. Christina Georgina Rossetti. **CP-RosC2**
No Churchman am I for to rail and to write. Song. Robert Burns. **CP-BurnR**
No cloud, no relique of the sunken day. Samuel Taylor Coleridge. **PBBP**, *ll.* 1–69; *Fr.* The Nightingale. **CP-ColeS**
No cloud, no relique of the sunken day. The Nightingale. Samuel Taylor Coleridge. **CP-ColeS**
No clouds out the window. Robert Creeley. **CP-CreeR**
No Color Man. Donald Hall. **CP-HallD**
No Coming to God without Christ. Robert Herrick. **CP-HerrR**
No Comment! John Hewitt. **CP-HewiJ**
No cool breezes, not a cloud. 1922. Stephen Berg. **SP-BergS**
No coward soul is mine. Emily Brontë. **CP-BronE**
No Cresta Run. John Hewitt. **CP-HewiJ**
No Crowd that has occurred. Emily Dickinson. **CP-DickE**
No Danger to Men Desperate. Robert Herrick. **CP-HerrR**
No dark in the body. Roy Fisher. **SP-FishR** *Fr.* Handsworth Liberties.
No, darling, the world is not ruled by sense, not sense. Alligators and Paris and North America. William Dickey. **SP-DickW**
No day is right for the apocalypse. The Waste Carpet. William Matthews. **SP-MattW**
No Deposit. Donald Hall. **CP-HallD**
No Despight to the Dead. Robert Herrick. **CP-HerrR**
No Difference. Shel Silverstein. **CP-SilS2**
No Difference in the Dark [*or* i'th'dark]. Robert Herrick. **CP-HerrR**
No dignity without chromium. Ballad of Faith. William Carlos Williams. **CP-WilW2**
No Doctors Today, Thank You. Ogden Nash. **CP-NashO**
No, don't ask me to give you. Moon Flock. James Dickey. **CP-DickJ**
No doubt but ye are the People—your throne is above the King's. The Islanders. Rudyard Kipling. **CP-KiplR**
No doubt he'd once had eyes to see. Archibald MacLeish. **CP-MacLA** *Fr.* The Happy Marriage.
No doubt I will end my life as poor as you. Talking to My Grandmother Who Died Poor. Alice Walker. **CP-WalkA**
No doubt she was a singer. The Girl Who Died #2. Alice Walker. **CP-WalkA**
No doubt the creation was something like this. Morning. Derek Mahon. *Fr.* Four Walks in the Country Near Saint-Brieuc. **SP-MahoD**
No doubt to-morrow I will hide. At Mass. Nicholas Vachel Lindsay. **CP-LindV**
No Druid can control a woman's longing. Druid Love. Robert Ranke Graves. **CP-GravR**
No dust have I to cover me. An Inscription by the Sea. Glaukos. **AWP; ChTr; ELU; FaBoEE** *Fr.* Variations of Greek Themes. **CP-RobiE**
No Earthly Enterprise. Edna St. Vincent Millay. **CP-MillE**
No empty bed blues. Madison, Wis., Remembering the Bloom of Monticello (1931). Louis Zukofsky. *Fr.* 29 Songs. **CP-ZukLS**
No empty bed blues. 29 Songs. Louis Zukofsky. **CP-ZukLS**
No Epitaph. Donald Davie. **CP-DavDo**
No Escaping the Scourging. Robert Herrick. **CP-HerrR**
No event of Wind or Bird. Emily Dickinson. **SP-DickE**
No faculty not ill at ease. After a Long Illness. Robert Duncan. **SP-DuncR**
No faith of partnership dominion owns. Lucan, *tr. by* Samuel Johnson. **CP-JohnS** *Fr.* Pharsalia.

No farther out / than in—. No. Robert Creeley. **CP-CreeR**

No fate, save by the victim's fault, is low. Ralph Waldo Emerson. **CP-EmerR**

No Fault in Women. Robert Herrick. **CP-HerrR**

No fiction was it of the antique age. The Faery Chasm. William Wordsworth. *Fr.* The River Duddon [A Series of Sonnets]. **CP-WorW2**

No fish passed this way this century. Italian Town Abandoned. Richard Hugo. **CP-HugoR**

No Fixed Place. Alice Walker. **CP-WalkA**

No flower grew where I was bred. The Slum Child. Walter de la Mare. **CP-DeLaW**

No flowers, please, in plastic hoods. Brief Encounter. Phoebe Hesketh. **SP-HeskP**

No foot could endure it. Night City. Elizabeth Bishop. **CP-BishE**

No, for I'll save it! Seven years since. Apparent Failure. Robert Browning. **CP-BroR1**

No Frog Prince ever had a pond. To a Waterbed. John Updike. **CP-UpdiJ**

No front yard to speak of. The House on Bishop Street. Rita Dove. **SP-DoveR**

No further from me than my hand. Edna St. Vincent Millay. **CP-MillE**

No gifts today. Last night no monster star. Christmas with Shepherds in Brefaro. Richard Hugo. **CP-HugoR**

No Good Too. William Carlos Williams. **CP-WilW2**

No grave for woe, yet earth my watrie teares devoures. *At. to* Thomas Campion *and to* Philip Rosseter. **CP-CampT**

No grief is grown so desperate, but the ill. The Will Makes the Work, or Consent Makes the Cure. Robert Herrick. **CP-HerrR**

No guidance can be found in ancient lore. A Major Port. Wystan Hugh Auden. *Fr.* A Voyage. **CP-AudeW**

No hawk at wrist, but blessed by sudden sun. Portrait of Mrs. Spaxton. Charles Tomlinson. **CP-TomlC**

No hawk hangs over in this air. The Snow Storm. Edna St. Vincent Millay. **CP-MillE**

No Hearing. Robert Lowell. **SP-LoweR**

No Hearing. Robert Lowell. **SP-LoweR**

No heart that broke but further went. Emily Dickinson. **SP-DickE**

No Heaven. David St. John. **SP-StJoD**

No hills. Raw wind unchecked, brings word. In Stafford Country. Richard Hugo. **CP-HugoR**

No Holy Wars for Them. Robert Frost. **CP-FrosR**

No hope in life; yet is there hope. What Good Shall My Life Do Me? Christina Georgina Rossetti. **CP-RosC3**

No hope, no change! The clouds have shut us in. Two Months. Rudyard Kipling. **CP-KiplR**

No hyacinthine imagination can express this clock of meat bleakly pining. Allen Ginsberg. **CP-GinsA**

No I don't know what your connection with the railroads is. There's Plenty of Anguish at the Railroad. Diane Wakoski. **SP-WakoD**

No, I don't like the rain either. Letter to comfort a friend. Jenny Joseph. *Fr.* Life and Turgid Times of A. Citizen. **SP-JoseJ**

No, I had set no prohibiting sign. Trespass. Robert Frost. **CP-FrosR**

No, I have never found. Places, Loved Ones. Philip Larkin. **CP-LarkP**

No, I have seen the mirage tremble, seen how thin. The Mirage. Kathleen Jessie Raine. *Fr.* Three Poems on Illusion. **SP-RainK**

No, I was wrecked here. Hayden Carruth. **CP-CarHS** *Fr.* The Clay Hill Anthology.

No, I will go alone. The Concert. Edna St. Vincent Millay. **CP-MillE**

No, I will never forget you and your great eyes. Song. May Sarton. **SP-SartM**

No idea, Gelli, spurred me to mirror you faithful. Catullus. *See* Carmen 91: "In this hopeless & wasting love of mine."

No in-between. The news is good or bad. Uig Registrar. Richard Hugo. **CP-HugoR**

No Infant Sotheby, Whose Dauntless Head. Byron. **CP-Byron**

No it didn't get too cold here too often. If you asked. John Yau. **SP-YauJo**

No it would not mean a damn (quick whim referred to pure. Catullus. *See* Carmen 97: "As God is my witness where is the difference between."

No Joy in Life. David Herbert Lawrence. **CP-LawrD**

No knightly sword to serve, nor harp of bard. George Meredith. *Fr.* The Sage Enamoured and the Honest Lady. **CP-MerG1**

No Kraken Shall Be Found Till Sought By Name. Malcolm Lowry. **CP-LowrM**

No Labor-Saving Machine. Walt Whitman. **CP-WhitW**

No lack of counsel from the shrewd and wise. Edna St. Vincent Millay. **CP-MillE**

No ladder needs the bird but skies. Emily Dickinson. **CP-DickE**

No lame excuses can gloss over. Green Rock, Winthrop Bay. Sylvia Plath. **CP-PlatS**

No Lamp Has Ever Shown Us Where to Look. Archibald MacLeish. **CP-MacLA**

No leaf stirs. I am alone. Kenneth Rexroth. **SP-RexrK** *Fr.* On Flower Wreath Hill.

No less fabulous than the carved marble inner. Leap of Faith. David St. John. **SP-StJoD**

No Letter. Robert Ranke Graves. **CP-GravR**

No Life can pompless pass away. Emily Dickinson. **CP-DickE**

No lift odd mere horror, harrowed (why boy?) that no woman will. Catullus. *See* Carmen 69: "Do not wonder when the wench declines."

No Loathsomnesse in Love. Robert Herrick. **CP-HerrR**

No Lock against Lechery. Robert Herrick. **CP-HerrR**

No longer burn the hands that seized. Stanza. Louise Bogan. **CP-BogaL**

No longer do the Brady loggers harry. Deserted Lumber Yard. Louise McNeill. **SP-McNeL**

No longer I follow a sound. Song on Peace. William Cowper. **CP-CowpW**

No longer mourn for me when I am dead. Sonnet 71. William Shakespeare. **AWP; EBEV; EIL; EnRePo; FaBoRV; GBL; GTBS; GTBS-6; GTBS-P; HAP; HBV; HeIP; IMW; ImPo; LO; LiTB; NAEL-1; NoP; NoSic; OAEP; OBSC; OXAEP-1; PAI; PPoe; PoRA; SCGP; SeCeV; Son; TEP; TFi; TrGrPo; TreFT; WHA** *Fr.* Sonnets. **CP-ShaWS**

No longer now the attitude's high profile. Function. John Hewitt. **CP-HewiJ**

No longer throne of a goddess to whom we pray. Full Moon. Robert Earl Hayden. **CP-HaydR**

No longer torn by what she knows. The Poor Relation. Edwin Arlington Robinson. **CP-RobiE**

No Loser, No Weeper. Maya Angelou. **SP-AngeM**

No love / no love cried the last fling. Grace Paley. **CP-PaleG**

No love by test, my love, 'll air then, time, say the care of all my time. Catullus. *See* Carmen 87: "No woman loved, in truth, Lesbia."

No love is so dear (quivered Cupid, fly!). 2.5. Ovid. **CP-MarlC,** *tr. by* Christopher Marlowe; *Fr.* Elegies.

No love without hurt? No lovesong without distortion? Hayden Carruth. *Fr.* The Sleeping Beauty. **CP-CarHL**

No lovelier hills than thine have laid. England. Walter de la Mare. **CP-DeLaW**

No lover ever found a cure for love. The Cure. Robert Ranke Graves. **CP-GravR**

No lover saith, I love, nor any other. The Paradox. John Donne. **CP-DonnJ**

No Luck in Love. Robert Herrick. **CP-HerrR**

No Man can compass a Despair. Emily Dickinson. **CP-DickE**

No man can see God except he be blind, *ad. from* Eckhart. Thomas Merton. *Fr.* Cables to the Ace. **CP-MertT**

No man comes late unto that place from whence. Never Too Late to Dye. Robert Herrick. **CP-HerrR**

No man is tempted so, but may o'recome. Temptations. Robert Herrick. **CP-HerrR**

No man may him hyde. Sun. Marianne Craig Moore. **CP-MoorM**

No man saw awe, nor to his house. Emily Dickinson. **CP-DickE**

No man should stand before the moon. A Sense of Humor. Nicholas Vachel Lindsay. **CP-LindV**

No man so well a Kingdom Rules, as He. *see also* Obedience. Robert Herrick. **CP-HerrR**

No man such rare paths hath, that he can swim. No Man Without Money. Robert Herrick. **CP-HerrR**

No man, unless he has died, and learned to be alone. Initiation Degrees. David Herbert Lawrence. **CP-LawrD**

No man was better, no more just than hee. Sir Walter Ralegh. **CP-RaleW** *Fr.* Metamorphoses.

No Man Without Money. Robert Herrick. **CP-HerrR**

No man, if men are gods;but if gods must. Edward Estlin Cummings. **CP-CummE; SP-CummE**

No manner of address will do. The Fear. Geoffrey Hill. *Fr.* Metamorphoses. **CP-HillG**

No manner of address will do. Metamorphoses. Geoffrey Hill. **CP-HillG**

No Map. Stephen Dobyns. **SP-DobyS**

No Map Available. Jenny Joseph. **SP-JoseJ**

No map traces the street. The Sleepers. Sylvia Plath. **CP-PlatS**

No, Mary, there was nothing—not a word. Lazarus. Edwin Arlington Robinson. **CP-RobiE**

No master I but able seaman. Exorcism. Jenny Joseph. **SP-JoseJ**

No matter how dull your soul, you cannot help. Playing Skittles. Howard Nemerov. **CP-NemeH**

No matter how gently, with what suspended. Once More for My Lady. Dabney Stuart. **SP-StuaD**

No matter how thick or how thin you slice it it's still baloney. Carl Sandburg. *Fr.* The People, Yes. **CP-SandC**

No Matter, Never Mind. Gary Snyder. **CP-SnydG**

No matter—now—Sweet. Emily Dickinson. **CP-DickE**

No Matter What, After All, and That Beautiful Word So. Hayden Carruth. **CP-CarHS**

No matter what color my pants are. Swinging Down Central. Robert Creeley. **CP-CreeR**

No matter what I am. The Poet Answers the Accuser. Kathleen Jessie Raine. **SP-RainK**

No matter what I say. Eel-Grass. Edna St. Vincent Millay. **CP-MillE**

No matter what life you lead. Snow White and the Seven Dwarfs. Anne Sexton. **CP-SextA**

No matter what you call it. James Whitcomb Riley. Paul Laurence Dunbar. **CP-DunbP**

No matter where the Saints abide. Emily Dickinson. **CP-DickE**

No matter which back route I took. South Bronx, 1939. Robert Pack. **SP-PackR**

No matter why, nor whence, nor when she came. The Story of the Ashes and the Flame. Edwin Arlington Robinson. **CP-RobiE**

No McTavish. Genealogical Reflection. Ogden Nash. **CP-NashO**

No Messiah. Robert Lowell. **SP-LoweR**

No metaphor reinvents the job of the nurture of children. Grace Paley. *Fr.* Stanzas: Old Age and the Conventions of Retirement Have Driven My Friends from the Work They Love. **CP-PaleG**

No mischief worthier of our fear. On Flatterers. *Unknown, tr. fr. Greek by* William Cowper. **CP-CowpW**

No! Mr Lawrence! David Herbert Lawrence. **CP-LawrD**

No, Mr. Lawrence, it's not like that! No! Mr Lawrence! David Herbert Lawrence. **CP-LawrD**

No money to bury him. Ballad of the Man Who's Gone. Langston Hughes. **SP-HughL**

No Moon Floods the Memory of that Night. Etheridge Knight. **SP-KnigE**

No more--no more--Oh! never more on me. My Days of Love Are Over. Byron. **OBNC** *Fr.* Canto the First. **EnRP; NAEL-2; NoP; OAEL-2; PoE** *Fr.* Don Juan. **CP-Byron**

No more / Thou little winged Archer, now no more. Sir Thomas Wortley's Sonnet Answered. Richard Lovelace. **CP-LoveR**

No more, / where the tidal river rushes. Maximus to Himself June 1964. Charles Olson. **SP-OlsoC** *Fr.* The Maximus Poems.

No More Access to Her Underpants. John Updike. *Fr.* Two Sonnets Whose Titles Came to Me Simultaneously. **CP-UpdiJ**

No more be grieved at that which thou hast done. Sonnet 35. William Shakespeare. **HeIP; ImPo; NAEL-1; NoSic; OXAEP-1; PeHV; PoE; SCGP; TEP; UnPo** *Fr.* Sonnets. **CP-ShaWS**

No more, blind god! for see, my heart. Truce in Love Intreated. Thomas Carew. **CP-CareT**

No More Doors Tonight. Al Young. **CP-YounA**

No More Elegies. Jane Cooper. *Fr.* March. **SP-CoopJ**

No more Fabian, no more like that. Fabian Bell—His Last Visit to Cuernavaca. Marsden Hartley. **CP-HartM**

No More Ghosts. Robert Ranke Graves. **CP-GravR**

No more let Greece her bolder fables tell. On the Famous Voyage. Ben Jonson. **CP-JonsB**

No more loud Fall / October is suddenly over / Sunk in snow. Early Blizzard. Thomas Merton. **CP-MertT**

No more, my dear, no more these counsels try. Sonnet 64. Sir Philip Sidney. **HBV 1-2; OBSC; SCGP** *Fr.* Astrophil and Stella. **SP-SidnP**

No more my Silvia, do I mean to pray. To Silvia. Robert Herrick. **CP-HerrR**

No more my visionary soul shall dwell. Pantisocracy. Samuel Taylor Coleridge. **CP-ColeS**

No more my wearied soul attempts to stray. To Mrs. ****. Charlotte Smith. **CP-SmitC**

No more, O my spirit. Euripides, *tr. by* Hilda Doolittle ("H.D."). **CP-DoolH** *Fr.* Hippolytus.

No more of talk where God or Angel Guest. John Milton. **EPCY; NOSC; OBS; TOF** *Fr.* Book IX. **FHYEP; NAEL-1; NAWM-1; NoP; OAEL-1** *Fr.* Paradise Lost. **CP-MiltJ**

(Higher Argument.) **NOSC**

(Subject of Heroic Song, The.) **OBS**

No more [of] talk where God or Angel Guest. Book IX. John Milton. **FHYEP; NAEL-1; NAWM-1; NoP; OAEL-1** *Fr.* Paradise Lost. **CP-MiltJ**

No more of your guests, be they titled or not. Robert Burns. *Fr.* To John Syme. **CP-BurnR**

No more of your titled acquaintances boast. Robert Burns. **CP-BurnR**

No More People. Stevie Smith. **CP-SmitS**

No more phrases, Swenson: I was once. Lions in Sweden. Wallace Stevens. **CP-StevW**

No More Sea. Louis MacNeice. **CP-MacNL**

No more shall hapless Celia's ears. Song. William Cowper. **CP-CowpW**

No more shall I, since I am driven hence. To Larr [or Lar]. Robert Herrick. **CP-HerrR**

No more shall meads be deckt [or deck'd] with flowers. The Protestation [A Sonnet]. Thomas Carew. **CP-CareT**

No more stalling. Saying Goodbye to Love. Charles Bukowski. **SP-BukC2**

No more summer for Molly and me. Molly Gone. Thomas Hardy. **CP-HardT**

No more: the end is sudden and abrupt. Apology. William Wordsworth. **CP-WorW2**

No more the quizzish Bewley's destin'd wife. Epiologue [B] to *What Is She?*. Charlotte Smith. **CP-SmitC** *Fr.* What is She?

No more the white refulgent streets. Elegy. Allen Tate. **CP-TateA**

No more the white refulgent streets. Euthanasia. Allen Tate. **CP-TateA**

No more these simple flowers belong. Burns. John Greenleaf Whittier. **CP-WhitJ**

No more thus brooding o'er yon heap. The Vanity of Wealth. Samuel Johnson. **CP-JohnS**

No more 'twixt conscience staggering and the Pope. Lines Suggested by the Last Words of Berengarius. Samuel Taylor Coleridge. **CP-ColeS**

No more violets. Pastorale. Hart Crane. **CP-CranH**

No more! while sun and planets fly. I See That All Things Come to an End. Christina Georgina Rossetti. **CP-RosC2**

No more wine? then we'll push back chairs and talk. Bishop Blougram's Apology. Robert Browning. **CP-BroR1**

No more with overflowing light. For a Dead Lady. Edwin Arlington Robinson. **CP-RobiE**

No more, ye warblers of the wood, no more. Sonnet on the Death of Robert Riddel, Esq. *of Glen Riddel, April 1794.* Robert Burns. **CP-BurnR**

No mortal man beneath the sky. Epitaph for George Moore. Thomas Hardy. **CP-HardT**

No mortal object did these eyes behold. Michelangelo Buonarroti, *tr. fr. Italian by* William Wordsworth. **CP-WorW1**

No moss nor mottle stains. No Epitaph. Donald Davie. **CP-DavDo**

No, Music, thou art not the "food of Love." Another Fragment to Music. Percy Bysshe Shelley. **CP-ShelP**

No Name. Margaret Atwood. **SP-AtwM2**

No need to get home early. Father's Voice. William Stafford. **SP-StafW**

No News. David Herbert Lawrence. **CP-LawrD**

No news in the *Times* to-day. Legetai Ti Khainon. Gerard Manley Hopkins. *Fr.* A Trio of Triolets. **CP-HopkG**

No news of navies burnt at seas. A New-Year's [or New-Yeares] Gift Sent to Sir Simeon Steward. Robert Herrick. **CP-HerrR**

No, no! / and the dirtyneck boy starts crying and running. Dreaming. Juan Ramón Jiménez. *Fr.* Ten Short Poems. **CP-WrigJ**

No; no; / It must not be so. Paths of Former Time. Thomas Hardy. **CP-HardT**

No, no, fair heretic[k], it needs must be. Song. Sir John Suckling. **AnAnS-2; BeJo; CABA; CaPo; LoBV; OBS; PrIm** *Fr.* Aglaura. **CP-SuckJ**

No, no,—forget your Cricket and your Ant. Leffingwell. Edwin Arlington Robinson. **CP-RobiE**

No, no! Go from me. I have left her lately. A Virginal. Ezra Pound. **SP-PounE**

No, no, go not to Lethe, neither twist. Ode on Melancholy. John Keats. **CP-KeatJ**

No, no. Guard thee. Get thee gone. Not that way. Walter de la Mare. **CP-DeLaW**

No No No No. Maya Angelou. **SP-AngeM**

No, no, the falling blossom is no sign. Song. George Meredith. **CP-MerG1**

No. No. The woman is cheerful, she smiles at her stomach. Eighth Psalm. Anne Sexton. *Fr.* O Ye Tongues. **CP-SextA**

No noise is here, or none that hinders thought. William Cowper. **PBBP** *Fr.* The Night was winter in his roughest mood. **EnRP; FHYEP; TEP** *Fr.* The Winter Walk at Noon. For The Task. **CP-CowpW**

No, not from this life, not from this life is any. Wystan Hugh Auden. **CP-AudWJ**

No. Not really red. Song for a Red Nightgown. Anne Sexton. **CP-SextA**

No, not that door—never! But. I Am Dreaming of a White Christmas: The Natural History of a Vision. Robert Penn Warren. **SP-WarrR**

No, not the downfall. Rumba! Rumba! William Carlos Williams. **CP-WilW2**

No—not where I shall make my own. Her Late Husband. Thomas Hardy. **CP-HardT**

No Notice gave She, but a Change. Emily Dickinson. **CP-DickE**

No novice / In those elaborate rituals. Miss Drake Proceeds to Supper. Sylvia Plath. **CP-PlatS**

No, now I wish the sunshine would stop. And Oh—That the Man I Am Might Cease to Be. David Herbert Lawrence. **CP-LawrD**

No, of course we were never. *Song*: Of Course. Robert Ranke Graves. **CP-GravR**

No one / Can teach us the deep-water. The Diving Ballet. Laurence Lieberman. **SP-LiebL**

No one / else in the room. Here. Robert Creeley. **CP-CreeR**

No one believes in the calm. Belief. Philip Levine. **SP-LeviP**

No one can boast herself so much belov'd. Catullus. *See* Carmen 87: "No woman loved, in truth, Lesbia."

No one can die twice of the same fever? Twice Of The Same Fever. Robert Ranke Graves. **CP-GravR**

No one can hear the loud voice of the city. The Ohio River—Louisville. Thomas Merton. **CP-MertT; SP-MertT**

No one can help him anymore. Company. Rita Dove. **SP-DoveR**

No one can hurt me. They've tried to kill me. Alone. "Anna Akhmatova", *tr. fr. Russian* by Stephen Berg. **SP-BergS**

No one can tell you why. William DeWitt Snodgrass. **ConAP; NePoEA** *Fr.* Heart's Needle. **SP-SnodW**

No One Can Watch the Wasichu. Alice Walker. **CP-WalkA**

No one could enter those vast fields. Fragments of an Old Song 2. Gilbert Sorrentino. **SP-SorrG**

No one escapes the perjury of time. An Old Photograph. Howard Nemerov. **CP-NemeH**

No One Ever Tried To Kiss Anna May Wong. John Yau. **SP-YauJo**

No one ever walking this our only earth, various, very clouded. He Had a Quality of Growth. Muriel Rukeyser. **CP-RukeM**

No one ever works alone. Kenneth Patchen. **CP-PatcK**

No one gives you a thought, as day by day. Neurotics. Philip Larkin. **CP-LarkP**

No one I meet is ever armed. Urban Hunting Scenes. Dabney Stuart. **SP-StuaD**

No One Inn. Louis Zukofsky. *Fr.* 29 Songs. **CP-ZukLS**

No one is here today, the streets. Times. Stephen Berg. **SP-BergS**

No one is left to eat by my fire. Signs. Audre Lorde. **SP-LordA**

No one is lovely. To a Woman Seen Once. William Carlos Williams. **CP-WilW2**

No one is missed in the garden. Nobody's there. Egoist. Pablo Neruda, *tr. fr. Spanish* by Ben Belitt. **SP-NeruP**

No one is perfection, yet. Absence. Stephen Spender. **CP-SpenS**

No one is pleased with himself. The Lemmings. John Haines. **SP-HainJ**

No one is "Woman" to another. Mother II. Marilyn Hacker. **SP-HackM**

No one knows, / the heart of a child. Hilda Doolittle. **CP-DoolH** *Fr.* Electra-Orestes.

No one knows yet. Violence. Adrienne Rich. **CP-RicAE**

No one, not even Cambridge, was to blame. A. E. Housman. Wystan Hugh Auden. **CP-AudeW**

No one, not even God, can put back a leaf on to a tree. Fatality. David Herbert Lawrence. **CP-LawrD**

No one now imagines you answer idle questions. Short Ode to the Cuckoo. Wystan Hugh Auden. **CP-AudeW**

No one prays for me. . . Giovanna or the others. Dante 3. Buonconte. Robert Lowell. **SP-LoweR**

No One Remembers. Philip Levine. **SP-LeviP**

No one waits for me. Jokes on the Poop. Malcolm Lowry. **CP-LowrM**

No one was in the fields. Tom's Angel. Walter de la Mare. **CP-DeLaW**

No one was looking at his lonely case. Any Size We Please. Robert Frost. **CP-FrosR**

No one was with me there. Estranged. Walter de la Mare. **CP-DeLaW**

No one will ever understand that evening. Evening Plaza, San Miguel. Muriel Rukeyser. **CP-RukeM**

No one's fated or doomed to love anyone. Adrienne Rich. *Fr.* Twenty-one Love Poems. **SP-RicA1; SP-RicA2**

No one's going to read. A Dance for Militant Dilettantes. Al Young. **CP-YounA**

No one's hangin' stockin's up. Merry. Shel Silverstein. **SP-SilS2**

No Other can reduce. Emily Dickinson. **CP-DickE**

No other such luxuriance: the. The Gentle Negress. William Carlos Williams. **CP-WilW2**

No Paines, No Gaines. Robert Herrick. **CP-HerrR**

No Passenger was known to flee. Emily Dickinson. **CP-DickE**

No people on the golf-links, not a crack. North Coast Recollections. Sir John Betjeman. **CP-BetjJ**

No physician has a balsam for my wo. Hafiz, *tr. by* Ralph Waldo Emerson. **CP-EmerR** *Fr.* Odes.

No Pindar I, but a poor gentleman. *English Vers. of* Antorcha y Corona, 1968. Robert Ranke Graves. **CP-GravR**

No pine so firmly set, no lofty towers. J.S. Bach. Wystan Hugh Auden. **CP-AudWJ**

No place for a lady, this. Sisterhood. Marilyn Hacker. **SP-HackM**

No, Plato, No. Wystan Hugh Auden. **CP-AudeW**

No Pleasure, Without Some Payne. Sir Walter Ralegh. **CP-RaleW**

No point in looking. The. Sunday Morning. Donald Davie. **CP-DavDo**

No porter guards the passage of your door. John Dryden. **EBEV** *Fr.* To My Honoured [*or* Honour'd] Kinsman, John Driden [of Chesterton in the County of Huntingdon, Esquire0. **SP-DrydJ**

No Possum, No Sop, No Taters. Wallace Stevens. **CP-StevW**

No prayer for the people. Malcolm Lowry. **CP-LowrM**

No pretense no more than the. Cézanne. William Carlos Williams. **CP-WilW2**

No Prisoner be. Emily Dickinson. **CP-DickE**

No protesting, dearest! Saint Martin's Summer. Robert Browning. **CP-BroR2**

No question but Dols cheecks wo'd soon rost dry. Upon Dol. Robert Herrick. **CP-HerrR**

No Rack can torture me. Emily Dickinson. **CP-DickE**

No real Style of Colouring ever appears. William Blake. **CP-BlakW**

No record tells of lance opposed to lance. William Wordsworth. *Fr.* The River Duddon [A Series of Sonnets]. **CP-WorW2**

No Regrets. Langston Hughes. **SP-HughL**

No Reply. The Beatles. **CP-Beatl**

No Reply at Christmas. Phoebe Hesketh. **SP-HeskP**

No Respect. Stevie Smith. **CP-SmitS**

No Resurrection. Robinson Jeffers. **CP-JefR2**

No ripening curve can be allowed to sag. Cherry Ripe. Donald Davie. **CP-DavDo**

No Road. Philip Larkin. **CP-LarkP**

No road in existence strikes such terror. Malcolm Lowry. *Fr.* The Roar of the Sea and the Darkness. **CP-LowrM**

No role in peace for such a restless captain. Legend in His Own Lifetime. John Hewitt. **CP-HewiJ**

No Romance sold unto. Emily Dickinson. **CP-DickE**

No roofes of golf o're riotous tables shining. *ad. fr. the Latin* Domus non Auratae Descriptio. Richard Crashaw. **CP-CrasR**

No room for nostalgia here. What would it look like? Location. Adrienne Rich. *Fr.* Turning the Wheel. **SP-RicA2**

No rose that in a garden ever grew. Edna St. Vincent Millay. **CP-MillE**

No Rose, yet felt myself a'bloom. Emily Dickinson. **SP-DickE**

No rustle. / Not a lip / stirs in the town square. Siesta. Laurence Lieberman. **SP-LiebL**

No salt here, old sea father, holy giant. The Far-removed Mountain Men. Hayden Carruth. **CP-CarHS**

No sculptur'd marble here, nor pompous lay. Epitaph. Here Lies Robert Fergusson, Poet. Robert Burns. **CP-BurnR**

No Second Troy. John Hewitt. **CP-HewiJ**

No Second Troy. William Butler Yeats. **CP-YeatW**

No sense of past. Did Serra. Mission in Carmel. Richard Hugo. **CP-HugoR**

No shark, the fin that scars a circle. Name the Mystery Fin and Win a Doll. Richard Hugo. **CP-HugoR**

No shields now / Cross the knoll. Iceland. Louis MacNeice. **CP-MacNL**

No ship of all that under sail or steam. Immigrants. Robert Frost. **CP-FrosR**

No Shipwrack of Vertue. To a Friend. Robert Herrick. **CP-HerrR**

No Shoes No Shirt No Service. Gary Snyder. **CP-SnydG**

No sir i would not like to sell. W. D. Attempts to Save Cock Robin. William DeWitt Snodgrass. **SP-SnodW**

No skilled hands. In Abeyance. Denise Levertov. **CP-LeveD**

No sleep. The sultriness pervades the air. The House-Top. Herman Melville. **SP-MelvH**

No smile so innocent or angelic. Against Witchcraft. Robert Ranke Graves. **CP-GravR**

No smoke says law light- / Ning arrest alarm for. Comedy Card for a Serious Case. Thomas Merton. **CP-MertT**

No smoke spreads out of this chimney-pot. Starlings on the Roof. Thomas Hardy. **CP-HardT**

No So. Not So. Anne Sexton. **CP-SextA**

No song nor dance I bring from yon great city. Prologue. Robert Burns. **CP-BurnR**

No song so tuneful, quoth the fox. Ralph Waldo Emerson. **CP-EmerR**

No sooner come [*or* came] but gone, and fallen [*or* fall'n] asleep. On My Dear Grandchild Simon Bradstreet, [Who Died on 16TH November, 1669, Being But A Month And One Day Old]. Anne Bradstreet. **CP-BradA**

No sooner had I left A. Midpoint. Charles Simic. **SP-SimiC**

No sooner had th' Almighty ceas't, but all. Heaven. John Milton. **OBS** *Fr.* Book III. *Fr.* Paradise Lost. **CP-MiltJ**

No Sorrow Peculiar to the Sufferer. Vincent Bourne, *tr. fr. Latin by* William Cowper. **CP-CowpW**

No sort of learning ever hurts his head. Lout, The. John Clare. **SP-ClarJ**

No sound falls. After. Maya Angelou. **SP-AngeM**

No sound of any storm that shakes. Hillcrest. Edwin Arlington Robinson. **CP-RobiE**

No spade for leagues had won a rood of earth. William Wordsworth. **CP-WorW1**

No Spartan tube, no Attic shell. Ode [for General Washington's Birthday]. Robert Burns. **CP-BurnR**

No specious splendour of this stone. The Cornelian. Byron. **CP-Byron**

No Speech from the Scaffold. Thom Gunn. **CP-GunnT**

No speed of wind or water rushing by. The Master Speed. Robert Frost. **CP-FrosR**

No spot of earth where men have so fiercely for ages of time. Antrim. Robinson Jeffers. **CP-JefR2**

No Spouse but a Sister. Robert Herrick. **CP-HerrR**

No spring, nor summer beauty hath such grace. The Autumnal[l]. John Donne. **InPS; JCP; NOSC; OAEP; PoEL-2; SeCV-1; TEP** *Fr.* Elegies. **CP-DonnJ**

No sprouted wheat and soya shoots. The Health-Food Diner. Maya Angelou. **SP-AngeM**

No state is enviable. To the luck alone. George Meredith. *Fr.* Modern Love. **CP-MerG1**

No Stewart art thou, Galloway. On Lord Galloway. Robert Burns. **FaBoEE** *Fr.* Epigrams on Lord Galloway. **CP-BurnR**

No strength of Nature can suffice. Love Constraining to Obedience. William Cowper. **NOCV** *Fr.* Olney Hymns. **CP-CowpW**

No Strings Attached. Al Young. **CP-YounA**

No sun these months. Ice-dark and cold. Robert Earl Hayden. **CP-HaydR** *Fr.* The Snow Lamp.

No sunlight ever. Bleak trees whisper ironies. Sunday in the Park. Louis MacNeice. **CP-MacNL**

No sunset, but a grey, great, struggling sky. Sonnet. Edward Estlin Cummings. **CP-CummE**

No Supervening Thought of Grace. Hayden Carruth. **CP-CarHS**

No swallows build their nests here my dear Toller. To Herr Toller, Who Hanged Himself. Malcolm Lowry. **CP-LowrM**

No Swan So Fine. Marianne Craig Moore. **CP-MoorM**

No, Thank You, John. Christina Georgina Rossetti. **CP-RosC1**

No, that carved angel whose still smile. The Chartres Annunciation. Kathleen Jessie Raine. **SP-RainK**

No that is not it. To Have Done Nothing. William Carlos Williams. **CP-WilW1**

No, the Christian faith, as at any rate I understood it. Claude to Eustace. Arthur Hugh Clough. **EnVR** *Fr.* Amours de Voyage. **SP-ClouA**

No, the night has gone. William Dickey. **SP-DickW** *Fr.* At Your Old House.

No, the serpent did not. Theology. Ted Hughes. **SP-HughT**

No, they are come; their horn is lifted up. Gerard Manley Hopkins. **CP-HopkG**

No thing is great on this side of the grave. Heaviness May Endure for a Night, But Joy Cometh in the Morning. Christina Georgina Rossetti. **CP-RosC2**

No thing less than one thing. Flowers. Robert Creeley. **CP-CreeR**

No, this guy told me you can go. The Hitchhiker. Jim Morrison. **SP-MorrJ**

No: this, my love, is neither you nor I. This Beast, This Angel. Adrienne Rich. **CP-RicAE**

No! those days are gone away. Robin Hood. John Keats. **CP-KeatJ**

No time ago / or else a life. Edward Estlin Cummings. **CP-CummE; SP-CummE**

No Time for Lamentation Now. John Milton. *See* Come, come, no time for lamentation now.

No Time in Eternity. Robert Herrick. **CP-HerrR**

No time, noe roome, noe thought, or writing can. Sonnet 7. Mary Sidney, Countess of Montgomery Wroth. *Fr.* Pamphilia to Amphilanthus. **CP-WrotM**

No, Time, thou shalt not boast that I do change. Sonnet 123. William Shakespeare. **OAEP; OBSC; OXAEP-1; Son; TrGrPo** *Fr.* Sonnets. **CP-ShaWS**

No Time to Stop and Think. Malcolm Lowry. **CP-LowrM**

No Time to Think. "Bob Dylan." **CP-DylaB**

No trail / can't be followed. Target Practice. Gary Snyder. **CP-SnydG**

No trellises, no vines. Iron Landscapes (and the Statue of Liberty). Thom Gunn. **CP-GunnT**

No trenchant parting this. Wystan Hugh Auden. **CP-AudWJ**

No Trespassing. Al Young. **CP-YounA**

No True Rhyme in English for "Silver." William Matthews. **SP-MattW**

No trump tells thy virtues—the grave where they rest. On Robert Emmet's Grave. Percy Bysshe Shelley. **CP-ShelP**

No trust to Metals nor to Marbles, when. Epitaph on the Tomb of Sir Edward Giles and His Wife in the South Aisle of Dean Prior Church. Robert Herrick. **CP-HerrR**

No unh-unh no hot sauce for me. The Rundown at Ned's Bar B.Q. Al Young. **CP-YounA**

No use hoping, or feeling vext. He Wonders about Himself. Thomas Hardy. **CP-HardT**

No use in my going. Blue Monday. Langston Hughes. **SP-HughL**

No use invoking Apollo in a case like theirs. The Epigoni. Wystan Hugh Auden. **CP-AudeW**

No use, no use, now, begging Recognize! Amnesiac. Sylvia Plath. **CP-PlatS**

No use to make a tape. The Sounds. Daniel Gerard Hoffman. **SP-HoffD**

No use to make any more. Lofty. Archie Randolph Ammons. **SP-AmmoA**

No use whistling for Lyonnesse! Lyonnesse. Sylvia Plath. **CP-PlatS**

No verse is free that has been sweated for. Vers Libre. John Hewitt. **CP-HewiJ**

No, Virgil, no. Secondary Epic. Wystan Hugh Auden. **CP-AudeW**

No vow once sworn may ever be annulled. The Vow. Robert Ranke Graves. **CP-GravR**

No Voyage. Mary Oliver. **SP-OlivM**

No vulture is here, hardly a hawk. The Low Sky. Robinson Jeffers. **CP-JefR2**

No Want Where There's Little. Robert Herrick. **CP-HerrR**

No waste is trackless: all terrain the lost. Sestina II. Howard Nemerov. **CP-NemeH**

No water is still, on top. The Movement of Fish. James Dickey. **CP-DickJ**

No water so still as the / dead fountains of Versailles. No swan. No Swan So Fine. Marianne Craig Moore. **CP-MoorM**

No whimsy of the purse is here. William Wordsworth. **CP-WorW1**

No White Bird Sings. John Ciardi. **SP-CiarJ**

No window in his suburb lights that bedroom where. Wystan Hugh Auden. *Fr.* The Quest. **CP-AudeW**

No wit (and none needed) but. The Atlantic City Convention. William Carlos Williams. **CP-WilW1**

No witnesses. Nobody driving. Witnesses. Daniel Gerard Hoffman. **SP-HoffD**

No Woe Is Gossamer to Mr. Bessemer. Ogden Nash. **CP-NashO**

No woman, if she is honest, can say that she's. Catullus. *See* Carmen 87: "No woman loved, in truth, Lesbia."

No woman loved, in truth, Lesbia. Carmen 87. Catullus. *Fr.* Carmina. **CP-Catul**

No wonder / The river Humber. The River Humber. Stevie Smith. **CP-SmitS**

No wonder it feared peace, the knees of years. Malcolm Lowry. **CP-LowrM**

No Wonder Our Fathers Died. Ogden Nash. **CP-NashO**

No wonder, shaggy saint, breast-deep in Jordan's. Salome. James Merrill. **SP-MerrJ**

No Word. Stephen Berg. **SP-BergS**

No Word. Stanley Jasspon Kunitz. **CP-KuniS**

No words assess, no pencil knows. Malcolm Lowry. **CP-LowrM**

NO WORK is master of the mine today. The Tunnel. Muriel Rukeyser. **CP-RukeM**

No, worldling, no, 'tis not thy gold. The Second Rapture. Thomas Carew. **CP-CareT**

No worst, there is none. Pitched past pitch of grief. Gerard Manley Hopkins. **CP-HopkG**

No wrath of Men, or rage of Seas. Purposes. Robert Herrick. **CP-HerrR**

No Yellow Jackets on the Mountain. Dabney Stuart. **SP-StuaD**

Noah drunken, taking. Dancing Measures. Donald Davie. **CP-DavDo**

Noah retrieves the dove again. After the Flood. Robert Ranke Graves. **CP-GravR**

Noah the first was (as Tradition sayes). The Fast, or Lent. Robert Herrick. **CP-HerrR**

Nobil rosa ancor non crebbe. L'Incognita. Christina Georgina Rossetti. **CP-RosC3**

Noble. David Herbert Lawrence. **CP-LawrD**

Noble, The. William Wordsworth. **ChTr** *Fr.* France (Concluded). *Fr.* The Prelude; Growth of a Poet's Mind [1850 vers.]. **CP-WorW3**

Noble and Ethereal. Stevie Smith. **CP-SmitS**

Noble beyond degree. The Anabasis. Allen Tate. **CP-TateA**

Noble City Full of Pigeons or Everyone a Hypocrite Including Me. Malcolm Lowry. **CP-LowrM**

Noble Englishman, The. David Herbert Lawrence. **CP-LawrD**

Noble hart, that harbours vertuous [*or* virtuous] thought, The. The Fight of the Red Cross Knight and the Heathen Sansjoy. Edmund Spenser. **FHYEP; FiP; NoSic** *Fr.* The Faerie Queene. **CP-Spens**

Noble in Nature, great in arms. Ode to General Draper. Christopher Smart. **SP-SmarC**

Noble Lady of the Italian shore, A. Sonnet on the Nuptials of the Marquis Antonio Cavalli with the Countess Clelia Rasponi of Ravenna. Byron. **CP-Byron**

Noble Lady's Tale, The. Thomas Hardy. **CP-HardT**

Noble Man, The. Richard Eberhart. **CP-EberR**

Noble Maxwels and their powers, The. Nithsdale's Welcome Hame. Robert Burns. **CP-BurnR**

Noble Mayde, still standing, all this vewd, The. Edmund Spenser. **PoEL-1** *Fr.* The Mask of Cupid. **OBSC** *Fr.* The Faerie Queene. **CP-Spens**

Noble Nature, The. Ben Jonson. *See* It Is Not Growing Like a Tree.

Noble sire fallen on evil days, The. Virginia—the West. Walt Whitman. **CP-WhitW**

Noble Sisters. Christina Georgina Rossetti. **CP-RosC1**

Noble theme demands a noble verse, A. To Mrs. Newton. William Cowper. **CP-CowpW**

Noblest Charis, you that are. His Discourse with Cupid. Ben Jonson. *Fr.* A Celebration of Charis in Ten Lyric[k] Pieces [*or* Peeces]. **CP-JonsB**

Nobly, nobly Cape Saint Vincent to the North-west died away. Home-Thoughts, from the Sea. Robert Browning. **CP-BroR1**

Nobody. Robert Ranke Graves. **CP-GravR**

Nobody, ancient mischief, nobody. Nobody. Robert Ranke Graves. **CP-GravR**

Nobody but Lester let Lester leap. Lester Leaps In. Al Young. **CP-YounA**

Nobody But You. "Lou Reed." **SP-ReedL**

Nobody can stop this dry wind. Sonora. Richard Shelton. **SP-ShelR**

Nobody 'Cept You. "Bob Dylan." **CP-DylaB**

Nobody Comes. Thomas Hardy. **CP-HardT**

Nobody could / in superhuman flights. Edward Estlin Cummings. **CP-CummE**

Nobody dies of love. You Are My Heart's Bouquet. Gilbert Sorrentino. **SP-SorrG**

Nobody feels any pain. Just Like a Woman. "Bob Dylan." **CP-DylaB**

Nobody heard him, the dead man. Not Waving but Drowning. Stevie Smith. **CP-SmitS**

Nobody hears me, nobody sees me. Widowhood or The Home-Coming of Lady Ross. Stevie Smith. **CP-SmitS**

Nobody home. Long threads of sunlight slant. Pierce Street. Thom Gunn. **CP-GunnT**

Nobody I know would like to be buried. Thanksgiving for a Habitat. Wystan Hugh Auden. **NYBP** *Fr.* Thanksgiving for a Habitat. **CP-AudeW**

Nobody in the lane, and nothing, nothing but blackberries. Blackberrying. Sylvia Plath. **CP-PlatS**

Nobody knows if the water will dry up. The Doomsday Books. Howard Nemerov. **CP-NemeH**

Nobody knows this little Rose. Emily Dickinson. **CP-DickE**

Nobody knows what I feel about Freddy. Freddy. Stevie Smith. **CP-SmitS**

Nobody loses all the time. Edward Estlin Cummings. **CP-CummE; SP-CummE**

Nobody loved this. Edward Estlin Cummings. **CP-CummE**

Nobody noogers the shaff of a sloo. On a Flimmering Floom You Shall Ride. Carl Sandburg. **CP-SandC**

Nobody picks a red rose when the winter wind. Red and White. Carl Sandburg. **CP-SandC**

Nobody planted roses, he recalls. Summertime and the Living. Robert Earl Hayden. **CP-HaydR**

Nobody says: Ah, that is the place. Places. Thomas Hardy. **CP-HardT**

Nobody steps into the same river twice. Heraclitus on Rivers. Derek Mahon. **SP-MahoD**

Nobody sucks blood in Translyvania anymore. Zimmer Fearing Anemia. Paul Zimmer. **SP-ZimmP**

Nobody there: / no body. On the Mountain. Charles Tomlinson. **CP-TomlC**

Nobody told me anything much. I was born. Bedlam Revisited. John Ciardi. **SP-CiarJ**

Nobody took any notice of her as she stood on the causey kerb. The Market-Girl. Thomas Hardy. *Fr.* At Casterbridge Fair. **CP-HardT**

Nobody understands so let the Rabbi. Prayer. Stephen Berg. **SP-BergS**

Nobody understood Juan. Juan's Twilight Dance. Marge Piercy. **SP-PierM**

Nobody wears a yellow. Edward Estlin Cummings. **CP-CummE**

Nobody's / with me this time. To the Being We Are. Stephen Berg. **SP-BergS**

Nobody's hero, George Vancouver, ever. Vancouver. Donald Davie. **CP-DavDo**

Noctivagi terror, ganeonis triste flagellum. *acc. by English translation.* Christopher Marlowe. **CP-MarlC**

Nocturn: "Night comes, an angel stands." Kathleen Jessie Raine. **SP-RainK**

Nocturn Cabbage. Carl Sandburg. **CP-SandC**

Nocturn IV: "Claims of the sea, of the tide, move out, The." Carl Sandburg. **CP-SandC**

Nocturnal. Charles Tomlinson. *Fr.* In Winter Woods. **CP-TomlC**

Nocturnal[l] upon Saint Lucy's [*or* S. Lucies] Day, Being the Shortest Day, A. John Donne. **CP-DonnJ**

Nocturne: "Appearing unannounced, the moon." Wystan Hugh Auden. **CP-AudeW**

Nocturne: "Dark blood of night-time, The." Louis MacNeice. **CP-MacNL**

Nocturne: "Dear Wanderer, on your unimagined journey." Frederick Morgan. **SP-MorgF**

Nocturne: "Do squamous and squiggling fish." Wystan Hugh Auden. **CP-AudeW**

Nocturne: "Earth, still heavy and warm with afternoon, The." Archibald MacLeish. **CP-MacLA**

Nocturne. Martin Edmunds. **SP-EdmuM**

Nocturne: "Night has a sea which quenches the machine." Thomas Merton. **CP-MertT**

Nocturne: "Their six-weeks-old daughter." Stephen Spender. **CP-SpenS**

Nocturne: "This evening Venus signs alone." Malcolm Lowry. **CP-LowrM**

Nocturne: "'Tis not my voice now speaks; but as a bird." Walter de la Mare. **CP-DeLaW**

Nocturne: "When the lithe moonlight silently." Edward Estlin Cummings. **CP-CummE**

Nocturne: "Where now has our young Adam." John Crowe Ransom. **SP-RansJ**

Nocturne for the Heirs of Light. Kenneth Patchen. **CP-PatcK**

Nocturne in a Deserted Brickyard. Carl Sandburg. **CP-SandC**

Nocturne Militaire. Thomas McGrath. **SP-McGrT**

Nod. Walter de la Mare. **CP-DeLaW**

Noddin' by de Fire. Paul Laurence Dunbar. **CP-DunbP**

Nodding. Tom Clark. **SP-ClarT**

Nodding. Stevie Smith. **CP-SmitS**

Nodding, its great head rattling like a gourd. Original Sin; a Short Story. Robert Penn Warren. **SP-WarrR**

Nodding promontories, and blue isles, The. Percy Bysshe Shelley. *Fr.* Ode to Liberty. **CP-ShelP**

Nodding tho' the lamps lit low. The Sheep Lady from Algiers. Patti Smith. **SP-SmitP**

Noël, Noël. Christmas Poem for Nancy. Delmore Schwartz. *Fr.* Occasional Poems. **SP-SchwD**

Noel, Noel. Occasional Poems. Delmore Schwartz. **SP-SchwD**

Noguchi. Muriel Rukeyser. **CP-RukeM**

Noire soeur. Samuel Beckett. **CP-BeckS**

Noise. Edward Estlin Cummings. **CP-CummE**

Noise of Battle. David Herbert Lawrence. **CP-LawrD**

Noise of death is in this desolate bar, The. Malcolm Lowry. **CP-LowrM** *Fr.* The Drunkards.

Noise of falls I am possessèd by, A. Gerard Manley Hopkins. **CP-HopkG**

Noise of Life, The. John Yau. **SP-YauJo**

Noise of the hollow ground, A. George Meredith. *Fr.* The Day of the Daughter of Hades. **CP-MerG1**

Noise of the vans woke us before we would. Narcissus Moving. John Berryman. **CP-BerrJ**

Noise of trampling, the wind of trumpets, The. Louis XVI. William Blake. **ChER** *Fr.* The French Revolution. **CP-BlakW**

Noise of water teased his literal ear[s], The. Persistent Explorer. John Crowe Ransom. **SP-RansJ**

Noise the Hairless Make, The. Stephen Dobyns. **SP-DobyS**

Noiseless patient spider, A. Walt Whitman. **CP-WhitW**

Noiselessly, the world has begun to defect. Jim Carroll. **SP-CarrJ**

Noises new to sea and land. The Big Tent Under the Roof. Ogden Nash. **CP-NashO**

Noli Me Tangere. David Herbert Lawrence. **CP-LawrD**

Nollekens. Randall Jarrell. **CP-JarrR**

Nomad Exquisite. Wallace Stevens. **CP-StevW**

Nomads. Dabney Stuart. **SP-StuaD**

Nombril Walketh on the Loam. Thomas Merton. **CP-MertT**

Nomine Dracus erat signatus ut incolat undas. *acc. by English translation.* Thomas Campion. **CP-CampT**

Non-action of the wise man is not inaction, The. Action and Non-Action. Chuang Tzu, *tr. fr. Chinese by* Thomas Merton. **CP-MertT**

Non Cogunt Astra. Robert Ranke Graves. **CP-GravR**

Non-communicant. Jenny Joseph. **SP-JoseJ**

Non ego hoc ferrem calida juventâ. At Thirty Years. Byron. **FiP** *Fr.* Canto the First. EnRP; NAEL-2; NoP; OAEL-2; PoE *Fr.* Don Juan. **CP-Byron**

Non-Entity, The. William Carlos Williams. **CP-WilW2**

Non Est Mortale Quod Opto. Sir John Suckling. **CP-SuckJ**

Non-Existence. David Herbert Lawrence. **CP-LawrD**

Non Nobis Domine! Rudyard Kipling. **CP-KiplR**

Non Omnis Moriar. Allen Tate. **CP-TateA**

Non Son Io La Rosa Ma Vi Stetti Appresso. Christina Georgina Rossetti. *Fr.* Il Rosseggiar Dell'Oriente Canzoniere. **CP-RosC3**

Non Ti Fidar. Louis Zukofsky. **CP-ZukLS**

Nona Domenica Garnaro sits in the sun. Poems from Italy. John Ciardi. **SP-CiarJ**

Nona poured oil on the water and saw the eye. The Evil Eye. John Ciardi. **SP-CiarJ**

Nonconformist, The. Donald Davie. **CP-DavDo**

Nondescript express in from the South, A. Gare du Midi. Wystan Hugh Auden. **CP-AudeW**

Nondum. Gerard Manley Hopkins. **CP-HopkG**

None. Hayden Carruth. **CP-CarHS**

None but a lioness moaned this, Libya's mountains. Catullus. *See* Carmen 60: "Hard. Hard. As she-cat whelped in desert mountains."

None but one beheld him dying. Emily Brontë. **CP-BronE**

None can experience stint. Emily Dickinson. **CP-DickE**

None could ever say that she. Catullus. *See* Carmen 75: "Reason blinded by sin, Lesbia."

None dares with impious steel the grove to rend. Lucan, *tr. by* Samuel Johnson. **CP-JohnS** *Fr.* Pharsalia.

None ever loved as Molly loved me then. The Strangling in Merrion Square. Robert Ranke Graves. **CP-GravR**

None ever shar'd the social feast. Sparrows Self-Domesticated. Vincent Bourne, *tr. fr. Latin by* William Cowper. **CP-CowpW**

None Free from Fault. Robert Herrick. **CP-HerrR**

None goes to warfare, but with this intent. Hope Heartens. Robert Herrick. **CP-HerrR**

None in our day has to such sure effect. Dedication of "The Rhyming Weavers." John Hewitt. **CP-HewiJ**

None in these days shall crutch my limping faith. Salute to Matthew Arnold. John Hewitt. **CP-HewiJ**

None, none can tell where I shall be. Where Is Thy Victory? Walter de la Mare. **CP-DeLaW**

None of my kindred now can tell. Emily Brontë. **CP-BronE**

None of the Books Have Time. Philip Larkin. **CP-LarkP**

None of the many words we summoned to our sides fitted what. Bare Sheets II. John Yau. **SP-YauJo**

None of us are as young. Wystan Hugh Auden. **ArLo** *Fr.* Shorts [1972–1973] ("None of us are as young"). **CP-AudeW**

None of us are as young. Shorts [1972–1973]. Wystan Hugh Auden. **CP-AudeW**

None Other Lamb None Other Name. Christina Georgina Rossetti. **CP-RosC2**

None spares another yet it pleases me. Ralph Waldo Emerson. **CP-EmerR**

None the Wiser. Robert Ranke Graves. **CP-GravR**

None then should through thy beawty, *Lawra,* pine. Epigram. Thomas Campion. *Fr.* Observations in the Art of English Poesie. **CP-CampT**

None Truly Happy Here. Robert Herrick. **CP-HerrR**

None who saw it ever told it. Emily Dickinson. **CP-DickE**

"None whole or clean," we cry, "or free from stain." The Last Department. Rudyard Kipling. **CP-KiplR**

None With Him. Christina Georgina Rossetti. **CP-RosC3**

None yet have been good jocund days. Spring 1974. Robert Ranke Graves. **CP-GravR**

Nonentity. David Herbert Lawrence. **CP-LawrD**

Nones. Wystan Hugh Auden. *Fr.* Horae Canonicae. **CP-AudeW**

Nones. John Berryman. **CP-BerrJ**

Nones. Donald Davie. *Fr.* Horae Canonicae. **CP-DavDo**

Nonne Preestes Tale, The, *see* Nun's Priest's Tale, The. Geoffrey Chaucer. *See* The Nun's Priest's Tale.

Nonsun blob a / cold to. Edward Estlin Cummings. **CP-CummE**

Noo lyart leaves blaw ower the green. Epistle to Charles Baxter. Robert Louis Stevenson. **CP-StevR**

Nooksack Valley. Gary Snyder. **CP-SnydG**

Noon. Paul Laurence Dunbar. **CP-DunbP**

Noon. Robinson Jeffers. **CP-JefR1**

Noon. Philip Levine. **SP-LeviP**

Noon. Nicholas Vachel Lindsay. *Fr.* An Indian Summer Day on the Prairie. **CP-LindV**

Noon. Adrienne Rich. **CP-RicAE**

Noon and Night Flower. Walter de la Mare. **CP-DeLaW**

Noon Apocrypha. James McAuley. **SP-McAuJ**

Noon casts no shadow. Any other time. Advice from the Holy Tomb. Howard Nemerov. **CP-NemeH**

Noon Hour. Carl Sandburg. **CP-SandC**

Noon in an English county. Hymn. John Hewitt. **CP-HewiJ**

Noon—is the Hinge of Day. Emily Dickinson. **CP-DickE**

Noon is the hour of choice. Frederick Morgan. *Fr.* The Gorge. **SP-MorgF**

Noon light on the jacaranda fans. Bicoastal Journal. Charles Wright. **SP-WrigC**

Noon of the Sunbather. Marge Piercy. **SP-PierM**

Noon Office. James Schuyler. **CP-SchuJ**

Noon. The tall trees uphold the sky. The Dragon-Fly. Charles Olson. **CP-OlsoC**

Noon Walk on the Asylum Lawn. Anne Sexton. **CP-SextA**

Noon was shady, and soft airs, The. The Dog and the Water-Lily. William Cowper. **CP-CowpW**

Noone and a star stand, am to am. Edward Estlin Cummings. **CP-CummE**

Noone-day and Midnight shall at once be seene. His Protestation to Perilla. Robert Herrick. **CP-HerrR**

"Noone"autumnal this great lady's gaze. Edward Estlin Cummings. **CP-CummE**

Nor any day gone. You, God. William Everson. **SP-EverW**

Nor art thou lesse esteem'd, that I have plac'd. To Doctor Alabaster. Robert Herrick. **CP-HerrR**

Nor Buying or Selling. Robert Herrick. **CP-HerrR**

Nor can ambition make this garden theirs. The Hidden Garden. Robert Ranke Graves. **CP-GravR**

Nor cold, nor swtern, my soul! yet I detest. Lines Composed in a Concert-Room. Samuel Taylor Coleridge. **CP-ColeS**

Nor delayed the wingèd saint. Raphael's Descent. John Milton. **NOSC** *Fr.* Book V. *Fr.* Paradise Lost. **CP-MiltJ**

Nor did Saint Cuthbert's daughters fail. The Saint of Holy Island. Sir Walter Scott. **SP-ScotW** *Fr.* Marmion.

Nor did the prophet. Louis Zukofsky. *Fr.* Songs of Degrees. **CP-ZukLS**

Nor do you think that their legs is all. Ben Jonson. **CP-JonsB** *Fr.* Christmas His Masque.

Nor dread nor hope attend. Death. William Butler Yeats. **CP-YeatW**

Nor from the compass-quarter of the rising sun. A Solis Ortus Cardine. Sedulius, *tr. fr. Latin by* Thomas Merton. **CP-MertT**

Nor Good Red Herring. Isabella Gardner. **CP-GardI**

Nor had saffron and sapphire and red. George Meredith. *Fr.* The Day of the Daughter of Hades. **CP-MerG1**

Nor happiness, nor majesty, nor fame. Sonnet: Political Greatness. Percy Bysshe Shelley. **CP-ShelP**

Nor is my Number full, till I inscribe. To His Worthy Kinsmen, Mr. Stephen Soame. Robert Herrick. **CP-HerrR**

Nor is this the setting for extravagance. Trees. Northern Spring. Charles Tomlinson. **CP-TomlC**

Nor jewelled phrase nor mere mellifluous rhyme. Edwin Arlington Robinson. *Fr.* Octaves. **CP-RobiE**

Nor judge me light, tho' light at times I seem. Robert Louis Stevenson. *Fr.* Sonnets. **CP-StevR**

Nor Mountain hinder Me. Emily Dickinson. **CP-DickE**

Nor oils of balmy scent produce. On Pallas Bathing. Callimachus, *tr. fr. Greek by* William Cowper. **CP-CowpW**

Nor scorn the aid which Fancy oft doth lend. Apology. William Wordsworth. *Fr.* Ecclesiastical Sonnets. **CP-WorW2**

Nor second he, that rode sublime. Thomas Gray. **EPCY** *Fr.* The Progress of Poesy. **CP-GrayT**

Nor shall my verse that elder bard forget. James Thomson. **EPCY** *Fr.* Summer. *Fr.* The Seasons. **CP-ThomJ**

Nor shall the eternal roll of praise reject. Clerical Integrity. William Wordsworth. *Fr.* Ecclesiastical Sonnets. **CP-WorW2**

Nor should this, perchance. William Wordsworth. **OxAEP-2** *Fr.* School-Time. *Fr.* The Prelude; Growth of a Poet's Mind [1805 vers.]. **CP-WorW3**

Nor skin nor hide nor fleece. Lethe. Hilda Doolittle. **CP-DoolH**

Nor Southerne heat nor Northerne snow. 3.24. Horace. **CP-RaleW**, *tr. by* Sir Walter Ralegh; *Fr.* Odes.

Nor think, in nature's state they blindly trod. Alexander Pope. **OAEL-1** *Fr.* An Essay on Man. **CP-PopeA**

Nor thinke that Thou in this my Booke art worst. To the Most Accomplisht Gentleman Master Michael Oulsworth. Robert Herrick. **CP-HerrR**

Nor travels my meand'ring eye. Written at Shurton Bars, near Bridgewater, September 1795, in Answer to a Letter from Bristol. Samuel Taylor Coleridge. *Fr.* Poetical Epistles. **CP-ColeS**

...for wants the cause the panic-striking aid. Saxon Conquest. William Wordsworth. *Fr.* Ecclesiastical Sonnets. **CP-WorW2**

...for was that final, for about that time. Wystan Hugh Auden. **CP-AudWJ**

...for was this fellowship vouchsaf'd to me. Wordsworth Skates on Esthwaite Water. William Wordsworth. **FaBoPP** *Fr.* Introduction—Childhood and School-Time. *Fr.* The Prelude; Growth of a Poet's Mind [1805 vers.]. **CP-WorW3**

...for We of Her to Him. Stevie Smith. **CP-SmitS**

...for woman / (just as it be). Edward Estlin Cummings. **CP-CummE**

...for yet, nor yet, O you in this night blessed. Ben Jonson. **CP-JonsB** *Fr.* Oberon, the Fairy Prince.

Nora: A Serenade. Paul Laurence Dunbar. **CP-DunbP**

Nora O'Kane. Louise McNeill. **SP-McNeL**

Nordeast. Barton Sutter. **SP-SuttB**

Norembega. John Greenleaf Whittier. **CP-WhitJ**

Norfolk. Sir John Betjeman. **CP-BetjJ**

Norfolk. Donald Davie. **CP-DavDo**

Norham Castle. Sir Walter Scott. **SP-ScotW** *Fr.* Marmion.

Norman, / the moon, like Mary-Beth's pleasing savories. Searching for the Canto Fermo. Diane Wakoski. **SP-WakoD**

Norman and Saxon. Rudyard Kipling. **CP-KiplR**

Norman Boy, The. William Wordsworth. **CP-WorW2**

Norman Conquest, The. William Wordsworth. *Fr.* Ecclesiastical Sonnets. **CP-WorW2**

Normandy Beach. Miller Williams. **SP-WillM**

NORMS / Grraa aa aa lll. Thomas Merton. *Fr.* A Selection of Concrete Poems. **CP-MertT**

Norsemen, The. John Greenleaf Whittier. **CP-WhitJ**

North, The. Wystan Hugh Auden. **CP-AudWJ**

North. Seamus Heaney. **SP-HeanS**

North. Richard Hugo. **CP-HugoR**

North. Louis MacNeice. *Fr.* Sleeping Winds. **CP-MacNL**

North. Thomas Merton. *Fr.* The Geography of Lograire. **CP-MertT**
    Kane Relief Expedition.
    Prologue: Why I Have a Wet Footprint on Top of My Mind.
    Queens Tunnel.
    Ranter and Their Pleads, The.
    "There is a grain of sand in Lambeth which Satan cannot find."

North American Sequence. Theodore Roethke. **CP-RoetT**
    Far Field, The. **NAAL-2; NoAM; NoP; PrIm; SeCeV**
    Journey to the Interior. **DiPo; PFL**
    Long Waters, The. **NYBP**
    Longing, The.
    Meditation at Oyster River. **CAPP; CMoP; MoAmPo; NYBP**
    Rose, The. **BiP; NOBA; NYBP; PPoe; TRP**

North American Time. Adrienne Rich. **SP-RicA1; SP-RicA2**

North & South. Donald Davie. **CP-DavDo**

North and South. Robert Herrick. **CP-HerrR**

North and South. Derek Walcott. **CP-WalcD**

North and the South, The. Elizabeth Barrett Browning. **CP-BroEB**

North Area. Roy Fisher. *Fr.* City. **SP-FishR**

North Atlantic. Carl Sandburg. **CP-SandC**

North Beach Alba. Gary Snyder. **CP-SnydG**

North Coast, The. Gary Snyder. **CP-SnydG**

North Coast Recollections. Sir John Betjeman. **CP-BetjJ**

North Country, The. David Herbert Lawrence. **CP-LawrD**

North Country Blues. "Bob Dylan." **CP-DylaB**

North Dublin. Donald Davie. **CP-DavDo**

North Haven. Elizabeth Bishop. **CP-BishE**

North Labrador. Hart Crane. **CP-CranH**

North of Alliance. Ted Kooser. **SP-KoosT**

North of 96th where the tracks come out from under. From a Diary. Frederick Morgan. **SP-MorgF**

North people known for silence. Long. They Accuse Me of Not Talking. Hayden Carruth. **CP-CarHS**

North Sea, The. Donald Davie. **CP-DavDo**

North Sea, The. Louis MacNeice. **CP-MacNL**

North Sea, in a Snowstorm, The. Donald Davie. **CP-DavDo**

North Sea Patrol, The. Rudyard Kipling. **CP-KiplR**

North Ship, The. Philip Larkin. **CP-LarkP**

North Star beams us cleanly down the Patuxent, The. Night Watch on the Chesapeake. Peter Meinke. **SP-MeinP**

North Star Whispers to the Blacksmith's Son, The. Nicholas Vachel Lindsay. **CP-LindV**

North Street. Archie Randolph Ammons. **SP-AmmoA**

North summer wind swept the hay, The. Meadow in Summer. Carl Sandburg. **CP-SandC**

North to the Pole, south to the Pole. The Chanting of the Whales. Nicholas Vachel Lindsay. *Fr.* Golden Whales of California. **CP-LindV**

North-West Passage. Robert Louis Stevenson. **CP-StevR**

North-West Passage: An Old Man Dying. John Hewitt. **CP-HewiJ**

North wind doth blow, The. Ma, What's a Banker? or, Hush, My Child. Ogden Nash. **CP-NashO**

North wind like a fine drill. China Journal. Charles Wright. **SP-WrigC**

North Wind: Portrush. Derek Mahon. **SP-MahoD**

North Winter. Hayden Carruth. **CP-CarHL**
    "After the thaw after."
    Afterword: What the Poet Had Written.
    "Arctic owl moved across the snowsmooth, The."
    "Astigmatism breaks."
    "Beginning with the palest and softest lavender."
    "Blizzard trampling past has left."
    "Brook has holes in its cover, The."
    "Caught in the briary stars."
    "Cold hunger tripped her but her years."
    "Coming of winter / is a beech sapling."
    "Day the brook went out, The."
    "Eons gone by the sea."
    "Eye of / the hut, The."
    "Five / jays / discuss / goodandevil."
    "Four greens / the poplar trunk."
    "Frozen / brook sprawls, The."
    "Gunmetal snow icecolored sky."
    "Harlequin / is said to assimilate himself to a condition."
    "Heavy gloves / or better."
    "In cold / the snow."
    "In freshfallen snow."
    "In late winter cold nights."
    "In spring this mountain was a fish."
    "In the snowy woods of morning."
    "Layer upon layer / late winter snow."
    "Lichen and liverwort."
    "Lichen is a hardy plant."
    "Like a frozen lake the sky in the bitterest."
    "Lover of balsam lover of white pine."
    "Morning ice on the window."
    "Night is a cauldron."
    "On Lincoln's birthday the forest."
    "One day music / begins."
    "Pale dawnlight spooks the mist."
    "Sky like fishblood."
    "Sky yellow sky."
    "Small things / hardest to believe."
    "Snow / ice / bitter wind."
    "Snow buntings whirling / on a snowy field."
    "Snow comes / bits / of light."
    "Snow's downstrokes climb softly up the conifer."
    "Song of the gray, The."
    "Spaniel flies with his ears, The."
    "Stronger than destiny is pain."
    "Tamarack with needles lost, The."
    "Think not of chaste snow always."
    "This wind this / screaming parrot."
    "Three sixteen seventy."
    "Tracks of the snowshoe rabbit across the."
    "Twenty-two degrees below zero."
    "Under the hill a winter twilight."
    "Wet fire / it turns out."
    "When conditions of frost and."
    "When some amazonian indians for whom."
    "Where the snow bank leans."
    "Where two boots labored yesterday across the."
    "Window / the icicle / the gleaming moon, The."
    "Winter's tale is told in, A."

Northamptonshire. Donald Davie. **CP-DavDo**

Northeast wind was the wind off the lake, The. Cook County. Archibald MacLeish. **CP-MacLA**

Norther—Key West, A. Elizabeth Bishop. **CP-BishE**

Northern April. Edna St. Vincent Millay. **CP-MillE**

Northern countryside of China, The. Spring in the Snow-Drenched Garden. Mao Tse-tung, *tr. fr. Chinese* by William Carlos Williams *with* David Rafael Wang. **CP-WilW2**

Northern Exposure. Charles Simic. **SP-SimiC**

Northern Farmer: New Style. Tennyson. **CP-TennA**

Northern Fields (For Carol). Chuck Miller. **SP-MillC**

Northern Heather. Robinson Jeffers. **CP-JefR2**

Northern Lass, The. Robert Burns. **CP-BurnR**

Northern Lights. Daniel Gerard Hoffman. **SP-HoffD**

Northern lights. I wouldn't have noticed them, The. I Know, I Remember, But How Can I Help You. Hayden Carruth. **CP-CarHS**

Northern Metres. Donald Davie. **CP-DavDo**

Northern Pike. James Wright. **CP-WrigJ**

Northern Snows, The. Randall Jarrell. **CP-JarrR**

Northern Spring. John Hewitt. **CP-HewiJ**

Northern Spring. Charles Tomlinson. **CP-TomlC**

Northern Stone. Phoebe Hesketh. **SP-HeskP**

Northfork October Return. John Clellon Holmes. **SP-HolmJ**

Northman. Ralph Waldo Emerson. *Fr.* Quatrains. **CP-EmerR**

Northumberland. Donald Davie. **CP-DavDo**

Northumberland House. Stevie Smith. **CP-SmitS**

Northward I came, and knocked in the coated wall. Rodez. Donald Davie. **CP-DavDo**

Northward, the black sky at dusk. Storm in the Ozarks. John Clellon Holmes. **SP-HolmJ**

Northwest Passage. Allen Ginsberg. **CP-GinsA**

Northwest Retrospective: Mark Tobey. Richard Hugo. **CP-HugoR**

Northwood Path. Louise Glück. **SP-GlücL**

Norumbega Hall. John Greenleaf Whittier. **CP-WhitJ**

Norwegian Wood. The Beatles. **CP-Beatl**

Nose, The. Samuel Taylor Coleridge. **CP-ColeS**

Nose. Donald Hall. **CP-HallD**

Nose and chin would shame a knocker. On Sam Rogers. Byron. **CP-Byron**

Nose and palate never doubt, The. Smelt and Tasted. Wystan Hugh Auden. **CP-AudeW**

Nose-end that twitches, the old imperfections, The. The Companionable Ills. Sylvia Plath. **CP-PlatS**

Nose, I am free. Metaphor. Wystan Hugh Auden. *Fr.* Shorts I ("Watch upon my wrist, The"). **CP-AudeW**

Nosegay, The. Donald Davie. **CP-DavDo**

Noses. Stephen Dobyns. **SP-DobyS**

Noses to grindstone! / Beaks to the Northstar! Sweet Good Night Poem to Our Beloved Hartebeeste from All the Little Animals. Malcolm Lowry. **CP-LowrM**

Nossis. Hilda Doolittle. **CP-DoolH**

Nostalgia. David Herbert Lawrence. **CP-LawrD**

Nostalgia. Louis MacNeice. **CP-MacNL**

Nostalgia. Charles Kenneth Williams. **SP-WillC**

Nostalgia for Edith Sitwell. Richard Eberhart. **CP-EberR**

Nostalgia for India. May Sarton. **SP-SartM**

Nostalgia, incantation, escape. Sports Page. Louis MacNeice. **CP-MacNL**

Nostalgia is only amnesia turned around. Hohokam. Adrienne Rich. *Fr.* Turning the Wheel. **SP-RicA2**

Nostalgia of old men. In Praise of Necessity. Thomas McGrath. **SP-McGrT**

Nostalgias. Derek Mahon. **SP-MahoD**

Noster was a ship of swank, The. Edward Estlin Cummings. **CP-CummE**

Nostrarum quoties prendit me nausea rerum. *acc. by English translation.* Thomas Campion. **CP-CampT**

Nostre Voluntà Quieti Virtù di Carità. Christina Georgina Rossetti. *Fr.* Il Rosseggiar Dell'Oriente Canzoniere. **CP-RosC3**

Not a breath of air. Airey-Force Valley. William Wordsworth. **CP-WorW2**

Not a derangement of the senses but yes there is an occult other. Poetry Disarranged. Robert Duncan. **SP-DuncR**

Not a flake assaults my birds. Emily Dickinson. **SP-DickE**

Not a flow'r can be found in the fields. The Innocent Thief. Vincent Bourne, *tr. fr. Latin by* William Cowper. **CP-CowpW**

Not a friend hated time. Wild Geranium. Louis Zukofsky. **CP-ZukLS**

Not a land, or like other lands, with trees coming out and the grass growing. The United States. Kay Boyle. **CP-BoylK**

Not a line of her writing have I. Thoughts of Phena. Thomas Hardy. **CP-HardT**

Not a Movie. Langston Hughes. **SP-HughL**

Not a *Paris Review* Interview. Frank Templeton Prince. **CP-PrinF**

Not a rat-hole, a cat-hole: the knife of time; on the ledge, overlooking. Charles Olson. **CP-OlsoC**

Not a Rootless Lily. Jenny Joseph. **SP-JoseJ**

Not a Second Time. The Beatles. **CP-Beatl**

Not a sigh was heard, not a tear was shed. The Death and Burial of McDonald Clarke, a Parody. Walt Whitman. **CP-WhitW**

Not a sound. The house could be. James McAuley. **SP-McAuJ** *Fr.* After the Blizzard.

Not a tree but the tree. There Is Only One of Everything. Margaret Atwood. **SP-AtwM1**

Not a vapour had stained the breezeless blue. Emily Brontë. **CP-BronE**

Not a word to each other; we kept the great pace. Robert Browning. **Poetr** *Fr.* How They Brought the Good News from Ghent to Aix. **CP-BroR1**

Not able to resist the spring. Jenny Joseph. *Fr.* Life and Turgid Times of A. Citizen. **SP-JoseJ**

Not Again. Robert Creeley. **CP-CreeR**

Not Aladdin magian. On Visiting Staffa. John Keats. **CP-KeatJ**

Not all die early, dying young. Emily Dickinson. **CP-DickE**

Not all of life to live, is it. Emily Dickinson. **SP-DickE**

Not all of my eyes see, wándering on the world. Ashboughs. Gerard Manley Hopkins. **CP-HopkG**

Not all of them were human. The Village Tudda. Kenneth Patchen. **CP-PatcK**

Not all of us were heroes said my brother wit. Malcolm Lowry. **CP-LowrM**

Not All That Bad. Charles Bukowski. **SP-BukC3**

Not All There. Robert Frost. **FaBoCo** *Fr.* Ten Mills. **CP-FrosR**

Not all thy flushing suns are set. An Ode to Master Endymion Porter, upon His Brother's Death. Robert Herrick. **CP-HerrR**

Not alone those camps of white, old comrades of the wars. Camps of Green. Walt Whitman. **CP-WhitW**

Not always as the whirlwind's rush. The Call of the Christian. John Greenleaf Whittier. **CP-WhitJ**

Not always should the tear's ambrosial dew. Pitt. Samuel Taylor Coleridge. *Fr.* Effusions. **CP-ColeS**

Not any flower that blows. Noon and Night Flower. Walter de la Mare. **CP-DeLaW**

Not any higher stands the Grave. Emily Dickinson. **CP-DickE**

Not any more to be lacked. Emily Dickinson. **CP-DickE**

Not any sunny tone. Emily Dickinson. **CP-DickE**

Not architecture, not. Gloucestershire. Donald Davie. **CP-DavDo**

Not argue, unless, that is, you are the kind. One Drunk Allegory. Robert Penn Warren. **SP-WarrR**

Not as a poor requital of the joy. To J. P. John Greenleaf Whittier. **CP-WhitJ**

Not as that dream Napoleon, rumour's dread and centre. Like a Vocation. Wystan Hugh Auden. **CP-AudeW**

Not as we are but as we must appear. Geoffrey Hill. **NoAM** *Fr.* Funeral Music. **CP-HillG**

Not as with Sundering of the Earth. Algernon Charles Swinburne. **SP-SwinA** *Fr.* Atalanta in Calydon.

Not At All What One Is Used To. Isabella Gardner. **CP-GardI**

Not at [the] first sight, nor with a dribbled shot. Sonnet 2. Sir Philip Sidney. **NAEL-1; OAEL-1** *Fr.* Astrophil and Stella. **SP-SidnP**

Not at Home. Samuel Taylor Coleridge. **CP-ColeS**

Not at Home. Robert Ranke Graves. **CP-GravR**

Not at Home to Callers. Emily Dickinson. **CP-DickE**

Not aware of it much of the time, but of course we are. Une Présence Absolue. Hayden Carruth. **CP-CarHS**

Not bad mouth / in bad mouth. Bad Mouth. Charles Kenneth Williams. **CP-WillC**

Not because of his eyes. The Turtle. William Carlos Williams. **CP-WilW2**

Not because they are far, but because so near. The Dead. Kathleen Jessie Raine. **SP-RainK**

Not boskiest bow'r. Epigraph to "The Woodlanders." Thomas Hardy. **CP-HardT**

Not by growth / But the. Drawing. George Oppen. **CP-OppeG**

Not by planning and not by choosing. The Bottom of the Glass. Stanley Jasspon Kunitz. **CP-KuniS**

Not Caesar's birth made Caesar to survive. Vertue the Best Monument. *Unknown, sometimes at. to* Sir Walter Ralegh. **CP-RaleW**

Not Caesar's deeds, nor all his honours won. To Clement Edmonds, on His *Caesar's Commentaries* Observed, and Translated. Ben Jonson. **CP-JonsB**

Not, Celia, that I look for rest. After Charles Sedley. Louis Zukofsky. **CP-ZukLS**

Not Christmas nor the new year white with snow. Poem for May First. Edwin Rolfe. **CP-RolfE**

Not comprehending half the Chairman says. Collector's Choice. John Hewitt. **CP-HewiJ**

Not content with eyes. Analyst. Phoebe Hesketh. **SP-HeskP**

Not counting the little kids. To My Daughter. Gary Gildner. **SP-GildG**

Not dawn but flown by glistening mares. Night Drive. Derek Mahon. **SP-MahoD**

Not deerpark, royal chase. Sylvae. Donald Davie. **CP-DavDo**

Not easy to state the change you made. Love Letter. Sylvia Plath. **CP-PlatS**

Not enough. The question: what is. Love ("Not enough. The question: what is"). Robert Creeley. **CP-CreeR**

Not envying Latian shades—if yet they throw. William Wordsworth. *Fr.* The River Duddon [A Series of Sonnets]. **CP-WorW2**

Not ere the bitter herb we taste. The Lesson of Grief. George Meredith. **CP-MerG1**

Not even for a moment. He knew, for one thing, what he was. Leda. Mona Van Duyn. **SP-VanDM**

Not Even for Brunch. Ogden Nash. **CP-NashO**

Not even if with a wizard force I might. Caput Mortuum. Edwin Arlington Robinson. **CP-RobiE**

Not even if you went on hands and knees. Reply to a Philistine. Phoebe Hesketh. **SP-HeskP**

Not even my pride will suffer much. Edna St. Vincent Millay. **SBG; VBLP** *Fr.* Theme and Variations. **CP-MillE**

Not ever, now, any more, upon this mildewed planet. If, in the Foggy Aleutians. Edna St. Vincent Millay. **CP-MillE**

Not Every Day Fit for Verse. Robert Herrick. **CP-HerrR**

Not every man has gentians in his house. Bavarian Gentians. David Herbert Lawrence. **CP-LawrD**

Not everyone has plenty of time to die in. Charles Henri Ford. *Fr.* Epigrams. **SP-FordC**

Not exactly disembodied, but speaking from no mouth. A Quiet Afternoon at Home. Mona Van Duyn. **SP-VanDM**

Not far advanc'd was morning day. Battle, The ("Not far advanc'd was morning day"). Sir Walter Scott. **SP-ScotW** *Fr.* Marmion.

Not far from hence. From yonder pointed hill. Orpheus. Percy Bysshe Shelley. **CP-ShelP**

Not far from Mellstock—so tradition saith. By the Barrows. Thomas Hardy. **CP-HardT**

Not faster in the summer's ray. Seneca, *tr. by* Samuel Johnson. **CP-JohnS** *Fr.* Hippolytus.

Not fat, not gross, just well fed and hefty he sits before / what's his. The Nine of Cups. Marge Piercy. *Fr.* Laying Down the Tower. **SP-PierM**

Not for a Nation. Edna St. Vincent Millay. **CP-MillE**

Not for me marring or making. Mariana. Christina Georgina Rossetti. **CP-RosC2**

Not for me, the crusader cross. Prologue. James McAuley. **SP-McAuJ** *Fr.* The Exile's Recurring Nightmare.

Not for myself I make this prayer. Pagan Prayer. Countee Cullen. **CP-CullC**

Not for the naked make I this my prayer. Ballade of Soul. Edward Estlin Cummings. **CP-CummE**

Not for these lovely blooms that prank your chambers did I come. Indeed. Rendezvous. Edna St. Vincent Millay. **CP-MillE**

Not forgetting Ko-jen, that. More Foreign Cities. Charles Tomlinson. **CP-TomlC**

Not Fortune's worshipper, nor Fashion's fool. Apologia pro Vita Sua. Alexander Pope. **NOBE** *Fr.* Epistle to Dr. Arbuthnot. **CP-PopeA**

Not from successful love alone. Halcyon Days. Walt Whitman. **CP-WhitW**

Not from that / could you get it. The City. Robert Creeley. **CP-CreeR**

Not from the stars do I my judgement pluck. Sonnet 14. William Shakespeare. **MasP; Son** *Fr.* Sonnets. **CP-ShaWS**

Not from This Anger. Dylan Thomas. **CP-ThomD**

Not George Washington's, Not Abraham Lincoln's, but Mine. Ogden Nash. **CP-NashO**

Not glad, like those that have new hopes, or suits. To the Same [Robert, Earl of Salisbury] [Upon the Accension of the Treasurership to Him]. Ben Jonson. **CP-JonsB**

Not God, / not God. Orestes Theme. Hilda Doolittle. **CP-DoolH**

Not Going Back. Leonard Cohen. **CP-CoheL**

Not good any more, not beautiful. The Face. Randall Jarrell. **CP-JarrR; SP-JarrR**

Not great, not / among the acerbic. Homage to John Lyly and Frankie Newton. Hayden Carruth. **CP-CarHS**

Not Hatred. Edwin Rolfe. **CP-RolfE**

Not he that flies the court for want of clothes. To Sir Ra[l]ph Shelton. Ben Jonson. **CP-JonsB**

Not heat nor soul—some spirit. Recipe. Raissa Maritain, *tr. fr. French by* Thomas Merton. **CP-MertT**

Not Heat Flames Up and Consumes. Walt Whitman. **CP-WhitW**

Not Heaving from My Ribb'd Breast Only. Walt Whitman. **CP-WhitW**

Not Her, She Aint No Gypsy. Al Young. **CP-YounA**

Not Here, O Apollo. Matthew Arnold. *See* Song of Callicles, The ("Through the black, rushing smoke-burst").

Not him I prize who poorly gains. Martial, *tr. by* Samuel Johnson. **CP-JohnS** *Fr.* Epigrams.

Not his that gaunt mask. Fool's comparison. 1957–1972. John Hewitt. **CP-HewiJ**

Not honey, / not the plunder of the bee. Fragment 113. Hilda Doolittle. **CP-DoolH**

Not hour after hour, / but grief after grief the day passes. Initial. Pablo Neruda, *tr. fr. Spanish by* Ben Belitt. **SP-NeruP**

Not house-proud: garden-proud are the people here. Carmel. Robinson Jeffers. **CP-JefR3**

Not hurled precipitous from steep to steep. William Wordsworth. *Fr.* The River Duddon [A Series of Sonnets]. **CP-WorW2**

Not, I keep being told, the Time. First Epistle. Donald Davie. *Fr.* Six Epistles to Eva Hesse. **CP-DavDo**

Not I, not I, but the wind that blows through me! David Herbert Lawrence. **CMoP; ChMP; CoBMV; GTBS-6; GTBS-P; InPS; LiTM; MeMBP; MoPo; OxBTC; PeFWW; PoE; RaBo; SeCeV; TRP** *Fr.* Song of a Man Who Has Come Through. **CP-LawrD**

Not I, not I, but the wind that blows through me! Song of a Man Who Has Come Through. David Herbert Lawrence. **CP-LawrD**

Not Ideas about the Thing but the Thing Itself. Wallace Stevens. **CP-StevW**

Not If He Has Any Sense, He Won't Be Back. Kenneth Patchen. **CP-PatcK**

Not, I'll not, carrion comfort, Despair, not feast on thee. Carrion Comfort. Gerard Manley Hopkins. **CP-HopkG**

Not in a gorgeous hall of pride / Mid tears of grief and friendship's sigh. *earlier vers. of* The Death of the Nature-Lover. Walt Whitman. **CP-WhitW**

Not in a gorgeous hall of pride / Where tears fall thick, and loved ones sigh. *for earlier vers. see* My Departure. Walt Whitman. **CP-WhitW**

Not in a silver casket cool with pearls. Edna St. Vincent Millay. **CP-MillE**

Not in Baedeker. Wystan Hugh Auden. **CP-AudeW**

Not in believing, but in pretending. Not in knowing, but in pretending. Imagining in Writing. Robert Duncan. **SP-DuncR**

Not in Marble Palaces. Pedro Salinas, *tr. fr. Spanish by* James Wright. **CP-WrigJ**

Not in our time, O Lord. Hilda Doolittle. **NOBA** *Fr.* Tribute to the Angels. **CP-DoolH**

Not in rich furniture, or fine array. The H[oly] Communion. George Herbert. **CP-HerbG**

Not in shyness but in disgust. This Morning Again It Was in the Dusty Pines. Mary Oliver. **SP-OlivM**

Not in the camp his victory lies. The Reformers. Rudyard Kipling. **CP-KiplR**

Not in the days of Adam and Eve, but when Adam. In the Days of Prismatic Color. Marianne Craig Moore. **CP-MoorM**

Not in the Lucid Intervals of Life. William Wordsworth. **CP-WorW2**

Not in the mines beyond the western main. To Cordelia M———. William Wordsworth. *Fr.* Poems Composed or Suggested During a Tour, in the Summer of 1833. **CP-WorW2**

Not in the rustle of water, the air's noise. Night in Martindale. Kathleen Jessie Raine. **SP-RainK**

Not in the streets, not in the white streets. Theory of Prayer. Thomas Merton. **CP-MertT**

Not in the thick of the fight. The Verdicts. Rudyard Kipling. **CP-KiplR**

Not in their houses stand the stars. To the Shah, from Enweri. "Anvari", *tr. fr. Persian by* Ralph Waldo Emerson. **CP-EmerR**

Not in this chamber only at my birth. Edna St. Vincent Millay. **CP-MillE**

Not in this grave. Defiance to Cupid. William Carlos Williams. **CP-WilW2**

Not in this World to see his face. Emily Dickinson. **CP-DickE**

Not in those climes where I have late been straying. To Ianthe. Byron. **FaBoEn; OBNC** *Fr.* Childe Harold's Pilgrimage. **CP-Byron**

Not in vain the distance beacons. Foreward, forward let us range. Tennyson. **FaBoEH** *Fr.* Locksley Hall. **CP-TennA**

Not it was no dream of coming death. Louis Zukofsky. **CP-ZukLS**

Not Kenesaw high-arching. The March to the Sea. Herman Melville. **SP-MelvH**

Not kind! to freeze me with forecast. Gerard Manley Hopkins. **CP-HopkG**

Not knowing he rose from earth, not having seen him rise. On First Having Heard the Skylark. Edna St. Vincent Millay. **CP-MillE**

Not knowing them in very heart. A Sketch. Herman Melville. **SP-MelvH** *Fr.* Clarel: A Poem and Pilgrimage in the Holy Land.

Not knowing when the Dawn will come. Emily Dickinson. **CP-DickE**

Not Knowing Where to Go. Leonard Cohen. **CP-CoheL**

Not Known. Thomas Hardy. **CP-HardT**

Not leaves, not lightning, not the greatness of rivers. Muriel Rukeyser. **CP-RukeM**

Not leaves, not lightning, not the greatness of rivers. Muriel Rukeyser. **CP-RukeM**

Not Leaving the House. Gary Snyder. **CP-SnydG**

Not less a Queen, because I wear. Queen Zuleima. George Meredith. **CP-MerG2**

Not less because in purple I descend, See also Tea at the Palaz of Hoon by Wallace Stevens. Magic Arrival No. 7. Tom Clark. **SP-ClarT**

Not less because in purple I descended. Tea at the Palaz of Hoon. Wallace Stevens. **CP-StevW**

Not like a beast borne on the flood of passion, boat without oars, but mindful of all his dignity. The Humanist's Tragedy. Robinson Jeffers. **CP-JefR1**

Not, like his great Compeers, indignantly. The Source of the Danube. William Wordsworth. *Fr.* Memorials of a Tour of the Continent; 1820. **CP-WorW2**

Not like That. Adrienne Rich. **CP-RicAE**

Not living for each other's sake. Knowledge. Howard Nemerov. **CP-NemeH**

Not locking onto. Charles Henri Ford. **SP-FordC** *Fr.* Emblems of Arachne.

Not long ago, the writer of these lines. To ———. Edgar Allan Poe. **CP-PoeEd**

Not long this transport held its place. The Third Voice. "Lewis Carroll." *Fr.* The Three Voices. **CP-CarrL**

Not Love, not War, nor the Tumultuous Swell. William Wordsworth. **CP-WorW2**

Not magnitude, not lavishness. Greek Architecture. Herman Melville. **SP-MelvH**

Not many enchant you (put to it) popular is he, Juventi. Catullus. *See* Carmen 81: "Surely, Iuventius, one of this throng in Rome."

Not Many Kingdoms Left. Kenneth Patchen. **CP-PatcK**

Not many years but long enough to see. Emily Brontë. **CP-BronE**

Not Marble nor the Gilded Monuments. Archibald MacLeish. **CP-MacLA**

Not marble, nor the gilded monuments. Sonnet 55. William Shakespeare. **AWP; BLPL; CABA; CTC; EPCY; EnRePo; FF; FaBoEn; FaFP; HeIL; HeIP; ImPo; InPK; LPA; LiTB; LoBV; MasP; NAEL-1; NIP; NOBE; NoP; NoSic; OAEL-1; OAEP; OBSC; OXAEP-1; PAI; PPoe; PeHV; PoE; PoEL-2; PoRA; Poetr; SCGP; SeCeV; Son; TEP; TrGrPo** *Fr.* Sonnets. **CP-ShaWS**

Not marching in the fields of Trasimene. Doctor Faustus. Christopher Marlowe.

Not Meagre, Latent Boughs Alone. Walt Whitman. **CP-WhitW**

Not Men Alone. Edwin Rolfe. **CP-RolfE**

Not 'mid the World's vain objects that enslave. Composed While the Author Was Engaged in Writing a Tract, Occasioned by the Convention of Cintra. William Wordsworth. **CP-WorW1**

Not mine own fears nor the prophetic soul. Sonnet 107. William Shakespeare. **AWP; CABA; CTC; EBEV; FiP; HAP; ImPo; LiTB; LoBV; MasP; NAEL-1; NoP; NoSic; OAEL-1; OAEP; OBSC; OXAEP-1; PPoe; SCGP; SeCeV** *Fr.* Sonnets. **CP-ShaWS**

Not much more than being. Louis Zukofsky. **PoE** *Fr.* 29 Poems. **CP-ZukLS**

Not My Enemies Ever Invade Me. Walt Whitman. **CP-WhitW**

Not my hands but green across you now. The Lady in Kicking Horse Reservoir. Richard Hugo. **CP-HugoR**

Not night now. Dawn. Six o'clock, a November morning. Hayden Carruth. *Fr.* Paragraphs. **CP-CarHS**

Not Now. Robert Creeley. **CP-CreeR**

Not o'er thy dust let there be spent. Whittier. Paul Laurence Dunbar. **CP-DunbP**

Not of father nor of mother. The Song of Blodeuwedd. Robert Ranke Graves. **CP-GravR**

Not of School Age. Robert Frost. **CP-FrosR**

Not of the dust, but of the wave. For Joseph Conrad. Countee Cullen. **CP-CullC**

Not of Works. William Cowper. *Fr.* Olney Hymns. **CP-CowpW**

Not on my knees praising God. Winter Daffodils. Phoebe Hesketh. **SP-HeskP**

Not on Penobscot's wooded bank the spires. Norumbega Hall. John Greenleaf Whittier. **CP-WhitJ**

Not One by Heaven defrauded stay. Emily Dickinson. **CP-DickE**

Not one corner of a foreign field. Fragment. Wilfred Owen. **CP-OwenW**

Not one not dandled a man high up in the air. White Pines, Felled 1984. Richard Eberhart. **CP-EberR**

Not one of my candidates won. Not one. November Seven, Nineteen Eighty-Four. Barton Sutter. **SP-SuttB**

Not one of your tall captains bred to rule. Minister. John Hewitt. **CP-HewiJ**

Not Only. Walter de la Mare. **CP-DeLaW**

Not only can I not remember anecdotes that are racy. What's in a Name? Some Letter I Always Forget. Ogden Nash. **CP-NashO**

Not Only I. Thomas Hardy. **CP-HardT**

Not only love plus awful grief. Edna St. Vincent Millay. **CP-MillE**

Not only sands and gravels. One Step Taken Backward. Robert Frost. **CP-FrosR**

Not only were you waiting. H₂O. Al Young. **CP-YounA**

Not Oral Roberts' city of heavenly glitz. Tulsa. John Updike. **CP-UpdiJ**

Not Our Good Luck. Robinson Jeffers. **CP-JefR1**

Not out of mercy / Did I launch this transaction. Epitaph for a Public Servant. Thomas Merton. **CP-MertT**

Not over-kind nor over-quick in study. Edna St. Vincent Millay. *Fr.* Sonnets from an Ungrafted Tree. **CP-MillE**

Not picnics or pageants or the improbable. Terror. Robert Penn Warren. **SP-WarrR**

Not power nor the casual [or storied] hand of God. Allen Tate. *Fr.* Sonnets of the Blood. **CP-TateA**

Not probable—The barest Chance. Emily Dickinson. **CP-DickE**

Not Quite So Soon. Charles Bukowski. **SP-BukC2**

Not Quite Social. Robert Frost. **CP-FrosR**

Not quite yet. First, / around the corner for a visit. Dining Out with Doug and Frank. James Schuyler. **CP-SchuJ**

Not "Revelation" 'tis, that waits. Emily Dickinson. **CP-DickE**

Not rose of death. Rose in the Afternoon. Jenny Joseph. **SP-JoseJ**

Not roses to the rose, I trow. Robert Louis Stevenson. **CP-StevR**

Not Sacco and Vanzetti. Countee Cullen. **CP-CullC**

Not sedentary all: there are who roam. Missions and Travels. William Wordsworth. *Fr.* Ecclesiastical Sonnets. **CP-WorW2**

Not seeing, still we know. Emily Dickinson. **CP-DickE**

Not seldom, clad in radiant vest. William Wordsworth. *Fr.* Inscriptions Supposed to Be Found in and near a Hermit's Cell; 1818. **CP-WorW2**

Not Sickness stains the Brave. Emily Dickinson. **CP-DickE**

Not slowly wrought, nor treasured for their form. Snowflakes. Howard Nemerov. **CP-NemeH**

Not So Far as the Forest. Edna St. Vincent Millay. **CP-MillE**

Not so he felt, who with her was to pay. The Condemned Felon. George Crabbe. **SP-CrabG** *Fr.* The Borough.

Not so that Pair whose youthful spirits dance. The Same Subject. William Wordsworth. *Fr.* The River Duddon [A Series of Sonnets]. **CP-WorW2**

Not so the infinite Relations—Below. Emily Dickinson. **CP-DickE**

Not solely that the Future she destroys. George Meredith. **GBL; TEP** *Fr.* Modern Love. **CP-MerG1**

Not solitarily in fields we find. Earth's Secret. George Meredith. **CP-MerG1**

Not, Stanhope! with the Patriot's doubtful name. To Earl Stanhope. Samuel Taylor Coleridge. *Fr.* Effusions. **CP-ColeS**

Not stone, not air, but something in the air. Man as Real (CITY; HUMAN). Jenny Joseph. *Fr.* Man as Matter. **SP-JoseJ**

Not strangeness, but strange likeness. Obstinate. Geoffrey Hill. **HAP; NoAM** *Fr.* Mercian Hymns. **CP-HillG**

Not surprisingly / I lost track of the seasons. Jim Carroll. **SP-CarrJ**

Not That. Stephen Berg. **SP-BergS**

Not that he goes—we love him more. Emily Dickinson. **CP-DickE**

Not that I look to my eyes more than your love. Catullus. *See* Carmen 14: "If, my irrepressible Calvus, I didn't."

Not that in colour it was like thy hair. The Bracelet. John Donne. *Fr.* Elegies. **CP-DonnJ**

Not that it matters, not that my heart's cry. Edna St. Vincent Millay. **CP-MillE**

Not that it was beautiful. For John, Who Begs Me Not to Enquire Further. Anne Sexton. **CP-SextA**

Not that light is holy, but that the holy is the light—. Kathleen Jessie Raine. *Fr.* To the Sun. **SP-RainK**

Not that, of course, you couldn't stick it out. To a Friend. Howard Nemerov. **CP-NemeH**

Not that she had no equal, not that she was. Fallgrief's Girlfriends. Ted Hughes. **SP-HughT**

Not that way. Walter de la Mare. **CP-DeLaW**

Not that we are not all. To a Man Dying on His Feet. William Carlos Williams. **CP-WilW2**

Not the action of rowing. A Christian Hero. Donald Davie. **CP-DavDo**

Not the Blood a Dreamer Kissed from My Mouth. Diane Wakoski. *Fr.* Fifteen Poems for a Lunar Eclipse None of Us Saw. **SP-WakoD**

Not the branches. All of December Toward New Year's. Louis Zukofsky. **CP-ZukLS**

Not the calm—the clarity. Nothing: a Divagation. Charles Tomlinson. *Fr.* Antecedents. **CP-TomlC**

Not the expression of collective emotion. A Note on War Poetry. Thomas Stearns Eliot. **CP-ElioT**

Not the least enviable of your many gifts. At the Cradle of Genius. Donald Davie. **CP-DavDo**

Not the Moon. Margaret Atwood. **SP-AtwM2**

Not the more. Fragment: Redundance. William Wordsworth. **CP-WorW1**

Not the Occult. Stephen Dunn. **SP-DunnS**

Not the Pilot. Walt Whitman. **CP-WhitW**

Not the sea-wave so bellows abroad when it bursts upon shingle. Clash in Arms of the Achaians and Trojans. Homer, *tr.* by George Meredith. **CP-MerG1** *Fr.* The Iliad.

Not the soft sighs of vernal gales. Song, A. Samuel Johnson. **CP-JohnS**

Not the symbol but the scene this pavement leads. George Oppen. **APSN** *Fr.* Route. **CP-OppeG**

Not the whole warbling grove in concert heard. To the Cuckoo. William Wordsworth. **CP-WorW2**

Not There. Tess Gallagher. **SP-GallT**

Not They Who Soar! Paul Laurence Dunbar. **CP-DunbP**

Not thine where marble-still and white. To Sydney. Robert Louis Stevenson. **CP-StevR**

Not this week nor this month dare I lie down. Training. Wilfred Owen. **CP-OwenW**

Not though you die to-night, O Sweet, and wail. Rudyard Kipling. **CP-KiplR** *Fr.* By Word of Mouth. *Fr.* Plain Tales from the Hills.

Not through the rational mind. The Recapitulation. Richard Eberhart. **CP-EberR**

Not time's how(anchored in what mountaining roots). Edward Estlin Cummings. **CP-CummE**

Not to admire, is all the Art I know. The Sixth Epistle of the First Book of Horace Imitated. Alexander Pope. **CP-PopeA**

Not to be Printed, Not to Be Said, Not to Be Thought. Muriel Rukeyser. **CP-RukeM**

Not to be shattered. Paxdominisit Sem Pervobiscum Etcumspiri Tutuo. Kenneth Patchen. **CP-PatcK**

Not to Be Trusted. Robert Penn Warren. **SP-WarrR**

Not to be without words in a season of effort. Thomas Merton. *Fr.* Cables to the Ace. **CP-MertT**

Not to Covet Much Where Little is the Charge. Robert Herrick. **CP-HerrR**

Not to discover weakness is. Emily Dickinson. **CP-DickE**

Not to exclude or demarcate, or pick out evils from their formidable masses (even to expose them,). L. of G.'s Purport. Walt Whitman. **CP-WhitW**

Not to have guessed is better: what is, ends. The Sphinx's Riddle to Oedipus. Randall Jarrell. **CP-JarrR**

Not to Keep. Robert Frost. **CP-FrosR**

Not to know vice at all, and keep[e] true state. Epode. Ben Jonson. **CP-JonsB**

Not to let ourselves know. Even Now You Are Leaving. Tess Gallagher. **SP-GallT**

Not to Live. John Berryman. **CP-BerrJ**

Not To Love. Robert Herrick. **CP-HerrR**

Not, to me, less lavish—though my dreams have been splendid. Edna St. Vincent Millay. **CP-MillE**

Not to mumble. You Must Remember. John Yau. **SP-YauJo**

Not to permit himself to be. Charles Olson. **CP-OlsoC**

Not to reduce the thing to nothing. George Oppen. **APSN** *Fr.* Route. **CP-OppeG**

Not to Sleep. Robert Ranke Graves. **CP-GravR**

Not to sleep all the night long, for pure joy. Not to Sleep. Robert Ranke Graves. **CP-GravR**

Not to thank dogwood nor. Basil Bunting. **CP-BuntB**

Not to the clouds, not to the cliff, he flew. The Dunlolly Eagle. William Wordsworth. *Fr.* Poems Composed or Suggested During a Tour, in the Summer of 1833. **CP-WorW2**

Not to the midnight of the gloomy past. On the Dedication of Dorothy Hall. Paul Laurence Dunbar. **CP-DunbP**

Not to the object specially designed. William Wordsworth. *Fr.* Sonnets upon the Punishment of Death. **CP-WorW2**

Not To Worry. Charles Bukowski. **SP-BukC3**

Not to You. Stephen Spender. **CP-SpenS**

Not to you, / Unborn generations. Sentiments for a Dedication. Archibald MacLeish. **CP-MacLA**

Not today, not tomorrow. Song: Yesterday Only. Robert Ranke Graves. **CP-GravR**

Not Transhistorical Death, or at Least Not Quite. Hayden Carruth. **CP-CarHS**

Not twice a twelvemonth [*or* twelve-month] you appear in Print. Epilogue to the Satires, in Two Dialogues. Alexander Pope. **CP-PopeA**

Not undelightful, friend, our rustic ease. Robert Louis Stevenson. *Fr.* Sonnets. **CP-StevR**

Not unto us, O Lord, not unto us. Psalm 115. Bible, *O.T. Fr.* Psalms. **CP-Psal**

Not unto us who did but seek. Hymn for the Celebration of Emancipation at Newburyport. John Greenleaf Whittier. **CP-WhitJ**

Not us, I say, not us. Bible, *O.T. See* Psalm 115: "Not unto us, O Lord, not unto us."

Not utterly unworthy to endure. Apology. William Wordsworth. *Fr.* Ecclesiastical Sonnets. **CP-WorW2**

Not vainly did old poets tell. Channing. John Greenleaf Whittier. **CP-WhitJ**

Not vainly doth the earnest voice of man. To Alex. Smith, the "Glasgow Poet," on His Sonnet to "Fame." George Meredith. **CP-MerG2**

Not vainly we waited and counted the hours. The Quakers Are Out. John Greenleaf Whittier. **CP-WhitJ**

Not very affectionate; she likes to kiss. Dog Under False Pretences. William Dickey. **SP-DickW**

Not want / jesus, The. The Sting. Charles Kenneth Williams. **CP-WillC**

Not Waving but Drowning. Stevie Smith. **CP-SmitS**

Not what / neutralizes by balance. A Grammar for Doctrine. Roy Fisher. **SP-FishR**

Not what I think / or see (I can't. Labor Day. James Schuyler. **CP-SchuJ**

Not what the stars have done. Emily Dickinson. **SP-DickE**

Not what We did, shall be the test. Emily Dickinson. **CP-DickE**

Not while, but long after he had told me. Each Bird Walking. Tess Gallagher. **SP-GallT**

Not with a Club, the Heart is broken. Emily Dickinson. **CP-DickE**

Not with an iron will, no. More like a whip. *see also* Dancer's Reply, The. Howard Nemerov. **CP-NemeH**

Not with an outcry to Allah nor any complaining. The Captive. Rudyard Kipling. **CP-KiplR**

Not with libations, but with shouts and laughter. Edna St. Vincent Millay. **CP-MillE**

Not with more glories, in th'ethereal plain. Alexander Pope. **EBEV; EBNV; ECEV; NOBE; NOEC; OXAEP-1; WHA** *Fr.* The Rape of the Lock[, an Heroi-Comical Poem]. **CP-PopeA**
(Voyage on the Thames, The.) **NOBE**

Not with the splendors of the days of old. Pennsylvania Hall. John Greenleaf Whittier. **CP-WhitJ**

Not without envy Wealth at times must look. The Problem. John Greenleaf Whittier. **CP-WhitJ**

Not without heavy grief of heart did He. Gabriello Chiabrera, *tr. fr. Italian by* William Wordsworth. **CP-WorW1**

Not writ in water[,] nor in mist. For John Keats, Apostle of Beauty. Countee Cullen. **CP-CullC** *Fr.* Four Epitaphs.

Not Yet. Muriel Rukeyser. **CP-RukeM**

Not yet did I know your laws, enticing Amathusia. Elegy 7. John Milton, *tr. fr. Latin by* John T. Shawcross. **CP-MiltJ**

Not yet enslaved, not wholly vile. O My Mother Isle! ("Not yet enslaved, not wholly vile"). Samuel Taylor Coleridge. **FaBoPP** *Fr.* Ode on the Departing Year. **CP-ColeS**

Not yet had History's Ætna smoked the skies. George Meredith. **FaPoB**, *sect.* 1–5; *Fr.* The Revolution. **CP-MerG1**

Not yet had History's Ætna smoked the skies. The Revolution. George Meredith. **CP-MerG1**

Not yet, my soul, these friendly fields desert. Robert Louis Stevenson. **CP-StevR**

Not yet the thirtieth year, the thirtieth. Fragment of a Meditation. Allen Tate. **CP-TateA**

Not you I fear but that other. Margaret Atwood. *Fr.* Circe / Mud Poems. **SP-AtwM1**

Not you, lean quarterlies and swarthy periodicals. To the Film Industry in Crisis. Frank O'Hara. **SP-OharF**

Not your dark poisons again. Sleep. Georg Trakl, *tr. fr. German by* James Wright. **CP-WrigJ**

Not your eyes, but what they disguise. Speech Out of Shadow. Ted Hughes. **SP-HughT**

Not Yours But You. Christina Georgina Rossetti. **CP-RosC3**

Not Youth Pertains to Me. Walt Whitman. **CP-WhitW**

Nota in una Bottiglia. Erica Jong. **SP-JongE**

Nota: man is the intelligence of his soil. The Comedian as the Letter C. Wallace Stevens. **CP-StevW**

Notations from a Muddled Indolence. Charles Bukowski. **SP-BukC2**

Note / as it gets darker. Elegy. Charles Simic. **SP-SimiC**

Note. James Liddy. *Fr.* A Munster Song of Love and War. **CP-LiddJ**

Note. Malcolm Lowry. **CP-LowrM**

Note, A. Malcolm Lowry. *See* The Wounded Bat.

Note. Charles Simic. **SP-SimiC**

Note, A. William Carlos Williams. **CP-WilW2**

Note for a Diary. Kenneth Patchen. **CP-PatcK**

Note For a Poem. Malcolm Lowry. **CP-LowrM**

Note from Capri to Richard Ryan on the Adriatic Floor. Richard Hugo. **CP-HugoR**

Note from St. Francis. Joseph Ceravolo. **SP-CeraJ**

Note in Honor of Machiavelli, A. Thomas Merton. **CP-MertT**

Note Left in Jimmy Leonard's Shack, A. James Wright. **CP-WrigJ**

Note on Commercial Theatre. Langston Hughes. **SP-HughL**

Note on Intellectuals. John Hewitt. **CP-HewiJ**

Note on Moonlight. Wallace Stevens. **CP-StevW**

Note on the Late Elections, A. Thomas McGrath. **SP-McGrT**

Note on War Poetry, A. Thomas Stearns Eliot. **CP-ElioT**

Note read re / letter of Lawrence's. Robert Creeley. **CP-CreeR**

Note Slipped Under a Door. Charles Simic. **SP-SimiC**

Note the stump, a peach tree. We had to cut it down. Places and Ways to Live. Richard Hugo. **CP-HugoR**

Note to Grandparents. Grace Paley. **CP-PaleG**

Note to La Fontaine, A. Jean Garrigue. **SP-GarrJ**

Note to Music: Brahms 1st Piano Concerto. William Carlos Williams. **CP-WilW2**

Note to Olga (1966), A. Denise Levertov. **CP-LeveD**

Note to R. H. from Strongsville. Richard Hugo. **CP-HugoR**

Note to subversives: Uncle has two extreme right hands and means business! Thomas Merton. *Fr.* Cables to the Ace. **CP-MertT**

Note to the Boys in the Back Room, A. Charles Bukowski. **SP-BukC3**

Note to the Previous Tenants. John Updike. **CP-UpdiJ**

Note to Wang Wei. John Berryman. **CP-BerrJ**

Note Upon the Love Letters of Beethoven. Charles Bukowski. **SP-BukC3**

Notebook / divine love is so. Picasso Laughing. Patti Smith. **SP-SmitP**

Notebook. Patti Smith. **SP-SmitP**

Notebooks indicate that this café, The. *see also* Café, The. Leonard Cohen. **CP-CoheL**

Noteless stream, the Birchbrook runs, A. Birchbrook Mill. John Greenleaf Whittier. **CP-WhitJ**

Notes for a Biography. Louis MacNeice. **CP-MacNL**

"Lavender blue for love, lavender green for youth."

"Oranges (sweet) and lemons (bitter) childhood, An."

"Splinters under the nails, weals on the buttocks."

"To the Lords of Convention'—The horses went by."

"White rolling battlements on rumbling lead."

Notes for a Little Play. Ted Hughes. **SP-HughT**

Notes for a New Liturgy. Thomas Merton. *Fr.* South. *Fr.* The Geography of Lograire. **CP-MertT**

Notes for a Poem. Muriel Rukeyser. **CP-RukeM**

Notes For Nobody. Donald Hall. **CP-HallD**

Notes for CXI: "I, one thing, as relation to one thing", See Canto 111, Notes for. Ezra Pound. *See* Canto 111, Notes for: "I, one thing, as relation to one thing."

Notes for CXVII et seq.: "For the blue flash and the moments / benedetta", *See* Canto 117 et seq., Notes for. Ezra Pound. *See* Canto 117 et seq., Notes for: "For the blue flash and the moments / benedetta."

Notes from a Suburban Heart. Mona Van Duyn. **SP-VanDM**

Notes from a Tunisian Journal. Rita Dove. **SP-DoveR**

Notes from India. May Sarton. **SP-SartM**

Notes from Robin Hill Cottage. Hayden Carruth. **CP-CarHS**

Notes from the Agent on Earth: How to be Human. Miller Williams. **SP-WillM**

Notes from the Childhood and the Girlhood. Gwendolyn Brooks. **SP-BrooG**

Ballad of the Late Annie, The.

Do Not Be Afraid of No.

Old Relative.

Parents: People Like Our Marriage Maxie and Andrew, The.

Pygmies Are Pygmies Still, Though Percht on Alps. **PoNe**

Sunday Chicken.

Throwing Out the Flowers.

Notes from the provinces always start. May Journal. Charles Wright. **SP-WrigC**

Notes I fall for fall from the lip of the sky, The. Spring Abstract. Charles Wright. **SP-WrigC**

Notes of a Parachute Jumper. Jorge Carrera Andrade, *tr. fr. Spanish by* Thomas Merton. **CP-MertT**

Notes on My Contemporaries. Michael Hartnett. **SP-HarMi**

Person as Dreamer: We Talk about the Future, The. **PBCIP**

Poet as Black Sheep, The.

Poet as Mastercraftsman, The.

Poet Down, The.

Poet Dreams and Resolves, The.

Notes on the Death of Nels Paulssen, Farmer, at the Ripe Old Age of 93. Ted Kooser. **SP-KoosT**

Notes on the tuned frame of strings. Sub Contra. Louise Bogan. **CP-BogaL**

Notes to a Neophyte. Sylvia Plath. **CP-PlatS**

Notes toward a Supreme Fiction. Wallace Stevens. **CP-StevW**

"And for what, except for you, do I feel love?" **NOBA**

It Must Be Abstract.

"Begin, ephebe, by perceiving the idea." **NOBA**

"First idea was not our own, The. Adam." **NOBA**

"It feels good as it is without the giant." **MoPo; NOBA**

"Major abstraction is the idea of man, The." **NOBA**

It Must Change.

"Bethou me, said sparrow, to the crackled blade." **LiTM; MoPo**

Great Statue of the General Du Puy, The. **LiTA**

President Ordains the Bee to Be, The. **LiTA**

Two Things of Opposite Natures Seem to Depend. **MeMAP**

It Must Give Pleasure.

Whistle Aloud, Too Weedy Wren. **LiTA**

"Soldier, there is a war between the mind." **LiTA; NePA; NoAM**

(Soldier, There Is a War between the Mind.) **LiTA; NePA**

Notes towards a Poem That Can Never Be Written. Margaret Atwood. **SP-AtwM2**

Notes towards a Video of Avondale House. James Liddy. **CP-LiddJ**

Notes Towards an Autobiography. Richard Shelton. **SP-ShelR**

Notes towards an Ivy Leaf Video. James Liddy. **CP-LiddJ**

Nothing. Margaret Atwood. **SP-AtwM2**

Nothing. James Fenton. **SP-FentJ**

Nothing. Robert Ranke Graves. **CP-GravR**

Nothing / substance utters or time. Basil Bunting. **CP-BuntB**

Nothing: a Divagation. Charles Tomlinson. *Fr.* Antecedents. **CP-TomlC**

Nothing below me moves except a fan blade. Through Glass. Stephen Berg. **SP-BergS**

Nothing But Change. Richard Eberhart. **CP-EberR**

Nothing but Nature. Ogden Nash. **CP-NashO**

Nothing but one life: all stands. Springhouse, Menses, Held Apple, House and Beyond. James Dickey. **CP-DickJ**

Nothing can be more loathsome, then to see. Cruelty Base in Commanders. Robert Herrick. **CP-HerrR**

Nothing can prevent the passing; like wind. Still Passing. Robert Pack. **SP-PackR**

Nothing comes Free-cost here; *Jove* will not let. Nothing Free-Cost. Robert Herrick. **CP-HerrR**

Nothing could make me sooner to confess[e]. The Second Anniversary [*or* Anniversarie]. John Donne. **ESCV; SeCP** *Fr.* Of the Progres[se] of the Soule; the Second Anniversarie. **CP-DonnJ**

Nothing day full of, A. Closed Gentian Distances. James Schuyler. **CP-SchuJ**

Nothing Down. Rita Dove. **SP-DoveR**

Nothing else in this song—only your face. Paula. Carl Sandburg. **CP-SandC**

Nothing endures, / Not even love. Countee Cullen. **CP-CullC**

Nothing exists that is not marred; therefore. Therefore. William Dickey. **SP-DickW**

Nothing false and possible is love. Edward Estlin Cummings. **CP-CummE; SP-CummE**

Nothing for a dirty man. All That Is Lovely in Men. Robert Creeley. **CP-CreeR**

Nothing For Tears. John Milton. **OtMeF** *Fr.* Samson Agonistes. **CP-MiltJ**

Nothing Free-Cost. Robert Herrick. **CP-HerrR**

Nothing Gold Can Stay. Robert Frost. **CP-FrosR**

Nothing grimmer than dawn at noon. Gilbert Sorrentino. **SP-SorrG**

Nothing hard, or harsh can prove. No Action Hard to Affection. Robert Herrick. **CP-HerrR**

Nothing I, The. Hayden Carruth. *Fr.* Contra Mortem. **CP-CarHL**

Nothing I Can Lose. Leonard Cohen. **CP-CoheL**

Nothing II, The. Hayden Carruth. *Fr.* Contra Mortem. **CP-CarHL**

Nothing in her Life became her. Emily Dickinson. **SP-DickE**

Nothing in life has been made by man for man's using. Untimely. Rudyard Kipling. **CP-KiplR** *Fr.* Debits and Credits.

Nothing in this bright region melts or shifts. From the Highest Camp. Thom Gunn. **CP-GunnT**

Nothing inclusive of a human Heart. Emily Dickinson. **SP-DickE**

Nothing is / as transient as sound. Audition. Dabney Stuart. **SP-StuaD**

Nothing is better, I well think. The Leper. Algernon Charles Swinburne. **SP-SwinA**

Nothing is better than seaweed on rocks. Frederick Morgan. *Fr.* Blue Hill Poems. **SP-MorgF**

NOTHING is circular. Nothing. Robert Ranke Graves. **CP-GravR**

Nothing is ever really lost, or can be lost. Continuities. Walt Whitman. **CP-WhitW**

Nothing is given which is not taken. Apollo Musagete, Poetry, and the Leader of the Muses. Delmore Schwartz. **SP-SchwD**

Nothing is glummer. Fahrenheit *Gesundheit*. Ogden Nash. **CP-NashO**

Nothing is happening / Nothing. Event. Charles Tomlinson. **CP-TomlC**

Nothing is here for tears, nothing to wail. Nothing For Tears. John Milton. **OtMeF** *Fr.* Samson Agonistes. **CP-MiltJ**

Nothing is more certain than the flower. Two Aspects of April. William Carlos Williams. **CP-WilW1**

Nothing is more exactly terrible than. Edward Estlin Cummings. **CP-CummE**

Nothing is new: we walk where others went. Nothing New. Robert Herrick. **CP-HerrR**

Nothing is re-enacted. Nothing. Elijah on Mount Carmel. Robert Penn Warren. **SP-WarrR**

Nothing is really any fun, to-day. Always This Paying. David Herbert Lawrence. **CP-LawrD**

Nothing Is Right. Alice Walker. **CP-WalkA**

Nothing is simple, / not even simplification. Throwing away the Mail. Wendell Berry. **CP-BerrW**

Nothing is so beautiful as Spring—. Spring. Gerard Manley Hopkins. **CP-HopkG**

Nothing is so magnificent. Opulence. Richard Eberhart. **CP-EberR**

Nothing is so sure that it. The Looking Glass. Walter de la Mare. **CP-DeLaW**

Nothing is to be seen. Reflections at Forty-Nine. Lewis Turco. **SP-TurcL**

Nothing like love to put blood. Nothing. Margaret Atwood. **SP-AtwM2**

Nothing like the freedom of vision. Life as Visionary Spirit. Richard Eberhart. **CP-EberR**

Nothing Matters Much. Thomas Hardy. **CP-HardT**

Nothing more simple. Among the tarnished. Louis MacNeice. *Fr.* Didymus. **CP-MacNL**

Nothing moves / or murmurs but ourselves, as light. Wreckage of the Pagoda Moons. Laurence Lieberman. **SP-LiebL**

Nothing moves. In its cage, the broken. Returning a Lost Child. Louise Glück. **SP-GlücL**

Nothing New. Robert Herrick. **CP-HerrR**

Nothing Now Astonishes. Robert Ranke Graves. **CP-GravR**

Nothing prolongs. Neither the bronze plaque. Memorial. Thomas McGrath. **SP-McGrT**

Nothing remained: Nothing, the wanton name. The Annihilation of Nothing. Thom Gunn. **CP-GunnT**

Nothing respects your solitude. The planes. Soledad. Edwin Rolfe. **CP-RolfE**

Nothing says that you must. The Dozens. Audre Lorde. **SP-LordA**

Nothing seemed so incongruous. Santa Claus in Oaxaca. Richard Eberhart. **CP-EberR**

Nothing seems right, not the monument too close. Culloden. Richard Hugo. **CP-HugoR**

Nothing Significant Was Really Said. Philip Larkin. **CP-LarkP**

Nothing so difficult as a beginning. Byron. **EnRP,** *canto* 4, *stanzas* 1–73; **FiP** *Fr.* Canto the Fourth. *Fr.* Don Juan. **CP-Byron**

(Romantic to Burlesque.) **FiP,** *canto* 4, *stanzas* 1–3;

Nothing so difficult as a beginning. Canto the Fourth. Byron. *Fr.* Don Juan. **CP-Byron**

Nothing so true as what you once let fall. Epistle [II,] to a Lady[: Of the Characters of Women]. Alexander Pope. **CP-PopeA**

Nothing so true as what you once let fall. Epistle [II,] to a Lady[: Of the Characters of Women]. Alexander Pope. **CP-PopeA**

Nothing so true as what you once let fall. Alexander Pope. **OxBoLi** *Fr.* Epistle [II,] to a Lady[: Of the Characters of Women]. **CP-PopeA**

Nothing Subtle. Charles Bukowski. **SP-BukC2**

"Nothing" the unjust man complained. Edward Estlin Cummings. **CP-CummE**

Nothing there? nothing up the sky alive? John Berryman. **BoLoP** *Fr.* Sonnets to Chris. **CP-BerrJ**

Nothing to Be Said. Philip Larkin. **CP-LarkP**

Nothing to grind? Then answer, and I'll go. Prologue: The Grinder. Alun Lewis. **CP-LewiA**

Nothing to it, man. Kicking. Al Young. **CP-YounA**

Nothing to Save. David Herbert Lawrence. **CP-LawrD**

Nothing to say to all those marriages! Place for a Third. Robert Frost. **CP-FrosR**

Nothing Was Delivered. "Bob Dylan." **CP-DylaB**

Nothing was heard in the room but the hurrying pen of the stripling. Love and Friendship. Henry Wadsworth Longfellow. **TreFS** *Fr.* The Courtship of Miles Standish. **SP-LongH**

Nothing was left of me. A Dream of Burial. James Wright. **CP-WrigJ**

Nothing was less than its seemed, my darling. Long Past Moncada. Muriel Rukeyser. **CP-RukeM**

Nothing whichful about / thick big this. Edward Estlin Cummings. **CP-CummE**

Nothing Will Cure the Sick Lion But To Eat an Ape. Marianne Craig Moore. **CP-MoorM**

Nothing will hold him much longer—let him go. The Sunken Crown. Edwin Arlington Robinson. **CP-RobiE**

Nothing Will Yield. Howard Nemerov. **CP-NemeH**

Nothing would sleep in that cellar, dank as a ditch. Root Cellar. Theodore Roethke. **CP-RoetT**

Nothingness. Stephen Berg. **SP-BergS**

Notice. Patti Smith. **SP-SmitP**

Notice how he has numbered the blue veins. Mr. Mine. Anne Sexton. **CP-SextA**

Notice that is called the Spring, The. Emily Dickinson. **CP-DickE**

Notice the convulsed orange inch of moon. Edward Estlin Cummings. **CP-CummE**

Notice 2. Patti Smith. **SP-SmitP**

Notions of freedom are tied up with drink. Malcolm Lowry. **CP-LowrM** *Fr.* The Drunkards.

NOTL. Margaret Atwood. *See* You Fit into Me.

Chickens in San Francisco. William Dickey. **SP-DickW**

Spinazzola: *Quella Cantina Là*. Richard Hugo. **CP-HugoR**

Notre Dame, I am afraid. Kerouac's Ronsard Dance. James Liddy. **CP-LiddJ**

Nottingham's New University. David Herbert Lawrence. **CP-LawrD**

Nottinghamshire. Donald Davie. **CP-DavDo**

Nought from my birth or ancestors I claim. Ovid, *tr. by* Samuel Johnson. **CP-JohnS** *Fr.* Metamorphoses.

Nought have I to bring / Tramping a-chill and shivering. November. Christina Georgina Rossetti. *Fr.* The Months: A Pageant. **CP-RosC2**

Nought is on earth more sacred or divine. Edmund Spenser. **OAEL-1** *Fr.* The Faerie Queene. **CP-Spens**

Nought is there under heav'ns wide hollownesse. Edmund Spenser. **FHYEP** *Fr.* The Faerie Queene. **CP-Spens**

Nought loves another as itself. Little Boy Lost, A. William Blake. **CP-BlakW** *Fr.* Songs of Experience.

Nought vnder heauen so strongly doth allure. Edmund Spenser. **NoSic** *Fr.* The Faerie Queene. **CP-Spens**

Nouns to nouns / wan / wan. Edward Estlin Cummings. **CP-CummE**

Nourish Me on an Egg. Stevie Smith. **CP-SmitS**

Nourish Your Heart. John Hewitt. **CP-HewiJ**

Nourishment before Battle. Homer, *tr. by* George Meredith. **CP-MerG2** *Fr.* The Iliad.

Nova. Robinson Jeffers. **CP-JefR2**

Nova Scotia. Stephen Dunn. **SP-DunnS**

Novel, The. Denise Levertov. **CP-LeveD**

Novel, The. Wallace Stevens. **CP-StevW**

Novelettes. Louis MacNeice. **CP-MacNL**
  Christina.
  Gardener, The. **FaBCIP; IIP**
  Les Sylphides. **BoLoP; CoBMV**
  Old Story, The.
  Preacher, The.
  Provence.

Novelist, The. Wystan Hugh Auden. **CP-AudeW**

Novelists. Howard Nemerov. **CP-NemeH**

Novella. Adrienne Rich. **CP-RicAE; SP-RicA2**

November. Margaret Atwood. **SP-AtwM1**

November. Martin Edmunds. **SP-EdmuM**

November. Robert Frost. **CP-FrosR**

November. Ted Hughes. **SP-HughT**

November. Archibald MacLeish. **CP-MacLA**

November. Christina Georgina Rossetti. *Fr.* The Months: A Pageant. **CP-RosC2**

November. James Schuyler. **CP-SchuJ**

November. Richard Shelton. **SP-ShelR**

November. Stevie Smith. **CP-SmitS**

November. Gary Snyder. *Fr.* Six Years. **CP-SnydG**

November. Edmund Spenser. **PoEL-1** *Fr.* The Shepheardes [*or* Shepeards *or* Shepherd's] Calender. **CP-Spens**
  Dido My Dear, Alas, Is Dead. **ChTr**

November. John Updike. **CP-UpdiJ**

November Seven, Nineteen Eighty-Four. Barton Sutter. **SP-SuttB**

November air, The. Hotel Sierra. David St. John. **SP-StJoD**

November always seemed to me. Emily Dickinson. **SP-DickE**

November at Weybourne. Wystan Hugh Auden. **CP-AudWJ**

NOVEMBER (*Boxing*). Rudyard Kipling. *Fr.* Verses on Games. **CP-KiplR**

(Boxing.) **OtMeF**

November by the Sea. David Herbert Lawrence. **CP-LawrD**

November chill blaws loud wi' angry sugh. Robert Burns. **OBEC** *Fr.* The Cotter's Saturday Night [Inscribed to Robert Aiken [*or* R. A****], Esq.]. **CP-BurnR**

November dawns and dewy-glooming downs. November in the Isle of Wight. Tennyson. **FaBoPP** *Fr.* Enoch Arden. **CP-TennA**

November Day at McClure's Beach. Robert Bly. **SP-BlyR**

November Days. John Gould Fletcher. **SP-FletJ**

November Dusk. Chuck Miller. **SP-MillC**

November dusk, at four o'clock. November Park. John Hewitt. **CP-HewiJ**

November, 1806. William Wordsworth. **CP-WorW1**

November, 1813. William Wordsworth. **CP-WorW1**

November, 1836. William Wordsworth. **CP-WorW2**

November 1st. Richard Shelton. **SP-ShelR**

November for Beginners. Rita Dove. **SP-DoveR**

November Ghosts, The. Randall Jarrell. **SP-JarrR**

November Graveyard. Sylvia Plath. **CP-PlatS**

November in afterpiece. Local Journal. Charles Wright. **SP-WrigC**

November in Ohio. Kenneth Patchen. **CP-PatcK**

November in the Isle of Wight. Tennyson. **FaBoPP** *Fr.* Enoch Arden. **CP-TennA**

November: Indian Summer. Hayden Carruth. **CP-CarHS**

November Jeans Song. Hayden Carruth. **CP-CarHS**

November 1968. Adrienne Rich. **CP-RicAE; SP-RicA2**

November, 1937, *sl. diff. vers. in sec.1*, The Cantinas line. Malcolm Lowry. *Fr.* The Lighthouse Invites the Storm. **CP-LowrM**

November 1. William Wordsworth. **CP-WorW2**

November Park. John Hewitt. **CP-HewiJ**

November rain with thin fingers tapping. Kathleen Jessie Raine. *Fr.* My Mother's Birthday. **SP-RainK**

November rips gold foil from the oak ridges. Damon's Lament for his Clorinda, Yorkshire 1654. Geoffrey Hill. *Fr.* An Apology for the Revival of Christian Architecture in England. **CP-HillG**

November sun invites me, The. Nutting Song. Paul Laurence Dunbar. **CP-DunbP**

November Surf. Robinson Jeffers. **CP-JefR2**

Nov. 23, 1963: Alone. Allen Ginsberg. **CP-GinsA**

November Wood. John Hewitt. **CP-HewiJ**

November's chill blast on the rough beach is howling. The Female Exile. Written at Brighthelmstone in November 1792. Charlotte Smith. **CP-SmitC**

Novice, The. John Hewitt. **CP-HewiJ**

Novice, The. Christina Georgina Rossetti. **CP-RosC3**

Novice, hear me what I say. Hafiz, *tr.* by Ralph Waldo Emerson. **CP-EmerR** *Fr.* Odes.

Novice was sitting on a cornice, A. Illustration. John Ashbery. **SP-AshbJ**

Novices, The. Denise Levertov. **CP-LeveD**

Novices. Marianne Craig Moore. **CP-MoorM**

Novitiates sing Ave. Miss Scarlet, Mr. Rhett and other Latter-Day Saints. Maya Angelou. **SP-AngeM**

Now. Charles Bukowski. **SP-BukC3**

NOW. Audre Lorde. **SP-LordA**

Now! / Not now! In a Balcony. Robert Browning. **CP-BroR1**

Now. Anne Sexton. **CP-SextA**

N(o)w / the / how / dis(appeared cleverly)world. Edward Estlin Cummings. **CP-CummE**

Now. Dylan Thomas. **CP-ThomD**

Now a conundrum Love propounds. Elizabeth Bishop. *Fr.* Three Valentines. **CP-BishE**

Now above all is the time for the minorities of men. Minorities in Danger. David Herbert Lawrence. **CP-LawrD**

Now, after all, let no man. The Phoenix Analysed. Ben Jonson. **CP-JonsB**

Now again and now for ever breaks the great illusion. The Gulf. David Herbert Lawrence. **CP-LawrD**

Now air is air and thing is thing:no bliss. Edward Estlin Cummings. **CP-CummE**

Now al is done; bring home the bride againe. Edmund Spenser. **FiP** *Fr.* Epithalamion: "Ye learned sisters, which have oftentimes." **CP-Spens**

Now all day long the man who is not dead. Mother and Son. Allen Tate. **CP-TateA**

Now all my words are bricks. The Way It Goes or the Proper Use of Leisure Time. Stephen Dobyns. **SP-DobyS**

Now all of change. Sir Thomas Wyatt. **CP-WyatT**

Now all our saws sing holy sonnets in this world of timber. Trappists, Working. Thomas Merton. **CP-MertT; SP-MertT**

Now all the fingers of this tree(darling)have. Edward Estlin Cummings. **CP-CummE; SP-CummE**

Now all the hosts are marching to the grave. Resurrection. David Herbert Lawrence. **CP-LawrD**

Now all the truth is out. To a Friend Whose Work Has Come to Nothing. William Butler Yeats. **CP-YeatW**

Now all the world she knew is dead. House of Rest. Sir John Betjeman. **CP-BetjJ**

Now all the world she knew is dead. House of Rest. Sir John Betjeman. **OxAEP-2** *Fr.* House of Rest. **CP-BetjJ**

Now an elderly person. No Cresta Run. John Hewitt. **CP-HewiJ**

Now and again. Virgin Youth. David Herbert Lawrence. **CP-LawrD**

Now and Then. James Schuyler. **CP-SchuJ**

Now, Antonius, in a smiling age. De M. Antonio. Robert Louis Stevenson. **CP-StevR**

Now Art has lost its mental Charms. William Blake. **CP-BlakW**

Now as a lover would. Alun Lewis. *Fr.* The Soldier. **CP-LewiA**

Now as at all times I can see in the mind's eye. The Magi. William Butler Yeats. **CP-YeatW**

Now, as desire and the things desired. Compline. Wystan Hugh Auden. *Fr.* Horae Canonicae. **CP-AudeW**

Now as from maple to elm the flittermice skitter and twirl. Idyll. Theodore Roethke. **CP-RoetT**

Now as he rolled these matters within him in heart & in spirit. Odysseus Encircled. Homer, *tr.* by George Meredith. **CP-MerG2** *Fr.* The Iliad.

Now as Heaven is my Lot, they're the Pests of the Nation! A Soliloquy on the Full Moon, She Being in a Mad Passion. Samuel Taylor Coleridge. **CP-ColeS**

Now as I was young and easy under the apple boughs. Fern Hill. Dylan Thomas. **CP-ThomD**

Now as I watch the progress of the plague. The Missing. Thom Gunn. **CP-GunnT**

Now as I watch you, strong of arm and endurance, battling and struggling. To the Swimmer. Countee Cullen. **CP-CullC**

Now as the train bears west. Night Journey. Theodore Roethke. **CP-RoetT**

Now as the year turns toward its darkness. Going Away. Howard Nemerov. **CP-NemeH**

Now, at last, / I carry nothing. Breathing Purely. Daniel Gerard Hoffman. **SP-HoffD**

Now at ninety this frail and lightsome woman. Examination of Psyche: Thoughts of Home. Richard Eberhart. **CP-EberR**

Now at our island's shining rim. Aubade: Bermuda. Thomas Merton. **CP-MertT**

Now at the end I smell the smell of spring. Exit Molloy. Derek Mahon. **POL** *Fr.* Four Walks in the Country Near Saint-Brieuc. **SP-MahoD**

Now, at the rising of Venus—the steady star. North and South. Derek Walcott. **CP-WalcD**

Now, at the time that was before agreed. Edmund Spenser. **OAEL-1** *Fr.* The Faerie Queene. **CP-Spens**

Now bare to the beholder's eye. Robert Louis Stevenson. **CP-StevR**

Now by a sudden shift of eye. The Olive-Yard. Robert Ranke Graves. **CP-GravR**

Now by the path I climbed, I journey back. Edna St. Vincent Millay. **CP-MillE**

Now, by the verdure on thy thousand hills. Adequacy. Elizabeth Barrett Browning. **CP-BroEB**

Now by this moon, before this moon shall wane. Edna St. Vincent Millay. **CP-MillE**

Now Came Still Evening On. John Milton. **FaBoRV** *Fr.* Book IV. **OAEL-1** *Fr.* Paradise Lost. **CP-MiltJ**

Now came still Ev'ning [*or* evening *or* Eevning] on, and Twilight gray [*or* grey]. John Milton. **PeECV**, *ll.* 598–688; **ChTr; FaBoEn; NOBE; TreFS** *Fr.* Book IV. **OAEL-1** *Fr.* Paradise Lost. **CP-MiltJ**

(Evening in Paradise.) **FaBoEn; TreFS**, *ll.* 598–609; **NOBE**, *ll.* 598–656;

(Moon and the Nightingale, The.) **ChTr**, *ll.* 598–609;

Now can you see the monument? It is of wood. The Monument. Elizabeth Bishop. **CP-BishE**

Now, Chatto, you're a dreary place. An Elegy upon James Therburn. James Thomson. **CP-ThomJ**

Now Chil the Kite brings home the night. Rudyard Kipling. **CP-KiplR** *Fr.* Mowgli's Brothers. *Fr.* The Jungle Book.

Now Close the Windows. Robert Frost. **CP-FrosR**

Now cocks crow coop to coop. Fayetteville Dawn (1). John Clellon Holmes. **SP-HolmJ**

Now come to me all men. Experience Evoked. Richard Eberhart. **CP-EberR**

Now comes the good rain farmers pray for(and). Edward Estlin Cummings. **CP-CummE**

Now cometh alle ye that ben ibroght. Huc omnes pariter. Boethius, *tr.* by John Walton. **OBMV** *Fr.* Consolation of Philosophy, The ("De Consolacione Philosophie"). **CP-ChauG**

Now constantly there is the sound. October 10. Wendell Berry. **CP-BerrW**

Now crows mill blackly above them. Young Owls. Brendan Galvin. **SP-GalvB**

Now Curll his shop from rubbish drains. Jonathan Swift. **PeLV** *Fr.* Verses on the Death of Dr. Swift, D.S.P.D. **CP-SwifJ**

Now *Dædalus*, behold, by fate assign'd. Ovid, *tr.* by Samuel Johnson. **CP-JohnS** *Fr.* The Art of Love.

Now dawns all waxen to your seal of life. George Meredith. **CP-MerG2**

Now dearest comrade, lift me to your face. To the Reader at Parting. Walt Whitman. **CP-WhitW**

Now deeply drunk, always where you have found him. G.F. Died 1954, Aged 27. William Dickey. **SP-DickW**

Now Dian, with her burning face. Ben Jonson. **CP-JonsB** *Fr.* The Masque of Blackness.

Now did you mark a falcon. Noble Sisters. Christina Georgina Rossetti. **CP-RosC1**

Now dis "daughter" uv eve(who aint precisely slim)sim. Edward Estlin Cummings. **CP-CummE**

Now do our eyes behold. Aeschylus. **CP-HousA** *Fr.* The Seven against Thebes.

Now do you know of Avalon. The Jingo and the Minstrel. Nicholas Vachel Lindsay. **CP-LindV**

Now does our world descend. Edward Estlin Cummings. **CP-CummE**

Now does Spain's fleet her spacious wings unfold. On the Victory Obtained by Blake over the Spaniards, in the Bay of Santa [*or* Sancta] Cruz, in the Island of Tenerife, 1657. Andrew Marvell. **CP-MarvA**

Now does *Spains* Fleet her spatious wings unfold. Andrew Marvell. **FaBoEH** *Fr.* On the Victory Obtained by Blake over the Spaniards, in the Bay of Santa [*or* Sancta] Cruz, in the Island of Tenerife, 1657. **CP-MarvA**

Now, don't sir! Don't expose me! Just this once! Mr Sludge, "The Medium." Robert Browning. **CP-BroR1**

Now dreary dawns the eastern light. Alfred Edward Housman. **CP-HousA**

Now dumb is he who waked the world to speak. On Hearing the News from Venice. George Meredith. **CP-MerG1**

Now Europe's balanc'd neither Side prevails. The Balance of Europe. Alexander Pope. **CP-PopeA**

Now fades the last long streak of snow. And buds and blossoms like the rest. Tennyson. **EBVV; FHYEP; FaBoEn; FaBoRV; GTBS-6; GTBS-P; NOBE; OBNC; SeCeV** *Fr.* In Memoriam A. H. H. **CP-TennA**

Now farewell to you! you are. Lines to a Friend Visiting America. George Meredith. **CP-MerG1**

Now fie upon that everlasting life, I dye! Valiant Love. Richard Lovelace. **CP-LoveR**

Now Finalè to the Shore. Walt Whitman. **CP-WhitW**

Now first of all he means the night. A Song for the Middle of the Night. James Wright. **CP-WrigJ**

Now for the first time on the night of your death your name is mentioned in convents, *ne cadas in obscurum.* An Elegy for Ernest Hemingway. Thomas Merton. **CP-MertT; SP-MertT**

Now for the spirit of the people. Here. Wystan Hugh Auden. **FaBoPV** *Fr.* Letter to Lord Byron. **CP-AudeW**

Now forth to meadow as the farmer goes. Edna St. Vincent Millay. *Fr.* Epitaph for the Race of Man. **CP-MillE**

Now from far eastern wolds, the bay. Wystan Hugh Auden. **CP-AudWJ**

Now from Leander's place she rose, and found. George Chapman. **EBEV** *Fr.* Hero and Leander. **CP-MarlC**

Now from my window-sill I watch the night. The Watchers. Wystan Hugh Auden. **CP-AudeW**

Now from our village we regard the moon. The Moon. John Hewitt. **CP-HewiJ**

Now from the meadow floods the wild duck clamours. Pastoral 5. George Meredith. *Fr.* Pastorals. **CP-MerG1**

Now frost has broken summer like a glass. Der Abschied. May Sarton. **SP-SartM**

Now ginnes this goodly frame of temperaunce. The Bower of Bliss. Edmund Spenser. **PoEL-1** *Fr.* The Faerie Queene. **CP-Spens**

Now give us lands where the olives grow. The North and the South. Elizabeth Barrett Browning. **CP-BroEB**

Now goes under, and I watch it go under, the sun. To a Friend Estranged from Me. Edna St. Vincent Millay. **CP-MillE**

Now grapes are plush upon the vines. Contrary Theses (I). Wallace Stevens. **CP-StevW**

Now green, now burning, I make a way for peace. Tenth Elegy. Elegy in Joy. Muriel Rukeyser. **CP-RukeM**

Now green, now burning, I malke a way for peace. Now Green, Now Burning. Muriel Rukeyser. **LPA** *Fr.* Tenth Elegy. Elegy in Joy. **CP-RukeM**

Now grey-ey'd hazy Eve's begun. Evening. John Clare. **SP-ClarJ**

Now had her glut of vengeance left her grey. George Meredith. *Fr.* The Revolution. **CP-MerG1**

Now had night measured with her shadowy cone. Then when I Am Thy Captive, Talk of Chains. John Milton. **WHA** *Fr.* Book IV. **OAEL-1** *Fr.* Paradise Lost. **CP-MiltJ**

Now had th' Almighty Father from above. John Milton. **NIP** *Fr.* Book III. *Fr.* Paradise Lost. **CP-MiltJ**

Now had the loophole of that dungeon, still. Ugolino. Dante Alighieri, *tr.* by Shelley. **CP-ShelP** *Fr.* Inferno. *Fr.* Divina Commedia.

Now had the seasons returned, when the nights grow colder and longer. Henry Wadsworth Longfellow. *Fr.* Part the First. *Fr.* Evangeline, a Tale of Acadie. **SP-LongH**

"In-doors, warm by the wide mouthed fireplace, idly the farmer." **APN-1**

Now hardly here and there a hackney coach. A Description of the Morning. Jonathan Swift. **CP-SwifJ**

Now hath Flora rob'd [*or* robbed] her bowers. Song. Thomas Campion. **OBSC** *Fr.* Lord Hay's Mask.

Now he has become one who upon that coast. His Head is Full of Faces. Muriel Rukeyser. **CP-RukeM**

Now He Knows All There Is to Know: Now He Is Acquainted With the Day and Night. Delmore Schwartz. **SP-SchwD**

Now he plays with the other children. Muriel Rukeyser. **CP-RukeM**

Now health forsakes that angel face. Fragment. Robert Burns. **CP-BurnR**

Now here is peace for one who knew. No Bird. Theodore Roethke. **CP-RoetT**

Now hollow fires burn out to black. Alfred Edward Housman. **CP-HousA**

Now homing tradesmen scatter through the streets. Place Pigalle. Richard Wilbur. **CP-WilbR**

Now honest William's gaen to Heaven. Elegy on Mister William Cruikshank A. M. Robert Burns. **CP-BurnR**

Now I am all. Mystery. David Herbert Lawrence. **CP-LawrD**

Now I am come again, to you who have so desired. Return. David Herbert Lawrence. **CP-LawrD**

Now I am dead you sing to me. An Upbraiding. Thomas Hardy. **CP-HardT**

Now I am going. The Thing Itself. Alice Walker. **CP-WalkA**

Now I am minded to take a pipe in hand. Gerard Manley Hopkins. **CP-HopkG**

Now I am old and free from time. Winter Paradise. Kathleen Jessie Raine. **SP-RainK**

Now I am out of element. Against Disaster. Theodore Roethke. **CP-RoetT**

Now I am surer where they were going. For W. H. Auden. Richard Wilbur. **CP-WilbR**

Now I am young and credulous. Wisdom Cometh with the Years. Countee Cullen. **CP-CullC**

Now I arise, impow'r'd by Thee. At Dressing in the Morning. Christopher Smart. *Fr.* Hymns for the Amusement of Children. **SP-SmarC**

Now I Become Myself. May Sarton. **SP-SartM**

Now I believe tradition, which doth call. Upon the Author. By a Known Friend. Benjamin Woodbridge. **CP-BradA**

Now I break the mask, repeal those years. Two Graves in a Day. Richard Hugo. **CP-HugoR**

Now I can be sure of my sleep. On the Hill below the Lighthouse. James Dickey. **CP-DickJ**

Now I can tell you. Hearing the shrill leaves. The Thrasher in the Willow by the Lake. Robert Pack. **SP-PackR**

Now I commend this body to this earth. It Is for Us the Living. Kenneth Patchen. **CP-PatcK**

Now I go down here and bring up a moon. Auctioneer. Carl Sandburg. **CP-SandC**

Now I have become a man. Ode: My 24th Year. Allen Ginsberg. **CP-GinsA**

Now I have thought the very thoughts of God! Jane Cooper. *Fr.* After the Bomb Tests. **SP-CoopJ**

Now I knew I lost her. Emily Dickinson. **CP-DickE**

Now I know. Delphi. Hilda Doolittle. **CP-DoolH**

Now I know I never shall. Ted Hughes. **SP-HughT** *Fr.* Prometheus on His Crag.

Now I lay me down to sleep. Compline. Donald Davie. *Fr.* Horae Canonicae. **CP-DavDo**

Now I lay thee down to Sleep. Emily Dickinson. **CP-DickE**

Now i lay(with everywhere around). Edward Estlin Cummings. **CP-CummE**

Now I long for the Pierian fountains. To My Father. John Milton, *tr. fr. Latin by* John T. Shawcross. **CP-MiltJ**

Now I must sit naked. The Sweat. Gary Snyder. **CP-SnydG**

Now I need to forget the pages I can't forget and can't read again. Mother Political. Stephen Berg. **SP-BergS**

Now I out walking. Away! Robert Frost. **CP-FrosR**

Now I remember: in our town the druggist. Serving with Gideon. William Stafford. **SP-StafW**

Now I remember life; and out of me. Injured Sire. John Crowe Ransom. *Fr.* Two Gentlemen in Bonds. **SP-RansJ**

Now I surveyed my native faculties. Fragment of a Poem on the Works and Wonders of Almighty Power. James Thomson. **CP-ThomJ**

Now, I try, oh for so awf'ly long. Sign on the Cross. "Bob Dylan." **CP-DylaB**

Now I want to return. The Other Garden. Jim Carroll. **SP-CarrJ**

Now I Went Down to the Ringside and Little Henry Armstrong Was There. Kenneth Patchen. **CP-PatcK**

Now I will abandon the route of my life. Mr. Wakeville on Interstate 90. Donald Hall. **CP-HallD**

Now I will do nothing but listen. Walt Whitman. **HoPM; SAmP** *Fr.* Song of Myself. **CP-WhitW**

Now I will shut you in a box. La Prisonnière. Thom Gunn. **CP-GunnT**

Now if ever it is time to cleanse Helicon. Ezra Pound. **CrMA; VGW** *Fr.* Homage to Sextus Propertius. **SP-PounE**

Now if thou hast one dram of Grace. Catullus. *See* Carmen 55: "Where / if it's not too much to ask."

Now If You. Kenneth Patchen. **CP-PatcK**

Now, if you love me, tell me. Nor Buying or Selling. Robert Herrick. **CP-HerrR**

Now, If You Were Teaching Creative Writing, He Asked, What Would You Tell Them? Charles Bukowski. **SP-BukC1**

Now I'll also tell what food. Gary Snyder. **CP-SnydG** *Fr.* Hunting. *Fr.* Myths and Texts.

Now I'll record my secret vision, impossible sight of the face of God. Psalm IV. Allen Ginsberg. **CP-GinsA**

Now I'm / into things. Progress Report. Archie Randolph Ammons. **SP-AmmoA**

Now I'm dead, load what's left on the wagon. The Right Madness on Skye. Richard Hugo. **CP-HugoR**

Now in a thought, now in a shadowed word. L'Envoi. Edwin Arlington Robinson. **CP-RobiE**

Now in her green mantle blythe nature arrays. My Nannie's Awa'. Robert Burns. **CP-BurnR**

Now in midsummer come and all fools slaughtered. Credences of Summer. Wallace Stevens. **CP-StevW**

Now in November nearer comes the sun. November by the Sea. David Herbert Lawrence. **CP-LawrD**

Now in the cheap motel, I lie, and. Night: The Motel down the Road from the Pen. Robert Penn Warren. *Fr.* Penological Study: Southern Exposure. **SP-WarrR**

Now in the helicopters the casual will. George Oppen. *Fr.* Of Being Numerous. **CP-OppeG**

Now, in the middle of the limpid evening. Evening. Thomas Merton. **CP-MertT; SP-MertT**

Now, in the night, all music haunts us here. Johnny Appleseed Speaks of the Appleblossom Amaranth That Will Come to This City. Nicholas Vachel Lindsay. **CP-LindV**

Now in the Spring. John Hewitt. **CP-HewiJ**

Now in the suburbs and the falling light. Father and Son. Stanley Jasspon Kunitz. **CP-KuniS**

Now in the turnings of the poem. Deluxe Assorted. Gilbert Sorrentino. **SP-SorrG**

Now in this evening land of fire and shadow. From Yellow Lake: An Interval. Mona Van Duyn. **SP-VanDM**

Now in Vienna there are ten pretty women. Take This Waltz (*After Lorca*). Leonard Cohen. **CP-CoheL**

Now incense fills the air. After Yeats. Allen Ginsberg. **CP-GinsA**

Now, innocent, within the deep. M., Singing. Louise Bogan. **CP-BogaL**

Now is a ship / which captain am. Edward Estlin Cummings. **CP-CummE**

Now Is the Air Made of Chiming Balls. Richard Eberhart. **CP-EberR**

Now is the day of our farewell in fear, lean pages. The Poet, to His Book. Thomas Merton. **CP-MertT**

Now is the globe shrunk tight. Snowdrop. Ted Hughes. **SP-HughT**

Now is the season / of hungry mice, / cold rabbits. Wolf Moon. Mary Oliver. **SP-OlivM**

Now is the season for dry smell of powder. September Shooting. Howard Nemerov. **CP-NemeH**

Now is the time, / the children grown. A Child Called *Morte*. Siv Cedering Fox. **SP-CedeS**

Now is the time for mirth. To Live Merrily, and To Trust to Good Verses. Robert Herrick. **CP-HerrR**

Now is the time, now is the hower. Another Dialogue, To Be Sung at the Same Time. Thomas Campion. *Fr.* The Ayres that Were Sung and Played, at *Brougham Castle* in *Westmerland*, in the Kings Entertainment. **CP-CampT**

Now is the time to. Thelonious: An Intro. Al Young. **CP-YounA**

Now is the time, when all the lights wax dim. To Anthea. Robert Herrick. **CP-HerrR**

Now is the time when weakness comes,—& strength goes. Salve Senescentem. Sadi, *tr. fr. Persian by* Ralph Waldo Emerson. **CP-EmerR**

Now is the tolling time. St. Luke's Summer. Phoebe Hesketh. **SP-HeskP**

Now is the world withdrawn all. Carol. Howard Nemerov. **CP-NemeH**

Now is your turne (my Dearest) to be set. To his deare Valentine, Mistresse Margaret Falconbrige. Robert Herrick. **CP-HerrR**

Now Israel may say, and that truly. Bible, *O.T. See* Psalm 124: "If it had not been the Lord who was on our side. . . ."

Now it begins: / sprays of forsythia against wet brick. Breaking Camp. Marge Piercy. **SP-PierM**

Now it has come to this, the little glen. The Mortal Place. John Hewitt. **CP-HewiJ**

Now it is almost night, from the bronzey soft sky. Storm in the Black Forest. David Herbert Lawrence. **CP-LawrD**

Now it is autumn and the falling fruit. The Ship of Death. David Herbert Lawrence. **CP-LawrD**

Now it is fifteen years you have lain in the meadow. Lines for an Interment. Archibald MacLeish. **CP-MacLA**

Now it is gone, all of it. Stones. Donald Hall. **CP-HallD**

Now it is June again, one of those. Sunday Morning. Ted Kooser. **SP-KoosT**

Now it is late winter. Two Spring Charms. James Wright. **CP-WrigJ**

Now, it is night and time. I Got the Fat Poet into a Corner. Kenneth Patchen. **CP-PatcK**

Now it is night, now in the brilliant room. De Anima. Howard Nemerov. **CP-NemeH**

Now it is no longer the war, but a war. 1914. Randall Jarrell. **CP-JarrR**

Now it is not good for the Christian's health to hustle the Aryan brown. Rudyard Kipling. **CP-KiplR** *Fr.* The Naulahka.

Now it is September and the web is woven. The Dwarf. Wallace Stevens. **CP-StevW**

Now it is the 27th. Poem. Frank O'Hara. **SP-OharF**

Now it is winter. / By winter I mean: white, silent. Margaret Atwood. *Fr.* Circe / Mud Poems. **SP-AtwM1**

Now it may happen that one. The Burning Book. William Everson. **SP-EverW** *Fr.* The Falling of the Grain.

Now it seems to me that since the Word Himself has come down from heaven to us, we no longer have any need for the schooling of men. The Logos Our Teacher. Clement of Alexandria, *tr. fr. Greek by* Thomas Merton. **CP-MertT**

Now it was noonday, fortieth of the flood. John Gould Fletcher. **SP-FletJ** *Fr.* Branches of Adam.

Now it was the ninth morning and the unseen God. John Gould Fletcher. **SP-FletJ** *Fr.* Branches of Adam.

Now it's Borodin. . . 4:18 A.M. Fleg. Charles Bukowski. **SP-BukC2**

Now it's clean. The whores seem healthy. Galleria Umberto I. Richard Hugo. **CP-HugoR**

Now It's Happened. David Herbert Lawrence. **CP-LawrD**

Now it's our turn. Three a.m. Jane Cooper. *Fr.* The Flashboat. **SP-CoopJ**

Now it's time to say good night good night sleep tight. Goodnight. The Beatles. **CP-Beatl**

Now it's Uncle Sam sitting on top of the world. Carl Sandburg. **OFD** *Fr.* Good Morning, America. **CP-SandC**

Now I've said all I would, mother. Life Out of Death. Christina Georgina Rossetti. **CP-RosC3**

Now Johnson would go up to join the [great] simulacra of men. Up Rising. Robert Duncan. **SP-DuncR** *Fr.* Passages.

Now Jones had left his new-wed bride to keep his house in order. A Code of Morals. Rudyard Kipling. **CP-KiplR**

Now, joy and thanks forevermore! Pæan. John Greenleaf Whittier. **CP-WhitJ**

Now Kennedy if foot or horse. To Mr. John Kennedy. Robert Burns. **CP-BurnR**

Now leaning over the salt nerve of our wave length we have decided to send you the frozen exports of a compromised musician. Thomas Merton. *Fr.* Cables to the Ace. **CP-MertT**

Now let all lovely things embark. Lament. Countee Cullen. **CP-CullC**

Now let forever the phlox and the rose be tended. The Hardy Garden. Edna St. Vincent Millay. **CP-MillE**

Now let her change and spare not. Thomas Campion. **CP-CampT**

Now let him go to sleep with history. Hitler. Leonard Cohen. **CP-CoheL**

Now let no man abide. The Bombarded City. Thomas Merton. **CP-MertT**

Now let the cycle sweep us here and there. Hilda Doolittle. **AnAn; VGW** Fr. Sigil. **CP-DoolH**

Now let the generations pass. Nicholas Vachel Lindsay. Fr. Shantung[, or The Empire of China is Crumbling Down]. **CP-LindV**

Now let the legless boy show the great lady. In the Children's Hospital. "Hugh MacDiarmid." **SP-MacDH**

Now let the mouth of wailing for a time. Edna St. Vincent Millay. **CP-MillE**

Now let us honor with violin and flute. Song. May Sarton. **SP-SartM**

Now let's imagine that I bought. Robot Romance. Robert Pack. **SP-PackR**

Now Lift Me Close. Walt Whitman. **CP-WhitW**

Now light is less; noon skies are wide and deep. Slow Season. Theodore Roethke. **CP-RoetT**

Now like a rose come tip-toe out of bud. David Herbert Lawrence. Fr. All of Roses. **CP-LawrD**

Now list to my morning's romanza, I tell the signs of the Answerer. Song of the Answerer. Walt Whitman. **CP-WhitW**

Now Listen to This. Jim Morrison. **SP-MorrJ**

Now littlely wandering. . . littlely dressed in rainment suitable to. Deathsong for a Maiden. Kenneth Patchen. **CP-PatcK**

Now Long Ago. Maya Angelou. **SP-AngeM**

Now look and see in yonder throne. Ben Jonson. **CP-JonsB** Fr. News from the New World.

Now look here. Altercation. David Herbert Lawrence. **CP-LawrD**

Now Lord, or never, they'l[l] believe [or beleeve] on Thee. On the Miracle of Loaves. Richard Crashaw. **CP-CrasR**

Now luck for us and a kind hearty pit. Prologue to The Spanish Friar. John Dryden. **SP-DrydJ** Fr. The Spanish Friar [or Fryar].

Now, Mary, you can face it good. Poem to Miss Mary. Ernest Hemingway. **CP-HemiE**

Now mind is clear. A Desolation. Allen Ginsberg. **CP-GinsA**

Now mist takes the hemlocks and nothing. Selectivity. John Ciardi. **SP-CiarJ**

Now more and more on my concern with the lifted waves of genius gaining. On the Ocean Floor. "Hugh MacDiarmid." **SP-MacDH**

Now more precisely touched in light and gloom. Gerard Manley Hopkins. Fr. Hopkg. **CP-HopkG**

Now Morn her rosie steps in th' eastern clime. John Milton. **OAEL-1,** ll. 1–128; **NAEL-1,** ll. 1–135; Fr. Book V. Fr. Paradise Lost. **CP-MiltJ**

Now Morn her rosie steps in th' Eastern Clime. Book V. John Milton. Fr. Paradise Lost. **CP-MiltJ**

Now Morning from her orient chamber came. Imitation of Spenser. John Keats. **CP-KeatJ**

Now, moving in, cartons on the floor. Autumn Perspective. Erica Jong. **SP-JongE**

Now must all satisfaction. Certain Mercies. Robert Ranke Graves. **CP-GravR**

Now must I learn to feign. Sir Thomas Wyatt. **CP-WyatT**

Now must I le[a]rn[e] to live [or lyve] at rest. Sir Thomas Wyatt. **CP-WyatT**

Now must I these three praise. Friends. William Butler Yeats. **CP-YeatW**

Now, my cunning lady moon. Ben Jonson. **CP-JonsB** Fr. Oberon, the Fairy Prince.

Now my father carries his old heart. Christmas Eve. Ted Kooser. **SP-KoosT**

Now my mind's been brought to such a state—and it's your fault. Catullus. See Carmen 75: "Reason blinded by sin, Lesbia."

Now my mind's been brought to such extremes—and it's your fault. Catullus. See Carmen 75: "Reason blinded by sin, Lesbia."

Now my October with the yellow leaf. Feathers on Turf. John Hewitt. Fr. Freehold. **CP-HewiJ**

Now nature cleeds the flowery lea. Lassie wi' the Lintwhite Locks. Robert Burns. **CP-BurnR**

Now Nature hangs her mantle green. Lament of Mary Queen of Scots on the Approach of Spring. Robert Burns. **CP-BurnR**

Now night perfumes lie upon the air. Summer Nocturne. Philip Larkin. **CP-LarkP**

Now, not a tear begun. A Woman Mourned by Daughters. Adrienne Rich. **CP-RicAE; SP-RicA2**

Now not every man has the makings of a barber. Ohio River Blues. Kenneth Patchen. **CP-PatcK**

Now—now, as low I stooped, thought I. The Snowdrop. Walter de la Mare. **CP-DeLaW**

Now, now begin to set. Ben Jonson. **CP-JonsB** Fr. Masque of Hymen.

Now, now the mirth comes. Twelfe Night, or King and Queene. Robert Herrick. **CP-HerrR**

Now, now, the world. Deciduous Spring. Robert Penn Warren. **ArNa** Fr. Love: Two Vignettes. **SP-WarrR**

Now, now's the time so oft by Truth. An Epithalamy to Sir Thomas Southwell and His Lady. Robert Herrick. **CP-HerrR**

Now o'er the sea from her old love comes she. I, 13. Elegy: Ad Auroram, ne properet. Ovid. **CP-MarlC,** tr. by Christopher Marlowe; Fr. Elegies.

Now on the great stage a silence falls. Proletarian in Abstract Light. Thomas McGrath. **SP-McGrT**

Now, on this bluest of mornings, we wake. Pastoral. Edwin Rolfe. **CP-RolfE**

Now on this out of season afternoon. Original Sin on the Sussex Coast. Sir John Betjeman. **CP-BetjJ**

Now on you is the hungry equinox. Rebuke of the Rocks. Robert Penn Warren. Fr. Kentucky Mountain Farm. **SP-WarrR**

Now once more gray mottled buckeye branches. Andrée Rexroth. Kenneth Rexroth. **SP-RexrK**

Now only beggars still go singing. Alun Lewis. Fr. Threnody for a Starry Night. **CP-LewiA**

Now Patrick with his footmanship has done. Upon Patrick a Footman. Robert Herrick. **CP-HerrR**

Now Pine-Needles. Stevie Smith. **CP-SmitS**

Now polish the crucible. Hilda Doolittle. **NALW** Fr. Tribute to the Angels. **CP-DoolH**

Now praise the Gods of Time and Chance. A Song of French Roads. Rudyard Kipling. **CP-KiplR**

Now Precedent Songs, Farewell. Walt Whitman. **CP-WhitW**

Now preye I to hem alle that herkne this. Chaucer's Retraction. Geoffrey Chaucer. Fr. The Canterbury Tales. **CP-ChauG**

Now ravel up the roots of workman oak trees. Dirge for the World Joyce Died In. Thomas Merton. **CP-MertT**

Now Returned Home. Robinson Jeffers. **CP-JefR2**

Now Robin lies in his last lair. Elegy on the Death of Robert Ruisseaux. Robert Burns. **CP-BurnR**

Now rockets pierce the limit of our air. Lecture. Richard Hugo. **CP-HugoR**

Now rosy May comes in wi' flowers. Dainty Davie. Robert Burns. **CP-BurnR**

Now secretness dies of the open. For the Nightly Ascent of the Hunter Orion over a Forest Clearing. James Dickey. **CP-DickJ**

Now seed their Magus (of Gelli's mother wrestling confounded). Catullus. See Carmen 90: "Let there stem (Gellius)."

Now sets his foot upon the eastern sill. Edna St. Vincent Millay. Fr. Epitaph for the Race of Man. **CP-MillE**

Now shall I make my soul. William Butler Yeats. **OBD** Fr. The Tower. **CP-YeatW**

Now shall I sing. The Prophetess. Thomas Hardy. **CP-HardT**

Now she burn[e]s as well as I. Thomas Carew. **CP-CareT** (To Her Again, She Burning in a Fever.) **CP-CareT**

Now She Dwells Here. Tom Clark. **SP-ClarT**

Now she is still not beautiful but more. Eve. Jane Cooper. **SP-CoopJ**

Now she will lean away to fold. A Girl in a Window. James Wright. **CP-WrigJ**

Now shut your eyes. The Old Orchard. David Herbert Lawrence. **CP-LawrD**

Now simmer blinks on flowery braes. Robert Burns. See Birks of Aberfeldy, The [Composed on the Spot].

Now sing, O slight girls. Euripides, tr. by Hilda Doolittle ("H.D."). **CP-DoolH** Fr. Iphigenia [or Iphigeneia] in Aulis.

Now sits the autumn cricket in the grass. Edna St. Vincent Millay. **CP-MillE**

Now sleeps he / With that old whore Death. Poem to Mary (Second Poem). Ernest Hemingway. **CP-HemiE**

Now sleeps the crimson petal, now the white. Tennyson. **ArLo; BLPL; BoLoP; CBLP; ChER; ChTr; CoGr; EBEV; EBVV; ELP; FHYEP; FaBoBe; FaPoB; FiP; GBL; GTBS-P; LLLT; MeMBP; NAEL-2; NIP; NOBE; NoP; OBEV; OBNC; OPOU; OXAEP-2; PPP; PlP; PoEL-5; SCGP; SCV; SeCePo; TFi; TrGrPo** Fr. So was their sanctuary violated. Fr. The Princess. **CP-TennA**

(Song: "Now sleeps the crimson petal, now the white.") **BLPL; FaBoBe; OPOU**

(Summer Night.) **OBEV; SeCePo**

Now small boys come to stare across the garden. The Murderer's House. Mary Oliver. **SP-OlivM**

Now soldiers we seem. Nicholas Vachel Lindsay. Fr. The Master of the Dance. **CP-LindV**

Now some men must get up and depart. Departure. David Herbert Lawrence. **CP-LawrD**

Now, sometimes in my sorrow shut. Tennyson. *Fr.* In Memoriam A. H. H. **CP-TennA**

Now somewhere in the black mountain hills of Dakota there lived a. Rocky Raccoon. The Beatles. **CP-Beatl**

Now Spring brings back the tepid breeze. Catullus. *See* Carmen 46: "Now spring bursts."

Now spring bursts. Carmen 46. Catullus. *Fr.* Carmina. **CP-Catul**

Now Spring has clad the grove in green. Scotch Song. Robert Burns. **CP-BurnR**

Now stamp the Lord's Prayer on a grain of rice. Dylan Thomas. **FaBoMo** *Fr.* Altarwise by Owl-Light. **CP-ThomD**

Now standing on this hedgeside path. Pastoral 3. George Meredith. *Fr.* Pastorals. **CP-MerG1**

Now, starflake frozen on the windowpane. Moment. Howard Nemerov. **CP-NemeH**

Now stir the fire, and close the shutters fast. Reading the Newspaper. William Cowper. **ECEV; FaBoDD** *Fr.* The Winter Evening. *Fr.* The Task. **CP-CowpW**

Now striding through the reaped and withered year. Sonnets in October. John Hewitt. **CP-HewiJ**

Now strike up a concert of action in the electric nest. A Tune for Festive Dances in the Nineteen Sixties. Thomas Merton. **CP-MertT**

Now strike your sailes, ye jolly mariners. Edmund Spenser. **EtS; MOS** *Fr.* The Faerie Queene. **CP-Spens**

Now sun rises in Ram sign. Addendum for C. Ezra Pound. *Fr.* Cantos. **CP-PoCan**

Now supposing the French or the Neopolitan soldier. Claude to Eustace. Arthur Hugh Clough. **PeLV** *Fr.* Amours de Voyage. **SP-ClouA**

Now Tell Me About Yourself. Ogden Nash. **CP-NashO**

Now tell me if we don't need a revolution! Black. Hayden Carruth. *Fr.* Paragraphs. **CP-CarHS**

Now tells the flower. Hafiz, *tr. by* Ralph Waldo Emerson. **CP-EmerR** *Fr.* Odes.

Now thanked be the great god *Pan, speech of Dametas.* Sir Philip Sidney. **SP-SidnP** *Fr.* Arcadia.

Now that a crimson rambler. Crimson Rambler. Carl Sandburg. **CP-SandC**

Now that a letter gives me ground at last. The Beach Head. Thom Gunn. **CP-GunnT**

Now that a Parthenon acends to crown. The Modern Athens. William Wordsworth. **CP-WorW2**

Now that all hearts are glad, all faces bright. November, 1813. William Wordsworth. **CP-WorW1**

Now that April with sweet rain. Wendell Berry. *Fr.* Window Poems. **CP-BerrW**

Now that at last I must forego. Frederick Morgan. **SP-MorgF**

Now that few people need. Not a *Paris Review* Interview. Frank Templeton Prince. **CP-PrinF**

Now that fierce few. Edward Estlin Cummings. **CP-CummE**

Now that first light has filled the sky. Jam Lucis Orto Sidere. *Unknown. Fr.* Four Medieval Latin Poems. **CP-MacNL**

Now that I am all but blind. Tribute to Neruda the Poet Collector of Seashells. William Carlos Williams. **CP-WilW2**

Now that I am fifty-six. Rondel. Muriel Rukeyser. **CP-RukeM**

Now That I Am Forever with Child. Audre Lorde. **SP-LordA**

Now That I Am in Madrid and Can Think. Frank O'Hara. **SP-OharF**

Now That I have cooled to you. Postlude. William Carlos Williams. **CP-WilW1**

Now that I have your face by heart, I look. Song for the Last Act. Louise Bogan. **CP-BogaL**

Now that I know. Knowledge. Louise Bogan. **CP-BogaL**

Now that I know you are gone. The Creation. Mona Van Duyn. **SP-VanDM**

Now that I, tying thy glass mask tightly. Laboratory, The [Ancien Régime]. Robert Browning. **CP-BroR1**

Now that I've wasted. My Alba. Allen Ginsberg. **CP-GinsA**

Now that my page is exiled,—doomed, maybe. To a Lady. Thomas Hardy. **CP-HardT**

Now that nothing has worked out. Ars Poetica. Al Young. **CP-YounA**

Now that of absence the most irksome night. Sonnet 89. Sir Philip Sidney. **NAEL-1** *Fr.* Astrophil and Stella. **SP-SidnP**

Now that our hero has come back to us. On Seeing Larry Rivers' *Washington Crossing the Delaware* at the Museum of Modern Art. Frank O'Hara. **SP-OharF**

Now that Robin Redbreast. Egg. Daniel Gerard Hoffman. **SP-HoffD**

Now that sea's over that island. Basil Bunting. **CP-BuntB**

Now that the bird of life. Voix Glauque. Lawrence Ferlinghetti. **SP-FerlL**

Now That the Book Is Finished. Alice Walker. **CP-WalkA**

Now that the cameras zero in from space. The Weather of the World. Howard Nemerov. **CP-NemeH**

Now that the clouds have come like cattle. Aubade—the City. Thomas Merton. **CP-MertT; SP-MertT**

Now that the day is done. Centaur Song. Hilda Doolittle. **CP-DoolH**

Now that the farewell tear is dried. Italian Itinerant, and the Swiss Goatherd, The. William Wordsworth. *Fr.* Memorials of a Tour of the Continent; 1820. **CP-WorW2**

Now that the hearth [*or* harth] is crowned [*or* crown'd] with smiling fire. Ode. To Sir William Sydney, on His Birthday. Ben Jonson. **CP-JonsB**

Now that the hillside woods are dense with summer. The Witnesses. Charles Tomlinson. **CP-TomlC**

Now that the night is here. Night. David Herbert Lawrence. **CP-LawrD**

Now that the river has changed, my dear. Muriel Rukeyser. **CP-RukeM**

Now that the salt has lost its savor. Howard Nemerov. *Fr.* Dialectical Songs. **CP-NemeH**

Now That the Shapes of Mist. Louis MacNeice. **CP-MacNL**

Now that the west is washed of clouds and clear. Edna St. Vincent Millay. **CP-MillE**

Now that the winter's gone, the earth hath lost. The Spring. Thomas Carew. **CP-CareT**

Now that they've abolished chrome work. Ask Daddy, He Won't Know. Ogden Nash. **CP-NashO**

Now that they've got it settled whose I be. The Pauper Witch of Grafton. Robert Frost. *Fr.* Two Witches. **CP-FrosR**

Now that thy servants all may sing. Ut Queant. Paul the Deacon, *tr. fr. Latin by* Thomas Merton. **CP-MertT**

Now that we sponsor the extirpation of folklore. The Peaceable Kingdom. Daniel Gerard Hoffman. **SP-HoffD**

Now that we're almost settled in our house. In Memory of Major Robert Gregory. William Butler Yeats. **CP-YeatW**

Now that you have gone. Except. Wendell Berry. **CP-BerrW**

Now that you have made your great renunciation. Anaktoria. Frederick Morgan. **SP-MorgF**

Now that your hopes are shamed, you stand. Afterward. Adrienne Rich. **CP-RicAE; SP-RicA1; SP-RicA2**

Now that you've written it. To a Romantic Novelist. Allen Tate. **CP-TateA**

Now that,more nearest even than your fate. Edward Estlin Cummings. **CP-CummE**

Now the active young attornies. Helter Skelter. Jonathan Swift. **CP-SwifJ**

Now the autumn shudders. Autumn Chant. Edna St. Vincent Millay. **CP-MillE**

Now the beginning: the block divided. Unit Assignment. Edwin Rolfe. **CP-RolfE**

Now the Blessed Virgin Mary is the one created who enacts and shows forth in her life all that is hidden in Sophia. Sunset. The Hour of Compline. Salve Regina. Thomas Merton. *Fr.* Hagia Sophia. **CP-MertT**

Now the bright morning Star, Dayes [*or* day's] harbinger. Song: on [*or* of] May Morning. John Milton. **CP-MiltJ**

Now the devout James coming from the remote north. On the Fifth of November. John Milton. **CP-MiltJ**

Now the flames they followed Joan of Arc. Joan of Arc. Leonard Cohen. **CP-CoheL**

Now the Fog. Edwin Rolfe. **CP-RolfE**

Now the Four-way Lodge is opened, now the Hunting Winds are loose. The Feet of the Young Men. Rudyard Kipling. **CP-KiplR**

Now the frog, all lean and weak. The Sweet o' the Year. George Meredith. **CP-MerG1**

Now the frost is on the pane. A Word about Winter. Ogden Nash. **CP-NashO**

Now the golden morn aloft. Thomas Gray. **GTBS; GTBS-6; GTBS-P; NOEC** *Fr.* Ode on the Pleasure Arising from Vicissitude. **CP-GrayT**

Now the golden morn aloft. Ode on the Pleasure Arising from Vicissitude. Thomas Gray. **CP-GrayT**

Now the Grass is Glass. Emily Dickinson. **SP-DickE**

Now the heat comes, I am demoralized. Barnsley Cricket Club. Donald Davie. *Fr.* Two Dedications. **CP-DavDo**

Now the keen rigour of the winter's o'er. A Town Eclogue. Jonathan Swift. **CP-SwifJ**

Now the last day of many days. To Jane: The Recollection. Percy Bysshe Shelley. **CP-ShelP**

Now the lean children of the God of armies. Rahab's House. Thomas Merton. **CP-MertT**

Now the leaves are falling fast. Autumn Song. Wystan Hugh Auden. *Fr.* Twelve Songs. **CP-AudeW**

Now the lone world is streaky as a wall of marble. Evening: Zero Weather. Thomas Merton. **CP-MertT; SP-MertT**

Now the meadows with crocus besprent. George Meredith. *Fr.* The Day of the Daughter of Hades. **CP-MerG1**

Now the midwinter grind. Middle Age. Robert Lowell. **SP-LoweR**

Now the New Year, reviving last Year's Debt. The Rupaiyat of Omar Kal'vin. Rudyard Kipling. **CP-KiplR**

Now the New Year reviving old desires. The Exiles' Line. Rudyard Kipling. **CP-KiplR**

Now the night is here. Blood. Gilbert Sorrentino. **SP-SorrG**

Now the North wind ceases. Tardy Spring. George Meredith. **CP-MerG1**

Now the official nerve is analyzed. Thomas Merton. **CP-MertT**

Now the official nerve is cauterized. And So Goodbye to Cities. Thomas Merton. **CP-MertT**

Now the old ways that have brought us. At a Country Funeral. Wendell Berry. **CP-BerrW**

Now the pain beginneth and the word is spoken. Zara. Christina Georgina Rossetti. **CP-RosC3**

Now the *Peace* is made at the Foes rate. Sonnet. To Generall Goring. Richard Lovelace. **CP-LoveR**

Now the preacher told Willie when he said his last prayer. Willie Francis and the Electric Chair. Charles Olson. **CP-OlsoC**

Now the rain. Gerard Manley Hopkins. *Fr.* Fragments. **CP-HopkG**

Now the seasons are closing their files. Year's End. Ted Kooser. **SP-KoosT**

Now the shadow of the wolf in him. Dog Love. Brendan Galvin. **SP-GalvB**

Now the singers leave the darkened garden. Lament for the Makers of Songs. Kenneth Patchen. **CP-PatcK**

Now the snow / lies on the ground. Winter. William Carlos Williams. **CP-WilW1**

Now the sordid tragedy crashes to a close. The Neutrals. Robinson Jeffers. **CP-JefR3**

Now the Starlit Moonless Spring. Kenneth Rexroth. **SP-RexrK**

Now the stone house on the lake front is finished and the workmen are beginning the fence. A Fence. Carl Sandburg. **CP-SandC**

Now the storm begins to lower. The Fatal Sisters. Thomas Gray, *after the Icelandic.* **CP-GrayT**

Now the summer perch flips twice and glides. Underwater Autumn. Richard Hugo. **CP-HugoR**

Now the sun-lit hours are o'er. Night and Death. Christina Georgina Rossetti. **CP-RosC3**

Now the swan it floated on the English River. The Traitor. Leonard Cohen. **CP-CoheL**

Now the tide is coming in, each long, low, hastening wave in the cove. A Poem of Gratitude. Kay Boyle. **CP-BoylK**

Now the time of year has come for the leaves to be burning. October 1954. Kay Boyle. **CP-BoylK**

Now the trees tempt. The Birth and Death of the Sun. Jim Carroll. **SP-CarrJ**

Now the trumpet sounds with a mighty voice calling the soldiers of the world to arms, announcing war. Soldiers of Peace. Clement of Alexandria, *tr. fr. Greek by* Thomas Merton. **CP-MertT**

Now the twin-light of my eyes. Bible, *O.T. See* Psalm 121: "I will lift up mine eyes unto the hills."

Now the unruly knowing. Thomas Merton. *Fr.* Cables to the Ace. **CP-MertT**

Now the valley in ruin of fields. George Meredith. *Fr.* The Day of the Daughter of Hades. **CP-MerG1**

Now the violets are all gone, the rhinoceroses, the cymbals. Poem. Frank O'Hara. **SP-OharF**

Now the winds are all composure. St. Philip and St. James. Christopher Smart. **LoBV; NOCV; NOEC** *Fr.* Hymns and Spiritual Songs for the Fasts and Festivals of the Church of England. **SP-SmarC**

Now the winter nights begin. Postcript to Iceland. Louis MacNeice. **CP-MacNL**

Now, the wry Rosenbloom is dead. Cortege for Rosenbloom. Wallace Stevens. **CP-StevW**

Now the youth footed swift to the dawn. George Meredith. *Fr.* The Day of the Daughter of Hades. **CP-MerG1**

Now the youth was not ware of the beams. George Meredith. *Fr.* The Day of the Daughter of Hades. **CP-MerG1**

Now Then. Robert Creeley. **CP-CreeR**

Now there are second thoughts. Evening News. Jim Carroll. **SP-CarrJ**

Now there is. Robert Creeley. **CP-CreeR**

Now there is a slit in the blue fabric of air. Fragments. Stephen Dobyns. **SP-DobyS**

Now there is nothing wrong with me. *parody of* Robert Louis Stevenson. Rudyard Kipling. **CP-KiplR** *Fr.* The Muse among the Motors.

Now, there's a certain thing. Open the Door, Homer. "Bob Dylan." **CP-DylaB**

Now there's nothing in this world. Sick Leave. Leonard Nathan. **SP-NathL**

Now they are all moving. Reading Translated Poets, Feb. 1. Thomas Merton. **CP-MertT**

Now they are resting. Fine Work with Pitch and Copper. William Carlos Williams. **CP-WilW1**

Now They Bury Her Again. Carl Sandburg. **CP-SandC**

Now they bury her and the clouds run scared. Digging Is an Art. Richard Hugo. **CP-HugoR**

Now They Desire. Christina Georgina Rossetti. **CP-RosC3**

Now They Desire a Better Country. Christina Georgina Rossetti. **CP-RosC2**

Now they have bridged the canyon of the Gauley. The River. Louise McNeill. **SP-McNeL**

Now, this is the cup the White Men drink. A Song of the White Men. Rudyard Kipling. **CP-KiplR**

Now this is the price of a stirrup-cup. *parody of a Border Ballad.* Rudyard Kipling. **CP-KiplR** *Fr.* The Muse among the Motors.

Now this is the tale of the Council the German Kaiser decreed. An Imperial Rescript. Rudyard Kipling. **CP-KiplR**

Now this particular girl. Spinster. Sylvia Plath. **CP-PlatS**

Now this remains: the thunder stopped. Country Excursion. Kenneth Patchen. **CP-PatcK**

Now this the Law of the Jungle—as old and as true as the sky. Rudyard Kipling. **CP-KiplR** *Fr.* How the Fear Came. *Fr.* The Second Jungle Book.

(Law of the Jungle, The.) **CP-KiplR**

Now, this, to my notion, is pleasant cheer. The Beggar's Soliloquy. George Meredith. **CP-MerG1**

Now thou art dead, no eye shall ever see. Upon His Spaniel[l] Tracie [*or* Tracy]. Robert Herrick. **CP-HerrR**

Now thou hast lov'd me one whole day. Woman's Constancy. John Donne. **CP-DonnJ**

Now thread my voice / with lies. How I Can Lie to You. Maya Angelou. **SP-AngeM**

Now time himself the master streamer. Grace Paley. **CP-PaleG**

Now Time's Andromeda on this rock rude. Andromeda. Gerard Manley Hopkins. **CP-HopkG**

Now 'tis Spring on wood and wold. Invitation to the Country. George Meredith. **CP-MerG1**

Now to dissolve in port. I take the train. Canto XII. Louis MacNeice. *Fr.* Autumn Sequel. **CP-MacNL**

Now to her lap the incestuous earth. Alfred Edward Housman. **CP-HousA**

Now to th'ascent of that steep savage hill. Satan Journeys to the Garden of Eden. John Milton. **ChTr** *Fr.* Book IV. **OAEL-1** *Fr.* Paradise Lost. **CP-MiltJ**

Now to the come of the poem, let me be worthy. Fragment 1956. Allen Ginsberg. **CP-GinsA**

Now Tomlinson gave up the ghost at his house in Berkeley Square. Tomlinson. Rudyard Kipling. **CP-KiplR**

Now, too much of nothing. Too Much of Nothing. "Bob Dylan." **CP-DylaB**

Now trust a heart that trusts in you. Emily Brontë. **CP-BronE**

Now twenty-four or maybe twenty-five. Inside and Outside. Allen Tate. **CP-TateA**

Now two old ladies sit peacefully knitting. Edward Estlin Cummings. **CP-CummE**

Now upon this piteous year. The Stranger. Jean Garrigue. **SP-GarrJ**

Now Vole art dead. To a Dead Vole. Stevie Smith. **CP-SmitS**

Now wars and waters, stars. The Book. Frank Templeton Prince. **CP-PrinF**

Now was her face white waves in the tempest's sharp flame-blink. George Meredith. *Fr.* The Revolution. **CP-MerG1**

Now was our heav'nly task deprived of the light, *speech of Philisides.* Sir Philip Sidney. **SP-SidnP** *Fr.* Arcadia.

"Now we approach the darkness of to-night!" Delmore Schwartz. **SP-SchwD** *Fr.* Genesis.

Now we are back to normal, now the mind is. Louis MacNeice. **CMoP; OXAEP-2** *Fr.* Autumn Journal. **CP-MacNL**

Now we are come to our Kingdom. The Kingdom. Rudyard Kipling. **CP-KiplR** *Fr.* The Naulahka.

Now we are tired of boisterous joy. Blind Highland Boy, The; A Tale Told by the Fire-side, After Returning to the Vale of Grasmere. William Wordsworth. **CP-WorW1**

Now we do most of the killing. George Oppen. *Fr.* Power, the Enchanted World. **CP-OppeG**

Now we have buried the face we never knew. Easter, 1968. May Sarton. **SP-SartM**

Now we have considered these things, each to each. Lull. Malcolm Lowry. *Fr.* The Moon in Scandinavia. **CP-LowrM**

Now we have taught our love to know. To His Rival. Sir John Suckling. **CP-SuckJ**

Now we remember all: the wild pear-tree. Pictures by Vuillard. Adrienne Rich. **CP-RicAE**

Now we, returning from the vaulted domes. Doom of Exiles. Sylvia Plath. **CP-PlatS**

Now we shall learn to live in the dark. Dusk of the Revolutionaries. John Haines. **SP-HainJ**

Now we shall open boxes and look. Keepsake Boxes. Carl Sandburg. **CP-SandC**

Now we will say it with a small poem. A poem that will not. Portrait of a Lady. Ernest Hemingway. **CP-HemiE**

Now Welcom[e], Somer [or Summer]. Geoffrey Chaucer. **HAP; OxBM; SeCePo** Fr. The Parlement of Foules. **CP-ChauG**

(Foules Rondel.) **TrGrPo**

(Qui Bien Aime a Tard Oublie.) **EnLoPo**

(Roundel: "Now welcom[e], Somer [or Summer] with thy sunne soft[e].") **CTC; OAEL-1; OPOU; OxBSP**

(Welcome, Summer.) **MeEL**

Now westlin winds, and slaught'ring guns. Song, Composed in August. Robert Burns. **CP-BurnR**

Now westward Sol had spent the richest beam[e]s. ad. fr. the Latin ofStrada. Richard Crashaw. **CP-CrasR**

Now we've no hope of going back. Basil Bunting. **CP-BuntB**

Now what is Love, I praie thee tell. A Description of Love. Sir Walter Ralegh. **CP-RaleW**

Now what were motionless move(exists no). Edward Estlin Cummings. **CP-CummE**

Now, when I / die, don't bury me. Last Words By "Slick." Etheridge Knight. **SP-KnigE**

Now when I lay me down to sleep. Insomnia the Gem of the Ocean. John Updike. **CP-UpdiJ**

Now when I walk around at lunchtime. Personal Poem. Frank O'Hara. **SP-OharF**

'Now when King Offa was alive and dead', they were. Geoffrey Hill. Fr. Mercian Hymns. **CP-HillG**

Now, when the cheerless empire of the sky. James Thomson. **OxBA** Fr. Winter. Fr. The Seasons. **CP-ThomJ**

Now when the flood of April. Log Drive. Louise McNeill. **SP-McNeL**

Now when the frogs. The Associate Professor Delivers an Exhortation to His Failing Students. Miller Williams. **SP-WillM**

Now when the Gods had crushed the Asian State. Virgil, tr. by William Wordsworth. **CP-WorW2** Fr. The Aeneid [or Eneados, Aeneis].

Now when the number of my years. Robert Louis Stevenson. **CP-StevR**

Now when the primrose makes a splendid show. Poor Robin. William Wordsworth. **CP-WorW2**

Now when the wars augment our woes and fears. Another, upon the Poems. John Pinchbacke. Fr. Commendatory Poems. **CP-LoveR**

Now when those girls, all thirty-six, go. The Rockettes. John Updike. **CP-UpdiJ**

Now where the hills of Languedoc are blue with vineyards. St. John's Night. Thomas Merton. **CP-MertT**

Now, whether it were by peculiar grace. William Wordsworth. **Par; UV** Fr. Resolution and Independence. **CP-WorW2**

Now, while the birds thus sing a joyous song. William Wordsworth. **Prf** Fr. Ode: Intimations of Immortality [from Recollections of Early Childhood]. **CP-WorW1**

Now while the moon pulls darkness. Richard Shelton. Fr. Dry Season. **SP-ShelR**

Now Whitehall's in the grave. A Mock Song. Richard Lovelace. **CP-LoveR**

Now who could take you off to tiny life. The Independent Man. Gwendolyn Brooks. Fr. A Street in Bronzeville. **SP-BrooG**

Now? Why— / whirlpools of. Virtue. William Carlos Williams. **CP-WilW1**

Now why would a visitation from the Isles. A Visitation. Daniel Gerard Hoffman. **SP-HoffD**

Now, will you play all night! Zeppelin Nights. David Herbert Lawrence. Fr. Bits. **CP-LawrD**

Now will you stand for me, in this cool light. Love in the Museum. Adrienne Rich. **CP-RicAE**

Now William pulled the lever down. William Blake. Allen Tate. **CP-TateA**

Now winging selves sing sweetly, while ghosts(there). Edward Estlin Cummings. **CP-CummE**

Now winter downs the dying of the year. Year's End. Richard Wilbur. **CP-WilbR**

Now Winter Nights Enlarge. Thomas Campion. **CP-CampT**

Now with no weak unballast wing. 2.20. Horace. **CP-JohnS,** tr. by Samuel Johnson; Fr. Odes.

Now with the bells through the apple bloom. Wantage Bells. Sir John Betjeman. **CP-BetjJ**

Now with the threat growing still greater within me. Fruit. Sir John Betjeman. **CP-BetjJ**

Now, with your palms on the blades of my shoulders. Dead Still. Andrei Voznesensky, tr. fr. Russian by Richard Wilbur. **CP-WilbR**

Now "W"—we'll call you "W." W. D. Sits in Kafka's Chair and Is Interrogated Concerning the Assumed Death of Cock Robin. William DeWitt Snodgrass. **SP-SnodW**

Now y'have oblieg'd the age. thy wel known Worth. To my best Brother on his Poems, called Lucasta. Francis Lovelace. Fr. Commendatory Poems. **CP-LoveR**

Now you are a priest. Priest. Hilda Doolittle. **CP-DoolH**

Now you are gone, and with your unreturning goes. Therefore, Adieu. Countee Cullen. **CP-CullC**

Now you are holding a book. Frederick Morgan. Fr. The River. **SP-MorgF**

Now you are holding my skull in your hand. A Meditation. Richard Eberhart. **CP-EberR**

Now you are mine, to-night at last I say it. New Year's Night. David Herbert Lawrence. **CP-LawrD**

Now you are ready to build your human brain. Cybernetics. Howard Nemerov. **CP-NemeH**

Now, you great stanza, you heroic mould. Single Sonnet. Louise Bogan. **CP-BogaL**

Now you have found the clay to live. With a Little Book of Pottery. John Hewitt. **CP-HewiJ**

Now you have freely given me leave to love. To a Lady, That Desired I Would Love Her. Thomas Carew. **CP-CareT**

Now you have read them all; or if not all. Rahel to Varnhagen. Edwin Arlington Robinson. **CP-RobiE**

Now you have stabbed her good. Kreutzer Sonata. Ted Hughes. **SP-HughT**

Now You Have to Push. Ted Hughes. **SP-HughT**

Now you, John Henry, 'tain't no use. Charity. Paul Laurence Dunbar. **CP-DunbP**

Now you lean over suicide's precipice. James McAuley. Fr. Aor Against the Ingrate Who Abused Our Hospitality. **SP-McAuJ**

Now You See It, Now I Don't. Ogden Nash. **CP-NashO**

Now you take ol Rufus. He beat drums. For Freckle-Faced Gerald. Etheridge Knight. **SP-KnigE**

Now you're here beside me, baby. Never Gonna Be the Same Again. "Bob Dylan." **CP-DylaB**

Nowadays everybody wants to be young. Old People. David Herbert Lawrence. **CP-LawrD**

Nowadays, to talk of humility is a sin against the Holy Ghost. Humility. David Herbert Lawrence. **CP-LawrD**

Nowhere. John Berryman. **CP-BerrJ**

("Traitoring words, tearing my thought across.") **CP-BerrJ**

Nowhere before you. Backwards. Robert Creeley. **CP-CreeR**

Nowhere. Hear the stormy spring. Roy Fisher. Fr. Five Morning Poems from a Picture by Manet. **SP-FishR**

Nowhere Man. The Beatles. **CP-Beatl**

Now(more near ourselves than we). Edward Estlin Cummings. **CP-CummE**

Now's the Time. Al Young. **CP-YounA**

Now's the time for mirth and play. For Saturday. Christopher Smart. **FaBoCh; LAuP; NOEC; OxBChV** Fr. Hymns for the Amusement of Children. **SP-SmarC**

Nuances of a Theme by Williams. Wallace Stevens. **CP-StevW**

Nubian in / Tangerine, carrying a, A. Charles Henri Ford. **SP-FordC** Fr. Emblems of Arachne.

Nuclear Winter. Thomas McGrath. **SP-McGrT**

Nuda Natens. John Updike. **CP-UpdiJ**

Nude bodies like peeled logs. Sonnet in Search of an Author. William Carlos Williams. **CP-WilW2**

Nude Swim, The. Anne Sexton. **CP-SextA**

Nudity at the Capital. Wallace Stevens. **CP-StevW**

Nudity in the Colonies. Wallace Stevens. **CP-StevW**

Nuisance, The. Marge Piercy. **SP-PierM**

Nuit Blanche. Edna St. Vincent Millay. **CP-MillE**

Nuit qui fais tant. Samuel Beckett. **CP-BeckS**

Nullus. David Herbert Lawrence. **CP-LawrD**

Numb. The limit of sin. Near the Finish. James McAuley. Fr. Ten-Mile Run. **SP-McAuJ**

Numb Your Ass and Your Brain and Your Heart—. Charles Bukowski. **SP-BukC1**

Numb(and / that was). Edward Estlin Cummings. **CP-CummE**

Number. Robert Pack. **SP-PackR**

Number 8 Fireman. Malcolm Lowry. **CP-LowrM**

Number Man. Carl Sandburg. **CP-SandC**

Number of Two, The. Robert Herrick. **CP-HerrR**

Number runner / Come to my door. Madam and the Number Writer. Langston Hughes. **SP-HughL**

Number, said the skull Pythagoras. Under the Bell Jar. Howard Nemerov. **CP-NemeH**

Number Song. Anne Waldman. **SP-WaldA**

No. 13 Hymn Written in Concord Sept. 1814. Ralph Waldo Emerson. **CP-EmerR**

Numbers. Robert Creeley. **CP-CreeR**

Numbers. Langston Hughes. **SP-HughL**

Numbers. Stevie Smith. **SP-SmitS**

Numbers and Faces. Wystan Hugh Auden. **CP-AudeW**

Numbers who can't even hear me. Math. James Dickey. **CP-DickJ**

Numerous host of dreaming saints succeed, A. Zimri: The Duke of Buckingham. John Dryden. **AWP; NOBE; OBSV; SeCePo** *Fr.* Absalom and Achitophel, Pt. I. **SP-DrydJ**

Numpholeptos. Robert Browning. **CP-BroR2**

Nun of St. Michan's, The. James McAuley. **SP-McAuJ**

Nunc Est Bibendum, Cleopatra's Death. Robert Lowell. **SP-LoweR**

Nunnery. William Wordsworth. *Fr.* Poems Composed or Suggested During a Tour, in the Summer of 1833. **CP-WorW2**

Nuns are allowed full liberty of conscience. Gooseflesh Abbey. Robert Ranke Graves. **CP-GravR**

Nun's Aspiration. Ralph Waldo Emerson. **CP-EmerR**

Nuns fret not at their convent's narrow room. William Wordsworth. **CP-WorW1**

Nuns in the Wind. Muriel Rukeyser. **CP-RukeM**

Nun's Priest's Prologue, The, *see* Prologue of the Nun's Priest's Tale, The. Geoffrey Chaucer. *See* The Prologue of the Nun's Priest's Tale.

Nun's Priest's Tale, The. Geoffrey Chaucer. **FHYEP; NAEL-1; NAWM-1; NoP; OAEL-1; TrGrPo** *Fr.* The Canterbury Tales. **CP-ChauG**

("Once a poor widow, aging year by year.") **NAWM-1**

("Once a poor widow, aging year by year.") **NAWM-1**

("Poore widwe [*or* widow], somdeel [*or* somedeal] stape in age, A.") **NAEL-1; NoP**

("Poore widwe [*or* widow], somdeel [*or* somedeal] stape in age, A.") **NAEL-1; NoP**

"His comb was redder than the fine coral." **PBBP**

"There liv'd, as Authors tell, in Days of Yore." **OBVE**

"This Chauntecleer stood hye up-on his toos." **FiP**

Nun's Song. William Carlos Williams. **CP-WilW2**

Nun's Well, Brigham. William Wordsworth. **CP-WorW2**

Nun's Well, Brigham. William Wordsworth. *Fr.* Poems Composed or Suggested During a Tour, in the Summer of 1833. **CP-WorW2**

Nuptial song, A. James Thomson. **CP-ThomJ**

Nuptiall Song, or Epithalamie, on Sir Clipseby Crew and His Lady, A. Robert Herrick. **CP-HerrR**

Nuptiall Verse to Mistresse Elizabeth Lee, Now Lady Tracie. Robert Herrick. **CP-HerrR**

Nuptials. Allen Tate. **CP-TateA**

Nuptials of Attila, The. George Meredith. **CP-MerG1**

"Flat as to an eagle's eye." **PeVV**

"Square along the couch, and stark." **PeVV**

"Under the thin hoop of gold."

Nurse. Leonard Nathan. **SP-NathL**

Nurse carried him up the stair, The. At Thomas Hardy's Birthplace, 1953. James Wright. **CP-WrigJ**

Nurse in Medea / Had the right idea?, The. A Passing Impatience With a Noble Country. Malcolm Lowry. **CP-LowrM**

Nurse is at the tree, and if I'm thirsty no one minds, The. The Christmas Roses. Randall Jarrell. **CP-JarrR**

Nurse on the battlefield, A. Dien Bien Phu. Adrienne Rich. **SP-RicA2**

Nursery Darling, A. "Lewis Carroll." **CP-CarrL**

Nursery Rhyme. Wystan Hugh Auden. **CP-AudeW**

Nursery Rhyme, A. Randall Jarrell. **CP-JarrR**

Nursery Rhyme. May Sarton. **SP-SartM**

Nursery Rhyme. Charles Simic. **SP-SimiC**

Nursery Rhyme No. 1. Isabella Gardner. **CP-GardI**

Nursery Rhyme No. 2. Isabella Gardner. **CP-GardI**

Nursery Tale. Philip Larkin. **CP-LarkP**

Nurses, The. Rudyard Kipling. **CP-KiplR** *Fr.* Land and Sea Tales.

Nurse's Song ("When the voices of children are heard on the green / And laughing is heard on the hill"). William Blake. **AWP; BLPL; CH; EnRP; FHYEP; FaBoBe; HBV; HBVY; HoFi; LauP; NAEL-2; OBEC; OxBChV; PeLV; SCGP** *Fr.* Songs of Innocence. **CP-BlakW**

(Play Time.) **FaPON**

Nurse's Song ("When the voices of children are heard on the green / And whisperings [*or* whisprings] are in the dale"). William Blake. **CP-BlakW** *Fr.* Songs of Experience.

Nurse's Song. Louise Glück. **SP-GlücL**

Nursing Sister, The. Rudyard Kipling. **CP-KiplR** *Fr.* The Naulahka.

Nursing You. Erica Jong. **SP-JongE**

Nursing your nerves / well; I've roused my own; well. The Afterwake. Adrienne Rich. **CP-RicAE; SP-RicA2**

Nusayris, The. Thomas Merton. *Fr.* East with Ibn Battuta. *Fr.* East. *Fr.* The Geography of Lograire. **CP-MertT**

Nut, The. Charles Kenneth Williams. **CP-WillC**

Nuthin but Brass. Edwin Rolfe. **CP-RolfE**

Nuts in May. Louis MacNeice. **CP-MacNL**

Nutting. William Wordsworth. **CP-WorW1**

Nutting Song. Paul Laurence Dunbar. **CP-DunbP**

Nw / O / h / S / LoW. Edward Estlin Cummings. **CP-CummE**

NW5 and N6. Sir John Betjeman. **CP-BetjJ**

Nyanu was appointed. Early Losses: a Requiem. Alice Walker. **CP-WalkA**

NYC—. Robert Creeley. **CP-CreeR**

Nymph and Her Fawn, The. Andrew Marvell. **FaBoCh** *Fr.* The Nymph Complaining for the Death of Her Faun [*or* Fawn]. **CP-MarvA**

(Girl and Her Fawn, The.) **BoTP**

Nymph and shepherd raise electric tridents. Chances "R." Allen Ginsberg. **CP-GinsA**

Nymph and swain, Sheelah and Dermot hight, A. A Pastoral Dialogue. Jonathan Swift. **CP-SwifJ**

Nymph and the Shepherd, or She Went That-a-Way, The. Ogden Nash. **CP-NashO**

Nymph Complaining for the Death of Her Faun [*or* Fawn], The. Andrew Marvell. **CP-MarvA**

Nymph and Her Fawn, The. **FaBoCh**

(Girl and Her Fawn, The.) **BoTP**

Nymph her graces here express'd may find, The. *in imitation of* Waller. Alexander Pope. **CP-PopeA**

Nymph must lose her female friend, The. The Lily and the Rose. William Cowper. **CP-CowpW**

Nymph of the downward smile, and sidelong glance. To Georgiana Augusta Wylie. John Keats. **CP-KeatJ**

Nymph of the forest, only in whose honour, The. Ambience. Robert Ranke Graves. **CP-GravR**

Nymph of the garden where all beauties be. Sonnet 82. Sir Philip Sidney. **InvP; PoE** *Fr.* Astrophil and Stella. **SP-SidnP**

Nymph of the rock! whose dauntless spirit braves. To Fortitude. Charlotte Smith. **CP-SmitC**

Nymph who wrote this in an amorous fit, The. The Answer to Vanessa's Rebus. Jonathan Swift. **CP-SwifJ**

Nymph, would you learn the only art. Lines from Cadenus to Vanessa. Jonathan Swift. **CP-SwifJ**

Nympha potens Thamesis soli cessura Dianae. *acc. by English translation.* Thomas Campion. **CP-CampT**

Nymphs and Graces Dancing, The. Edmund Spenser. **DIP** *Fr.* The Faerie Queene. **CP-Spens**

Nymphs and Shepherds dance no more. John Milton. **ELP; FiP** *Fr.* Arcades. **CP-MiltJ**

(Song from Arcades.) **FiP**

Nymphs bewail'd poor Daphnis hapless death, The. Translation of Virgil: Pastoral V. Virgil, *tr. by* Samuel Johnson. **CP-JohnS** *Fr.* Pastorals.

Nymphs of Himera—for you remember Daphnis and Hylas. Damon's Epitaph. John Milton, *tr. fr. Latin by* John T. Shawcross. **CP-MiltJ**

Nymph's Passion, A. Ben Jonson. **CP-JonsB**

O

Ö. Rita Dove. **SP-DoveR**

O. Charles Henri Ford. **SP-FordC**

O. Robert Ranke Graves. **CP-GravR**

O / nly this / darkness(in). Edward Estlin Cummings. **CP-CummE**

O / out of a bed of love. Holy Spring. Dylan Thomas. **CP-ThomD**

O / sure)but / nobody unders(no). Edward Estlin Cummings. **CP-CummE**

O / the round / little man we. Edward Estlin Cummings. **CP-CummE**

O / the sweet & aged people. oDE. Edward Estlin Cummings. **CP-CummE**

O! Al Young. **CP-YounA**

O a little lonely in Cambridge [all] that first Fall. Transit. John Berryman. **CP-BerrJ**

O a new song, a free song. Song of the Banner at Daybreak. Walt Whitman. **CP-WhitW**

O a' ye pious, godly flocks. The Holy Tulzie. Robert Burns. **CP-BurnR**

O absent presence, Stella is not here. Sonnet 106. Sir Philip Sidney. *Fr.* Astrophil and Stella. **SP-SidnP**

O Adolescence, O Adolescence. Tarkington, Thou Should'st Be Living in This Hour. Ogden Nash. **CP-NashO**

O ailing Love, compose your struggling wing! Edna St. Vincent Millay. **CP-MillE**

O All Down within the Pretty Meadow. Kenneth Patchen. **CP-PatcK**

O all ye exorcizers come and exorcize now, and ye clergymen draw. So Does Everybody Else, Only Not So Much. Ogden Nash. **CP-NashO**

O all ye fair ladies with your colours and your graces. The Revenant. Walter de la Mare. **CP-DeLaW**

O all your ages at the mercy of my loves. John Berryman. **NOBA** *Fr.* Homage to Mistress Bradstreet. **CP-BerrJ**

O! Americans. David Herbert Lawrence. **CP-LawrD**

O An Ye Were Dead Gudeman. Robert Burns. **CP-BurnR**

O and we sang then whose voices. Poem for Bob Leed. Robert Creeley. **CP-CreeR**

O apple-seed I planted in a silly shallow place. The Fairy from the Apple-Seed. Nicholas Vachel Lindsay. **CP-LindV**

O are you tangled up in yourself. Self-Conscious People. David Herbert Lawrence. **CP-LawrD**

O Ary Scheffer! when beneath thine eye. On a Prayer-Book. John Greenleaf Whittier. **CP-WhitJ**

O Attic shape! Fair attitude! with brede. John Keats. **GrIP** *Fr.* Ode on a Grecian Urn. **CP-KeatJ**

O Autumn, laden with fruit, and stained. To Autumn. William Blake. **CP-BlakW**

O Ay My Wife She Dang Me. Robert Burns. **CP-BurnR**

O Bacchus, what a world of toil, both now. The Cyclops. Euripides, *tr. fr. Greek by* Shelley. **CP-ShelP**

O be swift. The Helmsman. Hilda Doolittle. **CP-DoolH**

O beauteous daughter, the bright pitcher of death. All That Night Lights Were Seen Moving in Every Direction. Kenneth Patchen. **CP-PatcK**

O, beauteous is the earth! and fair. The Love That Is Hereafter. Walt Whitman. **CP-WhitW**

O beautiful Forever! I Saw Eternity. Louise Bogan. **CP-BogaL**

O beautiful, my relic bone. Song. Jean Garrigue. **SP-GarrJ**

O beautiful prey, / night-voice. Stanley Jasspon Kunitz. *Fr.* Meditations on Death. **CP-KuniS**

O Beauty, in a beauteous Body dight! The Veil of Spirit. Samuel Taylor Coleridge. **CP-ColeS**

O best oeconomist of life. Prudence. Christopher Smart. *Fr.* Hymns for the Amusement of Children. **SP-SmarC**

O between distress and pleasure. Song. Emily Brontë. **CP-BronE**

O bid me mount and sail up there. His Wildness. William Butler Yeats. *Fr.* A Man Young and Old. **CP-YeatW**

O Bitter Madrigal. Marsden Hartley. **CP-HartM**

O blessed body [*or* bodie]! Whither art thou thrown? Sepulchre. George Herbert. **CP-HerbG**

O blessed man, that in th' advice. Bible, *O.T. See* Psalm 1: "Blessed is the man that walketh. . . ."

O, blessed of the gods. 4.6. Horace. **CP-CummE,** *tr. by* E. E. Cummings; *Fr.* Odes.

O blessed Paul elect to grace, / Arise and wash away thy sin. Conversion of St. Paul. Christina Georgina Rossetti. **CP-RosC2**

O blessed, silent one, who speaks everywhere! Early Morning. The Hour of Prime. Thomas Merton. **CP-MertT** *Fr.* Hagia Sophia.

O blisful light, of which the beames clere. Wooing of Criseide, The, III. Geoffrey Chaucer. **PoEL-1** *Fr.* Troilus and Criseyde [*or* Criseide]. **CP-ChauG**

O blithe New-comer! I have heard. To the Cuckoo. William Wordsworth. **CP-WorW1**

O blow of the building. Midday Construction. Pablo Neruda, *tr. fr. Spanish by* Ben Belitt. **SP-NeruP**

O Blush Not So! O Blush Not So! John Keats. **CP-KeatJ**

O bonie was yon rosy brier. Scotish Song. Robert Burns. **CP-BurnR**

O Book! infinite sweetness! let my heart. The Holy Scriptures (1). George Herbert. **CP-HerbG**

O Boston city lecture-hearing. Ralph Waldo Emerson. **CP-EmerR**

O boy the blues! The Old Fashioned Cincinnati Blues. Al Young. **CP-YounA**

O Breath. Elizabeth Bishop. *Fr.* Four Poems. **CP-BishE**

O briar-scents, on yon wet wing. Breath of the Briar. George Meredith. **CP-MerG1**

O bright, O swift and bright. The Birds of Vietnam. Hayden Carruth. **CP-CarHS**

O [*or* Oh], Brignal[l] banks are wild and fair. Edmund's Songs. Sir Walter Scott. **SP-ScotW** *Fr.* Rokeby.

O but there is wisdom. *fr.* A Woman Young and Old. William Butler Yeats. **CP-YeatW**

O but we talked at large before. Sixteen Dead Men. William Butler Yeats. **CP-YeatW**

O by the by / has anybody seen. Edward Estlin Cummings. **CP-CummE; SP-CummE**

O Caesar, we who are about to die. Morituri Salutamus. Henry Wadsworth Longfellow. **SP-LongH**

O Caledonia! Sir Walter Scott. **FaBoPP** *Fr.* Breathes there the [*or a*] Man [with Soul So Dead]. **SP-ScotW** *Fr.* The Lay of the Last Minstrel.

O, call me not to justify the wrong. Sonnet 139. William Shakespeare. *Fr.* Sonnets. **CP-ShaWS**

O cam ye here the fight to shun. The Battle of Sherra-Moor. Robert Burns. **CP-BurnR**

O Captain! My Captain! Walt Whitman. **AA; APN-1; CBCWP; EBEvV; FPL; FaBV; FaBoBe; FaBoCh; FaFP; FaPON; FaPoR; GN; GOA; ImPo; InPK; LiTA; MOS; MeMAP; MoAmPo; OBCA; OHFP; OHIP; PAH; PBMP; PIP; PoLF; SAmP; TAP; TFi; TrGrPo** *Fr.* Memories of President Lincoln. **CP-WhitW**

O Carib Isle! Hart Crane. **CP-CranH**

O Charity! that couldst receive. Ash Wednesday. First Day of Lent. Christopher Smart. *Fr.* Hymns and Spiritual Songs for the Fasts and Festivals of the Church of England. **SP-SmarC**

O Chatterton, how very sad thy fate! To Chatterton. John Keats. **CP-KeatJ**

O Cheese. Donald Hall. **CP-HallD**

O chief director of the growing race. Ad Quintilianum. Robert Louis Stevenson. **CP-StevR**

O Childish Mind! Walter de la Mare. **CP-DeLaW**

O Christ my God Who seest the unseen. Christina Georgina Rossetti. **CP-RosC2**

O Christ of God! whose life and death. Vesta. John Greenleaf Whittier. **CP-WhitJ**

O Christ our All in each, our All in all! Christina Georgina Rossetti. **CP-RosC2**

O Christ our Light, Whom even in darkness we. Light of Light. Christina Georgina Rossetti. **CP-RosC2**

O Christ the Life, look on me where I lie / Ready to die. Half Dead. Christina Georgina Rossetti. **CP-RosC2**

O Christ the Vine with living Fruit. I Know You Not. Christina Georgina Rossetti. **CP-RosC3**

O! Christmas Day, Oh! happy day! Homeless. Samuel Taylor Coleridge. **CP-ColeS**

O ciliegia infiorita. Christina Georgina Rossetti. **CP-RosC3**

O clap your hands, all ye people. Psalm 47. Bible, *O.T. Fr.* Psalms. **CP-Psal**

O cloud-pale eyelids, dream-dimmed eyes. He Tells of the Perfect Beauty. William Butler Yeats. **CP-YeatW**

O Cold grey stones! What mighty warrior lies beneath thy shade? Arthur's Quoit, Dyffryn. Wystan Hugh Auden. **CP-AudWJ**

O Colonia, whose wishes build a long bridge to dance on. Catullus. *See* Carmen 17: "Cologna Veneta - / where the good folk."

O come again; what chains withhold. Emily Brontë. **CP-BronE**

O come, dearest Emma! the rose is full blown. To Emma. John Keats. **CP-KeatJ**

O come here! a sunflower! Day of Rabblement. Kenneth Patchen. **CP-PatcK**

O come, let us sing unto the Lord. Psalm 95. Bible, *O.T.* **AWP; OHIP** *Fr.* Psalms. **CP-Psal**

O come, soft rest of cares, come Night. Bridal Song. George Chapman. **NOBE; OBEV** *Fr.* Hero and Leander. **CP-MarlC**

O come with me, thus ran the song. Emily Brontë. **CP-BronE**

O could I give thee India's wealth. To Mr. McMurdo, with a Pound of Lundiefoot Snuff. Robert Burns. **CP-BurnR**

O Country People. John Hewitt. **CP-HewiJ**

O crimson salamander. The Ordeal. William Carlos Williams. **CP-WilW1**

O cross, more splendid than all the stars. Thomas Merton. **CP-MertT**

O cruel cloudless space. Nativity. May Sarton. **SP-SartM**

O cruel Death, give three things back. *fr.* Words for Music Perhaps. William Butler Yeats. **CP-YeatW**

O, cruel heart, where is thy faith? Sir Thomas Wyatt. **CP-WyatT**

O Cupid, that dost never cease my smart. 2.9. Ovid. **CP-MarlC,** *tr. by* Christopher Marlowe; *Fr.* Elegies.

O curlew, cry no more in the air. He Reproves the Curlew. William Butler Yeats. **CP-YeatW**

O Daedalus, Fly Away Home. Robert Earl Hayden. **CP-HaydR**

O dandelion, rich and haughty. The Dandelion. Nicholas Vachel Lindsay. **CP-LindV**

O darling (as we used to say). The Escape. Leonard Cohen. **CP-CoheL**

O David, highest in the list. Christopher Smart. **NOEC** *Fr.* A Song to David. **SP-SmarC**

O Day! he cannot die. A Death Scene. Emily Brontë. **CP-BronE**

O Day most calm, most bright. Sunday. George Herbert. **CP-HerbG**

O days and hours, your work is this. Tennyson. **HBV 1-2; PeECV** *Fr.* In Memoriam A. H. H. **CP-TennA**

O deadly rancour to a constant heart. Sonnet 2. Mary Sidney, Countess of Montgomery Wroth. *Fr.* Lindamira's Complaint. *Fr.* Part 1. *Fr.* Urania. **CP-WrotM**

O dear cool you couldn't be virile—you couldn't a parent he. Catullus. *See* Carmen 67: "Sweet entrance to a husband's pleasure."

O Dear Life, When Shall It Be? Sir Philip Sidney. *See* Tenth Song.

O dear life, when shall it be. Tenth Song. Sir Philip Sidney. **EnRePo** *Fr.* Astrophil and Stella. **SP-SidnP**

O dear Minny What Shall I Do? Robert Burns. **CP-BurnR**

O dear Mother outline of knowledge most sage. William Blake. **CP-BlakW** ("Then Reynolds said O woman most sage.") **CP-BlakW**

O dear sweet rosy. An Asphodel. Allen Ginsberg. **CP-GinsA**

O deare, that I with thee might live. Thomas Campion. **CP-CampT**

O dearer far than light and life are dear. To ———. William Wordsworth. **CP-WorW2**

O dearest bloom the seasons know. An Easter Flower Gift. John Greenleaf Whittier. **CP-WhitJ**

O dearest eyes the lights, and guids of love. Sonnet 43. Mary Sidney, Countess of Montgomery Wroth. *Fr.* Pamphilia to Amphilanthus. **CP-WrotM**

O dearly-bought revenge, yet glorious! Heroic Vengeance. John Milton. **OBS** *Fr.* Samson Agonistes. **CP-MiltJ**

O dearly loved! / And worthy of our love! No more. Daniel Wheeler. John Greenleaf Whittier. **CP-WhitJ**

O, Death! a black and pierceless pall. Time to Come. Walt Whitman. **CP-WhitW**

O Death, Death, He is come. Gerard Manley Hopkins. **CP-HopkG**

"O Death, great captain, lift anchor!". Delmore Schwartz. **SP-SchwD** *Fr.* Genesis.

O death, hadst thou but spar'd his life. Epigram on Said Occasion. Robert Burns. **CP-BurnR**

O death, so dear to me. Poem. James Dickey. **CP-DickJ**

O death! thou tyrant fell and bloody! Elegy on Captain Matthew Henderson [*or* Capt. M——— H———] [A *Gentleman* Who Held the Patent for His Honours Immediately from Almighty God!]. Robert Burns. **CP-BurnR**

O Death Where Is Thy Sting? Christina Georgina Rossetti. **CP-RosC3**

O destiny, destiny. Destiny. David Herbert Lawrence. **CP-LawrD**

O Deus, Ego Amo Te. Gerard Manley Hopkins. **CP-HopkG**

O Distinct / Lady of my unkempt adoration. Edward Estlin Cummings. **CP-CummE**

O Do Not Love Too Long. William Butler Yeats. **CP-YeatW**

O do not praise my beauty more. The Beauty. Thomas Hardy. **CP-HardT**

O do not use me / After my sin[ne]s! look not on my desert. Sighs and Groans [*or* Grones]. George Herbert. **CP-HerbG**

O dreadful Justice, what a fright and terror. Justice (2). George Herbert. **CP-HerbG**

O Dream, where art thou now? Emily Brontë. **CP-BronE**

"O Dreary life," we cry, "O dreary life!" Patience Taught by Nature. Elizabeth Barrett Browning. **CP-BroEB**

O dull cold northern sky. Robert Louis Stevenson. **CP-StevR**

O Duty, / Why hast thou not the visage of a sweetie or a cutie? Kind of an Ode to Duty. Ogden Nash. **CP-NashO**

O dwellers in the stately towns. June on the Merrimac. John Greenleaf Whittier. **CP-WhitJ**

O ear whose creatures cannot wish to fall. Wystan Hugh Auden. *Fr.* Anthem for St. Cecilia's Day. **CP-AudeW**

O early one morning I walked out like Agag. The Streets of Laredo. Louis MacNeice. **CP-MacNL**

O Earth! Earth! Earth heare thou my voice, and be. To His Paternall Countrey. Robert Herrick. **CP-HerrR**

O Earth, lie heavily upon her eyes. Rest. Christina Georgina Rossetti. **CP-RosC1**

O Earth Mother, who consents to everything, who forgives everything. You (V) (after Holderlin). Tom Clark. **SP-ClarT**

O Earth, unhappy planet born to die. Edna St. Vincent Millay. **HeIP; WoWa** *Fr.* Epitaph for the Race of Man. **CP-MillE**

O Ease My Spirit. "Hugh MacDiarmid." **SP-MacDH**

O—eh—lee! La—La! Sicilian Emigrant's Song. William Carlos Williams. **CP-WilW1**

O elegant whore! Carmen 43. Catullus. *Fr.* Carmina. **CP-Catul**

O embittered joy. Fiend's Weather. Louise Bogan. **CP-BogaL**

O England, may God punish thee! England to Germany in 1914. Thomas Hardy. **CP-HardT**

O epic-famed, god-haunted Central Sea. Genoa and the Mediterranean. Thomas Hardy. **CP-HardT**

O Eros, silently smiling one, hear me. Hymn to Eros. Denise Levertov. **CP-LeveD**

O evening, steal into the silent city. Invocation to Evening. John Gould Fletcher. **SP-FletJ**

O evening, why is thy light so sad? Emily Brontë. **CP-BronE**

O everlastingly self-deluded! Basil Bunting, *after the Persian of* Hafiz. **CP-BuntB**

O Everliving Queen! Kenneth Patchen. **CP-PatcK**

O eyes, which do the spheres of beauty move. Sonnet 42. Sir Philip Sidney. *Fr.* Astrophil and Stella. **SP-SidnP**

O face within the sky. The Cruelkind Swans. Kenneth Patchen. **CP-PatcK**

O fahter, fahter. Epigraph to *Call Me Ishmael.* Charles Olson. **CP-OlsoC**

O fair and stately maid, whose eyes. To Eva. Ralph Waldo Emerson. **CP-EmerR**

O fair is Love's first hope to gentle mind! First Advent of Love. Samuel Taylor Coleridge. **CP-ColeS**

O Fairest flower no sooner blown but blasted. On the Death of a Fair Infant Dying of a Cough. John Milton. **CP-MiltJ**

O fairest Pattern to a failing Age! Epitaph on John Knight, Who Died Oct. 2, 1733. Alexander Pope. **CP-PopeA**

O fall of the leaf I am tired. John Hewitt. *See* Leaf.

O farm, dear nest, or say Sabine, ah say Tibur's. Catullus. *See* Carmen 44: "It depends who's talking if you're a 'Sabine.' "

O fate, O fault, O curse, child of my bliss. Sonnet 93. Sir Philip Sidney. *Fr.* Astrophil and Stella. **SP-SidnP**

O father, answer me. Dialogue. Howard Nemerov. **CP-NemeH**

O Father, give the spirit power to climb. Boethius, *tr. fr. Latin.* **MLL,** *tr. by* Helen Waddell; *Fr.* Consolation of Philosophy, The ("De Consolacione Philosophie"). **CP-ChauG**

O favorable spirit, propitious guest. Adam Unfallen. John Milton. **NOCV** *Fr.* Book V. *Fr.* Paradise Lost. **CP-MiltJ**

O fields of the sun! The Age of Pericles. Kenneth Patchen. **CP-PatcK**

O fiery river / Flow out over the land. Kenneth Patchen. **CP-PatcK**

O fiery tiger walking down through the air. I Have No Place to Take Thee. Kenneth Patchen. **CP-PatcK**

O fill pull willand lean of that gleam. At the Entrance to the Other World. Kenneth Patchen. **CP-PatcK**

O Fill Your Sack with Tiger Cubs. Kenneth Patchen. **CP-PatcK**

O Firstfruits of our grain, / Infant and Lamb appointed to be slain. Feast of the Presentation. Christina Georgina Rossetti. **CP-RosC2**

O flag of the nation! O Red,White and Blue! Our Flag. Edward Estlin Cummings. **CP-CummE**

"O Flodden Field." Donald Hall. **CP-HallD**

O Florida, Venereal Soil. Wallace Stevens. **CP-StevW**

O flower of all that springs from gentle blood. Gabriello Chiabrera, *tr. fr. Italian by* William Wordsworth. **CP-WorW1**

O follow the sonnet's flight. Hafiz, *tr. by* Ralph Waldo Emerson. **CP-EmerR** *Fr.* Odes.

O foolish Soul! to make thy count / For languid falls and much forgiven. Christina Georgina Rossetti. **CP-RosC2**

O foolishnes of men! that lend their ears. Comus's Praise of Nature. John Milton. **PoEL-3** *Fr.* Comus; a Masque Presented at Ludlow Castle.

O for a dirge! But why complain? Elegiac Stanzas (Addressed to Sir G.H.B. upon the Death of His Sister-in-Law). William Wordsworth. **CP-WorW2**

O, for a kindling touch from that pure flame. Siege of Vienna Raised by John Sobieski February, 1816. William Wordsworth. **CP-WorW2**

O for a pair like turtles wear. Ecquis Binas. Gerard Manley Hopkins. **CP-HopkG**

O For a voice like thunder, and a tongue. Prologue, Intended for a Dramatic Piece of King Edward the Fourth. William Blake. **CP-BlakW**

O, for Ane-and-Twenty Tam. Robert Burns. **CP-BurnR**

O for doors to be open and an invite with gilded edges. Song of the Beggars. Wystan Hugh Auden. **PeLV** *Fr.* Twelve Songs. **CP-AudeW**

O for God's sake / they are connected. Islands. Muriel Rukeyser. **CP-RukeM**

O for my ain king, quo gude Wallace. Gude Wallace. Robert Burns. **CP-BurnR**

O, for my sake do you with Fortune chide. Sonnet 111. William Shakespeare. **OXAEP-1** *Fr.* Sonnets. **CP-ShaWS**

O for ten years, that I may overwhelm. John Keats. **NAEL-2; OAEL-2** *Fr.* Sleep and Poetry. **CP-KeatJ**

O for that warning voice which he who saw. John Milton. **TEP,** *ll.* 1–324; **OxAEP-1,** *ll.* 1–535; **NAEL-1,** *ll.* 1–775; **PoEL-3** *Fr.* Book IV. **OAEL-1** *Fr.* Paradise Lost. **CP-MiltJ**

(Prospect of Eden, The.) **PoEL-3**, *ll.* 1–775;

O for the help of Angels to complete. In the Cathedral at Cologne. William Wordsworth. *Fr.* Memorials of a Tour of the Continent; 1820. **CP-WorW2**

O for the time when I shall sleep. Emily Brontë. **OBD** *Fr.* Enough of Thought, Philosopher. **CP-BronE**

O for wings. Euripides, *tr.* by Hilda Doolittle ("H.D."). **CP-DoolH** *Fr.* Hippolytus.

O form'd t' illume a sunless world forlorn. To William Godwin. Samuel Taylor Coleridge. **CP-ColeS**

O fram'd at once to charm the ear and sight. To Mrs. Dacosta. Christopher Smart. **SP-SmarC**

O Frame the strains anew. Bible, *O.T. See* Psalm 98: "O sing unto the Lord a new song. . . ."

O friend blame not Hafiz. Hafiz, *tr.* by Ralph Waldo Emerson. **CP-EmerR** *Fr.* Odes.

O Friend! I know not which way I must look. Written in London, September, 1802. William Wordsworth. **CP-WorW1**

O Friend! O Teacher! God's great Gift to me! To W. Wordsworth. Samuel Taylor Coleridge. **CP-ColeS**

O friend, who hast attained thyself in her. S.T. Edward Estlin Cummings. **CP-CummE**

O friends! with whom my feet have trod. The Eternal Goodness. John Greenleaf Whittier. **CP-WhitJ**

O, from [*or* O! From] what power hast thou this powerful might. Sonnet 150. William Shakespeare. **OXAEP-1; SCGP** *Fr.* Sonnets. **CP-ShaWS**

O "fruitful and purified"—an identity in the Invisible! Nothing. A Time to Believe! Kenneth Patchen. **CP-PatcK**

O Future bards. A Prophecy. Allen Ginsberg. **CP-GinsA**

O Galloway Tam cam here to woo. Galloway Tam. Robert Burns. **CP-BurnR**

O gaudy Summer, veil thy blushing head. To Mr. Thomson, on his Blooming Winter. *Unknown, signed*Mira. **CP-ThomJ**

O generation of the thoroughly smug / and thoroughly uncomfortable. Salutation. Ezra Pound. **SP-PounE**

O[h,] gentle Love, do not forsake the guide. Upon Some Alterations in My Mistress, after My Departure into France. Thomas Carew. **CP-CareT**

O gentle Sleep! do they belong to thee. To Sleep ("O gentle Sleep! do they belong to thee"). William Wordsworth. **CP-WorW1**

O ghost in the bluehearing grove. Each Is Alone, Each Is Everything. Kenneth Patchen. **CP-PatcK**

O gie the lass her fairin' lad. Gie the Lass her Fairin'. Robert Burns. **CP-BurnR**

O Gin My Love Were Yon Red Rose. Robert Burns. **GBP** *Fr.* O Were My Love Yon Lilac[k] Fair. **CP-BurnR**

O give thanks unto the Lord; call upon his name. Psalm 105. Bible, *O.T. Fr.* Psalms. **CP-Psal**

O give thanks unto the Lord; for he is good: because his mercy endureth for ever. Psalm 118. Bible, *O.T.* **TrJP** *Fr.* Psalms. **CP-Psal**

O give thanks unto the Lord, for he is good: for his mercy endureth for ever. Psalm 107. Bible, *O.T. Fr.* Psalms. **CP-Psal**

O give thanks unto the Lord; for he is good [or gracious]: for his mercy endureth for ever. Psalm 136. Bible, *O.T.* **AWP; OHIP** *Fr.* Psalms. **CP-Psal**

O Give yee thanks unto the Lord. Bible, *O.T. See* Psalm 107: "O give thanks unto the Lord, for he is good: for. . . ."

O Gloriosa Domina, *ad. fr. the Medieval Latin* De Beata Virgine. Richard Crashaw. **CP-CrasR**

O glorious sea that in each climbing wave. Christina Georgina Rossetti. **CP-RosC3**

O[h] glorious spirits, who after all your bands. To All Angels and Saints. George Herbert. **CP-HerbG**

O God do I have to be Wordsworth. Thomas Merton. *Fr.* Cables to the Ace. **CP-MertT**

O God, I love thee, I love thee—. O Deus, Ego Amo Te. Gerard Manley Hopkins. **CP-HopkG**

O God, in the dream the terrible horse began. The Dream. Louise Bogan. **CP-BogaL**

O God, keep not Thou silence. Bible, *O.T. See* Psalm 83: "Keep not thou silence, O God."

O God! My God! have mercy now. Supposed Confessions of a Second-rate Sensitive Mind. Tennyson. **CP-TennA**

O God, my heart is fixed. Psalm 108. Bible, *O.T. Fr.* Psalms. **CP-Psal**

O God, O Venus, O Mercury, patron of thieves. The Lake Isle. Ezra Pound. **SP-PounE**

O, God of Columbia! O, Shield of the Free! Ode. Walt Whitman. **CP-WhitW**

O God of heaven! the dream of horror. Emily Brontë. **CP-BronE**

O God of my salvation. Psalm 88. Bible, *O.T. Fr.* Psalms. **CP-Psal**

O God, the heathen are come into thine inheritance. Psalm 79. Bible, *O.T.* **TrJP** *Fr.* Psalms. **CP-Psal**

O God, thou art my God; early will I seek thee. Psalm 63. Bible, *O.T. Fr.* Psalms. **CP-Psal**

O God, thou hast cast us off, thou hast scattered us. Psalm 60. Bible, *O.T. Fr.* Psalms. **CP-Psal**

O God, where do they tend--these struggling aims? Robert Browning. **WGRP** *Fr.* Pauline [*or* Pauline; A Fragment of a Confession]. **CP-BroR1**

O God, whose favourable eye. True and False Comforts. William Cowper. *Fr.* Olney Hymns. **CP-CowpW**

O God, why hast thou cast us off for ever? Psalm 74. Bible, *O.T. Fr.* Psalms. **CP-Psal**

O God, why hast thou thus / Repuls'd, and scatter'd us? Bible, *O.T. See* Psalm 74: "O God, why hast thou cast us off for ever?"

O goddess excellently bright. The She-Bear. Charles Olson. **CP-OlsoC**

O Goddess! hear these tuneless numbers, wrung. Ode to Psyche. John Keats. **CP-KeatJ**

O golden-tongued romance, with serene lute! On Sitting Down to Read "King Lear" Once Again. John Keats. **CP-KeatJ**

O gong of wept / O unviolet. Joseph Ceravolo. **SP-CeraJ**

O goodly golden chaine, wherewith yfere. Edmund Spenser. **FHYEP** *Fr.* The Faerie Queene. **CP-Spens**

O goodly hand. Sir Thomas Wyatt. **CP-WyatT**

O Gowdie, terror o' the whigs. Epistle to John Goldie in Kilmarnock, Author of, the Gospel Recovered. Robert Burns. **CP-BurnR**

O gracious Lord, how shall I know. The Holy Communion. George Herbert. **CP-HerbG**

O grammar rules, O now your virtues show. Sonnet 63. Sir Philip Sidney. **FaBoUs** *Fr.* Astrophil and Stella. **SP-SidnP**

O grande Amor possente. Amore E Dispetto. Christina Georgina Rossetti. **CP-RosC3**

O Grant. John Keats. *See* O grant that like to Peter I.

O grant that like to Peter I. John Keats. **CBNP; ChIV-2** *Fr.* Three Undated Fragments. **CP-KeatJ**

(O Grant.) **ChIV-2**

O great heart of God. Heart of God. Nicholas Vachel Lindsay. **CP-LindV**

O great world that trains me! that loses my. Passivation. Joseph Ceravolo. **SP-CeraJ**

O Griefe, how divers are they shapes wherein men languish! To The Most Sacred King James. Thomas Campion. **CP-CampT**

O griefe, O spight, to see poore Vertue scorn'd. Thomas Campion. **CP-CampT**

O gude ale comes and gude ale goes. Robert Burns. **CP-BurnR**

O guide my judgment and my taste. Taste. Christopher Smart. **ChIV-1; NOCV** *Fr.* Hymns for the Amusement of Children. **SP-SmarC**

O had the malt thy strength of mind. Robert Burns. *Fr.* To John Syme. **CP-BurnR**

O had truth power the guiltless could not fall. Sir Walter Ralegh's [*or* S.W. Raghlies] Petition to the Queene 1618. Sir Walter Ralegh. **CP-RaleW**

O Hafiz, give me thought. Hafiz, *tr.* by Ralph Waldo Emerson. **CP-EmerR** *Fr.* Odes.

O Hafiz! speak not of thy need. Hafiz, *tr.* by Ralph Waldo Emerson. **CP-EmerR** *Fr.* Odes.

O halcyon! O sea-conceiving bird! The Tenth Book. Archibald MacLeish. *Fr.* Conquistador. **CP-MacLA**

O half moon. Thalidomide. Sylvia Plath. **CP-PlatS**

O hand that smooths the air's flesh. Morning, My Prince—the Eye That Walks. Kenneth Patchen. **CP-PatcK**

O happy are they that have forgiveness got. Bible, *O.T. See* Psalm 32: "Blessed is he whose transgression is forgiven, whose sin is covered."

O Happy Dogs of England. Stevie Smith. **CP-SmitS**

O happy hour, and happier hours. Tennyson. **EnVR** *Fr.* O true and tried, so well and long. **OAEL-2** *Fr.* In Memoriam A. H. H. **CP-TennA**

O happy rose-bud blooming. Gone for Ever. Christina Georgina Rossetti. **CP-RosC1**

O happy Rose, red Rose, that bloomest lonely. The Solitary Rose. Christina Georgina Rossetti. **CP-RosC3**

O happy Thames, that didst my Stella bear. Sonnet 103. Sir Philip Sidney. **OXAEP-1** *Fr.* Astrophil and Stella. **SP-SidnP**

O happy they whose hearts receive. Arthur Hugh Clough. **SP-ClouA**

O happy time of youthful lovers (thus). Vaudracour and Julia. William Wordsworth. **CP-WorW1**

O have you seen my Tuck? my bonny bonny Tuck! George Meredith. **CP-MerG2**

O have you seen the thorn that grows. Song. Alun Lewis. **CP-LewiA**

O heart, be at peace, because. Against Unworthy Praise. William Butler Yeats. **CP-YeatW**

O heart, hold thee secure. Courage. Walter de la Mare. **CP-DeLaW**

O heart, small urn. Hilda Doolittle. **LLLT**, *sect.* 28; *Fr.* The Walls Do Not Fall. **CP-DoolH**

O Heart! the equal poise of love's both parts. Richard Crashaw. **GeHe; TrGrPo** *Fr.* The Flaming Heart. **CP-CrasR**

O Heart: this is a dream I had, or not a dream. Poem. Stanley Jasspon Kunitz. **CP-KuniS**

O Heart Uncovered. Joseph Ceravolo. **SP-CeraJ**

O Heaven, and thou most loving family. Arthur Hugh Clough. **SP-ClouA**

O height dispersed and head. Happiness in the Trees. Joseph Ceravolo. **SP-CeraJ**

O Hell! what do mine eyes with grief behold! Satan Beholds Adam and Eve in Eden. John Milton. **TW** *Fr.* Book IV. **OAEL-1** *Fr.* Paradise Lost. **CP-MiltJ**

O helpless few in my country. Ezra Pound. **SP-PounE** *Fr.* Lustra. (Rest, The.) **SP-PounE**

O Henley, in my hours of ease. Robert Louis Stevenson. **CP-StevR**

O Henriette / I remember yet. Henriette. David Herbert Lawrence. **CP-LawrD**

O he's suffering—maybe dying—and I not there to aid. The Telegram. Thomas Hardy. **CP-HardT**

O Hesperus! thou bringest all good things. Evening. Byron. **AWP; TrGrPo** *Fr.* Canto the Third. *Fr.* Don Juan. **CP-Byron**

O hide your eyes. Archibald MacLeish. **CP-MacLA** *Fr.* The Happy Marriage.

O hideous little bat, the size of snot. The Fly. Karl Shapiro. **SP-ShapK**

O high hilarity. The Bones of Coleridge. Richard Eberhart. **CP-EberR**

O hinder me by no delay. Emily Brontë. **CP-BronE**

O Holy Aether, and swift-wingèd Wings. The Wail of Prometheus Bound. Aeschylus. **WGRP** *Fr.* Prometheus Bound. **CP-BroEB**

O holy, blessèd, glorious Trinity. The Sinner's Sacrifice. Ben Jonson. **CP-JonsB**

O Holy Father! just and true. Hymn. John Greenleaf Whittier. **CP-WhitJ**

O Holy Ghost, whose temple I. The Holy Ghost. John Donne. **NOCV** *Fr.* A Litany. **CP-DonnJ**

O holy virgin! clad in purest white. To Morning. William Blake. **CP-BlakW**

O homesick, brood no more! Homesick. Walter de la Mare. **CP-DeLaW**

O Hope! thou soother sweet of human woes! To Hope. Charlotte Smith. **CP-SmitC**

O how came Love, that is himself a fire. Ben Jonson. **CP-JonsB** *Fr.* Love Restored.

O how can I be blythe and glad. The Bonie Lad That's Far Awa. Robert Burns. **CP-BurnR**

O how could this be done to me. The Blues. Jim Morrison. **SP-MorrJ**

O, how I faint when I of you do write. Sonnet 80. William Shakespeare. **OXAEP-1** *Fr.* Sonnets. **CP-ShaWS**

O! How I Love, on a Fair Summer's Eve. John Keats. **CP-KeatJ**

O how I love thy holy word. Afflictions Sanctified by the Word. William Cowper. *Fr.* Olney Hymns. **CP-CowpW**

O[h], how much more doth beauty beauteous seem. Sonnet 54. William Shakespeare. **AWP; EIL; OBEV; OBSC; PoE; SCGP** *Fr.* Sonnets. **CP-ShaWS**

O how shall I, unskilfu', try. Lovely Davies. Robert Burns. **CP-BurnR**

O, how sick and weary I. In a Myrtle [*or* Mirtle] Shade. William Blake. **CP-BlakW**

O how the pleasant airs of true love be. Sonnet 78. Sir Philip Sidney. *Fr.* Astrophil and Stella. **SP-SidnP**

O, how thy worth with manners may I sing. Sonnet 39. William Shakespeare. *Fr.* Sonnets. **CP-ShaWS**

O Howling Cells. Kenneth Patchen. **CP-PatcK**

O hurry where by water among the trees. The Ragged Wood. William Butler Yeats. **CP-YeatW**

O Husband! this word of care born &. Sonnet: O Husband! Anne Waldman. **SP-WaldA**

O hushed October morning mild. October. Robert Frost. **CP-FrosR**

O Hymen! O Hymenee! Walt Whitman. **CP-WhitW**

O I admire and sorrow! The heart's eye grieves. On the Portrait of Two Beautiful Young People. Gerard Manley Hopkins. **CP-HopkG**

O I am happy! O Swami Shivananda—a smile! Today. Allen Ginsberg. **CP-GinsA**

O! I do love thee, meek Simplicity! To Simplicity. Samuel Taylor Coleridge. *Fr.* Sonnets Attempted in the Manner of Contemporary Writers. **CP-ColeS**

O I forbid you, maidens a' [*or* all]. Tam Lin. *Unknown.* **CP-BurnR**

O! I had my gyp *prepare* that tea. Tea. John Berryman. **CP-BerrJ**

O I had such a wonderful dream, she said. The Dream. Leonard Cohen. **CP-CoheL**

O I say you Joe. William Blake. **CP-BlakW** *Fr.* An Island in the Moon.

O, I wad gang tae Harrogate. Perp. Revival i' the North. Sir John Betjeman. **CP-BetjJ**

O, I wad like to ken—to the beggar-wife says I. The Spaewife. Robert Louis Stevenson. **CP-StevR**

O I Won't Lead a Homely Life. Thomas Hardy. **CP-HardT**

O, if a flame is in you, be it so! Be It So. David Herbert Lawrence. **CP-LawrD**

O, ill-fated mother of the best of offspring, Five, O. Pros Karolon ton Basilea [To King Charles]. Andrew Marvell, *tr. fr. Greek by* William A. McQueen *and* Kiffin A. Rockwell. **CP-MarvA**

O, it is godlike to sit selfpossessed. Basil Bunting. **CP-BuntB**

O it is not lazy to be a messenger or to live out of the shadow of some town. Thomas Merton. *Fr.* Cables to the Ace. **CP-MertT**

O! it is pleasant, with a heart at ease. Fancy in Nubibus. Samuel Taylor Coleridge. **CP-ColeS**

O it was lovely round that other house. Balloons and Wooden Guns. John Hewitt. **CP-HewiJ**

O it was sad enough, weak enough, mad enough. The Going of the Battery. Thomas Hardy. **CP-HardT**

O it's I that am the captain of a tidy little ship. My Ship and I. Robert Louis Stevenson. **CP-StevR**

O It's Nice To Get Up In,the slipshod mucous kiss. Edward Estlin Cummings. **CP-CummE**

O it's so haggard, the face of the moon! Blurry. New Year's. Stephen Berg. **SP-BergS**

O Jealousie, that art. To Jealousie. Robert Herrick. **CP-HerrR**

O Jehovah our Lord, how wondrous great, *par. by* Milton. Bible, *O.T. See* Psalm 8: "O Lord our Lord, how excellent. . . ."

O Jesu, better than Thy gifts / Art Thou Thine only Self to us! The Chiefest among Ten Thousand. Christina Georgina Rossetti. **CP-RosC2**

O Jesu, gone so far apart / Only my heart can follow Thee. Vigil of St. Peter. Christina Georgina Rossetti. **CP-RosC2**

"O Jesus Christ! I'm hit," he said; and died. The Last Laugh. Wilfred Owen. **CP-OwenW**

O Jesus, thou who sittest up there on the right. Sonnet. Hayden Carruth. **CP-CarHS** *Fr.* Sonnets.

O joy! that in our embers. William Wordsworth. **PoPle; Prf** *Fr.* Ode: Intimations of Immortality [from Recollections of Early Childhood]. **CP-WorW1**

O joy, too high for my low style to show. Sonnet 69. Sir Philip Sidney. **NAEL-1; OXAEP-1; TrGrPo** *Fr.* Astrophil and Stella. **SP-SidnP**

O Joyes exceeding! Thomas Campion. *Fr.* A Relation of the Late Royall Entertainment Given by the Right Honourable the Lord *Knowles*, at *Cawsome*-House neere *Redding:* to Our Most *Gracious Queene, Queene* ANNE, *in her* Progresse toward the *Bathe*, upon *the Seven and Eight and Twentie Days of Aprill.* **CP-CampT**

O Jupiter, sho'd I speake ill. In Praise of Women. Robert Herrick. **CP-HerrR**

O Kangaroo, O Kangaroo. The Kangaroo. Ogden Nash. **CP-NashO**

O ken ye what Meg o' the mill has gotten. Robert Burns. **CP-BurnR**

O ken ye what Meg o' the mill has gotten. Ken Ye What Meg o' the Mill Has Gotten. Robert Burns. **CP-BurnR**

O Kenmure's on and awa, Willie. Robert Burns. **CP-BurnR**

O kind protecting Darkness! as a child. Arthur Hugh Clough. *Fr.* Blank Misgivings of a Creature Moving About in Worlds Not Realized. **SP-ClouA**

O kind watchers came. Kenneth Patchen. **CP-PatcK**

O Kindness, Kindness. These virtues are. Thank You. Robert Creeley. **CP-CreeR**

O king, if you make an end of me, a lawful person. A Philosopher on His Way to His Death Suddenly Sent This Message to a Certain King Who Had Unawares Condemned Him, Unrecognized and Innocent, When He Was Seized by Chance Among Criminals. John Milton, *tr. fr. Latin and Greek by* John T. Shawcross. **CP-MiltJ**

O kiss, which dost those ruddy gems impart. Sonnet 81. Sir Philip Sidney. **NAEL-1; Son** *Fr.* Astrophil and Stella. **SP-SidnP**

O know to end, as to begin. Ben Jonson. **CP-JonsB** *Fr.* Masque of Hymen.

O know you what I have done. The Brother. Thomas Hardy. **CP-HardT**

O Lady fair and sweet. Robert Louis Stevenson. **CP-StevR**

O Lady fair, these silks of mine are beautiful and rare. The Vaudois Teacher. John Greenleaf Whittier. **CP-WhitJ**

O Lady Mary Ann looks o'er the castle-wa'. My Bonie Laddie's Young but He's Growin Yet. Robert Burns. **CP-BurnR**

O Lady Moon. Christina Georgina Rossetti. **CP-RosC2**

O Lady Moon, your horns point toward the east. O Lady Moon. Christina Georgina Rossetti. **CP-RosC2**

O Lady, my city, and new flower of the prairie. After Reading the Sad Story of the Fall of Babylon. Nicholas Vachel Lindsay. **CP-LindV**

O lady of the lucent hair. To a Lady Passing Time Better Left Unpassed. Ogden Nash. **CP-NashO**

O lady, when the tipped cup of the moon blessed you. Song. Ted Hughes. **SP-HughT**

O land alive with miracles! Song: Contemplation. Thomas Merton. **CP-MertT**

O land of Empire, art and love. Resignation—to Faustus. Arthur Hugh Clough. **SP-ClouA**

O land of mine, O land I love. Apostrophe to the Land. Countee Cullen. **CP-CullC**

O lapwing, thou fliest around the heath. William Blake. **CP-BlakW**

O lassie art thou sleeping yet. Let Me in This Ae Night. Robert Burns. **CP-BurnR**

O Lay Thy Loof in Mine Lass. Robert Burns. **CP-BurnR**

O—lead me there. Water from the Rock. Marsden Hartley. **CP-HartM**

O leave novels, ye Mauchline belles. Robert Burns. **CP-BurnR**

O leeze me on my spinning-wheel. Bess[y] and Her Spinning-Wheel. Robert Burns. **CP-BurnR**

O Lelius, beauteous flower of gentleness. Gabriello Chiabrera, *tr. fr. Italian by* William Wordsworth. **CP-WorW1**

O! Lest the world should task you to recite. Sonnet 72. William Shakespeare. **OXAEP-1** *Fr.* Sonnets. **CP-ShaWS**

O let not fraud 'gainst me prevail. Justice. Christopher Smart. *Fr.* Hymns for the Amusement of Children. **SP-SmarC**

O let the seeds be planted. Rogation Sunday. William Carlos Williams. **CP-WilW2**

O let the solid ground. My Day. Tennyson. **NAEL-2; NOBVV** *Fr.* Maud [A Monodrama]. **CP-TennA**

O life! what letts thee from a quicke decease? I Dye Alive. Robert Southwell. **CP-SoutR**

O life with the sad seared face. To Life. Thomas Hardy. **CP-HardT**

O lift me—majestic Sire. Marsden Hartley. **CP-HartM**

O Light Invisible, we praise Thee!, fr. sect. 10. Thomas Stearns Eliot. **ILwL; OxBoCh; TrPWD** *Fr.* Choruses from "The Rock." **CP-ElioT**

O light of light, supreme delight. Geoffrey Hill. *Fr.* Tenebrae. **CP-HillG**

O li'l lamb out in de col'. Hymn. Paul Laurence Dunbar. **CP-DunbP**

O [or Oh] listen, listen, ladies gay! Rosabelle. Sir Walter Scott. **SP-ScotW** *Fr.* The Lay of the Last Minstrel.

O lithest Shirley! & the other worlds. Shirley & Auden. John Berryman. **CP-BerrJ**

"O little cloud," the virgin said, "I charge thee tell to me." William Blake. **OBD** *Fr.* The Book of Thel. **CP-BlakW**

O little forests, meekly. Love Winter When the Plant Says Nothing. Thomas Merton. **CP-MertT; SP-MertT**

O little ships that come and go. Little Ships. John Hewitt. **CP-HewiJ**

O littleblood, hiding from the mountains in the mountains. Littleblood. Ted Hughes. **SP-HughT** *Fr.* Crow.

O Living Always, Always Dying. Walt Whitman. **CP-WhitW**

O living will that shalt endure. Tennyson. **EBVV; EBVVPR; FaBoBe; MeMBP; OAEL-2; WGRP** *Fr.* In Memoriam A. H. H. **CP-TennA**

(Prayer, The: "O living will that shalt endure.") **WGRP**

O, Logan, sweetly didst thou glide. Song. Robert Burns. **CP-BurnR**

O lonely bay of Trinity. The Cable Hymn. John Greenleaf Whittier. **CP-WhitJ**

O lonely workman, standing there. In the Moonlight. Thomas Hardy. **NoAM** *Fr.* Satires of Circumstance in Fifteen Glimpses. **CP-HardT**

O Lord Almighty, Who hast formed us weak. Ascension Eve. Christina Georgina Rossetti. **CP-RosC2**

O Lord, as I thee have both prayed and pray. Bible, *O.T. See* Psalm 38: "O Lord, rebuke me not in thy wrath."

O Lord, fulfil Thy Will / Be the days few or many, good or ill. The Will of the Lord Be Done. Christina Georgina Rossetti. **CP-RosC2**

O Lord God, hear the silence of each soul, / Its cry unutterable of ruth and shame. I Will Come and Heal Him. Christina Georgina Rossetti. **CP-RosC2**

O Lord God, to whom vengeance belongeth. Psalm 94. Bible, *O.T. Fr.* Psalms. **CP-Psal**

O lord, he said, Japanese women. The Japanese Wife. Charles Bukowski. **SP-BukC2**

O Lord, how canst Thou say Thou lovest me? When My Heart Is Vexed, I Will Complain. Christina Georgina Rossetti. **CP-RosC1**

O Lord, I am ashamed to seek Thy Face / As tho' I loved Thee as Thy saints love Thee. Christina Georgina Rossetti. **CP-RosC2**

O Lord, I cannot plead my love of Thee. Christina Georgina Rossetti. **CP-RosC3**

O lord, I dred, and that I did not dred. Bible, *O.T. See* Psalm 6: "O Lord, rebuke me not in thine anger."

O Lord I Will Praise Thee. William Cowper. *Fr.* Olney Hymns. **CP-CowpW**

O Lord, in me there lieth nought, *par. by* Countess of Pembroke, Mary Sidney Herbert. Bible, *O.T. See* Psalm 139: "O Lord, thou hast searched me, and known me."

O Lord, it was all night. Sun. James Dickey. **CP-DickJ**

O Lord Jesus Christ, son of the living God. A Prayer. Richard Crashaw. **CP-CrasR**

O Lord, my best desire fulfil. William Cowper. **CP-CowpW; OxBoCh** *Fr.* Olney Hymns. **CP-CowpW**

(Submission.) **CP-CowpW**

O Lord my God, in thee do I put my trust. Psalm 7. Bible, *O.T. Fr.* Psalms. **CP-Psal**

O Lord! my sinne doth overchardge Thy breste. Synne's Heavy Loade. Robert Southwell. **CP-SoutR**

O Lord, on Whom we gaze and dare not gaze, / Increase our faith that gazing we may see. Christina Georgina Rossetti. **CP-RosC2**

O Lord our Lord, how excellent is thy name in all the earth! Psalm 8. Bible, *O.T.* **AWP; NAWM-1; PBMP; TrGrPo; TrJP** *Fr.* Psalms. **CP-Psal**

O Lord, oure Lord, thy name how merveillous. Prologue of the Prioress's Tale. Geoffrey Chaucer. *Fr.* The Canterbury Tales. **CP-ChauG**

O Lord, rebuke me not in thine anger. Psalm 6. Bible, *O.T. Fr.* Psalms. **CP-Psal**

O Lord, rebuke me not in thy wrath. Psalm 38. Bible, *O.T. Fr.* Psalms. **CP-Psal**

O Lord, seek us, O Lord, find us / In Thy patient care. Lord, Save Us, We Perish. Christina Georgina Rossetti. **CP-RosC2**

O Lord, since in my mouth thy mighty name. Bible, *O.T. See* Psalm 6: "O Lord, rebuke me not in thine anger."

O Lord, since we have feasted thus. Grace after Dinner. Robert Burns. **FaBoEE** *Fr.* After Dinner. Fr. Graces———at the Globe Tavern. **CP-BurnR**

O Lord, that rul'st the human heart, *par. by* Christopher Smart. Bible, *O.T. See* Psalm 8: "O Lord our Lord, how excellent. . . ."

O Lord, the hard-won miles. Prayer, A. Paul Laurence Dunbar. **CP-DunbP**

O Lord, thou God of bliss. St. Andrew. Christopher Smart. *Fr.* Hymns and Spiritual Songs for the Fasts and Festivals of the Church of England. **SP-SmarC**

O Lord, thou hast searched me, and known me. Psalm 139. Bible, *O.T. Fr.* Psalms. **CP-Psal**

O Lord, thou hearest my daily moan. In My Solitary Hours in My Dear Husband His Absence. Anne Bradstreet. **CP-BradA**

O Lord, thy land has favour found. Bible, *O.T. See* Psalm 85: "Lord, thou hast been favourable unto thy land."

O Lord, when hunger pinches sore. Before Dinner. Robert Burns. *Fr.* Graces———at the Globe Tavern. **CP-BurnR**

O Lord, when Thou didst call me, didst Thou know. Christina Georgina Rossetti. **CP-RosC2**

O Lord, why grievest Thou? By the Earth's Corpse. Thomas Hardy. **CP-HardT**

O Lorde oure gouvernoure, howe excellent is thy name, *par. by* Miles Coverdale. Bible, *O.T. See* Psalm 8: "O Lord our Lord, how excellent. . . ."

O Loss of sight, of thee I most complain. The Blindness of Samson. John Milton. **ImPo; LiTB** *Fr.* Samson Agonistes. **CP-MiltJ**

O love, be fed with apples while you may. Sick Love. Robert Ranke Graves. **CP-GravR**

O love is a deep thing. Deeper Than Love. David Herbert Lawrence. **CP-LawrD**

O love, love, hold me fast. The Hour and the Ghost. Christina Georgina Rossetti. **CP-RosC1**

O Love, Love, Love! O withering might! Fatima. Tennyson. **CP-TennA**

O Love! O Glory! what are you who fly. Byron. **OAEL-2** *Fr.* Canto the Seventh. *Fr.* Don Juan. **CP-Byron**

O Love! O Glory! what are you who fly. Canto the Seventh. Byron. *Fr.* Don Juan. **CP-Byron**

O Love, of pure and heav'nly birth! Truth and Divine Love Rejected by the World. Jeanne Marie Bouvier de la Motte-Guyon, *tr. fr. French by* William Cowper. **CP-CowpW**

O love sweet love. Francesca in Winter. Stevie Smith. **CP-SmitS**

O love, what hours were thine and mine. The Daisy. Tennyson. **CP-TennA**

O Love, where are thy Shafts, thy Quiver, and thy Bow? Thomas Campion. **CP-CampT**

O love, you airtight bird. Memo from the Cave. Louise Glück. **SP-GlücL**

O, loveliest throat of all sweet throats. Edna St. Vincent Millay. **OxBA** *Fr.* Memorial to D. C. **CP-MillE**

O lovely apple! Perfection. William Carlos Williams. **CP-WilW2**

O loyal to the royal in thyself. To the Queen. Tennyson. *Fr.* Idylls of the King. **CP-TennA**

O Lucifer, Son of the Morning! Christina Georgina Rossetti. **CP-RosC2**

O Lull Me, Lull Me. Theodore Roethke. **CP-RoetT**

O lurcher-loving collier, black as night. Wystan Hugh Auden. *Fr.* Twelve Songs. **CP-AudeW**

O luve will venture in where it daur na weel be seen. The Posie. Robert Burns. **CP-BurnR**

O magic sleep! O comfortable bird. Life Again. John Keats. **SeCePo** *Fr.* Endymion: Poetic Romance. **CP-KeatJ**

O Magnet-South. Walt Whitman. **CP-WhitW**

O maiden aunt, you have come to call. The Tour. Sylvia Plath. **CP-PlatS**

O Maiden! heir of kings! Victoria's Tears. Elizabeth Barrett Browning. **CP-BroEB**

O Make Me a Mask. Dylan Thomas. **CP-ThomD**

O Maker! of almighty skill. St. Stephen. Christopher Smart. *Fr.* Hymns and Spiritual Songs for the Fasts and Festivals of the Church of England. **SP-SmarC**

O Maker of the starry world. Boethius, *tr. fr. Latin.* **MLL**, *tr. by* Helen Waddell; *Fr.* Consolation of Philosophy, The ("De Consolacione Philosophie"). **CP-ChauG**

O Mally's Meek, Mally's Sweet. Robert Burns. **CP-BurnR**

O Mandragora / herbal puppet. Mandrake. Erica Jong. **SP-JongE**

O, many a panting, noble heart. Fame's Vanity. Walt Whitman. **CP-WhitW**

O marinaro che mi apporti tu? Christina Georgina Rossetti. **CP-RosC3**

O [or Oh] Mary, at the window be. Mary Morison. Robert Burns. **CP-BurnR**

O Mary Barrie, Mary Barrie. George Meredith. **CP-MerG2**

O Mary dear, that you were here. To Mary————. Percy Bysshe Shelley. **CP-ShelP**

O Mary, fragile mother. For the Year of the Insane. Anne Sexton. **CP-SextA**

O mater! O fils! Apostroph. Walt Whitman. **CP-WhitW**

O matutini rores, auræque salubres. Votum. William Cowper. **CP-CowpW**

O Maximilian stern and wild. Maximilian Esterhazy. Stevie Smith. **CP-SmitS**

O May, thy morn was ne'er sae sweet. Robert Burns. **CP-BurnR**

O me, man of slack faith so long. All Is Truth. Walt Whitman. **CP-WhitW**

O me, my pleasant rambles by the lake. Edwin Morris. Tennyson. **CP-TennA**

O Me! O Life! Walt Whitman. **CP-WhitW**

O[h] me[e], the time is [or has] come to part. Song. Mary Sidney, Countess of Montgomery Wroth. **NOSC** *Fr.* Pamphilia to Amphilanthus. **CP-WrotM**

O me! what eyes hath Love put in my head. Sonnet 148. William Shakespeare. **GTBS; GTBS-6; GTBS-P** *Fr.* Sonnets. **CP-ShaWS**

O meek attendant of Sol's setting blaze. To the Evening Star. Samuel Taylor Coleridge. **CP-ColeS**

O meikle thinks my luve o' my beauty. My Tocher's the Jewel. Robert Burns. **CP-BurnR**

O 'Melia, my dear, this does everything crown! The Ruined Maid. Thomas Hardy. **CP-HardT**

O Memory [or Memorie], could I but loose thee now. Sonnet. Mary Sidney, Countess of Montgomery Wroth. **WPE** *Fr.* Lindamira's Complaint. *Fr.* Part 1. *Fr.* Urania. **CP-WrotM**

O memory, where is now my youth. Memory and I. Thomas Hardy. **CP-HardT**

O mercy, O me miserable man! A Bitter Reflection. Samuel Taylor Coleridge. **CP-ColeS**

O merry hae I been teethin a heckle. Merry Hae I Been Teethin a Heckle. Robert Burns. **CP-BurnR**

O might I load my arms with thee. The Crown of Love. George Meredith. **CP-MerG1**

O might those sigh[e]s and tear[e]s return[e] again[e]. John Donne. **BiP; OBS** *Fr.* Divine Meditations. **CP-DonnJ** *Fr.* Holy Sonnets. **CP-DonnJ**

O mighty are the lights that shine above Isle Iranim. Isle Iranim. John Gould Fletcher. **SP-FletJ**

O mighty mind, in whose deep stream this age. Fragment: To Byron. Percy Bysshe Shelley. **CP-ShelP**

O Mighty *Nothing!* unto thee. Matthew 27; And He Answered Them Nothing. Bible, *N.T.* **CP-CrasR**, *tr. by* Richard Crashaw; *Fr.* St. Matthew.

O mighty One: / Let me not constrain. Prayer and Sermon of Ibn Abbad. Thomas Merton. *Fr.* Readings from Ibn Abbad. **CP-MertT**

O Miller Knox, whom we knew well. At the Mill. Thomas Hardy. **CP-HardT**

O mind, beset by music never for a moment quiet. Northern April. Edna St. Vincent Millay. **CP-MillE**

O mine enemy / Rejoice not over me! Christina Georgina Rossetti. **CP-RosC2**

O miserable sorrow withouten cure! Sir Thomas Wyatt. **CP-WyatT**

O mister Eckhart! calling. The Morning News. Charles Olson. **CP-OlsoC**

O-Mok-See at Nine Mile. Richard Hugo. **CP-HugoR**

O months of blossoming, months of transfigurations. The Lilacs and the Roses. Louis Aragon, *tr. fr. French by* Louis MacNeice. **CP-MacNL**

O Moon! if e'er I joyed when thy soft light. Written in a Grotto. William Wordsworth. **CP-WorW1**

O moon my mask. Enemy of Those Who Are Enemies of Sleep. Jean Garrigue. **SP-GarrJ**

O moon of illusion. Moonsong at Morning. Sylvia Plath. **CP-PlatS**

O Moon! the oldest shades 'mong oldest trees. John Keats. **EnRP** *Fr.* Endymion: Poetic Romance. **CP-KeatJ**

O Moon, Thou Cool. . . . Hart Crane. **CP-CranH**

O mortal man, who livest here by toil. James Thomson. **LAuP** *Fr.* The Castle of Indolence. **CP-ThomJ**

O most just Vizier, send away. The Sick King in Bokhara. Matthew Arnold. **SP-ArnoM**

O Mother Earth! Upon thy lap. Randolph of Roanoke. John Greenleaf Whittier. **CP-WhitJ**

O Mother Gaia. Gary Snyder. **CP-SnydG**

O mother, I am not regretting. Emily Brontë. **CP-BronE**

O mother, lay your hand on my brow! The Sick Child. Robert Louis Stevenson. **CP-StevR**

O mother maid, O maiden mother free! Two Invocations of the Virgin, II. Geoffrey Chaucer. **ACP** *Fr.* The Prioress's Prologue. *Fr.* The Canterbury Tales. **CP-ChauG**

O Mother Race! to thee I bring. Ode to Ethiopia. Paul Laurence Dunbar. **CP-DunbP**

O Mother State! the winds of March. Sumner. John Greenleaf Whittier. **CP-WhitJ**

O mount and go. The Captain's Lady. Robert Burns. **CP-BurnR**

O mountain Stream! the Shepherd and his Cot. William Wordsworth. *Fr.* The River Duddon [A Series of Sonnets]. **CP-WorW2**

O mud, mud, how fluid! Words Heard, by Accident, over the Phone. Sylvia Plath. **CP-PlatS**

O Muse! O Music! Voice and Lyre. On Gratitude. Christopher Smart. **SP-SmarC**

O Muse who willingly drags along with a limping step. To Salzilli, a Roman Poet, Being Ill. John Milton, *tr. fr. Latin by* John T. Shawcross. **CP-MiltJ**

O my body! I dare not desert the likes of you in other men and women, nor the likes of the parts of you. Walt Whitman. **ErPo** *Fr.* I sing the body electric. **CP-WhitW**

O my chief good. Good Friday. George Herbert. **CP-HerbG**

O my darling troubles heaven. Kenneth Patchen. **CP-PatcK**

O my dearest / While the sun still spends its fabulous money. For Miriam. Kenneth Patchen. **CP-PatcK**

O my dearest [or deerest], I shall grieve thee. The Complement. Thomas Carew. **CP-CareT**

O my eyes how do you lead. Mary Sidney, Countess of Montgomery Wroth. *Fr.* Love's Victorie. **CP-WrotM**

O my first Love! You are in my life forever. Of My First Love. "Hugh MacDiarmid." **SP-MacDH**

O my grey hairs! Spring. William Carlos Williams. **CP-WilW1**

O my heart's heart, and you who are to me. Christina Georgina Rossetti. *Fr.* Monna Innominata. **CP-RosC2**

O my Lord, I am not eloquent. Somber Prayer. John Berryman. **CP-BerrJ**

O my love / The pretty towns. Kenneth Patchen. **CP-PatcK**

O my lover! the night like a broad smooth wave. Shemselnihar. George Meredith. **CP-MerG1**

O[h] my luve's [or luve is or love is] like a red, red rose. Robert Burns. **CP-BurnR**

(Red, Red Rose, A.) **CP-BurnR**

O My Mother Isle! Samuel Taylor Coleridge. **FaBoPP** *Fr.* Fears in Solitude. **CP-ColeS**

O My Mother Isle! ("Not yet enslaved, not wholly vile"). Samuel Taylor Coleridge. **FaBoPP** *Fr.* Ode on the Departing Year. **CP-ColeS**

O My Name It Is Sam Hall. Randall Jarrell. **CP-JarrR**

O my pretty pink frock. The Pink Frock. Thomas Hardy. **CP-HardT**

O my sister remember the stars the tears the trains. To My Sister. Theodore Roethke. **CP-RoetT**

O My songs. Coda. Ezra Pound. **SP-PounE**

O my soul, keep the rest unknown! He Resolves to Say No More. Thomas Hardy. **CP-HardT**

O my thirteen pictures are in prison! 13 Pictures. David Herbert Lawrence. **CP-LawrD**

O my trade it is the rarest one. The Stranger's Song. Thomas Hardy. **CP-HardT**

O my wholly unwise and definite. Edward Estlin Cummings. **CP-CummE**

O Nash! more blest in ev'ry other thing. Alexander Pope. *Fr.* Epigrams Occasioned by Cibber's Verses in Praise of Nash. **CP-PopeA**

O native Britain! O my Mother Isle! O My Mother Isle! Samuel Taylor Coleridge. **FaBoPP** *Fr.* Fears in Solitude. **CP-ColeS**

O Nepos, twice my neighbour (since at home). Ad Nepotem. Robert Louis Stevenson. **CP-StevR**

O never girl beneath the skies of Italy. Feminine Charm. Stevie Smith. **CP-SmitS**

O never harm the dreaming world. Vegetation. Kathleen Jessie Raine. **SP-RainK**

O never rudely will I blame his faith. Mythology in an Age of Reason. Johann Christoph Friedrich von Schiller. **CP-ColeS** *Fr.* The Piccolomini.

O [or Oh], never say that I was false of heart. Sonnet 109. William Shakespeare. **EiL; GTBS; GTBS-6; GTBS-P; HBV; NOBE; OBEV; OBSC; OXAEP-1** *Fr.* Sonnets. **CP-ShaWS**

O never to be moved. Thomas Campion. **CP-CampT**

"O New York boy, this is Life, Life in which". Delmore Schwartz. **SP-SchwD** *Fr.* Genesis.

O night of admiration, full of choirs. The Dark Encounter. Thomas Merton. **CP-MertT**

O night, the ease of care, the pledge of pleasure. Sir Philip Sidney. **SP-SidnP** *Fr.* Arcadia.

O nightingale, best poet of the grove. To the Nightingale. James Thomson. **CP-ThomJ**

O nightingale! how hast thou learnt. To a Nightingale. George Meredith. **CP-MerG1**

O Nightingale, that on yon bloomy Spray. Sonnet 1. John Milton. **CP-MiltJ**

O Nightingale! thou surely art. William Wordsworth. **CP-WorW1**

O nimis semper mea vere amata. *acc. by English translation.* Thomas Campion. **CP-CampT**

O none but gods have power their love to hide. Christopher Marlowe. **OXAEP-1** *Fr.* Hero and Leander. **CP-MarlC**

O Norah, lay thy basket down. Kathleen. John Greenleaf Whittier. **CP-WhitJ**

O! nothing earthly save the ray. Al Aaraaf. Edgar Allan Poe. **CP-PoeEd**

O now, although the year be done. Robert Louis Stevenson. **CP-StevR**

O now that the genius of Bewick were mine. Two Thieves, The; or, the Last Stage of Avarice. William Wordsworth. **CP-WorW1**

O now the drenched land wakes. Kenneth Patchen. **CP-PatcK**

O now you've got a very different look. A Lost Poem. Kenneth Patchen. **CP-PatcK**

O ocean sea, for all your being vast. Does No One at All Ever Feel This Way in the Least? Robert Frost. **CP-FrosR**

O once I loved [or lov'd] a bonnie lass. Robert Burns. **CP-BurnR**

O only Source of all our light and life. Qui Laborat, Orat. Arthur Hugh Clough. **SP-ClouA**

O, open the door, some pity to show. The Palmer. Sir Walter Scott. **SP-ScotW**

O, Opportunity, thy guilt is great. Opportunity. William Shakespeare. **LiTB; NOBE; OBSC; PoEL-2** *Fr.* The Rape of Lucrece. **CP-ShaWS**

O out of that feast in the blond wood of the morning. Kenneth Patchen. *Fr.* Wanderers of the Pale Wood. **CP-PatcK**

O Outrider! / when you come to the threshold of the stars. Robert Duncan. **SP-DuncR** *Fr.* The Structure of Rime.

O painter of the fruits and flowers. Garden. John Greenleaf Whittier. **CP-WhitJ**

O Paleys [or palace], whylom [or whilom] croune [or crown] of houses all[e]. The Complaint of Troilus. Geoffrey Chaucer. **NOBE; OBEV** *Fr.* Troilus and Criseyde [or Criseide]. **CP-ChauG**

O parakeets & avocets, O immortelles. Old Man Goes South Again Alone. John Berryman. **CP-BerrJ**

O pardon, Cupid I confess my fault, sels. Mary Sidney, Countess of Montgomery Wroth. *Fr.* Pamphilia to Amphilanthus. **CP-WrotM**

O Passenger, pray list and catch. The Levelled Churchyard. Thomas Hardy. **CP-HardT**

O Peace! and dost thou with thy presence bless. On Peace. John Keats. **CP-KeatJ**

O Peace, that on a lilied bank dost love. Lines in the Manner of Spenser. Samuel Taylor Coleridge. *Fr.* Effusions. **CP-ColeS**

O peace! the fairest child of Heaven. To Peace. James Thomson *and* David Mallet. *Fr.* Alfred: A Masque. **CP-ThomJ**

O people-chosen! are ye not. To the Thirty-Ninth Congress. John Greenleaf Whittier. **CP-WhitJ**

O per se O, O per se O! O. Robert Ranke Graves. **CP-GravR**

O Personages. Daniel Gerard Hoffman. **SP-HoffD**

O Philly, happy be that day. Song. Robert Burns. **CP-BurnR**

O pillow cold and wet with tears! Cancelled Passage. Percy Bysshe Shelley. **CP-ShelP**

O Pino / What a bean-o! To Pino. David Herbert Lawrence. **CP-LawrD**

O pleasant exercise of hope and joy! William Wordsworth. **OBRV** *Fr.* Residence in France and French Revolution. *Fr.* The Prelude; Growth of a Poet's Mind [1805 vers.]. **CP-WorW3**

O[h!] pleasant exercise of hope and joy! William Wordsworth. **HAP; PoEL-4,** *book* 11, *ll.* 105–144; **FiP** *Fr.* France (Concluded). *Fr.* The Prelude; Growth of a Poet's Mind [1850 vers.]. **CP-WorW3**

(French Revolution, The.) **FiP,** *book* 11, *ll.* 105–144;

O pleasant port! O place of rest! Man to the Wound in Christ's Side. Robert Southwell. **CP-SoutR**

O pluck me quick the raven's quill. Melancholy. Christopher Smart. *Fr.* Hymns for the Amusement of Children. **SP-SmarC**

O Poesy! for thee I hold my pen. John Keats. **FHYEP** *Fr.* Sleep and Poetry. **CP-KeatJ**

O poet, come you haunting here. At a House in Hampstead. Thomas Hardy. **CP-HardT**

O poet rare and old! Astræa. John Greenleaf Whittier. **CP-WhitJ**

O poor Catullus, stupid long enough! Catullus. *See* Carmen 8: "Break off / fallen Catullus."

O poore distracted world, partly a slave. To the World. Thomas Campion. **CP-CampT**

O poortith cauld, and restless love. Song. Robert Burns. **CP-BurnR**

O pr / gress verily thou art m. Edward Estlin Cummings. **CP-CummE**

O praedestinata bis. May Lines. Gerard Manley Hopkins. **CP-HopkG**

O praise God in his holiness: praise him in the firmament of his power. Bible, *O.T. See* Psalm 150: "Praise ye the Lord. Praise God in his sanctuary."

O Praise the Lord, and bless his name. Bible, *O.T. See* Psalm 135: "Praise ye the Lord. Praise ye the name of the Lord; praise him, O ye servants of the Lord."

O praise ye the Lord, all ye nations. Psalm 117. Bible, *O.T. Fr.* Psalms. **CP-Psal**

O pretty village. . . aye, mine own home. To Say If You Love Someone. Kenneth Patchen. **CP-PatcK**

O prodigal son, O recreant daughter. Nicholas Vachel Lindsay. *Fr.* A Rhymed Address to All Renegade Campbellites, Exhorting Them to Return. *Fr.* Alexander Campbell. **CP-LindV**

O Pug! Stevie Smith. **CP-SmitS**

O purblind race of miserable men. Geraint and Enid. Tennyson. *Fr.* Idylls of the King. **CP-TennA**

O Purity, thou test. Annunciation of the Blessed Virgin. Christopher Smart. *Fr.* Hymns and Spiritual Songs for the Fasts and Festivals of the Church of England. **SP-SmarC**

O purple finch / please tell me why. Edward Estlin Cummings. **CP-CummE**

O Queen of Heaven. La Gretchen de Nos Jours (II). Stevie Smith. **CP-SmitS**

O Queen of virtues, whose sweet pow'r. Charity. Christopher Smart. *Fr.* Hymns for the Amusement of Children. **SP-SmarC**

O Qui Me—! Arthur Hugh Clough. **SP-ClouA**

O qui sonora coelites altos cheli. *?acc. by English translation.* Thomas Campion. **CP-CampT**

O quick floss silk of the Juventii, form. Catullus. *See* Carmen 24: "Best sprig of the clan."

O quick quick quick, quick hear the song-sparrow. Cape Ann. Thomas Stearns Eliot. **GoJo; NAEL-2; NoAM** *Fr.* Landscapes. **CP-ElioT**

O raging Fortune's withering blast. Robert Burns. **CP-BurnR**

O rain at seven. Virginia. Hart Crane. *Fr.* Three Songs. **NAAL-2** *Fr.* The Bridge. **CP-CranH**

O ram ridicule home, Cato, the jokes some. Catullus. *See* Carmen 56: "Matter for mirth, Cato, & a smile, A."

O rattlin, roarin Willie. Rattlin, Roarin Willie. Robert Burns. **CP-BurnR**

O Reader behold the Philosophers Grave. William Blake. **CP-BlakW**

O restless fingers—not that music make! Music. Walter de la Mare. **CP-DeLaW**

O river winding to the sea! Haverhill. John Greenleaf Whittier. **CP-WhitJ**

O rook your pearly gray ruff. The Convalescence. Charles Henri Ford. **SP-FordC**

O room of silences, alien land. The Mirror. Howard Nemerov. **CP-NemeH**

O Rose, thou art sick[!]. The Sick Rose. William Blake. **CP-BlakW** *Fr.* Songs of Experience.

O Rose, thou flower of flowers, thou fragrant wonder. The Rose. Christina Georgina Rossetti. **CP-RosC3**

O rose, who dares to name thee? A Dead Rose. Elizabeth Barrett Browning. **CP-BroEB**

O rosy fair and rosy sweet. The Ballad of the Lady Eglantine. George Meredith. **CP-MerG2**

O rough, rude, ready-witted R******. Epistle to J. R******, Enclosing Some Poems. Robert Burns. **CP-BurnR**

! / o(rounD)moon,how. Edward Estlin Cummings. **CP-CummE**

O Rourk's noble fare. *with music.* Hugh MacGowran, *tr. fr. Irish by* Jonathan Swift. **CP-SwifJ**

O ruined father dead, long sweetly rotten. For the Word Is Flesh. Stanley Jasspon Kunitz. **CP-KuniS**

O ruthless, perilous, imperious hate. Hilda Doolittle. *Fr.* Epigrams. **CP-DoolH**

O sacred Providence, who from end to end. George Herbert. **AngWe** *Fr.* Providence. **CP-HerbG**

O sacred Providence, who from end to end. Providence. George Herbert. **CP-HerbG**

O sad and heavy should I part. Sae Far Awa. Robert Burns. **CP-BurnR**

O sad man, now a long dead man. The Pair He Saw Pass. Thomas Hardy. **CP-HardT**

O sailor, come ashore. Christina Georgina Rossetti. **BoTP; FM** *Fr.* Sing-Song. **CP-RosC2**

O Sailor, Come Ashore. Christina Georgina Rossetti. **CP-RosC2**

O San Francisco lighting the truth of. Berkeley Pome. Al Young. **CP-YounA**

O! save ye Gods, omnipotent and kind. Seneca, *tr. by* Samuel Johnson. **CP-JohnS** *Fr.* Hercules Furens.

O saw ye bonny Lesley. Robert Burns. **CP-BurnR**

O saw ye my dearie, my Eppie Mcnab? Eppie McNab. Robert Burns. **CP-BurnR**

O saw ye my dearie, my Phely. Saw Ye My Phely (Quasi Dicat, Phillis). Robert Burns. **CP-BurnR**

O Saw Ye My Maggie. Robert Burns. **CP-BurnR**

O Scarlet Beauty with thy milk-white eyes. To a Toadstool. Wystan Hugh Auden. **CP-AudWJ**

O Sea!. . . 'Tis I, risen from death once more. To Helen. Paul Valéry, *tr. fr. French by* Delmore Schwartz. **SP-SchwD**

O seal the shining! this stillness binds the stars. The Firing. Kenneth Patchen. **CP-PatcK**

O seditious toxins of nostalgia. O. Charles Henri Ford. **SP-FordC**

O see what I have made! Homunculus. Louise Bogan. **CP-BogaL**

O Seraph, pause no more! The Seraphim. Elizabeth Barrett Browning. **CP-BroEB**

O shallow ground. Words to be Spoken. Archibald MacLeish. **CP-MacLA**

O She Is as Lovely-Often as Every Day. Kenneth Patchen. **CP-PatcK**

O she that made the brave appeal. George Meredith. *Fr.* France. **CP-MerG1**

O she was full of loving fuss. One of the Principal Causes of War. "Hugh MacDiarmid." **SP-MacDH**

O she whom I cannot abide. One Night in Oz. Ogden Nash. **CP-NashO**

O Shepherd with the bleeding Feet. The Good Shepherd. Christina Georgina Rossetti. **CP-RosC2**

O ship in a bottle. Ships in Bottles. David Herbert Lawrence. **CP-LawrD**

O shrive me Friar, my ghostly Friar! George Meredith. **CP-MerG2**

O shut your bright eyes that mine must endanger. At the Manger. Wystan Hugh Auden. *Fr.* For the Time Being; a Christmas Oratorio. **CP-AudeW**

O sight of pity, shame and dole! The Singer in the Prison. Walt Whitman. **CP-WhitW**

O, sing a new Song to the L———! A New Psalm for the Chapel of Kilmarnock, on the Thanksgiving-Day for His Majesty's Recovery. Robert Burns. **CP-BurnR**

O sing unto the Lord a new song; for he hath done marvellous [or marvelous] things. Psalm 98. Bible, O.T. **TrGrPo; TrJP** *Fr.* Psalms. **CP-Psal**

O sing unto the Lord a new song; let us make a joyful noise. Psalm 96. Bible, O.T. *Fr.* Psalms. **CP-Psal**

O Sister! couldst thou know as thou wilt know. Antigone. George Meredith. **CP-MerG1**

O sister of the shadow. Stanley Jasspon Kunitz. *Fr.* Meditations on Death. **CP-KuniS**

O sixteen hundred and ninety-one. The Two Witches. Robert Ranke Graves. **CP-GravR**

O skylark! I see thee and call thee joy! To a Skylark. George Meredith. **CP-MerG1**

O Slain for love of me, canst Thou be cold. Zion Said. Christina Georgina Rossetti. **CP-RosC3**

O sleep, the sky goes down behind the poplars. Louis Zukofsky. *Fr.* 29 Poems. **CP-ZukLS**

O sleeping falls the maiden snow. Kenneth Patchen. **CP-PatcK**

O Sleepless Night. James Schuyler. **CP-SchuJ**

O small St. Agnes, dressed in gold. A Prelude: For the Feast of St. Agnes. Thomas Merton. **CP-MertT**

O snake, you are an argument / for poetry. Psalm to Snake. Margaret Atwood. **SP-AtwM2**

O soft embalmer of the still midnight. To Sleep. John Keats. **CP-KeatJ**

O Solitude! If I Must With Thee Dwell. John Keats. **CP-KeatJ**

O Solitude! to thy sequester'd vale. By the Same. To Solitude. Charlotte Smith. **CP-SmitC**

O solo mio, hot diggety, nix 'I wather think I can'. Poem. Frank O'Hara. **SP-OharF**

O some will court and compliment. John Come Kiss Me Now. Robert Burns. **CP-BurnR**

O Son[ne] of God, who seeing two things. The Son. John Donne. **NOCV** *Fr.* A Litany. **CP-DonnJ**

O Sorrow! John Keats. *See* Song of the Indian Maid.

O Sorrow, cruel fellowship. Tennyson. **EBVVPR; EnVR; HAP; OAEL-2** *Fr.* In Memoriam A. H. H. **CP-TennA**

O sorrow it is. Kenneth Patchen. *Fr.* Wanderers of the Pale Wood. **CP-PatcK**

O Sorrow,/ Why dost borrow. Song of the Indian Maid. John Keats. **CH; NOBE; OAEP; OBEV** *Fr.* Endymion: Poetic Romance. **CP-KeatJ**

O Sorrow, wilt thou live with me. Tennyson. *Fr.* In Memoriam A. H. H. **CP-TennA**

O sovereign power of love! O grief! O balm! John Keats. **EnRP; OBNC** *Fr.* Endymion: Poetic Romance. **CP-KeatJ**

O sov'reign of an isle renown'd. On His Majesty's Sea Bathing. William Cowper. **CP-CowpW**

O Spirit, / spark my spark. Euripides, *tr. by* Hilda Doolittle ("H.D."). **CP-DoolH** *Fr.* Hippolytus.

O Spirit blest! / Whether th' eternal Throne around, *ll 80–90 of 1790 vers.* Samuel Taylor Coleridge. *Fr.* Monody on the Death of Chatterton. **CP-ColeS**

O spiteful bitter thought[!]. Assurance. George Herbert. **CP-HerbG**

O splendid to reach a craft and creed. The Magic Car. Kenneth Patchen. **CP-PatcK**

O stamping–ground of the shod Word! So hard. Shiloh Church, 1862: Twenty–Three Thousand. Geoffrey Hill. *Fr.* Locust Songs. **CP-HillG**

O Star of France (1870–71). Walt Whitman. **CP-WhitW**

O Star (the fairest one in sight). Robert Frost. **CP-FrosR** (Take Something Like a Star.) **CP-FrosR**

O staring eyes, searchlight disks. Van der Lubbe. Stephen Spender. **CP-SpenS**

O! Start a Revolution. David Herbert Lawrence. **CP-LawrD**

O State prayer-founded! never hung. To Pennsylvania. John Greenleaf Whittier. **CP-WhitJ**

O Statue of Liberty Spouse of Europa Destroyer of Past Present Future. Stotras to Kali Destroyer of Illusions. Allen Ginsberg. **CP-GinsA**

O stay mine eyes, shed nott thes fruitles tears. Sonnet 47. Mary Sidney, Countess of Montgomery Wroth. *Fr.* Pamphilia to Amphilanthus. **CP-WrotM**

O stay! sweet is the least delay. The Farewell Song. Thomas Campion. *Fr.* The Ayres that Were Sung and Played, *at* Brougham Castle *in* Westmerland, in the Kings Entertainment. **CP-CampT**

O stay, sweet warbling woodlark stay. Address to the Woodlark. Robert Burns. **CP-BurnR**

O stay that covetous hand! First turn all eye. Upon the Curtain[e] of Lucasta's Picture [It Was Thus Wrought]. Richard Lovelace. **CP-LoveR**

O stealing time, the subject of delay, *speech of Philoclea.* Sir Philip Sidney. **SP-SidnP** *Fr.* Arcadia.

O steer her up and "haud" her gaun. Robert Burns. **CP-BurnR**

O stiffly shapen houses that change not. Suburbs on a Hazy Day. David Herbert Lawrence. **CP-LawrD**

O storied vale of Merrimac. One of the Signers. John Greenleaf Whittier. **CP-WhitJ**

O stormy, stormy world. Happiness Makes Up in Height for What It Lacks in Length. Robert Frost. **CP-FrosR**

O strange devices that alone divide. Eyes. Walter de la Mare. **CP-DeLaW**

O stream, descending to the sea. Arthur Hugh Clough. **SP-ClouA**

Ô[h] strive not[t] still to heap[e] disdain[e] on me[e]. Sonnet 6. Mary Sidney, Countess of Montgomery Wroth. **NOSC** *Fr.* Pamphilia to Amphilanthus. **CP-WrotM**

O strong, upwelling prayers of faith. The Hermit of the Thebaid. John Greenleaf Whittier. **CP-WhitJ**

O Sun! Instigator of cocks! Salute. Archibald MacLeish. **CP-MacLA**

O Sun of Real Peace. Walt Whitman. **CP-WhitW**

O sun! take off thy hood of clouds. Ralph Waldo Emerson. **CP-EmerR**

O Sun! With your eye of a great bird. Maya Against Itzas. Charles Olson. **CP-OlsoC**

O sundown, sundown / Like blood on Sion! *ad. from* Micah 3. Thomas Merton. **CP-MertT**

O! Superstition is the Giant Shadow. Superstition. Samuel Taylor Coleridge. **CP-ColeS**

O Swallow, Swallow, flying, flying South. Tennyson. **CBLP; PIP** *Fr.* There sinks the nebulous star we call the Sun. *Fr.* The Princess. **CP-TennA**

O, sweep of stars over Harlem streets. Stars. Langston Hughes. **SP-HughL**

O sweet – attentive to the pray'r. Mercy. Christopher Smart. *Fr.* Hymns for the Amusement of Children. **SP-SmarC**

O sweet delight, O more than human[e] bliss[e]. Song. Thomas Campion. **CP-CampT**

O sweet escape! O smiling flight! The Communion. Thomas Merton. **CP-MertT**

O sweet everlasting Voices be still. The Everlasting Voices. William Butler Yeats. **CP-YeatW**

O Sweet Irrational Worship. Thomas Merton. **CP-MertT; SP-MertT**

O sweet sincerity!— / Where modern methods be. To Sincerity. Thomas Hardy. **CP-HardT**

O sweet spontaneous. Edward Estlin Cummings. **CP-CummE; SP-CummE**

O sweet To-morrow! Song of Hope. Thomas Hardy. **CP-HardT**

O sweet woods, the delight of solitariness! Sir Philip Sidney. **SP-SidnP** *Fr.* Arcadia.

     Sweetly Empty Woods. **CBCK**

O[h] sweet woods, the delight of solitariness! Sweetly Empty Woods. Sir Philip Sidney. **CBCK** *Fr.* O sweet woods, the delight of solitariness! **SP-SidnP** *Fr.* Arcadia.

O swiftly, re-light the flame. Hilda Doolittle. **NALW** *Fr.* Tribute to the Angels. **CP-DoolH**

O Sylvia, Sylvia. Sylvia's Death. Anne Sexton. **CP-SextA**

O take my gift. At Croton. Hilda Doolittle. **CP-DoolH**

O take my hand Walt Whitman! Salut au Monde! Walt Whitman. **CP-WhitW**

O Tan-Faced Prairie-Boy. Walt Whitman. **CP-WhitW**

O Taste and See. Denise Levertov. **CP-LeveD**

O te te nimis, & nimis beatum! *Eng. trans. included.* Richard Crashaw. **CP-CrasR**

O tears, no tears, but rain from beauty's skies. Sonnet 100. Sir Philip Sidney. **Son** *Fr.* Astrophil and Stella. **SP-SidnP**

O tell me, friends, while yet we part. Sectantem levia nervi deficiunt. Arthur Hugh Clough. **SP-ClouA**

O tell me, Harper, wherefore flow. On the Massacre of Glencoe, 1692. Sir Walter Scott. **SP-ScotW**

O tell me of the Russians, Communist, my son! Communist. John Berryman. **CP-BerrJ**

O tell me where, in lands or seas. Ballade of the Ladies of Time Past. François Villon, *tr. fr. French by* Richard Wilbur. **CP-WilbR**

O tenderly the haughty day. Ode Sung in the Town Hall. Ralph Waldo Emerson. **CP-EmerR**

O terrible is the highest thing. Kenneth Patchen. **CP-PatcK**

O th' oppressive, irksome weight. Uncertainty in Love. Samuel Taylor Coleridge. **CP-ColeS**

O that a chariot of cloud were mine! Percy Bysshe Shelley. **CP-ShelP**

O that a week could be an age, and we. To James Rice. John Keats. **CP-KeatJ**

O that I could a sin once see! Sin. George Herbert. **CP-HerbG**

O That I Had Ne'er Been Married. Robert Burns. **CP-BurnR**

O that I knew how all thy lights combine. The Holy Scriptures (2). George Herbert. **CP-HerbG**

O! that I might but now as senceles bee. Mary Sidney, Countess of Montgomery Wroth. *Fr.* Part 1. *Fr.* Urania. **CP-WrotM**

O That I Now. Algernon Charles Swinburne. **SP-SwinA** *Fr.* Atalanta in Calydon.

O that I were where Helen lies. *see also* Helen of Kirconnell. Robert Burns. **CP-BurnR**

O, that joy so soon should waste! Ben Jonson. **CP-JonsB** *Fr.* Cynthia's Revels.

"O that mastering tune!" And up in the bed. In the Nuptial Chamber. Thomas Hardy. **InPK** *Fr.* Satires of Circumstance in Fifteen Glimpses. **CP-HardT**

O! that noe day would ever more appeere. Sonnet 6. Mary Sidney, Countess of Montgomery Wroth. *Fr.* Pamphilia to Amphilanthus. **CP-WrotM**

O that our dreamings all, of sleep or wake. John Keats. **OAEL-2** *Fr.* To J. H. Reynolds, Esq. **CP-KeatJ**

O that the rain would come—the rain in big battalions. Precursors. Louis MacNeice. **CP-MacNL**

O[h] that 'twere possible. Tennyson. **BoLoP; HBV; IMW; NAEL-2; NOBE; NOBVV; OAEL-2; OBEV; OBVV; PoE** *Fr.* Maud [A Monodrama]. **CP-TennA**

O[h] that you were yourself! but, love, you are. Sonnet 13. William Shakespeare. **OAEP; TEP** *Fr.* Sonnets. **CP-ShaWS**

O that's the lassie o' my heart. Robert Burns. *See* Song: "O wat ye what that lo'es me."

O the beautiful garment. The Flowering of the Rod. Hilda Doolittle. **CP-DoolH**

O the bitter shame and sorrow. Hymn. Christina Georgina Rossetti. **CP-RosC3**

O the clammy cold November. Apathy and Enthusiasm. Herman Melville. **SP-MelvH**

O the clear moment, when from the mouth. Fragment of a Lost Poem. Robert Ranke Graves. **CP-GravR**

O the crossbones of Galway. Galway. Louis MacNeice. **OxBI** *Fr.* The Closing Album. **CP-MacNL**

O the dummies in the windows! Dummies. Randall Jarrell. **CP-JarrR**

O the gentle fool / He fell in love. Antipoem 1. Thomas Merton. **CP-MertT**

O the green glimmer of apples in the orchard. Ballad of Another Ophelia. David Herbert Lawrence. **CP-LawrD**

O the jungle is beautiful the jungle is wild. Recollection of Childhood. Richard Eberhart. **CP-EberR**

O the Lord is good. *ad. fr.* Psalm 71. Thomas Merton. **CP-MertT**

O the North is a wild land, a splendid and a fair. The North. Wystan Hugh Auden. **CP-AudW3**

O the old wall here! How I could pass. Prologue. Robert Browning. **CP-BroR2**

O the opal and the sapphire of that wandering western sea. Beeny Cliff. Thomas Hardy. **CP-HardT**

O the phoenix is gone and the unicorn. At the Zoo. Isabella Gardner. **CP-GardI**

O the precipice Titanic. A Canticle. Herman Melville. **SP-MelvH**

O the Sad Moon. Sir Philip Sidney. *See* Sonnet 31: "With how sad steps, O Moon, thou climb'st the skies."

O the sledbirds rides over the willow. Kenneth Patchen. **CP-PatcK**

O the slums of Dublin fermenting with children. Slum Song. Louis MacNeice. **CP-MacNL**

O the snows last so long. Despair. Richard Eberhart. **CP-EberR**

O the stale old dogs who pretend to guard. The Young and Their Moral Guardians. David Herbert Lawrence. **CP-LawrD**

O the sun comes up-up-up in the opening. Edward Estlin Cummings. **CP-CummE**

O the valley in the summer where I and my John. Wystan Hugh Auden. **PIP** *Fr.* Twelve Songs. **CP-AudeW**

(Johnny.) **PIP**

O the wind, the wind, the wind doth blow. Song. George Meredith. **CP-MerG2**

O Theos Meta Sou. Arthur Hugh Clough. **SP-ClouA**

O there is blessing in this gentle breeze. Introduction—Childhood and School-Time. William Wordsworth. **EnRP; FHYEP** *Fr.* The Prelude; Growth of a Poet's Mind [1850 vers.]. **CP-WorW3**

O there is blessing in this gentle breeze. Introduction—Childhood and School-Time. William Wordsworth. *Fr.* The Prelude; Growth of a Poet's Mind [1805 vers.]. **CP-WorW3**

O there is blessing in this gentle breeze. William Wordsworth. **OAEL-2** *Fr.* Introduction—Childhood and School-Time. **EnRP; FHYEP** *Fr.* The Prelude; Growth of a Poet's Mind [1850 vers.]. **CP-WorW3**

O there is peace here! There scarcely lifts a sound. The Mill. Wystan Hugh Auden. **CP-AudWJ**

O there's a laughy light. Absent from the United States. Al Young. **CP-YounA**

O these wakeful[l] wounds of thine! On the Wounds of Our Crucified Lord. Richard Crashaw. **CP-CrasR**

O they canna' do without it. Song. George Meredith. **CP-MerG2**

O th'hate I move love. Quarry it fact I am, for that's so re queries. Catullus. *See* Carmen 85: "I hate and I love. And if you ask me how."

O this is no my ain lassie. Song. Robert Burns. **CP-BurnR**

O This Is Not Spring. Kay Boyle. **CP-BerrW**

O thou bright Sun! beneath the dark blue line. Evening: To Harriet. Percy Bysshe Shelley. **CP-ShelP**

O thou dread Pow'r, who reign'st above! Lying at a Reverend Friend's House One Night, the Author Left the Following *Verses* in the Room Where He Slept. Robert Burns. **CP-BurnR**

O Thou, far off and here, whole and broken. To the Holy Spirit. Wendell Berry. **CP-BerrW**

O Thou Father of splendor, Giver of light. *tr. of* "O Tu Pater splendoris Dator luminis." Thomas Merton, *tr. fr. Latin by the author.* **CP-MertT**

O Thou, fierce God of armies, Mars the red. Queen Annelida and False Arcite. Geoffrey Chaucer. **CP-BroEB**

O Thou great Being! what Thou art. A Prayer, under the Pressure of Violent Anguish. Robert Burns. **CP-BurnR**

O thou immortal deity. Fragment. Percy Bysshe Shelley. **CP-ShelP**

O thou in heaven and earth the only place. The Plan of Salvation. John Milton. **WGRP** *Fr.* Book III. *Fr.* Paradise Lost. **CP-MiltJ**

O thou, in whom we live and move. Grace after Meat. Robert Burns. **CP-BurnR**

O thou Most High, who rulest all. Upon My Dear and Loving Husband His Going into England. Anne Bradstreet. **CP-BradA**

O thou Mother Oberoi / Crosseyed goddess of death. Songs of Experience; India, One. Thomas Merton. **CP-MertT**

O thou, my lovely boy, who in thy power. Sonnet 126. William Shakespeare. **HeIP; NAEL-1** *Fr.* Sonnets. **CP-ShaWS**

O Thou my monster, Thou my guide. Prayer in Mid-Passage. Louis MacNeice. **CP-MacNL**

O Thou my soule, Jehovah blesse, *fr.* Bay Psalm Book. Bible, *O.T. See* Psalm 103: "Bless the Lord, O my soul. . . ."

O Thou, of British Orators the chief. Catullus. *See* Carmen 49: "Silver-tongued among the sons of Rome."

O, Thou Opening, O. Theodore Roethke. **CP-RoetT**

O thou pale Orb, that silent shines. The Lament. Occasioned by the Unfortunate Issue of a Friend's Amour. Robert Burns. **CP-BurnR**

O thou that after toil and storm. Tennyson. **PeECV** *Fr.* In Memoriam A. H. H. **CP-TennA**

O thou that from thy mansion. For My Funeral. Alfred Edward Housman. **CP-HousA**

O thou that hearest the prayers of thine. In Thankful Acknowledgement for the Letters I Received from My Husband Out Of England. Anne Bradstreet. **CP-BradA**

O Thou, that in the heavens does dwell. Holy Willie's Prayer. Robert Burns. **CP-BurnR**

O thou, that sit'st upon a throne. Christopher Smart. **OxAEP-1** *Fr.* A Song to David. **SP-SmarC**

O Thou, that sit'st upon a throne. A Song to David. Christopher Smart. **SP-SmarC**

O[h] thou that swing'st [*or* swingest] upon the waving hair[e] [*or* ear *or* eare]. Richard Lovelace. **CP-LoveR**

(Grasse-Hopper, The.) **CP-LoveR**

O thou that with surpassing Glory crowned. Satan's Soliloquy. John Milton. **LiTB; OBS** *Fr.* Book IV. **OAEL-1** *Fr.* Paradise Lost. **CP-MiltJ**

O Thou, the first, the greatest friend. The *First Six Verses* of the Ninetieth Psalm. Robert Burns. **CP-BurnR**

O thou the span of whose Omnipotence. *ad. fr. the Latin of* Grotius. Richard Crashaw. **CP-CrasR**

O thou, the wonder of all day[e]s! The Dirge of Jephthah's Daughter. Robert Herrick. **CP-HerrR**

O Thou to whom the musical white spring. Edward Estlin Cummings. **CP-CummE**

O thou, to whose fury the nations are. King Edward the Third. William Blake. **CP-BlakW**

O thou undaunted daughter of desires! Richard Crashaw. **HAP; NOBE; OBEV** *Fr.* The Flaming Heart. **CP-CrasR**

(Upon the Book and Picture of the Seraphical Saint Teresa.) **NOBE; OBEV**

O Thou unknown, Almighty Cause. A Prayer, in the Prospect of Death. Robert Burns. **CP-BurnR**

O thou! whatever title suit thee. Address to the Deil. Robert Burns. **CP-BurnR**

O thou which to search out the secret parts. To Mr S. B. John Donne. **CP-DonnJ**

O thou who giving helm and sword. The Dreamer. Walter de la Mare. **CP-DeLaW**

O Thou, who kindly dost [*or* doth] provide. A Grace before Dinner, Extempore. Robert Burns. **CP-BurnR**

O Thou who movest onward with a mind. Gabriello Chiabrera, *tr. fr. Italian by* William Wordsworth. **CP-WorW1**

O thou, who passest through [*or* thro'] our valleys [*or* vallies] in. To Summer. William Blake. **CP-BlakW**

O thou who pausest here. The Thorn. Walter de la Mare. **CP-DeLaW**

O thou, who plumed with strong desire. The Two Spirits[: An Allegory]. Percy Bysshe Shelley. **CP-ShelP**

O thou! who rollest in yon azure field. A Version of Ossian's Address to the Sun. Byron. **CP-Byron**

O thou! who sleep'st where hazle-bands entwine. Supposed to Have Been Written in a Church-yard, over the Grave of a Young Woman of Nineteen. Charlotte Smith. **CP-SmitC**

O thou who tell'st me that all hope is over. Christina Georgina Rossetti. **CP-RosC3**

O tuou whom Poetry [*or* Poesy] abhors. Robert Burns. **CP-BurnR**

(To Mr. E—— on His Translation of and Commentaries on Martial.) **CP-BurnR**

O thou, whose all-creating hands sustain. Boethius. **CP-PopeA** *Fr.* Consolation of Philosophy, The ("De Consolacione Philosophie"). **CP-ChauG**

O Thou Whose Face Hath Felt the Winter's Wind. John Keats. **CP-KeatJ**

O thou! whose fancies from afar are brought. To H. C.[, Six Years Old]. William Wordsworth. **CP-WorW1**

O thou whose image in the shrine. Hymnos Aymnos. Arthur Hugh Clough. **SP-ClouA**

O thou, whose mighty palace roof doth hang. Hymn to Pan. John Keats. **ChER; MeMBP; OBRV; PoEL-4** *Fr.* Endymion: Poetic Romance. **CP-KeatJ**

O Thou! whose name too often is profaned. To Friendship. Charlotte Smith. **CP-SmitC**

O thou whose pow'r o'er moving worlds presides. Boethius, *tr. by* Samuel Johnson. **CP-JohnS; OBVE; TrPWD** *Fr.* Consolation of Philosophy, The ("De Consolacione Philosophie"). **CP-ChauG**

O Thou, whose presence went before. Hymn. John Greenleaf Whittier. **CP-WhitJ**

O Thou whose reason guides the universe. Boethius, *tr. fr. Latin.* **MLL,** *tr. by* Helen Waddell; *Fr.* Consolation of Philosophy, The ("De Consolacione Philosophie"). **CP-ChauG**

O thou whose tender serious eyes. To Myra. James Thomson. **CP-ThomJ**

O thou wild Fancy, check thy wing! No more. Written in Early Youth, the Time an Autumnal Evening. Samuel Taylor Coleridge. *Fr.* Effusions. **CP-ColeS**

O thou, with dewy locks, who lookest down. To Spring. William Blake. **CP-BlakW**

O thou yclep'd by vulgar sons of Men. Farewell Petition to J.C.H., Esq. Byron. **CP-Byron**

O thought, fly to her when the end of day. Old Memory. William Butler Yeats. **CP-YeatW**

O thrilling voice of Zeus. Oedipus Rex. Sophocles, *tr. by* Stephen Spender. **CP-SpenS** *Fr.* Oedipus the King [*or* Oedipus Rex].

O throw it away, throw it all away on the wind. Song for a Revolutionary Love. Sylvia Plath. **CP-PlatS**

O thy bright eyes must answer now. Emily Brontë. **CP-BronE**

("Oh, thy bright eyes must answer now.") **CP-BronE**

(Plead for Me.) **CP-BronE**

O thy flamed cheek, / Those locks with weeping wet. Forgiveness. Walter de la Mare. **CP-DeLaW**

O Time the fatal wrack of mortal things. Anne Bradstreet. **PBWP; WPOW** *Fr.* Contemplations. **CP-BradA**

O Time—the heedless child you are! The Moment. Walter de la Mare. **CP-DeLaW**

O Time, whence comes the Mother's moody look amid her labours. The Lacking Sense. Thomas Hardy. **CP-HardT**

O times most bad. Upon the Troublesome Times. Robert Herrick. **CP-HerrR**

O 'tis my delight / In the dead of the night. George Meredith. **CP-MerG2**

O to Be a Dragon. Marianne Craig Moore. **CP-MoorM**

O to be in finland. Edward Estlin Cummings. **CP-CummE; SP-CummE**

O to break loose, like the chinook. Waking Early Sunday Morning. Robert Lowell. **SP-LoweR**

O to make the most jubilant song! A Song of Joys. Walt Whitman. **CP-WhitW**

O tongue / licking. To an Old Jaundiced Woman. William Carlos Williams. **CP-WilW1**

O too dull brain, O unpiercing nerves. The Revenant. Archibald MacLeish. **CP-MacLA**

O transient voyager of heaven! To a Wreath of Snow. Emily Brontë. **CP-BronE**

O trip and skip, Elvire! Link arm in arm with me! Fifine at the Fair. Robert Browning. **CP-BroR2**

O truant Muse, what shall be thy amends. Sonnet 101. William Shakespeare. *Fr.* Sonnets. **CP-ShaWS**

O true and tried, so well and long. Tennyson. **OAEL-2** *Fr.* In Memoriam A. H. H. **CP-TennA**

"And, star and system rolling past." **ImOP**

"O happy hour, and happier hours." **EnVR**

O truly, Lily was a lulu. Pop Smash, Out of Echo Chamber. John Updike. **CP-UpdiJ**

O Tu Pater splendoris Dator luminis. *see also English tr.* Prayer of Thanksgiving Written for Victor Hammer, A ("O Thou Father of splendor, Giver of light"). Thomas Merton. **CP-MertT**

O universal Mother, who dost keep. Hymn to Earth the Mother of All. *Unknown.* **CP-ShelP** *Fr.* Homeric Hymns.

O uommibatto / Agil, giocondo. Christina Georgina Rossetti. **CP-RosC3**

O Urizen! Creator of men! mistaken Demon of heaven! Take Thy Bliss, O Man. William Blake. **EnRP** *Fr.* Visions of the Daughters of Albion. **CP-BlakW**

O Voice of Approbation, bless. Munificence and Modesty. Christopher Smart. **SP-SmarC**

O. W. Holmes on His Eightieth Birthday. John Greenleaf Whittier. **CP-WhitJ**

O wander not so far away! Emily Brontë. **CP-BronE**

O, wast thou with me, dearest, then. Tennyson. **MeMBP** *Fr.* In Memoriam A. H. H. **CP-TennA**

O wastfull Riot, never well content. Lucan, *tr.* by Sir Walter Ralegh. **CP-RaleW** *Fr.* Pharsalia.

O wat ye wha that lo'es me. Song. Robert Burns. **CP-BurnR**

O wat ye wha's in yon town. Song. Robert Burns. **CP-BurnR**

O Wave God who broke through me today. Burning Island. Gary Snyder. **CP-SnydG**

O, We Are the Outcasts. Charles Bukowski. **SP-BukC2**

O weary Champion of the Cross, lie still. Cardinal Newman. Christina Georgina Rossetti. **CP-RosC3**

O weary mariners, here shaded, fed. Randall Jarrell. **CP-JarrR**

O well for him whose will is strong! Will. Tennyson. **CP-TennA**

O were I on Parnassus hill. Robert Burns. **CP-BurnR**

O! were I one of the Olympian twelve. Extracts from an Opera. John Keats. **CP-KeatJ**

O Were My Love Yon Lilac[k] Fair. Robert Burns. **CP-BurnR**
  O Gin My Love Were Yon Red Rose. **GBP**

O [or Oh] Wert Thou in the Cauld Blast. Robert Burns. **CP-BurnR**

O wert thou, Love, but near me. Robert Burns. *See* English Song.

O Western Wind. George Oppen. **CP-OppeG**

O wha my babie-clouts will buy? The Rantin' Dog, the Daddie o't. Robert Burns. **CP-BurnR**

O wha will to Saint Stephen's house. The Fête Champetre. Robert Burns. **CP-BurnR**

O wha'll m-w me now, my jo. Wha'll M-w Me Now. Robert Burns. **CP-BurnR**

O whar did ye get that hauver-meal bannock? Bonie Dundee. Robert Burns. **CP-BurnR**

O[h] what a cunning guest. Confession. George Herbert. **CP-HerbG**

O what a loud and fearful shriek was there. Koskiusko. Samuel Taylor Coleridge. **EnRP** *Fr.* Effusions. **CP-ColeS**

"O what a mess of judgment we have made". Delmore Schwartz. **SP-SchwD** *Fr.* Genesis.

O what a physical effect it has on me. In Love with You. Kenneth Koch. **SP-KochK**

O What a Revolution! Kenneth Patchen. **CP-PatcK**

O what a silence is this wilderness! Gerard Manley Hopkins. **CP-HopkG**

O, what a thing is man! how far from power. Giddiness. George Herbert. **CP-HerbG**

O what an endelesse worke have I in hand. Edmund Spenser. **MOS** *Fr.* The Faerie Queene. **CP-Spens**

O what are heroes prophets men. Ralph Waldo Emerson. **CP-EmerR**

O what astonishment if you. Spite of Mirrors. Robert Ranke Graves. **CP-GravR**

O [or Oh or Ah], what can ail thee, knight-at-arms [or wretched wight]. La Belle Dame Sans Merci. John Keats. **CP-KeatJ**

O what could be more nice. Light Listened. Theodore Roethke. **CP-RoetT**

O what has made that sudden noise? The Ghost of Roger Casement. William Butler Yeats. **CP-YeatW**

O What have I to do. Ralph Waldo Emerson. **CP-EmerR**

O what is Heaven but the fellowship. Ralph Waldo Emerson. **CP-EmerR**

O What Is That Sound [Which So Thrills the Ear]. Wystan Hugh Auden. **CP-AudeW**

O what to me the little room. The Heart of the Woman. William Butler Yeats. **CP-YeatW**

O, what undeserved cruelty. Sir Thomas Wyatt. **CP-WyatT**

O what unhop't for sweet supply! Thomas Campion. **CP-CampT**

O what's the gain, my worthy Sir. The Forbidden Banns. Thomas Hardy. **CP-HardT**

O what's the weather in a Beard? Dinky. Theodore Roethke. **CP-RoetT**

O when I grunted, over lines and her. Images of Elspeth. John Berryman. **CP-BerrJ**

O when I take my love out walking. Kenneth Patchen. **CP-PatcK**

O when in San Fransisco do. Scenic. John Updike. **CP-UpdiJ**

O when she cam ben she bobbed fu' law. When She Cam Ben She Bobbed. Robert Burns. **CP-BurnR**

O when the world's at peace. The Mad Farmer's Love Song. Wendell Berry. **CP-BerrW**

O when you were little, you were really big. Duet. Theodore Roethke. **CP-RoetT**

O whence do you come. The Sailor's Mother. Thomas Hardy. **CP-HardT**

"O where are you going?" said reader to rider. Wystan Hugh Auden. **CMoP; CoGr; FaBoCh; LiTB; LiTM; MeMAP; NOBE; NoAM;**

OAEL-2; SoSe; UV *Fr.* Five Songs ("What's in your mind, my dove, my coney"). **CP-AudeW**

(Epilogue: " 'O where are you going?' said reader to rider.") **FaBoCh**

(Song: " 'O where are you going?' said reader to rider.") **OAEL-2**

O where hae ye been, Lord Ronald, my son? Lord Ronald My Son. Robert Burns. **CP-BurnR**

O where have I wandered—out. Marsden Hartley. **CP-HartM**

O where is it, the wilderness. Gerard Manley Hopkins. **CP-HopkG**

O where would those choleric boys. Wystan Hugh Auden. *Fr.* Shorts [1948–1957] ("At peace under this mandarin, sleep, Lucina"). **CP-AudeW**

O whistle, and I'll come to you [or ye], my lad. Robert Burns. **CP-BurnR**
  (Song: "O whistle, and I'll come to ye, my lad.") **CP-BurnR**

O who can ever gaze his fill. Death's Echo. Wystan Hugh Auden. **CP-AudeW**

O [or Oh], who shall from this dungeon raise. A Dialogue between the Soul and [the] Body. Andrew Marvell. **CP-MarvA**

O who will give me tears? Come all ye springs. Grief. George Herbert. **CP-HerbG**

O who will share with me. Epithalamion. John Hewitt. **CP-HewiJ**

O who will show me those delights on high? Heaven. George Herbert. **CP-HerbG**

O who'll get me a healthy child. A Practical Woman. Thomas Hardy. **CP-HardT**

O why did we uncover to view. The Clasped Skeleton. Thomas Hardy. **CP-HardT**

O, why judge Myrrhina. Myrrhina. Robert Ranke Graves. **CP-GravR**

O why the deuce should I repine. Extempore. Robert Burns. **CP-BurnR**

O Why Was I Born With a Different Face? William Blake. (To Thomas Butts, 16 August 1803.) **CP-BlakW**

O Wife Unmasked. Leonard Cohen. **CP-CoheL**

O Wild Chaos! Richard Eberhart. **CP-EberR**

O wild West Wind, thou breath of Autumn's being. Ode to the West Wind. Percy Bysshe Shelley. **CP-ShelP**

O Willie brew'd a peck o' maut. Willie Brew'd [or Brewed] a Peck o' Maut. Robert Burns. **CP-BurnR**

O wilt thou go wi' me, sweet Tibbie Dunbar. Tibbie Dunbar. Robert Burns. **CP-BurnR**

O wind, where have you been. Christina Georgina Rossetti. **CP-RosC2**

O wind, why do you never rest. Christina Georgina Rossetti. **CP-RosC2**

O Winter! bar thine adamantine doors. To Winter. William Blake. **CP-BlakW**

O winter, what a deadly foe. Impromptu on Winter. John Clare. **SP-ClarJ**

O withering seas. George Oppen. **NNaP** *Fr.* Some San Francisco Poems. **CP-OppeG**

O woe is me for the merry life. The Lament of the Border Cattle Thief. Rudyard Kipling. **CP-KiplR**

O women, kneeling by your altar-rails long hence. The Lover Speaks to the Hearers of His Songs in Coming Days. William Butler Yeats. **CP-YeatW**

O wonderful nonsense of lotions of Lucky Tiger. Haircut. Karl Shapiro. **SP-ShapK**

"O words are lightly spoken." The Rose Tree. William Butler Yeats. **CP-YeatW**

O words, which fall like summer dew on me!, *speech of Dametas.* Sir Philip Sidney. **SP-SidnP** *Fr.* Arcadia.

O world, I cannot hold thee close enough! God's World. Edna St. Vincent Millay. **CP-MillE**

O world! O life! O time! Lament, A. Percy Bysshe Shelley. **CP-ShelP**

O World of Many Worlds. Wilfred Owen. **CP-OwenW**

O worthy of belief I hold it was. Pan and Luna. Robert Browning. **CP-BroR2**

O ye red-blushing summer roses, ye. Floral Teaching. Christina Georgina Rossetti. **CP-RosC3**

O Ye Tongues. Anne Sexton. **CP-SextA**
  First Psalm.
  Second Psalm.
  Third Psalm. **NALW**
  Fourth Psalm.
  Fifth Psalm.
  Sixth Psalm.
  Seventh Psalm.
  Eighth Psalm.
  Ninth Psalm.
  Tenth Psalm.

O [or A or Oh] ye wha are sae guid yoursel. Address to the Unco Guid, or the Rigidly Righteous. Robert Burns. **CP-BurnR**

O ye, who are not dead and fit. Christina Georgina Rossetti. **CP-RosC2**

O ye who love today, / Turn away / From Patience with her silver ray. Christina Georgina Rossetti. **CP-RosC2**

O ye who tread the Narrow Way. Buddha at Kamakura. Rudyard Kipling. **CP-KiplR**

O ye whose cheek the tear of pity stains. For the Author's Father. Robert Burns. **CP-BurnR**

O years [or yeares]! and age! farewell. Eternity [or Eternitie]. Robert Herrick. **CP-HerrR**

O yes—you understand, I say. Hilda Doolittle. **NALW** *Fr.* Tribute to the Angels. **CP-DoolH**

O yet how early, and before her time. Ben Jonson. **CP-JonsB** *Fr.* Oberon, the Fairy Prince.

O you are sad on Twelfth Night. Burning the Holly. Thomas Hardy. **CP-HardT**

O you chorus of indolent reviewers. Hendecasyllabics. Tennyson. **CP-TennA**

O you Dr. Ycas you! A Bitter Life. John Updike. **CP-UpdiJ**

O you hard-boiled conservatives, and you soft-boiled liberals. Hard-Boiled Conservatives. David Herbert Lawrence. **CP-LawrD**

O you so long dead. To My Brother: Killed: Hammont Wood: October, 1918. Louise Bogan. **CP-BogaL**

O you that hear this voice. Sixth Song. Sir Philip Sidney. **OBSC** *Fr.* Astrophil and Stella. **SP-SidnP**

O! You the Virgins nine! Hymne to the Muses, A. Robert Herrick. **CP-HerrR**

O you who lose the art of hope. The Illinois Village. Nicholas Vachel Lindsay. *Fr.* A Gospel of Beauty. **CP-LindV**

O You Whom I Often and Silently Come. Walt Whitman. **CP-WhitW**

O younge [or yonge] fres[s]he folkes, he or she. Love Unfeigned. Geoffrey Chaucer. **LO; NOBE; OBEV; OxBM** *Fr.* Troilus and Criseyde [or Criseide]. **CP-ChauG**

O youth whose heart is right. The Sage to the Young Man. Alfred Edward Housman. **CP-HousA**

O yr facing reality now—. Broken Back Blues. Robert Creeley. **CP-CreeR**

Oa-xa-ca! Oa-xa-ca! Song for a Marimba. Malcolm Lowry. **CP-LowrM**

Oafishness Sells Good, Like an Advertisement Should. Ogden Nash. **CP-NashO**

Oak, The. Richard Eberhart. **CP-EberR**

Oak and Lily. Ben Jonson. *See* It Is Not Growing Like a Tree.

Oak and the Brere, The. Edmund Spenser. **OBSC** *Fr.* February. *Fr.* The Shepheardes [or Shepeards or Shepherd's] Calender. **CP-Spens**

Oak and the Broom, The; A Pastoral. William Wordsworth. **CP-WorW1**

Oak Arms. Carl Sandburg. **CP-SandC**

Oak burns steady and hot and long. Shadows of the Burning. Marge Piercy. **SP-PierM**

Oak grove's, The. Waking. Archie Randolph Ammons. **SP-AmmoA**

Oak inns creak in their joints as light declines, The. Derek Walcott. **CP-WalcD** *Fr.* Midsummer.

Oak-Leaves, The. Edna St. Vincent Millay. **CP-MillE**

Oak leaves as big as a gray squirrel's ear. Mountain Corn Song. Louise McNeill. **SP-McNeL**

Oak Leaves Are Hands. Wallace Stevens. **CP-StevW**

Oak oak! like like / it then. Drunken Winter. Joseph Ceravolo. **SP-CeraJ**

Oak of Guernica! Tree of holier power. William Wordsworth. **CP-WorW1**

Oak Openings. Donald Davie. **CP-DavDo**

Oak trees lean their elbows on, The. Blue Morning Glories. Peter Meinke. **SP-MeinP**

Oak twig drops, An. Acorns. Donald Hall. **CP-HallD**

Oaks and dark pines, remote, the northern forest. Hayden Carruth. *Fr.* The Sleeping Beauty. **CP-CarHL**

Oaks, how subtle and marine, The. Bearded Oaks. Robert Penn Warren. **SP-WarrR**

Oaks rooted in stone, The. A Day. Stephen Berg. **SP-BergS**

Oaks shone / gaunt gold, The. Lightning. Mary Oliver. **SP-OlivM**

Oath, The. Robert Ranke Graves. **CP-GravR**

Oath. Patti Smith. **SP-SmitP**

Oath, The. Allen Tate. **CP-TateA**

Oatmeal Deluxe. Stephen Dobyns. **SP-DobyS**

Oatwoman, The. Michael Hartnett. **SP-HarMi**

Oaxaca. Audre Lorde. **SP-LordA**

Oaxaca Bus, The. Charles Tomlinson. **CP-TomlC**

Ob-La-Di Ob-La-Da. The Beatles. **CP-Beatl**

Obedience. Rita Dove. **SP-DoveR**

Obedience. George Herbert. **CP-HerbG**

Obedience. Robert Herrick. **CP-HerrR**

Obedience in Subjects. Robert Herrick. **CP-HerrR**

Obedient, The. Rudyard Kipling. *Fr.* Epitaphs of the War [1914–1918]. **CP-KiplR**

Obedient daily dress. Skin. Philip Larkin. **CP-LarkP**

Oberon, the Fairy Prince. Ben Jonson.
    "Buzz [or buz], quoth the blue fly [orflie]." **CP-JonsB**
    "Gentle knights, / Know some measure of your nights." **CP-JonsB**
    "Melt earth to sea, sea flow to air." **CP-JonsB**
    "Nay, nay, / You must not stay." **CP-JonsB**
    "Nor yet, nor yet, O you in this night blessed." **CP-JonsB**
    "Now, my cunning lady moon." **CP-JonsB**
    "O yet how early, and before her time." **CP-JonsB**
    "Solemn rites are well begun, The." **CP-JonsB**

Oberon's Feast. Robert Herrick. **CP-HerrR**

Oberon's Palace. Robert Herrick. **CP-HerrR**

Obit. Robert Lowell. **SP-LoweR**

Obit. Charles Olson. **CP-OlsoC**

Obiter Dicta. Donald Davie. **CP-DavDo**

Obituary for Jan Masaryk. John Clellon Holmes. **SP-HolmJ**

Object, An. Ezra Pound. **SP-PounE**

Object adorable of charms. *A la Chabot. Unknown, tr. fr. French by* Richard Lovelace. **CP-LoveR**

Object among dreams, you sit here with your shoes off, An. A Girl in a Library. Randall Jarrell. **CP-JarrR; SP-JarrR**

Object in a Setting. Charles Tomlinson. **CP-TomlC**

Object Lesson. Charles Bukowski. **SP-BukC2**

Objection to Being Stepped On, The. Robert Frost. **CP-FrosR**

Objector. William Stafford. **SP-StafW**

Objects. Wystan Hugh Auden. **CP-AudeW**

Objects, The. Charles Olson. **CP-OlsoC**

Objects. Richard Wilbur. **CP-WilbR**

Objects & Apparitions. Octavio Paz, *tr. fr. Spanish by* Elizabeth Bishop. **CP-BishE**

Obligations. Jane Cooper. **SP-CoopJ**

Obligations of Civil to Religious Liberty. William Wordsworth. *Fr.* Ecclesiastical Sonnets. **CP-WorW2**

Obliged by frequent visits of this man. Flecknoe, an English Priest at Rome. Andrew Marvell. **CP-MarvA**

Oblique cloud of purple smoke, An. Woman Walking. William Carlos Williams. **CP-WilW1**

Oblique essence of the personal. A Solitary. Daniel Gerard Hoffman. **SP-HoffD**

Oblique Frontier. Marsden Hartley. **CP-HartM**

Oblique light on the trite, on brick and tile. Courtyards in Delft. Derek Mahon. **SP-MahoD**

Obliterate / mythology as you unwind. The Cavern. Charles Tomlinson. **CP-TomlC**

Obliterate Tomb, The. Thomas Hardy. **CP-HardT**

Oblivion. Stephen Berg. **SP-BergS**

Oblivion. Stevie Smith. **CP-SmitS**

Oblivion's Room. Archie Randolph Ammons. **SP-AmmoA**

O'Brien, most disconsolate of Men. Arthur Hugh Clough. **SP-ClouA**

Obscene Poem, An. Robert Creeley. **CP-CreeR**

Obscenity. David Herbert Lawrence. **CP-LawrD**

Obscure, unpriz'd, and dark, the magnet lies. Claudian, *tr. fr. Latin by* Samuel Johnson. **CP-JohnS**

Obscure Writer, An. John Donne. **CP-DonnJ**

Obscurely yet most surely called to praise. Praise in Summer. Richard Wilbur. **CP-WilbR**

Obscurest night involved [or involv'd] the sky. The Castaway. William Cowper. **CP-CowpW**

Obscurity has its tale to tell. Focus. Adrienne Rich. **CP-RicAE; SP-RicA1; SP-RicA2**

Obsequial Ode. David Herbert Lawrence. **CP-LawrD**

Obsequies to the Lady Anne Hay. Thomas Carew. **CP-CareT**

Obsequies to the Lord Harrington, Brother to the Lady Lucy, Countess of Bedford. John Donne. **CP-DonnJ**

Observance. Wendell Berry. **CP-BerrW**

Observant of the way she told. Tact. Edwin Arlington Robinson. **CP-RobiE**

Observation ("Jewes, when they built Houses [I have read], The"). Robert Herrick. **CP-HerrR**

Observation ("Virgin-Mother stood at distance [there], The"). Robert Herrick. **CP-HerrR**

Observation. Robert Herrick. **CP-HerrR**

Observation. Philip Larkin. **CP-LarkP**

Observation of Facts. Charles Tomlinson. **CP-TomlC**

Observation of October. Howard Nemerov. **CP-NemeH**

vation Post: Forward Area. Alun Lewis. **CP-LewiA**

rvation Tower, The. Lewis Turco. **SP-TurcL**

Observations in the Art of English Poesie. Thomas Campion. **CP-CampT**

Elegye, An: "Constant to none, but ever false to me." **AAS**

English *Sapphick*, The.

Epigram: "None then should through thy beawty, Lawra, pine."

Epigramme: "All in sattin Oteny will be suited."

Epigramme: "All wonders Barnzy speakes, all grosely faind."

Epigramme: "Arthure brooks only those that brooke not him."

Epigramme: "At all thou frankly throwst, while, Frank, thy wife."

Epigramme: "Barnzy stiffly vowes that hees no Cuckold."

Epigramme: "Buffe loves fat vians, fat ale, fat all things."

Epigramme: "Cease, fond wretch, to love, so oft deluded."

Epigramme: "Drue feasts no Puritans; the churles, he saith."

Epigramme: "Drue gives thee money, yet thou thankst not him."

Epigramme: "His late losse the Wireless Higs in order."

Epigramme: "If fancy can not erre which vertue guides."

Epigramme: "Kate can fancy only berdles husbands."

Epigramme: "Lockly spits apace, the rhewme he cals it."

Epigramme: "Phoebe all the rights Elisa claymeth."

Epigramme: "Smith, by sute divorst, the knowne adultres."

Epigramme: "Thou telst me, Barnzy, Dawson hath a wife."

Epigramme: "Tosts as snakes or as the mortall Henbane."

Epigramme: "What though Harry braggs, let him be noble."

Epigramme: "Why droopst thou, Trefeild? Will Hurst the Banker."

Epigramme: "Wiseman wary lives, yet most secure, A."

"Follow, follow[e] / Though with mischiefe." **EnLoPo**

"Goe, numbers, boldly passe, stay not for ayde."

"Greatest in thy wars."

"Just beguiler, / Kindest love, yet only chastest."

"Kind in every kinde."

"Raving warre, begot / In the thirstye sands." **AAS**

Rose-cheeked Laura[, Come]. **AAS; CP-CampT; EnLoPo; EnRePo; InPK; InPS; InvP; LoBV; NAEL-1; NOSC; NoP; OAEL-1; OAEP; PoE; PoEL-2; SeCeV; TFi; TRP; TrGrPo**

(Laura.) **EIL; NOBE; OBEV; OBSC; SeCePo; UnS**

("Rose-cheekt Lawra, come.") **AAS; CP-CampT**

"Some from the starry throne his fame derives."

Writer to his Booke, The. **OAEL**

("Whither thus hastes my little book so fast?") **OAEP**

Observations of P. Ovidus Naso on the Incidence of Sex in the Contemporary Novel. Archibald MacLeish. **CP-MacLA**

Observe how it will be at last. Summing Up in Italy. Elizabeth Barrett Browning. **CP-BroEB**

Observe how Miyanoshita cracked in two. Edna St. Vincent Millay. *Fr.* Epitaph for the Race of Man. **CP-MillE**

Observe. Ridged, raised, tactile, the horror. "Scream, The." Donald Hall. **CP-HallD**

Observe the cautious toadstools. Song. William DeWitt Snodgrass. **SP-SnodW**

Observe the dying father speak. The Faggot. Jonathan Swift. **CP-SwifJ**

Observed from down the beach, the seal. Seal in Nature. John Updike. **CP-UpdiJ**

Observer, The. Stephen Dunn. **SP-DunnS**

Observer, The. Adrienne Rich. **CP-RicAE; SP-RicA2**

Observer, The. William Carlos Williams. **CP-WilW2**

Obsessed, bewildered / By the shipwreck. George Oppen. *Fr.* Of Being Numerous. **CP-OppeG**

Obsolescent and His Deity (Polyptych), An. Bill Knott. **SP-KnotB**

Obsolete as books in leather bindings. Relics. Louis MacNeice. **CP-MacNL**

Obsolete Oxfordshire game of "A-All," The. James Fenton. *Fr.* Exempla. **SP-FentJ**

Obstructions. James Dickey. **CP-DickJ**

Obtaining but our own Extent. Emily Dickinson. **CP-DickE**

Obviously Five Believers. "Bob Dylan." **CP-DylaB**

Obviously, in a plutocracy. Childe Harold to the Round Tower Came. William Carlos Williams. **CP-WilW2**

Occasional Address, Spoken by Miss Fontenell, on Her Benefit-Night, Decr. 4th. 1793.—Written by Mr Burns. Robert Burns. **CP-BurnR**

Occasional Meditations: "By night, when others soundly slept." Anne Bradstreet. **CP-BradA**

Occasional Poem 7.1.72. Roy Fisher. **SP-FishR**

Occasional Poems. Delmore Schwartz. **SP-SchwD**

Christmas Poem for Nancy.

Rabbi to Preach.

Salute Valentine.

Occasional Prologue Delivered Previous to the Performance of "The Wheel of Fortune" at a Private Theatre, An. Byron. **CP-Byron**

Occasional Yarrow, The. Stevie Smith. **CP-SmitS**

Occasioned by Sir William Temple's Late Illness and Recovery. Jonathan Swift. **CP-SwifJ**

Occasioned by Some Verses of his Grace the Duke of Buckingham. Alexander Pope. **CP-PopeA**

Occasioned by the Battle of Waterloo February, 1816. William Wordsworth. **CP-WorW2**

Occasioned by the Battle of Waterloo (the Last Six Lines Intended for an Inscription) February, 1816. William Wordsworth. **CP-WorW2**

Occidit, O juvenis, pater et sub syrtibus his est. Full Fathom Five. Gerard Manley Hopkins. *Fr.* Songs from Shakespeare, in Latin and Greek. **CP-HopkG**

Occludes wild dawn. Up thro' green ragged clouds. Prime. John Berryman. **CP-BerrJ**

Occultation, The. Thomas Hardy. **CP-HardT**

Occultation of Orion, The. Henry Wadsworth Longfellow. **SP-LongH**

Occupation. David Markson. **CP-MarkD**

Occupations of Hell. John Milton. **NOSC** *Fr.* Book II. **FHYEP; NAEL-1; OxAEP-1** *Fr.* Paradise Lost. **CP-MiltJ**

Occurrences, The. George Oppen. **CP-OppeG**

Occurrences, The. George Oppen. **CP-OppeG**

Occurring "neither for self." George Oppen. *Fr.* Of Being Numerous. **CP-OppeG**

Ocean, The. Byron. **PoEL-4** *Fr.* Childe Harold's Pilgrimage. **CP-Byron**

(By the Deep Sea.) **OBNC**

"And I have loved thee, Ocean! and my joy." **OxBoS**

"Roll on, thou deep and dark blue ocean—roll!" **FaPON; GN; OxBoS; UV; WGRP**

(Roll On, Thou Deep and Dark Blue Ocean.) **FaPON**

(To the Ocean.) **GN; WGRP**

"There is a pleasure in the pathless woods." **BLPL; ChTr; FaBV; FaBoBe; FiP; GGP; ImPo; LiTB; MOS; MeMBP; OHFP; OXAEP-2; OxBoS; TFi; TrGrPo; WBLP**

(Apostrophe to the Ocean.) **OHFP; WBLP**

(Deep and Dark Blue Ocean.) **ChTr**

(Ocean, The.) **FaBV; MeMBP; TFi; TrGrPo**

(Roll On, Thou Deep and Dark Blue Ocean.) **FiP**

(Sea, The.) **BLPL; FaBoBe; GGP; ImPo; LiTB**

"Thou glorious mirror, where the Almighty's form." **OxBoS**

Ocean, The. Byron. *See* There is a pleasure in the pathless woods.

Ocean. Joseph Ceravolo. **SP-CeraJ**

Ocean. Robinson Jeffers. **CP-JefR1**

Ocean. Robinson Jeffers. **CP-JefR3**

Ocean / this morning, The. Braised Leeks & Framboise. Diane Wakoski. **SP-WakoD**

Ocean. John Greenleaf Whittier. **CP-WhitJ**

Ocean fooled me, The. California Poem. Jim Carroll. **SP-CarrJ**

Ocean glittered quietly in the moonlight, The. Rock Music. Derek Mahon. **SP-MahoD**

Ocean has befriended me, The. On Barbara's Shore. Diane Wakoski. **SP-WakoD**

Ocean has not been so quiet for a long while, The. Evening Ebb. Robinson Jeffers. **CP-JefR2**

Ocean is salt and the waters, The. Salt. Isabella Gardner. **CP-GardI**

Ocean-lights go flashing. Roy Fisher. **SP-FishR** *Fr.* Matrix.

Ocean, 1940. John Hewitt. **CP-HewiJ**

Ocean on Monday. Richard Hugo. **CP-HugoR**

Ocean Springs Missippy. Al Young. **CP-YounA** *Fr.* The Song Turning Back into Itself.

Ocean twanging away there, The. The Parting: I. Adrienne Rich. **CP-RicAE; SP-RicA2**

Ocean's Love to Cynthia, The. Sir Walter Ralegh.

11th: and Last Booke of the Ocean to Scinthia, The. **CP-RaleW**

End of the Boo[c]k[e]s, of the Ocean's Love to Cynthia [*or* Scinthia], and the Beginning[e] of the 12 [*or* 22] Boo[c]k, Entreating of Sorrow, The. **CP-RaleW**

Ocean's Tribute, The. Robinson Jeffers. **CP-JefR3**

Ochenaid Sant Francis Xavier, Apostol Yr Indiaid. Gerard Manley Hopkins. **CP-HopkG**

Ocius O flavas has, ocius O ad arenas. Come Unto These Yellow Sands. Gerard Manley Hopkins. *Fr.* Songs from Shakespeare, in Latin and Greek. **CP-HopkG**

Octaves. Edwin Arlington Robinson. **CP-RobiE**

"Forebodings are the fiends of Recreance."

"Guerdon of new childhood is reose, The."

"Here by the windy docks I stand alone."

"I grant you friendship is a royal thing."

"Like a white wall whereon forever breaks."

"Nor jewelled phrase nor mere mellifluous rhyme."

"Prophet of dead words defeats himself, The."

"Something as one with eyes that look below."

"Still through the dusk of dead, blank-legended."

"There is no loneliness:—no matter where."

"There is one battle-field whereon we fall."

"Though the sick beast infect us, we are fraught."

"To curse the chilled insistence of the dawn."

"To me the groaning of world-worshippers."

"To you that sit with Sorrow like chained slaves."

"Tumultuously void of a clean scheme."

"We lack the courage to be where we are."

"We thrill too strangely at the master's touch."

"When one that you and I had all but sworn."

"When we shall hear no more the cradle-songs."

"Where does a dead man go?—The dead man dies."

"While we are drilled in error, we are lost."

"With conscious eyes not yet sincere enough."

Octets. Osip Emilevich Mandelstam, *tr. fr. Russian* by Donald Davie. **CP-DavDo**

"Advise me, draftsman of the drifting sands."

"And of the sixth sense, the infinitesimal suffix."

"Butterfly-girl of the Mussulman, all."

"I come in out of Space, and with a rake."

"I love the way the weave, when two or three or."

"I love the way the weave, when two or three or."

"Schubert from water, from birdsong's gamut Mozart."

"Those plaguy; needling games of ours, where stooks."

"To get past harping on the laws of Nature."

"Well, but the saw-edged maple-leaf can suffer."

"When you have shoved aside the scribbled worksheet."

October. Tom Clark. **SP-ClarT**

October. Paul Laurence Dunbar. **CP-DunbP**

October. Robert Frost. **CP-FrosR**

October. Robert Earl Hayden. **CP-HaydR**

October. Denise Levertov. **CP-LeveD**

October. Audre Lorde. **SP-LordA**

October. Mary Oliver. **SP-OlivM**

October. Christina Georgina Rossetti. *Fr.* The Months: A Pageant. **CP-RosC2**

October. James Schuyler. **CP-SchuJ**

October. Gary Snyder. *Fr.* Six Years. **CP-SnydG**

October. Edmund Spenser. **NAEL-1; OAEL-1** *Fr.* The Shepheardes [*or* Shepeards *or* Shepherd's] Calender. **CP-Spens**

  (Contempt of Poetry, The.) **OBSC**

October. Charles Tomlinson. **CP-TomlC**

October. Charles Wright. **SP-WrigC**

October Afternoon. Marsden Hartley. **CP-HartM**

October—An Etching. Edna St. Vincent Millay. **CP-MillE**

October-Born. John Hewitt. **CP-HewiJ**

October Dawn. Ted Hughes. **SP-HughT**

October days / Red admirals. Late Butterflies. Howard Nemerov. **CP-NemeH**

October Dory Race. Brendan Galvin. **SP-GalvB**

October 18: Boston. John Ciardi. **SP-CiarJ**

October, 1803 ("One might believe that natural miseries"). William Wordsworth. **CP-WorW1**

October, 1803 ("These times strike monied worldlings with dismay"). William Wordsworth. **CP-WorW1**

October, 1803 ("When, looking on the present face of things"). William Wordsworth. **CP-WorW1**

October Evening. Robinson Jeffers. **CP-JefR1**

October 5, 1981. James Schuyler. **CP-SchuJ**

October Garden, An. Christina Georgina Rossetti. **CP-RosC2**

OCTOBER (*Golf*). Rudyard Kipling. *Fr.* Verses on Games. **CP-KiplR**

October hangs in grape. Evening Wind. James Schuyler. **CP-SchuJ**

October in Bloomsbury. Louis MacNeice. **CP-MacNL**

October in Hyde Park. Derek Mahon. **SP-MahoD**

October in Maine. The human touch. Frederick Morgan. *Fr.* Blue Hill Poems. **SP-MorgF**

October in New England. Spinsters. Marsden Hartley. **CP-HartM**

October is marigold, and yet. October Dawn. Ted Hughes. **SP-HughT**

October is the treasurer of the year. October. Paul Laurence Dunbar. **CP-DunbP**

October Maples, Portland. Richard Wilbur. **CP-WilbR**

October 1954. Kay Boyle. **CP-BoylK**

October-November. Hart Crane. **CP-CranH**

October Paint. Carl Sandburg. **CP-SandC**

October Salmon, An. Ted Hughes. **SP-HughT**

October 16[: The Raid]. Langston Hughes. **SP-HughL**

October slows thru me. The October Variations. Al Young. **CP-YounA**

October Sonnets. John Hewitt. **CP-HewiJ**

  "Her situation seemed a piteous thing."

  "I saw my father die. For two long years."

  "I've seen no more than three loved persons die."

  "My dear spouse died—a tumour on the brain."

  "Of course, the gruffest prompting comes from age."

  "This is the season I think most of death."

  "When my wife's sister's husband came to die."

October Sunset. Malcolm Lowry. **CP-LowrM**

October 10. Wendell Berry. **CP-BerrW**

October: the falling leaves resume the earth. Autumnal. Howard Nemerov. **CP-NemeH**

October Tragedy. William Everson. **SP-EverW**

October 21, 1905. George Meredith. **CP-MerG2**

October. Twilight / flutters like cloth of silver. Hayden Carruth. **CP-CarHS** *Fr.* The Clay Hill Anthology.

October Variations, The. Al Young. **CP-YounA**

October Week-End. Robinson Jeffers. **CP-JefR2**

October Window. Al Young. **CP-YounA**

October woods, wherein. Ralph Waldo Emerson. **CP-EmerR**

October's both, back in the Sooner State. John Berryman. *Fr.* Sonnets to Chris. **CP-BerrJ**

October's Child. John Hewitt. **CP-HewiJ**

October's completing light falls. A Beginning. Wendell Berry. *Fr.* Work Song. **CP-BerrW**

October's end, a blue still sky. The Lagan in October. John Hewitt. **CP-HewiJ**

Octets, The. James Merrill. **SP-MerrJ**

Octopus, An. Marianne Craig Moore. **CP-MoorM**

Octopus, The. Ogden Nash. **CP-NashO**

Octopus would be my model—, The. If I Could Be Like Wallace Stevens. William Stafford. **SP-StafW**

Octopus's Garden. "Ringo Starr." **CP-Beatl**

Odd music, / cutting through horn blasts and squawks of traffic, asserts. The Organist's Black Carnation. Laurence Lieberman. **SP-LiebL**

Odd stillness of your body, The. Clutter-up People. Alice Walker. **CP-WalkA**

Odd, that Mozart, the frock-coated. The XIX. Pablo Neruda, *tr. fr. Spanish* by Ben Belitt. **SP-NeruP**

Oddjob, a Bull Terrier. Derek Walcott. **CP-WalcD**

Oddly Lovely Day Alone, An. John Updike. **CP-UpdiJ**

Odds, The. Al Young. **CP-YounA**

Odds and Ends. "Bob Dylan." **CP-DylaB**

Odds & ends: / Enosburg Falls & Geof's cabin. Hayden Carruth. *Fr.* The Sleeping Beauty. **CP-CarHL**

Ode [for General Washington's Birthday]. Robert Burns. **CP-BurnR**

Ode: "Bards of passion and of mirth." John Keats. **CP-KeatJ**

Ode, An. Richard Barnfield. *See* As it fell upon a day.

Ode: "Idea of justice may be precious, An." Frank O'Hara. **SP-OharF**

Ode: "If men, and times were now." Ben Jonson. **CP-JonsB**

oDE: "O / the sweet & aged people." Edward Estlin Cummings. **CP-CummE**

Ode: "O, God of Columbia! O, Shield of the Free!" Walt Whitman. **CP-WhitW**

Ode: "So long as memory, valour, and faith endure." Rudyard Kipling. **CP-KiplR**

Ode: "Though aware of our rank and alert to obey orders." Wystan Hugh Auden. **CP-AudeW**

Ode: "To-night is so coarse with chocolate." Louis MacNeice. **CP-MacNL**

Ode: "Who rises on the banks of Seine." William Wordsworth. **CP-WorW2**

Ode: "You are deceiv'd; I sooner may dull fair." Richard Lovelace. **CP-LoveR**

Ode Allegoric. Ben Jonson. **CP-JonsB**

Ode, An: "Exalt me, Clio, to the skies." *Unknown.* *Fr.* Complimentary Pieces to Milton. **CP-CowpW**

Ode, An: "Helen, did Homer never see." Ben Jonson. **CP-JonsB**

Ode, An: "High-spirited friend, / I send not balms, nor corsives to your wound." Ben Jonson. **CP-JonsB**

Ode, An: "I'm going to write a novel, hey." John Updike. **CP-UpdiJ**

Ode, An: "Stern winter now, by spring repress'd." Samuel Johnson. **CP-JohnS**

Ode Composed on May Morning. William Wordsworth. **CP-WorW2**

Ode, De Skia Insula. Samuel Johnson. **CP-JohnS**

Ode: 1815. William Wordsworth. **CP-WorW2**

Ode: 1814. William Wordsworth. **CP-WorW2**

Ode Enthusiastic. Ben Jonson. **CP-JonsB**

Ode et Amo. Catullus. *See* Carmen 85: "I hate and I love. And if you ask me how."

Ode for Him, An. Robert Herrick. **CP-HerrR**

Ode for Memorial Day. Paul Laurence Dunbar. **CP-DunbP**

Ode for Music. Thomas Gray. **CP-GrayT**

Ode for Music on St. Cecilia's Day. Alexander Pope. **CP-PopeA** Descend, Ye Nine. **GN**

Ode for Ted. Sylvia Plath. **CP-PlatS**

Ode for the American Dead in Asia. Thomas McGrath. *See* God love you now, if no one else will ever.

Ode from the French. Byron. **CP-Byron**

Ode in the Manner of Anacreon, An. Samuel Taylor Coleridge. **CP-ColeS**

Ode, Inscribed to W. H. Channing. Ralph Waldo Emerson. **CP-EmerR**

Ode: Intimations of Immortality [from Recollections of Early Childhood]. William Wordsworth. **CP-WorW1**

"And O, ye Fountains, Meadows, Hills, and Groves."

"Behold the child among his new-born blisses."

"Earth fills her lap with pleasures of her own."

"Now, while the birds thus sing a joyous song." **Prf**

"O joy! that in our embers." **PoPle; Prf**

"Our birth is but a sleep and a forgetting." **ChTr; EaLo; FaBV; WGRP** (Intimations of Immortality.) **ChTr** (Our Birth Is But a Sleep.) **FaBV**

"Rainbow comes and goes, The."

"Then sing, ye Birds, sing, sing a joyous song!"

"There was a time when meadow, grove and stream." **HeIL; ImPo; NAEL-2; PBMP; SCGP; TFi; TOF; TRP**

"There was a time when meadow, grove, and stream." **FaPoB**

"Thou, whose exterior semblance doth belie."

"Ye blessed Creatures, I have heard the call."

Ode: My 24th Year. Allen Ginsberg. **CP-GinsA**

Ode on a Distant Prospect of Eton College. Thomas Gray. **CP-GrayT**

Ode on a Grecian Urn. John Keats. **CP-KeatJ**

Ode on a Grecian Urn. John Keats. **CP-KeatJ**

"Ah, happy, happy boughs! that cannot shed."

"Heard melodies are sweet, but those unheard."

"O Attic shape! Fair attitude! with brede." **GrIP**

"Thou still unravished bride of quietness."

"Who are these coming to the sacrifice?"

Ode on a Lady Leaving Her Place of Abode; Almost Impromptu, An. Samuel Johnson. **CP-JohnS**

Ode on a Prayer-Book. Richard Crashaw. **CP-CrasR**

Ode on Æolus's Harp, An. James Thomson. **CP-ThomJ**

Ode on Causality. Frank O'Hara. **SP-OharF**

Ode on Friendship, An. Samuel Johnson. **CP-JohnS**

Ode on Indolence. John Keats. **CP-KeatJ**

Ode on Melancholy. John Keats. **CP-KeatJ**

Ode on Nativity, An. Charles Olson. **CP-OlsoC; SP-OlsoC**

Ode on Necrophilia. Frank O'Hara. **SP-OharF**

Ode on *Sir Charles Grandison*. William Cowper. **CP-CowpW**

Ode on Solitude. Alexander Pope. **CP-PopeA**

Ode on the Birth of Our Saviour, An. Robert Herrick. **CP-HerrR**

Ode on the Death of a Favourite [*or* Favorite] Cat, Drowned in a Tub [*or* Bowl] of Gold Fishes. Thomas Gray. **CP-GrayT**

Ode on the Death of a Lady. Vincent Bourne, *tr. fr. Latin by* William Cowper. **CP-CowpW**

Ode on the Death of the Duke of Wellington. Tennyson. **CP-TennA** "Bury the Great Duke." **EBVVPR**

Ode on the Death of [Mr.] Thomson. William Collins. *See* In yonder grave a Druid lies.

Ode on the Departing Year. Samuel Taylor Coleridge. **CP-ColeS** O My Mother Isle! ("Not yet enslaved, not wholly vile"). **FaBoPP**

Ode on the Installation of His Royal Highness Prince Albert as Chancellor of the University of Cambridge, July, 1847. William Wordsworth. **CP-WorW2**

Ode on the Loss of the Titanic. Geoffrey Hill. *Fr.* Of Commerce and Society: Variations on a Theme. **CP-HillG**

Ode on the Marriage of a Friend. William Cowper. **CP-CowpW**

Ode on the Ottery and Tiverton Church Music. Samuel Taylor Coleridge. **CP-ColeS**

Ode on the Pleasure Arising from Vicissitude. Thomas Gray. **CP-GrayT** "Now the golden morn aloft." **GTBS; GTBS-6; GTBS-P; NOEC**

Ode on the Spring. Thomas Gray. **CP-GrayT**

Ode on Venice. Byron. **CP-Byron**

Ode, or Psalme, to God, An. Robert Herrick. **CP-HerrR**

Ode, or Song, by All the Muses, An. Ben Jonson. **CP-JonsB**

Ode, Sacred to the Memory of Mrs. —— of ——. Robert Burns. **CP-BurnR**

Ode: Salute to the French Negro Poets. Frank O'Hara. **SP-OharF**

Ode: Secundum Artem, An. William Cowper. **CP-CowpW**

Ode Sung in the Town Hall. Ralph Waldo Emerson. **CP-EmerR**

Ode: The Dying Christian to His Soul. Alexander Pope. *See* Vital spark of heavenly [*or* heav'nly] flame!

Ode: The Morning of the Day Appointed for a General Thanksgiving. January 18, 1816. William Wordsworth. **CP-WorW2**

Ode to a Lady Whose Lover Was Killed by a Ball, Which at the Same Time Shivered a Portrait next His Heart. Byron. **CP-Byron**

Ode to a Lebanese Crock of Olives. Diane Wakoski. **SP-WakoD**

Ode to a Lovesick Moose. Robert Pack. **SP-PackR**

Ode to a Maintenance Man and His Family. Kay Boyle. **CP-BoylK**

Ode to a Nightingale. John Keats. **CP-KeatJ** "Darkling I listen; and for many a time." **OBD** Magic Casements. **FaBV**

Ode to Admiral Sir George Pocock. Christopher Smart. **SP-SmarC**

Ode to All Rebels. "Hugh MacDiarmid." "I mind when ny first wife died." **SP-MacDH** "Think not that I forget a single pang." **SP-MacDH**

Ode to Apollo. William Cowper. **CP-CowpW**

Ode to Apollo ("God of the golden bow"). John Keats. **CP-KeatJ**

Ode to Apollo ("In thy western halls of gold"). John Keats. **CP-KeatJ**

Ode to Apollo. William Wordsworth. **CP-WorW1**

Ode to Arnold Schoenberg. Charles Tomlinson. **CP-TomlC**

Ode to Beauty. Ralph Waldo Emerson. **CP-EmerR** "Who gave thee, O Beauty." **PoEL-4**

Ode To Damon. "Lewis Carroll." **CP-CarrL**

Ode to Death. Charlotte Smith. **CP-SmitC**

Ode to Despair. Charlotte Smith. **CP-SmitC**

Ode to Dr. William Sancroft. Jonathan Swift. **CP-SwifJ**

Ode to Duty. William Wordsworth. **CP-WorW1**

Ode to Entropy. John Updike. *Fr.* Seven Odes to Seven Natural Processes. **CP-UpdiJ**

Ode to Ethiopia. Paul Laurence Dunbar. **CP-DunbP**

Ode to Failure. Allen Ginsberg. **CP-GinsA**

Ode to Fear. Allen Tate. **CP-TateA**

Ode to Gaea. Wystan Hugh Auden. **CP-AudeW**

Ode to General Draper. Christopher Smart. **SP-SmarC**

Ode to Georgiana, Duchess of Devonshire. Samuel Taylor Coleridge. **CP-ColeS**

Ode to Good Men Fallen Before Hero Come. Peter Meinke. **SP-MeinP**

Ode to Growth. John Updike. *Fr.* Seven Odes to Seven Natural Processes. **CP-UpdiJ**

Ode to Healing. John Updike. *Fr.* Seven Odes to Seven Natural Processes. **CP-UpdiJ**

Ode to Heaven. Percy Bysshe Shelley. **CP-ShelP**

Ode to Hengist and Horsa. Robinson Jeffers. **CP-JefR3**

Ode to H.I.M. Napoleon 3d. George Meredith. **CP-MerG2**

Ode to Himself. Ben Jonson. **CP-JonsB**

Ode. To Himself, An. Ben Jonson. **CP-JonsB**

Ode to James, Earl of Desmond, An. Ben Jonson. **CP-JonsB**

Ode (To Joseph Lesueur) on the Arrow That Flieth by Day. Frank O'Hara. **SP-OharF**

Ode to Joy. Daniel Gerard Hoffman. **SP-HoffD**

Ode to Lady Harriot. Christopher Smart. **SP-SmarC**

Ode to Laziness. Pablo Neruda, *tr. fr. Spanish by* William Carlos Williams. **CP-WilW2**

Ode to Liberty. Percy Bysshe Shelley. **CP-ShelP**

Ode to Liberty. Percy Bysshe Shelley. **CP-ShelP** Athens. **GrIP** "Come thou, but lead out of the inmost cave." "Eager hours and unreluctant years, The." "England yet sleeps: was she not called of old?" "From what Hyrcanian glen or frozen hill." "Glorious people vibrated again, A." "He who taught man to vanquish whatsoever." "Man, the imperial shape, then multiplied." "Nodding promontories, and blue isles, The."

"Oh, that the free would stamp the impious name."

"Oh, that the wise from their bright minds would kindle."

"Paused, and the Spirit of that mighty singing."

"Sun and the serenest Moon sprang forth:, The."

"Then Rome was, and from thy deep bosom fairest."

"Thou Heaven of earth! what spells could pall thee then."

"Thou huntress swifter than the Moon! thou terror."

"Thousand years the Earth cried, 'Where art thou?', A."

"Tomb of Arminius! render up thy dead."

"Within the surface of Time's fleeting river."

Ode to Lucasta: The Rose. Richard Lovelace. *See* Sweet serene sky[e]-like Flower.

Ode to Lycoris. William Wordsworth. **CP-WorW2**

Ode to Lycoris; May, 1817. William Wordsworth. **CP-WorW2**

Ode to Master Endymion Porter, upon His Brother's Death, An. Robert Herrick. **CP-HerrR**

Ode to May. Fragment. John Keats. *See* Mother of Hermes! and still youthful Maia!

Ode to Michael Goldberg ('s Birth and Other Births). Frank O'Hara. **SP-OharF**

Ode To My Lady H. Richard Lovelace. **CP-LoveR**

Ode to My shoes. Erica Jong. **SP-JongE**

Ode to Naples. Percy Bysshe Shelley. **CP-ShelP**

  At Pompeii. **FaBoPP**

Ode to Napoleon Buonaparte. Byron. **CP-Byron**

Ode to October Mist. Robert Pack. **SP-PackR**

Ode to Our Young Pro-consuls of the Air. Allen Tate. **CP-TateA**

Ode to Peace. William Cowper. **CP-CowpW**

Ode to Pleasure. Richard Wilbur. **CP-WilbR**

Ode to Psyche. John Keats. **CP-KeatJ**

Ode to Rot. John Updike. *Fr.* Seven Odes to Seven Natural Processes. **CP-UpdiJ**

Ode to Rouse. John Milton. *See* To John Rouse.

Ode to Silence. Richard Eberhart. **CP-EberR**

Ode to Silence. Edna St. Vincent Millay. **CP-MillE**

Ode to Sir Clipsebie Crew, An. Robert Herrick. **CP-HerrR**

Ode. To Sir William Sydney, on His Birthday. Ben Jonson. **CP-JonsB**

Ode to Sleep. Samuel Taylor Coleridge. **CP-ColeS**

Ode to Spring. Robert Burns. **CP-BurnR**

Ode to Tanaquil Leclercq. Frank O'Hara. **SP-OharF**

Ode to Terminus. Wystan Hugh Auden. **CP-AudeW**

Ode to the Athenian Society. Jonathan Swift. **CP-SwifJ**

Ode to the Chinese Paper Snake. Richard Eberhart. **CP-EberR**

Ode to the Confederate Dead. Allen Tate. **CP-TateA**

Ode to the Departed Regency-Bill—1789. Robert Burns. **CP-BurnR**

Ode to the Diencephalon. Wystan Hugh Auden. **CP-AudeW**

Ode to the Framers of the Frame Bill, An. Byron. **CP-Byron**

Ode to the Honourable Sir William Temple. Jonathan Swift. **CP-SwifJ**

Ode to the King. Jonathan Swift. **CP-SwifJ**

Ode to the Medieval Poets. Wystan Hugh Auden. **CP-AudeW**

Ode to the Missel Thrush. Charlotte Smith. **CP-SmitC**

Ode to the Olive Tree. Charlotte Smith. **CP-SmitC**

Ode to the Present Century. Thomas Merton. **CP-MertT**

Ode to the Rain, An. Samuel Taylor Coleridge. **CP-ColeS**

Ode to the Setting Sun. Allen Ginsberg. **CP-GinsA**

Ode to the Spirit of Earth in Autumn. George Meredith. **CP-MerG1**

Ode to the Swallow, *ad. fr.* Anacreon. Elizabeth Barrett Browning. **CP-BroEB**

Ode to the Trio Fruit Company of Missoula. Richard Hugo. **CP-HugoR**

Ode to the West Wind. Percy Bysshe Shelley. **CP-ShelP**

Ode to Tranquillity. Samuel Taylor Coleridge. **CP-ColeS**

Ode Written October, 1819, An. Percy Bysshe Shelley. **CP-ShelP**

Odes, *sels.* Hafiz, *tr. fr.* Persian.

  "Ah, could I hide me in my song." **CP-EmerR**

  "Alas! till now I had not known." **CP-EmerR**

  "All day the rain." **CP-EmerR**

  "And had Hafiz." **CP-EmerR**

  "And since round lines are drawn." **CP-EmerR**

  "Art thou wise, four things resign." **CP-EmerR**

  "Blame me not thou hoarse preacher." **CP-EmerR**

  "Boy bring the bowl full of wine." **CP-EmerR**

  "Bring wine release me." **CP-EmerR**

  "Builder of heaven, The." **CP-EmerR**

  "By breath of beds of roses drawn." **CP-EmerR**

  "Chemist of love, The." **CP-EmerR**

  "Come let us strew roses." **CP-EmerR**

"Come!—the palace of heaven rests on aëry pillars." **CP-EmerR**

"Desire no bread, forsake the guest hall of the earth." **CP-EmerR**

"Drink, hear my counsel, my son, that the world fret thee not." **CP-EmerR**

"Drink till the turbans are all unbound." **CP-EmerR**

"Drink wine, and the heaven." **CP-EmerR**

"Early after the night long revel." **CP-EmerR**

"Fair fall thy soft heart!" **CP-EmerR**

"Fit for the Pleiads' azure chord." **CP-EmerR**

"For his constant dwelling place has Hafiz." **CP-EmerR**

"Free thyself from wo." **CP-EmerR**

"Good is what goes on the road of Nature." **CP-EmerR**

"Hafiz since on the world." **CP-EmerR**

"Hafiz thou art from Eternity." **CP-EmerR**

"Has thine enemy slandered thy house." **CP-EmerR**

"Hear what the glass will tell thee." **CP-EmerR**

"High heart, O Hafiz! though not thine." **CP-EmerR**

"His learning truly lifted Hafiz to Heaven." **CP-EmerR**

"I am: what I am." **CP-EmerR**

"I batter the wheel of heaven." **CP-EmerR**

"I have no hoarded treasure." **CP-EmerR**

"I know this perilous love-can." **CP-EmerR**

"I never went out of my country." **CP-EmerR**

"I said to heaven that glowed above."

  From Hafiz. **CP-EmerR**

  "If my darling should depart." **CP-EmerR**

"I said to the East wind." **CP-EmerR**

"I shall go from my sickbed to heaven." **CP-EmerR**

"I will be drunk and down with wine." **CP-EmerR**

"If thy darling favor thee." **CP-EmerR**

"In bounding youth the night & train." **CP-EmerR**

"In the kingdom of Poesy Hafiz waves like a banner." **CP-EmerR**

"In thy holiday of life." **CP-EmerR**

"It is certain that who his mind." **CP-EmerR**

"Knowst thou the luck the friends face to see." **CP-EmerR**

"Lament not, o Hafiz, the distribution." **CP-EmerR**

"Lo! where from Heaven's high roof." **CP-EmerR**

"Loose the knots of the heart; never think on thy fate." **CP-EmerR**

"Many our needs, yet we spare prayers." **CP-EmerR**

"Ninefold table of Heaven, The." **CP-EmerR**

"No physician has a balsam for my wo." **CP-EmerR**

"Novice, hear me what I say." **CP-EmerR**

"Now tells the flower." **CP-EmerR**

"O follow the sonnet's flight." **CP-EmerR**

"O friend blame not Hafiz." **CP-EmerR**

"O Hafiz, give me thought." **CP-EmerR**

"O Hafiz! speak not of thy need." **CP-EmerR**

"Oft have I said, I say it once more." **CP-EmerR**

"Our Shah's counsel is the efflux." **CP-EmerR**

"Out of the East, and out of the West, no man understands me." **CP-EmerR**

Phoenix, The. **CP-EmerR**

"Plunge in yon angry waves." **CP-EmerR**

"Prince the ball of heaven should." **CP-EmerR**

"Reach me wine No counsel weakens the conclusion of the lot." **CP-EmerR**

"Red rose blooms, The." **CP-EmerR**

"Roguish wind and I, The." **CP-EmerR**

"Ruler after word & thought." **CP-EmerR**

"Secretly to love & to drink, what is it? tis a dissolute day's work." **CP-EmerR**

"See & hear the fraud, the malice of the change of fortune." **CP-EmerR**

"See how the roses burn!" **CP-EmerR**

"Should I shed my tears." **CP-EmerR**

"Since you set no worth on the heart." **CP-EmerR**

"So long as there's a trace." **CP-EmerR**

"Spare thou neither time nor blood for thy friend." **CP-EmerR**

"Stand up, that we may sacrifice the soul." **CP-EmerR**

"Stately bride is the shining world, A." **CP-EmerR**

"Take my heart in thy hand, O beautiful boy of Schiraz!" **CP-EmerR**

"There resides in the grieving." **CP-EmerR**

"They strew in the path of kings and czars." **CP-EmerR**

"This effervescing gentleman who despises a secret." **CP-EmerR**

"Thou who with thy long hair." **CP-EmerR**

"Thousand dangers of ruin has the street of love." **CP-EmerR**

"Thy poems Hafiz shame the rose leaves." **CP-EmerR**

"Thy songs O Hafiz." **CP-EmerR**

"'Tis write on Paradise's gate." **CP-EmerR**

"To be wise the dull brain so earnestly throbs." **CP-EmerR**

"To whom a glass full of red wine." **CP-EmerR**

"Treacherous wind pipes a lewd song, The." **CP-EmerR**

"Understanding's copper coin, The." **CP-EmerR**

"Untruth is become the mode." **CP-EmerR**

"Way of love is unlimited, The." **CP-EmerR**

"We wish like the glass." **CP-EmerR**

"We would do nought but good." **CP-EmerR**

"What lovelier forms things wear." **CP-EmerR**

"When in eternity the light." **CP-EmerR**

"Where o where is the message which today." **CP-EmerR**

"Who compares a poem." **CP-EmerR**

"Who dedicates himself to the glass." **CP-EmerR**

"Who ever suffered as I from separation?" **CP-EmerR**

"Who gave thy cheek the mixed tint." **CP-EmerR**

"Who royally bedded." **CP-EmerR**

"Wine resembles the Lord Jesus." **CP-EmerR**

"World is a bride superbly dressed, The." **CP-EmerR**

"Yet all comes out of this, that one door." **CP-EmerR**

Odes. Horace, *tr. fr. Latin.*

"Brasen tower[*or*Tower] with doors[*or*dores] close barred[*or*bar'd], The." **CP-RaleW**

1.1: To Maecenas. **SP-SmarC,** *tr. by* Christopher Smart;

1.2: How to Live. **SP-MahoD,** *tr. by* Derek Mahon;

1.4: "Fetters of winter are shattered,shatter, The." **CP-CummE,** *tr. by* E. E. Cummings;

1.4: To Sextius, a Person of Consular Dignity. **SP-SmarC,** *tr. by* Christopher Smart;

1.5: "What slender youth bedewed [*or* bedew'd] with liquid odours" ("Quis multa gracilis").

(Fifth Ode of Horace, The.) **CP-MiltJ,** *tr. by* Milton;

1.9: "Behold yon mountain's hoary height." ("Vides ut alta"). **CP-CowpW**

("See'st thou yon mountains laden with deep snow.") **CP-CowpW,** *tr. by* William Cowper;

1.22: Translations of Horace ("Integer vitae"). **CP-JohnS,** *tr. by* Samuel Johnson;

1.24: "I mist my end, and lost my way." **CP-JohnS,** *tr. by* Samuel Johnson;

1.24: "Who chides the tears that weep so dear a head?" **CP-CummE,** *tr. by* E. E. Cummings;

1.38: Simplicity. **CP-CowpW,** *tr. by* William Cowper;

("Ah child, no Persian—perfect art.") **CP-HopkG,** *tr. by* Gerard Manley Hopkins;

(Another Translation of the Same Ode.) **CP-CowpW,** *tr. by* William Cowper;

("Boy! I detest all Persian fopperies.") **CP-CowpW,** *tr. by* William Cowper;

(Horace: Persicos Odi, Puer, Apparatus.) **CP-HopkG**

("Persian pomps, boy, ever I renounce them.") **SP-SmarC,** *tr. by* Christopher Smart;

(To His Servant.) **SP-SmarC,** *tr. by* Christopher Smart;

2.1: "With heedless feet on fires you go." **CP-JohnS,** *tr. by* Samuel Johnson;

2.5: "Maid whom now you court in vain, The." **CP-JohnS,** *tr. by* Samuel Johnson;

2.9: Translation of Horace: *Odes* II ix. **CP-JohnS,** *tr. by* Samuel Johnson;

2.10: "Receive, dear friend, the truths I teach" ("Rectius vives"). **CP-CowpW,** *tr. by* William Cowper;

2.14: "Ah, Postumus, fleet-footed are the years!" **CP-CummE,** *tr. by* E. E. Cummings;

("Ah! Posthumus, the years, the years.") **SP-SmarC,** *tr. by* Christopher Smart;

(To Posthumus.) **SP-SmarC**

2.14: Translation of Horace *Odes* II xiv ("Eheu Fugaces"). **CP-JohnS,** *tr. by* Samuel Johnson;

2.15: Upon the Luxury of the Age He Lived in. **SP-SmarC,** *tr. by* Christopher Smart;

2.16: To Grosphus. **SP-SmarC,** *tr. by* Christopher Smart; **CP-CowpW**

("Ease is the weary merchant's pray'r.") **CP-CowpW,** *tr. by* William Cowper;

2.18: "Gold or iv'ry's not intended." **SP-SmarC,** *tr. by* Christopher Smart;

2.20: Translation of Horace: *Odes* II xx. **CP-JohnS,** *tr. by* Samuel Johnson;

3.1: "Tread back—and back, the lewd and lay!"

(Horace: Odi Profanum Volgus Et Arceo.) **CP-HopkG**

3.2: "Seldome the villaine, though much hast he make." **CP-RaleW,** *tr. by* Sir Walter Ralegh;

3.2: "Stranger to folly and to fear." **CP-JohnS,** *tr. by* Samuel Johnson;

3.4: "Who rules the duller earth, the wind-swolne streames." **CP-RaleW,** *tr. by* Sir Walter Ralegh;

3.7: "To taint th'attentive mind she tries." **CP-JohnS,** *tr. by* Samuel Johnson;

3.9: Dialogue between Horace and Lydia, A ("Donec gratus eram"). **CP-HerrR,** *tr. by* Robert Herrick;

3.9: To Lydia. Dialogue of Horace and Lydia. **CP-JonsB,** *tr. by* Ben Jonson;

3.12: To Neobule. **SP-SmarC,** *tr. by* Christopher Smart;

3.13: Translation of Horace's Ode III, xiii. **CP-WorW1,** *tr. by* William Wordsworth;

3.16: "By gifts the Macedon clave Gates a-sunder." **CP-RaleW,** *tr. by* Sir Walter Ralegh;

3.16: To Maecenas. **SP-SmarC,** *tr. by* Christopher Smart;

3.22: Pine Tree for Diana, The ("Montium custos nemorumque"). **SP-SmarC**

("Queen of the mountains far and near.") **SP-SmarC,** *tr. by* Christopher Smart;

3.23: "If rustic Phidyle her prayer renews." **CP-JohnS,** *tr. by* Samuel Johnson;

3.24: "He whom the dread of want ensnares." **CP-JohnS,** *tr. by* Samuel Johnson;

3.24: "Nor Southerne heat nor Northerne snow." **CP-RaleW,** *tr. by* Sir Walter Ralegh;

4.1: To Venus. **CP-JonsB**

4.2: Praise of Pindar, The ("Pindarum quisquis studet aemulari").

(To Antonius Julus, the Son of Mark Antony, tof the Triumvirate.) **SP-SmarC**

("Whoever vies with Pindar's strain.") **SP-SmarC,** *tr. by* Christopher Smart;

4.2: "Such as like heavenly wights doe come." **CP-RaleW,** *tr. by* Sir Walter Ralegh;

4.3: To Melpomene. **SP-SmarC,** *tr. by* Christopher Smart;

4.6: "O, blessed of the gods." **CP-CummE,** *tr. by* E. E. Cummings;

4.7: "Farewell,runaway snows! For the meadow is green,and the tree stands." **CP-CummE,** *tr. by* E. E. Cummings;

4.7: "Snow dissolvd no more is seen, The" ("Diffugere nives").

("Melted snow the verdure now restores, The.") **SP-SmarC,** *tr. by* Christopher Smart;

(To L. Manlius Torquatus.) **SP-SmarC,** *tr. by* Christopher Smart;

(Translation of Horace *Odes* IV vii ("Diffugere nives").) **CP-JohnS,** *tr. by* Samuel Johnson;

4.9: "Many by valour have deserved renown." **CP-RaleW,** *tr. by* Sir Walter Ralegh;

4.11: To Phyllis. **SP-SmarC,** *tr. by* Christopher Smart;

Out of Horace. **CP-CrasR,** *tr. by* Richard Crashaw;

Odi et Amo. Alun Lewis. **CP-LewiA**

Odin. Frederick Morgan. **SP-MorgF**

Odin's Song. Frederick Morgan. **SP-MorgF**

Odor is of sulphur and autumn, The. The Pharmacy. Lewis Turco. **SP-TurcL**

Odour from the flower is gone, The. On a Faded Violet. Percy Bysshe Shelley. **CP-ShelP**

Odour, The. (2 Corinthians 2). George Herbert. **CP-HerbG**

Odradek. Lewis Turco. **SP-TurcL**

O'Driscoll drove with a song. The Host of the Air. William Butler Yeats. **CP-YeatW**

Odysseus Encircled. Homer, *tr. by* George Meredith. **CP-MerG2** *Fr.* The Iliad.

Odysseus on Hermes. Thom Gunn. **CP-GunnT**

Odyssey. Homer, *tr. fr. Greek by* Robert Fitzgerald.

Daughters of Pandarus, The. **CP-BroEB,** *tr. by* Elizabeth Barrett Browning;

Gardens of Alcinous, The. **CP-PopeA**

"Mindes of men are ever so affected, The." **CP-RaleW,** *tr. by* Sir Walter Ralegh;

"Muse, / tell me of this man of wit." **CP-DoolH**

"Sun descending, the *Phæacian* train, The." **CP-PopeA**

Odyssey, The. Alun Lewis. **CP-LewiA**

Odyssey of error humbles the cosmopolitan, An. The Cosmopolitan Sense. Jim Carroll. **SP-CarrJ**

Oedipus. Richard Eberhart. **CP-EberR**

Oedipus at Colonus. Sophocles, *tr. fr. Ancient Greek.*

Colonus' Praise. **CP-YeatW**

"Stranger, this is shining Colonos." **CP-SpenS**

"What man is he that yearneth." **CP-HousA**

Oedipus Rex. Sophocles, *tr. by* Stephen Spender. **CP-SpenS** *Fr.* Oedipus the King [*or* Oedipus Rex].

Oedipus slew his father near this muddy field. On the Way to Delphi. John Updike. **CP-UpdiJ**

Oedipus the King [*or* Oedipus Rex]. Sophocles, *tr. fr.* Ancient Greek. Oedipus Rex. **CP-SpenS**

Oedipus Tyrannus; or, Swellfoot the Tyrant. Percy Bysshe Shelley. **CP-ShelP**

Œnone. Tennyson. **CP-TennA**

O'er faded heath-flowers spun, or thorny furze. The Gossamer. Charlotte Smith. **CP-SmitC**

O'er Ice the rapid Skaiter flies. Translations of Roy's Verses on Skaters. Samuel Johnson. **CP-JohnS**

O'er the bare woods, whose outstretched hands. The Last Walk in Autumn. John Greenleaf Whittier. **CP-WhitJ**

O'er the garden water goes the wind alone. "Anvari", *tr. fr.* Persian by Ralph Waldo Emerson. **CP-EmerR**

O'er the glad waters of the dark blue sea. Byron. *Fr.* The Corsair. **CP-Byron**

 "Unlike the heroes of each ancient race." **NOBRP**

O'er the glad waters of the dark blue sea. The Corsair. Byron. **CP-Byron**

O'er the high down the night-wind blew. Lydia. Charlotte Smith. **CP-SmitC**

O'er the raised earth the gales of evening sigh. Fragment. Samuel Taylor Coleridge. **CP-ColeS**

O'er the Water to Charlie. Robert Burns. **CP-BurnR**

O'er the wide earth, on mountain and on plain. William Wordsworth. **CP-WorW1**

O'er wayward childhood would'st thou hold firm rule. Love, Hope, and Patience in Education. Samuel Taylor Coleridge. **CP-ColeS**

O'erhung with yew, midway the Muses mount. A Mighty Fountain. Samuel Taylor Coleridge. **CP-ColeS**

O'erweening Statesmen have full long relied. 1810. William Wordsworth. **CP-WorW1**

O'erwhelm'd with sorrow, and sustaining long. Verses Intended to Have Been Prefixed to the Novel of Emmeline, but Then Suppressed. Charlotte Smith. **CP-SmitC**

Of: / my crow / Pluto. To Victor Hugo of My Crow Pluto. Marianne Craig Moore. **CP-MoorM**

Of a Drunkard. Quintus Catulus, *tr. fr. Latin* by Richard Lovelace. **CP-LoveR**

Of a few years. Of Years. Robert Creeley. **CP-CreeR**

Of a Lady Singing to Her Lute, *in imitation of* Waller. Alexander Pope. **CP-PopeA**

Of a Professor. John Hewitt. **CP-HewiJ**

Of a Son. Walter de la Mare. **CP-DeLaW**

Of a steady winking beat between. Paraphrase. Hart Crane. **CP-CranH**

Of A' the Airts [the Wind Can Blaw]. Robert Burns.
 (I Love My Jean.) **CP-BurnR**

Of a' the ills that flesh can fear. My Conscience! Robert Louis Stevenson. **CP-StevR**

Of all among the fallen from on high. Doctor of Billiards. Edwin Arlington Robinson. **CP-RobiE**

Of all disquiets sorrow is most serene. Reflexive. Hayden Carruth. **CP-CarHS**

Of all God's creatures give me man. Song for a Temperature of a Hundred and One. Ogden Nash. **CP-NashO**

Of all grandeur that was Solomon's. At the Wailing Wall in Jerusalem. Countee Cullen. **CP-CullC**

Of all green trees, I love a nevergreen. Blue Spruce. Muriel Rukeyser. **CP-RukeM**

Of all our bath-house thieves the cleverest one. Catullus. *See* Carmen 33: "Vibennius & son, renowned."

Of all our parts, the eyes expresse. Bashfulnesse. Robert Herrick. **CP-HerrR**

Of all returns in man's device. Lines with a Pocket Book. Christopher Smart. **SP-SmarC**

Of all sad words of tongue or pen. The Saddest Words. John Greenleaf Whittier. **ImPo** *Fr.* Maud Muller. **CP-WhitJ**

Of all that ever in extreme disease. Edna St. Vincent Millay. **CP-MillE**

Of all that Orient lands can vaunt. The Haschish. John Greenleaf Whittier. **CP-WhitJ**

Of all that weeks-long day, though call it back. John Berryman. *Fr.* Sonnets to Chris. **CP-BerrJ**

Of all the birds that rove and sing. Jenny Wren. Walter de la Mare. **CP-DeLaW**

Of all the blessings which to man. Edward Estlin Cummings. **CP-CummE; SP-CummE**

Of all the causes which conspire to blind. Alexander Pope. **OxAEP-1** *Fr.* An Essay on Criticism. **CP-PopeA**

Of all the cities in Romanian lands. Disdain Punished. John Dryden. **EBNV; NOSC** *Fr.* Theodore and Honoria, From [Fables Ancient and Modern from] Boccace. **SP-DrydJ**

Of all the cities in Romanian lands. Theodore and Honoria, From [Fables Ancient and Modern from] Boccace. John Dryden. **SP-DrydJ**

Of all the disgraceful and abominable things. This Is Disgraceful and Abominable. Stevie Smith. **CP-SmitS**

Of all the downfalls in the world, / The flutter of an Autumn leaf. Vanity of Vanities. Christina Georgina Rossetti. **CP-RosC2**

Of all the gifts thine hand bestows. Praise for Faith. William Cowper. *Fr.* Olney Hymns. **CP-CowpW**

Of all the good things whatsoe're we do. Robert Herrick. **CP-HerrR**

Of all the kings that ever here did reign. Sonnet 75. Sir Philip Sidney. **NoSic** *Fr.* Astrophil and Stella. **SP-SidnP**

Of all the nights, yours were greenest, Gene. Jungle Strut. Al Young. **CP-YounA**

Of all the numerous ills that hurt our peace. Remorse. Robert Burns. **CP-BurnR**

Of all the off'rings thanks can find. An Epistle to John Sherratt, Esq. Christopher Smart. **SP-SmarC**

Of all the rides since the birth of time. Skipper Ireson's Ride. John Greenleaf Whittier. **CP-WhitJ**

Of all the Souls that stand create. Emily Dickinson. **CP-DickE**

Of all the Sounds despatched abroad. Emily Dickinson. **CP-DickE**

Of all the things that I would rather. In Which the Poet Is Ashamed but Pleased. Ogden Nash. **CP-NashO**

Of all the thoughts of God that are. The Sleep. Elizabeth Barrett Browning. **CP-BroEB**

Of all the trees that grow so fair. A Tree Song. Rudyard Kipling. **CP-KiplR** *Fr.* Weland's Sword. *Fr.* Puck of Pook's Hill.

Of all the twice ten thousand bards. Ballad. Byron. **CP-Byron**

Of all the ways in which this country. American Cancer Society Or There Is More Than One Way to Skin a Coon. Audre Lorde. **SP-LordA**

Of all things, lady, be not proud. Advice to a Beauty. Countee Cullen. **CP-CullC**

Of all things under our. Edward Estlin Cummings. **CP-CummE**

Of all things which are living and can form a judgment. Euripides, *tr. by* Rex Warner. **GrIP** *Fr.* Medea. **CP-JefR3,** *tr. by* Robinson Jeffers.

Of all those discourses I have heard. Thomas Merton. *Fr.* The Legacy of Herakleitos. **CP-MertT**

Of all those three-brave-brothers, faln i'th'Warre. To the Right Gratious Prince, Lodwick, Duke of Richmond and Lenox. Robert Herrick. **CP-HerrR**

Of all who hail thy presence as the morning. To M. L. S——. Edgar Allan Poe. **CP-PoeEd**

Of Amlwch, / a pattern of fields and buildings. Patchworks. Steve Griffiths. **SP-GrifS**

Of an Evening Pulling Off a Little Experience (with the english language). Hart Crane. **CP-CranH**

Of an it ignoblest he, The. Edward Estlin Cummings. **CP-CummE**

Of asphodel, that greeny flower. Asphodel, That Greeny Flower. William Carlos Williams. **CP-WilW2**

Of asphodel, that greeny flower. William Carlos Williams. **CMoP; PP** *Fr.* Asphodel, That Greeny Flower. **CP-WilW2**

Of asphodel, that greeny flower, the least. Paterson, Book V: The River of Heaven. William Carlos Williams. **CP-WilW2**

Of Beginning Light. Charles Tomlinson. **CP-TomlC**

Of Being is a Bird. Emily Dickinson. **CP-DickE**

Of Being Numerous. George Oppen. **CP-OppeG**

 "*Amor fati* / The love of fate."

 "Approached the window as if to see."

 "Because the known and the unknown."

 "Behind their house, behind the back porch."

 "Chorus (androgynous): 'Find me'."

 "Clarity / In the sense of *transparence*."

 "Emotions are engaged, The."

 "For the people of that flow."

 "Great stone / Above the river, The."

 "Half free / And half mad."

 "He who will not work shall not eat."

 "I cannot even now / Altogether disengage myself."

 "In these explanations it is presumed."

 "In this nation." **GOA**

 "It is difficult now to speak of poetry." **NNaP**

 "It is *that* light."

 "It is the air of atrocity."

"Light / Of the closed pages, tightly closed, packed against each other, The."

"Like the wind in the trees and the bells."

"My daughter, my daughter, what can I say."

"Now in the helicopters the casual will."

"Obsessed, bewildered / By the shipwreck."

"Occurring 'neither for self'."

"Only that it should be beautiful."

"Or define / Man beyond rescue."

"Or, in that light, New arts!'"

"Roots of words, The."

"So spoke of the existence of things."

"Strange that the youngest people I know."

"There are things / We live among 'and to see them'."

"There can be a brick."

"They await / War, and the news."

"They carry nativeness / To a conclusion."

"Tho the world."

"Unable to begin / At the beginning, the fortunate."

"We are pressed, pressed on each other."

"Whether, as the intensity of seeing increases, one's distance."

"Which is ours, which is ourselves."

"Whitman: 'April 19, 1864'."

"You are the last."

Of both our Fortunes good and bad we find. Felicitie Knowes No Fence. Robert Herrick. **CP-HerrR**

Of bricks. . . Who built it? Like some crazy balloon. Our Youth. John Ashbery. **SP-AshbJ**

Of Bright & Blue Birds & the Gala Sun. Wallace Stevens. **CP-StevW**

Of Bronze—and Blaze. Emily Dickinson. **CP-DickE**

Of Brook and Stone. Hayden Carruth. **CP-CarHS**

Of Brussels—it was not. Emily Dickinson. **CP-DickE**

Of buildings, this building, / frame a stream of windows. Arches. James Schuyler. **CP-SchuJ**

Of Carthage he, that worthy warrior. Sir Thomas Wyatt. **CP-WyatT**

Of Cato. Pentadius, *tr. fr. Latin by* Richard Lovelace. **CP-LoveR**

Of Chloe all the town has rung. Strephon and Chloe. Jonathan Swift. **CP-SwifJ**

Of Colmcille, blood-arrogant and royal. Colmcille. John Hewitt. *Fr.* Two Irish Saints. **CP-HewiJ**

Of Coming-into-Being and Passing-Away. Geoffrey Hill. **CP-HillG**

Of Commerce and Society: Variations on a Theme. Geoffrey Hill. **CP-HillG**

Apostles: Versailles, 1919, The.

Death of Shelley, The.

   "Rivers bring down. The sea."

   "Slime; the residues of refined tears."

Lowlands of Holland, The.

Martyrdom of Saint Sebastian.

Ode on the Loss of the Titanic.

"Statesman have known visions. And, not alone."

Of Conscience. Isabella Gardner. **CP-GardI**

Of Consciousness, her awful Mate. Emily Dickinson. **CP-DickE**

Of course I may be remembering it all wrong. Santarém. Elizabeth Bishop. **CP-BishE**

Of Course—I prayed. Emily Dickinson. **CP-DickE**

Of course, if you make naughtiness nasty. Our Moral Age. David Herbert Lawrence. **CP-LawrD**

Of course it is all twisted. Gimlet. Gilbert Sorrentino. **SP-SorrG**

Of course it is snowing. Dear Old Stockholm. Al Young. **CP-YounA**

Of course it sounds cold. More Under Saturn. William Dickey. **SP-DickW**

Of course make love not. Hayden Carruth. **CP-CarHS** *Fr.* The Clay Hill Anthology.

Of course, mankind—and the brain of it, brawn of it. On Canann Mountain Meadow. Hayden Carruth. **CP-CarHS**

Of course, of course! Who else would die. The Germans Are Lunatics. Randall Jarrell. **CP-JarrR**

Of course the dead outnumber us. Death's Door. Thom Gunn. **CP-GunnT**

Of course, the entire effort is to put my [*or* one] self. Thoughts During an Air Raid. Stephen Spender. **CP-SpenS**

Of course, the gruffest prompting comes from age. John Hewitt. *Fr.* October Sonnets. **CP-HewiJ**

Of course the plane is late. The Poet Dreams of a Nice Warm Motel. Marge Piercy. **SP-PierM**

Of course, we were all fucked-up, I was suicidal but hitting the. The Old Gang. Charles Bukowski. **SP-BukC3**

Of course you must stop her. Say anything: "Hello!" "Good-bye!" Kenneth Koch. *Fr.* The Art of Love. **SP-KochK**

Of course you will always want to be. Mid-Life Crises: A Critical Review. Al Young. **CP-YounA**

Of course you're dreaming. Ghost of His Wife Comes to Tell Him How It Is. Miller Williams. **SP-WillM**

Of course Zimmer was late for the gig. The Duke Ellington Dream. Paul Zimmer. **SP-ZimmP**

Of De Witt Williams on His Way to Lincoln Cemetery. Gwendolyn Brooks. **NOBA; NoAM** *Fr.* A Street in Bronzeville. **SP-BrooG**

Of Death. Ben Jonson. **CP-JonsB**

Of death / the barber. Death the Barber. William Carlos Williams. **CP-WilW1**

Of Death I try to think like this. Emily Dickinson. **CP-DickE**

Of Distress Being Humiliated by the Classical Chinese Poets. Hayden Carruth. **CP-CarHS**

Of each sad word which is more sorrowful. Christina Georgina Rossetti. **CP-RosC2**

Of English blood, of Tuscan birth. A Child's Grave at Florence. Elizabeth Barrett Browning. **CP-BroEB**

Of Equality—as if it harm'd me, giving others the same chances and rights as myself—as if it were not indispensible to my own rights that others possess the same. Thought. Walt Whitman. **CP-WhitW**

Of Ever-Ever Land i speak. Edward Estlin Cummings. **CP-CummE; SP-CummE**

Of every land or east or west. My Native Land. David Herbert Lawrence. *Fr.* Songs I Learnt at School. **CP-LawrD**

Of evident invisibles / exquisite the hovering. Edward Estlin Cummings. **CP-CummE**

Of Experience. Howard Nemerov. **CP-NemeH**

Of falling leaves and melting. Artful Pose. Maya Angelou. **SP-AngeM**

Of Fields with dead bestrew'd around. Upon the Feast of St Simon and St Jude. Samuel Johnson. **CP-JohnS**

Of fire and of lust proceeds the world. Howard Nemerov. *Fr.* Four Sonnets. **CP-NemeH**

Of Fitness to Survive. Louise McNeill. **SP-McNeL**

Of Flanks and Chines of Beefe doth *Gorrell* boast. Great Boast, Small Rost. Robert Herrick. **CP-HerrR**

Of Flesh and Bone. Isabella Gardner. **CP-GardI**

Of Folly weary, shrinking from the view. To the Goddess of Botany. Charlotte Smith. **CP-SmitC**

Of foure teeth onely Bridget was possest. Upon Bridget. Robert Herrick. **CP-HerrR**

Of gentle Philips will I ever sing. The Three Gentle Shepherds. Alexander Pope. **CP-PopeA**

Of Glory not a Beam is left. Emily Dickinson. **CP-DickE**

Of God we ask one favor. Emily Dickinson. **CP-DickE**

Of gold the bread on which he banqueted. Caligula's Dream. John Updike. **CP-UpdiJ**

Of green and hexagonal glass. The Bottle. Walter de la Mare. **CP-DeLaW**

Of Grief. May Sarton. **SP-SartM**

Of Hartford in a Purple Light. Wallace Stevens. **CP-StevW**

Of H[ayley]s birth this was the happy lot. William Blake. **CP-BlakW**

Of Heaven Considered as a Tomb. Wallace Stevens. **CP-StevW**

Of her arms, this was her sin. Hutch. Anne Sexton. **CP-SextA**

Of Her Picture, *in imitation of* Waller. Alexander Pope. **CP-PopeA**

Of Her Sickness, *in imitation of* Waller. Alexander Pope. **CP-PopeA**

Of Her Sighing, *in imitation of* Waller. Alexander Pope. **CP-PopeA**

Of Her Walking in a Garden after a Shower, *in imitation of* Waller. Alexander Pope. **CP-PopeA**

Of heroes, history, grand events, premises, myths, poems. The Few Drops Known. Walt Whitman. **CP-WhitW**

Of Him I Love Day and Night. Walt Whitman. **CP-WhitW**

Of Him That Was Ready to Perish. Christina Georgina Rossetti. **CP-RosC2**

Of Himself. William Cowper. **CP-CowpW**

Of Hours. George Oppen. **CP-OppeG**

Of how that current ran in, and turned. Silhouette. John Ashbery. **SP-AshbJ**

Of ice. Deceptively reserved and flat. An Octopus. Marianne Craig Moore. **CP-MoorM**

Of interest to John Calvin and Thomas Aquinas. Why God Permits Evil: For Answers to This Question of Interest to Many Write Bible Answers Dept. E-7. Miller Williams. **SP-WillM**

Of it, the trees have the wind willing one thing—pretty feet. On My Side. Kenneth Patchen. **CP-PatcK**

Of Jacopo del Sellaio. Ezra Pound. **SP-PounE**

Of Jeoffry, His Cat. Christopher Smart. *See* For I will consider my Cat Jeoffry.

Of John Davidson. "Hugh MacDiarmid." **SP-MacDH**

Of Justice—as if Justice could be any thing but the same ample law, expounded by natural judges and saviors. Thought. Walt Whitman. **CP-WhitW**

Of keeping; the competition of brutal law. O Fill Your Sack with Tiger Cubs. Kenneth Patchen. **CP-PatcK**

Of Lady Grange. Charles Tomlinson. **CP-TomlC**

Of Lady, of Beauty, of Stream. Charles Olson. **CP-OlsoC**

Of late, in one of those most weary hours. The Garden of Boccaccio. Samuel Taylor Coleridge. **CP-ColeS**

Of late I've been talking to my shadow. Conversation Piece. Leonard Nathan. **SP-NathL**

Of late they leave the light on in my entry. Words for Muffin, a Guinea Pig. Robert Lowell. **SP-LoweR**

Of Late Two Dainties Were before Me Placed. John Keats. **CP-KeatJ**

Of lead and emerald. A Note to Olga (1966). Denise Levertov. **CP-LeveD**

Of Life and Death. Ben Jonson. **CP-JonsB**

Of Life to own. Emily Dickinson. **CP-DickE**

Of little use the man you may suppose. Alexander Pope. **EBEV** *Fr.* The First Epistle of the Second Book of Horace Imitated. **CP-PopeA**

Of Love ("Ile get me hence"). Robert Herrick. **CP-HerrR**

Of Love ("Instruct me now, what love will do"). Robert Herrick. **CP-HerrR**

Of Love: ("I do not love, nor can it be"). Robert Herrick. **CP-HerrR**

Of Love. A Sonnet. Robert Herrick. **CP-HerrR**

Of Manners gentle, of Affections mild. On Mr. Gay, in Westminster Abbey, 1732. Alexander Pope. **CP-PopeA**

Of Man's First Disobedience, and the Fruit. John Milton. **EBEVv; EPCY; FaBoRV; FiP; NAWM-1; NoP; PeECV; SCV; TOF; TreFS,** *ll.* 1–26; **EBEV,** *ll.* 1–270; **NIP,** *ll.* 1–49; **FaPoB,** *ll.* 1–74; **TEP,** *ll.* 1–75; **FaBoEn; NOSC; PoE; PoEL-3** *Fr.* Book I. **FHYEP; NAEL-1; OAEL-1; OxAEP-1** *Fr.* Paradise Lost. **CP-MiltJ**

(Induction, The.) **PoE,** *ll.* 1–26;

(Invocation.) **FaBoEn; NOSC; PoEL-3,** *ll.* 1–26;

Of Man's [*or* Mans] First Disobedience, and the Fruit. Book I. John Milton. **FHYEP; NAEL-1; OAEL-1; OxAEP-1** *Fr.* Paradise Lost. **CP-MiltJ**

Of Many a Smutch'd Deed Reminiscent. Walt Whitman. **CP-WhitW**

Of Margaret ("Frost, and a leaf has quit the tulip tree"). John Crowe Ransom. *Fr.* Sixteen Poems in Eight Pairings. **SP-RansJ**

Of Margaret ("With the fall of the first leaf that winds rend"). John Crowe Ransom. *Fr.* Sixteen Poems in Eight Pairings. **SP-RansJ**

Of Mathilde. Charles Olson. **CP-OlsoC**

Of me and of my theme think what thou wilt. My Theme. George Meredith. **CP-MerG1**

Of medium nature, this farouche extreme. The Bouquet. Wallace Stevens. **CP-StevW**

Of men he would have raised to light he fell. Gordon of Khartoum. George Meredith. **CP-MerG1**

Of Mercy. Isabella Gardner. **CP-GardI**

Of Merlin wise I learned a song. Merlin's Song. Ralph Waldo Emerson. **CP-EmerR**

Of moderate height. The Magician's Retreat. Marianne Craig Moore. **CP-MoorM**

Of Modern Poetry. Wallace Stevens. **CP-StevW**

Of Money. And the Past. Muriel Rukeyser. **CP-RukeM**

Of morning, Iowa City, blue. Poem. Ted Berrigan. **SP-BerrT**

Of mortal Justice if thou scorn the rod. Virgil, *tr.* by Samuel Johnson. **CP-JohnS** *Fr.* The Aeneid [*or* Eneados, Aeneis].

Of mortal parents is the Hero born. Hofer. William Wordsworth. **CP-WorW1**

Of mother of sex. When the Glass of My Body Broke. Anne Sexton. **CP-SextA**

Of music, in a cavernous house. Note to Music: Brahms 1st Piano Concerto. William Carlos Williams. **CP-WilW2**

Of my / soul a street is. Edward Estlin Cummings. **CP-CummE**

Of my city the worst that men will ever say is this. They Will Say. Carl Sandburg. **CP-SandC**

Of My First Love. "Hugh MacDiarmid." **SP-MacDH**

Of my grandmother / who at over eighty. The Teachings. Robert Creeley. **CP-CreeR**

Of My Life. Christina Georgina Rossetti. **CP-RosC3**

Of Nature I shall have enough. Emily Dickinson. **CP-DickE**

Of nearness to her sundered Things. Emily Dickinson. **CP-DickE**

Of Neptune's empire [*or* Empyre] let us sing. Thomas Campion. **CP-CampT**

(Hymne in Praise of Neptune, A.) **CP-CampT**

Of Nicolette. Edward Estlin Cummings. **CP-CummE**

Of noble minds and noble hearts. John Boyle O'Reilly. Paul Laurence Dunbar. **CP-DunbP**

Of nothing but me, me. Introduction. John Updike. *Fr.* Midpoint. **CP-UpdiJ**

Of obedience, faith, adhesiveness. Thought. Walt Whitman. **CP-WhitW**

Of olden time, when it came to pass. Blood-Money. Walt Whitman. **CP-WhitW**

Of One Dead. Tennyson. *See* If one should bring me this report.

Of one scrap of science I've evidence ocular. Verses Trivocular. Samuel Taylor Coleridge. **CP-ColeS**

Of ownership—as if one fit to own things could not at pleasure enter upon all, and incorporate them into himself or herself. Thoughts. Walt Whitman. **CP-WhitW**

Of Pacchiarotto, and How He Worked in Distemper. Robert Browning. **CP-BroR2**

Of Paradise' existence. Emily Dickinson. **CP-DickE**

Of Paradise, O hermit wise. Ghaselle. Hafiz, *tr. fr. Persian by* Ralph Waldo Emerson. **CP-EmerR**

Of Paul and Silas it is said. Emily Dickinson. **CP-DickE**

Of pearl light and blue shadows. Man in Old Blue Suit at the Plaza. Gilbert Sorrentino. *Fr.* Twelve Études for Voice and Kazoo. **SP-SorrG**

Of people running down the street. A Picture. Howard Nemerov. **CP-NemeH**

Of persons arrived at high positions, ceremonies, wealth, scholarships, and the like. Thought. Walt Whitman. **CP-WhitW**

Of public opinion. Thoughts. Walt Whitman. **CP-WhitW**

Of purpose Love chose first for to be blind. Sir Thomas Wyatt. **CP-WyatT**

Of Pushes Spalt has such a knottie race. Upon Spalt. Robert Herrick. **CP-HerrR**

Of rhymes I printed seven volumes. E Nihilo Nihil. Byron. **CP-Byron**

Of rights and of wrongs. Mrs. Choate's House-Warming. John Greenleaf Whittier. **CP-WhitJ**

Of Robert Frost. Gwendolyn Brooks. **SP-BrooG**

Of Robin Redbreast's babes I told. George Meredith. **CP-MerG2**

Of Rumor, of Clamor. Geoffrey Hill. *Fr.* Scenes with Harlequins. **CP-HillG**

Of sailors—those two Corsicans at Marseille. A Traveller Born. Hart Crane. **CP-CranH**

Of Schooners, Islands, and Maroons. Robert Louis Stevenson. **CP-StevR**

Of seven sparrows on a country wire. Minus One. John Ciardi. **SP-CiarJ**

Of Silken Speech and Specious Shoe. Emily Dickinson. **CP-DickE**

Of simple choice they are the villagers; their clothes come. Adrienne Rich. **HCAP; SP-RicA2** *Fr.* Shooting Script. **CP-RicAE**

Of so divine a Loss. Emily Dickinson. **CP-DickE**

Of *solanum tuberosum,* that vagrant vegetable. William Matthews. *Fr.* This Spud's for You. **SP-MattW**

Of speckled eggs the birdie sings. Singing. Robert Louis Stevenson. **CP-StevR**

Of such touch given. William Everson. **SP-EverW** *Fr.* The Blowing of the Seed.

Of Suicide. John Berryman. **CP-BerrJ**

Of That Blithe Throat of Thine. Walt Whitman. **CP-WhitW**

Of that short roll of friends writ in my heart. To Mr I. L. John Donne. **CP-DonnJ**

Of that world's conquest and the fortunate wars, The. True History of Bernál Díaz. Archibald MacLeish. *Fr.* Conquistador. **CP-MacLA**

Of the beast. . . an angel. The Everlasting Contenders. Kenneth Patchen. **CP-PatcK**

Of the Blessed Sacrament of the Altar [*or* Aulter]. Robert Southwell. **CP-SoutR**

Of the electric guitar as a percussion instrument. A Prayer to the Mountain. John Ciardi. **SP-CiarJ**

Of the Empirical Self and for Me. Roy Fisher. **SP-FishR**

Of the Four Ages of Man. Anne Bradstreet. **CP-BradA**

Of the Four Humors in Man's Constitution. Anne Bradstreet. **CP-BradA**

Of the four louts who threw him off the dock. A Finished Man. Richard Wilbur. **CP-WilbR**

Of the Francia. Malcolm Lowry. *Fr.* The Lighthouse Invites the Storm. **CP-LowrM**

Of the Great World he knew not much. Epitaph. Howard Nemerov. **CP-NemeH**

Of the handsome bluey-brown bodies, they might just as well be gutta-percha. Sea-Bathers. David Herbert Lawrence. **CP-LawrD**

Of the Heart that goes in, and closes the Door. Emily Dickinson. **CP-DickE**

Of the hospital with the news that. Coming Out. Ron Koertge. **SP-KoerR**

Of the incertain game. The Deposition. Howard Nemerov. **CP-NemeH**

Of the jungle / In the desecration of the iris. In the Gears. Jim Carroll. **SP-CarrJ**

Of the Lady Lu there were stories told. The Caricature. Thomas Hardy. **CP-HardT**

Of the Lady Who Could Not Sleep in a Stormy Night, *in imitation of* Waller. Alexander Pope. **CP-PopeA**

Of the many flowers you brought me. To Miss Rawlinson. Robert Louis Stevenson. **CP-StevR**

Of the million or two, more or less. Instans Tyrannus. Robert Browning. **CP-BroR1**

Of the no need. Hilda Doolittle. **NALW** *Fr.* Tribute to the Angels. **CP-DoolH**

Of the old heroes when the warlike shades. The Loyal Scot. Andrew Marvell. **CP-MarvA**

Of the primeval Priests assum'd power. The Book of Urizen [*or* First Book of Urizen]. William Blake. **CP-BlakW**

Of the Progres[se] of the Soule; the Second Anniversarie. John Donne. **CP-DonnJ**

Harbinger to the Progress, The.

Second Anniversary [*or* Anniversarie], The. **ESCV; SeCP**

Contemplation of Our State in Our Deathbed. **OBS**

Our Companie in the Next World. **OBS**

"Poor soul, in this thy flesh what dost thou know?" **OAEL-1**

("Poore soule, in this thy flesh what dost thou know?") **OBS**

(Soules Ignorance in This Life and Knowledge in the Next, The.) **OBS**

("We see in authors, too stiff to recant.") **NOSC**, *ll.* 281–300;

"We now lament not, but congratulate." **NOSC**

Of the right way. As to How Much. Louis Zukofsky. **CP-ZukLS**

Of the rights of each to zero. No, I mean the only. Hayden Carruth. *Fr.* Paragraphs. **CP-CarHS**

Of the same beauty were stars made. Kenneth Patchen. **CP-PatcK**

Of the Seasons. May Sarton. **SP-SartM**

Of the shadow cast by earth in the sun's light. Introspectional. Hayden Carruth. *Fr.* Poetical Abstracts. **CP-CarHS**

Of the Stones of the Place. Robert Frost. **CP-FrosR**

Of the Surface of Things. Wallace Stevens. **CP-StevW**

Of the Terrible Doubt of Appearances. Walt Whitman. **CP-WhitW**

Of the three voices, it is hers that stays. Die Älte Frau, Die Älte Marschallin. William Dickey. **SP-DickW**

Of the two cardinals the female is both bolder and more "beautiful." She comes. Meditation in the Presence of "Ostrich Walk." Hayden Carruth. **CP-CarHS**

Of the two, one / faces one. In. One Way. Robert Creeley. **CP-CreeR**

Of the United States. Charles Olson. **CP-OlsoC**

Of the visages of things—And of piercing through to the accepted hells beneath. Thoughts—I: Visages. Walt Whitman. **CP-WhitW**

Of the wholesome, lonesome ones. For the Shut Eye. Marsden Hartley. **CP-HartM**

Of the Winter Ball Game. Charles Tomlinson. **CP-TomlC**

Of thee (kind boy) I ask no red and white. Sonnet. Sir John Suckling. **CP-SuckJ**

Of their peculiar light. Emily Dickinson. **CP-DickE**

Of them, undefined / repetitions, the / inactual. It Is at Times. Robert Creeley. **CP-CreeR**

Of these the false Achitophel was first. John Dryden. **AWP; FaBoEH; FiP; HAP; InPS; NOBE; NOSC; OBS; PoEL-3; SeCePo; WHA** *Fr.* Absalom and Achitophel, Pt. I. **SP-DrydJ**

(Achitophel.) **AWP; SeCePo**

(Achitophel: The Earl of Shaftsbury.) **NOBE**

(False Achitophel, The.) **FiP**

(Shaft[e]sbury.) **NOSC; OBS**

Of these years I sing. Thoughts. Walt Whitman. **CP-WhitW**

Of this / all things. The Little Pin: Fragment. George Oppen. **CP-OppeG**

Of This All Things. . . . George Oppen. **CP-OppeG**

Of this aspiring burgher who disdained. Lasalle. Donald Davie. **CP-DavDo**

Of this day hovers. Over the Rim. Daniel Gerard Hoffman. **SP-HoffD**

Of this Ensuing Discourse. Thomas Campion. **CP-CampT**

Of this is Day composed. Emily Dickinson. **CP-DickE**

Of this profusion. Middle. William Carlos Williams. **CP-WilW1**

Of this sunset(which is so). Edward Estlin Cummings. **CP-CummE**

Of this wilting wall the colour drub. Edward Estlin Cummings. **CP-CummE**

Of those ambitions which incited me. The Poet's Trade. John Hewitt. **CP-HewiJ**

Of thousands grown climb head-on-head. "X." Louis Zukofsky. **CP-ZukLS**

Of tides that toss the souls of men. The Turnip-Hoer. Thomas Hardy. **CP-HardT**

Of Time & the Body. David St. John. *Fr.* Study for the World's Body. **SP-StJoD**

Of Tolling Bell I ask the cause? Emily Dickinson. **CP-DickE**

Of Tribulation, these are They. Emily Dickinson. **CP-DickE**

Of two fair virgins, modest, though admired. Jacopo Vittorelli, *tr. fr. Italian by* Byron. **CP-Byron**

(Translation from Vittorelli.) **CP-Byron**

Of virtues I most warmly bless. Gerard Manley Hopkins. **FaBoEE** *Fr.* Seven Epigrams. **CP-HopkG**

Of war and peace the truth just twists. Gates of Eden. "Bob Dylan." **CP-DylaB**

Of waste and again of waste, and of the waste of wasting, o void, o desolation. I Tell You For Several Years of My Madness I Heard the Voice of Lilith Singing in the Trees of Chicago. Hayden Carruth. **CP-CarHS**

Of wealthy lustre was the banquet-room. The Banquet. John Keats. **SeCePo** *Fr.* Lamia. **CP-KeatJ**

Of western New York state. As You Came from the Holy Land. John Ashbery. **SP-AshbJ**

Of what an easy quick access. Prayer (2). George Herbert. **CP-HerbG**

Of what I write from myself—As if that were not the resumé. Thoughts—6: "Of What I Write." Walt Whitman. **CP-WhitW**

Of what importance, O my lovely girls, my dancers, O my lovely boys. Edna St. Vincent Millay. **CP-MillE**

Of What Is Past. Charles Kenneth Williams. **CP-WillC; SP-WillC**

Of what mould did Nature frame me[?]. The Tinder. Thomas Carew. **CP-CareT**

Of where or how, I nothing know;. The Susquehanna and the Delaware. Robert Louis Stevenson. **CP-StevR**

Of which I am the sand—. This Florida: 1924. William Carlos Williams. **CP-WilW1**

Of white and tawny, black as ink. Variation on a Sentence. Louise Bogan. **CP-BogaL**

Of who we and all they are. The Grapevine. John Ashbery. **SP-AshbJ**

Of whom so dear. Emily Dickinson. **CP-DickE**

Of whom two will make love. What happens. Here There Are Three of Us Driving South in This Expensive Car. William Dickey. **SP-DickW**

Of Wickedness the Word. Herman Melville. **SP-MelvH** *Fr.* Clarel: A Poem and Pilgrimage in the Holy Land.

Of writing many books there is no end! Elizabeth Barrett Browning. **NOBVV** *Fr.* Aurora Leigh. **CP-BroEB**

Of Writings Unfinished. David Markson. **CP-MarkD**

Of Years. Robert Creeley. **CP-CreeR**

Of Yellow was the outer Sky. Emily Dickinson. **CP-DickE**

Of you, if anyone, it can be said. Catullus. *See* Carmen 98: "Same can be said of you, Victius, The."

Of your trouble, Ben, to ease me. Her Man Described by Her Own[e] Dictamen. Ben Jonson. *Fr.* A Celebration of Charis in Ten Lyric[k] Pieces [*or* Peeces]. **CP-JonsB**

Of yourself and your beginnings. John Haines. *Fr.* Daphne. **SP-HainJ**

Off a pane)the. Edward Estlin Cummings. **CP-CummE**

Off Cape Colona. Herman Melville. **SP-MelvH**

Off garbage outside the diner. Outside the Diner. Thom Gunn. **CP-GunnT**

Off Highway 106. Cherrylog Road. James Dickey. **CP-DickJ**

Off left in a hollow. Third Mile. James McAuley. *Fr.* Ten-Mile Run. **SP-McAuJ**

Off Point Lotus. Stanley Jasspon Kunitz. **CP-KuniS**

Off she goes, my little Red-Riding-Hood. Story. Jenny Joseph. *Fr.* Derivations. **SP-JoseJ**

Off Spectacle Island. Richard Eberhart. **CP-EberR**

Off that landspit of stony mouth-plugs. Medusa. Sylvia Plath. **CP-PlatS**

Off the coast of Ireland. Seascape. Langston Hughes. **SP-HughL**

Off the long headland, threshed about by round-backed breakers. The Black Rock. John Gould Fletcher. **SP-FletJ**

Off the Peg. Louis MacNeice. **CP-MacNL**

Off the Top of My Head. "Bob Dylan." **CP-DylaB**

Off the Trail. Gary Snyder. **CP-SnydG**

Offense, The. James Wright. **CP-WrigJ**

Offer 'em up to me—bullneck crook of the baths. Catullus. *See* Carmen 33: "Vibennius & son, renowned."

Offer it up plank it down. Ooftish. Samuel Beckett. **CP-BeckS**

Offer no borrowed proof or energy; the dust. That We Here Highly Resolve. Kenneth Patchen. **CP-PatcK**

Offer thy gift; but first the Law commands. To Julia . Robert Herrick. **CP-HerrR**

Offering. Siv Cedering Fox. **SP-CedeS**

Offering, An. George Herbert. **CP-HerbG**

Offering. Thomas McGrath. **SP-McGrT**

Offering. William Carlos Williams. **CP-WilW1**

Offering and Rebuff. Carl Sandburg. **CP-SandC**

Offering for Mr. Bluehart, An. James Wright. **CP-WrigJ**

Offering of the New Law, the One Oblation Once Offered, The. Christina Georgina Rossetti. **CP-RosC3**

Offerings. Walt Whitman. **CP-WhitW**

Office Love. Karl Shapiro. **SP-ShapK**

Office sunlight, edging back, protrudes, The. Winter Afternoon. Wystan Hugh Auden. **CP-AudWJ**

Officer wore a thin smile, The. Howard Nemerov. *Fr.* Seven Macabre Songs. **CP-NemeH**

Officers' Prison Camp Seen from a Troop-Train, An. Randall Jarrell. **CP-JarrR**

Official Piety. John Greenleaf Whittier. **CP-WhitJ**

Offscape, the in-folds, secreted, The. At the Edge. Charles Tomlinson. **CP-TomlC**

Offspring of Jove, Calliope, once more. Homer's Hymn to the Sun. *Unknown.* **CP-ShelP** *Fr.* Homeric Hymns.

Oft as I paced the deck. At Sea, September 1833. Ralph Waldo Emerson. **CP-EmerR**

Oft bend the Bow, and thou with ease shalt do. By Use Comes Easinesse. Robert Herrick. **CP-HerrR**

Oft did I wounder why the sweets of Love. Sonnet. Mary Sidney, Countess of Montgomery Wroth. *Fr.* Pamphilia to Amphilanthus. **CP-WrotM**

Oft has our Poet wisht [or wished], this happy Seat. John Dryden. **SP-DrydJ**
(Epilogue to the University of Oxford, 1674.) **SP-DrydJ**

Oft has the muse, with mean attempt, employed. A Poem to the Memory of Mr. Congreve. James Thomson. **CP-ThomJ**

Oft have I caught, upon a fitful breeze. Written in a Blank Leaf of MacPherson's *Ossian.* William Wordsworth. *Fr.* Poems Composed or Suggested During a Tour, in the Summer of 1833. **CP-WorW2**

Oft have I heard both Youths and Virgins say. To His Valentine, on S. Valentines Day. Robert Herrick. **CP-HerrR**

Oft have I looked on France with envy vain. To P.A. Labouchère Esq. George Meredith. **CP-MerG2**

Oft have I mused, but now at length I find. Sir Philip Sidney. **SP-SidnP**

Oft have I said, I say it once more. Hafiz, *tr.* by Ralph Waldo Emerson. **CP-EmerR** *Fr.* Odes.

Oft have I seen, ere Time had ploughed my cheek. Decay of Piety. William Wordsworth. **CP-WorW2**

Oft have I sigh'd for him that heares me not. Thomas Campion. **CP-CampT**

Oft have I wonder'd that on Irish ground. On Mr. Burke by an Opponent and a Friend to Mr. Hastings. Robert Burns. *Fr.* Dumfries Epigrams. **CP-BurnR**

Oft have you seen a swan superbly frowning. John Keats. **PBBP** *Fr.* To Charles Cowden Clarke. **CP-KeatJ**

Oft have you seen a swan superbly frowning. To Charles Cowden Clarke. John Keats. **CP-KeatJ**

Oft I had heard of Lucy Gray. Lucy Gray; or, Solitude. William Wordsworth. **CP-WorW1**

Oft in Danger yet alive. To Mrs Thrale [on Her Thirty-fifth Birthday]. Samuel Johnson. **CP-JohnS**

Oft in the stilly night. Who Did Which? or Who Indeed? Ogden Nash. **CP-NashO**

Oft is the medal faithful to its trust. Inscription in a Garden of Stone. William Wordsworth. **CP-WorW1**

Oft o'er my brain does that strange fancy roll. Sonnet Composed on a Journey Homeward; the Author Having Received Intelligence of the Birth of a Son, 20 September 1796. Samuel Taylor Coleridge. **CP-ColeS**

Oft, oft methinks, the while with thee. The Happy Husband. Samuel Taylor Coleridge. **CP-ColeS**

Oft-Repeated Dream, The. Robert Frost. **Poetr** *Fr.* The Hill Wife. **CP-FrosR**

Oft, through thy fair domains, illustrious Peer! William Wordsworth. *Fr.* The Excursion. **CP-WorW2**

Oft we enhance our ills by discontent. By Philemon. Philemon, *tr. fr. Greek* by William Cowper. **CP-CowpW**

Oft when I look I may descry. The Dart. Thomas Carew. **CP-CareT**

Oft when I'm sitting without anything to read. Lines to a World-famous Poet Who Failed to Complete a World-famous Poem; or, Come Clean, Mr. Guest! Ogden Nash. **CP-NashO**

Oft with true sighs, oft with uncalled tears. Sonnet 61. Sir Philip Sidney. **NAEL-1** *Fr.* Astrophil and Stella. **SP-SidnP**

Often, / around certain backwaters / like the ponds behind the oyster shacks. Great Blue. Brendan Galvin. **SP-GalvB**

Often an easterly churns. Letter from our Man in Blossomtime. Louise Glück. **SP-GlücL**

Often beneath the wave, wide from this ledge. At Melville's Tomb. Hart Crane. **CP-CranH**

Often dreaming on juicy fat tomatoes. Woman Irritable because of Her Menses. Gilbert Sorrentino. *Fr.* Twelve Études for Voice and Kazoo. **SP-SorrG**

Often, half-way to sleep. In Procession. Robert Ranke Graves. **CP-GravR**

Often I Am Permitted to Return to a Meadow. Robert Duncan. **SP-DuncR**

Often I leave my television set to listen to my wireless. This Is My Own, My Native Tongue. Ogden Nash. **CP-NashO**

Often I looked at you—started at the window I had started. *tr. fr. the German of* Rilke. Randall Jarrell. **CP-JarrR**

Often I meet, on walking from a door. The Signals. Theodore Roethke. **CP-RoetT**

Often I saw, as on my balcony. Christ Church Meadows, [Oxford]. Donald Hall. **CP-HallD**

Often I squinted my courage to see the spot. The Vanishing Point. Miller Williams. **SP-WillM**

Often I think of the beautiful town. My Lost Youth. Henry Wadsworth Longfellow. **SP-LongH**

Often I visit them where they slump. The Old Clothes. Brendan Galvin. **SP-GalvB**

Often I watched her lift it. Old Smoothing Iron. Seamus Heaney. **SP-HeanS** *Fr.* Shelf Life.

Often I would stand at the window. Grandmother. Louise Glück. *Fr.* Dedication to Hunger. **SP-GlücL**

Often, in these blue meadows. Pursuit from Under. James Dickey. **CP-DickJ**

Often it will start without me and come soon to where I once was. The Lesson in Composition. Roy Fisher. **SP-FishR**

Often rebuked, yet always back returning. Stanzas. Emily Brontë. **CP-BronE**

Often the man, alone shut, shall consider. Wystan Hugh Auden. **CP-AudWJ**

Often the mockingbird is only a mocker. Kansas Lessons. Carl Sandburg. **CP-SandC**

Often Was It. Kenneth Patchen. **CP-PatcK**

Often When Warring. Thomas Hardy. **CP-HardT**

Oggi. Christina Georgina Rossetti. *Fr.* Il Rosseggiar Dell'Oriente Canzoniere. **CP-RosC3**

Ogre, The. William Carlos Williams. **CP-WilW1**

Ogre does what ogres can, The. August 1968. Wystan Hugh Auden. **CP-AudeW**

Ogres and Pygmies. Robert Ranke Graves. **CP-GravR**

Oh / CRASH! / my / BASH! The Fourth. Shel Silverstein. **SP-SilS2**

Oh. Anne Sexton. **CP-SextA**

Oh / the sumac died. Some Simple Measures in the American Idiom and the Variable Foot. William Carlos Williams. **CP-WilW2**

Oh, a patch of green. Charles Henri Ford. **SP-FordC** *Fr.* Emblems of Arachne.

Oh Absalom, beloved, what can I say? Lament. Alun Lewis. **CP-LewiA**

Oh all the money that in my whole life I did spend. Restless Farewell. "Bob Dylan." **CP-DylaB**

O[h] *all ye,* who pass[e] by, whose eyes and mind[e]. The Sacrifice. George Herbert. **CP-HerbG**

Oh, America / The sun sets in you. The Evening Land. David Herbert Lawrence. **CP-LawrD**

Oh, Ammons rolled the octaves slow. An Expatiation on the Combining of Weathers at Thirty-Seventh and Indiana Where the Southern More or Less Crosses the Dog. Hayden Carruth. **CP-CarHS**

Oh and / Who is it unforlorn. Malcolm Lowry. **CP-LowrM**

Oh, Anne! your offences to me have been grievous. To Anne. Byron. **CP-Byron**

Oh, ask not what is love, she said. Arthur Hugh Clough. **SP-ClouA**

Oh, Auntie, isn't he a beauty! And is he a gentleman or a lady? Puss-Puss! David Herbert Lawrence. **CP-LawrD**

Oh, ban the books and save the children's lives. John Hewitt. *Fr.* Two Sonnets on the Free State of Censorship Bill. **CP-HewiJ**

"Oh! banish care"—such ever be. Epistle to a Friend. Byron. **CP-Byron**

Oh be a demon. Be a Demon! David Herbert Lawrence. **CP-LawrD**

Oh be thou blest with all that Heav'n can send. To Mrs. M. B. on Her Birth-Day. Alexander Pope. **CP-PopeA**

Oh, black Persian cat! Mujer. William Carlos Williams. **CP-WilW1**

Oh! bold bad Baronet / You need no coronet. Sir John Piers. Sir John Betjeman. **CP-BetjJ**

Oh Brittannia's got a baby, a baby, a baby. Brittannia's Baby. David Herbert Lawrence. **CP-LawrD**

Oh brother, put me in your pouch. The Child and the Soldier. David Herbert Lawrence. *Fr.* Bits. **CP-LawrD**

Oh but is it not hard, Dear? Mary Wollstonecraft and Fuseli. Robert Browning. **CP-BroR2**

Oh, but it is dirty! Filling Station. Elizabeth Bishop. **CP-BishE**

Oh but my doubt is a sea harsher than this that I see. Louis MacNeice. *Fr.* Didymus. **CP-MacNL**

Oh but, says one, tradition set aside. Tradition. John Dryden. **OBS** *Fr.* Religio Laici. **SP-DrydJ**

Oh, cabaret dancer, *I* know a dancer. How a Little Girl Danced. Nicholas Vachel Lindsay. **CP-LindV**

Oh, Castlereagh! thou art a patriot now. Epigrams. Byron. **CP-Byron**

Oh Christianity, Christianity. Stevie Smith. **CP-SmitS**

Oh cold and ferocious are the children of the cross. The Children of the Cross. Stevie Smith. **CP-SmitS**

Oh Colonel, you from Embaba. The Girl in Cairo. David Herbert Lawrence. *Fr.* Bits. **CP-LawrD**

Oh, come again to Astolat! Elaine. Edna St. Vincent Millay. **CP-MillE**

Oh come, let us sing unto Jehovah. Bible, *O.T. See* Psalm 95: "O come, let us sing unto the Lord."

Oh, come, my lad, or go, my lad. The Betrothal. Edna St. Vincent Millay. **CP-MillE**

Oh, comrade, comrade, I have missed you so! Comrade. Paul Laurence Dunbar. **CP-DunbP**

Oh, could I draw, my friend, thy genuine mind. On the Death of Mr. Aikman. James Thomson. **CP-ThomJ**

Oh! could Le Sage's demon's gift. Granta—A Medley. Byron. **CP-Byron**

Oh (cry'd the Goddess) for some pedant Reign! Alexander Pope. **FaBoEH** *Fr.* Yet, yet a moment, one dim ray of light. **NAEL-1; OAEL-1; PoEL-3** *Fr.* The Dunciad. **CP-PopeA**

Oh curse them not nor rail. Bureaucrats: Diggers. Thomas Merton. **CP-MertT**

Oh Daddy, look at that man, excuse my pointing, but just look at him! Machinery Doesn't Answer, Either, but You Aren't Married to It. Ogden Nash. **CP-NashO**

Oh! Darling. The Beatles. **CP-Beatl**

Oh, de clouds is mighty heavy. Keep a Song Up on de Way. Paul Laurence Dunbar. **CP-DunbP**

Oh, de grubbin'-hoe's a-rustin' in de co'nah. The Deserted Plantation. Paul Laurence Dunbar. **CP-DunbP**

Oh, de weathah it is balmy an' de breeze is sighin' low. Li'l' Gal. Paul Laurence Dunbar. **CP-DunbP**

Oh dead punk lady with the knack. The Victim. Thom Gunn. **CP-GunnT**

Oh dear, / the plane is so small the baggage. East Hampton—Boston by Air. John Updike. **CP-UpdiJ**

Oh dear, what can I do, baby's in black and I'm feeling blue. Baby's in Black. John Lennon *and* Paul McCartney. **CP-Beatl**

Oh death / about you I know nothing, nothing. Gladness of Death. David Herbert Lawrence. **CP-LawrD**

Oh, dere's lots o' keer an' trouble. A Banjo Song. Paul Laurence Dunbar. **CP-DunbP**

Oh! did those eyes, instead of fire. To M———. Byron. **CP-Byron**

Oh! did you ne'er hear of a jolly young Carpenter. The Jolly Young Carpenter. George Meredith. **CP-MerG2**

Oh! did you observe the Black Canon pass. Saint Edmond's Eve. Percy Bysshe Shelley. *Fr.* Original Poetry by Victor and Cazire. **CP-ShelP**

Oh dirty Maggie Mae they have taken her away. Maggie Mae. *Unknown.* **CP-Beatl**

Oh do not die, for I shall hate. A Fever. John Donne. **CP-DonnJ**

Oh, do not forget the day when we met. Ode To Damon. "Lewis Carroll." **CP-CarrL**

Oh, do not tell me the heavens as well are a wheel. The Wandering Cosmos. David Herbert Lawrence. **CP-LawrD**

Oh do[e] not wanton with those eyes. Ben Jonson. **CP-JonsB**

Oh down at the tavern. Portrait of an Old Woman on the College Tavern Wall. Anne Sexton. **CP-SextA**

Oh, dwarfed and wronged, and stained with ill. A Woman. John Greenleaf Whittier. **CP-WhitJ**

Oh, early every afternoon. Cat Naps Are Too Good for Cats. Ogden Nash. **CP-NashO**

Oh, East is East, and West is West, and never the twain shall meet. The Ballad of East and West. Rudyard Kipling. **CP-KiplR**

Oh factious viper! whose envenom'd tooth. Byron. **CP-Byron**

Oh fair enough are sky and plain. Alfred Edward Housman. **CP-HousA**

Oh fair Milly Brandon, a young maid, a fair maid! Brandons Both. Christina Georgina Rossetti. **CP-RosC2**

Oh, Fair To See. Christina Georgina Rossetti. **CP-RosC2**

Oh, Fair to See. Christina Georgina Rossetti. **CP-RosC2; FaPON; OHIP; TiPo** *Fr.* Sing-Song. **CP-RosC2**

Oh fallen star! a darkened light, / A glory hurtled form its car. O Lucifer, Son of the Morning! Christina Georgina Rossetti. **CP-RosC2**

Oh flame falling, as shaken, as the stories. The Fire. Robert Creeley. **CP-CreeR**

Oh, fond attempt to give a deathless lot. William Cowper. **CP-CowpW**

(On the Biographia Britannica.) **CP-CowpW**

Oh for a candle I could light. Love Magick. Erica Jong. **SP-JongE**

Oh! for a closer walk with God. Walking with God. William Cowper. **ECEV; EnRP; FiP; NOCV; NOEC; PeECV; PoEL-3; SCGP; TEP; TOF** *Fr.* Olney Hymns. **CP-CowpW**

Oh for a knight like Bayard. The Hero. John Greenleaf Whittier. **CP-WhitJ**

Oh for a lodge in some vast wilderness. William Cowper. **EnRP; NOEC; OAEP** *Fr.* The Time-piece. *Fr.* The Task. **CP-CowpW**

(Against Slavery.) **NOEC**

Oh for a lodge in some vast wilderness. The Time-piece. William Cowper. *Fr.* The Task. **CP-CowpW**

Oh for a poet—for a beacon bright. Sonnet. Edwin Arlington Robinson. **CP-RobiE**

Oh for boyhood's painless play. John Greenleaf Whittier. **AiP** *Fr.* The Barefoot Boy. **CP-WhitJ**

Oh! for imperial Polydamna's art. Nepenthe. Charlotte Smith. **CP-SmitC**

Oh for my love, my only love. A Dream. Christina Georgina Rossetti. **CP-RosC3**

O[h]! for some honest lover's ghost. Sonnet. Sir John Suckling. **CP-SuckJ**

Oh for the breath of the briny deep. A Sailor's Song. Paul Laurence Dunbar. **CP-DunbP**

Oh for the time gone by when thought of Christ. Come Unto Me. Christina Georgina Rossetti. **CP-RosC3**

Oh Forza Irresistibile Dell'umile Preghiera. Christina Georgina Rossetti. *Fr.* Il Rosseggiar Dell'Oriente Canzoniere. **CP-RosC3**

Oh, Friend, for ever loved, for ever dear! Epitaph on a Friend. Byron. **CP-Byron**

Oh Future! thou secreted peace. Emily Dickinson. **CP-DickE**

Oh, gallant was our galley from her carven steering-wheel. The Galley-Slave. Rudyard Kipling. **CP-KiplR**

Oh [*or* O] Galuppi, Baldassaro, this is very sad to find! A Toccata of Galuppi's. Robert Browning. **CP-BroR1**

Oh gentle Jesus of the hymnal once. Malcolm Lowry. **CP-LowrM**

Oh, gipsies, proud and stiff-necked and perverse. I Know All This When Gipsy Fiddles Cry. Nicholas Vachel Lindsay. **CP-LindV**

Oh give it Motion—deck it sweet. Emily Dickinson. **CP-DickE**

Oh, give us pleasure in the flowers today. A Prayer in Spring. Robert Frost. **CP-FrosR**

Oh, glorious are the guarded heights. The Wage-Slaves. Rudyard Kipling. **CP-KiplR**

Oh God help me now to cry out and bear witness. The Restless Night. Thomas McGrath. **SP-McGrT**

Oh god, let's go. / This is a poem for Kenneth Patchen. Please. Robert Creeley. **CP-CreeR**

Oh God said to Abraham, "Kill me a son." Highway 61 Revisited. "Bob Dylan." **CP-DylaB**

Oh God the Olney Hymns abound. Olney Hymns. Sir John Betjeman. **CP-BetjJ**

Oh, good gigantic smile o' the brown old earth. Among the Rocks. Robert Browning. **OxBSP** *Fr.* James Lee's Wife. **CP-BroR1**

Oh Grateful Colours, Bright Looks! Stevie Smith. **CP-SmitS**

Oh, greenly and fair in the lands of the sun. The Pumpkin. John Greenleaf Whittier. **CP-WhitJ**

Oh! had each SCOT of ancient times. On Miss J. Scott, of Ayr. Robert Burns. **CP-BurnR**

Oh! had my fate been join'd with thine. To a Lady. Byron. **CP-Byron**

Oh half as fearful for the yawning day. Terce. John Berryman. **CP-BerrJ**

Oh hand me down my old cigar with its Havana wrapper. What to Do until the Doctor Goes or It's Tomorrow Than You Think. Ogden Nash. **CP-NashO**

Oh Happy Days are here again. Good Luck. Malcolm Lowry. **CP-LowrM**

Oh happy happy land! Christian and Jew. A Dialogue. Christina Georgina Rossetti. **CP-RosC1**

Oh happy shades—to me unblest! The Shrubbery. William Cowper. **CP-CowpW**

Oh hard is the bed they have made him. Illic Jacet. Alfred Edward Housman. **CP-HousA**

Oh Have You Heard. Shel Silverstein. **SP-SilS2**

Oh, he *is* sweet. I do love him sometimes. Muriel Rukeyser. **CP-RukeM**

Oh hell, what do mine eyes. Milton by Firelight. Gary Snyder. **CP-SnydG**

Oh, help me in my weakness. Drifter's Escape. "Bob Dylan." **CP-DylaB**

Oh, here the air is sweet and still. The Little Hill. Edna St. Vincent Millay. **CP-MillE**

Oh, here we are at the mammoth banquet. The Banquet. Ogden Nash. **CP-NashO**

Oh ho uncircumcised Sadducee I see. A Jew Is Angry with His Friend Who Does Not Believe in Circumcision. Stevie Smith. **CP-SmitS**

Oh, honey of an hour. Emily Dickinson. **CP-DickE**

Oh [*or* O] how comely it is and how reviving. John Milton. **NOBE; NOCV; OBEV; OBS; OXAEP-1; SeCeV** *Fr.* Samson Agonistes. **CP-MiltJ**

(Deliverer, The.) **OBS**

Oh How I Wish That an Embargo. Byron. **CP-Byron**

Oh how the women. The Little Peasant. Anne Sexton. **CP-SextA**

Oh, how worried they are about my. Soul. Charles Bukowski. **SP-BukC1**

Oh how you used to walk. Just for a Time. Maya Angelou. **SP-AngeM**

Oh, Hubshee, carry your shoes in your hand and bow your head on your breast! Kitchener's School. Rudyard Kipling. **CP-KiplR**

Oh! hush thee, my baby, the night is behind us. Rudyard Kipling. **CP-KiplR** *Fr.* The White Seal. *Fr.* The Jungle Book.

Oh I am a cat that likes to. The Galloping Cat. Stevie Smith. **CP-SmitS**

Oh I am a chickie who lives in an egg. I Won't Hatch. Shel Silverstein. **SP-SilS2**

Oh, I am come to the low Countrie. The Highland Widow's Lament. Robert Burns. **CP-BurnR**

Oh, I am grown so free from care. The Merry Maid. Edna St. Vincent Millay. **CP-MillE**

Oh, I am hurt to death, my Love. One Life. Paul Laurence Dunbar. **CP-DunbP**

Oh I am of the people! Amo Sacrum Vulgus. David Herbert Lawrence. **CP-LawrD**

Oh I can praise a cloistered virtue, such. Three Moral Discoveries. Donald Davie. **CP-DavDo**

Oh, I des received a letter f'om de sweetest little gal. A Love Letter. Paul Laurence Dunbar. **CP-DunbP**

Oh, I do like a little bit of gossip. This Was Told Me in Confidence. Ogden Nash. **CP-NashO**

Oh, I have done those things that my Soul fears. Arthur Hugh Clough. **SP-ClouA**

Oh I have loved my fellow-men. But I Say unto You: Love One Another. David Herbert Lawrence. **CP-LawrD**

Oh, I have n't got long to live, for we all. A Border Ballad. Paul Laurence Dunbar. **CP-DunbP**

Oh, I have walked in Kansas. Kansas. Nicholas Vachel Lindsay. **CP-LindV**

Oh I know / if I'd practised the piano. Gradus ad Parnassum. Muriel Rukeyser. **CP-RukeM**

Oh I loved you Pete Brown. And you were a brother. Hayden Carruth. Jaz *Fr.* Paragraphs. **CP-CarHS**

Oh I suppose I should. Le Médecin Malgré Lui. William Carlos Williams. **CP-WilW1**

Oh I was bad. Ballad of a Bad Boy. Patti Smith. **SP-SmitP**

Oh I wish that there were some wing, some wing. I Wish. Stevie Smith. **CP-SmitS**

Oh if a thousand old folk looked askance. The Great Death. Hayden Carruth. *Fr.* Contra Mortem. **CP-CarHL**

Oh, If Only. Stevie Smith. **CP-SmitS**

Oh, if you're a bird, be an early bird. Early Bird. Shel Silverstein. **SP-SilS2**

Oh I'm a British bo—oy, Sir. The British Boy. David Herbert Lawrence. *Fr.* Songs I Learnt at School. **CP-LawrD**

Oh, I'm being eaten. Boa Constrictor. Shel Silverstein. **SP-SilS2**

Oh I'm Dirty Dan, the world's dirtiest man. The Dirtiest Man in the World. Shel Silverstein. **SP-SilS2**

Oh I'm going to ride on The Flying Festoon. The Flying Festoon. Shel Silverstein. **SP-SilS2**

Oh, I'm sailin' away my own true love. Boots of Spanish Leather. "Bob Dylan." **CP-DylaB**

Oh in a slim spaced forest. Alun Lewis. *Fr.* Pastorals. **CP-LewiA**

Oh, in the pen, oh, in the pen. Keep That Morphine Moving, Cap. Robert Penn Warren. *Fr.* Penological Study: Southern Exposure. **CP-WarrR**

Oh, in the world of the flesh of man. What Then Is Evil? David Herbert Lawrence. **CP-LawrD**

Oh is it the jar of nations. Alfred Edward Housman. **CP-HousA**

Oh it's fare thee well my darlin' true. Farewell. "Bob Dylan." **CP-DylaB**

Oh, I've never writ a ballad. How Ballad Writing Affects Our Seniors. Ernest Hemingway. **CP-HemiE**

Oh Jews, an' lords, an' moneymen. The Song of the Shipyard Men. John Hewitt. **CP-HewiJ**

Oh journeyman, Oh journeyman. Song. Alun Lewis. **CP-LewiA**

Oh! kangaroos, sequins, chocolate sodas! Today. Frank O'Hara. **SP-OharF**

O[h] King of grief! (a title strange, yet true). The Thanksgiving. George Herbert. **CP-HerbG**

Oh kiss me once before I go. Husband and Wife. Christina Georgina Rossetti. **CP-RosC3**

Oh knell of a passing time, / Will it never cease to chime? Christina Georgina Rossetti. **CP-RosC2**

Oh Lady! when I left the shore. To Florence. Byron. **CP-Byron**

Oh, late withdrawn from human-kind. *after* Horace Book 5, Ode 20. Rudyard Kipling. **CP-KiplR** *Fr.* Debits and Credits.

Oh, lay my ashes on the wind. The Curse. Edna St. Vincent Millay. **CP-MillE**

Oh, le petit rondelay! Chanson. Robert Creeley. **CP-CreeR**

Oh, let me not serve so, as those men serve. John Donne. *Fr.* Elegies. **CP-DonnJ**

Oh, let's go up the hill and scare ourselves. The Bonfire. Robert Frost. **CP-FrosR**

Oh Life! without thy chequered scene. After-Thought. William Wordsworth. *Fr.* Memorials of a Tour of the Continent; 1820. **CP-WorW2**

Oh, Light was the world that he weighed in his hands! A Song of Kabir. Rudyard Kipling. **CP-KiplR** *Fr.* The Miracle of Purun Bhagat. *Fr.* The Second Jungle Book.

Oh lion in a peculiar guise. The Roman Road. Stevie Smith. **CP-SmitS**

Oh listen, listen; for the Earth. The World's Harmonies. Christina Georgina Rossetti. **CP-RosC3**

Oh, little body, do not die. A Child Ill. Sir John Betjeman. **CP-BetjJ**

Oh, little did the Wolf-Child care. Romulus and Remus. Rudyard Kipling. **CP-KiplR**

Oh little fledgling out of the nest. Paul Laurence Dunbar. **CP-DunbP**

Oh, little rose tree, bloom! Three Songs from "The Lamp and the Bell." Edna St. Vincent Millay. **CP-MillE**

Oh, long had we paltered. Hymn of the Triumphant Airman. Rudyard Kipling. **CP-KiplR**

Oh Lord Cozens Hardy. Lord Cozens Hardy. Sir John Betjeman. **CP-BetjJ**

Oh Lord have mercy on my soul. Suicide's Epitaph. Stevie Smith. **CP-SmitS**

"Oh Lord, our Lord! how wondrously,"(quoth she. *mod. vers. by* William Wordsworth; *incl.* The Prioress' Prologue. Geoffrey Chaucer. **CP-WorW1** *Fr.* The Canterbury Tales. **CP-ChauG**

Oh Lord upon whose will dependeth my welfare, *par. by* Earl of Surrey, Henry Howard. Bible, *O.T. See* Psalm 88: "O God of my salvation."

Oh lost garden Paradise. An Afterthought. Christina Georgina Rossetti. **CP-RosC3**

Oh lov'd! but not enough—though dearer far. Glory to God Alone. Jeanne Marie Bouvier de la Motte-Guyon, *tr. fr. French by* William Cowper. **CP-CowpW**

Oh, Love. Robert Creeley. **CP-CreeR**

Oh love / Oh Shame, we are late. Malcolm Lowry. **CP-LowrM**

Oh Love, Love, thou that from the eyes diffusest. Robert Browning. **CP-BroR2**

Oh love! no habitant of earth thou art. Byron. **CBLP; OBNC** *Fr.* Childe Harold's Pilgrimage. **CP-Byron**

(Fatal Spell, The.) **OBNC**

Oh, Love—no, Love! All the noise below, Love. Epilogue. Robert Browning. **CP-BroR2**

Oh, love, why do we argue like this? A Curse against Elegies. Anne Sexton. **CP-SextA**

Oh, Lovely Rock. Robinson Jeffers. **CP-JefR2**

Oh lyre divine, what daring spirit. Thomas Gray. **EPCY** *Fr.* The Progress of Poesy. **CP-GrayT**

Oh Mabel. Robert Creeley. **CP-CreeR**

Oh, Mariamne! now for thee. Herod's Lament for Mariamne. Byron. **CP-Byron**

Oh master, let it be loose-all, it is enough! Foreign Sunset. David Herbert Lawrence. *Fr.* Bits. **CP-LawrD**

Oh Matchless Earth—We underrate. Emily Dickinson. **SP-DickE**

Oh men, living men, vivid men, ocean and fire. Hold Back! David Herbert Lawrence. **CP-LawrD**

Oh! might I kiss those eyes of fire. Catullus. *See* Carmen 48: "Iuventius, / were I allowed."

Oh mirk, mirk is this midnight hour. Lord Gregory. Robert Burns. **CP-BurnR**

Oh Mr. Pussy-Cat. Nipping Pussy's Feet in Fun. Stevie Smith. **CP-SmitS**

Oh most delightful hour by man. On a Similar Occasion for the Year 1789. William Cowper. **CP-CowpW**

Oh mother. Mothers. Anne Sexton. **CP-SextA**

Oh, Mother, / Virgin Mother. Jesus, the Actor, Plays the Holy ghost. Anne Sexton. **CP-SextA**

Oh, much maligned one, meager hunkerer. Spleen. Stephen Dobyns. **SP-DobyS**

Oh my bald head. Apostrophe to a Buddhist Monk. David Herbert Lawrence. **CP-LawrD**

Oh, my belovèd, have you thought of this. Edna St. Vincent Millay. **CP-MillE**

Oh my black[e] soul[e]! now thou art summoned. John Donne. **EBEV; JCP; OAEL-1; OBS; OxAEP-1; Poetr; Son; TEP; TOF** *Fr.* Divine Meditations. **CP-DonnJ** *Fr.* Holy Sonnets. **CP-DonnJ**

Oh my darling Goosey-Gander. The True Tyrant or the Spirit of Duty Rebuked. Stevie Smith. **CP-SmitS**

Oh my God what a bitter shame. And Jude the Obscure and His Beloved. David Herbert Lawrence. **CP-LawrD**

Oh! my heart, although it sounds better. A Poem in Envy of Cavalcanti. Frank O'Hara. **SP-OharF**

Oh my lamented Talbot! while with thee. Ancient and Modern Italy Compared. James Thomson. *Fr.* Liberty. **CP-ThomJ**

Oh!—my lonely—lonely—lonely Pillow! Stanzas. Byron. **CP-Byron**

"Oh My Love. . . ." Robert Creeley. **CP-CreeR**

Oh my love and my own deary! What to Do? Christina Georgina Rossetti. **CP-RosC3**

Oh my name it is nothin'. With God on Our Side. "Bob Dylan." **CP-DylaB**

Oh, my old darling, my dear one, my friend. Wife. Barton Sutter. **SP-SuttB**

Oh! mystery of man, from what a depth. William Wordsworth. **FiP** *Fr.* Imagination and Taste, How Impaired and Restored. **EnRP** *Fr.* The Prelude; Growth of a Poet's Mind [1850 vers.]. **CP-WorW3**

Oh never talk again to me. The Girl of Cadiz. Byron. **CP-Byron**

Oh never try to knock on rotten wood. Admonitions. Sylvia Plath. **CP-PlatS**

Oh No. Robert Creeley. **CP-CreeR**

Oh, no one can deny. Self's the Man. Philip Larkin. **CP-LarkP**

Oh noble, rich, glowing color of blood. That Noble Flower. Robinson Jeffers. **CP-JefR3**

Oh nobody's a long time. Lonesome Boy Blues. Kenneth Patchen. **CP-PatcK**

Oh, none in all the world before. Hymn Sung at Christmas by the Scholars of St. Helena's Island, S.C. John Greenleaf Whittier. **CP-WhitJ**

"Oh no,"said It: "her lifedoings." The Absolute Explains. Thomas Hardy. **CP-HardT**

Oh, not inexplicable. Death explains. Hemingway. Archibald MacLeish. **CP-MacLA**

Oh, not the loss of the accomplished thing! Two Poems from the War. Archibald MacLeish. **CP-MacLA**

Oh, oh, you will be sorry for that word! Edna St. Vincent Millay. **CP-MillE**

Oh old dry rose of God. An Imaginary Rose in a Book. Allen Ginsberg. **CP-GinsA**

Oh, on an early morning I think I shall live forever! Poem in Three Parts. Robert Bly. **SP-BlyR**

Oh on my breast in days hereafter. Alfred Edward Housman. **CP-HousA**

Oh, once I walked a garden. On the Garden Wall. Nicholas Vachel Lindsay. **CP-LindV**

Oh, once I walked in Heaven, all alone. How Johnny Appleseed Walked Alone in the Jungles of Heaven. Nicholas Vachel Lindsay. **CP-LindV**

Oh, once there lived in Kankakee. Tune for an Ill-Tempered Clavichord. Ogden Nash. **CP-NashO**

Oh, open the door, some pity to shew. Open the Door to Me, Oh! Robert Burns. **CP-BurnR**

"Oh, our manhood's prime vigour! no spirit feels waste." Robert Browning. **OtMeF** *Fr.* Saul. **CP-BroR1**

Oh, over the factory cities there seems to hover a doom. The Factory Cities. David Herbert Lawrence. **CP-LawrD**

Oh pity the dead that are dead, but cannot take. The Houseless Dead. David Herbert Lawrence. **CP-LawrD**

Oh! place me where the burning noon. From Petrarch. Petrarch, *tr. fr. Italian by* Charlotte Smith. **CP-SmitC**

Oh! place me where the burning noon, *see also* trans. by Henry Howard, Earl of Surrey "Set me whereas the sun doth parch the green." Petrarch, *tr. by* Charlotte Smith. **CP-SmitC** *Fr.* Sonnets to Laura.

Oh pleasant eventide! Twilight Calm. Christina Georgina Rossetti. **CP-RosC1**

Oh! pleasant exercise of hope and joy! French Revolution as It Appeared to Enthusiasts at Its Commencement. Reprinted from "The Friend." William Wordsworth. **CP-WorW1**

Oh, Please Don't Get Up! Ogden Nash. **CP-NashO**

Oh, poor Mary Ann / When she got to the top. Malcolm Lowry. **CP-LowrM**

Oh [or O], praise an' tanks! De Lord he come. Song of the Negro Boatmen. John Greenleaf Whittier. **GN** *Fr.* At Port Royal. **CP-WhitJ**

Oh, Prue she has a patient man. She Is Overheard Singing. Edna St. Vincent Millay. **CP-MillE**

Oh pudgy podgy pup! / Why *did* they wake you up? "Lewis Carroll." *Fr.* Two Poems to Rachel Daniel. **CP-CarrL**

Oh, pyre of Bierce and springboard of Hart Crane! Malcolm Lowry. *Fr.* Songs for Second Childhood. **CP-LowrM**

"Oh! Raining! Look!" she whispered. Episodes. Walter de la Mare. **CP-DeLaW**

Oh Raphael. Guardian angel. In love and crime. Seventh Heaven. Patti Smith. **SP-SmitP**

Oh read the verses of the loaded scourges. The Biography. Thomas Merton. **CP-MertT; SP-MertT**

Oh, "rorty" was a mid-Victorian word. You Can Be a Republican, I'm a Genocrat. Ogden Nash. **CP-NashO**

Oh roses for the flush of youth. Song. Christina Georgina Rossetti. **CP-RosC1**

Oh sad thy lot before I came. Light Love. Christina Georgina Rossetti. **CP-RosC1**

Oh, said the discontented check, you will indeed win like it says in the papers. Thomas Merton. *Fr.* Cables to the Ace. **CP-MertT**

Oh, saucy gold circle of fairyland silk. On Suddenly Receiving a Curl Long Refused. Nicholas Vachel Lindsay. *Fr.* This Section Is a Christmas Tree. **CP-LindV**

Oh, saw I there. The Daisy. Walter de la Mare. **CP-DeLaW**

Oh say not, sweet Anne, that the Fates have decreed. To the Same. Byron. **CP-Byron**

Oh see how thick the goldcup flowers. Alfred Edward Housman. **CP-HousA**

Oh seekers, when you leave off seeking. Seekers. David Herbert Lawrence. **CP-LawrD**

Oh Shadow on the Grass. Emily Dickinson. **CP-DickE**

Oh sharp diamond, my mother! Christmas Eve. Anne Sexton. **CP-SextA**

Oh, show me how a rose can shut and be a bud again! The Scholars. Rudyard Kipling. **CP-KiplR**

Oh, Shucks, Ma'am, I Mean Excuse Me. Ogden Nash. **CP-NashO**

Oh, sick I am to see you, will you never let me be? The New Mistress. Alfred Edward Housman. **CP-HousA**

Oh sing unto Jehovah a new song; for he hath done marvellous things, *diff. vers.* Bible, *O.T. See* Psalm 98: "O sing unto the Lord a new song. . . ."

Oh, Sister. "Bob Dylan" *and* Jacques Levy. **CP-DylaB**

Oh, sleep forever in the Latmian cave. Edna St. Vincent Millay. **CP-MillE**

Oh! Snatch'd Away in Beauty's Bloom. Byron. **CP-Byron**

Oh sock, sock, sock! The Brilliance. William Carlos Williams. **CP-WilW2**

Oh, some people grieve for New Year's Eve. The Middle of the Month. Ogden Nash. **CP-NashO**

Oh, sometimes I sit around and think, what would you do if you. How Now, Sirrah? Oh, Anyhow. Ogden Nash. **CP-NashO**

Oh, sometimes I wish I had the wings of an angel because then I. It's Snug to Be Smug. Ogden Nash. **CP-NashO**

Oh! soothing hour, when glowing day. Evening. Charlotte Smith. **CP-SmitC**

"Oh, soul," I sometimes—often—still say when I'm trying to convince my inner self of something. Thinking Thought. Charles Kenneth Williams. **SP-WillC**

Oh stay at home, my lad, and plough. Alfred Edward Housman. **CP-HousA**

Oh, Stop Being Thankful All over the Place. Ogden Nash. **CP-NashO**

Oh Storms / Oh The Seal! Malcolm Lowry. **CP-LowrM**

Oh strong-ridged and deeply hollowed. Smell. William Carlos Williams. **CP-WilW1**

Oh Stubborn Race of Cadmus' Seed. Stevie Smith. **CP-SmitS**

Oh, summer has clothed the earth. In Summer. Paul Laurence Dunbar. **CP-DunbP**

Oh Sumptuous moment. Emily Dickinson. **CP-DickE**

Oh! take the pure gem to where southerly breezes. On an Icicle That Clung to the Grass of a Grave. Percy Bysshe Shelley. **CP-ShelP**

Oh [or O], talk not to me of a name great in story. Stanzas Written on the Road between Florence and Pisa. Byron. **CP-Byron**

Oh tell me once and tell me twice. One Foot on Sea, and One on Shore. Christina Georgina Rossetti. **CP-RosC2**

Oh tempo tardo e amaro! Eppure Allora Venivi. Christina Georgina Rossetti. *Fr.* Il Rosseggiar Dell'Oriente Canzoniere. **CP-RosC3**

Oh thank you for giving me the chance. Thank You. Kenneth Koch. **SP-KochK**

Oh that horse I see so high. A Gift of Great Value. Robert Creeley. **CP-CreeR**

Oh that I had wings like a dove! Bible, *O.T. See* Psalm 55: "Give ear to my prayer, O God."

Oh, that last long ride is a. Widow Woman. Langston Hughes. **SP-HughL**

Oh! That my young life were a lasting dream! Dreams. Edgar Allan Poe. **CP-PoeEd**

Oh that Pieria's spring would thro' my breast. John Milton. *See* To My Father.

Oh! that the desert [*or* desart] were my dwelling-place. The Ocean. Byron. **OBNC; PoEL-4** *Fr.* Childe Harold's Pilgrimage. **CP-Byron**

Oh, that the free would stamp the impious name. Percy Bysshe Shelley. *Fr.* Ode to Liberty. **CP-ShelP**

Oh, that the wise from their bright minds would kindle. Percy Bysshe Shelley. *Fr.* Ode to Liberty. **CP-ShelP**

Oh, that this lashing wind was something more. Chaos in Motion and Not in Motion. Wallace Stevens. **CP-StevW**

Oh that those lips had language! Life has passed. Lines on Receiving His Mother's Picture. William Cowper. **CH; OHIP** *Fr.* On the Receipt of My Mother's Picture out of Norfolk [the Gift of My Cousin Ann Bodham]. **CP-CowpW; FiP**

Oh [*or* O] that those lips had language! Life has passed [*or* pass'd]. On the Receipt of My Mother's Picture out of Norfolk [the Gift of My Cousin Ann Bodham]. William Cowper. **CP-CowpW; FiP**

Oh, the age of the inmates. Walls of Red Wing. "Bob Dylan." **CP-DylaB**

Oh, the beautiful girl, too white. Gold Hair. Robert Browning. **CP-BroR1**

Oh, the benches were stained with tears and perspiration. Day of the Locusts. "Bob Dylan." **CP-DylaB**

Oh the breeze is blowin' balmy. Till the Wind Gets Right. Paul Laurence Dunbar. **CP-DunbP**

Oh the cheerful budding-time. Seasons. Christina Georgina Rossetti. **CP-RosC3**

Oh, the day has set me dreaming. Little Lucy Landman. Paul Laurence Dunbar. **CP-DunbP**

Oh the dreamer said. Grace Paley. **CP-PaleG**

Oh, the gentlemen are talking and the midnight moon is on the riverside. Dark Eyes. "Bob Dylan." **CP-DylaB**

Oh the good times! the laughter on the hill! The Last Question. Stanley Jasspon Kunitz. **CP-KuniS**

Oh the green glimmer of apples in the orchard. Another Ophelia. David Herbert Lawrence. **CP-LawrD**

Oh the happy ending, the happy ending. The Sphere. Kathleen Jessie Raine. **SP-RainK**

Oh the Harteebeeste is *dear* to us. Malcolm Lowry. **CP-LowrM**

Oh the innocent girl. The Jeune Fille. David Herbert Lawrence. **CP-LawrD**

Oh, the little bird is rocking in the cradle of the wind. The Farm Child's Lullaby. Paul Laurence Dunbar. **CP-DunbP**

Oh the maple! The Two Trees. Archibald MacLeish. **CP-MacLA**

Oh, the moist, full water-jar! Prisoners at Work in the Rain. David Herbert Lawrence. *Fr.* Bits. **CP-LawrD**

Oh, the poets may sing of their lady Irenes. To Louise. Paul Laurence Dunbar. **CP-DunbP**

Oh the Pyrrus boys are we. Malcolm Lowry. **CP-LowrM**

Oh, the ragman draws circles. Stuck Inside of Mobile with the Memphis Blues Again. "Bob Dylan." **CP-DylaB**

Oh the rose of England is a single rose. The Rose of England. David Herbert Lawrence. **CP-LawrD**

Oh the rose of keenest thorn! The Iniquity of the Fathers upon the Children. Christina Georgina Rossetti. **CP-RosC1**

Oh, the streets of Rome are filled with rubble. When I Paint My Masterpiece. "Bob Dylan." **CP-DylaB**

Oh the sun stood still above the Passport Office. Jericho. Louis MacNeice. **CP-MacNL**

Oh the thumb-sucker's thumb. Thumbs. Shel Silverstein. **SP-SilS2**

Oh the time will come up. When the Ship Comes In. "Bob Dylan." **CP-DylaB**

Oh, the wild joys of living! the leaping from rock up to rock. Robert Browning. **BoTP; FaBV** *Fr.* Saul. **CP-BroR1**

(Youth.) **BoTP**

Oh the year before I was born. Song Stanzas of Private Luck. Grace Paley. **CP-PaleG**

Oh then be nameless and be never seen! Resurrection of the Flesh. David Herbert Lawrence. **CP-LawrD**

Oh! there are spirits of the air. To ———. Percy Bysshe Shelley. **CP-ShelP**

Oh there hasn't been much change. The Grange. Stevie Smith. **CP-SmitS**

Oh, there is evil, there is an evil world-soul. The Evil World-Soul. David Herbert Lawrence. **CP-LawrD**

Oh there is much to speak of. Emily Dickinson. **SP-DickE**

Oh, thicker, deeper, darker growing. A Memorial. John Greenleaf Whittier. **CP-WhitJ**

Oh, think not I am faithful to a vow! Edna St. Vincent Millay. **CP-MillE**

Oh, this is the tale the grandmas tell. The Ballad of the Brown Girl. Countee Cullen. **CP-CullC**

Oh this world and oh this dear worldbody. The Woman's Genitals. Hayden Carruth. *Fr.* Contra Mortem. **CP-CarHL**

Oh thou, by long experience tried. The Soul That Loves God Finds Him Every Where. Jeanne Marie Bouvier de la Motte-Guyon, *tr. fr.* French *by* William Cowper. **CP-CowpW**

Oh! thou dead / And everlasting witness! whose unsinking. Byron. **ChIV-1** *Fr.* Cain: A Mystery. **CP-Byron**

Oh, thou! in Hellas deemed of heavenly birth. Byron. **NAEL-2** *Fr.* Childe Harold's Pilgrimage. **CP-Byron**

Oh thou, that dear and happy isle. Andrew Marvell. **OxBoLi** *Fr.* Upon Appleton House [To My Lord Fairfax]. **CP-MarvA**

Oh thou that liftest up thy hands in prayer. Belgium. Edward Estlin Cummings. **CP-CummE**

Oh! thou that roll'st above thy glorious Fire. Ossian's Address to the Sun in "Carthon." Byron. **CP-Byron**

Oh thou who art not above. Prayer. Malcolm Lowry. **CP-LowrM**

Oh thou who with a safety razor blade. To a Tragic Poetess. Ernest Hemingway. **CP-HemiE**

Oh thou, whose fixed bewildered eye. Septimi Gades. William Wordsworth. **CP-WorW1**

Oh, thy bright eyes must answer now. Emily Brontë. *See* O thy bright eyes must answer now.

Oh, 'tisn't manly, of course, 'tisin't manly, this method of / wooing;. Arthur Hugh Clough. **EBVVPR,** *canto* 2, 14; *Fr.* Amours de Voyage. **SP-ClouA**

Oh to be at Crowdieknowe. Crowdieknowe. "Hugh MacDiarmid." **SP-MacDH**

Oh, to be in England. Home-Thoughts, from Abroad. Robert Browning. **CP-BroR1**

Oh to be in England now that Winston's out, *subsel.* Ezra Pound. *See* Canto 80: "Ain' committed no federal crime."

Oh to Be Odd! Ogden Nash. **CP-NashO**

Oh, to be Orville Prescott. Tome-Thoughts, from the *Times.* John Updike. **CP-UpdiJ**

Oh to be seventeen years old. Kenneth Koch. *Fr.* Fresh Air. **SP-KochK**

Oh to have you in May. In May. Paul Laurence Dunbar. **CP-DunbP**

Oh, to vex me, contraries [*or* conraryes] meet in one. John Donne. **NOSC; OAEL-1; PoEL-2; SeCePo; Son** *Fr.* Divine Meditations. **CP-DonnJ** *Fr.* Holy Sonnets. **CP-DonnJ**

(Devout Fits.) **SeCePo**

("Oh, to vex me, two contraries meet in one.") **ChIV-2**

Oh, to vex me, two contraries meet in one. John Donne. *See* Oh, to vex me, contraries [*or* conraryes] meet in one.

Oh to what height will love of greatness drive. Upon Mr. Thomas Coryat's Crudities. John Donne. *Fr.* Satires. **CP-DonnJ**

Oh, tree outside my window, we are kin. To a Tree. Elizabeth Bishop. **CP-BishE**

Oh turn not in from marching. Alfred Edward Housman. **CP-HousA**

Oh Tyrant Love! hast thou possest. Chorus of Youths and Virgins. Alexander Pope. *Fr.* Two Chorus's to the Tragedy of Brutus. **CP-PopeA**

Oh, unapproachable One. Frederick Morgan. *Fr.* Blue Hill Poems. **SP-MorgF**

Oh unforgotten! / How long ago? one spirit saith. Unforgotten. Christina Georgina Rossetti. **CP-RosC3**

Oh vanity / makes everything a little lovelier. Wanting to Get Closer. Stephen Dunn. **SP-DunnS**

Oh Venice! Venice! when thy marble walls. Ode on Venice. Byron. **CP-Byron**

Oh virgin queen of mountain-side and woodland. 3.22. Horace. *Fr.* Odes.

Oh we are running! / The dear ducks are running! Welcome Home Oh Sweetest Harteebeeste with Quadruple Devotion from All the Little Animals. Malcolm Lowry. **CP-LowrM**

Oh, weep for Mr. and Mrs. Bryan! The Lion. Ogden Nash. **CP-NashO**

Oh weep for the glory departed. A Counsel. Christina Georgina Rossetti. **CP-RosC3**

Oh! Weep for Those. Byron. **CP-Byron**

Oh welcome Home /To thy cot by the foam. Malcolm Lowry. **CP-LowrM**

Oh well done Lord E———n! and better done R———r! An Ode to the Framers of the Frame Bill. Byron. **CP-Byron**

Oh! well I know your subtle Sex. To ———. Byron. **CP-Byron**

Oh, well may Essex sit forlorn. William Francis Bartlett. John Greenleaf Whittier. **CP-WhitJ**

Oh well, they had such a big garden. Mona Van Duyn. **SP-VanDM**

Oh, Wellington! (or "Villainton") for fame. Byron. **FiP; OBSV; OxAEP-2; OxBoLi** *Fr.* Canto the Ninth. *Fr.* Don Juan. **CP-Byron**

(On Wellington.) **FiP**

Oh, Wellington! (or "Villainton") for fame. Canto the Ninth. Byron. *Fr.* Don Juan. **CP-Byron**

Oh were he and I together. Alfred Edward Housman. **CP-HousA**

Oh we've got to trust. Trust. David Herbert Lawrence. **CP-LawrD**

Oh, what a dawn of day! A Lovers' Quarrel. Robert Browning. **CP-BroR1**

Oh what a Grace is this. Emily Dickinson. **CP-DickE**

Oh what a lad was Zimmer. A Zimmershire Lad. Paul Zimmer. **SP-ZimmP**

Oh, what a pity, Oh! don't you agree. Innocent England. David Herbert Lawrence. **CP-LawrD**

Oh, what a shining town were Death. Valentine. Edna St. Vincent Millay. **CP-MillE**

Oh what a syllabub. Chorale. Jenny Joseph. *Fr.* Life and Turgid Times of A. Citizen. **SP-JoseJ**

Oh What a Wreck! How Changed in Mien and Speech! William Wordsworth. **CP-WorW2**

Oh, what brings her out in the dark and night? Keepsakes. Robert Penn Warren. *Fr.* Ballad of a Sweet Dream of Peace. **SP-WarrR**

Oh what can be happening pray what are they at? Friskers, or, Gods and Men. Stevie Smith. **CP-SmitS**

Oh what comes over the sea. Song. Christina Georgina Rossetti. **CP-RosC1**

Oh what do you do, poor Angus. Poor Angus. Shel Silverstein. **SP-SilS2**

Oh what fools! what shattered fools we are. Our (American) Ragcademicians. William Carlos Williams. **CP-WilW1**

Oh, what in the world could be more fun. September Morn. Ogden Nash. **CP-NashO**

Oh what is earth, that we should build / Our houses here, and seek concealed. Then Whose Shall Those Things Be? Christina Georgina Rossetti. **CP-RosC2**

Oh what is that country. Mother Country. Christina Georgina Rossetti. **CP-RosC1**

Oh! what is the gain of restless care. Song: Translated from the Italian. Percy Bysshe Shelley. *Fr.* Original Poetry by Victor and Cazire. **CP-ShelP**

Oh what is the terrible thing he has done. Oh What Is The Thing He Done? Stevie Smith. **CP-SmitS**

Oh What Is The Thing He Done? Stevie Smith. **CP-SmitS**

Oh, what shall I do? I am wholly upset. The Disturber. Paul Laurence Dunbar. **CP-DunbP**

Oh, what we want on earth. Temples. David Herbert Lawrence. **CP-LawrD**

Oh what wealth of stucco flowers. Dirge for the City of Miami. Thomas Merton. **CP-MertT**

Oh! what's the matter? what's the matter? Goody Blake and Harry Gill. William Wordsworth. **CP-WorW1**

Oh! what's the matter? what's the matter? William Wordsworth. **Par** *Fr.* Goody Blake and Harry Gill. **CP-WorW1**

Oh, when I think of the industrial millions, when I see some of them. We Die Together. David Herbert Lawrence. **CP-LawrD**

Oh, when I was a little Ghost / A merry time had we! Canto IV: Hys Nouryture. "Lewis Carroll." *Fr.* Phantasmagoria. **CP-CarrL**

Oh, when I was in love with you. Alfred Edward Housman. **CP-HousA**

Oh when Mercury came to London. London Mercury. David Herbert Lawrence. **CP-LawrD**

Oh when my love, my darling / You've left me here alone. The Cockney Amorist. Sir John Betjeman. **CP-BetjJ**

Oh when shall the grave hide for ever my sorrow? To Caroline. Byron. **CP-Byron**

Oh when the early morning at the seaside. East Anglian Bathe. Sir John Betjeman. **CP-BetjJ**

Oh, when the grass flowers, the grass. Magnificent Democracy. David Herbert Lawrence. **CP-LawrD**

Oh, when the world is hopeless. What Is a Man to Do? David Herbert Lawrence. **CP-LawrD**

Oh when you're young. They Come No More, Those Words, Those Finches. Archibald MacLeish. **CP-MacLA**

Oh whence do you come, my dear friend, to me. The Poor Ghost. Christina Georgina Rossetti. **CP-RosC1**

Oh where are ye going ye human faces. Where Are You Going? Stevie Smith. **CP-SmitS**

Oh where are you going to, all you Big Steamers. Big Steamers. Rudyard Kipling. **CP-KiplR**

Oh where are you going with your lovelocks flowing. Amor Mundi. Christina Georgina Rossetti. **CP-RosC1**

Oh, where have you been, my blue-eyed son? A Hard Rain's A-Gonna Fall. "Bob Dylan." **CP-DylaB**

Oh where were these magazines. "Bob Dylan." *Fr.* 11 Outlined Epitaphs. **CP-DylaB**

Oh, whither is my fair sun fled. A Lady, Rescued from Death by a Knight, Who in the Instant Leaves Her, Complains Thus. Thomas Carew. **CP-CareT**

Oh who is / so cosy with. The End of the Day. Robert Creeley. **CP-CreeR**

Oh who is that young sinner with the handcuffs on his wrists? Alfred Edward Housman. **CP-HousA**

Oh, who is the Lord of the land of life. The Masters. Paul Laurence Dunbar. **CP-DunbP**

Oh, who would be sad tho' the sky be a-graying. Winter-Song. Paul Laurence Dunbar. **CP-DunbP**

Oh, who would live in a silent house. Little Feet. Ogden Nash. **CP-NashO**

Oh, Why? Walter de la Mare. **CP-DeLaW**

Oh, why did God, / Creator wise, that peopled highest Heaven. Adam Speaks. John Milton. **NU** *Fr.* Book X. **FHYEP** *Fr.* Paradise Lost. **CP-MiltJ**

Oh, why does man pursue the smelt? The Smelt. Ogden Nash. **CP-NashO**

Oh why is heaven built so far. De Profundis. Christina Georgina Rossetti. **CP-RosC2**

Oh, why should a *hen*. Trouvée. Elizabeth Bishop. **CP-BishE**

Oh wind I hear you faltering. From the Lookout Rock. Richard Wilbur. **CP-WilbR**

Oh, wind of the spring-time, oh, free wind of May. Roses. Paul Laurence Dunbar. **CP-DunbP**

Oh Wonderful Machine! David Herbert Lawrence. **CP-LawrD**

Oh wond'rous power of words, how sweet they are. The Young Wordsworth's London. William Wordsworth. **FaBoPP** *Fr.* Residence in London. *Fr.* The Prelude; Growth of a Poet's Mind [1805 vers.]. **CP-WorW3**

Oh would I could subdue the flesh. Senex. Sir John Betjeman. **CP-BetjJ**

Oh would I were a politician. Yes and No. Ogden Nash. **CP-NashO**

Oh would that I were a reliable spirit careering around. Longing for Death because of Feebleness. Stevie Smith. **CP-SmitS**

Oh! would that I were very far away. Wishes: Sonnet. Christina Georgina Rossetti. **CP-RosC3**

Oh, ye playboys and playgirls. Playboys and Playgirls. "Bob Dylan." **CP-DylaB**

Oh, ye who hold the written clue. Things and the Man. Rudyard Kipling. **CP-KiplR**

Oh ye! who teach the ingenuous youth of nations. Byron. **EnRP** *Fr.* Canto the Second. *Fr.* Don Juan. **CP-Byron**

Oh ye! who teach the ingenuous youth of nations. Canto the Second. Byron. *Fr.* Don Juan. **CP-Byron**

Oh yeah! All right! Are you gonna be in my dreams tonight? The End. John Lennon *and* Paul McCartney. **CP-Beatl**

Oh yeah, I'll tell you something. I Want to Hold Your Hand. The Beatles. **CP-Beatl**

Oh yeah, oh yeah, oh yeah, oh yeah. I'll Get You. The Beatles. **CP-Beatl**

Oh yellow head. Roy Fisher. **SP-FishR** *Fr.* Three Ceremonial Poems.

Oh, Yes. Charles Bukowski. **SP-BukC3**

Oh yes, I love you, book of my confessions. Chinese Tomb Guardians. Robert Bly. **SP-BlyR**

Oh yes, I will own we were dear to each other. To George, Earl Delawarr. Byron. **CP-Byron**

Oh, yes, I'd love to go to the play. Wednesday Matinee. Ogden Nash. **CP-NashO**

Oh yes it is intelligence. Thomas Merton. *Fr.* Cables to the Ace. **CP-MertT**

Oh, yes! they love through all this world of ours! Sonnet. Elizabeth Barrett Browning. *Fr.* Sonnets from the Portuguese. **CP-BroEB**

Oh! yet a few short years of useful life. William Wordsworth. **OBRV** *Fr.* Conclusion: "In one of these excursions, travelling then." *Fr.* The Prelude; Growth of a Poet's Mind [1805 vers.]. **CP-WorW3**

Oh Yet We Trust. Tennyson. **EBVV; EBVVPR; EaLo; EnVR; FHYEP; ImPo; LiTB; MeMBP; NoP; OAEL-2; OBNC; PeECV; TrGrPo** *Fr.* In Memoriam A. H. H. **CP-TennA**

(Larger Hope, The.) **WGRP**

O[h] yet we trust that somehow good. Oh Yet We Trust. Tennyson. **EBVV; EBVVPR; EaLo; EnVR; FHYEP; ImPo; LiTB; MeMBP; NoP; OAEL-2; OBNC; PeECV; TrGrPo; WGRP** *Fr.* In Memoriam A. H. H. **CP-TennA**

Oh you are kind and lavish with your pence. For Certain Subscribers to the Miners' Fund. John Hewitt. **CP-HewiJ**

Oh you brown bacon machine. Hog. Anne Sexton. **CP-SextA**

Oh, you can read out your Bible. Quit Your Low Down Ways. "Bob Dylan." **CP-DylaB**

Oh you stiff shapes, swift transformation seethes. Transformations. David Herbert Lawrence. **CP-LawrD**

Oh you, the sprightliest & most puggish, the brightest star. After Peire Vidal, & Myself. Ted Berrigan. **SP-BerrT**

Oh You, Who in All Names Can Tickle the Town. Byron. **CP-Byron**

Oh you'd think the British Public. Lucky Little Britisher. David Herbert Lawrence. **CP-LawrD**

Oh [or O], young Lochinvar is come out of the west. Lochinvar. Sir Walter Scott. **SP-ScotW** *Fr.* Marmion.

Oh young men oh young comrades. Us. Stephen Spender. **CP-SpenS**

Oh za ki tan ke parlay lot. Za Ki Tan Ke Parlay Lot. Audre Lorde. **SP-LordA**

Ohio. John Updike. **CP-UpdiJ**

Ohio River Blues. Kenneth Patchen. **CP-PatcK**

Ohio River—Louisville, The. Thomas Merton. **CP-MertT; SP-MertT**

Ohld song / you Know. Edward Estlin Cummings. **CP-CummE**

Oi! oi! *noli me tangere*, no argument. The Millipede. John Updike. **CP-UpdiJ**

Oibò, piccina / Tutto atterrita. Christina Georgina Rossetti. **CP-RosC3**

Oil. Gary Snyder. **CP-SnydG**

Oil and Blood. William Butler Yeats. **CP-YeatW**

Oil & Wine, / Sparkling gems, & rich attire. Ralph Waldo Emerson. **CP-EmerR**

Oil brown smog over Denver. Who Runs America? Allen Ginsberg. **CP-GinsA**

Oil Field. Louise McNeill. **SP-McNeL**

Oil for extreme unction must be blessed, The. The Rule. Richard Wilbur. **CP-WilbR**

Oil in wild Aladdin's lamp, The. A Rose in Candlelight. Walter de la Mare. **CP-DeLaW**

Oil is spilling down the little stream. The Breaking of Rainbows. Howard Nemerov. **CP-NemeH**

Oil Painting of the Artist as the Artist. Archibald MacLeish. **CP-MacLA**

Oil tel duh woil doi sez. Edward Estlin Cummings. **CP-CummE**

Oil Terminal. Steve Griffiths. **SP-GrifS**

Oilers for rivers: cargo ships for stars. Only God Knows How III. Malcolm Lowry. *Fr.* The Moon in Scandinavia. **CP-LowrM**

Oils, beasts, grasses, petrifactions, birds, incrustations. Canto 34. Ezra Pound. *Fr.* Cantos. **CP-PoCan**

Oily Weather. Ernest Hemingway. **CP-HemiE**

Ointment, The. Thomas Merton. **CP-MertT**

Oiran and Her Kamuso, An. John Gould Fletcher. **SP-FletJ**

Okay, Fulke Greville: "None can well behold". Hayden Carruth. *Fr.* The Sleeping Beauty. **CP-CarHL**

OK Neal. Elegy for Neal Cassady. Allen Ginsberg. **CP-GinsA**

Okay, you leaves up there, come clean. Call for Clues. William DeWitt Snodgrass. **SP-SnodW**

Okeanos rages, tears rocks back in his path. Maximus, at the Harbor. Charles Olson. **SP-OlsoC** *Fr.* The Maximus Poems.

Oklahoma. Ernest Hemingway. **CP-HemiE**

Oklahoma Ligno and Lithograph Co, The. Corporate Entity. Archibald MacLeish. **CP-MacLA**

Ol' black Bascom, don't break no mirrors. Tell Me, Momma. "Bob Dylan." **CP-DylaB**

Ol' Bunk's Band. William Carlos Williams. **CP-WilW2**

Ol' man Simon, planted a diamond. The Garden. Shel Silverstein. **SP-SilS2**

Ol' time's gone, de new time's hyeah, De. Long Ago. Paul Laurence Dunbar. **CP-DunbP**

Ol' Tunes, The. Paul Laurence Dunbar. **CP-DunbP**

Olbers' Paradox. Lawrence Ferlinghetti. **SP-FerlL**

Old. Paul Laurence Dunbar. **CP-DunbP**

Old. Thomas Merton. **CP-MertT**

Old. Anne Sexton. **CP-SextA**

Old. Louis Zukofsky. **CP-ZukLS**

Old Abbeys. William Wordsworth. *Fr.* Ecclesiastical Sonnets. **CP-WorW2**

Old Acquaintance, An. Lewis Turco. **SP-TurcL**

Old Adam, The. Denise Levertov. **CP-LeveD**

Old Age. Ralph Waldo Emerson. **CP-EmerR**

Old Age Compensation. James Wright. **CP-WrigJ**

Old age hath clawed me with his scaly clutch. Robinson Jeffers. **CP-JefR3**

Old age is. To Waken an Old Lady. William Carlos Williams. **CP-WilW1**

Old Age of Michelangelo, The. Frank Templeton Prince. **CP-PrinF**

Old Age of Queen Maeve, The. William Butler Yeats. **CP-YeatW**

Old Age Porch. Grace Paley. **CP-PaleG**

Old age sticks / up Keep. Edward Estlin Cummings. **CP-CummE**

Old Age's Lambent Peaks. Walt Whitman. **CP-WhitW**

Old Age's Ship & Crafty Death's. Walt Whitman. **CP-WhitW**

Old Amusement Park. Marianne Craig Moore. **CP-MoorM**

Old, and abandon'd by each venal friend. Impromptu. Thomas Gray. **CP-GrayT**

Old and New Year Ditties. Christina Georgina Rossetti. **CP-RosC1** "New Year met me somewhat sad."

Passing Away. **MeMBP; NoP; OAEL-2; OBNC; PFP; WPE** "Watch with me, men, women, and children dear."

Old and the New Masters, The. Randall Jarrell. **CP-JarrR; SP-JarrR**

Old Angler, The. Walter de la Mare. **CP-DeLaW**

Old Apple-Tree, The. Paul Laurence Dunbar. **CP-DunbP**

Old Apple Trees. William DeWitt Snodgrass. **SP-SnodW**

Old Archangels. David Herbert Lawrence. **CP-LawrD**

Old Archibald, in his eternal chair. Archibald's Example. Edwin Arlington Robinson. **CP-RobiE**

Old bag of bones. Self-Portrait in Shoulder Stand. Erica Jong. **SP-JongE**

Old Barn at the Bottom of the Fogs, The. Robert Frost. **CP-FrosR**

Old beast ended in this place, An. The Burnt-Out Spa. Sylvia Plath. **CP-PlatS**

Old Becker crawling in the night. The Coronation Murder. Robert Ranke Graves. **CP-GravR**

Old Ben. Walter de la Mare. **CP-DeLaW**

Old black dog comes in one evening, The. First Snow. Ted Kooser. **SP-KoosT**

Old black-man showed me, The. Canthara. William Carlos Williams. **CP-WilW1**

Old, black, rutting tomcat, An. Old Tom. Richard Eberhart. **CP-EberR**

Old Blake was warm, he got down to the hub. Malcolm Lowry. **CP-LowrM**

Old blanket. The crumbs of rubbed wool turning up, The. Adrienne Rich. **HCAP; SP-RicA2** *Fr.* Shooting Script. **CP-RicAE**

Old Boards. Robert Bly. **SP-BlyR**

Old Boys' blazers like a Mardi-Gras, The. John Berryman. *Fr.* Sonnets to Chris. **CP-BerrJ**

Old boys, the cracked boards spread before. Bread. James Dickey. **CP-DickJ**

Old brown hen and the old blue sky, The. Continual Conversation with a Silent Man. Wallace Stevens. **CP-StevW**

Old Brown Shoe. George Harrison. **CP-Beatl**

Old brown thorn-trees break in two high over Cummen Strand, The. Red Hanrahan's Song about Ireland. William Butler Yeats. **CP-YeatW**

Old Buddy, An. Charles Bukowski. **SP-BukC3**

Old Bug up There. Daniel Gerard Hoffman. **SP-HoffD**

Old Burying-Ground, The. John Greenleaf Whittier. **CP-WhitJ**

Old Cabin, The. Paul Laurence Dunbar. **CP-DunbP**

Old Care with Industry and Art. Care and Generosity. Christopher Smart. **SP-SmarC**

Old Catechism, The. Michael Hartnett. **SP-HarMi**

Old Chants. Walt Whitman. **CP-WhitW**

Old Chartist, The. George Meredith. **CP-MerG1**

Old Chimæras, old receipts, The. Robert Louis Stevenson. **CP-StevR**

Old church tower and garden wall, The. Emily Brontë. **CP-BronE**

Old Clothes, The. Brendan Galvin. **SP-GalvB**

Old Clothes Man, The. Stanley Jasspon Kunitz. **CP-KuniS**

Old coach-road through a common of furze, The. The Meeting. George Meredith. **CP-MerG1**

Old colleague, / Puritan New England's famous scholar. Night Watch in the City of Boston. Archibald MacLeish. **CP-MacLA**

Old Colliery, The. Wystan Hugh Auden. **CP-AudWJ**

Old Colonial Imperialist, An. Howard Nemerov. **CP-NemeH**

Old Corinth. John Hewitt. **CP-HewiJ**

Old Country, The. Howard Nemerov. **CP-NemeH**

Old Countryside. Louise Bogan. **CP-BogaL**

Old Couple. Charles Simic. **SP-SimiC**

Old Cracked Tune, An. Stanley Jasspon Kunitz. **CP-KuniS**

Old Cumberland Beggar, The. William Wordsworth. **CP-WorW1**

Old Dafydd, eyes like a bloodhound's red with age. Mid-Winter. Alun Lewis. **CP-LewiA**

Old Davis owned a solid mica mountain. A Fountain, a Bottle, a Donkey's Ears and Some Books. Robert Frost. **CP-FrosR**

Old Day the gardener seemed. A Figure of Time. Denise Levertov. **CP-LeveD**

Old Days, The. Howard Nemerov. **CP-NemeH**

Old dead builder, how wise you were. Maria Hat Geholfen. Wystan Hugh Auden. **CP-AudWJ**

Old Deep Sing-Song. Carl Sandburg. **CP-SandC**

Old desperation of the flesh, An. Observation of October. Howard Nemerov. **CP-NemeH**

Old Dichotomy: Choosing Sides. Richard Eberhart. **CP-EberR**

Old Doctor Ledlie brought me in this bag. The Doctor's Bag. John Hewitt. **CP-HewiJ**

Old dog barks backward without getting up, The. The Span of Life. Robert Frost. **GDP; HoPM; LiTM; SoSe** *Fr.* Ten Mills. **CP-FrosR**

Old Dog's Song, The. Grace Paley. **CP-PaleG**

Old Dutch Woman, The. Gary Snyder. **CP-SnydG**

Old Dwarf Heart. Anne Sexton. **CP-SextA**

Old Eben Flood, climbing alone one night. Mr. Flood's Party. Edwin Arlington Robinson. **CP-RobiE**

Old Eddie's face, wrinkled with river lights. The Glory Trumpeter. Derek Walcott. **CP-WalcD**

Old Ella Mason keeps cats, eleven at last count. Ella Mason and Her Eleven Cats. Sylvia Plath. **CP-PlatS**

Old Elm Tree by the River, The. Wendell Berry. **CP-BerrW**

Old emotions like powdery tenements. City Home Detroit. Al Young. **CP-YounA**

Old England. Anne Bradstreet. **KTR** *Fr.* A Dialogue between Old England and New. **CP-BradA**

Old Euclid drew a circle. Euclid. Nicholas Vachel Lindsay. **CP-LindV** *Fr.* Poems about the Moon.

Old Excursions. Thomas Hardy. **CP-HardT**

Old fabulous rendering up. The Flame of a Candle. Howard Nemerov. **CP-NemeH**

Old Farm in Northern Michigan. Gary Gildner. **SP-GildG**

Old farmers, travelers, workmen (no matter how crippled or bent). True Conquerors. Walt Whitman. **CP-WhitW**

Old-Fashioned Air. Ted Berrigan. **SP-BerrT**

Old Fashioned American Business Man, An. Richard Eberhart. **CP-EberR**

Old Fashioned Cincinnati Blues, The. Al Young. **CP-YounA**

Old-Fashioned German Christmas Card, An. William Carlos Williams. **CP-WilW2**

Old-Fashioned Lightning Rod. John Updike. **CP-UpdiJ**

Old-Fashioned Requited Love. Carl Sandburg. **CP-SandC**

Old-fashioned shadows hanging down, that difficulty in love too soon. 37 Haiku. John Ashbery. **SP-AshbJ**

Old fat fish of everlasting life. Lines on a Carp. Gary Snyder. **CP-SnydG**

Old Father Ocean calls my tide. A Song of the River Thames. John Dryden. **SP-DrydJ** *Fr.* Albion and Albanius.

Old fathers, great-grandfathers. *fr.* Words for Music Perhaps. William Butler Yeats. **CP-YeatW**

Old Fitz, who from your suburb grange. To E. Fitzgerald. Tennyson. **CP-TennA**

Old Flagman, The. Carl Sandburg. **CP-SandC**

Old flagman has great-grandchildren, The. The Old Flagman. Carl Sandburg. **CP-SandC**

Old Flame, The. Robert Lowell. **SP-LoweR**

Old Florist. Theodore Roethke. **CP-RoetT**

Old folks play a game, The. Traffic Signals. Charles Bukowski. **SP-BukC1**

Old Fools, The. Philip Larkin. **CP-LarkP**

Old Freighter in an Old Port, *sl. diff. fr.* On Reading R.L.S. Malcolm Lowry. **CP-LowrM**

Old friend, it's easy. However you behave. Anent Socrates, or Somebody. Hayden Carruth. **CP-CarHS**

Old friend, kind friend! lightly down. To My Old Schoolmaster. John Greenleaf Whittier. **CP-WhitJ**

Old friend, suppose luck grants to us. Martial, *tr. by* William Matthews. **SP-MattW** *Fr.* Epigrams.

Old friend, you may kneel as you read this. Magic Is Alive. Leonard Cohen. **CP-CoheL**

Old Friends. Sir John Betjeman. **CP-BetjJ**

In Memoriam: A. C., R. J. O., K. S. **CP-BetjJ**

Old Fritz, on this rotating bed. A Flat One. William DeWitt Snodgrass. **SP-SnodW**

Old Front Gate, The. Paul Laurence Dunbar. **CP-DunbP**

Old fun is too true for the truth. Old. Thomas Merton. **CP-MertT**

Old Furniture. Thomas Hardy. **CP-HardT**

Old Gang, The. Charles Bukowski. **SP-BukC3**

Old garden of grayish and ochre lichen. To the Rock that Will Be a Cornerstone of the House. Robinson Jeffers. **CP-JefR1**

Old Ghosts. Stevie Smith. **CP-SmitS**

Old Glory at halfmast. From the New World. Donald Davie. **CP-DavDo**

Old goatherds swear how all night long they hear. Goatsucker. Sylvia Plath. **CP-PlatS**

Old Gown, The. Thomas Hardy. **CP-HardT**

Old Gray Couple (1), The. Archibald MacLeish. **CP-MacLA**

Old Gray Couple (2), The. Archibald MacLeish. **CP-MacLA**

Old grey Alp has caught the cold, The. By the Rosanna. George Meredith. **CP-MerG1**

Old grey mother she thrummed on her knee, The. Margaret's Bridal-Eve. George Meredith. **CP-MerG1**

Old guy / next door, The. A Patriot of Life. Charles Bukowski. **SP-BukC3**

Old guy put down his beer, The. Do the Dead Know What Time It Is? Kenneth Patchen. **CP-PatcK**

Old half blinded hawk—but how can he hunt with only one eye?—, The. Robinson Jeffers. **CP-JefR3**

Old Hall of Elbë, ruined, lonely now. Emily Brontë. **CP-BronE**

Old he was but not yet wax. My Father's Face. Hayden Carruth. **CP-CarHL**

Old heavens, you used to tweak above us. John Ashbery. **SP-AshbJ** *Fr.* The Skaters.

Old High School and the New, The. Paul Laurence Dunbar. **CP-DunbP**

Old hill town in northern Pennsylvania, a missed connection for a bus, an hour to kill, an. Neglect. Charles Kenneth Williams. **SP-WillC**

Old Hokusai Print. Carl Sandburg. **CP-SandC**

Old Home Week. Donald Hall. **CP-HallD**

Old Homestead, The. Paul Laurence Dunbar. **CP-DunbP**

Old Hope. Steve Griffiths. **SP-GrifS**

Old Horn to All Atlantic said. Frankie's Trade. Rudyard Kipling. **CP-KiplR**

Old horse dies slow, The. When Structure Fails Rhyme Attempts to Come to the Rescue. William Carlos Williams. **CP-WilW2**

Old Horse in the City, The. Nicholas Vachel Lindsay. **CP-LindV**

Old hound wags his shaggy tail, The. Over the Hills. George Meredith. **CP-MerG2**

Old House, The. William Carlos Williams. **CP-WilW2**

Old house grows, adding rooms of silence, The. The House Growing. John Updike. **CP-UpdiJ**

Old Houses. Donald Hall. **CP-HallD**

Old houses, and new-fangled violence. Ransom. Robert Penn Warren. **SP-WarrR**

Old Hundredth, *metrical vers. by* William Kethe. Bible, *O.T. See* Psalm 100: "Make a joyful noise unto the Lord, all ye lands."

Old Idea of Sacrifice, The. David Herbert Lawrence. **CP-LawrD**

Old inventive Poets, had they seen, The. The Plain of Donnerdale. William Wordsworth. *Fr.* The River Duddon [A Series of Sonnets]. **CP-WorW2**

Old Ireland. Walt Whitman. **CP-WhitW**

Old Is for Books. Dorothy Nash. **CP-NashO**

Old is the song that I sing. Rudyard Kipling. *See* Army Headquarters.

Old Italians Dying, The. Lawrence Ferlinghetti. **SP-FerlL**

Old Jewelry. William DeWitt Snodgrass. **SP-SnodW**

Old King Cole. Edwin Arlington Robinson. **CP-RobiE**

Old King's New Jester, The. Edwin Arlington Robinson. **CP-RobiE**

Old ladders shorten, pulled down. John Haines. *Fr.* Homestead. **SP-HainJ**

Old Ladies' Home. Sylvia Plath. **CP-PlatS**

Old Lady, An. Derek Mahon. **SP-MahoD**

Old Lady in the Park. Marsden Hartley. **CP-HartM**

Old lady (so they say) but I, The. Robert Louis Stevenson. *Fr.* The Family. **CP-StevR**

Old lady writes me in a spidery style, An. A Letter from Brooklyn. Derek Walcott. **CP-WalcD**

Old Lambro pass'd unseen a private gate. Byron. **EnRP** *Fr.* Canto the Third. *Fr.* Don Juan. **CP-Byron**

Old Latimer preaching did fairly describe. On the Irish Bishops. Jonathan Swift. **CP-SwifJ**

Old Lead-mine, The. Wystan Hugh Auden. **CP-AudWJ**

Old Lean Over the Tombstones, The. Kenneth Patchen. **CP-PatcK**

Old Lewis thus the terms of peace to burnish. Jonathan Swift. **CP-SwifJ** *Fr.* Dunkirk to be Let.

Old liar, death, do you think I don't see you? The Challenger. Mona Van Duyn. **SP-VanDM**

Old Liberals, The. Sir John Betjeman. **CP-BetjJ**

Old *Life* photograph, An. A Sister by the Pond. Donald Hall. **CP-HallD**

Old Light. Al Young. **CP-YounA**

Old Likeness, An. Thomas Hardy. **CP-HardT**

Old Lutheran Bells at Home, The. Wallace Stevens. **CP-StevW**

Old, mad, blind, despised, and dying king, An. Percy Bysshe Shelley. **CP-ShelP**

(Sonnet: England in 1819.) **CP-ShelP**

Old, mad, dancing Mrs Dean. Education. Steve Griffiths. **SP-GrifS**

Old madhouse in Santiago stood tucked back, The. Walls To Put Up, Walls To Take Down. Stephen Dobyns. **SP-DobyS**

Old maid early eer I knew, An. William Blake. **CP-BlakW**

Old Man, The. John Clare. **SP-ClarJ**

Old Man. Kenneth Patchen. **CP-PatcK**

Old Man and the Child, The. "Ping Hsin", *tr. fr. Chinese by* William Carlos Williams *with* David Rafael Wang. **CP-WilW2**

Old man asked me: What is Love? I turned, An. Grown Cold. Christina Georgina Rossetti. **CP-RosC3**

Old Man Asleep, An. Wallace Stevens. **CP-StevW**

Old Man at Valdez. Charles Tomlinson. **CP-TomlC**

Old man bending I come among new faces, An. The Wound-Dresser. Walt Whitman. **CP-WhitW**

Old man cocked his ear upon a bridge, An. The Phases of the Moon. William Butler Yeats. **CP-YeatW**

Old man, come out in the sun. Bermuda. Jane Cooper. **SP-CoopJ**

Old man, Dead in a Room. Charles Bukowski. **SP-BukC2**

Old Man Drunk. James Wright. **CP-WrigJ**

Old Man Goes South Again Alone. John Berryman. **CP-BerrJ**

Old Man Going. Jenny Joseph. **SP-JoseJ**

Old man had his box and earned, The. The Scissors-Grinder. Nicholas Vachel Lindsay. **CP-LindV**

Old man in the crystal morning after snow. Poem. Delmore Schwartz. **SP-SchwD**

Old Man Is Older in History than in Time, The. Wendell Berry. *Fr.* The Handing Down. **CP-BerrW**

Old man, it's four flights up and for what? Doors, Doors, Doors. Anne Sexton. **CP-SextA**

Old man lives on, The. A Wilderness Starts towards Him. Wendell Berry. *Fr.* The Handing Down. **CP-BerrW**

Old Man of the Alps, The. Samuel Taylor Coleridge. **CP-ColeS**

Old man on the prison work release gang, The. Ghost in a Field of Mint. Richard Hugo. **CP-HugoR**

Old man planted and dug and tended, An. Disappointed. Paul Laurence Dunbar. **CP-DunbP**

Old Man Playing with Children. John Crowe Ransom. **SP-RansJ**

Old man remembers to old man. Old Home Week. Donald Hall. **CP-HallD**

Old man riding his slow bike, An. Crash. Gary Snyder. **CP-SnydG**

Old man sailin' in a dinghy boat. Apple Suckling Tree. "Bob Dylan." **CP-DylaB**

Old man sick with boyhood fears, The. The Man Upstairs. Stanley Jasspon Kunitz. **CP-KuniS**

Old man sits / In the shadow of a pine tree, An. Six Significant Landscapes. Wallace Stevens. **CP-StevW**

Old Man Stirs the Fire to a Blaze, An. William Butler Yeats. **RB** *Fr.* The Wanderings of Oisin. **CP-YeatW**

Old man to the child, The. The Old Man and the Child. "Ping Hsin", *tr. fr. Chinese by* William Carlos Williams *with* David Rafael Wang. **CP-WilW2**

Old Man to the Lizard, The. Archibald MacLeish. **CP-MacLA**

Old man waiting bare-headed in the rain, The. Certain Prospects and Spectacular Diversions. Leonard Nathan. **SP-NathL**

Old man who goes about, The. Pastoral 1. William Carlos Williams. **CP-WilW1**

Old man who had dug the small pit, The. Burial. May Sarton. **SP-SartM**

Old man whose black face, An. The Rainwalkers. Denise Levertov. **CP-LeveD**

Old man with a double-bit axe, An. The Inhumanist. Robinson Jeffers. *Fr.* The Double Axe. **CP-JefR3**

Old man, with hair made of newspaper cutting. The Public Son of a Public Man. Stephen Spender. **CP-SpenS**

Old man with whitening beard. The Man in the Moon. Gilbert Sorrentino. **SP-SorrG**

Old man Woolworth put up a building. Again? Carl Sandburg. **CP-SandC**

Old man, you surface seldom. Full Fathom Five. Sylvia Plath. **CP-PlatS**

Old Man's Beard. Charles Tomlinson. **CP-TomlC**

Old Man's Journey. Archibald MacLeish. **CP-MacLA**

Old Man's Road, The. Wystan Hugh Auden. **CP-AudeW**

Old Man's Thought of School, An. Walt Whitman. **CP-WhitW**

Old man's wasting brain, An; a ruined city. Life and Letters. Adrienne Rich. **CP-RicAE**

Old Man's Winter Night, An. Robert Frost. **CP-FrosR**

Old Mansion. John Crowe Ransom. **SP-RansJ**

Old Map of Barnstable County. Brendan Galvin. **SP-GalvB**

Old Map of Uhlerstown. Richard Hugo. **CP-HugoR**

Old maple hairytrunks root asphalt grass marge, November branches rare leaved. Have You Seen This Movie? Allen Ginsberg. **CP-GinsA**

Old Mary. Gwendolyn Brooks. **SP-BrooG**

Old Masters Abroad. Louis MacNeice. **CP-MacNL**

Old Meg. Thom Gunn. **CP-GunnT**

Old Meg she was a gipsy [*or* gypsy]. John Keats. **CP-KeatJ**
   (Old Meg She Was a Gipsy.) **CP-KeatJ**

Old Meg She Was a Gipsy. John Keats. *See* Old Meg she was a gipsy [*or* gypsy].

Old Memory, An. Paul Laurence Dunbar. **CP-DunbP**

Old Memory. William Butler Yeats. **CP-YeatW**

Old Men, The. Walter de la Mare. **CP-DeLaW**

Old Men, The. Rudyard Kipling. **CP-KiplR**

Old Men. David Herbert Lawrence. **CP-LawrD**

Old Men. Ogden Nash. **CP-NashO**

Old Men, The. William Carlos Williams. **CP-WilW1**

Old Men Admiring Themselves in the Water, The. William Butler Yeats. **CP-YeatW**

Old men and women walk by my window. Winter Afternoon. Grace Paley. **CP-PaleG**

Old Men at Pevensey. Rudyard Kipling. *Fr.* Puck of Pook's Hill. Runes on Weland's Sword, The. **CP-KiplR**

Old Men in the Leaf Smoke, The. Archibald MacLeish. **CP-MacLA**

Old men live a life. Hebrides. Archibald MacLeish. **CP-MacLA**

Old men rake the yards for winter, The. The Old Men in the Leaf Smoke. Archibald MacLeish. **CP-MacLA**

Old men say, The. Why the Telephone Wires Dip and the Poles Are Cracked and Crooked. John Updike. **CP-UpdiJ**

Old Men Sitting. John Hewitt. **CP-HewiJ**

Old men, son, drink whisky, for they know, The. Moonshine. Howard Nemerov. **CP-NemeH**

Old men wept when the Old Man in blue, The. Ancestor. John Berryman. **CP-BerrJ**

Old metal princes, copper-coloured, cool. Iron and Stone. John Hewitt. **CP-HewiJ**

Old Mill-Race, The. John Hewitt. **CP-HewiJ**

Old Mine, The. Wystan Hugh Auden. **CP-AudWJ**

Old mr ly / fresh from a fu. Edward Estlin Cummings. **CP-CummE**

Old monk is turned loose / And can travel!, The. Thomas Merton. **CP-MertT**

Old moon my eyes are new moon with human footprint. Poem Rocket. Allen Ginsberg. **CP-GinsA**

Old Mother Laidinwool. Rudyard Kipling. **CP-KiplR**

Old motorbike she was, The. An Old Lady. Derek Mahon. **SP-MahoD**

Old Mountain Road. Charles Simic. **SP-SimiC**

Old Mrs. Court and Her Quilt. Barton Sutter. **SP-SuttB**

Old Mrs. Kawabata. Yase: September. Gary Snyder. **CP-SnydG**

Old Music for Quiet Hearts. Carl Sandburg. **CP-SandC**

Old Neighbour and the New, The. Thomas Hardy. **CP-HardT**

Old New England. Derek Walcott. **CP-WalcD**

Old Nigger on One-Mule Cart Encountered Late at Night When Driving Home from Party in the Back Country. Robert Penn Warren. **SP-WarrR**

Old Nollekens? No, Little Nollekens. Nollekens. Randall Jarrell. **CP-JarrR**

Old Norbert with the flat blue cap. Leipzig. Thomas Hardy. **CP-HardT**

Old Nurse sits mending by the fire. In the Nursery. Wystan Hugh Auden. **CP-AudWJ**

Old Nursery. John Gould Fletcher. **SP-FletJ** *Fr.* The Ghosts of an Old House.

Old oak, old timber, sunk and rooted. G. M. B. Donald Davie. **CP-DavDo**

Old oblivion-book, that I lay open. Accountability. Gerrit Achterberg, *tr. fr. Dutch by* Adrienne Rich. **CP-RicAE**

Old, old widow Greedy needs wo'd wed, An. Upon Greedy. Robert Herrick. **CP-HerrR**

Old ones to the side. Psalm. Charles Simic. **SP-SimiC**

Old ones want to be young, and they aren't young, The. The Grudge of the Old. David Herbert Lawrence. **CP-LawrD**

Old O.O. Blues, The. Al Young. **CP-YounA**

Old Orchard, The. David Herbert Lawrence. **CP-LawrD**

Old orchard in the middle of the forest, The. Randall Jarrell. **CP-JarrR**

Old Osawatomie. Carl Sandburg. **CP-SandC**

Old pagan burials, uninscribed rock, The. Delusion of Saints. Robinson Jeffers. **CP-JefR2**

Old Paintings on Italian Walls. Kathleen Jessie Raine. **SP-RainK**

Old Pair of Shoes, An. Kenneth Patchen. **CP-PatcK**

Old Parson Beanes hunts six days [*or* dayes] of the week. Upon Parson Beanes. Robert Herrick. **CP-HerrR**

Old Penobscot Indian, The. Flux. Richard Eberhart. **CP-EberR**

Old People. Ron Koertge. **SP-KoerR**

Old People. David Herbert Lawrence. **CP-LawrD**

Old People Working (Garden, Car). Gwendolyn Brooks. **SaC** *Fr.* A Catch of Shy Fish. **SP-BrooG**

Old People's Home. Wystan Hugh Auden. **CP-AudeW**

Old person of Troy, An. First Limick. Ogden Nash. **CP-NashO**

Old Photograph, An. Ted Kooser. **SP-KoosT**

Old Photograph, An. Howard Nemerov. **CP-NemeH**

Old photograph shows you, An. Dabney Stuart. *Fr.* The Opposite Field. **SP-StuaD**

Old photographs would have her bookish, sitting. Ma. Paul Muldoon. **SP-MuldP**

Old Picture, An. Howard Nemerov. **CP-NemeH**

Old Pictures in Florence. Robert Browning. **CP-BroR1**

Old Pilot, The. Donald Hall. **CP-HallD**

Old Poems. Randall Jarrell. **CP-JarrR**

Old Poet Moves to a New Aprtment 14 Times, The. Louis Zukofsky. **CP-ZukLS**

Old Poet, Poetry's final subject glimmers months ahead. Don't Grow Old. Allen Ginsberg. **CP-GinsA**

Old poet, The / with his face full of lines. A Reading. Erica Jong. **SP-JongE**

Old Poet with Distant Admirers. Geoffrey Hill. *Fr.* Soliloquies. **CP-HillG**

Old Pond. Allen Ginsberg. **CP-GinsA**

Old pond—a frog jumps in, kerplunk, The. Old Pond. Allen Ginsberg. **CP-GinsA**

Old priest Peter Gilligan, The. The Ballad of Father Gilligan. William Butler Yeats. **CP-YeatW**

Old Professor and the Sphinx, The. Lewis Turco. **SP-TurcL**

Old Question. Richard Eberhart. **CP-EberR**

Old Reilly stole a stallion. Seven Curses. "Bob Dylan." **CP-DylaB**

Old Relative. Gwendolyn Brooks. *Fr.* Notes from the Childhood and the Girlhood. **SP-BrooG**

Old Reprobate. Daniel Gerard Hoffman. **SP-HoffD**

Old Roman sow / Bears a new litter now, The. Fable for a War. Thomas Merton. **CP-MertT**

Old, root-crowded cemetery, An. John Haines. *Fr.* The Stone Bear. **SP-HainJ**

Old Roscoff, *after* Corbière. Derek Mahon. **SP-MahoD**

Old Roses. Donald Hall. **CP-HallD**

Old Rotting Tree Trunk Down. Gary Snyder. **CP-SnydG**

Old rusty-belly thing will soon be gone. The Sappa Creek. Gary Snyder. **CP-SnydG**

Old Sailors, The. Lawrence Ferlinghetti. **SP-FerlL**

Old saints on millstones float with cats. Islands. Wystan Hugh Auden. *Fr.* Bucolics. **CP-AudeW**

Old Salt Kossabone. Walt Whitman. **CP-WhitW**

Old sandpiper contemplates his age, The. Summer's Early End at Hudson's Bay. Hayden Carruth. **CP-CarHS**

Old Saybrook House, The. John Clellon Holmes. **SP-HolmJ**

Old Saying, An. Algernon Charles Swinburne. **SP-SwinA**

Old Scene. Richard Hugo. **CP-HugoR**

Old self, The / like a dybbuk. Lullabye for a Dybbuk. Erica Jong. **SP-JongE**

Old ships are preserved. The Taste. George Oppen. **NNaP** *Fr.* Some San Francisco Poems. **CP-OppeG**

Old shoe, an old pot, an old skin, An. Autumn Sequence. Adrienne Rich. **CP-RicAE**

Old shoe, like a dog who sleeps besides my bed. Meditations on an Old Shoe. Chuck Miller. **SP-MillC**

Old sick green parrot, The. Parrot. Stevie Smith. **CP-SmitS**

Old sir, I think of you in this tardy spring. To Lu Chi. Howard Nemerov. **CP-NemeH**

Old sisters at our Maris Stella House. Mother Marie Therese. Robert Lowell. **SP-LoweR**

"Old Smoky" when you sing with Robin, Chris. John Berryman. *Fr.* Sonnets to Chris. **SP-BerrJ**

Old Smoothing Iron. Seamus Heaney. **SP-HeanS** *Fr.* Shelf Life.

Old Snaps, The. Derek Mahon. **SP-MahoD**

Old snapshot from Venice 1952. Robert Lowell. **SP-LoweR**

Old Soldiers' Home. Ted Kooser. **SP-KoosT**

Old Soldiers' Home, The. Howard Nemerov. **CP-NemeH**

Old son, he said. Old Reprobate. Daniel Gerard Hoffman. **SP-HoffD**

Old Song. Hart Crane. **CP-CranH**

Old Song. Robert Creeley. **CP-CreeR**

Old Song, An. Randall Jarrell. **CP-JarrR**

Old Song, An. Rudyard Kipling. **CP-KiplR**

Old Song. David Herbert Lawrence. **CP-LawrD**

Old song wanders round / on some lost errand sent, An. Lilibulero. John Hewitt. **CP-HewiJ**

Old soubrettes could always have, The. The Soubrettes. Alun Lewis. **CP-LewiA**

Old South, The. John Gould Fletcher. **SP-FletJ**

Old South Boston Aquarium stands, The. For the Union Dead. Robert Lowell. **SP-LoweR**

Old sow in the mud. Mother of the Buddhas, Queen of Heaven, Mother of the Sun; Marici, Goddess of the Dawn. Gary Snyder. **CP-SnydG**

Old spoon, An. Spoon. Charles Simic. **SP-SimiC**

Old Squire said, as he stood by his gate, The. Valuation. John Greenleaf Whittier. **CP-WhitJ**

Old Stoic, The. Emily Brontë. **CP-BronE**

(Old Stoic, The.) **CP-BronE**

Old Stoic, The. Emily Brontë. *See* The Old Stoic.

Old Stone Cross, The. William Butler Yeats. **CP-YeatW**

Old Stone-Mason, The. Robinson Jeffers. **CP-JefR3**

Old Story, The. Argentarius. **AWP** *Fr.* Variations of Greek Themes. **CP-RobiE**

Old Story, The. Paul Laurence Dunbar. **CP-DunbP**

Old Story, The. Louis MacNeice. *Fr.* Novelettes. **CP-MacNL**

Old Story, An. Howard Nemerov. *Fr.* Epigrams: "Wasp, climbing the window pane." **CP-NemeH**

Old Story, An. Edwin Arlington Robinson. **CP-RobiE**

Old story is true of charms fading, The. The Old Story. Louis MacNeice. *Fr.* Novelettes. **CP-MacNL**

Old story that you can't find out about, An. The Open Boat. Gilbert Sorrentino. **SP-SorrG**

Old Summerhouse, The. Walter de la Mare. **CP-DeLaW**

Old Susan. Walter de la Mare. **CP-DeLaW**

Old Sweet Dove of Wiveton, The. Stevie Smith. **CP-SmitS**

Old Tale. Gilbert Sorrentino. **SP-SorrG**

Old Tennis Player. Gwendolyn Brooks. **LiSp; SD** *Fr.* A Catch of Shy Fish. **SP-BrooG**

Old-Testament Gospel. William Cowper. **ChIV-2; TrCP** *Fr.* Olney Hymns. **CP-CowpW**

Old things need not be therefore true. Arthur Hugh Clough. **SP-ClouA**

Old timber ship steams down the Mersey, The. From Helsinki to Liverpool with Lumber. Malcolm Lowry. *Fr.* The Roar of the Sea and the Darkness. **CP-LowrM**

Old-Time Sea-Fight, An. Walt Whitman. *See* Would You Hear of an Old-Time [*or* Old-Fashioned] Sea fight?

Old Timers. Carl Sandburg. **CP-SandC**

Old Timer's Day. Donald Hall. *See* When the tall puffy.

Old Tom. Richard Eberhart. **CP-EberR**

Old Tom Again, *fr.* Words for Music Perhaps. William Butler Yeats. **CP-YeatW**

Old Toyota, green as a frog, coughs and clanks, The. Talking in the Woods with Karl Amorelli. Etheridge Knight. **SP-KnigE**

Old Trails. Edwin Arlington Robinson. **CP-RobiE**

Old Tree by the Penobscot. Richard Eberhart. **CP-EberR**

Old trees are witnesses. A Kind of Ethics. Thom Gunn. **CP-GunnT**

Old Trip by Dream Train, The. Brendan Galvin. **SP-GalvB**

Old Trostan holds his snow among the clouds. Late Spring. John Hewitt. **CP-HewiJ**

Old Village before I Die, The. Allen Ginsberg. **CP-GinsA**

Old voice of the ocean, the bird-chatter of little rivers, The. Natural Music. Robinson Jeffers. **CP-JefR1**

Old Walt. Langston Hughes. **SP-HughL**

Old War-Dreams. Walt Whitman. **CP-WhitW**

Old warder of these buried bones. Tennyson. **PeECV; PoEL-5** *Fr.* In Memoriam A. H. H. **CP-TennA**

Old Warplane, An. Howard Nemerov. **CP-NemeH**

Old Warrior Terror, The. Alice Walker. **CP-WalkA**

Old watch: their, The. Vapor Trail Reflected in the Frog Pond. Galway Kinnell. **SP-KinnG**

Old widow lady, and went out to do her chore, An. Mona Van Duyn. **SP-VanDM**

Old widow Prouse to do her neighbours evill. Upon an Old Woman. Robert Herrick. **CP-HerrR**

Old Widow Shopter, when so ere she cryes. Upon Shopter. Robert Herrick. **CP-HerrR**

Old Wife in High Spirits. "Hugh MacDiarmid." **SP-MacDH**

Old willow with hollow branches, An. Epitaph. William Carlos Williams. **CP-WilW1**

Old Winter, with his frosty beard. Impomptu, on Mrs. W. Riddell's Birthday, 4th Novr. 1793. Robert Burns. **CP-BurnR**

Old wives have often told, how they. Upon Cupid. Robert Herrick. **CP-HerrR**

Old Wives Prayer, The. Robert Herrick. **CP-HerrR**

Old Wolf My Father, The. Robinson Jeffers. **CP-JefR3**

Old Woman, The. Thom Gunn. **CP-GunnT**

Old Woman, The. Ted Kooser. **SP-KoosT**

Old Woman. Carl Sandburg. **CP-SandC**

Old Woman. Al Young. **CP-YounA**

Old woman across the way, The. The Whipping. Robert Earl Hayden. **CP-HaydR**

Old woman, asleep on her back, The. The Old Woman. Ted Kooser. **SP-KoosT**

Old Woman Nature. Gary Snyder. **CP-SnydG**

Old woman sits on a bench before the door and quarrels, The. Fawn's Foster-Mother. Robinson Jeffers. **CP-JefR1**

Old Woman Telling Another Version. Brendan Galvin. **SP-GalvB**

Old Woman who Buried Cats, The. Malcolm Lowry. **CP-LowrM**

Old women came from their caves to close the too many doors, The. Robert Duncan. **SP-DuncR** *Fr.* The Structure of Rime.

Old women come here to die. Nurses. In the Ward. Charles Tomlinson. **CP-TomlC**

Old wood stands uncut, of long years' space, An. 3.1. Ovid. **CP-MarlC,** *tr. by* Christopher Marlowe; *Fr.* Elegies.

Old Woodsroads. Brendan Galvin. **SP-GalvB**

Old words: *trust fidelity.* For Memory. Adrienne Rich. **SP-RicA1; SP-RicA2**

Old Workman, The. Thomas Hardy. **CP-HardT**

Old world moans and topes, The. Robert Louis Stevenson. **CP-StevR**

Old-World Thicket, An. Christina Georgina Rossetti. **CP-RosC2**

Old, worn harp that had been played, An. The Master-Player. Paul Laurence Dunbar. **CP-DunbP**

Old Worshipper, The. William Carlos Williams. **CP-WilW1**

Old yew, which graspest at the stones. Tennyson. **EBVV; EBVVPR; ELP; EnVR; GTBS-6; GTBS-P; NOBE; NoP; OAEL-2; OBNC; PAI; PoEL-5; SeCeV; UnPo** *Fr.* In Memoriam A. H. H. **CP-TennA**

Older girls taunted me into one of those. The Voice. Stephen Berg. **SP-BergS**

Older I grow the more ignorant I become, The. Ignorance. Philippe Jaccottet. *Fr.* Three Poems by Phillipe Jaccottet. **SP-MahoD**

Oldest Conversation, The. Kenneth Patchen. **CP-PatcK**

Oldest joke / in the world, The. My Father's Telescope. Rita Dove. **SP-DoveR**

Oldest Killed Lake in North America, The. Hayden Carruth. **CP-CarHS**

Oldest Soldier, The. Robert Ranke Graves. **CP-GravR**

Oldest Song, The. Rudyard Kipling. **CP-KiplR**

O'Leary was a poet—for a while. Shadrach O'Leary. Edwin Arlington Robinson. **CP-RobiE**

Oleaster, The. Robert Ranke Graves. **CP-GravR**

Oleo Strut. Gilbert Sorrentino. **SP-SorrG**

Oleum Misericordiae. John Ashbery. **SP-AshbJ**

Olga Poems. Denise Levertov. **CP-LeveD**

Olim fungus ego, silex verebar. *acc. by English translation.* Thomas Campion. **CP-CampT**

Olim te duro cernebam tempore Martis. *acc. by English translation.* Thomas Campion. **CP-CampT**

Olive, The. Alfred Edward Housman. **CP-HousA**

Olive Branch, The. Robert Herrick. **CP-HerrR**

Olive Branch, The. George Meredith. **CP-MerG1**

Olive Garden, The, *tr. fr. the German of* Rilke. Randall Jarrell. **CP-JarrR**

Olive-green, sky-blue, gravel-brown. September Landscape. Robert Ranke Graves. **CP-GravR**

Olive Grove. James Merrill. **SP-MerrJ**

Olive Grove, The. May Sarton. **SP-SartM**

Olive Tree, The. Karl Shapiro. **SP-ShapK**

Olive-Yard, The. Robert Ranke Graves. **CP-GravR**

Oliver wanted to write about reality. Make Big Money at Home! Write Poems in Spare Time! Howard Nemerov. **CP-NemeH**

Oliverio Girondo. Pablo Neruda, *tr. fr. Spanish by* Ben Belitt. **SP-NeruP**

Olives and Mountains. Elizabeth Barrett Browning. **FaBoPP; OBTV** *Fr.* Aurora Leigh. **CP-BroEB**

Olivet, Olivet! Where heaven robbed us. A Whitsun Canticle. Thomas Merton. **CP-MertT**

Ollie, Answer Me. Stephen Berg. **SP-BergS**

Olney Hymns. Sir John Betjeman. **CP-BetjJ**

Olney Hymns. William Cowper. **CP-CowpW**
   Abuse of the Gospel.
   Afflictions Sanctified by the Word.
   Christian, The.
   Contentment. **ChIV-2**
   Covenant, The.
   Dependance.
   Ephraim Repenting. **ChIV-1**
   Exhortation to Prayer. **NOCV**
   For the Poor.
   Future Peace and Glory of the Church, The.
     (Hymn 10.) **ChIV-1**

   Grace and Providence.
   Happy Change, The.
   Hatred of Sin.
   Heart Healed and Changed by Mercy, The.
   Hidden Life, The.
   House of Prayer, The. **ChIV-2**
   I Will Praise the Lord at All Times.
   Jehovah-Jesus.
   Jehovah-Jireh.
   Jehovah-Nissi.
   Jehovah Our Righteousness. **NOCV**
   Jehovah-Rophi.
   Jehovah-Shalom.
   Jehovah-Shammah.
   Jesus Hasting to Suffer.
   Joy and Peace in Believing. **NOCV; TRV**
   Light and Glory of the World, The.
   Light Shining out of Darkness. **EBEV; EBEvV; ECEV; ELP; EaLo; EnRP; FHYEP; FPL; FaBoCh; FiP; HeIP; ImPo; LiTB; NOBE; NOCV; NOEC; NoP; OBEC; PWR; PoEL-3; SCGP; SeCePo; TFi; TOF; TRV; TrGrPo; WGRP**
   Lively Hope, and Gracious Fear. **CP-CowpW**
   Living and a Dead Faith, A.
   Looking Upwards in a Storm.
   Lord Will Happiness Divine, The. **NOCV**
     (Contrite Heart, The.) **CP-CowpW**
   Love Constraining to Obedience. **NOCV**
   Lovest Thou Me? **ChIV-2; HBV 1-2; OBEC**
     "Lord, it is my chief complaint." **TrPWD**
   Mourning and Longing.
   "My former hopes are fled." **CP-CowpW; OxBoCh**
     (Shining Light, The.) **CP-CowpW**
   My Soul Thirsteth for God. **TrCP**
   Narrow Way, The.
   New Convert, The.
   Not of Works.
   O Lord I Will Praise Thee.
   "O Lord, my best desire fulfil." **CP-CowpW; OxBoCh**
     (Submission.) **CP-CowpW**
   Old-Testament Gospel. **ChIV-2; TrCP**
   On Opening a Place for Social Prayer.
   On the Death of a Minister.
   Peace after a Storm.
   Pleading for and with Youth.
   Praise for Faith.
   Praise for the Fountain Opened. **InPK**
     (Fountain, The.) **ChIV-1**
   Prayer for a Blessing.
   Prayer for Children.
   Prayer for Patience.
   Retirement.
   Sardis. **ChIV-2**
   Seeking the Beloved.
   Self-Acquaintance. **NOCV**
   Sower, The. **ChIV-2; SaC**
   Temptation.
   True and False Comforts.
   True Pleasures. **CP-CowpW**
   Valley of the Shadow of Death, The.
   Vanity of the World.
   Waiting Soul, The.
   Walking with God. **ECEV; EnRP; FiP; NOCV; NOEC; PeECV; PoEL-3; SCGP; TEP; TOF**
   Welcome Cross.
   Welcome to the Table.
   Wisdom. **ChIV-1**

Olor Iscanus queries: "Why should we." To Samuel E. Sewall and Harriet W. Sewall. John Greenleaf Whittier. **CP-WhitJ**

Olwen: / She said, 'Where is the horseman,'. Olwen and Taliesin. Alun Lewis. **CP-LewiA**

Olwen and Taliesin. Alun Lewis. **CP-LewiA**

Olympian, The. James Dickey. **CP-DickJ**

Olympian before the Olympics, that inhuman backdrop, An. The Noble Man. Richard Eberhart. **CP-EberR**

Olympian gods, mark now my bedside lamp. Edna St. Vincent Millay. **CP-MillE**

Olympic Girl, The. Sir John Betjeman. **CP-BetjJ**

Olympics have descended into, The. Big Beat. Allen Ginsberg. **CP-GinsA**

Olympus. John Berryman. **CP-BerrJ**

OM—the pride of perfumed money, food music from China, a place to sit. Thoughts Sitting Breathing. Allen Ginsberg. **CP-GinsA**

Omaha. Carl Sandburg. **CP-SandC**

Omega. John Updike. **CP-UpdiJ**

Omega ran to witness him; beseeched. A Surrealist and Omega. Gwendolyn Brooks. *Fr.* A Catch of Shy Fish. **SP-BrooG**

Omen, The. Walter de la Mare. **CP-DeLaW**

Omen. Frederick Morgan. **SP-MorgF**

Omens and Auguries. John Hewitt. **CP-HewiJ**

Ominous bird sang from its branch, An. Beware! Walter de la Mare. **CP-DeLaW**

On— / Thro' the gleaming gray. He Climbs the Hill Where the Tree Grows. Nicholas Vachel Lindsay. *Fr.* The Tree of Laughing Bells or The Wings of the Morning. **CP-LindV**

On a Bank of Flowers. Robert Burns. **CP-BurnR**

On a bare tree in a hollow place. Epigram on a Painting of Golgotha. Allen Ginsberg. **CP-GinsA**

On a Bath. Plato, *tr. fr. Greek by* William Cowper. **CP-CowpW**

On a Battered Beauty. *Unknown, tr. fr. Greek by* William Cowper. **CP-CowpW**

On a bed of gravel moving. A Folk Singer of the Thirties. James Dickey. **CP-DickJ**

On a Bed of Guernsey Lilies. Christopher Smart. **SP-SmarC**

On a bend in the road near St. Mary. John Haines. *Fr.* News from the Glacier. **SP-HainJ**

On a Bereaved Girl. Alun Lewis. **CP-LewiA**

On a Bird Singing in its Sleep. Robert Frost. **CP-FrosR**

On a bright blue day in October. Sky. Barton Sutter. **SP-SuttB**

On a Bright Day, Next Week. Maya Angelou. **SP-AngeM**

On a catafalque, draped in black, under bronze cannon. The Passing of the South. John Gould Fletcher. **SP-FletJ**

On a Cataract, *ad. fr. the German of* Stolberg. Samuel Taylor Coleridge. **CP-ColeS**

On a Celebrated Event in Ancient History, *see also* Upon the Same Event. William Wordsworth. **CP-WorW1**

On a Celebrated Ruling Elder. Robert Burns. **CP-BurnR**

On a Certain Engagement South of Seoul. Hayden Carruth. **CP-CarHS**

On a Certain Lady at Court. Alexander Pope. **CP-PopeA**

On a certain part of the lawn outside the. Loving Ugly. Ron Koertge. **SP-KoerR**

On a Change of Masters at a Great Public School. Byron. **CP-Byron**

On a Clean Book. Paul Laurence Dunbar. **CP-DunbP**

On a clear day how thin the horizon. Horizon. Robert Ranke Graves. **CP-GravR**

On a clear day, the jealous. The Danger of Loss. Robert Bly. **SP-BlyR**

On a clear spring windless sky. The Feathered Robe. Gary Snyder. **CP-SnydG**

On a cold evening, summer almost gone. The Loon's Cry. Howard Nemerov. **CP-NemeH**

On a Cold Night. Frank Templeton Prince. **CP-PrinF**

On a Columnar Self. Emily Dickinson. **CP-DickE**

On a Cornelian Heart Which Was Broken. Byron. **CP-Byron**

On a Country Bus Forty Years Ago. John Hewitt. **CP-HewiJ**

On a Country Life. James Thomson. **CP-ThomJ**

On a Daffodil, the First Flower the Author Had Seen That Year. Samuel Johnson. **CP-JohnS**

On a Damask[e] Rose, Sticking upon a Lady's Breast. Thomas Carew. **CP-CareT**

On a darkening planet. Flight to Catalina. Erica Jong. **SP-JongE**

On a day, alack the day!, *sl. diff. vers. also in* Love's Labours Lost, IV, iii. *Various Authors.* **CP-ShaWS** *Fr.* The Passionate Pilgrim. **CP-ShaWS**

On a Day in August. Thomas Merton. **CP-MertT**

On a day in fall, when high winds trouble the country. Hymn for the Feast of Duns Scotus. Thomas Merton. **CP-MertT**

On a day like this the rain comes. Fauré's Second Piano Quartet. James Schuyler. **CP-SchuJ**

On a day of dry wind. The Danger in the Air. Archibald MacLeish. **CP-MacLA**

On a day when the trees are exchanging the cured gold of the sun. In Early Autumn. Thomas McGrath. **SP-McGrT**

On a Diet. William Matthews. **SP-MattW**

On a Discovered Curl of Hair. Thomas Hardy. **CP-HardT**

On a Discovery Made Too Late. Samuel Taylor Coleridge. **EnRP; Son** *Fr.* Effusions. **CP-ColeS**

On a Distant View of the Village and School of Harrow on the Hill. Byron. **CP-Byron**

On a Dog of Lord Eglinton's. Robert Burns. **CP-BurnR**

On a Drawing by Flavio. Philip Levine. **SP-LeviP**

On a Drop of Dew, *see also* Ros. Andrew Marvell. **CP-MarvA**

On a Dunce Who Had Not a Word to Say for Himself. Gerard Manley Hopkins. *Fr.* Seven Epigrams. **CP-HopkG**

On a Faded Violet. Percy Bysshe Shelley. **CP-ShelP**

On a Fan of the Author's Design, in Which Was Painted the Story of CEPHALUS and PROCRIS, with the Motto, AURA VENI, *in imitation of* Waller. Alexander Pope. **CP-PopeA**

On a Ferry across Chesapeake Bay. Robert Bly. **SP-BlyR**

On a Fête at Carlton House: Fragment. Percy Bysshe Shelley. **CP-ShelP**

On a Fine Morning. Thomas Hardy. **CP-HardT**

On a flaked ridge of the desert. Bar-Room TV. Ted Hughes. *Fr.* Boom. **SP-HughT**

On a flat road runs the well-train'd runner. The Runner. Walt Whitman. **CP-WhitW**

On a Flimmering Floom You Shall Ride. Carl Sandburg. **CP-SandC**

On a Fly-Leaf of Longfellow's Poems. John Greenleaf Whittier. **CP-WhitJ**

On a Foule Morning, Being Then to Take a Journey. Richard Crashaw. **CP-CrasR**

On a Fowler. Isidorus, *tr. fr. Greek by* William Cowper. **CP-CowpW**

On a Goldfinch Starved to Death in His Cage. William Cowper. **CP-CowpW**

On a Good Man. *Unknown, tr. fr. Greek by* William Cowper. **CP-CowpW**

On a gray evening. History. Charles Simic. **SP-SimiC**

On a Greek Tomb Relief. Wystan Hugh Auden. **CP-AudWJ**

On a ground beaten gold by running and. A Game of Ball. Muriel Rukeyser. **CP-RukeM**

On a ground remarkable for lack of character. A Poem not a Picture. Roy Fisher. **SP-FishR**

On a Heath. Thomas Hardy. **CP-HardT**

On a high branch two. Charles Henri Ford. **SP-FordC** *Fr.* Emblems of Arachne.

On a High Part of the Coast in Cumberland. William Wordsworth. **CP-WorW2**

On a Horse Carved in Wood. Donald Hall. **CP-HallD**

On a hot summer Sunday. The Cemetery at Academy, California. Philip Levine. **SP-LeviP**

On a January Train Journey. John Hewitt. **CP-HewiJ**

On a kind of Christmas day. Reminiscent of a Wave At the Curl. Marianne Craig Moore. **CP-MoorM**

On a kitchen chair. News for the Ear. Roy Fisher. **SP-FishR**

On a Lady Who P-ssed [or P———st] at the Tragedy of Cato. Alexander Pope. **CP-PopeA**

On a Lady's Presenting a Sprig of Myrtle to a Gentleman. Samuel Johnson. **CP-JohnS**

On a Landscape by Li Ch'eng. Charles Tomlinson. **CP-TomlC**

On a Late Connubial Rupture in High Life. Samuel Taylor Coleridge. **CP-ColeS**

On a Leander Gem which Miss Reynolds, My Kind Friend, Gave Me. John Keats. **CP-KeatJ**

On a Letter of Miss Fanshawe. William Cowper. **CP-CowpW**

On a long block. Drawn to Perspective. Charles Simic. **SP-SimiC**

On a low cedar-bush. Eagle in New Mexico. David Herbert Lawrence. **CP-LawrD**

On a low couch reclining. The Spanish Lady. Walt Whitman. **CP-WhitW**

On a low Lorrainian knoll a leaning peasant sinking a pit. Attila. William Everson. **SP-EverW**

On a May Night. Charles Tomlinson. **CP-TomlC**

On a Mexican Straw Christ. Charles Tomlinson. **CP-TomlC**

On a mid-December day. Since. Wystan Hugh Auden. **CP-AudeW**

On a Midsummer Eve. Thomas Hardy. **CP-HardT**

On a Mischievous Bull. William Cowper. **CP-CowpW**

On a Miser. Lucilius. *See* They call thee rich; I deem thee poor.

On a Mistake in His Translation of Homer. William Cowper. **CP-CowpW**

On a morning sick as the day of doom. In a Waiting-Room. Thomas Hardy. **CP-HardT**

On a mound an Arab lay. Hermione. Ralph Waldo Emerson. **CP-EmerR**

On a mountain-side the real estate agents. Landscape. Carl Sandburg. **CP-SandC**

On a Mourner. Tennyson. **CP-TennA**

On a Night Like This. "Bob Dylan." **CP-DylaB**

On a Night of the Full Moon, *with music.* Audre Lorde. **SP-LordA**

On a Night You Don't Sleep. Charles Bukowski. **SP-BukC2**

On a Noisy Polemic. Robert Burns. **CP-BurnR**

On a Painting by Julius Olsson R.A. Sir John Betjeman. **CP-BetjJ**

On a Perfum'd Lady. Robert Herrick. **CP-HerrR**

On a Photo of Sgt. Ciardi a Year Later. John Ciardi. **SP-CiarJ**

On a Photograph of My Mother at Seventeen. Miller Williams. **SP-WillM**

On a Picture of a Black Centaur by Edmund Dulac. William Butler Yeats. **CP-YeatW**

On a piece of toilet paper. Bladder Song. Leonard Nathan. **SP-NathL**

On a Pig's Head. Charles Tomlinson. **CP-TomlC**

On a Plant of Virgin's Bower. William Cowper. **CP-CowpW**

On a Poetess. Gerard Manley Hopkins. **PP** *Fr.* Seven Epigrams. **CP-HopkG**

On a poet's lips I slept. Percy Bysshe Shelley. **ChER; ELP; EPCY; FiP; TOF,** *ll.* 737–751; **GTBS; GTBS-6; GTBS-P** *Fr.* Prometheus Unbound. **CP-ShelP**

(Poet's Dream, The.) **GTBS; GTBS-6; GTBS-P,** *ll.* 737–749;

On a Political Prisoner. William Butler Yeats. **CP-YeatW**

On a Portrait of a Deaf Man. Sir John Betjeman. **CP-BetjJ**

On a Portrait of the Duke of Wellington upon the Field of Waterloo, by Haydon. William Wordsworth. **CP-WorW2**

On a Portrait of Wordsworth by B. R. Haydon. Elizabeth Barrett Browning. **CP-BroEB**

On a Prayer-Book. John Greenleaf Whittier. **CP-WhitJ**

On a Printer's Being Sent to Newgate. Jonathan Swift. **CP-SwifJ**

On a Proposed Celebration of Ezra Pound. Donald Davie. **CP-DavDo**

On a Proposed Trip South. William Carlos Williams. **CP-WilW1**

On a Protestant Mystic. James Liddy. **CP-LiddJ**

On a Railroad Right of Way. Carl Sandburg. **CP-SandC**

On a rainy night / On a rainy night in April. April 4th 1968. Thomas Merton. **CP-MertT**

On a Raised Beach. "Hugh MacDiarmid." **SP-MacDH**

On a raisin stone. Ralph Waldo Emerson. **CP-EmerR**

On a relief map. Sioux Haiku. William Stafford. **SP-StafW**

On a Report That in Some Rest Homes Residents Who Are Depressed Will be Charged at a Higher Rate. Frank Templeton Prince. **CP-PrinF**

On a Review Condemning Thelyphthora. William Cowper. **CP-CowpW**

On a Robbery. Ben Jonson. **CP-JonsB**

On a rock, whose haughty brow. A Pindaric Ode. Thomas Gray. **SeCePo** *Fr.* Bard, The [A Pindaric Ode]. **CP-GrayT**

On a Royal Visit to the Vaults. Byron. **CP-Byron**

On a Ruined House in a Romantic Country. Samuel Taylor Coleridge. **FaBoPa; Par** *Fr.* Sonnets Attempted in the Manner of Contemporary Writers. **CP-ColeS**

(House That Jack Built, The.) **CBNP**

On a Schoolmaster in Cleish Parish, Fifeshire. Robert Burns. *See* Here lie Willie Michie's [*or* M—hie's] banes.

On a Scotch Bard Gone to the West Indies. Robert Burns. **CP-BurnR**

On a Shell-strewn Beach. Kathleen Jessie Raine. **SP-RainK**

On a shining day of October we remembered you, Commander. The Commander. Sir John Betjeman. **CP-BetjJ**

On a Similar Character. Lucianus. *See* You give your cheeks a rosy stain.

On a Similar Occasion for the Year 1788. William Cowper. **CP-CowpW**

On a Similar Occasion for the Year 1789. William Cowper. **CP-CowpW**

On a Similar Occasion for the Year 1790. William Cowper. **CP-CowpW**

On a Similar Occasion for the Year 1792. William Cowper. **CP-CowpW**

On a Similar Occasion for the Year 1793. William Cowper. **CP-CowpW**

On a snug evening I shall watch her fingers. Piano after War. Gwendolyn Brooks. **SP-BrooG**

On a Spaniel Called Beau Killing a Young Bird. William Cowper. **CP-CowpW**

On a Squirrel Crossing the Road in Autumn, in New England. Richard Eberhart. **CP-EberR**

On a stale morning. Hotel Breakfast. Archibald MacLeish. **CP-MacLA**

On a starred [*or* starr'd] night Prince Lucifer uprose. Lucifer in Starlight. George Meredith. **CP-MerG1**

On a still, silent night, scarce could I number. His Dream. Sir John Suckling. **CP-SuckJ**

On a summer's afternoon, hot. The Wounded Bat. Malcolm Lowry. **CP-LowrM**

On a summer's day as I sat by a stream. Song, A. Paul Laurence Dunbar. **CP-DunbP**

On a sunny brae alone I lay. A Day Dream. Emily Brontë. **CP-BronE**

On a Text: Jonah IV, xi. Howard Nemerov. **CP-NemeH**

On a theme fantastic, a light / *aria*, by some altogether monstrous woman in. The Trap. Robert Creeley. **CP-CreeR**

On a Theme of Pasternak. Charles Tomlinson. *Fr.* Four Kantian Lyrics. **CP-TomlC**

On a Thief. *Unknown, tr. fr. Greek by* William Cowper. **CP-CowpW**

On a Trailways Bus a Man Who Holds His Head Strangely Speaks to the Seat Behind Him. Miller Williams. **SP-WillM**

On a Tree Fallen across the Road. Robert Frost. **CP-FrosR**

On a True Friend. *Unknown, tr. fr. Greek by* William Cowper. **CP-CowpW**

On a Very Old Glass. Jonathan Swift. **CP-SwifJ**

On a Volunteer Singer. Samuel Taylor Coleridge. **CP-ColeS**

On a Wedding Anniversary. Dylan Thomas. **CP-ThomD**

On a wet pavement the white sky recedes. The Bitter World of Spring. William Carlos Williams. **CP-WilW2**

On a Winter Night. May Sarton. **SP-SartM**

On Acid. Robert Creeley. **CP-CreeR**

On Addison. Alexander Pope. *See* Atticus ("Peace to all such! but were there one whose fires").

On afternoons of drowsy calm. Afternoon Service at Mellstock. Thomas Hardy. **CP-HardT**

On Aging. Maya Angelou. **SP-AngeM**

On Albina. Christina Georgina Rossetti. **CP-RosC3**

On all fours around the roof. And I, Too, Am Something of a Stranger Here, My Friend. Kenneth Patchen. **CP-PatcK**

On All Sides. Charles Olson. **CP-OlsoC**

On all that strand. Roundelay. Samuel Beckett. **CP-BeckS**

On all the streetcorners the children are standing. The Flying Red Horse. Muriel Rukeyser. **CP-RukeM**

On almost the incendiary eve. Deaths and Entrances. Dylan Thomas. **CP-ThomD**

On alternating levels the world pounds in. The Overworld. Kenneth Patchen. **CP-PatcK**

On an Ancient Isle. Kathleen Jessie Raine. **SP-RainK**

On an Anthology of Chinese Poems. Robinson Jeffers. **CP-JefR3**

On an Eagle Confined in a College-Court. Christopher Smart. **SP-SmarC**

On an empty morning a small clerk. The Lake in the Park. Louis MacNeice. **CP-MacNL**

On an empty stomach I send you a wish for health. Elegy 6. John Milton, *tr. fr. Latin by* John T. Shawcross. **CP-MiltJ**

On an Icicle That Clung to the Grass of a Grave. Percy Bysshe Shelley. **CP-ShelP**

On an Infant. Lucianus. *See* Bewail not much, my parents! me, the prey.

On an Infant Which Died before Baptism. Samuel Taylor Coleridge. **CP-ColeS**

On an Innkeeper in Tarbolton. Robert Burns. **CP-BurnR**

On an Insignificant. Samuel Taylor Coleridge. **CP-ColeS**

On an Invitation to the United States. Thomas Hardy. **CP-HardT**

On an Island. John Updike. **CP-UpdiJ**

On an oak in autumn. Survivor. Archibald MacLeish. **CP-MacLA**

On an Old Acquaintance Who Seemed to Pass the Bard without Notice. Robert Burns. *Fr.* Dumfries Epigrams. **CP-BurnR**

"Dost blush, my dear Billy, asham'd of thyself."

"Dost hang thy head, Billy, asham'd that thou knowest me?"

On an Old-Fashioned Water-Colour of Oxford. Sir John Betjeman. **CP-BetjJ**

On an Old Horn. Wallace Stevens. **CP-StevW**

On an old shore, the vulgar ocean rolls. Somnambulisma. Wallace Stevens. **CP-StevW**

On an Old Woman. Lucilius, *tr. fr. Greek by* William Cowper. **CP-CowpW**

On an olive beach, beneath a turquoise sky. Sunglasses. John Updike. **CP-UpdiJ**

On an Ugly Fellow. *Unknown, tr. fr. Greek by* William Cowper. **CP-CowpW**

On and Off the Road. Charles Bukowski. **SP-BukC3**

On and on and on. Wystan Hugh Auden. *Fr.* Ten Songs. **CP-AudeW**

On and On and On. David Herbert Lawrence. **CP-LawrD**

On Andrew Turner. Robert Burns. **CP-BurnR**

On Another's Sorrow. William Blake. **AWP; EBCP; EnRP; FHYEP; FaBV; OXAEP-2; PoEL-4** *Fr.* Songs of Innocence. **CP-BlakW**

On Approaching the Staub-Bach, Lauterbrunnen. William Wordsworth. *Fr.* Memorials of a Tour of the Continent; 1820. **CP-WorW2**

On, as thou hast begunne, brave youth, and get. To His Nephew, to Be Prosperous in His Art of Painting. Robert Herrick. **CP-HerrR**

On bank and brake the moonshine quakes. The Miller. Randall Jarrell. **CP-JarrR**

On Bank the Usurer. Ben Jonson. **CP-JonsB**

On Banner Dome. John Haines. **SP-HainJ**

On Barbara's Shore. Diane Wakoski. **SP-WakoD**

On Bawds and Usurers. Ben Jonson. **CP-JonsB**

On Beauty. Kenneth Koch. **SP-KochK**

On Beauty [*or* Beauety]. James Thomson *and* David Mallet. **CP-ThomJ**

"This happy place with all delights abounds." **UV**

On Beechen Cliff self-commune I. Midnight on Beechen, 187–. Thomas Hardy. **CP-HardT**

On Being a Member of the Jury for a Poetry Prize. Howard Nemerov. **CP-NemeH**

On Being Asked for a Peace Poem. Howard Nemerov. **CP-NemeH**

On Being Asked for a War Poem. William Butler Yeats. **CP-YeatW**

On Being Asked to Leave a Place of Honor for One of Comfort, Preferably in the Northern Suburbs. Alice Walker. **CP-WalkA**

On Being Asked to Write a Poem Against the War in Vietnam. Hayden Carruth. **CP-CarHS**

On Being Asked What Was the "Origin of Love." Byron. **CP-Byron**

On Being Asked Why God Had Made Miss D—— So Little and Mrs A—— —— So Big. Robert Burns. **CP-BurnR**

On Being Cautioned against Walking on an Headland Overlooking the Sea, because It Was Frequented by a Lunatic. Charlotte Smith. **CP-SmitC**

On Being Chosen Poet of Vermont. Robert Frost. **CP-FrosR**

On Being Denied for Being Already Took. David Markson. **CP-MarkD**

On Being Given Time. May Sarton. **SP-SartM**

On Being Idolized. Robert Frost. **CP-FrosR**

On Being Recognized. Charles Bukowski. **SP-BukC3**

On Being Stranded near the Harbour of Boulogne. William Wordsworth. *Fr.* Memorials of a Tour of the Continent; 1820. **CP-WorW2**

On Being 20. Charles Bukowski. **SP-BukC3**

On Being Twenty-Six. Philip Larkin. **CP-LarkP**

On benches in front of the Old Soldiers' Home. Old Soldiers' Home. Ted Kooser. **SP-KoosT**

On Benjamin Disraeli. Robert Browning. **CP-BroR2**

On Bertrand Russell's "Portraits from Memory." Donald Davie. **CP-DavDo**

On board the Matsue Maru. Malcolm Lowry. **CP-LowrM**

On Boston Common a red star. A Winter's Tale. Sylvia Plath. **CP-PlatS**

On bravely through the sunshine & the showers. Ralph Waldo Emerson. **CP-EmerR**

On Britain Europe's safety lies. To Mr. Harley's Surgeon. Jonathan Swift. **CP-SwifJ**

On Building with Stone. Robinson Jeffers. **CP-JefR1**

On Burning a Dull Poem. Jonathan Swift. **CP-SwifJ**

On Burroughs' Work. Allen Ginsberg. **CP-GinsA**

On Canann Mountain Meadow. Hayden Carruth. **CP-CarHS**

On Cape Cod a Child Is Stolen. William Matthews. **SP-MattW**

On Captain Hazard the Cheater. Ben Jonson. **CP-JonsB**

On Captn. L————lles. Robert Burns. **CP-BurnR**

On Capt. W—— R-dd-ck of C-rb—ton. Robert Burns. **CP-BurnR**

On Cashiered Capt[ain] Surly. Ben Jonson. **CP-JonsB**

On Castle Hill. Marge Piercy. **SP-PierM**

On Censure. Jonathan Swift. **CP-SwifJ**

On Central Coast radio KTOM blasts. Watsonville after the Quake. Al Young. **CP-YounA**

On certain days I am not in love. Grace Paley. **CP-PaleG**

On Certain Wits. Howard Nemerov. **CP-NemeH**

On Cessnock banks a lassie dwells. Song. Robert Burns. **CP-BurnR**

On Cheveril. Ben Jonson. **CP-JonsB**

On Cheveril the Lawyer. Ben Jonson. **CP-JonsB**

On Chloris Requesting Me to Give Her a Spray of a Sloe-Thorn in Full Blossom. Robert Burns. **CP-BurnR**

On Choosing Some Verses for My Sister's Cremation. John Hewitt. **CP-HewiJ**

On Chuff, Banks the Usurer's Kinsman. Ben Jonson. **CP-JonsB**

On clear days here the sea is most clear. Maratea Antica. Richard Hugo. **CP-HugoR**

On cliffs above the town, high domes disdain. Port Townsend. Richard Hugo. **CP-HugoR**

On Climbing the Sierra Matterhorn Again after Thirty-One Years. Gary Snyder. **CP-SnydG**

On cold days. Becoming a Nun. Erica Jong. **SP-JongE**

On Colinward: The Scattering. John Hewitt. **CP-HewiJ**

On Combe Bottom: Surrey. George Meredith. **CP-MerG2**

On Commissary Goldie's Brains. Robert Burns. **CP-BurnR**

On Como. George Meredith. **CP-MerG2**

On Correggio. Robert Browning. **CP-BroR2**

On Court-Parrot. Ben Jonson. **CP-JonsB**

On Court-Worm[e]. Ben Jonson. **CP-JonsB**

On Critics. Robert Burns. **IHNG** *Fr.* To R***** G***** of F*****, Esq. **CP-BurnR**
  (Second Epistle to Robert Graham.) **DBV**

On Cruachan's plain slept he. *fr.* Words for Music Perhaps. William Butler Yeats. **CP-YeatW**

On Cupid's bow how are my heart-strings bent. Sonnet 19. Sir Philip Sidney. **NoSic** *Fr.* Astrophil and Stella. **SP-SidnP**

On Cutting Down the Old Thorn at Market Hill. Jonathan Swift. **CP-SwifJ**

On Dan Jackson's Picture. Jonathan Swift. **CP-SwifJ**

On days like these. Washing. Randall Jarrell. **CP-JarrR**

On Death. Percy Bysshe Shelley. **CP-ShelP**
  "Who telleth a tale of unspeaking death?" **OBD**

On December nights. Local Knowledge. Richard Shelton. **SP-ShelR**

On Deck. Sylvia Plath. **CP-PlatS**

On desperate wings and strong. He Starts on the Return Journey. Nicholas Vachel Lindsay. *Fr.* The Tree of Laughing Bells or The Wings of the Morning. **CP-LindV**

On Devenish I heard a snipe. At the Water's Edge. Seamus Heaney. *Fr.* Triptych. **SP-HeanS**

On distant sides of the bed. In the Child's Night. James Dickey. **CP-DickJ**

On Diverse Deviations. Maya Angelou. **SP-AngeM**

On Dr. Rundle. Jonathan Swift. **CP-SwifJ**

On Don Surly. Ben Jonson. **CP-JonsB**

On Donne's First Poem. Samuel Taylor Coleridge. **CP-ColeS**

On Donne's Poetry. Samuel Taylor Coleridge. **CP-ColeS**

On Dreams. Jonathan Swift. **CP-SwifJ**

On dreams, on mathematics, and on death. Du rêve, de la mathématique, et de la mort. Howard Nemerov. **CP-NemeH**

On Dunmore's Waste. John Hewitt. **CP-HewiJ**

On Dwelling. Robert Ranke Graves. **CP-GravR**

On ear and ear two noises too old to end. The Sea and the Skylark. Gerard Manley Hopkins. **CP-HopkG**

On earth are many sights of woe. We All Shall Rest at Last. Walt Whitman. **CP-WhitW**

On earth's wide thoroughfares below. Omar Khayyám, *tr. fr. Persian by* Ralph Waldo Emerson. **CP-EmerR**

On Easter morning two egrets. Two Egrets. John Ciardi. **SP-CiarJ**

On Edges. Adrienne Rich. **CP-RicAE; SP-RicA1; SP-RicA2**

On either side the river lie. The Lady of Shalott. Tennyson. **CP-TennA**

On Eleventh Street. Charles Tomlinson. **CP-TomlC**

On Embarkation. Alun Lewis. **CP-LewiA**
  "And so we wait the tide, and when the dark."
  "Before he sails a man may go on leave."
  "Consider this silent disciplined assembly."
  "In all the ways of going who can tell."

On English Monsieur. Ben Jonson. **CP-JonsB**

On Entering Douglas Bay, Isle of Man. William Wordsworth. *Fr.* Poems Composed or Suggested During a Tour, in the Summer of 1833. **CP-WorW2**

On Envy. *Unknown, tr. fr. Greek by* William Cowper. **CP-CowpW**

On evenings like this. Tango. Louise Glück. **SP-GlücL**

On every Friday afternoon. Der Tag. Malcolm Lowry. **CP-LowrM**

On every house is red. Chromatism in Red. Marsden Hartley. **CP-HartM**

On every thought I have the countless shadows fall. Light and Shadow. "Hugh MacDiarmid." **SP-MacDH**

On eyes embarked for sleep the only light. For Ellen. Richard Wilbur. **CP-WilbR**

On Fame ("Fame, like a wayward girl, will still be coy"). John Keats. *See* Fame, like a wayward girl, will still be coy.

On Fame ("How fever'd is the man who cannot look"). John Keats. *See* How fever'd is the man who cannot look.

On Faneuil Hall there squats a copper. Old Bug up There. Daniel Gerard Hoffman. **SP-HoffD**

On Fanny Godwin. Percy Bysshe Shelley. **CP-ShelP**

On Female Inconstancy. *Unknown, tr. fr. Greek by* William Cowper. **CP-CowpW**

On Fergusson. Robert Burns. **CP-BurnR**

On Finding a Fan. Byron. **CP-Byron**

On First Having Heard the Skylark. Edna St. Vincent Millay. **CP-MillE**

On First Looking into Chapman's Homer. John Keats. **CP-KeatJ**

On First Opening the Lyric Year. William Carlos Williams. **CP-WilW1**

On Flatterers. *Unknown, tr. fr. Greek by* William Cowper. **CP-CowpW**

On Flaxman and Stothard, On F[laxman] & S[tothard]. William Blake. **CP-BlakW**

On Flaxman's Penelope. William Cowper. **CP-CowpW**

On Flower Wreath Hill. Kenneth Rexroth.
  "Aging pilgram on a, An." **SP-RexrK**
  "No leaf stirs. I am alone." **SP-RexrK**
  "This world of ours, before we." **SP-RexrK**

On Flunking a Nice Boy out of School. John Ciardi. **SP-CiarJ**

On forelands high in heaven. Alfred Edward Housman. **CP-HousA**

On Fortune. Robert Herrick. **CP-HerrR**

On Forty-first Street. Neighbors. Carl Sandburg. **CP-SandC**

On Freedom's Ground. Richard Wilbur. **CP-WilbR**

On Gabriel Richardson. Robert Burns. **CP-BurnR**

On Gay Wallpaper. William Carlos Williams. **CP-WilW1**

On Gelli-Flowers Begotten. Robert Herrick. **CP-HerrR**

On Generous Lines. Donald Davie. **CP-DavDo**

On getting a card. Poem. William Carlos Williams. **CP-WilW2**

On Getting My Poems Back from the Typist. Chuck Miller. **SP-MillC**

On Getting Out Of Vietnam. Howard Nemerov. **CP-NemeH**

On Giles and Joan. Ben Jonson. **CP-JonsB**

On Giving. Robert Ranke Graves. **CP-GravR**

On glossy wires artistically bent. Waspish. Robert Frost. **BoAnP** *Fr.* Ten Mills. **CP-FrosR**

On Going Back to the Street after Viewing an Art Show. Charles Bukowski. **SP-BukC2**

On Going by Train to White River Junction, Vt. Jean Garrigue. **SP-GarrJ**

On Going Unnoticed. Robert Frost. **CP-FrosR**

On Gold. Samuel Johnson. **IHNG** *Fr.* The Vanity of Human Wishes [The Tenth Satire of Juvenal Imitated]. **CP-JohnS**

On golden seas of drink, so the Greek poet said. Alcohol. Louis MacNeice. **CP-MacNL**

On Gratitude. Christopher Smart. **SP-SmarC**

On Groin. Ben Jonson. **CP-JonsB**

On Gut. Ben Jonson. **CP-JonsB**

On gypsum slabs of preternatural whiteness. Animal, Vegetable and Mineral. Louise Bogan. **CP-BogaL**

On Gypsy. Ben Jonson. **CP-JonsB**

On Hare Mountain, Giuliano's lair. Montelepre. John Hewitt. **CP-HewiJ**

On Having Mis-identified a Wild Flower. Richard Wilbur. **CP-WilbR**

On H[ayley] the Pick Thank. William Blake. **CP-BlakW**

On H[ayle]ys Friendship. William Blake. **CP-BlakW**

On Hayley's Portrait. William Cowper. **CP-CowpW**

On he goes, the little one. Tortoise Family Connections. David Herbert Lawrence. **CP-LawrD**

On Hearing a Name Long Unspoken. Leonard Cohen. **CP-CoheL**

On Hearing a New Escalation. Richard Hugo. **CP-HugoR**

On Hearing a Symphony of Beethoven. Edna St. Vincent Millay. **CP-MillE**

On Hearing a Traveller's Tale of the Alps. John Hewitt. **CP-HewiJ**

On Hearing About the Death of Mitzi Mayfair. Miller Williams. **SP-WillM**

On Hearing Miss Thrale Deliberate about Her Hat. Samuel Johnson. **CP-JohnS**

On Hearing the Airlines Will Use a Psychological Profile to Catch Potential Skyjackers. Stephen Dunn. **SP-DunnS**

On Hearing the Full Peal of Ten Bells from Christ Church, Swindon, Wilts. Sir John Betjeman. **CP-BetjJ**

On Hearing the News from Venice. George Meredith. **CP-MerG1**

On Hearing the "Ranz des Vaches" on the Top of the Pass of St Gothard. William Wordsworth. *Fr.* Memorials of a Tour of the Continent; 1820. **CP-WorW2**

On Heaven. Robert Herrick. **CP-HerrR**

On Hellespont, guilty of true love's blood. Christopher Marlowe. **LoBV; NoSic; OAEL-1; OAEP; PoE; PoEL-2; SeCePo; TEP** *Fr.* Hero and Leander. **CP-MarlC**

On Her Endeavoring to Conceal Her Grief at Parting. William Cowper. **CP-CowpW**

On her great venture, Man. Earth and Man. George Meredith. **CP-MerG1**

On her lost arm love bade her look. George Meredith. *Fr.* Alsace-Lorraine. **CP-MerG1**

On her shut lids the lightning flickers. Rhea. Robert Ranke Graves. **CP-GravR**

On her side, reclining on her elbow. So-and-So Reclining on Her Couch. Wallace Stevens. **CP-StevW**

On her 36th birthday, Thomas had shown her. Wingfoot Lake. Rita Dove. **SP-DoveR**

On her white breast a sparkling cross she wore. Alexander Pope. **ACP** *Fr.* The Rape of the Lock[, an Heroi-Comical Poem]. **CP-PopeA**

On Hermocratia. *Unknown, tr. fr. Greek by* William Cowper. **CP-CowpW**

On High Feast-Days they were given a public airing. Rois Fainéants. Wystan Hugh Auden. **CP-AudeW**

On high hills top I saw a stately frame. Joachim Du Bellay. *Fr.* The Visions of Bellay. **CP-Spens**

On highest summits dawn comes soonest. Basil Bunting. **CP-BuntB**

On him the long enchained, released. George Meredith. *Fr.* Napoléon. **CP-MerG1**

On Himself ("Wearied Pilgrim, I have wandered here, A"). Robert Herrick. **CP-HerrR**

On Himselfe ("Lost to the world"). Robert Herrick. **CP-HerrR**

On Himselfe ("Weep for the dead, for they have lost this light"). Robert Herrick. **CP-HerrR**

On Himselfe: ("Born[e] I was to meet with Age"). Robert Herrick. **CP-HerrR**

On Himselfe ("Aske me, why I do not sing"). Robert Herrick. **CP-HerrR**

On Himselfe ("I will no longer kiss"). Robert Herrick. **CP-HerrR**

On Himselfe ("I'll write no more of Love; but now repent"). Robert Herrick. **CP-HerrR**

On Himselfe ("Ile sing no more, nor will I longer write"). Robert Herrick. **CP-HerrR**

On Himselfe ("Let me not live, if I not love"). Robert Herrick. **CP-HerrR**

On Himselfe ("Live by thy Muse thou shalt; when others die"). Robert Herrick. **CP-HerrR**

On Himselfe ("Love-sick I am, and must endure"). Robert Herrick. **CP-HerrR**

On Himselfe ("Some parts may perish; dye thou canst not all"). Robert Herrick. **CP-HerrR**

On Himselfe ("Work is done: young men, and maidens set, The"). Robert Herrick. **CP-HerrR**

On Himselfe ("Young I was, but [*or* who] now am old"). Robert Herrick. **CP-HerrR**

On Himselfe: ("If that my Fate has now fulfill'd my yeere"). Robert Herrick. **CP-HerrR**

On Himselfe ("Here down my wearyed limbs Ile lay"). Robert Herrick. **CP-HerrR**

On Himselfe ("I fear no Earthly Powers"). Robert Herrick. **CP-HerrR**

On Himselfe ("One Eare tingles; some there be"). Robert Herrick. **CP-HerrR**

On His Approaching Visit to Hayley. William Cowper. **CP-CowpW**

On His Booke ("Bound (almost) now of my book I see, The"). Robert Herrick. **CP-HerrR**

On His Grotto at Twickenham. Alexander Pope. **CP-PopeA**

On His Majesty's Sea Bathing. William Cowper. **CP-CowpW**

On His Mistress [*or* Mistris]. John Donne. **AnAnS-1; BoLoP; CBLP; EBEV; ESCV; LiTB; NAEL-1; NoSic; PoEL-2; SeCeV** *Fr.* Elegies. **CP-DonnJ**

(Elegie XVI: On His Mistress.) **OXAEP-1; SeCP**

(Elegy on His Mistress.) **GBL; LoBV; MeLP; MePo; SCGP; SeCV-1**

(To His Mistress Desiring to Travel with Him as His Page.) **NOBE**

On His Mistress[e] Going to Sea. Thomas Cary. **CP-CareT**

On his morning rounds the Master. Incident Characteristic of a Favourite Dog. William Wordsworth. **CP-WorW1**

On His Own Deafness. Jonathan Swift. **CP-SwifJ**

On His Pitiable Transformation. Robert Louis Stevenson. **CP-StevR**

On His Portrait. William Cowper. **CP-CowpW**

On his sides are recreated reeds. Bass. Richard Hugo. **CP-HugoR**

On Hope. Richard Crashaw. *See* Against Hope.

On hot nights the whole city. Gus in the Streets. Paul Zimmer. **SP-ZimmP**

On hot September nights, when sleep is scarce. My Father Dreams of Baseball. Laurence Lieberman. **SP-LiebL**

On Ignaz Moscheles. Robert Browning. **CP-BroR2**

On Illness. Allen Ginsberg. **CP-GinsA**

On Installing an American Kitchen in Lower Austria. Wystan Hugh Auden. *See* Grub First, Then Ethics.

On Invalids. *Unknown, tr. fr. Greek by* William Cowper. **CP-CowpW**

On Iona. Phoebe Hesketh. **SP-HeskP**

On its arc the bottle. Old Hope. Steve Griffiths. **SP-GrifS**

On its way I see. Kathleen Jessie Raine. **SP-RainK**

On Jas. Grieve, Laird of Boghead, Tarbolton. Robert Burns. *See* Here lies Boghead among the dead.

On Jane Street in October. An Arboreal Mystery. Grace Paley. **CP-PaleG**

On Jessy Lewars. Robert Burns. **CP-BurnR**

   "But rarely seen since Nature's birth."

   "Fill me with the rosy wine."

   "Say, sages, what's the charm on earth."

   "Talk not to me of savages."

On J-hn M-r-ne, Laird of L-gg-n. Robert Burns. **CP-BurnR**

On John McMurdo. Robert Burns. **CP-BurnR**

On Johnson's Opinion of Hampden. Robert Burns. **CP-BurnR**

On Jone. Robert Herrick. **CP-HerrR**

On Jordan's Banks. Byron. **CP-Byron**

On Journeys through the States. Walt Whitman. **CP-WhitW**

On Julia's Breath. Robert Herrick. **CP-HerrR**

On Julias Lips. Robert Herrick. **CP-HerrR**

On Julia's Picture. Robert Herrick. **CP-HerrR**

On June 5th, '90: / closed shops. Six Something. James Schuyler. **CP-SchuJ**

On Keats, 18 January, 1948 (Eve of St Agnes). Christina Georgina Rossetti. **CP-RosC3**

On page 1003 of the anatomy text. Gray's Apocrypha. Mona Van Duyn. **SP-VanDM**

On Pallas Bathing. Callimachus, *tr. fr. Greek by* William Cowper. **CP-CowpW**

On Parting. Byron. **CP-Byron**

On Passing Over a Dreary Tract of Country, and Near the Ruins of a Deserted Chapel, During a Tempest. Charlotte Smith. **CP-SmitC** *Fr.* Montalbert.

On Passion As a Literary Tradition. John Ciardi. **SP-CiarJ**

On Peace. John Keats. **CP-KeatJ**

On peace and rest my mind was bent. O Ay My Wife She Dang Me. Robert Burns. **CP-BurnR**

On Pedigree. *Unknown, tr. fr. Greek by* William Cowper. **CP-CowpW**

On pillow after pillow lies. Heads in the Women's Ward. Philip Larkin. **CP-LarkP**

On Playwright ("Playwright convict of public wrongs to men"). Ben Jonson. **CP-JonsB**

On Playwright ("Playwright, by chance, hearing some toys I had writ"). Ben Jonson. **CP-JonsB**

On Poet-Ape. Ben Jonson. **CP-JonsB**

On Poet Prat. Robert Herrick. **CP-HerrR**

On Poetry: a Rhapsody. Jonathan Swift. **CP-SwifJ**
  "All human race would fain be wits." **HAP; OBSV; PoEL-3**
  "Hobbes clearly proves that every creature." **HAP; SCV; SeCePo** (Critics.) **SeCePo**

On Portents. Robert Ranke Graves. **CP-GravR**

On prince or bride no diamond stone. Hafiz, *tr. fr. Persian by* Ralph Waldo Emerson. **CP-EmerR**

On Property. Louis MacNeice. *See* Property! Property! Let us extend.

On Psyche. Jonathan Swift. **CP-SwifJ**

On Rachmaninoff's Birthday ("Blue windows, blue rooftops"). Frank O'Hara. **SP-OharF**

On Rachmaninoff's Birthday. Frank O'Hara. **SP-OharF**

On Ragged Mountain birches twists from rifts in granite. Granite and Grass. Donald Hall. **CP-HallD**

On rainy days alone I dine. The Author's Manner of Living. Jonathan Swift. **CP-SwifJ**

On raw days Cherry stands at the back door and. Whippersnappers. Ron Koertge. **SP-KoerR**

On Reaching Forty. Maya Angelou. **SP-AngeM**

On Reaching the Age of Two Hundred. Donald Hall. **CP-HallD**

On Reading a Vast Anthology. Erica Jong. **SP-JongE**

On Reading Dr. Young's Satires. Jonathan Swift. **CP-SwifJ**

On Reading Edmund Wilson's Remarks about Rimbaud. Malcolm Lowry. *Fr.* The Moon in Scandinavia. **CP-LowrM**

On Reading, in a Newspaper, the Death of J———— McL————, Esq. Brother to a Young Lady, a Particular Friend of the Author's. Robert Burns. **CP-BurnR**

On Reading Omar Khayyam. Nicholas Vachel Lindsay. **CP-LindV**

On Reading Redburn, *also appears in* The Lighthouse Invites the Storm, *sl. diff. vers.* Malcolm Lowry. *Fr.* The Moon in Scandinavia. **CP-LowrM**

On Reading R.L.S. Malcolm Lowry. *Fr.* The Roar of the Sea and the Darkness. **CP-LowrM**

On Reading Terence de Vere White on Landor. John Hewitt. **CP-HewiJ**

On Reading "The Love and Death of Cornet Christopher Rilke." Howard Nemerov. **CP-NemeH**

On Reading Wallace Stevens' *Collected Poems* after Many Years. John Hewitt. **CP-HewiJ**

On Reading William Blake's "The Sick Rose." Allen Ginsberg. **CP-GinsA**

On Receiving a Christmas Card. Wystan Hugh Auden. **CP-AudWJ**

On Receiving a Curious Shell, and a Copy of Verses, from the Same Ladies. John Keats. **CP-KeatJ**

On Receiving a Laurel Crown from Leigh Hunt. John Keats. **CP-KeatJ**

On Receiving an Account That His Only Sister's Death Was Inevitable. Samuel Taylor Coleridge. **CP-ColeS**

On Receiving an Eagle's Quill from Lake Superior. John Greenleaf Whittier. **CP-WhitJ**

On Receiving from a Lady a Present of a Ring. George Crabbe. **SP-CrabG**

On Receiving from the Right Hon. the Lady Frances Shirley a Standish and Two Pens. Alexander Pope. **CP-PopeA**

On Receiving Hayley's Picture. William Cowper. **CP-CowpW**

On Receiving Heyne's Virgil. William Cowper. **CP-CowpW**

On Receiving One of Gloriana's Letters. Nicholas Vachel Lindsay. *Fr.* This Section Is a Christmas Tree. **CP-LindV**

On Reformed Gamester. Ben Jonson. **CP-JonsB**

On Religion's holy hill. Fragment of an Intended Poem on Milton, Written in the Copy of *Paradise Lost* Which Belonged to Wordsworth at Cambridge. William Wordsworth. **CP-WorW1**

On Returning to a Lake in Spring. Richard Eberhart. **CP-EberR**

On Revisiting Dunlolly Castle. William Wordsworth. *Fr.* Poems Composed or Suggested During a Tour, in the Summer of 1833. **CP-WorW2**

On Revisiting Harrow. Byron. **CP-Byron**

On Revisiting the Sea-Shore, after Long Absence. Samuel Taylor Coleridge. **CP-ColeS**

On Rico LeBrun's Crucifixion. Edwin Rolfe. **CP-RolfE**

On Rising Early. Robert Ranke Graves. **CP-GravR**

On roadsides, / in fall fields, / in rumpy bunches. Goldenrod. Mary Oliver. **SP-OlivM**

On roaring iron down the Holloway Road. The Sandemanian Meeting-House in Highbury Quadrant. Sir John Betjeman. **CP-BetjJ**

On Robert Emmet's Grave. Percy Bysshe Shelley. **CP-ShelP**

On Robert Riddel. Robert Burns. **CP-BurnR**

On Saint Paddy's Day, the jukebox plays. James McAuley. **SP-McAuJ** *Fr.* Green Beer.

On St. *Peter* Casting Away His Nets at Our Saviours Call. Richard Crashaw. **CP-CrasR**

On Saint Peter Cutting of Malchus His Eare. Richard Crashaw. **CP-CrasR**

On St. Winefred. Gerard Manley Hopkins. **CP-HopkG**

On Sam Rogers. Byron. **CP-Byron**

On Sanazar's Being Honoured. Richard Lovelace. **CP-LoveR**

On Saturday sailed from Bremen. Gerard Manley Hopkins. **SeCePo** *Fr.* The Wreck of the Deutschland. **CP-HopkG**

On Saturday, the power-mowers' whine. Suburban Prophecy. Howard Nemerov. **CP-NemeH**

On Scaring Some Waterfowl in Loch Turit, a Wild Scene among the Hills of Oughtertyre. Robert Burns. **CP-BurnR**

On Seeing a Lock of Milton's Hair. John Keats. **CP-KeatJ**

On Seeing a Needlecase in the Form of a Harp; the Work of E.M.S. William Wordsworth. **CP-WorW2**

On Seeing a Portrait of Mrs Montagu. Samuel Johnson. **CP-JohnS**

On Seeing a Wounded Hare Limp by Me, Which a Fellow Had Just Shot At. Robert Burns. **CP-BurnR**

On Seeing a Youth Affectionately Welcomed by a Sister. Samuel Taylor Coleridge. **CP-ColeS**

On Seeing an Egyptian Mummy in Berlin, 1932. Richard Eberhart. **CP-EberR**

On Seeing an Old Civil War Painting with My Love. Charles Bukowski. **SP-BukC2**

On Seeing an Old Poet in the Café Royal. Sir John Betjeman. **CP-BetjJ**

On Seeing Kabir's Poems on Her Dressing Table. Leonard Cohen. **CP-CoheL**

On Seeing Larry Rivers' *Washington Crossing the Delaware* at the Museum of Modern Art. Frank O'Hara. **SP-OharF**

On Seeing Miss Fontenelle in a Favourite Character. Robert Burns. **CP-BurnR**

On Seeing Mrs. Kemble in Yarico. Robert Burns. **CP-BurnR**

On seeing my own play. 15 Years Later. William Carlos Williams. **CP-WilW2**

On Seeing Some Dutch Pictures. Wystan Hugh Auden. **CP-AudWJ**

On Seeing Some Tourists of the Lakes Pass by Reading; a Practice Very Common. William Wordsworth. **CP-WorW1**

On Seeing the Beautiful County-Seat of Lord G————. Robert Burns. *Fr.* Epigrams on Lord Galloway. **CP-BurnR**

On Seeing the Black Male as #1 Sex Object in America. Etheridge Knight. **SP-KnigE**

On Seeing the Elgin Marbles. John Keats. **CP-KeatJ**

On Seeing the Royal Palace at Stirling in Ruins. Robert Burns. **DBV** *Fr.* Here Stewarts once in triumph reign'd. *Fr.* Lines on Stirling. **CP-BurnR**

On Seeing Verses Written upon Windows in Inns. Jonathan Swift. **CP-SwifJ**

On Sending You a Lock of My Hair. Erica Jong. **SP-JongE**

On Seventh Avenue, once upon. Myth. Peter Meinke. **SP-MeinP**

On Shakespear[e]. John Milton. **CP-MiltJ**

On shallow slates the pigeons shift together. Pigeons. Philip Larkin. **CP-LarkP**

On shallow straw, in shadeless glass. Take One Home for the Kiddies. Philip Larkin. **CP-LarkP**

On Sherman's Men. Herman Melville. **SP-MelvH**

On Shooting Particles beyond the World. Richard Eberhart. **CP-EberR**

On short, still days. Gathering Wood. Philip Larkin. **CP-LarkP**

On Sight. Alice Walker. **CP-WalkA**

On Sight of a Gentlewoman's Face in the Water. Thomas Carew. **CP-CareT**

On Silence, *in imitation of* John Wilmot, Earl of Rochester. Alexander Pope. **CP-PopeA**

On Singers. Robert Browning. **CP-BroR2**

On Sir Cod the Perfumed. Ben Jonson. **CP-JonsB**

On Sir John Roe ("In place of scutcheons, that should deck thy hearse"). Ben Jonson. **CP-JonsB**

On Sir John Roe ("What two brave perils of the private sword"). Ben Jonson. **CP-JonsB**

On Sir Voluptuous Beast. Ben Jonson. **CP-JonsB**

On Sitting Down to Read "King Lear" Once Again. John Keats. **CP-KeatJ**

On Some Ghostly Companions at a Spa. Robert Louis Stevenson. **CP-StevR**

On some night a train is going past the library. Chuck Miller. **SP-MillC**

On some rude fragment of the rocky shore. Written on the Sea Shore.—October, 1784. Charlotte Smith. **CP-SmitC**

On Some Such Morning. Siv Cedering Fox. **SP-CedeS**

On Something, That Walks [or Walkes] Somewhere. Ben Jonson. **CP-JonsB**

On souls robbed of their birth-right's better part. Edward Estlin Cummings. **CP-CummE**

On Spies. Ben Jonson. **CP-JonsB**

On St. Valentine's Day. William Carlos Williams. **CP-WilW2**

On starry heights. The Conflict of Convictions. Herman Melville. **SP-MelvH**

On Stella's Birthday, 1718/1719. Jonathan Swift. *See* Stella this day is thirty-four.

On Stephen Duck, the Thresher, and Favourite Poet. Jonathan Swift. **CP-SwifJ**

On stern Blencartha's perilous height. A Thought. Samuel Taylor Coleridge. **CP-ColeS**

On still days when country telephone. Troubleshooting. William Stafford. **SP-StafW**

On Stinsford Hill at Midnight. Thomas Hardy. **CP-HardT**

On storm-struck deck, wind sirens caterwaul. Channel Crossing. Sylvia Plath. **CP-PlatS**

On stormy nights. Richard Shelton. *Fr.* The Stone Garden. **SP-ShelR**

On Stothard. William Blake. **CP-BlakW**

On Stripping Bark from Myself. Alice Walker. **CP-WalkA**

On Sturminster Foot-Bridge. Thomas Hardy. **CP-HardT**

On such a day among the stones and the shafts. The Horse's Mouth. Steve Griffiths. **SP-GrifS**

On such a morning as this. In Memory of Basil, Marquess of Dufferin and Ava. Sir John Betjeman. **CP-BetjJ**

On such a night, or such a night. Emily Dickinson. **CP-DickE**

On Suddenly Receiving a Curl Long Refused. Nicholas Vachel Lindsay. *Fr.* This Section Is a Christmas Tree. **CP-LindV**

On summer evenings here. Boston: From the Embankment. Dabney Stuart. *Fr.* The Charles River. **SP-StuaD**

On Sunday at six, in the street that's call'd Gerrard. Alexander Pope. *Fr.* Epigrams Occasion'd by an Invitation to Court. **CP-PopeA**

On Sunday Walks. Wystan Hugh Auden. **CP-AudeW**

On sunny summer Sunday afternoons in Harlem. Passing. Langston Hughes. **SP-HughL**

On Susan's Birthday. Jim Carroll. **SP-CarrJ**

On Sutton Strand. Donald Davie. **CP-DavDo**

On Taking a Batchelor's Degree, *see also* Horace, Odes III, 30. Christopher Smart. **SP-SmarC**

On Taking from the Top to Broaden the Base. Robert Frost. **CP-FrosR**

On Taking Physicke, *sl. diff. vers.* Richard Crashaw. *See* Temperance or the Cheap Physitian upon the Translation of Lessius.

On Taking up Residence in Virginia. Kay Boyle. **CP-BoylK**

On Tam the Chapman. Robert Burns. *See* As Tam the chapman on a day.

On That Day. David Herbert Lawrence. **CP-LawrD**

On that dear Frame the Years had worn. Emily Dickinson. **CP-DickE**

On that gray night of mournful drone. A Man Was Drawing Near to Me. Thomas Hardy. **CP-HardT**

On that great night of her success. Aimée. George Meredith. **CP-MerG2**

On that last night before we went. Tennyson. **OAEL-2; PoEL-5** *Fr.* In Memoriam A. H. H. **CP-TennA**

On that night the poet went. Ralph Waldo Emerson. **CP-EmerR**

On that specific Pillow. Emily Dickinson. **CP-DickE**

On that water / Grey with morning. George Oppen. *Fr.* Image of the Engine. **CP-OppeG**

On the Adequacy of Landscape. Wallace Stevens. **CP-StevW**

On the Anniversary of My Baptism. Thomas Merton. **CP-MertT; SP-MertT**

On the anvil of love my flesh has been hammered out. How Long Is the Night? Stanley Jasspon Kunitz. **CP-KuniS**

On the Aphorism "L'Amitié est l'Amour sans Ailes." Charlotte Smith. **CP-SmitC**

On the Archbishop of Cashel and Bettesworth. Jonathan Swift. **CP-SwifJ**

On the Astrologers. *Unknown, tr. fr. Greek by* William Cowper. **CP-CowpW**

On the Atchafalaya. Henry Wadsworth Longfellow. **AA** *Fr.* It was the month of May. Far down the Beautiful River. *Fr.* Part the Second. *Fr.* Evangeline, a Tale of Acadie. **SP-LongH**

On the Author of Letters on Literature. William Cowper. **CP-CowpW**

On the Author, Work, and Translator. Ben Jonson. **CP-JonsB**

On the Avenue. Erica Jong. **SP-JongE**

On the Balcony. David Herbert Lawrence. **CP-LawrD**

On the Bank Street Pier. Grace Paley. **CP-PaleG**

On the Banks of a Rocky Stream. William Wordsworth. **CP-WorW2**

On the Banks of the Sumida. John Gould Fletcher. **SP-FletJ**

On the bare moorland / across the brown heather. Mist. John Hewitt. **CP-HewiJ**

On the base platform cold beneath the lamps. The Splendid Dawn. John Hewitt. **CP-HewiJ**

On the Beach. John Gould Fletcher. **SP-FletJ**

On the Beach at Night. Walt Whitman. **CP-WhitW**

On the Beach at Night Alone. Walt Whitman. **CP-WhitW**

On the beach where we had been idly. Gracious Goodness. Marge Piercy. **SP-PierM**

On the Belgian Expatriation. Thomas Hardy. **CP-HardT**

On the Best, Last, and Only Remaining Comedy of Mr. Fletcher. Richard Lovelace. **CP-LoveR**

On the Big Horn. John Greenleaf Whittier. **CP-WhitJ**

On the Biographia Britannica. William Cowper. *See* Oh, fond attempt to give a deathless lot.

On the Birth of a Black / Baby / Boy. Etheridge Knight. **SP-KnigE**

On the Birth of a Posthumous Child, Born in Peculiar Circumstances of Family Distress. Robert Burns. **CP-BurnR**

On the Birth of Good & Evil During the Long Winter of '28. Philip Levine. **SP-LeviP**

On the Birth of John William Rizzo Hoppner. Byron. **CP-Byron**

On the black stage he. Mime. John Updike. **CP-UpdiJ**

On the blackboard map your country. Comic Books vs. History. Margaret Atwood. **SP-AtwM1**

On the Bleeding Wounds of Our Crucified Lord. Richard Crashaw. **CP-CrasR**

"Jesu, no more! It is full tide." **TrGrPo**

On the Blessed Virgins Bashfulnesse. Richard Crashaw. **CP-CrasR**

On the Breakwater. Carl Sandburg. **CP-SandC**

On the Bridge of Sighs. Byron. *See* I stood in Venice on the Bridge of Sighs.

On the brink of sleep, stretched in a wide bed. Friday Night. Robert Ranke Graves. **CP-GravR**

On the broad mountain-top. Samuel Taylor Coleridge. *Fr.* Some Fragments, Mainly from Manuscripts of 1797–8. **CP-ColeS**

On the Building of Springfield. Nicholas Vachel Lindsay. **WHA** *Fr.* A Gospel of Beauty. **CP-LindV**

On the Burial of His Brother. Catullus. *See* Carmen 101: "Journeying over many seas and through many countries."

On the Burning of Lord Mansfield's Library. William Cowper. **CP-CowpW**

On the Burning of Whitehall in 1698. Jonathan Swift. **CP-SwifJ**

On the Canal. John Hewitt. **CP-HewiJ**

On the Card[e]s, and Dice. Sir Walter Ralegh. **CP-RaleW**

On the Castle of Chillon. Byron. *See* Sonnet on Chillon.

On the chamber, on the stairs. Ralph Waldo Emerson. **CP-EmerR**

On the Choice of a Title. John Hewitt. **CP-HewiJ**

On the Christening of a Friend's Child. Samuel Taylor Coleridge. **CP-ColeS**

On the Christmaswhite plains of the floured and flowering kitchen table. The Bread of this World; Praises III. Thomas McGrath. **SP-McGrT**

On the Circuit. Wystan Hugh Auden. **CP-AudeW**

On the City Ramparts of Cádiz. Juan Ramón Jiménez. *Fr.* Ten Short Poems. **CP-WrigJ**

On the coast of ARMORICA. A monastery. *tr. fr. the French of* Tristan Corbière. Randall Jarrell. **CP-JarrR**

On the coast of Chile where Neruda lived. The General Song of Humanity. Lawrence Ferlinghetti. **SP-FerlL**

On the cold waterfall, the flush of dawn gleams bright. Dawn. Wystan Hugh Auden. **CP-AudWJ**

On the Collar of Mrs. Dingley's Lap-Dog. Jonathan Swift. **CP-SwifJ**

On the Continent. Charles Bukowski. **SP-BukC1**

On the Coosawattee. James Dickey. **CP-DickJ**

By Canoe through the Fir Forest. **NYBP**

On the Corner. Philip Levine. **SP-LeviP**

On the counter among many. The Writings of the Mystics. Charles Simic. **SP-SimiC**

On the Countess of Burlington Cutting Paper. Alexander Pope. **CP-PopeA**

On the curving, dusty roads. Indonesia. Mary Oliver. **SP-OlivM**

On the Danger of War. George Meredith. **CP-MerG1**

On the Dark Height of Jura. Percy Bysshe Shelley. *Fr.* Poems from St. Irvyne, or, The Rosicrucian. **CP-ShelP**

On the day of breasts and small hips. Song for a Lady. Anne Sexton. **CP-SextA**

On the Day of Judgement. Jonathan Swift. *See* With a whirl of thought oppressed.

On the Day of the Destruction of Jerusalem by Titus. Byron. **CP-Byron**

On the day of the explosion. The Explosion. Philip Larkin. **CP-LarkP**

On the day the Magi came. On My Father's Hundredth Birthday. John Gould Fletcher. **SP-FletJ**

On the day when the Savoy. Projection. Langston Hughes. **SP-HughL**

On the day when youth is no more upon me. To Wish Myself Courage. William Carlos Williams. **CP-WilW1**

On the Death, after Lying Wounded in the Thigh for Twenty-Six Days, of the Author of "Astrophel and Stella." David Markson. **CP-MarkD**

On the Death-Bed. Thomas Hardy. *Fr.* Satires of Circumstance in Fifteen Glimpses. **CP-HardT**

On the Death of a Cat. Christina Georgina Rossetti. **CP-RosC3**

On the Death of a Fair Infant Dying of a Cough. John Milton. **CP-MiltJ**

On the Death of a German Philosopher. Stevie Smith. **CP-SmitS**

On the Death of a Middle-Aged Man. Miller Williams. **SP-WillM**

On the Death of a Minister. William Cowper. *Fr.* Olney Hymns. **CP-CowpW**

On the Death of a Young Lady. Byron. **CP-Byron**

On the Death of an Unfortunate Lady. William Wordsworth. **CP-WorW1**

On the Death of Damon. John Milton. *See* Damon's Epitaph.

On the Death of Dean Swift. Jonathan Swift. *See* The Time is not remote when I.

On the Death of Dr [*or* Mr] Robert Levet [a Practiser in Physic]. Samuel Johnson. **CP-JohnS**

On the Death of Donne. Thomas Carew. **NOBE** *Fr.* An Elegy upon the Death of the Dean of [St.] Paul's, Dr. John Donne.

On the Death of Echo, a Lap-Dog. Robert Burns. **CP-BurnR**

On the Death of Her Mother. Muriel Rukeyser. **CP-RukeM**

On the Death of His Majesty (George the Third). William Wordsworth. **CP-WorW2**

On the Death of his Mother. James Thomson. **CP-ThomJ**

On the Death of Mr. Aikman. James Thomson. **CP-ThomJ**

On the Death of Mr. John Haskins. Ralph Waldo Emerson. **CP-EmerR**

On the Death of Mrs. Elizabeth Filmer. Richard Lovelace. **CP-LoveR**

On the Death of My Dear Brother. Dudley Posthume Lovelace. *Fr.* Elegies, 1660. **CP-LoveR**

On the Death of My Student, the Poet Serafin. Kay Boyle. **CP-BoylK**

On the Death of Russell. William Cowper. **CP-CowpW**

On the Death of Sir J. Hunter Blair. Robert Burns. **CP-BurnR**

On the Death of the Bishop of Ely. John Milton, *tr. fr.* Latin by John T. Shawcross. **CP-CowpW; CP-MiltJ**

("My lids with grief were tumid yet.") **CP-CowpW**, *tr.* by William Cowper;

On the Death of the Late Lord President Dundas. Robert Burns. **CP-BurnR**

On the Death of the Vice-Chancellor, a Physician. John Milton, *tr. fr.* Latin by John T. Shawcross. **CP-CowpW; CP-MiltJ**

("Learn, ye nations of the earth.") **CP-CowpW**, *tr.* by William Cowper;

On the Death of W. C. Paul Laurence Dunbar. **CP-DunbP**

On the Decline of Oracles. Sylvia Plath. **CP-PlatS**

On the Dedication of Dorothy Hall. Paul Laurence Dunbar. **CP-DunbP**

On the Departure of Sir Walter Scott from Abbotsford, for Naples. William Wordsworth. **CP-WorW2**

On the Departure of the Nightingale. Charlotte Smith. **CP-SmitC**

On the Departure Platform. Thomas Hardy. **CP-HardT**

On the Detraction Which Followed the Publication of a Certain Poem. William Wordsworth. **CP-WorW2**

On the Difficulty of Conjuring Up a Dryad. Sylvia Plath. **CP-PlatS**

On the door you will not enter. Catarina to Camoens. Elizabeth Barrett Browning. **CP-BroEB**

On the Doorstep. Thomas Hardy. **CP-HardT**

On the Doorstep. Thomas Hardy. **CP-HardT**

On the Downs, in the Weald, on the Marshes. Very Many People. Rudyard Kipling. **CP-KiplR**

On the Dresser. James Schuyler. **CP-SchuJ**

On the Drum. David Herbert Lawrence. **CP-LawrD**

On the Duchess of Gordon's Reel Dancing. Robert Burns. **CP-BurnR**

On the Duke of Buckingham. Thomas Carew. **CP-CareT**

On the Duke of Buckingham. John Dryden. *See* Some of their chiefs were princes of the land.

On the Edge. Philip Levine. **SP-LeviP**

On the edge of woods. Igor Stravinsky. Charles Olson. **CP-OlsoC**

On the Embankment. Jenny Joseph. **SP-JoseJ**

On the Engraver of His Likeness. John Milton, *tr. fr.* Latin and Greek by John T. Shawcross. **CP-MiltJ**

On the Engraver of His Pourtrait. William Cowper. **CP-CowpW**

On the equator east of my son I Orion bequeath to him my riches. Charles Olson. **CP-OlsoC**

On the Esplanade. Walter de la Mare. **CP-DeLaW**

On the Esplanade. Thomas Hardy. **CP-HardT**

On the Eternity of the Supreme Being. Christopher Smart. **SP-SmarC**

On the eve of All-Souls' Day. A Night of Questionings. Thomas Hardy. **CP-HardT**

On the evening of July 25, 1936. Mediterranean. Muriel Rukeyser. **CP-RukeM**

On the evening of the third day. Richard Shelton. *Fr.* Angel and the Anchorite. **SP-ShelR**

On the Extinction of a Species. Daniel Gerard Hoffman. **SP-HoffD**

On the Extinction of the Venetian Republic. William Wordsworth. **CP-WorW1**

On the Eyes of an SS Officer. Richard Wilbur. **CP-WilbR**

On the Eyes of Miss A—— H——. Byron. **CP-Byron**

On the Failure of a Poet. Charles Bukowski. **SP-BukC2**

On the fair green hills of Rio. The Burglar of Babylon. Elizabeth Bishop. **CP-BishE**

On the Fall of Zalona. Emily Brontë. **CP-BronE**

On the Famous Voyage. Ben Jonson. **CP-JonsB**

"By this time had they reached the Stygian pool." **NOSC**

On the far side of water, high on a sand bar. Arkansas Traveller. Charles Wright. **SP-WrigC**

On the Father of Liberty. Allen Tate. *Fr.* Historical Epitaphs. **CP-TateA**

On the field of elm or slate the lines are far too close. Shove Halfpenny. Louis MacNeice. *Fr.* Indoor Sports. **CP-MacNL**

On the 15th day of November in the year of the motorcar. Ted Berrigan. **SP-BerrT** *Fr.* The Sonnets.

On the fifth day / the unicorn. Unicorn. Phoebe Hesketh. **SP-HeskP**

On the Fifth of November. John Milton. **CP-MiltJ**

On the Final Submission of the Tyrolese. William Wordsworth. **CP-WorW1**

On the fine wire of his whine he walked. Mosquito. John Updike. **CP-UpdiJ**

On the first day. How God Was Made. Kenneth Patchen. **CP-PatcK**

On the first eve of Carnival, the night of the Queen. Queen of the Billiards. Laurence Lieberman. **SP-LiebL**

On the first few nights of the new year, a week. Sex. Hayden Carruth. **CP-CarHS**

On the first hour of my first day. The Beginner. Rudyard Kipling. **FaBoTw** *Fr.* Epitaphs of the War [1914–1918]. **CP-KiplR**

On the first night. Nursing You. Erica Jong. **SP-JongE**

On the first of the Feast of Feasts. Epilogue. Robert Browning. **CP-BroR1**

On the first page of my dreambook. Empire of Dreams. Charles Simic. **SP-SimiC**

On the first Survival Day. Jours-Fixes. James Liddy. *Fr.* Glass after Oblivion. **CP-LiddJ**

On the first tree. Eve Explains Everything to the Thrush Who Repeats Everything. Archibald MacLeish. *Fr.* Songs for Eve. **CP-MacLA**

On the Firth of Clyde. William Wordsworth. *Fr.* Poems Composed or Suggested During a Tour, in the Summer of 1833. **CP-WorW2**

On the Five Ladies at Sot's Hole, with the Doctor at Their Head. Jonathan Swift. **CP-SwifJ**

On the flat road a man at last appears. A Light Snow-Fall after Frost. Thomas Hardy. **CP-HardT**

On the flood is of Babiloyne there we saten. Bible, *O.T. See* Psalm 137: "By the rivers of Babylon. . . ."

On the Fly-Leaf of Pound's Cantos. Basil Bunting. **CP-BuntB**

On the Forcers of Conscience. John Milton. *See* Because you have thrown off your Prelate Lord.

On the Founder of the Industrial System in the United States. Allen Tate. *Fr.* Historical Epitaphs. **CP-TateA**

On the Four Masters. Louis MacNeice. *Fr.* Dark Age Glosses. **CP-MacNL**

On the Fourth Floor. Grace Paley. **CP-PaleG**

On the Fourth of July at the beach. At the Beach. James Schuyler. **CP-SchuJ**

On the Fragility of Mind. Richard Eberhart. **CP-EberR**

On the frigid face of the heath-hemmed pond. At Rushy-Pond. Thomas Hardy. **CP-HardT**

On the frontier at dawn getting down. Wystan Hugh Auden. **CP-AudWJ**

On the Frontispiece of Isaacsons Chronologie Explained. Richard Crashaw. **CP-CrasR**

On the Frozen Lake. William Wordsworth. *See* And in the frosty season, when the sun.

On the Garden Wall. Nicholas Vachel Lindsay. **CP-LindV**

On the Goodness of the Supreme Being. Christopher Smart. **SP-SmarC**

On the gorgeous hills of morning. Robert Louis Stevenson. **CP-StevR**

On the Grand Dublin Canal: Musing on the "Two Nations" Theory. John Hewitt. **CP-HewiJ**

On the Grasshopper. *Unknown, tr. fr. Greek by* William Cowper. **CP-CowpW**

On the Grasshopper and [the] Cricket. John Keats. **CP-KeatJ**

On the grassy banks / Lambkins at their pranks. Christina Georgina Rossetti. **CP-RosC2**

On the Grave. Herman Melville. **SP-MelvH**

On the Great Atlantic Rainway. Kenneth Koch. **SP-KochK**

On the Great Conciliator: Now Honored in the Old Dominion. Allen Tate. *Fr. Historical Epitaphs.* **CP-TateA**

On the Great Encouragement Given By English Nobility & Gentry to Correggio Rubens Rembrandt Reynolds Gainsborough Catalani Ducrowe & Dilbury Doodle. William Blake. **CP-BlakW**

On the great streams the ships may go. The Canoe Speaks. Robert Louis Stevenson. **CP-StevR**

On the great streams the ships may go. Robert Louis Stevenson. **SD** *Fr.* The Canoe Speaks. **CP-StevR**

On the Great Wall. Rudyard Kipling. *Fr.* Puck of Pook's Hill. Song to Mithras, A. **CP-KiplR**

On the green / with lignum vitae balls and ivory markers. Bowls. Marianne Craig Moore. **CP-MoorM**

On the green a white boy goes / And he walks. Three ciphers and a faint fakir. Penn Station. Ted Berrigan. **SP-BerrT** *Fr.* The Sonnets.

On the green a white boy goes / We may read about all those radio waves. Ted Berrigan. **SP-BerrT** *Fr.* The Sonnets.

On the green margin of the brook. Song, A. William Cowper. **CP-CowpW**

On the green riverbank. The Old Sailors. Lawrence Ferlinghetti. **SP-FerlL**

On the green sheep-track, up the heathy hill. Samuel Taylor Coleridge. **OBNC** *Fr.* Fears in Solitude. **CP-ColeS**

On the Grettir Saga. Louis MacNeice. *Fr.* Dark Age Glosses. **CP-MacNL**

On the grey rock of Cashel the mind's eye. The Double Vision of Michael Robartes. William Butler Yeats. **CP-YeatW**

On the grey sand beside the shallow stream. Ego Dominus Tuus. William Butler Yeats. **CP-YeatW**

On the gulf in an airplane shack made of light everything looks. Autorotation without Gravity. Tom Clark. **SP-ClarT**

On the Gunpowder Plot. John Milton, tr. fr. Latin by John T. Shawcross. **CP-MiltJ**

On the Gunpowder-Treason. Richard Crashaw. **CP-CrasR**

On the Hall at Stowey. Charles Tomlinson. **CP-TomlC**

On the Heart's Beginning to Cloud the Mind. Robert Frost. **CP-FrosR**

On the High Price of Fish. William Cowper. **CP-CowpW**

On the Hill below the Lighthouse. James Dickey. **CP-DickJ**

On the hill is cool! Even the dead. Morning. William Carlos Williams. **CP-WilW1**

On the Hill Late at Night. Wendell Berry. **CP-BerrW**

On the Home Guards. Herman Melville. **SP-MelvH**

On the Honoured Poems of His Honoured Friend, Sir John Beaumont, Baronet. Ben Jonson. **CP-JonsB**

On the Hoop. James Thomson. **CP-ThomJ**

On the horizon, through the steam of exhausted blast furnaces fog yes. The Ax God:Sea Pursuit. James Dickey. **CP-DickJ**

On the hour he shuts the door and walks out of town. Face of the Dam: Vivian Jones. Muriel Rukeyser. **CP-SpenS**

On the housetop, the floor of the boundless. The New Roof. Wendell Berry. **CP-BerrW**

On the Ice Islands Seen Floating in the German Ocean. William Cowper. **CP-CowpW**

On the idle hill of summer. Alfred Edward Housman. **CP-HousA**

On the Immensity of the Supreme Being. Christopher Smart. **SP-SmarC**

On the Inclusion of Miniature Dinosaurs in Breakfast Cereal Boxes. John Updike. **CP-UpdiJ**

On the Inconstancy of Women. Catullus. *See* Carmen 70: "Lesbia says she'd rather marry me."

On the Industrial Highway. Daniel Gerard Hoffman. **SP-HoffD**

On the Inventor of Gunpowder. John Milton, tr. fr. Latin by John T. Shawcross. **CP-MiltJ**

(On the Inventor of Guns.) **CP-CowpW**, tr. by William Cowper;

("Praise in old times the sage Prometheus won.") **CP-CowpW**, tr. by William Cowper;

On the Inventor of Guns. John Milton. *See* On the Inventor of Gunpowder.

On the Irish Bishops. Jonathan Swift. **CP-SwifJ**

On the Irish Club. Jonathan Swift. **CP-SwifJ**

On the isle of Penikese. The Prayer of Agassiz. John Greenleaf Whittier. **CP-WhitJ**

On the jetty, our fingers shading. In the Beginning. Daniel Gerard Hoffman. **SP-HoffD**

On the King's Birthday. Ben Jonson. **CP-JonsB**

On the kitchen wall a flash. The World Outside. Denise Levertov. **CP-LeveD**

On the land and on the sea. For H.P. Christina Georgina Rossetti. **CP-RosC3**

On the last day of a rough but fortunate voyage, near the farthest end of the known world. Atlas and the Fatman. Thomas Merton. **CP-MertT**

On the Late Captain Grose's Peregrinations thro' Scotland, Collecting the Antiquities of That King. Robert Burns. **CP-BurnR**

On the Life of Man. Sir Walter Ralegh. *See* What is our life? a play of passion.

On the lips of the child Janet float changing dreams. Sixteen Months. Carl Sandburg. **CP-SandC**

On the little bank, below the orchard. At the Cearne. David Herbert Lawrence. **CP-LawrD**

On the Little House by the Churchyard of Castleknock. Jonathan Swift. **CP-SwifJ**

On the London Train. John Berryman. **CP-BerrJ**

On the long road of winding steel. Thomas Merton. *Fr.* Cables to the Ace. **CP-MertT**

On the long shore, lit by the moon. The Goose Fish. Howard Nemerov. **CP-NemeH**

On the Loss of the *Royal George*. William Cowper. **CP-CowpW**

On the low shore, alone, inordinate. The Real World. Dabney Stuart. **SP-StuaD**

On the Madam's best april the. Edward Estlin Cummings. **CP-CummE**

On the Magnetic Lady. Ben Jonson. **CP-JonsB**

On the Manner of Addressing Clouds. Wallace Stevens. **CP-StevW**

On the March. David Herbert Lawrence. **CP-LawrD**

On the Marginal Way. Richard Wilbur. **CP-WilbR**

On the Marriage of a Virgin. Dylan Thomas. **CP-ThomD**

On the Marriage of T. K. and C. C.: The Morning Stormy. Thomas Carew. **CP-CareT**

On the Martyr of Harpers Ferry. Allen Tate. *Fr.* Historical Epitaphs. **CP-TateA**

On the Massacre of Glencoe, 1692. Sir Walter Scott. **SP-ScotW**

On the Medusa of Leonardo da Vinci in the Florentine Gallery. Percy Bysshe Shelley. **CP-ShelP**

On the Miracle of Loaves. Richard Crashaw. **CP-CrasR**

On the Miracle of Multiplied [or Multiplyed] Loaves. Richard Crashaw. **CP-CrasR**

On the Morning of Christs Nativity. John Milton. **CP-MiltJ**

Hymn on the Morning of Christ's Nativity [or On the Morning of Christ's Nativity]. **FiP; NAEL-1; NOBE; OBEV; OtMeF**

"But peaceful was the night." **FaBoCh**

"Oracles are dumm, The." **GrIP**

Magi, The. **ChTr**

"This is the month, and this the happy morn." **FaBoCh**

On the morning of May. A Faith on Trial. George Meredith. **CP-MerG1**

On the morning of the crowning we chorused our. Geoffrey Hill. **HAP** *Fr.* Mercian Hymns. **CP-HillG**

On the morning you woke beside me—already thinking of going away. Mornings / of an impossible love. Alice Walker. **CP-WalkA**

On the Mountain. John Haines. **SP-HainJ**

On the Mountain. Charles Tomlinson. **CP-TomlC**

On the Move. Thom Gunn. **CP-GunnT**

On the Murder of Lieutenant José Del Castillo by the Falangist Bravo Martinez, July 12, 1936. Philip Levine. **SP-LeviP**

On the Nature of Scientific Law. Jenny Joseph. **SP-JoseJ**

On the Neglect of Figure Composition. Roy Fisher.

Prelude: "Hundreds upon hundreds of years of Lapiths." **SP-FishR**

Sketch for the First Exhibition of the New Heroic Art. **SP-FishR**

On the New Hot-House. Ben Jonson. **CP-JonsB**

On the New Motion. Ben Jonson. **CP-JonsB**

On the Night of a Friend's Wedding. Edwin Arlington Robinson. **CP-RobiE**

On the night of the Belgian surrender the moon rose. The Moon and the Night and the Men. John Berryman. **CP-BerrJ**

On the night that Mrs. Mandrill entered Nature. Mrs. Mandrill. Howard Nemerov. **CP-NemeH**

On the Njal Saga. Louis MacNeice. *Fr.* Dark Age Glosses. **CP-MacNL**

On the north side of the telephone pole wet snow stuck. Anniversary. Charles Olson. **CP-OlsoC**

On the note you do not send me. Christina Georgina Rossetti. **CP-RosC3**

On the Ocean Floor. "Hugh MacDiarmid." **SP-MacDH**

On the Omniscience of the Supreme Being. Christopher Smart. **SP-SmarC**

On the one hand, the railings. On the Embankment. Jenny Joseph. **SP-JoseJ**

On the one hand the steel works. Joliet. Carl Sandburg. **CP-SandC**

On the Open Side. Roy Fisher. **SP-FishR**

On the orchard of the sea far out are whitecaps. On a Ferry across Chesapeake Bay. Robert Bly. **SP-BlyR**

On the Orthodoxy and Creed of My Power Mower. John Ciardi. **SP-CiarJ**

On the Other Hand. Charles Kenneth Williams. **SP-WillC**

"On the other hand," said Gavin—or could have said. Canto II. Louis MacNeice. *Fr.* Autumn Sequel. **CP-MacNL**

On the other phone, Persephone: "He crushed me,—he creased my britches." The Allegory of Wealth. Charles Olson. **CP-OlsoC**

On the other side of the page. The Other Side of the Page. Erica Jong. **SP-JongE**

On the other side of the world's narrow lane. Fact of the Act. Robert Ranke Graves. **CP-GravR**

On the Other Side of Uji Bridge. Siv Cedering Fox. **SP-CedeS**

On the patchwork fairways of Rackham. Black Lotus of the Links. Laurence Lieberman. **SP-LiebL**

On the path. Under the Maud Moon. Galway Kinnell. **SP-KinnG**

On the Patio. John Ciardi. **SP-CiarJ**

On the paved parapet. Thetis. Hilda Doolittle. **CP-DoolH**

On the Photograph of Corps Commander. Herman Melville. **SP-MelvH**

On the Picture of a Sleeping Child. Vincent Bourne, *tr. fr. Latin by* William Cowper. **CP-CowpW**

On the plain is a tower. For Thieves and Beggars. Frank Templeton Prince. **CP-PrinF**

On the planet of Mars. The Planet of Mars. Shel Silverstein. **SP-SilS2**

On the Platform. Howard Nemerov. **CP-NemeH**

On the Platonic Idea as Aristotle Understood It. John Milton, *tr. fr. Latin by* John Shawcross. **CP-CowpW; CP-MiltJ**

("Ye sister pow'rs, who o'er the sacred groves.") **CP-CowpW,** *tr. by* William Cowper;

On the Plethora of Dryads. Sylvia Plath. **CP-PlatS**

On the Poems. Norris Jephson. *Fr.* Commendatory Poems. **CP-LoveR**

On the poop of a ship. Outward Bound. Malcolm Lowry. **CP-LowrM**

On the Porch at the Frost Place, Franconia, NH. William Matthews. **SP-MattW**

On the porch overlooking the eighteenth green. Greenwich 1930's, II. Frederick Morgan. **SP-MorgF**

On the Portrait of a Woman About to Be Hanged. Thomas Hardy. **CP-HardT**

On the Portrait of Two Beautiful Young People. Gerard Manley Hopkins. **CP-HopkG**

On the Power of Sound. William Wordsworth. **CP-WorW2**

On the Power of the Supreme Being. Christopher Smart. **SP-SmarC**

On the Preservation of Work Sheets. John Hewitt. **CP-HewiJ**

On the Principle of Blowclocks. Charles Tomlinson. **CP-TomlC**

On the Projected Kendal and Windermere Railway. William Wordsworth. **CP-WorW2**

On the Projects Playground. Etheridge Knight. **SP-KnigE**

On the Promotion of Thurlow. William Cowper. **CP-CowpW**

On the Prospect of Establishing a Pantisocracy in America. Samuel Taylor Coleridge. **CP-ColeS**

On the proud banks of great Euphrates' flood. Bible, *O.T. See* Psalm 137: "By the rivers of Babylon. . . ."

On the Quay. Theodore Roethke. **CP-RoetT**

On the Queens's Visit to London. William Cowper. **CP-CowpW**

On the Quotation "And My True Faith Can Alter Never, Though Thou Art Gone Perhaps Forever." Byron. **CP-Byron**

On the radio a canary bewailed her luck. Lightnin' Blues. Rita Dove. **SP-DoveR**

On the Railway Platform. Randall Jarrell. **CP-JarrR**

On the Ramblas / A Tree A Girl. Grace Paley. **CP-PaleG**

On the Receipt of My Mother's Picture out of Norfolk [the Gift of My Cousin Ann Bodham]. William Cowper. **CP-CowpW; FiP**

Lines on Receiving His Mother's Picture. **CH; OHIP**

On the Recently Minted Hundred-Cent Piece. John Updike. **CP-UpdiJ**

On the Reed. *Unknown, tr. fr. Greek by* William Cowper. **CP-CowpW**

On the Report that a Wooden Bridge. James Thomson. **CP-ThomJ**

On the Right Honourable and Virtuous Lord Weston, L[ord] High Treasurer of England, upon the Day He Was Made Earl of Portland, 17. Febr. 1632. To the Envious. Ben Jonson. **CP-JonsB**

On the River. Paul Laurence Dunbar. **CP-DunbP**

On the Road. Paul Laurence Dunbar. **CP-DunbP**

On the Road. John Haines. **SP-HainJ**

On the Road. Seamus Heaney. **SP-HeanS** *Fr.* Sweeney Redivivus.

On the Road. David Herbert Lawrence. **CP-LawrD**

On the Road Again. "Bob Dylan." **CP-DylaB**

On the Road Home. Wallace Stevens. **CP-StevW**

On the road of the self-contained. Poem for a Cold Journey. John Haines. **SP-HainJ**

On the road to Bangor, we spotted a domed stone. Bringing a Turtle Home. Robert Lowell. **SP-LoweR**

On the Road to Nowhere. Nicholas Vachel Lindsay. **CP-LindV**

On the Road to Wockensutter. John Crowe Ransom. **SP-RansJ**

On the Road to Woodlawn. Theodore Roethke. **CP-RoetT**

On the roads at night I saw the glitter of eyes. Eyes of Night-Time. Muriel Rukeyser. **CP-RukeM**

On the Roof. Charles Kenneth Williams. **CP-WillC**

On the Rush. Jim Carroll. **SP-CarrJ**

On the Same ["James derided the Purgatorial fire of the soul"]. John Milton, *tr. fr. Latin by* John T. Shawcross. **CP-MiltJ**

On the Same ["Thus did you strive to vouchsafe James to Heaven"]. John Milton, *tr. fr. Latin by* John T. Shawcross. **CP-MiltJ**

On the Same ["Whom impious Rome had just marked out for her curses"]. John Milton, *tr. fr. Latin by* John T. Shawcross. **CP-MiltJ**

On the Same, *see also* On the Burning of Lord Mansfield's Library. William Cowper. **CP-CowpW**

On the Same, *see also* Watching unto God in the Night-Season. Jeanne Marie Bouvier de la Motte-Guyon, *tr. fr. French by* William Cowper. **CP-CowpW**

On the Same, *see also* Watching unto God in the Night-Season. Jeanne Marie Bouvier de la Motte-Guyon, *tr. fr. French by* William Cowper. **CP-CowpW**

On the Same Beast. Ben Jonson. **CP-JonsB**

On the Same Nobleman. Robert Burns. *See* On Lord Galloway.

On the Same Occasion [on Seeing the Foundation Preparing for the Erection of Rydal Chapel]. William Wordsworth. **CP-WorW2**

On the Same Occasion. William Wordsworth. **CP-WorW2**

On the Same Picture. Walt Whitman. **CP-WhitW**

On the Sea. John Keats. **CP-KeatJ**

On the sea and at the Hogue, sixteen hundred ninety-two. Hervé Riel. Robert Browning. **CP-BroR2**

On the sea of motherhood and death you voyaged, waif of eternity. The Death. Hayden Carruth. *Fr.* Mother. **CP-CarHL**

On the Sea Wall. Paul Laurence Dunbar. **CP-DunbP**

On the Seas and Far Away. Robert Burns. **CP-BurnR**

On the secret map the assassins. Rivers and Mountains. John Ashbery. **SP-AshbJ**

On the sheep-cropped summit, under hot sun. Cat and Mouse. Ted Hughes. **SP-HughT**

On the Shore. Charles Olson. **CP-OlsoC**

On the Shortness of Life. William Cowper, *tr. fr. Latin of Dr. Jortin.* **CP-CowpW**

On the Sicilian strand a hare well wrought. Ausonius, *tr. fr. Latin by* Richard Lovelace. **CP-LoveR**

On the side of a road in Alabama. Fragments of an Old Song 1. Gilbert Sorrentino. **SP-SorrG**

On the sidewalk. Construction. William Carlos Williams. **CP-WilW2**

On the Sight of a Manse in the South of Scotland. William Wordsworth. **CP-WorW2**

On the sink of the Golden Motel washroom. Leonard Nathan. **SP-NathL** *Fr.* To Be Read to Yourself in a Public Place, July 4, 1976.

On the Skeleton of a Hound. James Wright. **CP-WrigJ**

On the Slain Collegians. Herman Melville. **SP-MelvH**

On the slow train time does not interfere & at the Arabian. Highway 61 Revisited (liner notes). "Bob Dylan." **CP-DylaB**

On the small marble-paved platform. Margrave. Robinson Jeffers. **CP-JefR2**

On the Solitary Fells around Hawkshead. William Wordsworth. *See* Fair seed-time had my soul, and I grew up.

On the South-West Coast of Erehwemos Stands a Romantic Little Village. Kenneth Patchen. **CP-PatcK**

On the southwest side of Capri. The Nude Swim. Anne Sexton. **CP-SextA**

On the Star of "The Legion of Honour." Byron. **CP-Byron**

On the Statue of *Cleopatra*, Made into a Fountain by *Leo* the Tenth. Baldassare, Count of Novilara Castiglione, *tr. fr. Latin by* Alexander Pope. **CP-PopeA**

On the steep slope by the drive he. Three Gardens. James Schuyler. **CP-SchuJ**

On the Steps. Stephen Berg. **SP-BergS**

On the stiff twig up there. Black Rook in Rainy Weather. Sylvia Plath. **CP-PlatS**

On the Still Surviving Markes of Our Saviours Wounds. Richard Crashaw. **CP-CrasR**

On the storm's wet tongue, greens. Suffering Does for the Character. Steve Griffiths. **SP-GrifS**

On "The Story of Rimini." John Keats. **CP-KeatJ**

On the street / Slung on his shoulder is a handle half way across. The Shovel Man. Carl Sandburg. **CP-SandC**

On the street I am met with constant hostility. Fragment, A. Robert Creeley. **CP-CreeR**

On the Subject of Roses. Diane Wakoski. **SP-WakoD**

On the Subtle Man. Richard Eberhart. **CP-EberR**

On the Subway Station. Grace Paley. **CP-PaleG**

On the summit: it stands on a fair summit. Grace's House. Thomas Merton. **CP-MertT; SP-MertT**

On the Symbolic Consideration of Hands and the Significance of Death. Miller Williams. **SP-WillM**

On the tallest day in time, the dead came back. V-J Day. John Ciardi. **SP-CiarJ**

On the television screen. Galway Kinnell. *Fr.* The Dead Shall Be Raised Incorruptible. **SP-KinnG**

On the third finger of my left hand. Ceremony. William Stafford. **SP-StafW**

On the threshold of heaven, the figures in the street. To an Old Philosopher in Rome. Wallace Stevens. **CP-StevW**

On the Threshold of His Greatness, the Poet Comes Down With a Sore Throat. Howard Nemerov. **CP-NemeH**

On the tidal mud, just before sunset. Daybreak. Galway Kinnell. **SP-KinnG**

On the Tlacolula Bus. Charles Tomlinson. **CP-TomlC**

On the top of my red banner. A Song for Elizabeth. Nicholas Vachel Lindsay. **CP-LindV**

On the Town's Honest Man. Ben Jonson. **CP-JonsB**

On the Towpath. John Ashbery. **SP-AshbJ**

On the tropical coast of Java. Canzone. Gilbert Sorrentino. **SP-SorrG**

On the Truly Honourable Coll. Richard Lovelace, Occasioned by the Publication of His Posthume-Poems. Symon Ognell. *Fr.* Elegies, 1660. **CP-LoveR**

On the Tune Called the Old-Hundred-and-Fourth. Thomas Hardy. **CP-HardT**

On the turf's edge—grass flashing like a knife. The Conscript. Stephen Spender. **CP-SpenS**

On the unbreathing sides of hills. Squatter's Children. Elizabeth Bishop. **CP-BishE**

On the Union. Ben Jonson. **CP-JonsB**

On the University Carrier Who Sick'n'd [*or* Sickened] in the Time of His Vacancy [, Being Forbid to go to London, by Reason of the Plague]. John Milton. **CP-MiltJ**

On the up-platform at Morpeth station. The Complaint of the Morpethshire Farmer. Basil Bunting. **CP-BuntB**

On the Use of Dialect Words. John Hewitt. **CP-HewiJ**

On the Venerable Bede. Louis MacNeice. *Fr.* Dark Age Glosses. **CP-MacNL**

On the Venetian Painter. William Blake. **CP-BlakW**

On the Verandah. John Gould Fletcher. **SP-FletJ**

On the Victory Obtained by Blake over the Spaniards, in the Bay of Santa [*or* Sancta] Cruz, in the Island of Tenerife, 1657. Andrew Marvell. **CP-MarvA**

"Now does *Spains* Fleet her spatious wings unfold." **FaBoEH**

On the Virginity of the Virgin Mary & Johanna Southcott. William Blake. **CP-BlakW**

On the Water of Our Lord's Baptism[e]. Richard Crashaw. **CP-CrasR**

On the Way. Thomas Hardy. **CP-HardT**

On the Way. Edwin Arlington Robinson. **CP-RobiE**

On the Way. Carl Sandburg. **CP-SandC**

On the Way Home From Nowhere, New Year's Eve. Miller Williams. **SP-WillM**

On the way to / the eternal sea. Immediacy. Archie Randolph Ammons. **SP-AmmoA**

On the way to a woman, I give. Into the Stone. James Dickey. **CP-DickJ**

On the way to Cottonwood, Minnesota. Whiteness. Stephen Dunn. **SP-DunnS**

On the Way to Delphi. John Updike. **CP-UpdiJ**

On the Way to the Planetarium. James Wright. *Fr.* Many of Our Waters: Variations on a Poem by a Black Child. **CP-WrigJ**

On the way up from Sheet I met some children. To Edward Thomas. Alun Lewis. **CP-LewiA**

On the weekend, the upholstery of a sofa was replaced. A Poem for the Students of Greece. Kay Boyle. **CP-BoylK**

On the Welsh Mountains. Alun Lewis. **CP-LewiA**

On the wheat-sacks sullen with the ceaseless damp. John Berryman. *Fr.* Sonnets to Chris. **CP-BerrJ**

On the Wide Heath. Edna St. Vincent Millay. **CP-MillE**

On the wide lawn the snow lay deep. Red Riding-Hood. John Greenleaf Whittier. **CP-WhitJ**

On the wide Texan and New Mexican ranches. Oysters. Robinson Jeffers. **CP-JefR3**

On the wide veranda white. A Corn-Song. Paul Laurence Dunbar. **CP-DunbP**

On the wind of January. The Wind of January. Christina Georgina Rossetti. **YeAr** *Fr.* A Year's Windfalls. **CP-RosC1**

On the wind of January. A Year's Windfalls. Christina Georgina Rossetti. **CP-RosC1**

On the wine label, monks, towers and wimples. It Don't Mean a Thing if it Ain't Got That Swing. William Matthews. **SP-MattW**

On the Wing. Christina Georgina Rossetti. **CP-RosC1**

On the Words "Brother Protestants and Fellow Christians." Jonathan Swift. **CP-SwifJ**

On the World you colored. Emily Dickinson. **CP-DickE**

On the Wounds of Our Crucified Lord. Richard Crashaw. **CP-CrasR**

On the Yard. Etheridge Knight. **SP-KnigE**

On thee has God conferred. Ralph Waldo Emerson. **CP-EmerR**

On these green banks, where falls too soon. An Outdoor Reception. John Greenleaf Whittier. **CP-WhitJ**

On things asleep, no balm. The Longing. Theodore Roethke. *Fr.* North American Sequence. **CP-RoetT**

On this bald hill the new year hones its edge. Parliament Hill Fields. Sylvia Plath. **CP-PlatS**

On this blest day may no dark cloud, or shower. To the Countess of A—. Written on the Anniversary of Her Marriage. Charlotte Smith. **CP-SmitC**

On this cold mercenary hill. Conscript's Song. Edwin Rolfe. **CP-RolfE**

On This Day I Complete My Thirty-sixth Year. Byron. **CP-Byron**

On this day man's disgust is known. On Shooting Particles beyond the World. Richard Eberhart. **CP-EberR**

On this day of crisis / when men march. August 1939. John Hewitt. **CP-HewiJ**

On this day tradition allots. A New Year Greeting. Wystan Hugh Auden. **CP-AudeW**

On this decline of Christmas Day. A Nightmare, and the Next Thing. Thomas Hardy. **CP-HardT**

On this dishonored, this perverted globe. Port Townsend, 1974. Richard Hugo. **CP-HugoR**

On this feast day, oh, cursèd day and hour! Love at First Sight. Christopher Marlowe. **NOBE** *Fr.* Hero and Leander. **CP-MarlC**

On this flashing afternoon of Ascension Thursday let me sit. Ceremony for Edward Dahlberg. Thomas Merton. **CP-MertT**

On This Island. Wystan Hugh Auden. **CP-AudeW**

On this kindly yellow day of mild low-travelling winter sun. A Spellbound Palace. Thomas Hardy. **CP-HardT**

On this lone island, whose unfruitful breast. Supposed to Have Been Written in the Hebrides. Charlotte Smith. **CP-SmitC**

On this long storm the Rainbow rose. Emily Dickinson. **CP-DickE**

On this map white. A state thick as a fist. A Map of Montana in Italy. Richard Hugo. **CP-HugoR**

On This Shore. Siv Cedering Fox. **SP-CedeS**

On This Side of the River. Stephen Berg. **SP-BergS**

On this side of the tapestry. The Tapestry. Howard Nemerov. **CP-NemeH**

On this they were in agreement. Long Term. Stephen Dunn. **SP-DunnS**

On this tree thrown up. Spindrift. Galway Kinnell. **SP-KinnG**

On this wondrous sea. Emily Dickinson. **CP-DickE**

On those islands / The west wind drops its message of indolence. The Hebrides. Louis MacNeice. **CP-MacNL**

On Those That Hated "The Playboy of the Western World," 1907. William Butler Yeats. **CP-YeatW**

On Thought in Harness. Edna St. Vincent Millay. **CP-MillE**

On thrones from China to Peru. A Model for the Laureate. William Butler Yeats. **CP-YeatW**

On Thurlow. William Cowper. **CP-CowpW**

On thy grey bark, in witness of my flame. Pietro Metastasio, *tr. fr. Italian by* Charlotte Smith. **CP-SmitC**

On thy stupendous summit, rock sublime! Beachy Head. Charlotte Smith. **CP-SmitC**

On thy wild banks, by frequent torrents worn. To the River Arun. Charlotte Smith. **CP-SmitC**

On Time. John Milton. **CP-MiltJ**

On to Iona!—What can she afford. Iona. William Wordsworth. *Fr.* Poems Composed or Suggested During a Tour, in the Summer of 1833. **CP-WorW2**

On Tomasin Parsons. Robert Herrick. **CP-HerrR**

On top of that if you know me I pronounce you an ignu. Ignu. Allen Ginsberg. **CP-GinsA**

On Tour. Jim Carroll. **SP-CarrJ**

On tram's top deck—in nineteen twenty-three. Encounter With R.J. Welch, The Antiquary. John Hewitt. **CP-HewiJ**

On Twelfth Street in Manhattan. Stanley Jasspon Kunitz. *Fr.* Signs and Portents. **CP-KuniS**

On two days it steads not to run from thy grave. Omar Khayyám, *tr. fr. Persian by* Ralph Waldo Emerson. **CP-EmerR**

On Ullsawater. William Wordsworth. *See* One evening (surely I was led by her).

On up the sea slant. Sea Slant. Carl Sandburg. **CP-SandC**

On Vacation. Robert Creeley. **CP-CreeR**

On vacation. Well / earned, twice and. You're. James Schuyler. **CP-SchuJ**

On Valentine's Day to Friends. Louis Zukofsky. **CP-ZukLS**

On vent'rous wing in quest of praise I go. Virgil, *tr. by* Samuel Johnson. **CP-JohnS** *Fr.* Georgics.

On Visiting Staffa. John Keats. **CP-KeatJ**

On Visiting the Tomb of Burns. John Keats. **CP-KeatJ**

On Vulture Peak. Gary Snyder. **CP-SnydG**

On W. R———, Esq. Robert Burns. *See* So vile was poor Wat, such a miscreant slave.

On Waking to the Third Rainy Morning of a Long Week End. Ogden Nash. **CP-NashO**

On Walking Slowly after an Accident. Stevie Smith. **CP-SmitS**

On Watching Politicians Perform at Martin Luther King's Funeral. Etheridge Knight. **SP-KnigE**

On Water. Charles Tomlinson. **CP-TomlC**

On Wee Johnie. Robert Burns. **CP-BurnR**

On Wellington ("You are 'the best of cut-throats' "). Byron. *See* You are "the best of cut-throats:"—do not start.

On Wellington. Byron. *See* Oh, Wellington! (or "Villainton") for fame.

On Wenlock Edge the wood's in trouble. Alfred Edward Housman. **CP-HousA**

On Wet Iota. John Ciardi. **SP-CiarJ**

On what foundation stands the warrior's pride. Samuel Johnson. **NOBE; OBWP** *Fr.* The Vanity of Human Wishes [The Tenth Satire of Juvenal Imitated]. **CP-JohnS**

(Charles XII of Sweden.) **NOBE**

On What Planet. Kenneth Rexroth. **SP-RexrK**

On which to shoot pool (that. A Table of Green Fields. James Schuyler. **CP-SchuJ**

On white linen the silk. The Ripple. Denise Levertov. **CP-LeveD**

On William Graham [*or* W——— Gr-h-m], Esq., of Mossknowe [*or* M-sskn-w]. Robert Burns. **CP-BurnR**

On Willie Chalmers. Robert Burns. **CP-BurnR**

On Windermere; Bowness Bay and Belle Isle. William Wordsworth. **FaBoPP** *Fr.* School-Time. *Fr.* The Prelude; Growth of a Poet's Mind [1805 vers.]. **CP-WorW3**

On wings too stiff to flap. The Milky Way Is a Cowpath. Robert Frost. **CP-FrosR**

On Winter's Margin. Mary Oliver. **SP-OlivM**

On Wisdom's Defeat in a Learned Debate. Jonathan Swift. **CP-SwifJ**

On with thy work[e], though thou beest hardly prest. Rest. Robert Herrick. **CP-HerrR**

On Woman. William Butler Yeats. **CP-YeatW**

On Wood the Ironmonger. Jonathan Swift. **CP-SwifJ**

On Working White Liberals. Maya Angelou. **SP-AngeM**

On yonder hills soft twilight dwells. The Longest Day. George Meredith. **CP-MerG1**

On you th' affections of your Fathers Friends. To My Worthy Friend, Mr. John Mounson, Sonne and Heyre to Sir Thomas Mounson, Knight and Baronet. Thomas Campion. **CP-CampT**

On your feet like paws and if a board might squeak. A Part of the Series on the Paths. Charles Olson. **CP-OlsoC**

On your midnight pallet lying. Alfred Edward Housman. **CP-HousA**

On Your Own. Tess Gallagher. **SP-GallT**

Once. / Always excited to say twice. Brim Beauvais. Gertrude Stein. **CP-SteiG**

Once, / I was afraid of dying. I Was Afraid of Dying. James Wright. **CP-WrigJ**

Once, / in August. Keeping the City. Anne Sexton. **CP-SextA**

Once. Christina Georgina Rossetti. **CP-RosC3**

Once / starving in Philadelphia. The Night I Fucked My Alarm Clock. Charles Bukowski. **SP-BukC1**

Once. Alice Walker. **CP-WalkA**

"I/ never liked/ white folks." **PoBA**

"It is true--/ I've always loved." **NMM; PoBA**

Once a dream did weave a shade. A Dream. William Blake. **CH; EnRP; FHYEP; HoFi; LAuP; NOBRP; PoPle** *Fr.* Songs of Innocence. **CP-BlakW**

Once a lively image of human nature. Epitaph on Miss Stanley. James Thomson. **CP-ThomJ**

Once a man killed another, to rob him. William Stafford. *Fr.* Stories to Live in the World With. **SP-StafW**

Once a man was traveling through the woods, and. Maximus Letter # Whatever. Charles Olson. **SP-OlsoC** *Fr.* The Maximus Poems.

Once a pair of savages found a stranded tree. The Junk and the Dhow. Rudyard Kipling. **CP-KiplR** *Fr.* Land and Sea Tales.

Once a poor widow, aging year by year. Geoffrey Chaucer. *See* The Nun's Priest's Tale.

Once a ripple came to land. A Ripple Song. Rudyard Kipling. **CP-KiplR** *Fr.* The Undertakers. *Fr.* The Second Jungle Book.

Once a week. Zimmer Guilty of the Burnt Girl. Paul Zimmer. **SP-ZimmP**

Once a year. Desert Water. Richard Shelton. **SP-ShelR**

Once a year at midnight. Reunion. Richard Shelton. **SP-ShelR**

Once, after long-drawn revel at The Mermaid. The Craftsman. Rudyard Kipling. **CP-KiplR**

Once, Again. Alice Walker. **CP-WalkA**

Once again after dawn before questions. Halves. Stephen Dunn. **SP-DunnS**

Once again the pine-tree sung. Ralph Waldo Emerson. **APN-1** *Fr.* Woodnotes II ("As sunbeams stream through liberal space"). **CP-EmerR**

Once again the Steamer at Calais— the tackles. Song of Seventy Horses. Rudyard Kipling. **CP-KiplR**

Once again they were dismayed. Exploits of a Machine Age. Thomas Merton. **CP-MertT**

Once again to wake, nor wish to sleep. But Thy Commandment Is Exceeding Broad. Christina Georgina Rossetti. **CP-RosC2**

Once again we live in a whole landscape. Summer Amnesty. Jenny Joseph. **SP-JoseJ**

Once Alien Here. John Hewitt. **CP-HewiJ**

Once and Again. Hayden Carruth. **CP-CarHS**

Once, and but once found in thy company. The Perfume. John Donne. **AnAnS-1; ESCV; NoSic; SeCP** *Fr.* Elegies. **CP-DonnJ**

Once and for all, have done with it. Have Done With It. David Herbert Lawrence. **CP-LawrD**

Once, as a boy of nine, he heard his teacher. Nineteen Sixteen, or the Terrible Beauty. John Hewitt. **CP-HewiJ**

Once as a Child I Had Bad Dreams. Paul Zimmer. **SP-ZimmP**

Once [*or* Ons], as methought, Fortune me kissed [*or* kist *or* kyst]. Sir Thomas Wyatt. **CP-WyatT**

Once as my carriage wearily dragg'd. The Three Gipsies. Nikolaus Lenau, *tr. fr. German by* George Meredith. **CP-MerG2**

Once at a country halt—now closed for years. Age and Youth. John Hewitt. **CP-HewiJ**

Once at Cold Mountain, troubles cease. Gary Snyder. **CP-SnydG**

Once at midnight in the fall. The Muse Considered As a Demon Lover. Frank O'Hara. **SP-OharF**

Once at Swanage. Thomas Hardy. **CP-HardT**

Once, at the Agricultural Show. The Pat of Butter. Thomas Hardy. **CP-HardT**

Once at the Plaza, looking out into the park. Three Bills. Randall Jarrell. **CP-JarrR**

Once below a Time. Dylan Thomas. **CP-ThomD**

Once branching light startles the hair of the coconuts. Hurucan. Derek Walcott. **CP-WalcD**

Once by a bitter candle. Later in Belleville: Career. Margaret Atwood. **SP-AtwM1**

Once by the Pacific. Robert Frost. **CP-FrosR**

Once did I heere an aged father say. Sonnet 24. Mary Sidney, Countess of Montgomery Wroth. *Fr.* Pamphilia to Amphilanthus. **CP-WrotM**

Once did She hold the gorgeous east in fee. On the Extinction of the Venetian Republic. William Wordsworth. **CP-WorW1**

Once down on my knees to growing plants. A Mood Apart. Robert Frost. **CP-FrosR**

Once Duffy's Circus had shaken out its tent. Duffy's Circus. Paul Muldoon. **SP-MuldP**

Once each year. Mexico. Richard Shelton. **SP-ShelR**

Once, early in the morning. The Devil's Walk. Percy Bysshe Shelley. **CP-ShelP**

Once Fairly Set Out on His Party of Pleasure. Byron. **CP-Byron**

Once fondly lov'd, and still rememb'red dear. Wrote on the Blank Leaf of a Copy of My First Edition, Which I Sent to an Old Sweetheart, Then Married. Robert Burns. **CP-BurnR**

Once for All. (Margaret). Christina Georgina Rossetti. **CP-RosC1**

Once for candy Cook had stolen. Wystan Hugh Auden. **PV** *Fr.* Shorts [1939–1947] ("Motionless, deep in his mind, lies the past the poet's forgotten"). **CP-AudeW**

Once from a big, big building. A Visit to the Asylum. Edna St. Vincent Millay. **CP-MillE**

Once he was seduced by the soft luxurious hill. The Puritan. May Sarton. **SP-SartM**

Once he went inside a pool hall. The Well-Ordered Life. Miller Williams. **SP-WillM**

Once hid in a fiery twist. The Scratch. James Dickey. **CP-DickJ**

Once I ached for thy dear sake: / Wilt thou cause Me now to ache? Monday in Holy Week. Christina Georgina Rossetti. **CP-RosC2**

Once I adopted / A little girl child. Madam and the Charity Child. Langston Hughes. **SP-HughL**

Once I am sure there's nothing going on. Church Going. Philip Larkin. **CP-LarkP**

Once I believed in you. The Spirit Wooed. Philip Larkin. **CP-LarkP**

Once I changed my name to race the rich. Memoirs. Richard Hugo. **CP-HugoR**

Once I Could Hail (Howe'er Serene the Sky). William Wordsworth. **CP-WorW2**

Once I had a Comrade. The Good Comrade. Ludwig Uhland, *tr. fr. German by* George Meredith. **CP-MerG2**

Once I had a pony, her name was Lucifer. New Pony. "Bob Dylan." **CP-DylaB**

Once I heard your voice. Kathleen Jessie Raine. **SP-RainK**

Once I knew, nothing in the leaf could see me. The Daughters. Stephen Berg. **SP-BergS**

Once I looked inside / the darkness. The Hermit Crab. Mary Oliver. **SP-OlivM**

Once I loved a fairy. Queen Mab in the Village. Nicholas Vachel Lindsay. **CP-LindV**

Once I loved a spider. The Spider and the Ghost of the Fly. Nicholas Vachel Lindsay. **CP-LindV**

Once I Pass'd through a Populous City. Walt Whitman. **CP-WhitW**

Once I rambled in a wood. The Dead City. Christina Georgina Rossetti. **CP-RosC3**

Once I said lightly. Ted Hughes. **SP-HughT** *Fr.* Gaudete.

Once I said three gulls are often four. Sailing from Naples. Richard Hugo. **CP-HugoR**

Once I saw a Devil in a flame of fire. Memorable Fancy, A. William Blake. *Fr.* The Marriage of Heaven and Hell. **CP-BlakW**

Once I saw a grown man fall from a tree. Death and the Maiden. Howard Nemerov. **CP-NemeH**

Once I spoke the language of the flowers. Forgotten Language. Shel Silverstein. **SP-SilS2**

Once I thought to sit so high. The Offering of the New Law, the One Oblation Once Offered. Christina Georgina Rossetti. **CP-RosC3**

Once I was a small grain. The Last Step. Philip Levine. **CP-LeviP**

Once I was immortal. The Maiden. Audre Lorde. **SP-LordA**

Once I was part of the music I heard. Youth in Age. George Meredith. **CP-MerG2**

Once I was water, full of scaly fish. Two Riddles from Aldhelm. Richard Wilbur. **CP-WilbR**

Once I wished I might rehearse. Freedom. Ralph Waldo Emerson. **CP-EmerR**

Once in a California Sierra. Auspex. Robert Frost. **CP-FrosR**

Once in a dark restaurant I caught the eyes of another. Behind the Mirror. Thom Gunn. **CP-GunnT**

Once in a dream (for once I dreamed of you). On the Wing. Christina Georgina Rossetti. **CP-RosC1**

Once in a dream I saw the flowers. Paradise. Christina Georgina Rossetti. **CP-RosC1**

Once in a lonely hamlet I sojourned. The Emigrant Mother. William Wordsworth. **CP-WorW1**

Once, in a night as black as ink. How Samson Bore Away the Gates of Gaza. Nicholas Vachel Lindsay. **CP-LindV**

Once in a showery summer, sick of war. Townland of Peace. John Hewitt. *Fr.* Freehold. **CP-HewiJ**

Once in a while / we'd find a patch. The Children. William Carlos Williams. **CP-WilW2**

Once in Canandaigua, hitchhiking from Ann Arbor. Faces. John Ciardi. **SP-CiarJ**

Once in life I watched a Star. The Penalty. Rudyard Kipling. **CP-KiplR**

Once, in Louisville on pass from basic training. The Curse of the Frogs. Paul Zimmer. **SP-ZimmP**

Once, in Our Quarreling. David Markson. **CP-MarkD**

Once-in-Passing, The. Louis MacNeice. **FaBCIP** *Fr.* A Hand of Snapshots. **CP-MacNL**

Once, in Rotterdam, a whore once, in a bar, a sailors' bar, a hooker bar, opened up her legs. Medusa. Charles Kenneth Williams. **SP-WillC**

"Once in so often," King Solomon said. Banquet Night. Rudyard Kipling. **CP-KiplR** *Fr.* Debits and Credits.

Once, in summer, / in the blueberries. Picking Blueberries, Austerlitz, New York, 1957. Mary Oliver. **SP-OlivM**

Once, in the city of Kalamazoo. Kalamazoo. Nicholas Vachel Lindsay. **CP-LindV**

Once in the wind of morning. The Merry Guide. Alfred Edward Housman. **CP-HousA**

Once in your grace I know I was. Sir Thomas Wyatt. **CP-WyatT**

Once it had gorged itself. On a Pig's Head. Charles Tomlinson. **CP-TomlC**

Once it made music, tiny, frail, yet sweet. Sallie's Musical Box. Walter de la Mare. **CP-DeLaW**

Once it smiled a silent dell. The Valley of Unrest. Edgar Allan Poe. **CP-PoeEd**

Once It Was the Colour of Saying. Dylan Thomas. **CP-ThomD**

Once like a broken bow Mark sprang aside. St. Mark. Christina Georgina Rossetti. **CP-RosC2**

Once like a lady / In a silken dress. To the Three for Whom the Book. Countee Cullen. **CP-CullC**

Once like a spark. Edward Estlin Cummings. **CP-CummE**

Once, long ago, set close beside a wood, *mod. vers. by* Frank Ernest Hill. Geoffrey Chaucer. *See* The Nun's Priest's Tale.

Once Love grew bold and arrogant of air. Love's Chastening. Paul Laurence Dunbar. **CP-DunbP**

Once made a fairy rooster from. For My Sister Molly Who in the Fifties. Alice Walker. **CP-WalkA**

Once men touch one another, then the modern industrial. Future States. David Herbert Lawrence. **CP-LawrD**

Once More. Hayden Carruth. **CP-CarHS**

Once more / the sun roaming on the carpenter's back. Is It True? Anne Sexton. **CP-SextA**

Once more / The yellow iris on the wrack-strewn shore. Kore. Kathleen Jessie Raine. **SP-RainK**

Once more, dear friends, you meet beneath. Anniversary Poem. John Greenleaf Whittier. **CP-WhitJ**

Once more evening on the earth. The Lake in the Sky. John Haines. **SP-HainJ**

Once More for My Lady. Dabney Stuart. **SP-StuaD**

Once more he turned to that which could not be fixed. Two Versions of the Same Poem. Wallace Stevens. **CP-StevW**

Once more I dare to rouse the sounding string. On the Immensity of the Supreme Being. Christopher Smart. **SP-SmarC**

Once more I go over your earthly body. Rediscovery. Thomas McGrath. **SP-McGrT**

Once more I saw him. In the lofty room. The Last Sight. Robert Louis Stevenson. **CP-StevR**

Once more I welcome Thee, and Thou, fair Plant. The Tuft of Primroses. William Wordsworth. **CP-WorW1**

Once more into my arid days like dew. Edna St. Vincent Millay. **CP-MillE**

Once more, my now bewildered Dove. Emily Dickinson. **CP-DickE**

Once more, O all-adjusting Death! Samuel J. Tilden. John Greenleaf Whittier. **CP-WhitJ**

Once more, O Mountains of the North, unveil. Mountain Pictures. John Greenleaf Whittier. **CP-WhitJ**

Once More, O Ye. Richard Eberhart. **CP-EberR**

Once more on yonder laurelled height. Our River. John Greenleaf Whittier. **CP-WhitJ**

Once more, sweet Stream! with slow foot wand'ring near. Lines to a Beautiful Spring in a Village. Samuel Taylor Coleridge. **CP-ColeS**

Once more the cauldron of the sun. The Sun on the Bookcase. Thomas Hardy. **CP-HardT**

Once more the Church is seized with sudden fear. Wicliffe. William Wordsworth. *Fr.* Ecclesiastical Sonnets. **CP-WorW2**

Once more the country calls. Ode to Our Young Pro-consuls of the Air. Allen Tate. **CP-TateA**

Once more the liberal year laughs out. Harvest Hymn. John Greenleaf Whittier. **OHIP** *Fr.* For an Autumn Festival. **CP-WhitJ**

Once More, the Round. Theodore Roethke. **CP-RoetT**

Once more the storm is howling, and half hid. A Prayer for My Daughter. William Butler Yeats. **CP-YeatW**

Once more the wonted road I tread. Arthur Hugh Clough. *Fr.* Blank Misgivings of a Creature Moving About in Worlds Not Realized. **SP-ClouA**

Once more thou art the rage oh good John Donne. Donne He's Regular. Malcolm Lowry. **CP-LowrM**

Once more upon the waters! yet once more! Byron. **FHYEP** *Fr.* Childe Harold's Pilgrimage. **CP-Byron**

Once more you've degraded yourself on the road. Goodbye, Iowa. Richard Hugo. **CP-HugoR**

Once, my father took me to the Rockaways. Regardless. Stephen Dunn. **SP-DunnS**

Once, on a glittering ice-field, ages and ages ago. The Story of Ung. Rudyard Kipling. **CP-KiplR**

Once on a Lord-Mayors day, in Cheapside, when. Way in a Crowd. Robert Herrick. **CP-HerrR**

Once on a night in spring. Hayden Carruth. **CP-CarHS** *Fr.* The Bloomingdale Papers.

Once on a Night in the Delta: A Report From Hell. Etheridge Knight. **SP-KnigE**

Once on a time, as old stories rehearse. A Ballad to the Tune of the Cutpurse [*or* "The Cut-Purse"]. Jonathan Swift. **CP-SwifJ**

Once on a time, the ancient legends tell. A Legend of Truth. Rudyard Kipling. **CP-KiplR** *Fr.* Debits and Credits.

Once on a time was a King anxious to understand. The King's Job. Rudyard Kipling. **CP-KiplR**

Once on a time when thought began. Drinking Song. Thomas Hardy. **CP-HardT**

Once on his star-gemmed, dazzling throne. The Punishment of Pride. Walt Whitman. **CP-WhitW**

Once on returning home, purse-proud and hale. The Auction. Theodore Roethke. **CP-RoetT**

Once on Saipan at the end of the rains. An Island Galaxy. John Ciardi. **SP-CiarJ**

Once on the kind of day called "weather breeder." An Encounter. Robert Frost. **CP-FrosR**

Once on the top of Tynwald's formal mound. Tynwald Hill. William Wordsworth. *Fr.* Poems Composed or Suggested During a Tour, in the Summer of 1833. **CP-WorW2**

Once, once, in Washington. Patriotic Tour and Postulate of Joy. Robert Penn Warren. **SP-WarrR**

Once. . . once upon a time. Martha. Walter de la Mare. **CP-DeLaW**

Once Only. Gary Snyder. **CP-SnydG**

Once only by the garden gate. Youth and Love I. Robert Louis Stevenson. **CP-StevR**

Once out of Eden, love learned its deviousness. Mona Van Duyn. *Fr.* Footnotes to "The Autobiography of Bertrand Russell." **SP-VanDM**

Once over water, to you borne brightly. The Faring. Robert Penn Warren. *Fr.* The True Nature of Time. **SP-WarrR**

Once owned a blind horse, a big gray who. My Father. Ron Koertge. **SP-KoerR**

Once Poore, Still Penurious. Robert Herrick. **CP-HerrR**

Once riding in Old Baltimore. Incident. Countee Cullen. **CP-CullC**

Once (says an Author, whom I need not say). Verbatim from Boileau. Alexander Pope. **CP-PopeA**

Once Seen, and No More. Robert Herrick. **CP-HerrR**

Once slain for Him Who first was slain for them. All Saints: Martyrs. Christina Georgina Rossetti. **CP-RosC2**

Once, so they say, pinetrees seeded on Pelion's peak swam. Basil Bunting, *after the Latin of* Catullus; Carmen 64. **CP-BuntB**

Once, taking a train into Chicago. Freight Cars. Stephen Dobyns. **SP-DobyS**

Once the broom has started. Sorting the Personae. Donald Davie. **CP-DavDo**

Once the fair Romance of story. George Meredith. **CP-MerG2**

Once the priest / Lived in an age. Ralph Waldo Emerson. **CP-EmerR**

Once there was a cabin here, and once there was a man. Stafford's Cabin. Edwin Arlington Robinson. **CP-RobiE**

Once there was a city where these marshes are. The City of God. Thomas Merton. *Fr.* The Tower of Babel—A Morality. **CP-MertT**

Once there was a couple named Mr. and Mrs. Pepperloaf. Frailty, Thy Name Is a Misnomer. Ogden Nash. **CP-NashO**

Once there was a fair young damsel and she early went. Rapunzel, Rapunzel, Let's Let Down Our Hair. Ogden Nash. **CP-NashO**

Once there was a girl named Miriam. Miriam's Lucky Day. Ogden Nash. **CP-NashO**

Once there was a Greek divinity of the sea named Ceto. Medusa and the Mot Juste. Ogden Nash. *Fr.* Fables Bullfinch Forgot. **CP-NashO**

Once there was a handsome man named Mr. Beamington and. Love Me but Leave My Dog Alone. Ogden Nash. **CP-NashO**

Once there was a lonely man named Mr. Powers. The Solitude of Mr. Powers. Ogden Nash. **CP-NashO**

Once there was a lyric writer named Mr. Amazon. The Strange Case of the Renegade Lyric Writer. Ogden Nash. **CP-NashO**

Once there was a man, and he was named Mr. Barcalow, to be exact. Mr. Barcalow's Breakdown. Ogden Nash. **CP-NashO**

Once there was a man named Jarvis Gravel who was just a man. The Individualist. Ogden Nash. **CP-NashO**

Once there was a man named Mr. Arents. Father, Dear Father, Go Jump in the Lake, or, You're Costlier than You Think. Ogden Nash. **CP-NashO**

Once there was a man named Mr. Culpepper Wood. The Strange Case of Mr. Wood's Frustration, or, A Team that Won't Be Beaten Better Stay off the Field. Ogden Nash. **CP-NashO**

Once there was a man named Mr. O'Banion. The Strange Case of Mr. O'Banion's Come-Uppance. Ogden Nash. **CP-NashO**

Once there was a man named Mr. Palliser and he asked his wife. The Strange Case of Mr. Palliser's Palate. Ogden Nash. **CP-NashO**

Once there was a man named Mr. Pauncefoot to whom Fate could. The Strange Case of Mr. Pauncefoot's Broad Mind. Ogden Nash. **CP-NashO**

Once there was a man named Mr. Peachey and he lived on Park. Mr. Peachey's Predicament or No Mot Parades. Ogden Nash. **CP-NashO**

Once there was a man named Mr. Train who wasn't called Choo-choo. The Happy Ending of Mr. Train. Ogden Nash. **CP-NashO**

Once there was a man named Mr. Artesian and his activity was tremendous. Mr. Artesian's Conscientiousness. Ogden Nash. **CP-NashO**

Once there was a man who lived by the ocean named Mr. Strawbridge. Poor Mr. Strawbridge. Ogden Nash. **CP-NashO**

Once there was a poem, and it was serious and not in jest. Birdies, Don't Make Me Laugh. Ogden Nash. **CP-NashO**

Once there was a spirit. Eat your Rose Hips, C'est La Vie. Diane Wakoski. *Fr.* Fifteen Poems for a Lunar Eclipse None of Us Saw. **SP-WakoD**

Once, there was a way to get back homeward. Golden Slumbers. The Beatles. **CP-Beatl**

Once there was an Archer. Version. Robert Frost. **CP-FrosR**

Once there was blood. The One-Legged Man. Anne Sexton. **CP-SextA**

Once there were some children and they were uninterested in chores. The Child Is Father to the Man, But with More Authority. Ogden Nash. **CP-NashO**

Once there were two men named Mr. Webster and Mr. Merriam. To Ee Is Human. Ogden Nash. **CP-NashO**

Once they were sticks and stones. Names. Robert Earl Hayden. **CP-HaydR**

Once those fences kept me in. Mr. Mote. School Days. William Matthews. **SP-MattW**

Once to the verge of yon steep barrier came. Home at Grasmere. William Wordsworth. **CP-WorW1** *Fr.* The Recluse; Home at Grasmere.

Once to the verge of yon steep barrier came. The Recluse; Home at Grasmere. William Wordsworth.

Once upon a midnight dreary, while I pondered [*or* ponder'd], weak and weary. The Raven. Edgar Allan Poe. **CP-PoeEd**

Once upon a time. The Boy and the Man. Edward Estlin Cummings. **CP-CummE**

Once upon a time does well enough. Casting. Dabney Stuart. **SP-StuaD**

Once upon a time there was a beautiful woman named Mrs. Geraldine. The Strange Case of the Dead Divorcee. Ogden Nash. **CP-NashO**

Once upon a time there was a boy named Robin Bideawee. The Strange Case of the Ambitious Caddy. Ogden Nash. **CP-NashO**

Once upon a time there was a flock of doves. The Strange Case of the Blackmailing Dove. Ogden Nash. **CP-NashO**

Once upon a time there was a man named Mr. Lionel Fortague. The Strange Case of Mr. Fortague's Disappointment. Ogden Nash. **CP-NashO**

Once upon a time there was a man named Mr. Sponsoon who was. The Strange Case of the Girl o' Mr. Sponsoon's Dreams. Ogden Nash. **CP-NashO**

Once upon a time there was a man named Mr. Donnybrook. The Strange Case of Mr. Donnybrooks's Boredom. Ogden Nash. **CP-NashO**

Once upon a time there was a man named Orlando Tregennis and he was in love with his wife. The Unselfish Husband. Ogden Nash. **CP-NashO**

Once upon a time there was a taxi-driver named Llewellyn Abdullah. The Strange Case of the Pleasing Taxi-Driver. Ogden Nash. **CP-NashO**

Once upon a time there was a young man named Harold Scrutiny. The Strange Case of the Irksome Prude. Ogden Nash. **CP-NashO**

Once upon a time there was an attorney named Mr. Ballantine. The Strange Case of Mr. Ballantine's Valentine. Ogden Nash. **CP-NashO**

Once upon a time there was an Italian. Columbus. Ogden Nash. **CP-NashO**

Once upon a time you dressed so fine. Like a Rolling Stone. "Bob Dylan." **CP-DylaB**

Once upon a today and yesterday and nevermore there were 7 men. Fable. Etheridge Knight. **SP-KnigE**

Once upon earth they stood. Dreams. Kathleen Jessie Raine. **SP-RainK**

Once, very sick, / late one night. Samoan Head. John Clellon Holmes. **SP-HolmJ**

Once was every woman the witch. Witches. Ted Hughes. **SP-HughT**

Once we feared The Beast—when he followed us we ran. Song of the Men's Side. Rudyard Kipling. **CP-KiplR**

Once we have driven past Mundo Nuevo trace. Crusoe's Journal. Derek Walcott. **CP-WalcD**

Once We Meant It. Thomas McGrath. **SP-McGrT**

Once we presumed to found ourselves for good. The Disappearing Island. Seamus Heaney. **SP-HeanS**

Once we were happy, we had no memories. Song of the River. Louise Glück. *Fr.* Marathon. **SP-GlücL**

Once we'd packed up your clothes. Partial Eclipse. William DeWitt Snodgrass. **SP-SnodW**

Once when I saw a cripple. Cripple. Carl Sandburg. **CP-SandC**

Once, when I wandered in the woods alone. Amaryllis. Edwin Arlington Robinson. **CP-RobiE**

Once when I was little and played on the hill. First Flight. Louise McNeill. **SP-McNeL**

Once when I was only eight or nine. First Funeral. John Hewitt. **CP-HewiJ**

Once when, like birds, we feared the hunter's gun. The Snare. Thomas Merton. **CP-MertT**

Once, when midnight smote the air. On Those That Hated "The Playboy of the Western World," 1907. William Butler Yeats. **CP-YeatW**

Once when my soul was newly shriven. The Light. Paul Laurence Dunbar. **CP-DunbP**

Once when our eyes were clean as noon, our rooms. Cana. Thomas Merton. **CP-MertT; SP-MertT**

Once, when the grand nudes, golden as fields of grain—. Trinc: Praises II. Thomas McGrath. **SP-McGrT**

Once when the snow of the year was beginning to fall. The Runaway. Robert Frost. **CP-FrosR**

Once when the white clouds praised you, Yorkshire. Rievaulx: St. Ailred. Thomas Merton. **CP-MertT**

Once when they found me, some refrain *"Quoi faire?".* John Berryman. *Fr.* Sonnets to Chris. **CP-BerrJ**

Once when we were younger. Simplicity. Gilbert Sorrentino. **SP-SorrG**

Once White & Gold / daisy in the dust. Edward Estlin Cummings. **CP-CummE**

Once with my mother and my grandmother. Brown's Bay, Islandmagee, Spring 1917. John Hewitt. **CP-HewiJ**

Once within, within for evermore: / There the long beatitudes begin. He Shall Go No More Out. Christina Georgina Rossetti. **CP-RosC2**

Once years ago / we listened to Bilbao. Camaradas Y Compañeros. John Hewitt. **CP-HewiJ**

Once you have let the first blade. The Salt Marsh. James Dickey. **CP-DickJ**

Once you said joking slyly, *If I'm killed.* The Faithful. Jane Cooper. **SP-CoopJ**

Ondumonde" / (first than caref. Edward Estlin Cummings. **CP-CummE**

One. Stephen Berg. **SP-BergS**

One. Tom Clark. **SP-ClarT**

One. Leonard Cohen. **CP-CoheL**

One, The. James Dickey. **CP-DickJ**

One. Langston Hughes. **SP-HughL**

One / man who will, The. Curse. Robert Creeley. **CP-CreeR**

One. Stephen Spender. **CP-SpenS**

One / t / hi / s / snowflake. Edward Estlin Cummings. **CP-CummE**

(One!) / the wisti-twisti barber. Edward Estlin Cummings. **CP-CummE**

One after 909. The Beatles. **CP-Beatl**

One after the other we consume one another. Men and Women (the Boltzmann Distribution). Chuck Miller. **SP-MillC**

One afternoon that May, just off the park. Agree. David Markson. **CP-MarkD**

One afternoon the last week in April. Axe Handles. Gary Snyder. **CP-SnydG**

One almost takes a hedge for granted. Stone Walls. Wystan Hugh Auden. **CP-AudWJ**

One among friends who stood above your grave. Auden's Funeral. Stephen Spender. **CP-SpenS**

One and. A Piece. Robert Creeley. **CP-CreeR**

One and One—are One. Emily Dickinson. **CP-DickE**

1 and 1 are 2—/ That's for me and you. Christina Georgina Rossetti. **CP-RosC2**

One, and then another, they settled before me like flakes of air. Dabney Stuart. **SP-StuaD**

(Killdeer.) **SP-StuaD**

One Anguish—in a Crowd. Emily Dickinson. **CP-DickE**

One ant turns backward. Hayden Carruth. **CP-CarHS** *Fr.* The Clay Hill Anthology.

One April dusk the. Edward Estlin Cummings. **CP-CummE**

One arch of the sky. Love in Labrador. Carl Sandburg. **CP-SandC**

One-armed, one-legged, and one-headed. Terms. Randall Jarrell. **CP-JarrR**

One Art. Elizabeth Bishop. **CP-BishE**

One ask'd me where the roses grew? The Rosarie. Robert Herrick. **CP-HerrR**

One before the Parthenon, before, The. Concluding Remarks. Leonard Nathan. **SP-NathL**

One Birth our Saviour had; the like none yet. Christs Birth. Robert Herrick. **CP-HerrR**

One Blessing had I than the rest. Emily Dickinson. **CP-DickE**

One bliss for which / There is no match. Taboo to Boot. Ogden Nash. **CP-NashO**

One Brief Hour of Grown-up Glory on the Gulf of Mexico. Nicholas Vachel Lindsay. *Fr.* Doctor Mohawk. **CP-LindV**

One by one I proclaim your songs. Three Nahuatl Poems. William Carlos Williams. **CP-WilW2**

One by one lights of a skyscraper fling their checkering cross work on the. The Skyscraper Loves Night. Carl Sandburg. **CP-SandC**

One by one the guests arrive. The Guests. Leonard Cohen. **CP-CoheL**

One by one, the words. Reading Hölderlin on the Patio with the Aid of a Dictionary. Rita Dove. **SP-DoveR**

One by one they appear in. My Sad Captains. Thom Gunn. **CP-GunnT**

One by Twachtman at the Frye. Richard Hugo. **CP-HugoR**

One called Next steps up, The. Hayden Carruth. *Fr.* Paragraphs. **CP-CarHS**

One can be tolerant with a bore. Tolerance. David Herbert Lawrence. **CP-LawrD**

One can do one begins to one can only. Reincarnation (II). James Dickey. **CP-DickJ**

One can say more of sunlight. Light is Speech. Marianne Craig Moore. **CP-MoorM**

One cannot lose what one has not possessed. Coplas. Geoffrey Hill. *Fr.* The Songbook of Sebastian Arrurruz. **CP-HillG**

One cannot now help thinking. Now It's Happened. David Herbert Lawrence. **CP-LawrD**

One can't / have it. Coming Right Up. Archie Randolph Ammons. **SP-AmmoA**

One cantaloupe is ripe and lush. The Cantaloupe. Ogden Nash. **CP-NashO**

One Certainty, The. Christina Georgina Rossetti. **CP-RosC1**

One chemical afternoon in mid-autumn. Contrary Theses (II). Wallace Stevens. **CP-StevW**

One Christmas Eve my grandmother fell ill. The Filled Stocking. John Hewitt. **CP-HewiJ**

One Christmas-time, / The day before the holidays began. William Wordsworth. **RB** Imagination, How Impaired and Restored. *Fr.* The Prelude; Growth of a Poet's Mind [1805 vers.]. **CP-WorW3**

One Circumlocution. Wystan Hugh Auden. **CP-AudeW**

One clear glass slipper; a slender blue single-rose vase. Cranston Near the City Line. Ted Berrigan. **SP-BerrT**

One cloud in the sky comes from Greece. Paestum. James Dickey. **CP-DickJ**

One Comes Back. Pablo Neruda, *tr. fr. Spanish by* Ben Belitt. **SP-NeruP**

One cop holds the spic delicately between thumb and forefinger. The Jet Must Be Hunting for Something. Robert Penn Warren. **SP-WarrR**

One creature, not the mollusk. Sleeping with You. John Updike. **CP-UpdiJ**

One crown that no one seeks. Emily Dickinson. **CP-DickE**

One Crucifixion is recorded—only. Emily Dickinson. **CP-DickE**

One damn time (7th inning), The. The Ball Game. Robert Creeley. **CP-CreeR**

One Day. Robert Creeley. **CP-CreeR**

One day / Marilyn marched. Chic Freedom's Reflection. Alice Walker. **CP-WalkA**

One Day ("One day I decided..."). Grace Paley. **CP-PaleG**

One Day ("One day lying on my stomach..."). Grace Paley. **CP-PaleG**

One Day. Christina Georgina Rossetti. **CP-RosC1**

One day 3 poets & 60 ears sat under a green-striped Chataqua tent in Aurora. Nagasaki Days. Allen Ginsberg. **CP-GinsA**

One day a nigger. Edward Estlin Cummings. **CP-CummE**

One Day a Woman. Miller Williams. **SP-WillM**

One day a woman picking peaches in Georgia. One Day a Woman. Miller Williams. **SP-WillM**

One day, along the electric wire. Rantoul. John Greenleaf Whittier. **CP-WhitJ**

One day, an obscure youth, a wanderer. Ambition. Walt Whitman. **CP-WhitW**

One day as he did raunge the fields abroad. The Vision of the Graces. Edmund Spenser. **NoSic** *Fr.* The Faerie Queene. **CP-Spens**

One day at a time. And one barn. Scene. Richard Hugo. **CP-HugoR**

One day at work he cried. Grace Paley. *Fr.* Stanzas: Old Age and the Conventions of Retirement Have Driven My Friends from the Work They Love. **CP-PaleG**

One day He. The Fury of God's Good-bye. Anne Sexton. *Fr.* The Furies. **CP-SextA**

One day, his mother took him on the tram. Portrait of the Artist I. Charles Tomlinson. **CP-TomlC**

One day I forgot Jerusalem and my right arm is withered. A Warning. Grace Paley. **CP-PaleG**

One day I wrote her name upon the strand. Edmund Spenser. **AWP; ArLo; BLPL; BoLoP; CABA; CBLP; EBEV; EPCY; EiL; FiP; GBL; HAP; HBV; HeiP; ImPo; InPS; LiTB; NAEL-1; NoP; NoSic; OAEL-1; OAEP; PAI; PBMP; PoE; SeCePo; SeCeV; Son; TFi; WeW** *Fr.* Amoretti. **CP-Spens**

One day in April. Softly Softly. Richard Shelton. **SP-ShelR**

One day in early Spring. Song: Fig Tree in Leaf. Robert Ranke Graves. **CP-GravR**

One day in Paradise. Quietness. William Carlos Williams. **CP-WilW1**

One Day is there of the Series. Emily Dickinson. **CP-DickE**

One day it thundered and lightened. Adam, Lilith, and Eve. Robert Browning. **CP-BroR2**

One day it will vanish. The Vanishings. Stephen Dunn. **SP-DunnS**

One day Moongod wanted to send a message to man. Hare's Message. Thomas Merton. *Fr.* Two Moralities. *Fr.* South. *Fr.* The Geography of Lograire. **CP-MertT**

One day music / begins. Hayden Carruth. *Fr.* North Winter. **CP-CarHL**

One Day of Autumn. Charles Tomlinson. **CP-TomlC**

One day out in right field. Thurman's Slumping Blues. Paul Zimmer. **SP-ZimmP**

One day Sun found a new canyon. People of the South Wind. William Stafford. **SP-StafW**

One day Sweeney went to Drum Iarann in Connacht. Sweeney in Connacht. Seamus Heaney. **SP-HeanS**

One day the god of fond desire. James Thomson. **CP-ThomJ**

(To the God of Fond Desire.) **CP-ThomJ**

One day the nouns were clustered in the street. Permanently. Kenneth Koch. **SP-KochK**

One day the water merchants came. Fable of the Water Merchants. Stephen Dunn. **SP-DunnS**

One day they argued whence their family name. The Covenanter's Grave. John Hewitt. **CP-HewiJ**

One day we lay beneath an apple tree. One Day We Played a Game. Countee Cullen. **CP-CullC**

One day we notice that the sun. Feeding the Sun. Bill Knott. **SP-KnotB**

One Day We Played a Game. Countee Cullen. **CP-CullC**

One day when I am written off as dead. The Half-Finished Letter. Robert Ranke Graves. **CP-GravR**

One day, whiles that my daylie cares did sleepe. Edmund Spenser. *Fr.* Visions of the World's Vanity [*or* Vanitie]. **CP-Spens**

One day you finally knew. The Journey. Mary Oliver. **SP-OlivM**

One day you'll look to see I've gone. I'll Follow the Sun. The Beatles. **CP-Beatl**

One debarred from enrollment at Harvard. In Lieu of the Lyre. Marianne Craig Moore. **CP-MoorM**

1. Deck the halls with git. Xmas. Gary Gildner. **SP-GildG**

One died, and the soul was wrenched out. Street Musicians. John Ashbery. **SP-AshbJ**

One dignity delays for all. Emily Dickinson. **CP-DickE**

One doctor in a Piper Cub. A Hot Night in Wheat Country. Ted Kooser. **SP-KoosT**

One does not expect to see them, out there. Sails on All Saints' Day. John Updike. **CP-UpdiJ**

One does not feel hatred. Not Hatred. Edwin Rolfe. **CP-RolfE**

One does not quarry this mountain. Whitman. John Gould Fletcher. **SP-FletJ**

One dot / Grainily shifting we at roadside and. The Bee. James Dickey. **CP-DickJ**

One Drunk Allegory. Robert Penn Warren. **SP-WarrR**

One Dull Thing You Did Was to Die, Fletcher, The. John Ciardi. **SP-CiarJ**

One Eare tingles; some there be. On Himselfe ("One Eare tingles; some there be"). Robert Herrick. **CP-HerrR**

One earring's smile. Summery Weather. Kenneth Koch. **SP-KochK**

One evening Eros took me by the hand. To the Bitter Sweet-heart: a Dream. Wilfred Owen. **CP-OwenW**

One evening (surely I was led by her). William Wordsworth. **FaBoPP; OBRV; RB** *Fr.* Introduction—Childhood and School-Time. *Fr.* The Prelude; Growth of a Poet's Mind [1805 vers.]. **CP-WorW3**

(Boat Stealing.) **RB**

(On Ullsawater.) **FaBoPP**

One ever hangs where shelled roads part. At a Calvary near the Ancre. Wilfred Owen. **CP-OwenW**

One Eye? a thousand rather, and a Thousand more. It Is Better To Go into Heaven with One Eye. Richard Crashaw. **CP-CrasR**

One-Eye, Two-Eyes, Three-Eyes. Anne Sexton. **CP-SextA**

One face looks out from all his canvas[s]es. In an Artist's Studio. Christina Georgina Rossetti. **CP-RosC3**

One face, two face, three. True Numbers. Charles Olson. **CP-OlsoC**

One failure on. Their Sex Life. Archie Randolph Ammons. **SP-AmmoA**

One fairest of the ripe unwedded left. George Meredith. *Fr.* The Sage Enamoured and the Honest Lady. **CP-MerG1**

One fairest of the ripe unwedded left. The Sage Enamoured and the Honest Lady. George Meredith. **CP-MerG1**

One faith is bondage. Two. A Homecoming. Wendell Berry. **CP-BerrW**

One feather is a bird. The Voice. Theodore Roethke. **CP-RoetT**

One feeds on Lard, and yet is leane. Littlenesse No Cause of Leanesse. Robert Herrick. **CP-HerrR**

One fellow turns all. Kingpin. Archie Randolph Ammons. **SP-AmmoA**

(One fine day) / let's take the train. Edward Estlin Cummings. **CP-CummE**

One fire than other burnes more forcibly, *ad. fr. Latin of* Pausanius. Sir Walter Ralegh. **CP-RaleW**

One flick of the wrist / and heat from the baseboards. Warmth. Brendan Galvin. **SP-GalvB**

One Flight Up. Jim Carroll. **SP-CarrJ**

One foot down, then hop! It's hot. Harlem Hopscotch. Maya Angelou. **SP-AngeM**

One Foot on Sea, and One on Shore. Christina Georgina Rossetti. **CP-RosC2**

One for Beauty. Leonard Nathan. **SP-NathL**

One for Old Snaggle-Tooth. Charles Bukowski. **SP-BukC1**

One for the Chevalier. Vir XI. James Liddy. *Fr.* Vir I–XII. **CP-LiddJ**

One for the Ladies at the Troy Laundry Who Cooled Themselves for Zimmer. Paul Zimmer. **SP-ZimmP**

One for the Old Boy. Charles Bukowski. **SP-BukC3**

One for the Road. Martin Edmunds. **SP-EdmuM**

One for the Rose. Philip Levine. **SP-LeviP**

One for the Roses. Jean Garrigue. **SP-GarrJ**

One for the Shoeshine Man. Charles Bukowski. **SP-BukC1**

One Forever Alien. Howard Nemerov. **CP-NemeH**

One friend. Louis Zukofsky. **CP-ZukLS**

1 from 9 is 8. Alice Faye at Ruby Foo's. James Schuyler. **CP-SchuJ**

One from the ends of the earth—gifts at an open door. The Song of the Sons. Rudyard Kipling. **CP-KiplR**

One gable towards the road, one towards the slope. Cushkib Fair. John Hewitt. **CP-HewiJ**

1. Get smart with general biggle in the quadrangle of math and fun. Twenty Three Point Prospectus for Small College in the Badlands. Thomas Merton. **CP-MertT**

One-gloved beasts in cleats, they come clattering. Golfers. John Updike. **CP-UpdiJ**

One gold, one silver, one lead: who thinks. The Theme of the Three Caskets. William Matthews. **SP-MattW**

One granite ridge. Piute Creek. Gary Snyder. **CP-SnydG**

One grief on me is laid. The Burden. Rudyard Kipling. **CP-KiplR** *Fr.* Debits and Credits.

One Guess. Robert Frost. *Fr.* Ten Mills. **CP-FrosR**

One had a fair body, / One a lovely face. Nettles of Offence. John Hewitt. **CP-HewiJ**

One had a lovely face. Memory. William Butler Yeats. **CP-YeatW**

One half / lives in sunlight; he is. Divided, the Man is Dreaming. John Haines. **SP-HainJ**

One half-dark night my father. Rudiments. Roy Fisher. **SP-FishR**

One hand washes the other. Ralph Waldo Emerson. **CP-EmerR**

I. "Happy ye leaves whenas those lily [*or* lilly] hands." Edmund Spenser. **EBEV; LoBV; NAEL-1; NIP; OAEL-1; PoE; Son** *Fr.* Amoretti. **CP-Spens**

One Hard Look. Robert Ranke Graves. **CP-GravR**

One has flippers. This one is like a seal. The Ones that Are Thrown Out. Miller Williams. **SP-WillM**

One Home. William Stafford. **SP-StafW**

One Hour to Madness and Joy. Walt Whitman. **CP-WhitW**

One human hellgrammite that I think we could all dispense with. King Leer. Ogden Nash. **CP-NashO**

One Hundred and Ninety-Nine Pounds of Clay Leaning Forward. Charles Bukowski. **SP-BukC2**

108 East 19th. William Stafford. **SP-StafW**

One hundred feet from off the ground. Long-Suffering of God. Christopher Smart. **LAuP; NOCV** *Fr.* Hymns for the Amusement of Children. **SP-SmarC**

107 Poems. Roy Fisher. **SP-FishR**

107th & Amsterdam. William Matthews. **SP-MattW**

I. 13. Elegy: Ad Auroram, ne properet. Ovid. **CP-MarlC**, *tr. by* Christopher Marlowe; *Fr.* Elegies.

103 Degrees. Charles Bukowski. **SP-BukC1**

125th Street. Langston Hughes. **SP-HughL**

One hundred years ago, the last of the Cæsars. 1921. John Gould Fletcher. **SP-FletJ** *Fr.* The Parables of Christ.

One hymn more, O my lyre! Hymns from the French of Lamartine. John Greenleaf Whittier. **CP-WhitJ**

One I Loved, The. John Hewitt. **CP-HewiJ**

1. I will tell you what you can do ask me if you do not understand what I just said. Proverbs. Thomas Merton. **CP-MertT**

One image of success. Cemaes Songs. Steve Griffiths. **SP-GrifS**

One imagines a surgeon to be. Surgeons. Robert Creeley. **CP-CreeR**

One imagines himself / addressing his peers. To C. T. George Oppen. **CP-OppeG**

One in my hand. The Juggler to His Audience. Bill Knott. **SP-KnotB**

One in the Public Gallery. Walter de la Mare. **CP-DeLaW**

One Inch Tall. Shel Silverstein. **SP-SilS2**

One Incident of Many. William Dickey. **SP-DickW**

One innocent spring. Now Long Ago. Maya Angelou. **SP-AngeM**

One instant of morning. The Greeting. Charles Tomlinson. **CP-TomlC**

One is large and lazy. The Furies. May Sarton. **SP-SartM**

One Jay at a Time. John Ciardi. **SP-CiarJ**

One joy of so much anguish. Emily Dickinson. **CP-DickE**

One kind of person when catching a train always wants to allow. We Don't Need to Leave Yet, Do We? Or, Yes We Do. Ogden Nash. **CP-NashO**

One kiss, dear Maid! I said and sigh'd. The Kiss. Samuel Taylor Coleridge. *Fr.* Effusions. **CP-ColeS**

One-l lama, / He's a priest, The. The Lama. Ogden Nash. **CP-NashO**

One lady poet was a nymphomaniac and wrote for Vanity Fair. The Lady Poets With Foot Notes. Ernest Hemingway. **CP-HemiE**

One last night under a pink sky. Dust. Stephen Berg. **SP-BergS**

One Law for the Lion and Ox is Oppression. Standings. Donald Davie. **CP-DavDo**

One leaf on a line. So Little It Can Take. Phoebe Hesketh. **SP-HeskP**

One leaves his leaves at home. Great Mullen. William Carlos Williams. **CP-WilW1**

One-Legged Man, The. Anne Sexton. **CP-SextA**

One lesson, Nature, let me learn of [*or* from] thee. Quiet Work. Matthew Arnold. **SP-ArnoM**

One Life. Paul Laurence Dunbar. **CP-DunbP**

One Life of so much Consequence! Emily Dickinson. **CP-DickE**

One likes to see a laggard rook's high. Combat Cultural. Marianne Craig Moore. **CP-MoorM**

One lives by commerce, said the guide. Guide to the Ruins. Howard Nemerov. **CP-NemeH**

One Look at the Creation. Martin Edmunds. **SP-EdmuM**

One look at this mill and the adjacent croft. Mill at Romesdal. Richard Hugo. **CP-HugoR**

One looks from the train. The Orient Express. Randall Jarrell. **CP-JarrR; SP-JarrR**

One loves the temporal, some unique manifestation. "Hugh MacDiarmid." **SP-MacDH** *Fr.* The Battle Continues.

One luncheon party in Andy's rooms in Magdalene. Meeting. John Berryman. **CP-BerrJ**

One lutenist played *look*; your through was *drink*. Louis Zukofsky. **CP-ZukLS**

One man except, the only son of light. The Flood. John Milton. **NOSC** *Fr.* Book XI. *Fr.* Paradise Lost. **CP-MiltJ**

One man in a house. To Landrum Guy, Beginning to Write at Sixty. James Dickey. **CP-DickJ**

One man in a thousand, Solomon says. The Thousandth Man. Rudyard Kipling. **CP-KiplR**

One man in me is locked inside an oakwomb. The Man Locked Inside the Oak. Robert Bly. **SP-BlyR**

One man killed another. The saying between them had been "I'd give you." Hate. Carl Sandburg. **CP-SandC**

One man repentant is of more esteem. A Position in the Hebrew Divinity. Robert Herrick. **CP-HerrR**

One man shall smile one day and say goodbye. Cambodia. James Fenton. **SP-FentJ**

One Man Walking a Deserted Platform. Philip Larkin. **CP-LarkP**

One Man's Meed Is Another Man's Overemphasis. Ogden Nash. **CP-NashO**

One master, aged, as I am, thirty-two. Marilyn Hacker. *Fr.* The Regent's Park Sonnets. **SP-HackM**

One may define eternity in various ways. The Touch. Frederick Morgan. **SP-MorgF**

One may say courage. A Kind of Garden: A Poem for my Sister. George Oppen. **CP-OppeG**

One memorial stone reads. Carl Sandburg. *Fr.* The People, Yes. **CP-SandC**

One midnight, after a day when lilies. Digging. Donald Hall. **CP-HallD**

One might believe that natural miseries. October, 1803 ("One might believe that natural miseries"). William Wordsworth. **CP-WorW1**

One might talk of the sanity of the atom. The Sane Universe. David Herbert Lawrence. **CP-LawrD**

One mile more is. News for Her Mother. Thomas Hardy. **CP-HardT**

One misty evening, one another's guide. Iris by Night. Robert Frost. **CP-FrosR**

One Modern Poet. Carl Sandburg. **CP-SandC**

One moment bid the horses wait. A Ballade of Jakko Hill. Rudyard Kipling. **CP-KiplR**

One Moment in Eternity. Howard Nemerov. **CP-NemeH**

One moment past our bodies cast. Morning Song in the Jungle. Rudyard Kipling. **CP-KiplR** *Fr.* Letting in the Jungle. *Fr.* The Second Jungle Book.

One moment you are stabbed with a white flag. The Butterfly and the Bull. Charles Henri Ford. **SP-FordC**

One Month. Muriel Rukeyser. **CP-RukeM**

One moonlight, in the simple-colored night, The. Note on Moonlight. Wallace Stevens. **CP-StevW**

One More Brevity. Robert Frost. **CP-FrosR**

One more by Thee, Love, and Desert have sent. To Mistresse Mary Willand. Robert Herrick. **CP-HerrR**

One more casualty. To Clio, Muse of History. Howard Nemerov. **CP-NemeH**

One More Cup of Coffee (Valley Below). "Bob Dylan." **CP-DylaB**

One more day gone, / done, found in / the form of days. Again. Robert Creeley. **CP-CreeR**

One More New Botched Beginning. Stephen Spender. **CP-SpenS**

One More Night. "Bob Dylan." **CP-DylaB**

One More Round. Maya Angelou. **SP-AngeM**

One More Time. Richard Shelton. **SP-ShelR**

One More Weekend. "Bob Dylan." **CP-DylaB**

One morn before me were three figures seen. Ode on Indolence. John Keats. **CP-KeatJ**

One Morning. John Ciardi. **SP-CiarJ**

One morning / the wind scouring. The Death of See. William Carlos Williams. **CP-WilW1**

One morning a great gaggle slid. When Angels Came to Zimmer. Paul Zimmer. **SP-ZimmP**

One morning a whole people. The Chosen. Leonard Nathan. **SP-NathL**

One morning early I met armoured cars. The Toome Road. Seamus Heaney. **SP-HeanS**

One morning I put in the pocket of my shirt. Believing in Symbols. Miller Williams. **SP-WillM**

One morning I shall find. Maisie. James Merrill. **SP-MerrJ**

One morning in my first winter. John Haines. *Fr.* Homestead. **SP-HainJ**

One morning in the month of June. The Blackbird. Derek Mahon. **SP-MahoD**

One morning of the first sad Fall. A Lay of Old Time. John Greenleaf Whittier. **CP-WhitJ**

One morning (raw it was and wet—). The Sailor's Mother. William Wordsworth. **CP-WorW1**

One morning the Grand Seigneur. The Great Horned Owl. Charles Simic. **SP-SimiC**

One morning you step out, still in pajamas. Saturday, March 6. John Ciardi. **SP-CiarJ**

One most like himself is not this mirror's, The. Himself. Daniel Gerard Hoffman. **SP-HoffD**

One mummy walks on snow. Mummies. Nicanor Parra, *tr. fr. Spanish by* Thomas Merton. **CP-MertT**

One musician is sure. The Harp. Ralph Waldo Emerson. **CP-EmerR**

One must have a mind of winter. The Snow Man. Wallace Stevens. **CP-StevW**

One name becomes two—Siegfried and Sassoon (or stop and shop. A Different Prince. John Yau. **SP-YauJo**

One need not be a Chamber—to be Haunted. Emily Dickinson. **CP-DickE**

One night as I did wander. Fragment, A. Robert Burns. **CP-BurnR**

One night he dreamed of a palace fair. Ralph Waldo Emerson. **CP-EmerR**

One Night I Burned. Leonard Cohen. **CP-CoheL**

One night I reached a cave: I slept, my head. Incident on a Journey. Thom Gunn. **CP-GunnT**

One night i' th' yeare [or in the year], my dearest Beauties, come. To His Lovely Mistresses. Robert Herrick. **CP-HerrR**

One night I thirsted like a prince. Diabetes. James Dickey. **CP-DickJ**

One night in a dream. Kathleen Jessie Raine. Fr. The Hollow Hill. **SP-RainK**

One night in Albany. Drunks. John Berryman. **CP-BerrJ**

One night in my room, still and beamless. The Phantom Kiss. Paul Laurence Dunbar. **CP-DunbP**

One Night in Oz. Ogden Nash. **CP-NashO**

One Night Ma / Lay with Pa. Charles Olson. **CP-OlsoC**

One Night Stand. Charles Bukowski. **SP-BukC2**

One night the water lay so deathly still. The Oldest Killed Lake in North America. Hayden Carruth. **CP-CarHS**

One night we find ourselves near the giant's house. Near the Giant's House. Robert Bly. **SP-BlyR**

One nonsufficiently inunderstood. Edward Estlin Cummings. **CP-CummE**

One noonday, at my window in the town. Ball's Bluff. Herman Melville. **SP-MelvH**

One note, a daisy, and a photograph. John Berryman. Fr. Sonnets to Chris. **CP-BerrJ**

1. Now you are all here you might as well know this is America we do what we like. Thomas Merton. **CP-MertT**

"One oak fool box";—the pun. Louis Zukofsky. **CP-ZukLS**

One o'clock in the letter-box. The Meeting. Muriel Rukeyser. **CP-RukeM**

One of Annie's forks is doing time. The Fork of Annie. Marsden Hartley. **CP-HartM**

One of God's creatures, just as much as you. Snake. Robert Lowell. **SP-LoweR**

One of her hands one of her cheeks lay under. A Supplement of an Imperfect Copy of Verses of Mr. William Shakespeare's, By the Author. Sir John Suckling. **CP-SuckJ**

One of Many. Stevie Smith. **CP-SmitS**

One of my wishes is that those dark trees. Into My Own. Robert Frost. **CP-FrosR**

One of the / things I found out by being. 1837 War in Retrospect. Margaret Atwood. **SP-AtwM1**

One of the Cherokees in Oklahoma, having a million or so from oil. Carl Sandburg. Fr. The People, Yes. **CP-SandC**

One of the Crowd on the Shore Tells How It Was. Miller Williams. **SP-WillM**

One of the Dead. Christina Georgina Rossetti. **CP-RosC3**

One of the five straight branches of my hand. Upon the Losse of His Finger. Robert Herrick. **CP-HerrR**

One of the foremost organs of beauty. The Back. Karl Shapiro. **SP-ShapK**

One of the hardest explanations to be found. I'm Sure She Said Six-Thirty. Ogden Nash. **CP-NashO**

One of the Hottest. Charles Bukowski. **SP-BukC1**

One of the Inhabitants of the West. Wallace Stevens. **CP-StevW**

One of the lizards. One. Leonard Cohen. **CP-CoheL**

One of the Muses. Charles Kenneth Williams. **CP-WillC**

One of the ones that Midas touched. Emily Dickinson. **CP-DickE**

One of the Principal Causes of War. "Hugh MacDiarmid." **SP-MacDH**

One of the Signers. John Greenleaf Whittier. **CP-WhitJ**

One of the Soldiers with a Spear Pierced His Side. Christina Georgina Rossetti. **CP-RosC2**

One of the surprises of nature. Tree Swallows. Richard Eberhart. **CP-EberR**

One of the two according to your choice. Haidee. Byron. SeCePo Fr. Canto the Fourth. Fr. Don Juan. **CP-Byron**

"One of the wits of the school" your chum would say. Your Birthday in Wisconsin You Are 140. John Berryman. **CP-BerrJ**

One of These Days. Leonard Cohen. **CP-CoheL**

One of These Days. Lawrence Ferlinghetti. **SP-FerlL**

One of These Nights. Derek Mahon. **SP-MahoD**

One of those great, garishly emerald flies that always look freshly generated from fresh excrement. My Fly. Charles Kenneth Williams. **SP-WillC**

One of those impossibly lonely. Still Lives. Al Young. **CP-YounA**

One of Those Rare Occurrences on a City Bus. Miller Williams. **SP-WillM**

One of Us Cannot Be Wrong. Leonard Cohen. **CP-CoheL**

One of Us Must Know (Sooner or Later). "Bob Dylan." **CP-DylaB**

One of us said, how odd. Hilda Doolittle. **NALW** Fr. Tribute to the Angels. **CP-DoolH**

One of us would spot his horse, same white. Time to Remember Sangster. Richard Hugo. **CP-HugoR**

One of you is a major, made of cord and catskin. Lent in a Year of War. Thomas Merton. **CP-MertT; SP-MertT**

One, one / Lives all alone. Perpetual Motion. Thomas McGrath. **SP-McGrT**

One onely fire has Hell; but yet it shall. Hell Fire. Robert Herrick. **CP-HerrR**

One or Two. I've Finished. Gertrude Stein. **CP-SteiG**

One or Two Things. Mary Oliver. **SP-OlivM**

One ought not to have to care. The Hill Wife. Robert Frost. **CP-FrosR**

One ought not to have to care. Loneliness. Robert Frost. **FaBoEn; VGW** Fr. The Hill Wife. **CP-FrosR**

One parson, one poet, one belman, one crier. William Cowper. **CP-CowpW**

One Parting. Carl Sandburg. **CP-SandC**

One passed me like a flash of lightning by. For One Sake. Christina Georgina Rossetti. **CP-RosC3**

One person present steps on his pedal of speech. The Talker. Mona Van Duyn. **SP-VanDM**

One petal to her mind. Passionate Rebuke. Marsden Hartley. **CP-HartM**

One poet used to take. Beauti-ful. Charles Bukowski. **SP-BukC3**

One Queen Artemisa, as old stories tell. Another [Epigram on Said Occasion]. Robert Burns. **CP-BurnR**

One Ralph Blossom Soliloquizes. Thomas Hardy. **CP-HardT**

One: recalling going somewhere. See America First. Gilbert Sorrentino. **SP-SorrG**

One Remains, The. Wilfred Owen. **CP-OwenW**

One remains, the many change and pass, The. Percy Bysshe Shelley. **SCV** Fr. Adonais; An Elegy on the Death of John Keats. **CP-ShelP**

One remembers hysterical laughter. Land of Cotton. Gilbert Sorrentino. **SP-SorrG**

One rope one single twist one sole man. Uncertain of the Crime. Paul Éluard, tr. fr. French by William Carlos Williams. **CP-WilW2**

One royal afternoon. Birdcage Walk. Thomas Merton. **CP-MertT; SP-MertT**

One said, because I saw the leaf. Raindrop. John Hewitt. **CP-HewiJ**

One Sea-Side Grave. Christina Georgina Rossetti. **CP-RosC2**

One seem'd all dark and red--a tract of sand. Tennyson. **UnPo** Fr. The Palace of Art. **CP-TennA**

One seems to have / a wheel and stick arrangment. The Last Open-Air Concert. Brendan Galvin. **SP-GalvB**

1 September 1939. John Berryman. **CP-BerrJ**

One should have known, I suppose, that you can't even trust. An Annual and Perennial Problem. Mona Van Duyn. **SP-VanDM**

"One Should Not Talk to a Skilled Hunter about What Is Forbidden by the Buddha", Hsiang-yen. Gary Snyder. **CP-SnydG**

One Side of the Story. Stephen Dunn. **SP-DunnS**

One sigh stretches heaven. O Lull Me, Lull Me. Theodore Roethke. **CP-RoetT**

One silent night of late. The Cheat of Cupid; or, The Ungentle Guest. Robert Herrick. **CP-HerrR**

One silver spoon shines in the house of Croot. Upon Croot. Robert Herrick. **CP-HerrR**

One simple and effective rhyme. Woodpigeons at Raheny. Donald Davie. **CP-DavDo**

One sister for sale! For Sale. Shel Silverstein. **SP-SilS2**

One Sister have I in our house. Emily Dickinson. **CP-DickE**

One slipslouch twi / tterstamp. Edward Estlin Cummings. **CP-CummE**

One small joy still left. Notes from Robin Hill Cottage. Hayden Carruth. **CP-CarHS**

One small soldier going towards the mountain. Another Old Tale. Jenny Joseph. **SP-JoseJ**

One Soldier. Muriel Rukeyser. **CP-RukeM**

One Son North to Naples. Richard Hugo. **CP-HugoR**

One Song, America, Before I Go. Walt Whitman. **CP-WhitW**

One sorrow more? I thought the tale complete. Whom the Lord Loveth He Chasteneth. Christina Georgina Rossetti. **CP-RosC2**

One sound. Then the hiss and whir. The Garden. Louise Glück. **SP-GlücL**

One spring the circus gave. A Hill of Beans. Rita Dove. **SP-DoveR**

One stabbe could not fierce Cato's Life unty. Pentadius, tr. fr. Latin by Richard Lovelace. **CP-LoveR**

One star in the dark pass of the houses. tr. fr. the German of Rilke. Randall Jarrell. **CP-JarrR**

One star is for Alaska. Flag. Shel Silverstein. **SP-SilS2**

One step more, and the race is ended; / One word more, and the lesson's done. Septuagesima. Christina Georgina Rossetti. **CP-RosC2**

One Step Taken Backward. Robert Frost. **CP-FrosR**

One Struggle More, and I Am Free. Byron. **CP-Byron**

One sudden week (the roads still salty,). Styles of Bloom. John Updike. **CP-UpdiJ**

One summer evening (led by her) I found. William Wordsworth. **FiP; NU** *Fr.* Introduction—Childhood and School-Time. **EnRP; FHYEP** *Fr.* The Prelude; Growth of a Poet's Mind [1850 vers.]. **CP-WorW3**

(Lines: "One summer evening (led by her) I found.") **NU**

One summer, like a stone. Stanley Jasspon Kunitz. *Fr.* What of the Night? **CP-KuniS**

One summer Sunday in the old Queen's time. A Victorian Steps Out. John Hewitt. **CP-HewiJ**

One summer they stayed with her family at their cabin; peeling paint. The Noise of Life. John Yau. **SP-YauJo**

One Sunday afternoon by the shuttered corner shop. Releases. Roy Fisher. **SP-FishR**

One Sunday in 1966. Isabella Gardner. **CP-GardI**

One sung of thee who left the tale untold. Fragment: A Tale Untold. Percy Bysshe Shelley. **CP-ShelP**

One Swallow Does Not Make a Summer. Christina Georgina Rossetti. **CP-RosC3**

One sweltering Sunday afternoon in August. Frederick Morgan. *Fr.* Death Mother. **SP-MorgF**

One that is ever kind said yesterday. The Folly of Being Comforted. William Butler Yeats. **CP-YeatW**

1. The shield. Three Functions of Irony. Thomas McGrath. **SP-McGrT**

One, the summer fire. The Two Fires. Margaret Atwood. **SP-AtwM1**

One thing / done, the. Robert Creeley. **CP-CreeR**

One thing about the past. Ho, Varlet! My Two Cents' Worth of Penny Postcard! Ogden Nash. **CP-NashO**

One Thing and Another. Archie Randolph Ammons. **SP-AmmoA**

One thing does not exist: Oblivion. Everness. Jorge Luis Borges, *tr. fr. Spanish by* Richard Wilbur. **CP-WilbR**

One thing has a shelving bank. A Drumlin Woodchuck. Robert Frost. **CP-FrosR**

One thing is certain, we've got to take hands off love. Love. David Herbert Lawrence. **CP-LawrD**

One thing of it we borrow. Emily Dickinson. **CP-DickE**

One thing that is bow-legged. Rainbow. David Herbert Lawrence. **CP-LawrD**

One thing the old will never understand, The. Stop It. David Herbert Lawrence. **CP-LawrD**

One Third of a Calendar. Ogden Nash. **CP-NashO**

One Thought Ever at the Fore. Walt Whitman. **CP-WhitW**

One thought the recurring "image" in the poet's song. Handbook of Versification. Gilbert Sorrentino. **SP-SorrG**

One thousand pounds per annuum. What Tottles Meant. "Lewis Carroll." **CP-CarrL** *Fr.* Sylvie and Bruno Concluded.

One time / there was Rene who. Ass But No Class. Charles Bukowski. **SP-BukC3**

One time I thought that sunset's flaming air. Fair Cuirass Shattered. Allen Tate. **CP-TateA**

One time I was invited to see Croce. Love among The Ruins. Richard Eberhart. **CP-EberR**

One time Wind World. Wind World. William Stafford. **SP-StafW**

One to one / walking talk, The. Walking the Dog. Robert Creeley. **CP-CreeR**

One to the Breastplate. Charles Bukowski. **SP-BukC1**

One Too Many Mornings. "Bob Dylan." **CP-DylaB**

One trouble with a cough. Can I Get You a Glass of Water? or, Please Close the Glottis after You. Ogden Nash. **CP-NashO**

One tug pounds to haul an afternoon. West Marginal Way. Richard Hugo. **CP-HugoR**

One, two, three, four / Can I have a little more. All Together Now. John Lennon *and* Paul McCartney. **CP-Beatl**

One two three four five, six and one, seven. Mad Poem: Wind Blowing Through the Shack. Malcolm Lowry. **CP-LowrM**

One used and butchered me: another spied. Raped and Revenged. Rudyard Kipling. *Fr.* Epitaphs of the War [1914–1918]. **CP-KiplR**

One Viceroy Resigns. Rudyard Kipling. **CP-KiplR**

One Volume Missing. Rita Dove. **SP-DoveR**

One Voter out of Sixteen. Robert Penn Warren. *Fr.* Fall Comes in Back-Country Vermont. **SP-WarrR**

One wading a Fall meadow finds on all sides. The Beautiful Changes. Richard Wilbur. **CP-WilbR**

One wants a Teller in a time like this. Gwendolyn Brooks. **SP-BrooG** *Fr.* The Womanhood.

One wants to say to them: even Florida, if they'd have just left even Florida alone. Every Man His Own Matador; or for That Matter Any Member of the Family. Charles Olson. **CP-OlsoC**

One was put in the lockup. My Poets. Philip Levine. **SP-LeviP**

One Way. Robert Creeley. **CP-CreeR**

One Way. Howard Nemerov. **CP-NemeH**

One way of going is to bang the door your last time. Wheel of Fortune. Richard Hugo. **CP-HugoR**

One Way of Love. Robert Browning. **CP-BroR1**

One way there was of muting in the mind. Edna St. Vincent Millay. *Fr.* Sonnets from an Ungrafted Tree. **CP-MillE**

One-Way Ticket. Langston Hughes. **SP-HughL**

One way to be very happy is to be very rich. Lines Indited with All the Depravity of Poverty. Ogden Nash. **CP-NashO**

One We Knew. Thomas Hardy. **CP-HardT**

One week of early morning sunshine, like a perfect rose frozen. Cannon Beach. Diane Wakoski. **SP-WakoD**

One West Coast. Al Young. **CP-YounA**

One whistle, a short husky breath. Not There. Tess Gallagher. **SP-GallT**

One who could repeat the Summer day, The. Emily Dickinson. **CP-DickE**

One who gave the warning with his wings, The. Exile. Karl Shapiro. **CRP** *Fr.* Adam and Eve. **SP-ShapK**

One who has loved the hills and died, a man. Pony Rock. Archibald MacLeish. **CP-MacLA**

One who lights the wood stove, The. February. Charles Simic. **SP-SimiC**

One Who Married above Him. Thomas Hardy. **CP-HardT**

One who sees giant Orion, the torches of winter midnight. Flight of Swans. Robinson Jeffers. **CP-JefR2**

One Who Stayed, The. Shel Silverstein. **SP-SilS2**

One Who Was Different, The. Randall Jarrell. **CP-JarrR**

One who was suffering tumult in his soul. Composed During a Storm. William Wordsworth. **CP-WorW2**

One winds through firs—their weeds are ferns. Leave. Randall Jarrell. **CP-JarrR**

One winter afternoon / (at the magical hour). Edward Estlin Cummings. **CP-CummE**

One winter morning as a child. A Vision of the Garden. James Merrill. **SP-MerrJ**

One winter night, at half-past nine. Canto I: The Trystyng. "Lewis Carroll." *Fr.* Phantasmagoria. **CP-CarrL**

One with eyes the fairest. Love Song. Euripides. **AWP** *Fr.* The Cyclops. **CP-ShelP**

One without looks in to-night [*or* tonight]. The Fallow Deer at the Lonely House. Thomas Hardy. **CP-HardT**

One woe is past. Come what come will. Christina Georgina Rossetti. **CP-RosC2**

One Woman to All Women. David Herbert Lawrence. **CP-LawrD**

One wondered who would see and date you next. Robert Lowell. *Fr.* Mermaid. **SP-LoweR**

One Word as the Complete Poem. Charles Olson. **CP-OlsoC**

One word is too often profaned. Percy Bysshe Shelley. **CP-ShelP**

(To ———: "One word is too often profaned.") **CP-ShelP**

One Word More. Robert Browning. **CP-BroR1**

"I shall never, in the years remaining." **EPCY**

Phases of the Moon. **ChTr**

One word—'tis all I ask of thee. The Dying Man to His Betrothed. Christina Georgina Rossetti. **CP-RosC3**

One World. Charles Tomlinson. **CP-TomlC**

One world you say. One World. Charles Tomlinson. **CP-TomlC**

One would be in less danger. Family Court. Ogden Nash. **CP-NashO**

One writes, that "Other friends remain." Tennyson. **EnVR; PoEL-5** *Fr.* In Memoriam A. H. H. **CP-TennA**

One Year. Gary Snyder. **CP-SnydG**

One Year ago—jots what? Emily Dickinson. **CP-DickE**

One year floods rose. Canto 9. Ezra Pound. **SP-PounE** *Fr.* Cantos. **CP-PoCan**

One-Year-Old, The. John Updike. **CP-UpdiJ**

One year, you gave us. The Classmate. Adrienne Rich. **CP-RicAE**

One young life lost, two happy young lives blighted. A Death of a First-Born. Christina Georgina Rossetti. **CP-RosC3**

One/the Sun / / Moon/one. Robert Creeley. **CP-CreeR**

One(Floatingly)arrive / (silent)one by(alive). Edward Estlin Cummings. **CP-CummE**

One's grand flights, one's Sunday baths. The Sense of the Sleight-of-Hand Man. Wallace Stevens. **CP-StevW**

One's not half two. It's two are halves of one. Edward Estlin Cummings. **CP-CummE; SP-CummE**

One's-Self I Sing. Walt Whitman. **CP-WhitW**

Ones that Are Thrown Out, The. Miller Williams. **SP-WillM**

Ones that disappeared are back, The. Emily Dickinson. **CP-DickE**

ones who camped on the slopes, below the bare summit, The. 7/13/68. Adrienne Rich. **CP-RicAE** *Fr.* Ghazals: Homage to Ghalib. **SP-RicA2**

Ongoing Story, The. John Ashbery. **SP-AshbJ**

Onion Days. Carl Sandburg. **CP-SandC**

Onions. William Matthews. **SP-MattW**

Onions. Jonathan Swift. *See* Onyons.

Only a Curl. Elizabeth Barrett Browning. **CP-BroEB**

Only a few faint elements of order hint. The Yellow of the Mask. Charles Olson. **CP-OlsoC**

Only a few top-heavy holly-hocks, wilting in arid beds. The Public Gardens. Alun Lewis. **CP-LewiA**

Only a Hobo. "Bob Dylan." **CP-DylaB**

Only [*or* Onely] a little more. His Poetry His Pillar. Robert Herrick. **CP-HerrR**

Only a madman could mistake. Arrow Shots. Robert Ranke Graves. **CP-GravR**

Only a man harrowing clods. In Time of "The Breaking of Nations." Thomas Hardy. **CP-HardT**

Only a Northern Song. George Harrison. **CP-Beatl**

Only a Pawn in Their Game. "Bob Dylan." **CP-DylaB**

Only a Shrine, but Mine. Emily Dickinson. **CP-DickE**

Only a smell had feelings to make known. Wystan Hugh Auden. *Fr.* Sonnets from China. **CP-AudeW**

Only a Woman's Hair. "Lewis Carroll." **CP-CarrL**

"Only a woman's hair!" Fling it aside! Only a Woman's Hair. "Lewis Carroll." **CP-CarrL**

Only accidents preserve. Athena in the Front Lines. Marge Piercy. **SP-PierM**

Only acquaintances / Seem do we. In the Street. Thomas Hardy. **CP-HardT**

Only as what(out of a flophouse)floats. Edward Estlin Cummings. **CP-CummE**

Only Balmless Wound, The. Emily Dickinson. **SP-DickE**

Only Bar in Dixon, The. Richard Hugo. **CP-HugoR**

Only Believe. Christina Georgina Rossetti. **CP-RosC3**

Only Bird That Sang, The. Kay Boyle. **CP-BoylK**

Only brooms / Know the devil. Brooms. Charles Simic. **SP-SimiC**

Only close up could you make out the wings on their horses. Evidence? What Evidence. . . ? Kenneth Patchen. **CP-PatcK**

Only comfort of my life, The. His Comfort. Robert Herrick. **CP-HerrR**

Only death remains. John Ledyard. Richard Eberhart. **CP-EberR**

Only from the back / could I be seen clearly. What's for Dinner. Robert Creeley. **CP-CreeR**

Only Ghost I ever saw, The. Emily Dickinson. **CP-DickE**

Only God—detect the Sorrow. Emily Dickinson. **CP-DickE**

Only God Knows How. Malcolm Lowry. *Fr.* The Moon in Scandinavia. **CP-LowrM**

Only God Knows How III. Malcolm Lowry. *Fr.* The Moon in Scandinavia. **CP-LowrM**

Only hope is the next drink, The. No Time to Stop and Think. Malcolm Lowry. **CP-LowrM**

Only hope is to catch the moment as it flies, The. The Truth. Richard Eberhart. **CP-EberR**

Only hungers left, The. Sacrifice. Audre Lorde. **SP-LordA**

Only Image, The. Roy Fisher. **SP-FishR**

Only in books the flat and final happens. Observation. Philip Larkin. **CP-LarkP**

Only in the Dream. Richard Eberhart. **CP-EberR**

Only joy, now here you are. Fourth Song. Sir Philip Sidney. **EiL; EnRePo; GBL; HAP; InvP; NAEL-1; NoP; NoSic; OBSC; UnTE** *Fr.* Astrophil and Stella. **SP-SidnP**

Only let it form within his hands once more. The Brandy Glass. Louis MacNeice. **CP-MacNL**

Only Love can wound. Emily Dickinson. **SP-DickE**

Only Man. David Herbert Lawrence. **CP-LawrD**

Only man I ever loved, The. Poem. Ernest Hemingway. **CP-HemiE**

Only man that eer I knew. William Blake. **CP-BlakW** (William Cowper Esqre.) **CP-BlakW**

Only my written word / I've sacrificed every thing, including sex and woman. Maximus of Gloucester. Charles Olson. **SP-OlsoC** *Fr.* The Maximus Poems.

Only News I know, The. Emily Dickinson. **CP-DickE**

Only one destiny. Charles Henri Ford. **SP-FordC** *Fr.* Secret Haiku.

Only parts of the body same, The. Eyes. William Matthews. **SP-MattW**

Only parts of the pain of living. Detroit 1958. Al Young. **CP-YounA**

Only people I ever heard talk about My Lady Poverty, The. Poverty. David Herbert Lawrence. **CP-LawrD**

Only people who should really sin, The. Inter-Office Memorandum. Ogden Nash. **CP-NashO**

Only Poem, The. Leonard Cohen. **CP-CoheL**

Only question to ask today, about man or woman, The. The Egoists. David Herbert Lawrence. **CP-LawrD**

Only Race There Is, The. Al Young. **CP-YounA**

Only reason for living is being fully alive, The. Being Alive. David Herbert Lawrence. **CP-LawrD**

Only Relic, The. Isabella Gardner. **CP-GardI**

Only salvation is to realise that we know nothing about it, The. Salvation. David Herbert Lawrence. **CP-LawrD**

Only some spires of bright green grass. Emily Brontë. **CP-BronE**

Only Son, An. Rudyard Kipling. *Fr.* Epitaphs of the War [1914–1918]. **CP-KiplR**

Only Son, The. Rudyard Kipling. **CP-KiplR**

Only stand high a long enough time your lightning will come; that is what blunts the peaks of redwoods. The Summit Redwood. Robinson Jeffers. **CP-JefR1**

Only target / is the eyeball, The. Roy Fisher. **SP-FishR** *Fr.* The Six Deliberate Acts.

Only teaching on Tuesdays, book-worming. Memories of West Street and Lepke. Robert Lowell. **SP-LoweR**

Only that it should be beautiful. George Oppen. *Fr.* Of Being Numerous. **CP-OppeG**

Only that lone man in the stone tower by the rough. The Habit of Mercy. John Hewitt. **CP-HewiJ**

Only the Arab stallion will I. To a Man on His Horse. Frank Templeton Prince. **CP-PrinF**

Only the Best Matters. David Herbert Lawrence. **CP-LawrD**

Only the dead have an enduring city. The Situation Does Not Change. Howard Nemerov. **CP-NemeH**

Only the diamond and the diamond's dust. Edna St. Vincent Millay. *Fr.* Epitaph for the Race of Man. **CP-MillE**

Only the female falcon is a true falcon. Peregrine Falcon. Siv Cedering Fox. **SP-CedeS**

Only the gods may act with perfect impudence—. Purana, Meaning Once Upon a Time. Hayden Carruth. **CP-CarHS**

Only the Irresistible Abides. Jean Garrigue. **SP-GarrJ**

Only the Japanese, the narrator said. For Those Who Pray for the Souls of Broken Dolls. Chuck Miller. **SP-MillC**

Only the little / town / remains beyond. Van Gogh: "The Starry Night." William DeWitt Snodgrass. **SP-SnodW**

Only the Polished Skeleton. Countee Cullen. **CP-CullC**

Only the priest. Charioteer. Hilda Doolittle. **CP-DoolH**

Only the prism's obstruction shows aright. Deaf and Dumb. Robert Browning. **CP-BroR1**

Only the Red Fox, Only the Crow. Charles Olson. **CP-OlsoC**

Only the rich remember the past. Arcades of Philadelphia the Past. Wallace Stevens. **CP-StevW**

Only their hands are living, to the wheel attracted. Casino. Wystan Hugh Auden. **CP-AudeW**

Only themselves understand themselves and the like of themselves. Perfections. Walt Whitman. **CP-WhitW**

Only these stone hut walls record their lives. Chysauster. Richard Hugo. **CP-HugoR**

Only thing for a man to do now, or a woman, The. What's to Be Done. David Herbert Lawrence. **CP-LawrD**

Only thing I have of Jane MacNaughton, The. The Leap. James Dickey. **CP-DickJ**

Only thing non / repetitious on the midway is, The. The Barker. Dabney Stuart. **SP-StuaD**

Only thing that Jack had, The. Malcolm Lowry. **CP-LowrM**

Only thing to be done, now, The. Be Still! David Herbert Lawrence. **CP-LawrD**

Only think, dearest Louisa, what fearful scenes we have witnessed! Arthur Hugh Clough. **EBVV** *Fr.* Amours de Voyage. **SP-ClouA**

Only this evening I saw again low in the sky. Martial Cadenza. Wallace Stevens. **CP-StevW**

Only thou livest. Centuries wheel and pass. Helen. Edward Estlin Cummings. **CP-CummE**

Only three things lengthen life. *Unknown, tr. fr. Persian by* Jean Chardin *and fr. French by* Ralph Waldo Emerson. **CP-EmerR**

Only 3 years ago it was 4 years ago. The Abacus. Malcolm Lowry. **CP-LowrM**

Only time, I swear, I ever fell more than abstractly in love with someone else's wife, The. Ethics. Charles Kenneth Williams. **SP-WillC**

Only time in Catholic church, empty in afternoon. Desert for All of Music to Take Place. Alice Notley. **SP-NotlA**

Only to have a grief. Peeling Onions. Adrienne Rich. **CP-RicAE; SP-RicA2**

Only Trouble, The. Robert Penn Warren. **SP-WarrR**

Only two African kopjes. Two Kopjes. Rudyard Kipling. **CP-KiplR**

Only until this cigarette is ended. Edna St. Vincent Millay. **CP-MillE**

Only water—. Louis Zukofsky. *Fr.* 29 Poems. **CP-ZukLS**

Only way it makes sense, The. The Undead. Charles Kenneth Williams. **CP-WillC**

Only way to be quiet, The. Poetry. Frank O'Hara. **SP-OharF**

Only way to settle the property question, The. The Way Out. David Herbert Lawrence. **CP-LawrD**

Only, when I am sudden loss. Promise Me. Stanley Jasspon Kunitz. **CP-KuniS**

Onna-E, Pictures of Women. Siv Cedering Fox. **SP-CedeS**

   Blanc de Blanc.

   Exposing Fox and Artifice.

   Sentence, A.

   Story of Toile, The.

   Susanna.

"Onora, Onora,"—her mother is calling. The Lay of the Brown Rosary. Elizabeth Barrett Browning. **CP-BroEB**

Onset, The. Robert Frost. **CP-FrosR**

Ontario. Paul Muldoon. **SP-MuldP**

Ontological Episode of the Asylum. Hayden Carruth. **CP-CarHS**

Onward led the road again. Hell Gate. Alfred Edward Housman. **CP-HousA**

Onyons. Jonathan Swift. **BlrV; FaBoUs** *Fr.* Verses Made for the Women Who Cry Apples, etc. **CP-SwifJ**

   (Onions.) **CP-SwifJ**

O.O. Gabugah writes that he "was born in a taxicab right". Boogie With O.O. Gabugah. Al Young. **CP-YounA**

Ooftish. Samuel Beckett. **CP-BeckS**

Oomba. Carl Sandburg. **CP-SandC**

Oomba went along years. Oomba. Carl Sandburg. **CP-SandC**

Oonts. Rudyard Kipling. **CP-KiplR**

Ooo I need your love babe, guess you know it's true. Eight Days a Week. John Lennon *and* Paul McCartney. **CP-Beatl**

Oooh Wheee, look at me. Underneath the Bottle. "Lou Reed." **SP-ReedL**

Oooo, moon you look so lovely. The Tutti Colori Quality of Light. Al Young. **CP-YounA**

Opals hiding in your lids, The. Jane Awake. Frank O'Hara. **SP-OharF**

Open— / and away. Roy Fisher. **SP-FishR** *Fr.* Handsworth Liberties.

Open-Air Museum. Adrienne Rich. **CP-RicAE; SP-RicA2**

Open any grate, any glass gate. Winter in Muscovy. Lewis Turco. **SP-TurcL**

Open Boat, The. Gilbert Sorrentino. **SP-SorrG**

Open city / uncluttered as a map. Night Taxi. Thom Gunn. **CP-GunnT**

Open Country. Richard Hugo. **CP-HugoR**

Open Door, The. Rudyard Kipling. **CP-KiplR**

Open door says, "Come in", An. Doors. Carl Sandburg. **CP-SandC**

Open Eye, The. John Hewitt. **CP-HewiJ**

Open Fire Near a Shed. Tess Gallagher. **SP-GallT**

Open green those / (dear). Edward Estlin Cummings. **CP-CummE**

Open his head, baby. Edward Estlin Cummings. **CP-CummE**

Open hither, open hence. George Meredith. *Fr.* The Woods of Westermain. **CP-MerG1**

Open horizons round. George Meredith. **CP-MerG2**

Open House. Theodore Roethke. **CP-RoetT**

Open Letter from a Constant Reader. Mona Van Duyn. **SP-VanDM**

Open Letter, Personal. Mona Van Duyn. **SP-VanDM**

Open Letter, Returning a Questionnaire Unanswered. Daniel Gerard Hoffman. **SP-HoffD**

Open Letter to the Poet Archibald MacLeish Who Has Forsaken His Massachusetts Farm to Make Propaganda for Freedom. Carl Sandburg. **CP-SandC**

Open Letter to Voyager II, An. John Updike. **CP-UpdiJ**

Open, love, open. Unclench Yourself. Marge Piercy. **SP-PierM**

Open-mouthed, the baby god. I Want, I Want. Sylvia Plath. **CP-PlatS**

Open my eyes on the welcome. Advent. James Schuyler. **CP-SchuJ**

Open Poem and the Closed Poem, The. Roy Fisher.

   "To come out ready capitalized, with outlines." **SP-FishR**

   "Winking drop on the lens." **SP-FishR**

Open Prospect. William Wordsworth. *Fr.* The River Duddon [A Series of Sonnets]. **CP-WorW2**

Open rosette flowering continually cyme. African Violet. Louis Zukofsky. **CP-ZukLS**

Open secret, the elementary chemistry of Greek fire. What is Worthless? Robinson Jeffers. **CP-JefR3**

Open the barn door, farm woman. She Opens the Barn Door Every Morning. Carl Sandburg. **CP-SandC**

Open the book of tales you knew by heart. Living Memory. Adrienne Rich. **SP-RicA1**

Open the door, Homer. "Bob Dylan." **CP-DylaB**

Open the door now. Pearl Fog. Carl Sandburg. **CP-SandC**

Open the Door, open the Door. Emily Dickinson. **SP-DickE**

Open the Door to Me, Oh! Robert Burns. **CP-BurnR**

Open the Gates. Stanley Jasspon Kunitz. **CP-KuniS**

Open the old cigar-box, get me a Cuba stout. The Betrothed. Rudyard Kipling. **CP-KiplR**

Open the trunk: She is there. The Girl You Thought You Loved. Lewis Turco. **SP-TurcL**

Open thy gates. To Heaven. Robert Herrick. **CP-HerrR**

Open water facing Bradbury snags fog in its spruce. Penobscot. James Schuyler. **CP-SchuJ**

Open Window on Chicago, An. Allen Ginsberg. **CP-GinsA**

Open with care the journal of those years. For Memory. Muriel Rukeyser. **CP-RukeM**

Open your gates, ye everlasting Piles! Cathedrals, etc. William Wordsworth. *Fr.* Ecclesiastical Sonnets. **CP-WorW2**

Open your heart: / i'll give you a treasure. Edward Estlin Cummings. **CP-CummE**

Open Your Mouth and Say. Gilbert Sorrentino. **SP-SorrG**

Opening a bus window in N.Y. You Might Get in Trouble. Allen Ginsberg. **CP-GinsA**

Opening and the Close, The. Emily Dickinson. **CP-DickE**

Opening Game, The. Ernest Hemingway. **CP-HemiE**

Opening like a marigold. I Will Not Be Your Sickness. Marge Piercy. **SP-PierM**

Opening of the chambers close. Edward Estlin Cummings. **CP-CummE**

Opening of the doors. Dark, The. The Sun-Artist. Muriel Rukeyser. **CP-RukeM**

Opening out and out, The. The Broken Ground. Wendell Berry. **CP-BerrW**

Opening the Door of a Barn I Thought Was Empty on New Year's Eve. Robert Bly. **SP-BlyR**

Opening the Window. Kenneth Patchen. **CP-PatcK**

Operation, The. Robert Creeley. **CP-CreeR**

Operation, The. Anne Sexton. **CP-SextA**

Operation, The. William DeWitt Snodgrass. **SP-SnodW**

Ophelia. Walter de la Mare. **CP-DeLaW**

Ophelia. John Hewitt. **CP-HewiJ**

Opinion is a flitting thing. Emily Dickinson. **CP-DickE**

Opinion is not worth a rush. Michael Robartes and the Dancer. William Butler Yeats. **CP-YeatW**

Opium and Hitler. Leonard Cohen. **CP-CoheL**

Opportunity. Paul Laurence Dunbar. **CP-DunbP**

Opportunity, The. Thomas Hardy. **CP-HardT**

Opportunity. Leonard Nathan. **SP-NathL**

Opportunity. William Shakespeare. **LiTB; OBSC; PoEL-2** *Fr.* The Rape of Lucrece. **CP-ShaWS**

   (Outcry upon Opportunity, An.) **NOBE**

Opposite Field, The. Dabney Stuart. **SP-StuaD**

   "Am I brother to you."

   "I had no thought to find." **NGP**

   "June, 1981. You are forty."

   Lyric Meditation on Sour Locker Rooms, A. **NGP**

   "Newer photograph shows you, A."

   "Old photograph shows you, An."

Opposite House, The. Robert Lowell. **SP-LoweR**

Opposition. Richard Eberhart. **CP-EberR**

Opposition Is True Friendship. William Blake. *Fr.* The Marriage of Heaven and Hell. **CP-BlakW**

   (Plate 21.)

Opposition lurks, An. The Menace. Thom Gunn. **CP-GunnT**

Oppositions, The. Frederick Morgan. **SP-MorgF**

Oppositions. Charles Tomlinson. **CP-TomlC**

Oppress'd with grief, oppress'd with care. Despondency, an Ode. Robert Burns. **CP-BurnR**

Oppression of the tumult—wrath and scorn, The. Monastery of Old Bangor. William Wordsworth. *Fr.* Ecclesiastical Sonnets. **CP-WorW2**

Optimism. Steve Griffiths. **SP-GrifS**

Optimist, The. David Herbert Lawrence. **CP-LawrD**

Opulence. Richard Eberhart. **CP-EberR**

Opus Dei. John Berryman. **CP-BerrJ**

Opusculum paedagogum. Study of Two Pears. Wallace Stevens. **CP-StevW**

Opusthirteen. Hayden Carruth. **CP-CarHS**

Or. Tom Clark. **SP-ClarT**

Or. Charles Kenneth Williams. **CP-WillC**

Or a Valentine. Louis Zukofsky. **CP-ZukLS**

Or Another Place. Richard Hugo. **CP-HugoR**

Or as the embryo, whose vital band. So Make Them Melt as the Dishouséd Snail. Donald Davie. **CP-DavDo**

Or Captain Philip Sheridan. The Civil War. Charles Olson. **CP-OlsoC**

Or define / Man beyond rescue. George Oppen. *Fr.* Of Being Numerous. **CP-OppeG**

Or else their cooings came from bays of trees. Gerard Manley Hopkins. **CP-HopkG**

Or else, there's no wife in the case. The Spoils of Youth. Robert Browning. **CBCK** *Fr.* A Likeness. **CP-BroR1**

Or ever the battered liners sank. The Changelings. Rudyard Kipling. **CP-KiplR** *Fr.* Debits and Credits.

Or ever the early stirrings of skylark. Gerard Manley Hopkins. *Fr.* Fragments. **CP-HopkG**

Or, from That Sea of Time. Walt Whitman. **CP-WhitW**

Or I could just say no I won't. Perfect Point. Alice Notley. **SP-NotlA**

Or I shall live your epitaph to make. Sonnet 81. William Shakespeare. **OAEP; OBSC; OXAEP-1** *Fr.* Sonnets. **CP-ShaWS**

Or: I work at the language as a spring of water works at the rock. Source. Robert Duncan. **SP-DuncR**

Or if I will not rape. The Pedigree. Robert Creeley. **CP-CreeR**

Or if I should delight my privat hours. John Milton. **PeECV** *Fr.* Book IV. *Fr.* Paradise Regained [*or* Regain'd]. **CP-MiltJ**

Or in My Throat. John Ashbery. **SP-AshbJ**

Or, in that light, New arts! George Oppen. *Fr.* Of Being Numerous. **CP-OppeG**

Or independence, call it what you blame well like. Hayden Carruth. *Fr.* The Sleeping Beauty. **CP-CarHL**

Or is really October in Houston? Houston in October. Al Young. **CP-YounA**

Or looked [*or* lookt] I back unto the times hence flown. To M. Denham, on His Prospective Poem. Robert Herrick. **CP-HerrR**

Or me wanting another man's / wife, etc. The Europeans. Robert Creeley. **CP-CreeR**

Or must I say, Vain Word, false thought! Alteram Partem. Arthur Hugh Clough. **SP-ClouA**

Or play the strong boy, spit in the world's face, shout. Archibald MacLeish. *Fr.* Hamlet of A. Macleish. **CP-MacLA**

Or scorn[e], or pity [*or* pittie] on me take. The Dream[e]. Ben Jonson. **CP-JonsB**

Or shall we run with Artemis. The Vital Choice. George Meredith. **CP-MerG1**

Or, Solitude. Donald Davie. **CP-DavDo**

Or the single path— / Which the cool moon sheds. George Meredith. **CP-MerG2**

Or: *They are come near me that.* Thou Art Near at Hand, O Lord. Donald Davie. **CP-DavDo**

Or To Perish Before Day. Robert Ranke Graves. **CP-GravR**

Or Traveller's Joy. Charles Tomlinson. **CP-TomlC**

Or were he a Jew or a. To My Friend Ezra Pound. William Carlos Williams. **CP-WilW2**

Or what is closer to the truth. When I Buy Pictures. Marianne Craig Moore. **CP-MoorM**

Or whether doth my mind, being crowned with you. Sonnet 114. William Shakespeare. **SCGP** *Fr.* Sonnets. **CP-ShaWS**

Or who and who. Edward Estlin Cummings. **CP-CummE**

Or will you let him live. Nicholas Vachel Lindsay. *Fr.* The Sea Serpent Chantey. **CP-LindV**

Or with a rush. Sluggishly. William Carlos Williams. **CP-WilW1**

"Or with the tangles" as one of our own said. Louis MacNeice. *Fr.* Memoranda to Horace. **CP-MacNL**

Oracle. Seamus Heaney. **SP-HeanS**

Oracle / High between the cliffs, The. The Oracle. Louis MacNeice. *Fr.* Out of the Picture. **CP-MacNL**

Oracle, The. Louis MacNeice. *Fr.* Out of the Picture. **CP-MacNL**

Oracle, The. Thomas Merton. **CP-MertT**

Oracle of the market! thence you drew. Camelus Saltat: Continued. George Meredith. **CP-MerG1**

Oracles, The. Alfred Edward Housman. **CP-HousA**

Oracles. Kathleen Jessie Raine. **SP-RainK**

Oracles are dumm, The. John Milton. **GrIP** *Fr.* Hymn on the Morning of Christ's Nativity [*or* On the Morning of Christ's Nativity]. **FiP; NAEL-**

1; **NOBE; OBEV; OtMeF** *Fr.* On the Morning of Christs Nativity. **CP-MiltJ**

O'Rahilly, The. William Butler Yeats. **CP-YeatW**

Oral Messages. Lawrence Ferlinghetti.

"I am waiting for my case to come up." **SP-FerlL**

Orananaoig, or, the Song of Death. Robert Burns. **CP-BurnR**

Orange Bears, The. Kenneth Patchen. **CP-PatcK**

Orange blossoms have dropped their threads. Landscape with Seated Figure and Olive Trees. Charles Wright. **SP-WrigC**

Orange Buds by Mail from Florida. Walt Whitman. **CP-WhitW**

Orange Clock, An. Ted Berrigan. **SP-BerrT**

Orange devours, An. In Earliest Morning. James Schuyler. **CP-SchuJ**

Orange hawkeye stronger than thought winking above a thousand thin grassblades. Independence Day. Allen Ginsberg. **CP-GinsA**

Orange in side walk, The. An Apple at Dawn. Jim Carroll. **SP-CarrJ**

Orange in the middle of a table. Against Still Life. Margaret Atwood. **SP-AtwM1**

Orange translucent butterflies are cruising. Above. Howard Nemerov. **CP-NemeH**

Orange tree, in various light, The. In a Green Night. Derek Walcott. **CP-WalcD**

Oranges. Jonathan Swift. *Fr.* Verses Made for the Women Who Cry Apples, etc. **CP-SwifJ**

Oranges Returned, The. Gilbert Sorrentino. **SP-SorrG**

Oranges (sweet) and lemons (bitter) childhood, An. Louis MacNeice. *Fr.* Notes for a Biography. **CP-MacNL**

Oratio Patris Condren: O Jesu Vivens in Maria. Gerard Manley Hopkins. **CP-HopkG**

Orator. Ralph Waldo Emerson. **OxBA** *Fr.* Quatrains. **CP-EmerR**

Orator dismal of Nottinghamshire, An. An Excellent New Song. Jonathan Swift. **CP-SwifJ**

Orb of all pervading light. Light of Night. Marsden Hartley. **CP-HartM**

Orbem bellis, urbem gabellis. Canto 55. Ezra Pound. *Fr.* Cantos. **CP-PoCan**

Orca. Robinson Jeffers. **CP-JefR3**

Orcas in the Eyes. Richard Hugo. **CP-HugoR**

Orchard. Archie Randolph Ammons. **SP-AmmoA**

Orchard. Hilda Doolittle. **CP-DoolH**

Orchard, The. Richard Eberhart. *Fr.* Burr Oaks. **CP-EberR**

Orchard. Richard Eberhart. **CP-EberR**

"And the first, the father, with indomitable will."

"Lovely were the fruit trees in the evening."

Orchard, The. William Carlos Williams. **CP-WilW2**

Orchard and the Heath, The. George Meredith. **CP-MerG1**

Orchard at Night in Rain Light, The. Al Young. **CP-YounA**

Orchard Country. John Hewitt. **CP-HewiJ**

Orchard Keeper, The. Robert Bly. **SP-BlyR**

Orchard Pathway, The. William Wordsworth. **CP-WorW1**

Orchard Trees, January. Richard Wilbur. **CP-WilbR**

Orchard's gorgeous, The. Real Estate. Barton Sutter. **SP-SuttB**

Orchards half the way, The. The First of May. Alfred Edward Housman. **CP-HousA**

Orchestra, The. William Carlos Williams. **CP-WilW2**

Orchestras have so long been speaking. Music Is International. Wystan Hugh Auden. **CP-AudeW**

Orchid. Robert Pack. **SP-PackR**

Orchid, The. Charles Kenneth Williams. **SP-WillC**

Orchids. Theodore Roethke. **CP-RoetT**

Ordeal, The. William Carlos Williams. **CP-WilW1**

Order of Saying, The. Charles Tomlinson. **CP-TomlC**

Order of Service, An. Geoffrey Hill. **CP-HillG**

Order of the small town on the riverbank, The. 8/1/68. Adrienne Rich. **CP-RicAE** *Fr.* Ghazals: Homage to Ghalib. **SP-RicA2**

Order. Order. The bottle contains. Divisions. Robert Creeley. **CP-CreeR**

Order to View. Louis MacNeice. **CP-MacNL**

Orderly hand of man, hollowing, The. Switzerland. John Updike. **CP-UpdiJ**

Orders for the Day. Theodore Roethke. **CP-RoetT**

Ordinary Days. Stephen Dunn. **SP-DunnS**

Ordinary Evening in Cleveland, An. Lewis Turco. **SP-TurcL**

Ordinary Evening in New Haven, An. Wallace Stevens. **CP-StevW**

Ordinary God. Donald Davie. **CP-DavDo**

Ordinary milkman brought that dawn, The. The Trial of Man. Sylvia Plath. **CP-PlatS**

Ordinary Miracles. Erica Jong. **SP-JongE**

Ordinary Morning, An. Philip Levine. **SP-LeviP**

Ordinary Newscaster, An. Robinson Jeffers. **CP-JefR3**

Ordinary people are peculiar too. Conversation. Louis MacNeice. **CP-MacNL**

Ordinary Poem. Diane Wakoski. **SP-WakoD**

Ordinary Women, The. Wallace Stevens. **SP-StevW**

Ordination, The. Robert Burns. **CP-BurnR**

Ordonnance. Thomas McGrath. **SP-McGrT**

O're [or O'er] the smooth enamel'd [or enameled or enamelled] green. John Milton. **OBEV; OxBSP; TrGrPo** Fr. Arcades. **CP-MiltJ**
(Song: "O'er the smooth enamelled green.") **OxBSP**

Oread. Hilda Doolittle. **CP-DoolH**

Oregon Message, An. William Stafford. **SP-StafW**

Orestes at Tauris. Randall Jarrell. **CP-JarrR**

Orestes Theme. Hilda Doolittle. **CP-DoolH**

Orfeo. James Merrill. **SP-MerrJ**

Orford. Donald Davie. **CP-DavDo**

Organ. Alfonso Cortes, tr. fr. Spanish by Thomas Merton. **CP-MertT**

Organ is moaning, The. Emily Dickinson. **SP-DickE**

Organ swells, the trumpets sound, The. Emily Brontë. **CP-BronE**

Organic Bloom. Stanley Jasspon Kunitz. **CP-KuniS**

Organist's Black Carnation, The. Laurence Lieberman. **SP-LiebL**

Organized knowledge in story and picture. From Morning-Glory to Petersburg. Adrienne Rich. **CP-RicAE; SP-RicA2**

Organs and War News. These States: Into L.A. Allen Ginsberg. **CP-GinsA**

Orgy. Muriel Rukeyser. **CP-RukeM**

Orhan Vele, Turkish listener to Istanbul, I'm cool. Moon Over Matter. Al Young. **CP-YounA**

Oriane. James Schuyler. **CP-SchuJ**

Orient and Immortal Wheat. Derek Walcott. **CP-WalcD**

Orient Express, The. Randall Jarrell. **CP-JarrR; SP-JarrR**

Orient Wheat. Adrienne Rich. **CP-RicAE**

Oriental Ballerina, The. Rita Dove. **SP-DoveR**

Oriental Maxims. John Greenleaf Whittier. **CP-WhitJ**

Oriental Visitor, An. Donald Davie. **CP-DavDo**

Orientation Week. Ron Koertge. **SP-KoerR**

Orientations. John Hewitt. **CP-HewiJ**

Origen. Thomas Merton. **CP-MertT**

Origin. Howard Nemerov. **CP-NemeH**

Origin of Baseball, The. Kenneth Patchen. **CP-PatcK**

Origin of Flattery, The. Charlotte Smith. **CP-SmitC**

Origin of Laughter, The. John Updike. **CP-UpdiJ**

"Origin of Love!"—Ah! why, The. On Being Asked What Was the "Origin of Love." Byron. **CP-Byron**

Origin of the Praise of God, The. Robert Bly. **SP-BlyR**

Original—"Apropos." Ralph Waldo Emerson. **CP-EmerR**

Original artist, you have become. Decorated Skull in a University Museum. Howard Nemerov. **CP-NemeH**

Original Child Bomb. Thomas Merton. **CP-MertT**

Original Poetry by Victor and Cazire. Percy Bysshe Shelley. **CP-ShelP**
Despair.
Fragment, or The Triumph of Conscience.
Ghasta; or, The Avenging Demon!!!
"Here I sit with my paper, my pen and my ink."
Irishman's Song, The.
Revenge.
Saint Edmond's Eve.
Song: "Cold, cold is the blast when December is howling."
Song: "Come [Harriet]! sweet is the hour."
Song: "Fierce roars the midnight storm."
Song: "To me this world's a dreary blank."
Song: Hope.
Song: To———[Harriet] ("Ah! sweet is the moonbeam. . . .")
Song: To——— [Harriet] ("Stern, stern is the voice. . . .")
Song: Translated from the German.
Song: Translated from the Italian.
To Miss — — [Harriet Grove] from Miss — — [Elizabeth Shelley].

Original Sin. Robinson Jeffers. **CP-JefR3**

Original Sin. Thomas Merton. Fr. Cables to the Ace. **CP-MertT**

Original Sin. Miller Williams. **SP-WillM**

Original Sin; a Short Story. Robert Penn Warren. **SP-WarrR**

Original Sin on the Sussex Coast. Sir John Betjeman. **CP-BetjJ**

Original Temptation, The. Jim Morrison. **SP-MorrJ**

Original Wrapper, The. "Lou Reed." **SP-ReedL**

Originators, The. Thomas Merton. **CP-MertT**

Origins. Derek Walcott. **CP-WalcD**

Oriole sings in the greening grove, The. Summer in the South. Paul Laurence Dunbar. **CP-DunbP**

Orioles live in the elms, and in classical verse. Summer Solstice. Stanley Jasspon Kunitz. **CP-KuniS**

Orion. William Everson. **SP-EverW**

Orion. Adrienne Rich. **CP-RicAE; SP-RicA1; SP-RicA2**

Orion Dead. Hilda Doolittle. **CP-DoolH**

Orion plunges like a drunken hunter. Adrienne Rich. **SP-RicA1** Fr. The Spirit of Place. **SP-RicA2**

Orion swung southward aslant. Before Marching and After. Thomas Hardy. **CP-HardT**

Orlando Furioso. Ludovico Ariosto, tr. fr. Italian.
"Orlando who great length of time had been." **CP-WorW1**

Orlando who great length of time had been. Ludovico Ariosto, tr. fr. Italian by William Wordsworth. **CP-WorW1** Fr. Orlando Furioso.

Ormerod was deeply troubled. Distractions and the Human Crowd. Stevie Smith. **CP-SmitS**

Ornithology. Siv Cedering Fox. **SP-CedeS**

Ornithology in a World of Flux. Robert Penn Warren. **SP-WarrR**

Orotava Road, The. Basil Bunting. **CP-BuntB**

O'Rourk's noble fare. The Description of an Irish Feast. Jonathan Swift. **CP-SwifJ**

Orphan, The. Thomas McGrath. **SP-McGrT**

Orphan Hours, the Year is dead. Dirge for the Year. Percy Bysshe Shelley. **CP-ShelP**

Orphan is looking for parents, The. The Orphan Reformed. Stevie Smith. **CP-SmitS**

Orphan Reformed, The. Stevie Smith. **CP-SmitS**

Orphaned Old Maid, The. Thomas Hardy. **CP-HardT**

Orphans of the heart must turn to thee, The. Ostia. David St. John. Fr. To Pasolini. **SP-StJoD**

Orpheus. Wystan Hugh Auden. **CP-AudeW**

Orpheus. Donald Davie. **CP-DavDo**

Orpheus. Stephen Dobyns. **SP-DobyS**

Orpheus. Robert Herrick. **CP-HerrR**

Orpheus. Muriel Rukeyser. **CP-RukeM**

Orpheus. Percy Bysshe Shelley. **CP-ShelP**

Orpheus. William DeWitt Snodgrass. **SP-SnodW**

Orpheus! an Orpheus! yes, Faith may grow bold, An. Power of Music. William Wordsworth. **CP-WorW1**

Orpheus and animus, / drawing back to journeys now. Marilyn Hacker. **SP-HackM** Fr. The Navigators.

Orpheus and Eurydice. Geoffrey Hill. **CP-HillG**

Orpheus and Eurydice. Virgil, tr. by William Wordsworth. **CP-WorW1** Fr. Georgics.

Orpheus and Pluto. Robert Herrick. **CP-HerrR**

Orpheus as a Christian Scientist. James Liddy. Fr. Glass after Oblivion. **CP-LiddJ**

Orpheus fertur et arbores canendo. Orpheus With His Lute Made Trees. Gerard Manley Hopkins. Fr. Songs from Shakespeare, in Latin and Greek. **CP-HopkG**

Orpheus, for so the Gentiles call'd thy name. On the Goodness of the Supreme Being. Christopher Smart. **SP-SmarC**

Orpheus he went (as poets tell). Orpheus. Robert Herrick. **CP-HerrR**

Orpheus in Connaught. James Liddy. Fr. Glass after Oblivion. **CP-LiddJ**

Orpheus in the Underground. Phoebe Hesketh. **SP-HeskP**

Orpheus liked the glad personal quality. Syringa. John Ashbery. **SP-AshbJ**

Orpheus (1). Margaret Atwood. **SP-AtwM2**

Orpheus to Beasts. Richard Lovelace. **CP-LoveR**

Orpheus to Eurydice. Frederick Morgan. **SP-MorgF**

Orpheus to Woods. Richard Lovelace. **CP-LoveR**

Orpheus (2). Margaret Atwood. **SP-AtwM2**

Orpheus With His Lute Made Trees. Gerard Manley Hopkins. Fr. Songs from Shakespeare, in Latin and Greek. **CP-HopkG**

Orphic Scenario. Howard Nemerov. **CP-NemeH**

Orson of the Muse, An. George Meredith. **CP-MerG1**

Orthodontia. John Updike. **CP-UpdiJ**

Orthodox, Orthodox, wha [or who] believe in John Knox. Robert Burns. **CP-BurnR**

O'Ryan. Charles Olson. **CP-OlsoC**

O'Ryan 11-15. Charles Olson. **CP-OlsoC**

Osawatomie. Carl Sandburg. **CP-SandC**

Oscar of Alva. Byron. **CP-Byron**

Osceola. Walt Whitman. **CP-WhitW**

Osiris pales; the palace walls. Dilemma in the Delta. John Updike. **CP-UpdiJ**

Osmund Dutch, and John Gallop, mariners, their wages. Maximus, in Gloucester Sunday, LXV. Charles Olson. **SP-OlsoC** *Fr.* The Maximus Poems.

Osprey Suicides, The. Laurence Lieberman. **SP-LiebL**

Ospreys in Cry. Richard Eberhart. **CP-EberR**

Ossian's Address to the Sun in "Carthon." Byron. **CP-Byron**

Ossian's Grave. Robinson Jeffers. **CP-JefR2**

Ossian's Grave, Lubitavish, County Antrim. John Hewitt. **CP-HewiJ**

Ossie Esmonde. James Liddy. *Fr.* His Resplendent Neighbours. **CP-LiddJ**
    After Life.
    City Life.
    Country Life.

Ostia. David St. John. *Fr.* To Pasolini. **SP-StJoD**

Ostrich, The. Ogden Nash. *Fr.* Nature-Walks, or, Not to Mention a Dopping of Sheldrakes. **CP-NashO**

Ostrich roams the great Sahara, The. The Ostrich. Ogden Nash. *Fr.* Nature-Walks, or, Not to Mention a Dopping of Sheldrakes. **CP-NashO**

Other, The. James Dickey. **CP-DickJ**

Other, The. Sylvia Plath. **CP-PlatS**

Other, The. Theodore Roethke. **CP-RoetT**

Other, The. Anne Sexton. **CP-SextA**

Other acquainted years. On Reaching Forty. Maya Angelou. **SP-AngeM**

Other Beaverbank, The. Richard Hugo. **CP-HugoR**

Other Benefits. William Wordsworth. *Fr.* Ecclesiastical Sonnets. **CP-WorW2**

Other Cambridge, The. John Berryman. **CP-BerrJ**

Other Cindy, The. John Ashbery. **SP-AshbJ**

Other day, The. The Day the Epileptic Spoke. Charles Bukowski. **SP-BukC3**

Other day a witch came to call, The. An Intruder. May Sarton. **SP-SartM**

Other day we spent, The. Carmen 50. Catullus. *Fr.* Carmina. **CP-Catul**

Other days still to come. Let's Wait. Pablo Neruda, *tr. fr. Spanish by* Ben Belitt. **SP-NeruP**

Other Garden, The. Jim Carroll. **SP-CarrJ**

Other Grave, The. Richard Hugo. **CP-HugoR**

Other guineahen, the. Edward Estlin Cummings. **CP-CummE**

Other Influences. William Wordsworth. *Fr.* Ecclesiastical Sonnets. **CP-WorW2**

Other Man, The. Rudyard Kipling. *Fr.* Plain Tales from the Hills. "When the earth was sick and the skies were grey." **CP-KiplR**

Other mens sins wee ever beare in mind. Our Owne Sinnes Unseen. Robert Herrick. **CP-HerrR**

Other night I saw. . . / Who did I see?, The. Rafael Alberti, *tr. by* Thomas Merton. **CP-MertT** *Fr.* Roman Nocturnes.

Other night we went to see Sam's play, The. Doin' the Things That We Want To. Lou Reed. **SP-ReedL**

Other Sea-Cities. Hilda Doolittle. **CP-DoolH**

Other Side, The. Seamus Heaney. **SP-HeanS**

Other Side, The. Charles Kenneth Williams. **CP-WillC**

Other Side of the Page, The. Erica Jong. **SP-JongE**

Other Side of the River, The. Charles Wright. **SP-WrigC**

Other Side: The Green Home, The. Kenneth Patchen. **CP-PatcK**

Other strangers than our own may remember. Shorts / Excerpts. Bill Knott. **SP-KnotB**

Other strangers than our own may remember. Shorts / Excerpts. Bill Knott. **SP-KnotB**

Other Tea, The. Charles Olson. **CP-OlsoC**

Other Than. Charles Olson. **CP-OlsoC**

Other than propaganda—. "Immediate Aim, The." Louis Zukofsky. *Fr.* 29 Songs. **CP-ZukLS**

Other Tradition, The. John Ashbery. **SP-AshbJ**

Other Two, The. Sylvia Plath. **CP-PlatS**

Other two, slight air and purging fire, The. Sonnet 45. William Shakespeare. *Fr.* Sonnets. **CP-ShaWS**

Other way Satan went down, Th'. John Milton. **NAEL-1** *Fr.* Book X. **FHYEP** *Fr.* Paradise Lost. **CP-MiltJ**

Other Wing, The. Louis MacNeice. **CP-MacNL**

Other Women Have Reared in Me. David Herbert Lawrence. **CP-LawrD**

Other World, The. Richard Shelton. **SP-ShelR**

Others abide our question. Thou art free. Shakespeare. Matthew Arnold. **SP-ArnoM**

Others beat timbrels with uplifted hands. History of a Malady. Charles Tomlinson. **CP-TomlC**

Others because you did not keep. A Deep-sworn Vow. William Butler Yeats. **CP-YeatW**

Others had found it prudent to withdraw. Wystan Hugh Auden. *Fr.* The Quest. **CP-AudeW**

Others, I am not the first. Alfred Edward Housman. **CP-HousA**

Others in museums pass them by. Roman Portrait Busts. John Updike. **CP-UpdiJ**

Others may need new life in Heaven. Speculative. Robert Browning. **CP-BroR2**

Others May Praise What They Like. Walt Whitman. **CP-WhitW**

Others taunt me with having knelt at well-curbs. For Once, Then, Something. Robert Frost. **CP-FrosR**

Others wore colours; I wore white. Emily Dickinson. Phoebe Hesketh. **SP-HeskP**

Otherwise. John Ashbery. **SP-AshbJ**

Otherwise considered being is a force. The Child. Hayden Carruth. *Fr.* Contra Mortem. **CP-CarHL**

Otherworld. Muriel Rukeyser. **CP-RukeM**

Otho, *see also* Fragments Supposed to Be Part of Otho. Percy Bysshe Shelley. **CP-ShelP**

Otho the Great. John Keats. **CP-KeatJ**

Otho's scooped nut its pusillanimity. Catullus. *See* Carmen 54: "If not by all that his friends boast."

O'Toole / attempting an entry of the *mons Parnassus*. Carmen 105. Catullus. *Fr.* Carmina. **CP-Catul**

O'Toole is generally accounted. Carmen 114. Catullus. *Fr.* Carmina. **CP-Catul**

O'Toole is the proud master of. Carmen 115. Catullus. *Fr.* Carmina. **CP-Catul**

Otra vez soy llamado al campo eterno. Primer Amor. Edwin Rolfe, *tr. fr. Spanish by* Jose Manuel Cabezas Cabello. **CP-RolfE**

Ottava Rima would, I know, be proper. Wystan Hugh Auden. **NOBL** *Fr.* Letter to Lord Byron. **CP-AudeW**

Otter, The. Seamus Heaney. **SP-HeanS**

Otter, An. Ted Hughes. **SP-HughT**

Otto. Theodore Roethke. **CP-RoetT**

Otto ore suonano: / Picchia il postino! Christina Georgina Rossetti. **CP-RosC3**

Où Sont IIs, Où, Vierge Souvrain? Gilbert Sorrentino. **SP-SorrG**

Ought we, Raphael, to join / The builders of this city? The Legend of the Tower. Thomas Merton. *Fr.* The Tower of Babel—A Morality. **CP-MertT**

Ouija. Sylvia Plath. **CP-PlatS**

Our / YOUR FRIEND CHARLIE pawnshop. Riot: 60's. Maya Angelou. **SP-AngeM**

Our (American) Ragcademicians. William Carlos Williams. **CP-WilW1**

Our April must replenish the delightful wells. An April Manifesto. Louis MacNeice. **CP-MacNL**

Our *argute* voices vied among the bracken. Hampshire. Donald Davie. **CP-DavDo**

Our arms sleep / Together under water. Pillow. Tom Clark. **SP-ClarT**

Our author by experience finds it true. Prologue. John Dryden. **FiP; OBS; OxBoLi; SeCV-2** *Fr.* Aureng-Zebe. **SP-DrydJ**

Our Autocrat. John Greenleaf Whittier. **CP-WhitJ**

Our Avenue. John Hewitt. **CP-HewiJ**

Our bane and physic the same earth bestows. Ovid, *tr. by* Samuel Johnson. **CP-JohnS** *Fr.* Remediae Amoris.

Our bard, to modern epilogue a foe. Epilogue to Agamemnon. James Thomson. **CP-ThomJ**

Our bark's on the water; come down, come down. Love and Death. Christina Georgina Rossetti. **CP-RosC3**

Our Bastard-children are but like to Plate. Bastards. Robert Herrick. **CP-HerrR**

Our Bias. Wystan Hugh Auden. **CP-AudeW**

Our Birth Is But a Sleep. William Wordsworth. *See* Our birth is but a sleep and a forgetting.

Our birth is but a sleep and a forgetting. William Wordsworth. **ChTr; EaLo; FaBV; WGRP** *Fr.* Ode: Intimations of Immortality [from Recollections of Early Childhood]. **CP-WorW1**
    (Intimations of Immortality.) **ChTr**
    (Our Birth Is But a Sleep.) **FaBV**

Our boat is asleep on Serchio's stream. The Boat on the Serchio. Percy Bysshe Shelley. **CP-ShelP**

Our boat is asleep on Serchio's stream. Percy Bysshe Shelley. **Mes** *Fr.* The Boat on the Serchio. **CP-ShelP**

Our Bodies. Denise Levertov. **CP-LeveD**

Our bodily life, some plead, that life the shrine. William Wordsworth. *Fr.* Sonnets upon the Punishment of Death. **CP-WorW2**

Our Bog is Dood. Stevie Smith. **CP-SmitS**

Our bond is no little economy based on the exchange. Wendell Berry. *Fr.* The Country of Marriage. **CP-BerrW**

Our brains ache, in the merciless iced east winds that knive us. Exposure. Wilfred Owen. **CP-OwenW**

Our brethren of England, who love us so dear. An Excellent New Ballad. Jonathan Swift. **CP-SwifJ**

Our brows are wreathed with spindrift and the weed is on our knees. The Coastwise Lights. Rudyard Kipling. **CP-KiplR**

Our canoe idles in the idling current. Floating. Kenneth Rexroth. **SP-RexrK**

Our chief amusement was to lie naked. Written after Reading an Item in the Paper about a Young Lady Who Went Mad upon Forsaking Her Lover. He Is Here Assumed to Speak. Kenneth Patchen. **CP-PatcK**

Our Child Doesn't Know Anything. Ogden Nash. **CP-NashO**

Our Children, Coming of Age. Wendell Berry. **CP-BerrW**

Our Church Palms are Budding Willow Twigs. Christina Georgina Rossetti. **CP-RosC2**

Our Companie in the Next World. John Donne. **OBS** *Fr.* The Second Anniversary [*or* Anniversarie]. **ESCV; SeCP** *Fr.* Of the Progres[se] of the Soule; the Second Anniversarie. **CP-DonnJ**

Our conversation was short and sweet. You're a Big Girl Now. "Bob Dylan." **CP-DylaB**

Our cookbook is bound like Whitman's *Leaves of Grass-*. Beethoven. Robert Lowell. **SP-LoweR**

Our Country. John Greenleaf Whittier. **CP-WhitJ**

Our courage is an old legend. The Defeated: for Wales. Alun Lewis. **CP-LewiA**

Our Crosses are no other then the rods. Crosses. Robert Herrick. **CP-HerrR**

Our Curious Position. Charles Bukowski. **SP-BukC3**

Our Daily Bread. César Vallejo, *tr. fr. Spanish by* James Wright. **CP-WrigJ**

Our Day Is Over. David Herbert Lawrence. **CP-LawrD**

Our Desires. Jim Carroll. **SP-CarrJ**

Our destiny takes us, and binds us and breaks us. That's What I Mean. Malcolm Lowry. **CP-LowrM**

Our divinations, / Mechanisms of angelic thought. One of the Inhabitants of the West. Wallace Stevens. **CP-StevW**

Our Doom to Bloom. Robert Frost. **CP-FrosR**

Our earth in 1969. Doggerel by a Senior Citizen. Wystan Hugh Auden. **CP-AudeW**

Our elder brother whom we had not seen. Allen Tate. *Fr.* Sonnets of the Blood. **CP-TateA**

Our England is a garden that is full of stately views. The Glory of the Garden. Rudyard Kipling. **CP-KiplR**

Our epoch takes a voluptuous satisfaction. Hypocrite Auteur. Archibald MacLeish. **CP-MacLA**

Our era is dying. The Death of Our Era. David Herbert Lawrence. **CP-LawrD**

Our Eunuch Dreams. Dylan Thomas. **CP-ThomD**

Our Euripedes, the human / With his droppings of warm tears. Balaustion's Adventure. Robert Browning. **CP-BroR1**

Our eyeless bark sails free. The Earth. Ralph Waldo Emerson. **CP-EmerR**

Our eyes by day are good enough: only the birds. Robinson Jeffers. **CP-JefR3**

Our faces are like other faces. The Dwarfs. Siv Cedering Fox. **SP-CedeS**

Our Family. Leo Vroman, *tr. fr. Dutch by* Adrienne Rich. **CP-RicAE**

Our farewells lack the plausibility of our departures. Shorts / Excerpts. Bill Knott. **SP-KnotB**

Our Father. James Schuyler. **CP-SchuJ**

Our father is three months dead. Woodcutting on Lost Mountain. Tess Gallagher. **SP-GallT**

Our father sleeps. It is the hour when they. Heaven and Earth. Byron. **CP-Byron**

Our Father, who art neither in heaven, nor on earth. The Prayer of the Antichrist. John Gould Fletcher. **SP-FletJ** *Fr.* The Parables of Antichrist.

Our Father, whose creative Will. Wystan Hugh Auden. **TrPWD** *Fr.* The Summons. *Fr.* For the Time Being; a Christmas Oratorio. **CP-AudeW**

Our Fathers Also. Rudyard Kipling. **CP-KiplR**

Our fathers claimed, by obvious madness moved. Period I. Ogden Nash. *Fr.* Period Period. **CP-NashO**

Our fathers' God! from out whose hand. Centennial Hymn. John Greenleaf Whittier. **CP-WhitJ**

Our Fathers in a wondrous age. The Heritage. Rudyard Kipling. **CP-KiplR**

Our fathers in their books and speech. Orient Wheat. Adrienne Rich. **CP-RicAE**

Our fathers liked to carry persian beards. Jean Sans Terre Reviews the Fathers. Iwan Goll, *tr. fr. French by* William Carlos Williams. **CP-WilW2**

Our Fathers of Old. Rudyard Kipling. **CP-KiplR**

Our feet shall tread upon the stars. Eye Hath Not Seen. Christina Georgina Rossetti. **CP-RosC3**

Our fellow-countrymen in chains! Expostulation. John Greenleaf Whittier. **CP-WhitJ**

Our first daylight drive to Bridgetown. . . The stream. Woman's Tongue. Laurence Lieberman. **SP-LiebL**

Our Flag. Edward Estlin Cummings. **CP-CummE**

Our flesh that was a battle-ground. The Litany of the Dark People. Countee Cullen. **CP-CullC**

Our foolish neighbor farther up the hill. Folk Custom. John Hewitt. **CP-HewiJ**

Our friend X brought me your letter. Letter to One Who Has Abandoned The Way. Thomas Merton. *Fr.* Readings from Ibn Abbad. **CP-MertT**

Our Future Lot. Walt Whitman. **CP-WhitW**

Our gaieties, our luxuries / Our pleasures and our glee. In Stratis Viarum II. Arthur Hugh Clough. **SP-ClouA**

Our global story is not yet completed. Wystan Hugh Auden. *Fr.* Sonnets from China. **CP-AudeW**

Our Gloves are stiff with the frozen blood. Angutivaun Taina. Rudyard Kipling. **CP-KiplR** *Fr.* Quiquern. *Fr.* The Second Jungle Book.

Our God was to be a breath, and not a postcard. The View from Pisgah. Howard Nemerov. **CP-NemeH**

Our good knight, Ted, girds his broadsword on. The Knight. Paul Laurence Dunbar. **CP-DunbP**

Our good old friend is gone, gone to his rest. Translation of Verses to Lloyd. William Cowper, *ad. fr. the Latin of Vincent Bourne.* **CP-CowpW**

Our grandfathers were strangers and their absurd notions. The Seekers. Thomas McGrath. **SP-McGrT**

Our Guardian Angels and Their Children. Nicholas Vachel Lindsay. **CP-LindV**

Our half-thought thoughts divide in sifted wisps. Train to Dublin. Louis MacNeice. **CP-MacNL**

Our hammock swung between Americas. Elegy. Derek Walcott. **CP-WalcD**

Our haughty life is crowned with darkness. London, from Hampstead Heath. William Wordsworth. **FaBoPP** *Fr.* Extempore Effusion upon the Death of James Hogg. **CP-WorW2**

Our Hearts. Kenneth Koch. **SP-KochK**

Our heaven must be within ourselves / Our home and heaven the work of faith. Christina Georgina Rossetti. **CP-RosC2**

Our Hells. Carl Sandburg. **CP-SandC**

Our hill has made its submission and the green. Homage to Clio. Wystan Hugh Auden. **CP-AudeW**

Our history is grave noble and tragic. Men. Archibald MacLeish. **CP-MacLA**

Our Hold on the Planet. Robert Frost. **CP-FrosR**

Our honeymoon. Bridal Piece. Louise Glück. **SP-GlücL**

Our Honours, and our Commendations be. Merits Make the Man. Robert Herrick. **CP-HerrR**

Our host, Don Tomás Morel—retired mayor. Eros at the World Kite Pageant. Laurence Lieberman. **SP-LiebL**

Our house is dead / It burned to the ground. Lament—June 1944. Malcolm Lowry. **CP-LowrM**

Our house resettles, waiting there. The Old Saybrook House. John Clellon Holmes. **SP-HolmJ**

Our houses are one step from the gutter. Plastic curtains. Derek Walcott. **CP-WalcD** *Fr.* Midsummer.

Our houses parted as that shutter fell. Consequences. John Hewitt. **CP-HewiJ**

Our Houshold-gods our Parents be. The Primitiæ to Parents. Robert Herrick. **CP-HerrR**

Our Hunting Fathers. Wystan Hugh Auden. **CP-AudeW**

Our infantry is combing the hideouts. Thomas Merton. *Fr.* Cables to the Ace. **CP-MertT**

Our Islet out of Helgoland, dismissed. Islet the Dachs. George Meredith. **CP-MerG1**

Our Johnie's deid. The mair's the pity! To Charles Baxter. Robert Louis Stevenson. **CP-StevR**

Our journey had advanced. Emily Dickinson. **CP-DickE**

Our Kind. William Stafford. **SP-StafW**

Our King went forth on pilgrimage. The King's Pilgrimage. Rudyard Kipling. **CP-KiplR**

Our Ladie's Nativity. Robert Southwell. **CP-SoutR**

Our Lady. Donald Davie. **CP-DavDo**

Our Lady of Ardboe. Paul Muldoon. **SP-MuldP**

Our Lady of Solitude. Leonard Cohen. **CP-CoheL**

Our Lady of the Sackcloth. Rudyard Kipling. **CP-KiplR**

Our Lady of the Snow. William Wordsworth. *Fr.* Memorials of a Tour of the Continent; 1820. **CP-WorW2**

Our Lady of the Snows. Rudyard Kipling. **CP-KiplR**

Our Lady of the Snows. Robert Louis Stevenson. **CP-StevR**

Our Ladye's Spousalls. Robert Southwell. **CP-SoutR**

Our Lady's [*or* Ladie's] Salutation. Robert Southwell. **CP-SoutR**

Our Lady's Winter Words. Theodore Roethke. **CP-RoetT**

Our last connection with the mythic. Planting Trees. John Updike. **CP-UpdiJ**

Our last morning in that long room. In the Last Few Moments Came the Old German Cleaning Woman. Jane Cooper. **SP-CoopJ**

Our Latin books, in motley row. A Lesson in Latin. "Lewis Carroll." **CP-CarrL**

Our leader / is a man of water. Margaret Atwood. *Fr.* Two-Headed Poems. **SP-AtwM2**

Our letters cross by nosing silver. Letter from India. Louis MacNeice. **CP-MacNL**

Our life is long. Not so, wise Angels say. Christina Georgina Rossetti. **CP-RosC2**

Our life is two fold: Sleep hath its own world. The Dream. Byron. **CP-Byron**

Our life splinters like the wood under my axe. For Judy. Chuck Miller. **SP-MillC**

Our little baby fell asleep. Christina Georgina Rossetti. **CP-RosC2**

Our little Kinsmen—after Rain. Emily Dickinson. **CP-DickE**

Our little secrets slink away. Emily Dickinson. **CP-DickE**

Our lives are Swiss. Emily Dickinson. **CP-DickE**

Our lives before hopelessly our mistake!—. John Berryman. *Fr.* Sonnets to Chris. **CP-BerrJ**

Our lives we do not weep. Men With Coats Thrashing. Malcolm Lowry. **CP-LowrM**

Our living proof that provokes the cat. Small Substantial Shadow. Steve Griffiths. **SP-GrifS**

Our Lord in His Circumcision to His Father. Richard Crashaw. **CP-CrasR**

Our Lord Who did the Ox command. Carol, A. Rudyard Kipling. **CP-KiplR**

Our lords are to the mountains gane. Hughie Graham. Robert Burns. **CP-BurnR**

Our love conducted as in tropic rain. John Berryman. *Fr.* Sonnets to Chris. **CP-BerrJ**

Our love has chosen its appropriate gesture. Lesson. Bill Knott. **SP-KnotB**

Our love is full of memorable things. Sonnet. John Hewitt. **CP-HewiJ**

Our love will not come back on fortune's wheel. Obit. Robert Lowell. **SP-LoweR**

Our man has mown today. Emily Dickinson. **SP-DickE**

Our marriage book, it. The Drill. Charles Bukowski. **SP-BukC1**

Our Martyred Soldiers. Paul Laurence Dunbar. **CP-DunbP**

Our Master. John Greenleaf Whittier. **CP-WhitJ**

"We may not climb the heavenly steeps." **BLRP; WBLP,** *ll.* 17–64;

Our Master lies asleep and is at rest. Mary Magdalene and the Other Mary. Christina Georgina Rossetti. **CP-RosC2**

Our meetings are no longer like a screening. Robert Lowell. *Fr.* Mermaid. **SP-LoweR**

Our mood had dissipated: a restless night. In Mexico. Frederick Morgan. **SP-MorgF**

Our Moral Age. David Herbert Lawrence. **CP-LawrD**

Our mortall parts may wrapt in Seare-cloths lye. Great Spirits Supervive. Robert Herrick. **CP-HerrR**

Our mother knew our worth---. Our Kind. William Stafford. **SP-StafW**

Our Mother Pocahontas. Nicholas Vachel Lindsay. **CP-LindV**

"Powhatan was conqueror / Powhatan was emperor."

"She heard the forest talking."

"We here renounce our Saxon blood."

Our mother, while she turned her wheel. Mother. John Greenleaf Whittier. **AA; OHIP** *Fr.* Snow-Bound [*or* Snow-Bound; a Winter Idyl]. **CP-WhitJ**

Our Mothers, lovely women pitiful; / Our sisters, gracious in their life and death. Christina Georgina Rossetti. **CP-RosC2**

Our news is seldom good: the heart. Wystan Hugh Auden. **FaBoRV** *Fr.* New Year Letter. **CP-AudeW**

Our Office Cat. Stevie Smith. **CP-SmitS**

Our Old Feuillage. Walt Whitman. **CP-WhitW**

Our Old Friend Dualism. Thomas Hardy. **CP-HardT**

Our one foreboding was: we might forget. Brief Reunion. Robert Ranke Graves. **CP-GravR**

Our orchestra / is the cat's nuts. Shoot It Jimmy! William Carlos Williams. **CP-WilW1**

Our own hearts too like, seems's-zo, whenever. Hayden Carruth. *Fr.* The Sleeping Beauty. **CP-CarHL**

Our own possessions—though our own. Emily Dickinson. **CP-DickE**

Our Owne Sinnes Unseen. Robert Herrick. **CP-HerrR**

Our Padre. Sir John Betjeman. **CP-BetjJ**

Our passions are most like to floods and stream[e]s. Sir Walter Ralegh to the Queen. Sir Walter Ralegh. **CP-RaleW**

Our play is done; and yours doth now begin. Epilogue. Sir John Suckling. *Fr.* Aglaura. **CP-SuckJ**

Our poor angel how sick. Hounding Mercy. Charles Kenneth Williams. **CP-WillC**

Our portion of fire. The Manichaeans. Gary Snyder. **CP-SnydG**

Our Prayer of Thanks. Carl Sandburg. **CP-SandC**

Our present Teares here (not our present laughter). Teares. Robert Herrick. **CP-HerrR**

Our Princess married. The Forlorn Sea. Stevie Smith. **CP-SmitS**

Our purple tongues that testify. For Proserpine. Stanley Jasspon Kunitz. **CP-KuniS**

Our River. John Greenleaf Whittier. **CP-WhitJ**

Our royal king and queen, God bless. Ben Jonson's Grace before King James. Ben Jonson. **CP-JonsB**

Our rural ancestors, with little blest. The Ideals of Satire. Alexander Pope. **FiP** *Fr.* The First Epistle of the Second Book of Horace Imitated. **CP-PopeA**

Our sainted great-great. Gallows Etiquette. Charles Simic. **SP-SimiC**

Our sardine fishermen work at night in the dark of the moon; daylight or moonlight. The Purse-Seine. Robinson Jeffers. **CP-JefR2**

Our second Eve putts on her mortall shrowde. The Conception of our Ladie. Robert Southwell. **CP-SoutR**

Our Self. Robert Ranke Graves. **CP-GravR**

Our set of strollers, wandering up and down. Billet to the Company of Players. Jonathan Swift. **CP-SwifJ**

Our shadows now grow long in the sun. Louis MacNeice. *Fr.* The Island. **CP-MacNL**

Our Shah's counsel is the efflux. Hafiz, *tr. by* Ralph Waldo Emerson. **CP-EmerR** *Fr.* Odes.

Our share of night to bear. Emily Dickinson. **CP-DickE**

Our shells clacked on the plates. Oysters. Seamus Heaney. **SP-HeanS**

Our ship (in this easy metaphor I employ. The Læstrygonians. William Dickey. **SP-DickW**

Our Singing Strength. Robert Frost. **CP-FrosR**

Our single purpose was to walk through snow. Polar Exploration. Stephen Spender. **CP-SpenS**

Our sister sayeth such and such. The Nursing Sister. Rudyard Kipling. **CP-KiplR** *Fr.* The Naulahka.

Our Sister Water. Louis MacNeice. **CP-MacNL**

"Back in the Seventeen-Seventies to Birmingham he came."

"Steam is a dry word; the best word is water."

"Water is beginning, is end, is pure, is pure gift."

"World's best is water; in the megrims of parched."

Our songs went up and out the chimney. At the Entering of the New Year. Thomas Hardy. **CP-HardT**

Our Stars Come from Ireland. Wallace Stevens. **CP-StevW**

Our State. John Greenleaf Whittier. **CP-WhitJ**

Our storm[e] is past, and that storm[e]'s tyrannous rage. The Calm[e]. John Donne. **CP-DonnJ**

Our summer's gone. My Life Has Turned to Blue. Maya Angelou. **SP-AngeM**

Our Sunday morning when dawn-priests were applying. John Berryman. *Fr.* Sonnets to Chris. **CP-BerrJ**

Our Sunday School Teacher. John Hewitt. **CP-HewiJ**

Our swans are now of such remorseless quill. Modern Poets. Gerard Manley Hopkins. *Fr.* Seven Epigrams. **CP-HopkG**

Our Sweetheart, Spring, came softly. Sweetheart Spring. Nicholas Vachel Lindsay. *Fr.* Sweethearts of the Year. **CP-LindV**

Our teachers teach that one and one make two. Christina Georgina Rossetti. *Fr.* Later Life: A Double Sonnet of Sonnets. **CP-RosC2**

Our tickets / won't be honored. A Trip. Daniel Gerard Hoffman. **SP-HoffD**

Our toothless chauffeur with the rubber face. Nicolai, Courier in Belgrade. John Hewitt. **CP-HewiJ**

Our touching hearts slenderly comprehend. Edward Estlin Cummings. **CP-CummE**

Our towns spill out, yet at the heart decay. The Ruins Answer. John Hewitt. **CP-HewiJ**

Our trees seem leaflesser. Around Here. Archie Randolph Ammons. **SP-AmmoA**

Our Twentieth Wedding Anniversary (Elizabeth). Robert Lowell. **SP-LoweR**

Our Two Worthies. John Crowe Ransom. **SP-RansJ**

Our uncrowned kings have no such regal rind. Melongène. Richard Wilbur. **CP-WilbR**

Our valentine the heart proposed by three. The Record. Louis Zukofsky. **CP-ZukLS**

Our vales are sweet with fern and rose. The Old Burying-Ground. John Greenleaf Whittier. **CP-WhitJ**

Our Walk in Yorkshire. Donald Hall. **CP-HallD**

Our walk was far among the ancient trees. To M. H. William Wordsworth. **CP-WorW1**

Our wealth has wasted all away. I Look for the Lord. Christina Georgina Rossetti. **CP-RosC3**

Our whistling son called his canary Hector. Boy, Cat, Canary. Stephen Spender. **CP-SpenS**

Our Whole Life. Adrienne Rich. **CP-RicAE; SP-RicA1; SP-RicA2**

Our Widowed Queen. Christina Georgina Rossetti. **CP-RosC3**

Our Willie had been sae lang awa'. The Wandering Burgess. "Lewis Carroll." **CP-CarrL**

Our young lady's a huntin gane. The Rowin 't in Her Apron. Robert Burns. **CP-BurnR**

Our Youth. John Ashbery. **SP-AshbJ**

Ourchestra. Shel Silverstein. **SP-SilS2**

Our[e] ho[o]ste saugh [or sey] wel that the brighte sonne. Introduction to the Man of Law's Tale. Geoffrey Chaucer. **FiP** *Fr.* The Canterbury Tales. **CP-ChauG**

Oure Hoste [or Hooste] gan to swere as he were wood. Introduction to the Pardoner's Tale. Geoffrey Chaucer. **FHYEP; NAEL-1; NoP; OAEL-1; PoE** *Fr.* The Canterbury Tales. **CP-ChauG**

Oure sweete Lord God of hevene, that no. The Parson's Tale. Geoffrey Chaucer. *Fr.* The Canterbury Tales. **CP-ChauG**

Ours is No Wedlock. Robert Ranke Graves. **CP-GravR**

Ours is the ancient story. For Daughters of Magdalen. Countee Cullen. **CP-CullC**

Ours was a short day. Decline of the West. John Clellon Holmes. **SP-HolmJ**

Ours yet not ours, being set apart. For Friends Only. Wystan Hugh Auden. *Fr.* Thanksgiving for a Habitat. **CP-AudeW**

Ourselves we do inter with sweet derision. Emily Dickinson. **CP-DickE**

Ourselves were wed one summer—dear. Emily Dickinson. **CP-DickE**

Out. Margaret Atwood. **SP-AtwM2**

Out. Robert Creeley. **CP-CreeR**

Out. Ted Hughes. **SP-HughT**

    "Dead man in his cave beginning to sweat, The."

    Dream Time, The.

    Remembrance Day.

Out, all the way, without. Applause. Charles Olson. **CP-OlsoC**

Out alone in the winter rain. The Thatch. Robert Frost. **CP-FrosR**

Out and In, *sels.* Kenneth Koch. *Fr.* Days and Nights. **SP-KochK**

Out and in the river is winding. The Red River Voyageur. John Greenleaf Whittier. **CP-WhitJ**

Out back of the sideshow. The Geek. Ted Kooser. **SP-KoosT**

Out-fleeced bushes like a spaniel's ear. Gerard Manley Hopkins. *See* Thick-fleeced bushes like a heifer's ear.

Out for a walk, after a week in bed. An Urban Convalescence. James Merrill. **SP-MerrJ**

Out from Behind This Mask. Walt Whitman. **CP-WhitW**

Out from Jerusalem / The king rode with his great. King Solomon and the Ants. John Greenleaf Whittier. **CP-WhitJ**

Out Here. Richard Shelton. **SP-ShelR**

Out here on Cottage Grove it matters. The galloping. Pyrography. John Ashbery. **SP-AshbJ**

Out here there are no hearthstones. Sleep in the Mojave Desert. Sylvia Plath. **CP-PlatS**

Out, hunchback! / I was born so, mother! The Deformed Transformed. Byron. **CP-ByroN**

Out in de night a sad bird moans. The Memory of Martha. Paul Laurence Dunbar. **CP-DunbP**

Out in the air, the statue. From the 'Town Guide'. Roy Fisher. **SP-FishR**

Out in the country. Vir IX. James Liddy. *Fr.* Vir I–XII. **CP-LiddJ**

Out in the early morning, by empty roads. Roy Fisher. **SP-FishR** *Fr.* New Diversions.

Out in the elegy country, summer evenings. Blue Suburban. Howard Nemerov. **CP-NemeH**

Out in the green sun-dancing cane a mad half-Spaniard. Fugitive. Thomas Merton. **CP-MertT**

Out in the Lane I Pause. Philip Larkin. **CP-LarkP**

Out in the late amber afternoon. In Shadow. Hart Crane. **CP-CranH**

Out in the rain a world is growing green. Easter Monday. Christina Georgina Rossetti. **CP-RosC2**

Out in the sky the great dark clouds are massing. Ships That Pass in the Night. Paul Laurence Dunbar. **CP-DunbP**

Out in the soundless / World that the window. Anxious View of a Tree. Hayden Carruth. **CP-CarHS**

Out in the visible city, the heart. At Italo's. David St. John. *Fr.* To Pasolini. **SP-StJoD**

Out in the visible city, the heart. To Pasolini. David St. John. **SP-StJoD**

Out in the yellow meadows, where the bee. George Meredith. **GBL** *Fr.* Modern Love. **CP-MerG1**

Out in this desert we are testing bombs. Trying to Talk with a Man. Adrienne Rich. **SP-RicA1; SP-RicA2**

Out in what we may as well term the dark. Everything Is a Still-Life. Gilbert Sorrentino. **SP-SorrG**

Out Is Out. Ogden Nash. **CP-NashO**

Out o' the wilderness, dusty an' dry. Columns. Rudyard Kipling. **CP-KiplR**

Out of a bellicose fore-time, thundering. River Profile. Wystan Hugh Auden. **CP-AudeW**

Out of a blow dryer Santa Ana rolling. Fireflies. Tom Clark. **SP-ClarT**

Out of a chaos of red chimney-pots. Elegy on London. John Gould Fletcher. **SP-FletJ**

Out of a dark into the dark she leaped. All the Beautiful are Blameless. James Wright. **CP-WrigJ**

Out of a descended generation. Fruits of Virtue. Steve Griffiths. **SP-GrifS**

Out of a Descended Generation. Steve Griffiths. **SP-GrifS**

Out of a Fever: For Robert Lowell (Sept. 13, 1977). John Clellon Holmes. **SP-HolmJ**

Out of a fired ship, which, by no way. A Burnt Ship. John Donne. **CP-DonnJ**

Out of a gothic North, the pallid children. Good-Bye to the Mezzogiorno. Wystan Hugh Auden. **CP-AudeW**

Out of a government grant to poets, I paid. Economics. Mona Van Duyn. **SP-VanDM**

Out of a half- / demolished church. To Transcend the Cat. Leonard Nathan. **SP-NathL**

Out of a quiet mood of night. Silences. Gilbert Sorrentino. **SP-SorrG**

Out of a sealed window. In Another Town. Miller Williams. **SP-WillM**

Out of a supermetamathical subpreincestures. Edward Estlin Cummings. **CP-CummE**

Out Of Bounds. Walter de la Mare. **CP-DeLaW**

Out of burlap sacks, out of bearing butter. They Feed They Lion. Philip Levine. **SP-LeviP**

Out of Catullus. Ausonius, *tr. fr. Latin by* Richard Crashaw. **CP-CrasR**

Out of Catullus. Catullus. *See* Carmen 5: "Lesbia / live with me."

Out of Darkness I Came. Tom Clark. **SP-ClarT**

Out of East Anglia. Donald Davie. **CP-DavDo**

Out of Egypt. Mary's Song. Anne Sexton. **CP-SextA**

Out of Euphormio, *fr. the Latin of* Euphormio. Richard Crashaw. **CP-CrasR**

Out of *Grotius* his Tragedy of *Christes* Sufferinges, *ad. fr. the Latin of*Grotius. Richard Crashaw. **CP-CrasR**

Out of her womb of pain my mother spat me. Audre Lorde. **SP-LordA** *Fr.* Story Books on a Kitchen Table.

(Story Books on a Kitchen Table.) **SP-LordA**

Out of him that I loved. Our Stars Come from Ireland. Wallace Stevens. **CP-StevW**

Out of Honolulu. Heading for Nandi. John Updike. **CP-UpdiJ**

Out of Horace, *Class. Gr. trans. incl.* Horace. **CP-CrasR,** *tr. by* Richard Crashaw; *Fr.* Odes.

Out of it steps our future, through this door. Wystan Hugh Auden. **Son** *Fr.* The Quest. **CP-AudeW**

(Door, The.) **Son**

Out of love, / No regrets. No Regrets. Langston Hughes. **SP-HughL**

Out of Martiall. Martial, *tr. fr. Latin by* Richard Crashaw. **CP-CrasR**

Out of May's Shows Selected. Walt Whitman. **CP-WhitW**

Out of midsummer's blazing most not night. Edward Estlin Cummings. **CP-CummE**

Out of mist, God's. Interjection #6: What You Sometimes Feel on Your Face at Night. Robert Penn Warren. **SP-WarrR**

Out o' Mobile I saw a '60 Ford. Plain. Miller Williams. **SP-WillM**

Out of more find than seeks. Edward Estlin Cummings. **CP-CummE**

Out of my flesh that happens. *with music.* Audre Lorde. **SP-LordA**

Out of my heart, one day, I wrote a song. Misapprehension. Paul Laurence Dunbar. **CP-DunbP**

Out of my heart, one treach'rous winter's day. Love and Grief. Paul Laurence Dunbar. **CP-DunbP**

Out of my own great woe. *ad.fr.*Heine. Elizabeth Barrett Browning. **CP-BroEB**

Out of my pen: curses ride down. Mother's Curse. Anne Waldman. **SP-WaldA**

Out of my poverty. Conversation by the Body's Light. Jane Cooper. **SP-CoopJ**

Out of My Soul's Depth. Thomas Campion. **CP-CampT**

Out of night's almosT Floats a colour(in). Edward Estlin Cummings. **CP-CummE**

Out of nothing. Hayden Carruth. *Fr.* The Sleeping Beauty. **CP-CarHL**

Out of Nothing. Robert Pack. **SP-PackR**

Out of our own mouths we are sentenced. Last Journal. Charles Wright. **SP-WrigC**

Out of Petronius. Petronius Arbiter, *tr. fr. Latin by* Richard Crashaw. **CP-CrasR**

Out of Phlegethon! Canto 75. Ezra Pound. *Fr.* Cantos. **CP-PoCan**

Out of poverty / to begin. Song, the Winds of Downhill. George Oppen. **CP-OppeG**

Out of poverty. White. Charles Simic. **SP-SimiC**

Out of puff / noonhot in tweeds and gray felt. Basil Bunting. *Fr.* Attis: Or, Something Missing. **CP-BuntB**

Out of shape, / my legs ache. The Walk. James Schuyler. **CP-SchuJ**

Out of Sight. Robert Creeley. **CP-CreeR**

Out of sight assuredly, not out of mind. Wystan Hugh Auden. **CP-AudWJ**

Out of Sight in the Direction of My Body. Paul Éluard, *tr. fr. French by* Samuel Beckett. **CP-BeckS**

Out of sight? What of that? Emily Dickinson. **CP-DickE**

Out of silence. Koto Music/Singing. Al Young. **CP-YounA**

Out of silence walks delight. Into Broad Daylight. Robert Penn Warren. **SP-WarrR**

Out of Sleep Awakened. Archibald MacLeish. **CP-MacLA**

Out of the Ash. William Everson. **SP-EverW**

Out of the bigg / est the knownun. Edward Estlin Cummings. **CP-CummE**

Out of the Blue. Charles Bukowski. **SP-BukC3**

Out of the blue, in plaster from wrist to bicep. Strato in Plaster. James Merrill. **SP-MerrJ**

Out of the bosom of the air. Snow-Flakes. Henry Wadsworth Longfellow. **SP-LongH**

Out of the cellar, scraping around for coal. Geranium. Jenny Joseph. *Fr.* Derivations. **SP-JoseJ**

Out of the church she followed [*or* follow'd] them. Maude Clare. Christina Georgina Rossetti. **CP-RosC1**

Out of the Cradle Endlessly Rocking. Walt Whitman. **CP-WhitW**

Out of the darkness, fretted sometimes in its sleeping. Blueness. David Herbert Lawrence. **CP-LawrD**

Out of the Deep. Christina Georgina Rossetti. **CP-RosC3**

Out of the depths [*or* deep] have I cried unto thee [*or* I called thee], O Lord. Psalm 130. Bible, O.T. **BLRP; TrGrPo; TrJP; WGRP** *Fr.* Psalms. **CP-Psal**

Out of the earth beneath the water. The Mud Turtle. Howard Nemerov. **CP-NemeH**

Out of the East, and out of the West, no man understands me. Hafiz, *tr. by* Ralph Waldo Emerson. **CP-EmerR** *Fr.* Odes.

Out of the filing cabinet of true steel. The Crucifix in the Filing Cabinet. Karl Shapiro. **SP-ShapK**

Out of the fire. Pool. Carl Sandburg. **CP-SandC**

Out of the fire out of the mouth. Stevens Song. Charles Olson. **SP-OlsoC** *Fr.* The Maximus Poems.

Out of the first warmth of spring. Celle Qui Fût Héaulmiette. Wallace Stevens. **CP-StevW**

Out of the foliage of sensual pride. Good Husbandry. Geoffrey Hill. *Fr.* Locust Songs. **CP-HillG**

Out of the garden. Hayden Carruth. **CP-CarHS** *Fr.* The Clay Hill Anthology.

Out of the Greeke Cupid's Cryer. Moschus, *tr. fr. Classical Greek by* Richard Crashaw. **CP-CrasR**

Out of the grey wet sand. Rotterdam. John Hewitt. **CP-HewiJ**

Out of the Italain. Giovanni Battista Marino, *tr. fr. Italian by* Richard Crashaw. **CP-CrasR**

Out of the Italian. Ammianus Marcellinus, *tr. fr. Italian by* Richard Crashaw. **CP-CrasR**

Out of the Italian; a Song, *ad.fr. the Italian of* Ceba. Richard Crashaw. **CP-CrasR**

Out of the lie of no. Edward Estlin Cummings. **CP-CummE**

Out of the light of Heaven the flower. Charles Olson. **SP-OlsoC** *Fr.* The Maximus Poems.

Out of the little chapel I burst. Christmas-Eve. Robert Browning. **CP-BroR1**

Out of the living word. The Book of Kells. Howard Nemerov. **CP-NemeH**

Out of the maternal watery blue lines. Ted Hughes. *Fr.* Curlews Lift. **SP-HughT**

Out of the mould from the molten flow. Any Page of Thomas Mann's. Marsden Hartley. **CP-HartM**

Out of the mountain of his soul comes. Edward Estlin Cummings. **CP-CummE**

Out of the mud two strangers came. Two Tramps in Mud Time. Robert Frost. **CP-FrosR**

Out of the murk of heaviest clouds. Spain, 1873–74. Walt Whitman. **CP-WhitW**

Out of the pants which cover me. Edward Estlin Cummings. **CP-CummE**

Out of the past there rises a week. The Change. Thomas Hardy. **CP-HardT**

Out of the Picture. Louis MacNeice. **CP-MacNL**
     Empty Shoes.
     Finale.
     Jingles of the Morning, The.
     Les Neiges d'Antan.
     Oracle, The.
     Pindar is Dead.
     Riding in Cars.
     War Heroes.

Out of the rain and the darkness and the depths, the bottomless holes in the green sea. Thomas Merton. *Fr.* The Early Legend. **CP-MertT**

Out of the Rainbow End. Carl Sandburg. **CP-SandC**

"Out of the Rolling Ocean, the Crowd . . . ." Robert Bly. **SP-BlyR**

Out of the Rolling Ocean the Crowd. Walt Whitman. **CP-WhitW**

Out of the seagull cries and wind. To Liberty. Hart Crane. **CP-CranH**

Out of the shut cell of that solitude there is. Something: a Direction. Charles Tomlinson. *Fr.* Antecedents. **CP-TomlC**

Out of the Sighs. Dylan Thomas. **CP-ThomD**

Out of the silence, the saying. Into. The Enclave. Robert Penn Warren. *Fr.* The True Nature of Time. **SP-WarrR**

Out of the small domestic jungle. The Junction, on a Warm Afternoon. Howard Nemerov. **CP-NemeH**

Out of the sump rise the marigolds. Marengo. Mary Oliver. **SP-OlivM**

Out of the sun and the dispersing stars. The Concert. Robert Duncan. **SP-DuncR** *Fr.* Passages.

Out of the sun, out of the blast. Our Lady of the Snows. Robert Louis Stevenson. **SP-StevR**

Out of the sunshine and out of the heat. The Dove. Paul Laurence Dunbar. **CP-DunbP**

Out of the table endlessly rocking. Just Friends. Robert Creeley. **CP-CreeR**

Out of the testimony of such relcutant lips, out of the oaths and mouths. High Conspiratorial Persons. Carl Sandburg. **CP-SandC**

Out of the tomb, we bring Badroulbadour. The Worms at Heaven's Gate. Wallace Stevens. **CP-StevW**

Out of the watercolored windows, when you look. Poem to Johann Sebastian Bach. Delmore Schwartz. **SP-SchwD**

Out of the waves they clomb, plant, insect, fish, and bird. John Gould Fletcher. **SP-FletJ** *Fr.* Branches of Adam.

Out of the weather, in the first room. The Trading Post. Lewis Turco. **SP-TurcL**

Out of the woods he came. Edward Thomas. Phoebe Hesketh. **SP-HeskP**

Out of the woods where pollen is a powder of gold. A Vision: Circa 1880. Robert Penn Warren. *Fr.* Mortmain. **SP-WarrR**

Out of the world he must, who once comes in. None Free from Fault. Robert Herrick. **CP-HerrR**

Out of the zero under sound, the pure. Allegro Vivace. James McAuley. *Fr.* The Exile's Fifth Symphony. **SP-McAuJ**

Out of Their Butchered Hearts. Gilbert Sorrentino. **SP-SorrG**

Out of this oubliette between the mountains. Misery. David Herbert Lawrence. **CP-LawrD**

Out of this sea of time, a hidden shape now rises. Journey Day. John Gould Fletcher. **SP-FletJ**

Out of those hallways. A March. Denise Levertov. **CP-LeveD**

Out of Time. Stevie Smith. **CP-SmitS**

Out of Time, Out of Tune. Robert Herrick. **CP-HerrR**

Out of Virgil, in the Praise of the Spring. Virgil. **CP-CrasR**, *tr. by* Richard Crashaw; *Fr.* Georgics.

Out of White Lips. Carl Sandburg. **CP-SandC**

Out on the high "bird islands," Ciboux and Hertford. Cape Breton. Elizabeth Bishop. **CP-BishE**

Out on the lawn I lie in bed. A Summer Night. Wystan Hugh Auden. **CP-AudeW**

Out, Out —. Robert Frost. **CP-FrosR**

Out, out, away! my blood boils up! The Hungarian Horse-Herd. Karl Beck, *tr. fr. German by* George Meredith. **CP-MerG2**

Out over the Forth, I look to the North. I Look to the North. Robert Burns. **CP-BurnR**

Out Picking up Corn. Robert Bly. **SP-BlyR**

Out shines again the glorious round sun. The Near Eclipse. Robert Ranke Graves. **CP-GravR**

Out—so this means you render them, ten sestertia, Silo. Catullus. *See* Carmen 103: "Either give me my hundred pounds back, Silo."

Out somewhere in the middle of the crickets. The School of Summer. Randall Jarrell. **CP-JarrR**

Out the same picture window the pine bow. The Clouds. Charles Olson. **CP-OlsoC**

Out the window, the cow out the window. The Simplicity of the Unknown Past. Kenneth Koch. **SP-KochK**

Out There. Anne Waldman. **SP-WaldA**

Out there in the dark, what's that horrible chomping? Go it, Granny—Go it, Hog! Robert Penn Warren. *Fr.* Ballad of a Sweet Dream of Peace. **SP-WarrR**

Out there in the fighting. What the Old Women Say. Archibald MacLeish. **CP-MacLA**

Out there, out there beyond the air. The Spy. Howard Nemerov. **CP-NemeH**

Out there. The mind of the river. Study of History. Adrienne Rich. **CP-RicAE; SP-RicA2**

Out there, we've walked quite friendly up to Death. The Next War. Wilfred Owen. **CP-OwenW**

Out through the fields and the woods. Reluctance. Robert Frost. **CP-FrosR**

Out to one side. Roy Fisher. **SP-FishR** *Fr.* Diversions.

Out to the yard a faintest bluish tinge. Warm Mountain Poem for Matt Liban. James Liddy. **CP-LiddJ**

Out, traitor absence: dar'st thou counsel me. Sonnet 88. Sir Philip Sidney. *Fr.* Astrophil and Stella. **SP-SidnP**

Out upon it! I have loved [*or* lov'd]. Sir John Suckling. **BeJo; CBLP; EBEvV; GGP; HeIP; ImPo; NBLV; NOSC; OxAEP-1; PBMP; PeLV; PoE; SeCV-1** *Fr.* A Poem with the Answer. **CP-SuckJ**

(Constant Lover, A [*or* The].) **CBLP; GGP; HeIP; ImPo; NOSC; OxAEP-1; PBMP**

(Sir S.J.) **SeCV-1**

Out walking in the frozen swamp one gray [*or* grey] day. The Wood-Pile. Robert Frost. **CP-FrosR**

Out-worn heart, in a time out-worn. Into the Twilight. William Butler Yeats. **CP-YeatW**

Outbound, your bark awaits you. Were I one. Godspeed. John Greenleaf Whittier. **CP-WhitJ**

Outcast, The. Samuel Taylor Coleridge. *Fr.* Effusions. **CP-ColeS**

Outcast. Richard Shelton. **SP-ShelR**

Outcast City on the Kennebec, The. Marsden Hartley. **CP-HartM**

Outcome of Mr. Buck's Superstition, The. Ogden Nash. **CP-NashO**

Outcrop stone is miserly. Still-Life. Ted Hughes. **SP-HughT**

Outcry. A circus on another planet. The hero does not trust the evidence of verbs. Thomas Merton. *Fr.* Cables to the Ace. **CP-MertT**

Outcry upon Opportunity, An. William Shakespeare. *See* Opportunity.

Outdoor Concert, The. Thom Gunn. **CP-GunnT**

Outdoor Reception, An. John Greenleaf Whittier. **CP-WhitJ**

Outer and Inner. George Meredith. **CP-MerG1**

Outer Banks, The. Muriel Rukeyser. **CP-RukeM**

Outer—from the Inner, The. Emily Dickinson. **CP-DickE**

Outlandish Agon. Mona Van Duyn. **SP-VanDM**

Outlandish as a circus, the ravaged face. The Ravaged Face. Sylvia Plath. **CP-PlatS**

Outlasting You. Robert Pack. **SP-PackR**

Outlaw, The. Sir Walter Scott. *See* Brignall Banks.

Outlaw Blues. "Bob Dylan." **CP-DylaB**

Outlaw of the Lowest Planet, The. Kenneth Patchen. **CP-PatcK**

Outlaws. Robert Ranke Graves. **CP-GravR**

Outlaws, The. Rudyard Kipling. **CP-KiplR**

Outlaws claw mostly to a riddled end. John Berryman. *Fr.* Sonnets to Chris. **CP-BerrJ**

Outlines / start to appear. Roy Fisher. **SP-FishR** *Fr.* Diversions.

Outlines for a Tomb. Walt Whitman. **CP-WhitW**

Outlivers (Harriet and Elizabeth). Robert Lowell. **SP-LoweR**

Outpost. Muriel Rukeyser. **CP-RukeM**

Outside, / the snow is falling into its past. Widower's Winter. Bill Knott. **SP-KnotB**

Outside Fargo, North Dakota. James Wright. **CP-WrigJ**

Outside: forecasts of humiliating storms. A Night with Cindy at Heitman's. Richard Hugo. **CP-HugoR**

Outside his library window he could see. Montaigne. Wystan Hugh Auden. **CP-AudeW**

Outside in the street I hear. Family Reunion. Sylvia Plath. **CP-PlatS**

Outside my senses, known as printed words. Hedgehog. John Hewitt. **CP-HewiJ**

Outside my window. The Night Rides of My Neighbor, Lorca, That Prevent Sleep. Diane Wakoski. **SP-WakoD**

Outside St. Louis. Etheridge Knight. *Fr.* Missouri Haiku. **SP-KnigE**

Outside, sun, frost, wind, rain. Kathleen Jessie Raine. *Fr.* The Hollow Hill. **SP-RainK**

Outside the Casement. Thomas Hardy. **CP-HardT**

Outside, the children play Ping-Pong. Ping-Pong. Peter Meinke. **SP-MeinP**

Outside, the crackhead who panhandles an eight. Little Blue Nude. William Matthews. **SP-MattW**

Outside the Creeds. John Hewitt. **CP-HewiJ**

Outside the Crowd. George Meredith. **CP-MerG2**

Outside the Diner. Thom Gunn. **CP-GunnT**

Outside the door, the noises of the sleugh. Zombie. Lewis Turco. **SP-TurcL**

Outside the factory window April came. April in a Town. Wystan Hugh Auden. **CP-AudWJ**

Outside the great clanging cathedrals of rust and smoke. A Poem Written under an Archway in a Discontinued Railroad Station, Fargo, North Dakota. James Wright. **CP-WrigJ**

Outside, the heirs of purity pick by. Violet and Jasper. Richard Wilbur. **CP-WilbR**

Outside the House. Le Singe qui swing. Stevie Smith. **CP-SmitS**

Outside the house an ash-tree hung its terrible whips. Discord in Childhood. David Herbert Lawrence. **CP-LawrD**

Outside, the last kids holler. Leaving the Motel. William DeWitt Snodgrass. **SP-SnodW**

Outside, the night is glowing. Second Language. Tess Gallagher. **SP-GallT**

Outside the porthole life, or what is. Flight. George Oppen. **CP-OppeG**

Outside the rain upon the street. A Musical. Paul Laurence Dunbar. **CP-DunbP**

Outside the vineyard is a caravan. Graffiti from the Gare Saint-Manqué. Marilyn Hacker. **SP-HackM**

Outside the Wall. Leonard Nathan. **SP-NathL**

Outside the window. Wendell Berry. *Fr.* Window Poems. **CP-BerrW**

Outside the Window. Thomas Hardy. *Fr.* Satires of Circumstance in Fifteen Glimpses. **CP-HardT**

Outside, to corpse and fish, means atmosphere. The Inside-Outside Game. Thom Gunn. **CP-GunnT**

Outside, upon warm air. The Death of the Infanta. Charles Tomlinson. **CP-TomlC**

Outside was the roar of the sea and the darkness. Malcolm Lowry. **CP-LowrM**

Outskirts, The. Walter de la Mare. **CP-DeLaW**

Outsong in the Jungle. Rudyard Kipling. **CP-KiplR** *Fr.* The Spring Running. *Fr.* The Second Jungle Book.

Outspoken buttocks in pink beads. National Winter Garden. Hart Crane. **ErPo; InPS; LiTM; NAAL-2; OxBA** *Fr.* Three Songs. **NAAL-2** *Fr.* The Bridge. **CP-CranH**

Outstraw green turns gold turns ashen and, The. Carl Sandburg. *Fr.* The People, Yes. **CP-SandC**

Outstretching flame-ward his upbraided hand. Cranmer. William Wordsworth. *Fr.* Ecclesiastical Sonnets. **CP-WorW2**

Outward Bound. Malcolm Lowry. **CP-LowrM**

Ouzo for Robin. James Merrill. **SP-MerrJ**

Ouzo Unclouded. Robert Ranke Graves. **CP-GravR**

Oval Portrait: Jessie Wilkie, The. Kathleen Jessie Raine. **SP-RainK**

Oval the golden moon. Kathleen Jessie Raine. **SP-RainK**

Ovando. Richard Hugo. **CP-HugoR**

Oven Bird, The. Robert Frost. **CP-FrosR**

Over-all picture is winter, The. The Hunters in the Snow. William Carlos Williams. **LCAP** *Fr.* Pictures from Brueghel. **CP-WilW2**

Over an ash-fawn beach fronting a sea which keeps. Fiascherino. Charles Tomlinson. **CP-TomlC**

Over and around   grass banked and packed short and holding back. Messages. James Dickey. **CP-DickJ**

Over and back. At Ithaca. Hilda Doolittle. **CP-DoolH**

Over and Done With. Archie Randolph Ammons. **SP-AmmoA**

Over and over. Hayden Carruth. **CP-CarHS** *Fr.* The Clay Hill Anthology.

Over and over I have heard. Portrait. Edna St. Vincent Millay. **CP-MillE**

Over and over it happens, my wife and I are. The Great House. Paul Zimmer. **SP-ZimmP**

Over and over, like a Tune. Emily Dickinson. **CP-DickE**

Over and over something would remain. For Proust. James Merrill. **SP-MerrJ**

Over and over thru the dull material world the call is made. Night Gleam. Allen Ginsberg. **CP-GinsA**

Over and through the burial chant. Interpolation Sounds. Walt Whitman. **CP-WhitW**

Over back where they speak of life as staying. The Investment. Robert Frost. **CP-FrosR**

Over Brooklyn Bridge. Charles Tomlinson. **CP-TomlC**

Over Denver Again. Allen Ginsberg. **CP-GinsA**

Over-dew / Became a dread name for Cynthia. The House of Over-Dew. Stevie Smith. **CP-SmitS**

Over Elizabeth Bridge: a Circumvention. Charles Tomlinson. **CP-TomlC**

Over forty years, and I haven't left your weather. First Flight. Mona Van Duyn. **SP-VanDM**

Over-Heart, The. John Greenleaf Whittier. **CP-WhitJ**

Over his head were the maple buds. Excelsior. Ralph Waldo Emerson. *Fr.* Quatrains. **CP-EmerR**

Over Kansas. Allen Ginsberg. **CP-GinsA**

Over knowledge of death. I Have Increased Power. Allen Ginsberg. **CP-GinsA**

Over Laramie. Allen Ginsberg. **CP-GinsA**

Over-logical fell for the witch, The. Wystan Hugh Auden. *Fr.* The Quest. **CP-AudeW**

Over my bed / My father stood. Fathers and Sons. Donald Hall. **CP-HallD**

Over my head, I see the bronze butterfly. Lying in a Hammock at William Duffy's Farm in Pine Island, Minnesota. James Wright. **CP-WrigJ**

Over my shoulder, to the left. Waking Up in Santa Cruz at Sea. Al Young. **CP-YounA**

Over night it had emerged. Moth in the Schoolroom. May Sarton. **SP-SartM**

Over oceans sped he, Attis, in the speediest of ships. Catullus. *See* Carmen 63: "Plunging towards Phrygia over violent water."

Over our heads, if we but knew. At a Party. Louise Bogan. **CP-BogaL**

Over Peoria we lost the sun. His Smile. Robert Penn Warren. **SP-WarrR**

Over silent waters / day descending. Finis. Edward Estlin Cummings. **CP-CummE**

Over Sir John's Hill. Dylan Thomas. **CP-ThomD**

Over stone walls and barns. Going Gone. Anne Sexton. **CP-SextA**

Over Switzerland broods the. Kenneth Rexroth. **CP-RexKL** *Fr.* The Dragon and the Unicorn.

Over the ankles in snow and numb past pain. The Secret Sharer. Thom Gunn. **CP-GunnT**

Over the Appalachian Barricade. Nicholas Vachel Lindsay. *Fr.* In Praise of Johnny Appleseed. **CP-LindV**

Over the Arafura sea, the China sea. For John Chappell. Gary Snyder. **CP-SnydG**

Over the ball of it. Pisgah-Sights. I. Robert Browning. **CP-BroR2**

Over the borders, a sin without pardon. Keepsake Mill. Robert Louis Stevenson. **CP-StevR**

Over the bright green rich with buttercups. Antrim April. John Hewitt. **CP-HewiJ**

Over the Carnage Rose Prophetic a Voice. Walt Whitman. **CP-WhitW**

Over the chessboard now. Artificial Intelligence. Adrienne Rich. **CP-RicAE; SP-RicA2**

Over the Coffin. Thomas Hardy. *Fr.* Satires of Circumstance in Fifteen Glimpses. **CP-HardT**

Over the dead line we have called to you. To a Dead Man. Carl Sandburg. **CP-SandC**

Over the Door at the Entrance into the Apollo. Ben Jonson. **CP-JonsB**

Over the dumb Campagna-sea. View Across the Roman Campagna. Elizabeth Barrett Browning. **CP-BroEB**

Over the edge of the purple down. The City of Sleep. Rudyard Kipling. **CP-KiplR**

Over the fence. Emily Dickinson. **CP-DickE**

Over the fence. Emily Dickinson. **CP-DickE**

Over the ferry, and over the ferry. Song. George Meredith. **CP-MerG2**

Over the flat land the clouds go. Even Over the Flat Land. Jenny Joseph. **SP-JoseJ**

Over the florid capitals. Randall Jarrell. **CP-JarrR**

Over the flowery, sharp pasture's edge. Flowers by the Sea. William Carlos Williams. **CP-WillW1**

Over the fountains and the orange-trees. Prisoner at Work in a Turkish Garden. David Herbert Lawrence. *Fr.* Bits. **CP-LawrD**

Over the gray, massed blunder of her face. Woman Waiting. Mona Van Duyn. **SP-VanDM**

Over the ground of slate and light gravel. The Sanctuary. Howard Nemerov. **CP-NemeH**

Over the half-finished houses. The Roofwalker. Adrienne Rich. **CP-RicAE; SP-RicA1; SP-RicA2**

Over the heart of the west, the Taos desert. The Red Wolf. David Herbert Lawrence. **CP-LawrD**

Over the heather the wet wind blows. Roman Wall Blues. Wystan Hugh Auden. **DTC; FaBoEH; NTP** *Fr.* Twelve Songs. **CP-AudeW**

Over the hill and over the dale. John Keats. **CP-KeatJ** (Over the Hill and Over the Dale.) **CP-KeatJ**

Over the Hill and Over the Dale. John Keats. *See* Over the hill and over the dale.

Over the Hills. Paul Laurence Dunbar. **CP-DunbP**

Over the Hills. George Meredith. **CP-MerG2**

Over the Hills. James Schuyler. **CP-SchuJ**

Over the hills in Shutesbury, Leverett. Adrienne Rich. *Fr.* The Spirit of Place. **SP-RicA2**

Over the ice she flies. DECEMBER (Skating). Rudyard Kipling. *Fr.* Verses on Games. **CP-KiplR**

Over the land is April. Robert Louis Stevenson. **CP-StevR**

Over the life of Man. The Annunciation. Wystan Hugh Auden. *Fr.* For the Time Being; a Christmas Oratorio. **CP-AudeW**

Over the local stations, one by one. Beyond the Snow Belt. Mary Oliver. **SP-OlivM**

Over the low, barnacled, elephant-colored rocks. Meditation at Oyster River. Theodore Roethke. **CAPP; CMoP; MoAmPo; NYBP** *Fr.* North American Sequence. **CP-RoetT**

Over the mauve there is smoke like a swan. Port Moody. Malcolm Lowry. **CP-LowrM**

Over the Medes and light Sabaeans reigns [*or* raignes]. Claudian. **CP-RaleW**, *tr. by* Sir Walter Ralegh; *Fr.* Against Eutropius.

Over the Mountain. Louise McNeill. **SP-McNeL**

Over the Rim. Daniel Gerard Hoffman. **SP-HoffD**

Over the rising waters. Flood Peak. William Matthews. *Fr.* Flood. **SP-MattW**

Over the roof-tops race the shadows of clouds. John Gould Fletcher. **SP-FletJ** *Fr.* Irradiations.

Over the roofs and cranes, blistered cupola and hungry smokestack. Louis MacNeice. **LiTM** *Fr.* The Kingdom. **CP-MacNL**

Over the rounded sides of the Rockies, the aspens of autumn. Autumn at Taos. David Herbert Lawrence. **CP-LawrD**

Over the sea our galleys went. The Wanderers. Robert Browning. **OBEV** *Fr.* Paracelsus. **CP-BroR1**

Over the snow at night. The Winter Lightning. Howard Nemerov. **CP-NemeH**

Over the snow wall her hand comes. Some with Wings, Some with Manes. Tess Gallagher. **SP-GallT**

Over the stones still rattling, up Pall Mall. Byron. **NOBL** *Fr.* Canto the Eleventh. **NOBRP** *Fr.* Don Juan. **CP-Byron**

Over the threshold of his pleasant home. Banished from Massachusetts. John Greenleaf Whittier. **CP-WhitJ**

Over the towers of autoerotic honey. Flag of Ecstasy. Charles Henri Ford. **SP-FordC**

Over the utmost hill at length I sped. Percy Bysshe Shelley. **OBWP** *Fr.* The Revolt of Islam. **CP-ShelP**

Over the water, where I lie alive. Song, from "Mr. Amazeen on the River." Muriel Rukeyser. **CP-RukeM**

Over the Western sea hither from Niphon come. A Broadway Pageant. Walt Whitman. **CP-WhitW**

Over the wharves at Provincetown. At Provincetown. Daniel Gerard Hoffman. **SP-HoffD**

Over the years these clouds have colored much. The Clouds of Uig. Richard Hugo. **CP-HugoR**

Over these brooks trusting to ease mine eyes, *speech of Cleophila.* Sir Philip Sidney. **SP-SidnP** *Fr.* Arcadia.

Over these cheekbones. Assuming Fine Feathers, W. D. Takes Flight. William DeWitt Snodgrass. **SP-SnodW**

Over 2000 Illustrations and a Complete Concordance. Elizabeth Bishop. **CP-BishE**

Over us if(as what dusk becomes). Edward Estlin Cummings. **CP-CummE**

Over what bridge-fours has that luscious sea. On a Painting by Julius Olsson R.A. Sir John Betjeman. **CP-BetjJ**

Over your body the clouds go. Gulliver. Sylvia Plath. **CP-PlatS**

Overall, mover of the unnumbered. O'Ryan. Charles Olson. **CP-OlsoC**

Overbold, The. Jenny Joseph. **SP-JoseJ**

Overcast, Hot. James Schuyler. **CP-SchuJ**

Overcome—O bitter sweetness. *fr.* A Woman Young and Old. William Butler Yeats. **CP-YeatW**

Overfaithful sword returns the user, The. The Pro-Consuls. Rudyard Kipling. **CP-KiplR**

Overgrown roses have speckled the granite sill, The. James McAuley. *Fr.* The Exile on His Failing Vision. **SP-McAuJ**

Overhead Mirrors. Charles Bukowski. **SP-BukC3**

Overhead the skull-hill rises. Galway Kinnell. *Fr.* Ruins under the Stars. **SP-KinnG**

Overheard. Denise Levertov. **CP-LeveD**

Overheard on a Bus (Miner's Wife). Louise McNeill. **SP-McNeL**

Overheard on a Bus (Woman with a Cleft Palate). Louise McNeill. **SP-McNeL**

Overland Mail, The. Rudyard Kipling. **CP-KiplR**

Overloaded circuit—lightning, An. Shimmering Pediment. John Yau. **SP-YauJo**

Overlooking the River Stour. Thomas Hardy. **CP-HardT**

Overlooking Yale. Richard Hugo. **CP-HugoR**

Overnight Projects with Woods. Diane Wakoski. **SP-WakoD**

Overnight, very / Whitely, discreetly. Mushrooms. Sylvia Plath. **CP-PlatS**

Overnights. Alice Walker. **CP-WalkA**

Overpopulation. Lawrence Ferlinghetti. **SP-FerlL**

Overruled. John Greenleaf Whittier. **CP-WhitJ**

Overseas Prayer. John Berryman. **CP-BerrJ**

Oversifted fine white flour / with little crust. Boer War Bread Strike. James Schuyler. **CP-SchuJ**

Overtakelessness of those, The. Emily Dickinson. **CP-DickE**

Overthrow of One o'Clock at Night, The. Muriel Rukeyser. **CP-RukeM**

Overture. Delmore Schwartz. **SP-SchwD**

Overture. A shutter opens. Down. Trees Listening to Bach. James Merrill. **SP-MerrJ**

Overture for an Ulster Literature. John Hewitt. **CP-HewiJ**

Overture: The Hostages. Randall Jarrell. **CP-JarrR**

Overture to a Dance of Locomotives. William Carlos Williams. **CP-WilW1**

Overtures. John Crowe Ransom. *Fr.* Sixteen Poems in Eight Pairings. **SP-RansJ**

Overweight Poem. Diane Wakoski. **SP-WakoD**

Overworld, The. Kenneth Patchen. **CP-PatcK**

Ovid. Siv Cedering Fox. **SP-CedeS**

OVID DIVO. Thomas Merton. *Fr.* A Selection of Concrete Poems. **CP-MertT**

Ovid forlorn by the Black Sea. Exile. Frederick Morgan. **SP-MorgF**

Ovid in Love. Ovid, *tr. by* Derek Mahon. **SP-MahoD** *Fr.* Amores. "Day being humid and my head, The."

Ovid in the Third Reich. Geoffrey Hill. **CP-HillG**

Ovid in Tomis. Derek Mahon. **SP-MahoD**

Ovid, Old Buddy, I Would Discourse with You a While. Hayden Carruth. **CP-CarHS**

Ovidian Elegiac Metre, The. Samuel Taylor Coleridge. **CP-ColeS**

Owen Aherne and His Dancers. William Butler Yeats. **CP-YeatW**

Owen at Play. James McAuley. **SP-McAuJ**

Owen's praise demands my song. The Triumphs of Owen. Thomas Gray. **CP-GrayT**

Owl, The. Wystan Hugh Auden. **CP-AudWJ**

Owl, The ("Door-bell..."). Walter de la Mare. **CP-DeLaW**

Owl. Phoebe Hesketh. **SP-HeskP**

Owl, The. John Hewitt. **CP-HewiJ**

Owl. Sylvia Plath. **CP-PlatS**

Owl / washes his claws, An. West Window. Ted Kooser. **SP-KoosT**

Owl and Phoenix. Chuang Tzu, *tr. fr. Chinese by* Thomas Merton. **CP-MertT**

Owl, and wagtail / and huo-hu, the fire-fox. Canto 112, From. Ezra Pound. **CP-PoCan** *Fr.* Cantos. **CP-PoCan**

Owl-car clatters along, dogged by the echo, The. Old Woman. Carl Sandburg. **CP-SandC**

Owl I hear, An. The Owl. Wystan Hugh Auden. **CP-AudWJ**

Owl in the Sarcophagus, The. Wallace Stevens. **CP-StevW**

Owl[e] is abroad, the bat, and the toad, The. Charm[e]. Ben Jonson. **CP-JonsB** *Fr.* The Witches' Charms. *Fr.* The Masque of Queens.

Owl King, The. James Dickey. **CP-DickJ**

  Call, The. **CoPo; NePoEA-2**

Owl Minerva, The. Donald Davie. **CP-DavDo**

Owl, owl, stop calling from the swamp, let. Dawn. Robert Penn Warren. *Fr.* Penological Study: Southern Exposure. **SP-WarrR**

Owl Song. Margaret Atwood. *Fr.* Songs of the Transformed. **SP-AtwM1**

Owl, The ("What If To Edge Of Dream"). Walter de la Mare. **CP-DeLaW**

Owl winks in the shadows, An. Mother Earth: Her Whales. Gary Snyder. **CP-SnydG**

Owlet pulls / Pieces of meat from between the, The. Charles Henri Ford. **SP-FordC** *Fr.* Secret Haiku.

Owls. William DeWitt Snodgrass. **SP-SnodW**

Owl's a clock-face without fingers, The. Owl. Phoebe Hesketh. **SP-HeskP**

Owl's Bedtime Story, The. Randall Jarrell. **CP-JarrR**

Owl's Song. Ted Hughes. **SP-HughT**

Owls that cry in the night. Hoot Owls. Richard Eberhart. **CP-EberR**

Owls–they whinny down the night. Outlaws. Robert Ranke Graves. **CP-GravR**

Owl's torches gutter. Chaos clouds the globe, The. Goats and Monkeys. Derek Walcott. **CP-WalcD**

Owning Everything. Leonard Cohen. **CP-CoheL**

Owre Hoost upon his stiropes stood anon. The Epilogue to the Man of Laws' Tale. Geoffrey Chaucer. *Fr.* The Canterbury Tales. **CP-ChauG**

Ox-Bow. Donald Davie. **CP-DavDo**

Ox Cart Man. Donald Hall. **CP-HallD**

Ox, long fed with musty hay, An. Recantation. Samuel Taylor Coleridge. **CP-ColeS**

Ox Mountain Parable, The. Mencius, *tr. fr. Chinese by* Thomas Merton. **CP-MertT**

Ox-Tamer, The. Walt Whitman. **CP-WhitW**

Oxalis. Louis Zukofsky. **CP-ZukLS**

Oxen, The. Thomas Hardy. **CP-HardT**

Oxen gone, the house is fallen where, The. The Trial. John Berryman. **CP-BerrJ**

Oxen: Ploughing at Fiesole. Charles Tomlinson. **CP-TomlC**

Oxen that rattle the yoke and chain or halt in the leafy shade. Walt Whitman. **FM** *Fr.* The Drayman. **PoNe** *Fr.* Song of Myself. **CP-WhitW**

Oxford. Wystan Hugh Auden. **CP-AudeW**

Oxford, May 30, 1820 ("Ye sacred Nurseries of blooming Youth!"). William Wordsworth. **CP-WorW2**

Oxford, May Thirtieth, Eighteen Twenty ("Shame on this faithless heart! that could allow"). William Wordsworth. **CP-WorW2**

Oxford: Sudden Illness at the Bus-stop. Sir John Betjeman. **CP-BetjJ**

Oxford, Thirty Years After. John Updike. **CP-UpdiJ**

Oxford Town. "Bob Dylan." **CP-DylaB**

Oxford Voice, The. David Herbert Lawrence. **CP-LawrD**

Oxfordshire. Donald Davie. **CP-DavDo**

Oya. Audre Lorde. **SP-LordA**

Oyster, The. Ogden Nash. **CP-NashO**

Oyster, cast upon the shore, An. The Poet, the Oyster, and Sensitive Plant. William Cowper. **CP-CowpW**

Oyster that went to bed x-million years ago, An. Goodnight. John Ciardi. **SP-CiarJ**

Oysters. Seamus Heaney. **SP-HeanS**

Oysters. Robinson Jeffers. **CP-JefR3**

Oysters. Anne Sexton. *Fr.* The Death of the Fathers. **CP-SextA**

Oysters. Jonathan Swift. *Fr.* Verses Made for the Women Who Cry Apples, etc. **CP-SwifJ**

Oysters and Hermits. Donald Hall. **CP-HallD**

Oysters we ate. Oysters. Anne Sexton. *Fr.* The Death of the Fathers. **CP-SextA**

Ozell, at Sanger's call, invok'd his muse. The Translator. Alexander Pope. **CP-PopeA**

Ozone. George lived for gas (the Comic Twilight), The. I.M. George Fitzpatrick. James Liddy. *Fr.* Love Songs of Corca Bascinn. **CP-LiddJ**

Ozymandias [of Egypt]. Percy Bysshe Shelley. **CP-ShelP**

Ozymandias. George Oppen. **CP-OppeG**

Ozymandias II. Howard Nemerov. **CP-NemeH**

P

Pa McCabe. Hayden Carruth. **CP-CarHS**

Pablo and Pedro, and black Serafin. Bacardi Spreads the Eagle's Wing. Hart Crane. **CP-CranH**

Pablo Casals. Archibald MacLeish. **CP-MacLA**

Pablo Neruda. Stephen Dobyns. **SP-DobyS**

Pablo Neruda stands on a corner next to a poster. Pablo Neruda. Stephen Dobyns. **SP-DobyS**

Pace is the Essence. Charles Bukowski. **SP-BukC3**

Pacer in the Fresco. John the Baptist, The. Donald Davie. **CP-DavDo**

Pacha sank at last upon his knee, The. The Giaour and the Pacha. Richard Wilbur. **CP-WilbR**

Pachuta, Mississippi/a Memoir. Al Young. **CP-YounA**

Pachysandra. Louis Zukofsky. **CP-ZukLS**

Pacific: in Russian as. Out of East Anglia. Donald Davie. **CP-DavDo**

Pacific is a feeble symbol of death. Malcolm Lowry. **CP-LowrM**

Pacific Lament. Charles Olson. **CP-OlsoC**

Pacific Telephone. Charles Bukowski. **SP-BukC1**

Pacifist's Song, The. John Berryman. **CP-BerrJ**

Pacing as with some consequent. Robert Creeley. **CP-CreeR**

Pacing that sunburnt lane, on either side. The Seedsman. John Hewitt. **CP-HewiJ**

Packed bus that brought me back glared and stunk, The. Malcolm Lowry. *Fr.* The Canadian Turned Back at the Border. **CP-LowrM**

Packet of Letters. Louise Bogan. **CP-BogaL**

Pact, The. Robert Ranke Graves. **CP-GravR**

Pact, A. Ezra Pound. **SP-PounE**

Pact that we made was the ordinary pact, The. From a Survivor. Adrienne Rich. **SP-RicA1; SP-RicA2**

Pad, Pad. Stevie Smith. **CP-SmitS**

Padding down the street, the. No Shoes No Shirt No Service. Gary Snyder. **CP-SnydG**

Pads in a quilted bathrobe to the door. The Callers. Marilyn Hacker. **SP-HackM**

Pæan. John Greenleaf Whittier. **CP-WhitJ**

Paestum. James Dickey. **CP-DickJ**

Paestum. Richard Hugo. **CP-HugoR**

Pagan. Alice Walker. **CP-WalkA**

Pagan Prayer. Countee Cullen. **CP-CullC**

Pagani's, November 8. Ezra Pound. **SP-PounE**

Pagan's myths through marble lips are spoken, The. Worship. John Greenleaf Whittier. **CP-WhitJ**

Page from a Tale. Wallace Stevens. **CP-StevW**

Page from the Koran. James Merrill. **SP-MerrJ**

Page Turner, The. Gary Gildner. **SP-GildG**

Page 256. Stephen Berg. **SP-BergS**

Pageant, The. John Greenleaf Whittier. **CP-WhitJ**

Pageant of Elizabeth, A. Rudyard Kipling. **CP-KiplR**

Pageant of the Seasons and the Months, The. Edmund Spenser. *See* The Mask of Mutability.

Pagett, M. P. Rudyard Kipling. **CP-KiplR**

Pagett, a schoolboy, got a sword, and then. Upon Pagget. Robert Herrick. **CP-HerrR**

Pagoda princes in blue silk. Willow Pattern. John Hewitt. **CP-HewiJ**

Paid on Both Sides. Wystan Hugh Auden. **CP-AudeW**
    "To throw away the key and walk away." **CMoP; CP-AudWJ; MoBrPo**
    (Chorus: "To throw away the key and walk away.") **MoBrPo**
    (Walking Tour, The.) **CMoP**

Paid Quarterly. John Hewitt. **CP-HewiJ**

Pail. Gilbert Sorrentino. **SP-SorrG**

Pail droops on chain, rotten, The. The Tree House. Louise Glück. **SP-GlücL**

Pain. Richard Shelton. **SP-ShelR**

Pain. John Updike. **CP-UpdiJ**

Pain and weariness, aching eyes and head. A Sick Child's Meditation. Christina Georgina Rossetti. **CP-RosC3**

Pain can make a whole winter bright. Humpty Dumpty. May Sarton. **SP-SartM**

Pain—expands the Time. Emily Dickinson. **CP-DickE**

Pain flattens the world—its bubbles. Pain. John Updike. **CP-UpdiJ**

Pain for a Daughter. Anne Sexton. **CP-SextA**

Pain—has an Element of Blank. Emily Dickinson. **CP-DickE**

Pain has but one Acquaintance. Emily Dickinson. **CP-DickE**

Pain in Pleasure. Elizabeth Barrett Browning. **CP-BroEB**

Pain Is an Eagle Clinging to Your Name. Pablo Antonio Cuadra, *tr. fr. Spanish by* Thomas Merton. **CP-MertT**

Pain is seen to have been transitory. On Seeing an Egyptian Mummy in Berlin, 1932. Richard Eberhart. **CP-EberR**

Pain-monger came home, The. The Failure of a Secular Life. Leonard Cohen. **CP-CoheL**

Pain of all pain, the most grievous pain. Sir Thomas Wyatt. **CP-WyatT**

Pain of love's a better fate, The. Sadi, *tr. fr. Persian by* Ralph Waldo Emerson. **CP-EmerR**

Pain of loving you, The. A Young Wife. David Herbert Lawrence. **CP-LawrD**

Pain Songs. Joseph Ceravolo. **SP-CeraJ**

Pain visits me. My Knees Go Before the Firing Squad at Dawn. Diane Wakoski. **SP-WakoD**

Pain was pulled down over his eyes like a fool's hat. A God. Ted Hughes. **SP-HughT**

Paine and Pleasure. Robert Herrick. **CP-HerrR**

Pain[e] Ends in Pleasure. Robert Herrick. **CP-HerrR**

Paines without Profit. Robert Herrick. **CP-HerrR**

Painfully grinning faces like dogs' or. Old Masters Abroad. Louis MacNeice. **CP-MacNL**

Painkillers. Thom Gunn. **CP-GunnT**

Pains enough thou hast given me. Tanck's Song About His Birthday. Hayden Carruth. **CP-CarHS** *Fr.* Songs About What Comes Down: The Complete Works of Mr. Septic Tank.

Pains of Sleep, The. Samuel Taylor Coleridge. **CP-ColeS**

Paint Box. Phoebe Hesketh. **SP-HeskP**

Paint Castlemaine in colours that will hold. Andrew Marvell. **OBSV** *Fr.* The Last Instructions to a Painter. **CP-MarvA**

Paint last the King, and a dead shade of night. Andrew Marvell. **OBS; OBSV** *Fr.* The Last Instructions to a Painter. **CP-MarvA**
    (Charles II.) **OBS**

Paint me a cavernous waste shore. Sweeney Erect. Thomas Stearns Eliot. **CP-ElioT**

Painted Head. John Crowe Ransom. **SP-RansJ**

Painted kings in the midst of the clearing. The Indians Worship Him, but He Hurries On. Nicholas Vachel Lindsay. *Fr.* In Praise of Johnny Appleseed. **CP-LindV**

Painted Lace. Gertrude Stein. **CP-SteiG**

Painted wind has sprung, A. Edward Estlin Cummings. **CP-CummE**

Painted Wives. John Updike. **CP-UpdiJ**

Painter, The. John Ashbery. **SP-AshbJ**

Painter Dreaming in the Scholar's House, The. Howard Nemerov. **CP-NemeH**

Painter in China once painted a hall, A. Body and Soul. "Anvari", *tr. fr. Persian by* Ralph Waldo Emerson. **CP-EmerR**

Painter Speaks—the Woman Answers, The. Kay Boyle. **CP-BoylK**

Painter, this likeness is too strong. Another ["Painter, this likeness is too strong"]. Unknown, *tr. fr. Greek by* William Cowper. **CP-CowpW**

Painter, you are come, but may be gone. The Mind. Ben Jonson. **GoBC** *Fr.* Eupheme. **CP-JonsB**

Painters. Muriel Rukeyser. **CP-RukeM**

Painter's Dream, The. Lawrence Ferlinghetti. **SP-FerlL**

Painter's eye follows relation out, The. The Painter Dreaming in the Scholar's House. Howard Nemerov. **CP-NemeH**

Painter's face—if, The. Frank Templeton Prince. *Fr.* Walks in Rome. **CP-PrinF**

Painters of Spain, The. Spanish School. Stevie Smith. **CP-SmitS**

Painter's Wife, The. David Herbert Lawrence. **CP-LawrD**

Painting, The. William Carlos Williams. **CP-WilW2**

Painting a Mountain Stream. Howard Nemerov. **CP-NemeH**

Painting and Sculpture. Ralph Waldo Emerson. **CP-EmerR**

Painting by Flashlight. Jim Carroll. **SP-CarrJ**

Painting by Winifred Nicholson, A. Kathleen Jessie Raine. **SP-RainK**

Painting Sometimes Permitted. Robert Herrick. **CP-HerrR**

Painting the North San Juan School. Gary Snyder. **CP-SnydG**

Painture [or Peinture]. Richard Lovelace. **CP-LoveR**

Pair He Saw Pass, The. Thomas Hardy. **CP-HardT**

Pair of crystal eyes will lead me, A. Ralph Waldo Emerson. **CP-EmerR**

Pair of frozen dice come, A. Chelsea May. Jim Carroll. **SP-CarrJ**

Pair of newlyweds, A. The Imperfect Lover. Nicanor Parra, *tr. fr. Spanish by* Thomas Merton. **CP-MertT**

Pair of Stays to mend the Shape, A. William Blake. **CP-BlakW**

Pairing Time Anticipated. William Cowper. **CP-CowpW**

Paisant Chronicle. Wallace Stevens. **CP-StevW**

Palace, The. Rudyard Kipling. **CP-KiplR**

Palace in smoky light. Canto 4. Ezra Pound. *Fr.* Cantos. **CP-PoCan**

Palace of Art, The. Tennyson. **CP-TennA**
    Lincolnshire Shores ("A still salt pool locked in with bars of sand"). **FaBoPP**
    "One seem'd all dark and red--a tract of sand." **UnPo**

Palace of the Babies. Wallace Stevens. **CP-StevW**

Palace of unreality, where the place. Airport. John Updike. **CP-UpdiJ**

Palace-roof of cloudless nights! Ode to Heaven. Percy Bysshe Shelley. **CP-ShelP**

Palaces and far pavilions / Beam upon the night. Life. John Gould Fletcher. **SP-FletJ**

Palais de justice of chambermaids, The. The Surprises of the Superhuman. Wallace Stevens. **CP-StevW**

Palais des Arts. Louise Glück. **SP-GlücL**

Palatine, The. John Greenleaf Whittier. **CP-WhitJ**

Pale at first and cold. The Finding of Love. Robert Ranke Graves. **CP-GravR**

Pale beech and pine so blue. Thomas Hardy. *See* In a Wood.

Pale Bliss. John Updike. **CP-UpdiJ**

Pale blossoms, each balanced on a single jointed stem. Carnations. Theodore Roethke. **CP-RoetT**

Pale Blue Eyes. "Lou Reed." **SP-ReedL**

Pale brows, still hands and dim hair. The Lover Mourns for the Loss of Love. William Butler Yeats. **CP-YeatW**

Pale bubbles, The. She Looks Back. David Herbert Lawrence. **CP-LawrD**

Pale cliffs and sky. Handfast Point. Frank Templeton Prince. **CP-PrinF**

Pale dawnlight spooks the mist. Hayden Carruth. *Fr.* North Winter. **CP-CarHL**

Pale Dream came to a Lady fair, A. Marianne's Dream. Percy Bysshe Shelley. **CP-ShelP**

Pale Genius roves alone. Ralph Waldo Emerson. **CP-EmerR**

Pale gold of the walls, gold. Gold. Donald Hall. **CP-HallD**

Pale green of the English Hymnal! Yattendon hymns. The Old Liberals. Sir John Betjeman. **CP-BetjJ**

Pale green-white, in a gallop across the sky. The Gale. John Gould Fletcher. *Fr.* Sand and Spray: A Sea-Symphony. **SP-FletJ**

Pale moon sails out blank, The. Variations 2. Gilbert Sorrentino. **SP-SorrG**

Pale on its stalk, the aster flower. The Aster Flower. John Gould Fletcher. **SP-FletJ**

Pale Panther, The. Louis MacNeice. **CP-MacNL**

Pale Roamer through the Night! thou poor Forlorn! The Outcast. Samuel Taylor Coleridge. *Fr.* Effusions. **CP-ColeS**

Pale sad face of her I wronged, The. Zara. Christina Georgina Rossetti. **CP-RosC3**

Pale sand edges England's Old. Virginia Britannia. Marianne Craig Moore. **CP-MoorM**

Pale, the cold, and the moony smile, The. On Death. Percy Bysshe Shelley. **CP-ShelP**

Paled in by many a lofty hill. The Magic Castle. Sir Walter Scott. **SP-ScotW** *Fr.* The Bridal of Trierman.

Palely intent, he urged his keel. At the Cannon's Mouth. Herman Melville. **SP-MelvH**

Paler, not quite so fair as in her life. One of the Dead. Christina Georgina Rossetti. **CP-RosC3**

Palestine. John Greenleaf Whittier. **CP-WhitJ**

Palimpsest. John Hewitt. **CP-HewiJ**

Palinode. Robinson Jeffers. *Fr.* The Broken Balance. **CP-JefR1**

Palladiums. Carl Sandburg. **CP-SandC**

Pallas, a goddess chaste and wise. The Storm. Jonathan Swift. **CP-SwifJ**

Pallas grew vap'rish once and odd. On the Countess of Burlington Cutting Paper. Alexander Pope. **CP-PopeA**

Pallas, observing Stella's wit. To Stella, Visiting Me in My Sickness. Jonathan Swift. **CP-SwifJ**

Pallas saw *Venus* arm'd, and streight she cry'd. Upon the Same. Ausonius, *tr. fr. Latin by* Richard Crashaw. **CP-CrasR**

Pallid, mis-shapen he stands. The World's grimed thumb. In the Dock. Walter de la Mare. **CP-DeLaW**

Pallid Wreath, The. Walt Whitman. **CP-WhitW**

Pallor of so many, The. Arlington. John Haines. **SP-HainJ**

Palm Drive Palo Alto. Al Young. **CP-YounA**

Palm of the Hand. Charles Tomlinson. **CP-TomlC**

Palm Sunday. Christina Georgina Rossetti. **CP-RosC2**

Palm-Tree, The. John Greenleaf Whittier. **CP-WhitJ**

Palm-tree, single and apart. Song: The Palm Tree. Robert Ranke Graves. **CP-GravR**

Palmer, The. Sir Walter Scott. **SP-ScotW**

Palmist, The. John Hewitt. **CP-HewiJ**

Palms for a Catholic Child. Kenneth Patchen. **CP-PatcK**

Palms of Mammon have disowned, The. The Revealer. Edwin Arlington Robinson. **CP-RobiE**

Palos Verdes Cliffs. Muriel Rukeyser. **CP-RukeM**

Pals. Carl Sandburg. **CP-SandC**

Paltry-Looking People. David Herbert Lawrence. **CP-LawrD**

Paltry Nude Starts on a Spring Voyage, The. Wallace Stevens. **CP-StevW**

Pambo. Robert Browning. **CP-BroR2**

Pamela. Rita Dove. **SP-DoveR**

Pamela was too simple to deceive. The Tree in Pamela's Garden. Edwin Arlington Robinson. **CP-RobiE**

Pamphilia to Amphilanthus, *sometimes appended to* Urania. Mary Sidney, Countess of Montgomery Wroth. **CP-WrotM**

  Crowne of Sonetts Dedicated to Love, A.

  Sonnet 1: "In this strang labourinth how shall I turne?"

  Sonnet 2: "Is to leave all, and take the thread of love."

  Sonnet 3: "His flames as joyes, his bands true lovers might."

  Sonnet 4: "And bee in his brave court a gloriouse light."

  Sonnet 5: "And burne, yett burning you will love the smart."

  Sonnet 6: "Hee may owr profitt, and out Tuter prove."

  Sonnet 7: "How blest bee they then, who his favors prove."

  Sonnet 8: "Hee that shunns love doth love him self the less."

  Sonnet 9: "But wher they may returne with honors grace."

  Sonnet 10: "Bee from court of Love, and reason torne."

  Sonnet 11: "Unprofitably pleasing, and unsound."

  Sonnet 12: "Bee given to him who triumphs in his right."

  Sonnet 13: "Free from all fogs butt shining faire, and cleere."

  Sonnet 14: "Except my hart which you beestow'd before."

"O pardon, Cupid I confess my fault."

Song: "Beeing past the paines of love."

Song: "Birds doe sing, day doth apeere, The."

Song: "Deerest if I by my deserving."

Song: "Fairest, and still truest eyes."

Song: "I, that ame of all most crost." **KTR**

Song: "Love a child is ever criing [*or* crying]." **KTR; NOSC**

Song: "Love as well can make abiding."

Song: "O[h] me[e] the time is [*or* has] come to part." **NOSC**

Song: "Say Venus how long have I lov'd, and serv'd you heere?"

Song: "Springing time of my first loving, The."

Song 1: "Spring now come att last, The."

Song 1: "Sweet lett mee injoye thy sight."

Song 2: "All night I weep[e], all day I cry, Ay me[e]." **NOSC**

Song 2: "Sweet Silvia in a shadie wood."

Song 3: "Come merry spring delight us."

Song 3: "Stay, my thoughts, do nott aspire."

Song 4: "Lovers learne to speake butt truthe."

Song 4: "Sweetest love returne againe."

Song 5: "Time only cause of my unrest."

Song 6: "You happy blessed eyes."

Song 7: "Sorrow, I yeeld, and grieve that I did miss."

Sonnet: "Can the lov'd Image of thy deerest face."

Sonnet: "Eyes, can you tell mee wher my hart remaines?"

Sonnet: "Fly traiter joye whose end brings butt dispaire."

Sonnet: "Lett griefe as farr bee from your deerest brest."

Sonnet: "Oft did I wounder why the sweets of Love."

Sonnet 1: "In night yett may wee see some kind of light."

Sonnet 1: "My hart is lost, what can I now expect."

Sonnet 1: "When night's [*or* nights] black mantle could most darknes prove." **Son**

Sonnet 2: "Deare eyes how well (indeed) you doe adorne."

Sonnet 2: "Late in the Forest I did Cupid see." **KTR**

Sonnet 2: "Love like a jugler, comes to play his prise."

Sonnet 3: "Juno still jealouse of her husband Jove."

Sonnet 3: "Most blessed Night, the happy time for love."

Sonnet 3: "Yett is ther hope: Then Love butt play thy part."

Sonnet 4: "Cruell suspition, O! bee now att rest."

Sonnet 4: "Forbeare darke night, my joyes now budd againe."

Sonnet 4: "When I beeheld the Image of my deere."

Sonnet 5: "Can pleasing sight, misfortune ever bring?"

Sonnet 5: "How many nights have I with paine indur'd."

Sonnet 5: "Like to huge clowds of smoke which well may hide."

Sonnet 6: "My pain[e], still smothered [*or* smother'd] in my grievèd bre[a]st." **NOSC**

Sonnet 6: "Ô strive nott still to heape disdaine on mee." **NOSC**

Sonnet 6: "O! that noe day would ever more appeere."

Sonnet 7: "End fond jealousie alas I know, An."

Sonnet 7: "Love leave to urge, thou know'st thou hast the hand."

Sonnet 07: "No time, noe roome, noe thought, or writing can."

Sonnet 8: "How gloewoorme like the sunn doth now apeere."

Sonnet 8: "Led by the powre of griefe, to waylings brought."

Sonnet 8: "Poore Love in chaines, and fetters like a thiefe."

Sonnet 9: "Be[e] you all pleased [*or* pleas'd]? your pleasures grieve not[t] me[e]." **BWW; NOSC**

Sonnet 9: "My muse now hapy, lay thy self to rest."

Sonnet 9: "'Pray doe nott use thes words I must bee gone."

Sonnet 10: "Folly would needs make mee a lover bee."

Sonnet 10: "Weary traveller who tired sought, The."

Sonnet 11: "You endless torments that my rest opress."

Sonnet 12: "Cloy'd with the torments of a tedious night."

Sonnet 13: "Deare fammish nott what you your self gave food."

Sonnet 14: "Am I thus conquered? [*or* conquer'd]? have I lost the powers." **NAEL-1; NOSC**

Sonnet 15: "Truly poore Night thou wellcome art to mee."

Sonnet 16: "Sleepe fy possess mee nott, nor doe nott fright."

Sonnet 17: "Sweet shades why doe you seeke to give delight."

Sonnet 18: "Which should I better like of, day, or night."

Sonnet 19: "Come darkest night, be[e]coming sorrow best." **NOSC**

Sonnet 20: "Sunn which glads, the earth att his bright sight, The."

Sonnet 21: "When last I saw thee, I did not[t] thee see."

Sonnet 22: "Like to the Indians, scorched with the sun[ne]." **NOSC**

Sonnet 23: "When every one to pleasing pastime hies." **WPE**

Sonnet 24: "Once did I heere an aged father say."

Sonnet 25: "Poore eyes bee blind, the light behold noe more."

Sonnet 26: "Deare cherish this, and with it[t] my soules will." **BWW**

Sonnet 27: "Fie [or Fy] tedious Hope, why do[e] you still rebel[l]?" **NOSC**

Sonnet 28: "Griefe, killing griefe: have nott my torments binn." **KTR**

Sonnet 29: "Fly hence O! joy noe longer heere abide." **KTR**

Sonnet 30: "You blessed shades, which give mee silent rest." **KTR**

Sonnet 31: "After long trouble in a taedious way." **KTR**

Sonnet 32: "How fast thou fliest, O Time, on loves swift wings."

Sonnet 33: "How many eyes poore Love hast thou to guard."

Sonnet 34: "Take heed mine eyes, how you your lookes doe cast."

Sonnet 35: "False [or Faulce] hope which feeds but[t] to destroy, and spill." **KTR; NAEL-1**

Sonnet 36: "How well poore hart thou wittnes canst I love."

Sonnet 37: "Night, welcome art thou to my mind destrest."

Sonnet 38: "What pleasure can a bannish'd creature have."

Sonnet 39: "Iff I were giv'n to mirthe 't'wowld be more cross."

Sonnet 40: "Itt is nott love which you poore fooles do deeme."

Sonnet 41: "You blessed starrs which doe heavns glory show."

Sonnet 42: "If ever love had force in huma[i]ne brest?" **BWW**

Sonnet 43: "O dearest eyes the lights, and guids of love."

Sonnet 44: "How fast thou hast'st (O spring) with sweetest speed."

Sonnet 45: "Good now bee still, and doe nott mee torment."

Sonnet 46: "Love, thou hast all, for now thou hast mee made."

Sonnet 47: "O stay mine eyes, shed nott thes fruitles tears."

Sonnet 48: "How like a fire doth love increase in me[e]." **NOSC**

"Venus unto the Gods a sure did move."

Pamphilia's Sonnet. Mary Sidney, Countess of Montgomery Wroth. *See* Loss[e] my molester at last patient be.

Pamphylian. Louis Zukofsky. **CP-ZukLS**

Pan and Luna. Robert Browning. **CP-BroR2**

Pan came out of the woods one day. Pan with Us. Robert Frost. **CP-FrosR**

Pan, Echo, and the Satyr. Moschus, *tr. fr. Greek by* Shelley. **CP-ShelP**

Pan in Vermont. Rudyard Kipling. **CP-KiplR**

Pan loved his neighbour Echo—but that child. Pan, Echo, and the Satyr. Moschus, *tr. fr. Greek by* Shelley. **CP-ShelP**

Pan with Us. Robert Frost. **CP-FrosR**

Panacea. Muriel Rukeyser. **CP-RukeM**

Pancake, The. Christina Georgina Rossetti. *See* Mix a Pancake.

Pancake? Shel Silverstein. **SP-SilS2**

Pandora. Robert Ranke Graves. **CP-GravR**

Pandora's Box, An Ode. Ted Berrigan. **SP-BerrT**

Pane Caldo. Erica Jong. **SP-JongE**

Panegyre, on the Happy Entrance of James, Our Sovreign, to His First High Session of Parliament in This Kingdom, the 19 of March, 1603, A. Ben Jonson. **CP-JonsB**

Panegyric on the Dean, A. Jonathan Swift. **CP-SwifJ**

Panegyric on the Reverend Dean Swift, A. Jonathan Swift. **CP-SwifJ**

Panegyric to Sir Lewis Pemberton, A. Robert Herrick. **CP-HerrR**

Panel board of the table, The. Nature Alive. Jorge Guillén, *tr. fr. Spanish by* James Wright. **CP-WrigJ**

Panels. Carl Sandburg. **CP-SandC**

Pang is more conspicuous in Spring, A. Emily Dickinson. **CP-DickE**

Pang More Sharp Than All, The. Samuel Taylor Coleridge. **CP-ColeS**

Pang of Reminiscence, A. David Herbert Lawrence. **CP-LawrD**

Pangloss's Song: A Comic-Opera Lyric. Richard Wilbur. **CP-WilbR**

Pangolin, The. Marianne Craig Moore. **CP-MoorM**

Pangur Ban. John Hewitt. **CP-HewiJ**

Panhandle (For Annette). Chuck Miller. **SP-MillC**

Panic Vine, The. Isabella Gardner. **CP-GardI**

Panoply of Paradise is mine. Ralph Waldo Emerson. **CP-EmerR**

Panorama, The. John Milton. **WHA** *Fr.* Book III. *Fr.* Paradise Lost. **CP-MiltJ**

Panorama, The. John Greenleaf Whittier. **CP-WhitJ**

Panorama of ruined houses, walls, A. Trial and Death, a Double Feature. Howard Nemerov. **CP-NemeH**

Panoramas are not what they used to be. Botanist on Alp (No. 1). Wallace Stevens. **CP-StevW**

Pansies. Charles Bukowski. **SP-BukC2**

Pansies, lilies, kingcups, daisies. To the Small Celandine. William Wordsworth. **CP-WorW1**

Panther, The. Ogden Nash. **CP-NashO**

Panther and the Antelope, The. Phoebe Hesketh. **SP-HeskP**

Panther, knowing that his spotted hide, The. Edmund Spenser. **EnRePo** *Fr.* Amoretti. **CP-Spens**

Panther sprang at the feet, A. Local Boys and Girls Small Town Stuff. Marsden Hartley. **CP-HartM**

Panthera. Thomas Hardy. **CP-HardT**

Pantisocracy. Samuel Taylor Coleridge. **CP-ColeS**

Pantoum. Marilyn Hacker. **SP-HackM**

Pantoum Approaching the Speed of Light. Robert Pack. **SP-PackR**

Panty Hose. Ron Koertge. **SP-KoerR**

Papa above! Emily Dickinson. **CP-DickE**

Papa and Mama Dance, The. Anne Sexton. **CP-SextA**

Papa called her Pearl when he came home. Taking in Wash. Rita Dove. **SP-DoveR**

Papa died in the gas chamber. Uses. Anne Sexton. **CP-SextA**

Papa eats bread. Sut Lovingood. Charles Olson. **CP-OlsoC**

Papa Joffre, the shoulders of him wide as the land of France. Memoir. Carl Sandburg. **CP-SandC**

Papa Love Baby. Stevie Smith. **CP-SmitS**

Papageno, *sl. diff. vers.* William DeWitt Snodgrass. *See* Far in the woods my stealthy flute.

Papal Abuses. William Wordsworth. *Fr.* Ecclesiastical Sonnets. **CP-WorW2**

Papal Dominion. William Wordsworth. *Fr.* Ecclesiastical Sonnets. **CP-WorW2**

Papas Blondine / Grew tall & wise. Ralph Waldo Emerson. **CP-EmerR**

Paper Anniversary. Muriel Rukeyser. **CP-RukeM**

Paper Bag, A. Margaret Atwood. **SP-AtwM2**

Paper Banners. John Hewitt. **CP-HewiJ**

Paper book is sent by Boyle, A. Jonathan Swift. **CP-SwifJ**

Paper by Maillol, no kiddin'. The End of the Rope. William Carlos Williams. **CP-WilW2**

Paper Cranes. Thomas Merton. **CP-MertT**

Paper Cuts. Erica Jong. **SP-JongE**

Paper is two kinds, to write on, to wrap with. Paper I. Carl Sandburg. **CP-SandC**

Paper Nautilus, The. Marianne Craig Moore. **CP-MoorM**

Paper I. Carl Sandburg. **CP-SandC**

Paper Palace, The. Edward Estlin Cummings. **CP-CummE**

Paper-Thin Hotel. Leonard Cohen. **CP-CoheL**

Paper II. Carl Sandburg. **CP-SandC**

Paperback Writer. The Beatles. **CP-Beatl**

Papers everywhere—piled onto tables and shelves—. James McAuley. **SP-McAuJ** *Fr.* Map.

Papers to sign and documents to read. Sa Majestá Très Chrétienne. Arthur Hugh Clough. **SP-ClouA**

Paphian Ball, The. Thomas Hardy. **CP-HardT**

Papilio et Limax. John Gay, *tr. fr. English by* William Cowper. **CP-CowpW**

Pappy Wants a Poppy. Ogden Nash. **CP-NashO**

Papylus had a dong so long. Martial, *tr. by* William Matthews. **SP-MattW** *Fr.* Epigrams.

Parable. Wystan Hugh Auden. **FaBoCo** *Fr.* Shorts I ("Watch upon my wrist, The"). **CP-AudeW**

Parable, A. Louise Glück. **SP-GlücL**

Parable. Alun Lewis. **CP-LewiA**

Parable. Thomas McGrath. **SP-McGrT**

Parable. Thomas McGrath. **SP-McGrT**

Parable. Richard Wilbur. **CP-WilbR**

Parable for Sports Writers, Society Columnists, Bond Salesmen, and Poets or Go Get a Reputation, A. Ogden Nash. **CP-NashO**

Parable of the Blind, The. William Carlos Williams. **CP-WilW2; LCAP; SAmP** *Fr.* Pictures from Brueghel. **CP-WilW2**

Parable of the Fictionist. Stephen Dunn. **SP-DunnS**

Parable of the Four-Poster. Erica Jong. **SP-JongE**

Parable of the Old Man and the Young, The. Wilfred Owen. **CP-OwenW**

Parables of Antichrist, The. John Gould Fletcher.
  Blessing of the Worms, The. **SP-FletJ**
  End of Job, The. **SP-FletJ**
  Hard Sayings. **SP-FletJ**
  Levite and the Samaritan, The. **SP-FletJ**
  New Beatitudes, The. **SP-FletJ**
  Prayer of the Antichrist, The. **SP-FletJ**

Parables of Christ, The. John Gould Fletcher.
  Birth of Christ, The. **SP-FletJ**
  Crucifixion, The. **SP-FletJ**
  Fragments of Eternity, The. **SP-FletJ**
  Last Judgment, The. **SP-FletJ**

1921. **SP-FletJ**

Procession, The. **SP-FletJ**

Paracelsus. Robert Browning. **CP-BroR1**

Awakening of Man, The. **WGRP**

"Heap cassia, sandal-buds and stripes." **OBEV**

Thus the Mayne Glideth. **OBEV**

Wanderers, The. **OBEV**

Parachuting / down through clouds. Unrequited. Erica Jong. **SP-JongE**

Parade. Langston Hughes. **SP-HughL**

Parade. Leonard Nathan. **SP-NathL**

Parade-Song of the Camp Animals. Rudyard Kipling. **CP-KiplR** *Fr.* Her Majesty's Servants. *Fr.* The Jungle Book.

Parades. Rattle of palm trees. The silver planes. Muriel Rukeyser. **CP-RukeM**

Paradigm, The. Allen Tate. **CP-TateA**

Paradise. George Herbert. **CP-HerbG**

Paradise. Robert Herrick. **CP-HerrR**

Paradise ("Another side, umbrageous Grots and Caves"). John Milton. **OBS** *Fr.* Book IV. **OAEL-1** *Fr.* Paradise Lost. **CP-MiltJ**

Paradise ("His fair large front and eye sublime declared"). John Milton. **PIP** *Fr.* Book IV. **OAEL-1** *Fr.* Paradise Lost. **CP-MiltJ**

Paradise ("In narrow room nature's whole wealth, yea more"). John Milton. **NOSC** *Fr.* Book IV. **OAEL-1** *Fr.* Paradise Lost. **CP-MiltJ**

Paradise. Christina Georgina Rossetti. **CP-RosC1**

Paradise. John Yau. **SP-YauJo**

Paradise, an / endless movie. You. Kingdoms of Heaven. Denise Levertov. **CP-LeveD**

Paradise: in a Symbol. Christina Georgina Rossetti. **CP-RosC3**

Paradise is (as from the Learn'd I gather). Paradise. Robert Herrick. **CP-HerrR**

Paradise is of the option. Emily Dickinson. **CP-DickE**

Paradise is that old mansion. Emily Dickinson. **CP-DickE**

Paradise Lost. John Milton. **CP-MiltJ**

Book I. **FHYEP; NAEL-1; OAEL-1; OxAEP-1**

"Anon out of the earth a fabric huge." **TreFS**

Council of Satan, The. **PoEL-3**

"Dungeon horrible, on all sides round, A." **OBD**

"If thou beest he; but O how fall'n! how chang'd." **SCV**

Immortal Hate. **NOBE**

"Is this the region, this the soil, the clime." **FF**, *ll.* 242–255; **TreFS**, *ll.* 242–263; **TEP**, *ll.* 242–270; **FiP**

(Fall of the Angels, The.) **FiP**, *ll.* 242–363;

Mulciber. **NOSC**

"Next came one / Who mourn'd in earnest, when the Captive Ark." **EBEV**

"Of Man's First Disobedience, and the Fruit." **EBEvV; EPCY; FaBoEn; FiP; NAWM-1; NoP; PeECV; SCV; TOF; TreFS**, *ll.* 1–26; **EBEV**, *ll.* 1–270; **NIP**, *ll.* 1–49; **FaPoB**, *ll.* 1–74; **TEP**, *ll.* 1–75; **FaBoEn; NOSC; PoE; PoEL-3**

(Induction, The.) **PoE**, *ll.* 1–26;

(Invocation.) **FaBoEn; NOSC; PoEL-3**, *ll.* 1–26;

Satan ("His pride / Had cast him out from Heaven, with all his host"). **TrGrPo**

Satan and His Host. **OBS**

Satan and the Fallen Angels. **LiTB; OBS**

(Satan ("He scarce had ceas't when the superior Fiend").) **SeCePo**

(Satan's Summons.) **NOSC**

Satan Defiant. **WHA**, *ll.* 44–109;

(Fallen Angels, The.) **FaBoEn**, *ll.* 44–74;

Satan's Legions and the Beech Leaves of the Casentino. **FaBoPP**, *ll.* 300–304;

(Summons, The.) **WHA**, *ll.* 300–587;

"So stretched out huge in length the Arch-Fiend lay." **TEP**

"There stood a hill not far whose grisly top."

What Though the Field Be Lost? **EaLo**

(Satan's Adjuration.) **FaBoEn**

Book II. **FHYEP; NAEL-1; OxAEP-1**

Hell ("At once with him they rose"). **OBS**

"High on a throne of royal state, which far." **OAEL-1**, *ll.* 1–309; **NIP**, *ll.* 1–42;

"Meanwhile [*or* Mean while] the Adversary of God and Man." **EBEV**, *ll.* 629–734; **DL**, *ll.* 629–841; **OBNV**

(Sin and Death.) **OBNV**, *ll.* 629–889;

Occupations of Hell. **NOSC**

"Pensive here I sat." **OBD**

Place of the Damned, The. **FaBoEn**

Satan ("He ceased; and Satan stayed not to reply"). **SeCePo**

(Satan Views the World.) **WHA**

Satan's Journey. **NOSC**

"Stygian council thus disolved; and forth, The." **OAEL-1**

"Thus Belial with words clothed in reason's garb." **FaBoPV**

"Thus saying, from her side the fatal Key." **EBEV**

Book III.

Atonement, The. **OBS**

"Hail holy Light, offspring [*or* offspring] of Heav'n [*or* Heaven] first-born." **OAEL-1; SCV; TOF**, *ll.* 1–55; **NAEL-1**, *ll.* 1–587; **PeECV**, *ll.* 1–69; **FaBoEn; FiP; ImPo; LiTB; NOBE; NOSC; OBEV; OBS; PIP; WHA**

(Hail, Holy Light[!].) **FiP; ImPo; WHA**, *ll.* 1–55; **PIP**, *ll.* 1–55, *abr.*;

(Holy Light.) **NOBE**, *ll.* 1–55;

(Hymn to Light.) **FaBoEn**, *ll.* 1–50;

(Invocation to Light.) **NOSC**, *ll.* 1–55;

(Light.) **LiTB; OBEV; OBS**, *ll.* 1–55;

Heaven. **OBS**

New Worlds.

"Now had th' Almighty Father from above." **NIP**

Panorama, The. **WHA**

Plan of Salvation, The. **WGRP**

"Thus they in Heav'n, above the starry Sphear." **EBEV**

Book IV. **OAEL-1**

"Beneath him with new wonder now he views." **PPP**

"Fiend / Saw undelighted all delight, all kind, The." **FaBoPV**

"Into thir inmost bower." **FF**, *ll.* 738–757; **TOF**, *ll.* 738–775;

"Me miserable! which way shall I fly." **PoE**

Now Came Still Evening On. **FaBoRV**

"Now came still Ev'ning [*or* evening *or* Eevning] on, and Twilight gray [*or* grey]." **PeECV**, *ll.* 598–688; **ChTr; FaBoEn; NOBE; TreFS**

(Evening in Paradise.) **FaBoEn; TreFS**, *ll.* 598–609; **NOBE**, *ll.* 598–656;

(Moon and the Nightingale, The.) **ChTr**, *ll.* 598–609;

"O for that warning voice which he who saw." **TEP**, *ll.* 1–324; **OxAEP-1**, *ll.* 1–535; **NAEL-1**, *ll.* 1–775; **PoEL-3**

(Prospect of Eden, The.) **PoEL-3**, *ll.* 1–775;

Paradise ("Another side, umbrageous Grots and Caves"). **OBS**

Paradise ("His fair large front and eye sublime declared"). **PIP**

Paradise ("In narrow room nature's whole wealth, yea more"). **NOSC**

Satan Beholds Adam and Eve in Eden. **TW**

Satan Journeys to the Garden of Eden. **ChTr**

Satan's Soliloquy. **LiTB; OBS**

"She as a veil down to the slender waist." **ErPo**, *ll.* 304–311; **NIP**

(Before the Fall.) **NIP**, *ll.* 304–355;

"So passed they naked on, nor shunned the sight." **PeECV**, *ll.* 319–334; **SeCePo**

(Adam and Eve.) **SeCePo**, *ll.* 319–355;

Their Wedded Love. **SeCePo**

(Unfallen Love.) **NOSC**

(Wedded Love.) **OBS**

Then when I Am Thy Captive, Talk of Chains. **WHA**

Thus Eve to Adam. **FaBV**

"Thus talking hand in hand alone they pass'd." **EBEV**

"Thus was this place, / A happy rural seat of various view." **PeECV**, *ll.* 246–275; **FaBoEn**

(Eden.) **FaBoEn**, *ll.* 246–268;

"Two of far nobler shape erect and tall." **PeECV**, *ll.* 288–299; **TreFS**, *ll.* 288–324;

"Which way I fly is Hell; my self am Hell." **TW**

"While thus he spake, th'Angelic Squadron bright." **SCV**

"With thee conversing I forget all time." **ArLo; ChTr; FaBoEn; GBL; TrGrPo; TreFS; UV; WiR**

(Eve Speaks to Adam.) **ArLo; ChTr**

(Eve to Adam.) **FaBoEn; TrGrPo**

Book V.

Adam Unfallen. **NOCV**

Ascent of Species. **NOSC**

"At once on th' Eastern cliff of Paradise." **PeECV**

Morning Hymn of Adam. **TrPWD**, *ll.* 153–208, *abr.*;

(Adam's Morning Hymn.) **WGRP**, *ll.* 153–210;

"Now Morn her rosie steps in th' eastern clime." **OAEL-1**, *ll.* 1–128; **NAEL-1**, *ll.* 1–135;

Raphael's Descent. **NOSC**

"So to the sylvan lodge." **NAEL-1**

Book VI.

"They ended parle, and both addressed for fight." **OBWP**

Book VII.

"And God created the great whales, and each." **MOS**

Creation. **NOSC,** *ll.* 387–516;

(Creation of the Animals.) **FM,** *ll.* 387–505;

"Descend from Heaven [*or* Heav'n], Urania, by that name." **EPCY,** *ll.* 1–31; **EBEV; NAEL-1; NOSC; OAEL-1; TOF,** *ll.* 1–39; **FiP; OBS**

(Invocation to Urania.) **FiP; OBS,** *ll.* 1–39;

"Earth was form'd, but in the womb as yet, The." **MOS**

"Forthwith the sounds and seas, each creek and bay." **ChIV-1**

"Half yet remains unsung, but narrower bound." **FaBoPV**

"Heaven opened wide / Her ever during gates, harmonious sound." **ChIV-1**

Leviathan. **AmMo**

"Meanwhile the tepid caves and fens and shores." **PBBP**

"Sixth and of creation last arose, The."

Standing on Earth. **ChTr**

"Thus God the Heav'n created, thus the Earth." **PeECV**

Book VIII.

"And thus he spake, each bird and beast behold." **OBF**

"For man to tell how human life began." **ChIV-1**

"Love thou saist." **TOF**

"So spake the godlike power, and thus our sire." **NAEL-1**

"To the Nuptial Bowre." **OxBM**

Book IX.   **FHYEP; NAEL-1; NAWM-1; NoP; OAEL-1**

"As when of old some orator renowed." **ChIV-1**

Fall, The.   **PoEL-3**

(Fall, The.)

"Her long with ardent look his Eye pursu'd." **UnPo**

"How shall I behold the face." **TOF**

"In bower and field he sought, where any tuft." **TEP,** *ll.* 417–792; **OBS**

(Eve.) **OBS,** *ll.* 417–466;

"No more of talk where God or Angel Guest." **EPCY; NOSC; OBS; TOF**

(Higher Argument.) **NOSC**

(Subject of Heroic Song, The.) **OBS**

"So spake the enemy of mankind, enclosed."

Temptation of Eve, The. **EBNV**

Tempter Disarmed, The. **NOSC**

Uncloistered Virtue. **NOSC**

What Words Have Passed. **TrCP**

Book X.   **FHYEP**

Adam Speaks. **NU**

"Be it so, for I submit; his doom is fair." **NAWM-1**

Eve Penitent. **OBS**

"Other way Satan went down, Th'." **NAEL-1**

"Such was thir song." **PeECV**

"Then both ourselves and seed at once to free." **OBD**

"Thus Adam himself lamented loud." **OAEL-1**

"Thus began / Outrage from lifeless things; but Discord first." **NAEL-1**

Book XI.

Flood, The. **NOSC**

"This most afflicts me, that departing hence." **PeECV**

"To whom the Father, without Cloud, serene." **PeECV**

"To whom thus Michael. Those whom last thou saw'st." **PeECV**

Book XII.

Adam Fallen ("Descended, Adam to the bower where Eve"). **NOCV**

"Egypt, divided buy the river Nile." **FaBoPV**

Expulsion from Eden, The. **OPOU**

Expulsion from Paradise. **ChTr**

"He ended, and they both descend the hill." **NAWM-1**

(Adam Fallen ("He ended, and they both descend the hill").)

"He ended; and thus *Adam* last reply'd." **HeIP; PoEL-3**

(Retreat from Paradise, The.) **PoEL-3**

"High in front advanced." **EBEvV**

Leave Taking. **FaBoEn**

"So spake our Mother Eve, and Adam heard." **FaBoRV; NOBE; NOSC; OBS**

(Banishment, The.) **NOBE; OBS**

(Exile.) **NOSC**

(Exit from Eden, The.) **FaBoRV**

"So spake the [*or* th'] Archangel Michael; then paused." **FaBoPV,** *ll.* 466–551; **NAEL-1; OAEL-1,** *ll.* 466–649;

Their Banishmnet. **SeCePo**

"This having learnt, thou hast attained the summe." **SCV**

"To whom thus also th' Angel last repli'd." **FiP; OxAEP-1; PeECV**

(Paradise Lost.) **FiP**

"To whom thus Michael. Justly thou abhorr'st." **FaBoPV**

Paradise Lost. John Milton. *See* To whom thus also th' Angel last repli'd.

Paradise might have appeared here. The Aristocracy. Wendell Berry. **CP-BerrW**

Paradise of Squares. Nicanor Parra, *tr. fr. Spanish by* Thomas Merton. **CP-MertT**

Paradise Re-entered. David Herbert Lawrence. **CP-LawrD**

Paradise Regained [*or* Regain'd]. John Milton. **CP-MiltJ**

Book I.

"At thy nativity a glorious quire." **PChr**

"I who erewhile the happy Garden sung." **PeECV**

Satan's Guile ("Whom thus answer'd th' Arch Fiend now undisguis'd"). **LiTB; OBS**

"So spake our morning star then in his rise." **PeECV**

"So they in Heav'n their odes and vigils tun'd." **PeECV,** *ll.* 182–195; **OBS**

(Messiah, The ("So they in Heav'n their odes and vigils tun'd").) **OBS,** *ll.* 182–293;

Book II.

Banquet, The. **NOSC**

"It was the hour of night, when thus the Son." **EBEV; PeECV**

"Set women in his eye and in his walk." **PeECV**

"Sometimes they thought he might be only shewn." **PeECV**

Table Richly Spread, A. **FaBoCh**

Book III.

Parthians, The. **OBS**

(Parthian Powers.) **NOSC,** *book* III, *ll.* 310–43;

True and False Glory. **LiTB; OBS**

Book IV.

"Look once more ere we leave this specular Mount." **PeECV,** *ll.* 236–271; **OBTV,** *ll.* 236–284; **NOSC; OBS**

(Athens.) **NOSC; OBS,** *ll.* 236–364;

"Or if I would delight my privat hours." **PeECV**

Rome ("He brought our saviour to the western side"). **NOSC**

Rome ("The City which thou seest no other deem"). **OBS**

"Therefore let pass, as they are transitory." **OAEL-1**

"To whom the fiend with fear abasht repli'd." **PeECV**

"To whom the Tempter impudent replied." **ChIV-2**

Paradox, The.   Robert Creeley. **CP-CreeR**

Paradox, The.   John Donne. **CP-DonnJ**

Paradox, The.   Paul Laurence Dunbar. **CP-DunbP**

Paradox.   Thomas Hardy. **CP-HardT**

Paradox, A.   Richard Lovelace. **CP-LoveR**

Paradox.   Robert Penn Warren. **SP-WarrR**

Paradoxes and Oxymorons. John Ashbery. **SP-AshbJ**

Paragon of Animals, The. Alexander Pope. *See* Know then thyself, presume not God to scan.

Paragraphs. Hayden Carruth. **CP-CarHS**

"All things lay in nature, even the plastic flowers."

"And I was past caring   so many, too many men."

"And so with paragraphics."

"And the water / the rising water."

"Another hard, hard morning with a hard snow."

"Arthritic gray snowlight hobbles down the valley westward."

"Begin right here. The Campground Road. Some calls it the."

"Day   very solid   February 12th, 1944, A." **Jaz**

"Exact beat from—, The." **Jaz**

"High above themselves. Above everything, flux, ooze." **Jaz**

"I am a fanatic lover of liberty, considering it."

"I was watching the telly not serious you know just looking."

"In filthy Puerto Rico lives a bird with no."

"It was the custom of my tribe to be silent."

"Ithiel Falls, below the Nazarene campground. A name."

"Keep going. *There's nothing else to do.* Past."

"Lamoille River Valley otherwise known, The."

"Not night now. Dawn. Six o'clock, a November morning."

"Now tell me if we don't need a revolution! Black."

"Of the rights of each to zero. No, I mean the only."

"Oh I loved you Pete Brown. And you were a brother." **Jaz**

"One called Next steps up, The."

"RAVAGE, v.t. To lay waste; to subject."

"Reading myself, old poems, their inside truth that was."

"Slums par excellence that were your farms! And all."

"There was this girl   18, 19   and slight."

"Ugly, evil, dying. The old soft lines."

"Why was the passenger pigeon exterminated?"

Parallel Invention. Muriel Rukeyser. **CP-RukeM**

Parallelism therefore is in fact Black Stone to Footstool of. For Mac Hammond. Charles Olson. **CP-OlsoC**

Parallels Never Meet. John Hewitt. **CP-HewiJ**

Paralytic. Sylvia Plath. **CP-PlatS**

Paranæticall, or Advisive Verse, to His Friend, M. John Wicks. Robert Herrick. **CP-HerrR**

Parang. Derek Walcott. **CP-WalcD**

Paraphrase. Hart Crane. **CP-CranH**

Paraphrase from Notebooks. Howard Nemerov. **CP-NemeH**

Paraphrase of Verses by Mayakovsky. John Hewitt. **CP-HewiJ**

Paraphrase on Psalm 114, A. John Milton. **CP-MiltJ**

Paraphrase on the Latter Part of the Sixth Chapter of St. Matthew's, A. James Thomson. **CP-ThomJ**

Paraphrases. Roy Fisher. **SP-FishR**

Parasceve, or Preparation, The. Robert Herrick. **CP-HerrR**

Parasol is the umbrella's daughter, The. Emily Dickinson. **CP-DickE**

Paratrooper. Mona Van Duyn. **SP-VanDM**

Parcæ, The; or, Three Dainty Destinies: The Armilet. Robert Herrick. **CP-HerrR**

Parcell-gil't-Poetry. Robert Herrick. **CP-HerrR**

Pardon. Wystan Hugh Auden. **CP-AudWJ**

Pardon, The. Robert Ranke Graves. **CP-GravR**

Pardon. Robert Herrick. **CP-HerrR**

Pardon, The. Richard Wilbur. **CP-WilbR**

Pardon a stranger hand that gives. Album Verses. John Greenleaf Whittier. **CP-WhitJ**

Pardon (blest shade) that I thus crowd to be. Sacred to the Memory of My Late Honoured Friend, Collonell Richard Lovelace. Eldred Revett. *Fr.* Elegies, 1660. **CP-LoveR**

Pardon, Lord, the lips that dare. John Greenleaf Whittier. *Fr.* Andrew Rykman's Prayer. **CP-WhitJ**

Pardon Me. Pablo Neruda, *tr. fr. Spanish by* Ben Belitt. **SP-NeruP**

Pardon me God, (once more I Thee intreat). To God. Robert Herrick. **CP-HerrR**

Pardon me if, to my eyes. Pardon Me. Pablo Neruda, *tr. fr. Spanish by* Ben Belitt. **SP-NeruP**

Pardon mine ears; both I and they do pray. Sonnet 51. Sir Philip Sidney. *Fr.* Astrophil and Stella. **SP-SidnP**

Pardon my injuries. Eve. William Carlos Williams. **CP-WilW1**

Pardon my trespasse (Silvia) I confesse. To Silvia . Robert Herrick. **CP-HerrR**

Pardon, oh, pardon, that my soul should make. Sonnet. Elizabeth Barrett Browning. *Fr.* Sonnets from the Portuguese. **CP-BroEB**

Pardon, old fathers, if you still remain. William Butler Yeats. **CP-YeatW**

Pardon the faults in me. Wife to Husband. Christina Georgina Rossetti. **CP-RosC1**

Pardoner's Prologue, The. Geoffrey Chaucer. **FHYEP; NAEL-1; NAWM-1; NoP; OAEL-1; PoE** *Fr.* The Canterbury Tales. **CP-ChauG**

(" 'In churches,' said the Pardoner, "when I preach.'") **NAWM-1**

(" 'In churches,' said the Pardoner, "when I preach.'") **NAWM-1**

Pardoner's Tale, The. Geoffrey Chaucer. **FHYEP; NAEL-1; NAWM-1; NoP; OAEL-1; PoE** *Fr.* The Canterbury Tales. **CP-ChauG**

("There was a company of young folk living.") **NAWM-1**

"But, sires, o word forgat I in my tale." **EBEV**

Death and the Three Revellers. **OBNV**

"It's of three rioters I have to tell." **SCV**

"This olde man gan looke in his visage." **OBD**

Three Rioters, The. **EBNV**

Pardons. Robert Herrick. **CP-HerrR**

Paregoric Babies. Jim Carroll. **SP-CarrJ**

Parent, The. Ogden Nash. **CP-NashO**

Parent and Prince of Heav'n O lead I pray. Cleanthes, *tr. fr. Latin by* Richard Lovelace. **CP-LoveR**

Parent of golden dreams, Romance! To Romance. Byron. **CP-Byron**

Parentage. William Stafford. **SP-StafW**

Parenthetical Address. Byron. **CP-Byron**

Parents. Stevie Smith. **CP-SmitS**

Parents of Beauty, The. Emily Dickinson. **SP-DickE**

Parents: People Like Our Marriage Maxie and Andrew, The. Gwendolyn Brooks. *Fr.* Notes from the Childhood and the Girlhood. **SP-BrooG**

Parergon. John Ashbery. **SP-AshbJ**

Paring the Apple. Charles Tomlinson. **CP-TomlC**

Paris. Al Young. **CP-YounA**

Paris and Diomedes. Homer, *tr. by* George Meredith. **CP-MerG1** *Fr.* The Iliad.

Paris came to Ida. Euripides, *tr. by* Hilda Doolittle ("H.D."). **CP-DoolH** *Fr.* Iphigenia [*or* Iphigeneia] in Aulis.

Paris—Christmas 1938. Edwin Rolfe. **CP-RolfE**

Paris Day. Anne Waldman. **SP-WaldA**

Paris Journal. Jim Morrison. **SP-MorrJ**

Paris Models. Leonard Cohen. **CP-CoheL**

Paris moon-drowned streets and the chestnuts blooming. Sappho in Paris. Gilbert Sorrentino. **SP-SorrG**

Paris, 7 A.M. Elizabeth Bishop. **CP-BishE**

Paris Transformations. Lawrence Ferlinghetti. **SP-FerlL**

Parish: A Satire, The. John Clare. **SP-ClarT**

Parish hind oppressions humble slave, The. The Parish: A Satire. John Clare. **SP-ClarT**

Parish Register, The. George Crabbe.

  Contented Peasant, The. **SP-CrabG**

  Phoebe Dawson. **SP-CrabG**

Parisina. Byron. **CP-Byron**

Paris's Second Judgement. Richard Lovelace. **CP-LoveR**

Paris;this April sunset completely utters. Edward Estlin Cummings. **CP-CummE**

Paris,thou art not. Edward Estlin Cummings. **CP-CummE**

Park, The. Ralph Waldo Emerson. **CP-EmerR**

Park, The. Roy Fisher. *Fr.* City. **SP-FishR**

Park, The. Louis MacNeice. **CP-MacNL**

Park, The. Charles Kenneth Williams. **SP-WillC**

Park at Villammare, The. Richard Hugo. **CP-HugoR**

Park. Let's walk the brief path back. Carloway Broch. Richard Hugo. **CP-HugoR**

Parked in the fields. The Forms of Love. George Oppen. **CP-OppeG**

Parker River, The. Richard Eberhart. **CP-EberR**

Parkinsons Shade to the House of Mr. Pallauicine Taking His Death Ill. Robert Herrick. **CP-HerrR**

Parklands, The. Stevie Smith. **CP-SmitS**

Parks & ponds are good by day. Ralph Waldo Emerson. **CP-EmerR**

Parlement of Foules, The, *see also* Parliament of Fowls, The. Geoffrey Chaucer. **CP-ChauG**

  Now Welcom[e], Somer [*or* Summer]. **HAP; OxBM; SeCePo**

  (Foules Rondel.) **TrGrPo**

  (Qui Bien Aime a Tard Oublie.) **EnLoPo**

  (Roundel: "Now welcom[e], Somer [*or* Summer] with thy sunne soft[e].") **CTC; OAEL-1; OPOU; OxBSP**

  (Welcome, Summer.) **MeEL**

  "There mighte men the royal eagle find." **PB; PBBP**

Parliament Hill Fields. Sir John Betjeman. **CP-BetjJ**

Parliament Hill Fields. Sylvia Plath. **CP-PlatS**

Parliament Hill in the Evening. David Herbert Lawrence. **CP-LawrD**

Parliament of Roses to Julia, The. Robert Herrick. **CP-HerrR**

Parliamentary Oscillators. Samuel Taylor Coleridge. **CP-ColeS**

Parnassus. Tennyson. **CP-TennA**

Parnell. William Butler Yeats. **CP-YeatW**

Parnell came down the road, he said to a cheering man. Parnell. William Butler Yeats. **CP-YeatW**

Parnell's Funeral. William Butler Yeats. **CP-YeatW**

Parochial Theme. Wallace Stevens. **CP-StevW**

Parodies of Bishop Percy's *Hermit of Warkworth*. Samuel Johnson. *See* I put my hat upon my head.

Parodies of Bishop Percy's *Hermit of Warkworth*. Samuel Johnson. *See* I therefore pray thee, Renny dear.

Parodies of Bishop Percy's *Hermit of Warkworth*. Samuel Johnson. *See* The Tender infant, meek and mild.

Parody [*or* Parodie], A. George Herbert. **CP-HerbG**

Parody of Alfred Austin. George Meredith. **CP-MerG2**

Parousia. George Oppen. *Fr.* Five Poems about Poetry. **CP-OppeG**

Parquet barely gleams, a lake, The. In the Hall of Mirrors. James Merrill. **SP-MerrJ**

Parrat protests 'tis he, and only he. Upon Parrat. Robert Herrick. **CP-HerrR**

Parrot, The. Vincent Bourne, *tr. fr. Latin by* William Cowper. **CP-CowpW**

Parrot, A. May Sarton. **SP-SartM**

Parrot. Stevie Smith. **CP-SmitS**

Parrot Fish, The. James Merrill. **SP-MerrJ**

Parrot, from east India to me sent, The. 2.6. Ovid. **CP-MarlC**, *tr. by* Christopher Marlowe; *Fr.* Elegies.

Parrot, The / Is eating a carrot. Who Killed Lawless Lean? Stevie Smith. **CP-SmitS**

Parsi Woman, The. Edna St. Vincent Millay. **CP-MillE**

Parsley. Rita Dove. **SP-DoveR**

Parsley. Further Reflection on Parsley. Ogden Nash. **CP-NashO**

Parsley for Vice-President! Ogden Nash. **CP-NashO**

Parsnip, The. Ogden Nash. **CP-NashO**

Parsnips. Charles Tomlinson. **CP-TomlC**

Parson him answered, "Benedicite!", The. Shipman, The. Geoffrey Chaucer. **ACP** *Fr.* The Epilogue to the Man of Laws' Tale. *Fr.* The Canterbury Tales. **CP-ChauG**

Parson of a country town was he, The, *mod. vers. by* H.C. Leonard. Geoffrey Chaucer. *See* A Good man ther[e] was of religioun [*or* religion].

Parson, these things is thy possessing. *in imitation of* Swift. Alexander Pope. **CP-PopeA**

Parson to his pallid spouse, The. Questions in a Wood. Robert Ranke Graves. **CP-GravR**

Parsonage, The, *sels.* William Wordsworth. *Fr.* The Excursion. **CP-WorW2**

Parsonage in Oxfordshire, A. William Wordsworth. **CP-WorW2**

Parson's Case, The. Jonathan Swift. **CP-SwifJ**

Parson's Prologue, The. Geoffrey Chaucer. *Fr.* The Canterbury Tales. **CP-ChauG**

Parson's Tale, The. Geoffrey Chaucer. *Fr.* The Canterbury Tales. **CP-ChauG**

Part, The. Denise Levertov. **CP-LeveD**

Part 1. Mary Sidney, Countess of Montgomery Wroth. *Fr.* Urania. **CP-WrotM**

"Adieu sweet Sun."

"As these drops fall: so Hope drops now on me."

"Beare part with me most straight and pleasant Tree."

("Bear part with me most straight and pleasant tree.") **WPE**

(Morea's Sonnet.) **WPE**

"Blame me not dearest, though grieved for your sake."

"Cruell Remembrance alas now be still."

"Deare Love, alas, how have I wronged thee."

"Deare, though unconstant, these I send to you."

Dialogue: Shepheard, and Sheapherdess.

"Did I boast of liberty?"

"Drowne me not you cruell teares."

"*Egypts* Pyramids inclose their Kings."

"Faithfull lovers keepe from hence."

"Fond aged man, why doe you on me gaze."

"From a long way, and Pilgrimage for Love."

"From victory in love I now am come."

"Have I lost my liberty."

"Heart drops distilling like a new cut-vine."

"Here all alone in silence might I mourne."

"How doe I find my soules extreamest anguish."

"I, who doe feele the highest part of griefe."

"If a clear [*or* cleere] fountain[e] still keeping a sad course." **WPE**

(Duke's Song, The.) **WPE**

"Infernall Spirits listen to my moanes."

"Joy you say the Heavens in motion trie, The."

Lindamira's Complaint.

Sonnet: "O Memory [*or* Memorie], could I but loose thee now." **BWW; WPE**

("Leave me vaine Hope too long thou hast possesst.") **BWW**

Sonnet 1: "Deare eyes farewell, my Sunne once, now my end."

Sonnet 2: "O deadly rancour to a constant heart."

Sonnet 3: "Surgeon I would aske, but 'tis too late."

Sonnet 5: "Leave me vain Hope, too long thou hast posses[s]t." **BWW**

Sonnet 6: "Though you forsake me, yet alas permit."

Sonnet 7: "Some doe, perhaps, both wrong my love, and care."

"Loss[e] my molester at last patient be." **WPE**

(Pamphilia's Sonnet.) **WPE**

"Love among the clouds did hover."

"Love farewell I now discover."

"Love growne proud with victory."

"Love peruse me, seeke, and finde."

"My thoughts thou hast supported without rest."

"O! that I might but now as senceles bee."

"Pray thee *Diana* tell mee, is it ill."

"Rise, rise from sluggishness, fly fast my Deere."

"Sheapherd who noe care did take, A."

Song: "Gon is my joy while heere I mourne."

Song: "Love what art thou? A vaine thought."

Song: "Who can blame mee if I love?"

Sonnet: "Unquiet griefe search farder, in my hart."

"Stay mine eyes, these floods of teares."

"Sunne hath no long journey now to goe, The."

"Sweete solitarines, joy to those hearts."

"Teares some times flow from mirth, as well as sorrow."

"That which to some their wishes ends present."

"This no wonder's of much weight."

"Unseene, unknowne, I here alone complaine."

"When I with trembling aske if you love still."

"Why doe you so much wish for raine, when I."

"You powers divine of love-commanding eyes."

"You pure and holy fire."

"You, who ending never saw."

Part 2. Mary Sidney, Countess of Montgomery Wroth. *Fr.* Urania. **CP-WrotM**

"Beehold this sacred fire."

"Come deere, lett's waulke into this spring."

"Come lusty gamesters of the sea."

"Fierce love, alas yett lett mee rest."

"Had I loved butt att that rate."

"Honor now injoye the day."

"Love butt a phantesie light, and vaine."

"Love lett mee live, ore lett mee dye."

"Lying upon the beach."

"Most deere, more hapy soverainsing harts."

"Most hapy memory bee ever blest."

"Returne my thoughts, why fly you soe?"

"Stay holy fires."

"This is Honor's holly day."

"This night the Moone eclipsed was."

"Was I to blame to trust."

"Were ever eyes of such devinitie."

"Why doe you thus torment my poorest hart?"

Part barn, part boxcar, part of a chicken shed. At the Bait Stand. Ted Kooser. **SP-KoosT**

Part fenced by man, part by a rugged steep. A Place of Burial in the South of Scotland. William Wordsworth. **CP-WorW2**

Part of a Letter. Richard Wilbur. **CP-WilbR**

Part of a Novel, Part of a Poem, Part of a Play. Marianne Craig Moore. Hero, The. **CP-MoorM**

Steeple-Jack, The. **CP-MoorM**

Part of a Summer, The. Jonathan Swift. **CP-SwifJ**

Part of a True Story. Marilyn Hacker. **SP-HackM**

Part of an Ode, A. Ben Jonson. *See* It Is Not Growing Like a Tree.

Part of the Darkness. Isabella Gardner. **CP-GardI**

Part of the Forest. George Oppen. **CP-OppeG**

Part of the Ninth Ode of Horace Imitated. Alexander Pope. **CP-PopeA**

Part of the Ninth Ode of the Fourth Book of Horace. Jonathan Swift. **CP-SwifJ**

Part of the Series on the Paths, A. Charles Olson. **CP-OlsoC**

Part of the work[e] remains [*or* remaines]; one part is past. The End of His Work. Robert Herrick. **CP-HerrR**

Part Song, With Concert of Recorders. William Dickey. **SP-DickW**

"And he lies dead—."

"And I, who lay so warm and quiet there—."

"Come, Doctor, we must fly someotherwhere."

"Doctor, I did not see that you were there."

"For we have gone a curious way from there."

"I did not know you when you came in there."

"Who made you come and find the door to there?"

Part where General Matthei leaves his office, The. General Matthei Drives Home through Santiago. Stephen Dobyns. **SP-DobyS**

Parta Quies. Alfred Edward Housman. **CP-HousA**

Partake as doth the Bee. Emily Dickinson. **CP-DickE**

Partaking of the miraculous. Apparition of Splendor. Marianne Craig Moore. **CP-MoorM**

Parted. Paul Laurence Dunbar. **CP-DunbP**

Parted. Paul Laurence Dunbar. **CP-DunbP**

Parted. Paul Laurence Dunbar. **CP-DunbP**

Parthenia. Allen Tate. **CP-TateA**

Parthenon, The. Herman Melville. **SP-MelvH**

Parthian Powers. John Milton. *See* The Parthians.

Parthians, The. John Milton. **OBS** *Fr.* Book III. *Fr.* Paradise Regained [*or* Regain'd]. **CP-MiltJ**

(Parthian Powers.) **NOSC**, *book* III, *ll.* 310–43;

Partial Analysis. Marilyn Hacker. **SP-HackM**

Partial Eclipse. William DeWitt Snodgrass. **SP-SnodW**

Partial Explanation, The. Charles Simic. **SP-SimiC**

Partial Muse, has from my earliest hours, The. Charlotte Smith. **CP-SmitC**

Partial Resemblance. Denise Levertov. **CP-LeveD**

Particular density: in the center, rises, A. Gilbert Sorrentino. **SP-SorrG**

Particular Lullaby. Stanley Jasspon Kunitz. **CP-KuniS**

Particularity. Adrienne Rich. *Fr.* Turning the Wheel. **SP-RicA2**

Particulars they want. Envoi. Robert Creeley. **CP-CreeR**

Parting. Stanley Jasspon Kunitz. **CP-KuniS**

Parting, *fr.* A Woman Young and Old. William Butler Yeats. **CP-YeatW**

Parting after parting, / Sore loss and gnawing pain. Christina Georgina Rossetti. **CP-RosC2**

Parting as Descent. John Berryman. **CP-BerrJ**

Parting at Dawn. John Crowe Ransom. **SP-RansJ**

Parting at Morning. Robert Browning. **CP-BroR1**

Parting, Celia Weeps. Thomas Carew. **CP-CareT**

Parting: I, The. Adrienne Rich. **CP-RicAE; SP-RicA2**

Parting, I take with me completed June. Parting. Stanley Jasspon Kunitz. **CP-KuniS**

Parting: II, The. Adrienne Rich. **CP-RicAE; SP-RicA2**

Parting is one of the exactions. Emily Dickinson. **SP-DickE**

Parting Lovers. Elizabeth Barrett Browning. **CP-BroEB**

Parting of the Columns, The. Rudyard Kipling. **CP-KiplR**

Parting-Scene, A. Thomas Hardy. **CP-HardT**

Parting up / down from / one on the shore, two egrets—. Hayden Carruth. **CP-CarHS** *Fr.* The Clay Hill Anthology.

Parting Verse, Or Charge to His Supposed Wife When He Travelled, The. Robert Herrick. **CP-HerrR**

Parting Verse, the Feast There Ended, The. Robert Herrick. **CP-HerrR**

Parting with Thee reluctantly. Emily Dickinson. **CP-DickE**

Parting, without a Sequel. John Crowe Ransom. **SP-RansJ**

Partition. Wystan Hugh Auden. **CP-AudeW**

Partly from reading the books and hearing the plays. Country Talk. John Hewitt. **CP-HewiJ**

Partly to think, more to be left alone. The Book of Annandale. Edwin Arlington Robinson. **CP-RobiE**

Partly work[e] and partly play. Saint Distaffs Day, or the Morrow after Twelfth Day. Robert Herrick. **CP-HerrR**

Partnership. Edwin Arlington Robinson. **CP-RobiE**

Partnership dissolved. Sale. Miller Williams. **SP-WillM**

Partridge. Phoebe Hesketh. **SP-HeskP**

Parts of an Opera, Parts of a Guitar, Part of Nowhere. Charles Bukowski. **SP-BukC2**

Party, The. Stephen Dobyns. **SP-DobyS**

Party, The. Paul Laurence Dunbar. **CP-DunbP**

Party, The. Phoebe Hesketh. **SP-HeskP**

Party, The. Ogden Nash. **CP-NashO**

Party Knee. John Updike. **CP-UpdiJ**

Party Next Door, The. Ogden Nash. **CP-NashO**

Party on Shipboard. George Oppen. **CP-OppeG**

Party Politics. Philip Larkin. **CP-LarkP**

Parva qudem regio, sed rellligione primorum. Samuel Johnson. **CP-JohnS**

Parvenu. Nicholas Vachel Lindsay. **CP-LindV**

(parvenue) delinquent, who will now. The Late Comer. Robert Creeley. **CP-CreeR**

Pas à pas. Samuel Beckett. **CP-BeckS**

Pas davantage. Samuel Beckett. **CP-BeckS**

Pas même Fréron / hais personne / pas même Fréron. Canto 114. Ezra Pound. *Fr.* Cantos. **CP-PoCan**

Pasa Thalassa Thalassa. Edwin Arlington Robinson. **CP-RobiE**

Paske, though his debt be due upon the day. Upon Paske a Draper. Robert Herrick. **CP-HerrR**

Pass forth, my wonted cries. Sir Thomas Wyatt. **CP-WyatT**

Pass, Friend. Carl Sandburg. **CP-SandC**

Pass now in metaphor beyond birds. Dancing Flame. Robert Ranke Graves. **CP-GravR**

Pass of Kirkstone, The. William Wordsworth. **CP-WorW2**

Pass of the Sierra, The. John Greenleaf Whittier. **CP-WhitJ**

Pass to thy Rendezvous of Light. Emily Dickinson. **CP-DickE**

Pass we from entertainments, that are such. William Wordsworth. **EnRP** *Fr.* Residence in London. *Fr.* The Prelude; Growth of a Poet's Mind [1850 vers.]. **CP-WorW3**

Pass we to another land. Song. George Meredith. **CP-MerG2**

Passage. Hart Crane. **CP-CranH**

Passage, The. Robert Creeley. **CP-CreeR**

Passage, The, *from the German of* J. L. Uhland. Paul Laurence Dunbar. **CP-DunbP**

Passage, The. Richard Eberhart. **CP-EberR**

Passage from John Wilson's The Angler's Tent. William Wordsworth. **CP-WorW1**

Passage from Mary Barker's *Lines Addressed to a Noble Lord* (His Lordship Will Know Why). William Wordsworth. **CP-WorW2**

Passage of the Apennines. Percy Bysshe Shelley. **CP-ShelP**

Passage of Time, The. Louise McNeill. **SP-McNeL**

Passage over Water. Robert Duncan. **SP-DuncR**

Passage Steamer. Louis MacNeice. **CP-MacNL**

Passage to godhead, fitfully glared upon. The Lynchings of Jesus. Muriel Rukeyser. **CP-RukeM**

Passage to India. Walt Whitman. **CP-WhitW**

"Ah, more than any priest, O soul, we too believe in God." **WGRP**

"Bathe me O God in thee, mounting to thee." **TrPWD**

Passage to Worship. Donald Hall. **CP-HallD**

Passages. Robert Duncan.

Architecture, The. **SP-DuncR**

Before the Judgment. **SP-DuncR**

Concert, The. **SP-DuncR**

Fire, The. **SP-DuncR**

In Blood's Domaine. **SP-DuncR**

Stage Directions. **SP-DuncR**

Torso, The. **SP-DuncR**

Tribal Memories. **SP-DuncR**

Up Rising. **SP-DuncR**

Passages. Thomas McGrath. **SP-McGrT**

Passaic, N.J. William Carlos Williams. **CP-WilW2**

Passed by the little fresh water pond. The Man the Father. Marsden Hartley. **CP-HartM**

Passed through the dark wall. The Long Hunter. Wendell Berry. **CP-BerrW**

Passenger Pigeons. Robinson Jeffers. **CP-JefR3**

Passenger who e're thou art. [Mr. Herrys,] His Epitaph. Richard Crashaw. **CP-CrasR**

Passer-By, The. Thomas Hardy. **CP-HardT**

Passer Domesticus. William Carlos Williams. **CP-WilW2**

Passer Mortuus Est. Edna St. Vincent Millay. **CP-MillE**

Passers-by. Carl Sandburg. **CP-SandC**

Passing. Langston Hughes. **SP-HughL**

Passing a Flemish village and a burning city. Brueghel: The Triumph of Time. Howard Nemerov. **CP-NemeH**

Passing a leathercraft shop in Mill Valley I see. The Scout. William Everson. **SP-EverW**

Passing and Glassing. Christina Georgina Rossetti. **CP-RosC2**

Passing at my pleasure's pace. No More People. Stevie Smith. **CP-SmitS**

Passing Away. Christina Georgina Rossetti. **MeMBP; NoP; OAEL-2; OBNC; PFP; WPE** *Fr.* Old and New Year Ditties. **CP-RosC1**

Passing away the bliss, / The anguish passing away. Christina Georgina Rossetti. **CP-RosC3**

Passing-Bell, A. David Herbert Lawrence. **CP-LawrD**

Passing by, he could be anybody. The Night Traveler. Mary Oliver. **SP-OlivM**

Passing Cloud, The. Stevie Smith. **CP-SmitS**

Passing cyclist winks; well, let her, let her!, A. Sears Roebuck. Randall Jarrell. **CP-JarrR**

Passing Glimpse, A. Robert Frost. **CP-FrosR**

Passing her in the day he had but dared. Archibald MacLeish. **CP-MacLA** *Fr.* The Happy Marriage.

Passing Impatience With a Noble Country, A. Malcolm Lowry. **CP-LowrM**

Passing into the wilderness of twisted trees. The Souvenir. Robert Creeley. **CP-CreeR**

Passing men in the street who are dead. Conclusion. Audre Lorde. **SP-LordA**

Passing my house in the suburbs. To a Chinese Woman. William Carlos Williams. **CP-WilW2**

Passing Newbridge-on-Wye. Roy Fisher. **SP-FishR**

Passing of Arthur, The. Tennyson. **FHYEP; NAEL-2; OBNC** *Fr.* Idylls of the King. **CP-TennA**

"And answer made King Arthur, breathing hard." **PeECV**, *ll.* 330–440;

"And slowly answered Arthur from the barge." **FaBoEH**

"But now farewell. I am going a long way." **FaBoRV**

Prayer: "Pray for my soul. More things are wrought by prayer." **WGRP**

"So all day long the noise of battle rolled." **FaBoRV**

"Then rose the King and moved his host by night." **PeVV**

Passing of the South, The. John Gould Fletcher. **SP-FletJ**

Passing of the Year, The. Edward Estlin Cummings. **CP-CummE**

Passing On. Adrienne Rich. **CP-RicAE**

Passing Remark. William Stafford. **SP-StafW**

Passing stranger! you do not know how longingly I look upon you. To a Stranger. Walt Whitman. **CP-WhitW**

Passing tall. Louis Zukofsky. *Fr.* 29 Poems. **CP-ZukLS**

Passing the Strait. Wendell Berry. **CP-BerrW**

"Dance passes beyond us, The."

"Forsaking all others, we."

"Past the strait of kept faith."

Passing the Word. Stephen Dobyns. **SP-DobyS**

Passing through huddled and ugly walls. The Harbor. Carl Sandburg. **CP-WilbR**

Passing Time. Maya Angelou. **SP-AngeM**

Passing Visit to Helen. David Herbert Lawrence. **CP-LawrD**

Passion. Robert Herrick. **CP-HerrR**

Passion. John Hewitt. **CP-HewiJ**

Passion, The. John Milton. **CP-MiltJ**

Passion and Love. Paul Laurence Dunbar. **CP-DunbP**

Passion Flower hath sprung up tall, The. Christina Georgina Rossetti. **CP-RosC2**

Passion for Roman order seized the plains, A. Indianapolis. John Updike. **CP-UpdiJ**

Passion for the Sky. Joseph Ceravolo. **SP-CeraJ**

Passion may call for a partner. The Evening Sunsets Witness and Pass On. Carl Sandburg. **CP-SandC**

Passion of the Mad Rabbit, The. Anne Sexton. **CP-SextA**

Passion Play. Gary Gildner. **SP-GildG**

Passion, too intemperate. Somewhere Else. Richard Eberhart. **CP-EberR**

Passion Week. William Everson. **SP-EverW**

Passion Week Monday after Palm Sunday. Martin Edmunds. **SP-EdmuM**

Passionate Man[']s Pilgrimage, The. Sir Walter Ralegh. **CP-RaleW**

Passionate Pagan and the Dispassionate Public, The. Ogden Nash. **CP-NashO**

Passionate Pilgrim, The. *Various Authors.* **CP-ShaWS**

"As it fell upon a day." **AWP; CH; CP-ShaWS; EIL; GBL; GTBS; GTBS-P; LoBV; NOBE; OBEV; OBSC; PBBP**

(Nightingale, The.) **AWP; GTBS; GTBS-P**

(Ode, An.) **EIL; LoBV; OBSC**

(Philomel.) **CH; NOBE; OBEV**

"Beauty is but a vain and doubtful good." **OBSC**

(Beauty.) **OBSC**

"Crabbed age and youth cannot live together." **EBEvV; EIL; FaBoEn; GBL; GTBS; GTBS-P; HBV 1-2; InPS; LiTB; NIP; NoSic; OBEV; OBSC; TreFS; UnTE**

(Age and Youth.) **EIL; FaBoEn**

(Crabbed Age and Youth.) **EBEvV; GBL; HBV 1-2; InPS; LiTB; NIP; NoSic; OBEV; TreFS; UnTE**

(Madrigal, A: "Crabbed age and youth.") **GTBS; GTBS-P; InPS**

(Youth and Age.) **OBSC**

"Did not the heavenly rhetoric of thine eye."

"Fair is my love, but not so fair as fickle." **EIL**

(Fair is My Love.) **EIL**

"Fair was the morn when the fair queen of love."

"Good night, good rest. Ah, neither be my share."

"If love make me forsworn, how shall I swear to love?"

"If music and sweet poetry agree."

"It was a lording's daughter, the fairest one of three." **CP-ShaWS; EIL**

(It Was a Lording's Daughter.) **EIL**

"Live with me, and be my love."

"Lord, how mine eyes throw gazes to the east!"

"My flocks feed not."

"On a day, alack the day!"

"Scarce had the sun dried up the dewy morn."

"Sweet Cytherea, sitting by a brook."

"Sweet rose, fair flower, untimely pluck'd, soon vaded." **EIL**

(Sweet Rose, Fair Flower.) **EIL**

"Two loves I have, of comfort and despair."

"Venus, with young Adonis sitting by her."

"When as thine eye hath chose the dame."

"When my love swears that she is made of truth."

Passionate Rebuke. Marsden Hartley. **CP-HartM**

Passionate Shepherd to His Love, The. Christopher Marlowe. **CP-MarlC**

Passion's Cry. Robert Burns. **CP-BurnR**

Passiontide. Christina Georgina Rossetti. **CP-RosC2**

Passivation. Joseph Ceravolo. **SP-CeraJ**

Passive and dark, dead river. Dead River. Howard Nemerov. **CP-NemeH**

Passive I lie, looking up through leaves. Seventh Day. Kathleen Jessie Raine. **SP-RainK**

Passive Partner, The. Roy Fisher. **SP-FishR**

Passport Officer, The. Basil Bunting. **CP-BuntB**

Past, The. Ralph Waldo Emerson. **CP-EmerR**

Past, The. William Matthews. **SP-MattW**

Past, The. Frederick Morgan. **SP-MorgF**

Past, The. Percy Bysshe Shelley. **CP-ShelP**

Past, The. Stevie Smith. **CP-SmitS**

Past, The. Charles Kenneth Williams. **SP-WillC**

Past all your knowing. Song. Wystan Hugh Auden. **CP-AudWJ**

Past and Coming Year, The. John Greenleaf Whittier. **CP-WhitJ**

Past and Future. Elizabeth Barrett Browning. **CP-BroEB**

Past Burwash and the White River delta. At Slim's River. John Haines. **SP-HainJ**

Past crag and scarp. History. Robert Penn Warren. **SP-WarrR**

Past Days of Gales. Philip Larkin. **CP-LarkP**

Past death / past rainy days. Deep Religious Faith. William Carlos Williams. **CP-WilW2**

Past exchanges have left orbits of rain around my face. An Apology. Diane Wakoski. **SP-WakoD**

Past is not a package, The. Emily Dickinson. **SP-DickE**

Past is past, and if one. Salute. James Schuyler. **CP-SchuJ**

Past is such a curious Creature, The. Emily Dickinson. **CP-DickE**

Past Is the Present, The. Marianne Craig Moore. **CP-MoorM**

Past mesas in yellow ruin. A Drive to Los Alamos. Thom Gunn. **CP-GunnT**

Past second cock-crow yacht masts in the harbor go slowly white. Masts at Dawn. Robert Penn Warren. **SP-WarrR**

Past Silver Durango Over Mexic Sierra-Wrinkles. Allen Ginsberg. **CP-GinsA**

Past Terre Haute, the diesels pound. Vital Statistics. Robert Penn Warren. *Fr.* Homage to Theodore Dreiser. **SP-WarrR**

Past the abandoned quarry. Stanley Jasspon Kunitz. *Fr.* The Testing-Tree. **CP-KuniS**

Past the angular maguey fields, a ride on the optic nerve. Into Mexico. Mona Van Duyn. **SP-VanDM**

Past the hills that peep. Epeisodia. Thomas Hardy. **CP-HardT**

Past the strait of kept faith. Wendell Berry. *Fr.* Passing the Strait. **CP-BerrW**

Past time—those. Here. Robert Creeley. **CP-CreeR**

Past towns, states, deserts, hills, and rivers borne. Catullus. *See* Carmen 101: "Journeying over many seas and through many countries."

Pastel Dresses. Stephen Dobyns. **SP-DobyS**

Pastime. Christina Georgina Rossetti. **CP-RosC2**

Pastime. James Schuyler. **CP-SchuJ**

Pastor, The. William Wordsworth. *Fr.* The Excursion. **CP-WorW2**

Pastor and Patriot!—at whose bidding rise. To a Friend. William Wordsworth. *Fr.* Poems Composed or Suggested During a Tour, in the Summer of 1833. **CP-WorW2**

Pastor Caballero, The. Wallace Stevens. **CP-StevW**

Pastor Errante. Donald Davie. **CP-DavDo**

Pastor, The / of grief and dreams. A Cure of Souls. Denise Levertov. **CP-LeveD**

Pastoral: "Dove walks with sticky feet, The." Kenneth Patchen. **CP-PatcK**

Pastoral: "Enquiring fields, courtesies, The." Allen Tate. **CP-TateA**

Pastoral: "I came to a meadow." Charles Simic. **SP-SimiC**

Pastoral: "If it were only still!" Edna St. Vincent Millay. **CP-MillE**

Pastoral: "Little sparrows, The." William Carlos Williams. **CP-WilW1**

Pastoral: "Lonely evening crouches, darkens as the hour, The." Edwin Rolfe. **CP-RolfE**

Pastoral: "Now, on this bluest of mornings, we wake." Edwin Rolfe. **CP-RolfE**

Pastoral; "If I say I have heard voices." William Carlos Williams. **CP-WilW1**

Pastoral; "When I was younger." William Carlos Williams. **CP-WilW1**

Pastoral 1; "Old man who goes about, The." William Carlos Williams. **CP-WilW1**

Pastoral 2: "If I talk to things." William Carlos Williams. **CP-WilW1**

Pastoral Between Thirsis and Corydon, upon the Death of Damon, A. James Thomson. **CP-ThomJ**

Pastoral Betwixt David, Thirsis, and the Angel Gabriel, upon the Birth of our Saviour, A. James Thomson. **CP-ThomJ**

Pastoral Character. William Wordsworth. *Fr.* Ecclesiastical Sonnets. **CP-WorW2**

Pastoral[l] Dialogue, A. Thomas Carew. **CP-CareT**

Pastoral[l] Dialogue, A. Thomas Carew. **CP-CareT**

Pastoral Dialogue, A. Frank O'Hara. **SP-OharF**

Pastoral Dialogue, A. Jonathan Swift. **CP-SwifJ**

Pastoral Dialogue between Richmond Lodge and Marble Hill, A. Jonathan Swift. **CP-SwifJ**

Pastoral Entertainment, A. James Thomson. **CP-ThomJ**

Pastoral Letter, The. John Greenleaf Whittier. **CP-WhitJ**

Pastoral—1954. Edwin Rolfe. **CP-RolfE**

Pastoral Nun, A. Wallace Stevens. **CP-StevW**

Pastorale. Hart Crane. **CP-CranH**

Pastorale: "Rushing darkness of the summer evening, The." Gilbert Sorrentino. **SP-SorrG**

Pastorall Aeglogue upon the Death of Sir Phillip Sidney, Knight, etc., A. Edmund Spenser. *Fr.* Astrophel. **CP-Spens**

Pastorall Sung to the King: Montano, Silvio, and Mirtillo, Shepards, A. Robert Herrick. **CP-HerrR**

Pastorall Upon the Birth of Prince Charles, A. Robert Herrick. **CP-HerrR**

Pastorals. Alun Lewis. **CP-LewiA**

  "Had I ever a young field."

  "Oh in a slim spaced forest."

Pastorals. George Meredith. **CP-MerG1**

  Pastoral 1: "How sweet on sunny afternoons."

  Pastoral 2: "Yon upland slope which hides the sun."

  Pastoral 3: "Now standing on this hedgeside path."

  Pastoral 4: "Lo, as a tree, whose wintry twigs."

  Pastoral 5: "Now from the meadow floods the wild duck clamours."

  Pastoral 6: "How barren would this valley be."

  Pastoral 7: "Summer glows warm on the meadows, and speedwell, and gold-cups, and daisies."

Pastorals. Alexander Pope. **CP-PopeA**

  Autumn, the Third Pastoral, or Hylas and Ægon.

  Spring, the First Pastoral, or Damon.

  Summer, The Second Pastoral, or Alexis.

  Sylvan Delights. **NOBE**

  Winter, the Fourth Pastoral, or Daphne.

Pastorals. Virgil, *tr. fr. Latin.*

  Translation of Virgil: Pastoral V. **CP-JohnS**

  Translation of Virgil: Pastoral I. **CP-JohnS**

Pasture, The. Richard Eberhart. *Fr.* Burr Oaks. **CP-EberR**

Pasture, The. Robert Frost. **CP-FrosR**

Pasture Alp is webbed with shade, The. George Meredith. **CP-MerG2**

Pasture is a field of changing vision, The. The Pasture. Richard Eberhart. *Fr.* Burr Oaks. **CP-EberR**

Pasture Line Fence. Louise McNeill. **SP-McNeL**

Pasture, stone wall, and steeple. Question in a Field. Louise Bogan. **CP-BogaL**

Pat Dugan. . . my grandfather. . . throat cancer. . . 1947. People Who Died. Ted Berrigan. **SP-BerrT**

Pat of Butter, The. Thomas Hardy. **CP-HardT**

Patch of meadow & upland, A. Ralph Waldo Emerson. **CP-EmerR**

Patch of Old Snow, A. Robert Frost. **CP-FrosR**

Patch Work. Thom Gunn. **CP-GunnT**

Patchworks. Steve Griffiths. **SP-GrifS**

Paternis suppar. Family Mottoes. Frank Templeton Prince. **CP-PrinF**

Paterson. Allen Ginsberg. **CP-GinsA**

Paterson. William Carlos Williams.

Paterson. William Carlos Williams. **CP-WilW1**

  "Better than flowers." **CP-WilW1**

  Episode 17. **CP-WilW1**

  "I bought a new." **CP-WilW1**

  "When I saw." **CP-WilW1**

  "Your lovely hands." **CP-WilW1**

Paterson, Book V: The River of Heaven. William Carlos Williams. **CP-WilW2**

Paterson: The Falls. William Carlos Williams. **CP-WilW2**

Path, The. Paul Laurence Dunbar. **CP-DunbP**

Path, The. James McAuley. **SP-McAuJ**

Path, The. Kathleen Jessie Raine. **SP-RainK**

Path Ahead, The. John Hewitt. **CP-HewiJ**

Path between two rows of pines; spring, A. Song of Four Dancers. Stephen Dobyns. **SP-DobyS**

Path by which we twain did go, The. Tennyson. **EBVV; PeECV; SCV** *Fr.* In Memoriam A. H. H. **CP-TennA**

Path crowded with thistle fern blue daisy. Bixby Canyon. Allen Ginsberg. **CP-GinsA**

Path in the Sky, The. Nicholas Vachel Lindsay. **CP-LindV**

Path of Roses, The. "Lewis Carroll." **CP-CarrL**

Path that passes is of mud, The. The Tavern. Lewis Turco. **SP-TurcL**

Path to Han-shan's place is laughable, The, *after* Han-shan. Gary Snyder. **CP-SnydG**

Pathfinding in the dark byways. Trout Kill on the Sacremento. Tom Clark. **SP-ClarT**

Pathos broods, a desolation glowers, A. Malcolm Lowry. *Fr.* The Canadian Turned Back at the Border. **CP-LowrM**

Paths and Thingscape. Margaret Atwood. **SP-AtwM1**

Paths of Former Time. Thomas Hardy. **CP-HardT**

Paths of Victory. "Bob Dylan." **CP-DylaB**

Pathway, The. Kenneth Patchen. **CP-PatcK**

Patience. Robert Ranke Graves. **CP-GravR**

Patience. Christopher Smart. *Fr.* Hymns for the Amusement of Children. **SP-SmarC**

Patience, for I have wrong. Sir Thomas Wyatt. **CP-WyatT**

Patience for my device. Sir Thomas Wyatt. **CP-WyatT**

Patience, Hard Thing! Gerard Manley Hopkins. *See* Patience, hard thing! the hard thing but to pray.

Patience, hard thing! the hard thing but to pray. Gerard Manley Hopkins. **CP-HopkG**

  (Patience, Hard Thing!) **CP-HopkG**

Patience—has a quiet Outer. Emily Dickinson. **CP-DickE**

Patience in Princes. Robert Herrick. **CP-HerrR**

Patience: In the Mill. James Dickey. **CP-DickJ**

Patience Is When You Stop Waiting. Charles Kenneth Williams. **CP-WillC**

Patience, little Heart! Forecast. David Herbert Lawrence. **CP-LawrD**

Patience must dwell with Love, for Love and Sorrow. Christina Georgina Rossetti. **CP-RosC2**

Patience of all my smart. Sir Thomas Wyatt. **CP-WyatT**

Patience of an Angel. Max Jacob, *tr. fr. French by* Elizabeth Bishop. **CP-BishE**

Patience of Hope. Christina Georgina Rossetti. **CP-RosC2**

Patience, or Comforts in Crosses. Robert Herrick. **CP-HerrR**

Patience Taught by Nature. Elizabeth Barrett Browning. **CP-BroEB**

Patience though I have not. Sir Thomas Wyatt. **CP-WyatT**

Patient brute was Balaam's Ass, A. The Ass of Balaam. George Meredith. **CP-MerG2**

Patient Chief, who lab'ring long, arriv'd, The. Fragment of *Brutus*, an Epic. Alexander Pope. **CP-PopeA**

Patient Griselda, *mod. vers. by* Edward Hodnett. Geoffrey Chaucer. **PoRA** *Fr.* The Clerk's Tale. *Fr.* The Canterbury Tales. **CP-ChauG**

Patient, in the fire of noon. Ariadne at the Labyrinth. Thomas Merton. **CP-MertT; SP-MertT**

Patient old cripple, A. Jenny Joseph. *Fr.* Life and Turgid Times of A. Citizen. **SP-JoseJ**

Patient Pan / Drunken with nectar, The. Ralph Waldo Emerson. **CP-EmerR**

Patient Stupidity / So, heavy, passive to the tempest's shocks. Robert Burns. *Fr.* Versicles on Sign-Posts. **CP-BurnR**

Patient things wait in nature. In Silence. Frederick Morgan. **SP-MorgF**

Patna-Benares Express. Allen Ginsberg. **CP-GinsA**

Patriarch, The. Robert Burns. **CP-BurnR**

Patriarchal bed with four posts, The. No More Ghosts. Robert Ranke Graves. **CP-GravR**

Patriarchal Poetry. Gertrude Stein. **CP-SteiG**

Patriarchs, The. John Donne. *Fr.* A Litany. **CP-DonnJ**

Patrick Kavanagh's Dublin. James Liddy. **CP-LiddJ**

Patriot Engineer, The. George Meredith. **CP-MerG1**

Patriot of Life, A. Charles Bukowski. **SP-BukC3**

Patriot, The [An Old Story]. Robert Browning. **CP-BroR1**

Patriotic Poem. Diane Wakoski. **SP-WakoD**

Patriotic Sympathies. William Wordsworth. *Fr.* Ecclesiastical Sonnets. **CP-WorW2**

Patriotic Tour and Postulate of Joy. Robert Penn Warren. **SP-WarrR**

Patriots informed with Apostolic light. Aspects of Christianity in America—Concluded—American Episcopacy. William Wordsworth. **PAH** *Fr.* Ecclesiastical Sonnets. **CP-WorW2**

Patrol, The. Alun Lewis. **CP-LewiA**

Patrolling Barnegat. Walt Whitman. **CP-WhitW**

Patron of all those luckless brains. Ode to Apollo. William Cowper. **CP-CowpW**

Patronymic. Robinson Jeffers. **CP-JefR3**

Patsy's / brother / Bill—. Home. Robert Creeley. **CP-CreeR**

Pattern, The. Robert Creeley. **CP-CreeR**

Pattern of Our Lives, The. Edwin Rolfe. **CP-RolfE**

Pattern of the sun, The. Emily Dickinson. **CP-DickE**

Patterns / of sounds, endless. A Method. Robert Creeley. **CP-CreeR**

Patting good-bye, doubtless they told the lad. S.I.W. Wilfred Owen. **CP-OwenW**

Paudeen. William Butler Yeats. **CP-YeatW**

Paul. William Carlos Williams. **CP-WilW2**

Paul. James Wright. **CP-WrigJ**

Paul Blackburn. Ted Berrigan. **SP-BerrT**

Paul Bunyan. Shel Silverstein. **SP-SilS2**

Paul, did you mention chicory? Chicory. Hayden Carruth. **CP-CarHS**

Paul Eluard. Anne Waldman. **SP-WaldA**

Paul, he began ill, but he ended well. Beginnings and Endings. Robert Herrick. **CP-HerrR**

Paul Klee. John Haines. **SP-HainJ**

Paul Laurence Dunbar. Robert Earl Hayden. **CP-HaydR**

Paul, pinked with dozing, stood from the couch wherein. Pink and Pale. John Crowe Ransom. *Fr.* Two Gentlemen in Bonds. **SP-RansJ**

Paul Revere's Ride (The Landlord's Tale). Henry Wadsworth Longfellow. *Fr.* Tales of a Wayside Inn.

   (Landlord's Tale: Paul Revere's Ride, The.) **SP-LongH**

Paul Valéry Stood on the Cliff and Confronted the Furious Energies of Nature. Robert Penn Warren. **SP-WarrR**

Paula. Carl Sandburg. **CP-SandC**

Paula Becker to Clara Westhoff. Adrienne Rich. **SP-RicA2**

Paula is digging and shaping the loam of a salvia. June. Carl Sandburg. **CP-SandC**

Pauline [or Pauline; A Fragment of a Confession]. Robert Browning. **CP-BroR1**

   "My God, my God, let me for once look on thee." **TrPWD**

   "Night, and one single ridge of narrow path." **EBVVPR**

   "O God, where do they tend--these struggling aims?" **WGRP**

   "Sun-treader, life and light be thine for ever!" **EPCY**

   "Thou wilt remember. Thou art not more dear." **OAEL-2**

Pauline, mine own, bend o'er me—thy soft breast. Pauline [or Pauline; A Fragment of a Confession]. Robert Browning. **CP-BroR1**

Paulinus. William Wordsworth. *Fr.* Ecclesiastical Sonnets. **CP-WorW2**

Pauls hands do give, what give they bread or meat. Upon Paul. Robert Herrick. **CP-HerrR**

Paul's Wife. Robert Frost. **CP-FrosR**

Paumanok. Walt Whitman. **CP-WhitW**

Paumanok Picture, A. Walt Whitman. **CP-WhitW**

Pauper, A. Allen Tate. **CP-TateA**

Pauper Witch of Grafton, The. Robert Frost. *Fr.* Two Witches. **CP-FrosR**

Pause. A. Christina Georgina Rossetti. **CP-RosC3**

Pause, The. William Carlos Williams. **CP-WilW2**

Pause, courteous Spirit!—Baldi supplicates. Gabriello Chiabrera, *tr. fr. Italian by* William Wordsworth. **CP-WorW1**

Pause here, and think: a monitory rhime. Inscription for the Tomb of Hamilton. William Cowper. **CP-CowpW**

Pause of Thought, A. Christina Georgina Rossetti. **CP-RosC1; CoGr; FaBoEn; NOBE;** *Fr.* Three Stages. **CP-RosC3**

Pause on the railroad overpass. Black November. Chuck Miller. **SP-MillC**

Pause, Traveller! Whosoe'er thou be. Inscribed upon a Rock. William Wordsworth. *Fr.* Inscriptions Supposed to Be Found in and near a Hermit's Cell; 1818. **CP-WorW2**

Paused, and the Spirit of that mighty singing. Percy Bysshe Shelley. *Fr.* Ode to Liberty. **CP-ShelP**

Paused at the more than Brocken summit. At the Trade Center. Charles Tomlinson. **CP-TomlC**

Pausing in my sixth decade. Kenneth Rexroth. **CP-RexKL; SP-RexrK** *Fr.* The Heart's Garden, the Garden's Heart.

Pavana Dolorosa. Geoffrey Hill. *Fr.* Lachrimae; or Seven Tears Figured in Seven Passionate Pavans. **CP-HillG**

Pavane for a Dead Professor. John Hewitt. **CP-HewiJ**

Pavement, The. Charles Olson. **CP-OlsoC**

Pavements are quiet under press of their feet, The. Heine, Too, Lived in Germany. Kenneth Patchen. **CP-PatcK**

Pavilion pierces the green sky, The. Solo. Li Po, *tr. fr. Chinese by* William Carlos Williams *with* David Rafael Wang. **CP-WilW2**

Pawn-shop man knows hunger, The. Street Window. Carl Sandburg. **CP-SandC**

Pawnbroker roared, The. She's Your Lover Now. "Bob Dylan." **CP-DylaB**

Paws there. Snout there as well. Mustiness. Mould. Midwinter Waking. Philip Larkin. **CP-LarkP**

Pax. David Herbert Lawrence. **CP-LawrD**

Paxdominisit Sem Pervobiscum Etcumspiri Tutuo. Kenneth Patchen. **CP-PatcK**

Pay. Robert Creeley. **CP-CreeR**

Pay me my price, Potters! and I will sing. An Epigram of Homer. Homer, *tr. fr. Greek by* William Cowper. **CP-CowpW**

Paying calls. Thomas Hardy. **CP-HardT**

Paying Some Attention to His Birthday the Associate Professor Goes About His Business Considering What He Sees and a Kind of Praise. Miller Williams. **SP-WillM**

Pays Perdu. Jean Garrigue. **SP-GarrJ**

Paysage Moralisé. Wystan Hugh Auden. *See* Hearing of harvests rotting in the valleys.

Pcheek pcheek pcheek pcheek pcheek. Galway Kinnell. **LiTM; NePoEA-2** *Fr.* The Avenue Bearing the Initial of Christ into the New World. **SP-KinnG**

Pea Brush. Robert Frost. **CP-FrosR**

Pea pods cling to stems. Pods. Carl Sandburg. **CP-SandC**

Peace. Ted Berrigan. **SP-BerrT**

Peace. Leonard Cohen. **CP-CoheL**

Peace. Robert Creeley. **CP-CreeR**

Peace. Walter de la Mare. **CP-DeLaW**

Peace. George Herbert. **CP-HerbG**

Peace. Gerard Manley Hopkins. **CP-HopkG**

Peace. David Herbert Lawrence. **CP-LawrD**

Peace. Alun Lewis. **CP-LewiA**

Peace. Adrienne Rich. **CP-RicAE**

Peace. Christopher Smart. *Fr.* Hymns for the Amusement of Children. **SP-SmarC**

Peace. Charles Kenneth Williams. **SP-WillC**

Peace. William Carlos Williams. **CP-WilW1**

Peace. William Butler Yeats. **CP-YeatW**

Peace after a Storm. William Cowper. *Fr.* Olney Hymns. **CP-CowpW**

Peace and Dunkirk. Jonathan Swift. **CP-SwifJ**

Peace and her huge invasion to these shores. To My Father. Robert Louis Stevenson. **CP-StevR**

Peace and War. David Herbert Lawrence. **CP-LawrD**

Peace Autumn, The. John Greenleaf Whittier. **CP-WhitJ**

Peace be to the souls of those. St. Simon and St. Jude. Christopher Smart. *Fr.* Hymns and Spiritual Songs for the Fasts and Festivals of the Church of England. **SP-SmarC**

Peace Between Wars. Carl Sandburg. **CP-SandC**

Peace; come away: the song of woe. Tennyson. **EBVV; EBVVPR; EnVR; FHYEP; IMW** *Fr.* In Memoriam A. H. H. **CP-TennA**

Peace Convention at Brussels, The. John Greenleaf Whittier. **CP-WhitJ**

Peace has unveil'd her smiling face. The Entire Surrender. Jeanne Marie Bouvier de la Motte-Guyon, *tr. fr. French by* William Cowper. **CP-CowpW**

Peace I have from the core of the atom, from the core of space. Wealth. David Herbert Lawrence. **CP-LawrD**

Peace I Leave wth You. Christina Georgina Rossetti. **CP-RosC2**

Peace in Our Time. Howard Nemerov. **CP-NemeH**

Peace in this green field. Kenneth Patchen. **CP-PatcK**

Peace in thy hands / Peace in thine eyes. The Ghost. Walter de la Mare. **CP-DeLaW**

Peace is a fiction of our Faith. Emily Dickinson. **CP-DickE**

Peace is at last confirmed for us. Solomon's Seal. Robert Ranke Graves. **CP-GravR**

Peace is declared, an' I return. The Return. Rudyard Kipling. **CP-KiplR**

Peace is written on the doorstep. Peace. David Herbert Lawrence. **CP-LawrD**

Peace. May he waken. Wendell Berry. *Fr.* Window Poems. **CP-BerrW**

Peace mutt'ring thoughts, and do not grudge to keep. Content. George Herbert. **CP-HerbG**

Peace, Night, Sleep. Carl Sandburg. **CP-SandC**

Peace not Permanent. Robert Herrick. **CP-HerrR**

Peace of Cities, The. Richard Wilbur. **CP-WilbR**

Peace of Dives, The. Rudyard Kipling. **CP-KiplR**

Peace of Europe, The. John Greenleaf Whittier. **CP-WhitJ**

Peace of great doors be for you, The. For You. Carl Sandburg. **CP-SandC**

Peace of green summer lay over this meadow so deeply once, The. Once and Again. Hayden Carruth. **CP-CarHS**

Peace of Mind. Kathleen Jessie Raine. **SP-RainK**

Peace-of-the-Heart, my own for long. Nicholas Vachel Lindsay. *Fr.* The Tale of the Tiger Tree. **CP-LindV**

Peace of Wild Things, The. Wendell Berry. **CP-BerrW**

Peace-Offering, The. Thomas Hardy. **CP-HardT**

Peace on Earth. Edwin Arlington Robinson. **CP-RobiE**

Peace on Earth. William Carlos Williams. **CP-WilW1**

Peace on New England, on the shingled white houses, on golden. Jehu. Louis MacNeice. **CP-MacNL**

Peace Pact. John Hewitt. **CP-HewiJ**

Peace, peace! he is not dead, he doth not sleep. Percy Bysshe Shelley. **FaBoEn; LO; NOBE; OBD; OBNC** *Fr.* Adonais; An Elegy on the Death of John Keats. **CP-ShelP**

   (Elegy on the Death of John Keats, An.) **OBNC**

   (Mourn Not for Adonais.) **NOBE**

Peace, peace, my friend; these subjects fly. George Crabbe. **PoEL-4** *Fr.* Sir Eustace Grey. **SP-CrabG**

Peace, peace, peace, do you say? First News from Villafranca. Elizabeth Barrett Browning. **CP-BroEB**

Peace Peal, The. Thomas Hardy. **CP-HardT**

Peace prat[t]ler, do not lour [*or* lowre]. Conscience. George Herbert. **CP-HerbG**

Peace the great meaning has not been defined. Muriel Rukeyser. **CP-RukeM**

Peace, the Wasp. César Vallejo, *tr. fr. Spanish by* Thomas Merton. **CP-MertT**

Peace, the wild valley streaked with torrents. The Straw. Robert Ranke Graves. **CP-GravR**

Peace to all such! but were there one whose fires. Atticus ("Peace to all such! but were there one whose fires"). Alexander Pope. **AWP; IHNG; InPK; NOBE; SeCePo; TRP; WHA** *Fr.* Epistle to Dr. Arbuthnot. **CP-PopeA**

Peace to Swift's faults! his wit hath made them pass. Byron. **EPCY** *Fr.* Hints from Horace. **CP-Byron**

Peace upon Earth, Goodwill to men. SEPTEMBER (*Shooting*). Rudyard Kipling. *Fr.* Verses on Games. **CP-KiplR**

"Peace upon earth!" was said. We sing it. Christmas: 1924. Thomas Hardy. **CP-HardT**

Peace Walk. William Stafford. **SP-StafW**

Peace, war, religion. This Tokyo. Gary Snyder. **CP-SnydG**

Peace, we have arrived. Meditation in My Favorite Position. Marge Piercy. *Fr.* Walking into Love. **SP-PierM**

Peace which others seek they find, The. The Forsaken. William Wordsworth. **CP-WorW1**

Peaceable Kingdom, The. Daniel Gerard Hoffman. **SP-HoffD**

Peaceable Kingdom, The. Marge Piercy. **SP-PierM**

Peaceful and slow, peaceful and slow. Truck-Garden Market-Day. Edna St. Vincent Millay. **CP-MillE**

Peaceful Kingdom. Charles Simic. **SP-SimiC**

Peaceful Shepherd, The. Robert Frost. **CP-FrosR**

Peaceful Trees. Charles Simic. **SP-SimiC**

Peaceful Western Wind, The. Thomas Campion. **CP-CampT** ("Peacefull westerne winde, The.") **CP-CampT**

Peacefull westerne winde, The. Thomas Campion. *See* The Peaceful Western Wind.

Peacefull westerne winde the wintrye stormes hath calmde, The, *see also* Peaceful Western Wind, The. Thomas Campion. **CP-CampT**

Peach. David Herbert Lawrence. **CP-LawrD**

Peach Blossoms. Carl Sandburg. **CP-SandC**

Peach tree on the southern wall, The. Christina Georgina Rossetti. **CP-RosC2**

Peaches. Siv Cedering Fox. **SP-CedeS**

Peacock. David Herbert Lawrence. **CP-LawrD**

Peacock, The. James Merrill. **SP-MerrJ**

Peacock, The. William Butler Yeats. **CP-YeatW**

Peacock has a score of eyes, The. Christina Georgina Rossetti. **CP-RosC2**

Peacock Room, The. Robert Earl Hayden. **CP-HaydR**

Peacock's Eye, The. Gerard Manley Hopkins. **CP-HopkG**

Peaked in an immortal flame. The World; The Lovers; Falling Stars. Thomas McGrath. **SP-McGrT**

Peaks of pleasure, peaks. Charles Henri Ford. **SP-FordC** *Fr.* Emblems of Arachne.

Peal of Bells, A. Christina Georgina Rossetti. **CP-RosC1**

Peanut-Butter Sandwich. Shel Silverstein. **SP-SilS2**

Peapes he do's strut, and pick his Teeth, as if. Upon Adam Peapes. Robert Herrick. **CP-HerrR**

Pear-Blossom. David Herbert Lawrence. **CP-LawrD**

Pear like a Potato, A. John Updike. **CP-UpdiJ**

Pear Tree. Hilda Doolittle. **CP-DoolH**

Pear Tree, The. Edna St. Vincent Millay. **CP-MillE**

Pear tree that last year, The. Shimmer. James Schuyler. **CP-SchuJ**

Pear tree, why blossom? Query. John Updike. **CP-UpdiJ**

Pearl, The. Robert Ranke Graves. **CP-GravR**

Pearl. Stevie Smith. **CP-SmitS**

Pearl, a Girl, A. Robert Browning. **CP-BroR2**

Pearl Avenue runs past the high-school lot. Ex-Basketball Player. John Updike. **CP-UpdiJ**

Pearl better, The. Without the Season of Structure, Modes Lie Like Gods Thrown Down, Helpless Before the Newness Upsets Genesis When the Young Men Pour In. Charles Olson. **CP-OlsoC**

Pearl Fog. Carl Sandburg. **CP-SandC**

Pearl, great sphere, and hollow. Canto 29. Ezra Pound. *Fr.* Cantos. **CP-PoCan**

Pearl Harbor. Robinson Jeffers. **CP-JefR3**

Pearl Horizons. Carl Sandburg. **CP-SandC**

Pearl. It's baroque. Regular-irregular. A bad dialectic, The. What's Wrong with Pindar. Charles Olson. **CP-OlsoC**

Pearl. Matthew 13:45, The. George Herbert. *See* I know the way[e]s of learning; both the head.

Pearl of Biloxi, The. Nicholas Vachel Lindsay. **CP-LindV**

Pearls. Rita Dove. **SP-DoveR**

Pears hang on the tree by stems. Sunday. James Schuyler. **CP-SchuJ**

Peasant of the Alps, The. Charlotte Smith. **CP-SmitC**

Peasant Song. Alun Lewis. **CP-LewiA**

Peasant to his lord pay'd yearly court, A. John Milton. *See* The Fable of the Peasant and the Overlord.

Peasants, The. Alun Lewis. **CP-LewiA**

Peasant's Confession, The. Thomas Hardy. **CP-HardT**

Pebbles. Herman Melville. **SP-MelvH**

Pebble's Story. Archie Randolph Ammons. **SP-AmmoA**

Pêcheur, pêcheur, avez-vous vu. Frederick Morgan. *Fr.* Poems of the Two Worlds. **SP-MorgF**

Peck of Gold, A. Robert Frost. **CP-FrosR**

Pedagogy Agog. Archie Randolph Ammons. **SP-AmmoA**

Pedantic Literalist. Marianne Craig Moore. **CP-MoorM**

Pedants all / They would be original. Ralph Waldo Emerson. **CP-EmerR**

Pedens, who re-walked the trails, hobbyists, The. Charles Olson. *Fr.* Two Poems. **CP-OlsoC**

Pedestrian. Thomas Hardy. **CP-HardT**

Pedestrian. George Oppen. **CP-OppeG**

Pediatric Reflection. Ogden Nash. **CP-NashO**

Pedicabo et irrumabo. Carmen 16. Catullus. *Fr.* Carmina. **CP-Catul**

Pedigree, The. Robert Creeley. **CP-CreeR**

Pedigree, The. Thomas Hardy. **CP-HardT**

Pedigree of Honey, The, vers. 1. Emily Dickinson. **CP-DickE**

Pedigree of Honey, The, vers. 2. Emily Dickinson. **CP-DickE**

Pediment of Appearance, The. Wallace Stevens. **CP-StevW**

Pedlar I am, that take great care, A. A Pedlar of Small-Wares. Sir John Suckling. **CP-SuckJ**

Pedlar of Small-Wares, A. Sir John Suckling. **CP-SuckJ**

Pedro is the when and the how. Pedro Is When. Pablo Neruda, *tr. fr. Spanish by* Ben Belitt. **SP-NeruP**

Pedro Is When. Pablo Neruda, *tr. fr. Spanish by* Ben Belitt. **SP-NeruP**

Pedro lives out of the Wilshire Hotel. Dirty Blvd. "Lou Reed." **SP-ReedL**

Peekaboo, I Almost See You. Ogden Nash. **CP-NashO**

Peeling Onions. Adrienne Rich. **CP-RicAE; SP-RicA2**

Peepers in Our Meadow, The. Archibald MacLeish. **CP-MacLA**

Peeping Tom. Walter de la Mare. **CP-DeLaW**

Peer re foot own his. Grecian Windflower. Louis Zukofsky. **CP-ZukLS**

Peering into your stout you see a past of lazybeds. The Left-Behind. Louis MacNeice. **FaBCIP** *Fr.* A Hand of Snapshots. **CP-MacNL**

Peeropolis; another Petersburg! Malcolm Lowry. *Fr.* Peter Gaunt and the Canals. **CP-LowrM**

Peg Nicholson was a good bay mare. Elegy on Peg Nicholson. Robert Burns. **CP-BurnR**

Peg said, "This one," and we bought it. Mother's Day. William Stafford. **SP-StafW**

Peggy Day. "Bob Dylan." **CP-DylaB**

Pelayo. William Wordsworth. **CP-WorW1**

Pelican, The. Richard Wilbur. **CP-WilbR**

Pelicans. Robinson Jeffers. **CP-JefR1**

Pelicans in the Wilderness (A Grave near Halfa). Rudyard Kipling. **PeFWW** *Fr.* Epitaphs of the War [1914–1918]. **CP-KiplR**

Pelion and Ossa flourish side by side. William Wordsworth. **CP-WorW1**

Pelion could one time prong its top worthy keel in pines. Catullus. *See* Carmen 64: "In old days / driving through soft waters."

Pellam the King, who held and lost with Lot. Balin and Balan. Tennyson. *Fr.* Idylls of the King. **CP-TennA**

Pelleas and Ettarre. Tennyson. **NAEL-2** *Fr.* Idylls of the King. **CP-TennA**

"Rose, but one, none other rose had I, A." **PoEL-5**

PELLICANUS is the word / For a certain breed of bird. The Pelican. Richard Wilbur. **CP-WilbR**

Pen—to register; a key, A. Memory. William Wordsworth. **CP-WorW2**

Penal Farm, The. Etheridge Knight. *Fr.* Indiana Haiku—2. **SP-KnigE**

Penalty, The. Rudyard Kipling. **CP-KiplR**

Penalty for desertion, The. Love Story. Jim Carroll. **SP-CarrJ**

Penance. Thomas Hardy. **CP-HardT**

Penance. James McAuley. **SP-McAuJ**

Penance, The. Leonard Nathan. **SP-NathL**

Penance. Charles Kenneth Williams. **CP-WillC**

Pencil continues to grieve with long questions in the same lounge full of sea walkers, The. Thomas Merton. *Fr.* Cables to the Ace. **CP-MertT**

Pencil Sketch of Self & Other. Jane Cooper. **SP-CoopJ**

Pencilled Heaven. Jim Morrison. **SP-MorrJ**

Pencils. Carl Sandburg. **CP-SandC**

Pencils / telling where the wind comes from. Pencils. Carl Sandburg. **CP-SandC**

Pendragon. John Hewitt. **CP-HewiJ**

Penelope. Donald Davie. **CP-DavDo**

Penelope, old dear, you write. Washing Socks. Leonard Nathan. **SP-NathL**

Penetration and Trust. George Meredith. **CP-MerG1**

P'eng That Was a K'un, The. Chuang Tzu, *tr. fr. Chinese by* Robert Graves. **CP-GravR**

Penicillin. Patti Smith. **SP-SmitP**

Peninsula, The. Seamus Heaney. **SP-HeanS**

Peninsular arm, Sirmio, insular arm, well. Catullus. *See* Carmen 31: "Apple of islands, Sirmio, & bright peninsulas, set."

Peninsulas are held by an ancient people, The. Land's End. Archibald MacLeish. **CP-MacLA**

Penitence ("Doctors"). Robert Herrick. **CP-HerrR**

Penitence ("Who After"). Robert Herrick. **CP-HerrR**

Penitencie ("Man's Transgression"). Robert Herrick. **CP-HerrR**

Penitent, The. Robert Creeley. **CP-CreeR**

Penitent, The. Edna St. Vincent Millay. **CP-MillE**

Penitent Considers Another Coming of Mary, A. Gwendolyn Brooks. **SP-BrooG**

Penitential Psalms. Sir Thomas Wyatt.
  Prologue: "Love, to give law unto his subject hearts." **CP-WyatT**

Penitential Thought, in the Hour of Remorse—Intended for a Tragedy, A. Robert Burns. **CP-BurnR**

Penmaen Pool. Gerard Manley Hopkins. **CP-HopkG**

Penn Station. Ted Berrigan. **SP-BerrT** *Fr.* The Sonnets.

Pennies of sun's fire jazzing like silver foil. Porec. Donald Davie. **CP-DavDo**

Pennsylvania. Carl Sandburg. **CP-SandC**

Pennsylvania Hall. John Greenleaf Whittier. **CP-WhitJ**

Pennsylvania Pilgrim, The. John Greenleaf Whittier. **CP-WhitJ**

Penny for a poor lass with a child, A. The Gipsy Girl. Wystan Hugh Auden. **CP-AudWJ**

Penny is heavier than the shrew, A. The Masked Shrew. Isabella Gardner. **CP-GardI**

Penny Lane. The Beatles. **CP-Beatl**

Penny, pity, for the runaway ass!, A. John Berryman. *Fr.* Sonnets to Chris. **CP-BerrJ**

Pennycandystore beyond the El, The. Lawrence Ferlinghetti. **SP-FerlL**

Penobscot. George Oppen. **CP-OppeG**

Penobscot. James Schuyler. **CP-SchuJ**

Penological Study: Southern Exposure. Robert Penn Warren. **SP-WarrR**
  Dawn.
  Keep That Morphine Moving, Cap.
  Night is Personal.
  Night: The Motel down the Road from the Pen.
  Tomorrow Morning.
  Wet Hair: If Now His Mother Should Come. **NoAM**
  Where They Come to Wait for the Body: A Ghost Story.

Penshurst Place. Derek Mahon. **SP-MahoD**

Pensive and Faltering. Walt Whitman. **CP-WhitW**

Pensive at eve on the hard world I mus'd [*or* mused]. Samuel Taylor Coleridge. *Fr.* Sonnets Attempted in the Manner of Contemporary Writers. **CP-ColeS**

Pensive gnu, the staid aardvark, The. For an Amorous Lady. Theodore Roethke. **CP-RoetT**

Pensive here I sat. John Milton. **OBD** *Fr.* Book II. **FHYEP; NAEL-1; OxAEP-1** *Fr.* Paradise Lost. **CP-MiltJ**

Pensive on Her Dead Gazing, Pensive on Her Dead Gazing [I Heard the Mother of All]. Walt Whitman. **CP-WhitW**

Pensive Sceptic of the lonely vale, The. The Parsonage. William Wordsworth. *Fr.* The Excursion. **CP-WorW2**

Pensive They Sit, and Roll Their Languid Eyes. John Keats. **CP-KeatJ**

Pensive we sat the silent hours. Bible, *O.T. See* Psalm 137: "By the rivers of Babylon. . . ."

Pentagon Exorcism. Allen Ginsberg. **CP-GinsA**

Pentagram. Gilbert Sorrentino. **SP-SorrG**

Pente cōst under the body of the gull flying directly over. Charles Olson. **CP-OlsoC**

Pentecost. Donald Davie. **CP-DavDo**

Pentecost Castle, The. Geoffrey Hill. **CP-HillG**
  "And you my spent heart's treasure." **HAP**
  "As he is wounded."
  "At dawn the Mass."
  "Down in the orchard." **HAP**
  "Goldfinch and hawk."
  "I shall go down." **HAP**
  "I went out early."
  "If the night is dark."
  "Married and not for love."
  "Slowly my heron flies."
  "Splendidly-shining darkness." **HAP**
  "St James and St John."
  "They slew by night." **HAP**
  "This love will see me dead."
  "You watchers on the wall."

Penthesileia. Robert Ranke Graves. **CP-GravR**

Pentucket. John Greenleaf Whittier. **CP-WhitJ**

Penumbrae. John Updike. **CP-UpdiJ**

Peograms. Charles Olson. **CP-OlsoC**

Peonies. Mary Oliver. **SP-OlivM**

Peony Stalks. Mona Van Duyn. **SP-VanDM**

People, The. Robert Creeley. **CP-CreeR**

People. Robert Creeley. **CP-CreeR**

People, The. David Herbert Lawrence. **CP-LawrD**

People. David Herbert Lawrence. **CP-LawrD**

People. David Herbert Lawrence. **CP-LawrD**

People. Ogden Nash. **CP-NashO**

People. Miller Williams. **SP-WillM**

People, The. William Butler Yeats. **CP-YeatW**

People along the sand, The. Neither Out Far nor In Deep. Robert Frost. **CP-FrosR**

People always make war when they say they love peace. Peace and War. David Herbert Lawrence. **CP-LawrD**

People and a Heron. Robinson Jeffers. **CP-JefR1**

People are chewing on wood. Wanting to Be Heavier. Stephen Berg. **SP-BergS**

People are like leaves, fluttering and gay on the bush of the globe. The Difference. David Herbert Lawrence. **CP-LawrD**

People are putting up storm windows now. Storm Windows. Howard Nemerov. **CP-NemeH**

People Are So Busy: Or: That's Life! Thomas McGrath. **SP-McGrT**

People are too noisy, too loud. The Listener. John Hewitt. **CP-HewiJ**

People are wading up the stream all day. The Cool Stream. Thom Gunn. *Fr.* The Geysers. **CP-GunnT**

People ask questions. Marge Piercy. *Fr.* Living in the Open. **SP-PierM**

People Asleep. Dabney Stuart. **SP-StuaD**

People burned, came apart, suffocated, melted. Hayden Carruth. *Fr.* The Sleeping Beauty. **CP-CarHL**

People buying and selling, consuming pleasures, talking in the archways, The. Reference to a Passage in Plutarch's Life of Sulla. Robinson Jeffers. **CrMA** *Fr.* The Broken Balance. **CP-JefR1**

People come from all over to consult me, bringing their limbs. Margaret Atwood. **NALW** *Fr.* Circe / Mud Poems. **SP-AtwM1**

People don't act / like they act. The Changes. Robert Creeley. **CP-CreeR**

People down / The hallway who, The. Poem. Jim Carroll. **SP-CarrJ**

People dressed in the styles. Frederick Morgan. *Fr.* Meditations for Autumn. **SP-MorgF**

People expect old men to die. Old Men. Ogden Nash. **CP-NashO**

People fell back, a field of wheat, The. John Haines. *Fr.* The Dream of the Police. **SP-HainJ**

People filling the street, The. In a Gradually Moving Car Somewhere in Calcutta. Miller Williams. **SP-WillM**

People Getting Divorced. Lawrence Ferlinghetti. **SP-FerlL**

People go on singing when they have no song in them. Keep It Up. David Herbert Lawrence. **CP-LawrD**

People have eaten fried fish. In Answer to Your Silly Question. Alice Walker. **CP-WalkA**

People here are not here, The. From the Day Room. Phoebe Hesketh. **SP-HeskP**

People I live among, unforgivingly, The. First Neighbours. Margaret Atwood. **SP-AtwM1**

People I love the best, The. To Be of Use. Marge Piercy. **SP-PierM**

People in Hell are clothed. Gilbert Sorrentino. **SP-SorrG**

People in My Family. Grace Paley. **CP-PaleG**

People in the elevator all, The. Fiction. Howard Nemerov. **CP-NemeH**

People in the houses behind Searsport are dancing, The. Dancing in Vacationland. Stephen Dobyns. **SP-DobyS**

People in the village. Macarius and the Pony. Thomas Merton. **CP-MertT**

People is a lighted believer and, The. Carl Sandburg. *Fr.* The People, Yes. **CP-SandC**

People is a myth, an abstraction, The. Carl Sandburg. *Fr.* The People, Yes. **CP-SandC**

People is Everyman, everybody, The. Carl Sandburg. *Fr.* The People, Yes. **CP-SandC**

People know what the land knows, The. Carl Sandburg. *Fr.* The People, Yes. **CP-SandC**

People learn, unlearn, learn, The. Carl Sandburg. *Fr.* The People, Yes. **CP-SandC**

People live forever in Jacksonville and St. Petersburg and Tampa. Come On In, the Senility Is Fine. Ogden Nash. **CP-NashO**

People made a ring, The. The Hemorrhage. Stanley Jasspon Kunitz. **CP-KuniS**

People meeting at parties. Naked Ostrich. Phoebe Hesketh. **SP-HeskP**

People moves as one spirit unfettered, The. De Jure Belli ac Pacis. Geoffrey Hill. **CP-HillG**

People of England, ye who toil and groan. Fragment: To the People of England. Percy Bysshe Shelley. **CP-ShelP**

People of Letters. Al Young. **CP-YounA**

People of the Eastern Ice, they are melting like the snow, The. Rudyard Kipling. **CP-KiplR** *Fr.* Quiquern. *Fr.* The Second Jungle Book.

People of the Eaves, I Wish You Good Morning. Carl Sandburg. **CP-SandC**

People of the South Wind. William Stafford. **SP-StafW**

People on the avenue at noon, The. Near the Old People's Home. Howard Nemerov. **CP-NemeH**

People on wheels hate people on feet. Hi-Ho the Ambulance-O. Ogden Nash. **CP-NashO**

People on whom I do not bother to dote. Election Day Is a Holiday. Ogden Nash. **CP-NashO**

People—people of my kind, my own, The. To the Lacedemonians. Allen Tate. **CP-TateA**

People protest in sprawling lightless ways. Gwendolyn Brooks. **SP-BrooG** *Fr.* The Womanhood.

People Rest after Conquests, The. Frank Templeton Prince. *Fr.* Chaka. **CP-PrinF**

People say his painting caught so much. A District in the City. Richard Hugo. **CP-HugoR**

People say that spiritism is a joke and a swizz, The. From the County Lunatic Asylum. Stevie Smith. **CP-SmitS**

People that build their houses inland. Inland. Edna St. Vincent Millay. **CP-MillE**

People, the People, The. George Oppen. **CP-OppeG**

People Trying to Love. Stephen Berg. **SP-BergS**

People upstairs, The. Ogden Nash. **CP-NashO**

People upstairs are cold, The. One Flight Up. Jim Carroll. **SP-CarrJ**

People were bathing and posturing themselves on the beach. The Gods! The Gods! David Herbert Lawrence. **CP-LawrD**

People who, The. Edward Estlin Cummings. **CP-CummE**

People who are always praising the past. The Past. Stevie Smith. **CP-SmitS**

People Who Care. David Herbert Lawrence. **CP-LawrD**

People who complain of loneliness must have lost something. The Uprooted. David Herbert Lawrence. **CP-LawrD**

People Who Died. Ted Berrigan. **SP-BerrT**

People who have no children can be hard. Gwendolyn Brooks. **SP-BrooG** *Fr.* The Children of the Poor. **SP-BrooG,** *sect.* I, *pt.* 1-5; *Fr.* The Womanhood.

People who have no children can be hard. The Children of the Poor. Gwendolyn Brooks. **SP-BrooG,** *sect.* I, *pt.* 1-5; *Fr.* The Womanhood.

People who have what they want are very fond of telling people. The Terrible People. Ogden Nash. **CP-NashO**

People Who Live. Erica Jong. **SP-JongE**

People Who Must. Carl Sandburg. **CP-SandC**

People Who See Bubbles Rise. James Schuyler. **CP-SchuJ**

People will live on, The. Carl Sandburg. **MoAB; MoAmPo; MoPo; NOBA; NePA; NoAM; OxBA; TrGrPo** *Fr.* The People, Yes. **CP-SandC**

People with Proud Chins. Carl Sandburg. **CP-SandC**

People without their own scene. Robert Creeley. **CP-CreeR**

People, Yes, The. Carl Sandburg. **CP-SandC**

People, yes, The / Born with bones. . . . Carl Sandburg. *Fr.* The People, Yes. **CP-SandC**

People, yes, The / Out of what. . . . Carl Sandburg. *Fr.* The People, Yes. **CP-SandC**

"Accordingly, they commenced by an insidious."

"Always the storm of propaganda blows."

"And you take hold of a handle."

"Aster, a farewell-summer flower, stays long in the last fall weeks, An."

"Australian mounted infantryman now teaches, The."

"Big fish eat the little fish, The."

"Big oil tanks squat next the railroad."

"Blood of all men of all nations being red, The."

"Bottom of the sea accomodates mountain ranges, The."

"Breathing of the earth, The."

"Chicago seems all fox and swine."

"Come on, superstition, and get my goat."

"Deep in the dusty chattels of the tombs."

" 'Drama of politics doesn't interest me,' said a news rewrite man, The."

"Englishman in the old days, An." **FYAP**

"Father sees a son nearing manhood, A."

"For sixty years the pine lumber barn."

"From Illinois and Indiana came a later myth."

"From the four corners of the earth." **CMoP**

"From the people the countries get their names?"

"From what graveyards and sepulchers have they come."

"Gang in its working clothes, The."

"Grass lives, goes to sleep, lives again, The."

"Great Sphinx and the Pyramids say, The."

"Have you seen men handed refusals."

"He was a king or a shah, an ahkoond or rajah."

"Hold down the skylines now with your themes."

"Hope is a tattered flag and a dream out of time."

"Hunger and only hunger changes worlds?"

"I am zero, naught, one ciper."

"I pledge my allegiance."

"If you can imagine love letters written back and forth between Mary."

"In a winter sunset near Springfield, Illinois."

"In paper sacks the customers carry away millions of tons of goods daily."

"In the chain store or the independent it is the people meeting the people."

"In the days of the cockade and the brass pistol."

"In the folded and quiet yesterdays."

"In the light of the cold glimmer of what everybody knows, why should the."

"In the long flat panhandle of Texas."

"Kindest and gentlest here are the, The."

" 'Lawyer,' hiccuped a disbarred member of the bar, "is a man who", A."

"Let the nickels and dimes explain."

"LINCOLN? / He was a mystery in smoke and flags."

"Man in the street is fed, The."

"Marshall Field the First was spick and span while alive."

"Mazuma, the jack, the shekels, the kale, The."

"Mildred Klinghofer whirled through youth in bloom."

"Neither wife nor child had Mr. Eastman and the manner of his death."

"Nickels click off fares in the slot machines of the subway, the elevated, The."

"No matter how thick or how thin you slice it it's still baloney."

"On Lang Syne Plantation they had a prayer."

"One memorial stone reads."

"One of the Cherokees on Oklahoma, having a million or so from oil."

"Outstraw green turns gold turns ashen and, The."

"People is a lighted believer and, The."

"People is a myth, an abstraction, The."

"People is Everyman, everybody, The."

"People know what the land knows, The."

"People learn, unlearn, learn, The."

"People will live on, The." **MoAB; MoAmPo; MoPo; NOBA; NePA; NoAM; OxBA; TrGrPo**

"People, yes, The."

"People, yes, The."

"People, yes, the people, The."

"People, yes, the people, The."

"Poobahs rise and hold their poobah sway, The."

"Record is a scroll of many indecipherable scrawls, The."

"Remembere the chameleon. He was a well-behaved chameleon."

"Response of wild birds, The."

"Sacred legion of the justborn, The."

"Sayings, sentences, what of them?"

"Scaffolding holds the arch in place, The."

"Sea moves always, the wind moves always, The."

"Sea only knows the bottom of the ship, The."

"Sleep is a suspension midway."

"So you want to divide all the money there is."

"Somebody has to make the tubs and pails."

"There have been thousands of Andy Adams."

"They have yarns / Of a skyscraper so tall they had to put hinges."
AmFN; LiTA; MoAmPo

"Transient tar-paper shack, The."

"Tumblers of the rapids go white, go green, The."

"Tylor believed it important; he put it down; he asks us to read it, to look."

"Unemployed / Without a stake in the country, The."

"Was he preaching or writing poetry or talking through his hat? He was."

"We live only once."

"We'll see what we'll see."

"What did Hiamovi, the red man, Chief of."

"What is a judge? A judge is a seated torso and head sworn before God."

"What other oaths are wanted now?"

"What the people learn out of lifting and hauling and waiting and losing."
OBAL

"When was it long ago the murmurings began."

"When we say fresh eggs we mean fresh."

"Who can make a poem of the depths of weariness."

"Who knows the people, the migratory harvest hands and berry pickers."

"Who made Paul Bunyan, who gave him birth as a myth, who joked him."

"Who shall speak for the people?"

"Who shall speak for the people?" **OxBA**

"Who was that antique Chinese crook who put over his revolution and."

"Who was that early sodbuster in Kansas? He leaned at the gatepost and."

"Who were those editors picking the most."

"Why did the children." **OBAL; PBMP**

"Why repeat? I heard you the first time." **OBAL**

"Why should any man try to find the distance to the moon by guessing."

"Wind in the corn leaves among the naked stalks, The."

"Without the daily chores of the people."

"You can drum on immense drums."

"You do what you must—this world and then the mext—one world at a."

"Your low birth puts you beneath me."

People, yes, the people, The / Everyone who got. . . . Carl Sandburg. *Fr.* The People, Yes. **CP-SandC**

People, yes, the people, The / Until the people. . . . Carl Sandburg. *Fr.* The People, Yes. **CP-SandC**

People! your chains are severing link by link. Composed after Reading a Newspaper of the Day. William Wordsworth. **CP-WorW2**

People's Cry, The. Kay Boyle. **CP-BoylK**

People's Surroundings. Marianne Craig Moore. **CP-MoorM**

Peopleshaped toomany-ness far too, A. Edward Estlin Cummings. **CP-CummE**

Per Preferenza. Christina Georgina Rossetti. *Fr.* Il Rosseggiar Dell'Oriente Canzoniere. **CP-RosC3**

Perceive. Gilbert Sorrentino. **SP-SorrG**

Perceiving that in the masked ball. Nothing Will Cure the Sick Lion But To Eat an Ape. Marianne Craig Moore. **CP-MoorM**

Perception as a Guided Missile. Richard Eberhart. **CP-EberR**

Perception of an object costs. Emily Dickinson. **CP-DickE**

Perch, The. Peter Meinke. **SP-MeinP**

Perch Less. Louis Zukofsky. **CP-ZukLS**

Perch less, bird. Perch Less. Louis Zukofsky. **CP-ZukLS**

Perchance she died in age--surviving all. Rome by Metella's Tomb. Byron. **FaBoPP** *Fr.* Childe Harold's Pilgrimage. **CP-Byron**

Perched at the railing of a Portuguese. Saudades: The Portuguese Blues. Al Young. **CP-YounA**

Perched on a nettled stump he stands. Early Morning. Wystan Hugh Auden. **CP-AudWJ**

Percivale's Quest. Tennyson. **OAEL-2** *Fr.* The Holy Grail. *Fr.* Idylls of the King. **CP-TennA**

Percussion. Dabney Stuart. **SP-StuaD**

Percy's Song. "Bob Dylan." **CP-DylaB**

Perdita. Louis MacNeice. **CP-MacNL**

Perdona al primo eccesso. Lisetta all' Amante. Christina Georgina Rossetti. **CP-RosC3**

Perdy [or Perdie or Perdye], I said[e] it [or yt] not. Sir Thomas Wyatt. **CP-WyatT**

Peregrine Falcon. Siv Cedering Fox. **SP-CedeS**

Perennial Answer, The. Adrienne Rich. **CP-RicAE; SP-RicA2**

Perfect. "Hugh MacDiarmid." **SP-MacDH**

Perfect act is empty. Who can see it?, The. Thomas Merton. *Fr.* Cables to the Ace. **CP-MertT**

Perfect beneath an eight-rayed sun you lie. La Mejicana. Robert Ranke Graves. **CP-GravR**

Perfect Husband, The. Ogden Nash. **CP-NashO**

Perfect is the word I can never hear. Rhymes. Charles Tomlinson. **CP-TomlC**

Perfect Joy. Chuang Tzu, *tr. fr. Chinese by* Thomas Merton. **CP-MertT**

Perfect Love Casteth Out Everything. Randall Jarrell. **CP-JarrR**

Perfect Love Casteth Out Fear. Christina Georgina Rossetti. **CP-RosC2**

Perfect Marriage, The. Nicholas Vachel Lindsay. **CP-LindV**

Perfect moon / I am calling. December. Patti Smith. **SP-SmitP**

Perfect oval. Sam Spade Haiku. John Yau. **SP-YauJo**

Perfect Poet, The. Erica Jong. **SP-JongE**

Perfect Point. Alice Notley. **SP-NotlA**

Perfect rainbow! a wide, A. The Storm. William Carlos Williams. **CP-WilW2**

Perfect reliance on the impossible. To Put It Simply. Robert Ranke Graves. **CP-GravR**

Perfect Sacrifice, The. Jeanne Marie Bouvier de la Motte-Guyon, *tr. fr. French by* William Cowper. **CP-CowpW**

Perfect swan upon the perfect lake, The. Proverbs of the Middle World. Thomas McGrath. **SP-McGrT**

Perfection, The. Charles Tomlinson. **CP-TomlC**

Perfection. Alice Walker. **CP-WalkA**

Perfection. William Carlos Williams. **CP-WilW2**

Perfection is terrible, it cannot have children. The Munich Mannequins. Sylvia Plath. **CP-PlatS**

Perfection now is tended and observed. At Hertford House. Adrienne Rich. **CP-RicAE**

Perfection, of a kind, was what he was after. Epitaph on a Tyrant. Wystan Hugh Auden. **CP-AudeW**

Perfection Wasted. John Updike. **CP-UpdiJ**

Perfectionists. Robert Ranke Graves. **CP-GravR**

Perfections. Walt Whitman. **CP-WhitW**

Perfectly a year,we watched Together les enfants jumping and. Edward Estlin Cummings. **CP-CummE**

Perfectly clear liquid like water, A. Triolet. Anne Waldman. **SP-WaldA**

Perfectly Free Association, A. Randall Jarrell. **CP-JarrR**

Performance, The. James Dickey. **CP-DickJ**

Performances. William Dickey. **SP-DickW**

Performances, assortments, résumés. The Tunnel. Hart Crane. **CMoP; HoFi; MAT; MoAB; MoAmPo; OxBA** *Fr.* The Bridge. **CP-CranH**

Performers, The. Robert Earl Hayden. **CP-HaydR**

Perfume, The. John Donne. **AnAnS-1; ESCV; NoSic; SeCP** *Fr.* Elegies. **CP-DonnJ**

Perfume, The. Robert Herrick. **CP-HerrR**

Perfume / of flowers! A haw, The. Charles Olson. **CP-OlsoC**

Perfume / of Flowers! A quinee, The. Charles Olson. **CP-OlsoC**

Perfume!, The. Charles Olson. **CP-OlsoC**

Perfume of the iris, sweet citron, The. The Words, the Words, the Words. William Carlos Williams. **CP-WilW2**

Perfumed soap / and a little Kabir. On Seeing Kabir's Poems on Her Dressing Table. Leonard Cohen. **CP-CoheL**

Perhaps. James Schuyler. **CP-SchuJ**

Perhaps. Stephen Spender. **CP-SpenS**

Perhaps / You will remember / John Brown. October 16[: The Raid]. Langston Hughes. **SP-HughL**

Perhaps for Eridanus. Malcolm Lowry. *Fr.* The Lighthouse Invites the Storm. **CP-LowrM**

Perhaps I always knew what they were saying. The Prophets. Wystan Hugh Auden. **CP-AudeW**

Perhaps I asked too large. Emily Dickinson. **CP-DickE**

Perhaps I may allow, the Dean. Jonathan Swift. **EPCY; FaBoEn; NOBE; PeLV** *Fr.* Verses on the Death of Dr. Swift, D.S.P.D. **CP-SwifJ**

Perhaps I was born kneeling. Cigarettes and Whiskey and Wild, Wild Women. Anne Sexton. **CP-SextA**

Perhaps I'll get good at forgetting what. Forgetting to Forget. Robert Pack. **SP-PackR**

Perhaps it is to avoid some great sadness. Sleeping on the Wing. Frank O'Hara. **SP-OharF**

Perhaps it is to feel strike. Edward Estlin Cummings. **CP-CummE**

Perhaps it isn't as we like to think, the last resort, the end of something, thwarted choice or attempt. Suicide: Anne. Charles Kenneth Williams. **SP-WillC**

Perhaps it was Myself sits down in this chair. There were two chairs,in fact. Edward Estlin Cummings. **CP-CummE**

Perhaps it's a question of what. Black Poppy (At the Temple). David St. John. **SP-StJoD**

Perhaps it's the color of the sun cut flat. Mama, You Been on My Mind. "Bob Dylan." **CP-DylaB**

Perhaps, long hence, when I have passed away. Thomas Hardy. *Fr.* She, to Him. **CP-HardT**

Perhaps Macabre. Marsden Hartley. **CP-HartM**

Perhaps Mr. Bessemer is not a pessimist but, last and first. No Woe Is Gossamer to Mr. Bessemer. Ogden Nash. **CP-NashO**

Perhaps six lines, to keep one's other lines alive. A.D. 2029. David Markson. **CP-MarkD**

Perhaps some needful service of the State. Gabriello Chiabrera, *tr. fr. Italian by* William Wordsworth. **CP-WorW1**

Perhaps the dear, grieved Heart. Emily Dickinson. **SP-DickE**

Perhaps the earth is floating. The Poet of Ignorance. Anne Sexton. **CP-SextA**

Perhaps there's time to write a poem. Perhaps. James Schuyler. **CP-SchuJ**

Perhaps they do not go so far. Emily Dickinson. **SP-DickE**

Perhaps thy lot in life is higher. Ralph Waldo Emerson. **CP-EmerR**

Perhaps we desire death: or why is poison so sweet? The Sirens. Robinson Jeffers. **CP-JefR3**

Perhaps we ought to feel with more imagination. The Recent Past. John Ashbery. **SP-AshbJ**

Perhaps what's wrong is simply lack of vitality. What's Wrong. David Herbert Lawrence. **CP-LawrD**

Perhaps you smile at me. Emily Dickinson. **SP-DickE**

Perhaps you think me stooping. Emily Dickinson. **CP-DickE**

Perhaps you'd like a marching song for the embattled prolet-. Ars Poetica: Or: Who Lives in the Ivory Tower? Thomas McGrath. **SP-McGrT**

Perhaps you'd like to buy a flower. Emily Dickinson. **CP-DickE**

Peri Poietikes. Louis Zukofsky. **CP-ZukLS**

Peri Tou Autou. John Harmarus. *Fr.* Commendatory Poems. **CP-LoveR**

Periander. George Meredith. **CP-MerG1**

Pericles. Ralph Waldo Emerson. *Fr.* Quatrains. **CP-EmerR**

Peril, The. Thomas Merton. **CP-MertT; SP-MertT**

Peril as a Possession. Emily Dickinson. **CP-DickE**

Peril of Hope. Robert Frost. **CP-FrosR**

Peril upon the paths of this desire. Edna St. Vincent Millay. **CP-MillE**

Perimeters. Allen Tate. **CP-TateA**

Period I. Ogden Nash. *Fr.* Period Period. **CP-NashO**

Period Period. Ogden Nash. **CP-NashO**

  Period I.

  Period II.

Period Piece: 1834. William Carlos Williams. **CP-WilW2**

Period II. Ogden Nash. *Fr.* Period Period. **CP-NashO**

Periodicity. John Hewitt. **CP-HewiJ**

Periodicity: the crack. Roy Fisher. **SP-FishR** *Fr.* Diversions.

Perirrhanterium. George Herbert. **CP-HerbG**

Perish their names, however great or brave. Robert Burns. *Fr.* Annotations in Verse. **CP-BurnR**

Perishable Women. Erica Jong. **SP-JongE**

Perished have safe small. Edward Estlin Cummings. **CP-CummE**

Perjury Excused. Sir John Suckling. **CP-SuckJ**

Permanence. Archie Randolph Ammons. **SP-AmmoA**

Permanent Migrations, The. Kenneth Patchen. **CP-PatcK**

Permanent Way, A. Wystan Hugh Auden. **CP-AudeW**

Permanently. Kenneth Koch. **SP-KochK**

Permeo terras, ubi nuda rupes. Ode, De Skia Insula. Samuel Johnson. **CP-JohnS**

Permit me, Julia, now to goe away. To Julia. Robert Herrick. **CP-HerrR**

Permit me refuge in a region of your brain. Bon Voyage. Edwin Rolfe. **CP-RolfE**

Permit mine eyes to see. On Heaven. Robert Herrick. **CP-HerrR**

Permitted to assist you, let me see. Marianne Craig Moore. **CP-MoorM** (Saint Valentine.) **CP-MoorM**

Perp. Revival i' the North. Sir John Betjeman. **CP-BetjJ**

Perpetual Migration, The. Marge Piercy. **SP-PierM**

Perpetual Motion. Thomas McGrath. **SP-McGrT**

Perpetuum mobile of my, The. Sleepwalker's Way. Tom Clark. **SP-ClarT**

Perpetuum Mobile: The City. William Carlos Williams. **CP-WilW1**

Perplex'd and troubl'd at his bad success. Book IV. John Milton. *Fr.* Paradise Regained [*or* Regain'd]. **CP-MiltJ**

Perplexed Music. Elizabeth Barrett Browning. **CP-BroEB**

Persecution. William Wordsworth. *Fr.* Ecclesiastical Sonnets. **CP-WorW2**

Persecution of the Scottish Covenanters. William Wordsworth. *Fr.* Ecclesiastical Sonnets. **CP-WorW2**

Persecutions Profitable. Robert Herrick. **CP-HerrR**

Persecutions Purifie. Robert Herrick. **CP-HerrR**

Persecutor was redeem'd, The. King Charles the Martyr. Christopher Smart. *Fr.* Hymns and Spiritual Songs for the Fasts and Festivals of the Church of England. **SP-SmarC**

Persephone. Stevie Smith. **CP-SmitS**

Persephone and Dis, Dis, have mercy upon her. Ezra Pound. **MeMAP** *Fr.* Homage to Sextus Propertius. **SP-PounE**

Persephone Returns. Jenny Joseph. **SP-JoseJ**

Perseus. Robert Earl Hayden. **CP-HaydR**

Perseus. Louis MacNeice. **CP-MacNL**

Perseus. Sylvia Plath. **CP-PlatS**

Perseverance. George Herbert. **CP-HerbG**

Perseverance. Robert Herrick. **CP-HerrR**

Pershore Station, or a Liverish Journey First Class. Sir John Betjeman. **CP-BetjJ**

Persian, The. Stevie Smith. **CP-SmitS**

Persian Lesson, A. Walt Whitman. **CP-WhitW**

Persian pomps, boy, ever I renounce them. Horace. *See* 1.38: Simplicity.

Persian Version, The. Robert Ranke Graves. **CP-GravR**

Persian's flowery gifts, the shrine, The. For an Autumn Festival. John Greenleaf Whittier. **CP-WhitJ**

Persimmon wind, lost names raining. Thwart. Hayden Carruth. *Fr.* The Asylum. **CP-CarHL**

Persimmons, The. Gary Snyder. **CP-SnydG**

Persistence of 1937. Donald Hall. **CP-HallD**

Persistent Explorer. John Crowe Ransom. **SP-RansJ**

Persistent is the thought for me of that. Sonnet. Hayden Carruth. **CP-CarHS** *Fr.* Sonnets.

Persistent through the brazen chorus round. George Meredith. *Fr.* Napoléon. **CP-MerG1**

Person. Robert Creeley. **CP-CreeR**

Person as Dreamer: We Talk about the Future, The. Michael Hartnett. **PBCIP** *Fr.* Notes on My Contemporaries. **SP-HarMi**

Person crowns the Place; your lot doth fall, The. To His Sister in Law, M. Susanna Herrick. Robert Herrick. **CP-HerrR**

Person speaking now isn't, The. Feeding the Ducks. Leonard Nathan. **SP-NathL**

Person Who Eats Meat, A. Leonard Cohen. **CP-CoheL**

Personable shadow, you follow me into this. Corona. Tess Gallagher. **SP-GallT**

Personae seek provisional assent. Mamertinus on Rhetoric, A.D. 291. Donald Davie. **CP-DavDo**

Personage is seen, A. Landscape. Thomas Merton. **CP-MertT; SP-MertT**

Personal. Langston Hughes. **SP-HughL**

Personal. Malcolm Lowry. **CP-LowrM**

Personal Angel Glimpsed. Tom Clark. **SP-ClarT**

Personal Helicon. Seamus Heaney. **SP-HeanS**

Personal idiom of a corn shock staisfies me, The. Personalia. Carl Sandburg. **CP-SandC**

Personal Odyssey. James Liddy. **CP-LiddJ**

Personal Packaging, Inc. Robert Ranke Graves. **CP-GravR**

Personal Poem. Frank O'Hara. **SP-OharF**

Personal Poem #9, *sl. diff.* Ted Berrigan. *See* It's 8:54 a.m. in Brooklyn it's the 28th [*or* 26th] of July [and].

Personal Talk. William Wordsworth. **CP-WorW1**

Personalia. Carl Sandburg. **CP-SandC**

Personality. Carl Sandburg. **CP-SandC**

Personality and dourness of winter, The. Charles Olson. **CP-OlsoC**

Personally I don't care whether a detective-story writer was. Don't Guess, Let Me Tell You. Ogden Nash. **CP-NashO**

Personas propriis recte virtutibus ornas. *accompanied by Eng. translation.* Thomas Campion. **CP-CampT**

Persons. Robert Creeley. **CP-CreeR**

Persons wane and fade, they fade out of meaning. Personal greatness, The. Teheran. Robinson Jeffers. **CP-JefR3**

Persons who have something to say like to talk about the arts and politics and economics. Never Mind the Overcoat, Button Up That Lip. Ogden Nash. **CP-NashO**

Perspective betrays with its dichotomy. Love Is a Parallax. Sylvia Plath. **CP-PlatS**

Perspective never withers from their eyes. Quaker Hill. Hart Crane. **LiTM** *Fr.* The Bridge. **CP-CranH**

Perspectives. Denise Levertov. **CP-LeveD**

Perspectives. Louis MacNeice. **CP-MacNL**

Perspiration: A Travelling Eclogue. Samuel Taylor Coleridge. **CP-ColeS**

Persuaded you walk alone, alone walk naked, what veins of Ireland. Angels for Djuna Barnes. Kay Boyle. **CP-BoylK**

Persuasion, A. Hart Crane. **CP-CranH**

Persuasion. William Wordsworth. *Fr.* Ecclesiastical Sonnets. **CP-WorW2**

Persuasions to Enjoy. Thomas Carew. **CP-CareT**

Pertinax. Robert Frost. *Fr.* Ten Mills. **CP-FrosR**

Pertussin. Allen Ginsberg. **CP-GinsA**

Peruse my leaves through every part. Verses Wrote in a Lady's Ivory Table-Book. Jonathan Swift. **CP-SwifJ**

Perusing Mallarmé in Maine. Marsden Hartley. **CP-HartM**

Perverse habit of cat-goddesses—, A. Cat-Goddesses. Robert Ranke Graves. **CP-GravR**

Pervigilium Veneris. *Unknown. See* The Vigil of Venus.

Pesano rena e pena. Christina Georgina Rossetti. **CP-RosC3**

Peschiera. Arthur Hugh Clough. **SP-ClouA**

Pet Lamb, The; A Pastoral. William Wordsworth. **CP-WorW1**

Pet-Name, The. Elizabeth Barrett Browning. **CP-BroEB**

Pet-name, a common name. Best-selling brand, curt, A. Geoffrey Hill. **NoAM** *Fr.* Mercian Hymns. **CP-HillG**

Pet Shop, The. John Hewitt. **CP-HewiJ**

Pet Shop. Louis MacNeice. **CP-MacNL**

Pet shops were advertising non-rabid bats, The. The Week That Was. John Ciardi. **SP-CiarJ**

Pet was never mourned as you. Last Words to a Dumb Friend. Thomas Hardy. **CP-HardT**

Petal, colorless and without form, A. The Flower. William Carlos Williams. **CP-WilW1**

Petal of white rose. Kathleen Jessie Raine. **SP-RainK**

Petals of a soft yellow rose, The. In the Deep Green Vase. Jim Carroll. **SP-CarrJ**

Pete Brown's Old Eggs Still Hatch. Roy Fisher. **SP-FishR**

Peter. James Merrill. **SP-MerrJ**

Peter. Marianne Craig Moore. **CP-MoorM**

Peter. Richard Wilbur. **CP-WilbR**

Peter and Paul. "Lewis Carroll." **CP-CarrL** *Fr.* Sylvie and Bruno.

Peter Bell; a Tale. William Wordsworth. **CP-WorW1**

Peter Bell the Third. Percy Bysshe Shelley. **CP-ShelP**
  "All things that Peter saw and felt." **EPCY**
  "Among the guests who often stayed." **ChER**
  "Devil now knew his proper cue, The." **OBSV**
  "He was a might poet—and." **EPCY**
  "Hell is a city much like London." **OBD; OBSV**

Peter Bells, one, two and three. Peter Bell the Third. Percy Bysshe Shelley. **CP-ShelP**

Peter complains, that God has given. Epigram. Alexander Pope. **CP-PopeA**

Peter Gaunt and the Canals. Malcolm Lowry. **CP-LowrM**
  "After all, the vision was like but subtly sea-changed."
  "And lights a cigarette, noting, far off."
  "De Lesseps, he said, was not the only one."
  "Extravagance of nature took his mind, The."
  "Jig, like Noah's donkey in the Ark, The."
  "Lake, a sea itself, whose gentle crash, A."
  "Let us give him the benefit of some doubts."
  "Liverpool to Manchester via Runcorn."
  "Peeropolis; another Petersburg!"
  "Peter Gaunt, as Gynt then, climbs a dune."
  "Sees he the new city, the really better land."
  "So when flesh feels slighted by the present."
  "What was that story of an older dream."

Peter Gaunt, as Gynt then, climbs a dune. Malcolm Lowry. *Fr.* Peter Gaunt and the Canals. **CP-LowrM**

Peter Grump. Christina Georgina Rossetti. **CP-RosC3**

"Peter is poor," said noble Paul. Peter and Paul. "Lewis Carroll." **CP-CarrL** *Fr.* Sylvie and Bruno.

Peter Jackson was a-preaching. When Peter Jackson Preached in the Old Church. Nicholas Vachel Lindsay. **CP-LindV**

Peter-penny, The. Robert Herrick. **CP-HerrR**

Peter Peri (1899-1967). John Hewitt. **CP-HewiJ**

Peter Quince at the Clavier. Wallace Stevens. **CP-StevW**

Peterborough. Marilyn Hacker. **SP-HackM**

Peter's Diary in Goodentown. Kenneth Patchen. **CP-PatcK**

Pethox the Great. Jonathan Swift. **CP-SwifJ**

Petit Poème en Prose. Frank O'Hara. **SP-OharF**

Petition Concerning the Death-Wish. John Clellon Holmes. **SP-HolmJ**

Petitions. Leonard Cohen. **CP-CoheL**

Petrolio, vaunting his Mercedes' power. *parody of* Matthew Prior. Rudyard Kipling. **CP-KiplR** *Fr.* The Muse among the Motors.

Petrus Aponensis—there was a magician! *with music.* Robert Browning. **CP-BroR2**

Pettius no more I verses write. Translation of Horace: Epode xi. Horace, *tr. by* Samuel Johnson. **CP-JohnS** *Fr.* Epodes.

Petty fury, The. The Drunk and the Sailor. William Carlos Williams. **CP-WilW2**

Petty sneaking Knave I knew, A. William Blake. **CP-BlakW**

Petty Thing, A. Stephen Dunn. **SP-DunnS**

Petunia, The. William Carlos Williams. **CP-WilW2**

Petunia. Louis Zukofsky. **CP-ZukLS**

Phaedra. Hilda Doolittle. **CP-DoolH**

Phaedra. Algernon Charles Swinburne. **SP-SwinA**

Phaedra in the Farm House. Thom Gunn. **CP-GunnT**

Phaéthôn. George Meredith. **CP-MerG1**

Phalanx of cabs surges uptown in tune, A. 107th & Amsterdam. William Matthews. **SP-MattW**

Phaneron. Muriel Rukeyser. **CP-RukeM**

Phantasia for Elvira Shatayev. Adrienne Rich. **SP-RicA1; SP-RicA2**

Phantasmagoria. "Lewis Carroll." **CP-CarrL**
  Canto I: The Trystyng.
  Canto II: Hys Fyve Rules.
  Canto III: Scarmoges.
  Canto IV: Hys Nouryture.
  Canto V: Byckerment.
  Canto VI: Dyscomfyture.
  Canto VII: Sad Souvenaunce.

Phantasmagoria, The. Hayden Carruth. *Fr.* Mother. **CP-CarHL**

Phantasmal fears, / And the flap of the flame. A New Year's Eve in War Time. Thomas Hardy. **CP-HardT**

Phantasy. George Meredith. **CP-MerG1**

Phantom. Samuel Taylor Coleridge, *Unknown, sometimes at. to.* **CP-ColeS**

Phantom, The. Walter de la Mare. **CP-DeLaW**

Phantom Horsewoman, The. Thomas Hardy. **CP-HardT**

Phantom Kiss, The. Paul Laurence Dunbar. **CP-DunbP**

Phantom or Fact? Samuel Taylor Coleridge. **CP-ColeS**

Pharaoh and the Sergeant. Rudyard Kipling. **CP-KiplR**

Pharaoh has seen me in the hovels of Israel. Alun Lewis. *Fr.* The Captivity. **CP-LewiA**

Pharaohs were sealed up in their own dust, The. Crocodile at the Ancient Tombs. Howard Nemerov. **CP-NemeH**

Pharmacy, The. Lewis Turco. **SP-TurcL**

Pharoahs Sacrifice Themselves before Her, The. Tom Clark. **SP-ClarT**

Pharsalia. Lucan, *tr. fr. Latin.*
  "Amid the storms of war, with curious eyes." **CP-JohnS**
  In the French Translation of Lucan by Monsieur De Brebeuf Are These Verses: Lib 3. **CP-MarvA**
  In the French Translation of Lucan by Monsieur De Brebeuf Are These Verses: Lib 3. **CP-MarvA**
  "Just and fit actions, Ptolemy (he saith)." **CP-JonsB**
  (Speech out of Lucan, A.) **CP-JonsB**
  "Moist[e]ned Osyer [or osier] of the hoarie Willow, The." **CP-RaleW**
  "No faith of partnership dominion owns." **CP-JohnS**
  "None dares with impious steel the grove to rend." **CP-JohnS**
  "O wastfull Riot, never well content." **CP-RaleW**
  "Phoenicians first (if Fame may credit have)." **CP-RaleW,** *tr. by* Sir Walter Ralegh;
  "Wars worse than civil on Thessalian plains." **CP-MarlC**

Phases of the Moon. Robert Browning. **ChTr** *Fr.* One Word More. **CP-BroR1**

Phases of the Moon, The. William Butler Yeats. **CP-YeatW**

Pheasant. Sylvia Plath. **CP-PlatS**

Phebe drest like beauties Queen. William Blake. **CP-BlakW** *Fr.* An Island in the Moon.

Phèdre. Stevie Smith. **CP-SmitS**

Pheidippides. Robert Browning. **CP-BroR2**

Phekda. Siv Cedering Fox. *Fr.* Seven Letters to Zakarias. **SP-CedeS**

Phenomena. Robinson Jeffers. **CP-JefR1**

Phenomena. John Updike. **CP-UpdiJ**

Phenomenal Survivals of Death in Nantucket. Louise Glück. **SP-GlücL**

Phenomenal Woman. Maya Angelou. **SP-AngeM**

Phenomenology of Anger, The. Adrienne Rich. **SP-RicA1; SP-RicA2**

Philadelphia. Rudyard Kipling. **CP-KiplR**

Philadelphia city lights boiling under the. These States: to Miami Presidential Convention. Allen Ginsberg. **CP-GinsA**

Philadelphia: 1978. Charles Kenneth Williams. **SP-WillC**

Philai Te Kou Philai. George Oppen. **CP-OppeG**

Philander. Theodore Roethke. **CP-RoetT**

Philemon and Baucis. Thom Gunn. **CP-GunnT**

P[hillips] loved me, not as he loved his Friends. William Blake. **CP-BlakW**

Phillips! the suff'rer less by law than pow'r. A Sonnet Addressed to Mr. Phillips. William Cowper. **CP-CowpW**

Phillips, whose touch harmonious could remove. Samuel Johnson. **CP-JohnS**

(Epitaph on Claudy Phillips, a Musician, An.) **CP-JohnS**

Phillis the Fair. Robert Burns. **CP-BurnR**

Philo Vance. Literary Reflection. Ogden Nash. **CP-NashO**

Philo, with twelve years' study, hath been grieved. An Obscure Writer. John Donne. **CP-DonnJ**

Philodendron's ear-leaf, The. Night Post. Archie Randolph Ammons. **SP-AmmoA**

Philological. John Updike. **CP-UpdiJ**

Philology Recapitulates Ontology, Poetry Is Ontology. Delmore Schwartz. **SP-SchwD**

Philomel. Richard Barnfield. *See* As it fell upon a day.

Philomela. John Crowe Ransom. **SP-RansJ**

Philomena Andronico. William Carlos Williams. **CP-WilW2**

Philosopher, The. Emily Brontë. *See* Enough of Thought, Philosopher.

Philosopher, The. Robert Ranke Graves. **CP-GravR**

Philosopher, The. Edna St. Vincent Millay. **CP-MillE**

Philosopher and the King, The. William Cowper. **CP-CowpW**

Philosopher on His Way to His Death Suddenly Sent This Message to a Certain King Who Had Unawares Condemned Him, Unrecognized and Innocent, When He Was Seized by Chance Among Criminals, A. John Milton, *tr. fr. Latin and Greek by* John T. Shawcross. **CP-MiltJ**

Philosopher! 'tis said you wail. George Meredith. **CP-MerG2**

Philosophers, The. Thomas Merton. **CP-MertT**

Philosophers are lined with eyes within. Ralph Waldo Emerson. **CP-EmerR**

Philosophers have measured [*or* measur'd] mountains. The Agony [*or* Agonie]. George Herbert. **CP-HerbG**

Philosophers say, The: one, the few, the many. Canto 68. Ezra Pound. *Fr.* Cantos. **CP-PoCan**

Philosophia Perennis. Anne Waldman. **SP-WaldA**

Philosophical Fantasy, A. Thomas Hardy. **CP-HardT**

Philosophical Trinity, The. Samuel Taylor Coleridge. **CP-ColeS**

Philosophus et Phasiani. John Gay, *tr. fr. English by* William Cowper. **CP-CowpW**

Philosophy. Paul Laurence Dunbar. **CP-DunbP**

Philosophy. Howard Nemerov. **CP-NemeH**

Philosophy, baptised. William Cowper. **EPCY** *Fr.* The Garden. *Fr.* The Task. **CP-CowpW**

Phizzog. Carl Sandburg. **CP-SandC**

Phlebas the Phoenician, a fortnight dead. Death by Water. Thomas Stearns Eliot. **OBVE** *Fr.* The Waste Land. **CP-ElioT**

Phlox. Louis Zukofsky. **CP-ZukLS**

Phoebe all the rights *Elisa* claymeth. Epigramme. Thomas Campion. *Fr.* Observations in the Art of English Poesie. **CP-CampT**

Phoebe Dawson. George Crabbe. **SP-CrabG** *Fr.* The Parish Register.

Phoebe's Nest, A. William DeWitt Snodgrass. **SP-SnodW**

Phoebus and Dian, queen of bow'rs. Charles Hubert Sisson. *See* Carmen Saeculare.

Phœbus asleep forbad me Wine to take. Of a Drunkard. Quintus Catulus, *tr. fr. Latin by* Richard Lovelace. **CP-LoveR**

Phoebus farewell, a sweeter saint I serve, *speech of Basilius.* Sir Philip Sidney. **SP-SidnP** *Fr.* Arcadia.

Phoebus, make haste, the day's too long, be gone. Another. Anne Bradstreet. **CP-BradA**

Phoebus now shortening every shade. Apollo Outwitted. Jonathan Swift. **CP-SwifJ**

PHOEBUS, Phoebus, ere thou slay. Sophocles. **SP-PounE** *Fr.* Women of Trachis.

Phoebus was judge between Jove, Mars, and Love. Sonnet 13. Sir Philip Sidney. *Fr.* Astrophil and Stella. **SP-SidnP**

Phœbus! when that I a Verse. To Apollo. Robert Herrick. **CP-HerrR**

Phoebus with Admetus. George Meredith. **CP-MerG1**

Phoenicians first (if Fame may credit have). Lucan. **CP-RaleW**, *tr. by* Sir Walter Ralegh; *Fr.* Pharsalia.

Phœnissae. Euripides, *tr. fr. Greek.*

"Exiles, the proverb says, subsist on hope." **CP-JohnS**

Phoenix, The. Hafiz, *tr. by* Ralph Waldo Emerson. **CP-EmerR** *Fr.* Odes.

Phoenix. David Herbert Lawrence. **CP-LawrD**

Phœnix, The. Ogden Nash. **CP-NashO**

Phoenix, The. Howard Nemerov. **CP-NemeH**

Phoenix, The. May Sarton. **SP-SartM**

Phoenix Analysed, The. Ben Jonson. **CP-JonsB**

Phoenix and the Tortoise, The, *sels.* Kenneth Rexroth.

"Dark within dark I cling to sleep." **CP-RexKL; SP-RexrK**

"I am cold in my folded blanket." **CP-RexKL**

"I am cold in my folded blanket." **SP-RexrK**

"Softly and singly an owl." **CP-RexKL**

"Webs of misery spread in the brain." **CP-RexKL**

"Webs of misery spread in the brain." **SP-RexrK**

Phoenix and the Tortoise, The. William Carlos Williams. **CP-WilW2**

Phoenix and the Turtle, The. William Shakespeare. **CP-ShaWS**

Phoenix Lyrics. Delmore Schwartz. **SP-SchwD**

"If nature is life, nature is death."

"Purple black cloud at sunset: it is late August."

"When a hundred years had passed nature seemed to man / a clock."

Phoenix Undying, *sel.* Kuo Mo-jo, *tr. fr. Chinese by* William Carlos Williams *with* David Rafael Wang. **CP-WilW2**

Phone. Hayden Carruth. **CP-CarHS**

Phone. Robert Creeley. **CP-CreeR**

Phone Booth. Andrei Voznesensky, *tr. fr. Russian by* Richard Wilbur. **CP-WilbR**

Phone for the fish-knives, Norman. How to Get On in Society. Sir John Betjeman. **CP-BetjJ**

Phone rings, The. Macho Man. Charles Bukowski. **SP-BukC3**

Phonecall from Frank O'Hara, A. Anne Waldman. **SP-WaldA**

Phoning from Sweathouse Creek. Richard Hugo. **CP-HugoR**

Phonograph may(if it likes)be prophe, The. Edward Estlin Cummings. **CP-CummE**

Phonograph's voice like a keen spider skipping, The. Edward Estlin Cummings. **CP-CummE**

Phosphor Reading by His Own Light. Wallace Stevens. **CP-StevW**

Photo. Robert Creeley. **CP-CreeR**

Photo of Emily, The. Lawrence Ferlinghetti. **SP-FerlL**

Photo of Miners, A. Brendan Galvin. **SP-GalvB**

Photo of someone else's childhood, A. The Old Adam. Denise Levertov. **CP-LeveD**

Photo of the Author with a Favorite Pig. William Matthews. **SP-MattW**

Photograph, The. Leonard Cohen. **CP-CoheL**

Photograph, The. Paul Laurence Dunbar. **CP-DunbP**

Photograph, The. Thomas Hardy. **CP-HardT**

Photograph, A. James Schuyler. **CP-SchuJ**

Photograph, The. Stevie Smith. **CP-SmitS**

Photograph, The. Stephen Spender. **CP-SpenS**

Photograph, The. Lewis Turco. **SP-TurcL**

Photograph Album, The. Stephen Dunn. **SP-DunnS**

Photograph in the Hallway, The. Stephen Dunn. **SP-DunnS**

Photograph of a Boy in Costume, The. Wystan Hugh Auden. **CP-AudWJ**

Photograph of a Girl, The. Howard Nemerov. **CP-NemeH**

Photograph of a Lighthouse Through Fog. Tess Gallagher. **SP-GallT**

Photograph of the Unmade Bed, The. Adrienne Rich. **CP-RicAE; SP-RicA2**

Photograph where we smile, The. February 21st. Anne Sexton. **CP-SextA**

Photographer's Model, The. James McAuley. **SP-McAuJ**

Photographic chamber of the eye, The. Tale of a Tub. Sylvia Plath. **CP-PlatS**

Photographic plate is blurred, The. The Magellanic Clouds. Diane Wakoski. **SP-WakoD**

Photographs. Charles Bukowski. **SP-BukC1**

Photographs. Mona Van Duyn. **SP-VanDM**

Photographs, fading already, recall my discomfort. Getting It Wrong, Again. Steve Griffiths. **SP-GrifS**

Photographs of China. Donald Hall. **CP-HallD**

Photography Extraordinary. "Lewis Carroll." **CP-CarrL**

Photon or wave, bullet or billow riding? Light. Louise McNeill. **SP-McNeL**

Photos, The. Diane Wakoski. **SP-WakoD**

Photosynthesis. Archie Randolph Ammons. **SP-AmmoA**

Phryne. John Donne. **CP-DonnJ**

Phryne, *in imitation of* Earl of Dorset. Alexander Pope. **CP-PopeA**

Phyllis [*or* Phillis *or* Progress of Love, The]. Jonathan Swift. **CP-SwifJ**

Phyllis. Paul Laurence Dunbar. **CP-DunbP**

Phyllis, ah, Phyllis, my life is a gray day. Phyllis. Paul Laurence Dunbar. **CP-DunbP**

Phyllis Corydon clutched to him. Carmen 45. Catullus. **BoLoP** *Fr.* Carmina. **CP-Catul**

Phyllis, Tomalin, away. Second Song. Andrew Marvell. *Fr.* Two Songs at the Marriage of the Lord Fauconberg and the Lady Mary Cromwell. **CP-MarvA**

Phyllis Wounded. Marge Piercy. **SP-PierM**

Physical world is meaningless tonight, The. Jouga. Wallace Stevens. **CP-StevW**

Physician Nature! let my spirit blood! To Fanny. John Keats. **CP-KeatJ**

Physician's Tale, The. Geoffrey Chaucer. *Fr.* The Canterbury Tales. **CP-ChauG**

Physics. Pablo Neruda, *tr. fr. Spanish* by Ben Belitt. **SP-NeruP**

Physics of Loneliness, The. Al Young. **CP-YounA**

Physitians. Robert Herrick. **CP-HerrR**

Physitians say Repletion springs. Repletion. Robert Herrick. **CP-HerrR**

Pianist Joe Sullivan, The. The Thing About Joe Sullivan. Roy Fisher. **SP-FishR**

Piano, The. David Herbert Lawrence. **CP-LawrD**

Piano. David Herbert Lawrence. **CP-LawrD**

Piano after War. Gwendolyn Brooks. **SP-BrooG**

Piano di Sorrento. Robert Browning. **FaBoPP; SeCePo** *Fr.* The Englishman in Italy. **CP-BroR1**

(Englishman in Italy, The ["Time for rain! for your long hot dry autumn"].) SeCePo

Piano Practice. Derek Walcott. **CP-WalcD**

Piano ripples a delicate, The. The Dying Swan. James McAuley. **SP-McAuJ**

Piano, so long untuned, A. Arroyo Seco. Charles Tomlinson. **CP-TomlC**

Piano Solo. Nicanor Parra, *tr. fr. Spanish* by William Carlos Williams. **CP-WilW2**

Piano Tuner, Untune Me That Tune. Ogden Nash. **CP-NashO**

Piazza di Spagna, Early Morning. Richard Wilbur. **CP-WilbR**

Piazza Piece. John Crowe Ransom. **SP-RansJ**

Pibroch. Ted Hughes. **SP-HughT**

Pibroch of Donuil Dhu. Sir Walter Scott. **SP-ScotW**

Pibroch's note, discountenanced or mute. William Wordsworth. **CP-WorW2**

Picasso / you give us Things. Edward Estlin Cummings. **CP-CummE**

Picasso Laughing. Patti Smith. **SP-SmitP**

Picasso made me tough and quick, and the world. Memorial Day 1950. Frank O'Hara. **SP-OharF**

Piccadilly Circus at Night. David Herbert Lawrence. **CP-LawrD**

Piccola Commedia. Richard Wilbur. **CP-WilbR**

Piccolomini, The. Johann Christoph Friedrich von Schiller, *tr. fr. German by* Samuel Taylor Coleridge.
Mythology in an Age of Reason. **CP-ColeS**

Pick a quarrel, go to war. Wystan Hugh Auden. **PV** *Fr.* Shorts [1927–1932] ("Pick a quarrel, go to war"). **CP-AudeW**

Pick-Offs. Carl Sandburg. **CP-SandC**

Pick Up the Evening Paper. Kenneth Patchen. **CP-PatcK**

Picker. Miller Williams. **SP-WillM**

Pickers. John Haines. **SP-HainJ**

Pickin Em Up and Layin Em Down. Maya Angelou. **SP-AngeM**

Picking and Choosing. Marianne Craig Moore. **CP-MoorM**

Picking Blueberries, Austerlitz, New York, 1957. Mary Oliver. **SP-OlivM**

Picking the wax to crumbs in the iron lip of the candelabrum. Adrienne Rich. *Fr.* Shooting Script. **CP-RicAE**

Picking thru ruins with a stick. Italy. Patti Smith. **SP-SmitP**

Pickle Belt. Theodore Roethke. **CP-RoetT**

Picnic, The. Robert Creeley. **CP-CreeR**

Picnic. Adrienne Rich. **CP-RicAE; SP-RicA2**

Picnic Boat. Carl Sandburg. **CP-SandC**

Picnic Cantata, A. James Schuyler. **CP-SchuJ**

Picnic in the Saracen Ruin, The. Richard Hugo. **CP-HugoR**

Picnic Remembered. Robert Penn Warren. **SP-WarrR**

Pict Song, A. Rudyard Kipling. **CP-KiplR** *Fr.* The Winged Hats. *Fr.* Puck of Pook's Hill.

Pictor Ignotus. Robert Browning. **CP-BroR1**

Picture, The. Samuel Taylor Coleridge. **CP-ColeS**

Picture, A. Robert Creeley. **CP-CreeR**

Picture, A. Malcolm Lowry. **CP-LowrM**

Picture, A. Howard Nemerov. **CP-NemeH**

Picture, The. Charles Olson. **CP-OlsoC**

Picture and book remain. An Acre of Grass. William Butler Yeats. **CP-YeatW**

Picture Book. John Yau. **SP-YauJo**

Picture-Books in Winter. Robert Louis Stevenson. **CP-StevR**

Picture-frame for you to fill, A. To Minnie (With a Hand-Glass). Robert Louis Stevenson. **CP-StevR**

Picture in the Paper, A. Randall Jarrell. **CP-JarrR**

Picture is simply chile relleno, The. The Night before Michael Was Born. Al Young. **CP-YounA**

Picture of a Black Child with a White Doll. Thomas Merton. **CP-MertT**

Picture of a Nativity. Geoffrey Hill. **CP-HillG**

Picture of a Nude in a Machine Shop. William Carlos Williams. **CP-WilW2**

Picture of Daniel in the Lions' Den, at Hamilton Palace. William Wordsworth. **CP-WorW2**

Picture of Her Mind, The. Ben Jonson. *See* The Mind.

Picture of J. T. in a Prospect of Stone, The. Charles Tomlinson. **CP-TomlC**

Picture of Lee Ying, A. Thomas Merton. **CP-MertT; SP-MertT**

Picture of Little J. A. in a Prospect of Flowers, The. John Ashbery. **SP-AshbJ**

Picture of Little Rory in a Municipal Park, The. Robert Penn Warren. **SP-WarrR**

Picture of Little T. C. in a Prospect of Flowers, The. Andrew Marvell. **CP-MarvA**

Picture of the Body, The. Ben Jonson. **NOSC** *Fr.* Eupheme. **CP-JonsB**

Picture of the pretty Home, The. Emily Dickinson. **SP-DickE**

Picture Showing. William Carlos Williams. **CP-WilW1**

Picture some Isle smiling green 'mid the white-foaming ocean. The Poetry of Shakespeare. George Meredith. **CP-MerG1**

Picture this. I'll play the killer. 16 millimeter. K.O.D.A.K. Patti Smith. **SP-SmitP**

Picture yourself in a boat on a river with tangerine trees and marmalade skies. Lucy in the Sky with Diamonds. The Beatles. **CP-Beatl**

Pictures. Walt Whitman. **CP-WhitW**

Pictures. John Greenleaf Whittier. **CP-WhitJ**

Pictures by Vuillard. Adrienne Rich. **CP-RicAE**

Pictures from Brueghel. William Carlos Williams. **CP-WilW2**
Corn Harvest, The. **ArNa; PPP**
Haymaking. **NoAM**
Hunters in the Snow, The. **LCAP**
Landscape with the Fall of Icarus. **LCAP; NAAL-2; NoAM; PPP**
Parable of the Blind, The. **CP-WilW2; LCAP; SAmP**
Self-Portrait. **LCAP**

Pictures From Tofukuji. Anne Waldman. **SP-WaldA**

Pictures in the air have few visitors, The. Self-Portait. Charles Wright. **SP-WrigC**

Pictures of Philippa. Donald Hall. **CP-HallD**

Pictures of the People in the War. Louise Glück. **SP-GlücL**

Pictures of the Rhine. George Meredith. **CP-MerG1**

"Picturesque / common lot" the unwarranted light, The. Anniversary Poem. George Oppen. **APSN; NNaP** *Fr.* Some San Francisco Poems. **CP-OppeG**

Pidgin Moon. Al Young. **CP-YounA**

Pie-wedge petals / deeply pinked and. Yellow Flowers. James Schuyler. **CP-SchuJ**

Piece, A. Robert Creeley. **CP-CreeR**

Piece by piece I seem. Necessities of Life. Adrienne Rich. **CP-RicAE; SP-RicA1; SP-RicA2**

Piece of flesh gives off, A. Galway Kinnell. *Fr.* The Dead Shall Be Raised Incorruptible. **SP-KinnG**

Piece of me, curiously. Billfold. Robert Creeley. **CP-CreeR**

Piece of sky, A. Sky Seasoning. Shel Silverstein. **SP-SilS2**

Piece of thread ripped-out from a fierce design, A. 8/8/68: ii. Adrienne Rich. **CP-RicAE** *Fr.* Ghazals: Homage to Ghalib. **SP-RicA2**

Piecemeal the summer dies. Exeunt. Richard Wilbur. **CP-WilbR**

Pieces. Robert Creeley. **CP-CreeR**

Pieces. Adrienne Rich. **CP-RicAE; SP-RicA2**

Pieces. Wallace Stevens. **CP-StevW**

Pieces(in darker / than small is dirtiest). Edward Estlin Cummings. **CP-CummE**

Pieces of a piece. The face in the window larger. John Yau. **SP-YauJo** *Fr.* Scenes from the Life of Boullee.

Pieces of animals, pieces of all my friends. Ninth Elegy. The Antagonists. Muriel Rukeyser. **CP-RukeM**

Pieces of cake crumbling. Robert Creeley. **CP-CreeR**

Pieces of that steel. Charles and Arthur. Gilbert Sorrentino. **SP-SorrG**

Pied Beauty. Gerard Manley Hopkins. **CP-HopkG**

Pied Piper, The. John Ashbery. **SP-AshbJ**

Pied Piper of Hamelin, The. Robert Browning. **CP-BroR1**
"Into the street the Piper stept." **BoTP; OXAEP-2**

Pier-Glass, The. Robert Ranke Graves. **CP-GravR**

Pier: Under Pisces, The. James Merrill. **SP-MerrJ**

Pierce Street. Thom Gunn. **CP-GunnT**

Piero Luca, known of all the town. The Brother of Mercy. John Greenleaf Whittier. **CP-WhitJ**

Pierrot Le Fou. Adrienne Rich. **CP-RicAE; SP-RicA2**

Piers are pummelled by the waves, The. The Fall of Rome. Wystan Hugh Auden. **CP-AudeW**

Piet. Rudyard Kipling. **CP-KiplR**

Pietà. Donald Davie. **CP-DavDo**

Pietà. Louise Glück. **SP-GlücL**

Pietá. David Herbert Lawrence. *Fr.* Bits. **CP-LawrD**

Pietà, Rhenish, 14th C., the Cloisters, The. Mona Van Duyn. **SP-VanDM**

Pietro has twenty red and blue balloons on a string. Five Cent Balloons. Carl Sandburg. **CP-SandC**

Pietro of Abano, *with music.* Robert Browning. **CP-BroR2**

Piety. Charles Simic. **SP-SimiC**

Pievish doth boast, that he's the very first. Upon Pievish. Robert Herrick. **CP-HerrR**

Pig. Rudyard Kipling. *Fr.* Plain Tales from the Hills. "Go, stalk the red dear o'er the heather." **CP-KiplR**

Pig, The. Ogden Nash. **CP-NashO**

Pig, if I am not mistaken, The. The Pig. Ogden Nash. **CP-NashO**

Pig is a young sow or boar. Pigs—For T.H. Malcolm Lowry. **CP-LowrM**

Pig lay on a barrow dead, The. View of a Pig. Ted Hughes. **SP-HughT**

Pig pig she cries. Thom Gunn. *Fr.* Jack Straw's Castle. **CP-GunnT**

Pig Song. Margaret Atwood. **NoP** *Fr.* Songs of the Transformed. **SP-AtwM1**

Pig-Tale, The. "Lewis Carroll." **CP-CarrL** *Fr.* Sylvie and Bruno Concluded.

Melancholy Pig, The. **FaPON**

Pig-Tale, The, *incl. in* Pig-Tale, The. "Lewis Carroll." *See* Little Birds are dining.

Pigeon. Carl Sandburg. **CP-SandC**

Pigeon flies to her resting place, The. Five P.M. Ted Kooser. **SP-KoosT**

Pigeon purrs in the wood; the wood has gone, The. Idylls of the King. Geoffrey Hill. **FaBoRV; NoAM; PoE** *Fr.* An Apology for the Revival of Christian Architecture in England. **CP-HillG**

Pigeon, who are to me. The Reckoning. Stanley Jasspon Kunitz. **CP-KuniS**

Pigeons. Philip Larkin. **CP-LarkP**

Pigeons, The. Edna St. Vincent Millay. **CP-MillE**

Pigeons, The. Karl Shapiro. **SP-ShapK**

Pigeons riddle the London air, The, *sels.* Louis MacNeice. *Fr.* Autumn Journal. **CP-MacNL**

Pigeons shake their wings on the copper church roof. Fourth Floor, Dawn, Up All Night Writing Letters. Allen Ginsberg. **CP-GinsA**

Pigeons, thirty-five in a. Filling in the Dots. Archie Randolph Ammons. **SP-AmmoA**

Piggies. George Harrison. **CP-Beatl**

Piggy to Joey. Stevie Smith. **CP-SmitS**

Pigheaded Poet. William Carlos Williams. **CP-WilW2**

Pigling, pigling, burning bland. Malcolm Lowry. *Fr.* Songs for Second Childhood. **CP-LowrM**

Pigmy Scraper wi' his Fiddle, A. Robert Burns. *Fr.* The Jolly Beggars.

Pigmy seraphs—gone astray. Emily Dickinson. **CP-DickE**

Pignus Amoris. Byron. **CP-Byron**

Pigs—For T.H. Malcolm Lowry. **CP-LowrM**

Pijijiapan. Malcolm Lowry. *Fr.* The Lighthouse Invites the Storm. **CP-LowrM**

Pike. Ted Hughes. **SP-HughT**

Pike, The. Theodore Roethke. **CP-RoetT**

Pike Place Market. Richard Hugo. **CP-HugoR**

Pike, three inches long, perfect. Pike. Ted Hughes. **SP-HughT**

Pilas volare qui iubebat impius. *acc. by English translation.* Thomas Campion. **CP-CampT**

Pilate. Donald Davie. **CP-DavDo**

Pilate, Fragments. Gerard Manley Hopkins. **CP-HopkG**

Pile high the hickory and the light. Winter Night. Edna St. Vincent Millay. **CP-MillE**

Pile of Years is not so high, The. Emily Dickinson. **CP-DickE**

Pile the bodies high at Austerlitz and Waterloo. Grass. Carl Sandburg. **CP-SandC**

Piles of rock balls used for ammo then. Castel Sant'Angelo. Richard Hugo. **CP-HugoR**

"Pilfer" is true enough for me. No True Rhyme in English for "Silver." William Matthews. **SP-MattW**

Pilgrim, The. Charlotte Smith. **CP-SmitC**

Pilgrim, The. William Butler Yeats. **CP-YeatW**

Pilgrim disposition—, The. Roy Fisher. **SP-FishR** *Fr.* Diversions.

Pilgrim Fathers, The. William Wordsworth. *See* Aspects of Christianity in America—Concluded—American Episcopacy.

Pilgrim Fathers, The. William Wordsworth. *See* Aspects of Christianity in America—Continued.

Pilgrim Fathers, The. William Wordsworth. *See* Aspects of Christianity in America—the Pilgrim Fathers.

Pilgrim Fish Heads. Robert Bly. **SP-BlyR**

Pilgrim passes swiftly, The. Three Postcards from the Monastery. Thomas Merton. **CP-MertT; SP-MertT**

Pilgrim passes through the town by night, A. Malcolm Lowry. **CP-LowrM**

Pilgrim, when the summer day, A. The Pilgrim's Dream; or, The Star and the Glow-Worm. William Wordsworth. **CP-WorW2**

Pilgrimage, The. George Herbert. **CP-HerbG**

Pilgrimage, and the Game Warden, The. Marsden Hartley. **CP-HartM**

Pilgrims, The. Ralph Waldo Emerson. **CP-EmerR**

Pilgrim's Dream; or, The Star and the Glow-Worm, The. William Wordsworth. **CP-WorW2**

Pilgrim's Song, The. Bible, *O.T. See* Psalm 121: "I will lift up mine eyes unto the hills."

Pilgrims' Song. Thomas Merton. **CP-MertT**

Pilgrim's Way, A. Rudyard Kipling. **CP-KiplR**

Pili's Wall. Philip Levine. **SP-LeviP**

Pillar and the Post, The. Hart Crane. **CP-CranH**

Pillar at Sebzevar, A. Robert Browning. **CP-BroR2**

Pillar of Fame, The. Robert Herrick. **CP-HerrR**

Pillar of Trajan, The. William Wordsworth. *Fr.* Memorials of a Tour in Italy, 1837. **CP-WorW2**

Pillar [*or* Piller] perished [*or* pearisht] is whe[a]rto I le[a]nt, The. Sir Thomas Wyatt, *after the Italian of* Petrarch. **CP-WyatT**

Pillars. Raissa Maritain, *tr. fr. French by* Thomas Merton. **CP-MertT**

Pillow. Tom Clark. **SP-ClarT**

Pillow, The. Charles Simic. **SP-SimiC**

Pillow. John Updike. **CP-UpdiJ**

Pillows are going insane, The. Flat. Charles Kenneth Williams. **CP-WillC; SP-WillC**

Pilot, The. Edwin Arlington Robinson. **CP-RobiE**

Pilot, The. Lewis Turco. **SP-TurcL**

Pilot from the Carrier, A. Randall Jarrell. **CP-JarrR; SP-JarrR**

Pilot looked out of the cockpit window and (as the city vanished, The. Flying Inland. John Yau. **SP-YauJo**

Pilot, returned, sees the village, The. In the Sleep of Reason. Thomas McGrath. **SP-McGrT**

Pilots, Man Your Planes. Randall Jarrell. **CP-JarrR**

Primitiæ to Parents, The. Robert Herrick. **CP-HerrR**

Pin has a head, but has no hair, A. Christina Georgina Rossetti. **CP-RosC2**

Pin-swin or spine-swine, The. His Shield. Marianne Craig Moore. **CP-MoorM**

Pinch-penny light, rifted, pitied light. On the Failure of a Poet. Charles Bukowski. **CP-BukC2**

Pin'd I am, and like to die. Thomas Campion. **CP-CampT**

Pindar is Dead. Louis MacNeice. *Fr.* Out of the Picture. **CP-MacNL**

Pindar is imitable by none. 4.2. Horace. *Fr.* Odes.

Pindaric Ode, A. Thomas Gray. **SeCePo** *Fr.* Bard, The [A Pindaric Ode]. **CP-GrayT**

Píndaro no soy, sino caballero. *spanish vers. of* Torch and Crown, 1968. Robert Ranke Graves. **CP-GravR**

Pine. James Dickey. **CP-DickJ**

Pine-Apple and the Bee, The. William Cowper. **CP-CowpW**

Pine-apples, in triple row, The. The Pine-Apple and the Bee. William Cowper. **CP-CowpW**

Pine Creek Parish Hall. Barton Sutter. **SP-SuttB**

Pine Forest of the Cascine Near Pisa, The. Percy Bysshe Shelley. **CP-ShelP**

Pine needles receive our bones. Island with Army, Pines and Wind. Steve Griffiths. **SP-GrifS**

Pine of Monte Mario at Rome, The. William Wordsworth. *Fr.* Memorials of a Tour in Italy, 1837. **CP-WorW2**

Pine Planters, The. Thomas Hardy. **CP-HardT**

Pine River. Gary Snyder. **CP-SnydG**

Pine-Tree, The. John Greenleaf Whittier. **CP-WhitJ**

Pine tree is perfect, The. January. Gary Snyder. *Fr.* Six Years. **CP-SnydG**

Pine Tree Tops. Gary Snyder. **CP-SnydG**

Pine-trees bend to listen to the autumn wind as it mutters, The. At the Window. David Herbert Lawrence. **CP-LawrD**

Pine trees cast their needles softly, The. Wood Song. Alun Lewis. **CP-LewiA**

Pine with gray tips is moist still, The. Summer Landscape. Richard Eberhart. **CP-EberR**

Pines are darkly swaying, The. Schubert's "Farewell." George Meredith. **CP-MerG2**

Pines. The white, ochre-pocked houses. Sky unflawed. Upon so. Another August. James Merrill. **SP-MerrJ**

Pines, under pines. Gary Snyder. **CP-SnydG** *Fr.* Logging. *Fr.* Myths and Texts.

Pines were dark on Ramoth hill, The. My Playmate. John Greenleaf Whittier. **CP-WhitJ**

Pines were swaying in the serious wind, The. Honesty. Stephen Dunn. **SP-DunnS**

Pines write a Chinese poem upon the white-gold sun. Malcolm Lowry. **CP-LowrM**

Ping-Pong. Peter Meinke. **SP-MeinP**

Pink and Pale. John Crowe Ransom. *Fr.* Two Gentlemen in Bonds. **SP-RansJ**

Pink as a dawn in Galilee. Choral: The Pink Church. William Carlos Williams. **CP-WilW2**

Pink-cheeked Jesus, The. Cold Blue Tinge. Charles Simic. **SP-SimiC**

Pink confused with white. The Pot of Flowers. William Carlos Williams. **CP-WilW1**

Pink Dog. Elizabeth Bishop. **CP-BishE**

Pink Dominoes. Rudyard Kipling. **CP-KiplR**

("'They are fools who kiss and tell'.") **CP-KiplR**

Pink Dress, The. Diane Wakoski. **SP-WakoD**

Pink Frock, The. Thomas Hardy. **CP-HardT**

Pink Locust, The. William Carlos Williams. **CP-WilW2**

Pink may, double may, dead laburnum. Myfanwy at Oxford. Sir John Betjeman. **CP-BetjJ**

Pink nipples of the earth in springtime, The. Carl Sandburg. *Fr.* Timesweep. **CP-SandC**

Pink primrose from the plant he knows, A. The Unplanted Primrose. Thomas Hardy. **CP-HardT**

Pink—small—and punctual. Emily Dickinson. **CP-DickE**

Pink tits, or grace of white thighs. Long Distance. Charles Olson. **CP-OlsoC**

Pinky Brown must marry Rose Wilson. Brighton Rock by Graham Greene. Bill Knott. **SP-KnotB**

Pinned to Mrs R———'s Carriage. Robert Burns. *See* If you rattle along like your mistress's tongue.

Pioneer. John Hewitt. **CP-HewiJ**

Pioneer Lullaby. Rennie McOwan. **SP-McNeL**

Pioneers! O Pioneers! Walt Whitman. **CP-WhitW**

Pious Cat, The. Basil Bunting. **CP-BuntB**

Pious Horse to church may trot, The. AUGUST (*Coaching*). Rudyard Kipling. *Fr.* Verses on Games. **CP-KiplR**

Pious magistrate! sound his praise throughout, A. Official Piety. John Greenleaf Whittier. **CP-WhitJ**

Pipe Dreams. Ogden Nash. **SP-NashO**

Pipe the Gaelic back for one last dance. Piping to You on Skye from Lewis. Richard Hugo. **CP-HugoR**

Piper, The. William Blake. *See* Piping Down the Valleys Wild.

Piper, The. Robert Louis Stevenson. **CP-StevR**

Pipes at Lucknow, The. John Greenleaf Whittier. **CP-WhitJ**

Pipes of the misty moorlands. The Pipes at Lucknow. John Greenleaf Whittier. **CP-WhitJ**

Piping, beaus, I'll go *whoosh* and I'll rumble you. Catullus. *See* Carmen 16: "Pedicabo et irrumabo."

Piping Down the Valleys Wild. William Blake. **ClHu; EnRP; FaBV; FaBoBe; FaBoCh; GoJo; HeIP; HoFi; InPS; InvP; NAEL-2; NAWM-2; NIP; NOBE; NOEC; NoP; OAEL-2; OBNC; OnUR; PoE; PoEL-4; RHPC; SoSe; TEP; TFi; TrGrPo** *Fr.* Songs of Innocence. **CP-BlakW**

(Introduction: "Piping down the valleys wild.") **NOBRP; PFP**

(Piper, The.) **AWP; OxBChV; PDV**

(Reeds of Innocence.) **ImPo; LiTB; OBEV**

Piping to You on Skye from Lewis. Richard Hugo. **CP-HugoR**

Pipit sate upright in her chair. A Cooking Egg. Thomas Stearns Eliot. **CP-ElioT**

Pipling. Theodore Roethke. **OBCoV; TW** *Fr.* Three Epigrams. **CP-RoetT**

Pippa Passes. Robert Browning. **CP-BroR1**

Service. **TrGrPo**

Song: "Give her but a least excuse to love me!" **ViBoPo**

"Year's at the spring, The." **ArNa; BLPA; BLPL; BoTP; CoGr; EBCP; EBEvV; FHYEP; FaBV; FaBoBe; FaFP; FaPON; GoJo; HBV; HBVY; ImPo; LiTB; NTCP; OBEV; OBVV; OHIP; PAI; PDV; PoPl; PoToHe; SoSe; TEP; TFi; TRV; TrCP; TrGrPo; TreF; UnPo; WGRP; YeAr**

(Pippa's Song.) **BLPL; BoTP; CoGr; EBCP; FaFP; FaPON; GoJo; ImPo; LiTB; NTCP; OBEV; OBVV; OHIP; PDV; TEP; TRV; TrCP; TreF; UnPo**

(Song: "Year's at the Spring, The.") **EBEvV; FHYEP; HBV; HBVY; PoPl; SoSe; TFi; TrGrPo**

Pippa's Song. Robert Browning. *See* The Year's at the spring.

Pirate Captain Jim. Shel Silverstein. **SP-SilS2**

Pirate Poem. Frederick Morgan. **SP-MorgF**

Pirate Story. Robert Louis Stevenson. **CP-StevR**

Pirates in England, The. Rudyard Kipling. **CP-KiplR**

Pirouette. Audre Lorde. **SP-LordA**

("I saw your hands.") **SP-LordA**

Pisa's Leaning Tower. Herman Melville. **SP-MelvH**

Pisgah-Sights. I. Robert Browning. **CP-BroR2**

Pisgah-Sights. II. Robert Browning. **CP-BroR2**

Pishkun. Richard Hugo. **CP-HugoR**

Pishkun Reservoir. Richard Hugo. **CP-HugoR**

Piso's own comates, his, corps an inane as. Catullus. *See* Carmen 28: "In Piso's suite / are empty pockets."

Piss Factory. Patti Smith. **SP-SmitP**

Pissing off the Back of the Boat into the Nivernais Canal. William Matthews. **SP-MattW**

Pistol shots ring out in the barroom night. Hurricane. "Bob Dylan" *and* Jacques Levy. **CP-DylaB**

Pistols for Pleasure—Guitars for Defense. Marsden Hartley. **CP-HartM**

Pit, The. Theodore Roethke. **NAAL-2** *Fr.* The Lost Son. **CP-RoetT**

Pit—but Heaven over it, A. Emily Dickinson. **CP-DickE**

Pit where the buffalo cooled his hide. Rudyard Kipling. **CP-KiplR** *Fr.* Cupid's Arrows. *Fr.* Plain Tales from the Hills.

Pitch here the tent, while the old horse grazes. Juggling Jerry. George Meredith. **CP-MerGl**

Pitch Pines. Brendan Galvin. **SP-GalvB**

Pitched high above the shallows of the sea. Loss and Gain. Geoffrey Hill. *Fr.* An Apology for the Revival of Christian Architecture in England. **CP-HillG**

Pitcher, how / exactly is. Charles Olson. **CP-OlsoC**

Pitcher of Milk, The. John Haines. **SP-HainJ**

Pitcher that went to the well too often, The. The Need for Stoicism in the Stoa of Attalus. Thomas McGrath. **SP-McGrT**

Pite, that I have sought so yore agoo. The Complaint unto Pity. Geoffrey Chaucer. **CP-ChauG**

Piteous my rhyme is / What while I muse of love and pain. Christina Georgina Rossetti. **CP-RosC2**

Piteous sobs that choke the Virgin's breath, The. Sonnet [to Charles Lloyd]. Samuel Taylor Coleridge. **CP-ColeS**

Pithos. Rita Dove. **SP-DoveR**

Pitia a Damone. Christina Georgina Rossetti. **CP-RosC3**

Pitie to the Prostrate. Robert Herrick. **CP-HerrR**

Pitiful Case, A. William Blake. **CP-BlakW**

Pitiful dupes of old illusion, lost. Sparrows in a Hillside Drift. James Wright. **CP-WrigJ**

Pitiful lovers broken by your loves. Twelve Line Poem. William Carlos Williams. **CP-WilW2**

Pitmirk the nicht: God's waukrife yet. The Dying Earth. "Hugh MacDiarmid." **SP-MacDH**

Pitt. Samuel Taylor Coleridge. *Fr.* Effusions. **CP-ColeS**

Pitt-Rivers Museum, Oxford, The. James Fenton. **FaBoMo** *Fr.* Exempla. **SP-FentJ**

Pittie, and Punishment. Robert Herrick. **CP-HerrR**

Pity. Samuel Taylor Coleridge. *Fr.* Effusions. **CP-ColeS**

Pity. Robert Ranke Graves. **CP-GravR**

Pity. Richard Wilbur. **CP-WilbR**

Pity and Fear. Miller Williams. **SP-WillM**

Pity beyond all telling, A. The Pity of Love. William Butler Yeats. **CP-YeatW**

Pity could be no more. *see also* The Human Abstract. William Blake. **CP-BlakW**

Pity for Poor Africans. William Cowper. **CP-CowpW**

Pity his how illimitable plight. Edward Estlin Cummings. **CP-CummE**

Pity, if true. Hearts-Of-Gold. Herman Melville. **SP-MelvH**

Pity me not because the light of day. Edna St. Vincent Millay. **CP-MillE**

Pity! mourn in plaintive tone. Catullus. *See* Carmen 3: "Who loves beauty / vel her statues."

Pity mourns in plaintive tone. Catullus. *See* Carmen 3: "Who loves beauty / vel her statues."

Pity not! The Army gave. Ex-Clerk. Rudyard Kipling. *Fr.* Epitaphs of the War [1914–1918]. **CP-KiplR**

Pity of It, The. Thomas Hardy. **CP-HardT**

Pity of Love, The. William Butler Yeats. **CP-YeatW**

Pity of the Leaves, The. Edwin Arlington Robinson. **CP-RobiE**

Pity, says the Theban Bard. On Envy. *Unknown, tr. fr. Greek by* William Cowper. **CP-CowpW**

Pity the blind and the halt but yet pity. Song. Malcolm Lowry. **CP-LowrM**

Pity the deep in love. Countee Cullen. **CP-CullC**

Pity the Man Who English Lacks, *after the Irish of* David O'Bruaidar. Michael Hartnett. **SP-HarMi**

Pity the sorrows of a poor old Dog. A Word for the Dumb. Christina Georgina Rossetti. **CP-RosC3**

Pity this busy monster, manunkind. Edward Estlin Cummings. **CP-CummE; SP-CummE**

Pity would be no more. The Human Abstract. William Blake. **CP-BlakW** *Fr.* Songs of Experience.

Pity's Sake. Archibald MacLeish. **CP-MacLA**

Piute Creek. Gary Snyder. **CP-SnydG**

Pivot, The. Stanley Jasspon Kunitz. **CP-KuniS**

Pizza, The. Ogden Nash. *Fr.* Table Talk. **CP-NashO**

Pizzeria S. Biagio. Richard Hugo. **CP-HugoR**

Placard for a Poll Bearing an Old Shirt. William Wordsworth. **CP-WorW2**

Placation of Reality. Richard Eberhart. **CP-EberR**

Place, A. Robert Creeley. **CP-CreeR**

Place, The. Robert Creeley. **CP-CreeR**

Place. Robert Creeley. **CP-CreeR**

Place. Robert Creeley. **CP-CreeR**

Place. Robert Creeley. **CP-CreeR**

Place, The. Richard Eberhart. **CP-EberR**

Place. Robert Pack. **SP-PackR**

Place, The. Charles Simic. **SP-SimiC**

Place and Time. Robert Penn Warren. **SP-WarrR**

Place (Any Place) to Transcend All Places, A. William Carlos Williams. **CP-WilW2**

Place at Albert Bay, The. Muriel Rukeyser. **CP-RukeM**

Place between Us, The. Stephen Dobyns. **SP-DobyS**

Place-bound and time-bound in evening rain. Human Arrangement. Wallace Stevens. **CP-StevW**

Place Didn't Look Bad, The. Charles Bukowski. **SP-BukC1**

Place for a Third. Robert Frost. **CP-FrosR**

Place for No Story, The. Robinson Jeffers. **CP-JefR2**

Place, for the Marshal of the Masque! Charles the First. Percy Bysshe Shelley. **CP-ShelP**

Place: Fragments, A. Margaret Atwood. **SP-AtwM1**

Place in Kansas, A. Ted Kooser. **SP-KoosT**

Place in Maine, A. Stephen Dobyns. **SP-DobyS**

Place in which he lived, / Is called Scete, The. Macarius the Younger. Thomas Merton. **CP-MertT**

Place in which to, A. Charles Henri Ford. **SP-FordC** *Fr.* Emblems of Arachne.

Place is forgotten now; when I was a child, The. The Quarry. Howard Nemerov. **CP-NemeH**

Place is public—a thronged station, The. Danse Macabre. William Everson. **SP-EverW**

Place is the focus. What is the language. In Defence of Metaphysics. Charles Tomlinson. **CP-TomlC**

Place it, / make the space. The Edge. Robert Creeley. **CP-CreeR**

Place Names. Thomas Merton. **ChIV-1** *Fr.* East. *Fr.* The Geography of Lograire. **CP-MertT**

Place of a Skull. Louis MacNeice. **CP-MacNL**

Place of Burial in the South of Scotland, A. William Wordsworth. **CP-WorW2**

Place of clear concepts is taken by images, *anima telluris*, The. The Writ. Charles Olson. **CP-OlsoC**

Place of Death, The. Randall Jarrell. **CP-JarrR**

Place of the Damned [*or* Damn'd], The. Jonathan Swift. **CP-SwifJ**

Place of the Damned, The. John Milton. **FaBoEn** *Fr.* Book II. **FHYEP; NAEL-1; OxAEP-1** *Fr.* Paradise Lost. **CP-MiltJ**

Place of the Skull, The. James Dickey. **CP-DickJ**

Place of the Solitaires, The. Wallace Stevens. **CP-StevW**

Place of Value, The. Howard Nemerov. **CP-NemeH**

Place on the Map, The. Thomas Hardy. **CP-HardT**

Place Pigalle. Richard Wilbur. **CP-WilbR**

Place-Rituals. Muriel Rukeyser. **CP-RukeM**

Place so / hostile it does, A. There. Robert Creeley. **CP-CreeR**

Place this bunch of mignonette. Dirge. Paul Laurence Dunbar. **CP-DunbP**

Place Where a Great City Stands, The. Walt Whitman. **ImGa** *Fr.* Song of the Broad-Axe [*or* Broad-Ax]. **CP-WhitW**

Place Where Nothing Is, A. Robert Penn Warren. **SP-WarrR**

Place Where the Boy Pointed, The. Robert Penn Warren. **SP-WarrR**

Place Where the Rainbow Ends, The. Paul Laurence Dunbar. **CP-DunbP**

Place without associations, A. The End of the World. Louise Glück. **SP-GlücL**

Place yes a silver and golden face. Scott Rautmann, Saturday Night. James Liddy. **CP-LiddJ**

Placed on this isthmus of a middle state. Alexander Pope. **WeW** *Fr.* An Essay on Man. **CP-PopeA**

Places. Robert Creeley. **CP-CreeR**

Places. Thomas Hardy. **CP-HardT**

Places. Carl Sandburg. **CP-SandC**

Places and Ways to Live. Richard Hugo. **CP-HugoR**

Places, Loved Ones. Philip Larkin. **CP-LarkP**

Places of Worship. William Wordsworth. *Fr.* Ecclesiastical Sonnets. **CP-WorW2**

Placet Experiri. Mona Van Duyn. **SP-VanDM**

Placid lake that rested far below, The. Passage from John Wilson's The Angler's Tent. William Wordsworth. **CP-WorW1**

Placid Man's Epitaph, A. Thomas Hardy. **CP-HardT**

Placing a $2 Bet for a Man Who Will Never Go to the Horse Races Any More. Diane Wakoski. **SP-WakoD**

Plagiarist, The. Malcolm Lowry. **CP-LowrM**

Plague, The. Christina Georgina Rossetti. **CP-RosC3**

Plague and sores beyond relief. Les Congés du Lépreux. Frank Templeton Prince. **CP-PrinF**

Plague of Starlings, A. Robert Earl Hayden. **CP-HaydR**

Plague on your languages, German and Norse!, A. Written in Germany on One of the Coldest Days of the Century. William Wordsworth. **CP-WorW1**

Plague take all your pedants, say I! Sibrandus Schafnaburgensis. Robert Browning. **CTC; EBVV; TEP** *Fr.* Garden Fancies. **CP-BroR1**

Plagued Journey, A. Maya Angelou. **SP-AngeM**

Plagues of a Country Life. Jonathan Swift. *Fr.* Verses from Quilica. **CP-SwifJ**

Plaid Dress, The. Edna St. Vincent Millay. **CP-MillE**

Plain. Miller Williams. **SP-WillM**

Plain as the glistering planets shine. Robert Louis Stevenson. **CP-StevR**

Plain be the phrase, yet apt the verse. A Utilitarian View of the Monitor's Fight. Herman Melville. **SP-MelvH**

Plain black cotton dress, A. Piety. Charles Simic. **SP-SimiC**

Plain Fools. Alexander Pope. **OBSV** *Fr.* An Essay on Criticism. **CP-PopeA**

Plain in front of me, A. The Weary Walker. Thomas Hardy. **CP-HardT**

Plain of Donnerdale, The. William Wordsworth. *Fr.* The River Duddon [A Series of Sonnets]. **CP-WorW2**

Plain Sense of Things, The. Wallace Stevens. **CP-StevW**

Plain Song for Comadre, A. Richard Wilbur. **CP-WilbR**

Plain Speaking. Louis MacNeice. **CP-MacNL**

Plain Tales from the Hills, *sels.* Rudyard Kipling.

  Bank Fraud, A.

    "He drank strong waters and his speech was coarse." **CP-KiplR**

  Beyond the Pale.

    Love Song of Har Dyal, The. **CP-KiplR**

  Bisara of Pooree, The.

    "Little Blind Fish, thou art marvellous wise!" **CP-KiplR**

  Broken-Link Handicap, The.

    "While the snaffle holds or the long-neck stings." **CP-KiplR**

  Bronkhorst Divorce Case, The.

    "In the daytime, when she moved about me." **CP-KiplR**

  By Word of Mouth.

    "Not though you die to-night, O Sweet, and wail." **CP-KiplR**

  Consequences.

    "Rosicrucian subtleties / In the Orient had rise." **CP-KiplR**

  Conversion of Aurelian McGoggin, The.

    "Ride with an idle whip, ride with an unused heel." **CP-KiplR**

  Cupid's Arrows.

    "Pit where the buffalo cooled his hide." **CP-KiplR**

  False Dawn.

    "To-night, God knows what thing shall tide." **CP-KiplR**

  Germ-Destroyer, A.

    "Pleasant it is for the Little Tin Gods." **CP-KiplR**

  Hadramauti. **CP-KiplR**

  His Chance in Life.

    "Then a pile of heads he laid." **CP-KiplR**

  His Wedded Wife.

    "Cry 'Murder' in the market-place, and each." **CP-KiplR**

  In Error.

    "They burnt a corpse upon the sand." **CP-KiplR**

  In the House of Suddhoo.

"Stone's throw out on either hand, A." **CP-KiplR**

In the Pride of His Youth.
"'Stopped in the straight when the race was his own." **CP-KiplR**

Kidnapped.
"There is a tide in the affairs of men." **CP-KiplR**

Lispeth.
"Look, you have cast out Love! What Gods are these." **CP-KiplR**

Other Man, The.
"When the earth was sick and the skies were grey." **CP-KiplR**

Pig.
"Go, stalk the red dear o'er the heather." **CP-KiplR**

Rescue of Pluffles, The.
"Thus, for a season, they fought it fair." **CP-KiplR**

Rout of the White Hussars, The.
"It was not in the open fight." **CP-KiplR**

Taking of Lungtungpen, The.
"So we loosed a bloomin' volley." **CP-KiplR**

Thrown Away.
"And some are sulky, while some will plunge." **CP-KiplR**

To Be Filed for Reference.
By the Hoof of the Wild Goat. **CP-KiplR**

Tod's Amendment.
"World hath set its heavy yoke, The." **CP-KiplR**

Wressley of the Foreign Office.
Tarrant Moss. **CP-KiplR**

Plain tilt-bonnet on her head, A. In the Days of Crinoline. Thomas Hardy. **CP-HardT**

Plain was grassy, wild and bare, The. The Dying Swan. Tennyson. **CP-TennA**

Plain ye, mine eyes. Accompany my heart. Sir Thomas Wyatt. **CP-WyatT**

Plain youth, Lady, and a simple lover, A. Sonnet Translated from the Italian of Milton. William Wordsworth. **CP-WorW1**

Plainness in Diversity. John Ashbery. **SP-AshbJ**

Plains. Wystan Hugh Auden. **NePA** *Fr.* Bucolics. **CP-AudeW**

Plains ignore us, The. Visiting Mountains. Ted Kooser. **SP-KoosT**

Plains of snow. The buntings whirl like rung. Hayden Carruth. *Fr.* The Sleeping Beauty. **CP-CarHL**

Plaint. Charles Henri Ford. **SP-FordC**

Plaint. Theodore Roethke. **CP-RoetT**

Plaint to Man, A. Thomas Hardy. **CP-HardT**

Plaited Like the Generations of Men. "Hugh MacDiarmid."
"All life's million conflicting interests and relationships." **SP-MacDH**
"Come, follow me into the realms of music. Here is the gate." **SP-MacDH**
"Everlasting layers / Of ideas, images, feelings." **SP-MacDH**

Plan, The. Wendell Berry. **CP-BerrW**

Plan, The. Robert Creeley. **CP-CreeR**

Plan du Centre de Paris à Vol D'Oiseau. Lawrence Ferlinghetti. **SP-FerlL**

Plan Is the Body, The. Robert Creeley. **CP-CreeR**

Plan of Salvation, The. John Milton. **WGRP** *Fr.* Book III. *Fr.* Paradise Lost. **CP-MiltJ**

Plan of Self-Subjection, A. Thom Gunn. **CP-GunnT**

Plane. Howard Nemerov. **CP-NemeH**

Plane goes by, / and the sky takes hold, A. Sky Writing. Charles Tomlinson. **CP-TomlC**

Plane leaves, The. Autumn Rain. David Herbert Lawrence. **CP-LawrD**

Plane rose loudly and rammed west, The. Mea Culpa. Isabella Gardner. **CP-GardI**

Plane Ticket. Robert Lowell. **SP-LoweR**

Plane Tree, The. Wystan Hugh Auden. **CP-AudWJ**

Planes arc like arrows through the highest sky. Plotted. Robert Lowell. **SP-LoweR**

Planes Are Groaning Mothers. Jim Morrison. **SP-MorrJ**

Plane's flight your helix, transcontinental blood. Birth's Obituary. Charles Olson. **CP-OlsoC**

Planes, trains, lorries simmer through the garden. In the Mail. Robert Lowell. **SP-LoweR**

Planet Actions. Archie Randolph Ammons. **SP-AmmoA**

Planet of Mars, The. Shel Silverstein. **SP-SilS2**

Planet on the Table, The. Wallace Stevens. **CP-StevW**

Planet over Eastern Parkway, The. Thomas Merton. *Fr.* Cables to the Ace. **CP-MertT**

Planetarium. Adrienne Rich. **CP-RicAE; SP-RicA1; SP-RicA2**

Planh for the Young English King, *From the Provençal of Bertrans de Born.* Ezra Pound. **SP-PounE**

Planners, The. Robert Frost. **CP-FrosR**

Planning the Perfect Evening. Rita Dove. **MAYP** *Fr.* A Suite for Augustus. **SP-DoveR**

Plans for Altering the River. Richard Hugo. **CP-HugoR**

Planster's Vision, The. Sir John Betjeman. **CP-BetjJ**

Plant and Phantom. Louis MacNeice. **CP-MacNL**

Plant Magic dust / expect hope doubt. Edward Estlin Cummings. **CP-CummE**

Plant of noble stemme, forward and faire, A. Upon the Death of Mister Herrys. Richard Crashaw. **CP-CrasR**

Plantation a Beginning, A. Charles Olson. **SP-OlsoC** *Fr.* The Maximus Poems.

Plantation Child's Lullaby, The. Paul Laurence Dunbar. **CP-DunbP**

Plantation Melody, A. Paul Laurence Dunbar. **CP-DunbP**

Plantation Portrait, A. Paul Laurence Dunbar. **CP-DunbP**

Planted deeper than roots. A Stone Church Damaged by a Bomb. Philip Larkin. **CP-LarkP**

Planters, The. Margaret Atwood. **SP-AtwM1**

Planting. Philip Levine. **SP-LeviP**

Planting a Mailbox. John Updike. **CP-UpdiJ**

Planting Crocuses. Wendell Berry. **CP-BerrW**

Planting Trees. Wendell Berry. **CP-BerrW**

Planting Trees. John Updike. **CP-UpdiJ**

Planting trees early in spring. For the Future. Wendell Berry. **CP-BerrW**

Plants against the light, The. Dec. 28, 1974. James Schuyler. **CP-SchuJ**

Plants and trees made poore and old, The, *ad. fr. Latin of* Albinovanus. *Unknown, tr. by* Sir Walter Ralegh. **CP-RaleW,** *tr. by* Sir Walter Ralegh;

Plants went into camp last night, The. Emily Dickinson. **SP-DickE**

Plaster. Carl Sandburg. **CP-SandC**

Plastic surgeon who has, The. Poem. William Carlos Williams. **CP-WilW2**

Plate 21. William Blake. *See* Opposition Is True Friendship.

Plate Glass Window, A. Charles Bukowski. **SP-BukC1**

Plate in light upon a table is not a plate of hunger, A. Salvages: An Evening Place. Robert Duncan. **SP-DuncR**

Plate of Steaming Fish, A. Kenneth Patchen. **CP-PatcK**

Plated Life—diversified, A. Emily Dickinson. **CP-DickE**

Platform, The. Adrienne Rich. **CP-RicAE**

Platinum sun rising. / Platinum frost on porch. Malcolm Lowry. **CP-LowrM**

Platitudinous Reflection. Ogden Nash. **CP-NashO**

Plato says that in Heaven there is. Frank Templeton Prince. *Fr.* Memoirs in Oxford. **CP-PrinF**

Plato told / him:he couldn't. Edward Estlin Cummings. **CP-CummE; SP-CummE**

Platypus, The. Ogden Nash. *Fr.* The Astigmatic Naturalist. **CP-NashO**

Plaudite, or End of Life, The. Robert Herrick. **CP-HerrR**

Play, The. Richard Eberhart. **CP-EberR**

Play, The. Anne Sexton. **CP-SextA**

Play. William Carlos Williams. **CP-WilW1**

Play full smiles around the dimpled mouth, The. On Lady Mary Wortley Montagu's Portrait. Alexander Pope. **CP-PopeA**

Play-Ground, The. Walt Whitman. **CP-WhitW**

Play I could once; but, gentle friend, you see. To His Friend, on the Untunable Times. Robert Herrick. **CP-HerrR**

Play it across the table. Cahoots. Carl Sandburg. **CP-SandC**

Play me a game like Blind Man's dance. Bump d'Bump. Maya Angelou. **SP-AngeM**

Play of Memory, The. John Updike. *Fr.* Midpoint. **CP-UpdiJ**

Play, Phoebus, on thy lute. A Canticle to Apollo. Robert Herrick. **CP-HerrR**

Play seems out for an almost infinite run, The. It Bids Pretty Fair. Robert Frost. **CP-FrosR**

Play the blues for me. Misery. Langston Hughes. **SP-HughL**

Play their offensive and defensive parts. Good Christians. Robert Herrick. **CP-HerrR**

Play Time. William Blake. *See* Nurse's Song ("When the voices of children are heard on the green / And laughing is heard on the hill").

Playboy. Richard Wilbur. **CP-WilbR**

Playboy of the dawn. Gone Boy. Langston Hughes. **SP-HughL**

Playboys and Playgirls. "Bob Dylan." **CP-DylaB**

Played-Out Game, A. David Herbert Lawrence. **CP-LawrD**

Player Piano, The. Randall Jarrell. **CP-JarrR; SP-JarrR**

Player Piano. John Updike. **CP-UpdiJ**

Players Ask for a Blessing on the Psalteries and on Themselves, The. William Butler Yeats. **CP-YeatW**

Playful birches in the / Where the mind goes off in austerity. Four Exposures. Richard Eberhart. **CP-EberR**

Playing a phonograph record of a windy morning. From the Duck-Pond to the Carousel. Muriel Rukeyser. **CP-RukeM**

Playing alone / Drunk and bored. Malcolm Lowry. **CP-LowrM**

Playing alone, I found the wall. And I'd Love You to Be in It. John Ashbery. **SP-AshbJ**

Playing at bob cherry / Tom and Nell and Hugh. Christina Georgina Rossetti. **CP-RosC2**

Playing Cards, The. Alexander Pope. ChTr *Fr.* The Rape of the Lock[, an Heroi-Comical Poem]. **CP-PopeA**

Playing It Out. Charles Bukowski. **SP-BukC3**

Playing Shuffleboard, Drunk, in Key West, Fla. Peter Meinke. **SP-MeinP** *Fr.* Lines from Key West.

Playing Skittles. Howard Nemerov. **CP-NemeH**

Playing the Inventions. Howard Nemerov. **CP-NemeH**

Playing the quarter slots. Gambling at Reno. William Dickey. **SP-DickW**

Playmate, The. Rudyard Kipling. **CP-KiplR**

Plays are like feasts; and every act should be. Epilogue. Sir John Suckling. *Fr.* The Fifth Act of Aglaura As Presented to the Court. *Fr.* Aglaura. **CP-SuckJ**

Playwright, by chance, hearing some toys I had writ. On Playwright. Ben Jonson. **CP-JonsB**

Playwright convict of public wrongs to men. On Playwright. Ben Jonson. **CP-JonsB**

Playwright me reads, and still my verses damns. To Playwright. Ben Jonson. **CP-JonsB**

Plea, A. Paul Laurence Dunbar. **CP-DunbP**

Plea for a League of Sleep, A. Ogden Nash. **CP-NashO**

Plea for Authors, May, 1838, A. William Wordsworth. **CP-WorW2**

Plea for Mercy, A. William Carlos Williams. **CP-WilW2**

Plea for the Historian. William Wordsworth. *Fr.* Memorials of a Tour in Italy, 1837. **CP-WorW2**

Plea of the Simla Dancers, The. Rudyard Kipling. **CP-KiplR** ("Too late, alas! the song.") **CP-KiplR**

Plea to Boys and Girls, A. Robert Ranke Graves. **CP-GravR**

Plead for Me. Emily Brontë. *See* O thy bright eyes must answer now.

Plead my cause, O Lord, with them that strive with me. Psalm 35. Bible, O.T. *Fr.* Psalms. **CP-Psal**

Pleading for and with Youth. William Cowper. *Fr.* Olney Hymns. **CP-CowpW**

Pleasant isle of Rügen looks the Baltic water o'er, The. The Brown Dwarf of Rügen. John Greenleaf Whittier. **CP-WhitJ**

Pleasant it is for the Little Tin Gods. Rudyard Kipling. **CP-KiplR** *Fr.* A Germ-Destroyer. *Fr.* Plain Tales from the Hills.

Pleasant music floats along the Mere, A. Canute. William Wordsworth. *Fr.* Ecclesiastical Sonnets. **CP-WorW2**

Pleasant northeast wind, 2 monarch. Day Detail—Low Light of Afternoon. Tom Clark. **SP-ClarT**

Pleasant river gushes, The. Robert Louis Stevenson. **CP-StevR**

Pleasant sight it was when, having clomb. Summer Vacation. William Wordsworth. *Fr.* The Prelude; Growth of a Poet's Mind [1805 vers.]. **CP-WorW3**

Pleasant smell of frying sausages, A. Mixed Feelings. John Ashbery. **SP-AshbJ**

Pleasant the snaffle of Courtship, improving the manners and carriage. Rudyard Kipling. *Fr.* Certain Maxims of Hafiz. **CP-KiplR**

Pleasant Thought from Whitehead, A. Frank O'Hara. **SP-OharF**

Pleasantly rose next morn the sun on the village of Grand-Pré. Henry Wadsworth Longfellow. *Fr.* Part the First. *Fr.* Evangeline, a Tale of Acadie. **SP-LongH**

Pleas'd in these lines, *Belinda*, you may view. *see also* Rape of the Lock, The. Alexander Pope. **CP-PopeA**

Please. Robert Creeley. **CP-CreeR**

Please / do not / make f / un of. A Poem on the Neck of a Running Giraffe. Shel Silverstein. **SP-SilS2**

Please do not tell me there is no voodoo. Exposure. John Updike. **CP-UpdiJ**

Please don't anybody ask me to decide anything. Suppose He Threw It in Your Face. Ogden Nash. **CP-NashO**

Please give me room, Howard! I've tried before. Trying to Separate. Robert Pack. **SP-PackR**

Please Keep on Forwarding. Ogden Nash. **CP-NashO**

Please keep your icecream hands. Poem to a Most Affectionate Lady. Charles Bukowski. **SP-BukC2**

Please Leave Father Alone. Ogden Nash. **CP-NashO**

Please Like Me. Jim Morrison. **SP-MorrJ**

Please Master. Allen Ginsberg. **CP-GinsA**

Please master can I touch your cheek. Please Master. Allen Ginsberg. **CP-GinsA**

Please, Mrs. Henry. "Bob Dylan." **CP-DylaB**

Please Open the Window and Let Me In. Allen Ginsberg. **CP-GinsA**

Please Pass the Biscuit. Ogden Nash. **CP-NashO**

Please Please Me. The Beatles. **CP-Beatl**

Please rest the Life so many own. Emily Dickinson. **SP-DickE**

Please stop gushing about his pink. Basil Bunting, *after the Latin of* Horace. **CP-BuntB**

Please your Grace, from out your store. The Beggar to Mab, the Fairy [*or* Fairie] Queen. Robert Herrick. **CP-HerrR**

Please yourself how you have it. Loggerheads. David Herbert Lawrence. **CP-LawrD**

Pleasing form, a firm, yet cautious mind, A. Epitaph on Sir William Trumbal. Alexander Pope. **CP-PopeA**

Pleasing was his shape. The Temptation of Eve. John Milton. **EBNV** *Fr.* Book IX. **FHYEP; NAEL-1; NAWM-1; NoP; OAEL-1** *Fr.* Paradise Lost. **CP-MiltJ**

Pleasure boat, pleasure boat where has it gone? Charles Henri Ford. *Fr.* Epigrams. **SP-FordC**

Pleasure Island. Wystan Hugh Auden. **CP-AudeW**

Pleasure of Hope, The. Alexander Pope. **ACP** *Fr.* An Essay on Man. **CP-PopeA**

Pleasure of the wit sustains, The. For W.C.W. Robert Creeley. **CP-CreeR**

Pleasure Reconciled to Virtue. Ben Jonson.
"Come on, come on! And where you go." **CP-JonsB**
"Eye of looking back were well, An." **CP-JonsB**
Hymn: "Room, room, make room for the bouncing belly." **CP-JonsB**
"It follows now you are to prove." **CP-JonsB**

Pleasure Seas. Elizabeth Bishop. **CP-BishE**

Pleasure, whom had we lacked from earliest hour, *fr. the French of* La Fontaine. Ode to Pleasure. Richard Wilbur. **CP-WilbR**

Pleasures. Robinson Jeffers. **CP-JefR3**

Pleasures newly found are sweet. To the Same Flower [The Small Celandine]. William Wordsworth. **CP-WorW1**

Pleasures of Exile, The. John Yau. **SP-YauJo**

Pleasures of Friendship, The. Stevie Smith. **CP-SmitS**

Pleasures of Merely Circulating, The. Wallace Stevens. **CP-StevW**

Pleasures of pain. Robert Creeley. **CP-CreeR**

Pleasures of Peace, The. Kenneth Koch. **SP-KochK**

Pleasures of This Gentle Day. Kenneth Patchen. **CP-PatcK**

Pleasures Pernicious. Robert Herrick. **CP-HerrR**

Pledging My Time. "Bob Dylan." **CP-DylaB**

Plena Timoris. Thomas Hardy. **CP-HardT**

Plenteous Redemption. Christopher Smart. *Fr.* Hymns for the Amusement of Children. **SP-SmarC**

Plentiful sacrifice and believers in redemption. When the Saints Come Marching In. Audre Lorde. **SP-LordA**

Plessy vs Ferguson: Theme and Variations. Thomas Merton. **CP-MertT**

Plingen plangen auf gefangen. Malcolm Lowry. **CP-LowrM**

Ploche, or the Doubler. Sir Walter Ralegh. *Fr.* The Arte of English Poesie. **CP-RaleW**

Plod! Plod! Elephants Plodding. David Herbert Lawrence. **CP-LawrD**

Plodding down the road, past. A Stone. Daniel Gerard Hoffman. **SP-HoffD**

Plot Against Hitler, The. Stanley Jasspon Kunitz. *Fr.* Around Pastor Bonhoeffer. **CP-KuniS**

Plot against the Giant, The. Wallace Stevens. **CP-StevW**

Plot-Culture. Robert Browning. **CP-BroR2**

Plotless tale: the passing hours, A. Rower. Charles Tomlinson. **CP-TomlC**

Plots Not Still Prosperous. Robert Herrick. **CP-HerrR**

Plotted. Robert Lowell. **SP-LoweR**

Plough of Time, The. Lawrence Ferlinghetti. **SP-FerlL**

Ploughing. Wystan Hugh Auden. **CP-AudWJ**

Ploughing on Sunday. Wallace Stevens. **CP-StevW**

Ploughland has gone to bent, The. Gin the Goodwife Stint. Basil Bunting. **CP-BuntB**

Ploughman, The, *see also* The Ploughman *author unknown.* Robert Burns. **CP-BurnR**

Ploughman, The. John Hewitt. **CP-HewiJ**

Ploughman he's a bony lad, The. *see also* The Ploughman *author unknown.* Robert Burns. **CP-BurnR**

Plover. Marsden Hartley. **CP-HartM**

Plovers. Peter Meinke. **SP-MeinP**

Plow Cemetery. John Updike. **CP-UpdiJ**

Plow Horses. Kenneth Patchen. **CP-PatcK**

Plow of tamarisk wood which is shared with black copper, The. The Shallow Grass. Archibald MacLeish. *Fr.* The Pot of Earth. **CP-MacLA**

Plow: one of the three-mile inns that nicked, The. Plow Cemetery. John Updike. **CP-UpdiJ**

Plow over bars of sea plowing. Fins. Carl Sandburg. **CP-SandC**

Plow, they say, to plow the snow, A. Plowmen. Robert Frost. **CP-FrosR**

Plowboy. Carl Sandburg. **CP-SandC**

Plowdens, Finns. Robert Earl Hayden. **CNA** *Fr.* Beginnings. **CP-HaydR**

Plowmen. Robert Frost. **CP-FrosR**

Pluck the florets from. Song. William Carlos Williams. **CP-WilW2**

Plum Gatherer, The. Edna St. Vincent Millay. **CP-MillE**

Plumet Basilisk, The. Marianne Craig Moore. **CP-MoorM**

Pluming himself upon a sense of sin. Portrait of the Artist as a Farmyard Fowl. Donald Davie. *Fr.* A Dissentient Voice. **CP-DavDo**

Plump mate to my head, you alone absorb. Pillow. John Updike. **CP-UpdiJ**

Plump Mr. Pl'f is washing his hands of America, The. Oil Painting of the Artist as the Artist. Archibald MacLeish. **CP-MacLA**

Plunder, The. Robert Herrick. **CP-HerrR**

Plunge, The. Thom Gunn. **CP-GunnT**

Plunge beneath the ledge of coral. The Reef Fisher. Archibald MacLeish. **CP-MacLA**

Plunge in yon angry waves. Hafiz, *tr.* by Ralph Waldo Emerson. **CP-EmerR** *Fr.* Odes.

Plunger. Carl Sandburg. **CP-SandC**

Plunging and labouring on in a tide of visions. In Front of the Landscape. Thomas Hardy. **CP-HardT**

Plunging donkey puberty devi. Go Round. Gary Snyder. **CP-SnydG**

Plunging towards Phrygia over violent water. Carmen 63. Catullus. **OBVE** *Fr.* Carmina. **CP-Catul**

Plunking the Skagit. Richard Hugo. **CP-HugoR**

Plural of "Jack-in-the-Box,"The. John Ashbery. **SP-AshbJ**

Plural the verdicts we cast on the creatures we have to shake hands with. Talking to Mice. Wystan Hugh Auden. **CP-AudeW**

Plurality. Louis MacNeice. **CP-MacNL**

Plus loin un autre commémore. Samuel Beckett. **CP-BeckS**

Plutonian Ode. Allen Ginsberg. **CP-GinsA**

Plymouth. Philip Larkin. **CP-LarkP**

Po Chu-i, balding old politician. As I Step over a Puddle at the End of Winter, I Think of an Ancient Chinese Governor. James Wright. **CP-WrigJ**

Po-sy, a Po-sy, A. Charles Olson. **CP-OlsoC**

Pock-marked player of the accordion, The. Wedding Party. Donald Hall. **CP-HallD**

Pocket handkerchief to hem, A. Christina Georgina Rossetti. **CP-RosC2**

Pocket Poem. Ted Kooser. **SP-KoosT**

Pocket Song. Leonard Nathan. **SP-NathL**

Pocket watch, I tick well. Gigolo. Sylvia Plath. **CP-PlatS**

Pockets. Howard Nemerov. **CP-NemeH**

Pockets of our greatcoats full of barley, The. Requiem for the Croppies. Seamus Heaney. **SP-HeanS**

Pocoangelini 1 ("Pocoangelini sat"). Lewis Turco. **SP-TurcL**

Pocoangelini 5 ("Pocoangelini said"). Lewis Turco. **SP-TurcL**

Pocoangelini 7 ("Sir. Your Head. It is stuck into the sand"). Lewis Turco. **SP-TurcL**

Pocoangelini 8 ("First thing in the morning, The"). Lewis Turco. **SP-TurcL**

Pocoangelini 12 ("She is caught in her frail house"). Lewis Turco. **SP-TurcL**

Pocoangelini 26 ("In the empty stadium he stood"). Lewis Turco. **SP-TurcL**

Pocoangelini 38 ("You have many wrinkles"). Lewis Turco. **SP-TurcL**

Pocomania. Derek Walcott. **CP-WalcD**

Pod of the Milkweed. Robert Frost. *See* Calling all butterflies of every race.

Pods. Carl Sandburg. **CP-SandC**

Poem: "About the size of an old-style dollar bill." Elizabeth Bishop. **CP-BishE**

Poem: "And tomorrow morning at 8 o'clock in Springfield, Massachusetts." Frank O'Hara. **SP-OharF**

Poem: "As the cat." William Carlos Williams. **CP-WilW1**

Poem: "At night Chinamen jump." Frank O'Hara. **SP-OharF**

Poem: "Beach holds and sifts us through her dreaming fingers, The." Bill Knott. **SP-KnotB**

Poem: "Clear objects / one grows to love. The clarity, The." Gilbert Sorrentino. **SP-SorrG**

Poem: "*Consciousness*, said Don Miguel, *is a disease*." Edwin Rolfe. **CP-RolfE**

Poem: "Consider Wordsworth in his withered age." John Hewitt. **CP-HewiJ**

Poem: "Daniel Boone, the father of Kentucky." William Carlos Williams. **CP-WilW1**

Poem: "Down the small and crooked road." Thomas McGrath. **SP-McGrT**

Poem: "Eager note on my door said "Call me", The." Frank O'Hara. **SP-OharF**

Poem: "Every morning I forget how it is." Charles Simic. **SP-SimiC**

Poem: "Faithful to your commands, o consciousness, o." Delmore Schwartz. **SP-SchwD**

Poem: "Feeling chilled in that cold country." Kenneth Patchen. **CP-PatcK**

Poem: "For having left the birds that left me." James Dickey. **CP-DickJ**

Poem: "Friend o' the Poet, tired and leal." Robert Burns. **CP-BurnR**

Poem: "Girl lashed to the stake, The." Edwin Rolfe. **CP-RolfE**

Poem: "Green going through the jungle of those years." Muriel Rukeyser. **CP-RukeM**

Poem: "Hate is only one of many responses." Frank O'Hara. **SP-OharF**

Poem: "Here is the man of the islands." Thomas Merton. **CP-MertT**

Poem: "How about an oak leaf." James Schuyler. **CP-SchuJ**

Poem: "How could I have come so far?" Thomas McGrath. **SP-McGrT**

Poem: "I do not always understand what you say." James Schuyler. **CP-SchuJ**

Poem: "I don't know as I get what D.H. Lawrence is driving at." Frank O'Hara. **SP-OharF**

Poem: "I got my hair cut." James Schuyler. **CP-SchuJ**

Poem: "I heard of a man." Leonard Cohen. **CP-CoheL**

Poem: "I lived in the first century of world wars." Muriel Rukeyser. **CP-RukeM**

Poem: "I ran through the snow like a young Czarevitch!" Frank O'Hara. **SP-OharF**

Poem: "I saw the mountains in a rose-fire light." Jean Garrigue. **SP-GarrJ**

Poem: "I snatch a grape from her breast." Jim Carroll. **SP-CarrJ**

Poem: "I watched an armory combing its bronze bricks." Frank O'Hara. **SP-OharF**

Poem: "Immense sadness / of approaching winter, The." John Haines. **SP-HainJ**

Poem: "In a high wind the." Archie Randolph Ammons. **SP-AmmoA**

Poem: "In the early evening, as now, a man is bending." Louise Glück. **SP-GlücL**

Poem: "In the list of one thousand false addresses." Thomas McGrath. **SP-McGrT**

Poem: "In the morning, when it was raining." Delmore Schwartz. **SP-SchwD**

Poem: "Instant coffee with slightly sour cream." Frank O'Hara. **SP-OharF**

Poem: It falls onto my page like rain. Charles Tomlinson. **CP-TomlC**

Poem: "It is time to write a poem." Lewis Turco. **SP-TurcL**

Poem: "It's sad this vision required." Jim Carroll. **SP-CarrJ**

Poem: "Ivy is trembling in the hammock, The." Frank O'Hara. **SP-OharF**

Poem: "Khrushchev is coming on the right day!" Frank O'Hara. **SP-OharF**

Poem: "Let's take a walk, you." Frank O'Hara. **SP-OharF**

Poem: "Light clarity avocado salad in the morning." Frank O'Hara. **SP-OharF**

Poem: "Light flares from the tombstones. . . ." Thomas McGrath. **SP-McGrT**

Poem: "Light plays like a radio in the iron tree." Thomas Merton. **CP-MertT**

(Poem): "Like a room." Bill Knott. **SP-KnotB**

Poem: "Living friends live / in the past so they bore us." Gilbert Sorrentino. **SP-SorrG**

Poem: "Long wound of the summer—, The." Thomas McGrath. **SP-McGrT**

Poem: "Looking up, of a sudden." William Carlos Williams. **CP-WilW2**

Poem: "Love, I shall perfect for you the child." Seamus Heaney. **SP-HeanS**

Poem: "Muscles which move the eyeballs." Charles Tomlinson. **CP-TomlC**

Poem: "My daughter and I lie in the snow." Gary Gildner. **SP-GildG**

Poem: "My father writes all day, all night." Charles Simic. **SP-SimiC**

Poem: "My footsteps in the shallow." Jim Carroll. **SP-CarrJ**

Poem: "My little son comes running with open arms!" Thomas McGrath. **SP-McGrT**

Poem: "My little son, laughing, singing. . . ." Thomas McGrath. **SP-McGrT**

Poem: "My name is Revolution—let me speak." John Hewitt. **CP-HewiJ**

Poem: "Now it is the 27th." Frank O'Hara. **SP-OharF**

Poem: "Now the violets are all gone, the rhinoceroses, the cymbals." Frank O'Hara. **SP-OharF**

Poem: "O death, so dear to me." James Dickey. **CP-DickJ**

Poem: "O Heart: this is a dream I had, or not a dream." Stanley Jasspon Kunitz. **CP-KuniS**

Poem: "O sole mio, hot diggety, nix 'I wather think I can.' " Frank O'Hara. **SP-OharF**

Poem: "Of morning, Iowa City, blue." Ted Berrigan. **SP-BerrT**

Poem: "Old man in the crystal morning after snow." Delmore Schwartz. **SP-SchwD**

Poem: "On getting a card." William Carlos Williams. **CP-WilW2**

Poem: "Only man I ever loved, The." Ernest Hemingway. **CP-HemiE**

Poem: "People down / The hallway who, The." Jim Carroll. **SP-CarrJ**

Poem: "Plastic surgeon who has, The." William Carlos Williams. **CP-WilW2**

Poem: "Remember midsummer: the fragrance of box, of white roses." Delmore Schwartz. **SP-SchwD**

Poem: "Rose fades, The." William Carlos Williams. **CP-WilW2**

Poem: "St. Marks Place caught at night in hot summer." Alice Notley. **SP-NotlA**

Poem: "Small / poem / the unit of feeling, The." Roy Fisher. **SP-FishR**

Poem: "So many echoes in my head." Frank O'Hara. **SP-OharF**

Poem: "Some trust the wolf." Jim Carroll. *Fr.* 3 Short Poems. **SP-CarrJ**

Poem: "Space / window / that looks into itself." Charles Tomlinson. **CP-TomlC**

Poem: "Tea is boiling, The." Jim Carroll. **SP-CarrJ**

Poem: "That's not a cross look it's a sign of life." Frank O'Hara. **SP-OharF**

Poem: "There I could never be a boy." Frank O'Hara. **SP-OharF**

Poem: "Thing / To do / Is organize / The Sea, The." Kenneth Koch. **SP-KochK**

Poem: "This beauty that I see." James Schuyler. **CP-SchuJ**

Poem: "This country invades me." Jim Carroll. **SP-CarrJ**

Poem: "Through the fog / The gulls." Thomas McGrath. **SP-McGrT**

Poem: "To be idiomatic in a vacumm." Frank O'Hara. **SP-OharF**

Poem: "Twin spheres full of fur and noise." Frank O'Hara. **SP-OharF**

Poem: "Upended, it crouches on broken limbs." Charles Tomlinson. **CP-TomlC**

Poem: "Wakening with the window over fields." Charles Tomlinson. **CP-TomlC**

Poem: "Watching, among the rifled branches, for the sun, our hero." Thomas Merton. **CP-MertT; SP-MertT**

Poem: "We are very much a part of the boredom." Jim Carroll. **SP-CarrJ**

Poem: "Wet streets in Liverpool." Malcolm Lowry. **CP-LowrM**

Poem: "When drunk he crawled home on his knees." Malcolm Lowry. **CP-LowrM**

Poem: "When I am feeling depressed and anxious sullen." Frank O'Hara. **SP-OharF**

Poem: "When I carry my little son in the cold." Thomas McGrath. **SP-McGrT**

Poem: "Willing to die, / you give up." Wendell Berry. **CP-BerrW**

Poem: "Wind tears up the sun, The." James Schuyler. **CP-SchuJ**

Poem: "Window winter." Delmore Schwartz. **SP-SchwD**

Poem: "With the toys of your nape." Bill Knott. **SP-KnotB**

Poem: "Yesterday you past / into your lips. . . your hips." Jim Carroll. **SP-CarrJ**

Poem: "You hear that heroic big land music?" Alice Notley. **SP-NotlA**

Poem: "You, my photographer, you, most aware." Delmore Schwartz. **SP-SchwD**

Poem: "You out there, so secret." Thomas McGrath. **SP-McGrT**

Poem: "Your enchantment / enchants me, stretched." James Schuyler. **CP-SchuJ**

Poem, A: "If the water forms." Robert Creeley. **CP-CreeR**

Poem, A: "Tags of songs, like salvaged buttons." James Schuyler. **CP-SchuJ**

Poem: A Reminder. Robert Ranke Graves. **CP-GravR**

Poem: A Reminder. Robert Ranke Graves. **CP-GravR**

Poem about a poem that can't be written, A. Malcolm Lowry. *Fr.* The Comedian. **CP-LowrM**

Poem About Birch Trees. John Haines. **SP-HainJ**

Poem about Black Power, A. Kay Boyle. **CP-BoylK**

Poem about Breasts, A. James Wright. **CP-WrigJ**

Poem about George Doty in the Death House, A. James Wright. **CP-WrigJ**

Poem about Oxford. Philip Larkin. **CP-LarkP**

Poem About Storytelling, A. Grace Paley. **CP-PaleG**

Poem about the Jews, A. Kay Boyle. **CP-BoylK**

Poem and Prayer for an Invading Army. Edna St. Vincent Millay. **CP-MillE**

Poem as Abstract. Donald Davie. **CP-DavDo**

Poem as Mask, The. Muriel Rukeyser. **CP-RukeM**

Poem as object; communicable; naked, The. Passing the Word. Stephen Dobyns. **SP-DobyS**

Poem as Trajectory, The. Richard Eberhart. **CP-EberR**

Poem at Thirty-nine. Alice Walker. **CP-WalkA**

Poem Beginning "The." Louis Zukofsky. **CP-ZukLS**

Poem Beginning with a Line by Pindar, A. Robert Duncan. **SP-DuncR**

Poem by Garnie Braxton, A. James Wright. **CP-WrigJ**

Poem by the Bridge at Ten-shin, *fr. the Chinese of* Li Po (701-62). Ezra Pound. **SP-PounE**

Poem Circling Hamtramck, Michigan, All Night in Search of You, The. Philip Levine. **SP-LeviP**

Poem for a Birthday. Sylvia Plath. **CP-PlatS**

Poem For a Certain Lady on Her 33rd Birthday, The. Etheridge Knight. **SP-KnigE**

Poem for a Class Re-Union. Robert Louis Stevenson. **CP-StevR**

Poem for a Cold Journey. John Haines. **SP-HainJ**

Poem for a Far Land. John Updike. **CP-UpdiJ**

Poem for a Little Boy on the Buddha's Birthday. Diane Wakoski. **SP-WakoD**

Poem for a Painter Bent on Suicide. Kay Boyle. **CP-BoylK**

Poem for a Painter Who Drinks Wine. Kay Boyle. **CP-BoylK**

Poem for a Poet, A. Audre Lorde.
   ("I think of a coffin's quiet.") **SP-LordA**
   (Poem for a Poet.) **SP-LordA**

Poem for a Poet. Audre Lorde. *See* A Poem for a Poet.

Poem for Arthur, A. Kay Boyle. **CP-BoylK**

Poem for Beginners. Robert Creeley. **CP-CreeR**

Poem for Benn's Graduation from High School, A. John Ciardi. **SP-CiarJ**

Poem for Bhain, A. John Berryman. **SP-BerrJ**

Poem for Black Relocation Centers, A. Etheridge Knight. **SP-KnigE** *Fr.* Two Poems for Black Relocation Centers.

Poem for Bob Leed. Robert Creeley. **CP-CreeR**

Poem for D. H. Lawrence. Robert Creeley. **CP-CreeR**

Poem for Dorothy Dandridge, A. Al Young. **CP-YounA**

Poem for Dylan Thomas, A. Al Young. **CP-YounA**

Poem for Emily, A. Miller Williams. **SP-WillM**

Poem for February First 1975, A. Kay Boyle. **CP-BoylK**

Poem for J. Wendell Berry. **CP-BerrW**

Poem for Jacques Maritain and Leon Trotzky. Delmore Schwartz. **SP-SchwD**

Poem for Kathleen Ferrier. James Wright. **CP-WrigJ**

Poem for Lara, 10. Michael Hartnett. **SP-HarMi**

Poem for Lena Horne, A. Al Young. **CP-YounA**

Poem for Liz. Charles Bukowski. **SP-BukC2**

Poem for May First. Edwin Rolfe. **CP-RolfE**

Poem for Molly's Fortieth Birthday. Erica Jong. **SP-JongE**

Poem for My Father. Charles Tomlinson. **CP-TomlC**

Poem for My 43rd Birthday. Charles Bukowski. **SP-BukC2**

Poem for My Mother. Siv Cedering Fox. **SP-CedeS**

Poem for My Sister Nora, at the Reading. James Liddy. **CP-LiddJ**

Poem for My Wife, A. Gilbert Sorrentino. **SP-SorrG**

Poem for Myself (or Blues for a Mississippi Black Boy), A. Etheridge Knight. **SP-KnigE**

Poem for Norman Macleod, A. William Carlos Williams. **CP-WilW1**

Poem for Old Walt. Lawrence Ferlinghetti. **SP-FerlL**

Poem for Omar Khayyam (1050?-1123? A.D.) Al Young. **CP-YounA**

Poem for Paul Eluard. Charles Henri Ford. **SP-FordC**

Poem for Players, A. Al Young. **CP-YounA**

Poem for Samuel Beckett, A. Kay Boyle. **CP-BoylK**

Poem for Someone Killed in Spain, A. Randall Jarrell. **CP-JarrR**

Poem for the Governments, A. Charles Kenneth Williams. **CP-WillC**

Poem for the Liberation of Southern Africa. Etheridge Knight. **SP-KnigE**

Poem for the Students of Greece, A. Kay Boyle. **CP-BoylK**

Poem for the Teesto Diné of Arizona, A. Kay Boyle. **CP-BoylK**

Poem for the Time of Change. Archibald MacLeish. **CP-MacLA**

Poem for Vida Hadjebi Tabrizi, A. Kay Boyle. **CP-BoylK**

Poem for Willard Motley, A. Al Young. **CP-YounA**

Poem for Women in Rage, A. Audre Lorde. **SP-LordA**

Poem for Zen Hofman. Richard Hugo. **CP-HugoR**

Poem Found Emptying Out My Pockets. Al Young. **CP-YounA**

Poem: "He watched with all his organs of concern." Wystan Hugh Auden. *See* He watched with all his organs of concern.

Poem her belly marched through me as, The. Edward Estlin Cummings. **CP-CummE**

Poem (How I Lost My Pen-Name). Bill Knott. **SP-KnotB**

Poem: How Marvelous Man's Kind Is. Delmore Schwartz. **SP-SchwD**

Poem in Envy of Cavalcanti, A. Frank O'Hara. **SP-OharF**

Poem In January. Frank O'Hara. **SP-OharF**

Poem in May. John Hewitt. **CP-HewiJ**

Poem in October. Dylan Thomas. **CP-ThomD**

Poem in One Sentence, A. Kay Boyle. **CP-BoylK**

Poem in Prose. Louise Bogan. **CP-BogaL**

Poem in Prose. Archibald MacLeish. **CP-MacLA**

Poem in Stretching, A. Robert Duncan. **SP-DuncR**

Poem in the ancient mode for you. When I Wrote a Little. Hayden Carruth. **CP-CarHS**

Poem in the Form of a Letter: to Lauro de Bosis. Kenneth Patchen. **CP-PatcK**

Poem in the Modern Manner. Ted Berrigan. **SP-BerrT** *Fr.* The Sonnets.

Poem in the Rain and the Sun. Thomas Merton. **CP-MertT**

Poem in the Traditional Manner. Ted Berrigan. **SP-BerrT** *Fr.* The Sonnets.

Poem in Three Parts. Robert Bly. **SP-BlyR**

Poem in Translation, A. Tess Gallagher. **SP-GallT**

Poem Influenced By John Davenport and Cervantes. Malcolm Lowry. **CP-LowrM**

Poem Inspired By Auden and Clare's Snail. Malcolm Lowry. **CP-LowrM**

Poem is a dancing: it goes out of a mouth to your ears, A. The Three of Cups. Marge Piercy. *Fr.* Laying Down the Tower. **SP-PierM**

Poem is a Painting, A. Phoebe Hesketh. **SP-HeskP**

Poem is bare-chested, black and, The. Song of the Wrong Response. Stephen Dobyns. **SP-DobyS**

Poem Is By Maera, The. Ernest Hemingway. **CP-HemiE**

Poem is less an orange than a grid, A. Poem as Abstract. Donald Davie. **CP-DavDo**

Poem is this, The. The Poet and His Poems. William Carlos Williams. **CP-WilW2**

Poem Left in Sourdough Mountain Lookout. Gary Snyder. **CP-SnydG**

Poem moves. / After the fierce intention, The. Hayden Carruth. *Fr.* The Sleeping Beauty. **CP-CarHL**

Poem moves forward, A. The Journey of a Poem Compared to All the Sad Variety of Travel. Delmore Schwartz. **SP-SchwD**

Poem moves north, The. Hayden Carruth. *Fr.* The Sleeping Beauty. **CP-CarHL**

Poem must not charm us like a play [*or* film] , The. Against the False Magicians. Thomas McGrath. **SP-McGrT**

Poem must resist the intelligence, The. Man Carrying Thing. Wallace Stevens. **CP-StevW**

Poem: 1939. Thomas Merton. **CP-MertT**

Poem, 1928. Ernest Hemingway. **CP-HemiE**

Poem not a Picture, A. Roy Fisher. **SP-FishR**

Poem of Attrition, A. Etheridge Knight. **SP-KnigE**

Poem of Flight, The. Philip Levine. **SP-LeviP**

Poem of God's Mercy, A. Malcolm Lowry. *Fr.* The Roar of the Sea and the Darkness. **CP-LowrM**

Poem of Gratitude, A. Kay Boyle. **CP-BoylK**

Poem of Love, A. Kay Boyle. **CP-BoylK**

Poem of Margery Kempe, A. Howard Nemerov. **CP-NemeH**

Poem of Night. Galway Kinnell. **SP-KinnG**

Poem of Remembrances for a Girl or a Boy of These States. Walt Whitman. **CP-WhitW**

Poem of Sir Walter Rawleighs, A. Sir Walter Ralegh. **CP-RaleW**

Poem of Thanks, A. Wendell Berry. **CP-BerrW**

Poem of the Forgotten. John Haines. **SP-HainJ**

Poem of the Gold Coin. Frederick Morgan. **SP-MorgF**

Poem of the mind in the act of finding, The. Of Modern Poetry. Wallace Stevens. **CP-StevW**

Poem of the Self. Frederick Morgan. **SP-MorgF**

Poem of Women. Kadya Molodovsky. *See* The Faces of women long dead, of our family.

Poem on America, A. Allen Ginsberg. **CP-GinsA**

Poem on Eloquence by R. W. Emerson. Ralph Waldo Emerson. **CP-EmerR**

Poem on Getting up Early in the Morning (or Even Late in the Morning), When One is Old. Kay Boyle. **CP-BoylK**

Poem On Gold. Malcolm Lowry. **CP-LowrM**

Poem on His Birthday. Dylan Thomas. **CP-ThomD**

Poem on Life. Robert Burns. **CP-BurnR**

Poem on My Son's Birthday. Jim Carroll. **SP-CarrJ**

Poem on the Middle East "Peace Process", A. Etheridge Knight. **SP-KnigE**

Poem on the Neck of a Running Giraffe, A. Shel Silverstein. **SP-SilS2**

Poem, or Beauty Hurts Mr. Vinal. Edward Estlin Cummings. **CP-CummE; SP-CummE**

Poem Out of Childhood. Muriel Rukeyser. **CP-RukeM**

Poem Put into My Lady Laiton's Pocket by Sr W. Rawleigh, A. Sir Walter Ralegh. *See* Lady, farewell, whom[e] I in silence serve.

Poem Read at Joan Mitchell's. Frank O'Hara. **SP-OharF**

Poem Rocket. Allen Ginsberg. **CP-GinsA**

Poem Sent Me by Sir William Burlase, A. Ben Jonson. **CP-JonsB**

Poem should be palpable and mute, A. Ars Poetica. Archibald MacLeish. **CP-MacLA**

Poem so hard it has no heart, A. Why. Richard Eberhart. **CP-EberR**

Poem, Spoken Before the ΦBK Society, August, 1834. Ralph Waldo Emerson. **CP-EmerR**

Poem taken by the New Yorker, A. Snowy Owl. Richard Eberhart. **CP-EberR**

Poem That Took the Place of a Mountain, The. Wallace Stevens. **CP-StevW**

Poem, The: "Arriving at last." Daniel Gerard Hoffman. **SP-HoffD**

Poem, The / is a discipline. The Self. William Carlos Williams. **CP-WilW2**

Poem, The: "It discovers by night." Donald Hall. **CP-HallD**

Poem, The: "It's all in / the sound. A song." William Carlos Williams. **CP-WilW2**

Poem (the Starfish One). Bill Knott. **SP-KnotB**

Poem to a Most Affectionate Lady. Charles Bukowski. **SP-BukC2**

Poem to be Placed at the Conclusion of a Long Obscure Passionate and Eloquent Book of Poems. Malcolm Lowry. **CP-LowrM**

Poem to Be Watched, A. Roy Fisher. **SP-FishR**

Poem: To Brooklyn Bridge. Hart Crane. *See* To Brooklyn Bridge.

Poem To Delight My Friends Who Laugh at Science-Fiction, A. Edwin Rolfe. **CP-RolfE**

Poem to Galway Kinnell, A. Etheridge Knight. **SP-KnigE**

Poem to Johann Sebastian Bach. Delmore Schwartz. **SP-SchwD**

Poem to Mary (Second Poem). Ernest Hemingway. **CP-HemiE**

Poem to Miss Mary. Ernest Hemingway. **CP-HemiE**

Poem to Read in August, A. Gilbert Sorrentino. **SP-SorrG**

Poem to the Memory of Mr. Congreve, A. James Thomson. **CP-ThomJ**

Poem to the Memory of the Righ Honourable the Lord Talbot, A. James Thomson. **CP-ThomJ**

Poem—Unfinished Poem. Thomas McGrath. **SP-McGrT**

Poem upon the Death of His Late Highness the Lord Protector, A. Andrew Marvell. *See* A Poem upon the Death of Oliver Cromwell.

Poem upon the Death of Oliver Cromwell, A. Andrew Marvell.
 (Poem upon the Death of His Late Highness the Lord Protector, A.) **CP-MarvA**
 "I saw him dead, a leaden slumber lyes [*or* lies]." **ChTr; FaBoEH; JCP; OBS**
 (Cromwell Dead.) **ChTr**

Poem upon the page is as massive as, The. Ted Berrigan. **SP-BerrT** *Fr.* The Sonnets.

Poem V (F) W. Frank O'Hara. **SP-OharF**

Poem White Page White Page Poem. Muriel Rukeyser. **CP-RukeM**

Poem:"Who do I want to tell it." Alice Notley. **SP-NotlA**

Poem with Levels of Meaning. Gary Gildner. **SP-GildG**

Poem with No Ending, A. Philip Levine.
 "Across the world / in the high mountains of the West." **SP-LeviP**
 "How many lives were torn apart." **SP-LeviP**
 "I reenter a day in a late summer." **SP-LeviP**
 "Memory of rain falling slowly, The." **SP-LeviP**
 "To get west you go east." **SP-LeviP**
 "We sat by the shore." **SP-LeviP**

Poem With One Fact. Donald Hall. **CP-HallD**

Poem with Orange. Al Young. **CP-YounA**

Poem with Rhythms. Wallace Stevens. **CP-StevW**

Poem with the Answer, A. Sir John Suckling. **CP-SuckJ**
 "Out upon it! I have loved [*or* lov'd]." **BeJo; CBLP; EBEvV; GGP; HeIP; ImPo; NBLV; NOSC; OxAEP-1; PBMP; PeLV; PoE; SeCV-1**
 (Constant Lover, A [*or* The].) **CBLP; GGP; HeIP; ImPo; NOSC; OxAEP-1; PBMP**
 (Sir S.J.) **SeCV-1**
 Sir Toby Matthews. **SeCV-1**

Poem without a Title. Charles Simic. **SP-SimiC**

Poem Written after Reading Certain Poets Sired by the English School and Bitched by the C.P. Kenneth Patchen. **CP-PatcK**

Poem Written at Morning. Wallace Stevens. **CP-StevW**

Poem Written under an Archway in a Discontinued Railroad Station, Fargo, North Dakota, A. James Wright. **CP-WrigJ**

Poema de assumptione b.v.m. Robert Southwell. **CP-SoutR**

Poeme en Forme de la Bouche. Anne Waldman. **SP-WaldA**

Poemless Rhymes for the Times. Charles Olson. **CP-OlsoC**

POEM(or "the divine right of majorities, that illegitimate offspring of the divine right of kings" Homer Lea. Edward Estlin Cummings. **CP-CummE**

Poems. Gary Gildner. **SP-GildG**

Poems about the Moon. Nicholas Vachel Lindsay.
 Euclid. **CP-LindV**
 Yet Gentle Will the Griffin Be. **CP-LindV**

Poems come from incomplete knowledge. With Words. Diane Wakoski. **SP-WakoD**

Poems Composed or Suggested During a Tour, in the Summer of 1833. William Wordsworth. **CP-WorW2**

  Address from the Spirit of Cockermouth Castle.

  "Adieu Rydalian Laurels! that have grown."

  At Bala-Sala, Isle of Man.

  At Sea off the Isle of Man.

  Black Stones of Iona, The.

  By a Retired Mariner (A Friend of the Author).

  By the Sea-Shore, Isle of Man.

  Cave of Staffa ("Thanks for the lessons of this Spot—fit school").

  Cave of Staffa ("We saw, but surely, in the motley crowd"). **VLP**

  Cave of Staffa ("Ye shadowy Beings, that have rights and claims"). **VLP**

  "Desire we past illusions to recall?"

  "Despond who will—*I* heard a voice exclaim."

  Dunlolly Eagle, The.

  Flowers on the Top of the Pillars at the Entrance of the Cave.

  Greenock.

  "Homeward we turn. Isle of Columba's Cell."

  In Sight of the Town of Cockermouth.

  In the Channel, between the Coast of Cumberland and the Isle of Man.

  In the Firth of Clyde, Ailsa Crag.

  Iona ("How sad a welcome! To each voyager").

  Iona ("On to Iona!—What can she afford").

  Isle of Man ("Youth too certain of his power to wade, A").

  Isle of Man ("Youth too certain of his power to wade, A").

  Lowther.

  Mary Queen of Scots.

  Monument Commonly Called Long Meg and Her Daughters, near the River Eden, The.

  Monument of Mrs Howard.

  Most Sweet It Is with Unuplifted Eyes. **EnRP**

  (Inner Vision, The.) **GTBS; GTBS-6; GTBS-P**

  Nunnery.

  Nun's Well, Brigham.

  On Entering Douglas Bay, Isle of Man.

  On Revisiting Dunlolly Castle.

  On the Firth of Clyde.

  River Eden, Cumberland, The.

  Somnambulist, The.

  Stanzas Suggested in a Steamboat off Saint Bees' Head, on the Coast of Cumberland.

  Steamboats, Viaducts and Railways. **NAEL-2; VLP**

  Suggested by the Foregoing [Monument of Mrs Howard].

  " 'There!' said a Stripling, pointing with meet pride."

  "They called Thee MERRY ENGLAND, in old time."

  To a Friend.

  To Cordelia M———.

  To the Earl of Lonsdale.

  To the River Derwent.

  To the River Greta, near Keswick.

  Tynwald Hill.

  "Why should the Enthusiast, journeying through this Isle."

  Written in a Blank Leaf of MacPherson's *Ossian.*

Poems Done on a Late Night Car. Carl Sandburg. **CP-SandC**

Poems Don't Love Us Any More, The. Leonard Cohen. **CP-CoheL**

Poems from Italy. John Ciardi. **SP-CiarJ**

Poems from St. Irvyne, or, The Rosicrucian. Percy Bysshe Shelley. **CP-ShelP**

  Bereavement.

  Drowned Lover, The.

  On the Dark Height of Jura.

  Sister Rosa: A Ballad.

  St. Irvyne's Tower.

  Victoria.

Poems from the Chinese. Alun Lewis. **CP-LewiA**

  Civil Servant, The.

  Country Gentleman, The.

  Merchants Wife, The.

  Mine Host.

  Poet, The.

Poems, like lives, are doing what we can. Esthetic Theories: Art as Expression. Randall Jarrell. **CP-JarrR**

Poems of others he clipped and saved in those distant summers, The. Uses of the Lost Poets. Thomas McGrath. **SP-McGrT**

Poems of Our Climate, The. Wallace Stevens. **CP-StevW**

Poems of the Two Worlds. Frederick Morgan. **SP-MorgF**

  "Beginning is a cold wind, The."

  "Dark one crouching in his cave alone, The."

  "From the Crab's whirl."

  "Komë Berenikes floating."

  "Pêcheur, pêcheur, avez-vous vu."

  "Rose dawn, in smoke, over the East River, A."

Poems, Potatoes. Sylvia Plath. **CP-PlatS**

Poems rise in my brain. Reading French Poetry. Allen Ginsberg. **CP-GinsA**

"Poems", says the title. George Meredith. **CP-MerG2**

Poems should be made out of cedar, axe. Note. Malcolm Lowry. **CP-LowrM**

Poems Speaking of Buddha, Prince Siddartha. Nicholas Vachel Lindsay. **CP-LindV**

  Firemen's Ball, The.

  To Buddha.

  With a Bouquet of Twelve Roses.

Poems to a Brown Cricket. James Wright. **CP-WrigJ**

Poems which are written by the soul. Kenneth Patchen. **CP-PatcK**

Poesie Abrutie. Wallace Stevens. **CP-StevW**

Poesie to Prove Affection is Not Love, A. Sir Walter Ralegh. **CP-RaleW**

Poet, The. Elizabeth Barrett Browning. **CP-BroEB**

Poet, The. Hayden Carruth. **CP-CarHS**

Poet, The. Countee Cullen. **CP-CullC**

Poet, The. Hilda Doolittle. **CP-DoolH**

Poet, The. Paul Laurence Dunbar. **CP-DunbP**

Poet, The. Richard Eberhart. **CP-EberR**

Poet ("Ever the poet *from* the land"). Ralph Waldo Emerson. *Fr.* Quatrains. **CP-EmerR**

Poet ("To clothe the fiery thought"). Ralph Waldo Emerson. **OxBA; OxBSP; PCP; Spl** *Fr.* Quatrains. **CP-EmerR**

Poet, A. Thomas Hardy. **CP-HardT**

Poet, The. John Keats. **CP-KeatJ**

Poet, The. Alun Lewis. *Fr.* Poems from the Chinese. **CP-LewiA**

Poet. Archibald MacLeish. **CP-MacLA**

Poet. Louise McNeill. **SP-McNeL**

Poet, The. Delmore Schwartz. **SP-SchwD**

Poet. Karl Shapiro. **SP-ShapK**

Poet! Stevie Smith. **CP-SmitS**

Poet, The. Walt Whitman. **MoAmPo** *Fr.* By Blue Ontario's Shore. **CP-WhitW**

Poet alone, The / is writing an ode. Ode to My shoes. Erica Jong. **SP-JongE**

Poet and friend of poets, if thy glass. To E. C. S. John Greenleaf Whittier. **CP-WhitJ**

Poet and His Book, The. Edna St. Vincent Millay. **CP-MillE**

Poet and His Poems, The. William Carlos Williams. **CP-WilW2**

Poet and His Song, The. Paul Laurence Dunbar. **CP-DunbP**

Poet and the Baby, The. Paul Laurence Dunbar. **CP-DunbP**

Poet and the Bird, The. Elizabeth Barrett Browning. **CP-BroEB**

Poet and the Caged Turtledove, The. William Wordsworth. **CP-WorW2**

Poet and the Children, The. John Greenleaf Whittier. **CP-WhitJ**

Poet and the World, The. Byron. **SeCePo** *Fr.* Childe Harold's Pilgrimage. **CP-Byron**

Poet Answers the Accuser, The. Kathleen Jessie Raine. **SP-RainK**

Poet appointed dare not decline. Basil Bunting. *Fr.* Briggflatts [An Autobiography]. **CP-BuntB**

"Loaded with mail of linked lies." **FaBoEH**

Poet as Black Sheep, The. Michael Hartnett. *Fr.* Notes on My Contemporaries. **SP-HarMi**

Poet as Eagle Scout, The. Howard Nemerov. **CP-NemeH**

Poet As Equestrian, The. Richard Shelton. **SP-ShelR**

Poet as Fisherman. Lawrence Ferlinghetti. **SP-FerlL**

Poet as Mastercraftsman, The. Michael Hartnett. *Fr.* Notes on My Contemporaries. **SP-HarMi**

Poet at Carpenter's Bench. Diane Wakoski. **SP-WakoD**

Poet at Forty, The. Howard Nemerov. **CP-NemeH**

Poet, be seated at the piano. Mozart, 1935. Wallace Stevens. **CP-StevW**

Poet bred in Saadi's school. Proteus. Ralph Waldo Emerson. **CP-EmerR**

Poet Burns to be Honored, the headline read. My Wife Reads the Paper at Breakfast on the Birthday of the Scottish Poet. Miller Williams. **SP-WillM**

Poet comes with his white pain to save mankind, The. Broken Wing Theory. Richard Eberhart. **CP-EberR**

Poet could not sleep aright, A. A Vision of Poets. Elizabeth Barrett Browning. **CP-BroEB**

Poet Down, The. Michael Hartnett. *Fr.* Notes on My Contemporaries. **SP-HarMi**

Poet Dreams and Resolves, The. Michael Hartnett. *Fr.* Notes on My Contemporaries. **SP-HarMi**

Poet Dreams of a Nice Warm Motel, The. Marge Piercy. **SP-PierM**

Poet Hath Lost His Pipe, The. Robert Herrick. **CP-HerrR**

Poet hath the child's sight in his breast, The. The Poet. Elizabeth Barrett Browning. **CP-BroEB**

Poet!—He Hath Put His Heart to School, A. William Wordsworth. **CP-WorW2**

Poet Hin, The. Stevie Smith. **CP-SmitS**

Poet hunched, so, whom the worlds admire, The. John Berryman. *Fr.* Sonnets to Chris. **CP-BerrJ**

Poet I'm too near your and my sod daily. Catullus. *See* Carmen 35: "Fetch, papyrus / our soft-measured poet."

Poet in his lone yet genial hour, The. Apologia pro Vita Sua. Samuel Taylor Coleridge. **CP-ColeS**

Poet in Residence. Karl Shapiro. **SP-ShapK**

Poet is at home, A. Ralph Waldo Emerson. **CP-EmerR**

Poet is born, A. An Elegy on the Death of Kenneth Patchen. Lawrence Ferlinghetti. **SP-FerlL**

Poet Is Dead, The. William Everson. **SP-EverW**

Poet is of those, The. Kathleen Jessie Raine. **SP-RainK**

Poet is priest. Death to Van Gogh's Ear! Allen Ginsberg. **CP-GinsA**

Poet is the dreamer, The. Loneliness. Al Young. **CP-YounA**

Poet Loves a Mistress, but Not to Marry, The. Robert Herrick. **CP-HerrR**

Poet must rescue etymology from among the footnotes, The. Oppositions. Charles Tomlinson. **CP-TomlC**

Poet named Robert Browning eloped with a poetess named Elizabeth Barrett, A. Old Is for Books. Dorothy Nash. **CP-NashO**

Poet of Ignorance, The. Anne Sexton. **CP-SextA**

Poet of nature, thou hast wept to know. To Wordsworth. Percy Bysshe Shelley. **CP-ShelP**

Poet of nouns has left my attic, The. Message for the Sinecurist. Tess Gallagher. **SP-GallT**

Poet of poets / Is Time, the distiller. Ralph Waldo Emerson. **CP-EmerR**

Poet of the Prison Isle: Ritsos Against the Colonels, The. Thomas McGrath. **SP-McGrT**

Poet, oracle, and wit. Wystan Hugh Auden. *Fr.* The Quest. **CP-AudeW**

Poet Pleads with the Elemental Powers, The. William Butler Yeats. **CP-YeatW**

Poet, poet, what is your task. The Poet. Countee Cullen. **CP-CullC**

Poet Redeemed & Dead. Donald Davie. **CP-DavDo**

Poet Ridiculed by Hysterical Academics, The. William DeWitt Snodgrass. **SP-SnodW**

Poet Shadwell, The. John Dryden. *See* All human[e] things are subject to decay.

Poet, tagged by bourbon, The. Death Drag (The Elegist). John Clellon Holmes. **SP-HolmJ**

Poet, the Oyster, and Sensitive Plant, The. William Cowper. **CP-CowpW**

Poet, thou art dead and damned. Poet! Stevie Smith. **CP-SmitS**

Poet Tires of Those Who Disparage His City, The. Gilbert Sorrentino. **SP-SorrG**

Poet to His Beloved, A. William Butler Yeats. **CP-YeatW**

Poet, to His Book, The. Thomas Merton. **CP-MertT**

Poet to His Grandchild; Sequel to "A Plea for Authors." William Wordsworth. **CP-WorW2**

Poet to His Tongue, The. Peter Meinke. **SP-MeinP**

Poet, to whose mighty heart, The. Matthew Arnold. **EPCY** *Fr.* Resignation. **SP-ArnoM**

Poet, Trying to Surprise God, The. Peter Meinke. **SP-MeinP**

Poet Turned Lawyer, The. John Donne. *See* Satire 2: "Sir: though (I thank God for it) I do hate."

Poet would a-wishing go, A. A-Wishing Well. Robert Frost. **CP-FrosR**

Poet Writes in *I*, The. Erica Jong. **SP-JongE**

Poet wrote a long story with the first name, A. Claims. Louis Zukofsky. **CP-ZukLS**

Poeta Fit, Non Nascitur. "Lewis Carroll." **CP-CarrL**

Poetaster, The. Ben Jonson.
"Blush, folly, blush: here's none that fears." **CP-JonsB**
"If I freely may discover." **CP-JonsB**
"Love is blind, and a wanton." **CP-JonsB**
"Swell me a bowl with lusty wine." **CP-JonsB**
"Wake! Our mirth begins to die." **CP-JonsB**

Poetaster. Theodore Roethke. **CP-RoetT**

Poetic Pains. William Cowper. **FiP; PP** *Fr.* The Time-piece. *Fr.* The Task. **CP-CowpW**

Poetical Abstracts. Hayden Carruth. **CP-CarHS**
Chronological.
Classical.
Introspectional.
Metaphysical.
Rhopaloceral.

Poetical Commandments. Byron. **FiP; OBRV; OxBoLi; PeLV,** *canto* 1, *stanzas* 204–206; *Fr.* Canto the First. **EnRP; NAEL-2; NoP; OAEL-2; PoE** *Fr.* Don Juan. **CP-Byron**
(Poet's Credo.) **SeCePo,** *canto* 1, *stanzas* 204–207;

Poetical Epistle to Dr. Sheridan, A. Jonathan Swift. **CP-SwifJ**

Poetical Epistle to Sir William Bennet, Bart. of Grubbat. James Thomson. **CP-ThomJ**

Poetical Epistles. Samuel Taylor Coleridge. **CP-ColeS**
Silver Thimble, The.
To a Friend, in Answer to a Melancholy Letter.
To the Author of Poems.
Written after a Walk before Supper.
Written at Shurton Bars, near Bridgewater, September 1795, in Answer to a Letter from Bristol.

Poetical Inscription, for an Altar to Independence at Kerrouchtry, the Seat of Mr. Heron, Written in Summer 1795. Robert Burns. **CP-BurnR**

Poetical Numbers. Alexander Pope. *See* But most by numbers judge a poet's song.

Poetical Remains. Archibald MacLeish. **CP-MacLA**

Poetics. Robert Browning. **CP-BroR2**

Poetry. Ernest Hemingway. **CP-HemiE**

Poetry / like a bent ray. After Visiting Arl at the Hospital. Al Young. **CP-YounA**

Poetry. Marianne Craig Moore. **CP-MoorM**
("I, too, dislike it. / Reading it, however, with a perfect contempt for it, one discovers in.") **CP-MoorM**

Poetry. Frank O'Hara. **SP-OharF**

Poetry. Al Young. **CP-YounA**

Poetry, a Natural Thing. Robert Duncan. **SP-DuncR**

Poetry and Games. Richard Eberhart. **CP-EberR**

Poetry and Science. "Hugh MacDiarmid." **SP-MacDH**

Poetry and the Melancholy Man. John Milton. **EPCY** *Fr.* Il Penseroso. **CP-MiltJ**

Poetry As Continuity. Jane Cooper. **SP-CoopJ**

Poetry as salutation; taste. History as Poetry. Geoffrey Hill. **CP-HillG**

Poetry Disarranged. Robert Duncan. **SP-DuncR**

Poetry Ends with Me. Nicanor Parra, *tr. fr. Spanish by* Thomas Merton. **CP-MertT**

Poetry full of *cynghanedd*, and hair-trigger relationships, A. "Hugh MacDiarmid." **SP-MacDH** *Fr.* The Kind of Poetry I Want.

Poetry if / not the. Theory Center. Archie Randolph Ammons. **SP-AmmoA**

Poetry in which all connections will constantly render such services, A. "Hugh MacDiarmid." **SP-MacDH** *Fr.* The Kind of Poetry I Want.

Poetry Is a Destructive Force. Wallace Stevens. **CP-StevW**

Poetry is a projection across silence of cadences arranged to break that silence. Tentative (First Model) Definitions of Poetry. Carl Sandburg. **CP-SandC**

Poetry is dead? So they say. Now They Bury Her Again. Carl Sandburg. **CP-SandC**

Poetry is like fishing. Deep Fishing. Richard Eberhart. **CP-EberR**

Poetry is not instruments. To Gottfried Benn. Frank O'Hara. **SP-OharF**

Poetry is the supreme fiction, madame. A High-Toned Old Christian Woman. Wallace Stevens. **CP-StevW**

Poetry? It's a hobby. What the Chairman Told Tom. Basil Bunting. **CP-BuntB**

Poetry like a lance at rest, A. "Hugh MacDiarmid." **SP-MacDH** *Fr.* Further Passages from The Kind of Poetry I Want.

Poetry like the barrel of a gun, A. "Hugh MacDiarmid." **SP-MacDH** *Fr.* Further Passages from The Kind of Poetry I Want.

Poetry like the character of Indian culture, a. "Hugh MacDiarmid." **SP-MacDH** *Fr.* The Kind of Poetry I Want.

Poetry like the hope of achieving ere very long. "Hugh MacDiarmid." **SP-MacDH** *Fr.* The Kind of Poetry I Want.

Poetry, music, I have loved, and yet. The Spirit Medium. William Butler Yeats. **CP-YeatW**

Poetry of Chaucer, The. George Meredith. **CP-MerG1**

Poetry of Coleridge, The. George Meredith. **CP-MerG1**

Poetry of Departures. Philip Larkin. **CP-LarkP**
Ultimatum. **FL**

Poetry of earth is never dead, The. On the Grasshopper and [the] Cricket. John Keats. **CP-KeatJ**

Poetry of Keats, The. George Meredith. **CP-MerG1**

Poetry of Milton, The. George Meredith. **CP-MerG1**

Poetry of Shakespeare, The. George Meredith. **CP-MerG1**

Poetry of Shelley, The. George Meredith. **CP-MerG1**

Poetry of Southey, The. George Meredith. **CP-MerG1**

Poetry of Spenser, The. George Meredith. **CP-MerG1**

Poetry of such an integration as cannot be effected. "Hugh MacDiarmid." **SP-MacDH** *Fr.* The Kind of Poetry I Want.

Poetry of tragedy is never dead, The. Am I My Neighbor's Keeper. Richard Eberhart. **CP-EberR**

Poetry of Wordsworth, The. George Meredith. **CP-MerG1**

Poetry: I. Adrienne Rich. **SP-RicA1**

Poetry Perpetuates the Poet. Robert Herrick. **CP-HerrR**

Poetry Suit, The. Erica Jong. **SP-JongE**

Poetry that goes all the way, A. "Hugh MacDiarmid." **SP-MacDH** *Fr.* The Kind of Poetry I Want.

Poetry that never for a moment forgets, A. "Hugh MacDiarmid." **SP-MacDH** *Fr.* The Kind of Poetry I Want.

Poetry the quality of which, A. "Hugh MacDiarmid." **SP-MacDH** *Fr.* The Kind of Poetry I Want.

Poetry, the Unpredictable. Diane Wakoski. *Fr.* Fifteen Poems for a Lunar Eclipse None of Us Saw. **SP-WakoD**

Poetry, Then. . . . John Hewitt. **CP-HewiJ**

Poetry: III. Adrienne Rich. **SP-RicA1**

Poetry to the Rescue. Archie Randolph Ammons. **SP-AmmoA**

Poetry, Wadsworth / wrote, will have no. Terminator Too. Tom Clark. **SP-ClarT**

Poetry's a tree. Yes, the Secret Mind Whispers. Al Young. **CP-YounA**

Poets. Kay Boyle. **CP-BoylK**

Poets. Robert Herrick. **CP-HerrR**

Poets! / Madness is a gift. Grace Paley. **CP-PaleG**

Poets, The. Chuck Miller. **SP-MillC**

Poet's age is sad: for why?, The. Prologue. Robert Browning. **CP-BroR2**

Poets, and Painters have some near relation. To the Honorable, Valiant, and Ingenious Colonel Richard Lovelace, on His Exquisite Poems. Francis Lenton. *Fr.* Commendatory Poems. **CP-LoveR**

"Poets are born"—and so are whores—the trade is. John Clare. **SP-ClarJ** *Fr.* Don Juan.

Poets are colorpots. Ralph Waldo Emerson. **CP-EmerR**

Poets are dying because they are told to die, The. Occasional Poem 7.1.72. Roy Fisher. **SP-FishR**

Poets are Godlike in that they. Malcolm Lowry. **CP-LowrM**

Poets are guardians. The Title of Poet. Robert Ranke Graves. **CP-GravR**

Poets Are Silent, The. Stevie Smith. **CP-SmitS**

Poets aren't very useful. Everybody Makes Poets. Ogden Nash. **CP-NashO**

Poets attempt the noblest task they can. In Memory of John Thorton. William Cowper. **CP-CowpW**

Poet's cat, sedate and grave, A. The Retired Cat. William Cowper. **CP-CowpW**

Poets, come out of your closets. *see also* Ferlinghetti, "Sons of Whitman sons of Poe." Lawrence Ferlinghetti. **SP-FerlL**

Poet's Credo. Byron. *See* Poetical Commandments.

Poet's Curse, The. Robert Ranke Graves. **CP-GravR**

Poet's Dream, The. Percy Bysshe Shelley. *See* On a poet's lips I slept.

Poet's Dream, The, *sequel to* The Norman Boy. William Wordsworth. **CP-WorW2**

Poet's Epitaph, A. William Wordsworth. **CP-WorW1**

Poet's eye obscenely seeing, The. Lawrence Ferlinghetti. **SP-FerlL**

Poet's fancy takes from Flora's realm, The. Sent to the Honorable Mistress O'Neill, with Painted Flowers. Charlotte Smith. **CP-SmitC**

Poet's Final Instructions, The. John Berryman. **CP-BerrJ**

Poets, from paupers to well-heeled. Letter to John Fuller. James Fenton. **SP-FentJ**

Poets Good Wishes for the Most Hopefull and Handsome Prince, the Duke of Yorke, The. Robert Herrick. **CP-HerrR**

Poet's hope: to be, A. Shorts II. Wystan Hugh Auden. **CP-AudeW**

Poet's House Preserved as a Museum, The. Leonard Nathan. **SP-NathL**

Poet's Laughter. Archibald MacLeish. **CP-MacLA**

Poet's lie!, A. Wild Boar Clough. Donald Davie. **CP-DavDo**

Poets light but Lamps, The. Emily Dickinson. **CP-DickE**

Poet's Message, The. Roy Fisher. **SP-FishR**

Poets, minor or major, should arrange to remain slender. Poets. Kay Boyle. **CP-BoylK**

Poet's New-Year's Gift, The. William Cowper. **CP-CowpW**

Poets of the Land of Indra write, The. Godhulivela. Hayden Carruth. **CP-CarHS**

Poets pour us wine, The. Epilogue. Robert Browning. **CP-BroR2**

Poet's soul was with me at that time, The. William Wordsworth. **EnRP** *Fr.* Cambridge and the Alps. *Fr.* The Prelude; Growth of a Poet's Mind [1850 vers.]. **CP-WorW3**

Poet's Tale: The Birds of Killingworth, The. Henry Wadsworth Longfellow. *See* Birds of Killingworth, The (The Poet's Tale).

Poets tell us of an age of unalloyed felicity, The. The Golden Age. Wystan Hugh Auden. **CP-AudeW** *Fr.* Man of La Mancha.

Poet's Thoughts, A. Thomas Hardy. **CP-HardT**

Poets to Come. Walt Whitman. **CP-WhitW**

Poet's Trade, The. John Hewitt. **CP-HewiJ**

Poet's Vow, The. Elizabeth Barrett Browning. **CP-BroEB**

Poet's Welcome to His Love-Begotten Daughter [the First Instance that Entitled Him to the Venerable Appellation of Father], A. Robert Burns. **CP-BurnR**

Poets with whom I'd learned my trade. The Grey Rock. William Butler Yeats. **CP-YeatW**

Poets yeggs and thirsties. Edward Estlin Cummings. **CP-CummE**

Poets, your subjects, have their parts assigned. Prologue to the University of Oxford, 1674. John Dryden. **SP-DrydJ**

Poignance of a quarrel in the post!, The. A Quarrel. Malcolm Lowry. **CP-LowrM**

Point, The. Hayden Carruth. **CP-CarHS**

Point, The. Robert Earl Hayden. **CP-HaydR**

Point, The. Charles Simic. **SP-SimiC**

Point at Issue, The. William Wordsworth. *Fr.* Ecclesiastical Sonnets. **CP-WorW2**

"Point is Fixed. . . , A." Tom Clark. **SP-ClarT**

Point is (maybe) that the woman's face was *made*, The. Hayden Carruth. *Fr.* The Sleeping Beauty. **CP-CarHL**

Point Joe. Robinson Jeffers. **CP-JefR1**

Point No Point. Richard Hugo. **CP-HugoR**

Point of Age, A. John Berryman. **CP-BerrJ**

Point of life between my Parents' dust, A. In Sight of the Town of Cockermouth. William Wordsworth. *Fr.* Poems Composed or Suggested During a Tour, in the Summer of 1833. **CP-WorW2**

Point of No Return. Robert Ranke Graves. **CP-GravR**

Point of Taste, The. George Meredith. **CP-MerG1**

Point of View. Richard Shelton. **SP-ShelR**

Point of View. Shel Silverstein. **SP-SilS2**

Point Pinos and Point Lobos. Robinson Jeffers. **CP-JefR1**

Point-pushed by the wind, rain. Richard Eberhart. *Fr.* Four Lakes' Days. **CP-EberR**

Point Reyes. Gary Snyder. **CP-SnydG**

Point Shirley. Sylvia Plath. **CP-PlatS**

Poised for the leap she. 3 Stances. William Carlos Williams. **CP-WilW2**

Poised impossibly on the high tight-rope. Acrobats. Robert Ranke Graves. **CP-GravR**

Poised upside down on its duncecap. In the Cold Kingdom. Mona Van Duyn. **SP-VanDM**

Poison. David Herbert Lawrence. **CP-LawrD**

Poison, The. James Liddy. **CP-LiddJ**

Poison of Asps. Rudyard Kipling. **CP-KiplR**

Poison Tree, A. William Blake. **CP-BlakW** *Fr.* Songs of Experience. (Christian Forbearance.) **CP-BlakW**

"I was angry with my friend." **OBF**

Poisoned Air Befouled the Whole Decade, The. Edwin Rolfe. **CP-RolfE**

Poisoned Day. Robert Ranke Graves. **CP-GravR**

Poisoned in Nassau. John Updike. **CP-UpdiJ**

Poisoned Man, The. James Dickey. **CP-DickJ**

Poland, France, Judea ran in her veins. An Electric Sign Goes Dark. Carl Sandburg. **CP-SandC**

Polar Bear, The. William Carlos Williams. **CP-WilW2**

Polar Exploration. Stephen Spender. **CP-SpenS**

Polar ice-caps are melting, the mountain glaciers, The. Robinson Jeffers. **CP-JefR3**

Pole Star. Archibald MacLeish. *See* Where the wheel of light is turned.

Police are probing tonight for the bodies, The. Miners. James Wright. **CP-WrigJ**

Police dog eating grass, A. The Variant. Charles Simic. **SP-SimiC**

Police Spies. David Herbert Lawrence. **CP-LawrD**

Policeman buys shoes slow and careful, the. Psalm of Those Who Go Forth before Daylight. Carl Sandburg. **CP-SandC**

Policeman in front of a bank 3A.M.. . . lonely. Stripes. Carl Sandburg. **CP-SandC**

Polish girls singing, in the wind's soughing. Alun Lewis. *Fr.* Threnody for a Starry Night. **CP-LewiA**

Polish Rider, The. Derek Walcott. **CP-WalcD**

Polish'd with endless toil, my lays. Publius Papinius Statius, *tr.* by Samuel Johnson. **CP-JohnS** *Fr.* Sylvae.

Politely like Snakes in the Oats. Richard Hugo. **CP-HugoR**

Political passion is the poorest coin. An Irish Bull. James McAuley. **SP-McAuJ**

Political Prisoner 123456789. Edwin Rolfe. **CP-RolfE**

Political Reflection. Ogden Nash. **CP-NashO**

Political Reflexion [*or* Reflection]. Howard Nemerov. **ELU** *Fr.* Epigrams: "Wasp, climbing the window pane." **CP-NemeH**

    (Epigram: Political Reflexion.) **NIP**

    (Sparrow in the Zoo, The.) **MoP**

Political Song for the Year's End. Thomas McGrath. **SP-McGrT**

Politician is an arse upon, A. A . Edward Estlin Cummings. **CP-CummE; SP-CummE**

Politics. Ralph Waldo Emerson. **CP-EmerR**

Politics. Charles Kenneth Williams. **SP-WillC**

Politics. William Butler Yeats. **CP-YeatW**

Politics As History. Al Young. **CP-YounA**

Politics of This Book, The. Leonard Cohen. **CP-CoheL**

Pollen / fly makes, A. Hype. Archie Randolph Ammons. **SP-AmmoA**

Pollen. Brendan Galvin. **SP-GalvB**

Pollicie in Princes. Robert Herrick. **CP-HerrR**

Pollie. Walter de la Mare. **CP-DeLaW**

Polluted tide, / Desecrated earth destroyed. Kathleen Jessie Raine. **SP-RainK**

Polly—An Almost-True Story. Kenneth Patchen. **CP-PatcK**

Polly had a kind of electric beauty—it flashed out of her eye and. Polly—An Almost-True Story. Kenneth Patchen. **CP-PatcK**

Polly Red Top Thermos is with us. With Frank and George at Lexington. James Schuyler. **CP-SchuJ**

Polly's Tree. Sylvia Plath. **CP-PlatS**

Polonius. Walter de la Mare. **CP-DeLaW**

Polonius Passing Through a Stage. Howard Nemerov. **CP-NemeH**

Polterguest, My Polterguest. Ogden Nash. **CP-NashO**

Polyglot, albeit illiterate. Louis MacNeice. *Fr.* As In Their Time. **CP-MacNL**

Polyphiloprogenitive / The sapient sutlers of the Lord. Mr. Eliot's Sunday Morning Service. Thomas Stearns Eliot. **CP-ElioT**

Polythene Pam. The Beatles. **CP-Beatl**

Pomade. Rita Dove. **SP-DoveR**

Pomander Bracelet, The. Robert Herrick. **CP-HerrR**

Pomegranate. Louise Glück. **SP-GlücL**

Pomegranate. David Herbert Lawrence. **CP-LawrD**

Pomegranates. Siv Cedering Fox. **SP-CedeS**

Pomme arac. Derek Walcott. **FaBoVe** *Fr.* Sainte Lucie. **CP-WalcD**

Pompeii. John Updike. **CP-UpdiJ**

Ponce de León: A Morning Walk. Al Young. **CP-YounA**

Pond, The. Louise Glück. **SP-GlücL**

Pond, The. Edna St. Vincent Millay. **CP-MillE**

Pond, The. Howard Nemerov. **CP-NemeH**

Ponder, darling, these busted statues. Edward Estlin Cummings. **CP-CummE**

Ponder my words, if so that any be. An Request to the Graces. Robert Herrick. **CP-HerrR**

Ponds, The. Mary Oliver. **SP-OlivM**

Pondy Woods. Robert Penn Warren. **SP-WarrR**

Ponte dell' Angelo, Venice. Robert Browning. **CP-BroR2**

Ponte Veneziano. Charles Tomlinson. **CP-TomlC**

Ponti profundis clausa recessibus. Skia, An Ode on the Isle of Skye. Samuel Johnson. **CP-JohnS**

Pontiac. Donald Davie. **CP-DavDo**

Pontoosuce. Herman Melville. **SP-MelvH**

Pontormo there, for anatomic truth. History and Theory of Art. David Markson. **CP-MarkD**

Pony Rock. Archibald MacLeish. **CP-MacLA**

Poobahs rise and hold their poobah sway, The. Carl Sandburg. *Fr.* The People, Yes. **CP-SandC**

Pooem. John Updike. **CP-UpdiJ**

Pool, The. Robert Creeley. **CP-CreeR**

Pool, The. Hilda Doolittle. **CP-DoolH**

Pool, The. Paul Laurence Dunbar. **CP-DunbP**

Pool. Carl Sandburg. **CP-SandC**

Pool at the Y. James McAuley. **SP-McAuJ**

Pool of Bethesda. Carl Sandburg. **CP-SandC**

Pools where it offers to our curiosity, The. James Liddy. *Fr.* Shore. **CP-LiddJ**

Pools where it offers to our curiosity, The. Shore. James Liddy. **CP-LiddJ**

Poolville, N.Y. Charles Tomlinson. **CP-TomlC**

Poor, The. William Carlos Williams. **CP-WilW1**

Poor, The. William Carlos Williams. **CP-WilW1**

Poor and desperate men. Revisionist Poem: Machado. Thomas McGrath. **SP-McGrT**

Poor and inadequate the shadow-play. At Eventide. John Greenleaf Whittier. **CP-WhitJ**

Poor and Their Dwellings, The. George Crabbe. **SP-CrabG** *Fr.* The Borough.

Poor Angus. Shel Silverstein. **SP-SilS2**

Poor Bejamin Bunnn / From Wilmington. Benjamin Bunnn. Shel Silverstein. **SP-SilS2**

Poor Bit of a Wench! David Herbert Lawrence. **CP-LawrD**

Poor Boy Blues. "Bob Dylan." **CP-DylaB**

Poor But TerFLY / went(flesh is grass). Edward Estlin Cummings. **CP-CummE**

Poor Butterfly that stamped. Malcolm Lowry. **CP-LowrM**

Poor Child with the Hooked Hands, The. Kenneth Patchen. **CP-PatcK**

Poor child, you were kissed so much you thought you were walked on;. Robert Lowell. **SP-LoweR** *Fr.* Mexico.

Poor church / but an obstinate devotion, A. In Michoacán. Charles Tomlinson. **CP-TomlC**

Poor damned Catullus, here's no time for nonsense. Catullus. *See* Carmen 8: "Break off / fallen Catullus."

Poor dying thing; it was my dog, not I. To a Snake. Edna St. Vincent Millay. **CP-MillE**

Poor floating isle, tossed on ill fortune's waves. *see also* William Ewart Gkladstone's "Oh ship! new billows sweep thee out." Jonathan Swift. **CP-SwifJ**

Poor flowers in geometric beds. Fernando Pessoa. *Fr.* Twelve Poems from *The Keeper of the Flocks.* **CP-MertT**

Poor Ghost, The. Christina Georgina Rossetti. **CP-RosC1**

Poor Girl. Maya Angelou. **SP-AngeM**

Poor Gorrel. Kenneth Patchen. **CP-PatcK**

Poor heart, lament. The Method. George Herbert. **CP-HerbG**

Poor Honest Men. Rudyard Kipling. **CP-KiplR**

Poor Hope. Charles Kenneth Williams. **CP-WillC**

Poor human race that must. So to Fatness Come. Stevie Smith. **CP-SmitS**

Poor in my youth, and in life's later scenes. On Late-acquired Wealth *or* Riches. *Unknown, tr. fr. Greek by* William Cowper. **CP-CowpW**

Poor john, who joined in make of wrong. Welcome the Wrath. Stanley Jasspon Kunitz. **CP-KuniS**

Poor Julia's heart was in an awkward state. Byron. **NOBRP** *Fr.* Canto the First. **EnRP; NAEL-2; NoP; OAEL-2; PoE** *Fr.* Don Juan. **CP-Byron**

Poor ladies! Though their business be to play. The Hardship Put upon Ladies. Jonathan Swift. **CP-SwifJ**

Poor little book, *The Sleeping Beauty* died. Sonnet. Hayden Carruth. **CP-CarHS** *Fr.* Sonnets.

Poor little Foal of an oppressed Race! To a Young Ass. Samuel Taylor Coleridge. **EnRP; OBEC; OxAEP-2** *Fr.* Effusions. **CP-ColeS**

Poor little Heart! Emily Dickinson. **CP-DickE**

Poor Mailie's Elegy. Robert Burns. **CP-BurnR**

Poor Man and a Lady, A. Thomas Hardy. **CP-HardT**

Poor man weeps—here G———N sleeps, The. For G. H. Esq. Robert Burns. **CP-BurnR**

Poor man went to the rich man's doors, The. Precedent. Paul Laurence Dunbar. **CP-DunbP**

Poor melancholy bird—that all night long. To a Nightingale. Charlotte Smith. **CP-SmitC**

Poor Merry-andrew, in the [*or* a] neuk. Robert Burns. **OBCoV** *Fr.* The Jolly Beggars.

Poor Mr. Strawbridge. Ogden Nash. **CP-NashO**

Poor mother, my martyr. Mother. Ussin Kerim, *tr. fr. Bulgarian by* William Matthews. **SP-MattW**

Poor Myrtle would sigh, "Sweet my Coz." Goo Girl. Theodore Roethke. **CP-RoetT**

Poor nation, whose sweet sap and juice. The Jews. George Herbert. **CP-HerbG**

Poor noble Ghost that comes from place of pain. King Hamlet's Ghost. Stevie Smith. **CP-SmitS**

Poor old Abner, poor old white-haired nigger! Time the Hangman. William Carlos Williams. **CP-WilW1**

Poor Others. Robert Ranke Graves. **CP-GravR**

Poor parched man, we had to squeeze. Words for Some Ash. Thom Gunn. **CP-GunnT**

Poor Poet-Ape, that would be thought our chief. On Poet-Ape. Ben Jonson. **CP-JonsB**

Poor procurator, why do you ask someone else. Reply to Papini. Wallace Stevens. **CP-StevW**

Poor Relation, The. Edwin Arlington Robinson. **CP-RobiE**

Poor Robin. William Wordsworth. **CP-WorW2**

Poor Sam's a cold in Montparnasse. Vir. James Liddy. *Fr.* Vir I–XII. **CP-LiddJ**

Poor Sam's a cold in Montparnasse. Vir V. James Liddy. *Fr.* Vir I–XII. **CP-LiddJ**

Poor savages / Of ghost and glitter. Merely rolling now. The Mayan Ground. George Oppen. **CP-OppeG**

Poor sheepish plaything. For Sale. Robert Lowell. **SP-LoweR**

Poor Sherry, inglorious. Sheridan's Submission. Jonathan Swift. **CP-SwifJ**

Poor silly soul, whose hope and head lies low. Vanity (2). George Herbert. **CP-HerbG**

Poor soul, in this thy flesh what dost thou know? John Donne. **OAEL-1** *Fr.* The Second Anniversary [*or* Anniversarie]. **ESCV; SeCP** *Fr.* Of the Progres[se] of the Soule; the Second Anniversarie. **CP-DonnJ**

("Poore soule, in this thy flesh what dost thou know?") **OBS**

(Soules Ignorance in This Life and Knowledge in the Next, The.) **OBS**

("We see in authors, too stiff to recant.") **NOSC**, *ll.* 281–300;

Poor Soul, Poor Girl! Stevie Smith. **CP-SmitS**

Poor soul! Softy, whisperer. Basil Bunting, *after the Latin of* the Emperor Hadrian. **CP-BuntB**

Poor[e] soul[e], the centre of my sinful[l] earth. Sonnet 146. William Shakespeare. **AWP; BiP; CABA; EaLo; EiL; EnRePo; FaBoEn; GTBS; GTBS-6; GTBS-P; GoBC; HAP; HBV; HeIP; ImPo; InPS; LiTB; MasP; NAEL-1; NIP; NOBE; NOCV; NoP; OAEL-1; OBEV; OBSC; OXAEP-1; OxBoCh; PPP; PPoe; PoE; PoEL-2; SCGP; SeCeV; Son; TFi; TrGrPo; WHA** *Fr.* Sonnets. **CP-ShaWS**

Poor talker mouthperson. In France. Grace Paley. **CP-PaleG**

Poor the pleasure / Doled out by measure. Memento Mori. Christina Georgina Rossetti. **CP-RosC2**

Poor things! we know not what they suffer. George Meredith. *Fr.* Fragments for "The Harvest Home" and "The Doe." **CP-MerG2**

Poor Tom, wilt thou never accept a defiance. Swift to Sheridan. Jonathan Swift. **CP-SwifJ**

Poor torn heart, a tattered heart, A. Emily Dickinson. **CP-DickE**

Poor twisted lady, what can the world seem like. Lady. Jenny Joseph. *Fr.* Derivations. **CP-JoseJ**

Poor Vestris, griev'd beyond all measure. A Card. William Cowper. **CP-CowpW**

Poor Voter on Election Day, The. John Greenleaf Whittier. **CP-WhitJ**

"Poor wanderer," said the leaden sky. The Subalterns. Thomas Hardy. **CP-HardT**

Poor Washed Up by Chicago Winter, The. James Wright. **CP-WrigJ**

Poor Withered Rose. Paul Laurence Dunbar. **CP-DunbP**

Poor Young Things. David Herbert Lawrence. **CP-LawrD**

Poore eyes bee blind, the light behold noe more. Sonnet 25. Mary Sidney, Countess of Montgomery Wroth. *Fr.* Pamphilia to Amphilanthus. **CP-WrotM**

Poore Love in chaines, and fetters like a thiefe. Sonnet 8. Mary Sidney, Countess of Montgomery Wroth. *Fr.* Pamphilia to Amphilanthus. **CP-WrotM**

Poore Mans Part, The. Robert Herrick. **CP-HerrR**

Poore soule, in this thy flesh what dost thou know? John Donne. *See* Poor soul, in this thy flesh what dost thou know?

Poore widwe [*or* widow], somdeel [*or* somedeal] stape in age, A. Geoffrey Chaucer. *See* The Nun's Priest's Tale.

Poores Portion, The. Robert Herrick. **CP-HerrR**

Pooters walked to Watney Lodge, The. Thoughts on "The Diary of a Nobody." Sir John Betjeman. **CP-BetjJ**

Pop Smash, Out of Echo Chamber. John Updike. **CP-UpdiJ**

Popcorn peanuts clams and gum. Bar-Room Matins. Louis MacNeice. **CP-MacNL**

Pope and the Net, The. Robert Browning. **CP-BroR2**

Pope has the talent well to speak. Dr. Swift to Mr. Pope. Jonathan Swift. **CP-SwifJ**

Pope he was saying the high, high mass. The Gray Brother. Sir Walter Scott. **SP-ScotW**

Pope of Rome he could not win, The. APRIL (*Rowing*). Rudyard Kipling. *Fr.* Verses on Games. **CP-KiplR**

Pope on Christmas Day, The. Christmas Gifts. Elizabeth Barrett Browning. **CP-BroEB**

Popish Plot, The. John Dryden. **ACP** *Fr.* Absalom and Achitophel, Pt. I. **SP-DrydJ**

Poplar, absolute danseuse. Poplar, Sycamore. Richard Wilbur. **CP-WilbR**

Poplar and Elm. Carl Sandburg. **CP-SandC**

Poplar Field, The. William Cowper. **CP-CowpW**

Poplar, Sycamore. Richard Wilbur. **CP-WilbR**

Poplar tree under the stars, A. Stems. Denise Levertov. **CP-LeveD**

Poplars, The. Roy Fisher. *Fr.* City. **SP-FishR**

Poplars are felled [*or* fell'd], farewell to the shade, The. The Poplar Field. William Cowper. **CP-CowpW**

Popovich our guide is old and roads he knew. Spinning the Sava. Richard Hugo. **CP-HugoR**

Poppies. Mary Oliver. **SP-OlivM**

Poppies. Carl Sandburg. **CP-SandC**

Poppies in July. Sylvia Plath. **CP-PlatS**

Poppies in October. Sylvia Plath. **CP-PlatS**

Poppies of the Red Year. John Gould Fletcher. **SP-FletJ**

Poppy Anemone. Louis Zukofsky. **CP-ZukLS**

Poppy is a wound, the poppy is the mouth, The. Remembrance Day. Ted Hughes. *Fr.* Out. **SP-HughT**

Popular Demand. James Merrill. *Fr.* Topics. **SP-MerrJ**

Popular Heart is a Cannon first, The. Emily Dickinson. **CP-DickE**

Popular Personage at Home, A. Thomas Hardy. **CP-HardT**

Popular Revivals 1956. John Updike. **CP-UpdiJ**

Popular Songs. John Ashbery. **SP-AshbJ**

Popularity. Robert Browning. **SP-BroR1**

Population. George Oppen. **CP-OppeG**

Population Drifts. Carl Sandburg. **CP-SandC**

Population Explosion. Archibald MacLeish. **CP-MacLA**

Populist Manifesto, *see also* Ferlinghetti, "Sons of Whitman sons of Poe." Lawrence Ferlinghetti. **SP-FerlL**

Porcelain Bowl. Louise Glück. **SP-GlücL**

Porch, The. Gary Gildner. **SP-GildG**

Porch over the River, The. Wendell Berry. **CP-BerrW**

Porco la zucca / Fitta in parrucca! Christina Georgina Rossetti. **CP-RosC3**

Porcupine, The. Galway Kinnell. **SP-KinnG**

Porcupine, The. Ogden Nash. **CP-NashO**

Porcupine. Anne Sexton. **CP-SextA**

Porcupine Meditation. Margaret Atwood. **SP-AtwM2**

Porcupine skin, A. Along with Youth. Ernest Hemingway. **CP-HemiE**

Porcupine Tree. Margaret Atwood. **SP-AtwM2**

Porec. Donald Davie. **CP-DavDo**

Poring over calendars is apt to give people round shoulders. There Are More Ways to Roast a Pig than Burning the House Down or You Can Always Stick Your Head in a Volcano. Ogden Nash. **CP-NashO**

Porky & porkie. Edward Estlin Cummings. **CP-CummE**

Porky and Socration, two-eye sins as try. Catullus. *See* Carmen 47: "Lucius Calpurnius Piso Caesoninus."

Pornographic Poem. Marilyn Hacker. **SP-HackM**

Porous. William Carlos Williams. **CP-WilW1**

Porphyria's Lover. Robert Browning. **CP-BroR1**

Porphyro in Akron. Hart Crane. **CP-CranH**

Porpoise, The. Ogden Nash. **CP-NashO**

Porpoise was grandma. The Mohawk was doctor, The. Being My Notion, as a Ferocious Small-Boy, of My Ancestral Protector. Nicholas Vachel Lindsay. *Fr.* Doctor Mohawk. **CP-LindV**

Port Bou. Stephen Spender. **CP-SpenS**

Port Caradoc. Frederick Morgan. **SP-MorgF**

Port has a sweeter name than Saigon, The. Malcolm Lowry. **CP-LowrM**

Port Moody. Malcolm Lowry. **CP-LowrM**

Port of Call: Brazil. Alun Lewis. **CP-LewiA**

Port of Embarkation. Randall Jarrell. **CP-JarrR**

Port of Peace has many Coves, The. Emily Dickinson. **SP-DickE**

Port Town. Langston Hughes. **SP-HughL**

Port Townsend. Richard Hugo. **CP-HugoR**

Port Townsend, 1974. Richard Hugo. **CP-HugoR**

Portal as of shadowy adamant, A. An Allegory. Percy Bysshe Shelley. **CP-ShelP**

Portals. Walt Whitman. **CP-WhitW**

Portcullis, The. Roy Fisher. **SP-FishR** *Fr.* Inscriptions for Bluebeard's Castle.

Portent, The, *after* Horace Book 5, Ode 20. Rudyard Kipling. **CP-KiplR** *Fr.* Debits and Credits.

Portent, The. Herman Melville. **SP-MelvH**

Portent. William Carlos Williams. **CP-WilW1**

Portentous change when History can appear. In Allusion to Various Recent Histories and Notices of the French Revolution. William Wordsworth. **CP-WorW2**

Portents. Thomas McGrath. **SP-McGrT**

Porter. Langston Hughes. **SP-HughL**

Portion of this yew. Transformations. Thomas Hardy. **CP-HardT**

Portions of Manslayer. Charles Kenneth Williams. **CP-WillC**

Portland. Donald Davie. **CP-DavDo**

Portland Coliseum. Allen Ginsberg. **CP-GinsA**

Portland, 1968. Louise Glück. **SP-GlücL**

"Portly & middleaged" can never. Malcolm Lowry. **CP-LowrM**

Portobello Carnival 1973. Charles Tomlinson. **CP-TomlC**

Portrait. Wystan Hugh Auden. **CP-AudWJ**

Portrait. Louise Bogan. **CP-BogaL**

Portrait, A. Elizabeth Barrett Browning. **CP-BroEB**

Portrait, A. Walter de la Mare. **CP-DeLaW**

Portrait, The. John Gould Fletcher. **CP-FletJ**

Portrait. Louise Glück. **SP-GlücL**

Portrait, The. Robert Ranke Graves. **CP-GravR**

Portrait, The. John Hewitt. **CP-HewiJ**

Portrait, The. Stanley Jasspon Kunitz. **CP-KuniS**

Portrait. Philip Larkin. **CP-LarkP**

Portrait, The. William Matthews. **SP-MattW**

Portrait. Edna St. Vincent Millay. **CP-MillE**

Portrait, A. Christina Georgina Rossetti. **CP-RosC1**

Portrait. Carl Sandburg. **CP-SandC**

Portrait, A. Robert Louis Stevenson. **CP-StevR**

Portrait by a Neighbour. Edna St. Vincent Millay. **CP-MillE**

Portrait by Holbein. May Sarton. **SP-SartM**

Portrait d'une Femme. Ezra Pound. **SP-PounE**

Portrait from the Life, A. Jonathan Swift. **CP-SwifJ**

Portrait in Greys, A. William Carlos Williams. **CP-WilW1**

Portrait in Stone. Charles Tomlinson. **CP-TomlC**

Portrait of a Child Settling Down for an Afternoon Nap. Carl Sandburg. **CP-SandC**

Portrait of a Death. Edwin Rolfe. **CP-RolfE**

Portrait of a Girl. Leonard Cohen. **CP-CoheL**

Portrait of a Lady. Thomas Stearns Eliot. **CP-ElioT**

Portrait of a Lady. Ernest Hemingway. **CP-HemiE**

Portrait of a Lady. William Carlos Williams. **CP-WilW1**

Portrait of a Man, with a Background of Holdings. Muriel Rukeyser. **CP-RukeM**

Portrait of a Motorcar. Carl Sandburg. **CP-SandC**

Portrait of a Woman at Her Bath. William Carlos Williams. **CP-WilW2**

Portrait of a Woman in Bed. William Carlos Williams. **CP-WilW1**

Portrait of a Young Man with a Bad Heart. William Carlos Williams. **CP-WilW1**

Portrait of an Old Woman on the College Tavern Wall. Anne Sexton. **CP-SextA**

Portrait of Mary. Etheridge Knight. **SP-KnigE**

Portrait of Mrs. Spaxton. Charles Tomlinson. **CP-TomlC**

Portrait of my mother, The. The Virtuoso. Stevie Smith. **CP-SmitS**

Portrait of Rilke. Richard Eberhart. **CP-EberR**

Portrait of the Artist, A. Derek Mahon. **SP-MahoD**

Portrait of the Artist as a Farmyard Fowl. Donald Davie. *Fr.* A Dissentient Voice. **CP-DavDo**

Portrait of the Artist as a Prematurely Old Man. Ogden Nash. **CP-NashO**

Portrait of the Artist as an Interior Decorator. Kenneth Patchen. **CP-PatcK**

Portrait of the Artist I. Charles Tomlinson. **CP-TomlC**

Portrait of the Artist II. Charles Tomlinson. **CP-TomlC**

Portrait of the Artist with Hart Crane. Charles Wright. **SP-WrigC**

Portrait of the Artist with Li Po. Charles Wright. **SP-WrigC**

Portrait of the Author. William Carlos Williams. **CP-WilW1**

Portrait of the Queen in Tears. Louise Glück. **SP-GlücL**

Portrait of the Times, A. William Carlos Williams. **CP-WilW2**

Portrait of Three Conspirators. Howard Nemerov. **CP-NemeH**

Portrait on an American Theme. Kenneth Patchen. **CP-PatcK**

Portrait (I). Stevie Smith. **CP-SmitS**

Portrait (II). Stevie Smith. **CP-SmitS**

Portraits. David Herbert Lawrence. **CP-LawrD**

Portraits. Christina Georgina Rossetti. **CP-RosC3**

Portraits are to daily faces. Emily Dickinson. **CP-DickE**

Portraits on the Walls. John Hewitt. **CP-HewiJ**

Ports of death are sins; of life, good deeds, The. Of Life and Death. Ben Jonson. **CP-JonsB**

Portstewart, 1914. John Hewitt. **CP-HewiJ**

Portstewart, July 1914. John Hewitt. **CP-HewiJ**

Poseidon's Law. Rudyard Kipling. **CP-KiplR**

Poses like a young man. The Age of War. Richard Shelton. *Fr.* The Seven Ages of Man. **SP-ShelR**

Posie, The. Robert Burns. **CP-BurnR**

Posies from a Second Childhood, or, Hark How Gaffer Do Chaffer. Ogden Nash. **CP-NashO**

  Absentees, The.

  Boy's Will is the Wind's Will?, A.

  Daddy's Home, See You Tomorrow.

Position in the Hebrew Divinity, A. Robert Herrick. **CP-HerrR**

Position is where you. The Window. Robert Creeley. **CP-CreeR**

Position without a Magnitude. Charles Simic. **SP-SimiC**

Positively 4th Street. "Bob Dylan." **CP-DylaB**

Possesions. Robert Herrick. **CP-HerrR**

Possessed, The. John Berryman. **CP-BerrJ**

Possessed. Robert Ranke Graves. **CP-GravR**

Possession. Paul Laurence Dunbar. **CP-DunbP**

Possession. Daniel Gerard Hoffman. **SP-HoffD**

Possessions. Hart Crane. **CP-CranH**

Possessions. Pablo Neruda, *tr. fr. Spanish by* Ben Belitt. **SP-NeruP**

Possessions Are Nine Points of Conversation. Ogden Nash. **CP-NashO**

Possibil non sarebbe. Oggi. Christina Georgina Rossetti. *Fr.* Il Rosseggiar Dell'Oriente Canzoniere. **CP-RosC3**

Possibilities. Rudyard Kipling. **CP-KiplR**

Possible / To use. George Oppen. *Fr.* A Language of New York. **CP-OppeG**

Possibles we dare!, The. Love's Progress. Theodore Roethke. **CP-RoetT**

Possibly. Robert Ranke Graves. **CP-GravR**

Possibly because she's striking—tall, well dressed, very clear, pure skin. Hooks. Charles Kenneth Williams. **SP-WillC**

Possibly is not a monosyllable. Possibly. Robert Ranke Graves. **CP-GravR**

Possibly thrice we glimpsed. Edward Estlin Cummings. **CP-CummE**

Possum. Paul Laurence Dunbar. **CP-DunbP**

Possum Trot. Paul Laurence Dunbar. **CP-DunbP**

Possum's a greasy critter, The. Roast Possum. Rita Dove. **SP-DoveR**

Post-Boy, The. William Cowper. *See* Arrival of the Mail.

Post-boy drove with fierce career, The. Alice Fell; or, Poverty. William Wordsworth. **CP-WorW1**

Post Cards. Robert Creeley. **CP-CreeR**

Post-historic herbivore, A. On the Inclusion of Miniature Dinosaurs in Breakfast Cereal Boxes. John Updike. **CP-UpdiJ**

Post Imperial. Steve Griffiths. **SP-GrifS**

Post-Impressionist Susurration for the First of November, 1983, A. Hayden Carruth. **CP-CarHS**

Post-Modernism. Jim Carroll. **SP-CarrJ**

Post Mortem. Robinson Jeffers. **CP-JefR1**

Post Mortem. William Shakespeare. *See* Sonnet 32: "If thou survive my well-contented day."

Post-Script: for Gweno. Alun Lewis. **CP-LewiA**

Post That Fitted, The. Rudyard Kipling. **CP-KiplR**

("Though tangled and twisted the course of true love.") **CP-KiplR**

Post the Lake Poets Ballad. Frank O'Hara. **SP-OharF**

Post-Therapy Room. William Dickey. **SP-DickW**

Post Virginal, The. Charles Olson. **CP-OlsoC**

Postal authorities of the United States of America, The. Legal Reflection. Ogden Nash. **CP-NashO**

Postcard. Margaret Atwood. **SP-AtwM2**

Postcard. Adrienne Rich. **CP-RicAE**

Postcard from Berlin, A. Derek Mahon. **SP-MahoD**

Postcard from John Ashbery, A. Frank O'Hara. **SP-OharF**

Postcard from the Garden. Marge Piercy. **SP-PierM**

Postcard from the Volcano, A. Wallace Stevens. **CP-StevW**

Postcards: A Triptych, The. Denise Levertov. **CP-LeveD**

Postcards are fragments of an encyclopedia; and typical of one an- / nouncing. John Yau. **SP-YauJo** *Fr.* Two Meditations on Guanajuato.

Postcards from Cape Split. Mona Van Duyn. **SP-VanDM**

Postcards from Nebraska. John Yau. **SP-YauJo**

Postcards from Soviet Cities. John Updike. **CP-UpdiJ**

  Kiev.

  Leningrad.

  Moscow.

  Tbilisi.

  Yerevan.

Postcript. Stanley Jasspon Kunitz. **CP-KuniS**

Postcript to Iceland. Louis MacNeice. **CP-MacNL**

Posterity. Philip Larkin. **CP-LarkP**

Posthumous Fragments of Margaret Nicholson. Percy Bysshe Shelley. **CP-ShelP**

  Despair.

  Fragment: " 'Tis midnight now—athwart the murky air."

Fragment: "Yes! all is past—swift time has fled away."

Melody to a Scene of Former Times.

Spectral Horseman, The.

War.

Posthumous Letter to Gilbert White. Wystan Hugh Auden. **CP-AudeW**

Posthumous Tales. George Crabbe.

Ancient Mansion, The. **SP-CrabG**

Postillion, The. Nikolaus Lenau, *tr. fr. German* by George Meredith. **CP-MerG2**

Posting to Printing. Robert Herrick. **CP-HerrR**

Postlude. William Carlos Williams. **CP-WilW1**

Postman comes when I am still in bed, The. A Sick Child. Randall Jarrell. **CP-JarrR; SP-JarrR**

Postponement. Thomas Hardy. **CP-HardT**

Postquam, tartarei spoliis ditatus Averni. In festum pentecostes, anno domini 1580, 21 maii. Robert Southwell. **CP-SoutR**

Postscript [To W. S*****n, Ochiltree]. Robert Burns. **CP-BurnR**

Postscript. Wystan Hugh Auden. *Fr.* The Sea and the Mirror. **CP-AudeW**

Postscript, A. Hart Crane. **CP-CranH**

Postscript. Hart Crane. **CP-CranH**

Postscript, 1984. John Hewitt. **CP-HewiJ**

Postscript to a War. Edwin Rolfe. **CP-RolfE**

Posture of the tree, The. Lovers in Winter. Robert Ranke Graves. **CP-GravR**

Postures. Geoffrey Hill. *Fr.* The Songbook of Sebastian Arrurruz. **CP-HillG**

Posy [*or* Posie], The. George Herbert. **CP-HerbG**

Pot-au-feu. Mona Van Duyn. **SP-VanDM**

Pot-Luck among the Casuals. Marsden Hartley. **CP-HartM**

Pot of Earth, The. Archibald MacLeish. **CP-MacLA**

Carrion Spring, The.

"For if the sun breed maggots in a dead."

Shallow Grass, The.

Sowing of the Dead Corn, The.

Pot of Flowers, The. William Carlos Williams. **CP-WilW1**

Pot of gold at the rainbow end, The. Gold Mud. Carl Sandburg. **CP-SandC**

Pot Of Musk, A. Walter de la Mare. **CP-DeLaW**

Potato. Richard Wilbur. **CP-WilbR**

Potato Blossom Songs and Jigs. Carl Sandburg. **CP-SandC**

Potatoes' Dance, The. Nicholas Vachel Lindsay. **CP-LindV**

" 'Down cellar,' said the cricket."

"Potatoes were the waiters."

"There was just one sweet potato."

Potatoes were the waiters. Nicholas Vachel Lindsay. *Fr.* The Potatoes' Dance. **CP-LindV**

Potent tiller reck to copper. Cinquefoil. Louis Zukofsky. **CP-ZukLS**

Potentates. Robert Herrick. **CP-HerrR**

Potflower on the windowsill says to me, The. The Power of Suicide. Muriel Rukeyser. **CP-RukeM**

Potherbs (Of the Edible Wild Plants My Granny Taught Me). Louise McNeill. **SP-McNeL**

Potion, The. Charles Tomlinson. *Fr.* Three Wagnerian Lyrics. **CP-TomlC**

Potiphar Gubbins, C. E. Study of an Elevation, in Indian Ink. Rudyard Kipling. **CP-KiplR**

Potomac River Mist. Carl Sandburg. **CP-SandC**

Potomac Town in February. Carl Sandburg. **CP-SandC**

Potpourri from a Surrey Garden. Sir John Betjeman. **CP-BetjJ**

Potted fern / in a Vine St apartment, A. 2 takes from *Love in Los Angeles*. Al Young. **CP-YounA**

Potter nor iron-founder. The "Sculpture" of Rhyme. Donald Davie. **CP-DavD**

Pound at Spoleto. Lawrence Ferlinghetti. **SP-FerlL**

Pound pound pound / on thy cold grey corona oh P. Edward Estlin Cummings. **CP-CummE**

[dP]. S. D. Robert Ranke Graves. **CP-GravR**

Pounded spice [*or* spise] both tast[e] and s[c]ent doth please, The. Robert Southwell. **CP-SoutR**

(Decease, Release.) **CP-SoutR**

Pounding on wood. The woodpecker, A. Address to the Migrations. Jean Garrigue. **SP-GarrJ**

Pour Away That Youth. Philip Larkin. **CP-LarkP**

Pour Hélène. Pierre de Ronsard, *tr. fr. French* by John Hewitt. **CP-HewiJ**

Pour l'Election de Son Sepulchre, I-V. Ezra Pound. *See* For three years, out of key with his time.

Pour the unhappiness out. Another Weeping Woman. Wallace Stevens. **CP-StevW**

Pour the wine! pour the wine! Ralph Waldo Emerson. **CP-EmerR**

Pour wine and dance if manhood still have pride. The Mountain Tomb. William Butler Yeats. **CP-YeatW**

Poured streams of Europe's veins the flood. George Meredith. *Fr.* Napoléon. **CP-MerG1**

Pouring Milk Away. Muriel Rukeyser. **CP-RukeM**

Poussin. Louis MacNeice. **CP-MacNL**

Poverty. David Herbert Lawrence. **CP-LawrD**

Poverty and Riches. Robert Herrick. **CP-HerrR**

Poverty is always / Imaginary. The. Charles Henri Ford. **SP-FordC** *Fr.* Secret Haiku.

Poverty Programs, The. Howard Nemerov. **CP-NemeH**

Poverty the Greatest Pack. Robert Herrick. **CP-HerrR**

Povre widwe [*or* wyde], somde[e]l stape in age, A. The Nun's Priest's Tale. Geoffrey Chaucer. **FHYEP; OAEL-1; OBNV; TrGrPo** *Fr.* The Canterbury Tales. **CP-ChauG**

Powder, chunks of road, twisted. Bringing to Light. Thom Gunn. **CP-GunnT**

Power. Hart Crane. *See* Nasal whine of power whips a new universe.

Power. Ralph Waldo Emerson. *Fr.* Quatrains. **CP-EmerR** (Self-Reliance.) **APN-1**

Power. Daniel Gerard Hoffman. **SP-HoffD**

Power. Adrienne Rich. **SP-RicA1; SP-RicA2**

Power. Muriel Rukeyser. **CP-RukeM**

Power! / The power alone., The. The Appian Way. Kenneth Patchen. **CP-PatcK**

Power and Glory of Language, The. Delmore Schwartz. **SP-SchwD**

Power and Light. James Dickey. **CP-DickJ**

Power and Peace. Robert Herrick. **CP-HerrR**

Power blown, a candle, The. Like A Green Branch. Martin Edmunds. **SP-EdmuM**

Power-house, A. Classic Scene. William Carlos Williams. **CP-WilW1**

Power in the People, The. Robert Herrick. **CP-HerrR**

Power is a familiar growth. Emily Dickinson. **CP-DickE**

Power is mute (the trees tell me). This Is Simple. Pablo Neruda, *tr. fr. Spanish* by Ben Belitt. **SP-NeruP**

Power never dominion. / Some other power. Muriel Rukeyser. **CP-RukeM**

Power of a beautiful face lifts me to heaven, The. Michelangelo Buonarroti, *tr. fr. Italian* by Ralph Waldo Emerson. **CP-EmerR**

Power of Armies is a visible thing, The. 1811 ("Power of Armies is a visible thing, The"). William Wordsworth. **CP-WorW1**

Power of Music. William Wordsworth. **CP-WorW1**

Power of Positive Drinking, The. "Lou Reed." **SP-ReedL**

Power of Prayer, The. Samuel Johnson. **NOBE** *Fr.* The Vanity of Human Wishes [The Tenth Satire of Juvenal Imitated]. **CP-JohnS**

Power of Princes rests in the Consent, The. Obedience. Robert Herrick. **CP-HerrR**

Power of Ridicule, The. Alexander Pope. *See* Ask you what provocation I have had?

Power of Suicide, The. Muriel Rukeyser. **CP-RukeM**

Power of the Dog, The. Rudyard Kipling. **CP-KiplR**

Power of Time, The. Jonathan Swift. **CP-SwifJ**

Power of war leads to a plan of lives, The. Muriel Rukeyser. **CP-RukeM**

Power rigs drift like lights out past the breakwater. A Journal of True Confessions. Charles Wright. **SP-WrigC**

Power ruptures at a thousand holes. George Oppen. *Fr.* Power, the Enchanted World. **CP-OppeG**

Power, the Enchanted World. George Oppen. **CP-OppeG**

"Now we do most of the killing."

"Power ruptures at a thousand holes."

"Power, which hides what it can."

"Streets, in a poor district."

"That come before the swallow dares."

Power to be true to You, The. Emily Dickinson. **CP-DickE**

Power to fly is sweet, The. Emily Dickinson. **SP-DickE**

Power to the People. Howard Nemerov. **CP-NemeH**

Power, which hides what it can. George Oppen. *Fr.* Power, the Enchanted World. **CP-OppeG**

Powerful and armed, neutral in the midst of madness, we might have held. Shine, Empire. Robinson Jeffers. **CP-JefR3**

Powerful Little Stove, A. Leonard Nathan. **SP-NathL**

Powerless emperor, The. The Hard Listener. William Carlos Williams. **CP-WilW1; CP-WilW2**

Power's good; life is not always good but power's good. To the Children. Robinson Jeffers. *Fr.* The Broken Balance. **CP-JefR1**

Powers Unconfessed. Robert Ranke Graves. **CP-GravR**

Powers whose name and shape no living creature knows, The. The Poet Pleads with the Elemental Powers. William Butler Yeats. **CP-YeatW**

Powhatan was conqueror / Powhatan was emperor. Nicholas Vachel Lindsay. *Fr.* Our Mother Pocahontas. **CP-LindV**

Powhatan's Daughter. Hart Crane. *Fr.* The Bridge. **CP-CranH**

Dance, The. **LiTM; MoAB; MoAmPo; OxBA**

Harbor Dawn, The. **AP; AmPP; CMoP; CoBMV; CrMA; FaBV; GOA; LiTM; MoAB; MoAmPo; NOBA; NYP; NePA; NoAM; OxBA; PrIm; SeCeV; TrGrPo; TwAmPo**

Indiana.

River, The. **AmPP; CMoP; GOA; MoAB; MoAmPo; NOBA; OxBA; PrIm**

"Down, down—born pioneers in time's despite." **TrGrPo**

Van Winkle. **AmPP; FaBV; MoAB; MoAmPo**

Practical Mysticism. John Hewitt. **CP-HewiJ**

Practical People. Robinson Jeffers. **CP-JefR1**

Practical Program for Monks, A. Thomas Merton. **CP-MertT; SP-MertT**

Practical Woman, A. Thomas Hardy. **CP-HardT**

"Practically all you newspaper people." The Clown. Donald Hall. **CP-HallD**

Practically speaking / the great words of great men. A Trick to Dull Our Bleeding. Charles Bukowski. **CP-BukC2**

Practice. Charles Bukowski. **SP-BukC2**

Practice. Charles Bukowski. **SP-BukC3**

Practice makes perfect, the old folks said. Magic. Rita Dove. **SP-DoveR**

Practice of Oratory. Gertrude Stein. **CP-SteiG**

Prado: Bosch: S. Antonio, The. Richard Hugo. **CP-HugoR**

Prado: Number 2671, Anonimo Español, The. Richard Hugo. **CP-HugoR**

Praeludium. Charles Tomlinson. *Fr.* Antecedents. **CP-TomlC**

Pragmatical old Capulet, the head. The Bride of Reason. Donald Davie. **CP-DavDo**

Prague, or Novotny, If You Remember Him. John Hewitt. **CP-HewiJ**

Prairie, The. Rudyard Kipling. **CP-KiplR**

Prairie. Carl Sandburg. **CP-SandC**

Prairie Battlements, The. Nicholas Vachel Lindsay. **CP-LindV**

Prairie-Grass Dividing, The. Walt Whitman. **CP-WhitW**

Prairie States, The. Walt Whitman. **CP-WhitW**

Prairie Sunset, A. Walt Whitman. **CP-WhitW**

Prairie Town. William Stafford. **SP-StafW**

Prairie Waters by Night. Carl Sandburg. **CP-SandC**

Prairie Woodland. Carl Sandburg. **CP-SandC**

Praise, A. Wendell Berry. **CP-BerrW**

Praise. Wendell Berry. **CP-BerrW**

Praise. Jane Cooper. **SP-CoopJ**

Praise. Christopher Smart. **OxBChV** *Fr.* Hymns for the Amusement of Children. **SP-SmarC**

Praise for All Dancers. Robert Bly. **SP-BlyR**

Praise for an Urn. Hart Crane. **CP-CranH**

Praise for Death. Donald Hall. **CP-HallD**

Praise for Faith. William Cowper. *Fr.* Olney Hymns. **CP-CowpW**

Praise for the Fountain Opened. William Cowper. **InPK** *Fr.* Olney Hymns. **CP-CowpW**

(Fountain, The.) **ChIV-1**

Praise him for the place he picked. Death in the Aquarium. Richard Hugo. **CP-HugoR**

Praise in old times the sage Prometheus won. John Milton. *See* On the Inventor of Gunpowder.

Praise in Summer. Richard Wilbur. **CP-WilbR**

Praise Is Traditional and Appropriate. Delmore Schwartz. **SP-SchwD**

Praise it—'tis dead. Emily Dickinson. **CP-DickE**

Praise Life. Robinson Jeffers. **CP-JefR2**

Praise, my soul, the King of heaven, *par. by* Henry Francis Lyte. Bible, *O.T. See* Psalm 103: "Bless the Lord, O my soul. . . ."

Praise, my soul, the King of heaven. Bible, *O.T. See* Psalm 103: "Bless the Lord, O my soul. . . ."

Praise, O Syon! praise thy Saviour. Saint Thomas of Aquines Hymne Read on Corpus Christy Daye. Robert Southwell. **CP-SoutR**

Praise of Love. Christina Georgina Rossetti. **CP-RosC3**

Praise [or prayse] of meaner wits this work[e] like profit brings, The. Another of the Same. Sir Walter Ralegh *and* George Clifford. **CP-RaleW** *Fr.* Commendatory Verses to Edmund Spenser's Fairy Queen.

Praise of the Committee. Muriel Rukeyser. **CP-RukeM**

Praise (1). George Herbert. **CP-HerbG**

Praise the spells and bless the charms. Always Marry an April Girl. Ogden Nash. **CP-NashO**

Praise they that will Times past, I joy to see. The Present Time But Pleaseth. Robert Herrick. **CP-HerrR**

Praise (3). George Herbert. **CP-HerbG**

Praise to the End! Theodore Roethke. **CP-RoetT**

"Mips and ma the mooly moo." **CBNP; NBLV; RB**

Praise (2). George Herbert. **CP-HerbG**

Praise waiteth for thee, O God, in Sion. Psalm 65. Bible, *O.T. Fr.* Psalms. **CP-Psal**

"Praise Woman still!" his Lordship says. To Maria. Robert Burns. **CP-BurnR**

Praise ye the Lord. Blessed is the man that feareth the Lord. Psalm 112. Bible, *O.T. Fr.* Psalms. **CP-Psal**

Praise ye the Lord: for it is good to sing praises unto our God. Psalm 147. Bible, *O.T.* **FaPON** *Fr.* Psalms. **CP-Psal**

Praise ye the Lord. I will praise the Lord. Psalm 111. Bible, *O.T. Fr.* Psalms. **CP-Psal**

Praise ye the Lord. O give thanks unto the Lord. Psalm 106. Bible, *O.T. Fr.* Psalms. **CP-Psal**

Praise ye the Lord. Praise God in his sanctuary. Psalm 150. Bible, *O.T.* **TRV** *Fr.* Psalms. **CP-Psal**

Praise ye the Lord. Praise, O ye servants of the Lord. Psalm 113. Bible, *O.T. Fr.* Psalms. **CP-Psal**

Praise ye the Lord. Praise the Lord, O my soul. Psalm 146. Bible, *O.T. Fr.* Psalms. **CP-Psal**

Praise ye the Lord. Praise ye the Lord from the heavens. Psalm 148. Bible, *O.T.* **TrGrPo** *Fr.* Psalms. **CP-Psal**

Praise ye the Lord. Praise ye the name of the Lord; praise him, O ye servants of the Lord. Psalm 135. Bible, *O.T. Fr.* Psalms. **CP-Psal**

Praise ye the Lord. Sing unto the Lord a new song. Psalm 149. Bible, *O.T. Fr.* Psalms. **CP-Psal**

Praise youth's hot blood if you will, I think that happiness. Age in Prospect. Robinson Jeffers. **CP-JefR1**

Prais[e]d be Diana[']s fair[e] and harmles[s] light. Sir Walter Ralegh. **CP-RaleW**

Praised be the God of love. Antiphon (2). George Herbert. **CP-HerbG**

Praised be the Rivers, from their mountain springs. William Wordsworth. *Fr.* Ecclesiastical Sonnets. **CP-WorW2**

Praised by the Art whose subtle power could stay. Upon the Sight of a Beautiful Picture. William Wordsworth. **CP-WorW1**

Praisers of women in their proud and beautiful poems, The. Not Marble nor the Gilded Monuments. Archibald MacLeish. **CP-MacLA**

Praises. Thomas McGrath. **SP-McGrT**

Praises, The. Charles Olson. **CP-OlsoC**

Praises IV. Thomas McGrath. **SP-McGrT**

Praises of a Country Life, The. Horace, *tr. by* Ben Jonson. **CP-JonsB** *Fr.* Epodes.

Praising the Poets of That Country. Howard Nemerov. **CP-NemeH**

Prank of the Heart at play on the Heart, The. Emily Dickinson. **SP-DickE**

Prat he writes Satyres; but herein's the fault. On Poet Prat. Robert Herrick. **CP-HerrR**

Pray / pay / no attention to my greatness. Brief Lief. William Carlos Williams. **CP-WilW2**

Pray and Prosper. Robert Herrick. **CP-HerrR**

Pray Billy Pitt explain thy rigs. On Mr. Pitt's [*or* Pit's] Hair-Powder Tax. Robert Burns. **CP-BurnR**

Pray, butcher, spare yon tender calf. The Calf. Ogden Nash. **CP-NashO**

'Pray doe nott use thes words I must bee gone. Sonnet 9. Mary Sidney, Countess of Montgomery Wroth. *Fr.* Pamphilia to Amphilanthus. **CP-WrotM**

Pray for my soul. More things are wrought by prayer. Prayer. Tennyson. **WGRP** *Fr.* The Passing of Arthur. **FHYEP; NAEL-2; OBNC** *Fr.* Idylls of the King. **CP-TennA**

Pray give the "Atlantic." To Lucy Larcom. John Greenleaf Whittier. **CP-WhitJ**

Pray Ladies breath awhile lay by. Clitophon and Lucippe. Achilles Tatius, *tr. fr. Greek by* Richard Lovelace. **CP-LoveR**

Pray, Reader, have you eaten ortolans. Prologue. Robert Browning. **CP-BroR2**

Pray Remember the Poor. Christopher Smart. **NOEC** *Fr.* Hymns for the Amusement of Children. **SP-SmarC**

Pray steal me not, I'm Mrs. Dingley's. On the Collar of Mrs. Dingley's Lap-Dog. Jonathan Swift. **CP-SwifJ**

Pray thee *Diana* tell mee, is it ill. Mary Sidney, Countess of Montgomery Wroth. *Fr.* Part 1. *Fr.* Urania. **CP-WrotM**

Pray, thee, take care, that tak'st my book[e] in hand. To the Reader. Ben Jonson. **CP-JonsB**

Pray, what can dreams avail. Dream Song II. Paul Laurence Dunbar. **CP-DunbP**

Pray, what is this Bank of which the town rings? The Bank Thrown Down. Jonathan Swift. **CP-SwifJ**

Pray who are these *Natives* the Rabble so ven'rate, *sels.* Robert Burns. *Fr.* Dumfries Epigrams. **CP-BurnR**

Pray why are you so bare, so bare. The Haunted Oak. Paul Laurence Dunbar. **CP-DunbP**

Pray without ceasing (says the Saint). Prayer. Christopher Smart. *Fr.* Hymns for the Amusement of Children. **SP-SmarC**

Pray You Young Woman. Hayden Carruth. **CP-CarHS**

Prayed in the ghetto with my face in the cement. The Groom's Still Waiting at the Altar. "Bob Dylan." **CP-DylaB**

Prayer. Wystan Hugh Auden. **CP-AudWJ**

Prayer, A. Richard Crashaw. **CP-CrasR**

Prayer, A. Robert Creeley. **CP-CreeR**

Prayer, A. Walter de la Mare. **CP-DeLaW**

Prayer: "Give me the moon at my feet." David Herbert Lawrence. **CP-LawrD**

Prayer: "Give way, you fiends, and give that man some happiness", *incl. in* Perhaps for Eridanus. Malcolm Lowry. *Fr.* The Moon in Scandinavia. **CP-LowrM**

Prayer. Robert Herrick. **CP-HerrR**

Prayer: "I ask good things that I detest." Robert Louis Stevenson. **CP-StevR**

Prayer: "I ask you this." Langston Hughes. **SP-HughL**

Prayer: "I pray that I may form a prayer, oh Lord." Malcolm Lowry. **CP-LowrM**

Prayer: "If I must of my Senses lose." Theodore Roethke. **CP-RoetT**

Prayer, The. Denise Levertov. **CP-LeveD**

Prayer, A: "God give those drunkards. . ." Malcolm Lowry. **CP-LowrM**

Prayer: "Oh thou who art not above." Malcolm Lowry. **CP-LowrM**

Prayer: "More things are wrought by prayer." Tennyson. **BLRP** *Fr.* Morte d'Arthur. **DL; EBNV; EBVVPR; FaBoBe; FiP; NIP; NOBVV; OAEL-2; OBNV; OXAEP-2; PoEL-5** *Fr.* Morte d'Arthur. **CP-TennA**

Prayer: "Nobody understands so let the Rabbi." Stephen Berg. **SP-BergS**

Prayer: "Pray for my soul. More things are wrought by prayer." Tennyson. **WGRP** *Fr.* The Passing of Arthur. **FHYEP; NAEL-2; OBNC** *Fr.* Idylls of the King. **CP-TennA**

Prayer. Christopher Smart. *Fr.* Hymns for the Amusement of Children. **SP-SmarC**

Prayer. Patti Smith. **SP-SmitP**

Prayer, A. Dabney Stuart. **SP-StuaD**

Prayer: "Summe Deus, cui caeca patent penetralia cordis." Samuel Johnson. **CP-JohnS**

Prayer: "White, O white face." Hilda Doolittle. **CP-DoolH**

Prayer, A: "O lord, the hard-won miles." Paul Laurence Dunbar. **CP-DunbP**

Prayer After All, A. John Berryman. **CP-BerrJ**

Prayer after Eating. Wendell Berry. **CP-BerrW**

Prayer after World War. Carl Sandburg. **CP-SandC**

Prayer against the Curse Bomb. Laurence Lieberman. **SP-LiebL**

Prayer and Sermon of Ibn Abbad. Thomas Merton. *Fr.* Readings from Ibn Abbad. **CP-MertT**

Prayer at Death. Michael Hartnett. **SP-HarMi**

Prayer at Morning, A. Randall Jarrell. **CP-JarrR**

Prayer at the End of a Rope. Ogden Nash. **CP-NashO**

Prayer before Birth. Louis MacNeice. **CP-MacNL**

Prayer before Study. Theodore Roethke. **CP-RoetT**

Prayer before Work. May Sarton. **SP-SartM**

Prayer for a Blessing. William Cowper. *Fr.* Olney Hymns. **CP-CowpW**

Prayer for Children. William Cowper. *Fr.* Olney Hymns. **CP-CowpW**

Prayer for Messiah. Leonard Cohen. **CP-CoheL**

Prayer for my Daughter. Marilyn Hacker. **SP-HackM**

Prayer for My Daughter, A. William Butler Yeats. **CP-YeatW**

Prayer for My Father. Gary Gildner. **SP-GildG**

Prayer for My Son, A. William Butler Yeats. **CP-YeatW**

Prayer for Old Age, A. William Butler Yeats. **CP-YeatW**

Prayer for Patience. William Cowper. *Fr.* Olney Hymns. **CP-CowpW**

Prayer for Prayer. Robert Pack. **SP-PackR**

Prayer for Sun. Phoebe Hesketh. **SP-HeskP**

Prayer for the Great Family. Gary Snyder. **CP-SnydG**

Prayer for the Self, A. John Berryman. **PPP** *Fr.* Eleven Addresses to the Lord. **CP-BerrJ**

Prayer from the Wicket Gate for Forty One Doors for Forty Two. Malcolm Lowry. **CP-LowrM**

Prayer in Bad Weather. Charles Bukowski. **SP-BukC1**

Prayer in Mid-Passage. Louis MacNeice. **CP-MacNL**

Prayer in My Sickness, A. James Wright. **CP-WrigJ**

Prayer in Spring, A. Robert Frost. **CP-FrosR**

Prayer, in the Prospect of Death, A. Robert Burns. **CP-BurnR**

Prayer is the little implement. Emily Dickinson. **CP-DickE**

Prayer Meeting. Langston Hughes. **SP-HughL**

Prayer Not To Go to Paradise with the Asses. Kenneth Patchen. **CP-PatcK**

Prayer of Agassiz, The. John Greenleaf Whittier. **CP-WhitJ**

Prayer of Columbus. Walt Whitman. **CP-WhitW**

"Thou knowest my years entire, my life." **TrPWD**

Prayer of Miriam Cohen, The. Rudyard Kipling. **CP-KiplR**

Prayer of Nature, The. Byron. **CP-Byron**

Prayer of Thanksgiving Written for Victor Hammer, A ("O Thou Father of splendor, Giver of light"), *tr. of* "O Tu Pater splendoris Dator luminis." Thomas Merton, *tr. fr. Latin by the author.* **CP-MertT**

Prayer of Thanksgiving Written for Victor Hammer, A ("O Tu Pater splendoris Dator luminis"), *see also English tr.* Prayer of Thanksgiving Written for Victor Hammer, A ("O Thou Father of splendor, Giver of light"). Thomas Merton. **CP-MertT**

Prayer of the Antichrist, The. John Gould Fletcher. **SP-FletJ** *Fr.* The Parables of Antichrist.

Prayer of the Middle-Aged Man, The. John Berryman. **CP-BerrJ**

Prayer on Going into My House. William Butler Yeats. **CP-YeatW**

Prayer (1): "Prayer the Church's banquet, Angels' age." George Herbert. *See* Prayer the Church's banquet, Angels' age.

Prayer-Seeker, The. John Greenleaf Whittier. **CP-WhitJ**

Prayer, The: "My brother kneels, so saith Kabir." Rudyard Kipling. **CP-KiplR**

Prayer, The: "O living will that shalt endure." Tennyson. *See* O living will that shalt endure.

Prayer the Church's banquet, Angels' age. George Herbert. **CP-HerbG** (Prayer (1): "Prayer the Church's banquet, Angels' age.") **CP-HerbG**

Prayer to All the Dead Among Mine Own People, A. Nicholas Vachel Lindsay. **CP-LindV**

Prayer to Escape from the Market Place, A. James Wright. **CP-WrigJ**

Prayer to Go to Paradise with the Donkeys, A. Francis Jammes, *tr. fr. French by* Richard Wilbur. **CP-WilbR**

Prayer to Persephone. Edna St. Vincent Millay. *Fr.* Memorial to D. C. **CP-MillE**

Prayer to Saint Anatole. Thomas Merton. *Fr.* Cables to the Ace. **CP-MertT**

Prayer to the Lord Ramakrishna, A. James Wright. **CP-WrigJ**

Prayer to the Mountain, A. John Ciardi. **SP-CiarJ**

Prayer to the Snowy Owl. John Haines. **SP-HainJ**

Prayer to the Sun, A. Geoffrey Hill. **PRA** *Fr.* Four Poems Regarding the Endurance of Poets. **CP-HillG**

Prayer to the Wind, A. Thomas Carew. **CP-CareT**

Prayer to Venus. Edmund Spenser. *See* Address to Venus.

Prayer (2). George Herbert. **CP-HerbG**

Prayer, under the Pressure of Violent Anguish, A. Robert Burns. **CP-BurnR**

Prayers and Praises are those spotless two. Gods Prt. Robert Herrick. **CP-HerrR**

Prayers and Sayings of the Mad Farmer. Wendell Berry. **CP-BerrW**

"At night make me one with the darkness." **EaPr**

"Beware of the machinery of longevity. When a man's life is over."

"By the excellence of his work the workman is a neighbor. By."

"Don't own so much clutter that you will be relieved to see your."

"Don't pray for the rain to stop."

"Don't worry and fret about the crops. After you have done all you can for them, let them stand in the weather on their own."

"If a man finds it necessary to eat garbage, he should resist the."

"It is presumptuous and irresponsible to pray for other people. A."

"Let me wake in the night."

"Let my marriage be brought to the ground."

"Put your hands into the mire."

"Sowing the seed, / my hand is one with the earth." **EaPr**

"When I rise up." **EaPr**

Prayers I make will then be sweet indeed, The. Michelangelo Buonarroti, *tr. fr. Italian by* William Wordsworth. **CP-WorW1** (To the Supreme Being.) **CP-WorW1**

Prayers Must Have Poise. Robert Herrick. **CP-HerrR**

Prayers of a Pagan. James Liddy. **CP-LiddJ**

Prayers of Steel. Carl Sandburg. **CP-SandC**

Praying Always. Christina Georgina Rossetti. **CP-RosC2**

Praying answers prayer. Figuring Belief. Archie Randolph Ammons. **SP-AmmoA**

Praying Mantis. Jim Carroll. **SP-CarrJ**

Praying Mantis, The. Ogden Nash. *Fr.* Nature-Walks, or, Not to Mention a Dopping of Sheldrakes. **CP-NashO**

Praying on a 707. Anne Sexton. **CP-SextA**

Praying to Big Jack. Anne Sexton. **CP-SextA**

P.R.B., The. Christina Georgina Rossetti. **CP-RosC3**

Pre-Amphibian. Margaret Atwood. **SP-AtwM1**

Pre-puberty boys. Charles Henri Ford. **SP-FordC** *Fr.* Emblems of Arachne.

Pre-Raphaelite Notebook, A. Geoffrey Hill. **CP-HillG**

Preach me no preachments John Ruskin. Vezelay. Daniel Gerard Hoffman. **SP-HoffD**

Preacher, The. Louis MacNeice. *Fr.* Novelettes. **CP-MacNL**

Preacher, The. John Greenleaf Whittier. **CP-WhitJ**

Preacher: Ruminates Behind the Sermon, The. Gwendolyn Brooks. **PBMP** *Fr.* A Street in Bronzeville. **SP-BrooG**

Preaching from a Spanish Ballad, A. George Meredith. **CP-MerG1**

Preamble. Muriel Rukeyser. **CP-RukeM**

Precaution. Robert Frost. *Fr.* Ten Mills. **CP-FrosR**

Precedent. Paul Laurence Dunbar. **CP-DunbP**

Precepts. Robert Herrick. **CP-HerrR**

Precious Angel. "Bob Dylan." **CP-DylaB**

Precious Five. Wystan Hugh Auden. **CP-AudeW**

Precious in the light of the early sun the Housatonic. From a Train Window. Edna St. Vincent Millay. **CP-MillE**

Precious—moldering pleasure—'tis, A. Emily Dickinson. **CP-DickE**

Precious Moments. Carl Sandburg. **CP-SandC**

Precious to Me—She still shall be. Emily Dickinson. **CP-DickE**

Precious Weak Fields. Archie Randolph Ammons. **SP-AmmoA**

Precise counterpart, The. The Orchestra. William Carlos Williams. **CP-WilW2**

Precise yet furtive etiquette of dogs, The. Dogs in the Park. Louis MacNeice. **CP-MacNL**

Precisely as unbig a why as i'm. Edward Estlin Cummings. **CP-CummE**

Precisely, Not Violets. Diane Wakoski. **SP-WakoD**

Precision. Diane Wakoski. **SP-WakoD**

Precognition. Margaret Atwood. **SP-AtwM2**

Precursors. Louis MacNeice. **CP-MacNL**

Predators removed their harnesses, and vanished into the exposed, The. Manhattan Miniature. John Yau. **SP-YauJo**

Predecessor of Perseus, A. Howard Nemerov. **CP-NemeH**

Predella ("Blue Woolen..."). John Yau.

Predella. John Yau. **SP-YauJo**

"After removing the anodized plate, the two electricians discover an." **SP-YauJo**

"Beneath sky's broken tiles, ancient barns are embedded in plaster." **SP-YauJo**

"Blessed flagellants set forth, mounted on tatters of flaming horses, The." **SP-YauJo**

"Box mountain of hardened tears is hoisted up the scaffold, two, A." **SP-YauJo**

"Charred hansom is discovered on Bubbling Well Road. In the shade." **SP-YauJo**

"I learn to count without pointing at my fingers. This is Pinocchio." **SP-YauJo**

"She descends the stairway of the last ditch beyond the horizon. I." **SP-YauJo**

Predestination. Robert Herrick. **CP-HerrR**

Predicter of Famine, The. William Carlos Williams. **CP-WilW2**

Preexistence. Archie Randolph Ammons. **SP-AmmoA**

Preface: "Aged catch their breath, The." Wystan Hugh Auden. **LiTA** *Fr.* The Sea and the Mirror. **CP-AudeW**

Preface. Diane Wakoski. **SP-WakoD**

Preface, A: "To all to whom this little book may come." Rudyard Kipling. **CP-KiplR** *Fr.* Land and Sea Tales.

Preface to a Love Poem. Derek Mahon. **SP-MahoD**

Preface to "Bob Taylor's Birthday." Nicholas Vachel Lindsay. **CP-LindV**

Preface to "High and Low." Sir John Betjeman. **CP-BetjJ**

Preface to the Past. Ogden Nash. **CP-NashO**

Prefatory Poem to My Brother's Sonnets. Tennyson. **CP-TennA**

Preference, A. Paul Laurence Dunbar. **CP-DunbP**

Preference. Langston Hughes. **SP-HughL**

Preference of Metre. David Markson. **CP-MarkD**

Preferred pain of the Western World, The. Hangover. Al Young. **CP-YounA**

Preferring laxatives to wine. America's Plutonic Ecstasies. Hart Crane. **CP-CranH**

Pregnant again with th' old twins hope, and fear. To Mr. T. W. John Donne. **CP-DonnJ**

Pregnant, I Come. Joseph Ceravolo. **SP-CeraJ**

Pregnant moon of August, A. One of These Nights. Derek Mahon. **SP-MahoD**

Prejudged by foes determined not to spare. Laud. William Wordsworth. *Fr.* Ecclesiastical Sonnets. **CP-WorW2**

Prejudice, The. Robert Creeley. **CP-CreeR**

Prejudice against the Past, The. Wallace Stevens. **CP-StevW**

Prell. Jim Carroll. **SP-CarrJ**

Prelude: "Along the roadside, like the flowers of gold." John Greenleaf Whittier. **AP; APN-1; NAAL-1; NAAL-3; OxBA; PoEL-4** *Fr.* Among the Hills. **CP-WhitJ**

Prelude: "Before the beginning of things." John Gould Fletcher. **SP-FletJ**

Prelude: "By sunny market-place and street." Robert Louis Stevenson. **CP-StevR**

Prelude: "Hundreds upon hundreds of years of Lapiths." Roy Fisher. **SP-FishR** *Fr.* On the Neglect of Figure Composition.

Prelude: "I drew solitude over me, on the lone shore." Robinson Jeffers. **CP-JefR1**

Prelude: "I, with legs crossed along the daylight, watch." Derek Walcott. **CP-WalcD**

Prelude, A. Charles Tomlinson. **CP-TomlC**

Prelude. Al Young. **CP-YounA**

Prelude, A; "I know only the bare rocks of today." William Carlos Williams. **CP-WilW1**

Prelude: "And did those feet in ancient time." William Blake. *See* And Did Those Feet in Ancient Time.

Prelude and Fugue. Alun Lewis. **CP-LewiA**

Prelude: "England! awake! awake! awake!" William Blake. *See* England! awake! awake! awake!

Prelude: "Fields from Islington to Marybone, The." William Blake. *See* The Fields from Islington to Marybone.

Prelude: For the Feast of St. Agnes, A. Thomas Merton. **CP-MertT**

Prelude; Growth of a Poet's Mind [1805 vers.], The, *see also* The Prelude; Growth of a Poet's Mind [1850 vers.]. William Wordsworth. **CP-WorW3**

Prelude; Growth of a Poet's Mind [1850 vers.], The, *see also* The Prelude; Growth of a Poet's Mind [1805 vers.]. William Wordsworth. **CP-WorW3**

Books.

Books.

"Gracious spirit o'er this earth presides, A." **OBRV**

"He, who in his youth." **TOF**

There Was a Boy. **CP-WorW1; ChER; FHYEP; FaBoRV; MeMBP; NOBRP; OBRV; PoEL-4,** *book* 5, *ll.* 364–397;

(Boy of Winander, The.) **PoE,** *book* 5, *ll.* 364–388;

(Winander Lake.) **FiP,** *book* 5, *ll.* 364–388;

There Was a Boy. **RB,** *book* 5, *ll.* 389–422;

"These mighty workmen of our later age." **EnRP**

"Thirteen years / Or haply less, I might have seen, when first." **OxAEP-2**

"When Contemplation, like the night-calm felt." **OAEL-2**

"Wherupon I told, / That once in the stillness of a summer's moon." **PoEL-4**

Cambridge and the Alps.

Cambridge and the Alps.

"Brook and road, The." **OBRV**

"But 'twas a time when Europe was rejoiced." **FaBoPV**

Coleridge's Mind a Life Unto Itself. **EPCY**

"Far different dejection once was mine." **OBTV,** *book* 6, *ll.* 491–657; **RB**

(Crossing the Alps.) **RB,** *book* 6, *ll.* 491–572;

"I, too, have been a Wanderer; but, alas!" **OxAEP-2**

Imagination. **FiP**

"Melancholy slackening that ensued." **PoEL-4**

"Poet's soul was with me at that time, The." **EnRP**

"Single tree, A." **OBRV**

"'Tis told by one whom stormy waters threw." **ImOP**

Types and Symbols of Eternity. **CBCK**

"When from the Vallais we had turned, and clomb." **TOF**

"When the third summer freed us from restraint." **OAEL-2**

Conclusion: "In one of these excursions, travelling then."

"In one of these excursions, travelling then." **OxAEP-2,** *book* 13, *ll.* 1–65; **FaBoPP; FaBoRV**

(Climb to Snowdon, The.) **FaBoRV,** *book* 13;

(Snowdon Sunrise, The.) **FaBoPP,** *book* 13, *ll.* 1–65;

"It was a Summer's night, a close warm night." **OBNC**

"Oh! yet a few short years of useful life." **OBRV**

Conclusion: "In one of those excursions (may they ne'er)." **OAEL-2; OBNC**

"In one of those excursions (may they ne'er)." **EBEV,** *book* 14, *ll.* 1–119;

"It was a close, warm, breezeless summer night." **PoEL-4**

France (Concluded).

"It hath been told." **EnRP**

Noble, The. **ChTr**

"O[h!] pleasant exercise of hope and joy!" **HAP; PoEL-4,** *book* 11, *ll.* 105–144; **FiP**

(French Revolution, The.) **FiP**, *book* 11, *ll.* 105–144;

Imagination and Taste, How Impaired and Restored. **EnRP**

"In such strange passion, if I may once more." **OAEL-2**

"Oh! mystery of man, from what a depth." **FiP**

"There are in our existence spots of time." **PoEL-4; TOF**, *book* 12, *ll.* 208–335; **PoE**

(Spots of Time.) **PoE**, *book* 12, *ll.* 208–282;

Imagination, How Impaired and Restored.

"One Christmas-time, / The day before the holidays began." **RB**

"Ye motions of delight, that through the fields." **OBNC**

Introduction—Childhood and School-Time.

Introduction—Childhood and School-Time. **EnRP; FHYEP**

"And in the frosty season, when the sun." **FaBoCh; PlP**

(On the Frozen Lake.) **FaBoCh**

"Dust as we are, the immortal spirit grows." **SCV**

"Ere I had told / Ten birthdays when among the mountain-slopes." **TOF**

"Fair seed time had my soul, and I grew up." **NoP**, *book* 1, *ll.* 301–646;

"Fair seed-time had my soul, and I grew up." **OBNC; OxAEP-2**, *book* 1, *ll.* 305–489; **FaBoPP**

(On the Solitary Fells around Hawkshead.) **FaBoPP**, *book* 1, *ll.* 305–350;

Fishing. **SD**

In Patterdale. **FaBoRV**

Influence of Natural Objects [in Calling Forth and Strengthening the Imagination in Boyhood and Early Youth]. **AWP; CP-WorW1; OBRV**

"O there is blessing in this gentle breeze." **OAEL-2**

"One evening (surely I was led by her)." **FaBoPP; OBRV; RB**

(Boat Stealing.) **RB**

(On Ullswater.) **FaBoPP**

"One summer evening (led by her) I found." **FiP; NU**

(Lines: "One summer evening (led by her) I found.") **NU**

Skating. **CH; SD**

"Was it for this." **RB**

"Wisdom and Spirit of the universe!" **NOBE**

Wordsworth Skates on Esthwaite Water. **FaBoPP**

Residence at Cambridge.

Residence at Cambridge.

"Beside the pleasant Mills of Trompington." **OBRV**

"Evangelist St John my patron was, The." **HAP**, *book* 3, *ll.* 46–63; **FaBoRV**

(Newton's Statue.) **FaBoRV**, *book* 3, *ll.* 46–63;

Gentle Spenser. **EPCY**

"It was a dreary morning when the chaise." **FaBoPP; OxAEP-2**

Newton. **ImOP**

Wordsworth Reading Chaucer. **EPCY**

Residence in France ("As oftentimes a river, it might seem").

Residence in France ("Even as a river,—partly (it might seem)").

"Among that band of Officers was one." **ChER**, *book* 9, *ll.* 288–585;

"France lured me forth; the realm that I had crossed." **FaBoPV**

"I quitted and betook myself to France." **OxAEP-2**

Residence in France and French Revolution.

Residence in France and French Revolution.

"Cheered with this hope, to Paris I returned." **EnRP**, *book* 10, *ll.* 48–480, *abr;*

"In France, the Men who for their desperate ends." **OBRV**

"It pleased me more." **OAEL-2**

"It was a beautiful and silent day." **OxAEP-2**, *book* 10, *ll.* 1–736, *abr.;*

"O pleasant exercise of hope and joy!" **OBRV**

"State, as if to stamp the final seal, The." **FaBoPV**

To Coleridge in Sicily. **OBNC**

"When the proud fleet that bears the red-cross flag." **FaBoPV**

Residence in London.

Residence in London.

"As the black storm upon the mountain-top." **PoEL-4**

"Genius of Burke! forgive the pen seduced." **FaBoPV**

"Pass we from entertainments, that are such." **EnRP**

"Rise up, thou monstrous ant-hill on the plain." **HAP**, *book* 7, *ll.* 149–730, *much abr.;*

"Those days are now." **OxAEP-2**

Young Wordsworth's London, The. **FaBoPP**

Retrospect Love of Nature Leading to Love of Mankind.

Retrospect Love of Nature Leading to Love of Mankind.

"But lovelier far than this, the paradise." **OAEL-2**

Fair below Helvellyn, The. **FaBoPP**

Shepherd, The. **OBNC**

"What sounds are those, Helvellyn, that are heard." **EnRP**

Same subject (Continued) [Imagination and Taste, How Impaired and Restored].

Same Subject (Continued) [Imagination].

"From Nature doth emotion come, and moods." **EnRP**

"From Nature doth emotion come, and moods." **OBNC**

School-Time.

School-Time. **FHYEP**

"Blest the infant Babe." **TOF**

"But who shall parcel out." **TOF**

"For I would walk alone." **OBRV**

Intimations of Sublimity. **OBNC**

"Nor should this, perchance." **OxAEP-2**

On Windermere; Bowness Bay and Belle Isle. **FaBoPP**

"Those incidental charms which first attached." **OAEL-2**

"Thus were my sympathies enlarged, and thus." **EnRP**

Summer Vacation.

Summer Vacation.

Consummate Happiness. **OBNC**

Dedicated Spirit, A. **SeCePo**

"Favourite pleasure hath it been with me, A." **OBRV**

"In a throng, / A festal company of Maids and Youths." **EBEV; OBRV**

"It seemed the very garments that I wore." **OAEL-2**

"When first I made." **EnRP**

"When first I made." **OBRV**

"While thus I wander'd, step by step led on." **OxAEP-1**

"Wildly he wandered on." **TOF**

"Yet in spite / Of pleasure won, and knowledge not withheld." **PoEL-4**

Prelude in Boricua. Luis Palés Matos, *tr. fr. Spanish by* William Carlos Williams. **CP-WilW2**

Prelude in Darkness. James McAuley. **SP-McAuJ**

Prelude, Prefixed to the Volume Entitled "Poems Chiefly of Early and Late Years." William Wordsworth. **CP-WorW2**

Prelude to a Parting. Maya Angelou. **SP-AngeM**

Prelude to an Evening, *"A" version.* John Crowe Ransom. **AP; CoBMV; EAS; MoAB; MoAmPo; MoPo; MoVE; NePA; OxBA; PoCh** *Fr.* Sixteen Poems in Eight Pairings. **SP-RansJ**

Prelude to an Evening, *"B" version.* John Crowe Ransom. *Fr.* Sixteen Poems in Eight Pairings. **SP-RansJ**

Prelude to an Ode for Barnum. John Hewitt. **CP-HewiJ**

Prelude to Another Drink. Malcolm Lowry. **CP-LowrM**

Prelude to Consternation. John Hewitt. **CP-HewiJ**

Prelude to "Departmental Ditties." Rudyard Kipling. **CP-KiplR**

Prelude To Mammon. Malcolm Lowry. **CP-LowrM**

Prelude to Objects. Wallace Stevens. **CP-StevW**

Prelude to Winter. William Carlos Williams. **CP-WilW2**

Preludes (I–IV). Thomas Stearns Eliot. **CP-ElioT**

"His soul stretched tight across the skies."

"Morning comes to consciousness, The."

"Winter evening settles down, The." **MoShBr; OPOU**

"You tossed a blanket from the bed."

Prelusive. Herman Melville. **SP-MelvH** *Fr.* Clarel: A Poem and Pilgrimage in the Holy Land.

Premature Ejaculation. William Matthews. **SP-MattW**

Premises. Karl Shapiro. **SP-ShapK**

Premonition. Paul Laurence Dunbar. **CP-DunbP**

Premonition, The. Theodore Roethke. **CP-RoetT**

Premonitions. Thomas Hardy. **CP-HardT**

Premonitory July. John Clellon Holmes. **SP-HolmJ**

Prentys whilom dwelled in oure citee, A. The Cook's Tale. Geoffrey Chaucer. **BXAP** *Fr.* The Canterbury Tales. **CP-ChauG**

Preoccupation's Gift. Donald Davie. **CP-DavDo**

Preparation. Paul Laurence Dunbar. **CP-DunbP**

Preparation for the Highest Being. Kenneth Patchen. **CP-PatcK**

Prepare for death. But how can you prepare. Speculation. Howard Nemerov. **CP-NemeH**

Prepare for Songs; He's come, He's come. The New-Yeeres Gift, or Circumcisions Song, Sung to the King in the Presence at White Hall. Robert Herrick. **CP-HerrR**

Prepare, prepare, the iron helm of war. A War Song [to Englishmen]. William Blake. **CP-BlakW**

Prepare the ground when maple buds have burst. Planting a Mailbox. John Updike. **CP-UpdiJ**

Prepared for death and unprepared. Two Poems of the Military. James Dickey. **CP-DickJ**

Prepared Statement, The. Robert Ranke Graves. **CP-GravR**

Preparing for Exile. Derek Walcott. **CP-WalcD**

Preparing to Leave. Phoebe Hesketh. **SP-HeskP**

Preposterous is that Government, (and rude). Ill Government. Robert Herrick. **CP-HerrR**

Prepost'rous is that order, when we run. First Work, and Then Wages. Robert Herrick. **CP-HerrR**

Presage and caveat not only seem. The Window Sill. Robert Ranke Graves. **CP-GravR**

Prescience. Maya Angelou. **SP-AngeM**

Prescience. Robert Herrick. **CP-HerrR**

Prescription of Painful Ends. Robinson Jeffers. **CP-JefR3**

Presence, The. Robert Ranke Graves. **CP-GravR**

Presence, The. Denise Levertov. **CP-LeveD**

Presence. Dabney Stuart. **SP-StuaD**

Presence and Absence. Robert Herrick. **CP-HerrR**

Presence of Love, The. Samuel Taylor Coleridge. **CP-ColeS**

Presences. William Butler Yeats. **CP-YeatW**

Presences are always said to brood. Tuscan Morning. Donald Davie. **CP-DavDo**

Present. Tess Gallagher. **SP-GallT**

Present again / present present. "Follow the Drinking Gourd. . . ." Robert Creeley. **CP-CreeR**

Present and Future. Christina Georgina Rossetti. **CP-RosC3**

Present Government Grievous. Robert Herrick. **CP-HerrR**

Present is a gift, The. Fort Collins, Colorado. Al Young. **CP-YounA**

Present is a secure place to inhabit, The. The First Man. Thom Gunn. *Fr.* Misanthropos. **CP-GunnT**

Present: or, The Bag of the Bee, The. Robert Herrick. **CP-HerrR**

Present Time But Pleaseth, The. Robert Herrick. **CP-HerrR**

Present to the Sun, A. Marsden Hartley. **CP-HartM**

Presentation, The. Robert Southwell. **CP-SoutR**

Presentation of Christ in the Temple, The. Christopher Smart. *Fr.* Hymns and Spiritual Songs for the Fasts and Festivals of the Church of England. **SP-SmarC**

Presentation of Two Birds to My Son, A. James Wright. **CP-WrigJ**

Presentation Piece. Marilyn Hacker. **SP-HackM**

Presentation Verses to Nathaniel Pigott. Alexander Pope. **CP-PopeA**

Presentiment—is that long Shadow—on the Lawn. Emily Dickinson. **CP-DickE**

Presentiments. William Wordsworth. **CP-WorW2**

Presenting a *Lark, in imitation of* Cowley. Alexander Pope. **CP-PopeA**

Presently at our touch the teacup stirred. Voices from the Other World. James Merrill. **SP-MerrJ**

Preserve me, O God: for in thee do I put my trust. Psalm 16. Bible, *O.T. Fr.* Psalms. **CP-Psal**

Preserver of the church, thy spouse. The Presentation of Christ in the Temple. Christopher Smart. *Fr.* Hymns and Spiritual Songs for the Fasts and Festivals of the Church of England. **SP-SmarC**

President and Poet. Donald Hall. **CP-HallD**

President appeared to me in dreams, A. President Poem. Frederick Morgan. **SP-MorgF**

President awakens in the night, The. A Presidential Poem. Ted Kooser. **SP-KoosT**

President of my country his face flushed, The. The Nickname of Hell. Charles Kenneth Williams. **CP-WillC; SP-WillC**

President Ordains the Bee to Be, The. Wallace Stevens. **LiTA** *Fr.* It Must Change. *Fr.* Notes toward a Supreme Fiction. **CP-StevW**

President Poem. Frederick Morgan. **SP-MorgF**

Presidentiad, The. Donald Hall. **CP-HallD**

Presidential Address to a Party of Exiles. Howard Nemerov. **CP-NemeH**

Presidential flags! and the General is here. John Berryman. *Fr.* Sonnets to Chris. **CP-BerrJ**

Presidential Poem, A. Ted Kooser. **SP-KoosT**

President's Speech, The. Hayden Carruth. **CP-CarHS**

Press, The. Rudyard Kipling. **CP-KiplR**

Press Conference: King James Version. James McAuley. **SP-McAuJ**

Press is Peculiar, The. Carl Sandburg. **CP-SandC**

Press[e] me not to take more pleasure. The Rose. George Herbert. **CP-HerbG**

Press on the thought till every word is proved. Ars Poetica. John Hewitt. **CP-HewiJ**

Press onward, quickened souls, who mounting move. Christina Georgina Rossetti. *Fr.* Faint, Yet Pursuing. **CP-RosC3**

Press reports the enemy in power: the solo, The. Fields of Earth. Kenneth Patchen. **CP-PatcK**

Pressed by the Moon, Mute Arbitress of Tides. Charlotte Smith. (Written in the Church-yard at Middleton in Sussex.) **CP-SmitC**

Pressed Gentian, The. John Greenleaf Whittier. **CP-WhitJ**

Pressed with conflicting thoughts of love and fear. St Paul's. William Wordsworth. **CP-WorW1**

Pressing down I remember. In Your Own Words Without Lying Tell Something of Your Background With Particular Attention to Anything Relating to the Position For Which You Are Applying. Press Down. Miller Williams. **SP-WillM**

Pressing On. "Bob Dylan." **CP-DylaB**

Pressure as it crushes gags the moan, The. The Iceberg. Randall Jarrell. **CP-JarrR**

Pressure of sun on the rockslide. Water. Gary Snyder. **CP-SnydG**

Prest by the load of life, the weary mind. Prologue to Goldsmith's The Good Natur'd Man. Samuel Johnson. **CP-JohnS**

Prest her cold finger closer to her lips. John Keats. **EnRP** *Fr.* The Fall of Hyperion. **CP-KeatJ**

Prestidigitator makes things disappear, A. The Prestidigitator 1. Al Young. **CP-YounA**

Prestidigitator 1, The. Al Young. **CP-YounA**

Prestidigitator 2, The. Al Young. **CP-YounA**

Prestige. David Herbert Lawrence. **CP-LawrD**

Prestige. George Meredith. **CP-MerG2**

  "Full sooth he was a jewel bird to own."

  "His plunge matched the waters poured aglow."

  "In Eastern climes was once a cock, whose fame."

Presumption has it's Affliction. Emily Dickinson. **SP-DickE**

Presumptuous bard! How could you dare. An Answer to a Scandalous Poem. Jonathan Swift. **CP-SwifJ**

Presumptuous Poet, could you dare, *diff. vers.* Jonathan Swift. *See* An Answer to a Scandalous Poem.

Pretension has it / you can't. For the Graduation. Robert Creeley. **CP-CreeR**

Pretension's. Robert Creeley. **CP-CreeR**

Pretty. Stevie Smith. **CP-SmitS**

Pretty. Louis Zukofsky. **CP-ZukLS**

Pretty a day, A. Edward Estlin Cummings. **CP-CummE; SP-CummE**

Pretty boarders are leaving the trees, The. Emily Dickinson. **SP-DickE**

Pretty Epigram for [Those] the Entertainment of Those Who [Pay] Have Paid Great Sums in the Venetian & Flemish Ooze, A. William Blake. **CP-BlakW**

Pretty glow on the water. Kenneth Patchen. **CP-PatcK**

Pretty Halcyon Days. Ogden Nash. **CP-NashO**

Pretty little three / Sparrows in a tree. April. Christina Georgina Rossetti. *Fr.* The Months: A Pageant. **CP-RosC2**

Pretty Love, I Must Outlive You. Edna St. Vincent Millay. **CP-MillE**

Pretty party for people, a. And. Robert Creeley. **CP-CreeR**

Pretty, pretty girl, A. Profile of a Lady. Tu Fu, *tr. fr. Chinese by* William Carlos Williams *with* David Rafael Wang. **CP-WilW2**

Pretty Rain from those sweet Eaves, The. Emily Dickinson. **CP-DickE**

Pretty Redhead, The. Guillaume Apollinaire, *tr. fr. French by* James Wright. **CP-WrigJ**

Pretty Woman, A. Robert Browning. **CP-BroR1**

Pretty women wonder where my secret lies. Phenomenal Woman. Maya Angelou. **SP-AngeM**

Prevalence of the. Charles Henri Ford. **SP-FordC** *Fr.* Emblems of Arachne.

Prevalent At One Time. Marianne Craig Moore. **CP-MoorM**

Prevision, or Provision. Robert Herrick. **CP-HerrR**

Prey swooped up, the iron love seat shudders. Up and Down. James Merrill. **SP-MerrJ**

Price, The. Wystan Hugh Auden. **CP-AudeW**

Price, The. Charles Bukowski. **SP-BukC1**

Price, The. James Liddy. **CP-LiddJ**

Price of Experience, The. William Blake. **EnRP; Prf** *Fr.* Vala; or The Four Zoas. **CP-BlakW**

  (Night II (Enion's Lament).) **PoE**

Price of This Book, The. Leonard Cohen. **CP-CoheL**

Prickles is waspish, and puts forth his sting. Upon Prickles. Robert Herrick. **CP-HerrR**

Pride. Wystan Hugh Auden. **CP-AudWJ**

Pride. Wystan Hugh Auden. **CP-AudWJ**

Pride Allowable in Poets. Robert Herrick. **CP-HerrR**

Pride Goeth Before a Raise or Ah, There, Mrs. Cadwallader-Smith. Ogden Nash. **CP-NashO**

Pride in your history is pride. Louis MacNeice. *Fr.* Suite for Recorders. **CP-MacNL**

Pride, Malice, Folly, against Dryden rose. Alexander Pope. **EPCY** *Fr.* An Essay on Criticism. **CP-PopeA**

Pride of Love. Robert Ranke Graves. **CP-GravR**

Pride of Progeny. Robert Ranke Graves. **CP-GravR**

Pride of the Dead, The. Thomas Merton. **CP-MertT**

Pride of the Peacock, The. William Blake. **FF; RaBo** *Fr.* Proverbs of Hell. **MeMBP** *Fr.* The Marriage of Heaven and Hell. **CP-BlakW**

Priest. Hilda Doolittle. **CP-DoolH**

Priest Goes through the Motions of the Play, The. John Hewitt. **CP-HewiJ**

Priestcraft and Private Judgement. John Dryden. **OBS** *Fr.* Religio Laici. **SP-DrydJ**

Priesthood, The. George Herbert. **CP-HerbG**

Priestley. Samuel Taylor Coleridge. *Fr.* Effusions. **CP-ColeS**

Priest's Curse on Dancing, The. Howard Nemerov. **CP-NemeH**

Priests of the Old Gods, The. Clement of Alexandria, *tr. by* Thomas Merton. **CP-MertT** *Fr.* Diatribe Against the Old Gods.

Prig now drinks Water, who before drank Beere. Upon Prig. Robert Herrick. **CP-HerrR**

Prigg, when he comes to houses, oft doth use. Upon Prigg. Robert Herrick. **CP-HerrR**

Primacy of Dullness, The. John Dryden. *See* All human[e] things are subject to decay.

Primal Passions, The. David Herbert Lawrence. **CP-LawrD**

Primary Considerations. Ron Koertge. **SP-KoerR**

Primavera, The. Hayden Carruth. *Fr.* Contra Mortem. **CP-CarHL**

Prime. Wystan Hugh Auden. **CMoP; PoE** *Fr.* Horae Canonicae. **CP-AudeW**

Prime. John Berryman. **CP-BerrJ**

Prime. Donald Davie. *Fr.* Horae Canonicae. **CP-DavDo**

Prime Minister. John Hewitt. **CP-HewiJ**

Primer. Charles Simic. **SP-SimiC**

Primer Amor. Edwin Rolfe, *tr. fr. Spanish by* Jose Manuel Cabezas Cabello. **CP-RolfE**

Primer for Statesmen. John Crowe Ransom. *Fr.* Two Gentlemen in Bonds. **SP-RansJ**

Primer for Swimming at Black Point, A. Stephen Dunn. **SP-DunnS**

Primer for the Nuclear Age. Rita Dove. **SP-DoveR**

Primer Lesson. Carl Sandburg. **CP-SandC**

Primer of Plato. Jean Garrigue. **SP-GarrJ**

Primer of the Daily Round, A. Howard Nemerov. **CP-NemeH**

Primeval heathland spattered with the bones of mice. Geoffrey Hill. *Fr.* Mercian Hymns. **CP-HillG**

Primitive. George Oppen. **CP-OppeG**

Primitive head, That. Bad Island, The—Easter. Robert Frost. **CP-FrosR**

Primitive Journal. Charles Wright. **SP-WrigC**

Primitive Journal II. Charles Wright. **SP-WrigC**

Primitive like an Orb, A. Wallace Stevens. **CP-StevW**

Primitive Saxon Clergy. William Wordsworth. *Fr.* Ecclesiastical Sonnets. **CP-WorW2**

Primordial locutions and ventures. Seven Archaic Images. Thomas Merton. **CP-MertT**

Primrose, The. Robert Burns. **CP-BurnR**

Primrose[, Being at Montgomery Castle, upon the Hill, on Which It Is Situate], The. John Donne. **CP-DonnJ**

Primrose, The. Robert Herrick. **CP-HerrR**

Primrose. William Carlos Williams. **CP-WilW1**

Primrose Bed, The. Robert Ranke Graves. **CP-GravR**

Primrose of the Rock, The. William Wordsworth. **CP-WorW2**

Primrose petal's edge, A. Ted Hughes. *Fr.* Gaudete.

Primrose shape was printed on His mind, The. Imagination. Phoebe Hesketh. **SP-HeskP**

Primroses; salutations; the miry skull. A Pre-Raphaelite Notebook. Geoffrey Hill. **CP-HillG**

Prince, The. Randall Jarrell. **CP-JarrR**

Prince Arthur. Edmund Spenser. **OBSC** *Fr.* The Faerie Queene. **CP-Spens**

Prince Athanase; a Fragment. Percy Bysshe Shelley. **CP-ShelP**

Prince Harry turns from Percy's pouring sides. Up, Jack. Richard Wilbur. **CP-WilbR**

Prince Hohenstiel-Schwangau, Saviour of Society. Robert Browning. **CP-BroR1**

Prince leans to the girl in scarlet heels, The. Cinderella. Sylvia Plath. **CP-PlatS**

Prince of Bards was old Aneurin. Aneurin's Harp. George Meredith. **CP-MerG1**

Prince of calm, treasure of fascinating cuts on my arm. The Spirit Ink. Frank O'Hara. **SP-OharF**

Prince of the church whose lofty mind. Acknowledgement. Archibald MacLeish. **CP-MacLA**

Prince Rupert's Drop. Gilbert Sorrentino. **SP-SorrG**

Prince Rupert's drop, paper muslin ghost. Pedantic Literalist. Marianne Craig Moore. **CP-MoorM**

Prince the ball of heaven should. Hafiz, *tr. by* Ralph Waldo Emerson. **CP-EmerR** *Fr.* Odes.

Prince Wen Hui's cook. Cutting up an Ox. Chuang Tzu, *tr. fr. Chinese by* Thomas Merton. **CP-MertT**

Princely cockroach, inheritor. Kneeling at the Pipes. Marge Piercy. **SP-PierM**

Princes and Favourites. Robert Herrick. **CP-HerrR**

Princes of Exile, The. Richard Shelton. **SP-ShelR**

Princes of Mercia were badger and raven, The. Geoffrey Hill. **HAP; NAEL-2; NoAM; NoP; PoE** *Fr.* Mercian Hymns. **CP-HillG**

Prince's Progress, The. Christina Georgina Rossetti. **CP-RosC1**

  Bride Song. **OBEV; OBVV; WPE**

  (Too Late.) **OtMeF**

Princes run downward on to the shore, The. Bank Holiday. Wystan Hugh Auden. **CP-AudWJ**

Princess, The. Tennyson. **CP-TennA**

  "As through the land at eve we went." **ImPo; LiTB; PoToHe; SCGP**

  (Reconciliation, The.)

  (We Kiss'd Again with Tears.) **PoToHe**

  "Ask me no more: the moon may draw the sea." **CBLP; GBL; ImPo; LiTB; MeMBP; NAEL-2; OBNC; PoEL-5; TrGrPo**

  "Bright is the moon on the deep." **PIP**

  "Home they brought her warrior dead." **OXAEP-2; TrGrPo**

  Prologue: "Sir Walter Vivian all a summer's day."

  Sir Walter Vivian's House. **CBCK**

  "So was their sanctuary violated."

    " 'Blame not thyself too much,' I said, "nor blame."" **NAEL-2**

  "Come down, O maid, from yonder mountain height." **EBVV; FF; GTBS-P; MeMBP; NAEL-2; NOBVV; OAEL-2; OBEV; OBNC; PIP; SCGP; TrGrPo**

  (Idyl, An: "Come down, O maid, from yonder mountain height.") **TrGrPo**

  "Now sleeps the crimson petal, now the white." **ArLo; BLPL; BoLoP; CBLP; ChER; ChTr; CoGr; EBEV; EBVV; ELP; FHYEP; FaBoBe; FaPoB; FiP; GBL; GTBS-P; LLLT; MeMBP; NAEL-2; NIP; NOBE; NoP; OBEV; OBNC; OPOU; OXAEP-2; PPP; PIP; PoEL-5; SCGP; SCV; SeCePo; TFi; TrGrPo**

  (Song: "Now sleeps the crimson petal, now the white.") **BLPL; FaBoBe; OPOU**

  (Summer Night.) **OBEV; SeCePo**

  "So she low-toned; while with shut eyes I lay." **EBVV**

  "Splendor falls on castle walls, The." **AWP; BLPL; CH; ChTr; ClHu; CoGr; EBEvV; EBVV; ELP; FHYEP; FaBV; FaBoCh; FaBoPP; FaFP; FaPON; FiP; GN; GoJo; HeIL; HeIP; ImPo; InPK; LiTB; MeMBP; NAEL-2; NOBE; NoP; OAEL-2; OBEV; OBNC; PeVV; PoEL-5; PrIm; TFi; TrGrPo; UnPo; UnS; WSC; WiR**

  (Blow, Bugle, Blow.) **BLPL; ChTr; FaFP; ImPo; LiTB; NOBE; OBEV; UnPo; UnS; WiR**

  (Bugle Song.) **FaPON; GN**

  (He Hears the Bugle at Killarney.) **FaBoPP**

  (Splendour Falls, The.) **CoGr; TFi**

  "Sweet and low, sweet and low." **BLPL; BoTP; FHYEP; FaBoBe; FaPON; MOS; NAEL-2; OxBChV; PIP; PoLF; SCGP; TrGrPo**

  (Lullaby: "Sweet and low, sweet and low.") **PoLF**

  "There sinks the nebulous star we call the Sun."

  "O Swallow, Swallow, flying, flying South." **CBLP; PIP**

  "Tears, idle tears, I know not what they mean." **AWP; EBEvV; EBVV; ELP; EnVR; FPL; FaBoRV; FaFP; FaPoR; FiP; GTBS-P; HAP; ImPo; InPS; InvP; LiTB; MeMBP; NAEL-2; NIP; NOBE; NoP; OAEL-2; OBNC; OXAEP-2; PPP; PIP; PoE; PoEL-5; Poetr; SCGP; TEP; TFi; TrGrPo; UnPo; WeW**

  "Thy voice is heard through rolling drums." **TrGrPo**

Princess and the Goblins, The. Sylvia Plath. **CP-PlatS**

Princess Casamassima, The. Daniel Gerard Hoffman. **SP-HoffD**

Princess Di. James Schuyler. **CP-SchuJ**

Princess in the eastern tale, A. The Sleeping City. George Meredith. **CP-MerG1**

Princesse Löysa drawing. Richard Lovelace. **CP-LoveR**

Princess Recalls Her One Adventure, The. Edna St. Vincent Millay. **CP-MillE**

Princess, the poem is born and you have woken. Hayden Carruth. *Fr.* The Sleeping Beauty. **CP-CarHL**

Princess Wakes in the Wood, The. Randall Jarrell. **CP-JarrR**

Principle of all things; entrails made. Lucretius, *tr. fr. Latin* by Ralph Waldo Emerson. **CP-EmerR**

Print from a Lucite Block. Kay Boyle. **CP-BoylK**

Print is too small, distressing me, The. The Last Decision. Maya Angelou. **SP-AngeM**

Print-Out Song. Daniel Gerard Hoffman. **SP-HoffD**

Prints from the book club swelled, The. Speakers from the Vietnam War. Dabney Stuart. **SP-StuaD**

Prioress' Tale—A Modernization, The, *mod. vers.* by William Wordsworth; *incl.* The Prioress' Prologue. Geoffrey Chaucer. **CP-WorW1** *Fr.* The Canterbury Tales. **CP-ChauG**

Prioress's Prologue, The. Geoffrey Chaucer. *Fr.* The Canterbury Tales. **CP-ChauG**

   Two Invocations of the Virgin, II. **ACP**

Prioress's Tale, The. Geoffrey Chaucer. **ACP** *Fr.* The Canterbury Tales. **CP-ChauG**

Priory of St Saviour, Glendalough, The. Donald Davie. **CP-DavDo**

Priscilla. Henry Wadsworth Longfellow. **TreFS** *Fr.* The Courtship of Miles Standish. **SP-LongH**

Prism. James Merrill. **SP-MerrJ**

Prism. Howard Nemerov. **CP-NemeH**

Prison gets to be a friend, A. Emily Dickinson. **CP-DickE**

Prison Island. James Fenton. **SP-FentJ**

Prison Life. Charles Henri Ford. **SP-FordC**

Prison Walls. Robert Ranke Graves. **CP-GravR**

Prisoner. Maya Angelou. **SP-AngeM**

Prisoner, The, *see also* Julian M. and A.G. Rochelle *and* The Visionary. Emily Brontë. **CP-BronE**

   "He comes with western winds, with evening's wandering airs." **ELP**

   "Still, let my tyrants know, I am not doomed to wear." **ChER; NOBE; NoP; OBEV; OBNC; OBVV**

Prisoner, The. Elizabeth Barrett Browning. **CP-BroEB**

Prisoner, The. Erica Jong. **SP-JongE**

Prisoner, The. Raissa Maritain, *tr. fr. French* by Thomas Merton. **CP-MertT**

Prisoner, The. Charles Simic. **SP-SimiC**

Prisoner at a Desk. May Sarton. **SP-SartM**

Prisoner at Work in a Turkish Garden. David Herbert Lawrence. *Fr.* Bits. **CP-LawrD**

Prisoner for Debt, The. John Greenleaf Whittier. **CP-WhitJ**

Prisoner in this space perpetually narrow, A. When. James Dickey. **CP-DickJ**

Prisoner of Chillon, The. Byron. **CP-Byron**

   "Kind of change came in my fate, A." **NOBE**

   Sonnet on Chillon. **FiP; LiTB; LoBV; MeMBP; OAEP; OBRV; PBMP; SeCeV; TrGrPo; TreFS**

   (On the Castle of Chillon.) **GTBS; GTBS-6; GTBS-P**

Prisoner of Zenda, The. Richard Wilbur. **CP-WilbR**

Prisoner ran forward. First his head, The. Essay on Death. Hayden Carruth. **CP-CarHS**

Prisoners. Hilda Doolittle. **CP-DoolH**

Prisoners. Michael Hartnett. **SP-HarMi**

Prisoners, The. Robert Earl Hayden. **CP-HaydR**

Prisoners. Randall Jarrell. **CP-JarrR**

Prisoners, The. Adrienne Rich. **CP-RicAE; SP-RicA2**

Prisoners, The. Stephen Spender. **CP-SpenS**

Prisoners at Work in the Rain. David Herbert Lawrence. *Fr.* Bits. **CP-LawrD**

Prisoners of infinite choice, The. Leaves. Derek Mahon. **SP-MahoD**

Prisoners of Naples, The. John Greenleaf Whittier. **CP-WhitJ**

Prisoners on the Roof, The. John Hewitt. **CP-HewiJ**

Prithee, Gentle Lady, List. William Wordsworth. **CP-WorW2**

Private Dining Room, The. Ogden Nash. **CP-NashO**

Private Eye, The. Howard Nemerov. **CP-NemeH**

Private faces in public places. Wystan Hugh Auden. **FaBoEE; PV; PeLV** *Fr.* Shorts [1927–1932] ("Pick a quarrel, go to war"). **CP-AudeW**

   (Dedication: "Private faces in public places.") **PeLV**

Private First Class. Charles Bukowski. **SP-BukC1**

Private Ground. Sylvia Plath. **CP-PlatS**

Private Life of the Sphinx. Muriel Rukeyser. **CP-RukeM**

Private Man on Public Men, A. Thomas Hardy. **CP-HardT**

Private Means Is Dead. Stevie Smith. **CP-SmitS**

Private Ortheris's Song. Rudyard Kipling. **CP-KiplR** *Fr.* The Courting of Dinah Shadd. *Fr.* Life's Handicap.

Privato commune bonum, Lea, cum melius fit. *acc. by English translation.* Thomas Campion. **CP-CampT**

Privet. Louis Zukofsky. **CP-ZukLS**

Privilege. Stephen Dunn. **SP-DunnS**

Prized memorial this slight work may prove, A. With a Small Present. William Wordsworth. **CP-WorW2**

Pro-Consuls, The. Rudyard Kipling. **CP-KiplR**

Pro Nobis. George Oppen. **CP-OppeG**

Pro Tanto Quid Retribuamas. John Hewitt. **CP-HewiJ**

Pro Veritate. . . / curtiliagia teneant. Canto 109. Ezra Pound. *Fr.* Cantos. **CP-PoCan**

Probably death fits all right in the world. This Day. Charles Kenneth Williams. **CP-WillC**

Probably the most important person I met in Vancouver. West 6. Charles Olson. *Fr.* West. **CP-OlsoC**

Probably two thieves, but why a stone this big. Kilmuir Cemetery: Stone with Two Skulls and No Name. Richard Hugo. **CP-HugoR**

Probatur Aliter. Jonathan Swift. **CP-SwifJ**

Probing the deepest selves. Stanley Jasspon Kunitz. *Fr.* Meditations on Death. **CP-KuniS**

Problem, The. Robert Creeley. **CP-CreeR**

Problem, The. Ralph Waldo Emerson. **CP-EmerR**

   "Hand that rounded Peter's dome, The." **EyDe**

Problem, The. Thomas Hardy. **CP-HardT**

Problem, The. Jonathan Swift. **CP-SwifJ**

Problem, The. John Greenleaf Whittier. **CP-WhitJ**

Problem, The. William Carlos Williams. **CP-WilW2**

Problem from Milton, A. Richard Wilbur. **CP-WilbR**

Problem. I cannot come among Your saints. Nones. John Berryman. **CP-BerrJ**

Problem in Spatial Composition, A. Robert Penn Warren. **SP-WarrR**

Problem in the pool is plain, The. Dytiscus. "Hugh MacDiarmid." **SP-MacDH**

Problem is urgent, yes, for this hot light, The. To a Woman. John Berryman. **CP-BerrJ**

Problem of Identity, The. Al Young. **CP-YounA**

Problem, unstated until now, is how, The. Adrienne Rich. **SP-RicA1** *Fr.* Contradictions: Tracking Poems.

Problem was to get first things, The. Grace to Be Said before Committee Meetings. Howard Nemerov. **CP-NemeH**

Problem with so many modern poems, friend, The. Prosody. David Markson. **CP-MarkD**

Problems About the Other Woman. Charles Bukowski. **SP-BukC1**

Problems of Gender. Robert Ranke Graves. **CP-GravR**

Problems of Knowledge. Daniel Gerard Hoffman. **SP-HoffD**

Procedures for Underground. Margaret Atwood. **SP-AtwM1**

Process, A. Charles Tomlinson. **CP-TomlC**

Process. Al Young. **CP-YounA**

Process in the Weather of the Heart, A. Dylan Thomas. **CP-ThomD**

Process of time worketh such wonder. Sir Thomas Wyatt. **CP-WyatT**

Processes of generation; deeds of settlement. The. Geoffrey Hill. **NoP** *Fr.* Mercian Hymns. **CP-HillG**

Procession, The. John Gould Fletcher. **SP-FletJ** *Fr.* The Parables of Christ.

Procession. James Schuyler. **CP-SchuJ**

Procession. Allen Tate. **CP-TateA**

Procession of Dead Days, A. Thomas Hardy. **CP-HardT**

Procession winds like a little snake, The. Island Funeral. "Hugh MacDiarmid." **SP-MacDH**

Processionals in the exemplary cave. Geoffrey Hill. *Fr.* Funeral Music. **CP-HillG**

Processions Suggested on a Sabbath Morning in the Vale of Chamouny. William Wordsworth. *Fr.* Memorials of a Tour of the Continent; 1820. **CP-WorW2**

Processions that lack high stilts have nothing that catches the eye. High Talk. William Butler Yeats. **CP-YeatW**

Proclamation, The. Henry Wadsworth Longfellow. **PAH** *Fr.* Act II. *Fr.* John Endicott. **SP-LongH**

Proclamation, The. John Greenleaf Whittier. **CP-WhitJ**

Proclaymèd queene and mother of a god. The Visitation. Robert Southwell. **CP-SoutR**

Procne, Philomela, and Itylus. Philomela. John Crowe Ransom. **SP-RansJ**

Procrastination Is All of the Time. Ogden Nash. **CP-NashO**

Prodigal, The. Elizabeth Bishop. **CP-BishE**

Prodigal of loves and barbecues. To the (Supposed) Patron. Geoffrey Hill. **CP-HillG**

Prodigal Son, The. Robert Bly. **SP-BlyR**

Prodigal Son, The. Rudyard Kipling. **CP-KiplR** *Fr.* Kim.

Prodigal Son, A. Christina Georgina Rossetti. **CP-RosC2**

Prodigal Son is kneeling in the husks, The. The Prodigal Son. Robert Bly. **SP-BlyR**

Prodigal speaks: / I have no forgiveness in my soul The. Exile's Return. Malcolm Lowry. **CP-LowrM**

Prodigall Chyld's Soule Wracke, The. Robert Southwell. **CP-SoutR**

Prodigious goals—Flakes boat starmarsh—Great Highone I care. I Care What Happens. Kenneth Patchen. **CP-PatcK**

Prodigious Madness of the writing Race! Prologue to Garrick's *Lethe*. Samuel Johnson. **CP-JohnS**

Prodigious this! the Frail-one of our Play. Epilogue to Mr. Rowe's *Jane Shore*. Alexander Pope. **CP-PopeA**

Prodigy. Charles Simic. **SP-SimiC**

Prodigy, The. Charles Kenneth Williams. **SP-WillC**

Product. George Oppen. **CP-OppeG**

Products of my Farm are these, The. Emily Dickinson. **CP-DickE**

Proem: "I love the old melodious lays." John Greenleaf Whittier. **CP-WhitJ**

PROEM: *Against metaphor—but how then?*. Jenny Joseph. *Fr.* Life and Turgid Times of A. Citizen. **SP-JoseJ**

Proensa. Charles Olson. **CP-OlsoC**

Professionals see the signs in the dice, the signs in the cards and clouds, The. Muriel Rukeyser. **CP-RukeM**

Professor Varder handles Dante. Humanities Course. John Updike. **CP-UpdiJ**

Professors, The. Charles Bukowski. **SP-BukC1**

Professor's Song, A. John Berryman. **CP-BerrJ**

Proffered Love Rejected. Sir John Suckling. **CP-SuckJ**

Profile. Wystan Hugh Auden. **CP-AudeW**

Profile of a Lady. Tu Fu, *tr. fr. Chinese by* William Carlos Williams *with* David Rafael Wang. **CP-WilW2**

Profile of a man who waits, The. Shaving at Night. Charles Simic. **SP-SimiC**

Profit and Batten. Villains. Stevie Smith. **CP-SmitS**

Profiteers. Alexander Pope. *See* Well, if a King's a lion, at the least.

Profound and thrilling vibration of justice, sense of ultimate justice, The. Vibration of Justice. David Herbert Lawrence. **CP-LawrD**

Profound sensual experience of truth: Yea, this *is*! Satisfaction. David Herbert Lawrence. **CP-LawrD**

Profound stillness in the greystone. The Spark in the Tinder of Knowing. Kenneth Rexroth. **CP-RexKL**

Profoundest of all our sensualitites, The. The Deepest Sensuality. David Herbert Lawrence. **CP-LawrD**

Profumo. Paul Muldoon. **SP-MuldP**

Prognosis. Louis MacNeice. **CP-MacNL**

Prognosis. Theodore Roethke. **CP-RoetT**

Prognostick, A. Robert Herrick. **CP-HerrR**

Programme Note. Charles Tomlinson. **CP-TomlC**

Progress. Wystan Hugh Auden. **CP-AudWJ**

Progress? Wystan Hugh Auden. **CP-AudeW**

Progress, The. Gwendolyn Brooks. **SP-BrooG**

Progress, The. Robert Ranke Graves. **CP-GravR**

Progress. Peter Meinke. **SP-MeinP**

Progress. George Meredith. **CP-MerG1**

Progress. Alexander Pope. ECEV *Fr.* Windsor-Forest [*or* Windsor Forest]. **CP-PopeA**

Progress is/ The law of life, man is not Man as yet. The Awakening of Man. Robert Browning. WGRP *Fr.* Paracelsus. **CP-BroR1**

Progress of Beauty, The. Jonathan Swift. **CP-SwifJ**

Progress of Error, The. William Cowper. **CP-CowpW**

"From school to Cam or Isis, and thence home." **OBTV**

Progress of Faust, The. Karl Shapiro. **SP-ShapK**

Progress of Marriage, The. Jonathan Swift. **CP-SwifJ**

Progress of Œnia, The. Allen Tate. **CP-TateA**

Divagation.

Epilogue to Œnia.

In Wintertime.

Madrigale: "Seed in your heart, warm dust transmuted."

Vigil.

Progress of Poesy, The. Thomas Gray. **CP-GrayT**

Progress of Poesy, The. Thomas Gray. **CP-GrayT**

"Behold, where Dryden's less presumptuous car." **EPCY**

"Far from the sun and summer gale." **EPCY**

"In climes beyond the solar road." **OXAEP-1**

"Nor second he, that rode sublime." **EPCY**

"Oh lyre divine, what daring spirit." **EPCY**

Progress of Poetry, The. Jonathan Swift. **CP-SwifJ**

Progress[e] of the Soul[e], The. John Donne. **CP-DonnJ**

"Great Destiny the commissary of God." **OxBoCh**

"It quickened [*or* quicknd] next a toyful[l] ape, and so." **PoEL-2**

Whale, The. **ChTr**

Progress of the Soul, The. Thomas McGrath. **SP-McGrT**

Progress of the Spark, The, *parody of* John Donne. Rudyard Kipling. **CP-KiplR** *Fr.* The Muse among the Motors.

Progress Report. Archie Randolph Ammons. **SP-AmmoA**

Progress Report. Audre Lorde. **SP-LordA**

Progress Report. Leonard Nathan. **SP-NathL**

Progress to a View of Life. Kenneth Patchen. **CP-PatcK**

Progress you have made is very remarkable, The. Wystan Hugh Auden. *Fr.* Man of La Mancha.

("Ladies and gentlemen, you have made most remarkable.") **CP-AudeW** (Recitative by Death.) **CP-AudeW**

Progression. George Meredith. **CP-MerG2**

Progression. Stevie Smith. **CP-SmitS**

Progressive Insanities of a Pioneer. Margaret Atwood. **SP-AtwM1**

Prohibition, The. John Donne. **CP-DonnJ**

Prohibition, The. Robert Ranke Graves. **CP-GravR**

Project, The. Richard Eberhart. **CP-EberR**

Projected from the bilious Childe. Manfred. George Meredith. **CP-MerG1**

Projected Slide of an Unknown Soldier. Margaret Atwood. **SP-AtwM1**

Projected X-rays. Northern Lights. Daniel Gerard Hoffman. **SP-HoffD**

Projection. Langston Hughes. **SP-HughL**

Projection. Howard Nemerov. **CP-NemeH**

Projector. Hilda Doolittle. **CP-DoolH**

Projector II. Hilda Doolittle. **CP-DoolH**

Prokofiev's sick prince can't laugh. The Love for One Orange. Randall Jarrell. **CP-JarrR**

Prolegomenon to a Theodicy, A, *sels.* Kenneth Rexroth.

"Asking is / Dream of deign." **CP-RexKL**

"Asking is / Dream of deign."

"Bell / Too softly and too slowly tolled, The." **CP-RexKL**

"Bell / Too softly and too slowly tolled, The." **SP-RexrK**

"They were in an unstable condition." **SP-RexrK**

"Black / Blue Black / Blue." **CP-RexKL**

"Casual reverberation is not restitution, The." **CP-RexKL**

"Casual reverberation is not restitution, The."

"Grammar of cause, The." **CP-RexKL**

"In those days / In a pool of noise." **CP-RexKL**

"In those days / In a pool of noise."

"Light / Light / The sliver in the firmament." **SP-RexrK**

"It is now a decline." **CP-RexKL**

"This is the winter of the hardest year." **CP-RexKL; SP-RexrK**

"This the mortared stone." **CP-RexKL**

"This the mortared stone."

"We were interested in ways of being." **CP-RexKL; SP-RexrK**

Proletarian in Abstract Light. Thomas McGrath. **SP-McGrT**

Proletarian Portrait. William Carlos Williams. **CP-WilW1**

Proletariat for your Messiah, the poor and many are to seize power, The. Blind Horses. Robinson Jeffers. **CP-JefR2**

Prolific Spell, The. Donald Davie. **CP-DavDo**

Prologo. Thomas Merton. **CP-MertT**

Prologue: "And the way goes on in the worn earth." Archibald MacLeish. NoAM *Fr.* Conquistador. **CP-MacLA**

Prologue: "Delusions of the days that once have been." Henry Wadsworth Longfellow. **PAH** *Fr.* Giles Corey of the Salem Farms. **SP-LongH**

Prologue: "Fore love, a mighty session; and (I fear)." Sir John Suckling. *Fr.* The Fifth Act of Aglaura As Presented to the Court. *Fr.* Aglaura. **CP-SuckJ**

Prologue: "In these stern times of ours, when crimson strife." Thomas Hardy. **CP-HardT** *Fr.* The Dynasts.

Prologue: "I've thought upon't; and cannot tell which way." Sir John Suckling. *Fr.* Aglaura. **CP-SuckJ**

Prologue: "Ladies and Gentlemen seems stiff and cold." "Lewis Carroll." **CP-CarrL**

Prologue: "Love, to give law unto his subject hearts." Sir Thomas Wyatt. **CP-WyatT** *Fr.* Penitential Psalms.

Prologue: "Narcissus, speaking in the first person." Delmore Schwartz. **SP-SchwD**

Prologue: "No song nor dance I bring from yon great city." Robert Burns. **CP-BurnR**

Prologue: "Not for me, the crusader cross." James McAuley. **SP-McAuJ** *Fr.* The Exile's Recurring Nightmare.

Prologue: "O the old wall here! How I could pass." Robert Browning. **CP-BroR2**

Prologue: "Our author by experience finds it true." John Dryden. FiP; **OBS; OxBoLi; SeCV-2** *Fr.* Aureng-Zebe. **SP-DrydJ**

Prologue: "Poet's age is sad: for why?, The." Robert Browning. **CP-BroR2**

Prologue: "Pray, Reader, have you eaten ortolans." Robert Browning. **CP-BroR2**

Prologue: "Sir Walter Vivian all a summer's day." Tennyson. *Fr.* The Princess. **CP-TennA**
Sir Walter Vivian's House. **CBCK**

Prologue: "Starting with little in mind." Jim Carroll. **SP-CarrJ**

Prologue: "To-night we strive to read, as we may best." Henry Wadsworth Longfellow. *Fr.* John Endicott. **SP-LongH**

Prologue: "To sing of wars, of captain[e]s, and of kings." Anne Bradstreet. **CP-BradA**

Prologue: "When by a generous Public's kind acclaim." Robert Burns. **CP-BurnR**

Prologue: "Wiffie! I'm *sure* that something *is* the matter." "Lewis Carroll." **CP-CarrL**

Prologue: "Wit in a prologue poets justly may." Sir John Suckling. *Fr.* The Goblins. **CP-SuckJ**

Prologue at Sixty. Wystan Hugh Auden. **CP-AudeW**

Prologue Design'd for Mr. Durfy's Last Play. Alexander Pope. **CP-PopeA**

Prologue for an Evening at the Whitefriars. John Hewitt. **CP-HewiJ**

Prologue in Heaven, *See also* Randall Jarrell's *The Archangels' Song.* Johann Wolfgang von Goethe, *tr.* by Shelley. **CP-ShelP** *Fr.* Faust.
"Sun makes music as of old, The." **AWP; OBVE**
(Chorus of the Archangels, The.) **OBVE**

Prologue, Intended for a Dramatic Piece of King Edward the Fourth. William Blake. **CP-BlakW**

Prologue: Letter to an Indolent Norn. John Ciardi. **SP-CiarJ**

Prologue of the Author's to a Masque at Witten, A. Sir John Suckling. **CP-SuckJ**

Prologue of the Monk's Tale, The. Geoffrey Chaucer. *Fr.* The Canterbury Tales. **CP-ChauG**

Prologue of the Nun's Priest's Tale, The, *sels.* Geoffrey Chaucer. *Fr.* The Canterbury Tales. **CP-ChauG**
(" 'Stop!' cried the Knight. "No more of this, good sir!"") **NAWM-1**

Prologue of the Prioress's Tale. Geoffrey Chaucer. *Fr.* The Canterbury Tales. **CP-ChauG**

Prologue Spoken by Mr[.] Garrick at the Opening of the Theatre in Drury Lane, 1747. Samuel Johnson. **CP-JohnS**
"Then, crushed by rules, and weakened as refined." **EPCY**
"Then Jonson came, instructed from the school." **EPCY**

Prologue: The Birth of Architecture. Wystan Hugh Auden. *Fr.* Thanksgiving for a Habitat. **CP-AudeW**
"From gallery-grave and the hunt of a wren-king." **EyDe**
"Some thirty inches from my nose." **FaBoEE; IHNG**

Prologue: The Endless Inscription, *sels.* Thomas Merton. *Fr.* The Geography of Lograire. **CP-MertT**

Prologue: The Grinder. Alun Lewis. **CP-LewiA**

Prologue to a Play for Mr. Dennis's Benefit, in 1733, when He Was Old, Blind, and in Great Distress, a Little before His Death, A. Alexander Pope. **CP-PopeA**

Prologue to *Don Sebastian.* John Dryden. **SP-DrydJ** *Fr.* Don Sebastian.

Prologue to Garrick's *Lethe.* Samuel Johnson. **CP-JohnS**

Prologue to Goldsmith's *The Good Natur'd Man.* Samuel Johnson. **CP-JohnS**

Prologue to Hugh Kelly's *A Word to the Wise.* Samuel Johnson. **CP-JohnS**

Prologue to King John. William Blake. **CP-BlakW**

Prologue to "La Guida Di Bragia." "Lewis Carroll." **CP-CarrL**

Prologue to Mallet's Mustapha. James Thomson. **CP-ThomJ**

Prologue to Mr. Addison's *Tragedy of Cato.* Alexander Pope. **CP-PopeA**

Prologue to "Rhymes to be Traded for Bread." Nicholas Vachel Lindsay. **CP-LindV**

Prologue to Sir Thopas. Geoffrey Chaucer. **NAEL-1; Par** *Fr.* The Canterbury Tales. **CP-ChauG**

Prologue to Sir Thopas, *see* Introduction to the Tale of Sir Thopas, The. Geoffrey Chaucer. *See* Prologue to Sir Thopas.

Prologue to Spring. Sylvia Plath. **CP-PlatS**

Prologue to Tancred and Sigismunda. James Thomson. **CP-ThomJ**

Prologue to the Court ("'Tis strange, perchance you'll think, that she, that died"). Sir John Suckling. *Fr.* The Fifth Act of Aglaura As Presented to the Court. *Fr.* Aglaura. **CP-SuckJ**

Prologue to the Court ("Those common passions, hopes, and fears, that still"). Sir John Suckling. *Fr.* Aglaura. **CP-SuckJ**

Prologue to the Franklin's Tale, The, *see* Franklin's Prologue, The. Geoffrey Chaucer. *See* The Franklin's Prologue.

Prologue to the Friar's Tale, The, *see* Friar's Prologue, The. Geoffrey Chaucer. *See* The Friar's Prologue.

Prologue to the Miller's Tale, The, *see* Miller's Prologue, The. Geoffrey Chaucer. *See* The Miller's Prologue.

Prologue to the Pardoner's Tale, The, *see* Pardoner's Prologue, The. Geoffrey Chaucer. *See* The Pardoner's Prologue.

Prologue to the Scholars, A. Richard Lovelace. **CP-LoveR**

Prologue to *The Spanish Friar.* John Dryden. **SP-DrydJ** *Fr.* The Spanish Friar [*or* Fryar].

Prologue to *The Tempest* [*or The Enchanted Island*]. John Dryden. **SP-DrydJ**

Prologue to the *Three Hours after Marriage.* Alexander Pope. **CP-PopeA**

Prologue to the University of Oxford, 1673. John Dryden. **SP-DrydJ**

Prologue to the University of Oxford, 1674. John Dryden. **SP-DrydJ**

Prologue to the Wife of Bath's Tale, The, *see* Wife of Bath's Prologue, The. Geoffrey Chaucer. *See* The Wife of Bath's Prologue.

Prologue to *What is She?* A Comedy, in Five Acts. Charlotte Smith. **CP-SmitC** *Fr.* What is She?

Prologue to Wiley on November 17, 1941. Randall Jarrell. **CP-JarrR**

Prologue to William Godwin, *Antonio: or, The Soldier's Return.* Charlotte Smith. **CP-SmitC**

Prologue: Why I Have a Wet Footprint on Top of My Mind. Thomas Merton. *Fr.* North. *Fr.* The Geography of Lograire. **CP-MertT**

Prologues are over. It is a question, now, The. Asides on the Oboe. Wallace Stevens. **CP-StevW**

Prologues to What Is Possible. Wallace Stevens. **CP-StevW**

Proludium. Ben Jonson. **CP-JonsB**

Promenade. Charles Bukowski. **SP-BukC3**

Promenade. William Carlos Williams. **CP-WilW1**

Promenade, the plage, the paysage, The. Le Rendez-Vous des Paysages. Charles Tomlinson. *Fr.* Two Poems on titles proposed by Octavio and Marie José Paz. **CP-TomlC**

Promenading their / skirted galleons of sex. The Return to Work. William Carlos Williams. **CP-WilW1**

Prometheus. Byron. **CP-Byron**

Prometheus. Paul Laurence Dunbar. **CP-DunbP**

Prometheus. Richard Eberhart. **CP-EberR**

Prometheus. Robert Ranke Graves. **CP-GravR**

Prometheus. Jonathan Swift. **CP-SwifJ**

Prometheus. Charles Tomlinson. **CP-TomlC**

Prometheus Bound. Aeschylus, *tr. fr.* Greek by Elizabeth Barrett Browning. **CP-BroEB**
"Bright light, swift-winged winds, springs of the rivers, numberless." **GrIP**
"But Fortune governed all their works[,] till when." **CP-RaleW; SiPSBD,** *tr.* by Sir Walter Ralegh;
"Divinity of air, fleet-feather'd gales." **PBBP**
Wail of Prometheus Bound, The. **WGRP**

Prometheus brought down fire to men. Native Water-Carrier (M.E.F.) Rudyard Kipling. *Fr.* Epitaphs of the War [1914–1918]. **CP-KiplR**

Prometheus in Straits. John Crowe Ransom. **SP-RansJ**

Prometheus on His Crag. Ted Hughes.
"Now I know I never shall." **SP-HughT**
"Prometheus on his crag." **SP-HughT**
"Prometheus on his crag." **SP-HughT**

Prometheus stole from Heaven the sacred fire. Prometheus. Paul Laurence Dunbar. **CP-DunbP**

Prometheus Unbound. Percy Bysshe Shelley. **CP-ShelP**
"As I have said, I floated to the earth." **FHYEP**
"Canst thou imagine where those spirits live." **WSC**
"Crawling glaciers pierce me with the spears." **FHYEP**
"Eagle so caught in some bursting cloud, An." **PBBP**
"I wandering went / Among the haunts and dwellings of mankind." **FiP** Life of Life. **CH; FiP; MeMBP; NOBE; PoE; PoEL-4**
(Hymn to the Spirit of Nature.) **GTBS; GTBS-6; GTBS-P**
"Loud deep calls me home even now to feed it, The." **ChER**
"Monarch of Gods and Dæmons, and all Spirits." **FiP; NAEL-2; OAEL-2**
"My soul is enchanted boat." **FHYEP**
"On a poet's lips I slept." **ChER; ELP; EPCY; FiP; TOF,** *ll.* 737–751; **GTBS; GTBS-6; GTBS-P**
(Poet's Dream, The.) **GTBS; GTBS-6; GTBS-P,** *ll.* 737–749;
"Soon as the sound had ceased whose thunder filled." **ChER**
"Sphere, which is as many thousand spheres, a." **ImOP**
"There the voluptuous nightingales." **PBBP**
"This is the day, which down the void abysm." **FHYEP**
"Thou, Earth, calm empire of a happy soul." **FaBoRV; PeECV**
"Thou knowest that toads and snakes and loathly worms." **PoE** Variation of the Song of the Moon.
Who Reigns? **SeCePo**

Promise, The. Charles Bukowski. **SP-BukC1**

Promise. Leonard Cohen. **CP-CoheL**

Promise. Paul Laurence Dunbar. **CP-DunbP**

Promise, The. Frederick Morgan. **SP-MorgF**

Promise, A. Charles Olson. **CP-OlsoC**

Promise, The. Charles Tomlinson. **CP-TomlC**

Promise / Within a cloud. . . Rain?, The. Eugene, Orgeon. Jim Carroll. **SP-CarrJ**

Promise in Disturbance, The. George Meredith. **CP-MerG1**

Promise is firmer than a Hope, A. Emily Dickinson. **SP-DickE**

Promise Me. Stanley Jasspon Kunitz. **CP-KuniS**

Promise me no promises, / So will I not promise you. Promises like Pie-Crust. Christina Georgina Rossetti. **CP-RosC3**

Promise This, When You be Dying. Emily Dickinson. **CP-DickE**

Promise to California, A. Walt Whitman. **CP-WhitW**

Promise was broken too freely, The. Galway Kinnell. **NaP** *Fr.* The Avenue Bearing the Initial of Christ into the New World. **SP-KinnG**

Promised Ballad, The. Robert Ranke Graves. **CP-GravR**

Promisers, The. Wilfred Owen. **CP-OwenW**

Promises. Rita Dove. **SP-DoveR**

Promises. Jim Morrison. **SP-MorrJ**

Promises. Richard Shelton. **SP-ShelR**

Promises like Pie-Crust. Christina Georgina Rossetti. **CP-RosC3**

Promises made drunk should be kept drunk. Malcolm Lowry. **CP-LowrM**

Promises, Promises. Paul Muldoon. **SP-MuldP**

Promotion, The. Miller Williams. **SP-WillM**

Prompt—executive Bird is the Jay, A. Emily Dickinson. **CP-DickE**

Prompt sadness of Schumann and Tchaikovsky. From Bowling Green. Al Young. **CP-YounA**

Prompt transformation works the novel Lore. Conversion. William Wordsworth. *Fr.* Ecclesiastical Sonnets. **CP-WorW2**

Promptress of unnumber'd sighs. To Fortune. Samuel Taylor Coleridge. **CP-ColeS**

Pronouncing My Name. Ron Koertge. **SP-KoerR**

Proof, The. Wystan Hugh Auden. *See* When rites and melodies begin.

Proof, The. Richard Wilbur. **CP-WilbR**

Proof and Disproof. Elizabeth Barrett Browning. **CP-BroEB**

Proof to No Purpose. Robert Herrick. **CP-HerrR**

Prop. LXI. Louis Zukofsky. *Fr.* 29 Songs. **CP-ZukLS**

Proper authorities served us with precautions. Jim Carroll. *Fr.* Morning. **SP-CarrJ**

Proper Pride. David Herbert Lawrence. **CP-LawrD**

Proper Soul / in the Proper Body, The. Charles Olson. **CP-OlsoC**

Proper Study of Mankind, The. Alexander Pope. *See* Know then thyself, presume not God to scan.

Proper way to eat a fig, in society, The. Figs. David Herbert Lawrence. **CP-LawrD**

Property and No-Property. David Herbert Lawrence. **CP-LawrD**

Property is now Solomon's baby. Solomon's Baby. David Herbert Lawrence. **CP-LawrD**

Property of Jesus. "Bob Dylan." **CP-DylaB**

Property! Property! Let us extend. Louis MacNeice. **IHNG** *Fr.* Jigsaws. **CP-MacNL**

(On Property.) **IHNG**

Property Question, The. David Herbert Lawrence. **CP-LawrD**

Prophecy, A. William Blake. **FaBoEH** *Fr.* America; a Prophecy. **CP-BlakW**

Prophecy, A. Allen Ginsberg. **CP-GinsA**

Prophecy. Luigi Pulci. **PAH** *Fr.* The Morgante Maggiore. **CP-Byron**

Prophecy. Tennyson. *See* For I Dipped [*or* Dipt] into the Future.

Prophecy February, 1807, A. William Wordsworth. **CP-WorW1**

Prophecy in Stone. Edwin Rolfe. **CP-RolfE**

Prophecy of Dante, The. Byron. **CP-Byron**

Prophecy of Samuel Sewall, The. John Greenleaf Whittier. **CP-WhitJ**

Prophecy on Lethe. Stanley Jasspon Kunitz. **CP-KuniS**

Prophesying. Reading water or words, signs are cards in their multi-. A Poem in Stretching. Robert Duncan. **SP-DuncR**

Prophet. David Herbert Lawrence. **CP-LawrD**

Prophet. Thomas Merton. **CP-MertT**

Prophet, The. Alice Notley. **SP-NotlA**

Prophet, The. Richard Shelton. **SP-ShelR**

Prophet at Creation's door, The. Creation and the Prophet. George Meredith. **CP-MerG2**

Prophet beware: there is a tricky urchin in nature. The Urchin. Robinson Jeffers. **CP-JefR3**

Prophet in a Landscape of Immemorial Time. Bill Knott. **SP-KnotB**

Prophet in the Rose Garden, The. David Herbert Lawrence. **CP-LawrD**

Prophet of dead words defeats himself, The. Edwin Arlington Robinson. *Fr.* Octaves. **CP-RobiE**

Prophet of disaster ceased to shout, The. The Broken Drought. Robert Frost. **CP-FrosR**

Prophet stood, The. The Deity. John Greenleaf Whittier. **CP-WhitJ**

Prophetess, The. Thomas Hardy. **CP-HardT**

Prophetess. John Greenleaf Whittier. **AA** *Fr.* Snow-Bound [*or* Snow-Bound; a Winter Idyl]. **CP-WhitJ**

Prophets, The. Wystan Hugh Auden. **CP-AudeW**

Prophets, The. John Donne. *Fr.* A Litany. **CP-DonnJ**

Prophets, The. Richard Shelton. **SP-ShelR**

Prophets at Home. Rudyard Kipling. **CP-KiplR** *Fr.* Hal o' the Draft. *Fr.* Puck of Pook's Hill.

Prophets have honour all over the Earth. Prophets at Home. Rudyard Kipling. **CP-KiplR** *Fr.* Hal o' the Draft. *Fr.* Puck of Pook's Hill.

Prophets Isaiah and Ezekiel dined with me, and, The. Memorable Fancy, A. William Blake. *Fr.* The Marriage of Heaven and Hell. **CP-BlakW**

Proposal for Recycling Wastes, A. Marge Piercy. **SP-PierM**

Propositions. Richard Eberhart. *Fr.* Aesthetics after War. **CP-EberR**

Propriety. Marianne Craig Moore. **CP-MoorM**

Props. Carl Sandburg. **CP-SandC**

Props assist the House, The. Emily Dickinson. **CP-DickE**

Pros Karolon ton Basilea [To King Charles]. Andrew Marvell, *tr. fr. Greek by* William A. McQueen *and* Kiffin A. Rockwell. **CP-MarvA**

Prose in Advent Time, *tr. from* "Jubilemus omnes una Deo nostro qui creavit omnia." *Unknown, tr. fr. Latin by* Thomas Merton. **CP-MertT**

Prose Poem. Charles Tomlinson. **CP-TomlC**

Prosody. David Markson. **CP-MarkD**

Prosopopoia: or Mother Hubberds Tale. Edmund Spenser. **CP-Spens**

Prospect, The. Elizabeth Barrett Browning. **CP-BroEB**

Prospect, The. Thomas Hardy. **CP-HardT**

Prospect. Louis MacNeice. **CP-MacNL**

Prospect. Sylvia Plath. **CP-PlatS**

Prospect, The. Adrienne Rich. **CP-RicAE**

Prospect, The. James Thomson. *Fr.* Liberty. **CP-ThomJ**

Prospect of Eden, The. John Milton. *See* O for that warning voice which he who saw.

Prospective Immigrants Please Note. Adrienne Rich. **CP-RicAE; SP-RicA1; SP-RicA2**

Prospects of Nostradamus, The. Thomas Merton. *Fr.* Cables to the Ace. **CP-MertT**

Prospectus, *identical to lines 754–860 of* The Recluse; Home at Grasmere. William Wordsworth. **EnRP; FHYEP; NoP; PoE** *Fr.* The Excursion. **CP-WorW2**

Prosperity has stolen stupor from me. Sleepless in Scarsdale. John Updike. **CP-UpdiJ**

Prospero and Sycorax. Ted Hughes. **SP-HughT**

Prospero to Ariel, *sels.* Wystan Hugh Auden. *Fr.* The Sea and the Mirror. **CP-AudeW**

Prospero's Isle. Isabella Gardner. **CP-GardI**

Prosperous and beautiful, The. The Park. Ralph Waldo Emerson. **CP-EmerR**

Prospice. Robert Browning. **CP-BroR1**

Protagonists. Richard Eberhart. **CP-EberR**

Protean Lover. Phoebe Hesketh. **SP-HeskP**

Protean Maiden, The. Thomas Hardy. **CP-HardT**

Protect us help us forgive us help give. Archibald MacLeish. *Fr.* Hamlet of A. Macleish. **CP-MacLA**

Protection of Jehovah, The. Bible, *O.T. See* Psalm 23: "Lord is my shepherd, I shall not want, The."

Protest. Countee Cullen. **CP-CullC**

Protest. Paul Laurence Dunbar. **CP-DunbP**

Protest against the Ballot. William Wordsworth. **CP-WorW2**

Protestant Churches, The. David Herbert Lawrence. **CP-LawrD**

Protestant Easter. Anne Sexton. **CP-SextA**

Protestant shadow on the overpass, The. Vir VI. James Liddy. *Fr.* Vir I–XII. **CP-LiddJ**

Protestants often live beneath. Big Brown Eyes. Gilbert Sorrentino. **SP-SorrG**

Protestation [A Sonnet], The. Thomas Carew. **CP-CareT**

Protesters in their houses built of placards, The. Washington: Tourist View. John Updike. **CP-UpdiJ**

Proteus. Ralph Waldo Emerson. **CP-EmerR**

Proteus. May Sarton. **SP-SartM**

Prothalamion. May Sarton. **SP-SartM**

Prothalamion. Edmund Spenser. **CP-Spens**

"Calm was the day, and through the trembling air." **EBEvV; EnRePo; ImPo; SCGP**

("Calme was the day, and through the trembling ayre.") **OXAEP-1**

"With that I saw two swans of goodly hue." **PBBP**

Protocols. Randall Jarrell. **CP-JarrR**

Proton Decay. Robert Pack. **SP-PackR**

Protus. Robert Browning. **CP-BroR1**

Proud and Beautiful. Carl Sandburg. **CP-SandC**

Proud as Apollo on his forked hill. Bufo. Alexander Pope. **OBEC; OBSV** *Fr.* Epistle to Dr. Arbuthnot. **CP-PopeA**

Proud Death with Swelling Port. Stevie Smith. **CP-SmitS**

Proud elephant, by accident of bulk. The High-Hearts. John Updike. **CP-UpdiJ**

Proud Farmer, The. Nicholas Vachel Lindsay. *Fr.* A Gospel of Beauty. **CP-LindV**

Proud Heart, The. Countee Cullen. **CP-CullC**

Proud men / Eternally / Go about. Nicholas Vachel Lindsay. *Fr.* The Kallyope Yell. **CP-LindV**

Proud Music of the Storm. Walt Whitman. **CP-WhitW**

Proud of his scientific attitude. Edward Estlin Cummings. **CP-CummE; SP-CummE**

Proud of my broken heart, since thou didst break it. Emily Dickinson. **CP-DickE**

Proud of Their Rags. Carl Sandburg. **CP-SandC**

Proud Songsters. Thomas Hardy. **CP-HardT**

Proud Torsos. Carl Sandburg. **CP-SandC**

Proud Were Ye, Mountains, When, in Times of Old. William Wordsworth. **CP-WorW2**

Proudest now is but my peer, The. The Poor Voter on Election Day. John Greenleaf Whittier. **CP-WhitJ**

Proudest pearl of the wide world. The Pearl of Biloxi. Nicholas Vachel Lindsay. **CP-LindV**

Proudly, the fedoras march on the heads of the somewhat. Sky Pieces. Carl Sandburg. **CP-SandC**

Proust, doing penance. Les Saints Nouveaux. John Updike. **CP-UpdiJ**

Prove whether I do change, my dear. Sir Thomas Wyatt. **CP-WyatT**

Proved Etherege prudish, selfish, hypocrite, heartless. Gerard Manley Hopkins. **CP-HopkG**

Provence. Louis MacNeice. *Fr.* Novelettes. **CP-MacNL**

Proverbs. Thomas Merton. **CP-MertT**

Proverbs: "What shul these clothes thus manyfold." Geoffrey Chaucer. **CP-ChauG**

Proverbs of Corca Bascinn. James Liddy. *Fr.* Love Songs of Corca Bascinn. **CP-LiddJ**

Proverbs of Hell. William Blake. **MeMBP** *Fr.* The Marriage of Heaven and Hell. **CP-BlakW**

In Seed Time Learn. **FF**

Pride of the Peacock, The. **FF; RaBo**

Proverbs of the Middle World. Thomas McGrath. **SP-McGrT**

Provide, Provide. Robert Frost. **CP-FrosR**

Provide. That their mouths may bleed into the cinders. The Armoury. Roy Fisher. **SP-FishR** *Fr.* Inscriptions for Bluebeard's Castle.

Provide your friend with almanacs. Song. Howard Nemerov. **CP-NemeH**

Providence. Archie Randolph Ammons. **SP-AmmoA**

Providence. George Herbert. **CP-HerbG**

"O sacred Providence, who from end to end." **AngWe**

Providence. Charles Tomlinson. **CP-TomlC**

Providence 1. John Hewitt. **CP-HewiJ**

Providence 2. John Hewitt. **CP-HewiJ**

Providence 3. John Hewitt. **CP-HewiJ**

Providence, Rhode Island. Al Young. **CP-YounA**

Province, The. Robert Creeley. **CP-CreeR**

Province, The. William Carlos Williams. **CP-WilW2**

Province of the Saved, The. Emily Dickinson. **CP-DickE**

Provincial town-boy he,—frail, lame. The Boy's Dream. Thomas Hardy. **CP-HardT**

Provision. Roy Fisher. **SP-FishR**

Provocation of the Dream, The. Marge Piercy. **SP-PierM**

Prowess, vanity, mutual regard. Geoffrey Hill. *Fr.* Funeral Music. **CP-HillG**

Prudence. Ralph Waldo Emerson. **CP-EmerR**

("Motto to 'Prudence'.") **CP-EmerR**

Prudence. Christopher Smart. *Fr.* Hymns for the Amusement of Children. **SP-SmarC**

Prudence Caution and Foresight: A Story of Avignon. Gertrude Stein. **CP-SteiG**

Prudence is a tedious one. Emily Dickinson. **SP-DickE**

Prudent Hind intent on Gain, The. Boethius, *tr. by* Samuel Johnson. **CP-JohnS** *Fr.* Consolation of Philosophy, The ("De Consolacione Philosophie"). **CP-ChauG**

Prudent Simplicity. William Cowper, *tr. fr. the Latin of Owen.* **CP-CowpW**

Prue, my dearest maid, is sick. Upon Prudence Baldwin Her Sickness[e]. Robert Herrick. **CP-HerrR**

Prune us serried teen sear. Chokecherry. Louis Zukofsky. **CP-ZukLS**

Pruned Roses, The. William Dickey. **SP-DickW**

P.S. I Love You. The Beatles. **CP-Beatl**

P.S. i.e. almost dreamt. No One Inn. Louis Zukofsky. *Fr.* 29 Songs. **CP-ZukLS**

Psalm: "In the small beauty of the forest." George Oppen. **CP-OppeG**

Psalm: "Old ones to the side." Charles Simic. **SP-SimiC**

Psalm: "Their shoes are stuccoed with sawdust and blood." Grace Paley. **CP-PaleG**

Psalm, A: "When psalms surprise me with their music." Thomas Merton. **CP-MertT; SP-MertT**

Psalm I. Allen Ginsberg. **CP-GinsA**

Psalm II: "Ah, still Lord, ah sweet Divinity." Allen Ginsberg. **CP-GinsA**

Psalm III: "To God: to illuminate all men. Beginning with Skid Road." Allen Ginsberg. **CP-GinsA**

Psalm IV. Allen Ginsberg. **CP-GinsA**

Ps/alm 23 Revisited. Patti Smith. **SP-SmitP**

Psalm 55: Exaudi, Deus, *par. by* Countess of Pembroke, Mary Sidney Herbert. Bible, *O.T. See* Psalm 55: "Give ear to my prayer, O God."

Psalm 58: Si Vere Utique, *par. by* Countess of Pembroke, Mary Sidney Herbert. Bible, *O.T. See* Psalm 58: "Do ye indeed speak righteousness, O congregation?"

Psalm CIV Paraphrased. James Thomson. **CP-ThomJ**

Psalm 114. John Milton, *tr. fr. Greek by* John T. Shawcross. **CP-MiltJ**

Psalm 132: A Modern Monastic Revision. Thomas Merton. **CP-MertT**

Psalm 136. John Milton. **CP-MiltJ**

Psalm 139: Domine, Probasti, *par. by* Countess of Pembroke, Mary Sidney Herbert. Bible, *O.T. See* Psalm 139: "O Lord, thou hast searched me, and known me."

Psalm Concerning the Castle. Denise Levertov. **CP-LeveD**

Psalm of Life, A. Henry Wadsworth Longfellow. **SP-LongH**

Life. **GN**

"Tell me not in mournful numbers." **AH**

Psalm of the Bloodbank. Carl Sandburg. **CP-SandC**

Psalm of Those Who Go Forth before Daylight. Carl Sandburg. **CP-SandC**

Psalme or Hymne to the Graces, A. Robert Herrick. **CP-HerrR**

Psalm Praising the Hair of Man's Body, A. Denise Levertov. **CP-LeveD**

Psalm to Snake. Margaret Atwood. **SP-AtwM2**

Psalms. Bible, *O.T.* **CP-Psal**

Psalm 1: "Blessed is the man that walketh. . . ." **AWP; BiP; CP-MiltJ; EnlH; SCAP**

(Happy Is the Man.) **TrJP**

("O blessed man, that in th' advice.") **SCAP**

(Tree and the Chaff, The.) **WGRP**

Psalm 2: "Why do the heathen rage." **CP-MiltJ; NAAL-1; NAAL-3; OBVE**

Psalm 3: "Lord, how are the increased. . . ." **CP-MiltJ; OBVE**

Psalm 4: "Hear me when I call, O God of my righteousness." **CP-MiltJ**

Psalm 5: "Give ear to my words, O Lord, consider my meditation." **CP-MiltJ**

Psalm 6: "O Lord, rebuke me not in thine anger." **CP-MiltJ; CP-WyatT; OBVE**

("O lord, I dred, and that I did not dred.") **OBVE**

("O Lord, since in my mouth thy mighty name.") **CP-WyatT**

Psalm 7: "O Lord my God, in thee do I put my trust." **CP-MiltJ**

Psalm 8: "O Lord our Lord, how excellent. . . ." **AWP; CP-MiltJ; FaPON; ImOP; NAWM-1; OBVE; PBMP; TrPWD**

(How Glorious Is Thy Name.) **TrJP**

(What Is Man?) **TrGrPo**

("When I consider thy heavens, the work of thy fingers.") **FaPON; ImOP**

Psalm 9: "I will praise thee, O Lord. . . ."

Psalm 10: "Why standest thou afar off, O Lord?"

Psalm 11: "In the name of the Lord. . . ." **OBVE**

Psalm 12: "Help, Lord; for the godly man ceaseth." **SP-SidnP**

("Lord, help, it is high time for me to call.") **SP-SidnP**

Psalm 13: "How long wilt thou forget me, O Lord?" **NoSic; OBVE**

Psalm 14: "Fool hath said in his heart, The. . . ." **TrJP**

Psalm 15: "Lord, who shall abide in thy tabernacle?"

Psalm 16: "Preserve me, O God: for in thee do I put my trust."

Psalm 17: "Hear the right, O Lord. . . ." **OBVE**

Psalm 18: "I will love thee, O Lord, my strength." **SP-SmarC**

("Thee will I love, O Lord, my tow'r.") **SP-SmarC**, *tr. by* Christopher Smart;

Psalm 19: "Heavens declare the glory of God, The." **AWP; BLRP; BiP; ChIV-1; EnlH; FaPON; NAWM-1; OBVE; SCAP; TOF; TRV; WBLP**

(God's Glory.) **TrGrPo**

(Heavens, The.) **ChTr**

Psalm 20: "Lord hear thee in the day of trouble, The."

Psalm 21: "King shall rejoice in thy strength, O Lord, The."

Psalm 22: "My God, my God, why hast thou forsaken me?"

    (Cry in Distress, A.) **TrGrPo**

Psalm 23: "Lord is my shepherd, I shall not want, The." **AH; AMV-81; AWP; BLPL; BiP; CP-CrasR; ChIV-1; FPL; FaBoBe; FaPON; FaPoB; JCP; NAWM-1; NIP; OBCA; OBVE; OHIP; PoLF; PoPl; SP-SidnP; ScCV; TFi; TRP; TRV; TrGrPo; TrJP; WBLP**

    ("Lord is my shepherd, The; / I have everything I need.") **TRP**

    ("Lord, the Lord my shepherd is, The.") **SP-SidnP**

    ("Lord's my shepherd, I'll not want, The.") **AH; ScCV; TRP; WBLP**

    (Protection of Jehovah, The.) **WGRP**

    (Trusting God.) **WBLP**

Psalm 24: "Earth is the Lord's and the fulness thereof, The." **AWP; EaLo; FaPON; SP-SmarC; TrJP; TreFT**

    ("Earth is God's, with all she bears, The.") **SP-SmarC**, *tr. by* Christopher Smart;

    (Lift Up Your Heads.) **TrGrPo**

Psalm 25: "Unto thee, O Lord, do I lift up my soul." **SP-SmarC**

    ("Lord and Master, to thine altar.") **SP-SmarC**, *tr. by* Christopher Smart;

Psalm 26: "Judge me, O Lord; for I have walked in mine integrity."

Psalm 27: "Lord is my light and my salvation, The. . . ."

    (Deliverance of Jehovah, The.) **WGRP**

Psalm 28: "Unto thee will I cry, O Lord my rock." **SP-SidnP**

    ("To Thee, Lord, my cry I send.") **SP-SidnP**

Psalm 29: "Give unto the Lord, O ye mighty." **AWP**

Psalm 30: "I will extol thee, O Lord; for thou hast lifted me up."

Psalm 31: "In thee, O Lord, do I put my trust. . . ."

Psalm 32: "Blessed is he whose transgression is forgiven, whose sin is covered." **CP-WyatT**

    ("O happy are they that have forgiveness got.") **CP-WyatT**

Psalm 33: "Rejoice in the Lord, O ye righteous. . . ." **SP-SmarC**

    ("Rejoice in God, ye saints above.") **SP-SmarC**, *tr. by* Christopher Smart;

Psalm 34: "I will bless the Lord at all times."

Psalm 35: "Plead my cause, O Lord, with them that strive with me." **SP-SidnP**

    ("Speak Thou for me against wrong-speaking foes.") **SP-SidnP**

Psalm 36: "Transgression of the wicked. . . ."

Psalm 37: "Fret not thyself because of evildoers." **BLRP; CP-WyatT**

    ("Although thou see th'outrageous climb aloft.") **CP-WyatT**

Psalm 38: "O Lord, rebuke me not in thy wrath." **CP-WyatT**

    ("O Lord, as I thee have both prayed and pray.") **CP-WyatT**

Psalm 39: "I said, I will take heed to my ways."

    (Lord, Make Me to Know Mine End.) **TrJP**

Psalm 40: "I waited patiently for the Lord."

Psalm 41: "Blessed is he that considereth the poor."

Psalm 42: "As the hart panteth after the water brooks." **AWP; TRV; TrJP**

    (My Soul Thirsteth for God.) **TrGrPo**

Psalm 43: "Judge me, O God. . . ."

Psalm 44: "We have heard with our ears, O God."

Psalm 45: "My heart is inditing a good matter."

Psalm 46: "God is our refuge and strength. . . ." **AWP; TRV; TreFT**

    (Though the Earth Be Removed.) **TrGrPo**

Psalm 47: "O clap your hands, all ye people."

Psalm 48: "Great is the Lord. . . ."

Psalm 49: "Hear this, all ye people. . . ."

Psalm 50: "Mighty God, even the Lord, hath spoken, The." **BrRo**

Psalm 51: "Have mercy upon me, O God. . . ." **CP-WyatT**

    ("Rue on me, Lord, for thy goodness and grace.") **CP-WyatT**

Psalm 52: "Why boastest thou thyself in mischief. . . ." **NoSic; OBVE**

Psalm 53: "Fool hath said in his heart, The. . . ."

Psalm 54: "Save me, O God, by thy name. . . ."

Psalm 55: "Give ear to my prayer, O God." **AWP; OBVE**

    ("Oh that I had wings like a dove!") **FaPON**

    (Wings.) **FaPON**

Psalm 56: "Be merciful unto me. . . ."

Psalm 57: "Be merciful unto me, O God. . . ."

Psalm 58: "Do ye indeed speak righteousness, O congregation?" **NOCV; NoSic**

Psalm 59: "Deliver me from mine enemies, O my God." **NoSic**

Psalm 60: "O God, thou hast cast us off. . . ."

Psalm 61: "Hear my cry, O God. . . ."

Psalm 62: "Truly my soul waiteth upon God." **PBWP**

Psalm 63: "O God, thou art my God. . . ."

Psalm 64: "Hear my voice, O God, in my prayer."

Psalm 65: "Praise waiteth for thee, O God, in Sion." **OHIP**

Psalm 66: "Make a joyful unto God, all ye lands."

Psalm 67: "God be merciful unto us, and bless us."

Psalm 68: "Let God arise, let his enemies be scattered." **SP-SmarC**

    ("Arouse—and let thy foes disperse.") **SP-SmarC**, *tr. by* Christopher Smart;

Psalm 69: "Save me, O God. . . ."

Psalm 70: "Make haste, O God, to deliver me."

Psalm 71: "In thee, O Lord, do I put my trust. . . ."

Psalm 72: "Give the king thy judgments, O God." **OBVE**

Psalm 73: "Truly God is good to Israel." **NoSic**

Psalm 74: "O God, why hast thou cast us off for ever?" **NOCV**

    ("O God, why hast thou thus / Repuls'd, and scatter'd us?") **NOCV**

Psalm 75: "Unto thee, O God, do we give thanks."

Psalm 76: "In Judah is God known. . . ."

Psalm 77: "I cried unto God with my voice. . . ." **AWP; MOS**

    ("Waters saw thee, O God, The.") **MOS**

Psalm 78: "Give ear, O my people, to my law." **OBVE**

Psalm 79: "O God, the heathen are come. . . ."

    (Heathen Are Come into Thine Inheritance, The.) **TrJP**

Psalm 80: "Give ear, O Shepherd of Israel. . . ." **CP-MiltJ**

Psalm 81: "Sing aloud unto God our strength." **CP-MiltJ**

Psalm 82: "God standeth in the congregation of the mighty." **CP-MiltJ**

Psalm 83: "Keep not thou silence, O God." **CP-MiltJ**

    (Keep Not Thou Silence.) **TrJP**

    ("O God, keep not Thou silence.") **TrJP**

Psalm 84: "How amiable are thy tabernacles. . . ." **CP-MiltJ; TRV; TrJP; TrPWD**

    (Sparrow, The.) **FaPON**

    ("How Lovely are thy dwellings fair!," *par. by* Milton.) **CP-MiltJ; TrPWD**

    "How lovely are thy tabernacles." **TrJP**

    Sparrow, The. **FaPON**

Psalm 85: "Lord, thou hast been favourable unto thy land." **CP-MiltJ; SP-SmarC**

    ("O Lord, thy land has favour found.") **SP-SmarC**, *tr. by* Christopher Smart;

Psalm 86: "Bow down thine ear, O Lord, hear me." **CP-MiltJ**

Psalm 87: "His foundation is in the holy mountains." **CP-MiltJ**

Psalm 88: "O God of my salvation." **CP-MiltJ**

Psalm 89: "I will sing of the mercies of the Lord for ever."

Psalm 90: "Lord, thou hast been our dwelling place in all generations." **AWP; DL; EaLo**

Psalm 91: "He that dwelleth in the secret place. . . ." **AWP; CP-PopeA**

    (Mighty Fortress, A.) **TrGrPo**

Psalm 92: "It is a good thing to give thanks unto the Lord."

Psalm 93: "Lord reigneth, The. . . ."

Psalm 94: "O Lord God, to whom vengeance belongeth."

Psalm 95: "O come, let us sing unto the Lord." **AWP; BLRP; OHIP**

    ("Oh come, let us sing unto Jehovah.") **BLRP**

Psalm 96: "O sing unto the Lord a new song."

Psalm 97: "Lord reigneth, The; let the earth rejoice."

Psalm 98: "O sing unto the Lord a new song. . . ." **BLRP; SP-SmarC; TrGrPo; TrJP**

    (Floods Clap Their Hands, The.) **TrGrPo**

    ("O Frame the strains anew.") **SP-SmarC**, *tr. by* Christopher Smart;

Psalm 100: "Make a joyful noise unto the Lord, all ye lands." **OFD; OHIP; OtMeF; SUS; TRV**

    (Be Thankful unto Him.) **FaPON**

    (Scotch Te Deum.) **WGRP**

Psalm 101: "I will sing of mercy and judgment."

Psalm 102: "Hear my prayer, O Lord, and let my cry. . . " ["*Domine exaudi orationem meam*"]. **BiP; CP-WyatT; OBVE**

    ("Lord hear [*or* here] my prayer [*or* prayre] and let my cry[e] pass[e].") **CP-WyatT; OBVE**

Psalm 103: "Bless the Lord, O my soul. . . ." **AWP; NOCV; SCAP**

    ("Praise, my soul, the King of heaven.")

Psalm 104: "Bless the Lord, O my soul. . . ." **EnlH; MOS; NAWM-1; OHIP; TrJP**

    (Hymn of the World Without.) **WGRP**

    ("So is this great wide sea, wherein are things creeping innumerable.") **MOS**

    ("Unnamable God, you are fathomless.") **EnlH**

Psalm 105: "O give thanks unto the Lord. . . ."

Psalm 106: "Praise ye the Lord. O give thanks. . . ."

Psalm 107: "O give thanks unto the Lord, for he is good: for. . . ."
  ChTr; FaPON; MOS; OxBoS; SCAP
  ("O Give yee thanks unto the Lord.") **SCAP**
  ("They that go down to the sea in ships.") **ChTr; FaPON; MOS;**
    OxBoS
Psalm 108: "O God, my heart is fixed."
Psalm 109: "Hold not thy peace, O God of my praise."
Psalm 110: "Lord said unto my Lord, The."
Psalm 111: "Praise ye the Lord. I will praise. . . ."
Psalm 112: "Praise ye the Lord. Blessed. . . ."
Psalm 113: "Praise ye the Lord. Praise, O ye servants. . . ."
Psalm 114: "When Israel went out of Egypt." **OBVE**
  ("When Israel came from Egypt's coast.") **OBVE**
Psalm 115: "Not unto us, O Lord, not unto us." **NOCV**
  ("Not us, I say, not us.") **NOCV**
Psalm 116: "I love the Lord. . . ."
Psalm 117: "O praise the Lord, all ye nations."
Psalm 118: "O give thanks unto the Lord; for he is good: because. . . ."
  TrJP
Psalm 119: "Blessed are the undefiled in the way."
Psalm 120: "In my distress I cried unto the Lord. . . ."
Psalm 121: "I will lift up mine eyes unto the hills." **AWP; FaPON;**
  GePo; OBCA
  ("I to the hills lift up mine eyes.") **OBCA**
  ("Now the twin-light of my eyes.") **GePo**
  (Pilgrim's Song, The.) **WGRP**
  (Song of Trust, A.) **TrGrPo**
Psalm 122: "I was glad when they said unto me. . . ." **TRV**
Psalm 123: "Unto thee lift I up mine eyes. . . ."
Psalm 124: "If it had not been the Lord who was on our side. . . ."
  ScCV
  ("Now Israel may say, and that truly.") **ScCV**
Psalm 125: "They that trust in the Lord shall be as mount Zion."
Psalm 126: "When the Lord turned again the captivity of Zion. . . ."
  (Like unto Them That Dream.) **TrJP**
  ("When the Lord brought back those that returned to Zion.") **TrJP**
Psalm 127: "Except the Lord build the house." **BiP; SP-SmarC; TRV;**
  TrJP; TreF
  ("If the work be not direct.") **SP-SmarC**, *tr. by* Christopher Smart;
  ("They shall not be put to shame, / When they speak with their enemies
    in the gate.") **TrJP**
Psalm 128: "Blessed is every one that feareth the Lord." **TRV**
Psalm 129: "Many a time have they afflicted me from my youth. . . ."
Psalm 130: "Out of the depths have I cried unto thee, O Lord." **CP-**
  WyatT; NoSic; OBVE; ScCV; TrJP
  (De Profundis ("From depth of grief").) **SiPSBD**
  (De Profundis ("Out of the depths have I cried unto thee, O Lord").)
    BLRP; WGRP
  ("Deep sunk in floods of grief.") **ScCV**
  ("F[f]rom depth of[f] sin[n] and from a deep despair [*or* diepe
    dispaire].") **CP-WyatT; NoSic; OBVE**
  (Song of Supplication, A.) **TrGrPo**
Psalm 131: "Lord, my heart is not haughty, nor mine eyes lofty." **EnlH**
Psalm 132: "Lord, remember David, and all his afflictions."
Psalm 133: "Behold, how good and how pleasant it is." **AWP; OBVE**
  ("Beholde, how good and joyfull a thinge it is, brethren to dwell to
    gether in unitye.") **OBVE**
  (To Dwell Together in Unity.) **TrJP**
Psalm 134: "Behold, bless ye the Lord, all ye servants of the Lord."
  NoSic; SP-SmarC
  ("Attend to the music divine.") **SP-SmarC**, *tr. by* Christopher Smart;
Psalm 135: "Praise ye the Lord. Praise ye the name of the Lord; praise
  him, O ye servants of the Lord." **SP-SmarC**
  ("O Praise the Lord, and bless his name.") **SP-SmarC**, *tr. by*
    Christopher Smart;
Psalm 136: "O give thanks unto the Lord. . . ." **AWP; FL; OHIP**
Psalm 137: "By the rivers of Babylon. . . ." **AWP; CP-CowpW; CP-**
  CrasR; ChIV-1; NAWM-1; OAEL-1; OBS; OBVE; SP-SmarC; TrJP
  ("As by the streams of Babylon.") **OAEL-1**
  ("As on Euphrates shady banks we lay.") **OBS**
  ("By the rivers of Babel we sate.") **OAEL-1**
  ("By the waters of Babylon we sat downe and weapte, when we
    remembered the, O Syon.") **OBVE**
  ("Nigh where the river flows.") **OAEL-1**
  ("On the flood is of Babiloyne there we saten.") **OAEL-1**
  ("On the proud banks of great Euphrates' flood.") **CP-CrasR; OAEL-1**
  ("Pensive we sat the silent hours.") **SP-SmarC**, *tr. by* Christopher

Smart;
  (Song of Exile, A.) **TrGrPo**
  ("To Babylon's proud waters brought.") **CP-CowpW**, *tr. by* William
    Cowper;
  ("Upon the rivers of Babylon, there we sat and wept.") **OAEL-1**
  ("When as we sat all sad and desolate.") **OAEL-1**
  ("When on Euphrates' banks we sate.") **OAEL-1**
  ("When we, our weary limbs to rest.") **OAEL-1**
  ("Whenas we sat in Babylon.") **OAEL-1**
Psalm 138: "I will praise thee with my whole heart."
Psalm 139: "O Lord, thou hast searched me, and known me." **NOCV;**
  NoSic; OBSC; OBVE; OxBoCh
Psalm 140: "Deliver me, O Lord, from the evil man."
Psalm 141: "Lord, I cry unto thee. . . ."
Psalm 142: "I cried unto the Lord with my voice."
Psalm 143: "Hear my prayer, O Lord, give ear. . . ." **CP-WyatT**
  ("Hear my prayer, O Lord, hear my request.") **CP-WyatT**
Psalm 144: "Blessed be the Lord my strength."
Psalm 145: "I will extol thee, my God, O king."
Psalm 146: "Praise ye the Lord. Praise the Lord. . . ."
Psalm 147: "Praise ye the Lord: for it is good. . . ." **FaPON; NOCV;**
  OHIP
Psalm 148: "Praise ye the Lord. Praise ye the Lord from the heavens."
  OBVE; SP-SmarC; TrJP
  ("Hallelujah! kneel and sing / Praises to the heav'nly king.") **SP-**
    SmarC, *tr. by* Christopher Smart; **OBVE**
  ("Hallelujah. Praise ye the Lord from the heavens.") **TrJP**
  (Song of Praise, A.) **TrGrPo**
Psalm 149: "Praise ye the Lord. Sing unto the Lord a new song." **SP-**
  SmarC
  ("Hosanna! God be prais'd.") **SP-SmarC**, *tr. by* Christopher Smart;
Psalm 150: "Praise ye the Lord. Praise God in his sanctuary." **SP-SmarC;**
  TRV
  ("Hosanna! praise the Lord, and bless.") **SP-SmarC**, *tr. by* Christopher
    Smart;
  (Laudate Dominum.) **ChTr**
  ("O praise God in his holiness: praise him in the firmament of his
    power.") **ChTr**
Psalms of Assize. Geoffrey Hill. **CP-HillG**
"Ascend through declension."
"Why should I strike you with my name."
Psalmus 1, *Eng. trans. included*. Richard Crashaw. **CP-CrasR**
Pseudetai hostis ephe; dolichos chronos oiden ameiben. Exastichon. Villiers
  Harington. *Fr.* Commendatory Poems. **CP-LoveR**
Pseudo-Questions. Wystan Hugh Auden. **CP-AudeW**
Psyche. Samuel Taylor Coleridge. **CP-ColeS**
Psyche. Hilda Doolittle. **CP-DoolH**
Psyche and Cerberus, *verse tr. fr.* Metamorphoses by Apuleius. Elizabeth
  Barrett Browning. **CP-BroEB**
Psyche and Pan, *verse tr. fr.* Metamorphoses by Apuleius. Elizabeth Barrett
  Browning. **CP-BroEB**
Psyche and Proserpine, *verse tr.fr.* Metamorphoses by Apuleius. Elizabeth
  Barrett Browning. **CP-BroEB**
Psyche and the Eagle, *verse tr. fr.* Metamorphoses by Apuleius. Elizabeth
  Barrett Browning. **CP-BroEB**
Psyche and Venus, *verse tr.fr.* Metamorphoses by Apuleius. Elizabeth Barrett
  Browning. **CP-BroEB**
Psyche Gazing on Cupid, *verse tr. fr.* Apuleius' Metamorphoses. Elizabeth
  Barrett Browning. **CP-BroEB**
Psyche Propitiating Ceres, *verse tr. fr.* Metamorphoses by Apuleius. Elizabeth
  Barrett Browning. **CP-BroEB**
Psyche Wafted by Zephyrus, *verse tr. fr.* Metamorphoses by Apuleius.
  Elizabeth Barrett Browning. **CP-BroEB**
Psyche with the Candle. Archibald MacLeish. **CP-MacLA**
Psychodrama: Tokyo Mime Film. Laurence Lieberman. **SP-LiebL**
Psychological Profile. Robert Penn Warren. *Fr.* Homage to Theodore
  Dreiser. **SP-WarrR**
Psychometrist's Remarkable Forecast, The. John Hewitt. **CP-HewiJ**
Psychopathology of Everyday Life, The. William Matthews. **SP-MattW**
Psychopharmacological drugs. James Fenton. *Fr.* Exempla. **SP-FentJ**
Puberty. William Matthews. **SP-MattW**
Public Affairs. Thomas Merton. **CP-MertT**
Public Bath, The. Gary Snyder. **CP-SnydG**
Public Garden, The. Robert Lowell. **SP-LoweR**
Public Gardens, The. Alun Lewis. **CP-LewiA**
Public House Drunk. Sir John Betjeman. **SP-BetjJ**
Public Letter to Emily Dickinson. Carl Sandburg. **CP-SandC**
Public silence indeed is nothing. Monument. George Oppen. **CP-OppeG**

Public Son of a Public Man, The. Stephen Spender. **CP-SpenS**

Public sorrow, the acquired. Autumnal. Louise Glück. **SP-GlücL**

Public Square, The. Wallace Stevens. **CP-StevW**

Public Waste. Rudyard Kipling. **CP-KiplR**
("Walpole talks of 'a man and his price'.") **CP-KiplR**

Publication—is the Auction. Emily Dickinson. **CP-DickE**

Publius Vergilius Maro, the Madison Avenue Hick. John Updike. **CP-UpdiJ**

Puccini was Latin, and Wagner Teutonic. The Birds. Ogden Nash. **CP-NashO**

Puck Lost and Found. "Lewis Carroll." **CP-CarrL**

Puck of Pook's Hill, *sels.* Rudyard Kipling.
Centurion of the Thirtieth, A.
British-Roman Song, A. **CP-KiplR**
Cities and Thrones and Powers. **CP-KiplR**
Dymchurch Flit.
Bee-Boy's Song, The. **CP-KiplR**
Three-Part Song, A. **CP-KiplR**
Hal o' the Draft.
Prophets at Home. **CP-KiplR**
Smuggler's Song, A. **CP-KiplR**
Knights of the Joyous Venture, The.
Harp Song of the Dane Women. **CP-KiplR**
Thorkild's Song. **CP-KiplR**
Land of Our Birth.
Old Men at Pevensey.
Runes on Weland's Sword, The. **CP-KiplR**
On the Great Wall.
Song to Mithras, A. **CP-KiplR**
Puck's Song. **CP-KiplR**
Rimini. **CP-KiplR**
Treasure and the Law, The.
Song of the Fifth River. **CP-KiplR**
Weland's Sword.
Tree Song, A. **CP-KiplR**
Winged Hats, The.
Pict Song, A. **CP-KiplR**
Young Men at the Manor.
Sir Richard's Song. **CP-KiplR**

Puck's Song. Rudyard Kipling. **CP-KiplR** *Fr.* Puck of Pook's Hill.

Pueblo Pot. Edna St. Vincent Millay. **CP-MillE**

Puella Mea. Edward Estlin Cummings. **CP-CummE**

Puella Parvula. Wallace Stevens. **CP-StevW**

Puff of air or dry or damp, A. Ralph Waldo Emerson. **CP-EmerR**

Puisque je suis / Imaginaire. *see also English tr.* The Secret: "Since I am / Somebody's dream." Thomas Merton. **CP-MertT**

Pulchro pulchra datur, sociali foedere amanti, *accompanied by English translation.* Thomas Campion. *Fr.* Description of a Maske: Presented in the Banqueting Roome at *Whitehall*, on Saint Stephens Night Last, at the Marriage of the Right Honourable the Earle of *Somerset:* and the Right Noble the Lady FRANCES *Howard.* **CP-CampT**

Pull back the curtains, quick now that we've caught the mood of. Hymn to the Virgin. Elizabeth Bishop. **CP-BishE**

"Pull! crew" 's convenient to reprobate kin hides. Catullus. *See* Carmen 57: "Caesar Mamurraque! / A peerless pair of brazen buggers."

Pull my arm back, Seymour. Seymour and Chantelle or Un Peu de Vice. Stevie Smith. **CP-SmitS**

Pull my daisy. Fie My Fum. Allen Ginsberg. **CP-GinsA**

Pull My Daisy. Allen Ginsberg, Neal Cassady *and* Jack Kerouac. **CP-GinsA**

Pull of Memory, The. Richard Eberhart. *Fr.* Aesthetics after War. **CP-EberR**

Pull out the pissed-on clinkers. Form. James Dickey. **CP-DickJ**

Pull the rose apart. What Is a Person? Phoebe Hesketh. **SP-HeskP**

Pull up the bell-flow'rs of the spring. St. Mark. Christopher Smart. *Fr.* Hymns and Spiritual Songs for the Fasts and Festivals of the Church of England. **SP-SmarC**

Pulley, The. George Herbert. **CP-HerbG**

Pulse, The. Denise Levertov. **CP-LeveD**

Pulsing stops where time has been, The. The Bed. Thom Gunn. **CP-GunnT**

Puñal. Denise Levertov. **CP-LeveD**

Pumpernickel. Leonard Nathan. **SP-NathL**

Pumping away pumping away / now everyone is pumping away. For a Screaming Lady. Robert Creeley. **CP-CreeR**

Pumping Engine, Cashwell, The. Wystan Hugh Auden. **CP-AudWJ**

Pumpkin, / freshly scraped out of its tightly adhering. Pumpkin Pie, Or Reassurances Are Always Fake Though We Love Them, Only Physics Counts. Diane Wakoski. **SP-WakoD**

Pumpkin, The. John Greenleaf Whittier. **CP-WhitJ**

Pumpkin Pie, Or Reassurances Are Always Fake Though We Love Them, Only Physics Counts. Diane Wakoski. **SP-WakoD**

Punch Rubicundus. Thom Gunn. **CP-GunnT**

Punchard. Wystan Hugh Auden. **CP-AudWJ**

Punching the bag, running to the basket. Light-Heavy at Prayer. Marsden Hartley. **CP-HartM**

Punctuality. "Lewis Carroll." **CP-CarrL**

Puncture. John Crowe Ransom. **SP-RansJ**

Puncture: this is when. Pail. Gilbert Sorrentino. **SP-SorrG**

Pungent atom in the Air, The. Emily Dickinson. **CP-DickE**

Punisher, The, *also stands as sl. diff. separate poem.* David Herbert Lawrence. *Fr.* The Schoolmaster [A]. **CP-LawrD**

Punisher, The. David Herbert Lawrence. **CP-LawrD**

Punishing the Myth. John Ashbery. **SP-AshbJ**

Punishment. Seamus Heaney. **SP-HeanS**

Punishment of Pride, The. Walt Whitman. **CP-WhitW**

Punk Rock Your My Big Crybaby. Allen Ginsberg. **CP-GinsA**

Punt, The. Ernest Hemingway. **CP-HemiE**

Pupils of the eye expand, The. Or To Perish Before Day. Robert Ranke Graves. **CP-GravR**

Puppet Show, The. Jenny Joseph. **SP-JoseJ**

Puppeteer. Jenny Joseph. **SP-JoseJ**

Purana, Meaning Once Upon a Time. Hayden Carruth. **CP-CarHS**

Purché si cominci a ricordare la guerra di merda. Canto 72. Ezra Pound. *Fr.* Cantos. **CP-PoCan**

Purdah. Sylvia Plath. **CP-PlatS**

Pure air trembles, O pitiless God, The. Noon. Robinson Jeffers. **CP-JefR1**

Pure beauty is pure being and pure being. The Book. Hayden Carruth. *Fr.* Contra Mortem. **CP-CarHL**

Pure contralto sings in the organloft, The. Walt Whitman. **TTTS** *Fr.* Song of Myself. **CP-WhitW**

Pure Death. Robert Ranke Graves. **CP-GravR**

Pure element of waters! wheresoe'er. Suggested by Mr W. Westall's Views of the Caves, etc., in Yorkshire. William Wordsworth. **CP-WorW2**

Pure fasted faces draw unto this feast. Easter Communion. Gerard Manley Hopkins. **CP-HopkG**

Pure Fury, The. Theodore Roethke. **CP-RoetT**

Pure gold lily, but by the pure gold lily, A. Gerard Manley Hopkins. *Fr.* Fragments. **CP-HopkG**

Pure Good of Theory, The. Wallace Stevens. **CP-StevW**

Pure melody, love without alteration. Testament. Robert Ranke Graves. **CP-GravR**

Pure products of America, The. To Elsie. William Carlos Williams. **CP-WilW1**

Pure? What does it mean? Fever 103°. Sylvia Plath. **CP-PlatS**

Pure whiteness spreading, A. Dawn. Chuck Miller. **SP-MillC**

Purely Local. Adrienne Rich. **CP-RicAE**

Purer than purest pure. Edward Estlin Cummings. **CP-CummE**

Purest of Occasions. Leonard Cohen. **CP-CoheL**

Purest soul that e'er was sent, The. Another [Epitaph on the Lady Mary Villiers]. Thomas Carew. **CP-CareT**

Purgation ("Before and after the eye, grasses go over the long fields"), *second vers.* James Dickey. **CP-DickJ**

Purgation ("Beyond the eye, grasses go over the long fields"), *first vers.* James Dickey. **CP-DickJ**

Purgatorio. Hart Crane. **CP-CranH**

Purgatorio. Dante Alighieri. *Fr.* Divina Commedia. Matilda Gathering Flowers. **CP-ShelP**

Purgatory. John Berryman. **CP-BerrJ**

Purgatory. Robert Herrick. **CP-HerrR**

Purgatory Blind. Charles Olson. **CP-OlsoC**

Purification, A. Wendell Berry. *See* At start of spring I open a trench.

Purification. Robert Ranke Graves. **CP-GravR**

Purification of St. Mary the Virgin, The. Christina Georgina Rossetti. **CP-RosC2**

Purifying the Language of the Tribe. William Stafford. **SP-StafW**

Purist, The. Ogden Nash. **CP-NashO**

Purists Will Object. John Ashbery. **SP-AshbJ**

Puritan, The. May Sarton. **SP-SartM**

Puritan Ethos, The. Robert Creeley. **CP-CreeR**

Puritan is insane, The. Sane and Insane. David Herbert Lawrence. **CP-LawrD**

Puritans, The. Richard Wilbur. **CP-WilbR**

Purity. Reflection On a Wicked World. Ogden Nash. **CP-NashO**

Purity born of a Maid: / Was such a Virgin defiled? The Purification of St. Mary the Virgin. Christina Georgina Rossetti. **CP-RosC2**

Purloining while you played in honeyed youth. Carmen 99. Catullus. *Fr. Carmina.* **CP-Catul**

Purple— / Color of a Queen, is this, The. Emily Dickinson. **CP-DickE**

Purple! / for months unknown. The Petunia. William Carlos Williams. **CP-WilW2**

Purple. Wilfred Owen. **CP-OwenW**

Purple Anemones. David Herbert Lawrence. **CP-LawrD**

Purple black cloud at sunset: it is late August. Delmore Schwartz. *Fr. Phoenix Lyrics.* **SP-SchwD**

Purple—is fashionable twice. Emily Dickinson. **CP-DickE**

Purple Martins. Carl Sandburg. **CP-SandC**

Purposes. Robert Herrick. **CP-HerrR**

Purpurea rosa / Dolce, odorosa. Christina Georgina Rossetti. **CP-RosC3**

Purse-Seine, The. Robinson Jeffers. **CP-JefR2**

Pursued, The. Daniel Gerard Hoffman. **SP-HoffD**

Pursuing you in your transitions. Emily Dickinson. **CP-DickE**

Pursuit. Hilda Doolittle. **CP-DoolH**

Pursuit. Sylvia Plath. **CP-PlatS**

Pursuit. Robert Penn Warren. **SP-WarrR**

Pursuit from Under. James Dickey. **CP-DickJ**

Pursuit of Happiness, The. John Ashbery. **SP-AshbJ**

Push yourself in on others. Boy, the. Robert Creeley. **CP-CreeR**

Pusher, The. Maya Angelou. **SP-AngeM**

Pushkin. A Didactic Poem. Donald Davie. **CP-DavDo**

Puss-Puss! David Herbert Lawrence. **CP-LawrD**

Pusse and her Prentice both at Draw-gloves play. Upon Pusse and her Prentice. Robert Herrick. **CP-HerrR**

Pussy Blues. Allen Ginsberg. **CP-GinsA**

Pussy can sit by the fire and sing. Rudyard Kipling. **CP-KiplR** *Fr.* The Cat That Walked by Himself. *Fr.* Just-So Stories.

Pussy has a whiskered face, / Kitty has such pretty ways. Christina Georgina Rossetti. **CP-RosC2**

Pussy put her paw into the pail of paint. Epithalamion. Ted Berrigan. **SP-BerrT**

Pussy Willow. Louis Zukofsky. **CP-ZukLS**

Pussycat on Causeway Street is closed, The. In Memoriam Felis Felis. John Updike. **CP-UpdiJ**

Put a dog in a bottle. It won't bark. Keeping. John Ciardi. **SP-CiarJ**

Put a sun in Sunday, Sunday. Yet Dish. Gertrude Stein. **CP-SteiG**

Put Back Those Whiskers, I Know You. Ogden Nash. **CP-NashO**

Put by thy days like withered flowers. Unregarding. Walter de la Mare. **CP-DeLaW**

Put forth thy leaf, thou lofty plane. Arthur Hugh Clough. **SP-ClouA** (In Stratis Viarum IV.) **SP-ClouA**

Put forth to watch, unschooled, alone. Rudyard Kipling. **CP-KiplR**

Put him this way. Charles Olson. **CP-OlsoC**

Put in, drive home the sightless wedges. Ralph Waldo Emerson. **CP-EmerR**

Put it down! I say; put it down,—here, give it to me, I know. Tristan. Edna St. Vincent Millay. **CP-MillE**

Put it there, Mr. Longwell, put it there! Two Songs for a Boss Named Mr. Longwell. Ogden Nash. **CP-NashO**

Put mommy on the front steps. Creams. Charles Kenneth Williams. **CP-WillC**

Put Not Your Trust in Princes. Donald Davie. **CP-DavDo**

"Put off that mask of burning gold." The Mask. William Butler Yeats. **CP-YeatW**

Put Off the Wedding Five Times and Nobody Comes to It. Carl Sandburg. **CP-SandC**

Put off Thy robe of purple, then go on. Good Friday: Rex Tragicus, or, Christ Going to His Cross[e]. Robert Herrick. **CP-HerrR**

Put off your faces,Death:for day is over. Edward Estlin Cummings. **CP-CummE**

Put on a clean shirt. Clothes. Anne Sexton. **CP-SextA**

Put on thy *Holy Fillitings,* and so. Julia's Churching, or Purification. Robert Herrick. **CP-HerrR**

Put on your silks, and piece by piece. To His Mistresses. Robert Herrick. **CP-HerrR**

Put out that Light. The Light of Life. Stevie Smith. **CP-SmitS**

Put the broidery-frame away. Bertha in the Lane. Elizabeth Barrett Browning. **CP-BroEB**

Put the rest away, O put the rest away! Kenneth Patchen. **CP-PatcK**

Put this artificer of *chiaroscuro.* On Reading Wallace Stevens' *Collected Poems* after Many Years. John Hewitt. **CP-HewiJ**

Put up my lute! Emily Dickinson. **CP-DickE**

"Put up the sword!" The voice of Christ once more. Disarmament. John Greenleaf Whittier. **CP-WhitJ**

Put your / self out. Chasm. Archie Randolph Ammons. **SP-AmmoA**

Put your hands into the mire. Wendell Berry. *Fr.* Prayers and Sayings of the Mad Farmer. **CP-BerrW**

Putrefaction. Robert Herrick. **CP-HerrR**

Puts on a lacy blouse. The Transvestite. Siv Cedering Fox. **SP-CedeS**

Puttin' the Baby Away. Paul Laurence Dunbar. **CP-DunbP**

Putting in the Seed. Robert Frost. **CP-FrosR**

Putting It All Away. Stephen Dobyns. **SP-DobyS**

Putting out the candles. My Father after Work. Gary Gildner. **SP-GildG**

Putting out the light. Trees at Night. Charles Simic. **SP-SimiC**

Putting the skis down. The Color of Snow. Erica Jong. **SP-JongE**

Putting to Sea. Louise Bogan. **CP-BogaL**

Putting Up Snow Fence. Chuck Miller. **SP-MillC**

Puzzle, The. Charles Bukowski. **SP-BukC3**

Puzzle. "Lewis Carroll." **CP-CarrL**

Puzzle, The. Erica Jong. **SP-JongE**

Puzzle, The. Howard Nemerov. **CP-NemeH**

Puzzle assembled, The. The Solution. George Oppen. **CP-OppeG**

Puzzle faces in the dying elms. "Mystery Boy" Looks for Kin in Nashville. Robert Earl Hayden. **CP-HaydR**

Puzzled. Langston Hughes. **SP-HughL**

Puzzled Game-Birds, The. Thomas Hardy. **CP-HardT**

Puzzler, The. Rudyard Kipling. **CP-KiplR**

Puzzles from Wonderland. "Lewis Carroll." **CP-CarrL**

Puzzles.

   "Dreaming of apples on a wall."

   "John gave his brother James a box."

   "Said the Moon to the Sun."

   "Stick I found that weighed two pound, A."

   "Three sisters at breakfast were feeding the cat."

   "What is most like a bee in May?"

   "When the King found that his money was nearly all."

Solutions.

   "As curly-headed Jemmy was sleeping in bed."

   "Five seeing, and seven blind."

   "In Shylock's bargain for the flesh was found."

   " 'In these degenerate days,' we oft hear said."

   "Ten."

   "That salmon and sole Puss should think very grand."

   "'Twixt 'Perhaps' and 'May be.' "

Pygmalion. Hilda Doolittle. **CP-DoolH**

Pygmies Are Pygmies Still, Though Percht on Alps, *Quote fr. Edward Young.* Gwendolyn Brooks. **PoNe** *Fr.* Notes from the Childhood and the Girlhood. **SP-BrooG**

Pylons, The. Stephen Spender. **CP-SpenS**

Pyramids, Arches, Obelisks, were but the irregularity of vainglory. The Fauré Ballade. James Schuyler. **CP-SchuJ**

Pyramids of flesh sweated pyramids of stone. The Track of the Master Builder. Marge Piercy. **SP-PierM**

Pyramids rooted in a rubble of beggars and bored camels, The. Sonnet to Man-Made Grandeur. John Updike. **CP-UpdiJ**

Pyramus and Thisbe. John Donne. **CP-DonnJ**

Pyrography. John Ashbery. **SP-AshbJ**

Pyrra, jugo tandem vitulum junges-ne leoni? Jugum Improbum. Robert Ranke Graves. **CP-GravR**

Pythagoras planned it. Why did the people stare? The Statues. William Butler Yeats. **CP-YeatW**

Pythian Odes. Pindar. *tr. fr. Greek.*

   "For not the brave, or wise, or great." **CP-JohnS**

Q

Q:dwo / we know of anything which can. Edward Estlin Cummings. **CP-CummE**

QPP, The. Alice Walker. **CP-WalkA**

Qua Cursum Ventus. Arthur Hugh Clough. **SP-ClouA**

Quadroon mermaids, Afro angels, black saints. A Ballad of Remembrance. Robert Earl Hayden. **CP-HaydR**

Quæ lenta accedit, quam velox præterit hora! Motto on the King's Clock. William Cowper. **CP-CowpW**

Quae linquam, aut nihil, aut nihili, aut vix sunt mea. Sordes. Epitaphium Testamentarium. Samuel Taylor Coleridge. **CP-ColeS**

Quae ratio, aut quis te furor impulit, improbe Sanni. *acc. by English translation.* Thomas Campion. **CP-CampT**

Quaerendo Invenietis. Howard Nemerov. **CP-NemeH**
  "I am the combination to a door."
  "It is a spiral way that trues my arc."
  "Without my meaning nothing, nothing means."
Quai d'Orléans. Elizabeth Bishop. **CP-BishE**
Quail. Charles Olson. **CP-OlsoC**
Quail, The. James Wright. **CP-WrigJ**
Quail, and the wild mountain aster, The. Obit. Charles Olson. **CP-OlsoC**
Quail flutters like a forlorn castle falling, The. The Quantity of Mercy. Kenneth Patchen. **CP-PatcK**
Quaint Mazes. Geoffrey Hill. **NoAM** *Fr.* An Apology for the Revival of Christian Architecture in England. **CP-HillG**
Quake last night was nothing personal, The. Earth Tremors Felt in Missouri. Mona Van Duyn. **SP-VanDM**
Quake, quake, let us turn Quaker all! George Meredith. **CP-MerG2**
Quaker Alumni, The. John Greenleaf Whittier. **CP-WhitJ**
Quaker Graveyard in Nantucket, The. Robert Lowell. **SP-LoweR**
Quaker Hill. Hart Crane. **LiTM** *Fr.* The Bridge. **CP-CranH**
Quaker of the Olden Time, The. John Greenleaf Whittier. **CP-WhitJ**
Quakers Are Out, The. John Greenleaf Whittier. **CP-WhitJ**
Quales aërii montis de vertice nubes. Translation of a Simile in Paradise Lost. John Milton, *tr. fr. English by* William Cowper. **CP-CowpW**
Quality of Heaven, The. William Carlos Williams. **CP-WilW2**
Quality of Mercy. Allen Tate. **CP-TateA**
Quality of these trees, green height; of the sky, shining; of water, The. Shine, Republic. Robinson Jeffers. **CP-JefR2**
Qualm. John Ashbery. **SP-AshbJ**
Quand on n'a pas ce que l'on aime, il faut aimer ce que l'on a—. Stevie Smith. **CP-SmitS**
Quandary. Robert Frost. **CP-FrosR**
Quando il tempo avverrà che partiremo. Iddio C'illumini! Christina Georgina Rossetti. *Fr.* Il Rosseggiar Dell'Oriente Canzoniere. **CP-RosC3**
Quando para mucho mi amore defelice corazon. Sun King. The Beatles. **CP-Beatl**
Quanta. Richard Eberhart. **CP-EberR**
Quantity of Mercy, The. Kenneth Patchen. **CP-PatcK**
Quanto a Lei grata io sono. Christina Georgina Rossetti. **CP-RosC3**
Quarai. Charles Tomlinson. **CP-TomlC**
Quarrel, The. Stanley Jasspon Kunitz. **CP-KuniS**
Quarrel, A. Malcolm Lowry. **CP-LowrM**
Quarrel. Grace Paley. **CP-PaleG**
Quarrel in Old Age. William Butler Yeats. **CP-YeatW**
Quarrel with a Cloud. Richard Eberhart. **CP-EberR**
Quarrels make up, quarrels end. With Great Love Oh Beloved Harteebeeste from El Leon. Malcolm Lowry. **CP-LowrM**
Quarried from snow, the dark walks lead to doors. Windows. Randall Jarrell. **CP-JarrR; SP-JarrR**
Quarry, The. Walter de la Mare. **CP-DeLaW**
Quarry, The. Howard Nemerov. **CP-NemeH**
Quarry, The. Charles Tomlinson. **CP-TomlC**
Quarry Hills. Roy Fisher. **SP-FishR**
Quarter, The. James Liddy. **CP-LiddJ**
Quarter of pleasures where the rich are always waiting. The Capital. Wystan Hugh Auden. **CP-AudeW**
Quarterly, is it, money reproaches me. Money. Philip Larkin. **CP-LarkP**
Quartermaster at the Wheel. Malcolm Lowry. *Fr.* The Roar of the Sea and the Darkness. **CP-LowrM**
Quartermasters and filibusterers. War on the Mind in a Time of Love. Charles Olson. **CP-OlsoC**
Quartz opens its eyes in the snow. Pablo Neruda, *tr. fr. Spanish by* Ben Belitt. **SP-NeruP** *Fr.* Skystones.
Quasars. Robert Pack. **SP-PackR**
Quatrain: "Do not, at this high time, desert." Charles Olson. **CP-OlsoC**
Quatrain? Is that, A. The Sound of Waves. William Carlos Williams. **CP-WilW2**
Quatrains. Ralph Waldo Emerson. **CP-EmerR**
'ΑΔΑΚΡΥΝ ΝΕΜΟΝΤΑΙ ΑΙΩΝΑ.
  A.H.
  Artist.
  Borrowing from the French.
    (Needless Worry.) **TreFT**
  Botanist.
  Casella.
  Climacteric.
  Excelsior.
  Fate ("Her planted eye to-day controls"). **APN-1**

  Forester.
  From Alcuin.
  Gardener. **OxBA**
  Hafiz.
  Heri, Cras, Hodie.
  Horoscope.
  Hush!
  Love.
  Memory. **APN-1**
  Nature.
  Nature in Leasts.
  Northman.
  Orator. **OxBA**
  Pericles.
  Poet ("Ever the poet *from* the land").
  Poet ("To clothe the fiery thought"). **OxBA; OxBSP; PCP; Spl**
  Power.
    (Self-Reliance.) **APN-1**
  Sacrifice.
    (Faith.) **OtMeF**
  S.H.
  Shakspeare.
  Suum Cuique ("Wilt thou seal up the avenues of ill?"). **APN-1**
Quattrocento. Margaret Atwood. **SP-AtwM2**
Quavering cry. Screech-owl? A. Night, Death, Mississippi. Robert Earl Hayden. **CP-HaydR**
Quay recedes, The. Hurrah! Ahead we go! The Colonel's Soliloquy. Thomas Hardy. **CP-HardT**
Que ferais-je sans ce monde sans visage sans questions, *Author's own French vers. of his* "What would I do without this world faceless incurious." Samuel Beckett. **CP-BeckS**
Que J'ay Dit Devant. Louis Zukofsky. **CP-ZukLS**
Quebec Suite. Mona Van Duyn. **SP-VanDM**
Queen and huntress, chaste and fair. Ben Jonson. **CP-JonsB** *Fr.* Cynthia's Revels.
Queen and the Young Princess, The. Stevie Smith. **CP-SmitS**
Queen Annelida and False Arcite. Geoffrey Chaucer. **CP-BroEB**
Queen-Anne's-Lace. William Carlos Williams. **CP-WilW1**
Queen Anne's Lace. Louis Zukofsky. **CP-ZukLS**
Queen Bess was Harry's daughter. Stand forward partners all! The Looking Glass. Rudyard Kipling. **CP-KiplR**
Queen Caroline to Her Guests. Thomas Hardy. **CP-HardT**
Queen Djenira. Walter de la Mare. **CP-DeLaW**
Queen Guinevere had fled the court, and sat. Guinevere. Tennyson. *Fr.* Idylls of the King. **CP-TennA**
Queen has lately lost a part, The. Verses Said to Be Written on the Union. Jonathan Swift. **CP-SwifJ**
Queen Is in the Parlor, The. Ogden Nash. **CP-NashO**
Queen Jane Approximately. "Bob Dylan." **CP-DylaB**
Queen Mab. Percy Bysshe Shelley. **CP-ShelP**
  Magic Car Moved On, The. **GN**
  War Is the Statesman's Game. **FF; PPON**
Queen Mab in the Village. Nicholas Vachel Lindsay. **CP-LindV**
Queen Nefertiti–Small Fragment of Nose and Mouth Only. Marsden Hartley. **CP-HartM**
Queen of Bubbles, The. Nicholas Vachel Lindsay. **CP-LindV**
Queen of Hearts, The. Christina Georgina Rossetti. **CP-RosC1**
Queen of Pentacles, The. Marge Piercy. *Fr.* Laying Down the Tower. **SP-PierM**
Queen of Sharon in the valley. Song: To a Rose. Robert Ranke Graves. **CP-GravR**
Queen of Sheba came, The. King Solomon and the Queen of Shiba. Nicholas Vachel Lindsay. *Fr.* The Booker Washington Trilogy. **CP-LindV**
Queen of the Billiards. Laurence Lieberman. **SP-LiebL**
Queen of the Crabs, accept this claw. With the Gift of a Lion's Claw. Robert Ranke Graves. **CP-GravR**
Queen of the mountains far and near. Horace. *See* 3.22: Pine Tree for Diana, The ("Montium custos nemorumque").
Queen of the silver bow!—by thy pale beam. To the Moon. Charlotte Smith. **CP-SmitC**
Queen of the stars!—so gentle, so benign. To the Moon (Rydal). William Wordsworth. **CP-WorW2**
Queen of wit and beauty, Betty. To Betty the Grisette. Jonathan Swift. **CP-SwifJ**
Queen rejoices in her peers, A. Ralph Waldo Emerson. **CP-EmerR**
Queen Rose. Christina Georgina Rossetti. **CP-RosC3**

Queen she sent to look for me, The. Grenadier. Alfred Edward Housman. **CP-HousA**

Queen Theodolind has built. The Song of Theodolinda. George Meredith. **CP-MerG1**

Queen Venus, come now, be my heroine. The Flying House, and the May Queen Eternal. Nicholas Vachel Lindsay. **CP-LindV**

Queen Victoria and Me. Leonard Cohen. **CP-CoheL**

Queen Virtue's court, which some call Stella's face. Sonnet 9. Sir Philip Sidney. **NAEL-1** *Fr.* Astrophil and Stella. **SP-SidnP**

Queen Wasp, A. Walter de la Mare. **CP-DeLaW**

Queen Zuleima. George Meredith. **CP-MerG2**

Queene anone commands the waightie bowle, The. Virgil, *tr.* by Sir Walter Ralegh. **CP-RaleW** *Fr.* The Aeneid [*or* Eneados, Aeneis].

Queens Cemetery, Setting Sun. Lawrence Ferlinghetti. **SP-FerlL**

Queen's Complaint, The. Sylvia Plath. **CP-PlatS**

Queen's Crowning, The. Gerard Manley Hopkins. **CP-HopkG**

Queen's Men, The. Rudyard Kipling. **CP-KiplR**

Queens of Hell had lissome necks to crane, The. The Tall Girl. John Crowe Ransom. **SP-RansJ**

Queens Tunnel. Thomas Merton. *Fr.* North. *Fr.* The Geography of Lograire. **CP-MertT**

Queer are the ways of a man I know. The Phantom Horsewoman. Thomas Hardy. **CP-HardT**

Queer Client and the Forest-Inn, The. Kenneth Patchen. **CP-PatcK**

Queer Poem. Malcolm Lowry. **CP-LowrM**

Queer thing about those waters: there are no, A. Across the Bay. Donald Davie. **CP-DavDo**

Quenching the Red. Kathleen Jessie Raine. **SP-RainK**

Quentin Durward. Sir Walter Scott.
Serenade, A: "Ah! County Guy, the hour is nigh."
(County Guy.) **SP-ScotW**

Querencia. Stephen Dobyns. **SP-DobyS**

Queries to Casuists. Byron. **CP-Byron**

Queries to My Seventieth Year. Walt Whitman. **CP-WhitW**

Queries, you ask how many times must I kiss. Catullus. *See* Carmen 7: "Curious to learn / how may kiss- / es of your lips."

Query. John Updike. **CP-UpdiJ**

Query: was ever a quainter. Of Pacchiarotto, and How He Worked in Distemper. Robert Browning. **CP-BroR2**

Quest, The. Wystan Hugh Auden. **CP-AudeW**
"All had been ordered weeks before the start."
"Ashamed to be the darling of his grief."
"Fresh addenda are published every day."
"He parried every question that they hurled."
"He watched with all his organs of concern." **PoA**
(Poem: "He watched with all his organs of concern.") **PoA**
"His library annoyed him with its look."
"His peasant parents killed themselves with toil."
"In villages from which their childhoods came."
"Incredulous, he stared at the amused."
"No window in his suburb lights that bedroom where."
"Others had found it prudent to withdraw."
"Out of it steps our future, through this door." **Son**
(Door, The.) **Son**
"Over-logical fell for the witch, The."
"Poet, oracle, and wit."
"Spinning upon their central thirst like tops."
"Suppose he's listened to the erudite committee."
"They noticed that virginity was needed."
"This is an architecture for the odd."
"Two friends who met here and embraced are gone."
"Within these gates all opening begins."

Quest, The. Rudyard Kipling. **CP-KiplR**

Quest, The. Alun Lewis. **CP-LewiA**

Quest, The. James Wright. **CP-WrigJ**

Quest of the Purple-Fringed, The. Robert Frost. **CP-FrosR**

Question, The. Robert Creeley. **CP-CreeR**

Question, A. Paul Laurence Dunbar. **CP-DunbP**

Question, A. Robert Frost. **CP-FrosR**

Question. Langston Hughes. **SP-HughL**

Question, The. Rudyard Kipling. **CP-KiplR**

Question. David Herbert Lawrence. **CP-LawrD**

Question. Grace Paley. **CP-PaleG**

Question, The. Frank Templeton Prince. **CP-PrinF**

Question, The. Muriel Rukeyser. **CP-RukeM**

Question, The. Percy Bysshe Shelley. **CP-ShelP**

Question: / Tell me, where do fairy queens, The. Cold Sunbeams. Nicholas Vachel Lindsay. **CP-LindV**

Question, The. Charles Tomlinson. **CP-TomlC**

Question, The. Charles Tomlinson. **CP-TomlC**

Question, The. Charles Kenneth Williams. **SP-WillC**

Question and Answer. Elizabeth Barrett Browning. **CP-BroEB**

Question and Answer. William Carlos Williams. **CP-WilW1**

Question Answered, The [*or* A]. William Blake. *See* What is it men in women do require?

Question Book. Pablo Neruda.
"And why is the sun such a poor friend." **SP-NeruP**
"Are the salt and the sugar at work." **SP-NeruP**
"At whom is the rice grinning." **SP-NeruP**
"Can't you think death lives." **SP-NeruP**
"Do you hear yellow detonations." **SP-NeruP**
"Don't you also feel danger." **SP-NeruP**
"How long would a rhinoceros last." **SP-NeruP**
"If all rivers are sweet." **SP-NeruP**
"If I'm dead and don't know it." **SP-NeruP**
"Is all peace a dove's peace?" **SP-NeruP**
"Is 4 always 4 for everybody?" **SP-NeruP**
"Is it true that amber contains." **SP-NeruP**
"Is there anything crazier in this life." **SP-NeruP**
"Spelling book, can you love me." **SP-NeruP**
"Tell me, is the rose really naked." **SP-NeruP**
"That solemn Senator / who claimed I had castles." **SP-NeruP**
"To whom does the raggedy condor." **SP-NeruP**
"What are you hiding under your hump?" **SP-NeruP**
"What can it mean to endure." **SP-NeruP**
"What forced labor / for Hitler in Hell?" **SP-NeruP**
"What will the Poles think of my hat." **SP-NeruP**
"When does the butterfly read." **SP-NeruP**
"Where is the child that I was." **SP-NeruP**
"Who can persuade the sea." **SP-NeruP**
"Whom can I ask / what I meant to achieve in this world?" **SP-NeruP**
"Won't our life be a tunnel." **SP-NeruP**

Question in a Field. Louise Bogan. **CP-BogaL**

Question is: how does one hold an apple, The. The Gesture. George Oppen. **NNaP** *Fr.* Five Poems about Poetry. **CP-OppeG**

Question Is, Who Is Afraid of What, The? Kenneth Patchen. **CP-PatcK**

? Edward Estlin Cummings. **CP-CummE**

Question Mark. Richard Eberhart. **CP-EberR**

Question of Anatomy. David Markson. **CP-MarkD**

Question of Identity, A. Stephen Spender. **CP-SpenS**

Question of Libel, A. Alexander Pope. **PrIm** *Fr.* The First Satire of the Second Book of Horace [Imitated]. **CP-PopeA**

Question of Marriage, A. Thomas Hardy. **CP-HardT**

Question, The: "All of us believe." Wystan Hugh Auden. **CP-AudeW**

Question, The ("To ask the hard question is simple"). Wystan Hugh Auden. **CP-AudeW**

Question Whither, The. George Meredith. **CP-MerG1**

Questionable old man wanders, The. Sleepwalker. Dabney Stuart. **SP-StuaD**

Questioner Who Sits So Sly, The. Wystan Hugh Auden. **CP-AudeW**

Questioning Faces. Robert Frost. **CP-FrosR**

Questionnaire. Carl Sandburg. **CP-SandC**

Questions. Hayden Carruth. **CP-CarHS**

Questions. Howard Nemerov. **CP-NemeH**

Questions Are Remarks. Wallace Stevens. **CP-StevW**

Questions for my Grandfather. James McAuley. **SP-McAuJ**

Questions in a Wood. Robert Ranke Graves. **CP-GravR**

Questions of Life. John Greenleaf Whittier. **CP-WhitJ**

Questions of Travel. Elizabeth Bishop. **CP-BishE**

Quetzalcoatl Looks Down on Mexico. David Herbert Lawrence. **CP-LawrD**

Qui Bien Aime a Tard Oublie. Geoffrey Chaucer. *See* Now Welcom[e], Somer [*or* Summer].

Qui Laborat, Orat. Arthur Hugh Clough. **SP-ClouA**

Qui subito ex imis rerum in fastigia surgit. Papilio et Limax. John Gay, *tr. fr. English by* William Cowper. **CP-CowpW**

Quia Absurdum. Robinson Jeffers. **CP-JefR3**

Quibbling Elegy on the Worshipful Judge Boat, A. Jonathan Swift. **CP-SwifJ**

Quick! a last poem before I go. On Rachmaninoff's Birthday. Frank O'Hara. **SP-OharF**

Quick and yet he moves like silt. Trout. Richard Hugo. **CP-HugoR**

Quick bird sings and pierces me, The. Song. George Meredith. **CP-MerG2**

Quick death, Catullus! what more horrors may hurry! Catullus. *See* Carmen 52: "Drop dead, Catullus, lie right down & die."

Quick, Hammacher, My Stomacher! Ogden Nash. **CP-NashO**

Quick, Henry, the Flit! James Schuyler. **CP-SchuJ**

Quick i the death of thing. Edward Estlin Cummings. **CP-CummE**

Quick nine holes, A. Woodenbridge Golf Club. James Liddy. **CP-LiddJ**

Quick on my feet in those Novembers of my loneliness. A Mad Fight Song for William S. Carpenter, 1966. James Wright. **CP-WrigJ**

Quick, painter, quick the moment seize. Currente Calamo. Arthur Hugh Clough. **SP-ClouA** *Fr.* Mari Magno.

Quick sparks on the gorse bushes are leaping, The. The Wild Common. David Herbert Lawrence. **CP-LawrD**

Quick-Step. Robert Creeley. **CP-CreeR**

Quick sun brings, exciting mountains warm, The. Power. Muriel Rukeyser. **CP-RukeM**

Quick talk / their speech—. Robert Creeley. **CP-CreeR**

Quick! there's that. A Turn of the Head. Denise Levertov. **CP-LeveD**

Quickening of St. John the Baptist, The. Thomas Merton. **CP-MertT**

Quicker / than that, can't. A Sight. Robert Creeley. **CP-CreeR**

Quicker deceit dies, The. Emily Dickinson. **SP-DickE**

Quickly, my letter, run through the boundless deep. Elegy 4. John Milton, *tr. fr. Latin by* John T. Shawcross. **CP-MiltJ**

Quicksand Years. Walt Whitman. **CP-WhitW**

Quicquid in adversis potuit constantia rebus. *acc. by English translation.* Thomas Campion. **CP-CampT**

Quid conclamato jacis irrita vota sepulchro? Elegia IX. Robert Southwell. **CP-SoutR**

Quid, fact it is Gelli? quick'ning mother, at (queer) sis, all three. Catullus. *See* Carmen 88: "What, Gellius, of the man."

Quid Hic Agis? Thomas Hardy. **CP-HardT**

Quid tu te numeris immisces? anne medentem. *accompanied by English translation.* Thomas Campion. *Fr.* Lord Hay's Mask.

Quidditie [*or* Quiddity], The. George Herbert. **CP-HerbG**

Quiddity, Gelli, quarry, rosy as these too lips belie. Catullus. *See* Carmen 80: "How is it, Gellius."

Quiet. Walter de la Mare. **CP-DeLaW**

Quiet afternoon, A. Compulsory Chapel. Alice Walker. **CP-WalkA**

Quiet Afternoon at Home, A. Mona Van Duyn. **SP-VanDM**

Quiet as is proper for such places. Return. Robert Creeley. **CP-CreeR**

Quiet Clean Girls in Gingham Dresses. . . . Charles Bukowski. **SP-BukC1**

Quiet deepens. You will not persuade, The. Farewell to Van Gogh. Charles Tomlinson. **CP-TomlC**

Quiet Enemy, The. Walter de la Mare. **CP-DeLaW**

Quiet fading out of life, The. Magnolia Flowers. Langston Hughes. **SP-HughL**

Quiet Glades of Eden, The. Robert Ranke Graves. **CP-GravR**

Quiet Life and a Good Name, A. Jonathan Swift. **CP-SwifJ**

Quiet light out the window. For Mike and Kim. Chuck Miller. **SP-MillC**

Quiet Normal Life, A. Wallace Stevens. **CP-StevW**

Quiet now, sorrow; relax. Calm down, fear. Meditation. David St. John. **SP-StJoD**

Quiet pastures where they graze, The. Traveler and Old Sorrel. Louise McNeill. **SP-McNeL**

Quiet setting the rough hairy roots. At the Core. Marge Piercy. **SP-PierM**

Quiet Talk with Oneself, A. Charles Simic. **SP-SimiC**

Quiet voice, / In the midst of those blazing. Echo for the Promise of Georg Trakl's Life. James Wright. **CP-WrigJ**

Quiet Work. Matthew Arnold. **SP-ArnoM**

Quieter the people are, The. The Sign Board. Robert Creeley. **CP-CreeR**

Quietly I lay awake upon my bed. After Reading Keats' Ode. Wystan Hugh Auden. **CP-AudWJ**

Quietly pacifist peaceful, The. The QPP. Alice Walker. **CP-WalkA**

Quietly, quietly, why have I been waiting? To Wang Wei. Meng Hao Jan, *tr. fr. Chinese by* William Carlos Williams *with* David Rafael Wang. **CP-WilW2**

Quietness. William Carlos Williams. **CP-WilW1**

Quietness clings to the air. The Snow Fall. Archibald MacLeish. **CP-MacLA**

Quietude. David Markson. **CP-MarkD**

Quietude of a soft wind, The. The Creditor. Louis MacNeice. **CP-MacNL**

Quilt-Pattern, A. Randall Jarrell. **CP-JarrR**

Quilting, The. Paul Laurence Dunbar. **CP-DunbP**

Quilts the pond and / out from under its plumped-upness. Rain. James Schuyler. **CP-SchuJ**

Quin etiam nostros non aspernata labores. Gerard Manley Hopkins. *Fr.* Fragments on St. Winefred. **CP-HopkG**

Quinn the Eskimo. "Bob Dylan." **CP-DylaB**

Quinnapoxet. Stanley Jasspon Kunitz. **CP-KuniS**

Quinquagesima. Christina Georgina Rossetti. **CP-RosC2**

Quinque, *Latin vers. of* Five. Robert Ranke Graves. **CP-GravR**

Quinque tibi luces vibrant in nomine: quinque. *Latin vers. of* Five. Robert Ranke Graves. **CP-GravR**

Quinquereme of Nineveh from distant Ophir. Wystan. Paul Muldoon. *Fr.* 7, Middagh Street. **SP-MuldP**

Quintell, The. Robert Herrick. **CP-HerrR**

Quinti, see if't be wish of cool eyes day bear your Catullus. Catullus. *See* Carmen 82: "My eyes in your pledge, Quintius."

Quintia is handsome, fair, tall, straight, all these. Catullus. *See* Carmen 86: "We have heard of Quintia's beauty. To me she is tall, slender."

Quintia's *foremost* to multitudes; my eye can deed her *long, e*—. Catullus. *See* Carmen 86: "We have heard of Quintia's beauty. To me she is tall, slender."

Quintius if you'll endear Catullus eyes. Catullus. *See* Carmen 82: "My eyes in your pledge, Quintius."

Quip, The. George Herbert. **CP-HerbG**

Quips and players, seeming to vend astringency off-hours. Second Avenue. Frank O'Hara. **SP-OharF**

Quique Amavit. Wystan Hugh Auden. **CP-AudWJ**

Quique haec membra malis vis esse obnoxia multis. Gerard Manley Hopkins. **CP-HopkG**

Quiquern. Rudyard Kipling. *Fr.* The Second Jungle Book.

　Angutivaun Taina. **CP-KiplR**

　"People of the Eastern Ice, they are melting like the snow, The." **CP-KiplR**

Quisnam adeo, mortale genus, praecordia versat? *see also* The Garden. Andrew Marvell. **CP-MarvA**

Quit That. Archie Randolph Ammons. **SP-AmmoA**

Quit the hut, frequent the palace. Artist. Ralph Waldo Emerson. *Fr.* Quatrains. **CP-EmerR**

Quit writing / and in Morocco. Africa. William Carlos Williams. **CP-WilW1**

Quit Your Low Down Ways. "Bob Dylan." **CP-DylaB**

Quite empty, quite at rest. Emily Dickinson. **CP-DickE**

Quite Forsaken. David Herbert Lawrence. **CP-LawrD**

Quite outside and beyond the personal. Ace of Destiny. Tom Clark. **SP-ClarT**

Quite suddenly they flew. Buzzards. Wystan Hugh Auden. **CP-AudWJ**

Quite unexpectedly as Vasserot. The End of the World. Archibald MacLeish. **CP-MacLA**

Quivering wings of the winter ant, The. Winter Poem. Robert Bly. **SP-BlyR**

Quiz, The. Ron Koertge. **SP-KoerR**

Quo rubeant dulcesve rosae vel pomifer aestas? Gerard Manley Hopkins. *Fr.* Elegiacs. **CP-HopkG**

Quòd festas luces juvat instaurare Beatis. Ad Episcopum Salopiensem. Gerard Manley Hopkins. **CP-HopkG**

Quod nostros, Davisi, laudas recitasque libellos. *acc. by English translation.* Thomas Campion. **CP-CampT**

Quondam was I in my lady's grace. Sir Thomas Wyatt. **CP-WyatT**

Quoof. Paul Muldoon. **SP-MuldP**

Quotations. George Oppen. **CP-OppeG**

Quotations. Carl Sandburg. **CP-SandC**

Quoth an inquirer, "Praise the Merciful!" Mihrab Shah. Robert Browning. **CP-BroR2**

Quoth King Robin, our ribbons I see are too few. Verses on the Revival of the Order of the Bath. Jonathan Swift. **CP-SwifJ**

Quoth one: "Sir, solve a scruple! No true sage." Two Camels. Robert Browning. **CP-BroR2**

Quoth Saadi, when I stood before. Ralph Waldo Emerson. **CP-EmerR**

Quoth the thief to the dog; "let me into your door." The Dog and the Thief. Jonathan Swift. **CP-SwifJ**

R

R. Alcona to J. Brenzaida. Emily Brontë. *See* Remembrance.

R. C. Dallas. Byron. **CP-Byron**

R. G. E. Richard Eberhart. **CP-EberR**

R. L. S. Alfred Edward Housman. **CP-HousA**

r-p-o-p-h-e-s-s-a-g-r. Edward Estlin Cummings. **CP-CummE**

R R Bums, The. William Carlos Williams. **CP-WilW2**

R. S. S., at Deer Island on the Merrimac. John Greenleaf Whittier. **CP-WhitJ**

R. Usher. Malcolm Lowry. **CP-LowrM**

R². Charles Olson. **CP-OlsoC**

Rabbi, The. Robert Earl Hayden. **CP-HaydR**

Rabbi Ben Ezra. Robert Browning. **CP-BroR1**

"Grow old along with me!" **FaBV; ImPo; LPA; PoToHe**
Why Time Spins Fast. **FaBoDD**
Rabbi Ishmael. John Greenleaf Whittier. **CP-WhitJ**
Rabbi Nathan twoscore years and ten, The. The Two Rabbins. John Greenleaf Whittier. **CP-WhitJ**
Rabbi Robert Raaba will preach. Rabbi to Preach. Delmore Schwartz. *Fr.* Occasional Poems. **SP-SchwD**
Rabbi to Preach. Delmore Schwartz. *Fr.* Occasional Poems. **SP-SchwD**
Rabbi told me: On the day allowed, A. Doctor———. Robert Browning. **CP-BroR2**
Rabbi, we Gadarenes. Matthew VIII, 28 ff. Richard Wilbur. **CP-WilbR**
Rabbi's Song, The. Rudyard Kipling. **CP-KiplR**
Rabbit, The. Edna St. Vincent Millay. **CP-MillE**
Rabbit, The. Mary Oliver. **SP-OlivM**
Rabbit as King of the Ghosts, A. Wallace Stevens. **CP-StevW**
Rabbit Catcher, The. Sylvia Plath. **CP-PlatS**
Rabbit Fights for His Life the Leopard Eats Lunch, The. Charles Kenneth Williams. **CP-WillC**
Rabbit Hunter, The. Robert Frost. **CP-FrosR**
Rabbit hurries to the brim of its wood, The. Randall Jarrell. **CP-JarrR**
Rabbit in his burrow keeps, The. Haunted. Walter de la Mare. **CP-DeLaW**
Rabbit loves his hoppity and the wallaby loves his hippity, The. Don't Look for the Silver Lining, Just Wait for It. Ogden Nash. **CP-NashO**
Rabbit Snared in the Night. David Herbert Lawrence. **CP-LawrD**
Rabbit who used to belong to Matthew, The. Sojourners. Marge Piercy. **SP-PierM**
Rabbits, The. Ogden Nash. **CP-NashO**
Rabbits breed, flies breed, said the virgin lady. Unborn Song. Muriel Rukeyser. **CP-RukeM**
Rabbit's dreamy eyes grow dreamier, The. A Bulletin Has Just Come In. Ogden Nash. **CP-NashO**
(..rabid or dog-dull.) Let me tell you how. A Professor's Song. John Berryman. **CP-BerrJ**
Raccoon, A. Siv Cedering Fox. **SP-CedeS**
Raccoon. Kenneth Rexroth. **NNaP; SP-RexrK; ZA** *Fr.* A Bestiary. **SP-RexrK**
(Racoon.) **FiBHP**
Raccoon. Anne Sexton. **CP-SextA**
Raccoon lies broken, A. A Raccoon. Siv Cedering Fox. **SP-CedeS**
Raccoon wears a black mask, The. Raccoon. Kenneth Rexroth. **FiBHP; NNaP; SP-RexrK; ZA** *Fr.* A Bestiary. **SP-RexrK**
Raccoons have invaded the crawl space. In the Old Neighborhood. Rita Dove. **SP-DoveR**
Race, The. Howard Nemerov. **CP-NemeH**
Race, The. Charles Tomlinson. **CP-TomlC**
Race and Battle. David Herbert Lawrence. **CP-LawrD**
Race is not to the swift, The. Race and Battle. David Herbert Lawrence. **CP-LawrD**
Race of the Flood, The. Charles Kenneth Williams. **CP-WillC**
Race of Veterans. Walt Whitman. **CP-WhitW**
Race with the sun as he downed, A. Cynic's Epitaph. Thomas Hardy. **CP-HardT**
Racer's Widow, The. Louise Glück. **SP-GlücL**
Racetrack, The. Jane Cooper. *Fr.* Acceptances. **SP-CoopJ**
Rachel. Walter de la Mare. **CP-DeLaW**
Rachel sings sweet— / Oh, yes, at night. Rachel. Walter de la Mare. **CP-DeLaW**
Rachmaninoff's Third. James Schuyler. **CP-SchuJ**
Racist Poem. Bill Knott. **SP-KnotB**
Racists. Charles Kenneth Williams. **SP-WillC**
Rack of Paperbacks, A. John Updike. **CP-UpdiJ**
Rackman and victim twist: sounds all these weeks. John Berryman. *Fr.* Sonnets to Chris. **CP-BerrJ**
Racoon. Kenneth Rexroth. *See* Raccoon.
Radar and rocket-plane, the applications of chemistry, the tricks of. Staggering Back Toward Life. Robinson Jeffers. **CP-JefR3**
Raddle me riddle. Adam's Riddle. Archibald MacLeish. *Fr.* Songs for Eve. **CP-MacLA**
Raddle me riddle. Eve's Riddle. Archibald MacLeish. *Fr.* Songs for Eve. **CP-MacLA**
Raderus. John Donne. **CP-DonnJ**
Radiance comes from. Wiring. Archie Randolph Ammons. **SP-AmmoA**
Radiance in a Dark Wood, The. Kenneth Patchen. **CP-PatcK**
Radiant Silhouette I. John Yau. **SP-YauJo**
Radiant Silhouette II. John Yau. **SP-YauJo**
Radiant Silhouette III. John Yau. **SP-YauJo**
Radiant Silhouette IV. John Yau. **SP-YauJo**

Radiant Silhouette V. John Yau. **SP-YauJo**
Radiation is like oppression. The Long Death. Marge Piercy. **SP-PierM**
Radiator's hissing hot, The. Studio up over in Your Ear. Al Young. **CP-YounA**
Radiator's last hiss and steam-clang done, he, The. Reading Late at Night, Thermometer Falling. Robert Penn Warren. **SP-WarrR**
Radicals. Jorge Carrera Andrade, *tr. fr. Spanish by* Thomas Merton. **CP-MertT**
Radio. Tom Clark. **SP-ClarT**
Radio. Frank O'Hara. **SP-OharF**
Radio Madrid—1937. Edwin Rolfe. **CP-RolfE**
Radio predicts the first hard frost, The. The First Hard Frost. Barton Sutter. **SP-SuttB**
Radio silence of aircraft over the dense ocean. Muriel Rukeyser. **CP-RukeM**
Radiometer. James Merrill. **SP-MerrJ**
R.A.F. Hilda Doolittle. **CP-DoolH**
R.A.F. (Aged Eighteen). Rudyard Kipling. **PoWW** *Fr.* Epitaphs of the War [1914–1918]. **CP-KiplR**
Rafael Sublime Majestic Graceful Wise. William Blake. **CP-BlakW**
Raft, The. Robert Ranke Graves. **CP-GravR**
Raft, The. Nicholas Vachel Lindsay. *Fr.* Three Poems About Mark Twain. **CP-LindV**
Rafters, The. James Dickey. **CP-DickJ**
Rafts, The. Adrienne Rich. **CP-RicAE**
Rag Man, The. Robert Earl Hayden. **CP-HaydR**
Rage. Peter Meinke. **SP-MeinP**
Rage. Mary Oliver. **SP-OlivM**
Rage. Alice Walker. **CP-WalkA**
Rage and regret are tireless to explain. Geoffrey Hill. *Fr.* The Mystery of the Charity of Charles Péguy. **CP-HillG**
Rage swept them across the Vistula, Danube, Elbe. James McAuley. **SP-McAuJ** *Fr.* Map.
Ragged and thrashing. Jane Cooper. *Fr.* Messages. **SP-CoopJ**
Ragged boys / lift sweets, haggle. Market. Robert Earl Hayden. *Fr.* An Inference of Mexico. **CP-HaydR**
Ragged Island. Edna St. Vincent Millay. **CP-MillE**
Ragged Wood, The. William Butler Yeats. **CP-YeatW**
Raggs. Robert Herrick. **CP-HerrR**
Raging from every quarter. Wreath of Women. Muriel Rukeyser. **CP-RukeM**
Raging of the Rose, The. William Everson. **SP-EverW** *Fr.* The Rose of Solitude.
Raging on Duneneeny while the smoke. MacDonnell's Question. John Hewitt. **CP-HewiJ**
Rahab's House. Thomas Merton. **CP-MertT**
Rahel to Varnhagen. Edwin Arlington Robinson. **CP-RobiE**
Rahere. Rudyard Kipling. **CP-KiplR** *Fr.* Debits and Credits.
Rahere, King Henry's Jester, feared by all the Norman Lords. Rahere. Rudyard Kipling. **CP-KiplR** *Fr.* Debits and Credits.
Raid, The. William Everson. **SP-EverW**
Raid, The. Alun Lewis. **CP-LewiA**
Raiders' Dawn. Alun Lewis. **CP-LewiA**
Rail ends do not meet, The. Ernest Hemingway. **CP-HemiE**
Rail on, Rail on, ye heartless Crew! To a Knot of Ungenerous Critics. Byron. **CP-Byron**
Railroad Avenue. Langston Hughes. **SP-HughL**
Railroad track is miles away, The. Travel. Edna St. Vincent Millay. **CP-MillE**
Railroad yard in San Jose. In Back of the Real. Allen Ginsberg. **CP-GinsA**
Rails pause barely to tie the horizons, The. The Depot. Lewis Turco. **SP-TurcL**
Rails shine like new wire, The. The Trestle. Lewis Turco. **SP-TurcL**
Railway bore him through, The. After a Romantic Day. Thomas Hardy. **CP-HardT**
Railway Children, The. Seamus Heaney. **SP-HeanS**
Railway Junction, The. Walter de la Mare. **CP-DeLaW**
Railway Stationery, The. Kenneth Koch. **SP-KochK**
Railway stationery lay upon. The Railway Stationery. Kenneth Koch. **SP-KochK**
Railway stations of our daily plight. The Platform. Adrienne Rich. **CP-RicAE**
Rain. Wystan Hugh Auden. **CP-AudWJ**
Rain. Wendell Berry. **CP-BerrW**
Rain, The. Robert Creeley. **CP-CreeR**
Rain / Drips down / O'er fields, The. Early Summer Sketch. Edward Estlin Cummings. **CP-CummE**

Rain. The Beatles. **CP-Beatl**

Rain. Mary Oliver. **SP-OlivM**

Rain. John Crowe Ransom. *Fr.* Two Gentlemen in Bonds. **SP-RansJ**

Rain. James Schuyler. **CP-SchuJ**

Rain. Shel Silverstein. **SP-SilS2**

Rain. Robert Louis Stevenson. **CP-StevR**

Rain. William Carlos Williams. **CP-WilW1**

Rain. James Wright. **CP-WrigJ**

Rain, all night, taps the holly. Holly and Hickory. Robert Penn Warren. **SP-WarrR**

Rain always follows the cattle. How to Foretell a Change in the Weather. Ted Kooser. **SP-KoosT**

Rain, and then / the cool pursed. Mushrooms. Mary Oliver. **SP-OlivM**

Rain and thunder beat down and flooded the streets. Cartagena. Gary Snyder. **CP-SnydG**

Rain baptizes the ravaged counties. Midlands. Charles Tomlinson. **CP-TomlC**

Rain-beaten stones: great tussocks of dead grass. The Wind-bags. "Hugh MacDiarmid." **SP-MacDH**

Rain comes flapping through the yard, The. Gathering Mushrooms. Paul Muldoon. **SP-MuldP**

Rain Downriver. Philip Levine. **SP-LeviP**

Rain-drop on the eyelids of the earth, A. Sonnet. Edward Estlin Cummings. **CP-CummE**

Rain drums down like red ants, The. The Fury of Rain Storms. Anne Sexton. *Fr.* The Furies. **CP-SextA**

Rain extravagantly that morning kept us. The Story of a Citizen. Tess Gallagher. **SP-GallT**

Rain falls / down down and jumps, The. Down. Joseph Ceravolo. **SP-CeraJ**

Rain falls like knives, The. Derek Walcott. **PBCV** *Fr.* Another Life. **CP-WalcD**

Rain falls on the trash burning in an old oil drum and does not put it out. Moneses Uniflora. James Schuyler. *Fr.* The Cenotaph. **CP-SchuJ**

Rain Fell Heavily, The. Malcolm Lowry. **CP-LowrM**

Rain Glass, The. John Haines. **SP-HainJ**

Rain Guitar, The. James Dickey. **CP-DickJ**

Rain, hail and brutal sun, the plow in the roots. Robinson Jeffers. *Fr.* The Broken Balance. **CP-JefR1**

Rain has spoiled the farmer's day, The. Suum Cuique. Ralph Waldo Emerson. **CP-EmerR**

Rain has stopped. The waterfall will roar like that all, The. Giant Snail. Elizabeth Bishop. *Fr.* Rainy Season; Sub-Tropics. **CP-BishE**

Rain held off. They came to turn the laps, The. Haymaking in the Low Meadow. John Hewitt. **CP-HewiJ**

Rain imprinted the step's wet shine, The. On the Doorstep. Thomas Hardy. **CP-HardT**

Rain in Ohio. Mary Oliver. **SP-OlivM**

Rain in the Desert. John Gould Fletcher. *Fr.* Arizona Poems. **SP-FletJ**

Rain Is a Handsome Animal, The. Edward Estlin Cummings. **CP-CummE**

Rain is a long susurrance; makes no loud. Rain. John Crowe Ransom. *Fr.* Two Gentlemen in Bonds. **SP-RansJ**

Rain is My Home, The. Erica Jong. **SP-JongE**

Rain is over and done, The. Robert Louis Stevenson. **CP-StevR**

Rain is raining all around, The. Quick, Henry, the Flit! James Schuyler. **CP-SchuJ**

Rain is raining all around, The. Rain. Robert Louis Stevenson. **CP-StevR**

Rain it rains without a stay, The. The Floods. Rudyard Kipling. **CP-KiplR**

Rain, it streams on stone and hillock, The. Alfred Edward Housman. **CP-HousA**

Rain, its tiny pressure, The. Romanze, or the Music Students. Frank O'Hara. **SP-OharF**

Rain, now as all night, is tapping. Seattle Uplift. John Updike. **CP-UpdiJ**

Rain of Blood, The. Adrienne Rich. **CP-RicAE**

Rain of bombs, well placed, A. The Snow Begins. William Carlos Williams. **CP-WilW2**

Rain of London pimples, The. London Rain. Louis MacNeice. **CP-MacNL**

Rain on a Grave. Thomas Hardy. **CP-HardT**

Rain on South-East England. Donald Davie. **CP-DavDo**

Rain on That Morning, The. William Everson. **SP-EverW**

Rain on the West Side Highway. Adrienne Rich. **NAAL-2** *Fr.* Twenty-one Love Poems. **SP-RicA1; SP-RicA2**

Rain on the windows, creaking doors. The Division. Thomas Hardy. **CP-HardT**

Rain or hail / sam done. Edward Estlin Cummings. **CP-CummE; SP-CummE**

Rain or Shine. Charles Bukowski. **SP-BukC1**

Rain patters on a sea that tilts and sighs. Absences. Philip Larkin. **CP-LarkP**

Rain pools in the old lumber yard, The. Lumber Yard Pools at Sunset. Carl Sandburg. **CP-SandC**

Rain, pour down, pour down. Dust in the East. David Herbert Lawrence. *Fr.* Bits. **CP-LawrD**

Rain pumped snakes from their holes. Record Flood. William Matthews. *Fr.* Flood. **SP-MattW**

Rain, rain, and sun! a rainbow in the sky. Merlin's Riddling. Tennyson. **FaBoRV** *Fr.* The Coming of Arthur. *Fr.* Idylls of the King. **CP-TennA**

Rain set early in tonight, The. Porphyria's Lover. Robert Browning. **CP-BroR1**

Rain-shafts splintered on me, The. Christmastide. Thomas Hardy. **CP-HardT**

Rain slants from the clouded light, The. The November Ghosts. Randall Jarrell. **CP-JarrR**

Rain smites more and more, The. A January Night. Thomas Hardy. **CP-HardT**

Rain Song. Stephen Dobyns. **SP-DobyS**

Rain Song. Jean Garrigue. **SP-GarrJ**

Rain-Songs. Paul Laurence Dunbar. **CP-DunbP**

Rain stops. I look round: a square of floor, The. Thom Gunn. *Fr.* Jack Straw's Castle. **CP-GunnT**

Rain streams down like harp-strings from the sky, The. Rain-Songs. Paul Laurence Dunbar. **CP-DunbP**

Rain that ripens oranges, The. And Now, the Weather. . . . Karl Shapiro. **SP-ShapK**

Rain, the earliest creature. The Jaguar Myth. Pablo Antonio Cuadra, *tr. fr. Spanish by* Thomas Merton. **CP-MertT**

Rain the Stones the Darkness, The. Richard Shelton. **SP-ShelR**

Rain ("Things one sees through"). Robert Creeley. **CP-CreeR**

Rain to the wind said, The. Lodged. Robert Frost. **CP-FrosR**

Rain Towards Morning. Elizabeth Bishop. *Fr.* Four Poems. **CP-BishE**

Rain (2) ("Thoughtful of you, I was / anticipating change in"). Robert Creeley. **CP-CreeR**

Rain upon the window, rain upon the day. Lucubration. Richard Eberhart. **CP-EberR**

Rain-Wet Asphalt Heat, Garbage Curbed Cans Overflowing. Allen Ginsberg. **CP-GinsA**

Rain Winds Blow Doors Open. Carl Sandburg. **CP-SandC**

Rainbow, The. Robert Herrick. **CP-HerrR**

Rainbow, The. Gerard Manley Hopkins. **CP-HopkG**

Rainbow. Max Jacob, *tr. fr. French by* Elizabeth Bishop. **CP-BishE**

Rainbow, The. David Herbert Lawrence. **CP-LawrD**

Rainbow. David Herbert Lawrence. **CP-LawrD**

Rainbow appeared with its promises, A. An American Film. Stephen Dunn. **SP-DunnS**

Rainbow at Evening. Archibald MacLeish. **CP-MacLA**

Rainbow, beautiful and clear light, A. Kathleen Jessie Raine. **SP-RainK**

Rainbow Body. Gary Snyder. **CP-SnydG**

Rainbow comes and goes, The. William Wordsworth. *Fr.* Ode: Intimations of Immortality [from Recollections of Early Childhood]. **CP-WorW1**

Rainbow Grocery, The. William Dickey. **SP-DickW**

Rainbow never tells me, The. Emily Dickinson. **CP-DickE**

Rainbow; or Curious Covenant, The. Robert Herrick. **CP-HerrR**

Rainbow over evening, my. Rainbow at Evening. Archibald MacLeish. **CP-MacLA**

Raindrop. John Hewitt. **CP-HewiJ**

Raindrops on a Briar. William Carlos Williams. **CP-WilW2**

Raindrops on the tin roof. Falling Asleep. Wendell Berry. **CP-BerrW**

Rainer, / the man who was about to celebrate his 52nd birthday. The Death of Europe. Charles Olson. **CP-OlsoC; SP-OlsoC**

Raining here / in little pieces. Funny. Robert Creeley. **CP-CreeR**

Raining in Magens Bay. John Updike. **CP-UpdiJ**

Rainless darkness drew o'er the lake, A. On Como. George Meredith. **CP-MerG2**

Rainless winter; week on week sun edging the hills, A. Rattlesnake August. William Everson. **SP-EverW**

Rain's all right. The boys who physic. Biography of Southern Rain. Kenneth Patchen. **CP-PatcK**

Rains at length have ceased, the winds are stilled, The. William Wordsworth. **CP-WorW1**

Rain's lovely gray daughter has lost her tall lover. Fog. Kenneth Patchen. **CP-PatcK**

Rains, the rains, The. Louis Zukofsky. **CP-ZukLS**

Rainsweet / s / tillnes / s. Edward Estlin Cummings. **CP-CummE**

Rainwalkers, The. Denise Levertov. **CP-LeveD**

Rainy Afternoon, A. Wystan Hugh Auden. **CP-AudWJ**

Rainy Day Women # 12 & 35. "Bob Dylan." **CP-DylaB**

Rainy 4th. Marge Piercy. **SP-PierM**

Rainy Morning. Archie Randolph Ammons. **SP-AmmoA**

Rainy Pleiads wester, The. Alfred Edward Housman. **CP-HousA**

Rainy Season; Sub-Tropics. Elizabeth Bishop. **CP-BishE**
  Giant Snail.
  Giant Toad.
  Strayed Crab.

Rainy vacations / Try people's patience. Tomorrow, Partly Cloudy. Ogden Nash. **CP-NashO**

Raise from these rocky cliffs your heads. The First Song. Thomas Carew. **CP-CareT** Fr. Carew's Masque. **CP-CareT**

Raise me; undraw the curtain; that is well. Ellen Middleton. Christina Georgina Rossetti. **CP-RosC3**

Raise the shade. Edward Estlin Cummings. **CP-CummE; SP-CummE**

Raised are the dripping oars. The Youth of Nature. Matthew Arnold. **SP-ArnoM**

Raised are the dripping oars. The Youth of Nature: Wordsworth's Country. Matthew Arnold. **FaBoPP** Fr. The Youth of Nature. **SP-ArnoM**

Raisin, The. Donald Hall. **CP-HallD**

Rake-hell Muses. Thomas Hardy. **CP-HardT**

Rakeoff and the Getaway, The. Carl Sandburg. **CP-SandC**

Rakob is dead, what is left of him travels. Funeral in Hungary. Kay Boyle. **CP-BoylK**

Raleigh Was Right. William Carlos Williams. **CP-WilW2**

Rally and form in your squads. Paraphrase of Verses by Mayakovsky. John Hewitt. **CP-HewiJ**

Rallying-Point. David Herbert Lawrence. **CP-LawrD**

Ralph pares his nayles, his warts, his cornes, and Raph. Upon Ralph . Robert Herrick. **CP-HerrR**

Ralph Waldo's Aunt Mary. Mary Moody Emerson, R.I.P. Lewis Turco. **SP-TurcL**

Ralphius. John Donne. **CP-DonnJ**

Ram wears a cowboy. Charles Henri Ford. **SP-FordC** Fr. Emblems of Arachne.

Rambler, The. Thomas Hardy. **CP-HardT**

Ramblin' outa the wild West. Talking New York. "Bob Dylan." **CP-DylaB**

Rambling, Gambling Willie. "Bob Dylan." **CP-DylaB**

Rambling I looked for an old abode. Life Laughs Onward. Thomas Hardy. **CP-HardT**

Ramona, come closer, / Shut softly your watery eyes. To Ramona. "Bob Dylan." **CP-DylaB**

Rampage, The. Charles Kenneth Williams. **CP-WillC; SP-WillC**

Ram's Horn, The. John Hewitt. **CP-HewiJ**

Ran. Frederick Morgan. **SP-MorgF**

Randall Jarrell 1. October 1965. Robert Lowell. **SP-LoweR**

Randall Jarrell 2. Robert Lowell. **SP-LoweR**

Randall Jarrell 3. Robert Lowell. **SP-LoweR**

Randall Jarrell, Office Hours 10-11. Randall Jarrell. **CP-JarrR**

Randolph of Roanoke. John Greenleaf Whittier. **CP-WhitJ**

Randy old / woman said, The. In Her Burning. Muriel Rukeyser. **CP-RukeM**

Rang and rang, rang in a small boy's head. Muriel Rukeyser. **CP-RukeM**

Range after range of mountains. On Climbing the Sierra Matterhorn Again after Thirty-One Years. Gary Snyder. **CP-SnydG**

Range-finding. Robert Frost. **CP-FrosR**

Range in the Desert, The. Randall Jarrell. **CP-JarrR**

Ranger, The. John Greenleaf Whittier. **CP-WhitJ**

Ranges / of clinker heaps. John Maydew or The Allotment. Charles Tomlinson. **CP-TomlC**

Ranging the heights of Scawfell or Blackcomb. In the Channel, between the Coast of Cumberland and the Isle of Man. William Wordsworth. Fr. Poems Composed or Suggested During a Tour, in the Summer of 1833. **CP-WorW2**

Rank-and-Filer, The. John Hewitt. **CP-HewiJ**

Rannoch, by Glencoe. Thomas Stearns Eliot. **FaBoPP; NAEL-2; PoSH** Fr. Landscapes. **CP-ElioT**

Ransom. Robert Penn Warren. **SP-WarrR**

Ransomed of the Lord, The. Christina Georgina Rossetti. **CP-RosC2**

Ranstead yellow fringes dragon clusters. Butter-and-Eggs. Louis Zukofsky. **CP-ZukLS**

Rant, A. Frank O'Hara. **SP-OharF**

Ranter and Their Pleads, The. Thomas Merton. Fr. North. Fr. The Geography of Lograire. **CP-MertT**

Rantin' Dog, the Daddie o't, The. Robert Burns. **CP-BurnR**

Rantin Laddie, The. Robert Burns. **CP-BurnR**

Rantoul. John Greenleaf Whittier. **CP-WhitJ**

Rape. Adrienne Rich. **SP-RicA2**

Rape. Patti Smith. **SP-SmitP**

Rape of Aurora, The. George Meredith. **CP-MerG1**
  [Before the Rape]. **NoSic**

Rape of Lucrece, The. William Shakespeare. **CP-ShaWS**
  "Come, Philomele, that sing'st of ravishment." **PBBP**
  Lucrece's Death. **NoSic**
  Midnight. **OBSC**
  "Mis-shapen Time, copesmate of ugly Night." **OAEL-1**
  Opportunity. **LiTB; OBSC; PoEL-2**
    (Outcry upon Opportunity, An.) **NOBE**
  Time's Glory. **ChTr**
  Troy Depicted. **OBSC**

Rape of the Cataract, The. Richard Eberhart. **CP-EberR**

Rape of the Lock[, an Heroi-Comical Poem], The, see also To Belinda on the Rape of the Lock. Alexander Pope. **CP-PopeA**
  "And now, unveiled, the toilet stands displayed." **ECEV; NOBE; OBEC; OXAEP-1**
    (Toilet, The.) **NOBE; OBEC**
  "But anxious cares the pensive nymph oppressed." **EBNV; OXAEP-1**
  "But when to mischief mortals bend their will." **OXAEP-1**
  "Close by those meads, for ever crowned with flow'rs." **EBEvV; EBNV; FaBoEH; FaBoPP; FiP; OBSV; OxBoLi**
    (Hampton Court.) **FaBoPP; OBSV**
  "For lo! the board with cups and spoons is crown'd." **UV**
  "Hither the heroes and the nymphs resort." **ECEV**
  "Not with more glories, in th'ethereal plain." **EBEV; EBNV; ECEV; NOBE; NOEC; OXAEP-1; WHA**
    (Voyage on the Thames, The.) **NOBE**
  "On her white breast a sparkling cross she wore." **ACP**
  Playing Cards, The. **ChTr**
  "'Restore the lock!' she cries; and all around." **OXAEP-1**
  "'Say why are beauties praised and honoured most'." **ECEV**
  "She said: the pitying audience melt in tears." **EBNV, canto V, abr.;**
  "Sol through white curtains shot a tim'rous ray." **ECEV**
  "What dire offence from am'rous causes springs." **EBNV; NOEC; Poetr**

Rape of the Swan, The. Archibald MacLeish. **CP-MacLA**

Rape Poem. Marge Piercy. **SP-PierM**

Raped and Revenged. Rudyard Kipling. Fr. Epitaphs of the War [1914–1918]. **CP-KiplR**

Raper from Passenack, The. William Carlos Williams. **CP-WilW1**

Raphael. John Greenleaf Whittier. **CP-WhitJ**

Raphael's Descent. John Milton. **NOSC** Fr. Book V. Fr. Paradise Lost. **CP-MiltJ**

Rapid Transit. William Carlos Williams. **CP-WilW1**

Rapidly cruising or lying on the air there is a bird. The Frigate Pelican. Marianne Craig Moore. **CP-MoorM**

Rapids shake the low hung limbs like hair. Where Mission Creek Runs Hard for Joy. Richard Hugo. **CP-HugoR**

Rapine Brings Ruine. Robert Herrick. **CP-HerrR**

Rapine has yet tooke nought from me. To God, in Time of Plundering. Robert Herrick. **CP-HerrR**

Rapt above earth by power of one fair face. ad. fr. the Italian of Michelangelo Buonarotti. William Wordsworth. Fr. Memorials of a Tour in Italy, 1837. **CP-WorW2**

Rapt with the rage of mine own ravisht thought. An Hymne of Heavenly Beautie. Edmund Spenser. **PeECV** Fr. Fowre Hymnes. **CP-Spens**

Rapture, A. Thomas Carew. **CP-CareT**

Rapture. Marsden Hartley. Fr. Boston Portrait Projections. **CP-HartM**

Rapunzel. Anne Sexton. **CP-SextA**

Rapunzel Rapunzel let down your hair. The After-Thought. Stevie Smith. **CP-SmitS**

Rapunzel, Rapunzel, Let's Let Down Our Hair. Ogden Nash. **CP-NashO**

Rare are thy cheeks, Susanna, which do show. Upon Mistresse Susanna Southwell, Her Cheeks. Robert Herrick. **CP-HerrR**

Rare Gist, The. William Carlos Williams. **CP-WilW2**

Rare is the voice it selfe; but when we sing. The Voice and Violl. Robert Herrick. **CP-HerrR**

Rare-sweet the air in that unimagined country. The Unfinished Dream. Walter de la Mare. **CP-DeLaW**

Rare temples thou hast seen, I know. The Fairy Temple; or, Oberon's Chapel. Robert Herrick. **CP-HerrR**

Rarely, rarely, comest thou. Song. Percy Bysshe Shelley. **CP-ShelP**

Rarity and value of scientific knowledge, The. Poetry and Science. "Hugh MacDiarmid." **SP-MacDH**

Rash Bride, The. Thomas Hardy. **CP-HardT**

Rash flower / Gazing, now you have topped the wall. Rose. Jenny Joseph. *Fr.* Derivations. **SP-JoseJ**

Rash mortal, and slanderous Poet, thy name. Robert Burns. *Fr.* Lines on Stirling. **CP-BurnR**

Raspberries in My Driveway, The. Erica Jong. **SP-JongE**

Raspberry. Louis Zukofsky. **CP-ZukLS**

Raspberry thickets leaping, splashing. His Dream. Hayden Carruth. *Fr.* The Fifth Version. *Fr.* The Mythology of Dark and Light. **CP-CarHL**

Raspe playes at Nine-holes; and 'tis known he gets. Upon Raspe. Robert Herrick. **CP-HerrR**

Rastignac at 45. Thom Gunn. **CP-GunnT**

Rat, The. Edwin Arlington Robinson. **CP-RobiE**

Rat, The, "For order" at all cost. William Carlos Williams. **CP-WilW2**

Rat came on stage, A. Note. Charles Simic. **SP-SimiC**

Rat is in the trap, it is in the trap, The. Ted Hughes. **SP-HughT** (Rat's Dance, The.) **SP-HughT**

Rat is the conciesest Tenant, The. Emily Dickinson. **CP-DickE**

Rat Riddles. Carl Sandburg. **CP-SandC**

Rat Rises, A. Charles Bukowski. **SP-BukC2**

Rat sits up and works his, The. "For order" at all cost. William Carlos Williams. **CP-WilW2**

Rat Song. Margaret Atwood. **NIP** *Fr.* Songs of the Transformed. **SP-AtwM1**

Rat surrendered here, A. Emily Dickinson. **CP-DickE**

Rat-tat-tat-tash of shields upon Ida. The Other Wing. Louis MacNeice. **CP-MacNL**

Rather arid delight. Emily Dickinson. **CP-DickE**

"Rather dead than spotted"; and believe it. Then the Ermine. Marianne Craig Moore. **CP-MoorM**

Rather notice, mon cher. To a Solitary Disciple. William Carlos Williams. **CP-WilW1**

Rather than permit him. An Early Martyr. William Carlos Williams. **CP-WilW1**

Rather than that, I'd go down to the bar. Alternative. Malcolm Lowry. **CP-LowrM**

Rather the flying bird, leaving no trace. Fernando Pessoa. *Fr.* Twelve Poems from *The Keeper of the Flocks*. **CP-MertT**

Rathlin. Derek Mahon. **SP-MahoD**

Rationality. George Oppen. **CP-OppeG**

Rats. Daniel Gerard Hoffman. **CP-HoffD**

Rats, The. Georg Trakl, *tr. fr.* German by James Wright. **CP-WrigJ**

Rats. John Updike. **CP-UpdiJ**

Rat's Dance, The. Ted Hughes. *See* The Rat is in the trap, it is in the trap.

Rats Live on No Evil Star. Anne Sexton. **CP-SextA**

Rats move swiftly along a wall. Nightpiece. Gilbert Sorrentino. **SP-SorrG**

Rattle, rattle. There is no question. He Speaks to His Arguing Friends and to Himself. Miller Williams. **SP-WillM**

Rattlesnake August. William Everson. **SP-EverW**

Rattlesnake Country. Robert Penn Warren. **SP-WarrR**

Rattlesnakes I've had them. Abiquiu. Charles Tomlinson. **CP-TomlC**

Rattlin, Roarin Willie. Robert Burns. **CP-BurnR**

RAVAGE, v.t. To lay waste; to subject. Hayden Carruth. *Fr.* Paragraphs. **CP-CarHS**

Ravaged Face, The. Sylvia Plath. **CP-PlatS**

Ravaged Villa, The. Herman Melville. **SP-MelvH**

Raven, The. Samuel Taylor Coleridge. **CP-ColeS**

Raven, The. Nicarchus of Alexandria. **AWP; FaBoEE; OBAL** *Fr.* Variations of Greek Themes. **CP-RobiE**

Raven, The. Edgar Allan Poe. **CP-PoeEd**

Raven, The. Adrienne Rich. **CP-RicAE**

Raven, Don't Stay Away from My Door—A Chant for April First. Ogden Nash. **CP-NashO**

Raven once an Acorn took, A. Against Despair. Christopher Smart. *Fr.* Hymns for the Amusement of Children. **SP-SmarC**

Raven, while with glossy breast, A. Fable, A. William Cowper. **CP-CowpW**

Ravening through the persistent bric-à-brac. On the Difficulty of Conjuring Up a Dryad. Sylvia Plath. **CP-PlatS**

Ravenna. Louis MacNeice. **CP-MacNL**

Ravenous the flock. Maine Winter. Charles Tomlinson. **CP-TomlC**

Ravenousness of fondness, The. Emily Dickinson. **SP-DickE**

Ravens. Ted Hughes. **SP-HughT**

Ravine, The. Hayden Carruth. **CP-CarHS**

Raving warre, begot / In the thirstye sands. Thomas Campion. **AAS** *Fr.* Observations in the Art of English Poesie. **CP-CampT**

Raving winds around her blowing. Robert Burns. **CP-BurnR**

Raw as a New Town / the translation incomplete. Agrigento, Sicily. John Hewitt. **CP-HewiJ**

Raw-boned and an ignorant man, A. St. Christopher. Louise Bogan. **CP-BogaL**

Raw, red haze gnaws, A. December Frost. Martin Edmunds. **SP-EdmuM**

Rawdon Brown. Robert Browning. **CP-BroR2**

Ray. Hayden Carruth. **CP-CarHS**

Ray Wells, a big Nisqually, and I. Gary Snyder. **CP-SnydG** *Fr.* Logging. *Fr.* Myths and Texts.

Raze these long blocks of brick and stone. The Truce of Piscataqua. John Greenleaf Whittier. **CP-WhitJ**

Razor-Tailed Wren, The. Shel Silverstein. **SP-SilS2**

Razzle dazzle maggots are summary, The. Easter. Frank O'Hara. **SP-OharF**

Razzmatazz. Gilbert Sorrentino. **SP-SorrG**

R.C. Emily Brontë. *Fr.* The Two Children. **CP-BronE**

Re-Acquaintance. Hayden Carruth. **CP-CarHS**

Re-birth of Venus, The. Geoffrey Hill. **NePoEA** *Fr.* Metamorphoses. **CP-HillG**

Re C—. Robert Creeley. **CP-CreeR**

Re-Enactment, The. Thomas Hardy. **CP-HardT**

Re-entry, without pillow, dear and the pieces. Examples—for Richard Bridgeman. Charles Olson. **CP-OlsoC**

Re-forming the Crystal. Adrienne Rich. **SP-RicA1; SP-RicA2**

Re-place me in the firmament. Saturn. Hilda Doolittle. **CP-DoolH** *Fr.* Temple of the Sun.

Re-statement of Romance. Wallace Stevens. **CP-StevW**

Reach me a blue pencil of the moon. Ur Burial. Richard Eberhart. **CP-EberR**

Reach me a quill, pluckt from the flaming wing. Upon the Gunpowder Treason. Richard Crashaw. **CP-CrasR**

Reach me wine No counsel weakens the conclusion of the lot. Hafiz, *tr. by* Ralph Waldo Emerson. **CP-EmerR** *Fr.* Odes.

Reach Over. David Herbert Lawrence. **CP-LawrD**

Reach, with your whiter hands, to me. To the Water Nymphs, Drinking at the Fountain. Robert Herrick. **CP-HerrR**

Reaching down arm-deep into bright water. Shells. Kathleen Jessie Raine. **SP-RainK**

Reaching For the Gun. Richard Shelton. **SP-ShelR**

Reaching my gate, a narrow. Josef Weinheber. Wystan Hugh Auden. *Fr.* Eleven Occasional Poems. **CP-AudeW**

Reaching my own block. Walking Home at Night. Allen Ginsberg. **CP-GinsA**

Reaching Out with the Hands of the Sun. Diane Wakoski. **SP-WakoD**

Read by Moonlight. Thomas Hardy. **CP-HardT**

Read here: / This is the story of Evarra-man. Evarra and His Gods. Rudyard Kipling. **CP-KiplR**

Read here the moral roundly writ. NOVEMBER (*Boxing*). Rudyard Kipling. **OtMeF** *Fr.* Verses on Games. **CP-KiplR**

Read history: so learn your place in Time. Edna St. Vincent Millay. **CP-MillE**

Read history: thus learn how small a space. Edna St. Vincent Millay. **CP-MillE**

Read in the paper about a man killed with a sword. My Friend George. "Lou Reed." **SP-ReedL**

Read in these roses the sad story. Red and White Roses. Thomas Carew. **CP-CareT**

Read Me a Lesson, Muse, and Speak It Loud. John Keats. **CP-KeatJ**

Read me Euripides. The Follies of Adam. Theodore Roethke. **CP-RoetT**

Read (Reader) gently, gently ore, The. On the Death of My Dear Brother. Dudley Posthume Lovelace. *Fr.* Elegies, 1660. **CP-LoveR**

Read—Sweet—how others—strove. Emily Dickinson. **CP-DickE**

Read thou my lines, my Swetnaham, if there be. To M. Laurence Swetnaham. Robert Herrick. **CP-HerrR**

Reade, you that have some teares left yet unspent. An Elegie upon the Untimely Death of Prince *Henry*. Thomas Campion. **CP-CampT**

Reader, The, *tr. fr. the German of* Rilke. Randall Jarrell. **CP-JarrR**

Reader, The. Thomas Merton. **CP-MertT; SP-MertT**

Reader, The. Wallace Stevens. **CP-StevW**

Reader! behold a monument. *see also* Inscription for a Stone. William Cowper. **CP-CowpW**

Reader over My Shoulder, The. Robert Ranke Graves. **CP-GravR**

Reader, stay, / And if I had no more to say. An Epitaph on Master Philip Gray. Ben Jonson. **CP-JonsB**

Reader, when these dumb stones have told. Another [On the Duke of Buckingham]. Thomas Carew. **CP-CareT**

Readers of poetry, the writers of, The. Redwing. Tess Gallagher. **SP-GallT**

Readers of the *Boston Evening Transcript*, The. The *Boston Evening Transcript*. Thomas Stearns Eliot. **CP-ElioT**

Readers wee entreat ye pray. Purgatory. Robert Herrick. **CP-HerrR**

Readie Pome. William Carlos Williams. **CP-WilW1**

Readinesse. Robert Herrick. **CP-HerrR**

Readinesse of doing, doth expresse, The. Readinesse. Robert Herrick. **CP-HerrR**

Reading. Archie Randolph Ammons. **SP-AmmoA**

Reading. Elizabeth Barrett Browning. **GN** *Fr.* Aurora Leigh. **CP-BroEB**

Reading. John Hewitt. **CP-HewiJ**

Reading, A. Erica Jong. **SP-JongE**

Reading a Letter. David Herbert Lawrence. **CP-LawrD**

Reading Aloud. Tess Gallagher. **SP-GallT**

Reading an Anglo-Saxon love poem in its extravagance. The Good Silence. Robert Bly. **SP-BlyR**

Reading and Talking. Louis Zukofsky. **CP-ZukLS**

Reading Apollinaire by the Rogue River. Lawrence Ferlinghetti. **SP-FerlL**

Reading at the Local High School. Ron Koertge. **SP-KoerR**

Reading at the Old Federal Courts Building, St. Paul. Richard Hugo. **CP-HugoR**

Reading: Early Sorrow. Charles Kenneth Williams. **SP-WillC**

Reading French Poetry. Allen Ginsberg. **CP-GinsA**

Reading *Genesis* to a Blind Child. James Dickey. **CP-DickJ**

Reading Hölderlin on the Patio with the Aid of a Dictionary. Rita Dove. **SP-DoveR**

Reading how even the Swiss had thrown the sponge. Beyond the Alps. Robert Lowell. **SP-LoweR**

Reading in Fall Rain. Robert Bly. **SP-BlyR**

Reading in Li Po. After the Last Dynasty. Stanley Jasspon Kunitz. **CP-KuniS**

Reading in the Evening. David Herbert Lawrence. **CP-LawrD**

Reading Late at Night, Thermometer Falling. Robert Penn Warren. **SP-WarrR**

Reading Myself. Robert Lowell. **SP-LoweR**

Reading myself, old poems, their inside truth that was. Hayden Carruth. *Fr.* Paragraphs. **CP-CarHS**

Reading Nijinsky's Diary. Al Young. **CP-YounA**

Reading of an Ever-Changing Tale, The. John Yau. **SP-YauJo**

Reading of History, A. Leonard Nathan. **SP-NathL**

Reading of Rex Stout, A. Mona Van Duyn. **SP-VanDM**

Reading Room, The New York Public Library. Richard Eberhart. **CP-EberR**

Reading the Names of the Vietnam War Dead. Thomas McGrath. **SP-McGrT**

Reading the Newsapaper on Microfilm. Miller Williams. **SP-WillM**

Reading the Newspaper. William Cowper. **ECEV** *Fr.* The Winter Evening. *Fr.* The Task. **CP-CowpW**

(Hissing Urn, The.) **FaBoDD**

Reading their story I follow and agree. Frank Templeton Prince. *Fr.* Drypoints of the Hasidim. **CP-PrinF**

Reading this, you are waiting for the curtain. Programme Note. Charles Tomlinson. **CP-TomlC**

Reading Time : 1 Minute 26 Seconds. Muriel Rukeyser. **CP-RukeM**

Reading Translated Poets, Feb. 1. Thomas Merton. **CP-MertT**

Reading: Winter. Charles Kenneth Williams. **SP-WillC**

Reading X's Collected Works. Basil Bunting. **CP-BuntB**

Reading Yeats I do not think. Lawrence Ferlinghetti. **SP-FerlL**

Readings from Ibn Abbad. Thomas Merton. **CP-MertT**

Burial Place of Ibn Abbad, The.

Desolation.

Ibn Abbad Described by a Friend (Ibn Qunfud).

Letter to a Sufi Who Has Abandoned Sufism to Study Law.

Letter to One Who Has Abandoned The Way.

Prayer and Sermon of Ibn Abbad.

To a Novice ("Avoid three kinds of Master").

To a Novice ("Be a son of this instant").

To a Novice ("Fool is one, The").

To Belong to Allah.

Readings in French. Thom Gunn. **CP-GunnT**

Readings in those college towns were hell, The. The Hustle. Charles Bukowski. **SP-BukC3**

Readings of History. Adrienne Rich. **CP-RicAE**

Ready page, with hurried mead, The. The Bale-Fire. Sir Walter Scott. **SP-ScotW** *Fr.* The Lay of the Last Minstrel.

Ready to Kill. Carl Sandburg. **CP-SandC**

Ready to Roll. Allen Ginsberg. **CP-GinsA**

Real, The. Charles Olson. **CP-OlsoC**

Real and Half Real. Robinson Jeffers. **CP-JefR3**

Real as a dream. Understand That This Is a Dream. Allen Ginsberg. **CP-GinsA**

Real Avenue News. Carl Sandburg. **CP-SandC**

Real Democracy. David Herbert Lawrence. **CP-LawrD**

Real dreams. More real than. Charles Henri Ford. **SP-FordC** *Fr.* Emblems of Arachne.

Real Estate. John Hewitt. **CP-HewiJ**

Real Estate. Barton Sutter. **SP-SuttB**

Real immorality, as far as I can see it, The. Immorality. David Herbert Lawrence. **CP-LawrD**

Real Question, The. Paul Laurence Dunbar. **CP-DunbP**

Real things move. Roy Fisher. **SP-FishR** *Fr.* Glenthorne Poems.

Real Time. Al Young. **CP-YounA**

Real Work, The. Gary Snyder. **CP-SnydG**

Real World, The. Dabney Stuart. **SP-StuaD**

Realism. Tom Clark. **SP-ClarT**

Realism. Al Young. **CP-YounA**

Realists, The. William Butler Yeats. **CP-YeatW**

Realities. Howard Nemerov. **CP-NemeH**

Reality. Richard Eberhart. *Fr.* Aesthetics after War. **CP-EberR**

Reality is a question. The Terms in Which I Think of Reality. Allen Ginsberg. **CP-GinsA**

Reality is and is. For Selma Gubin's Umbrellas. Louis Zukofsky. **CP-ZukLS**

Reality is to be sought, not in concrete. Aesthetic. Charles Tomlinson. **CP-TomlC**

Reality of Peace, 1916. David Herbert Lawrence. **CP-LawrD**

Reality! said the stone-minded man. Maia. Howard Nemerov. **CP-NemeH**

Realization / Of fantasy, yes. This, A. Charles Henri Ford. **SP-FordC** *Fr.* Emblems of Arachne.

Realizing that any certainty is an old one. John Yau. **SP-YauJo** *Fr.* Scenes from the Life of Boullee.

Really, it is not the. In This Age of Hard Trying, Nonchalance Is Good and. Marianne Craig Moore. **CP-MoorM**

Really, must you. You. Wystan Hugh Auden. **CP-AudeW**

Realms quake by turns: proud Arbitress of grace. An Interdict. William Wordsworth. *Fr.* Ecclesiastical Sonnets. **CP-WorW2**

Reaper, The. Robert Duncan. **SP-DuncR**

Reaper. William Everson. **SP-EverW**

Reape's eyes so rawe are, that (it seemes) the flyes. Upon Reape. Robert Herrick. **CP-HerrR**

Rearmament. Robinson Jeffers. **CP-JefR2**

Rearrange a "Wife's" affection! Emily Dickinson. **CP-DickE**

Reas'ning at every step he treads. The Doves. William Cowper. **CP-CowpW**

Reason. Samuel Taylor Coleridge. **CP-ColeS**

Reason, A. Robert Creeley. **CP-CreeR**

Reason. George Meredith. **CP-MerG2**

Reason, The. Stevie Smith. **CP-SmitS**

Reason and Imagination. William Blake. **EnRP** *Fr.* Milton. **CP-BlakW**

Reason and Imagination. Christopher Smart. **SP-SmarC**

Reason and Religion. John Dryden. *See* Dim, as the borrow'd beams of moon and stars.

Reason and Revelation. John Dryden. *See* Dim, as the borrow'd beams of moon and stars.

Reason blinded by sin, Lesbia. Carmen 75. Catullus. *Fr.* Carmina. **CP-Catul**

Reason for Love's Blindness. Samuel Taylor Coleridge. **CP-ColeS**

Reason for Skylarks, The. Kenneth Patchen. **CP-PatcK**

Reason I Write, The. Leonard Cohen. **CP-CoheL**

Reason, in faith thou art well served, that still. Sonnet 10. Sir Philip Sidney. **NAEL-1** *Fr.* Astrophil and Stella. **SP-SidnP**

Reason let others give and realness bring. Edward Estlin Cummings. **CP-CummE**

Reason, tell me thy mind, if here be reason, *speech of Cleophila.* Sir Philip Sidney. **SP-SidnP** *Fr.* Arcadia.

Reason will not decide at last; the sword will decide. Contemplation of the Sword. Robinson Jeffers. **CP-JefR2**

Reasonable Constitution, A. Herman Melville. **SP-MelvH**

Reasonable, reasonable, reasonable . . . we walked through. The Hangman. Anne Sexton. **CP-SextA**

Reasons. Daniel Gerard Hoffman. **SP-HoffD**

Reasons for Attendance. Philip Larkin. **CP-LarkP**

Reasons for Music. Archibald MacLeish. **CP-MacLA**

Reassurance, The. Thom Gunn. **CP-GunnT**

Reassurance. Alice Walker. **CP-WalkA**

Reawakening, The. Walter de la Mare. **CP-DeLaW**

Rebecca at Play. Miller Williams. **SP-WillM**

Rebecca's Hymn. Sir Walter Scott. **SP-ScotW** *Fr.* Ivanhoe.

Rebel, The. John Hewitt. **CP-HewiJ**

Rebel, The. Rudyard Kipling. *Fr.* Epitaphs of the War [1914–1918]. **CP-KiplR**

Rebel Color-Bearers at Shiloh. Herman Melville. **SP-MelvH**

Rebellion, The. Leonard Cohen. **CP-CoheL**

Rebellion is my theme all day. The Modern Patriot. William Cowper. **CP-CowpW**

Rebellious. Living. The Nature of This Flower Is to Bloom. Alice Walker. **CP-WalkA**

Rebels, The. Lawrence Ferlinghetti. **SP-FerlL**

Rebirth. Rudyard Kipling. **CP-KiplR**

Rebuke of the Rocks. Robert Penn Warren. *Fr.* Kentucky Mountain Farm. **SP-WarrR**

Rebuked. David Herbert Lawrence. **CP-LawrD**

Recalcitrance / of whorl-wheel fossils, The. Near Corinium. Charles Tomlinson. **CP-TomlC**

Recalcitrants, The. Thomas Hardy. **CP-HardT**

Recall, The. Rudyard Kipling. **CP-KiplR**

Recall it you? That Kiss in the Dark. Thomas Hardy. **CP-HardT**

Recall, now, the omens of childhood. The Stone Man. Geoffrey Hill. *Fr.* Soliloquies. **CP-HillG**

Recalled. Edwin Arlington Robinson. **CP-RobiE**

Recantation. Samuel Taylor Coleridge. **CP-ColeS**

Recantation, A. Rudyard Kipling. **CP-KiplR**

Recantation. Sylvia Plath. **CP-PlatS**

Recapitulation, The. Richard Eberhart. **CP-EberR**

Recapitulation. Phoebe Hesketh. **SP-HeskP**

Receipt to Restore Stella's Youth, A. Jonathan Swift. **CP-SwifJ**

Receive, dear friend, the truths I teach. 2.10. Horace. **CP-CowpW,** *tr. by* William Cowper; *Fr.* Odes.

Received from Nadab and Abihu as they cried with one voice. The Transmission. Leonard Cohen. **CP-CoheL**

Receivers of the World's Attention. Stephen Dobyns. **SP-DobyS**

Receiving the Stigmata. Rita Dove. **SP-DoveR**

Recent Past, The. John Ashbery. **SP-AshbJ**

Recently he has turned to us and said: "It's bizzare to think about". Marco Polo. John Yau. **SP-YauJo**

Recently in the south of England. Ode to Hengist and Horsa. Robinson Jeffers. **CP-JefR3**

Recently regilded / General Sherman marches bravely. Sherman's March Reglitterized. Lawrence Ferlinghetti. **SP-FerlL**

Recessional. Rudyard Kipling. **CP-KiplR**

Réchauffé. Louis MacNeice. **CP-MacNL**

Recipe. Raissa Maritain, *tr. fr. French by* Thomas Merton. **CP-MertT**

Recipe For A Hippopotamus Sandwich. Shel Silverstein. **SP-SilS2**

Reciprocal Kindness the Primary Law of Nature. Vincent Bourne, *tr. fr. Latin by* William Cowper. **CP-CowpW**

Recital. John Updike. **CP-UpdiJ**

Recital? "Concert" is the word. Rescue With Yul Brynner. Marianne Craig Moore. **CP-MoorM**

Recitation before Bed. David Markson. **CP-MarkD**

Recitative. Hart Crane. **CP-CranH**

Recitative by Death. Wystan Hugh Auden. *See* The Progress you have made is very remarkable.

Reciting Adrienne Rich on Cole and Haight. The Differences. Thom Gunn. **CP-GunnT**

Recklessly you offered me your all. The Hoopoe Tells Us How. Robert Ranke Graves. **CP-GravR**

Reckoning, The. Stanley Jasspon Kunitz. **CP-KuniS**

Reckoning, The. Theodore Roethke. **CP-RoetT**

Reclaimed. Phoebe Hesketh. **SP-HeskP**

Reclamation at Coloma. Richard Hugo. **CP-HugoR**

"Reclining Figure." Donald Hall. **CP-HallD**

Recluse, The. Stevie Smith. **CP-SmitS**

Recluse; Home at Grasmere, The. William Wordsworth. Home at Grasmere. **CP-WorW1**

Recluse Hsu Su Kwei had come to see Prince Wu, The. Advising the Prince. Chuang Tzu, *tr. fr. Chinese by* Thomas Merton. **CP-MertT**

Recognition, The. Wendell Berry. **CP-BerrW**

Recognition. Richard Eberhart. **CP-EberR**

Recognition. Robert Ranke Graves. **CP-GravR**

Recognition, A. May Sarton. **SP-SartM**

Recognition, The. Johann N. Vogl, *tr. fr. German by* George Meredith. **CP-MerG2**

Recognition Not Enough. Stevie Smith. **CP-SmitS**

Recognition of Eve, The. Karl Shapiro. **ChIV-1; MoAB** *Fr.* Adam and Eve. **SP-ShapK**

Recognition of Region. Marsden Hartley. **CP-HartM**

Recognized by the others. The Prophet. Richard Shelton. **SP-ShelR**

Recognizing That My Wrists Always Have Salmon Leaping for Spring in Them. Diane Wakoski. **SP-WakoD**

Recoil. John Yau. **SP-YauJo**

Recollect the Face of me. Emily Dickinson. **CP-DickE**

Recollection of Childhood. Richard Eberhart. **CP-EberR**

Recollection of the Portrait of King Henry Eighth, Trinity Lodge, Cambridge. William Wordsworth. **CP-WorW2**

Recollection of the Stone Circle near Keswick, A. John Keats. **FaBoPP** *Fr.* Hyperion; a Fragment. **CP-KeatJ**

Recollections. Ussin Kerim, *tr. fr. Bulgarian by* William Matthews. **SP-MattW**

Recollections of George Oppen in a Letter to an English Friend. Donald Davie. **CP-DavDo**

Recollections of Love. Samuel Taylor Coleridge. **CP-ColeS**

Recommendation, The. Richard Crashaw. **CP-CrasR**

Recompence, The. Robert Herrick. **CP-HerrR**

Recompence. Robert Herrick. **CP-HerrR**

Recompense, The. Charles Tomlinson. **CP-TomlC**

Reconcilation, The. Tennyson. *See* As through the land at eve we went.

Reconciliation. Walter de la Mare. **CP-DeLaW**

Reconciliation. Walt Whitman. **CP-WhitW**

Reconciliation. William Butler Yeats. **CP-YeatW**

Reconsidering the Madman. Richard Hugo. **CP-HugoR**

Reconstructions. William DeWitt Snodgrass. **SP-SnodW**

Record, The. Louis Zukofsky. **CP-ZukLS**

Record Flood. William Matthews. *Fr.* Flood. **SP-MattW**

Record is a scroll of many indecipherable scrawls, The. Carl Sandburg. *Fr.* The People, Yes. **CP-SandC**

Record Stride, A. Robert Frost. **CP-FrosR**

Record we too, with just and faithful pen. Monks and Schoolmen. William Wordsworth. *Fr.* Ecclesiastical Sonnets. **CP-WorW2**

'Recorded ambience'—this. In the Studio. Charles Tomlinson. **CP-TomlC**

Recorders Ages Hence. Walt Whitman. **CP-WhitW**

Recorders in Italy. Adrienne Rich. **CP-RicAE**

Recording. Archie Randolph Ammons. **SP-AmmoA**

Records. Robert Ranke Graves. **CP-GravR**

Records. Robert Lowell. **SP-LoweR**

Records. Allen Tate. **CP-TateA**

Recovered from the Sea. Jenny Joseph. **SP-JoseJ**

Recovering. Muriel Rukeyser. **CP-RukeM**

Recovery. Archie Randolph Ammons. **SP-AmmoA**

Recovery. Maya Angelou. **SP-AngeM**

Recovery. John Berryman. **CP-BerrJ**

Recovery. Rita Dove. **SP-DoveR**

Recovery. Mona Van Duyn. **SP-VanDM**

Recovery. William Wordsworth. *Fr.* Ecclesiastical Sonnets. **CP-WorW2**

Recovery Room. William Matthews. **SP-MattW**

Recruit, The. Alfred Edward Housman. **CP-HousA**

Recruit. Edwin Rolfe. **CP-RolfE**

Rectangular, rearing / Black windows into daylight: the sound. George Oppen. *Fr.* Tourist Eye. **CP-OppeG**

Rectitude, and the terrible upstanding member. Washington in Love. John Berryman. **CP-BerrJ**

Rector's Memory, A. Rudyard Kipling. **CP-KiplR**

Rector's pallid neighbor at The Firs, The. The Villagers and Death. Robert Ranke Graves. **CP-GravR**

Recuerdo. Edna St. Vincent Millay. **CP-MillE**

Recurrently he also dreams. Hayden Carruth. *Fr.* The Sleeping Beauty. **CP-CarHL**

Recurring Dream, The. Lewis Turco. **SP-TurcL**

Red. David Herbert Lawrence. **CP-LawrD**

Red and black biplane, The. The Whole Point. Erica Jong. **SP-JongE**

Red and the Black, The. Roy Fisher. **SP-FishR**

Red and White. Carl Sandburg. **CP-SandC**

Red and White Roses. Thomas Carew. **CP-CareT**

Red apples hang like globes of light. Autumn 1964. Sir John Betjeman. **CP-BetjJ**

Red as the banner which enshrouds. Metacom. John Greenleaf Whittier. **CP-WhitJ**

Red balloon will collapse, my sweet, The. Waltz for Accordion. Isabella Gardner. *Fr.* Saloon Suite. **CP-GardI**

Red barns and red heifers spot the green. Omaha. Carl Sandburg. **CP-SandC**

Red beans in to soak. Roy Fisher. **SP-FishR** *Fr.* Metamorphoses.

Red—Blaze—is the Morning, The. Emily Dickinson. **CP-DickE**

Red Branch, The. Donald Hall. **CP-HallD**

Red Brick and Brown Stone. James Schuyler. **CP-SchuJ**

Red brick monastery in, The. The Semblables. William Carlos Williams. **CP-WilW2**

Red bridge fastening this city to the forest, A. Muriel Rukeyser. **CP-RukeM**

Red butterflies are so beautiful!, The. Minim. Howard Nemerov. *Fr.* Gnomes. **CP-NemeH**

Red cheeked boyfriends tenderly kiss me sweet mouthed. Tethnakin D'oligo Pideuis Fainom Alaia. Allen Ginsberg. **CP-GinsA**

Red cliffs arise. And up them service lifts. NW5 and N6. Sir John Betjeman. **CP-BetjJ**

Red Cloud (DAB) succeeded. As of Bozeman. Charles Olson. *Fr.* West. **CP-OlsoC**

Red Coats & the Blue, The. George Meredith. **CP-MerG2**

Red Cotton Night-Cap Country. Robert Browning. **CP-BroR2**
  "Accordingly, on weighty business bound." **EBVVPR**
  "And now let pass a week. Once more behold." **EBVVPR,** *sect.* III;
  " 'Thus I bestride the railing, leg o'er leg'." **EBVVPR,** *sect.* IV;

Red cradle of the night. Portent. William Carlos Williams. **CP-WilW1**

Red Dance, The. Anne Sexton. **CP-SextA**

Red Dog. Rudyard Kipling. *Fr.* The Second Jungle Book. Chil's Song. **CP-KiplR**
  "For our white and our excellent nights—for the nights of swift running." **CP-KiplR**

Red drips from my chin where I have been eating. Fight. Carl Sandburg. **CP-SandC**

Red Dust. Philip Levine. **SP-LeviP**

Red Earl, and will ye take for guide. The Ballad of the Red Earl. Rudyard Kipling. **CP-KiplR**

Red face / Texas. The Good Loser. Charles Bukowski. **SP-BukC1**

Red fence, The. Snow Fence. Ted Kooser. **SP-KoosT**

Red Fern, The. Wallace Stevens. **CP-StevW**

Red Fish-of-Bones, The. Charles Olson. **CP-OlsoC**

Red flower falls to its dim reflection, A. A Kiss. David Herbert Lawrence. **CP-LawrD**

Red fool, my laughing comrade. To a Comrade in Arms. Alun Lewis. **CP-LewiA**

Red Fountain. John Yau. **SP-YauJo**

Red fox, the vixen, The. Abnegation. Adrienne Rich. **CP-RicAE; SP-RicA2**

Red Front, The. Edward Estlin Cummings, *tr. from the French of Louis Aragon.* **CP-CummE**

Red Garland interpreting Bird's "Constellation." Moodsville. Tom Clark. **SP-ClarT**

Red Geranium and Godly Mignonette. David Herbert Lawrence. **CP-LawrD**

Red Geraniums. Stephen Dobyns. **SP-DobyS**

Red gold of pools. Harvest Sunset. Carl Sandburg. **CP-SandC**

Red granite and black diorite, with the blue. The Skeleton of the Future. "Hugh MacDiarmid." **SP-MacDH**

Red grapes shielded from the sun by thick, velvety leaves. Vines with Their. Kenneth Patchen. **CP-PatcK**

Red Guards battling country workers. Returning North of Vortex. Allen Ginsberg. **CP-GinsA**

Red hair / real. Red Up and Down. Charles Bukowski. **SP-BukC1**

Red Hanrahan's Song about Ireland. William Butler Yeats. **CP-YeatW**

Red-Headed Restaurant Cashier. Carl Sandburg. **CP-SandC**

Red-Herring. David Herbert Lawrence. **CP-LawrD**

Red Hook: December. George Oppen. **CP-OppeG**

Red-hot needle, A. Hornet. Anne Sexton. **CP-SextA**

Red Huitzilopochtli / Keeps day and night apart. Huitzilopochtli's Watch. David Herbert Lawrence. **CP-LawrD**

Red Jacket (from Aloft). Walt Whitman. **CP-WhitW**

Red Jacket's Grave. James Wright. **CP-WrigJ**

Red leaf. And beside it, a red leaf alive. Salamander. Muriel Rukeyser. **CP-RukeM**

Red Leaves take the Green Leaves place, The. Emily Dickinson. **SP-DickE**

Red Lily, The. William Carlos Williams. **CP-WilW1**

Red lips are not so red. Greater Love. Wilfred Owen. **CP-OwenW**

Red Mallows. Charles Olson. **CP-OlsoC**

Red Man told me, "Your father." The Dance, of the Grizzly Bear. Charles Olson. **CP-OlsoC**

Red mills and farms clumped soothingly here and there. A Battlefield. Donald Davie. **CP-DavDo**

Red moon hung above the pines that night, A. Travelling South. John Berryman. **CP-BerrJ**

Red Moon-Rise. David Herbert Lawrence. **CP-LawrD**

Red Mountain. Robinson Jeffers. **CP-JefR2**

Red Mullet, The. Robert Penn Warren. **SP-WarrR**

Red paper box, The. Composition. William Carlos Williams. **CP-WilW1**

Red Queen's Lullaby, The. "Lewis Carroll." **CP-CarrL** *Fr.* Through the Looking-Glass.

Red-rag and pink-flag. Edward Estlin Cummings. **CP-CummE; SP-CummE**

Red rain spatter under the redhaw, The. Redhaw Rain. Carl Sandburg. **CP-SandC**

Red, Red Rose, A. Robert Burns. *See* O[h] my luve's [*or* luve is *or* love is] like a red, red rose.

Red-Riding Hood. Anne Sexton. **CP-SextA**

Red Riding-Hood. John Greenleaf Whittier. **CP-WhitJ**

Red river, red river. Virginia. Thomas Stearns Eliot. **InPK** *Fr.* Landscapes. **CP-ElioT**

Red River Voyageur, The. John Greenleaf Whittier. **CP-WhitJ**

Red Rock of Utah. Donald Davie. **CP-DavDo**

Red room with the giant bed, The. To Minnie. Robert Louis Stevenson. **CP-StevR**

Red rose loosens, The. Hafiz, *tr. by* Ralph Waldo Emerson. **CP-EmerR** *Fr.* Odes.

Red Rose, proud Rose, sad Rose of all my days! To the Rose upon the Rood of Time. William Butler Yeats. **CP-YeatW**

Red Roses. Anne Sexton. **CP-SextA**

Red Roses for Bronze. Hilda Doolittle. **CP-DoolH**

Red Runner. Diane Wakoski. **SP-WakoD**

Red Scabies on the Skin. Smoke Rolling Down Street. Allen Ginsberg. **CP-GinsA**

"Red Sea," indeed! Talk not to me. Emily Dickinson. **CP-DickE**

Red Shift. Ted Berrigan. **SP-BerrT**

Red Shift, The. Robert Pack. **SP-PackR**

Red Shirt, A. Margaret Atwood. **SP-AtwM2**

Red Shoes, The. Anne Sexton. **CP-SextA**

Red Shower, The. Robert Ranke Graves. **CP-GravR**

Red Silk Blouse, A. William Matthews. **SP-MattW**

Red, soft-rock strata cut a line. Villa-Famès, August 1986. Steve Griffiths. **SP-GrifS**

Red Son, The. Carl Sandburg. **CP-SandC**

Red Stains. Allen Tate. **CP-TateA**

Red Stone. Richard Hugo. **CP-HugoR**

Red Sun. Joseph Ceravolo. **SP-CeraJ**

Red sun is going down somewhere, A. Gilbert Sorrentino. **SP-SorrG**

Red-tailed hawk, A. First Mile. James McAuley. *Fr.* Ten-Mile Run. **SP-McAuJ**

Red targets blowing. Marsden Hartley. *Fr.* Ironies out of St. George's. **CP-HartM**

Red Trees in the Wind. John Haines. **SP-HainJ**

Red tulips / living into their death. The Tulips. Denise Levertov. **CP-LeveD**

Red Up and Down. Charles Bukowski. **SP-BukC1**

Red varnish / Warm flitch. Two Dedications: Tibor Serly. Louis Zukofsky. *Fr.* 29 Poems. **CP-ZukLS**

Red velvet zinnias, small ones, across the room. Red Zinnias. Alice Notley. **SP-NotlA**

Red Weed. Stephen Berg. **SP-BergS** *Fr.* For My Father.

Red Wheelbarrow, The. William Carlos Williams. **CP-WilW1**

Red Wine and Yellow Hair. Kenneth Patchen. **CP-PatcK**

Red-Wing Blackbird, The. William Carlos Williams. **CP-WilW2**

Red Wing Church, The. Ted Kooser. **SP-KoosT**

Red Wolf, The. David Herbert Lawrence. **CP-LawrD**

Red woman, / (Keep Christ out). Navajo. William Carlos Williams. **CP-WilW2**

Red Zinnias. Alice Notley. **SP-NotlA**

Redbird, nesting, The. Glass Speciality. Archie Randolph Ammons. **SP-AmmoA**

Redbreast, The [Suggested in a Westmoreland Cottage]. William Wordsworth. **CP-WorW2**
  "Driven in by autumn's sharpening air." **PBBP**

Redbreast Chasing the Butterfly, The. William Wordsworth. **CP-WorW1**

Redbreast, early in the morning. Emily Brontë. **CP-BronE**

Redeem the surrogate goodbyes. Da Tagte Es. Samuel Beckett. **CP-BeckS**

Redeemer, A. Robinson Jeffers. **CP-JefR1**

Redeeming the Time. Christina Georgina Rossetti. **CP-RosC2**

Redemption. Richard Eberhart. **CP-EberR**

Redemption. George Herbert. **CP-HerbG**

Redemptrice of all vows and fealties, Dame. Geoffrey Hill. *Fr.* Hymns to Our Lady of Chartres. **CP-HillG**

Redeployment. Howard Nemerov. **CP-NemeH**

Redhaw Rain. Carl Sandburg. **CP-SandC**

Rediscovered Diary Entry. Al Young. **CP-YounA**

Rediscovery. Thomas McGrath. **SP-McGrT**

Redoubted King of courage leonine. Richard I. William Wordsworth. *Fr.* Ecclesiastical Sonnets. **CP-WorW2**

Redoubted knights, and honorable Dames. Edmund Spenser. **NoP** *Fr.* The Faerie Queene. **CP-Spens**

Reduced Sentence, A. Robert Ranke Graves. **CP-GravR**

Reduced to This. Thomas Merton. **CP-MertT**

Redwing. Tess Gallagher. **SP-GallT**

Redwing [*or*Red-winged] blackbird, The. Bay Bank. Archie Randolph Ammons. **SP-AmmoA**

Reed, A. Elizabeth Barrett Browning. **CP-BroEB**

Reed, / slashed and torn. Sea Lily. Hilda Doolittle. **CP-DoolH**

Reed-roof'd Village, still bepatch'd with snow, The. Samuel Taylor Coleridge. *Fr.* Some Fragments, Mainly from Manuscripts of 1797–8. **CP-ColeS**

Reeds. Charles Tomlinson. **CP-TomlC**

Reeds give, The. Small Song. Archie Randolph Ammons. **SP-AmmoA**

Reeds of Innocence. William Blake. *See* Piping Down the Valleys Wild.

Reeds of Runnymede, The. Rudyard Kipling. **CP-KiplR**

Reef, The. David St. John. **SP-StJoD**

Reef Fisher, The. Archibald MacLeish. **CP-MacLA**

Reel. John Updike. **CP-UpdiJ**

Reel o' Stumpie, The. Robert Burns. **CP-BurnR**

Reeve's Prologue, The. Geoffrey Chaucer. *Fr.* The Canterbury Tales. **CP-ChauG**

Reeve's Tale, The. Geoffrey Chaucer. *Fr.* The Canterbury Tales. **CP-ChauG**

   Bedroom Farce. **FaBoDD**

Reference, The. John Hewitt. **CP-HewiJ**

Reference Back. Philip Larkin. *See That was a pretty one,* I heard you call.

Reference to a Passage in Plutarch's Life of Sulla. Robinson Jeffers. **CrMA** *Fr.* The Broken Balance. **CP-JefR1**

Refined Man, The. Rudyard Kipling. **FaBoEE; FaBoTw; MMA; PeFWW** *Fr.* Epitaphs of the War [1914–1918]. **CP-KiplR**

Refining Mallarmé at last destroyed. Readings in French. Thom Gunn. **CP-GunnT**

Reflected light reflected again on snow. The Moon. Hayden Carruth. *Fr.* Contra Mortem. **CP-CarHL**

Reflecting Trees of Being and Not Being, The. Kenneth Rexroth. **SP-RexrK** *Fr.* Seven Poems for Marthe, My Wife.

Reflection, The. Frederick Morgan. **SP-MorgF**

Reflection. Christina Georgina Rossetti. **CP-RosC3**

Reflection by a Mailbox. Stanley Jasspon Kunitz. **CP-KuniS**

Reflection On of the Fallibility of Nemesis. Ogden Nash. **CP-NashO**

Reflection On a Wicked World. Ogden Nash. **CP-NashO**

Reflection on Babies. Ogden Nash. **CP-NashO**

Reflection on Caution. Ogden Nash. **CP-NashO**

Reflection on Ingenuity. Ogden Nash. **CP-NashO**

Reflection on the Foregoing Ode, *see also* Horace's Odes 2.10. William Cowper. **CP-CowpW**

Reflection on the Passage of Time, Its Inevitability and Its Quirks. Ogden Nash. **CP-NashO**

Reflection to Windward. Malcolm Lowry. **CP-LowrM**

Reflections. Walter de la Mare. **CP-DeLaW**

Reflections. Phoebe Hesketh. **SP-HeskP**

Reflections. Daniel Gerard Hoffman. **SP-HoffD**

Reflections. Louis MacNeice. **CP-MacNL**

Reflections. Charles Tomlinson. **CP-TomlC**

Reflections. William Wordsworth. *Fr.* Ecclesiastical Sonnets. **CP-WorW2**

Reflections at Forty-Nine. Lewis Turco. **SP-TurcL**

Reflections at Lake Louise. Allen Ginsberg. **CP-GinsA**

Reflections in a Forest. Wystan Hugh Auden. **CP-AudeW**

Reflections in an Old House. Allen Tate. **CP-TateA**

Reflections in Sleepy Eye. Allen Ginsberg. **CP-GinsA**

Reflections in the forest of the dying child, The. 1938: Tales from the Vienna Woods. Randall Jarrell. **CP-JarrR**

Reflections on Deafness. Donald Davie. **CP-DavDo**

Reflections on Having Left a Place of Retirement. Samuel Taylor Coleridge. **CP-ColeS**

Reflections on Ice-breaking. Ogden Nash. **CP-NashO**

Reflections on Reading a Life of Dickens. Robert Browning. **CP-BroR2**

Reflections on Some Drawings of Plants. Charlotte Smith. **CP-SmitC**

Reflections on the Vernacular. Ogden Nash. **CP-NashO**

Reflective. Archie Randolph Ammons. **SP-AmmoA**

Reflex, A. Robert Frost. **CP-FrosR**

Reflex. Marsden Hartley. **CP-HartM**

Reflexion of a Novelist. Howard Nemerov. **CP-NemeH**

Reflexions on suicide, & on my father, possess me. Of Suicide. John Berryman. **CP-BerrJ**

Reflexions on the Seizure of the Suez, and on a Proposal to Line the Banks of That Canal with Billboard Advertisements. Howard Nemerov. **CP-NemeH**

Reflexive. Hayden Carruth. **CP-CarHS**

Reforestation. Louise McNeill. **SP-McNeL**

Reformer, The. John Greenleaf Whittier. **CP-WhitJ**

Reformers, The. Rudyard Kipling. **CP-KiplR**

Refrain. Rita Dove. **SP-DoveR**

Refrain. Allen Ginsberg. **CP-GinsA**

Refrains. Richard Eberhart. **CP-EberR**

Refrigerator falls silent, The. Night in the Kitchen. Adrienne Rich. **CP-RicAE**

Refuge, Serpent-Riders. Charles Kenneth Williams. **CP-WillC**

Refugee Blues. Wystan Hugh Auden. *See* Say this city has ten million souls.

Refugee in America. Langston Hughes. **SP-HughL**

Refugees. Steve Griffiths. **SP-GrifS**

Refugees, The. Randall Jarrell. **CP-JarrR**

Refugees. Louis MacNeice. **CP-MacNL**

Refusal. Maya Angelou. **SP-AngeM**

Refusal, A. Thomas Hardy. **CP-HardT**

Refusal, The. James Wright. **CP-WrigJ**

Refusal of a Kindness Offered. Howard Nemerov. **CP-NemeH**

Refusal to Mourn, A. Derek Mahon. **SP-MahoD**

Refusal to Mourn the Death, by Fire, of a Child in London, A. Dylan Thomas. **CP-ThomD**

Refused Friendship. David Herbert Lawrence. **CP-LawrD**

Refuses / To refuse the racket, to mutter No to the net. Old Tennis Player. Gwendolyn Brooks. **LiSp; SD** *Fr.* A Catch of Shy Fish. **SP-BrooG**

Refusing Silence. Tess Gallagher. **SP-GallT**

Refusing the Necessary. Stephen Dobyns. **SP-DobyS**

Refusing to fall in love with God, he gave. Didymus. Louis MacNeice. **EaLo** *Fr.* Entered in the Minutes. **CP-MacNL**

Regard Me. Charles Bukowski. **SP-BukC2**

Regard of Tangents. Stanley Jasspon Kunitz. **CP-KuniS**

Regard the capture here, O Janus-faced. Recitative. Hart Crane. **CP-CranH**

Regarding Chainsaws. Hayden Carruth. **CP-CarHS**

Regarding Wave. Gary Snyder. **CP-SnydG**

Regardless. Stephen Dunn. **SP-DunnS**

Regatta, The. Richard Wilbur. **CP-WilbR**

Regent's Park Sonnets, The. Marilyn Hacker. **SP-HackM**

   "Another poet, woman and alive."

   Coda.

   "Gino hummed an epthialamium."

   "One master, aged, as I am, thirty-two."

   "Some table talk at lunch, of memory."

   " 'That was in another country,' but the wench."

   "Thursday, the eighth of August, four o'clock."

   " 'What's in a park they warn girls out of?' "Queers.""

   "You rang me up this morning from Marseilles."

Reggae thumps, a hangover. Post Imperial. Steve Griffiths. **SP-GrifS**

Reggie's Version. Al Young. **CP-YounA**

Regraduating the Lute. William DeWitt Snodgrass. **SP-SnodW**

Regression Spoiles Resolution. Robert Herrick. **CP-HerrR**

Regret, The. Thomas Merton. **CP-MertT; SP-MertT**

Regret Not Me. Thomas Hardy. **CP-HardT**

Regretfully, I proffer my excuses. Lines Declining a Transatlantic Dinner Invitation. Marilyn Hacker. **SP-HackM**

Regrets. William Wordsworth. *Fr.* Ecclesiastical Sonnets. **CP-WorW2**

Regularly I visited. Sickroom. Michael Hartnett. **SP-HarMi**

Regulars, The. Charles Kenneth Williams. **CP-WillC; SP-WillC**

Rehabilitation & Treatment in the Prisons of America. Etheridge Knight. **SP-KnigE**

Rehearsal, The. Stevie Smith. **CP-SmitS**

Rehearsal to Ourselves. Emily Dickinson. **CP-DickE**

Rehearse to me, ye sacred sisters nine. The Teares of the Muses. Edmund Spenser. **CP-Spens**

Reichsmarschall Hermann Göring ("And why, Herr Reichsmarschall, is Italy"). William DeWitt Snodgrass. **SP-SnodW**

Reichsmarschall Hermann Göring ("Dear friends, the moment's come to ask"). William DeWitt Snodgrass. **SP-SnodW**

Reign of Chaos, The. Alexander Pope. **EBEV; FaBoPV; SCV** *Fr.* Yet, yet a moment, one dim ray of light. **NAEL-1; OAEL-1; PoEL-3** *Fr.* The Dunciad. **CP-PopeA**

(Chaos.) **LoBV**

(Reign of Chaos, The.) **FiP**

(Triumph of Dulness [*or* Dulness], The.) **NOBE; NoP**

Reign of Chaos, The. Alexander Pope. *See* The Reign of Chaos.

Reincarnation (I) ["Still, passed through the spokes of an old wheel, on and around"]. James Dickey. **CP-DickJ**

Reincarnation (II). James Dickey. **CP-DickJ**

Reincarnation of Captain Cook, The. Margaret Atwood. **SP-AtwM1**

Reiteration, The. Robert Ranke Graves. **CP-GravR**

Reject me not if I should say to you. Love Song, A. David Herbert Lawrence. **CP-LawrD**

Rejected Member's Wife, The. Thomas Hardy. **CP-HardT**

Rejoice in God, O ye Tongues; give the glory to the Lord, and the Lamb. Fragment A. Christopher Smart. *Fr.* Jubilate Agno. **SP-SmarC**

Rejoice in God, O ye Tongues; give the glory to the Lord, and the Lamb. Christopher Smart. FaBoVe, *ll.* 1–22; *Fr.* Fragment A. *Fr.* Jubilate Agno. **SP-SmarC**

Rejoice in God, O ye Tongues; give the glory to the Lord, and the Lamb. Christopher Smart. PoE, *ll.* 1–11; *Fr.* Rejoice in God, O ye Tongues; give the glory to the Lord, and the Lamb. FaBoVe, *ll.* 1–22; *Fr.* Fragment A. *Fr.* Jubilate Agno. **SP-SmarC**

"Rejoice in God, O ye Tongues; give the glory to the Lord, and the Lamb." PoE, *ll.* 1–11;

Rejoice in God, ye saints above. Bible, *O.T. See* Psalm 33: "Rejoice in the Lord, O ye righteous. . . ."

Rejoice in the Abyss. Stephen Spender. **CP-SpenS**

Rejoice in the clefts of Gehenna. A Drama of Exile. Elizabeth Barrett Browning. **CP-BroEB**

Rejoice in the Lord, O ye righteous: for praise is comely for the upright. Psalm 33. Bible, *O.T. Fr.* Psalms. **CP-Psal**

Rejoice, mackerel, and whosoever is of the fish in the deep. Verse from Defensio Secunda. John Milton, *tr. fr. Latin by* John T. Shawcross. **CP-MiltJ**

Rejoice with Me. Christina Georgina Rossetti. **CP-RosC2**

Rejoinder to a Critic. Donald Davie. **CP-DavDo**

Relation of Art and Life, A. Howard Nemerov. **CP-NemeH**

Relation of the Late Royall Entertainment Given by the Right Honourable the Lord *Knowles*, at *Cawsome-House neere Redding:* to Our Most *Gracious Queene, Queene* ANNE, *in her* Progresse toward the *Bathe*, upon *the Seven and Eight and Twentie Dayes of Aprill*, A. Thomas Campion. **CP-CampT**

"Can you, the Author of our joy, / So soone depart?"

"Dance now and sing the joy and love we owe."

"Night as well as brightest day hath her delight."

"O Joyes exceeding!"

"Welcome to this flowrie place."

Relation seemed ordained for us. Song. Wystan Hugh Auden. **CP-AudWJ**

Relations. John Berryman. **CP-BerrJ**

Relationships. Mona Van Duyn. **SP-VanDM**

Relative and an Absolute, A. Mona Van Duyn. **SP-VanDM**

Relative to cost, the high figures / of production. The Surf: An Elegy. Robert Creeley. **CP-CreeR**

Relatives. John Updike. **CP-UpdiJ**

Relativity. David Herbert Lawrence. **CP-LawrD**

Relax, Maestro, put your baton down. Metalogue to The Magic Flute. Wystan Hugh Auden. *Fr.* Three Occasional Poems. **CP-AudeW**

Release. Archie Randolph Ammons. **SP-AmmoA**

Release, The. Thom Gunn. **CP-GunnT**

Release. David Herbert Lawrence. **CP-LawrD**

Release of Demonic Energies in the name of, The. Spel Against Demons. Gary Snyder. **CP-SnydG**

Release Time. Audre Lorde. **SP-LordA**

Releases. Roy Fisher. **SP-FishR**

Relentless man loved France, A. Is There Any Easy Road to Freedom? Carl Sandburg. **CP-SandC**

Relevance. David Markson. **CP-MarkD**

Relevant Is Different Points on the Circle. Audre Lorde. **SP-LordA**

Relic, The. John Donne. **CP-DonnJ**

Relic. Ted Hughes. **SP-HughT**

Relic, The. John Greenleaf Whittier. **CP-WhitJ**

Relic of Memory. Seamus Heaney. **SP-HeanS**

Relic taken, what avails the shrine?, The. Robert Louis Stevenson. **CP-StevR**

Relics. Louis MacNeice. **CP-MacNL**

Relief. Langston Hughes. **SP-HughL**

Relief of putting your fingers on the keyboard, The. Thanking My Mother for Piano Lessons. Diane Wakoski. **SP-WakoD**

Relieved, I let the book fall behind a stone. Depressed by a Book of Bad Poetry, I Walk toward an Unused Pasture and Invite the Insects to Join Me. James Wright. **CP-WrigJ**

Religio Laici. John Dryden. **SP-DrydJ**

"But if there be a power too just and strong." **NOCV**

"Dim, as the borrow'd beams of moon and stars." FiP; NOSC; OAEL-1; OBS; OxBoCh

(Reason and Religion.) **FiP**

(Reason and Revelation.) **OBS**

Priestcraft and Private Judgement. **OBS**

Scriptures, The. **OBS**

"Thus man by his own strength to Heaven would soar." **NOCV; WGRP**

Tradition. **OBS**

Religion. John Donne. *See* Satire 3: "Kind pity [*or* Kinde pitty] chokes my spleen[e]; brave scorn forbids."

Religion. Paul Laurence Dunbar. **CP-DunbP**

Religion. David Herbert Lawrence. **CP-LawrD**

Religion? Huh! Whenever I hear the word. Two Memories. "Hugh MacDiarmid." **SP-MacDH**

Religion Is That I Love You. Kenneth Patchen. **CP-PatcK**

Religious Articles. Donald Hall. **CP-HallD**

Religious faith is a most filling vapor. Innate Helium. Robert Frost. **CP-FrosR**

Religious garden. Roy Fisher. **SP-FishR** *Fr.* Matrix.

Religious Man, A. Stevie Smith. **CP-SmitS**

Religious Musings. Samuel Taylor Coleridge. **CP-ColeS**

"Lovely was the death." **EnRP**

"There is one Mind, one omnipresent Mind." **WGRP**

Reliquary. Adrienne Rich. **CP-RicAE**

Relishing this health, this singleness. The Night Skater. Frederick Morgan. **SP-MorgF**

Reluctance. Paul Laurence Dunbar. **CP-DunbP**

Reluctance. Robert Frost. **CP-FrosR**

Reluctant call it was; the rite delayed. Upon the Late General Fast. March, 1832. William Wordsworth. **CP-WorW2**

Reluctant Confession. Thomas Hardy. **CP-HardT**

Remains. Robert Pack. **SP-PackR**

Remark the empty bandstand in the park. Bandstand. John Hewitt. **CP-HewiJ**

Remarkably all this March first. March First. Louis Zukofsky. *Fr.* Songs of Degrees. **CP-ZukLS**

Remarked Robinson Jefferson. Edward Estlin Cummings. **CP-CummE**

Rembrandt. Robert Lowell. **SP-LoweR**

Rembrandt—Rouault—Piero. Marsden Hartley. **CP-HartM**

Rembrandt to Rembrandt. Edwin Arlington Robinson. **CP-RobiE**

Remediae Amoris. Ovid, *tr. fr. Latin.*

"At busy hearts in vain love's arrows fly." **CP-JohnS**

"Man will surely fail who dares delay, The." **CP-JohnS**

"Our bane and physic the same earth bestows." **CP-JohnS**

Remedies, Maladies, Reasons. Mona Van Duyn. **SP-VanDM**

Remember [Me]. Christina Georgina Rossetti. **CP-RosC1**

Remember? Alice Walker. **CP-WalkA**

Remember all those renowned generations. Three Marching Songs. William Butler Yeats. **CP-YeatW**

Remember, and already the lapse in. Croce e Delizia al Cor. Tess Gallagher. **SP-GallT**

Remember Graham. Richard Hugo. **CP-HugoR**

Remember Him Whom Passion's Power. Byron. **CP-Byron**

Remember how / Twenty-five years ago in Cincinnati. Remembering Cincinnati, 1953. Stephen Spender. **CP-SpenS**

Remember how, at seven years, the decrees. Fidelities. Geoffrey Hill. *Fr.* An Apology for the Revival of Christian Architecture in England. **CP-HillG**

Remember how Daylight Saving used to end. The Old Days. Howard Nemerov. **CP-NemeH**

Remember how, my watchful twin. Walnut. Robert Pack. **SP-PackR**

Remember how unimportant. Milkweed. Philip Levine. **SP-LeviP**

Remember, if I claim too much of you. By Way of Remembrance. Christina Georgina Rossetti. **CP-RosC3**

Remember, master, I asked you / to take this child Godfrey, my kinsman. News from the School at Chartres. Thomas Merton. **CP-MertT**

Remember me? Remember? Alice Walker. **CP-WalkA**

Remember me? I was the one. Hood. Charles Kenneth Williams. **CP-WillC; SP-WillC**

"Remember me" implored the Thief! Emily Dickinson. **CP-DickE**

Remember me when I am gone away. Remember [Me]. Christina Georgina Rossetti. **CP-RosC1**

Remember midsummer: the fragrance of box, of white roses. Poem. Delmore Schwartz. **SP-SchwD**

Remember: not making. Walter Armistead. James Dickey. **CP-DickJ**

Remember now, my Love, what piteous thing. A Carrion. Charles Baudelaire, *tr. fr. French by* Allen Tate. **CP-TateA**

Remember Ralph who ran so fast and far? Letter to the Patrol Twenty Years After. Leonard Nathan. **SP-NathL**

Remember something you never saw. A True Account of Talking to Judy Holiday, October 13. Alice Notley. **SP-NotlA**

Remember that breakfast one November. Between Two Wars. Kenneth Rexroth. **SP-RexrK**

Remember that farmer down in Maine. A Marriage. Daniel Gerard Hoffman. **SP-HoffD**

Remember the chameleon. He was a well-behaved chameleon. Carl Sandburg. *Fr.* The People, Yes. **CP-SandC**

Remember the days of our first happiness. Summer. Louise Glück. *Fr.* Marathon. **CP-GlücL**

Remember the old peasant of. As It Was. Frederick Morgan. **SP-MorgF**

Remember the story of Columbus and the orange? Gilbert Sorrentino. **SP-SorrG**

Remember the teacher who inspired them to great leaps of learning. If Other Students. Ron Koertge. **SP-KoerR**

Remember the way we bore our bodies to the pond. Puberty. William Matthews. **SP-MattW**

Remember the way you. The Flower. Robert Creeley. **CP-CreeR**

Remember Thee! Remember Thee! Byron. **CP-Byron**

Remember those awful parties. Brighton Beach. Derek Mahon. **SP-MahoD**

Remember those wingovers and loops and spins? The Dream of Flying Comes of Age. Howard Nemerov. **CP-NemeH**

Remember what a night of storm. George Meredith. **CP-MerG2**

Remember when I draped. Poem for My Mother. Siv Cedering Fox. **SP-CedeS**

Remember your manners. Standing on Ceremony. "Lou Reed." **SP-ReedL**

Rememberance for a great man is this. In a Back Alley. Carl Sandburg. **CP-SandC**

Remembered. Paul Laurence Dunbar. **CP-DunbP**

Remembered as octagonal, dark-panelled. Room 28. John Updike. **CP-UpdiJ**

Remembered Women. Carl Sandburg. **CP-SandC**

Remembering. Maya Angelou. **SP-AngeM**

Remembering. Denise Levertov. **CP-LeveD**

Remembering. William Stafford. **SP-StafW**

Remembering a Conversation: Itzik Manger at the PEN Conference, Edinburgh, 1950. John Hewitt. **CP-HewiJ**

Remembering and Forgetting. Stephen Berg. **SP-BergS**

Remembering Brother Bob. William Stafford. **SP-StafW**

Remembering Cincinnatti, 1953. Stephen Spender. **CP-SpenS**

Remembering how thou didst beguile. Elegy Written in the Same Place upon the Same Occasion. William Wordsworth. **CP-WorW1**

Remembering Loves and Deaths. Thomas McGrath. **SP-McGrT**

Remembering movies   love. Song: Remembering Movies. Muriel Rukeyser. **CP-RukeM**

Remembering the Children of Auschwitz. Thomas McGrath. **SP-McGrT**

Remembering the Strait of Belle Isle or. Large Bad Picture. Elizabeth Bishop. **CP-BishE**

Remembering the 'Thirties. Donald Davie. **CP-DavDo**

Remembering Williams. Charles Tomlinson. **CP-TomlC**

Remember'st thou. Hungarian Air. George Meredith. **CP-MerG2**

Remembrance. Maya Angelou. **SP-AngeM**

Remembrance. Emily Brontë. **CP-BronE**

(R. Alcona to J. Brenzaida.) **CP-BronE**

Remembrance. Byron. **CP-Byron**

Remembrance. Walter de la Mare. **CP-DeLaW**

Remembrance. William Shakespeare. *See* Sonnet 30: "When to the sessions of sweet silent thought."

Remembrance. Percy Bysshe Shelley. **CP-ShelP**

Remembrance. John Greenleaf Whittier. **CP-WhitJ**

Remembrance Day. Ted Hughes. *Fr.* Out. **SP-HughT**

Remembrance has a Rear and Front. Emily Dickinson. **CP-DickE**

Remembrance of Collins, Composed upon the Thames near Richmond. William Wordsworth. **CP-WorW1**

Remind Me Not, Remind Me Not. Byron. **CP-Byron**

Reminded of Bougainville. Donald Davie. **CP-DavDo**

Reminded of One of Those Girls I Never Was. Diane Wakoski. **SP-WakoD**

Reminder, A. Wystan Hugh Auden. *Fr.* Six Commissioned Texts. **CP-AudeW**

Reminder, The. Thomas Hardy. **CP-HardT**

Reminder. David Herbert Lawrence. **CP-LawrD**

Reminder, The. Theodore Roethke. **CP-RoetT**

Reminiscences of a Dancing Man. Thomas Hardy. **CP-HardT**

Reminiscent of a Wave At the Curl. Marianne Craig Moore. **CP-MoorM**

Reminiscent Reflection. Ogden Nash. **CP-NashO**

Remnant Water. James Dickey. **CP-DickJ**

Remonstrance, The. Walter de la Mare. **CP-DeLaW**

Remora. James Merrill. **SP-MerrJ**

Remorse. Robert Burns. **CP-BurnR**

Remorse. Samuel Taylor Coleridge.

    Invocation, An: "Hear, sweet spirit, hear the spell." **CP-ColeS**

Remorse. Carl Sandburg. **CP-SandC**

Remorse for Intemperate Speech. William Butler Yeats. **CP-YeatW**

Remorse for Time, The. Howard Nemerov. **CP-NemeH**

Remorse—is Memory—awake. Emily Dickinson. **CP-DickE**

Remorse upbraides my faultes. Saint Peter's Remorse. Robert Southwell. **CP-SoutR**

Remote and beyond, lonely farms on the shoulders of hills. Orion. William Everson. **SP-EverW**

Remote Farm on the Dubrovnik-Sarajevo Run. Richard Hugo. **CP-HugoR**

Remote from scenes, where the o'erwearied mind. Flora. Charlotte Smith. **CP-SmitC**

Remote, it lives now in a tiny glass. Looking Glass. Thom Gunn. **CP-GunnT**

Remove away that blackning church. An Ancient Proverb. William Blake. **CP-BlakW**

Remove—from Accident of Loss. Emily Dickinson. **CP-DickE**

Remove me from this land of slaves. Ireland. Jonathan Swift. **CP-SwifJ**

Removed from Natural Habitat. Diane Wakoski. **SP-WakoD**

Removing the Plate of the Pump on the Hydraulic System of the Backhoe. Gary Snyder. **CP-SnydG**

Renaissance. Hayden Carruth. **CP-CarHS**

Renaissance, *sl. diff. vers.* David Herbert Lawrence. *See* Renascence.

Renaming the Kings. Philip Levine. **SP-LeviP**

Renascence. David Herbert Lawrence. **CP-LawrD**

Renascence. Edna St. Vincent Millay. **CP-MillE**

    "All I could see from where I stood." **FaFP; MoAB; MoAmPo; OHFP; PDV; PFP**

Renato O. Jones, you maintain my beliefs. Ode to a Maintenance Man and His Family. Kay Boyle. **CP-BoylK**

Rencontres Funestes. Stevie Smith. **CP-SmitS**

Rend hearts and rend not garments for our sins. Christina Georgina Rossetti. *Fr.* Later Life: A Double Sonnet of Sonnets. **CP-RosC2**

Rendezvous. Kay Boyle. **CP-BoylK**

Rendezvous. Edna St. Vincent Millay. **CP-MillE**

Rendezvous. William Carlos Williams. **CP-WilW1**

Rendition, The. John Greenleaf Whittier. **CP-WhitJ**

Renewal. Alun Lewis. **CP-LewiA**

Renewal, A. James Merrill. **SP-MerrJ**

Renewal, The. Theodore Roethke. **CP-RoetT**

Renouncing an Epigram. Frank Templeton Prince. **CP-PrinF**

Renovated Temple, The. Archibald MacLeish. **CP-MacLA**

Renowned author of, The. Basil Bunting. *Fr.* Aus Dem Zweiten Reich. **CP-BuntB**

Rent. Jane Cooper. **SP-CoopJ**

Rent in the Screen, The. Howard Nemerov. **CP-NemeH**

Rent man knocked, The. Madam and the Rent Man. Langston Hughes. **SP-HughL**

Rentrer / À la nuit. Samuel Beckett. **CP-BeckS**

Renunciation—is a piercing Virtue. Emily Dickinson. **CP-DickE**

Reorganization. Archie Randolph Ammons. **SP-AmmoA**

Repairing the House, the Church, Restoring the Music. Richard Hugo. **CP-HugoR**

Repeat and repeat till they say what you. Brainwashing. Carl Sandburg. **CP-SandC**

Repeat blue words like gloom; to hold their hue. Villanelle for Pamela. Robert Pack. **SP-PackR**

Repeat that, repeat. Gerard Manley Hopkins. **CP-HopkG**

    (Repeat That, Repeat.) **CP-HopkG**

Repeat That, Repeat. Gerard Manley Hopkins. *See* Repeat that, repeat.

Repeated Journey, The. Thomas McGrath. **SP-McGrT**

Repeated Shapes, The. Donald Hall. **CP-HallD**

Repeating fly, blueback, thumbthick—so gross, A. Harriet. Robert Lowell. **SP-LoweR**

Repentance. George Chapman. **OBSC** *Fr.* Hero and Leander. **CP-MarlC**

Repentance. George Herbert. **CP-HerbG**

Repentance; A Pastoral Ballad. William Wordsworth. **CP-WorW1**

Repentance of Lady T, The. Stevie Smith. **CP-SmitS**

Repetition of the name made known, The. Martha, Martha. Robert Herrick. **CP-HerrR**

Repetitions. Carl Sandburg. **CP-SandC**

Repetitions of a Young Captain. Wallace Stevens. **CP-StevW**

Rephan. Robert Browning. **CP-BroR2**

Repining. Christina Georgina Rossetti. **CP-RosC3**

Repletion. Robert Herrick. **CP-HerrR**

Replies to Challenges to Rhyme. Robert Browning. **CP-BroR2**

Reply, The. Allen Ginsberg. **CP-GinsA**

Reply, The. Theodore Roethke. **CP-RoetT**

Reply of the County of Surrey to the Poet's Pathetic Address in Dispraise of Jean. George Meredith. **CP-MerG2**

Reply of the Friend, The. James Liddy. **CP-LiddJ**

Reply to a Lady Editor. Theodore Roethke. **CP-RoetT**

Reply to a Philistine. Phoebe Hesketh. **SP-HeskP**

Reply to Censure. Theodore Roethke. **CP-RoetT**

Reply to Impromptu Verses by Baretti, A. Samuel Johnson. *See* At sight of sparkling Bowls or beauteous Dames.

Reply to Mr. Wordsworth. Archibald MacLeish. **CP-MacLA**
"Space-time, our scientists tell us, is impervious." **ImOP**

Reply to Papini. Wallace Stevens. **CP-StevW**

Reply to Robert Riddell. Robert Burns. **CP-BurnR**

Reply to Some Verses of J.M.B. Pigot, Esq., on the Cruelty of His Mistress. Byron. **CP-Byron**

Report has come from the panel of tasters, The. The Lemonade Panel. Gilbert Sorrentino. **SP-SorrG**

Report of an Adjudged Case. William Cowper. **CP-CowpW**

Report of Health. John Updike. **CP-UpdiJ**

Report on a Happening in Washington Square San Francisco, A. Lawrence Ferlinghetti. **SP-FerlL**

Report on August. Roy Fisher. **SP-FishR**

Report on Conditions. Malcolm Lowry. **CP-LowrM**

Report to Crazy Horse. William Stafford. **SP-StafW**

Report to the Mother. Etheridge Knight. **SP-KnigE**

Report Upon the Consumption of Myself, A. Charles Bukowski. **SP-BukC2**

Reported Missing. Jenny Joseph. **SP-JoseJ**

Reportless Subjects, to the Quick. Emily Dickinson. **CP-DickE**

Repose in God. Jeanne Marie Bouvier de la Motte-Guyon, *tr. fr. French by* William Cowper. **CP-CowpW**

Repose of Rivers. Hart Crane. **CP-CranH**

Representing the Universe. Alice Walker. **CP-WalkA**

Repression. Charles Kenneth Williams. **SP-WillC**

Reprieve, The. Frederick Morgan. **SP-MorgF**

Reprieve and Admixture. Charles Bukowski. **SP-BukC2**

Reprimand, The. Elizabeth Bishop. **CP-BishE**

Reprisal[l], The. George Herbert. **CP-HerbG**

Reproach, The. Louise Glück. **SP-GlücL**

Reproach. Robert Ranke Graves. **CP-GravR**

Reproach to Dead Poets. Archibald MacLeish. **CP-MacLA**

Reproach we may the living; not the dead. No Despight to the Dead. Robert Herrick. **CP-HerrR**

Reproof. William Wordsworth. *Fr.* Ecclesiastical Sonnets. **CP-WorW2**

Reproof and Reply, The. Samuel Taylor Coleridge. **CP-ColeS**

Reproof Deserved; or After the Lecture. Sir John Betjeman. **CP-BetjJ**

Reprove not love, though fondly thou hast lost. *At.* to Thomas Campion *and* to Philip Rosseter. **CP-CampT**

Republic 1939, The. James Liddy. **CP-LiddJ**

Republicans? We've got a few. In fact. Hayden Carruth. *Fr.* Vermont. **CP-CarHL**

Repulse the staring eye. Reply to Censure. Theodore Roethke. **CP-RoetT**

Repulsed. David Herbert Lawrence. **CP-LawrD**

Request. Maya Angelou. **SP-AngeM**

Request. Richard Eberhart. **CP-EberR**

Request. Langston Hughes. **SP-HughL**

Request, The. Charles Tomlinson. **CP-TomlC**

Request for Offering. Richard Eberhart. **CP-EberR**

Request to the Graces, An. Robert Herrick. **CP-HerrR**

Requested journey to a planned occasion. Clogh-Oir: September 1971. John Hewitt. **CP-HewiJ**

Requiem: "In the sudden white silence, where are you?" Jean Garrigue. **SP-GarrJ**

Requiem. James McAuley. **SP-McAuJ**
"Alle Herrlichkeit Des Menschen."
Blessing.
Creed.
Glory.
Labor and Tribulation.
Mourners.
Secret.
Survivors.
Vigil.

Requiem: "There was a young belle of old Natchez." Ogden Nash. **CP-NashO**

Requiem: "Under the wide and starry sky." Robert Louis Stevenson. **CP-StevR**

Requiem: "We will see no more." Wendell Berry. **CP-BerrW**

Requiem: "Where faces are hueless, where eyelids are dewless." George Meredith. **CP-MerG1**

Requiem for a Non-Croppy. James Liddy. **CP-LiddJ**

Requiem for a Twentieth-Century Outlaw. John Gould Fletcher. **SP-FletJ**

Requiem for Sonora. Richard Shelton. **SP-ShelR**

Requiem for the Croppies. Seamus Heaney. **SP-HeanS**

Requiem for the Death of a Boy, *tr. fr. the German of* Rilke. Randall Jarrell. **CP-JarrR**

Requiem for the Plantagenet Kings. Geoffrey Hill. **CP-HillG**

Requiem for the Spanish Dead. Kenneth Rexroth. **SP-RexrK**

Requiescam. Countee Cullen. **CP-CullC**

Requiescat. Matthew Arnold. **SP-ArnoM**

Requirement. John Greenleaf Whittier. **CP-WhitJ**

Requiring something lovely on his arm. Labor Day. Louise Glück. **SP-GlücL**

Requisitioning. John Ciardi. **SP-CiarJ**

Requital. John Greenleaf Whittier. **CP-WhitJ**

Requite this angel whose. Geoffrey Hill. *Fr.* Tenebrae. **CP-HillG**

Rescue. Siv Cedering Fox. **SP-CedeS**

Rescue, The. Robert Creeley. **CP-CreeR**

Rescue, The. Frederick Morgan. **SP-MorgF**

Rescue. Dabney Stuart. **SP-StuaD**

Rescue of Pluffles, The. Rudyard Kipling. *Fr.* Plain Tales from the Hills. "Thus, for a season, they fought it fair." **CP-KiplR**

Rescue Poem. Diane Wakoski. **SP-WakoD**

Rescue With Yul Brynner. Marianne Craig Moore. **CP-MoorM**

Rescued! new-white. The Old House. William Carlos Williams. **CP-WilW2**

Rescued Year, The. William Stafford. **SP-StafW**

Rescuing gate is wide, The. Like a Mourningless Child. Kenneth Patchen. **CP-PatcK**

Research, Again. Gilbert Sorrentino. **SP-SorrG**

Research and Development: Classified. Robert Ranke Graves. **CP-GravR**

Research Team in the Mountains, The. William Stafford. **SP-StafW**

Resemblance, The. William Carlos Williams. **CP-WilW2**

Resembles Life what once was deem'd of Light. What Is Life? Samuel Taylor Coleridge. **CP-ColeS**

Resentment. Charles Kenneth Williams. **SP-WillC**

Reservations. Richard Shelton. **SP-ShelR**

Reserved. Walter de la Mare. **CP-DeLaW**

Residence at Cambridge. William Wordsworth. *Fr.* The Prelude; Growth of a Poet's Mind [1805 vers.]. **CP-WorW3**

Residence at Cambridge. William Wordsworth. *Fr.* The Prelude; Growth of a Poet's Mind [1850 vers.]. **CP-WorW3**
"Beside the pleasant Mills of Trompington." **OBRV**
"Evangelist St John my patron was, The." **HAP**, book 3, *ll.* 46–63; **FaBoRV**
(Newton's Statue.) **FaBoRV**, book 3, *ll.* 46–63;
Gentle Spenser. **EPCY**
"It was a dreary morning when the chaise." **FaBoPP; OxAEP-2**
Newton. **ImOP**
Wordsworth Reading Chaucer. **EPCY**

Residence in France ("As oftentimes a river, it might seem"). William Wordsworth. *Fr.* The Prelude; Growth of a Poet's Mind [1805 vers.]. **CP-WorW3**

Residence in France ("Even as a river,—partly (it might seem)"). William Wordsworth. *Fr.* The Prelude; Growth of a Poet's Mind [1850 vers.]. **CP-WorW3**
"Among that band of Officers was one." **ChER**, book 9, *ll.* 288–585;
"France lured me forth; the realm that I had crossed." **FaBoPV**
"I quitted and betook myself to France." **OxAEP-2**

Residence in France and French Revolution. William Wordsworth. *Fr.* The Prelude; Growth of a Poet's Mind [1805 vers.]. **CP-WorW3**

Residence in France and French Revolution. William Wordsworth. *Fr.* The Prelude; Growth of a Poet's Mind [1850 vers.]. **CP-WorW3**
"Cheered with this hope, to Paris I returned." **EnRP**, book 10, *ll.* 48–480, *abr;*

"In France, the Men who for their desperate ends." **OBRV**

"It pleased me more." **OAEL-2**

"It was a beautiful and silent day." **OxAEP-2**, *book* 10, *ll.* 1–736, *abr.*;

"O pleasant exercise of hope and joy!" **OBRV**

"State, as if to stamp the final seal, The." **FaBoPV**

To Coleridge in Sicily. **OBNC**

"When the proud fleet that bears the red-cross flag." **FaBoPV**

Residence in London. William Wordsworth. *Fr.* The Prelude; Growth of a Poet's Mind [1805 vers.]. **CP-WorW3**

Residence in London. William Wordsworth. *Fr.* The Prelude; Growth of a Poet's Mind [1850 vers.]. **CP-WorW3**

"As the black storm upon the mountain-top." **PoEL-4**

"Genius of Burke! forgive the pen seduced." **FaBoPV**

"Pass we from entertainments, that are such." **EnRP**

"Rise up, thou monstrous ant-hill on the plain." **HAP**, *book* 7, *ll.* 149–730, *much abr.*

"Those days are now." **OxAEP-2**

Young Wordsworth's London, The. **FaBoPP**

Residencies. Thomas McGrath. **SP-McGrT**

Resident Dispenser of Bromides, The. Being Called. John Ciardi. **SP-CiarJ**

Residual Years, The. William Everson. **SP-EverW**

Resign the rhapsody, the dream. To the Muse. Robert Louis Stevenson. **CP-StevR**

Resignation. Matthew Arnold. **SP-ArnoM**

"Poet, to whose mighty heart, The." **EPCY**

Resignation. Paul Laurence Dunbar. **CP-DunbP**

Resignation—to Faustus. Arthur Hugh Clough. **SP-ClouA**

Resign'd to live, prepar'd to die. To Mr. Thomas Southern, on His Birth-Day, 1742. Alexander Pope. **CP-PopeA**

Resistance Meeting: Boston Common. Jean Garrigue. **SP-GarrJ**

Resolution. Daniel Gerard Hoffman. **SP-HoffD**

Resolution and Independence. William Wordsworth. **CP-WorW1**

"Now, whether it were by peculiar grace." **Par; UV**

We Poets in Our Youth. **FaBoRV**

Resolutions. Donald Davie. **CP-DavDo**

Resolve. Archie Randolph Ammons. **SP-AmmoA**

Resolve, The. Denise Levertov. **CP-LeveD**

Resolve. Sylvia Plath. **CP-PlatS**

Resolved my annual verse to pay. Stella's Birthday (1723). Jonathan Swift. **CP-SwifJ**

Resolved my gratitude to show. A Panegyric on the Dean. Jonathan Swift. **CP-SwifJ**

Resort. George Oppen. **CP-OppeG**

Resound my voice [*or* voyse], ye woods [*or* wodes] that hear [*or* here] me plain. Sir Thomas Wyatt. **CP-WyatT**

Resource. John Hewitt. **CP-HewiJ**

Resources. John Milton. **FaBoDD** *Fr.* Comus; a Masque Presented at Ludlow Castle.

Respect his obstinacy of undefeat. The Traditionalist. Robert Ranke Graves. **CP-GravR**

Respect my faith, regard my service past. Thomas Campion. **CP-CampT**

Respectability. Robert Browning. **CP-BroR1**

Respectable Burgher, The. Thomas Hardy. **CP-HardT**

Respondez! Walt Whitman. **CP-WhitW**

Response. Paul Laurence Dunbar. **CP-DunbP**

Response, The. John Hewitt. **CP-HewiJ**

Response. John Greenleaf Whittier. **CP-WhitJ**

Response of wild birds, The. Carl Sandburg. *Fr.* The People, Yes. **CP-SandC**

Response to a Letter from France. Stephen Dunn. **SP-DunnS**

Response to a Translation by Longfellow. Robert Browning. **CP-BroR2**

Responsibilities roost on our fingers and toes. Under the Grind. Marge Piercy. **SP-PierM**

Responsibility. Grace Paley. **CP-PaleG**

Responsibilty fell at my feet. And the Scars Will Be Covered. Richard Shelton. **SP-ShelR**

Responsory, A. Thomas Merton. **CP-MertT**

Responsory, 1948, A. Thomas Merton. **CP-MertT; SP-MertT**

Respublica. Geoffrey Hill. **CP-HillG**

Rest. / A violin bow, a breeze. Jane Cooper. *Fr.* The Weather of Six Mornings. **SP-CoopJ**

Rest, The. Margaret Atwood. **SP-AtwM2**

Rest. Robert Herrick. **CP-HerrR**

Rest, The. Ezra Pound. *See* O helpless few in my country.

Rest. Christina Georgina Rossetti. **CP-RosC1**

Rest and Be Thankful! William Wordsworth. **CP-WorW2**

Rest, heart of the tired world. Kenneth Patchen. **CP-PatcK**

Rest House, The. Louis MacNeice. **CP-MacNL**

"Rest is not our business." Come the end or, The. Reminded of Bougainville. Donald Davie. **CP-DavDo**

Rest me with Chinese colours. A Song of the Degrees. Ezra Pound. **SP-PounE**

Rest Refreshes. Robert Herrick. **CP-HerrR**

Rest remains when all is done, / Work and vigil, prayer and fast. There Remaineth Therefore a Rest to the People of God. Christina Georgina Rossetti. **CP-RosC2**

Rest, rest, perturbèd Earth! Invocation to the Earth; February, 1816. William Wordsworth. **CP-WorW2**

Rest, rest; the troubled breast. The Dream. Christina Georgina Rossetti. **CP-RosC3**

Rest you by this various planet. Light & Shadow. Anne Waldman. **SP-WaldA**

Restaurant Car. Louis MacNeice. **CP-MacNL**

Restaurant serving Char-Broiled Meats, The. Ice Cream at Blauenberg. Charles Tomlinson. **CP-TomlC**

Restaurant's expensive and German, but, The. Sugar. Tess Gallagher. **SP-GallT**

Restful place, reviver of my smart, The. Sir Thomas Wyatt. **CP-WyatT**

Resting Figure. Denise Levertov. **CP-LeveD**

Resting-Place, The. William Wordsworth. *Fr.* The River Duddon [A Series of Sonnets]. **CP-WorW2**

Restless Farewell. "Bob Dylan." **CP-DylaB**

Restless Ghost, A. Robert Ranke Graves. **CP-GravR**

Restless Night, The. Thomas McGrath. **SP-McGrT**

Restlessness. David Herbert Lawrence. **CP-LawrD**

Restoration of the Pictures, The. Raissa Maritain, *tr. fr. French by* Thomas Merton. **CP-MertT**

Restore my truth, love, or have done for good. The Poet's Curse. Robert Ranke Graves. **CP-GravR**

'Restore the lock!' she cries; and all around. Alexander Pope. **OXAEP-1** *Fr.* The Rape of the Lock[, an Heroi-Comical Poem]. **CP-PopeA**

Restored, The. Theodore Roethke. **CP-RoetT**

Rests at Night. Emily Dickinson. **CP-DickE**

Result. Charles Bukowski. **SP-BukC3**

Resulting from Magnetic Interference. Richard Hugo. **CP-HugoR**

Results of Thought, The. William Butler Yeats. **CP-YeatW**

Resume unequal days in chilly thrall. Perception as a Guided Missile. Richard Eberhart. **CP-EberR**

Resurgam. Christina Georgina Rossetti. **CP-RosC2**

Resurgam. Allen Tate. **CP-TateA**

Resurgemus, *1850 vers. of* Europe, the 72d and 73d Years of These States. Walt Whitman. **CP-WhitW**

Resurgent sorrow is a sea in the cave, *sl. diff. vers. incl. in* Pijijiapan. Malcolm Lowry. *Fr.* The Comedian. **CP-LowrM**

Resurrection. Margaret Atwood. **SP-AtwM1**

Resurrection. John Donne. **ESCV; OBS** *Fr.* La Corona. **ChIV-2; ESCV; OBS; Son** *Fr.* Holy Sonnets. **CP-DonnJ**

("Moyst with one drop of thy blood, my dry soule.") **ESCV; OBS**

Resurrection, The. Stephen Dunn. **SP-DunnS**

Resurrection, The. Robert Herrick. **CP-HerrR**

Resurrection. Robinson Jeffers. **CP-JefR2**

Resurrection. David Herbert Lawrence. **CP-LawrD**

Resurrection, The. William Butler Yeats.

Two Songs from a Play. **CP-YeatW**, *sect.* 1-2;

Resurrection Eve. Christina Georgina Rossetti. **CP-RosC3**

Resurrection, Imperfect. John Donne. **CP-DonnJ**

Resurrection of the Flesh. David Herbert Lawrence. **CP-LawrD**

Resurrection of the Right Side. Muriel Rukeyser. **CP-RukeM**

Resurrection, Possible, and Probable, The. Robert Herrick. **CP-HerrR**

Resurrections. Archie Randolph Ammons. **SP-AmmoA**

Retaliation. William Cowper, *tr. fr. the Latin of Owen.* **CP-CowpW**

Reticent volcano keeps, The. Emily Dickinson. **CP-DickE**

Reticulations creep upon the slack stream's face. On Sturminster Foot-Bridge. Thomas Hardy. **CP-HardT**

Retire abandon world sd Swami Bhaktivedanta my age 47 approaching half-century. What I'd Like to Do. Allen Ginsberg. **CP-GinsA**

Retired Ballerinas, Central Park West. Lawrence Ferlinghetti. **SP-FerlL**

Retired Cat, The. William Cowper. **CP-CowpW**

Retired Colonel, The. Ted Hughes. **SP-HughT**

Retired [*or* Retyrèd] thought[e]s enjoy their own[e] delight[e]s. Look[e] Home. Robert Southwell. **CP-SoutR**

Retired, with purpose your fair worth to praise. To His Lady, Then Mrs Cary. Ben Jonson. **CP-JonsB**

Retirement. William Cowper. **CP-CowpW**

Retirement. William Cowper. *Fr.* Olney Hymns. **CP-CowpW**

"How sweet, how passing sweet, is solitude!" **OBF**

"I praise the Frenchman, his remark was shrewd." **BLPA**

London Suburbs. **FaBoPP**

Retirement. Karl Shapiro. **SP-ShapK**

Retirement. William Wordsworth. **CP-WorW2**

Retort. Paul Laurence Dunbar. **CP-DunbP**

Retort to Jesus. David Herbert Lawrence. **CP-LawrD**

Retort to Whitman. David Herbert Lawrence. **CP-LawrD**

Retreaded Rhymes. John Hewitt. **CP-HewiJ**

Retreat, The. Charles Bukowski. **SP-BukC1**

Retreat. Phoebe Hesketh. **SP-HeskP**

Retreat by dawn but love this bed—this cult—this wolf & cell of smelling. Alternatives to College. "Bob Dylan." **CP-DylaB**

Retreat from Paradise, The. John Milton. *See* He ended; and thus *Adam* last reply'd.

Retreat of Ita Cagney, The. Michael Hartnett. **SP-HarMi**

Retro. Tom Clark. **SP-ClarT**

Retroduction to American History. Allen Tate. **CP-TateA**

Retrospect Love of Nature Leading to Love of Mankind. William Wordsworth. *Fr.* The Prelude; Growth of a Poet's Mind [1805 vers.]. **CP-WorW3**

Retrospect Love of Nature Leading to Love of Mankind. William Wordsworth. *Fr.* The Prelude; Growth of a Poet's Mind [1850 vers.]. **CP-WorW3**

"But lovelier far than this, the paradise." **OAEL-2**

Fair below Helvellyn, The. **FaBoPP**

Shepherd, The. **OBNC**

"What sounds are those, Helvellyn, that are heard." **EnRP**

Retrospect, The: CWM Elan, 1812. Percy Bysshe Shelley. **CP-ShelP**

Retrospection. Paul Laurence Dunbar. **CP-DunbP**

Retrospective Forelook. Richard Eberhart. **CP-EberR**

Retty used to shake her head. Retty's Phases. Thomas Hardy. **CP-HardT**

Retty's Phases. Thomas Hardy. **CP-HardT**

Return. Robert Creeley. **CP-CreeR**

Return, The. Stephen Dunn. **SP-DunnS**

Return, The. Richard Eberhart. **CP-EberR**

Return, The. Louise Glück. **SP-GlücL**

Return. Robert Ranke Graves. **CP-GravR**

Return, The. Robert Earl Hayden. **CP-HaydR**

Return. Phoebe Hesketh. **SP-HeskP**

Return, The. John Hewitt. **CP-HewiJ**

Return. Robinson Jeffers. **CP-JefR2**

Return, The. Rudyard Kipling. **CP-KiplR**

Return. David Herbert Lawrence. **CP-LawrD**

Return. Audre Lorde. **SP-LordA**

Return. Archibald MacLeish. **CP-MacLA**

Return, The. Louis MacNeice. **CP-MacNL**

Return, The. Thomas McGrath. **SP-McGrT**

Return, The. Edna St. Vincent Millay. **CP-MillE**

Return, The. Mary Oliver. **SP-OlivM**

Return, The. Charles Olson. **CP-OlsoC**

Return. George Oppen. **CP-OppeG**

Return, The. Ezra Pound. **SP-PounE**

Return, The. Kathleen Jessie Raine. **SP-RainK**

Return, The. Theodore Roethke. **CP-RoetT**

Return, The. Theodore Roethke. **NAAL-2** *Fr.* The Lost Son. **CP-RoetT**

Return, The. Muriel Rukeyser. **CP-RukeM**

Return. May Sarton. **SP-SartM**

Return, The. Dabney Stuart. **SP-StuaD**

Return / to brush / their hair. Dead Women. Siv Cedering Fox. **SP-CedeS**

Return, The. Robert Penn Warren. *Fr.* Kentucky Mountain Farm. **SP-WarrR**

Return. William Wordsworth. **HAP** *Fr.* The River Duddon [A Series of Sonnets]. **CP-WorW2**

Return Alpheus, the dread voice is past. John Milton. **PeECV** *Fr.* Lycidas. **CP-MiltJ**

Return: An Elegy, The. Robert Penn Warren. **SP-WarrR**

Return, Content! for fondly I pursued. William Wordsworth. *Fr.* The River Duddon [A Series of Sonnets]. **CP-WorW2**

Return (1885), The. John Hewitt. **CP-HewiJ**

Return from Town, The. Edna St. Vincent Millay. **CP-MillE**

Return of Aphrodite, The. May Sarton. **SP-SartM**

Return of Imray, The. Rudyard Kipling. *Fr.* Life's Handicap.

"Doors were wide, the story saith, The." **CP-KiplR**

Return of Morgan and Fingal, The. Edwin Arlington Robinson. **CP-RobiE**

Return of Odysseus, The. Richard Eberhart. **CP-EberR**

Return of Returns. David Herbert Lawrence. **CP-LawrD**

Return of the Children, The. Rudyard Kipling. **CP-KiplR**

Return of the Evening Grosbeaks, The. Adrienne Rich. **CP-RicAE**

Return of the Goddess [Artemis]. Robert Ranke Graves. **CP-GravR**

Return of the Heroes, The. Walt Whitman. **CP-WhitW**

Return of the Hunters, The. John Yau. **SP-YauJo**

Return of the Native. Marsden Hartley. **CP-HartM**

Return of the Nightingale. Written in May 1791, The. Charlotte Smith. **CP-SmitC**

Return of Ulysses I. John Yau. **SP-YauJo**

Return of Ulysses II. John Yau. **SP-YauJo**

Return, return to Ealing. Lines Written to Martyn Skinner Before His Departure from Oxfordshire in Search of Quiet—1961. Sir John Betjeman. **CP-BetjJ**

Return to D'Ennery; Rain. Derek Walcott. **CP-WalcD**

Return to Hinton. Charles Tomlinson. **CP-TomlC**

Return to Lahore. Louis MacNeice. **CP-MacNL**

Return to Love. Hayden Carruth. **CP-CarHS**

Return to Marsh Street. Thomas McGrath. **SP-McGrT**

Return to Work, The. William Carlos Williams. **CP-WilW1**

Returne my thoughts, why fly you soe? Mary Sidney, Countess of Montgomery Wroth. *Fr.* Part 2. *Fr.* Urania. **CP-WrotM**

Returned from my far-near country, my erstwhile. Louis MacNeice. *Fr.* Memoranda to Horace. **CP-MacNL**

Returned to desk and book, pad and pen, the eyes. James McAuley. *Fr.* The Exile on His Failing Vision. **SP-McAuJ**

Returned to Say. William Stafford. **SP-StafW**

Returning. Wendell Berry. **CP-BerrW**

Returning. Robert Lowell. **SP-LoweR**

Returning a Lost Child. Louise Glück. **SP-GlücL**

Returning after I left my home in childhood. Ho Ch'e Ch'ang, *tr. fr.* Chinese *by* William Carlos Williams *with* David Rafael Wang. **CP-WilW2**

Returning at dawn from the city. The Anniversary Deer. Peter Meinke. **SP-MeinP**

Returning each morning from a timeless world. The Dark Years. Wystan Hugh Auden. **CP-AudeW**

Returning from a swim. Invincible Summer. Chuck Miller. **SP-MillC**

Returning from Church. Kathleen Jessie Raine. **SP-RainK**

Returning from its daily quest, my Spirit. Guido Cavalcanti, *tr. fr. Italian by* Shelley. **CP-ShelP**

(Sonnet: From the Italian of Guido Cavalcanti. Cavalcanti to Dante Alighieri.) **CP-ShelP**

Returning, I find her just the same. Passing Visit to Helen. David Herbert Lawrence. **CP-LawrD**

Returning I live with a huge space. Steve Griffiths. *Fr.* Hymns and Backward Glances. **SP-GrifS**

Returning Janus now prepares. A New Year's Gift for Bec. Jonathan Swift. **CP-SwifJ**

Returning Native. John Updike. **CP-UpdiJ**

Returning North of Vortex. Allen Ginsberg. **CP-GinsA**

Returning to Europe. Howard Nemerov. **CP-NemeH**

Returning to Glasgow after long exile. Glasgow, 1960. "Hugh MacDiarmid." **SP-MacDH**

Returning to Paris with Pissarro. Lawrence Ferlinghetti. **SP-FerlL**

Returning to that house. Birthplace: New Rochelle. George Oppen. **CP-OppeG**

Returning to the Country for a Brief Visit. Allen Ginsberg. **CP-GinsA**

Returning to the room: / I notice how. Margaret Atwood. *Fr.* The Circle Game. **SP-AtwM1**

Returning Turtle. Robert Lowell. **SP-LoweR**

Returns like an expatriate, a defector. April. Richard Shelton. **SP-ShelR**

Returns to a small village. The Age of Miracles. Richard Shelton. *Fr.* The Seven Ages of Man. **SP-ShelR**

Returns to punishment and, we all return, in agonized initiation. Chapman. Muriel Rukeyser. **CP-RukeM**

Reuben Bright. Edwin Arlington Robinson. **CP-RobiE**

Reunion. Charles Bukowski. **SP-BukC2**

Reunion. John Gould Fletcher. **SP-FletJ**

Reunion, A. James Schuyler. **CP-SchuJ**

Reunion. Richard Shelton. **SP-ShelR**

Reunion, The. John Greenleaf Whittier. **CP-WhitJ**

Rêve / sans fin. Samuel Beckett. **CP-BeckS**

Reveal the dragon thro' the human; coursing swift as fire. William Blake. **CP-BlakW**

Revealer, The. Edwin Arlington Robinson. **CP-RobiE**

Reveals to the halting ear. The Voice of the Woodthrush, Played at Half Speed. Daniel Gerard Hoffman. **SP-HoffD**

Reveille. Alfred Edward Housman. **CP-HousA**

Reveille. Malcolm Lowry. **CP-LowrM**

Reveille for a Rockinghorse Poet. Isabella Gardner. **CP-GardI**

Revelation, The. Robert Creeley. **CP-CreeR**

Revelation. Robert Frost. **CP-FrosR**

Revelation. John Updike. **CP-UpdiJ**

Revelation. Robert Penn Warren. **SP-WarrR**

Revelation. John Greenleaf Whittier. **CP-WhitJ**

Revelation, The. William Carlos Williams. **CP-WilW1**

Revelation, The. James Wright. **CP-WrigJ**

Revelation came on Jane, A. Jump-to-Glory Jane. George Meredith. **CP-MerG1**

Revelations every two hours on the Lounge. I Know. John Berryman. **CP-BerrJ**

Revenant, The. Walter de la Mare. **CP-DeLaW**

Revenant. John Hewitt. **CP-HewiJ**

Revenant, The. Archibald MacLeish. **CP-MacLA**

Revenant, The. Louis MacNeice. **CP-MacNL**

Revenge. Robert Herrick. **CP-HerrR**

Revenge. Percy Bysshe Shelley. *Fr.* Original Poetry by Victor and Cazire. **CP-ShelP**

Revenge for Love. Donald Davie. **CP-DavDo**

Revered, beloved—O you that hold. To the Queen. Tennyson. **CP-TennA**

Revered Defender of beauteous Stuart. Epistle to Mr Tytler of Woodhouselee, Author of a Defence of Mary Queen of Scots. Robert Burns. **CP-BurnR**

Reverence. Robert Herrick. **CP-HerrR**

Reverence to Riches. Robert Herrick. **CP-HerrR**

Reverend Butler came by. Madam and the Minister. Langston Hughes. **SP-HughL**

Rev. Dr. Barclay outgrew his profession, The. The Women at Point Sur. Robinson Jeffers. **CP-JefR1**

Rev. Royal Filkin preaches, The. Left Hand Canyon. William Matthews. **SP-MattW**

Reverie. Robert Browning. **CP-BroR2**

Reverie. Edward Estlin Cummings, *tr. from Sophocles'* Electra. **CP-CummE**

Reverie. Walter de la Mare. **CP-DeLaW**

Reverie and Invocation. William Carlos Williams. **CP-WilW2**

Reverie of Poor Susan, The. William Wordsworth. **CP-WorW1**

Reverie on the Harlem River. Langston Hughes. **SP-HughL**

Reversals. Walt Whitman. **CP-WhitW**

Reverse cannot befall. Emily Dickinson. **CP-DickE**

Reverse on the Back Side, The. Ben Jonson. **CP-JonsB**

Reverses. Maya Angelou. **SP-AngeM**

Reversing. Robert Pack. **SP-PackR**

Reversionary. Stevie Smith. **CP-SmitS**

Reversions, always. Hayden Carruth. **CP-CarHS** *Fr.* The Clay Hill Anthology.

Reviewing me without undue elation. A Choice of Weapons. Stanley Jasspon Kunitz. **CP-KuniS**

Revision for Clarinda. Robert Burns. **CP-BurnR**

Revisionist Poem: Machado. Thomas McGrath. **SP-McGrT**

Revisionist Poem—Octavio Paz. Thomas McGrath. **SP-McGrT**

Revisitation, The. Thomas Hardy. **CP-HardT**

Revisited. John Greenleaf Whittier. **CP-WhitJ**

Revival Meeting for Wheelchairs and Stretchers. Leonard Nathan. **SP-NathL**

Revival of Popery. William Wordsworth. *Fr.* Ecclesiastical Sonnets. **CP-WorW2**

Revivalist in Boston, A. Adrienne Rich. **CP-RicAE**

Revivals. Denise Levertov. **CP-LeveD**

Revives in Escudero's constant of the plumbline. Style. Marianne Craig Moore. **CP-MoorM**

Revolt of Islam, The. Percy Bysshe Shelley. **CP-ShelP**
　Child of Twelve, A. **GN**
　Ever as We Sailed. **SeCePo**
　"I could not choose but gaze; a fascination." **ChER**
　"Islands and the mountains in the day, The." **ChER**
　"Lifting the thunder of their acclamation." **ChER**
　"Over the utmost hill at length I sped." **OBWP**
　" 'Soldiers, our brethren and our friends are slain.'." **OBF**
　To Mary. **EnRP**

Revolution, The. Donald Hall. **CP-HallD**

Revolution. Alfred Edward Housman. **CP-HousA**

Revolution. The Beatles. **CP-Beatl**

Revolution, The. George Meredith. **CP-MerG1**
　"Amid the plash of scarlet mud."
　"As mighty thews burst manacles, she went mad."
　"Banners from East, from South."
　"Banners from South, from East."
　"Lo, where hurricane flocks of the North-wind rattle their thunder."
　"Not yet had History's Ætna smoked the skies." **FaPoB,** *sect.* 1–5;
　"Now had her glut of vengeance left her grey."
　"Now was her face white waves in the tempest's sharp flame-blink."
　"She drank what makes man demon at the draught."

Revolution. Anne Waldman. **SP-WaldA**

Revolution at Market Hill, The. Jonathan Swift. **CP-SwifJ**

Revolution in the Revolution in the Revolution. Gary Snyder. **CP-SnydG**

Revolution Is One Form of Social Change. Audre Lorde. **SP-LordA**

Revolution is the Pod. Emily Dickinson. **CP-DickE**

Revolution of the Children. Archibald MacLeish. **CP-MacLA**

"Revolution," said Mr. Adams, The. Canto 32. Ezra Pound. *Fr.* Cantos. **CP-PoCan**

"Revolution" said Mr Adams "took place in the." Canto 50. Ezra Pound. *Fr.* Cantos. **CP-PoCan**

Revolution shall be a toy of peace to you. Child and Mother. Muriel Rukeyser. **CP-RukeM**

Revolution, The / is accomplished. A Poem for Norman Macleod. William Carlos Williams. **CP-WilW1**

Revolutionary, The. David Herbert Lawrence. **CP-LawrD**

Revolutionary Petunias. Alice Walker. **CP-WalkA**

Revolutionists Stop for Orangeade, The. Wallace Stevens. **CP-StevW**

Revolutions. William Shakespeare. *See* Sonnet 60: "Like as the waves make towards the pebbled shore."

Revolutions as Such! David Herbert Lawrence. **CP-LawrD**

Revolving in oval loops of solar speed. The Dead. Sylvia Plath. **CP-PlatS**

Revolving Meditation. Stanley Jasspon Kunitz. **CP-KuniS**

Revulsion. Donald Davie. **CP-DavDo**

Revulsion. Thomas Hardy. **CP-HardT**

Rewaking, The. William Carlos Williams. **CP-WilW2**

Reward, The. John Greenleaf Whittier. **CP-WhitJ**

Rewarded porters opening their smiles, The. On the Railway Platform. Randall Jarrell. **CP-JarrR**

Rewards. Robert Herrick. **CP-HerrR**

Rewards and Punishments. Robert Herrick. **CP-HerrR**

Rex. Ralph Waldo Emerson. **CP-EmerR**

Rexroth and Patchen and Fearing—their mothers. Kenneths. John Updike. **CP-UpdiJ**

Rexroth's face reflecting human. Scribble. Allen Ginsberg. **CP-GinsA**

Reynolds, come, thy pencil prove. *after* Anacreon, Ode 69; *see also* "Painter, by unmatch'd desert." William Wordsworth. **CP-WorW1**

Rhapsody. Frank O'Hara. **SP-OharF**

Rhapsody of Life's Progress, A. Elizabeth Barrett Browning. **CP-BroEB**

Rhapsody on a Windy Night. Thomas Stearns Eliot. **CP-ElioT**

Rhapsody on Irish Themes, A. Randall Jarrell. **CP-JarrR**

Rhea. Robert Ranke Graves. **CP-GravR**

Rhenish Winter. Charles Tomlinson. **CP-TomlC**

Rhetoric. Marilyn Hacker. **SP-HackM**

Rhine-Land. George Meredith. **CP-MerG2**

Rhinoceros, The. Ogden Nash. **CP-NashO**

Rhodes Memorial, Table Mountain. Rudyard Kipling. **CP-KiplR**

Rhododendrons. Tess Gallagher. **SP-GallT**

Rhodora, The [On Being Asked Whence Is the Flower]. Ralph Waldo Emerson. **CP-EmerR**

Rhondda, The. Alun Lewis. **CP-LewiA**

Rhopaloceral. Hayden Carruth. *Fr.* Poetical Abstracts. **CP-CarHS**

Rhyme. Louise Bogan. **CP-BogaL**

Rhyme, The. Robert Creeley. **CP-CreeR**

Rhyme. Sylvia Plath. **CP-PlatS**

Rhyme About an Electrical Advertising Sign, A. Nicholas Vachel Lindsay. **CP-LindV**

Rhyme? and Reason? "Lewis Carroll." **CP-CarrL**

Rhyme for a Child Viewing a Naked Venus in a Painting of "The Judgement of Paris." Robert Browning. **CP-BroR2**

Rhyme for All Zionists, A. Nicholas Vachel Lindsay. **CP-LindV**
　"Ahasuerus in his prime."
　"He harried lions up the peaks."

Rhyme for Blake, A. John Hewitt. **CP-HewiJ**

Rhyme for Christmas Morning, A. John Hewitt. **CP-HewiJ**

Rhyme is after, The. For W.C.W. Robert Creeley. **CP-CreeR**

Rhyme of the Duchess May. Elizabeth Barrett Browning. **CP-BroEB**

Rhyme of the poet, The. Ralph Waldo Emerson. **PoEL-4** *Fr.* Merlin. **CP-EmerR**

Rhyme of the Three Captains, The. Rudyard Kipling. **CP-KiplR**

Rhyme of the Three Sealers, The. Rudyard Kipling. **CP-KiplR**

Rhyme on Edward Burne-Jones. Robert Browning. **CP-BroR2**

Rhyme [*or* Rime], the rack of finest wits. A Fit of Rhyme [*or* Rime] against Rhyme [*or* Rime]. Ben Jonson. **CP-JonsB**

Rhymed Address: The Lobster. William Carlos Williams. **CP-WilW1**

Rhymed Address to All Renegade Campbellites, Exhorting Them to Return, A. Nicholas Vachel Lindsay. *Fr.* Alexander Campbell. **CP-LindV**
"As I built cob-houses with small cousins on the floor."
"I walk the forest by the Daniel Boone trail."
"Like the woods of old Kentucky."
"O prodigal son, O recreant daughter."

Rhymer's Reply: Incense and Splendor, The. Nicholas Vachel Lindsay. *Fr.* An Argument. **CP-LindV**

Rhymes. Charles Tomlinson. **CP-TomlC**

Rhyming Exercises. Robert Browning. **CP-BroR2**

Rhythm, The. Robert Creeley. **CP-CreeR**

Rhythmic pincer-jaws clench. I Give Death to a Son. Phoebe Hesketh. **SP-HeskP**

Rib, The. James Dickey. **CP-DickJ**

Ribblesdale. Gerard Manley Hopkins. **CP-HopkG**

Ribbons. Charles Kenneth Williams. **CP-WillC**

Ribbons of the Year. Emily Dickinson. **CP-DickE**

Ribh at the Tomb of Baile and Aillinn. William Butler Yeats. **CP-YeatW**

Ribh Considers Christian Love Insufficient. William Butler Yeats. **CP-YeatW**

Ribh Denounces Patrick. William Butler Yeats. **CP-YeatW**

Ribh in Ecstasy. William Butler Yeats. **CP-YeatW**

Rice. Mary Oliver. **SP-OlivM**

Rich, The. Charles Tomlinson. **CP-TomlC**

Rich and poor / of every color and idea. Boilermakers. Gilbert Sorrentino. **SP-SorrG**

Rich fools there be, whose base and filthy heart. Sonnet 24. Sir Philip Sidney. *Fr.* Astrophil and Stella. **SP-SidnP**

Rich Georgian farmers send their sons. Tbilisi. John Updike. *Fr.* Postcards from Soviet Cities. **CP-UpdiJ**

Rich have money; Give to the Rich!, The. October. Gary Snyder. *Fr.* Six Years. **CP-SnydG**

Rich labour is the struggle to be wise. The Discipline of Wisdom. George Meredith. **CP-MerG1**

Rich *Lazarus!* richer in those gems, thy teares. Upon Lazarus His Teares. Richard Crashaw. **CP-CrasR**

Rich man, poor man, beggarman, thief. Malcolm Lowry. **CP-LowrM**

Rich man wanted breakfast, The. White Lemons. Gilbert Sorrentino. **SP-SorrG**

Rich man's Heir, his father's spirit fled, The. The Grief of an Heir. William Cowper. **CP-CowpW**

Rich profusion of familiar flowers, A. The Garden of Childhood. May Sarton. **SP-SartM**

Rich, thou hadst many lovers—poor, hast none. On Female Inconstancy. *Unknown, tr. fr. Greek by* William Cowper. **CP-CowpW**

Richard, Fragments. Gerard Manley Hopkins. **CP-HopkG**

Richard. Gerard Manley Hopkins. **CP-HopkG**

Richard Coeur-de-Lion. Louis Aragon, *tr. fr. French by* Louis MacNeice. **CP-MacNL**

Richard Cory. Edwin Arlington Robinson. **CP-RobiE**

Richard Hunt's "Arachne." Robert Earl Hayden. **CP-HaydR**

Richard Jefferies. Wystan Hugh Auden. **CP-AudWJ**

Richard Lionheart. George Meredith. **CP-MerG2**

Richard, Oremus. James Liddy. **CP-LiddJ**

Richard Roe and John Doe. Robert Ranke Graves. **CP-GravR**

Richard Roe wished himself Solomon. Richard Roe and John Doe. Robert Ranke Graves. **CP-GravR**

Richard Rolle. Marsden Hartley. **CP-HartM**

Richard I. William Wordsworth. *Fr.* Ecclesiastical Sonnets. **CP-WorW2**

Richard would wait till George the tale should ask. Ruth. George Crabbe. **SP-CrabG** *Fr.* Tales of the Hall.

Richard's Youth. George Crabbe. **SP-CrabG** *Fr.* Tales of the Hall.

Richer than Miser o'er his countless hoards. Lines Written at the King's Arms, Ross, Formerly the House of the "Man of Ross." Samuel Taylor Coleridge. **CP-ColeS**

Riches. William Blake. **CP-BlakW**

Riches. David Herbert Lawrence. **CP-LawrD**

Riches and Poverty. Robert Herrick. **CP-HerrR**

Riches I hold in light esteem. The Old Stoic. Emily Brontë. **CP-BronE**

Riches of the poet are equal to his poetry, The. The Poet. Delmore Schwartz. **SP-SchwD**

Riches we find inside will be in rich light, The. Approaching the Castle. Richard Hugo. **CP-HugoR**

Richest moment / is at the very beginning, The. Contractions. Steve Griffiths. **SP-GrifS**

Richmond. John Updike. **CP-UpdiJ**

Rick De Travaille. Lewis Turco. **SM** *Fr.* Bordello. **SP-TurcL**

Ricky was "L" but he's home with the flu. Love. Shel Silverstein. **SP-SilS2**

Rid of a vexing and a heavy load. Michelangelo Buonarroti, *tr. fr. Italian by* William Wordsworth. **CP-WorW1**

Riddle, The. Wystan Hugh Auden. **CP-AudeW**

Riddle, A. "Lewis Carroll." **CP-CarrL**

Riddle, The. Robert Creeley. **CP-CreeR**

Riddle, A. Walter de la Mare. **CP-DeLaW**

Riddle, The. Thomas Hardy. **CP-HardT**

Riddle: "I am just two and two, I am warm, I am cold." William Cowper. **CP-CowpW**

Riddle, The. Louis MacNeice. **CP-MacNL**

Riddle, A. Richard Wilbur. **CP-WilbR**

Riddle for Men, The. George Meredith. **CP-MerG1**

Riddle in the Garden. Robert Penn Warren. **SP-WarrR**

Riddle me raddle. The Babe's Riddle. Archibald MacLeish. *Fr.* Songs for Eve. **CP-MacLA**

Riddle me raddle. The Serpent's Riddle. Archibald MacLeish. *Fr.* Songs for Eve. **CP-MacLA**

Riddle of the World. Alexander Pope. *See* Know then thyself, presume not God to scan.

Riddle: "So small it is, there must be at least two." William DeWitt Snodgrass. **SP-SnodW**

Riddle Song, A. Walt Whitman. **CP-WhitW**

Riddle the Sphinx Forgot, A. Howard Nemerov. **CP-NemeH**

Riddle we can guess, The. Emily Dickinson. **CP-DickE**

Riddlers, The. Walter de la Mare. **CP-DeLaW**

Riddles. Jonathan Swift. **CP-SwifJ**
"All-ruling tyrant of the earth."
"Because I am by nature blind."
"By fate exalted high in place."
"Deprived of root, and branch, and rind."
Gulf of All Human Possessions, The.
"In youth exalted high in air."
"Joy of man, the pride of brutes, The."
Louisa to Strephon.
"Though I, alas! a prisoner be."

Riddles and Whims. Carl Sandburg. **CP-SandC**

Riddling Letter, A ("Sir, / Pray discruciate what follows: / The dullest beast, and gentleman's liquor"). Jonathan Swift. **CP-SwifJ**

Ride, The. Stevie Smith. **CP-SmitS**

Ride, The. Richard Wilbur. **CP-WilbR**

Ride a black horse with tan feet. Striped Cats, Old Men and Proud Stockings. Carl Sandburg. **CP-SandC**

Ride 'em, and, by the ride, down all night, all. Adamo Me. Charles Olson. **CP-OlsoC**

Ride to Stirling, The. Sir Walter Scott. **SP-ScotW** *Fr.* The Lady of the Lake.

Ride with an idle whip, ride with an unused heel. Rudyard Kipling. **CP-KiplR** *Fr.* The Conversion of Aurelian McGoggin. *Fr.* Plain Tales from the Hills.

"Ride you this fair cool morning?" said the Squire. Ellen. George Crabbe. **SP-CrabG** *Fr.* Tales of the Hall.

Riders. Robert Frost. **CP-FrosR**

Riders, The. John Hewitt. **CP-HewiJ**

Riders of the wind, The. Bitter Summer Thoughts. Carl Sandburg. **CP-SandC**

Riders to the Blood-Red Wrath. Gwendolyn Brooks. **SP-BrooG**

Rides into town. The Age of Despair. Richard Shelton. *Fr.* The Seven Ages of Man. **SP-ShelR**

Ridiculous Rose. Shel Silverstein. **SP-SilS2**

Riding a horse up a narrow gorge I pick. The Black Hills. William Everson. **SP-EverW**

Riding against the east. To Beachey, 1912. Carl Sandburg. **CP-SandC**

Riding along in the beautiful day (there go two. Letter Poem #2. James Schuyler. **CP-SchuJ**

Riding from Topeka, Kansas, to Manhattan, Kansas. Mockers Go to Kansas in Spring. Carl Sandburg. **CP-SandC**

Riding home from credulous blue domes. Terminal. Sylvia Plath. **CP-PlatS**

Riding in Cars. Louis MacNeice. *Fr.* Out of the Picture. **CP-MacNL**

Riding in glittering machines they didn't build. In the Parking Lot of the Supermarket. Chuck Miller. **SP-MillC**

Riding on a Railroad Train. Ogden Nash. **CP-NashO**

Riding out of the built-up. Roy Fisher. **SP-FishR** *Fr.* Handsworth Liberties.

Riding slowly along the banks of a canal. The Ride. Stevie Smith. **CP-SmitS**

Riding the black express from heaven to hell. Lucifer in the Train. Adrienne Rich. **CP-RicAE**

Riding the bus in the evening again. Chuck Miller. **SP-MillC**

Riding the Elevator into the Sky. Anne Sexton. **CP-SextA**

Riding the horse as was my wont. Don't Sign Anything. Robert Creeley. **CP-CreeR**

Riding to Town. Paul Laurence Dunbar. **CP-DunbP**

Riding whip, a glove wait on the table, A. 1911. Stephen Berg. **SP-BergS**

Ridway robbed Duncote of three hundred pound. On a Robbery. Ben Jonson. **CP-JonsB**

Rien nul / n'aura été. Samuel Beckett. **CP-BeckS**

Rievaulx: St. Ailred. Thomas Merton. **CP-MertT**

Rifkin Movement. Richard Eberhart. **CP-EberR**

Rifle goes up: / Does what a rifle does. The Soldier and the Star. Kenneth Patchen. **CP-PatcK**

Rifles are rammed full; / Bowie knives are sharpened. The Song of Natchez Under the Hill. John Gould Fletcher. **SP-FletJ**

Rift, The. Thomas Hardy. **CP-HardT**

Rigamarole. William Carlos Williams. **CP-WilW1**

Rigged poker-stiff on her back. All the Dead Dears. Sylvia Plath. **CP-PlatS**

Right. William Matthews. **SP-MattW**

Right after the Moon was got rid of, a moon was brought on. The. Moon "Continued." Kenneth Patchen. **CP-PatcK**

Right Arm, The. Paul Muldoon. **CP-MuldP**

Right arm: a many-splendored. Peter. James Merrill. **SP-MerrJ**

Right down the shocked street with a siren-blast. A Fire-Truck. Richard Wilbur. **CP-WilbR**

Right foot lets / The left know, The. Ninth Mile. James McAuley. *Fr.* Ten-Mile Run. **SP-McAuJ**

Right fresshe flowr, whos I ben have and shal. The Sorrow of Troilus. Geoffrey Chaucer. **PoEL-1** *Fr.* Troilus and Criseyde [*or* Criseide]. **CP-ChauG**

Right from the start he is dressed in his best—his blacks and his whites. A March Calf. Ted Hughes. **SP-HughT**

Right Hand, The. Robert Herrick. **CP-HerrR**

Right here the other night something. Edward Estlin Cummings. **CP-CummE**

Right in My Eye. Charles Olson. **CP-OlsoC**

Right in the track where Sherman. Howard at Atlanta. John Greenleaf Whittier. **CP-WhitJ**

Right in the Trail. Gary Snyder. **CP-SnydG**

Right Lads, The. Donald Davie. **CP-DavDo**

Right Madness on Skye, The. Richard Hugo. **CP-HugoR**

Right of Way, The. William Carlos Williams. **CP-WilW1**

Right off we started inflicting history. This Is a Sin. Charles Kenneth Williams. **CP-WillC**

Right on that branch we saw the snowy owl. The Cracked Apple Tree. Robert Pack. **SP-PackR**

Right out / of / Das Kapital. Song—3/4 time. Louis Zukofsky. *Fr.* 29 Songs. **CP-ZukLS**

Right Possessor, The. Thom Gunn. **CP-GunnT**

Right, Sir! your text I'll prove it true. The Calf. Robert Burns. **CP-BurnR**

Right Thing, The. Theodore Roethke. **CP-RoetT**

Right Thinking Man. Marge Piercy. **SP-PierM**

Right to Die, The. Paul Laurence Dunbar. **CP-DunbP**

Right to Grief, The. Carl Sandburg. **CP-SandC**

Right to Life. Marge Piercy. **SP-PierM**

Right to Life, The: What Can the White Man Say to the Black Woman? Alice Walker. **CP-WalkA**

Right to perish might be thought, The. Emily Dickinson. **CP-DickE**

Right to the end, that man, he was so hot. The Miracle. Thom Gunn. **CP-GunnT**

Right true it is and said full yore ago. Sir Thomas Wyatt. **CP-WyatT**

Right trusty, and so forth,—We let you to know. Apollo to the Dean. Jonathan Swift. **CP-SwifJ**

Right under their noses, the green. The Dusk of Horses. James Dickey. **CP-DickJ**

Right up there this side the Five Chimneys Corners. Block. Hayden Carruth. **CP-CarHS**

Right up under our noses, roses. Intimacy. Al Young. **CP-YounA**

Right well I wote [*or* wrote] most mighty Soueraine [*or* soveraine]. Edmund Spenser. **NoSic; OAEL-1** *Fr.* The Faerie Queene. **CP-Spens**

Right Wing Sympathies. Donald Davie. **CP-DavDo**

Rights of Woman—Spoken by Miss Fontenelle on Her Benefit Night, The. Robert Burns. **CP-BurnR**

Right's Security. Paul Laurence Dunbar. **CP-DunbP**

Rigid and bald as a dead rat's tail. Aor Against the Bad Reviewer. James McAuley. **SP-McAuJ**

Rigid sleeps the house in darkness, I alone. Late at Night. David Herbert Lawrence. **CP-LawrD**

Rigidity nonlife the meaning neither of life. The Thaw. Hayden Carruth. *Fr.* Contra Mortem. **CP-CarHL**

Rigor Vitus. Bill Knott. **SP-KnotB**

Rigorists. Marianne Craig Moore. **CP-MoorM**

Rijl. Tess Gallagher. **SP-GallT**

Rikki-Tikki-Tavi. Rudyard Kipling. *Fr.* The Jungle Book.
   "At the hole where he went in." **CP-KiplR**
   Darzee's Chaunt. **CP-KiplR**

Rilke, if you had known that I was trying. To Rilke. Alun Lewis. **CP-LewiA**

Rilke thought it was the human part. The Infinite Reason. Archibald MacLeish. **CP-MacLA**

Rilke's Epitaph. Thomas Merton. **CP-MertT**

Rillons, Rillettes. Richard Wilbur. **CP-WilbR**

Rillons, Rillettes, they taste the same. Rillons, Rillettes. Richard Wilbur. **CP-WilbR**

Rimbaud. Wystan Hugh Auden. **CP-AudeW**

Rimbaud Dead. Patti Smith. **SP-SmitP**

Rime Intrinsica, Fontmell Magna, Sturminster Newton and Melbury Bubb. Dorset. Sir John Betjeman. **CP-BetjJ**

Rime of the Ancient Mariner, The. Samuel Taylor Coleridge. **CP-ColeS**
   "Farewell, farewell! but this I tell." **PFP**
   "For when it dawn'd—they dropp'd their arms." **UnS**
   He Prayeth Best. **FaPON**
   He Prayeth Well. **BoTP**
   "This Hermit good lives in that wood." **Poetr**

Rimini. Rudyard Kipling. **CP-KiplR** *Fr.* Puck of Pook's Hill.

Rimmon. Rudyard Kipling. **CP-KiplR**

Rimrock, Where It Is. Hayden Carruth. **CP-CarHS**

Ring, The. Kathleen Jessie Raine. *Fr.* The Marriage of Psyche. **SP-RainK**

Ring, The. Diane Wakoski. **SP-WakoD**

Ring my friend I said you'd call Doctor Robert. Doctor Robert. John Lennon *and* Paul McCartney. **CP-Beatl**

Ring of, The. Charles Olson. **CP-OlsoC; SP-OlsoC**

Ring of a doorbell, The. Being Here. Miller Williams. **SP-WillM**

Ring of Irony, The. Diane Wakoski. **SP-WakoD**

Ring Out the Old, Ring In the New. Tennyson. *See* Ring out, wild bells, to the wild sky.

Ring out the Old, Ring in the New, but Don't Get Caught in Between. Ogden Nash. **CP-NashO**
   First Chime.
   Second Chime.

Ring out, wild bells, to the wild sky. Tennyson. **FaPON**, *sect.* 106, *ll.* 1–8; **BLPL; EBEvV; EBVV; FHYEP; FaFP; FaPoR; FiP; HBV; ImPo; LiTB; MeMBP; OAEL-2; OFD; OXAEP-2; PGD; PeECV; PlP; SBVL; SeCeV; TRV; TrGrPo; WBLP** *Fr.* In Memoriam A. H. H. **CP-TennA**
   (Ring Out the Old, Ring In the New.) **WBLP**

Ring out, ye bells! Christmas Carol. Paul Laurence Dunbar. **CP-DunbP**

Ring Posy, A. Christina Georgina Rossetti. **CP-RosC1**

Ring Presented to Julia, A. Robert Herrick. **CP-HerrR**

Ring the big bells. Contemporary Announcement. Maya Angelou. **SP-AngeM**

Ring to me Cecilia sends, A. On Receiving from a Lady a Present of a Ring. George Crabbe. **SP-CrabG**

Ring upon her finger, / Walks the bride, A. Christina Georgina Rossetti. **CP-RosC2**

"Ring us up when you want to see us. . . "—"Sure." John Berryman. *Fr.* Sonnets to Chris. **CP-BerrJ**

Ringed / with monstrous / a doomed. Edward Estlin Cummings. **CP-CummE**

Ringing the Bells. Anne Sexton. **CP-SextA**

Ringless. Diane Wakoski. **SP-WakoD**

Ringling. Muriel Rukeyser. **CP-RukeM**

Ringling Brothers, Barnum and Bailey. Mona Van Duyn. **SP-VanDM**

Rings of iron gray smoke; a woman's steel face. . . looking. . . looking. Fog Portrait. Carl Sandburg. **CP-SandC**

Rinsing our mouths. A Good Man in a Bad Time. Archibald MacLeish. **CP-MacLA**

Rintrah roars & shakes his fires in the burdend air. The Argument. William Blake. *Fr.* The Marriage of Heaven and Hell. **CP-BlakW**

Rio de Janeiro. Four Sambas. *Unknown, tr. fr. Portuguese by* Elizabeth Bishop. **CP-BishE**

Rio de Janeiro. John Updike. **CP-UpdiJ**

Riot: 60's. Maya Angelou. **SP-AngeM**

RIP. James Wright. **CP-WrigJ**

Rip, whoosh, wing-whistle: and out of. Sunset Walk in Thaw-Time in Vermont. Robert Penn Warren. **SP-WarrR**

Riparian origins. . . did you know. Amazonian. Donald Davie. **CP-DavDo**

Riparto d'Assalto. Ernest Hemingway. **CP-HemiE**

Ripe apples were caught like red fish in the nets. The Great Scarf of Birds. John Updike. **CP-UpdiJ**

Ripe Corn. Carl Sandburg. **CP-SandC**

Ripe grassheads bend in the starlight, The. On the Hill Late at Night. Wendell Berry. **CP-BerrW**

Ripe 'sparagrass. Asparagus. Jonathan Swift. *Fr.* Verses Made for the Women Who Cry Apples, etc. **CP-SwifJ**

Ripening. Wendell Berry. **CP-BerrW**

Ripening there / among the entanglement of leaves. Green Quinces. Charles Tomlinson. **CP-TomlC**

Ripetizione. Christina Georgina Rossetti. *Fr.* Il Rosseggiar Dell'Oriente Canzoniere. **CP-RosC3**

Riposte. Marilyn Hacker. **SP-HackM**

Riposte. William Carlos Williams. **CP-WilW1**

Ripple, The. Denise Levertov. **CP-LeveD**

Ripple Song, A. Rudyard Kipling. **CP-KiplR** *Fr.* The Undertakers. *Fr.* The Second Jungle Book.

Ripples on the Surface. Gary Snyder. **CP-SnydG**

Rippling eyelids. Robert Creeley. **CP-CreeR**

Riprap. Gary Snyder. **CP-SnydG**

Rise. Phoebe Hesketh. **SP-HeskP**

Rise, crowned with light, imperial Salem, rise! Alexander Pope. **GoBC; WGRP** *Fr.* Messiah [a Sacred Eclogue, in Imitation of Virgil's Pollio]. **CP-PopeA**

Rise from your bed of langour. Company. Stevie Smith. **CP-SmitS**

Rise heart; thy Lord is risen. Sing his praise. Easter. George Herbert. **CP-HerbG**

Rise, Heire of fresh Eternity. Easter Day. Richard Crashaw. **CP-CrasR**

Rise, Household-gods, and let us goe. To His Household Gods. Robert Herrick. **CP-HerrR**

Rise in the World, A. David Herbert Lawrence. **CP-LawrD**

Rise O Days from Your Fathomless Deeps. Walt Whitman. **CP-WhitW**

Rise, oh, rise! The daylight dies. Bruno's Song. "Lewis Carroll." **CP-CarrL** *Fr.* Sylvie and Bruno.

Rise, rise from sluggishness, fly fast my Deere. Mary Sidney, Countess of Montgomery Wroth. *Fr.* Part 1. *Fr.* Urania. **CP-WrotM**

Rise, Royall SION! rise and sing. *ad. fr. the Medieval* De Venerabili Sacramento. Richard Crashaw. **CP-CrasR**

Rise then, immortall maid! *Religion* rise! Upon the Ensuing Treatises [of Mr. Shelford]. Richard Crashaw. **CP-CrasR**

Rise!—they *have* risen: of brave Aneurin ask. Struggle of the Britons against the Barbarians. William Wordsworth. *Fr.* Ecclesiastical Sonnets. **CP-WorW2**

Rise, thou best and brightest morning! Hymn for New Year's Day. Richard Crashaw. **CP-CrasR**

Rise to capture the. Charles Henri Ford. **SP-FordC** *Fr.* Secret Haiku.

Rise up and proclaim themselves, and his skin. Hayden Carruth. *Fr.* The Sleeping Beauty. **CP-CarHL**

Rise up, poets, phalanx of the just. The Killer. Richard Eberhart. **CP-EberR**

Rise up, thou monstrous ant-hill on the plain. William Wordsworth. **HAP,** book 7, ll. 149–730, *much abr.*; *Fr.* Residence in London. *Fr.* The Prelude; Growth of a Poet's Mind [1850 vers.]. **CP-WorW3**

Risen. Ted Hughes. **SP-HughT**

Risen by weaving works to this. Webbe. Roy Fisher. **SP-FishR** *Fr.* Five Pilgrims in the Prologue to the Canterbury Tales.

Risen Christ! Once more, The. Geoffrey Hill. *Fr.* Scenes with Harlequins. **CP-HillG**

Risen Image Shines, The. Muriel Rukeyser. **CP-RukeM**

Risen in a / welter of waters. The Birth of Venus. Muriel Rukeyser. **CP-RukeM**

Risen Lord, The. David Herbert Lawrence. **CP-LawrD**

Rises at five, just when a late moon. The Insomniac Sleeps Well for Once and. Hayden Carruth. **CP-CarHS**

Risest thou thus, dim dawn, again. Tennyson. **EBVV** *Fr.* In Memoriam A. H. H. **CP-TennA**

Risest thou thus, dim dawn, again. Tennyson. **OBNC; PeECV; PoEL-5** *Fr.* In Memoriam A. H. H. **CP-TennA**

Risible nice go when from mud a crony. Catullus. *See* Carmen 53: "I laughed. Calvus. I laughed today."

Rising. Wendell Berry. **CP-BerrW**
 "And that is our story."
 "Any man's death could end the story."
 "Boy must learn the man, The."
 "Ended, a story is history."
 "Having danced until nearly."
 "I worked by will then, he."

Rising a Little. Kenneth Patchen. **CP-PatcK**

Rising cost of heart attacks. Different, The. John Yau. **SP-YauJo** *Fr.* Scenes from the Life of Boullee.

Rising early and walking in the garden. On Rising Early. Robert Ranke Graves. **CP-GravR**

Rising hills, the slopes, The. For the Children. Gary Snyder. **CP-SnydG**

Rising in the morning. Pane Caldo. Erica Jong. **SP-JongE**

Rising in the strained, gloomy dawn. Rising Up. Chuck Miller. **SP-MillC**

Rising of the Storm, The. Paul Laurence Dunbar. **CP-DunbP**

Rising out of the summer woods. The Colony. Lewis Turco. **SP-TurcL**

Rising Over Night-Blackened Detroit Streets. Allen Ginsberg. **CP-GinsA**

Rising Sun, The. Randall Jarrell. **CP-JarrR**

Rising, the river. Wendell Berry. *Fr.* Window Poems. **CP-BerrW**

Rising Up. Chuck Miller. **SP-MillC**

Risk. Joseph Ceravolo. **SP-CeraJ**

Risk, The. Robert Ranke Graves. **CP-GravR**

Risk, The. Anne Sexton. **CP-SextA**

Risk is the Hair that holds the Tun. Emily Dickinson. **CP-DickE**

Risks of Immortality, The. Emily Dickinson. **SP-DickE**

Rita Hayworth & Stan Getz. Motion, 1953. Tom Clark. **SP-ClarT**

Rita May. "Bob Dylan" *and* Jacques Levy. **CP-DylaB**

Rite. John Hewitt. **CP-HewiJ**

Rite. Muriel Rukeyser. **CP-RukeM**

Rite, Lubitavish, Glenaan. John Hewitt. **CP-HewiJ**

Rites, The. Robert Creeley. **CP-CreeR**

Rites deriv'd from ancient days, The. Translations from the *Medea* of Euripedes. Euripides, *tr. by* Samuel Johnson. **CP-JohnS** *Fr.* Medea. **CP-JefR3,** *tr. by* Robinson Jeffers;

Rites for Cousin Vit, The. Gwendolyn Brooks. **SP-BrooG** *Fr.* The Womanhood.

Rites for the Extrusion of a Leper. Thomas Merton. **CP-MertT**

Rites of Darkness, The. Kenneth Patchen. **CP-PatcK**

Rites of Passage. Thom Gunn. **CP-GunnT**

Rites of Passage. Audre Lorde. **SP-LordA**

Rites of War. Louis MacNeice. **CP-MacNL**

Ritner. John Greenleaf Whittier. **CP-WhitJ**

Ritornelli. Geoffrey Hill. **CP-HillG**

Ritornello. Charles Tomlinson. **CP-TomlC**

Ritratto. Erica Jong. **SP-JongE**

Ritual. Bill Knott. **SP-KnotB**

Ritual. James McAuley. **SP-McAuJ**

Ritual of Memories, The. Tess Gallagher. **SP-GallT**

Ritual to Read to Each Other, A. William Stafford. **SP-StafW**

Ritualists, The. William Carlos Williams. **CP-WilW2**

Rituals. Miller Williams. **SP-WillM**

Rival, The. Thomas Hardy. **CP-HardT**

Rival, The. Sylvia Plath. **CP-PlatS**

Rivals, The. Paul Laurence Dunbar. **CP-DunbP**

Rivals, The. Phoebe Hesketh. **SP-HeskP**

Rivals. Christina Georgina Rossetti. **CP-RosC3**

River, The. John Ciardi. **SP-CiarJ**

River, The. Hart Crane. **AmPP; CMoP; GOA; MoAB; MoAmPo; NOBA; OxBA; PrIm** *Fr.* Powhatan's Daughter. *Fr.* The Bridge. **CP-CranH**
 "Down, down—born pioneers in time's despite." **TrGrPo**

River, The. Louise McNeill. **SP-McNeL**

River, The. Frederick Morgan. **SP-MorgF**
 "As the sun dims we begin to think."
 "Decisions of afternoon: as."
 "Fresh June morning, A."
 "Morning. A river view."
 "Now you are holding a book."
 "Sleeping, we boarded a boat."
 "Sun tells stories, The."

"Two bodies in the river."

"Voice spoke in the night, A."

River, The, *in imitation of* Cowley. Alexander Pope. **CP-PopeA**

River, The. Dabney Stuart. **SP-StuaD**

River and Light. Siv Cedering Fox. **SP-CedeS**

River at Clone its direction, The. The Roses of Parnell & Mellowes. James Liddy. **CP-LiddJ**

River Bridged and Forgot, The. Wendell Berry. **CP-BerrW**

River Deben, The. Stevie Smith. **CP-SmitS**

River Down Home, The. James Wright. **CP-WrigJ**

River Duddon [A Series of Sonnets], The. William Wordsworth. **CP-WorW2**

   American Tradition.

   Change Me, Some God, Into That Breathing Rose! **Son**

   "Child of the clouds! remote from every taint."

   Conclusion: "But here no cannon thunders to the gale."

   Faery Chasm, The.

   "Fallen, and diffused into a shapeless heap."

   Flowers.

   "From this deep chasm, where quivering sunbeams play."

   Hints for the Fancy.

   "How shall I paint thee?—Be this naked stone."

   "I thought of Thee, my partner and my guide." **EnRP; FaBoPP; FaBoRV; NOBE; OBEV; OBNC; SeCePo**

   (After-Thought.) **EnRP; OBNC; SeCePo**

   (To the River Duddon: After-Thought.) **FaBoPP**

   (Valediction to the River Duddon.) **NOBE**

   (Valedictory Sonnet to the River Duddon.) **OBEV**

   Journey Renewed.

   "KIRK OF ULPHA to the pilgrim's eye, The."

   "Methinks 'twere no unprecedented feat."

   "No record tells of lance opposed to lance."

   "Not envying Latian shades—if yet they throw."

   "Not hurled precipitous from steep to steep."

   "O mountain Stream! the Shepherd and his Cot."

   Open Prospect.

   Plain of Donnerdale, The.

   Resting-Place, The.

   Return. **HAP**

   "Return, Content! for fondly I pursued."

   Same Subject, The.

   Seathwaite Chapel.

   Sheep-Washing.

   "Sole listener, Duddon! to the breeze that played."

   Stepping-Stones, The.

   "Take, cradled Nursling of the mountains, take."

   To the Rev. Dr Wordsworth (with the Sonnets to the River Duddon, and Other Poems in This Collection, 1820).

   Tradition.

   Tributary Stream.

   "What aspect bore the Man who roved or fled."

   "Whence that low voice?—A whisper from the heart."

   "Who swerves from innocence, who mkes divorce."

River Eden, Cumberland, The. William Wordsworth. *Fr.* Poems Composed or Suggested During a Tour, in the Summer of 1833. **CP-WorW2**

River falls and over the walls the coffins of cold funerals, The. River in Spate. Louis MacNeice. **CP-MacNL**

River-fog will do for privacy, The. Adrienne Rich. *Fr.* The Spirit of Place. **SP-RicA2**

River glides out of the grass. A river or a serpent, A. The Long Alley. Theodore Roethke. **CP-RoetT**

River God, The. Stevie Smith. **CP-SmitS**

River hemmed with leaning trees, The. A Mystery. John Greenleaf Whittier. **CP-WhitJ**

River Humber, The. Stevie Smith. **CP-SmitS**

River in its abundance, The. Eros at Temple Stream. Denise Levertov. **CP-LeveD**

River in Spate. Louis MacNeice. **CP-MacNL**

River in the dream, The. Frederick Morgan. *Fr.* The Gorge. **SP-MorgF**

River in the Valley. Gary Snyder. **CP-SnydG**

River Incident. Theodore Roethke. **CP-RoetT**

River irises, The. Grass. James Merrill. **SP-MerrJ**

River is full, The. Solstice. William Carlos Williams. **CP-WilW1**

River is gold under a sunset of Illinois, The. Letter S. Carl Sandburg. **CP-SandC**

River is rising, The. Wendell Berry. *Fr.* Window Poems. **CP-BerrW**

River is within us, the sea is all about us, The. Thomas Stearns Eliot. **OxBoS** *Fr.* The Dry Salvages. **AiP; LiTB; NoP; OxBA; SeCePo** *Fr.* Four Quartets. **CP-ElioT**

River-mirror mirrors the cold sky, The. Mists over the River. William Carlos Williams. **CP-WilW2**

River Moon. Carl Sandburg. **CP-SandC**

River Moons. Carl Sandburg. **CP-SandC**

River Now, The. Richard Hugo. **CP-HugoR**

River of green stone. Renaming the Kings. Philip Levine. **SP-LeviP**

River of long standing, bridge abut-ment. Chuck Miller. **SP-MillC**

River of Mist, The. Edward Estlin Cummings. **CP-CummE**

River of our substance. George Oppen. *Fr.* A Narrative. **CP-OppeG**

River of Rivers in Connecticut, The. Wallace Stevens. **CP-StevW**

River of Ruin, The. Paul Laurence Dunbar. **CP-DunbP**

River of sweetness that runs through the meadow of lies, The. Hill Dream of Youth, Thirty Years Later. Richard Eberhart. **CP-EberR**

River Path, The. John Greenleaf Whittier. **CP-WhitJ**

River Poem. James Merrill. **SP-MerrJ**

River Profile. Wystan Hugh Auden. **CP-AudeW**

River Rhyme. William Carlos Williams. **CP-WilW2**

River Rhyme II. William Carlos Williams. **CP-WilW2**

River Rising in India. Jenny Joseph. **SP-JoseJ**

River Road. Stanley Jasspon Kunitz. **CP-KuniS**

River Roads. Carl Sandburg. **CP-SandC**

River-Root: A Syzygy. William Everson.

   "River-Root: as even under high drifts, those fierce wind-grappled cuts of the Rockies." **SP-EverW**

River-Root: as even under high drifts, those fierce wind-grappled cuts of the Rockies. William Everson. **SP-EverW** *Fr.* River-Root: A Syzygy.

River Roses. David Herbert Lawrence. **CP-LawrD**

River Rouge, 1932. John Berryman. **CP-BerrJ**

River seems to sour and we can't recall, The. The Other Beaverbank. Richard Hugo. **CP-HugoR**

River sleeps beneath the sky, The. Sunset. Paul Laurence Dunbar. **CP-DunbP**

River Song, The, *ad. fr.* Rihaku (Li T'ai Po). Ezra Pound. **SP-PounE**

River Still To Be Found, A. Lawrence Ferlinghetti. **SP-FerlL**

River Streets, The. John Hewitt. **CP-HewiJ**

River Styx, Ohio, The. Mary Oliver. **SP-OlivM**

River takes the land, and leaves nothing, The. The Slip. Wendell Berry. **CP-BerrW**

River Temple: Wai, The. Alun Lewis. **CP-LewiA**

River Thames (?). Christina Georgina Rossetti. **CP-RosC3**

River That Is East, The. Galway Kinnell. **SP-KinnG**

River, that rollest by the ancient walls. Stanzas to the Po. Byron. **CP-Byron**

River turns, The. The Pike. Theodore Roethke. **CP-RoetT**

River Video, The. James Liddy. **CP-LiddJ**

River Water Music. Richard Eberhart. **CP-EberR**

River whispers the way, The. Homing. Barton Sutter. **SP-SuttB**

Riverbank, the long rigs. Broagh. Seamus Heaney. **SP-HeanS**

Rivergut girlriver damn drowned. I Was Born to Hustle Roses Down the Avenues of the Dead. Charles Bukowski. **SP-BukC2**

Riverly is a flower. Edward Estlin Cummings. **CP-CummE**

Riverman, The. Elizabeth Bishop. **CP-BishE**

Rivermouth Rocks are fair to see. The Wreck of Rivermouth. John Greenleaf Whittier. **CP-WhitJ**

Rivers and Mountains. John Ashbery. **SP-AshbJ**

Rivers and winds among the twisted hills. Robert Louis Stevenson. **CP-StevR**

"As with heaped bees at hiving time." **NOBVV**

Rivers Are Running Beneath Us. Steve Griffiths. **SP-GrifS**

Rivers bring down. The sea. Geoffrey Hill. *Fr.* The Death of Shelley. *Fr.* Of Commerce and Society: Variations on a Theme. **CP-HillG**

Rivers Come to the Hall of Proteus for the Marriage of the Thames and the Medway, The. Edmund Spenser. **FaBoPP** *Fr.* The Faerie Queene. **CP-Spens**

River's mirrorings remake a world. Below Tintern. Charles Tomlinson. **CP-TomlC**

Rivers of Ireland, The. Edmund Spenser. **CBCK** *Fr.* The Faerie Queene. **CP-Spens**

River's Tale, The. Rudyard Kipling. **CP-KiplR**

Rivers were made by the commingling. A Theory of Nato-geography as Advanced by the Tiaphidian Man, With a Comment on the Character of His Penal System. Kenneth Patchen. **CP-PatcK**

Riverside Park. Etheridge Knight. *Fr.* Indiana Haiku. **SP-KnigE**

Rivulet crossing my ground. Tennyson. *Fr.* Maud [A Monodrama]. **CP-TennA**

R.K. John Hewitt. **CP-HewiJ**

R.M.D. Hayden Carruth. **CP-CarHS**

Roach, foulest of creatures. Cockroach. Anne Sexton. **CP-SextA**

Roaches spit out, The. In a Neighborhood of Murder. Charles Bukowski. **SP-BukC1**

Road, The. Muriel Rukeyser. **CP-RukeM**

Road ahead, The. On the Road. Seamus Heaney. **SP-HeanS** *Fr.* Sweeney Redivivus.

Road and the End, The. Carl Sandburg. **CP-SandC**

Road at My Door, The. William Butler Yeats. **BIrV; CP-YeatW; LiTB; NOBE; PoE** *Fr.* Meditations in Time of Civil War. **CP-YeatW**

Road at the top of the rise, The. The Middleness of the Road. Robert Frost. **CP-FrosR**

Road Back, The. Anne Sexton. **CP-SextA**

Road back has been covered with many winds, The. The Ninth Book. Archibald MacLeish. *Fr.* Conquistador. **CP-MacLA**

Road Behind the Last Dune, The. Marge Piercy. **SP-PierM** *Fr.* Sand Roads.

Road deepening in the north, A. The Stone Harp. John Haines. **SP-HainJ**

Road Ends at Tahola. Richard Hugo. **CP-HugoR**

Road extended o'er a heath, The. William Wordsworth. **CP-WorW1**

Road from Glastonbury, The. Jenny Joseph. **SP-JoseJ**

Road had steepened and the sun sharpened on the high ridges; the stream probably was dry, The. A Redeemer. Robinson Jeffers. **CP-JefR1**

Road in Kentucky, A. Robert Earl Hayden. **CP-HaydR**

Road is a hard road, The. Driving to Passalacqua, 1960. Charles Wright. **SP-WrigC**

Road Map, The. Thom Gunn. **CP-GunnT**

Road Not Taken, The. Robert Frost. **CP-FrosR**

Road of Excess, The. Contra Blake. Wystan Hugh Auden. *Fr.* Shorts I ("Watch upon my wrist, The"). **CP-AudeW**

Road ran downhill into Spain, The, *sels.* Louis MacNeice. *Fr.* Autumn Journal. **CP-MacNL**

Road Song of the *Bandar-Log*. Rudyard Kipling. **CP-KiplR** *Fr.* Kaa's Hunting. *Fr.* The Jungle Book.

Road that had wound us 20,000 miles, A. Homecoming. Hayden Carruth. **CP-CarHS**

Road to Avallon, The. Ernest Hemingway. **CP-HemiE**

Road to Avrillé, The. Edna St. Vincent Millay. **CP-MillE**

Road to En-dor is easy to tread, The. En-dor. Rudyard Kipling. **CP-KiplR**

Road to Larissa, The. Leonard Cohen. **CP-CoheL**

Road to Paradise is plain, The. Emily Dickinson. **CP-DickE**

Road to the great canyon always feels, The. Adrienne Rich. **SP-RicA1; SP-RicA2** *Fr.* Turning the Wheel. **SP-RicA2** (Turning the Wheel.) **SP-RicA2**

Road to the Past, The. Edna St. Vincent Millay. **CP-MillE**

Road Up. Stevie Smith. **CP-SmitS**

Road was lit with Moon and star, The. Emily Dickinson. **CP-DickE**

Road winds down through autumn hills, The. Tour 5. Robert Earl Hayden. **CP-HaydR**

Roads. Robert Creeley. **CP-CreeR**

Roads, The. Louise McNeill. **SP-McNeL**

Roads Also, The. Wilfred Owen. **CP-OwenW**

Roads getting emptier, air in a steadily purer, The. Dudwood. Donald Davie. **CP-DavDo**

Roads in That Town Have No Name, The. Siv Cedering Fox. **SP-CedeS**

Road's Your Place, The. Wystan Hugh Auden. **CP-AudWJ**

Roadside Stand, A. Robert Frost. **CP-FrosR**

Roadway, A. Paul Laurence Dunbar. **CP-DunbP**

Roadway, The. Adrienne Rich. **CP-RicAE**

Roadways. John Haines. **SP-HainJ**
  "It is morning again in the west."
  "Many times bound outward."
  "These images and their hidden voices."
  "Years ago my father read to me."

Roaming in Thought. Walt Whitman. **CP-WhitW**

Roan Stallion. Robinson Jeffers. **CP-JefR1**

Roar and clatter, The. Man and Nature. William Carlos Williams. **CP-WilW1**

Roar of red wood racer eats field. Green breakaway go cars light lanes. Thomas Merton. *Fr.* South. *Fr.* The Geography of Lograire. **CP-MertT**

Roar of the Sea and the Darkness, The, *sl. diff. vers. incl. in* Pijijiapan. Malcolm Lowry. *Fr.* The Roar of the Sea and the Darkness. **CP-LowrM**

Roar of the Sea and the Darkness, The. Malcolm Lowry. **CP-LowrM**
  "Black thunderclouds mass up against the wind."
  "Christ, slashed with an axe, in the humped church."
  From Helsinki to Liverpool with Lumber.
  Fyrb[do]oterer.
  Iron Thoughts Sail Out at Evening.
  "Lighthouse invites the storm and lights it, The." **NOBC** (Lighthouse Invites the Storm, The.) **NOBC**
  Lines Written on Reading Dostoievski.
  "Lying awake beside a sleeping girl."
  "No road in existence strikes such terror."
  On Reading R.L.S.
  Poem of God's Mercy, A.
  Quartermaster at the Wheel.
  Roar of the Sea and the Darkness, The.
  Ship is Turning Homeward, The.
  "Ship of war sails in the grey morning, The."
  "So he would rather have written those lines."
  Song about Madrid, Useful Any Time.
  Tashtego Believed Red.
  There Is a Metallurgy.
  Vigil Forget.
  "We likened one man to a ship adrift."
  "You cannot, must not, Orpheus, look back, my soul."

Roar through the Tall Twin Elm-Trees, A. George Meredith. **CP-MerG1**

Roaring. Robert Herrick. **CP-HerrR**

Roaring alongside he takes for granted, The. Sandpiper. Elizabeth Bishop. **CP-BishE**

Roaring company that festive night, A. The Dark and the Fair. Stanley Jasspon Kunitz. **CP-KuniS**

Roaring Tinker if you like, The. Three Songs to the One Burden. William Butler Yeats. **CP-YeatW**

Roast Possum. Rita Dove. **SP-DoveR**

Rob Roy's Grave. William Wordsworth. **CP-WorW1**

Robbed by Death—but that was easy. Emily Dickinson. **CP-DickE**

Robber Bridegroom, The. Margaret Atwood. **SP-AtwM2**

Robber Bridegroom, The. Allen Tate. **CP-TateA**

Robber Woman, The. Marilyn Hacker. **SP-HackM**

Robbers' Den. Robert Ranke Graves. **CP-GravR**

Robbie's Dance, The. Al Young. **CP-YounA**

Robert Bresson. Patti Smith. **SP-SmitP**

Robert Bruce's March to Bannockburn. Robert Burns. *See* Scots, wha hae wi' Wallace bled.

Robert Burns' Answer [to Epistle from a Taylor]. Robert Burns. **CP-BurnR**

Robert Frost. Robert Lowell. **SP-LoweR**

Robert Frost in Warsaw. Peter Meinke. **SP-MeinP**

Robert Gould Shaw. Paul Laurence Dunbar. **CP-DunbP**

Robert Graves. Ernest Hemingway. **CP-HemiE**

Robert Herrick. John Yau. **SP-YauJo**

Robert Rawlin!—Frosts were falling. The Ranger. John Greenleaf Whittier. **CP-WhitJ**

Robert Schumann. Mary Oliver. **SP-OlivM**

Robert Schumann, Or: Musical Genius Begins with Affliction. Rita Dove. **SP-DoveR**

Robes of the judges are magnificent, The. The Summons. Charles Simic. **SP-SimiC**

Robespierre and Mozart as Stage. Robert Lowell. **SP-LoweR**

Robespierre could live with himself: "The Republic." Robespierre and Mozart as Stage. Robert Lowell. **SP-LoweR**

Robin, The. Wystan Hugh Auden. **CP-AudWJ**

Robin, A. Walter de la Mare. **CP-DeLaW**

Robin, The. Thomas Hardy. **CP-HardT**

Robin, The. John Greenleaf Whittier. **CP-WhitJ**

Robin and Harry. Jonathan Swift. **CP-SwifJ**

Robin cam to the wren's nest, The. The Wren's Nest. Robert Burns. **CP-BurnR**

Robin cries: *rain!*, The. Rain in Ohio. Mary Oliver. **SP-OlivM**

Robin for the Crumb, The. Emily Dickinson. **CP-DickE**

Robin Hood. John Keats. **CP-KeatJ**

Robin Hood Cove—Georgetown, Maine. Marsden Hartley. **CP-HartM**

Robin is a Gabriel, The. Emily Dickinson. **CP-DickE**

Robin is a lovely lad. The Dance. Thomas Campion. **CP-CampT; EIL; FaBoCh; LoBV** *Fr.* The Ayres that Were Sung and Played, at *Brougham Castle* in *Westmerland*, in the Kings Entertainment. **CP-CampT**

Robin is the One, The. Emily Dickinson. **CP-DickE**

Robin Redbreast. Stanley Jasspon Kunitz. **CP-KuniS**

Robin Redbreast in a cage, A. William Blake. **FaPON; MoShBr; OxBoLi** *Fr.* Auguries of Innocence. **CP-BlakW**

(Three Things to Remember.) **FaPON; MoShBr**

Robin said: The Spring will never come, A. A Wintry Sonnet. Christina Georgina Rossetti. **CP-RosC2**

Robin Shure in Hairst. Robert Burns. **CP-BurnR**

Robin, to beggars, with a curse. Robin and Harry. Jonathan Swift. **CP-SwifJ**

Robins' green-blue eggs, The. Morning. Louise Bogan. **CP-BogaL**

Robin's my Criterion for Tune, The. Emily Dickinson. **CP-DickE**

Robins sang in the orchard, the buds into blossoms grew, The. Marguerite. John Greenleaf Whittier. **CP-WhitJ**

"Robins?" They are writing now, The. Emily Dickinson. **SP-DickE**

Robin's whistled stave, The. Speech. Walter de la Mare. **CP-DeLaW**

Robot. Robert Pack. **SP-PackR**

Robot-Democracy. David Herbert Lawrence. **CP-LawrD**

Robot Feelings. David Herbert Lawrence. **CP-LawrD**

Robot Romance. Robert Pack. **SP-PackR**

Roc. Lewis Turco. **SP-TurcL**

Rock. Kathleen Jessie Raine. **SP-RainK**

Rock, The. Wallace Stevens. **SP-StevW**

Rock. Miller Williams. **SP-WillM**

Rock, a leaf, mud, even the grass, A. The Concealment: Ishi, the Last Wild Indian. William Stafford. **SP-StafW**

Rock and Hawk. Robinson Jeffers. **CP-JefR2**

Rock and precipice. Landscape. Octavio Paz, *tr. fr. Spanish by* Charles Tomlinson. **CP-TomlC**

Rock Climbing. Jane Cooper. **SP-CoopJ**

Rock drops in a bucket, A. Waters. Donald Hall. **CP-HallD**

Rock Flow, River Mix. Muriel Rukeyser. **CP-RukeM**

Rock Has Not Learned. Ted Hughes. **SP-HughT**

"Rock" in El Ghor, The. John Greenleaf Whittier. **CP-WhitJ**

Rock insults us, hard and so boldly browed. Giacometti. Richard Wilbur. **CP-WilbR**

Rock is written with the sign, The. Kathleen Jessie Raine. *Fr.* The Hollow Hill. **SP-RainK**

Rock, juniper, and wind. Return of the Native. Marsden Hartley. **CP-HartM**

Rock, like sculpture, is the solid body of a dream. The Salvation of Rock. Patti Smith. **SP-SmitP**

Rock Music. Derek Mahon. **SP-MahoD**

Rock 'N' Roll. "Lou Reed." **SP-ReedL**

Rock of Rubies: and The Quarrie of Pearls, The. Robert Herrick. **CP-HerrR**

Rock-Old Dogma, The. William Carlos Williams. **CP-WilW2**

Rock reproduces rock / In miniature. Gli Scafari. Charles Tomlinson. **CP-TomlC**

Rock shot chasms / Promise unplanned flight. Thomas Merton. *Fr.* Cables to the Ace. **CP-MertT**

Rock-Study with Wanderer. John Berryman. **CP-BerrJ**

Rock the boat to a fare-thee-well. Rites of Passage. Audre Lorde. **SP-LordA**

Rock there is whose homely front, A. The Primrose of the Rock. William Wordsworth. **CP-WorW2**

Rock-Tomb of Bradore, The. John Greenleaf Whittier. **CP-WhitJ**

Rocker, The. Donald Hall. **CP-HallD**

Rockettes, The. John Updike. **CP-UpdiJ**

Rocking across the lapis lazuli sea. Epitaph in Three Parts. Sylvia Plath. **CP-PlatS**

Rocking-chairs, The. Sunday at Key West. Elizabeth Bishop. **CP-BishE**

Rocking Woman, The. William Carlos Williams. **CP-WilW2**

Rocks, The. Stephen Berg. **SP-BergS**

Rocks, The. Robert Creeley. **CP-CreeR**

Rocks and the firm roots of trees. Spirituals. Langston Hughes. **SP-HughL**

Rocks and trees in silence stood, The. Will Man Ever Face Fact and Not Feel Flat? Stevie Smith. **CP-SmitS**

Rocks chilled to whiteness. Les Baux. Marsden Hartley. **CP-HartM**

Rocks here, if they sang, The. Creed. James McAuley. *Fr.* Requiem. **SP-McAuJ**

Rocksie Ann was a Roxy and she live on Histon, Eng. Malcolm Lowry. **CP-LowrM**

Rocky Acres. Robert Ranke Graves. **CP-GravR**

Rocky nook with hill-tops three, The. Boston. Ralph Waldo Emerson. **CP-EmerR**

Rococo compostions of decay. Via Portello. Donald Davie. **CP-DavDo**

Rod, The. Robert Herrick. **CP-HerrR**

Rod was but a harmless wand, The. The Virtues of Sid Hamet the Magician's Rod. Jonathan Swift. **CP-SwifJ**

Rode in the train all night, in the sick light. A bird. All Night, All Night. Delmore Schwartz. **SP-SchwD**

Roderick Usher rose at six. R. Usher. Malcolm Lowry. **CP-LowrM**

Rodez. Donald Davie. **CP-DavDo**

Rodin's Orpheus, floodlit, hacked. Postcard. Adrienne Rich. **CP-RicAE**

Rodric Lesley. 1830. Emily Brontë. **CP-BronE**

Roe (and my joy to name) th'art now, to go. To William Roe. Ben Jonson. **CP-JonsB**

Roe-Deer. Ted Hughes. **SP-HughT**

Roe Deer, The. Charles Tomlinson. **CP-TomlC**

Rogation Sunday. William Carlos Williams. **CP-WilW2**

Rogationtide. Christina Georgina Rossetti. **CP-RosC2**

Roger Casement. William Butler Yeats. **CP-YeatW**

Roger Clay's Proposal. James Merrill. **SP-MerrJ**

Rogers Group, A. Robert Frost. **CP-FrosR**

Rogo vos Amor unde sit, Camenae. Tell Me Where Is Fancy Bred. Gerard Manley Hopkins. *Fr.* Songs from Shakespeare, in Latin and Greek. **CP-HopkG**

Roguish wind and I, The. Hafiz, *tr. by* Ralph Waldo Emerson. **CP-EmerR** *Fr.* Odes.

Rois Fainéants. Wystan Hugh Auden. **CP-AudeW**

Rojo. Tom Clark. **SP-ClarT**

Rokeby, *sels.* Sir Walter Scott.

  Dawn and Sunrise. **SP-ScotW**

  Edmund's Songs. **SP-ScotW**

    Brignall Banks. **EnRP; HBV 1-2; OAEP; OBEV; OBRV**

    (Edmund's Song.) **PoRA**

    (Outlaw, The.) **GTBS; GTBS-6; GTBS-P; OtMeF**

    (Song: Brignal Banks.) **OxAEP-2**

  Evening. **SP-ScotW**

  Thorsgill. **SP-ScotW**

Roland Hayes Beaten (Georgia: 1942). Langston Hughes. **SP-HughL**

Roland Navarro (1939-1961). Al Young. **CP-YounA**

Roll Call. John Hewitt. **CP-HewiJ**

Roll of drums and the bugle's wailing, The. Revisited. John Greenleaf Whittier. **CP-WhitJ**

Roll On, Thou Deep and Dark Blue Copy Writer—Roll! Ogden Nash. **CP-NashO**

Roll On, Thou Deep and Dark Blue Ocean. Byron. *See* There is a pleasure in the pathless woods.

Roll on, thou deep and dark blue ocean—roll! Byron. **FaPON; GN; OxBoS; UV; WGRP** *Fr.* The Ocean. **PoEL-4** *Fr.* Childe Harold's Pilgrimage. **CP-Byron**

  (Roll On, Thou Deep and Dark Blue Ocean.) **FaPON**

  (To the Ocean.) **GN; WGRP**

Roll open this rug; a minx is. Props. Carl Sandburg. **CP-SandC**

Roll stones down on our head! On Taking from the Top to Broaden the Base. Robert Frost. **CP-FrosR**

Roll up! Roll up! For the magical mystery tour. Magical Mystery Tour. The Beatles. **CP-Beatl**

Rolled in the grass. The Grandfather-Father Poem. Charles Olson. **CP-OlsoC**

Rolled in the trough of thick desire. Edna St. Vincent Millay. *Fr.* Theme and Variations. **CP-MillE**

Rolled over on Europe: the sharp dew frozen to stars. Cornet Cornelius Rilke. Stephen Spender. **CP-SpenS**

Rolling along through Ohio. Ohio. John Updike. **CP-UpdiJ**

Rolling Back. John Haines. **SP-HainJ**

Rolling mill / Though day is dead, The. Daily Bread. Wystan Hugh Auden. **CP-AudWJ**

Rolling Stone, The. Moss. Al Young. **CP-YounA**

Rolling Thunder Stones. Allen Ginsberg. **CP-GinsA**

Rollo says, "I can bring down rain." Rollo's Miracle. Paul Zimmer. **SP-ZimmP**

Rollo's Miracle. Paul Zimmer. **SP-ZimmP**

Roma I. Charles Wright. **SP-WrigC**

Roma II. Charles Wright. **SP-WrigC**

Roman Antiquities. William Wordsworth. **CP-WorW2**

Roman Antiquities Discovered at Bishopstone, Hereforshire. William Wordsworth. **CP-WorW2**

Roman Centurion's Song, The. Rudyard Kipling. **CP-KiplR**

Roman Consul doomed his sons to die, The. William Wordsworth. *Fr.* Sonnets upon the Punishment of Death. **CP-WorW2**

Roman Dream. Jane Cooper. **SP-CoopJ**

Roman Fort, The. John Hewitt. **CP-HewiJ**

Roman Fountain. Louise Bogan. **CP-BogaL**

Roman Gravemounds, The. Thomas Hardy. **CP-HardT**

Roman had an, A / artist, a freedman. The Jerboa. Marianne Craig Moore. **CP-MoorM**

Roman had an, A / artist, a freedman. Too Much. Marianne Craig Moore. **CMoP** *Fr.* The Jerboa. **CP-MoorM**

Roman Master stands on the Grecian ground, A. On a Celebrated Event in Ancient History. William Wordsworth. **CP-WorW1**

Roman Morn. Lawrence Ferlinghetti. **SP-FerlL**

Roman Nocturnes. Rafael Alberti, *tr. fr. Spanish.*

  "From empty windows / Voice of dead eyes." **CP-MertT**

  "Nights belong to / What hurts." **CP-MertT**

  "Other night I saw. . . / Who did I see?, The." **CP-MertT**

  "Take, O take the key of Rome." **CP-MertT**

  "You did not come to Rome to dream." **CP-MertT**

Roman Portrait Busts. John Updike. **CP-UpdiJ**

Roman Road, The. Thomas Hardy. **CP-HardT**

Roman Road, The. Stevie Smith. **CP-SmitS**

Roman Virgil [*or* Vergil], thou that singest. To Virgil [*or* Vergil]. Tennyson. **CP-TennA**

Roman Wall Blues. Wystan Hugh Auden. **DTC; FaBoEH; NTP** *Fr.* Twelve Songs. **CP-AudeW**

Romance, A. Stephen Dunn. **SP-DunnS**

Romance. Edgar Allan Poe. **CP-PoeEd**

Romance. Anne Waldman. **SP-WaldA**

Romance. Al Young. **CP-YounA**

Romance in Durango. "Bob Dylan." **CP-DylaB**

Romance Moderne. William Carlos Williams. **CP-WilW1**

Romance of a Youngest Daughter. John Crowe Ransom. **SP-RansJ**

Romance of Science, The. Randall Jarrell. **CP-JarrR**

Romance of the Ganges, A. Elizabeth Barrett Browning. **CP-BroEB**

Romance of the precise is not the elision, The. Adult Epigram. Wallace Stevens. **CP-StevW**

Romance [*or* Romaunt] of the Rose, The. Guillaume de Lorris *and* Jean de Meun, *tr. fr. French,* Geoffrey Chaucer. **CP-ChauG**

  Garden of Amour, The. **PoEL-1**

  "Short space my feet had traversed ere." **OAEL-1**

  "There is no place in paradise." **PBBP**

Romance of the Swan's Nest, The. Elizabeth Barrett Browning. **CP-BroEB**

Romance was always young. To Lady Jane. Nicholas Vachel Lindsay. **CP-LindV**

Romance, who loves to nod and sing. Romance. Edgar Allan Poe. **CP-PoeEd**

Romance Without Finance. Al Young. **CP-YounA**

Romancing with Our Beasts. John Ciardi. **SP-CiarJ**

Romans Angry about the Inner World. Robert Bly. **SP-BlyR**

Romantic, The. Louise Bogan. **CP-BogaL**

Romantic, The. John Hewitt. **CP-HewiJ**

Romantic to Burlesque. Byron. *See* Nothing so difficult as a beginning.

Romany Girl, The. Ralph Waldo Emerson. **CP-EmerR**

Romanze, or the Music Students. Frank O'Hara. **SP-OharF**

Romatic Portrait. Louis Zukofsky. *Fr.* Michtam. **CP-ZukLS**

Romaunt of Margret, The. Elizabeth Barrett Browning. **CP-BroEB**

Romaunt of the Page, The. Elizabeth Barrett Browning. **CP-BroEB**

Rome. Arthur Hugh Clough. *See* Rome disappoints me still; but I shrink and adapt myself to it.

Rome ("He brought our saviour to the western side"). John Milton. **NOSC** *Fr.* Book IV. *Fr.* Paradise Regained [*or* Regain'd]. **CP-MiltJ**

Rome ("The City which thou seest no other deem"). John Milton. **OBS** *Fr.* Book IV. *Fr.* Paradise Regained [*or* Regain'd]. **CP-MiltJ**

Rome. James Thomson. *Fr.* Liberty. **CP-ThomJ**

Rome: At the Pyramid of Cestius near the Graves of Shelley and Keats. Thomas Hardy. **CP-HardT**

Rome: Building a New Street in the Ancient Quarter. Thomas Hardy. **CP-HardT**

Rome by Metella's Tomb. Byron. **FaBoPP** *Fr.* Childe Harold's Pilgrimage. **CP-Byron**

Rome disappoints me much,--St. Peter's, perhaps, in especial. Rome ("Rome disappoints me much"). Arthur Hugh Clough. **FaBoPP** *Fr.* Amours de Voyage. **SP-ClouA**

Rome disappoints me still; but I shrink and adapt myself to it. Arthur Hugh Clough. **EBVV; EBVVPR; FaBoPP; OBTV; OXAEP-2** *Fr.* Amours de Voyage. **SP-ClouA**

  (Rome.) **FaBoPP**

Rome has fallen, ye see it lying. Fragment: Rome and Nature. Percy Bysshe Shelley. **CP-ShelP**

Rome never looks where she treads. A Pict Song. Rudyard Kipling. **CP-KiplR** *Fr.* The Winged Hats. *Fr.* Puck of Pook's Hill.

Rome: On the Palatine. Thomas Hardy. **CP-HardT**

Rome ("Rome disappoints me much"). Arthur Hugh Clough. **FaBoPP** *Fr.* Amours de Voyage. **SP-ClouA**

Rome Sunday[,] June 1960. John Hewitt. **CP-HewiJ**

Rome: The Vatican: Sala delle Muse. Thomas Hardy. **CP-HardT**

Rome will not suit me, Eustace; the priests and soldiers possess / it;. Arthur Hugh Clough. **EBVVPR,** *canto* 5, 10; *Fr.* Amours de Voyage. **SP-ClouA**

Romeo Had Juliette. "Lou Reed." **SP-ReedL**

Romney! expert infallibly to trace. To Romney. William Cowper. **CP-CowpW**

Romulus and Remus. Rudyard Kipling. **CP-KiplR**

Ron Padgett is holding two birthday gifts. Jim Carroll. *Fr.* Birthday Poem. **SP-CarrJ**

Ronalds of the Bennals, The. Robert Burns. **CP-BurnR**

Rondeau: "Year has cast its cloak away, The." Charles, Duc d'Orléans, *tr. fr. French by* Richard Wilbur. **CP-WilbR**

Rondeau of a Conscientious Objector. David Herbert Lawrence. **CP-LawrD**

Rondel: "Kissing her hair." Algernon Charles Swinburne. *See* Kissing Her Hair.

Rondel: "Now that I am fifty-six." Muriel Rukeyser. **CP-RukeM**

Rondel of Merciles Beaute, A. Geoffrey Chaucer. *See* Merciless Beauty.

Rondel of Merciless Beauty, A, *mod. vers. by* Louis Untermeyer. Geoffrey Chaucer. *See* Merciless Beauty.

Rondels. Robert Louis Stevenson. **CP-StevR**

  "Far have you come, my lady, from the town."

  "Since I am sworn to live my life."

  "We'll walk the woods no more."

Rondo of the Familiar. Robert Pack. **SP-PackR**

Roof Garden. James Schuyler. **CP-SchuJ**

Roof overwoven by a soft tussle of leaves. Wellfleet: The House. Richard Wilbur. **CP-WilbR**

Roof shaped like a strawberry. Hurriedly torn. John Yau. **SP-YauJo** *Fr.* Scenes from the Life of Boullee.

Roofless and eyeless, weed-sodden, dank, old, cold. An Abandoned Church. Walter de la Mare. **CP-DeLaW**

Roofless houses, cartons of chalk. The Sahara Bus Trip. Rita Dove. **SP-DoveR**

Roofless, the wreck of a house and byre. Idrigill. Charles Tomlinson. **CP-TomlC**

Roofs. Philip Levine. **SP-LeviP**

Roof's peak is eye. Sitting Here. Robert Creeley. **CP-CreeR**

Rooftop, The. Thom Gunn. **CP-GunnT**

Roofwalker, The. Adrienne Rich. **CP-RicAE; SP-RicA1; SP-RicA2**

Rook[e] he sells feathers, yet he still doth cry. Upon Rook: Epigram. Robert Herrick. **CP-HerrR**

Rookery, The. Wystan Hugh Auden. **CP-AudWJ**

Rookhope (Weardale, Summer 1922). Wystan Hugh Auden. **CP-AudWJ**

Rooks In October. Walter de la Mare. **CP-DeLaW**

Rooks rose cawing noisily with fright, The. Sparrowhawk. John Hewitt. **CP-HewiJ**

Room, The. Stephen Dobyns. **SP-DobyS**

Room. Charles Kenneth Williams. **SP-WillC**

Room above the Square, The. Stephen Spender. **CP-SpenS**

Room after room, / I hunt the house through. Love in a Life. Robert Browning. **CP-BroR1**

Room all the way across america, A. Bringing It Home. Charles Kenneth Williams. **CP-WillC**

Room and the World, The. Stephen Dunn. **SP-DunnS**

Room darkened, darkened until, The. The Blessing. John Updike. **CP-UpdiJ**

Room designed by Orreryy receives, A. Dublin Georgian. Donald Davie. **CP-DavDo**

"Room for manoeuvre," I say. Intervals in a Busy Life. Donald Davie. **CP-DavDo**

"Room for the spheres!"—then first they shined. The Three Dimensions. Ralph Waldo Emerson. **CP-EmerR**

Room in a Penitentiary. Chuck Miller. **SP-MillC**

Room in Rome, A. Karl Shapiro. **SP-ShapK**

Room in the soft lamp glow, The. Farglow. Wystan Hugh Auden. **CP-AudWJ**

Room is all a stupid quietness, The. Happy Families. Louis MacNeice. **CP-MacNL**

Room is full of you!—As I came in, The. Interim. Edna St. Vincent Millay. **CP-MillE**

Room is like a cave, the webs of night, The. The Clock. Thom Gunn. **CP-GunnT**

Room of My Life, The. Anne Sexton. **CP-SextA**

Room of the guilty one / Evil place of bad luck. Aegeus in Prison. Alfonso Cortes, *tr. fr. Spanish by* Thomas Merton. **CP-MertT**

Room on room, we poke debris for fun. 1614 Boren. Richard Hugo. **CP-HugoR**

Room, room, make room for the bouncing belly. Hymn. Ben Jonson. **CP-JonsB** *Fr.* Pleasure Reconciled to Virtue.

Room 28. John Updike. **CP-UpdiJ**

Room was room enough for one, The. The Room and the World. Stephen Dunn. **SP-DunnS**

Room was small but neat and when I visited him, The. Result. Charles Bukowski. **SP-BukC3**

Room was suddenly rich and the great bay-window was, The. Snow. Louis MacNeice. **CP-MacNL**

Room with open windows facing a street, A. John Yau. **SP-YauJo** *Fr.* Scenes from the Life of Boullee.

Room with Revolutionists. Edwin Rolfe. **CP-RolfE**

Rooming Houses are Old Women. Audre Lorde. **SP-LordA**

Roominghouse, Winter. Margaret Atwood. **SP-AtwM1**

Rooms are grotesque with furniture of snow. The Return. Robert Earl Hayden. **CP-HaydR**

Rooms in Bloomsbury. Marilyn Hacker. **SP-HackM**

Roomy Eternity / Casts her schemes rarely. Ralph Waldo Emerson. **CP-EmerR**

Roosevelt. Ernest Hemingway. **CP-HemiE**

Roosevelt. Nicholas Vachel Lindsay. **CP-LindV**

Roosevelt died and met Wilson, who said, "I blundered into it". Wilson in Hell. Robinson Jeffers. **CP-JefR3**

Roosevelt, Renaissance, Gem, Alhambra, The. Movies. Langston Hughes. **SP-HughL**

Rooster, The. Ogden Nash. **CP-NashO**

Roosters. Elizabeth Bishop. **CP-BishE**

Roosters corn wooden dentures. D. C. Rita Dove. *Fr.* A Suite for Augustus. **SP-DoveR**

Root   an acceptable connection, The. What Appears to Be Yours. Frank O'Hara. **SP-OharF**

Root Canal, The. Marge Piercy. **SP-PierM**

Root Cellar. Theodore Roethke. **CP-RoetT**

Root-light, or the Lawyer's Daughter. James Dickey. **CP-DickJ**

Root of Our Evil, The. David Herbert Lawrence. **CP-LawrD**

Root of our present evil is that we buy and sell, The. The Root of Our Evil. David Herbert Lawrence. **CP-LawrD**

Rooted in doubt, you. The Tree. Frederick Morgan. **SP-MorgF**

Rootless. Stephen Dobyns. **SP-DobyS**

Roots. Charles Henri Ford. *Fr.* For Djuna Barnes. **SP-FordC**

Roots. Phoebe Hesketh. **SP-HeskP**

Roots. Adrienne Rich. **CP-RicAE; SP-RicA2**

Roots. Gary Snyder. **CP-SnydG**

Roots and Branches. Robert Duncan. **SP-DuncR**

Roots and Leaves Themselves Alone. Walt Whitman. **CP-WhitW**

Roots, go deep: wrap your coils; fasten your knots:. Wind Horses. Carl Sandburg. **CP-SandC**

Roots had no money; yet he went o'th score. Upon Roots. Robert Herrick. **CP-HerrR**

Roots of words, The. George Oppen. *Fr.* Of Being Numerous. **CP-OppeG**

Roots out of the ground and ongoing. Craters. James Dickey. **CP-DickJ**

Rope's End, The. Howard Nemerov. **CP-NemeH**

Ropewalk, The. Henry Wadsworth Longfellow. **SP-LongH**

Ropewalk, The. Lewis Turco. **SP-TurcL**

Ros, *see also* On a Drop of Dew. Andrew Marvell. **CP-MarvA**

Rosa Mystica. Gerard Manley Hopkins. **CP-HopkG**

Rosabelle. Sir Walter Scott. *Fr.* The Lay of the Last Minstrel. (Harold's Song.) **SP-ScotW**

Rosalia. Charles Simic. **SP-SimiC**

   "Especially forlorn human specimen, An." **SP-SimiC**

   (Dimly Outlined by a Police Artist.) **PPR**

   ("Especially forlorn specimen, An.") **PPR**

   "Rosalia and her mother moved away."

   "She saw the Archangel Michael, too."

Rosalia and her mother moved away. Charles Simic. *Fr.* Rosalia. **SP-SimiC**

Rosalind. George Meredith. **CP-MerG2**

Rosalind. Christina Georgina Rossetti. **CP-RosC3**

Rosalind and Helen; A Modern Eclogue. Percy Bysshe Shelley. **CP-ShelP**

Rosarie, The. Robert Herrick. **CP-HerrR**

Rosary Beads. Herman Melville. **SP-MelvH**

Rose, The. Leonard Cohen. **CP-CoheL**

Rose, The. Samuel Taylor Coleridge. *Fr.* Effusions. **CP-ColeS**

Rose, The. William Cowper. **CP-CowpW**

Rose, The. Robert Creeley. **CP-CreeR**

Rose. Walter de la Mare. **CP-DeLaW**

Rose, The. Robert Ranke Graves. **CP-GravR**

Rose, The. George Herbert. **CP-HerbG**

Rose, The. Robert Herrick. **CP-HerrR**

Rose / is dying the, The. Edward Estlin Cummings. **CP-CummE**

Rose. Jenny Joseph. *Fr.* Derivations. **SP-JoseJ**

Rose. Kathleen Jessie Raine. **SP-RainK**

Rose, The. John Crowe Ransom. **SP-RansJ**

Rose / red sunlight, A. Destroying Beauty. Charles Bukowski. **SP-BukC2**

Rose, The. Theodore Roethke. **BiP; NOBA; NYBP; PPoe; TRP** *Fr.* North American Sequence. **CP-RoetT**

Rose, The ("Gentle, Gentle"). Christina Georgina Rossetti. **CP-RosC3**

Rose, The ("O Rose"). Christina Georgina Rossetti. **CP-RosC3**

Rose, The ("First the warmth"). William Carlos Williams. **CP-WilW1**

Rose, The ("The rose is obsolete"). William Carlos Williams. **CP-WilW1**

Rose, The. William Carlos Williams. **CP-WilW2**

Rose, a lily, and the Face of Christ, A. Thou Art Fairer Than the Children of Men. Christina Georgina Rossetti. **CP-RosC2**

Rose and Cabbage. David Herbert Lawrence. **CP-LawrD**

Rose and other Fragrant Flowers smell best, The. Upon the Posthume and Precious Poems of the Nobly Extracted Gentleman Mr. R.L. James Howell. *Fr.* Elegies, 1660. **CP-LoveR**

Rose-Ann. Thomas Hardy. **CP-HardT**

Rose at the edge of my tax structure, The. On the Patio. John Ciardi. **SP-CiarJ**

Rose Bawn. Carl Sandburg. **CP-SandC**

Rose, but one, none other rose had I, A. Tennyson. **PoEL-5** *Fr.* Pelleas and Ettarre. **NAEL-2** *Fr.* Idylls of the King. **CP-TennA**

Rose-cheeked Laura[, Come]. Thomas Campion. **AAS; CP-CampT; EnLoPo; EnRePo; InPK; InPS; InvP; LoBV; NAEL-1; NOSC; NoP; OAEL-1; OAEP; PoE; PoEL-2; SeCeV; TFi; TRP; TrGrPo** *Fr.* Observations in the Art of English Poesie. **CP-CampT**

   (Laura.) **EIL; NOBE; OBEV; OBSC; SeCePo; UnS**

   ("Rose-cheekt Lawra, come.") **AAS; CP-CampT**

Rose dawn, in smoke, over the East River, A. Frederick Morgan. *Fr.* Poems of the Two Worlds. **SP-MorgF**

Rose did caper on her cheek, The. Emily Dickinson. **CP-DickE**

Rose fades, The. Poem. William Carlos Williams. **CP-WilW2**

Rose Family, The. Robert Frost. **CP-FrosR**

Rose had been wash'd, just wash'd in a shower, The. The Rose. William Cowper. **CP-CowpW**

Rose, harsh rose. Sea Rose. Hilda Doolittle. **CP-DoolH**

Rose has thorns as well as honey, A. Christina Georgina Rossetti. **CP-RosC2**

Rose-hips. Charles Tomlinson. **CP-TomlC**

Rose in a mystery, where is it found?, The. Rosa Mystica. Gerard Manley Hopkins. **CP-HopkG**

Rose in Candlelight, A. Walter de la Mare. **CP-DeLaW**

Rose, in tatters on the garden path, A. The Answer. Rudyard Kipling. **CP-KiplR**

Rose in the Afternoon. Jenny Joseph. **SP-JoseJ**

Rose in the park. 10/14. William Carlos Williams. **CP-WilW2**

Rose in Water, A. Walter de la Mare. **CP-DeLaW**

Rose is a rose, The. The Rose Family. Robert Frost. **CP-FrosR**

Rose is Love's own flower, and Love's no less, The. To My Fior-Di-Lisa. Christina Georgina Rossetti. **CP-RosC3**

Rose Is Not a Cabbage, A. David Herbert Lawrence. **CP-LawrD**

Rose late: the jarring and whining. Morning. Donald Davie. **CP-DavDo**

Rose, like dim battlements, the hills and reared. Macbeth. Walter de la Mare. **CP-DeLaW**

Rose, O pure / Contradiction / Longing to be nobody's. Rilke's Epitaph. Thomas Merton. **CP-MertT**

Rose of all Roses, Rose of all the World! The Rose of Battle. William Butler Yeats. **CP-YeatW**

Rose of All the World. David Herbert Lawrence. **CP-LawrD**

Rose of all the world is not for me, The. The Little White Rose. "Hugh MacDiarmid." **SP-MacDH**

Rose of Battle, The. William Butler Yeats. **CP-YeatW**

Rose of England, The. David Herbert Lawrence. **CP-LawrD**

Rose of Marion, The. James Schuyler. **CP-SchuJ**

Rose of Midnight, The. Nicholas Vachel Lindsay. **CP-LindV**

Rose of Peace, The. William Butler Yeats. **CP-YeatW**

Rose-of-Sharon. Louis Zukofsky. **CP-ZukLS**

Rose of Solitude, The. William Everson.

Rose of Solitude, The. William Everson. **SP-EverW** *Fr.* The Rose of Solitude.

Canticle of the Rose, The. **SP-EverW**

Kiss of the Cross, The. **SP-EverW**

"I cry. / Once of this world."

Raging of the Rose, The. **SP-EverW**

Rose of Solitude, The. **SP-EverW**

Vision of Felicity, The. **SP-EverW**

Rose of spirit, rose of light. On Reading William Blake's "The Sick Rose." Allen Ginsberg. **CP-GinsA**

Rose of the Sea. Juan Ramón Jiménez. *Fr.* Ten Short Poems. **CP-WrigJ**

Rose of the World, The. William Butler Yeats. **CP-YeatW**

Rose, on this terrace fifty years ago. The Roses on the Terrace. Tennyson. **CP-TennA**

Rose once grew within, A. A Lay of the Early Rose. Elizabeth Barrett Browning. **CP-BroEB**

Rose Plant in Jericho, A. Christina Georgina Rossetti. **CP-RosC1**

Rose Pogonias. Robert Frost. **CP-FrosR**

Rose Room. Gilbert Sorrentino. **SP-SorrG**

Rose, Rose. Charles Bukowski. **SP-BukC2**

Rose sericea: its red. Of Coming-into-Being and Passing-Away. Geoffrey Hill. **CP-HillG**

Rose that blushes rosy red, The. Christina Georgina Rossetti. **CP-RosC2**

Rose that drinks the fountain dew, The. To Constantia. Percy Bysshe Shelley. **CP-ShelP**

Rose Tree, The. William Butler Yeats. **CP-YeatW**

Rose was sick and smiling died [*or* di'd], The. The Funeral[l] Rites of the Rose. Robert Herrick. **CP-HerrR**

Rose which spied one swallow, A. One Swallow Does Not Make a Summer. Christina Georgina Rossetti. **CP-RosC3**

Rose with such a bonny blush, The. Christina Georgina Rossetti. **CP-RosC2**

Rosebay willow herb pushing. Nottinghamshire. Donald Davie. **CP-DavDo**

Roseblade's Visitants and Mine. John Hewitt. **CP-HewiJ**

Rosebud, The. Robert Burns. **CP-BurnR**

Rosebud by my early walk, A. The Rosebud. Robert Burns. **CP-BurnR**

Rosebud, knot of worms. Words for a Nursery. Sylvia Plath. **CP-PlatS**

Rosebush in an Unlikely Garden, A. William Carlos Williams. **CP-WilW2**

Rosebushes. Juan Ramón Jiménez. *Fr.* Ten Short Poems. **CP-WrigJ**

Rosemarie Branch, The. Robert Herrick. **CP-HerrR**

Rosemary. Edna St. Vincent Millay. **CP-MillE**

Rosemary. Marianne Craig Moore. **CP-MoorM**

Roses. Stephen Berg. **SP-BergS**

Roses. Thomas Campion. *See* Song: "Now hath Flora rob'd [*or*robbed] her bowers."

Roses. Rita Dove. **SP-DoveR**

Roses. Paul Laurence Dunbar. **CP-DunbP**

Roses. David Herbert Lawrence. **CP-LawrD**

Roses. Mary Oliver. **SP-OlivM**

Roses. Louis Zukofsky. **CP-ZukLS**

Roses and gold. Places. Carl Sandburg. **CP-SandC**

Roses and lilies grow above the place. Life Hidden. Christina Georgina Rossetti. **CP-RosC3**

Roses and Pearls. Paul Laurence Dunbar. **CP-DunbP**

Roses are sweet to smell and see. April Moon. Walter de la Mare. **CP-DeLaW**

Roses are things which Christmas is not a bed of them. April Yule, Daddy! Ogden Nash. **CP-NashO**

Roses at first were white. How Roses Came Red. Robert Herrick. **CP-HerrR**

Roses bloom too late for me. I Do Set My Bow in the Cloud. Christina Georgina Rossetti. **CP-RosC3**

Roses blushing red and white, / For delight. Christina Georgina Rossetti. **CP-RosC2**

Roses covered Lorca's breast. For Michael, Armoured with Roses. Diane Wakoski. *Fr.* Fifteen Poems for a Lunar Eclipse None of Us Saw. **SP-WakoD**

Roses glowed in the room, and she wrote by rose light. Her, The. Light. Diane Wakoski. *Fr.* Fifteen Poems for a Lunar Eclipse None of Us Saw. **SP-WakoD**

Roses hardy as clover return. Roses. Louis Zukofsky. **CP-ZukLS**

Roses, Late Summer. Mary Oliver. **SP-OlivM**

Roses lift from the strawberry-like leaves, The. A Bouquet of Ten Roses. Robert Bly. **SP-BlyR**

Roses lingered in her cheeks, The. On Albina. Christina Georgina Rossetti. **CP-RosC3**

Roses of irony blossom, The. The Nosegay. Donald Davie. **CP-DavDo**

Roses of Life, The. Kenneth Patchen. **CP-PatcK**

Roses of love glad the garden of life, The. Love's Last Adieu. Byron. **CP-Byron**

Roses of my brother's eyes, The. Five Stanzas for My Two Brothers. Siv Cedering Fox. **SP-CedeS**

Roses of Parnell & Mellowes, The. James Liddy. **CP-LiddJ**

Roses on a brier, / Pearls from out the bitter sea. Christina Georgina Rossetti. **CP-RosC2**

Roses on the Breakfast Table. David Herbert Lawrence. **CP-LawrD**

Roses on the Terrace, The. Tennyson. **CP-TennA**

Roses red and roses white. Blue Roses. Rudyard Kipling. **CP-KiplR** *Fr.* The Light That Failed.

Roses slanted crimson sobs, The. Testimony Regarding a Ghost. Carl Sandburg. **CP-SandC**

Roses Were Talking, The. Diane Wakoski. *Fr.* Fifteen Poems for a Lunar Eclipse None of Us Saw. **SP-WakoD**

Roses with the scent bred out. In Lieu. Louis MacNeice. **CP-MacNL**

Roses, you can never die. To Roses in Julia's Bosome. Robert Herrick. **CP-HerrR**

Rosetree,rosetree / —you're a song to see:whose. Edward Estlin Cummings. **CP-CummE**

Roshi, *see also* Roshi Again. Leonard Cohen. **CP-CoheL**

Roshi Again, *see also* Roshi. Leonard Cohen. **CP-CoheL**

Rosicrucian subtleties / In the Orient had rise. Rudyard Kipling. **CP-KiplR** *Fr.* Consequences. *Fr.* Plain Tales from the Hills.

Rosie sits inside a bar smoking a large man's cigar. Letters to the Vatican. "Lou Reed." **SP-ReedL**

Rosina. Emily Brontë. **CP-BronE**

Rosny. Robert Browning. **CP-BroR2**

Ross-shire Hills, The. "Hugh MacDiarmid." **SP-MacDH**

Rosy. Louise Glück. **SP-GlücL**

Rosy-fingered dawn, The. Easter in Neuchâtel. Peter Meinke. **SP-MeinP**

Rosy, It Was. Charles Olson. **CP-OlsoC**

Rosy maiden Winifred, / With a milkpail on her head. Christina Georgina Rossetti. **CP-RosC2**

ROTC March: / Drums roll and die. White blossoms. Mizzu. Etheridge Knight. *Fr.* Missouri Haiku. **SP-KnigE**

Rotha, my Spiritual Child! this head was grey. To Rotha Q—. William Wordsworth. **CP-WorW2**

Rothebât. Stevie Smith. **CP-SmitS**

Rotten thing is after you've been pushed around, The. Kilmuir Cemetery: The Knight in Blue-Green Relief. Richard Hugo. **CP-HugoR**

Rotterdam. John Hewitt. **CP-HewiJ**

Rotting Ginsberg, I stared in the mirror naked today. Mescaline. Allen Ginsberg. **CP-GinsA**

Rou-cou spoke the dove. Song of Fixed Accord. Wallace Stevens. **CP-StevW**

Rough Outline. Charles Simic. **SP-SimiC**

Rough Song of Animals Dying. Lawrence Ferlinghetti. **SP-FerlL**

Rough Times. Marge Piercy. **SP-PierM**

Rough wind, that moanest loud. Dirge, A. Percy Bysshe Shelley. **CP-ShelP**

Roughhousing. Stephen Dobyns. **SP-DobyS**

Roughly figured, this man of moderate habits. Life Cycle of Common Man. Howard Nemerov. **CP-NemeH**

Roughly-silvered leaves that are the snow. A Song from Armenia. Geoffrey Hill. *Fr.* The Songbook of Sebastian Arrurruz. **CP-HillG**

Round: "Body of a child lay in the pool, The." Jenny Joseph. **SP-JoseJ**

Round, The. Walter de la Mare. **CP-DeLaW**

Round a so moon could dream(i sus). Edward Estlin Cummings. **CP-CummE**

Round & a Canon, A. Charles Olson. **CP-OlsoC**

Round and a Hope for Smithgirls, A. Thomas Merton. **CP-MertT**

Round and round / again, and. For the Graduation: Bolinas, 1972. Robert Creeley. **CP-CreeR**

Round and Round. Thom Gunn. **CP-GunnT**

Round and smooth, my body in the bath, The. Young Woman's Song. John Berryman. **CP-BerrJ**

Round clouds roll in the arms of the wind. Come Spring, Come Sorrow. David Herbert Lawrence. **CP-LawrD**

Round face near the top of the stairs, A. Edward Estlin Cummings. **CP-CummE**

Round moon suffocates the neighbouring stars, A. Lure of Murder. Robert Ranke Graves. **CP-GravR**

Round of gold, The. A Girl's Ring. Edward Estlin Cummings. **CP-CummE**

Round Robin, A. Robert Browning. **CP-BroR2**

Round Susan, somewhere Susan. Trajectory of the Traveling Susan. Marge Piercy. **SP-PierM**

Round the cape of a sudden came the sea. Parting at Morning. Robert Browning. **CP-BroR1**

Round the Corner. Louis MacNeice. **CP-MacNL**

Round the green fountain thick with women. Adult Bookstore. Karl Shapiro. **SP-ShapK**

Round the house were lilacs and strawberries. Twenty Years Ago. David Herbert Lawrence. **CP-LawrD**

Round the three actors in any blessed event. Blessed Event. Wystan Hugh Auden. **CP-AudeW**

Round the wide earth, from the red field your valour has won. The Conquerors. Paul Laurence Dunbar. **CP-DunbP**

Round the wondrous globe I wander wild. Two Acrostics: Round the wondrous globe / Maidens, if a maid you meet. "Lewis Carroll." **CP-CarrL**

Round Thurlow's head in early youth. On the Promotion of Thurlow. William Cowper. **CP-CowpW**

Round Trip. Stephen Dunn. **SP-DunnS**

Roundabout hours of air, slanting past Massachusetts above the. Lat. 10 Degrees North, Long. 45 Degrees West. Muriel Rukeyser. **CP-RukeM**

Roundclouds occluding patches of the. Struggle of Wings. William Carlos Williams. **CP-WilW1**

Rounded Catalogue Divine Complete, The. Walt Whitman. **CP-WhitW**

Rounded world is fair to see, The. Ralph Waldo Emerson. **CP-EmerR**
   (Motto to "Nature" ("Rounded world is fair to see, The").) **CP-EmerR**

Roundel. Archie Randolph Ammons. **SP-AmmoA**

Roundel: "Now welcom[e], Somer [or Summer] with thy sunne soft[e]." Geoffrey Chaucer. See Now Welcom[e], Somer [or Summer].

Roundel seems to fit a round of days, A. Christina Georgina Rossetti. **CP-RosC3**

Roundelay: "Blood-red bird with one green eye, A." Isabella Gardner. **CP-GardI**

Roundelay: "On all that strand." Samuel Beckett. **CP-BeckS**

Roundelay, A: "It fell upon a holy eve." Edmund Spenser. See It Fell upon a Holy [or Holly] Eve.

Rouse for Stevens, A. Theodore Roethke. **CP-RoetT**

Rouse now, my dullard, and thy wits awake. The Imp Within. Walter de la Mare. **CP-DeLaW**

Rouse up thyself, my gentle muse. On the King's Birthday. Ben Jonson. **CP-JonsB**

Roused by importunate knocks. Arthur Hugh Clough. Fr. Blank Misgivings of a Creature Moving About in Worlds Not Realized. **SP-ClouA**

Roused from a double. Roy Fisher. **SP-FishR** Fr. Diversions.

Rousseau in His Day. Donald Davie. **CP-DavDo**

Rousseau, Voltaire, our Gibbon, and De Staël. Sonnet to Lake Leman. Byron. **CP-Byron**

Rout of the White Hussars, The. Rudyard Kipling. Fr. Plain Tales from the Hills.
   "It was not in the open fight." **CP-KiplR**

Route. Joseph Ceravolo. **SP-CeraJ**

Route. George Oppen. **CP-OppeG**
   "And if at 80." **APSN**
   "Cars on the highway filled with speech." **APSN**
   "Cars run in a void of utensils, The." **APSN**
   "Department of Plants and Structures— obsolete, the old name." **APSN**
   "In Alsace, during the war." **APSN**
   "Not the symbol but the scene this pavement leads." **APSN**
   "Not to reduce the thing to nothing." **APSN**
   "Tell the beads of the chromosomes like a rosary." **APSN**
   "Tell the life of the mind, the mind creates the finite." **APSN**
   "There was no other guarantee." **APSN**
   "To insist that what is true is good, no matter, no matter." **APSN**
   "Troubled that you are not, as they say." **APSN**
   "Wars that are just? A simpler question: In the event." **APSN**
   "Words cannot be wholly transparent. And that is the." **APSN**

Route Marchin'. Rudyard Kipling. **CP-KiplR**

Route of Evanescence, A. Emily Dickinson. **CP-DickE**

Route Six. Stanley Jasspon Kunitz. **CP-KuniS**

Route 66 curves. Outside St. Louis. Etheridge Knight. Fr. Missouri Haiku. **SP-KnigE**

Route Two. Howard Nemerov. **CP-NemeH**

Routine Things Around the House, The. Stephen Dunn. **SP-DunnS**

Rover. Stanley Jasspon Kunitz. **CP-KuniS**

Rover Come Home, The. Thomas Hardy. **CP-HardT**

Roving boy comes, staff in hand, A. The Recognition. Johann N. Vogl, tr. fr. German by George Meredith. **CP-MerG2**

Roving, roving, as it seems. Una. Ralph Waldo Emerson. **CP-EmerR**

Row after row with strict impunity. Ode to the Confederate Dead. Allen Tate. **CP-TateA**

Row us out from Desenzano, to your Sirmione row! Frater Ave Atque Vale. Tennyson. **CP-TennA**

Rowan like a lip-sticked girl, A. Song. Seamus Heaney. **SP-HeanS**

Rowdy wind pushed out the sky, A. The Regatta. Richard Wilbur. **CP-WilbR**

Rower. Charles Tomlinson. **CP-TomlC**

Rowers, The. Rudyard Kipling. **CP-KiplR**

Rowin 't in Her Apron, The. Robert Burns. **CP-BurnR**

Rowing. Anne Sexton. **CP-SextA**

Rowing between Pond and Western Islands. A Loon Call. Richard Eberhart. **CP-EberR**

Rowing Endeth, The. Anne Sexton. **CP-SextA**

Rowing, I reach'd a rock—the sea was low. Gerard Manley Hopkins. **ChTr** Fr. A Vision of the Mermaids. **CP-HopkG**

Rowle of Parchment Clunn about him beares, A. Upon Clunn. Robert Herrick. **CP-HerrR**

Roxy. James Schuyler. **CP-SchuJ**

Royal and Dower-royal, I the Queen. The Song of the Cities. Rudyard Kipling. **CP-KiplR**

Royal Love Child, The. Marsden Hartley. **CP-HartM**

Royal MAB, dethroned, discrowned, The. To M. A. B. "Lewis Carroll." **CP-CarrL**

Royal Palm. Hart Crane. **CP-CranH**

Royal Princess, A. Christina Georgina Rossetti. **CP-RosC1**

Royal roads were cow paths, The. The First Kingdom. Seamus Heaney. **SP-HeanS** Fr. Sweeney Redivivus.

Royal Sponsors. Thomas Hardy. **CP-HardT**

Royals. James Schuyler. **CP-SchuJ**

Royce Newport Money. Ron Koertge. **SP-KoerR**

R.P.M. John Hewitt. **CP-HewiJ**

R.S.S. William Cowper. **CP-CowpW**

R.S.S. Written in a Fit of Illness. William Cowper. **CP-CowpW**

Rub thou thy battered lamp: nor claim nor beg. The State of Age. George Meredith. **CP-MerG1**

Rubaiyat for Sue Ella Tucker. Miller Williams. **SP-WillM**

Rubber Rats. Stephen Berg. **SP-BergS**

Rubbing her mouth along my mouth she lost. Eleutheria. James Wright. **CP-WrigJ**

Rubbing her sable with long thoughtful. John Yau. **SP-YauJo** Fr. Scenes from the Life of Boullee.

Rubbing of the sleeping bag on my ear made me dream, The. The Ant Mansion. Robert Bly. **SP-BlyR**

Rubens had been a Statesman or a Saint. William Blake. See I Rubens am a Statesman & a Saint.

Rubh An' Dunain. Charles Tomlinson. **CP-TomlC**

Rubies. Ralph Waldo Emerson. **CP-EmerR**

Ruby and Amethyst. Robert Ranke Graves. **CP-GravR**

Ruby Brown. Langston Hughes. **SP-HughL**

Ruby Daggett. Richard Eberhart. **CP-EberR**

Ruby Tells All. Miller Williams. **SP-WillM**

Ruby wine is drunk by knaves. Heroism. Ralph Waldo Emerson. **CP-EmerR**

Rucksack braced on a board, lashed tight on back. September. Gary Snyder. Fr. Six Years. **CP-SnydG**

Ruddy drop of manly blood, A. Friendship. Ralph Waldo Emerson. **CP-EmerR**

Rude is this Edifice, and Thou hast seen. Written with a Pencil upon a Stone in the Wall of the House (an Out-House), on the Island at Grasmere. William Wordsworth. **CP-WorW1**

Rude man, 'tis vain thy damsel to commend. 3.4. Ovid. **CP-MarlC**, tr. by Christopher Marlowe; Fr. Elegies.

Rude wind is singing, The. Fragment. Percy Bysshe Shelley. **CP-ShelP**

Rudel to the Lady of Tripoli. Robert Browning. **CP-BroR1**

Rudiments. Roy Fisher. **SP-FishR**

Rudolph Reed was oaken. The Ballad of Rudolph Reed. Gwendolyn Brooks. **SP-BrooG**

Rudy Flesh. Shel Silverstein. **SP-SilS2**

Rudyerd, as lesser dames, to great ones use. To Benjamin Rudyerd. Ben Jonson. **CP-JonsB**

Rue Carpenter. Archibald MacLeish. **CP-MacLA**

Rue Conti where Jim, Hank, I. The Quarter. James Liddy. **CP-LiddJ**

Rue de Vaugirard. Samuel Beckett. **CP-BeckS**

Rue on me, Lord, for thy goodness and grace. Bible, O.T. See Psalm 51: "Have mercy upon me, O God. . . ."

Rufey my how frustrate unquickened and craved the tie I'm equal. Catullus. See Carmen 77: "Whom I have trusted to no end (Rufus)."

Rufus Woodpecker visited the President. Charles Olson. **CP-OlsoC**

Rugged forhead that with grave foresight, The. Edmund Spenser. **OAEL-1; OBSC** Fr. The Faerie Queene. **CP-Spens**
   (Love.) **OBSC**

Ruhr-Gebiet. Allen Ginsberg. **CP-GinsA**

"Too much industry." **EaPr**

Ruin. Christina Georgina Rossetti. **CP-RosC3**

Ruin, The. Charles Tomlinson. **CP-TomlC**

Ruin seize thee, ruthless King! Bard, The [A Pindaric Ode]. Thomas Gray. **CP-GrayT**

Ruination. David Herbert Lawrence. **CP-LawrD**

Ruined convent on the Breton coast, A. *after* Corbière. Derek Mahon. **SP-MahoD**

Ruined Cross, The. Christina Georgina Rossetti. **CP-RosC3**

Ruined Maid, The. Thomas Hardy. **CP-HardT**

Ruined, time ruined, all these once good things. Rimrock, Where It Is. Hayden Carruth. **CP-CarHS**

Ruines of Time, The. Edmund Spenser. **CP-Spens**

Ruins Answer, The. John Hewitt. **CP-HewiJ**

Ruins of a Great House. Derek Walcott. **CP-WalcD**

Ruins of Rome. Joachim Du Bellay, *tr. fr. French by* Edmund Spenser. **CP-Spens**

   "He that has seen a great oak dry and dead." **FaBoPP**

   "Hope ye, my verses, that posterity." **PoE**

   "Thou stranger, which for Rome in Rome here seekest." **FaBoPP; OBVE**

   "Thou that at Rome astonished doth behold." **FaBoPP**

   "Who list the Romane greatnes forth to figure." **OBVE**

Ruins under the Stars. Galway Kinnell. **SP-KinnG**

   "All day under acrobat."

   "Just now I had a funny sensation."

   "Overhead the skull-hill rises."

   "Sometimes I see them." **RFM**

   "This morning I watched."

Rule, The. Richard Wilbur. **CP-WilbR**

Rule, Britannia! James Thomson *and* David Mallet. **CP-ThomJ** *Fr.* Alfred: A Masque.

Rule of the majority is / strictly enforced in all matters, The. Hayden Carruth. **CP-CarHS** *Fr.* The Bloomingdale Papers.

Rule which by obeying grows. Intellect. Ralph Waldo Emerson. **CP-EmerR**

Ruler after word & thought. Hafiz, *tr. by* Ralph Waldo Emerson. **CP-EmerR** *Fr.* Odes.

Rules and Ranges for Ian Tyson. Roy Fisher. **SP-FishR**

Rules and Regulations. "Lewis Carroll." **CP-CarrL**

Rules break like a thermometer, The. Adrienne Rich. *Fr.* Twenty-one Love Poems. **SP-RicA1; SP-RicA2**

Rules for Our Reach. Robert Herrick. **CP-HerrR**

Rules to men made evident, The. Ralph Waldo Emerson. **CP-EmerR**

Rum asks—see, fortune won't molest you. Catullus. *See* Carmen 55: "Where / if it's not too much to ask."

Rum tiddy um, / tiddy um. Potato Blossom Songs and Jigs. Carl Sandburg. **CP-SandC**

Rumba! Rumba! William Carlos Williams. **CP-WilW2**

Rumbling under blackened girders, Midland, bound for Cricklewood. Parliament Hill Fields. Sir John Betjeman. **CP-BetjJ**

Ruminant pillows! Gregarious soft boulders! The Black Faced Sheep. Donald Hall. **CP-HallD**

Rumination. Richard Eberhart. **CP-EberR**

Rummage. Hayden Carruth. **CP-CarHS**

Rumor Unverified Stop Can You Confirm Stop. Robert Penn Warren. *Fr.* Ballad of a Sweet Dream of Peace. **SP-WarrR**

Rumors. John Yau. **SP-YauJo**

Rumors of liberation. We could not believe it. Richard Eberhart. *Fr.* Brotherhood of Men. **CP-EberR**

Rumour. Charles Tomlinson. **CP-TomlC**

Rump-Trumpet, the Critic. Refusal of a Kindness Offered. Howard Nemerov. **CP-NemeH**

Rumpe is a Turne-broach, yet he seldome can. Upon Rumpe. Robert Herrick. **CP-HerrR**

Rumpelstiltskin. Anne Sexton. **CP-SextA**

Rumpled river, The. River Rhyme. William Carlos Williams. **CP-WilW2**

Rumpled sheet, A. The Term. William Carlos Williams. **CP-WilW1**

Run before Dawn. William Stafford. **SP-StafW**

Run for Your Life. The Beatles. **CP-Beatl**

Run go get out of here. "Bob Dylan." *Fr.* Some Other Kinds of Songs. **CP-DylaB**

Run-In, The. Alun Lewis. **CP-LewiA**

Run of the Downs, The. Rudyard Kipling. **CP-KiplR**

Run on, you still dead to the sound of a name. Louis Zukofsky. **CP-ZukLS** *Fr.* 29 Poems. **CP-ZukLS**

Run out the boat, my broken comrades. Thalassa. Louis MacNeice. **CP-MacNL**

Run upon the Bankers, The. Jonathan Swift. **CP-SwifJ**

Runagate Runagate. Robert Earl Hayden. **CP-HaydR**

Runaway, The. Robert Frost. **CP-FrosR**

Runaway Colors. Carl Sandburg. **CP-SandC**

Runaway Slave, The. Walt Whitman. **PoNe** *Fr.* Song of Myself. **CP-WhitW**

Runaway Slave at Pilgrim's Point, The. Elizabeth Barrett Browning. **CP-BroEB**

Runaway Sun. Pablo Neruda, *tr. fr. Spanish by* Ben Belitt. **SP-NeruP**

Runaway Team (Written a Few Days After John Glenn's Space Flight), The. Louise McNeill. **SP-McNeL**

Rundown at Ned's Bar B.Q, The. Al Young. **CP-YounA**

Rune. Muriel Rukeyser. **CP-RukeM**

Rune of the Finland Woman. Marilyn Hacker. **SP-HackM**

Runes, The. Denise Levertov. **CP-LeveD**

Runes. Howard Nemerov. **CP-NemeH**

   "About Ulysses, the learned have reached two."

   "Consider how the seed lost by a bird."

   "Fat time of the year is also time, The."

   "Holy man said to me, 'Split the stick', A."

   "In this dehydrated time of digests, pills."

   "Seed sleeps in the furnaces of death, The."

   "Sunflowers, traders rounding the horn of time."

   "There is a threshold, that meniscus where."

   "There sailed out on the river, Conrad saw."

   "This is about the stillness in moving things."

   "To go low, to be as nothing, to die."

   "To watch water, to watch running water."

   "Unstable as water, thou shalt not excel."

   "White water now in the snowflake's prison."

   "White water, white water, feather of a form."

Runes on Weland's Sword, The. Rudyard Kipling. **CP-KiplR** *Fr.* Old Men at Pevensey. *Fr.* Puck of Pook's Hill.

Rungs. Charles Kenneth Williams. **SP-WillC**

Runner. Wystan Hugh Auden. *Fr.* Six Commissioned Texts. **CP-AudeW**

   "All visible, visibly." **SD**

Runner, The. Gary Gildner. **SP-GildG**

Runner. Daniel Gerard Hoffman. **SP-HoffD**

Runner, The. Walt Whitman. **CP-WhitW**

Runners, The. Jim Carroll. **SP-CarrJ**

   "Here, every lost act."

   "Their voice, as one, was heavy."

   "Thick as milk from a peasant's breast."

   "You hear the call."

Runners, The. Rudyard Kipling. **CP-KiplR**

Runners going from one to the other, The. Dusk. Chuck Miller. **SP-MillC**

Running. Brendan Galvin. **SP-GalvB**

Running. Richard Wilbur. **CP-WilbR**

Running again / through the woods. Down the Lanes and Paths (For Stack). Chuck Miller. **SP-MillC**

Running ahead beside the sea. Paradox. Robert Penn Warren. **SP-WarrR**

Running and standing still at once. Painting a Mountain Stream. Howard Nemerov. **CP-NemeH**

Running Barefoot, *also stands as sl. diff. and separate poem* A Baby Running Barefoot. David Herbert Lawrence. *Fr.* Baby-Movements. **CP-LawrD**

Running Changes, The. Roy Fisher. **SP-FishR**

Running Footsteps. James Schuyler. **CP-SchuJ**

Running from the shadow-coach. Entry. Edwin Rolfe. **CP-RolfE**

Running in Snow. James McAuley. **SP-McAuJ**

Running into Things. Miller Williams. **SP-WillM**

Running of the Grunion, The. Muriel Rukeyser. **CP-RukeM**

Running peoples on their bloody way, The. Fear. Randall Jarrell. **CP-JarrR**

Running through the thick wiry grasses to the pond. Shore. Jean Garrigue. **SP-GarrJ**

Running to Paradise. William Butler Yeats. **CP-YeatW**

Running Water Music. Gary Snyder. **CP-SnydG**

Running Water Music II. Gary Snyder. **CP-SnydG**

Running with the Hyenas. Peter Meinke. **SP-MeinP**

Runs falls rises stumbles on from darkness into darkness. Runagate Runagate. Robert Earl Hayden. **CP-HaydR**

Rupaiyat of Omar Kal'vin, The. Rudyard Kipling. **CP-KiplR**

Rural Architecture. William Wordsworth. **CP-WorW1**

Rural Ceremony. William Wordsworth. *Fr.* Ecclesiastical Sonnets. **CP-WorW2**

Rural Delivery. Charles Simic. **SP-SimiC**

Rural Illusions. William Wordsworth. **CP-WorW2**

Rural Life. George Crabbe. *See* Truth in Poetry.

Rural Mailboxes. Brendan Galvin. **SP-GalvB**

Rural Reflections. Adrienne Rich. **CP-RicAE; SP-RicA2**

Rural Sights and Sounds. William Cowper. *See* For I have lov'd the rural walk through lanes.

Rush of rain against the glass, The. New England Spring, 1942. Edna St. Vincent Millay. **CP-MillE**

Rush saves his shooes, in wet and snowie wether. Upon Rush. Robert Herrick. **CP-HerrR**

Rushes in a watery place, / And reeds in a hollow. Christina Georgina Rossetti. **CP-RosC2**

Rushing darkness of the summer evening, The. Pastorale. Gilbert Sorrentino. **SP-SorrG**

Rushing music, seizing on her dance, A. L'Etoile. Richard Wilbur. **CP-WilbR**

Russell Flint, A. Sir John Betjeman. **CP-BetjJ**

Russia. William Carlos Williams. **CP-WilW2**

Russia and America circle each other. A Woman Unconscious. Ted Hughes. **SP-HughT**

Russia, most feminine of lands. Poem for a Far Land. John Updike. **CP-UpdiJ**

Russia! Russia! you might say. Song. William Carlos Williams. **CP-WilW2**

Russia to the Pacifists. Rudyard Kipling. **CP-KiplR**

Russia, your white nights. White Nights, 1938. Martin Edmunds. **SP-EdmuM**

Russian Fugitive, The. William Wordsworth. **CP-WorW2**

Russian has three an' a half red eyes, A. "Bob Dylan." *Fr.* 11 Outlined Epitaphs. **CP-DylaB**

Russian Jew, for you. Mandelstam, on Dante. Donald Davie. **CP-DavDo**

Rust. Limewash. The iron tyres. Roy Fisher. **SP-FishR** *Fr.* New Diversions.

Rusted pundit, throttled chin. Genghis Chan: Private Eye IV. John Yau. **SP-YauJo**

Rustication. Adrienne Rich. **CP-RicAE**

Rustice, sta, paucis dum te moror, auribus adsis. *acc. by English translation.* Thomas Campion. **CP-CampT**

Rusticity's ungainly form. Robert Burns. **CP-BurnR**

Rustle of whispering wind over leaves, A. Kingfisher Flat. William Everson. **SP-EverW**

Rustling a Hog. Gary Gildner. **SP-GildG**

Rustum Beg of Kolazai—slightly backward Native State. A Legend of the Foreign Office. Rudyard Kipling. **CP-KiplR**

Rusty Crimson. Carl Sandburg. **CP-SandC**

Rusty-gold green trees, The. The Non-Entity. William Carlos Williams. **CP-WilW2**

Rusty Man, The. Herman Melville. **SP-MelvH**

Ruth [or, The Influences of Nature]. William Wordsworth. **CP-WorW1**

Ruth. George Crabbe. **SP-CrabG** *Fr.* Tales of the Hall.

Ruth of soups and balm of sauces, The. On a Diet. William Matthews. **SP-MattW**

Ruthie? That you? Well, how's it go- / ing back there, good? Yeah. Look. Phone. Hayden Carruth. **CP-CarHS**

Ruthlessly gentle, gently ruthless we move. Thom Gunn. *Fr.* Tom-Dobbin. **CP-GunnT**

Rutland. Donald Davie. **CP-DavDo**

Ruyter the while, that had our ocean curbed. The Dutch in the Medway. Andrew Marvell. **FaBoEH; OBS** *Fr.* The Last Instructions to a Painter. **CP-MarvA**

Ryder. John Haines. **SP-HainJ**

Ryder. Muriel Rukeyser. **CP-RukeM**

(Ryokan's scroll). Louis Zukofsky. **CP-ZukLS**

S

S(/ these out of in). Edward Estlin Cummings. **CP-CummE**

S. Dead. Marge Piercy. **SP-PierM**

S M. Alice Walker. **CP-WalkA**

S. Miniato: One by Aretino. Richard Hugo. **CP-HugoR**

S. R. Ralph Waldo Emerson. **CP-EmerR**

S-sss-ss-sh! Langston Hughes. **SP-HughL**

S. Thomae Aquinatis Rhythmus ad SS. Sacramentum. Gerard Manley Hopkins. **CP-HopkG**

Sa Majestá Très Chrétienne. Arthur Hugh Clough. **SP-ClouA**

Saadi. Ralph Waldo Emerson. **CP-EmerR**

Saadi held the Muse in awe. Ralph Waldo Emerson. **CP-EmerR**

Saadi loved the new & old. Ralph Waldo Emerson. **CP-EmerR**

Saadians, Marble, Tile, and Flower, The. James Liddy. **CP-LiddJ**

Sabbath, The. Wystan Hugh Auden. **CP-AudeW**

Sabbath bells renew the inviting peal, The. Visitation of the Sick. William Wordsworth. **CP-WorW2**

Sabbath evening privacy at home. Eben Haëzer. Gerrit Achterberg, *tr. fr. Dutch* by Adrienne Rich. **CP-RicAE**

Sabbath Morning at Sea, A. Elizabeth Barrett Browning. **CP-BroEB**

Sabbath of Mutual Respect, The. Marge Piercy. **SP-PierM**

Sabbath Scene, A. John Greenleaf Whittier. **CP-WhitJ**

Sabbaths. Robert Herrick. **CP-HerrR**

Sabbaths are threefold, (as S. Austine sayes:). Sabbaths. Robert Herrick. **CP-HerrR**

Sabbaths, W.I. Derek Walcott. **CP-WalcD**

Sabotage? Yes, he took it up to Manhattan. Canto 19. Ezra Pound. *Fr.* Cantos. **CP-PoCan**

Sabrina. John Milton. **OBS** *Fr.* Comus; a Masque Presented at Ludlow Castle.

Sabrina. John Milton. *See* Sabrina Fair.

Sabrina Fair. John Milton. **EBEV; ELP; FaBoCh; GN; PoEL-3** *Fr.* Comus; a Masque Presented at Ludlow Castle.

(Sabrina.) **CH; NOBE; OBEV**

(Song.) **OXAEP-1**

Sabrina fair. Sabrina Fair. John Milton. **CH; EBEV; ELP; FaBoCh; GN; NOBE; OBEV; OXAEP-1; PoEL-3** *Fr.* Comus; a Masque Presented at Ludlow Castle.

Sabrina's Song. John Milton. **NOSC** *Fr.* Comus; a Masque Presented at Ludlow Castle.

Saccharesent, lying in glucose, The. Canto 15. Ezra Pound. *Fr.* Cantos. **CP-PoCan**

Sacco Writes to His Son. Alun Lewis. **CP-LewiA**

Sacheverel. William Wordsworth. *Fr.* Ecclesiastical Sonnets. **CP-WorW2**

Sack of the Gods, The. Rudyard Kipling. **CP-KiplR** *Fr.* The Naulahka.

Sacrament. William Wordsworth. *Fr.* Ecclesiastical Sonnets. **CP-WorW2**

Sacred, blithesome, undenied, / With benisons from East and West. A Kiss to the Bride. Walt Whitman. **CP-WhitW**

Sacred England, stagnant pool. England Again. John Gould Fletcher. **SP-FletJ**

Sacred Fount, The. Daniel Gerard Hoffman. **SP-HoffD**

Sacred Goddess, Mother Earth. Song of Proserpine. Percy Bysshe Shelley. **CP-ShelP**

Sacred Heart. Thom Gunn. **CP-GunnT**

Sacred Heart 2. Thomas Merton. **CP-MertT**

Sacred is secret: at the confluence. The. Howard Nemerov. **CP-NemeH**

Sacred Lake. Muriel Rukeyser. **CP-RukeM**

Sacred legion of the justborn, The. Carl Sandburg. *Fr.* The People, Yes. **CP-SandC**

Sacred Objects. Louise Glück. *Fr.* Dedication to Hunger. **SP-GlücL**

Sacred? or sacrosanct? The Ironist. Donald Davie. **CP-DavDo**

Sacred Religion! "mother of form and fear." Seathwaite Chapel. William Wordsworth. *Fr.* The River Duddon [A Series of Sonnets]. **CP-WorW2**

Sacred song that on mine ear, The. To the Hon. Mrs. George Lamb. Byron. **CP-Byron**

Sacred sycamore and the odor of cedar wood (the odor of the buried boat). The Boat. Charles Olson. **CP-OlsoC**

Sacred to the Memory. Thomas Hardy. **CP-HardT**

Sacred to the Memory. Stanley Jasspon Kunitz. *Fr.* Words for the Unknown Makers: A Garland of Commemorative Verses. **CP-KuniS**

Sacred to the Memory of My Late Honoured Friend, Collonell Richard Lovelace. Eldred Revett. *Fr.* Elegies, 1660. **CP-LoveR**

Sacred watcher, wave thy bells! To the Bluebell. Emily Brontë. **CP-BronE**

Sacrifice, The. Richard Eberhart. **CP-EberR**

Sacrifice. Ralph Waldo Emerson. *Fr.* Quatrains. **CP-EmerR**

(Faith.) **OtMeF**

Sacrifice, The. George Herbert. **CP-HerbG**

Sacrifice. Audre Lorde. **SP-LordA**

Sacrifice, by Way of Discourse betwixt Himselfe and Julia, The. Robert Herrick. **CP-HerrR**

Sacrifice of Er-Heb, The. Rudyard Kipling. **CP-KiplR**

Sacrificed—and still no sound from the sea. Iphigenia in Aulis. Agamemnon Speaks. Malcolm Lowry. **CP-LowrM**

Sacrificed Author, A. Howard Nemerov. *Fr.* Gnomes. **CP-NemeH**

Sacrilege, The. Thomas Hardy. **CP-HardT**

Sad and lovely face, with upturned eyes, A. Sonnet to a Picture by Lucca Giordano in the Mureo Borbonico at Naples. William Wordsworth. **CP-WorW2**

Sad as he sits on the white sea-stone. Tarantella. David Herbert Lawrence. **CP-LawrD**

Sad Children's Song, The. Grace Paley. **CP-PaleG**

Sad Dust Glories. Allen Ginsberg. **CP-GinsA**

Sad-Eyed Lady of the Lowlands. "Bob Dylan." **CP-DylaB**

Sad-Eyed Mules of Men. Charles Bukowski. **SP-BukC2**

Sad-faced, heavy scholar / who, in spite of exemplary diligence, A. Pavane for a Dead Professor. John Hewitt. **CP-HewiJ**

Sad Heart, The. Stevie Smith. **CP-SmitS**

Sad heart, the gymnast of inertia, does not count. The Sad Indian. Hart Crane. **CP-CranH**

Sad Hesper o'er the buried sun. Tennyson. **EBVV; EnVR; NoP** *Fr.* In Memoriam A. H. H. **CP-TennA**

Sad Hour of Your Peace, The. Al Young. **CP-YounA**

Sad I'm a-sittin' on the railroad track. Ballad for a Friend. "Bob Dylan." **CP-DylaB**

Sad Indian, The. Hart Crane. **CP-CranH**

Sad Invective. Stephen Berg. **SP-BergS**

Sad is old Ben Tristlewaite. Old Ben. Walter de la Mare. **CP-DeLaW**

Sad little lake, your. The Exercise. Thom Gunn. **CP-GunnT**

Sad lot, to have no Hope! Though lowly kneeling. The Visionary Hope. Samuel Taylor Coleridge. **CP-ColeS**

Sad man on a summer day, A. Man and Nature. Elizabeth Barrett Browning. **CP-BroEB**

Sad Mayflower! watched by winter stars. The Mayflowers. John Greenleaf Whittier. **CP-WhitJ**

Sad Mother, The. Stevie Smith. **CP-SmitS**

Sad One, The. Sir John Suckling. **CP-SuckJ**
    Song to a Lute, A.

Sad Poem, A. Charles Bukowski. **SP-BukC3**

Sad seamstress, The. House Guest. Elizabeth Bishop. **CP-BishE**

Sad Shepherd, The. Ben Jonson.
    "Though I am young, and cannot tell." **CP-JonsB**

Sad Shepherd, The. William Butler Yeats. **CP-YeatW**

Sad Singing in Darkness. Michael Hartnett. **SP-HarMi**

Sad Song. "Lou Reed." **SP-ReedL**

Sad Steps. Philip Larkin. **CP-LarkP**

Sad Strains of a Gay Waltz. Wallace Stevens. **CP-StevW**

Sad thoughts, avaunt!—partake we their blithe cheer. Sheep-Washing. William Wordsworth. *Fr.* The River Duddon [A Series of Sonnets]. **CP-WorW2**

Sad thy tale, thou idle page. On Reading, in a Newspaper, the Death of J—— McL———, Esq. Brother to a Young Lady, a Particular Friend of the Author's. Robert Burns. **CP-BurnR**

Sad to say there's more than one—loneliness. The Body's Curse. Stephen Dobyns. **SP-DobyS**

Saddest Day, The. David Herbert Lawrence. **CP-LawrD**

Saddest noise, the sweetest noise, The. Emily Dickinson. **CP-DickE**

Saddest Words, The. John Greenleaf Whittier. **ImPo** *Fr.* Maud Muller. **CP-WhitJ**

Saddhu of Couva, The. Derek Walcott. **CP-WalcD**

Saddle and ride, I heard a man say. Alternative Song for the Severed Head in "The King of the Great Clock Tower." William Butler Yeats. **CP-YeatW**

S'addormentò la nostra figliolina. Christina Georgina Rossetti. **CP-RosC3**

Sade, misunderstood, went to jail. Sade on Calvary. John Clellon Holmes. **SP-HolmJ**

Sade on Calvary. John Clellon Holmes. **SP-HolmJ**

Sadie and Maud. Gwendolyn Brooks. **InPK; MoP; NOBA; NoAM; TAP** *Fr.* A Street in Bronzeville. **SP-BrooG**

Sadly I walk't within the field. The Olive Branch. Robert Herrick. **CP-HerrR**

Sadness is so much a part of me. Malcolm Lowry. **CP-LowrM**

Sadness of the Sea, The. William Carlos Williams. **CP-WilW1**

Sadness of Things for Sappho's Sickness, The. Robert Herrick. **CP-HerrR**

Sadness we bring back from sleep, The. Waking. Archibald MacLeish. **CP-MacLA**

Sae Far Awa. Robert Burns. **CP-BurnR**

Sae flaxen were her ringlets. She Says She Lo'es Me Best of A'. Robert Burns. **CP-BurnR**

Safari. Daniel Gerard Hoffman. **SP-HoffD**

Safe Despair it is that raves. Emily Dickinson. **CP-DickE**

Safe in their Alabaster Chambers. Emily Dickinson. **CP-DickE**

Safe upon the solid rock the ugly houses stand. Second Fig. Edna St. Vincent Millay. **CP-MillE**

Safe where I cannot lie yet, / Safe where I hope to lie too. Christina Georgina Rossetti. **CP-RosC2**

Safety Man, The. Ernest Hemingway. **HemiE**

Safety on the Shore. Robert Herrick. **CP-HerrR**

Safety To Look to Ones Selfe. Robert Herrick. **CP-HerrR**

Saffron. Stevie Smith. **CP-SmitS**

Sagacity. Richard Eberhart. **CP-EberR**

Sage, The. Edwin Arlington Robinson. **CP-RobiE**

Sage Enamoured and the Honest Lady, The. George Meredith. **CP-MerG1**
    "Across his path the spouseless Lady cast."
    "He passed her through the sermon's dull defile."
    "No knightly sword to serve, nor harp of bard."
    "One fairest of the ripe unwedded left."
    "So spake she her first utterance on the rack."

Sage of Darien, The. Ogden Nash. **CP-NashO**

Sage to the Young Man, The. Alfred Edward Housman. **CP-HousA**

Sage, who said he should be proud, The. On Seeing Verses Written upon Windows in Inns. Jonathan Swift. **CP-SwifJ**

Sagest of women, even of widows, she. Byron. **NOBL; PeLV** *Fr.* Canto the First. **EnRP; NAEL-2; NoP; OAEL-2; PoE** *Fr.* Don Juan. **CP-Byron**

Saginaw Song, The. Theodore Roethke. **CP-RoetT**

Sagittarius, Scorpio Rising. William Dickey. **SP-DickW**

Sahara Bus Trip, The. Rita Dove. **SP-DoveR**

Sahara doth not keep her livid hell. On the Road to Wockensutter. John Crowe Ransom. **SP-RansJ**

Said a people to a poet—"Go out from among us straightway!" The Poet and the Bird. Elizabeth Barrett Browning. **CP-BroEB**

Said a wistful daw in Saint Peter's tower. The Peace Peal. Thomas Hardy. **CP-HardT**

Said Abner, "At last thou art come! Ere I tell, ere thou speak." Saul. Robert Browning. **CP-BroR1**

Said Adam. Charles Olson. **CP-OlsoC**

Said Death to Passion. Emily Dickinson. **CP-DickE**

Said England unto Pharaoh, "I must make a man of you." Pharaoh and the Sergeant. Rudyard Kipling. **CP-KiplR**

Said Eve; / That Fall began. The Fall! Archibald MacLeish. *Fr.* Songs for Eve. **CP-MacLA**

Said General Clay to General Gore. The Generals. Shel Silverstein. **SP-SilS2**

Said Harvey Swados to Herbert Gold. A Vision. John Updike. **CP-UpdiJ**

Said Jim X. . . . Ezra Pound. *See* Canto 12: "And we sit here / under the wall."

Said John Quinn. All at Sea. Ezra Pound. **FaBoDD** *Fr.* Canto 12: "And we sit here / under the wall." **NAs** *Fr.* Cantos. **CP-PoCan**

Said lady once to lover. The Three Bushes. William Butler Yeats. **CP-YeatW**

Said red-ribboned Evans. A Squib on Colonel Evans. William Wordsworth. **CP-WorW2**

Said Rinpoche Chögyam Trungpa Tulku in the marble glittering apartment lobby. What Would You Do If You Lost It. Allen Ginsberg. **CP-GinsA**

Said Secrecy to Cowardice and Fraud. William Wordsworth. **CP-WorW2**

Said Set, the Great Accuser: "You poisoned your young brothers." She Becomes a Soul, Flowering Toward Egyptian Resurrection, B.C. 29. Nicholas Vachel Lindsay. *Fr.* The Trial of the Dead Cleopatra in Her Beautiful and Wonderful Tomb. **CP-LindV**

Said she didn't know anything about ovens. Gretel. Ron Koertge. **SP-KoerR**

Said the grave Dean of Westminster. A Refusal. Thomas Hardy. **CP-HardT**

Said the lady, Can you do. Question. Langston Hughes. **SP-HughL**

Said the Moon to the Sun. "Lewis Carroll." *Fr.* Puzzles. *Fr.* Puzzles from Wonderland. **CP-CarrL**

Said the panama hat to the fedora. Quotations. Carl Sandburg. **CP-SandC**

Said the Poet to the Analyst. Anne Sexton. **CP-SextA**

Said the red-cloaked crone. Signs and Tokens. Thomas Hardy. **CP-HardT**

Said the Undertaker to the Overtaker. Tweedledee and Tweedledoom. Ogden Nash. **CP-NashO**

Said the Watcher by the Way. The Town Down the River. Edwin Arlington Robinson. **CP-RobiE**

Said, "What the devil!" when he dropped. My Father. Ron Koertge. **SP-KoerR**

Sail and Oar. Robert Ranke Graves. **CP-GravR**

Sail before the morning breeze. The Archipelago. Herman Melville. **SP-MelvH**

Sail, Monarchs, rising and falling. Roots and Branches. Robert Duncan. **SP-DuncR**

Sail Out for Good, Eidólon Yacht! Walt Whitman. **CP-WhitW**

Sailboats. John Gould Fletcher. **SP-FletJ** *Fr.* Sand and Spray: A Sea-Symphony. **SP-FletJ**

Sailing after Lunch. Wallace Stevens. **CP-StevW**

Sailing at dawn into the Narrows. The Arrival. Charles Tomlinson. **CP-TomlC**

Sailing Dalmatia. Richard Hugo. **CP-HugoR**

Sailing from Naples. Richard Hugo. **CP-HugoR**

Sailing Home. Erica Jong. **SP-JongE**

Sailing Home from Rapallo. Robert Lowell. **SP-LoweR**

Sailing of the Mayflower, The. Henry Wadsworth Longfellow. *Fr.* The Courtship of Miles Standish. **SP-LongH**

Expedition to Wessagusset, The. **PAH**

"There with his boat was the Master, already a little impatient." **TreFS**

Sailing Orders. Louis MacNeice. **CP-MacNL**

Sailing Pine, The; the Cedar, proud and tall. Kinds of Trees to Plant. Edmund Spenser. **OHIP** *Fr.* The Faerie Queene. **CP-Spens**

Sailing Sailing / under the creatura ridge. Floating Gardens. Joseph Ceravolo. **SP-CeraJ**

Sailing thru the straits of Demos. Lawrence Ferlinghetti. **SP-FerlL**

Sailing to Buck's Harbor. Richard Eberhart. **CP-EberR**

Sailing to Byzantium. William Butler Yeats. **CP-YeatW**

Sailing to Tauris: the pitchy cave. Orestes at Tauris. Randall Jarrell. **CP-JarrR**

Sailor cannot see the North, The. Emily Dickinson. **SP-DickE**

Sailor dreamt of loss, The. The Snowmass Cycle. Stephen Dunn. **SP-DunnS**

Sailor in Africa, The. Rita Dove. **SP-DoveR**

Sailors, The. Malcolm Lowry. *Fr.* Songs for Second Childhood. **CP-LowrM**

Sailor's Mother, The. Thomas Hardy. **CP-HardT**

Sailor's Mother, The. William Wordsworth. **CP-WorW1**

Sailor's Song, A. Paul Laurence Dunbar. **CP-DunbP**

Sailors there are of gentlest breed. Commemorative of a Naval Victory. Herman Melville. **SP-MelvH**

Sailors who come ashore, The. Fleet Visit. Wystan Hugh Auden. **CP-AudeW**

Sailor's Wife, The. "Lewis Carroll." **CP-CarrL**

Sails on All Saints' Day. John Updike. **CP-UpdiJ**

Saint. Frank O'Hara. **SP-OharF**

Saint About to Fall, A. Dylan Thomas. **CP-ThomD**

St. Agnes: A Responsory. Thomas Merton. **CP-MertT; SP-MertT**

St. Agnes' Eve—Ah, bitter chill it was! The Eve of St. Agnes. John Keats. **CP-KeatJ**

St. Alberic. Thomas Merton. **CP-MertT; SP-MertT**

Saint and demon blindly stare. Europe. Howard Nemerov. **CP-NemeH**

Saint and the Hunchback, The. William Butler Yeats. **CP-YeatW**

St. Andrew. Christopher Smart. *Fr.* Hymns and Spiritual Songs for the Fasts and Festivals of the Church of England. **SP-SmarC**

St. Andrew's Church. Christina Georgina Rossetti. **CP-RosC3**

Saint Anthony and the Rose of Life. Stevie Smith. **CP-SmitS**

St. Anthony, my father's holy man. Temptation. John Ciardi. **SP-CiarJ**

St Antony of Padua. Robert Ranke Graves. **CP-GravR**

Saint-Apollinaire. Daniel Gerard Hoffman. **SP-HoffD**

St. Armorer's Church from the Outside. Wallace Stevens. **CP-StevW**

St. Barnabas. Christina Georgina Rossetti. **CP-RosC2**

St. Barnabas. Christopher Smart. *Fr.* Hymns and Spiritual Songs for the Fasts and Festivals of the Church of England. **SP-SmarC**

St. Barnabas, with John his sister's son. St. Barnabas. Christina Georgina Rossetti. **CP-RosC2**

St. Bartholomew. Christina Georgina Rossetti. **CP-RosC2**

St. Bartholomew. Christopher Smart. *Fr.* Hymns and Spiritual Songs for the Fasts and Festivals of the Church of England. **SP-SmarC**

Saint Cadoc. Sir John Betjeman. **CP-BetjJ**

St Catherine of Ledbury. William Wordsworth. **CP-WorW2**

Saint Cecilia: / between / man as vehicle traversed. Nashville Mornings. Donald Davie. **CP-DavDo**

St. Christopher. Louise Bogan. **CP-BogaL**

St. Clement's: Harris. Richard Hugo. **CP-HugoR**

Saint Distaffs Day, or the Morrow after Twelfth Day. Robert Herrick. **CP-HerrR**

St. Dorothea, *For shorter and diff. vers., see also* For a Picture of Saint Dorothea *and* Lines for a Picture of St. Dorothea. Gerard Manley Hopkins. **CP-HopkG**

Saint Edmond's Eve. Percy Bysshe Shelley. *Fr.* Original Poetry by Victor and Cazire. **CP-ShelP**

St. Elizabeth of Hungary. Christina Georgina Rossetti. **CP-RosC3**

St. Eustace. Derek Mahon. **SP-MahoD**

Saint Francis and the Sow. Galway Kinnell. **SP-KinnG**

St. Francis, Buddha, Tolstoi, and St. John. Above the Battle's Front. Nicholas Vachel Lindsay. **CP-LindV**

St. Francis of San Francisco. Nicholas Vachel Lindsay. *Fr.* Golden Whales of California. **CP-LindV**

St George's, Hardwicke Street. North Dublin. Donald Davie. **CP-DavDo**

Saint Gregory's Guest. John Greenleaf Whittier. **CP-WhitJ**

Saint Harmony, many / years I have stript. Freedom and Discipline. Hayden Carruth. **CP-CarHS**

St. Helena Lullaby, A. Rudyard Kipling. **CP-KiplR**

St. Ignatius Where the Salish Wail. Richard Hugo. **CP-HugoR**

St. James. Christopher Smart. *Fr.* Hymns and Spiritual Songs for the Fasts and Festivals of the Church of England. **SP-SmarC**

Saint Jason. Thomas Merton. **CP-MertT; SP-MertT**

Saint Jerome and his lion. Leonardo Da Vinci's. Marianne Craig Moore. **CP-MoorM**

St John. David Herbert Lawrence. **CP-LawrD**

St. John. John Greenleaf Whittier. **CP-WhitJ**

Saint John and the Back-Ache. Wallace Stevens. **CP-StevW**

St. John Baptist. Thomas Merton. **CP-MertT**

St.-John Perse. Charles Henri Ford. *Fr.* Four Elegies. **SP-FordC**

St. John tells how, at Cana's wedding-feast. A Wedding Toast. Richard Wilbur. **CP-WilbR**

St. John the Evangelist. Christopher Smart. *Fr.* Hymns and Spiritual Songs for the Fasts and Festivals of the Church of England. **SP-SmarC**

St. John, whose love indulg'd my labours past. The First Epistle of the First Book of Horace Imitated. Alexander Pope. **CP-PopeA**

St. John's Chapel. Richard Hugo. **CP-HugoR**

St. John's Night. Thomas Merton. **CP-MertT**

St. Johnswort! Grace Paley. **CP-PaleG**

Saint Judas. James Wright. **CP-WrigJ**

Saint-Just 1767–93. Robert Lowell. **SP-LoweR**

St. Launce's Revisited. Thomas Hardy. **CP-HardT**

Saint Leon of Ripe. From *The Gleanings of a Gadwall.* Malcolm Lowry. **CP-LowrM**

Saint-Lô. Samuel Beckett. **CP-BeckS**

St Luke. David Herbert Lawrence. **CP-LawrD**

St. Luke. Christopher Smart. *Fr.* Hymns and Spiritual Songs for the Fasts and Festivals of the Church of England. **SP-SmarC**

St. Luke's Summer. Phoebe Hesketh. **SP-HeskP**

St. Maedoc. Thomas Merton. **CP-MertT**

St. Malachy. Thomas Merton. **CP-MertT; SP-MertT**

St Mark. David Herbert Lawrence. **CP-LawrD**

St. Mark. Christina Georgina Rossetti. **CP-RosC2**

St. Mark. Christopher Smart. *Fr.* Hymns and Spiritual Songs for the Fasts and Festivals of the Church of England. **SP-SmarC**

St. Marks Place caught at night in hot summer. Poem. Alice Notley. **SP-NotlA**

St. Martin and the Beggar. Thom Gunn. **CP-GunnT**

Saint Martin's Summer. Robert Browning. **CP-BroR2**

St. Martin's Summer. Robert Louis Stevenson. **CP-StevR**

St. Martin's Summer. John Greenleaf Whittier. **CP-WhitJ**

St Matthew. David Herbert Lawrence. **CP-LawrD**

St. Matthew. Christopher Smart. *Fr.* Hymns and Spiritual Songs for the Fasts and Festivals of the Church of England. **SP-SmarC**

Saint Matthew and All. William Stafford. **SP-StafW**

St. Matthias. Christopher Smart. *Fr.* Hymns and Spiritual Songs for the Fasts and Festivals of the Church of England. **SP-SmarC**

St. Michael and all Angels. Christina Georgina Rossetti. **CP-RosC2**

St. Michael and All Angels. Christopher Smart. *Fr.* Hymns and Spiritual Songs for the Fasts and Festivals of the Church of England. **SP-SmarC**

Saint Monica. Charlotte Smith. **CP-SmitC**

Saint Nicholas. Marianne Craig Moore. **CP-MoorM**

Saint of Holy Island, The. Sir Walter Scott. **SP-ScotW** *Fr.* Marmion.

Saint on the pillar stands, The. Stylite. Louis MacNeice. **CP-MacNL**

Saint Orpheus. James Liddy. **CP-LiddJ**

Saint Patrick. John Hewitt. *Fr.* Two Irish Saints. **CP-HewiJ**

St. Patrick bound unto himself. The Comforter. Donald Davie. **CP-DavDo**

Saint Patrick, slave to Milcho of the herds. The Proclamation. John Greenleaf Whittier. **CP-WhitJ**

Saint Patrick was a proper man, a man to be admired. It's a Grand Parade It Will Be, Modern Design. Ogden Nash. **CP-NashO**

St. Paul. Thomas Merton. **CP-MertT; SP-MertT**

St. Paul and All That. Frank O'Hara. **SP-OharF**

St. Paul never saw a sight like this. United 555. Richard Eberhart. **CP-EberR**

St. Peter. Christina Georgina Rossetti. **CP-RosC2**

St. Peter. Christopher Smart. *Fr.* Hymns and Spiritual Songs for the Fasts and Festivals of the Church of England. **SP-SmarC**

St. Peter once: "Lord, dost Thou wash my feet?" Christina Georgina Rossetti. **CP-RosC2**

Saint Peter sat by the celestial gate. Byron. **FHYEP; OBSV; OXAEP-2; OxBoLi** *Fr.* The Vision of Judgment. **CP-Byron**

(Vision of Judgment, The.) **OXAEP-2**

Saint Peter sat by the celestial gate. The Vision of Judgment. Byron. **CP-Byron**

Saint Peter's Afflicted Mynde. Robert Southwell. **CP-SoutR**

Saint Peter's Complaint. Robert Southwell. **CP-SoutR**

    Fear. **CBCK**

    Sleep. **CBCK**

    Stanzas from Saint Peter's Complaint. **ACP**

Saint Peter's Remorse. Robert Southwell. **CP-SoutR**

St. Philip and St. James. Christopher Smart. **LoBV; NOCV; NOEC** *Fr.* Hymns and Spiritual Songs for the Fasts and Festivals of the Church of England. **SP-SmarC**

St. Philip's Church in Antigua. Archibald MacLeish. **CP-MacLA**

St. Roach. Muriel Rukeyser. **CP-RukeM**

St Rosalie: Monte Pellegrino. John Hewitt. **CP-HewiJ**

Saint sat down with the sinner, The. Fusion. George Meredith. **CP-MerG2**

Saint Sex. Charles Kenneth Williams. **CP-WillC; SP-WillC**

St. Simeon Stylites. Tennyson. **CP-TennA**

St. Simon and St. Jude. Christopher Smart. *Fr.* Hymns and Spiritual Songs for the Fasts and Festivals of the Church of England. **SP-SmarC**

St. Stephen. Christopher Smart. *Fr.* Hymns and Spiritual Songs for the Fasts and Festivals of the Church of England. **SP-SmarC**

St Stephen's Day. John Hewitt. **CP-HewiJ**

Saint Theresa. Jim Carroll. **SP-CarrJ**

St. Thérèse. George Meredith. **CP-MerG2**

St. Thomas. Christopher Smart. **ChIV-2** *Fr.* Hymns and Spiritual Songs for the Fasts and Festivals of the Church of England. **SP-SmarC**

St. Thomas Aquinas. Thomas Merton. **CP-MertT**

St. Thomas Aquinas thought. Vulture. Kenneth Rexroth. **NNaP; SP-RexrK** *Fr.* A Bestiary. **SP-RexrK**

Saint Thomas of Aquines Hymne Read on Corpus Christy Daye. Robert Southwell. **CP-SoutR**

Saint Valentine, / although late, would "some interested law". For February 14th. Marianne Craig Moore. **CP-MoorM**

Saint Valentine. Marianne Craig Moore. *See* Permitted to assist you, let me see.

St. Valentine's Day 1881. Christina Georgina Rossetti. **CP-RosC3**

St. Winefred's Well, Fragment. Gerard Manley Hopkins. **CP-HopkG**

Sainte Anne De Beaupré. Richard Eberhart. **CP-EberR**

Sainte Lucie. Derek Walcott. **CP-WalcD**

    "Pomme arac." **FaBoVe**

Sainte-Nitouche. Edwin Arlington Robinson. **CP-RobiE**

Saintly Youth has ceased to rule, discrowned, The. Revival of Popery. William Wordsworth. *Fr.* Ecclesiastical Sonnets. **CP-WorW2**

Saints, The. Robert Creeley. **CP-CreeR**

Saints. William Wordsworth. *Fr.* Ecclesiastical Sonnets. **CP-WorW2**

Saints and Angels. Christina Georgina Rossetti. **CP-RosC1**

Saints are like roses when they flush rarest. I Gave a Sweet Smell. Christina Georgina Rossetti. **CP-RosC2**

Saints-bell calls; and, Julia, I must read, The. To Julia. Robert Herrick. **CP-HerrR**

Saints Come Marching In, The. Anne Sexton. **CP-SextA**

Saints should never be dismay'd, The. Jehovah-Jireh. William Cowper. *Fr.* Olney Hymns. **CP-CowpW**

Sakyamuni Coming Out from the Mountain. Allen Ginsberg. **CP-GinsA**

Salad, The. William Cowper, *ad. fr. Virgil's tr. of Parthenius.* **CP-CowpW**

Salad-and-sand sandwiches. The Last Resort. Derek Mahon. *Fr.* Autobiographies. **SP-MahoD**

Salamander. Muriel Rukeyser. **CP-RukeM**

Salami. Philip Levine. **SP-LeviP**

Sale. Theodore Roethke. **CP-RoetT**

Sale. Miller Williams. **SP-WillM**

Sale, The. William Carlos Williams. **CP-WilW2**

Salem. Richard Eberhart. **CP-EberR**

Salesman, The. Ted Kooser. **SP-KoosT**

Salesman is an it that stinks excuse, A. Edward Estlin Cummings. **CP-CummE; SP-CummE**

Saleswomen in Bakery Shops. Mona Van Duyn. **SP-VanDM**

Salisbury Plain and Stonehenge. William Wordsworth. **FaBoPP** *Fr.* Guilt and Sorrow; or Incidents upon Salisbury Plain. **CP-WorW1**

Sallie's Musical Box. Walter de la Mare. **CP-DeLaW**

Sallow Bird, The. Stevie Smith. **CP-SmitS**

Sally. Phoebe Hesketh. **SP-HeskP**

Salmon Drowns Eagle. Malcolm Lowry. **CP-LowrM**

Salmon Eggs. Ted Hughes. **SP-HughT**

Salmon Fishing. Robinson Jeffers. **CP-JefR1**

Salmon, in silver flip wing majesty, The. The Enchanter of Yellow Gold to the Old Friend. James Liddy. **CP-LiddJ**

Salmon were just down there—, The. Salmon Eggs. Ted Hughes. **SP-HughT**

Salmon west leapt soft, spawned wild to sunset, The. Summer Evening. Isabella Gardner. **CP-GardI**

Salmoneus, as the Grecian tale is. On Wood the Ironmonger. Jonathan Swift. **CP-SwifJ**

Salome. James Merrill. **SP-MerrJ**

Salonikan Grave. Rudyard Kipling. *Fr.* Epitaphs of the War [1914–1918]. **CP-KiplR**

Saloon is gone up the creek, The. Hemmed-in Males. William Carlos Williams. **CP-WilW1** *Fr.* A Folded Skyscraper.

Saloon Suite. Isabella Gardner. **CP-GardI**

    Jig for Harmonica.

    Tango for Zither.

    Waltz for Accordion.

Salt. Isabella Gardner. **CP-GardI**

Salt. David Herbert Lawrence. **CP-LawrD**

Salt and water, / beach sloped form. Sea. Robert Creeley. **CP-CreeR**

Salt creek mouths unflushed by the sea. The South Coast. William Everson. **SP-EverW**

Salt Garden, The. Howard Nemerov. **CP-NemeH**

Salt grass silent of hooves, the lake stinks. Basil Bunting. *Fr.* Vestiges. **CP-BuntB**

Salt hacks, tavern boys, what skews, can't you burn alleys. Catullus. *See* Carmen 37: "Nine posts, five doors, up the Clivus."

Salt Marsh, The. James Dickey. **CP-DickJ**

Salt of the Earth. David Herbert Lawrence. **CP-LawrD**

Salt seas, mountains, deserts. Toward Climax. Gary Snyder. **CP-SnydG**

Salt shining behind its glass cylinder. Morning. Mary Oliver. **SP-OlivM**

Salt starts falling from my tongue. Seance Music. John Yau. **SP-YauJo**

Salt Water Story. Richard Hugo. **CP-HugoR**

Salt weather on the East River, A. For the Squadron. Howard Nemerov. **CP-NemeH**

Salta, ranocchio, e mostrati. Christina Georgina Rossetti. **CP-RosC3**

Saltcod Red. Laurence Lieberman. **SP-LiebL**

Salted and Pierced and sucked-in side. *Vigil: She Tarries, Far-Off, in a Strange Anguish, The.* Alun Lewis. *Fr.* War Wedding. **CP-LewiA**

Salts and Oils. Philip Levine. **SP-LeviP**

Salts work their way. The Only Image. Roy Fisher. **SP-FishR**

Salut au Monde! Walt Whitman. **CP-WhitW**

Salutation. Robert Herrick. **CP-HerrR**

Salutation. Ezra Pound. **SP-PounE**

Salutations to a Mouse. Marsden Hartley. **CP-HartM**

Salute. Archie Randolph Ammons. **SP-AmmoA**

Salute. John Hewitt. **CP-HewiJ**

Salute. Archibald MacLeish. **CP-MacLA**

Salute. James Schuyler. **CP-SchuJ**

Salute Gravettian-Aurignacian. Ancient Song Rising. Anne Waldman. **SP-WaldA**

Salute the last and everlasting day. Ascension [*or* Ascention]. John Donne. *Fr.* La Corona. **ChIV-2; ESCV; OBS; Son** *Fr.* Holy Sonnets. **CP-DonnJ**

Salute to Matthew Arnold. John Hewitt. **CP-HewiJ**

Salute us all, Christus with your iron. Geoffrey Hill. *Fr.* The Mystery of the Charity of Charles Péguy. **CP-HillG**

Salute Valentine. Delmore Schwartz. *Fr.* Occasional Poems. **SP-SchwD**

Salvador. Paul Muldoon. *Fr.* 7, Middagh Street. **SP-MuldP**

Salvage. Robinson Jeffers. **CP-JefR3**

Salvage. Carl Sandburg. **CP-SandC**

Salvaged Parts. William Stafford. **SP-StafW**

Salvages: An Evening Place. Robert Duncan. **SP-DuncR**

Salvation. David Herbert Lawrence. **CP-LawrD**

Salvation of Rock, The. Patti Smith. **SP-SmitP**

Salvation to all that will is nigh. Annunciation. John Donne. **TrCP** *Fr.* La Corona. **ChIV-2; ESCV; OBS; Son** *Fr.* Holy Sonnets. **CP-DonnJ**

Salvationists. Ezra Pound. **SP-PounE**

Salvé, next, minimal, poor little nosey. Catullus. *See* Carmen 43: "O elegant whore!"

Salve, quae fingis proprio modulamine carmen. Christopher Smart. *See* Inscriptions on an Aeolian Harp.

Salve Senescentem. Sadi, *tr. fr.* Persian by Ralph Waldo Emerson. **CP-EmerR**

Salzburg is like a crystal palace in the winter. A Winter Fable. Kay Boyle. **CP-BoylK**

Sam and Poll Go Back to the City. Hayden Carruth. **CP-CarHS**

Sam so cold in Montparnasse. Vir III. James Liddy. *Fr.* Vir I–XII. **CP-LiddJ**

Sam Spade Haiku. John Yau. **SP-YauJo**

Sam the whorehouse man. Little Tigers Everywhere. Charles Bukowski. **SP-BukC1**

Sam was lyin' in the jungle. Xmas in February. "Lou Reed." **SP-ReedL**

Sam wishes a blazing kiss was the lighthouse. Vir VIII. James Liddy. *Fr.* Vir I–XII. **CP-LiddJ**

Same. Robert Creeley. **CP-CreeR**

Same can be said of you, Victius, The. Carmen 98. Catullus. *Fr.* Carmina. **CP-Catul**

Same faces, and then the same scandels, The. Wind in the Street. Thom Gunn. **CP-GunnT**

Same Fragment—Second Look. Marsden Hartley. **CP-HartM**

Same gold of summer was on the winter hills, The. Winter Gold. Carl Sandburg. **CP-SandC**

Same grey path covered with last year's leaves, The. Frank Templeton Prince. *Fr.* Drypoints of the Hasidim. **CP-PrinF**

Same in Blues. Langston Hughes. **SP-HughL** *Fr.* Lenox Avenue Mural.

Same Kiss After Many Years, The. Tess Gallagher. **SP-GallT**

Same leaves over and over again, The! In Hardwood Groves. Robert Frost. **CP-FrosR**

Same old baffling questions! O my friend, The. Trust. John Greenleaf Whittier. **CP-WhitJ**

Same Story. Pablo Neruda, *tr. fr. Spanish by* Ben Belitt. **SP-NeruP**

Same Subject, The. William Wordsworth. *Fr.* The River Duddon [A Series of Sonnets]. **CP-WorW2**

Same subject (Continued) [Imagination and Taste, How Impaired and Restored]. William Wordsworth. *Fr.* The Prelude; Growth of a Poet's Mind [1850 vers.]. **CP-WorW3**

Same Subject (Continued) [Imagination]. William Wordsworth. *Fr.* The Prelude; Growth of a Poet's Mind [1805 vers.]. **CP-WorW3**

  "From Nature doth emotion come, and moods." **EnRP**

  "From Nature doth emotion come, and moods." **OBNC**

Same Subject, The [Dissolution of the Monasteries]. William Wordsworth. *Fr.* Ecclesiastical Sonnets. **CP-WorW2**

Same, The [Eminent Reformers]. William Wordsworth. *Fr.* Ecclesiastical Sonnets. **CP-WorW2**

Same, The [Inside of King's College Chapel, Cambridge]. William Wordsworth. *Fr.* Ecclesiastical Sonnets. **CP-WorW2**

Same tunes hang on pegs in the cloakrooms of the mind, The. Off the Peg. Louis MacNeice. **CP-MacNL**

Same, who crownes the Conquerour, will be, The. Comforts in Contentions. Robert Herrick. **CP-HerrR**

Samedi répit. Samuel Beckett. **CP-BeckS**

Sammy Lou of Rue. Revolutionary Petunias. Alice Walker. **CP-WalkA**

Samoan Head. John Clellon Holmes. **SP-HolmJ**

Samson. Frederick Morgan. **SP-MorgF**

Samson. John Milton. **CP-MiltJ**

  All Is Best. **NOBE; NOSC; OBEV; OBS; SeCePo**

  As Lords. **FaBoDD**

  Blindness of Samson, The. **ImPo; LiTB**

  "I, dark in light, exposed." **TrGrPo**

  "But see here comes thy reverend Sire." **EBEV**

  "But what is strength without a double share." **ChIV-1**

  "Come, come, no time for lamentation now." **ChTr; FaBoRV; FiP**

  (Death of Samson.) **ChTr**

  (No Time for Lamentation Now.) **FaBoRV**

  Delilah. **SeCePo**

  Desire of Wine. **FaBoDD**

  "Feast and noon grew high, and Sacrifice, The." **EBEV**

  Heroic Vengeance. **OBS**

  "Let me obtain forgiveness of thee, Samson." **EBEV**

  "Little onward lend thy guiding hand, A." **FaBoPV; OXAEP-1**

  (Samson before the Prison in Gaza.) **FaBoPV**

  Nothing For Tears. **OtMeF**

  "Oh [*or* O] how comely it is and how reviving." **NOBE; NOCV; OBEV; OBS; OXAEP-1; SeCeV**

  (Deliverer, The.) **OBS**

  Samson's Complaint. **NOSC**

  "This, this is he; softly a while." **OBS; UnPo**

  (Samson Fallen.) **OBS**

  Transcendence of God, The. **OBS**

  Ways of God to Men, The. **OBS**

  "Wilt thou then serve the Philistines with that gift." **EBEV**

  Woman. **OBS**

Samson Agonistes. Ogden Nash. **CP-NashO**

Samson before the Prison in Gaza. John Milton. *See* A Little onward lend thy guiding hand.

Samson Fallen. John Milton. *See* This, this is he; softly a while.

Samson stark at Dagon's knee. Ralph Waldo Emerson. **CP-EmerR**

Samson to His De[*or* a]lilah. Richard Crashaw. **CP-CrasR**

Samson's Complaint. John Milton. **NOSC** *Fr.* Samson Agonistes. **CP-MiltJ**

Samuel Beckett's Dublin. Donald Davie. **CP-DavDo**

Samuel E. Sewall. John Greenleaf Whittier. **CP-WhitJ**

Samuel J. Tilden. John Greenleaf Whittier. **CP-WhitJ**

Samuel Pepys. Rudyard Kipling. **CP-KiplR**

San Fancisco chronicle, A. Head Lines. Louis Zukofsky. **CP-ZukLS**

San Francisco Streets. Thom Gunn. **CP-GunnT**

San Fruttuoso. Charles Tomlinson. **CP-TomlC**

San Jose Symphony Reception. Lawrence Ferlinghetti. **SP-FerlL**

San Juan's Day. Richard Shelton. **SP-ShelR**

San Sebastian. Thomas Hardy. **CP-HardT**

Sanazar's Hexaflick. *Unknown, tr. fr. Latin by* Richard Lovelace. **CP-LoveR**

Sancta Maria Dolorum, *ad. fr. the Medieval* Stabat Mater Dolorosa. Richard Crashaw. **CP-CrasR**

Sancti Dominici Pallium. Samuel Taylor Coleridge. **CP-ColeS**

Sanctity, The. Charles Kenneth Williams. **CP-WillC; SP-WillC**

Sanctuary. John Berryman. **CP-BerrJ**

Sanctuary. John Hewitt. **CP-HewiJ**

Sanctuary, The. Howard Nemerov. **CP-NemeH**

Sand and Spray: A Sea-Symphony. John Gould Fletcher. **SP-FletJ**

  Calm, The.

  Gale, The.

  Groundswell, The.

  Gulls, The.

  Night of Stars.

  Night Wind, The.

  Sailboats. **SP-FletJ**

  Sands, The.

  Snow at Sea.

  Steamers.

  Tide, The.

  Tide of Storms.

  Wreck, The.

Sand Dollar. John Updike. **CP-UpdiJ**

Sand Dunes. Robert Frost. **CP-FrosR**

Sand: For the cigarette finished, The. Louis Zukofsky. *Fr.* 29 Songs. **CP-ZukLS**

Sand in the Air. Louis MacNeice. **CP-MacNL**

Sand-Man, The. Paul Laurence Dunbar. **CP-DunbP**

Sand Man, The. Thom Gunn. **CP-GunnT**

Sand-man he's a jolly old fellow, The. Johnny Speaks. Paul Laurence Dunbar. **CP-DunbP**

Sand of the sea runs red. Flux. Carl Sandburg. **CP-SandC**

Sand-Quarry with Moving Figures. Muriel Rukeyser. **CP-RukeM**

Sand Roads. Marge Piercy.

  Development, The. **SP-PierM**

  Road Behind the Last Dune, The. **SP-PierM**

Sand, sand; hills of sand. The Mermaids. Walter de la Mare. **CP-DeLaW**

Sand Scribblings. Carl Sandburg. **CP-SandC**

Sand tears fall; time's tears always falling. The Face of the Earth. Charles Henri Ford. **SP-FordC**

Sand upon the Red Sea shore, or on the beach, The. Delmore Schwartz. **SP-SchwD** *Fr.* Genesis.

Sandbanks, The. Richard Hugo. **CP-HugoR**

Sandbanks climb and curve until. First South and Cambridge. Richard Hugo. **CP-HugoR**

Sandemanian Meeting-House in Highbury Quadrant, The. Sir John Betjeman. **CP-BetjJ**

Sanders Theater. Richard Eberhart. **CP-EberR**

Sandhill People. Carl Sandburg. **CP-SandC**

Sandhills. James Liddy. **CP-LiddJ**

  "Donn, / though you are cousin."

  "Donn na Duimche."

  "Spring tide swept 'em to the hills."

  "Unlike the moon."

  "Waters by this music."

Sandinista Avioncitos. Lawrence Ferlinghetti. **SP-FerlL**

Sandman, I'd tear you limb from limb. Charles Henri Ford. *Fr.* Epigrams. **SP-FordC**

Sandmartins' nests were loopholes of darkness in the riverbank, The. Nesting-Ground. Seamus Heaney. **SP-HeanS**

Sandpiper. Elizabeth Bishop. **CP-BishE**

Sandpipers. Howard Nemerov. **CP-NemeH**

Sandpipers. Carl Sandburg. **CP-SandC**

Sandpipers at the margin. Point Reyes. Gary Snyder. **CP-SnydG**

Sandra. Charles Bukowski. **SP-BukC1**

Sandra's seen a leprechaun. Magic. Shel Silverstein. **SP-SilS2**

Sands, The. John Gould Fletcher. *Fr.* Sand and Spray: A Sea-Symphony. **SP-FletJ**

Sands darkened by insects. An Early Morning Crucifixion. Jim Carroll. **SP-CarrJ**

Sand's still blue with the receding water, sky topples, The. Formosa. Muriel Rukeyser. **CP-RukeM**

Sands, sunset, toilets. Kitville. Frank O'Hara. **SP-OharF**

Sandstone Keepsake. Seamus Heaney. **SP-HeanS**

Sandwich and a beer might cure these ills, A. Love. Howard Nemerov. *Fr.* Gnomes. **CP-NemeH**

Sandy and Jockie. Robert Burns. *See* Twa bonny [*or* bony] lads were Sandy and Jockie.

Sandy wall and trees. White Cloud, White Blossom. Roy Fisher. **SP-FishR**

Sandy's Sunday Best. Ted Berrigan. **SP-BerrT**

Sandys's Ghost, or a Proper New Ballad on the New Ovid's Metamorphosis as it Was Intended to Be. Alexander Pope. **CP-PopeA**

Sane and Insane. David Herbert Lawrence. **CP-LawrD**

Sane, random, negligent hours. Supplement Hours. Walt Whitman. **CP-WhitW**

Sane Revolution, A. David Herbert Lawrence. **CP-LawrD**

Sane Universe, The. David Herbert Lawrence. **CP-LawrD**

Sang from the Heart, Sire. Emily Dickinson. **CP-DickE**

Sang old Tom the lunatic. *fr.* Words for Music Perhaps. William Butler Yeats. **CP-YeatW**

Sang Solomon to Sheba. Solomon to Sheba. William Butler Yeats. **CP-YeatW**

Sanies I. Samuel Beckett. **CP-BeckS**

Sanies II. Samuel Beckett. **CP-BeckS**

Sanine to Leda. Robert Creeley. **CP-CreeR**

Sank through easeful. The Diver. Robert Earl Hayden. **CP-HaydR**

Sans. David Markson. **CP-MarkD**

Sans Name. Charles Olson. **CP-OlsoC**

Sanskrit root word, The. Hayden Carruth. **CP-CarHS** *Fr.* The Clay Hill Anthology.

Santa. Anne Sexton. *Fr.* The Death of the Fathers. **CP-SextA**

Santa and the Reindeer. Shel Silverstein. **SP-SilS2**

Santa Claus. Howard Nemerov. **CP-NemeH**

Santa Claus in Oaxaca. Richard Eberhart. **CP-EberR**

Santa Fe Sketches. Carl Sandburg. **CP-SandC**

Santa-Fé Trail (A Humoresque), The. Nicholas Vachel Lindsay. **CP-LindV** In Which a Racing Auto Comes from the East. In Which Many Autos Pass Westward.

Santa Maria delle Nevi. Charles Tomlinson. **CP-TomlC**

Santaigo: In Praise of Community. Stephen Dobyns. **SP-DobyS**

Santana. Laurence Lieberman. **SP-LiebL**

Santarém. Elizabeth Bishop. **CP-BishE**

Santiago: Five Men in the Street: Number One. Stephen Dobyns. **SP-DobyS**

Santiago: Five Men in the Street: Number Two. Stephen Dobyns. **SP-DobyS**

Santiago: Forestal Park. Stephen Dobyns. **SP-DobyS**

Santiago: la Avenida Pedro de Valdivia. Stephen Dobyns. **SP-DobyS**

Santiago: Market Day in Winter. Stephen Dobyns. **SP-DobyS**

Santo. James Merrill. **SP-MerrJ**

Santorini: Stopping the Leak. James Merrill. **SP-MerrJ**

São Paulo. John Updike. **CP-UpdiJ**

Sap in the Sticks Again. John Hewitt. **CP-HewiJ**

Sap of the sullen moor is blood of my blood. Northern Stone. Phoebe Hesketh. **SP-HeskP**

Sap rises from the sodden ditch. For Jane Myers. Louise Glück. **SP-GlücL**

Sapessi Pure! Christina Georgina Rossetti. *Fr.* Il Rosseggiar Dell'Oriente Canzoniere. **CP-RosC3**

Sapho, I will chuse to go. To Sapho. Robert Herrick. **CP-HerrR**

Sapling springs, the milkweed blooms, The: obsolete Nature. Adrienne Rich. **CP-RicAE**

Sappa Creek, The. Gary Snyder. **CP-SnydG**

Sappers. Rudyard Kipling. **CP-KiplR**

Sapphic Fragment, fr. the Greek of Sappho. Thomas Hardy. **CP-HardT**

Sapphics. Edward Estlin Cummings. **CP-CummE**

Sapphics. Algernon Charles Swinburne. **SP-SwinA**

Sappho / and the Venus de Milo. In Longfellow's Library. Charles Tomlinson. **CP-TomlC**

Sappho. Catullus. *See* Carmen 51: "Godlike the man who."

Sappho. Christina Georgina Rossetti. **CP-RosC3**

Sappho. Sappho, *tr. fr.* Ancient Greek *by* William Carlos Williams. **CP-WilW2**

Sappho. James Wright. **CP-WrigJ**

Sappho, Be Comforted. William Carlos Williams. **CP-WilW2**

Sappho Crosses the Dark River into Hades. Edna St. Vincent Millay. **CP-MillE**

Sappho in Paris. Gilbert Sorrentino. **SP-SorrG**

Sappho, Sappho, Sappho! initiate. To a Lovely Old Bitch. William Carlos Williams. **CP-WilW2**

Sappho to Phaon. Alexander Pope. **CP-PopeA**

Sappho to Philaenis. John Donne. **FaBoBl** *Fr.* Elegies. **CP-DonnJ**

Sara. "Bob Dylan." **CP-DylaB**

Sara in Her Father's Arms. George Oppen. **CP-OppeG**

Sarabande. Howard Nemerov. **CP-NemeH**

Sarah Cynthia Sylvia Stout Would Not Take the Garbage Out. Shel Silverstein. **SP-SilS2**

Sarah Greenleaf, of eighteen years. The Home-Coming of the Bride. John Greenleaf Whittier. **CP-WhitJ**

Sarah's Letter to Peter. Carl Sandburg. **CP-SandC**

Sarajevo. Howard Nemerov. **CP-NemeH**

Sarajevo Moon. Al Young. **CP-YounA**

Sarajevo Moonlight. Al Young. **CP-YounA**

Sarcastic Science, she would like to know. Why Wait for Science. Robert Frost. **CP-FrosR**

Sarcophagus. John Hewitt. **CP-HewiJ**

Sardanapalus. Byron. **CP-Byron**

Sardines in Striped Dresses. Charles Bukowski. **SP-BukC3**

Sardis. William Cowper. **ChIV-2** *Fr.* Olney Hymns. **CP-CowpW**

Saris go by me from the embassies, The. The Woman at the Washington Zoo. Randall Jarrell. **CP-JarrR; SP-JarrR**

Sarolla's women in their picture hats. Lawrence Ferlinghetti. **SP-FerlL**

Saroyan on his deathbed said. Our Curious Position. Charles Bukowski. **SP-BukC3**

Sartre said Francis Ponge had a moss-complex. Thomas Merton. *Fr.* Cables to the Ace. **CP-MertT**

Sash the faces of lust. An Orange Clock. Ted Berrigan. **SP-BerrT**

Sasquatch. Lewis Turco. **SP-TurcL**

Satan. Robert Herrick. **CP-HerrR**

Satan ("He ceased; and Satan stayed not to reply"). John Milton. **SeCePo** *Fr.* Book II. **FHYEP; NAEL-1; OxAEP-1** *Fr.* Paradise Lost. **CP-MiltJ**

(Satan Views the World.) **WHA**

Satan ("His pride / Had cast him out from Heaven, with all his host"). John Milton. **TrGrPo** *Fr.* Book I. **FHYEP; NAEL-1; OAEL-1; OxAEP-1** *Fr.* Paradise Lost. **CP-MiltJ**

Satan ("He scarce had ceas't when the superior Fiend"). John Milton. *See* Satan and the Fallen Angels.

Satan and His Host. John Milton. **OBS** *Fr.* Book I. **FHYEP; NAEL-1; OAEL-1; OxAEP-1** *Fr.* Paradise Lost. **CP-MiltJ**

Satan and the Fallen Angels. John Milton. **LiTB; OBS** *Fr.* Book I. **FHYEP; NAEL-1; OAEL-1; OxAEP-1** *Fr.* Paradise Lost. **CP-MiltJ**

(Satan ("He scarce had ceas't when the superior Fiend").) **SeCePo**

(Satan's Summons.) **NOSC**

Satan Beholds Adam and Eve in Eden. John Milton. **TW** *Fr.* Book IV. **OAEL-1** *Fr.* Paradise Lost. **CP-MiltJ**

Satan Defiant. John Milton. **WHA**, *ll.* 44–109; *Fr.* Book I. **FHYEP; NAEL-1; OAEL-1; OxAEP-1** *Fr.* Paradise Lost. **CP-MiltJ**

(Fallen Angels, The.) **FaBoEn**, *ll.* 44–74;

Satan from hence now on the lower stair. The Panorama. John Milton. **WHA** *Fr.* Book III. *Fr.* Paradise Lost. **CP-MiltJ**

Satan Journeys to the Garden of Eden. John Milton. **ChTr** *Fr.* Book IV. **OAEL-1** *Fr.* Paradise Lost. **CP-MiltJ**

Satan Views the World. John Milton. *See* Satan ("He ceased; and Satan stayed not to reply").

Satan's Adjuration. John Milton. *See* What Though the Field Be Lost?

Satan's Guile ("Whom thus answer'd th' Arch Fiend now undisguis'd"). John Milton. **LiTB; OBS** *Fr.* Book I. *Fr.* Paradise Regained [*or* Regain'd]. **CP-MiltJ**

Satan's Journey. John Milton. **NOSC** *Fr.* Book II. **FHYEP; NAEL-1; OxAEP-1** *Fr.* Paradise Lost. **CP-MiltJ**

Satan's Legions and the Beech Leaves of the Casentino. John Milton. **FaBoPP**, *ll.* 300–304; *Fr.* Book I. **FHYEP; NAEL-1; OAEL-1; OxAEP-1** *Fr.* Paradise Lost. **CP-MiltJ**

(Summons, The.) **WHA**, *ll.* 300–587;

Satan's Soliloquy. John Milton. **LiTB; OBS** *Fr.* Book IV. **OAEL-1** *Fr.* Paradise Lost. **CP-MiltJ**

Satan's Summons. John Milton. *See* Satan and the Fallen Angels.

Sather Gate Illumination. Allen Ginsberg. **CP-GinsA**

Satin-Clad. Stevie Smith. **CP-SmitS**

Satin Shoes, The. Thomas Hardy. **CP-HardT**

Satire, The. Walter de la Mare. **CP-DeLaW**

Satire IV of Dr. John Donne, Versified. Alexander Pope. **CP-PopeA**

Satire on an Inconstant Lover. A. Jonathan Swift. **CP-SwifJ**

Satire II of Dr. John Donne, Versified. Alexander Pope. **CP-PopeA**

Satires. John Donne. **CP-DonnJ**

Satire 1: "Away thou fondling motley humourist."
(London Street, A.) **NoSic**

Satire 2: "Sir: though (I thank God for it) I do hate."
(Poet Turned Lawyer, The.) **OBSV**

Satire 3: "Kind pity [*or* Kinde pitty] chokes my spleen[e]; brave scorn forbids." **EBEV; ESCV; FHYEP; JCP; OAEL-1; OBS; PoEL-2; SeCV-1**

(Religion.) **NoP**

(Satyre [*or* Satire] III.) **MeLP; OXAEP-1**

(Satyre III: On Religion.) **NAEL-1; SeCP**

(Satyre: Of Religion.) **MePo; PoE**

(Search for True Religion, The.) **NoSic**

("Though Truth and Falsehood be.") **NOBE**

(Truth.) **SeCePo**

Satire 4: "Well, I may now receive, and die: my sin." **OBSV**

Satire 5: "Thou shalt not laugh in this leaf, Muse, nor they." **OBSV**
Upon Mr. Thomas Coryat's Crudities.

Satires. Horace, *tr. fr. Latin.*

1.1: "What doating bigot to his faults so blind." **CP-JohnS**

1.5: "'Twas a long journey lay before us." **CP-CowpW**

1.9: "Saunt'ring along the street one day." **CP-CowpW**

2.1: "In books the various scenes of life he drew." **CP-JohnS**

2.6: "This was the summit of my views." **SP-SmarC,** *tr. by* Christopher Smart; **CP-JohnS**

("Chearful sage, when solemn dictatees fail.") **CP-JohnS,** *ll.* 77, *tr. by* Samuel Johnson;

2.13: "Thirsting Tantalus doth catch at stream[e]s that from him flee, The." **CP-RaleW**

Satires. Juvenal, *tr. fr. Latin.*

"Beasts of each kind their fellows spare." **CP-JohnS**

"Egyptians [*or* Aegyptians] think[e] it sin[ne] to root[e] up, or to bite." **CP-RaleW**

"Fickle crowd with fortune comes and goes, The." **CP-JohnS**

"Mind of mortals, in perverseness strong, The." **CP-JohnS**

"More safely truth to urge her claim presumes." **CP-JohnS**

"See the wild purchase of the bold and vain." **CP-JohnS**

"Vain man runs headlong, to caprice resign'd." **CP-JohnS**

Satires. Sir Thomas Wyatt.

"Mine [*or* Myne] own[e] John Poyntz, since [*or* sins] ye delight to know." **CP-WyatT**

"My mother's maids [*or* maydes] when they did sew [*or* sowe] and spin [*or* spynne]." **CP-WyatT**

"Spending hand that alway poureth [*or* powreth] out [*or* owte], A." **CP-WyatT**

Satires of Circumstance in Fifteen Glimpses. Thomas Hardy. **CP-HardT**

At a Watering-Place. **CMoP**

At Tea.

At the Altar-Rail. **MoAB; MoBrPo**

At the Draper's. **MoAB; MoBrPo; OBD; OxBM**

By Her Aunt's Grave. **MoAB; MoBrPo**

In Church. **IHNG; InPK; MoAB; MoBrPo; SCV**

In the Cemetery. **InPK; Son**

In the Moonlight. **NoAM**

In the Nuptial Chamber. **InPK**

In the Restaurant. **MoAB; MoBrPo**

In the Room of the Bride-Elect. **InPK**

In the Study.

On the Death-Bed.

Outside the Window.

Over the Coffin.

Satirical Elegy on the Death of a Late Famous General, A. Jonathan Swift. **CP-SwifJ**

Satirical Shrub, A. Ben Jonson. **CP-JonsB**

Satirist, The. Louis MacNeice. **CP-MacNL**

Satisfaction. David Herbert Lawrence. **CP-LawrD**

Satisfaction Coal Company, The. Rita Dove. **SP-DoveR**

Satisfaction for Sufferings. Robert Herrick. **CP-HerrR**

Satisfaction—is the Agent. Emily Dickinson. **CP-DickE**

Satisfactions of the Mad Farmer, The. Wendell Berry. **CP-BerrW**

Satisfied loves eat big breakfasts. I. Marilyn Hacker. **SP-HackM** *Fr.* Separations.

Saturated meadow, A. Rose Pogonias. Robert Frost. **CP-FrosR**

Saturday. Marsden Hartley. **CP-HartM**

Saturday. Charles Kenneth Williams. **CP-WillC**

Saturday Afternoon. Robert Creeley. **CP-CreeR**

Saturday, April 26, 1973. A Poem to Galway Kinnell. Etheridge Knight. **SP-KnigE**

Saturday, March 6. John Ciardi. **SP-CiarJ**

Saturday Market, The. Erica Jong. **SP-JongE**

Saturday Morning Journal. Charles Wright. **SP-WrigC**

Saturday morning—no school today. Chestnut Orchard. Louise McNeill. **SP-McNeL**

Saturday Night. James Schuyler. **CP-SchuJ**

Saturday Night (1890-1910). Louise McNeill. **SP-McNeL**

Saturday Night (1930s). Louise McNeill. **SP-McNeL**

Saturday night and the Brady loggers. Saturday Night (1890-1910). Louise McNeill. **SP-McNeL**

Saturday Night at the Elk's Club. Richard Shelton. **SP-ShelR**

Saturday Night: Horses Going to Pasture. John Gould Fletcher. **SP-FletJ**

Saturday night I buy a soda. I Like to Collapse. Joseph Ceravolo. **SP-CeraJ**

Saturday Night in the Parthenon. Kenneth Patchen. **CP-PatcK**

Saturday night on the streets of Swago. Saturday Night (1930s). Louise McNeill. **SP-McNeL**

Saturday night outsider / looking in through lighted windows. Single Footprints. Phoebe Hesketh. **SP-HeskP**

Saturday Sweeping. Philip Levine. **SP-LeviP**

Saturday's Child. Countee Cullen. **CP-CullC**

Saturn. Hilda Doolittle. **CP-DoolH** *Fr.* Temple of the Sun.

Saturn. John Keats. *See* Deep in the shady sadness of a vale.

Saturnalia. Louise Glück. **SP-GlücL**

Saturnalia. Thom Gunn. **CP-GunnT**

Saturne to be the fatter is not knowne, *ad. fr. Greek of* Lycophron. Sir Walter Ralegh. **CP-RaleW**

Satyr spied a Goddess in her bath, A. The Teaching of the Nude. George Meredith. **CP-MerG1**

Satyre [*or* Satire] III. John Donne. *See* Satire 3: "Kind pity [*or* Kinde pitty] chokes my spleen[e]; brave scorn forbids."

Satyre III: On Religion. John Donne. *See* Satire 3: "Kind pity [*or* Kinde pitty] chokes my spleen[e]; brave scorn forbids."

Satyre: Of Religion. John Donne. *See* Satire 3: "Kind pity [*or* Kinde pitty] chokes my spleen[e]; brave scorn forbids."

Satyrs dance! All the deformities take wing. Tribute to the Painters. William Carlos Williams. **CP-WilW2**

Sauce for Sorrowes. Robert Herrick. **CP-HerrR**

Saucer holds a Cup, A. Emily Dickinson. **CP-DickE**

Sauchs in the Reuch Heuch Hauch, The. "Hugh MacDiarmid." **SP-MacDH**

Saudades: The Portuguese Blues. Al Young. **CP-YounA**

Saul. Robert Browning. **CP-BroR1**

" 'Oh, our manhood's prime vigour! no spirit feels waste,'." **OtMeF**

"Oh, the wild joys of living! the leaping from rock up to rock." **BoTP; FaBV**

(Youth.) **BoTP**

"Then I tuned my harp—took off the lilies we twine round its chords." **FiP**

"Yea, my King." **WGRP**

Saul. Byron. **CP-Byron**

Saul at Gilboa. Robert Penn Warren. **SP-WarrR**

"Before the knowledge in me, he, beautiful, down in the dirt, kneels."

"Death I have entered is a death, The."

"From landscape the color of lions."

"How beautiful are the young, walking."

"I am the past time, am old, but."

"I do not say that I will annoint against him that boy."

"I had once poured oil on his head."

"South shoulder of the pass, The."

"Woman, who had cried out, 'O thou, The'."

Sauntering the pavement or riding the country by-road, lo, such faces! Faces. Walt Whitman. **CP-WhitW**

Saunt'ring along the street one day. 1.9. Horace, *tr. by* William Cowper. **CP-CowpW** *Fr.* Satires.

Savage Beast, The. William Carlos Williams. **CP-WilW2**

Savage Bubbles. Jim Carroll. **SP-CarrJ**

Savage I was sitting in my house, late, lone. The Householder. Robert Browning. **CP-BroR2**

Savage's romance, The. New York. Marianne Craig Moore. **CP-MoorM**

Savannah. Donald Davie. **CP-DavDo**

Savantism. Walt Whitman. **CP-WhitW**

Save for a lusterless honing-stone of moon. The Olive Tree. Karl Shapiro. **SP-ShapK**

Save me from such as me assail, *par. by* Countess of Pembroke, Mary Sidney Herbert. Bible, *O.T. See* Psalm 59: "Deliver me from mine enemies, O my God."

Save me from the idolatry. Emily Dickinson. **SP-DickE**

Save me, O God, by thy name, and judge me by thy strength. Psalm 54. Bible, *O.T. Fr.* Psalms. **CP-Psal**

Save me, O God; for the waters are come in unto my soul. Psalm 69. Bible, *O.T. Fr.* Psalms. **CP-Psal**

Save that the optimistic ones are worse. Malcolm Lowry. **CP-LowrM**

Save thou, my rose; in it thou art my all. Gypsy. Paul Muldoon. *Fr.* 7, Middagh Street. **SP-MuldP**

Saved. "Bob Dylan." **CP-DylaB**

Saving Grace. "Bob Dylan." **CP-DylaB**

Saving the Appearances. Charles Tomlinson. **CP-TomlC**

Saving Way, The. Hayden Carruth. **CP-CarHS**

Savior! I've no one else to tell. Emily Dickinson. **CP-DickE**

Savior looked on Peter. Ay, no word, The. The Look. Elizabeth Barrett Browning. **CP-BroEB**

Savior must have been, The. Emily Dickinson. **CP-DickE**

Savior's only signature, The. Emily Dickinson. **SP-DickE**

Saviour hides his face!, The. Mourning and Longing. William Cowper. *Fr.* Olney Hymns. **CP-CowpW**

Saviour! what a noble flame, The. Jesus Hasting to Suffer. William Cowper. *Fr.* Olney Hymns. **CP-CowpW**

Savoir Faire. Carl Sandburg. **CP-SandC**

Savoy. Frank O'Hara. **SP-OharF**

Savoy Truffle. George Harrison. **CP-Beatl**

Saw Carrara's marble mountains. Carrara, Looking Seaward. Lawrence Ferlinghetti. **SP-FerlL**

Saw 'er at a temple on the outskirts of Hangzhou. Chuck Miller. **SP-MillC**

Saw I Never the Righteous Forsaken. Donald Davie. **CP-DavDo**

Saw ye my Maggie? O Saw Ye My Maggie. Robert Burns. **CP-BurnR**

Saw Ye My Phely (Quasi Dicat, Phillis). Robert Burns. **CP-BurnR**

Sawdust-spattered plank floor is a stage, The. Loves of the Peacocks. Laurence Lieberman. **SP-LiebL**

Sawmill, The. Wystan Hugh Auden. **CP-AudWJ**

Saxon Conquest. William Wordsworth. *Fr.* Ecclesiastical Sonnets. **CP-WorW2**

Saxon Monasteries, and Lights and Shades of the Religion. William Wordsworth. *Fr.* Ecclesiastical Sonnets. **CP-WorW2**

Say a mass for my soul's repose, my brother. The Murdered Lover. Paul Laurence Dunbar. **CP-DunbP**

Say a master of the track. When This Clangor in the Brain. Adrienne Rich. **CP-RicAE**

Say a prayer for the cowboy, his mare's run away. Ballad of the Absent Mare. Leonard Cohen. **CP-CoheL**

Say, but did you love so long? Sir Toby Matthews. Sir John Suckling. **SeCV-1** *Fr.* A Poem with the Answer. **CP-SuckJ**

Say, goddesses, guardians of the sacred groves. On the Platonic Idea as Aristotle Understood It. John Milton, *tr. fr. Latin by* John Shawcross. **CP-MiltJ**

Say Good-bye to Big Daddy. Randall Jarrell. **CP-JarrR**

Say goodbye to the help, the ranks. Dr. Joseph Goebbels ("Say goodbye to the help, the ranks"). William DeWitt Snodgrass. **CAPP** *Fr.* The Führer Bunker. **SP-SnodW**

Say I was where in dream I seemed to be. The Elementals. Kathleen Jessie Raine. **SP-RainK**

Say in what country, where. Dames du Temps Jadis. Robert Lowell. **SP-LoweR**

Say it depends on the interpretation. Muriel Rukeyser. **CP-RukeM**

Say It Has Been Snowing. Siv Cedering Fox. **SP-CedeS**

Say, lad, have you things to do? Alfred Edward Housman. **CP-HousA**

Say life is the one-way trip, the one-way flight. Watchmaker God. Robert Lowell. **SP-LoweR**

Say, lovely youth, that dost my heart command. Sappho to Phaon. Alexander Pope. **CP-PopeA**

Say, Mister! / Uh-huh? On the Projects Playground. Etheridge Knight. **SP-KnigE**

Say never the strong heart. The Eagle. Allen Tate. **CP-TateA**

Say not Eve needed Adam's pardon. He Digs, He Dug, He Has Dug. Ogden Nash. **CP-NashO**

Say not of me that weakly I declined. Robert Louis Stevenson. **CP-StevR**

Say not the mermaid is a myth. The Mermaid. Ogden Nash. **CP-NashO**

Say not the struggle nought [*or* naught] availeth. Arthur Hugh Clough. **SP-ClouA**

Say nothing: let us sit within arm's reach. Meeting. George Meredith. **CP-MerG2**

Say of the gulls that they are flying. Variations on a Summer Day. Wallace Stevens. **CP-StevW**

Say over again, and yet once over again. Sonnet. Elizabeth Barrett Browning. **HBV 1-2; NAEL-2** *Fr.* Sonnets from the Portuguese. **CP-BroEB**

Say, Robin, what can Traulus mean. Traulus. Jonathan Swift. **CP-SwifJ**

Say, sages, what's the charm on earth. Robert Burns. *Fr.* On Jessy Lewars. **CP-BurnR**

Say something, man, say something before the nations and. Class of 1934. Kenneth Patchen. **CP-PatcK**

Say something warm. Hello. The world. High Grass Prairie. Richard Hugo. **CP-HugoR**

Say, tell me true, what is the doleful cause. A Pastoral Between Thirsis and Corydon, upon the Death of Damon. James Thomson. **CP-ThomJ**

Say that inside this shell, some live. A Seashell. William DeWitt Snodgrass. **SP-SnodW**

Say that it is a crude effect, black reds. Bouquet of Roses in Sunlight. Wallace Stevens. **CP-StevW**

Say that the men of the old black tower. The Black Tower. William Butler Yeats. **CP-YeatW**

Say that these are the fireworks of water. For the Fountains and Fountaineers of Villa d'Este. Jean Garrigue. **SP-GarrJ**

Say that thou didst forsake me for some fault. Sonnet 89. William Shakespeare. **OAEP; OXAEP-1** *Fr.* Sonnets. **CP-ShaWS**

Say that We Saw Spain Die. Edna St. Vincent Millay. **CP-MillE**

Say that you're / lonely—and want / something to. Chicago. Robert Creeley. **CP-CreeR**

Say the word and you'll be free. The Word. The Beatles. **CP-Beatl**

Say the young man among. Cautious Circumspection Does Not Win the West. Gilbert Sorrentino. **SP-SorrG**

Say this city has ten million souls. Wystan Hugh Auden. **LiTA; LiTM; NYBP; OxAEP-2** *Fr.* Ten Songs. **CP-AudeW**

(Refugee Blues.) **LiTA; OxAEP-2**

(Song: "Say this city has ten million souls.") **NYBP**

Say to me only. Sotto Voce. Stanley Jasspon Kunitz. **CP-KuniS**

Say Venus how long have I lov'd, and serv'd you heere? Song. Mary Sidney, Countess of Montgomery Wroth. *Fr.* Pamphilia to Amphilanthus. **CP-WrotM**

Say we we were pushed to name a time. Tune. Al Young. **CP-YounA**

Say, what is Honour?—"Tis the finest sense." William Wordsworth. **CP-WorW1**

Say What Is Love—To Live In Vain. Song. John Clare. **SP-ClarJ** *Fr.* Child Harold.

Say, what is the spell, when her fledgelings are cheeping. A Song of Love. "Lewis Carroll." **CP-CarrL** *Fr.* Sylvie and Bruno Concluded.

Say what we like, our civilisation has learnt a great lesson. The Young Are Not Greedy. David Herbert Lawrence. **CP-LawrD**

Say what you will, and scratch my heart to find. Edna St. Vincent Millay. **CP-MillE**

Say, whose is this fair picture, which the light. The Missionary. John Greenleaf Whittier. **CP-WhitJ**

"Say why are beauties praised and honoured most." Alexander Pope. **ECEV** *Fr.* The Rape of the Lock[, an Heroi-Comical Poem]. **CP-PopeA**

Say, ye apostate and profane. Ode on *Sir Charles Grandison*. William Cowper. **CP-CowpW**

Say, ye far-travelled clouds, far-seeing hills. On the Sight of a Manse in the South of Scotland. William Wordsworth. **CP-WorW2**

Say Yes! Wystan Hugh Auden. **CP-AudWJ**

Say you're drunk or drugged and something hums. Sound Track Conditional. Richard Hugo. **CP-HugoR**

Saying. Frederick Morgan. **SP-MorgF**

Saying Farewell at the Monastery After Hearing the Old Master Lecture on "Return to the Source." Gary Snyder. **CP-SnydG**

Saying Good-bye. Thomas Hardy. **CP-HardT**

Saying Goodbye to Love. Charles Bukowski. **SP-BukC2**

Saying Goodbye to Mrs. Noraine. Richard Hugo. **CP-HugoR**

Saying Her Name. Brendan Galvin. **SP-GalvB**

Saying It to Keep It from Happening. John Ashbery. **SP-AshbJ**

Saying of Farewell, A. James Dickey. **CP-DickJ**

Sayings from the Northern Ice. William Stafford. **SP-StafW**

Sayings of Henry Stephens. Carl Sandburg. **CP-SandC**

Sayings, sentences, what of them? Carl Sandburg. *Fr.* The People, Yes. **CP-SandC**

Says. Walt Whitman. **CP-WhitW**

Says ol man no body. Edward Estlin Cummings. **CP-CummE**

Says the pipe to the snuff-box, I can't understand. To Mr. Newton. William Cowper. **CP-CowpW**

Scab / is a beautiful thing—a coin, A. Ode to Healing. John Updike. *Fr. Seven Odes to Seven Natural Processes.* **CP-UpdiJ**

Scaffolding holds the arch in place, The. Carl Sandburg. *Fr.* The People, Yes. **CP-SandC**

Scala Coeli. Kathleen Jessie Raine. **SP-RainK**

Scalded cat, / claws, arched back and blistered pride. Night Letter. Marge Piercy. **SP-PierM**

Scales of the Eyes, The. Howard Nemerov. **CP-NemeH**

Scales of the monster, The. Heaven and Earth. Kenneth Patchen. **CP-PatcK**

Scaling small rocks, exhaling smog. Central Park. Robert Lowell. **SP-LoweR**

Scaling your words like crags I found. Mentor. Audre Lorde. **SP-LordA**

Scallop Song. Anne Waldman. **SP-WaldA**

Scamp. Paul Laurence Dunbar. **CP-DunbP**

Scan the heavens of our future, comrades. Three Who Died. Edwin Rolfe. **CP-RolfE**

Scandal. John Clare. **SP-ClarJ**

Scapegoat. Phoebe Hesketh. **SP-HeskP**

Scapegoats and Rabies. Ted Hughes. **SP-HughT**
    Haunting, A.
    Mascot, The.
    "So the leaves trembled."
    Two Minute's Silence.
    Wit's End.

Scar, The. John Hewitt. **CP-HewiJ**

Scar, The. Charles Tomlinson. **CP-TomlC**

Scar. Charles Kenneth Williams. **SP-WillC**

Scar[e]-Fire, The. Robert Herrick. **CP-HerrR**

Scarce had the solemn Sabbath-bell. A Sabbath Scene. John Greenleaf Whittier. **CP-WhitJ**

Scarce had the sun dried up the dewy morn. *Various Authors.* **CP-ShaWS** *Fr.* The Passionate Pilgrim. **CP-ShaWS**

Scarce images of life, one here, one there. A Recollection of the Stone Circle near Keswick. John Keats. **FaBoPP** *Fr.* Hyperion; a Fragment. **CP-KeatJ**

Scarce tolerable life, which all life long. Christina Georgina Rossetti. **CP-RosC2**

Scarcely Disfigured. Paul Éluard, *tr. fr. French by* Samuel Beckett. **CP-BeckS**

Scarcely speaking: it becomes as a. Geoffrey Hill. *Fr.* The Songbook of Sebastian Arrurruz. **CP-HillG**

Scarecrow. Archie Randolph Ammons. **SP-AmmoA**

Scarecrow, The. Walter de la Mare. **CP-DeLaW**

Scared Child, The. Robert Ranke Graves. **CP-GravR**

Scarf of June, The. Richard Eberhart. **CP-EberR**

Scarlatina. John Hewitt. **CP-HewiJ**

Scarlet. Charles Bukowski. **SP-BukC1**

Scarlet and green, the dahlias. The Dahlias. John Gould Fletcher. **SP-FletJ**

Scarlet Tanager. James Schuyler. **CP-SchuJ**

Scarlet the sunset, crimson the dawn. Psalm of the Bloodbank. Carl Sandburg. **CP-SandC**

Scarred Girl, The. James Dickey. **CP-DickJ**

Scars Remaining, The. Samuel Taylor Coleridge. **OBNC** *Fr.* Christabel. **CP-ColeS**

Scars take us back to places we have been, The. Memoranda. William Dickey. **SP-DickW**

Scars upon the day, The. Await. James Schuyler. **CP-SchuJ**

Scatter a few cold cinders into the empty grate. Making a fire. Walter de la Mare. **CP-DeLaW**

Scatter a fragrant flower. Emily Dickinson. **SP-DickE**

Scattered / In the barnyard. George Washington Slept Here. Diane Wakoski. **SP-WakoD**

Scattered Moluccas. Ezra Pound. *Fr.* Mauberly (1920). *Fr.* Hugh Selwyn Mauberley. (Life and Contacts). **SP-PounE**

Scatterghost, / it can't float away. The Rabbit. Mary Oliver. **SP-OlivM**

Scattering, The. John Hewitt. **CP-HewiJ**

Scattering, like birds escaped the fowler's net. English Reformers in Exile. William Wordsworth. *Fr.* Ecclesiastical Sonnets. **CP-WorW2**

Scavai la neve,—sì che scavai! Christina Georgina Rossetti. **CP-RosC3**

Scene. Paul Éluard, *tr. fr. French by* Samuel Beckett. **CP-BeckS**

Scene. Richard Hugo. **CP-HugoR**

Scene from a Drama. John Gould Fletcher. **SP-FletJ**

Scene from "Tasso", *see also* Song for "Tasso." Percy Bysshe Shelley. **CP-ShelP**

Scene in Venice. William Wordsworth. *Fr.* Ecclesiastical Sonnets. **CP-WorW2**

Scene is the fore-court of a noble dwelling on the island of Rhodes, The. At the Fall of an Age. Robinson Jeffers. **CP-JefR2**

Scene on the Lake of Brientz. William Wordsworth. *Fr.* Memorials of a Tour of the Continent; 1820. **CP-WorW2**

Scene stands stubborn, The: skinflint trees. November Graveyard. Sylvia Plath. **CP-PlatS**

Scene Twelve: Take Seven. John Ciardi. **SP-CiarJ**

Scene, which 'wildered fancy viewed, A. Retrospect, The: CWM Elan, 1812. Percy Bysshe Shelley. **CP-ShelP**

Scenes Favourable to Meditation. Jeanne Marie Bouvier de la Motte-Guyon, *tr. fr. French by* William Cowper. **CP-CowpW**

Scenes from Politian. Edgar Allan Poe. **CP-PoeEd**

Scenes from the Life of Boullee. John Yau.
    "Casual solitude that is beyond casualness, A." **SP-YauJo**
    "Certainty of being part of the atmosphere, The." **SP-YauJo**
    "Counting the times as if they added up." **SP-YauJo**
    "Pieces of a piece. The face in the window larger." **SP-YauJo**
    "Realizing that any certainty is an old one." **SP-YauJo**
    "Rising cost of heart attacks. Different, The." **SP-YauJo**
    "Roof shaped like a strawberry. Hurriedly torn." **SP-YauJo**
    "Room with open windows facing a street, A." **SP-YauJo**
    "Rubbing her sable with long thoughtful." **SP-YauJo**
    "Scotch tape scars on the wall. Scared, The." **SP-YauJo**
    "Sheets dangling from the line, The." **SP-YauJo**
    "So much of the proscenium burned." **SP-YauJo**
    "Stuffing yourself into a blizzard." **SP-YauJo**
    "Stumbling blocks are realigned, The." **SP-YauJo**
    "Without noticing the fire descending into the." **SP-YauJo**
    "Zebra-striped pillow. The restlessness." **SP-YauJo**

Scenes of Childhood. James Merrill. **SP-MerrJ**

Scenes with Harlequins. Geoffrey Hill. **CP-HillG**
    "Beautiful lady, / in reverence."
    "Day clacks and birds, The."
    "Decembrist blood! We are taxed."
    "Distance is on edge."
    "Even now one is amazed."
    "Of Rumor, of Clamor."
    "Risen Christ! Once more, The."

Scenic. John Updike. **CP-UpdiJ**

Scenic View. Donald Hall. **CP-HallD**

Scenic View. William Matthews. **SP-MattW**

Scent / from the apple-loft! The Farmer's Wife: at Fostons Ash. Charles Tomlinson. **CP-TomlC**

Scent of Irises. David Herbert Lawrence. **CP-LawrD**

Scent of ripeness from over a wall, A. Unharvested. Robert Frost. **CP-FrosR**

Scent of weak lilac, cheap caporal, The. Why the Heart Has Dreams Is Why the Mind Goes Mad. Jean Garrigue. **SP-GarrJ**

Scented Herbage of My Breast. Walt Whitman. **CP-WhitW**

Schad paced the length of his studio. Agosta the Winged Man and Rasha the Black Dove. Rita Dove. **SP-DoveR**

Scheherazade. John Ashbery. **SP-AshbJ**

Scherzo. Randall Jarrell. **CP-JarrR**

Scherzo. James McAuley. *Fr.* The Exile's Fifth Symphony. **SP-McAuJ**

Schiller! that hour I would have wish'd to die. To the Author of "The Robbers." Samuel Taylor Coleridge. *Fr.* Effusions. **CP-ColeS**

Schinden. Patti Smith. **SP-SmitP**

Schism, A / Nurtured by foppery and barbarism. John Keats. **EPCY** *Fr.* Sleep and Poetry. **CP-KeatJ**

Schizophrene. Louis MacNeice. **CP-MacNL**

Schizophrenic, wrenched by two styles. Codicil. Derek Walcott. **CP-WalcD**

Scholar-Gipsy, The. Matthew Arnold. **SP-ArnoM**
    At Some Lone Alehouse. **FaBoDD**

Scholar is a ball thats spent. Ralph Waldo Emerson. **CP-EmerR**

Scholars, The. Rudyard Kipling. **CP-KiplR**

Scholars, The. William Butler Yeats. **CP-YeatW**

Scholars at the Orchid Pavilion. John Berryman. **CP-BerrJ**

Scholars call the masculine swan a cob. The Swan. Ogden Nash. **CP-NashO**

Scholar's Life, The. Samuel Johnson. *See* When first the college rolls receive his name.

School. William Matthews. **SP-MattW**

School Boy, The. William Blake. **CP-BlakW** *Fr.* Songs of Experience.

School Children, The. Louise Glück. **SP-GlücL**

School children, The. Upon First Reading the Immortal Literature of the World—. Charles Bukowski. **SP-BukC3**

School Days. William Matthews. **SP-MattW**

School Drawing. Lewis Turco. **SP-TurcL**

School Figures. William Matthews. **SP-MattW**

School for Dark Thoughts. Charles Simic. **SP-SimiC**

School in August, The. Philip Larkin. **CP-LarkP**

School is over. It is too hot. The Lonely Street. William Carlos Williams. **CP-WilW1**

School Lesson Based on Word of Tragic Death of Entire Gillum Family. Robert Penn Warren. **SP-WarrR**

School of Beauty's a tavern now, The. Southeast Corner. Gwendolyn Brooks. VGW *Fr.* A Street in Bronzeville. **SP-BrooG**

School of Summer, The. Randall Jarrell. **CP-JarrR**

School on the Outskirts. David Herbert Lawrence. **CP-LawrD**

School or Perl of Putney, the Mistress of All Singular Manners, Mistresse Portman, The. Robert Herrick. **CP-HerrR**

School Play, The. James Merrill. **SP-MerrJ**

School Song, A. Rudyard Kipling. **CP-KiplR**

School-Time. William Wordsworth. **FHYEP** *Fr.* The Prelude; Growth of a Poet's Mind [1850 vers.]. **CP-WorW3**

School-Time. William Wordsworth. *Fr.* The Prelude; Growth of a Poet's Mind [1805 vers.]. **CP-WorW3**

"Blest the infant Babe." **TOF**

"But who shall parcel out." **TOF**

"For I would walk alone." **OBRV**

Intimations of Sublimity. **OBNC**

"Nor should this, perchance." **OxAEP-2**

On Windermere; Bowness Bay and Belle Isle. **FaBoPP**

"Those incidental charms which first attached." **OAEL-2**

"Thus were my sympathies enlarged, and thus." **EnRP**

School Upstairs, The. John Hewitt. **CP-HewiJ**

Schoolbell rings and dies before, The. Camas Prairie School. Richard Hugo. **CP-HugoR**

Schoolboy's Complaint, The. Malcolm Lowry. **CP-LowrM**

Schoolboys in blazers infiltrate the aisles. The Battle of Hastings. Daniel Gerard Hoffman. **SP-HoffD**

Schoolboys with Dog, Winter. William Matthews. **SP-MattW**

Schoolchildren. Wystan Hugh Auden. **CP-AudeW**

Schoolcraft's Diary Written on the Missouri: 1830. Robert Bly. **SP-BlyR**

Schoolgirl at Seola. Richard Hugo. **CP-HugoR**

Schoolgirls in pantyhose. Girls in Pantyhose. Charles Bukowski. **SP-BukC1**

Schoolhouse, The. Galway Kinnell. **SP-KinnG**

Schoolmaster [A], The. David Herbert Lawrence. **CP-LawrD**

Schoolmaster [B], The. David Herbert Lawrence. **CP-LawrD**

  Afternoon / The Last Lesson.

  Afternoon in School / The Last Lesson.

  Best of School, The.

  Best of School, The.

  Evening.

  "How can I teach you when your blue." **CP-LawrD**

  Morning / Scripture Lesson.

  Punisher, The.

  Snowy Day in School, A.

  Snowy Day in School, A.

Schoolmaster. Philip Larkin. **CP-LarkP**

Schooner, The. Lewis Turco. **SP-TurcL**

Schooner Flight, The. Derek Walcott. **CP-WalcD**

Schreckhorn, The. Thomas Hardy. **CP-HardT**

Schubert from water, from birdsong's gamut Mozart. Osip Emilevich Mandelstam. *Fr.* Octets. **CP-DavDo**

Schubert's "Farewell." George Meredith. **CP-MerG2**

Schumann Adds Trombones to His Second Symphony After Mendelssohn Conducts the First Performance. Miller Williams. **SP-WillM**

Schwarzwald. Ernest Hemingway. **CP-HemiE**

Science. Robinson Jeffers. **CP-JefR1**

Science in God. Robert Herrick.

  (Knowledge.) **CP-HerrR**

Science of the Night, The. Stanley Jasspon Kunitz. **CP-KuniS**

Science outstrips. Exotic. Archie Randolph Ammons. **SP-AmmoA**

Science puffs up, says Gut, when either Pease. Upon Gut. Robert Herrick. **CP-HerrR**

Science—so the Savants say, A. Emily Dickinson. **CP-DickE**

Science, that gives man hope to live without lies. Curb Science? Robinson Jeffers. **CP-JefR3**

Science, that makes wheels turn, cities grow. Triad. Robinson Jeffers. **CP-JefR2**

Science, that simple saint, cannot be bothered. Dr. Sigmund Freud Discovers the Sea Shell. Archibald MacLeish. **CP-MacLA**

Science! true daughter of Old Time thou art! Sonnet—To Science. Edgar Allan Poe. **CP-PoeEd**

Science will not trust us. Emily Dickinson. **SP-DickE**

Scientific Doctor, The. David Herbert Lawrence. **CP-LawrD**

Scientists are in terror, The. Canto 115, From. Ezra Pound. **APSN; CP-PoCan; FaBoMo** *Fr.* Cantos. **CP-PoCan**

Scissors cut the long-grown hair, The. Upon Shaving Off One's Beard. John Updike. **CP-UpdiJ**

Scissors For a One-Armed Tailor. John Hewitt. **CP-HewiJ**

Scissors-Grinder, The. Nicholas Vachel Lindsay. **CP-LindV**

Scobble for whoredom[e] whips his wife, and cries [*or* cryes]. Upon Scobble [Epigram]. Robert Herrick. **CP-HerrR**

Scoffing, amorous maidens and young men. Canzone. John Milton, *tr. fr. Italian* by John T. Shawcross. **CP-MiltJ**

Sconset. Charles Tomlinson. **CP-TomlC**

Score of airy miles will smooth, A. Ralph Waldo Emerson. **CP-EmerR**

Score of years had come and gone, A. John Underhill. John Greenleaf Whittier. **CP-WhitJ**

Score tied in the 8th, the only fans, bison. The Ballpark at Moiese. Richard Hugo. **CP-HugoR**

Scorn Not the Sonnet [Critic, You Have Frowned]. William Wordsworth. **CP-WorW2**

Scorne Not the Leaste. Robert Southwell. **CP-SoutR**

Scorned, to be scorned by one that I scorn. Tennyson. *Fr.* Maud [A Monodrama]. **CP-TennA**

Scorpio. Ted Berrigan. **SP-BerrT**

Scorpion. Stevie Smith. **CP-SmitS**

Scotch Drink. Robert Burns. **CP-BurnR**

Scotch Mary. Frederick Morgan. **SP-MorgF**

Scotch Song. Robert Burns. **CP-BurnR**

Scotch tape scars on the wall. Scared, The. John Yau. **SP-YauJo** *Fr.* Scenes from the Life of Boullee.

Scotch Te Deum. Bible, *O.T. See* Psalm 100: "Make a joyful noise unto the Lord, all ye lands."

Scotish Ballad. Robert Burns. **CP-BurnR**

Scotish Song. Robert Burns. **CP-BurnR**

Scotish Song. Robert Burns. **CP-BurnR**

Scotland. "Hugh MacDiarmid." **SP-MacDH**

Scotland Small? "Hugh MacDiarmid." **SP-MacDH**

Scots Ballad. Robert Burns. **CP-BurnR**

Scots Poem. John Berryman. **CP-BerrJ**

Scots Prologue, *For Mrs. Sutherland's Benefit Night*, Spoken at the Theatre Dumfries. Robert Burns. **CP-BurnR**

Scots steel tempered wi' Irish fire. The Weapon. "Hugh MacDiarmid." **SP-MacDH**

Scots, wha hae wi' Wallace bled. Robert Burns. **CP-BurnR**

  (Robert Bruce's March to Bannockburn.) **CP-BurnR**

Scotsman's Return from Abroad, The. Robert Louis Stevenson. **CP-StevR**

Scott Rautmann, Saturday Night. James Liddy. **CP-LiddJ**

Scottish Broom on Birdnest brae, The. A Help for the Memory of the Grand Independent; A New Song. William Wordsworth. **CP-WorW2**

Scottish hinds, too poor to house, The. A Receipt to Restore Stella's Youth. Jonathan Swift. **CP-SwifJ**

Scottish Interlude. John Hewitt. **CP-HewiJ**

Scottsboro, Too, Is Worth Its Song. Countee Cullen. **CP-CullC**

Scour, The. Archie Randolph Ammons. **SP-AmmoA**

Scour the Mind. Jim Morrison. **SP-MorrJ**

Scoured like a conch. The Night Rider. William Carlos Williams. **CP-WilW2**

Scourge, The. Stanley Jasspon Kunitz. **CP-KuniS**

Scourge of life, and death's extreme disgrace, The. Sir Philip Sidney. **SP-SidnP**

Scouring, The. Richard Eberhart. **CP-EberR**

Scout, The. William Everson. **SP-EverW**

Scram, Lion! Ogden Nash. **CP-NashO**

Scraping in the cokehouse. One red car, A. 107 Poems. Roy Fisher. **SP-FishR**

Scraps. Louise Glück. **SP-GlücL**

Scratch, The. James Dickey. **CP-DickJ**

Scratch on the Scratch Pad. Philip Larkin. **CP-LarkP**

"Scream, The." Donald Hall. **CP-HallD**

Scream, The. Charles Tomlinson. **CP-TomlC**

Scream, The. Robert Penn Warren. **SP-WarrR**

Scream of the Butterfly. Patti Smith. **SP-SmitP**

Scream to the Editor, A. Charles Olson. **CP-OlsoC**

Screamed the far sea-mew. On the mirroring sands. Flotsam. Walter de la Mare. **CP-DeLaW**

Screams round the Arch-druid's brow the sea-mew—white. Trepidation of the Druids. William Wordsworth. **Son** *Fr.* Ecclesiastical Sonnets. **CP-WorW2**

Screech-Owl. Donald Davie. **CP-DavDo**

Screed of the Flesh, The. William Everson. **SP-EverW**

Screen of supreme good fortune curved, The. The Young Son. John Ashbery. **SP-AshbJ**

Screen with the Face with the Voice, The. Ogden Nash. **CP-NashO**

Screendoor whines, clacks, The. Night on Hatchet Cove. Denise Levertov. **CP-LeveD**

Screened Porch in the Country, A. James Dickey. **CP-DickJ**

Screw, a Technical Love Poem. Diane Wakoski. **SP-WakoD**

Screw-Guns. Rudyard Kipling. **CP-KiplR**

Scribble. Allen Ginsberg. **CP-GinsA**

Scribe, The. Walter de la Mare. **CP-DeLaW**

Scribe. Hilda Doolittle. **CP-DoolH**

Scribes, The. Seamus Heaney. **SP-HeanS** *Fr.* Sweeney Redivivus.

Scriblerian Verses. Jonathan Swift. **CP-SwifJ**

Scribner's Sons. Malcolm Lowry. **CP-LowrM**

Script of trees before the hill, A. Winter Spring. Richard Wilbur. **CP-WilbR**

Scriptsmith. Carl Sandburg. **CP-SandC**

Scripture. Carl Sandburg. **CP-SandC**

Scriptures, The. John Dryden. **OBS** *Fr.* Religio Laici. **SP-DrydJ**

Scritch, scratch, saith the frozen spring snow. Upon the Last Day of His Forty-Ninth Year. John Updike. **CP-UpdiJ**

Scroggam. Robert Burns. **CP-BurnR**

Scroll, The. Leonard Nathan. **SP-NathL**

Scroll. Carl Sandburg. **CP-SandC**

Scroll is defaced; the worm, The. Some Shires Revisited. Donald Davie. **CP-DavDo**

Scrolls from the Dead. Daniel Gerard Hoffman. **SP-HoffD**

Scrotum tumescit Pandaro; tremat scortum. *acc. by English translation.* Thomas Campion. **CP-CampT**

Scrub. Edna St. Vincent Millay. **CP-MillE**

Scrutinize the Scorpion constellation. Almanac. Carl Sandburg. **CP-SandC**

Scrutiny [*or* Scrutinie], The. Richard Lovelace. **CP-LoveR**

Scudamor in the Temple of Venus. Edmund Spenser. **PoE** *Fr.* The Faerie Queene. **CP-Spens**

Scuffed snout, infected ear, ticks like interest. Dog Life. William Matthews. **SP-MattW**

Sculptor. Sylvia Plath. **CP-PlatS**

Sculptor?—Nameless, though once dear to fame. Inscription for a Bust of Homer. William Cowper. **CP-CowpW**

Sculpture, The. Bill Knott. **SP-KnotB**

"Sculpture" of Rhyme, The. Donald Davie. **CP-DavDo**

Sculptures in Hungary. Donald Davie. **CP-DavDo**

Scum has come, The. Lament, for Cocoa. John Updike. **CP-UpdiJ**

Scuts of froth swirled from the discharge pipe. The Milk Factory. Seamus Heaney. **SP-HeanS**

Scyros. Karl Shapiro. **SP-ShapK**

Scythe, The. John Gould Fletcher. **SP-FletJ**

Scythe, The. Lewis Turco. **SP-TurcL**

Scythian Charioteers, The. Donald Davie. **CP-DavDo**

Se Cossi Fosse. Christina Georgina Rossetti. *Fr.* Il Rosseggiar Dell'Oriente Canzoniere. **CP-RosC3**

Se Fossi Andata a Hastings. Christina Georgina Rossetti. *Fr.* Il Rosseggiar Dell'Oriente Canzoniere. **CP-RosC3**

Se t'insegnasse Iddio. Lassuso Il Caro Fiore. Christina Georgina Rossetti. *Fr.* Il Rosseggiar Dell'Oriente Canzoniere. **CP-RosC3**

Sea: / And in its flaw the sprung silence. William Everson. **SP-EverW** *Fr.* Chronicle of Division.

Sea, The. Byron. *See* There is a pleasure in the pathless woods.

Sea, The. Robert Creeley. **CP-CreeR**

Sea. Robert Creeley. **CP-CreeR**

Sea, The. Donald Hall. **CP-HallD**

Sea / Is not distinguished by. James Liddy. *Fr.* Birds. **CP-LiddJ**

Sea, The. David Herbert Lawrence. **CP-LawrD**

Sea, The. Louis MacNeice. *Fr.* Nature Notes. **CP-MacNL**

Sea, The. Mary Oliver. **SP-OlivM**

Sea / Pouring, The. Injured Choriant or Paeonic. Malcolm Lowry. **CP-LowrM**

Sea, The. William Carlos Williams. **CP-WilW1**

Sea, a body of mysterious calls, The. Homecoming. Christian J. Van Geel, *tr. fr.* Dutch *by* Adrienne Rich. **CP-RicAE**

Sea: A Summer and Winter View, The. George Crabbe. **SP-CrabG** *Fr.* The Borough.

Sea always arriving, The. The Farmer and the Sea. Wendell Berry. **CP-BerrW**

Sea and a crescent strip of beach, The. And Their Winter and Night in Disguise. George Oppen. **APSN; NNaP** *Fr.* Some San Francisco Poems. **CP-OppeG**

Sea and Ourselves at Cape Ann, The. Lawrence Ferlinghetti. **SP-FerlL**

Sea and the Hills, The. Rudyard Kipling. **CP-KiplR**

Sea and the Mirror, The. Wystan Hugh Auden. **CP-AudeW**
  Caliban to the Audience.
  Postscript.
  Preface: "Aged catch their breath, The." **LiTA**
  Prospero to Ariel.
  Supporting Cast, Sotto Voce, The.
    "At Dirty Dick's and Sloppy Joe's." **BoLoP; DTC; FaBoTw; MOS**
    (Song of the Master and Boatswain.) **BoLoP; DTC; MOS**
    "My Dear One is mine as mirrors are lonely." **NoAM**

Sea and the Skylark, The. Gerard Manley Hopkins. **CP-HopkG**

Sea at evening moves across the sand, The. Soldiers Bathing. Frank Templeton Prince. **CP-PrinF**

Sea at its worst drives a white foam up, The. Chasers. Carl Sandburg. **CP-SandC**

Sea at sunset can reflect, The. Edna St. Vincent Millay. **CP-MillE**

Sea-Bathers. David Herbert Lawrence. **CP-LawrD**

Sea Battle. Jim Carroll. **SP-CarrJ**

Sea-beast for sky-worshippers, the whale. The Whale Knot. Roy Fisher. **SP-FishR**

Sea-beauty! stretch'd and basking! Paumanok. Walt Whitman. **CP-WhitW**

Sea-born Goddesse, let me be. A Hymne to Venus, and Cupid. Robert Herrick. **CP-HerrR**

Sea Burial. John Ciardi. **SP-CiarJ**

Sea Burial from the Cruiser *Reve.* Richard Eberhart. **CP-EberR**

Sea called, The. Loss. Hilda Doolittle. **CP-DoolH**

Sea Calm. Langston Hughes. **CP-HughL**

Sea Canes. Derek Walcott. **CP-WalcD**

Sea Change. Charles Tomlinson. **CP-TomlC**

Sea-Chantey, A. Derek Walcott. **CP-WalcD**

Sea Chest. Carl Sandburg. **CP-SandC**

Sea-Choros. Euripides, *tr. by* Hilda Doolittle ("H.D."). *Fr.* Hecuba. **CP-DoolH**

Sea-coast looks at the sea, and the cities pour, The. After Melville. Muriel Rukeyser. **CP-RukeM**

Sea Coming Indoors, The. Marilyn Hacker. **SP-HackM**

Sea Corpse, The. Anne Sexton. **CP-SextA**

Sea crawls evenly, and every inch, The. Recovered from the Sea. Jenny Joseph. **SP-JoseJ**

Sea cries with its meaningless voice, The. Pibroch. Ted Hughes. **SP-HughT**

Sea dances its morning, The. Sea Mercy. Muriel Rukeyser. **CP-RukeM**

Sea designed these cliffs. Stone is cut, The. Cape Nothing. Richard Hugo. **CP-HugoR**

Sea desires deep hulls—, The. Oily Weather. Ernest Hemingway. **CP-HemiE**

Sea Dirge, A. "Lewis Carroll." **CP-CarrL**

Sea Dream, A. John Greenleaf Whittier. **CP-WhitJ**

Sea-Elephant, The. William Carlos Williams. **CP-WilW1**

Sea Engraving—Style of 1880. Marsden Hartley. **CP-HartM**

Sea Fight, The. Thomas Hardy. **CP-HardT**

Sea Fogs at the Chequammitt Inn. Brendan Galvin. **SP-GalvB**

Sea full of fishes in shoals, the woods that let, The. Mountains Covered with Cats. Wallace Stevens. **CP-StevW**

Sea Gods. Hilda Doolittle. **CP-DoolH**

Sea Grapes. Derek Walcott. **CP-WalcD**

Sea-Gull, The. Ogden Nash. **CP-NashO**

Sea Has Caves and Urns, The. Kenneth Patchen. *Fr.* Eight Early Poems. **CP-PatcK**

Sea has opened, the limit of his dream, The. Muriel Rukeyser. **CP-RukeM**

Sea-Hawk. Richard Eberhart. **CP-EberR**

Sea here used to look, The. At Darien Bridge. James Dickey. **CP-DickJ**

Sea Heroes. Hilda Doolittle. **CP-DoolH**

Sea Hold, The. Carl Sandburg. **CP-SandC**

Sea Horse, The. Robert Ranke Graves. **CP-GravR**

Sea Huns. Brendan Galvin. **SP-GalvB**

Sea in Winter, The. Derek Mahon. **SP-MahoD**

Sea Iris. Hilda Doolittle. **CP-DoolH**

Sea is a circuit of holes, The. The Coral Reef. Laurence Lieberman. **SP-LiebL**

Sea is a wilderness of waves, The. Long Trip. Langston Hughes. **SP-HughL**

Sea is all that they say: it wreaks death one way only, The. Our Lady. Donald Davie. **CP-DavDo**

Sea / is an archaeology: eight fathom down, on Dogger Bank, the bones, The. Charles Olson. **CP-OlsC**

Sea is awash with roses O they blow, The. For Miriam. Kenneth Patchen. **CP-PatcK**

Sea is calm tonight [or to-night], The. Dover Beach. Matthew Arnold. **SP-ArnoM**

Sea Is Calm Tonight, The. Lawrence Ferlinghetti. **SP-FerlL**

Sea is emormous, The. On the City Ramparts of Cádiz. Juan Ramón Jiménez. *Fr.* Ten Short Poems. **CP-WrigJ**

Sea is History, The. Derek Walcott. **CP-WalcD**

Sea is increasingly, The. For the Irish Sea. Steve Griffiths. **SP-GrifS**

Sea is large, The. The Sea Hold. Carl Sandburg. **CP-SandC**

Sea is never still, The. Young Sea. Carl Sandburg. **CP-SandC**

Sea is Open to the Light, The. Charles Tomlinson. **CP-TomlC**

Sea is the road of the bold, The. From Alcuin. Alcuin, *tr. fr. Latin by* Ralph Waldo Emerson. *Fr.* Quatrains. **CP-EmerR**

Sea is wild and black and black, The. What Is Sacrament. Marsden Hartley. **CP-HartM**

Sea Knell. John Updike. **CP-UpdiJ**

Sea laments with appeasable / Hankering wail of loss, The. Was Thy Wrath against the Sea? Christina Georgina Rossetti. **CP-RosC2**

Sea Level. Joseph Ceravolo. **SP-CeraJ**

Sea Level. Al Young. **CP-YounA**

Sea Lily. Hilda Doolittle. **CP-DoolH**

Sea-lions and birds. The Real Work. Gary Snyder. **CP-SnydG**

Sea-lions loafed in the swinging tide in the inlet, long fluent creatures. Orca. Robinson Jeffers. **CP-JefR3**

Sea-Magic. Walter de la Mare. **CP-DeLaW**

Sea Marshes in Winter. John Ciardi. **SP-CiarJ**

Sea Mercy. Muriel Rukeyser. **CP-RukeM**

Sea-Mew, The. Elizabeth Barrett Browning. **CP-BroEB**

Sea Monsters. Edmund Spenser. **ChTr; FaBoEn** *Fr.* The Faerie Queene. **CP-Spens**

Sea moves always, the wind moves always, The. Carl Sandburg. *Fr.* The People, Yes. **CP-SandC**

Sea Nymphs, The. Edmund Spenser. **CBCK** *Fr.* The Faerie Queene. **CP-Spens**

Sea only knows the bottom of the ship, The. Carl Sandburg. *Fr.* The People, Yes. **CP-SandC**

Sea opened its lips / blue with cold, The. Amy Lowell Thoughts. James Schuyler. **CP-SchuJ**

Sea otter dived, The. Translations from the Esquimaux: There Are Seasons. Ernest Hemingway. **CP-HemiE**

Sea Poem. Charles Tomlinson. **CP-TomlC**

Sea Poppies. Hilda Doolittle. **CP-DoolH**

Sea-preserved, heaped with sea-spoils. Picture of a Nativity. Geoffrey Hill. **CP-HillG**

Sea Raised Up, The. Hart Crane. **CP-CranH**

Sea reflects the rosy sky, The. Ralph Waldo Emerson. **CP-EmerR**

Sea repeats itself in light flourishes, The. Moment of Equilibrium among the Islands. Richard Eberhart. **CP-EberR**

Sea roars, the storm whistles, The. The Way of the World. Carl Sandburg. **CP-SandC**

Sea rocks have a green moss, The. Home Thoughts. Carl Sandburg. **CP-SandC**

Sea Rose. Hilda Doolittle. **CP-DoolH**

Sea-Ruck. Richard Eberhart. **CP-EberR**

Sea runs back against itself, The. Winter Seascape. Sir John Betjeman. **CP-BetjJ**

Sea said "Come" to the Brook, The. Emily Dickinson. **CP-DickE**

Sea-scut, bayberries, aquamarine. Northfork October Return. John Clellon Holmes. **SP-HolmJ**

Sea Serpent Chantey, The. Nicholas Vachel Lindsay. **CP-LindV**
"Dive, mermaids, with sharp swords."
"He waits by the door of his cave."
"Or will you let him live."
"There's a snake on the western wave."

Sea-Shore. Ralph Waldo Emerson. **CP-EmerR**

Sea-shouldering Ithaca. Canal. Muriel Rukeyser. **CP-RukeM**

Sea Side. Robert Ranke Graves. **CP-GravR**

Sea-side walk, A. Elizabeth Barrett Browning. **CP-BroEB**

Sea Slant. Carl Sandburg. **CP-SandC**

Sea-Sounding Bells. John Gould Fletcher. **SP-FletJ**

Sea speaks a language polite people never repeat, The. Two Nocturns. Carl Sandburg. **CP-SandC**

Sea speaks to me of you, The. Paul Laurence Dunbar. **CP-DunbP**

Sea Storm. Richard Eberhart. **CP-EberR**

Sea sucks at its own, The. Landcrab II. Margaret Atwood. **SP-AtwM2**

Sea Surface Full of Clouds. Wallace Stevens. **CP-StevW**

Sea that encloses her young body, The. The Sea. William Carlos Williams. **CP-WilW1**

Sea, the Sea, The. David Herbert Lawrence. **CP-LawrD**

Sea Took Pity, The. Gerard Manley Hopkins. **CP-HopkG**

Sea-Trout and Butterfish. William Carlos Williams. **CP-WilW1**

Sea Unicorns and Land Unicorns. Marianne Craig Moore. **CP-MoorM**

Sea unlocks a child's castle and an angel's, The. The Sea Has Caves and Urns. Kenneth Patchen. *Fr.* Eight Early Poems. **CP-PatcK**

Sea View. Frank Templeton Prince. **CP-PrinF**

Sea View, The. Charlotte Smith. **CP-SmitC**

Sea Violet. Hilda Doolittle. **CP-DoolH**

Sea-Violins. John Gould Fletcher. **SP-FletJ**

Sea-ward, white-gleaming thro' [or through] the busy Scud. Looking Seaward. Samuel Taylor Coleridge. **CP-ColeS**

Sea was always the sea, The. Sea Wisdom. Carl Sandburg. **CP-SandC**

Sea was born of the earth without sweet union of love Hesiod says, The. Maximus, from Dogtown-1. Charles Olson. **SP-OlsoC** *Fr.* The Maximus Poems.

Sea-Wash. Carl Sandburg. **CP-SandC**

Sea-wash never ends, The. Sea-Wash. Carl Sandburg. **CP-SandC**

Sea waves are green and wet. Sand Dunes. Robert Frost. **CP-FrosR**

Sea-Weed. David Herbert Lawrence. **CP-LawrD**

Sea-Widow, The. Stevie Smith. **CP-SmitS**

Sea-Wife, The. Rudyard Kipling. **CP-KiplR**

Sea will wash in, The. Seafarer. William Carlos Williams. **CP-WilW2**

Sea Wisdom. Carl Sandburg. **CP-SandC**

Seabattle of Salamis Took Place off Perama. Allen Ginsberg. **CP-GinsA**

Seabed, The. Thom Gunn. *Fr.* Three for Children. **CP-GunnT**

Seacoast late at night and a wheel of wind, A. On the Death of Her Mother. Muriel Rukeyser. **CP-RukeM**

Seacorps hint imbues blues *blue.* Chicory. Louis Zukofsky. **CP-ZukLS**

Seadove in a shroud. This Portrait of a Seadove—Dead. Marsden Hartley. **CP-HartM**

Seafarer. Archibald MacLeish. **CP-MacLA**

Seafarer, The, *For other tr., see* "I can sing a true song about myself." Ezra Pound, *tr. fr. Anglo-Saxon.* **SP-PounE**

Seafarer. William Carlos Williams. **CP-WilW2**

Seagulls. John Updike. **CP-UpdiJ**

Seahorse. Charles Bukowski. **SP-BukC2**

Seal. Anne Sexton. **CP-SextA**

Seal and all the fishes green, The. A Mysterious Hint. Malcolm Lowry. **CP-LowrM**

Seal in Nature. John Updike. **CP-UpdiJ**

Seal swims like a poodle through the sheet, A. The Flaw. Robert Lowell. **SP-LoweR**

Sealed inside the anemone. The Pulse. Denise Levertov. **CP-LeveD**

Sealed into the cocoon. At the Café Parnasse. Donald Davie. **CP-DavDo**

Sealion, salmon, offshore. Gary Snyder. **CP-SnydG** *Fr.* Hunting. *Fr.* Myths and Texts.

Seals. Robert Lowell. **SP-LoweR**

Seals and porpoises present. Off Spectacle Island. Richard Eberhart. **CP-EberR**

Seals at play off Western Isle, The. Seals, Terns, Time. Richard Eberhart. **CP-EberR**

Seals in Penobscot Bay, The. Daniel Gerard Hoffman. **SP-HoffD**

Seals in the Inner Harbor. Brendan Galvin. **SP-GalvB**

Seals, Terns, Time. Richard Eberhart. **CP-EberR**

Seaman's Ditty. Gary Snyder. **CP-SnydG**

Seamless Garment, The. "Hugh MacDiarmid." **SP-MacDH**

Seance Music. John Yau. **SP-YauJo**

Search, The. John Berryman. **CP-BerrJ**

Search, The, *comprises* Psalms 42 *and* 43. Bible, *O.T. See* Psalm 42: "As the hart panteth after the water brooks."

Search, The, *comprises* Psalms 42 *and* 43. Bible, *O.T. See* Psalm 43: "Judge me, O God. . . ."

Search, The. George Herbert. **CP-HerbG**

Search, The. John Hewitt. **CP-HewiJ**

Search, The. Malcolm Lowry. **CP-LowrM**

Search. Pablo Neruda, *tr. fr. Spanish by* Ben Belitt. **SP-NeruP**

Search, The. Shel Silverstein. **SP-SilS2**

Search for Love. David Herbert Lawrence. **CP-LawrD**

Search for nothing any more, nothing. Search for Truth. David Herbert Lawrence. **CP-LawrD**

Search for Sound Free from Motion. Wallace Stevens. **CP-StevW**

Search for True Religion, The. John Donne. *See* Satire 3: "Kind pity [*or* Kinde pitty] chokes my spleen[e]; brave scorn forbids."

Search for Truth. David Herbert Lawrence. **CP-LawrD**

Search Party, The. William Matthews. **SP-MattW**

Search thou my heart. Confessional. Paul Laurence Dunbar. **CP-DunbP**

Search under every veil. Basil Bunting. **CP-BuntB**

Searching. Robert Lowell. **SP-LoweR**

Searching / Not Searching. Muriel Rukeyser. **CP-RukeM**

Searching auld wives' barrels. An Extemporaneous Effusion on Being Appointed to the Excise. Robert Burns. **CP-BurnR**

Searching for the Canto Fermo. Diane Wakoski. **SP-WakoD**

Searching in a ravaged heart for anguish. Malcolm Lowry. *Fr.* The Comedian. **CP-LowrM**

Searching it goes. Shorts / Excerpts. Bill Knott. **SP-KnotB**

Searching my heart for its true sorrow. Exiled. Edna St. Vincent Millay. **CP-MillE**

Searching once I found a flower. Indian Pipe. Richard Eberhart. **CP-EberR**

Searchlight, The. Isabella Gardner. **CP-GardI**

Sears Roebuck. Randall Jarrell. **CP-JarrR**

Seas netted with ambushes, The. Two Christmas-Cards. Robinson Jeffers. **CP-JefR3**

Seasalt has rusted the ironwork trellis. San Fruttuoso. Charles Tomlinson. **CP-TomlC**

Seascape. Elizabeth Bishop. **CP-BishE**

Seascape. Langston Hughes. **SP-HughL**

Seascape. Stephen Spender. **CP-SpenS**

Seascape for an Engraver. Kay Boyle. **CP-BoylK**

Seascape shifts, The. Distinctions. Charles Tomlinson. **CP-TomlC**

Seashell, A. William DeWitt Snodgrass. **SP-SnodW**

Seashore. Ralph Waldo Emerson. **CP-EmerR**

Seashore through Dark Glasses (Atlantic City). Langston Hughes. **SP-HughL**

Seaside Golf. Sir John Betjeman. **CP-BetjJ**

Seaside Serenade. Ogden Nash. **CP-NashO**

Seaside Town, A. John Hewitt. **CP-HewiJ**

Season late, day late, sun just down, and the sky. Birth of Love. Robert Penn Warren. **SP-WarrR**

Season of Death. Edwin Rolfe. **CP-RolfE**

Season of mists and mellow fruitfulness[!]. To Autumn. John Keats. **CP-KeatJ**

Season of mists and migraines, rich catarrhs. Portrait of the Artist II. Charles Tomlinson. **CP-TomlC**

Season of my purest pleasure. *see also* Watching unto God in the Night-Season. Jeanne Marie Bouvier de la Motte-Guyon, *tr. fr.* French *by* William Cowper. **CP-CowpW**

Season of Phantasmal Peace, The. Derek Walcott. **CP-WalcD**

Season Opens on Wild Boar in Chianti. Robert Penn Warren. **SP-WarrR**

Season stalls, unseasonably fair, The. Indian Summer at Land's End. Stanley Jasspon Kunitz. **CP-KuniS**

Season 'tis, my lovely lambs, the. Edward Estlin Cummings. **CP-CummE**

Season was the childhood of sweet June, The. Fiordispina. Percy Bysshe Shelley. **CP-ShelP**

Seasoning Barn. William DeWitt Snodgrass. **SP-SnodW**

Seasonless, The. James Wright. **CP-WrigJ**

Seasons, The. Richard Eberhart. **CP-EberR**
  Man of Autumn, The.
  Man of Summer, The.
  Spring Man.
  "Spring was never his fort. Suspect at first."

Seasons ("Crocuses and snowdrops wither"). Christina Georgina Rossetti. **CP-RosC3**

Seasons ("In Springtime when the leaves. . ."). Christina Georgina Rossetti. **CP-RosC3**

Seasons ("Oh the cheerful budding-time"). Christina Georgina Rossetti. **CP-RosC3**

Seasons, The. Edmund Spenser. *See* The Mask of Mutability.

Seasons, The. James Thomson. **CP-ThomJ**
  Autumn.
    "Cormorant on high, The." OxBoS
  Hymn on the Seasons, A. **EnRP; LAuP; OxBoCh**
  Spring.
    "As rising from the vegetable World." **PoEL-3**
    "Behold yon breathing prospect bids the Muse." **PoE**

"Flushed by the spirit of the genial year." **OxAEP-1**
    "Lend me your song, ye nightingales! oh, pour." **PBBP**
    "Should I my steps turn to the rural seat." **FM; ScCV**
  Spring Flowers. **NOBE**
  Summer.
    "And what, my thoughtless sons, should fire you more." **ECEV**
    Happy Britannica. **OBEC; SeCePo**
    (Britannia.) **FaBoPP,** *ll.* 1–19;
    "His was the treasure of two thousand years." **EPCY**
    "Home from his morning task the swain retreats." **FM**
    "Nor shall my verse that elder bard forget." **EPCY**
    "Still let me pierce into the midnight depth." **EnRP**
    "'Tis raging noon; and vertical, the sun." **EBEV; OAEL-1**
    Wild Shakespeare. **EPCY**
  Winter.
    "As thus the snows arise, and foul and fierce." **ECEV; SeCePo**
    (Winter Tragedy, A.) **ECEV**
    "Drooping, the labourer-ox." **FM**
    "Fowls of heaven, The." **PBBP**
    "Keener tempests come, The: and fuming dun." **EBEV; EnRP; NoP**
    "Now, when the cheerless empire of the sky." **OxBA**
    "See, Winter comes, to rule the varied year." **NOEC; TEP**
    "'Tis done! Dread Winter spreads his latest glooms." **OxAEP-1**
    "What art thou, frost? and whence are thy keen stores." **OxBS**
    "When from the pallid sky the sun descends." **OAEL-1; OxBS**
  Winter Night, A. **NOBE**

Seasons are a series of transparencies, The. In Four Seasons. Jim Carroll. **SP-CarrJ**

Season's End. John Hewitt. **CP-HewiJ**

Season's Greetings. Leonard Nathan. **SP-NathL**

Seasons have plunged past my destiny, The. A Minstrel in Labrador. Malcolm Lowry. **CP-LowrM**

Seasons of Her Year, The. Thomas Hardy. **CP-HardT**

Seasons of the Soul. Allen Tate. **CP-TateA**

Season's Return. John Hewitt. **CP-HewiJ**

Seasons revolve and the years change, The. Another Spring. Kenneth Rexroth. **SP-RexrK**

Seated above the dead. Wind of the Village. William Carlos Williams. **CP-WilW1**

Seated after breakfast. The Geography of the House. Wystan Hugh Auden. *Fr.* Thanksgiving for a Habitat. **CP-AudeW**

Seated Figure. Louise Glück. **SP-GlücL**

Seated Man. George Oppen. **CP-OppeG**

Seated one day at the dictionary I was pretty weary and also pretty. Where There's a Will, There's Velleity. Ogden Nash. **CP-NashO**

Seathwaite Chapel. William Wordsworth. *Fr.* The River Duddon [A Series of Sonnets]. **CP-WorW2**

Seattle Uplift. John Updike. **CP-UpdiJ**

Seattle's still behind me now, and yet. Leaving Home for Home. Al Young. **CP-YounA**

Seaweed. Henry Wadsworth Longfellow. **SP-LongH**

Seclusion. William Wordsworth. *Fr.* Ecclesiastical Sonnets. **CP-WorW2**

Second after, / the first boat touched the shore, A. The Settlers. Margaret Atwood. **SP-AtwM1**

Second Air Force. Randall Jarrell. **CP-JarrR**

Second Anniversary [*or* Anniversarie], The. John Donne. **ESCV; SeCP** *Fr.* Of the Progres[se] of the Soule; the Second Anniversarie. **CP-DonnJ**
  Contemplation of Our State in Our Deathbed. **OBS**
  Our Companie in the Next World. **OBS**
  "Poor soul, in this thy flesh what dost thou know?" **OAEL-1**
  ("Poore soule, in this thy flesh what dost thou know?") **OBS**
  (Soules Ignorance in This Life and Knowledge in the Next, The.) **OBS**
  ("We see in authors, too stiff to recant.") **NOSC,** *ll.* 281–300;
  "We now lament not, but congratulate." **NOSC**

Second Attempt, A. Thomas Hardy. **CP-HardT**

Second Avenue. Frank O'Hara. **SP-OharF**

Second-Best. Robinson Jeffers. **CP-JefR2**

Second-Best Bed, The. Howard Nemerov. **CP-NemeH**

Second Book, The. Archibald MacLeish. *Fr.* Conquistador. **CP-MacLA**

Second Chances. Richard Hugo. **CP-HugoR**

Second Childhood. Phoebe Hesketh. **SP-HeskP**

Second Chime. Ogden Nash. *Fr.* Ring out the Old, Ring in the New, but Don't Get Caught in Between. **CP-NashO**

Second Chorus from Seneca's Tragedy "Thyestes", The. Seneca, *tr. fr. Latin by* Andrew Marvell. **CP-MarvA** *Fr.* Thyestes.

Second Coming, The. William Butler Yeats. **CP-YeatW**

Second Didactic Poem. Denise Levertov. **CP-LeveD**

Second Elegy. Age of Magicians. Muriel Rukeyser. **CP-RukeM**

Second Epistle. Donald Davie. *Fr.* Six Epistles to Eva Hesse. **CP-DavDo**

Second Epistle of the Second Book of Horace Imitated, The. Alexander Pope. **CP-PopeA**
"Bred up at home, full early I begun."
"But grant I may relapse, for want of grace."

Second Epistle to Davie. Robert Burns. **CP-BurnR**

Second Epistle to John Lapraik. Robert Burns.
(To the Same [John Lapraik].) **CP-BurnR**
"For thus the royal *Mandate* ran." **OBF**

Second Epistle to Robert Graham. Robert Burns. *See* On Critics.

Second-Fated, The. Robert Ranke Graves. **CP-GravR**

Second Fig. Edna St. Vincent Millay. **CP-MillE**

Second Front: Double Summertime, July 1943. John Hewitt. **CP-HewiJ**

Second Glance at a Jaguar. Ted Hughes. **SP-HughT**

Second Hymn to Lenin, *sels.* "Hugh MacDiarmid."
"Ah, Lenin, you were right. But I'm a poet."
"Are my poems spoken in the factories and fields." **SP-MacDH**

Second Jungle Book, The, *sels.* Rudyard Kipling.
How the Fear Came.
"Now this the Law of the Jungle—as old as and as true as the sky." **CP-KiplR**
(Law of the Jungle, The.) **CP-KiplR**
King's Ankus, The.
Song of the Little Hunter, The. **CP-KiplR**
"These are the four that are never content, that have never been filled since the Dews began." **CP-KiplR**
Letting in the Jungle.
Morning Song in the Jungle. **CP-KiplR**
Mowgli's Song against People. **CP-KiplR**
"Veil them, cover them, wall them round." **CP-KiplR**
Miracle of Purun Bhagat, The.
"Night we felt the earth would move, The." **CP-KiplR**
Song of Kabir, A. **CP-KiplR**
Quiquern.
Angutivaun Taina. **CP-KiplR**
"People of the Eastern Ice, they are melting like the snow, The." **CP-KiplR**
Red Dog.
Chil's Song. **CP-KiplR**
"For our white and our excellent nights—for the nights of swift running." **CP-KiplR**
Spring Running, The.
"Man goes to Man! Cry the challenge though the Jungle!" **CP-KiplR**
Outsong in the Jungle. **CP-KiplR**
Tiger-Tiger.
"What of the hunting, hunter bold?" **CP-KiplR**
Undertakers, The.
Ripple Song, A. **CP-KiplR**
"When ye say to Tabaqui, 'My Brother!' when ye call the Hyena to meat." **CP-KiplR**

Second Language. Tess Gallagher. **SP-GallT**

Second Limick. Ogden Nash. **CP-NashN**

Second Month It's Not Itemized, The. Ogden Nash. **CP-NashO**

2nd Musical Form, for Dave Young, A. Charles Olson. **CP-OlsoC**

Second Nature. Paul Éluard, *tr. fr. French by* Samuel Beckett. **CP-BeckS**
"In honour of the dumb the blind the deaf." **RHTwFP**

Second Night, The. Thomas Hardy. **CP-HardT**

2nd Novel, The. Charles Bukowski. **SP-BukC1**

Second Nun's Prologue, The. Geoffrey Chaucer. *Fr.* The Canterbury Tales. **CP-ChauG**
Two Invocations of the Virgin, I. **ACP**

Second Nun's Tale, The. Geoffrey Chaucer. *Fr.* The Canterbury Tales. **CP-ChauG**

Second Party. Archie Randolph Ammons. **SP-AmmoA**

Second People, The. Kenneth Patchen. **CP-PatcK**

Second Psalm. Anne Sexton. *Fr.* O Ye Tongues. **CP-SextA**

Second Rapture, The. Thomas Carew. **CP-CareT**

Second Satire of the First Book of Horace Imitated, The. Alexander Pope. **CP-PopeA**

Second Satire of the Second Book of Horace Imitated, The. Alexander Pope. **CP-PopeA**
"With all a woman's virtues but the pox." **OBSV**

Second Shaman Song. Gary Snyder. **CP-SnydG** *Fr.* Burning. *Fr.* Myths and Texts.

Second Sight (My Son's First Springtime). Louise McNeill. **SP-McNeL**

Second Song. Louise Bogan. **CP-BogaL**

Second Song, The. Thomas Carew. **CP-CareT** *Fr.* Carew's Masque. **CP-CareT**

Second Song. Andrew Marvell. *Fr.* Two Songs at the Marriage of the Lord Fauconberg and the Lady Mary Cromwell. **CP-MarvA**

Second Song. Sir Philip Sidney. **NoSic** *Fr.* Astrophil and Stella. **SP-SidnP**

Second Song of Huitzilopochtli. David Herbert Lawrence. **CP-LawrD**

Second Stanza, A. Donald Hall. **CP-HallD**

Second Universe. Diane Wakoski. *Fr.* The Universes. **SP-WakoD**

Second Version, The. Hayden Carruth. *Fr.* The Mythology of Dark and Light. **CP-CarHL**

Second Visit, The. Thomas Hardy. **CP-HardT**

Second Voice, The. "Lewis Carroll." *Fr.* The Three Voices. **CP-CarrL**

Second Voyage, The. Rudyard Kipling. **CP-KiplR**

Secondary Epic. Wystan Hugh Auden. **CP-AudeW**

Seconds. Louise Glück. **SP-GlücL**

Secrecy. Robert Ranke Graves. **CP-GravR**

Secrecy [or Secresie] Protested. Thomas Carew. **CP-CareT**

Secret, The. Paul Laurence Dunbar. **CP-DunbP**

Secret, The. Kenneth Koch. *Fr.* Days and Nights. **SP-KochK**

Secret, The. Denise Levertov. **CP-LeveD**

Secret. James McAuley. *Fr.* Requiem. **SP-McAuJ**

Secret, The, *tr. of* Le Secret. Thomas Merton, *tr. fr. French by* William Davis. **CP-MertT**

Secret, A. Sylvia Plath. **CP-PlatS**

Secret Agent, The. Wystan Hugh Auden. *See* Control of the passes was, he saw, the key.

Secret amusement, the inward smile. Her Dream. Hayden Carruth. *Fr.* The Fifth Version. *Fr.* The Mythology of Dark and Light. **CP-CarHL**

Secret child walks down the street, The. Christmas Eve. Muriel Rukeyser. **CP-RukeM**

Secret drops of love run through my mind, The. The Moonflower. Frank Templeton Prince. **CP-PrinF**

Secret Garden, The. Rita Dove. **SP-DoveR**

Secret Gratitude, A. James Wright. **CP-WrigJ**

Secret Haiku. Charles Henri Ford.
"Activity without / Attachment. One link with the." **SP-FordC**
"After the drama." **SP-FordC**
"And no night visitors." **SP-FordC**
"And the Path of Least." **SP-FordC**
"Baby on the way!" **SP-FordC**
"Bedraggled rose, The." **SP-FordC**
"Before his father." **SP-FordC**
"Break up conventional." **SP-FordC**
"Brought in tame from the." **SP-FordC**
"Day has twenty-four hours, The." **SP-FordC**
"Death's-head moth, A." **SP-FordC**
"Dreaming of walking." **SP-FordC**
"First owl of the evening." **SP-FordC**
"Fortune's Wheel. In the." **SP-FordC**
"Garden flooded with." **SP-FordC**
"He has a luminous." **SP-FordC**
"Heartfelt installations. / Beginnings are benevolent." **SP-FordC**
"He's out on the loggia." **SP-FordC**
"I do put art before." **SP-FordC**
"I felt my forefinger." **SP-FordC**
"I thought I heard Indra's." **SP-FordC**
"I'd like to linger." **SP-FordC**
"I'm attached, and he's." **SP-FordC**
"In my hair he's put." **SP-FordC**
"Indra needs a haircut." **SP-FordC**
"Like a wild bird he." **SP-FordC**
"Little boys, faces smeared." **SP-FordC**
"Modesty, chastity." **SP-FordC**
"Only one destiny." **SP-FordC**
"Owlet pulls / Pieces of meat from between, the, The." **SP-FordC**
"Poverty is always / Imaginary. The." **SP-FordC**
"Rise to capture the." **SP-FordC**
"Seeking out corpses." **SP-FordC**
"Some flowers wickedly." **SP-FordC**
"Someone made up my eyes." **SP-FordC**
"That first and last word." **SP-FordC**
"Theatre of winter, The." **SP-FordC**
"There's a howling stray." **SP-FordC**
"These days of small but." **SP-FordC**

"This dream of burnt ivory." **SP-FordC**

"This year's jackfruit hang." **SP-FordC**

"Through him (The Diamond)." **SP-FordC**

"Two people can be." **SP-FordC**

"Typhoid and smallpox." **SP-FordC**

"Unwashed, unbedded. / He has fine bones and a." **SP-FordC**

"What am I dreaming of?" **SP-FordC**

"When you close your eyes." **SP-FordC**

Secret Heart, The. Richard Eberhart. **CP-EberR**

Secret I take it a commitment hushed to feed amic—. Catullus. *See* Carmen 102: "If, Cornelius, we entrust our secrets."

Secret Land, The. Robert Ranke Graves. **CP-GravR**

Secret Life, A. Stephen Dunn. **SP-DunnS**

Secret Love; or, The Maiden Queen. John Dryden.

    Song: "I feed a flame within, which so torments me." **SP-DrydJ**

Secret Love or Two I Must Confess[e], A. Thomas Campion. **CP-CampT**

Secret my heart keeps, The. Hermetic Poem. Stanley Jasspon Kunitz. **CP-KuniS**

Secret of the Burning Stars, The. Pablo Antonio Cuadra, *tr. fr. Spanish by* Thomas Merton. **CP-MertT**

Secret of the Machines, The. Rudyard Kipling. **CP-KiplR**

Secret of these hills was stone, and cottages, The. The Pylons. Stephen Spender. **CP-SpenS**

Secret Rose, The. William Butler Yeats. **CP-YeatW**

Secret Sharer, The. Thom Gunn. **CP-GunnT**

Secret Sits, The. Robert Frost. **CP-FrosR**

Secret that should not be blown, The, *after the Persian*. Ralph Waldo Emerson. **CP-EmerR**

Secret Theatre. Robert Ranke Graves. **CP-GravR**

Secret told, A. Emily Dickinson. **CP-DickE**

Secret Waters, The. David Herbert Lawrence. **CP-LawrD**

Secretary Chant, The. Marge Piercy. **SP-PierM**

Secretly to love & to drink, what is it? tis a dissolute day's work. Hafiz, *tr. by* Ralph Waldo Emerson. **CP-EmerR** *Fr.* Odes.

Secrets. Wystan Hugh Auden. **CP-AudeW**

Secrets. Robert Pack. **SP-PackR**

Secrets. Charles Kenneth Williams. **SP-WillC**

"Secrets" is a daily word. Emily Dickinson. **CP-DickE**

Secrets of American Civilization. Muriel Rukeyser. **SP-RukeM**

Secrets of Divine Love Are To Be Kept, The. Jeanne Marie Bouvier de la Motte-Guyon, *tr. fr. French by* William Cowper. **CP-CowpW**

Secrets of the Earth, The. William Blake. **NOBE** *Fr.* The Book of Thel. **CP-BlakW**

Secrets of the Old, The. William Butler Yeats. *Fr.* A Man Young and Old. **CP-YeatW**

Sectantem levia nervi deficiunt. Arthur Hugh Clough. **SP-ClouA**

Secular Masque, The. John Dryden. **SP-DrydJ**

    ("Chronos, Chronos, mend thy pace.") **SP-DrydJ**

    All, All of a Piece Throughout. **ChTr; CoGr; ELP; ELU; HAP; ImPo; InPS**

    (Chorus to the Gods.) **OxBSP**

    (Song: "All, all of a piece throughout.") **WeW**

    Diana's Hunting-Song. **NOBE; SeCePo**

    Momus' Song to Mars. **OxBSP**

    "Sound the trumpet, beat the drum." **FaBoRV**

Secular Ode, The. Charles Hubert Sisson. *See* Carmen Saeculare.

Secular Signs. Thomas Merton. **CP-MertT**

Secured by sooted windows. Through the Inner City to the Suburbs. Maya Angelou. **SP-AngeM**

Securely, after days. *after Horace, Book 5, Ode 22.* Rudyard Kipling. **CP-KiplR** *Fr.* Debits and Credits.

Securely sunning in a forest glade. A Fable. Richard Wilbur. **CP-WilbR**

Securer a bo? no sacred armpits lair hops as that he-goat's. Catullus. *See* Carmen 71: "If every anyone / was deservedly plagued by a goat under his armpits."

Sedative Reflection. Ogden Nash. **CP-NashO**

Sedge. Tom Clark. **SP-ClarT**

Seductive Piece of Business, A. Randall Jarrell. **CP-JarrR**

Seductive Waltz!—though on thy native shore. Byron. **DIP** *Fr.* The Waltz. **CP-Byron**

See, / how they trace. Birds in Snow. Hilda Doolittle. **CP-DoolH**

See / it was like this when. Lawrence Ferlinghetti. **SP-FerlL**

See America First. Gilbert Sorrentino. **SP-SorrG**

See & hear the fraud, the malice of the change of fortune. Hafiz, *tr. by* Ralph Waldo Emerson. **CP-EmerR** *Fr.* Odes.

See, and not see; and if thou chance t' espy [*or* espie]. To the Generous Reader. Robert Herrick. **CP-HerrR**

See, as the prettiest graves will do in time. Fame. Robert Browning. **PP; SoSe** *Fr.* Earth's Immortalities. **CP-BroR1**

See, Comini, popular arbitrer turned on uncanny senescence. Catullus. *See* Carmen 108: "If, by general consent, it should be decided."

See could we quit coveting hope taunting where hope hid and. Catullus. *See* Carmen 107: "If ever anyone anywhere, Lesbia, is looking."

See dis pictyah in my han'? The Photograph. Paul Laurence Dunbar. **CP-DunbP**

See-er of Cities, The. Randall Jarrell. **CP-JarrR**

See! from the brake the whirring Pheasant springs. Alexander Pope. **ECEV; FHYEP; FM; PoEL-3** *Fr.* Windsor-Forest [*or* Windsor Forest]. **CP-PopeA**

    (Hunting and Fishing.) **ECEV**

See her austere beauty bend. Necessity. Richard Eberhart. **CP-EberR**

See here a Shadow from that setting Sunne. Richard Crashaw. *See* Upon Bishop Andrewes's [*or* Andrewes His] Picture before His Sermons.

See here an easy [*or* easie] Feast that know[e]s no wound. On the Miracle of Multiplied [*or* Multiplyed] Loaves. Richard Crashaw. **CP-CrasR**

See, here's the workbox, little wife. The Workbox. Thomas Hardy. **CP-HardT**

See his black nose snubbed back, pressed over like a whale's blow-holes. He-Goat. David Herbert Lawrence. **CP-LawrD**

See how from far upon the eastern road. The Magi. John Milton. **ChTr** *Fr.* On the Morning of Christs Nativity. **CP-MiltJ**

See how Romance adheres. Ralph Waldo Emerson. **CP-EmerR**

See how she snuggles against my neck. Baby Songs Ten Months Old. David Herbert Lawrence. **CP-LawrD**

See how Spring opens with disabling cold. Gerard Manley Hopkins. **CP-HopkG**

See how the archèd earth does here. Upon the Hill and Grove at Bilbrough. Andrew Marvell. **CP-MarvA**

See how the flowers, as at parade. Andrew Marvell. **OBEV; TrGrPo** *Fr.* Upon Appleton House [To My Lord Fairfax]. **CP-MarvA**

    (Garden, A.) **OBEV**

See how the generations pass. Nicholas Vachel Lindsay. *Fr.* Shantung[, *or* The Empire of China is Crumbling Down]. **CP-LindV**

See how the heights of Almscliff. Epigramma in Duos Montes Amosclivium et Bilboreum: Farfacio [Epigram on Two Mountains, Almscliff and Bilbrough: To Fairfax]. Andrew Marvell, *tr. fr. Latin by* William A. McQueen *and* Kiffin A. Rockwell. **CP-MarvA**

See how the orient dew. *see also* Ros. Andrew Marvell. **CP-MarvA**

See how the poore do waiting stand. Upon Her Almes. Robert Herrick. **CP-HerrR**

See how the red name faded hard to sorry. Ode to the Trio Fruit Company of Missoula. Richard Hugo. **CP-HugoR**

See how the roses burn! Hafiz, *tr. by* Ralph Waldo Emerson. **CP-EmerR** *Fr.* Odes.

See how the sun in dusky skies. *in imitation of* Waller. Alexander Pope. **CP-PopeA**

See how these masses mill and swarm. Edna St. Vincent Millay. **CP-MillE**

See, I put them. No. Hilda Doolittle. *Fr.* Child Poems. **CP-DoolH**

See, it is all one thing, now, this meadow. Meeting Up. Jenny Joseph. **SP-JoseJ**

See, now, this filigree: 'tis snow. The Snowflake. Walter de la Mare. **CP-DeLaW**

See on one hand. The Rainbow. Gerard Manley Hopkins. **CP-HopkG**

See quick calm moot as gratifying the tombed—sepulchres. Catullus. *See* Carmen 96: "If, Calvus, effects of grief."

See, See, Moon. Al Young. **CP-YounA**

See Sir, how as the sun's hot masculine flame. To E. of D. with Six Holy Sonnets. John Donne. **CP-DonnJ**

See! some strange comfort every state attend. Life's Poor Play. Alexander Pope. **OBEC; SeCePo** *Fr.* An Essay on Man. **CP-PopeA**

See Susan Read. David Markson. **CP-MarkD**

See that horseman from the distant land. The Visitor. Li Po, *tr. fr. Chinese by* William Carlos Williams *with* David Rafael Wang. **CP-WilW2**

See that lady / Dressed so fine? Lady's Boogie. Langston Hughes. **SP-HughL**

See the calm exit of the aged Saint. On the Death of Mr. John Haskins. Ralph Waldo Emerson. **CP-EmerR**

See the chariot at hand here of Love. Her Triumph. Ben Jonson. **CBLP; CTC; EBEV; ELP; EIL; InvP; JCP; LiTB; NOBE; NOSC; NoP; OBEV; OPOP; PoEL-2; PrIm; SeCV-1; TFi** *Fr.* A Celebration of Charis in Ten Lyric[k] Pieces [*or* Peeces]. **CP-JonsB**

See the Condemned alone within his cell. William Wordsworth. *Fr.* Sonnets upon the Punishment of Death. **CP-WorW2**

See! the faint green tinge from the western sky has. Arthur Hugh Clough. **SP-ClouA**

See the high birds! Is their's the song. The Sowing of Meanings. Thomas Merton. **CP-MertT; SP-MertT**

See the kitten on the wall. The Kitten at Play. William Wordsworth. **FaPON; PCat** *Fr.* The Kitten and [the] Falling Leaves. **CP-WorW1**

See. The lamp is adjusted. The ash tray. Now. Anne Sexton. **CP-SextA**

See, the Ship in the Bay Is Riding. John Keats. **CP-KeatJ**

See. See the smoking bowl before us. Robert Burns. **GoTS; PoE** *Fr.* The Jolly Beggars.

(Drinking Song.) **TrGrPo**

("Fig for those by law protected!, A.") **TrGrPo**

See the star yonder. George Meredith. **CP-MerG2**

See the stars, love. In a Boat. David Herbert Lawrence. **CP-LawrD**

See, the sun hath risen! The Martyr. Christina Georgina Rossetti. **CP-RosC3**

See the sweet women, friend, that lean beneath. A Ballad of Fair Ladies in Revolt. George Meredith. **CP-MerG1**

See the trees lean to the wind's way of learning. Landscape. Carl Sandburg. **CP-SandC**

See the wild purchase of the bold and vain. Juvenal, *tr.* by Samuel Johnson. **CP-JohnS** *Fr.* Satires.

See the wild Waste of all-devouring years! Epistle V, to Mr. Addison. Alexander Pope. **CP-PopeA**

See! Their verses are laid. Basil Bunting. **CP-BuntB**

See them in snow under a full moon they told me. The Standing Stones of Callanish. Richard Hugo. **CP-HugoR**

See! There are tears upon her face. The Sailor's Wife. "Lewis Carroll." **CP-CarrL**

See, they return; ah, see the tentative. The Return. Ezra Pound. **SP-PounE**

See this arm, the rivers have good names—. A Map of the Peninsula. Richard Hugo. **CP-HugoR**

See this house, how dark it is. The Empty House. Walter de la Mare. **CP-DeLaW**

See what a clouded majesty, and eyes. To My Worthy Friend Mr. Peter Lely [or Lilly]. Richard Lovelace. **CP-LoveR**

See what a lovely shell. Tennyson. **GN** *Fr.* Maud [A Monodrama]. **CP-TennA**

(Shell, The.) **GN**

See! what an undisturbed teare. Lucasta Paying Her Obsequies. Richard Lovelace. **CP-LoveR**

See what delights in sylvan scenes appear! Sylvan Delights. Alexander Pope. **NOBE** *Fr.* Summer, The Second Pastoral, or Alexis. *Fr.* Pastorals. **CP-PopeA**

See what gay wild flowers deck this earth-built Cot. Highland Hut. William Wordsworth. **CP-WorW2**

See where Capella with her golden kids. Edna St. Vincent Millay. **CMoP; MoAB; MoAmPo** *Fr.* Epitaph for the Race of Man. **CP-MillE**

See where, gathered, the wharves. By Cure of—Sulfa. Charles Olson. **CP-OlsoC**

See, where his difficult way that Old Man wins. In Lombardy. William Wordsworth. *Fr.* Memorials of a Tour in Italy, 1837. **CP-WorW2**

See Where She Flies. Thomas Campion. **CP-CampT**

See where she sits upon the grassie [or grassy] green[e]. Ditty, A: In Praise of Eliza, Queen of the Shepherds. Edmund Spenser. **FaBoCh; OBEV** *Fr.* Aprill. **NAEL-1; OBEV; OBSC; PoEL-1** *Fr.* The Shepheardes [or Shepeards or Shepherd's] Calender. **CP-Spens**

See Where the Thames, the Purest Stream. William Cowper. **CP-CowpW**

See who ne'er was or will be half read! Verses to Be Placed under the Picture of England's Arch-Poet: Containing a Compleat Catalogue of His Works. Alexander Pope. **CP-PopeA**

See, Winter comes, to rule the varied year. James Thomson. **NOEC; TEP** *Fr.* Winter. *Fr.* The Seasons. **CP-ThomJ**

See, Winter comes, to rule the varied year. Winter. James Thomson. *Fr.* The Seasons. **CP-ThomJ**

See with how little motion, now, the noon wind. Calypso's Island. Thomas Merton. **CP-MertT; SP-MertT**

See, with strong heart, O youth, the change. To a Youth. Robert Louis Stevenson. **CP-StevR**

See with the eyes of a horse. Point of View. Richard Shelton. **SP-ShelR**

See with what constant motion. Gratiana Dancing [or Dauncing] and [or &] Singing. Richard Lovelace. **CP-LoveR**

See with what simplicity. The Picture of Little T. C. in a Prospect of Flowers. Andrew Marvell. **CP-MarvA**

See yon opening flower. Song from the Wandering Jew. Percy Bysshe Shelley. **CP-ShelP**

See yonder leafless trees against the sky. Ralph Waldo Emerson. **CP-EmerR**

See you the ferny ride that steals. Puck's Song. Rudyard Kipling. **CP-KiplR** *Fr.* Puck of Pook's Hill.

See you yond' motion? Not the old fading. On the New Motion. Ben Jonson. **CP-JonsB**

Seeal'd up with Night-gum, Loach each morning lyes. Upon Loach. Robert Herrick. **CP-HerrR**

Seed-at-Zero, The. Dylan Thomas. **CP-ThomD**

Seed Cutters, The. Seamus Heaney. **FaBCIP; PNI** *Fr.* Mossbawn. **SP-HeanS**

Seed in your heart, warm dust transmuted. Madrigale. Allen Tate. *Fr.* The Progress of Œnia. **CP-TateA**

Seed is costly, The. Peasant Song. Alun Lewis. **CP-LewiA**

Seed Leaves. Richard Wilbur. **CP-WilbR**

Seed sleeps in the furnaces of death, The. Howard Nemerov. *Fr.* Runes. **CP-NemeH**

Seed-Time. George Meredith. **CP-MerG1**

Seed-Time and Harvest. John Greenleaf Whittier. **CP-WhitJ**

Seeded, brown beyond admiration. Comparison with a Sunflower. Phoebe Hesketh. **SP-HeskP**

Seeding Time. John Hewitt. **CP-HewiJ**

Seedling, The. Paul Laurence Dunbar. **CP-DunbP**

Seedlings in the Mail. Marge Piercy. **SP-PierM**

Seeds, The. Wendell Berry. **CP-BerrW**

Seeds begin abstract as their species, The. The Seeds. Wendell Berry. **CP-BerrW**

Seeds of treason choake up as they spring, The. Treason. Robert Herrick. **CP-HerrR**

Seedsman, The. John Hewitt. **CP-HewiJ**

Seedtime. Denise Levertov. **CP-LeveD**

See'est thou a Skylark whose glistening winglets ascending. The Poetry of Shelley. George Meredith. **CP-MerG1**

Seeing. Archibald MacLeish. **CP-MacLA**

Seeing. Archibald MacLeish. **CP-MacLA**

Seeing a chipmunk in the yard. An August Evening Outside of Nashville. Miller Williams. **SP-WillM**

Seeing death bobbled by destiny, touched. In the Dark Mountains, Brilliant. Tom Clark. **SP-ClarT**

Seeing dogwood trees in bloom. The Dogwood Trees. Robert Earl Hayden. **CP-HaydR**

Seeing Eye to Eye Is Believing. Ogden Nash. **CP-NashO**

Seeing Her Leave. Donald Davie. **CP-DavDo**

Seeing his stale vocabulary blind. Limited Achievement. Donald Davie. **CP-DavDo**

Seeing how I love you utterly. To Elinor Wylie. Edna St. Vincent Millay. **CP-MillE**

Seeing is Deceiving. Richard Eberhart. **CP-EberR**

Seeing it first, eye filled with. To H.C. Marsden Hartley. **CP-HartM**

Seeing Off a Friend. Stephen Dobyns. **SP-DobyS**

Seeing the Moon Rise. Thomas Hardy. **CP-HardT**

Seeing the Real You at Last. "Bob Dylan." **CP-DylaB**

Seeing the snowman standing all alone. Boy at the Window. Richard Wilbur. **CP-WilbR**

Seeing Thee Soame, I see a Goodly man. To His Kinsman, Sir Tho. Soame. Robert Herrick. **CP-HerrR**

Seeing them again, now in their final form. On Getting My Poems Back from the Typist. Chuck Miller. **SP-MillC**

Seeing Things. Howard Nemerov. **CP-NemeH**

Seeing thou art fair, I bar not thy false playing. 3.13. Ovid. **CP-MarlC,** *tr.* by Christopher Marlowe; *Fr.* Elegies.

Seeing we never spied frail Fairyland. To a Comrade in Flanders. Wilfred Owen. **CP-OwenW**

Seeing You Have. . . . William DeWitt Snodgrass. **SP-SnodW**

Seeing you have a woman. Seeing You Have. . . . William DeWitt Snodgrass. **SP-SnodW**

Seek[e] Flowers of Heaven. Robert Southwell. **CP-SoutR**

Seek not for favour of women. So shall you find it indeed. Rudyard Kipling. *Fr.* Certain Maxims of Hafiz. **CP-KiplR**

Seek not in me the big I capital. Iota Subscript. Robert Frost. **CP-FrosR**

Seek not the spirit, if it hide. Sursum Corda. Ralph Waldo Emerson. **CP-EmerR**

Seek[e] not to know my love, for she. To One That Desired to Know My Mistress [or Mistris]. Thomas Carew. **CP-CareT**

Seek or record then the benefactor—pree or voluptuous. Catullus. *See* Carmen 76: "If evocations of past kindness shed."

Seek the Lord. Thomas Campion. **CP-CampT**

("Seeke the Lord, and in his wayes persever.") **CP-CampT**

Seek True Religion!, *shorter vers.* John Donne. *See* Satire 3: "Kind pity [or Kinde pitty] chokes my spleen[e]; brave scorn forbids."

Seek true religion. O[,] where? Mirreus, *shorter vers.* John Donne. *See* Satire 3: "Kind pity [or Kinde pitty] chokes my spleen[e]; brave scorn forbids."

Seek who will delight in fable. The Westmoreland Girl. William Wordsworth. **CP-WorW2**

Seek ye Love, ye fairy-sprites? Love among the Roses. "Lewis Carroll." **CP-CarrL**

Seek[e] and Find[e]. Robert Herrick. **CP-HerrR**

Seeke the Lord, and in his wayes persever. Thomas Campion. *See* Seek the Lord.

Seeker of truth / follow no path. Edward Estlin Cummings. **CP-CummE**

Seekers. David Herbert Lawrence. **CP-LawrD**

Seekers, The. Thomas McGrath. **SP-McGrT**

Seeking. James Schuyler. **CP-SchuJ**

Seeking from women nurturance, feedback, idea. Marge Piercy. *Fr.* The Homely War. **SP-PierM**

Seeking of the Waterfall, The. John Greenleaf Whittier. **CP-WhitJ**

Seeking out corpses. Charles Henri Ford. **SP-FordC** *Fr.* Secret Haiku.

Seeking Rest. Christina Georgina Rossetti. **CP-RosC3**

Seeking the Beloved. William Cowper. *Fr.* Olney Hymns. **CP-CowpW**

Seeking the Chosen. James Dickey. **CP-DickJ**

Seele im Raum. Randall Jarrell. **CP-JarrR; SP-JarrR**

Seemed enough ambition for anyone with sense. To Be Charmed. Kenneth Patchen. **CP-PatcK**

Seemed, tho' the soft sheen all enchants. Ralph Waldo Emerson. **CP-EmerR**

Seemed to me—never maid. Ralph Waldo Emerson. **CP-EmerR**

Seeming, The. Muriel Rukeyser. **CP-RukeM**

Seems lak folks is mighty curus. Foolin' wid de Seasons. Paul Laurence Dunbar. **CP-DunbP**

Seems like a long time. The Partial Explanation. Charles Simic. **SP-SimiC**

Seems like only yesterday. Love Is Just a Four-Letter Word. "Bob Dylan." **CP-DylaB**

Seems So Long Ago, Nancy. Leonard Cohen. **CP-CoheL**

Seen by the Waits. Thomas Hardy. **CP-HardT**

Seen from above / The foam in the curving bay is a goose-quill. Under the Mountain. Louis MacNeice. **CP-MacNL**

Seen from the train. Kathleen Jessie Raine. *Fr.* Monessie Gorge. **SP-RainK**

Seen my lady home las' night. A Negro Love Song. Paul Laurence Dunbar. **CP-DunbP**

Seen on the sea, no sign; no sign, no sign. The Dead Wingman. Randall Jarrell. **CP-JarrR; SP-JarrR**

Seen through the windshield of a car. Goshen Pass: Winter. Dabney Stuart. **SP-StuaD**

Seen, too clear and historic within us, our sins of omission. The Main Regret. George Meredith. **CP-MerG1**

Seen when nights are silent. Wystan Hugh Auden. *Fr.* Five Songs ("What's in your mind, my dove, my coney"). **CP-AudeW**

Seen you down at chu'ch las' night. Discovered. Paul Laurence Dunbar. **CP-DunbP**

Seene? and yet hated thee? they did not see. But Now They Have Seen, and Hated. Richard Crashaw. **CP-CrasR**

Seer interprets the ministry of the stars, the broken gear of a bird, A. Thomas Merton. *Fr.* Cables to the Ace. **CP-MertT**

Seeress of the misty Norland. To Fredrika Bremer. John Greenleaf Whittier. **CP-WhitJ**

Sees he the new city, the really better land. Malcolm Lowry. *Fr.* Peter Gaunt and the Canals. **CP-LowrM**

Seesaw. Thom Gunn. **CP-GunnT**

See'st thou that Cloud as silver cleare. Her Bed. Robert Herrick. **CP-HerrR**

Seest thou that Cloud which rides in State. The Cloud. Robert Herrick. **CP-HerrR**

Seest thou those diamonds which she wears. Robert Herrick. **CP-HerrR**

See'st thou yon mountains laden with deep snow. Horace. *See* 1.9: "Behold yon mountain's hoary height." ("Vides ut alta").

Seething in my inmost guts with corrosive anger. Meum Est Propositum. Archipoeta. *Fr.* Four Medieval Latin Poems. **CP-MacNL**

Segre Song. Muriel Rukeyser. **CP-RukeM**

Seine / "transcend, be real," The. The Grand Duo. James Schuyler. **CP-SchuJ**

Seis Hermanos. Charles Henri Ford. *Fr.* For Djuna Barnes. **SP-FordC**

16 heures / l'Etoile. Edward Estlin Cummings. **CP-CummE**

Seize structure / Correspond with the real. The Six Canons. Muriel Rukeyser. **CP-RukeM**

Seize the bow, old swarthy fiddler! To an Old Gipsy. Johann N. Vogl, *tr. fr. German by* George Meredith. **CP-MerG2**

Seizures of power. Usurper. Richard Eberhart. **CP-EberR**

Seldom "can't," / Seldom "don't." Christina Georgina Rossetti. **CP-RosC2**

"Seldom we find," says Solomon Don Dunce. An Enigma. Edgar Allan Poe. **CP-PoeEd**

Seldom Yet Now. Robert Ranke Graves. **CP-GravR**

Seldom yet now: the quality. Seldom Yet Now. Robert Ranke Graves. **CP-GravR**

Seldome the villaine, though much hast he make. 3.2. Horace. **CP-RaleW**, *tr. by* Sir Walter Ralegh; *Fr.* Odes.

Select the stone. Incise the words. For Stonecutters. John Hewitt. **CP-HewiJ**

Selecting a Reader. Ted Kooser. **SP-KoosT**

Selection of Concrete Poems, A. Thomas Merton. **CP-MertT**
 "AWFULMUSICAW."
 "BROnze fasHIONs / ONZEfa shIONS BR."
 Found Macaronic Antipoem.
 "HURLUB / ERL UH."
 "Natur / aabho / rrret / vacuu / uuuum."
 "NORMS / Grraa aa aa lll."
 "OVID DIVO."
 Semiotic Poem from Racine's "Iphigenie."
 "THWPRVNCL."
 "Vicovicovicovicovico."
 "WHISKE / WHI SK."
 "Wundiwundiwundiwundiwundiwundi."

Selectivity. John Ciardi. **SP-CiarJ**

Selectric II. Al Young. **CP-YounA**

Selene Afterwards. Archibald MacLeish. **CP-MacLA**

Self. Archie Randolph Ammons. **SP-AmmoA**

Self. Kathleen Jessie Raine. **SP-RainK**

Self, The. William Carlos Williams. **CP-WilW2**

Self-Acquaintance. William Cowper. **NOCV** *Fr.* Olney Hymns. **CP-CowpW**

Self-Condemnation. George Herbert. **CP-HerbG**

Self-Conscious People. David Herbert Lawrence. **CP-LawrD**

Self-contemplation is a curse. Lines upon Leaving a Sanitarium. Theodore Roethke. **CP-RoetT**

Self Criticism. Countee Cullen. **CP-CullC**

Self-Criticism in February. Robinson Jeffers. **CP-JefR2**

Self crowned the day displays its plumage. Hymn Among the Ruins. Octavio Paz, *tr. fr. Spanish by* William Carlos Williams. **CP-WilW2**

Self-Dependence. Matthew Arnold. **SP-ArnoM**

Self-Diffidence. Jeanne Marie Bouvier de la Motte-Guyon, *tr. fr. French by* William Cowper. **CP-CowpW**

Self-drivers may curse their luck. A Permanent Way. Wystan Hugh Auden. **CP-AudeW**

Self-educated WILLIAM BLAKE. Wystan Hugh Auden. **EPCY** *Fr.* New Year Letter. **CP-AudeW**

Self-Effacement of Electra Thorne, The. Ogden Nash. **CP-NashO**

Self-Glamourer, A. Thomas Hardy. **CP-HardT**

Self-hatred. Adrienne Rich. *Fr.* Turning the Wheel. **SP-RicA2**

Self in 1958. Anne Sexton. **CP-SextA**

Self-Interrogation. Emily Brontë. *See* The Evening passes fast away.

Self is empty, as empty, The. The Body of Desire. David St. John. *Fr.* Study for the World's Body. **SP-StJoD**

Self-Knowledge. Samuel Taylor Coleridge. **CP-ColeS**

Self Love. John Donne. **CP-DonnJ**

Self-Love and Truth Incompatible. Jeanne Marie Bouvier de la Motte-Guyon, *tr. fr. French by* William Cowper. **CP-CowpW**

Self-Pity. David Herbert Lawrence. **CP-LawrD**

Self-Pity Is a Kind of Lying, Too. James Schuyler. **CP-SchuJ** ("It's / snowing defective.") **CP-SchuJ**

Self-Portrait ("In Murray, Kentucky, I lay once"). Charles Wright. **SP-WrigC**

Self-Portrait ("Pictures in the air have few visitors, The"). Charles Wright. **SP-WrigC**

Self-Portrait. William Carlos Williams. **LCAP** *Fr.* Pictures from Brueghel. **CP-WilW2**

Self-Portrait ("Charles on the Trevisan, night bridge"). Charles Wright. **SP-WrigC**

Self-Portrait ("Marostica, Val di Ser. Bassano del Grappa"). Charles Wright. **SP-WrigC**

Self-Portrait ("Someday they'll find me out, and my lavish hands"). Charles Wright. **SP-WrigC**

Self-Portrait 1. William Carlos Williams. **CP-WilW1**

Self-Portrait 2. William Carlos Williams. **CP-WilW1**

Self-Portrait as a Bear. Donald Hall. **CP-HallD**

Self-Portrait at Six. Stephen Berg. **SP-BergS**

Self-Portrait at Thirty-Nine. Ted Kooser. **SP-KoosT**

Self-Portrait: David, A. Charles Tomlinson. **CP-TomlC**

Self-Portrait: Holding On. Al Young. **CP-YounA**

Self-Portrait in a Convex Mirror. John Ashbery. **SP-AshbJ**

Self-Portrait in Shoulder Stand. Erica Jong. **SP-JongE**

Self-Portraits and Their Mirrors. Roy Fisher. **SP-FishR**

Self Prepares for an Unwilling Journey, The. William Dickey. **SP-DickW**

Self-Protection. David Herbert Lawrence. **CP-LawrD**

Self-Reliance. Ralph Waldo Emerson. *See* Power.

Self-Sacrifice ("Self-sacrifice, after all"). David Herbert Lawrence. **CP-LawrD**

Self-Sacrifice ("Self-sacrifice is"). David Herbert Lawrence. **CP-LawrD**

Self-Seeker, The. Robert Frost. **CP-FrosR**

Self-Service. John Updike. **CP-UpdiJ**

Self to self. Walter de la Mare. **CP-DeLaW**

Self-Unconscious. Thomas Hardy. **CP-HardT**

Self-Unseeing, The. Thomas Hardy. **CP-HardT**

Self[e] Accuser, A. John Donne. **CP-DonnJ**

Self's the Man. Philip Larkin. **CP-LarkP**

Selfsame Song, The. Thomas Hardy. **CP-HardT**

Selfsame toothless voice for death or bridal, The. Bell Speech. Richard Wilbur. **CP-WilbR**

Selina, Countess of Huntingdon. Donald Davie. **CP-DavDo**

Sell me a violin, mister, of old mysterious wood. Kreisler. Carl Sandburg. **CP-SandC**

Seltzer. Jim Carroll. **SP-CarrJ**

Selva Oscura. Louis MacNeice. **CP-MacNL**

Selves. Thom Gunn. **CP-GunnT**

Semantic Drift. Chuck Miller. **SP-MillC**

Semblables, The. William Carlos Williams. **CP-WilW2**

Semi-Centennial. John Crowe Ransom. *Fr.* Sixteen Poems in Eight Pairings. **SP-RansJ**

Semi-Detached. Robert Ranke Graves. **CP-GravR**

Semi-Lunatics of Kilmuir, The. Richard Hugo. **CP-HugoR**

Semi-Revolution, A. Robert Frost. **CP-FrosR**

Semi-Spring. Edward Estlin Cummings. **CP-CummE**

Semiotic Poem from Racine's "Iphigenie." Thomas Merton. *Fr.* A Selection of Concrete Poems. **CP-MertT**

Semiramis. Anne Bradstreet. **KTR** *Fr.* The Four[e] Monarchies. **CP-BradA**

Semite. George Oppen. **CP-OppeG**

Senator Explains a Vote, The. Miller Williams. **SP-WillM**

Senator Smoot (Republican, Ut.) Invocation. Ogden Nash. **CP-NashO**

Send home my long strayed [*or* long-strayed *or* long-strayd] eyes to me[e]. The Message. John Donne. **CP-DonnJ**

Send me some token, that my hope may live. Sonnet. The Token. John Donne. **CP-DonnJ**

Send No Money. Philip Larkin. **CP-LarkP**

Send-Off, The. Wilfred Owen. **CP-OwenW**

Send peace on all the lands and flickering corn. Anashuya and Vijaya. William Butler Yeats. **CP-YeatW**

Send regards to Ida the bitch. Louis Zukofsky. **CP-ZukLS**

Send this man to the mine, this to the battle. Argument for Suicide. William Wordsworth. **CP-WorW1**

Seneca. Thomas Merton. **CP-MertT**

Senescence begins / And middle age ends. Crossing the Border. Ogden Nash. **CP-NashO**

Senescente Mundo. Thomas Merton. **CP-MertT; SP-MertT**

Senex. Sir John Betjeman. **CP-BetjJ**

Senex, an oak. To Return to the Trees. Derek Walcott. **CP-WalcD**

Sengekontacket. Brendan Galvin. **SP-GalvB**

Senior school seemed vast, an oblong space, The. The Big Room. John Hewitt. **CP-HewiJ**

Señor, I am glad you recognize me. Letter from the Snake Woman. Siv Cedering Fox. **SP-CedeS**

Señor, señor, do you know where we're headin'? Señor (Tales of Yankee Power). "Bob Dylan." **CP-DylaB**

Señor (Tales of Yankee Power). "Bob Dylan." **CP-DylaB**

Señora, it is true the Greeks are dead. Invocation to the Social Muse. Archibald MacLeish. **CP-MacLA**

Senorita's Bouquet, A. Gilbert Sorrentino. **SP-SorrG**

Sense and Spirit. George Meredith. **CP-MerG1**

Sense of danger must not disappear, The. Leap Before You Look. Wystan Hugh Auden. **CP-AudeW**

Sense of disguise is a, The. Follow That Stagecoach. Diane Wakoski. **SP-WakoD**

Sense of Distance, A. Charles Tomlinson. **CP-TomlC**

Sense of Humor, A. Nicholas Vachel Lindsay. **CP-LindV**

Sense of the Sleight-of-Hand Man, The. Wallace Stevens. **CP-StevW**

Sense of the world is short, The. Eros. Ralph Waldo Emerson. **CP-EmerR**

Sense of Truth. David Herbert Lawrence. **CP-LawrD**

Sense that sits in the thin skins of lips, The. The Betrayal. Thomas Merton. **CP-MertT**

Senseless school, where we must give, A. A Young Man's Epigram on Existence. Thomas Hardy. **CP-HardT**

Senses loving Earth or well or ill, The. Sense and Spirit. George Meredith. **CP-MerG1**

Senses of Insecurity. Maya Angelou. **SP-AngeM**

Senses of one's / life begin, The. An Illness. Robert Creeley. **CP-CreeR**

Sensibility how charming. Song. Robert Burns. **CP-BurnR**

Sensibility! O La! Theodore Roethke. **CP-RoetT**

Sensible, coarse, and moral; in decent brown. John Berryman. *Fr.* Sonnets to Chris. **CP-BerrJ**

Sensitive Plant, The. Percy Bysshe Shelley. **CP-ShelP**

"Whether the sensitive plant, or that." **OAEL-2**

Sensual heat on the heavy leaves, A. Taking Shelter. Steve Griffiths. **SP-GrifS**

Sensual mind in the wreaths of wine, The. Alun Lewis. *Fr.* The Madman. **CP-LewiA**

Sensualist, The. John Updike. **CP-UpdiJ**

Sensualists, The. Theodore Roethke. **CP-RoetT**

Sent straight from suns. Lamplight. John Updike. **CP-UpdiJ**

Sent to George Lyttleton, Esq., Soon After the Death of His Wife. James Thomson. **CP-ThomJ**

Sent to the Honorable Mistress O'Neill, with Painted Flowers. Charlotte Smith. **CP-SmitC**

Sentence, A. Siv Cedering Fox. *Fr.* Onna-E, Pictures of Women. **SP-CedeS**

Sentence, The. Robert Creeley. **CP-CreeR**

Sentence, The. Robert Ranke Graves. **CP-GravR**

Sentence of John L. Brown, The. John Greenleaf Whittier. **CP-WhitJ**

Sentence undulates, The. The End of the Parade. William Carlos Williams. **CP-WilW2**

Sentence uttered makes a world appear, A. Words. Wystan Hugh Auden. **CP-AudeW**

Sentencing goes blithely on its way, The. In a Poem. Robert Frost. **CP-FrosR**

Sententious Man, The. Theodore Roethke. **CP-RoetT**

Sentience. Al Young. **CP-YounA**

Sentiment, Oeconomy, and Greed. A Triad of British Evils. George Meredith. **CP-MerG2**

Sentimental Delusion, A. Mona Van Duyn. **SP-VanDM**

Sentimental is just outside the door, The. Diaghilev Did Not Say "Étonnez-Moi." Gilbert Sorrentino. **SP-SorrG**

Sentimentalist sends his mauve balloon, The. The Celebration in the Plaza. Adrienne Rich. **CP-RicAE**

Sentiments are nice, "The Lonely Crowd." John Button Birthday. Frank O'Hara. **SP-OharF**

Sentiments for a Dedication. Archibald MacLeish. **CP-MacLA**

Sentinel robins two / guard me and you. Edward Estlin Cummings. **CP-CummE**

Sentinels, The. Robert Duncan. **SP-DuncR**

Sentry, The. Alun Lewis. **CP-LewiA**

Sentry, The. Wilfred Owen. **CP-OwenW**

Sentry. Edwin Rolfe. **CP-RolfE**

Sepal, petal, and a thorn, A. Emily Dickinson. **CP-DickE**

Separate Lives. Marilyn Hacker. **SP-HackM**

Separate place between the thought and felt, A. The Corridor. Thom Gunn. **CP-GunnT**

Separate Rose, The. Pablo Neruda.

Island (VII), The. **SP-NeruP**

Island (VIII), The. **SP-NeruP**

Island (XII), The. **SP-NeruP**

Island (XVII), The. **SP-NeruP**

Island (XX), The. **SP-NeruP**

Men (II), The. **SP-NeruP**

Men (IV), The. **SP-NeruP**

Men (IX), The. **SP-NeruP**

Men (XVIII), The. **SP-NeruP**

Men (XIX), The. **SP-NeruP**

Separate Time, A. Stephen Dobyns. **SP-DobyS**

Separated. David Herbert Lawrence. **CP-LawrD**

Separation, The. Thom Gunn. **CP-GunnT**

Separation, The. Stanley Jasspon Kunitz. **CP-KuniS**

Separation, A. Alun Lewis. **CP-LewiA**

Separation. Audre Lorde. **SP-LordA**

Separation from Asra. Samuel Taylor Coleridge. **CP-ColeS**

Separation of Lovers. Thomas Carew. *Fr.* Four Songs, by Way of Chorus To a Play. **CP-CareT**

Separations. Stephen Dobyns. **SP-DobyS**

Separations. Marilyn Hacker.

"Culled from the brambled ceiling of my wide." **SP-HackM**

"February of the merely real, A." **SP-HackM**

"Friend (this is an imaginary letter)." **SP-HackM**

"I still balk at my preference for rhyme." **SP-HackM**

"I'll dabble in specifics in my bath." **SP-HackM**

"More circumspect good friend, if by 'deceive'." **SP-HackM**

"Satisfied loves eat big breakfasts. I." **SP-HackM**

"This is a high and sprawling wooden flat." **SP-HackM**

Sepia Fashion Show. Maya Angelou. **SP-AngeM**

September. Wystan Hugh Auden. **CP-AudWJ**

September. Christina Georgina Rossetti. *Fr.* The Months: A Pageant. **CP-RosC2**

September. James Schuyler. **CP-SchuJ**

September. William DeWitt Snodgrass. **SP-SnodW**

September. Gary Snyder. *Fr.* Six Years. **CP-SnydG**

September Afternoon at Four O'Clock. Marge Piercy. **SP-PierM**

September, and the butterflies are drifting. The Crossing. Howard Nemerov. **CP-NemeH**

September comes smoking over the hills. The Tobacco Shed. Lewis Turco. **SP-TurcL**

September, 1815. William Wordsworth. *See* While not a leaf seems faded; while the fields.

September, 1819 ("Departing summer hath assumed"). William Wordsworth. **CP-WorW2**

September, 1819 ("Sylvan slopes with corn-clad fields, The"). William Wordsworth. **CP-WorW2**

September, 1802. Near Dover. William Wordsworth. *See* Inland, within a hollow Vale, I stood.

September has come and I wake. Louis MacNeice. *Fr.* Autumn Journal. **CP-MacNL**

September in Kittery. Gilbert Sorrentino. **SP-SorrG**

September in the Park. William DeWitt Snodgrass. **SP-SnodW**

September Is Summer, Too. Ogden Nash. **CP-NashO**

September Landscape. Robert Ranke Graves. **CP-GravR**

September Lull. John Hewitt. **CP-HewiJ**

September Morn. Ogden Nash. **CP-NashO**

September 1961. Denise Levertov. **CP-LeveD**

September 1913. William Butler Yeats. **CP-YeatW**

September Ode. Donald Hall. **CP-HallD**

September on Jessore Road, *with music.* Allen Ginsberg. **CP-GinsA**

September 1, 1802. William Wordsworth. **CP-WorW1**

SEPTEMBER (*Shooting*). Rudyard Kipling. *Fr.* Verses on Games. **CP-KiplR**

September Shooting. Howard Nemerov. **CP-NemeH**

September Song. Geoffrey Hill. **CP-HillG**

September sunlight. Saint-Apollinaire. Daniel Gerard Hoffman. **SP-HoffD**

September, the First Day of School. Howard Nemerov. **CP-NemeH**

September, the fugue of dry weather. Primitive Journal II. Charles Wright. **SP-WrigC**

September 21. Adrienne Rich. **CP-RicAE**

September twenty-second, Sir: today. After the Surprising Conversions. Robert Lowell. **SP-LoweR**

September 2, 1969. Wendell Berry. **CP-BerrW**

September's Baccalaureate. Emily Dickinson. **CP-DickE**

September's Book. Alice Notley. **SP-NotlA**

Septentrion. René Char, *tr. fr. French by* Thomas Merton. **CP-MertT**

Septic Tanck. Hayden Carruth. **CP-CarHS**

Septimi Gades. William Wordsworth. **CP-WorW1**

Septimius and Acme. Catullus. *See* Carmen 45: "Phyllis Corydon clutched to him."

Septimius thus his love addressed. Catullus. *See* Carmen 45: "Phyllis Corydon clutched to him."

Septuagenarian, The. Robert Ranke Graves. **CP-GravR**

Septuagesima. Christina Georgina Rossetti. **CP-RosC2**

Sepulchral, *parody of an epigram from* The Greek Anthology. Rudyard Kipling. **CP-KiplR** *Fr.* The Muse among the Motors.

Sepulchre. George Herbert. **CP-HerbG**

Sequal. Ernest Hemingway. **CP-HemiE**

Sequel, The. Theodore Roethke. **CP-RoetT**

Sequel, the Conclusion, the Endlessness, The. Delmore Schwartz. **SP-SchwD**

Sequel to *Beggars* Composed Many Years After. William Wordsworth. **CP-WorW2**

Sequence, A. Denise Levertov. **CP-LeveD**

Sequence 1944-6. Louis Zukofsky. **CP-ZukLS**

"But lose patience."

Flushing Meadows.

"Having outlived self-offense."

"Heart too human."

"I look at the pines on the hillside."

Seraph. William Carlos Williams. **CP-WilW1**

Seraph and Poet, The. Elizabeth Barrett Browning. **CP-BroEB**

Seraph scanned the murderer in the dock, The. One in the Public Gallery. Walter de la Mare. **CP-DeLaW**

Seraph sings before the manifest, The. The Seraph and Poet. Elizabeth Barrett Browning. **CP-BroEB**

Seraphic shame generosity causes, The. Emily Dickinson. **SP-DickE**

Seraphim, The. Elizabeth Barrett Browning. **CP-BroEB**

Seraphs! around th'Eternal's seat who throng. Anthem for the Children of Christ's Hospital. Samuel Taylor Coleridge. **CP-ColeS**

Sere ring a pipe wood. Lilac. Louis Zukofsky. **CP-ZukLS**

Serena I. Samuel Beckett. **CP-BeckS**

Serena II. Samuel Beckett. **CP-BeckS**

Serena III. Samuel Beckett. **CP-BeckS**

Serenade ("Come, wander forth with me! The orange flowers"). Christina Georgina Rossetti. **CP-RosC3**

Serenade: "Windows reflect the fuscous clouds." John Yau. **SP-YauJo**

Serenade, A: "Ah! County Guy, the hour is nigh." Sir Walter Scott. *Fr.* Quentin Durward.

(County Guy.) **SP-ScotW**

Serenade at the Villa, A. Robert Browning. **CP-BroR1**

Serenade to Leonor. Charles Henri Ford. **SP-FordC**

Serene, and fitted to embrace. Dion. William Wordsworth. **CP-WorW2**

Serene and purple twilight of the South. Procession. James Schuyler. **CP-SchuJ**

Serene immediate silliest and whose. Edward Estlin Cummings. **CP-CummE**

Serene in his unconquerable might. Fragment: Pater Omnipotens. Percy Bysshe Shelley. **CP-ShelP**

Serene night cold November. The News and the Weather. Thomas McGrath. **SP-McGrT**

Serenely in the crystal jet, *subsel.* Ezra Pound. *See* Canto 74: "Enormous tragedy of the dream in the peasant's bent shoulders, The."

Serenity of Faith, The, *vv. 7–14 of diff. tr., by* McFadyen. Bible, *O.T. See* Psalm 27: "Lord is my light and my salvation, The. . . ."

Serfs are glad through Lara's wide domain, The. Byron. *Fr.* Lara. **CP-Byron**

"In him inexplicably mixed appeared." **NOBRP; OAEL-2**

Serfs are glad through Lara's wide domain. Lara. Byron. **CP-Byron**

Sergeant of the Lawe, war and wys, A. Geoffrey Chaucer. **CTC** *Fr.* The General Prologue. **FHYEP; NAWM-1; OAEL-1; PoE** *Fr.* The Canterbury Tales. **CP-ChauG**

Sgt. Pepper's Lonely Hearts Club Band. The Beatles. **CP-Beatl**

Sgt. Pepper's Lonely Hearts Club Band (Reprise). The Beatles. **CP-Beatl**

Sergeant says that eight and twenty wagons, The. The Young Soldier with Bloody Spurs. David Herbert Lawrence. **CP-LawrD**

Sgt. stands so fluently in leather, The. On a Photo of Sgt. Ciardi a Year Later. John Ciardi. **SP-CiarJ**

Sergeant Valentine Function, at Hollyfort. James Liddy. **CP-LiddJ**

Sergeant's Song, The. Thomas Hardy. **CP-HardT**

Sergeant's Weddin', The. Rudyard Kipling. **CP-KiplR**

(Sergey) (Yesenin) Speaking (Isadora) (Duncan). Bill Knott. **SP-KnotB**

Serious Case, A. Mona Van Duyn. **SP-VanDM**

Serious historians care for coins and weapons. Makers of History. Wystan Hugh Auden. **CP-AudeW**

Serious moment for the water is when it boils, A. The Boiling Water. Kenneth Koch. **SP-KochK**

Serious Poem upon William Wood, A. Jonathan Swift. **CP-SwifJ**

Serious Step Taken Lightly, A. Robert Frost. **CP-FrosR**

Sermon of the Twelve Acknowledgements, The. Anne Sexton. **CP-SextA**

Serpent, The. Robert Lowell. **SP-LoweR**

Serpent. Robert Lowell. **SP-LoweR**

Serpent, The. Theodore Roethke. **CP-RoetT**

Serpent does not crouch at Athene's feet, The. Helios and Athene. Hilda Doolittle. **CP-DoolH**

Serpent is shut out from Paradise, The. To Edward Williams. Percy Bysshe Shelley. **CP-ShelP**

Serpent, Ouroboros / Whose tail is in his mouth: he is the root. George Oppen. *Fr.* A Narrative. **CP-OppeG**

Serpent's Cradle Song, The. Archibald MacLeish. *Fr.* Songs for Eve. **CP-MacLA**

Serpent's Riddle, The. Archibald MacLeish. *Fr.* Songs for Eve. **CP-MacLA**

Serpent's Tail. Robert Ranke Graves. **CP-GravR**

Servant, A. Rudyard Kipling. **PeFWW** *Fr.* Epitaphs of the War [1914–1918]. **CP-KiplR**

Servant Girl's Bed. "Hugh MacDiarmid." **SP-MacDH**

Servant of Stars, The. Leonard Nathan. **SP-NathL**

Servant to Servants, A. Robert Frost. **CP-FrosR**

Servant When He Reigneth, A. Rudyard Kipling. **CP-KiplR**

Servants of the Emperor, The. Siv Cedering Fox. **SP-CedeS**

Service. Robert Browning. **TrGrPo** *Fr.* Pippa Passes. **CP-BroR1**

Service. David Herbert Lawrence. **CP-LawrD**

Service and strength, God's Angels and Archangels. St. Michael and all Angels. Christina Georgina Rossetti. **CP-RosC2**

Service Man, The. Rudyard Kipling. **CP-KiplR**

Service, or Latin *sorbus*, European. The Life of Service. Donald Davie. **CP-DavDo**

Service without Hope, The. Emily Dickinson. **CP-DickE**

Servile Herd, The. Alexander Pope. **OBSV** *Fr.* An Essay on Criticism. **CP-PopeA**

Serving man. Curled my hair, A. Thom Gunn. **OxBC** *Fr.* Memoirs of the World. *Fr.* Misanthropos. **CP-GunnT**

Serving no haughty Muse, my hands have here. Valedictory Sonnet. William Wordsworth. **CP-WorW2**

Serving the Curve. Marsden Hartley. **CP-HartM**

Serving with Gideon. William Stafford. **SP-StafW**

Sessile, unseeing. Progress? Wystan Hugh Auden. **CP-AudeW**

Session[s] of the Poets, A. Sir John Suckling. **CP-SuckJ**

"First that broke silence was good old Ben, The." **EPCY**

Session was held the other day, A. A Session[s] of the Poets. Sir John Suckling. **CP-SuckJ**

Sessions of Gaole delivery held in the Old Bayley. The Ranter and Their Pleads. Thomas Merton. *Fr.* North. *Fr.* The Geography of Lograire. **CP-MertT**

Sestets. Marsden Hartley. **CP-HartM**

Sestina: "Coming to Spain on the first day of the fighting." Muriel Rukeyser. *Fr.* Letter to the Front. **CP-RukeM**

Sestina: "For a week now our bodies have whispered." Marilyn Hacker. **SP-HackM**

Sestina: "Hang it all, Ezra Pound, there is only the one sestina." Donald Hall. **CP-HallD**

Sestina: "I die, no matter what I do I die." Richard Eberhart. **CP-EberR**

Sestina: "I have reached, alas, the long shadow", *tr. of* *XIT* / Dante's "Al poco giorno. . . ". James Schuyler. **CP-SchuJ**

Sestina: "September rain falls on the house." Elizabeth Bishop. **CP-BishE**

Sestina: Altaforte. Ezra Pound. **SP-PounE**

Sestina for Warm Seasons. Mona Van Duyn. **SP-VanDM**

Sestina from the Home Gardener. Diane Wakoski. **SP-WakoD**

Sestina in a Cantina. Malcolm Lowry. **CP-LowrM**

Sestina of the Tramp-Royal. Rudyard Kipling. **CP-KiplR**

Sestina I: "Thickness of paint or flesh cannot deface." Howard Nemerov. **CP-NemeH**

Sestina II: "No waste is trackless: all terrain the lost." Howard Nemerov. **CP-NemeH**

Set fire to the City, burn the City down. What Had to Go. Charles Olson. **CP-OlsoC**

Set not thy foot on graves. To J. W. Ralph Waldo Emerson. **CP-EmerR**

Set of phrases learned [*or* learnt] by rote, A. The Furniture of a Woman's Mind. Jonathan Swift. **CP-SwifJ**

Set of Seasons, A. Donald Hall. **CP-HallD**

Set over Orontes. De Los Cantares. Charles Olson. **CP-OlsoC**

Set the foot down with distrust upon the crust of the world—it is thin. Underground System. Edna St. Vincent Millay. **CP-MillE**

Set the table and sweep the floor. Myself to Me. May Sarton. **SP-SartM**

Set the tall white candles burning. Host. John Hewitt. **CP-HewiJ**

Set women in his eye and in his walk. John Milton. **PeECV** *Fr.* Book II. *Fr.* Paradise Regained [*or* Regain'd]. **CP-MiltJ**

Seta cangiante. Eyes. James Schuyler. **CP-SchuJ**

Sets. Roy Fisher. **SP-FishR**

Setting a trotline after sundown. In the Deep Channel. William Stafford. **SP-StafW**

Setting for joy is rarely, The. Meditation on Two Themes. Stephen Dunn. **SP-DunnS**

Setting his camera to blink a frame. A Thanks to a Botanist. John Ciardi. **SP-CiarJ**

Setting in the wine-house. Wine-O. Langston Hughes. **SP-HughL**

Setting Out. Wendell Berry. **CP-BerrW**

Setting Out. William DeWitt Snodgrass. **SP-SnodW**

Setting out East on rain bright highways. Auto Poesy: On the Lam from Bloomington. Allen Ginsberg. **CP-GinsA**

Settlement. Archie Randolph Ammons. **SP-AmmoA**

Settlement of love, A. Invitation to a Hay. Jean Garrigue. **SP-GarrJ**

Settler, The. Rudyard Kipling. **CP-KiplR**

Settlers, The. Margaret Atwood. **SP-AtwM1**

Seur, near Blois. Donald Davie. **CP-DavDo**

Seurat and Juan Gris combine this season. Ted Berrigan. **SP-BerrT** *Fr.* The Sonnets.

Seven against Thebes, The. Aeschylus, *tr. fr.* Greek by A. E. Housman. "Now do our eyes behold." **CP-HousA**

Seven Ages of Man, The. Richard Shelton. **SP-ShelR**

Age of Desire, The.

Age of Despair, The.

Age of Elegance, The.

Age of Miracles, The.

Age of Progress, The.

Age of Romance, The.

Age of War, The.

Seven and Ten addyd to nyne. Jonathan Swift. **CP-SwifJ** *Fr.* A Famous Prediction of Merlin.

Seven Archaic Images. Thomas Merton. **CP-MertT**

Seven Attempted Moves. Roy Fisher. **SP-FishR**

Seven bulls of a Sunday. Theory of Regress. Charles Tomlinson. **CP-TomlC**

Seven buxom women abreast, and arm in arm. Ice on the Highway. Thomas Hardy. **CP-HardT**

Seven Curses. "Bob Dylan." **CP-DylaB**

Seven Daughters had Lord Archibald. The Seven Sisters, or, the Solitude of Binnorie. William Wordsworth. **CP-WorW1**

Seven Day is an unknown country where aspirins come from. Sewende (Seven Day). Thomas Merton. *Fr.* East. *Fr.* The Geography of Lograire. **CP-MertT**

Seven Days. "Bob Dylan." **CP-DylaB**

Seven days all fog, all mist, and the turbines pounding through high seas. Baltic Fog Notes. Carl Sandburg. **CP-SandC**

Seven days and six nights the hero watched relentlessly. The Amazing Tale of Skunkdog. Patti Smith. **SP-SmitP**

Seven days, seven more days she'll be comin'. Seven Days. "Bob Dylan." **CP-DylaB**

Seven Dungeon Songs. Ted Hughes.

"Dead, she became space-earth." **SP-HughT**

"Earth locked out the light, The." **SP-HughT**

"Face was necessary—I found face." **SP-HughT**

"I walk / Unwind with activity of legs." **SP-HughT**

"If mouth could open its cliff." **SP-HughT**

Seven Eleven. Carl Sandburg. **CP-SandC**

Seven Epigrams. Gerard Manley Hopkins. **CP-HopkG**

By One of the Old School Who Was Bid to Follow Mr. Browning's Flights.

Modern Poets.

"Of virtues I most warmly bless." **FaBoEE**

On a Dunce Who Had Not a Word to Say for Himself.

On a Poetess. **PP**

On One Who Borrowed His Sermons.

"You ask why can't Clarissa hold her tongue."

7:47 a.m. Now's the Time. Al Young. **CP-YounA**

7.IV.64. Gary Snyder. **CP-SnydG**

Seven ladies / and seventeen gentlemen. Parade. Langston Hughes. **SP-HughL**

Seven Letters to Zakarias. Siv Cedering Fox. **SP-CedeS**

Alioth.

Alkaid.

Alkor/Mizar.

Dubhe.

Megrez.

Merak.

Phekda.

Seven Macabre Songs. Howard Nemerov. **CP-NemeH**

Bluebeard's Wife.

Dream, A.

From the Last Dream of a Dying Woman Aged Eighty.

"It is forbidden to go further."

"My death with a nail in his foot."

"Officer wore a thin smile, The."

"Under the pie crust."

Seven maidens 'neath the midnight. A Romance of the Ganges. Elizabeth Barrett Browning. **CP-BroEB**

Seven men from all the world back to Docks again. The Ballad of the "Bolivar." Rudyard Kipling. **CP-KiplR**

7, Middagh Street. Paul Muldoon. **SP-MuldP**
Ben.
Carson.
Chester.
Gypsy.
Louis.
Salvador.
Wystan.
Seven millions stand / Emaciate, in that ancient Delta-land. An Appeal to America on Behalf of the Belgian Destitute. Thomas Hardy. **CP-HardT**
Seven nations stood with their hands on the jaws of death. Jaws. Carl Sandburg. **CP-SandC**
Seven New Ways of Looking at the Moon. John Updike. **CP-UpdiJ**
Seven Odes to Seven Natural Processes. John Updike. **CP-UpdiJ**
Ode to Entropy.
Ode to Growth.
Ode to Healing.
Ode to Rot.
To Crystallization.
To Evaporation.
To Fragmentation.
Seven of Pentacles, The. Marge Piercy. **CrSp** *Fr.* Laying Down the Tower. **SP-PierM**
Seven Pilgrims: A Clerk. Geoffrey Chaucer. *See* A Clerk ther was of Oxenford also.
Seven Pilgrims: A Knight. Geoffrey Chaucer. *See* A Knight [orKnyght] ther[e] was, and that a worthy man.
Seven Pilgrims: A Miller. Geoffrey Chaucer. **TrGrPo** *Fr.* The General Prologue. **FHYEP; NAWM-1; OAEL-1; PoE** *Fr.* The Canterbury Tales. **CP-ChauG**
Seven Pilgrims: A Monk. Geoffrey Chaucer. *See* A Monk ther was, a fair for the maistrye [or maistrie].
Seven Pilgrims: A Prioress[e]. Geoffrey Chaucer. *See* Ther[e] was also a Nonne [or nun], a Prioress[e].
Seven Pilgrims: A Squire [or Squyer]. Geoffrey Chaucer. **TrGrPo** *Fr.* The General Prologue. **FHYEP; NAWM-1; OAEL-1; PoE** *Fr.* The Canterbury Tales. **CP-ChauG**
Seven Pilgrims: A Student, *mod. vers. by* Louis Untermeyer. Geoffrey Chaucer. *See* A Clerk ther was of Oxenford also.
Seven Pilgrims: A Wife of Bath, *mod. vers. by* Louis Untermeyer. Geoffrey Chaucer. *See* A Good Wyf [or Wif] was ther of bisyde [or biside] Bathe.
Seven Pilgrims: A Wyf of Bathe. Geoffrey Chaucer. *See* A Good Wyf [or Wif] was ther of bisyde [or biside] Bathe.
Seven Poems. Charles Henri Ford.
"Is he a blood relation of yourd." **SP-FordC**
"This is the story of fire without flames." **SP-FordC**
Seven Poems for Marthe, My Wife. Kenneth Rexroth.
Dialogue of Watching, A. **SP-RexrK**
Marthe Away (She is Away). **SP-RexrK**
Reflecting Trees of Being and Not Being, The. **SP-RexrK**
Seven Preludes to Silence. Richard Shelton. **SP-ShelR**
Seven Sages, The. William Butler Yeats. **CP-YeatW**
Seven Seals. David Herbert Lawrence. **CP-LawrD**
7:VII. Gary Snyder. **CP-SnydG**
Seven-Sided Poem. Carlos Drummond de Andrade, *tr. fr. Portuguese by* Elizabeth Bishop. **CP-BishE**
Seven Sisters, or, the Solitude of Binnorie, The. William Wordsworth. **CP-WorW1**
Seven Songs, The. Charles Olson. **CP-OlsoC**
Seven Sonnets. Arthur Hugh Clough. **SP-ClouA**
"But if as (not by that the soul desired." **SP-FordC**
"But whether in the uncoloured light of truth."
"If it is thou whose casual hand withdraws."
"Shall I decide it by a random shot?"
"That children in their loveliness should die."
"That there are better things within the womb."
"To see the rich autumnal tints depart."
Seven Spiritual Ages of Mrs. Marmaduke Moore, The. Ogden Nash. **CP-NashO**
Seven Stanzas at Easter. John Updike. **CP-UpdiJ**
Seven thousand acres of grass have faded yellow. Farmer, Dying. Richard Hugo. **CP-HugoR**
Seven Times, The. Thomas Hardy. **CP-HardT**
Seven vials hold Thy wrath: but what can hold. Christina Georgina Rossetti. **CP-RosC2**
Seven Watchmen. Rudyard Kipling. **CP-KiplR**

Seven Years. Robert Ranke Graves. **CP-GravR**
Seven years' curse is ended now, The. Return. Robert Ranke Graves. **CP-GravR**
7 Years from Somewhere. Philip Levine. **SP-LeviP**
Seven years I had to think it over. Nebuchadnezzar, Solus. Howard Nemerov. **CP-NemeH**
Seven years I watched the next-door. Late Snow. Louise Glück. **SP-GlücL**
Seven years' words wasted. Long Live the Spiderweb. Allen Ginsberg. **CP-GinsA**
1789–1939. Randall Jarrell. **CP-JarrR**
Seventeen Months. Carl Sandburg. **CP-SandC**
Seventeen seventy one / and two. In those years the fame. July, 1773. Wendell Berry. **CP-BerrW**
Seventeen Warnings in Search of a Feminist Poem. Erica Jong. **SP-JongE**
Seventeen Years. Wendell Berry. **CP-BerrW**
17th century men / who founded this land. Charles Olson. **CP-OlsoC**
Seventh April. Al Young. **CP-YounA**
Seventh Avenue. Muriel Rukeyser. *See* This is the cripples' hour on Seventh Avenue.
Seventh Book, The. Archibald MacLeish. *Fr.* Conquistador. **CP-MacLA**
Seventh Day. Kathleen Jessie Raine. **SP-RainK**
Seventh dragon turned to his wife, The. Where Two O'clock Came From. Kenneth Patchen. **CP-PatcK**
Seventh Elegy. Dream-Singing Elegy. Muriel Rukeyser. **CP-RukeM**
Seventh Epistle of the First Book of Horace Imitated, The. Alexander Pope. **CP-PopeA**
Seventh Heaven. Patti Smith. **SP-SmitP**
Seventh of November, The. Robert Burns. *See* The Day returns, my bosom burns.
Seventh Psalm. Anne Sexton. *Fr.* O Ye Tongues. **CP-SextA**
Seventh Sign, The. Audre Lorde. **SP-LordA**
Seventh Song. Sir Philip Sidney. *Fr.* Astrophil and Stella. **SP-SidnP**
Seventieth Birthday. Robinson Jeffers. **CP-JefR3**
Seventy Feet Down. Philip Larkin. **RB** *Fr.* Livings. **CP-LarkP**
Seventy-four and Twenty. Thomas Hardy. **CP-HardT**
LXXIV. "Most happy letters framed by skilfull trade." Edmund Spenser. **NAEL-1** *Fr.* Amoretti. **CP-Spens**
LXX. "Fresh Spring, the herald of love's mighty king." Edmund Spenser. **AWP; CABA; ChTr; EiL; FF; FaBoEn; HAP; HBV; InPS; NoP; OBEV; OBSC; PoE; SeCeV; Son; ViBoPo** *Fr.* Amoretti. **CP-Spens**
(Fresh Spring, the Herald.) **LiTB**
LXXIX. "Men call you fair [or fayre], and you do[e] credit it." Edmund Spenser. **AWP; FaBoBe; NAEL-1; NoP; Son** *Fr.* Amoretti. **CP-Spens**
(Sonnet: "Men call you fair, and you do credit it.") **BLPL**
LXXI. "I joy to see how, in your drawen work." Edmund Spenser. **PoE** *Fr.* Amoretti. **CP-Spens**
LXXVII. "Was it a dream, or did I see it plain?" Edmund Spenser. **CBLP; NIP** *Fr.* Amoretti. **CP-Spens**
LXXVI. "Fair bosom! fraught with virtue's richest treasure." Edmund Spenser. **NIP** *Fr.* Amoretti. **CP-Spens**
LXXII. "Oft when my spirit doth spread her bolder wings." Edmund Spenser. **OAEP; OBSC; Son** *Fr.* Amoretti. **CP-Spens**
Seventy years ago my mother labored to bear me. Birthday (Autobiography). Robinson Jeffers. **CP-JefR3**
Several faiths / bid him leap—. Opium and Hitler. Leonard Cohen. **CP-CoheL**
Several Pieces for Jose Garcia Villa. Marsden Hartley. **CP-HartM**
"Like a lustrous bird threading the maze."
"Villa—I would be brief, yet say—."
Several Questions Answered. William Blake. **CP-BlakW**
Eternity ("He who binds [or bends] to himself a joy"). **AWP; ArNa; EBEV; EnlH; FaBoEE; ImPo; LAuP; LoBV; MeMBP; NOBE; NTP; NoP; OBNC; OxBSP; PFP; Poetr; RB; SCGP; SoSe; Spl; TrGrPo**
"Look of love alarms, The."
"Soft deceit & idleness."
("Which are beauties sweetest dress.")
"What is it men in women do require?" **ErPo; FaBoEE; GBL; MeMBP; NoP; OAEL-2; OxBM**
(Question Answered, The [or A].) **ErPo; FaBoEE; GBL; MeMBP; NoP; OxBM**
Several Voices Out of a Cloud. Louise Bogan. **CP-BogaL**
Severe lady, / your nets are out. Ran. Frederick Morgan. **SP-MorgF**
Severer Service of myself. Emily Dickinson. **CP-DickE**
Severnside. Charles Tomlinson. **CP-TomlC**
Sew. Donald Hall. **CP-HallD**
Sew the Flags Together. Nicholas Vachel Lindsay. **CP-LindV**

Sewende (Seven Day). Thomas Merton. *Fr.* East. *Fr.* The Geography of Lograire. **CP-MertT**

Sewerplant Grows In Harlem Or I'm a Stranger Here Myself. . . . Audre Lorde. **SP-LordA**

Sex. Charles Bukowski. **SP-BukC1**

Sex. Hayden Carruth. **CP-CarHS**

Sex and Trust. David Herbert Lawrence. **CP-LawrD**

Sex and/or Love. Charles Bukowski. **SP-BukC3**

Sex, as they harshly call it. Adrienne Rich. **NIP; NOBA; TAP** *Fr.* Two Songs. **CP-RicAE; SP-RicA2**

Sex floated like a moon. A Circle, a Square, a Triangle and a Ripple of Water. Jane Cooper. **SP-CoopJ**

Sex For You. Jim Morrison. **SP-MorrJ**

Sex Isn't Sin. David Herbert Lawrence. **CP-LawrD**

Sex Object. Ron Koertge. **SP-KoerR**

Sex Won't Work. David Herbert Lawrence. **CP-LawrD**

Sexagesima. Christina Georgina Rossetti. **CP-RosC2**

Sexist Stanza. David Markson. **CP-MarkD**

Sexless, my brother flies. Song. Summer. Rita Dove. **SP-DoveR**

Sexpot. Charles Bukowski. **SP-BukC1**

Sext. Wystan Hugh Auden. *Fr.* Horae Canonicae. **CP-AudeW**

Sext. John Berryman. **CP-BerrJ**

Sext. Donald Davie. *Fr.* Horae Canonicae. **CP-DavDo**

Sexton at Longpuddle, The. Thomas Hardy. **CP-HardT**

Sexton! My Master's sleeping here. Emily Dickinson. **CP-DickE**

Sexual Disappointments. Dabney Stuart. **SP-StuaD**

Sexual intercourse began. Annus Mirabilis. Philip Larkin. **CP-LarkP**

Sexy Sadie. The Beatles. **CP-Beatl**

Seyd planted where the deluge ploughed. Ralph Waldo Emerson. **CP-EmerR**

Seymour and Chantelle or Un Peu de Vice. Stevie Smith. **CP-SmitS**

Sez the Junior Orderly Sergeant. The Shut-Eye Sentry. Rudyard Kipling. **CP-KiplR**

S.F. Southward. Allen Ginsberg. **NAAL-2** *Fr.* Continuation of a Long Poem of These States. **CP-GinsA**

S.F.D. Edward Estlin Cummings. **CP-CummE**

S.H. Ralph Waldo Emerson. *Fr.* Quatrains. **CP-EmerR**

Sh estiffl / ystrut sal. Edward Estlin Cummings. **CP-CummE**

Shabby little bird. Passer Domesticus. William Carlos Williams. **CP-WilW2**

Shabby, tweedy, academic, he was old enough to be her father and I thought he was her father. The Dirty Talker: D Line, Boston. Charles Kenneth Williams. **SP-WillC**

Shack and a few trees, The. After Work. Gary Snyder. **CP-SnydG**

Shacks are brown, big where things were sold. Ghosts at Garnet. Richard Hugo. **CP-HugoR**

Shad, The. Ogden Nash. *Fr.* Table Talk. **CP-NashO**

Shad-Blow Tree, The. Louise Glück. **SP-GlücL**

Shad-Time. Richard Wilbur. **CP-WilbR**

Shadder in de valley. Noon. Paul Laurence Dunbar. **CP-DunbP**

Shade, The. Walter de la Mare. **CP-DeLaW**

Shade, The. Charles Kenneth Williams. **CP-WillC; SP-WillC**

Shade confounds shadows now. Blue. Nocturnal. Charles Tomlinson. *Fr.* In Winter Woods. **CP-TomlC**

Shade for me, but over thee, The. The Sisters: A Picture by Barry. John Greenleaf Whittier. **CP-WhitJ**

Shade of Caractacus, if spirits love. The Eagle and the Dove. William Wordsworth. **CP-WorW2**

Shade upon the mind there passes, A. Emily Dickinson. **CP-DickE**

Shaded lamp and a waving blind, A. An August Midnight. Thomas Hardy. **CP-HardT**

Shades. David Herbert Lawrence. **CP-LawrD**

Shades of Callimachus, Coan ghosts of Philetas. Homage to Sextus Propertius. Ezra Pound. **SP-PounE**

Shades of Callimachus, Coan ghosts of Philetas. Ezra Pound. **CMoP; HAP; MoAB; MoVE; NOBA; OBVE; OxBA; PP** *Fr.* Homage to Sextus Propertius. **SP-PounE**

Shading Flight In. Archie Randolph Ammons. **SP-AmmoA**

Shadow. Walter de la Mare. **CP-DeLaW**

Shadow. Walter de la Mare. **CP-DeLaW**

Shadow. Kathleen Jessie Raine. *Fr.* Eileann Chanaidh. **SP-RainK**

Shadow / ran before it lengthening, The. Up at La Serra. Charles Tomlinson. **CP-TomlC**

Shadow. David St. John. **SP-StJoD**

Shadow, The. William Carlos Williams. **CP-WilW1**

Shadow and light both strove to be. The Bells. Walter de la Mare. **CP-DeLaW**

Shadow and Shade. Allen Tate. **CP-TateA**

Shadow and the Light, The. John Greenleaf Whittier. **CP-WhitJ**

"All souls that struggle and aspire." **TrPWD**

Shadow and the Real, The. James Wright. **CP-WrigJ**

Shadow does not move. It is the water moves, The. The Well Disciplined Bargeman. William Carlos Williams. **CP-WilW2**

Shadow faces / In the shadow night. Chord. Langston Hughes. **SP-HughL**

Shadow his father makes with joined hands, A. Alphabets. Seamus Heaney. **SP-HeanS**

Shadow is floating through the moonlight, A. The Bird of Night. Randall Jarrell. **CP-JarrR**

Shadow of a bird / upon the yard upon, The. In Wiry Winter. James Schuyler. **CP-SchuJ**

Shadow of a pine-branch quivered, The. Words. Thom Gunn. **CP-GunnT**

Shadow of a poplar tree, The. The Massacre. Walter de la Mare. **CP-DeLaW**

Shadow of Death, The. David Herbert Lawrence. **CP-LawrD**

Shadow of her face upon the wall, The. Two Sketches. Elizabeth Barrett Browning. **CP-BroEB**

Shadow of the little fishing launch, The. The Parrot Fish. James Merrill. **SP-MerrJ**

Shadow of the Venetian blind on the painted wall, The. Forties Flick. John Ashbery. **SP-AshbJ**

Shadow of War. Stephen Spender. **CP-SpenS**

Shadow on the Stone, The. Thomas Hardy. **CP-HardT**

Shadow Play For Guilt, A. Marge Piercy. **SP-PierM**

"Always you were dancing before the altar of guilt."

"Man can lie to himself, A."

"Many people have a thing they want to protect."

"You speak of the collective."

Shadow, shadow on the wall. Three Nuns. Christina Georgina Rossetti. **CP-RosC3**

Shadow sprang out, The. Hayden Carruth. **CP-CarHS** *Fr.* The Clay Hill Anthology.

Shadow streamed into the wall, The. Shadow and Shade. Allen Tate. **CP-TateA**

Shadow was so black, The. Conviction (iii). Stevie Smith. **CP-SmitS**

Shadow Wash. Shel Silverstein. **SP-SilS2**

Shadowes before the shining sunne do vanish. Thomas Campion. **CP-CampT**

Shadowes darkning our intents, The. Song. Thomas Campion. *Fr.* The Ayres that Were Sung and Played, at *Brougham Castle* in *Westmerland*, in the Kings Entertainment. **CP-CampT**

Shadows. David Herbert Lawrence. **CP-LawrD**

Shadows. Alun Lewis. **CP-LewiA**

Shadows. Charles Kenneth Williams. **SP-WillC**

Shadows. William Carlos Williams. **CP-WilW2**

Shadows and Spring Flowers. Kenneth Patchen. **CP-PatcK**

Shadows cast by the street light. Shadows. William Carlos Williams. **CP-WilW2**

Shadows Coming. Jenny Joseph. **SP-JoseJ**

Shadows Fall Blue on the Mountains. Carl Sandburg. **CP-SandC**

Shadows gather round me, while you are in the sun, The. Next of Kin. Christina Georgina Rossetti. **CP-RosC3**

Shadows grow and deepen round me, The. What the Traveller Said at Sunset. John Greenleaf Whittier. **CP-WhitJ**

Shadows have their seasons, too, The. Penumbrae. John Updike. **CP-UpdiJ**

Shadows in his eye sockets like shades, The. Richmond. John Updike. **CP-UpdiJ**

Shadows in the room. Strange objects. The gladiolas on the coffee table, for instance. Survival as Tao, Beginning at 5:00 A.M. Hayden Carruth. **CP-CarHS**

Shadows of my chimneys stretch afar, The. Evening Shadows. Thomas Hardy. **CP-HardT**

Shadows of the ash-trees stride across the hay, The. The Death of the Baron. David Herbert Lawrence. **CP-LawrD**

Shadows of the banisters march march, The. Intimations of Mortality. Louis MacNeice. **CP-MacNL**

Shadows of the Burning. Marge Piercy. **SP-PierM**

Shadows of the ships, The. Sketch. Carl Sandburg. **CP-SandC**

Shadows on the wall. Life Doesn't Frighten Me. Maya Angelou. **SP-AngeM**

Shadows round the inland sea, The. The Lakeside. John Greenleaf Whittier. **CP-WhitJ**

Shadows Today. Christina Georgina Rossetti. **CP-RosC2**

Shadows today, while shadows show God's Will. Shadows Today. Christina Georgina Rossetti. **CP-RosC2**

Shadowy arch calling the clouds of the sun, A. Gold Leaf. Muriel Rukeyser. **CP-RukeM**

Shadowy daughter of Urthona stood before red Orc, The. America; a Prophecy. William Blake. **CP-BlakW**

Shadowy Room. James Schuyler. **CP-SchuJ**

Shadowy Waters, The. William Butler Yeats. **CP-YeatW**

Shadrach O'Leary. Edwin Arlington Robinson. **CP-RobiE**

Shadwell Stair. Wilfred Owen. **CP-OwenW**

Shady friend—for Torrid days, A. Emily Dickinson. **CP-DickE**

Shaft, The. John Ciardi. **SP-CiarJ**

Shaft, The. Charles Tomlinson. **CP-TomlC**

Shaft[e]sbury. John Dryden. *See* Of these the false Achitophel was first.

Shag-Bark Hickory. Carl Sandburg. **CP-SandC**

Shaggy and heavily natural, they stand. The Horses. Jorge Guillén, *tr. fr. Spanish by* Richard Wilbur. **CP-WilbR**

Shah Abbas. Robert Browning. **CP-BroR2**

Shah Sandschar, whose lowest slave. "Anvari", *tr. fr. Persian by* Ralph Waldo Emerson. **CP-EmerR**

Shake back your hair, O red-headed girl. Red-Headed Restaurant Cashier. Carl Sandburg. **CP-SandC**

Shake hands, we shall never be friends, all's over. Alfred Edward Housman. **CP-HousA**

Shake of the electric fan above our village;. 1930's. Robert Lowell. **SP-LoweR**

Shake out the ruffle, turn and go. To a Hostess Saying Goodnight. James Wright. **CP-WrigJ**

Shake, Well Before Using. Hayden Carruth. **CP-CarHS**

Shaken, / The blossoms of lilac. Follies. Carl Sandburg. **CP-SandC**

Shaker. James Schuyler. **CP-SchuJ**

Shaker, Why Don't You Sing? Maya Angelou. **SP-AngeM**

Shakespeare. Matthew Arnold. **SP-ArnoM**

Shakespeare Say. Rita Dove. **SP-DoveR**

Shakespeare should have come to Acapulco. Malcolm Lowry. *Fr.* The Cantinas. **CP-LowrM**

Shakespeare!—to such name's sounding, what succeeds. The Names. Robert Browning. **CP-BroR2**

Shakespeare (whom and every playhouse bill). Alexander Pope. **EPCY** *Fr.* The First Epistle of the Second Book of Horace Imitated. **CP-PopeA**

Shakespearean fish swam the sea, far away from land. Three Movements. William Butler Yeats. **CP-YeatW**

Shakespeare's Grave. Robinson Jeffers. **CP-JefR2**

Shakespeare's house is safe and sound. Malcolm Lowry. **CP-LowrM**

Shaking the head from / side to side, arms. The Animal. Robert Creeley. **CP-CreeR**

Shaking the President's Hand. Daniel Gerard Hoffman. **SP-HoffD**

Shakspeare. Ralph Waldo Emerson. *Fr.* Quatrains. **CP-EmerR**

Shakspeare-Bacon's Cipher. Walt Whitman. **CP-WhitW**

Shakspere. Gerard Manley Hopkins. **CP-HopkG**

Shal I come, if I swim? wide are the waves, you see. Thomas Campion. *See* Shall I come, if I swim? wide are the waves, you see.

Shale and water thrown together so-so first of all, The. Jug. Carl Sandburg. **CP-SandC**

Shall Christ hang on the Cross, and we not look? Behold the Man! Christina Georgina Rossetti. **CP-RosC2**

Shall Earth no more inspire thee. Emily Brontë. **CP-BronE**

Shall gentle Coleridge pass unnoticed here. Byron. **EPCY** *Fr.* English Bards and Scotch Reviewers. **CP-Byron**

Shall Gods Be Said to Thump The Clouds. Dylan Thomas. **CP-ThomD**

Shall he then finally "put away childish things." Hayden Carruth. *Fr.* The Sleeping Beauty. **CP-CarHL**

Shall hearts that beat no base retreat. The Enthusiast. Herman Melville. **SP-MelvH**

Shall I a daily Begger be. The Begger. Robert Herrick. **CP-HerrR**

Shall I again have Lilac week? George Meredith. **CP-MerG2**

Shall I be prisoner till my pulses stop. Edna St. Vincent Millay. **CP-MillE**

Shall I begin with *Ah*, or *Oh*? An Ode: Secundum Artem. William Cowper. **CP-CowpW**

Shall I come, if I swim? wide are the waves, you see. Thomas Campion. ("Shal I come, if I swim? wide are the waves, you see.") **CP-CampT**

Shall I Come, Sweet Love. Thomas Campion. **CP-CampT**

Shall I compare her to a summer play? Sonnet on Famous and Familiar Sonnets and Experiences. Delmore Schwartz. **SP-SchwD**

Shall I compare thee to a summer's day? Sonnet 18. William Shakespeare. **ArLo; BoLoP; CTC; ClHu; EiL; EnLoPo; FPL; FaBV; FaBoBe; FaFP; FaPoB; FiP; GBL; GTBS; GTBS-6; GTBS-P; HAP; HeiL; HeiP; ImPo; InPK; InPS; InvP; LPA; LiTB; MAT; NIP; NOBE; NoP; NoSic; OAEL-1; OBEV; OBSC; PBMP; PIP; PoE; PoEL-2; PoLF; PoRA; PrIm; SCGP; SCV; SeCePo; Son; TEP; TFi; TrGrPo; WeW** *Fr.* Sonnets. **CP-ShaWS**

Shall I counsel the moon in her ascending? Song of Ruark to Bhanavar the Beautiful. George Meredith. **CP-MerG2**

Shall I decide it by a random shot? Arthur Hugh Clough. *Fr.* Seven Sonnets. **SP-ClouA**

Shall I despise you that your colourless tears. To a Young Girl. Edna St. Vincent Millay. **CP-MillE**

Shall I Forget? Christina Georgina Rossetti. **CP-RosC1**

Shall I go all my bright days singing. Self Criticism. Countee Cullen. **CP-CullC**

Shall I go to love and tell. To Electra. Robert Herrick. **CP-HerrR**

Shall I leave you behind me. Tragedian to Tragedienne. Thomas Hardy. **CP-HardT**

Shall I let myself be caught. Pygmalion. Hilda Doolittle. **CP-DoolH**

Shall I, [(]like an hermit[)], dwell. *Unknown, sometimes at. to* Sir Walter Ralegh. **CP-RaleW**

Shall I, Like an Hermit, Dwell. Sir Walter Ralegh. **CP-RaleW**

Shall I love God for causing me to be? The Proof. Richard Wilbur. **CP-WilbR**

Shall I never make him look at me again? As a World Would Have It. Edwin Arlington Robinson. **CP-RobiE**

Shall I sonnet-sing you about myself? House. Robert Browning. **CP-BroR2**

Shall I stroke your thighs. "I Would Not Change For Thine." William Carlos Williams. **CP-WilW2**

Shall I Subsume. . . . Hart Crane. **CP-CranH**

Shall I sulk because my love has a double heart? Basil Bunting, *after a qasida of* Manuchehri. **CP-BuntB**

Shall I take thee, the Poet said. Emily Dickinson. **CP-DickE**

Shall I tell you again the new word. The New Word. David Herbert Lawrence. **CP-LawrD**

Shall I tell you the signs of a New Age coming? The New Age. Stevie Smith. **CP-SmitS**

Shall I tell you, then, how it is? Shades. David Herbert Lawrence. **CP-LawrD**

Shall I then hope when faith is fled? Thomas Campion. **CP-CampT**

Shall I then praise the heavens, the trees, the earth. Anne Bradstreet. **NOSC; PBWP** *Fr.* Contemplations. **CP-BradA**

Shall life be the victor. Song about Madrid, Useful Any Time. Malcolm Lowry. *Fr.* The Roar of the Sea and the Darkness. **CP-LowrM**

Shall not the Judge of all the earth do right? Christina Georgina Rossetti. **CP-RosC2**

Shall she never out of my mind. Sir Thomas Wyatt. **CP-WyatT**

Shall soldiers tread the murderous path of war. Prologue to "La Guida Di Bragia." "Lewis Carroll." **CP-CarrL**

Shall the great soul of Newton quit this earth. To the Memory of Sir Isaac Newton. James Thomson. **CP-ThomJ**

Shall the Muse sing for thousands & not sing. Ralph Waldo Emerson. **CP-EmerR**

Shall then a traiterous kis or a smile. *At. to* Thomas Campion *and to* Philip Rosseter. **CP-CampT**

Shall we address it. A Birthday. Robert Creeley. **CP-CreeR**

Shall we assume that the world. To Poets' Worksheets in the Air-Conditioned Vault of a Library. Mona Van Duyn. **SP-VanDM**

"Shall we come back?" the gamblers asked. The Rakeoff and the Getaway. Carl Sandburg. **CP-SandC**

Shall we come out of it all, some day, as one does from a tunnel? Claude to Eustace. Arthur Hugh Clough. **EBVVPR** *Fr.* Amours de Voyage. **SP-ClouA**

Shall we conceal the Case, or tell it. The Problem. Thomas Hardy. **CP-HardT**

Shall we ever find the face again. Find the Face. Marsden Hartley. **CP-HartM**

Shall we let go. To Let Go Or to Hold on—? David Herbert Lawrence. **CP-LawrD**

Shall we remember the jingles of the morning. The Jingles of the Morning. Louis MacNeice. *Fr.* Out of the Picture. **CP-MacNL**

Shall we roam, my love. To the Queen of My Heart. Percy Bysshe Shelley. **CP-ShelP**

Shall we win at love or shall we lose. Hôtel Transylvanie. Frank O'Hara. **SP-OharF**

Shallot, A. Richard Wilbur. **CP-WilbR**

Shallow, dangerous, but without sensation. Commuter. Roy Fisher. **SP-FishR**

Shallow folds of the wood, The. Woods in Spring. Gerard Manley Hopkins. **CP-HopkG**

Shallow Grass, The. Archibald MacLeish. *Fr.* The Pot of Earth. **CP-MacLA**

Shallow or deep, snows on Soracte won't. To an American Classicist. Donald Davie. **CP-DavDo**

Shallow pools of water / Are drinking up the sky. The Sands. John Gould Fletcher. *Fr.* Sand and Spray: A Sea-Symphony. **SP-FletJ**

Shallow stream, from fountains, A. Voyage of the Jettie. John Greenleaf Whittier. **CP-WhitJ**

Shallows, brighter, The. The Pier: Under Pisces. James Merrill. **SP-MerrJ**

Shalom. Denise Levertov. **CP-LeveD**

Shalt thou be dug or left as pasture land. The Terrible Choice. John Hewitt. **CP-HewiJ**

Shamanism, Dalston. Steve Griffiths. **SP-GrifS**

Shambling urban prospect, A. Draft Balance Sheet. James McAuley. **SP-McAuJ**

Shame, The. Robert Creeley. **CP-CreeR**

Shame. Frederick Morgan. *Fr.* Enigmas. **SP-MorgF**

Shame. Karl Shapiro. *Fr.* Adam and Eve. **SP-ShapK**

Shame. Richard Wilbur. **CP-WilbR**

Shame. Charles Kenneth Williams. **SP-WillC**

Shame checks our first attempts, but then 'tis proved. Sins Loathed, and Yet Loved. Robert Herrick. **CP-HerrR**

Shame is a shadow cast by sin: yet shame. Christina Georgina Rossetti. *Fr.* Later Life: A Double Sonnet of Sonnets. **CP-RosC2**

Shame is the shawl of Pink. Emily Dickinson. **CP-DickE**

Shame, No Statist. Robert Herrick. **CP-HerrR**

Shame of mans face is no more, The. Another. Robert Herrick. **CP-HerrR**

Shame of thy mother soyle! ill-nurtur'd tree! *Class. Gr. trans. incl.* Horace. **CP-CrasR,** *tr. by* Richard Crashaw; *Fr.* Odes.

Shame on this faithless heart! that could allow. Oxford, May Thirtieth, Eighteen Twenty. William Wordsworth. **CP-WorW2**

Shame on You. Langston Hughes. **SP-HughL**

Shampoo, The. Elizabeth Bishop. **CP-BishE**

Shane O'Neill's Cairn. Robinson Jeffers. **CP-JefR2**

Shang Cup. Louis Zukofsky. **CP-ZukLS**

Shang Dynasty Oracle Bone 2 Say. Charles Olson. **CP-OlsoC**

Shanghai Shenanigans. John Yau. **SP-YauJo**

Shank-end of day, spit of snow, the call. The Dream He Never Knew the End of. Robert Penn Warren. *Fr.* Audubon. **SP-WarrR**

Shantung[, or The Empire of China is Crumbling Down]. Nicholas Vachel Lindsay. **CP-LindV**

"Always the generations pass."

"Confucius, Confucius, how great was Confucius."

"Now let the generations pass."

"See how the generations pass."

"Slowly the generations pass."

Shapcot, to thee the Fairy [*or* faery] State. Oberon's Feast. Robert Herrick. **CP-HerrR**

Shape a couple out of mist. Thaw. Frederick Morgan. *Fr.* Enigmas. **SP-MorgF**

Shape of the Fire, The. Theodore Roethke. **CP-RoetT**

Shape of the gesture, The. The Abstraction. Gilbert Sorrentino. **SP-SorrG**

Shape of the world is either a box or a bag, The. Atlas, How Have You Been? Carl Sandburg. **CP-SandC**

Shape the lips to an *o*, say *a*. Ö. Rita Dove. **SP-DoveR**

Shapes. Kenneth Patchen. **CP-PatcK**

Shapes and Intensities of This Man, This Confucius, The. Kenneth Patchen. **CP-PatcK**

Shapes of change take their time, The. Man the Moon Shooter. Carl Sandburg. **CP-SandC**

Shapes of Winter. Gilbert Sorrentino. **SP-SorrG**

Shaping Spirit, The. Phoebe Hesketh. **SP-HeskP**

Sharaku Dreams. John Gould Fletcher. **SP-FletJ**

Sharded in black, like beetles. Old Ladies' Home. Sylvia Plath. **CP-PlatS**

Share-Croppers. Langston Hughes. **SP-HughL**

Sharing what sharing quickly who. Knock. James Dickey. **CP-DickJ**

Shark, The. Ogden Nash. **CP-NashO**

Shark Island. Richard Hugo. **CP-HugoR**

Shark Meat. Gary Snyder. **CP-SnydG**

Shark, when he goes to any publick feast. Upon Shark. Robert Herrick. **CP-HerrR**

Shark, with your mouth tucked under. Cannibal. Thom Gunn. *Fr.* Three for Children. **CP-GunnT**

Shark's Parlor, The. James Dickey. **CP-DickJ**

Sharp and silent in the. Heavy Date. Wystan Hugh Auden. **CP-AudeW**

Sharp eyes, hoodlum skin. Charles Henri Ford. **SP-FordC** *Fr.* Emblems of Arachne.

Sharp is the night, but stars with frost alive. Winter Heavens. George Meredith. **CP-MerG1**

Sharp Ridge, The. Robert Ranke Graves. **CP-GravR**

Sharp Words in the Men's Room. Dabney Stuart. **SP-StuaD**

Shattered crystal of his mind, The. Alun Lewis. *Fr.* The Madman. **CP-LewiA**

Shattered Image. Sir John Betjeman. **CP-BetjJ**

Shattered water made a misty din, The. Once by the Pacific. Robert Frost. **CP-FrosR**

Shaven heads, rubber. Charles Henri Ford. **SP-FordC** *Fr.* Emblems of Arachne.

Shaving. Stephen Dobyns. **SP-DobyS**

Shaving at Night. Charles Simic. **SP-SimiC**

Shaving Mirror. John Updike. **CP-UpdiJ**

Shaving out the bathroom window. Holden, a Thought From Abroad. James Liddy. **CP-LiddJ**

She. Margaret Atwood. **SP-AtwM2**

She. Ted Berrigan. **SP-BerrT**

She: / I died into his eyes. A Separation. Alun Lewis. **CP-LewiA**

She. Charles Olson. **CP-OlsoC**

She. Theodore Roethke. **CP-RoetT**

She, *with music.* Richard Wilbur. **CP-WilbR**

She, a beautician, came to see her friend. The Beautician. Thom Gunn. **CP-GunnT**

She, a woman of abrupt features. Ruby Daggett. Richard Eberhart. **CP-EberR**

She alters all our lives for the better, merely. She (Not to be confused with she, a girl). Ted Berrigan. **SP-BerrT**

She always had to burn a light. Five Nocturnes. Robert Frost. **CP-FrosR**

She always had to burn a light. The Night Light. Robert Frost. *Fr.* Five Nocturnes. **CP-FrosR**

She always said "*tu*" in such a way. A Dark Portrait. Lawrence Ferlinghetti. **SP-FerlL**

She answers the bothersome telephone, takes the message, forgets the message, forgets who called. Alzheimer's: The Wife. Charles Kenneth Williams. **SP-WillC**

She appeared in Triad—Youth, Truth, Beauty. Tousled Pillow. Robert Ranke Graves. **CP-GravR**

She arrives at the volcano almost dead. The Heroine. William Dickey. **SP-DickW**

She as a veil down to the slender waist. John Milton. **ErPo,** *ll.* 304–311; **NIP** *Fr.* Book IV. **OAEL-1** *Fr.* Paradise Lost. **CP-MiltJ**

(Before the Fall.) **NIP,** *ll.* 304–355;

She at His Funeral. Thomas Hardy. **CP-HardT**

She bade me follow to her garden, where. Snap-Dragon. David Herbert Lawrence. **CP-LawrD**

She bade the moon stand still. Two Moon Fantasies. Carl Sandburg. **CP-SandC**

She-Bear, The. Charles Olson. **CP-OlsoC**

She-Bear (II), The. Charles Olson. **CP-OlsoC**

She Becomes a Goddess. Nicholas Vachel Lindsay. *Fr.* The Trial of the Dead Cleopatra in Her Beautiful and Wonderful Tomb. **CP-LindV**

She Becomes a Soul, Flowering Toward Egyptian Resurrection, B.C. 29. Nicholas Vachel Lindsay. *Fr.* The Trial of the Dead Cleopatra in Her Beautiful and Wonderful Tomb. **CP-LindV**

She began to think that jealousy was only an excuse, a front, for something even more rapacious. The Image. Charles Kenneth Williams. **SP-WillC**

She begins as if memory were faultles. Old Woman Telling Another Version. Brendan Galvin. **SP-GalvB**

She being Brand. Edward Estlin Cummings. **CP-CummE; SP-CummE**

She being most zealously in love with her. This Lady Rides a Languid Dromedary toward Her Dear-God. Marsden Hartley. *Fr.* Boston Portrait Projections. **CP-HartM**

She beheld herself to have gone through tall gateways. Rose Bawn. Carl Sandburg. **CP-SandC**

She believed in love, but was it. Louis MacNeice. **POL** *Fr.* As In Their Time. **CP-MacNL**

She Belongs to Me. "Bob Dylan." **CP-DylaB**

She bent over the side of the bed. The Promise. Charles Bukowski. **SP-BukC1**

She Bitches About Boys. Marilyn Hacker. **SP-HackM**

She blinks above her sunglasses at the man. Everything Is Fine Here How Are You. Miller Williams. **SP-WillM**

She bore it till the simple veins. Emily Dickinson. **CP-DickE**

—She by a sycamore. Fragment. Gerard Manley Hopkins. **CP-HopkG**

She by the river sate, and sitting there. Another upon Her Weeping. Robert Herrick. **CP-HerrR**

She came among us from the South. Enrica, 1865. Christina Georgina Rossetti. **CP-RosC1**

She came and stood in the Old South Church. In the "Old South." John Greenleaf Whittier. **CP-WhitJ**

She came crying down to me. A Summer Memory in the Crowded City. James Wright. **CP-WrigJ**

She came every morning to draw water. A Drink of Water. Seamus Heaney. **SP-HeanS**

She Came from The Uttermost Part of the Earth. Christina Georgina Rossetti. **CP-RosC2**

She came home running. The Mothering Blackness. Maya Angelou. **SP-AngeM**

She came in from the snowing air. Ice. Stephen Spender. **CP-SpenS**

She Came in Through the Bathroom Window. The Beatles. **CP-Beatl**

She Came Out of the Bathroom With Her Flaming Red Hair and Said—. Charles Bukowski. **SP-BukC1**

She came—she is gone—we have met. Catharina. William Cowper. **CP-CowpW**

She came to alter sky with glass. Schoolgirl at Seola. Richard Hugo. **CP-HugoR**

She came to the village church. Tennyson. **EBVV; NAEL-2** *Fr.* Maud [A Monodrama]. **CP-TennA**

She came up to him at closing time. Contact. Steve Griffiths. **SP-GrifS**

She can be as wise as we. Marian. George Meredith. **CP-MerG1**

She cannot leave it alone. The New Toy. Thomas Hardy. **CP-HardT**

She carried a book, either to imply. Hilda Doolittle. **NALW** *Fr.* Tribute to the Angels. **CP-DoolH**

She carries her handkerchief, her gloves. *tr. fr. the German of* Rilke. Randall Jarrell. **CP-JarrR**

She Charged Me. Thomas Hardy. **CP-HardT**

She cleaned house, and then lay down long. A Secret Gratitude. James Wright. **CP-WrigJ**

She comes, and straight therewith her shining twins do move. Sonnet 76. Sir Philip Sidney. *Fr.* Astrophil and Stella. **SP-SidnP**

She comes as in a dream with west wind eggs. Poem in the Modern Manner. Ted Berrigan. **SP-BerrT** *Fr.* The Sonnets.

She comes at me in red tights. Red Runner. Diane Wakoski. **SP-WakoD**

She comes home steaming. Sex Object. Ron Koertge. **SP-KoerR**

She comes level with him at. Donahue's Sister. Thom Gunn. **CP-GunnT**

She comes! she comes! the sable throne behold. Alexander Pope. **ECEV** *Fr.* Yet, yet a moment, one dim ray of light. **NAEL-1; OAEL-1; PoEL-3** *Fr.* The Dunciad. **CP-PopeA**

She Comes To Him in the Night. Alun Lewis. *Fr.* War Wedding. **CP-LewiA**

She confessed to me. I Fall into It Without Trying. Charles Bukowski. **SP-BukC3**

She Considers Evading Him. Margaret Atwood. **SP-AtwM1**

She Contrasts with Herself Hippolyta. Hilda Doolittle. **CP-DoolH**

She could bind the world's winds in a single strand. Rune of the Finland Woman. Marilyn Hacker. **SP-HackM**

She could hold me with stories, even. Present. Tess Gallagher. **SP-GallT**

She could not live upon the Past. Emily Dickinson. **CP-DickE**

She coulda been somethin. Ho. Al Young. **CP-YounA**

She cut my toenails the night before. 103 Degrees. Charles Bukowski. **SP-BukC1**

She dealt her pretty words like Blades. Emily Dickinson. **CP-DickE**

She-death, my green mother, you. Roman Dream. Jane Cooper. **SP-CoopJ**

She descends the stairway of the last ditch beyond the horizon. I. John Yau. **SP-YauJo** *Fr.* Predella.

She did good. She stood up like a. Grace Paley. *Fr.* Stanzas: Old Age and the Conventions of Retirement Have Driven My Friends from the Work They Love. **CP-PaleG**

She did not answer him again. Undine. Christina Georgina Rossetti. **CP-RosC3**

She did not know that she was dead. Dinah in Heaven. Rudyard Kipling. **CP-KiplR**

She Did Not Turn. Thomas Hardy. **CP-HardT**

She died at play, / Gambolled away. Emily Dickinson. **CP-DickE**

She died in the upstairs bedroom. Death in Leamington. Sir John Betjeman. **CP-BetjJ**

She died—this was the way she died. Emily Dickinson. **CP-DickE**

She drank from a bottle called DRINK ME. Alice. Shel Silverstein. **SP-SilS2**

She drank what makes man demon at the draught. George Meredith. *Fr.* The Revolution. **CP-MerG1**

She dreamed long of waters. American Wedding. James Wright. **CP-WrigJ**

She dreamed the doctors arrived. Morning Song. Leonard Cohen. **CP-CoheL**

She dreams the baby's so small she keeps. Motherhood. Rita Dove. **SP-DoveR**

She dreamt of a lady in light green. Conversation Galante. Charles Olson. **CP-OlsoC**

She drew back; he was calm. The Subverted Flower. Robert Frost. **CP-FrosR**

She dried her tears, and they did smile. Emily Brontë. **CP-BronE**

She drives into the parking lot while. Turnabout. Charles Bukowski. **SP-BukC1**

She dropped the bar, she shot the bolt, she fed the fire anew. The Only Son. Rudyard Kipling. **CP-KiplR**

She dwelleth in the Ground. Emily Dickinson. **CP-DickE**

She dwelt among the untrodden ways. William Wordsworth. **AWP; BLPA; BoLoP; CABA; EBEvV; ELP; EnLoPo; EnRP; FF; FPL; FaBV; FaBoEn; GTBS; GTBS-6; GTBS-P; HAP; HBVY; HeIL; HeIP; IMW; ImPo; LiTB; LoBV; MeMBP; NIP; NOBRP; NoP; OAEP; OBRV; OXAEP-2; OxBSP; PAI; PBMP; PPP; PWR; Poetr; PrIm; SpRo; TEP; TreF; UV; UnPo; WHA; WeW** *Fr.* Lucy. **CP-WorW1**

(Lost Love, The.) **GTBS; GTBS-6; GTBS-P**

(Song: "She dwelt among the untrodden ways.") **NOBRP**

She even thinks that up in heaven. For a Lady I Know. Countee Cullen. **CP-CullC** *Fr.* Four Epitaphs.

She fanned herself with a violet fan. In a Spanish Tram-Car. David Herbert Lawrence. **CP-LawrD**

She fears him, and will always ask. Eros Turannos. Edwin Arlington Robinson. **CP-RobiE**

She fell asleep among the flowers. The Watchers. Christina Georgina Rossetti. **CP-RosC3**

She fell away in her first ages spring. Edmund Spenser. **OBEV; PoPle** *Fr.* Daphnaïda. **CP-Spens**

She felt, as she left the station. James McAuley. **SP-McAuJ** *Fr.* Witness.

She filled her arms with wood, and set her chin. Edna St. Vincent Millay. *Fr.* Sonnets from an Ungrafted Tree. **CP-MillE**

She foots it forward down the town. The Third Kissing-Gate. Thomas Hardy. **CP-HardT**

She gave a rose. She Gave Me a Rose. Paul Laurence Dunbar. **CP-DunbP**

She Gave Me a Rose. Paul Laurence Dunbar. **CP-DunbP**

She gave me childhood's flowers. Heirloom. Kathleen Jessie Raine. **SP-RainK**

She gave me the flowers—. In Maceio. Tess Gallagher. **SP-GallT**

She gave up beauty in her tender youth. A Portrait. Christina Georgina Rossetti. **CP-RosC1**

She gave with joy her virgin breast. Translation of a Passage in Ottfried's Metrical Paraphrase of the Gospel. Samuel Taylor Coleridge. **CP-ColeS**

She gives him his eyes, she found them. Bride and Groom Lie Hidden for Three Days. Ted Hughes. **SP-HughT**

She gives most dangerous sight. For a Marriage. Louise Bogan. **CP-BogaL**

She-Goat. David Herbert Lawrence. **CP-LawrD**

She greeted us with open arms but I hardly noticed. Florence. Patti Smith. **SP-SmitP**

She grew up in bedeviled southern wilderness. The Ballad of Sue Ellen Westerfield. Robert Earl Hayden. **CP-HaydR**

She had a box. Love Beyond Keeping. Carl Sandburg. **CP-SandC**

She had a coarse and common grace. Homo Sum, Nihil Humani—. Arthur Hugh Clough. **SP-ClouA**

She had a horror he would die at night. Edna St. Vincent Millay. *Fr.* Sonnets from an Ungrafted Tree. **CP-MillE**

She had a little time to think. Leda Reconsidered. Mona Van Duyn. **SP-VanDM**

She had a secret—bonny Bess! George Meredith. **CP-MerG2**

She had a tall man's height or more. Beggars. William Wordsworth. **CP-WorW1**

She had a way of doing. Marsden Hartley. *Fr.* Ironies out of St. George's. **CP-HartM**

She had already kissed Antony's dead lips. Cleopatra. "Anna Akhmatova", *tr. fr. Russian by* Stanley Kunitz. **CP-KuniS**

She had amid her ringlets bound. Treachery. Walter de la Mare. **CP-DeLaW**

She had climbed into sleep halfway. Parade. Leonard Nathan. **SP-NathL**

She had come, like the river. Eternity. William Carlos Williams. **CP-WilW2**

She Had Concealed Him in a Deep Dark Cave. Kenneth Patchen. **CP-PatcK**

She had forgotten how the August night. Edna St. Vincent Millay. *Fr.* Sonnets from an Ungrafted Tree. **CP-MillE**

She had her mind on the main. Louis MacNeice. *Fr.* As In Their Time. **CP-MacNL**

She had huge thighs. The Place Didn't Look Bad. Charles Bukowski. **SP-BukC1**

She had no saying dark enough. The Oft-Repeated Dream. Robert Frost. **Poetr** *Fr.* The Hill Wife. **CP-FrosR**

She had on a sweet vermillion gown. Variations 3. Gilbert Sorrentino. **SP-SorrG**

She had quickly learned to show. Tanck's Song About Women. Hayden Carruth. **CP-CarHS** *Fr.* Songs About What Comes Down: The Complete Works of Mr. Septic Tank.

She had that softness which is falsity. Edward Estlin Cummings. **CP-CummE**

She had thought the studio would keep itself. Living in Sin. Adrienne Rich. **SP-RicA1**

She had wealth of mornings in her year. Ralph Waldo Emerson. **CP-EmerR**

She hailed him Saint. George Meredith. *Fr.* Alsace-Lorraine. **CP-MerG1**

She has been condemned to death by hanging. Marrying the Hangman. Margaret Atwood. **SP-AtwM2**

She has decided that she no longer loves me. The Wind in the Tree. Frank Templeton Prince. **CP-PrinF**

She has finished and sealed the letter. Parting, without a Sequel. John Crowe Ransom. **SP-RansJ**

She Has Given Me the Bullet, *see also* Commentary—She Has Given Me the Bullet. Leonard Cohen. **CP-CoheL**

She has left. A Daughter Moves Out. Lewis Turco. **SP-TurcL**

She has lost both her money and her figure. The Gibbous Moon. Richard Shelton. *Fr.* Five Lies About the Moon. **SP-ShelR**

She has no need to fear the fall. Portrait. Louise Bogan. **CP-BogaL**

She has put her hand. Sinking, Swimming. Gilbert Sorrentino. **SP-SorrG**

She has this magical bidet. Hygiene. David Markson. **CP-MarkD**

She has three pills left in the bottle. Richard Shelton. *Fr.* The Stone Garden. **SP-ShelR**

She hastens out and scarcely pins her clothes. Scandal. John Clare. **SP-ClarJ**

She heard the forest talking. Nicholas Vachel Lindsay. *Fr.* Our Mother Pocahontas. **CP-LindV**

She heard the gates of autumn. The Oatwoman. Michael Hartnett. **SP-HarMi**

She heard with patience all unto the end. Prince Arthur. Edmund Spenser. **OBSC** *Fr.* The Faerie Queene. **CP-Spens**

She hears me strike the board and say. *fr.* A Woman Young and Old. William Butler Yeats. **CP-YeatW**

She Hears the Storm. Thomas Hardy. **CP-HardT**

She held it out. "But you can't have it," she said. The Hatband. Thomas Hardy. **CP-HardT**

She Hid in the Trees from the Nurses. James Wright. **CP-WrigJ**

She hideth Her the last. Emily Dickinson. **CP-DickE**

She holds a lily in her hand. Within the Veil. Christina Georgina Rossetti. **CP-RosC3**

She, I, and They. Thomas Hardy. **CP-HardT**

She I love leaves me, and I leave my friends. False Bay. Frank Templeton Prince. **CP-PrinF**

She in the hurling night. Compassion. Alun Lewis. **CP-LewiA**

She is a bald-headed woman. When someone. The Full Daytime Moon. Richard Shelton. *Fr.* Five Lies About the Moon. **SP-ShelR**

She is a grotesque. Carnival 1927. Kay Boyle. **CP-BoylK**

She is a winsome wee thing. My Wife's a Winsome Wee Thing. Robert Burns. **CP-BurnR**

She is again with child. Blessed Event. Marsden Hartley. **CP-HartM**

She is all there. For My Lover, Returning to His Wife. Anne Sexton. **CP-SextA**

She is always two blue eyes. She. Ted Berrigan. **SP-BerrT**

She is an iris. Court Lady Standing under Cherry Tree. John Gould Fletcher. **SP-FletJ**

She is as in a field a silken tent. The Silken Tent. Robert Frost. **CP-FrosR**

She is asleep: one breast, uncovered. Night World. Edwin Rolfe. **CP-RolfE**

She is caught in her frail house. Pocoangelini 12. Lewis Turco. **SP-TurcL**

She is dead. Hilda Doolittle. **CP-DoolH** *Fr.* Electra-Orestes.

She [*or* Shee] is dead; and all which die. The Dissolution. John Donne. **CP-DonnJ**

She is devout and plump, but not happy. A Baroque Gravure. Thomas Merton. **CP-MertT**

She is foremost of those that I would hear praised. Her Praise. William Butler Yeats. **CP-YeatW**

She is gamesome and good. Nature 2. Ralph Waldo Emerson. **CP-EmerR**

She is gone by the Hilda. Coronach. "Lewis Carroll." **CP-CarrL**

She is large and matronly. Lui et Elle. David Herbert Lawrence. **CP-LawrD**

She Is Lifted with the Old Gods into the Western Sky. Nicholas Vachel Lindsay. *Fr.* The Trial of the Dead Cleopatra in Her Beautiful and Wonderful Tomb. **CP-LindV**

She is like that man. Jane Cooper. *Fr.* A Mission with the Night. **SP-CoopJ**

She is lying on my outstretched arm. Harrowed by These Apprehensions He Resolved to Commit Himself to the Mercy of the Storm. Kenneth Patchen. **CP-PatcK**

She is madonna in an art. Nicholas Vachel Lindsay. *Fr.* Mae Marsh, Motion Picture Actress. **CP-LindV**

She is neither pink nor pale. Witch-Wife. Edna St. Vincent Millay. **CP-MillE**

She Is No Liar. Robert Ranke Graves. **CP-GravR**

She is not easy to see. She wears. Virginia Woolf Gathers Mushrooms. William Dickey. **SP-DickW**

She is not Folly—that I know. The Playmate. Rudyard Kipling. **CP-KiplR**

She is not Indian, she's ill. To a Lady in a Train. Stevie Smith. **CP-SmitS**

She is not wearing / shoes or a dress   I begin to change. Sea Level. Joseph Ceravolo. **SP-CeraJ**

She is now water and air. Sea Burial from the Cruiser *Reve*. Richard Eberhart. **CP-EberR**

She Is Overheard Singing. Edna St. Vincent Millay. **CP-MillE**

She Is Raggedy Ann at seventy-six. Old Mrs. Court and Her Quilt. Barton Sutter. **SP-SuttB**

She is standing on my lids. Lady Love. Paul Éluard, *tr. fr. French.* **CP-BeckS,** *tr. by* Samuel Beckett.

She is still, she is cold. Percy Bysshe Shelley. **ChER** *Fr.* Ginevra. **CP-ShelP**

She is struggling through grass-mesh—not flying. A Cranefly in September. Ted Hughes. **SP-HughT**

She is sweet and soft-throated. A Decision. David Herbert Lawrence. **CP-LawrD**

She is that kind of a wife. She can see. Gertrude Stein. **VBLP** *Fr.* A Sonatina Followed by Another. **CP-SteiG**

She is the darkness where I wander. Madrigal. Howard Nemerov. **CP-NemeH**

She is the Lane to the Indes. Emily Dickinson. **SP-DickE**

She is the one you call sister. The Mirror in Which Two Are Seen as One. Adrienne Rich. **SP-RicA2**

She is the prettiest of creatures. Kenneth Patchen. **CP-PatcK**

She is young and elegantly this. She goes. The Waning Crescent Moon. Richard Shelton. *Fr.* Five Lies About the Moon. **SP-ShelR**

She issues radiant from her dressing-room. George Meredith. **EnVR; NOBVV** *Fr.* Modern Love. **CP-MerG1**

She keeps her clavichord. The Clavichord. May Sarton. **SP-SartM**

She kept her songs, they took so little space. Love Songs in Age. Philip Larkin. **CP-LarkP**

She kiltit up her kirtle weel. On the Duchess of Gordon's Reel Dancing. Robert Burns. **CP-BurnR**

She kneels on the floor, snip snip. Sew. Donald Hall. **CP-HallD**

She knows, like Ophelia. Prospero and Sycorax. Ted Hughes. **SP-HughT**

She laid her docile Crescent down. Emily Dickinson. **CP-DickE**

She lay as if at play. Emily Dickinson. **CP-DickE**

She lay like a book. Hayden Carruth. **CP-CarHS** *Fr.* The Clay Hill Anthology.

She leans across a golden table. Epitaph. Countee Cullen. **CP-CullC**

She leans forward; he is lying exhausted. The Artist, Reclining. James McAuley. **SP-McAuJ**

She left me at the silent time. Lines Written in the Bay of Lerici. Percy Bysshe Shelley. **CP-ShelP**

She let her golden ball fall down the well. The Frog and the Golden Ball. Robert Ranke Graves. **CP-GravR**

She let them leave their jellies at the door. Edna St. Vincent Millay. *Fr.* Sonnets from an Ungrafted Tree. **CP-MillE**

She lies, her head beneath her knees. La Belle au Bois Dormant. Randall Jarrell. **CP-JarrR**

She lies in the grass and spreads her golden hair. Rebecca at Play. Miller Williams. **SP-WillM**

She lies on her left side her flank golden. Landscape as a Nude. Archibald MacLeish. **CP-MacLA**

She liked mornings the best—Thomas gone. Weathering Out. Rita Dove. **SP-DoveR**

She liked the blue drapes. They made a star. The Couple in the Next Room. John Ashbery. **SP-AshbJ**

She listened like a cushat dove. Listening. Christina Georgina Rossetti. **CP-RosC3**

She listened to his voice urgently pleading. What Did You Say? Robert Ranke Graves. **CP-GravR**

She lived in Galveston and was into. T.M. Charles Bukowski. **SP-BukC1**

She lived in storm and strife. That the Night Come. William Butler Yeats. **CP-YeatW**

She looked like a bird from a cloud. At the Word "Farewell." Thomas Hardy. **CP-HardT**

She looked over his shoulder. The Shield of Achilles. Wystan Hugh Auden. **CP-AudeW**

She Looks Back. David Herbert Lawrence. **CP-LawrD**

She looks far west towards Carmel, shading her eyes with her hand. An Evening in Galilee. Thomas Hardy. **CP-HardT**

She looks from the window: still it pours down direly. Henley Regatta. Thomas Hardy. **CP-HardT**

She loved her husband. The day he left her. The Half-Moon. Richard Shelton. *Fr.* Five Lies About the Moon. **SP-ShelR**

She loves blood-red poppies for a garden to walk in. Poppies. Carl Sandburg. **CP-SandC**

She Loves You. The Beatles. **CP-Beatl**

She mark'd where I and Fabian met. Continuation of R. Garnett's *Nix.* Gerard Manley Hopkins. **CP-HopkG**

She marries the knight she loves. George Meredith. **CP-MerG2**

She may be rash, may flounder now and then. Agitator. John Hewitt. **CP-HewiJ**

She might, so noble from head. A Thought from Propertius. William Butler Yeats. **CP-YeatW**

She must have been kicked unseen or brushed by a car. Dog's Death. John Updike. **CP-UpdiJ**

She never comes to me. Ralph Waldo Emerson. **CP-EmerR**

She (Not to be confused with she, a girl). Ted Berrigan. **SP-BerrT**

She of the Dancing Feet Sings. Countee Cullen. **CP-CullC**

She of the shining eyes. The Astonished Heart. Lawrence Ferlinghetti. **SP-FerlL**

She often lies with her hands behind her head. For My Daughter. Ron Koertge. **SP-KoerR**

She Opened the Door. Thomas Hardy. **CP-HardT**

She opened the lower button of her blouse. James McAuley. *Fr.* Three Acts from a Play. **SP-McAuJ**

She Opens the Barn Door Every Morning. Carl Sandburg. **CP-SandC**

She packs the flower beds with leaves. For Fran. Philip Levine. **SP-LeviP**

She paints with white & red the moors. Ralph Waldo Emerson. **CP-EmerR**

She phoned me from a far away. Out of the Blue. Charles Bukowski. **SP-BukC3**

She pulled her dress off. Fuck. Charles Bukowski. **SP-BukC1**

She puts down the handmirror. "Look at"arranging. Mame. Edward Estlin Cummings. *Fr.* Five Americans. **CP-CummE**

She read my hand and told me patent lies. The Palmist. John Hewitt. **CP-HewiJ**

She Rebukes Hippolyta. Hilda Doolittle. **CP-DoolH**

She Remains. Alun Lewis. *Fr.* War Wedding. **CP-LewiA**

She rested by the Broken Brook. Unforgotten II, The. Robert Louis Stevenson. **CP-StevR**

She Revisits Alone the Church of Her Marriage. Thomas Hardy. **CP-HardT**

She rides her hips as. Mounted as an Amazon. William Carlos Williams. **CP-WilW2**

She rides in the park on a prancing bay. George Meredith. **CP-MerG2**

She rose as high as His Occasion. Emily Dickinson. **CP-DickE**

She rose to His Requirement—dropt. Emily Dickinson. **CP-DickE**

She rushed to meet him: the nurse following. Hector and Andromache. Homer. **CP-BroEB,** *tr.* by Elizabeth Barrett Browning; *Fr.* The Iliad.

She Said. . . . Stevie Smith. **CP-SmitS**

She Said. Charles Bukowski. **SP-BukC3**

She Said. Alice Walker. **CP-WalkA**

She said, and for her lost Galanthis sighs. The Fable of Dryope. Ovid, *tr.* by Alexander Pope. **CP-PopeA** *Fr.* Metamorphoses.

She Said as Well to Me. David Herbert Lawrence. **CP-LawrD**

She said 'How tiring the lights are!'. Consequences. Wystan Hugh Auden. **CP-AudWJ**

She said, "I came a weary way". The Encounter. Alun Lewis. **CP-LewiA**

She said, "I cannot come." The Cenci's Curse upon His Daughter. Percy Bysshe Shelley. **TW** *Fr.* The Cenci. **CP-ShelP**

She said I know what it's like to be dead. She Said She Said. The Beatles. **CP-Beatl**

She Said She Said. The Beatles. **CP-Beatl**

She said: the pitying audience melt in tears. Alexander Pope. **EBNV,** *canto* V, *abr.*; *Fr.* The Rape of the Lock[, an Heroi-Comical Poem]. **CP-PopeA**

She said to me, He lay there sleeping. The Watchers. Muriel Rukeyser. **CP-RukeM**

She said: "When I was with him." She Said:. Alice Walker. **CP-WalkA**

She sang alone, ere womanhood had known. Lydia H. Sigourney. John Greenleaf Whittier. **CP-WhitJ**

She sang, and I listened the whole song thro'. Remembered. Paul Laurence Dunbar. **CP-DunbP**

She sang beyond the genius of the sea. The Idea of Order at Key West. Wallace Stevens. **CP-StevW**

She sat alway thro' the long day. Repining. Christina Georgina Rossetti. **CP-RosC3**

She sat and sang alway. Song. Christina Georgina Rossetti. **CP-RosC1**

She sat and sewed that hath done me the wrong. Sir Thomas Wyatt. **CP-WyatT**

She sat by the window. Girl with Sampler. Stanley Jasspon Kunitz. *Fr.* Words for the Unknown Makers: A Garland of Commemorative Verses. **CP-KuniS**

She sat in her cool parlour. The Miner's Wife. Wystan Hugh Auden. **CP-AudWJ**

She sat upon a mountain. Rosalind. Christina Georgina Rossetti. **CP-RosC3**

She sat watching the moth at the candle. Death of the Hired Zimmer. Paul Zimmer. **SP-ZimmP**

She sat with a Warwick Deeping. Station Syren. Sir John Betjeman. **CP-BetjJ**

She Sauntered Most Elegantly Down. Marsden Hartley. *Fr.* City Vignettes. **CP-HartM**

She saw herself a lady. Imaginings. Thomas Hardy. **CP-HardT**

She Saw Him, She Said. Thomas Hardy. **CP-HardT**

She saw the Archangel Michael, too. Charles Simic. *Fr.* Rosalia. **SP-SimiC**

She says: *Seek help!* Ha-ha Ha-ha & Christ. No. John Berryman. **CP-BerrJ**

She says she believes in reincarnation. Red Geraniums. Stephen Dobyns. **SP-DobyS**

She Says She Lo'es Me Best of A'. Robert Burns. **CP-BurnR**

She scarce has a word for Papa. George Meredith. **CP-MerG2**

She Schools the Flighty Pupils of Her Eyes. Gerard Manley Hopkins. **CP-HopkG**

She sends me news of bluejays, frost. A Letter from Home. Mary Oliver. **SP-OlivM**

She Shall Be Brought unto the King. Christina Georgina Rossetti. **CP-RosC2**

She shall rise worthier of her prototype. George Meredith. *Fr.* France. **CP-MerG1**

She shall sing me a song. A Song Composed for Fanny Burney. Samuel Johnson. **CP-JohnS**

She, she is dead; she's dead: when thou knowest [*or* know'st] this. John Donne. **JCP** *Fr.* The First Anniversary [*or* Anniversarie]. **AnAnS-1; FaBoRV; MasP; SeCV-1** *Fr.* Anatomy [*or* Anatomie] of the World, An[: The First Anniversary]. **CP-DonnJ**

She shook him and the boy tumbled down the stairs, bouncing oddly from side to side. The Phantasmagoria. Hayden Carruth. *Fr.* Mother. **CP-CarHL**

"She shoots up in the neck," she told. Junkies. Charles Bukowski. **SP-BukC1**

She should never have looked at me. Cristina. Robert Browning. **CP-BroR1**

She sights a Bird—she chuckles. Emily Dickinson. **CP-DickE**

She sings by her wheel at that low cottage-door. The Yankee Girl. John Greenleaf Whittier. **CP-WhitJ**

She sits behind the wooden shutters. Portrait of a Girl. Leonard Cohen. **CP-CoheL**

She sits dropping on a caret of clenched arms. Edward Estlin Cummings. **CP-CummE**

She sits in her night-dress without the door. On the Doorstep. Thomas Hardy. **CP-HardT**

She sits in the dust at the walls. Noon Hour. Carl Sandburg. **CP-SandC**

She sits in the tawny vapour. A Wife in London. Thomas Hardy. **CP-HardT**

She sits on the recreation ground. Reading a Letter. David Herbert Lawrence. **CP-LawrD**

She sits up there. Gloomy Lady. Charles Bukowski. **SP-BukC1**

She sits with. Young Woman at a Window. William Carlos Williams. **CP-WilW1**

She sits with one hand poised against her head, the. Dialogue. Adrienne Rich. **SP-RicA2**

She sitteth still who used to dance. Today For Me. Christina Georgina Rossetti. *Fr.* The German-French Campaign, 1870–1871. **CP-RosC1**

She skimmed the yellow water like a moth. My Grandmother's Ghost. James Wright. **CP-WrigJ**

She sleepeth: would ye wake her if ye could? O Death Where Is Thy Sting? Christina Georgina Rossetti. **CP-RosC3**

She sleeps, in the day, in the silence. Roy Fisher. **SP-FishR** *Fr.* Metamorphoses.

She sleeps on soft, last breaths; but no ghost looms. The Kind Ghosts. Wilfred Owen. **CP-OwenW**

She slept beneath a tree. Emily Dickinson. **CP-DickE**

She smiled as. The Treatment. Charles Olson. **CP-OlsoC**

She snatched at heaven's flame of old. George Meredith. *Fr.* France. **CP-MerG1**

She sought the Studios, beckoning to her side. Heiress and Architect. Thomas Hardy. **CP-HardT**

She speaks always in her own voice. The Portrait. Robert Ranke Graves. **CP-GravR**

She sped as Petals of a Rose. Emily Dickinson. **CP-DickE**

She sped through the door. The Glimpse. Thomas Hardy. **CP-HardT**

She spends her money in the desert, at the movies. Confessions. John Yau. **SP-YauJo**

She springs from the ground-clinging thicket, her face. Veneris Venefica Agrestis. Lucio Piccolo, *tr. fr. Italian by* Charles Tomlinson. **CP-TomlC**

She staked her Feathers—Gained an Arc. Emily Dickinson. **CP-DickE**

She stands / In the quiet darkness. Troubled Woman. Langston Hughes. **SP-HughL**

She stands as pale as Parian statues stand. A Study.(A Soul). Christina Georgina Rossetti. **CP-RosC3**

She stands before you naked. Light as the Breeze. Leonard Cohen. **CP-CoheL**

She stands between the trees and holds. She Hid in the Trees from the Nurses. James Wright. **CP-WrigJ**

She stands in the dead center like a star. The Mother. William DeWitt Snodgrass. **SP-SnodW**

She stands now, shy among the destinies. Maiden with Orb and Planets. Howard Nemerov. **CP-NemeH**

She stayed over after. Last Words of My Grandmother. William Carlos Williams. **CP-WilW1**

She steps into the dark swamp. A Meeting. Mary Oliver. **SP-OlivM**

She still cries over that dead child. Dim House, Bright Face. Tess Gallagher. **SP-GallT**

She stood against the kitchen sink, and looked. In the Home Stretch. Robert Frost. **CP-FrosR**

She stood at the window. There was / a sound, a light. Goodbye. Robert Creeley. **CP-CreeR**

She sweeps the kitchen floor of the river bed her husband saw fit. Pomade. Rita Dove. **SP-DoveR**

She sweeps with many-colored Brooms. Emily Dickinson. **CP-DickE**

She talked of you before she went. Emily Dickinson. **SP-DickE**

She talks too loud, her face. Aunt. Al Young. **CP-YounA**

She taught him the gods. Was it teaching? He went on. The Embrace. Louise Glück. **SP-GlücL**

She tells: / Sing I chant I. A Ballad Theme. Muriel Rukeyser. **CP-RukeM**

She Tells Her Love while Half Asleep. Robert Ranke Graves. **CP-GravR**

She that but little patience knew. On a Political Prisoner. William Butler Yeats. **CP-YeatW**

She that should most, perceiveth least. Sir Thomas Wyatt. **CP-WyatT**

She, then, like snow in a dark night. Like Snow. Robert Ranke Graves. **CP-GravR**

She thinks she was hurt this summer. The Battered Wife. Donald Davie. **CP-DavDo**

She thought, without the benefit of knowing. First Meeting with a Possible Mother-in-Law. Thom Gunn. **CP-GunnT**

She, Thus. Charles Olson. **CP-OlsoC**

She to Him. Robert Ranke Graves. **CP-GravR**

She, to Him. Thomas Hardy. **CP-HardT**

"I will be faithful to thee; aye, I will!"

"Perhaps, long hence, when I have passed away."

"This love puts all humanity from me." **TOF**

"When you shall see me in the toils of Time." **OxBTC**

She Told Her Beads. Paul Laurence Dunbar. **CP-DunbP**

She told him that she could not do this thing. Wanda and the Fish. Paul Zimmer. **SP-ZimmP**

She told him, "You were in my dream last night." Realities. Howard Nemerov. **CP-NemeH**

She told how they used to form for the country dances. One We Knew. Thomas Hardy. **CP-HardT**

She told the story, and the whole world wept. Harriet Beecher Stowe. Paul Laurence Dunbar. **CP-DunbP**

She took the belt I offered, closed her eyes. The Psychometrist's Remarkable Forecast. John Hewitt. **CP-HewiJ**

She turned in the high pew, until her sight. A Church Romance. Thomas Hardy. **CP-HardT**

She turned round to me with her steadfast eyes. The Last Answer. Christina Georgina Rossetti. **CP-RosC3**

She turns her head. She Who Turns Her Head. William Carlos Williams. **CP-WilW1**

She twists scraps of her hair in unshelled snails. Marilyn Hacker. **SP-HackM** *Fr.* Taking Notice.

She used to let her golden hair fly free. Petrarch, *tr. by* Morris Bishop. *Fr.* Sonnets to Laura.

("Loose to the wind her golden tresses stream'd.") **CP-SmitC,** *tr. by* Charlotte Smith.

She Used to Water the Plants. Siv Cedering Fox. **SP-CedeS**

She Wakes Early, While He Still Sleeps. Alun Lewis. *Fr.* War Wedding. **CP-LewiA**

She walked alone, as she did every morning. Spy. Rita Dove. **SP-DoveR**

She walked in flowers around my field. Ralph Waldo Emerson. **CP-EmerR**

She walks beside the river. Two Ghosts Together. Kenneth Patchen. **CP-PatcK**

She Walks in Beauty. Byron. **CP-Byron**

She walks in beauty like a lake. The Bed. Robert Creeley. **CP-CreeR**

She walks in while. Writing Is a State of Trance. Charles Bukowski. **SP-BukC3**

She wanted a little room for thinking. Daystar. Rita Dove. **SP-DoveR**

She wants to hear. Sunday Greens. Rita Dove. **SP-DoveR**

She was a bundle of statistics, her skin. Louis MacNeice. **POL** *Fr.* As In Their Time. **CP-MacNL**

She was a dog-rose kind of girl. Sally. Phoebe Hesketh. **SP-HeskP**

She was a fair young girl, on her brow. The Fair Quakeress. John Greenleaf Whittier. **CP-WhitJ**

She Was a Good Little Wife. David Herbert Lawrence. **CP-LawrD**

She was a phantom of delight. William Wordsworth. **CP-WorW1**

She was a short one. Sleep. Charles Bukowski. **SP-BukC2**

She was a working girl. Honey Pie. The Beatles. **CP-Beatl**

She was afraid of men. Chicken-Licken. Maya Angelou. **SP-AngeM**

She was [*or* is] all around me. The Blue Wing. Donald Hall. **CP-HallD**

She was an agèd woman; and the years. Tale of Society As It Is, A: From Facts, 1811. Percy Bysshe Shelley. **CP-ShelP**

She was as sweet as violets in the Spring. A Dirge. Christina Georgina Rossetti. **CP-RosC3**

She was blushing in the misty green of August. Good Night! Gilbert Sorrentino. **SP-SorrG**

She was brought up manly for a woman. As If It Happened. Tess Gallagher. **SP-GallT**

She was cleaning—there is always. Black Silk. Tess Gallagher. **SP-GallT**

She was cut-luggit, painch-lippit. The Auld Man's Mare's Dead. Robert Burns. **CP-BurnR**

She was famous for kindness, Geneva. Geneva. Barton Sutter. **SP-SuttB**

She was fifteen—had great eyes. Robert Browning. **CP-BroR2**

She was given crystal flesh for a home. Variations on a Theme. Carl Sandburg. **CP-SandC**

She was, Grandfather said, *a fly-by-night.* Hattie Bloom. Mary Oliver. **SP-OlivM**

She was herself, not his, not anything. Archibald MacLeish. **CP-MacLA** *Fr.* The Happy Marriage.

She was just about to say. Table Talk. Leonard Nathan. **SP-NathL**

She was most like a rose, when it flushes rarest. Gone Before. Christina Georgina Rossetti. **CP-RosC3**

"She was", my father said (in an aside). From My Diary. Stephen Spender. **CP-SpenS**

She was my harbour, larder, / and my lexicon. E.H. John Hewitt. **CP-HewiJ**

She was not always so unkind I swear. Portrait (I). Stevie Smith. **CP-SmitS**

She was not as pretty as women I know. My Kate. Elizabeth Barrett Browning. **CP-BroEB**

She was O'Kane and O'Kanes were white trash. Nora O'Kane. Louise McNeill. **SP-McNeL**

She was pretty swacked by the time she. Dinner at George & Katie Schneeman's. Ted Berrigan. **SP-BerrT**

She was round and warm and brown. Partridge. Phoebe Hesketh. **SP-HeskP**

She was round, full, ripe, a maid immaculate. Epithalamion of a Peach. John Crowe Ransom. *Fr.* Two Gentlemen in Bonds. **SP-RansJ**

She was searching for a sign and listening. Exodus with Children. Peter Meinke. **SP-MeinP**

She was sitting in the window. Liberty. Charles Bukowski. **SP-BukC1**

She was so young, so like a tigress. Her Daughter. Marsden Hartley. **CP-HartM**

She was tangled up in her own self-conceit, a woman. The Painter's Wife. David Herbert Lawrence. **CP-LawrD**

She was taught desire in the street. The Trap. Nicholas Vachel Lindsay. **CP-LindV**

She was the one who lived up country. After Reading "The Country of the Pointed Firs." Jean Garrigue. **SP-GarrJ**

She was the rose of Sharon from paradise lost. Caribbean Wind. "Bob Dylan." **CP-DylaB**

She was whiter than the ermine. Once. Christina Georgina Rossetti. **CP-RosC3**

She was young and beautiful. Ruby Brown. Langston Hughes. **SP-HughL**

She wears gold carelessly, because it is. The Full Harvest Moon. Richard Shelton. *Fr.* Five Lies About the Moon. **SP-ShelR**

She wears old clothes she holds a borrowed handkerchief and her sorrow shows us the papers have bad news again today. A Picture of Lee Ying. Thomas Merton. **CP-MertT; SP-MertT**

She welcomes him with pretty impatience. The Visit. Ogden Nash. **CP-NashO**

She went as quiet as the Dew. Emily Dickinson. **CP-DickE**

She went to bed. Siesta. Stevie Smith. **CP-SmitS**

She went to buy a brand new hat. Colors. Countee Cullen. **CP-CullC**

She Went to Stay. Robert Creeley. **CP-CreeR**

She wept.—Life's purple tide began to flow. Sonnet on Seeing Miss Helen Maria Williams Weep at a Tale of Distress. William Wordsworth. **CP-WorW1**

She Wept, She Railed. Stanley Jasspon Kunitz. **CP-KuniS**

She wept upon her cheeks, and weeping so. Upon Her Weeping. Robert Herrick. **CP-HerrR**

She who has power to call her man. An Unsaid Word. Adrienne Rich. **CP-RicAE; SP-RicA1; SP-RicA2**

She Who Hits at Will. Charles Olson. **CP-OlsoC**

She, who last felt young during the war. Bluebells. Louis MacNeice. **CP-MacNL**

She Who Saw Not. Thomas Hardy. **CP-HardT**

She who to lift her heavy eyes had tried. Virgil, *tr.* by William Wordsworth. **CP-WorW2** *Fr.* The Aeneid [*or* Eneados, *Aeneis*].

She Who Turns Her Head. William Carlos Williams. **CP-WilW1**

She who was burned more than half her body skipped out of death. The Praises. Charles Olson. **CP-OlsoC**

She who weighs pearls, who plays lutes. A Figure for J.V. Meer. Jean Garrigue. **SP-GarrJ**

She who with innocent and tender hands. The Monstrous Marriage. William Carlos Williams. **CP-WilW2**

She who yielded once. On a Bereaved Girl. Alun Lewis. **CP-LewiA**

She whom no one ever found. Gilbert Sorrentino. **SP-SorrG**

"She will change," I cried. *fr.* Words for Music Perhaps. William Butler Yeats. **CP-YeatW**

She will jilt a lover. The Father's Thought of His Daughter. John Gould Fletcher. **SP-FletJ**

She will never know I cried for her. Country & Western. Marilyn Hacker. **SP-HackM**

She will not die, they say. Betrayal. Walter de la Mare. **CP-DeLaW**

She wished of him a lover's kiss and. Communication I. Maya Angelou. **SP-AngeM**

She with her thighs harder than hooves. The Changeling. Theodore Roethke. **CP-RoetT**

She woke at length, but not as sleepers wake. The Death of Haidée. Byron. **FiP** *Fr.* Canto the Fourth. *Fr.* Don Juan. **CP-Byron**

She wore a cloche hat. The Photo of Emily. Lawrence Ferlinghetti. **SP-FerlL**

She wore a new "terra-cotta" dress. A Thunderstorm in Town. Thomas Hardy. **CP-HardT**

She wore a platinum blond wig. One of the Hottest. Charles Bukowski. **SP-BukC1**

She wore high sea-boots and a wave-dowsed shirt. Mary Hagan, Islandmagee, 1919. John Hewitt. **CP-HewiJ**

She would come back, dripping thick water, from the green bog. Her Grave. Mary Oliver. **SP-OlivM**

She would like to roll down the aisles. My Aunt Ella Meets the Buddha on His Birthday. Diane Wakoski. **SP-WakoD**

She would plunge all poets in the ninth circle. An Afterwards. Seamus Heaney. **SP-HeanS**

She Would Welcome Old Tribulations. Thomas Hardy. **CP-HardT**

She wouldn't believe / This pencil has. Magical Eraser. Shel Silverstein. **SP-SilS2**

She wrapped her soul in a lace of lies. Parted. Paul Laurence Dunbar. **CP-DunbP**

She wreathed bright flower-wreaths in her hair. The Ruined Cross. Christina Georgina Rossetti. **CP-RosC3**

She writes: you'll. Moaning and Groaning. Charles Bukowski. **SP-BukC1**

She wrote me for years. Artists. Charles Bukowski. **SP-BukC1**

She wrote, "They were making love / up against the gymnasium wall." Decorum. Stephen Dunn. **SP-DunnS**

She yields: my Lady in her noblest mood. George Meredith. *Fr.* Modern Love. **CP-MerG1**

Sheapherd who noe care did take, A. Mary Sidney, Countess of Montgomery Wroth. *Fr.* Part 1. *Fr.* Urania. **CP-WrotM**

Shears, The. Robinson Jeffers. **CP-JefR3**

Sheath of sleep in the black of the bed. True Night. Gary Snyder. **CP-SnydG**

Sheath pierces the turf / and the flower unfurls: drooping, The. The Snowdrop. James Schuyler. **CP-SchuJ**

She'd look upon us, if she could. The Voice of Age. Edwin Arlington Robinson. **CP-RobiE**

Shed no tear! O, shed no tear! John Keats. **CP-KeatJ**
(Faery Bird's Song.) **CP-KeatJ**

Shed no tears o'er that tomb. Emily Brontë. **CP-BronE**

She'd said let's have tea. My Tea with Madame Descartes. David St. John. **SP-StJoD**

She'd thrust the canyon out of her mind; she never thought of the whispering fall, the ferns, the hawk-haunted. Home. Robinson Jeffers. **CP-JefR1**

Shedding of Blood. David Herbert Lawrence. **CP-LawrD**

Sheds left out in the darkness. Cornpicker Poem. Robert Bly. **SP-BlyR**

Shee brought her to her joyous paradize. The Garden of Adonis. Edmund Spenser. **NOBE; PoEL-1** *Fr.* The Faerie Queene. **CP-Spens**

Sheep. Ted Hughes. **SP-HughT**
"Mothers have come back, The."
"Sheep has stopped crying, The."
"When we sat his mother on her tail, he mouthed her teat." **OBD**

Sheep. Carl Sandburg. **CP-SandC**

Sheep. Anne Sexton. **CP-SextA**

Sheep-Boy, The. Thomas Hardy. **CP-HardT**

Sheep-boy whistled loud, and lo!, The. Elegiac Verses in Memory of My Brother, John Wordsworth. William Wordsworth. **CP-WorW1**

Sheep Child, The. James Dickey. **CP-DickJ**

Sheep dog standing in the rain. Hey Bulldog. The Beatles. **CP-Beatl**

Sheep Fair, A. Thomas Hardy. **CP-HardT**

Sheep Fair. John Hewitt. **CP-HewiJ**

Sheep families are out in the meadow, The. Families. Grace Paley. **CP-PaleG**

Sheep graze where the cemetery was. The Town. Charles Olson. **CP-OlsoC**

Sheep has stopped crying, The. Ted Hughes. *Fr.* Sheep. **SP-HughT**
"When we sat his mother on her tail, he mouthed her teat." **OBD**

Sheep in Fog. Sylvia Plath. **CP-PlatS**

Sheep in the Ruins, The. Archibald MacLeish. **CP-MacLA**

Sheep is blind; a passing Owl, The. The Blind Sheep. Randall Jarrell. **CP-JarrR**

Sheep Lady from Algiers, The. Patti Smith. **SP-SmitP**

Sheep like soldiers, The. Lower Field—Enniscorthy. Charles Olson. **CP-OlsoC**

Sheep move on the grass. The Kill. Donald Hall. **CP-HallD**

Sheep mutter as we pass. Our Walk in Yorkshire. Donald Hall. **CP-HallD**

Sheep Skull, The. John Hewitt. **CP-HewiJ**

Sheep start galloping in moon-blind wheels. Man and Woman. Robert Lowell. **SP-LoweR**

Sheep-Washing. William Wordsworth. *Fr.* The River Duddon [A Series of Sonnets]. **CP-WorW2**

Sheer naked rock. From the high cliff-cut. Stone Face Falls. William Everson. **SP-EverW**

Sheer over to the other side,—for see. The Idiot. Hart Crane. **CP-CranH**

Sheets dangling from the line, The. John Yau. **SP-YauJo** *Fr.* Scenes from the Life of Boullee.

Sheets of night mist travel a long valley, The. Mist Forms. Carl Sandburg. **CP-SandC**

Sheets were frozen hard, and they cut the naked hand, The. Christmas at Sea. Robert Louis Stevenson. **CP-StevR**

Shelf Life. Seamus Heaney.
Granite Chip. **SP-HeanS**
Old Smoothing Iron. **SP-HeanS**
Stone from Delphi. **SP-HeanS**

Shell. Daniel Gerard Hoffman. **SP-HoffD**

Shell, The. Peter Meinke. **SP-MeinP**

Shell, / sitting still. Wingaersheek Beach. Marsden Hartley. **CP-HartM**

Shell, The. Tennyson. *See* See what a lovely shell.

Shell, The. Charles Tomlinson. **CP-TomlC**

Shell arched under my toes, A. River Incident. Theodore Roethke. **CP-RoetT**

Shell of a doll's head, The. Modigliani's Death Mask. John Updike. **CP-UpdiJ**

Shelley and jazz and lieder and love and hymn-tunes. Louis MacNeice. **NOBL** *Fr.* Autumn Journal. **CP-MacNL**

Shelley was drowned near here. Arms at his side. Lerici. Thom Gunn. **CP-GunnT**

Shelley's Skylark. Thomas Hardy. **CP-HardT**

Shells. Howard Nemerov. **CP-NemeH**

Shells. Kathleen Jessie Raine. **SP-RainK**

Shells. Charles Kenneth Williams. **CP-WillC**

Shells. Charles Kenneth Williams. **SP-WillC**

Shells from the Coast mistaking. Emily Dickinson. **CP-DickE**

Shelter from the Storm. "Bob Dylan." **CP-DylaB**

Shelter this candle from the wind. To the Wife of a Sick Friend. Edna St. Vincent Millay. **CP-MillE**

Sheltered Garden. Hilda Doolittle. **CP-DoolH**

Shemselnihar. George Meredith. **CP-MerG1**

Shenandoah. Charles Olson. **CP-OlsoC**

Shenandoah. Carl Sandburg. **CP-SandC**

Shenandoah Journey. Carl Sandburg. **CP-SandC**

Shepeheards boye (no better doe him call), A. January Eclogue. Edmund Spenser. **FiP** *Fr.* The Shepheardes [*or* Shepeards *or* Shepherd's] Calender. **CP-Spens**

Shepheardes [*or* Shepeards *or* Shepherd's] Calender, The. Edmund Spenser. **CP-Spens**

Aprill. **NAEL-1; OBEV; OBSC; PoEL-1**

("Tell me, good Hobbinoll, what garres thee greete?") **OBEV; OBSC; PoEL-1**

Ditty, A: In Praise of Eliza, Queen of the Shepherds. **OBEV**

(Ditty, A: "See where she sits upon the grassy green.") **FaBoCh**

Elisa ("Ye dainty nymphs, that in this blessed brook"). **OBSC**

(Lay to Eliza, The.) **NOBE**

August.

It Fell upon a Holy [*or* Holly] Eve. **CBLP; InvP**

(Roundelay, A: "It fell upon a holy eve.") **EIL**

February.

Oak and the Brere, The. **OBSC**

January Eclogue. **FiP**

November. **PoEL-1**

Dido My Dear, Alas, Is Dead. **ChTr**

October. **NAEL-1; OAEL-1**

(Contempt of Poetry, The.) **OBSC**

Shepheards boy (best known by that name), The. Colin Clouts Come Home Againe. Edmund Spenser. **CP-Spens**

Shepheards, that wont on pipes of oaten reed. Astrophel. Edmund Spenser. *Fr.* Astrophel. **CP-Spens**

Shepherd, The. William Blake. **BoTP; EnRP; FHYEP; HBV; LoBV; OBEC; PFP; TiPo** *Fr.* Songs of Innocence. **CP-BlakW**

Shepherd, The. Hilda Doolittle. **CP-DoolH**

Shepherd, The. William Wordsworth. **OBNC** *Fr.* Retrospect Love of Nature Leading to Love of Mankind. *Fr.* The Prelude; Growth of a Poet's Mind [1805 vers.]. **CP-WorW3**

Shepherd and Goatherd. William Butler Yeats. **CP-YeatW**

Shepherd, looking eastward softly said, The. William Wordsworth. **CP-WorW1**

Shepherd of the morning. Marsden Hartley. *Fr.* Ironies out of St. George's. **CP-HartM**

Shepherd stands by a gate in a white smock-frock, A. An Unkindly May. Thomas Hardy. **CP-HardT**

Shepherd touch'd his reed; sweet Philomel, The. Strada's Nightingale. Vincent Bourne, *tr. fr. Latin by* William Cowper. **CP-CowpW**

Shepherd, with his eye on hazy South, The. Earth and a Wedded Woman. George Meredith. **CP-MerG1**

Shepherds and the nymphs were seen, The. Cadenus and Vanessa. Jonathan Swift. **CP-SwifJ**

Shepherds armed with staff and sling. Carol of Patience. Robert Ranke Graves. **CP-GravR**

Shepherd's Boy (he seeks no better name), A. Summer, The Second Pastoral, or Alexis. Alexander Pope. *Fr.* Pastorals. **CP-PopeA**

Shepherd's Brow, The. Gerard Manley Hopkins. **CP-HopkG**

Shepherd's [*or* Shepheards] Calendar, The. John Clare.

August. **SP-ClarJ**

February.

(February: A Thaw.) **SP-ClarJ**

("Snow is gone from cottage tops, The.") **SP-ClarJ**

January: A Winters Day. **SP-ClarJ**

Shepherds Had an Angel, The. Christina Georgina Rossetti.

(Christmas Carol, for My Godchildren, A.) **CP-RosC3**

Shepherd's Hymn, The ("We saw Thee in Thy balmy nest"). Richard Crashaw. **ACP; TrGrPo** *Fr.* In the Holy Nativity of Our Lord God.

(Verses from the Shepherd's Hymn.) **OBEV**

Shepherds' Hymn, The. Richard Crashaw. **NOBE** *Fr.* In the Holy Nativity of Our Lord God.

Shepherds watch their flocks by night, The. A Hymn for Christmas Day. Christina Georgina Rossetti. **CP-RosC3**

Shepherds went their hasty way, The. Christmas Carol, A. Samuel Taylor Coleridge. **CP-ColeS**

Shepherd's Wife, The. Robert Burns. **CP-BurnR**

Shepherd's wife cries o'er the knowe, The. The Shepherd's Wife. Robert Burns. **CP-BurnR**

Sheridan, a Goose. Jonathan Swift. **CP-SwifJ**

Sheridan at Cedar Creek. Herman Melville. **SP-MelvH**

Sheridan's Submission. Jonathan Swift. **CP-SwifJ**

Sherman's March Reglitterized. Lawrence Ferlinghetti. **SP-FerlL**

She's a Woman. The Beatles. **CP-Beatl**

She's All My Fancy Painted Him. "Lewis Carroll." **CP-CarrL**

She's combed his neckties out of her hair. A Widow. Ted Kooser. **SP-KoosT**

"She's coming," the farmer said to the owl. The Farmer and the Queen. Shel Silverstein. **SP-SilS2**

She's dreaming / of salt again. Nightmare. Rita Dove. **SP-DoveR**

She's fair and fause that causes my smart. Robert Burns. **CP-BurnR**

She's from Texas and weighs. Texan. Charles Bukowski. **SP-BukC1**

She's gone. She was my love, my moon or more. Complaint. James Wright. **CP-WrigJ**

She's got everything she needs. She Belongs to Me. "Bob Dylan." **CP-DylaB**

She's got my heart and I've got hers. Two Hearts. Anne Waldman. **SP-WaldA**

She's happy, with a new Content. Emily Dickinson. **CP-DickE**

She's in a room full of letters, dressed in white. The Little Robber Girl Gets On in the Wide World. Marilyn Hacker. **SP-HackM**

She's late. He mixes another drink. Husband. Miller Williams. **SP-WillM**

She's Leaving Home. The Beatles. **CP-Beatl**

She's not a girl who misses much. Happiness Is a Warm Gun. The Beatles. **CP-Beatl**

She's not for you, man. Longshot. Charles Bukowski. **SP-BukC1**

She's pretty to walk with. Sir John Suckling. *Fr.* Brennoralt. **CP-SuckJ**

She's the girl. No Good Too. William Carlos Williams. **CP-WillW2**

She's trying to find a way to turn her cup. No One Ever Tried To Kiss Anna May Wong. John Yau. **SP-YauJo**

She's up seeing my doctor. Don't Touch the Girls. Charles Bukowski. **SP-BukC1**

She's wearing a cotton dress. Backdrop With Lovers, 1931. Tess Gallagher. **SP-GallT**

She's Your Lover Now. "Bob Dylan." **CP-DylaB**

She,straddling my lap. Edward Estlin Cummings. **CP-CummE**

Shew me a man who's seemingly at peace. Old Men Sitting. John Hewitt. **CP-HewiJ**

Shewes and nightly revels, signes of joy and peace. Thomas Campion. *Fr.* Lord Hay's Mask.

Shield of Achilles, The. Wystan Hugh Auden. **CP-AudeW**

Shield of Achilles, The. Homer, *tr. by* George Meredith. **CP-MerG2** *Fr.* The Iliad.

Shield of Faith, The. Nicholas Vachel Lindsay. **CP-LindV**

Shielded, vague soldiers, visored, crouch alert. Bogside, Derry, 1971. John Hewitt. **CP-HewiJ**

Shift[,] here, in town, not meanest among squires. On Lieutenant Shift. Ben Jonson. **CP-JonsB**

Shift now has cast his clothes: got all things new. Upon Shift. Robert Herrick. **CP-HerrR**

Shift of Scene, A. Robert Ranke Graves. **CP-GravR**

Shillin' a Day. Rudyard Kipling. **CP-KiplR**

Shilling life will give you all the facts, A. Who's Who. Wystan Hugh Auden. **CP-AudeW**

Shillington. John Updike. **CP-UpdiJ**

Shiloh [A Requiem]. Herman Melville. **SP-MelvH**

Shiloh Church, 1862: Twenty–Three Thousand. Geoffrey Hill. *Fr.* Locust Songs. **CP-HillG**

Shimmer. James Schuyler. **CP-SchuJ**

Shimmer at the ear: a sheen, A. A Little Night Music. Charles Tomlinson. **CP-TomlC**

Shimmer of Evil, The. Theodore Roethke. **CP-RoetT**

Shimmering Pediment. John Yau. **SP-YauJo**

Shine alone, shine nakedly, shine like bronze. Nuances of a Theme by Williams. Wallace Stevens. **CP-StevW**

Shine, Empire. Robinson Jeffers. **CP-JefR3**

Shine miraculous / mottled river. River Rhyme II. William Carlos Williams. **CP-WilW2**

Shine on, majestic soul, abide. *see also* To the Lady Elizabeth Queen of Bohemia. George Herbert. **CP-HerbG**

Shine on, O moon of summer. Back Yard. Carl Sandburg. **CP-SandC**

Shine, Perishing Republic. Robinson Jeffers. **CP-JefR1**

Shine, Republic. Robinson Jeffers. **CP-JefR2**

Shines / in the mind of heaven God [*or* heaven God]. Canto 51. Ezra Pound. **SP-PounE** *Fr.* Cantos. **CP-PoCan**

Shines, billowing cold and gold from Cumnor Hurst. On an Old-Fashioned Water-Colour of Oxford. Sir John Betjeman. **CP-BetjJ**

Shines coldly away. Roy Fisher. **SP-FishR** *Fr.* Handsworth Liberties.

Shines on top of Mountains where Grey Stone monastery sits & blinks at the sky. Man's Glory. Allen Ginsberg. **CP-GinsA**

Shines the last age, the next with hope is seen. Heri, Cras, Hodie. Ralph Waldo Emerson. *Fr.* Quatrains. **CP-EmerR**

Shining Diamonds & Sequins glitter. December 31, 1978. Allen Ginsberg. **CP-GinsA**

Shining Light, The. William Cowper. *See* My former hopes are fled.

Shining neutral summer has no voice, The. In Memory of Ernst Toller. Wystan Hugh Auden. **CP-AudeW**

Shining wave, A. The Wave. Elizabeth Bishop. **CP-BishE**

Shinking Song. Ogden Nash. **CP-NashO**

Shiny record albums scattered over. As You Leave Me. Etheridge Knight. **SP-KnigE**

Shiny, shiny, shiny boots of leather. Venus in Furs. "Lou Reed." **SP-ReedL**

Ship, The. Wystan Hugh Auden. *Fr.* A Voyage. **CP-AudeW**

Ship, The. Hayden Carruth. *Fr.* Mother. **CP-CarHL**

Ship. Malcolm Lowry. **CP-LowrM**

Ship, The. Edwin Rolfe. **CP-RolfE**

Ship, a forest of guilty masts, A. Welcome. Thomas Merton. **CP-MertT**

Ship Ahoy! Walt Whitman. **CP-WhitW**

Ship-Builders, The. John Greenleaf Whittier. **CP-WhitJ**

Ship Burning and a Comet All in One Day, A. Richard Eberhart. **CP-EberR**

Ship, called the most holy *Trinidada*, The. Byron. **OxBoS** *Fr.* Canto the Second. *Fr.* Don Juan. **CP-Byron**

Ship glides steadily on, The. Midsummer Dawn at Sea. John Gould Fletcher. **SP-FletJ**

Ship in the Tomb. Archibald MacLeish. **CP-MacLA**

Ship is Turning Homeward, The, *sl. diff. vers. in* Pijijiapan. Malcolm Lowry. *Fr.* The Roar of the Sea and the Darkness. **CP-LowrM**

Ship lies black against the wharf, The. Ship. Malcolm Lowry. **CP-LowrM**

Ship long laid up is a filthy thing, A. Look Out! The Bloody Bosun. Malcolm Lowry. **CP-LowrM**

Ship moves, the. 4th of July. William Carlos Williams. **CP-WilW1**

Ship of Death, *draft vers.* David Herbert Lawrence. **CP-LawrD**

Ship of Death, The, *draft vers.* David Herbert Lawrence. **CP-LawrD**

Ship of Death, The. David Herbert Lawrence. **CP-LawrD**

Ship of Fools. Archibald MacLeish. **CP-MacLA**

Ship of war sails in the grey morning, The. Malcolm Lowry. *Fr.* The Roar of the Sea and the Darkness. **CP-LowrM**

Ship stands drawn like a jewelled dagger, A. Malcolm Lowry. **CP-LowrM**

Ship Starting, The. Walt Whitman. **CP-WhitW**

Ship Translated Being La Paquebot, The. Ernest Hemingway. **CP-HemiE**

Ship went on with solemn face, The. A Sabbath Morning at Sea. Elizabeth Barrett Browning. **CP-BroEB**

Ship will sail again, the watches sing, The. Malcolm Lowry. **CP-LowrM**

Ship-Wrack. Robert Herrick. **CP-HerrR**

Shipbored. John Updike. **CP-UpdiJ**

Shipbuilder, The. Siv Cedering Fox. **SP-CedeS**

Shipman, The ("Parson him answered, 'Benedcite!,' The"). Geoffrey Chaucer. **ACP** *Fr.* The Epilogue to the Man of Laws' Tale. *Fr.* The Canterbury Tales. **CP-ChauG**

Shipman, The ("Shipman was ther, woning fer by weste, A"). Geoffrey Chaucer. **MOS** *Fr.* The General Prologue. **FHYEP; NAWM-1; OAEL-1; PoE** *Fr.* The Canterbury Tales. **CP-ChauG**

Shipman was ther, woning fer by weste, A. Shipman, The. Geoffrey Chaucer. **MOS** *Fr.* The General Prologue. **FHYEP; NAWM-1; OAEL-1; PoE** *Fr.* The Canterbury Tales. **CP-ChauG**

Shipman's Tale, The. Geoffrey Chaucer. *Fr.* The Canterbury Tales. **CP-ChauG**

Ships? / Sure I'll sail them. Call Letters: Mrs. V.B. Maya Angelou. **SP-AngeM**

Ships destroy us above, The. Tin Fish. Rudyard Kipling. **CP-KiplR**

Ships in Bottles. David Herbert Lawrence. **CP-LawrD**

Ship's Log. Archibald MacLeish. **CP-MacLA**

Ship's Orchestra, The. Roy Fisher. **SP-FishR**

Ships That Pass in the Night. Paul Laurence Dunbar. **CP-DunbP**

Ship's Waiters. Charles Tomlinson. **CP-TomlC**

Shipwreck of Idomeneus, The. George Meredith. **CP-MerG1**

Shirland Road. Marilyn Hacker. **SP-HackM**

Shirley & Auden. John Berryman. **CP-BerrJ**

Shirley came to town with a broken leg. A Change of Habit. Charles Bukowski. **SP-BukC1**

Shirt ("I remember once I ran. . ."). Carl Sandburg. **CP-SandC**

Shirt ("My shirt is a token and a symbol. . ."). Carl Sandburg. **CP-SandC**

Shirt. Charles Simic. **SP-SimiC**

Shirt, britches, paper. Hayden Carruth. **CP-CarHS** *Fr.* The Clay Hill Anthology.

Shit Time. Charles Bukowski. **SP-BukC1**

Shiv and the Grasshopper. Rudyard Kipling. **CP-KiplR** *Fr.* Toomai of the Elephants. *Fr.* The Jungle Book.

Shiv, who poured the harvest and made the winds to blow. Shiv and the Grasshopper. Rudyard Kipling. **CP-KiplR** *Fr.* Toomai of the Elephants. *Fr.* The Jungle Book.

Shiva. Robinson Jeffers. **CP-JefR2**

Shiver, The. Thomas Hardy. **CP-HardT**

Shivering in the darkness. A Portrait of the Artist. Derek Mahon. **SP-MahoD**

Shivering native who, by Tenglio's side, The. The Laplander. Charlotte Smith. **CP-SmitC**

Shlup, shlup, the dog. Denise Levertov. **HeIL; HeIP; InPK; Poetr** *Fr.* Six Variations. **CP-LeveD**

Shoal rocks with the sea, The. His Foreboding. Theodore Roethke. **CP-RoetT**

Shoaled on this shingle. Ship of Fools. Archibald MacLeish. **CP-MacLA**

Shock, A. Wystan Hugh Auden. **CP-AudeW**

Shock. Rudyard Kipling. *Fr.* Epitaphs of the War [1914–1918]. **CP-KiplR**

"Shock? Is that what you're asking? My dear, I was a". Hayden Carruth. *Fr.* The Sleeping Beauty. **CP-CarHL**

Shock Troops. Ernest Hemingway. **CP-HemiE**

Shocks Brakes (For Kurt and Yansky). Chuck Miller. **SP-MillC**

Sho'd I not put on Blacks, when each one here. Upon M. William Lawes, the Rare Musitian. Robert Herrick. **CP-HerrR**

Shoe Shop. Barton Sutter. **SP-SuttB**

Shoe that I forgot to tie, A. An Old Song. Randall Jarrell. **CP-JarrR**

Shoe the steed with silver. Sheridan at Cedar Creek. Herman Melville. **SP-MelvH**

Sho[o]e Tying, The. Robert Herrick. **CP-HerrR**

Shoe with legs, A. Lobster. Anne Sexton. **CP-SextA**

Shoebox upon shoebox—the elderly dawdle. A Place in Maine. Stephen Dobyns. **SP-DobyS**

Shoemakers, The. John Greenleaf Whittier. **CP-WhitJ**

Shoes In Rain Jungle. Robert Penn Warren. **SP-WarrR**

Shoes of Travel. Carl Sandburg. **CP-SandC**

Shoes, secret face of my inner life. My Shoes. Charles Simic. **SP-SimiC**

Shoes, table, light, and telephone. The Bath Room. Richard Eberhart. *Fr.* Suite in Prison. **CP-EberR**

Shoeshine. Stephen Berg. **SP-BergS**

Sholto Peach Harrison you are no son of mine. Correspondence between Mr. Harrison in Newcastle and Mr. Sholto Peach Harrison in Hull. Stevie Smith. **CP-SmitS**

Shook down shook up on these trees they have come. Lord in the Air, the. James Dickey. **CP-DickJ**

Shoot It Jimmy! William Carlos Williams. **CP-WilW1**

Shooting a Farmhouse. Ted Kooser. **SP-KoosT**

Shooting Gallery. Muriel Rukeyser. **CP-RukeM**

Shooting Incident, The. Stevie Smith. **CP-SmitS**

Shooting of Levellers, Burford, 1649. Steve Griffiths. **SP-GrifS**

Shooting Script. Adrienne Rich. **CP-RicAE**

Ghazal V. **SP-RicA2**

"I was looking for a way out of a lifetime's consolations." **SP-RicA2**

"In my imagination I was the pivot of a fresh beginning." **SP-RicA2**

"Mare's skeleton in the clearing: another sign of life, The." **FaBoWP; SP-RicA2**

Newsreel. **FaBoWP; HCAP; SP-RicA2**

"Of simple choice they are the villagers; their clothes come." **HCAP; SP-RicA2**

"Old blanket. The crumbs of rubbed wool turning up, The." **HCAP; SP-RicA2**

"Picking the wax to crumbs in the iron lip of the candelabrum."

"They come to you with their descriptions of your soul." **HCAP; SP-RicA2**

"We are driven to odd attempts; once it would not have occurred to." **HCAP; SP-RicA1; SP-RicA2**

"We were bound on the wheel of an endless conversation." **SP-RicA1; SP-RicA2**

"Whatever it was: the grains of the glacier caked in the boot-cleats." **FaBoWP; HCAP; SP-RicA1; SP-RicA2**

"Woman waking behind grimed blinds slatted across a courtyard, A." **SP-RicA1**

"You are beside me like a wall; I touch you with my fingers and." **SP-RicA2**

Shooting Season. Robinson Jeffers. **CP-JefR2**

Shop. Robert Browning. **CP-BroR2**

Shops take down their awnings. An Almanac. James Schuyler. **CP-SchuJ**

Shore. Jean Garrigue. **SP-GarrJ**

Shore. James Liddy. **CP-LiddJ**

  "As in poetry."

  May Day Song.

  "Pools where it offers to our curiosity, The."

  Song about Sinn Fein for Serena.

  "Tips of the fronds become swollen, The."

Shore, The. David St. John. **SP-StJoD**

Shore is cabbage green and reeks, The. Early Morning on the Tel Aviv-Haifa Freeway. Rita Dove. **SP-DoveR**

Shore looked wild, without a trace of man, The. Byron. **HAP** *Fr.* Canto the Second. *Fr.* Don Juan. **CP-Byron**

Shoring up the ocean. A railroad track. Blood-Sister. Adrienne Rich. **SP-RicA2**

Shorn moon trembling indistinct on her path, The. Brother and Sister. David Herbert Lawrence. **CP-LawrD**

Short afternoon ends, and the year is over, The. New Year. Philip Larkin. **CP-LarkP**

Short and Long Both Likes. Robert Herrick. **CP-HerrR**

Short Days, The. John Updike. **CP-UpdiJ**

Short direction / To avoid dejection, A. Rules and Regulations. "Lewis Carroll." **CP-CarrL**

Short History of British India (I), A. Geoffrey Hill. *Fr.* An Apology for the Revival of Christian Architecture in England. **CP-HillG**

Short History of British India (II), A. Geoffrey Hill. *Fr.* An Apology for the Revival of Christian Architecture in England. **CP-HillG**

Short History of British India (III), A. Geoffrey Hill. *Fr.* An Apology for the Revival of Christian Architecture in England. **CP-HillG**

Short Hymne to Larr, A. Robert Herrick. **CP-HerrR**

Short Hymne to Venus, A. Robert Herrick. **CP-HerrR**

Short is time, and only time is bleak. Christina Georgina Rossetti. **CP-RosC2**

Short Journeys Before Daybreak. James McAuley. **SP-McAuJ**

Short Ode to a Philologist, A. Wystan Hugh Auden. *Fr.* Eleven Occasional Poems. **CP-AudeW**

Short Ode to the Cuckoo. Wystan Hugh Auden. **CP-AudeW**

Short Poem. William Carlos Williams. **CP-WilW2**

Short Poem in Color, A. Kay Boyle. **CP-BoylK**

Short Reminder, A. Jim Carroll. **SP-CarrJ**

Short Rides. Stephen Dobyns. **SP-DobyS**

Short Run to Camborne. Donald Davie. **CP-DavDo**

Short Song of Congratulation [*or* To a Young Heir], A. Samuel Johnson. **CP-JohnS**

Short space my feet had traversed ere. Guillaume de Lorris *and* Jean de Meun, *tr. by* F. S. Ellis. **OAEL-1** *Fr.* The Romance [*or* Romaunt] of the Rose. **CP-ChauG**

Short spit from Strangeways, A. The Meths Men. Phoebe Hesketh. **SP-HeskP**

Short Story. Edna St. Vincent Millay. **CP-MillE**

Short Story on a Painting of Gustav Klimt. Lawrence Ferlinghetti. **SP-FerlL**

Short Summary. Louise Bogan. **CP-BogaL**

Short Walk along the Coast, A. Nicholas Vachel Lindsay. *Fr.* Golden Whales of California. **CP-LindV**

Shortened Day, The. John Hewitt. **CP-HewiJ**

Shortening Days at the Homestead. Thomas Hardy. **CP-HardT**

Shortest Way Home, The. Muriel Rukeyser. **CP-RukeM**

Shorts [1927–1932] ("Pick a quarrel, go to war"). Wystan Hugh Auden. **CP-AudeW**

Shorts [1939–1947] ("Motionless, deep in his mind, lies the past the poet's forgotten"). Wystan Hugh Auden. **CP-AudeW**

Shorts [1948–1957] ("At peace under this mandarin, sleep, Lucina"). Wystan Hugh Auden. **CP-AudeW**

Shorts [1972–1973] ("None of us are as young"). Wystan Hugh Auden. **CP-AudeW**

"As the poets have mournfully sung." **CBCK; FaBoBl; NBLV; OBAL; OBCoV; PeLi**

  (Aesthetic Point of View, The.) **NBLV; OBAL; OBCoV**

  (Comprehensive Death.) **CBCK**

  (Limerick: "As the poets have mournfully sung.") **FaBoBl; PeLi**

"Babies in their mothers' arms."

"Base words are uttered only by the base." **OxBSP; PeLV**

  (Words.) **PeLV**

"Behold the manly mesomorph." **OxBSP**

"Bull-roarers cannot keep up the annual rain."

"Champion smiles, The—What Personality!"

"Do we want to return to the womb? Not at all."

"Don't you dream of a world, a society, with no coercion?"

Epitaph for the Unknown Soldier. **FaBoCo**

"Fair is Middle-Earth nor changes, though to Age."

"Friends of the born nurse, The."

"From bad lands where eggs are small and dear."

"Give me a doctor, partridge-plump." **OBCoV**

  (Give Me A Doctor.) **OBCoV**

"Guard, Civility, with guns."

"Hans-in-Kelder, Hans-in-Kelder."

"His ageing nature is the same."

"I'm afraid there's many a spectacled sod."

"I'm beginning to lose patience." **PV**

In Memoriam L. K.-A. 1950–1952.

"Let us honour if we can." **PeLV**

  (Dedication: "Let us honour if we can.") **PeLV**

"Motionless, deep in his mind, lies the past the poet's forgotten."

"None of us are as young." **ArLo**

"O where would those choleric boys."

"Once for candy Cook had stolen." **PV**

"Pick a quarrel, go to war." **PV**

"Private faces in public places." **FaBoEE; PV; PeLV**

  (Dedication: "Private faces in public places.") **PeLV**

"Standing among the ruins, the horror-struck conqueror exclaimed."

"These had stopped seeking."

"These public men who seem so to enjoy their dominion."

"Those who will not reason."

"To the man-in-the-street who, I'm sorry to say." **FiBHP; PoPl**

"When he is well."

"When Statesmen gravely say, 'We must be realistic'." **FaBoCo; OBCoV; PV**

  (Statesmen.) **OBCoV**

"Whether conditioned by God or their neural structure, still."

"Who will cure the nation's ill?"

"Why are the public buildings so high? How come you don't know?" **FaBoCo**

"With what conviction the young man spoke." **PV**

"Young Person came out of the mists, A."

"You're a long way off becoming a saint."

Shorts / Excerpts ("Hope. . . goosestep"). Bill Knott. **SP-KnotB**

Shorts / Excerpts ("I keep a TV monitor on my chest"). Bill Knott. **SP-KnotB**

Shorts / Excerpts ("I write these lines to cripple the dead"). Bill Knott. **SP-KnotB**

Shorts / Excerpts ("Night, in whose death did your ennui take refuge?"). Bill Knott. **SP-KnotB**

Shorts / Excerpts ("Other strangers than our own may remember"). Bill Knott. **SP-KnotB**

Shorts / Excerpts ("Our farewells lack the plausibility of our departures"). Bill Knott. **SP-KnotB**

Shorts / Excerpts ("Searching it goes"). Bill Knott. **SP-KnotB**

Shorts I / Excerpts ("Suddenly I understood"). Bill Knott. **SP-KnotB**

Shorts I ("Watch upon my wrist, The"). Wystan Hugh Auden. **CP-AudeW**

  "At Twenty we find our friends for ourselves, but it takes Heaven."

  "Between those happenings that prefigure it."

  Contra Blake.

  Economics.

  Lost. **FaBoEE**

  Metaphor.

  "Moon profaned by, A."

  Parable. **FaBoCo**

  To Goethe: a Complaint.

  "We've covered enough ground since that awkward day."

Shorts II [1958–1971] ("Poet's hope: to be, A"). Wystan Hugh Auden. **CP-AudeW**

Shot. Robert Creeley. **CP-CreeR**

Shot, The. Robert Ranke Graves. **CP-GravR**

Shot: from crag to crag, A. Hunting Season. Wystan Hugh Auden. **CP-AudeW**

Shot gold, maroon and violet, dazzling silver, fawn. A Prairie Sunset. Walt Whitman. **CP-WhitW**

Shot of Love. "Bob Dylan." **CP-DylaB**

Shot? so quick, so clean an ending? Alfred Edward Housman. **CP-HousA**

Shots were heard last night / Out by the burial ground. Ernesto Cardenal, tr. by Thomas Merton. **CP-MertT** Fr. Three Epigrams.

Should all our churchmen foam in spite. At Farringford. Tennyson. **FaBoPP** Fr. To the Rev. F. D. Maurice. **CP-TennA**

Should auld acquaintance be forgot. Auld Lang Syne. Robert Burns. **CP-BurnR**

Should Be Sufficient. Kenneth Patchen. **CP-PatcK**

Should every creature be as I have been. Elegy. Theodore Roethke. **CP-RoetT**

Should every object claim a place to fit. It Seems You Never Were. Charles Henri Ford. **SP-FordC**

Should far this from mankind's unmysteries. Edward Estlin Cummings. **CP-CummE**

Should he escape the slaughter of thine Eyes. Robert Burns. Fr. Dumfries Epigrams. **CP-BurnR**

Should I Care. Robert Ranke Graves. **CP-GravR**

Should i entirely ask of god why. Fran. Edward Estlin Cummings. Fr. Five Americans. **CP-CummE**

Should I my steps turn to the rural seat. James Thomson. **FM; ScCV** Fr. Spring. Fr. The Seasons. **CP-ThomJ**

Should I presume to separate you now. To the Right Vertuous, and Honorable, the Lord and Lady Hayes. Thomas Campion. Fr. Lord Hay's Mask.

Should I say, my people? I turned [to] stone. Maratea Porto: Saying Good-bye to the Vitolos. Richard Hugo. **CP-HugoR**

Should I shed my tears. Hafiz, tr. by Ralph Waldo Emerson. **CP-EmerR** Fr. Odes.

Should I treat it as my own. The Discarded Love Poem. Robert Ranke Graves. **CP-GravR**

Should I wander with no frown, these idle days. The Unpenned Poem. Robert Ranke Graves. **CP-GravR**

Should I worry about choosing. Begging on North Main. Dabney Stuart. **SP-StuaD**

Should Lanterns Shine. Dylan Thomas. **CP-ThomD**

Should not the white lie and the unkept promise. The Pardon. Robert Ranke Graves. **CP-GravR**

Should one of us remember, / And one of us forget. He and She. Christina Georgina Rossetti. **CP-RosC2**

Should the building totter, run for an archway! The Fallen Tower of Siloam. Robert Ranke Graves. **CP-GravR**

Should the lone Wanderer, fainting on his way. Charlotte Smith. **CP-SmitC**

Should the shade of Plato. Grub First, Then Ethics. Wystan Hugh Auden. **NYBP** Fr. Thanksgiving for a Habitat. **CP-AudeW**

Should they not have the best of both worlds? Mules. Paul Muldoon. **SP-MuldP**

Should this fool die. Edward Estlin Cummings. **CP-CummE**

Should thy love die; / O bury it not under ice-blue eyes! Song. George Meredith. **CP-MerG1**

Should unknown messengers appear. Song: From Otherwhere or Nowhere. Robert Ranke Graves. **CP-GravR**

Should you but fail at—Sea. Emily Dickinson. **CP-DickE**

Should you go to Centre Harbor. A Legend of the Lake. John Greenleaf Whittier. **CP-WhitJ**

Shoulders sag, / The pull of weighted needling. Junkie Monkey Reel. Maya Angelou. **SP-AngeM**

Shout. Langston Hughes. **SP-HughL**

Shout, The. Anne Sexton. **CP-SextA**

Shout, The. Charles Tomlinson. **CP-TomlC**

Shout, for a mighty Victory is won! Anticipation. October, 1803. William Wordsworth. **CP-WorW1**

Shout for those whose course is done. Song. Ralph Waldo Emerson. **CP-EmerR**

Shout of a King is common among them. One day may I be, The. What Hath God Wrought! Christina Georgina Rossetti. **CP-RosC2**

Shout to the Sheperds, A. Ralph Waldo Emerson. **CP-EmerR**

Shouting of the sea and the storm storming, The. The Famous Resort in Late Autumn. Delmore Schwartz. **SP-SchwD**

Shove Halfpenny. Louis MacNeice. Fr. Indoor Sports. **CP-MacNL**

Shove off from the wharf-edge! Steady. Song of the Red War-Boat. Rudyard Kipling. **CP-KiplR**

Shovel Man, The. Carl Sandburg. **CP-SandC**

Shovel of his ashes took, A. Fragment of a Ghost Story. Percy Bysshe Shelley. **CP-ShelP**

Show, The. Wilfred Owen. **CP-OwenW**

Show is not the Show, The. Emily Dickinson. **CP-DickE**

Show me again the time. Lines to a Movement in Mozart's E-Flat Symphony. Thomas Hardy. **CP-HardT**

Show me, dear Christ, Thy Spouse, so bright and clear. John Donne. See Show me dear[e] Christ, thy spouse, so bright and clear.

Show me dear[e] Christ, thy spouse, so bright and clear. John Donne. **MeLP; NAEL-1; NOSC; NoP; OAEP; OBS; PoE; Son** Fr. Divine Meditations. **CP-DonnJ** Fr. Holy Sonnets. **CP-DonnJ**

("Show me, dear Christ, Thy Spouse, so bright and clear.") **PeECV**

Show me Eternity, and I will show you Memory. Emily Dickinson. **SP-DickE**

Show me himselfe, himselfe (bright Sir) O show. Matthew 28; Come See the Place where the Lord Lay. Bible, N.T. **CP-CrasR**, tr. by Richard Crashaw; Fr. St. Matthew.

Show me the noblest Youth of present time. The Triad. William Wordsworth. **CP-WorW2**

Show [or Shew] me thy feet; show [or shew] me thy legs, thy thighs. To Dianeme. Robert Herrick. **CP-HerrR**

Show Saturday. Philip Larkin. **CP-LarkP**

Show the runner coming through the shadows. The Runner. Gary Gildner. **SP-GildG**

Show thee as I thought thee. To Outer Nature. Thomas Hardy. **CP-HardT**

Shower of black infants across the infected landscape, The. August. Jim Carroll. **SP-CarrJ**

Showered, shaved, splashed / (Ajaccio Violets) I. Ajaccio Violets. James Schuyler. **CP-SchuJ**

Showery summer afternoon: the leaves, A. Memories. Frederick Morgan. **SP-MorgF**

Showing that our ways agreed. For an Evolutionist and His Opponent. Countee Cullen. **CP-CullC**

Showing the girl. Giovanni's Rape of the Sabine Women at Wildenstein's. George Oppen. **CP-OppeG**

Showre of Blossomes, The. Robert Herrick. **CP-HerrR**

Showre of Roses, The. Robert Herrick. **CP-HerrR**

Shows. David Herbert Lawrence. **CP-LawrD**

Shows you in a London / room: books, a painting. A Photograph. James Schuyler. **CP-SchuJ**

Shrew. Daniel Gerard Hoffman. **SP-HoffD**

Shrike, The. Sylvia Plath. **CP-PlatS**

Shrine, The. Hilda Doolittle. **CP-DoolH**

Shrinking Horizon. Steve Griffiths. **SP-GrifS**

Shropshire. Donald Davie. **CP-DavDo**

Shropshire Lad, A. Sir John Betjeman. **CP-BetjJ**

Shroud, The. Edna St. Vincent Millay. **CP-MillE**

Shroud is yet unspread, The. The Young Queen. Elizabeth Barrett Browning. **CP-BroEB**

Shroud of Color, The. Countee Cullen. **CP-CullC**

Shrouded maidens sleep on the wave. Fog Over the Sea and the Sun Going Down. Kenneth Patchen. **CP-PatcK**

Shrouded Stranger, The. Allen Ginsberg. **CP-GinsA**

Shrouded Stranger, The. Allen Ginsberg. **CP-GinsA**

Shrubbery, The. William Cowper. **CP-CowpW**

Shrugging in the flight of its leaves. The Old Elm Tree by the River. Wendell Berry. **CP-BerrW**

Shrunken world, A. Epistle. To Enrique Caracciolo Trejo. Donald Davie. **CP-DavDo**

Shudder [, The]. Donald Hall. **CP-HallD**

Shuddring the Spectre howls, his howlings terrify the night. William Blake. **OAEL-2** Fr. Jerusalem; The Emanation of the Giant Albion. **CP-BlakW**

Shuffle and cut. What was so large and one. Aftermath. Louis MacNeice. **CP-MacNL**

Shuffle and shudder of Autumn, The. Autumn Imagined. Donald Davie. **CP-DavDo**

Shuffle up the stairs betrays our age, The. Academy. John Updike. **CP-UpdiJ**

Shun[ne] delay[e]s, they breed[e] remorse. Loss[e] in Delay[e]. Robert Southwell. **CP-SoutR**

Shun not this rite, neglected, yea abhorred. The Commination Service. William Wordsworth. Fr. Ecclesiastical Sonnets. **CP-WorW2**

Shun passion, fold the hands of thrift. Ralph Waldo Emerson. **CP-EmerR**

Shun—shun the Bowl! That fatal, facile drink. Rudyard Kipling. See The Man Who Could Write.

Shunga. Siv Cedering Fox. **SP-CedeS**

Shut-Eye Sentry, The. Rudyard Kipling. **CP-KiplR**

Shut in from all the world without. John Greenleaf Whittier. **OBCP**, *ll.* 155–163; **AA** *Fr.* Snow-Bound [*or* Snow-Bound; a Winter Idyl]. **CP-WhitJ**

(Firelight.) **AA**

Shut in kept off. Charles Olson. **CP-OlsoC**

Shut not me alive away. The Commuted Sentence. Stevie Smith. **CP-SmitS**

Shut not so soon; the dull-eyed night. To Daisies, Not to Shut So Soon[e]. Robert Herrick. **CP-HerrR**

Shut Not Your Doors. Walt Whitman. **CP-WhitW**

Shut Out. Christina Georgina Rossetti. **CP-RosC1**

Shut Out That Moon. Thomas Hardy. **CP-HardT**

Shut, shut the door, good John! [fatigu'd I said]. *in imitation of* Horace (*Satires*, Prologue). Alexander Pope. **CP-PopeA**

Shut, shut the door, good *John*! fatigu'd, I said. Alexander Pope. **OBCoV** *Fr.* Epistle to Dr. Arbuthnot. **CP-PopeA**

Shut your eyes then. Nursery Rhyme. May Sarton. **SP-SartM**

Shutter of time darkening ceaselessly, The. August. Louis MacNeice. **CP-MacNL**

Shuttle, The. John Updike. **CP-UpdiJ**

Shuttles of trains going north, going south, drawing threads of blue. Morning Sun. Louis MacNeice. **CP-MacNL**

Shy at first but quick. Return to Love. Hayden Carruth. **CP-CarHS**

Shy defiers of the existential world. Eyelids. Stephen Dobyns. **SP-DobyS**

Shy Man, The. Theodore Roethke. **CP-RoetT**

Shy one, shy one. To an Isle in the Water. William Butler Yeats. **CP-YeatW**

Shy Roofer, The. Gary Gildner. **SP-GildG**

Sì che il fratello s'ha falconcello. Christina Georgina Rossetti. **CP-RosC3**

Si monumentum requiris. . . the church in which we are sitting. In Memory of George Whitby, Architect. Sir John Betjeman. **CP-BetjJ**

Si Peu Séduisante. Stevie Smith. **CP-SmitS**

Si Rimanda La Tocca-Caldaja. Christina Georgina Rossetti. *Fr.* Il Rosseggiar Dell'Oriente Canzoniere. **CP-RosC3**

Si tam longinquis rogites quis scripsit ab oris. Filii prodigi porcos pascentis ad patrem epistola. Robert Southwell. **CP-SoutR**

Siamese twins: one, maddened by. Twins. Robert Ranke Graves. **CP-GravR**

Sibb when she saw her face how hard it was. Upon Sibb. Robert Herrick. **CP-HerrR**

Sibelius in Silence. Michael Hartnett. **SP-HarMi**

Sibrandus Schafnaburgensis. Robert Browning. **CTC; EBVV; TEP** *Fr.* Garden Fancies. **CP-BroR1**

Sibyl. Seamus Heaney. *Fr.* Triptych. **SP-HeanS**

Sic a Wife as Willie Had. Robert Burns. **CP-BurnR**

Sic Semper Mr. Sherman's Temper, or Kindly Place Your Order in English. Ogden Nash. **CP-NashO**

Sic transit gloria mundi. Emily Dickinson. **CP-DickE**

Sic transit gloria Scotiae—a' the floo'ers. A Drunk Man Looks at the Thistle. "Hugh MacDiarmid." **FaBoDD** *Fr.* A Drunk Man Looks at the Thistle. **SP-MacDH**

Sicilian Cyclamens. David Herbert Lawrence. **CP-LawrD**

Sicilian Emigrant's Song. William Carlos Williams. **CP-WilW1**

Sicilian Vespers, The. John Greenleaf Whittier. **CP-WhitJ**

Sick. Robert Creeley. **CP-CreeR**

Sick. David Herbert Lawrence. **CP-LawrD**

Sick. Robert Lowell. **SP-LoweR**

Sick. Shel Silverstein. **SP-SilS2**

Sick African. William Carlos Williams. **CP-WilW1**

Sick, am I sick of a jealous dread? Tennyson. *Fr.* Maud [A Monodrama]. **CP-TennA**

Sick as I am. An Exercise. William Carlos Williams. **CP-WilW2**

Sick Battle-God, The. Thomas Hardy. **CP-HardT**

Sick Child, A. Randall Jarrell. **CP-JarrR; SP-JarrR**

Sick Child, The. Robert Louis Stevenson. **CP-StevR**

Sick Child's Meditation, A. Christina Georgina Rossetti. **CP-RosC3**

Sick grapes on the chair by the bed lie prone; at the window, The. Malade. David Herbert Lawrence. **CP-LawrD**

Sick is Anthea, sickly is the spring. To Anthea. Robert Herrick. **CP-HerrR**

Sick King in Bokhara, The. Matthew Arnold. **SP-ArnoM**

Sick Leave. Leonard Nathan. **SP-NathL**

Sick Love. Robert Ranke Graves. **CP-GravR**

Sick Man in the Sun. Pablo Neruda, *tr. fr. Spanish by* Ben Belitt. **SP-NeruP**

Sick Man Looks at Flowers. Gwendolyn Brooks. *Fr.* A Catch of Shy Fish. **SP-BrooG**

Sick morning. . . school kids. Back Home. Jim Carroll. **SP-CarrJ**

Sick Nought, The. Randall Jarrell. **CP-JarrR**

Sick of the self. To a Transatlantic Mirror. Erica Jong. **SP-JongE**

Sick of You. "Lou Reed." **SP-ReedL**

Sick of your arms. The Head-Aim. James Dickey. **CP-DickJ**

Sick Rose, The. William Blake. **CP-BlakW** *Fr.* Songs of Experience.

Sick sparrow, stiffening in my hands, The. Learning Experience. Leonard Nathan. **SP-NathL**

Sick with the flu. Trench Warfare. Charles Bukowski. **SP-BukC1**

Sick with the lightning lay my sister-in-law. The Lightning. John Berryman. **CP-BerrJ**

Sickness, The. Charles Bukowski. **SP-BukC3**

Sickness. Daniel Gerard Hoffman. **SP-HoffD**

Sickness. David Herbert Lawrence. **CP-LawrD**

Sickness Blues. Allen Ginsberg. **CP-GinsA**

Sickness brought me this. A Friend's Illness. William Butler Yeats. **CP-YeatW**

Sickness may seem a falling out of love. Pity. Robert Ranke Graves. **CP-GravR**

Sickness of Adam, The. Karl Shapiro. **AP; CRP; CoBMV; MoAB** *Fr.* Adam and Eve. **SP-ShapK**

Sickness of this World it most occasions, A. Emily Dickinson. **CP-DickE**

Sickness poured through the roads, The. Slow Death of the Dragon. Muriel Rukeyser. **CP-RukeM**

Sickness, the minister of Death, doth lay. Upon the King's Sickness. Thomas Carew. **CP-CareT**

Sickness unto Death, The. Anne Sexton. **CP-SextA**

Sickroom. Michael Hartnett. **SP-HarMi**

Sicut et acre piper, mordax epigramma palato. *acc. by English translation.* Thomas Campion. **CP-CampT**

Side by Side. Thomas Hardy. **CP-HardT**

Side by Side. Adrienne Rich. **CP-RicAE**

Side by side, their faces blurred. An Arundel Tomb. Philip Larkin. **CP-LarkP**

Side-Step, O Sons of Men! David Herbert Lawrence. **CP-LawrD**

Side streets of my world in order ran, The. The River Streets. John Hewitt. **CP-HewiJ**

Sidekicks. Ron Koertge. **SP-KoerR**

(Sideshow). Bill Knott. **SP-KnotB**

Sidewalkers Moved, The. Jim Morrison. **SP-MorrJ**

Sidling upon the river, the white boat. The Puritans. Richard Wilbur. **CP-WilbR**

Sidney's Complaynt. Anne Waldman. **SP-WaldA**

Siege. Edna St. Vincent Millay. **CP-MillE**

Siege, The. Sir John Suckling. *See* 'Tis now, since I sat[e] down before.

Siege of Corinth, The. Byron. **CP-Byron**

Siege of Vienna Raised by John Sobieski February, 1816. William Wordsworth. **CP-WorW2**

Siege Perilous. Edwin Arlington Robinson. **CP-RobiE**

Siegfried. Randall Jarrell. **CP-JarrR**

Siena. Charles Olson. **CP-OlsoC**

Siena Mi Fe'; Disfecemi Maremma. Ezra Pound. **MoAmPo** *Fr.* Hugh Selwyn Mauberley. (Life and Contacts). **SP-PounE**

Siesta. Laurence Lieberman. **SP-LiebL**

Siesta. Stevie Smith. **CP-SmitS**

Siesta in Xbalba, And Return to the States. Allen Ginsberg. **CP-GinsA**

Sigh, The. Samuel Taylor Coleridge. *Fr.* Effusions. **CP-ColeS**

Sigh, The. Thomas Hardy. **CP-HardT**

Sigh as it ends. I keep an eye on your. John Berryman. *Fr.* Sonnets to Chris. **CP-BerrJ**

Sigh No More. David Herbert Lawrence. **CP-LawrD**

Sigh paid to be studious when I moved went on to (queer) once. Catullus. *See* Carmen 116: "Conscientiously bringing my mind to bear on this problem."

Sigh that heaves the grasses, The. Alfred Edward Housman. **CP-HousA**

Sigh, you seven seas. Hayden Carruth. **CP-CarHS** *Fr.* The Clay Hill Anthology.

Sighed Rawdon Brown: "Yes, I'm departing, Toni!" Rawdon Brown. Robert Browning. **CP-BroR2**

Sighed the wind to the wheat. Gold. Walter de la Mare. **CP-DeLaW**

Sighing, bursting: steam—sulfur—lava. Arktos. Gary Snyder. **CP-SnydG**

Sighing I see yon little troop at play. Charlotte Smith. **CP-SmitC**

Sighs. David Herbert Lawrence. *Fr.* Bits. **CP-LawrD**

Sighs and Groans [or Grones]. George Herbert. **CP-HerbG**

Sighs are my food, drink are my tears. Sir Thomas Wyatt. **CP-WyatT**

Sight, A. Robert Creeley. **CP-CreeR**

Sight and Flight. Charles Tomlinson. **CP-TomlC**

Sight in Camp [*or*] Sight in Camp in the Daybreak Gray and Dim, A. Walt Whitman. **CP-WhitW**

Sight of God, The. David Herbert Lawrence. **CP-LawrD**

Sightseeing. Rita Dove. **SP-DoveR**

Sightseers, The. Paul Muldoon. **SP-MuldP**

Sightseers. Howard Nemerov. **CP-NemeH**

Sigil. Hilda Doolittle. **CP-DoolH**
  "Are these ashes in my hand." **AnAn**
  "Are we unfathomable night." **AnAn**
  "But it won't be that way." **AnAn**
  "I could say, / red." **AnAn**
  " 'I love you,' / spoken in rhapsodic metre." **AnAn**
  "If you take the moon in your hands." **AnAn; BoWoP; FaBoWP; NYBP**
    (Moon in Your Hands, The.) **BoWoP; NYBP**
  "Let me be / a splinter in your side." **AnAn**
  "Now let the cycle sweep us here and there." **AnAn; VGW**
  "So if you love me." **AnAn**
  "There is no sign-post to say." **AnAn**
  "Time breaks the barrier." **AnAn**
  "You'll go on, talking away." **AnAn**

Sign. Robert Creeley. **CP-CreeR**

Sign, A. Walter de la Mare. **CP-DeLaW**

Sign, The. Roy Fisher. **SP-FishR**

Sign, The. Randall Jarrell. **CP-JarrR**

Sign. Marge Piercy. **SP-PierM**

Sign Board, The. Robert Creeley. **CP-CreeR**

Sign *Faehre nach Wilm*, The. Stephen Spender. **CP-SpenS**

Sign Language. "Bob Dylan." **CP-DylaB**

Sign on the Cross. "Bob Dylan." **CP-DylaB**

Sign on the Window. "Bob Dylan." **CP-DylaB**

Sign-Post. Robinson Jeffers. **CP-JefR2**

Sign-Seeker, A. Thomas Hardy. **CP-HardT**

Sign Whereby He Knew, The. Robert Penn Warren. *Fr.* Audubon. **SP-WarrR**

Signal, The. Archibald MacLeish. **CP-MacLA**

Signal from the House, The. Stanley Jasspon Kunitz. **CP-KuniS**

Signal light of the firefly in the rose, The. Fireflies. Charles Tomlinson. **CP-TomlC**

Signals, The. Theodore Roethke. **CP-RoetT**

Signature for Tempo. Archibald MacLeish. **CP-MacLA**

Signature of All Things, The. Kenneth Rexroth. **SP-RexrK**

Signature of our behavior. The. Moralizing. Marsden Hartley. **CP-HartM**

Signatures. Daniel Gerard Hoffman. **SP-HoffD**

Signatures, / written down in careless hand. Signatures of Multiple Things. Marsden Hartley. **CP-HartM**

Signatures of Multiple Things. Marsden Hartley. **CP-HartM**

Signes of shame that stayne my blushinge face, The. Mary Magdalen's Blushe. Robert Southwell. **CP-SoutR**

Signorina Angeli, veteran of *Vogue*. South of the Alps. John Updike. **CP-UpdiJ**

Signs. Audre Lorde. **SP-LordA**

Signs. James McAuley. **SP-McAuJ**

Signs. Charles Olson. **CP-OlsoC**

Signs. Charles Kenneth Williams. **SP-WillC**

Signs and Portents. Stanley Jasspon Kunitz. **CP-KuniS**
  "At the Porch of the Caryatids."
  "Children at play in a field."
  "Jonathan, the last of the giant tortoises."
  "On Twelfth Street in Manhattan."
  "Three thousand years ago."

Signs and Tokens. Thomas Hardy. **CP-HardT**

Signs have appeared in heaven, that dog is one. The second. The Dog in the Sky. Robinson Jeffers. **CP-JefR3**

Signs of the Times. Paul Laurence Dunbar. **CP-DunbP**

Signs of the Times. David Herbert Lawrence. **CP-LawrD**

Signs of the times are always disquieting. Presence. Dabney Stuart. **SP-StuaD**

Silence / and a deeper silence. Summer Haiku. Leonard Cohen. **CP-CoheL**

Silence, The. Wendell Berry. **CP-BerrW**

Silence, The. Wendell Berry. **CP-BerrW**

Silence. Hayden Carruth. **CP-CarHS**

Silence. Walter de la Mare. **CP-DeLaW**

Silence. Stephen Dobyns. **SP-DobyS**

Silence. Paul Laurence Dunbar. **CP-DunbP**

Silence. Ralph Waldo Emerson. **CP-EmerR**

Silence. Robert Herrick. **CP-HerrR**

Silence / .is / a / looking. Edward Estlin Cummings. **CP-CummE**

Silence. Stanley Jasspon Kunitz. **CP-KuniS**

Silence ("Come, holy Silence. . ."). David Herbert Lawrence. **CP-LawrD**

Silence ("Since I lost you. . ."). David Herbert Lawrence. **CP-LawrD**

Silence. Marianne Craig Moore. **CP-MoorM**

Silence. Theodore Roethke. **CP-RoetT**

Silence, The. Anne Sexton. **CP-SextA**

Silence. Christopher Smart. *Fr.* Hymns for the Amusement of Children. **SP-SmarC**

Silence, The. Charles Kenneth Williams. **SP-WillC**

Silence. William Carlos Williams. **CP-WilW2**

Silence and Tears. Stevie Smith. **CP-SmitS**

Silence, and whirling worlds afar. Night. Paul Laurence Dunbar. **CP-DunbP**

Silence augmenteth grief, writing encreaseth rage. Another of the Same. Edmund Spenser. *Fr.* Astrophel. **CP-Spens**

Silence! calm, venerable majesty. Address to Silence. William Wordsworth. **CP-WorW1**

Silence! coeval with Eternity. *in imitation of* John Wilmot, Earl of Rochester. Alexander Pope. **CP-PopeA**

Silence does not know how to veil her face. Vir IV. James Liddy. *Fr.* Vir I–XII. **CP-LiddJ**

Silence is a great blue bell. The Choir and Music of Solitude and Silence. Delmore Schwartz. **SP-SchwD**

Silence is a shape that has passed. The Green Plant. Wallace Stevens. **CP-StevW**

Silence is all we dread. Emily Dickinson. **CP-DickE**

Silence' oblation to the Ear. Emily Dickinson. **SP-DickE**

Silence o'er sea and earth. The Sicilian Vespers. John Greenleaf Whittier. **CP-WhitJ**

Silence of a City—How awful at midnight, The. A Silent City. Samuel Taylor Coleridge. **CP-ColeS**

Silence of preluded song—, The. South-West Wind in the Woodland. George Meredith. **CP-MerG1**

Silence of the ether, The. Morning Radio. Derek Mahon. **SP-MahoD**

Silence of the Lambs, The. Tom Clark. **SP-ClarT**

Silence of the world's despair, The. The Heart of Joy. John Hewitt. **CP-HewiJ**

Silence of the Year, The. This hour the streets. Landscape of the Star. Adrienne Rich. **CP-RicAE**

Silence of Volcanoes. Muriel Rukeyser. **CP-RukeM**

Silence! Oh, well are Death and Sleep and Thou. Fragment: Apostrophe to Silence. Percy Bysshe Shelley. **CP-ShelP**

Silence tel que ce qui fut. Samuel Beckett. **CP-BeckS**

Silence, The / of nature. Without. Gary Snyder. **CP-SnydG**

Silence. The man defined. The Hand at Callow Hill Farm. Charles Tomlinson. **CP-TomlC**

Silence, words into foolishness fading. The Black Goddess. Robert Ranke Graves. **CP-GravR**

Silences. Thomas Hardy. **CP-HardT**

Silences. Gilbert Sorrentino. **SP-SorrG**

Silent alone, where none or saw, or heard. Anne Bradstreet. **PBWP** *Fr.* Contemplations. **CP-BradA**

Silent and amazed even when a little boy. A Child's Amaze. Walt Whitman. **CP-WhitW**

Silent City, A. Samuel Taylor Coleridge. **CP-ColeS**

Silent I sat, dejected, and alone. John Milton. *See* Elegy 3: On the Death of the Bishop of Winchester.

Silent Icicles, The. Samuel Taylor Coleridge. *See* All Seasons Shall Be Sweet.

Silent in America. Philip Levine. **SP-LeviP**

Silent is the House—all are laid asleep. *see also* The Visionary *and* The Prisoner. Emily Brontë. **CP-BronE**

Silent is the house: all are laid asleep. *see also* Julian M. and A.G. Rochelle *and* The Prisoner. Emily Brontë. **CP-BronE**

Silent Journal. Charles Wright. **SP-WrigC**

Silent Shepherds, The. Robinson Jeffers. **CP-JefR3**

Silent Silent Night. William Blake. **CP-BlakW**

Silent Slain, The. Archibald MacLeish. *See* We too, we too, descending once again.

Silent unday by silently not night. Edward Estlin Cummings. **CP-CummE**

Silent Visit. Robert Ranke Graves. **CP-GravR**

Silent Weekend. "Bob Dylan." **CP-DylaB**

Silent woods with desarts shade. Mary Sidney, Countess of Montgomery Wroth. *Fr.* Love's Victorie. **CP-WrotM**

Silently . . . / she was quieter than breathing now. Juliet's Garden. Charles Tomlinson. **CP-TomlC**

Silently fell / The snow on the waters. Snow at Sea. John Gould Fletcher. *Fr.* Sand and Spray: A Sea-Symphony. **SP-FletJ**

Silently I ascend the western pavilion. Li Yü, *tr. fr. Chinese by* William Carlos Williams *with* David Rafael Wang. **CP-WilW2**

Silently I footed by an uphill road. The Last Signal. Thomas Hardy. **CP-HardT**

Silently if,out of not knowable. Edward Estlin Cummings. **CP-CummE**

Silently little blue elephant shyly(he was terri), The. Edward Estlin Cummings. **CP-CummE**

Silently on the sliding Nile. The Sowing of the Dead Corn. Archibald MacLeish. *Fr.* The Pot of Earth. **CP-MacLA**

Silently without my window. Melancholia. Paul Laurence Dunbar. **CP-DunbP**

Silhouette. John Ashbery. **SP-AshbJ**

Silhouette. Langston Hughes. **SP-HughL**

Silk Ascot for the Terrorist, A. Gilbert Sorrentino. **SP-SorrG**

Silk glove at my window, A. The Glove. Raissa Maritain, *tr. fr. French by* Thomas Merton. **CP-MertT**

Silk Worm, The. Vincent Bourne, *tr. fr. Latin by* William Cowper. **CP-CowpW**

Silken Snake, The. Robert Herrick. **CP-HerrR**

Silken Tent, The. Robert Frost. **CP-FrosR**

Silly boy, 'tis ful[l] moon[e] yet, thy night as day shines clearly [*or* clearely]. First Love. Thomas Campion. **CP-CampT**

Silly fool, the silly fool, The. Happy Ending. Wystan Hugh Auden. **CP-AudeW**

Silly girls your heads full of boys. Plainness in Diversity. John Ashbery. **SP-AshbJ**

Silo, The. Lewis Turco. **SP-TurcL**

Siloam. Donald Davie. **CP-DavDo**

Silvanus long in love, and long in vain, *dialogue of Espilus and Therion.* Sir Philip Sidney. **SP-SidnP** *Fr.* The Lady of May.

Silver. Diane Wakoski. **SP-WakoD**

Silver Age, The. Thom Gunn. **CP-GunnT**

Silver as / the needle's eye. George Oppen. **NNaP** *Fr.* Some San Francisco Poems. **CP-OppeG**

Silver bark of beech, and sallow. Counting-out Rhyme. Edna St. Vincent Millay. **CP-MillE**

Silver bird is E backward in cool pond water, The. Thomas Merton. **CP-MertT**

Silver burbles of the frogs wind and swirl, The. Frog Songs. Carl Sandburg. **CP-SandC**

Silver Creek Falls. William Dickey. **SP-DickW**

Silver dust. Pear Tree. Hilda Doolittle. **CP-DoolH**

Silver Fish, The. Shel Silverstein. **SP-SilS2**

Silver grapes in sleeves. Uncle Sam in the White House. Diane Wakoski. **SP-WakoD**

Silver jet, A. Sitting Down, Looking Up. Archie Randolph Ammons. **SP-AmmoA**

Silver Jubilee, The. Gerard Manley Hopkins. **CP-HopkG**

Silver key of the fountain of tears. A Fragment: To Music. Percy Bysshe Shelley. **CP-ShelP**

Silver leaves of the last summer. Poplar and Elm. Carl Sandburg. **CP-SandC**

Silver Mirrors. Jim Carroll. **SP-CarrJ**

Silver Nails. Carl Sandburg. **CP-SandC**

Silver of one star, The. Star Silver. Carl Sandburg. **CP-SandC**

Silver Point. Carl Sandburg. **CP-SandC**

Silver point of an evening star, The. Silver Point. Carl Sandburg. **CP-SandC**

Silver Poplars. William DeWitt Snodgrass. **SP-SnodW**

Silver scarce-call-silver gloss, A. Gerard Manley Hopkins. **CP-HopkG**

Silver shadow where the line falls grey, The. Upcountry. Adrienne Rich. **SP-RicA1; SP-RicA2**

Silver Ship, my King, was her name, The. To Kalakaua. Robert Louis Stevenson. **CP-StevR**

Silver spoons, The / were warbling. Here Comes. Erica Jong. **SP-JongE**

Silver Stag, The. Kathleen Jessie Raine. **SP-RainK**

Silver Star. Richard Hugo. **CP-HugoR**

Silver Swan, The. Kenneth Rexroth.

   "Drowned moon plunges, The." **SP-RexrK**

   "Hototogisu—horobirete." **SP-RexrK**

   "Under the half moon." **SP-RexrK**

Silver Thimble, The. Samuel Taylor Coleridge. *Fr.* Poetical Epistles. **CP-ColeS**

Silver-tongued among the sons of Rome. Carmen 49. Catullus. *Fr.* Carmina. **CP-Catul**

Silver Was the Barbèd Hook. John Hewitt. **CP-HewiJ**

Silver Wind. Carl Sandburg. **CP-SandC**

Silverpoint. Louise Glück. **SP-GlücL**

Simaetha. Hilda Doolittle. **CP-DoolH**

Simile, A. Jonathan Swift. **CP-SwifJ**

Simile for Her Smile, A. Richard Wilbur. **CP-WilbR**

Simile Latinised, A. *Unknown, tr. fr. English by* William Cowper. **CP-CowpW**

Similes for Two Political Characters of 1819. Percy Bysshe Shelley. **CP-ShelP**

Simmer's a Pleasant Time. Robert Burns.

   (Ay Waukin O.) **CP-BurnR**

Simon calls. It seems his new. Primary Considerations. Ron Koertge. **SP-KoerR**

Simon Judson. Lewis Turco. **SM** *Fr.* Bordello. **SP-TurcL**

Simon Lee [the Old Huntsman]. William Wordsworth. **CP-WorW1**

Simon Legree—A Negro Sermon. Nicholas Vachel Lindsay. **HBMV; InMe; LiTA; MeMAP; MoVE; NePA; TAP** *Fr.* The Booker Washington Trilogy. **CP-LindV**

   (Negro Sermon—Simon Legree, A.) **MoAmPo**

Simon the Cyrenian Speaks. Countee Cullen. **CP-CullC**

Simone Signoret. James Schuyler. **CP-SchuJ**

Simpering sideways under a picture-hat. Lincolnshire. Donald Davie. **CP-DavDo**

Simple. Hayden Carruth. **CP-CarHS**

Simple and fresh and fair from winter's close emerging. The First Dandelion. Walt Whitman. **CP-WhitW**

Simple Autumnal. Louise Bogan. **CP-BogaL**

Simple Bard, rough at the rustic plough, The. The Brigs of Ayr, a Poem. Inscribed to J. B*********, Esq; Ayr. Robert Burns. **CP-BurnR**

Simple child, dear brother Jim, A. We Are Seven. William Wordsworth. **CP-WorW1**

Simple Experiment, A. Muriel Rukeyser. **CP-RukeM**

Simple goatherd between Alp and sky, The. Mountaineer and Poet. Elizabeth Barrett Browning. **CP-BroEB**

Simple is madness, like a kick in the pants. Charles Henri Ford. *Fr.* Epigrams. **SP-FordC**

Simple like all dream-wishes, they employ. Wystan Hugh Auden. *Fr.* Sonnets from China. **CP-AudeW**

Simple Location. Roy Fisher. **SP-FishR**

Simple-Minded Christian, The. John Hewitt. **CP-HewiJ**

Simple misery of survival, The. 9 Rings. Charles Bukowski. **SP-BukC2**

Simple nosegay! was that much to ask?, A. The Troll's Nosegay. Robert Ranke Graves. **CP-GravR**

Simple people each with basket or tool, The. Ralph Waldo Emerson. **CP-EmerR**

Simple ring with a single stone, A. A Pearl, a Girl. Robert Browning. **CP-BroR2**

Simple Seabird's Tribute to Her Harteebeeste, A. Malcolm Lowry. **CP-LowrM**

Simple Sonatina. Tess Gallagher. **SP-GallT**

Simple-Song. Marge Piercy. **SP-PierM**

Simple, spontaneous, curious, two souls interchanging. For Us Two, Reader Dear. Walt Whitman. **CP-WhitW**

Simple Trust. Jeanne Marie Bouvier de la Motte-Guyon, *tr. fr. French by* William Cowper. **CP-CowpW**

Simple Twist of Fate. "Bob Dylan." **CP-DylaB**

Simple was I and was young. After Reading Psalms XXXIX, XL, etc. Thomas Hardy. **CP-HardT**

Simplest / Words say the grass blade, The. The Occurrences. George Oppen. **CP-OppeG**

Simplex Sigilum Veri: A Catalogue. William Carlos Williams. **CP-WilW1**

Simplicity. Gilbert Sorrentino. **SP-SorrG**

Simplicity of Everything in Viet Nam, The. Charles Bukowski. **SP-BukC2**

Simplicity of the Unknown Past, The. Kenneth Koch. **SP-KochK**

Simplicity yea even to write. Confections. Paul Éluard, *tr. fr. French by* Samuel Beckett. **CP-BeckS**

Simplification, A. Richard Wilbur. **CP-WilbR**

Simplon Pass, The. William Wordsworth. **CP-WorW1**

Simply because of a question, my life is implicated. Private Life of the Sphinx. Muriel Rukeyser. **CP-RukeM**

Simultaneously, as soundlessly. Prime. Wystan Hugh Auden. **CMoP; PoE** *Fr.* Horae Canonicae. **CP-AudeW**

Sin ("Sin leads the way, but as it goes, it feels"). Robert Herrick. **CP-HerrR**

Sin ("Sin never slew a soule, unlesse there went"). Robert Herrick. **CP-HerrR**

Sin ("Sin no Existence; Nature none it hath"). Robert Herrick. **CP-HerrR**

Sin ("Sin once reacht up to Gods eternall Sphere"). Robert Herrick. **CP-HerrR**

Sin ("There is no evill that we do commit"). Robert Herrick. **CP-HerrR**

Sin. Robert Herrick. **CP-HerrR**

Sin: "O that I could a sin once see!" George Herbert. **CP-HerbG**

Sin against the Holy. . . though what, The. The Blasphemies. Louis MacNeice. **CP-MacNL**

Sin and Death. John Milton. *See* Meanwhile [*or* Mean while] the Adversary of God and Man.

Sin and Strife. Robert Herrick. **CP-HerrR**

Sin City, D.C. John Updike. **CP-UpdiJ**

Sin enslav'd me many years. The Heart Healed and Changed by Mercy. William Cowper. *Fr.* Olney Hymns. **CP-CowpW**

Sin has undone our wretched race. Pleading for and with Youth. William Cowper. *Fr.* Olney Hymns. **CP-CowpW**

Sin is an act so free, that if we shall. Another. Robert Herrick. **CP-HerrR**

Sin is inferiority. The mother's cooperation in the birth of her daughter. Charles Olson. **CP-OlsoC**

Sin is the cause of death; and sin's alone. Another. Robert Herrick. **CP-HerrR**

Sin leads the way, but as it goes, it feels. Sin. Robert Herrick. **CP-HerrR**

Sin no Existence; Nature none it hath. Sin. Robert Herrick. **CP-HerrR**

Sin [*or* Sinne] of self-love [*or* selfe-love] possesseth all mine eye [*or* eie]. Sonnet 62. William Shakespeare. **EBEV; EnRePo; OXAEP-1; PoEL-2** *Fr.* Sonnets. **CP-ShaWS**

Sin once reacht up to Gods eternall Sphere. Sin. Robert Herrick. **CP-HerrR**

Sin (1). George Herbert. **CP-HerbG**

Sin recognized—but that—may keep us humble. Recognition Not Enough. Stevie Smith. **CP-SmitS**

Sin Seen. Robert Herrick. **CP-HerrR**

Sin Severely Punisht. Robert Herrick. **CP-HerrR**

Sinbad. Allen Tate. **CP-TateA**

Sinbu put order in Sun land, Nippon, in the beginning of all things. Canto 58. Ezra Pound. *Fr.* Cantos. **CP-PoCan**

Since / And the rain since. De Votre Bonheur Il ne Reste Que Vos Photos. Archibald MacLeish. **CP-MacLA**

Since. Wystan Hugh Auden. **CP-AudeW**

Since all of your work was really an effort to appease. Derek Walcott. **CP-WalcD** *Fr.* Midsummer.

Since all that beat about in Nature's range. Constancy to an Ideal Object. Samuel Taylor Coleridge. **CP-ColeS**

Since all the Riches of this World. William Blake. **CP-BlakW**

Since as in night's deck-watch ye show. Herman Melville. **APN-2; SP-MelvH** *Fr.* John Marr. **SP-MelvH**

Since Athens first began to draw mankind. Prologue to Mallet's Mustapha. James Thomson. **CP-ThomJ**

Since, Bacchus, thou art father. The Dedication of the King's New Cellar. To Bacchus. Ben Jonson. **CP-JonsB**

Since Brass, Nor Stone, Nor Earth. William Shakespeare. *See* Sonnet 65: "Since brass, nor stone, nor earth, nor boundless sea."

Since brass, nor stone, nor earth, nor boundless sea. Sonnet 65. William Shakespeare. **AWP; CABA; EnRePo; FF; FaFP; FiP; GTBS; GTBS-6; GTBS-P; HAP; ImPo; InPS; LiTB; MasP; NAEL-1; NOBE; NoP; NoSic; OXAEP-1; PoRA; RaBo; SCGP; SeCeV; Son; TFi; UnPo** *Fr.* Sonnets. **CP-ShaWS**

Since brooding men put beauty in a rime. Sonnet. John Hewitt. **CP-HewiJ**

Since Christ embraced the Cross itself, dare I. The Cross. John Donne. **CP-DonnJ**

Since Christmas they have lived with us. Balloons. Sylvia Plath. **CP-PlatS**

Since death is there in the light of the sun, in the song of the. Carl Sandburg. *Fr.* Timesweep. **CP-SandC**

Since depth of love is never gauged. Depth of Love. Robert Ranke Graves. **CP-GravR**

Since every sound moves memories. A Duettist to her Pianoforte. Thomas Hardy. **CP-HardT**

Since every tree begins to blossom now. A Letter Written by Sir H. G. and J. D. alternis vicibus. John Donne. **CP-DonnJ**

Since feeling is first. Edward Estlin Cummings. **CP-CummE; SP-CummE**

Since first break of dawn the fiend. The Tempter Disarmed. John Milton. **NOSC** *Fr.* Book IX. **FHYEP; NAEL-1; NAWM-1; NoP; OAEL-1** *Fr.* Paradise Lost. **CP-MiltJ**

Since first the White Horse Banner blew free. A Departure. Rudyard Kipling. **CP-KiplR** *Fr.* Land and Sea Tales.

Since, for the charity they knew. Of Wickedness the Word. Herman Melville. **SP-MelvH** *Fr.* Clarel: A Poem and Pilgrimage in the Holy Land.

Since for thy full deserts (with all the rest). To His Peculiar Friend Sir Edward Fish, Knight Baronet. Robert Herrick. **CP-HerrR**

Since Gander did his prettie Youngling wed. Upon Gander. Robert Herrick. **CP-HerrR**

Since Half the World is H$_2$O. "Lou Reed." **SP-ReedL**

Since he had few intimate friends, and little. "Women of Color" Have Rarely Had the Opportunity to Write about Their Love Affairs. Alice Walker. **CP-WalkA**

Since he is older than Hamlet or Stavrogin. A Predecessor of Perseus. Howard Nemerov. **CP-NemeH**

Since his sharp sight has taught you. A Valediction. William DeWitt Snodgrass. **SP-SnodW**

Since I am / Somebody's dream. *tr. of* Le Secret. Thomas Merton, *tr. fr. French by* William Davis. **CP-MertT**

Since I am coming [*or* comming] to that holy room[e]. Hymn[e] to God My God, In My Sickness[e]. John Donne. **CP-DonnJ**

Since I am sworn to live my life. Robert Louis Stevenson. *Fr.* Rondels. **CP-StevR**

Since I cannot persuade you from this mood. Edna St. Vincent Millay. **CP-MillE**

Since I do trust Jehova still, *par. by* Sir Philip Sidney. Bible, O.T. *See* Psalm 11: "In the name of the Lord. . . ."

Since I Have Lacked the Comfort. Edmund Spenser. **EnRePo** *Fr.* Amoretti. **CP-Spens**

Since I have lacked the comfort of that light. Since I Have Lacked the Comfort. Edmund Spenser. **EnRePo** *Fr.* Amoretti. **CP-Spens**

Since I left the city's heat. At Loafing-Holt. Paul Laurence Dunbar. **CP-DunbP**

Since I left you, mine eye is in my mind. Sonnet 113. William Shakespeare. **SCGP; WeW** *Fr.* Sonnets. **CP-ShaWS**

Since I lost you, I am silence-haunted. Silence. David Herbert Lawrence. **CP-LawrD**

Since I lost you, my darling, the sky has come near. Call into Death. David Herbert Lawrence. **CP-LawrD**

Since I no longer speak I. Silent in America. Philip Levine. **SP-LeviP**

Since I was minutely hurt. Minutely Hurt. Countee Cullen. **CP-CullC**

Since *Jack* and *Jill* both wicked be. Jack and Jill. Robert Herrick. **CP-HerrR**

Since Josh was in the Northwest woods with Clark. Martha MacElmain. Louise McNeill. **SP-McNeL**

Since June was hot on head and hand. John Hewitt. *Fr.* Three Horatian Odes. **CP-HewiJ**

Since life in sorrow must be spent. The Love of God the End of Life. Jeanne Marie Bouvier de la Motte-Guyon, *tr. fr. French by* William Cowper. **CP-CowpW**

Since long ago, a child at home. To an Island Princess. Robert Louis Stevenson. **CP-StevR**

Since, Lord, to thee / A narrow way and little gate. Holy Baptism (2). George Herbert. **CP-HerbG**

Since louely sweete, much like unto a Dewe. Elegy. Robert Herrick. **CP-HerrR**

Since love is an astonished always. The Theme of Death. Robert Ranke Graves. **CP-GravR**

Since love is such that, as ye wot. Sir Thomas Wyatt. **CP-WyatT**

Since Love will needs that I shall love. Sir Thomas Wyatt. **CP-WyatT**

Since man's life is nothing but a bit of action at a distance. Piano Solo. Nicanor Parra, *tr. fr. Spanish by* William Carlos Williams. **CP-WilW2**

Since men grow diffident at last. Youth Sings a Song of Rosebuds. Countee Cullen. **CP-CullC**

Since men have left to do praiseworthy things. To Thomas, Earl of Suffolk. Ben Jonson. **CP-JonsB**

Since much at home on. *Song:* The Sundial's Lament. Robert Ranke Graves. **CP-GravR**

Since Munich, what? A tangle of black film. The News-Reel. Louis MacNeice. **CP-MacNL**

Since my girlhood, in that small boat. Boat Ride. Tess Gallagher. **SP-GallT**

Since my old friend is grown so great. A Dialogue. Alexander Pope. **CP-PopeA**

Since Nature's works be good, and death doth serve, *speech of Musidorus.* Sir Philip Sidney. **SP-SidnP** *Fr.* Arcadia.

Since no one knows the why of the weather. The Why of the Weather. Robert Ranke Graves. **CP-GravR**

Since now I dare not ask. The Sharp Ridge. Robert Ranke Graves. **CP-GravR**

Since now in every public place. The Sea Horse. Robert Ranke Graves. **CP-GravR**

Since now the hour is come at last. To Emma. Byron. **CP-Byron**

Since now those clouds, that lately over-cast. To My Honourable Friend, Sr. Thomas Mounson, *Knight and Baronet.* Thomas Campion. **CP-CampT**

Since of no creature living the last breath. Edna St. Vincent Millay. **CP-MillE**

Since our Country, our God—Oh, my Sire! Jephtha's Daughter. Byron. **CP-Byron**

Since Persia fell at Marathon. Villanelle of Change. Edwin Arlington Robinson. **CP-RobiE**

Since Reason, with itself dissatisfied. Reason. George Meredith. **CP-MerG2**

Since Reverend Doctors now declare. The Respectable Burgher. Thomas Hardy. **CP-HardT**

Since risen from ocean, ocean to defy. In the Firth of Clyde, Ailsa Crag. William Wordsworth. *Fr.* Poems Composed or Suggested During a Tour, in the Summer of 1833. **CP-WorW2**

Since she, ev'n shee, for whom I liv'd. Thomas Campion. **CP-CampT**

Since she must go, and I must mourn, come night. His Parting from Her. John Donne. **EBEV; OBS** *Fr.* Elegies. **CP-DonnJ**

Since she whom I loved [or lov'd] hath paid [or payd] her last debt. John Donne. **JCP; MePo; NAEL-1; NOSC; OAEP; Son** *Fr.* Divine Meditations. **CP-DonnJ** *Fr.* Holy Sonnets. **CP-DonnJ**

Since shed or Cottage I have none. To His Peculiar Friend M. Jo: Wicks. Robert Herrick. **CP-HerrR**

Since she's been gone I want no one to talk to me. Don't Bother Me. George Harrison. **CP-Beatl**

Since, shunning pain, I ease can never find. Sir Philip Sidney. **SP-SidnP**

Since so mine eyes are subject to your sight, *speech of Dorus.* Sir Philip Sidney. **SP-SidnP** *Fr.* Arcadia.

Since so ye please to hear me plain. Sir Thomas Wyatt. **CP-WyatT**

Since that last evening we have fallen indeed. Adam and Eve. Arthur Hugh Clough. **SP-ClouA**

Since that my language without eloquence. Sir Thomas Wyatt. **CP-WyatT**

speech of Cleophila. Sir Philip Sidney. **SP-SidnP** *Fr.* Arcadia.

Since the Autumn day. Wystan Hugh Auden. **CP-AudWJ**

Since the devil hopping on. Ralph Waldo Emerson. **CP-EmerR**

Since the Majority of Me. Philip Larkin. **CP-LarkP**

Since the night in which you stole. The Watch. Robert Ranke Graves. **CP-GravR**

Since the refinement of this polish'd age. An Occasional Prologue Delivered Previous to the Performance of "The Wheel of Fortune" at a Private Theatre. Byron. **CP-Byron**

Since the splendour of MacDonnell of the cliffs. James Liddy. *Fr.* Cliffs. **CP-LiddJ**

Since then I have arrived here. Wendell Berry. *Fr.* History. **CP-BerrW**

Since there are people who complain. Dialogue between an Eminent Lawyer and Dr. Swift, Dean of St. Patrick's. Jonathan Swift. **CP-SwifJ**

Since this is the last night I keep you home. Seven Seals. David Herbert Lawrence. **CP-LawrD**

Since thou hast given me this good hope, O God. Robert Louis Stevenson. **CP-StevR**

Since to look at earth through his eyes. Second Sight (My Son's First Springtime). Louise McNeill. **SP-McNeL**

Since to th'Country first I came. To Sir Clipsebie Crew. Robert Herrick. **CP-HerrR**

Since Tuck is faithless found, no more. Madrigal. George Meredith. **CP-MerG2**

Since very soon it is required of you. Noguchi. Muriel Rukeyser. **CP-RukeM**

Since wailing is a bud of causeful sorrow, *speech of Agelastus.* Sir Philip Sidney. **SP-SidnP** *Fr.* Arcadia.

Since we agreed to let the road between us. No Road. Philip Larkin. **CP-LarkP**

Since we can't go back to Tuscany, Dinty. To My Baby Paul. Louis Zukofsky. **CP-ZukLS**

Since we had changed. Message. Allen Ginsberg. **CP-GinsA**

Since we have become so cerebral. Touch. David Herbert Lawrence. **CP-LawrD**

Since we're not young, weeks have to do time. Adrienne Rich. **UnAS; VBLP** *Fr.* Twenty-one Love Poems. **SP-RicA1; SP-RicA2**

Since what you want, not what you ought. I Could Let Tom Go—But What about the Children. Stevie Smith. **CP-SmitS**

Since Without Thee We Do No Good. Elizabeth Barrett Browning. **CP-BroEB**

Since ye delight to know. Sir Thomas Wyatt. **CP-WyatT**

Since ye distemper and defile. *parody of* Robert Herrick. Rudyard Kipling. **CP-KiplR** *Fr.* The Muse among the Motors.

Since years ago for evermore. Robert Louis Stevenson. **CP-StevR**

Since you and I became engines. Thomas Merton. *Fr.* Cables to the Ace. **CP-MertT**

Since you are going to begin to-day. Venus Will Now Say a Few Words. Wystan Hugh Auden. **CP-AudeW**

Since you are in your element of fire. Virgo. Malcolm Lowry. **CP-LowrM**

Since you ask, most days I cannot remember. Wanting to Die. Anne Sexton. **CP-SextA**

Since You Asked Me. Mona Van Duyn. **SP-VanDM**

Since you did depart. The Inheritance. David Herbert Lawrence. **CP-LawrD**

Since you first drew my irresistible wave. Cliff and Wave. Robert Ranke Graves. **CP-GravR**

Since you must go, and I must bid farewell. Elegy, An. Ben Jonson. **CP-JonsB**

Since you packed your rubber bottom boots. Early Hours. Carl Sandburg. **CP-SandC**

Since you remember Nimmo, and arrive. Nimmo. Edwin Arlington Robinson. **CP-RobiE**

Since you set no worth on the heart. Hafiz, *tr.* by Ralph Waldo Emerson. **CP-EmerR** *Fr.* Odes.

Since you will needs that I shall sing. Sir Thomas Wyatt. **CP-WyatT**

Since you would claim the sources of my thought. Sonnet. Louise Bogan. **CP-BogaL**

Since you've been gone. Living the Blues. "Bob Dylan." **CP-DylaB**

Sincèrement. Robert Ranke Graves. **CP-GravR**

Sincerity. Robert Herrick. **CP-HerrR**

Sincerity. Thomas Merton. **CP-MertT**

Sine Prole. Thomas Hardy. **CP-HardT**

Sinecure for P. Whalen, A. Gary Snyder. **CP-SnydG**

Sinful painter drapes his goddess warm, The. Painting and Sculpture. Ralph Waldo Emerson. **CP-EmerR**

Sing a song of critics. Valentine. Ernest Hemingway. **CP-HemiE**

Sing a song of joy. Thomas Campion. **CP-CampT**

Sing a Song of Singapore. Al Young. **CP-YounA**

Sing a song of 'sistence. Two Conceits. Allen Tate. **CP-TateA**

Sing a song of slaughter. Nursery Rhyme No. 1. Isabella Gardner. **CP-GardI**

Sing a song of sunlight. Truant. Phoebe Hesketh. **SP-HeskP**

Sing aloud that she is mine. George Meredith. **CP-MerG2**

Sing aloud unto God our strength. Psalm 81. Bible, *O.T. Fr.* Psalms. **CP-Psal**

Sing, Ballad-singer, raise a hearty tune. At Casterbridge Fair. Thomas Hardy. **CP-HardT**

Sing clearlier, Muse, or evermore be still. Robert Louis Stevenson. **CP-StevR**

Sing heav'nly moose, you baffler of behaviorists. Ode to a Lovesick Moose. Robert Pack. **SP-PackR**

Sing; how 'a would sing! Julie-Jane. Thomas Hardy. **CP-HardT**

Sing in me, Muse, and through me tell the story. Odyssey. Homer, *tr. fr. Greek by* Robert Fitzgerald.

Sing it. Utter the phrase, the fine word. Bard. William Everson. **SP-EverW**

Sing Laura, sing, whilst silent are the Sphears. A Dialogue. Lute and Voice. Richard Lovelace. **CP-LoveR**

Sing like a bird at the open. That Land. George Oppen. *Fr.* Five Poems about Poetry. **CP-OppeG**

Sing me a hero! Quench my thirst. Tray. Robert Browning. **CP-BroR2**

Sing me a song— / What shall I sing? Christina Georgina Rossetti. **CP-RosC2**

Sing me a song of a lad that is gone. Robert Louis Stevenson. **CP-StevR**

Sing me a thrush, bone. The Fury of Beautiful Bones. Anne Sexton. *Fr.* The Furies. **CP-SextA**

Sing me at morn but only with your laugh. Song of Songs. Wilfred Owen. **CP-OwenW**

Sing me to death; for til thy voice be cleare. Upon a Hoarse Singer. Robert Herrick. **CP-HerrR**

Sing miserere / For the men who must die. Litany. Thomas Merton. **CP-MertT**

Sing, Mister, Sing. Charles Olson. **CP-OlsoC**

Sing, muse, (if such a theme, so dark, so long). The Progress of Error. William Cowper. **CP-CowpW**

Sing, Muse, the son of Maia and of Jove. Hymn to Mercury. *Unknown.* **CP-ShelP** *Fr.* Homeric Hymns.

Sing now no hymn nor chant a dirge. To a Prodigal Old Maid. Allen Tate. **CP-TateA**

Sing of a love lost and forgotten. Two Parted. Christina Georgina Rossetti. **CP-RosC3**

Sing of the O'Rahilly. The O'Rahilly. William Butler Yeats. **CP-YeatW**

Sing on, sweet thrush, upon the leafless bough. Sonnet—On Hearing a Thrush Sing on a Morning Walk in January. Robert Burns. **CP-BurnR**

Sing out pent soul[e]s, sing cheerfully! The Vintage to the Dungeon. Richard Lovelace. **CP-LoveR**

Sing praise for statuary. Touch-and-Go. Sylvia Plath. **CP-PlatS**

Sing Song. Robert Creeley. **CP-CreeR**

Sing-Song. Christina Georgina Rossetti. **CP-RosC2**

"Brown and furry." **BoTP; FaBoVe; FaPON; GoJo; OxBChV; RHPC; SUS; SiSoPo; SoPo**

(Caterpillar, The.) **BoTP; FaPON; GoJo; OxBChV; RHPC; SUS; SiSoPo; SoPo**

City Mouse and the Garden Mouse, The. **BoTP; FaBoBe; FaPON; HBV; HBVY; NTCP**

Ferry Me across the Water. **BiP; ChTr; GoJo; NTP; OxBChV; PDV; SUS; TLR**

(Ferryman, The.) **BoTP; SoPo**

Flint. **OxBChV; RHPC; TiPo**

"Horses of the sea, The." **FaPON; GoJo; NTCP; SUS**

Hurt No Living Thing. **FM; FaPON; OTCP; PDV; RHPC; SiSoPo; SiSoSe; SoPo; TSS**

Let's Be Merry. **FaPON; TLR; TiPo**

Minnie and Mattie. **GoJo; InvP**

Mix a Pancake. **NTCP**

(Pancake, The.) **BoTP**

"O sailor, come ashore." **BoTP; FM**

Oh, Fair to See. **CP-RosC2; FaPON; OHIP; TiPo**

Sing-Song of Old Man Kangaroo, The. Rudyard Kipling. *Fr.* Just-So Stories.

"This is the mouth-filling song of the race that was run by a Boomer." **CP-KiplR**

Sing the song of death, O sing it! Song of Death. David Herbert Lawrence. **CP-LawrD**

Sing to me / weather about / one bird. So Good. James Schuyler. **CP-SchuJ**

Sing to the Lord, for what can better be, *par.* by Countess of Pembroke, Mary Sidney Herbert. Bible, *O.T. See* Psalm 147: "Praise ye the Lord: for it is good. . . ."

Sing unto the Lord a New Song. Donald Davie. **CP-DavDo**

Sing unto the Lord with Thanksgiving, *sel., vv. 7–9, 12, of sl. diff. vers.* Bible, *O.T. See* Psalm 147: "Praise ye the Lord: for it is good. . . ."

Sing you for love and idleness. Another Immorality. Malcolm Lowry. **CP-LowrM**

Sing your new song in the winepress where these bloody pence. The Victory. Thomas Merton. **CP-MertT**

Singapore. Mary Oliver. **SP-OlivM**

Singer, The. John Greenleaf Whittier. **CP-WhitJ**

Singer and tailor am I. Darzee's Chaunt. Rudyard Kipling. **CP-KiplR** *Fr.* Rikki-Tikki-Tavi. *Fr.* The Jungle Book.

Singer Asleep, A. Thomas Hardy. **CP-HardT**

Singer in the Prison, The. Walt Whitman. **CP-WhitW**

Singer Must Die, A. Leonard Cohen. **CP-CoheL**

Singer Will Not Sing, The. Maya Angelou. **SP-AngeM**

Singers are gone from the Cornmarket-place, The. After the Fair. Thomas Hardy. **CMoP; HAP; VLP** *Fr.* At Casterbridge Fair. **CP-HardT**

Singer's House, The. Seamus Heaney. **SP-HeanS**

Singing. Daniel Gerard Hoffman. **SP-HoffD**

Singing. Robert Louis Stevenson. **CP-StevR**

Singing. / The morning bird. / (Humphum!). Malcolm Lowry. **CP-LowrM**

Singing across the orchard. To a Wood Thrush. William Carlos Williams. **CP-WilW1**

Singing Cat, The. Stevie Smith. **CP-SmitS**

Singing in the Rain. Countee Cullen. **CP-CullC**

Singing Is Fire. Charles Bukowski. **SP-BukC2**

Singing Kettle & the purring Cat, The. The Happy Home. Samuel Taylor Coleridge. **CP-ColeS**

Singing Lovers. Thomas Hardy. **CP-HardT**

Singing my days. Passage to India. Walt Whitman. **CP-WhitW**

Singing Nigger. Carl Sandburg. **CP-SandC**

Singing School. Seamus Heaney. **SP-HeanS**

Singing smell of tar, of the highway, A. Malcolm Lowry. *Fr.* The Canadian Turned Back at the Border. **CP-LowrM**

Singing Woman, The. Thomas Hardy. **CP-HardT**

Singing-Woman from the Wood's Edge, The. Edna St. Vincent Millay. **CP-MillE**

Single cap pistol, A. Spotfire. William Everson. **SP-EverW**

Single clenched fist lifted and ready, The. Choose. Carl Sandburg. **CP-SandC**

Single clover Plank, A. Emily Dickinson. **CP-DickE**

Single creature leads a partial life, The. Wystan Hugh Auden. *Fr.* Ten Songs. **CP-AudeW**

Single dog, A. Dog. Charles Bukowski. **SP-BukC1**

Single egg hatched every shape that swarms, A. Resolution. Daniel Gerard Hoffman. **SP-HoffD**

Single Fare. Richard Graves. **CP-GravR**

Single Footprints. Phoebe Hesketh. **SP-HeskP**

Single Life Most Secure. Robert Herrick. **CP-HerrR**

Single man stands like a bird-watcher, A. The Mouth of the Hudson. Robert Lowell. **SP-LoweR**

Single Screw of Flesh, A. Emily Dickinson. **CP-DickE**

Single shine broods gloomily, A. A Victorian Rehearsal. Thomas Hardy. **CP-HardT**

Single Sonnet. Louise Bogan. **CP-BogaL**

Single soul of a pair of twins, The. The Soul of Twins. Ted Kooser. **SP-KoosT**

Single stalk climbed up, A. The White Iris. Philip Levine. **SP-LeviP**

Single tree, A. William Wordsworth. **OBRV** *Fr.* Cambridge and the Alps. *Fr.* The Prelude; Growth of a Poet's Mind [1805 vers.]. **CP-WorW3**

Single Vision. Stanley Jasspon Kunitz. **CP-KuniS**

Single Witness, The. Thomas Hardy. **CP-HardT**

Singleness in Love. Robert Ranke Graves. **CP-GravR**

Singular Metamorphosis, A. Howard Nemerov. **CP-NemeH**

Singular Yen, A. Al Young. **CP-YounA**

Sink, thou strange heart, unto thy rest. Futility. Walter de la Mare. **CP-DeLaW**

Sinking down by the gate I discern the thin moon. The Difference. Thomas Hardy. **CP-HardT**

Sinking Like Sediment through the Day. Philip Larkin. **CP-LarkP**

Sinking, Swimming. Gilbert Sorrentino. **SP-SorrG**

Sinner, The. George Herbert. **CP-HerbG**

Sinner. Langston Hughes. **SP-HughL**

Sinners. Robert Herrick. **CP-HerrR**

Sinners. David Herbert Lawrence. **CP-LawrD**

Sinners confounded are a twofold way. Sinners. Robert Herrick. **CP-HerrR**

Sinner's own fault? So it was, The. Christina Georgina Rossetti. **CP-RosC2**

Sinner's Rue. Alfred Edward Housman. **CP-HousA**

Sinner's Sacrifice, The. Ben Jonson. **CP-JonsB**

Sins Loathed, and Yet Loved. Robert Herrick. **CP-HerrR**

Sins of Kalamazoo, The. Carl Sandburg. **CP-SandC**

Sins of Kalamazoo are neither scarlet nor crimson, The. The Sins of Kalamazoo. Carl Sandburg. **CP-SandC**

Sin's Round. George Herbert. **CP-HerbG**

Sinuously winding through the room. Carmen de Boheme. Hart Crane. **CP-CranH**

Sinverguenza. Robinson Jeffers. **CP-JefR2**

S'io t'incontrassi nell'eterna pace. "Blumine" Risponde. Christina Georgina Rossetti. *Fr.* Il Rosseggiar Dell'Oriente Canzoniere. **CP-RosC3**

Sion. George Herbert. **CP-HerbG**

Sioux Haiku. William Stafford. **SP-StafW**

Sioux sat around their wigwam fires, The. Crossing the Paces. Carl Sandburg. **CP-SandC**

Sipping grog one day at sea. Robert Browning. **CP-BroR2**

Sir, / Delany reports it, and he has a shrewd tongue. A Left-Handed Letter to Dr. Sheridan. Jonathan Swift. **CP-SwifJ**

Sir, / Ere you pass this threshold, stay. To the King, at His Entrance into Saxham: By Master John Crofts. Thomas Carew. **CP-CareT**

Sir, / in reading your letter alone in my hackney. Dean Swift's Answer to the Reverend Dr. Sheridan. Jonathan Swift. **CP-SwifJ**

Sir, / Our times are much degenerate from those. To His Noble Friend Mr. Richard Lovelace upon His Poems. Andrew Marvell. *Fr.* Commendatory Poems. **CP-LoveR**

Sir, / Our times are much degenerate from those. To His Noble Friend, Mr Richard Lovelace, upon His Poems. Andrew Marvell. **CP-MarvA**

Sir, / Pray discruciate what follows: / The dullest beast, and gentleman's liquor. Riddling Letter, A ("Sir, / Pray discruciate what follows: / The dullest beast, and gentleman's liquor"). Jonathan Swift. **CP-SwifJ**

Sir, / That the abusing of your ear's a crime. Epilogue for the Court. Sir John Suckling. *Fr.* Aglaura. **CP-SuckJ**

Sir, / When I left you, I found myself of the grape's juice sick. To Dr. Helsham. Jonathan Swift. **CP-SwifJ**

Sir, / When I saw you today, as I went with Lord Anglesey. The Dean to Thomas Sheridan. Jonathan Swift. **CP-SwifJ**

Sir, / Whether these lines do find you out. Sir John Suckling. **CP-SuckJ**

Sir. Miller Williams. **SP-WillM**

Sir, as your mandate did request. The Inventory. Robert Burns. **CP-BurnR**

Sir: Cruising for profit. The Slave Ship. Louise Glück. **SP-GlücL**

Sir: drinking is a problem without doubt. Prelude To Mammon. Malcolm Lowry. **CP-LowrM**

Sir Eustace Grey. George Crabbe. **SP-CrabG**

Frenzy. **NOBE**

"Peace, peace, my friend; these subjects fly." **PoEL-4**

"Then those ill-favour'd Ones, whom none." **ELP**

Sir Eustace Grey. Christina Georgina Rossetti. **CP-RosC3**

ir Galahad [or The Purple Heart]. Tennyson. **CP-TennA**

ir, I admit your general [or gen'ral] Rule. Epigram from the French. Alexander Pope, *also at.* to Matthew Prior *and to* Samuel Taylor Coleridge. **CP-PopeA**

ir, I am thankful, first, to heaven, for you. Epistle to a Friend, An. Ben Jonson. **CP-JonsB**

ir, I arrest you at your country's suit. To Master W. Montague. Thomas Carew. **CP-CareT**

ir Inigo doth fear it as I hear. To a Friend, an Epigram of Him. Ben Jonson. **CP-JonsB**

ir, it is raining tonight in Towson, Maryland. Memo: Preliminary Draft of a Prayer to God the Father. John Ciardi. **SP-CiarJ**

ir John Cope trode the north right far. Johnie Cope. Robert Burns. **CP-BurnR**

ir John Piers. Sir John Betjeman. **CP-BetjJ**

ir John Suckling's Answer. Sir John Suckling. **CP-SuckJ**

ir John was entombed, and the crypt was closed, and she. The Inscription. Thomas Hardy. **CP-HardT**

ir John Wingfield. John Donne. **CP-DonnJ**

ir Jo[s]hua praised Rubens with a Smile. William Blake. **CP-BlakW**

ir Joshua Praises Michael Angelo. William Blake. **CP-BlakW**

ir Joshua sent his own Portrait to. Florentine Ingratitude. William Blake. **CP-BlakW**

ir Launcelot and Queen Guinevere. Tennyson. **CP-TennA**

ir Luckless, troth, for luck's sake pass by one. To the Same [Sir Luckless Woo-All]. Ben Jonson. **CP-JonsB**

ir, more than kisses, letters mingle souls. To Sir Henry Wotton. John Donne. **CP-DonnJ**

ir Nameless, once of Athelhall, declared. The Children and Sir Nameless. Thomas Hardy. **CP-HardT**

ir, now unravelled [or unravell'd] is the Golden Fleece. To Dr. F. B. on His Book of Chess[e]. Richard Lovelace. **CP-LoveR**

ir, o'er a gill I gat your card. Extempore Epistle to Mr. McAdam of Craigengillian, (Wrote in Nanse Tinnock's, Mauchline) in Answer to an Obliging Letter He Sent in the Commencement of My Poetic Career. Robert Burns. **CP-BurnR**

Sir Richard's Song. Rudyard Kipling. **CP-KiplR** *Fr.* Young Men at the Manor. *Fr.* Puck of Pook's Hill.

Sir Rider Haggard / Was completely staggered. Wystan Hugh Auden. **FaBoCo** *Fr.* Academic Graffiti. **CP-AudeW**

Sir Robert wearied by Will Pulteney's teasings. On Mr. Pulteney Being Put Out of the Council. Jonathan Swift. **CP-SwifJ**

Sir S.J. Sir John Suckling. *See* Out upon it! I have loved [or lov'd].

Sir Thomas More. Robert Lowell. **SP-LoweR**

Sir Thomas Wortley's Sonnet Answered. Richard Lovelace. **CP-LoveR**

Sir Thopas. Geoffrey Chaucer. *Fr.* The Canterbury Tales. **CP-ChauG** (Tale of Sir Thopas, The.) **Par,** *ll.* 1–247; **BXAP,** *ll.* 1–248; **NAEL-1,** *ll.* 1–252;

Sir: though (I thank God for it) I do hate. Satire 2. John Donne. **OBSV** *Fr.* Satires. **CP-DonnJ**

Sir Toby Matthews. Sir John Suckling. **SeCV-1** *Fr.* A Poem with the Answer. **CP-SuckJ**

Sir W. Ralegh, on the Snuff of a Candle the Night Before He Died. Sir Walter Ralegh. *See* Cowards fear to die, but Courage stout.

Sir Walter Ra[u]le[i]gh to His Son[ne]. Sir Walter Ralegh. **CP-RaleW**

Sir Walter Ralegh to the Queen. Sir Walter Ralegh. **CP-RaleW**

Sir Walter Ralegh's [or S.W. Raghlies] Petition to the Queene 1618. Sir Walter Ralegh. **CP-RaleW**

Sir Walter Rawly made this rime upon the name of a gallant one Mr. Noel. Noe L. From the Diary of John Manningham of the Middle Temple. Sir Walter Ralegh. **CP-RaleW**

Sir Walter Vivian all a summer's day. Prologue. Tennyson. *Fr.* The Princess. **CP-TennA**

Sir Walter Vivian's House. Tennyson. **CBCK** *Fr.* Prologue: "Sir Walter Vivian all a summer's day." *Fr.* The Princess. **CP-TennA**

Sir! when I flew to seize the bird. Beau's Reply. William Cowper. **CP-CowpW**

Sir, will you let me give you a ride? The Pedestrian. Thomas Hardy. **CP-HardT**

Sir William MacGregor / Representative of Her Majesty the Queen. Cargo Songs. Thomas Merton. *Fr.* East. *Fr.* The Geography of Lograire. **CP-MertT**

Sir Winter. Christina Georgina Rossetti. **CP-RosC3**

Sir Wisdom's a fool when he's fou. Robert Burns. **OBCoV** *Fr.* The Jolly Beggars.

Sir, you were a credit to whatever. To a Teacher of French. Donald Davie. **CP-DavD0**

Sir. Your Head. It is stuck into the sand. Pocoangelini 7. Lewis Turco. **SP-TurcL**

Sir your sad absence I complain, as Earth (birth. The Triumphs of Philamore and Amoret. Richard Lovelace. **CP-LoveR**

"Sire Clerk of Oxenford," oure Hoost sayde. The Clerk's Prologue. Geoffrey Chaucer. *Fr.* The Canterbury Tales. **CP-ChauG**

"Sire Nonnes Preest," our Hoost seide anoon. Epilogue to the Nun's Priest's Tale. Geoffrey Chaucer. *Fr.* The Canterbury Tales. **CP-ChauG**

Siren. James McAuley. *Fr.* Ten-Mile Run. **SP-McAuJ**

Siren Song. Margaret Atwood. **HAP; NIP; PoA; WeW** *Fr.* Songs of the Transformed. **SP-AtwM1**

Sirens, The. Robinson Jeffers. **CP-JefR3**

Sirens, The. Richard Wilbur. **CP-WilbR**

Sirius: / what mystery is this? Hilda Doolittle. **PBWP** *Fr.* The Walls Do Not Fall. **CP-DoolH**

Sirmio. Catullus. *See* Carmen 31: "Apple of islands, Sirmio, & bright peninsulas, set."

Sirmio, thou dearest dear of strands. Catullus. *See* Carmen 31: "Apple of islands, Sirmio, & bright peninsulas, set."

Sirocco. Robert Penn Warren. *Fr.* To a Little Girl, One Year Old, in a Ruined Fortress. **SP-WarrR**

Sirocco at Deyá. Robert Ranke Graves. **CP-GravR**

Sirocco brings the minor devils. Cattivo Tempo. Wystan Hugh Auden. **CP-AudeW**

Sirs! may I shake your hands? The Patriot Engineer. George Meredith. **CP-MerG1**

Sirs, when you are in your last extremity. Gone Away Blues. Thomas McGrath. **SP-McGrT**

Siskins, The. Theodore Roethke. **CP-RoetT**

Sisley / Walked so nicely. Bag-Snatching in Dublin. Stevie Smith. **CP-SmitS**

Sister. Stephen Dunn. **SP-DunnS**

Sister, The. Marsden Hartley. **CP-HartM**

Sister. Langston Hughes. **SP-HughL**

Sister. John Greenleaf Whittier. **AA** *Fr.* Snow-Bound [or Snow-Bound; a Winter Idyl]. **CP-WhitJ**

Sister, a sister calling. Gerard Manley Hopkins. **FaBoVe** *Fr.* The Wreck of the Deutschland. **CP-HopkG**

Sister and mother and diviner love. To the One of Fictive Music. Wallace Stevens. **CP-StevW**

Sister Ann. Stephen Berg. **SP-BergS**

Sister Beach, Sister Garden. James Liddy. **CP-LiddJ**

Sister by the Pond, A. Donald Hall. **CP-HallD**

Sister hands it to me—the pod, The. Kennedy's Inauguration. Robert Bly. **SP-BlyR**

Sister Hours in circles linked, The. Alsace-Lorraine. George Meredith. **CP-MerG1**

Sister Hours in circles linked, The. George Meredith. *Fr.* Alsace-Lorraine. **CP-MerG1**

Sister I never had, The. Sister. Stephen Dunn. **SP-DunnS**

Sister in the snow, I took another family. Another Family. Leonard Cohen. **CP-CoheL**

Sister Maude. Christina Georgina Rossetti. **CP-RosC1**

Sister, Morning Is a Time for Miracles. Audre Lorde. **SP-LordA**

Sister of love-lorn Poets, Philomel! To the Nightingale. Samuel Taylor Coleridge. *Fr.* Effusions. **CP-ColeS**

Sister of Ophir. Emily Dickinson. **CP-DickE**

Sister, oh holy Sister. Litany of Grey Nurses. David Herbert Lawrence. *Fr.* Bits. **CP-LawrD**

Sister on the Tracks, A. Donald Hall. **CP-HallD**

Sister Rosa: A Ballad. Percy Bysshe Shelley. *Fr.* Poems from St. Irvyne, or, The Rosicrucian. **CP-ShelP**

Sister, sister, go to bed! Brother and Sister. "Lewis Carroll." **CP-CarrL**

Sister, tha knows while we was on th' planks. Violets. David Herbert Lawrence. **CP-LawrD**

Sister to Brother. Look, there it is—I'm sure that is the oak. Robert Pack. **SP-PackR**

Sister who told fortunes prophesied, The. From the Cupola. James Merrill. **SP-MerrJ**

Sister, you're ten today. Your first decade. Birthday. Dabney Stuart. **SP-StuaD**

Sisterhood. Marilyn Hacker. **SP-HackM**

Sisters. Adrienne Rich. **CP-RicAE; SP-RicA2**

Sisters. Anne Waldman. **SP-WaldA**

Sisters, The. John Greenleaf Whittier. **CP-WhitJ**

Sisters, I am sorry for this foreign man. David Herbert Lawrence. *Fr.* Bits. **CP-LawrD**

Sisters of Mercy. Leonard Cohen. **CP-CoheL**

Sisters! sisters! who sent you here? Fire, Famine, and Slaughter. Samuel Taylor Coleridge. **CP-ColeS**

Sister's Son. David Markson. **CP-MarkD**

Sisters: A Picture by Barry, The. John Greenleaf Whittier. **CP-WhitJ**

Sistine eye / The twisted thigh. If, The. Dead Salamander's Song. Jim Carroll. **SP-CarrJ**

Sit by the Window and Refuse. Charles Olson. **CP-OlsoC**

Sit doon by me, my canty freend. Robert Louis Stevenson. **CP-StevR**

Sit Down in the Lowest Room. Christina Georgina Rossetti. **CP-RosC2**

Sit Down, Master. Leonard Cohen. **CP-CoheL**

Sit, friend. We'll be drinking and I'll tell you why. Kostas Tympakianákis. James Merrill. **SP-MerrJ**

Sit further, and make room for thine own fame. *see also* Dignissimo Suo Amico Doctori Witty. Andrew Marvell. **CP-MarvA**

Sit like snaps. Your Nipples. Siv Cedering Fox. **SP-CedeS**

Sit on the bed. I'm blind, and three parts shell. A Terre. Wilfred Owen. **CP-OwenW**

Sitalkas. Hilda Doolittle. **CP-DoolH**

Site decoded from the air, The. The Roman Fort. John Hewitt. **CP-HewiJ**

Site echoes, The. At Delphi. May Sarton. **SP-SartM**

Sith I myself displease thee. Sir Thomas Wyatt. **CP-WyatT**

Sith it is so that I am thus refused. Sir Thomas Wyatt. **CP-WyatT**

Sith my life from life is parted. Mary Magdalen's Complaint at Christ's Death. Robert Southwell. **CP-SoutR**

Sitôt sorti de l'ermitage. Samuel Beckett. **CP-BeckS**

Sits on a hill. The Age of Romance. Richard Shelton. *Fr.* The Seven Ages of Man. **SP-ShelR**

Sittin' here thinkin' / Where does the money go. Money Blues. "Bob Dylan" *and* Jacques Levy. **CP-DylaB**

Sitting again on the front porch of the first cabin. Charles Wright. *Fr.* Three Poems of Departure. **SP-WrigC**

Sitting airborne on the. The Shuttle. John Updike. **CP-UpdiJ**

Sitting All Evening Alone in the Kitchen. Ted Kooser. **SP-KoosT**

Sitting alone (as one forsook). The Vision. Robert Herrick. **CP-HerrR**

Sitting Alone at Sunrise: Problems in the Space-Time Continuum. Miller Williams. **SP-WillM**

Sitting alone of a summer's evening. Brickenden, Hertfordshire. Stevie Smith. **CP-SmitS**

Sitting among the bluebells. Wendell Berry. *Fr.* The Strait. **CP-BerrW**

Sitting, and ready to be drawn. The Picture of the Body. Ben Jonson. NOSC *Fr.* Eupheme. **CP-JonsB**

Sitting and resting on the crest, looking far. May. Gary Snyder. *Fr.* Six Years. **CP-SnydG**

Sitting at the top of the stadium. Harvard Stadium. Richard Eberhart. **CP-EberR**

Sitting behind you in that rented city. Fireworks. Dabney Stuart. **SP-StuaD**

Sitting between the sea and the buildings. The Painter. John Ashbery. **SP-AshbJ**

Sitting by a Bush in Broad Sunlight. Robert Frost. **CP-FrosR**

Sitting by the streams that glide, *par. by* Thomas Carew. Bible, *O.T. See* Psalm 137: "By the rivers of Babylon. . . ."

Sitting Down. Pablo Neruda, *tr. fr. Spanish by* Ben Belitt. **SP-NeruP**

Sitting Down, Looking Up. Archie Randolph Ammons. **SP-AmmoA**

Sitting Here. Robert Creeley. **CP-CreeR**

Sitting here / doing nothing. Summer Twilight. Stephen Berg. **SP-BergS**

Sitting here in my house. Suburban Madrigal. John Updike. **CP-UpdiJ**

Sitting in a Sandwich Joint. Charles Bukowski. **SP-BukC1**

Sitting in a Small Screenhouse on a Summer Morning. James Wright. **CP-WrigJ**

Sitting in a tree-. Edward Estlin Cummings. **CP-CummE**

Sitting in the depths of this prison. For Han Shan on His Cold Mountain. Chuck Miller. **SP-MillC**

Sitting in the kitchen. Self-Portrait: Holding On. Al Young. **CP-YounA**

Sitting next to you. But You. Robert Creeley. **CP-CreeR**

Sitting on a Barbed-Wire Fence. "Bob Dylan." **CP-DylaB**

Sitting on a bench by the Rogue River, Oregon. Two Immortals. Gary Snyder. **CP-SnydG**

Sitting on a tree stump with half cup of tea. Cabin in the Rockies. Allen Ginsberg. **CP-GinsA**

Sitting on my kitchen table. Un Morceau en Forme de Poire. Diane Wakoski. **SP-WakoD**

Sitting on Some Rocks in Shaw Cove. Robert Bly. **SP-BlyR**

Sitting on the Bridge. Thomas Hardy. **CP-HardT**

Sitting once more outside the British Museum. Time for a Smoke. Louis MacNeice. **SP-MacNL**

Sitting up to fill pages. Robert Creeley. **CP-CreeR**

Sitting with the professors. The Professors. Charles Bukowski. **SP-BukC1**

Situation. Langston Hughes. **SP-HughL**

Situation Does Not Change, The. Howard Nemerov. **CP-NemeH**

Situation is blue and white, The. The Crucifixion of Noel. Marsden Hartley. **CP-HartM**

Situation of feeling increasingly. Robert Creeley. **CP-CreeR**

Sive canis silvas, Spencere, vel horrida belli. *acc. by English translation.* Thomas Campion. **CP-CampT**

S.I.W. Wilfred Owen. **CP-OwenW**

Siwashing It Out Once in Siuslaw Forest. Gary Snyder. *Fr.* Four Poems fo Robin. **CP-SnydG**

Six / are in a room's dark around). Edward Estlin Cummings. **CP-CummE**

Six, The. James Dickey. **CP-DickJ**

6 A.M. Charles Bukowski. **SP-BukC2**

Six A.M. / Sat down on excavation gravel. Magpie's Song. Gary Snyder. **CP-SnydG**

Six bells stopped, and in the dark I heard, The. Calvinistic Evensong. Sir John Betjeman. **CP-BetjJ**

Six blind women bustle along with arms linked. Santaigo: In Praise of Community. Stephen Dobyns. **SP-DobyS**

Six Boards, The. Thomas Hardy. **CP-HardT**

Six brothers in an autumn boat called me. Seis Hermanos. Charles Henri Ford. *Fr.* For Djuna Barnes. **SP-FordC**

Six calices yellow gold. Kathleen Jessie Raine. **SP-RainK**

Six Canons, The. Muriel Rukeyser. **CP-RukeM**

Six changeful years have vanished since I first. Residence in London. William Wordsworth. *Fr.* The Prelude; Growth of a Poet's Mind [1850 vers.]. **CP-WorW3**

Six Commissioned Texts. Wystan Hugh Auden. **CP-AudeW**

  Ballad of Barnaby, The. **OBNV**

  Moralities.

  Reminder, A.

  Runner.

   "All visible, visibly." **SD**

  Twelve, The.

  United Nations Hymn.

Six days and two thousand miles. The Way Back. Alun Lewis. **CP-LewiA**

Six days out of all the days. The Destruction of Carthage. Kenneth Patchen. **CP-PatcK**

Six Deliberate Acts, The. Roy Fisher.

  "Emptying his bowel / he sat. . . ." **SP-FishR**

  "Emptying his bowel / in the toilet. . . ." **SP-FishR**

  "He is going to the woman." **SP-FishR**

  "Only target / is the eyeball, The." **SP-FishR**

  "To see the film you buy a ticket." **SP-FishR**

  "Today / let us think." **SP-FishR**

Six demons came and cut down three tall trees. Hypocrite! Oxford Grouper! Yahoo! Malcolm Lowry. **CP-LowrM**

Six Epistles to Eva Hesse. Donald Davie. **CP-DavDo**

  Fifth Epistle.

  First Epistle.

  Fourth Epistle.

  Second Epistle.

  Sixth Epistle.

  Third Epistle.

Six feet from One to One. Amor Vincit Omnia. Wystan Hugh Auden. **CP-AudWJ**

6 Foot Goddess, The. Charles Bukowski. **SP-BukC1**

Six-foot nest of the sea-hawk, The. Sea-Hawk. Richard Eberhart. **CP-EberR**

Six hours a day I lay me down. Meditation in Hydrotherapy. Theodore Roethke. **CP-RoetT**

Six hundred years ago, more or less. After a Brubeck Concert. Miller Williams. **SP-WillM**

Six Inch Chapter—in Verse, A. Charles Olson. **CP-OlsoC**

Six larks are not so sweet as one. Arithmetic. John Hewitt. **CP-HewiJ**

Six leaves there are of these. Geometric Death. Marsden Hartley. **CP-HartM**

Six long days was the unseen God in labour with the earth. John Gould Fletcher. **SP-FletJ** *Fr.* Branches of Adam.

Six Maidens, The. Alexander Pope. **CP-PopeA**

Six miasmic women in green. Couples. Carl Sandburg. **CP-SandC**

Six month child, The. Slippery. Carl Sandburg. **CP-SandC**

Six months to six years added he remained. Epitaph. William Wordsworth. **CP-WorW1**

Six Naps in One Day. Donald Hall. **CP-HallD**

Six o'clock and / the sun rises. Love Poem. Miller Williams. **SP-WillM**

Six o'clock in Princes Street. Wilfred Owen. **CP-OwenW**

Six o'clock reveille: Scamblers Farm. July 2nd, 1916. Phoebe Hesketh. **SP-HeskP**

Six pigs at the breast of their mother, The. More Country People. Carl Sandburg. **CP-SandC**

Six Poems on Moving. Stephen Dobyns. **SP-DobyS**

Six Significant Landscapes. Wallace Stevens. **CP-StevW**

Six Something. James Schuyler. **CP-SchuJ**

Six street ends come together here. Blue Island Intersection. Carl Sandburg. **CP-SandC**

Six thankful weeks,—& let it be. Written in a Volume of Goethe. Ralph Waldo Emerson. **CP-EmerR**

Six thousand veterans practised in war's game. Sonnet in the Pass of Killicranky. William Wordsworth. **CP-WorW1**

6/21. Adrienne Rich. **SP-RicA1**

Six Variations. Denise Levertov. **CP-LeveD**

"Shlup, shlup, the dog." **HeIL; HeIP; InPK; Poetr**

Six whittled chickens. A Chinese Toy. William Carlos Williams. **CP-WilW1**

Six Winter Privacy Poems. Robert Bly. **SP-BlyR**

"About four, a few flakes."

Listening to Bach.

"More of the fathers are dying each day."

"My shack has two rooms; I use one."

On Meditation.

"When I woke, a new snow had fallen."

Six Years. Gary Snyder. **CP-SnydG**

April.

August.

December. **InPS**

Envoy to Six Years.

February.

January.

July.

June.

March.

May.

November.

October.

September.

Six Years Later. Joseph Brodsky, *tr. fr. Russian by* Richard Wilbur. **CP-WilbR**

Six Young Men. Ted Hughes. **SP-HughT**

Six/Nine/Forty-Four. David St. John. **SP-StJoD**

"Sixpence a week," says the girl to her lover. By Her Aunt's Grave. Thomas Hardy. **MoAB; MoBrPo** *Fr.* Satires of Circumstance in Fifteen Glimpses. **CP-HardT**

Sixteen and time to pay off I got this job in a piss factory. Piss Factory. Patti Smith. **SP-SmitP**

Sixteen Dead Men. William Butler Yeats. **CP-YeatW**

16 February. Patti Smith. **SP-SmitP**

1614 Boren. Richard Hugo. **CP-HugoR**

16 Lines. Gilbert Sorrentino. **SP-SorrG**

Sixteen Months. Carl Sandburg. **CP-SandC**

16. ix. 65. James Merrill. **SP-MerrJ**

XVI. "One day as I unwarily did gaze." Edmund Spenser. **OAEL-1** *Fr.* Amoretti. **CP-Spens**

Sixteen Poems in Eight Pairings. John Crowe Ransom. **SP-RansJ**

Agitato Ma Non Troppo ("I have a grief"). **OxBA**

Agitato Ma Non Troppo ("This is what the man said").

Birthday of an Aging Seer.

Conrad Sits in Twilight.

(Conrad in Twilight.) **MeMAP; OxBA**

Here Lies a Lady.

Here Lies a Lady. **AWP; CMoP; CoBMV; EvOK; HAP; HBMV; InvP; LiTM; MeMAP; MoAB; MoAmPo; MoP; NAAL-2; NoAM; PoRA; RB; TAP; TwAmPo; VGW**

Master's in the Garden Again.

Of Margaret ("Frost, and a leaf has quit the tulip tree").

Of Margaret ("With the fall of the first leaf that winds rend").

Overtures.

Prelude to an Evening.

Prelude to an Evening. **AP; CoBMV; EAS; MoAB; MoAmPo; MoPo; MoVE; NePA; OxBA; PoCh**

Semi-Centennial.

Tom, Tom, the Piper's Son.

Two Gentlemen Scholars.

Vanity of the Bright Boys, The.

Sixteen years, / Sixteen banners united over the field. Changing of the Guards. "Bob Dylan." **CP-DylaB**

16 years old. My Old Man. Charles Bukowski. **SP-BukC1**

Sixteen years. The narrow rough-gullied backroads. Sources. Adrienne Rich. **SP-RicA1**

Sixth and of creation last arose, The, *sels.* John Milton. *Fr.* Book VII. *Fr.* Paradise Lost. **CP-MiltJ**

Sixth Book, The. Archibald MacLeish. *Fr.* Conquistador. **CP-MacLA**

Sixth Elegy. River Elegy. Muriel Rukeyser. **CP-RukeM**

Sixth Epistle. Donald Davie. *Fr.* Six Epistles to Eva Hesse. **CP-DavDo**

Sixth Epistle of the First Book of Horace Imitated, The. Alexander Pope. **CP-PopeA**

Sixth-Month Song in the Foothills. Gary Snyder. **CP-SnydG**

Sixth Night: Waking, The. Muriel Rukeyser. **CP-RukeM**

Sixth Psalm. Anne Sexton. *Fr.* O Ye Tongues. **CP-SextA**

Sixth Satire of the Second Book of Horace Imitated, The. Alexander Pope. **CP-PopeA**

Sixth Song. Sir Philip Sidney. **OBSC** *Fr.* Astrophil and Stella. **SP-SidnP**

Sixth was August, being rich arrayed, The. August. Edmund Spenser. **GN** *Fr.* The Faerie Queene. **CP-Spens**

Sixth Winter, The. Edwin Rolfe. **CP-RolfE**

Sixty Five. William Everson. **SP-EverW**

LXV. "Doubt which ye misdeeme, fayre love, is vaine, The." Edmund Spenser. **NAEL-1** *Fr.* Amoretti. **CP-Spens**

Sixty odd years of poaching and drink. The Carter's Funeral. Wystan Hugh Auden. **CP-AudWJ**

LXI. "Glorious image of the Maker's beauty, The." Edmund Spenser. **Son** *Fr.* Amoretti. **CP-Spens**

Sixty, seventy, eighty: I would see you mellow. Randall Jarrell 1. October 1965. Robert Lowell. **SP-LoweR**

LXIII. "After long storms and tempests sad assay." Edmund Spenser. **FaBoEn; OAEL-1; OAEP; OBSC** *Fr.* Amoretti. **CP-Spens**

LXII. "Weary year his race now having run, The." Edmund Spenser. **OBSC** *Fr.* Amoretti. **CP-Spens**

60 Yard Pass. Charles Bukowski. **SP-BukC3**

Size, The. George Herbert. **CP-HerbG**

Size and Tears. "Lewis Carroll." **CP-CarrL**

Size circumscribes—it has no room. Emily Dickinson. **CP-DickE**

Size of a small skull, and like a skull segmented. To a Box Turtle. John Updike. **CP-UpdiJ**

Size of Song, The. John Ciardi. **SP-CiarJ**

Sizing. Archie Randolph Ammons. **SP-AmmoA**

Sizzle of the Coleman, The. The Voyeur. Mona Van Duyn. **SP-VanDM**

Skagway. John Haines. **SP-HainJ**

Skald's Death. "Hugh MacDiarmid." **SP-MacDH**

Skateboard. Thom Gunn. **CP-GunnT**

Skateboard Throne: an Ode to Citizen Amputees, The. Laurence Lieberman. **SP-LiebL**

Skaters, The. John Ashbery.

"Old heavens, you used to tweak above us." **SP-AshbJ**

"Wind thrashes the maple seed-pods, The." **SP-AshbJ**

Skaters, The. Charles Bukowski. **SP-BukC3**

Skaters, The. Randall Jarrell. **CP-JarrR**

Skating. Edward Estlin Cummings. **CP-CummE**

Skating. William Wordsworth. **CH; SD** *Fr.* Introduction—Childhood and School-Time. **EnRP; FHYEP** *Fr.* The Prelude; Growth of a Poet's Mind [1850 vers.]. **CP-WorW3**

Skein bottoms them together, A. Charlock per Winkle. Louis Zukofsky. **CP-ZukLS**

Skeleton, The. Robert Creeley. **CP-CreeR**

Skeleton Bride. Phoebe Hesketh. **SP-HeskP**

Skeleton in Armor [*or* Armour], The. Henry Wadsworth Longfellow. **SP-LongH**

Skeleton in the Closet, The. Ted Kooser. **SP-KoosT**

Skeleton of the Future, The. "Hugh MacDiarmid." **SP-MacDH**

Skeleton produces flesh enemy, The. Solipsism While Dying. Margaret Atwood. **SP-AtwM1**

Skelpick. Donald Davie. **CP-DavDo**

Skeptic, The. Ralph Waldo Emerson. **CP-EmerR**

Skeptic. Robert Frost. **CP-FrosR**

Skerryvore. Robert Louis Stevenson. **CP-StevR**

Skerryvore: the Parallel. Robert Louis Stevenson. **CP-StevR**

Sketch. Stephen Berg. **SP-BergS**

Sketch. Robert Burns. **CP-BurnR**

Sketch, A. Byron. *See* A Sketch from Private Life.

Sketch, A. Herman Melville. **SP-MelvH** *Fr.* Clarel: A Poem and Pilgrimage in the Holy Land.

Sketch, A. Christina Georgina Rossetti. **CP-RosC3**

Sketch. Carl Sandburg. **CP-SandC**

Sketch, A. Richard Wilbur. **CP-WilbR**

Sketch for a Portrait of Henry Ford. William Carlos Williams. **CP-WilW2**

Sketch for a Portrait of Mme. G————M————. Archibald MacLeish. **CP-MacLA**

Sketch for an Elegy. Robert Burns. **CP-BurnR**

Sketch for the First Exhibition of the New Heroic Art. Roy Fisher. **SP-FishR** *Fr.* On the Neglect of Figure Composition.

Sketch from Private Life, A. Byron. **CP-Byron** (Sketch, A.) **CP-Byron**

Sketch. Inscribed to the Rt. Hon. Ch. J. Fox Esq. Robert Burns. **CP-BurnR**

Sketch. New Year's Day. To Mrs. Dunlop. Robert Burns. **CP-BurnR**

Sketch of a Poet. Carl Sandburg. **CP-SandC**

Sketch of His Own Character. Thomas Gray. **CP-GrayT**

Sketch of the Great Dejection, A. Thom Gunn. **CP-GunnT**

Sketch of the Ultimate Politician. Wallace Stevens. **CP-StevW**

Skew Lines. Denise Levertov. **CP-LeveD**

Ski-rails run down the sugar-loaf. January 1938. Randall Jarrell. **CP-JarrR**

Skia, An Ode on the Isle of Skye. Samuel Johnson. **CP-JohnS**

Skier, The. Diane Wakoski. **SP-WakoD**

Skier and the Mountain, The. Richard Eberhart. **CP-EberR**

Skiers. Robert Penn Warren. **SP-WarrR**

Skies can't keep their secret!, The. Emily Dickinson. **CP-DickE**

Skies may be blue;yes. Edward Estlin Cummings. **CP-CummE**

Skies remind you of those mounds of custard, The. James Fenton. *See* Lollipops of the Pomeranian Baroque.

Skies they were ashen and sober, The. Ulalume [*or* Ulalume—a Ballad]. Edgar Allan Poe. **CP-PoeEd**

Skimming, bruising, overloading, / diverting the traffic of signs. Words. Phoebe Hesketh. **SP-HeskP**

Skimming lightly, wheeling still. Shiloh [A Requiem]. Herman Melville. **SP-MelvH**

Skimpy Day at the Solstice. Marge Piercy. **SP-PierM**

Skin. Philip Larkin. **CP-LarkP**

Skin / of my poems, The. Genesis. Etheridge Knight. **SP-KnigE**

Skin-Flying into the Storm Center. Laurence Lieberman. **SP-LiebL**

Skin is broken, The. The hotel breakfast china. Houseboat Days. John Ashbery. **SP-AshbJ**

Skin of the sea, The. In Sylvia Plath Country. Erica Jong. **SP-JongE**

Skin seethes in the heat, The. A Sunday Drive. Margaret Atwood. **SP-AtwM2**

Skin Song. Laurence Lieberman. **SP-LiebL**

Skinful of bowls, he bowls them. Second Glance at a Jaguar. Ted Hughes. **SP-HughT**

Skink, The. Ogden Nash. **CP-NashO**

Skinned corpse of a lion, The. The Manifold Fusions. Kenneth Patchen. **CP-PatcK**

Skinns he din'd well to day; how do you think? Upon Skinns. Robert Herrick. **CP-HerrR**

Skinny. Shel Silverstein. **SP-SilS2**

Skinny kids in shorts get cups. In the House of the Rising Sun. Gary Snyder. **CP-SnydG**

Skinny voice / of the leatherfaced, The. Edward Estlin Cummings. **CP-CummE**

Skinny waterfalls, footpaths, The. Lastness. Galway Kinnell. **SP-KinnG**

Skip, The. James Fenton. **SP-FentJ**

Skipper Ireson's Ride. John Greenleaf Whittier. **CP-WhitJ**

Skirting the river road, (my forenoon walk, my rest,). The Dalliance of the Eagles. Walt Whitman. **CP-WhitW**

Skis won't creak again, The. This Cold. Stephen Berg. **SP-BergS**

Skoles stinks so deadly, that his Breeches loath. Upon Skoles. Robert Herrick. **CP-HerrR**

Skreak and skritter of evening gone, The. Autumn Refrain. Wallace Stevens. **CP-StevW**

Skrew lives by shifts; yet sweares by no small oathes. Upon Skrew. Robert Herrick. **CP-HerrR**

Skull. David Markson. **CP-MarkD**

Skull, / museum object. Waking Alone. Anne Sexton. **CP-SextA**

Skulls, The. Frederick Morgan. **SP-MorgF**

Skulls. Finalities. They emerge. Skullshapes. Charles Tomlinson. **CP-TomlC**

Skullshapes. Charles Tomlinson. **CP-TomlC**

Skunk, The. Seamus Heaney. **SP-HeanS**

Skunk Cabbage. Mary Oliver. **SP-OlivM**

Skunk Hour. Robert Lowell. **SP-LoweR**

Skunks. Robinson Jeffers. **CP-JefR3**

Skurffe by his Nine-bones sweares, and well he may. Upon Skurffe. Robert Herrick. **CP-HerrR**

Sky. Tom Clark. **SP-ClarT**

Sky. Leonard Cohen. **CP-CoheL**

Sky. Barton Sutter. **SP-SuttB**

Sky / was   can dy / lu   mi, The, *See also* The / sky. . .). Edward Estlin Cummings. **CP-CummE**

Sky a silver, The. Edward Estlin Cummings. **CP-CummE**

Sky and sea, horizon-hinged. The Hermit at Outermost House. Sylvia Plath. **CP-PlatS**

Sky and the sea put on a show, The. Thimble Islands. Carl Sandburg. **CP-SandC**

Sky begins to lower and thick'ning Clouds, The. A Thunder Storm. William Cowper. **CP-CowpW**

Sky behind the farthest shore, The. Water Night. Muriel Rukeyser. **CP-RukeM**

Sky black black clouds and black rain falls. That blond wound. The Builders. Kenneth Patchen. **CP-PatcK**

Sky-born and royal. Hercules and Antaeus. Seamus Heaney. **SP-HeanS**

Sky brims with the ghost of a great rage, The. Frank Templeton Prince. *Fr.* Apollo and the Sibyl. **CP-PrinF**

Sky-coloured bird, blue wings with no more spots of spotless white. Edna St. Vincent Millay. **CP-MillE**

Sky darkened watching you, The. Jack. Randall Jarrell. **CP-JarrR**

Sky Eats Up the Trees, The. James Schuyler. **CP-SchuJ**

Sky full of blue nothing toward which the Magi. Birds. Tom Clark. **SP-ClarT**

Sky has given over, The. Spring Storm. William Carlos Williams. **CP-WilW1**

Sky has murder in the eye, and I, The. The Nature of a Mirror. Robert Penn Warren. **SP-WarrR**

Sky immense, bejewelled with rain of stars, The. Night of Stars. John Gould Fletcher. *Fr.* Sand and Spray: A Sea-Symphony. **SP-FletJ**

Sky in the trees, the trees mixed up, The. Landscape at the End of the Century. Stephen Dunn. **SP-DunnS**

Sky is alone tonight, The. The Naked Surgeon. Michael Hartnett. **SP-HarMi**

Sky is changed!—and such a change! Oh night, The. Byron. **NOBRP** *Fr.* Is thy face like thy mother's, my fair child. *Fr.* Childe Harold's Pilgrimage. **CP-Byron**

Sky is green, and there is no book to tell us what it means, The. John Yau. *See* Engines of Gloom and Affection.

Sky is lead, and our faces are red, The. Rudyard Kipling. **CP-KiplR** *Fr.* At the End of the Passage. *Fr.* Life's Handicap.

Sky is low—the Clouds are mean, The. Emily Dickinson. **CP-DickE**

Sky is overcast, The. A Night-Piece. William Wordsworth. **CP-WorW1**

Sky is pitiless I beg, The. The Dog Wants His Dinner. James Schuyler. **CP-SchuJ**

Sky is ruddy in the east, The. The Ship-Builders. John Greenleaf Whittier. **CP-WhitJ**

Sky is torn across, The. On a Wedding Anniversary. Dylan Thomas. **CP-ThomD**

Sky is unmistakeable. Not lurid, not low, not black, The. Haying Before Storm. Muriel Rukeyser. **CP-RukeM**

Sky like fishblood. Hayden Carruth. *Fr.* North Winter. **CP-CarHL**

Sky minted into golden sequins, The. Gerard Manley Hopkins. *Fr.* Fragments. **CP-HopkG**

Sky of brightest gray seems dark, The. Comparison. Paul Laurence Dunbar. **CP-DunbP**

Sky of gray is eaten in six places, The. Broken Sky. Carl Sandburg. **CP-SandC**

Sky, paid to be blue, The. Raining in Magens Bay. John Updike. **CP-UpdiJ**

Sky Pieces. Carl Sandburg. **CP-SandC**

Sky-Prospect—From the Plain of France. William Wordsworth. *Fr.* Memorials of a Tour of the Continent; 1820. **CP-WorW2**

Sky Seasoning. Shel Silverstein. **SP-SilS2**

Sky seemed so small that winter day, The. Two Illustrations That the World Is What You Make of It. Wallace Stevens. **CP-StevW**

Sky Sign. Charles Bukowski. **SP-BukC3**

Sky sinks its blue teeth, The. For an Earth-Landing. Erica Jong. **SP-JongE**

Sky Talk. Carl Sandburg. **CP-SandC**

Sky, the Sea, The. Roy Fisher. **SP-FishR**

Sky too hot for photographs, A. In Provence. Daniel Gerard Hoffman. **SP-HoffD**

Sky was cold December blue with great tumbling clouds, and the, The. Steelhead, Wild Pig, the Fungus. Robinson Jeffers. **CP-JefR2**

Sky was glowering so thick that day in Keokuk. Keokuk. Richard Hugo. **CP-HugoR**

Sky was like a waterdrop, The. Remembrance. Walter de la Mare. **CP-DeLaW**

Sky, Water. Charles Kenneth Williams. **CP-WillC**

Sky widens to Cornwall, The. A sense of sea. In Memoriam: A. C., R. J. O., K. S. Sir John Betjeman. **CP-BetjJ** *Fr.* Old Friends. **CP-BetjJ**

Sky widens to Cornwall, The. A sense of sea. Old Friends. Sir John Betjeman. **CP-BetjJ**

Sky Writing. Charles Tomlinson. **CP-TomlC**

Sky yellow sky. Hayden Carruth. *Fr.* North Winter. **CP-CarHL**

Skyey Developments. John Updike. **CP-UpdiJ**

Skykomish River Running. Richard Hugo. **CP-HugoR**

Skylarks. Ted Hughes. **SP-HughT**

"All the dreary Sunday morning." **HAP**, *sect.* 6;

"Crueller than owl or eagle." **HAP**

"I suppose you just gape and let your gaspings." **HAP**

"Lark begins to go up, The." **HAP**

"Like those flailing flames." **HAP**, *sect.* 7;

"Manacled with blood."

"My idleness curdles." **HAP**, *sect.* 5;

"You stop to rest, far up, you teeter."

Skylike limpid eyes, The. Brennbaum. Ezra Pound. **MoAmPo** *Fr.* Hugh Selwyn Mauberley. (Life and Contacts). **SP-PounE**

Skypiece. John Hewitt. **CP-HewiJ**

Skyreholme Mill. Wystan Hugh Auden. **CP-AudWJ**

Skyreholme Mill. Wystan Hugh Auden. **CP-AudWJ**

Sky's blue and clear usually, The. It Is. Stephen Berg. **SP-BergS**

Skyscraper. Carl Sandburg. **CP-SandC**

Skyscraper Loves Night, The. Carl Sandburg. **CP-SandC**

Skyscrapers of the Financial District Dance with Gasman, The. Marge Piercy. **SP-PierM**

Skyscrapers Stand Proud. Carl Sandburg. **CP-SandC**

Skystones. Pablo Neruda.

"From the breach to the iron explosion." **SP-NeruP**

"I entered the cave of the amethysts." **SP-NeruP**

"I want the jailed / light to awaken: I want." **SP-NeruP**

"Quartz opens its eyes in the snow." **SP-NeruP**

"Stone, toppled by water and mountain, The." **SP-NeruP**

"When all turned to altitude." **SP-NeruP**

Slabs of the Sunburnt West. Carl Sandburg. **CP-SandC**

Slag pile seeps into the sulphured stream, The. Winter Day (Coal Country). Louise McNeill. **SP-McNeL**

Slain for man, slain for me, O Lamb of God, look down. Slain from the Foundation of the World. Christina Georgina Rossetti. **CP-RosC2**

Slain from the Foundation of the World. Christina Georgina Rossetti. **CP-RosC2**

Slain in their high places: fallen on rest. Christina Georgina Rossetti. **CP-RosC2**

Slants at Buffalo, New York. Carl Sandburg. **CP-SandC**

Slash of angular blacks, A. The Public Square. Wallace Stevens. **CP-StevW**

Slash of Blue, A. Emily Dickinson. **CP-DickE**

Slave Coffle. Maya Angelou. **SP-AngeM**

Slave Quarters. James Dickey. **CP-DickJ**

Slave Ship, The. Louise Glück. **SP-GlücL**

Slave-Ships, The. John Greenleaf Whittier. **CP-WhitJ**

Slave Singing at Midnight, The. Henry Wadsworth Longfellow. **SP-LongH**

Slave that Cinna's named his cook, The. Martial, *tr.* by William Matthews. **SP-MattW** *Fr.* Epigrams.

Slave to a God whose sole known verb is *Flatter!* He. Howard Nemerov. **CP-NemeH**

Slave to love's unbounded sway, A. O Lay Thy Loof in Mine Lass. Robert Burns. **CP-BurnR**

Slave yet wearing on my head a crown, A. Epitaph. Christina Georgina Rossetti. **CP-RosC3**

Slavery. Robert Herrick. **CP-HerrR**

Slave's Critique of Practical Reason, The. Rita Dove. **SP-DoveR**

Slave's Lament, The. Robert Burns. **CP-BurnR**

Slaves of Martinique, The. John Greenleaf Whittier. **CP-WhitJ**

Slay with your eyes, Greek. Toward the Piraeus. Hilda Doolittle. **CP-DoolH**

Sled Burial, Dream Ceremony. James Dickey. **CP-DickJ**

Sleds of the children, The. The Rites of Darkness. Kenneth Patchen. **CP-PatcK**

Sleek as a lizard at round of a stone. Penetration and Trust. George Meredith. **CP-MerG1**

Sleep. Wendell Berry. **CP-BerrW**

Sleep, The. Elizabeth Barrett Browning. **CP-BroEB**

Sleep. Charles Bukowski. **SP-BukC2**

Sleep. Robert Creeley. **CP-CreeR**

Sleep. Walter de la Mare. **CP-DeLaW**

Sleep. John Haines. **SP-HainJ**

Sleep. Ron Koertge. **SP-KoerR**

Sleep. David Herbert Lawrence. **CP-LawrD**

Sleep. William Matthews. **SP-MattW**

Sleep. James Schuyler. **CP-SchuJ**

Sleep. James Schuyler. **CP-SchuJ**

Sleep. Sir Philip Sidney. *See* Sonnet 39: "Come sleep, O sleep, the certain knot of peace."

Sleep. Robert Southwell. **CBCK** *Fr.* Saint Peter's Complaint. **CP-SoutR**

Sleep. Georg Trakl, *tr. fr. German by* James Wright. **CP-WrigJ**

Sleep after Toil. Edmund Spenser. *See* He there now does enjoy eternal rest.

Sleep and Poetry. John Keats. **CP-KeatJ**

"And can I ever bid these joys farewell?" **TOF**

"Could all this be forgotten? Yes, a schism." **ChER**

"O for ten years, that I may overwhelm." **NAEL-2; OAEL-2**

"O Poesy! for thee I hold my pen." **FHYEP**

"Schism, A / Nurtured by foppery and barbarism." **EPCY**

"Stop and consider! life is but a day." **OBRV; SeCePo; TreFT**

Sleep and Waking. David Herbert Lawrence. **CP-LawrD**

Sleep, Angry Beauty. Thomas Campion. **CP-CampT**

Sleep, angry beauty, sleep, and fear[e] not me. Sleep, Angry Beauty. Thomas Campion. **CP-CampT**

Sleep at last has fled these eyes. Watching unto God in the Night-Season. Jeanne Marie Bouvier de la Motte-Guyon, *tr. fr. French by* William Cowper. **CP-CowpW**

Sleep at noon. Window blind. Hurricane. Archibald MacLeish. **CP-MacLA**

Sleep at Sea. Christina Georgina Rossetti. **CP-RosC1**

Sleep brings no joy to me. Emily Brontë. **CP-BronE**

Sleep by the Hot Stream. Thom Gunn. *Fr.* The Geysers. **CP-GunnT**

Sleep, Ellen Aubrey, sleep, and dream of me. Tennyson. **CBLP** *Fr.* Audley Court. **CP-TennA**

Sleep-Gummed Eyes. James Schuyler. **CP-SchuJ**

Sleep half sleep half silence and with reasons. Ted Berrigan. **SP-BerrT** *Fr.* The Sonnets.

Sleep: here's your bed. . . You'll not come, any more, to ours. *ad. fr. the French of* Tristan Corbière. Randall Jarrell. **CP-JarrR**

Sleep, morns of a snail. Sleepwalking. Christian J. Van Geel, *tr. fr. Dutch by* Adrienne Rich. **CP-RicAE**

Sleep Impression. Carl Sandburg. **CP-SandC**

Sleep in the Mojave Desert. Sylvia Plath. **CP-PlatS**

Sleep is a maker of makers. Birds sleep. Feet cling to a perch. Look at. Sleepyheads. Carl Sandburg. **CP-SandC**

Sleep is a suspension midway. Carl Sandburg. *Fr.* The People, Yes. **CP-SandC**

Sleep is supposed to be. Emily Dickinson. **CP-DickE**

Sleep is the gift of many spiders. Drowsy. Carl Sandburg. **CP-SandC**

Sleep, kinsman thou to death and trance. Tennyson. *Fr.* In Memoriam A. H. H. **CP-TennA**

Sleep, let me sleep, for I am sick of care. Looking Forward. Christina Georgina Rossetti. **CP-RosC3**

Sleep, little babe, on my knee. Void in Law. Elizabeth Barrett Browning. **CP-BroEB**

Sleep, little Baby, sleep, / The holy angels love thee. Holy Innocents. Christina Georgina Rossetti. **CP-RosC3**

Sleep, my body, sleep, my ghost. Louis MacNeice. *Fr.* Autumn Journal. **CP-MacNL**

"Sleep serene, avoid the backward." **CMoP**

Sleep, my darling, sleep. Louis MacNeice. **CP-MacNL**

(Cradle Song for Eleanor.) **CP-MacNL**

Sleep, my son, and smile in sleep. Lullaby: Smile in Sleep. Robert Penn Warren. **SP-WarrR**

Sleep not, dream not; this bright day. Emily Brontë. **CP-BronE**

(A.A.A.) **CP-BronE**

Sleep of this night deepens, The. Under Stars. Tess Gallagher. **SP-GallT**

Sleep on, baby, on the floor. Sleeping and Watching. Elizabeth Barrett Browning. **CP-BroEB**

Sleep serene, avoid the backward. Louis MacNeice. **CMoP** *Fr.* Sleep, my body, sleep, my ghost. *Fr.* Autumn Journal. **CP-MacNL**

Sleep, Sleep Happy Child; All Creation Slept and Smiled. Christina Georgina Rossetti. **CP-RosC3**

Sleep Sleep; in thy sleep. William Blake. *See* Cradle Song, A: "Sleep, sleep, beauty bright."

Sleep, sleep, mine Holy One! The Virgin Mary to the Child Jesus. Elizabeth Barrett Browning. **CP-BroEB**

Sleep sleep old sun, thou canst not have repast [*or* repassed].   Resurrection, Imperfect.   John Donne.   **CP-DonnJ**

Sleep, sleep on! forget thy pain.   The Magnetic Lady to Her Patient.   Percy Bysshe Shelley.   **CP-ShelP**

Sleep softly. . . eagle forgotten. . . under the stone.   The Eagle That Is Forgotten.   Nicholas Vachel Lindsay.   **CP-LindV**

Sleep Song.   Carl Sandburg.   **CP-SandC**

Sleep, sweet babe! my cares beguiling.   *tr. from anonymous Latin print.*   Samuel Taylor Coleridge.   **CP-ColeS**

Sleep, that knits up the ravell'd sleeve of care.   The Winter Night.   Charlotte Smith.   **CP-SmitC**

Sleep till death.   Nicolas-Sébastien Roch Chamfort, *tr. fr. French by* Samuel Beckett.

Sleep, unforgotten sorrow, sleep awhile.   Acme.   Christina Georgina Rossetti.   **CP-RosC3**

Sleep-Worker, The.   Thomas Hardy.   **CP-HardT**

Sleepe, Death's allye, oblivion of teares.   Sleep.   Robert Southwell.   **CBCK** *Fr.* Saint Peter's Complaint.   **CP-SoutR**

Sleepe fy possess mee nott, nor doe nott fright.   Sonnet 16.   Mary Sidney, Countess of Montgomery Wroth.   *Fr.* Pamphilia to Amphilanthus.   **CP-WrotM**

Sleeper, The ("As Ann came in. . .").   Walter de la Mare.   **CP-DeLaW**

Sleeper, The ("The Lovely sleeping. . .").   Walter de la Mare.   **CP-DeLaW**

Sleeper, The.   Edgar Allan Poe.   **CP-PoeEd**

Sleepers.   James Dickey.   **CP-DickJ**

Sleepers, The.   Sylvia Plath.   **CP-PlatS**

Sleepers, The.   Walt Whitman.   **CP-WhitW**

Sleeping.   Donald Hall.   **CP-HallD**

Sleeping and Watching.   Elizabeth Barrett Browning.   **CP-BroEB**

Sleeping at last, the trouble and tumult over.   Christina Georgina Rossetti.   **CP-RosC3**

Sleeping Beauty, The.   Hayden Carruth.   **CP-CarHL**

"Ain't that something? Why, I knowed old Tom."

"And he stood at his window and shook his fist at a cloud."

"And in the town, in neon-blaring twilight."

"And there in the sky is the known face half-hidden."

"Any fire will do - you who are sleeping."

"As doctor Peter said."

"As movement seen, so is the sound, the singing."

"As Rousseau was another, singing."

"As the broken front differential pops and jumps."

"*As you or I, but at least he fights hard to get.*"

"Back of Budbill's where it dreens offn the ledges. Snugger."

"*Better, goddamn it. Why, whenever I see folks.*"

"Bleakness in the town."

"Blizzard in the mountains. Dusk. The cabin's light."

"Border is what creates illegal aliens, The."

"Called him 'Big Joe' yes and Joe Turner it was his name."

"Came in upon him once how he might find."

"Death, he thinks. In fact he has thought it every day."

"Destinies, destinations: In Morrisville."

"Dornröschen, princess."

"Down there like. Maybe not the same, of course."

" 'For fifteen years he never knew I never'."

"Full of the moon. In pine woods a snowlight, The."

" 'Good-bye,' they always whisper, "oh God," clinging."

"*Hah! not what's wrote down, I reckon. I'm leaving.*"

"Half-turned, as if reluctant, the lady of water."

"He decided to live. Alone. One room. Quaking."

"He goes out with his chainsaw into the cold bright."

"He reads: / 'That is one of the great tragedies'."

"He reads there, only a boy, fifteen, in the dingy."

"He remembers: / There was this big house they called the Hatch."

"He said: / All right then, I *was*, o.k.? Screwing."

"He thinks how, often when his semen spews."

"He thinks in wonder how love was all that was."

"He thinks of classical women."

"He used to think his escape was in lucidity."

"He was a soldier, he was a madman, he was a hermit."

"His body, caught there in the mirror, lean."

"His dream: / He is dressed in a white sheet, riding."

"House out to sea."

"In France, through archways, the archaic stonework."

"In the exigencies of consciousness."

"In the mind's house of heaven the great night never."

"In wavering shadow and silted with soot, her face."

"It was Catlett driving, de Paris blowing strong."

"It's awful, Amos."

"Jays shrieking in the fir clump, a world enraged."

"*La colline du mystère.* Solitary here. The stone."

"Late. The back road 'slicker than owl shit.' Snow."

"Making love in the cabin, not to himself."

"Maybe because they're so damn frigging rich."

"Mingled, windows stuffed with grainsacks, 'Lots'."

" 'My mother did it. She had to,' she said. She took."

"Named she was a Smith, born Smith, but how related."

"Near Addison now."

"Nine, he thinks, and every one a failure."

"No love without hurt? No lovesong without distortion?"

"Oaks and dark pines, remote, the northern forest."

"Odds & ends: / Enosburg Falls & Geof's cabin."

"Okay, Fulke Greville: 'None can well behold'."

"*Or independence, call it what you blame well like.*"

"Our own hearts too like, seems's-zo, whenever."

"Out of nothing."

"People burned, came apart, suffocated, melted."

"Plains of snow. The buntings whirl like rung."

"Poem moves. / After the fierce intention, The."

"Poem moves north, The."

"Point is (maybe) that the woman's face was *made*, The."

"Princess, the poem is born and you have woken."

"Recurrently he also dreams."

"Rise up and proclaim themselves, and his skin."

"Shall he then finally 'put away childish things'."

" 'Shock? Is that what you're asking? My dear, I was a'."

"Slows. A bent figure in the dark, thickly clothed."

"Some don't get much, Amos."

"Spirit / let there be even in the last hour."

"Spirit / whatever you are wherever."

"Springtime so impetuous. Already pink blossoms, The."

"*Store, more'n likely, in one of those tenements.*"

" 'Thee knows. Must thee not knowe?' I so saying."

"Then from beyond, from nowhere, from the wilderness."

"Then here was where it began, dear sleeping princess."

"Then rapture is self in itself entranced. And love?"

"There where pines darken the water above the brookbed."

" 'They tossed my baby like a cat in the air'."

"Three persons are here, of whom the first."

"To her, to *be* her, that her hurt and wrong be mine."

"Upward through the dark, this."

"Voided by too many hopes betrayed, too many."

"Was she innocent? Too beautiful for that."

"We thought the château was safe. The men were gone."

"When them old hooters had plenty eating material."

"*Which ain't much barn at that, maybe twenty head.*"

"Why dost thou tear me? Had I done thee hurt?"

"Why is the face in the water a woman? Because."

"Wind in the pines, a dark, damp, Novemb'ring wind."

"Wind sighing, crying, singing in the pines. Who knows."

"You, Amos? But you're dead now."

"You are the dreamer who dreams the world, and yet."

"You know what?"

"You lay there on that couch as if in effigy."

"You then. Your eyes hooded, shrewd a little."

"Your dream: / At first its name is Heliopolis."

"Your dream: / Her name was Hestia, sister of God."

"Your dream: / His name is Heraclitus, and he is huge."

"Your dream: / His name was Hannibal, i.e., by Baal's."

"Your dream: / His name was Harlequin. He wore the mask."

"Your dream: / His name was Heathcliff, and he was clearly."

"Your dream: / His name was Hegel, a dear sweet man."

"Your dream: / His name was Hendryk Hudson. And oh, the glory!"

"Your dream: / His name was Hermann, tender, quiet."

"Your dream: / His name was Hermes, and he was all to all."

"Your dream: / His name was Hero, and his other name."

"Your dream: / His name was Herod. No? How close."

"Your dream: / His name was Hesiod, a darkish man."

"Your dream: / His name was Hilarity but he never laughed."

"Your dream: / His name was Hitler and he lived over."

"Your dream: / His name was Hölderlin. Ah, name, name!"

"Your dream: / His name was Homer. He was blind."

"Your dream: / His name was Husband, his title Herr."

"Your dream: / His name was unheard of, very strange."

"Your dream: / Its name apparently is Honeywell."

"Your dream: / Its peculiar name is Hydrogen Bomb."

"Your dream: / The letters HIV appear."

"Your dream is Hamlet again."

Sleeping Beauty. Howard Nemerov. **CP-NemeH**

Sleeping Beauty, The. Wilfred Owen. **CP-OwenW**

Sleeping Beauty: Variation of the Prince, The. Randall Jarrell. **CP-JarrR**

Sleeping Brute, The. William Carlos Williams. **CP-WilW2**

Sleeping Cat. Ted Kooser. **SP-KoosT**

Sleeping City, The. George Meredith. **CP-MerG1**

Sleeping dog before the stove, The. The Response. John Hewitt. **CP-HewiJ**

Sleeping face folds down over this human country, The. Boxers Hit Harder When Women Are Around. Kenneth Patchen. **CP-PatcK**

Sleeping Fury, The. Louise Bogan. **CP-BogaL**

Sleeping Giant, The. Donald Hall. **CP-HallD**

Sleeping House, The. Tennyson. **FaBoEn; OBNC** *Fr.* Maud has a garden of roses. **FHYEP** *Fr.* Maud [A Monodrama]. **CP-TennA**

Sleeping in fever, I am unfit. For God While Sleeping. Anne Sexton. **CP-SextA**

Sleeping in the Forest. Mary Oliver. **SP-OlivM**

Sleeping map lay green, and we who were never much, The. The Leasing of September. John Ashbery. **SP-AshbJ**

Sleeping on the Ceiling. Elizabeth Bishop. **CP-BishE**

Sleeping on the Wing. Frank O'Hara. **SP-OharF**

Sleeping Out at Easter. James Dickey. **CP-DickJ**

Sleeping Over. Charles Kenneth Williams. **CP-WillC**

Sleeping Sardines. Shel Silverstein. **SP-SilS2**

Sleeping Standing Up. Elizabeth Bishop. **CP-BishE**

Sleeping, turning in turn like planets. Adrienne Rich. **PeHV; TRP** *Fr.* Twenty-one Love Poems. **SP-RicA1; SP-RicA2**

Sleeping, we boarded a boat. Frederick Morgan. *Fr.* The River. **SP-MorgF**

Sleeping Winds. Louis MacNeice. **CP-MacNL**

   East.

   North.

   South.

   West.

Sleeping with Women. Kenneth Koch. **SP-KochK**

Sleeping with You. John Updike. **CP-UpdiJ**

Sleeping woman dreams she wakes, A. Nightmare. Isabella Gardner. **CP-GardI**

Sleeping Woodman. Written in April 1790, The. Charlotte Smith. **CP-SmitC**

Sleeping Youth, A. John Keats. **SeCePo** *Fr.* Endymion: Poetic Romance. **CP-KeatJ**

Sleepless. Robert Lowell. **SP-LoweR**

Sleepless. Stephen Spender. **CP-SpenS**

Sleepless at Crown Point. Richard Wilbur. **CP-WilbR**

Sleepless, I stare. The Broken Dark. Robert Earl Hayden. **CP-HaydR**

Sleepless in Scarsdale. John Updike. **CP-UpdiJ**

Sleepless Night, A. Philip Levine. **SP-LeviP**

Sleeplessness. Jim Carroll. **SP-CarrJ**

Sleepmonger / deathmonger. The Addict. Anne Sexton. **CP-SextA**

Sleepness Night of Eugene Delacroix, The. John Yau. **SP-YauJo**

Sleep's huge soft instruments rustle. Ecstasy of the Pure. Kenneth Patchen. **CP-PatcK**

Sleep'st thou, or wauk'st thou, fairest creature. The Lover's Morning Salute to His Mistress. Robert Burns. **CP-BurnR**

Sleepwalker. Tom Clark. **SP-ClarT**

Sleepwalker. Dabney Stuart. **SP-StuaD**

Sleepwalker can never die. Forty Days. Tom Clark. **SP-ClarT**

Sleepwalker is henry hill, the wiseguy who survives. Sleepwalker. Tom Clark. **SP-ClarT**

Sleepwalker, though you toted your dead comrade's M-Sixty. Sleepwalker's Fate. Tom Clark. **SP-ClarT**

Sleepwalker's Fate. Tom Clark. **SP-ClarT**

Sleepwalker's Way. Tom Clark. **SP-ClarT**

Sleepwalking. Christian J. Van Geel, *tr. fr. Dutch by* Adrienne Rich. **CP-RicAE**

Sleepy Day at Half Moon Bay. Al Young. **CP-YounA**

Sleepy giant, / You've been resting awhile. Africa. Langston Hughes. **SP-HughL**

Sleepy Sentinel, The. Rudyard Kipling. *Fr.* Epitaphs of the War [1914–1918]. **CP-KiplR**

Sleepy sound of a tea-time tide, The. A Bay in Anglesey. Sir John Betjeman. **CP-BetjJ**

Sleepyheads. Carl Sandburg. **CP-SandC**

Sleeve, picked out with gold and stones of rare design, of interest. Worn on the. Kenneth Patchen. **CP-PatcK**

Slender finger of light, A. Haiku 1. Etheridge Knight. **SP-KnigE**

Slender maiden found me sleeping, The. Nicholas Vachel Lindsay. *Fr.* Johnny Appleseed's Wife of the Mind. **CP-LindV**

SLEPT / folded in girls. Song of the Slip. Gary Snyder. **CP-SnydG**

Slice of Wedding Cake, A. Robert Ranke Graves. **CP-GravR**

Slicing Oranges for Jeremiah. Diane Wakoski. **SP-WakoD**

Slick. Daniel Gerard Hoffman. **SP-HoffD**

Slide, The. "Lou Reed." **SP-ReedL**

Sliding Mountain, The. Stevie Smith. **CP-SmitS**

Sliding the tongue-leaved. Roy Fisher. **SP-FishR** *Fr.* Diversions.

Slight hole opened in the sky, A. A Hole in the Sky. Robert Pack. **SP-PackR**

Slight Relax of Air Where Cold Was, A. Philip Larkin. **CP-LarkP**

Slight wander of innocence. Anywhere. Robert Creeley. **CP-CreeR**

Slightly before the middle of Congressman Pudd. Edward Estlin Cummings. **CP-CummE**

Sligo and Mayo. Louis MacNeice. **FaBoPP** *Fr.* The Closing Album. **CP-MacNL**

Slim / young fascist, A. On the Yard. Etheridge Knight. **SP-KnigE**

Slim and singing copper girl, A. Early Copper. Carl Sandburg. **CP-SandC**

Slim dragonfly / too rapid for the eye. Arthur Mitchell. Marianne Craig Moore. **CP-MoorM**

Slim inquirer, while the old fathers sleep. Earthworm. Anne Sexton. **CP-SextA**

Slim sunburnt girls adorn. Lines on a Tudor Mansion. Alun Lewis. **CP-LewiA**

Slime, in the grains of the State. Next to Last Things. Stanley Jasspon Kunitz. *Fr.* Around Pastor Bonhoeffer. **CP-KuniS**

Slime of all my yesterdays, The. April 18. Sylvia Plath. **CP-PlatS**

Slime; the residues of refined tears. Geoffrey Hill. *Fr.* The Death of Shelley. *Fr.* Of Commerce and Society: Variations on a Theme. **CP-HillG**

Sling Along. Paul Laurence Dunbar. **CP-DunbP**

Sling me under the sea. Bones. Carl Sandburg. **CP-SandC**

Slinking by the jug-and-bottle. Basil Bunting. *Fr.* The Well of Lycopolis. **CP-BuntB**

Slip, The. Wendell Berry. **CP-BerrW**

Slip back, Time! St. Launce's Revisited. Thomas Hardy. **CP-HardT**

Slipperwort. Louis Zukofsky. **CP-ZukLS**

Slippery. Carl Sandburg. **CP-SandC**

Slippin' and slidin' like a weasel on the run. One More Weekend. "Bob Dylan." **CP-DylaB**

Slipping Away. Stephen Dobyns. **SP-DobyS**

Slipping in blood, by his own hand, through pride. To an Artist, to Take Heart. Louise Bogan. **CP-BogaL**

Slips of the last rose of summer, The. Emily Dickinson. **SP-DickE**

Sliver. Langston Hughes. **SP-HughL**

Sliver of Sermon. Langston Hughes. **SP-HughL**

Slivers of rain upon the pane. Echoes. Hart Crane. **CP-CranH**

Sloe Gin. Seamus Heaney. **SP-HeanS**

Sloe was lost in flower, The. Alfred Edward Housman. **CP-HousA**

Slog of travelling it, The. Human Hymn. Vasil Sotirov, *tr. fr. Bulgarian by* William Matthews. **SP-MattW**

Sloop of Amber slips away, A. Emily Dickinson. **CP-DickE**

Slope of the heavy woods, The. The Source. William Carlos Williams. **CP-WilW1**

Slope woods' snows melt. Easter Sunday. Allen Ginsberg. **CP-GinsA**

Slopeshouldered shape from scurrying burdens, A. &. Richard Wilbur. **CP-WilbR**

Sloping and tapering away. Roy Fisher. **SP-FishR** *Fr.* Mystery Poems.

Sloth. Stephen Dobyns. **SP-DobyS**

Sloth, The. Isabella Gardner. **CP-GardI**

Sloth, The. Theodore Roethke. **CP-RoetT**

Slothful Sleep. John Milton, *tr. fr. Latin by* John T. Shawcross. **CP-MiltJ**

Slouch he packs up. and goes to sev'rall Faires. Upon Slouch. Robert Herrick. **CP-HerrR**

Slough. Sir John Betjeman. **CP-BetjJ**

Slough of Despond: Or the House of Hope, The. Malcolm Lowry. **CP-LowrM**

Slough of unamiable liars, The. Ezra Pound. *See* Canto 14: "Io venni luogo d'ogni luce muto."

Slovak Tongue, The. James Liddy. **CP-LiddJ**

Slow, / Over the sombre prairie, on the darkening earth below. Symphony of Snow. John Gould Fletcher. **SP-FletJ**

Slow Boat Ride. Richard Eberhart. **CP-EberR**

Slow Child, The. Peter Meinke. **SP-MeinP**

Slow circular flail of fan, A. Eternally Undismayed Are the Poolshooters. William Matthews. **SP-MattW**

Slow cooking in a world on the move. Cook. Roy Fisher. **SP-FishR** *Fr.* Five Pilgrims in the Prologue to the Canterbury Tales.

Slow Dance. David St. John. **SP-StJoD**

Slow de night's a-fallin'. Whip-Poor-Will and Katy-Did. Paul Laurence Dunbar. **CP-DunbP**

Slow Death of the Dragon. Muriel Rukeyser. **CP-RukeM**

Slow Dialogue between Pain and Roosevelt. Muriel Rukeyser. **CP-RukeM**

Slow Down, Mr. Ganderdonk, You're Late. Ogden Nash. **CP-NashO**

Slow in the Wintry Morn, the struggling light. The Emigrants. Charlotte Smith. **CP-SmitC**

Slow in the Wintry Morn, the struggling light, *sels.* Charlotte Smith. *Fr.* The Emigrants. **CP-SmitC**

Slow Life. Tom Clark. **SP-ClarT**

Slow May. Spring in These Hills. Archibald MacLeish. **CP-MacLA**

Slow Movement. Louis MacNeice. **CP-MacNL**

Slow Movement. William Carlos Williams. **CP-WilW1**

Slow moves the pageant of a climbing race. Slow through the Dark. Paul Laurence Dunbar. **CP-DunbP**

Slow Nature, The. Thomas Hardy. **CP-HardT**

Slow Potomac, tarnished water. At the Lincoln Memorial. Archibald MacLeish. **CP-MacLA**

Slow Program. Carl Sandburg. **CP-SandC**

Slow pulse in a den of roots. John Haines. *Fr.* The Stone Bear. **SP-HainJ**

Slow-rolling beauty. The Mountains of California: Part 2. Al Young. **CP-YounA**

Slow Season. Theodore Roethke. **CP-RoetT**

Slow sinks, more lovely ere his race be run. The Curse of Minerva. Byron. **CP-Byron**

Slow sinks, more lovely ere his race be run. Sunset over the Aegean. Byron. **OBNC; OBRV** *Fr.* The Corsair. **CP-Byron**

Slow, slow, fresh fount, keep time with my salt tears. Ben Jonson. **CP-JonsB** *Fr.* Cynthia's Revels.

Slow slowing—. Robert Creeley. **CP-CreeR**

Slow Starter, The. Louis MacNeice. **CP-MacNL**

Slow, the chill that gravitates. Flu. Al Young. **CP-YounA**

Slow through the dark. Paul Laurence Dunbar. **CP-DunbP**

Slow Train. "Bob Dylan." **CP-DylaB**

Slow Waker. Thom Gunn. **CP-GunnT**

("I look at the nephew.") **CP-GunnT**

Slower now, less sure of my footing. On the Canal. John Hewitt. **CP-HewiJ**

Slowly / the dried up pond. A Vermont Diary. James Schuyler. **CP-SchuJ**

Slowly. Anne Waldman. **SP-WaldA**

Slowly I Married Her. Leonard Cohen. **CP-CoheL**

Slowly I smoke and hug my knee. Ballade by the Fire. Edwin Arlington Robinson. **CP-RobiE**

Slowly my heron flies. Geoffrey Hill. *Fr.* The Pentecost Castle. **CP-HillG**

Slowly, Prometheus. Always the Same. Adrienne Rich. **CP-RicAE**

Slowly rising, slowly strengthening moon. A La Lune. William Carlos Williams. **CP-WilW1**

Slowly slowly / Comes Christ through the garden. Thomas Merton. *Fr.* Cables to the Ace. **CP-MertT**

Slowly stroking your fingers where they lie. Always. Robert Ranke Graves. **CP-GravR**

Slowly the generations pass. Nicholas Vachel Lindsay. *Fr.* Shantung[, or The Empire of China is Crumbling Down]. **CP-LindV**

Slowly the moon is rising out of the ruddy haze. Aware. David Herbert Lawrence. **CP-LawrD**

Slowly the passenger pigeons increased, then suddenly their numbers. Passenger Pigeons. Robinson Jeffers. **CP-JefR3**

Slowly the salt of the earth becomes salt of the sea. Salt of the Earth. David Herbert Lawrence. **CP-LawrD**

Slowly the sun from the mist arises. Matin sur le Port. Albert Samain, *tr. fr. French by* John Hewitt. **CP-HewiJ**

Slowly the toiling images will rise. Stage Directions. Robert Duncan. **SP-DuncR** *Fr.* Passages.

Slowly the women file to where he stands. Faith Healing. Philip Larkin. **CP-LarkP**

Slowly with bleeding nose and aching wrists. The Hero. Robert Ranke Graves. **CP-GravR**

Slowly, without sun, the day sinks. Fairbanks Under the Solstice. John Haines. **SP-HainJ**

Slows. A bent figure in the dark, thickly clothed. Hayden Carruth. *Fr.* The Sleeping Beauty. **CP-CarHL**

Slug, The. Alun Lewis. **CP-LewiA**

Slug. Theodore Roethke. **CP-RoetT**

Slug and the rat possess the dead, The. Burial Ground. Charles Olson. **CP-OlsoC**

Slug had climbed, when first I shut the door, The. The Slug. Alun Lewis. **CP-LewiA**

Sluggishly. William Carlos Williams. **CP-WilW1**

Slum Child, The. Walter de la Mare. **CP-DeLaW**

Slum Song. Louis MacNeice. **CP-MacNL**

Slumber did my spirit seal, A. William Wordsworth. **AWP; BLPL; BiP; CABA; EBEvV; ELP; EnLoPo; FaBoCh; GGP; GTBS; GTBS-6; GTBS-P; HAP; HelP; ImPo; InPK; InPS; InvP; MeMBP; NIP; NOBRP; NoP; PBMP; PPP; PoEL-4; PoRA; PrIm; SCV; TEP; TreFS; UnPo; WeW** *Fr.* Lucy. **CP-WorW1**

Slumped under the impressive genitals. Boston Common. John Berryman. **CP-BerrJ**

Slums, The. Kenneth Patchen. **CP-PatcK**

Slums par excellence that were your farms! And all. Hayden Carruth. *Fr.* Paragraphs. **CP-CarHS**

Slung from the gantries cranes. Steel. Charles Tomlinson. **CP-TomlC**

Slurred and drawled and crooning sounds, The. A Toast. Louis MacNeice. **CP-MacNL**

Small / poem / the unit of feeling, The. Poem. Roy Fisher. **SP-FishR**

Small, The. Theodore Roethke. **CP-RoetT**

Small Action Poem. Charles Tomlinson. **CP-TomlC**

Small and emptied woman you lie here a thousand years dead. In the Museum. Isabella Gardner. **CP-GardI**

Small as a peanut. No Difference. Shel Silverstein. **SP-SilS2**

Small barking sounds—. Sunday. William Carlos Williams. **CP-WilW1**

Small birds flew from tree to tree, The. A Hunter Went Killing: A Fable. Edwin Rolfe. **CP-RolfE**

Small birds rejoice in the green leaves returning, The. Song. Robert Burns. **CP-BurnR**

Small birds swirl around, The. The Small. Theodore Roethke. **CP-RoetT**

Small Birds, to Agree with the Leaves, Come in the Fall. Charles Olson. **CP-OlsoC**

Small black goat with, A. Charles Henri Ford. **SP-FordC** *Fr.* Emblems of Arachne.

Small blind street off East Commercial Road, A. An East-End Curate. Thomas Hardy. **CP-HardT**

Small blue flowers like points. The Voice. Philip Levine. **SP-LeviP**

Small Blue Heron, The. James Wright. **CP-WrigJ**

Small boy drove the shaggy ass, The. Turf-Carrier [*or* Turf Carrier] on Aranmore. John Hewitt. **CP-HewiJ**

Small boy in a black hat walks among streaky shadows. Cold Spring in Essex. Donald Davie. **CP-DavDo**

Small bronze figure lips a silent flute, The. Chinese Fluteplayer. John Hewitt. **CP-HewiJ**

Small brook gushed on stones hard by, A. An Interlude. Walter de la Mare. **CP-DeLaW**

Small, busy flames play through the fresh-laid coals. To My Brothers. John Keats. **CP-KeatJ**

Small but Brilliant Fire Blazed in the Grate, A. Kenneth Patchen. **CP-PatcK**

Small Cabin, The. Margaret Atwood. **SP-AtwM1**

Small Celandine, The. William Wordsworth. *See* There is a flower, the Lesser Celandine.

Small child of a wind, A. Requiem for Sonora. Richard Shelton. **SP-ShelR**

Small-City People. John Updike. **CP-UpdiJ**

Small dawn, sailor. First light glints, A. Here, but Unable to Answer. Richard Hugo. **CP-HugoR**

Small Excursion, A. Mona Van Duyn. **SP-VanDM**

Small fact and fingers and farthest one from me. A Poem for Emily. Miller Williams. **SP-WillM**

Small Farm, A. Michael Hartnett. **SP-HarMi**

Small fawn edging through the underbrush. Gemela. James Wright. *Fr.* Many of Our Waters: Variations on a Poem by a Black Child. **CP-WrigJ**

Small Fig Tree, A. Donald Hall. **CP-HallD**

Small fish entwined by their tentacles. May Day Song. James Liddy. *Fr.* Shore. **CP-LiddJ**

Small flame pointing, shadowing, picking out. Interiors. Howard Nemerov. **CP-NemeH**

Small Frogs Killed on the Highway. James Wright. **CP-WrigJ**

Small Garden Near a Field. Tess Gallagher. **SP-GallT**

Small girls hurried to the hilltop church, The. Whit Monday. John Hewitt. **CP-HewiJ**

Small gnats that fly. One Hard Look. Robert Ranke Graves. **CP-GravR**

Small Hands, Relinquish All. Edna St. Vincent Millay. **CP-MillE**

Small Homes. Carl Sandburg. **CP-SandC**

Small householder now comes out warily, The. Spring Voices. Louis MacNeice. **CP-MacNL**

Small is the trust when love is green. Robert Louis Stevenson. **CP-StevR**

Small, just / a room, / the altar. A Chapel. James Schuyler. **CP-SchuJ**

Small knowledge have we that by knowledge met. Modernities. Edwin Arlington Robinson. **CP-RobiE**

Small Lady, The. Stevie Smith. **CP-SmitS**

Small Moment. Howard Nemerov. **CP-NemeH**

Small Moon. Howard Nemerov. **CP-NemeH**

Small Oil Left in the House We Rented in Boulder, The. Richard Hugo. **CP-HugoR**

Small Plane in Kansas. Thom Gunn. **CP-GunnT**

Small porch of imitation, The. Taylor Street. Thom Gunn. **CP-GunnT**

Small Room, The. Roy Fisher. **SP-FishR** *Fr.* Interiors with Various Figures.

Small room, the varnished floor, A. A Theological Definition. George Oppen. **CP-OppeG**

Small service is true service while it lasts. To a Child [Written in Her Album]. William Wordsworth. **CP-WorW2**

Small Soldiers with Drum in Large Landscape. Robert Penn Warren. *Fr.* Mexico Is a Foreign Country: Four Studies in Naturalism. **SP-WarrR**

Small Song. Archie Randolph Ammons. **SP-AmmoA**

Small Song. James Dickey. **CP-DickJ**

Small-soul-pleasing, loved with condescension. Ivana. Robert Lowell. **SP-LoweR**

Small spurts of green, flowers like lavender. The Saadians, Marble, Tile, and Flower. James Liddy. **CP-LiddJ**

Small Substantial Shadow. Steve Griffiths. **SP-GrifS**

Small the Theme of My Chant. Walt Whitman. **CP-WhitW**

Small things / hardest to believe. Hayden Carruth. *Fr.* North Winter. **CP-CarHL**

Small Town. Rita Dove. **SP-DoveR**

Small Town. "Lou Reed." **SP-ReedL**

Small town slanted on a slight hill, A. In Your Small Dream. Richard Hugo. **CP-HugoR**

Small Towns of Ireland, The. Sir John Betjeman. **CP-BetjJ**

Small type of great ones, that do hum. A Fly Caught in a Cobweb. Richard Lovelace. **CP-LoveR**

Small vellum environment, A. Page from the Koran. James Merrill. **SP-MerrJ**

Small, viewless Æronaut, that by the line. To the Insect of the Gossamer. Charlotte Smith. **CP-SmitC**

Small voice is fretting my house in the night, A. The Smallish Son. Hayden Carruth. **CP-CarHS**

Small weight is obnoxious, A. Emily Dickinson. **SP-DickE**

Small wheel, A. Watch Repair. Charles Simic. **SP-SimiC**

Small White Flower that Contains the Sun, The. Barton Sutter. **SP-SuttB**

Small White House. Robert Penn Warren. **SP-WarrR**

Small wind, A. The Cat and the Wind. Thom Gunn. **CP-GunnT**

Small Wire. Anne Sexton. **CP-SextA**

Small, yellow grass-onion, The. To Be Hungry Is to Be Great. William Carlos Williams. **CP-WilW1**

Smaller, older *Girl at a Sewing Machine*, The. Two Hoppers. John Updike. **CP-UpdiJ**

Smallest flower, The. Compleynt Blossoms April to July. Charles Olson. **CP-OlsoC**

Smalley Bar. Marge Piercy. **SP-PierM**

Smallish Son, The. Hayden Carruth. **CP-CarHS**

Smart. Robert Herrick. **CP-HerrR**

Smart. Shel Silverstein. **SP-SilS2**

Smart gain, The. Pedagogy Agog. Archie Randolph Ammons. **SP-AmmoA**

Smart sends his compliments and pray'rs. Epistle to Dr. Nares. Christopher Smart. **SP-SmarC**

Smart, stupid—let me tell you how to do it. Bravado. Stephen Dobyns. **SP-DobyS**

Smash down the cities. And They Obey. Carl Sandburg. **CP-SandC**

Smashed, and brought up against. After an Accident. Donald Davie. **CP-DavDo**

Smashed bones. Gristle of ribs. Encounter at Nightfall. Kenneth Patchen. **CP-PatcK**

Smashed weirdness of the raving cadenzas of God, The. Realism. Tom Clark. **SP-ClarT**

Smell. William Carlos Williams. **CP-WilW1**

Smell of apricots that brings a place, A. The Memory. Gilbert Sorrentino. **SP-SorrG**

Smell of burning like a noise erupts—, A. Figure in a Landscape. Jenny Joseph. **SP-JoseJ**

Smell of further honey, A. Song of the Foolish Bees. Martinus Nijhoff, *tr. fr. Dutch by* Adrienne Rich. **CP-RicAE**

Smell of gum wrappers as of Saturday afternoon at movies. Robert Creeley. **CP-CreeR**

Smell of Lebanon, The. Alice Walker. **CP-WalkA**

Smell of snow, stinging in nostrils as the wind lifts it from a beach, The. The Crystal Lithium. James Schuyler. **CP-SchuJ**

Smell of stale air, The. Robert Creeley. **CP-CreeR**

Smell of the heat is boxwood, The. To Daphne and Virginia. William Carlos Williams. **CP-WilW2**

Smell of the Sacrifice, The. Robert Herrick. **CP-HerrR**

Smell of the sea in my nostrils, The. The Mystic Sea. Paul Laurence Dunbar. **CP-DunbP**

Smells, / sounds. Robert Creeley. **CP-CreeR**

Smells are surer than sounds or sights. Lichtenberg. Rudyard Kipling. **CP-KiplR**

Smells of ordinariness, The. Night Drive. Seamus Heaney. **SP-HeanS**

Smelt, The. Ogden Nash. **CP-NashO**

Smelt and Tasted. Wystan Hugh Auden. **CP-AudeW**

Smelt Fishing. Robert Earl Hayden. **CP-HaydR**

Smelting-mill stack is crumbling, no smoke is alive there, The. Allendale. Wystan Hugh Auden. **CP-AudWJ**

Smile, The. William Blake. **CP-BlakW**

Smile, The. Robert Frost. *Fr.* The Hill Wife. **CP-FrosR**

Smile, The. James Merrill. **SP-MerrJ**

Smile, The. Stevie Smith. **CP-SmitS**

Smile and a Sigh, A. Christina Georgina Rossetti. **CP-RosC1**

Smile because the nights are short!, A. A Smile and a Sigh. Christina Georgina Rossetti. **CP-RosC1**

Smile fell in the grass, A. The Night Dances. Sylvia Plath. **CP-PlatS**

Smile of iceboxes annihilates me, The. An Appearance. Sylvia Plath. **CP-PlatS**

Smile of the Moon!—for so I name. Lament of Mary Queen of Scots on the Eve of a New Year. William Wordsworth. **CP-WorW2**

Smile, Smile, Smile. Wilfred Owen. **CP-OwenW**

Smiles. Stephen Dunn. **SP-DunnS**

Smiling back from Coronation. Emily Dickinson. **CP-DickE**

Smiling Dane, A. William Carlos Williams. **CP-WilW2**

Smiling Morne had newly wak't the Day, The. The Beginning of Heliodorus. Heliodorus, *tr. fr. Classical Greek by* Richard Crashaw. **CP-CrasR**

Smiling through my own memories of painful excitement your wide eyes. Ode to Tanaquil Leclercq. Frank O'Hara. **SP-OharF**

Smiling spring comes in rejoicing, The. Bonie Bell. Robert Burns. **CP-BurnR**

Smith, by sute divorst, the knowne adultres. Epigramme. Thomas Campion. *Fr.* Observations in the Art of English Poesie. **CP-CampT**

Smith makes me, A. The Runes on Weland's Sword. Rudyard Kipling. **CP-KiplR** *Fr.* Old Men at Pevensey. *Fr.* Puck of Pook's Hill.

Smog trucks mile after mile high wire. Bayonne Entering NYC. Allen Ginsberg. **CP-GinsA**

Smoke. Robert Creeley. **CP-CreeR**

Smoke. Carl Sandburg. **CP-SandC**

Smoke and Steel. Carl Sandburg. **CP-SandC**

"Bar of steel—it is only, A." **AiP**

"Smoke of the fields in spring is one." **MoAmPo**

Smoke Blue. Carl Sandburg. **CP-SandC**

Smoke-color; haze thinly over the hills, low hanging. August. William Everson. **SP-EverW**

Smoke for a sign my people as the churn of, The. The Eleventh Book. Archibald MacLeish. *Fr.* Conquistador. **CP-MacLA**

Smoke from the train-gulf hid by hoardings blunders upward. Birmingham. Louis MacNeice. **CP-MacNL**

Smoke of an orange corona corona, The. The Crown. Gilbert Sorrentino. **SP-SorrG**

Smoke of autumn is on it all. Three Pieces on the Smoke of Autumn. Carl Sandburg. **CP-SandC**

Smoke of our campfire lowers, The. Spring Rain. Kenneth Rexroth. **SP-RexrK** *Fr.* Mary and the Seasons. **SP-RexrK**

Smoke of the fields in spring is one. Carl Sandburg. **MoAmPo** *Fr.* Smoke and Steel. **CP-SandC**

Smoke of these landscapes has gone God knows where. Runaway Colors. Carl Sandburg. **CP-SandC**

Smoke Rolling Down Street. Allen Ginsberg. **CP-GinsA**

Smoke Rose Gold. Carl Sandburg. **CP-SandC**

Smoke Shapes. Carl Sandburg. **CP-SandC**

Smoke Shop Owner's Daughter, The. Jean Garrigue. **SP-GarrJ**

Smoke upon your Altar dies, The. L'Envoi; Departmental Ditties. Rudyard Kipling. **CP-KiplR**

Smokin' my pipe on the mountings, sniffin' the mornin'-cool. Screw-Guns. Rudyard Kipling. **CP-KiplR**

Smoking Pot on the Bus. Thom Gunn. **CP-GunnT**

Smoky autumn night, stars up in the sky. Golden Loom. "Bob Dylan." **CP-DylaB**

Smoky rain riddles the ocean plains, A. My Father Paints the Summer. Richard Wilbur. **CP-WilbR**

Smooth as a snail, this little parson. Liquid Paper. Peter Meinke. **SP-MeinP**

Smooth between sea and land. Alfred Edward Housman. **CP-HousA**

Smooth Gnarled Crape Myrtle. Marianne Craig Moore. **CP-MoorM**

Smooth it slides upon its travel. Looking-Glass River. Robert Louis Stevenson. **CP-StevR**

Smooth light: all bronze. Brilliant Silence. Charles Tomlinson. **CP-TomlC**

Smooth mink, the swift seal, The. Welcome Home—Oh Most Beloved Harteebeeste. Malcolm Lowry. **CP-LowrM**

Smooth quill and bristle down. Lullaby: The Comforting of Cock Robin. William DeWitt Snodgrass. **SP-SnodW**

Smooth smell of Manhattan taxis, The. Dance of the Infidels. Al Young. **CP-YounA**

Smooth was the Sea, and seem'd to call. Faire Shewes Deceive. Robert Herrick. **CP-HerrR**

Smoothing soft the nestling head. The Two Loves. John Greenleaf Whittier. **CP-WhitJ**

Smooths and burdens. Snow. Robert Earl Hayden. **CP-HaydR**

Smouldering embers blush, The. Emily Dickinson. **CP-DickE**

Smudged eyeballs. Breakfast in a Bowling Alley in Utica, New York. Adrienne Rich. **CP-RicAE**

Smudging. Diane Wakoski. **SP-WakoD**

Smugglers and Poachers. George Crabbe. **SP-CrabG** *Fr.* Tales of the Hall.

Smuggler's Song, A. Rudyard Kipling. **CP-KiplR** *Fr.* Hal o' the Draft. *Fr.* Puck of Pook's Hill.

Snail [*or* Snayl], The. Richard Lovelace. **CP-LoveR**

Snail, The. Vincent Bourne, *tr. fr. Latin by* William Cowper. **CP-CowpW**

Snail. Langston Hughes. **SP-HughL**

Snail. Anne Sexton. **CP-SextA**

Snail gives off stillness, The. Evening. Charles Simic. **SP-SimiC**

Snail moves like a, The. Hedgehog. Paul Muldoon. **SP-MuldP**

Snail pushes through a green, The. Considering the Snail. Thom Gunn. **CP-GunnT**

Snails lead slow idyllic lives. The Widow's Yard. Isabella Gardner. **CP-GardI**

Snake, The. Wendell Berry. **CP-BerrW**

Snake. David Herbert Lawrence. **CP-LawrD**

"He drank enough." **RR**

"Snake came to my water-trough, A." **UV**

Snake. Robert Lowell. **SP-LoweR**

Snake, The. William Matthews. **SP-MattW**

Snake. Theodore Roethke. **CP-RoetT**

Snake. Anne Sexton. **CP-SextA**

Snake, The. Robert Penn Warren. *Fr.* Boy's Will, Joyful Labor without Pay, and Harvest Home (1918). **SP-WarrR**

Snake came to my water-trough, A. David Herbert Lawrence. **UV** *Fr.* Snake. **CP-LawrD**

Snake came to my water-trough, A. Snake. David Herbert Lawrence. **CP-LawrD**

Snake Charming. Leonard Nathan. **SP-NathL**

Snake enters your dreams through paintings:, The. Quattrocento. Margaret Atwood. **SP-AtwM2**

Snake hunts and sinews, The. She. Margaret Atwood. **SP-AtwM2**

Snake is one name of God, The. After Heraclitus. Margaret Atwood. **SP-AtwM2**

Snake is the love of a thumb, A. The Snake. William Matthews. **SP-MattW**

Snake Woman. Margaret Atwood. **SP-AtwM2**

Snakebite. James Dickey. **CP-DickJ**

Snakecharmer. Sylvia Plath. **CP-PlatS**

Snakes are weeping on the rocks. The Valley-sleeper, the Children, the Snakes, and the Giant. Kenneth Patchen. **CP-PatcK**

Snakes, Mongooses, Snake-Charmers, and the Like. Marianne Craig Moore. **CP-MoorM**

Snap-Comb Wilderness, The. Robert Ranke Graves. **CP-GravR**

Snap-Dragon. David Herbert Lawrence. **CP-LawrD**

Snap the blind; I am not blind. Aubade for Infants. Louis MacNeice. **CP-MacNL**

Snapped Thread, The. Robert Ranke Graves. **CP-GravR**

Snapshot of 15th S.W., A. Richard Hugo. **CP-HugoR**

Snapshot of the Auxiliary, A. Richard Hugo. **CP-HugoR**

Snapshot of Uig in Montana, A. Richard Hugo. **CP-HugoR**

Snapshots. John Updike. **CP-UpdiJ**

Snapshots of a Daughter-in-Law. Adrienne Rich. **CP-RicAE; SP-RicA1; SP-RicA2**

Snare, The. Thomas Merton. **CP-MertT**

Snare, ten i'th'hundred calls his wife; and why? Upon Snare, an Usurer. Robert Herrick. **CP-HerrR**

Snares of Varuna, The. "Hugh MacDiarmid."

"As I have often told." **SP-MacDH**

Snark Was a Boojum Was a Prawn, The. Ogden Nash. **CP-NashO**

Snarleyow. Rudyard Kipling. **CP-KiplR**

Snatch of Sliphorn Jazz. Carl Sandburg. **CP-SandC**

Snatches for Charles Ives. Daniel Gerard Hoffman. **SP-HoffD**

Sneape has a face so brittle, that it breaks. Upon Sneape. Robert Herrick. **CP-HerrR**

Sneosdal. Richard Hugo. **CP-HugoR**

Sniff of the real, that's, The. Autobiography. Thom Gunn. **CP-GunnT**

Sniffle, The. Ogden Nash. **CP-NashO**

SNO / a white idea(Listen). Edward Estlin Cummings. **CP-CummE**

Snoqualmie. Richard Hugo. **CP-HugoR**

Snorkeling in the Caribbean. Dabney Stuart. **SP-StuaD**

Snorting hippopotamus at the lake's bottom, all snoot. A Winter's Tale, by a Wife. Mona Van Duyn. **SP-VanDM**

Snow / began here / this morning and all day, The. First Snow. Mary Oliver. **SP-OlivM**

Snow, / blessed snow. Snow. Anne Sexton. **CP-SextA**

Snow, The. Hayden Carruth. **CP-CarHS**

Snow / coming / to my window, going up. Hotel Steinplatz, Berlin, December 25 (1966). Charles Olson. **SP-OlsoC** *Fr.* The Maximus Poems.

Snow, The. Robert Creeley. **CP-CreeR**

SNOW / cru / is / ingw Hi. Edward Estlin Cummings. **CP-CummE**

Snow. Walter de la Mare. **CP-DeLaW**

Snow. Robert Frost. **CP-FrosR**

Snow, The. Donald Hall. **CP-HallD**

Snow. Robert Earl Hayden. **CP-HaydR**

Snow. Daniel Gerard Hoffman. **SP-HoffD**

Snow / ice / bitter wind. Hayden Carruth. *Fr.* North Winter. **CP-CarHL**

Snow. Philip Levine. **SP-LeviP**

Snow. Louis MacNeice. **CP-MacNL**

Snow. William Matthews. **SP-MattW**

Snow, The. Charles Olson. **CP-OlsoC**

Snow. Adrienne Rich. **CP-RicAE**

Snow. Carl Sandburg. **CP-SandC**

Snow, The. James Schuyler. **CP-SchuJ**

Snow. Anne Sexton. **CP-SextA**

Snow. Anne Waldman. **SP-WaldA**

Snow: / years of anger following. Blizzard. William Carlos Williams. **CP-WilW1**

Snow air in the wind. It stings our lunch sacks. Dog Lake with Paula. Richard Hugo. **CP-HugoR**

Snow and Stars. Wallace Stevens. **CP-StevW**

Snow, and the silence of snow, heavy on the rousing day. A Snowy Day at School. David Herbert Lawrence. **CP-LawrD**

Snow Angels. Louise McNeill. **SP-McNeL**

Snow at Sea. John Gould Fletcher. *Fr.* Sand and Spray: A Sea-Symphony. **SP-FletJ**

Snow Begins, The. William Carlos Williams. **CP-WilW2**

Snow beneath whose chilly softness. Emily Dickinson. **CP-DickE**

Snow-blizzard sowing. Car Crash. Allen Ginsberg. **CP-GinsA**

Snow-Bound [*or* Snow-Bound; a Winter Idyl]. John Greenleaf Whittier. **CP-WhitJ**

Mother. **AA; OHIP**

Prophetess. **AA**

"Shut in from all the world without." **OBCP,** *ll.* 155–163; **AA**

(Firelight.) **AA**

Sister. **AA**

Winter Night. **TrGrPo**

World Transformed, The. **AA**

Snow-bound in woodland, a mournful word. Postponement. Thomas Hardy. **CP-HardT**

Snow brings into view the far hills. Appearance. Charles Tomlinson. **CP-TomlC**

Snow buntings whirling / on a snowy field. Hayden Carruth. *Fr.* North Winter. **CP-CarHL**

Snow came down last night like moths, The. First Snow in Alsace. Richard Wilbur. **CP-WilbR**

Snow came to us in the week of Thanksgiving. Essay on Marriage. Hayden Carruth. **CP-CarHS**

Snow Cascades. Richard Eberhart. **CP-EberR**

Snow comes / bits / of light. Hayden Carruth. *Fr.* North Winter. **CP-CarHL**

Snow comes down on New York City. Snow. Anne Waldman. **SP-WaldA**

Snow dissolv'd no more is seen, The. 4.7. Horace. **CP-JohnS** *Fr.* Odes.

Snow-Drop, The. Samuel Taylor Coleridge. **CP-ColeS**

Snow Fall, The. Archibald MacLeish. **CP-MacLA**

Snow falling and night falling fast, oh, fast. Desert Places. Robert Frost. **CP-FrosR**

Snow falls deep; the forest lies alone, The. Gipsies. John Clare. **SP-ClarJ**

Snow falls in the buffet of Aldersgate station. Monody on the Death of Aldersgate Street Station. Sir John Betjeman. **CP-BetjJ**

Snow falls in the dusk of Connecticut. The stranger. The Sound of Snow. Hayden Carruth. **CP-CarHS**

Snow fell forward forever. Ask the Roses. Philip Levine. **SP-LeviP**

Snow Fence. Ted Kooser. **SP-KoosT**

Snow Fences, The. Charles Tomlinson. **CP-TomlC**

Snow flakes / I counted till they danced so. Emily Dickinson. **CP-DickE**

Snow-Flakes. Henry Wadsworth Longfellow. **SP-LongH**

Snow-freaked rocks the eagle alone questions. Contemplation of Dead Reckoning. Malcolm Lowry. **CP-LowrM**

Snow Geese. Robert Bly. **SP-BlyR**

Snow Globe, The. Howard Nemerov. **CP-NemeH**

Snow had buried Stuyvesant, The. Inauguration Day: January 1953. Robert Lowell. **SP-LoweR**

Snow-happy hicks of a boy's world. Twelfth Night. Louis MacNeice. **CP-MacNL**

Snow has fallen on snow for two days behind the Keillen farmhouse. The Orchard Keeper. Robert Bly. **SP-BlyR**

Snow has left the cottage top, The. February. John Clare. *Fr.* The Shepherd's [*or* Shepheards] Calendar.

Snow in May. Marge Piercy. **SP-PierM**

Snow in the Suburbs. Thomas Hardy. **CP-HardT**

Snow is deep on the ground, The. Kenneth Patchen. **CP-PatcK**

Snow is durable and deceiving. It can be shaped into a wall. Cenotaph of Snow. John Yau. **SP-YauJo**

Snow Is Falling. Leonard Cohen. **CP-CoheL**

Snow is gone from cottage tops, The. John Clare. *See* February.

Snow is in the oak. The Snow. Donald Hall. **CP-HallD**

Snow is thin and wet, The. The Covered Bridge. Lewis Turco. **SP-TurcL**

Snow King, The. Rita Dove. **SP-DoveR**

Snow Lamp, The. Robert Earl Hayden.
"Across lunar wastes of wind and snow." **CP-HaydR**
"It is beginning oh." **CP-HaydR**
"No sun these months. Ice-dark and cold." **CP-HaydR**

Snow Leopard, The. Stephen Dunn. **SP-DunnS**

Snow Leopard. Phoebe Hesketh. **SP-HeskP**

Snow-Leopard, The. Randall Jarrell. **CP-JarrR**

Snow, less intransigeant than their marble, The. At the Grave of Henry James. Wystan Hugh Auden. **CP-AudeW**

Snow lies deep upon the ground, The. Christmas in the Heart. Paul Laurence Dunbar. **CP-DunbP**

Snow Light, The. May Sarton. **SP-SartM**

Snow Man, The. Louis MacNeice. **CP-MacNL**

Snow Man, The. Wallace Stevens. **CP-StevW**

Snow means that / life is a black cannonadin. Edward Estlin Cummings. **CP-CummE**

Snow mountain fields. Teton Village. Allen Ginsberg. **CP-GinsA**

Snow names a wreath *snowdrop*. Snowdrop. Louis Zukofsky. **CP-ZukLS**

Snow nearly hard as hail. Hunting Moon. Lewis Turco. **SP-TurcL**

Snow on a Southern State. James Dickey. **CP-DickJ**

Snow on the ground. A day in March. River Rouge, 1932. John Berryman. **CP-BerrJ**

Snow on the mountain—water in. A Song in the Manner of Flannery O'Connor. William Stafford. **SP-StafW**

Snow: I. Charles Kenneth Williams. **SP-WillC**

Snow, out over the elephant's rump. Landscape Winter. Anne Sexton. **CP-SextA**

Snow packs the roadside, sends dunes. The Bus to Alliston, Ontario. Margaret Atwood. **SP-AtwM2**

Snow Party, The. Derek Mahon. **SP-MahoD**

Snow-piles in dark places are gone, The. Just Before April Came. Carl Sandburg. **CP-SandC**

Snow Poem. Richard Hugo. **CP-HugoR**

Snow polished, The. Twangs & Little Twists. Archie Randolph Ammons. **SP-AmmoA**

Snow Queen, The. Adrienne Rich. **CP-RicAE; SP-RicA2**

Snow Roost. Archie Randolph Ammons. **SP-AmmoA**

Snow Sequence. Charles Tomlinson. *Fr.* In Winter Woods. **CP-TomlC**

Snow Signs. Charles Tomlinson. **CP-TomlC**

Snow, Snow. Marge Piercy. **SP-PierM**

Snow starts at twilight. All night the house. Twelve Seasons. Donald Hall. **CP-HallD**

Snow-Storm, The. Ralph Waldo Emerson. **CP-EmerR**

Snow Storm, The. Edna St. Vincent Millay. **CP-MillE**

Snow that never drifts, The. Emily Dickinson. **CP-DickE**

Snow thick and wet, porous. Spring. James Schuyler. **CP-SchuJ**

Snow Thickets. James Dickey. **CP-DickJ**

Snow took us away from the smoke valleys into white mountains, we saw. Snow. Carl Sandburg. **CP-SandC**

Snow: II. Charles Kenneth Williams. **SP-WillC**

Snow was falling, The. Front Lawn. Leonard Cohen. **CP-CoheL**

Snow White and the Seven Dwarfs. Anne Sexton. **CP-SextA**

Snow-white ray. Pietà. Donald Davie. **CP-DavDo**

Snow White was always waiting for The Prince. Charles Olson. **CP-OlsoC**

Snow would be the easy. November for Beginners. Rita Dove. **SP-DoveR**

Snow wounds squirting along my arteries. Deaths and Electrocutions. James Liddy. *Fr.* Glass after Oblivion. **CP-LiddJ**

Snow-Wreath. Louis Zukofsky. **CP-ZukLS**

Snowbanks North of the House. Robert Bly. **SP-BlyR**

Snowdon Sunrise, The. William Wordsworth. *See* In one of these excursions, travelling then.

Snowdrop, The. Walter de la Mare. **CP-DeLaW**

Snowdrop. Ted Hughes. **SP-HughT**

Snowdrop, The. James Schuyler. **CP-SchuJ**

Snowdrop. Louis Zukofsky. **CP-ZukLS**

Snowdrop is the prophet of the flowers, The. The Wild Rose and the Snowdrop. George Meredith. **CP-MerG1**

Snowdrops. Charlotte Smith. **CP-SmitC**

Snowdrops 1987. John Updike. **CP-UpdiJ**

Snowfall, A. Richard Eberhart. **CP-EberR**

Snowfall in March. For Lew Welch in a Snowfall. Gary Snyder. **CP-SnydG**

Snowfall in the Afternoon. Robert Bly. **SP-BlyR**

Snowflake, The. Walter de la Mare. **CP-DeLaW**

Snowflake. Louis Zukofsky. **CP-ZukLS**

Snowflake Which Is Now and Hence Forever, The. Archibald MacLeish. **CP-MacLA**

Snowflakes. Howard Nemerov. **CP-NemeH**

Snowflakes rise and fall on the wind. From the Japanese, V. John Gould Fletcher. **SP-FletJ**

Snowheart. Tess Gallagher. **SP-GallT**

Snowin'. Paul Laurence Dunbar. **CP-DunbP**

Snowing. Walter de la Mare. **CP-DeLaW**

Snowman. Shel Silverstein. **SP-SilS2**

Snowman, The. Barton Sutter. **SP-SuttB**

Snowman on the Moor, The. Sylvia Plath. **CP-PlatS**

Snowmass Cycle, The. Stephen Dunn. **SP-DunnS**

fr. Horace *Odes iv 7.* Diffugere Nives. Alfred Edward Housman. **CP-HousA**

Snow's downstrokes climb softly up the conifer. Hayden Carruth. *Fr.* North Winter. **CP-CarHL**

Snows' night's winds on the window rattling. Louis Zukofsky. *Fr.* 29 Songs. **CP-ZukLS**

Snows of February had buried Christmas, The. The Christmas Robin. Robert Ranke Graves. **CP-GravR**

Snow's on the fellside, look! How deep. Basil Bunting, *after the Latin of* Horace. **CP-BuntB**

Snow's our winter brightening. Crinkling Trails. Archie Randolph Ammons. **SP-AmmoA**

Snow)says!Says / over un / graves. Edward Estlin Cummings. **CP-CummE**

Snowshoe Hare, The. Mary Oliver. **SP-OlivM**

Snowstorms high-traveling. Down Low. Archie Randolph Ammons. **SP-AmmoA**

Snowstorms in the Midwest. James Wright. **CP-WrigJ**

Snowy curtain / slides up the sky, A. Noon Office. James Schuyler. **CP-SchuJ**

Snowy Day at School, A. David Herbert Lawrence. **CP-LawrD**

Snowy Day in School, A, *also incl. in* The Schoolmaster [B]. David Herbert Lawrence. *Fr.* The Schoolmaster [A]. **CP-LawrD**

Snowy Day in School, A, *also incl. in* The Schoomaster [A]. David Herbert Lawrence. *Fr.* The Schoolmaster [B]. **CP-LawrD**

Snowy Day in School, A. David Herbert Lawrence. **CP-LawrD**

Snowy Night. John Haines. **SP-HainJ**

Snowy Owl. Richard Eberhart. **CP-EberR**

Snowy Owl, The. Robert Pack. **SP-PackR**

Snub nose, the guts of twenty mules are in your cylinders and transmission. New Farm Tractor. Carl Sandburg. **CP-SandC**

So / mucked up with. Charles Kenneth Williams. **CP-WillC**

So? Leonard Nathan. **SP-NathL**

So / we sailed out from the island to Cozumél. The Second Book. Archibald MacLeish. *Fr.* Conquistador. **CP-MacLA**

So / zoom / your Special Spot. For a Brookline Lady I Love. Etheridge Knight. **SP-KnigE**

So a new similitude is given us. The Spoonbait. Seamus Heaney. **SP-HeanS**

So about twelve at night, the punk. Dean's Answer to "Upon Stealing a Crown," The. Jonathan Swift. **CP-SwifJ**

So Abram rose, and clave the wood, and went. The Parable of the Old Man and the Young. Wilfred Owen. **CP-OwenW**

So active they seem passive, little sheep. Grace. Richard Wilbur. **CP-WilbR**

So all day long the noise of battle rolled. *incorporated in* Idylls of the King *with changes, as* The Passing of Arthur. Tennyson. **DL; EBNV; EBVVPR; FaBoBe; FiP; NIP; NOBVV; OAEL-2; OBNV; OXAEP-2; PoEL-5** *Fr.* Morte d'Arthur. **CP-TennA**

So all day long the noise of battle rolled. Tennyson. **FaBoRV** *Fr.* The Passing of Arthur. **FHYEP; NAEL-2; OBNC** *Fr.* Idylls of the King. **CP-TennA**

So am I as the rich, whose blessed key. Sonnet 52. William Shakespeare. **OBSC; OXAEP-1** *Fr.* Sonnets. **CP-ShaWS**

So an age ended, and its last deliverer died. Wystan Hugh Auden. **CMoP; PoE** *Fr.* Sonnets from China. **CP-AudeW**

("And the age ended, and the last deliverer died.") **Son**

So-and-so is sick of all the shit. *see also* Commentary—It's Probably Spring. Leonard Cohen. **CP-CoheL**

So-and-So Reclining on Her Couch. Wallace Stevens. **CP-StevW**

So are you to my thoughts as food to life. Sonnet 75. William Shakespeare. **PoEL-2** *Fr.* Sonnets. **CP-ShaWS**

So art thou broken in upon me, Apollo. An After Song. William Carlos Williams. **CP-WilW1**

So, art thou feathered, art thou flown. The Fledgling. Edna St. Vincent Millay. **CP-MillE**

So as they travelled, the drouping night. Edmund Spenser. **OAEL-1** *Fr.* The Faerie Queene. **CP-Spens**

So at last at least. "Bob Dylan." *Fr.* 11 Outlined Epitaphs. **CP-DylaB**

So back you have come from the town, Nan, dear! A Military Appointment. Thomas Hardy. **CP-HardT**

So Bartas-like thy fine spun poems been. An Anagram. *Unknown.* **CP-BradA**

So bashful when I spied her! Emily Dickinson. **CP-DickE**

So Be It. Kenneth Patchen. **CP-PatcK**

So beauty on the waters stood. Ben Jonson. **CP-JonsB** *Fr.* The Masque of Beauty.

So began our one flirtation with winter. The Path. James McAuley. **SP-McAuJ**

So Big. Robert Creeley. **CP-CreeR**

So big / the *out there*. For Chuck Hinman. Robert Creeley. **CP-CreeR**

So breaks the sun earth's rugged chains. Ben Jonson. **CP-JonsB** *Fr.* The Irish Masque.

So brief a life, and then an endless life / Or endless death. All Flesh Is Grass. Christina Georgina Rossetti. **CP-RosC2**

So, butterfly, / you and the leaf you sit on. That the Unexamined Life Is Not Worth Living. Leonard Nathan. **SP-NathL**

So-called poet of love, The. Robert Creeley. **CP-CreeR**

So Can Anger. Stevie Smith. **CP-SmitS**

"So careful of the type?" but no. Tennyson. **EBVV; EBVVPR; EnVR; FF; FHYEP; HAP; HBV; LoBV; NoP; OAEL-2; OBNC; TOF** *Fr.* In Memoriam A. H. H. **CP-TennA**

So; caught you in, my fine young fellow? W. D. Meets Mr. Evil while Removing the Record of Bartok and Replacing It with a Recent Recording by the Everly Brothers in Order to Create a Mood Conducive to Searching for Cock Robin. William DeWitt Snodgrass. **SP-SnodW**

So, Conor, take our thanks for what you've done. William Conor RHA, 1881–1968. John Hewitt. **CP-HewiJ**

So country-alone, and O so very friendly. Careless Night. Robert Lowell. **SP-LoweR**

So dark a mind within me dwells, *sels.* Tennyson. *Fr.* Maud [A Monodrama]. **CP-TennA**

So daylight dies. The Moon's Last Quarter. Robert Ranke Graves. **CP-GravR**

So delicate a diffidence. Emily Dickinson. **SP-DickE**

So did we pray: and took arms: and we marched: and. The Sixth Book. Archibald MacLeish. *Fr.* Conquistador. **CP-MacLA**

So different, this man. Marriage. William Carlos Williams. **CP-WilW1**

So, Doctor, tell me what it means. Archeology. Robert Pack. **SP-PackR**

So does a man's voice speak from the dream that bears his. The First Book. Archibald MacLeish. *Fr.* Conquistador. **CP-MacLA**

So Does Everybody Else, Only Not So Much. Ogden Nash. **CP-NashO**

So Dream Thy Sails. . . . Hart Crane. *See* So dream thy sails, O phantom bark.

So dream thy sails, O phantom bark. Hart Crane. **CP-CranH**

(So Dream Thy Sails. . . .) **CP-CranH**

So early into a big bed stowed out of sight. Bedtime Stories. Mona Van Duyn. **SP-VanDM**

So ended Saturn; and the God of the Sea. John Keats. **FHYEP** *Fr.* Hyperion; a Fragment. **CP-KeatJ**

So Fair, So Sweet, Withal So Sensitive. William Wordsworth. **CP-WorW2**

So fallen! so lost! the light withdrawn. Ichabod[!]. John Greenleaf Whittier. **CP-WhitJ**

So Far, and So Far, and On toward the End. Walt Whitman. **CP-WhitW**

So far as our story approaches the end. A Light Woman. Robert Browning. **CP-BroR1**

So feeble is the thread that doth the burden stay. Petrarch, *tr. fr. Italian by* Sir Thomas Wyatt. **CP-WyatT**

So few particles of bodyhood engine. Survival of a Heart. Tess Gallagher. **SP-GallT**

So, forth issued [*or* issew'd] the Seasons of the year(e). The Mask of Mutability. Edmund Spenser. **GN; OBSC; OXAEP-1** *Fr.* The Faerie Queene. **CP-Spens**

So forth she comes, and to her coche does clyme. Edmund Spenser. **NAEL-1; OAEL-1** *Fr.* The Faerie Queene. **CP-Spens**

So, Fortinbras: Alas is now the keyword here. Rites of War. Louis MacNeice. **CP-MacNL**

So, friend, your shop was all your house! Shop. Robert Browning. **CP-BroR2**

So from defeat I learn. Defeat. John Hewitt. **CP-HewiJ**

So from the mould / Scarlet and Gold. Emily Dickinson. **CP-DickE**

So from the pregnant braine of Jove did rise. To My Noble and Most Ingenious Friend, Col. Richard Lovelace, upon His Lucasta. John Pinchbacke. *Fr.* Commendatory Poems. **CP-LoveR**

So from the years their gifts were showered: each. Wystan Hugh Auden. **CMoP** *Fr.* Sonnets from China. **CP-AudeW**

So from the years their gifts were showered: each. Sonnets from China. Wystan Hugh Auden. **CP-AudeW**

So gay a Flower. Emily Dickinson. **CP-DickE**

So gentle Ellen now no more. William Wordsworth. **ChER** *Fr.* The Three Graves. **CP-WorW1**

So give me back to Death. Emily Dickinson. **CP-DickE**

So glad we are—a Stranger'd deem. Emily Dickinson. **CP-DickE**

So Going Around Cities. Ted Berrigan. **SP-BerrT**

So going away slowly now. Mary Sleeth. Muriel Rukeyser. **CP-RukeM**

So Good. James Schuyler. **CP-SchuJ**

So good luck came, and on my roof[e] did light. The Coming of Good Luck. Robert Herrick. **CP-HerrR**

So Great a Cloud of Witnesses. Christina Georgina Rossetti. **CP-RosC2**

So great our palaces are now. 2.15. Horace. **SP-SmarC,** *tr. by* Christopher Smart; *Fr.* Odes.

So grieves th' advent'rous merchant, when he throws. My Mistress Commanding Me to Return Her Letters. Thomas Carew. **CP-CareT**

So guns and strong explosives. Murderous Weapons. David Herbert Lawrence. **CP-LawrD**

So has a Daisy vanished. Emily Dickinson. **CP-DickE**

So hath myn herte caught in remembraunce. Womanly Noblesse. Geoffrey Chaucer. **CP-ChauG**

So having ended, silence long ensewed. Nature's Reply to Mutability. Edmund Spenser. **NOBE** *Fr.* The Faerie Queene. **CP-Spens**

So he that saileth in this world of pleasure. Anne Bradstreet. **WPOW** *Fr.* Contemplations. **CP-BradA**

So he took her as anointed. April Treason. John Crowe Ransom. **SP-RansJ**

So he, with a clear shout of laughter. Paris and Diomedes. Homer, *tr.* by George Meredith. **CP-MerG1** *Fr.* The Iliad.

So, he would pay his "debt to medicine." Chekhov on Sakhalin. Seamus Heaney. **SP-HeanS**

So he would rather have written those lines. Malcolm Lowry. *Fr.* The Roar of the Sea and the Darkness. **CP-LowrM**

So he wouldn't think of his children. The Worrier. Stephen Dunn. **SP-DunnS**

So help me God, I couldn't choose between. Catullus. *See* Carmen 97: "As God is my witness where is the difference between."

So here the great man stood. On the Porch at the Frost Place, Franconia, NH. William Matthews. **SP-MattW**

So here's your Empire. No more wine, then? Good. One Viceroy Resigns. Rudyard Kipling. **CP-KiplR**

So him in dream. William Everson. *Fr.* In the Fictive Wish. **SP-EverW**

So huge is God's despair. Death of an Oaxaqueñian. Malcolm Lowry. **CP-LowrM**

So, I am safe emergèd from these broils! Otho the Great. John Keats. **CP-KeatJ**

So I began my walk of life; no stop. Christina Georgina Rossetti. **CP-RosC3**

So I grew half delirious and quite sick. Christina Georgina Rossetti. **CP-RosC3**

So, I have seen a man killed! Arthur Hugh Clough. **EBVV; PeVV** *Fr.* Amours de Voyage. **SP-ClouA**

So I have seen the maids in vain. Impromptu ["So I have seen the maids in vain"]. William Cowper. **CP-CowpW**

So I have written this that men may know. He Suggests a Solution. John Hewitt. *Fr.* Two Sonnets. **CP-HewiJ**

So I may say. Epitaph. Hilda Doolittle. **CP-DoolH**

So I move through the black doorway. The Loft. Jim Carroll. **SP-CarrJ**

So I must go my way. Wystan Hugh Auden. **CP-AudWJ**

So I pull my Stockings off. Emily Dickinson. **CP-DickE**

So I renewed my shaken marriage vow. Letter to My Widow. Robert Pack. **SP-PackR**

So I resigned from the Chu Chin Chowder and Marching Club. Ogden Nash. **CP-NashO**

So, I shall see her in three days. In Three Days. Robert Browning. **CP-BroR1**

So I would hear out those lungs. Buckdancer's Choice. James Dickey. **CP-DickJ**

So if she dies / And if you write of it. Sequal. Ernest Hemingway. **CP-HemiE**

So if you love me. Hilda Doolittle. **AnAn** *Fr.* Sigil. **CP-DoolH**

So I'm an alcoholic Catholic mother-lover. Jack Would Speak through the Imperfect Medium of Alice. Alice Notley. **SP-NotlA**

So I'm antiquated. I still like to see. Tanck's Song About November. Hayden Carruth. **CP-CarHS** *Fr.* Songs About What Comes Down: The Complete Works of Mr. Septic Tank.

So in evening there is still light. Chuck Miller. **SP-MillC**

So Intricately Is This World Resolved. Stanley Jasspon Kunitz. **CP-KuniS**

So is it not with me as with that Muse. Sonnet 21. William Shakespeare. **HeIP; InvP; OBSC** *Fr.* Sonnets. **CP-ShaWS**

So is there life on you, moon? Al Young. **CP-YounA**

So is this great wide sea, wherein are things creeping innumerable. Bible, *O.T. See* Psalm 104: "Bless the Lord, O my soul. . . ."

So isn't small one littlest why. Edward Estlin Cummings. **CP-CummE**

So It Ends. Kenneth Patchen. **CP-PatcK**

So it has come to this. The Ambition Bird. Anne Sexton. **CP-SextA**

So justware lord, may all your judgements be. An Epigram. To Thomas Lo[rd] Ellsmere, the Last Term He Sat Chancellor. Ben Jonson. **CP-JonsB**

So large a morning[,] so itself[,] to lean. Song, The. Wystan Hugh Auden. **CP-AudeW**

So large my Will / The little that I may. Emily Dickinson. **CP-DickE**

So late, for whom, to whom. Kathleen Jessie Raine. *Fr.* Testimony. **SP-RainK**

So late in Autumn half the world's asleep. Christina Georgina Rossetti. *Fr.* Later Life: A Double Sonnet of Sonnets. **CP-RosC2**

So Let Me Live. David Herbert Lawrence. **CP-LawrD**

So let the world chant on. There is harsh fruit in the garden. Louis MacNeice. *Fr.* The Stygian Banks. **CP-MacNL**

So Let's Live—Really Live! Catullus. *See* Carmen 5: "Lesbia / live with me."

So let's live—really live!—for love and loving. Catullus. *See* Carmen 5: "Lesbia / live with me."

So like a quiet pigeon in a hollowed rock. Mosaic: St. Praxed's. Raissa Maritain, *tr. fr. French by* Thomas Merton. **CP-MertT**

So, like a switchblade / quivering in its mark. Nocturne. Martin Edmunds. **SP-EdmuM**

So, like him, we cry *"l'honneur des hommes: Saint Langage"*. "Hugh MacDiarmid." **SP-MacDH** *Fr.* In Memoriam James Joyce.

So like, they seem the same. On an Ancient Isle. Kathleen Jessie Raine. **SP-RainK**

So little he is. Edward Estlin Cummings. **CP-CummE**

So Little It Can Take. Phoebe Hesketh. **SP-HeskP**

So live, so love, so use that fragile hour. Robert Louis Stevenson. **CP-StevR**

So Long. Langston Hughes. **SP-HughL**

So long, / So far away. Afro-American Fragment. Langston Hughes. **SP-HughL**

So long / So long as the void. Apollo. James Dickey. **CP-DickJ**

So Long. William Stafford. **SP-StafW**

So Long! Walt Whitman. **CP-WhitW**

So long adrift, so fast aground. The Wise Brothers. Edwin Arlington Robinson. **CP-RobiE**

So long ago that was called Jimmy Yancey. For Papa. Hayden Carruth. **CP-CarHS**

So long as memory, valour, and faith endure. Ode. Rudyard Kipling. **CP-KiplR**

So long as 'neath the Kalka hills. An Old Song. Rudyard Kipling. **CP-KiplR**

So long as there's a trace. Hafiz, *tr. by* Ralph Waldo Emerson. **CP-EmerR** *Fr.* Odes.

So long as we speak the same language and never understand each other. Useless Words. Carl Sandburg. **CP-SandC**

So long had life together been that now. Six Years Later. Joseph Brodsky, *tr. fr. Russian by* Richard Wilbur. **CP-WilbR**

So long having foreseen these convulsions, forecast the hemorrhagic. The Blood-Guilt. Robinson Jeffers. **CP-JefR3**

So long (it seem'd) as Maries Faith was small. Upon Woman and Mary. Robert Herrick. **CP-HerrR**

So Long It's Been Good to Know You. Chuck Miller. **SP-MillC**

So Long, Marianne. Leonard Cohen. **CP-CoheL**

So long you did not sing, or touch your Lute. Upon a Gentlewoman with a Sweet Voice. Robert Herrick. **CP-HerrR**

So look the mornings when the Sun. The Maiden-Blush. Robert Herrick. **CP-HerrR**

So looks Anthea, when in bed she lyes. To Anthea Lying in Bed. Robert Herrick. **CP-HerrR**

So Love, emergent out of chaos, brought. Euclia's Hymn. Ben Jonson. **CP-JonsB** *Fr.* Love's Triumph through Callipolis.

So lovely, now, the day / quiets. What one hoped. For Benny and Sabina. Robert Creeley. **CP-CreeR**

So Make Them Melt as the Dishoused Snail. Donald Davie. **CP-DavDo**

So Many Blood-Lakes. Robinson Jeffers. **CP-JefR3**

So many convolutions and not enough simplicity! To Marina. Kenneth Koch. **SP-KochK**

So many crickets tonight—. Sure Signs. Ted Kooser. **SP-KoosT**

So many crutches. Now even the daylight. A Landscape with Crutches. Charles Simic. **SP-SimiC**

So many different kinds. Loneliness. Stephen Dunn. **SP-DunnS**

So many echoes in my head. Poem. Frank O'Hara. **SP-OharF**

So many fruits come from roses. Grapes. David Herbert Lawrence. **CP-LawrD**

So many loves have I neglected. Thomas Campion. **CP-CampT**

So many minds in search of bodies. Adrienne Rich. **CP-RicAE**

So many nights the solitary lamp had burned. Rousseau in His Day. Donald Davie. **CP-DavDo**

So many others have lived in me! Residencies. Thomas McGrath. **SP-McGrT**

So many painted boxes. Circles and Squares. John Haines. **SP-HainJ**

So many poems about the deaths of animals. Essay. Hayden Carruth. **CP-CarHS**

So many roses in the garden. A Dream of Roses. Kathleen Jessie Raine. **SP-RainK**

So many selves(so many fiends and gods). Edward Estlin Cummings. **CP-CummE**

So many things happen. Four Ways of Knowledge. Robert Bly. **SP-BlyR**

So many tortoises. The Race. Howard Nemerov. **CP-NemeH**

So many women are murdered because some man. Body Count. Leonard Nathan. **SP-NathL**

So many worlds, so much to do. Tennyson. **HBV 1-2** *Fr.* In Memoriam A. H. H. **CP-TennA**

So many years have passed. Disillusion with the French Revolution. Charlotte Smith. **ECWP** *Fr.* Long wintry months are past; the Moon that now. *Fr.* The Emigrants. **CP-SmitC**

So months of cool flowers close in these arms. Jim Carroll. *Fr.* Living at the Movies. **SP-CarrJ**

So much depends. The Red Wheelbarrow. William Carlos Williams. **CP-WilW1**

So much for taupe and beige and eggshell. A Red Silk Blouse. William Matthews. **SP-MattW**

So much for the elves' wergild, the true governance. Geoffrey Hill. **NoAM** *Fr.* Mercian Hymns. **CP-HillG**

So much forgetten already. Paris Journal. Jim Morrison. **SP-MorrJ**

So much he had from fashion and no more. The Troublesome Reign. Geoffrey Hill. **CP-HillG**

So much is parchment where I gloom. The Black Mesa. James Merrill. **SP-MerrJ**

So much of Heaven has gone from Earth. Emily Dickinson. **CP-DickE**

So much of the proscenium burned. John Yau. **SP-YauJo** *Fr.* Scenes from the Life of Boullee.

So much rain / to make the mud again. A Wish. Robert Creeley. **CP-CreeR**

So much rain, so much life like the swollen sky. Dark August. Derek Walcott. **CP-WalcD**

So much slipping by. The Business. Charles Olson. **CP-OlsoC**

So much Summer. Emily Dickinson. **CP-DickE**

So Near—And Yet. Kenneth Patchen. **CP-PatcK**

So near to air and water merely. Celery. John Updike. **CP-UpdiJ**

So neck to stubborn neck, and obstinate knee to knee. Antaeus: A Fragment. Wilfred Owen. **CP-OwenW**

So nigh is grandeur to our dust. Duty. Ralph Waldo Emerson. **FaFP; GN; HBV 1-2; HBVY; TRV; TreF; TreFS; YaD** *Fr.* In an Age of Fops and Toys. **FPL; LiTA; PoLF** *Fr.* Voluntaries. **CP-EmerR**

So, nightly, hourly, I violate my mind. The Artist Speaks. . . the Woman Answers. Kay Boyle. **CP-BoylK**

So now, / Alive / John Daughty Dead. Defense of Luxembourg. Ernest Hemingway. **CP-HemiE**

So now, / Loseing the three last night. Poetry. Ernest Hemingway. **CP-HemiE**

So, now I have confess'd that he is thine. Sonnet 134. William Shakespeare. **HeIP; InvP; OXAEP-1** *Fr.* Sonnets. **CP-ShaWS**

So now it's your turn. Instructions to the Double. Tess Gallagher. **SP-GallT**

So now my summer task is ended, Mary. The Revolt of Islam. Percy Bysshe Shelley. **CP-ShelP**

So now my summer task is ended, Mary. *Dedication to* The Revolt of Islam. Percy Bysshe Shelley. **EnRP** *Fr.* The Revolt of Islam. **CP-ShelP**

So now the horses of Aiakides, off wide of the war-ground. The Horses of Achilles. Homer, *tr. by* George Meredith. **CP-MerG1** *Fr.* The Iliad.

So now the very bones of you are gone. Doricha. Posidippus. **AWP; FaBoEE; OBVE** *Fr.* Variations of Greek Themes. **CP-RobiE**

So oft as I with state of present time. Edmund Spenser. **OAEL-1** *Fr.* The Faerie Queene. **CP-Spens**

So oft I invoked thee for my Muse. Sonnet 78. William Shakespeare. *Fr.* Sonnets. **CP-ShaWS**

So often and with such cruel fascination I have dreamed the implacable void that contains dream. Charles Kenneth Williams. **SP-WillC**

(Gap, The.) **SP-WillC**

So often artists have painted a woman. January 18, 1979. John Yau. **SP-YauJo**

So often, so long I have thought of death. Song: So Often, So Long I Have Thought. Hayden Carruth. **CP-CarHS**

So old, so delicate, so small. Pablo Casals. Archibald MacLeish. **CP-MacLA**

So on she goes, and in her idle flight. Christopher Marlowe. **PoE** *Fr.* Hero and Leander. **CP-MarlC**

So on the seventh day. Apple Tragedy. Ted Hughes. **SP-HughT**

So once again, hearing the tired aunts. In the House of the Dying. Jane Cooper. **SP-CoopJ**

So, overmasterful, to sea! The Furious Voyage. Robert Ranke Graves. **CP-GravR**

So parted you as if the world for ever. To the Most Princely and Vertuous the Lady Elizabeth. Thomas Campion. **CP-CampT**

So passed they naked on, nor shunned the sight. John Milton. **PeECV**, *ll.* 319–334; **SeCePo** *Fr.* Book IV. **OAEL-1** *Fr.* Paradise Lost. **CP-MiltJ**

(Adam and Eve.) SeCePo, *ll.* 319–355;

So, passing through the rustic gate. The Burnt Bridge. Louis MacNeice. **CP-MacNL**

So Patrick once, striding the flogging weathers. Saint Patrick. John Hewitt. *Fr.* Two Irish Saints. **CP-HewiJ**

So pawed, / by this long last Bear-son. To Gerhardt, There, among Europe's Things of Which He Has Written Us in His "Brief an Creely und Olson." Charles Olson. **CP-OlsoC; SP-OlsoC**

So Penseroso. Ogden Nash. **CP-NashO**

So Phoebus makes me worthy of his bays. To Sir Thomas Overbury. Ben Jonson. **CP-JonsB**

So, Pound, you have found the gallows tree. A Lustrum for You, E.P. Charles Olson. **CP-OlsoC**

So proud she was to die. Emily Dickinson. **CP-DickE**

So Quicke, So Hot, So Mad is Thy Fond Sute. Thomas Campion. **CP-CampT**

So quickly, and so slowly. . . In the tiny elevator of the flat you'd borrowed on the Rue de Pondichery. Le Petit Salvié. Charles Kenneth Williams. **SP-WillC**

So quiet. Even the dogs. Playing Shuffleboard, Drunk, in Key West, Fla. Peter Meinke. **SP-MeinP** *Fr.* Lines from Key West.

So ran the schoolday, full of time and stress. Childhood. Rainer Maria Rilke, *tr. fr. German by* Howard Nemerov. **CP-NemeH**

So, remotely, in your part of the world. A Letter from Armenia. Geoffrey Hill. *Fr.* The Songbook of Sebastian Arrurruz. **CP-HillG**

So, salt is the boundary mark between Fire that burns, and the Wet. The Boundary Stone. David Herbert Lawrence. **CP-LawrD**

So *Satan spake*, and him *Bëelzebub*. The Council of Satan. John Milton. **PoEL-3** *Fr.* Book I. **FHYEP; NAEL-1; OAEL-1; OxAEP-1** *Fr.* Paradise Lost. **CP-MiltJ**

"So say the foolish!" Say the foolish so, Love? Poetics. Robert Browning. **CP-BroR2**

So set its Sun in Thee. Emily Dickinson. **CP-DickE**

So several factions from this first ferment. Achitophel: The Earl of Shaftsbury. John Dryden. **NOBE** *Fr.* Absalom and Achitophel, Pt. I. **SP-DrydJ**

So shall I live, supposing thou art true. Sonnet 93. William Shakespeare. **InvP; MasP** *Fr.* Sonnets. **CP-ShaWS**

So shall this book wax like unto a well. Robert Louis Stevenson. *Fr.* Sonnets. **CP-StevR**

So she came back into his house again. Edna St. Vincent Millay. *Fr.* Sonnets from an Ungrafted Tree. **CP-MillE**

So she low-toned; while with shut eyes I lay. Tennyson. **EBVV** *Fr.* So was their sanctuary violated. *Fr.* The Princess. **CP-TennA**

So she must have been pleased with us. Hilda Doolittle. **NALW** *Fr.* Tribute to the Angels. **CP-DoolH**

So She Said. James Wright. **CP-WrigJ**

So shy shy shy(and with a). Edward Estlin Cummings. **CP-CummE**

So small it is, there must be at least two. Riddle. William DeWitt Snodgrass. **SP-SnodW**

So smell those odours that do rise. To the Most Fair and Lovely Mistress Anne Soame, Now Lady Abdie. Robert Herrick. **CP-HerrR**

So smooth, so sweet, so silv'ry is thy voice. Upon Julia's Voice. Robert Herrick. **CP-HerrR**

So, so, break[e] off this last lamenting kiss[e]. The Expiration. John Donne. **CP-DonnJ**

So soft streams meet, so springs with gladder smiles. The Welcome to Sack. Robert Herrick. **CP-HerrR**

So soon as day, forth dawning from the East. Artegall and Radigund. Edmund Spenser. **OBSC** *Fr.* The Faerie Queene. **CP-Spens**

So soon as ever your mazed spirit descends. Instructions to the Orphic Adept. Robert Ranke Graves. **CP-GravR**

So sounds grass, and if it is sun or no sun. Louis Zukofsky. **CP-ZukLS**

So spake Esaias: so, in words of flame. To George B. Cheever. John Greenleaf Whittier. **CP-WhitJ**

So spake he, supplicating; and him heard Phoibos Apollo. The Vengeance of Apollo. Homer, *tr. by* George Meredith. **CP-MerG2** *Fr.* The Iliad.

So spake our morning star then in his rise. John Milton. **PeECV** *Fr.* Book I. *Fr.* Paradise Regained [*or* Regain'd]. **CP-MiltJ**

So spake our Mother Eve, and Adam heard. John Milton. **FaBoRV; NOBE; NOSC; OBS** *Fr.* Book XII. *Fr.* Paradise Lost. **CP-MiltJ**

(Banishment, The.) **NOBE; OBS**

(Exile.) **NOSC**

(Exit from Eden, The.) **FaBoRV**

So spake she her first utterance on the rack. George Meredith. *Fr.* The Sage Enamoured and the Honest Lady. **CP-MerG1**

So spake the [*or* th'] Archangel Michael; then paused. John Milton. **FaBoPV**, *ll.* 466–551; **NAEL-1; OAEL-1**, *ll.* 466–649; *Fr.* Book XII. *Fr.* Paradise Lost. **CP-MiltJ**

So spake the enemy of mankind, enclosed. John Milton. *Fr.* Book IX. **FHYEP; NAEL-1; NAWM-1; NoP; OAEL-1** *Fr.* Paradise Lost. **CP-MiltJ**

So spake the godlike power, and thus our sire. John Milton. **NAEL-1** *Fr.* Book VIII. *Fr.* Paradise Lost. **CP-MiltJ**

So spake the Son of God, and Satan stood. Book III. John Milton. *Fr.* Paradise Regained [*or* Regain'd]. **CP-MiltJ**

So spake the Voice; and, as with a single life. Alcaics. Arthur Hugh Clough. **SP-ClouA**

So spoke of the existence of things. George Oppen. *Fr.* Of Being Numerous. **CP-OppeG**

So squeezed, wince you I scream? I love you & hate. John Berryman. **FF** *Fr.* Homage to Mistress Bradstreet. **CP-BerrJ**

So standing.our eyes filled with the wind,and the. Edward Estlin Cummings. **CP-CummE**

So stood of old the holy Christ. The Healer. John Greenleaf Whittier. **CP-WhitJ**

So stretched out huge in length the Arch-Fiend lay. John Milton. **TEP** *Fr.* Book I. **FHYEP; NAEL-1; OAEL-1; OxAEP-1** *Fr.* Paradise Lost. **CP-MiltJ**

So summer comes in the end to these few stains. The Beginning. Wallace Stevens. **CP-StevW**

So sung the BARD—and Nansie's waws. Robert Burns. **PoE** *Fr.* The Jolly Beggars.

So sweet / the body. Robert Creeley. **CP-CreeR**

So sweet is thy discourse to me. Thomas Campion. **CP-CampT**

So That Even a Lover. Louis Zukofsky. **CP-ZukLS**

So that the vines burst from my fingers. Canto 17. Ezra Pound. **InPS; MeMAP; NAAL-2; OBMV; SP-PouneE** *Fr.* Cantos. **CP-PoCan**

So that Tien-tan chose bulls, a thousand. Canto 54. Ezra Pound. *Fr.* Cantos. **CP-PoCan**

So that's what it's like to be a wheel. The Ballad of the Wheel. Charles Simic. **SP-SimiC**

So That's Who I Remind Me Of. Ogden Nash. **CP-NashO**

So the Chosunese would imagine the earth to be flat. Chosun. James Fenton. **SP-FentJ**

So the church Christ was hit and buried. Le Christianisme. Wilfred Owen. **CP-OwenW**

So the distances are Galatea. The Distances. Charles Olson. **CP-OlsoC; SP-OlsoC**

So the Eyes accost—and sunder. Emily Dickinson. **CP-DickE**

So the Jesuits brought in astronomy. Canto 60. Ezra Pound. *Fr.* Cantos. **CP-PoCan**

So the leaves trembled. Ted Hughes. *Fr.* Scapegoats and Rabies. **SP-HughT**

So the Norse / were neurotic. Charles Olson. **CP-OlsoC**

So the plastic conduits for the new. Cracking a Few Hundred Million Years. Archie Randolph Ammons. **SP-AmmoA**

So the rain falls. Cornkind. Frank O'Hara. **SP-OharF**

So the sea stands up to the shore, banging his chains. William Everson. *Fr.* Tendril in the Mesh. **SP-EverW**

So the storms bore the daughters of Pandarus out into thrall, *diff. vers.* Homer. *See* The Daughters of Pandarus.

So the strong will prevailed, and Alden went on his errand. The Lover's Errand. Henry Wadsworth Longfellow. **TreFS** *Fr.* The Courtship of Miles Standish. **SP-LongH**

So, the three Court-ladies began. Which? Robert Browning. **CP-BroR2**

So, the tide forgets, as morning. The Shore. David St. John. **SP-StJoD**

So, the water gate. Roy Fisher. **SP-FishR** *Fr.* Matrix.

So, the year's done with! Love. Robert Browning. **ArLo; EnLoPo** *Fr.* Earth's Immortalities. **CP-BroR2**

So then—the Vandals of our isle. On the Burning of Lord Mansfield's Library. William Cowper. **CP-CowpW**

So There! David Herbert Lawrence. **CP-LawrD**

So there are the clouds, do not believe them. Maytime. Gilbert Sorrentino. **SP-SorrG**

So there sat they. Side by Side. Thomas Hardy. **CP-HardT**

So there you are. The Poet of the Prison Isle: Ritsos Against the Colonels. Thomas McGrath. **SP-McGrT**

So they in Heav'n their odes and vigils tun'd. John Milton. **PeECV**, *ll.* 182–195; **OBS** *Fr.* Book I. *Fr.* Paradise Regained [*or* Regain'd]. **CP-MiltJ**

(Messiah, The ("So they in Heav'n their odes and vigils tun'd").) **OBS**, *ll.* 182–293;

So, this is all,—the utmost reach. The Pastoral Letter. John Greenleaf Whittier. **CP-WhitJ**

So this is death that I. Death. William Carlos Williams. **CP-WilW2**

So this is Glastonbury. A green hill far away. Canto XXII. Louis MacNeice. *Fr.* Autumn Sequel. **CP-MacNL**

So this is (may we take it) Mitteleuropa. Canto 35. Ezra Pound. *Fr.* Cantos. **CP-PoCan**

So This Is Nebraska. Ted Kooser. **SP-KoosT**

So this is what's become of the idea. Funeral Homes. William Matthews. **SP-MattW**

So this was what the day had waited for. Helen. Wystan Hugh Auden. **CP-AudWJ**

So Thomas Edison. Lines to Be Embroidered on a Bib, or, The Child Is Father of the Man, but Not for Quite a While. Ogden Nash. **CP-NashO**

So through that unripe day you bore your head. Philip Larkin. **CP-LarkP**

So through the darkness and the cold we flew. Skating. William Wordsworth. **CH; SD** *Fr.* Introduction—Childhood and School-Time.

EnRP; FHYEP *Fr.* The Prelude; Growth of a Poet's Mind [1850 vers.]. **CP-WorW3**

So, Time. Thomas Hardy. **CP-HardT**

So Tir'd Are All My Thoughts. Thomas Campion. **CP-CampT**

So tired. Robert Creeley. **CP-CreeR**

So tired am I, so weary of today. Christina Georgina Rossetti. *Fr.* Later Life: A Double Sonnet of Sonnets. **CP-RosC2**

So to celebrate the kingdom: it grows. The Herefordshire Carol. Geoffrey Hill. *Fr.* An Apology for the Revival of Christian Architecture in England. **CP-HillG**

So to Fatness Come. Stevie Smith. **CP-SmitS**

So to Speak. Carl Sandburg. **CP-SandC**

So to the sylvan lodge. John Milton. **NAEL-1** *Fr.* Book V. *Fr.* Paradise Lost. **CP-MiltJ**

So to the tented ground where showmen come. Prelude to an Ode for Barnum. John Hewitt. **CP-HewiJ**

So treat me, even dead. Wendell Berry. *Fr.* Testament. **CP-BerrW**

So Uncle Sam was truly Prospero. The Magician. John Hewitt. **CP-HewiJ**

So unwarely was never no man caught. Sir Thomas Wyatt. **CP-WyatT**

So valiant is the intimacy. Emily Dickinson. **SP-DickE**

So Various. Thomas Hardy. **CP-HardT**

So Venus does hang and glitter in the prepared sky. The Objects. Charles Olson. **CP-OlsoC**

So vile was poor Wat, such a miscreant slave. Robert Burns. **CP-BurnR** (On W. R———, Esq.) **CP-BurnR**

So was their sanctuary violated. Tennyson. *Fr.* The Princess. **CP-TennA**
" 'Blame not thyself too much,' I said, "nor blame."" **NAEL-2**
"Come down, O maid, from yonder mountain height." **EBVV; FF; GTBS-P; MeMBP; NAEL-2; NOBVV; OAEL-2; OBEV; OBNC; PIP; SCGP; TrGrPo**
(Idyl, An: "Come down, O maid, from yonder mountain height.") **TrGrPo**
"Now sleeps the crimson petal, now the white." **ArLo; BLPL; BoLoP; CBLP; ChER; ChTr; CoGr; EBEV; EBVV; ELP; FHYEP; FaBoBe; FaPoB; FiP; GBL; GTBS-P; LLLT; MeMBP; NAEL-2; NIP; NOBE; NoP; OBEV; OBNC; OPOU; OXAEP-2; PPP; PIP; PoEL-5; SCGP; SCV; SeCePo; TFi; TrGrPo**
(Song: "Now sleeps the crimson petal, now the white.") **BLPL; FaBoBe; OPOU**
(Summer Night.) **OBEV; SeCePo**
"So she low-toned; while with shut eyes I lay." **EBVV**

So we came again to the sea water. The Third Book. Archibald MacLeish. *Fr.* Conquistador. **CP-MacLA**

So we loosed a bloomin' volley. Rudyard Kipling. **CP-KiplR** *Fr.* The Taking of Lungtungpen. *Fr.* Plain Tales from the Hills.

So we must say Goodbye, my darling. Goodbye. Alun Lewis. **CP-LewiA**

So we settled it all when the storm was done. Rudyard Kipling. **CP-KiplR** *Fr.* The Light That Failed.

So we shall never hear him any more. W.R. Rodgers. John Hewitt. **CP-HewiJ**

So we started walking along the passage. Eurydice to Orpheus. Jenny Joseph. **SP-JoseJ**

So we, who've supped the self-same cup. After the Quarrel. Paul Laurence Dunbar. **CP-DunbP**

So We'll Go No More a Roving. Byron. **CP-Byron**

So well that I can live without. Emily Dickinson. **CP-DickE**

So we're drinking and we're dancing. Closing Time. Leonard Cohen. **CP-CoheL**

So We've Come at Last to Freud. Alice Walker. **CP-WalkA**

So what, if Lance the Leftist, did shout once for "Arms for Spain"? Where Did That One Go to, 'Erbert. Malcolm Lowry. **CP-LowrM**

So what is a body but a man. Face While Shaving. Charles Bukowski. **SP-BukC2**

So what is the use of poetry these days. Uses of Poetry. Lawrence Ferlinghetti. **SP-FerlL**

So what said the others and the sun went down. Mrs. Alfred Uruguay. Wallace Stevens. **CP-StevW**

So what the door was guarded. Curfew. Paul Éluard, *tr. fr. French by* William Carlos Williams. **CP-WilW2**

So when flesh feels slighted by the present. Malcolm Lowry. *Fr.* Peter Gaunt and the Canals. **CP-LowrM**

So when she lay beside me. As She Was Thus Alone in the Clear Moonlight. Kenneth Patchen. **CP-PatcK**

So while the blear-eyed pimp beside me walked. Easter Day II. Arthur Hugh Clough. **SP-ClouA**

So white I was, he would have me cry. The Dead Bride. Geoffrey Hill. **TW** *Fr.* Three Baroque Meditations. **CP-HillG**

So why does this dead carnation hold. Song: So Why Does This Dead Carnation. Hayden Carruth. **CP-CarHS**

So with sweet oaths converting the salt earth. The Emblem. Geoffrey Hill. *Fr.* Locust Songs. **CP-HillG**

So you are lost to me! Bread upon the Waters. David Herbert Lawrence. **CP-LawrD**

So you aren't Tolstoy or Saint Francis. So? Leonard Nathan. **SP-NathL**

So You Have Been, Despite Parental Ban. Philip Larkin. **CP-LarkP**

So you have swept me back. Hilda Doolittle. **NALW; VBLP; VGW** *Fr.* Eurydice. **CP-DoolH**

So you have swept me back. Eurydice. Hilda Doolittle. **CP-DoolH**

So you haven't got a drum, just beat you belly. Ourchestra. Shel Silverstein. **SP-SilS2**

So you thought those gorgeous lips were for you to use? The Goddess of Nature's Diatribe to her People. Jenny Joseph. **SP-JoseJ**

So you turn up like an old. The Lansing Bad Penny Come Again Blues. Marge Piercy. **SP-PierM**

So you want to divide all the money there is. Carl Sandburg. *Fr.* The People, Yes. **CP-SandC**

So you'd eat the ear of Van Gogh! Charles Henri Ford. *Fr.* Epigrams. **SP-FordC**

So your belly feels hungry. Syracuse Nights. Stephen Dobyns. **SP-DobyS**

So you're hunting for ann well i'm looking for will. Edward Estlin Cummings. **CP-CummE**

So youre playing / Macbeth in Singapore. Identities. Al Young. **CP-YounA**

So zestfully canst thou sing? The Blinded Bird. Thomas Hardy. **CP-HardT**

Soaker. Archie Randolph Ammons. **SP-AmmoA**

Soaking leaves, green yellow, hold like rubber, The. Robert Lowell. *Fr.* Fall Weekend at *Milgate*. **SP-LoweR**

Soap-Pig, The. Paul Muldoon. **SP-MuldP**

Soap Suds. Louis MacNeice. **CP-MacNL**

Soar[e] up[p], my soul[e], unto thy rest[e]. Seek[e] Flowers of Heaven. Robert Southwell. **CP-SoutR**

Soaring lark is blest as proud, The. Gold and Silver Fishes in a Vase. William Wordsworth. **CP-WorW2**

Sobbing of the Bells, The. Walt Whitman. **CP-WhitW**

Sober I rode into the brand new dawn. Sunrise. Malcolm Lowry. **CP-LowrM**

Sober laverock, warbling wild, The. Robert Burns. **PBBP** *Fr.* The Humble Petition of Bruar Water to the Noble Duke of Athole. **CP-BurnR**

Sobieski's Shield. Geoffrey Hill. **CP-HillG**

Sobriety in Search. Robert Herrick. **CP-HerrR**

Social. Charles Bukowski. **SP-BukC1**

Socialist Realism & Capitalist Realism. Realism. Al Young. **CP-YounA**

Society. Robert Herrick. **CP-HerrR**

Society. George Meredith. **CP-MerG1**

Society for me my misery. Emily Dickinson. **CP-DickE**

Society of gnats, A. Gnats. Richard Eberhart. **CP-EberR**

Sociology of Toyotas and Jade Chrysanthemums, The. Hayden Carruth. **CP-CarHS**

Socrates on the frozen lake. Alun Lewis. *Fr.* Threnody for a Starry Night. **CP-LewiA**

Socratic. Hilda Doolittle. **HoPM** *Fr.* Child Poems. **CP-DoolH**

Soda Fountains. Nicanor Parra, *tr. fr. Spanish by* Thomas Merton. **CP-MertT**

Sodden sleep from which we open like umbrellas, The. Fellow Oddballs. William Matthews. **SP-MattW**

See I may gaine thy death, my life I'le give. Matthew 16:25; Whosoever Shall Loose His Life. Bible, *N.T.* **CP-CrasR,** *tr. by* Richard Crashaw; *Fr.* St. Matthew.

Soeur Louise De La Miséricorde. Christina Georgina Rossetti. **CP-RosC2**

Sofa, The, *sels.* William Cowper. *Fr.* The Task. **CP-CowpW**

    Ease. **TEP**

    "For I have lov'd the rural walk through lanes." **EnRP; NOEC**

    (Rural Sights and Sounds.) **NOEC,** *book* 1, *ll.* 109–210; God Made the Country. **FiP; PoEL-3**

    "Thou knowest my praise of nature most sincere." **NAEL-1**

Soft and softlier hold me, friends! Maiden Speech of the Æolian Harp. Ralph Waldo Emerson. **CP-EmerR**

Soft As a Cloud Is Yon Blue Ridge. William Wordsworth. **CP-WorW2**

Soft as the bed in the earth. The Shadow. William Carlos Williams. **CP-WilW1**

Soft as the massacre of Suns. Emily Dickinson. **CP-DickE**

Soft cat and the scratchy cat, The. Concord Cats. Richard Eberhart. **CP-EberR**

Soft deceit & idleness. William Blake. *Fr.* Several Questions Answered. **CP-BlakW**

    ("Which are beauties sweetest dress.")

Soft earth turns straight up. Uluru Wild Fig Song. Gary Snyder. **CP-SnydG**

Soft grey ghosts crawl up my sleeve. Remembering. Maya Angelou. **SP-AngeM**

Soft May mists are here again. May, 1972. James Schuyler. **CP-SchuJ**

Soft Musick. Robert Herrick. **CP-HerrR**

Soft night–wind went laden to death, The. George Meredith. *Fr.* The Young Princess. **CP-MerG1**

Soft Parade, The. Jim Morrison. **SP-MorrJ**

Soft rain on the. Straits of Malacca 24 Oct 1957. Gary Snyder. **CP-SnydG**

Soft rainsqualls on the swells. Oil. Gary Snyder. **CP-SnydG**

Soft Sea washed around the House, A. Emily Dickinson. **CP-DickE**

Soft Snow. William Blake. **CP-BlakW**

Soft songs, like birds, die in poison air. Apology for Apostasy? Etheridge Knight. **SP-KnigE**

Soft, subtle fire, thou soul of art. Ben Jonson. **CP-JonsB** *Fr.* Mercury Vindicated.

Soft unclouded blue of air, The. Lines. Emily Brontë. **CP-BronE**

Soft voluptuous opiate shades, The. Twilight. Walt Whitman. **CP-WhitW**

Soft, where the shadow glides. Autumnal. James Wright. **CP-WrigJ**

Soft white lamb in the daisy meadow. Ballad. Christina Georgina Rossetti. **CP-RosC3**

Soft wind, A. No One Remembers. Philip Levine. **SP-LeviP**

Soft Wood. Robert Lowell. **SP-LoweR**

Soft you day, be velvet soft. The Gamut. Maya Angelou. **SP-AngeM**

Softening the marbles, day. Dream (Escape from the Sculpture Museum) and Waking. James Merrill. **SP-MerrJ**

Softens the air so cold & rude. Ralph Waldo Emerson. **CP-EmerR**

Softly along the road of evening. Nod. Walter de la Mare. **CP-DeLaW**

Softly and singly an owl. Kenneth Rexroth. **CP-RexKL** *Fr.* The Phoenix and the Tortoise.

Softly croons the radiogram, loudly hoot the owls. Invasion Exercise on the Poultry Farm. Sir John Betjeman. **CP-BetjJ**

Softly from its still lair in Plympton Street. Edward Estlin Cummings. **CP-CummE**

Softly, in the dusk, a woman is singing to me. Piano. David Herbert Lawrence. **CP-LawrD**

Softly Softly. Richard Shelton. **SP-ShelR**

Softly the civilized. Raiders' Dawn. Alun Lewis. **CP-LewiA**

Softly the evening came. The sun from the western horizon. Henry Wadsworth Longfellow. **APN-1** *Fr.* It was the month of May. Far down the Beautiful River. *Fr.* Part the Second. *Fr.* Evangeline, a Tale of Acadie. **SP-LongH**

Softly, Then, Softly. David Herbert Lawrence. **CP-LawrD**

Softly wanton the wind. Eros in May at MacDowell. Isabella Gardner. **CP-GardI**

Sohl. Patti Smith. **SP-SmitP**

Sohrab and Rustum. Matthew Arnold.

    "But the majestic river floated on." **SP-ArnoM**

Soil now gets a rumpling soft and damp, The. The Strong Are Saying Nothing. Robert Frost. **CP-FrosR**

Soil of Flint, if steady tilled. Emily Dickinson. **CP-DickE**

Soil sandy and the plow light, neither, The. Basil Bunting. **CP-BuntB**

Soiled city oblongs stand sprawling, The. City Number. Carl Sandburg. **CP-SandC**

Soiled Dove. Carl Sandburg. **CP-SandC**

Soirée. Charles Bukowski. **SP-BukC2**

Sojourn in the Whale. Marianne Craig Moore. **CP-MoorM**

Sojourner Truth. Robert Earl Hayden. **CNA** *Fr.* Stars. **CP-HaydR**

Sojourners. Marge Piercy. **SP-PierM**

Sojourning through a southern realm in youth. The Sleeping Beauty. Wilfred Owen. **CP-OwenW**

Sol Brady. Louise McNeill. **SP-McNeL**

Sol through white curtains shot a tim'rous ray. Alexander Pope. **ECEV** *Fr.* The Rape of the Lock[, an Heroi-Comical Poem]. **CP-PopeA**

Solace. Richard Eberhart. **CP-EberR**

Solace of kisses and cookies and cabbage. Last Words. Theodore Roethke. **CP-RoetT**

Solar. Philip Larkin. **CP-LarkP**

Solar emeralds melt and blend. Eos. Tom Clark. **SP-ClarT**

Solar floes / big as continents. Transducer. Archie Randolph Ammons. **SP-AmmoA**

Solar insect on the wing. Ralph Waldo Emerson. **CP-EmerR**

Soldier [T. P.]. Randall Jarrell. **CP-JarrR**

Soldier, A. Robert Frost. **CP-FrosR**

Soldier, The. Gerard Manley Hopkins. **CP-HopkG**

Soldier, The. Randall Jarrell. **CP-JarrR**

Soldier, The. Alun Lewis. **CP-LewiA**
  "I within me holding."
  "Now as a lover would."
Soldier, A. Sir John Suckling. **CP-SuckJ**
Soldier an' Sailor Too. Rudyard Kipling. **CP-KiplR**
Soldier and the Star, The. Kenneth Patchen. **CP-PatcK**
Soldier Dear to Us, A. Stevie Smith. **CP-SmitS**
Soldier from the wars returning. Alfred Edward Housman. **CP-HousA**
Soldier may forget his Sword, The. The Press. Rudyard Kipling. **CP-KiplR**
Soldier on His Knees in the Snow. Marsden Hartley. **CP-HartM**
Soldier, past full retreat, is marching out of the grave, The. Go Ask the Dead. Thomas McGrath. **SP-McGrT**
Soldier Rejects His Times Addressing His Contemporaries, A. Richard Eberhart. **CP-EberR**
Soldier, rest! thy warfare o'er. Ellen's Song. Sir Walter Scott. **SP-ScotW** Fr. The Lady of the Lake.
Soldier runs home, A. Planting. Philip Levine. **SP-LeviP**
Soldier, Soldier. Rudyard Kipling. **CP-KiplR**
Soldier, there is a war between the mind. Wallace Stevens. **LiTA; NePA; NoAM** Fr. Notes toward a Supreme Fiction. **CP-StevW**
(Soldier, There Is a War between the Mind.) **LiTA; NePA**
Soldier, There Is a War between the Mind. Wallace Stevens. See Soldier, there is a war between the mind.
Soldier Walks under the Trees of the University, The. Randall Jarrell. **CP-JarrR**
Soldier Who Lived Through the War, The. Howard Nemerov. **CP-NemeH**
Soldiers are marching singing down the lane. A Haunting. Ted Hughes. Fr. Scapegoats and Rabies. **SP-HughT**
Soldiers Bathing. Frank Templeton Prince. **CP-PrinF**
Soldier's boots, beautifully bulled, The. Two Minute's Silence. Ted Hughes. Fr. Scapegoats and Rabies. **SP-HughT**
Soldier's Dream. Wilfred Owen. **CP-OwenW**
Soldiers never do die well. Champs d'Honneur. Ernest Hemingway. **CP-HemiE**
Soldiers of Peace. Clement of Alexandria, tr. fr. Greek by Thomas Merton. **CP-MertT**
"Soldiers, our brethren and our friends are slain." Percy Bysshe Shelley. **OBF** Fr. The Revolt of Islam. **CP-ShelP**
Soldiers Returning, The. Richard Shelton. **SP-ShelR**
Soldiers walk around. Charles Henri Ford. **SP-FordC** Fr. Emblems of Arachne.
Soldiers with Green Leggings. Peter Meinke. **SP-MeinP**
Soldier's Wound, The. Wallace Stevens. See How red the rose that is the soldier's wound.
Sole listener, Duddon! to the breeze that played. William Wordsworth. Fr. The River Duddon [A Series of Sonnets]. **CP-WorW2**
Sole Maid, associate sole, to me beyond. Her Thoughts. Samuel Taylor Coleridge. **CP-ColeS**
Sole Positive of Night! Ne Plus Ultra. Samuel Taylor Coleridge. **CP-ColeS**
Sole watchman of the flying stars, guard me. John Berryman. **UnPo** Fr. Eleven Addresses to the Lord. **CP-BerrJ**
Soledad. Robert Earl Hayden. **CP-HaydR**
Soledad. Edwin Rolfe. **CP-RolfE**
Soleil d'automne. Do. Charles Henri Ford. **SP-FordC** Fr. Emblems of Arachne.
Solemn-breathing air is ended, The. Ad Lyram. Samuel Taylor Coleridge. **CP-ColeS**
Solemn dreams / Dreams beautiful as the fair hues that lie. Fragments from the Alfoxden Note-Book (II). William Wordsworth. **CP-WorW1**
Solemn League and Covenant, The. Robert Burns. **CP-BurnR**
Solemn light in morning drizzle early. Mist Sleeve Flight. Tom Clark. **SP-ClarT**
Solemn Music. Thomas Merton. Fr. Cables to the Ace. **CP-MertT**
Solemn Music. Leonard Nathan. **SP-NathL**
Solemn plain-faced child stands gazing there, A. A Portrait. Walter de la Mare. **CP-DeLaW**
Solemn rites are well begun, The. Ben Jonson. **CP-JonsB** Fr. Oberon, the Fairy Prince.
Solemn thing—it was—I said, A. Emily Dickinson. **CP-DickE**
Solemn thing within the Soul, A. Emily Dickinson. **CP-DickE**
Solemnity of a bemused tiger, there in his eyes. Green Eyes. William Carlos Williams, tr. fr. Spanish by William Carlos Williams. **CP-WilW2**
Soles. Derek Mahon. **SP-MahoD**
Solfeggietto. Adrienne Rich. **SP-RicA1**
Solid, The. Charles Kenneth Williams. **SP-WillC**

Solid, Ironical, Rolling Orb. Walt Whitman. **CP-WhitW**
Solid Rock. "Bob Dylan." **CP-DylaB**
Solid shimmer of his prose, The. Nabokov's Death. William Matthews. **SP-MattW**
Solid, solid universe, The. Cupido. Ralph Waldo Emerson. **CP-EmerR**
Solid Sprite Who Stands Alone, The. Edna St. Vincent Millay. **CP-MillE**
Soliloquies. Charles Kenneth Williams. **SP-WillC**
Soliloquies. Geoffrey Hill. **CP-HillG**
  Old Poet with Distant Admirers.
  Stone Man, The.
Soliloquy ("August and laurelled have been. . ."). Robinson Jeffers. **CP-JefR1**
Soliloquy. James McAuley. **SP-McAuJ**
Soliloquy: "Whenever I am got under my gravestone." Ted Hughes. **SP-HughT**
Soliloquy in Circles. Ogden Nash. **CP-NashO**
Soliloquy in Dogtown, Cape Ann. Marsden Hartley. **CP-HartM**
Soliloquy of a Bard in the Country. Byron. **CP-Byron**
Soliloquy of a Turkey. Paul Laurence Dunbar. **CP-DunbP**
Soliloquy of One of the Spies Left in the Wilderness, A. Gerard Manley Hopkins. **CP-HopkG**
Soliloquy of the Solipsist. Sylvia Plath. **CP-PlatS**
Soliloquy of the Spanish Cloister. Robert Browning. **CP-BroR1**
Soliloquy on the Full Moon, She Being in a Mad Passion, A. Samuel Taylor Coleridge. **CP-ColeS**
Soliloquy Upon Love. Kathleen Jessie Raine. **SP-RainK**
Solipsism. Karl Shapiro. **SP-ShapK**
Solipsism & Solecism. Howard Nemerov. **CP-NemeH**
Solipsism While Dying. Margaret Atwood. **SP-AtwM1**
Solipsist. Stephen Spender. **CP-SpenS**
Solitaire. John Updike. **CP-UpdiJ**
Solitary, A. Daniel Gerard Hoffman. **SP-HoffD**
Solitary, The. Percy Bysshe Shelley. **CP-ShelP**
Solitary, The. William Wordsworth. Fr. The Excursion. **CP-WorW2**
  "Homeward the / Shepherds moved." **EnRP**
  "I could not, ever and anon, forbear." **EnRP**
Solitary are obsessed, The. George Oppen. Fr. Tourist Eye. **CP-OppeG**
Solitary Life. Thomas Merton. **CP-MertT**
Solitary Man Discovered in a Field of Daisies. Gilbert Sorrentino. Fr. Twelve Études for Voice and Kazoo. **SP-SorrG**
Solitary Observation Brought Back from a Sojourn in Hell. Louise Bogan. **CP-BogaL**
Solitary Pond, The. John Updike. **CP-UpdiJ**
Solitary Reaper, The. William Wordsworth. **CP-WorW1**
Solitary Rose, The. Christina Georgina Rossetti. **CP-RosC3**
Solitary Travel. Louis MacNeice. **CP-MacNL**
Solitude. "Lewis Carroll." **CP-CarrL**
Solitude. Walter de la Mare. **CP-DeLaW**
Solitude, A. Denise Levertov. **CP-LeveD**
Solitude. Charles Simic. **SP-SimiC**
Solitude is kind. Marsden Hartley. **CP-HartM**
Solitude Late at Night in the Woods. Robert Bly. **SP-BlyR**
Solitude of Mr. Powers, The. Ogden Nash. **CP-NashO**
Solo. Li Po, tr. fr. Chinese by William Carlos Williams with David Rafael Wang. **CP-WilW2**
Solo for Saturday Night Guitar. Carl Sandburg. **CP-SandC**
Solomon and Balkis. Robert Browning. **CP-BroR2**
Solomon and the Witch. William Butler Yeats. **CP-YeatW**
Solomon King of the Jews and the Queen of Sheba, Balkis. Solomon and Balkis. Robert Browning. **CP-BroR2**
Solomon most glorious in array / Put not on his glories without care. Consider the Lilies of the Field. Christina Georgina Rossetti. **CP-RosC2**
Solomon to Sheba. William Butler Yeats. **CP-YeatW**
Solomon's Baby. David Herbert Lawrence. **CP-LawrD**
Solomon's Mines. Geoffrey Hill. **CP-HillG**
Solomon's Seal. Robert Ranke Graves. **CP-GravR**
Solon. George Meredith. **CP-MerG1**
Solstice. Louise Glück. **SP-GlücL**
Solstice. Robinson Jeffers. **CP-JefR2**
Solstice. Louis MacNeice. **CP-MacNL**
Solstice. William Carlos Williams. **CP-WilW1**
Solstice of the dark, the absolute. Out of the Ash. William Everson. **SP-EverW**
Solstice Poem. Margaret Atwood. **SP-AtwM2**
  "As for the women, who did not."
  "Beyond the white hill which maroons us."

"In this house (in a dying orchard." **CrSp**

"My daughter crackles paper, blows."

"Tree hulks in the living-, A."

Solution. Ralph Waldo Emerson. **CP-EmerR**

Solution. George Oppen. **CP-OppeG**

Solutions, to Puzzles from Wonderland. "Lewis Carroll." Fr. Puzzles from Wonderland. **CP-CarrL**

"As curly-headed Jemmy was sleeping in bed."

"Five seeing, and seven blind."

"In Shylock's bargain for the flesh was found."

" 'In these degenerate days,' we oft hear said."

"Ten."

"That salmon and sole Puss should think very grand."

" 'Twixt 'Perhaps' and "May be.""

Solving the Riddle. Charles Simic. **SP-SimiC**

Solvitur Acris Hiems. Horace. Fr. Three Odes of Horace. **CP-MacNL**

Somber figures that wander off into the night. You Must Have Some Idea Where They've Gone. Kenneth Patchen. **CP-PatcK**

Somber Prayer. John Berryman. **CP-BerrJ**

Some act of Love's bound to rehearse. Why I Write Not of Love. Ben Jonson. **CP-JonsB**

Some Afternoon. Robert Creeley. **CP-CreeR**

Some ancient authors wisely write. A Poetical Epistle to Dr. Sheridan. Jonathan Swift. **CP-SwifJ**

Some angels were standing on the ground. The Angels. Richard Eberhart. **CP-EberR**

Some are bewildered in the maze of Schools. Plain Fools. Alexander Pope. **OBSV** Fr. An Essay on Criticism. **CP-PopeA**

Some Are Born. Stevie Smith. **CP-SmitS**

Some are home-sick—some two or three. The Delinquent Travellers. Samuel Taylor Coleridge. **CP-ColeS**

Some are in prison; some are dead. The Chums. Theodore Roethke. **CP-RoetT**

Some are laughing, some are weeping. Sound Sleep. Christina Georgina Rossetti. **CP-RosC1**

Some are teethed on a silver spoon. Saturday's Child. Countee Cullen. **CP-CullC**

Some Arrows slay but whom they strike. Emily Dickinson. **CP-DickE**

Some ask praise of their fellows. Edward Estlin Cummings. **CP-CummE**

Some asked me where the rubies grew. The Rock of Rubies: and The Quarrie of Pearls. Robert Herrick. **CP-HerrR**

Some Aspects of Immortality. Archibald MacLeish. **CP-MacLA**

Some awful / grating sound. Sounds. Robert Creeley. **CP-CreeR**

Some Beasts. Pablo Neruda, tr. fr. Spanish by James Wright. **CP-WrigJ**

Some beating in there. Night Bird. James Dickey. **CP-DickJ**

Some beauties yet no precepts can declare. Alexander Pope. **HAP** Fr. An Essay on Criticism. **CP-PopeA**

Some Bloody Mutiny. Thomas Merton. **CP-MertT**

Some books are lies frae end to end. Death and Doctor Hornbook [A True Story]. Robert Burns. **CP-BurnR**

Some boys ar playing cards but I dont feal. Gary Gildner. Fr. Letters from Vicksburg. **SP-GildG**

Some breath breathes out Adonais & Canto General. On Neruda's Death. Allen Ginsberg. **CP-GinsA**

Some Brilliant Sky. Diane Wakoski. **SP-WakoD**

Some by their friends, more by themselves thought wise. John Dryden. **ChIV-1; OBSV** Fr. Absalom and Achitophel, Pt. I. **SP-DrydJ**

Some call that deep-deep bell. Hilda Doolittle. **NALW** Fr. Tribute to the Angels. **CP-DoolH**

Some came in chains. Captives. Ernest Hemingway. **CP-HemiE**

Some can flatter, some can faine. Thomas Campion. **CP-CampT**

Some can gaze and not be sick. Alfred Edward Housman. **CP-HousA**

Some candle clear burns somewhere I come by. The Candle Indoors. Gerard Manley Hopkins. **CP-HopkG**

Some certified nut. John Ashbery. **SP-AshbJ** Fr. Litany. **SP-AshbJ**

Some Colinæus praise, some Bleau. Verses to be Prefix'd before Bernard Lintot's New Miscellany. Alexander Pope. **CP-PopeA**

Some Collisions Bring Luck. Marge Piercy. **SP-PierM**

Some Comfort in Calamity. Robert Herrick. **CP-HerrR**

Some Constantly Besieged Castle. Diane Wakoski. **SP-WakoD**

Some Creature. Pablo Neruda, tr. fr. Spanish by Ben Belitt. **SP-NeruP**

Some critic tried to put me down. Gary Snyder. **CP-SnydG**

Some day—can it be believed? Ode to Entropy. John Updike. Fr. Seven Odes to Seven Natural Processes. **CP-UpdiJ**

Some day I will go to Aarhus. The Tollund Man. Seamus Heaney. **SP-HeanS**

Some day in six inches of. Kenneth Rexroth. **SP-RexrK** Fr. Love Poems of Marichiko.

Some day our town will grow old. The Springfield of the Far Future. Nicholas Vachel Lindsay. **CP-LindV**

Some day soon this rhyming volume, if you learn with proper speed. To My Name-Child. Robert Louis Stevenson. **CP-StevR**

Some day when you are picked up. Ernest Hemingway. **CP-HemiE**

Some days / the sunlight has a clarity. Chuck Miller. **SP-MillC**

Some days a shadow through. Men Are a Mockery of Angels. Geoffrey Hill. Fr. Four Poems Regarding the Endurance of Poets. **CP-HillG**

Some days before death / When food's tasting sour on my tongue. Good-bye. Sir John Betjeman. **CP-BetjJ**

Some days I am lonesome I want to talk to my mother. Grace Paley. **CP-PaleG**

Some Days retired from the rest. Emily Dickinson. **CP-DickE**

Some days the tick of two protestant clocks. Greystone Cottage. Richard Hugo. **CP-HugoR**

Some days the wind comes. The Wind. Chuck Miller. **SP-MillC**

Some days when you look out, the land. Mr. or Mrs. Nobody. William Stafford. **SP-StafW**

Some days you're finished. Not even eels. Why Sapri Will Never Be Italian. Richard Hugo. **CP-HugoR**

Some departure from the norm. Saying It to Keep It from Happening. John Ashbery. **SP-AshbJ**

Some desperation of the sense. The Birth of the Spirit. Richard Eberhart. **CP-EberR**

Some detectives in worn suits slide at my door. Jim Carroll. **SP-CarrJ**

Some dichty folks. Weekend Glory. Maya Angelou. **SP-AngeM**

Some die too late and some too soon. The Lost Occasion. John Greenleaf Whittier. **CP-WhitJ**

Some doe, perhaps, both wrong my love, and care. Sonnet 7. Mary Sidney, Countess of Montgomery Wroth. Fr. Lindamira's Complaint. Fr. Part 1. Fr. Urania. **CP-WrotM**

Some dogs who sleep at night. Eulogy to a Hell of a Dame—. Charles Bukowski. **SP-BukC3**

Some don't get much, Amos. Hayden Carruth. Fr. The Sleeping Beauty. **CP-CarHL**

Some Dreams They Forgot. Elizabeth Bishop. **CP-BishE**

Some drink! what, boy, some drink! Sir John Suckling. Fr. The Goblins. **CP-SuckJ**

Some Echoes. Robert Creeley. **CP-CreeR**

Some evenings, there are ghosts. There are. Ghosts. Ghosts. Miller Williams. **SP-WillM**

Some fat son-of-a-bitch with. Charles Bukowski. Fr. Horsemeat. **SP-BukC3**

Some fathers may have some consideration. Left out of vacation. Robert Lowell. **SP-LoweR**

Some fires are heard most truly. Blowgun and Rattlesnake. James Dickey. **CP-DickJ**

Some fish we peel back, leaving only the bones. Others devour us. John Yau. **SP-YauJo** Fr. Carp and Goldfish.

Some flowers come up. Charles Henri Ford. **SP-FordC** Fr. Emblems of Arachne.

Some flowers wickedly. Charles Henri Ford. **SP-FordC** Fr. Secret Haiku.

Some flushed-earth-color pueblo. Sacred Lake. Muriel Rukeyser. **CP-RukeM**

Some folks t'inks hit's right an' p'opah. Noddin' by de Fire. Paul Laurence Dunbar. **CP-DunbP**

Some for a little while do love, and some for long. Sonnet. Countee Cullen. **CP-CullC**

Some for their looks. Rue Carpenter. Archibald MacLeish. **CP-MacLA**

Some foreign freighter crawls a blue path north. Guns at Fort Flagler. Richard Hugo. **CP-HugoR**

Some Foreign Letters. Anne Sexton. **CP-SextA**

Some forty years ago or maybe more. Broken Neck. Robert Ranke Graves. **CP-GravR**

Some fowls there be that have so perfect sight. Petrarch, tr. by Sir Thomas Wyatt. **CP-WyatT** Fr. Sonnets to Laura.

Some Fragments, Mainly from Manuscripts of 1797–8. Samuel Taylor Coleridge. **CP-ColeS**

"Behind the thin / Grey cloud that cover'd but not hid the sky."

"Broad-breasted Pollards with broad-branching head."

"Long deep Lane / So overshadow'd, it might seem one bower, A."

"On the broad mountain-top."

"Reed-roof'd Village, still bepatch'd with snow, The."

"Sun-shine lies on the cottage-wall, The."

"Swallows interweaving there mid the paired, The."

"Terrible and loud / As the strong Voice that from the Thunder-cloud."

"'Twas not a mist, nor was it quite a cloud."

"'Twas sweet to know it only possible."

Some Frenchmen. John Updike. **CP-UpdiJ**

Some Friends from Pascagoula. Wallace Stevens. **CP-StevW**

Some from the starry throne his fame derives. Thomas Campion. *Fr.* Observations in the Art of English Poesie. **CP-CampT**

Some future day, when what is now is not. Mari Magno I. Arthur Hugh Clough. **SP-ClouA**

Some Future Moon. Donald Davie. **CP-DavDo**

Some General Instructions. Kenneth Koch. **CP-KochK**

Some ghosts are women. Ghosts. Anne Sexton. **CP-SextA**

Some glory in their birth, some in their skill. Sonnet 91. William Shakespeare. *Fr.* Sonnets. **CP-ShaWS**

Some Good News. Charles Olson. **SP-OlsoC** *Fr.* The Maximus Poems.

Some have [*or* hae] meat and cannot [*or* canna] eat. Robert Burns. **CP-BurnR**

  (Burns Grace at Kirkudbright.) **CP-BurnR**

Some hawk-nosed man. Gilbert Sorrentino. **SP-SorrG**

Some Herons. Mary Oliver. **SP-OlivM**

Some I perceive, content. Advent. Donald Davie. **CP-DavDo**

Some ideas hit. Sizing. Archie Randolph Ammons. **SP-AmmoA**

Some in the Godspeed, the Susan C. Enough. Marianne Craig Moore. **CP-MoorM**

Some insects feed on rosebuds. Bugs. Ogden Nash. **CP-NashO**

Some keep the Sabbath going to Church. Emily Dickinson. **CP-DickE**

Some kind of relaxed and beautiful thing. Dogfish. Mary Oliver. **SP-OlivM**

Some kind of ritual / for your dwindling. Margaret Atwood. *Fr.* Five Poems for Grandmothers. **SP-AtwM2**

Some Kinda Love. "Lou Reed." **SP-ReedL**

Some kinds of love. Some Kinda Love. "Lou Reed." **SP-ReedL**

Some ladies dress in muslin full and white. Christina Georgina Rossetti. **CP-RosC3**

Some ladies smoke too much and some ladies drink too much and some ladies pray too much. Curl Up and Diet. Ogden Nash. **CP-NashO**

Some leading thoroughfares of man. Via Crucis. Herman Melville. **SP-MelvH** *Fr.* Clarel: A Poem and Pilgrimage in the Holy Land.

Some leaves hang late, some fall. The Soughing Wind. William Carlos Williams. **CP-WilW1**

Some like wine and some like hops. The Power of Positive Drinking. "Lou Reed." **SP-ReedL**

Some Lines Finished Just Before Dawn at the Bedside of a Dying Student / It has Snowed All Night. Miller Williams. **SP-WillM**

Some look. to see the sweet Outlines. William Blake. **CP-BlakW**

Some Loss. Roy Fisher. **SP-FishR**

Some Love. Allen Ginsberg. **CP-GinsA**

Some lovers speak, when they their Muses entertain. Sonnet 6. Sir Philip Sidney. **NAEL-1; NoSic; Son** *Fr.* Astrophil and Stella. **SP-SidnP**

"Some lower branches haven't lost their green." Unburying the Birch. Robert Pack. **SP-PackR**

Some lucky day each November great waves awake and are drawn. November Surf. Robinson Jeffers. **CP-JefR2**

Some man unworthy to be possessor. Confined Love. John Donne. **CP-DonnJ**

Some may have blamed you that you took away. Reconciliation. William Butler Yeats. **CP-YeatW**

Some may say that the electric world. Thomas Merton. *Fr.* Cables to the Ace. **CP-MertT**

Some melodies are popular as well as classical, which I suppose makes them popsicles. Everybody's Mind to Me a Kingdom Is, or, A Great Big Wonderful World It's. Ogden Nash. **CP-NashO**

Some Men created for destruction come. William Blake. **CP-BlakW**

Some men of books or friends not speaking right. To My Truly-Beloved Friend, Mr Browne: on His Pastorals. Ben Jonson. **CP-JonsB**

Some minds have room alone for pageant stories. Motto Intended for Poems on the Naming of Places. William Wordsworth. **CP-WorW1**

Some Moments with Locatelli. Marsden Hartley. **CP-HartM**

Some monster bird, the barn. Cows, a Vision. Tess Gallacher. **SP-GallT**

Some moralist or mythological poet. William Butler Yeats. **PoE** *Fr.* Nineteen Hundred and Nineteen. **CP-YeatW**

Some must employ the scythe. The Dedicated. Philip Larkin. **CP-LarkP**

Some ne'er advance a judgment of their own. The Servile Herd. Alexander Pope. **OBSV** *Fr.* An Essay on Criticism. **CP-PopeA**

Some night I wish they'd knock. Because We Are Not Taken Seriously. Stephen Dunn. **SP-DunnS**

Some nights, a fearful. Robert Creeley. **CP-CreeR**

Some nights when you're off. The Avenues. David St. John. **SP-StJoD**

Some Objects of Wood and Stone. Margaret Atwood. **SP-AtwM1**

Some Oddities. Donald Hall. **SP-HallD**

Some of My Best Friends Are Children. Ogden Nash. **CP-NashO**

Some of My Readers. Charles Bukowski. **SP-BukC3**

Some of the sky is grey and some of it is white. Moving. Randall Jarrell. **CP-JarrR; SP-JarrR**

Some of the Things I See for You. Anne Waldman. **SP-WaldA**

Some of the young men. George Oppen. *Fr.* A Narrative. **CP-OppeG**

Some of their chiefs were princes of the land. John Dryden. **AWP; EBEV; IHNG; SCV** *Fr.* Absalom and Achitophel, Pt. I. **SP-DrydJ**

  (On the Duke of Buckingham.) **IHNG**

  (Zimri: "Some of their chiefs were princes of the land.") **AWP**

Some of what came and some were poor. All This Changing Trouble Luck and Suddenness. John Yau. **SP-YauJo**

Some of you may know, others perhaps can guess. Around the Mountain. Robert Ranke Graves. **CP-GravR**

Some of you will be glad I did what I did. Not Quite Social. Robert Frost. **CP-FrosR**

Some of your hurts you have cured. Borrowing from the French. Ralph Waldo Emerson. **TreFT** *Fr.* Quatrains. **CP-EmerR**

Some old Auruncans, I remember well. Virgil, *tr. by* Sir Walter Ralegh. **CP-RaleW** *Fr.* The Aeneid [*or* Eneados, *Aeneis*].

Some old Egyptian joke is in the air. By Nilus Once I Knew. Hart Crane. **CP-CranH**

Some old Mexico Lisbon set. Dream Take: 22. Al Young. **CP-YounA**

Some Old Tires. John Ashbery. **SP-AshbJ**

Some one prepared this mighty show. Emily Dickinson. **CP-DickE**

Some one who hears the bugle neigh will know. Dirge. Thomas Merton. **CP-MertT**

Some Other Kinds of Songs. "Bob Dylan." **CP-DylaB**

  "Amazon chick / with an amazin' pancho villa face, An."

  "Baby black's / been had."

  "For francoise hardy / at the seine's edge."

  "High treachery sails / unveils."

  "I could make you crawl."

  "I used t' hate enzo."

  "Jack o' diamonds / jack o' diamonds."

  "Johnny (little johnny) / with his father's hammer."

  "Michelangelo would've wept."

  "Run go get out of here."

  "You tell me about politics."

Some Painful Butterflies Pass Through. Tess Gallacher. **SP-GallT**

Some part of us lives. The Fourth Dimension. Leonard Nathan. **SP-NathL**

Some partial cloudiness will flow locally, mostly. Charles Olson. **CP-OlsoC**

Some parts may perish; dye thou canst not all. On Himselfe. Robert Herrick. **CP-HerrR**

Some peers, perhaps, have skill to judge, 'tis true. To Mr. Thomson. Aaron Hill. **CP-ThomJ**

Some people, / they just don't hate enough yet. Beyond. Charles Kenneth Williams. **CP-WillC**

Some people admire the work of a Fool. William Blake. **CP-BlakW**

Some people, and it doesn't matter whether they are paupers or millionaires. Possessions Are Nine Points of Conversation. Ogden Nash. **CP-NashO**

Some people are born simply to pay postage due. Please Keep on Forwarding. Ogden Nash. **CP-NashO**

Some people are do-it-some-other-timers and other people are do-it-nowers. Splash! Ogden Nash. **CP-NashO**

Some people are in favor of compromising, while other people. The Strange Case of the Lucrative Compromise. Ogden Nash. **CP-NashO**

Some people are popular with other people because their wit is. People. Ogden Nash. **CP-NashO**

Some people don't want to be doctors because they think doctors. Cousin Euphemia Knows Best, or, Physician, Heal Somebody Else. Ogden Nash. **CP-NashO**

Some people get savage and bitter when to backbiters they refer. Hush, Here They Come. Ogden Nash. **CP-NashO**

Some people hang portraits up. A Likeness. Robert Browning. **CP-BroR1**

Some people lead a feverish life. A Plea for a League of Sleep. Ogden Nash. **CP-NashO**

Some people like to hitch and hike. Riding on a Railroad Train. Ogden Nash. **CP-NashO**

Some people look to the future and others look days of yore-wards. Now You See It, Now I Don't. Ogden Nash. **CP-NashO**

Some people put their trust in art, others. The General and the Tango Singer. Stephen Dobyns. **SP-DobyS**

Some people relate anecdotes about Samuel Goldwyn and Gregory Ratoff. Doctor Fell? I Thought So. Ogden Nash. **CP-NashO**

Some people set themselves tasks. Life. Grace Paley. **CP-PaleG**

Some people shave before bathing. And Three Hundred and Sixty-Six in Leap Year. Ogden Nash. **CP-NashO**

Some people think that they can beat three two's with a pair of aces. How Long Has This Been Going On? Oh, Quite Long. Ogden Nash. **CP-NashO**

Some people think the nose of the Sphinx was flattened. The Thirteenth Labor of Hercules. Ogden Nash. *Fr.* Fables Bullfinch Forgot. **CP-NashO**

Some people understand all about machinery. Up from the Wheelbarrow. Ogden Nash. **CP-NashO**

Some Picnic. Charles Bukowski. **SP-BukC1**

Some pimps wear summer hats. What? Langston Hughes. **SP-HughL**

Some Place. Robert Creeley. **CP-CreeR**

Some Power Company Employee. The Man. Charles Simic. **SP-SimiC**

Some primal termite knocked on wood. The Termite. Ogden Nash. **CP-NashO**

Some Questions You Might Ask. Mary Oliver. **SP-OlivM**

Some quickly-weathering rock, perhaps. Twilight on the Waste Lands. Donald Davie. **CP-DavDo**

Some Rainbow—coming from the Fair! Emily Dickinson. **CP-DickE**

Some Recent Fiction. Al Young. **CP-YounA**

Some Riddles from Symphosius. Richard Wilbur. **CP-WilbR**

Some rule of birds kills off the song. The Size of Song. John Ciardi. **SP-CiarJ**

Some salve to every sore, we may apply. Upon Love. Robert Herrick. **CP-HerrR**

Some San Francisco Poems. George Oppen. **CP-OppeG**
  And Their Winter and Night in Disguise. **APSN; NNaP**
  Anniversary Poem. **APSN; NNaP**
  But So As by Fire. **NNaP**
  Impossible Poem, The. **NNaP**
  Morality Play: Preface, A. **APSN; NNaP**
  "Moving over the hills, crossing the irrigation." **APSN; NNaP**
  "O withering seas." **NNaP**
  "Silver as / The needle's eye." **NNaP**
  Taste, The. **NNaP**
  Translucent Mechanics, The. **NNaP**

Some Sap Sings a Poor Pantoum. Gilbert Sorrentino. *Fr.* Twelve Études for Voice and Kazoo. **SP-SorrG**

Some say acceptance is the heart of it, or grief, the "true self" or the here and now. Not That. Stephen Berg. **SP-BergS**

Some say goodnight—at night. Emily Dickinson. **CP-DickE**

Some say it was radiation, some say there was acid on the microphone. Legionnaire's Disease. "Bob Dylan." **CP-DylaB**

Some say that handsome raider still at large. Wystan Hugh Auden. **CP-AudWJ**

Some say that love and joy are one: and so. Sonnet. Christina Georgina Rossetti. **CP-RosC3**

Some say that love's a little boy. Wystan Hugh Auden. **PAW** *Fr.* Twelve Songs. **CP-AudeW**

Some say the fastest living creature is the cheetah. Mrs. Purvis Dreads Room Service. Ogden Nash. **CP-NashO**

Some say the spot is banned: that the pillar Cross-and-Hand. The Lost Pyx. Thomas Hardy. **CP-HardT**

Some say the tarn is bottomless. The Tarn. Wystan Hugh Auden. **CP-AudWJ**

Some say the world will end in fire. Fire and Ice. Robert Frost. **CP-FrosR**

Some say thy fault is youth, some wantonness. Sonnet 96. William Shakespeare. *Fr.* Sonnets. **CP-ShaWS**

Some Science Fiction. Robert Frost. **CP-FrosR**

Some Shadows. William Stafford. **SP-StafW**

Some shapes cannot be seen in a glass. Holding the Mirror Up to Nature. Howard Nemerov. **CP-NemeH**

Some Shires Revisited. Donald Davie. **CP-DavDo**

Some simple / virtue of silence. For Joel. Robert Creeley. **CP-CreeR**

Some Simple Measures in the American Idiom and the Variable Foot. William Carlos Williams. **CP-WilW2**

Some singers sing of ladies' eyes. The Clean Platter. Ogden Nash. **CP-NashO**

Some sit and stare. The Common Grave. James Dickey. **CP-DickJ**

Some sketch sweat' out, unwilling swift & crude. John Berryman. *Fr.* Sonnets to Chris. **CP-BerrJ**

Some Spice for Jack Spicer. Al Young. **CP-YounA**

Some such Butterfly be seen. Emily Dickinson. **CP-DickE**

Some sway for long and then decline. The Oak. Richard Eberhart. **CP-EberR**

Some table talk at lunch, of memory. Marilyn Hacker. *Fr.* The Regent's Park Sonnets. **SP-HackM**

Some take their walks at night. Invitation. Marsden Hartley. **CP-HartM**

Some that have deeper digged love's mine than [*or* myne then] I. Love's Alchemy [*or* Alchemie]. John Donne. **CP-DonnJ**

Some things / are so. Teleology. Archie Randolph Ammons. **SP-AmmoA**

Some Things Are Dark. Edna St. Vincent Millay. **CP-MillE**

Some things are never clear. Voice Ways. Robert Frost. **CP-FrosR**

Some things are truly lost. Think of a sun-hat. The Mind-Reader. Richard Wilbur. **CP-WilbR**

Some things, by their affinity light's token. Sunlight. Thom Gunn. **CP-GunnT**

Some Things I Like about My Triple Bloods. Alice Walker. **CP-WalkA**

Some Things I Wanted to Say to You. Stephen Dunn. **SP-DunnS**

Some things, niño, some things are like this. Of Bright & Blue Birds & the Gala Sun. Wallace Stevens. **CP-StevW**

Some things that fly there be. Emily Dickinson. **CP-DickE**

Some things you say how sweet to. A widowed aunt's. The Park at Villammare. Richard Hugo. **CP-HugoR**

Some think that in the Christian scheme. Mutual Subjection. Christopher Smart. **NOCV; OxBChV** *Fr.* Hymns for the Amusement of Children. **SP-SmarC**

Some thirty inches from my nose. Wystan Hugh Auden. **FaBoEE; IHNG** *Fr.* Prologue: The Birth of Architecture. *Fr.* Thanksgiving for a Habitat. **CP-AudeW**

Some time ago a crazy dream came to me. Talkin' World War III Blues. "Bob Dylan." **CP-DylaB**

Some time ago there was a rich old codger, *mod. vers. by* Nevill Coghill. Geoffrey Chaucer. *See* The Miller's [*or* Milleres] Tale.

Some time has gone. Louis Zukofsky. **CP-ZukLS**

Some time is longer than the rest. Emily Dickinson. **SP-DickE**

Some time now I have felt outside life. Hand over Hand. John Hewitt. **CP-HewiJ**

Some time when the river is ice ask me. Ask Me. William Stafford. **SP-StafW**

Some to Conceit alone their taste confine. Alexander Pope. **OxAEP-1,** *ll.* 289–393; *Fr.* An Essay on Criticism. **CP-PopeA**

Some, too fragile for winter winds. Emily Dickinson. **CP-DickE**

Some Trees. John Ashbery. **SP-AshbJ**

Some trees loft their heads. Pitch Pines. Brendan Galvin. **SP-GalvB**

Some trust the wolf. Poem. Jim Carroll. *Fr.* 3 Short Poems. **SP-CarrJ**

Some virtue in. Brilliance. Donald Davie. **CP-DavDo**

Some we see no more, Tenements of Wonder. Emily Dickinson. **CP-DickE**

Some weeks ago I heard that you were dead. Hesitant Memorial. John Hewitt. **CP-HewiJ**

Some weep to find the Golden Pear. Colored Blues Singer. Countee Cullen. **CP-CullC**

Some white academy of grace. Michael Hartnett. *Fr.* Anatomy of a Cliché. **SP-HarMi**

Some who are uncertain compel me. They fear. At This Moment of Time. Delmore Schwartz. **SP-SchwD**

Some winters, taking leave. A Storm in April. Richard Wilbur. **CP-WilbR**

Some with Wings, Some with Manes. Tess Gallagher. **SP-GallT**

Some women live for the idiotic furniture of their houses. Furniture. David Herbert Lawrence. **CP-LawrD**

Some women marry houses. Housewife. Anne Sexton. **CP-SextA**

Some Words. John Ashbery. **SP-AshbJ**

Some—Work for Immortality. Emily Dickinson. **CP-DickE**

Some would distinguish nothing here but oaks. A Wood. Richard Wilbur. **CP-WilbR**

Some would know / Why I so. His Answer to a Question. Robert Herrick. **CP-HerrR**

Some Wretched creature, savior take. Emily Dickinson. **CP-DickE**

Some years ago he started to escape. Malcolm Lowry. **CP-LowrM**

Some years back I worked a strip mine. Lester Tells of Wanda and the Big Snow. Paul Zimmer. **SP-ZimmP**

Some years the birds. Richard Shelton. *Fr.* Dry Season. **SP-ShelR**

Somebody Always Breaking My Dainty Solitude. . . . Charles Bukowski. **SP-BukC2**

Somebody and Somebody Else and You. Edwin Rolfe. **CP-RolfE**

Somebody deep in my bones. Birthday. Ted Kooser. **SP-KoosT**

Somebody Died. Robert Creeley. **CP-CreeR**

Somebody dies every four minutes. Rapid Transit. William Carlos Williams. **CP-WilW1**

Somebody has endlessly postponed. The Last Time. Marilyn Hacker. **SP-HackM**

Somebody has to make the tubs and pails. Carl Sandburg. *Fr.* The People, Yes. **CP-SandC**

Somebody is shooting at something in our town. The Swarm. Sylvia Plath. **CP-PlatS**

Somebody keeps track of how many times. Innings. Charles Kenneth Williams. **CP-WillC**

Somebody knew Lincoln somebody Xerxes. Edward Estlin Cummings. **CP-CummE**

Somebody left a ladder. Negligence These Days. Archie Randolph Ammons. **SP-AmmoA**

Somebody long ago. The Hedge of Hemlocks. Edna St. Vincent Millay. **CP-MillE**

Somebody loses whenever somebody wins. Crapshooters. Carl Sandburg. **CP-SandC**

Somebody said for killing one. The Bats. Brendan Galvin. **SP-GalvB**

Somebody who should have been born. The Abortion. Anne Sexton. **CP-SextA**

Somebody's grandmother glides through the bracken. Metempsychosis. Margaret Atwood. **SP-AtwM2**

Somebody's knockin' at th' door. The Collier's Wife. David Herbert Lawrence. **CP-LawrD**

Somebody's little girl—how easy to make a sob story over who she was once. Crabapple Blossoms. Carl Sandburg. **CP-SandC**

Somebody's shout displaces the horizon. The Shout. Charles Tomlinson. **CP-TomlC**

Someday, if you are lucky. Man. Kenneth Rexroth. **SP-RexrK** *Fr.* A Bestiary. **SP-RexrK**

Someday they'll find me out, and my lavish hands. Self-Portrait. Charles Wright. **SP-WrigC**

Somehow. Marge Piercy. **SP-PierM**

Somehow for me, at this slow hour and in this mood. The Living Landscape. John Hewitt. **CP-HewiJ**

Somehow I cannot let it go yet, funeral though it is. The Pallid Wreath. Walt Whitman. **CP-WhitW**

Somehow it has all. A Song Sparrow Singing in the Fall. Wendell Berry. **CP-BerrW**

Somehow myself survived the Night. Emily Dickinson. **CP-DickE**

Someone / gave me a copy of. Sunflowers. Siv Cedering Fox. **SP-CedeS**

Someone a long way off is using my blood. Lure. Jenny Joseph. **SP-JoseJ**

Someone at a table under a brown metal lamp. Poetry: I. Adrienne Rich. **SP-RicA1**

Someone ate the baby. Dreadful. Shel Silverstein. **SP-SilS2**

Someone else's Leica sitting on the table. Essay on Style. Frank O'Hara. **SP-OharF**

Someone had been walking in and out. The Origin of Baseball. Kenneth Patchen. **CP-PatcK**

Someone has fallen to the earth. An Examination into Life and Death. Kenneth Patchen. **CP-PatcK**

Someone has frozen the many-storeyed houses. Easter Sunday. Tom Clark. **SP-ClarT**

Someone has gathered a shell. The Triumph of the Shell. Archibald MacLeish. **CP-MacLA**

Someone has set up a gate here. The Gate. Charles Tomlinson. **CP-TomlC**

Someone in ancient Mas d'Avil. A Missive Missile. Robert Frost. **CP-FrosR**

Someone is actually playing a dulcimer. A Backyard in California. Hayden Carruth. **CP-CarHS**

Someone is always trying to feel something. Trying to Feel Something. John Ciardi. **SP-CiarJ**

Someone is always willing. To You. Richard Shelton. **SP-ShelR**

Someone is dead. Lament. Anne Sexton. **SP-SextA**

Someone is loose is Moscow who won't stop. Phone Booth. Andrei Voznesensky, *tr. fr. Russian by* Richard Wilbur. **CP-WilbR**

Someone is present / On the earth are laid the crowns. The Watcher. Kenneth Patchen. **CP-PatcK**

Someone is sitting in the red house. Small Town. Rita Dove. **SP-DoveR**

Someone left green plastic bags full of leaves. In the 20th Century. Stephen Dunn. **SP-DunnS**

Someone like I / across the pale water. Mosquitoes in New Jersey. Gilbert Sorrentino. **SP-SorrG**

Someone lives in a cave. The Fury of Abandonment. Anne Sexton. *Fr.* The Furies. **CP-SextA**

Someone made up my eyes. Charles Henri Ford. **SP-FordC** *Fr.* Secret Haiku.

Someone may be a horse. Should Be Sufficient. Kenneth Patchen. **CP-PatcK**

Someone moves through the jungle. The Drowned Man: Death Between Two Rivers. Thomas McGrath. **SP-McGrT**

Someone must make out the cards. What *Was* Her Name. John Ciardi. **SP-CiarJ**

Someone said that shoes had personality. Empty Shoes. Louis MacNeice. *Fr.* Out of the Picture. **CP-MacNL**

Someone Talking to Himself. Richard Wilbur. **CP-WilbR**

Someone we both know, Rufus, looked me. Martial, *tr. by* William Matthews. **SP-MattW** *Fr.* Epigrams.

Someone Will Enter between the Gates. David Herbert Lawrence. **CP-LawrD**

Someone's been up here nights. In a Country Cemetery in Iowa. Ted Kooser. **SP-KoosT**

Someone's Blood. Rita Dove. **SP-DoveR**

Someone's got it in for me, they're planting stories in the press. Idiot Wind. "Bob Dylan." **CP-DylaB**

Someplace in Arizona. Dogs. Charles Bukowski. **SP-BukC3**

Somersby. Richard Hugo. **CP-HugoR**

Somersby, Lincolnshire; after Leaving the Refectory. Tennyson. *See* Unwatched [*or* unwatch'd], the garden bough shall sway.

Somerset. Donald Davie. **CP-DavDo**

Something. Charles Bukowski. **SP-BukC1**

Something / cold is in the air. The Fury of Sunsets. Anne Sexton. *Fr.* The Furies. **CP-SextA**

Something. Robert Creeley. **CP-CreeR**

Something. Stephen Dunn. **SP-DunnS**

Something. George Harrison. **CP-Beatl**

Something: a Direction. Charles Tomlinson. *Fr.* Antecedents. **CP-TomlC**

Something Amazing Just Happened. Ted Berrigan. **SP-BerrT**

Something approaches, about. The Old Woman. Thom Gunn. **CP-GunnT**

Something as one with eyes that look below. Edwin Arlington Robinson. *Fr.* Octaves. **CP-RobiE**

Something breathless hangs in the air. The Breathless. Richard Eberhart. **CP-EberR**

Something broken Something / I need By someone. Nightbreak. Adrienne Rich. **CP-RicAE; SP-RicA1; SP-RicA2**

Something brought them here. It was an outcropping of peace. Haunted Landscape. John Ashbery. **SP-AshbJ**

Something Childish, but Very Natural. Samuel Taylor Coleridge. *See* If I Had but Two Little Wings.

Something comes crawling from St. James's Park. Lullaby for a Summer Recess. James Fenton. **SP-FentJ**

Something do I see. The Head above the Fog. Thomas Hardy. **CP-HardT**

Something fallen out of the air, some. A Difference. Tom Clark. **SP-ClarT**

Something far off buried deep and free. The Flash. James Dickey. **CP-DickJ**

Something for a long time has gone wrong. Turning Away. James Dickey. **CP-DickJ**

Something for Easter. Robert Creeley. **CP-CreeR**

Something for Hope. Robert Frost. **CP-FrosR**

Something forgotten for twenty years: though my fathers. A Map of the Western Part of the County of Essex in England. Denise Levertov. **CP-LeveD**

Something gnaws inside my head. Kirilov on a Skyscraper. Randall Jarrell. **CP-JarrR**

Something gone, something gone out with Nelson. Suffolk. Donald Davie. **CP-DavDo**

Something had cracked in her mouth as she slept. The Gap in the White. Thomas Hardy. **CP-HardT**

Something hangs in back of me. The Wings. Denise Levertov. **CP-LeveD**

Something has left itself scattered. The Rib. James Dickey. **CP-DickJ**

Something has to happen here. Roy Fisher. **SP-FishR** *Fr.* Handsworth Liberties.

Something I saw or thought I saw. On the Heart's Beginning to Cloud the Mind. Robert Frost. **CP-FrosR**

Something I should like to know is, which. Visitors Laugh at Locksmiths or, Hospital Doors Haven't Got Locks Anyhow. Ogden Nash. **CP-NashO**

Something immense and lonely. Foreboding. John Haines. **SP-HainJ**

Something in a summer's Day, A. Emily Dickinson. **CP-DickE**

Something in me has always known. Empathy. Robert Pack. **SP-PackR**

Something in me hates being here. Crutches. Stephen Berg. **SP-BergS**

Something in the light of this March afternoon. A Tenancy. James Merrill. **SP-MerrJ**

Something in the way she moves. Something. George Harrison. **CP-Beatl**

Something inspires the only cow of late. The Cow in Apple Time. Robert Frost. **CP-FrosR**

Something is burning, baby, are you aware? Something's Burning, Baby. "Bob Dylan." **CP-DylaB**

Something is calling to me. In the Corners of Fields. Ted Kooser. **SP-KoosT**

Something is definitely *not*. A Civilization Constantly Worrying about Itself as It Goes on Doing What It Is Worrying About That It Is Doing. Jean Garrigue. **SP-GarrJ**

Something is dying, but without blood or. Simple Sonatina. Tess Gallagher. **SP-GallT**

Something Is Dying Here. Thomas McGrath. **SP-McGrT**

Something Is Going to Happen. Robert Penn Warren. **SP-WarrR**

Something is taking place. Rites of Passage. Thom Gunn. **CP-GunnT**

Something is there. And teacher here at home. The Dream of Waking. Randall Jarrell. **CP-JarrR**

Something is very gently. The Thread. Denise Levertov. **CP-LeveD**

Something Like Happiness. Stephen Dunn. **SP-DunnS**

Something like the way. Look Good, Smell Good, Feel. Al Young. **CP-YounA**

Something occurred after the operation. Surgical Ward: Men. Robert Ranke Graves. **CP-GravR**

Something of glass about her, of dead water. Circe. Louis MacNeice. **CP-MacNL**

Something of yesterday clings to today. Today Isn't Everything. Pablo Neruda, *tr. fr. Spanish by* Ben Belitt. **SP-NeruP**

Something old and tyrannical burning there. A Coal Fire in Winter. Thomas McGrath. **SP-McGrT**

Something plus something else is not one thing. Gilbert Sorrentino. **SP-SorrG**

Something primal in our spine makes the child swing. Derek Walcott. **CP-WalcD** *Fr.* Midsummer.

Something removed roars in the ears of this house. Missing the Sea. Derek Walcott. **CP-WalcD**

Something said: You have nothing to fear. Heard by a Girl. Louise Bogan. **CP-BogaL**

Something Similar. John Ashbery. **SP-AshbJ**

Something spoke in the creek-ice. The Sun Now or Never (For Barbara). Chuck Miller. **SP-MillC**

Something startles me where I thought I was safest. This Compost. Walt Whitman. **CP-WhitW**

Something Still Lives. Edwin Rolfe. **CP-RolfE**

Something strange is creeping across me. Daffy Duck in Hollywood. John Ashbery. **SP-AshbJ**

Something strange is creeping across me. A Hollywood Everything. John Ashbery. **CBCK** *Fr.* Daffy Duck in Hollywood. **SP-AshbJ**

Something Tapped. Thomas Hardy. **CP-HardT**

Something tells him he is off-limits. Retirement. Karl Shapiro. **SP-ShapK**

Something that Saved Him, The. Thomas Hardy. **CP-HardT**

Something There, *Author's own English vers. of his* "Hors crâne seul dedans." Samuel Beckett. **CP-BeckS**

Something There Is About You. "Bob Dylan." **CP-DylaB**

Something there is that doesn't love a frost. Birches. David Markson. **CP-MarkD**

Something there is that doesn't love a wall. Mending Wall. Robert Frost. **CP-FrosR**

Something this foggy day, a something which. Christina Georgina Rossetti. **NAEL-2** *Fr.* Later Life: A Double Sonnet of Sonnets. **CP-RosC2**

Something to dip myself into. Acids. Charles Kenneth Williams. **CP-WillC**

Something to Say. Robert Ranke Graves. **CP-GravR**

Something unkempt about it. Grant's Tomb Revisited. Karl Shapiro. **SP-ShapK**

Something will be hanging from the ceiling. Event Without Particulars. James Merrill. *Fr.* Five Old Favorites. **SP-MerrJ**

Something wrong with my desk the desk. Two Romance Poems. George Oppen. **CP-OppeG**

Something's Burning, Baby. "Bob Dylan." **CP-DylaB**

Sometime during eternity / some guys show up. Lawrence Ferlinghetti. **SP-FerlL**

Sometime I fled the fire that me brent. Sir Thomas Wyatt. **CP-WyatT**

Sometime I must try to write the truth. No Messiah. Robert Lowell. **SP-LoweR**

Sometime I sigh, sometime I sing. Sir Thomas Wyatt. **CP-WyatT**

Sometime I'll lay down my wrath. Sometime Jailhouse Blues. Allen Ginsberg. **CP-GinsA**

Sometime Jailhouse Blues. Allen Ginsberg. **CP-GinsA**

Sometime let gorgeous Tragedy. Poetry and the Melancholy Man. John Milton. **EPCY** *Fr.* Il Penseroso. **CP-MiltJ**

Sometime Sportsman Greets the Spring, The. John Updike. **CP-UpdiJ**

Sometime the pride of my assured truth. Argument, Th'. Sir Thomas Wyatt. **CP-WyatT**

Sometime turns inside out. Memorial III—from a Phone Booth on Broadway. Audre Lorde. **SP-LordA**

Sometime,perhaps in Paris we will. Edward Estlin Cummings. **CP-CummE**

Sometimes / A night funeral. Dead in There. Langston Hughes. **SP-HughL**

Sometimes / in)Spring a someone will lie(glued). Edward Estlin Cummings. **CP-CummE**

Sometimes. Ron Koertge. **SP-KoerR**

Sometimes. Thomas McGrath. **SP-McGrT**

Sometimes / on this green hill. In Hanoi 1969. Grace Paley. **CP-PaleG**

Sometimes. James Schuyler. **CP-SchuJ**

Sometimes. John Yau. **SP-YauJo**

Sometimes a crumb falls. Luck. Langston Hughes. **SP-HughL**

Sometimes a lantern moves along the night. The Lantern Out of Doors. Gerard Manley Hopkins. **CP-HopkG**

Sometimes a light surprizes. Joy and Peace in Believing. William Cowper. **NOCV; TRV** *Fr.* Olney Hymns. **CP-CowpW**

Sometimes a maple seed. Bride. Archie Randolph Ammons. **SP-AmmoA**

Sometimes a wild thing. Yours Truly. Leonard Nathan. **SP-NathL**

Sometimes a word will start it, like. Variant. John Ashbery. **SP-AshbJ**

Sometimes after you get your ass. About Cranes. Charles Bukowski. **SP-BukC1**

Sometimes, apart in sleep, by chance. The Trance. Stephen Spender. **CP-SpenS**

Sometimes are living those who have been seen. Veer-Voices: Two Sisters under Crows. James Dickey. **CP-DickJ**

Sometimes as I drive by the factory. A Street off Sunset. Randall Jarrell. *Fr.* The Lost World. **CP-JarrR; SP-JarrR**

Sometimes as I woke, the branches beside the stars. New Georgia. Randall Jarrell. **CP-JarrR**

Sometimes at night I think of how we did. My Life Before Dawn. Louise Glück. **SP-GlücL**

Sometimes at the beggining of a movie. A Little Poem About Jazz. Al Young. **CP-YounA**

Sometimes at the mouth of this river. A Poem for Willard Motley. Al Young. **CP-YounA**

Sometimes deeply immured in white-washed tower. The Tingling Back. Karl Shapiro. **SP-ShapK**

Sometimes Even My Knees Smile. Diane Wakoski. **SP-WakoD**

Sometimes goldfinches one by one will drop. John Keats. **GN; PBBP** *Fr.* I Stood Tip-Toe upon a Little Hill. **CP-KeatJ** (Goldfinches.) **GN**

Sometimes he thinks the earth. Wendell Berry. *Fr.* Window Poems. **CP-BerrW**

Sometimes he would try to write a poem. Style. Miller Williams. **SP-WillM**

Sometimes I almost go hours without crying. Villanelle of the Suicide's Mother. Charles Kenneth Williams. **SP-WillC**

Sometimes i am alive because with. Edward Estlin Cummings. **CP-CummE**

Sometimes I am embarrassed. Not Again. Robert Creeley. **CP-CreeR**

Sometimes I dip my pen and find the bottle full of fire. An Apology for the Bottle Volcanic. Nicholas Vachel Lindsay. **CP-LindV**

Sometimes I envy others, fear them. The Cure. William Carlos Williams. **CP-WilW2**

Sometimes I envy those. The Mole. John Haines. **SP-HainJ**

Sometimes I feel so bad. Family Of. Alice Walker. **CP-WalkA**

Sometimes I feel so happy. Pale Blue Eyes. "Lou Reed." **SP-ReedL**

Sometimes I feel so low-down and disgusted. Slow Train. "Bob Dylan." **CP-DylaB**

Sometimes I have supposed seals. Soft Wood. Robert Lowell. **SP-LoweR**

Sometimes I hear my father's voice, sometimes my son's, in mine. Frederick Morgan. **SP-MorgF**

Sometimes I play a game that is of interest only to me. Mr. Burgess, Meet Mr. Barmecide. Ogden Nash. **CP-NashO**

Sometimes I play the music of Charlie Byrd. Kinaesthesia. Richard Eberhart. **CP-EberR**

Sometimes I see them. Galway Kinnell. **RFM** *Fr.* Ruins under the Stars. **SP-KinnG**

Sometimes I think of your father in his neat gangster shoes. Screw, a Technical Love Poem. Diane Wakoski. **SP-WakoD**

Sometimes I think that as he aged. The Grandfather Cap. Ted Kooser. **SP-KoosT**

Sometimes i want to take them in. Chuck Miller. **SP-MillC**

Sometimes I'm in the mood, I wanna leave my lonesome home. Baby, I'm in the Mood for You. "Bob Dylan." **CP-DylaB**

Sometimes in moods of gloom—like mist. Mist. Walter de la Mare. **CP-DeLaW**

Sometimes in our sleep. John Haines. *Fr.* The Fossil. **SP-HainJ**

Sometimes it comes, a gloomy flap of lightning. Ted Hughes. **SP-HughT** *Fr.* Gaudete.

Sometimes it happens. The Porch. Gary Gildner. **SP-GildG**

Sometimes it is like a beast. A Trucker. Thom Gunn. **CP-GunnT**

Sometimes it occurs to me in the moonlit. Gods. Hayden Carruth. **CP-CarHS**

Sometimes it seems to be the inmost land. On Being Given Time. May Sarton. **SP-SartM**

Sometimes It Turns Dry and the Leaves Fall before They Are Beautiful. William Carlos Williams. **CP-WilW2**

Sometimes it's difficult, isn't it, not to grow grim and rancorous. A Necessary Dirge. Ogden Nash. **CP-NashO**

Sometimes it's the flagrant accentuation. Jazz as Was. Al Young. **CP-YounA**

Sometimes it's the look of love. Big Sur. Al Young. **CP-YounA**

Sometimes it's the way the blues hits you. More Clues to the Blues. Al Young. **CP-YounA**

Sometimes men are kissing. Men are sometimes kissing. Men. Gertrude Stein. **CP-SteiG**

Sometimes, oh, often, indeed, in the midst of ugly adversity, beautiful. Edna St. Vincent Millay. **CP-MillE**

Sometimes our life reminds me. Wendell Berry. *Fr.* The Country of Marriage. **CP-BerrW**

Sometimes, reading late, I glimpse. Widow at "Whaleroad's End," The. Brendan Galvin. **SP-GalvB**

Sometimes, riding in a car, in Wisconsin. Three Kinds of Pleasures. Robert Bly. **SP-BlyR**

Sometimes she'd begin to sing to herself before she was out of bed, before, I can remember thinking. Mornings: Catherine. Charles Kenneth Williams. **SP-WillC**

Sometimes the light falls here too as at Florence. The Old Age of Michelangelo. Frank Templeton Prince. **CP-PrinF**

Sometimes the Longing for Death. Richard Eberhart. **CP-EberR**

Sometimes the night echoes to prideless wailing. John Berryman. NoAM *Fr.* Sonnets to Chris. **CP-BerrJ**

Sometimes the pencil, in cool airy halls. James Thomson. PoEL-3 *Fr.* The Castle of Indolence. **CP-ThomJ**

Sometimes the ridge across. Rainy Morning. Archie Randolph Ammons. **SP-AmmoA**

Sometimes the river. The Mind Hesitant. William Carlos Williams. **CP-WilW2**

Sometimes the sun beats up the rocks of capes. Crusoe. Thomas Merton. **CP-MertT; SP-MertT**

Sometimes the sun is still trying. Desert. Richard Shelton. **SP-ShelR**

Sometimes the sun turns hostile to men. The Hostile Sun. David Herbert Lawrence. **CP-LawrD**

Sometimes there's a wind in the Georgia dusk. Georgia Dusk. Langston Hughes. **SP-HughL**

Sometimes they thought he might be only shewn. John Milton. PeECV *Fr.* Book II. *Fr.* Paradise Regained [*or* Regain'd]. **CP-MiltJ**

Sometimes, though the sun is high. Vision. Peter Meinke. **SP-MeinP**

Sometimes up out of this land. Bi-Focal. William Stafford. **SP-StafW**

Sometimes waking, sometimes sleeping. Nestus Gurley. Randall Jarrell. **CP-JarrR; SP-JarrR**

Sometimes, walking for hours through the woods. 1945—1985: Poem for the Anniversary. Mary Oliver. **SP-OlivM**

Sometimes walking late at night. Butcher Shop. Charles Simic. **SP-SimiC**

Sometimes want makes touch too much. Warmth. Barton Sutter. **SP-SuttB**

Sometimes we don't say anything. Sometimes. Silence. Hayden Carruth. **CP-CarHS**

Sometimes we remember kisses. By the Spring at Sunset. Nicholas Vachel Lindsay. **CP-LindV**

Sometimes we see astonishingly clearly. One Circumlocution. Wystan Hugh Auden. **CP-AudeW**

Sometimes when I am wearied suddenly. Edna St. Vincent Millay. **CP-MillE**

Sometimes when I'm lonely. Hope. Langston Hughes. **SP-HughL**

Sometimes When Lovers Lie Quietly Together, Unexpectedly One of Them Will Feel the Other's Pulse. Hayden Carruth. **CP-CarHS**

Sometimes when my eyes are red. My Sad Self. Allen Ginsberg. **CP-GinsA**

Sometimes with One I Love. Walt Whitman. **CP-WhitW**

Sometimes with the Heart. Emily Dickinson. **CP-DickE**

Sometimes With the Waves. Al Young. **CP-YounA**

Sometimes you are liked for all the wrong. Funny. Charles Bukowski. **SP-BukC3**

Sometimes you have hardly been born. Bashing the Babies. John Ciardi. **SP-CiarJ**

Sometimes you hear, fifth-hand. Poetry of Departures. Philip Larkin. **CP-LarkP**

Sometimes you love someone. Winter Leaves. Al Young. **CP-YounA**

Sometimes your face. The Words Are Said, the Love Is Made. Marge Piercy. *Fr.* Walking into Love. **SP-PierM**

Somewhat apart from the village, and nearer the Basin of Minas. Evangeline in Acadie. Henry Wadsworth Longfellow. **AA** *Fr.* In the Acadian land, on the shores of the Basin of Minas. *Fr.* Part the First. *Fr.* Evangeline, a Tale of Acadie. **SP-LongH**

Somewhat, to hope for. Emily Dickinson. **CP-DickE**

Somewhere / a black bear / has just risen from sleep. Spring. Mary Oliver. **SP-OlivM**

Somewhere. Robert Creeley. **CP-CreeR**

Somewhere. Howard Nemerov. **CP-NemeH**

Somewhere. John Updike. **CP-UpdiJ**

Somewhere a king walks in his gallery. The Captives—a Psalm. Thomas Merton. **CP-MertT; SP-MertT**

Somewhere a white wall faces a white wall. Two Walls. Robert Lowell. **SP-LoweR**

Somewhere afield here something lies. Shelley's Skylark. Thomas Hardy. **CP-HardT**

Somewhere behind the lanes, over the map. The Mascot. Ted Hughes. *Fr.* Scapegoats and Rabies. **SP-HughT**

Somewhere beneath that piano's superb sleek black. The Piano. David Herbert Lawrence. **CP-LawrD**

Somewhere between bells the right angles staggered. Mangham. James Dickey. **CP-DickJ**

Somewhere between Greenfield and Holyoke. In the Bus. Grace Paley. **CP-PaleG**

Somewhere, between the coming. Marsden Hartley. **CP-HartM**

Somewhere Else. Richard Eberhart. **CP-EberR**

Somewhere I have never travelled, gladly beyond. Edward Estlin Cummings. **CP-CummE; SP-CummE**

Somewhere in a Turrent. Marilyn Hacker. **SP-HackM**

Somewhere in Africa. Anne Sexton. **CP-SextA**

Somewhere in Kansas, a friend found. A Place in Kansas. Ted Kooser. **SP-KoosT**

Somewhere in Mauriac a girl. Frank Templeton Prince. PeSAV *Fr.* Memoirs in Oxford. **CP-PrinF**

Somewhere in Russia I have heard. In Russia. Hayden Carruth. **CP-CarHS**

Somewhere in the hour. R.M.D. Hayden Carruth. **CP-CarHS**

Somewhere inside me / perhaps under my left shoulder. Guevara. John Haines. **SP-HainJ**

Somewhere, inside the wintry colonnade. The House of Caiphas. Thomas Merton. **CP-MertT; SP-MertT**

Somewhere Is Such a Kingdom. John Crowe Ransom. **SP-RansJ**

Somewhere It Still Moves. Stephen Dobyns. **SP-DobyS**

Somewhere on his travels the strange Child. Santa Claus. Howard Nemerov. **CP-NemeH**

Somewhere or Other. Christina Georgina Rossetti. **CP-RosC1**

Somewhere someone is traveling furiously toward you. At North Farm. John Ashbery. **SP-AshbJ**

Somewhere the long mellow note of the blackbird. Study. David Herbert Lawrence. **CP-LawrD**

Somewhere upon the general Earth. Emily Dickinson. **CP-DickE**

Somewhere, you and I remember we came. Throwbacks. Carl Sandburg. **CP-SandC**

Somme toute / tout compte fait. Samuel Beckett. **CP-BeckS**

Somnambulism. Tom Clark. **SP-ClarT**

Somnambulisma. Wallace Stevens. **CP-StevW**

Somnambulist, The. William Wordsworth. *Fr.* Poems Composed or Suggested During a Tour, in the Summer of 1833. **CP-WorW2**

Somnambulists along the promenade. Yánnina. James Merrill. **SP-MerrJ**

Somno compositam iacere Clytham. *acc. by English translation.* Thomas Campion. **CP-CampT**

Somonour was ther with us in that place, A. Geoffrey Chaucer. **OBCoV** *Fr.* The General Prologue. **FHYEP; NAWM-1; OAEL-1; PoE** *Fr.* The Canterbury Tales. **CP-ChauG**

Somtyme this world was so stedfast and stable. Lak of Stedfastnesse. Geoffrey Chaucer. **CP-ChauG**

Son, The. Hayden Carruth. *Fr.* Mother. **CP-CarHL**

Son, The. John Donne. NOCV *Fr.* A Litany. **CP-DonnJ**

Son, The. Rita Dove. **SP-DoveR**

Son[ne], The. George Herbert. **CP-HerbG**

Son, A. Rudyard Kipling. ChMP; FaBoEE; PeFWW *Fr.* Epitaphs of the War [1914–1918]. **CP-KiplR**

Son, The. Denise Levertov. **CP-LeveD**

Son, The. Louise McNeill. **SP-McNeL**

Son. Al Young. **CP-YounA**

Son Altesse. Robert Ranke Graves. **CP-GravR**

Son, and my friend, I had not called you so. Epigram. To a Friend and Son. Ben Jonson. **CP-JonsB**

Son[ne] of God hear[e] us, and since thou. John Donne. *Fr.* A Litany. **CP-DonnJ**

Son of Love and Lord of War I sing, The. The Conquest. Byron. **CP-Byron**

Son of Melancholy, The. Walter de la Mare. **CP-DeLaW**

Son of my buried Son, while thus thy hand. Poet to His Grandchild; Sequel to "A Plea for Authors." William Wordsworth. **CP-WorW2**

Son of my woman's body, you go, to the drum and fife. Mater Triumphans. Robert Louis Stevenson. **CP-StevR**

Son of the dark solstice descends the tree. A Christmas Crown. Marilyn Hacker. **SP-HackM**

Son of the Morning Star. David Herbert Lawrence. **CP-LawrD**

Son of the old moon-mountains African! To the Nile. John Keats. **CP-KeatJ**

Son ombre une nuit. Samuel Beckett. **CP-BeckS**

Son, Remember. Christina Georgina Rossetti. **CP-RosC2**

"Son," said my mother. The Ballad of the Harp-Weaver. Edna St. Vincent Millay. **CP-MillE**

Sonatina Followed by Another, A. Gertrude Stein. **CP-SteiG**

"She is that kind of a wife. She can see." **VBLP**

Sonatina to Hans Christian. Wallace Stevens. **CP-StevW**

Song, [A]: "Ask[e] me no more where Jove bestows." Thomas Carew. *See* Ask[e] Me No More Where Jove Bestow[e]s.

Song: "Adown winding Nith I did wander." Robert Burns. **CP-BurnR**

Song: "Ae fond kiss, and then we sever." Robert Burns. *See* Ae fond kiss, and then we sever.

Song: "Again rejoicing Nature sees." Robert Burns. **CP-BurnR**

Song: "Age is when to a man." Samuel Beckett. **CP-BeckS** *Fr.* Words and Music.

Song: "Ah fading joy, how quickly art thou past!" John Dryden. *See* Ah fading joy, how quickly art thou past!

Song: "Anna, thy charms my bosom fire." Robert Burns. **CP-BurnR**

Song: "As I cam down by yon castle wa' ." Robert Burns. **CP-BurnR**

Song: "As I stood by yon roofless tower." Robert Burns. **CP-BurnR**

Song: "Beautiful Dove, come back to us in April." Edna St. Vincent Millay. **CP-MillE**

Song: "Beauty is a shell." William Carlos Williams. **CP-WilW2**

Song: "Beeing past the paines of love." Mary Sidney, Countess of Montgomery Wroth. *Fr.* Pamphilia to Amphilanthus. **CP-WrotM**

Song: "Behind yon hills where Lugar flows." Robert Burns. **CP-BurnR**

Song: "Behold the hour, the boat arrive." Robert Burns. **CP-BurnR**

Song: "Birds doe sing, day doth apeere, The." Mary Sidney, Countess of Montgomery Wroth. *Fr.* Pamphilia to Amphilanthus. **CP-WrotM**

Song: "Black-winged gull, The." William Carlos Williams. **CP-WilW1**

Song: "Blythe hae I been on yon hill." Robert Burns. **CP-BurnR**

Song: "Bottom of the sea has come, The." Thomas Merton. **CP-MertT; SP-MertT**

Song: "Breeze of the night in gentler sighs." Byron. **CP-Byron**

Song: "Burne or drowne me." Robert Herrick. **CP-HerrR**

Song: "But we've the may / (for you are in love)." Edward Estlin Cummings. **CP-CummE**

Song: "Buy, buy, buy." George Meredith. **CP-MerG2**

Song: "Can life be a blessing." John Dryden. *See* Can Life be a blessing.

Song: "Cold, cold is the blast when December is howling." Percy Bysshe Shelley. *Fr.* Original Poetry by Victor and Cazire. **CP-ShelP**

Song: "Come [Harriet]! sweet is the hour." Percy Bysshe Shelley. *Fr.* Original Poetry by Victor and Cazire. **CP-ShelP**

Song: "Come into the garden, Maud." Tennyson. *See* Come into the garden, Maud.

Song: "Come to me in any shape!" George Meredith. **CP-MerG1**

Song: "Come where the grieving rivers of the night." Thomas Merton. **CP-MertT**

Song: "Contented wi' little, and cantie wi' mair." Robert Burns. *See* Contented wi' Little.

Song: "Crafty boy that had full oft assay'd, The." Sir John Suckling. **CP-SuckJ**

Song: "Crocus stars the border, The." Wystan Hugh Auden. **CP-AudWJ**

Song: "Daisy now is out upon the green, The." George Meredith. **CP-MerG1**

Song: "De bee hit sip some honey f'om de matermony vine." Paul Laurence Dunbar. **CP-DunbP**

Song: "Deerest if I by my deserving." Mary Sidney, Countess of Montgomery Wroth. *Fr.* Pamphilia to Amphilanthus. **CP-WrotM**

Song: "Deftly, admiral, cast your fly." Wystan Hugh Auden. *See* Deftly, admiral, cast your fly.

Song: "Devastation / of being, The." Frederick Morgan. **SP-MorgF**

Song: "Does Pity give, tho' Fate denies." Charlotte Smith. **CP-SmitC**

Song: "Dying gales of sweet even." John Clare. **SP-ClarJ** *Fr.* Child Harold.

Song: "Fair and false! No dawn will greet." George Meredith. **CP-MerG1**

Song: "Fair, sweet and young, receive a prize." John Dryden. **SP-DrydJ**

Song: "Fairest, and still truest eyes." Mary Sidney, Countess of Montgomery Wroth. *Fr.* Pamphilia to Amphilanthus. **CP-WrotM**

Song: "Fairest isle, all isles excelling." John Dryden. *See* Song of Venus.

Song: "Farewell fair Arminda, my joy and my grief." John Dryden. **SP-DrydJ**

Song: "Farewell, thou stream that winding flows." Robert Burns. **CP-BurnR**

Song: "Farewell ungrateful[l] traitor [or traytor]." John Dryden. *See* Farewell ungrateful[l] traitor [or traytor], / Farewell my perjured swain.

Song: "Fierce roars the midnight storm." Percy Bysshe Shelley. *Fr.* Original Poetry by Victor and Cazire. **CP-ShelP**

Song: "Flower unfolds its dawning cup, The." George Meredith. **CP-MerG1**

Song: "Fresh from the dewy hill, the merry year." William Blake. **CP-BlakW**

Song: "From thee, ELIZA, I must go." Robert Burns. **CP-BurnR**

Song: "From whence cometh song?" Theodore Roethke. **CP-RoetT**

Song: "Fruit of Aurora's tears, fair Rose." François-Joachim Pierre de, Cardinal Bernis, *tr. fr. French by* Charlotte Smith. **CP-SmitC**

Song: "Full of thy glory am I." George Meredith. **CP-MerG2**

Song: "Full well thou knowest I love thee dear." Robert Burns. **CP-BurnR** ("Fairest maid on Devon banks.") **CP-BurnR**

Song: "Give her but a least excuse to love me!" Robert Browning. **ViBoPo** *Fr.* Pippa Passes. **CP-BroR1**

Song: "Gloomy night is gath'ring fast, The." Robert Burns. **CP-BurnR**

Song: "Go, and catch a falling star." John Donne. **CP-DonnJ**

Song: "Go tell Amynta, gentle swain." John Dryden. **SP-DrydJ** *Fr.* Sylvae.

Song: "God bless the little Island!" George Meredith. **CP-MerG2**

Song: "God give you pardon from gratitue." Robert Creeley. **CP-CreeR**

Song: "Gon is my joy while heere I mourne." Mary Sidney, Countess of Montgomery Wroth. *Fr.* Part 1. *Fr.* Urania. **CP-WrotM**

Song: "Gone, gone again is Summer the lovely." Edna St. Vincent Millay. **CP-MillE**

Song: "Grit / of things, The." Robert Creeley. **CP-CreeR**

Song: "Had I a cave on some wild, distant shore." Robert Burns. **CP-BurnR**

Song: "Here I am yours, and here, and here." Jane Cooper. **SP-CoopJ**

Song: "Honest lover whosoever." Sir John Suckling. **CP-SuckJ**

Song: "How happy the lover." John Dryden. **SP-DrydJ** *Fr.* King Arthur.

Song: "How simply / for another." Robert Creeley. **CP-CreeR**

Song: "How sweet I roamed [or roam'd] from field to field." William Blake. *See* How Sweet I Roamed [or roam'd] from Field to Field.

Song: "Hush, hush! tread softly! hush, hush my dear." John Keats. **CP-KeatJ**

Song: "I almost went to bed." Leonard Cohen. **CP-CoheL**

Song: "I cannot lose thee for a day." George Meredith. **CP-MerG1**

Song: "I feed a flame within, which so torments me." John Dryden. **SP-DrydJ** *Fr.* Secret Love; or, The Maiden Queen.

Song: "I had a dove and the sweet dove died." John Keats. **CP-KeatJ**

Song: "I have a little book." Wystan Hugh Auden. **CP-AudWJ**

Song: "I have loved you for long years Ellen." Christina Georgina Rossetti. **CP-RosC3**

Song: "I lay in sheets of softest linen." Alun Lewis. **CP-LewiA**

Song: "I love the jocund dance." William Blake. **CP-BlakW**

Song: "I murder hate by field or flood." Robert Burns. **NCEP** *Fr.* Lines Written on the Windows of the Globe Tavern, Dumfries. **CP-BurnR**

Song: "I peeled bits of straw and I got switches too." John Clare. **SP-ClarJ**

("I peeled bits o strews and I got switches too.") **SP-ClarJ**

Song: "I prithee send me back my heart." Sir John Suckling. **CP-SuckJ**

Song: "I prithee spare me, gentle boy." Sir John Suckling. **CP-SuckJ**

Song: "I saw her; she was lovely." Christina Georgina Rossetti. **CP-RosC3**

Song: "I tell my love in rhyme." Wendell Berry. **CP-BerrW**

Song: "I, that ame of all most crost." Mary Sidney, Countess of Montgomery Wroth. **KTR** *Fr.* Pamphilia to Amphilanthus. **CP-WrotM**

Song: "I would be the bounding deer." George Meredith. **CP-MerG2**

Song: "I would I were the drop of rain." George Meredith. **CP-MerG1**

Song: "I wouldn't / embarrass you." Robert Creeley. **CP-CreeR**

Song: "I'd rather read an account." William Carlos Williams. **CP-WilW2**

Song: "If I / could count the silence." William Carlos Williams. **CP-WilW2**

Song: "If you refuse me once and think again." Sir John Suckling. **CP-SuckJ**

Song: "I'll tell you a tale of a wife." Robert Burns. **CP-BurnR**

Song: "I'm about to go shopping." James Schuyler. **CP-SchuJ**

Song: "In Mauchline there dwells six proper young Belles." Robert Burns. **CP-BurnR**

Song: "In mine one [or own] monument I lie [or lye]." Richard Lovelace. **CP-LoveR**

Song: "In minute gestures / that jet wetly slight." Jim Carroll. **SP-CarrJ**

Song: "Is it dirty." Frank O'Hara. **SP-OharF**

Song: "It goes, it / Goes." Jim Carroll. **SP-CarrJ**

Song: "It is not for her even brow." Christina Georgina Rossetti. **CP-RosC3**

Song: "It is not now I learn." Louise Bogan. **CP-BogaL**

Song: "It was upon a Lammas night." Robert Burns. *See* It was upon a Lammas night.

Song: "Joyful / And woful." Johann Wolfgang von Goethe, *tr. fr. German by* George Meredith. **CP-MerG2**

Song: "Keep the dream alive and growing always." Edwin Rolfe. **CP-RolfE**

Song: "King Julius left the south country." Emily Brontë. **CP-BronE**

Song: "Let not Woman e'er complain." Robert Burns. **CP-BurnR**

Song: "Light foot and tight foot." Robert Louis Stevenson. **CP-StevR**

Song: "Light lies layered in the leaves, The." James Schuyler. **CP-SchuJ**

Song: "Linnet in the rocky dells, The." Emily Brontë. **CP-BronE**

Song: "Lord, when the sense of Thy sweet grace." Richard Crashaw. **CP-CrasR**

Song: "Love a child is ever criing [*or* crying]." Mary Sidney, Countess of Montgomery Wroth. **KTR; NOSC** *Fr.* Pamphilia to Amphilanthus. **CP-WrotM**

Song: "Love and harmony combine." William Blake. **CP-BlakW**

Song: "Love as well can make abiding." Mary Sidney, Countess of Montgomery Wroth. *Fr.* Pamphilia to Amphilanthus. **CP-WrotM**

Song: "Love what art thou? A vaine thought." Mary Sidney, Countess of Montgomery Wroth. *Fr.* Part 1. *Fr.* Urania. **CP-WrotM**

Song: "Love within the lover's breast." George Meredith. **CP-MerG1**

Song: "Make this night loveable." Wystan Hugh Auden. *See* Make this night loveable.

Song: "Mark yonder pomp of costly fashion." Robert Burns. **CP-BurnR**

Song: "Memory, hither come." William Blake. **CP-BlakW**

Song: "Merriest cuckoo / Which haunted us in May, The." Wystan Hugh Auden. **CP-AudWJ**

Song: "Might I lie where leans her lute." George Meredith. **CP-MerG2**

Song. John Milton. *See* Sabrina Fair.

Song: "Moon is alone in the sky, The." George Meredith. **CP-MerG1**

Song. Vinícius de Moraes, *tr. fr. Portuguese by* Richard Wilbur. **CP-WilbR**

Song: "My chosen bride shall bless the plough." George Meredith. **CP-MerG2**

Song: "My darling's love shall close me up." George Meredith. **CP-MerG2**

Song: "My father was a farmer upon the Carrick border O." Robert Burns. **CP-BurnR**

Song: "My girl she's airy, she's buxom and gay." Robert Burns. **CP-BurnR**

Song: "My heart to thy heart." Paul Laurence Dunbar. **CP-DunbP**

Song: "My silks and fine array." William Blake. **CP-BlakW**

Song: "My wrath, where's the edge." Theodore Roethke. **CP-RoetT**

Song: "Nay but you, who do not love her." Robert Browning. **CP-BroR1**

Song: "'Neath blue-bell or streamer." Edgar Allan Poe. **AmPP; AnAmPo; OxBA** *Fr.* Song: "Young flowers were whispering in melody." **NOBA** *Fr.* Al Aaraaf. **CP-PoeEd**

Song: "No Churchman am I for to rail and to write." Robert Burns. **CP-BurnR**

Song: "No, I will never forget you and your great eyes." May Sarton. **SP-SartM**

Song: "No more shall hapless Celia's ears." William Cowper. **CP-CowpW**

Song: "No, no, fair heretic[k], it needs must be." Sir John Suckling. **AnAnS-2; BeJo; CABA; CaPo; LoBV; OBS; PrIm** *Fr.* Aglaura. **CP-SuckJ**

Song: "No, no, the falling blossom is no sign." George Meredith. **CP-MerG1**

Song: "Now hath Flora rob'd [*or* robbed] her bowers." Thomas Campion. *Fr.* Lord Hay's Mask.
(Roses.) **OBSC**

Song: "Now let us honor with violin and flute." May Sarton. **SP-SartM**

Song: "Now sleeps the crimson petal, now the white." Tennyson. *See* Now sleeps the crimson petal, now the white.

Song: "O beautiful, my relic bone." Jean Garrigue. **SP-GarrJ**

Song: "O between distress and pleasure." Emily Brontë. **CP-BronE**

Song: "O have you seen the thorn that grows." Alun Lewis. **CP-LewiA**

Song: "O lady, when the tipped cup of the moon blessed you." Ted Hughes. **SP-HughT**

Song: "O, Logan, sweetly didst thou glide." Robert Burns. **CP-BurnR**

Song: "O Philly, happy be that day." Robert Burns. **CP-BurnR**

Song: "O poortith cauld, and restless love." Robert Burns. **CP-BurnR**

Song: "O sweet delight, O more than human[e] bliss[e]." Thomas Campion. **CP-CampT**

Song: "O the wind, the wind, the wind doth blow." George Meredith. **CP-MerG2**

Song: "O they canna' do without it." George Meredith. **CP-MerG2**

Song: "O this is no my ain lassie." Robert Burns. **CP-BurnR**

Song: "O wat ye wha's in yon town." Robert Burns. **CP-BurnR**

Song: "O wat ye what that lo'es me." Robert Burns. **CP-BurnR** ("O that's the lassie o' my heart.") **CP-BurnR**

Song: "O whistle, and I'll come to ye, my lad." Robert Burns. *See* O whistle, and I'll come to you [*or* ye], my lad.

Song: "Observe the cautious toadstools." William DeWitt Snodgrass. **SP-SnodW**

Song: "O'er the smooth enamelled green." John Milton. *See* O're [*or* O'er] the smooth enamel'd [*or* enameled *or* enamelled] green.

Song: "Oh journeyman, Oh journeyman." Alun Lewis. **CP-LewiA**

Song: "Oh roses for the flush of youth." Christina Georgina Rossetti. **CP-RosC1**

Song: "Oh what comes over the sea." Christina Georgina Rossetti. **CP-RosC1**

Song: "O[h] me[e] the time is [*or* has] come to part." Mary Sidney, Countess of Montgomery Wroth. **NOSC** *Fr.* Pamphilia to Amphilanthus. **CP-WrotM**

Song: "On Cessnock banks a lassie dwells." Robert Burns. **CP-BurnR**

Song: "Over the ferry, and over the ferry." George Meredith. **CP-MerG2**

Song: "Pass we to another land." George Meredith. **CP-MerG2**

Song: "Past all your knowing." Wystan Hugh Auden. **CP-AudWJ**

Song: "Pity the blind and the halt but yet pity." Malcolm Lowry. **CP-LowrM**

Song: "Pluck the florets from." William Carlos Williams. **CP-WilW2**

Song: "Provide your friend with almanacs." Howard Nemerov. **CP-NemeH**

Song: "Quick bird sings and pierces me, The." George Meredith. **CP-MerG2**

Song: "Rarely, rarely, comest thou." Percy Bysshe Shelley. **CP-ShelP**

Song: "Relation seemed ordained for us." Wystan Hugh Auden. **CP-AudWJ**

Song: "Rowan like a lip-sticked girl, A." Seamus Heaney. **SP-HeanS**

Song: "Russia! Russia! you might say." William Carlos Williams. **CP-WilW2**

Song: "Say this city has ten million souls." Wystan Hugh Auden. *See* Say this city has ten million souls.

Song: "Say Venus how long have I lov'd, and serv'd you heere?" Mary Sidney, Countess of Montgomery Wroth. *Fr.* Pamphilia to Amphilanthus. **CP-WrotM**

Song: "Say What Is Love—To Live In Vain." John Clare. **SP-ClarJ** *Fr.* Child Harold.

Song: "Sensibility how charming." Robert Burns. **CP-BurnR**

Song: "Shadowes darkning our intents, The." Thomas Campion. *Fr.* The Ayres that Were Sung and Played, at *Brougham Castle* in *Westmerland*, in the Kings Entertainment. **CP-CampT**

Song: "She dwelt among the untrodden ways." William Wordsworth. *See* She dwelt among the untrodden ways.

Song: "She sat and sang alway." Christina Georgina Rossetti. **CP-RosC1**

Song: "Should thy love die; / O bury it not under ice-blue eyes!" George Meredith. **CP-MerG1**

Song: "Shout for those whose course is done." Ralph Waldo Emerson. **CP-EmerR**

Song: "Small birds rejoice in the green leaves returning, The." Robert Burns. **CP-BurnR**

Song: "Song tells us of our old way of living, The." John Ashbery. **SP-AshbJ**

Song: "Spirit haunts the last year's hours, A." Tennyson. *See* A Spirit haunts the year's last hours.

Song: "Spirit here that reignest!" John Keats. **CP-KeatJ**

Song: "Springing time of my first loving, The." Mary Sidney, Countess of Montgomery Wroth. *Fr.* Pamphilia to Amphilanthus. **CP-WrotM**

Song: "Stay, ruby-breasted warbler, stay." John Keats. **CP-KeatJ**

Song: "Stop all the clocks, cut off the telephone." Wystan Hugh Auden. *See* Stop all the clocks, cut off the telephone.

Song: "Stranger, you who hide my love." Stephen Spender. **CP-SpenS**

Song: "Stream moaneth as it floweth, The." Christina Georgina Rossetti. **CP-RosC3**

Song: "Strive not, vain Lover, to be fine." Richard Lovelace. **CP-LoveR**

Song: "Summer burns on the edges of day." Hayden Carruth. **CP-CarHS**

Song: "Summer is over upon the sea." Elizabeth Bishop. **CP-BishE**

Song: "Sunny shaft did I behold, A." Samuel Taylor Coleridge. *See* Glycine's Song.

Song: "Sweet beast, I have gone prowling." William DeWitt Snodgrass. **SP-SnodW**

Song: "Sweetest Love, I Do Not Go." John Donne. **CP-DonnJ**

Song: "Their groves o' sweet myrtle let Foreign Lands reckon." Robert Burns. **CP-BurnR**

Song: "There is indeed now reason for rejoicing." Edwin Rolfe. **CP-RolfE**

Song: "This fair parcel of summer's." Theodore Roethke. **CP-RoetT**

Song: "Tho' women's minds, like winter winds." Robert Burns. **CP-BurnR**

Song: "Those rivers run from that land." Robert Creeley. **CP-CreeR**

Song: "Thou steppest from thy splendour." George Meredith. **CP-MerG2**

Song: "Thou to me art such a spring." George Meredith. **CP-MerG1**

Song: "Thou tremblest O my love! thy hand in mine." George Meredith. **CP-MerG2**

Song: "Though veiled in spires of myrtle wreath." Samuel Taylor Coleridge. **CP-ColeS**

Song: "Through all the cowering world, crouching, shrinking." Edwin Rolfe. **CP-RolfE**

Song: "Thyrsis, when we parted, swore." Thomas Gray. **CP-GrayT**

Song: "Tibby I hae seen the day." Robert Burns. **CP-BurnR**

Song: "To me this world's a dreary blank." Percy Bysshe Shelley. *Fr. Original Poetry by Victor and Cazire.* **CP-ShelP**

Song: " 'Twas na her bonie blue e'e was my ruin." Robert Burns. **CP-BurnR**

Song: "Twelve arrows, and a bow, and spear." George Meredith. **CP-MerG2**

Song: "Two doves upon the selfsame branch." Christina Georgina Rossetti. **CP-RosC1**

Song: "Two wedded lovers watched the rising moon." George Meredith. **CP-MerG1**

Song: "Under boughs of breathing May." George Meredith. **CP-MerG1**

Song: "Under the yellow sea." Delmore Schwartz. *Fr. Two Lyrics from Kilroy's Carnival: A Masque.* **SP-SchwD**

Song: "Unjust decrees, that do at once exact." Sir John Suckling. **CP-SuckJ**

Song: "Up in the high." David Herbert Lawrence. **CP-LawrD**

Song: "Voice flew out of the river as morning flew, A." Muriel Rukeyser. **CP-RukeM**

Song: "We buried her among the flowers." Christina Georgina Rossetti. **CP-RosC3**

Song: "Weight of the world, The." Allen Ginsberg. **CP-GinsA**

Song: "Were I myself more blithe." Robert Creeley. **CP-CreeR**

Song: "What do you / want, love. To be." Robert Creeley. **CP-CreeR**

Song: "What I took in my hand." Robert Creeley. **CP-CreeR**

Song: "When all within is peace." William Cowper. **CP-CowpW**

Song: "When blooming spring." James Thomson. **CP-ThomJ**

Song: "When, dearest, I but think on [or of] thee." Sir John Suckling *and* Owen Feltham. **CP-SuckJ**

Song: "When early morn walks forth in sober grey." William Blake. **CP-BlakW**

Song: "When I am dead, my dearest." Christina Georgina Rossetti. **CP-RosC1**

Song: "When on my faithful charger." George Meredith. **CP-MerG2**

Song: "When rain, (sings light) rain has devoured my house." Thomas Merton. **CP-MertT**

Song: "Wherever I am, and whatever I do." John Dryden. **SP-DrydJ** *Fr. The Conquest of Granada.*

Song: "Who can blame mee if I love?" Mary Sidney, Countess of Montgomery Wroth. *Fr. Part 1. Fr. Urania.* **CP-WrotM**

Song: "Who says, she is in danger." George Meredith. **CP-MerG2**

Song: "Why so pale and wan, fond lover?" Sir John Suckling. *See* Why so pale and wan, fond lover?

Song: "Wild trees have bought me." Audre Lorde. **SP-LordA**

Song: "Will ye go to the Indies, my Mary." Robert Burns. **CP-BurnR**

Song: "Wintah, summah, snow er shine." Paul Laurence Dunbar. **CP-DunbP**

Song: "Woo me now & you'll win me." George Meredith. **CP-MerG2**

Song: "World is full of colored / people, The." Alice Walker. **CP-WalkA**

Song: "World is full of loss; bring, wind, my love, The." Muriel Rukeyser. **CP-RukeM**

Song: "Year's at the Spring, The." Robert Browning. *See* The Year's at the spring.

Song: "Yestreen I had a pint o' wine." Robert Burns. *See* Yestreen I had a pint o' wine.

Song: "You are as gold." Hilda Doolittle. **CP-DoolH**

Song: "You are forever April." William Carlos Williams. **CP-WilW2**

Song: "You charmed me not with that fair face." John Dryden. **SP-DrydJ** *Fr. An Evening's Love.*

Song: "You look out and you see people." Robert Creeley. **CP-CreeR**

Song: "Young flowers were whispering in melody." Edgar Allan Poe. **NOBA** *Fr. Al Aaraaf.* **CP-PoeEd**

Song: "Neath blue-bell or streamer." **AmPP; AnAmPo; OxBA**

Song: "You're wondering if I'm lonely." Adrienne Rich. **SP-RicA2**

Song 1: "Spring now came att last, The." Mary Sidney, Countess of Montgomery Wroth. *Fr. Pamphilia to Amphilanthus.* **CP-WrotM**

Song 1: "Sweet lett mee injoye thy sight." Mary Sidney, Countess of Montgomery Wroth. *Fr. Pamphilia to Amphilanthus.* **CP-WrotM**

Song 2: "All night I weep[e], all day I cry, Ay me[e]." Mary Sidney, Countess of Montgomery Wroth. **NOSC** *Fr. Pamphilia to Amphilanthus.* **CP-WrotM**

Song 2: "Sweet Silvia in a shadie wood." Mary Sidney, Countess of Montgomery Wroth. *Fr. Pamphilia to Amphilanthus.* **CP-WrotM**

Song 3: "Come merry spring delight us." Mary Sidney, Countess of Montgomery Wroth. *Fr. Pamphilia to Amphilanthus.* **CP-WrotM**

Song 3: ("Stay, my thoughts, do nott aspire"). Mary Sidney, Countess of Montgomery Wroth. *Fr. Pamphilia to Amphilanthus.* **CP-WrotM**

Song 4: "Lovers learne to speake butt truthe." Mary Sidney, Countess of Montgomery Wroth. *Fr. Pamphilia to Amphilanthus.* **CP-WrotM**

Song 4: "Sweetest love returne againe." Mary Sidney, Countess of Montgomery Wroth. *Fr. Pamphilia to Amphilanthus.* **CP-WrotM**

Song 5: "Time only cause of my unrest." Mary Sidney, Countess of Montgomery Wroth. *Fr. Pamphilia to Amphilanthus.* **CP-WrotM**

Song 6: "You happy blessed eyes." Mary Sidney, Countess of Montgomery Wroth. *Fr. Pamphilia to Amphilanthus.* **CP-WrotM**

Song 7: "Sorrow, I yeeld, and grieve that I did miss." Mary Sidney, Countess of Montgomery Wroth. *Fr. Pamphilia to Amphilanthus.* **CP-WrotM**

Song, A: "As at the bottom of a seething well." Richard Wilbur. **CP-WilbR**

Song, A: "Beneath thy skies, November!" John Greenleaf Whittier. **CP-WhitJ**

Song, A: "Come away; bring thy golden theft." Thomas Campion. *Fr. The Lords Mask[e].*

Song, A: "Come, let us here enjoy the shade." Ben Jonson. **CP-JonsB**

Song, A: "I had wanted a quiet testament." Robert Creeley. **CP-CreeR**

Song, A: "Loose no time nor youth but be." Robert Herrick. **CP-HerrR**

Song, A: "Not the soft sighs of vernal gales." Samuel Johnson. **CP-JohnS**

Song, A: "On a summer's day as I sat by a stream." Paul Laurence Dunbar. **CP-DunbP**

Song, A: "On the green margin of the brook." William Cowper. **CP-CowpW**

Song, A: "Sparkling eye, the mantling cheek." William Cowper. **CP-CowpW**

Song, A: "Thou art the soul of a summer's day." Paul Laurence Dunbar. **CP-DunbP**

Song, A: "Thou lingering Star with lessening ray." Robert Burns. *See* Thou Ling'ring Star.

Song, A: "When it was day, we heard the panes of windows." Thomas Merton. **CP-MertT**

Song, A: "Widow bird sate mourning for her love, A." Percy Bysshe Shelley. *See* A Widow bird sate mourning for her love.

Song, A; "I thought no more was needed." William Butler Yeats. **CP-YeatW**

Song: A Phoenix Flame. Robert Ranke Graves. **CP-GravR**

Song, a poem of itself—the word itself a dirge, A. Yonnondio. Walt Whitman. **CP-WhitW**

Song about Madrid, Useful Any Time. Malcolm Lowry. *Fr. The Roar of the Sea and the Darkness.* **CP-LowrM**

Song about Myself, A. John Keats. **CP-KeatJ**

"There was a naughty boy." **BoTP; CBNP; FHYEP; FaBoCh; FaBoCo; LiTB; MeMBP; MoShBr; OBCoV; OnUR; OxBChV**

(Song about Myself, A.) **MeMBP**

Song about Myself, A. John Keats. *See* There was a naughty boy.

Song about Sinn Fein for Serena. James Liddy. *Fr. Shore.* **CP-LiddJ**

Song about the happy-go-lucky fellow who hasn't time, The. I Burn Money. Ogden Nash. **CP-NashO**

Song against Singing, A. Elizabeth Barrett Browning. **CP-BroEB**

Song: "All, all of a piece throughout." John Dryden. *See* All, All of a Piece Throughout.

Song, Altered from an Old English One. Robert Burns. *See* It was the charming month of May.

Song at Cock-Crow, A. Rudyard Kipling. **CP-KiplR**

Song at Dawn. Robert Louis Stevenson. **CP-StevR**

Song at Shannon's, A. Edwin Arlington Robinson. **CP-RobiE**

Song at Sunset. Walt Whitman. **CP-WhitW**

Song at the Feast of Brougham Castle upon the Restoration of Lord Clifford, the Shepherd, to the Estates and Honours of His Ancestors. William Wordsworth. **CP-WorW1**

Song at the Ruin'd Inn. Tennyson. **PoEL-5** *Fr.* The Vision of Sin. **CP-TennA**

Song at the Winepresses, A. Kenneth Rexroth. **CP-RexKL**

Song: Autumn. George Meredith. **CP-MerG1**

Song: Basket of Blossom. Robert Ranke Graves. **CP-GravR**

Song: Beautiful Mistress, A. Thomas Carew. *See* If when the sun at noon displays.

Song Before Breakfast. Ogden Nash. **CP-NashO**

Song: Beyond Giving. Robert Ranke Graves. **CP-GravR**

Song: Brignal Banks. Sir Walter Scott. *See* Brignall Banks.

Song by Comus and Three Peasants, A. John Dryden. *See* Harvest Home.

Song By J. Brenzaida To G.S. Emily Brontë. **CP-BronE**

Song by Julius Angora. Emily Brontë. **CP-BronE**

Song By Julius Brenzaida To G.S. Emily Brontë. **CP-BronE**

Song by Klipstein and Krumpacker, Snow and Swarts as before. Thomas Stearns Eliot. *Fr.* Two Songs from *Sweeny Agonistes*. **UnPo** *Fr.* Sweeney Agonistes. **CP-ElioT**

Song by Wauchope and Horsfall, Snow as Tambo. Swarts as Bones. Thomas Stearns Eliot. *Fr.* Two Songs from *Sweeny Agonistes*. **UnPo** *Fr.* Sweeney Agonistes. **CP-ElioT**

Song: Cherries or Lilies. Robert Ranke Graves. **CP-GravR**

Song: Come, Enjoy Your Sunday! Robert Ranke Graves. **CP-GravR**

Song.—Composed at Auchtertyre on Miss Euphemia Murray of Lentrose. Robert Burns. *See* Blythe Was She.

Song Composed for Fanny Burney, A. Samuel Johnson. **CP-JohnS**

Song, Composed in August. Robert Burns. **CP-BurnR**

Song: Contemplation. Thomas Merton. **CP-MertT**

Song Contest. Geoffrey Hill. **CP-HillG**

Song: Crown of Stars. Robert Ranke Graves. **CP-GravR**

Song-Day in Autumn. David Herbert Lawrence. **CP-LawrD**

Song: Dew-Drop and Diamond. Robert Ranke Graves. **CP-GravR**

Song: Dream Warning. Robert Ranke Graves. **CP-GravR**

Song, ex improviso. Samuel Taylor Coleridge. **CP-ColeS**

Song: Fig Tree in Leaf. Robert Ranke Graves. **CP-GravR**

Song 1st By a Shepherd. William Blake. **CP-BlakW**

Song for a Birth Day in Exile. Edwin Rolfe. **CP-RolfE**

Song for a Dark Girl. Langston Hughes. **SP-HughL**

Song for a Dark Voice. Denise Levertov. **CP-LeveD**

Song for a Lady. Anne Sexton. **CP-SextA**

Song for a Lyre. Louise Bogan. **CP-BogaL**

Song for a Marimba. Malcolm Lowry. **CP-LowrM**

Song for a Red Nightgown. Anne Sexton. **CP-SextA**

Song for a Revolutionary Love. Sylvia Plath. **CP-PlatS**

Song for a Slight Voice. Louise Bogan. **CP-BogaL**

Song for a Summer's Day. Sylvia Plath. **CP-PlatS**

Song for a Temperature of a Hundred and One. Ogden Nash. **CP-NashO**

Song—For A' That and A' That. Robert Burns. *See* Is there, for honest poverty.

Song for a Thin Sister. Audre Lorde. **SP-LordA**

Song for Abraham Klein. Leonard Cohen. **CP-CoheL**

Song for All Seas, All Ships. Walt Whitman. **CP-WhitW**

Song for an Allegorical Play. John Ciardi. **SP-CiarJ**

Song for Apollo. Matthew Arnold. *See* Song of Callicles, The ("Through the black, rushing smoke-burst").

Song for Billie Holiday. Langston Hughes. **SP-HughL**

Song for "Buvez les Vins du Postillion"—Advt. Jean Garrigue. **SP-GarrJ**

Song for Certain Congressmen. Walt Whitman. **CP-WhitW**

Song for Champagne Saturday. Dabney Stuart. **SP-StuaD**

Song for Dead Children. Muriel Rukeyser. **CP-RukeM**

Song for Ditherers. Ogden Nash. **CP-NashO**

Song for Elizabeth, A. Nicholas Vachel Lindsay. **CP-LindV**

Song for Happy Feast Days, A. Hart Crane. **CP-CranH**

Song for Ishtar. Denise Levertov. **CP-LeveD**

Song for Making the Birds Come. Stephen Dobyns. **SP-DobyS**

Song for May Day. John Hewitt. **CP-HewiJ**

Song for My Assassin. Leonard Cohen. **CP-CoheL**

Song for My Wife. Malcolm Lowry. **CP-LowrM**

Song for Nobody. Thomas Merton. **CP-MertT; SP-MertT**

Song for Occupations, A. Walt Whitman. **CP-WhitW**

"Will you seek afar off? you surely come back at last." **ChIV-1**

Song for Our Lady of Cobre. Thomas Merton. **CP-MertT; SP-MertT**

Song for Pier Something or Other. Ogden Nash. **CP-NashO**

Song for Rustam, A. Basil Bunting. **CP-BuntB**

Song for St Cecilia's Day [1687], A. John Dryden. **SP-DrydJ**

Fife and Drum. **GN**

Song for Simeon, A. Thomas Stearns Eliot. **CP-ElioT**

Song for "Tasso", *see also* Scene from "Tasso." Percy Bysshe Shelley. **CP-ShelP**

Song for the Blessed Sacrament. Thomas Merton. **CP-MertT**

Song for the Death of Averroës. Thomas Merton. **CP-MertT**

Song for the Last Act. Louise Bogan. **CP-BogaL**

Song for the Least of All Saints, A. Christina Georgina Rossetti. **CP-RosC2**

Song for the Middle of the Night, A. James Wright. **CP-WrigJ**

Song for the Old Ones. Maya Angelou. **SP-AngeM**

Song for the Ragged Schools of London, A. Elizabeth Barrett Browning. **CP-BroEB**

Song for the Rainy Season. Elizabeth Bishop. **CP-BishE**

Song for the Spinning Wheel (Founded upon a Belief Prevalent among the Pastoral Vales of Westmoreland). William Wordsworth. **CP-WorW1**

Song for the Squeeze-Box. Theodore Roethke. **CP-RoetT**

Song for the Time, A. John Greenleaf Whittier. **CP-WhitJ**

Song for the unsung heroes who rose in the country's need, A. The Unsung Heroes. Paul Laurence Dunbar. **CP-DunbP**

Song for the Wandering Jew. William Wordsworth. **CP-WorW1**

Song for the Women, The. Rudyard Kipling. **CP-KiplR**

Song for the Year's End, A. Louis Zukofsky. **CP-ZukLS**

Song for Young Lovers in a City. Edna St. Vincent Millay. **CP-MillE**

Song: "Forever." George Meredith. **CP-MerG2**

Song (4). Wendell Berry. **CP-BerrW**

Song from Arcades. John Milton. *See* Nymphs and Shepherds dance no more.

Song from Armenia, A. Geoffrey Hill. *Fr.* The Songbook of Sebastian Arrurruz. **CP-HillG**

Song from "Cleopatra." John Berryman. **CP-BerrJ**

Song from Heine. Thomas Hardy. **CP-HardT**

Song, from "Mr. Amazeen on the River." Muriel Rukeyser. **CP-RukeM**

Song: From Otherwhere or Nowhere. Robert Ranke Graves. **CP-GravR**

Song from *Puck Fair*. Muriel Rukeyser. **CP-RukeM**

Song from the French. *Unknown, tr. fr. French by* Charlotte Smith. **CP-SmitC**

Song from "The Player Queen,"A. William Butler Yeats. **CP-YeatW**

Song from the Wandering Jew. Percy Bysshe Shelley. **CP-ShelP**

Song: Hope. Percy Bysshe Shelley. *Fr.* Original Poetry by Victor and Cazire. **CP-ShelP**

Song: How Can I Care? Robert Ranke Graves. **CP-GravR**

Song: If You Seek. Thomas Merton. **CP-MertT**

Song in a cornfield, A. Songs in a Cornfield. Christina Georgina Rossetti. **CP-RosC1**

Song in a Year of Catastrophe. Wendell Berry. **CP-BerrW**

Song in July, A. Nicholas Vachel Lindsay. **CP-LindV**

Song in Sligo. Jean Garrigue. **SP-GarrJ**

Song in Spite of Myself. Countee Cullen. **CP-CullC**

Song in Storm, A. Rudyard Kipling. **CP-KiplR**

Song.—In the Character of a Ruined Farmer. Robert Burns. **CP-BurnR**

Song in the Desert, A. Rudyard Kipling. **CP-KiplR**

Song in the Front Yard, A. Gwendolyn Brooks. **IDB; NAAL-2; NOBA; NoAM; PoBA** *Fr.* A Street in Bronzeville. **SP-BrooG**

Song in the Manner of Flannery O'Connor, A. William Stafford. **SP-StafW**

Song: In the Shows of the Round Ox. Thomas Merton. **CP-MertT; SP-MertT**

Song in the Songless. George Meredith. **CP-MerG1**

Song is but a little thing, A. The Poet and His Song. Paul Laurence Dunbar. **CP-DunbP**

Song: Just Friends. Robert Ranke Graves. **CP-GravR**

Song: Lift-Boy. Robert Ranke Graves. **CP-GravR**

Song: Love in Whose Rich Honor. Muriel Rukeyser. **CP-RukeM**

Song: Luxury. Hayden Carruth. **CP-CarHS**

Song: Lying in Daylight. Muriel Rukeyser. **CP-RukeM**

Song: "Moth's kiss, first, The!" Robert Browning. *See* Moth's kiss, first, The!

Song: Murdering Beauty. Thomas Carew. *See* I'll gaze no more on her bewitching face.

Song: Not There. Randall Jarrell. **CP-JarrR**

Song: " 'O where are you going?' said reader to rider." Wystan Hugh Auden. *See* "O where are you going?" said reader to rider.

Song of a Camera. Thom Gunn. **CP-GunnT**

Song of a Man Who Has Come Through, The. David Herbert Lawrence. **CP-LawrD**

"Not I, not I, but the wind that blows through me!" **CMoP; ChMP; CoBMV; FaBoMo; GTBS-6; GTBS-P; InPS; LiTM; MeMBP; MoPo; OxBTC; PeFWW; PoE; RaBo; SeCeV; TRP**

Song of a Man Who Is Loved. David Herbert Lawrence. **CP-LawrD**

Song of a Man Who Is Not Loved. David Herbert Lawrence. **CP-LawrD**

Song of a nightingale sent thro' a slumbrous valley, The. The Poetry of Keats. George Meredith. **CP-MerG1**

Song of a Second April. Edna St. Vincent Millay. **CP-MillE**

Song of Albert Graeme. Sir Walter Scott. **SP-ScotW** *Fr.* The Lay of the Last Minstrel.

Song of Another Tribe, A. Muriel Rukeyser. **CP-RukeM**

Song of Autumn, A. Joseph Ceravolo. **SP-CeraJ**

Song of Bananas, A. Rudyard Kipling. **CP-KiplR**

Song of Bliss. Edmund Spenser. *See* The Whiles someone did chant this lovely lay.

Song of Blodeuwedd, The. Robert Ranke Graves. **CP-GravR**

Song of Callicles, The ("Through the black, rushing smoke-burst"). Matthew Arnold. **NOBE; OAEL-2; OBEV; OBVV** *Fr.* Empedocles on Etna. **SP-ArnoM**

   (Callicles' Song.) **ChTr; LoBV**

   (Not Here, O Apollo.) **FaBoRV**

   (Song for Apollo.) **FiP**

   (Song of the Muses, The.) **WiR**

Song of Callicles, The ("Far, far from here"). Matthew Arnold. *See* Far far from here.

Song of canaries, The. The Canary. Ogden Nash. **CP-NashO**

Song of Contrariety. Robert Ranke Graves. **CP-GravR**

Song: Of Course. Robert Ranke Graves. **CP-GravR**

Song of Courtesy, The. George Meredith. **CP-MerG1**

Song of Death. David Herbert Lawrence. **CP-LawrD**

Song of Degrees, A. Howard Nemerov. **CP-NemeH**

Song of Diego Valdez, The. Rudyard Kipling. **CP-KiplR**

Song of Don Ramon, The. David Herbert Lawrence. **CP-LawrD**

Song of Drab, The. George Meredith. **CP-MerG2**

Song of Enitharmon. William Blake. **OAEL-2** *Fr.* Vala; or The Four Zoas. **CP-BlakW**

Song of Exile, A. Bible, *O.T.* *See* Psalm 137: "By the rivers of Babylon. . . ."

Song of Fixed Accord. Wallace Stevens. **CP-StevW**

Song of Flight, A. Christina Georgina Rossetti. **CP-RosC2**

Song of Four Dancers. Stephen Dobyns. **SP-DobyS**

Song of Four Faeries. John Keats. **CP-KeatJ**

Song of French Roads, A. Rudyard Kipling. **CP-KiplR**

Song of Harvest, A. John Greenleaf Whittier. **CP-WhitJ**

Song of Hiawatha, The, *sels.* Henry Wadsworth Longfellow.

   Hiawatha's Childhood. **SP-LongH**

      "By the shores of Gitche[e] Gumee." **EBEvV; FaPON; FaPoB; OHFP; PFP; WBLP**

   Hiawatha's Fasting. **SP-LongH**

Song of Hope. Thomas Hardy. **CP-HardT**

Song of Invisible Boundaries. Louise Glück. **SP-GlücL** *Fr.* Marathon. **SP-GlücL**

Song of Joys, A. Walt Whitman. **CP-WhitW**

Song of Kabir, A. Rudyard Kipling. **CP-KiplR** *Fr.* The Miracle of Purun Bhagat. *Fr.* The Second Jungle Book.

Song of Liberty, A. William Blake. *Fr.* The Marriage of Heaven and Hell. **CP-BlakW**

Song of Los, The. William Blake. **CP-BlakW**

Song of Love, A. "Lewis Carroll." **CP-CarrL** *Fr.* Sylvie and Bruno Concluded.

Song of Love and Death, The. Tennyson. **OBNC** *Fr.* Lancelot and Elaine. *Fr.* Idylls of the King. **CP-TennA**

Song of Mercy and Judgment, A. William Cowper. **CP-CowpW**

Song of Myself. Walt Whitman. **CP-WhitW**

   "All goes onward and outward, nothing collapses." **IMW**

   "Alone far in the wilds and mountains I hunt." **SAmP**

   "Child said *What is the grass?*, A." **AA; BLPL; ImPo; NoP; SAmP**

      (Grass.) **BLPL; ImPo**

   Drayman, The. **PoNe**

   "Oxen that rattle the yoke and chain or halt in the leafy shade." **FM**

   "Flaunt of the sunshine I need not your bask." **TrGrPo**

   Gigantic Beauty of a Stallion, A. **ASP; ImGa; PDV**

   Has Any One Supposed It Lucky to Be Born? **NAs**

   "Houses and rooms are full of perfumes." **EBEvV; TrGrPo; UnPo**

   I Am of Old and Young. **ImGa**

   "I am the poet of the Body and I am the poet of the Soul." **BiP; SeCeV; WeW**

   I Am He That Walks with the Tender and Growing Night. **ChTr**

   "I believe a leaf of grass is no less than the journey-work of the stars." **EaPr; PDV; SAmP; SeCeV; TRV; TiPo**

   "I believe in the flesh and the appetites." **Prf**

   "I believe in you my soul." **Prf**

   Swiftly Arose. **TrCP**

   "I celebrate myself, and sing myself." **AA; BLPL; FaBoBe; FaBoVe; MeMAP; NAWM-2; NTP; NoAM; NoP; PoE; RaBo; SAmP**

      ("I celebrate myself, / And what I assume you shall assume.") **HeIP**

      (Myself.) **BLPL; FaBoBe**

   "I have said that the soul is not more than the body." **EnlH; FaFP; ImPo**

      (Hub of the Universe, The.) **FaFP; ImPo**

   "I hear and behold God in every object, yet understand God not in the least." **WGRP**

   "I think I could turn and live awhile with animals." **EaPr; FaFP; HAP; ImPo; NU; PDV; PFP; SAmP; TrGrPo; WGRP; WeW**

      (Animals.) **FaFP; ImPo**

   "I understand the large hearts of heroes." **AA; SAmP**

      (Heroes.) **AA**

   Infinity. **AA**

   "Little one sleeps in its cradle, The." **SAmP; TrGrPo**

   "My signs are a rain-proof coat, good shoes, a staff cut from the woods." **Prf**

   "Now I will do nothing but listen." **HoPM; SAmP**

   "Pure contralto sings in the organloft, The." **TTTS**

   Runaway Slave, The. **PoNe**

   "Spotted hawk swoops by and accuses me, The." **NoP; SAmP**

   "Trippers and askers surround me." **EnlH; UnPo**

   "Twenty-eight young men bathe by the shore." **HAP; LPA; NoP; SAmP**

   Walt Whitman. **BiP; NoAM**

   "Walt Whitman, a kosmos, of Manhattan the son." **NoP; SAmP; SCV**

   "Who goes there? hankering, gross, mystical, nude." **TrGrPo**

   "With music strong I come, with my cornets and my drums." **TrGrPo**

   Would You Hear of an Old-Time [*or* Old-Fashioned] Sea fight? **SAmP, *sect.* XXXV; ImGa, *sect.* XXXV–XXXVI;**

      (Battle of the *Bonhomme Richard* and the *Serapis.*) **MOS; RB; UnPo, *sect.* XXXV–XXXVI;**

      (Old-Time Sea-Fight, An.) **OnMSP**

   Wounded Person, The. **PoNe**

   "You sea! I resign myself to you also—I guess what you mean." **OxBoS**

Song of Natchez Under the Hill, The. John Gould Fletcher. **SP-FletJ**

Song of Nature. Ralph Waldo Emerson. **CP-EmerR**

Song of Obstacles. Louise Glück. *Fr.* Marathon. **SP-GlücL**

Song of Paternal Care, A. John Updike. **CP-UpdiJ**

Song of Praise, A. Bible, *O.T.* *See* Psalm 148: "Praise ye the Lord. Praise ye the Lord from the heavens."

Song of Praise, A. Countee Cullen. **CP-CullC**

Song of Praise. Countee Cullen. **CP-CullC**

Song of Proserpine. Percy Bysshe Shelley. **CP-ShelP**

Song of Prudence. Walt Whitman. **CP-WhitW**

Song of Purification. Carlos Drummond de Andrade, *tr. fr.* Portuguese by Thomas Merton. **CP-MertT**

Song of Rahéro: A Legend of Tahiti, The. Robert Louis Stevenson. **CP-StevR**

Song of Ruark to Bhanavar the Beautiful. George Meredith. **CP-MerG2**

Song of Saul before His Last Battle. Byron. **CP-Byron**

Song of Seven Cities, The. Rudyard Kipling. **CP-KiplR**

Song of Seventy Horses. Rudyard Kipling. **CP-KiplR**

Song of Seyd [*or* Seid] Nimetollah of Kuhistan. Seid Nimatullah, *tr. fr.* Persian by Ralph Waldo Emerson. **CP-EmerR**

Song of Slaves in the Desert. John Greenleaf Whittier. **CP-WhitJ**

Song of Songs. Wilfred Owen. **CP-OwenW**

Song of Sour Grapes, A. Countee Cullen. **CP-CullC**

Song of Summer. Paul Laurence Dunbar. **CP-DunbP**

Song of Supplication, A. Bible, *O.T.* *See* Psalm 130: "Out of the depths have I cried unto thee, O Lord."

Song of Taliesin. Taliesin, Ralph Waldo Emerson's *ad. of English tr., fr. the Welsh of* Taliesin, by David William Nash. **CP-EmerR**

Song of the Ackworth Clock, The. Basil Bunting. **CP-BuntB**

Song of the Aged Mother which shook the heavens with wrath, The. Vala; or The Four Zoas. William Blake. **CP-BlakW**

Song of the Answerer. Walt Whitman. **CP-WhitW**

Song of the Banjo, The. Rudyard Kipling. **CP-KiplR**

Song of the Banner at Daybreak. Walt Whitman. **CP-WhitW**

Song of the Beggars. Wystan Hugh Auden. **PeLV** *Fr.* Twelve Songs. **CP-AudeW**

Song of the Borderguard, The. Robert Duncan. **SP-DuncR**

Song of the Bowmen of Shu. Ezra Pound, after the Chinese. **SP-PounE**

Song of the Bridegroom, The. John Berryman. **CP-BerrJ**

Song of the Broad-Axe [*or* Broad-Ax]. Walt Whitman. **CP-WhitW**

   Broad-Ax, The. **MoAmPo**

   Place Where a Great City Stands, The. **ImGa**

Song of the Camel, The. Charles Edward Carryl. *Fr.* The Admiral's Caravan. **SP-RexrK**
  Unicorn. **SP-RexrK**
Song of the Cities, The. Rudyard Kipling. **CP-KiplR**
Song of the Dead, The. Rudyard Kipling. **CP-KiplR**
Song of the Dead. David Herbert Lawrence. **CP-LawrD**
Song of the degrees, A. Except the Lord Build the House. Donald Davie. **CP-DavDo**
Song of the Degrees, A. Ezra Pound. **SP-PounE**
Song of the Demented Priest, The. John Berryman. **CP-BerrJ**
Song of the Devil. Wystan Hugh Auden. *Fr.* Two Songs. **CP-AudeW**
Song of the Drowned Boy. Stephen Dobyns. **SP-DobyS**
Song of the Drowned Ghost in the Pool's, The. Tom Clark. **SP-ClarT**
Song of the Dynamo. Rudyard Kipling. **CP-KiplR**
Song of the English, A. Rudyard Kipling. **CP-KiplR**
Song of the Exposition. Walt Whitman. **CP-WhitW**
  Muse in the New World, The. **MoAmPo**
Song of the Fifth River. Rudyard Kipling. **CP-KiplR** *Fr.* The Treasure and the Law. *Fr.* Puck of Pook's Hill.
Song of the Foolish Bees. Martinus Nijhoff, *tr. fr. Dutch by* Adrienne Rich. **CP-RicAE**
Song of the Fox. Margaret Atwood. *Fr.* Songs of the Transformed. **SP-AtwM1**
Song of the Fucked Duck. Marge Piercy. **SP-PierM**
Song of the Galley-Slaves. Rudyard Kipling. **CP-KiplR**
Song of the Garden-Toad, The. Nicholas Vachel Lindsay. **CP-LindV**
Song of the gray, The. Hayden Carruth. *Fr.* North Winter. **CP-CarHL**
Song of the Grey Dog, The. David Herbert Lawrence. **CP-LawrD**
Song of the Happy Shepherd, The. William Butler Yeats. **CP-YeatW**
Song of the Hen's Head. Margaret Atwood. *Fr.* Songs of the Transformed. **SP-AtwM1**
Song of the Hogan. Richard Shelton. **SP-ShelR**
Song of the Indian Maid ("O, Sorrow..."). John Keats. **NOBE; OAEP; OBEV** *Fr.* Endymion: Poetic Romance. **CP-KeatJ**
  (O Sorrow!) **CH**
Song of the Indian Maid, The ("Beneath my palm-trees, by the riverside"). John Keats. **NOBE** *Fr.* Endymion: Poetic Romance. **CP-KeatJ**
Song of the Lathes, The. Rudyard Kipling. **CP-KiplR**
Song of the Little Hunter, The. Rudyard Kipling. **CP-KiplR** *Fr.* The King's Ankus. *Fr.* The Second Jungle Book.
Song of the Lotus-Eaters. Tennyson. *See* There is sweet music here that softer falls.
Song of the Man Forsaken and Obsessed. John Berryman. **CP-BerrJ**
Song of the Master and Boatswain. Wystan Hugh Auden. *See* At Dirty Dick's and Sloppy Joe's.
Song of the Men's Side. Rudyard Kipling. **CP-KiplR**
Song of the Moderns. John Gould Fletcher. **SP-FletJ**
Song of the Moon, A. Ben Jonson. **CP-JonsB**
Song of the Muses, The. Matthew Arnold. *See* Song of Callicles, The ("Through the black, rushing smoke-burst").
Song of the Negro Boatmen. John Greenleaf Whittier. **GN** *Fr.* At Port Royal. **CP-WhitJ**
Song of the New Zealander among the Ruins of Old London. George Meredith. **CP-MerG2**
Song of the Ogres. Wystan Hugh Auden. **RHPC** *Fr.* Two Songs. **CP-AudeW**
Song of the Old Guard, The. Rudyard Kipling. **CP-KiplR**
Song of the Old Mother, The. William Butler Yeats. **CP-YeatW**
Song of the Open Fireplace. John Updike. **CP-UpdiJ**
Song of the Open Road. Ogden Nash. **CP-NashO**
Song of the Open Road. Walt Whitman. **CP-WhitW**
  "Afoot and light-hearted I take to the open road." **RFM**
Song of the Red War-Boat. Rudyard Kipling. **CP-KiplR**
Song of the Redwood-Tree. Walt Whitman. **CP-WhitW**
Song of the River. Louise Glück. *Fr.* Marathon. **SP-GlücL**
Song of the River Thames, A. John Dryden. **SP-DrydJ** *Fr.* Albion and Albanius.
Song of the Road, A. Robert Louis Stevenson. **CP-StevR**
Song of the Rolling Earth, A. Walt Whitman. **CP-WhitW**
Song of the Rose. Sappho, *tr. fr. Greek by* Elizabeth Barrett Browning. **CP-BroEB**
Song of the Shipyard Men, The. John Hewitt. **CP-HewiJ**
Song of the Slip. Gary Snyder. **CP-SnydG**
Song of the Soldiers' Wives and Sweethearts. Thomas Hardy. **CP-HardT**
Song of the Sons, The. Rudyard Kipling. **CP-KiplR**
Song of the Star, The. Christina Georgina Rossetti. **CP-RosC3**
Song of the Sturdy Snails, The. Nicholas Vachel Lindsay. **CP-LindV**

Song of the Tangle. Gary Snyder. **CP-SnydG**
Song of the Taste. Gary Snyder. **CP-SnydG**
Song of the Thrush. Laurence Lieberman. **SP-LiebL**
Song of the Tortured Girl, The. John Berryman. **CP-BerrJ**
Song of the Traveller, The. Thomas Merton. **CP-MertT**
Song of the Two Crows. Hayden Carruth. **CP-CarHS**
Song of the Universal. Walt Whitman. **CP-WhitW**
  "And thou, America, / For the scheme's culmination." **PGD**
Song of the Vermonters, 1779, The. John Greenleaf Whittier. **CP-WhitJ**
Song of the White Men, A. Rudyard Kipling. **CP-KiplR**
Song of the Wise Children. Rudyard Kipling. **CP-KiplR**
Song of the Worms. Margaret Atwood. *Fr.* Songs of the Transformed. **SP-AtwM1**
Song of the Wrong Response. Stephen Dobyns. **SP-DobyS**
Song of the Young Hawaiian, The. John Berryman. **CP-BerrJ**
Song of Theodolinda, The. George Meredith. **CP-MerG1**
Song of Travel, A. Rudyard Kipling. **CP-KiplR**
Song of Troylus, The. Geoffrey Chaucer. *See* If no love is, O God, what fele I so.
Song of Trust, A. Bible, *O.T. See* Psalm 121: "I will lift up mine eyes unto the hills."
Song of Venus. John Dryden. *Fr.* King Arthur.
  (Song: "Fairest isle, all isles excelling.") **SP-DrydJ**
Song of Wandering Aengus, The. William Butler Yeats. **CP-YeatW**
Song of Welcome to King Charles, A. Ben Jonson. **CP-JonsB**
Song: Olive Tree. Robert Ranke Graves. **CP-GravR**
Song—(On Chloris Being Ill). Robert Burns. **CP-BurnR**
Song: on [*or* of] May Morning. John Milton. **CP-MiltJ**
Song. On Miss P—— K——, A. Robert Burns. **CP-BurnR**
Song. On Miss W. A. Robert Burns. **CP-BurnR**
Song on Peace. William Cowper. **CP-CowpW**
Song (On Seeing Dead Bodies Floating Off the Cape). Alun Lewis. **CP-LewiA**
Song: Once More. Robert Ranke Graves. **CP-GravR**
Song (1). Wendell Berry. **CP-BerrW**
Song: Reconciliation. Robert Ranke Graves. **CP-GravR**
Song: Remembering Movies. Muriel Rukeyser. **CP-RukeM**
Song 2nd By a Young Shepherd. William Blake. **CP-BlakW**
Song: Sensation Time at the Home, A. Thomas Merton. **CP-MertT**
Song: Seven Fresh Years. Robert Ranke Graves. **CP-GravR**
Song skips around, The. Al Young. **CP-YounA** *Fr.* The Song Turning Back into Itself.
Song: So Often, So Long I Have Thought. Hayden Carruth. **CP-CarHS**
Song: So Why Does This Dead Carnation. Hayden Carruth. **CP-CarHS**
Song Sparrow Singing in the Fall, A. Wendell Berry. **CP-BerrW**
Song sparrow's limited creativity. To the Poets. Howard Nemerov. **CP-NemeH**
Song: Spring. George Meredith. **CP-MerG1**
Song Stanzas of Private Luck. Grace Paley. **CP-PaleG**
Song: Sullen Moods. Robert Ranke Graves. **CP-GravR**
Song. Summer. Rita Dove. **SP-DoveR**
Song: Sword and Rose. Robert Ranke Graves. **CP-GravR**
Song tells us of our old way of living, The. Song. John Ashbery. **SP-AshbJ**
Song That Sounds like This, The. James Fenton. **SP-FentJ**
Song. That Women Are But Men's Shadows. Ben Jonson. **CP-JonsB**
Song, The: "Did not want the air." Ted Hughes. **SP-HughT**
Song, The: "I met a ragged man." Theodore Roethke. **CP-RoetT**
Song, The: "It still makes sense." Robert Creeley. **CP-CreeR**
Song, The: "More than the sennet of the solstice pipe." Charles Olson. **CP-OlsoC; SP-OlsoC**
Song, The: "My soul, lost in the music's mist." Paul Laurence Dunbar. **CP-DunbP**
Song, The: "So large a morning[,] so itself[,] to lean." Wystan Hugh Auden. **CP-AudeW**
Song, The: "Wooe her, and win her, he that can." Thomas Campion. *Fr.* The Lords Mask[e].
Song the Body Dreamed in the Spirit's Mad Behest, The. William Everson. **SP-EverW**
Song, the Brain-Coral. Muriel Rukeyser. **CP-RukeM**
Song: The Clocks of Time. Robert Ranke Graves. **CP-GravR**
Song: The Famous Vision of America. Hayden Carruth. **CP-CarHS**
Song: The Far Side of Your Moon. Robert Ranke Graves. **CP-GravR**
Song: The Old, Old Man. Hayden Carruth. **CP-CarHS**
Song: The Palm Tree. Robert Ranke Graves. **CP-GravR**
Song: The Promise. Robert Ranke Graves. **CP-GravR**
Song: The Queen of Time. Robert Ranke Graves. **CP-GravR**

Song: The Sigil. Robert Ranke Graves. **CP-GravR**

Song: The Star in the Nets of Heaven. Muriel Rukeyser. **CP-RukeM**

Song: The Sundial's Lament. Robert Ranke Graves. **CP-GravR**

Song, the Winds of Downhill. George Oppen. **CP-OppeG**

Song: The Wren. George Meredith. **CP-MerG2**

Song: The Young Man with the Guitar, Testing. Hayden Carruth. **CP-CarHS**

Song Theme. Louis Zukofsky. *Fr.* 29 Poems. **CP-ZukLS**

Song 3rd By an Old Shepherd. William Blake. **CP-BlakW**

Song: Though Once True Lovers. Robert Ranke Graves. **CP-GravR**

Song (3). Wendell Berry. **CP-BerrW**

Song—3/4 time. Louis Zukofsky. *Fr.* 29 Songs. **CP-ZukLS**

Song: Three Rings for Her. Robert Ranke Graves. **CP-GravR**

Song: Time Drawes Neere. Anne Waldman. **SP-WaldA**

Song to a Fair Young Lady, Going Out of the Town in the Spring. John Dryden. **SP-DrydJ**

Song to a Lute, A. Sir John Suckling. *Fr.* The Sad One. **CP-SuckJ**

Song: To a Rose. Robert Ranke Graves. **CP-GravR**

Song to A.A. Emily Brontë. **CP-BronE**

Song to an Old Burden. Thomas Hardy. **CP-HardT**

Song to Aurore. Thomas Hardy. **CP-HardT**

Song to Be Sung by the Father of Infant Female Children. Ogden Nash. **CP-NashO**

Song: To Become Each Other. Robert Ranke Graves. **CP-GravR**

Song to Celia. Catullus. *See* Carmen 5: "Lesbia / live with me."

Song. To Celia: ("Come my Celia, let us prove"). Ben Jonson. **CP-JonsB** *Fr.* Volpone.

Song. To Celia ("Drink to me only with thine eyes"). Ben Jonson. **CP-JonsB**

Song to David, A. Christopher Smart. **SP-SmarC**

  Beauteous, Yea Beauteous More than These. **EaLo**

  "Glorious the sun in mid career." **FaBoCh**

  "O David, highest in the list." **NOEC**

  "O thou, that sit'st upon a throne." **OxAEP-1**

  "Strong is the horse upon his speed." **LiTB; OtMeF; UV**

  (Man of Prayer, The.) **LiTB**

  (Strength.) **OtMeF**

  "Strong is the lion – like a coal." **HAP**

  "Sublime – invention ever young." **OBEV**

  "Tell them, I AM, Jehovah said." **WGRP**

Song: To———[Harriet] ("Ah! sweet is the moonbeam. . . ."). Percy Bysshe Shelley. *Fr.* Original Poetry by Victor and Cazire. **CP-ShelP**

Song: To——— [Harriet] ("Stern, stern is the voice. . . "). Percy Bysshe Shelley. *Fr.* Original Poetry by Victor and Cazire. **CP-ShelP**

Song to Make Me Still. Leonard Cohen. **CP-CoheL**

Song to Mithras, A. Rudyard Kipling. **CP-KiplR** *Fr.* On the Great Wall. *Fr.* Puck of Pook's Hill.

Song to the Maskers, A. Robert Herrick. **CP-HerrR**

Song to the Men of England. Percy Bysshe Shelley. **CP-ShelP**

Song to the Suliotes. Byron. **CP-Byron**

Song to the Tune of *La Cucaracha*. David Herbert Lawrence. **CP-LawrD**

Song to Woody. "Bob Dylan." **CP-DylaB**

Song: Translated from the German. Percy Bysshe Shelley. *Fr.* Original Poetry by Victor and Cazire. **CP-ShelP**

Song: Translated from the Italian. Percy Bysshe Shelley. *Fr.* Original Poetry by Victor and Cazire. **CP-ShelP**

Song Turning Back into Itself, The. Al Young. **CP-YounA**

  "Again / Who am I?" **CP-YounA**

  "Always it's either." **CP-YounA**

  "Breathing in morning." **CP-YounA**

  "Get that feeling sometimes." **CP-YounA**

  "I violinize peace." **CP-YounA**

  "Ocean Springs Missippy." **CP-YounA**

  "Song skips around, The." **CP-YounA**

Song Turning Back Into Itself 1. Al Young. **CP-YounA**

Song: Twinned Heart. Robert Ranke Graves. **CP-GravR**

Song (2). Wendell Berry. **CP-BerrW**

Song upon Silvia, A. Robert Herrick. **CP-HerrR**

Song: Victims of Calumny. Robert Ranke Graves. **CP-GravR**

Song: Wherever We May Be. Robert Ranke Graves. **CP-GravR**

Song without Forgiveness. David St. John. **SP-StJoD**

Song: Yesterday Only. Robert Ranke Graves. **CP-GravR**

Songbirds giggling all across California. Maya. Al Young. **CP-YounA**

Songbook of Sebastian Arrurruz, The. Geoffrey Hill. **CP-HillG**

  Coplas.

  From the Latin.

Letter from Armenia, A.

  "Love, oh my love, it will come."

  Postures.

  "Scarcely speaking: it becomes as a."

  Song from Armenia, A.

  "Ten years without you. For so it happens."

  To His Wife.

  "What other men do with other women."

  "Workable fancy. Old petulant, A."

Songe d'Athalie. Stevie Smith. **CP-SmitS**

Songe Made by Sir Walter Rawley, A. *Unknown, sometimes at. to* Sir Walter Ralegh. **CP-RaleW**

Songless. Alice Walker. **CP-WalkA**

Songlet. Archie Randolph Ammons. **SP-AmmoA**

Songs. Paul Laurence Dunbar. **CP-DunbP**

Songs. Thomas Merton. **CP-MertT**

Songs About What Comes Down: The Complete Works of Mr. Septic Tanck. Hayden Carruth.

  Tanck's Brag. **CP-CarHS**

  Tanck's Epilogue. **CP-CarHS**

  Tanck's Prolegomenon. **CP-CarHS**

  Tanck's Song About Brains. **CP-CarHS**

  Tanck's Song About Dying Young. **CP-CarHS**

  Tanck's Song About Earl Hines. **CP-CarHS**

  Tanck's Song About Fear of Falling. **CP-CarHS**

  Tanck's Song About His Birthday. **CP-CarHS**

  Tanck's Song About His Unicameral Mind. **CP-CarHS**

  Tanck's Song About November. **CP-CarHS**

  Tanck's Song About Pride. **CP-CarHS**

  Tanck's Song About Silence. **CP-CarHS**

  Tanck's Song About Survival. **CP-CarHS**

  Tanck's Song About the Jinx. **CP-CarHS**

  Tanck's Song About the Transportation Business. **CP-CarHS**

  Tanck's Song About the Younger Generation. **CP-CarHS**

  Tanck's Song About Women. **CP-CarHS**

  Tanck's Song About Youth and Age. **CP-CarHS**

Songs for a Colored Singer. Elizabeth Bishop. **CP-BishE**

  "Lullaby. / Adult and child."

  "Time has come to call a halt, The."

  "Washing hangs upon the line, A." **FaBoVe; FaBoWP**

  "What's that shining in the leaves."

Songs for Eve. Archibald MacLeish. **CP-MacLA**

  Adam in the Evening.

  Adam's Jealousy: Eve's Answer.

  Adam's Riddle.

  Babe's Riddle, The.

  Eve Answers the Burdock.

  Eve Explains Everything to the Thrush Who Repeats Everything.

  Eve in the Dawn.

  Eve Old.

  Eve Quiets Her Children.

  Eve to the Storm of Thunder.

  Eve's Child.

  Eve's Exile.

  Eve's First Prophecy.

  Eve's Now-I-Lay-Me.

  Eve's Rebuke to Her Child.

  Eve's Riddle.

  Eve's Second Prophecy.

  Fall!, The.

  Serpent's Cradle Song, The.

  Serpent's Riddle, The.

  What Adam Said.

  What Eve Said.

  What Eve Sang.

  What the Green Tree Said.

  What the Lion Said to the Child.

  What the Serpent Said to Adam. **ChIV-1; MeMAP; NePA**

  What the Vine Said to Eve.

  What the Wind Said to the Water: What the Water Replied.

Songs for Second Childhood. Malcolm Lowry. **CP-LowrM**

  "Another than Wordsworth dropped his live work."

  "As the poor end of each dead day drew near."

  Curse.

  "Dead man sat in the sun, The."

Delirium in Los Angeles.

Devil was a Gentleman, The.

"Gentleness of rain is in the wind, The."

"He plays the piano with a razor."

"He wrote for the dead, but the ubiquitous dead."

"Lead were their feet, and lead their heart and bone."

"Loathing as as beautiful as the scourge."

"Oh, pyre of Bierce and springboard of Hart Crane!"

"Pigling, pigling, burning bland."

Sailors, The.

"Stone must be rolled away from self's pain, The."

"Sun shines; where is the lyric!, The."

"Time entered the stuffed court, slowly swearing."

"Tortures of hell are stern, their fires burn fiercely, The."

"Where do you come from? The land of Epigram."

Songs for the Night. Alun Lewis. **CP-LewiA**

"Black dog barking at the moon."

"Stars seem gilded nipples."

"Under each starry leafless tree."

Songs from Cyprus. Hilda Doolittle. **CP-DoolH**

"Gather for festival." **MoAmPo**

"Where is the nightingale." **MoAmPo**, *sect.* 2;

Songs from Shakespeare, in Latin and Greek. Gerard Manley Hopkins. **CP-HopkG**

Come Unto These Yellow Sands.

Full Fathom Five.

Orpheus With His Lute Made Trees.

Tell Me Where Is Fancy Bred.

Unfinished Rendering of "When Icicles Hang by the Wall."

While You Here Do Snoring Lie.

Songs I Learnt at School. David Herbert Lawrence. **CP-LawrD**

British Boy, The.

My Native Land.

Neptune's Little Affair with Freedom.

13,000 People.

Songs I Sing, The. John Hewitt. **CP-HewiJ**

Songs I wrote when I was young and ardent, The. Boethius, *tr. fr. Latin.* **MLL**, *tr. by* Helen Waddell; *Fr.* Consolation of Philosophy, The ("De Consolacione Philosophie"). **CP-ChauG**

Songs in a Cornfield. Christina Georgina Rossetti. **CP-RosC1**

Songs in Absence. Arthur Hugh Clough.

"Where lies the land to which the ship would go?" **SP-ClouA**

(Mari Magno II.) **SP-ClouA**

Songs of Degrees. Louis Zukofsky. **CP-ZukLS**

Happiest February.

March First.

Nor did the prophet.

William Carlos Williams Alive!

Wish, A.

With a Valentine (the 12 February).

With a Valentine (the 14 February).

Songs of Experience. William Blake.

Ah, Sun-Flower [*or* Ah! Sun-Flower]. **CP-BlakW**

Angel, The. **CP-BlakW**

Chimney Sweeper, The ("A little black thing among the snow"). **CP-BlakW**

Clod and [*or* &] the Pebble, The. **CP-BlakW**

Earth's Answer. **CP-BlakW**

Garden of Love, The. **CP-BlakW**

Holy Thursday ("Is this a holy thing to see"). **CP-BlakW**

Human Abstract, The. **CP-BlakW**

Infant Sorrow. **CP-BlakW**

Introduction: "Hear the voice of the Bard!" **CP-BlakW**

Lily, The. **CP-BlakW**

Little Boy Lost, A ("Nought loves another as itself"). **CP-BlakW**

Little Fly. **CP-BlakW**

(Fly, The.) **CP-BlakW**

("Woe alas my guilty hand.") **CP-BlakW**

Little Girl Found, The. **CP-BlakW**

Little Girl Lost, A. **CP-BlakW**

Little Girl Lost, The. **CP-BlakW**

Little Vagabond, The. **CP-BlakW**

London ("I wander through each chartered street"). **CP-BlakW**

("I wander tho each dirty street.") **CP-BlakW**

My Pretty Rose Tree. **CP-BlakW**

Nurse's Song ("When the voices of children are heard on the green / And

whisperings [*ot* whisprings] are in the dale"). **CP-BlakW**

Poison Tree, A. **CP-BlakW**

(Christian Forbearance.) **CP-BlakW**

"I was angry with my friend." **OBF**

School Boy, The. **CP-BlakW**

Sick Rose, The. **CP-BlakW**

Tiger [*or* Tyger][!], The. **CP-BlakW**

To Tirzah. **CP-BlakW**

Voice of the Ancient Bard, The. **CP-BlakW**

Songs of Experience; India, One. Thomas Merton. **CP-MertT**

Songs of Innocence. William Blake. **CP-BlakW**

Blossom, The. **FHYEP; GoJo; PB; PBBP**

Chimney Sweeper, The ("When my mother died I was very young"). **CH; EnRP; FF; FHYEP; FaBoPV; HeIP; HoFi; InPK; LAuP; NAEL-2; NAWM-2; NOEC; OAEL-2; OXAEP-2; OxBChV; PAI; PPP; PPoe; PoE; Poetr; SCGP; SaC; SoSe; TEP; TFi**

Cradle Song, A: "Sweet dreams, form a shade." **EnRP; FHYEP; LAuP; OAEP; OBCP; SBVL**

Divine Image, The ("To Mercy, Pity, Peace, and Love"). **BoTP; CoGr; EBCP; EnRP; FHYEP; FaBoEn; HoFi; LAuP; LO; MeMBP; NAEL-2; NOBE; NOBRP; NOEC; NoP; OAEL-2; OAEP; OBEC; OBNC; OxBoCh; PFP; PPP; PeECV; PoE; PoEL-4; TEP; TRV; WGRP**

Dream, A. **CH; EnRP; FHYEP; HoFi; LAuP; NOBRP; PoPle**

Echoing [*or* Ecchoing] Green, The. **BoTP; CABA; CH; FHYEP; HoFi; LAuP; NAEL-2; NTP; OBEC; OXAEP-2; PoE; PoSC; UnPo; WiR**

Holy Thursday (" 'Twas on a Holy Thursday, their innocent faces clean"). **CH; EnRP; FHYEP; HBV; HoFi; InPS; LAuP; MeMBP; NAEL-2; NAWM-2; NOBE; NOBRP; NOEC; NoP; OAEL-2; OAEP; OBEC; OFD; PeECV; PoE; SCV; TEP; TFi; TrCP**

Infant Joy. **FHYEP; FaPON; GoJo; HBV; HBVY; LAuP; LoBV; NAEL-2; NAs; NTP; OXAEP-2; OxBSP; PoLF; SiSoSe; TEP**

Lamb, The. **BLPL; BoTP; CABA; CH; ChIV-2; EBCP; EBEvV; EaLo; EnRP; FHYEP; FaBoBe; FaBoCh; FaPON; GoJo; HBV; HeIL; HeIP; ImPo; InPS; LAuP; LiTB; LoBV; MeMBP; NAEL-2; NAWM-2; NIP; NOBRP; NOEC; NoP; OAEL-2; OAEP; OBEC; OXAEP-2; OxBChV; OxBoCh; PAI; PoE; PoPl; Poetr; SBVL; SUS; SeCeV; SoSe; TEP; TFi; TRP; TRV; TrCP; TrGrPo; TreF; UnPo; WGRP; WHA**

Little Black Boy, The. **AWP; BiP; CABA; CH; EnRP; FHYEP; HBV; HeIP; HoFi; InPK; LAuP; NAEL-2; NAWM-2; NOBRP; NOEC; NoP; OAEL-2; OAEP; OBEC; OBEV; OBNC; OxBChV; OxBoCh; PeECV; PoE; PoEL-4; PoNe; SCGP; SeCeV; TFi; TrGrPo; TreFS**

Little Boy Found, The. **EnRP; FHYEP; LAuP; NoP**

Little Boy Lost, The ("Father, father, where are you going?"). **EnRP; FHYEP; LAuP; NoP; TiPo**

Little Girl Found, The. **CP-BlakW; FHYEP; NOBRP**

Little Girl Lost, The. **CP-BlakW; FHYEP; NOBRP**

Night. **BLPL; BoNaP; BoTP; CH; EnRP; FHYEP; FaBoBe; FaPON; HBV; HBVY; HoFi; MeMBP; OBEC; OBEV; OxBChV; OxBoCh; PoLF; TreFT; WiR**

Nurse's Song ("When the voices of children are heard on the green / And laughing is heard on the hill"). **AWP; BLPL; CH; EnRP; FHYEP; FaBoBe; HBV; HBVY; HoFi; LAuP; NAEL-2; OBEC; OxBChV; PeLV; SCGP**

(Play Time.) **FaPON**

On Another's Sorrow. **AWP; EBCP; EnRP; FHYEP; FaBV; OXAEP-2; PoEL-4**

Piping Down the Valleys Wild. **ClHu; EnRP; FaBV; FaBoBe; FaBoCh; GoJo; HeIP; HoFi; InPS; InvP; NAEL-2; NAWM-2; NIP; NOBE; NOEC; NoP; OAEL-2; OBNC; OnUR; PoE; PoEL-4; RHPC; SoSe; TEP; TFi; TrGrPo**

(Introduction: "Piping down the valleys wild.") **NOBRP; PFP**

(Piper, The.) **AWP; OxBChV; PDV**

(Reeds of Innocence.) **ImPo; LiTB; OBEV**

Shepherd, The. **BoTP; EnRP; FHYEP; HBV; LoBV; OBEC; PFP; TiPo**

Spring. **BoTP; FHYEP; FaBoCh; FaPON; MoShBr; NTP; TTTS**

When the Green Woods Laugh. **CH; EnRP; GoJo; HoFi; LAuP; NBLV; OxBChV; PoSC; SUS; SoPo; TiPo**

(Laughing Song.) **BoTP; FHYEP; NAEL-2**

Songs of Praise. Derek Mahon. **SP-MahoD**

Songs of Sleep. Alun Lewis. **CP-LewiA**

Songs of small birds fade away, The. The Sorrel Filly. Wendell Berry. **CP-BerrW**

Songs of the Pixies. Samuel Taylor Coleridge. **CP-ColeS**

Songs of the Transformed. Margaret Atwood. **SP-AtwM1**

Bull Song.

Corpse Song.

Crow Song.

Owl Song.

Pig Song. **NoP**

Rat Song. **NIP**

Siren Song. **HAP; NIP; PoA; WeW**

Song of the Fox.

Song of the Hen's Head.

Song of the Worms.

Songs that break. Gypsy Melodies. Langston Hughes. **SP-HughL**

Songs We Know Best, The. John Ashbery. **SP-AshbJ**

Songster, The. Stevie Smith. **CP-SmitS**

Songsters of the air repair, The. Lines to a Persian Cat. Thomas Stearns Eliot. *Fr.* Five-Finger Exercises. **CP-ElioT**

Sonic Boom. John Updike. **CP-UpdiJ**

Sonnet [to Charles Lloyd]. Samuel Taylor Coleridge. **CP-ColeS**

Sonnet [on the Death of Mr. Richard West]. Thomas Gray. **CP-GrayT**

Sonnet: "Accuse me not, beseech thee, that I wear." Elizabeth Barrett Browning. *Fr.* Sonnets from the Portuguese. **CP-BroEB**

Sonnet: "All revolutions in modern times have led." Hayden Carruth. **CP-CarHS** *Fr.* Sonnets.

Sonnet: "Among the many selves that throng my flesh." John Hewitt. **CP-HewiJ**

Sonnet: "And therefore if to love can be desert." Elizabeth Barrett Browning. *Fr.* Sonnets from the Portuguese. **CP-BroEB**

Sonnet: "And wilt thou have me fashion into speech." Elizabeth Barrett Browning. **BWW; BrRo; EnVR** *Fr.* Sonnets from the Portuguese. **CP-BroEB**

Sonnet: "And yet, because thou overcomest so." Elizabeth Barrett Browning. *Fr.* Sonnets from the Portuguese. **CP-BroEB**

Sonnet: "April is here but when will Easter come?" Wystan Hugh Auden. **CP-AudWJ**

Sonnet: "At the hospital where I had the echocardiagram." Hayden Carruth. **CP-CarHS** *Fr.* Sonnets.

Sonnet: "August, tasting of ripe grapes and afternoon sleep." James Schuyler. **CP-SchuJ**

Sonnet: "Be slowly lifted up, thou long black arm." Wilfred Owen. **CP-OwenW**

Sonnet: "Because thou hast the power and own'st the grace." Elizabeth Barrett Browning. *Fr.* Sonnets from the Portuguese. **CP-BroEB**

Sonnet: "Beloved, my beloved, when I think." Elizabeth Barrett Browning. **OAEP; Son; WPE** *Fr.* Sonnets from the Portuguese. **CP-BroEB**

Sonnet: "Beloved, thou hast brought me many flowers." Elizabeth Barrett Browning. **EBVV; EnVR; OAEP; OBNC; WPE** *Fr.* Sonnets from the Portuguese. **CP-BroEB**

Sonnet "First time that the sun rose on thine oath, The." Elizabeth Barrett Browning. **EnVR; NAEL-2; WPE** *Fr.* Sonnets from the Portuguese. **CP-BroEB**

Sonnet: "But only three in all God's universe." Elizabeth Barrett Browning. *Fr.* Sonnets from the Portuguese. **CP-BroEB**

Sonnet: "But still, still. . . / In stillness mystery calls." Hayden Carruth. **CP-CarHS** *Fr.* Sonnets.

Sonnet: "By the sea's edge, on gravel and on sand." John Hewitt. **CP-HewiJ**

Sonnet: "Can it be right to give what I can give." Elizabeth Barrett Browning. **CTC; HBV; OHCV; Son** *Fr.* Sonnets from the Portuguese. **CP-BroEB**

Sonnet: "Can the lov'd Image of thy deerest face." Mary Sidney, Countess of Montgomery Wroth. *Fr.* Pamphilia to Amphilanthus. **CP-WrotM**

Sonnet: "Caught—the bubble." Elizabeth Bishop. **CP-BishE**

Sonnet: "Cindy, I've used my writing all my life." Hayden Carruth. **CP-CarHS** *Fr.* Sonnets.

Sonnet: "Cindy, the secret's out. Yes, you're addict-." Hayden Carruth. **CP-CarHS** *Fr.* Sonnets.

Sonnet: "Could I be sure that I shall see the day." Allen Tate. **CP-TateA**

Sonnet: "Dark, underground, is furnished with the bone." Louise Bogan. **CP-BogaL**

Sonnet: "Dearest, I never knew such loving. There." Hayden Carruth. **CP-CarHS** *Fr.* Sonnets.

Sonnet: "Depose your finger of that Ring." Richard Lovelace. **CP-LoveR**

Sonnet: "Dost see how unregarded now." Sir John Suckling. **CP-SuckJ**

Sonnet: "Emblem of blasted hope and lost desire." Paul Laurence Dunbar. **CP-DunbP**

Sonnet: "Each servant stamps the reader with a look." John Ashbery. **SP-AshbJ**

Sonnet: "Ere elfish Night shall sift another day." Hart Crane. **CP-CranH**

Sonnet: "Eyes, calm beside thee, (Lady couldst thou know!)." Robert Browning. **CP-BroR2**

Sonnet: "Eyes, can you tell mee wher my hart remaines?" Mary Sidney, Countess of Montgomery Wroth. *Fr.* Pamphilia to Amphilanthus. **CP-WrotM**

Sonnet: "Face of all the world is changed, I think, The." Elizabeth Barrett Browning. **CTC; HBV; OAEP; VLP** *Fr.* Sonnets from the Portuguese. **CP-BroEB**

Sonnet: "Fear of falling is why the old men walk." Hayden Carruth. **CP-CarHS** *Fr.* Sonnets.

Sonnet: "First time he kissed me, he but only kissed." Elizabeth Barrett Browning. **BLPA; BLPL; CTC; FaBoBe; HBV; PoPl** *Fr.* Sonnets from the Portuguese. **CP-BroEB**

Sonnet: "Fly traiter joye whose end brings butt dispaire." Mary Sidney, Countess of Montgomery Wroth. *Fr.* Pamphilia to Amphilanthus. **CP-WrotM**

Sonnet: "For that I have forgot the world these days." Edward Estlin Cummings. **CP-CummE**

Sonnet: "Form of Christ cut from dark wood, the pale, A." Howard Nemerov. **CP-NemeH**

Sonnet: "Freedom in love? It has been questioned. Think." Hayden Carruth. **CP-CarHS** *Fr.* Sonnets.

Sonnet: "From our very high window at the Sheraton." Hayden Carruth. **CP-CarHS** *Fr.* Sonnets.

Sonnet: "Go from me. Yet I feel that I shall stand." Elizabeth Barrett Browning. **BLPL; BWW; CBLP; HBV; OBEV; OBVV; OXAEP-2; TrGrPo; TreFS** *Fr.* Sonnets from the Portuguese. **CP-BroEB**

Sonnet: "Hateful are those false themes of speculation." George Meredith. **CP-MerG2**

Sonnet: "Heavy heart, Beloved, have I borne, A." Elizabeth Barrett Browning. *Fr.* Sonnets from the Portuguese. **CP-BroEB**

Sonnet: "Honey, darling, baby. . . but no endearments." Hayden Carruth. **CP-CarHS** *Fr.* Sonnets.

Sonnet: "How do I love thee? Let me count the ways." Elizabeth Barrett Browning. **ArLo; BWW; BoLoP; CTC; EBEvV; EBVV; EnVR; FF; FPL; FaBV; FaBoBe; FaFP; FaPoB; HBV; HeIP; HoPM; InPK; LPA; LiTB; NAEL-2; NALW; NIP; NoP; OAEP; OHCV; OLR; OXAEP-2; OxBM; PoE; PoLF; PoPl; PoRA; Poetr; Son; TEP; TFi; TRV; TrGrPo; TreF; UV; UnPo; WHA; WPE** *Fr.* Sonnets from the Portuguese. **CP-BroEB**

(How Do I Love Thee?) **ImPo; PoToHe**

(Sonnet from the Portuguese.) **OPOU**

Sonnet: "How is it, tell me, that this new self can be—." Hayden Carruth. **CP-CarHS** *Fr.* Sonnets.

Sonnet: "I am in need of music that would flow." Elizabeth Bishop. **CP-BishE**

Sonnet: "I dreamed I was among the conquerors." Edward Estlin Cummings. **CP-CummE**

Sonnet: "I follow thought and what the world announces." Delmore Schwartz. **SP-SchwD**

Sonnet: "I have no time to worship. I must live." John Hewitt. **CP-HewiJ**

Sonnet: "I have not loved you in the noblest 'way." Countee Cullen. **CP-CullC**

Sonnet: "I know now how a man whose blood is hot." Countee Cullen. **CP-CullC**

Sonnet: "I lift my heavy heart up solemnly." Elizabeth Barrett Browning. **NALW** *Fr.* Sonnets from the Portuguese. **CP-BroEB**

Sonnet: "I lived with visions for my company." Elizabeth Barrett Browning. **BWW** *Fr.* Sonnets from the Portuguese. **CP-BroEB**

Sonnet: "I love to see the summer beaming forth." John Clare. **SP-ClarJ**

Sonnet: "I never gave a lock hair away." Elizabeth Barrett Browning. **EBVV; HAP; HBV** *Fr.* Sonnets from the Portuguese. **CP-BroEB**

Sonnet: "I see thine image through my tears tonight." Elizabeth Barrett Browning. *Fr.* Sonnets from the Portuguese. **CP-BroEB**

Sonnet: "I thank all who have loved me in their hearts." Elizabeth Barrett Browning. *Fr.* Sonnets from the Portuguese. **CP-BroEB**

Sonnet: "I think continually of the differences." Hayden Carruth. **CP-CarHS** *Fr.* Sonnets.

Sonnet: "I think of Glasgow, where reluctantly." John Hewitt. **CP-HewiJ**

Sonnet: "I think of thee! My thoughts do twine and bud." Elizabeth Barrett Browning. *Fr.* Sonnets from the Portuguese. **CP-BroEB**

Sonnet: "I thought once how Theocritus had sung." Elizabeth Barrett Browning. **BWW; EBVV; EnVR; GBL; HBV; NOBE; NoP; OAEP; OBEV; OBNC; OXAEP-2; TreFT; WPE** *Fr.* Sonnets from the Portuguese. **CP-BroEB**

Sonnet: "I thought tonight of all the lovers gone." John Hewitt. **CP-HewiJ**

Sonnet: "I want to do a complaint now. Which is to say." Hayden Carruth. **CP-CarHS** *Fr.* Sonnets.

Sonnet: "I wish I could remember the first day." Christina Georgina Rossetti. *See* I wish I could remember the [or that] first day.

Sonnet: "If grief dismiss me not to them that rest." Petrarch, *tr. fr. Italian by* William Wordsworth. **CP-WorW1**

Sonnet: "If I die today, which statistically speaking." Hayden Carruth. **CP-CarHS** *Fr.* Sonnets.

Sonnet: "If I leave all for thee, wilt thou exchange." Elizabeth Barrett Browning. **Son** *Fr.* Sonnets from the Portuguese. **CP-BroEB**

Sonnet: "If thou must love me, let it be for nought." Elizabeth Barrett Browning. **BWW; CTC; FaFP; HBV; HeIP; InPS; LiTB; OBEV; OBNC; OBVV; OHCV; OXAEP-2; PFP; SoSe; TrGrPo; TreFS; WHA** *Fr.* Sonnets from the Portuguese. **CP-BroEB**

(For Love's Sake Only.) **PoToHe**

Sonnet: "If you see a child that shivers when it hears." Hayden Carruth. **CP-CarHS** *Fr.* Sonnets.

Sonnet: "In the mind of the kiss occurs a thought so rich." Hayden Carruth. **CP-CarHS** *Fr.* Sonnets.

Sonnet: "Indeed this very love which is my boast." Elizabeth Barrett Browning. **HBV 1-2** *Fr.* Sonnets from the Portuguese. **CP-BroEB**

Sonnet: "Is it indeed so? If I lay here dead." Elizabeth Barrett Browning. *Fr.* Sonnets from the Portuguese. **CP-BroEB**

Sonnet: "It seems to be the trouble, everyone." Howard Nemerov. **CP-NemeH**

Sonnet: "It's said by the thoughtful masters that to know death." Hayden Carruth. **CP-CarHS** *Fr.* Sonnets.

Sonnet: "Key-reist, I am fed and sick unto death with this." Hayden Carruth. **CP-CarHS** *Fr.* Sonnets.

Sonnet: "Last night, I don't know if from habit or intent." Hayden Carruth. **CP-CarHS** *Fr.* Sonnets.

Sonnet: "Let the world's sharpness, like a clasping knife." Elizabeth Barrett Browning. **NOBWV** *Fr.* Sonnets from the Portuguese. **CP-BroEB**

Sonnet: "Lett griefe as farr bee from your deerest brest." Mary Sidney, Countess of Montgomery Wroth. *Fr.* Pamphilia to Amphilanthus. **CP-WrotM**

Sonnet: "Lift not the painted veil which those who live." Percy Bysshe Shelley. **CP-ShelP**

Sonnet: "Like the magnificent stationary animal it is." Hayden Carruth. **CP-CarHS** *Fr.* Sonnets.

Sonnet: "Long since, the flicker brushed with shameless wing." Edward Estlin Cummings. **CP-CummE**

Sonnet: "Master and the slave go hand in hand, The." Edwin Arlington Robinson. **CP-RobiE**

Sonnet: "Most brainy woman, the sexuality of your thought." Hayden Carruth. **CP-CarHS** *Fr.* Sonnets.

Sonnet: "Must genius always struggle, always exaggerate." Hayden Carruth. **CP-CarHS** *Fr.* Sonnets.

Sonnet: "My future will not copy fair my past." Elizabeth Barrett Browning. **EnVR** *Fr.* Sonnets from the Portuguese. **CP-BroEB**

Sonnet: "My God, where is that ancient heat towards Thee." George Herbert. **CP-HerbG**

Sonnet: "My letters! All dead paper, mute and white." Elizabeth Barrett Browning. **HAP; HBV; OXAEP-2** *Fr.* Sonnets from the Portuguese. **CP-BroEB**

Sonnet: "My own Beloved, who hast lifted me." Elizabeth Barrett Browning. *Fr.* Sonnets from the Portuguese. **CP-BroEB**

Sonnet: "My poet, thou canst touch on all the notes." Elizabeth Barrett Browning. **BrRo; HBV; VLP; WHA** *Fr.* Sonnets from the Portuguese. **CP-BroEB**

Sonnet: "No sunset, but a grey, great, struggling sky." Edward Estlin Cummings. **CP-CummE**

Sonnet: "O Jesus, thou who sittest up there on the right." Hayden Carruth. **CP-CarHS** *Fr.* Sonnets.

Sonnet: "O Memory [or Memorie], could I but loose thee now." Mary Sidney, Countess of Montgomery Wroth. **BWW; WPE** *Fr.* Lindamira's Complaint. *Fr.* Part 1. *Fr.* Urania. **CP-WrotM**

("Leave me vaine Hope, too long thou hast possess't.") **BWW**

Sonnet: "Of thee (kind boy) I ask no red and white." Sir John Suckling. **CP-SuckJ**

Sonnet: "Oft did I wounder why the sweets of Love." Mary Sidney, Countess of Montgomery Wroth. *Fr.* Pamphilia to Amphilanthus. **CP-WrotM**

Sonnet: "Oh for a poet—for a beacon bright." Edwin Arlington Robinson. **CP-RobiE**

Sonnet: "Oh! for some honest lover's ghost." Sir John Suckling. **CP-SuckJ**

Sonnet: "Oh, yes! they love through all this world of ours." Elizabeth Barrett Browning. *Fr.* Sonnets from the Portuguese. **CP-BroEB**

Sonnet: "Our love is full of memorable things." John Hewitt. **CP-HewiJ**

Sonnet: "Pardon, oh, pardon, that my soul should make." Elizabeth Barrett Browning. *Fr.* Sonnets from the Portuguese. **CP-BroEB**

Sonnet: "Persistent is the thought for me of that." Hayden Carruth. **CP-CarHS** *Fr.* Sonnets.

Sonnet: "Poor little book, *The Sleeping Beauty* died." Hayden Carruth. **CP-CarHS** *Fr.* Sonnets.

Sonnet: "Rain-drop on the eyelids of the earth, A." Edward Estlin Cummings. **CP-CummE**

Sonnet: "Say over again, and yet once over again." Elizabeth Barrett Browning. **HBV 1-2; NAEL-2** *Fr.* Sonnets from the Portuguese. **CP-BroEB**

Sonnet: "Since brooding men put beauty in a rime." John Hewitt. **CP-HewiJ**

Sonnet: "Since you would claim the sources of my thought." Louise Bogan. **CP-BogaL**

Sonnet: "Some for a little while do love, and some for long." Countee Cullen. **CP-CullC**

Sonnet: "Some say that love and joy are one: and so." Christina Georgina Rossetti. **CP-RosC3**

Sonnet: "Soul's Rialto hath its merchandise, The." Elizabeth Barrett Browning. *Fr.* Sonnets from the Portuguese. **CP-BroEB**

Sonnet: "Sure Lord, there is enough in thee to dry." George Herbert. **CP-HerbG**

Sonnet: "The Bo was three when we slugged through Arizona." Hayden Carruth. **CP-CarHS** *Fr.* Sonnets.

Sonnet: "The hubbub of the Hall of Languages, our Babel." Hayden Carruth. **CP-CarHS** *Fr.* Sonnets.

Sonnet: "The loving mind in this death-haunted body." Hayden Carruth. **CP-CarHS** *Fr.* Sonnets.

Sonnet: "The Word for Today is 'panoptic,' which the goddamn." Hayden Carruth. **CP-CarHS** *Fr.* Sonnets.

Sonnet: "There in the lonely quarry where at dawn." John Hewitt. **CP-HewiJ**

Sonnet: "These are no wind-blown rumors, soft say-sos." Countee Cullen. **CP-CullC**

Sonnet: "This is our perfect silver maple's day." Hayden Carruth. **CP-CarHS** *Fr.* Sonnets.

Sonnet: "This ruin now, where moonlight walks alone." Malcolm Lowry. **CP-LowrM**

Sonnet: "This world is full of lovely things." Wystan Hugh Auden. **CP-AudWJ**

Sonnet: "Thou comest! all is said without a word." Elizabeth Barrett Browning. **BWW** *Fr.* Sonnets from the Portuguese. **CP-BroEB**

Sonnet: "Thou hast thy calling to some palace floor." Elizabeth Barrett Browning. **OXAEP-2; Son** *Fr.* Sonnets from the Portuguese. **CP-BroEB**

Sonnet: "Thy sting sufficeth, Death. If Heidegger first." Hayden Carruth. **CP-CarHS** *Fr.* Sonnets.

Sonnet: "Time, that renews the tissues of this frame." Edna St. Vincent Millay. **CP-MillE**

Sonnet: "To have been Diogenes. Why not? Or de Sade." Hayden Carruth. **CP-CarHS** *Fr.* Sonnets.

Sonnet: "To rebel is suitable philosophical tactics." Hayden Carruth. **CP-CarHS** *Fr.* Sonnets.

Sonnet: "To rebel. So I have saved my life, not once." Hayden Carruth. **CP-CarHS** *Fr.* Sonnets.

Sonnet: "To see a woman long oppressed by fear." Hayden Carruth. **CP-CarHS** *Fr.* Sonnets.

Sonnet: "To the aged, trembling, illiterate woman yesterday." Hayden Carruth. **CP-CarHS** *Fr.* Sonnets.

Sonnet: "Unlike are we, unlike, O princely heart!" Elizabeth Barrett Browning. **BWW; EnVR; HBV; OAEP; OBEV; OBVV; OXAEP-2; TrGrPo** *Fr.* Sonnets from the Portuguese. **CP-BroEB**

Sonnet: "Unquiet griefe search farder, in my hart." Mary Sidney, Countess of Montgomery Wroth. *Fr.* Part 1. *Fr.* Urania. **CP-WrotM**

Sonnet: "Was Yahweh chosen by the chosen people?" Hayden Carruth. **CP-CarHS** *Fr.* Sonnets.

Sonnet: "Way the world is not, The." Bill Knott. **SP-KnotB**

Sonnet: "Well, Jim says that the couplet at the end." Hayden Carruth. **CP-CarHS** *Fr.* Sonnets.

Sonnet: "Well, she told me I had an aura. 'What?' I said." Hayden Carruth. **CP-CarHS**

Sonnet: "What can I give thee back, O liberal." Elizabeth Barrett Browning. **BWW; HBV 1-2; OBVV; OXAEP-2** *Fr.* Sonnets from the Portuguese. **CP-BroEB**

Sonnet: "What I am saying now was said before." Countee Cullen. **CP-CullC**

Sonnet: "What if the psychologians, those grand old frauds." Hayden Carruth. **CP-CarHS** *Fr.* Sonnets.

Sonnet: "When I by Thy Faire Shape Did Sweare." Richard Lovelace. **CP-LoveR**

Sonnet: "When I have read your hard and lively words." John Hewitt. **CP-HewiJ**

Sonnet: "When our two souls stand up erect and strong." Elizabeth Barrett Browning. **BWW; BoWoP; EnVR; GGP; NAEL-2; NALW; NOBE; OBEV; PFP; TrGrPo; VBLP; WPE** *Fr.* Sonnets from the Portuguese. **CP-BroEB**

Sonnet: "When we can all so excellently give." Edwin Arlington Robinson. **CP-RobiE**

Sonnet: "When we first met and loved, I did not build." Elizabeth Barrett Browning. *Fr.* Sonnets from the Portuguese. **CP-BroEB**

Sonnet: "Where didst thou find, young Bard, thy sounding lyre?" John Keats. **CP-KeatJ**

Sonnet: "While you stood talking at the counter, cutting." Hayden Carruth. **CP-CarHS** *Fr.* Sonnets.

Sonnet: " 'Whut do you spose thet thing is,' Oi said. 'Whut?' " Hayden Carruth. **CP-CarHS**

Sonnet: "Why complain, brothers, to you, my writing." Hayden Carruth. **CP-CarHS** *Fr.* Sonnets.

Sonnet: "Why extremely do we observe more of." Hayden Carruth. **CP-CarHS** *Fr.* Sonnets.

Sonnet: "Why should we weep or mourn, Angelic boy." William Wordsworth. **CP-WorW2**

Sonnet. Richard Wilbur. **CP-WilbR**

Sonnet: "With the same heart, I said, I'l answer thee." Elizabeth Barrett Browning. *Fr.* Sonnets from the Portuguese. **CP-BroEB**

Sonnet: "Women in anger, it seems, become theatrical." Hayden Carruth. **CP-CarHS** *Fr.* Sonnets.

Sonnet: "Ye hasten to the grave! What seek ye there." Percy Bysshe Shelley. **CP-ShelP**

Sonnet: "Yes. After all my arguments with myself." Hayden Carruth. **CP-CarHS** *Fr.* Sonnets.

Sonnet: "Yes, call me by my pet-name! let me hear." Elizabeth Barrett Browning. *Fr.* Sonnets from the Portuguese. **CP-BroEB**

Sonnet: "Yet, love, mere love, is beautiful indeed." Elizabeth Barrett Browning. **BWW; CTC; HBV; OHCV; OXAEP-2; VLP** *Fr.* Sonnets from the Portuguese. **CP-BroEB**

Sonnet: "You in a tallness slenderly, as a lone." Hayden Carruth. **CP-CarHS** *Fr.* Sonnets.

Sonnet: "You rose from our embrace and the small light spread." Hayden Carruth. **CP-CarHS** *Fr.* Sonnets.

Sonnet 1: "O Nightingale, that on yon bloomy spray." John Milton. **CP-MiltJ**

Sonnet 2: "Charming lady, she whose beautiful name honors." John Milton, *tr. fr. Italian by* John T. Shawcross. **CP-CowpW; CP-MiltJ**

("Fair Lady! whose harmonious name the Rhine.") **CP-CowpW,** *tr. by* William Cowper;

Sonnet 3: "As on a rugged mountain at the darkening of evening." John Milton, *tr. fr. Italian by* John T. Shawcross. **CP-CowpW; CP-MiltJ**

("As on a hill-top rude, when closing day.") **CP-CowpW,** *tr. by* William Cowper;

Sonnet 5: "In truth your fair eyes, my lady." John Milton, *tr. fr. Italian by* John T. Shawcross. **CP-CowpW; CP-MiltJ**

("Lady! It cannot be, but that thine eyes.") **CP-CowpW,** *tr. by* William Cowper;

Sonnet 6: "Young, gentle, and candid lover that I am." John Milton, *tr. fr. Italian by* John T. Shawcross. **CP-CowpW; CP-MiltJ**

("Enamour'd, artless, young, on foreign ground.") **CP-CowpW,** *tr. by* William Cowper;

Sonnet 7: "How soon hath Time the suttle theef of youth." John Milton. *See* How soon hath Time the suttle [*or* subtle] theef [*or* thief] of youth.

Sonnet 8: "Captain or Colonel, or Knight in Arms." John Milton. *See* Captain or Colonel, or Knight in Arms.

Sonnet 10: "Daughter to that good Earle, once President." John Milton. *See* Daughter to that good Earl[e], once President.

Sonnet 11: "I did but prompt the age to quit their [*or* thir] clogs." John Milton. *See* I did but prompt the age to quit their [*or* thir] clogs.

Sonnet 12: "Book was writt of late call'd Tetrachordon, A." John Milton. *See* A Book was writ[t] of late called [*or* call'd] *Tetrachordon.*

Sonnet 13: "Harry, whose tunefull and well-measur'd song." John Milton. *See* Harry, whose tuneful[l] and well-measured [*or* well-measur'd] song.

Sonnet 14: "When Faith and Love which parted from thee never." John Milton. *See* When Faith and Love which parted from thee never.

Sonnet 15: "Fairfax, whose name in armes through Europe rings." John Milton. *See* Fairfax, whose name in armes through Europe rings.

Sonnet 16: "Cromwell, our cheif of men, who through a cloud." John Milton. *See* Cromwell, our chief [*or* cheif] of men, who through a cloud.

Sonnet 17: "Vane, young in yeares, but in sage counsell old." John Milton. *See* Vane, young in yeares, but in sage counsell old.

Sonnet 18: "Avenge O Lord thy slaughter'd Saints, whose bones." John Milton. *See* Avenge O Lord thy slaughtered [*or* slaughter'd] Saints, whose bones.

Sonnet 20: "Lawrence of vertuous Father vertuous Son." John Milton. *See* Lawrence of virtuous [*or* vertuous] Father virtuous [*or* vertuous] Son.

Sonnet 21: "Cyriack, whose Grandsire on the Royal Bench." John Milton. *See* Cyriack, whose Grandsire on the Royal Bench.

Sonnet 22: "Cyriack, this three years day these eyes, though clear." John Milton. *See* Cyriack, this three years['] day these eyes, though clear.

Sonnet 23: "Mee thought I saw my late espoused saint." John Milton. *See* Methought [*or* Mee thought] I saw my late espoused saint.

Sonnet 1: "Deare eyes farewell, my Sunne once, now my end." Mary Sidney, Countess of Montgomery Wroth. *Fr.* Lindamira's Complaint. *Fr.* Part 1. *Fr.* Urania. **CP-WrotM**

Sonnet 1: "In night yett may wee see some kind of light." Mary Sidney, Countess of Montgomery Wroth. *Fr.* Pamphilia to Amphilanthus. **CP-WrotM**

Sonnet 1: "In this strang labourinth how shall I turne?" Mary Sidney, Countess of Montgomery Wroth. *Fr.* A Crowne of Sonetts Dedicated to Love. *Fr.* Pamphilia to Amphilanthus. **CP-WrotM**

Sonnet 1: "My hart is lost, what can I now expect." Mary Sidney, Countess of Montgomery Wroth. *Fr.* Pamphilia to Amphilanthus. **CP-WrotM**

Sonnet 1: "When night's [*or* nights] black mantle could most darknes prove." Mary Sidney, Countess of Montgomery Wroth. **Son** *Fr.* Pamphilia to Amphilanthus. **CP-WrotM**

Sonnet 2: "Deare eyes how well (indeed) you doe adorne." Mary Sidney, Countess of Montgomery Wroth. *Fr.* Pamphilia to Amphilanthus. **CP-WrotM**

Sonnet 2: "Is to leave all, and take the thread of love." Mary Sidney, Countess of Montgomery Wroth. *Fr.* A Crowne of Sonetts Dedicated to Love. *Fr.* Pamphilia to Amphilanthus. **CP-WrotM**

Sonnet 2: "Late in the Forest I did Cupid see." Mary Sidney, Countess of Montgomery Wroth. **KTR** *Fr.* Pamphilia to Amphilanthus. **CP-WrotM**

Sonnet 2: "Love like a jugler, comes to play his prise." Mary Sidney, Countess of Montgomery Wroth. *Fr.* Pamphilia to Amphilanthus. **CP-WrotM**

Sonnet 2: "O deadly rancour to a constant heart." Mary Sidney, Countess of Montgomery Wroth. *Fr.* Lindamira's Complaint. *Fr.* Part 1. *Fr.* Urania. **CP-WrotM**

Sonnet 3: "His flames ar joyes, his bands true lovers might." Mary Sidney, Countess of Montgomery Wroth. *Fr.* A Crowne of Sonetts Dedicated to Love. *Fr.* Pamphilia to Amphilanthus. **CP-WrotM**

Sonnet 3: "Juno still jealouse of her husband Jove." Mary Sidney, Countess of Montgomery Wroth. *Fr.* Pamphilia to Amphilanthus. **CP-WrotM**

Sonnet 3: "Most blessed Night, the happy time for love." Mary Sidney, Countess of Montgomery Wroth. *Fr.* Pamphilia to Amphilanthus. **CP-WrotM**

Sonnet 3: "Surgeon I would aske, but 'tis too late." Mary Sidney, Countess of Montgomery Wroth. *Fr.* Lindamira's Complaint. *Fr.* Part 1. *Fr.* Urania. **CP-WrotM**

Sonnet 3: "Yett is ther hope: Then Love butt play thy part." Mary Sidney, Countess of Montgomery Wroth. *Fr.* Pamphilia to Amphilanthus. **CP-WrotM**

Sonnet 4: "And bee in his brave court a gloriouse light." Mary Sidney, Countess of Montgomery Wroth. *Fr.* A Crowne of Sonetts Dedicated to Love. *Fr.* Pamphilia to Amphilanthus. **CP-WrotM**

Sonnet 4: "Cruell suspition, O! bee now att rest." Mary Sidney, Countess of Montgomery Wroth. *Fr.* Pamphilia to Amphilanthus. **CP-WrotM**

Sonnet 4: "Forbeare darke night, my joyes now budd againe." Mary Sidney, Countess of Montgomery Wroth. *Fr.* Pamphilia to Amphilanthus. **CP-WrotM**

Sonnet 4: "When I beeheld the Image of my deere." Mary Sidney, Countess of Montgomery Wroth. *Fr.* Pamphilia to Amphilanthus. **CP-WrotM**

Sonnet 5: "And burne, yett burning you will love the smart." Mary Sidney, Countess of Montgomery Wroth. *Fr.* A Crowne of Sonetts Dedicated to Love. *Fr.* Pamphilia to Amphilanthus. **CP-WrotM**

Sonnet 5: "Can pleasing sight, misfortune ever bring?" Mary Sidney, Countess of Montgomery Wroth. *Fr.* Pamphilia to Amphilanthus. **CP-WrotM**

Sonnet 5: "How many nights have I with paine indur'd." Mary Sidney, Countess of Montgomery Wroth. *Fr.* Pamphilia to Amphilanthus. **CP-WrotM**

Sonnet 5: "Leave me vain Hope, too long thou hast posses[s]t." Mary Sidney, Countess of Montgomery Wroth. **BWW** *Fr.* Lindamira's Complaint. *Fr.* Part 1. *Fr.* Urania. **CP-WrotM**

Sonnet 5: "Like to huge clowds of smoke which well may hide." Mary Sidney, Countess of Montgomery Wroth. *Fr.* Pamphilia to Amphilanthus. **CP-WrotM**

Sonnet 6: "Hee may owr profitt, and out Tuter prove." Mary Sidney, Countess of Montgomery Wroth. *Fr.* A Crowne of Sonetts Dedicated to Love. *Fr.* Pamphilia to Amphilanthus. **CP-WrotM**

Sonnet 6: "My pain[e], still smothered [*or* smother'd] in my grievèd bre[a]st." Mary Sidney, Countess of Montgomery Wroth. **NOSC** *Fr.* Pamphilia to Amphilanthus. **CP-WrotM**

Sonnet 6: "Ô strive nott still to heape disdaine on mee." Mary Sidney, Countess of Montgomery Wroth. **NOSC** *Fr.* Pamphilia to Amphilanthus. **CP-WrotM**

Sonnet 6: "O! that noe day would ever more appeere." Mary Sidney, Countess of Montgomery Wroth. *Fr.* Pamphilia to Amphilanthus. **CP-WrotM**

Sonnet 6: "Though you forsake me, yet alas permit." Mary Sidney, Countess of Montgomery Wroth. *Fr.* Lindamira's Complaint. *Fr.* Part 1. *Fr.* Urania. **CP-WrotM**

Sonnet 7: "End fond jealousie alas I know, An." Mary Sidney, Countess of Montgomery Wroth. *Fr.* Pamphilia to Amphilanthus. **CP-WrotM**

Sonnet 7: "How blest bee they then, who his favors prove." Mary Sidney, Countess of Montgomery Wroth. *Fr.* A Crowne of Sonetts Dedicated to Love. *Fr.* Pamphilia to Amphilanthus. **CP-WrotM**

Sonnet 7: "Love leave to urge, thou know'st thou hast the hand." Mary Sidney, Countess of Montgomery Wroth. *Fr.* Pamphilia to Amphilanthus. **CP-WrotM**

Sonnet 7: "No time, noe roome, noe thought, or writing can." Mary Sidney, Countess of Montgomery Wroth. *Fr.* Pamphilia to Amphilanthus. **CP-WrotM**

Sonnet 7: "Some doe, perhaps, both wrong my love, and care." Mary Sidney, Countess of Montgomery Wroth. *Fr.* Lindamira's Complaint. *Fr.* Part 1. *Fr.* Urania. **CP-WrotM**

Sonnet 8: "Hee that shunns love doth love him self the less." Mary Sidney, Countess of Montgomery Wroth. *Fr.* A Crowne of Sonetts Dedicated to Love. *Fr.* Pamphilia to Amphilanthus. **CP-WrotM**

Sonnet 8: "How gloewoorme like the sunn doth now apeere." Mary Sidney, Countess of Montgomery Wroth. *Fr.* Pamphilia to Amphilanthus. **CP-WrotM**

Sonnet 8: "Led by the powre of griefe, to waylings brought." Mary Sidney, Countess of Montgomery Wroth. *Fr.* Pamphilia to Amphilanthus. **CP-WrotM**

Sonnet 8: "Poore Love in chaines, and fetters like a thiefe." Mary Sidney, Countess of Montgomery Wroth. *Fr.* Pamphilia to Amphilanthus. **CP-WrotM**

Sonnet 9: "Be[e] you all pleased [*or* pleas'd]? your pleasures grieve not[t] me[e]." Mary Sidney, Countess of Montgomery Wroth. **BWW; NOSC** *Fr.* Pamphilia to Amphilanthus. **CP-WrotM**

Sonnet 9: "But wher they may returne with honors grace." Mary Sidney, Countess of Montgomery Wroth. *Fr.* A Crowne of Sonetts Dedicated to Love. *Fr.* Pamphilia to Amphilanthus. **CP-WrotM**

Sonnet 9: "My muse now hapy, lay thy self to rest." Mary Sidney, Countess of Montgomery Wroth. *Fr.* Pamphilia to Amphilanthus. **CP-WrotM**

Sonnet 9: "'Pray doe nott use thes words I must bee gone." Mary Sidney, Countess of Montgomery Wroth. *Fr.* Pamphilia to Amphilanthus. **CP-WrotM**

Sonnet 10: "Bee from court of Love, and reason torne." Mary Sidney, Countess of Montgomery Wroth. *Fr.* A Crowne of Sonetts Dedicated to Love. *Fr.* Pamphilia to Amphilanthus. **CP-WrotM**

Sonnet 10: "Folly would needs make mee a lover bee." Mary Sidney, Countess of Montgomery Wroth. *Fr.* Pamphilia to Amphilanthus. **CP-WrotM**

Sonnet 10: "Weary traveller who tired sought, The." Mary Sidney, Countess of Montgomery Wroth. *Fr.* Pamphilia to Amphilanthus. **CP-WrotM**

Sonnet 11: "Unprofitably pleasing, and unsound." Mary Sidney, Countess of Montgomery Wroth. *Fr.* A Crowne of Sonetts Dedicated to Love. *Fr.* Pamphilia to Amphilanthus. **CP-WrotM**

Sonnet 11: "You endless torments that my rest opress." Mary Sidney, Countess of Montgomery Wroth. *Fr.* Pamphilia to Amphilanthus. **CP-WrotM**

Sonnet 12: "Bee given to him who triumphs in his right." Mary Sidney, Countess of Montgomery Wroth. *Fr.* A Crowne of Sonetts Dedicated to Love. *Fr.* Pamphilia to Amphilanthus. **CP-WrotM**

Sonnet 12: "Cloy'd with the torments of a tedious night." Mary Sidney, Countess of Montgomery Wroth. *Fr.* Pamphilia to Amphilanthus. **CP-WrotM**

Sonnet 13: "Deare fammish nott what you your self gave food." Mary Sidney, Countess of Montgomery Wroth. *Fr.* Pamphilia to Amphilanthus. **CP-WrotM**

Sonnet 13: "Free from all fogs butt shining faire, and cleere." Mary Sidney, Countess of Montgomery Wroth. *Fr.* A Crowne of Sonetts Dedicated to Love. *Fr.* Pamphilia to Amphilanthus. **CP-WrotM**

Sonnet 14: "Am I thus conquered? [*or* conquer'd]? have I lost the powers." Mary Sidney, Countess of Montgomery Wroth. **NAEL-1; NOSC** *Fr.* Pamphilia to Amphilanthus. **CP-WrotM**

Sonnet 14: "Except my hart which you beestow'd before." Mary Sidney, Countess of Montgomery Wroth. *Fr.* A Crowne of Sonetts Dedicated to Love. *Fr.* Pamphilia to Amphilanthus. **CP-WrotM**

Sonnet 15: "Truly poore Night thou wellcome art to mee." Mary Sidney, Countess of Montgomery Wroth. *Fr.* Pamphilia to Amphilanthus. **CP-WrotM**

Sonnet 16: "Sleepe fy possess mee nott, nor doe nott fright." Mary Sidney, Countess of Montgomery Wroth. *Fr.* Pamphilia to Amphilanthus. **CP-WrotM**

Sonnet 17: "Sweet shades why doe you seeke to give delight." Mary Sidney, Countess of Montgomery Wroth. *Fr.* Pamphilia to Amphilanthus. **CP-WrotM**

Sonnet 18: "Which should I better like of, day, or night." Mary Sidney, Countess of Montgomery Wroth. *Fr.* Pamphilia to Amphilanthus. **CP-WrotM**

Sonnet 19: "Come darkest night, be[e]coming sorrow best." Mary Sidney, Countess of Montgomery Wroth. **NOSC** *Fr.* Pamphilia to Amphilanthus. **CP-WrotM**

Sonnet 20: "Sunn which glads, the earth att his bright sight, The." Mary Sidney, Countess of Montgomery Wroth. *Fr.* Pamphilia to Amphilanthus. **CP-WrotM**

Sonnet 21: "When last I saw thee, I did not[t] thee see." Mary Sidney, Countess of Montgomery Wroth. *Fr.* Pamphilia to Amphilanthus. **CP-WrotM**

Sonnet 22: "Like to the Indians, scorched with the sun[ne]." Mary Sidney, Countess of Montgomery Wroth. **NOSC** *Fr.* Pamphilia to Amphilanthus. **CP-WrotM**

Sonnet 23: "When every one to pleasing pastime hies." Mary Sidney, Countess of Montgomery Wroth. **WPE** *Fr.* Pamphilia to Amphilanthus. **CP-WrotM**

Sonnet 24: "Once did I heere an aged father say." Mary Sidney, Countess of Montgomery Wroth. *Fr.* Pamphilia to Amphilanthus. **CP-WrotM**

Sonnet 25: "Poore eyes bee blind, the light behold noe more." Mary Sidney, Countess of Montgomery Wroth. *Fr.* Pamphilia to Amphilanthus. **CP-WrotM**

Sonnet 26: "Deare cherish this, and with it[t] my soules will." Mary Sidney, Countess of Montgomery Wroth. **BWW** *Fr.* Pamphilia to Amphilanthus. **CP-WrotM**

Sonnet 27: "Fie [*or* Fy] tedious Hope, why do[e] you still rebel[l]?" Mary Sidney, Countess of Montgomery Wroth. **NOSC** *Fr.* Pamphilia to Amphilanthus. **CP-WrotM**

Sonnet 28: "Griefe, killing griefe: have nott my torments binn." Mary Sidney, Countess of Montgomery Wroth. **KTR** *Fr.* Pamphilia to Amphilanthus. **CP-WrotM**

Sonnet 29: "Fly hence O! joy noe longer heere abide." Mary Sidney, Countess of Montgomery Wroth. **KTR** *Fr.* Pamphilia to Amphilanthus. **CP-WrotM**

Sonnet 30: "You blessed shades, which give mee silent rest." Mary Sidney, Countess of Montgomery Wroth. **KTR** *Fr.* Pamphilia to Amphilanthus. **CP-WrotM**

Sonnet 31: "After long trouble in a taedious way." Mary Sidney, Countess of Montgomery Wroth. **KTR** *Fr.* Pamphilia to Amphilanthus. **CP-WrotM**

Sonnet 32: "How fast thou fliest, O Time, on loves swift wings." Mary Sidney, Countess of Montgomery Wroth. *Fr.* Pamphilia to Amphilanthus. **CP-WrotM**

Sonnet 33: "How many eyes poore Love hast thou to guard." Mary Sidney, Countess of Montgomery Wroth. *Fr.* Pamphilia to Amphilanthus. **CP-WrotM**

Sonnet 34: "Take heed mine eyes, how you your lookes doe cast." Mary Sidney, Countess of Montgomery Wroth. *Fr.* Pamphilia to Amphilanthus. **CP-WrotM**

Sonnet 35: "False [*or* Faulce] hope which feeds but[t] to destroy, and spill." Mary Sidney, Countess of Montgomery Wroth. **KTR; NAEL-1** *Fr.* Pamphilia to Amphilanthus. **CP-WrotM**

Sonnet 36: "How well poore hart thou wittnes canst I love." Mary Sidney, Countess of Montgomery Wroth. *Fr.* Pamphilia to Amphilanthus. **CP-WrotM**

Sonnet 37: "Night, welcome art thou to my mind destrest." Mary Sidney, Countess of Montgomery Wroth. *Fr.* Pamphilia to Amphilanthus. **CP-WrotM**

Sonnet 38: "What pleasure can a bannish'd creature have." Mary Sidney, Countess of Montgomery Wroth. *Fr.* Pamphilia to Amphilanthus. **CP-WrotM**

Sonnet 39: "Iff I were giv'n to mirthe 't'wowld be more cross." Mary Sidney, Countess of Montgomery Wroth. *Fr.* Pamphilia to Amphilanthus. **CP-WrotM**

Sonnet 40: "Itt is nott love which you poore fooles do deeme." Mary Sidney, Countess of Montgomery Wroth. *Fr.* Pamphilia to Amphilanthus. **CP-WrotM**

Sonnet 41: "You blessed starrs which doe heavns glory show." Mary Sidney, Countess of Montgomery Wroth. *Fr.* Pamphilia to Amphilanthus. **CP-WrotM**

Sonnet 42: "If ever love had force in huma[i]ne brest?" Mary Sidney, Countess of Montgomery Wroth. **BWW** *Fr.* Pamphilia to Amphilanthus. **CP-WrotM**

Sonnet 43: "O dearest eyes the lights, and guids of love." Mary Sidney, Countess of Montgomery Wroth. *Fr.* Pamphilia to Amphilanthus. **CP-WrotM**

Sonnet 44: "How fast thou hast'st (O spring) with sweetest speed." Mary Sidney, Countess of Montgomery Wroth. *Fr.* Pamphilia to Amphilanthus. **CP-WrotM**

Sonnet 45: "Good now bee still, and doe nott mee torment." Mary Sidney, Countess of Montgomery Wroth. *Fr.* Pamphilia to Amphilanthus. **CP-WrotM**

Sonnet 46: "Love, thou hast all, for now thou hast mee made." Mary Sidney, Countess of Montgomery Wroth. *Fr.* Pamphilia to Amphilanthus. **CP-WrotM**

Sonnet 47: "O stay mine eyes, shed nott thes fruitles tears." Mary Sidney, Countess of Montgomery Wroth. *Fr.* Pamphilia to Amphilanthus. **CP-WrotM**

Sonnet 48: "How like a fire doth love increase in me[e]." Mary Sidney, Countess of Montgomery Wroth. **NOSC** *Fr.* Pamphilia to Amphilanthus. **CP-WrotM**

Sonnet, A: "Ile dote noe more, nor shall mine eyes." Robert Herrick. **CP-HerrR**

Sonnet (Aboard a Troopship) to Gweno. Alun Lewis. **CP-LewiA**

Sonnet Addressed to Mr. Phillips, A. William Cowper. **CP-CowpW**

Sonnet at Easter. Howard Nemerov. **CP-NemeH**

Sonnet Autumnal. Wilfred Owen. **CP-OwenW**

Sonnet beloved of doctors, clergymen. After Reading *Sonnets* by Rev. Charles Turner (1864) and *The New Day*, Sonnets by Dr T. Gordon Hake (1890). John Hewitt. **CP-HewiJ**

Sonnet Composed at—Castle. William Wordsworth. *See* Degenerate Douglas! O [*or* oh,] the unworthy lord!

Sonnet Composed on a Journey Homeward; the Author Having Received Intelligence of the Birth of a Son, 20 September 1796. Samuel Taylor Coleridge. **CP-ColeS**

Sonnet: [From the Italian of Dante.] Dante Alighieri to Guido Cavalcanti. Dante Alighieri. *See* Guido, I would that Lapo, thou, and I.

Sonnet Dialogue. Countee Cullen. **CP-CullC**

Sonnet: England in 1819. Percy Bysshe Shelley. *See* An Old, mad, blind, despised, and dying king.

Sonnet entitled how to run the world). Edward Estlin Cummings. **CP-CummE; SP-CummE**

Sonnet for Jane Freilicher, A. Frank O'Hara. **SP-OharF**

Sonnet for My Acquaintances. Isabella Gardner. **CP-GardI**

Sonnet 4: "Diodati, and I will say it to you with wonder." John Milton, *tr. fr. Italian by* John T. Shawcross. **CP-CowpW; CP-MiltJ**

("Charles—and I say it wond'ring—thou must know.") **CP-CowpW,** *tr. by* William Cowper;

Sonnet: From the Italian of Guido Cavalcanti. Cavalcanti to Dante Alighieri. Guido Cavalcanti. *See* Returning from its daily quest, my Spirit.

Sonnet from the Portuguese. Elizabeth Barrett Browning. *See* Sonnet: "How do I love thee? Let me count the ways."

Sonnet from the Psalms. Christina Georgina Rossetti. **CP-RosC3**

Sonnet I: "There was desolate silence on the world." Wystan Hugh Auden. **CP-AudWJ**

Sonnet II: "It matters not that we shall cease to be." Wystan Hugh Auden. **CP-AudWJ**

Sonnet in Autumn. John Hewitt. **CP-HewiJ**

Sonnet in Search of an Author. William Carlos Williams. **CP-WilW2**

Sonnet in the Pass of Killicranky. William Wordsworth. **CP-WorW1**

Sonnet: "Late Gracie Allen was a very lucid comedienne, The." Alice Notley. **SP-NotlA**

Sonnet: "Men call you fair, and you do credit it." Edmund Spenser. *See* LXXIX. "Men call you fair [*or* fayre], and you do[e] credit it."

Sonnet:"My thoughts through yours refracted into speech." Muriel Rukeyser. **CP-RukeM**

Sonnet 9: "Ladie, that in the prime of earliest youth." John Milton. **CP-MiltJ**

Sonnet 19: "When I consider how my light is spent." John Milton. *See* When I consider how my light is spent.

Sonnet: O Husband! Anne Waldman. **SP-WaldA**

Sonnet of Intimacy. Vinícius de Moraes, *tr. fr. Portuguese by* Elizabeth Bishop. **CP-BishE**

Sonnet of Michel Angelo Buonaroti. Michelangelo Buonarroti, *tr. fr. Italian by* Ralph Waldo Emerson. **CP-EmerR**

Sonnet of Perilla, A. Robert Herrick. **CP-HerrR**

Sonnet on Chillon. Byron. **FiP; LiTB; LoBV; MeMBP; OAEP; OBRV; PBMP; SeCeV; TrGrPo; TreFS** *Fr.* The Prisoner of Chillon. **CP-Byron**

(On the Castle of Chillon.) **GTBS; GTBS-6; GTBS-P**

Sonnet on Famous and Familiar Sonnets and Experiences. Delmore Schwartz. **SP-SchwD**

Sonnet—On Hearing a Thrush Sing on a Morning Walk in January. Robert Burns. **CP-BurnR**

Sonnet: On Launching Some Bottles Filled with Knowledge into the Bristol Channel. Percy Bysshe Shelley. **CP-ShelP**

Sonnet on Milton. William Wordsworth. **CP-WorW1**

Sonnet on Quitting Christ's Hospital. Samuel Taylor Coleridge. **CP-ColeS**

Sonnet on Receiving a Letter Informing Me of the Birth of a Son. Samuel Taylor Coleridge. **CP-ColeS**

Sonnet on Seeing Miss Helen Maria Williams Weep at a Tale of Distress. William Wordsworth. **CP-WorW1**

Sonnet on the Death of Robert Riddel, Esq. *of Glen Riddel, April* 1794. Robert Burns. **CP-BurnR**

Sonnet on the Death of the Man Who Invented Plastic Roses. Peter Meinke. **SP-MeinP**

Sonnet on the Nuptials of the Marquis Antonio Cavalli with the Countess Clelia Rasponi of Ravenna. Byron. **CP-Byron**

Sonnet: Political Greatness. Percy Bysshe Shelley. **CP-ShelP**

Sonnet, she told the crowd of bearded, The. Sonnet, The. Daniel Gerard Hoffman. **SP-HoffD**

Sonnet—Silence. Edgar Allan Poe. **CP-PoeEd**

Sonnet: Sin. Hayden Carruth. **CP-CarHS** *Fr.* Sonnets.

Sonnet Suggested by Homer, Chaucer, Shakespeare, Edgar Allan Poe, Paul Valéry, James Joyce, et al. Delmore Schwartz. **SP-SchwD**

Sonnet, The: "Sonnet, she told the crowd of bearded, The." Daniel Gerard Hoffman. **SP-HoffD**

Sonnet: The Recollected Actual Voices of Romanticism. Hayden Carruth. **CP-CarHS** *Fr.* Sonnets.

Sonnet. The Token. John Donne. **CP-DonnJ**

Sonnet: To a Balloon Laden with Knowledge. Percy Bysshe Shelley. **CP-ShelP**

Sonnet, to a Child. Wilfred Owen. **CP-OwenW**

Sonnet to a Friend Who Asked[,] How I Felt When the Nurse First Presented My Infant to Me. Samuel Taylor Coleridge. **CP-ColeS**

Sonnet to a Picture by Lucca Giordano in the Mureo Borbonico at Naples. William Wordsworth. **CP-WorW2**

Sonnet (To an Octogenarian). William Wordsworth. **CP-WorW2**

Sonnet to Beauty. Allen Tate. **CP-TateA**

Sonnet: To Byron. Percy Bysshe Shelley. **CP-ShelP**

Sonnet: To Eva. Sylvia Plath. **CP-PlatS**

Sonnet to Gath. Edna St. Vincent Millay. **CP-MillE**

Sonnet. To Generall Goring. Richard Lovelace. **CP-LoveR**

Sonnet, to Genevra. Byron. **CP-Byron**

Sonnet to Henry Cowper. William Cowper. **CP-CowpW**

Sonnet to J.M. George Meredith. **CP-MerG2**

Sonnet to Lake Leman. Byron. **CP-Byron**

Sonnet to Man-Made Grandeur. John Updike. **CP-UpdiJ**

Sonnet to Mrs. Unwin. William Cowper. *See* Mary! I want a lyre with other strings.

Sonnet to Satan. Sylvia Plath. **CP-PlatS**

Sonnet—To Science. Edgar Allan Poe. **CP-PoeEd**

Sonnet to the Forest Ytene. Charlotte Smith. **CP-SmitC**

Sonnet to the Noble Lady, the Lady Mary Wroth, A. Ben Jonson. **CP-JonsB**

Sonnet to the Prince Regent. Byron. **CP-Byron**

Sonnet to the River Otter. Samuel Taylor Coleridge. **CP-ColeS**

Sonnet, to the Same. Byron. **CP-Byron**

Sonnet to the Virgin. William Wordsworth. *See* The Virgin.

Sonnet: To Time. Sylvia Plath. **CP-PlatS**

Sonnet to Wilberforce. William Cowper. *See* Thy country, Wilberforce, with just disdain.

Sonnet to William Linley. Samuel Taylor Coleridge. **CP-ColeS**

Sonnet to Zante. Ugo Foscolo, *tr. fr. Greek by* Edgar Allen Poe. **CP-PoeEd**

Sonnet Translated from the Italian of Milton. William Wordsworth. **CP-WorW1**

Sonnet upon Sonnets, A. Robert Burns. **CP-BurnR**

Sonnet with X's. Gilbert Sorrentino. **SP-SorrG**

Sonnet Written by Mr — Immediately after the Death of His Wife. William Wordsworth. **CP-WorW1**

Sonnet: Zimmer Imagines Himself Being Poet-in-Residence. Paul Zimmer. **SP-ZimmP**

Sonnets, The. Ted Berrigan.

"Academy of the future is opening its doors, The." **SP-BerrT**

"Banging around in a cigarette she isn't 'in love'." **SP-BerrT**

"Banging around in a cigarette she isn't 'in love' / She murmurs of signs to her fingers." **SP-BerrT**

"Bulbs burn phosphorescent, white, The." **SP-BerrT**

"Clarity! clarity! a semblance of motion, omniscience. / There is no such thing as a breakdown." **SP-BerrT**

"DEAR CHRIS / It is 3:17 a.m. in New York city, yes, it is." **SP-BerrT**

"Dear Margie, hello. It is 5:15 a.m." **SP-BerrT**

"Dear Ron: hello. Your name is now a household name." **SP-BerrT**

"Dear Ron: Keats was a baiter of bears etc." **SP-BerrT**

"Each tree stands alone in stillness." **SP-BerrT**

Final Sonnet, A. **SP-BerrT**

"Grace to be born and live as variously as possible." **SP-BerrT**

"Harum-scarum haze on the Pollock streets / Where Snow White sleeps among the silent dwarfs." **SP-BerrT**

"His piercing pince-nez. Some dim frieze." **SP-BerrT**

"How strange to be gone in a minute / Bearden is dead Gallup is dead

Margie is dead." **SP-BerrT**

"I like to beat people up." **SP-BerrT**

"In Joe Brainard's collage its white arrow." **SP-BerrT**

"In my paintings for they are present." **SP-BerrT**

"Into the closed air of the slow." **SP-BerrT**

"It is a human universe: & I." **SP-BerrT**

"It is night. You are asleep. And beautiful tears." **SP-BerrT**

"It was summer. We were there. And THERE WAS NO." **SP-BerrT**

"It's 8:54 a.m. in Brooklyn it's the 28th [or 26th] of July [and]." **SP-BerrT**

Lines for Lauren Owen. **SP-BerrT**

"Lord, it is time. Summer was very great." **SP-BerrT**

"Mountains of twine and." **SP-BerrT**

"Musick strides through these poems." **SP-BerrT**

"My dream a drink with Lonnie Johnson we discuss the code." **SP-BerrT**

"On the 15th day of November in the year of the motorcar." **SP-BerrT**

"On the green a white boy goes / We may read about all those radio waves." **SP-BerrT**

Penn Station. **SP-BerrT**

Poem in the Modern Manner. **SP-BerrT**

Poem in the Traditional Manner. **SP-BerrT**

"Poem upon the page is as massive as, The." **SP-BerrT**

"Seurat and Juan Gris combine this season." **SP-BerrT**

"Sleep half sleep half silence and with reasons." **SP-BerrT**

"Stronger than alcohol, more great than song." **SP-BerrT**

"Summer so histrionic, marvelous dirty days." **SP-BerrT**

"Sweeter than sour apples flesh to boys." **SP-BerrT**

Sonnets. Hayden Carruth.

Sonnet: "All revolutions in modern times have led." **CP-CarHS**

Sonnet: "At the hospital where I had the echocardiogram." **CP-CarHS**

Sonnet: "But still, still. . . / In stillness mystery calls." **CP-CarHS**

Sonnet: "Cindy, I've used my writing all my life." **CP-CarHS**

Sonnet: "Cindy, the secret's out. Yes, you're addict-." **CP-CarHS**

Sonnet: "Dearest, I never knew such loving. There." **CP-CarHS**

Sonnet: "Fear of falling is why the old men walk." **CP-CarHS**

Sonnet: "Freedom in love? It has been questioned. Think." **CP-CarHS**

Sonnet: "From our very high window at the Sheraton." **CP-CarHS**

Sonnet: "Honey, darling, baby. . . but no endearments." **CP-CarHS**

Sonnet: "How is it, tell me, that this new self can be—." **CP-CarHS**

Sonnet: "I think continually of the differences." **CP-CarHS**

Sonnet: "I want to do a complaint now. Which is to say." **CP-CarHS**

Sonnet: "If I die today, which statistically speaking." **CP-CarHS**

Sonnet: "If you see a child that shivers when it hears." **CP-CarHS**

Sonnet: "In the mind of the kiss occurs a thought so rich." **CP-CarHS**

Sonnet: "It's said by the thoughtful masters that to know death." **CP-CarHS**

Sonnet: "Key-reist, I am fed and sick unto death with this." **CP-CarHS**

Sonnet: "Last night, I don't know if from habit or intent." **CP-CarHS**

Sonnet: "Like the magnificent stationary animal it is." **CP-CarHS**

Sonnet: "Most brainy woman, the sexuality of your thought." **CP-CarHS**

Sonnet: "Must genius always struggle, always exaggerate." **CP-CarHS**

Sonnet: "O Jesus, thou who sittest up there on the right." **CP-CarHS**

Sonnet: "Persistent is the thought for me of that." **CP-CarHS**

Sonnet: "Poor little book, *The Sleeping Beauty* died." **CP-CarHS**

Sonnet: "The Bo was three when we slugged through Arizona." **CP-CarHS**

Sonnet: "The hubbub of the Hall of Languages, our Babel." **CP-CarHS**

Sonnet: "The loving mind in this death-haunted body." **CP-CarHS**

Sonnet: "The Word for Today is 'panoptic,' which the goddamn." **CP-CarHS**

Sonnet: "This is our perfect silver maple's day." **CP-CarHS**

Sonnet: "Thy sting sufficeth, Death. If Heidegger first." **CP-CarHS**

Sonnet: "To have been Diogenes. Why not? Or de Sade." **CP-CarHS**

Sonnet: "To rebel is suitable philosophical tactics." **CP-CarHS**

Sonnet: "To rebel. So I have saved my life, not once." **CP-CarHS**

Sonnet: "To see a woman long oppressed by fear." **CP-CarHS**

Sonnet: "To the aged, trembling, illiterate woman yesterday." **CP-CarHS**

Sonnet: "Was Yahweh chosen by the chosen people?" **CP-CarHS**

Sonnet: "Well, Jim says that the couplet at the end." **CP-CarHS**

Sonnet: "What if the psychologians, those grand old frauds." **CP-CarHS**

Sonnet: "While you stood talking at the counter, cutting." **CP-CarHS**

Sonnet: "Why complain, brothers, to you, my writing." **CP-CarHS**

Sonnet: "Why extremely do we observe more of." **CP-CarHS**

Sonnet: "Women in anger, it seems, become theatrical." **CP-CarHS**

Sonnet: "Yes. After all my arguments with myself." **CP-CarHS**

Sonnet: "You in a tallness slenderly, as a lone." **CP-CarHS**

Sonnet: "You rose from our embrace and the small light spread." **CP-CarHS**

Sonnet: Sin. **CP-CarHS**

Sonnet: The Recollected Actual Voices of Romanticism. **CP-CarHS**

Sonnets. William Shakespeare. **CP-ShaWS**

Sonnet 1: "From fairest creatures we desire increase." **CTC; FaBoEn; HeIP; ImPo; LiTB; MasP; OAEP; OBSC; TrGrPo**

Sonnet 2: "When forty winters shall besiege thy brow." **BLPL; FF; HeIP; ImPo; LiTB; NoSic; OBSC; Son; TEP**

Sonnet 3: "Look in thy glass, and tell the face thou viewest." **CABA; EnRePo; ImPo; LiTB; MasP; NAEL-1; OBSC; SCGP**

Sonnet 4: "Unthrifty loveliness, why dost thou spend."

Sonnet 5: "Those hours, that with gentle work did frame." **TEP**

Sonnet 6: "Then let not winter's ragged hand deface." **MasP**

Sonnet 7: "Lo! in the orient when the gracious light."

Sonnet 8: "Music[k] to hear[e], why hear'st thou music[k]." **PoEL-2**

Sonnet 9: "Is it for fear to wet a widow's eye." **MasP**

Sonnet 10: "For shame! deny that thou bear'st love to any." **MasP**

Sonnet 11: "As fast as thou shall wane, so fast thou growest."

Sonnet 12: "When I do count the clock that tells the time." **AWP; EIL; EnRePo; HeIP; InPS; MasP; NAEL-1; NoP; NoSic; OAEL-1; OBSC; SCGP; Son; TEP**

(When I Do Count the Clock.) **FaFP**

Sonnet 13: "Oh [or O] that you were yourself! but, love, you are." **OAEP; TEP**

Sonnet 14: "Not from the stars do I my judgement pluck." **MasP; Son**

Sonnet 15: "When I consider everything that grows." **AWP; BLPL; MasP; NAEL-1; NoSic; OAEP; OBSC; SCGP; Son; TEP; TrGrPo**

Sonnet 16: "But wherefore do not you a mightier way." **FaBoEn**

Sonnet 17: "Who will believe my verse in time to come." **OBSC**

Sonnet 18: "Shall I compare thee to a summer's day?" **ArLo; BoLoP; CTC; ClHu; EIL; EnLoPo; FPL; FaBV; FaBoBe; FaFP; FaPoB; FiP; GBL; HAP; HeIL; HeIP; ImPo; InPK; InPS; InvP; LPA; LiTB; MAT; NIP; NOBE; NoP; NoSic; OAEL-1; OBEV; OBSC; PBMP; PIP; PoE; PoEL-2; PoLF; PoRA; PrIm; SCGP; SCV; SeCePo; Son; TEP; TFi; TrGrPo; WeW**

(To His Love ("Shall I compare thee to a summer's day?").) **GTBS; GTBS-6; GTBS-P**

Sonnet 19: "Devouring Time, blunt thou the lion's paws." **AWP; ChTr; EBEV; HeIP; ImPo; MAT; NAEL-1; NoSic; OAEL-1; OBSC; OXAEP-1; PoE; PoEL-2; SCGP; TrGrPo; WHA**

Sonnet 20: "Woman's face with Nature's own hand painted, A." **ErPo; HeIP; InvP; MasP; NAEL-1; NoSic; OAEL-1; OXAEP-1; PeHV**

Sonnet 21: "So is it not with me as with that Muse." **HeIP; InvP; OBSC**

Sonnet 22: "My glass shall not persuade me I am old." **OBSC; Son**

Sonnet 23: "As an unperfect actor on the stage." **BiP; HBV; InvP; NoSic; OAEP; Son**

Sonnet 24: "Mine eye hath play'd the painter, and hath stell'd." **EyDe**

Sonnet 25: "Let those who are in favour with their stars." **OBSC; OXAEP-1; PAW; SCGP**

Sonnet 26: "Lord of my love, to whom in vassalage." **HeIP**

Sonnet 27: "Weary with toil, I haste me to my bed." **HeIP; NoSic; OBSC; PIP; SCGP**

Sonnet 28: "How can I then return in happy plight." **OBSC**

Sonnet 29: "When, in disgrace with fortune and men's eyes." **AWP; CTC; EBEV; EIL; FaBV; FaBoEn; FaPoB; GBL; HAP; HBV; HeIL; HeIP; ImPo; InPK; InPS; InvP; LiTB; LoBV; MasP; NAEL-1; NOBE; NoP; NoSic; OAEL-1; OAEP; OBEV; OBSC; OPOP; OPOU; OXAEP-1; PeHV; PoEL-2; PoPl; Poetr; SCGP; Son; TFi; WeW**

(Consolation, A.) **GTBS; GTBS-6; GTBS-P**

(When, in Disgrace.) **PFP**

Sonnet 30: "When to the sessions of sweet silent thought." **AWP; ArLo; BiP; CABA; CTC; ClHu; EBEV; EBEvV; EIL; EnRePo; FF; FPL; FaBV; FaBoEn; FaBoRV; FaPoB; GBL; HAP; HBV; HeIP; ImPo; InPS; LiTB; LoBV; MasP; NAEL-1; NOBE; NoP; NoSic; OAEL-1; OAEP; OBEV; OBSC; OXAEP-1; PAI; PPP; PoE; PoEL-2; PoLF; PoPle; PoRA; PrIm; SCGP; SeCeV; TEP; TFi; TrGrPo; TreFS; WHA**

(Remembrance.) **FaFP; GTBS; GTBS-6; GTBS-P; TRV**

Sonnet 31: "Thy bosom is endeared with all hearts." **NOBE; OBEV; OBSC; PoEL-2**

Sonnet 32: "If thou survive my well-contented day." **EIL; HBV; OBSC; PP**

(Post Mortem.) **GTBS; GTBS-6; GTBS-P**

Sonnet 33: "Full many a glorious morning have I seen[e]." **AWP; EBEV; EBEvV; EIL; FaBoEn; HAP; HBV; ImPo; LiTB; LoBV; NIP; NoP; NoSic; OAEL-1; OAEP; OBSC; OXAEP-1; OtMeF; PPP; PoRA; SCGP; SeCePo; SeCeV; Son; TEP; TFi; TrGrPo; TreFS; WeW**

(Full Many a Glorious Morning.) **FaFP**

Sonnet 34: "Why didst thou promise such a beauteous day." **HeIP; OBSC; OXAEP-1**

Sonnet 35: "No more be grieved at that which thou hast done." **HeIP; ImPo; NAEL-1; NoSic; OXAEP-1; PeHV; PoE; SCGP; TEP; UnPo**

Sonnet 36: "Let me confess that we two must be twain." **HeIP; OAEP; PeHV**

Sonnet 37: "As a decrepit father takes delight."

Sonnet 38: "How can my muse want subject to invent."

Sonnet 39: "O, how thy worth with manners may I sing."

Sonnet 40: "Take all my loves, my Love, yea, take them all." **HeIP; InvP; OBSC; OXAEP-1; SCGP**

Sonnet 41: "Those petty [or pretty] wrongs that liberty commits." **InvP; OXAEP-1**

Sonnet 42: "That thou hast her, it is not all my grief[e]." **CBLP; HeIP; InvP; OXAEP-1**

Sonnet 43: "When most I wink, then do mine eyes best see."

Sonnet 44: "If the dull substance of my flesh were thought." **Son**

Sonnet 45: "Other two, slight air and purging fire, The."

Sonnet 46: "Mine eye and heart are at a mortal war." **EyDe; HeIP**

Sonnet 47: "Betwixt mine eye and heart a league is took." **EyDe**

Sonnet 48: "How careful was I, when I took my way."

Sonnet 49: "Against that time, if ever that time come." **OXAEP-1**

Sonnet 50: "How heavy do I journey on the way." **OXAEP-1**

Sonnet 51: "Thus can my love excuse the slow offence."

Sonnet 52: "So am I as the rich, whose blessed key." **OBSC; OXAEP-1**

Sonnet 53: "What is your substance, whereof are you made." **CTC; EBEV; EIL; EnRePo; FaFP; ImPo; LiTB; MasP; NoSic; OAEL-1; OAEP; OBEV; OBSC; OXAEP-1; PeHV; SCGP**

Sonnet 54: "O [or Oh], how much more doth beauty beauteous seem." **AWP; EIL; OBEV; OBSC; PoE; SCGP**

Sonnet 55: "Not marble, nor the gilded monuments." **AWP; BLPL; CABA; CTC; EPCY; EnRePo; FF; FaBoEn; FaFP; HeIL; HeIP; ImPo; InPK; LPA; LiTB; LoBV; MasP; NAEL-1; NIP; NOBE; NoP; NoSic; OAEL-1; OAEP; OBSC; OXAEP-1; PAI; PPoe; PeHV; PoE; PoEL-2; PoRA; Poetr; SCGP; SeCeV; Son; TEP; TrGrPo**

Sonnet 56: "Sweet love, renew thy force; be it not said." **PoLF; SCGP**

Sonnet 57: "Being your slave, what should I do[e] but tend." **HAP; NoSic; OBEV; PeHV; PoEL-2**

(Absence.) **GTBS; GTBS-6; GTBS-P**

Sonnet 58: "That god forbid that made me first your slave."

Sonnet 59: "If there be nothing new, but that which is."

Sonnet 60: "Like as the waves make towards the pebbled shore." **ChTr; EBEV; EIL; EnRePo; FPL; FaBoEn; FaPoB; HBV; LiTB; LoBV; NIP; NOBE; NoSic; OBSC; OXAEP-1; PeHV; PoRA; SCGP; SeCeV; Son; TEP; TFi; UnPo**

(Like as the Waves.) **FaFP; ImPo**

(Revolutions.) **GTBS; GTBS-6; GTBS-P**

Sonnet 61: "Is it thy will thy image should keep open." **PoEL-2**

Sonnet 62: "Sin [or Sinne] of self-love [or selfe-love] possesseth all mine eye [or eie]." **EBEV; EnRePo; OXAEP-1; PoEL-2**

Sonnet 63: "Against my love shall be, as I am now." **OBSC**

Sonnet 64: "When I have seen by Time's fell hand defac'd." **AWP; BLPL; CABA; EIL; EnLoPo; EnRePo; FaFP; HAP; HeIP; ImPo; LO; LiTB; NOBE; NoP; NoSic; OAEL-1; OBSC; OXAEP-1; PPoe; PIP; PoE; PoRA; SCGP; SeCeV; Son**

(Time and Love, I.) **GTBS; GTBS-6; GTBS-P**

Sonnet 65: "Since brass, nor stone, nor earth, nor boundless sea." **AWP; CABA; EnRePo; FF; FiP; HAP; InPS; LiTB; MasP; NAEL-1; NOBE; NoP; NoSic; OXAEP-1; PoRA; RaBo; SCGP; SeCeV; Son; TFi; UnPo**

(Since Brass, Nor Stone, Nor Earth.) **FaFP; ImPo**

(Time and Love, II.) **GTBS; GTBS-6; GTBS-P**

Sonnet 66: "Tired [or Tyr'd, or Tir'd] with all these, for restful death I cry." **AWP; CTC; CoGr; EBEV; FaBoPV; FaFP; HAP; InPS; LiTB; NOBE; NoSic; OAEL-1; OBSC; OXAEP-1; PoEL-2; SeCeV; TFi; TrGrPo; WHA; WeW**

(Tired With All These.) **CBCK; ImPo**

(World's Way, The.) **GTBS; GTBS-6; GTBS-P**

Sonnet 67: "Ah! wherefore with infection should he live." **PeHV; SCGP**

Sonnet 68: "Thus is his cheek the map of days outworn." **OBSC; SCGP**

Sonnet 69: "Those parts of thee that the world's eye doth view."

Sonnet 70: "That thou art blamed shall not be thy defect." **OXAEP-1; SCGP**

Sonnet 71: "No longer mourn for me when I am dead." **AWP; EBEV; EIL; EnRePo; FaBoRV; GBL; HAP; HBV; HeIP; IMW; ImPo; LO; LiTB; NAEL-1; NoP; NoSic; OAEP; OBSC; OXAEP-1; PAI; PPoe; PoRA; SCGP; SeCeV; Son; TEP; TFi; TrGrPo; TreFT; WHA**

(Triumph of Death, The.) **GTBS; GTBS-6; GTBS-P**

Sonnet 72: "O! Lest the world should task you to recite." **OXAEP-1**

Sonnet 73: "That time of year thou may'st [or maist] in me behold." **AWP; ArNa; BoLoP; CTC; ChTr; ClHu; EBEV; EIL; EnRePo; FaPoB; GTBS; GTBS-P; HAP; HeIP; HoPM; ImPo; InPK; InPS; InvP; LiTB; NAEL-1; NIP; NOBE; NoP; NoSic; OAEL-1; OBD; OBEV; OHFP; PBMP; PPP; PIP; PoE; PoEL-2; PoRA; PrIm; QFR; SCGP; SoSe; Son; TEP; TFi; TrGrPo; UnPo; WeW**

Sonnet 74: "But be contented: when that fell arrest." **NAEL-1; OBSC; OXAEP-1; Son**

Sonnet 75: "So are you to my thoughts as food to life." **PoEL-2**

Sonnet 76: "Why is my verse so barren of new pride." **EBEV; InvP; NoSic; OXAEP-1; PP**

Sonnet 77: "Thy glass will show thee how thy beauties wear." **EnRePo; HeIP; QFR**

Sonnet 78: "So oft I invoked thee for my Muse."

Sonnet 79: "Whilst I alone did call upon thy aid."

Sonnet 80: "O, how I faint when I of you do write." **OXAEP-1**

Sonnet 81: "Or I shall live your epitaph to make." **OAEP; OBSC; OXAEP-1**

Sonnet 82: "I grant thou wert not married to my Muse."

Sonnet 83: "I never saw that you did painting need."

Sonnet 84: "Who is it that says most? which can say more."

Sonnet 85: "My tongue-tied Muse in manners holds her still." **Son**

Sonnet 86: "Was it the proud full sail of his great verse." **InvP; NoSic; OAEL-1; OAEP; OXAEP-1; SCGP; Son; TEP**

Sonnet 87: "Farewell! Thou art too dear[e] for my possessing." **CBLP; EBEV; EBEvV; EIL; GTBS; GTBS-6; GTBS-P; ImPo; InPS; InvP; LiTB; MasP; NAEL-1; NoSic; OAEL-1; OAEP; OBEV; OBSC; OXAEP-1; PeHV; PoEL-2; QFR; Son; TFi; TrGrPo**

Sonnet 88: "When thou shalt be dispos'd to set me light." **OXAEP-1**

Sonnet 89: "Say that thou didst forsake me for some fault." **OAEP; OXAEP-1**

Sonnet 90: "Then hate me when thou wilt; if ever, now." **AWP; EBEV; EIL; NOBE; NoSic; OBEV; OBSC; OXAEP-1; PoEL-2; WHA**

Sonnet 91: "Some glory in their birth, some in their skill."

Sonnet 92: "But do thy worst to steal thyself away."

Sonnet 93: "So shall I live, supposing thou art true." **InvP; MasP**

Sonnet 94: "They that have power to hurt[e], and will do[e] none." **BLPL; CABA; CBLP; EIL; FaBoEn; ImPo; InPS; LiTB; MasP; NAEL-1; NOBE; NoP; NoSic; OAEL-1; OBEV; OXAEP-1; PPP; PPoe; PeHV; PoE; PoEL-2; SCGP; SCV; Son; TEP; TRP; TrGrPo**

(Life without Passion, The.) **GTBS; GTBS-6; GTBS-P**

Sonnet 95: "How sweet and lovely dost thou make the shame." **HeIP; MasP; SCGP; TrGrPo**

Sonnet 96: "Some say thy fault is youth, some wantonness."

Sonnet 97: "How like a winter hath my absence been[e]." **AWP; CABA; EIL; EnLoPo; EnRePo; EyDe; FaBoEn; GTBS; GTBS-6; GTBS-P; HeIP; NAEL-1; NOBE; NoSic; OAEL-1; OBEV; OBSC; OXAEP-1; PoRA; Son; TEP; TFi; TrGrPo**

Sonnet 98: "From you have I been absent in the spring." **AWP; ChTr; EBEV; EIL; ImPo; LiTB; NAEL-1; NOBE; NoSic; OBEV; OBSC; OXAEP-1; PoPle; TEP**

Sonnet 99: "Forward violet thus did I chide, The." **OAEP; OBSC; OXAEP-1**

Sonnet 100: "Where art thou, Muse, that thou forget'st so long." **OBSC**

Sonnet 101: "O truant Muse, what shall be thy amends."

Sonnet 102: "My love is strengthen'd, though more weak in seeming." **AWP; EIL; OAEP; OBEV; OBSC**

Sonnet 103: "Alack, what poverty my Muse brings forth."

Sonnet 104: "To me, fair[e] friend, you never can be old." **EIL; EnRePo; FPL; FaBoEn; GBL; GTBS; GTBS-6; GTBS-P; HeIP; NoSic; OBEV; OBSC; OXAEP-1; PeHV; Prf; SCGP**

Sonnet 105: "Let not my love be call'd idolatry."

Sonnet 106: "When in the chronicle of wasted time." **AWP; BLPL; CTC; EBEvV; EIL; EnLoPo; EnRePo; FaBV; FaBoCh; FiP; ImPo; LiTB; NAEL-1; NOBE; NoP; NoSic; OBEV; OBSC; OXAEP-1; PoRA; SCGP; Son; TEP; TrGrPo**

(To His Love ("When in the chronicle of wasted time").) **GTBS; GTBS-6; GTBS-P**

Sonnet 107: "Not mine own fears nor the prophetic soul." **AWP; CABA; CTC; EBEV; FiP; HAP; ImPo; LiTB; LoBV; MasP; NAEL-1; NoP; NoSic; OAEL-1; OAEP; OBSC; OXAEP-1; PPoe; SCGP; SeCeV**

Sonnet 108: "What's in the brain that ink may character."

Sonnet 109: "O [or Oh], never say that I was false of heart." **EIL; HBV; NOBE; OBEV; OBSC; OXAEP-1**

(Unchangeable, The.) **GTBS; GTBS-6; GTBS-P**

Sonnet 110: "Alas, 'tis true I have gone here and there." **EBEV; NoSic; OAEP; OBSC; OXAEP-1; PeHV**

Sonnet 111: "O, for my sake do you with Fortune chide." **OXAEP-1**

Sonnet 112: "Your love and pity doth the impression fill."

Sonnet 113: "Since I left you, mine eye is in my mind." **SCGP; WeW**

Sonnet 114: "Or whether doth my mind, being crowned with you." SCGP

Sonnet 115: "Those lines that I before have writ do lie."

Sonnet 116: "Let me not to the marriage of true minds." **AWP; ArLo; ClHu; EBEvV; EIL; EnLoPo; EnRePo; FPL; FaBV; FaFP; FaPoB; GBL; GGP; HAP; HeIL; HeIP; InPS; InvP; LiTB; NAEL-1; NIP; NOBE; NoP; NoSic; OAEL-1; OBEV; OBSC; OXAEP-1; OxBM; PBMP; PPP; PeHV; PoE; PoEL-2; PoRA; Poetr; PrIm; SCGP; SCV; SeCePo; SoSe; Son; TEP; TFi; TRP; TrGrPo; UnPo; WeW**

(Marriage of True Minds, The.) ImPo; PlP

(True Love.) **GTBS; GTBS-6; GTBS-P**

Sonnet 117: "Accuse me thus; that I have scanted all."

Sonnet 118: "Like as, to make our appetites more keen." **CABA; SCGP**

Sonnet 119: "What potions have I drunk of Siren tears." **OXAEP-1; WHA**

Sonnet 120: "That you were once unkind befriends me now." **InvP; OXAEP-1**

Sonnet 121: "'Tis better to be vile than vile esteem'd." **InvP; NoSic; OAEL-1; OXAEP-1; PoEL-2; SCGP**

Sonnet 122: "Thy gift, thy tables, are within my brain."

Sonnet 123: "No, Time, thou shalt not boast that I do change." **OAEP; OBSC; OXAEP-1; Son; TrGrPo**

Sonnet 124: "If my dear love were but the child of state." **NoSic**

Sonnet 125: "Were't aught to me I bore the canopy." **NoSic**

Sonnet 126: "O thou, my lovely boy, who in thy power." **HeIP; NAEL-1**

Sonnet 127: "In the old age black was not counted fair." **OXAEP-1**

Sonnet 128: "How oft, when thou, my music, music play'st." **EIL; NAEL-1; OXAEP-1; PoE**

Sonnet 129: "Expense of spirit in a waste of shame, The [or Th']." **AWP; BiP; CABA; EBEV; EnRePo; ErPo; FaBoEn; GBL; HAP; HeIP; ImPo; InPS; LiTB; LoBV; MasP; NAEL-1; NIP; NOBE; NoP; NoSic; OAEL-1; OBEV; OBSC; OXAEP-1; OtMeF; PAI; PPP; PPoe; PoE; PoEL-2; Poetr; QFR; SCGP; SCV; SeCePo; SeCeV; Son; TEP; TFi; TrGrPo; UnPo; WHA; WeW**

(Lust in Action.) PlP

(Sonnet 129.) CoGr

Sonnet 130: "My mistress' eyes are nothing like the sun." **AWP; BiP; BoLoP; CABA; EBEV; FF; HAP; HBV; HeIP; HoPM; ImPo; InPK; InPS; InvP; LiTB; NAEL-1; NIP; NoP; NoSic; OAEL-1; OAEP; OXAEP-1; OtMeF; PAI; PBMP; PP; PPP; PlP; PoE; PoPle; Poetr; PrIm; SeCeV; SoSe; Son; TEP; TFi; WeW**

Sonnet 131: "Thou art as tyrannous, so as thou art."

Sonnet 132: "Thine eyes I love, and they, as pitying me." **OAEP; OBSC; OXAEP-1**

Sonnet 133: "Beshrew that heart that makes my heart to groan." **InvP; OXAEP-1**

Sonnet 134: "So, now I have confess'd that he is thine." **HeIP; InvP; OXAEP-1**

Sonnet 135: "Whoever hath her wish, thou hast thy Will." **NAEL-1; OAEL-1**

Sonnet 136: "If thy soul check thee that I come so near."

Sonnet 137: "Thou blind fool, Love, what dost thou to mine eyes." **WeW**

Sonnet 138: "When my love swears [or sweares] that she is made of truth." **AWP; BiP; CABA; EBEV; HeIP; NAEL-1; NoP; NoSic; OAEL-1; OAEP; OXAEP-1; PAI; PPP; PlP; PoEL-2; Poetr; SoSe; TEP; TrGrPo**

Sonnet 139: "O, call me not to justify the wrong."

Sonnet 140: "Be wise as thou art cruel; do not press." **NoSic**

Sonnet 141: "In faith, I do[e] not love thee with mine eyes." **HeIP; OXAEP-1; PoEL-2; TrGrPo**

Sonnet 142: "Love is my sin and thy dear virtue hate."

Sonnet 143: "Lo! as a careful housewife runs to catch." **BiP; InPK; OAEP; SCGP**

Sonnet 144: "Two loves I have of comfort and despair." **CABA; EBEV; HeIP; InvP; LoBV; NAEL-1; NIP; OAEL-1; OAEP; PeHV; PoEL-2; Son**

(Two Loves I Have.) PFP

Sonnet 145: "Those lips that Love's own hand did make." Son

Sonnet 146: "Poor[e] soul[e], the centre of my sinful[l] earth." **AWP; BiP; CABA; EaLo; EIL; EnRePo; FaBoEn; HAP; HBV; HeIP; ImPo; InPS; LiTB; MasP; NAEL-1; NIP; NOBE; NOCV; NoP; OAEL-1; OBEV; OBSC; OXAEP-1; OxBoCh; PPP; PPoe; PoE; PoEL-2; SCGP; SeCeV; Son; TFi; TrGrPo; WHA**

(Soul and Body.) **GTBS; GTBS-6; GoBC**

Sonnet 147: "My love is as a fever [or feaver], longing still." **EBEV; HoPM; NAEL-1; OXAEP-1; PoEL-2; TEP**

Sonnet 148: "O me, what eyes hath Love put in my head."

(Blind Love.) **GTBS; GTBS-6; GTBS-P**

Sonnet 149: "Canst thou, O cruel! say I love thee not."

Sonnet 150: "O! from [or O! From] what power hast thou this powerful might." **OXAEP-1; SCGP**

Sonnet 151: "Love is too young to know what conscience is." **EBEV; HeIP; NoSic; OXAEP-1; PoE; PoEL-2**

Sonnet 152: "In loving thee thou know'st I am forsworn." **HeIP**

Sonnet 153: "Cupid laid by his brand, and fell asleep."

Sonnet 154: "Little love-god lying once asleep, The."

Sonnets. Robert Louis Stevenson. CP-StevR

"As Daniel, bird-alone, in that far land."

"As in the hostel by the bridge, I sate."

"As starts the absent dreamer, when a train."

"I have a hoard of treasure in my breast."

"Nor judge me light, tho' light at times I seem."

"Not undelightful, friend, our rustic ease."

"So shall this book wax like unto a well."

"Strong man's hand, the snow-cool head of age, The."

Sonnets are full of love, and this my tome. Christina Georgina Rossetti. **CP-RosC2**

Sonnets at Christmas. Allen Tate. CP-TateA

"Ah, Christ, I love you rings to the wild sky." PoNe; Son

"This is the day His hour of life draws near." **NAAL-2; Son**

Sonnets Attempted in the Manner of Contemporary Writers. Samuel Taylor Coleridge. CP-ColeS

On a Ruined House in a Romantic Country. FaBoPa; Par

(House That Jack Built, The.) CBNP

"Pensive at eve on the hard world I mus'd [or mused]."

To Simplicity.

Sonnets for Roberta (1954). John Hewitt. CP-HewiJ

"And, by that act of giving, my slow hand."

"How have I served you? I have let you waste." **CP-HewiJ; PNI**

"If I had given you that love and care." PNI

"Take the intention then and let me live."

"To such a gap as this our love has come."

Sonnets from an Ungrafted Tree. Edna St. Vincent Millay. CP-MillE

"Doctor asked her what she wanted done, The."

"From the wan dream that was her waking day."

"Gazing upon him now, severe and dead." SBG

"It came into her mind, seeing how the snow."

"Last white sawdust on the floor was grown, The."

"Not over-kind nor over-quick in study."

"One way there was of muting in the mind."

"She filled her arms with wood, and set her chin."

"She had a horror he would die at night."

"She had forgotten how the August night."

"She let them leave their jellies at the door."

"So she came back into his house again."

"Tenderly, in those times, as though she fed."

"Then cautiously she pushed the cellar door."

"There was upon the sill a pencil mark."

"Wagon stopped before the house, A; she heard."

"White bark writhed and sputtered like a fish, The."

Sonnets from China. Wystan Hugh Auden. CP-AudeW

"As evening fell the day's oppression lifted."

"Certainly praise: let song mount again and again."

"Chilled by the Present, its gloom and its noise." PPP

"Far from a cultural centre he was used." **CMoP; NoAM**

"He looked in all His wisdom from His throne."

"He stayed, and was imprisoned in possession." CMoP

"He turned his field into a meeting-place." **PoPl; SCV**

"He was their servant (some say he was blind)." CMoP

"He watched the stars and noted birds in flight." CMoP

"Here war is harmless like a monument." OBWP

"His care-free swagger was a fine invention." CMoP

"Only a smell had feelings to make known."

"Our global story is not yet completed."

"Simple like all dream-wishes, they employ."

"So an age ended, and its last deliverer died." **CMoP; PoE**

("And the age ended, and the last deliverer died.") Son

"So from the years their gifts were showered: each." CMoP

"They are and suffer; that is all they do."

"They wondered why the fruit had been forbidden." **CMoP; ChIV-1; Son**

"Though Italy and King's are far away."

"When all our apparatus of report."

"Who needs their names? Another genus built."

Sonnets from the Portuguese. Elizabeth Barrett Browning. CP-BroEB

Sonnet "First time that the sun rose on thine oath, The." **EnVR; NAEL-2; WPE**

Sonnet: "Accuse me not, beseech thee, that I wear."

Sonnet: "And therefore if to love can be desert."

Sonnet: "And wilt thou have me fashion into speech." **BWW; BrRo; EnVR**

Sonnet: "And yet, because thou overcomest so."

Sonnet: "Because thou hast the power and own'st the grace."

Sonnet: "Beloved, my beloved, when I think." **OAEP; Son; WPE**

Sonnet: "Beloved, thou hast brought me many flowers." **EBVV; EnVR; OAEP; OBNC; WPE**

Sonnet: "But only three in all God's universe."

Sonnet: "Can it be right to give what I can give." **CTC; HBV; OHCV; Son**

Sonnet: "Face of all the world is changed, I think, The." **CTC; HBV; OAEP; VLP**

Sonnet: "First time he kissed me, he but only kissed." **BLPA; BLPL; CTC; FaBoBe; HBV; PoPl**

Sonnet: "Go from me. Yet I feel that I shall stand." **BLPL; BWW; CBLP; HBV; OBEV; OBVV; OXAEP-2; TrGrPo; TreFS**

Sonnet: "Heavy heart, Beloved, have I borne, A."

Sonnet: "How do I love thee? Let me count the ways." **ArLo; BWW; BoLoP; CTC; EBEvV; EBVV; EnVR; FF; FPL; FaBV; FaBoBe; FaFP; FaPoB; HBV; HeIP; HoPM; InPK; LPA; LiTB; NAEL-2; NALW; NIP; NoP; OAEP; OHCV; OLR; OXAEP-2; OxBM; PoE; PoLF; PoPl; PoRA; Poetr; Son; TEP; TFi; TRV; TrGrPo; TreF; UV; UnPo; WHA; WPE**

(How Do I Love Thee?) **ImPo; PoToHe**

(Sonnet from the Portuguese.) **OPOU**

Sonnet: "I lift my heavy heart up solemnly." **NALW**

Sonnet: "I lived with visions for my company." **BWW**

Sonnet: "I never gave a lock hair away." **EBVV; HAP; HBV**

Sonnet: "I see thine image through my tears tonight."

Sonnet: "I thank all who have loved me in their hearts."

Sonnet: "I think of thee! My thoughts do twine and bud."

Sonnet: "I thought once how Theocritus had sung." **BWW; EBVV; EnVR; GBL; HBV; NOBE; NoP; OAEP; OBEV; OBNC; OXAEP-2; TreFT; WPE**

Sonnet: "If I leave all for thee, wilt thou exchange." **Son**

Sonnet: "If thou must love me, let it be for nought." **BWW; CTC; FaFP; HBV; HeIP; InPS; LiTB; OBEV; OBNC; OBVV; OHCV; OXAEP-2; PFP; SoSe; TrGrPo; TreFS; WHA**

(For Love's Sake Only.) **PoToHe**

Sonnet: "Indeed this very love which is my boast." **HBV 1-2**

Sonnet: "Is it indeed so? If I lay here dead."

Sonnet: "Let the world's sharpness, like a clasping knife." **NOBVV**

Sonnet: "My future will not copy fair my past." **EnVR**

Sonnet: "My letters! All dead paper, mute and white." **HAP; HBV; OXAEP-2**

Sonnet: "My own Beloved, who hast lifted me."

Sonnet: "My poet, thou canst touch on all the notes." **BrRo; HBV; VLP; WHA**

Sonnet: "Oh, yes! they love through all this world of ours."

Sonnet: "Pardon, oh, pardon, that my soul should make."

Sonnet: "Say over again, and yet once over again." **HBV 1-2; NAEL-2**

Sonnet: "Soul's Rialto hath its merchandise, The."

Sonnet: "Thou comest! all is said without a word." **BWW**

Sonnet: "Thou hast thy calling to some palace floor." **OXAEP-2; Son**

Sonnet: "Unlike are we, unlike, O princely heart!" **BWW; EnVR; HBV; OAEP; OBEV; OBVV; OXAEP-2; TrGrPo**

Sonnet: "What can I give thee back, O liberal." **BWW; HBV 1-2; OBVV; OXAEP-2**

Sonnet: "When our two souls stand up erect and strong." **BWW; BoWoP; EnVR; GGP; NAEL-2; NALW; NOBE; OBEV; PFP; TrGrPo; VBLP; WPE**

Sonnet: "When we first met and loved, I did not build."

Sonnet: "With the same heart, I said, I'l answer thee."

Sonnet: "Yes, call me by my pet-name! let me hear."

Sonnet: "Yet, love, mere love, is beautiful indeed." **BWW; CTC; HBV; OHCV; OXAEP-2; VLP**

Sonnets in October. John Hewitt. **CP-HewiJ**

Sonnets of the Blood. Allen Tate. **CP-TateA**

"Captains of industry, your aimless power."

"Fire I praise was once perduring flame, The." **PoA**

"Near to me as perfection in the blood."

("Near to me as my flesh, my flesh and blood.") **PoA**

"Not power nor the casual [or storied] hand of God."

"Our elder brother whom we had not seen."

"Then, brother, you would never think me vain."

"These generations that have sealed your heart."

"This message hastens lest we both go down."

"Times have changed. Why do you make a fuss, The."

("Times have changed, there is not left to us, The.") **PoA**

"What is this flesh and blood compounded of."

Sonnets to Chris. John Berryman. **CP-BerrJ**

"Ah when you drift hover before you kiss."

"All I did wrong, all the Grand Guignol years."

"All we were going strong last night this time." **FaBoMo**

"And does the old wound shudder open? Shall."

"And Plough-month peters out. . .its thermal power."

"Anomalous I linger, and ignore."

"*Are we?* You murmur 'not.' What of the night."

"As usual I'm up before the sun."

"Astronomies and slangs to find you, dear."

"Audacities and fetes of the drunken weeks!"

"Because I'd seen you not believe your lover."

"Began with swirling, blind, unstilled oh still."

"Bell to sore knees vestigial crowds, let crush."

"Boy twenty-one, in Donne, shied like a blow."

"'Broken heart'. but *can* a heart break, now?, A."

"Cambridge friend put in,—one whom I used, A."

"Christian to Try: 'I am so coxed in it'."

"Clots of age, grovel and palsy, crave, The."

"Cold rewards trail in, when the man is blind, The."

"College of cocktails, a few gentlemen."

"Crouched on a ridge sloping to where you pour."

"Darling I wait O in my upstairs box."

"Demand me again what Kafka's riddles mean."

"Dew is drying fast, a last drop glistens, The."

"Faith like the warrior ant swarming, enslaving."

"Fall and rise of her midriff bells. I watch."

"For you am I collared to quit my dear."

"For you an idyl, was it not, so far."

"Four oval shadows, paired, ringed each by sun."

"Great citadels whereon the gold sun falls."

"He made, a thousand years ago, a-many songs."

"Here too you came and sat a time once, drinking."

"How far upon these songs with my strict wrist."

"How shall I do, to pass the weary time."

"How shall I sing, western & dry & thin."

"I am interested alone in making ready."

"I break my pace now for a sonic boom."

"'*I couldn't leave* you' you confessed next day."

"I didn't see anyone else, I just saw Lies."

"I dreamt he drove me back to the asylum."

"I expect you from the North. The path winds in."

"I lift—lift you five States away your glass." **FaBoDD**

(At Six O'Clock.) **FaBoDD**

"I owe you, do I not, a roofer: though."

"I say *I laid siege—you enchanted me.*"

"I wished, all the mild days of middle March."

"If long enough I sit here, she, she'll pass."

"If not white shorts—then in a princess gown."

"Impossible to speak to her, and worse."

"In a poem made by Cummings, long since, his."

"Infallible symbolist!—Tanker driven ashore."

"Is it possible, poor kids, you must not come out?"

"It was the sky all day I grew to and saw."

"It will seem strange, no more this range on range."

"Itself a lightning-flash ripping the dark."

"I've found out why, that day, that suicide." **PoE**

"I've met your friend at last, your violent friend."

"Keep your eyes open when you kiss: do: when."

"Languid the songs I wish I willed . I try."

"Loves are the summer's. Summer like a bee."

"Mallarmé siren upside down,—rootedly!"

"Man who made her let me climb the derrick, The."

"Marble nor monuments where of then we spoke."

"Ménage à trois, like Tristan's,—difficult."

"Most strange, my change, this nervous interim—."

"Moths white as ghosts among these hundreds cling."

"Murmuration of the shallow, Crane, A."

"Musculatures and skulls. Later some throng."

"Mutinous in the half-light, & malignant, grind."

"Nothing there? nothing up the sky alive." **BoLoP**

"October's both, back in the Sooner State."

"Of all that weeks-long day, though call it back."
"Old Boys' blazers like a Mardi-Gras, The."
" 'Old Smoky' when you sing with Robin, Chris."
"On the wheat-sacks sullen with the ceaseless damp."
"Once when they found me, some refrain *Quoi faire?'.*"
"One note, a daisy, and a photograph."
"Our lives before hopelessly our mistake!—.'"
"Our love conducted as in tropic rain."
"Our Sunday morning when dawn-priests were applying."
"Outlaws claw mostly to a riddled end."
"Penny, pity, for the runaway ass!, A."
"Poet hunched, so, whom the worlds admire, The."
"Presidential flags! and the General is here."
"Rackman and victim twist: sounds all these weeks."
" 'Ring us up when you want to see us. . . '—'Sure'."
"Sensible, coarse, and moral; in decent brown."
"Sigh as it ends. . .I keep an eye on your."
"Some sketch sweat' out, unwilling swift & crude."
"Sometimes the night echoes to prideless wailing." **NoAM**
"Spendthrift Urethra—Sphincter, frugal one—."
"Spot of poontang on a five-foot piece, A."
"Still it pleads and rankles: 'Why do you love *me*?'."
"Sullen brook hardly would satisfy, A."
"Sunderings and luxations, *luxe*, and grief."
"Swarthy when young; who took the tonsure; sign."
"They come too thick, hail-hard, and all beside."
"They may, because I would not cloy your ear."
"Three, almost, now into the ass's years."
"Thrice, or I moved to sack, I saw you: how."
"Today is it? Is it today? I shudder."
"Tongue there is wags, down in the dark wood O, A."
"Troubling are masks. . .the faces of friends, my face."
"Two plantations Greatgrandmother brought, The."
"Tyranny of your car—so far resembles."
"Wasp skims nearby up the bright warm air, A."
"What can to you this music wakes my years."
"What was Ashore, then?. Cargoed with Forget."
"When I recall I could believe you'd go."
"Where the lane from the highway swerves the first drops fell."
"Who for those ages ever without some blood."
"Whom undone David upto the dire van sent."
"Why can't, Chris, why shouldn't *they* fall in love?"
"You, Chris, *contrite* I never thought to see."
"You come blonde visiting through the black air."
"You in your stone home where the sycamore."
"You sailed in sky-high, with your speech askew."
"You should be gone in winter, that Nature mourn."
"Your shining—where?—rays my wide room with gold."
Sonnets to Laura. Petrarch, *tr. fr. Italian.*
"I find no peace and all my war[r] is done." **CP-WyatT**
"Long[e] love that in my thought do[e]th [*or* I] harbour [*or* harber *or* harbar], The." **CP-WyatT**
"My galley [*or* galy] charged with forgetfulness." **CP-WyatT**
"Oh! place me where the burning noon." **CP-SmitC**
"She used to let her golden hair fly free."
("Loose to the wind her golden tresses stream'd.") **CP-SmitC,** *tr. by* Charlotte Smith;
"Some fowls there be that have so perfect sight." **CP-WyatT**
"Where the green leaves exclude the summer beam." **CP-SmitC**
"Ye vales and woods! fair scenes of happier hours." **CP-SmitC**
Sonnets upon the Punishment of Death. William Wordsworth. **CP-WorW2**
"Ah, think how one compelled for life to abide."
Apology.
"Before the world had past her time of youth."
Conclusion: "Yes, though He well may tremble at the sound."
"Fit retribution, by the moral code."
"Is *Death*, when evil against good has fought."
"Not to the object specially designed."
"Our bodily life, some plead, that life the shrine."
"Roman Consul doomed his sons to die, The."
"See the Condemned alone within his cell."
Suggested by the View of Lancaster Castle (on the Road from the South).
"Tenderly do we feel by Nature's law."
"Though to give timely warning and deter."
"Ye brood of conscience—Spectres! that frequent."

Sonora. Richard Shelton. **SP-ShelR**
Sonora Desert-Edge. Allen Ginsberg. **CP-GinsA**
Sonora for Sale. Richard Shelton. **SP-ShelR**
Sons and lovers into Hell. Orpheus in Connaught. James Liddy. *Fr.* Glass after Oblivion. **CP-LiddJ**
Sons of *Greece*, The. Samuel Johnson. **CP-JohnS** *Fr.* Irene.
Sons of Martha, The. Rudyard Kipling. **CP-KiplR**
Sons of Mary seldom bother, for they have inherited that good part, The. The Sons of Martha. Rudyard Kipling. **CP-KiplR**
Sons of men, from the wombs of wistful women. Side-Step, O Sons of Men! David Herbert Lawrence. **CP-LawrD**
Sons of Old Killie, The. Robert Burns. **CP-BurnR**
Sons of the Greeks, arise! Translation of the Famoue Greek War Song *Deute Paides Tov Ellenon.* Byron. **CP-Byron**
Sons of Whitman sons of Poe. *see also* Ferlinghetti, "Poets, come out of your closets." Lawrence Ferlinghetti. **SP-FerlL**
Son's Portrait, The. Thomas Hardy. **CP-HardT**
Sons, seek not me among these polished stones. Charles Cavendish to His Posterity. Ben Jonson. **CP-JonsB**
Soon. Charles Kenneth Williams. **CP-WillC**
Soon as / you stop. Cleavage. Archie Randolph Ammons. **SP-AmmoA**
Soon as *Glumdalclitch* miss'd her pleasing Care. The Lamentation of Glumdalclitch for the Loss of Grildrig. Alexander Pope. **CP-PopeA**
Soon as the sound had ceased whose thunder filled. Percy Bysshe Shelley. **ChER** *Fr.* Prometheus Unbound. **CP-ShelP**
Soon did the Almighty Giver of all rest. Upon Perusing the "Epistle [To Sir George Howland Beaumont"] Thirty Years after Its Composition. William Wordsworth. **CP-WorW2**
Soon fades the rose; once past the fragrant hour, *tr. fr. the Greek Anthology.* Samuel Johnson. **CP-JohnS**
Soon felt she in her shivered frame. George Meredith. *Fr.* Napoléon. **CP-MerG1**
Soon it must come, the great charge. Lorca. Richard Eberhart. **CP-EberR**
Soon It Will. Kenneth Patchen. **CP-PatcK**
Soon our friends perish. Robert Louis Stevenson. **CP-StevR**
Soon Shall the Winter's Foil Be Here. Walt Whitman. **CP-WhitW**
Soone after this I saw an elephant. Edmund Spenser. *Fr.* Visions of the World's Vanity [*or* Vanitie]. **CP-Spens**
Sooner let nightmares whinny, if we cannot. Dreams in Middle Age. Louis MacNeice. **CP-MacNL**
Sooner or late—in earnest or in jest. The Hour of the Angel. Rudyard Kipling. **CP-KiplR** *Fr.* Land and Sea Tales.
Sooner or later. The Rewaking. William Carlos Williams. **CP-WilW2**
Sooner or later: yet at last / The Jordan must be past. Christina Georgina Rossetti. **CP-RosC2**
Soonest Mended. John Ashbery. **SP-AshbJ**
Soonest mended, nothing said; / And help my rise from east or west, The. A Fisher-Wife. Christina Georgina Rossetti. **CP-RosC2**
Soot drifted from the engines to the marble, The. The Carnegie Library, Juvenile Division. Randall Jarrell. **CP-JarrR; SP-JarrR**
Soot, house-dust, and tar didn't go far. Painted Wives. John Updike. **CP-UpdiJ**
Soothing sanity and blitheness of completion, The. An Ended Day. Walt Whitman. **CP-WhitW**
Sopa. Robert Creeley. **CP-CreeR**
Sorcerer Bids Farewell to Seem, A. Sylvia Plath. **CP-PlatS**
Sorcerer's Daughter, The. Louise Bogan. **CP-BogaL**
Sorceress!, The. Nicholas Vachel Lindsay. **CP-LindV**
Sorcery. Walter de la Mare. **CP-DeLaW**
Sordello. Robert Browning. **CP-BroR1**
"In Mantua-territory half is slough." **EBVVPR**
Sorer the joints, The. Charles Henri Ford. **SP-FordC** *Fr.* Emblems of Arachne.
Sorrel. Geoffrey Hill. **CP-HillG**
Sorrel Filly, The. Wendell Berry. **CP-BerrW**
Sorrow. John Gould Fletcher. **SP-FletJ**
Sorrow. David Herbert Lawrence. **CP-LawrD**
Sorrow. Edna St. Vincent Millay. **CP-MillE**
Sorrow, The. Charles Kenneth Williams. **CP-WillC**
Sorrow almost resents love. Emily Dickinson. **SP-DickE**
Sorrow, benighted with Fathoms. Emily Dickinson. **SP-DickE**
Sorrow hath a double voice, / Sharp today but sweet tomorrow. Christina Georgina Rossetti. **CP-RosC2**
Sorrow, I yeeld, and grieve that I did miss. Song 7. Mary Sidney, Countess of Montgomery Wroth. *Fr.* Pamphilia to Amphilanthus. **CP-WrotM**
Sorrow is my own yard. The Widow's Lament in Springtime. William Carlos Williams. **CP-WilW1**

Sorrow of Love, The ("Brawling of a sparrow in the eaves, The"), *see also* The Sorrow of Love ("The quarrel of the sparrows in the eaves"). William Butler Yeats. **CP-YeatW**

Sorrow of Obedience, The. John Ciardi. **SP-CiarJ**

Sorrow of saints is sorrow of a day. Thy Servant Will Go and Fight with This Philistine. Christina Georgina Rossetti. **CP-RosC2**

Sorrow of Troilus, The. Geoffrey Chaucer. **PoEL-1** *Fr.* Troilus and Criseyde [or Criseide]. **CP-ChauG**

Sorrow Song, The. Hayden Carruth. **CP-CarHS**

Sorrow, who to this house scarce knew the way. Elegy on the L. C. John Donne. **CP-DonnJ**

Sorrowes. Robert Herrick. **CP-HerrR**

Sorrowes divided amongst many, lesse. Griefe. Robert Herrick. **CP-HerrR**

Sorrowes our portion are: Ere hence we goe. Sorrowes. Robert Herrick. **CP-HerrR**

Sorrowful dreams remembered after waking. Edna St. Vincent Millay. **CP-MillE**

Sorrowful Girl, The. Stevie Smith. **CP-SmitS**

Sorrows and Joys. George Meredith. **CP-MerG1**

Sorrows have come before and have stood mute. George Sterling's Death. Robinson Jeffers. **CP-JefR1**

Sorrows Succeed. Robert Herrick. **CP-HerrR**

Sorry. Leonard Nathan. **SP-NathL**

Sorry I am, my God, sorry I am. Sin's Round. George Herbert. **CP-HerbG**

Sors adversa gerit stimulum, sed tendit et alas. A Simile Latinised. *Unknown, tr. fr. English by* William Cowper. **CP-CowpW**

Sort of a Song, A. William Carlos Williams. **CP-WilW2**

Sort of anxiousness crystal in crystal has, A. The Song of the Bridegroom. John Berryman. **CP-BerrJ**

Sort of girl I like to see, The. The Olympic Girl. Sir John Betjeman. **CP-BetjJ**

Sort of roll develops out of the bay, A. Calm Day at Drake's Bay. Robert Bly. **SP-BlyR**

Sort of sexual trauma, A. Café Notre Dame. Lawrence Ferlinghetti. **SP-FerlL**

Sortes Vergilianae. John Ashbery. **SP-AshbJ**

Sorting out letters and piles of my old. Mementos, 1. William DeWitt Snodgrass. **SP-SnodW**

Sorting the Personae. Donald Davie. **CP-DavDo**

Sorting, Wrapping, Packing, Stuffing. James Schuyler. **CP-SchuJ**

S.O.S Sinking fast by both bow and stern. Malcolm Lowry. **CP-LowrM**

Sospetto d'Herode. Giovanni Battista Marino. **CP-CrasR** *Fr.* Strage degli innocenti, La.
"Mongst all the Palaces in Hells command."

Soto! Explore thyself! Emily Dickinson. **CP-DickE**

Sotto Voce. Walter de la Mare. **CP-DeLaW**

Sotto Voce. Stanley Jasspon Kunitz. **CP-KuniS**

Soubrettes, The. Alun Lewis. **CP-LewiA**

Soughing Wind, The. William Carlos Williams. **CP-WilW1**

Soul, The. Stephen Berg. **SP-BergS**

Soul. Charles Bukowski. **SP-BukC1**

Soul. Richard Eberhart. **CP-EberR**

Soul, A. Randall Jarrell. **CP-JarrR**

Soul, The. Malcolm Lowry. **CP-LowrM**

Soul, The. George Meredith. **CP-MerG2**

Soul, The. Charles Olson. **CP-OlsoC**

Soul, The. Jelaluddin Rumi, *tr. fr. Persian by* Ralph Waldo Emerson. **CP-EmerR**

Soul and Body. William Shakespeare. *See* Sonnet 146: "Poor[e] soul[e], the centre of my sinful[l] earth."

Soul and Body of John Brown, The. Muriel Rukeyser. **CP-RukeM**

Soul as full of Worth, as void of Pride, A. Epistle to James Craggs, Esq., Secretary of State. Alexander Pope. **CP-PopeA**

Soul, Geologically, A. Margaret Atwood. **SP-AtwM1**

Soul has Bandaged moments, The. Emily Dickinson. **CP-DickE**

Soul has many motions, body one, The. The Motion. Theodore Roethke. **CP-RoetT**

Soul, he said, is composed, The. Anecdote of Men by the Thousand. Wallace Stevens. **CP-StevW**

Soul in Migration. Joseph Ceravolo. **SP-CeraJ**

Soul Is the Salt, The. Robert Herrick. **CP-HerrR**

Soul itself its awful witness is, The. Oriental Maxims. John Greenleaf Whittier. **CP-WhitJ**

Soul Kitchen. Jim Morrison. **SP-MorrJ**

Soul lonely comes and goes; for each our theme. Lachesis. Kathleen Jessie Raine. **SP-RainK**

Soul Longs to Return Whence It Came, The. Richard Eberhart. **CP-EberR**

Soul must go by Death alone, The. Emily Dickinson. **SP-DickE**

Soul, O ganders, flies beyond the parks, The. Invective against Swans. Wallace Stevens. **CP-StevW**

Soul of a Butterfly, The. Nicholas Vachel Lindsay. **CP-LindV**

Soul of a Spider, The. Nicholas Vachel Lindsay. **CP-LindV**

Soul of my soul, in the ancestral wood. Invocation. Stanley Jasspon Kunitz. **CP-KuniS**

Soul of Spain with McAlmon and Bird the Publishers, The. Ernest Hemingway.
"After a while there were no bull fights. What the hell." **CP-HemiE**
"Estocada stuck well stuck. They run round in circles." **CP-HemiE**
"In the rain in the rain in the rain in the rain in Spain." **CP-HemiE**
"There is no night life in Spain. They stay up late but." **CP-HemiE**
"We got on a train and went somewhere else." **CP-HemiE**
"You come to Spain but do not remain. Anna Veronica." **CP-HemiE**

Soul of the City Receives the Gift of the Holy Spirit, The. Nicholas Vachel Lindsay. **CP-LindV**

Soul of Twins, The. Ted Kooser. **SP-KoosT**

Soul rudderless, unbraced. Christina Georgina Rossetti. **CP-RosC3**

Soul selects her own Society, The. Emily Dickinson. **CP-DickE**

Soul should always stand ajar, The. Emily Dickinson. **CP-DickE**

Soul, take thy risk. Emily Dickinson. **CP-DickE**

Soul that hath a Guest, The. Emily Dickinson. **CP-DickE**

Soul That Loves God Finds Him Every Where, The. Jeanne Marie Bouvier de la Motte-Guyon, *tr. fr. French by* William Cowper. **CP-CowpW**

Soul unto itself, The. Emily Dickinson. **CP-DickE**

Soul, Wilt thou toss again? Emily Dickinson. **CP-DickE**

Soul within his pastoral, The. Parable. Alun Lewis. **CP-LewiA**

Soulages's space is deep and wide. The Moderate. John Updike. **CP-UpdiJ**

Soule, The. Robert Herrick. **CP-HerrR**

Soules Ignorance in This Life and Knowledge in the Next, The. John Donne. *See* Poor soul, in this thy flesh what dost thou know?

Souls. Charles Kenneth Williams. **SP-WillC**

Soul's Calm Sunshine, The. Alexander Pope. **FaBoRV** *Fr.* An Essay on Man. **CP-PopeA**

Soul's Desert, The. Robinson Jeffers. **CP-JefR3**

Soul's distinct connection, The. Emily Dickinson. **CP-DickE**

Soul's Expression, The. Elizabeth Barrett Browning. **CP-BroEB**

Souls in virginity joined together. Virgin Mirror. Robert Ranke Graves. **CP-GravR**

Soul's joy, bend not those morning stars from me. Sonnet 48. Sir Philip Sidney. **NoP** *Fr.* Astrophil and Stella. **SP-SidnP**

Soul's joy, when thou art gone. A Parody [or Parodie]. George Herbert. **CP-HerbG**

Souls of Poets dead and gone. Lines on the Mermaid Tavern. John Keats. **CP-KeatJ**

Souls of the day's dead fly up like birds, big sister, The. Composition in Grey and Pink. Charles Wright. **SP-WrigC**

Souls of the Slain, The. Thomas Hardy. **CP-HardT**

Soul's Pentonville, The. Malcolm Lowry. **CP-LowrM**

Soul's Rialto hath its merchandise, The. Sonnet. Elizabeth Barrett Browning. *Fr.* Sonnets from the Portuguese. **CP-BroEB**

Soul's Seas. Archie Randolph Ammons. **SP-AmmoA**

Souls smell in hades. Thomas Merton. *Fr.* The Legacy of Herakleitos. **CP-MertT**

Soul's Superior instants, The. Emily Dickinson. **CP-DickE**

Souls to Save. David Herbert Lawrence. **CP-LawrD**

Soul's Travelling, The. Elizabeth Barrett Browning. **CP-BroEB**

Sound. Robert Creeley. **CP-CreeR**

Sound as if from bells of silver, A. The Pageant. John Greenleaf Whittier. **CP-WhitJ**

Sound forth, cælestiall Organs, lett heavens quire. Upon the Kings Coronation. Richard Crashaw. **CP-CrasR**

Sound in the Night, A. Thomas Hardy. **CP-HardT**

Sound now the trumpet warningly! A Frémont Campaign Song. John Greenleaf Whittier. **CP-WhitJ**

Sound of a Moment at Scariff, The. James Liddy. **CP-LiddJ**

Sound of gongs, the songs of birds, The. Kenneth Rexroth. **CP-RexKL**; **SP-RexrK** *Fr.* The Heart's Garden, the Garden's Heart.

Sound of many running feet, The. In the Railway Hotel at Cordoba. Steve Griffiths. **SP-GrifS**

Sound of music in the house. A House of Music. Kathleen Jessie Raine. **SP-RainK**

Sound of passing cars, (if a car comes), The. Ernesto Cardenal, *tr. by* Thomas Merton. **CP-MertT** *Fr.* Gethsemani, KY.

Sound of screaming for thirteen centuries, A. Muriel Rukeyser. **CP-RukeM**

Sound of Snow, The. Hayden Carruth. **CP-CarHS**

Sound of That Wind, The. Robert Penn Warren. *Fr.* Audubon. **SP-WarrR**

Sound of the closing outside door was all, The. The Valley's Singing Day. Robert Frost. **CP-FrosR**

Sound of Time, The. Charles Tomlinson. **CP-TomlC**

Sound of Trees, The. Robert Frost. **CP-FrosR**

Sound of tumult troubles all the air, A. What of the Day? John Greenleaf Whittier. **CP-WhitJ**

Sound of Waves, The. William Carlos Williams. **CP-WilW2**

Sound of weeping is preferable, The. Solitary Man Discovered in a Field of Daisies. Gilbert Sorrentino. *Fr.* Twelve Études for Voice and Kazoo. **SP-SorrG**

Sound over all waters, reach out from all lands. A Christmas Carmen. John Greenleaf Whittier. **CP-WhitJ**

Sound Sleep. Christina Georgina Rossetti. **CP-RosC1**

Sound slender, quasi tinnula. Canto 20. Ezra Pound. *Fr.* Cantos. **CP-PoCan**

Sound, sound aloud / The welcome of the orient flood. Ben Jonson. **CP-JonsB** *Fr.* The Masque of Blackness.

Sound Teeth has Lucie, pure as Pearl, and small. Upon Lucie. Robert Herrick. **CP-HerrR**

Sound the deep waters. Sleep at Sea. Christina Georgina Rossetti. **CP-RosC1**

Sound the flute! Spring. William Blake. **BoTP; FHYEP; FaBoCh; FaPON; MoShBr; NTP; TTTS** *Fr.* Songs of Innocence. **CP-BlakW**

Sound the invisible trumps. In circuit vast. Break of Morning. Walter de la Mare. **CP-DeLaW**

Sound the trumpet, beat the drum. John Dryden. **FaBoRV** *Fr.* The Secular Masque. **SP-DrydJ**

Sound Track Conditional. Richard Hugo. **CP-HugoR**

Sound was like one made by a board, The. The Event. Robert Penn Warren. **SP-WarrR**

Sounding cataract, The/ Haunted me like a passion. William Wordsworth. **FaBoEn; WGRP** *Fr.* Lines Composed a Few Miles above Tintern Abbey on Revisiting the Banks of the Wye during a Tour, July 13, 1798. **CP-WorW1**

Sounding Chinese at Inspiration Point. Tom Clark. **SP-ClarT**

Soundings, The. Leonard Nathan. **SP-NathL**

Soundless is the Winter Darkness. Alone. Wystan Hugh Auden. **CP-AudWJ**

Soundless the moth-flit, crisp the death-watch tick. Maerchen. Walter de la Mare. **CP-DeLaW**

Sounds. Elizabeth Barrett Browning. **CP-BroEB**

Sounds. Robert Creeley. **CP-CreeR**

Sounds, The. Daniel Gerard Hoffman. **SP-HoffD**

Sounds Like Pearls. Maya Angelou. **SP-AngeM**

Sounds of a Devon Village. Donald Davie. **CP-DavDo**

Sounds of night in the country of the opposites. Muriel Rukeyser. **CP-RukeM**

Sounds of the Winter. Walt Whitman. **CP-WhitW**

Sounds sum and summon the remembering of summer. Summer Remembered. Isabella Gardner. **CP-GardI**

Soup. Robert Creeley. **CP-CreeR**

Soup. Carl Sandburg. **CP-SandC**

Soup, The. Charles Simic. **SP-SimiC**

Soup Jar, The. Dabney Stuart. **SP-StuaD**

Sour Milk. Diane Wakoski. **SP-WakoD**

Sour smell, The. Getting in the Wood. Gary Snyder. **CP-SnydG**

Source. Robert Duncan. **SP-DuncR**

Source, The. George Oppen. **CP-OppeG**

Source, The. William Carlos Williams. **CP-WilW1**

Source of love, and light of day. Self-Diffidence. Jeanne Marie Bouvier de la Motte-Guyon, *tr. fr. French by* William Cowper. **CP-CowpW**

Source of Love, my brighter Sun. Necessity of Self-Abasement. Jeanne Marie Bouvier de la Motte-Guyon, *tr. fr. French by* William Cowper. **CP-CowpW**

Source of the Danube, The. William Wordsworth. *Fr.* Memorials of a Tour of the Continent; 1820. **CP-WorW2**

Sources. Philip Levine. **SP-LeviP**

Sources. Adrienne Rich. **SP-RicA1**

Sourdough mountain called a fire in. The Text. Gary Snyder. **CP-SnydG** *Fr.* Burning. *Fr.* Myths and Texts.

Sours of the Hills. Gary Snyder. **CP-SnydG**

Sours of the Hills. Gary Snyder. **CP-SnydG**

Souterrain, The. John Hewitt. **CP-HewiJ**

South, The. Langston Hughes. **SP-HughL**

South. Louis MacNeice. *Fr.* Sleeping Winds. **CP-MacNL**

South. Thomas Merton. *Fr.* The Geography of Lograire. **CP-MertT**

  Ce Xochitl: The Sign of FLowers.

  Chilam Balam.

  Clever Strategem: Or, How to Handle Mystics, A.

  Dzules.

  Hymns of Lograire.

  Ladies of Tlatilco, The.

  Miami You Are About to Be Surprised.

  Notes for a New Liturgy.

  "Roar of red wood racer eats field. Green breakaway go cars light lanes."

  Two Moralities.

    Hare's Message.

    Thonga Lament.

  "Will a narrow lane / Save Cain?"

South Africa. Rudyard Kipling. **CP-KiplR**

South and far south below the Line. With Drake in the Tropics. Rudyard Kipling. **CP-KiplR**

South Bronx, 1939. Robert Pack. **SP-PackR**

South Coast, The. William Everson. **SP-EverW**

South Italy, Remote and Stone. Richard Hugo. **CP-HugoR**

South-land boasts its teeming cane, The. Our State. John Greenleaf Whittier. **CP-WhitJ**

South Lodge is blue. A Kensington Notebook. Derek Mahon. **SP-MahoD**

South London Sketch, 1844. Sir John Betjeman. **CP-BetjJ**

South London Sketch, 1944. Sir John Betjeman. **CP-BetjJ**

South of Boston, south of Washington. Robert Lowell. **SP-LoweR** *Fr.* Mexico.

South of the Alps. John Updike. **CP-UpdiJ**

South of the Bridge on Seventeenth. Fifteen. William Stafford. **SP-StafW**

South of the Line, inland from far Durban. A Christmas Ghost-Story. Thomas Hardy. **CP-HardT**

South Parks Road. James Fenton. *Fr.* Exempla. **SP-FentJ**

South Sea King was Act-on-Your-Hunch, The. Two Kings and No-Form. Chuang Tzu, *tr. fr. Chinese by* Thomas Merton. **CP-MertT**

South shoulder of the pass, The. Robert Penn Warren. *Fr.* Saul at Gilboa. **SP-WarrR**

South: The Name of Home. Alice Walker. **CP-WalkA**

South-West Wind in the Woodland. George Meredith. **CP-MerG1**

South-Wester, The. George Meredith. **CP-MerG1**

South Wind. Ralph Waldo Emerson. **CP-EmerR**

South Wind. John Haines. **SP-HainJ**

South wind / striking in—torn. Advent of Today. William Carlos Williams. **CP-WilW1**

South-wind brings, The. Threnody. Ralph Waldo Emerson. **CP-EmerR**

South Wind—has a pathos, A. Emily Dickinson. **CP-DickE**

South Wind Says So, The. Carl Sandburg. **CP-SandC**

South Window. Grace Paley. **CP-PaleG**

South Winds jostle them. Emily Dickinson. **CP-DickE**

Southeast Arkanasia. Maya Angelou. **SP-AngeM**

Southeast Corner. Gwendolyn Brooks. **VGW** *Fr.* A Street in Bronzeville. **SP-BrooG**

Southend at Dusk. Alun Lewis. **CP-LewiA**

Southern Cross. Hart Crane. *Fr.* Three Songs. **NAAL-2** *Fr.* The Bridge. **CP-CranH**

Southern Cross, The. Charles Wright. **SP-WrigC**

Southern gentle lady, / Do not swoon. Silhouette. Langston Hughes. **SP-HughL**

Southern Mammy Sings. Langston Hughes. **SP-HughL**

Southern Night. David Herbert Lawrence. **CP-LawrD**

Southern Pacific. Carl Sandburg. **CP-SandC**

Southern Sunrise. Sylvia Plath. **CP-PlatS**

Southey and Wordsworth. Byron. **TrGrPo** *Fr.* Dedication: "Bob Southey! You're a poet--poet-laureate." **CTC; EnRP; OAEL-2; OBSV** *Fr.* Don Juan. **CP-Byron**

Southey! thy melodies steal o'er mine ear. To Robert Southey. Samuel Taylor Coleridge. **CP-ColeS**

Southward floated over. To Florida. Louise Glück. **SP-GlückL**

Southwest of Buffalo. Donald Hall. **CP-HallD**

Southwest of True North. Isabella Gardner. **CP-GardI**

Southwind, tell her what. Basil Bunting. **CP-BuntB**

Souvenir, The. Robert Creeley. **CP-CreeR**

Souvenir. Edna St. Vincent Millay. **CP-MillE**

Souvenir. Edwin Arlington Robinson. **CP-RobiE**

Souvenir de Monsieur Poop. Stevie Smith. **CP-SmitS**

Souvenirs. Jane Cooper. *Fr.* Dispossessions. **SP-CoopJ**

Souvenirs of Democracy, *earlier vers. of* My Legacy. Walt Whitman. **CP-WhitW**

Sovereign of the wilderness! Kenneth Patchen. **CP-PatcK**

Soviet Souvenir. Ted Berrigan. **SP-BerrT**

Sow. Sylvia Plath. **CP-PlatS**

Sowed shut with humus / and scuts of moss. Old Woodsroads. Brendan Galvin. **SP-GalvB**

Sower, The. Wystan Hugh Auden. **CP-AudWJ**

Sower, The. William Cowper. **ChIV-2; SaC** *Fr.* Olney Hymns. **CP-CowpW**

Sowing. Wendell Berry. **CP-BerrW**

Sowing. Audre Lorde. **SP-LordA**

Sowing of Meanings, The. Thomas Merton. **CP-MertT; SP-MertT**

Sowing of the Dead Corn, The. Archibald MacLeish. *Fr.* The Pot of Earth. **CP-MacLA**

Sowing the seed, / my hand is one with the earth. Wendell Berry. **EaPr** *Fr.* Prayers and Sayings of the Mad Farmer. **CP-BerrW**

Sown in dishonor! Emily Dickinson. **CP-DickE**

Soy Sauce. Gary Snyder. **CP-SnydG**

Sozzled, Mo-tsu, after a silence, vouchsafed. Scholars at the Orchid Pavilion. John Berryman. **CP-BerrJ**

Space. David Herbert Lawrence. **CP-LawrD**

Space / window / that looks into itself. Poem. Charles Tomlinson. **CP-TomlC**

Space being(don't forget to remember)Curved. Edward Estlin Cummings. **CP-CummE**

Space Creatures. Charles Bukowski. **SP-BukC3**

Space is ample, east and west. Unity. Ralph Waldo Emerson. **CP-EmerR**

Space mildews at our touch. Moth Hour. Adrienne Rich. **CP-RicAE; SP-RicA2**

Space of the world is immense, before me and around me, The. Song of a Man Who Is Not Loved. David Herbert Lawrence. **CP-LawrD**

Space—shroud and swaddle—you wore. You, Hart Crane. Charles Olson. **CP-OlsoC**

Space Song. Alfonso Cortes, *tr. fr. Spanish by* Thomas Merton. **CP-MertT**

Space-time / Is all there is of space and time. What Eve Sang. Archibald MacLeish. *Fr.* Songs for Eve. **CP-MacLA**

Space-time, our scientists tell us, is impervious. Archibald MacLeish. **ImOP** *Fr.* Reply to Mr. Wordsworth. **CP-MacLA**

Spaceship. Archie Randolph Ammons. **SP-AmmoA**

Spacious firmament on high, The, *par. by* Joseph Addison. Bible, *O.T. See* Psalm 19: "Heavens declare the glory of God, The."

Spade a Spade (Grocery for the Poor), A. Chuck Miller. **SP-MillC**

Spade! with which Wilkinson hath tilled his lands. To the Spade of a Friend (An Agriculturist). William Wordsworth. **CP-WorW1**

Spades take up leaves. Gathering Leaves. Robert Frost. **CP-FrosR**

Spaewife, The. Robert Louis Stevenson. **CP-StevR**

Spaghetti. Shel Silverstein. **SP-SilS2**

Spain, 1873–74. Walt Whitman. **CP-WhitW**

Spain frightened you. Spain. You Hated Spain. Ted Hughes. **SP-HughT**

Spain Sits Like a Hidden Flower in My Coffeepot. Charles Bukowski. **SP-BukC2**

Spake the fire-tinged bramble, bossed with gleaming fruit. Thus Her Tale. Walter de la Mare. **CP-DeLaW**

Span of Life, The. Robert Frost. **GDP; HoPM; LiTM; SoSe** *Fr.* Ten Mills. **CP-FrosR**

Spangled, mauve, The. Touching. Archie Randolph Ammons. **SP-AmmoA**

Spaniel, Beau, that fares like you, A. On a Spaniel Called Beau Killing a Young Bird. William Cowper. **CP-CowpW**

Spaniel flies with his ears, The. Hayden Carruth. *Fr.* North Winter. **CP-CarHL**

Spanish. Carl Sandburg. **CP-SandC**

Spanish Friar [*or* Fryar], The. John Dryden.

  "Farewell ungrateful[l] traitor [*or* traytor], / Farewell my perjured swain." **SP-DrydJ**

  (Song: "Farewell ungrateful[l] traitor [*or* traytor].") **SP-DrydJ**

  Prologue to *The Spanish Friar.* **SP-DrydJ**

Spanish Guerillas 1811. William Wordsworth. **CP-WorW1**

Spanish Harlem Incident. "Bob Dylan." **CP-DylaB**

Spanish Lady, The. Walt Whitman. **CP-WhitW**

Spanish Lie, The. Archibald MacLeish. **CP-MacLA**

Spanish Privilege. David Herbert Lawrence. **CP-LawrD**

Spanish Providence, A. Steve Griffiths. **SP-GrifS**

Spanish School. Stevie Smith. **CP-SmitS**

Spanish Sonnets. John Updike. **CP-UpdiJ**

  "All crises pass, though not the condition of crisis."

  "By the light of insomnia, truths."

  "Each day's tour, I gather sandy castles."

  "He omits, Goya, not even the good news."

  "Land is dry enough to make the rivers, The."

  "*Neumático punturado*—we stopped."

  "These islands of history amid traffic snarls."

  "Yes, self-obsession fills our daily clothes."

Spanish Wife, The. David Herbert Lawrence. **CP-LawrD**

Spare me, dread angel of reproof. The Answer. John Greenleaf Whittier. **CP-WhitJ**

Spare me thy vengeance, G———. To the Same, on the Author Being Threatened with His Resentment. Robert Burns. *Fr.* Epigrams on Lord Galloway. **CP-BurnR**

Spare then the person, and expose the vice. Alexander Pope. **OBSV** *Fr.* Epilogue to the Satires, in Two Dialogues. **CP-PopeA**

Spare thou neither inner nor blood for thy friend. Hafiz, *tr. by* Ralph Waldo Emerson. **CP-EmerR** *Fr.* Odes.

Spark, The. Walter de la Mare. **CP-DeLaW**

Spark, The. Louise McNeill. **SP-McNeL**

Spark in the Tinder of Knowing, The. Kenneth Rexroth. **CP-RexKL**

Spark of Godhead! child. The Soul. George Meredith. **CP-MerG2**

Spark of Laurel, A. Stanley Jasspon Kunitz. **CP-KuniS**

Spark Poetry. Malcolm Lowry. **CP-LowrM**

Sparkle sparkle, little verse. Fourth Epistle. Donald Davie. *Fr.* Six Epistles to Eva Hesse. **CP-DavDo**

Sparkles from the Wheel. Walt Whitman. **CP-WhitW**

Sparkling eye, the mantling cheek, The. Song, A. William Cowper. **CP-CowpW**

Sparks. Charles Bukowski. **SP-BukC3**

Sparks. Denise Levertov. **CP-LeveD**

Sparks. James Schuyler. **CP-SchuJ**

Sparky air, The. Gerard Manley Hopkins. *Fr.* Fragments. **CP-HopkG**

Sparrow. Wendell Berry. **CP-BerrW**

Sparrow, The. Bible, *O.T.* **FaPON** *Fr.* Psalm 84: "How amiable are thy tabernacles, O Lord of hosts!" **CP-MiltJ; TRV; TrPWD** *Fr.* Psalms. **CP-Psal**

Sparrow, The. Bible, *O.T. See* Psalm 84: "How amiable are thy tabernacles. . . ."

Sparrow, The. Paul Laurence Dunbar. **CP-DunbP**

Sparrow, The. Thom Gunn. **CP-GunnT** *Fr.* Three Songs.

Sparrow, The. William Carlos Williams. **CP-WilW2**

Sparrow and the Robin on a toot, The. The Tiger on Parade. Nicholas Vachel Lindsay. **CP-LindV**

Sparrow dips in his wheel-rut bath, The. The Five Students. Thomas Hardy. **CP-HardT**

Sparrow hath found an house, The. The Sparrow. Bible, *O.T.* **FaPON** *Fr.* Psalm 84: "How amiable are thy tabernacles, O Lord of hosts!" **CP-MiltJ; TRV; TrPWD** *Fr.* Psalms. **CP-Psal**

Sparrow in the cobbled street. Stranger's Child. George Oppen. **CP-OppeG**

Sparrow in the Zoo, The. Howard Nemerov. *See* Political Reflexion [*or* Reflection].

Sparrow is / his hunger organized, A. Sparrow. Wendell Berry. **CP-BerrW**

Sparrow is rich in her nest, The. Ralph Waldo Emerson. **CP-EmerR**

Sparrow, my girl's pleasure, delight of my girl. Catullus. *See* Carmen 2: "Lesbia's sparrow! / Lesbia's plaything!"

Sparrow took a Slice of Twig, A. Emily Dickinson. **CP-DickE**

Sparrowhawk / flies hard to, The. Anxiety. Archie Randolph Ammons. **SP-AmmoA**

Sparrowhawk. John Hewitt. **CP-HewiJ**

Sparrows. Hayden Carruth. **CP-CarHS**

Sparrows among Dry Leaves. William Carlos Williams. **CP-WilW2**

Sparrows by the iron fence post, The. Sparrows among Dry Leaves. William Carlos Williams. **CP-WilW2**

Sparrows in a Hillside Drift. James Wright. **CP-WrigJ**

Sparrow's Nest, The. William Wordsworth. **CP-WorW1**

Sparrows quarreled outside our window. Waking an Angel. Philip Levine. **SP-LeviP**

Sparrows Self-Domesticated. Vincent Bourne, *tr. fr. Latin by* William Cowper. **CP-CowpW**

Spartan, his companion slain, A. From Julianus. Emperor Julian, *tr. fr. Greek by* William Cowper. **CP-CowpW**

Spartan 'scaping from the fight, A. By Palladas. Palladas, *tr. fr. Greek by* William Cowper. **CP-CowpW**

Spattering of the rain upon pale terraces, The. John Gould Fletcher. **SP-FletJ** *Fr.* Irradiations.

Spaulding and Francois. Gwendolyn Brooks. *Fr.* A Catch of Shy Fish. **SP-BrooG**

Speak. James Wright. **CP-WrigJ**

Speak—Alice / speak. Alice Miriam. Marsden Hartley. **CP-HartM**

Speak and tell us, our Ximena, looking northward far away. The Angels of Buena Vista. John Greenleaf Whittier. **CP-WhitJ**

Speak, did the Bloud of Abel cry. Abels Bloud. Robert Herrick. **CP-HerrR**

Speak earth and bless me with what is richest. Love Poem. Audre Lorde. **SP-LordA**

Speak gently to your husband, ma'am. A Warning to Wives. Ogden Nash. **CP-NashO**

Speak, God of visions, plead for me. Requiem for a Non-Croppy. James Liddy. **CP-LiddJ**

Speak, Gracious Lord, oh speak; thy Servant hears. A Paraphrase on Thomas à Kempis. Alexander Pope. **CP-PopeA**

Speak low to me, my Saviour, low and sweet. Comfort. Elizabeth Barrett Browning. **CP-BroEB**

Speak, Memory! Mona Van Duyn. **SP-VanDM**

Speak not—whisper not. The Sunken Garden. Walter de la Mare. **CP-DeLaW**

Speak Now for Peace. Nicholas Vachel Lindsay. *Fr.* To Jane Addams at the Hague. **CP-LindV**

Speak peace and toleration. Moderate. Memorandum for the Moderates. John Hewitt. **CP-HewiJ**

Speak roughly to your little boy. "Lewis Carroll." **CP-CarrL** *Fr.* Alice's Adventures in Wonderland.
(Duchess's Lullaby, The.) **CP-CarrL**

Speak, sir, and be wise. Basket. Carl Sandburg. **CP-SandC**

Speak softly; sun going down. Fall of the Evening Star. Kenneth Patchen. **CP-PatcK**

Speak! speak! thou fearful guest! The Skeleton in Armor [*or* Armour]. Henry Wadsworth Longfellow. **SP-LongH**

Speak thou and speed, where will or power ought [*or* aught] help'th. Sir Thomas Wyatt. **CP-WyatT**

Speak Thou for me against wrong-speaking foes. Bible, *O.T. See* Psalm 35: "Plead my cause, O Lord, with them that strive with me."

Speak to me friend! Or is the world so wide. W.H.W., Jr. Edward Estlin Cummings. **CP-CummE**

Speak to me. Take my hand. What are you now? Effort at Speech between Two People. Muriel Rukeyser. **CP-RukeM**

Speak! yellow men who grub for gold. Josepha. George Meredith. **CP-MerG2**

Speake in Season. Robert Herrick. **CP-HerrR**

Speaker and hearer, words. The Conversation. Wendell Berry. *Fr.* The Handing Down. **CP-BerrW**

Speaker in this case, The. The Gold Key. Anne Sexton. **CP-SextA**

Speakers from the Vietnam War. Dabney Stuart. **SP-StuaD**

Speakin' at de Cou't-House. Paul Laurence Dunbar. **CP-DunbP**

Speakin' in general, I 'ave tried 'em all. Sestina of the Tramp-Royal. Rudyard Kipling. **CP-KiplR**

Speakin' o' Christmas. Paul Laurence Dunbar. **CP-DunbP**

Speaking Bitterness. Anne Sexton. **CP-SextA**

Speaking for Them. Hayden Carruth. **CP-CarHS**

Speaking mouth's a hearse of wasted days, The. Leaflet (One). Kenneth Patchen. **CP-PatcK**

Speaking of death / and decay. Exercises on Themes from Life. Alice Walker. **CP-WalkA**

Speaking of love(of). Edward Estlin Cummings. **CP-CummE**

Speaking Tree, The. Muriel Rukeyser. **CP-RukeM**

Spearing, The. Laurence Lieberman. **SP-LiebL**

Spearmint. Louis Zukofsky. **CP-ZukLS**

Special continuations: the Gethsemani racetrack. Thomas Merton. **CP-MertT**

Special Effects. Charles Henri Ford. **SP-FordC**

Special Starlight. Carl Sandburg. **CP-SandC**

Special Train, A. Daniel Gerard Hoffman. **SP-HoffD**

Species of common garden cat, who are. The Lady of Shalott, Her Mirror Broken. William Dickey. **SP-DickW**

Species of thistle no one had ever seen before appeared almost overnight in all the meadows, A. Drought. Charles Kenneth Williams. **SP-WillC**

Specific light, / water, ground. Wanting You. Robert Creeley. **CP-CreeR**

Specifically, a writer of music. Louis Zukofsky. *Fr.* 29 Songs. **CP-ZukLS**

Specifications for a Perfect Lover. Richard Crashaw. **CBCK** *Fr.* Wishes. To His (Supposed) Mistresse. **CP-CrasR**

Specimen of an Induction to a Poem. John Keats. **CP-KeatJ**

Speck that would have been beneath my sight, A. A Considerable Speck. Robert Frost. **CP-FrosR**

Speckled cat and a tame hare, A. Two Songs of a Fool. William Butler Yeats. **CP-YeatW**

Speckled frogs leap from my mouth. Fantasy and Conversation. Audre Lorde. **SP-LordA**

Spectacle of the New York Yacht Club, The. Sailing to Buck's Harbor. Richard Eberhart. **CP-EberR**

Spectacle of Truth, The. John Hewitt. **CP-HewiJ**

Spectral Horseman, The. Percy Bysshe Shelley. *Fr.* Posthumous Fragments of Margaret Nicholson. **CP-ShelP**

Spectral Lovers. John Crowe Ransom. **SP-RansJ**

Spectre, The. Walter de la Mare. **CP-DeLaW**

Spectres That Grieve. Thomas Hardy. **CP-HardT**

Speculate with all our might. Emily Dickinson. **SP-DickE**

Speculation. Howard Nemerov. **CP-NemeH**

Speculative. Robert Browning. **CP-BroR2**

Sped by the British Council. The Test. John Hewitt. **CP-HewiJ**

Speech. Wystan Hugh Auden. **CP-AudWJ**

Speech. Walter de la Mare. **CP-DeLaW**

Speech. Carl Sandburg. **CP-SandC**

Speech According to Horace, A. Ben Jonson. **CP-JonsB**

Speech after long silence; it is right. *fr.* Words for Music Perhaps. William Butler Yeats. **CP-YeatW**

Speech at Soli, The. George Oppen. **CP-OppeG**

Speech for the Assistant, from Houdini. Muriel Rukeyser. **CP-RukeM**

Speech for the Repeal of the McCarran Act. Richard Wilbur. **CP-WilbR**

"Speech"—is a prank of Parliament. Emily Dickinson. **CP-DickE**

Speech is one symptom of Affection. Emily Dickinson. **CP-DickE**

Speech of the Mother, from "The Middle of the Air." Muriel Rukeyser. **CP-RukeM**

Speech out of Lucan, A. Lucan. *See* Just and fit actions, Ptolemy (he saith).

Speech Out of Shadow. Ted Hughes. **SP-HughT**

Speech Presented unto King James at a Tilting in the Behalf of the Two Noble Brothers S[ir] Robert and S[ir] Henry Rich, Now Earls of Warwick and Holland, A. Ben Jonson. **CP-JonsB**

Speech to a Crowd. Archibald MacLeish. **CP-MacLA**

Speech to the Detractors. Archibald MacLeish. **CP-MacLA**

Speech to Those Who Say Comrade. Archibald MacLeish. **CP-MacLA**

Speeches. Donald Hall. **CP-HallD**

Speeches for Dr Frankenstein. Margaret Atwood. **SP-AtwM1**

Speechless statue of the Virgin stands, The. The Adoration of the Virgin. Robert Duncan. **SP-DuncR**

Speed, Malise, speed! the lake is past. The Fiery Cross. Sir Walter Scott. **SP-ScotW** *Fr.* The Lady of the Lake.

Speed of Darkness, The. Muriel Rukeyser. **CP-RukeM**

Speed, We Say. Muriel Rukeyser. **CP-RukeM**

Speed, we say of our time: racing my writing word. Speed, We Say. Muriel Rukeyser. **CP-RukeM**

Speeding from city, feeling day. Driveway. Muriel Rukeyser. **CP-RukeM**

Speeds down the freeway. The Age of Progress. Richard Shelton. *Fr.* The Seven Ages of Man. **SP-ShelR**

Spel Against Demons. Gary Snyder. **CP-SnydG**

Spell, The. Robert Herrick. **CP-HerrR**

Spell. Dabney Stuart. **SP-StuaD**

Spell Against Sorrow. Kathleen Jessie Raine. **SP-RainK**

Spell before Winter, A. Howard Nemerov. **CP-NemeH**

Spell cannot be tattered, A. Emily Dickinson. **SP-DickE**

Spell Eva back[e] and Ave shall you [*or* yowe] find[e]. Our Lady's [*or* Ladie's] Salutation. Robert Southwell. **CP-SoutR**

Spell Is Broke, the Charm is Flown, The. Byron. **CP-Byron**

Spell of Conjunctivitis, A. Mona Van Duyn. **SP-VanDM**

Spell of Sleep. Kathleen Jessie Raine. **SP-RainK**

Spell of the Rose, The. Thomas Hardy. **CP-HardT**

Spell to Bring Lost Creatures Home. Kathleen Jessie Raine. **SP-RainK**

Spellbound Palace, A. Thomas Hardy. **CP-HardT**

Spellin'-Bee, The. Paul Laurence Dunbar. **CP-DunbP**

Spelling book, can you love me. Pablo Neruda. *tr. fr. Spanish by* Ben Belitt. **SP-NeruP** *Fr.* Question Book.

Spells and Incantation (a Fragment). Wilfred Owen. **CP-OwenW**

Spelt from Sibyl's Leaves. Gerard Manley Hopkins. **CP-HopkG**

Spend Harmless shade thy nightly Houres. Upon a Virgin. Robert Herrick. **CP-HerrR**

Spend the years of learning squandering. Gnome. Samuel Beckett. **CP-BeckS**

Spending beyond their income on gifts for Christmas. Christmas Shopping. Louis MacNeice. **CP-MacNL**

Spending hand that alway poureth [*or* powreth] out [*or* owte], A. Sir Thomas Wyatt. **CP-WyatT** *Fr.* Satires.

Spendthrift. Isabella Gardner. **CP-GardI**

Spendthrift Urethra—Sphincter, frugal one—. John Berryman. *Fr.* Sonnets to Chris. **CP-BerrJ**

Spenke has a strong breath, yet short Prayers saith. Upon Spenke. Robert Herrick. **CP-HerrR**

Spenser! A Jealous Honourer of Thine. John Keats. **CP-KeatJ**

Spenser has Britomart on guard in the enchanter's house. A Last Attachment. Frank Templeton Prince. **CP-PrinF**

Spenser's Ireland. Marianne Craig Moore. **CP-MoorM**

Spent purpose of a perfectly marvellous, The. In Favor of One's Time. Frank O'Hara. **SP-OharF**

Spermologies fallen on stony ground. Stone of relentlessness, stone of crime. Louis MacNeice. *Fr.* Areopagus. **CP-MacNL**

Sphere, The. Kathleen Jessie Raine. **SP-RainK**

Sphere, which is as many thousand spheres, A. Percy Bysshe Shelley. **ImOP** *Fr.* Prometheus Unbound. **CP-ShelP**

Sphinx, The. Wystan Hugh Auden. *Fr.* A Voyage. **CP-AudeW**

Sphinx. Richard Eberhart. **CP-EberR**

Sphinx, The. Ralph Waldo Emerson. **CP-EmerR**

Sphinx. Robert Earl Hayden. **CP-HaydR**

Sphinx. David Herbert Lawrence. **CP-LawrD**

Sphinx, A. Carl Sandburg. **CP-SandC**

Sphinx's Riddle to Oedipus, The. Randall Jarrell. **CP-JarrR**

Spice-Tree, The. Nicholas Vachel Lindsay. **CP-LindV**

Spices in the plants that run. Ralph Waldo Emerson. **CP-EmerR**

Spider, The. Charles Bukowski. **SP-BukC1**

Spider, The. Richard Eberhart. **CP-EberR**

Spider. Sylvia Plath. **CP-PlatS**

Spider, The. Robert Penn Warren. **SP-WarrR**

Spider and the Ghost of the Fly, The. Nicholas Vachel Lindsay. **CP-LindV**

Spider as an Artist, The. Emily Dickinson. **CP-DickE**

Spider, dashing from, The. Planet Actions. Archie Randolph Ammons. **SP-AmmoA**

Spider expects the cold of winter, The. The Spider. Richard Eberhart. **CP-EberR**

Spider holds a Silver Ball, The. Emily Dickinson. **CP-DickE**

Spider Mums, The. Karl Shapiro. **SP-ShapK**

Spider mums are yellow, The. The Spider Mums. Karl Shapiro. **SP-ShapK**

Spider or Ribbon Plant. Louis Zukofsky. **CP-ZukLS**

Spider pendulously waits, The. Breaking Webs. Louis MacNeice. **CP-MacNL**

Spider Psyche. Charles Kenneth Williams. **SP-WillC**

Spider sewed at Night, A. Emily Dickinson. **CP-DickE**

Spider, spider, twisting tight. Louis MacNeice. *Fr.* Autumn Journal. **CP-MacNL**

Spider spreads her webs, whether she be, The. Letter to Maria Gisborne. Percy Bysshe Shelley. **CP-ShelP**

Spider, you have long silver legs. Sun Dancer. Carl Sandburg. **CP-SandC**

Spiders. Delmore Schwartz. **SP-SchwD**

Spiderweb. Malcolm Lowry. **CP-LowrM**

Spiel of [the] Three Mountebanks. John Crowe Ransom. **SP-RansJ**

Spies' March, The. Rudyard Kipling. **CP-KiplR**

Spies, you are lights in state, but of base stuff. On Spies. Ben Jonson. **CP-JonsB**

Spiked sun. The Hudson's. Early December in Croton-on-Hudson. Louise Glück. **SP-GlücL**

Spikehorn. William Everson. **SP-EverW**

Spikes of new smell driven up nostrils. Gary Snyder. **CP-SnydG** *Fr.* Burning. *Fr.* Myths and Texts.

Spilling the Salt. David Herbert Lawrence. **CP-LawrD**

Spilt Milk. William Butler Yeats. **CP-YeatW**

Spin, Spell, Spill. John Yau. **SP-YauJo**

Spin the ball! I reel, I burn. Song of Seyd [or Seid] Nimetollah of Kuhistan. Seid Nimatullah, *tr. fr. Persian by* Ralph Waldo Emerson. **CP-EmerR**

Spindle Song, The. Sir Walter Scott. **SP-ScotW**

Spindrift. Galway Kinnell. **SP-KinnG**

Spine hog, / how do you grow? Porcupine. Anne Sexton. **CP-SextA**

Spinney's sparse and thinner now, The. The Path Ahead. John Hewitt. **CP-HewiJ**

Spinning Heart, The. John Berryman. **CP-BerrJ**

Spinning hymns downstream is fun. The worm spins. Bad Eyes Spinning the Rock. Richard Hugo. **CP-HugoR**

Spinning on his heel, the traveller. A Flashing Cliff. Muriel Rukeyser. **CP-RukeM**

Spinning the Sava. Richard Hugo. **CP-HugoR**

Spinning upon their central thirst like tops. Wystan Hugh Auden. *Fr.* The Quest. **CP-AudeW**

Spinning-Wheel, The. Henry Wadsworth Longfellow. *Fr.* The Courtship of Miles Standish. **SP-LongH**

"Month after month passed away, and in autumn the ships of the merchants." **TreFS**

Spinster. Sylvia Plath. **CP-PlatS**

Spinsters. Marsden Hartley. **CP-HartM**

Spiral Flame. David Herbert Lawrence. **CP-LawrD**

Spiral of green hay on the end of a rake, A. Last before America. Louis MacNeice. **CP-MacNL**

Spiral Shell, A. Howard Nemerov. *Fr.* Epigrams: "Wasp, climbing the window pane." **CP-NemeH**

Spirals and Fugues. Muriel Rukeyser. **CP-RukeM**

Spire Cranes, The. Dylan Thomas. **CP-ThomD**

Spirea. Louis Zukofsky. **CP-ZukLS**

Spirit / let there be even in the last hour. Hayden Carruth. *Fr.* The Sleeping Beauty. **CP-CarHL**

Spirit. Leonard Nathan. **SP-NathL**

Spirit / whatever you are wherever. Hayden Carruth. *Fr.* The Sleeping Beauty. **CP-CarHL**

Spirit and nature beat in one breast-bone—. The Sententious Man. Theodore Roethke. **CP-RoetT**

Spirit blows from the home cliff with gulls, The. Hunger. Malcolm Lowry. **CP-LowrM**

Spirit breathes upon the word, The. The Light and Glory of the World. William Cowper. *Fr.* Olney Hymns. **CP-CowpW**

Spirit colossal / (& daunted by always). Edward Estlin Cummings. **CP-CummE**

Spirit cried Go up higher, The. Extremity. Richard Eberhart. **CP-EberR**

Spirit Epiloguizes, The. John Milton. *See* To the ocean now I fly.

Spirit from Perfecter Ages. Arthur Hugh Clough. *See* Is it illusion? or does there a spirit from perfecter ages.

Spirit has an impregnable tower, The. The Tower of the Spirit. Chuang Tzu, *tr. fr. Chinese by* Thomas Merton. **CP-MertT**

Spirit has infinite facets, but the body, The. Tossing and Turning. John Updike. **CP-UpdiJ**

Spirit haunts the year's last hours, A. Tennyson. **CP-TennA**

(Song: "Spirit haunts the last year's hours, A.") **CP-TennA**

Spirit here that reignest! Song. John Keats. **CP-KeatJ**

Spirit Ink, The. Frank O'Hara. **SP-OharF**

Spirit is the Conscious Ear, The. Emily Dickinson. **CP-DickE**

Spirit lasts, but in what mode, The. Emily Dickinson. **CP-DickE**

Spirit Medium, The. William Butler Yeats. **CP-YeatW**

Spirit moves, The. A Light Breather. Theodore Roethke. **CP-RoetT**

Spirit of Air, The. Walter de la Mare. **CP-DeLaW**

Spirit of Antiquity—enshrined, The. Bruges. William Wordsworth. *Fr.* Memorials of a Tour of the Continent; 1820. **CP-WorW2**

Spirit of Noplace, The. Kenneth Patchen. **CP-PatcK**

Spirit of Place, The. Adrienne Rich. **SP-RicA2**

"Mountain laurel in bloom, The."

"Orion plunges like a drunken hunter." **SP-RicA1**

"Over the hills in Shutesbury, Leverett."

"River-fog will do for privacy, The."

"Strangers are an endangered species."

Spirit of Plato. *Unknown, tr. fr. Greek by* Shelley. **CP-ShelP**

Spirit of quickness reading *slipperwort*. Slipperwort. Louis Zukofsky. **CP-ZukLS**

Spirit of romance dies not to those, The. Pictures of the Rhine. George Meredith. **CP-MerG1**

Spirit of Russia, now has come. The Crisis. George Meredith. **CP-MerG2**

Spirit of '76. William Carlos Williams. **CP-WilW1**

Spirit of Shakespeare, The. George Meredith. **CP-MerG1**

Spirit of Shakespeare: Continued, The. George Meredith. **CP-MerG1**

Spirit of the Crusades. Lawrence Ferlinghetti. **SP-FerlL**

Spirit of the frozen North. The Spirit of the North. John Greenleaf Whittier. **CP-WhitJ**

Spirit of the North, The. John Greenleaf Whittier. **CP-WhitJ**

Spirit Pass'd Before Me, A. Byron. **CP-Byron**

Spirit seems to pass, A. Lausanne: In Gibbon's Old Garden: 11–12 p.m. Thomas Hardy. **CP-HardT**

Spirit That Form'd This Scene. Walt Whitman. **CP-WhitW**

Spirit the Triumph, The. Charles Kenneth Williams. **CP-WillC; SP-WillC**

Spirit who sweepest the wild Harp of Time! Ode on the Departing Year. Samuel Taylor Coleridge. **CP-ColeS**

Spirit Whose Work Is Done. Walt Whitman. **CP-WhitW**

Spirit Wooed, The. Philip Larkin. **CP-LarkP**

Spirited people make a thousand jewels in verse and prose, and the restlessness of talent. Vices. Robinson Jeffers. **CP-JefR1**

Spirits and illusions have died. Life from the Lifeless. Robinson Jeffers. **CP-JefR2**

Spirits Are Organized Men. Marsden Hartley. *Fr.* Un Recuerdo—Hermano—Hart Crane R.I.P. **CP-HartM**

Spirit's Epilogue, The. John Milton. *See* To the ocean now I fly.

Spirits of the abnormally born. October. Audre Lorde. **SP-LordA**

Spirits of the Dead. Edgar Allan Poe. **CP-PoeEd**

Spirits of the wise, sit on the clouds, The. Ralph Waldo Emerson. **CP-EmerR**

Spirits of well-shot woodcock, partridge, snipe. Sir John Betjeman. **CP-BetjJ**

(Death of King George V.) **CP-BetjJ**

Spirit's Song. Louise Bogan. **CP-BogaL**

Spirits Summoned West. David Herbert Lawrence. **CP-LawrD**

Spiritual. Tom Clark. **SP-ClarT**

Spiritual, A. Paul Laurence Dunbar. **CP-DunbP**

Spiritual Chickens. Stephen Dobyns. **SP-DobyS**

Spiritual Explorations. Stephen Spender. **CP-SpenS**

Spiritual Laws. Ralph Waldo Emerson. **CP-EmerR**

Spiritual Life. William Matthews. **SP-MattW**

Spiritual Manifestation, A. John Greenleaf Whittier. **CP-WhitJ**

Spiritual Woman, A, *diff. vers.* David Herbert Lawrence. *See* These Clever Women.

Spirituals. Langston Hughes. **SP-HughL**

Spit. Charles Kenneth Williams. **CP-WillC; SP-WillC**

Spit in my face ye [*or* you] Jew[e]s, and pierce my side. John Donne. **JCP; OBS; OxBoCh; Son; TOF** *Fr.* Divine Meditations. **CP-DonnJ** *Fr.* Holy Sonnets. **CP-DonnJ**

Spite. Stephen Dobyns. **SP-DobyS**

Spite Fence. Richard Eberhart. **CP-EberR**

Spite hath no power to make me sad. Sir Thomas Wyatt. **CP-WyatT**

Spite of Dutch friends and English foes. Peace and Dunkirk. Jonathan Swift. **CP-SwifJ**

Spite of Mirrors. Robert Ranke Graves. **CP-GravR**

Spite of their spite which they in vain. Sir Thomas Wyatt. **CP-WyatT**

Splash! Ogden Nash. **CP-NashO**

Spleen. Stephen Dobyns. **SP-DobyS**

Spleen. Frank O'Hara. **SP-OharF**

Splendid Dawn, The. John Hewitt. **CP-HewiJ**

Splendidly-shining darkness. Geoffrey Hill. **HAP** *Fr.* The Pentecost Castle. **CP-HillG**

Splendor falls on castle walls, The. Tennyson. **AWP; BLPL; CH; ChTr; ClHu; CoGr; EBEvV; EBVV; ELP; FHYEP; FaBV; FaBoCh; FaBoPP; FaFP; FaPON; FiP; GN; GoJo; HeIL; HeIP; ImPo; InPK; LiTB; MeMBP; NAEL-2; NOBE; NoP; OAEL-2; OBEV; OBNC; PeVV; PoEL-5; PrIm; TFi; TrGrPo; UnPo; UnS; WSC; WiR** *Fr.* The Princess. **CP-TennA**

(Blow, Bugle, Blow.) **BLPL; ChTr; FaFP; ImPo; LiTB; NOBE; OBEV; UnPo; UnS; WiR**

(Bugle Song.) **FaPON; GN**

(He Hears the Bugle at Killarney.) **FaBoPP**

(Splendor Falls, The.) **CoGr; TFi**

Splendor of ended day floating and filling me. Song at Sunset. Walt Whitman. **CP-WhitW**

Splendor Paternae Gloriae. Saint Ambrose, *tr. fr. Latin by* Thomas Merton. **CP-MertT**

Splendour Falls, The. Tennyson. *See* The Splendor falls on castle walls.

Splendour! O more than mortal. Ode Enthusiastic. Ben Jonson. **CP-JonsB**

Splendour of life so splendidly contained. The Masque of Blackness. Geoffrey Hill. **NoAM** *Fr.* Lachrimae; or Seven Tears Figured in Seven Passionate Pavans. **CP-HillG**

Splendour of the kindling day, The. Fluttered Wings. Christina Georgina Rossetti. **CP-RosC2**

Splendour's fondly-fostered child! Ode to Georgiana, Duchess of Devonshire. Samuel Taylor Coleridge. **CP-ColeS**

Splinter. Carl Sandburg. **CP-SandC**

Splinter, flicked, A. New Moon in January. Ted Hughes. **SP-HughT**

Splinters under the nails, weals on the buttocks. Louis MacNeice. *Fr.* Notes for a Biography. **CP-MacNL**

Split-cedar / smoked salmon, The. The Way West, Underground. Gary Snyder. **CP-SnydG**

Split: 1962. Stephen Dunn. **SP-DunnS**

Split the Lark—and you'll find the Music. Emily Dickinson. **CP-DickE**

Splitting a bottle of white wine. Pale Bliss. John Updike. **CP-UpdiJ**

Splitting from Jack Delany's, Sheridan Square. God Rest Ye Merry, Gentlemen. Derek Walcott. **CP-WalcD**

Splittings. Adrienne Rich. **SP-RicA1; SP-RicA2**

Spoiler's Return, The. Derek Walcott. **CP-WalcD**

Spoiling daylight inched along the bar-top, The. The Mill. Richard Wilbur. **CP-WilbR**

Spoils, The. Basil Bunting. **CP-BuntB**

"All things only of earth and water."

"Man's life so little worth."

"They filled the eyes of the vaulting."

Spoils. Robert Ranke Graves. **CP-GravR**

Spoils of Youth, The. Robert Browning. **CBCK** *Fr.* A Likeness. **CP-BroR1**

Spokane Perspective. James McAuley. **SP-McAuJ**

Spoke joe to jack. Edward Estlin Cummings. **CP-CummE; SP-CummE**

Spokes when he sees a rosted Pig, he swears. Upon Spokes. Robert Herrick. **CP-HerrR**

Sponge Full of Vinegar, The. Thomas Merton. **CP-MertT**

Sponsors. William Wordsworth. *Fr.* Ecclesiastical Sonnets. **CP-WorW2**

Spontaneous Me. Walt Whitman. **CP-WhitW**

Spontaneous overflows of powerful feeling. Barren Leaves. Thom Gunn. **CP-GunnT**

Spook's Sabbath, Five Bowings. Louis Zukofsky. **CP-ZukLS**

Spooky summer on the horizon I'm gazing at. Revolution. Anne Waldman. **SP-WaldA**

Spoon. Charles Simic. **SP-SimiC**

Spoonbait, The. Seamus Heaney. **SP-HeanS**

Spoons with Realistic Dead Flies on Them. Charles Simic. **SP-SimiC**

Sport of Kings, The. Ernest Hemingway. **CP-HemiE**

Sporting people, The. Free Fantasia: Tiger Flowers. Robert Earl Hayden. **CP-HaydR**

Sports and gallantries, the stage, the arts, the antics of dancers. Boats in a Fog. Robinson Jeffers. **CP-JefR1**

Sports Page. Louis MacNeice. **CP-MacNL**

Sports without Blood—a Letter to Dylan Thomas (1948). Thomas Merton. **CP-MertT**

Sporus. Alexander Pope. *See* Let Sporus tremble--"What? That thing of silk."

Sposa velata, / Innanellata. Christina Georgina Rossetti. **CP-RosC3**

Spot, A. Thomas Hardy. **CP-HardT**

Spot of my youth! whose hoary branches sigh. Lines Written beneath an Elm in the Churchyard of Harrow. Byron. **CP-Byron**

Spot of poontang on a five-foot piece, A. John Berryman. *Fr.* Sonnets to Chris. **CP-BerrJ**

Spotfire. William Everson. **SP-EverW**

Spotlight her face her face has no light in it. Movie. Muriel Rukeyser. **CP-RukeM**

Spots of Time. William Wordsworth. *See* There are in our existence spots of time.

Spotted fawn / Awoke in small leaf-netted suns, The. The First Day. Phoebe Hesketh. **SP-HeskP**

Spotted hawk swoops by and accuses me, The. Walt Whitman. **NoP; SAmP** *Fr.* Song of Myself. **CP-WhitW**

Spotting the moonlight at my bedside. Li Po, *tr. fr. Chinese by* William Carlos Williams *with* David Rafael Wang. **CP-WilW2**

Spouse, The. Gilbert Sorrentino. **SP-SorrG**

Spouse! Sister! Angel! Pilot of the Fate. Percy Bysshe Shelley. **CBLP; ChER** *Fr.* Epipsychidion. **CP-ShelP**

Spouts. William Carlos Williams. **CP-WilW1**

S.P.Q.R. A Letter from Rome. John Ciardi. **SP-CiarJ**

Sprawled / on our faces in the spring. The Hen Flower. Galway Kinnell. **SP-KinnG**

Sprawled, / on the bottom. To the She-Bear: *The 1st Song.* Charles Olson. **CP-OlsoC**

Sprawled in the pigsty. For a Young Artist. Robert Earl Hayden. **CP-HaydR**

Spray. David Herbert Lawrence. **CP-LawrD**

Spray. Carl Sandburg. **CP-SandC**

Spray of sound, The. Walking to Bells. Charles Tomlinson. **CP-TomlC**

Spray sprang up across the cusps of the moon, The. Once at Swanage. Thomas Hardy. **CP-HardT**

Spread back across the air, wings wide. Gulls Land and Cease to Be. John Ciardi. **SP-CiarJ**

Spread beneath me it lies—lean upland. Flying Above California. Thom Gunn. **CP-GunnT**

Spread hand of black trees, A. Necessaries. Roy Fisher. **SP-FishR**

Spreading herbs, and flowerets bright. Melrose by Moonlight. Sir Walter Scott. **SP-ScotW** *Fr.* The Lay of the Last Minstrel.

Sprengeri. Louis Zukofsky. **CP-ZukLS**

Spring. William Blake. **BoTP; FHYEP; FaBoCh; FaPON; MoShBr; NTP; TTTS** *Fr.* Songs of Innocence. **CP-BlakW**

Spring. Kay Boyle. **CP-BoylK**

Spring, The. Thomas Carew. **CP-CareT**

Spring. Joseph Ceravolo. **SP-CeraJ**

Spring. Robert Creeley. **CP-CreeR**

Spring. Ralph Waldo Emerson. **OtMeF** *Fr.* April. **CP-EmerR**

Spring. Gerard Manley Hopkins. **CP-HopkG**

Spring. Kenneth Koch. **SP-KochK**

Spring. Philip Larkin. **CP-LarkP**

Spring. Edna St. Vincent Millay. **CP-MillE**

Spring. Mary Oliver. **SP-OlivM**

Spring. Mary Oliver. **SP-OlivM**

Spring, The. Ezra Pound. **SP-PounE**

Spring, The. Rainer Maria Rilke, *tr. fr. German by* Delmore Schwartz. **SP-SchwD**

Spring. Christina Georgina Rossetti. **CP-RosC1**

Spring. James Schuyler. **CP-SchuJ**

Spring, The. Gary Snyder. **CP-SnydG**

Spring. James Thomson. *Fr.* The Seasons. **CP-ThomJ**

  "As rising from the vegetable World." **PoEL-3**

  "Behold yon breathing prospect bids the Muse." **PoE**

  "Flushed by the spirit of the genial year." **OxAEP-1**

  "Lend me your song, ye nightingales! oh, pour." **PBBP**

  "Should I my steps turn to the rural seat." **FM; ScCV**

  Spring Flowers. **NOBE**

Spring. William Carlos Williams. **CP-WilW1**

Spring, a toy trumpet to her lips. Easter Monday. Wystan Hugh Auden. **CP-AudWJ**

Spring Abstract. Charles Wright. **SP-WrigC**

Spring again, can I stand it. Margaret Atwood. **SP-AtwM1**

Spring and All. William Carlos Williams. **CP-WilW1**

Spring and Death. Gerard Manley Hopkins. **CP-HopkG**

Spring and Fall. Gerard Manley Hopkins. **CP-HopkG**

Spring, and not a Blue Bird. Emily Dickinson. **SP-DickE**

Spring and the Fall, The. Edna St. Vincent Millay. **CP-MillE**

Spring: another / joke. / This run-down. Charles Kenneth Williams. **CP-WillC**

Spring Azures. Mary Oliver. **SP-OlivM**

Spring birds wing to the feeding tray. Dreams Dreamed. Kay Boyle. **CP-BoylK**

Spring bursts today, / For Christ is risen and all the earth's at play. An Easter Carol. Christina Georgina Rossetti. **CP-RosC2**

Spring Call, The. Thomas Hardy. **CP-HardT**

Spring Carol. Robert Louis Stevenson. **CP-StevR**

Spring Carries Surprises. Carl Sandburg. **CP-SandC**

Spring Cleaning. Louis MacNeice. **CP-MacNL**

Spring Clearing. Archie Randolph Ammons. **SP-AmmoA**

Spring comes and autumn goes. Sparrows. Hayden Carruth. **CP-CarHS**

Spring comes on the World. Emily Dickinson. **CP-DickE**

Spring Comes to Murray Hill. Ogden Nash. **CP-NashO**

Spring Cries. Carl Sandburg. **CP-SandC**

Spring crosses over into summer. Crisscross. Carl Sandburg. **CP-SandC**

Spring Day. John Ashbery. **SP-AshbJ**

Spring day in the weeds, A. Dog Yoga. Charles Wright. **SP-WrigC**

SPRING DUSK DARK SHORE. Poem for Old Walt. Lawrence Ferlinghetti. **SP-FerlL**

Spring Fancies. Christina Georgina Rossetti. **CP-RosC3**

  "All the world is out in leaf."

  "If it's weary work to live."

  Spring Quiet. **ArNa; BoNaP; BoTP; CH; CP-RosC1; GTBS-6; GTBS-P; InPS; LoBV; MeMBP; PoE; PoEL-5; WPE**

Spring Fashions. Allen Ginsberg. **CP-GinsA**

Spring Fever. Paul Laurence Dunbar. **CP-DunbP**

Spring finally comes though bitten with cold. For Richard Hopper (Dies 1978). Chuck Miller. **SP-MillC**

Spring Flowers. James Thomson. **NOBE** *Fr.* Spring. *Fr.* The Seasons. **CP-ThomJ**

Spring flowers, autumn moon—when will you end? Bella Donna Iu. Li Yü, *tr. fr. Chinese by* William Carlos Williams *with* David Rafael Wang. **CP-WilW2**

"Spring-flowers"! While you still delay to take. To Mary Boyle. Tennyson. **CP-TennA**

Spring Grass. Carl Sandburg. **CP-SandC**

Spring grass, there is a dance to be danced. Spring Grass. Carl Sandburg. **CP-SandC**

Spring had been bulldozed under. Killing the Spring. Anne Sexton. **CP-SextA**

Spring has been exquisite and the, The. Edward Estlin Cummings. **CP-CummE**

Spring has come; I look up and see. Robert Bly. **SP-BlyR** *Fr.* Four Seasons in American Woods.

Spring has come with its smell of Nicaragua. Ernesto Cardenal, *tr. by* Thomas Merton. **CP-MertT** *Fr.* Gethsemani, KY.

Spring has returned! Everything has returned! The Spring. Rainer Maria Rilke, *tr. fr. German by* Delmore Schwartz. **SP-SchwD**

Spring Images. James Wright. **CP-WrigJ**

Spring in the Classroom. Mary Oliver. **SP-OlivM**

Spring in the Garden. Edna St. Vincent Millay. **CP-MillE**

Spring in the Snow-Drenched Garden. Mao Tse-tung, *tr. fr. Chinese by* William Carlos Williams *with* David Rafael Wang. **CP-WilW2**

Spring in These Hills. Archibald MacLeish. **CP-MacLA**

Spring in This World of Poor Mutts. Joseph Ceravolo. **SP-CeraJ**

Spring is a happiness so beautiful. Emily Dickinson. **SP-DickE**

Spring is come again not as at first. Christina Georgina Rossetti. **CP-RosC3**

Spring is Here Again, Sir. William Carlos Williams. **CP-WilW2**

Spring is like a perhaps hand. Edward Estlin Cummings. **CP-CummE; SP-CummE**

Spring is not so beautiful there, The. Water-Front Streets. Langston Hughes. **SP-HughL**

Spring is past, and Summer's past. Skating. Edward Estlin Cummings. **CP-CummE**

Spring is the Period. Emily Dickinson. **CP-DickE**

Spring is when the grass turns green and glad. Lines Written for Gene Kelly to Dance To. Carl Sandburg. **CP-SandC**

Spring lingers-out its arrival in these woods. The Hesitation. Charles Tomlinson. **CP-TomlC**

Spring Man. Richard Eberhart. *Fr.* The Seasons. **CP-EberR**

Spring: Monastery Farm. Thomas Merton. **CP-MertT**

Spring Morning. Alfred Edward Housman. **CP-HousA**

Spring Morning. David Herbert Lawrence. **CP-LawrD**

Spring Mountain Climb. Richard Eberhart. **CP-EberR**

Spring moved to summer—the rude cold rain. Harriet. Robert Lowell. **SP-LoweR**

Spring Night in Shokoku-ji, A. Gary Snyder. **ArLo; VGW** *Fr.* Four Poems for Robin. **CP-SnydG**

Spring 1974. Robert Ranke Graves. **CP-GravR**

Spring 1967. Hayden Carruth. **CP-CarHS**

Spring Notes from Robin Hill. Hayden Carruth. **CP-CarHS**

Spring now come att last, The. Song 1. Mary Sidney, Countess of Montgomery Wroth. *Fr.* Pamphilia to Amphilanthus. **CP-WrotM**

Spring of the Year. John Hewitt. **CP-HewiJ**

Spring Offensive. Wilfred Owen. **CP-OwenW**

Spring Offensive of the Snail, The. Marge Piercy. **SP-PierM**

Spring omnipotent goddess thou dost. Edward Estlin Cummings. **CP-CummE**

Spring People. Audre Lorde. **SP-LordA**

Spring Plowing. Ted Kooser. **SP-KoosT**

Spring Pools. Robert Frost. **CP-FrosR**

Spring pricks a little. I get out the maps. A Spring Song. Donald Davie. **CP-DavDo**

Spring Quiet. Christina Georgina Rossetti. **ArNa; BoNaP; BoTP; CH; CP-RosC1; GTBS-6; GTBS-P; InPS; LoBV; MeMBP; PoE; PoEL-5; WPE** *Fr.* Spring Fancies. **CP-RosC3**

Spring Rain. Stephen Dobyns. **SP-DobyS**

Spring Rain. Kenneth Rexroth. **SP-RexrK** *Fr.* Mary and the Seasons. **SP-RexrK**

Spring, rainbows, / ordinary miracles. Ordinary Miracles. Erica Jong. **SP-JongE**

Spring Reminiscence. Countee Cullen. **CP-CullC**

Spring Restored, The. John Hewitt. **CP-HewiJ**

Spring rides no horses down the hill. The Goose-Girl. Edna St. Vincent Millay. **CP-MillE**

Spring Running, The. Rudyard Kipling. *Fr.* The Second Jungle Book.

  "Man goes to Man! Cry the challenge though the Jungle!" **CP-KiplR** Outsong in the Jungle. **CP-KiplR**

Spring-Shock. James Dickey. **CP-DickJ**

Spring Snow. William Matthews. **SP-MattW**

Spring Song, A. Donald Davie. **CP-DavDo**

Spring Song. Paul Laurence Dunbar. **CP-DunbP**

Spring Song. Li Po, *tr. fr. Chinese by* William Carlos Williams *with* David Rafael Wang. **CP-WilW2**

Spring Song. Edna St. Vincent Millay. **CP-MillE**

Spring Song. Ogden Nash. **CP-NashO**

Spring Song. Robert Louis Stevenson. **CP-StevR**

Spring Song. Dabney Stuart. **SP-StuaD**

Spring Song. John Updike. **CP-UpdiJ**

Spring Song. William Carlos Williams. **CP-WilW1**

Spring Song for Cagli, A. Charles Olson. **CP-OlsoC**

Spring Song II. Jean Garrigue. **SP-GarrJ**

Spring spreads one green lap of flowers, The. Death-Watches. Christina Georgina Rossetti. **CP-RosC2**

Spring Storm. Thomas Merton. **CP-MertT; SP-MertT**

Spring Storm. William Carlos Williams. **CP-WilW1**

Spring Strains. William Carlos Williams. **CP-WilW1**

Spring Sunshine. Louis MacNeice. **CP-MacNL**

Spring Symphony, The. Charles Tomlinson. **CP-TomlC**

Spring: the first morning when that one true block of sweet, laminar, complex scent arrives. From My Window. Charles Kenneth Williams. **CP-WillC; SP-WillC**

Spring, the First Pastoral, or Damon, *sels.* Alexander Pope. *Fr.* Pastorals. **CP-PopeA**

Spring this year in Austria started off benign. Talking to Myself. Wystan Hugh Auden. **CP-AudeW**

Spring Thunder. Adrienne Rich. **CP-RicAE**

Spring tide swept 'em to the hills. James Liddy. *Fr.* Sandhills. **CP-LiddJ**

Spring-time, Summer and Fall: days to behold a world. In Due Season. Wystan Hugh Auden. **CP-AudeW**

Spring Tornado. Archie Randolph Ammons. **SP-AmmoA**

Spring unsettles sleeping partnerships, The. Wystan Hugh Auden. **CP-AudWJ**

Spring Voices. Louis MacNeice. **CP-MacNL**

Spring Warning. Philip Larkin. **CP-LarkP**

Spring was never his fort. Suspect at first. Richard Eberhart. *Fr.* The Seasons. **CP-EberR**

Spring water in the green creek is clear, *after* Han-shan. Gary Snyder. **CP-SnydG**

Spring will come, The. Wystan Hugh Auden. **CP-AudWJ**

Spring Wind. Carl Sandburg. **CP-SandC**

Spring wind blowing, A. The Thought of Something Else. Wendell Berry. **CP-BerrW**

Spring with its thrusting leaves and jargling birds is here again. Unpredictable but Providential. Wystan Hugh Auden. **CP-AudeW**

Spring with the Larke, most comely Bride, and meet. Nuptiall Verse to Mistresse Elizabeth Lee, Now Lady Tracie. Robert Herrick. **CP-HerrR**

Spring Wooing, A. Paul Laurence Dunbar. **CP-DunbP**

Springboard, The. Louis MacNeice. **CP-MacNL**

Springboard, The. Adrienne Rich. **CP-RicAE**

Springer Mountain. James Dickey. **CP-DickJ**

Springfield Magical. Nicholas Vachel Lindsay. **CP-LindV**

Springfield of the Far Future, The. Nicholas Vachel Lindsay. **CP-LindV**

Springhouse, Menses, Held Apple, House and Beyond. James Dickey. **CP-DickJ**

Springing time of my first loving, The. Song. Mary Sidney, Countess of Montgomery Wroth. *Fr.* Pamphilia to Amphilanthus. **CP-WrotM**

Spring!may— / everywhere's here. Edward Estlin Cummings. **CP-CummE**

Springs, The. Wendell Berry. **CP-BerrW**

Spring's dewy hand on this fair summit weaves. Written in Farm Wood, South Downs, in May 1784. Charlotte Smith. **CP-SmitC**

Spring's first conviction is a wealth. Emily Dickinson. **SP-DickE**

Spring(side / walks are)is. Edward Estlin Cummings. **CP-CummE**

Springtime so impetuous. Already pink blossoms, The. Hayden Carruth. *Fr.* The Sleeping Beauty. **CP-CarHL**

Sprinkler on the lawn, The. The Megalopsych. Wystan Hugh Auden. **CP-AudWJ**

Sprinter at Forty, The. James Dickey. **CP-DickJ**

Spruce Woods. Archie Randolph Ammons. **SP-AmmoA**

Sprung of the father blood, the mother brain. Foresight and Patience. George Meredith. **CP-MerG1**

Spry Arms of the Wind, The. Emily Dickinson. **CP-DickE**

Spry, wry, and gray as these March sticks. Among the Narcissi. Sylvia Plath. **CP-PlatS**

Spunge makes his boasts that he's the onely man. Upon Spunge. Robert Herrick. **CP-HerrR**

Spunta la margherita. Christina Georgina Rossetti. **CP-RosC3**

Spur, The. William Butler Yeats. **CP-YeatW**

Spur jingles now, and sweares by no meane oathes. Upon Spur. Robert Herrick. **CP-HerrR**

Spurn the temerity. Emily Dickinson. **CP-DickE**

Spurred altering wake toss Attis his craft racing till marled in the. Catullus. *See* Carmen 63: "Plunging towards Phrygia over violent water."

Spy. Rita Dove. **SP-DoveR**

Spy. The. Howard Nemerov. **CP-NemeH**

Spyres Curten, The. Thomas Campion. **CP-CampT**

Squab, The. Ogden Nash. *Fr.* Nature-Walks, or, Not to Mention a Dopping of Sheldrakes. **CP-NashO**

Squad of soldiers lies beside a river, A. The Twentieth Century. Daniel Gerard Hoffman. **SP-HoffD**

Squall. George Oppen. **CP-OppeG**

Squall Ball. Archie Randolph Ammons. **SP-AmmoA**

Squalls rounder. Squall Ball. Archie Randolph Ammons. **SP-AmmoA**

Squalor spreads its hideous length. The Tribute. Hilda Doolittle. **CP-DoolH**

Square, The. Charles Tomlinson. **CP-TomlC**

Square along the couch, and stark. George Meredith. **PeVV** *Fr.* The Nuptials of Attila. **CP-MerG1**

Square Dance for a Square, A. Kay Boyle. **CP-BoylK**

Square Matthew Hale's young grafted apple tree. The Gold Hesperidee. Robert Frost. **CP-FrosR**

Square sheets—they saw the marble only into. Island Quarry. Hart Crane. **CP-CranH**

Squat in swamp shadows. Second Shaman Song. Gary Snyder. **CP-SnydG** *Fr.* Burning. *Fr.* Myths and Texts.

Squatter on Company Land, The. Richard Hugo. **CP-HugoR**

Squatter's Children. Elizabeth Bishop. **CP-BishE**

Squatting a day in the sun. Fire in the Hole. Gary Snyder. **CP-SnydG**

Squatting, serious, / His small hand locked on my middle finger. The Changeling. Thomas McGrath. **SP-McGrT**

Squaw Lilies: Some Notes. Margaret Atwood. **SP-AtwM2**

Squeal. Allen Ginsberg. **CP-GinsA**

Squeal of brakes, A. Stopped Dead. Sylvia Plath. **CP-PlatS**

Squib on Colonel Evans, A. William Wordsworth. **CP-WorW2**

Squid, The. Ogden Nash. *Fr.* Nature-Walks, or, Not to Mention a Dopping of Sheldrakes. **CP-NashO**

Squid, frightened or angry, shoots darkness, The. Ink-Sack. Robinson Jeffers. **CP-JefR3**

Squier, com neer, if it youre wille be. Introduction to the Squire's Tale. Geoffrey Chaucer. *Fr.* The Canterbury Tales. **CP-ChauG**

Squince. Derek Mahon. **SP-MahoD**

Squinting eyes / against the hilly snow. The Skier. Diane Wakoski. **SP-WakoD**

Squinting through smoked glass, the moon. Dark of the Moon. Daniel Gerard Hoffman. **SP-HoffD**

Squints a blond / job at her. Edward Estlin Cummings. **CP-CummE**

Squire Hooper. Thomas Hardy. **CP-HardT**

Squireless Kate. George Meredith. **CP-MerG2**

Squire's Tale, The. Geoffrey Chaucer. *Fr.* The Canterbury Tales. **CP-ChauG**

Squirrel, The. Ogden Nash. **CP-NashO**

Squirrel, bunching branches, The. Winter Sanctuaries. Archie Randolph Ammons. **SP-AmmoA**

Squirrels. Al Young. **CP-YounA**

Squirrels Mating. John Updike. **CP-UpdiJ**

S.S.K. John Hewitt. **CP-HewiJ**

S.T. Edward Estlin Cummings. **CP-CummE**

St. Barnabas, Oxford. Sir John Betjeman. **CP-BetjJ**

St. Francis Einstein of the Daffodils. William Carlos Williams. **CP-WilW1**

St. Francis Einstein of the Daffodils. William Carlos Williams. **CP-WilW1**

St George and the Dragon. David Herbert Lawrence. **CP-LawrD**

St. Irvyne's Tower. Percy Bysshe Shelley. *Fr.* Poems from St. Irvyne, or, The Rosicrucian. **CP-ShelP**

St James and St John. Geoffrey Hill. *Fr.* The Pentecost Castle. **CP-HillG**

St. John. Bible, *N.T.*

John 15; Upon Our Lords Last Comfortable Discourse with His Disciples. **CP-CrasR,** *tr. by* Richard Crashaw;

John 16; Verily I Say unto You, Yee Shall Weep and Lament. **CP-CrasR,** *tr. by* Richard Crashaw;

John 3; But Men Loved Darknesse Rather than Light. **CP-CrasR,** *tr. by* Richard Crashaw;

St. John, Apostle. Christina Georgina Rossetti. **CP-RosC2**

St. Louis Out of Time. Audre Lorde. **SP-LordA**

St. Luke. Bible, *N.T.*

Blessed be the Paps which Thou hast Sucked.
(Luke 11; Blessed Be the Paps Which Thou Hast Sucked.) **CP-CrasR**

Luke 10; And a Certaine Priest Comming that Way Looked on Him and Passed by. **CP-CrasR,** *tr. by* Richard Crashaw;

Luke 11; Upon the Dumbe Devill Cast Out, and the Slanderous Jewes Put to Silence. **CP-CrasR,** *tr. by* Richard Crashaw;

Luke 15; On the Prodigall. **CP-CrasR,** *tr. by* Richard Crashaw;

Luke 16; Dives *Asking a Drop.* **CP-CrasR,** *tr. by* Richard Crashaw;

Luke 2; Quærit Jesum Suum Maria. **CP-CrasR,** *tr. by* Richard Crashaw;

Luke 7; She Began To Wash His Feet with Teares and Wipe Them with the Haires of Her Head. **CP-CrasR,** *tr. by* Richard Crashaw;

St. Mark. Bible, *N.T.*

Mark 10; The Blind Cured by the Word of Our Saviour. **CP-CrasR,** *tr. by* Richard Crashaw;

Mark 12; (Give to Cæsar———) (And to God———). **CP-CrasR,** *tr. by* Richard Crashaw;

Mark 4; Why Are Yee Afraid, O Yee of Little Faith? **CP-CrasR,** *tr. by* Richard Crashaw;

Mark 7; The Dumbe Healed, and the People Enjoyned Silence. **CP-CrasR,** tr. by Richard Crashaw;

St. Matthew. Bible, N.T.

Matthew 16:25; Whosoever Shall Loose His Life. **CP-CrasR,** tr. by Richard Crashaw;

Matthew 22; Neither Durst Any Man from that Day Aske Him Any More Questions. **CP-CrasR,** tr. by Richard Crashaw;

Matthew 23; Yee Build the Sepulchres of the Prophets. **CP-CrasR,** tr. by Richard Crashaw;

Matthew 27; And He Answered Them Nothing. **CP-CrasR,** tr. by Richard Crashaw;

Matthew 28; Come See the Place where the Lord Lay. **CP-CrasR,** tr. by Richard Crashaw;

Matthew 8; I Am Not Worthy that Thou Should'st Come Under my Roofe. **CP-CrasR,** tr. by Richard Crashaw;

St Paul's. William Wordsworth. **CP-WorW1**

St. Saviour's, Aberdeen Park, Highbury, London, N. Sir John Betjeman. **CP-BetjJ**

St. Thecla. Gerard Manley Hopkins. **CP-HopkG**

St. Valentine. William Carlos Williams. **CP-WilW2**

Stable, The. Lewis Turco. **SP-TurcL**

Stable-lamp is lighted, A. A Christmas Hymn. Richard Wilbur. **CP-WilbR**

Stable yields a stercoraceous heap, The. How to Grow Cucumbers. William Cowper. **FaBoUs** Fr. The Garden. Fr. The Task. **CP-CowpW**

Staff[e] is now greased [or greas'd], The. Hag[g], The. Robert Herrick. **CP-HerrR**

Staff of Aesculapius, The. Marianne Craig Moore. **CP-MoorM**

Staffe and Rod, The. Robert Herrick. **CP-HerrR**

Stafford's Cabin. Edwin Arlington Robinson. **CP-RobiE**

Staffordshire. Donald Davie. **CP-DavDo**

Staffordshire Murderer, A. James Fenton. **SP-FentJ**

Staffordshire Red. Roy Fisher. **SP-FishR**

Stage Directions. Robert Duncan. **SP-DuncR** Fr. Passages.

Stage is about to be swept of corpses, The. Horatian Epode to the Duchess of Malfi. Allen Tate. **CP-TateA**

Stage-lit streets. Continuation of a Long Poem of These States. Allen Ginsberg. **CP-GinsA**

Stages on a Journey Westward. James Wright. **CP-WrigJ**

Staggering Back Toward Life. Robinson Jeffers. **CP-JefR3**

Staggering homeward between the stream and the trees the unhappy. New Year's Eve. Robinson Jeffers. **CP-JefR2**

Staggering, you know / they fall. Comfort. Robert Creeley. **CP-CreeR**

Stagnant pleasure like a Pool, A. Emily Dickinson. **CP-DickE**

Stagnant this wintry gloom. Afar. Fog. Walter de la Mare. **CP-DeLaW**

Stairs lead to the room as bleak as glass, The. Iphigenia: Politics. Thomas Merton. **CP-MertT**

Stairs will forget your footsteps, The. Love Passes Beyond the Incredible Hawk of Innocence. Diane Wakoski. **SP-WakoD**

Stairway, face, window. The Undermining of the Defense Economy. James Wright. **CP-WrigJ**

Stairway is not, The. The Jacob's Ladder. Denise Levertov. **CP-LeveD**

Stalag Luft. Randall Jarrell. **CP-JarrR**

Stalemated their armies stood, with tottering banners. The Snowman on the Moor. Sylvia Plath. **CP-PlatS**

Stalin. Robert Lowell. **SP-LoweR**

Stalking the Wild Mushroom. Barton Sutter. **SP-SuttB**

Stallion. John Hewitt. **CP-HewiJ**

Stallion, The. Barton Sutter. **SP-SuttB**

Stallions go leap, and rimfire knows. The Young Girl of the Mississippi Valley. Muriel Rukeyser. **CP-RukeM**

Stan and / Monica. Monica and Stan. Met last year. Courtship of the Jersey Lineman. Laurence Lieberman. **SP-LiebL**

Stand at the grave's head. Last Poem. Frank Templeton Prince. **CP-PrinF**

Stand back, make way, you mindless scum. Dr. Joseph Goebbels ("Stand back, make way, you mindless scum"). William DeWitt Snodgrass. **SP-SnodW** Fr. The Führer Bunker. **SP-SnodW**

Stand back, make way, you mindless scum. William DeWitt Snodgrass. **TW** Fr. Dr. Joseph Goebbels ("Say goodbye to the help, the ranks"). **CAPP** Fr. The Führer Bunker. **SP-SnodW**

"Stand, Bayard, stand!"—The steed obey'd. The Ride to Stirling. Sir Walter Scott. **SP-ScotW** Fr. The Lady of the Lake.

Stand by the Magick of my powerfull Rhymes. To His Honour'd Friend, Sir Thomas Heale. Robert Herrick. **CP-HerrR**

Stand fast, my child, and after all. Fortitude. Christopher Smart. **ChIV-2** Fr. Hymns for the Amusement of Children. **SP-SmarC**

Stand forth brave man, since Fate has made thee here. To Sir John Berkeley, Governour of Exeter. Robert Herrick. **CP-HerrR**

Stand forth,John Keats! On earth thou knew'st me not. Fame Speaks. Edward Estlin Cummings. **CP-CummE**

Stand-Ins, The. Anne Sexton. **CP-SextA**

Stand near the gates of the desert. The Princes of Exile. Richard Shelton. **SP-ShelR**

Stand of people, A. Autumn. William Carlos Williams. **CP-WilW1**

Stand off, Mother, let me go! N'est-ce pas assez de ne me point haïr? Stevie Smith. **CP-SmitS**

Stand on the highest pavement of the stair. La Figlia Che Piange. Thomas Stearns Eliot. **CP-ElioT**

Stand still, and I will read to thee. A Lecture upon the Shadow. John Donne. **CP-DonnJ**

Stand still in the middle of the world. Alive in the World. John Haines. **SP-HainJ**

Stand still, my soul, in the silent dark. My Soul and I. John Greenleaf Whittier. **CP-WhitJ**

Stand still, true poet that you are! Popularity. Robert Browning. **CP-BroR1**

Stand still, you floods! do[e] not deface. On Sight of a Gentlewoman's Face in the Water. Thomas Carew. **CP-CareT**

Stand There Listening. Jim Morrison. **SP-MorrJ**

Stand there on the rock. Coming Down to the Desert at Lordsburg, N.M. Hayden Carruth. **CP-CarHS**

Stand Up! David Herbert Lawrence. **CP-LawrD**

Stand Up. Adrienne Rich. **CP-RicAE**

Stand up and lift your hand and bless. The Saint and the Hunchback. William Butler Yeats. **CP-YeatW**

Stand up, stand up, thou May Janet. May Janet. Algernon Charles Swinburne. **CP-SwinA**

Stand up, that we may sacrifice the soul. Hafiz, tr. by Ralph Waldo Emerson. **CP-EmerR** Fr. Odes.

Stand whoso list upon the slipper top. Sir Thomas Wyatt. **CP-WyatT**

Stand with thy Graces forth, Brave man, and rise. To Worthy Friend, M. Tho. Falconbirge. Robert Herrick. **CP-HerrR**

Stand with your lover on the ending earth. Edward Estlin Cummings. **CP-CummE**

Standards, The. Richard Eberhart. **CP-EberR**

Standin' at de winder. Blue. Paul Laurence Dunbar. **CP-DunbP**

Standin' on the corner. Sweet Jane. "Lou Reed." **SP-ReedL**

Standing. Shel Silverstein. **SP-SilS2**

Standing, a little figure alone in the middle of a. The Safety Man. Ernest Hemingway. **CP-HemiE**

Standing Afar Off for the Fear of Her Torment. Christina Georgina Rossetti. **CP-RosC2**

Standing against the gorge, he sees the slides of light. Portrait of a Man, with a Background of Holdings. Muriel Rukeyser. **CP-RukeM**

Standing alone on a fence in a spasm. The Cousin. Stevie Smith. **CP-SmitS**

Standing aloof in giant ignorance. To Homer. John Keats. **CP-KeatJ**

Standing among the ruins, the horror-struck conqueror exclaimed. Wystan Hugh Auden. **Fr.** Shorts [1939–1947] ("Motionless, deep in his mind, lies the past the poet's forgotten"). **CP-AudeW**

Standing and Watching. James Schuyler. **CP-SchuJ**

Standing at the Door. Diane Wakoski. **SP-WakoD**

Standing between the sun and moon preserves. Einstein. Archibald MacLeish. **CP-MacLA**

Standing by the Mantlepiece. Thomas Hardy. **CP-HardT**

Standing Ground, A. Wendell Berry. **CP-BerrW**

Standing high on the shoulders of all things, all things. The Place at Albert Bay. Muriel Rukeyser. **CP-RukeM**

Standing in front of my students. Paying Some Attention to His Birthday the Associate Professor Goes About His Business Considering What He Sees and a Kind of Praise. Miller Williams. **SP-WillM**

Standing in high grass at home imagining farm. Grace Paley. **CP-PaleG**

Standing in the dock at Southampton. The Ballad of John and Yoko. John Lennon and Paul McCartney. **CP-Beatl**

Standing in the kitchen, ready to rip open the tinfoil. An Essay on Criticism. Mona Van Duyn. **SP-VanDM**

Standing on a stepladder. Soy Sauce. Gary Snyder. **CP-SnydG**

Standing on Ceremony. "Lou Reed." **SP-ReedL**

Standing on Earth. John Milton. **ChTr** Fr. Book VII. Fr. Paradise Lost. **CP-MiltJ**

Standing on my elbow. Standing. Shel Silverstein. **SP-SilS2**

Standing on the corner / until Tatum passed. On the Corner. Philip Levine. **SP-LeviP**

Standing on the garden. Charles Henri Ford. **SP-FordC** Fr. Emblems of Arachne.

Standing on the Highway. "Bob Dylan." **CP-DylaB**

Standing on the waters casting your bread. Jokerman. "Bob Dylan." **CP-DylaB**

Standing on top of the hay. The Farm. Donald Hall. **CP-HallD**

Standing on your window, honey. Temporary Like Achilles. "Bob Dylan." **CP-DylaB**

Standing Stones of Callanish, The. Richard Hugo. **CP-HugoR**

Standing there with Tony Sorce. The Velocity of Cows. Stephen Dobyns. **SP-DobyS**

Standing under the fobbed. Send No Money. Philip Larkin. **CP-LarkP**

Standing up eating a pan of oatmeal and rice. For Barbara. Chuck Miller. **SP-MillC**

Standing up on lifted, folded rock. By Frazier Creek Falls. Gary Snyder. **CP-SnydG**

Standing where the city and the forest. Leaves and Ashes. John Haines. **SP-HainJ**

Standings. Donald Davie. **CP-DavDo**

Stands the Spring! heralded by its bright-clothed. Fragment from May. Philip Larkin. **CP-LarkP**

Stanger Minstrel, A. Samuel Taylor Coleridge. **CP-ColeS**

Stanley Kunitz. Mary Oliver. **SP-OlivM**

Stanley Kunitz once said, somewhere. Hartnett in Worcester. David Markson. **CP-MarkD**

Stanza: "If I walk in Autumn's even." Percy Bysshe Shelley. **CP-ShelP**

Stanza: "No longer burn the hands that seized." Louise Bogan. **CP-BogaL**

Stanza from a Translation of the Marseillaise Hymn. Percy Bysshe Shelley. **CP-ShelP**

Stanza, Written at Bracknell. Percy Bysshe Shelley. **CP-ShelP**

Stanzas: "Ah! think'st thou, Laura, then, that wealth." Charlotte Smith. **CP-SmitC**

Stanzas: "At length, my soul! thy fruitless hopes give o'er." François de Malherbe, tr. fr. French by Alexander Pope. **CP-PopeA**

Stanzas: "Bind up thy tresses, thou beautiful one." John Greenleaf Whittier. **CP-WhitJ**

Stanzas: "Chill and mirk is the nightly blast." Byron. **CP-Byron**

Stanzas: "Could Love for ever." Byron. **CP-Byron**

Stanzas: "How often we forget all time, when lone." Edgar Allan Poe. **CP-PoeEd**

Stanzas: "I heard thy fate without a tear." Byron. **CP-Byron**

Stanzas: "I may sing; but minstrel's singing." Elizabeth Barrett Browning. **CP-BroEB**

Stanzas: "I'll not weep that thou art going to leave me." Emily Brontë. *See* I'll not weep that thou art going to leave me.

Stanzas: "Often rebuked, yet always back returning." Emily Brontë. **CP-BronE**

Stanzas: "Oh!—my lonely—lonely—lonely Pillow!" Byron. **CP-Byron**

Stanzas: "Through cloudless skies, in silvery sheen." Byron. **CP-Byron**

Stanzas: "You say you love; but with a voice." John Keats. **CP-KeatJ**

Stanzas—April, 1814. Percy Bysshe Shelley. **CP-ShelP**

Stanzas Composed in the Simplon Pass. William Wordsworth. *Fr.* Memorials of a Tour of the Continent; 1820. **CP-WorW2**

Stanzas for Music ("There be none of Beauty's daughters"). Byron. **CP-Byron**

Stanzas for Music ("There's not a joy the world can give like that it takes away"). Byron. **CP-Byron**

Stanzas for Music. Byron. **CP-Byron**

Stanzas for Music. Byron. **CP-Byron**

Stanzas for the Times. John Greenleaf Whittier. **CP-WhitJ**

Stanzas from Saint Peter's Complaint. Robert Southwell. **ACP** *Fr.* Saint Peter's Complaint. **CP-SoutR**

Stanzas from the Grande Chartreuse. Matthew Arnold. **SP-ArnoM**

"For rigorous teachers seized my youth." **FHYEP**

Stanzas in Meditation. Gertrude Stein. **CP-SteiG**

"Full well I know that she is there." **PoA**

"How I wish I were able to say what I think." **PBWP**

Stanzas in Memory of the Author of "Obermann." Matthew Arnold. **SP-ArnoM**

Stanzas: Old Age and the Conventions of Retirement Have Driven My Friends from the Work They Love. Grace Paley. **CP-PaleG**

"Every day he went out, forsaking."

"Job of hunting of shooting in hunting season of, The."

"Muncipal center / the morning of anger, The."

"No metaphor reinvents the job of the nurture of children."

"One day at work he cried."

"She did good. She stood up like a."

"When she was young she wanted."

Stanzas on Milton's Remains. William Cowper. **CP-CowpW**

Stanzas on Some Skulls in Beauly Abbey, Near Inverness. John Keats. **CP-KeatJ**

Stanzas on the Same Occasion [in the Prospect of Death]. Robert Burns. **CP-BurnR**

Stanzas Printed on Bills of Mortality 1787–1790, 1792, 1793, *see also* On a Similar Occasion for the Year 1788, 1789, 1790, 1792, 1793. William Cowper. *See* While thirteen moons saw smoothly run.

Stanzas Suggested in a Steamboat off Saint Bees' Head, on the Coast of Cumberland. William Wordsworth. *Fr.* Poems Composed or Suggested During a Tour, in the Summer of 1833. **CP-WorW2**

Stanzas to———. Emily Brontë. **CP-BronE**

Stanzas to a Lady on Leaving England. Byron. **CP-Byron**

Stanzas to a Lady, with the Poems of Camoëns. Byron. **CP-Byron**

Stanzas to Augusta. Byron. **CP-Byron**

Stanzas to Augusta. Byron. **CP-Byron**

Stanzas to Jessy. Byron. **CP-Byron**

Stanzas to Mr Richard Bentley. Thomas Gray. *See* In silent gaze the tuneful choir among.

Stanzas to the Po. Byron. **CP-Byron**

Stanzas Written at Night in Radio City. Allen Ginsberg. **CP-GinsA**

Stanzas Written in Dejection, near Naples [or —December 1818, near Naples]. Percy Bysshe Shelley. **CP-ShelP**

Stanzas Written in My Pocket-Copy of Thomson's "Castle of Indolence." William Wordsworth. **CP-WorW1**

Stanzas Written on the Road between Florence and Pisa. Byron. **CP-Byron**

Star, The. Wendell Berry. **CP-BerrW**

Star, The. Charles Bukowski. **SP-BukC3**

Star[re], The. George Herbert. **CP-HerbG**

Star. Pablo Neruda, tr. fr. Spanish by Ben Belitt. **SP-NeruP**

Star, The. Kathleen Jessie Raine. **SP-RainK**

Star. Derek Walcott. **CP-WalcD**

Star and coronal and bell. Spring Morning. Alfred Edward Housman. **CP-HousA**

Star-Apple Kingdom, The. Derek Walcott. **CP-WalcD**

Star by Day. Hilda Doolittle. *Fr.* Two Poems for Christmas, 1937. **CP-DoolH**

Star dissolved in evening—the one star, The. Ancestral. Archibald MacLeish. **CP-MacLA**

Star-eyes of books he elaborated, The. Tray-Carrier of Laurels, Liam Miller. James Liddy. **CP-LiddJ**

Star-filled seas are smooth to-night, The. The Isle of Portland. Alfred Edward Housman. **CP-HousA**

Star Fish Gluttony. Jim Morrison. **SP-MorrJ**

Star-Gazer. Louis MacNeice. **CP-MacNL**

Star-Gazers. William Wordsworth. **CP-WorW1**

"What crowd is this? what have we here! we must not pass it by." **Poetr**

Star hit in the hills behind our house, A. The Star in the Hills. William Stafford. **SP-StafW**

Star in a Stoneboat, A. Robert Frost. **CP-FrosR**

Star in the Hills, The. William Stafford. **SP-StafW**

Star in the nets of heaven blazed past your breastbone, The. Song: The Star in the Nets of Heaven. Muriel Rukeyser. **CP-RukeM**

Star in the sky. How many words and tears, A. "Nikolai Nikolaevich Morshen." *Fr.* Two Poems. **CP-WilbR**

Star looks down at me, A. Waiting Both. Thomas Hardy. **CP-HardT**

Star most spiritual, principal, preeminent, A. Gerard Manley Hopkins. *Fr.* Fragments. **CP-HopkG**

Star-Nosed Mole. Anne Sexton. **CP-SextA**

Star of Bethlehem. Kathleen Jessie Raine. **SP-RainK**

Star of Bethlehem, The. John Greenleaf Whittier. **CP-WhitJ**

Star of My Heart. Nicholas Vachel Lindsay. **CP-LindV**

Star of the brave!—whose beam hath shed. On the Star of "The Legion of Honour." Byron. **CP-Byron**

Star seer Copernicus / Only could earn a curse. Ralph Waldo Emerson. **CP-EmerR**

Star Silver. Carl Sandburg. **CP-SandC**

Star Sirius, The. George Meredith. **CP-MerG1**

Star Sirius and the Pole Star dwell afar. Christina Georgina Rossetti. *Fr.* Later Life: A Double Sonnet of Sonnets. **CP-RosC2**

Star Song. Joseph Ceravolo. **SP-CeraJ**

Star-Song; a Carol to the King; Sung at White-Hall, The. Robert Herrick. **CP-HerrR**

Star-stricken still / we lie under them. The Rebels. Lawrence Ferlinghetti. **SP-FerlL**

Star System, The. Richard Wilbur. **NBLV** *Fr.* Flippancies. **CP-WilbR**

Star that beams on Anna's breast, The. To a Lady ["Star that beams on Anna's breast, The"]. William Cowper. **CP-CowpW**

Star That Bids the Shepherd Fold, The. John Milton. **FaBoCh; OBEV; PPoe; WHA** *Fr.* Comus; a Masque Presented at Ludlow Castle. (Comus' Invocation to His Readers.) **TrGrPo**

(Comus Speaks.) **NOBE**

(Comus' Summons.) **NOSC**

(Invocation of Comus, The.) **OBS**

(Light Fantastic Round, A.) **FaBoDD**

(Mask, A.) **FiP**

Star, that looked so long among the stones. The Meteorite. Randall Jarrell. **CP-JarrR; SP-JarrR**

Star two ash stow, A. Aster. Louis Zukofsky. **CP-ZukLS**

Star which comes at close of day to shine, The. To I.F. William Wordsworth. **CP-WorW2**

Starched unbending candles stir, The. The Bidden Guest. Geoffrey Hill. **CP-HillG**

Stare at the monster: remark. Famous Poet. Ted Hughes. **SP-HughT**

Stare of the Man from the Provinces, The. Howard Nemerov. **CP-NemeH**

Stare's Nest by My Window, The. William Butler Yeats. **BIrV; CP-YeatW; FaBoPV; GTBS-6; GTBS-P; InPS; LiTB; NOBE** *Fr.* Meditations in Time of Civil War. **CP-YeatW**

("Bees in the crevices, The.") **FaBoPV**

Starfish, The. Robert Bly. **SP-BlyR**

Starfish. Mary Oliver. **SP-OlivM**

Stargazing. Robert Penn Warren. *See* The Stars are only a backdrop for.

Starglow. Louis Zukofsky. **CP-ZukLS**

Staring at my picture book. Sad Song. "Lou Reed." **SP-ReedL**

Staring she / kindles. Weasel Snout. William Carlos Williams. **CP-WilW1**

Stark bewölkt. Wystan Hugh Auden. **CP-AudeW**

Stark Major. Hart Crane. **CP-CranH**

Stark rock bulk of Gottéron ravine rises, The. Gottéron Landscape. Stephen Dobyns. **SP-DobyS**

Starlight. Philip Levine. **SP-LeviP**

Starlight and Non-Being. Chuang Tzu, *tr. fr. Chinese by* Thomas Merton. **CP-MertT**

Starlight Night, The. Gerard Manley Hopkins. **CP-HopkG**

Starling, The. Stevie Smith. **CP-SmitS**

Starling and a willow-wren, A. Wystan Hugh Auden. **FaBoMo** *Fr.* Five Songs ("Deftly, admiral, cast your fly"). **CP-AudeW**

Starling drops / from branch to / branch, it's cold, A. Deep Winter. James Schuyler. **CP-SchuJ**

Starlings. Phoebe Hesketh. **SP-HeskP**

Starlings gather on the eaves, The. November at Weybourne. Wystan Hugh Auden. **CP-AudWJ**

Starlings have good ears. Starlings. Phoebe Hesketh. **SP-HeskP**

Starlings on the Roof. Thomas Hardy. **CP-HardT**

Starred Coverlet, The. Robert Ranke Graves. **CP-GravR**

Starry Night, A. Paul Laurence Dunbar. **CP-DunbP**

Starry Night, The. Anne Sexton. **CP-SextA**

Starry night shall tidings bring, The. Emily Brontë. **CP-BronE**

Stars. Emily Brontë. *See* Ah! why, because the dazzling sun.

Stars, The. John Gould Fletcher. **SP-FletJ**

Stars. Robert Frost. **CP-FrosR**

Stars. Robert Earl Hayden. **CP-HaydR** Sojourner Truth. **CNA**

Stars. Langston Hughes. **SP-HughL**

Stars. Carl Sandburg. **CP-SandC**

· Stars and grass. Weeds. James Dickey. **CP-DickJ**

Stars are dropping thick as stones into the twiggy. Stars over the Dordogne. Sylvia Plath. **CP-PlatS**

Stars are forth, the moon above the tops, The. Byron. **OAEL-2** *Fr.* Manfred: A Dramatic Poem. **CP-Byron**

Stars Are Mansions Built by Nature's Hand, The. William Wordsworth. **CP-WorW2**

Stars are old, that stood for me, The. Emily Dickinson. **CP-DickE**

Stars are only a backdrop for, The. Robert Penn Warren. **SP-WarrR** (Stargazing.) **SP-WarrR**

Stars are too many to count, The. Stars. Carl Sandburg. **CP-SandC**

Stars at Tallapoosa. Wallace Stevens. **CP-StevW**

Stars Dance, The. Thomas Campion. **OBSC** *Fr.* The Lords Mask[e].

Stars dwindle / they will not reward me. Separation. Audre Lorde. **SP-LordA**

Stars from five wars, scars. At a VA Hospital in the Middle of the United States of America: An Act in a Play. Etheridge Knight. **SP-KnigE**

Stars Go Over the Lonely Ocean, The. Robinson Jeffers. **CP-JefR3**

Stars go to sleep so peacefully, The. Kenneth Patchen. **CP-PatcK**

Stars have not dealt me the worst they could do, The. Alfred Edward Housman. **CP-HousA**

Stars have simple paradigms, The. Malcolm Lowry. **CP-LowrM**

Stars hidden by dark clouds. Boethius, *tr. fr. Latin.* **MLL,** *tr. by* Helen Waddell; *Fr.* Consolation of Philosophy, The ("De Consolacione Philosophie"). **CP-ChauG**

Stars, I have seen them fall. Alfred Edward Housman. **CP-HousA**

Stars, in their unchecked lust. For John Donne. Jim Carroll. **SP-CarrJ**

Stars may dissolve, and the fountain of light, The. The Irishman's Song. Percy Bysshe Shelley. *Fr.* Original Poetry by Victor and Cazire. **CP-ShelP**

Stars of the Great Bear drift apart, The. A Lesson in Geography. Kenneth Rexroth. **SP-RexrK**

Stars over the Dordogne. Sylvia Plath. **CP-PlatS**

Stars point in all directions, The. Richard Shelton. *Fr.* Angel and the Anchorite. **SP-ShelR**

Stars put out their pale opinions, one by one, The. St. Thomas Aquinas. Thomas Merton. **CP-MertT**

Stars seem gilded nipples. Alun Lewis. *Fr.* Songs for the Night. **CP-LewiA**

Stars, Songs, Faces. Carl Sandburg. **CP-SandC**

Stars, that are small lights, The. At Night. William Carlos Williams. **CP-WilW1**

Stars that open and shut, The. Nonentity. David Herbert Lawrence. **CP-LawrD**

Stars waving their indivisible rays. Gerard Manley Hopkins. *Fr.* Fragments. **CP-HopkG**

Stars were brighter than the fireworks, The. Fourth of July. Peter Meinke. **SP-MeinP**

Stars were packed so close that night, The. Gerard Manley Hopkins. **CP-HopkG**

Stars were wild that summer evening, The. Two Seasons. Galway Kinnell. **SP-KinnG**

Stars wheel in purple, yours is not so rare. Hilda Doolittle. **MoAmPo; NOBA; TAP** *Fr.* Let Zeus Record. **CP-DoolH**

Starspangled cowboy / sauntering out of the almost. Backdrop Addresses Cowboy. Margaret Atwood. **SP-AtwM1**

Start a system of official spying. Police Spies. David Herbert Lawrence. **CP-LawrD**

Start Again. Jim Morrison. **SP-MorrJ**

Start not—nor deem my spirit fled. Lines Inscribed upon a Cup Formed from a Skull. Byron. **CP-Byron**

Start not! upon the minister wall. Emily Brontë. **CP-BronE**

Start such a fire in England, Master Ridley. Oxfordshire. Donald Davie. **CP-DavDo**

Start up in gray, / in moist green. Birds. James Schuyler. **CP-SchuJ**

Start Up the Music Again. Chuck Miller. **SP-MillC**

Start with the brightest star. Finding the Andromeda Nebula. Siv Cedering Fox. **SP-CedeS**

Starting Back. Richard Hugo. **CP-HugoR**

Starting from black or. The Painting. William Carlos Williams. **CP-WilW2**

Starting from fish-shape Paumanok where I was born. Starting from Paumanok. Walt Whitman. **CP-WhitW**

Starting from Paumanok. Walt Whitman. **CP-WhitW**

Starting to Make a Tree. Roy Fisher. *Fr.* City. **SP-FishR**

Starting with eyeball kicks. Over Kansas. Allen Ginsberg. **CP-GinsA**

Starting with little in mind. Prologue. Jim Carroll. **SP-CarrJ**

Startled by his own thoughts, he looked around. Percy Bysshe Shelley. **OxBoS** *Fr.* Alastor; or, The Spirit of Solitude. **CP-ShelP**

Starvation. Maya Angelou. **SP-AngeM**

Starved eye devours the seascape for the morsel, The. The Castaway. Derek Walcott. **CP-WalcD**

Starved Lovers. Archibald MacLeish. **CP-MacLA**

Stasis in darkness. Ariel. Sylvia Plath. **CP-PlatS**

State, The. Randall Jarrell. **CP-JarrR**

State, as if to stamp the final seal, The. William Wordsworth. **FaBoPV** *Fr.* Residence in France and French Revolution. *Fr.* The Prelude; Growth of a Poet's Mind [1850 vers.]. **CP-WorW3**

State Funeral: March 31, 1969. Archibald MacLeish. **CP-MacLA**

State of Age, The. George Meredith. **CP-MerG1**

State of the Nation, The. Kenneth Patchen. **CP-PatcK**

State with the prettiest name, The. Florida. Elizabeth Bishop. **CP-BishE**

State you must dare not enter, A. Happiness. Stephen Dunn. **SP-DunnS**

Stately bride is the shining world, A. Hafiz, *tr. by* Ralph Waldo Emerson. **CP-EmerR** *Fr.* Odes.

Stately flower in my garden grows, A. To A.M. George Meredith. **CP-MerG2**

Stately Goddesse, do thou please. An Hymne to Juno. Robert Herrick. **CP-HerrR**

Statement by Willkie after Returning from England. Muriel Rukeyser. **CP-RukeM**

Statement for El Greco and William Carlos Williams, A. Kay Boyle. **CP-BoylK**

Statement: Philippa Allen. Muriel Rukeyser. **CP-RukeM**

Statements in a Personal Winter. John Clellon Holmes. **SP-HolmJ**

States! Walt Whitman. **CP-WhitW**

States strong enough to do good are but few. No Holy Wars for Them. Robert Frost. **CP-FrosR**

States when they black out and lie there rolling when they turn, The. Falling. James Dickey. **CP-DickJ**

Statesman have known visions. And, not alone. Geoffrey Hill. *Fr.* Of Commerce and Society: Variations on a Theme. **CP-HillG**

Statesman, I thank thee! and, if yet dissent. To William H. Seward. John Greenleaf Whittier. **CP-WhitJ**

Statesman is an easy man, A. The Old Stone Cross. William Butler Yeats. **CP-YeatW**

Statesman, yet Friend to Truth! of Soul sincere. Epitaph on James Craggs, Esq., in Westminster Abbey. Alexander Pope. **CP-PopeA**

Statesmen. Wystan Hugh Auden. *See* When Statesmen gravely say, "We must be realistic."

Static. Barton Sutter. **SP-SuttB**

Static forces / not a ball of silver, The. On the Principle of Blowclocks. Charles Tomlinson. **CP-TomlC**

Station Island. Seamus Heaney. **SP-HeanS**

"Black water. White waves. Furrows snowcapped." **NoAM**

"I had come to the edge of the water." **FaBCIP; PBCIP**

"Like a convalescent, I took the hand." **FaBoPV; NAEL-2; NoAM; TOF**

"My brain dried like spread turf, my stomach." **CIP**

Station Syren. Sir John Betjeman. **CP-BetjJ**

Stationary sense. . . as, I suppose, A. Maturity. Philip Larkin. **CP-LarkP**

Stations. Ted Hughes. **SP-HughT**

"I can understand the haggard eyes." **NoAM**

"Suddenly his poor body." **NoAM**

"They have sunk into deeper service. They have gone down." **NoAM**

"Whether you say it, think it, know it." **NoAM**

"You are a wild look—out of an egg." **NoAM**, *sect.* 4;

Stations of the West, The. Seamus Heaney. **SP-HeanS**

Statistics. Gary Gildner. **SP-GildG**

Statistics. Carl Sandburg. **CP-SandC**

Statistics. William Butler Yeats. **CP-YeatW**

Statistics say the heart is a long-stemmed glass. Statistics. Gary Gildner. **SP-GildG**

Statue. Gerrit Achterberg, *tr. fr.* Dutch by Adrienne Rich. **CP-RicAE**

Statue, The. John Berryman. **CP-BerrJ**

Statue, The. Tom Clark. **SP-ClarT**

Statue, The. Robert Creeley. **CP-CreeR**

Statue against a Clear Sky. Wallace Stevens. **EyDe** *Fr.* New England Verses. **CP-StevW**

Statue and Birds. Louise Bogan. **CP-BogaL**

Statue and the Bust, The. Robert Browning. **CP-BroR1**

"There's a palace in Florence, the world knows well." **Mes**

Statue of Liberty. Richard Eberhart. **CP-EberR**

Statue of Liberty, The. Thomas Hardy. **CP-HardT**

Statue of Liberty. Karl Shapiro. **SP-ShapK**

Statue of Old Andrew Jackson, The. Nicholas Vachel Lindsay. **CP-LindV**

Statue of the founder wears a green, The. Generic College. John Updike. **CP-UpdiJ**

Statue stood, The. Newton. William Wordsworth. **ImOP** *Fr.* Residence at Cambridge. *Fr.* The Prelude; Growth of a Poet's Mind [1850 vers.]. **CP-WorW3**

Statue, tolerant through years of weather, The. The Statue. John Berryman. **CP-BerrJ**

Statues. Kathleen Jessie Raine. **SP-RainK**

Statues. Richard Wilbur. **CP-WilbR**

Statues, The. William Butler Yeats. **CP-YeatW**

Statues in the Public Gardens, The. Howard Nemerov. **CP-NemeH**

Statues with exposed hearts and barbed-wire crowns. The Mud Vision. Seamus Heaney. **SP-HeanS**

Status indeed and protocol I pay. Church of Ireland. Donald Davie. **CP-DavDo**

Stave of Roving Tim, A. George Meredith. **CP-MerG1**

Stay. Leonard Cohen. **CP-CoheL**

Stay beautiful / but dont stay down underground too long. For Poets. Al Young. **CP-YounA**

Stay, bold Adventurer; rest awhile thy limbs. Written with a Slate Pencil on a Stone, on the Side of the Mountain of Black Comb. William Wordsworth. **CP-WorW1**

Stay close, little tortoise, dig in. Jenny Joseph. *Fr.* Fables. **SP-JoseJ**

Stay, coward blood, and do not yield. On Mistress N. Thomas Carew. **CP-CareT**

Stay here, fond youth, and ask no more, be wise. Against Fruition. Sir John Suckling. **CP-SuckJ**

Stay holy fires. Mary Sidney, Countess of Montgomery Wroth. *Fr.* Part 2. *Fr.* Urania. **CP-WrotM**

Stay Home. Wendell Berry. **CP-BerrW**

Stay, if you list, O passer by the way. Epitaph, An. Alfred Edward Housman. **CP-HousA**

Stay in line. stay in step. people. Advice for Geraldine on Her Miscellaneous Birthday. "Bob Dylan." **CP-DylaB**

Stay mine eyes, these floods of teares. Mary Sidney, Countess of Montgomery Wroth. *Fr.* Part 1. *Fr.* Urania. **CP-WrotM**

Stay, my Charmer, can you leave me. Robert Burns. **CP-BurnR**

Stay, my thoughts, do nott aspire. Song 3. Mary Sidney, Countess of Montgomery Wroth. *Fr.* Pamphilia to Amphilanthus. **CP-WrotM**

Stay near me—do not take thy flight! To a Butterfly. William Wordsworth.

Stay near me—do not take thy flight! William Wordsworth. **CP-WorW1** *Fr.* To a Butterfly.

Stay, ruby-breasted warbler, stay. Song. John Keats. **CP-KeatJ**

Stay, silver-footed Came, strive not to wed. An Elegie on the Death of Doctor Porter. Richard Crashaw. **CP-CrasR**

Stay, twist, or buy. Ace is eleven or one. Vingt-et-un. Louis MacNeice. *Fr.* Indoor Sports. **CP-MacNL**

Stay, view this stone: and, if thou beest not such. Ben Jonson. **CP-JonsB**

Stay while ye will, or goe. To Carnations. Robert Herrick. **CP-HerrR**

Stay with me, Ariel, while I pack, and with your first free act. Prospero to Ariel. Wystan Hugh Auden. *Fr.* The Sea and the Mirror. **CP-AudeW**

Stayed in her room when. The Bright Crown of Freedom. James Liddy. **CP-LiddJ**

Stayed No Longer in the Place Than to Hire a Guide for the Next Stage. Kenneth Patchen. **CP-PatcK**

Staying. Miller Williams. **SP-WillM**

Staying here, we turn inflexible. Setting Out. William DeWitt Snodgrass. **SP-SnodW**

Staying overnight in a friend's house. Overnights. Alice Walker. **CP-WalkA**

Stealer, The. Thom Gunn. **CP-GunnT**

Stealing a dollar once just before dawn. In Blue Light. Stephen Berg. **SP-BergS**

Stealing the Christmas Greens. Brendan Galvin. **SP-GalvB**

Stealing Trout on a May Morning. Ted Hughes. *See* I park the car half in the ditch and switch off and sit.

Stealth and Subtleties of Growth. Richard Eberhart. **CP-EberR**

Steam Crane, The. Roy Fisher. **SP-FishR** *Fr.* Interiors with Various Figures.

Steam in Sacrifice. Robert Herrick. **CP-HerrR**

Steam is a dry word; the best word is water. Louis MacNeice. *Fr.* Our Sister Water. **CP-MacNL**

Steamboat Whistle, The. Archibald MacLeish. **CP-MacLA**

Steamboats, Viaducts and Railways. William Wordsworth. **NAEL-2; VLP** *Fr.* Poems Composed or Suggested During a Tour, in the Summer of 1833. **CP-WorW2**

Steamboats, Viaducts, and Railways. William Wordsworth. **CP-WorW2**

Steamer, steamer, outward bound. Song for Pier Something or Other. Ogden Nash. **CP-NashO**

Steamers. John Gould Fletcher. *Fr.* Sand and Spray: A Sea-Symphony. **SP-FletJ**

Steaming Ties. James Schuyler. **CP-SchuJ**

Steaming ties, cutting rue. Steaming Ties. James Schuyler. **CP-SchuJ**

Steatopygous, sow-dugged. Dame Kind. Wystan Hugh Auden. **CP-AudeW**

Steel. Charles Tomlinson. **CP-TomlC**

Steel doors—guillotine gates. The Prisoners. Robert Earl Hayden. **CP-HaydR**

Steel edge of plough. Dusk. Stephen Spender. **CP-SpenS**

Steel worker on the girder, The. The Building of the Skyscraper. George Oppen. **CP-OppeG**

Steelhead. William Everson. **SP-EverW**

Steelhead, Wild Pig, the Fungus. Robinson Jeffers. **CP-JefR2**

Steely Silence. Diane Wakoski. **SP-WakoD**

Steep and black the mountain to the graying sky; no star but the morning. Dawn. Robinson Jeffers. **CP-JefR3**

Steep roads, a tunnel through chalk downs, are the approaches. Dover. Wystan Hugh Auden. **CP-AudeW**

Steep turn down, A. Roy Fisher. **SP-FishR** *Fr.* Glenthorne Poems.

Steep up in Lubitavish townland stands. Ossian's Grave. Robinson Jeffers. **CP-JefR2**

Steeple bush, hardhack. Hayden Carruth. **CP-CarHS** *Fr.* The Clay Hill Anthology.

Steeple-Jack, The. Marianne Craig Moore. **CP-MoorM** *Fr.* Part of a Novel, Part of a Poem, Part of a Play.

Steeple on the House, A. Robert Frost. **CP-FrosR**

Steepletop. Edna St. Vincent Millay. **CP-MillE**

Steering my little boat towards a misty islet. Meng Hao Jan, *tr. fr. Chinese by* William Carlos Williams *with* David Rafael Wang. **CP-WilW2**

Stelae, The. Adrienne Rich. **CP-RicAE; SP-RicA2**

Stella at Woodpark. Jonathan Swift. **CP-SwifJ**

Stella Dallas. William Dickey. **SP-DickW**

Stella in Mourning. Samuel Johnson. **CP-JohnS**

Stella is sick, and in that sick-bed lies. Sonnet 101. Sir Philip Sidney. *Fr.* Astrophil and Stella. **SP-SidnP**

Stella oft sees the very face of woe. Sonnet 45. Sir Philip Sidney. **InPS; NAEL-1; NoSic; PoE** *Fr.* Astrophil and Stella. **SP-SidnP**

Stella, since thou so right a Princess art. Sonnet 107. Sir Philip Sidney. **HBV; NoP; OXAEP-1** *Fr.* Astrophil and Stella. **SP-SidnP**

Stella stands in the rain, outside the great house. Stella Dallas. William Dickey. **SP-DickW**

Stella, the fullness of my thoughts of thee. Sonnet 50. Sir Philip Sidney. *Fr.* Astrophil and Stella. **SP-SidnP**

Stella, the only planet of my light. Sonnet 68. Sir Philip Sidney. **OBSC** *Fr.* Astrophil and Stella. **SP-SidnP**

Stella, think not that I by verse seek fame. Sonnet 90. Sir Philip Sidney. **NoSic; OBSC** *Fr.* Astrophil and Stella. **SP-SidnP**

Stella this day is thirty-four. Jonathan Swift. **CP-SwifJ**
(On Stella's Birthday, 1718/1719.) **CP-SwifJ**

Stella, whence doth this new assault arise. Sonnet 36. Sir Philip Sidney. *Fr.* Astrophil and Stella. **SP-SidnP**

Stella, while now by honour's cruel might. Sonnet 91. Sir Philip Sidney. **NAEL-1; PoE** *Fr.* Astrophil and Stella. **SP-SidnP**

Stellar Thanksgiving. Robert Pack. **SP-PackR**

Stella's Birthday (1725). Jonathan Swift. **CP-SwifJ**

Stella's Birthday ([March 13,] 1727). Jonathan Swift. **CP-SwifJ**

Stella's Birthday (1723). Jonathan Swift. **CP-SwifJ**

Stella's Birthday; Written in the Year 1720–21. Jonathan Swift. **CP-SwifJ**

Stella's Kiss. Sir Philip Sidney. *See* Sonnet 79: "Sweet kiss, thy sweets I fain would sweetly indite."

Stellenbosch. Rudyard Kipling. **CP-KiplR**

Stem of a departed Flower, The. Emily Dickinson. **CP-DickE**

Stempclasp becomes two *cross you.* Jade. Louis Zukofsky. **CP-ZukLS**

Stems. Denise Levertov. **CP-LeveD**

Steorra, stir / by the bird's whir. X to the Nth. Charles Olson. **CP-OlsoC**

Step, A. Robert Creeley. **CP-CreeR**

Step, A. Robert Creeley. **CP-CreeR**

Step, The. Frederick Morgan. **SP-MorgF**

Step Away from Them, A. Frank O'Hara. **SP-OharF**

Step into my room tonight. People Trying to Love. Stephen Berg. **SP-BergS**

Step lightly on this narrow spot. Emily Dickinson. **CP-DickE**

Step me now a bridal measure. To Dan. Paul Laurence Dunbar. **CP-DunbP**

Step off the road and in a hollow place. The Little Glen. John Hewitt. **CP-HewiJ**

Step very softly, sweet Quiet-foot. Mrs. Grundy. Walter de la Mare. **CP-DeLaW**

Step wid de banjo an' glide wid de fiddle. Christmas. Paul Laurence Dunbar. **CP-DunbP**

Stepfather, I wanted / to spit in your mouth. Compassion. Jim Carroll. *Fr.* 3 Short Poems. **SP-CarrJ**

Stephen and Barberie, Fragment. Gerard Manley Hopkins. **CP-HopkG**

Stephen Spender, I write about your face. Face, Ocean. Richard Eberhart. **CP-EberR**

Stepping Backward. Hayden Carruth. **CP-CarHS**

Stepping Backward. Adrienne Rich. **CP-RicAE; SP-RicA2**

Stepping down was like being born. Change. Tom Clark. **SP-ClarT**

Stepping Out. Robert Pack. **SP-PackR**

Stepping Outside. Tess Gallagher. **SP-GallT**

Stepping-Stones, The. William Wordsworth. *Fr.* The River Duddon [A Series of Sonnets]. **CP-WorW2**

Stepping-stones, once, The. A Dance. Wendell Berry. **CP-BerrW**

Stepping Westward. Denise Levertov. **CP-LeveD**

Stepping Westward. William Wordsworth. **CP-WorW1**

Steps. Frank O'Hara. **SP-OharF**

Steps for a Dancer, *see also* Dancer's Reply, The. Howard Nemerov. **CP-NemeH**

Sterile faces squeezed out from squalid tubes of. Mercy, Wherever You Are, Come Running in to Me and Grab Me in Your Good Arms—. Charles Bukowski. **SP-BukC2**

Sterile these stones. The Corner Stone. Walter de la Mare. **CP-DeLaW**

Stern Daughter of the Voice of God! Ode to Duty. William Wordsworth. **CP-WorW1**

Stern, stern is the voice of fate's fearful command. Song: To——— [Harriet] ("Stern, stern is the voice. . . "). Percy Bysshe Shelley. *Fr.* Original Poetry by Victor and Cazire. **CP-ShelP**

Stern winter now, by spring repress'd. Ode, An. Samuel Johnson. **CP-JohnS**

Stethoscope Case, A. Charles Bukowski. **SP-BukC1**

Stethoscope tells what everyone fears, The. Academic. Theodore Roethke. **CP-RoetT**

Stevens Song. Charles Olson. **SP-OlsoC** *Fr.* The Maximus Poems.

Stevenson. Ernest Hemingway. **CP-HemiE**

Stick, The. Anne Waldman. **SP-WaldA**

Stick I found that weighed two pound, A. "Lewis Carroll." *Fr.* Puzzles. *Fr.* Puzzles from Wonderland. **CP-CarrL**

Stick of Incense, A. William Butler Yeats. **CP-YeatW**

Stick of the blind man, The. Parable. Thomas McGrath. **SP-McGrT**

Stick the finger inside. Black Mail. Alice Walker. **CP-WalkA**

Stick your patent name on a signboard. The River. Hart Crane. **AmPP; CMoP; GOA; MoAB; MoAmPo; NOBA; OxBA; PrIm** *Fr.* Powhatan's Daughter. *Fr.* The Bridge. **CP-CranH**

Sticks. Stephen Berg. **SP-BergS**

Sticks and Stones. Dabney Stuart. **SP-StuaD**

Sticks-in-a-drowse droop over sugary loam. Cuttings ("Sticks-in-a-drowse droop over sugary loam"). Theodore Roethke. **CP-RoetT**

Stiff spokes of this wheel, The. July in Washington. Robert Lowell. **SP-LoweR**

Stigmata of Fact, The. Kenneth Rexroth. **CP-RexKL** *Fr.* The Homestead Called Damascus.
"Morphology repeats ontology." **SP-RexrK**

Still. Robert Creeley. **CP-CreeR**

Still, / I would leap too. Small Frogs Killed on the Highway. James Wright. **CP-WrigJ**

Still a full hour before dusk. The Creole Mephistopheles. Laurence Lieberman. **SP-LiebL**

Still after the clapper cracked the bell. The Fall. Hayden Carruth. *Fr.* Contra Mortem. **CP-CarHL**

Still and blanched and cold and lone. The Mountains. Walter de la Mare. **CP-DeLaW**

Still anxious to secure your partial favor. Occasional Address, Spoken by Miss Fontenell, on Her Bnefit-Night, Decr. 4th. 1793.—Written by Mr Burns. Robert Burns. **CP-BurnR**

Still as a mountain with dark pines and sun. Goliath. Walter de la Mare. **CP-DeLaW**

Still, as of old, in Beavor's Vale. Revelation. John Greenleaf Whittier. **CP-WhitJ**

Still as she looked the iron clouds. Emily Brontë. **CP-BronE**

Still as the Profile of a Tree. Emily Dickinson. **SP-DickE**

Still beside that dreary water. Emily Brontë. **CP-BronE**

Still, Citizen Sparrow. Richard Wilbur. **CP-WilbR**

Still, citizen sparrow, this vulture which you call. Still, Citizen Sparrow. Richard Wilbur. **CP-WilbR**

Still dark. / The unknown bird sits on his usual branch. Five Flights Up. Elizabeth Bishop. **CP-BishE**

Still days of late November. November Days. John Gould Fletcher. **SP-FletJ**

Still, Dear, it is incredible to me. Her Second Husband Hears Her Story. Thomas Hardy. **CP-HardT**

Still Do I Keep My Look, My Identity. Gwendolyn Brooks. **SP-BrooG**

Still explosions on the rocks, The. The Shampoo. Elizabeth Bishop. **CP-BishE**

Still Frame. Archie Randolph Ammons. **SP-AmmoA**

Still from those years two incidents remain. Two Spectres Haunt Me. John Hewitt. **CP-HewiJ**

Still go funny, in the face of him. Issue, Mood. Charles Olson. **CP-OlsoC**

Still green with bays each ancient altar stands. Alexander Pope. **EPCY** *Fr.* An Essay on Criticism. **CP-PopeA**

Still half drunk, after a night at cards. A Day on the Big Branch. Howard Nemerov. **CP-NemeH**

Still haunted / by the kookahs. Hookah. Chuck Miller. **SP-MillC**

Still haunted by the cycle of the moon. The Morning Moon. Derek Walcott. **CP-WalcD**

Still heavy with may, and the sky ready to fall. Before Invasion, 1940. Sir John Betjeman. **CP-BetjJ**

Still Here. Langston Hughes. **SP-HughL**

Still I bring flowers. Ad Infinitum. William Carlos Williams. **CP-WilW1**

Still I love to rhyme, and still more, rhyming, to wander. Robert Louis Stevenson. **CP-StevR**

Still I Rise. Maya Angelou. **SP-AngeM**

Still in the now of then they remain. After Fifty-five Years. Kathleen Jessie Raine. **SP-RainK**

Still in thy streets, O Paris! doth the stain. The Peace Convention at Brussels. John Greenleaf Whittier. **CP-WhitJ**

Still, it is dear defiance now to carry. Gwendolyn Brooks. **SP-BrooG** (Love Note II: Flags.) **SP-BrooG**

Still it pleads and rankles: "Why do you love *me*?" John Berryman. *Fr.* Sonnets to Chris. **CP-BerrJ**

Still let me pierce into the midnight depth. James Thomson. **EnRP** *Fr.* Summer. *Fr.* The Seasons. **CP-ThomJ**

Still, let my tyrants know, I am not doomed to wear. Emily Brontë. **ChER; NOBE; NoP; OBEV; OBNC; OBVV** *Fr.* The Prisoner. **CP-BronE**

Still Life. Louise Glück. **SP-GlücL**

Still Life. Thom Gunn. **CP-GunnT**

Still-Life. Ted Hughes. **SP-HughT**

Still Life. George Oppen. **CP-OppeG**

Still Life. Carl Sandburg. **CP-SandC**

Still Life. Charles Kenneth Williams. **CP-WillC**

Still Life. William Carlos Williams. **CP-WilW2**

Still Life I. Howard Nemerov. **CP-NemeH**

Still Life Or. Robert Creeley. **CP-CreeR**

Still Life III. Howard Nemerov. **CP-NemeH**

Still Life II. Howard Nemerov. **CP-NemeH**

Still Life with Tulips. Erica Jong. **SP-JongE**

Still Lifes. William Carlos Williams. **CP-WilW2**

Still linger in our noon of time. Child-Songs. John Greenleaf Whittier. **CP-WhitJ**

Still Lives. Al Young. **CP-YounA**

Still marveling at the light. The Return. Richard Eberhart. **CP-EberR**

Still Moment at Dun Laoghaire. Tess Gallagher. **SP-GallT**

Still must I hear?—shall hoarse Fitzgerald bawl. English Bards and Scotch Reviewers. Byron. **CP-Byron**

Still Must I Love You. Edwin Rolfe. **CP-RolfE**

Still must the poet as of old. To Kathleen. Edna St. Vincent Millay. **CP-MillE**

Still night. The old clock Ticks. Last Night in Calcutta. Allen Ginsberg. **CP-GinsA**

Still on the spot Lord Marmion stay'd. Edinburgh from the Pentland Hills. Sir Walter Scott. **SP-ScotW** *Fr.* Marmion.

Still onward winds the dreary way, *sels.* Tennyson. *Fr.* In Memoriam A. H. H. **CP-TennA**

Still own thee—still thou art. Emily Dickinson. **CP-DickE**

Still, passed through the spokes of an old wheel, on and around. Reincarnation (I) ["Still, passed through the spokes of an old wheel, on and around"]. James Dickey. **CP-DickJ**

Still Passing. Robert Pack. **SP-PackR**

Still pressed for cash to pay his son's remaining. Clayfeld's Son Selects His Specialty. Robert Pack. **SP-PackR**

Still Reading Fairy Stories. Jenny Joseph. **SP-JoseJ**

Still salt pool locked in with bars of sand, A. Lincolnshire Shores. Tennyson. **FaBoPP** *Fr.* The Palace of Art. **CP-TennA**

Still sits the school-house by the road. In School-Days. John Greenleaf Whittier. **CP-WhitJ**

Still skies, still seas. Kathleen Jessie Raine. **SP-RainK**

Still sleeping, he heard. Wendell Berry. *Fr.* Window Poems. **CP-BerrW**

Still small voice spake unto me, A. The Two Voices. Tennyson. **CP-TennA**

Still sometimes in my secret heart of hearts. Cor Mio. Christina Georgina Rossetti. **CP-RosC3**

Still speeding to your heart. Malcolm Lowry. **CP-LowrM**

Still, still without ceasing. Simple Trust. Jeanne Marie Bouvier de la Motte-Guyon, *tr. fr. French by* William Cowper. **CP-CowpW**

Still stone / In heart of hill. Stone on High Crag. Kathleen Jessie Raine. *Fr.* Eileann Chanaidh. **SP-RainK**

Still take advice; though counsels when they flye. Advice the Best Actor. Robert Herrick. **CP-HerrR**

Still the Mind Smiles. Robinson Jeffers. **CP-JefR2**

Still the same / day? Still. Robert Creeley. **CP-CreeR**

Still the world is wondrous large,—seven seas from marge to marge. The Wide, Wide World. Rudyard Kipling. **OtMeF** *Fr.* In the Neolithic Age. **CP-KiplR**

Still Though the One I Sing. Walt Whitman. **CP-WhitW**

Still through the dusk of dead, blank-legended. Edwin Arlington Robinson. *Fr.* Octaves. **CP-RobiE**

Still Time, The. Galway Kinnell. **SP-KinnG**

Still to be neat, still to be dressed [*or* Drest]. Ben Jonson. **CP-JonsB** *Fr.* Epicoene; or, The Silent Woman.

Still to our gains our chief respect is had. Rewards. Robert Herrick. **CP-HerrR**

Still Too Quick to Hold. Steve Griffiths. **SP-GrifS**

Still turn, and imitate the heaven. Ben Jonson. **CP-JonsB** *Fr.* The Masque of Beauty.

Still up at midnight, addled. Midnight Oil. John Clellon Holmes. **SP-HolmJ**

Still—Volcano—Life, A. Emily Dickinson. **CP-DickE**

Still Wet From. Jim Morrison. **SP-MorrJ**

Still, when the wind is right. Treblinka. Martin Edmunds. **SP-EdmuM**

Still will I harvest beauty where it grows. Edna St. Vincent Millay. **CP-MillE**

Still you stand, still you listen, still you smile! Numpholeptos. Robert Browning. **CP-BroR2**

Stillborn. Sylvia Plath. **CP-PlatS**

Stille Nacht, Heilege Nacht. Peter Meinke. **SP-MeinP**

Stillness, A. Daniel Gerard Hoffman. **SP-HoffD**

Stillness, / of the wood, The. The Figures. Robert Creeley. **CP-CreeR**

Stillness. William Carlos Williams. **CP-WilW1**

Stillness and moonlight, with. Loneliness[: An Outburst of Hexasyllables]. Hayden Carruth. **CP-CarHS**

Stillness! Down the dripping ride. Tunstall Forest. Donald Davie. **CP-DavDo**

Stillness of the rose, The. The Rose. William Carlos Williams. **CP-WilW2**

Stills. Archie Randolph Ammons. **SP-AmmoA**

Stimulus, beyond the Grave, The. Emily Dickinson. **CP-DickE**

Stimulus of Loss, The. Emily Dickinson. **SP-DickE**

Sting, The. Charles Kenneth Williams. **CP-WillC**

Sting of bees took away my father, The. Sylvia Plath. **CP-PlatS**

Stinging / gold swarms. Edward Estlin Cummings. **CP-CummE**

Stinging nettles on my wrists woke me, The. The Chief Mystery. David Herbert Lawrence. **CP-LawrD**

Stings. Sylvia Plath. **CP-PlatS**

Stinking city full of stinking, A. Gilbert Sorrentino. **SP-SorrG**

Stirred. . . the fur-toothed graves. The Battle of Unameit. Kenneth Patchen. **CP-PatcK**

Stirring suddenly from long hibernation. Mid-Winter Waking. Robert Ranke Graves. **CP-GravR**

Stirrup Cup, The. Paul Laurence Dunbar. **CP-DunbP**

S.ti:rst;hiso,nce;ma:n. Edward Estlin Cummings. **CP-CummE**

Stitch Too Late Is My Fate, A. Ogden Nash. **CP-NashO**

Stoat, The. John Hewitt. **CP-HewiJ**

Stoat danced on the lawns here, A. Strawberry Hill. Ted Hughes. **SP-HughT**

Stocking feet or barefoot. Prayer. Patti Smith. **SP-SmitP**

Stockyard, The. Lewis Turco. **SP-TurcL**

Stoic. David Herbert Lawrence. **CP-LawrD**

Stoic (Circa 1907). Louise McNeill. **SP-McNeL**

Stoker Tom's Ukulele. Malcolm Lowry. **CP-LowrM**

Stolen. Charles Bukowski. **SP-BukC1**

Stolen Child, The. William Butler Yeats. **CP-YeatW**

Stolen Clothes. Robert Pack. **SP-PackR**

Stolen Heart, The. Frank Templeton Prince. **CP-PrinF**

Stolen Jewel. Robert Ranke Graves. **CP-GravR**

Stolen lady was coming on board, A. The Discovery of the Madeiras. Robert Frost. **CP-FrosR**

Stolen Waters. "Lewis Carroll." **CP-CarrL**

Stomach-foot's about it, / one of those glitches in the Plan. War in the Garden. Brendan Galvin. **SP-GalvB**

Stomach of goat, crushed. Salami. Philip Levine. **SP-LeviP**

Stomping with Catullus. Robert Creeley. **CP-CreeR**

Stone, The. Hayden Carruth. *Fr.* Contra Mortem. **CP-CarHL**

Stone. Martin Edmunds. **SP-EdmuM**

Stone. John Hewitt. **CP-HewiJ**

Stone, A. Daniel Gerard Hoffman. **SP-HoffD**

Stone, The. Ted Hughes. **SP-HughT**

Stone, / like stillness. After Mallarmé. Robert Creeley. **CP-CreeR**

Stone. Charles Simic. **SP-SimiC**

Stone against stone, they are building back. The Churchyard Wall. Charles Tomlinson. **CP-TomlC**

Stone Age Figure Far Below, A. Derek Mahon. **SP-MahoD**

Stone and Flower Series. Charles Olson. **CP-OlsoC**

Stone and Shadow. Lewis Turco. **SP-TurcL**

Stone Arabia Farm. Brendan Galvin. **SP-GalvB**

Stone Axe, The. Robinson Jeffers. **CP-JefR2**

Stone Bear, The. John Haines. **SP-HainJ**
"I left the graveyard by a chosen path."

"Old, root-crowded cemetery, An."

"Slow pulse in a den of roots."

Stone, bronze, stone, steel, stone, oakleaves, horses' heels. Triumphal March. Thomas Stearns Eliot. **OBWP; WaaP** *Fr.* Coriolan. **CP-ElioT**

Stone Church Damaged by a Bomb, A. Philip Larkin. **CP-LarkP**

Stone Crock, The. William Carlos Williams. **CP-WilW2**

Stone-cutters fighting time with marble, you foredefeated. To the Stone-Cutters. Robinson Jeffers. **CP-JefR1**

Stone Face Falls. William Everson. **SP-EverW**

Stone face higher than six horses stood five thousand years gazing. The Has-Been. Carl Sandburg. **CP-SandC**

Stone-flake and salmon. Gary Snyder. **CP-SnydG** *Fr.* Burning. *Fr.* Myths and Texts.

Stone from Delphi. Seamus Heaney. **SP-HeanS** *Fr.* Shelf Life.

Stone Garden, The. Richard Shelton. **SP-ShelR**

"Everything is quiet in the garden."

"He is ill."

"On stormy nights."

"She has three pills left in the bottle."

"Widow has burned her book, The."

"Wife sits all afternoon, The."

Stone goes straight, The. Washington Monument by Night. Carl Sandburg. **CP-SandC**

Stone Harp, The. John Haines. **SP-HainJ**

Stone in my tread, The. Holding On. Archie Randolph Ammons. **SP-AmmoA**

Stone Knife, A. James Schuyler. **CP-SchuJ**

Stone lips to the unspoken cave. Orpheus. William DeWitt Snodgrass. **SP-SnodW**

Stone Man, The. Geoffrey Hill. *Fr.* Soliloquies. **CP-HillG**

Stone must be rolled away from self's pain, The. Malcolm Lowry. *Fr.* Songs for Second Childhood. **CP-LowrM**

Stone on High Crag. Kathleen Jessie Raine. *Fr.* Eileann Chanaidh. **SP-RainK**

Stone Pietà / for which the city. Geoffrey Hill. *Fr.* Churchill's Funeral. **CP-HillG**

Stone Speech. Charles Tomlinson. **CP-TomlC**

Stone, steel, dominions pass. Alfred Edward Housman. **CP-HousA**

Stone steps, a solid. Hard Times. William Carlos Williams. **CP-WilW2**

Stone tablet they found in the mound at Grave Creek, The. The Grave Creek Inscribed Stone. Louise McNeill. **SP-McNeL**

Stone Telling. Shel Silverstein. **SP-SilS2**

Stone, toppled by water and mountain, The. Pablo Neruda, *tr. fr. Spanish by* Ben Belitt. **SP-NeruP** *Fr.* Skystones.

Stone turns over slowly, The. A Fit against the Country. James Wright. **CP-WrigJ**

Stone Verdict, The. Seamus Heaney. **SP-HeanS**

Stone Walls. Wystan Hugh Auden. **CP-AudWJ**

Stone Walls. Wystan Hugh Auden. **CP-AudWJ**

Stone Walls. Donald Hall. **CP-HallD**

Stone Walls. May Sarton. **SP-SartM**

Stone Walls: at Chew Magna. Charles Tomlinson. **CP-TomlC**

Stone walls emerge from leafy ground. Stone Walls. Donald Hall. **CP-HallD**

Stonecarver's Poem, The. Denise Levertov. **CP-LeveD**

Stoned & / singing Indian scat. A River Still To Be Found. Lawrence Ferlinghetti. **SP-FerlL**

Stones, The. Wendell Berry. **CP-BerrW**

Stones. John Haines. **SP-HainJ**

Stones. Donald Hall. **CP-HallD**

Stones, The. Richard Shelton. **SP-ShelR**

Stones are falling from the sky. Roc. Lewis Turco. **SP-TurcL**

Stones, brown tufted grass, but no water. The Ravine. Hayden Carruth. **CP-CarHS**

Stones huddled together on the ramparts, The. Faction du Muet. René Char, *tr. fr. French by* Thomas Merton. **CP-MertT**

Stones of a Seventeenth Century Village, The. Kay Boyle. **CP-BoylK**

Stones of kin and friend, The. Lorelei. James Merrill. **SP-MerrJ**

Stones of spring, The. Under Libra: Weights and Measures. James Merrill. **SP-MerrJ**

Stones of Time, The. Kenneth Koch. **NoAM** *Fr.* Days and Nights. **SP-KochK**

Stones only, the disjecta membra of this Great House. Ruins of a Great House. Derek Walcott. **CP-WalcD**

Stones that rolled in the sea for a thousand years. The Old Stone-Mason. Robinson Jeffers. **CP-JefR3**

Stone's throw out on either hand, A. Rudyard Kipling. **CP-KiplR** *Fr.* In the House of Suddhoo. *Fr.* Plain Tales from the Hills.

Stones to Wind. Marsden Hartley. **CP-HartM**

Stones trip Coquet burn. Basil Bunting. **CP-BuntB**

Stones you have gathered, of diverse shapes, The. Consortium of Stones. Robert Ranke Graves. **CP-GravR**

Stonewall Jackson. Herman Melville. **SP-MelvH**

Stoney Wales / with its slate-grey roofs. Spirit of the Crusades. Lawrence Ferlinghetti. **SP-FerlL**

Stoning Stone. Archie Randolph Ammons. **SP-AmmoA**

Stony Limits. "Hugh MacDiarmid." **SP-MacDH**

Stony Lonesome. Langston Hughes. **SP-HughL**

Stood there then among. Stars. Robert Earl Hayden. **CP-HaydR**

Stool-Ball. Robert Herrick. **CP-HerrR**

Stool Pigeon Blues. Allen Ginsberg. **CP-GinsA**

Stop. Richard Wilbur. **CP-WilbR**

Stop all the clocks, cut off the telephone. Wystan Hugh Auden. **MoBrPo; OPOU; RB** *Fr.* Twelve Songs. **CP-AudeW**

     (Song: "Stop all the clocks, cut off the telephone.") **MoBrPo; OPOU**

Stop and consider! life is but a day. John Keats. **OBRV; SeCePo; TreFT** *Fr.* Sleep and Poetry. **CP-KeatJ**

Stop, Christian passer-by!—Stop, child of God. Epitaph. Samuel Taylor Coleridge. **CP-ColeS**

"Stop!" cried the Knight. "No more of this, good sir!" Geoffrey Chaucer. *See* The Prologue of the Nun's Priest's Tale.

Stop fingering your tie; walk slower. Chloe to Daphnis in Hyde Park. Wystan Hugh Auden. **CP-AudWJ**

Stop! for thy tread is on an empire's dust! Byron. **InPS** *Fr.* Childe Harold's Pilgrimage. **CP-Byron**

Stop It. David Herbert Lawrence. **CP-LawrD**

Stop, let me have the truth of that! Dîs Aliter Visum; or, Le Byron de Nos Jours. Robert Browning. **CP-BroR1**

Stop look & / listen Venezia: incline mine. Memorabilia. Edward Estlin Cummings. **CP-CummE; SP-CummE**

Stop playing, poet! May a brother speak? Transcendentalism: A Poem in Twelve Books. Robert Browning. **CP-BroR1**

Stop rowing! This one of our bye-canals. Ponte dell' Angelo, Venice. Robert Browning. **CP-BroR2**

Stop the chafed boar, or play. Separation of Lovers. Thomas Carew. *Fr.* Four Songs, by Way of Chorus To a Play. **CP-CareT**

Stop the Deathwish! Stop It! Stop! Daniel Gerard Hoffman. **SP-HoffD**

"Stop thief!" dame Nature call'd to Death. On William Graham [*or* W—— — Gr-h-m], Esq., of Mossknowe [*or* M-sskn-w]. Robert Burns. **CP-BurnR**

Stopped Dead. Sylvia Plath. **CP-PlatS**

Stopped Frames and Set-Pieces. Roy Fisher. **SP-FishR**

'Stopped in the straight when the race was his own. Rudyard Kipling. **CP-KiplR** *Fr.* In the Pride of His Youth. *Fr.* Plain Tales from the Hills.

Stopping a Kaleidoscope. Richard Eberhart. **CP-EberR**

Stopping by Woods on a Snowy Evening. Robert Frost. **CP-FrosR**

Stopping on the bus from Novi Pazar in the rain. Defending the Faith. Allen Ginsberg. **CP-GinsA**

Stopping the diary. Forget What Did. Philip Larkin. **CP-LarkP**

Stopwatch and an Ordnance Map, A. Stephen Spender. **CP-SpenS**

Store, more'n likely, in one of those tenements. Hayden Carruth. *Fr.* The Sleeping Beauty. **CP-CarHL**

Store of courage to me grant. A Vow to Mars. Robert Herrick. **CP-HerrR**

Stores, The / guarded / by the lynx-eyed. Christmas 1950. William Carlos Williams. **CP-WilW2**

Stories. Donald Hall. **CP-HallD**

Stories at Evening (A Suburban Mother Tells Stories to Her Son). Louise McNeill. **SP-McNeL**

Stories to Live in the World With. William Stafford. **SP-StafW**

"At a little pond in the woods."

"Long rope of gray smoke was, A."

"Once a man killed another, to rob him."

Storks like elbows had a fit of falling, The. There's No Place to Sleep in This Bed, Tanguy. Charles Henri Ford. **SP-FordC**

Storm[e], The. John Donne. **CP-DonnJ**

Storm at Sea, A. **NOBE**

Storm. Hilda Doolittle. **CP-DoolH**

Storm, The. George Herbert. **CP-HerbG**

Storm, The. John Hewitt. **CP-HewiJ**

Storm. Wilfred Owen. **CP-OwenW**

Storm, The. Theodore Roethke. **CP-RoetT**

Storm. Robert Louis Stevenson. **CP-StevR**

Storm, The. Jonathan Swift. **CP-SwifJ**

Storm. Alice Walker. **CP-WalkA**

Storm, The. Charles Kenneth Williams. **SP-WillC**

Storm, The. William Carlos Williams. **CP-WilW2**

Storm and disorder and the giant emotions. The Two Illuminations. Muriel Rukeyser. **CP-RukeM**

Storm and peril overpast, The. Garrison. John Greenleaf Whittier. **CP-WhitJ**

Storm and strife and stress. Death. Paul Laurence Dunbar. **CP-DunbP**

Storm and unconscionable winds once cast. The Wreck. Walter de la Mare. **CP-DeLaW**

Storm at Night, The. Thomas Merton. **CP-MertT**

Storm at Sea, A. John Donne. **NOBE** *Fr.* The Storm[e]. **CP-DonnJ**

Storm-beaten old watch-tower, A. Symbols. William Butler Yeats. **CP-YeatW**

Storm blowing up, rain and dark weather and the roaring wind, The. Robinson Jeffers. **CP-JefR3**

Storm came Monday night. On Wednesday we, The. Études de Plusiers Paysages de l'Âme. Hayden Carruth. **CP-CarHS**

Storm Cone, The. Rudyard Kipling. **CP-KiplR**

Storm-dances of gulls, the barking game of seals, The. Divinely Superfluous Beauty. Robinson Jeffers. **CP-JefR1**

Storm, darkness, a cracked hurdle of lightning, The. Lightning Storm on Fuji. Howard Nemerov. **CP-NemeH**

Storm Fear. Robert Frost. **CP-FrosR**

Storm-Flower, The. Nicholas Vachel Lindsay. **CP-LindV**

Storm has passed and now the sun, The. The Walk. Wystan Hugh Auden. **CP-AudWJ**

Storm in Acquafredda. Richard Hugo. **CP-HugoR**

Storm in April, A. Richard Wilbur. **CP-WilbR**

Storm in the Black Forest. David Herbert Lawrence. **CP-LawrD**

Storm in the Ozarks. John Clellon Holmes. **SP-HolmJ**

Storm is done, the sun shines out, The. *Song*: Reconciliation. Robert Ranke Graves. **CP-GravR**

Storm is over, and the land has forgotten the storm, ; the trees are still, The. Cap D'Antibes. Edna St. Vincent Millay. **CP-MillE**

Storm is over; too bad, I say, The. Ordinary Days. Stephen Dunn. **SP-DunnS**

Storm mixed and fell upon the lake, The. Entering the Storm, Unable to Swim, Zimmer, Rollo, and Cecil Are Saved. Paul Zimmer. **SP-ZimmP**

Storm of Angels, A. May Sarton. **SP-SartM**

Storm of white petals, A. The Year. Carl Sandburg. **CP-SandC**

Storm on Lake Asquam. John Greenleaf Whittier. **CP-WhitJ**

Storm raged among the live oaks, A. The Lady speaks. William Carlos Williams. **CP-WilW2**

Storm rehearses through the bewildered fields, The. The Winter's Tale. Randall Jarrell. **CP-JarrR**

Storm-Surge. William Everson. **SP-EverW**

Storm that downed, The. Leaning Up. Archie Randolph Ammons. **SP-AmmoA**

Storm that needed a mountain, A. Found in a Storm. William Stafford. **SP-StafW**

Storm Warnings. Adrienne Rich. **CP-RicAE; SP-RicA1; SP-RicA2**

Storm was coming, but the winds were still, A. Merlin and Vivien. Tennyson. *Fr.* Idylls of the King. **CP-TennA**

Storm wind / was tearing at sleep: as it struck, The. The Awakening. Charles Tomlinson. **CP-TomlC**

Storm Windows. Howard Nemerov. **CP-NemeH**

Stormclouds / give their morose faces to the sea. Juan Ramón Jiménez. *Fr.* Ten Short Poems. **CP-WrigJ**

Stormed at with shot and shell. Tennyson. **Poetr** *Fr.* The Charge of the Light Brigade. **CP-TennA**

Storms Begin Far Back. Carl Sandburg. **CP-SandC**

Storm's cold javelins constrain, The. By the Gateway of India: Bombay. Alun Lewis. **CP-LewiA**

Storms have beaten on this point of land. Cumulatives. Carl Sandburg. **CP-SandC**

Stormy. William Carlos Williams. **CP-WilW2**

Stormy evening closes now in vain, The. Robert Louis Stevenson. **CP-StevR**

Stormy Nights. Robert Louis Stevenson. **CP-StevR**

Story, The. Robert Creeley. **CP-CreeR**

Story, A. Randall Jarrell. **CP-JarrR**

Story. Jenny Joseph. *Fr.* Derivations. **SP-JoseJ**

Story. Philip Larkin. **CP-LarkP**

Story, A. Charles Olson. **CP-OlsoC**

Story, A. Muriel Rukeyser. **CP-RukeM**

Story, The. Miller Williams. **SP-WillM**

Story, a story!, A. Rowing. Anne Sexton. **CP-SextA**

Story Books on a Kitchen Table. Audre Lorde. "Out of her womb of pain my mother spat me." **SP-LordA**

(Story Books on a Kitchen Table.) **SP-LordA**

Story Books on a Kitchen Table. Audre Lorde. *See* Out of her womb of pain my mother spat me.

Story for Rose on the Midnight Flight to Boston, A. Anne Sexton. **CP-SextA**

Story I Have Told, The. Stevie Smith. **CP-SmitS**

Story of a Citizen, The. Tess Gallagher. **SP-GallT**

Story of a Cock and a Bull, A. Christopher Smart. **SP-SmarC**

Story of an Olson, and Bad Thing, The. Charles Olson. **CP-OlsoC**

Story of Baucis & Philemon, The. Jonathan Swift. *See* Baucis and Philemon.

Story of Ida, The. John Greenleaf Whittier. **CP-WhitJ**

Story of Isaac. Leonard Cohen. **CP-CoheL**

Story of My Life, The. John Updike. **CP-UpdiJ**

Story of Richard Maxfield, The. Diane Wakoski. **SP-WakoD**

Story of Sir Arnulph, The. George Meredith. **CP-MerG2**

Story of the Ashes and the Flame, The. Edwin Arlington Robinson. **CP-RobiE**

Story of the Gadsbys, The. Rudyard Kipling. Winners, The. **CP-KiplR**

Story of Toile, The. Siv Cedering Fox. *Fr.* Onna-E, Pictures of Women. **SP-CedeS**

Story of Ung, The. Rudyard Kipling. **CP-KiplR**

Story of Uriah, The. Rudyard Kipling. **CP-KiplR**

Story That Could Be True, A. William Stafford. **SP-StafW**

Story thread runs out through your hands, The. The Tire. Tom Clark. **SP-ClarT**

S[tothard] in Childhood on the Nursery floor. William Blake. **CP-BlakW**

Stotras to Kali Destroyer of Illusions. Allen Ginsberg. **CP-GinsA**

Stout and well-knit in fact. Mandelstam's Hope for the Best. Donald Davie. **CP-DavDo**

Stout marches lead to certain ends. Robert Louis Stevenson. **CP-StevR**

Stout Sparta shrined the god of Laughter. Ralph Waldo Emerson. **CP-EmerR**

Stove it is—well—patcheable, The. With Sweetest Love and Welcome from All the Little Animals. Malcolm Lowry. **CP-LowrM**

Stowaway, The. Malcolm Lowry. **CP-LowrM**

Strada's Nightingale. Vincent Bourne, *tr. fr. Latin by* William Cowper. **CP-CowpW**

Strafed by the Milky Way. The Lists. Leonard Cohen. **CP-CoheL**

Strafford. Frank Templeton Prince. **CP-PrinF**

Strage degli innocenti, La, *sels.* Giovanni Battista Marino, *tr. fr. Italian by* Richard Crashaw. Sospetto d'Herode. **CP-CrasR** "Mongst all the Palaces in Hells command."

Strahan, Tonson, Lintot of the times. Byron. **CP-Byron** (Strahan, Tonson, Lintot of the Times.) **CP-Byron**

Strahan, Tonson, Lintot of the Times. Byron. *See* Strahan, Tonson, Lintot of the times.

Straight and slender. *with music.* Allen Ginsberg. **CP-GinsA**

Straight-Creek—Great Burn. Gary Snyder. **CP-SnydG**

Straight down from Amarillo. Drifting South. Gilbert Sorrentino. **SP-SorrG**

Straight into the sea fog. Roy Fisher. **SP-FishR** *Fr.* Glenthorne Poems.

Straight Life. William Matthews. **SP-MattW**

Straight, the swift, the debonair, The. Magnets. Countee Cullen. **CP-CullC**

Straightway let it be done! Aristodemus the Messenian. Thomas Hardy. **CP-HardT**

Strait, The. Wendell Berry. **CP-BerrW** "I have come to the end." "Sitting among the bluebells." "Valley holds its shadow, The." "World's one song is passing, The."

Straitjacket, straitjacket, straitjacket. Uprising. Stephen Dobyns. **SP-DobyS**

Straits of Malacca 24 Oct 1957. Gary Snyder. **CP-SnydG**

Strambotti. Frank Templeton Prince. **CP-PrinF**

Strambotto. Gilbert Sorrentino. **SP-SorrG**

Strand, The. Louis MacNeice. **CP-MacNL**

Strand at Lough Beg, The. Seamus Heaney. **SP-HeanS**

Stranded here in Ishmael's November. Dire Coasts. John Clellon Holmes. **SP-HolmJ**

Stranded in the middle of the nation like this. Wake. Rita Dove. *Fr.* A Suite for Augustus. **SP-DoveR**

Stranded late at night when the blackout came. The Door. Frederick Morgan. **SP-MorgF**

Strange / Distorted blades of grass. Garden. Langston Hughes. **SP-HughL**

Strange about shadows, but the sun. Solipsism & Solecism. Howard Nemerov. **CP-NemeH**

Strange are the ways of men. Robert Louis Stevenson. **CP-StevR**

Strange—as I sat brooding here. Lucy. Walter de la Mare. **CP-DeLaW**

Strange bed, whose recurrent dream we are, The. Hotel de l'Univers et Portugal. James Merrill. **SP-MerrJ**

Strange bird, / His song remains secret. Youth. James Wright. **CP-WrigJ**

Strange Calendar. Stanley Jasspon Kunitz. **CP-KuniS**

Strange Case of Mr. Ballantine's Valentine, The. Ogden Nash. **CP-NashO**

Strange Case of Mr. Fortague's Disappointment, The. Ogden Nash. **CP-NashO**

Strange Case of Mr. Niobob's Transmogrification, The. Ogden Nash. **CP-NashO**

Strange Case of Mr. O'Banion's Come-Uppance, The. Ogden Nash. **CP-NashO**

Strange Case of Mr. Palliser's Palate, The. Ogden Nash. **CP-NashO**

Strange Case of Mr. Pauncefoot's Broad Mind, The. Ogden Nash. **CP-NashO**

Strange Case of Mr. Wood's Frustration, or, A Team that Won't Be Beaten Better Stay off the Field, The. Ogden Nash. **CP-NashO**

Strange Case of Mr. Donnybrooks's Boredom, The. Ogden Nash. **CP-NashO**

Strange Case of the Ambitious Caddy, The. Ogden Nash. **CP-NashO**

Strange Case of the Blackmailing Dove, The. Ogden Nash. **CP-NashO**

Strange Case of the Cautious Motorist, The. Ogden Nash. **CP-NashO**

Strange Case of the Dead Divorcee, The. Ogden Nash. **CP-NashO**

Strange Case of the Entomologist's Heart, The. Ogden Nash. **CP-NashO**

Strange Case of the Girl o' Mr. Sponsoon's Dreams, The. Ogden Nash. **CP-NashO**

Strange Case of the Irksome Prude, The. Ogden Nash. **CP-NashO**

Strange Case of the Lovelorn Letter Writer, The. Ogden Nash. **CP-NashO**

Strange Case of the Lucrative Compromise, The. Ogden Nash. **CP-NashO**

Strange Case of the Pleasing Taxi-Driver, The. Ogden Nash. **CP-NashO**

Strange Case of the Renegade Lyric Writer, The. Ogden Nash. **CP-NashO**

Strange church smelled a bit 'high,' of censers, The. Geoffrey Hill. **PoE** *Fr.* Mercian Hymns. **CP-HillG**

Strange Erratum in all the Editions, A. To the Royal Academy. William Blake. **CP-BlakW**

Strange fabled face! From sterile shore to shore. Mirage. Walter de la Mare. **CP-DeLaW**

Strange fits of passion have I known. William Wordsworth. **EBEV; EnRP; FiP; GBL; LO; LiTB; NAEL-2; NOBE; NOBRP; OAEL-2; OAEP; OBEV; OBNC; OBRV; PPP; PoE; TEP; TrGrPo** *Fr.* Lucy. **CP-WorW1**

Strange Fruit. Seamus Heaney. **SP-HeanS**

Strange House, The. Thomas Hardy. **CP-HardT**

Strange Hurt. Langston Hughes. **SP-HughL**

Strange Meeting. Wilfred Owen. **CP-OwenW**

Strange memorable objects. Rose Room. Gilbert Sorrentino. **SP-SorrG**

Strange metamorphosis! It was but now. Upon the Kings Coronation. Richard Crashaw. **CP-CrasR**

Strange Metamorphosis of Poets. Howard Nemerov. **CP-NemeH**

Strange Moment, A. Charles Bukowski. **SP-BukC3**

Strange, Moving Lights of People Handle Holinesses Unknown, The. Kenneth Patchen. **CP-PatcK**

Strange New Cottage in Berkeley, A. Allen Ginsberg. **CP-GinsA**

Strange Night. David Markson. **CP-MarkD**

Strange now to think of you, gone without corsets & eyes. Kaddish. Allen Ginsberg. **CP-GinsA**

Strange place—where all men gain. Inner Distance. Marsden Hartley. **CP-HartM**

Strange Spirit, The. Walter de la Mare. **CP-DeLaW**

Strange that I did not know him then. An Old Story. Edwin Arlington Robinson. **CP-RobiE**

Strange, that I felt so gay. Tennyson. *Fr.* Maud [A Monodrama]. **CP-TennA**

Strange that sexual jealousy should be so much like sex itself: the same engrossing reveries. Soliloquies. Charles Kenneth Williams. **SP-WillC**

Strange that the youngest people I know, *sl. diff. vers. incl. in* Of Being Numerous. George Oppen. *Fr.* A Language of New York. **CP-OppeG**

Strange that the youngest people I know. George Oppen. *Fr.* Of Being Numerous. **CP-OppeG**

Strange that their dog. The Complexity. William Carlos Williams. **CP-WilW2**

Strange thing I said to Sam is the way they die, The. Man Is to Man a Beast. Kenneth Patchen. **CP-PatcK**

Strange thing I said to Sam is the way they die, The. Kenneth Patchen. **CP-PatcK**

Strange thing surely that my Heart, when love had come unsought, A. Owen Aherne and His Dancers. William Butler Yeats. **CP-YeatW**

Strange thing that I, by nature nothing prone. Edna St. Vincent Millay. **CP-MillE**

Strange, those lighted windows on. Gawain. Frederick Morgan. **SP-MorgF**

Strange to conceive, how the same objects strike. Occasioned by Sir William Temple's Late Illness and Recovery. Jonathan Swift. **CP-SwiftJ**

Strange to know nothing, never to be sure. Ignorance. Philip Larkin. **CP-LarkP**

Strange / To reach that age. Louis Zukofsky. **CP-ZukLS**

Strange voices sing among the planets which. Christina Georgina Rossetti. **CP-RosC3**

Strange walkers! See their processional. The Mushroom Gatherers. Donald Davie. **CP-DavDo**

Strange wind off the night, A. The Face. Philip Levine. **SP-LeviP**

Strange winds from the uttermost heavens swept the tomb. She Becomes a Goddess. Nicholas Vachel Lindsay. *Fr.* The Trial of the Dead Cleopatra in Her Beautiful and Wonderful Tomb. **CP-LindV**

Strangely radiant skies have come, The. March-Mad. May Sarton. **SP-SartM**

Strangeness. Robert Ranke Graves. **CP-GravR**

Strangeness, come again. Muse Wooing: A Song. John Clellon Holmes. **SP-HolmJ**

Stranger, The. Walter de la Mare. **CP-DeLaW**

Stranger, The. Walter de la Mare. **CP-DeLaW**

Stranger, The. Jean Garrigue. **SP-GarrJ**

Stranger, The. Rudyard Kipling. **CP-KiplR**

Stranger, The. Thomas Merton. **CP-MertT**

Stranger, The. Kenneth Patchen. **CP-PatcK**

Stranger, The. Adrienne Rich. **CP-RicAE**

Stranger, The. Adrienne Rich. **SP-RicA1**

Stranger. Richard Shelton. **SP-ShelR**

Stranger. Allen Tate. **CP-TateA**

Stranger across the road, The. Timeshare. Dabney Stuart. **SP-StuaD**

Stranger! behold, interr'd together. Epitaph for Joseph Blacket. Byron. **CP-Byron**

Stranger calling a dog whistled, A. Grace Paley. **CP-PaleG**

Stranger came to the door at eve, A. Love and a Question. Robert Frost. **CP-FrosR**

Stranger from the noisy inn, The. Good Company. Walter de la Mare. **CP-DeLaW**

Stranger has come, A. Love in the Asylum. Dylan Thomas. **CP-ThomD**

Stranger, I threaded sunken-hearted, A. The Woman I Met. Thomas Hardy. **CP-HardT**

Stranger, if you passing meet me and desire to speak to me, why should you not speak to me? To You. Walt Whitman. **CP-WhitW**

Stranger, ignore yon loud bassoon. That's Funny, Wasn't It? No, It Won't Be. Ogden Nash. **CP-NashO**

Stranger lives in the Sages' mansion, A. Tillie Sage (1). Louise McNeill. **SP-McNeL**

Stranger Song, The. Leonard Cohen. **CP-CoheL**

Stranger, striding down the paths of spring, The. The Old Man. John Clare. **SP-ClarJ**

Stranger, the bark you see before you says. Catullus. *See* Carmen 4: "My bean-pod boat you see here."

Stranger, the wages that we earned. For the Madrid Road. Randall Jarrell. **CP-JarrR**

Stranger, the world expected You for long days. Messias. Thomas Merton. **CP-MertT**

Stranger! this hillock of mis-shapen stones. Written with a Slate Pencil upon a Stone, the Largest of a Heap Lying near a Deserted Quarry, upon One of the Islands at Rydal. William Wordsworth. **CP-WorW1**

Stranger, this is shining Colonos. Sophocles, *tr.* by Stephen Spender. **CP-SpenS** *Fr.* Oedipus at Colonus.

Stranger to folly and to fear. 3.2. Horace. **CP-JohnS,** *tr.* by Samuel Johnson; *Fr.* Odes.

Stranger! whose eyes a look of pity shew. The Old Man of the Alps. Samuel Taylor Coleridge. **CP-ColeS**

Stranger within my gate, The. The Stranger. Rudyard Kipling. **CP-KiplR**

Stranger, you who hide my love. Song. Stephen Spender. **CP-SpenS**

Strangers. Philip Larkin. **CP-LarkP**

Strangers. May Sarton. **SP-SartM**

Strangers. Richard Shelton. **SP-ShelR**

Strangers and Neighbors. John Hewitt. **CP-HewiJ**

Strangers are an endangered species. Adrienne Rich. *Fr.* The Spirit of Place. **SP-RicA2**

Stranger's Child. George Oppen. **CP-OppeG**

Strangers drawn from the ends of the earth, jewelled and plumed were we. The Sack of the Gods. Rudyard Kipling. **CP-KiplR** *Fr.* The Naulahka.

Stranger's Song, The. Thomas Hardy. **CP-HardT**

Strangest is their reality. Dream Objects. John Updike. **CP-UpdiJ**

Strangest Sight You Ever Did See—, The. Charles Bukowski. **SP-BukC1**

Strangling in Merrion Square, The. Robert Ranke Graves. **CP-GravR**

Strapped at the center of the blazing wheel. A Pilot from the Carrier. Randall Jarrell. **CP-JarrR; SP-JarrR**

Strapped helpless, monarchs and prelates, round they swung. The Wheel of Fortune. Thom Gunn. **CP-GunnT**

Stratagem, The. Walter de la Mare. **CP-DeLaW**

Stratford on Avon. Donald Davie. **CP-DavDo**

Stratford-on-Avon. Louis Zukofsky. **CP-ZukLS**

Strathallan's Lament. Robert Burns. **CP-BurnR**

Strathnaver. Donald Davie. **CP-DavDo**

Strato in Plaster. James Merrill. **SP-MerrJ**

Stratosphere was once where angels were, The. Christmas 1944. Hilda Doolittle. **CP-DoolH**

Stravinsky looks upon the mountain. Mountain Impasse. John Updike. **CP-UpdiJ**

Straw, The. Robert Ranke Graves. **CP-GravR**

Straw Hat. Rita Dove. **SP-DoveR**

Straw-stuff'd hamper with his ruthless steel, The. Lines after the Manner of Homer. William Cowper. **CP-CowpW**

Strawberries, pears, fingers, the eyes. Another Elegy. Margaret Atwood. **SP-AtwM2**

Strawberry Fields Forever. The Beatles. **CP-Beatl**

Strawberry Hill. Ted Hughes. **SP-HughT**

Strawberry Moon. Mary Oliver. **SP-OlivM**

Strawberry Shrub, The. Edna St. Vincent Millay. **CP-MillE**

Strawman. "Lou Reed." **SP-ReedL**

Stray Pleasures. William Wordsworth. **CP-WorW1**

Strayed Crab. Elizabeth Bishop. *Fr.* Rainy Season; Sub-Tropics. **CP-BishE**

Strayed Message, The. Robert Ranke Graves. **CP-GravR**

Strayed Village, The. Adrienne Rich. **CP-RicAE**

Streaking (A Phenomenon Following the Sixties). Alice Walker. **CP-WalkA**

Stream, The. Charles Simic. **SP-SimiC**

Stream, The. Mona Van Duyn. **SP-VanDM**

Stream and Sun at Glendalough. William Butler Yeats. **CP-YeatW**

Stream, go hide yourself. On a Railroad Right of Way. Carl Sandburg. **CP-SandC**

Stream I think persuaded me at first, The. The Road's Your Place. Wystan Hugh Auden. **CP-AudWJ**

Stream moaneth as it floweth, The. Song. Christina Georgina Rossetti. **CP-RosC3**

Stream of my fathers! sweetly still. The Merrimac. John Greenleaf Whittier. **CP-WhitJ**

STREAM, to mingle with your favourite Dee, A. To the Lady E.B. and the Hon. Miss P. William Wordsworth. **CP-WorW2**

Stream with languid murmur creeps, The. Imitated from Ossian. Samuel Taylor Coleridge. *Fr.* Effusions. **CP-ColeS**

Streams. Wystan Hugh Auden. *Fr.* Bucolics. **CP-AudeW**

Streams that glide in orient plains. Castle Gordon—*Intended to Be Sung to Morag.* Robert Burns. **CP-BurnR**

Street, The. Stephen Dobyns. **SP-DobyS**

Street. George Oppen. **CP-OppeG**

Street Called Crooked, The. Countee Cullen. **CP-CullC**

Street Corner College. Kenneth Patchen. **CP-PatcK**

Street Corner Dialogue. Grace Paley. **CP-PaleG**

Street corner to corner he will talk all day. Muriel Rukeyser. **CP-RukeM**

Street Has Changed, The. Randall Jarrell. **CP-JarrR**

Street Hassle: Street Hassle. "Lou Reed." **SP-ReedL**

Street Hassle: Waltzing Matilda. "Lou Reed." **SP-ReedL**

Street in Bronzeville, A. Gwendolyn Brooks. **SP-BrooG**
 Ballad of Chocolate Mabbie, The. **CAPP**
 Hunchback Girl: She Thinks of Heaven.
 Independent Man, The.
 Kitchenette Building. **BPo; FF; FaBoWP; NAAL-2; NoP; PoE; PoNe; Poetr; UnPo**
 Mother, The. **CrDW; CrSp; MDDM; NALW**
 Of De Witt Williams on His Way to Lincoln Cemetery. **NOBA; NoAM**
 Preacher: Ruminates Behind the Sermon, The. **PBMP**
 Sadie and Maud. **InPK; MoP; NOBA; NoAM; TAP**
 Song in the Front Yard, A. **IDB; NAAL-2; NOBA; NoAM; PoBA**
 Southeast Corner. **VGW**

Vacant Lot, The. **NAAL-2; NOBA; NoAM**

Street Lamps. Philip Larkin. **CP-LarkP**

Street Lamps. David Herbert Lawrence. **CP-LawrD**

Street Meeting. Lewis Turco. **SP-TurcL**

Street Musicians. John Ashbery. **SP-AshbJ**

Street Names. John Hewitt. **CP-HewiJ**

Street off Sunset, A. Randall Jarrell. *Fr.* The Lost World. **CP-JarrR; SP-JarrR**

Street Scene. Louis MacNeice. **CP-MacNL**

Street Song. Thom Gunn. **CP-GunnT**

Street Song. Langston Hughes. **SP-HughL**

Street Song. Sylvia Plath. **CP-PlatS**

Street sounds to the soldiers' tread, The. Alfred Edward Housman. **CP-HousA**

Street Window. Carl Sandburg. **CP-SandC**

Streetcars. Leonard Cohen. **CP-CoheL**

Streetlight. Stephen Dobyns. **SP-DobyS**

Streetlight from my parents' bed at night split, The. Streetlight. Stephen Dobyns. **SP-DobyS**

Streetlights bent / the sleet streams as I went, The. Two Cities. Marilyn Hacker. **SP-HackM**

Streetlights wreathed under saffron curls. It's My Town! Kenneth Patchen. **CP-PatcK**

Streets are new, the harbour, The. Visit to Toronto, with Companions. Margaret Atwood. **SP-AtwM1**

Streets as ever blocky, grey—square sense of rectangular enclosures. NYC—. Robert Creeley. **CP-CreeR**

Streets, guns, machines. Wendell Berry. *Fr.* The Clearing. **CP-BerrW**

Streets, in a poor district. George Oppen. *Fr.* Power, the Enchanted World. **CP-OppeG**

Streets of Laredo, The. Louis MacNeice. **CP-MacNL**

Streets of San Francisco, The. Niece. George Oppen. **CP-OppeG**

Streets. Of the mind. Whose gangs, The. First Invention on the Theme of the Adam. Robert Duncan. **SP-DuncR**

Streets Too Old. Carl Sandburg. **CP-SandC**

Streetsweeper, The. Ron Koertge. **SP-KoerR**

Streetwalking woman. Harlem. Etheridge Knight. *Fr.* Indiana Haiku—2. **SP-KnigE**

STRENGTH / inked with a light brush. Hymn to Alias Thor. Basil Bunting. **CP-BuntB**

Strength. Christopher Smart. *See* Strong is the horse upon his speed.

Strength of Baptisme, that's within, The. Baptisme. Robert Herrick. **CP-HerrR**

Strength of Fields, The. James Dickey. **CP-DickJ**

Strength of my country, whilst I bring to view. To True Soldiers. Ben Jonson. **CP-JonsB**

Strength of the Lonely, The. Nicholas Vachel Lindsay. **CP-LindV**

Strength of twice three thousand horse, The. The Destroyers. Rudyard Kipling. **CP-KiplR**

Strength Thy service cannot tire, A. Lines from a Letter to a Young Clerical Friend. John Greenleaf Whittier. **CP-WhitJ**

Strength to Support Soveraignty. Robert Herrick. **CP-HerrR**

Strengthened to live, strengthened to die for. In Distrust of Merits. Marianne Craig Moore. **CP-MoorM**

Strengthening as secret manna. What? Christina Georgina Rossetti. **CP-RosC3**

Strephon and Chloe. Jonathan Swift. **CP-SwifJ**

Stress of his anger set me back. The Revelation. James Wright. **CP-WrigJ**

Stretch towards the moonless midnight of the trees. To Dorothy Wellesley. William Butler Yeats. **CP-YeatW**

Stretch'd on a moulder'd Abbey's broadest wall. Melancholy. Samuel Taylor Coleridge. **CP-ColeS**

Stretched on the dying Mother's lap, lies dead. Monument of Mrs Howard. William Wordsworth. *Fr.* Poems Composed or Suggested During a Tour, in the Summer of 1833. **CP-WorW2**

Stretched out under the oak, in the wood's new leaves. *after Eduard Mörike.* Randall Jarrell. **CP-JarrR**

Stretching away to westward the great river lies quiet beneath me. The River of Mist. Edward Estlin Cummings. **CP-CummE**

Stretching eyes west / Over the sea. The Riddle. Thomas Hardy. **CP-HardT**

Stretching of the Belly, The. Etheridge Knight. **SP-KnigE**

Strew on her roses, roses. Requiescat. Matthew Arnold. **SP-ArnoM**

Stricken Deer, The. William Cowper. *See* I was a stricken deer, that left the herd.

Strictly Bucolic. Charles Simic. **SP-SimiC**

Strident high / civic trumpeting, The. Respublica. Geoffrey Hill. **CP-HillG**

Strife. David Herbert Lawrence. **CP-LawrD**

Strife between the Poet and Ambition, The. Thomas Merton. **CP-MertT**

Strife is grown between Virtue and Love, A. Sonnet 52. Sir Philip Sidney. **NAEL-1; NoP** *Fr.* Astrophil and Stella. **SP-SidnP**

Strike, churl; hurl, cheerless wind, then; heltering hail. Gerard Manley Hopkins. **CP-HopkG**

Strike home, strong-hearted man! To Ronge. John Greenleaf Whittier. **CP-WhitJ**

Strike not thy dog with a stick! To Children. George Meredith. **CP-MerG1**

Strike of the Night, The. Jean Garrigue. **SP-GarrJ**

Strike the bells wantonly. A Peal of Bells. Christina Georgina Rossetti. **CP-RosC1**

Striking like lightning to the quick of the real world. Duns Scotus. Thomas Merton. **CP-MertT; SP-MertT**

String, The. James Dickey. **CP-DickJ**

String of the scarlet rubies of Ceylon, A. 1945. Donald Davie. **CP-DavDo**

Strings' excitement, the applauding drum, The. Family Ghosts. Wystan Hugh Auden. **CP-AudeW**

Strings of her instrument become, The. The Harpist's Dream. Dabney Stuart. **SP-StuaD**

Strip off kindness. Where Dream Begins. May Sarton. **SP-SartM**

Strip to the waist and have a seat. The doctor. Words. Miller Williams. **SP-WillM**

Striped blouse in a clearing by Bazille, A. Ceremony. Richard Wilbur. **CP-WilbR**

Striped Cats, Old Men and Proud Stockings. Carl Sandburg. **CP-SandC**

Stripes. Carl Sandburg. **CP-SandC**

Stripes justly given yerk us (with their fall). Smart. Robert Herrick. **CP-HerrR**

Stripped / you're beginning to float free. November 1968. Adrienne Rich. **CP-RicAE; SP-RicA2**

Stripped more or less, they wrestle among the furniture on his. The Wrestler. Roy Fisher. **SP-FishR** *Fr.* Interiors with Various Figures.

Stripped of its horns and skin. The Moosehead. John Haines. **SP-HainJ**

Strive not, vain Lover, to be fine. Song. Richard Lovelace. **CP-LoveR**

Stroke, The. Rita Dove. **SP-DoveR**

Stroke, The. Stevie Smith. **CP-SmitS**

Stroke a flint, and there is nothing to admire. Christina Georgina Rossetti. **CP-RosC2**

Stroke by / stroke my / body remembers that life and cries for. The Sea. Mary Oliver. **SP-OlivM**

Stroke by stroke, in the country of the fragile. The Blue Flower. Muriel Rukeyser. **CP-RukeM**

Stroke the small silk with your whispering hands. The Eve of St Mark. Geoffrey Hill. *Fr.* An Apology for the Revival of Christian Architecture in England. **CP-HillG**

Stroller. William Carlos Williams. **CP-WilW1**

Strolling along / By the teeming docks. Docks. Carl Sandburg. **CP-SandC**

Strong am I among mortals, not without a name. Hippolytus. Euripides, *tr. fr.* Classical Greek by Rex Warner.

Strong and mighty Angel, A. The Mantle of St. John de Matha. John Greenleaf Whittier. **CP-WhitJ**

Strong and slippery / built for the midnight grass-party. Peter. Marianne Craig Moore. **CP-MoorM**

Strong Are Saying Nothing, The. Robert Frost. **CP-FrosR**

Strong Draughts of Their Refreshing Minds. Emily Dickinson. **CP-DickE**

Strong enough to be neutral—as is now proved, now American power. Historical Choice. Robinson Jeffers. **CP-JefR3**

Strong I stand, though I have borne. Emily Brontë. **CP-BronE**

Strong Ilion thou shalt see with walls and towers high. Ovid, *tr. by* Sir Walter Ralegh. **CP-RaleW** *Fr.* Heroides.

Strong is the horse upon his speed. Christopher Smart. **LiTB; OtMeF; UV** *Fr.* A Song to David. **SP-SmarC**

(Man of Prayer, The.) **LiTB**

(Strength.) **OtMeF**

Strong is the lion – like a coal. Christopher Smart. **HAP** *Fr.* A Song to David. **SP-SmarC**

Strong man's hand, the snow-cool head of age, The. Robert Louis Stevenson. *Fr.* Sonnets. **CP-StevR**

Strong men, The. Beach Trip. Charles Bukowski. **SP-BukC1**

Strong men keep coming on, The. Upstream. Carl Sandburg. **CP-SandC**

Strong Men, Riding Horses. Gwendolyn Brooks. **SP-BrooG**

Strong rocks hold up the riksdag bridge. . . always strong river waters. Two Items. Carl Sandburg. **CP-SandC**

Strong Son of God, immortal Love. Tennyson. **EBVV; EBVVPR; EaLo; EnVR; HAP; HBV; LiTB; MeMBP; NAWM-2; OAEL-2; SeCeV; TRV; TrCP; TrGrPo; TrPWD; TreF; WGRP; WHA** *Fr.* In Memoriam A. H. H. **CP-TennA**

Strong song tows, A. Basil Bunting. **OAEL-2** *Fr.* Briggflatts [An Autobiography]. **CP-BuntB**

Strong sun, that bleach. The Plaid Dress. Edna St. Vincent Millay. **CP-MillE**

Strong woman is a woman who is straining, A. For Strong Women. Marge Piercy. **SP-PierM**

Stronger Lessons. Walt Whitman. **CP-WhitW**

Stronger than alcohol, more great than song. Ted Berrigan. **SP-BerrT** *Fr.* The Sonnets.

Stronger than destiny is pain. Hayden Carruth. *Fr.* North Winter. **CP-CarHL**

Strongly it bears us along in swelling and limitless billows. The Homeric Hexameter. Samuel Taylor Coleridge. **CP-ColeS**

Strophe of green leaves. The Linden Branch. Archibald MacLeish. **CP-MacLA**

Struck head to. Oblivion's Room. Archie Randolph Ammons. **SP-AmmoA**

Struck, was I, not yet by Lightning. Emily Dickinson. **CP-DickE**

Struck with the rising scene, thus I, amazed. Britain. James Thomson. *Fr.* Liberty. **CP-ThomJ**

Structure is rising. It takes on shape, it takes on meaning, A. Muriel Rukeyser. **CP-RukeM**

Structure of Rime, The. Robert Duncan.

"Back to the figure." **SP-DuncR**

"Best of ways. That there be a law the Earth gives and the Mountain." **SP-DuncR**

"Erecting beyond the boundaries of all government." **SP-DuncR**

"I ask the unyielding Sentence that shows Itself forth in the language." **SP-DuncR**

"Master of Rime told me, You must learn to lose heart, The." **SP-DuncR**

"O Outrider! / when you come to the threshold of the stars." **SP-DuncR**

"Old women came from their caves to close the too many doors, The." **SP-DuncR**

"There are memories everywhere then. Rememberd, we go out, as in." **SP-DuncR**

"This potion is love's portion. This herb." **SP-DuncR**

"What of the structure of Rime? I said." **SP-DuncR**

Structure of the Plane, The. Muriel Rukeyser. **CP-RukeM**

Structure,miraculous challenge,devout am. Edward Estlin Cummings. **CP-CummE**

Struggle of the Britons against the Barbarians. William Wordsworth. *Fr.* Ecclesiastical Sonnets. **CP-WorW2**

Struggle of Wings. William Carlos Williams. **CP-WilW1**

Struggling. Joseph Ceravolo. **SP-CeraJ**

Struggling Rill insensibly is grown, The. The Stepping-Stones. William Wordsworth. *Fr.* The River Duddon [A Series of Sonnets]. **CP-WorW2**

Strumpet Song. Sylvia Plath. **CP-PlatS**

Strut, once a Fore-man of a Shop we knew. Upon Strut. Robert Herrick. **CP-HerrR**

Stubbing the cloud-fields—the searchlight, high. Louis Zukofsky. **CP-ZukLS** *Fr.* 29 Poems. **CP-ZukLS**

Stubborn hidalgo, rusting in his mail. The Sacred Fount. Daniel Gerard Hoffman. **SP-HoffD**

Stubborn man put out to sea, A. The Scouring. Richard Eberhart. **CP-EberR**

Stubborne Author of the trifle, Crime, The. Epilogue, The. Richard Lovelace. **CP-LoveR**

Stubby Carrot. Laurence Lieberman. **SP-LiebL**

Stuck in the mud they are saying: "We were sad." Basil Bunting. *Fr.* The Well of Lycopolis. **CP-BuntB**

Stuck Inside of Mobile with the Memphis Blues Again. "Bob Dylan." **CP-DylaB**

Student, The. Elizabeth Barrett Browning. **CP-BroEB**

Student, The. Marianne Craig Moore. **CP-MoorM**

Student, The. Dabney Stuart. **SP-StuaD**

Student / The dust of ancient pages, The. Communication II. Maya Angelou. **SP-AngeM**

Student all the way down, The. Writing Class. Stephen Berg. **SP-BergS**

Student came from Oxford town also, A, *mod. vers. by* Louis Untermeyer. Geoffrey Chaucer. *See* A Clerk ther was of Oxenford also.

Student Dies in 100 Yard Dash. Howard Nemerov. **CP-NemeH**

Student here, from Ballintoy, A. The Clink of Rhyme. John Hewitt. **CP-HewiJ**

Student Revolution. Erica Jong. **SP-JongE**

Students listen to the tapes. June. Gary Snyder. *Fr.* Six Years. **CP-SnydG**

Students, The / went out / of their way. Streaking (A Phenomenon Following the Sixties). Alice Walker. **CP-WalkA**

Studies. Roy Fisher.

"Civic water / with lilies and flies." **SP-FishR**

"Convalescent / to get along the shop fronts." **SP-FishR**

Studies by the Sea. Charlotte Smith. **CP-SmitC**

Studies for a Self-Portrait at Forty. James McAuley.
   "Better the big NOW, singular." **SP-McAuJ**
   "Cock the right eyebrow: Heredity." **SP-McAuJ**
   Episodes for a Panel. **SP-McAuJ**
   "Leave the hair white, uncombed." **SP-McAuJ**
   "You'd hardly notice at first how everything." **SP-McAuJ**

Studies for an Actress. Jean Garrigue. **SP-GarrJ**

Studies of man's friendly competitor the rat have shown. Thomas Merton.
   Fr. Cables to the Ace. **CP-MertT**

Studies themselves will languish and decay. Studies to Be Supported.
   Robert Herrick. **CP-HerrR**

Studies to Be Supported. Robert Herrick. **CP-HerrR**

Studio, The. Derek Mahon. **SP-MahoD**

Studio up over in Your Ear. Al Young. **CP-YounA**

Studiously by lamp-light I appraised. Man Does, Woman Is. Robert Ranke
   Graves. **CP-GravR**

Study. David Herbert Lawrence. **CP-LawrD**

STUDY: *A Lady in her Bedroom* (Bonnard). Jenny Joseph. *Fr.* Altarpiece (A
   Meditation on Lust, Desire and Love). **SP-JoseJ**

Study. (A Soul), A. Christina Georgina Rossetti. **CP-RosC3**

Study for the World's Body. David St. John. **SP-StJoD**
   Body of Desire, The.
   Of Time & the Body.

Study in a Late Subway. Muriel Rukeyser. **CP-RukeM**

Study Nature. Gertrude Stein. **CP-SteiG**

Study of an Elevation, in Indian Ink. Rudyard Kipling. **CP-KiplR**
   ("This ditty is a string of lies.") **CP-KiplR**

Study of History. Adrienne Rich. **CP-RicAE; SP-RicA2**

Study of Images I. Wallace Stevens. **CP-StevW**

Study of Images II. Wallace Stevens. **CP-StevW**

Study of Reading Habits, A. Philip Larkin. **CP-LarkP**

Study of Two Pears. Wallace Stevens. **CP-StevW**

Study the irregular verb. Note For a Poem. Malcolm Lowry. **CP-LowrM**

Study to Deserve Death. Stevie Smith. **CP-SmitS**

Studying the Signs. Allen Ginsberg. **CP-GinsA**

Stuff of the moon. Nocturne in a Deserted Brickyard. Carl Sandburg. **CP-SandC**

Stuffing, O'Toole naturally stuffs with his tool. Carmen 94. Catullus. *Fr.*
   Carmina. **CP-Catul**

Stuffing yourself into a blizzard. John Yau. **SP-YauJo** *Fr.* Scenes from
   the Life of Boullee.

Stumble into the great red sunset. Chuck Miller. **SP-MillC**

Stumbling and weeping. Chuck Miller. **SP-MillC**

Stumbling blocks are realigned, The. John Yau. **SP-YauJo** *Fr.* Scenes
   from the Life of Boullee.

Stumbling up an unfamiliar stairway. Song: The Sigil. Robert Ranke
   Graves. **CP-GravR**

Stump. Donald Hall. **CP-HallD**

Stun. James Schuyler. **CP-SchuJ**

Stunned in that first estrangement. What We Said. William DeWitt
   Snodgrass. **SP-SnodW**

Stunt Flier, The. John Updike. **CP-UpdiJ**

Stupefying images of grief-in-dream. Geoffrey Hill. *Fr.* Tenebrae. **CP-HillG**

Stupid? Of course that older lot were stupid. In and Come In. Archibald
   MacLeish. **CP-MacLA**

Stupid painter paints. He, The. Gilbert Sorrentino. **SP-SorrG**

Stupid tranquility, to be most sure. Zero. Tess Gallagher. **SP-GallT**

Stupor of knowledge lacking inwardness—. The Pure Fury. Theodore
   Roethke. **CP-RoetT**

Sturdy Legs, That. Kenneth Patchen. **CP-PatcK**

Stygian Banks, The. Louis MacNeice. **CP-MacNL**
   "And take me then! In the dawn under the high window."
   "And what when the glass breaks when the Note sounds?"
   "Fantasy holds the child in the man, the lover in the monk, the monk in
   the lover."
   "So let the world chant on. There is harsh fruit in the garden."
   "That is the end of the news. The humanist."
   "That roses are red is home—and homesickness."
   "To keep themselves young—Is that why people have children?"

Stygian council thus disolved; and forth, The. John Milton. **OAEL-1** *Fr.*
   Book II. **FHYEP; NAEL-1; OxAEP-1** *Fr.* Paradise Lost. **CP-MiltJ**

Style. Leonard Cohen. **CP-CoheL**

Style. Roy Fisher. **SP-FishR**

Style. John Hewitt. **CP-HewiJ**

Style. Marianne Craig Moore. **CP-MoorM**

Style. Howard Nemerov. **CP-NemeH**

Style. Carl Sandburg. **CP-SandC**

Style. Miller Williams. **SP-WillM**

Style—go ahead talking about style. Style. Carl Sandburg. **CP-SandC**

Style? I couldn't begin. Style. Roy Fisher. **SP-FishR**

Style is the perfection of a point of view. Meditation Two. Richard
   Eberhart. **CP-EberR**

Style is the water out of Homer. The Garden God. Richard Eberhart. **CP-EberR**

Styles of Bloom. John Updike. **CP-UpdiJ**

Stylist, The. William Carlos Williams. **CP-WilW2**

Stylite. Louis MacNeice. **CP-MacNL**

Styro. Jim Carroll. **SP-CarrJ**

Sub Contra. Louise Bogan. **CP-BogaL**

Sub Specie Aeternitatis. Robert Earl Hayden. **AmPP** *Fr.* An Inference of
   Mexico. **CP-HaydR**

Sub Terra. William Carlos Williams. **CP-WilW1**

Subalterns, The. Thomas Hardy. **CP-HardT**

Subaltern's Love-Song, A. Sir John Betjeman. **CP-BetjJ**

Subcommittee submits, The. The Bill. Muriel Rukeyser. **CP-RukeM**

Subject-Cases: The Background of a Detective Story. Gertrude Stein. **CP-SteiG**

Subject for Eisenstein. Constitution Day. Charles Tomlinson. **CP-TomlC**

Subject, Object, Sentence. Stephen Spender. **CP-SpenS**

Subject of Heroic Song, The. John Milton. *See* No more of talk where God
   or Angel Guest.

Subject thought: because he had a verb, A. Subject, Object, Sentence.
   Stephen Spender. **CP-SpenS**

Subject To Like Passions as We Are. Christina Georgina Rossetti. **CP-RosC2**

Subjected Earth. Robinson Jeffers. **CP-JefR2**

Sublime – invention ever young. Christopher Smart. **OBEV** *Fr.* A Song to
   David. **SP-SmarC**

Submerged Dragon. Thomas Merton. **CP-MertT**

Submergence. David Herbert Lawrence. **CP-LawrD**

Submission. William Cowper. *See* O Lord, my best desire fulfil.

Submission. George Herbert. **CP-HerbG**

Subscription. Jenny Joseph. *Fr.* Life and Turgid Times of A. Citizen. **SP-JoseJ**

Substance and Shadow. John Hewitt. **CP-HewiJ**

Substantial Planes. Archie Randolph Ammons. **SP-AmmoA**

Substitute, The. Stephen Dunn. **SP-DunnS**

Substitute for an Epitaph. Byron. **CP-Byron**

Substitution. Elizabeth Barrett Browning. **CP-BroEB**

Subterranean Homesick Blues. "Bob Dylan." **CP-DylaB**

Subtle chain of countless rings, A. Ralph Waldo Emerson. **CP-EmerR**
   (Motto to "Nature" ("Subtle chain of countless rings, A").) **CP-EmerR**

Subtle, clever brain, wiser than I am. Play. William Carlos Williams. **CP-WilW1**

Subtle man, meaning the subtle woman too, The. On the Subtle Man.
   Richard Eberhart. **CP-EberR**

Subtle power in perfume found, The. Sweet Fern. John Greenleaf Whittier.
   CP-WhitJ

Suburb. John Hewitt. **CP-HewiJ**

Suburb. Stevie Smith. **CP-SmitS**

Suburb lies like a hand tonight, The. The Wind at Night. Roy Fisher. *Fr.*
   City. **SP-FishR**

Suburban. John Ciardi. **SP-CiarJ**

Suburban Classes, The. Stevie Smith. **CP-SmitS**

Suburban Madrigal. John Updike. **CP-UpdiJ**

Suburban Prophecy. Howard Nemerov. **CP-NemeH**

Suburban Sicilian Sketches. Carl Sandburg. **CP-SandC**

Suburban Spring in Warwickshire. John Hewitt. **CP-HewiJ**

Suburban villas, highway-side retreats. London Suburbs. William Cowper.
   FaBoPP *Fr.* Retirement. **CP-CowpW**

Suburbs of a Secret, The. Emily Dickinson. **CP-DickE**

Suburbs on a Hazy Day. David Herbert Lawrence. **CP-LawrD**

Subversive leaves, you fall. John Haines. *Fr.* The End of the Summer.
   SP-HainJ

Subverted Flower, The. Robert Frost. **CP-FrosR**

Subway. Carl Sandburg. **CP-SandC**

Subway, The. Allen Tate. **CP-TateA**

Subway from New Britain to the Bronx, The. Randall Jarrell. **CP-JarrR**

Subway Rush Hour. Langston Hughes. **SP-HughL**

Succeeding years thy early frame destroy. Ovid, *tr.* by Samuel Johnson. **CP-JohnS** *Fr.* Heroides.

Success is a played-out game, success, success! A Played-Out Game. David Herbert Lawrence. **CP-LawrD**

Success is counted sweetest. Emily Dickinson. **CP-DickE**

Success is dust, but an aim. Emily Dickinson. **SP-DickE**

Success is like some horrible disaster. Malcolm Lowry. **CP-LowrM**

Success Story. Archie Randolph Ammons. **SP-AmmoA**

Success Story. Philip Larkin. **CP-LarkP**

Succession. Howard Nemerov. **CP-NemeH**

Succession of Kings, The. Christina Georgina Rossetti. **CP-RosC3**

Succession of the Foure Sweet Months, The. Robert Herrick. *See* First, April, she with mellow show[e]rs.

Successions. Pablo Neruda, *tr. fr. Spanish* by Ben Belitt. **SP-NeruP**

Succourful daughters of men are the rosed and starred. George Meredith. *Fr.* Alsace-Lorraine. **CP-MerG1**

Succubus, The. Robert Ranke Graves. **CP-GravR**

Such a day such a day when the rain. Tom's a-Cold. Stephen Spender. **CP-SpenS**

Such a fine pullet ought to go. A Blue Ribbon at Amesbury. Robert Frost. **CP-FrosR**

Such a hubbub in the nests, / Such a bustle and squeak! Freaks of Fashion. Christina Georgina Rossetti. **CP-RosC2**

Such a Parcel of Rogues in a Nation. Robert Burns. **CP-BurnR**

Such a reasonable irrational fellow goodhumored. The Sun. Hayden Carruth. *Fr.* Contra Mortem. **CP-CarHL**

Such a starved bank of moss. Robert Browning. **CP-BroR2**

Such age how beautiful! O Lady bright. To —, in Her Seventieth Year. William Wordsworth. **CP-WorW2**

Such an alarm / as was raised last night. The Fox. Paul Muldoon. **SP-MuldP**

Such another peerless queen. Ralph Waldo Emerson. **CP-EmerR**

Such apt names befall great men. In Legationem Domini Oliveri St John ad Provincias Foederatas [On the Embassy of Lord Oliver St John to the United Provinces]. Andrew Marvell, *tr. fr. Latin* by William A. McQueen *and* Kiffin A. Rockwell. **CP-MarvA**

Such are the inlets of the mind. Emily Dickinson. **CP-DickE**

Such As in Ships. Rudyard Kipling. **CP-KiplR**

Such as like heavenly wights doe come. 4.2. Horace. **CP-RaleW,** *tr. by* Sir Walter Ralegh; *Fr.* Odes.

Such as the cause was of two husbands' war. 1.10. Ovid. **CP-MarlC,** *tr. by* Christopher Marlowe; *Fr.* Elegies.

Such as thou art, my faithful Lyre. To My Lyre. Charlotte Smith. **CP-SmitC**

Such Counsels You Gave to Me. Robinson Jeffers. **CP-JefR2**

Such dayes as weare the badge of holy red. To the Right, Noble, and Vertuous, Henry Lord Clifford, Sonne and Heyre to the Right Honourable, Francis, Earle of Cumberland. Thomas Campion. **CP-CampT**

Such earnestness! such wear and tear. Ungar and Rolfe. Herman Melville. **SP-MelvH** *Fr.* Clarel: A Poem and Pilgrimage in the Holy Land.

Such eviedence I have of indifference. Voice from the Tomb (3). Stevie Smith. **CP-SmitS**

Such figures if they succeed are beautiful. The Wheel of Being II. Hayden Carruth. *Fr.* Contra Mortem. **CP-CarHL**

Such fruitless questions may not long beguile. American Tradition. William Wordsworth. *Fr.* The River Duddon [A Series of Sonnets]. **CP-WorW2**

Such hap as I am happed in. Sir Thomas Wyatt. **CP-WyatT**

Such hope, as is the sick despair of good. Fragment. Percy Bysshe Shelley. **CP-ShelP**

Such is Love, it comforts in extremity. Charity Never Faileth. Christina Georgina Rossetti. **CP-RosC2**

Such is the course that nature's kind hath wrought. Sir Thomas Wyatt. **CP-WyatT**

Such is the Force of Happiness. Emily Dickinson. **CP-DickE**

Such love as mourning Husbands have. Life in Death. Samuel Taylor Coleridge. **CP-ColeS**

Such perfection / of dream would. The Dream. Robert Creeley. **CP-CreeR**

Such places are too still for history. Deep Woods. Howard Nemerov. **CP-NemeH**

Such pleasure as the teeming earth. To the Right Hon[oura]ble Hierome, L[ord] Weston. An Ode Gratulatory for His Return from His Embassy. 1632. Ben Jonson. **CP-JonsB**

Such shameless bards we have; and yet 'tis true. The Bookful Blockhead. Alexander Pope. **OBSV** *Fr.* An Essay on Criticism. **CP-PopeA**

Such should this day be, so the sun should hide. On the Marriage of T. K. and C. C.: The Morning Stormy. Thomas Carew. **CP-CareT**

Such Simple Love. Thomas McGrath. **SP-McGrT**

Such skill, matcht with such courage as he had. Edmund Spenser. **OBWP** *Fr.* Astrophel. **CP-Spens**

Such strains as, mingled with the lyre. Epilogue to Horace's *Carmen Seculare*. Samuel Johnson. **CP-JohnS**

Such strangeness of mind I know. Robert Creeley. **CP-CreeR**

Such syllables flicker out of grass. Basil Bunting. **CP-BuntB**

Such things there are, we don't know. Mona Van Duyn. **SP-VanDM**

Such vain thought as wonted to mislead me. Sir Thomas Wyatt. **CP-WyatT**

Such Verse as Bowles, heart-honour'd Poet, sang. Lines to Thomas Poole. Samuel Taylor Coleridge. **CP-ColeS**

Such was the circumstance of our first love. Coronet of Moonlight. Robert Ranke Graves. **CP-GravR**

Such was the power of sleep over him, his unfolded heart swaying. The Black Panther and the Little Boy. Kenneth Patchen. **CP-PatcK**

Such was the time when Waltz might best maintain. Byron. **DIP** *Fr.* The Waltz. **CP-Byron**

Such was thir song. John Milton. **PeECV** *Fr.* Book X. **FHYEP** *Fr.* Paradise Lost. **CP-MiltJ**

Such were the gifts inflicted upon us who trembled. The People Rest after Conquests. Frank Templeton Prince. *Fr.* Chaka. **CP-PrinF**

Such were the notes thy once-lov'd Poet sung. Epistle to Robert Earl of Oxford and Earl Mortimer. Alexander Pope. **CP-PopeA**

Such were the trophies, that, in earlier days. John Milton. *See* I with foolish mind and heedless zeal formerly.

Suchness. Kenneth Rexroth. **SP-RexrK**

Sudden / loss of hope, A. Echoes. Robert Creeley. **CP-CreeR**

Sudden Attack. Jim Morrison. **SP-MorrJ**

Sudden blow: the great wings beating still, A. Leda and the Swan. William Butler Yeats. **CP-YeatW**

Sudden chasm of ghastly light, A. Emily Brontë. **CP-BronE**

Sudden conflict rises from the swell, A. Sacheverel. William Wordsworth. *Fr.* Ecclesiastical Sonnets. **CP-WorW2**

Sudden Journey. Tess Gallagher. **SP-GallT**

Sudden Light and the Trees, The. Stephen Dunn. **SP-DunnS**

Sudden mildness, like the heart of May, A. A Country Walk in March. John Hewitt. **CP-HewiJ**

Sudden the desert changes. Bridge-Guard in the Karroo. Rudyard Kipling. **CP-KiplR**

Sudden upriseth from her stately palace. Edmund Spenser. **PPP** *Fr.* The Faerie Queene. **CP-Spens**

Suddenly / I touch upon wordlessness. The Curative Powers of Silence. Al Young. **CP-YounA**

Suddenly. James Schuyler. **CP-SchuJ**

Suddenly, at last, the bitter wind veers round. Arrow on the Vane. Robert Ranke Graves. **CP-GravR**

Suddenly Christ closed his eyes. No Avail. Michael Hartnett. **SP-HarMi**

Suddenly discovering in the eyes of the very beautiful Normande cocotte. Pagani's, November 8. Ezra Pound. **SP-PounE**

Suddenly he awoke and was running—raw. Bayonet Charge. Ted Hughes. **SP-HughT**

Suddenly his poor body. Ted Hughes. **NoAM** *Fr.* Stations. **SP-HughT**

Suddenly his virtues became universal. Death by Radio. William Carlos Williams. **CP-WilW2**

Suddenly I remember the holes. The Holes. Stephen Berg. **SP-BergS**

Suddenly I saw the cold and rook-delighting heaven. The Cold Heaven. William Butler Yeats. **CP-YeatW**

Suddenly I see it. Behold: A Relationship. Marge Piercy. *Fr.* Walking into Love. **SP-PierM**

Suddenly I understood. Shorts / Excerpts. Bill Knott. **SP-KnotB**

Suddenly in the night the sirens. Ernesto Cardenal, *tr.* by Thomas Merton. **CP-MertT** *Fr.* Three Epigrams.

Suddenly. Is. Now not what was *not*. Dawn. Robert Penn Warren. *Fr.* Two Poems about Suddenly and a Rose. **SP-WarrR**

Suddenly it is late night, there are people in the basement. The Colour Machine. Thom Gunn. **CP-GunnT**

Suddenly night crushed out the day and hurled. The Unreturning. Wilfred Owen. **CP-OwenW**

Suddenly, not long before. Long Last. Philip Larkin. **CP-LarkP**

Suddenly, nothing was left of all those. Jason Potter. Lewis Turco. *Fr.* Bordello. **SP-TurcL**

Suddenly, out of its still and drowsy air, the air of slaves. *1850 vers. of* Europe, the 72d and 73d Years of These States. Walt Whitman. **CP-WhitW**

Suddenly out of its still and drowsy lair, the lair of slaves. Europe, the 72d and 73d Year of These States. Walt Whitman. **CP-WhitW**

Suddenly, suddenly, everything. Intuition. Robert Penn Warren. *Fr.* Two Poems about Suddenly and a Rose. **SP-WarrR**

Suddenly the cherry has opened. Cherry. Jenny Joseph. *Fr.* Derivations. **SP-JoseJ**

Suddenly the drizzle lifts. Taken at the Flood. William Matthews. *Fr.* Flood. **SP-MattW**

Suddenly they came flying, like a long scarf of smoke. The Thing. Theodore Roethke. **CP-RoetT**

Sudds launders bands in piss[e]; and starches them. Upon Sudds, a Laundress[e]. Robert Herrick. **CP-HerrR**

Sue Ella Tucker was barely in her teens. Rubaiyat for Sue Ella Tucker. Miller Williams. **SP-WillM**

Sueño Real. Lawrence Ferlinghetti. **SP-FerlL**

Suffenus is, stay Varus,—whom you've proven—is the. Catullus. *See* Carmen 22: "I must, Varus, tell you."

Suffenus, whom so well you know. Catullus. *See* Carmen 22: "I must, Varus, tell you."

Suffenus whom you know, the Witty. Catullus. *See* Carmen 22: "I must, Varus, tell you."

Suffer the Children. Audre Lorde. **SP-LordA**
   ("He is forever trapped.") **SP-LordA**

Suffer Thou that Canst not Shift. Robert Herrick. **CP-HerrR**

Suffer thy legs, but not thy tongue to walk. Silence. Robert Herrick. **CP-HerrR**

Sufferance. Robert Herrick. **CP-HerrR**

Sufferance of her race is shown, The. Formerly a Slave. Herman Melville. **SP-MelvH**

Suffering / lament, sorrow and wild. Lyric, The. Tom Clark. **SP-ClarT**

Suffering Does for the Character. Steve Griffiths. **SP-GrifS**

Suffering in sorrow, in hope to attain. Sir Thomas Wyatt. **CP-WyatT**

Suffering through the winter months, with food. The Guerrillas. Edwin Rolfe. **CP-RolfE**

Sufferings. Robert Herrick. **CP-HerrR**

Sufficed not, madame, that you did tear. Sir Thomas Wyatt. **CP-WyatT**

Sufficeth it to you [*or* yow] my joy[e]s interred. The 11th: and Last Booke of the Ocean to Scinthia. Sir Walter Ralegh. **CP-RaleW** *Fr.* The Ocean's Love to Cynthia.

Suffolk. Donald Davie. **CP-DavDo**

Sugar. Tess Gallagher. **SP-GallT**

Sugar flowers. Roy Fisher. **SP-FishR** *Fr.* Matrix.

Sugar I am CALLING you. Not. The Islander. Louise Glück. **SP-GlücL**

Suggested at Tyndrum in a Storm. William Wordsworth. **CP-WorW2**

Suggested by a Picture of the Bird of Paradise. William Wordsworth. **CP-WorW2**

Suggested by a View from an Eminence in Inglewood Forest. William Wordsworth. **CP-WorW2**

Suggested by Mr W. Westall's Views of the Caves, etc., in Yorkshire. William Wordsworth. **CP-WorW2**

Suggested by the Foregoing [Monument of Mrs Howard]. William Wordsworth. *Fr.* Poems Composed or Suggested During a Tour, in the Summer of 1833. **CP-WorW2**

Suggested by the View of Lancaster Castle (on the Road from the South). William Wordsworth. *Fr.* Sonnets upon the Punishment of Death. **CP-WorW2**

Suggestion for a Telegraphic Birthday Greeting. Robert Browning. **CP-BroR2**

Suggestion for an Arrangement. Charles Bukowski. **SP-BukC3**

Suggestions for the Improvement of a Sunset. Charles Tomlinson. **CP-TomlC**

Suicide. Charles Bukowski. **SP-BukC2**

Suicide, The. Walter de la Mare. **CP-DeLaW**

Suicide, The. Alun Lewis. **CP-LewiA**

Suicide, The. Louis MacNeice. **CP-MacNL**

Suicide, The. Edna St. Vincent Millay. **CP-MillE**

Suicide. Allen Tate. **CP-TateA**

Suicide. Alice Walker. **CP-AudeW**

Suicide. Al Young. **CP-YounA**

Suicide: Anne. Charles Kenneth Williams. **SP-WillC**

Suicide applicant, A. Ant Dodger. Bill Knott. **SP-KnotB**

Suicide Blues. Muriel Rukeyser. **CP-RukeM**

Suicide, far from content, The. The Suicide in The Copse. Robert Ranke Graves. **CP-GravR**

Suicide in The Copse, The. Robert Ranke Graves. **CP-GravR**

Suicide Note. Jane Cooper. **SP-CoopJ**

Suicide Note. Richard Eberhart. **CP-EberR**

Suicide Note. Anne Sexton. **CP-SextA**

Suicide off Egg Rock. Sylvia Plath. **CP-PlatS**

Suicide on Junction Road Station after Abstention from Evening Communion in North London. Sir John Betjeman. **CP-BetjJ**

Suicide's Argument, The. Samuel Taylor Coleridge. **CP-ColeS**

Suicide's Epitaph. Stevie Smith. **CP-SmitS**

Suicide's Note. Langston Hughes. **SP-HughL**

Suit, The. Philip Levine. **SP-LeviP**

Suitable entrance to this village, A. The Permanent Migrations. Kenneth Patchen. **CP-PatcK**

Suitcase Strapped with a Rope, A. Charles Simic. **SP-SimiC**

Suite. Tom Clark. **SP-ClarT**
   "Got to be there, so that she'll know."
   "Her voice is heard, and then the child's."
   "I draw a head. You ask."
   "Then again by day fog drapes the boats."
   "Thought is surrounded by a halo."
   "Tones of voice are petty, The."
   "Warm ripe days. The sun floods the ridge with color."
   "What the picture tells me is itself."

Suite. Jean Garrigue. **SP-GarrJ**

Suite. Patti Smith. **SP-SmitP**

Suite for Augustus, A. Rita Dove. **SP-DoveR**
   Augustus Observes the Sunset.
   Back.
   D. C.
   1963.
   Planning the Perfect Evening. **MAYP**
   Wake.

Suite for Lord Timothy Dexter. Muriel Rukeyser. **CP-RukeM**

Suite for Recorders. Louis MacNeice. **CP-MacNL**
   "Come, my sheep, my goats, graze where the shoots are tender."
   "If shepherd to nymph were the whole story."
   "In a little room, a little plot, a little lifetime."
   "Pride in your history is pride."

Suite in Prison. Richard Eberhart. **CP-EberR**
   Address to you.
   Bath Room, The.
   "Grave's a seed will get some monstrous bloom, The."
   "I turned where the sun came up and he held my hand."
   "Incarcerating sunlight, world damnation."
   "Lord, stabilise me. My legs."

Suite of Imitations Written After Reading Translations of Poems by Li He And Li Shang-yin, A. John Yau. **SP-YauJo**

Suitor, The. Paul Laurence Dunbar. **CP-DunbP**

Suitors sinn'd, but with a fair excuse, The. On Flaxman's Penelope. William Cowper. **CP-CowpW**

Sulkily the sticks burn, and though they crackle. Under the Pot. Robert Ranke Graves. **CP-GravR**

Sullen brook hardly would satisfy, A. John Berryman. *Fr.* Sonnets to Chris. **CP-BerrJ**

Sullen hot noon, a loop of wire. The Hill behind the Town. Roy Fisher. *Fr.* City. **SP-FishR**

Sulmo, Peligny's third part, me contains. 2.16. Ovid. **CP-MarlC,** *tr. by* Christopher Marlowe; *Fr.* Elegies.

Sulpicia to Cerinthus. Tibullus, *tr. fr. Latin by* Allen Tate. **CP-TateA**

Sultry summer day is done, The. Evening. Sir Walter Scott. **SP-ScotW** *Fr.* Rokeby.

Sum, The. Paul Laurence Dunbar. **CP-DunbP**

Sum of all the parts of Such—, The. Synthetic Such. Robert Ranke Graves. **CP-GravR**

Sumach and Birds. Carl Sandburg. **CP-SandC**

Summa. Gerard Manley Hopkins. **CP-HopkG**

Summah is de lovin' time. A Summer Night. Paul Laurence Dunbar. **CP-DunbP**

Summah night an' sighin' breeze. Lover's Lane. Paul Laurence Dunbar. **CP-DunbP**

Summah's nice, wif sun a-shinin'. Time to Tinker 'Roun'! Paul Laurence Dunbar. **CP-DunbP**

Summe, and the Satisfaction, The. Robert Herrick. **CP-HerrR**

Summe Deus, cui cæca patent penetralia cordis. Prayer. Samuel Johnson. **CP-JohnS**

Summe Pater, quodcunque tuum de corpore Numen. On Losing the Power of Speech. Samuel Johnson. **CP-JohnS**

Summer. John Ashbery. **SP-AshbJ**

Summer, The. Hayden Carruth. *Fr.* Contra Mortem. **CP-CarHL**

Summer. Louise Glück. *Fr.* Marathon. **SP-GlücL**

Summer ("Come, Cuckoo, Come"). Christina Georgina Rossetti. **CP-RosC1**

Summer ("Hark to the song. . ."). Christina Georgina Rossetti. **CP-RosC3**

Summer ("Winter is Cold-hearted"). Christina Georgina Rossetti. **CP-RosC3**

Summer. Edmund Spenser. **GN** *Fr.* The Faerie Queene. **CP-Spens**

Summer! / The painting is organized. The Corn Harvest. William Carlos Williams. **ArNa; PPP** *Fr.* Pictures from Brueghel. **CP-WilW2**

Summer. James Thomson. *Fr.* The Seasons. **CP-ThomJ**

"And what, my thoughtless sons, should fire you more." **ECEV**

Happy Britannica. **OBEC; SeCePo**

(Britannica.) **FaBoPP,** *ll.* 1–19;

"His was the treasure of two thousand years." **EPCY**

"Home from his morning task the swain retreats." **FM**

"Nor shall my verse that elder bard forget." **EPCY**

"Still let me pierce into the midnight depth." **EnRP**

"'Tis raging noon; and vertical, the sun." **EBEV; OAEL-1**

Wild Shakespeare. **EPCY**

Summer. Al Young. **CP-YounA**

Summer Afternoon an Old Man Gives Some Thought to the Central Questions, A. Miller Williams. **SP-WillM**

Summer again; / in the mirrors of this room. Margaret Atwood. *Fr.* The Circle Game. **SP-AtwM1**

Summer Amnesty. Jenny Joseph. **SP-JoseJ**

Summer and Spring. William Butler Yeats. *Fr.* A Man Young and Old. **CP-YeatW**

Summer and Winter. Percy Bysshe Shelley. **CP-ShelP**

Summer and winter close commune. In St. Paul's a While Ago. Thomas Hardy. **CP-HardT**

Summer apples, showy and sugary, mealy and touchy. Jelly Jelly. James Schuyler. **CP-SchuJ**

Summer Arcady. John Hewitt. **CP-HewiJ**

Summer, be seen no more within this wood. Edna St. Vincent Millay. **CP-MillE**

Summer begins to have the look. Emily Dickinson. **CP-DickE**

Summer Breezes. Frank O'Hara. **SP-OharF**

Summer burns on the edges of day. Song. Hayden Carruth. **CP-CarHS**

Summer by the Lakeside. John Greenleaf Whittier. **CP-WhitJ**

Summer cloud / Seeming to pause, seeming to look at yourself. Cloud. Jenny Joseph. *Fr.* Derivations. **SP-JoseJ**

Summer cloud in summer blue, The. Cloud and Flame. John Berryman. **CP-BerrJ**

Summer cold. No rash. No fever. Nothing. But a dozen times during the night I wake, A. The Shade. Charles Kenneth Williams. **CP-WillC; SP-WillC**

Summer dawn breaks over the city, A. Thursday. James Schuyler. **CP-SchuJ**

Summer Day, The. Mary Oliver. **SP-OlivM**

Summer day on which you came, The. Emily Dickinson. **SP-DickE**

Summer ends now; now, barbarous in beauty, the stooks [a]rise. Hurrahing in Harvest. Gerard Manley Hopkins. **CP-HopkG**

Summer Evening. Isabella Gardner. **CP-GardI**

Summer Evening. Marsden Hartley. **CP-HartM**

Summer Evening. Chuck Miller. **SP-MillC**

Summer Evening (Calumet Avenue). Langston Hughes. **SP-HughL**

Summer Evening Churchyard, A. Percy Bysshe Shelley. **CP-ShelP**

Summer fading, winter comes. Picture-Books in Winter. Robert Louis Stevenson. **CP-StevR**

Summer for prose and lemons, for nakedness and languor. Bleecker Street, Summer. Derek Walcott. **CP-WalcD**

Summer for thee, grant I may be. Emily Dickinson. **CP-DickE**

Summer glows warm on the meadows, and speedwell, and gold-cups, and daisies. Pastoral 7. George Meredith. *Fr.* Pastorals. **CP-MerG1**

Summer Grass. Carl Sandburg. **CP-SandC**

Summer grass aches and whispers. Summer Grass. Carl Sandburg. **CP-SandC**

Summer grows old, cold-blooded mother. Frog Autumn. Sylvia Plath. **CP-PlatS**

Summer Haiku. Leonard Cohen. **CP-CoheL**

Summer hail flings crystals on the window. Death of Anne Boleyn. Robert Lowell. **SP-LoweR**

Summer has been wide and deep, The. Emily Dickinson. **SP-DickE**

Summer has two Beginnings. Emily Dickinson. **CP-DickE**

Summer Holiday. Robinson Jeffers. **CP-JefR1**

Summer Home. Seamus Heaney. **SP-HeanS**

Summer in the South. Paul Laurence Dunbar. **CP-DunbP**

Summer in the trees! "It is time to strangle several bad poets." Kenneth Koch. *Fr.* Fresh Air. **SP-KochK**

Summer is done—. Marsden Hartley. **CP-HartM**

Summer Is Ended, The. Christina Georgina Rossetti. **CP-RosC3**

Summer Is Ended. Christina Georgina Rossetti. **CP-RosC2**

Summer is fading. Afternoons. Philip Larkin. **CP-LarkP**

Summer is gone with all its roses. Bitter for Sweet. Christina Georgina Rossetti. **CP-RosC1**

Summer is over / —it's no use demanding. Edward Estlin Cummings. **CP-CummE**

Summer is over upon the sea. Song. Elizabeth Bishop. **CP-BishE**

Summer is shorter than any one. Emily Dickinson. **CP-DickE**

Summer laid her simple Hat. Emily Dickinson. **CP-DickE**

Summer Landscape. Richard Eberhart. **CP-EberR**

Summer lies thick along the hedgerows. Rise. Phoebe Hesketh. **SP-HeskP**

Summer Lightning. Donald Davie. **CP-DavDo**

Summer like a rajah dies, The. Kipling's Vermont. Ogden Nash. **CP-NashO**

Summer Malison, The. Gerard Manley Hopkins. **CP-HopkG**

Summer Memory in the Crowded City, A. James Wright. **CP-WrigJ**

Summer Morning. Charles Simic. **SP-SimiC**

Summer Morning, A. Richard Wilbur. **CP-WilbR**

Summer morning is risen. Ballad. John Clare. **SP-ClarJ** *Fr.* Child Harold.

Summer Night, A. Matthew Arnold. **SP-ArnoM**

Summer Night, A. Wystan Hugh Auden. **CP-AudeW**

Summer Night, A. Paul Laurence Dunbar. **CP-DunbP**

Summer Night, A. Randall Jarrell. **CP-JarrR**

Summer Night, A. Ted Kooser. **SP-KoosT**

Summer Night. Robert Louis Stevenson. **CP-StevR**

Summer Night. Tennyson. *See* Now sleeps the crimson petal, now the white.

Summer nights are short, / Where northern days are long, The. Christina Georgina Rossetti. **CP-RosC2**

Summer Nocturne. Philip Larkin. **CP-LarkP**

Summer of nineteen eighteen, The. The Bad Old Days. Kenneth Rexroth. **SP-RexrK**

Summer Oracle. Audre Lorde. **SP-LordA**

Summer Park. John Hewitt. **CP-HewiJ**

Summer Pastoral, A. Paul Laurence Dunbar. **CP-DunbP**

Summer People, The. James Merrill. **SP-MerrJ**

Summer Pilgrimage, A. John Greenleaf Whittier. **CP-WhitJ**

Summer quickens grass, The. Wystan Hugh Auden. **CP-AudWJ**

Summer Remembered. Isabella Gardner. **CP-GardI**

Summer Schemes. Thomas Hardy. **CP-HardT**

Summer School. Brendan Galvin. **SP-GalvB**

Summer Serenade. Ogden Nash. **CP-NashO**

Summer Shirt Sale. Carl Sandburg. **CP-SandC**

Summer shirt sale of a downtown haberdasher is glorified in a show, The. Summer Shirt Sale. Carl Sandburg. **CP-SandC**

Summer Silence. Edward Estlin Cummings. **CP-CummE**

Summer so histrionic, marvelous dirty days. Ted Berrigan. **SP-BerrT** *Fr.* The Sonnets.

Summer Solstice. Daniel Gerard Hoffman. **SP-HoffD**

Summer Solstice. Stanley Jasspon Kunitz. **CP-KuniS**

Summer Song. Edward Estlin Cummings. **CP-CummE**

Summer Song. Li Po, *tr. fr. Chinese by* William Carlos Williams *with* David Rafael Wang. **CP-WilW2**

Summer Song. William Carlos Williams. **CP-WilW1**

Summer Stars. Carl Sandburg. **CP-SandC**

Summer Storm (Circa 1916), and God's Grace. Robert Penn Warren. **SP-WarrR**

Summer Sun. Robert Louis Stevenson. **CP-StevR**

Summer sun ray, The. Noon Walk on the Asylum Lawn. Anne Sexton. **CP-SextA**

Summer sun shone round me, The. Robert Louis Stevenson. **CP-StevR**

Summer. Sunset. Someone is playing. Transient Barracks. Randall Jarrell. **CP-JarrR; SP-JarrR**

Summer that we did not prize, The. Emily Dickinson. **CP-DickE**

Summer, the Sacramento. Muriel Rukeyser. **CP-RukeM**

Summer, The Second Pastoral, or Alexis. Alexander Pope. *Fr.* Pastorals. **CP-PopeA**

Sylvan Delights. **NOBE**

Summer, this is our flesh. Seasons of the Soul. Allen Tate. **CP-TateA**

Summer thunder darkens, and its climbing. Prometheus. Charles Tomlinson. **CP-TomlC**

Summer Twilight. Stephen Berg. **SP-BergS**

Summer Vacation. William Wordsworth. *Fr.* The Prelude; Growth of a Poet's Mind [1805 vers.]. **CP-WorW3**

Summer Vacation. William Wordsworth. *Fr.* The Prelude; Growth of a Poet's Mind [1850 vers.]. **CP-WorW3**

Consummate Happiness. **OBNC**

Dedicated Spirit, A. **SeCePo**

"Favourite pleasure hath it been with me, A." **OBRV**

"In a throng, / A festal company of Maids and Youths." **EBEV; OBRV**

"It seemed the very garments that I wore." **OAEL-2**

"When first I made." **EnRP**

"When first I made." **OBRV**

"While thus I wander'd, step by step led on." **OxAEP-1**

"Wildly he wandered on." **TOF**

"Yet in spite / Of pleasure won, and knowledge not withheld." **PoEL-4**

ummer warmth has left the sky, The. Hazel Blossoms. John Greenleaf Whittier. **CP-WhitJ**

ummer was another country, where the birds. Holiday. Adrienne Rich. **CP-RicAE**

ummer was dead and Autumn was expiring. The Zucca. Percy Bysshe Shelley. **CP-ShelP**

ummer was the problem of the universal. Spring Man. Richard Eberhart. *Fr.* The Seasons. **CP-EberR**

ummer—we all have seen. Emily Dickinson. **CP-DickE**

ummer: West Side. John Updike. **CP-UpdiJ**

ummer wilderness, a blue light. The Loon on Forrester's Pond. Hayden Carruth. **CP-CarHS**

ummer Wish. Louise Bogan. **CP-BogaL**

ummer Wish, A. Christina Georgina Rossetti. **CP-RosC1**

ummergreen for President. Ogden Nash. **CP-NashO**

ummerhouse, The. Daniel Gerard Hoffman. **SP-HoffD**

ummers Ago. Isabella Gardner. **CP-GardI**

ummer's coming's summer's going. Circling Splinters. Archie Randolph Ammons. **SP-AmmoA**

ummer's Dream, A. Elizabeth Bishop. **CP-BishE**

ummer's Early End at Hudson's Bay. Hayden Carruth. **CP-CarHS**

ummer's Elegy. Howard Nemerov. **CP-NemeH**

ummer's last half moon waning high. 16. ix. 65. James Merrill. **SP-MerrJ**

ummer's last sun nigh unto setting shines. The Last Eve of Summer. John Greenleaf Whittier. **CP-WhitJ**

ummer's Night, A. Paul Laurence Dunbar. **CP-DunbP**

ummers of bloom—and months of frost. Emily Dickinson. **CP-DickE**

ummers they sit among pine trees. Ice Shanties. Gary Gildner. **SP-GildG**

ummertime and the Living. Robert Earl Hayden. **CP-HaydR**

ummertime dogs. Bravo. Charles Bukowski. **SP-BukC3**

ummery Weather. Kenneth Koch. **SP-KochK**

ummery Windermere, sweet lake! Richard Eberhart. **MiAP** *Fr.* Four Lakes' Days. **CP-EberR**

(Four Lakes' Days, The.) **MiAP**, *sect.* 1;

umming-up, The. Stanley Jasspon Kunitz. **CP-KuniS**

umming Up in Italy. Elizabeth Barrett Browning. **CP-BroEB**

ummit, The. Frederick Morgan. **SP-MorgF**

ummit, The. Kathleen Jessie Raine. *Fr.* Bheinn Naomh. **SP-RainK**

ummit Redwood, The. Robinson Jeffers. **CP-JefR1**

ummoned from offices and homes, we came. The Disciple. John Berryman. **CP-BerrJ**

ummoned to desolation by the dawn. Morning Hymn to a Dark Girl. James Wright. **CP-WrigJ**

ummoner's Prologue, The. Geoffrey Chaucer. *Fr.* The Canterbury Tales. **CP-ChauG**

ummoner's Tale, The. Geoffrey Chaucer. *Fr.* The Canterbury Tales. **CP-ChauG**

ummoning, The. Bill Knott. **SP-KnotB**

ummoning artists to participate. For John F. Kennedy; His Inauguration. Robert Frost. **CP-FrosR**

ummoning the Muse to a New House. Erica Jong. **SP-JongE**

ummons, The. Wystan Hugh Auden. *Fr.* For the Time Being; a Christmas Oratorio. **CP-AudeW**

   "Great is Caesar: He has conquered Seven Kingdoms." **LiTM**

   "Our Father, whose creative Will." **TrPWD**

ummons, The. James Dickey. **CP-DickJ**

ummons, The. John Milton. *See* Satan's Legions and the Beech Leaves of the Casentino.

ummons, The. Charles Simic. **SP-SimiC**

ummons, A. John Greenleaf Whittier. **CP-WhitJ**

ummons, The. John Greenleaf Whittier. **CP-WhitJ**

ummons because the marvelous prey is fleeing, A. Eraser. Charles Simic. **SP-SimiC**

ummons was urgent: and forth I went, The. Her Death and After. Thomas Hardy. **CP-HardT**

ummum Bonum. Robert Browning. **CP-BroR2**

umner. John Greenleaf Whittier. **CP-WhitJ**

ums. Donald Hall. **CP-HallD**

un, The. Robert Browning. **CP-BroR2**

un, The. Hayden Carruth. *Fr.* Contra Mortem. **CP-CarHL**

Sun. James Dickey. **CP-DickJ**

Sun / Flashed from blades of salix of chitin of stone. Sun. Kathleen Jessie Raine. *Fr.* Bheinn Naomh. **SP-RainK**

Sun, The. Donald Hall. **CP-HallD**

Sun. Marianne Craig Moore. **CP-MoorM**

Sun, The. Mary Oliver. **SP-OlivM**

Sun, The. Marge Piercy. **WPOW** *Fr.* Laying Down the Tower. **SP-PierM**

   (Total Influence of Outcome of the Matter: The Sun, The.) **WPOW**

Sun. Kathleen Jessie Raine. *Fr.* Bheinn Naomh. **SP-RainK**

Sun, The. Anne Sexton. **CP-SextA**

Sun. Diane Wakoski. **SP-WakoD**

Sun, The. William Carlos Williams. **CP-WilW1**

Sun, Aeroplane, Lovers. Malcolm Lowry. **CP-LowrM**

Sun again unearthed, colours come up fresh, The. After Cumae. Geoffrey Hill. **CP-HillG**

Sun always setting behind us, The. Twelve Hours Out of New York After Twenty-Five Days at Sea. Gary Snyder. **CP-SnydG**

Sun and Air. Richard Wilbur. **CP-WilbR**

Sun and Fog contested, The. Emily Dickinson. **CP-DickE**

Sun and Moon must make their haste, The. Emily Dickinson. **CP-DickE**

Sun and softness. Sun Song. Langston Hughes. **SP-HughL**

Sun and the serenest Moon sprang forth:, The. Percy Bysshe Shelley. *Fr.* Ode to Liberty. **CP-ShelP**

Sun arises from the sea, The. Easter Morning. Christina Georgina Rossetti. **CP-RosC3**

Sun arises in the East, The. Day. William Blake. **CP-BlakW**

Sun-Artist, The. Muriel Rukeyser. **CP-RukeM**

Sun at last will stand and stare, The. Eve's Second Prophecy. Archibald MacLeish. *Fr.* Songs for Eve. **CP-MacLA**

Sun at noon to higher air, The. March. Alfred Edward Housman. **CP-HousA**

Sun athwart the cloud thought it no sin, The. Ralph Waldo Emerson. **CP-EmerR**

Sun attacks in white on the reef outside the window, The. Wedding Photograph. Steve Griffiths. **SP-GrifS**

Sun Bathers, The. William Carlos Williams. **CP-WilW1**

Sun-beams [*or* Sun-beames] in the east are spred [*or* spred], The. Epithalamion Made at Lincoln's Inn [*or* Lincolnes Inne]. John Donne. **CP-DonnJ**

Sun, bedded in mud, The. November. Martin Edmunds. **SP-EdmuM**

Sun Boat. May Sarton. **SP-SartM**

Sun breaks over the eucalyptus. Marin-An. Gary Snyder. **CP-SnydG**

Sun burns in the sky like the Face of God, The. High Morning. The Hour of Tierce. Thomas Merton. *Fr.* Hagia Sophia. **CP-MertT**

Sun Cab, A. James Schuyler. **CP-SchuJ**

Sun Came, The. Etheridge Knight. **SP-KnigE**

Sun came up, bigger than all my sorrow. West Country Song. Edna St. Vincent Millay. **CP-MillE**

Sun Dancer. Carl Sandburg. **CP-SandC**

Sun, dark sun. Tropic. David Herbert Lawrence. **CP-LawrD**

Sun descending in the west, The. Night. William Blake. **BLPL; BoNaP; BoTP; CH; EnRP; FHYEP; FaBoBe; FaPON; HBV; HBVY; HoFi; MeMBP; OBEC; OBEV; OxBChV; OxBoCh; PoLF; TreFT; WiR** *Fr.* Songs of Innocence. **CP-BlakW**

Sun descending, the *Phœacian* train, The. Homer, *tr.* by Alexander Pope. **CP-PopeA** *Fr.* Odyssey.

Sun does [*or* doth] arise, The. The Echoing [*or* Ecchoing] Green. William Blake. **BoTP; CABA; CH; FHYEP; HoFi; LAuP; NAEL-2; NTP; OBEC; OXAEP-2; PoE; PoSC; UnPo; WiR** *Fr.* Songs of Innocence. **CP-BlakW**

Sun-Face and Moon-Face. Robert Ranke Graves. **CP-GravR**

Sun falls behind Wales, The; the towns and hills. Midsummer Night, 1940. Philip Larkin. **CP-LarkP**

Sun floats in sublime, The. Frank Templeton Prince. *Fr.* Walks in Rome. **CP-PrinF**

Sun from the west glares back, The. Coming Up Oxford Street: Evening. Thomas Hardy. **CP-HardT**

Sun gives not directly, The. Sunshine. Nicholas Vachel Lindsay. **CP-LindV**

Sun goes down, and with him takes, The. The Romany Girl. Ralph Waldo Emerson. **CP-EmerR**

Sun goes down, each minute the air darker, The. The Upward Moon and the Downward Moon. Robert Bly. **SP-BlyR**

Sun goes down in the dusty April night, The. An Evening When the Full Moon Rose as the Sun Set. Robert Bly. **SP-BlyR**

Sun goes slowly blind, The. Love in the Valley. Derek Walcott. **CP-WalcD**

Sun, great giver of all that is. Kathleen Jessie Raine. *Fr.* To the Sun. **SP-RainK**

Sun Hacks, The. Roy Fisher. *Fr.* City. **SP-FishR**

Sun had clos'd the winter-day, The. Robert Burns. **BSV** *Fr.* Duan First. *Fr.* The Vision. **CP-BurnR**

Sun had clos'd the winter-day, The. Robert Burns. **OxBS** *Fr.* Duan First. *Fr.* The Vision. **CP-BurnR**

Sun had clos'd the winter-day, The. Duan First. Robert Burns. *Fr.* The Vision. **CP-BurnR**

Sun had not gone down. The new moon, The. The Journey. Charles Tomlinson. **CP-TomlC**

Sun had rais'd above the mead, The. The Country Squire and the Mandrake. Christopher Smart. **SP-SmarC**

Sun had stained the roofs with blood, The. The Sower. Wystan Hugh Auden. **CP-AudWJ**

Sun had wheeled from Grey's to Dammer's Crest, The. The Burghers. Thomas Hardy. **CP-HardT**

Sun Has Burst the Sky, The. Jenny Joseph. **SP-JoseJ**

Sun has climbed the hill, the day is on the downward slope, The. The Mid-Day Verse. David Herbert Lawrence. **CP-LawrD**

Sun has fired my face to terra-cotta, The. Derek Walcott. **CP-WalcD** *Fr.* Midsummer.

Sun has long been set, The. William Wordsworth. **CP-WorW1**

Sun has lost its heat, dahlias, The. Homo Sapiens. Jenny Joseph. **SP-JoseJ**

Sun has set, and the long grass now, The. The . Emily Brontë. **CP-BronE**

Sun has slipped his tether, The. Waiting. Paul Laurence Dunbar. **CP-DunbP**

Sun has sucked and beat the encircling hills, The. In Hospital: Poona (2). Alun Lewis. **CP-LewiA**

Sun hath shed its kindly light, The. A Thanksgiving Poem. Paul Laurence Dunbar. **CP-DunbP**

Sun he is sunk in the west, The. Song.—In the Character of a Ruined Farmer. Robert Burns. **CP-BurnR**

Sun hit shine an' de win' hit blow, De. Winter's Approach. Paul Laurence Dunbar. **CP-DunbP**

Sun immense and rosy, The. Elegy. David Herbert Lawrence. **CP-LawrD**

Sun, in clownish yellow, but not a clown, The. Wallace Stevens. **NOBA** *Fr.* Esthétique du Mal. **CP-StevW**

Sun in Me. David Herbert Lawrence. **CP-LawrD**

Sun in our sails, our hooker wheels again. Shark Island. Richard Hugo. **CP-HugoR**

Sun in reining to the West, The. Emily Dickinson. **CP-DickE**

Sun is a huntress young, The. In the Beginning. Nicholas Vachel Lindsay. *Fr.* An Indian Summer Day on the Prairie. **CP-LindV**

Sun is a smoldering fire, The. Mid-Morning. Nicholas Vachel Lindsay. *Fr.* An Indian Summer Day on the Prairie. **CP-LindV**

Sun is a wounded deer, The. Noon. Nicholas Vachel Lindsay. *Fr.* An Indian Summer Day on the Prairie. **CP-LindV**

Sun is an eagle old, The. Sunset. Nicholas Vachel Lindsay. *Fr.* An Indian Summer Day on the Prairie. **CP-LindV**

Sun is blazing and the sky is blue, The. Pink Dog. Elizabeth Bishop. **CP-BishE**

Sun is bleeding its fires upon the mist, The. Ruination. David Herbert Lawrence. **CP-LawrD**

Sun is caked on vertical tan stone, The. Index. Richard Hugo. **CP-HugoR**

Sun is couched, the sea-fowl gone to rest, The. By the Sea-Side. William Wordsworth. **CP-WorW2**

Sun is Dead—ye heard the curfew toll, The. Sonnet Written by Mr — Immediately after the Death of His Wife. William Wordsworth. **CP-WorW1**

Sun is down hopeless, The. Hopeless and Felons. Thomas Merton. **CP-MertT**

Sun is gay or stark, The. Goldsworthy Lowes Dickinson. **CP-DickE**

Sun is gone from mid-heaven, the soldiers are gone from hence, The. Mesopotamia. David Herbert Lawrence. *Fr.* Bits. **CP-LawrD**

Sun is like an open furnace door, The. Last Look round St. Martin's Fair. Thomas Hardy. **CP-HardT**

Sun is low, The. On the River. Paul Laurence Dunbar. **CP-DunbP**

Sun is not abed when I, The. The Sun's Travels. Robert Louis Stevenson. **CP-StevR**

Sun is not yet risen, The. Alice Du Clos. Samuel Taylor Coleridge. **CP-ColeS**

Sun is one—and on the Tare, The. Emily Dickinson. **CP-DickE**

Sun is set; the swallows are asleep, The. Evening: Ponte al Mare, Pisa. Percy Bysshe Shelley. **CP-ShelP**

Sun is shining in my backdoor, The. Myself When I Am Real. Al Young. **CP-YounA**

Sun is so bright on the snow, The. No More Elegies. Jane Cooper. *Fr.* March. **SP-CoopJ**

Sun is the center of the universe, The. Nicholas Copernicus (1473–1543). Siv Cedering Fox. *Fr.* Letters from the Astronomers. **SP-CedeS**

Sun is the sole inconsumable fire, The. Ralph Waldo Emerson. **CP-EmerR**

Sun is warm, the sky is clear, The. Stanzas Written in Dejection, near Naples [*or* —December 1818, near Naples]. Percy Bysshe Shelley. **CP-ShelP**

Sun just / went behind the / ridge and turned, The. Sunset. James Schuyler. **CP-SchuJ**

Sun just risen, The. Gerard Manley Hopkins. *Fr.* Fragments. **CP-HopkG**

Sun—just touched the Morning, The. Emily Dickinson. **CP-DickE**

Sun keeps its promises, The. John Haines. *Fr.* The End of the Summer. **SP-HainJ**

Sun kept setting—setting—still, The. Emily Dickinson. **CP-DickE**

Sun kept stooping—stooping—low!, The. Emily Dickinson. **CP-DickE**

Sun King. The Beatles. **CP-Beatl**

Sun kings / their faces sagging like the combs of cocks. Geriatrics. Steve Griffiths. **SP-GrifS**

Sun like an orange mousse through the trees. Dog Day Vespers. Charles Wright. **SP-WrigC**

Sun made a late and lamented, The. The Pale Panther. Louis MacNeice. **CP-MacNL**

Sun makes music as of old, The. Johann Wolfgang von Goethe. **AWP; OBVE** *Fr.* Prologue in Heaven. **CP-ShelP** *Fr.* Faust. (Chorus of the Archangels, The.) **OBVE**

Sun makes music as of old, The. *See also* Randall Jarrell's *The Archangels' Song.* Johann Wolfgang von Goethe, *tr. by* Shelley. **CP-ShelP** *Fr.* Faust.

Sun May Set, The. Catullus. *See* The Sunne may set and rise.

Sun-Men. David Herbert Lawrence. **CP-LawrD**

Sun Now or Never (For Barbara), The. Chuck Miller. **SP-MillC**

Sun of July beats down on the small white house, The. Small White House. Robert Penn Warren. **SP-WarrR**

Sun of the Sleepless! Byron. **CP-Byron**

Sun on the Bookcase, The. Thomas Hardy. **CP-HardT**

Sun on the city morning high on walls. City Morning. John Hewitt. **CP-HewiJ**

Sun on the faces. On the knotted rocks. Muriel Rukeyser. **CP-RukeM**

Sun on the Letter, The. Thomas Hardy. **CP-HardT**

Sun on their naked shoulders. Weekend Bathers. Kenneth Patchen. **CP-PatcK**

Sun on Your Shoulder, The. John Haines. **SP-HainJ**

Sun, perhaps three of them, one black one red, you know, and her dancing, The. Alma. Frank O'Hara. **SP-OharF**

Sun Ra / Roi / Ho. The Myth Science of Our Time. Al Young. **CP-YounA**

Sun retired to a cloud, The. Emily Dickinson. **CP-DickE**

Sun rises at midday, The. Unmeasured Tempo. Maya Angelou. **SP-AngeM**

Sun[ne] Rising, The. John Donne. **CP-DonnJ**

Sun rose today, and, The. Birthday Poem. Etheridge Knight. **SP-KnigE**

Sun rushed up the sky; the taxi flew, The. Parting as Descent. John Berryman. **CP-BerrJ**

Sun said, watching my watering-pot, The. The Tenant-for-Life. Thomas Hardy. **CP-HardT**

Sun saw that widening shore, The. Sainte Anne De Beaupré. Richard Eberhart. **CP-EberR**

Sun Says His Prayers, The. Nicholas Vachel Lindsay. **CP-LindV**

Sun set, but set not his hope, The. Character. Ralph Waldo Emerson. **CP-EmerR**

Sun sets / in a wall that holds the sky, The. Dusk. Roy Fisher. **SP-FishR**

Sun sets out the autumn crocuses, The. Autumn Sunshine. David Herbert Lawrence. **CP-LawrD**

Sun sets unevenly and the people / go to bed, The. Chasing the Bird. Robert Creeley. **CP-CreeR**

Sun sets wide the yellow crocuses, The. Amour. David Herbert Lawrence. **CP-LawrD**

Sun-shine lies on the cottage-wall, The. Samuel Taylor Coleridge. *Fr.* Some Fragments, Mainly from Manuscripts of 1797–8. **CP-ColeS**

Sun shines, The. Tommies in the Train. David Herbert Lawrence. **CP-LawrD**

Sun shines easy, sun shines gay. Louis MacNeice. *Fr.* Autumn Journal. **CP-MacNL**

Munich Agreement, The. **FaBoEH**

Sun shines on the gliding river, The. Frank Templeton Prince. *Fr.* Memoirs in Oxford. **CP-PrinF**

Sun shines warm on seven old soldiers, The. The Oldest Soldier. Robert Ranke Graves. **CP-GravR**

Sun shines; where is the lyric!, The. Malcolm Lowry. *Fr.* Songs for Second Childhood. **CP-LowrM**

Sun shone all day, The. Will Somers. Lewis Turco. *Fr.* Bordello. **SP-TurcL**

'sun shoots high. . . ", The. Tom Clark. **SP-ClarT**

Sun sings out, as of old, The. *tr. fr.* Goethe's *Faust.* Randall Jarrell. **CP-JarrR**

Sun sits back, watches the street, The. A Child Growing Up with the Sun. Jim Carroll. **SP-CarrJ**

Sun smudge on the smoky water. Autumn. Archibald MacLeish. **CP-MacLA**

Sun Song. Langston Hughes. **SP-HughL**

Sun splits into two, The. Judging the Pageant. Jim Carroll. **SP-CarrJ**

Sun! stay thy course, this moment stay. The Secrets of Divine Love Are To Be Kept. Jeanne Marie Bouvier de la Motte-Guyon, *tr. fr. French by* William Cowper. **CP-CowpW**

Sun struts over the asphalt world, The. Noon of the Sunbather. Marge Piercy. **SP-PierM**

Sun Tan at Dusk. James Wright. **CP-WrigJ**

Sun tells stories, The. Frederick Morgan. *Fr.* The River. **SP-MorgF**

Sun, that brave man, The. The Brave Man. Wallace Stevens. **CP-StevW**

Sun that brief December day, The. Snow-Bound [*or* Snow-Bound; a Winter Idyl]. John Greenleaf Whittier. **CP-WhitJ**

Sun that never rose has now gone down, The. October Sunset. Malcolm Lowry. **CP-LowrM**

Sun, that seemed so mildly to retire, The. On a High Part of the Coast in Cumberland. William Wordsworth. **CP-WorW2**

Sun the Blond Out. Anne Waldman. **SP-WaldA**

Sun the thunder and the hunher grow, The. Alun Lewis. *Fr.* Indian Day. **CP-LewiA**

Sun, the warm man renting boats, The. Lone Lake, Whidbey. Richard Hugo. **CP-HugoR**

Sun This March, The. Wallace Stevens. **CP-StevW**

Sun threw down a radiant spot, The. The Sun's Last Look on the Country Girl. Thomas Hardy. **CP-HardT**

Sun-treader, life and light be thine for ever! Robert Browning. **EPCY** *Fr.* Pauline [*or* Pauline; A Fragment of a Confession]. **CP-BroR1**

Sun. Tree. Beginning. God in a thicket. Crown. Two Portraits of Sex. Philip Larkin. **CP-LarkP**

Sun Up. Phoebe Hesketh. **SP-HeskP**

Sun was almost shining, The. Malcolm Lowry. **CP-LowrM**

Sun was shining on the sea, The. The Walrus and the Carpenter. "Lewis Carroll." **CP-CarrL** *Fr.* Through the Looking-Glass.

Sun was strong enough today, The. A Courtyard Thaw. Richard Wilbur. **CP-WilbR**

Sun went down—no Man looked on, The. Emily Dickinson. **CP-DickE**

Sun Wields Mercy, The. Charles Bukowski. **SP-BukC2**

Sun will rise in me, A. Sun in Me. David Herbert Lawrence. **CP-LawrD**

Sun with Hands for Rays. Diane Wakoski. *Fr.* Fifteen Poems for a Lunar Eclipse None of Us Saw. **SP-WakoD**

Sun woke me this morning loud, The. A True Account of Talking to the Sun at Fire Island. Frank O'Hara. **SP-OharF**

Sun-Women. David Herbert Lawrence. **CP-LawrD**

Sun, you may send your haze gold. Haze Gold. Carl Sandburg. **CP-SandC**

Sunbeam on the well-waxed oak, A. The Chink. Robert Ranke Graves. **CP-GravR**

Sunburst. Donald Davie. **CP-DavDo**

Sunburst / in crystal, unleashed and surprised, The. Possessions. Pablo Neruda, *tr. fr. Spanish by* Ben Belitt. **SP-NeruP**

Sunburst. Dabney Stuart. **SP-StuaD**

Sunclad, steel-shod eremite. Richard Rolle. Marsden Hartley. **CP-HartM**

Sunday, A. Walter de la Mare. **CP-DeLaW**

Sunday. George Herbert. **CP-HerbG**

Sunday. Ron Koertge. **SP-KoerR**

Sunday. Howard Nemerov. **CP-NemeH**

Sunday. James Schuyler. **CP-SchuJ**

Sunday. James Schuyler. **CP-SchuJ**

Sunday. John Updike. **CP-UpdiJ**

Sunday. William Carlos Williams. **CP-WilW1**

Sunday afternoon, / and couples walk the breakwater. Veracruz. Robert Earl Hayden. **AmNP** *Fr.* An Inference of Mexico. **CP-HaydR**

Sunday Afternoon. Stephen Berg. **SP-BergS**

Sunday Afternoon in Italy. David Herbert Lawrence. **CP-LawrD**

Sunday Afternoon Service in St. Enodoc Church, Cornwall. Sir John Betjeman. **CP-BetjJ**

Sunday again / Never a week without Sunday. One Sunday in 1966. Isabella Gardner. **CP-GardI**

Sunday at Key West. Elizabeth Bishop. **CP-BishE**

Sunday at the End of Summer. Howard Nemerov. **CP-NemeH**

Sunday Before Advent. Christina Georgina Rossetti. **CP-RosC2**

Sunday by the Combination. Langston Hughes. **SP-HughL**

Sunday Chicken. Gwendolyn Brooks. *Fr.* Notes from the Childhood and the Girlhood. **SP-BrooG**

Sunday Drive, A. Margaret Atwood. **SP-AtwM2**

Sunday Evening. Adrienne Rich. **CP-RicAE**

Sunday Evening Revery. Edwin Rolfe. **CP-RolfE**

Sunday, first day of summer. George Trakl Journal. Charles Wright. **SP-WrigC**

Sunday, 4 A.M. Elizabeth Bishop. **CP-BishE**

Sunday Greens. Rita Dove. **SP-DoveR**

Sunday Illumination. Al Young. **CP-YounA**

Sunday in Boston. John Updike. **CP-UpdiJ**

Sunday in Inwood Park. Picnic. Adrienne Rich. **CP-RicAE; SP-RicA2**

Sunday in October. Richard Eberhart. **CP-EberR**

Sunday in the Park. Louis MacNeice. **CP-MacNL**

Sunday lamb cracks in its fat, The. Mary's Song. Sylvia Plath. **CP-PlatS**

Sunday Lemons. Derek Walcott. **CP-WalcD**

Sunday, mid-afternoon, radiator pipes knocking. The Living Room. Stephen Dobyns. **SP-DobyS**

Sunday Morning. Wystan Hugh Auden. **CP-AudWJ**

Sunday Morning. Donald Davie. **CP-DavDo**

Sunday Morning. Ted Kooser. **SP-KoosT**

Sunday Morning. Louis MacNeice. **CP-MacNL**

Sunday Morning. Wallace Stevens. **CP-StevW**

Sunday Morning Apples. Hart Crane. **CP-CranH**

Sunday Morning, King's Cambridge. Sir John Betjeman. **CP-BetjJ**

Sunday Morning Prophecy. Langston Hughes. **SP-HughL**

Sunday Morning Tragedy, A. Thomas Hardy. **CP-HardT**

Sunday: My Throat Afire. Laurence Lieberman. **SP-LiebL**

Sunday night and the park policemen tell each other it is dark as a. Picnic Boat. Carl Sandburg. **CP-SandC**

Sunday Night at Grandfather's. Rita Dove. **SP-DoveR**

Sunday. Nothing to do. I park. Gratitude. Stephen Berg. **SP-BergS**

Sunday papers are on the streets, The. The Truth of the Matter. Howard Nemerov. **CP-NemeH**

Sunday Rain. John Updike. **CP-UpdiJ**

Sunday shuts down on this twentieth-century evening. Boy with His Hair Cut Short. Muriel Rukeyser. **CP-RukeM**

Sunday Sonnet for My Mother's Mother, A. Al Young. **CP-YounA**

Sunday the only day we don't work. A Walk. Gary Snyder. **CP-SnydG**

Sundays Kill More Men Than Bombs. Charles Bukowski. **SP-BukC2**

Sundays óf Satin-Legs Smith, The. Gwendolyn Brooks. **SP-BrooG**

Sundays, They Sleep Late. Muriel Rukeyser. **CP-RukeM**

Sundays too my father got up early. Those Winter Sundays. Robert Earl Hayden. **CP-HaydR**

Sunderings and luxations, *luxe,* and grief. John Berryman. *Fr.* Sonnets to Chris. **CP-BerrJ**

Sunderland. Howard Nemerov. **CP-NemeH**

Sundew, The. Algernon Charles Swinburne. **SP-SwinA**

Sundial, The. Jane Cooper. *Fr.* Acceptances. **SP-CoopJ**

Sundial on a Wet Day, The. Thomas Hardy. **CP-HardT**

Sundown. Alfonso Cortes, *tr. fr. Spanish by* Thomas Merton. **CP-MertT**

Sundown, *ad. from* Micah 3. Thomas Merton. **CP-MertT**

Sundown and Starlight. James Merrill. *Fr.* Five Old Favorites. **SP-MerrJ**

SUNDOWN, NASTY COUNTRY—over a stony plain in armored cars, like dogs nosing a rhinorceros. Diary of Desert War. Tom Clark. **SP-ClarT**

Sundown, white with ecstasy, hold. Sundown. Alfonso Cortes, *tr. fr. Spanish by* Thomas Merton. **CP-MertT**

Sundowner. Phoebe Hesketh. **SP-HeskP**

Sunflower. John Updike. **CP-UpdiJ**

Sunflower Sutra. Allen Ginsberg. **CP-GinsA**

Sunflowers. Siv Cedering Fox. **SP-CedeS**

Sunflowers, The. Mary Oliver. **SP-OlivM**

Sunflowers. William Carlos Williams. **CP-WilW2**

Sunflowers: An Ode. James McAuley.

  "Beyond the crowding spires of pine, the hill." **SP-McAuJ**

  "I lounge on the warm step, watching the child." **SP-McAuJ**

  "I planned a little fountain." **SP-McAuJ**

Sunflowers, traders rounding the horn of time. Howard Nemerov. *Fr.* Runes. **CP-NemeH**

Sung badly hymns are loaded with remorse. A Chapel Further West than Most. Richard Hugo. **CP-HugoR**

Sunglasses, The. Howard Nemerov. **CP-NemeH**

Sunglasses. John Updike. **SP-UpdiJ**

Sunjuice. Erica Jong. **SP-JongE**

Sunk Lyonesse. Walter de la Mare. **CP-DeLaW**

Sunk were his eyes, his voice was harsh and loud. John Dryden. **FaBoEH** *Fr. Absalom and Achitophel, Pt. I.* **SP-DrydJ**

Sunken Crown, The. Edwin Arlington Robinson. **CP-RobiE**

Sunken Garden, The. Walter de la Mare. **CP-DeLaW**

Sunken Lane, The. Wystan Hugh Auden. **CP-AudWJ**

Sunlicht still on me, you row'd in clood, The. At My Father's Grave. "Hugh MacDiarmid." **SP-MacDH**

Sunlight. Thom Gunn. **CP-GunnT**

Sunlight. Seamus Heaney. *See* Mossbawn Sunlight.

Sunlight catches a wall. Sea View. Frank Templeton Prince. **CP-PrinF**

Sunlight climbs the snowpeak. Late October Camping in the Sawtooths. Gary Snyder. **CP-SnydG**

Sunlight glitters clean and bright, The. Hampton Beach. John Greenleaf Whittier. **CP-WhitJ**

Sunlight in a, The. At the Faucet of June. William Carlos Williams. **CP-WilW1**

Sunlight Is Imagination. Richard Wilbur. **CP-WilbR**

Sunlight lies along my table. Jane Cooper. *Fr.* The Weather of Six Mornings. **SP-CoopJ**

Sunlight, like Rouault, draws a line, The. Tourists at Ensenada. Thomas McGrath. **SP-McGrT**

Sunlight on the Garden, The. Louis MacNeice. **CP-MacNL**

Sunlight once played upon the granite ledges. Wordsworth's Old Age. Phoebe Hesketh. **SP-HeskP**

Sunlight so blurred with clouds we couldn't tell. Wide France. Donald Davie. *Fr.* Two Dedications. **CP-DavDo**

Sunlight strikes a glass of grapefruit juice. Morning in the Hospital Solarium. Sylvia Plath. **CP-PlatS**

Sunlight struck before us. John Haines. *Fr.* News from the Glacier. **SP-HainJ**

Sunlight the tall women may never have seen. Children, the Sandbar, That Summer. Muriel Rukeyser. **CP-RukeM**

Sunlight to the river. Ariadne To Theseus. Christina Georgina Rossetti. **CP-RosC3**

Sunlight upon Judæa's hills! The Crucifixion. John Greenleaf Whittier. **CP-WhitJ**

Sunlight was over. Edward Estlin Cummings. **CP-CummE**

Sunlit green of a late summer hayfield. A Painting by Winifred Nicholson. Kathleen Jessie Raine. **SP-RainK**

Sunlit, the lashes fringe the half-closed eyes. The Window. Walter de la Mare. **CP-DeLaW**

Sunn which glads, the earth att his bright sight, The. Sonnet 20. Mary Sidney, Countess of Montgomery Wroth. *Fr.* Pamphilia to Amphilanthus. **CP-WrotM**

Sunne hath no long journey now to goe, The. Mary Sidney, Countess of Montgomery Wroth. *Fr.* Part 1. *Fr.* Urania. **CP-WrotM**

Sunne may set and rise, The. Catullus. **CP-RaleW; FaBoEE; NoSic; OBVE,** *tr. by Sir Walter Ralegh;* **EnRePo; FaBoRV; SiPS** *Fr.* Carmen 5: "Lesbia / live with me." **CP-ZukLS; NAWM 1-2; STV** *Fr.* Carmina. **CP-Catul**

(Lines from Catullus.) **EnRePo; SiPS,** *tr. by Sir Walter Ralegh.*

(Sun May Set, The.) **FaBoRV,** *tr. by Sir Walter Ralegh.*

Sunned in the South, and here to-day. To Flowers from Italy in Winter. Thomas Hardy. **CP-HardT**

Sunny day's complete Poussiniana, A. Poem Written at Morning. Wallace Stevens. **CP-StevW**

Sunny Prestatyn. Philip Larkin. **CP-LarkP**

Sunny shaft did I behold, A, *ad. fr. Tieck's* Herbstlied. Glycine's Song. Samuel Taylor Coleridge. **CP-ColeS** *Fr.* Zapolya.

Sunnyside Child. George Oppen. **CP-OppeG**

Sunripe. Jenny Joseph. *Fr.* Life and Turgid Times of A. Citizen. **SP-JoseJ**

Sunrise. Walter de la Mare. **CP-DeLaW**

Sunrise. Robert Lowell. **SP-LoweR**

Sunrise. Malcolm Lowry. **CP-LowrM**

Sunrise. George Meredith. **CP-MerG1**

Sunrise. Mary Oliver. **SP-OlivM**

Sunrise runs for Both, The. Emily Dickinson. **CP-DickE**

Sunrise wakes the lark to sing, The. Bird Raptures. Christina Georgina Rossetti. **CP-RosC1**

Sun's / sky in / form of, The. Water. Robert Creeley. **CP-CreeR**

Sun's angle's so, The. Worky Shallows. Archie Randolph Ammons. **SP-AmmoA**

Sun's Last Look on the Country Girl, The. Thomas Hardy. **CP-HardT**

Suns of eighteen centuries have shone, The. The Gallows. John Greenleaf Whittier. **CP-WhitJ**

Sun's shadows at dawn lay a splint on, The. In Time, AIDS. Jim Carroll. **SP-CarrJ**

Suns that set, and moons that wane. On the Shortness of Life. William Cowper, *tr. fr. Latin of Dr. Jortin.* **CP-CowpW**

Sun's Travels, The. Robert Louis Stevenson. **CP-StevR**

Sun's white in the high fog, The. The Heights. Louis Zukofsky. **CP-ZukLS**

Sun's wind, The. Photosynthesis. Archie Randolph Ammons. **SP-AmmoA**

Sunset, A. Samuel Taylor Coleridge. **CP-ColeS**

("Upon the mountain's Edge all lightly resting.") **CP-ColeS**

Sunset. Robert Creeley. **CP-CreeR**

Sunset. Edward Estlin Cummings. **CP-CummE**

Sunset. Paul Laurence Dunbar. **CP-DunbP**

Sunset. Allen Ginsberg. **CP-GinsA**

Sunset. John Hewitt. **CP-HewiJ**

Sunset. David Herbert Lawrence. **CP-LawrD**

Sunset. Nicholas Vachel Lindsay. *Fr.* An Indian Summer Day on the Prairie. **CP-LindV**

Sunset. James McAuley. **SP-McAuJ**

Sunset. James Schuyler. **CP-SchuJ**

Sunset, The. Percy Bysshe Shelley. **CP-ShelP**

Sunset and evening star. Crossing the Bar. Tennyson. **CP-TennA**

Sunset and Sunrise. William Cowper, *tr. fr. the Latin of Owen.* **CP-CowpW**

Sunset at Night—is natural. Emily Dickinson. **CP-DickE**

Sunset from Omaha Hotel Window. Carl Sandburg. **CP-SandC**

Sunset II. Margaret Atwood. **SP-AtwM2**

Sunset. Look away to the airbase, far. For the Humanism Class at Fairchild Airforce Base, in Place of a Session on the Book of Job. James McAuley. **SP-McAuJ**

Sunset, now that we're finally in it. Sunset II. Margaret Atwood. **SP-AtwM2**

Sunset of the City, A. Gwendolyn Brooks. **SP-BrooG**

Sunset on the Bearcamp. John Greenleaf Whittier. **CP-WhitJ**

Sunset over Glenaan. John Hewitt. **CP-HewiJ**

Sunset over the Aegean. Byron. **OBNC; OBRV** *Fr.* The Corsair. **CP-Byron**

Sunset Piece, The. Archibald MacLeish. **CP-MacLA**

Sunset S.S. Azemour. Allen Ginsberg. **CP-GinsA**

Sunset stopped on Cottages, The. Emily Dickinson. **CP-DickE**

Sunset swept / To the valley's west, you remember, The. Valley Song. Carl Sandburg. **CP-SandC**

Sunset that screens, reveals. Emily Dickinson. **CP-DickE**

Sunset. The Hour of Compline. Salve Regina. Thomas Merton. *Fr.* Hagia Sophia. **CP-MertT**

Sunset Verse, The. David Herbert Lawrence. **CP-LawrD**

Sunset Walk in Thaw-Time in Vermont. Robert Penn Warren. **SP-WarrR**

Sunset worn to its last vermilion he. Union in Disseverance. George Meredith. **CP-MerG1**

Sunset)edges become swiftly. Edward Estlin Cummings. **CP-CummE**

Sunsets. Carl Sandburg. **CP-SandC**

Sunshade, The. Thomas Hardy. **CP-HardT**

Sunshine. Wystan Hugh Auden. **CP-AudWJ**

Sunshine. Nicholas Vachel Lindsay. **CP-LindV**

Sunshine / makes shade / acid blue. Buttered Greens. James Schuyler. **CP-SextA**

Sunshine. Christina Georgina Rossetti. **CP-RosC3**

Sunshine in morning field. Childhood Memory. Kathleen Jessie Raine. **SP-RainK**

Sunshine on medders. A Warm Day in Winter. Paul Laurence Dunbar. **CP-DunbP**

Sunshine on Sandstone. John Updike. **CP-UpdiJ**

Sunshine was he, *after the Arabic.* Ralph Waldo Emerson. **CP-EmerR**

Sunstroke. Ted Hughes. **SP-HughT**

Sunt Leones. Stevie Smith. **CP-SmitS**

Superballs. Tom Clark. **SP-ClarT**

Superficial among the superficial. Reaching For the Gun. Richard Shelton. **SP-ShelR**

Superfluous were the Sun. Emily Dickinson. **CP-DickE**

Superiorities. Richard Wilbur. **CP-WilbR**

Superiority to Fate. Emily Dickinson. **CP-DickE**

Superliminare. George Herbert. **CP-HerbG**

Superman. John Updike. **CP-UpdiJ**

Supermarket. Peter Meinke. **SP-MeinP**

Supermarket in California, A. Allen Ginsberg. **CP-GinsA**

Superseded, The. Thomas Hardy. **CP-HardT**

Superstition. Samuel Taylor Coleridge. **CP-ColeS**

Superstition. Robert Ranke Graves. **CP-GravR**

Supine the Wanderer lay. William Wordsworth. **NOBRP** *Fr.* The Wanderer. **EnRP** *Fr.* The Excursion. **CP-WorW2**

Supper after the Last, The. Galway Kinnell. **SP-KinnG**

Supper Before Last, The. Stanley Jasspon Kunitz. **CP-KuniS**

Supper with Lindsay. Theodore Roethke. **CP-RoetT**

Supplanter, The. Thomas Hardy. **CP-HardT**

Supplanting, The. Wendell Berry. **CP-BerrW**

Supple, determined V of geese, A. Tŷ Newydd. Steve Griffiths. **SP-GrifS**

Supple haft, the helve, The. William Adams Delano. Archibald MacLeish. **CP-MacLA**

Supplement Hours. Walt Whitman. **CP-WhitW**

Supplement of an Imperfect Copy of Verses of Mr. William Shakespeare's, By the Author, A. Sir John Suckling. **CP-SuckJ**

Supplication for Love, A. Elizabeth Barrett Browning. **CP-BroEB**

Supplication of the Black Aberdeen. Rudyard Kipling. **CP-KiplR**

Supplication to the Muses on a Trying Day. Hart Crane. **CP-CranH**

Supported now by Clouds descend. A Full Song. Thomas Campion. *Fr.* The Lords Mask[e].

Supporting Cast, Sotto Voce, The. Wystan Hugh Auden. *Fr.* The Sea and the Mirror. **CP-AudeW**

"At Dirty Dick's and Sloppy Joe's." **BoLoP; DTC; FaBoTw; MOS** (Song of the Master and Boatswain.) **BoLoP; DTC; MOS**

"My Dear One is mine as mirrors are lonely." **NoAM**

Supports, The. Rudyard Kipling. **CP-KiplR** *Fr.* Debits and Credits.

Suppose—. Roy Fisher. **SP-FishR**

Suppose. Paul Laurence Dunbar. **CP-DunbP**

Suppose / Life is an old man carrying flowers on his head. Edward Estlin Cummings. **CP-CummE; SP-CummE**

Suppose he had been Tabled at thy Teates. Blessed be the Paps which Thou hast Sucked. Bible, *N.T., tr. by* Richard Crashaw. **CP-CrasR** *Fr.* St. Luke.

Suppose He Threw It in Your Face. Ogden Nash. **CP-NashO**

Suppose he wishes balloon routes. Wanting the Impossible. Carl Sandburg. **CP-SandC**

Suppose he's listened to the erudite committee. Wystan Hugh Auden. *Fr.* The Quest. **CP-AudeW**

Suppose I Darken Your Door. Ogden Nash. **CP-NashO**

Suppose I move a factory. To Market. Charles Kenneth Williams. **CP-WillC**

Suppose me dead; and then suppose. Jonathan Swift. **LoBV; NOBE; NOEC; OxBoLi; PeLV; PoEL-3; TEP** *Fr.* Verses on the Death of Dr. Swift, D.S.P.D. **CP-SwifJ**

Suppose some peddler offered. The Market Economy. Marge Piercy. **SP-PierM**

Suppose, suppose the lion closed a fist on the calendar. An Afternoon with André Breton. Charles Henri Ford. **SP-FordC**

Suppose that once in a while. Suppose—. Roy Fisher. **SP-FishR**

Suppose that we part (work done, comes play). Pambo. Robert Browning. **CP-BroR2**

Suppose the Ceiling went Outside. The Ceiling. Theodore Roethke. **CP-RoetT**

Suppose the dead could crown their wit. A Responsory, 1948. Thomas Merton. **CP-MertT; SP-MertT**

Suppose they met, the inevitable procedure. Wystan Hugh Auden. **CP-AudWJ**

Suppose they sweltered here three thousand years. A Short History of British India (II). Geoffrey Hill. *Fr.* An Apology for the Revival of Christian Architecture in England. **CP-HillG**

Suppose this was the root of everything. A Golden Woman in a Silver Mirror. Wallace Stevens. **CP-StevW**

Suppose you stood facing. Pierrot Le Fou. Adrienne Rich. **CP-RicAE; SP-RicA2**

Suppose you want to leave your life. What You Need. William Matthews. **SP-MattW**

Supposed Confessions of a Second-rate Sensitive Mind. Tennyson. **CP-TennA**

Supposed Dancer, The. Roy Fisher. **SP-FishR**

Supposed of Pamphylax the Antiochene. A Death in the Desert. Robert Browning. **CP-BroR1**

Supposed To Be Written by Werter. Charlotte Smith. **CP-SmitC**

Supposed to Have Been Written in a Church-yard, over the Grave of a Young Woman of Nineteen. Charlotte Smith. **CP-SmitC**

Supposed To Have Been Written in America. Charlotte Smith. **CP-SmitC**

Supposed to Have Been Written in the Hebrides. Charlotte Smith. **CP-SmitC**

Supposing i dreamed this). Edward Estlin Cummings. **CP-CummE**

Supposing I say: dogs are my neighbours. As Thyself! David Herbert Lawrence. **CP-LawrD**

Supposing that one walks out into the air. Kenneth Koch. **OBCoV** *Fr.* Fresh Air. **SP-KochK**

Sup'rabundance of my store, The. The Poores Portion. Robert Herrick. **CP-HerrR**

Supremacy. Edwin Arlington Robinson. **CP-RobiE**

Supreme Authority of the Imagination, The. Richard Eberhart. **CP-EberR**

Supreme Fortune Falls Soonest. Robert Herrick. **CP-HerrR**

Supreme in the distance, veiled. The Unreturning Hosts. Kenneth Patchen. **CP-PatcK**

Sure. Jim Carroll. **SP-CarrJ**

Sure, / Herbert—. Ice Cream. Robert Creeley. **CP-CreeR**

Sure a seaman's los is bless'd. St. James. Christopher Smart. *Fr.* Hymns and Spiritual Songs for the Fasts and Festivals of the Church of England. **SP-SmarC**

Sure. All the time I come upon the evil. Nameless. James Dickey. **CP-DickJ**

Sure, deck your lower limbs in pants. What's the Use. Ogden Nash. **CP-NashO**

Sure enough, moving, the thunder became men. Thunder by the Musician. Wallace Stevens. **CP-StevW**

Sure Lord, there is enough in thee to dry. Sonnet. George Herbert. **CP-HerbG**

Sure never did man see. My Lady's Lamentation and Complaint against the Dean. Jonathan Swift. **CP-SwifJ**

Sure never was heard so berhymed & beriddled! Time. George Meredith. **CP-MerG2**

"Sure," Said Benny Goodman. Hayden Carruth. **CP-CarHS**

Sure Signs. Ted Kooser. **SP-KoosT**

Sure There Is Food. Kenneth Patchen. **CP-PatcK**

Sure there's some wondrous joy in doing good. Ode to the King. Jonathan Swift. **CP-SwifJ**

Surely / Cued / motif smites truly to Beautifully, The, *See also* Newly / cued. . . . Edward Estlin Cummings. **CP-CummE** ("Newly, The / cued / motif smites truly to beautifully.") **CP-CummE**

Surely among a rich man's flowering lawns. Ancestral Houses. William Butler Yeats. **CP-YeatW; LiTB; OAEL-2** *Fr.* Meditations in Time of Civil War. **CP-YeatW**

Surely among a rich man's flowering lawns. Meditations in Time of Civil War. William Butler Yeats. **CP-YeatW**

Surely He Hath Borne Our Griefs. Christina Georgina Rossetti. **CP-RosC2**

Surely he'd outwitted them, outdistanced them and earned. The Pursued. Daniel Gerard Hoffman. **SP-HoffD**

Surely I pass most signs without seeing them. Driving North from Savannah on My Birthday. Paul Zimmer. **SP-ZimmP**

Surely I will be disquieted. August 17th. Anne Sexton. **CP-SextA**

Surely in your language. Margaret Atwood. *Fr.* Two-Headed Poems. **SP-AtwM2**

Surely it has some virtue, having none. Red Rock of Utah. Donald Davie. **CP-DavDo**

Surely it is time for the true grace of women. Muriel Rukeyser. *Fr.* Letter to the Front. **CP-RukeM**

Surely, Iuventius, one of this throng in Rome. Carmen 81. Catullus. *Fr.* Carmina. **CP-Catul**

Surely one of my finest days, I'd just. Extract from Memoirs. Howard Nemerov. **CP-NemeH**

Surely there, among the great docks, is peace, my mind. In Harbor. William Carlos Williams. **CP-WilW1**

Surely there is an aching void within. Christina Georgina Rossetti. **CP-RosC3**

Surely there was, at first, some love of letters. A Full Professor. Howard Nemerov. **CP-NemeH**

Surely we knew our darkling shore. The Birth of Venus. Hayden Carruth. **CP-CarHS**

Surely you paused at this roadside oasis. A Garage in Co. Cork. Derek Mahon. **SP-MahoD**

Surely you stay my certain own, you stay. Love Note I: Surely. Gwendolyn Brooks. **SP-BrooG**

Surely you've trodden straight. Obsequial Ode. David Herbert Lawrence. **CP-LawrD**

Surest thing there is is we are riders. Riders. Robert Frost. **CP-FrosR**

Surf: An Elegy, The. Robert Creeley. **CP-CreeR**

Surface shine, the inner steel of track, The. The Young Men. Muriel Rukeyser. **CP-RukeM**

Surfaces. Peter Meinke. **SP-MeinP**

Surfaces of childhood give off a faint, The. A Few Bars Over Again. Steve Griffiths. **SP-GrifS**

Surfeits. Robert Herrick. **CP-HerrR**

Surgeon, The. Anne Sexton. **CP-SextA**

Surgeon at 2 A.M., The. Sylvia Plath. **CP-PlatS**

Surgeon I would aske, but 'tis too late. Sonnet 3. Mary Sidney, Countess of Montgomery Wroth. *Fr.* Lindamira's Complaint. *Fr.* Part 1. *Fr.* Urania. **CP-WrotM**

Surgeons. Robert Creeley. **CP-CreeR**

Surgeons cutting a hole. Last Elegy. Stephen Berg. **SP-BergS**

Surgeons must be very careful. Emily Dickinson. **CP-DickE**

Surgery. Richard Shelton. **SP-ShelR**

Surgery of the Sea, The. Erica Jong. **SP-JongE**

Surgical Ward: Men. Robert Ranke Graves. **CP-GravR**

Surly One, The. Theodore Roethke. **CP-RoetT**

Surly's old whore in her new silks doth swim. On Cashiered Capt[ain] Surly. Ben Jonson. **CP-JonsB**

Surprise. Leonard Nathan. **SP-NathL**

Surprise is like a thrilling—pungent. Emily Dickinson. **CP-DickE**

Surprise me on some ordinary day. John Berryman. *Fr.* Eleven Addresses to the Lord. **CP-BerrJ**

Surprise Package. Marsden Hartley. **CP-HartM**

Surprised by Evening. Robert Bly. **SP-BlyR**

Surprised by Joy [Impatient as the Wind]. William Wordsworth. *See* Surprised by Joy—impatient as the wind.

Surprised by Joy—impatient as the wind. William Wordsworth. **CP-WorW1**

(Surprised by Joy [Impatient as the Wind].) **CP-WorW1**

Surprised one day, I watched Belfast's Lord Mayor. The YCVS and the Ulster Division. John Hewitt. **CP-HewiJ**

Surprises of the Superhuman, The. Wallace Stevens. **CP-StevW**

Surrealist and Omega, A. Gwendolyn Brooks. *Fr.* A Catch of Shy Fish. **SP-BrooG**

Surreptitious you at bay doom loot is, my little Juventi. Catullus. *See* Carmen 99: "Purloining while you played in honeyed youth."

Surrey. Donald Davie. **CP-DavDo**

Surrounded, The. Muriel Rukeyser. **CP-RukeM**

Surrounded by eunuchs and limp as a tissue. Martial, *tr.* by William Matthews. **SP-MattW** *Fr.* Epigrams.

Surrounded by tigers. The Life of the Wolf. Gary Gildner. **SP-GildG**

Surrounded by Wild Turkeys. Gary Snyder. **CP-SnydG**

Surrounded by your glance. Tout Entouré de Mon Regard. Charles Tomlinson. **CP-TomlC**

Sursum Corda. Ralph Waldo Emerson. **CP-EmerR**

Sursum Corda. Christina Georgina Rossetti. **CP-RosC2**

Survey of Literature. John Crowe Ransom. **SP-RansJ**

Surveyor straightens from his theodolite, The. Guyana. Derek Walcott. **CP-WalcD**

Surview [*or* Surview: Cogitavi Vias Meas]. Thomas Hardy. **CP-HardT**

Survival. Phoebe Hesketh. **SP-HeskP**

Survival. John Hewitt. **CP-HewiJ**

Survival, The. Rudyard Kipling. **CP-KiplR** *Fr.* Debits and Credits.

Survival. Richard Shelton. **SP-ShelR**

Survival as Tao, Beginning at 5:00 A.M. Hayden Carruth. **CP-CarHS**

Survival in Missouri. John Ciardi. **SP-CiarJ**

Survival: Infantry. George Oppen. **CP-OppeG**

Survival Is of the Essence. Edwin Rolfe. **CP-RolfE**

Survival is the Word. Survival. Phoebe Hesketh. **SP-HeskP**

Survival of a Heart. Tess Gallagher. **SP-GallT**

Surviving Love. John Berryman. **CP-BerrJ**

Survivor, The. Robert Ranke Graves. **CP-GravR**

Survivor. Archibald MacLeish. **CP-MacLA**

Survivor, The. Miller Williams. **SP-WillM**

Survivor among Graves, The. Randall Jarrell. **CP-JarrR**

Survivor sole, and hardly such, of all. Yardley Oak. William Cowper. **CP-CowpW**

Survivors. Phoebe Hesketh. **SP-HeskP**

Survivors, The. John Clellon Holmes. **SP-HolmJ**

Survivors. James McAuley. *Fr.* Requiem. **SP-McAuJ**

Survivors, The. William DeWitt Snodgrass. **SP-SnodW**

Susan O'Kane. Louise McNeill. **SP-McNeL**

Susan Sontag says. See Susan Read. David Markson. **CP-MarkD**

Susanna. Siv Cedering Fox. *Fr.* Onna-E, Pictures of Women. **SP-CedeS**

Sushi. Paul Muldoon. **SP-MuldP**

Suspended in a moving night. Corner Seat. Louis MacNeice. **CP-MacNL**

Suspended lion face. Solar. Philip Larkin. **CP-LarkP**

Suspense. Thomas Hardy. **CP-HardT**

Suspense. David Herbert Lawrence. **CP-LawrD**

Suspense—is Hostiler than Death. Emily Dickinson. **CP-DickE**

Suspension. Audre Lorde. **SP-LordA**

Suspicion, Discontent, and Strife. Single Life Most Secure. Robert Herrick. **CP-HerrR**

Suspicion Makes Secure. Robert Herrick. **CP-HerrR**

Suspition upon His Over-much Familiarity with a Gentlewoman, The. Robert Herrick. **CP-HerrR**

Susquehanna and the Delaware, The. Robert Louis Stevenson. **CP-StevR**

Sussex. Donald Davie. **CP-DavDo**

Sussex. Rudyard Kipling. **CP-KiplR**

Sussex Men are Noted Fools, The. William Blake. **CP-BlakW**

Sustainment. James Dickey. **CP-DickJ**

Sut Lovingood. Charles Olson. **CP-OlsoC**

Sutors o' Selkirk. Robert Burns. **CP-BurnR**

Suum Cuique ("Rain has spoiled the farmer's day, The"). Ralph Waldo Emerson. **CP-EmerR**

Suum Cuique ("Wilt thou seal up the avenues of ill?"). Ralph Waldo Emerson. **APN-1** *Fr.* Quatrains. **CP-EmerR**

Suzanne. William Carlos Williams. **CP-WilW2**

Suzanne [Takes You Down]. Leonard Cohen. **CP-CoheL**

Suzy. William Carlos Williams. **CP-WilW2**

Suzy Q, The. John Clellon Holmes. **SP-HolmJ**

Swaddled to his nose against the chill. The Vigil of Corpus Christi. Thom Gunn. **CP-GunnT**

Swaggering Gait, The. William Carlos Williams. **CP-WilW2**

Swain, Hind, Knight; I fed, till'd, did command, A. Pentadius, *tr. fr.* Latin by Richard Lovelace. **CP-LoveR**

Swallow, The. Jeanne Marie Bouvier de la Motte-Guyon, *tr. fr. French by* William Cowper. **CP-CowpW**

Swallow, The. Charlotte Smith. *See* The Gorse is yellow on the heath.

Swallow came from over the sea, The. George Meredith. **CP-MerG2**

Swallow has set her six young on the rail, The. In the Doorway. Robert Browning. **SCGP** *Fr.* James Lee's Wife. **CP-BroR1**

Swallow, my sister, O sister swallow. Itylus. Algernon Charles Swinburne. **SP-SwinA**

Swallow, privileged above the rest, The. John Dryden. **SP-DrydJ** *Fr.* The Hind and the Panther.

Swallow—rebuilding, The. Ted Hughes. **SP-HughT** *Fr.* Gaudete.

Swallows. Marsden Hartley. **CP-HartM**

Swallows are nesting in the hovels of Israel, The. Alun Lewis. *Fr.* The Captivity. **CP-LewiA**

Swallows flew in the curves of an eight, The. Overlooking the River Stour. Thomas Hardy. **CP-HardT**

Swallows Flown. Walter de la Mare. **CP-DeLaW**

Swallows in their torpid state, The. To the Rev. Mr. Newton. William Cowper. **CP-CowpW**

Swallows interweaving there mid the paired, The. Samuel Taylor Coleridge. *Fr.* Some Fragments, Mainly from Manuscripts of 1797–8. **CP-ColeS**

Swallows Return, The. Richard Eberhart. **CP-EberR**

Swallows travel to and fro. Robert Louis Stevenson. **CP-StevR**

Swallows' twisting southward-turning flock, The. Zeno. Randall Jarrell. **CP-JarrR**

Swallowtail, swallowtail. Backcountry Blues. Kenneth Patchen. **CP-PatcK**

Swamp, The. Derek Walcott. **CP-WalcD**

Swampstrife and spatterdock. The Marsh. William DeWitt Snodgrass. **SP-SnodW**

Swan. Donald Hall. **CP-HallD**

Swan. John Hewitt. **CP-HewiJ**

Swan. David Herbert Lawrence. **CP-LawrD**

Swan, The. Ogden Nash. **CP-NashO**

Swan, The. Mary Oliver. **SP-OlivM**

Swan, The. Theodore Roethke. **CP-RoetT**

Swan at Sheffield Park, The. David St. John. **SP-StJoD**

Swan I see upon the sullen water, The. Swan. John Hewitt. **CP-HewiJ**

Swan is the signet, heraldic joy, The. The Banners. Robert Duncan. **SP-DuncR**

Swan of the heavens, The. The Bird-Queen. Kenneth Patchen. **CP-PatcK**

Swan Song of Parson Avery, The. John Greenleaf Whittier. **CP-WhitJ**

Swans. Louise Glück. **SP-GlücL**

Swans, The. May Sarton. **SP-SartM**

Swans. I watch them. Canal. Charles Tomlinson. **CP-TomlC**

Swan's Nest. John Hewitt. **CP-HewiJ**

Swans on the River Ayr. Mary Oliver. **SP-OlivM**

Swans sing before they die—'twere no bad thing. On a Volunteer Singer. Samuel Taylor Coleridge. **CP-ColeS**

Swans Walk My Brain in April It Rains, The. Charles Bukowski. **SP-BukC2**

Swan's Way, The. Alun Lewis. **CP-LewiA**

Swarm, The. Sylvia Plath. **CP-PlatS**

Swarthy when young; who took the tonsure; sign. John Berryman. *Fr.* Sonnets to Chris. **CP-BerrJ**

Swatara, Swatara, black river. The Countryman. Wallace Stevens. **CP-StevW**

Swath of light climbs up the skyscraper, The. Evening Questions. Carl Sandburg. **CP-SandC**

Swathe Uncut, The. John Hewitt. **CP-HewiJ**

Swathed round in mist and crown'd with cloud. George Meredith. **CP-MerG1**

Swear by what the sages spoke. Under Ben Bulben. William Butler Yeats. **CP-YeatW**

Swear to love and cherish her? To a Bridegroom. Thomas Hardy. **CP-HardT**

Sweat. Stephen Dobyns. **SP-DobyS**

Sweat, The. Gary Snyder. **CP-SnydG**

Sweater. Charles Bukowski. **SP-BukC3**

Sweater of Vladimir Ussachevsky, The. John Haines. **SP-HainJ**

Sweating under the intense Corinthian sun. Old Corinth. John Hewitt. **CP-HewiJ**

Sweaty Day in August, A. Charles Bukowski. **SP-BukC3**

Sweaty redfaced laughter of drunken friends!, The. Andante Cantabile. James McAuley. Fr. The Exile's Fifth Symphony. **SP-McAuJ**

Sweden. Lapp. Pouch made from a blackthroated diver. James Fenton. Fr. Exempla. **SP-FentJ**

Swedish Lesson. Barton Sutter. **SP-SuttB**

Sweeney. Anne Sexton. **CP-SextA**

Sweeney Agonistes. Thomas Stearns Eliot. **CP-ElioT**
  Fragment of an Agon. **LiTB**
  Two Songs from *Sweeny Agonistes.* **UnPo**
    Song by Klipstein and Krumpacker.
    Song by Wauchope and Horsfall.
    "You'll be my little seven stone missionary!"
  "Well here again that don't apply." **FaBoVe**

Sweeney among the Nightingales. Thomas Stearns Eliot. **CP-ElioT**

Sweeney Astray. Seamus Heaney. **SP-HeanS**

Sweeney Erect. Thomas Stearns Eliot. **CP-ElioT**

Sweeney in Connacht. Seamus Heaney. **SP-HeanS**

Sweeney Praises the Trees. Seamus Heaney. **SP-HeanS**

Sweeney Redivivus. Seamus Heaney.
  Artist, An. **SP-HeanS**
  Cleric, The. **SP-HeanS**
  Drifting Off. **SP-HeanS**
  First Flight, The. **SP-HeanS**
  First Kingdom, The. **SP-HeanS**
  Holly. **SP-HeanS**
  In Illo Tempore. **SP-HeanS**
  In the Beech. **SP-HeanS**
  Master, The. **SP-HeanS**
  On the Road. **SP-HeanS**
  Scribes, The. **SP-HeanS**

Sweeney's Lament on Alisa Craig. Seamus Heaney. **SP-HeanS**

Sweeney's Last Poem. Seamus Heaney. **SP-HeanS**

Sweep the house. The Dead Baby. William Carlos Williams. **CP-WilW1**

Sweep the house clean. Love Song. William Carlos Williams. **CP-WilW1**

Sweeper of Ways, The. Howard Nemerov. **CP-NemeH**

Sweeper said Karanje had a temple, The. Karanje Village. Alun Lewis. **CP-LewiA**

Sweeping past the florist's came the baby and the girl. Girl and Baby Florist Sidewalk Pram Nineteen Seventy Something. Kenneth Koch. **SP-KochK**

Sweeping Wendy: Study in Fugue. Carl Sandburg. **CP-SandC**

Sweet, a delicate white mouse, A. The Waltzer in the House. Stanley Jasspon Kunitz. **CP-KuniS**

Sweet Acclamation of Death divulges it, The. Emily Dickinson. **SP-DickE**

Sweet after showers, ambrosial air. Tennyson. **EBVV** Fr. In Memoriam A. H. H. **CP-TennA**

Sweet Alice S. Morris, I *am* pleased, of course. Reply to a Lady Editor. Theodore Roethke. **CP-RoetT**

Sweet Amarillis, by a spring's. Upon Mistress Elizabeth Wheeler under the Name of Amarillis. Robert Herrick. **CP-HerrR**

Sweet and low, sweet and low, *see also alt. vers.* "Bright is the moon on the deep." Tennyson. **BLPL; BoTP; FHYEP; FaBoBe; FaPON; MOS; NAEL-2; OxBChV; PlP; PoLF; SCGP; TrGrPo** Fr. The Princess. **CP-TennA**
  (Lullaby: "Sweet and low, sweet and low.") **PoLF**

Sweet and soft as summer, Darlings. Emily Dickinson. **SP-DickE**

Sweet and various the woodlark. Lawrence Ferlinghetti. **SP-FerlL**

Sweet Anna Gram is not. That'll Be the Day. Dabney Stuart. **SP-StuaD**

Sweet are my Julia's lips and cleane. On Julias Lips. Robert Herrick. **CP-HerrR**

Sweet are the pleasures that to verse belong. To George Felton Mathew. John Keats. **CP-KeatJ**

Sweet as Eden is the air. Woodland Peace. George Meredith. **CP-MerG1**

Sweet babe, whose image here express'd. On the Picture of a Sleeping Child. Vincent Bourne, *tr. fr. Latin by* William Cowper. **CP-CowpW**

Sweet, be not proud of those two eyes. To Dianeme. Robert Herrick. **CP-HerrR**

Sweet beast, I have gone prowling. Song. William DeWitt Snodgrass. **SP-SnodW**

Sweet bird that shunn'st the noise of folly. John Milton. **CH** Fr. Il Penseroso. **CP-MiltJ**

Sweet bird, whom the winter constrains. Invitation to the Redbreast. Vincent Bourne, *tr. fr. Latin by* William Cowper. **CP-CowpW**

Sweet Boy, Gimme Yr Ass. Allen Ginsberg. **CP-GinsA**

Sweet Briars of the Stairways. Nicholas Vachel Lindsay. **CP-LindV**

Sweet Bridget blusht, & therewithall. Upon His Kinswoman Mistresse Bridget Herrick. Robert Herrick. **CP-HerrR**

Sweet brother, if I do not sleep. For My Brother: Reported Missing In Action, 1943. Thomas Merton. **CP-MertT; SP-MertT**

Sweet Charity. John Clellon Holmes. **SP-HolmJ**

Sweet child, / little girl with well-shaped legs. The Ogre. William Carlos Williams. **CP-WilW1**

Sweet closes the evening on Craigieburn-wood. Craigieburn-Wood—A Song. Robert Burns. **CP-BurnR**

Sweet country life, to such unknown. The Country Life, to the Honored Mr. Endymion Porter[, Groome of the Bed-Chamber to His Maj.]. Robert Herrick. **CP-HerrR**

Sweet cyder is a great thing. Great Things. Thomas Hardy. **CP-HardT**

Sweet Cytherea, sitting by a brook. *Various Authors.* **CP-ShaWS** Fr. The Passionate Pilgrim. **CP-ShaWS**

Sweet Dancer. William Butler Yeats. **CP-YeatW**

Sweet day, so cool, so calm, so bright. Virtue [*or* Vertue]. George Herbert. **CP-HerbG**

Sweet Death. Christina Georgina Rossetti. **CP-RosC1**

Sweet disorder in the dress[e], A. Delight in Disorder. Robert Herrick. **CP-HerrR**

Sweet Dorothy, I know you're still. A Poem for Dorothy Dandridge. Al Young. **CP-YounA**

Sweet dreams form a shade. Cradle Song, A. William Blake. **EnRP; FHYEP; LAuP; OAEP; OBCP; SBVL** Fr. Songs of Innocence. **CP-BlakW**

Sweet dreams, sweet memories, sweet taste of earth. *with music.* Stephen Dobyns. **SP-DobyS**

Sweet earth, he ran and changed his shoes to go. Arrangements with Earth for Three Dead Friends. James Wright. **CP-WrigJ**

Sweet Echo, sweetest Nymph, that livest unseen. Echo. John Milton. **ELP; LoBV; NOBE; OBEV; OBS; SeCeV; TrGrPo** Fr. Comus; a Masque Presented at Ludlow Castle.

Sweet entrance to a husband's pleasure. Carmen 67. Catullus. Fr. Carmina. **CP-Catul**

Sweet everlasting Love, daughter of God. Gregory Nazianzen. Frank Templeton Prince. **CP-PrinF**

Sweet, exclude me[e] not, nor be divided. Bar Not the Door. Thomas Campion. **CP-CampT**

Sweet fa's the eve on Craigieburn. Robert Burns. **CP-BurnR**

Sweet Fern. John Greenleaf Whittier. **CP-WhitJ**

Sweet fish tinned in the innocence of sleep. Night Flight, over Ocean. John Updike. **CP-UpdiJ**

Sweet Florentine, sea-spawned. *He Gives Her Botticelli's Birth of Venus as a Wedding Gift.* Alun Lewis. Fr. War Wedding. **CP-LewiA**

Sweet Flower! belike one day to have. To the Daisy. William Wordsworth. **CP-WorW1**

Sweet flower! that peeping from thy russet stem. On Observing a Blossom on the First of February 1796. Samuel Taylor Coleridge. **CP-ColeS**

Sweet floweret, pledge o' meikle love. On the Birth of a Posthumous Child, Born in Peculiar Circumstances of Family Distress. Robert Burns. **CP-BurnR**

Sweet girl! though only once we met. To a Beautiful Quaker. Byron. **CP-Byron**

Sweet glove, the witness of my secret bliss, *speech of Dorus.* Sir Philip Sidney. **SP-SidnP** Fr. Arcadia.

Sweet Good Night Poem to Our Beloved Hartebeeste from All the Little Animals. Malcolm Lowry. **CP-LowrM**

Sweet Highland Girl, a very shower. To the Highland Girl of Inversneyde. William Wordsworth. **CP-WorW1**

Sweet hours have perished here. Emily Dickinson. **CP-DickE**

Sweet Hussy, The. Thomas Hardy. **CP-HardT**

Sweet is it as Life. Emily Dickinson. **SP-DickE**

"Sweet is the holiness of Youth"—so felt. Edward VI. William Wordsworth. **EPCY** Fr. Ecclesiastical Sonnets. **CP-WorW2**

Sweet is the light of infancy, and sweet. Infancy and Age. George Meredith. **CP-MerG2**

Sweet is the swamp with its secrets. Emily Dickinson. **CP-DickE**

Sweet is true love tho' given in vain, in vain. The Song of Love and Death. Tennyson. **OBNC** *Fr.* Lancelot and Elaine. *Fr.* Idylls of the King. **CP-TennA**

Sweet is your antique body, not yet young. Sonnet, to a Child. Wilfred Owen. **CP-OwenW**

Sweet Jane. "Lou Reed." **SP-ReedL**

Sweet Jesus, talking / his melancholy madness. Maybe. Mary Oliver. **SP-OlivM**

Sweet Justice of Norbiton, neighbour of Jones. George Meredith. **CP-MerG2**

Sweet kiss, thy sweets I fain would sweetly indite. Sonnet 79. Sir Philip Sidney. **CBCK; NoSic** *Fr.* Astrophil and Stella. **SP-SidnP**

"Sweet land" / at last! St. Francis Einstein of the Daffodils. William Carlos Williams. **CP-WilW1**

Sweet Land of Liberty. Emily Dickinson. **SP-DickE**

Sweet lett mee injoye thy sight. Song 1. Mary Sidney, Countess of Montgomery Wroth. *Fr.* Pamphilia to Amphilanthus. **CP-WrotM**

Sweet Levinsky. Allen Ginsberg. **CP-GinsA**

Sweet Life is dead.— / Not so. May. Christina Georgina Rossetti. **CP-RosC3**

Sweet lips, there are songs about kisses now. Counting. Carl Sandburg. **CP-SandC**

Sweet love, renew thy force; be it not said. Sonnet 56. William Shakespeare. **PoLF; SCGP** *Fr.* Sonnets. **CP-ShaWS**

Sweet love, sweet thorn, when lightly to my heart. Edna St. Vincent Millay. **CP-MillE**

Sweet Marie, she loves just me. Just Me, Just Me. Shel Silverstein. **SP-SilS2**

Sweet Mary the first time she ever was there. Mary. William Blake. **CP-BlakW**

Sweet Meat Has Sour Sauce. William Cowper. **CP-CowpW**

Sweet Mercy! how my very heart has bled. Pity. Samuel Taylor Coleridge. *Fr.* Effusions. **CP-ColeS**

Sweet mildness of the late December day. The Rent in the Screen. Howard Nemerov. **CP-NemeH**

Sweet Mother Chruch, beleaguered on the hill. Alun Lewis. *Fr.* Threnody for a Starry Night. **CP-LewiA**

Sweet Mountains—Ye tell Me no lie. Emily Dickinson. **CP-DickE**

Sweet muse / with bitter milk. Insomnia & Poetry. Erica Jong. **SP-JongE**

Sweet Music. Charles Bukowski. **SP-BukC1**

Sweet naïveté of feature. On Seeing Miss Fontenelle in a Favourite Character. Robert Burns. **CP-BurnR**

Sweet night / And sleep then, A. Malcolm Lowry. **CP-LowrM**

Sweet Night Bleeds From Zimmer, The. Paul Zimmer. **SP-ZimmP**

Sweet night nursing a neighbor—. Night Watch. May Sarton. **SP-SartM**

Sweet nymph, who art, it seems, accused. To a Young Lady Who Stole a Pen. William Cowper. **CP-CowpW**

Sweet o' the Year, The. George Meredith. **CP-MerG1**

Sweet Oenone, doe but say. To Oenone. Robert Herrick. **CP-HerrR**

Sweet of dreams, The. Canta Naranja. Gilbert Sorrentino. **SP-SorrG**

Sweet Old Man. Marsden Hartley. **CP-HartM**

Sweet peace, where dost thou dwell? I humbly crave. Peace. George Herbert. **CP-HerbG**

Sweet Peas. John Keats. **FHYEP; GN** *Fr.* I Stood Tip-Toe upon a Little Hill. **CP-KeatJ**

Sweet peas, pale diapers, The. Air. Tom Clark. **SP-ClarT**

Sweet Piece from Fontal. Richard Hugo. **CP-HugoR**

Sweet Pirate of the heart. Emily Dickinson. **CP-DickE**

Sweet poet of the woods, a long adieu! On the Departure of the Nightingale. Charlotte Smith. **CP-SmitC**

Sweet pretty things are in bed now of course, The. Tombstone Blues. "Bob Dylan." **CP-DylaB**

Sweet Rose, Fair Flower. William Shakespeare. *See* Sweet rose, fair flower, untimely pluck'd, soon vaded.

Sweet rose, fair flower, untimely pluck'd, soon vaded. William Shakespeare. **CP-ShaWS; EIL** *Fr.* The Passionate Pilgrim. **CP-ShaWS**

(Sweet Rose, Fair Flower.) **EIL**

Sweet, sad / nostalgia—. Robert Creeley. **CP-CreeR**

Sweet—safe—Houses. Emily Dickinson. **CP-DickE**

Sweet Sally took a cardboard box. The Ballad of the Light-Eyed Little Girl. Gwendolyn Brooks. **SP-BrooG** *Fr.* The Womanhood.

Sweet serene sky[e]-like Flower. Richard Lovelace. **CP-LoveR**

(Ode to Lucasta: The Rose.) **CP-LoveR**

Sweet shades why doe you seeke to give delight. Sonnet 17. Mary Sidney, Countess of Montgomery Wroth. *Fr.* Pamphilia to Amphilanthus. **CP-WrotM**

Sweet-Shop Round The Corner, The. Robert Ranke Graves. **CP-GravR**

Sweet Silvia in a shadie wood. Song 2. Mary Sidney, Countess of Montgomery Wroth. *Fr.* Pamphilia to Amphilanthus. **CP-WrotM**

Sweet Sixteen Lines. Al Young. **CP-YounA**

Sweet Skepticism of the Heart. Emily Dickinson. **CP-DickE**

Sweet, sleeky Doctor, dear pacific soul. The Incomparable Soporific Doctor. James Thomson. **CP-ThomJ**

Sweet soul, do you with me as thou wilt. Tennyson. *Fr.* In Memoriam A. H. H. **CP-TennA**

Sweet sounds, begone— / Whose music on my ear. Music Unheard. Walter de la Mare. **CP-DeLaW**

Sweet sounds, oh, beautiful music, do not cease! On Hearing a Symphony of Beethoven. Edna St. Vincent Millay. **CP-MillE**

Sweet spring day is glad with music, The. To Lydia Maria Child. John Greenleaf Whittier. **CP-WhitJ**

Sweet spring is your. Edward Estlin Cummings. **CP-CummE; SP-CummE**

Sweet star, which gleaming o'er the darksome scene. To a Star. Percy Bysshe Shelley. **CP-ShelP**

Sweet stream, that winds through [or thro'] yonder glade. William Cowper. **CP-CowpW**

(Another [Addressed to a Young Lady].) **CP-CowpW**

Sweet streamlet bason! at thy side. Arthur Hugh Clough. **SP-ClouA**

Sweet summer days had past & gone. Wandering Willie. George Meredith. **CP-MerG2**

Sweet Swan of Avon! what a sight it were. Ben Jonson. **ChTr** *Fr.* To the Memory of My Beloved, the Author Mr [or Master] William Shakespeare[: And What He Hath Left Us]. **CP-JonsB**

Sweet, sweet, is sleep,—Ah! sweeter, to be stone. Michelangelo Buonarroti, *tr. fr. Italian by* Ralph Waldo Emerson. **CP-EmerR**

Sweet, Sweet Is the Greeting of Eyes. John Keats. **CP-KeatJ**

Sweet sweet sound of distant waters falling. For Advent. Christina Georgina Rossetti. **CP-RosC3**

Sweet swelling lip, well mayst thou swell in pride. Sonnet 80. Sir Philip Sidney. *Fr.* Astrophil and Stella. **SP-SidnP**

Sweet tenants of this grove! Joy in Martyrdom. Jeanne Marie Bouvier de la Motte-Guyon, *tr. fr. French by* William Cowper. **CP-CowpW**

Sweet Things. Thom Gunn. **CP-GunnT**

Sweet, thou art pale. The Three Enemies. Christina Georgina Rossetti. **CP-RosC1**

Sweet, thou hast trod on a heart. A False Step. Elizabeth Barrett Browning. **CP-BroEB**

Sweet, to have had them lost. Emily Dickinson. **CP-DickE**

Sweet toil for smitten hands. Emily Dickinson. **SP-DickE**

Sweet tones of the stream, The. Sergeant Valentine Function, at Hollyfort. James Liddy. **CP-LiddJ**

Sweet tooth taught us to admire, A. Bestiaries Are Out. Wystan Hugh Auden. **CP-AudeW**

Sweet Tyrant Love. James Thomson. **CP-ThomJ**

"Sweet Valley, Say." James Thomson *and* David Mallet. **CP-ThomJ** *Fr.* Alfred: A Masque.

Sweet Violets! from your humble beds. Violets. Charlotte Smith. **CP-SmitC**

Sweet virgin, that I do not set. Upon His Kinswoman Mistris Elizabeth Herrick. Robert Herrick. **CP-HerrR**

Sweet was the walk along the narrow lane. William Wordsworth. **CP-WorW1**

Sweet were the day[e]s, when thou didst lodge with Lot. Decay. George Herbert. **CP-HerbG**

Sweet [or Swete] were the sauce would please e[a]ch kind of tast[e]. Sir Walter Ralegh. **CP-RaleW**

(Walter Rawley [or Ralegh or Rawely] of the Middle Temple, in Commendation of the Steel[e] Glass[e].) **CP-RaleW**

Sweet western wind, whose luck it is. To the Western Wind. Robert Herrick. **CP-HerrR**

Sweet Will. Philip Levine. **SP-LeviP**

Sweet—You forgot—but I remembered. Emily Dickinson. **CP-DickE**

Sweetbread, The. Ogden Nash. *Fr.* Table Talk. **CP-NashO**

Sweete, come againe. *At. to* Thomas Campion *and to* Philip Rosseter. **CP-CampT**

Sweete solitarines, joy to those hearts. Mary Sidney, Countess of Montgomery Wroth. *Fr.* Part 1. *Fr.* Urania. **CP-WrotM**

Sweeten these bitter wild crabapples, Illinois. Crabapples. Carl Sandburg. **CP-SandC**

Sweeter than sour apples flesh to boys. Ted Berrigan. **SP-BerrT** *Fr.* The Sonnets.

Sweeter was loss than silver coins to spend. Edna St. Vincent Millay. *Fr.* Epitaph for the Race of Man. **CP-MillE**

Sweetest blossoms die, The. Sweet Death. Christina Georgina Rossetti. **CP-RosC1**

Sweetest Elizabeth, accept I pray. To My Friend Elizabeth. Christina Georgina Rossetti. **CP-RosC3**

Sweetest Heresy received, The. Emily Dickinson. **CP-DickE**

Sweetest Loue since wee must part. Farewell, The. Robert Herrick. **CP-HerrR**

Sweetest love, I do not go[e]. Song. John Donne. **CP-DonnJ**

Sweetest love returne againe. Song 4. Mary Sidney, Countess of Montgomery Wroth. *Fr.* Pamphilia to Amphilanthus. **CP-WrotM**

Sweetest May. Robert Burns. **CP-BurnR**

Sweetest of all childlike dreams. The Vanishers. John Greenleaf Whittier. **CP-WhitJ**

Sweetest of sweets, I thank you: when displeasure. Church-Music[k]. George Herbert. **CP-HerbG**

Sweetest of the flowers a-blooming. The Lily of the Valley. Paul Laurence Dunbar. **CP-DunbP**

Sweetest Saviour, if my soul. A Dialogue. George Herbert. **CP-HerbG**

Sweetest way I think of you, The. Emily Dickinson. **SP-DickE**

Sweetgum avenue leads to a college of charm, The. Thomas Merton. *Fr.* Cables to the Ace. **CP-MertT**

Sweetheart. Alice Notley. **SP-NotlA**

Sweetheart Autumn. Nicholas Vachel Lindsay. *Fr.* Sweethearts of the Year. **CP-LindV**

Sweetheart, do not love too long. O Do Not Love Too Long. William Butler Yeats. **CP-YeatW**

Sweetheart, I beg you to renew and seal. For Ever. Robert Ranke Graves. **CP-GravR**

Sweetheart Like You. "Bob Dylan." **CP-DylaB**

Sweetheart of the Csikos, The. Johann N. Vogl, *tr. fr. German by* George Meredith. **CP-MerG2**

Sweetheart Spring. Nicholas Vachel Lindsay. *Fr.* Sweethearts of the Year. **CP-LindV**

Sweetheart Summer. Nicholas Vachel Lindsay. *Fr.* Sweethearts of the Year. **CP-LindV**

Sweetheart Winter. Nicholas Vachel Lindsay. *Fr.* Sweethearts of the Year. **CP-LindV**

Sweethearts of the Year. Nicholas Vachel Lindsay. **CP-LindV**

    Sweetheart Autumn.

    Sweetheart Spring.

    Sweetheart Summer.

    Sweetheart Winter.

Sweetly Empty Woods. Sir Philip Sidney. **CBCK** *Fr.* O sweet woods, the delight of solitariness! **SP-SidnP** *Fr.* Arcadia.

Sweetmeat, what we need is a tune. Needsong. Brendan Galvin. **SP-GalvB**

Sweetness. Stephen Dunn. **SP-DunnS**

Sweetness of England, The. Elizabeth Barrett Browning. **OXAEP-2** *Fr.* Aurora Leigh. **CP-BroEB**

Sweetness of rest when Thou sheddest rest. Christina Georgina Rossetti. **CP-RosC2**

Sweetness of temper unsurpassed and unforgettable, A. A Watering-Place Lady Inventoried. Thomas Hardy. **CP-HardT**

Sweetnesse in Sacrifice. Robert Herrick. **CP-HerrR**

Sweets of Evening, The. Christopher Smart. **SP-SmarC**

Sweets of Pillage, can be known, The. Emily Dickinson. **CP-DickE**

Sweets you were glittering this morning. Dear Arl. Al Young. **CP-YounA**

Sweet[e] were the joy[e]s that both might like and last. No Pleasure, Without Some Payne. Sir Walter Ralegh. **CP-RaleW**

Swell me a bowl with lusty wine. Ben Jonson. **CP-JonsB** *Fr.* The Poetaster.

Swell People. Carl Sandburg. **CP-SandC**

Swelld limbs with no outline that you can descry. William Blake. **CP-BlakW**

Swells then thy feeling heart, and streams thine eye. The Dead Beggar, an Elegy Addressed to a Lady. Charlotte Smith. **CP-SmitC**

Swept from his fleet upon that fatal night. The Shipwreck of Idomeneus. George Meredith. **CP-MerG1**

Swerving east, from rich industrial shadows. Here. Philip Larkin. **CP-LarkP**

Swi[/ across!gold's / rouNdly. Edward Estlin Cummings. **CP-CummE**

Swich fyn hath, lo, this Troilus for love! Geoffrey Chaucer. **NOCV** *Fr.* Troilus and Criseyde [*or* Criseide]. **CP-ChauG**

Swift and sure the swallow. Christina Georgina Rossetti. **CP-RosC2**

Swift as a spirit hastening to his task. The Triumph of Life. Percy Bysshe Shelley. **CP-ShelP**

Swift cloud / across still cloud. Into Distance. Charles Tomlinson. **CP-TomlC**

Swift Comes the Swift, The. Ted Hughes. **SP-HughT**

Swift curve of the lip, nose, forehead. Head against White. Margaret Atwood. **SP-AtwM1**

Swift fall the blows, and men upbraid. George Meredith. *Fr.* France. **CP-MerG1**

Swift fleet the billowy clouds along the sky. On Passing Over a Dreary Tract of Country, and Near the Ruins of a Deserted Chapel, During a Tempest. Charlotte Smith. **CP-SmitC** *Fr.* Montalbert.

Swift has sailed into his rest. Swift's Epitaph. William Butler Yeats. **CP-YeatW**

Swift red flash, a winter king, The. The Dance. Hart Crane. **LiTM; MoAB; MoAmPo; OxBA** *Fr.* Powhatan's Daughter. *Fr.* The Bridge. **CP-CranH**

Swift to Sheridan. Jonathan Swift. **CP-SwifJ**

Swifter far than summer's flight—. Remembrance. Percy Bysshe Shelley. **CP-ShelP**

Swifter than aught 'neath the sun the car of Simonides moved him. *parody of an epigram from* The Greek Anthology. Rudyard Kipling. **CP-KiplR** *Fr.* The Muse among the Motors.

Swiftly Arose. Walt Whitman. **TrCP** *Fr.* I believe in you my soul. **Prf** *Fr.* Song of Myself. **CP-WhitW**

Swiftly re-light the flame. Hilda Doolittle. **NALW** *Fr.* Tribute to the Angels. **CP-DoolH**

Swiftly turn the murmuring wheel! Song for the Spinning Wheel (Founded upon a Belief Prevalent among the Pastoral Vales of Westmoreland). William Wordsworth. **CP-WorW1**

Swiftly walk o'er the western wave. To Night. Percy Bysshe Shelley. **CP-ShelP**

Swifts. Ted Hughes. **SP-HughT**

Swift's Epitaph. William Butler Yeats. **CP-YeatW**

Swim little king-fish Leap small salmon. Canzonetta. Isabella Gardner. **CP-GardI**

Swim so now million many worlds in each. Edward Estlin Cummings. **CP-CummE**

Swimmer, The. Louise Glück. **SP-GlücL**

Swimmer, The. Alun Lewis. **CP-LewiA**

Swimmer at Lake Edward, The. Richard Hugo. **CP-HugoR**

Swimmers, The. Allen Tate. **CP-TateA**

Swimming. Byron. **GN** *Fr.* The Two Foscari. **CP-Byron**

Swimming by Night. James Merrill. **SP-MerrJ**

Swimming Chenango Lake. Charles Tomlinson. **CP-TomlC**

Swimming in the last of September. Chuck Miller. **SP-MillC**

Swimming in the memorial. September. James Schuyler. **CP-SchuJ**

Swimming Lesson, The. Mary Oliver. **SP-OlivM**

Swimming Pool Pastoral. Laurence Lieberman. **SP-LiebL**

Swimming through the air, in schools upon the highways. Charles Olson. **SP-OlsoC** *Fr.* The Maximus Poems.

Swinburne on the Playing Fields. James Liddy. **CP-LiddJ**

Swing, The. Robert Louis Stevenson. **CP-StevR**

Swing by starwhite bones and. How to Enter a Big City. Thomas Merton. **CP-MertT**

Swing has its bold rhythm, The. The Young Sibyl. Robert Ranke Graves. **CP-GravR**

Swing low so I. Gospel. Rita Dove. **SP-DoveR**

Swing-Song. Louis MacNeice. **CP-MacNL**

Swing Song of a Girl and a Soldier. David Herbert Lawrence. *Fr.* Bits. **CP-LawrD**

Swing yo' lady roun' an' roun'. A Frolic. Paul Laurence Dunbar. **CP-DunbP**

Swinging / and the colored afghan. Just Inside the Vigil of Christmas. Charles Olson. **CP-OlsoC**

Swinging Bridge, The. Richard Eberhart. **CP-EberR**

Swinging Down Central. Robert Creeley. **CP-CreeR**

Swinging mill bell changed its rate, The. A Lone Striker. Robert Frost. **CP-FrosR**

Swirl. Carl Sandburg. **CP-SandC**

Swirl in the air where your head was once, A. Swirl. Carl Sandburg. **CP-SandC**

Swirl sleeping in the waterfall! Chomei at Toyama. Basil Bunting. **CP-BuntB**

Swirls of Black Dust on Avenue D. Allen Ginsberg. **CP-GinsA**

Swirls of brown, dark, swaying. Sestets. Marsden Hartley. **CP-HartM**

Switch on lights yellow as the sun. City Midnight Junk Strains. Allen Ginsberg. **CP-GinsA**

Switzerland. Matthew Arnold.

    Farewell, A: "My horse's feet beside the lake." **SP-ArnoM**

    Isolation: To Marguerite. **SP-ArnoM**

Lake, The.
  (Meeting.) **SP-ArnoM**
To Marguerite—Continued. **SP-ArnoM**
Switzerland. John Updike. **CP-UpdiJ**
Switzerland. Robert Penn Warren. **SP-WarrR**
Swoggled. Archie Randolph Ammons. **SP-AmmoA**
Swoon of noon, a trance of tide, A. In a Bye-Canal. Herman Melville. **SP-MelvH**
(Swooning)a pillar of youngly. Edward Estlin Cummings. **CP-CummE**
Swooning swim to less and less. Buddha. Herman Melville. **SP-MelvH**
Sword, The. Charles Bukowski. **SP-BukC3**
Sword. Marilyn Hacker. **SP-HackM**
Sword and the Sickle, The. William Blake. *See* The Sword sang [*or* sung] on the barren heath.
Sword bites for peace, The. Another Voice. Richard Wilbur. **CP-WilbR**
Sword in a Cloud of Light, A. Kenneth Rexroth. **SP-RexrR** *Fr.* The Lights in the Sky are Stars.
Sword in his right hand, a stone in his left hand, A. The Bronze David of Donatello. Randall Jarrell. **CP-JarrR; SP-JarrR**
Sword in length a reaping-hook amain. King Harald's Trance. George Meredith. **CP-MerG1**
Sword of Castruccio Castracani, The. Elizabeth Barrett Browning. **CP-BroEB**
Sword of Common Sense!—. To the Comic Spirit. George Meredith. **CP-MerG1**
Sword of sorrow, whetted sharp for me, The. The Complaint of Annelida to False Arcite. Geoffrey Chaucer. **CP-BroEB**
Sword sang [*or* sung] on the barren heath, The. William Blake. **ChTr; FaBoEE; TrGrPo** *Fr.* Gnomic Verses. **CP-BlakW**
  (Sword and the Sickle, The.) **ChTr**
Sword was sheathed: in April's sun, The. The Vow of Washington. John Greenleaf Whittier. **CP-WhitJ**
Swordfish, I know you are tired: tiredout with the sharpness of your face. Undersea Fragment in Colons. James Dickey. **CP-DickJ**
Sycamore, The. Wendell Berry. **SP-BerrW**
Sycamore. Robert Frost. **CP-FrosR**
Sycamore, The. Marianne Craig Moore. **CP-MoorM**
Sycamore, by the heap of dead, The. Foreboding. Walter de la Mare. **CP-DeLaW**
Sycamore gathers / out of the sky, white, The. Wendell Berry. *Fr.* Window Poems. **CP-BerrW**
Sycamores, The. John Greenleaf Whittier. **CP-WhitJ**
Sylo pray pay me my ten Sesterces. Catullus. *See* Carmen 103: "Either give me my hundred pounds back, Silo."
Sylph was it? or a Bird more bright. Rural Illusions. William Wordsworth. **CP-WorW2**
Sylvae. Donald Davie. **CP-DavDo**
Sylvae. John Dryden.
  Song: "Go tell Amynta, gentle swain." **SP-DrydJ**
Sylvae. Publius Papinius Statius, *tr. fr. Latin.*
  "Polish'd with endless toil, my lays." **CP-JohnS**
Sylvan Delights. Alexander Pope. **NOBE** *Fr.* Summer, The Second Pastoral, or Alexis. *Fr.* Pastorals. **CP-PopeA**
Sylvan meant savage in those primal woods. Woods. Wystan Hugh Auden. *Fr.* Bucolics. **CP-AudeW**
Sylvan slopes with corn-clad fields, The. September, 1819. William Wordsworth. **CP-WorW2**
Sylvester's Dying Bed. Langston Hughes. **SP-HughL**
Sylvia's Death. Anne Sexton. **CP-SextA**
Sylvie and Bruno. "Lewis Carroll."
  Acrostic: Is all our Life, then, but a dream. **CP-CarrL**
  Bruno's Song. **CP-CarrL**
  Lady Muriel's Song. **CP-CarrL**
  Mad Gardener's Song, The. **CP-CarrL**
  Peter and Paul. **CP-CarrL**
  Three Badgers, The. **CP-CarrL**
  Warden's Charm, The. **CP-CarrL**
Sylvie and Bruno Concluded. "Lewis Carroll."
  Acrostic: Dreams, that elude the Waker's frenzied grasp—. **CP-CarrL**
  King-Fisher [*or* King-Fisher's] Song, The. **CP-CarrL**
  Little Birds.
    "Little Birds are dining." **CP-CarrL**
    Little Birds Are Playing. **OxBoLi; PeLV**
  Little Man That Had a Little Gun, The. **CP-CarrL**
  Matilda Jane. **CP-CarrL**
  Pig-Tale, The. **CP-CarrL**
    Melancholy Pig, The. **FaPON**

Song of Love, A. **CP-CarrL**
What Tottles Meant. **CP-CarrL**
Symbol from the first, of mastery, A. The Staff of Aesculapius. Marianne Craig Moore. **CP-MoorM**
Symbol of war, a war, The. All That is Perfect in Woman. William Carlos Williams. **CP-WilW2**
Symbols. Christina Georgina Rossetti. **CP-RosC1**
Symbols. William Butler Yeats. **CP-YeatW**
Symbols jostle for their breathing space, The. Those Swans Remember; A Poem. John Hewitt. **CP-HewiJ**
Symmetries & Asymmetries. Wystan Hugh Auden. **CP-AudeW**
Symon Gray. Robert Burns. *Fr.* To Symon Gray. **CP-BurnR**
Sympathetic. William Matthews. **SP-MattW**
Sympathetic Magic. Stephen Dunn.
  Chipping Away at Death. **SP-DunnS**
  Lovers. **SP-DunnS**
  Traveling. **SP-DunnS**
Sympathetic Portrait of a Child. William Carlos Williams. **CP-WilW1**
Sympathy, *sl. diff.* Emily Brontë. *See* There should be no despair for you.
Sympathy. Paul Laurence Dunbar. **CP-DunbP**
Sympathy. Paul Laurence Dunbar. **CP-DunbP**
Sympathy. David Herbert Lawrence. **CP-LawrD**
Sympathy, a Welcome, A. John Berryman. **CP-BerrJ**
Sympathy in White Major. Philip Larkin. **CP-LarkP**
Symphony for a Sea Bird. Chuang Tzu, *tr. fr. Chinese by* Thomas Merton. **CP-MertT**
Symphony of Snow. John Gould Fletcher. **SP-FletJ**
Symptom of the Gale, The. Emily Dickinson. **CP-DickE**
Symptoms. Robert Lowell. **SP-LoweR**
Symptoms of Love, The. William Cowper. **CP-CowpW**
Symptoms of Love. Robert Ranke Graves. **CP-GravR**
Synagogue, The. Karl Shapiro. **SP-ShapK**
Synagogue dispirits the deep street, The. The Synagogue. Karl Shapiro. **SP-ShapK**
Synne's Heavy Loade. Robert Southwell. **CP-SoutR**
Synthetic Such. Robert Ranke Graves. **CP-GravR**
Syphillitic selling violets calmly, The. Moment Fugue. Hart Crane. **CP-CranH**
Syracuse Nights. Stephen Dobyns. **SP-DobyS**
Syria. Thomas Merton. *Fr.* East with Ibn Battuta. *Fr.* East. *Fr.* The Geography of Lograire. **CP-MertT**
Syringa. John Ashbery. **SP-AshbJ**
Syrinx. James Merrill. **SP-MerrJ**
System, The. John Ashbery. **SP-AshbJ**
System, The. Stanley Jasspon Kunitz. **CP-KuniS**
System. Robert Louis Stevenson. **CP-StevR**
System was breaking down, The. The one who had wandered alone past so. The System. John Ashbery. **SP-AshbJ**
Szostak. Gary Gildner. **SP-GildG**

T

'T is better to sit here beside the sea. Silence. Paul Laurence Dunbar. **CP-DunbP**
'T is done—and shivering in the gale. Stanzas to a Lady on Leaving England. Byron. **CP-Byron**
'T is done—but yesterday a King! Ode to Napoleon Buonaparte. Byron. **CP-Byron**
'T is done!—I saw it in my dreams. Remembrance. Byron. **CP-Byron**
'T is fifty years, and yet their fray. The Duel. Byron. **CP-Byron**
'T is midnight—but it is not dark. Venice. Byron. **CP-Byron**
'T is over, Moses! All is lost! A Letter. John Greenleaf Whittier. **CP-WhitJ**
'T is said that in the Holy Land. My Thanks. John Greenleaf Whittier. **CP-WhitJ**
'T is the noon of the spring-time, yet never a bird. April. John Greenleaf Whittier. **CP-WhitJ**
'T is [*or* 'Tis] time this heart should be unmoved. On This Day I Complete My Thirty-sixth Year. Byron. **CP-Byron**
T' snow is witherin' off'n th' gress—. The Drained Cup. David Herbert Lawrence. **CP-LawrD**
T the Great. Wystan Hugh Auden. **CP-AudeW**
'T was after dread Pultowa's day. Mazeppa. Byron. **CP-Byron**
'T was night. The tranquil moonlight smile. Toussaint L'Ouverture. John Greenleaf Whittier. **CP-WhitJ**
'T was now the noon of night, and all was still. Soliloquy of a Bard in the Country. Byron. **CP-Byron**

'T were extreme folly should I dare attempt. Upon the Author. *Unknown,* poem signed "C. B." **CP-BradA**

Ta / ppin / g / toe / hip. Edward Estlin Cummings. **CP-CummE**

Tabernacle. David Herbert Lawrence. **CP-LawrD**

Tabitha dressed for her wedding. The Wedding Morning. Thomas Hardy. **CP-HardT**

Table, The. Carlos Drummond de Andrade, *tr. fr. Portuguese by* Elizabeth Bishop. **CP-BishE**

Table, The. Donald Hall. **CP-HallD**

Table describes, The. The Dish of Fruit. William Carlos Williams. **CP-WilW2**

Table hurled itself, to our surprise, The. Lingard and the Stars. Edwin Arlington Robinson. **CP-RobiE**

Table is cleared of my place, The. Hold Me. Philip Levine. **SP-LeviP**

Table of Green Fields, A. James Schuyler. **CP-SchuJ**

Table Richly Spread, A. John Milton. **FaBoCh** *Fr.* Book II. *Fr.* Paradise Regained [*or* Regain'd]. **CP-MiltJ**

Table Talk. William Cowper. **CP-CowpW**
 "Contemporaries all surpassed, see one." **EPCY**
 "Then Pope, as harmony itself exact." **EPCY**
 "When Cromwell fought for power, and while he reigned." **EPCY**

Table Talk. Derek Mahon. **SP-MahoD**

Table Talk. Ogden Nash. **CP-NashO**
 Pizza, The.
 Shad, The.
 Sweetbread, The.
 Yorkshire Pudding.

Table Talk. Leonard Nathan. **SP-NathL**

Tableau. Countee Cullen. **CP-CullC**

Tableau at Twilight. Ogden Nash. **CP-NashO**

Tableau de l'Inconstance des Mauvais Anges. Stevie Smith. **CP-SmitS**

Tableau Vivant. Tess Gallagher. **SP-GallT**

Tables Turned, The. William Wordsworth. **CP-WorW1**

Taboo to Boot. Ogden Nash. **CP-NashO**

Tabula Rasa. Hayden Carruth. **CP-CarHS**

Taciturn, The. Walter de la Mare. **CP-DeLaW**

Tackle, The. Ernest Hemingway. **CP-HemiE**

Taconite Harbor. Barton Sutter. **SP-SuttB**

Tact. Ralph Waldo Emerson. **CP-EmerR**

Tact. Edwin Arlington Robinson. **CP-RobiE**

Tag. Langston Hughes. **SP-HughL**

Tags of songs, like salvaged buttons. Poem, A. James Schuyler. **CP-SchuJ**

Tagus farewell, that westward with thy streams. Sir Thomas Wyatt. **CP-WyatT**

Tagus is finer than the creek, The. Fernando Pessoa. *Fr.* Twelve Poems from *The Keeper of the Flocks*. **CP-MertT**

Tahola. Richard Hugo. **CP-HugoR**

Tail lights turn off the quarry road. Quarry Hills. Roy Fisher. **SP-FishR**

Tail-spinning from the shelves of sky. Jubilo. Allen Tate. **CP-TateA**

Tail, the waist, the nose turret or the ball gunner, The. Reality. Richard Eberhart. *Fr.* Aesthetics after War. **CP-EberR**

Tailor, The. Walter de la Mare. **CP-DeLaW**

Tailpiece. Samuel Beckett. **CP-BeckS**

Tailpiece. William Carlos Williams. **CP-WilW2**

Tails. Charles Kenneth Williams. **CP-WillC**

Take a hold now. Pals. Carl Sandburg. **CP-SandC**

Take a lunatic. Iron Hans. Anne Sexton. **CP-SextA**

Take a model of the world so big. The Rescued Year. William Stafford. **SP-StafW**

Take a red book called Telephone. Telephone. Anne Sexton. **CP-SextA**

Take a trip with me. A Small Excursion. Mona Van Duyn. **SP-VanDM**

Take all away. Emily Dickinson. **CP-DickE**

Take all away from me, but leave me Ecstasy. Emily Dickinson. **CP-DickE**

Take all my loves, my Love, yea, take them all. Sonnet 40. William Shakespeare. **HeIP; InvP; OBSC; OXAEP-1; SCGP** *Fr.* Sonnets. **CP-ShaWS**

Take away all this crystal and silver. Bowls. David Herbert Lawrence. **CP-LawrD**

Take away your knowledge, Doktor. The Doctor of the Heart. Anne Sexton. **CP-SextA**

Take Care Of Him. Christina Georgina Rossetti. **CP-RosC2**

Take care of this. It's all there is. I. Kenneth Rexroth. **SP-RexrK** *Fr.* A Bestiary. **SP-RexrK**

Take care when you speak to me. When You Speak to Me. Tess Gallagher. **SP-GallT**

Take, cradled Nursling of the mountains, take. William Wordsworth. *Fr.* The River Duddon [A Series of Sonnets]. **CP-WorW2**

Take determination, take it apart; stamp out the music from its means. World Tour. Kay Boyle. **CP-BoylK**

Take down its ears first. Dismantling the Silence. Charles Simic. **SP-SimiC**

Take for example this. Edward Estlin Cummings. **CP-CummE**

Take from me something. Chance Meeting. Hilda Doolittle. **CP-DoolH**

Take from the mind its little bitterness. Breastplate. John Hewitt. **CP-HewiJ**

Take heed betime, lest ye be spied. Sir Thomas Wyatt. **CP-WyatT**

Take heed mine eyes, how you your lookes doe cast. Sonnet 34. Mary Sidney, Countess of Montgomery Wroth. *Fr.* Pamphilia to Amphilanthus. **CP-WrotM**

Take heed of loving me[e]. The Prohibition. John Donne. **CP-DonnJ**

Take It. Charles Bukowski. **SP-BukC3**

Take it away, and swallow it yourself. An Island. Edwin Arlington Robinson. **CP-RobiE**

Take it from me kiddo. Poem, or Beauty Hurts Mr. Vinal. Edward Estlin Cummings. **CP-CummE; SP-CummE**

Take it out in vile whiskey, take it out. Impromptu: The Suckers. William Carlos Williams. **CP-WilW1**

Take me, Lieutenant, to that Surrey homestead! Love in a Valley. Sir John Betjeman. **CP-BetjJ**

Take me or leave me, cries. Melody Grundy. Denise Levertov. **CP-LeveD**

Take mine advise, and go not neere. To his Booke. Robert Herrick. **CP-HerrR**

Take my heart in thy hand, O beautiful boy of Schiraz! Hafiz, *tr. by* Ralph Waldo Emerson. **CP-EmerR** *Fr.* Odes.

Take my love, it is not true. Complaint of the Skeleton to Time. Allen Ginsberg. **CP-GinsA**

Take No Thought for The Morrow. Christina Georgina Rossetti. **CP-RosC2**

Take not my hand as mine alone. Robert Louis Stevenson. **CP-StevR**

Take, O take the key of Rome. Rafael Alberti, *tr. by* Thomas Merton. **CP-MertT** *Fr.* Roman Nocturnes.

Take of English earth as much. A Charm. Rudyard Kipling. **CP-KiplR**

Take off your cloak and your hat. December Night. David Herbert Lawrence. **CP-LawrD**

Take off your clothes, love. Old Song. Robert Creeley. **CP-CreeR**

Take off your hat five minutes every day. Atlas. John Hewitt. **CP-HewiJ**

Take One Home for the Kiddies. Philip Larkin. **CP-LarkP**

Take our hands, James Russell Lowell. A Welcome to Lowell. John Greenleaf Whittier. **CP-WhitJ**

Take out of time that moment when you stood. The Sundial. Jane Cooper. *Fr.* Acceptances. **SP-CoopJ**

Take some one in England with brains enough. Genesis. William Carlos Williams. **CP-WilW1**

Take Something Like a Star. Robert Frost. *See* O Star (the fairest one in sight).

Take that, damn you; and that! Mezzo Forte. William Carlos Williams. **CP-WilW1**

Take the broken ankles of consciousness. For César Vallejo and his Profound Oxides of Sadness. Chuck Miller. **SP-MillC**

Take the cloak from his face, and at first. After. Robert Browning. **CP-BroR1**

Take the general mumble. Notes to a Neophyte. Sylvia Plath. **CP-PlatS**

Take the hands / off of. The Hands. Robert Creeley. **CP-CreeR**

Take the intention then and let me live. John Hewitt. *Fr.* Sonnets for Roberta (1954). **CP-HewiJ**

Take the letter "H" from a Spanish. El Hombre del Ombre. Jim Carroll. **SP-CarrJ**

Take the lump in your throat. The Soup. Charles Simic. **SP-SimiC**

Take the useful events. Instructions for Angels. Kenneth Patchen. **CP-PatcK**

Take the word butterfly. *see also* Commentary—How to Speak Poetry. Leonard Cohen. **CP-CoheL**

Take, then, my answer. The K. Charles Olson. **CP-OlsoC**

Take these, times tardy truants, sent by me. Upon Two Greene Apricockes Sent to Cowley by Sir Crashaw. Richard Crashaw. **CP-CrasR**

Take this kiss upon the brow! A Dream within a Dream. Edgar Allan Poe. **CP-PoeEd**

Take this Longing. Leonard Cohen. **CP-CoheL**

Take this old man with the soldierly straight back. Louis MacNeice. *Fr.* The Kingdom. **CP-MacNL**

Take this, the nexus. The Love Charm. William Carlos Williams. **CP-WilW2**

Take This Waltz (*After Lorca*). Leonard Cohen. **CP-CoheL**

Take thought, man, tonight. Thomas Merton. *Fr.* The Early Legend. **CP-MertT**

Take Thy Bliss, O Man. William Blake. **EnRP** *Fr.* Visions of the Daughters of Albion. **CP-BlakW**

Take thy lute and sing. The Flower of the Ruins. George Meredith. **CP-MerG1**

Take time as lubricant or. Continuing. Al Young. **CP-YounA**

Take Time Out. Maya Angelou. **SP-AngeM**

Take to thy bosom, gentle earth, a swain. Another ["Take to thy bosom, gentle earth, a swain"]. *Unknown, tr. fr. Greek by* William Cowper. **CP-CowpW**

Take up the White Man's burden. The White Man's Burden. Rudyard Kipling. **CP-KiplR**

Take up your load and go, lad. Envoi. Wystan Hugh Auden. **CP-AudWJ**

Take what you want, we'll throw the rest away. Photographs. Mona Van Duyn. **SP-VanDM**

Take wings of fancy, and ascend. Tennyson. *Fr.* In Memoriam A. H. H. **CP-TennA**

Take your fill of intimate remorse, perfumed sorrow. The Right to Grief. Carl Sandburg. **CP-SandC**

Take Your Heaven further on. Emily Dickinson. **CP-DickE**

Taken at the Flood. William Matthews. *Fr.* Flood. **SP-MattW**

Taken for Granted. Louis MacNeice. **CP-MacNL**

Taken from men—this morning. Emily Dickinson. **CP-DickE**

Taker, The. Anne Sexton. **CP-SextA**

Takes time where wild the. Thyme. Louis Zukofsky. **CP-ZuklS**

Taking a Walk with You. Kenneth Koch. **SP-KochK**

Taking, giving back their lives. The Field Hospital. Paul Muldoon. **SP-MuldP**

Taking in Wash. Rita Dove. **SP-DoveR**

Taking infection from the vulgar air. The Words of the Preacher. Stanley Jasspon Kunitz. **CP-KuniS**

Taking into consideration all your loveliness. The Papa and Mama Dance. Anne Sexton. **CP-SextA**

Taking Leave of a Friend, *fr. the Chinese of* Li Po (701-62). Ezra Pound. **SP-PounE**

Taking Notice. Marilyn Hacker.
  "And I shout at Iva, whine at you. Easily." **SP-HackM**
  "Angry, I speak, and pass the hurt to you." **SP-HackM**
  "As yoked to her by absence as by prescence." **SP-HackM**
  "Grizzled doorman lets the doctors' wives, The." **SP-HackM**
  "I will never be only a Lesbian." **SP-HackM**
  "If we talk, we're too tired to make love; if we." **SP-HackM**
  "I'll tell you what I don't want: an affair." **SP-HackM**
  "Morning: the phone jangles me from words: you." **SP-HackM**
  "My child wants dolls, a tutu, that girls' world made." **SP-HackM**
  "No better lost than any other woman." **SP-HackM**
  "She twists scraps of her hair in unshelled snails." **SP-HackM**
  "When I read poems to the art students." **SP-HackM**
  "When that jackbooted choreography." **SP-HackM**

Taking of Lungtungpen, The. Rudyard Kipling. *Fr.* Plain Tales from the Hills.
  "So we loosed a bloomin' volley." **CP-KiplR**

Taking off at dawn. If I Take the Wings of the Morning. Donald Davie. **CP-DavDo**

Taking off from Kennedy. The Grave the Well. Donald Hall. **CP-HallD**

Taking One's Students to Avondale. James Liddy. **CP-LiddJ**

Taking Shelter. Steve Griffiths. **SP-GrifS**

Taking Sides. Dabney Stuart. **SP-StuaD**

Taking the tram to Boudry was an adventure. Hôtel Lion d'Or. Peter Meinke. **SP-MeinP**

Taking the Wheel. Dabney Stuart. **SP-StuaD**

Taking up the fair Ideal. Emily Dickinson. **CP-DickE**

Taking what is, and seeing it as it is. Vermeer. Howard Nemerov. **CP-NemeH**

Talbot Road. Thom Gunn. **CP-GunnT**
  "Between the pastel boutiques."
  "But I came back, after the last bus."
  "Glamorous and difficult friend."
  "London returned to after twelve years, A."
  "That was fifteen years ago."

Tale, A. Wystan Hugh Auden. **CP-AudWJ**

Tale, A. Louise Bogan. **CP-BogaL**

Tale, A. Robert Burns. **CP-BurnR**

Tale. Howard Nemerov. **CP-NemeH**

Tale, A: "In Scotland's realm, where trees are few." William Cowper. **CP-CowpW**

Tale for Roman guides to tell, A. Saint Gregory's Guest. John Greenleaf Whittier. **CP-WhitJ**

Tale, Founded on a Fact, A. William Cowper. **CP-CowpW**

Tale of a Citizen and His Wife, A. John Donne. *Fr.* Elegies. **CP-DonnJ**

Tale of a Tub. Sylvia Plath. **CP-PlatS**

Tale of Acadie, A. Henry Wadsworth Longfellow. **MeMAP** *Fr.* Evangeline, a Tale of Acadie. **SP-LongH**
  "This is the forest primeval. The murmuring pines and the hemlocks." **APN-1; UV**

Tale of Custard the Dragon, The. Ogden Nash. **CP-NashO**

Tale of Melibee, The. Geoffrey Chaucer. *Fr.* The Canterbury Tales. **CP-ChauG**

Tale of Sir Thopas, The. Geoffrey Chaucer. *See* Sir Thopas.

Tale of Society As It Is, A: From Facts, 1811. Percy Bysshe Shelley. **CP-ShelP**

Tale of the Nun's Priest, The, *see* Nun's Priest's Tale, The. Geoffrey Chaucer. *See* The Nun's Priest's Tale.

Tale of the Tiger Tree, The. Nicholas Vachel Lindsay. **CP-LindV**
  "Beware of the trumpeting swine."
  "Gray king died in his hour, The."
  "Peace-of-the-Heart, my own for long."
  "This is the tale of the Tiger Tree."
  "This was the end of the battle."

Tale of Time. Robert Penn Warren. **SP-WarrR**
  Answer Yes or No.
  Insomnia.
  Interim, The.
  Mad Druggest, The.
  What Happened.
  What Were You Thinking Dear Mother?

Tale of Two Cities, A. Rudyard Kipling. **CP-KiplR**

Tale of Villafranca, A. Elizabeth Barrett Browning. **CP-BroEB**

Tale-Teller, The. Daniel Gerard Hoffman. **SP-HoffD**

Tale Told by an Idiot, A. David Herbert Lawrence. **CP-LawrD**

Talent is what they say. For the Young Who Want To. Marge Piercy. **SP-PierM**

Talented creatures, on the defensive because. Insignificant Elephants. Wystan Hugh Auden. **CP-AudeW**

Talented old gentleman painting a hedge, A. When Walking. Stevie Smith. **CP-SmitS**

Tales. George Crabbe.
  Edward Shore. **SP-CrabG**
  Frank Courtship, The. **SP-CrabG**
  Mother, The. **SP-CrabG**
  Wager, The. **SP-CrabG**

Tales. David Herbert Lawrence. *Fr.* Bits. **CP-LawrD**

Tales of a Wayside Inn, *sels.* Henry Wadsworth Longfellow.
  Birds of Killingworth, The (The Poet's Tale).
    (Poet's Tale: The Birds of Killingworth, The.) **SP-LongH**
    "Do you ne'er think what wondrous beings these?" **WBLP**
  Paul Revere's Ride (The Landlord's Tale).
    (Landlord's Tale: Paul Revere's Ride, The.) **SP-LongH**
  Theologian's Tale: Torquemada, The. **SP-LongH**

Tales of Arabia. Robert Louis Stevenson. **CP-StevR**

Tales of the American Night. Jim Morrison. **SP-MorrJ**

Tales of the Hall. George Crabbe.
  Ellen. **SP-CrabG**
  Lady Barbara; or, The Ghost. **SP-CrabG**
  Richard's Youth. **SP-CrabG**
  Ruth. **SP-CrabG**
  Smugglers and Poachers. **SP-CrabG**

Tales of the Islands. Derek Walcott. **CP-WalcD**

Talk. David Herbert Lawrence. **CP-LawrD**

Talk about the mother tongue. Swedish Lesson. Barton Sutter. **SP-SuttB**

Talk not of sad November, when a day. A Day. John Greenleaf Whittier. **CP-WhitJ**

Talk not to me of savages. Robert Burns. *Fr.* On Jessy Lewars. **CP-BurnR**

Talk not to me of Summer Trees. Emily Dickinson. **CP-DickE**

Talk of energy. Mayan sub-flower. Dangers of the Journey to the Happy Land. Joseph Ceravolo. **SP-CeraJ**

Talk of Faith. David Herbert Lawrence. **CP-LawrD**

Talk of Loyalty. David Herbert Lawrence. **CP-LawrD**

Talk of the Paintings. Peter Meinke. **SP-MeinP**

Talk turned this evening on the end of man. Immortality. John Hewitt. **CP-HewiJ**

Talk with prudence to a Beggar. Emily Dickinson. **CP-DickE**

Talker, The. Mona Van Duyn. **SP-VanDM**

Talkin' John Birch Paranoid Blues. "Bob Dylan." **CP-DylaB**

Talkin' World War III Blues. "Bob Dylan." **CP-DylaB**

Talking. Stephen Berg. **SP-BergS**

Talking Bear Mountain Picnic Massacre Blues. "Bob Dylan." **CP-DylaB**

Talking in Bed. Philip Larkin. **CP-LarkP**

Talking in the Woods with Karl Amorelli. Etheridge Knight. **SP-KnigE**

Talking Late with the Governor about the Budget. Gary Snyder. **CP-SnydG**

Talking Myself to Sleep at One More Hilton. John Ciardi. **SP-CiarJ**

Talking New York. "Bob Dylan." **CP-DylaB**

Talking of death / is like talking of. Eat. Charles Bukowski. **SP-BukC2**

Talking to Clare as. James Liddy. *Fr.* A Munster Song of Love and War. **CP-LiddJ**

Talking to Dogs. Wystan Hugh Auden. **CP-AudeW**

Talking To Grandpa Eastman. Barton Sutter. **SP-SuttB**

Talking to Mice. Wystan Hugh Auden. **CP-AudeW**

Talking to My Grandmother Who Died Poor. Alice Walker. **CP-WalkA**

Talking to My Mailbox. . . . Charles Bukowski. **SP-BukC3**

Talking to Myself. Wystan Hugh Auden. **CP-AudeW**

Talking to Sheep. Anne Sexton. **CP-SextA**

Tall and singularly dark you pass among the breakers—. Louis Zukofsky. *Fr.* 29 Poems. **CP-ZukLS**

Tall as a guardsman, pale as the east at dawn. Robert Louis Stevenson. *Fr.* The Family. **CP-StevR**

Tall Atlas, Jupiter, Hercules, Thor. Deities and Beasts. John Updike. **CP-UpdiJ**

Tall birds have come into the cove tonight. Not swans. A Dialogue of Birds for Howard Nemerov. Kay Boyle. **CP-BoylK**

Tall, black, Nubian nanny, The. Going Out to Look at the Year's First Blossoms. Martin Edmunds. **SP-EdmuM**

Tall blonde dabbing scent behind her ears, The. On the Njal Saga. Louis MacNeice. *Fr.* Dark Age Glosses. **CP-MacNL**

Tall buildings swayed / in downtown San Francisco. Shadowy Room. James Schuyler. **CP-SchuJ**

Tall camels of the spirit, The. "World without Objects Is a Sensible Emptiness, A." Richard Wilbur. **CP-WilbR**

Tall dark handsome man who lived next door, The. Paid Quarterly. John Hewitt. **CP-HewiJ**

Tall Girl, The. John Crowe Ransom. **SP-RansJ**

Tall lean young negroes in Paris. Art and Technology. John Hewitt. **CP-HewiJ**

Tall Man, A. Carl Sandburg. **CP-SandC**

Tall man, A / Without clothes. Karamojongs. Alice Walker. **CP-WalkA**

Tall man spilled his cards, The. Passion. John Hewitt. **CP-HewiJ**

Tall marigolds darken, The. The Fear of Darkness. Wendell Berry. **CP-BerrW**

Tall oaks are / Speckled yellow. At Beaulieu. Frank Templeton Prince. **CP-PrinF**

Tall place, The. Roy Fisher. **SP-FishR** *Fr.* Handsworth Liberties.

Tall, sallow guardsmen their horsetails have spread, The. From Perugia. John Greenleaf Whittier. **CP-WhitJ**

Tall story over a dark sanctum, A. Louis MacNeice. *Fr.* Areopagus. **CP-MacNL**

Tall Timber. Carl Sandburg. **CP-SandC**

Tall timber stood here once. Improved Farm Land. Carl Sandburg. **CP-SandC**

Tall woman wants the tall story, The. The Story. Robert Creeley. **CP-CreeR**

Talla spales, The. Servant Girl's Bed. "Hugh MacDiarmid." **SP-MacDH**

Taller To-day. Wystan Hugh Auden. *See* Taller to-day, we remember similar evenings.

Taller to-day, we remember similar evenings. Wystan Hugh Auden. **CP-AudWJ; CP-AudeW**

(Taller To-day.) **CP-AudeW**

Tally, A. Robert Creeley. **CP-CreeR**

Tally of forces, consequent, A. A Tally. Robert Creeley. **CP-CreeR**

T.A.M. Edward Estlin Cummings. **CP-CummE**

Tam Cari Capitis. Louis MacNeice. **CP-MacNL**

Tam Cari Capitis. Louis Zukofsky. *Fr.* 29 Poems. **CP-ZukLS**

Tam Glen. Robert Burns. **CP-BurnR**

Tam Lin. *Unknown.* **CP-BurnR**

Tam o' Shanter [A Tale]. Robert Burns. **CP-BurnR**

Tam Samson's Elegy. Robert Burns. **CP-BurnR**

Tamar. Robinson Jeffers. **CP-JefR1**

Tamarack with needles lost, The. Hayden Carruth. *Fr.* North Winter. **CP-CarHL**

Tambourine Life. Ted Berrigan. **SP-BerrT**

Tambourines. Langston Hughes. **SP-HughL**

Tame Cat. Ezra Pound. **SP-PounE**

Tamed by *Miltown*, we lie on Mother's bed. Man and Wife. Robert Lowell. **SP-LoweR**

Tamely frail body abstain today; today. Upon the Annunciation and Passion Falling upon One Day. 1608. John Donne. **CP-DonnJ**

Tamer and Hawk. Thom Gunn. **CP-GunnT**

Tamerlane. Edgar Allan Poe. **CP-PoeEd**

Tampa Stomp. John Berryman. **CP-BerrJ**

Tanck's Brag. Hayden Carruth. **CP-CarHS** *Fr.* Songs About What Comes Down: The Complete Works of Mr. Septic Tank.

Tanck's Epilogue. Hayden Carruth. **CP-CarHS** *Fr.* Songs About What Comes Down: The Complete Works of Mr. Septic Tank.

Tanck's Prolegomenon. Hayden Carruth. **CP-CarHS** *Fr.* Songs About What Comes Down: The Complete Works of Mr. Septic Tank.

Tanck's Song About Brains. Hayden Carruth. **CP-CarHS** *Fr.* Songs About What Comes Down: The Complete Works of Mr. Septic Tank.

Tanck's Song About Dying Young. Hayden Carruth. **CP-CarHS** *Fr.* Songs About What Comes Down: The Complete Works of Mr. Septic Tank.

Tanck's Song About Earl Hines. Hayden Carruth. **CP-CarHS** *Fr.* Songs About What Comes Down: The Complete Works of Mr. Septic Tank.

Tanck's Song About Fear of Falling. Hayden Carruth. **CP-CarHS** *Fr.* Songs About What Comes Down: The Complete Works of Mr. Septic Tank.

Tanck's Song About His Birthday. Hayden Carruth. **CP-CarHS** *Fr.* Songs About What Comes Down: The Complete Works of Mr. Septic Tank.

Tanck's Song About His Unicameral Mind. Hayden Carruth. **CP-CarHS** *Fr.* Songs About What Comes Down: The Complete Works of Mr. Septic Tank.

Tanck's Song About November. Hayden Carruth. **CP-CarHS** *Fr.* Songs About What Comes Down: The Complete Works of Mr. Septic Tank.

Tanck's Song About Pride. Hayden Carruth. **CP-CarHS** *Fr.* Songs About What Comes Down: The Complete Works of Mr. Septic Tank.

Tanck's Song About Silence. Hayden Carruth. **CP-CarHS** *Fr.* Songs About What Comes Down: The Complete Works of Mr. Septic Tank.

Tanck's Song About Survival. Hayden Carruth. **CP-CarHS** *Fr.* Songs About What Comes Down: The Complete Works of Mr. Septic Tank.

Tanck's Song About the Jinx. Hayden Carruth. **CP-CarHS** *Fr.* Songs About What Comes Down: The Complete Works of Mr. Septic Tank.

Tanck's Song About the Transportation Business. Hayden Carruth. **CP-CarHS** *Fr.* Songs About What Comes Down: The Complete Works of Mr. Septic Tank.

Tanck's Song About the Younger Generation. Hayden Carruth. **CP-CarHS** *Fr.* Songs About What Comes Down: The Complete Works of Mr. Septic Tank.

Tanck's Song About Women. Hayden Carruth. **CP-CarHS** *Fr.* Songs About What Comes Down: The Complete Works of Mr. Septic Tank.

Tanck's Song About Youth and Age. Hayden Carruth. **CP-CarHS** *Fr.* Songs About What Comes Down: The Complete Works of Mr. Septic Tank.

Taneum Creek. Richard Hugo. **CP-HugoR**

T'ang Notebook. Charles Wright. **SP-WrigC**

Tangibles. Carl Sandburg. **CP-SandC**

Tangled [*or* Tanglid] I was [*or* was I] in [*or* yn] Love's snare. Sir Thomas Wyatt. **CP-WyatT**

Tangled Up in Blue. "Bob Dylan." **CP-DylaB**

Tango. Louise Glück. **SP-GlücL**

Tango for Zither. Isabella Gardner. *Fr.* Saloon Suite. **CP-GardI**

Tango-ing. Diane Wakoski. **SP-WakoD**

Tanker slips behind a distant ridge, The. Being Born. Thom Gunn. **CP-GunnT**

Tannhäuser wandered in the Venusberg. Liebestod. Charles Tomlinson. *Fr.* Three Wagnerian Lyrics. **CP-TomlC**

Tanto e Amara. Charles Olson. **CP-OlsoC**

Tao. Chuang Tzu, *tr. fr. Chinese* by Thomas Merton. **CP-MertT**

Tao in the Yankee Stadium Bleachers. John Updike. **CP-UpdiJ**

Taos. Martin Edmunds. *Fr.* The High Road to Taos. **SP-EdmuM**

Tap (better known then trusted) as we heare. Upon Tap. Robert Herrick. **CP-HerrR**

Taped to the wall of my cell are 47 pictures: 47 black. The Idea of Ancestry. Etheridge Knight. **SP-KnigE**

Tapers. Robert Herrick. **CP-HerrR**

Tapestry. John Ashbery. **SP-AshbJ**

Tapestry, The. Howard Nemerov. **CP-NemeH**

Tapestry. Charles Simic. **SP-SimiC**

Tapestry and Sail. James Dickey. **CP-DickJ**

Tapestry, with Unicorn. Erica Jong. **SP-JongE**

Tapicer. Roy Fisher. **SP-FishR** *Fr.* Five Pilgrims in the Prologue to the Canterbury Tales.

Tapiola. William Carlos Williams. **CP-WilW2**

Tar. Brendan Galvin. **SP-GalvB**

Tar. Charles Kenneth Williams. **CP-WillC; SP-WillC**

Tarantella. David Herbert Lawrence. **CP-LawrD**

Tarantula rattling at the lily's foot, The. O Carib Isle! Hart Crane. **CP-CranH**

Tarbolton Lasses, The. Robert Burns. **CP-BurnR**

Tardy. William Matthews. **SP-MattW**

Tardy Poet: 1978. David Markson. **CP-MarkD**

Tardy Spring. George Meredith. **CP-MerG1**

Tares make the corn to grow. By the Road to Upper Midhope. Donald Davie. **CP-DavDo**

Target Practice. Muriel Rukeyser. **CP-RukeM**

Target Practice. Gary Snyder. **CP-SnydG**

Tarkington, Thou Should'st Be Living in This Hour. Ogden Nash. **CP-NashO**

Tarn, The. Wystan Hugh Auden. **CP-AudWJ**

Tarpaper and wind / a street rolling stones. John Haines. *Fr.* The Mirror. **SP-HainJ**

Tarpaper shack and the red rose bush, The. Muriel Rukeyser. **CP-RukeM**

Tarpon. Laurence Lieberman. **SP-LiebL**

Tarpon. Derek Walcott. **CP-WalcD**

Tarquin. Frank O'Hara. **SP-OharF**

Tarquinia. Charles Tomlinson. **CP-TomlC**

Tarrant Moss. Rudyard Kipling. **CP-KiplR** *Fr.* Wressley of the Foreign Office. *Fr.* Plain Tales from the Hills.

Tarry, delight, so seldom met. Alfred Edward Housman. **CP-HousA**

Tarry sweete love. Thomas Campion. **CP-CampT**

Tarrying Bridegroom, The. Thomas Hardy. **CP-HardT**

Tartar horsemen shake their spears, The. Dialogue. Frederick Morgan. *Fr.* Eight Triolets. **SP-MorgF**

Tartine, for All Her Bulk. Laurence Lieberman. **SP-LiebL**

Tartine, Strumming Her Opera. Laurence Lieberman. **SP-LiebL**

Tartine's Banishment. Laurence Lieberman. **SP-LiebL**

Tarts. David Herbert Lawrence. **CP-LawrD**

Tartuffe, *Act I, Scene 4.* Molière, *tr. fr. French by* Richard Wilbur. **CP-WilbR**

Tashkent Blossoms, 1944. Stephen Berg. **SP-BergS**

Tashtego Believed Red. Malcolm Lowry. *Fr.* The Roar of the Sea and the Darkness. **CP-LowrM**

Task, The. John Ashbery. **SP-AshbJ**

Task, The. William Cowper. **CP-CowpW**

  Garden, The.

    How to Grow Cucumbers. **FaBoUs**

    "I was a stricken deer, that left the herd." **EnRP; FaBoRV; FiP; LoBV; NAEL-1; OAEP; OxBoCh; PAI; PoE**

    ("Morning finds the self-sequestr'd man, The.") **PoE**

    (Stricken Deer, The.) **FiP; LoBV**

    "Philosophy, baptised." **EPCY**

  Sofa, The.

    Ease. **TEP**

    "For I have lov'd the rural walk through lanes." **EnRP; NOEC**

    (Rural Sights and Sounds.) **NOEC,** book 1, *ll.* 109–210;

    God Made the Country. **FiP; PoEL-3**

    "Thou knowest my praise of nature most sincere." **NAEL-1**

  Time-piece, The.

    Effeminate Englishmen. **EBEvV; ECEV**

    (England.) **FiP**

    "Oh for a lodge in some vast wilderness." **EnRP; NOEC; OAEP**

    (Against Slavery.) **NOEC**

    Poetic Pains. **FiP; PP**

  Winter Evening, The.

    Arrival of the Mail. **ECEV**

    (Post-Boy, The.) **FiP**

    "Come evening once again, season of peace." **NAEL-1**

    "Just when our drawing-rooms begin to blaze." **NOEC**

    Reading the Newspaper. **ECEV**

    (Hissing Urn, The.) **FaBoDD**

    "Thee too, enamoured of the life I loved." **EPCY**

  Winter Morning Walk, The.

    "'Tis morning' and the sun with ruddy orb." **LAuP; NOEC; PoEL-3**

    (Frosty Morning, A.) **NOEC**

    "Whose freedom is by suff'rance, and at will." **EnRP**

  Winter Walk at Noon, The.

    "Groans of nature in this nether world, The." **NoP**

    "Lord of all, himself through all diffused, The." **OAEL-1**

    "Night was winter in his roughest mood, The." **EnRP; FHYEP; TEP**

"No noise is here, or none that hinders thought." **PBBP**

Tasker Norcross. Edwin Arlington Robinson. **CP-RobiE**

Tasso and Leonora. Christina Georgina Rossetti. **CP-RosC3**

Taste, The. George Oppen. **NNaP** *Fr.* Some San Francisco Poems. **CP-OppeG**

Taste. Christopher Smart. **ChIV-1; NOCV** *Fr.* Hymns for the Amusement of Children. **SP-SmarC**

Taste. John Updike. **CP-UpdiJ**

Taste of time is sweet at first, The. Eve Old. Archibald MacLeish. *Fr.* Songs for Eve. **CP-MacLA**

Tata, Baba, Great Spirit—. The Sorrow Song. Hayden Carruth. **CP-CarHS**

Tattered and ragg'd, with greatcoat tied in strings. The Mole-Catcher. John Clare. **SP-ClarJ**

Tattered Kaddish. Adrienne Rich. **SP-RicA1**

Tattoo. Wallace Stevens. **CP-StevW**

Tattooed Desert, The. Richard Shelton. **SP-ShelR**

Tattooed Lady, The. Ted Kooser. **SP-KoosT**

Tattooed Man, The. Robert Earl Hayden. **CP-HaydR**

Tauler. James Fenton. **SP-FentJ**

Tauler. John Greenleaf Whittier. **CP-WhitJ**

Taurean reaper of the wild apple field. Tattered Kaddish. Adrienne Rich. **SP-RicA1**

Tautog. Brendan Galvin. **SP-GalvB**

Tavern. Edna St. Vincent Millay. **CP-MillE**

Tavern, The. Edwin Arlington Robinson. **CP-RobiE**

Tavern, The. Lewis Turco. **SP-TurcL**

Tawny. Carl Sandburg. **CP-SandC**

Tawny are the leaves turned, but they still hold. Antique Harvesters. John Crowe Ransom. **SP-RansJ**

Tawny in a pasture by the true sea. The Forgotten Rock. Richard Eberhart. **CP-EberR**

Tax-Free Encounter. John Updike. **CP-UpdiJ**

Tax not the royal Saint with vain expense. Inside of King's College Chapel, Cambridge. William Wordsworth. **EnRP; GTBS; GTBS-6; GTBS-P; OBNC** *Fr.* Ecclesiastical Sonnets. **CP-WorW2**

Taxis, The. Louis MacNeice. **CP-MacNL**

Taxis toot whirl people moving perhaps laugh into the slowly. Edward Estlin Cummings. **CP-CummE**

Taxis were beyond us. Mother. Donald Davie. **CP-DavDo**

Taxman. George Harrison. **CP-Beatl**

Taylor, The. Robert Burns. **CP-BurnR**

Taylor fell thro' the bed, thimble an' a', The. Robert Burns. **CP-BurnR**

Taylor he cam here to sew, The. The Taylor. Robert Burns. **CP-BurnR**

Taylor Street. Thom Gunn. **CP-GunnT**

Tbilisi. John Updike. *Fr.* Postcards from Soviet Cities. **CP-UpdiJ**

Te escribo cartas, Che / En la sazón de lluvias. Letters to Che: Canto Bilingue. Thomas Merton. **CP-MertT**

Tea. John Berryman. **CP-BerrJ**

Tea. Wallace Stevens. **CP-StevW**

Tea at the Palaz of Hoon. Wallace Stevens. **CP-StevW**

Tea drinking, garden viewing. Kenneth Rexroth. **CP-RexKL** *Fr.* The Heart's Garden, the Garden's Heart.

Tea for two / And two for tea. Eva Braun. William DeWitt Snodgrass. **CAPP** *Fr.* The Führer Bunker. **SP-SnodW**

Tea is boiling, The. Poem. Jim Carroll. **SP-CarrJ**

Tea leaves I've given up. Recantation. Sylvia Plath. **CP-PlatS**

Tea-rose tea-gown, etc., The. Ezra Pound. **MoAmPo; NOBE** *Fr.* Hugh Selwyn Mauberley. (Life and Contacts). **SP-PounE**

Tea Shop, The. Ezra Pound. **SP-PounE**

Tea-time in November. Wystan Hugh Auden. **CP-AudWJ**

Teach Him—When He makes the names. Emily Dickinson. **CP-DickE**

Teach me / to be like you, to take. Stone. Martin Edmunds. **SP-EdmuM**

Teach me I am forgotten by the dead. Ralph Waldo Emerson. **CP-EmerR**

Teach me, my God and King. The Elixir [*or* Elixer]. George Herbert. **CP-HerbG**

Teach me your mood, O patient stars! Ralph Waldo Emerson. **CP-EmerR**

Teach the Gifted Children. "Lou Reed." **SP-ReedL**

Teach Us to Number Our Days. Rita Dove. **SP-DoveR**

Teach your child to earn his meal. *Unknown, tr. fr. Persian by* Jean Chardin *and fr. French by* Ralph Waldo Emerson. **CP-EmerR**

Teacher. Audre Lorde. **SP-LordA**

Teacher and friend, what you restored to me. Instead of an Essay. Charles Tomlinson. **CP-TomlC**

Teacher Answering Young Radicals. Stephen Dunn. **SP-DunnS**

Teacher, the preacher, my mother, a mouse, The. Overture: The Hostages. Randall Jarrell. **CP-JarrR**

Teachers. Leonard Cohen. **CP-CoheL**

Teacher's Residence, The. John Hewitt. **CP-HewiJ**

Teaching. Al Young. **CP-YounA**

Teaching of the Blows of Fortune, The. George Meredith. **CP-MerG2**

Teaching of the Nude, The. George Meredith. **CP-MerG1**

Teaching Poetry at a Country School in Florida. Peter Meinke. **SP-MeinP**

Teachings, The. Robert Creeley. **CP-CreeR**

Teage has told lyes so long, that when Teage tells. Upon Teage. Robert Herrick. **CP-HerrR**

Teamster's Farewell, A. Carl Sandburg. **CP-SandC**

Tear, The. Byron. **CP-Byron**

Tear[e], The. Richard Crashaw. **CP-CrasR**

Tear another's tears bring forth, The. Sympathy. Paul Laurence Dunbar. **CP-DunbP**

Tear Gas. Adrienne Rich. **CP-RicAE; SP-RicA2**

Tear Is an Intellectual Thing, A. Marsden Hartley. *Fr.* Un Recuerdo—Hermano—Hart Crane R.I.P. **CP-HartM**

Tear off the calendar. The Month's Calendar. Thomas Hardy. **CP-HardT**

Tear which mourn'd a brother's fate scarce dry, The. On Receiving an Account That His Only Sister's Death Was Inevitable. Samuel Taylor Coleridge. **CP-ColeS**

Teare Sent to Her from Stanes, The. Robert Herrick. **CP-HerrR**

Teares ("Teares most prevaile; with teares too thou mayst move"). Robert Herrick. **CP-HerrR**

Teares: ("God from our eyes all teares. . . "). Robert Herrick. **CP-HerrR**

Teares: ("Our present Teares here (not our present laughter)"). Robert Herrick. **CP-HerrR**

Teares: ("Teares of Saints more sweet by farre, The"). Robert Herrick. **CP-HerrR**

Teares, and Laughter. Robert Herrick. **CP-HerrR**

Teares are Tongues. Robert Herrick. **CP-HerrR**

Teares most prevaile; with teares too thou mayst move. Teares . Robert Herrick. **CP-HerrR**

Teares of Saints more sweet by farre, The. Teares. Robert Herrick. **CP-HerrR**

Teares of the Muses, The. Edmund Spenser. **CP-Spens**

Teares quickly drie: griefes will in time decay. Faire after Foule. Robert Herrick. **CP-HerrR**

Teares some times flow from mirth, as well as sorrow. Mary Sidney, Countess of Montgomery Wroth. *Fr.* Part 1. *Fr.* Urania. **CP-WrotM**

Teares, though th'are here below the sinners brine. Upon Teares. Robert Herrick. **CP-HerrR**

Tearing and tearing / ripped-up bits of paper. Blizzard. James Schuyler. **CP-SchuJ**

Tearing Down the Hotel. Miller Williams. **SP-WillM**

Tears. Maya Angelou. **SP-AngeM**

Tears. Elizabeth Barrett Browning. **CP-BroEB**

Tears. Allen Ginsberg. **CP-GinsA**

Tears. Walt Whitman. **CP-WhitW**

Tears are for what can be mended. A Song for Rustam. Basil Bunting. **CP-BuntB**

Tears flow, and cease not, where the good man lies. Epitaph on Mr. Chester. William Cowper. **CP-CowpW**

Tears for the long-gone times. Soul's Seas. Archie Randolph Ammons. **SP-AmmoA**

Tears from our eyes. Three Words Only. Robert Ranke Graves. **CP-GravR**

Tears, idle tears, I know not what they mean. Tennyson. **AWP; EBEvV; EBVV; ELP; EnVR; FPL; FaBoRV; FaFP; FaPoR; FiP; GTBS-P; HAP; ImPo; InPS; InvP; LiTB; MeMBP; NAEL-2; NIP; NOBE; NoP; OAEL-2; OBNC; OXAEP-2; PPP; PlP; PoE; PoEL-5; Poetr; SCGP; TEP; TFi; TrGrPo; UnPo; WeW** *Fr.* There sinks the nebulous star we call the Sun. *Fr.* The Princess. **CP-TennA**

Tears in Sleep. Louise Bogan. **CP-BogaL**

Tears of a Muse in America, The. Frank Templeton Prince. **CP-PrinF**

Tears of a Painter, The. Vincent Bourne, *tr. fr. Latin by* William Cowper. **CP-CowpW**

Tears of delight that on my name-day. Name Day. Robert Ranke Graves. **CP-GravR**

Tears of man in various measure gush, The. Edward Signing the Warrant for the Execution of Joan of Kent. William Wordsworth. *Fr.* Ecclesiastical Sonnets. **CP-WorW2**

Tears of Rage. "Bob Dylan." **CP-DylaB**

Tears of the widow of the military man, The. Silence and Tears. Stevie Smith. **CP-SmitS**

Tears of the widower, when he sees. Tennyson. **PeHV** *Fr.* In Memoriam A. H. H. **CP-TennA**

Tears! tears! tears! / In the night, in solitude, tears. Tears. Walt Whitman. **CP-WhitW**

Tears, that have been stagnant. The Old Catechism. Michael Hartnett. **SP-HarMi**

Tears, the firebursts and the vows, The. Cracked Looking Glass. Jean Garrigue. **SP-GarrJ**

Tease. David Herbert Lawrence. **CP-LawrD**

Technically it was liquid asphalt. Tar. Brendan Galvin. **SP-GalvB**

Technologies. George Oppen. **CP-OppeG**

Tecumseh. Mary Oliver. **SP-OlivM**

Ted Roethke was a tearing man. Was a Man. John Ciardi. **SP-CiarJ**

Tedded hay, the first fruits of the soil, The. The Keepsake. Samuel Taylor Coleridge. **CP-ColeS**

Teddy said it was a hat. Hat. Shel Silverstein. **SP-SilS2**

Tedium of déjà—vu of home. Christmas. Robert Lowell. **SP-LoweR**

Ted's studio burnt down, with all his poems. Martial, *tr. by* William Matthews. **SP-MattW** *Fr.* Epigrams.

Teen-age boy in training pants, A. Kai, Today. Gary Snyder. **CP-SnydG**

Teenagers and oldsters, married couples and lovers. Santiago: Forestal Park. Stephen Dobyns. **SP-DobyS**

Teeth Mother Naked at Last, The. Robert Bly. **SP-BlyR**

Teeth of These Mountains, The. Richard Shelton. **SP-ShelR**

Teetotal Master. John Hewitt. **CP-HewiJ**

Teevo cheevo cheevio chee. The Woodlark. Gerard Manley Hopkins. **CP-HopkG**

Teheran. Robinson Jeffers. **CP-JefR3**

Tek a cool night, good an' cleah. Hunting Song. Paul Laurence Dunbar. **CP-DunbP**

Telegram, The. Thomas Hardy. **CP-HardT**

Telegram. Carl Sandburg. **CP-SandC**

Telegram says you have gone away, The. Denouement. Sylvia Plath. **CP-PlatS**

Teleology. Archie Randolph Ammons. **SP-AmmoA**

Telephone, The. Maya Angelou. **SP-AngeM**

Telephone, The. Robert Frost. **CP-FrosR**

Telephone, The. Isabella Gardner. **CP-GardI**

Telephone. Anne Sexton. **CP-SextA**

Telephone Call, The. John Yau. **SP-YauJo**

Telephone line goes cold, A. The Farm on the Great Plains. William Stafford. **SP-StafW**

Telephone Poles. John Updike. **CP-UpdiJ**

Telephus Sedum. Louis Zukofsky. **CP-ZukLS**

Telescope picks off star dust, The. Pick-Offs. Carl Sandburg. **CP-SandC**

Telesila. Hilda Doolittle. **CP-DoolH**

Telesphere, The. Charles Olson. **SP-OlsoC** *Fr.* The Maximus Poems.

Television cameras vacillate from Monticello. Inauguration Day. Jim Carroll. **SP-CarrJ**

TV Off. Ted Hughes. **SP-HughT**

Television set hung, The. The Terminal Bar. Derek Mahon. **SP-MahoD**

Television Speaks. Etheridge Knight. **SP-KnigE**

Television Was a Baby Crawling toward That Deathchamber. Allen Ginsberg. **CP-GinsA**

Tell, acquaint me. French Hill. Hayden Carruth. **CP-CarHS**

Tell all my mourners. Wake. Langston Hughes. **SP-HughL**

Tell all the Truth but tell it slant. Emily Dickinson. **CP-DickE**

Tell as a Marksman—were forgotten. Emily Dickinson. **CP-DickE**

Tell, if thou canst, (and truly) whence doth come. Upon Julia's Unlacing Her Self. Robert Herrick. **CP-HerrR**

Tell in the wind of the singing of sorrow. Monongah (December 6, 1907, Marion County, West Virginia, on the Monongahela River). Louise McNeill. **SP-McNeL**

Tell It to the Eskimos or Tell it to the Esquimaux. Ogden Nash. **CP-NashO**

Tell it to the locked-up trees. Cuckoo Song. Rudyard Kipling. **CP-KiplR**

Tell It to Your Heart. "Lou Reed." **SP-ReedL**

Tell Me. Langston Hughes. **SP-HughL**

Tell Me a Story. Robert Penn Warren. **MT** *Fr.* Audubon. **SP-WarrR**

Tell me a word. Conundrums. David Herbert Lawrence. **CP-LawrD**

Tell me about yourself they. A Word in Edgeways. Charles Tomlinson. **CP-TomlC**

Tell me again the birds are flying southward. Backward Flight. Louise McNeill. **SP-McNeL**

Tell me *Alexis* what this parting is. Dialogue. Lucasta, Alexis. Richard Lovelace. **CP-LoveR**

Tell me bright Boy, tell me my golden Lad. Luke 15; On the Prodigall. Bible, *N.T.* **CP-CrasR**, *tr. by* Richard Crashaw; *Fr.* St. Luke.

Tell me: doth it not grieve thee to lie here. Death Is Swallowed Up in Victory. Christina Georgina Rossetti. **CP-RosC3**

Tell me, Eutresia, since my fate. Methodus Amandi. Thomas Cary. **CP-CareT**

Tell me, gentle howre of night. Thomas Campion. *Fr.* Lord Hay's Mask.

Tell me good Hobbinoll, what garres thee greete? Aprill. Edmund Spenser. **NAEL-1; PoEL-1** *Fr.* The Shepheardes [*or* Shepeards *or* Shepherd's] Calender. **CP-Spens**

Tell me, good Hobbinoll, what garres thee greete? Edmund Spenser. *See* Aprill.

Tell me, is the rose really naked. Pablo Neruda, *tr. fr. Spanish by* Ben Belitt. **SP-NeruP** *Fr.* Question Book.

Tell me maiden dost thou use. Ralph Waldo Emerson. **CP-EmerR**

Tell Me, Momma. "Bob Dylan." **CP-DylaB**

Tell me more of the eagle, Cotton. Some Friends from Pascagoula. Wallace Stevens. **CP-StevW**

Tell me, my love, since Hymen tied [*or* ty'ed]. An Hymeneal[l] Dialogue. Thomas Carew. **CP-CareT**

Tell me, my patient friends, awaiters of messages. Speech to a Crowd. Archibald MacLeish. **CP-MacLA**

Tell me not here, it needs not saying. Alfred Edward Housman. **CP-HousA**

Tell me not how electricity or. Edward Estlin Cummings. **CP-CummE**

Tell me not in mournful numbers. Henry Wadsworth Longfellow. **AH** *Fr.* A Psalm of Life. **SP-LongH**

Tell me not in mournful numbers. A Psalm of Life. Henry Wadsworth Longfellow. **SP-LongH**

Tell me not, Sweet, I am unkind[e]. To Lucasta, [on] Going to the War[re]s. Richard Lovelace. **CP-LoveR**

Tell me not that death of grief. Hope in Grief. Christina Georgina Rossetti. **CP-RosC3**

Tell me, O Octopus, I begs. The Octopus. Ogden Nash. **CP-NashO**

Tell me, on what holy ground. Domestic Peace. Samuel Taylor Coleridge. *Fr.* Effusions. **CP-ColeS**

Tell me, Perigot, what shalbe the game. August. Edmund Spenser. *Fr.* The Shepheardes [*or* Shepeards *or* Shepherd's] Calender. **CP-Spens**

Tell me Pippididdledum. Group Life: Letchworth. Sir John Betjeman. **CP-BetjJ**

Tell me rich man, for what intent. The Poore Mans Part. Robert Herrick. **CP-HerrR**

Tell me something / you say. Mother-in-Law. Adrienne Rich. **SP-RicA2**

Tell Me, Tell Me. Marianne Craig Moore. **CP-MoorM**

Tell me, tell me, / Unknown stranger. The Galliass. Walter de la Mare. **CP-DeLaW**

Tell me, tell me, smiling child. Emily Brontë. **CP-BronE**

Tell Me That It Isn't True. "Bob Dylan." **CP-DylaB**

"Tell me the truth, Mark," you insist. Martial, *tr. by* William Matthews. **SP-MattW** *Fr.* Epigrams.

Tell me the truths which you hear of our constant young lady. Difference of Opinion with Lygdamus. Ezra Pound. **MeMAP** *Fr.* Homage to Sextus Propertius. **SP-PounE**

Tell me, thou soul of her I love. To Her I Love. James Thomson. **CP-ThomJ**

Tell me, thou Star, whose wings of light. The World's Wanderers. Percy Bysshe Shelley. **CP-ShelP**

"Tell me to touch your breast," I wanted to say: "Please, please, please touch me breast." The Orchid. Charles Kenneth Williams. **SP-WillC**

Tell me to what conclusion or in aid. Geoffrey Chaucer. **OxBM** *Fr.* The Wife of Bath's Prologue. **FHYEP; NAEL-1; OAEL-1,** *ll.* 1–862 *complete; Fr.* The Canterbury Tales. **CP-ChauG**

Tell me, watcher, is it winter? Gleneden's Dream. Emily Brontë. **CP-BronE**

Tell me, what needs those rich deceits. Upon Julia's Haire, Bundled up in a Golden Net. Robert Herrick. **CP-HerrR**

Tell Me What You See. The Beatles. **CP-Beatl**

Tell me what you see in it. Black Pine Tree in an Orange Light. Sylvia Plath. **CP-PlatS**

Tell me what you're doing over here, John Gorham. John Gorham. Edwin Arlington Robinson. **CP-RobiE**

Tell me what you're gonna do. Whatcha Gonna Do. "Bob Dylan." **CP-DylaB**

Tell me, where do ghosts in love. Ghosts in Love. Nicholas Vachel Lindsay. **CP-LindV**

Tell Me Where Is Fancy Bred. Gerard Manley Hopkins. *Fr.* Songs from Shakespeare, in Latin and Greek. **CP-HopkG**

Tell me who can. The Toucan. Shel Silverstein. **SP-SilS2**

Tell Me Why. The Beatles. **CP-Beatl**

Tell me, ye juster deities. The Expostulation. Sir John Suckling. **CP-SuckJ**

Tell me, ye subtill Judges in Loves Treasury. Ode To My Lady H. Richard Lovelace. **CP-LoveR**

Tell me, ye Zephyrs! that unfold. A Flower Garden at Coleorton Hall, Leicestershire. William Wordsworth. **CP-WorW2**

Tell me, you years I had for my life. Remembering Brother Bob. William Stafford. **SP-StafW**

Tell me young man, or did the Muses bring. To his Worthy Friend M. John Hall, Student of Grayes-Inne. Robert Herrick. **CP-HerrR**

Tell men what they knew before. Ralph Waldo Emerson. **CP-EmerR**

Tell of us sedum comic. Telephus Sedum. Louis Zukofsky. **CP-ZukLS**

Tell that Brave Man, fain thou wo'dst have access. To His Muse, Another to the Same. Robert Herrick. **CP-HerrR**

Tell the beads of the chromosomes like a rosary. George Oppen. **APSN** *Fr.* Route. **CP-OppeG**

Tell the jury your name. The Doctors. Muriel Rukeyser. **CP-RukeM**

Tell the life of the mind, the mind creates the finite. George Oppen. **APSN** *Fr.* Route. **CP-OppeG**

Tell the story. Think. Robert Creeley. **CP-CreeR**

Tell the whole history which I crave. Two Gentlemen Scholars. John Crowe Ransom. *Fr.* Sixteen Poems in Eight Pairings. **SP-RansJ**

Tell them, I AM, Jehovah said. Christopher Smart. **WGRP** *Fr.* A Song to David. **SP-SmarC**

Tell them, though 'tis an awful thing to die. Concluding Lines of Epitaph on Mrs Mason. Thomas Gray. **CP-GrayT**

Tell this to ladies: how a hero man. Man without Sense of Direction. John Crowe Ransom. **SP-RansJ**

Tell us / how we'll be together in that time. When/Then. Adrienne Rich. **SP-RicA2**

Tell us about the wolves again—you know. Around the Fire. Leonard Nathan. **SP-NathL**

Tell us, O pilgrim, what strange She. The Decoy. Walter de la Mare. **CP-DeLaW**

Tell us, streaming lady. James Liddy. **CIP** *Fr.* Love Songs of Corca Bascinn. **CP-LiddJ**

(History.) **CIP**

Tell us, thou clear [*or* cleere] and heavenly tongue. The Star-Song; a Carol to the King; Sung at White-Hall. Robert Herrick. **CP-HerrR**

Tell your love where the roses blow. Diplomacy. Paul Laurence Dunbar. **CP-DunbP**

Telling. Alice Walker. **CP-WalkA**

Telling the Bees. John Greenleaf Whittier. **CP-WhitJ**

Telling You True, About My Fantasy Life. Diane Wakoski. **SP-WakoD**

Tell's Birth-Place, *ad. fr. the German of* Stolberg. Samuel Taylor Coleridge. **CP-ColeS**

Tèma con Variazioni. "Lewis Carroll." **CP-CarrL**

Temeraire, The. Herman Melville. **SP-MelvH**

Temper, The. Robert Creeley. **CP-CreeR**

Temper of chums, the love of your wife, and a new piano's tune, The. Rudyard Kipling. *Fr.* Certain Maxims of Hafiz. **CP-KiplR**

Temper of Time. Sylvia Plath. **CP-PlatS**

Temper (1), The. George Herbert. **CP-HerbG**

Temper (2), The. George Herbert. **CP-HerbG**

Temperament. Robert Frost. *See* With anyone to death, comes so far short.

Temperance. Christopher Smart. *Fr.* Hymns for the Amusement of Children. **SP-SmarC**

Temperance and Virginity. John Milton. **OBS** *Fr.* Comus; a Masque Presented at Ludlow Castle.

Temperance or the Cheap Physitian upon the Translation of Lessius. Richard Crashaw. **CP-CrasR**

Temperat aestiva fessis sua balnea membris. In S. Winefridam. Gerard Manley Hopkins. **CP-HopkG**

Tempest and terror below; but Christ the Almighty above. God Is Our Hope and Strength. Christina Georgina Rossetti. **CP-RosC2**

Tempest cracked on the theatre, A. Quickly. Repetitions of a Young Captain. Wallace Stevens. **CP-StevW**

Tempest over and gone, the calm begun, The. Easter Even. Christina Georgina Rossetti. **CP-RosC2**

Tempest plucks the wood at last; on high, The. Job. Wystan Hugh Auden. **CP-AudWJ**

Tempest tossed and sore afflicted, sin defiled and care oppressed. Robert Louis Stevenson. **CP-StevW**

Temple, *sels.* John Donne. *Fr.* La Corona. **ChIV-2; ESCV; OBS; Son** *Fr.* Holy Sonnets. **CP-DonnJ**

Temple, The. Robert Herrick. **CP-HerrR**

Temple, A. Kenneth Patchen. **CP-PatcK**

Temple of Fame, The, *see also Chaucer's* House of Fame. Alexander Pope. **CP-PopeA**

Temple of the body crumbles, The. Refrains. Richard Eberhart. **CP-EberR**

Temple of the Sun. Hilda Doolittle.

Saturn. **CP-DoolH**

Zeus-Provider. **CP-DoolH**

Temple of Venus, The. Edmund Spenser. **EIL; WHA** *Fr.* The Faerie Queene. **CP-Spens**

Temple stood, holy and perfect, The. Myth. May Sarton. **SP-SartM**

Temples. David Herbert Lawrence. **CP-LawrD**

Temples he built and palaces of air. The Dreamer. Paul Laurence Dunbar. **CP-DunbP**

Temporall Goods. Robert Herrick. **CP-HerrR**

Temporarily. Stephen Dunn. **SP-DunnS**

Temporary Like Achilles. "Bob Dylan." **CP-DylaB**

Temporary the All, The. Thomas Hardy. **CP-HardT**

Temporary Thing. "Lou Reed." **SP-ReedL**

Temporis interpres, parvum congestus in orbem. *acc. by English translation.* Thomas Campion. **CP-CampT**

Temptation. John Ciardi. **SP-CiarJ**

Temptation. William Cowper. *Fr.* Olney Hymns. **CP-CowpW**

Temptation. Paul Laurence Dunbar. **CP-DunbP**

Temptation of Eve, The. John Milton. **EBNV** *Fr.* Book IX. **FHYEP; NAEL-1; NAWM-1; NoP; OAEL-1** *Fr.* Paradise Lost. **CP-MiltJ**

Temptation of St. Joseph, The, *sels.* Wystan Hugh Auden. *Fr.* For the Time Being; a Christmas Oratorio. **CP-AudeW**

Temptations ("No man is tempted so, but may o'recome"). Robert Herrick. **CP-HerrR**

Temptations ("Temptations hurt not, though they have accesse"). Robert Herrick. **CP-HerrR**

Temptations ("Those Saints, which God loves best"). Robert Herrick. **CP-HerrR**

Temptations from Roman Refinements. William Wordsworth. *Fr.* Ecclesiastical Sonnets. **CP-WorW2**

Tempter Disarmed, The. John Milton. **NOSC** *Fr.* Book IX. **FHYEP; NAEL-1; NAWM-1; NoP; OAEL-1** *Fr.* Paradise Lost. **CP-MiltJ**

Tempus Fugit. Christina Georgina Rossetti. **CP-RosC2**

Tempus loquendi, / tempus tacendi. Canto 31. Ezra Pound. *Fr.* Cantos. **CP-PoCan**

Ten. "Lewis Carroll." *Fr.* Solutions. *Fr.* Puzzles from Wonderland. **CP-CarrL**

10 August '77. . . Raft trip today. Hilarious God. Lawrence Ferlinghetti. **SP-FerlL**

Ten Below. Charles Kenneth Williams. **CP-WillC; SP-WillC**

("It is bad enough crying for children.") **CP-WillC**

Ten Days Leave. William DeWitt Snodgrass. **SP-SnodW**

Ten Feet of Rope. Stephen Dobyns. **SP-DobyS**

Ten fifty eight *may* arrive. Malcolm Lowry. **CP-LowrM**

Ten hours' light is abating, The. At Day-Close in November. Thomas Hardy. **CP-HardT**

Ten hundred times. The Vow. David Markson. **CP-MarkD**

10 Lions and the End of the World. Charles Bukowski. **SP-BukC2**

Ten men, nine alive. State Funeral: March 31, 1969. Archibald MacLeish. **CP-MacLA**

Ten-Mile Run. James McAuley. **SP-McAuJ**

Downhill.

Fifth Mile.

First Mile.

Near the Finish.

Ninth Mile.

Siren.

Third Mile.

Uphill.

Ten miles from home. On Banner Dome. John Haines. **SP-HainJ**

Ten miles of flat land along the sea. Sandpipers. Carl Sandburg. **CP-SandC**

Ten miles out of Cherbourg, a blind ship broke the fog. Last Words. Dabney Stuart. **SP-StuaD**

Ten Mills. Robert Frost. **CP-FrosR**

Evil Tendencies Cancel.

Hardship of Accounting, The. **FaBoCh; FaBoCo; FaFP; OBAL; WhC**

In Divés' Dive. **VGW**

Not All There. **FaBoCo**

One Guess.

Pertinax.

Precaution.

Span of Life, The. **GDP; HoPM; LiTM; SoSe**

Waspish. **BoAnP**

Wrights' Biplane, The. **WeW**

Ten minutes before post time. Charles Bukowski. *Fr.* Horsemeat. **SP-BukC3**

Ten minutes now I have been looking at this. Ready to Kill. Carl Sandburg. **CP-SandC**

Ten more miles, it is South Dakota. Sitting in a Small Screenhouse on a Summer Morning. James Wright. **CP-WrigJ**

Ten p.m. Half lit, Lenny Benson. Night Out. Barton Sutter. **SP-SuttB**

Ten Short Poems, (from the Spanish of Juan Ramón Jiminez). Juan Ramón Jiménez, *tr. fr.* Spanish *by* James Wright. **CP-WrigJ**

"Dawn brings with it, The."

Dreaming.

"How close to becoming spirit something is."

Life.

Moguer.

On the City Ramparts of Cádiz.

Rose of the Sea.

Rosebushes.

"Stormclouds / give their morose faces to the sea."

"To the bridge of love."

Ten Songs. Wystan Hugh Auden. **CP-AudeW**

Calypso.

"Carry her over the water." **FaBoTw; RB**

Domesday Song.

"Eyes look into the well."

"My second thoughts condemn."

"On and on and on."

"Say this city has ten million souls." **LiTA; LiTM; NYBP; OxAEP-2**

(Refugee Blues.) **LiTA; OxAEP-2**

(Song: "Say this city has ten million souls.") **NYBP**

"Single creature leads a partial life, The."

"Though determined Nature can."

"Warm are the still and lucky miles."

Ten Songs. John Yau. **SP-YauJo**

10,000 men / on the / pasadena. The Caboose Factory. Ron Koertge. **SP-KoerR**

Ten thousand things are getting out of hand, The. The Way. Frederick Morgan. **SP-MorgF**

Ten times a year you're ill, Malingerus. Martial, *tr. by* William Matthews. **SP-MattW** *Fr.* Epigrams.

X. "Unrighteous Lord of love, what law is this." Edmund Spenser. **NoP** *Fr.* Amoretti. **CP-Spens**

Ten years / and will you be. Return to Hinton. Charles Tomlinson. **CP-TomlC**

Ten years a widow, my old mother's mind. My Widowed Mother. John Hewitt. **CP-HewiJ**

Ten years ago it seemed impossible. In Progress. Christina Georgina Rossetti. **CP-RosC3**

Ten years ago this minute, he possibly sat. The Days. Donald Hall. **CP-HallD**

Ten Years Since. Thomas Hardy. **CP-HardT**

Ten years together without yet a cloud. Firelight. Edwin Arlington Robinson. **CP-RobiE**

Ten years without you. For so it happens. Geoffrey Hill. *Fr.* The Songbook of Sebastian Arrurruz. **CP-HillG**

10/14. William Carlos Williams. **CP-WilW2**

Tenancy, A. James Merrill. **SP-MerrJ**

Tenant-for-Life, The. Thomas Hardy. **CP-HardT**

Tended by Faustina. Faustina, or Rock Roses. Elizabeth Bishop. **CP-BishE**

Tender as the sweets of Spring. Lines on a Portrait of a Lady. Samuel Taylor Coleridge. **CP-ColeS**

Tender blows the leaf, tender drops the eye. Charles Henri Ford. *Fr.* Epigrams. **SP-FordC**

Tender child of summers three, A. The Light That Is Felt. John Greenleaf Whittier. **CP-WhitJ**

Tender infant, meek and mild, The. Samuel Johnson. **CP-JohnS**

(Parodies of Bishop Percy's *Hermit of Warkworth*.) **CP-JohnS**

Tender Island Night. Jim Morrison. **SP-MorrJ**

Tender Love's mother, a new poet get. 3.14. Ovid. **CP-MarlC**, *tr. by* Christopher Marlowe; *Fr.* Elegies.

Tender meat were you to snouted boys. Curse. Malcolm Lowry. *Fr.* Songs for Second Childhood. **CP-LowrM**

Tender Only to One. Stevie Smith. **CP-SmitS**

Tender Reverence. David Herbert Lawrence. **CP-LawrD**

Tender, semi- / articulate flickers. For My Mother: Genevieve Jules Creeley. Robert Creeley. **CP-CreeR**

Tender stranger. gentle stranger. why strangle the rose. Jet Flakes. Patti Smith. **SP-SmitP**

Tenderloin. Thom Gunn. **CP-GunnT**

Tenderly. Stephen Dobyns. **SP-DobyS**

Tenderly do we feel by Nature's law. William Wordsworth. *Fr.* Sonnets upon the Punishment of Death. **CP-WorW2**

Tenderly, in those times, as though she fed. Edna St. Vincent Millay. *Fr.* Sonnets from an Ungrafted Tree. **CP-MillE**

Tenderness. Stephen Dunn. **SP-DunnS**

Tenderness, ache on me, and lay your neck. James Dickey. **TAP** *Fr.* The Zodiac. **CP-DickJ**

Tenderness and Resolution. Hart Crane. **CP-CranH**

Tenderness has not a Date. Emily Dickinson. **SP-DickE**

Tending. Dabney Stuart. **SP-StuaD**

Tendril. Leonard Nathan. **SP-NathL**

Tendril in the Mesh. William Everson. **SP-EverW**

    "And it creams: from under her elbow a suffix of light, a sheen of kept being."

    "And the storm swings in from the sea with a smashing of floats."

    "Dark God of Eros, Christ of the buried brood."

    "Daughter of earth and child of the wave be appeased." **NoAM**

    "Man of God. Tall man, man of oath. Mad man of ignorant causes."

    "So the sea stands up to the shore, banging his chains."

Tenebrae. Geoffrey Hill. **CP-HillG**

    "And you, who with your soft but searching voice."

    "He wounds with ecstasy. All."

    "Music survives, composing her own sphere."

    "O light of light, supreme delight."

    "Requite this angel whose."

    "Stupefying images of grief-in-dream."

    "This is the ash-pit of the lily-fire."

    "Veni Redemptor, but not in our time."

Tenemeny twilightish landscape. Charles Olson. **CP-OlsoC**

Tenor Solo on St. Cecilia's Day. James McAuley. **SP-McAuJ**

Tent-lights glimmer on the land, The. At Port Royal. John Greenleaf Whittier. **CP-WhitJ**

Tent on the Beach, The. John Greenleaf Whittier. **CP-WhitJ**

Tentative (First Model) Definitions of Poetry. Carl Sandburg. **CP-SandC**

Tenth Book, The. Archibald MacLeish. *Fr.* Conquistador. **CP-MacLA**

Tenth Elegy. Elegy in Joy. Muriel Rukeyser. **CP-RukeM**

    Now Green, Now Burning. **LPA**

Tenth Muse. Robert Lowell. **SP-LoweR**

Tenth Muse, Oh my heart-felt Sloth. Tenth Muse. Robert Lowell. **SP-LoweR**

Tenth Psalm. Anne Sexton. *Fr.* O Ye Tongues. **CP-SextA**

Tenth Song. Sir Philip Sidney. *Fr.* Astrophil and Stella. **SP-SidnP**

    (O Dear Life, When Shall It Be?) **EnRePo**

Tenth Try, The. Jim Carroll. **SP-CarrJ**

Tenth year we came upon immense sunlight, a relief, The. Archipelago. Louise Glück. **SP-GlücL**

Tents pegged, the beds unrolled. The End of the World. John Hewitt. **CP-HewiJ**

Tenuous and Precarious. Stevie Smith. **CP-SmitS**

Tenzone. John Ciardi. **SP-CiarJ**

Tenzone. Ezra Pound. **SP-PounE** *Fr.* Contemporania.

Teotihuacán. Charles Tomlinson. **CP-TomlC**

Terce. Wystan Hugh Auden. **CMoP; PoE** *Fr.* Horae Canonicae. **CP-AudeW**

Terce. John Berryman. **CP-BerrJ**

Terce. Donald Davie. *Fr.* Horae Canonicae. **CP-DavDo**

Tercets of the Triad. Allen Tate. **CP-TateA**

Terence, This Is Stupid Stuff. Alfred Edward Housman. **CP-HousA**

Teresa. Richard Wilbur. **CP-WilbR**

Teresa, ah, Teresita! The King's Gift. Elizabeth Barrett Browning. **CP-BroEB**

Terez and Deanne elude me. Far from the Soil. Leonard Cohen. **CP-CoheL**

Term, The. William Carlos Williams. **CP-WilW1**

Terminal. Thom Gunn. **CP-GunnT**

Terminal. Sylvia Plath. **CP-PlatS**

Terminal Bar, The. Derek Mahon. **SP-MahoD**

Terminal Days at Beverly Farms. Robert Lowell. **SP-LoweR**

Terminal Moraine, A. James Fenton. **SCBI** *Fr.* Exempla. **SP-FentJ**

Terminal Tramps. Charles Tomlinson. **CP-TomlC**

Terminator Too. Tom Clark. **SP-ClarT**

Terminology. Charles Bukowski. **SP-BukC3**

Terminus ("For thought & not praise"). Ralph Waldo Emerson. **CP-EmerR**

Terminus ("It is time to be old"). Ralph Waldo Emerson. **CP-EmerR**

Terminus. Seamus Heaney. **SP-HeanS**

Termite, The. Ogden Nash. **CP-NashO**

Terms. Randall Jarrell. **CP-JarrR**

Terms, The, *sl. diff. vers.* Charles Simic. *See* A Child crying in the night.

Terms in Which I Think of Reality, The. Allen Ginsberg. **CP-GinsA**

Ternarie of Littles, upon a Pipkin of Jellie [*or* Jelly] Sent to a Lady, A. Robert Herrick. **CP-HerrR**

Terra. Hayden Carruth. *Fr.* Journey to a Known Place. **CP-CarHL**

Terra Incognita. David Herbert Lawrence. **CP-LawrD**

Terrace, The. Richard Wilbur. **CP-WilbR**

Terraced streets, her intricate perms. Hairdresser, Age 55, Dalston. Steve Griffiths. **SP-GrifS**

Terraced Valley, The. Robert Ranke Graves. **CP-GravR**

Terraces of Rain. David St. John. **SP-StJoD**

Terre, A. Wilfred Owen. **CP-OwenW**

Terre des Hommes, consider how strong your voice is. Dedicated to *Terre des Hommes.* Kay Boyle. **CP-BoylK**

Terrestrial Cuckoo, A. Frank O'Hara. **SP-OharF**

Terribilis Est Locus Iste; *Gaugin and the Pont-Aven School.* Geoffrey Hill. **CP-HillG**

Terrible and loud / As the strong Voice that from the Thunder-cloud. Samuel Taylor Coleridge. *Fr.* Some Fragments, Mainly from Manuscripts of 1797–8. **CP-ColeS**

Terrible Choice, The. John Hewitt. **CP-HewiJ**

Terrible People, The. Ogden Nash. **CP-NashO**

Terrible streets, the manichee hell of twilight. The Peace of Cities. Richard Wilbur. **CP-WilbR**

Terrible temper of the day gone dim, The. The Sunglasses. Howard Nemerov. **CP-NemeH**

Terrible trains crawl seaward thro' the South, The. Have a Genuine American Horror-&-Mist on the Rocks. John Berryman. **CP-BerrJ**

Terrifying are the attent sleek thrushes on the lawn. Thrushes. Ted Hughes. **SP-HughT**

Territorial Rights. Richard Shelton. **SP-ShelR**

Terror. Robert Penn Warren. **SP-WarrR**

Terror finally becomes almost. There Once Was a Woman Who Put Her Head into an Oven. Charles Bukowski. **SP-BukC1**

Terror in the house does roar. William Blake. **CP-BlakW**

Terror of the country, The. Winter in the Country. Mary Oliver. **SP-OlivM**

Terror of the serene plane is in their eyes, The. About Eyes. Edwin Rolfe. **CP-RolfE**

Terrors are to come. The earth. To My Children, Fearing for Them. Wendell Berry. **CP-BerrW**

Terrors of the scenery, The. The Sliding Mountain. Stevie Smith. **CP-SmitS**

Terrors that bayed upon my track. The Hounds. Louise McNeill. **SP-McNeL**

Terse Verse. Robert Browning. **CP-BroR2**

Tess's Lament. Thomas Hardy. **CP-HardT**

Test, The. Ralph Waldo Emerson. **CP-EmerR**

Test, The. John Hewitt. **CP-HewiJ**

Test of Love—is Death, The. Emily Dickinson. **CP-DickE**

Test of Manhood, The. George Meredith. **CP-MerG1**

Test of the poet is knowledge of love. Casella. Ralph Waldo Emerson. *Fr.* Quatrains. **CP-EmerR**

Testament. Wendell Berry. **CP-BerrW**

    "Beneath this stone a Berry is planted."

    "But do not let your ignorance."

    "Dear relatives and friends, when my last breath."

    "So treat me, even dead."

Testament, A. Robert Creeley. **CP-CreeR**

Testament, A. Richard Eberhart. **CP-EberR**

Testament. Robert Ranke Graves. **CP-GravR**

Testament. Daniel Gerard Hoffman. **SP-HoffD**

Testament. Carl Sandburg. **CP-SandC**

Testament for My Students, 1968–1969. Kay Boyle. **CP-BoylK**

Testament of Perpetual Change, The. William Carlos Williams. **CP-WilW2**

Testament to a Flowering Race. Edwin Rolfe. **CP-RolfE**

Testimonial. Langston Hughes. **SP-HughL**

Testimony. Richard Eberhart. **CP-EberR**

Testimony. Kathleen Jessie Raine. **SP-RainK**

    "I am old, I am alone."

    "So late, for whom, to whom."

    "What can I tell you, future ones."

Testimony, A. Christina Georgina Rossetti. **CP-RosC1**

Testimony of Divine Adoption, The. Jeanne Marie Bouvier de la Motte-Guyon, *tr. fr. French by* William Cowper. **CP-CowpW**

Testimony Regarding a Ghost. Carl Sandburg. **CP-SandC**

Testing the soul's mettle. New England Winter. Erica Jong. **SP-JongE**

Testing-Tree, The. Stanley Jasspon Kunitz. **CP-KuniS**

    "Around the bend / that tried to loop me home."

    "In the recurring dream."

    "On my way home from school."

    "Past the abandoned quarry."

Tests. Walt Whitman. **CP-WhitW**

Tests are good, The. You need a million of them. Wooden Buildings. John Ashbery. **SP-AshbJ**

Tether of the aeons holds them, The. The Dogs of Zimmer. Paul Zimmer. **SP-ZimmP**

Tethnakin D'oligo Pideuis Fainom Alaia. Allen Ginsberg. **CP-GinsA**

Teton Village. Allen Ginsberg. **CP-GinsA**

Texan. Charles Bukowski. **SP-BukC1**

Texas. John Greenleaf Whittier. **CP-WhitJ**

Texas Sprawl. John Yau. **SP-YauJo**

Text, The. Gary Snyder. **CP-SnydG** *Fr.* Burning. *Fr.* Myths and Texts.

Th' ast dar'd too farre; but Furie now forbeare. To the Fever, Not To Trouble Julia. Robert Herrick. **CP-HerrR**

Th' Astrologers did all alike presage. On the Astrologers. *Unknown, tr. fr. Greek by* William Cowper. **CP-CowpW**

Th' have left thee naked Lord, O that they had. On Our Crucified Lord Naked, and Bloody. Richard Crashaw. **CP-CrasR**

Th' old man, our amiable old is gone. *see also* Translation of Verses to Lloyd. William Cowper, *ad. fr. the Latin of* Vincent Bourne. **CP-CowpW**

Thalassa. Louis MacNeice. **CP-MacNL**

Thalia, tell in sober lays. The Part of a Summer. Jonathan Swift. **CP-SwifJ**

Thalidomide. Sylvia Plath. **CP-PlatS**

Thames. William Blake. *See* Why Should I Care for the Men of Thames?

Thames flows proudly to the sea, The. The Banks of Nith. Robert Burns. **CP-BurnR**

Than a choice of subject. Château de Muzot. Charles Tomlinson. **CP-TomlC**

Than Heaven more remote. Emily Dickinson. **CP-DickE**

Than his chaste wife, though Beast now know no more. On the Same Beast. Ben Jonson. **CP-JonsB**

Than I. Robert Creeley. **CP-CreeR**

Than which not any could be found other. Louis MacNeice. *Fr.* The Trolls. **CP-MacNL**

Than which not any. Time. Louis MacNeice. *Fr.* The Trolls. **CP-MacNL**

Than(by yon sunset's wintry glow). Edward Estlin Cummings. **CP-CummE**

Thank God, bless God, all ye who suffer not. Tears. Elizabeth Barrett Browning. **CP-BroEB**

Thank God for Alleys. Charles Bukowski. **SP-BukC2**

Thank God for rest, where none molest. The Peace Autumn. John Greenleaf Whittier. **CP-WhitJ**

Thank God for the old Jewish ladies. Street Corner Dialogue. Grace Paley. **CP-PaleG**

Thank God for the token! one lip is still free. Ritner. John Greenleaf Whittier. **CP-WhitJ**

Thank God Life Came For Me, Nerthus Gathered Me Up For Her Annual. This Year. Charles Olson. **CP-OlsoC**

Thank God my Afflictions are such. An Eighteenth-Century Calvinistic Hymn. Sir John Betjeman. **CP-BetjJ**

Thank God, thank God, we do believe. Christmas Carol, A. Christina Georgina Rossetti. **CP-RosC3**

Thank God there is a world. Emily Dickinson. **SP-DickE**

Thank God who made the British Isles. JUNE (*Cricket*). Rudyard Kipling. *Fr.* Verses on Games. **CP-KiplR**

Thank God Who spared me what I feared! For a Mercy Received. Christina Georgina Rossetti. **CP-RosC3**

Thank Heaven! the crisis. For Annie. Edgar Allan Poe. **CP-PoeEd**

Thank heaven there are trees that bare—. Perhaps Macabre. Marsden Hartley. **CP-HartM**

Thank her dear power for having come. Emily Dickinson. **SP-DickE**

Thank the gods thy governors. Ralph Waldo Emerson. **CP-EmerR**

Thank the stars for the translators. Translators. Patti Smith. **SP-SmitP**

Thank You. Robert Creeley. **CP-CreeR**

Thank You. Kenneth Koch. **SP-KochK**

Thank You. Stevie Smith. **CP-SmitS**

Thank you, dear Clarinda. To Clarinda. David Herbert Lawrence. **CP-LawrD**

"Thank you" ebbs between us. Emily Dickinson. **SP-DickE**

Thank You, Fog. Wystan Hugh Auden. **CP-AudeW**

Thank you for leaving the bar of soap. Note to the Previous Tenants. John Updike. **CP-UpdiJ**

Thank You for Not Cooperating. John Ashbery. **SP-AshbJ**

Thank you for your letter. Ilford Rose Book. James Schuyler. **CP-SchuJ**

Thank You Girl. The Beatles. **CP-Beatl**

Thank you in my heart obstructs, The. Emily Dickinson. **SP-DickE**

"Thank You," it said when she uncovered it. Homunculus. Lewis Turco. **SP-TurcL**

Thank You, Lord. Maya Angelou. **SP-AngeM**

Thank-You Note. Elizabeth Bishop. **CP-BishE**

Thank You, O Lord. Jim Morrison. **SP-MorrJ**

Thank you. Thank you very much. I'm pleased. Untoward Occurance at Embassy Poetry Reading. Marilyn Hacker. **SP-HackM**

Thank you very much, how often I have thanked you, how. A Sonatina Followed by Another. Gertrude Stein. **CP-SteiG**

"Thank you, whatever comes." And then she turned. Erat Hora. Ezra Pound. **SP-PounE**

Thanking My Mother for Piano Lessons. Diane Wakoski. **SP-WakoD**

Thankless for favours from on high. On a Similar Occasion for the Year 1792. William Cowper. **CP-CowpW**

Thanks for a Gift of Pheasants. William Cowper. **CP-CowpW**

Thanks for the lessons of this Spot—fit school. Cave of Staffa. William Wordsworth. *Fr.* Poems Composed or Suggested During a Tour, in the Summer of 1833. **CP-WorW2**

Thanks for thy gift. To Avis Keene. John Greenleaf Whittier. **CP-WhitJ**

Thanks in Old Age. Walt Whitman. **CP-WhitW**

Thanks, Nature, for Your gift. Beating Time. Robert Pack. **SP-PackR**

Thanks to a Botanist, A. John Ciardi. **SP-CiarJ**

Thanks to Industrial Essex. Donald Davie. **CP-DavDo**

Thanks to the huger stars. Stellar Thanksgiving. Robert Pack. **SP-PackR**

Thanks to the morning light. The World-Soul. Ralph Waldo Emerson. **CP-EmerR**

Thanks to those who go & come. Ralph Waldo Emerson. **CP-EmerR**

Thanksgiving, A. Wystan Hugh Auden. **CP-AudeW**

Thanksgiving. Louise Glück. **SP-GlücL**

Thanksgiving. Louise Glück. **SP-GlücL**

Thanksgiving, The. George Herbert. **CP-HerbG**

Thanksgiving. Robert Herrick. **CP-HerrR**

Thanksgiving. Kenneth Koch. **SP-KochK**

Thanksgiving after Childbirth. William Wordsworth. *Fr.* Ecclesiastical Sonnets. **CP-WorW2**

Thanksgiving: Detroit. John Berryman. **CP-BerrJ**

Thanksgiving Dinner. Edna St. Vincent Millay. **CP-MillE**

Thanksgiving dinner's sad and thankless. Point of View. Shel Silverstein. **SP-SilS2**

Thanksgiving for a former, doth invite. Thanksgiving. Robert Herrick. **CP-HerrR**

Thanksgiving for a Habitat. Wystan Hugh Auden. **CP-AudeW**

Thanksgiving for a Habitat. Wystan Hugh Auden. **NYBP** *Fr.* Thanksgiving for a Habitat. **CP-AudeW**

  Cave of Making, The.

  Cave of Nakedness, The.

  Common Life, The.

  Down There.

  Encomium Balnei.

  For Friends Only.

  Geography of the House, The.

  Grub First, Then Ethics.

    (On Installing an American Kitchen in Lower Austria.) **NYBP**

  Prologue: The Birth of Architecture.

    "From gallery-grave and the hunt of a wren-king." **EyDe**

    "Some thirty inches from my nose." **FaBoEE; IHNG**

  Thanksgiving for a Habitat. **NYBP**

  To-night at Seven-thirty.

  Up There. **OxBTC**

Thanksgiving for My Father, A. William Stafford. **SP-StafW**

Thanksgiving night: Third Avenue was dead. Thanksgiving's Over. Robert Lowell. **SP-LoweR**

Thanksgiving (1956). Edward Estlin Cummings. **CP-CummE**

Thanksgiving Poem, A. Paul Laurence Dunbar. **CP-DunbP**

Thanksgiving to God for His House, A. Robert Herrick. **CP-HerrR**

Thanksgiving's Over. Robert Lowell. **SP-LoweR**

Th'art hence removing, (like a Shepherds tent). Upon Himself. Robert Herrick. **CP-HerrR**

That a pansy is transitive. Emily Dickinson. **SP-DickE**

That a toss of wheat-ears lapping. Seur, near Blois. Donald Davie. **CP-DavDo**

That Actor Kiss. Michael Hartnett. **SP-HarMi**

That affable, vital, inspired even, and well-paid. Tenzone. John Ciardi. **SP-CiarJ**

That after Horror—that 'twas us. Emily Dickinson. **CP-DickE**

That afternoon I had been fishing alone. A Dream of Retarded Children. Robert Bly. **SP-BlyR**

That aged woman with the bass voice. The Great-Grandmother. Robert Ranke Graves. **CP-GravR**

That all night, eaves-high, the snow will press. Afterwards. Robert Penn Warren. *Fr.* Fall Comes in Back-Country Vermont. **SP-WarrR**

That any just to long for. Root-light, or the Lawyer's Daughter. James Dickey. **CP-DickJ**

That art is evil (stale). Tolstoy. William Carlos Williams. **CP-WilW2**

That at last the illustrious child. The Intention. Frank Templeton Prince. **CP-PrinF**

That auto horn sounds familiar. Ernesto Cardenal, *tr. by* Thomas Merton. **CP-MertT** *Fr.* Gethsemani, KY.

That bag was opened in the top front room. Scarlatina. John Hewitt. **CP-HewiJ**

That Bareheaded life under the grass. Emily Dickinson. **SP-DickE**

That bleeding beginning that every mourner knows. Emily Dickinson. **SP-DickE**

That blue hole, Heaven, carry its tide over the wounded within. Kenneth Patchen. *Fr.* The Hunted City. **CP-PatcK**

That blue, that dark, dark, green-dark blue. Invocation to Old Windylocks. Jean Garrigue. **SP-GarrJ**

That box, fair mistress, which thou gavest to me. Sir John Suckling. *Fr.* Brennoralt. **CP-SuckJ**

That boy took my love away. This Boy. The Beatles. **CP-Beatl**

That bright black boy whom I love. On the Way to the Planetarium. James Wright. *Fr.* Many of Our Waters: Variations on a Poem by a Black Child. **CP-WrigJ**

That bright chimeric beast. Countee Cullen. **CP-CullC**

That chair / isn't yours anymore. Coup. Leonard Nathan. **SP-NathL**

That children in their loveliness should die. Arthur Hugh Clough. *Fr.* Seven Sonnets. **SP-ClouA**

That chill is in the air. Not So Far as the Forest. Edna St. Vincent Millay. **CP-MillE**

That Chinese restaurant was a joke. The Will to Change. Adrienne Rich. **CP-RicAE**

That Christ did die, the Pagan saith. The Resurrection. Robert Herrick. **CP-HerrR**

That civilisation may not sink. Long-legged Fly. William Butler Yeats. **CP-YeatW**

That cloud—ambiguous, not. The Descent of Mr. Aldez. John Updike. **CP-UpdiJ**

That Cod can get no widow, yet a knight. On Sir Cod the Perfumed. Ben Jonson. **CP-JonsB**

That come before the swallow dares. George Oppen. *Fr.* Power, the Enchanted World. **CP-OppeG**

That Common Moth. Isabella Gardner. **CP-GardI**

That conversation we were always on the edge. Adrienne Rich. **BoWoP; NoAM** *Fr.* Twenty-one Love Poems. **SP-RicA1; SP-RicA2**

That Country. Grace Paley. *See* This is about the women of that country.

That country spire—Samuel Palmer knew. Returning from Church. Kathleen Jessie Raine. **SP-RainK**

That coursing on, whate'er men's speculations. The Calming Thought of All. Walt Whitman. **CP-WhitW**

That "Craning of the Neck." Isabella Gardner. **CP-GardI**

That crazed girl improvising her music. A Crazed Girl. William Butler Yeats. **CP-YeatW**

That crude little old logcabin. A Vanishing Institution. Kenneth Patchen. **CP-PatcK**

That cry's from the first cuckoo of the year. Shepherd and Goatherd. William Butler Yeats. **CP-YeatW**

That Curfew Tower in Cushendall. The Curfew Tower. John Hewitt. **CP-HewiJ**

That Day. Archie Randolph Ammons. **SP-AmmoA**

That Day. Elizabeth Barrett Browning. **CP-BroEB**

That day / in an oak tree—. Robert Creeley. **CP-CreeR**

That Day. Rudyard Kipling. **CP-KiplR**

That Day. Anne Sexton. **CP-SextA**

That day in the canoe. The Perch. Peter Meinke. **SP-MeinP**

That day of wrath, that dreadful day. Hymn for the Dead. Sir Walter Scott. **SP-ScotW** *Fr.* The Lay of the Last Minstrel.

That day, so innocent appeared. Picnic Remembered. Robert Penn Warren. **SP-WarrR**

That day the eggshell of appearance split. Transfigured Bird. James Merrill. **SP-MerrJ**

That day, the house was so much a ship. The Faring. Charles Tomlinson. **CP-TomlC**

That day the sails of the ship were torn. Lament for Tadhg Cronin's Children. Michael Hartnett. **SP-HarMi**

That day when oats were reaped, and wheat was ripe, and barley ripening. When Oats Were Reaped. Thomas Hardy. **CP-HardT**

That day would skin a fairy. A Dying Art. Derek Mahon. **SP-MahoD**

That dim shattering character of nerves. Going to Bed. Robert Creeley. **CP-CreeR**

That Distance was between Us. Emily Dickinson. **CP-DickE**

That dragonfly, bloated, pinned. Definition in the Face of Unnamed Fury. Rita Dove. **SP-DoveR**

That dreary lake, that midnight sky. Emily Brontë. **CP-BronE**

That each should in his house abide. Ralph Waldo Emerson. **CP-EmerR**

That each, who seems a separate whole. Tennyson. *Fr.* In Memoriam A. H. H. **CP-TennA**

That early training. Lesson. Al Young. **CP-YounA**

That Eden of earth's sunrise cannot vie. Christina Georgina Rossetti. **CP-RosC2**

That elephantine bray in the upper register, that sagacious rumbling down below. What a Wonder Among the Instruments Is the Walloping Tramboone! Hayden Carruth. **CP-CarHS**

That evening Sinda thought she heard the drums. The Dream. Robert Earl Hayden. **CP-HaydR**

That famous fatheads find that each. Edward Estlin Cummings. **CP-CummE**

That far-off day the leaves in flight. The Wind and the Rain. Robert Frost. **CP-FrosR**

That fawn-skin-dappled hair of hers. A Pretty Woman. Robert Browning. **CP-BroR1**

That fell and iced / the walks and streets. The Snow. James Schuyler. **CP-SchuJ**

That fellow on the boattrain who insisted. Lawrence Ferlinghetti. **SP-FerlL**

That filly couldn't carry a rider nor. Basil Bunting, *after the Latin of* Horace. **CP-BuntB**

That first and last word. Charles Henri Ford. **SP-FordC** *Fr.* Secret Haiku.

That first Day, when you praised Me, Sweet. Emily Dickinson. **CP-DickE**

That first green night of their dreaming, asleep beneath the. The Sixth Night: Waking. Muriel Rukeyser. **CP-RukeM**

That flattering glass, whose smooth face wears. A Looking-Glass. Thomas Carew. **CP-CareT**

That flow of Gallants which approach. Men Mind No State in Sicknesse. Robert Herrick. **CP-HerrR**

That flower unseen, that gem of purest ray. In a Churchyard. Richard Wilbur. **CP-WilbR**

That for seven lustres [*or* lusters] I did never come. To the Reverend Shade of His Religious Father. Robert Herrick. **CP-HerrR**

That frantic error [*or* Frantick Errour] I adore. The Apostasy of One and But One Lady. Richard Lovelace. **CP-LoveR**

That frown, *Aminta* now hath drown'd. Courante Monsieur. Richard Lovelace. **CP-LoveR**

That gaiety oh. Lear Is Gay. Robert Earl Hayden. **CP-HaydR**

That Garden of sedate Philosophy. The Garden of Epicurus. George Meredith. **CP-MerG1**

That girl upstream was diced by scaling knives—. Duwamish Head. Richard Hugo. **CP-HugoR**

That gleaming boat they took the time and grief. Prayer for My Father. Gary Gildner. **SP-GildG**

That gloomy cave, that gothic niche. Written in Mrs Field's Album opposite a Pen-and-Ink Sketch in the Manner of a Rembrandt Etching Done by Edmund Field. William Wordsworth. **CP-WorW2**

That god forbid that made me first your slave. Sonnet 58. William Shakespeare. *Fr.* Sonnets. **CP-ShaWS**

That God is colouring Newton does shew. To Venetian Artists. William Blake. **CP-BlakW**

That God of ours, the Great Geometer. Grace to Be Said at the Supermarket. Howard Nemerov. **CP-NemeH**

That goose died in opaque dream. Again, Kapowsin. Richard Hugo. **CP-HugoR**

That grandiose colossus who. Letter to a Purist. Sylvia Plath. **CP-PlatS**

That grey droning note. Whistle Buoy. Tom Clark. **SP-ClarT**

That guy three lots down on the oth- / er side? Name of Crawford. Shake, Well Before Using. Hayden Carruth. **CP-CarHS**

That gypsy strain is. Head of a Woman. Al Young. **CP-YounA**

That hackney'd judge of human life. On Marriage. Robert Burns. **CP-BurnR**

That had a swivel / mirror, a swivel. On the Dresser. James Schuyler. **CP-SchuJ**

That Happines do's still the longest thrive. Happinesse. Robert Herrick. **CP-HerrR**

That happy gleam of vernal eyes. The Gleaner (Suggested By a Picture). William Wordsworth. **CP-WorW2**

That he had no writ nor right to lie in that country. The Fourth Book. Archibald MacLeish. *Fr.* Conquistador. **CP-MacLA**

That he knows more of love than you, by far. The Gentleman. Robert Ranke Graves. **CP-GravR**

That heat! / That terrible heat. The Marriage of Souls. William Carlos Williams. **CP-WilW2**

That her acts / Olga's acts / of beauty. Fragment (1966). Ezra Pound. *Fr.* Cantos. **CP-PoCan**

That her serene influence should spread. Two Loves. Richard Eberhart. **CP-EberR**

That heresies should strike (if truth be scanned). Dissensions. William Wordsworth. *Fr.* Ecclesiastical Sonnets. **CP-WorW2**

That hero my allegiance earns. Everything's Haggis in Hoboken, or, Scots Wha Hae Hae. Ogden Nash. **CP-NashO**

That his fast-flowing hours with sandy silt. St. Thecla. Gerard Manley Hopkins. **CP-HopkG**

That holy Hymnes with Lovers cares are knit. To the Reader. Thomas Campion. **CP-CampT**

That honoured name! Lady Cochrane. Donald Davie. **CP-DavDo**

That houses forme within was rude and strong. The House of Richesse. Edmund Spenser. **CH** *Fr.* The Faerie Queene. **CP-Spens**

That huge stale smile you give—. Truants. Roy Fisher. **SP-FishR** *Fr.* Interiors with Various Figures.

That hump of a man bunching chrysanthemums. Old Florist. Theodore Roethke. **CP-RoetT**

That I cannot take. The Crisis. Gilbert Sorrentino. **SP-SorrG**

That I did always love. Emily Dickinson. **CP-DickE**

That I Had Had Courage When Young. Hayden Carruth. **CP-CarHS**

That I, hereafter, do not think the bar. An Epigram to the Coucillor That Pleaded and Carried the Cause. Ben Jonson. **CP-JonsB**

That insect, without antennae, over its. The Crane. Charles Tomlinson. **CP-TomlC**

That is a quiet place. The House of Silence. Thomas Hardy. **CP-HardT**

That is no country for old men. The young. Sailing to Byzantium. William Butler Yeats. **CP-YeatW**

That is solemn we have ended. Emily Dickinson. **CP-DickE**

That is the end of the news. The humanist. Louis MacNeice. *Fr.* The Stygian Banks. **CP-MacNL**

That is the face I wore. The Photograph Album. Stephen Dunn. **SP-DunnS**

That is the way you are, always given. The Narrows. Jim Carroll. **SP-CarrJ**

That is what they say, who were broken off from love. Muriel Rukeyser. **LCAP** *Fr.* Eighth Elegy. Children's Elegy. **CP-RukeM**

That is work of waste and ruin. Foresight. William Wordsworth. **CP-WorW1**

That it is true, Master. Emily Dickinson. **SP-DickE**

That it will never come again. Emily Dickinson. **CP-DickE**

That Jealousy may rule a mind. Not at Home. Samuel Taylor Coleridge. **CP-ColeS**

That kid's my buddy. Buddy. Langston Hughes. **SP-HughL**

That kind of summer's day when music comes. A Falling Out. Michael Hartnett. **SP-HarMi**

That Kind of Thing. Tess Gallagher. **SP-GallT**

That Kiss in the Dark. Thomas Hardy. **CP-HardT**

That kiss meant to sear my heart forever. Time Lapse with Tulips. Tess Gallagher. **SP-GallT**

That Land. George Oppen. *Fr.* Five Poems about Poetry. **CP-OppeG**

That lateness of the season here. The Blossomed Thorn. John Hewitt. **CP-HewiJ**

That lavished sunlight, where. Two Songs in a Stanza of Beddoes'. Richard Wilbur. **CP-WilbR**

That learning, thine ambassador. John Donne. *Fr.* A Litany. **CP-DonnJ**

That light blood-loving weasel, a tongue of yellow. Robinson Jeffers. *Fr.* The Broken Balance. **CP-JefR1**

That lime-tree—no, what is it? mulberry? Recollections of George Oppen in a Letter to an English Friend. Donald Davie. **CP-DavDo**

That line is the horizon line. Shipbored. John Updike. **CP-UpdiJ**

That little Negro's married and got a kid. Sister. Langston Hughes. **SP-HughL**

That little pretty [or prettie] bleeding part. To His Savior [or Saviour]. The New Years [or yeers] Gift. Robert Herrick. **CP-HerrR**

That lively organ, palpitant and red. The Proud Heart. Countee Cullen. **CP-CullC**

That living law, the magistrate. John Donne. *Fr.* A Litany. **CP-DonnJ**

That lofty monarch, Monarch Mind. Natural History. Sylvia Plath. **CP-PlatS**

That Love at length should find me out and bring. Edna St. Vincent Millay. **CP-MillE**

That Love is all there is. Emily Dickinson. **CP-DickE**

That Love last long; let it thy first care be. A Caution. Robert Herrick. **CP-HerrR**

That love 'twixt men do's ever longest last. On Love. Robert Herrick. **CP-HerrR**

That lovely spot which thou dost see. Upon a Mole in Celia's Bosom. Thomas Carew. **CP-CareT**

That lover of a night. *fr.* Words for Music Perhaps. William Butler Yeats. **CP-YeatW**

That love's a bitter sweet, I ne'er conceive. Elegy, An. Ben Jonson. **CP-JonsB**

That love's dull smart distressed my heart. Her Secret. Thomas Hardy. **CP-HardT**

That low keening you hear is me bemoaning my fate. Second Chime. Ogden Nash. *Fr.* Ring out the Old, Ring in the New, but Don't Get Caught in Between. **CP-NashO**

That luscious look of something becoming. Yes, I Know—Yes. Marsden Hartley. **CP-HartM**

That man is peer of the gods, who. Sappho. Sappho, *tr. fr. Ancient Greek by* William Carlos Williams. **CP-WilW2**

That Manna, which God on His people cast. Manna. Robert Herrick. **CP-HerrR**

That march of the funereal Past behold. Il y a Cent Ans. George Meredith. **CP-MerG2**

That mare stood in the field. All through the Rains. Gary Snyder. **CP-SnydG**

That matter of the murder is hushed up. The Cenci. Percy Bysshe Shelley. **CP-ShelP**

That me alone you lov'd, you once did say. Catullus. *See* Carmen 72: "There was a time, Lesbia, when."

That melancholy / fellow'll play / his handorgan. Edward Estlin Cummings. **CP-CummE**

That mid-fall morning, driving north. John Haines. *Fr.* News from the Glacier. **SP-HainJ**

That midwinter day / you could almost. The Birds. Dabney Stuart. **SP-StuaD**

That miracle / of science the Half. The Hermaphrodite. Dabney Stuart. **SP-StuaD**

That mirror / Which makes of men a transparency. Moments of Vision. Thomas Hardy. **CP-HardT**

That Moment. Thomas Hardy. **CP-HardT**

That Moment. Ted Hughes. **SP-HughT** *Fr.* Crow.

That moment when the high-wire walker suddenly begins to falter, wobble, sway, arms flailing. Vehicle: Conscience. Charles Kenneth Williams. **SP-WillC**

That month he was broke. Whiplash. William Matthews. **SP-MattW**

That morn[e] which saw me made a Bride. Upon a Maid That Died [or Dyed] the Day She Was Married [or Marryed]. Meleager, *tr. fr. Greek by* Robert Herrick. **CP-HerrR**

That Morning. Daniel Gerard Hoffman. **SP-HoffD**

That Morning. Ted Hughes. **SP-HughT**

That morning when I trod the town. The Chimes. Thomas Hardy. **CP-HardT**

That Music Always Round Me. Walt Whitman. **CP-WhitW**

That must be a silver bell. Emily Dickinson. **SP-DickE**

That Nature Is a Heraclitean Fire and of the Comfort of the Resurrection. Gerard Manley Hopkins. **CP-HopkG**

That neither fame nor love might wanting be. To Sir Henry Cary. Ben Jonson. **CP-JonsB**

That night, / winter, / rain. Charles Kenneth Williams. **CP-WillC; SP-WillC**

That night came on in Egypt with a step. The First-Born of Egypt. Robert Browning. **CP-BroR2**

That night, that night, / That song, that song! A Bygone Occasion. Thomas Hardy. **CP-HardT**

That Night. Moon came out full, you could see the white breathing of the. Kenneth Patchen. **CP-PatcK**

That night, the great tree split. The Scar. Charles Tomlinson. **CP-TomlC**

That night when joy began. Wystan Hugh Auden. **OxBTC; PAI; SoSe** *Fr.* Five Songs ("What's in your mind, my dove, my coney"). **CP-AudeW**

That night, when through the mooring-chains. Rudyard Kipling. *See* The Ballad of Fisher's Boardinghouse.

That night your great guns, unawares. Channel Firing. Thomas Hardy. **CP-HardT**

That nine-foot doughboy, were the sculptor good. Antiques in Ellettsville. Richard Hugo. **CP-HugoR**

That no fair woman will, wonder not why. Catullus. *See* Carmen 69: "Do not wonder when the wench declines."

That no man schemed it is my hope. The Blow. Thomas Hardy. **CP-HardT**

That No Man Take Thy Crown. Christina Georgina Rossetti. **CP-RosC2**

That Noble Flower. Robinson Jeffers. **CP-JefR3**

That none beguiled be by time's quick flowing. Sir John Suckling. **CP-SuckJ**

(Lover's Clock, The.) **CP-SuckJ**

That, not a pair of friends each other see. To Mime. Ben Jonson. **CP-JonsB**

That note you hold, narrowing and rising, shakes. For Sidney Bechet. Philip Larkin. **CP-LarkP**

That Nova was a moderate star like our good sun; it stored no doubt a. Nova. Robinson Jeffers. **CP-JefR2**

That oblong book's the Album; hand it here! The Inn Album. Robert Browning. **CP-BroR2**

That ocean you of late surveyed. To Mr. Newton [on His Return from Ramsgate]. William Cowper. **CP-CowpW**

That odd old man is dead a year. Emily Dickinson. **CP-DickE**

That old black goober that I ate. Sopa. Robert Creeley. **CP-CreeR**

That "old last act"! / And yet sometimes. Adrienne Rich. **NIP; NOBA; TAP** Fr. Two Songs. **CP-RicAE; SP-RicA2**

That on her lap she casts her humble Eye. On the Blessed Virgins Bashfulnesse. Richard Crashaw. **CP-CrasR**

That, once sighted. Wish. Roy Fisher. **SP-FishR**

That one who is the dreamer lies mostly in her left arm. Angina. James Dickey. **CP-DickJ**

That Other World. Robert Ranke Graves. **CP-GravR**

That our ears' sickness we [or eares sicknesse wee] may cure. John Donne. Fr. A Litany. **CP-DonnJ**

That our senses lie and our minds trick us is true, but in general. Advice to Pilgrims. Robinson Jeffers. **CP-JefR3**

That out of sight is out of mind. Arthur Hugh Clough. **SP-ClouA**

That pack of scoundrels. The System. Stanley Jasspon Kunitz. **CP-KuniS**

That pale face stretches across the centuries. Yes, I Know. Stevie Smith. **CP-SmitS**

That "part / Of consciousness." Debt. George Oppen. **CP-OppeG**

That Particular Air. Lewis Turco. **SP-TurcL**

That phrase in the head—that snatch repeated. Melody. Charles Tomlinson. **CP-TomlC**

That plastic Buddha jars out a Karate screech. Do Not Pick Up the Telephone. Ted Hughes. **SP-HughT**

That plush hair Fabulla wears? Martial, tr. by William Matthews. **SP-MattW** Fr. Epigrams.

That poets are far rarer births than kings. To Elizabeth, Countess of Rutland. Ben Jonson. **CP-JonsB**

That Possession fairest lies. Emily Dickinson. **SP-DickE**

That Prince must govern with a gentle hand. Gentlenesse. Robert Herrick. **CP-HerrR**

That Prince takes some enough the Victors roome. Prevision, or Provision. Robert Herrick. **CP-HerrR**

That Prince, who may doe nothing but what's just. A King and No King. Robert Herrick. **CP-HerrR**

That Princeling. Isabella Gardner. **CP-GardI**

That Princes may possesse a surer seat. Pollicie in Princes. Robert Herrick. **CP-HerrR**

That prodigal road! By rampant hawthorns you braked. Journey With a Conjuror. James McAuley. **SP-McAuJ** Fr. The Exile's Recurring Nightmare.

That profound cleft. June 9. William Carlos Williams. **CP-WilW2**

That Providence which had so long the care. A Poem upon the Death of Oliver Cromwell. Andrew Marvell. **CP-MarvA**

That public men publish falsehoods. Be Angry at the Sun. Robinson Jeffers. **CP-JefR3**

That quiet point of light. Letters. Jane Cooper. **SP-CoopJ**

That Reminds Me. Ogden Nash. **CP-NashO**

That ring-necked pheasant, feather-worn. Iowa City Zoo. Jean Garrigue. **SP-GarrJ**

That rising, of the first, you cause. Of Lady, of Beauty, of Stream. Charles Olson. **CP-OlsoC**

That rock shaped like a ship might scare us now. The Picnic in the Saracen Ruin. Richard Hugo. **CP-HugoR**

That roses are red is home—and homesickness. Louis MacNeice. Fr. The Stygian Banks. **CP-MacNL**

That row of icicles along the gutter. Beyond Words. Robert Frost. **CP-FrosR**

That sacred Closet when you sweep. Emily Dickinson. **CP-DickE**

That "Sacred to the Memory." Sacred to the Memory. Thomas Hardy. **CP-HardT**

That sail which leans on light. Sea Grapes. Derek Walcott. **CP-WalcD**

That salmon and sole Puss should think very grand. "Lewis Carroll." Fr. Solutions. Fr. Puzzles from Wonderland. **CP-CarrL**

That same first fiddler who leads the orchéstra to-night. At Madame Tussaud's in Victorian Years. Thomas Hardy. **CP-HardT**

That Saturday Without a Car. Stephen Dunn. **SP-DunnS**

That sculptor we knew, the passionate-eyed son of a quarryman. An Artist. Robinson Jeffers. **CP-JefR1**

That second time they hunted me. The Italian in England. Robert Browning. **CP-BroR1**

That Shadow My Likeness. Walt Whitman. **CP-WhitW**

That she could cook. Malcolm Lowry. **CP-LowrM**

That she forgot me was the least. Emily Dickinson. **CP-DickE**

That shining moon—watched by that one faint star. Night. Walter de la Mare. **CP-DeLaW**

That short—potential stir. Emily Dickinson. **CP-DickE**

That short-sleeved man, our. A Modest Mound of Bones. John Updike. **CP-UpdiJ**

That should be obvious. The Slums. Kenneth Patchen. **CP-PatcK**

That shrewd character Will Percy in. The University of the South. Donald Davie. **CP-DavDo**

That shy angle of his daughter's head. Variation on Gaining a Son. Rita Dove. **SP-DoveR**

That smokestack, for instance. Obedience. Rita Dove. **SP-DoveR**

That sneaky Thomas Cranmer! Widower. Donald Davie. **CP-DavDo**

That snowless, warmthless January sucked. Frost. John Updike. **CP-UpdiJ**

That solemn Senator / who claimed I had castles. Pablo Neruda, tr. fr. Spanish by Ben Belitt. **SP-NeruP** Fr. Question Book.

That "something far more deeply interfused." Elegy on Tintern Abbey. John Gould Fletcher. **SP-FletJ**

That Song of Songs which is Solomon's. In the Day of His Espousals. Christina Georgina Rossetti. **CP-RosC2**

That Sorrow dare to touch the Loved. Emily Dickinson. **SP-DickE**

That sound, everywhere about us, of the sea. Ce bruit da la mer. Denise Levertov. **CP-LeveD**

That story which the bold Sir Bedivere. The Passing of Arthur. Tennyson. **FHYEP; NAEL-2; OBNC** Fr. Idylls of the King. **CP-TennA**

That strange flower, the sun. Gubbinal. Wallace Stevens. **CP-StevW**

That Such have died enable Us. Emily Dickinson. **CP-DickE**

That Summer. Gary Gildner. **SP-GildG**

That summer midnight under her aurora. The Transgress. Muriel Rukeyser. **CP-RukeM**

That summer noonday, zenith, was too brief. Grandfather Robinson Dies in 1898. John Hewitt. **CP-HewiJ**

That summer when I worked in the frozen foods plant. Life Moving More Rapidly Than Hands Can Manage. William Dickey. **SP-DickW**

That sweet Physician, an approaching spring. Emily Dickinson. **SP-DickE**

That sweet sinewy green nymph. Laocoön is the Name of the Figure. Marge Piercy. **SP-PierM**

That sweetbread gazing up at me. The Sweetbread. Ogden Nash. Fr. Table Talk. **CP-NashO**

That terrible white light he could not shut out. Lazarus. Jenny Joseph. **SP-JoseJ**

That the Divine has been human. Emily Dickinson. **SP-DickE**

That the glass would melt in heat. The Glass of Water. Wallace Stevens. **CP-StevW**

That the Night Come. William Butler Yeats. **CP-YeatW**

That the Pear Delights Me Now. Daniel Gerard Hoffman. **SP-HoffD**

That the Unexamined Life Is Not Worth Living. Leonard Nathan. **SP-NathL**

That the world / is going. Charles Kenneth Williams. **CP-WillC; SP-WillC**

That the world will never be quite—what a cliché—the same again. Tam Cari Capitis. Louis MacNeice. **CP-MacNL**

That then becomes you Have. Assuming the Soul Is a Bitch. Charles Olson. **CP-OlsoC**

That there are better things within the womb. Arthur Hugh Clough. Fr. Seven Sonnets. **SP-ClouA**

That there are powers above us I admit. Arthur Hugh Clough. **SP-ClouA**

That there is falsehood in his looks. Robert Burns. **CP-BurnR**

(Epigram on Doctor Babington.) **CP-BurnR**

(In Answer to One Who Affirmed of a Well Known Character Here, Dr B——, That There Was Falsehood in His Very Looks.) **CP-BurnR**

That there's a God, we all do know. Another. Robert Herrick. **CP-HerrR**

That this is I. The Hills. George Oppen. **CP-OppeG**

That this is the gift. The Gift. Charles Bukowski. **SP-BukC2**

That this should feel the need of Death. Emily Dickinson. **CP-DickE**

That this wondering two-footed / notion of abeyance should. Persons. Robert Creeley. **CP-CreeR**

That thou art blamed shall not be thy defect. Sonnet 70. William Shakespeare. **OXAEP-1; SCGP** Fr. Sonnets. **CP-ShaWS**

That thou art loved of God, this work is done. To My L[ord] the King, on the Christening His Second Son James. Ben Jonson. **CP-JonsB**

That thou hast her, it is not all my grief[e]. Sonnet 42. William Shakespeare. **CBLP; HeIP; InvP; OXAEP-1** *Fr.* Sonnets. **CP-ShaWS**

That thou hast kept thy love, increased thy will. To the Same [Sir Thomas Roe]. Ben Jonson. **CP-JonsB**

That thou mayst injure no man, dove-like be. Prudent Simplicity. William Cowper, *tr. fr. the Latin of Owen.* **CP-CowpW**

That time I made the winter journey. The Authority of Krajova. Kenneth Patchen. **CP-PatcK**

That time I thought I was in love. Each from Different Heights. Stephen Dunn. **SP-DunnS**

That time is dead for ever, child! Lines. Percy Bysshe Shelley. **CP-ShelP**

That time of the early year. Back of Affluence. Donald Davie. **CP-DavDo**

That time of year thou may'st [*or* maist] in me behold. Sonnet 73. William Shakespeare. **AWP; ArNa; BoLoP; CTC; ChTr; ClHu; EBEV; EIL; EnRePo; FaPoB; GTBS; GTBS-P; HAP; HeIP; HoPM; ImPo; InPK; InPS; InvP; LiTB; NAEL-1; NIP; NOBE; NoP; NoSic; OAEL-1; OBD; OBEV; OBSC; OHFP; PBMP; PPP; PIP; PoE; PoEL-2; PoRA; PrIm; QFR; SCGP; SoSe; Son; TEP; TFi; TrGrPo; UnPo; WeW** *Fr.* Sonnets. **CP-ShaWS**

That time that mirth did steer my ship. Sir Thomas Wyatt. **CP-WyatT**

That, true to the contours which round it. Derbyshire Turf. Donald Davie. **CP-DavDo**

That unripe side of earth, that heavy clime. To the Countess of Huntingdon. John Donne. **CP-DonnJ**

That vast communicative Mind. Generosity. Christopher Smart. *Fr.* Hymns for the Amusement of Children. **SP-SmarC**

That vast wheel turning. Cranes. John Haines. **SP-HainJ**

That violent song of the twilight! Galway Kinnell. *Fr.* The Avenue Bearing the Initial of Christ into the New World. **SP-KinnG**

That volatile poet called Jonathan. Basil Bunting. **CP-BuntB**

That wandering fire to me appears. Ralph Waldo Emerson. **CP-EmerR**

That was a place, when I was young. An Offering for Mr. Bluehart. James Wright. **CP-WrigJ**

That was a pretty one, I heard you call. Philip Larkin. **CP-LarkP** (Reference Back.) **CP-LarkP**

That was by the door. Broken Promise. Archibald MacLeish. **CP-MacLA**

That was fifteen years ago. Thom Gunn. *Fr.* Talbot Road. **CP-GunnT**

That was I, you heard last night. A Serenade at the Villa. Robert Browning. **CP-BroR1**

"That was in another country," but the wench. Marilyn Hacker. *Fr.* The Regent's Park Sonnets. **SP-HackM**

That was in 1875, and we come through. Mona Van Duyn. **SP-VanDM**

That was in 1875, then we moved here. Mona Van Duyn. **SP-VanDM**

That was my grandfather, nearly went to prison. Mona Van Duyn. **SP-VanDM**

That was once her casement. In the Mind's Eye. Thomas Hardy. **CP-HardT**

That was the chirp of Ariel. Wind on the Lyre. George Meredith. **CP-MerG1**

That was the day they invited. Beethoven Attends the C Minor Seminar. Charles Tomlinson. **CP-TomlC**

That Was the Night. Robert Ranke Graves. **CP-GravR**

That was the proverb. Let my mistress[e] be. Long and Lazy [*or* Lazie]. Robert Herrick. **CP-HerrR**

That was the year / of the black nights and clear. Craigvara House. Derek Mahon. **SP-MahoD**

That was the year. A Poem To Delight My Friends Who Laugh at Science-Fiction. Edwin Rolfe. **CP-RolfE**

That was the year of the bad war. The others—. Interjection #4: Bad Year, Bad War: A New Year's Card, 1969. Robert Penn Warren. **SP-WarrR**

That Was Then. Isabella Gardner. **CP-GardI**

That way look, my Infant, lo! The Kitten and [the] Falling Leaves. William Wordsworth. **CP-WorW1**

That we are always glad. Secrets. Wystan Hugh Auden. **CP-AudeW**

That we are permanent. Emily Dickinson. **SP-DickE**

That We Here Highly Resolve. Kenneth Patchen. **CP-PatcK**

That we[e] may change to evenness[e]. John Donne. *Fr.* A Litany. **CP-DonnJ**

That we the loss might know, and thou our love. To King James. Ben Jonson. **CP-JonsB**

That week the fall was opulent. Vendanges. 1956. Daniel Gerard Hoffman. **SP-HoffD**

That well yourself had known, could know. A Tear Is an Intellectual Thing. Marsden Hartley. *Fr.* Un Recuerdo—Hermano—Hart Crane R.I.P. **CP-HartM**

That Where I Am, There Ye May Be Also. Christina Georgina Rossetti. **CP-RosC2**

That which brings it. Description. Charles Simic. **SP-SimiC**

That which eludes this verse and any verse. A Riddle Song. Walt Whitman. **CP-WhitW**

That which gives me to see. The Virtuous Agent. William Carlos Williams. **CP-WilW2**

That Which Hath Been Is Named Already, and It Is Known That It Is Man. Christina Georgina Rossetti. **CP-RosC2**

That which I have myself seen and the fighting. Bernál Díaz' Preface to his Book. Archibald MacLeish. *Fr.* Conquistador. **CP-MacLA**

That which is at your East, your heart, I cannot. Address to you. Richard Eberhart. *Fr.* Suite in Prison. **CP-EberR**

That which is inside me. Bloodbirth. Audre Lorde. **SP-LordA**

That which is marred at birth Time shall not mend. Gertrude's Prayer. Rudyard Kipling. **CP-KiplR**

That which pushes upward. Consulting I Ching Smoking Pot Listening to the Fugs Sing Blake. Allen Ginsberg. **CP-GinsA**

That which to some their wishes ends present. Mary Sidney, Countess of Montgomery Wroth. *Fr.* Part 1. *Fr.* Urania. **CP-WrotM**

That which we dare invoke to bless. Tennyson. **EBVV; FHYEP; NOCV; OAEL-2; TOF; WGRP** *Fr.* In Memoriam A. H. H. **CP-TennA**

That which we who're alive in spite of mirrors. Edward Estlin Cummings. **CP-CummE**

That whiskey will cook the egg. Bar. Langston Hughes. **SP-HughL**

That whisper takes the voice. In a Whispering Gallery. Thomas Hardy. **CP-HardT**

That white coconut, the sun. Cloud Shadows. John Updike. **CP-UpdiJ**

That Whitsun, I was late getting away. The Whitsun Weddings. Philip Larkin. **CP-LarkP**

That wind, I used to hear it swelling. Emily Brontë. **CP-BronE**

That wind's still there that I remember afire. The Agrigentum Road. Salvatore Quasimodo, *tr. fr. Italian by* Richard Wilbur. **CP-WilbR**

That winking, glimmering like the wings. Silver Poplars. William DeWitt Snodgrass. **SP-SnodW**

That winter I stopped loving the President. 1963. Rita Dove. *Fr.* A Suite for Augustus. **SP-DoveR**

That winter I stopped loving the President. A Suite for Augustus. Rita Dove. **SP-DoveR**

That winter night round the blazing turf. The Fairy Thresher. John Hewitt. **CP-HewiJ**

That winter of the war, every day. In Camp. William Stafford. **SP-StafW**

That winter when this thought came—how the river. Living on the Plains. William Stafford. **SP-StafW**

That with this bright believing band. The Impercipient. Thomas Hardy. **CP-HardT**

That would be waving and that would be crying. Waving Adieu, Adieu, Adieu. Wallace Stevens. **CP-StevW**

That year, March began in April. Discrepancies. Charles Tomlinson. **CP-TomlC**

That year of the cloud, when my marriage failed. River Road. Stanley Jasspon Kunitz. **CP-KuniS**

That year the news. Time Capsule. William Stafford. **SP-StafW**

That you allow yourself this vast neglect of me. Gilbert Sorrentino. *Fr.* Elegiacs of Sulpicia. **SP-SorrG**

That you are fair or wise is vain. Fate. Ralph Waldo Emerson. **CP-EmerR**

That you Captain? Sure. Galway Kinnell. *Fr.* The Dead Shall Be Raised Incorruptible. **SP-KinnG**

That you, friend Marcus, like a Stoic. The Parson's Case. Jonathan Swift. **CP-SwifJ**

That you have seen the pride, beheld the sport. Epigram, An. Ben Jonson. **CP-JonsB**

That you return to us alive. Emily Dickinson. **SP-DickE**

That you should send. On Receiving a Christmas Card. Wystan Hugh Auden. **CP-AudWJ**

That you should still send / yourself to me, that you should. Valentine. Hayden Carruth. **CP-CarHS**

That you were once unkind befriends me now. Sonnet 120. William Shakespeare. **InvP; OXAEP-1** *Fr.* Sonnets. **CP-ShaWS**

That you will take the meaning of this verse. To R.H.H. with Daphne. George Meredith. **CP-MerG2**

That your loved Confederate and yourself. Emily Dickinson. **SP-DickE**

Thatch, The. Robert Frost. **CP-FrosR**

Thatch dripped soot, The. A Visit to Croom, 1745. Michael Hartnett. **SP-HarMi**

Thatch white walls white roses creeping. Cottage by the Bridge. James Liddy. **CP-LiddJ**

Thatcher. Seamus Heaney. **SP-HeanS**

That'll Be the Day. Dabney Stuart. **SP-StuaD**

That's a place I've been. The town. The Small Oil Left in the House We Rented in Boulder. Richard Hugo. **CP-HugoR**

That's Dostoyevsky's skull beside my desk. Skull. David Markson. **CP-MarkD**

That's Funny, Wasn't It? No, It Won't Be. Ogden Nash. **CP-NashO**

That's good to hear, Professor Pagels, now. Out of Nothing. Robert Pack. **SP-PackR**

That's just your way, sweet April, smile and sigh. May. Christina Georgina Rossetti. *Fr.* The Months: A Pageant. **CP-RosC2**

That's Mexican for O youre too much! Malagueña Salerosa. Al Young. **CP-YounA**

That's my last Duchess painted on the wall. My Last Duchess [Ferrara]. Robert Browning. **CP-BroR1**

That's my mind out nines in coke. Sun the Blond Out. Anne Waldman. **SP-WaldA**

That's my younger brother with his Navy wings. Family Group. Archibald MacLeish. **CP-MacLA**

That's not a cross look it's a sign of life. Poem. Frank O'Hara. **SP-OharF**

That's our last look at the green canal. The Bridge of Sighs. Richard Hugo. **CP-HugoR**

That's the condition o't or near. "Hugh MacDiarmid." **SP-MacDH** *Fr.* Frae Anither Window in Thrums.

That's the down-town frieze. The Common Life. Wallace Stevens. **CP-StevW**

That's the girl in the middle, the one who will show you. Thomas Merton. *Fr.* Cables to the Ace. **CP-MertT**

That's the kind of books. Drugstore Library. William Carlos Williams. **CP-WilW2**

That's the Naples packet slipping out of the harbour. Prison Island. James Fenton. **SP-FentJ**

That's the only image. A Wall. Charles Simic. **SP-SimiC**

That's the sawmill—everyone can hear it. The Sawmill. Wystan Hugh Auden. **CP-AudWJ**

That's the Story of My Life. "Lou Reed." **SP-ReedL**

That's What I Mean. Malcolm Lowry. **CP-LowrM**

That's what misery is. Poetry Is a Destructive Force. Wallace Stevens. **CP-StevW**

That's what poetry is. A Poem is a Painting. Phoebe Hesketh. **SP-HeskP**

Thaw, The. Hayden Carruth. *Fr.* Contra Mortem. **CP-CarHL**

Thaw. Hayden Carruth. **CP-CarHS**

Thaw. Daniel Gerard Hoffman. **SP-HoffD**

Thaw. Philip Larkin. **CP-LarkP**

Thaw. Frederick Morgan. *Fr.* Enigmas. **SP-MorgF**

The. Robert Creeley. **CP-CreeR**

The / nimble / heat / had. Edward Estlin Cummings. **CP-CummE**

The / sky / was / can   dy   lu, *See also* Sky / was. . .). Edward Estlin Cummings. **CP-CummE**

The(/ Wistfully / dead seem generous)don't. Edward Estlin Cummings. **CP-CummE**

The. Louis Zukofsky. **CP-ZukLS**

The Truly Great. Stephen Spender. *See* I Think Continually of Those Who Were Truly Great.

Theatre. Tom Clark. **SP-ClarT**

Theatre of winter, The. Charles Henri Ford. **SP-FordC** *Fr.* Secret Haiku.

Theatrical Reflection. Ogden Nash. **CP-NashO**

Thebaid. Robinson Jeffers. **CP-JefR2**

Thebais. Publius Papinius Statius, *tr. fr. Latin.* "Fraternal Rage, the guilty Thebes alarms." **CP-PopeA**

Thee, dear friend, a brother soothes. To Rhea. Ralph Waldo Emerson. **CP-EmerR**

Thee for my recitative. To a Locomotive in Winter. Walt Whitman. **CP-WhitW**

Thee, God, I come from, to thee go. Gerard Manley Hopkins. **CP-HopkG**

'Thee knows. Must thee not knowe?' I so saying. Hayden Carruth. *Fr.* The Sleeping Beauty. **CP-CarHL**

Thee! lucid arbiter 'twixt day and night. To the Morning Star. Written Near the Sea. Charlotte Smith. **CP-SmitC**

Thee, Queen of Shadows!—shall I still invoke. To Fancy. Charlotte Smith. **CP-SmitC**

Thee sacrosanct, Thee sweet, Thee crystalline. Firstly Inclined to Take What It Is Told. Gwendolyn Brooks. **SP-BrooG**

Thee too, enamoured of the life I loved. William Cowper. **EPCY** *Fr.* The Winter Evening. *Fr.* The Task. **CP-CowpW**

Thee, whose refulgent staff, and summons clear. John Milton. *See* Elegy 2: On the Death of the Beadle of Cambridge University.

Thee will I love, O Lord, my tow'r. Bible, *O.T. See* Psalm 18: "I will love thee, O Lord, my strength."

Thee will i praise between those rivers whose. Edward Estlin Cummings. **CP-CummE**

Their Attitudes Differ. Margaret Atwood. **SP-AtwM1**

Their Banishmnet. John Milton. **SeCePo** *Fr.* Book XII. *Fr.* Paradise Lost. **CP-MiltJ**

Their barbarism did not assuage the grief. The Retreat of Ita Cagney. Michael Hartnett. **SP-HarMi**

Their Barricade against the Sky. Emily Dickinson. **CP-DickE**

Their Beauty Has More Meaning. Robinson Jeffers. **CP-JefR3**

Their brains are smooth machines that colonize. The Masters. Hart Crane. **CP-CranH**

Their dappled importunity. Emily Dickinson. **CP-DickE**

Their Day. John Ashbery. **SP-AshbJ**

Their faces are like fine watches. Zimmer Loathing the Gentry. Paul Zimmer. **SP-ZimmP**

Their faces are still there. The Long Goodbye. Dabney Stuart. **SP-StuaD**

Their faces, safe as an interior. The Middle-aged. Adrienne Rich. **CP-RicAE; SP-RicA2**

Their feet on London, their heads in the grey clouds. Whit Monday. Louis MacNeice. **CP-MacNL**

Their footless dance. Love and Knowledge. Robert Penn Warren. *Fr.* Audubon. **SP-WarrR**

Their garden has a silent tall stone-wall. Caserta Garden. Richard Wilbur. **CP-WilbR**

Their groves o' sweet myrtle let Foreign Lands reckon. Song. Robert Burns. **CP-BurnR**

Their hair, pomaded, faces jaded. Sepia Fashion Show. Maya Angelou. **SP-AngeM**

Their Heads Bent Toward Each Other Like Flowers. Tess Gallagher. **SP-GallT**

Their Height in Heaven comforts not. Emily Dickinson. **CP-DickE**

Their hesitant circling / their precarious ribs. Deer. Dabney Stuart. **SP-StuaD**

Their high heels catching sweetly in their long sweet skirts. Verlaine's Innocents. Gilbert Sorrentino. **SP-SorrG**

Their Laureate to an Academy Class Dinner Club. Robert Louis Stevenson. **CP-StevR**

Their learned kings bent down to chat with frogs. Nursery Rhyme. Wystan Hugh Auden. **CP-AudeW**

Their life, collapsed like unplayed cards. Moving in Winter. Adrienne Rich. **CP-RicAE; SP-RicA2**

Their Lonely Betters. Wystan Hugh Auden. **CP-AudeW**

Their marriage is a good one. In our eyes. The Common Wisdom. Howard Nemerov. **CP-NemeH**

Their most prized possession. The R R Bums. William Carlos Williams. **CP-WilW2**

Their Rectitude Their Beauty. Donald Davie. **CP-DavDo**

Their relationship consisted. Jamesian. Thom Gunn. **CP-GunnT**

Their sense is with their senses all mixed in. George Meredith. **NAEL-2; NoP; OAEL-2; OAEP; SCGP** *Fr.* Modern Love. **CP-MerG1**

Their Sex Life. Archie Randolph Ammons. **SP-AmmoA**

Their sex life was their own business. The Cities of the Plain. Mona Van Duyn. **SP-VanDM**

Their Shadows. John Yau. **SP-YauJo**

Their shoes are stuccoed with sawdust and blood. Psalm. Grace Paley. **CP-PaleG**

Their six-weeks-old daughter lies. Nocturne. Stephen Spender. **CP-SpenS**

Their spades grafted through the variably-resistant. Geoffrey Hill. **PoE** *Fr.* Mercian Hymns. **CP-HillG**

Their supply-lines cut, / The leaves go down to defeat. Alatus. Richard Wilbur. **CP-WilbR**

Their time past, pulled down. Burning the Christmas Greens. William Carlos Williams. **CP-WilW2**

Their verdure dare not show. . . their verdure dare not show. Valediction. Louis MacNeice. **CP-MacNL**

Their voice, as one, was heavy. Jim Carroll. *Fr.* The Runners. **SP-CarrJ**

Their voices heard, I stumble suddenly, remembering. One More New Botched Beginning. Stephen Spender. **CP-SpenS**

Their Voices Rang. Charles Tomlinson. **CP-TomlC**

Their war-boots said big shots to the plank floor. Behold, One of Several Little Christs. Kenneth Patchen. **CP-PatcK**

Their Wedded Love. John Milton. **SeCePo** *Fr.* Book IV. **OAEL-1** *Fr.* Paradise Lost. **CP-MiltJ**

(Unfallen Love.) **NOSC**

(Wedded Love.) **OBS**

Theirs is a perfection of pure form. Ants. Daniel Gerard Hoffman. **SP-HoffD**

Theirs is a trade for egomaniacs. Novelists. Howard Nemerov. **CP-NemeH**

Thel. William Blake. *Fr.* The Book of Thel. **CP-BlakW**

Thelonious: An Intro. Al Young. **CP-YounA**

Thel's Motto. William Blake. **ChTr** *Fr.* The Book of Thel. **CP-BlakW**

Them, Crying. James Dickey. **CP-DickJ**

Them which despair. Edward Estlin Cummings. **CP-CummE**

Theme and Variation. Robert Earl Hayden. **CP-HaydR**

Theme and Variations. Edna St. Vincent Millay. **CP-MillE**
  "And do you think that love itself."
  "Heart, do not bruise the breast."
  "I had not thought so tame a thing."
  "Not even my pride will suffer much." **SBG; VBLP**
  "Rolled in the trough of thick desire."

Theme for English B. Langston Hughes. **SP-HughL**

Theme in Yellow. Carl Sandburg. **CP-SandC**

Theme of Death, The. Robert Ranke Graves. **CP-GravR**

Theme of the Three Caskets, The. William Matthews. **SP-MattW**

Themes in Contrast. Carl Sandburg. **CP-SandC**

Themself are all I have. Emily Dickinson. **CP-DickE**

Then. Frederick Morgan. **SP-MorgF**

Then. Muriel Rukeyser. **CP-RukeM**

Then. Richard Wilbur. **CP-WilbR**

Then a partridge-shaped cloud over dust storm, *subsel. See* Canto 113: "Thru the 12 Houses of Heaven." Luis Cabalquinto.

Then a pile of heads he laid. Rudyard Kipling. **CP-KiplR** *Fr.* His Chance in Life. *Fr.* Plain Tales from the Hills.

Then after Eden. New World. Derek Walcott. **CP-WalcD**

Then again by day fog drapes the boats. Tom Clark. *Fr.* Suite. **SP-ClarT**

Then again in disorderly woods. George Meredith. *Fr.* The Day of the Daughter of Hades. **CP-MerG1**

Then all astoined with this mighty ghoast. Joachim Du Bellay. *Fr.* The Visions of Bellay. **CP-Spens**

Then all the nations of birds lifted together. The Season of Phantasmal Peace. Derek Walcott. **CP-WalcD**

Then and Now. Paul Laurence Dunbar. **CP-DunbP**

Then and now. Thomas Hardy. **CP-HardT**

Then at last the Lovers began to speak together. Kenneth Patchen. *Fr.* Wanderers of the Pale Wood. **CP-PatcK**

Then at the very end. Three Songs. Hayden Carruth. **CP-CarHS**

Then Bacchus' subtle speech her sorrow crossed. How Bacchus Comforts Ariadne. Nonnus. **CP-BroEB** *Fr.* Dionysiaca.

Then, blessing all, "Go, children of my care!" The Triumph of Dullness. Alexander Pope. **NOEC** *Fr.* Yet, a moment, one dim ray of light. **NAEL-1; OAEL-1; POEL-3** *Fr.* The Dunciad. **CP-PopeA**

Then both ourselves and seed at once to free. John Milton. **OBD** *Fr.* Book X. **FHYEP** *Fr.* Paradise Lost. **CP-MiltJ**

Then, brother, you would never think me vain. Allen Tate. *Fr.* Sonnets of the Blood. **CP-TateA**

Then call me traitor if you must. To Certain Critics. Countee Cullen. **CP-CullC**

Then came a time of great guilt, that I inhabited. Frank Templeton Prince. *Fr.* Apollo and the Sibyl. **CP-PrinF**

Then came fair May, the fairest maid on ground. May. Edmund Spenser. **GN** *Fr.* The Faerie Queene. **CP-Spens**

Then Came Flowers. Rita Dove. **SP-DoveR**

Then came jolly Summer, being dight. Summer. Edmund Spenser. **GN** *Fr.* The Faerie Queene. **CP-Spens**

Then came, Oscar, the time of the guns. Long Guns. Carl Sandburg. **CP-SandC**

Then came the Autumn all in yellow clad. Autumn. Edmund Spenser. **GN** *Fr.* The Faerie Queene. **CP-Spens**

Then cautiously she pushed the cellar door. Edna St. Vincent Millay. *Fr.* Sonnets from an Ungrafted Tree. **CP-MillE**

Then cried the American poet where she lay supine. Pearl. Stevie Smith. **CP-SmitS**

Then, crushed by rules, and weakened as refined. Samuel Johnson. **EPCY** *Fr.* Prologue Spoken by Mr[.] Garrick at the Opening of the Theatre in Drury Lane, 1747. **CP-JohnS**

Then did a sharped spyre of diamond bright. Joachim Du Bellay. *Fr.* The Visions of Bellay. **CP-Spens**

Then did I live when I did see. A Sonnet of Perilla. Robert Herrick. **CP-HerrR**

Then did the wind move sunful fingers through her hair. Kenneth Patchen. *Fr.* Wanderers of the Pale Wood. **CP-PatcK**

Then fled, O brethren, the wicked juba. The Ballad of Nat Turner. Robert Earl Hayden. **CP-HaydR**

Then forth issewed (great goddesse) great Dame Nature. Dame Nature. Edmund Spenser. **POEL-1** *Fr.* The Faerie Queene. **CP-Spens**

Then from beyond, from nowhere, from the wilderness. Hayden Carruth. *Fr.* The Sleeping Beauty. **CP-CarHL**

Then from their poverty they rose. The Ordinary Women. Wallace Stevens. **CP-StevW**

Then from Tomorrow. Thomas Merton. **CP-MertT**

Then Guidwife Count the Lawin. Robert Burns. **CP-BurnR**

Then hate me when thou wilt; if ever, now. Sonnet 90. William Shakespeare. **AWP; EBEV; EIL; NOBE; NoSic; OBEV; OBSC; OXAEP-1; POEL-2; WHA** *Fr.* Sonnets. **CP-ShaWS**

Then he invented the running wolf behind the wind. The Winter Runner. Brendan Galvin. **SP-GalvB**

Then he laid down the bow of his violin. Red. David Herbert Lawrence. **CP-LawrD**

Then heavenly branches did I see arise. Petrarch. *Fr.* The Visions of Petrarch. **CP-Spens**

Then here was where it began, dear sleeping princess. Hayden Carruth. *Fr.* The Sleeping Beauty. **CP-CarHL**

Then hey, for a lass wi' a tocher, then hey, for a lass wi' a tocher. Robert Burns. *See* Hey for a Lass wi' a Tocher.

Then I came to Harriet Monroe. To Harriet Monroe. Richard Eberhart. **CP-EberR**

Then I came to the house of wood. The Incurable Home. John Haines. **SP-HainJ**

Then I Commended Mirth. Christina Georgina Rossetti. **CP-RosC2**

Then I cried out upon him: Cease. Christina Georgina Rossetti. **PeVV** *Fr.* Despised and Rejected. **CP-RosC1**

Then I do not know what. The Trash Book. James Schuyler. **CP-SchuJ**

Then I forget / The star in the nets of heaven. Muriel Rukeyser. **CP-RukeM**

Then, I had no doubt. Exile. Kathleen Jessie Raine. *Fr.* Three Poems on Illusion. **SP-RainK**

Then I raised my head. Winter Sunset. William Carlos Williams. **CP-WilW1**

Then I Saw What the Calling Was. Muriel Rukeyser. **CP-RukeM**

Then I tuned my harp—took off the lilies we twine round its chords. Robert Browning. **FiP** *Fr.* Saul. **CP-BroR1**

Then if this clay thing calls. The Executions in Moscow. Kenneth Patchen. **CP-PatcK**

Then it came to pass that a pestilence fell on the city. The Finding of Gabriel. Henry Wadsworth Longfellow. **AA** *Fr.* In that delightful land which is washed by the Delaware's waters. *Fr.* Part the Second. *Fr.* Evangeline, a Tale of Acadie. **SP-LongH**

Then it snowed. I / saw it when I let. Afterward. James Schuyler. **CP-SchuJ**

Then it was dusk in Illinois, the small boy. First Song. Galway Kinnell. **SP-KinnG**

Then Jonson came, instructed from the school. Samuel Johnson. **EPCY** *Fr.* Prologue Spoken by Mr[.] Garrick at the Opening of the Theatre in Drury Lane, 1747. **CP-JohnS**

Then Jove commanded the god Mercury. *verse tr.fr.* Metamorphoses *by* Apuleius. Elizabeth Barrett Browning. **CP-BroEB**

Then, land!--then, England! oh, the frosty cliffs. Elizabeth Barrett Browning. **FaBoPP; NAEL-2** *Fr.* Aurora Leigh. **CP-BroEB**

Then let not winter's ragged hand deface. Sonnet 6. William Shakespeare. **MasP** *Fr.* Sonnets. **CP-ShaWS**

Then loudly cried the bold Sir Bedivere. Tennyson. **TOF** *Fr.* Morte d'Arthur. **DL; EBNV; EBVVPR; FaBoBe; FiP; NIP; NOBVV; OAEL-2; OBNV; OXAEP-2; POEL-5** *Fr.* Morte d'Arthur. **CP-TennA**

Then Mama, Papa, were the names we used. The Names We Used. John Hewitt. **CP-HewiJ**

Then marking this my sacred speech, but truly lend. Saint Justin Martyr. **CP-RaleW,** *tr. by* Sir Walter Ralegh; *Fr.* Hortatory Address to the Greeks.

Then Milton rose up from the heaven of Albion ardorous! William Blake. **OAEL-2** *Fr.* Milton. **CP-BlakW**

Then mother Ceres from afar beheld her. *verse tr. fr.* Metamorphoses *by* Apuleius. Elizabeth Barrett Browning. **CP-BroEB**

Then must I punish you with trustfulness. Nightmare of Senility. Robert Ranke Graves. **CP-GravR**

"Then, must it be." Elizabeth Barrett Browning. **NALW** *Fr.* Aurora Leigh. **CP-BroEB**

Then niest outspak a raucle carlin. Robert Burns. *Fr.* The Jolly Beggars.

Then night was shaken from me. Boethius, *tr. fr. Latin.* **MLL,** *tr. by* Helen Waddell; *Fr.* Consolation of Philosophy, The ("De Consolacione Philosophie"). **CP-ChauG**

Then night will come, though not the "sable" night. After the Blast. Louise McNeill. **SP-McNeL**

Then one woman spoke About my son. In San Salvador (II). Grace Paley. **CP-PaleG**

Then Pope, as harmony itself exact. William Cowper. **EPCY** *Fr.* Table Talk. **CP-CowpW**

Then Psyche entered in to Proserpine. *verse tr.fr.* Metamorphoses *by* Apuleius. Elizabeth Barrett Browning. **CP-BroEB**

Then Psyche, weak in body and soul, put on. *verse tr. fr.* Apulieus' Metamorphoses. Elizabeth Barrett Browning. **CP-BroEB**

Then rapture is self in itself entranced. And love? Hayden Carruth. *Fr.* The Sleeping Beauty. **CP-CarHL**

Then Reynolds said O woman most sage. William Blake. *See* O dear Mother outline of knowledge most sage.

Then Rome was, and from thy deep bosom fairest. Percy Bysshe Shelley. *Fr.* Ode to Liberty. **CP-ShelP**

Then rose the King and moved his host by night. Tennyson. **PeVV** *Fr.* The Passing of Arthur. **FHYEP; NAEL-2; OBNC** *Fr.* Idylls of the King. **CP-TennA**

Then said she, quick as the cries. George Meredith. *Fr.* The Day of the Daughter of Hades. **CP-MerG1**

Then said that royall Pere in sober wise. Edmund Spenser. **OAEL-1** *Fr.* The Faerie Queene. **CP-Spens**

Then saw they how there hove a dusky barge. Tennyson. **FaPoB** *Fr.* Morte d'Arthur. **DL; EBNV; EBVVPR; FaBoBe; FiP; NIP; NOBVV; OAEL-2; OBNV; OXAEP-2; PoEL-5** *Fr.* Morte d'Arthur. **CP-TennA**

Then see it! in distressing. The Last Turn. William Carlos Williams. **CP-WilW2**

Then seek your job with thankfulness and work till further orders. Rudyard Kipling. **EBCP** *Fr.* The Glory of the Garden. **CP-KiplR**

Then Shall Perceive. Walt Whitman. **CP-WhitW**

Then Shall Ye Shout. Christina Georgina Rossetti. **CP-RosC2**

Then sing, ye Birds, sing, sing a joyous song! William Wordsworth. *Fr.* Ode: Intimations of Immortality [from Recollections of Early Childhood]. **CP-WorW1**

Then some calm and formal portrait. Roy Fisher. **SP-FishR** *Fr.* Diversions.

Then the archangels all together abandoned the black menacing sky. John Gould Fletcher. **SP-FletJ** *Fr.* Branches of Adam.

Then the Brother of the Wind. Charles Kenneth Williams. **CP-WillC**

Then the Cynic sung. William Blake. **CP-BlakW** *Fr.* An Island in the Moon.

Then the eighty-year old lady with a sparkle. How It Is. Richard Eberhart. **CP-EberR**

Then the Ermine. Marianne Craig Moore. **CP-MoorM**

Then the flowers became very wild. Grace Paley. **CP-PaleG**

Then the knee of the wave. "Reclining Figure." Donald Hall. **CP-HallD**

Then the long sunlight lying on the sea. The Insusceptibles. Adrienne Rich. **CP-RicAE**

Then the old man flamed and prayed. Christina. Thomas Merton. **CP-MertT**

Then the wise hours, suddenly discovered. 3 A. M. in a War Year. Mona Van Duyn. **SP-VanDM**

Then Thel astonish'd view'd the Worm upon its dewy bed. William Blake. *Fr.* The Book of Thel. **CP-BlakW**

Then there was Johann. The Little Tear Gland That Says. Charles Simic. **SP-SimiC**

Then there was the time in. The Spider. Charles Bukowski. **SP-BukC1**

Then They That Feared the Lord Spake Often One to Another. Christina Georgina Rossetti. **CP-RosC3**

Then thick as locusts black'ning the ground. Carnations and Butterflies. Alexander Pope. **NOEC** *Fr.* Yet, yet a moment, one dim ray of light. **NAEL-1; OAEL-1; PoEL-3** *Fr.* The Dunciad. **CP-PopeA**

Then thou ill-favour'd Ones, whom none. George Crabbe. **ELP** *Fr.* Sir Eustace Grey. **SP-CrabG**

Then, to conclude these pleasant acts. Andrew Marvell. **CBNP** *Fr.* Upon Appleton House [To My Lord Fairfax]. **CP-MarvA**

Then to the well-trod stage anon. Mirth and Poetry. John Milton. **EPCY** *Fr.* L'Allegro. **CP-MiltJ**

Then ultimately asylum is the soul. Hayden Carruth. *Fr.* The Asylum. **CP-CarHL**

Then unto him responding answered fleet-foot Achilles. Nourishment before Battle. Homer, *tr. by* George Meredith. **CP-MerG2** *Fr.* The Iliad.

Then Urizen wept & thus his lamentation poured forth. Urizen's Curse upon His Children. William Blake. **TW** *Fr.* Vala; or The Four Zoas. **CP-BlakW**

Then Vera stopped at the flower called fireweed. Grace Paley. **CP-PaleG**

Then was I cast from out my state. Frenzy. George Crabbe. **NOBE** *Fr.* Sir Eustace Grey. **SP-CrabG**

Then Was My Neophyte. Dylan Thomas. **CP-ThomD**

Then was the faire Dodonian tree far seene. Joachim Du Bellay. *Fr.* The Visions of Bellay. **CP-Spens**

Then was there heard a most celestial sound. The Rivers Come to the Hall of Proteus for the Marriage of the Thames and the Medway. Edmund Spenser. **FaBoPP** *Fr.* The Faerie Queene. **CP-Spens**

Then we brought the lances down—then the trumpets blew. Rudyard Kipling. **CP-KiplR** *Fr.* The Light That Failed.

Then we stood where we could see. Nicholas Vachel Lindsay. *Fr.* Bryan, Bryan, Bryan, Bryan. **CP-LindV**

Then what do I seek? The Challenge. William Everson. **SP-EverW**

Then, what do you say to the poem of Mizpah? Dialogue between Father and Daughter. Robert Browning. **CP-BroR2**

Then what is the answer?—Not to be deluded by dreams. The Answer. Robinson Jeffers. **CP-JefR2**

Then, when an hour was twenty hours, he lay. Drowned under Grass. Stephen Spender. *Fr.* Lost Days. **CP-SpenS**

Then when I Am Thy Captive, Talk of Chains. John Milton. **WHA** *Fr.* Book IV. **OAEL-1** *Fr.* Paradise Lost. **CP-MiltJ**

Then when the ample season. Then. Richard Wilbur. **CP-WilbR**

Then, when the child was gone. Empty House. Stephen Spender. **CP-SpenS**

Then when the flame forked like a sudden path. Log. James Merrill. **SP-MerrJ**

Then Whose Shall Those Things Be? Christina Georgina Rossetti. **CP-RosC2**

Then will I not repine. Emily Dickinson. **SP-DickE**

"Then write," she said. "By all means, if that's." Assignment. Hayden Carruth. **CP-CarHS**

Thence forward by that painfull way they pas. Edmund Spenser. **OAEL-1** *Fr.* The Faerie Queene. **CP-Spens**

Thence passing forth, they shortly do arive. Edmund Spenser. **FiP** *Fr.* The Bower of Bliss. **PoEL-1** *Fr.* The Faerie Queene. **CP-Spens**

Theniel Menzies' Bony Mary. Robert Burns. **CP-BurnR**

Theodore and Honoria, From [Fables Ancient and Modern from] Boccace. John Dryden. **SP-DrydJ**

Disdain Punished. **EBNV; NOSC**

Theogony. Hesiod, *tr. fr.* Greek.

Bacchus and Ariadne. **CP-BroEB**, *tr. by* Elizabeth Barrett Browning; **SP-LongH** *Fr.* Tales of a Wayside Inn.

Theologian's Tale: Torquemada, The. Henry Wadsworth Longfellow. **SP-LongH** *Fr.* Tales of a Wayside Inn.

Theological Definition, A. George Oppen. **CP-OppeG**

Theology. Paul Laurence Dunbar. **CP-DunbP**

Theology. Ted Hughes. **SP-HughT**

The(oo)is / lOOk / (aliv / e)e / yes. Edward Estlin Cummings. **CP-CummE**

Theophilus. Edwin Arlington Robinson. **CP-RobiE**

Theorem. Carl Sandburg. **CP-SandC**

Theory, A. Thomas McGrath. **SP-McGrT**

Theory. Wallace Stevens. **CP-StevW**

Theory Center. Archie Randolph Ammons. **SP-AmmoA**

Theory if you hold it hard enough, A. Etherealizing. Robert Frost. **CP-FrosR**

Theory of Evil. Robert Earl Hayden. **CP-HaydR**

Theory of Flight. Muriel Rukeyser. **CP-RukeM**

Theory of Nato-geography as Advanced by the Tiaphidian Man, With a Comment on the Character of His Penal System, A. Kenneth Patchen. **CP-PatcK**

Theory of Poetry. Archibald MacLeish. **CP-MacLA**

Theory of Prayer. Thomas Merton. **CP-MertT**

Theory of Prosody, A. Philip Levine. **SP-LeviP**

Theory of Regress. Charles Tomlinson. **CP-TomlC**

Theory of the Universe, A. Tom Clark. **SP-ClarT**

Theory of Truth. Robinson Jeffers. **CP-JefR2**

Ther' ain't no use in all this strife. An Easy-Goin' Feller. Paul Laurence Dunbar. **CP-DunbP**

Ther is, at the west syde of Ytaille. The Clerk's Tale. Geoffrey Chaucer. *Fr.* The Canterbury Tales. **CP-ChauG**

Ther nys so high comfort to my pleasaunce. The Complaint of Venus. Geoffrey Chaucer. **CP-ChauG**

Ther was, as telleth Titus Livius. The Physician's Tale. Geoffrey Chaucer. *Fr.* The Canterbury Tales. **CP-ChauG**

There / are / Black men in the south. On Seeing the Black Male as #1 Sex Object in America. Etheridge Knight. **SP-KnigE**

"There. . . ." Robert Creeley. **CP-CreeR**

There. Robert Creeley. **CP-CreeR**

There. Daniel Gerard Hoffman. **SP-HoffD**

There / is / no moon tonight. The Keeping of a Promise. Etheridge Knight. **SP-KnigE**

There / is someone I can bear. W. S. Landor. Marianne Craig Moore. **CP-MoorM**

There. Howard Nemerov. **CP-NemeH**

There / Why / There / Why. One or Two. I've Finished. Gertrude Stein. **CP-SteiG**

There. William Butler Yeats. **CP-YeatW**

There ain't no pay beneath the sun. One More Round. Maya Angelou. **SP-AngeM**

There all the barrel-hoops are knit. There. William Butler Yeats. **CP-YeatW**

There all the golden codgers lay. News for the Delphic Oracle. William Butler Yeats. **CP-YeatW**

There also was a nun, a Prioress. Geoffrey Chaucer. *See* Ther[e] was also a Nonne [*or* nun], a Prioress[e].

There always is another way to say it. Saying. Frederick Morgan. **SP-MorgF**

There, an evening star, there again. Above. Tabula Rasa. Hayden Carruth. **CP-CarHS**

There are / No clocks on the wall. End. Langston Hughes. **SP-HughL**

There are afternoons in jazz. The Art of Benny Carter. Al Young. **CP-YounA**

There are astronomers, mathematicians, men of science, who believe. Explosion. Robinson Jeffers. **CP-JefR3**

There are beggars in Iran and Araby. Ralph Waldo Emerson. **CP-EmerR**

There are borders toward which. Almost Everyone. Stephen Dunn. **SP-DunnS**

There are brilliant heights of sorrow. Paul Laurence Dunbar. **CP-DunbP**

There are certain things—as, a spider, a ghost. A Sea Dirge. "Lewis Carroll." **CP-CarrL**

There are cloudlets and things of cool silver in our dream. Spaulding and Francois. Gwendolyn Brooks. *Fr.* A Catch of Shy Fish. **SP-BrooG**

There are depths even in a household. The Whale in the Blue Washing Machine. John Haines. **SP-HainJ**

There Are Different Gardens. Carl Sandburg. **CP-SandC**

There are different ways of dying without. After the Revolution. Marilyn Hacker. **SP-HackM**

There are few of us now, soon. For Eli Jacobson. Kenneth Rexroth. **SP-RexrK**

There are few songs for domesticity. Hidden Ice. Louis MacNeice. **CP-MacNL**

There are fields beyond. The world there obeys. The Survivor among Graves. Randall Jarrell. **CP-JarrR**

There are five people in this room. Representing the Universe. Alice Walker. **CP-WalkA**

There are forked branches of trees. Little Sketch. Carl Sandburg. **CP-SandC**

There are four good legs to my Father's Chair. My Father's Chair. Rudyard Kipling. **CP-KiplR**

There are four men mowing down by the Isar. A Youth Mowing. David Herbert Lawrence. **CP-LawrD**

There are four vibrators, the world's exactest clocks. Four Quartz Crystal Clocks. Marianne Craig Moore. **CP-MoorM**

There are hikers on all the roads—. Pindar is Dead. Louis MacNeice. *Fr.* Out of the Picture. **CP-MacNL**

There are (I scarce can think it, but [I] am told). The First Satire of the Second Book of Horace [Imitated]. Alexander Pope. **CP-PopeA**

There are in our existence spots of time. William Wordsworth. **PoEL-4; TOF**, book 12, *ll.* 208–335; **PoE** *Fr.* Imagination and Taste, How Impaired and Restored. **EnRP** *Fr.* The Prelude; Growth of a Poet's Mind [1850 vers.]. **CP-WorW3**

(Spots of Time.) **PoE**, book 12, *ll.* 208–282;

There are leaves. We Are Leaves. James Schuyler. **CP-SchuJ**

There are lights soft as milk striking. Winter Fires. David St. John. **SP-StJoD**

There are lilies for her sisters. To the End. Christina Georgina Rossetti. **CP-RosC3**

There are lips as strange and soft. Child Face. Carl Sandburg. **CP-SandC**

There are longings to kill that cannot be seen. As the Asian War Begins. Robert Bly. **SP-BlyR**

There are lovers who recall that. Part of the Forest. George Oppen. **CP-OppeG**

There are many hearts baking on this altar. *see also* Altar, The. Leonard Cohen. **CP-CoheL**

There are many intricate pieces of workmanship. Instruments. Richard Eberhart. *Fr.* Aesthetics after War. **CP-EberR**

There are many monsters that a glassen surface. The Octopus. James Merrill. **SP-MerrJ**

There are many more Good Fridays. Unkept Good Fridays. Thomas Hardy. **CP-HardT**

There are many single women in the world. Imagination and Reality. Charles Bukowski. **SP-BukC1**

There are many sounds which are neither music nor voice. The Ear. Louis MacNeice. **CP-MacNL**

There are many ways now of being a young man. Career. Kay Boyle. **CP-BoylK**

There are many ways to die. History among the Rocks. Robert Penn Warren. **CBCWP; GOA; MoAmPo; MoVE** *Fr.* Kentucky Mountain Farm. **SP-WarrR**

There are many who think of Quintia in terms of beauty. Catullus. *See* Carmen 86: "We have heard of Quintia's beauty. To me she is tall, slender."

There are masses, and there are classes. Masses and Classes. David Herbert Lawrence. **CP-LawrD**

There are memories everywhere then. Rememberd, we go out, as in. Robert Duncan. **SP-DuncR** *Fr.* The Structure of Rime.

There are men and. Hey Red! William Carlos Williams. **CP-WilW2**

There are moments a man turns from us. Drowning with Others. James Dickey. **CP-DickJ**

There are more accidents in the home than on the roads. Jenny Joseph. *Fr.* Life and Turgid Times of A. Citizen. **SP-JoseJ**

There are more than a hundred Turkish poems. The Eggplant Epithalamion. Erica Jong. **SP-JongE**

There are More Ways to Roast a Pig than Burning the House Down or You Can Always Stick Your Head in a Volcano. Ogden Nash. **CP-NashO**

There are never any suicides in the quarter among people one knows. Montparnasse. Ernest Hemingway. **CP-HemiE**

There are no angels yet. Gabriel. Adrienne Rich. **CP-RicAE**

There are no bears among the roses. The Virgin Carrying a Lantern. Wallace Stevens. **CP-StevW**

There are no beaten paths to Glory's height. The Path. Paul Laurence Dunbar. **CP-DunbP**

There are no colours in the fairest sky. Walton's Book of Lives. William Wordsworth. *Fr.* Ecclesiastical Sonnets. **CP-WorW2**

There are no constellations, only. Far-Off Light. Daniel Gerard Hoffman. **SP-HoffD**

There are no crosses / on the Hopi graves. They lie. A Death in the Desert. Charles Tomlinson. **CP-TomlC**

There are no dry bones. The Bones of My Father. Etheridge Knight. **SP-KnigE**

There Are No Gods. David Herbert Lawrence. **CP-LawrD**

There are no handles upon a language. Languages. Carl Sandburg. **CP-SandC**

There are no imperfect answers from perfect data. Requisitioning. John Ciardi. **SP-CiarJ**

There are no leaders to lead us to honour, and yet without leaders we sally. The Spies' March. Rudyard Kipling. **CP-KiplR**

There are no leaf-eating snakes. Bad Mouth. Margaret Atwood. **SP-AtwM2**

There are no losses. Kenneth Patchen. **CP-PatcK**

There are no more shopping days to Christmas. Eve. Howard Nemerov. **CP-NemeH**

There Are No Names. Marsden Hartley. **CP-HartM**

There are no peacocks in my house. Etude. Frederick Morgan. **SP-MorgF**

There are no roads. What is Life? John Haines. **SP-HainJ**

There are no roads but the frost. Old Age Compensation. James Wright. **CP-WrigJ**

There Are No Rocks and Trees. Marsden Hartley. **CP-HartM**

There are no rooms here. So Be It. Kenneth Patchen. **CP-PatcK**

There are no stars tonight. My Grandmother's Love Letters. Hart Crane. **CP-CranH**

There Are No Such Trees in Alpine, California. John Haines. **SP-HainJ**

There are no tigers. Alice Walker. **CP-WalkA**

There Are No Traitors. Leonard Cohen. **CP-CoheL**

There are not leaves enough to cover the face. United Dames of America. Wallace Stevens. **CP-StevW**

There are not many meteors over the flat country. Farmers. James Dickey. **CP-DickJ**

There are only a few games played by a pair. Essay on Chess. Karl Shapiro. **SP-ShapK**

There are only two men I can really. Playing It Out. Charles Bukowski. **SP-BukC3**

There are only two things now. New Year's Eve. David Herbert Lawrence. **CP-LawrD**

There are peaches, you know, and there are girls. Sunripe. Jenny Joseph. *Fr.* Life and Turgid Times of A. Citizen. **SP-JoseJ**

There are people so near nothing. Anywhere and Everywhere People. Carl Sandburg. **CP-SandC**

There are people there, beyond the Rockies. Beyond the Rockies. David Herbert Lawrence. **CP-LawrD**

There are people whose sex. Saint Sex. Charles Kenneth Williams. **CP-WillC; SP-WillC**

There are places / garden. My Mother: 33 Years Later. Grace Paley. **CP-PaleG**

There are places I go when I am strong. Haunts. Carl Sandburg. **CP-SandC**

There are places I remember. In My Life. The Beatles. **CP-Beatl**

There are portraits and still-lifes. Paring the Apple. Charles Tomlinson. **CP-TomlC**

There are possibly 2 1/2 or impossibly 3. Edward Estlin Cummings. **CP-CummE**

There are rivers lapsing down. River Thames (?). Christina Georgina Rossetti. **CP-RosC3**

There Are Roughly Zones. Robert Frost. **CP-FrosR**

There are several attitudes towards Christmas. The Cultivation of Christmas Trees. Thomas Stearns Eliot. **CP-ElioT**

There are several differences between me and Samuel Taylor Coleridge. I Can Hardly Wait for the Sandman. Ogden Nash. **CP-NashO**

There are several generally recognized grounds for divorce. Boop-Boop-Adieup, Little Group! Ogden Nash. **CP-NashO**

There are several people who I can claim I am glad I am not. How Do You Say Ha-Ha in French. Ogden Nash. **CP-NashO**

There are several robins here. Immature Pebbles. Louis Zukofsky. *Fr.* 29 Songs. **CP-ZukLS**

There are several things in life that keep me guessing. Unanswered by Request. Ogden Nash. **CP-NashO**

There are similarities / I notice: that the hills. Journey to the Interior. Margaret Atwood. **SP-AtwM1**

There are 6 doors. Edward Estlin Cummings. **CP-CummE**

There are sixteen bodies of lifeless men. Georgia Nightmare. Edwin Rolfe. **CP-RolfE**

There are sleeping dreams and waking dreams. A Ballad of Boding. Christina Georgina Rossetti. **CP-RosC2**

There are so many roots to the tree of anger. Who Said It Was Simple. Audre Lorde. **SP-LordA**

There are so many things I want. Margaret Atwood. *Fr.* Circe / Mud Poems. **SP-AtwM1**

There are so many tictoc. Edward Estlin Cummings. **CP-CummE**

There are some birds in these valleys. The Decoys. Wystan Hugh Auden. **CP-AudeW**

There are some coasts. Tides. Jenny Joseph. **SP-JoseJ**

There are some days the happy ocean lies. Seascape. Stephen Spender. **CP-SpenS**

There are some fiestas that the moment you arrive at them you. There's Always an Ubblebub. Ogden Nash. **CP-NashO**

There are some heights in Wessex, shaped as if by a kindly hand. Wessex Heights. Thomas Hardy. **CP-HardT**

There are Some Men. Leonard Cohen. **CP-CoheL**

There are some nights when. Insomniac. Maya Angelou. **SP-AngeM**

There are some people of whom I would certainly like to be one. A Stitch Too Late Is My Fate. Ogden Nash. **CP-NashO**

There are some people who are very resourceful. Hearts of Gold. Ogden Nash. **CP-NashO**

There are some qualities—some incorporate things. Sonnet—Silence. Edgar Allan Poe. **CP-PoeEd**

There are some words carry a curse with them:. Forbidden Words. Robert Ranke Graves. **CP-GravR**

There Are Sounds. Charles Olson. **CP-OlsoC**

There are still clefts cut in the earth. Staffordshire Red. Roy Fisher. **SP-FishR**

There are streams which are famous in history's story. The Vale of the Merrimac. John Greenleaf Whittier. **CP-WhitJ**

There are Such Springlike Nights. Kadya Molodovsky, *tr. fr. Yiddish by* Adrienne Rich. **CP-RicAE**

There are sunsets who whisper a good-by. Sunsets. Carl Sandburg. **CP-SandC**

There are Sweets of Pathos. Emily Dickinson. **SP-DickE**

There are the Alps. What is there to say about them? On the Fly-Leaf of Pound's Cantos. Basil Bunting. **CP-BuntB**

There are the feminine aspects. Of This All Things. . . . George Oppen. **CP-OppeG**

There are the few we hear of. Linoleum. Tess Gallagher. **SP-GallT**

There Are the Local. . . . Hart Crane. **CP-CranH**

There are things / We live among "and to see them". George Oppen. *Fr.* Of Being Numerous. **CP-OppeG**

There Are Things I Tell to No One. Galway Kinnell. **SP-KinnG**

There are those days, vivid and pure. Pays Perdu. Jean Garrigue. **SP-GarrJ**

There are those to whom place is unimportant. The Rose. Theodore Roethke. **BiP; NOBA; NYBP; PPoe; TRP** *Fr.* North American Sequence. **CP-RoetT**

There are those who speak of confusion today. Under the Capitol Dome. Carl Sandburg. **CP-SandC**

There are those who teach only the sweet lessons of peace and safety. Lessons. Walt Whitman. **CP-WhitW**

There are three degrees of bliss. The Jester. Rudyard Kipling. **CP-KiplR**

There are three folk driving in a quaint old chaise. The Interloper. Thomas Hardy. **CP-HardT**

There are three names. National Security. Archibald MacLeish. **CP-MacLA**

There are times of archaic splendor that you saw. Van Black, an Old Farmer in His Dell. Richard Eberhart. **CP-EberR**

There are times when. May Sarton. **SRLS,** *sect.* 1; *Fr.* The Invocation to Kali. **SP-SartM**

There are too many of you. Presidential Address to a Party of Exiles. Howard Nemerov. **CP-NemeH**

There Are Too Many People. David Herbert Lawrence. **CP-LawrD**

There are too many poems. Cat. Kenneth Rexroth. **SP-RexrK** *Fr.* A Bestiary. **SP-RexrK**

There are too many poems where. April Fool. Siv Cedering Fox. **SP-CedeS**

There are too many waterfalls here; the crowded streams. Questions of Travel. Elizabeth Bishop. **CP-BishE**

There are tracks which belong to wheels. In the Lupanar at Pompeii. James Dickey. **CP-DickJ**

There Are Two. Kenneth Patchen. **CP-PatcK**

There are two classes of men. Classes. David Herbert Lawrence. **CP-LawrD**

There are two different kinds, I believe, of human attraction. Claude to Eustace. Arthur Hugh Clough. **GTBS-6** *Fr.* Amours de Voyage. **SP-ClouA**

There are two facing peacocks. Chenille. James Dickey. **CP-DickJ**

There are two islands / at least, they do not exclude each other. Margaret Atwood. *Fr.* Circe / Mud Poems. **SP-AtwM1**

There are two kinds of people who blow through life like a breeze. I Have It on Good Authority. Ogden Nash. **CP-NashO**

There are two Mays. Emily Dickinson. **CP-DickE**

There are two Ripenings—one—of sight. Emily Dickinson. **CP-DickE**

There are two sides to it. A Waterfront for Allan Ross MacDougall. Kay Boyle. **CP-BoylK**

There are two trees in a lonely field. Emily Brontë. **CP-BronE**

There are two vaults left in St. Mark's-on-the-Bouwerie. During the Passaic Strike of 1926. Louis Zukofsky. *Fr.* 29 Poems. **CP-ZukLS**

There are two white captains. The Sailor in Africa. Rita Dove. **SP-DoveR**

There are vast realms of consciousness still undreamed of. Terra Incognita. David Herbert Lawrence. **CP-LawrD**

There are weeds that flower forth in fall. Seedtime. Denise Levertov. **CP-LeveD**

There are, who to my person pay their court. Alexander Pope. **OBF** *Fr.* Epistle to Dr. Arbuthnot. **CP-PopeA**

There are whose study is of smells. *after* Horace, *Book* 5, *Ode* 3. Rudyard Kipling. **CP-KiplR**

There are wolves in the next room waiting. The Wolves. Allen Tate. **CP-TateA**

There are words like *Freedom*. Refugee in America. Langston Hughes. **SP-HughL**

There are worse things than. Oh, Yes. Charles Bukowski. **SP-BukC3**

There as I bent above the broken pot from the mesa pueblo. Pueblo Pot. Edna St. Vincent Millay. **CP-MillE**

There at Dusk I Found You. Edna St. Vincent Millay. **CP-MillE**

There at the story's close. Peter. Richard Wilbur. **CP-WilbR**

There await men when they die. Thomas Merton. *Fr.* The Legacy of Herakleitos. **CP-MertT**

There be none of Beauty's daughters. Stanzas for Music. Byron. **CP-Byron**

There be three Badgers on a mossy stone. The Three Badgers. "Lewis Carroll." **CP-CarrL** *Fr.* Sylvie and Bruno.

There be two men of all mankind. Two Men. Edwin Arlington Robinson. **CP-RobiE**

There be who say, in these enlightened days. Byron. **EPCY** *Fr.* English Bards and Scotch Reviewers. **CP-Byron**

There Blooms No Bud in May. Walter de la Mare. **CP-DeLaW**

There, breathless, with his digging nails he clung. Byron. **OxAEP-2** *Fr.* Canto the Second. *Fr.* Don Juan. **CP-Byron**

There by some wrinkled stones round a leafless tree. The Twelve. Allen Tate. **CP-TateA**

There came a boy. The Last Arrow. Walter de la Mare. **CP-DeLaW**

There came a Day at Summer's full. Emily Dickinson. **CP-DickE**

There came a night I slept for hate of day. It Was Not I. Phoebe Hesketh. **SP-HeskP**

There came a Wind like a Bugle. Emily Dickinson. **CP-DickE**

There came, for lack of sleep. New York in August. Donald Davie. **CP-DavDo**

There came one day soon. The Oldest Conversation. Kenneth Patchen. **CP-PatcK**

There came such clear opening of the night sky. Night Sky. Kathleen Jessie Raine. **SP-RainK**

There can be a brick, *incl. in* Of Being Numerous. George Oppen. *Fr.* A Language of New York. **CP-OppeG**

There can be a brick. George Oppen. *Fr.* Of Being Numerous. **CP-OppeG**

There can be certain potions. The Big Boots of Pain. Anne Sexton. **CP-SextA**

There can be no anniversary. To a Poet Who Read in Gloucester Before the Cape Ann Historical Literary and Scientific Society. Charles Olson. **CP-OlsoC**

There comes a warning like a spy. Emily Dickinson. **CP-DickE**

There comes an hour when begging stops. Emily Dickinson. **CP-DickE**

There could be a book without nations in its chapters. A Book of Resemblances. Robert Duncan. **SP-DuncR**

There died a myriad. Ezra Pound. **FF; FaBoEH; MoAmPo; NOBE; PoE; TRP; WaaP** *Fr.* Hugh Selwyn Mauberley. (Life and Contacts). **SP-PounE**

There dwells a mighty pair. Doom and She. Thomas Hardy. **CP-HardT**

There dwells a wife by the Northern Gate. The Sea-Wife. Rudyard Kipling. **CP-KiplR**

There dwelt a widow learned and devout. The Hearth Eternal. Nicholas Vachel Lindsay. **CP-LindV**

There fell a sudden rain. George Meredith. **CP-MerG2**

There floated the sounds of church-chiming. At the Wicket-Gate. Thomas Hardy. **CP-HardT**

There goes the Lady Vi. How well. Lady Vi. Thomas Hardy. **CP-HardT**

There goes the Wapiti. The Wapiti. Ogden Nash. **CP-NashO**

There grew a goodly tree him faire beside. Balme. Edmund Spenser. **CH** *Fr.* The Faerie Queene. **CP-Spens**

There grew an aged tree on the green. The Oak and the Brere. Edmund Spenser. **OBSC** *Fr.* February. *Fr.* The Shepheardes [*or* Shepeards *or* Shepherd's] Calender. **CP-Spens**

There grew, within a favour'd vale. The Glastonbury Thorn. George Meredith. **CP-MerG2**

There grows a bonie brier-bush in our kail-yard. Robert Burns. **CP-BurnR**

There had been no such music here until. Girl with 'Cello. May Sarton. **SP-SartM**

There had been quiet all that afternoon. In Emanuel's Nightmare: Another Coming of Christ. Gwendolyn Brooks. **SP-BrooG**

There had been years of Passion—scorching, cold. And There Was a Great Calm. Thomas Hardy. **CP-HardT**

There has been so much noise. Erinnyes. David Herbert Lawrence. **CP-LawrD**

There has to be a hero who is not. Homage to John L. Stephens. Donald Davie. **CP-DavDo**

There Has to Be a Jail for Ladies. Thomas Merton. **CP-MertT; SP-MertT**

There hasn't been a book like this. *see also* Death to This Book. Leonard Cohen. **CP-CoheL**

There hasn't been any rain. Sleeping Over. Charles Kenneth Williams. **CP-WillC**

There haunts in Time's bare house an active ghost. Polonius. Walter de la Mare. **CP-DeLaW**

There have been so many gods. Spiral Flame. David Herbert Lawrence. **CP-LawrD**

There have been thousands of Andy Adams. Carl Sandburg. *Fr.* The People, Yes. **CP-SandC**

There have been times when I well might have passed and the ending have come. Thomas Hardy. **OAEL-2** *Fr.* In Tenebris. **CP-HardT**

There have been two strangers. Strangers. May Sarton. **SP-SartM**

There Hugo Wolf is buried: fully formed. In a Viennese Cemetery. James Wright. **CP-WrigJ**

There I could never be a boy. Poem. Frank O'Hara. **SP-OharF**

There I was, here I am: a foot in air. A Picture in the Paper. Randall Jarrell. **CP-JarrR**

There in a bare place, in among the rocks. The Little Lough. John Hewitt. **CP-HewiJ**

There in New Guinea, by the grounded metal. The Baggage King. James Dickey. **CP-DickJ**

There in the lonely quarry where at dawn. Sonnet. John Hewitt. **CP-HewiJ**

There in the meadow where we'll lap the hay. Easter Flock. John Hewitt. **CP-HewiJ**

There, in the order of traffic. The Liberator Explodes. James Dickey. **CP-DickJ**

There is / a heart. Finally a Valentine. Louis Zukofsky. **CP-ZukLS**

There is / a silence. The Hole. Robert Creeley. **CP-CreeR**

There is / A welcome at the door to which no one comes? Angel Surrounded by Paysans. Wallace Stevens. **CP-StevW**

There Is. Robert Creeley. **CP-CreeR**

There is / One great society alone on earth. The Noble. William Wordsworth. **ChTr** *Fr.* France (Concluded). *Fr.* The Prelude; Growth of a Poet's Mind [1850 vers.]. **CP-WorW3**

There is a / moon sole. Edward Estlin Cummings. **CP-CummE**

There is a ballad rooted in the Glens. The True Smith of Tieveragh. John Hewitt. **CP-HewiJ**

There is a band of dull gold in the west, and say what you like. Sunset. David Herbert Lawrence. **CP-LawrD**

There is a band playing in the early night. Listen to the Band! David Herbert Lawrence. **CP-LawrD**

There is a bareness in the images. Substance and Shadow. John Hewitt. **CP-HewiJ**

There is a bird. Richard Shelton. *Fr.* Dry Season. **SP-ShelR**

There is a bird in the poplars. Metric Figure. William Carlos Williams. **CP-WilW1**

There is a bird who builds his mate a bower. The New Guinea Gardener Bird. Malcolm Lowry. **CP-LowrM**

There is a bird who, by his coat. The Jackdaw. Vincent Bourne, *tr. fr. Latin by* William Cowper. **CP-CowpW**

There is a blue star, Janet. Baby Toes. Carl Sandburg. **CP-SandC**

There is a bondage worse, far worse, to bear. William Wordsworth. **CP-WorW1**

There is a book, which we may call. A Manual. Vincent Bourne, *tr. fr. Latin by* William Cowper. **CP-CowpW**

There is a boy who walks with a fish. A Spring Song for Cagli. Charles Olson. **CP-OlsoC**

There is a Bread which You and I propose. Early Mass. Thomas Merton. **CP-MertT**

There Is a Budding Morrow in Midnight. Christina Georgina Rossetti. **CP-RosC2**

There is a certain power in his book. *see also* Commentary—The Altar. Leonard Cohen. **CP-CoheL**

There is a change—and I am poor. A Complaint. William Wordsworth. **CP-WorW1**

There is a child. He comes from far. A Story. Muriel Rukeyser. **CP-RukeM**

There is a city whose fair houses wizen. Amsterdam. James Merrill. **SP-MerrJ**

"There is a cloud," / Fairfield used to say. Gray Day. James Schuyler. **CP-SchuJ**

There is a cop who is both prowler and father. Rape. Adrienne Rich. **SP-RicA2**

There is a country to cross you will. For My Young Friends Who Are Afraid. William Stafford. **SP-StafW**

There is a Dark River. Jean Garrigue. **SP-GarrJ**

There is a deep brooding. My Arkansas. Maya Angelou. **SP-AngeM**

There is a despair one comes to. The Prejudice. Robert Creeley. **CP-CreeR**

There is a desperate lovliness to be seen. Bright Conversation with Saint-Ex. Carl Sandburg. **CP-SandC**

There is a door. The Door. Lewis Turco. **SP-TurcL**

There is a drear and lonely tract of hell. Supremacy. Edwin Arlington Robinson. **CP-RobiE**

There is a face I know too well. The Face. Stevie Smith. **CP-SmitS**

There is a fearful solitude. Forgot! Stevie Smith. **CP-SmitS**

There is a fearsome path in the West Country. High Devil, Deep Pit. Jenny Joseph. **SP-JoseJ**

There is a fenceless garden overgrown. The Garden. Edwin Arlington Robinson. **CP-RobiE**

There is a field through which I often pass. The Needless Alarm. William Cowper. **CP-CowpW**

There is a finished feeling. Emily Dickinson. **CP-DickE**

There is a fish that quivers in the pool. In the Beck. Kathleen Jessie Raine. **SP-RainK**

There is a flower that Bees prefer. Emily Dickinson. **CP-DickE**

There is a flower, the Lesser Celandine. William Wordsworth. **CP-WorW1** (Small Celandine, The.) **CP-WorW1**

There is a fountain fill'd with blood. Praise for the Fountain Opened. William Cowper. **ChIV-1; InPK** *Fr.* Olney Hymns. **CP-CowpW**

There is a garden grey. Myself. Walter de la Mare. **CP-DeLaW**

There Is a Garden in Her Face. Thomas Campion. **CP-CampT**

There is a gentle nymph not far from hence. Sabrina. John Milton. **OBS** *Fr.* Comus; a Masque Presented at Ludlow Castle.

There is a giving beyond giving. Song: Beyond Giving. Robert Ranke Graves. **CP-GravR**

There is a god in whom I do not believe. God the Eater. Stevie Smith. **CP-SmitS**

There is a goddess who walks shrouded by day. The Stars. John Gould Fletcher. **SP-FletJ**

There is a grain of sand in Lambeth which Satan cannot find. Thomas Merton. *Fr.* North. *Fr.* The Geography of Lograire. **CP-MertT**

There is a great amount of poetry in unconscious. Critics and Connoisseurs. Marianne Craig Moore. **CP-MoorM**

There is a tide in the affairs of men. Rudyard Kipling. **CP-KiplR** *Fr.* Kidnapped. *Fr.* Plain Tales from the Hills.

There is a tide in the affairs of men. Malcolm Lowry. *Fr.* The Comedian. **CP-LowrM**

There is a time to admit how much the sword decides. Ischia. Wystan Hugh Auden. **CP-AudeW**

There is a train inside this iris. Iris. David St. John. **SP-StJoD**

There is a travelling fury in his feet. The Progress. Robert Ranke Graves. **CP-GravR**

There is a truth that travel brings. Familiar Things. George Meredith. **CP-MerG2**

There is a very life in our despair. Byron. **NOBRP** *Fr.* Is thy face like thy mother's, my fair child. *Fr.* Childe Harold's Pilgrimage. **CP-Byron**

There is a vicious laughter of. Laughter of Steel 2. Marsden Hartley. **CP-HartM**

There is a villa avenue. Suburb. John Hewitt. **CP-HewiJ**

There is a Void, outside of Existence, which if entered into. Jerusalem; The Emanation of the Giant Albion. William Blake. **CP-BlakW**

There is a wall that runs right through the summer. Outside the Wall. Leonard Nathan. **SP-NathL**

There Is a War. Leonard Cohen. **CP-CoheL**

There is a warm and gentle atmosphere. Fragment: Love's Tender Atmosphere. Percy Bysshe Shelley. **CP-ShelP**

There Is a Way, *ad. fr.* Isaiah 35:8–10. Thomas Merton. **CP-MertT**

There is a way the moon looks into the timber at night. Timber Moon. Carl Sandburg. **CP-SandC**

There is a way to enter a field. Receiving the Stigmata. Rita Dove. **SP-DoveR**

There is a well into whose bottomless eye. Edna St. Vincent Millay. **CP-MillE**

There is a white wood house near Hampstead Heath. On Sending You a Lock of My Hair. Erica Jong. **SP-JongE**

There is a wind on 91st St. all night. For Sue's Birthday. Jim Carroll. **SP-CarrJ**

There is a wind that seeks the crevice. Our Desires. Jim Carroll. **SP-CarrJ**

There is a wind where the rose was. Autumn. Walter de la Mare. **CP-DeLaW**

There is a wolf in me. . . fangs pointed for tearing gashes. Wilderness. Carl Sandburg. **CP-SandC**

There is a woman on Michigan Boulevard keeps a parrot and goldfish. White Ash. Carl Sandburg. **CP-SandC**

There is a word / Which bears a sword. Emily Dickinson. **CP-DickE**

There is a word you often see, pronounce it as you may. Ubique. Rudyard Kipling. **CP-KiplR**

There is a world. "There. . . ." Robert Creeley. **CP-CreeR**

There is a world outside the one you know. Wilful-Missing. Rudyard Kipling. **CP-KiplR**

There is a world somewhere else that is unendurable. Dimensions. Charles Kenneth Williams. **CP-WillC; SP-WillC**

There is a Yew-tree, pride of Lorton Vale. Yew-Trees. William Wordsworth. **CP-WorW1**

There is a Zone whose even Years. Emily Dickinson. **CP-DickE**

There is, all around us, / this country. Humpbacks. Mary Oliver. **SP-OlivM**

There is almost no sound. . . only the redundant stir. Easter Season. Louise Glück. **SP-GlücL**

There Is Always a Little Wind. Ted Kooser. **SP-KoosT**

There is always enough daylight in hell to blind;. Sunrise. Robert Lowell. **SP-LoweR**

There is always something to be made of pain. Love Poem. Louise Glück. **SP-GlücL**

There is an ancient landscape of green branches. Geoffrey Hill. *Fr.* The Mystery of the Charity of Charles Péguy. **CP-HillG**

There is an ancient myth behind every place. A Garland of Red. Tom Clark. **SP-ClarT**

There is an arid Pleasure. Emily Dickinson. **CP-DickE**

There is an Eminence,—of these our hills. William Wordsworth. **CP-WorW1**

There is an emotion to which we are most of us adduced. A Clean Conscience Never Relaxes. Ogden Nash. **CP-NashO**

There is an evening coming in. Going. Philip Larkin. **CP-LarkP**

There Is an Evil in the Air. Richard Eberhart. **CP-EberR**

There is an excited nonserious species of snowstorm. Flurry. John Updike. **CP-UpdiJ**

There Is an Island. Marsden Hartley. **CP-HartM**

There is an island, wester'd in the main. Gerard Manley Hopkins. *Fr.* Fragments. **CP-HopkG**

There is an old / statue in the courtyard. Dawn at Saint Patrick's. Derek Mahon. **SP-MahoD**

There is an old pine tree facing Penobscot bay. Old Tree by the Penobscot. Richard Eberhart. **CP-EberR**

There is another Loneliness. Emily Dickinson. **CP-DickE**

There is another sky. Emily Dickinson. **CP-DickE**

There is another world above this one; or outside of this one. Through the Smoke Hole. Gary Snyder. **CP-SnydG**

There is at least one thing I would less rather have in the. What's the Matter, Haven't You Got Any Sense of Humor? Ogden Nash. **CP-NashO**

There is but one May in the year. Christina Georgina Rossetti. **CP-RosC2**

There is eating one's self. Sure There Is Food. Kenneth Patchen. **CP-PatcK**

There is enough treachery, hatred. The Genius of the Crowd. Charles Bukowski. **SP-BukC2**

There is far too much of the suburban classes. The Suburban Classes. Stevie Smith. **CP-SmitS**

There is, first, the road. The Townsfolk. Lewis Turco. **SP-TurcL**

There is for me no sweeter holiday. George Meredith. **CP-MerG2**

There is great peace to be earned. Malcolm's Messasge. Al Young. **CP-YounA**

There is greatness in you, greater than your shoulders. Eyes of a Boy. Edwin Rolfe. **CP-RolfE**

There is grey in your hair. Broken Dreams. William Butler Yeats. **CP-YeatW**

There is her mother's letter on the table. These Words Also. Howard Nemerov. **CP-NemeH**

There is in age. Guest Room. George Oppen. **CP-OppeG**

There is in all the sons of men. Ralph Waldo Emerson. **CP-EmerR**

There is in all things an invisible fecundity. Dawn. The Hour of Lauds. Thomas Merton. *Fr.* Hagia Sophia. **CP-MertT**

There is in souls a sympathy with sounds. The Winter Walk at Noon. William Cowper. *Fr.* The Task. **CP-CowpW**

There is in space a small black hole. Cosmic Comics. Howard Nemerov. **CP-NemeH**

There is indeed now reason for rejoicing. Song. Edwin Rolfe. **CP-RolfE**

There is joy. Welcome Morning. Anne Sexton. **CP-SextA**

There is love, and it is a deep thing. Deeper Than Love. David Herbert Lawrence. **CP-LawrD**

There is love only. Variations. Robert Creeley. **CP-CreeR**

There is moonrise under your fingernail—. Guiffre's Nightmusic. Thomas McGrath. **SP-McGrT**

There is more to Fury. Crash. Allen Ginsberg. **CP-GinsA**

There is my country under glass. At the Tourist Centre in Boston. Margaret Atwood. **SP-AtwM1**

There is no architect. The House. Ralph Waldo Emerson. **CP-EmerR**

There is no beauty in New England like the boats. Product. George Oppen. **CP-OppeG**

There is no bravery in flight. The Acrobat. Siv Cedering Fox. **SP-CedeS**

There is no cause for love in such a script. Blue Movie. John Ciardi. **SP-CiarJ**

There is no "cure." Rationality. George Oppen. **CP-OppeG**

There is no decision. Nothing final. Snoqualmie. Richard Hugo. **CP-HugoR**

There is no difference between being raped. Rape Poem. Marge Piercy. **SP-PierM**

There is no distinction in the encounter, Sweet. Translation. William Carlos Williams. **CP-WilW2**

There is no drug can shock you into pain. To the Memory of John Wheelwright. Howard Nemerov. **CP-NemeH**

There is no dusk to be. An Eternity. Archibald MacLeish. **CP-MacLA**

There is no evil but can speak. Ralph Waldo Emerson. **CP-EmerR**

There is no evill that we do commit. Sin. Robert Herrick. **CP-HerrR**

There is no fall that wouldn't break itself. Afraid. Al Young. **CP-YounA**

There is no first, or last, in Forever. Emily Dickinson. **SP-DickE**

There is no first, or last, in Forever. Emily Dickinson. **SP-DickE**

There is no fool like an old fool. Fools. Robert Ranke Graves. **CP-GravR**

There is no Frigate like a Book. Emily Dickinson. **CP-DickE**

There is no God but God; he is all that exists. Robinson Jeffers. **CP-JefR3**

"There is no God," the foolish saith. Convinced by Sorrow. Elizabeth Barrett Browning. **BLRP; WBLP** *Fr.* The Cry of the Human. **CP-BroEB**

"There is no God," the wicked saith. Arthur Hugh Clough. **SP-ClouA** *Fr.* Dipsychus [and the Spirit].

There is no government so worthy as your son who fishes with you in silence beside the forest pool. Wendell Berry. *Fr.* To a Siberian Woodsman. **CP-BerrW**

There is no great and no small. History. Ralph Waldo Emerson.

There is no great and no small. Mottoes to "History." Ralph Waldo Emerson. **CP-EmerR** *Fr.* History.

There is no greater moon to contemplate. Carolina Moon. Al Young. **CP-YounA**

There is no instance that was not love. Gilbert Sorrentino. **SP-SorrG**

There Is No Language of Destruction. Philip Larkin. **CP-LarkP**

"There is no life worth living." The Royal Love Child. Marsden Hartley. **CP-HartM**

There is no loneliness:—no matter where. Edwin Arlington Robinson. *Fr.* Octaves. **CP-RobiE**

There is no longer any reason to confuse. Heads. James Dickey. **CP-DickJ**

There is no mail / There is no hope. Scribner's Sons. Malcolm Lowry. **CP-LowrM**

There is no man can take. Magician [Master]. Hilda Doolittle. **CP-DoolH**

There is no more for me to hope. La Revanche. Byron. **CP-Byron**

There is no name for brother. Hail to the Sons of Roosevelt. Nicholas Vachel Lindsay. **CP-LindV**

There Is No Natural Religion. William Blake. **CP-BlakW**

There is no night life in Spain. They stay up late but. Ernest Hemingway. **CP-HemiE** *Fr.* The Soul of Spain with McAlmon and Bird the Publishers.

There is now for us but always. Envoi. Robert Ranke Graves. **CP-GravR**

There is no one. This Is War. Leonard Cohen. **CP-CoheL**

There is no one here. Matisse: "The Red Studio." William DeWitt Snodgrass. **SP-SnodW**

There is no passion in my life. The Worm Turns. David Herbert Lawrence. **CP-LawrD**

There is no pity at sea. Jokes Amidships. Malcolm Lowry. **CP-LowrM**

There is no pity at sea. Jokes in the Galley. Malcolm Lowry. **CP-LowrM**

There is no place in paradise. Guillaume de Lorris *and* Jean de Meun. **PBBP** *Fr.* The Romance [*or* Romaunt] of the Rose. **CP-ChauG**

There is no place in this dark. Radiant Silhouette II. John Yau. **SP-YauJo**

"There is no place to turn," she said. The Sensualists. Theodore Roethke. **CP-RoetT**

There is no poetry when you live there. Malcolm Lowry. **CP-LowrM**

There is no point in work. Work. David Herbert Lawrence. **CP-LawrD**

There is no R in the month of May. What, No Oysters? Ogden Nash. **CP-NashO**

There is no race of men. Boethius, *tr. fr. Latin.* **MLL,** *tr. by* Helen Waddell; *Fr.* Consolation of Philosophy, The ("De Consolacione Philosophie"). **CP-ChauG**

There is no reason for the surcharge to bother you. Unctuous Platitudes. John Ashbery. **SP-AshbJ**

There Is No River Which Is Called Lethe. Charles Olson. **CP-OlsoC**

There is no sign-post to say. Hilda Doolittle. **AnAn** *Fr.* Sigil. **CP-DoolH**

There is no Silence in the Earth—so silent. Emily Dickinson. **CP-DickE**

There is no sinning against God, what does God care about sin! God and the Holy Ghost. David Herbert Lawrence. **CP-LawrD**

There is no sky today. Echoes of birds. Counterparts. Stephen Dobyns. **SP-DobyS**

There is no sorrow / Time heals never. Away. Walter de la Mare. **CP-DeLaW**

There is no substitute for mind. We Never Close. Dabney Stuart. **SP-StuaD**

There Is No Time. "Lou Reed." **SP-ReedL**

There is no warning rattle at the door. A Plagued Journey. Maya Angelou. **SP-AngeM**

There is no way here, shepherds, read the wooden sign. Eclogue by a Five-Barred Gate. Louis MacNeice. **CP-MacNL**

There is no way out. The Habitation. Lewis Turco. **SP-TurcL**

There Is No Way Out. David Herbert Lawrence. **CP-LawrD**

There is no weather in my room. Ward F4. Phoebe Hesketh. **SP-HeskP**

There is no where in you a paradise that is no place and there. The Fall. Thomas Merton. **CP-MertT; SP-MertT**

There is nobody on the road. The Wanderer. Thomas Hardy. **CP-HardT**

There is none like her, none. Tennyson. **FaBoEn; OBNC** *Fr.* I have led her home, my love, my only friend. **CBLP; ChER; EBVV; ELP; FiP; MeMBP; NAEL-2; NOBVV** *Fr.* Maud [A Monodrama]. **CP-TennA**

There Is None, O None but You. Thomas Campion. **CP-CampT**

There is not much about the hamster. The Hamster. Ogden Nash. *Fr.* The Astigmatic Naturalist. **CP-NashO**

There is not much that I can do. At the Railway Station, Upway. Thomas Hardy. **CP-HardT**

There is not so much Life as talk of Life. Emily Dickinson. **SP-DickE**

There is nothing / to turn from. Going. Robert Creeley. **CP-CreeR**

There is nothing false in thee. Kenneth Patchen. **CP-PatcK**

There is nothing for Death. An Empty Place. Ted Kooser. **SP-KoosT**

There is nothing more perky. The Turkey. Ogden Nash. **CP-NashO**

There is nothing more that they can do. Easter Even. Christina Georgina Rossetti. **CP-RosC3**

There is nothing now. To learn. The Fortress. Louise Glück. **SP-GlücL**

There is nothing sweeter than Honor, but Love. Emily Dickinson. **SP-DickE**

There is nothing to be afraid of. Night Poem. Margaret Atwood. **SP-AtwM2**

There is nothing to be said for you. Guard. To Statecraft Embalmed. Marianne Craig Moore. **CP-MoorM**

There is nothing to look at anymore. Tourists. David Herbert Lawrence. **CP-LawrD**

There is nothing to save, now all is lost. Nothing to Save. David Herbert Lawrence. **CP-LawrD**

There is now not a single. Winter Scene. Archie Randolph Ammons. **SP-AmmoA**

There is one battle-field whereon we fall. Edwin Arlington Robinson. *Fr.* Octaves. **CP-RobiE**

There is one country / and no shame to it. A Letter to Francis Picabia. Kay Boyle. **CP-BoylK**

There is one country and no shame to it. A Letter to Archibald Craig. Kay Boyle. **CP-BoylK**

There is one devil in the lexicon. Merax & Mullin. Wystan Hugh Auden. **CP-AudeW**

There is one fault that I must find with the twentieth century. Put Back Those Whiskers, I Know You. Ogden Nash. **CP-NashO**

There is one form of life to which I unconditionally surrender. Oh, Please Don't Get Up! Ogden Nash. **CP-NashO**

There is one Mind, one omnipresent Mind. Samuel Taylor Coleridge. **WGRP** *Fr.* Religious Musings. **CP-ColeS**

There is one phase of life that I have never heard discussed in any seminar. Who Understands Who Anyhow? Ogden Nash. **CP-NashO**

There is one story and one story only. To Juan at the Winter Solstice. Robert Ranke Graves. **CP-GravR**

There is one that has a head without an eye. Christina Georgina Rossetti. **CP-RosC2**

There is one thing I do not understand. Do Sphinxes Think? Dorothy Nash. **CP-NashO**

There is one thing that ought to be taught in all the colleges. Just Keep Quiet and Nobody Will Notice. Ogden Nash. **CP-NashO**

There Is One Who Watches. Kenneth Patchen. **CP-PatcK**

There is only one horse on the earth. Carl Sandburg. *Fr.* Timesweep. **CP-SandC**

There is only one love. Sappho, Be Comforted. William Carlos Williams. **CP-WilW2**

There Is Only One of Everything. Margaret Atwood. **SP-AtwM1**

There Is Only One Story. Erica Jong. **SP-JongE**

There is only time to say the first word. Meetings Like Hungry Beaks. Marge Piercy. **SP-PierM**

There is piping on the hills of Caledonia. Canticle for October. Marsden Hartley. **CP-HartM**

There is pleasure in the wet, wet clay. Rudyard Kipling. **CP-KiplR** *Fr.* The Naulahka.

There Is Rain in Me. David Herbert Lawrence. **CP-LawrD**

There is rust in my mouth. The Lost Lie. Anne Sexton. **CP-SextA**

There is silence that saith, "Ah, me!" Golden Silences. Christina Georgina Rossetti. **CP-RosC2**

There is so little that is close and warm. Debris of Life and Mind. Wallace Stevens. **CP-StevW**

There is so little to remember. Sunday Evening Revery. Edwin Rolfe. **CP-RolfE**

There is so much that I can share with you. Wystan Hugh Auden. **CP-AudWJ**

There is so much to look forward to. Sonnet: Zimmer Imagines Himself Being Poet-in-Residence. Paul Zimmer. **SP-ZimmP**

There is some beauty in sorrow. Placing a $2 Bet for a Man Who Will Never Go to the Horse Races Any More. Diane Wakoski. **SP-WakoD**

There is some sentry at the rim of winter. The Messenger. Thomas Merton. **CP-MertT; SP-MertT**

There is something. Mobile of Birds. John Updike. **CP-UpdiJ**

There is something about a hornet. Hornets by the Sill. Richard Eberhart. **CP-EberR**

There is something about a Martini. A Drink with Something in It. Ogden Nash. **CP-NashO**

There is something going on. The Wave of the Nineties. James Liddy. *Fr.* Glass after Oblivion. **CP-LiddJ**

There is something terrible. Eleventh Avenue Racket. Carl Sandburg. **CP-SandC**

There is something there. The Hoarder. Anne Sexton. **CP-SextA**

There is something to be said for the Victorians. Don't Look Now. Ogden Nash. **CP-NashO**

There is sorrow enough in the natural way. The Power of the Dog. Rudyard Kipling. **CP-KiplR**

There Is Spit upon the Daisy Stem. Marsden Hartley. **CP-HartM**

There is stone in me that knows stone. Rock. Kathleen Jessie Raine. **SP-RainK**

There is such sorrow here in these old orchards. Threnody for Old Orchards. Louise McNeill. **SP-McNeL**

There is sweet music here that softer falls. Tennyson. **FaBV; FaFP; GGP; HeIP; ImPo; NOBE; OBEV; OBNC** *Fr.* The Lotus-Eaters.

(Choric Song: "There is sweet music here that softer falls.") **HeIP; OBNC**

(Choric Song of the Lotos-Eaters.) **ImPo**

(Choric Song of the Lotos-Eaters.) **FaFP**

(Song of the Lotus-Eaters.) **GGP; NOBE; OBEV**

There is that in love. The Sentence. Robert Creeley. **CP-CreeR**

There is that moment when. The Perfection. Charles Tomlinson. **CP-TomlC**

There is that sound like the wind. Summer. John Ashbery. **SP-AshbJ**

There is the bullet but there is no death. *see also* She Has Given Me the Bullet. Leonard Cohen. **CP-CoheL**

There is the hand that has nothing attached to it, no arm no chest. Kenneth Patchen. **CP-PatcK**

There is the mirror and in it the pale dawn. Man as Matter. Jenny Joseph. **SP-JoseJ**

There is the mirror and in it the pale dawn. Man as Matter (ISLAND; PHYSICS). Jenny Joseph. *Fr.* Man as Matter. **SP-JoseJ**

There is the organic connection, like leaves that belong to a tree. Fallen Leaves. David Herbert Lawrence. **CP-LawrD**

There is the other universe, of the heart of man. The Heart of Man. David Herbert Lawrence. **CP-LawrD**

There is the sense of neurotic coherence. Ode on Causality. Frank O'Hara. **SP-OharF**

There is the sign of / the flower—. The Rhyme. Robert Creeley. **CP-CreeR**

There is the silence of a copse or croft. Silences. Thomas Hardy. **CP-HardT**

There is the sky and here. Update. Stephen Dunn. **SP-DunnS**

There is the star bloom of the moss. Forest. Jean Garrigue. **SP-GarrJ**

There is the world, the dream, and the one law. Unscientific Postscript. Howard Nemerov. **CP-NemeH**

There is this cave. The Jewel. James Wright. **CP-WrigJ**

There is this infinite energy, the power of God forever working. Robinson Jeffers. **CP-JefR3**

There is this long still knife somehow like a. The Literary Life. Charles Bukowski. **SP-BukC2**

There is this other element that shines. The Night Pool. James Dickey. **CP-DickJ**

There is this white wall, above which the sky creates itself. Apprehensions. Sylvia Plath. **CP-PlatS**

There is too much stuff here. Not able to resist the spring. Jenny Joseph. *Fr.* Life and Turgid Times of A. Citizen. **SP-JoseJ**

There is unknown dust that is near us. Surprised by Evening. Robert Bly. **SP-BlyR**

There is—whoe'er will know a bawd aright. 1.8. Ovid. **CP-MarlC**, *tr. by* Christopher Marlowe; *Fr.* Elegies.

There it is, a block of leaping marble. Cousin Florence. Richard Eberhart. **CP-EberR**

"There it is!/ You play beside a death-bed like a child." Elizabeth Barrett Browning. **BrRo** *Fr.* Aurora Leigh. **CP-BroEB**

There it stands, though alas, what a little of her. The Marble Tablet. Thomas Hardy. **CP-HardT**

There it was, all along. Missing the Point. Adrienne Rich. **CP-RicAE**

There it was I saw what I shall never forget. The Fawn. Edna St. Vincent Millay. **CP-MillE**

There it was, word for word. The Poem That Took the Place of a Mountain. Wallace Stevens. **CP-StevW**

There late was One whose subtle being. The Sunset. Percy Bysshe Shelley. **CP-ShelP**

There lay she all her length and kiss'd his feet. Tennyson. **EBVVPR** *Fr.* Merlin and Vivien. *Fr.* Idylls of the King. **CP-TennA**

There let thy bleeding branch atone. Emily Brontë. **CP-BronE**

There Leviathan / Hugest of living creatures, on the deep. Leviathan. John Milton. **AmMo** *Fr.* Book VII. *Fr.* Paradise Lost. **CP-MiltJ**

There lies a vale in Ida, lovelier. Œnone. Tennyson. **CP-TennA**

There liv'd a man in yonder glen. Johnie Blunt. Robert Burns. **CP-BurnR**

There liv'd, as Authors tell, in Days of Yore. Geoffrey Chaucer. **OBVE** *Fr.* The Nun's Priest's Tale. **FHYEP; NAEL-1; NAWM-1; NoP; OAEL-1; TrGrPo** *Fr.* The Canterbury Tales. **CP-ChauG**

There liv'd in Lombardy, as authors write. *see also* Merchant's Tale, The. Geoffrey Chaucer. **CP-PopeA** *Fr.* The Canterbury Tales. **CP-ChauG**

There lived a carl in Kellyburnbraes. Kellyburnbraes. Robert Burns. **CP-BurnR**

There lurked a dread that you had gone. Emily Dickinson. **SP-DickE**

There might be working some kind of throwaway. Meadow Bridge. James Dickey. **CP-DickJ**

There mighte men the royal eagle find. Geoffrey Chaucer. **PB; PBBP** *Fr.* The Parlement of Foules. **CP-ChauG**

There mounts in squalls a sort of rusty mire. The Exile's Return. Robert Lowell. **SP-LoweR**

There mournful cypress grew in greatest store. The Garden of Proserpina. Edmund Spenser. **ChTr** *Fr.* The Faerie Queene. **CP-Spens**

There must be / Moments when we see right through. Poet. Archibald MacLeish. **CP-MacLA**

There must be a place. Alone and Not Alone. Carl Sandburg. **CP-SandC**

There must be more for you to do. Margaret Atwood. *Fr.* Circe / Mud Poems. **SP-AtwM1**

"There must be some way out of here," said the joker to the thief. All Along the Watchtower. "Bob Dylan." **CP-DylaB**

There must be time when you, too, dream. Memory. Richard Eberhart. **CP-EberR**

There must have been a moment after the expulsion. Long Story. Stephen Dobyns. **SP-DobyS**

There never breathed a man who, when his life. Gabriello Chiabrera, *tr. fr. Italian by* William Wordsworth. **CP-WorW1**

There never yet was honest man. Loving and Beloved. Sir John Suckling. **CP-SuckJ**

There never yet was woman made. Sir John Suckling. **CP-SuckJ**

There now, she's passed—that slight. Two Romantic Pieces. Hayden Carruth. **CP-CarHS**

There now, where the first crumb. Solitude. Charles Simic. **SP-SimiC**

There on the top of the down. June Bracken and Heather. Tennyson. **CP-TennA**

There once, on that goat island, I. Robert Penn Warren. **NOBA** *Fr.* Tiberius on Capri. **SP-WarrR**

There Once was a Cow with a Double Udder. The Cow. Theodore Roethke. **CP-RoetT**

There once was a girl named Myrtle. Myrtle. Theodore Roethke. **CP-RoetT**

There Once Was a Woman Who Put Her Head into an Oven. Charles Bukowski. **SP-BukC1**

There ought to be a wedding. Jingle. William Carlos Williams. **CP-WilW2**

There overtook me and drew me in. The Gum-Gatherer. Robert Frost. **CP-FrosR**

There pass the careless people. Alfred Edward Housman. **CP-HousA**

There pipes the woodlark, and the song[-]thrush there. Thomas Gray. **CP-GrayT**

(Couplet about Birds.) **CP-GrayT**

There, quick, a crowd was on me. Jugglers, giants. Her Dream, Half Remembered. Charles Olson. **CP-OlsoC**

There Remaineth Therefore a Rest. Christina Georgina Rossetti. **CP-RosC3**

There Remaineth Therefore a Rest for the People of God ("Come blessed sleep. . ."). Christina Georgina Rossetti. **CP-RosC3**

There Remaineth Therefore a Rest to the People of God ("Rest remains when all is done. . ."). Christina Georgina Rossetti. **CP-RosC2**

There resides in the grieving. Hafiz, *tr. by* Ralph Waldo Emerson. **CP-EmerR** *Fr.* Odes.

There rolls the deep where grew the tree. Tennyson. **FaBoRV; HAP; NOBE; OAEL-2; SeCePo; SeCeV** *Fr.* In Memoriam A. H. H. **CP-TennA**

There runs a crisscross pattern of small leaves. Ophelia. Walter de la Mare. **CP-DeLaW**

There runs a road by Merrow Down. Merrow Down. Rudyard Kipling. **CP-KiplR** *Fr.* Just-So Stories.

There runs no road except the towpath through the valley. The Canal, Froghall. Wystan Hugh Auden. **CP-AudWJ**

"There!" said a Stripling, pointing with meet pride. William Wordsworth. *Fr.* Poems Composed or Suggested During a Tour, in the Summer of 1833. **CP-WorW2**

There sailed out on the river, Conrad saw. Howard Nemerov. *Fr.* Runes. **CP-NemeH**

There sandy seems the golden sky. A Cliff Dwelling. Robert Frost. **CP-FrosR**

There Seemed a Strangeness. Thomas Hardy. **CP-HardT**

There seems a spectral power. Emily Dickinson. **SP-DickE**

There set out, slowly, for a Different World. A War. Randall Jarrell. **CP-JarrR; SP-JarrR**

There Shall Be No More Sea. Kathleen Jessie Raine. **SP-RainK**

There she goes up the street with her book in her hand. Martin's Puzzle. George Meredith. **CP-MerG1**

There she lay so still and pale. The Dead Bride. Christina Georgina Rossetti. **CP-RosC3**

There she was. While the flare. Anima. Hayden Carruth. **CP-CarHS**

There shines the moon, at noon of night. Emily Brontë. **CP-BronE**

There should be no despair for you. Emily Brontë. **CP-BronE**

There sinks the nebulous star we call the Sun. Tennyson. *Fr.* The Princess. **CP-TennA**

"O Swallow, Swallow, flying, flying South." **CBLP; PIP**

"Tears, idle tears, I know not what they mean." **AWP; EBEvV; EBVV; ELP; EnVR; FPL; FaBoRV; FaFP; FaPoR; FiP; GTBS-P; HAP; ImPo; InPS; InvP; LiTB; MeMBP; NAEL-2; NIP; NOBE; NoP; OAEL-2; OBNC; OXAEP-2; PPP; PIP; PoE; PoEL-5; Poetr; SCGP; TEP; TFi; TrGrPo; UnPo; WeW**

There, spring lambs jam the sheepfold. In air. Watercolor of Grantchester Meadows. Sylvia Plath. **CP-PlatS**

There stands a singer in the street. London by Lamplight. George Meredith. **CP-MerG1**

There stands death, a bluish liquid. *tr. fr. the German of* Rilke. Randall Jarrell. **CP-JarrR**

There still is coal in many houses. The Sixth Winter. Edwin Rolfe. **CP-RolfE**

There stood a hill not far whose grisly top. John Milton. *Fr.* Book I. **FHYEP; NAEL-1; OAEL-1; OxAEP-1** *Fr.* Paradise Lost. **CP-MiltJ**

There stood in her street a poor exile of Queen Je'n. George Meredith. **CP-MerG2**

There stood the citadel—nothing left. The Ants of Argos. Rita Dove. **SP-DoveR**

There swept adown that dreary glen. Emily Brontë. **CP-BronE**

There the companions of his fall, o'erwhelmed. Immortal Hate. John Milton. **NOBE** *Fr.* Book I. **FHYEP; NAEL-1; OAEL-1; OxAEP-1** *Fr.* Paradise Lost. **CP-MiltJ**

There the four doctors were, sitting in comical attitudes. After Fever. Jane Cooper. **SP-CoopJ**

There, the moon, just appearing. The Joy and Agony of Improvisation. Hayden Carruth. **CP-CarHS**

There the most daintie Paradise on ground. Edmund Spenser. **EBEV** *Fr.* The Faerie Queene. **CP-Spens**

There the voluptuous nightingales. Percy Bysshe Shelley. **PBBP** *Fr.* Prometheus Unbound. **CP-ShelP**

There, there, sir. You have every cause. Through the Nursery Window. William DeWitt Snodgrass. **SP-SnodW**

There, there where those black spruces crowd. Ragged Island. Edna St. Vincent Millay. **CP-MillE**

There there's a place where I can go. There's a Place. The Beatles. **CP-Beatl**

There they are. The Fury of Cocks. Anne Sexton. *Fr.* The Furies. **CP-SextA**

There they are, my fifty men and women. One Word More. Robert Browning. **CP-BroR1**

There they are now. Three Sentences for a Dead Swan. James Wright. **CP-WrigJ**

There they dismounting, drew their weapons bold. Britomart in the House of Busirane. Edmund Spenser. **FiP** *Fr.* The Legend of Britomartis, or of Chastitie. **NAEL-1** *Fr.* The Faerie Queene. **CP-Spens**

There they slept. They left the train. Muriel Rukeyser. **CP-RukeM**

There they were. April is the Saddest Month. William Carlos Williams. **CP-WilW2**

There they were. Charles Olson. **CP-OlsoC**

There they were, as if our memory hatched them. After a Killing. Seamus Heaney. *Fr.* Triptych. **SP-HeanS**

There they were, as if our memory hatched them. Triptych. Seamus Heaney. **SP-HeanS**

There 'tis the Shepherd's task the winter long. The Shepherd. William Wordsworth. **OBNC** *Fr.* Retrospect Love of Nature Leading to Love of Mankind. *Fr.* The Prelude; Growth of a Poet's Mind [1805 vers.]. **CP-WorW3**

There trudges one to a merry-making. An Autumn Rain-Scene. Thomas Hardy. **CP-HardT**

There used to be a rich old oaf. Geoffrey Chaucer. *See* The Miller's [*or* Milleres] Tale.

There used to be gods in everything, and now they've gone. The Companions. Howard Nemerov. **CP-NemeH**

There walked in 1942 into my big home running water. His Refugees. James Liddy. *Fr.* His Resplendent Neighbours. **CP-LiddJ**

There was / what we call "words." Speech. Carl Sandburg. **CP-SandC**

There was a battle in the north. Geordie [An Old Ballad]. *Unknown.* **CP-BurnR**

There was a bicycle, a fine. The Bicycle. Derek Mahon. *Fr.* Autobiographies. **SP-MahoD**

There was a big blond uncle-bear. Stanley Jasspon Kunitz. *Fr.* Journal for My Daughter. **CP-KuniS**

There Was a Bonie Lass. Robert Burns. **CP-BurnR**

There Was a Boy. William Wordsworth. **CP-WorW1; ChER; FHYEP; FaBoRV; MeMBP; NOBRP; OBRV; PoEL-4,** *book* 5, *ll.* 364–397; *Fr.* Books. *Fr.* The Prelude; Growth of a Poet's Mind [1850 vers.]. **CP-WorW3**

(Boy of Winander, The.) **PoE,** *book* 5, *ll.* 364–388.

(Winander Lake.) **FiP,** *book* 5, *ll.* 364–388.

There Was a Boy. William Wordsworth. **RB,** *book* 5, *ll.* 389–422; *Fr.* Books. *Fr.* The Prelude; Growth of a Poet's Mind [1805 vers.]. **CP-WorW3**

There was a boy in our town with long hair. The Long-Haired Boy. Shel Silverstein. **SP-SilS2**

There was a cat named Crazy Christian. To Crazy Christian. Ernest Hemingway. **CP-HemiE**

There was a Child. Courage, a Tale. Thom Gunn. **CP-GunnT**

There Was a Child Went Forth. Walt Whitman. **CP-WhitW**

"There was a child went forth every day." **RFM,** *ll.* 1–10;

There was a child went forth every day. Walt Whitman. **RFM,** *ll.* 1–10; *Fr.* There Was a Child Went Forth. **CP-WhitW**

There was a company of young folk living. Geoffrey Chaucer. *See* The Pardoner's Tale.

There was a contest. Peaches. Siv Cedering Fox. **SP-CedeS**

There was a day. The White Snake. Anne Sexton. **CP-SextA**

There was a dog called Clanworthy. Mrs. Blow and her Animals. Stevie Smith. **CP-SmitS**

There was a fair footman of Torrington Square. George Meredith. **CP-MerG2**

There was a Fairy—flake of winter. The Fairy in Winter. Walter de la Mare. **CP-DeLaW**

There was a frost. The Frozen Greenhouse. Thomas Hardy. **CP-HardT**

There Was a Gay Bird Named Christine. David Herbert Lawrence. **CP-LawrD**

There was a girl / who danced in the city that night. The Red Dance. Anne Sexton. **CP-SextA**

There was a glorious time. He Fears His Good Fortune. Thomas Hardy. **CP-HardT**

There was a gray rat looked at me. Rat Riddles. Carl Sandburg. **CP-SandC**

There was a great Captain with Mary in his sails. Christopher Columbus. Thomas Merton. **CP-MertT**

There was a green branch hung with many a bell. Dedication to a Book of Stories Selected from the Irish Novelists. William Butler Yeats. **CP-YeatW**

There was a happy land. Sanies II. Samuel Beckett. **CP-BeckS**

There was a hardness of stone. The Harsh Country. Theodore Roethke. **CP-RoetT**

There was a high majestic fooling. Laughing Corn. Carl Sandburg. **CP-SandC**

There was a joke. The Joke. Robert Creeley. **CP-CreeR**

There was a jolly gauger, a gauging he did ride. The Jolly Gauger. Robert Burns. **CP-BurnR**

There was a lad was born in Kyle. Robert Burns. **CP-BurnR**

There was a landau deep and wide. *parody of* W.M. Praed. Rudyard Kipling. **CP-KiplR** *Fr.* The Muse among the Motors.

There was a landscape in my childhood. Autobiography. Archibald MacLeish. **CP-MacLA**

There was a lass and she was fair. Ballad, A. Robert Burns. **CP-BurnR**

There was a lass, they ca'd her Meg. Duncan Davison. Robert Burns. **CP-BurnR**

There was a late autumn cricket. Buckwheat. Carl Sandburg. **CP-SandC**

There was a light inside the mountain. Saint Orpheus. James Liddy. **CP-LiddJ**

There was a lion in Judah. St Mark. David Herbert Lawrence. **CP-LawrD**

There was a little fliv of a woman loved one man and lost out. And she. Ambassadors of Grief. Carl Sandburg. **CP-SandC**

There was a little lawny islet. The Isle. Percy Bysshe Shelley. **CP-ShelP**

There was a little turtle. The Little Turtle. Nicholas Vachel Lindsay. **CP-LindV**

There was a man, born like. The Anatomy of Melancholy. Thomas Merton. **CP-MertT**

There was a man walked out. Chillicothe. Carl Sandburg. **CP-SandC**

There was a man who was blown down by the wind. A Man Who Was Blown Down by the Wind. Richard Eberhart. **CP-EberR**

There was a man whom Sorrow named his friend. The Sad Shepherd. William Butler Yeats. **CP-YeatW**

There was a most Monstrous Whale. The Whale. Theodore Roethke. **CP-RoetT**

There was a most odious Yak. The Yak. Theodore Roethke. **CP-RoetT**

There was a mutter of rain on the leaves and we went back in the. Waiting Can Be Pretty Lousy. Kenneth Patchen. **CP-PatcK**

There was a naughty boy. John Keats. **BoTP; CBNP; FHYEP; FaBoCh; FaBoCo; LiTB; MeMBP; MoShBr; OBCoV; OnUR; OxBChV** *Fr.* A Song about Myself. **CP-KeatJ**

(Song about Myself, A.) **MeMBP**

There was a naughty boy. A Song about Myself. John Keats. **CP-KeatJ**

There was a path. Place. Robert Creeley. **CP-CreeR**

There was a Pig that sat alone. The Melancholy Pig. "Lewis Carroll." **FaPON** *Fr.* The Pig-Tale. **CP-CarrL** *Fr.* Sylvie and Bruno Concluded.

There was a Pig that sat alone. The Pig-Tale. "Lewis Carroll." **CP-CarrL** *Fr.* Sylvie and Bruno Concluded.

There was a poet whose untimely tomb. Percy Bysshe Shelley. **FHYEP; TOF** *Fr.* Alastor; or, The Spirit of Solitude. **CP-ShelP**

There was a pool that rippled in the silence of the north. John Gould Fletcher. **SP-FletJ** *Fr.* Branches of Adam.

There was a priest at Philæ. Our Lady of the Sackcloth. Rudyard Kipling. **CP-KiplR**

There was a river overhung with trees. In a Notebook. James Fenton *and* John Fuller. **SP-FentJ**

There was a river under First and Main. Prairie Town. William Stafford. **SP-StafW**

There was a road ran past our house. The Unexplorer. Edna St. Vincent Millay. **CP-MillE**

There was a roaring in the wind all night. Resolution and Independence. William Wordsworth. **CP-WorW1**

There was a row in Silver Street that's near to Dublin Quay. Belts. Rudyard Kipling. **CP-KiplR**

There Was a Saviour. Dylan Thomas. **CP-ThomD**

There was a Serpent who had to sing. The Serpent. Theodore Roethke. **CP-RoetT**

There was a singing woman. The Singing Woman. Thomas Hardy. **CP-HardT**

There was a sky-painter at Folkestone. Folkestone Limerick. Robert Browning. **CP-BroR2**

There was a small house that existed. Fairy Tale. Stephen Dunn. **SP-DunnS**

There was a sound of revelry by night. Byron. **BeLS; EBEV; EBEvV; FaBV; FaBoBe; FaBoCh; FaBoEH; FaBoEn; FaFP; FiP; GN; HBV; NOBE; OBNC; OBWP; OXAEP-2; OtMeF; TFi; TrGrPo; TreF; WBLP; WaaP** *Fr.* Childe Harold's Pilgrimage. **CP-Byron**

(Battle of Waterloo, The.) **FaFP; TreF**

(Eve of Waterloo, The.) **BeLS; EBEvV; FaBV; FaBoBe; FaBoCh; FaBoEn; HBV; NOBE; OBNC; OtMeF**

(Night before the Battle of Waterloo, The.) **WBLP**

(Night before Waterloo, The.) **GN**

(There Was a Sound of Revelry by Night.) **TFi**

(Waterloo.) **FiP; TrGrPo; WaaP**

There Was a Sound of Revelry by Night. Byron. *See* There was a sound of revelry by night.

There was a spot. William Wordsworth. **CP-WorW1**

There was a strife 'twixt man and maid. Rudyard Kipling. **CP-KiplR** *Fr.* The Naulahka.

There was a stunted handpost just on the crest. Near Lanivet, 1872. Thomas Hardy. **CP-HardT**

There was a sunlit absence. Mossbawn Sunlight. Seamus Heaney. **BIrV; FaBCIP; NoP** *Fr.* Mossbawn.

There was a tall slough grass. Man and Dog on an Early Winter Morning. Carl Sandburg. **CP-SandC**

There was a time for discoveries. Voyage West. Archibald MacLeish. **CP-MacLA**

There Was a Time, I Need Not Name. Byron. **CP-Byron**

There was a time in former years. She Hears the Storm. Thomas Hardy. **CP-HardT**

There was a time, Lesbia, when. Carmen 72. Catullus. *Fr.* Carmina. **CP-Catul**

There was a time when Ætna's silent fire. Heroism. William Cowper. **CP-CowpW**

There was a time when I preferred. Sweeney's Last Poem. Seamus Heaney. **SP-HeanS**

There was a time when ignorance made our innocence strong. The Calm before the Storm. "Lou Reed." **SP-ReedL**

There was a time when meadow, grove, and stream. Ode: Intimations of Immortality [from Recollections of Early Childhood]. William Wordsworth. **CP-WorW1**

There was a time when meadow, grove and stream. William Wordsworth. **HeIL; ImPo; NAEL-2; PBMP; SCGP; TFi; TOF; TRP** *Fr.* Ode: Intimations of Immortality [from Recollections of Early Childhood]. **CP-WorW1**

There was a time when meadow, grove, and stream. William Wordsworth. **FaPoB** *Fr.* Ode: Intimations of Immortality [from Recollections of Early Childhood]. **CP-WorW1**

There was a time when my cheek burned. Emily Brontë. **CP-BronE**

There was a time when the young girls. From the Second Chapter of a Verse History of the World. Thomas Merton. **CP-MertT**

There was a tower that went before a fall. Babel. Louis MacNeice. **CP-MacNL**

There was a tree of stars sprang up on a vertical panel of the south. Monkey of Stars. Carl Sandburg. **CP-SandC**

There was a veil between them. A Veil. Leonard Cohen. **CP-CoheL**

There was a whispering in my hearth. Miners. Wilfred Owen. **CP-OwenW**

There was a wicked messenger. The Wicked Messenger. "Bob Dylan." **CP-DylaB**

There was a wicked woman called Malady Festing. Angel Boley. Stevie Smith. **CP-SmitS**

There was a Widow in the village known. Smugglers and Poachers. George Crabbe. **SP-CrabG** *Fr.* Tales of the Hall.

There was a Wife from Bath, a well-appearing, *mod. vers. by* Louis Untermeyer. Geoffrey Chaucer. *See* A Good Wyf [*or* Wif] was ther of bisyde [*or* biside] Bathe.

There was a wife wonn'd in Cockpen. Scroggam. Robert Burns. **CP-BurnR**

There was a wild pigeon came often to Hinkley's timber. Timber Wings. Carl Sandburg. **CP-SandC**

There was a woman / Who moved crablike. Inverts. Jenny Joseph. *Fr.* Life and Turgid Times of A. Citizen. **SP-JoseJ**

There was a woman in Ithaca. Toast. Leonard Nathan. **SP-NathL**

There was a woman loved a man. Sea Chest. Carl Sandburg. **CP-SandC**

There was a woman tore off a red velvet gown. Woman with a Past. Carl Sandburg. **CP-SandC**

There was a worthy, but a simple Pair. The Mother. George Crabbe. **SP-CrabG** *Fr.* Tales.

There was a young belle of old Natchez. Requiem. Ogden Nash. **CP-NashO**

There was a young fellow named Crane. A Young Fellow Named Crane. Malcolm Lowry. **CP-LowrM**

There was a young lady of station. A Limerick. "Lewis Carroll." **CP-CarrL**

There was a young man from Oaxaca. The Young Man From Oaxaca. Malcolm Lowry. **CP-LowrM**

There was a young poet of Chelsea. George Meredith. **CP-MerG2**

There was a youth, who, as with toil and travel. Prince Athanase; a Fragment. Percy Bysshe Shelley. **CP-ShelP**

There Was a Youth Whose Name Was Thomas Granger. Charles Olson. **CP-OlsoC**

There was absolutely no reason after the centaur had pawed her and tried to mount her. Hercules, Deianira, Nessus. Charles Kenneth Williams. **SP-WillC**

Ther[e] was also a Nonne [*or* nun], a Prioress[e]. Geoffrey Chaucer. **CTC; NOBE; TrGrPo** *Fr.* The General Prologue. **FHYEP; NAWM-1; OAEL-1; PoE** *Fr.* The Canterbury Tales. **CP-ChauG**

(Madame Eglantine.) **NOBE**

(Seven Pilgrims: A Prioress[e].) **TrGrPo**

("There also was a nun, a Prioress.") **TrGrPo**

There was an ancient City, stricken down. "Lewis Carroll." *Fr.* Four Riddles. **CP-CarrL**

There was an ease of mind that was like being alone in a boat at sea. Prologues to What Is Possible. Wallace Stevens. **CP-StevW**

There was an infidel who. Water Walker. Richard Wilbur. **CP-WilbR**

There was an old Consul called Firmin. Malcolm Lowry. **CP-LowrM**

There was an old Dutch lady. For Example. Gary Snyder. **CP-SnydG**

There was an old farmer of Readall. Melodies. "Lewis Carroll." **CP-CarrL**

There was an old man of Calcutta. Arthur. Ogden Nash. **CP-NashO**

There was an old man of Scoharie. Drusilla. Ogden Nash. **CP-NashO**

There was an old miser named Clarence. Fragonard. Ogden Nash. **CP-NashO**

There was an old poop from Poughkeepsie. John Updike. *Fr.* Two Limericks after Lear.

There was an old woman who lived in a nice. The Old Woman who Buried Cats. Malcolm Lowry. **CP-LowrM**

There was an unwanted child. End, Middle, Beginning. Anne Sexton. **CP-SextA**

There was another, too. Graph. William Carlos Williams. **CP-WilW2**

There was calm rapture in the way she spoke. John Ashbery. **SP-AshbJ** *Fr.* The New Realism.

There was darkness under Heaven. Helen All Alone. Rudyard Kipling. **CP-KiplR**

There was desolate silence on the world. Sonnet I. Wystan Hugh Auden. **CP-AudWJ**

There was five Carlins in the South. The Five Carlins—A Ballad—Tune, Chevy Chase. Robert Burns. **CP-BurnR**

There Was Glass and There Are Stars. Randall Jarrell. **CP-JarrR**

There was Ike and Tony and Jaque and me. Ernest Hemingway. **CP-HemiE**

Ther[e] was in Asia [or Asye], in a great [or greet] city [or citee]. The Prioress's Tale. Geoffrey Chaucer. **ACP** *Fr.* The Canterbury Tales. **CP-ChauG**

There was just one sweet potato. Nicholas Vachel Lindsay. *Fr.* The Potatoes' Dance. **CP-LindV**

There was merry-making. The Man with a Past. Thomas Hardy. **CP-HardT**

There was never a queen like Balkis. Rudyard Kipling. **CP-KiplR** *Fr.* The Butterfly That Stamped. *Fr.* Just-So Stories.

There was never a sound beside the wood but one. Mowing. Robert Frost. **CP-FrosR**

There was never any worry about bread or even butter. Not At All What One Is Used To. Isabella Gardner. **CP-GardI**

There was never danger in this black sad water. Crinan Canal. Richard Hugo. **CP-HugoR**

There was never file half so well filed. Sir Thomas Wyatt. **CP-WyatT**

There was never naught. A Never Naught Song. Robert Frost. **CP-FrosR**

There was never nothing more me pained [or payned]. Sir Thomas Wyatt. **CP-WyatT**

There was no bulldozer handy, so. Frederick Morgan. *Fr.* Death Mother. **SP-MorgF**

There was no more than shadow where. The Shadow and the Real. James Wright. **CP-WrigJ**

There was no one like 'im, 'Orse or Foot. Follow Me 'Ome. Rudyard Kipling. **CP-KiplR**

There was no other guarantee. George Oppen. **APSN** *Fr.* Route. **CP-OppeG**

There was no place on that plain for a city. The Shortest Way Home. Muriel Rukeyser. **CP-RukeM**

There was no trace of Heaven. Bivouac. Alun Lewis. **CP-LewiA**

There was nought in the Valley. Time Passes. Walter de la Mare. **CP-DeLaW**

There was on a time, but old Time was then young. Caledonia. Robert Burns. **CP-BurnR**

There was once upon a time a little owl. The Owl's Bedtime Story. Randall Jarrell. **CP-JarrR**

There was once was a time when I loved. The Faithless Shepherdess. Christina Georgina Rossetti. **CP-RosC3**

There was one man and he was not an Irishman but he might have been one. A Comeallye for Robert Carlton Brown. Kay Boyle. **CP-BoylK**

There was one Syrian, with his bicycle, in our town. Derek Walcott. **CP-WalcD** *Fr.* Midsummer.

There was, perhaps, a time. Siv Cedering Fox. *Fr.* In Search of a Love Poem. **SP-CedeS**

There was rain early in November but afterwards. Seventieth Birthday. Robinson Jeffers. **CP-JefR3**

There was rebellion, Father, and the door was slammed. Father. Robert Lowell. **SP-LoweR**

There was Rundle, Station Master. The Mother-Lodge. Rudyard Kipling. **CP-KiplR**

There was simply / nothing to look at. Shaker. James Schuyler. **CP-SchuJ**

There was so much talk of the dead. An Untenable Situation. Pablo Neruda, *tr. fr. Spanish by* Ben Belitt. **SP-NeruP**

There was something obscene about wrestling that baby-faced boy. Outlandish Agon. Mona Van Duyn. **SP-VanDM**

There was such speed in her little body. Bells for John Whiteside's Daughter. John Crowe Ransom. **SP-RansJ**

There was the butcher's hand. A Weak Mind in the Mountains. Wallace Stevens. **CP-StevW**

There was the mechanicalism. Spook's Sabbath, Five Bowings. Louis Zukofsky. **CP-ZukLS**

There was the Strike; the shipyard engineers. The "Forty-Four Hours" Strike, 1919. John Hewitt. **CP-HewiJ**

There was this character come in. How Come He Got Canned at the Ribbon Factory. Allen Ginsberg. **CP-GinsA**

There was this girl 18, 19 and slight. Hayden Carruth. *Fr.* Paragraphs. **CP-CarHS**

There was this glittering fuzz. Bar Games. Gilbert Sorrentino. **SP-SorrG**

There was this lady once she used to grow. Tails. Charles Kenneth Williams. **CP-WillC**

There was this man and he was the strongest. The Contender. Ted Hughes. **SP-HughT**

There was this road. The Legs. Robert Ranke Graves. **CP-GravR**

There was this time in Boston. The Wedding Night. Anne Sexton. **CP-SextA**

There was three kings into the east. John Barleycorn [a Ballad]. Robert Burns. **CP-BurnR**

There was twa wives, and twa witty wives. Robert Burns. **CP-BurnR**

There was upon the sill a pencil mark. Edna St. Vincent Millay. *Fr.* Sonnets from an Ungrafted Tree. **CP-MillE**

There we were in the vaulted tunnel running. The Underground. Seamus Heaney. **SP-HeanS**

There were always little tragedies. Transformation and Disfiguration. Charles Bukowski. **SP-BukC3**

There were faces to remember in the Valley of the Shadow. The Valley of the Shadow. Edwin Arlington Robinson. **CP-RobiE**

There were five howling virgins / Who came. *English tr. of* Les Cinq Vierges. Thomas Merton, *tr. fr. French by* William Davis. **CP-MertT**

There were four apples on the bough. August. Algernon Charles Swinburne. **SP-SwinA**

There were four crates of chickens. The Man with the Golden Adam's Apple. Kenneth Patchen. **CP-PatcK**

There were ghosts that returned to earth to hear his phrases. Large Red Man Reading. Wallace Stevens. **CP-StevW**

There Were Giants in Those Days or Maybe There Weren't. Ogden Nash. **CP-NashO**

There were lead-mines here before the Romans. Not in Baedeker. Wystan Hugh Auden. **CP-AudeW**

There were majesties. / Rain tilted his shining spears. I Sent a Mental to My Love. Kenneth Patchen. **CP-PatcK**

There were many houses like that in Canlin. Investigation of Certain Interesting Questions. Kenneth Patchen. **CP-PatcK**

There were moons O there were moons. The New Mode of Production. Al Young. **CP-YounA**

There were more dirty / things They were dirty. Route. Joseph Ceravolo. **SP-CeraJ**

There were no antelope on the balcony. Midnight Special. Kenneth Patchen. **CP-PatcK**

There were no undesirables or girls in my set. Commander Lowell. Robert Lowell. **SP-LoweR**

There were none of my blood in this battle. Wildwest. Archibald MacLeish. **CP-MacLA**

There were only two things anyone would want. Cleveland, Oh? Kenneth Patchen. **CP-PatcK**

There were open boxes of fine cigars. Nicholas Vachel Lindsay. *Fr.* Billboards and Galleons. **CP-LindV**

There were others; their bodies. Epithalamium. Louise Glück. **SP-GlücL**

There were over me three hawks. Poem for the Time of Change. Archibald MacLeish. **CP-MacLA**

There were palm trees. Alice Walker. **CP-WalkA**

There were poems all over Broadway that morning. Before Danger. Muriel Rukeyser. **CP-RukeM**

There were sea-horses and mer-men. The Poet. Hilda Doolittle. **CP-DoolH**

There were several hundred fools. I Cannot Stand Tears. Charles Bukowski. **SP-BukC2**

There were some dirty plates. The Last Words of My English Grandmother. William Carlos Williams. **CP-WilW1**

There were still shards of an ancient pastoral. The Star-Apple Kingdom. Derek Walcott. **CP-WalcD**

There were the roses, in the rain. The Act. William Carlos Williams. **CP-WilW2**

There were thirty million English who talked of England's might. The Last of the Light Brigade. Rudyard Kipling. **CP-KiplR**

There were those who spoke and listened. After Kraske. James Liddy. **CP-LiddJ**

There were thoughts that came to Phil. Night Thoughts. Stevie Smith. **CP-SmitS**

There were three cherry trees once. The Three Cherry Trees. Walter de la Mare. **CP-DeLaW**

There were three eagles percht on a rock. The Three Eagles and the Sleepy Lion. George Meredith. **CP-MerG2**

There were three friends / Discussing life. Three Friends. Chuang Tzu, *tr. fr. Chinese by* Thomas Merton. **CP-MertT**

There were three friends that buried the fourth. Rudyard Kipling. **CP-KiplR** *Fr.* The Light That Failed.

There were three in the meadow by the brook. The Code. Robert Frost. **CP-FrosR**

There were three kings and a jolly three too. The first one. John Wesley Harding (Liner Notes). "Bob Dylan." **CP-DylaB**

There were three maidens met on the highway. The Three Maidens. George Meredith. **CP-MerG1**

There were three of them that night. Orgy. Muriel Rukeyser. **CP-RukeM**

There were twelve ragged children. November in Ohio. Kenneth Patchen. **CP-PatcK**

There were two brothers at Twyford school. The Two Brothers. "Lewis Carroll." **CP-CarrL**

There were two men to be hanged. To Will Davies. Ernest Hemingway. **CP-HemiE**

There were two youths of equal age. The Two Men. Thomas Hardy. **CP-HardT**

There were years vague of measure. Her Apotheosis. Thomas Hardy. **CP-HardT**

There when the water was not potable. Louis Zukofsky. *Fr.* Chloride of Lime and Charcoal. **CP-ZukLS**

There when the water was not potable. Louis Zukofsky. *Fr.* There when the water was not potable. *Fr.* Chloride of Lime and Charcoal. **CP-ZukLS**

   "How sweet is the sun, is the sun."

   "There when the water was not potable."

   "Zinnias you look so much like Gentiles."

There where pines darken the water above the brookbed. Hayden Carruth. *Fr.* The Sleeping Beauty. **CP-CarHL**

There where the course is. At Galway Races. William Butler Yeats. **CP-YeatW**

There where the deepe did show his sandy flore, *sel. of par. by* Countess of Pembroke, Mary Sidney Herbert. Bible, *O.T. See* Psalm 78: "Give ear, O my people, to my law."

There where the land of love. Robert Louis Stevenson. **CP-StevR**

There where the woodcock his long bill among the alders. October—An Etching. Edna St. Vincent Millay. **CP-MillE**

There! Whitman's skull—. Hayden Carruth. **CP-CarHS** *Fr.* The Clay Hill Anthology.

There will always be a father of all things, in some shape, in our minds. Gods. David Herbert Lawrence. **CP-LawrD**

There will always be an issue: doctrine, dogma, differences of conscience, politics, or creed. Interrogation II. Charles Kenneth Williams. **SP-WillC**

There will always be monkeys and peacocks. Swell People. Carl Sandburg. **CP-SandC**

There will be a rusty gun on the wall, sweetheart. A. E. F. Carl Sandburg. **CP-SandC**

There Will Be a Talking. Michael Hartnett. **SP-HarMi**

There will be little enough to forget. 1892—19—. Archibald MacLeish. **CP-MacLA**

There will be much to remember. Harvest. John Haines. **SP-HainJ**

There will be mud on the carpet tonight. The Wifebeater. Anne Sexton. **CP-SextA**

There will be no evil. Where Every Prospect. Kenneth Patchen. **CP-PatcK**

There will be no examination in Long Term Suffering. Long Term Suffering. Richard Eberhart. **CP-EberR**

There Will Be No Peace. Wystan Hugh Auden. **CP-AudeW**

There will be no simple. The Window. Robert Creeley. **CP-CreeR**

There will be no speech from. No Speech from the Scaffold. Thom Gunn. **CP-GunnT**

There will be people left over. Call the Next Witness. Carl Sandburg. **CP-SandC**

There will be rose and rhododendron. Elegy before Death. Edna St. Vincent Millay. **CP-MillE**

There will, indeed, be modification of landscape. Modification of Landscape. Robert Penn Warren. *Fr.* Infant Boy at Midcentury. **SP-WarrR**

There with his boat was the Master, already a little impatient. Henry Wadsworth Longfellow. **TreFS** *Fr.* The Sailing of the Mayflower. *Fr.* The Courtship of Miles Standish. **SP-LongH**

There would be far less masculine gaming and boozing. Thoughts Thought on an Avenue. Ogden Nash. **CP-NashO**

There would come up many idle men to sit with the strangers. He Compares Old Customs with Those of His Kingdom. Frank Templeton Prince. *Fr.* Chaka. **CP-PrinF**

There would have been things to say, quietness. From the Latin. Geoffrey Hill. *Fr.* The Songbook of Sebastian Arrurruz. **CP-HillG**

There would he stand. Fragments from the Alfoxden Notebook (I). William Wordsworth. **CP-WorW1**

There you are in the dark. A Forgotten Miniature. Thomas Hardy. **CP-HardT**

There! You shed a ray. He Wrote the History Book. Marianne Craig Moore. **CP-MoorM**

There You Were. Anne Sexton. **CP-SextA**

Thereafter on that cold. John Haines. *Fr.* In the Middle of America. **SP-HainJ**

Therefore. William Dickey. **SP-DickW**

Therefore, Adieu. Countee Cullen. **CP-CullC**

Therefore all seasons shall be sweet to thee. All Seasons Shall Be Sweet. Samuel Taylor Coleridge. **BoTP** *Fr.* Frost at Midnight. **CP-ColeS**

Therefore let pass, as they are transitory. John Milton. **OAEL-1** *Fr.* Book IV. *Fr.* Paradise Regained [*or* Regain'd]. **CP-MiltJ**

Therefore myself is that one only thing. Christina Georgina Rossetti. *Fr.* The Thread of Life. **CP-RosC2**

Therefore the constant powers do not lessen. The Climate of War. Kenneth Patchen. **CP-PatcK**

Therefore the hand of God. Delivery to the Secular Arm, The: A Scene During the Existence of the Spanish Inquisition at Antwerp, 1570. Robert Browning. **CP-BroR2**

Therefore to us, time's / final lesson: be content. Hayden Carruth. **CP-CarHS** *Fr.* The Clay Hill Anthology.

Therefore with thee triumpheth there. The Confessors. John Donne. *Fr.* A Litany. **CP-DonnJ**

There'll Always Be a War between the Sexes, or, A Woman Can Be Sometimes Pleased, but Never Satisfied. Ogden Nash. **CP-NashO**

There'll be all the requisites. Invitation. Al Young. **CP-YounA**

There'll Never Be Peace Till Jamie Comes Hame. Robert Burns. **CP-BurnR**

There's a bear in the Truro woods. The Truro Bear. Mary Oliver. **SP-OlivM**

There's a belief to fix. It feels strong. Roy Fisher. **SP-FishR** *Fr.* New Diversions.

There's a big Zulu runs the congregation. Notes for a New Liturgy. Thomas Merton. *Fr.* South. *Fr.* The Geography of Lograire. **CP-MertT**

There's a breathless hush on the freeway tonight. Wild Dreams of a New Beginning. Lawrence Ferlinghetti. **SP-FerlL**

There's a certain Slant of light. Emily Dickinson. **CP-DickE**

There's a click like a piece of chalk. Furnace. Ted Kooser. **SP-KoosT**

There's a convict more in the Central Jail. Rudyard Kipling. **CP-KiplR** *Fr.* The Head of the District. *Fr.* Life's Handicap.

There's a crack in this glass so fine we can't see it. Minuscule Things. William Matthews. **SP-MattW**

There's a curve in the road, and a slow curve in the land. Lonesome Pine Special. Charles Wright. **SP-WrigC**

There's a downtown fairy singing out "Proud Mary." The Halloween Parade. "Lou Reed." **SP-ReedL**

There's a fabulous story. The Place Where the Rainbow Ends. Paul Laurence Dunbar. **CP-DunbP**

There's a family of wrens who live upstairs. Upstairs. Shel Silverstein. **SP-SilS2**

There's a fog up on L.A. Blue Jay Way. George Harrison. **CP-Beatl**

There's a footstep coming; look out and see. The Ghost's Petition. Christina Georgina Rossetti. **CP-RosC1**

There's a Grandfather's Clock in the Hall. Robert Penn Warren. **SP-WarrR**

There's a hockey puck in front of the air on the window sill. Cough Syrup. Jim Carroll. **SP-CarrJ**

There's a hole in the bottom of the sea. Do You Want Affidavits? Carl Sandburg. **CP-SandC**

There's a howling stray. Charles Henri Ford. **SP-FordC** *Fr.* Secret Haiku.

There's a kind of white moth, I don't know. The Moths. Mary Oliver. **SP-OlivM**

There's a Legion that never was 'listed. The Lost Legion. Rudyard Kipling. **CP-KiplR**

There's a little monkey maiden looking eastward toward the sea. Kipling. Ernest Hemingway. **CP-HemiE**

There's a little red-faced man. Bobs. Rudyard Kipling. **CP-KiplR**

There's a little sunshine in my heart. Sunshine. Christina Georgina Rossetti. **CP-RosC3**

There's a long-distance train rolling through the rain, tears on the letter I write. Where Are You Tonight? (Journey through Dark Heat). "Bob Dylan." **CP-DylaB**

There's a long-legged girl. Pickin Em Up and Layin Em Down. Maya Angelou. **SP-AngeM**

There's a man / who sits on a bench in the park nearby. In Washington Square. Stephen Berg. **SP-BergS**

There's a memory keeps a-runnin'. The Old Apple-Tree. Paul Laurence Dunbar. **CP-DunbP**

There's a mighty sound a-comin'. For Theodore Roosevelt. Paul Laurence Dunbar. **CP-DunbP**

There's a mystery. Gin. David St. John. **SP-StJoD**

There's a naked bug at Cold Mountain, *after* Han-shan. Gary Snyder. **CP-SnydG**

There's a palace in Florence, the world knows well. Robert Browning. **Mes** *Fr.* The Statue and the Bust. **CP-BroR1**

There's a palace in Florence, the world knows well. The Statue and the Bust. Robert Browning. **CP-BroR1**

There's a pasture in a valley where the hanging woods divide. Alnaschar and the Oxen. Rudyard Kipling. **CP-KiplR** *Fr.* Debits and Credits.

There's a patch of old snow in a corner. A Patch of Old Snow. Robert Frost. **CP-FrosR**

There's a Place. The Beatles. **CP-Beatl**

There's a place called Faraway Meadow. The Last Mowing. Robert Frost. **CP-FrosR**

There's a pub here called *The Burnt Post*. The Burnt Post. John Hewitt. **CP-HewiJ**

There's a raw blue haze. First Cold. Stephen Berg. **SP-BergS**

There's a ripple of fountains. The Land o' Used to Be. Paul Laurence Dunbar. **CP-DunbP**

There's a seat, I see, still empty? The Carrier. Thomas Hardy. **CP-HardT**

There's a secret boundary hidden in the waving grasses. Two Poems. Adrienne Rich. **CP-RicAE**

There's a slow fire in my eyes. Untitled Poem. Ussin Kerim, *tr. fr. Bulgarian by* William Matthews. **SP-MattW**

There's a snake on the western wave. Nicholas Vachel Lindsay. *Fr.* The Sea Serpent Chantey. **CP-LindV**

There's a solitude I fear but know. A Powerful Little Stove. Leonard Nathan. **SP-NathL**

Theres a sort of. Sunflowers. William Carlos Williams. **CP-WilW2**

There's a time, finally. Roy Fisher. **SP-FishR** *Fr.* Matrix.

There's a tractor in the doorway of a church. The Red Wing Church. Ted Kooser. **CP-KoosT**

There's a Train Leaving Soon. Kenneth Patchen. **CP-PatcK**

There's a volcano snow-capped in the air some twenty miles. Resort. George Oppen. **CP-OppeG**

There's a whisper down the field where the year has shot her yield. Rudyard Kipling. **CP-KiplR**

(Long Trail, The.) **CP-KiplR**

There's a widow in sleepy Chester. The Grave of the Hundred Dead. Rudyard Kipling. **CP-KiplR**

There's a youth in this city, it were a great pity. Robert Burns. **CP-BurnR**

There's all sorts of gods, all sorts and every sort. All Sorts of Gods. David Herbert Lawrence. **CP-LawrD**

There's Always an Ubblebub. Ogden Nash. **CP-NashO**

There's an iron train a-travelin' that's been a-rollin' through the years. Train A-Travelin'. "Bob Dylan." **CP-DylaB**

There's auld Rob Morris that wons in yon glen. Auld Rob Morris. Robert Burns. **CP-BurnR**

There's been a Death, in the Opposite House. Emily Dickinson. **CP-DickE**

There's been an eagle on a nickel. Fact. Langston Hughes. **SP-HughL**

There's blacks with knives and whites with clubs. Hold On. "Lou Reed." **SP-ReedL**

There's blood between us, love, my love. The Convent Threshold. Christina Georgina Rossetti. **CP-RosC1**

There's Blood in the Streets. Jim Morrison. **SP-MorrJ**

There's Chamfort. He's a sample. Chamfort. Carl Sandburg. **CP-SandC**

There's death in the cup—sae beware! Inscription on a Goblet. Robert Burns. **CP-BurnR**

There's Einstein riding on a ray of light. Einstein's Pegasus. Robert Pack. **SP-PackR**

There's enough wind. From an English Sensibility. Roy Fisher. **SP-FishR**

There's four men mowing down by the river. The Mowers. David Herbert Lawrence. **CP-LawrD**

There's George Fisher, Charles Fleming, and Reginald Shore. Rural Architecture. William Wordsworth. **CP-WorW1**

There's grit in the road, and pumice. Straight Life. William Matthews. **SP-MattW**

There's guns across the river aimin' at ya. Billy. "Bob Dylan." **CP-DylaB**

There's heaven above, and night by night. Johannes Agricola in Meditation. Robert Browning. **CP-BroR1**

There's in my mind a woman. In Mind. Denise Levertov. **CP-LeveD**

There's just a twinkle in your eye. Ne Sit Ancillae Tibi Amor Pudori. Robert Louis Stevenson. **CP-StevR**

There's many a strong farmer. The Happy Townland. William Butler Yeats. **CP-YeatW**

There's my things. Portrait of a Woman in Bed. William Carlos Williams. **CP-WilW1**

There's nane sall ken, there's nane sall guess. I'll Ay[e] Ca' in by Yon Town. Robert Burns. **CP-BurnR**

There's naw—thing. It's a Gay Li-ife. Louis Zukofsky. *Fr.* 29 Songs. **CP-ZukLS**

There's never an end to dust. Carrie. Ted Kooser. **SP-KoosT**

There's News Lasses News. Robert Burns. **CP-BurnR**

There's no accounting for. *with music.* Robert Pack. **SP-PackR**

There's no color like the color of an orange. It's Nothing to Laugh About. Charles Bukowski. **SP-BukC2**

There's no constraint to do amisse. Sin. Robert Herrick. **CP-HerrR**

There's no more to be done, or feared, or hoped. After the Last Breath. Thomas Hardy. **CP-HardT**

There's no need to hurry. He Takes His Time. Wendell Berry. *Fr.* The Handing Down. **CP-BerrW**

There's no new spirit abroad. The Poets Are Silent. Stevie Smith. **CP-SmitS**

There's no no like money's. The Matter. Charles Kenneth Williams. **CP-WillC**

There's No Place to Sleep in This Bed, Tanguy. Charles Henri Ford. **SP-FordC**

There's no replying / To the Wind's sighing. Hollow-Sounding and Mysterious. Christina Georgina Rossetti. **CP-RosC2**

There's no sense of going further—it's the edge of cultivation. The Explorer. Rudyard Kipling. **CP-KiplR**

There's no such thing as a student. Teaching. Al Young. **CP-YounA**

There's no such thing as death everybody. Then the Brother of the Wind. Charles Kenneth Williams. **CP-WillC**

There's no way you can know how it beginss. Moving, Merging, Fading, Standing Still. Al Young. **CP-YounA**

There's no wind among these seas. Thorkild's Song. Rudyard Kipling. **CP-KiplR** *Fr.* The Knights of the Joyous Venture. *Fr.* Puck of Pook's Hill.

There's no winsome woman so winsome as she. A Winsome Woman. Thomas Hardy. **CP-HardT**

There's not a chance now that I might recover. The Scar. John Hewitt. **CP-HewiJ**

There's not a joy the world can give like that it takes away. Stanzas for Music. Byron. **CP-Byron**

There's not a nook within this solemn Pass. The Trosachs. William Wordsworth. **CP-WorW2**

There's not an Echo round me. A Child of God Longing To See Him Beloved. Jeanne Marie Bouvier de la Motte-Guyon, *tr. fr. French by* William Cowper. **CP-CowpW**

There's not enough air in the sky for his lungs to gulp. Runner. Daniel Gerard Hoffman. **SP-HoffD**

There's Nothing Like Instinct, Fortunately. Ogden Nash. **CP-NashO**

There's nothing like the sun, not even rain or children; see the grass. Sunshine. Wystan Hugh Auden. **CP-AudWJ**

There's nothing 'round here I believe in. Nobody 'Cept You. "Bob Dylan." **CP-DylaB**

There's nothing so weak as a lamb's first cry. A Rhyme for Blake. John Hewitt. **CP-HewiJ**

There's nothing to love in this. Warmth. Joseph Ceravolo. **SP-CeraJ**

There's Plenty of Anguish at the Railroad. Diane Wakoski. **SP-WakoD**

There's reason good, that you good laws should make. To the Parliament. Ben Jonson. **CP-JonsB**

There's sax eggs in the pan, gudeman. O An Ye Were Dead Gudeman. Robert Burns. **CP-BurnR**

There's Snow on the Fields. Christina Georgina Rossetti. **CP-RosC2**

There's so little of swift time, and what time. Tardy. William Matthews. **SP-MattW**

There's some wrong that can't be salved. Wrong. William Matthews. **SP-MattW**

There's somebody who's dying. They Warned Him Then They Threw Him Away. Charles Kenneth Williams. **CP-WillC**

There's Someone At the Door. Jim Morrison. **SP-MorrJ**

There's something burning, you said, when we were hammering. Malcolm Lowry. **CP-LowrM**

There's something dreadful about ghosts in new houses. Ghosts in New Houses. Malcolm Lowry. **CP-LowrM**

There's something in a flying horse. Peter Bell; a Tale. William Wordsworth. **CP-WorW1**

There's something in a stupid ass. Epilogue. Byron. **CP-Byron**

There's something or maybe even. Improvisation. Al Young. **CP-YounA**

There's something quieter than sleep. Emily Dickinson. **CP-DickE**

There's still some life left in an old red barn. Barn in Wisconsin. Edwin Rolfe. **CP-RolfE**

There's talk, says Illinois. Colloquy for the States. Archibald MacLeish. **CP-MacLA**

There's teuch sauchs growin' i' the Reuch Heuch Hauch. The Sauchs in the Reuch Heuch Hauch. "Hugh MacDiarmid." **SP-MacDH**

There's that praying. Charles Henri Ford. **SP-FordC** *Fr.* Emblems of Arachne.

There's the Battle of Burgoyne. Emily Dickinson. **CP-DickE**

There's this shape, black as the entrance to a cave. October. Mary Oliver. **SP-OlivM**

There's this to a good day's sweat. Tree Trimming. John Ciardi. **SP-CiarJ**

There's *this* to Remember about the Gnu. The Gnu. Theodore Roethke. **CP-RoetT**

There's three true gude fellows. Three Gude Fellows Ayont Yon Glen. Robert Burns. **CP-BurnR**

There's too much to consecrate. Leonard Nathan. **SP-NathL** *Fr.* To Be Read to Yourself in a Public Place, July 4, 1976.

There've been times I've thought worms. Afterlife. Stephen Dunn. **SP-DunnS**

Thermometer. Charles Bukowski. **SP-BukC2**

Thermometer. Ralph Waldo Emerson. **CP-EmerR**

Thermopylae is a well. The Empire of Persia. Kenneth Patchen. **CP-PatcK**

Thermos. Patti Smith. **SP-SmitP**

These / admonitory images. Maillol. Charles Tomlinson. **CP-TomlC**

These. William Carlos Williams. **CP-WilW1**

These acres, always again lost. Lost Acres. Robert Ranke Graves. **CP-GravR**

These All Wait upon Thee. Christina Georgina Rossetti. *See* Innocent eyes not ours / Are made to look on flowers.

These alternate nights and days, these seasons. Lines for a Prologue. Archibald MacLeish. **CP-MacLA**

These americans just looking. Three Seasons and a Gorilla. Charles Kenneth Williams. **CP-WillC**

These are amazing: each. Some Trees. John Ashbery. **SP-AshbJ**

These are days of sickness and forgetting. To Pull into Oneself as into a Locked Room. Stephen Dobyns. **SP-DobyS**

These are her angels! An Improvisation upon the Theme of the Lady and the Unicorn. Jean Garrigue. **SP-GarrJ**

These are men! the gaunt, unforesold, the vocal. Ol' Bunk's Band. William Carlos Williams. **CP-WilW2**

These are my great ones. Kenneth Patchen. **CP-PatcK**

These are no wind-blown rumors, soft say-sos. Sonnet. Countee Cullen. **CP-CullC**

These are not dewdrops, these are tears. Epitaph on a Free but Tame Redbreast. William Cowper. **CP-CowpW**

These are not words set down for the rejected. A Communication to Nancy Cunard. Kay Boyle. **CP-BoylK**

These are our brave, these with their hands in on the work. Citation for Horace Gregory. Muriel Rukeyser. **CP-RukeM**

These are *our* regulations. A Boy Scouts' Patrol Song. Rudyard Kipling. **CP-KiplR**

These are prices and costs. Theorem. Carl Sandburg. **CP-SandC**

These are savannas bluer than your dreams. Deep South. Thomas McGrath. **SP-McGrT**

These are some canyons. Indian Caves in the Dry Country. William Stafford. **SP-StafW**

These are stone jetties. Facing Africa. James Dickey. **CP-DickJ**

These are strange shores. No sand. Resulting from Magnetic Interference. Richard Hugo. **CP-HugoR**

These Are the Clouds. William Butler Yeats. **CP-YeatW**

These are the days I want to. The Gentle Rejoinder. William Carlos Williams. **CP-WilW2**

These are the days of elfs and fays. The Discovery. Paul Laurence Dunbar. **CP-DunbP**

These are the days of yellow and red. Vermont Idyll. Richard Eberhart. **CP-EberR**

These are the days that Reindeer love. Emily Dickinson. **CP-DickE**

These are the days when Birds come back—. Emily Dickinson. **CP-DickE**

These are the facts. The uncle, the elder brother, the squire. Claude to Eustace. Arthur Hugh Clough. **FaBoVe** *Fr.* Amours de Voyage. **SP-ClouA**

These are the fields I called for. You Shall Have Homes. Carl Sandburg. **CP-SandC**

These are the first days of fall. The wind. How To Like It. Stephen Dobyns. **SP-DobyS**

These are the four that are never content, that have never been filled since the Dews began. Rudyard Kipling. **CP-KiplR** *Fr.* The King's Ankus. *Fr.* The Second Jungle Book.

These are the houses of farmers. Houses at the Edge of Town. Ted Kooser. **SP-KoosT**

These are the Idiots chiefest arts. William Blake. **CP-BlakW**

These are the lines on which a committee is formed. Praise of the Committee. Muriel Rukeyser. **CP-RukeM**

These are the names of the companies that have made money from this war. War Profit Litany. Allen Ginsberg. **CP-GinsA**

These are the Nights that Beetles love. Emily Dickinson. **CP-DickE**

These are the original monies of the earth. A Cabinet of Seeds Displayed. Howard Nemerov. **CP-NemeH**

These are the places. Spring. Robert Creeley. **CP-CreeR**

These are the problems he inherits. The Fruit-Grower in War-time (and Some of His Enemies). James Fenton. *Fr.* Exempla. **SP-FentJ**

These are the proper names. Naming for Love. Hayden Carruth. **CP-CarHS**

These are the roads to take when you think of your country. The Road. Muriel Rukeyser. **CP-RukeM**

These are the Signs to Nature's Inns. Emily Dickinson. **CP-DickE**

These are the sins for which they cast out angels. Annotation for an Epitaph. Adrienne Rich. **CP-RicAE**

These are the small resorts. The *City of Keansburg*. George Oppen. **CP-OppeG**

These are the surface shapes upon my mind. Comment on Verse. John Hewitt. **CP-HewiJ**

These are the tawny days: your face comes back. Tawny. Carl Sandburg. **CP-SandC**

These are the times when all our feminine notables are beautified. Anybody Else Hate Nicknames? Ogden Nash. **CP-NashO**

These are the voices of the pastors calling. The Old Lutheran Bells at Home. Wallace Stevens. **CP-StevW**

These are thy glorious works, Parent of good. Morning Hymn of Adam. John Milton. **TrPWD**, *ll.* 153–208, *abr.*; **WGRP** *Fr.* Book V. *Fr.* Paradise Lost. **CP-MiltJ**

These are two friends whose lives were undivided. Epitaph. Percy Bysshe Shelley. **CP-ShelP**

These, as they change, Almighty Father, these. A Hymn on the Seasons. James Thomson. **EnRP**; **LAuP**; **OxBoCh** *Fr.* The Seasons. **CP-ThomJ**

These bald mountains. Reservations. Richard Shelton. **SP-ShelR**

These beautifully grown men. These hungerers. Cheever's People. Erica Jong. **SP-JongE**

These beds of bracken, climax of the summer's growth. Bracken Hills in Autumn. "Hugh MacDiarmid." **SP-MacDH**

These bones once held together. The Skeleton in the Closet. Ted Kooser. **SP-KoosT**

These brief imperfect meetings. Emily Dickinson. **SP-DickE**

These bulbs forgotten in a cellar. Christmas Letter to a Psychiatrist. May Sarton. **SP-SartM**

These Carols. Walt Whitman. **CP-WhitW**

These Chairs they have no words to utter. Fragments from Dove Cottage Manuscript 44 (II). William Wordsworth. **CP-WorW1**

These children playing at statues fill. Statues. Richard Wilbur. **CP-WilbR**

These children singing in stone a. Edward Estlin Cummings. **CP-CummE**; **SP-CummE**

These Clever Women. David Herbert Lawrence. **CP-LawrD**

These clothes, of which I now divest. At Undressing in the Evening. Christopher Smart. *Fr.* Hymns for the Amusement of Children. **SP-SmarC**

These coins and calendars stood for the moon, young boys. Of Money. And the Past. Muriel Rukeyser. **CP-RukeM**

These critics, who to faith no quarter grant. Lines Written in the Monthly Review. William Cowper. **CP-CowpW**

These Days. Charles Olson. **CP-OlsoC**

These days / only the telephone men are spurred. A Gloss. Charles Olson. **CP-OlsoC**

These Days. Alice Walker. **CP-WalkA**

These days are long before I die. Yet a Little While. Christina Georgina Rossetti. **CP-RosC3**

These days are misty, insulated, mute. Louis MacNeice. **CMoP** *Fr.* Autumn Journal. **CP-MacNL**

These days I think of Belvie. These Days. Alice Walker. **CP-WalkA**

These days of disinheritance, we feast. Cuisine Bourgeoise. Wallace Stevens. **CP-StevW**

These days of small but. Charles Henri Ford. **SP-FordC** *Fr.* Secret Haiku.

These days the air is thick with bitter cries. The Anglo-Irish Accord. John Hewitt. **CP-HewiJ**

These Deathy Leaves. Allen Tate. **CP-TateA**

These demonstrations of the one God. The Mountains of California: Part 1. Al Young. **CP-YounA**

These dirt mounds make the dead seem fat. Indian Graves at Jocko. Richard Hugo. **CP-HugoR**

These do generally ingender gross humours. The Menu of Melancholy. Lewis Turco. **SP-TurcL**

These dried-out paint brushes which fell from my lips have been removed. Sestina from the Home Gardener. Diane Wakoski. **SP-WakoD**

These dry, bright winter days. In March. Charles Tomlinson. **CP-TomlC**

These dulcet euphonies of autumn now begun. October Afternoon. Marsden Hartley. **CP-HartM**

These exquisite mementos. Marsden Hartley. **CP-HartM**

These faces make a chapel where worship comes easy. English Train Compartment. John Updike. **CP-UpdiJ**

These Fevered Days—to take them to the Forest. Emily Dickinson. **CP-DickE**

These few deep strongholds. Each with generator. Popular Demand. James Merrill. *Fr.* Topics. **SP-MerrJ**

These five, stepping to the scythes. Five Women. Marsden Hartley. **CP-HartM**

These flowers are I, poor Fanny Hurd. Voices from Things Growing in a Churchyard. Thomas Hardy. **CP-HardT**

These fought in any case. Ezra Pound. **FF; FaBoEH; HeIL; HeIP; MoAmPo; NOBE; OBWP; PoE; PoWW; TRP; VGW; WaaP** *Fr.* Hugh Selwyn Mauberley. (Life and Contacts). **SP-PounE**

These fragments you have shelved (shored). Canto 8. Ezra Pound. *Fr.* Cantos. **CP-PoCan**

These fresh beauties (we can prove). Why Flowers Change Color. Robert Herrick. **CP-HerrR**

These from my mother's greatgrandmother's rosebush white. Edward Estlin Cummings. **CP-CummE**

These generations that have sealed your heart. Allen Tate. *Fr.* Sonnets of the Blood. **CP-TateA**

These glistening brown eyes that shine. Violet Grape—and Shadowy Myrtle Leaf. Marsden Hartley. **CP-HartM**

These golden heads, these common suns. Dandelions. Howard Nemerov. **CP-NemeH**

These Gothic windows, how they wear me out. The Young Glass-Stainer. Thomas Hardy. **CP-HardT**

These grand and fatal movements toward death. Rearmament. Robinson Jeffers. **CP-JefR2**

These graves never fit a standard hymn. Antisocial Easter. Richard Hugo. **CP-HugoR**

These guys, it's hard to believe these guys. Funny. Stephen Dobyns. **SP-DobyS**

These had stopped seeking. Wystan Hugh Auden. *Fr.* Shorts [1927–1932] ("Pick a quarrel, go to war"). **CP-AudeW**

These hands so well articulated. Ceci est digne de gens sans dieu. Stevie Smith. **CP-SmitS**

These Have Gone with Silent Hands, Seeking. Kenneth Patchen. **CP-PatcK**

These have I set up. Dream Forest. Donald Davie. **CP-DavDo**

These have no Christ to spit and stoop. Black Magdalens. Countee Cullen. **CP-CullC**

These held their Wick above the West. Emily Dickinson. **CP-DickE**

These here are words of radical advice for a young man looking for a job. Will Consider Situation. Ogden Nash. **CP-NashO**

These heretics hate all true believers and when orderd by the Sultan. The Nusayris. Thomas Merton. *Fr.* East with Ibn Battuta. *Fr.* East. *Fr.* The Geography of Lograire. **CP-MertT**

These Heroics. Leonard Cohen. **CP-CoheL**

These hills, to hurt me more. Mist in the Valley. Edna St. Vincent Millay. **CP-MillE**

These Houres, and that which hover's o're my END. The Recommendation. Richard Crashaw. **CP-CrasR**

These I assume were words so deeply meant. The Ingenuities of Debt. Robert Frost. **CP-FrosR**

These I Singing in Spring. Walt Whitman. **CP-WhitW**

These images and their hidden voices. John Haines. *Fr.* Roadways. **SP-HainJ**

These Images Remain. May Sarton. **SP-SartM**

These images will parade until the morning. Shooting Gallery. Muriel Rukeyser. **CP-RukeM**

These, in the day when heaven was falling. Epitaph on an Army of Mercenaries. Alfred Edward Housman. **CP-HousA**

These Indian-Summer Days. Emily Dickinson. **SP-DickE**

These Indians explain away their hair. A Night at the Napi in Browning. Richard Hugo. **CP-HugoR**

These islands of history amid traffic snarls. John Updike. *Fr.* Spanish Sonnets. **CP-UpdiJ**

These legs need to run. I Kneel. Charles Bukowski. **SP-BukC2**

These locks on doors have brought me happiness. Locks. Kenneth Koch. **SP-KochK**

These locks, which fondly thus entwine. To a Lady Who Presented to the Author a Lock of Hair Braided with His Own, and Appointed a Night in December to Meet Him in the Garden. Byron. **CP-Byron**

These locusts by day, these crickets by night. Things of August. Wallace Stevens. **CP-StevW**

These loves are the helpless or wanted bliss. 1938: The Spring Dances. Randall Jarrell. **CP-JarrR**

These magnificent words that I read today. Magnificent Words. Stevie Smith. **CP-SmitS**

These market-dames, mid-aged, with lips thin-drawn. Former Beauties. Thomas Hardy. **CBLP; FaBoEn; NoAM; OBMV; OBNC** *Fr.* At Casterbridge Fair. **CP-HardT**

These massed grey shadows. Mothball Fleet: Benicia, California. John Haines. **SP-HainJ**

These memories of what. The Visionary Picnic. William Matthews. **SP-MattW**

These Men Are Revolution. Edwin Rolfe. **CP-RolfE**

These men were kings, albeit they were black. Black Majesty. Countee Cullen. **CP-CullC**

These men who do not die, but send to death. Not Sacco and Vanzetti. Countee Cullen. **CP-CullC**

These mighty workmen of our later age. William Wordsworth. **EnRP** *Fr.* Books. *Fr.* The Prelude; Growth of a Poet's Mind [1850 vers.]. **CP-WorW3**

These miracles of Paris. Marsden Hartley. **CP-HartM**

These Mornings of Rain. Alice Walker. **CP-WalkA**

These mysteries do point to three more great. The Reverse on the Back Side. Ben Jonson. **CP-JonsB**

These nuts, that I keep in the back of the nest. My Treasures. Robert Louis Stevenson. **CP-StevR**

These nymphs, whom I itch to perpetuate—. Afternoon of a Faun. Stéphane Mallarmé, *tr. fr. French by* Hayden Carruth. **CP-CarHS**

These of living emanate a formidable light. The Cloth of the Tempest. Kenneth Patchen. **CP-PatcK**

These open years, the river. For Jennifer, 6, on the Teton. Richard Hugo. **CP-HugoR**

These people are bowling, these people are living. In the Bowling Alley. James Liddy. **CP-LiddJ**

These people discuss spirits as if spirits. Like Us, Maybe. Leonard Nathan. **SP-NathL**

These people facing me—masons, architects, plumbers, bankers, painters— represent all the trades. Bread. Stephen Berg. **SP-BergS**

These people have not heard your name. In a Cathedral City. Thomas Hardy. **CP-HardT**

These people socalled were not given hearts. Edward Estlin Cummings. **CP-CummE**

These people, with their illegible diplomas. Metamorphoses. Howard Nemerov. **CP-NemeH**

These pines, these fall oaks, these rocks. After Drinking All Night with a Friend, We Go Out in a Boat at Dawn to See Who Can Write the Best Poem. Robert Bly. **CP-BlyR**

These pink-white acres of overcast. From Above. John Updike. **CP-UpdiJ**

These poems do not live: it's a sad diagnosis. Stillborn. Sylvia Plath. **CP-PlatS**

These pools that, though in forests, still reflect. Spring Pools. Robert Frost. **CP-FrosR**

These poplars dream. Consolation Sonata. Carl Sandburg. **CP-SandC**

These psalms are the workings of the vision haunted mind. Psalm I. Allen Ginsberg. **CP-GinsA**

These public men who seem so to enjoy their dominion. Wystan Hugh Auden. *Fr.* Shorts [1939–1947] ("Motionless, deep in his mind, lies the past the poet's forgotten"). **CP-AudeW**

These Pure Arches. May Sarton. **SP-SartM**

These Purists. William Carlos Williams. **CP-WilW2**

These quiet months of watching for. Song: Once More. Robert Ranke Graves. **CP-GravR**

These ravings, observations, etc. come from one who. Notice. Patti Smith. **SP-SmitP**

These rescues of the will in the will's. Keeping Clear. Dabney Stuart. **SP-StuaD**

These rings, O my beloved pair. Robert Louis Stevenson. *Fr.* The Family. **CP-StevR**

These rioteres three of which I tell. Death and the Three Revellers. Geoffrey Chaucer. **OBNV** *Fr.* The Pardoner's Tale. **FHYEP; NAEL-1; NAWM-1; NoP; OAEL-1; PoE** *Fr.* The Canterbury Tales. **CP-ChauG**

These rising chords / Will dance in time. Scherzo. James McAuley. *Fr.* The Exile's Fifth Symphony. **SP-McAuJ**

These roads will take you into your own country. The Book of the Dead. Muriel Rukeyser. **CP-RukeM**

These rolling flowing plunging breaking everlasting weaving waters. There Shall Be No More Sea. Kathleen Jessie Raine. **SP-RainK**

These Russian heavies are all wrong. W. D. Lifts Ten Times the Weight of His Own Body. William DeWitt Snodgrass. **SP-SnodW**

These sacks of flesh piled in a pile. Women on a Bus. Randall Jarrell. **CP-JarrR**

These—saw Visions. Emily Dickinson. **CP-DickE**

These secretly are going to some place. Grand Central, with Soldiers, in Early Morning. Howard Nemerov. **CP-NemeH**

These shacks are tricks. A simple smoke. Between the Bridges. Richard Hugo. **CP-HugoR**

These shells are paradox. Marsden Hartley. **CP-HartM**

These Six or Several Houses. Marsden Hartley. **CP-HartM**

These small West Country towns where year by year. From the Great Western. Sir John Betjeman. **CP-BetjJ**

These softs and solids, this clear, that rough. Cefalù. Frank Templeton Prince. **CP-PrinF**

These spasms and chrysanthemums of light. Fireworks. John Updike. **CP-UpdiJ**

These spectres resting on plastic stools. Café in Warsaw. Allen Ginsberg. **CP-GinsA**

These Springs were Maidens once that lov'd. How Springs Came First. Robert Herrick. **CP-HerrR**

These States: Into L.A. Allen Ginsberg. **CP-GinsA**

These States: to Miami Presidential Convention. Allen Ginsberg. **CP-GinsA**

These Strangers, in a foreign World. Emily Dickinson. **CP-DickE**

These Streets. Philip Levine. **SP-LeviP**

"These Students Couldn't Write Their Way out of a Paper Bag"—Anonymous. Ron Koertge. **SP-KoerR**

These suggestions by Asians are not taken seriously. Asian Peace Offers Rejected without Publication. Robert Bly. **SP-BlyR**

These summer-birds did with thy master stay. To His Maid Prew. Robert Herrick. **CP-HerrR**

These summer landscapes—clump, and croft, and copse. At the Royal Academy. Thomas Hardy. **CP-HardT**

These tarnished islands—set. Corniche—Marseille. Marsden Hartley. **CP-HartM**

These tears flooding my eyes, are they of pain. The Wand. Robert Ranke Graves. **CP-GravR**

These temp'rall goods God (the most Wise)commends. Temporall Goods. Robert Herrick. **CP-HerrR**

These tested Our Horizon. Emily Dickinson. **CP-DickE**

These, the unequalled, vicious. The Penitent. Robert Creeley. **CP-CreeR**

These, the Wings of the Morning. The Indian Girl Who Made Them. Nicholas Vachel Lindsay. *Fr.* The Tree of Laughing Bells or The Wings of the Morning. **CP-LindV**

These, then, he left, and away where ranks were now clashing the thickest. Agamemnon in the Fight. Homer, *tr. by* George Meredith. **CP-MerG1** *Fr.* The Iliad.

These, these are they. Ben Jonson. **CP-JonsB** *Fr.* Masque of Hymen.

These three men are friends. Three Friends: Outline for a Picture. Marsden Hartley. **CP-HartM**

These times strike monied worldlings with dismay. October, 1803 ("These times strike monied worldlings with dismay"). William Wordsworth. **CP-WorW1**

These to His Memory—since he held them dear. Dedication. Tennyson. *Fr.* Idylls of the King. **CP-TennA**

These Tourists, heaven preserve us! needs must live. The Brothers. William Wordsworth. **CP-WorW1**

These tracings from a world that's dead. Basil Bunting. **CP-BuntB**

These trees like tho'ts that to visions congeal. Ralph Waldo Emerson. **CP-EmerR**

These Trees Stand. William DeWitt Snodgrass. **SP-SnodW**

These two by the stone wall. Burghers of Petty Death. Wallace Stevens. **CP-StevW**

These two cats guard the grapes. Their claws. Bassetti's Lions. Richard Hugo. **CP-HugoR**

These umbered cliffs and gnarls of masonry. Rome: Building a New Street in the Ancient Quarter. Thomas Hardy. **CP-HardT**

These Unreturning Destinies. Kenneth Patchen. **CP-PatcK**

These vales were saddened with no common gloom. Epitaph in Grasmere Church. William Wordsworth. **CP-WorW2**

These verses also, Manso, the Pierides are meditating. Manso. John Milton, *tr. fr. Latin by* John T. Shawcross. **CP-MiltJ**

These verses also to thy praise the Nine. John Milton. *See* Manso.

These vulgar ways that round me be. Arthur Hugh Clough. **SP-ClouA**

These walls they knew those shadows. Wall Shadows. Carl Sandburg. **CP-SandC**

These waters run secretively until. The Race. Charles Tomlinson. **CP-TomlC**

These watery diamond spheres. Kathleen Jessie Raine. **SP-RainK**

These, we are told (in an hour of legends). The Expectant Shelters. Kenneth Patchen. **CP-PatcK**

These Were Her Nightly Journeys. May Sarton. **SP-SartM**

These were my companions going forth by night. Chil's Song. Rudyard Kipling. **CP-KiplR** *Fr.* Red Dog. *Fr.* The Second Jungle Book.

These were never your true love's eyes. The Oldest Song. Rudyard Kipling. **CP-KiplR**

These were our children who died for our lands: they were dear in our sight. The Children. Rudyard Kipling. **CP-KiplR**

These were the days I saw my future wife. My Future Wife. John Hewitt. **CP-HewiJ**

These wet rocks where the tide has been. Low-Tide. Edna St. Vincent Millay. **CP-MillE**

These wheels within wheels. Carl Sandburg. *Fr.* Timesweep. **CP-SandC**

These Winds. Robert Lowell. **SP-LoweR**

These women are supposed to come. Blue Cheese and Chili Peppers. Charles Bukowski. **SP-BukC1**

These wonderful things. A Last World. John Ashbery. **SP-AshbJ**

These woods are too impersonal. On a Day in August. Thomas Merton. **CP-MertT**

These Words Also. Howard Nemerov. **CP-NemeH**

These Years a Winter. Thomas Merton. **CP-MertT**

Theseus and Ariadne. Robert Ranke Graves. **CP-GravR**

Theseus, if he did destroy the Minotaur. On Getting Out Of Vietnam. Howard Nemerov. **CP-NemeH**

Theseus Within the Labyrinth. Stephen Dobyns. **SP-DobyS**

These(whom;pretends / blue nothing). Edward Estlin Cummings. **CP-CummE**

Thesis and Antithesis. Arthur Hugh Clough. **SP-ClouA**

Thesis, though sincerely meant, A. Fifth Epistle. Donald Davie. *Fr.* Six Epistles to Eva Hesse. **CP-DavDo**

Thethe / the pink / Tartskids with. Edward Estlin Cummings. **CP-CummE**

Thetis. Hilda Doolittle. **CP-DoolH**

Thetis. Hilda Doolittle. **CP-DoolH**

Th'expense in odours is a most vain sin. To the Same Sir Cod. Ben Jonson. **CP-JonsB**

They / are the light-hearted races. The Laughing Ones. Charles Olson. **CP-OlsoC**

They. Wystan Hugh Auden. **CP-AudeW**

They. Robert Creeley. **CP-CreeR**

They. Robert Creeley. **CP-CreeR**

They abuse no maiden universe. O Everliving Queen! Kenneth Patchen. **CP-PatcK**

They Accuse Me of Not Talking. Hayden Carruth. **CP-CarHS**

They, after the slow building of the house. Geoffrey Hill. **CP-HillG** (Asmodeus.) **CP-HillG**

They all came, some wore sentiments. The Other Tradition. John Ashbery. **SP-AshbJ**

They all kept looking at each other's eyes. Elizabeth Bishop. *Fr.* Three Sonnets for the Eyes. **CP-BishE**

They All Made Peace—What Is Peace? Ernest Hemingway. **CP-HemiE**

They All Want to Play Hamlet. Carl Sandburg. **CP-SandC**

They answer one's questions. People's Surroundings. Marianne Craig Moore. **CP-MoorM**

They are above us all the time. The Angels. John Updike. **CP-UpdiJ**

They are afraid of climbing down from this idiotic tin-pot heaven of ours. Climbing Down. David Herbert Lawrence. **CP-LawrD**

They are all gone away. The House on the Hill. Edwin Arlington Robinson. **CP-RobiE**

They are all gone upstairs into the world. Thomas Prologizes. Wystan Hugh Auden. **CP-AudWJ**

They are all round me in the dark. After Midnight. Derek Mahon. *Fr.* Four Walks in the Country Near Saint-Brieuc. **SP-MahoD**

They are allowed to inherit. The Immigrants. Margaret Atwood. **SP-AtwM1**

They are always with us, the thin people. The Thin People. Sylvia Plath. **CP-PlatS**

They are and suffer; that is all they do. Wystan Hugh Auden. *Fr.* Sonnets from China. **CP-AudeW**

They are at the track every. Space Creatures. Charles Bukowski. **SP-BukC3**

They are chanting now the service of All the Dead. All Souls. David Herbert Lawrence. **CP-LawrD**

They are closing the auto plants. Fall Out. Charles Bukowski. **SP-BukC3**

They are cowshit farmers, these New Englanders. Marshall Washer. Hayden Carruth. **CP-CarHS**

They are crying salt tears. Repetitions. Carl Sandburg. **CP-SandC**

They are dragging me back. The Tunnel. Phoebe Hesketh. **SP-HeskP**

They are dreaming existence. Stones. John Haines. **SP-HainJ**

They are fencing the upland against. The Snow Fences. Charles Tomlinson. **CP-TomlC**

They are flocking from the East / And the West. All Saints. Christina Georgina Rossetti. **CP-RosC2**

"They are fools who kiss and tell." Rudyard Kipling. *See* Pink Dominoes.

They Are Great Trees. Thomas Hardy. **CP-HardT**

They are here again. Seventeen Years. Wendell Berry. **CP-BerrW**

"They are his new boots," she pursued. The New Boots. Thomas Hardy. **CP-HardT**

They Are Hostile Nations. Margaret Atwood. **SP-AtwM1**

They are hunting the boar in the vineyards. Season Opens on Wild Boar in Chianti. Robert Penn Warren. **SP-WarrR**

They are kneeling upright on a flowered bed. Short Story on a Painting of Gustav Klimt. Lawrence Ferlinghetti. **SP-FerlL**

They are light as flakes of dandruff with scrawny legs. Crabs. Marge Piercy. **SP-PierM**

They are massing at the bank. A Waking Dream. Thom Gunn. **CP-GunnT**

They are murdering all the young men. Thou Shalt Not Kill. Kenneth Rexroth. **SP-RexrK**

They are not all beasts. St Matthew. David Herbert Lawrence. **CP-LawrD**

They are not dead, they are not dead! The Argonauts. David Herbert Lawrence. **CP-LawrD**

They are not fashioned with a weary look. Spirits Are Organized Men. Marsden Hartley. *Fr.* Un Recuerdo—Hermano—Hart Crane R.I.P. **CP-HartM**

They are not, sir, worst owers, that do pay. Epistle to a Friend. Ben Jonson. **CP-JonsB**

They are not those, are present with their face. To the Most Noble, and above His Titles, Robert, Earl of Somerset. Ben Jonson. **CP-JonsB**

They are not those who used to feed us. The Puzzled Game-Birds. Thomas Hardy. **CP-HardT**

They are old over there, older than we are. Turn of the Wheel. Carl Sandburg. **CP-SandC**

They are pounded into the earth. It Is This Way with Men. Charles Kenneth Williams. **CP-WillC; SP-WillC**

They are preparing to begin again. The Task. John Ashbery. **SP-AshbJ**

They are rattling breakfast plates in basement kitchens. Morning at the Window. Thomas Stearns Eliot. **CP-ElioT**

They are so like. Dolls. David St. John. **SP-StJoD**

They are standing, or stalking, in clouds. Flamingos of the Soda Lakes. Laurence Lieberman. **SP-LiebL**

They are taking all my letters, and they. The Dishonest Mailmen. Robert Creeley. **CP-CreeR**

They are taking down the beautiful houses once built with loving hands. Lament in the Pacific Northwest. Malcolm Lowry. **CP-LowrM**

They are tearing down Penn Station. Her Hat. Robert Penn Warren. **SP-WarrR**

They are tearing down the oldest hotel. Tearing Down the Hotel. Miller Williams. **SP-WillM**

They are the last romantics, these candles. Candles. Sylvia Plath. **CP-PlatS**

They are the oldest living captive race. Ginkgoes in Fall. Howard Nemerov. **CP-NemeH**

They are warming up the old horrors; and all that they say is echoes of. The Soul's Desert. Robinson Jeffers. **CP-JefR3**

They are with her now, and in her ears, and known. George Meredith. *Fr.* France. **CP-MerG1**

They are with us always, but they have the wit. The Distances They Keep. Howard Nemerov. **CP-NemeH**

They are writing our names in the sky. The Bad Angels. Stephen Dunn. **SP-DunnS**

They arrive inside. Explorers. Charles Simic. **SP-SimiC**

They ascend into themselves. The Elect. Dabney Stuart. **SP-StuaD**

They ask but our Delight. Emily Dickinson. **CP-DickE**

They Ask Each Other Where They Came From. Carl Sandburg. **CP-SandC**

They ask for a knife. Help Wanted. Charles Simic. **SP-SimiC**

They Ask: Is God, Too, Lonely. Carl Sandburg. **CP-SandC**

They ask me how I feel. I Believe in You. "Bob Dylan." **CP-DylaB**

They ask me to handle bronzes. Bronzes. Carl Sandburg. **CP-SandC**

They await / War, and the news. George Oppen. *Fr.* Of Being Numerous. **CP-OppeG**

They bear him to his resting-place. She at His Funeral. Thomas Hardy. **CP-HardT**

They bear, in place of classic names. The Trade. Rudyard Kipling. **CP-KiplR**

They bespoke doomsday and they meant it by. Geoffrey Hill. *Fr.* Funeral Music. **CP-HillG**

They bid me sing to thee. A Song against Singing. Elizabeth Barrett Browning. **CP-BroEB**

They both spilled the salt. No doubt about that. Who Spilled the Salt? Isabella Gardner. **CP-GardI**

They bound her in white linen, smeared rich spice. Sarcophagus. John Hewitt. **CP-HewiJ**

They brood through vaults of notebooks. The Death of Mathmaticians. James Liddy. **CP-LiddJ**

They brought her to the place where Christ stood by. Pardon. Wystan Hugh Auden. **CP-AudWJ**

They brought him in on a stretcher from the world. Grandfather. Derek Mahon. **SP-MahoD**

They brought his coffin home and laid it on. Carnations. John Hewitt. **CP-HewiJ**

They brought me rubies from the mine. Rubies. Ralph Waldo Emerson. **CP-EmerR**

They buried Abel at sunset in the red wet earth. John Gould Fletcher. **SP-FletJ** *Fr.* Branches of Adam.

They burned lime on the hill and dropped it down here in an iron car. Bixby's Landing. Robinson Jeffers. **CP-JefR1**

They burnt a corpse upon the sand. Rudyard Kipling. **CP-KiplR** *Fr.* In Error. *Fr.* Plain Tales from the Hills.

They Buy with an Eye to Looks. Carl Sandburg. **CP-SandC**

They call all experience of the senses *mystic*, when the experience is considered. Mystic. David Herbert Lawrence. **CP-LawrD**

They call me and I go. Complaint. William Carlos Williams. **CP-WilW1**

They call me crafty, I robbed my brother. Louis MacNeice. *Fr.* Day of Returning. **CP-MacNL**

They call thee rich; I deem thee poor. Lucilius, *tr. fr. Greek by* William Cowper. **CP-CowpW**

(On a Miser.) **CP-CowpW**

They called across to ask me to get some beer and come up and. Opening the Window. Kenneth Patchen. **CP-PatcK**

They called it Annandale—and I was there. How Annandale Went Out. Edwin Arlington Robinson. **CP-RobiE**

They called it Neosho, meaning. By a River in the Osage Country. William Stafford. **SP-StafW**

They called me to the Window, for. Emily Dickinson. **CP-DickE**

They called the place Lookout Farm. Memoirs of a Spinach-Picker. Sylvia Plath. **CP-PlatS**

They called Thee MERRY ENGLAND, in old time. William Wordsworth. *Fr.* Poems Composed or Suggested During a Tour, in the Summer of 1833. **CP-WorW2**

They called us. The Charm. Rita Dove. **SP-DoveR**

They called us to a change of heart. Muriel Rukeyser. *Fr.* Letter to the Front. **CP-RukeM**

They came / Next to meadows abundant, pierced with flowers. Gerard Manley Hopkins. *Fr.* Fragments. **CP-HopkG**

They came furtively. Chuck Miller. **SP-MillC**

They came on ponies, barefoot. Bolsheviks. Aba Shtoltsenberg, *tr. fr. Yiddish by* Stanley Kunitz. **CP-KuniS**

They came out of the sun undetected. The Raid. William Everson. **SP-EverW**

They came, the brothers, and took two chairs. The Announcement. Thomas Hardy. **CP-HardT**

They came to live in me. The Tree that Became a House. John Haines. **SP-HainJ**

They Came to Me and Said, "There Is a Child." Muriel Rukeyser. **Son** *Fr.* Nine Poems for the Unborn Child. **CP-RukeM**

They came to the end of the road. Three Children Looking Over the Edge of the World. Frederick Morgan. **SP-MorgF**

They came to Tísip / With pepper in their speech. Chilam Balam. Thomas Merton. *Fr.* South. *Fr.* The Geography of Lograire. **CP-MertT**

They can be fists punching the water. Sky, Water. Charles Kenneth Williams. **CP-WillC**

They can tell me the soul rises to its perch. The Soul. Stephen Berg. **SP-BergS**

They capped their heads with feathers, masked. Charivari. Margaret Atwood. **SP-AtwM1**

They carry nativeness / To a conclusion. George Oppen. *Fr.* Of Being Numerous. **CP-OppeG**

They christened my brother of old. The Bell Buoy. Rudyard Kipling. **CP-KiplR**

They clatter past; only the red rear light. Trippers. Wystan Hugh Auden. **CP-AudWJ**

They climbed a mountain in the afternoon. Say Yes! Wystan Hugh Auden. **CP-AudWJ**

They clock out and wait, worn out. Night Shift: the Composing Room. Barton Sutter. **SP-SuttB**

They come, *Author's own English vers. of his* "Elles viennent." Samuel Beckett. **CP-BeckS**

They come closer together, vines. Who Walks There? Kenneth Patchen. **CP-PatcK**

They come down from the mountains, proud of their rags. Proud of Their Rags. Carl Sandburg. **CP-SandC**

They come in tiny boats. . . . Passages. Thomas McGrath. **SP-McGrT**

They come in low, wings like dark bandages. Autumn Is the Crows' Time. Kenneth Patchen. **CP-PatcK**

They come into your life. The Desperate. Chuck Miller. **SP-MillC**

They Come No More, Those Words, Those Finches. Archibald MacLeish. **CP-MacLA**

They come on to my clean. The Fallen Angels. Anne Sexton. **CP-SextA**

They come to us but once in life. Holidays. George Meredith. **CP-MerG2**

They come to you with their descriptions of your soul. Adrienne Rich. **HCAP; SP-RicA2** *Fr.* Shooting Script. **CP-RicAE**

They come together for a time. Harvesters. Chuck Miller. **SP-MillC**

They come too thick, hail-hard, and all beside. John Berryman. *Fr.* Sonnets to Chris. **CP-BerrJ**

They conspired to paint the air. The Impressionists. Erica Jong. **SP-JongE**

They could bend low. Light and Moonbells. Carl Sandburg. **CP-SandC**

They could not carry much, as soldiers. Gigantomachia. Wallace Stevens. **CP-StevW**

They cross the frontier as their names cross your pages. The New Emigration. Kay Boyle. **CP-BoylK**

They cross the yard. From the Suburbs. Louise Glück. **FaBoWP; GeTw; NALW** *Fr.* Dedication to Hunger. **SP-GlücL**

They crush together—a rustling heap of flesh. The Ballet. Thomas Hardy. **CP-HardT**

They cut it in squares. Socratic. Hilda Doolittle. **HoPM** *Fr.* Child Poems. **CP-DoolH**

They Desire a Better Country. Christina Georgina Rossetti. **CP-RosC1**

They did not hear my children. God Said "They Did Not Hear. . . ." Thomas Merton. **CP-MertT**

They Die Over and Over. In the Movies. Gilbert Sorrentino. **SP-SorrG**

They die—the dead return not—Misery. Death. Percy Bysshe Shelley. **CP-ShelP**

They do not believe they visited islands that never existed. Return of Ulysses I. John Yau. **SP-YauJo**

They do not come separately. So Can Anger. Stevie Smith. **CP-SmitS**

They do say said. The Instance. Charles Tomlinson. **CP-TomlC**

They done took Cordelia. Stony Lonesome. Langston Hughes. **SP-HughL**

They don't come back, he said. Nitrate. Philip Levine. **SP-LeviP**

They don't say gully, cove, cut, gulch. Crow's Mark. Hayden Carruth. **CP-CarHS**

They don't smoke pot. Prospero's Isle. Isabella Gardner. **CP-GardI**

They dreamt not of a perishable home. Continued [Inside of King's College Chapel, Cambridge]. William Wordsworth. *Fr.* Ecclesiastical Sonnets. **CP-WorW2**

They drift unobtrusively into the dream, they linger, then they depart, but they emanate, always. Shadows. Charles Kenneth Williams. **SP-WillC**

They dropped like Flakes. Emily Dickinson. **CP-DickE**

They drowned her kittens only yesterday. The Cat. Wystan Hugh Auden. **CP-AudWJ**

They dug a trench, and threw him in a grave. A Young Greek, Killed In The Wars. Richard Eberhart. **CP-EberR**

They dug up the grave, while a banjo and two guitars. Muriel Rukeyser. **CP-RukeM**

They dunked me in the creek. Baptism. Alice Walker. **CP-WalkA**

They eat beans mostly, this old yellow pair. The Bean Eaters. Gwendolyn Brooks. **SP-BrooG**

They Eat Out. Margaret Atwood. **SP-AtwM1**

They ended parle, and both addressed for fight. John Milton. **OBWP** *Fr.* Book VI. *Fr.* Paradise Lost. **CP-MiltJ**

They enter as animals from the outer. Years. Sylvia Plath. **CP-PlatS**

They enter the bare wood, drawn. The Novices. Denise Levertov. **CP-LeveD**

They escape before, but their shadows walk behind. The Surrounded. Muriel Rukeyser. **CP-RukeM**

They face us in sea-noon sun, just as he saw them waiting. Suite for Lord Timothy Dexter. Muriel Rukeyser. **CP-RukeM**

They fall through my life and surround me. The Twin Falls. James Dickey. **CP-DickJ**

They Feed They Lion. Philip Levine. **SP-LeviP**

They filled the eyes of the vaulting. Basil Bunting. *Fr.* The Spoils. **CP-BuntB**

They fle[e] from me that sometime [*or* sometyme] did me se[e]k[e]. Sir Thomas Wyatt. **CP-WyatT**

They fought in heavy armor. The Gladiators. Stanley Jasspon Kunitz. **CP-KuniS**

They found him in the fields and called him back to music. Bunk Johnson Blowing. Muriel Rukeyser. **CP-RukeM**

They fuck you up, your mum and dad. This Be the Verse. Philip Larkin. **CP-LarkP**

They gathered from half the countryside. The Lifting. John Hewitt. **CP-HewiJ**

They gathered round in prayer, had preachers brought. My Great-Grandfather's Refusal. John Hewitt. **CP-HewiJ**

They gathered shouting crowds along the road. An Old Story. Howard Nemerov. *Fr.* Epigrams: "Wasp, climbing the window pane." **CP-NemeH**

They gave her a whip and colander. Some Sap Sings a Poor Pantoum. Gilbert Sorrentino. *Fr.* Twelve Études for Voice and Kazoo. **SP-SorrG**

They gave him a crown of bays and dressed him up. The Crown of Bays. Stevie Smith. **CP-SmitS**

They gave him an overdose. Loyal. William Matthews. **SP-MattW**

They gave me in trust. Hayden Carruth. **CP-CarHS** *Fr.* The Clay Hill Anthology.

They gave them royal names. The Rivals. Phoebe Hesketh. **SP-HeskP**

They get drunk, these Great-Sledmakers. Their copper mugs. The Great-Sledmakers. Kenneth Patchen. **CP-PatcK**

They get to Benvenuti's. There are booths. I Love Those Little Booths at Benvenuti's. Gwendolyn Brooks. **SP-BrooG** *Fr.* The Womanhood.

They get up on their garage roof. 2 Outside, As Bones Break in My Kitchen. Charles Bukowski. **SP-BukC2**

They give me a bad. Crows. Marge Piercy. **SP-PierM**

They go on writing. An Unkind Poem. Charles Bukowski. **SP-BukC1**

They had built it up—but not for this the lean. Débâcle. Louis MacNeice. **CP-MacNL**

They had come in on a carriage (which. The Epic Expands. Robert Creeley. **CP-CreeR**

They had eleven children of their own. The Return (1885). John Hewitt. **CP-HewiJ**

They had got used to him. But when they brought. *tr. from the German of* Rilke. Randall Jarrell. **CP-JarrR**

They had long met o' Zundays—her true love and she. The Bride-Night Fire. Thomas Hardy. **CP-HardT**

They had never had one in the house before. Bronzeville Woman in a Red Hat. Gwendolyn Brooks. **SP-BrooG**

They had supposed their formula was fixed. White Troops Had Their Orders but the Negroes Looked Like Men. Gwendolyn Brooks. **SP-BrooG**

They had taken off their sandals. My Coat Is Dirty. Kenneth Patchen. **CP-PatcK**

They had the Boston Bull before I was born. Growing Up Askew. Mona Van Duyn. **SP-VanDM**

They Had Torn Off My Face at the Office. Ted Kooser. **SP-KoosT**

They hail me as one living. The Dead Man Walking. Thomas Hardy. **CP-HardT**

They happened in us. . . . Remembering Loves and Deaths. Thomas McGrath. **SP-McGrT**

They hauled him many times. Vapid Transit. Gilbert Sorrentino. **SP-SorrG**

They Have. John Berryman. **CP-BerrJ**

They have a little Odor—that to me. Emily Dickinson. **CP-DickE**

They have all died and their souls are extinguished; three remnant images. Dear Judas. Robinson Jeffers. **CP-JefR2**

They have an innocence the words. The Evening Grass. Kay Boyle. **CP-BoylK**

They have been with us a long time. Telephone Poles. John Updike. **CP-UpdiJ**

They have brought gold and spices to my King. All Saints. Christina Georgina Rossetti. **CP-RosC3**

They have carried the mahogany chair and the cane rocker. Mourning Picture. Adrienne Rich. **CP-RicAE; SP-RicA2**

They have clipped the wings of my doves, my messengers. Alun Lewis. *Fr.* The Captivity. **CP-LewiA**

They have come again to graze the orchard. Thanksgiving. Louise Glück. **SP-GlücL**

They have come back from Russia. A Confession to Eugene Jolas. Kay Boyle. **CP-BoylK**

They have fenced in the dirt road. Burial. Alice Walker. **CP-WalkA**

They have gone / into the green hill, by doors without hinges. Apples. Donald Hall. **CP-HallD**

They have gone into the gray hills quilled with birches. Mined Country. Richard Wilbur. **CP-WilbR**

They have green tram in Florence now. À La Maniere De D. H. Lawrence. David Herbert Lawrence. **CP-LawrD**

They have hung the sky with arrows. Edward Estlin Cummings. **CP-CummE**

They have lived together for twenty years. Richard Shelton. *Fr.* Angel and the Anchorite. **SP-ShelR**

They have made for Leonora this low dwelling in the ground. Leonora. Edwin Arlington Robinson. **CP-RobiE**

They have no song, the sedges dry. Song in the Songless. George Meredith. **CP-MerG1**

"They have not chosen me," he said. Emily Dickinson. **CP-DickE**

They have only to look at each other to laugh. The Old Gray Couple (1). Archibald MacLeish. **CP-MacLA**

They have painted and sung. Women Washing Their Hair. Carl Sandburg. **CP-SandC**

They have removed a building to make. The United Front. William Carlos Williams. **CP-WilW2**

They have space enough, however cramped their quarters. Dreaming Children. Robert Ranke Graves. **CP-GravR**

They have sunk into deeper service. They have gone down. Ted Hughes. *Fr.* Stations. **SP-HughT**

They have taken Sun from Woman. Robbers' Den. Robert Ranke Graves. **CP-GravR**

They have taken the ball of earth. Leather Leggings. Carl Sandburg. **CP-SandC**

They have their moments, and if one loved them they ought to die in. Moments of Glory. Robinson Jeffers. **CP-JeffR3**

They Have Turned the Church Where I Ate God. Gary Gildner. **SP-GildG**

They have yarns / Of a skyscraper so tall they had to put hinges. Carl Sandburg. **AmFN; LiTA; MoAmPo** *Fr.* The People, Yes. **CP-SandC**

They haven't found the W. News from the Underworld. John Updike. **CP-UpdiJ**

They hear Thee not, O God! nor see. Ezekiel. John Greenleaf Whittier. **CP-WhitJ**

They hold their public meetings where. The Three Monuments. William Butler Yeats. **CP-YeatW**

They hunch their heads against the fable of the night. The Dolls Play at Hansel and Gretel. William Dickey. **SP-DickW**

They hurt no one. They rove the North. In Fur. William Stafford. **SP-StafW**

They improve their inimitable wire. Thomas Merton. *Fr.* Cables to the Ace. **CP-MertT**

They in their cruel traps, and we in ours. Thoughts in a Zoo. Countee Cullen. **CP-CullC**

They intimately know just how our fortune lies. Business Acquaintances. John Updike. **CP-UpdiJ**

They killed a Child to please the Gods. Rudyard Kipling. **CP-KiplR**

They killed him, just to really see. A Present to the Sun. Marsden Hartley. **CP-HartM**

They killed him on the gallows tree. Galán. Archibald MacLeish. **CP-MacLA**

They know the wilings of the world. Not Known. Thomas Hardy. **CP-HardT**

They lean against the cooling car, backs pressed. The Discovery of the Pacific. Thom Gunn. **CP-GunnT**

They lean over the path. Orchids. Theodore Roethke. **CP-RoetT**

They leave us so to the way we took. In Neglect. Robert Frost. **CP-FrosR**

They leave us with the Infinite. Emily Dickinson. **CP-DickE**

They left their home of summer ease. The Seeking of the Waterfall. John Greenleaf Whittier. **CP-WhitJ**

They lie at rest asleep and dead. My Old Friends. Christina Georgina Rossetti. **CP-RosC3**

They lie at rest, our blessed dead. Christina Georgina Rossetti. **CP-RosC2**

They live by attenuation. Maples in a Spruce Forest. John Updike. **CP-UpdiJ**

They live down by the sea. . . these men. The Gypsies Near Del Mar. Charles Bukowski. **SP-BukC2**

They lived long, and were faithful. A Marriage, an Elegy. Wendell Berry. **CP-BerrW**

They lived, Pompeiians. Pompeii. John Updike. **CP-UpdiJ**

They locked into each other. The Puzzle. Erica Jong. **SP-JongE**

They locked up a man. The Wrong Man. Leonard Cohen. **CP-CoheL**

They look like big dogs badly drawn, drawn wrong. Wolves in the Zoo. Howard Nemerov. **CP-NemeH**

They look like fact, the bath, the wall, the knife. Marat Dead. Charles Tomlinson. **CP-TomlC**

They look shabby and crazy but not. Small-City People. John Updike. **CP-UpdiJ**

They look surreal. Cronkhite Beach. Charles Tomlinson. **CP-TomlC**

They look twisted / because / they draw fruit from under earth. The Apple Trees. Brendan Galvin. **SP-GalvB**

They look up with their pale and sunken faces. Elizabeth Barrett Browning. **NBM; OBD** *Fr.* The Cry of the Children. **CP-BroEB**

They looked soft floating down[. White puffs that glowed]. Invasion North. Richard Hugo. **CP-HugoR**

They made a myth of you, professor. Mr. Attila. Carl Sandburg. **CP-SandC**

They made the chamber sweet with flowers and leaves. A Pause. Christina Georgina Rossetti. **CP-RosC3**

They made themselves so tiny. A Suitcase Strapped with a Rope. Charles Simic. **SP-SimiC**

They made very little of such events—*Horses rising out of the.* It Takes Few Kinds. Kenneth Patchen. **CP-PatcK**

They made you complicated. The Coats. Tess Gallagher. **SP-GallT**

They make a pretty pair of debauchees. Catullus. *See* Carmen 57: "*Caesar Mamurraque!* / A peerless pair of brazen buggers."

They make me wince, such vivid dreams rise up. Stone Walls. May Sarton. **SP-SartM**

They march at God's. Canaan. Geoffrey Hill. **CP-HillG**

They may, because I would not cloy your ear. John Berryman. *Fr.* Sonnets to Chris. **CP-BerrJ**

They may talk of the *goddesses* in *Ida* veils. Alexander Pope. *Fr.* Epigrams Occasion'd by an Invitation to Court. **CP-PopeA**

They met, and overwhelming her distrust. Job the Rejected. Edwin Arlington Robinson. **CP-RobiE**

They Met Young. Carl Sandburg. **CP-SandC**

They might have waited had they been aware. A House Demolished. John Hewitt. **CP-HewiJ**

They might not need me—yet they might. Emily Dickinson. **CP-DickE**

They mock my toil—the nymphs and am'rous swains. John Milton. *See* Canzone: "Scoffing, amorous maidens and young men."

They more than we are what we are. Statues. Kathleen Jessie Raine. **SP-RainK**

They move at maximum velocity. Hide & Seek. Howard Nemerov. **CP-NemeH**

They move beneath it. The Totem. Gilbert Sorrentino. **SP-SorrG**

They move between the jagged edge. The Planters. Margaret Atwood. **SP-AtwM1**

They must not go alone. Poem and Prayer for an Invading Army. Edna St. Vincent Millay. **SP-MillE**

They must to keep their certainty accuse. The Leaders of the Crowd. William Butler Yeats. **CP-YeatW**

They need no other. Charles Henri Ford. **SP-FordC** *Fr.* Emblems of Arachne.

They nickname Lesbia's brother 'pulcher'. Carmen 79. Catullus. *Fr.* Carmina. **CP-Catul**

They noticed that virginity was needed. Wystan Hugh Auden. *Fr.* The Quest. **CP-AudeW**

They offer you many things. Choices. Carl Sandburg. **CP-SandC**

They Part at Daybreak, Returning Their Inevitable Ways. Alun Lewis. *Fr.* War Wedding. **CP-LewiA**

They parted—a pallid, trembling pair. Cross-Currents. Thomas Hardy. **CP-HardT**

They passed beneath the College gate. The Majesty of Justice. "Lewis Carroll." **CP-CarrL**

They photograph you on your porch. Photographs. Charles Bukowski. **SP-BukC1**

They photographed me young upon a tiger skin. The Photograph. Stevie Smith. **CP-SmitS**

They played in the beautiful garden. The Warden. Stevie Smith. **CP-SmitS**

They please me not—these solemn songs. A Choice. Paul Laurence Dunbar. **CP-DunbP**

They pointed me out on the highway, and they said. The Traveller. John Berryman. **CP-BerrJ**

They pray. Security against oldness. Muriel Rukeyser. **CP-RukeM**

They prefer to sleep on tiny colored stones. The Tribes of Rakala. Kenneth Patchen. **CP-PatcK**

They pretend that there's nothing to believe in anymore! Yellow Stones—Sea of Majestic Doves. Kenneth Patchen. **CP-PatcK**

They put ma body in the ground. Judgment Day. Langston Hughes. **SP-HughL**

They put their finger on their lips. Silence. Ralph Waldo Emerson. **CP-EmerR**

They Put Their Trust in Thee, and Were Not Confounded. Christina Georgina Rossetti. **CP-RosC2**

  "Together once, but never more / While Time and Death run out their runs."

  "Whatso it be, howso it be, Amen. / Blessed it is, believing, not to see."

They put up big wooden gods. Manufactured Gods. Carl Sandburg. **CP-SandC**

They put Us far apart. Emily Dickinson. **CP-DickE**

They ran for their lives up the nightslope, gained the car. Mary Stuart. Robert Lowell. **SP-LoweR**

They recall the promises in the books and the. The German Girls! The German Girls! Archibald MacLeish. **CP-MacLA**

They rise into mind. For an Exchange of Rings. Donald Hall. **CP-HallD**

They rocked on iron benches on the sand. Turner. Kenneth Patchen. **CP-PatcK**

They roused him with muffins--they roused him with ice. The Baker's Tale. "Lewis Carroll." **EBEV; NAEL-2; OXAEP-2** *Fr.* The Hunting of the Snark. **CP-CarrL**

They rule out of our justice and our despair. Muriel Rukeyser. **CP-RukeM**

They sadly travelled thus, until they came. Arthur's Fight with Orgoglio and Duessa. Edmund Spenser. **EBNV** *Fr.* The Faerie Queene. **CP-Spens**

They said: / she is high and far and blind. For Bryher and Perdita. Hilda Doolittle. *Fr.* Hymen. **CP-DoolH**

They said I got away in a boat. After the Titanic. Derek Mahon. **SP-MahoD**

They said that Fame her clarion dropped. On Sherman's Men. Herman Melville. **SP-MelvH**

They said this mystery shall never cease. William Blake. **TrGrPo** *Fr.* Gnomic Verses. **CP-BlakW**

They said to us, or tried to say, and failed. The Innocents. Adrienne Rich. **CP-RicAE**

They sat in silent watchfulness. The Cypress-Tree of Ceylon. John Greenleaf Whittier. **CP-WhitJ**

They sat. They stood about. The Apostles: Versailles, 1919. Geoffrey Hill. *Fr.* Of Commerce and Society: Variations on a Theme. **CP-HillG**

They sat together in the park. Simple Twist of Fate. "Bob Dylan." **CP-DylaB**

They sate to meat, and Satyrane his chaunce. Edmund Spenser. **OAEL-1** *Fr.* The Faerie Queene. **CP-Spens**

They saw rivers flow west and hoped again. West Virginia. Muriel Rukeyser. **CP-RukeM**

They Say. Robert Creeley. **CP-CreeR**

They say a / woman passes at. Photo. Robert Creeley. **CP-CreeR**

They say *Argyll*'s a wit, for what? Alexander Pope. *Fr.* Epigrams Occasion'd by an Invitation to Court. **CP-PopeA**

They Say Etna. Basil Bunting. **CP-BuntB**

They say ev'rything can be replaced. I Shall Be Released. "Bob Dylan." **CP-DylaB**

They say eyes clear with age. Long Sight in Age. Philip Larkin. **CP-LarkP**

They say he didn't have an enemy. Last Great American Whale. "Lou Reed." **SP-ReedL**

They say I have a circus soul. they call me. The Ballad of Hagan Waker. Patti Smith. **SP-SmitP**

They say I was arrogant. Galileo Galilei (1564–1642). Siv Cedering Fox. *Fr.* Letters from the Astronomers. **SP-CedeS**

They say I wrote a naughty book. My Naughty Book. David Herbert Lawrence. **CP-LawrD**

They say ideal beauty cannot enter. Hiram Powers' "Greek Slave." Elizabeth Barrett Browning. **CP-BroEB**

They say it is very difficult. Fresh Water. David Herbert Lawrence. **CP-LawrD**

They say it is waiting for more, the snow. Snow Signs. Charles Tomlinson. **CP-TomlC**

They say it's over. Poem, 1928. Ernest Hemingway. **CP-HemiE**

They say love is a great heat. Certain Weathers. Jenny Joseph. **SP-JoseJ**

They say my mother is a witch. Johannes Kepler (1571–1630). Siv Cedering Fox. *Fr.* Letters from the Astronomers. **SP-CedeS**

They say my verse is sad: no wonder. Alfred Edward Housman. **CP-HousA**

They say one king is mad. Perhaps. Who knows? Who Knows? Nicholas Vachel Lindsay. **CP-LindV**

They say that absence conquers. Emily Dickinson. **SP-DickE**

They say that God lives very high. A Child's Thought of God. Elizabeth Barrett Browning. **CP-BroEB**

They say that Hope is happiness. Stanzas for Music. Byron. **CP-Byron**

They say, that Pity in Love's service dwells. George Meredith. *Fr.* Modern Love. **CP-MerG1**

They say that reality exists only in the spirit. Demiurge. David Herbert Lawrence. **CP-LawrD**

They say that "Time assuages." Emily Dickinson. **CP-DickE**

They say that trees scream. High Frequency. Marge Piercy. **SP-PierM**

They say the ground precisely swept. For the Felling of an Elm in the Harvard Yard. Adrienne Rich. **CP-RicAE**

They Say the Sea Is Loveless. David Herbert Lawrence. **CP-LawrD**

They say the war is over. But water still. Redeployment. Howard Nemerov. **CP-NemeH**

They say the wells. Winter News. John Haines. **SP-HainJ**

They say there is a dying star which is travelling in two directions. The Prophet. Alice Notley. **SP-NotlA**

They say there is a sweeter air. A Carriage from Sweden. Marianne Craig Moore. **CP-MoorM**

They say there is no hope. Sea Gods. Hilda Doolittle. **CP-DoolH**

They say they are one flesh. Archibald MacLeish. **CP-MacLA** *Fr.* The Happy Marriage.

They say, through patience, chalk. Hafiz, *tr. fr. Persian by* Ralph Waldo Emerson. **CP-EmerR**

They say to me, "There is." Idyl. William Carlos Williams. **CP-WilW1**

They saw we devour our men. To the Man Who Watches Spiders. Siv Cedering Fox. **SP-CedeS**

They say you are not for me. Forbidden Things. Alice Walker. **CP-WalkA**

They say you can't think and hit at the same time. Masterful. William Matthews. **SP-MattW**

They scarcely waked before they slept. Holy Innocents. Christina Georgina Rossetti. **CP-RosC2**

They scatter me from church to gutter. Avarice and Ambition Only Were the First Builders of Towns and Founders of Empire. Kenneth Patchen. **CP-PatcK**

They see his face! The Departed. Donald Davie. **CP-DavDo**

They seek, are sought; to daily battle led. Spanish Guerillas 1811. William Wordsworth. **CP-WorW1**

They seem hundreds of years away. Breughel. The Seed Cutters. Seamus Heaney. **FaBCIP; PNI** *Fr.* Mossbawn. **SP-HeanS**

They sent him back to her. The letter came. Not to Keep. Robert Frost. **CP-FrosR**

They sentenced me to twenty years of boredom. First We Take Manhattan. Leonard Cohen. **CP-CoheL**

They set their angels dancing on a pin. The Tumbling Spore. John Hewitt. **CP-HewiJ**

They set up stones to show where time has ended. Conway Burying Ground. Archibald MacLeish. **CP-MacLA**

They shall arise in the States. Mediums. Walt Whitman. **CP-WhitW**

They Shall Be as White as Snow. Christina Georgina Rossetti. **CP-RosC2**

They shall have breath that never were. Alfred Edward Housman. **CP-HousA**

They shall not be put to shame, / When they speak with their enemies in the gate. Bible, *O.T. See* Psalm 127: "Except the Lord build the house."

They shall not return to us, the resolute, the young. Mesopotamia. Rudyard Kipling. **CP-KiplR**

They should have called the thistle. Thistle. William Carlos Williams. **CP-WilW1**

They shut me up in Prose. Emily Dickinson. **CP-DickE**

They shut the road through the woods. The Way through the Woods. Rudyard Kipling. **CP-KiplR**

They sing in the darkness. Pistols for Pleasure—Guitars for Defense. Marsden Hartley. **CP-HartM**

They sing their dearest songs. During Wind and Rain. Thomas Hardy. **CP-HardT**

They sit and smoke on the esplanade. At a Watering-Place. Thomas Hardy. **CMoP** *Fr.* Satires of Circumstance in Fifteen Glimpses. **CP-HardT**

They sit in a room. Outside the world revolves. Portrait of Three Conspirators. Howard Nemerov. **CP-NemeH**

They sit in a row. The Fury of Overshoes. Anne Sexton. *Fr.* The Furies. **CP-SextA**

They sit up late / weighing synonyms. Brain Child. Phoebe Hesketh. **SP-HeskP**

They slew by night. Geoffrey Hill. **HAP** *Fr.* The Pentecost Castle. **CP-HillG**

They slew him, the women. The Leader. Charles Olson. **CP-OlsoC**

They smile and bring the food. Windy Night. Charles Bukowski. **SP-BukC3**

They snarl Over Spain like cur-dogs over a bone, then look at each other. Sinverguenza. Robinson Jeffers. **CP-JefR2**

They sought it with thimbles, they sought it with care. Fit the Fifth: The Beaver's Lesson. "Lewis Carroll." *Fr.* The Hunting of the Snark. **CP-CarrL**

They sought it with thimbles, they sought it with care. Fit the Seventh: The Banker's Fate. "Lewis Carroll." *Fr.* The Hunting of the Snark. **CP-CarrL**

They sought it with thimbles, they sought it with care. Fit the Sixth: The Barrister's Dream. "Lewis Carroll." **EBNV** *Fr.* The Hunting of the Snark. **CP-CarrL**

They sought it with thimbles, they sought it with care. The Vanishing. "Lewis Carroll." **OXAEP-2** *Fr.* The Hunting of the Snark. **CP-CarrL**

They speak to you, give their love. Out of Their Butchered Hearts. Gilbert Sorrentino. **SP-SorrG**

They spoke of the horse alive. The Horse. Philip Levine. **SP-LeviP**

They sprang up out of darkness, shouting! Kentucky. Edwin Rolfe. **CP-RolfE**

They spread their legs as a toad. Waking into Sleep. Kenneth Patchen. **CP-PatcK**

They stand confronting, the coffin between. Over the Coffin. Thomas Hardy. *Fr.* Satires of Circumstance in Fifteen Glimpses. **CP-HardT**

They stand contentedly, chewing. Plow Horses. Kenneth Patchen. **CP-PatcK**

They stand in a corner, on a shadowy shelf. Beginner's Guide. Howard Nemerov. **CP-NemeH**

They stand in the clearing of Kingfisher Flat. The High Embrace. William Everson. **SP-EverW**

They stand like monuments or trees, not women. Women at Streatham Hill. Jenny Joseph. **SP-JoseJ**

They stand there weeping in the stained daylight. Fresco: Departure for an Imperialist War. Thomas McGrath. **SP-McGrT**

They still seem G.I., the uniform lines. G. I. Graves in Tuscany. Richard Hugo. **CP-HugoR**

They stood at the foot of the figure. At a Pause in a Country Dance. Thomas Hardy. **CP-HardT**

They stopped singing because. Why They Stopped Singing. Roy Fisher. **SP-FishR**

They strew in the path of kings and czars. Hafiz, *tr.* by Ralph Waldo Emerson. **CP-EmerR** *Fr.* Odes.

They sucked us in. To Good Guys Dead. Ernest Hemingway. **CP-HemiE**

They sweep up, crying, riding the wind. Rooks In October. Walter de la Mare. **CP-DeLaW**

They take no shame for dark defeat. The Fortitude of the North. Herman Melville. **CP-MelvH**

They talk as slow as Legends grow. Emily Dickinson. **CP-DickE**

They talk down through / the centuries to us. On Going Back to the Street after Viewing an Art Show. Charles Bukowski. **SP-BukC2**

They talk of fencing, and the use of arms. An Epigram. To William, Earl of Newcastle. Ben Jonson. **CP-JonsB**

They talk of the triumph of the machine. The Triumph of the Machine. David Herbert Lawrence. **CP-LawrD**

They talk to each other, and he holds her hand. Muriel Rukeyser. **CP-RukeM**

They tell me, lady, that to-day. To Miss Cornish. Robert Louis Stevenson. **CP-StevR**

They tell me, Lucy, thou art dead. Lucy Hooper. John Greenleaf Whittier. **CP-WhitJ**

They tell me on the morrow I must leave. On a Proposed Trip South. William Carlos Williams. **CP-WilW1**

They tell me that euphoria is the feeling of feeling wonderful, well. No Doctors Today, Thank You. Ogden Nash. **CP-NashO**

They tell me that these British moral birds. British Sincerity. David Herbert Lawrence. **CP-LawrD**

They tell me 'tis decided you depart. Byron. **CBLP** *Fr.* Canto the First. **EnRP; NAEL-2; NoP; OAEL-2; PoE** *Fr.* Don Juan. **CP-Byron**

They tell me 'tis decided; you depart. Byron. **NOBRP** *Fr.* Canto the First. **EnRP; NAEL-2; NoP; OAEL-2; PoE** *Fr.* Don Juan. **CP-Byron**

"They tell me, your carpenters," quoth I to my friend the Russ. Ivàn Ivànovitch. Robert Browning. **CP-BroR2**

They that go down to the sea in ships. Bible, *O.T.* *See* Psalm 107: "O give thanks unto the Lord, for he is good: for. . . ."

They that have power to hurt[e], and will do[e] none. Sonnet 94. William Shakespeare. **BLPL; CABA; CBLP; EIL; FaBoEn; GTBS; GTBS-6; GTBS-P; ImPo; InPS; LiTB; MasP; NAEL-1; NOBE; NoP; NoSic; OAEL-1; OBEV; OXAEP-1; PPP; PPoe; PeHV; PoE; PoEL-2; SCGP; SCV; Son; TEP; TRP; TrGrPo** *Fr.* Sonnets. **CP-ShaWS**

They that love not—are they not as blind camels that behold no. George Meredith. *Fr.* Arabic Poems. **CP-MerG2**

They that trust in the Lord shall be as mount Zion. Psalm 125. Bible, *O.T.* *Fr.* Psalms. **CP-Psal**

They then to fountain-abundant Ida, mother of wild beasts. Hypnos on Ida. Homer, *tr.* by George Meredith. **CP-MerG1** *Fr.* The Iliad.

They think it's easy to be dead, those. Tableau Vivant. Tess Gallagher. **SP-GallT**

They throng from the east and the west, / The north and the south, with a song. As the Doves to Their Windows. Christina Georgina Rossetti. **CP-RosC2**

They throw in Drummer Hodge, to rest. Drummer Hodge. Thomas Hardy. **CP-HardT**

They tied his arms behind his back to teach him how to swim. The Blue Mask. "Lou Reed." **SP-ReedL**

They, to Me. Donald Davie. **CP-DavDo**

They Toil Not, Neither Do They Spin. Christina Georgina Rossetti. **CP-RosC2**

They Told Me. Walter de la Mare. **CP-DeLaW**

They told me I might hold the fairest one. Easy Rider. Kenneth Patchen. **CP-PatcK**

They told me in an old book. Two Women. Carl Sandburg. **CP-SandC**

They told me this story a long time ago. Sleeping Beauty. Howard Nemerov. **CP-NemeH**

They told me you had been to her. Evidence Read at the Trial of the Knave of Hearts. "Lewis Carroll." **CP-CarrL** *Fr.* Alice's Adventures in Wonderland.

They took me out. Ku Klux. Langston Hughes. **SP-HughL**

They took my man off the street. Private First Class. Charles Bukowski. **SP-BukC1**

"They tossed my baby like a cat in the air". Hayden Carruth. *Fr.* The Sleeping Beauty. **CP-CarHL**

They trace their ancestry. The Legend of Paper Plates. John Haines. **SP-HainJ**

They tried to hand it to us on a platter. Two Humpties. Carl Sandburg. **CP-SandC**

They turn every heart to stone O for the love. All the Roses of the World. Kenneth Patchen. **CP-PatcK**

They turned together with a shocked surprise—. Joseph and Mary. Robert Ranke Graves. **CP-GravR**

They (2). Robert Creeley. **CP-CreeR**

They walk foward now into this death. Those Upon Whom God Has Labored. Kenneth Patchen. **CP-PatcK**

They walk in and fall into. The Time. Robert Creeley. **CP-CreeR**

They walk on the waves at night—. Two Drowned at the Gateway. Marsden Hartley. **CP-HartM**

They walked beside the wave-worn beach. The Second Voice. "Lewis Carroll." *Fr.* The Three Voices. **CP-CarrL**

They want to caress. My Hands Are My Enemies. Richard Shelton. **SP-ShelR**

They wanted me to tell the truth. What They Wanted. Stephen Dunn. **SP-DunnS**

They wanted water. Once there'd been a spring. The Spring Restored. John Hewitt. **CP-HewiJ**

They Warned Him Then They Threw Him Away. Charles Kenneth Williams. **CP-WillC**

They wash you / when. Charles Kenneth Williams. **CP-WillC**

They watch me, those informers to the Fates. The Fates. Wilfred Owen. **CP-OwenW**

They Went Home. Maya Angelou. **SP-AngeM**

They were all inaccurate. Margaret Atwood. **SP-AtwM1**

They were all spared to tell their stories. A Morality. Howard Nemerov. **CP-NemeH**

They were alone once more; for them to be. Byron. **EBEV** *Fr.* Canto the Fourth. *Fr.* Don Juan. **CP-Byron**

They were both still. Lamentations. Louise Glück. **SP-GlücL**

They were calling certain styles of whiskers by the name of "lilacs." Alley Rats. Carl Sandburg. **CP-SandC**

They were confused at first, being well warned. A Reduced Sentence. Robert Ranke Graves. **CP-GravR**

They were human, they suffered, wore long black coat and gold watch chain. Founding Fathers, Nineteenth-Century Style, Southeast U.S.A. Robert Penn Warren. **SP-WarrR**

They were in an unstable condition. Kenneth Rexroth. **SP-RexrK** *Fr.* The Bell / Too softly and too slowly tolled. **CP-RexKL** *Fr.* A Prolegomenon to a Theodicy.

They were intense people, given to migraine. Proteus. May Sarton. **SP-SartM**

They were into the lambing, up late. The Birth (Near Port William). Wendell Berry. **CP-BerrW**

They were introduced in a grave glade. The Introduction. Louis MacNeice. **CP-MacNL**

They were kept in a wooden trunk. The Man in the Yellow Gloves. David St. John. **SP-StJoD**

They were never handsome and often came. Sidekicks. Ron Koertge. **SP-KoerR**

They were not painting about suffering. William Matthews. *Fr.* In Memory of W. H. Auden. **SP-MattW**

They were putting up the statue. Lawrence Ferlinghetti. **SP-FerlL**

They were sitting on the thin mattress. Wavelength. David St. John. **SP-StJoD**

They were so amply beautiful, the maps. Projection. Howard Nemerov. **CP-NemeH**

They were so mean they could not between them. Louis MacNeice. **POL** *Fr.* As In Their Time. **CP-MacNL**

They were talking about the war. The Place. Charles Simic. **SP-SimiC**

They Were There. . . . Hart Crane. **CP-CranH**

They were trying to catch up. They (2). Robert Creeley. **CP-CreeR**

They were waiting here to say. The Way It Is. Daniel Gerard Hoffman. **SP-HoffD**

They were wedded at midnight. The Queen's Crowning. Gerard Manley Hopkins. **CP-HopkG**

They were weeding out the dead at the funeral home. The Invasion of Sleep Walkers. John Ciardi. **SP-CiarJ**

They Were Welcome to Their Belief. Robert Frost. **CP-FrosR**

They were women then. Women. Alice Walker. **GOA; WPOW** *Fr.* In These Dissenting Times. **CP-WalkA**

They weren fully glad of their gude hap. John Keats. *Fr.* Three Undated Fragments. **CP-KeatJ**

They weren't so bright, or clean, or clever. School Lesson Based on Word of Tragic Death of Entire Gillum Family. Robert Penn Warren. **SP-WarrR**

They Who Feel Death. Alice Walker. **CP-WalkA**

They who have best succeeded on the stage. Epilogue to the Second Part of *The Conquest of Granada.* John Dryden. **SP-DrydJ** *Fr.* The Conquest of Granada.

They—who have seen the noble Roman's scorn. At Rome. William Wordsworth. *Fr.* Memorials of a Tour in Italy, 1837. **CP-WorW2**

They will be ashamed after they are dead. Malcolm Lowry. **CP-LowrM**

They will catch me. On Hearing the Airlines Will Use a Psychological Profile to Catch Potential Skyjackers. Stephen Dunn. **SP-DunnS**

They Will Say. Carl Sandburg. **CP-SandC**

They will soon be down. For the Last Wolverine. James Dickey. **CP-DickJ**

They wondered why the fruit had been forbidden. Wystan Hugh Auden. **CMoP; ChIV-1; Son** *Fr.* Sonnets from China. **CP-AudeW**

They Won't Believe, on New Year's Eve, that New Year's Day Will Come What May. Ogden Nash. **SP-NashO**

They won't frown always—some sweet Day. Emily Dickinson. **CP-DickE**

They won't go away, the sea perch. Dwelling. Richard Hugo. **CP-HugoR**

They won't let you in there for no seven cents. It's Because Your Heart Is Pure, Honey. Kenneth Patchen. **CP-PatcK**

They work with herbs. Doctors. Anne Sexton. **CP-SextA**

They worshipped Joe. Joe Louis. Langston Hughes. **SP-HughL**

They would be none the wiser, even could they overhear. None the Wiser. Robert Ranke Graves. **CP-GravR**

They Would Not Come. Thomas Hardy. **CP-HardT**

They'd come around and. The 2nd Novel. Charles Bukowski. **SP-BukC1**

They'd make you believe that your problem is one of sex. The New Being. Kenneth Patchen. **CP-PatcK**

They'll never find me hidden. W. D. Disguised as Cock Robin and Hidden Deep in Crimson. William DeWitt Snodgrass. **SP-SnodW**

They're altogether otherworldly now. Grandparents. Robert Lowell. **SP-LoweR**

They're at that stage where so much desire streams between them, so much frank need and want. Love: Beginnnings. Charles Kenneth Williams. **SP-WillC**

They're denying whites the beach. The tribe says. Changes in Policy at Taholah. Richard Hugo. **CP-HugoR**

They're discussing the political situation they've been watching evolve in a faraway country. Politics. Charles Kenneth Williams. **SP-WillC**

They're kindly here, to let us linger so late. Holy Thursday. Paul Muldoon. **SP-MuldP**

They're nice—one would never dream of going over. A Healthy Spot. Wystan Hugh Auden. **CP-AudeW**

They're out of the dark's ragbag, these two. Blue Moles. Sylvia Plath. **CP-PlatS**

They're selling postcards of the hanging. Desolation Row. "Bob Dylan." **CP-DylaB**

They're taking down a tree at the front door. Learning by Doing. Howard Nemerov. **CP-NemeH**

They're taking her children away. The Kids. "Lou Reed." **SP-ReedL**

They're waiting to be murdered. Old Couple. Charles Simic. **SP-SimiC**

Theys sO alive. Edward Estlin Cummings. **CP-CummE**

They've covered his face, & he's lost to us. C B M. George Meredith. **CP-MerG2**

They've got some pretty horses up in the long dark mountains. Now I Went Down to the Ringside and Little Henry Armstrong Was There. Kenneth Patchen. **CP-PatcK**

They've tricked you, these boundaries. A Short Reminder. Jim Carroll. **SP-CarrJ**

Thick as milk from a peasant's breast. Jim Carroll. *Fr.* The Runners. **SP-CarrJ**

Thick-fleeced bushes like a heifer's ear. Gerard Manley Hopkins. *Fr.* Fragments. **CP-HopkG**
  ("Out-fleeced bushes like a spaniel's ear.")

Thick lids of night closed upon me, The. The Souls of the Slain. Thomas Hardy. **CP-HardT**

Thick mist-sheet lies over the broken wheat, A. Mutilation. David Herbert Lawrence. **CP-LawrD**

Thick night fell, the folding table unfolded, The. The Rest House. Louis MacNeice. **CP-MacNL**

Thick-shanked, broad-flanked Purves. Blair Purves: Bluenose Portrait Effect #2. Marsden Hartley. **CP-HartM**

Thick-Sprinkled Bunting. Walt Whitman. **CP-WhitW**

Thick veins on the back of my forearm. Jim Carroll. **SP-CarrJ**

Thickest night, surround my dwelling! Strathallan's Lament. Robert Burns. **CP-BurnR**

Thickness of paint or flesh cannot deface. Sestina I. Howard Nemerov. **CP-NemeH**

Thief, The. Wendell Berry. **CP-BerrW**

Thief. Robert Ranke Graves. **CP-GravR**

Thief, The. Stanley Jasspon Kunitz. **CP-KuniS**

Thief. Alice Walker. **CP-WalkA**

Thief, and a murderer! stop her who can!, A. The Hue and Cry of John Lewars. Robert Burns. **CP-BurnR**

Thief in the Night. David Herbert Lawrence. **CP-LawrD**

Thief's Journal, The. Charles Tomlinson. **CP-TomlC**

Thiers. John Greenleaf Whittier. **CP-WhitJ**

Thieves, The. Robert Ranke Graves. **CP-GravR**

Thigh-deep in sedge and marigolds. The Other Side. Seamus Heaney. **SP-HeanS**

Thighs, *trees*— / you want / a place to stand. Trees. Robert Creeley. **CP-CreeR**

Thimble Islands. Carl Sandburg. **CP-SandC**

Thimbleberry redcap odor art whose. Raspberry. Louis Zukofsky. **CP-ZukLS**

Thin Air. John Updike. **CP-UpdiJ**

Thin blue smoke of our campfire, The. For the Boy Who Was Dodger Point Lookout Fifteen Years Ago. Gary Snyder. **CP-SnydG**

Thin brown orphan in his washed-out blue, A. Dublin Georgian (2). Donald Davie. **CP-DavDo**

Thin brown stain, A. Running Footsteps. James Schuyler. **CP-SchuJ**

Thin Edge of Your Pride, The. Kenneth Rexroth. **SP-RexrK**

Thin, foul scattering of grim, grey snow, A. Semi-Spring. Edward Estlin Cummings. **CP-CummE**

Thin green salient aimed at the heart of London, A. Buckinghamshire. Donald Davie. **CP-DavDo**

Thin Ice. Gary Snyder. **CP-SnydG**

Thin moonlight with trickling ray, The. The Tired Cupid. Walter de la Mare. **CP-DeLaW**

Thin People, The. Sylvia Plath. **CP-PlatS**

Thin Rain, whom are you haunting. Wraith. Edna St. Vincent Millay. **CP-MillE**

Thin sheets of blue smoke among white slabs. . . near the shingle mill. Hemlock and Cedar. Carl Sandburg. **CP-SandC**

Thin smoke, A. Roy Fisher. **SP-FishR** *Fr.* Handsworth Liberties.

Thin Strips. Carl Sandburg. **CP-SandC**

Thin wind winds off the water. Touch of Spring. John Updike. **CP-UpdiJ**

Thine am I, my Chloris fair. Robert Burns. **CP-BurnR**

Thine are all the gifts, O God! Hymn of the Children. John Greenleaf Whittier. **CP-WhitJ**

Thine be the volumes, Jessy fair. To a Young Lady, *Miss Jessy L———, Dumfries; with Books which the Bard Presented Her.* Robert Burns. **CP-BurnR**

Thine be those motions strong and sanative. To Coleridge in Sicily. William Wordsworth. **OBNC** *Fr.* Residence in France and French Revolution. *Fr.* The Prelude; Growth of a Poet's Mind [1805 vers.]. **CP-WorW3**

Thine emulous fond flowers are dead, too. My Butterfly. Robert Frost. **CP-FrosR**

Thine eyes' blue tenderness, thy long fair hair. Sonnet, to Genevra. Byron. **CP-Byron**

Thine eyes I love, and they, as pitying me. Sonnet 132. William Shakespeare. **OAEP; OBSC; OXAEP-1** *Fr.* Sonnets. **CP-ShaWS**

Thine Eyes Still Shined. Ralph Waldo Emerson. **CP-EmerR**

Thine is a grief, the depth of which another. To My Friend on the Death of His Sister. John Greenleaf Whittier. **CP-WhitJ**

Thine is a painted face, for all thy wings. The Dragon-fly. Wystan Hugh Auden. **CP-AudWJ**

Thine is my all, how little when 'tis told. To My Mother. Walter de la Mare. **CP-DeLaW**

Thine is the gentle day of love. On Mrs. Mendez' Birthday. James Thomson. **CP-ThomJ**

Thing, The. Theodore Roethke. **CP-RoetT**

Thing / To do / Is organize / The sea, The. Poem. Kenneth Koch. **SP-KochK**

Thing, The. William Carlos Williams. **CP-WilW2**

Thing About Joe Sullivan, The. Roy Fisher. **SP-FishR**

Thing about which I know the least, The. So I resigned from the Chu Chin Chowder and Marching Club. Ogden Nash. **CP-NashO**

Thing comes / of itself, The. Love ("Thing comes / of itself, The"). Robert Creeley. **CP-CreeR**

Thing Itself, The. Alice Walker. **CP-WalkA**

Thing most new complete fragile intense, A. Edward Estlin Cummings. **CP-CummE**

Thing no is(of). Edward Estlin Cummings. **CP-CummE**

Thing O say a sixteenth of an inch, A. They Have. John Berryman. **CP-BerrJ**

Thing of Beauty, A. John Keats. **BLPL; CTC; EBEvV; EnRP; FHYEP; FaBV; FaFP; FiP; ImPo; LiTB; MeMBP; NIP; NOBRP; NTP; OAEP; OBNC; OBRV; OXAEP-2; PoPl; PrIm; TRV; TreF** *Fr.* Endymion: Poetic Romance. **CP-KeatJ**

Thing of beauty is a joy forever, A. A Thing of Beauty. John Keats. **BLPL; CTC; EBEvV; EnRP; FHYEP; FaBV; FaFP; FiP; ImPo; LiTB; MeMBP; NIP; NOBRP; NTP; OAEP; OBNC; OBRV; OXAEP-2; PoPl; PrIm; TRV; TreF** *Fr.* Endymion: Poetic Romance. **CP-KeatJ**

Thing of beauty is joy for ever, A. Endymion: Poetic Romance. John Keats. **CP-KeatJ**

Thing that arrests me is, The. Waking in the Dark. Adrienne Rich. **SP-RicA1; SP-RicA2**

Thing that breaks Hell's prison bars, The. The Soul of a Butterfly. Nicholas Vachel Lindsay. **CP-LindV**

Thing That Eats the Heart, The. Stanley Jasspon Kunitz. **CP-KuniS**

Thing that eats the rotting stars, The. The Soul of a Spider. Nicholas Vachel Lindsay. **CP-LindV**

Thing to do is try for that sweet skin, The. Catch What You Can. Jean Garrigue. **SP-GarrJ**

Thing to know is how to write a verse, The. Malcolm Lowry. **CP-LowrM**

Thing Unplanned, The. Thomas Hardy. **CP-HardT**

Thing Was Moving, The. Charles Olson. **CP-OlsoC; SP-OlsoC**

Things / come and go. A Step. Robert Creeley. **CP-CreeR**

Things / come and go. A Step. Robert Creeley. **CP-CreeR**

Things. Jane Cooper. *Fr.* Dispossessions. **SP-CoopJ**

Things About You. Tom Clark. **SP-ClarT**

Things and people goodbye / It is not that I prefer. Thomas Merton. **CP-MertT**

Things and the Man. Rudyard Kipling. **CP-KiplR**

Things are / changing; things are starting to. Last Days. Mary Oliver. **SP-OlivM**

Things are better in Milan. The Next One. Leonard Cohen. **CP-CoheL**

Things are so changed since last we met. A Year Afterwards. Christina Georgina Rossetti. **CP-RosC3**

Things are uncertain, and the more we get. Things Mortal Still Mutable. Robert Herrick. **CP-HerrR**

Things as they are / are as they are because. A Child's Guide to Philosophy. Phoebe Hesketh. **SP-HeskP**

Things concentrate at the edges; the pond-surface. Marginalia. Richard Wilbur. **CP-WilbR**

Things do not explode. Endings. Derek Walcott. **CP-WalcD**

Things have their own lives here. The hall chairs. Things. Jane Cooper. *Fr.* Dispossessions. **SP-CoopJ**

Things he had loved because he knew them lost. Archibald MacLeish. **CP-MacLA** *Fr.* The Happy Marriage.

Things I Learned Last Week. William Stafford. **SP-StafW**

Things Kept. William Dickey. **SP-DickW**

Things Made by Iron. David Herbert Lawrence. **CP-LawrD**

Things Men Have Made. David Herbert Lawrence. **CP-LawrD**

Things Mortal Still Mutable. Robert Herrick. **CP-HerrR**

Things of August. Wallace Stevens. **CP-StevW**

Things of Choice, Long a Comming. Robert Herrick. **CP-HerrR**

Things O this world. The Illusion of Eternity. Richard Eberhart. **CP-EberR**

Things of which we want the proof, The. Emily Dickinson. **SP-DickE**

Things oft miscalling, as the hen-. Ralph Waldo Emerson. **CP-EmerR**

Things one sees through / a blurred sheet of glass. Rain ("Things one sees through"). Robert Creeley. **CP-CreeR**

Things out of perfection sail. *fr.* Words for Music Perhaps. William Butler Yeats. **CP-YeatW**

Things placed there. Obstructions. James Dickey. **CP-DickJ**

Things seem empty. On Vacation. Robert Creeley. **CP-CreeR**

Things that divine us we never touch. The Southern Cross. Charles Wright. **SP-WrigC**

Things That Fly. Jim Carroll. **SP-CarrJ**
   "Misery may be folded."
   "My blond niece speaks in riddles."

Things that make the happier life, are these, The. *See also Sir Richard Fanshawe's* "Things that make a life to please, The." Ben Jonson, *ad. fr. the Latin of Martial.* **CP-JonsB**

Things that never can come back, are several, The. Emily Dickinson. **CP-DickE**

Things, the work of dust and summer flies, upstairs over the. The Attic. Lewis Turco. **SP-TurcL**

Things they did together, no one knew, The. 1904. Frederick Morgan. **SP-MorgF**

Things thus agreed: Titan made Saturne sweare, *ad. fr. Latin of* Sibylla. Sir Walter Ralegh. **CP-RaleW**

Things to Do. James Schuyler. **CP-SchuJ**

Things To Do in Anne's Room. Ted Berrigan. **SP-BerrT**

Things To Do in New York (City). Ted Berrigan. **SP-BerrT**

Things to Do in Providence. Ted Berrigan. **SP-BerrT**

Things we place or do not place our faith in. A Celebration of Sorts. Gilbert Sorrentino. **SP-SorrG**

Things We Said Today. The Beatles. **CP-Beatl**

Things we thought that we should do, The. Emily Dickinson. **CP-DickE**

Think—! David Herbert Lawrence. **CP-LawrD**

Think. Robert Creeley. **CP-CreeR**

Think about it at will: there is that. The Meaning of Life. Allen Tate. **CP-TateA**

Think, Delia, with what cruel haste. Written in a Quarrel. William Cowper. **CP-CowpW**

Think For Yourself. George Harrison. **CP-Beatl**

Think how a peacock in a forest of high trees. Peacock. David Herbert Lawrence. **CP-LawrD**

Think how we touch each other when we sight land. Bay of Resolve. Richard Hugo. **CP-HugoR**

Think, if at seventy the news is. Finis Coronat Opus. Frank Templeton Prince. **CP-PrinF**

Think: if Ludwig were alive today. Note Upon the Love Letters of Beethoven. Charles Bukowski. **SP-BukC3**

Think It Over. "Lou Reed." **SP-ReedL**

Think me not unkind and rude. The Apology. Ralph Waldo Emerson. **CP-EmerR**

Think no more, lad; laugh, be jolly. Alfred Edward Housman. **CP-HousA**

Think no more of me. A Soldier Rejects His Times Addressing His Contemporaries. Richard Eberhart. **CP-EberR**

Think not, because I wonder where you fled. Another Dark Lady. Edwin Arlington Robinson. **CP-RobiE**

Think[e] not 'cause men flattering [or flatt'ring] say. To A. L.; Persuasions [or Perswasions] to Love. Thomas Carew. **CP-CareT**

Think not I have not heard. Menses. Edna St. Vincent Millay. **CP-MillE**

Think not my Phebe [or Phœbe], cause a cloud. To His Mistress [or Mistris] Confined. James Shirley. **CP-CareT**

Think not, nor for a moment let your mind. Edna St. Vincent Millay. **CP-MillE**

Think not of chaste snow always. Hayden Carruth. *Fr.* North Winter. **CP-CarHL**

Think Not of It, Sweet One, So. John Keats. **CP-KeatJ**

Think not, should your husband swear. George Meredith. **CP-MerG2**

Think not that I forget a single pang. "Hugh MacDiarmid." **SP-MacDH** *Fr.* Ode to All Rebels.

Think not that incense-smoke has had its day. Incense. Nicholas Vachel Lindsay. **CP-LindV**

Think not the gods receive thy prayer. Ralph Waldo Emerson. **CP-EmerR**

Think, O my soul. Phaedra. Hilda Doolittle. **CP-DoolH**

Think of an opening page illuminèd. Gerard Manley Hopkins. **CP-HopkG**

Think of how in a hurricane the winds. Form and Theory of Poetry. Miller Williams. **SP-WillM**

Think of it:not so long ago. Edward Estlin Cummings. **CP-CummE**

Think of man praying. He raises his hands to God. Death in the Mines. Richard Eberhart. **CP-EberR**

Think of sweet and chocolate. The Anniad. Gwendolyn Brooks. **SP-BrooG**

Think of that great courageous place. Emily Dickinson. **SP-DickE**

Think of the beds. Beds, Toilets, You and Me—. Charles Bukowski. **SP-BukC1**

Think of the minute amount a mouse eats. Jenny Joseph. **SP-JoseJ** *Fr.* Fables. **SP-JoseJ**

Think of the Soul. Walt Whitman. **CP-WhitW**

Think of the storm roaming the sky uneasily. Little Exercise. Elizabeth Bishop. **CP-BishE**

Think of those big trout, Bud, fifty years. Pishkun Reservoir. Richard Hugo. **CP-HugoR**

Think Tank. James Merrill. **SP-MerrJ**

Think that this world against the wind of time. Signature for Tempo. Archibald MacLeish. **CP-MacLA**

Think! Think hard. Try to remember. Loss, of Perhaps Love, in Our World of Contingency. Robert Penn Warren. **SP-WarrR**

Think yet how night doth waste. Ben Jonson. **CP-JonsB** *Fr.* Masque of Hymen.

Thinke then, my soule, that death is but a groome. Contemplation of Our State in Our Deathbed. John Donne. **OBS** *Fr.* The Second Anniversary [or Anniversarie]. **ESCV; SeCP** *Fr.* Of the Progres[se] of the Soule; the Second Anniversarie. **CP-DonnJ**

Thinker, The. William Carlos Williams. **CP-WilW1**

Thinking. Robert Creeley. **CP-CreeR**

Thinking. Robert Creeley. **CP-CreeR**

Thinking about Bill, Dead of AIDS. Miller Williams. **SP-WillM**

Thinking again of a weekend trip to Ferrara. Italian Days. Charles Wright. **SP-WrigC**

Thinking Back Toward Christmas: A Statement for the Virgin. William Carlos Williams. **CP-WilW2**

Thinking, Drinking. John Crowe Ransom. *Fr.* Two Gentlemen in Bonds. **SP-RansJ**

Thinking for Berky. William Stafford. **SP-StafW**

Thinking Friday Night with a Gothic Storm Going About Final Causes and Logos and Mitzi Mayfair. Miller Williams. **SP-WillM**

Thinking how it is. The Bent. Donald Davie. **CP-DavDo**

Thinking in terms of one. Counting. Philip Larkin. **CP-LarkP**

Thinking more and more. Practice. Charles Bukowski. **SP-BukC3**

Thinking not much of fish, idly at evening. Catch. Jenny Joseph. **SP-JoseJ**

Thinking of / Billy. William Carlos Williams Alive! Louis Zukofsky. *Fr.* Songs of Degrees. **CP-ZukLS**

Thinking of a Relation between the Images of Metaphors. Wallace Stevens. **CP-StevW**

Thinking of Inis Oírr in Cambridge, Mass. Derek Mahon. **SP-MahoD**

Thinking of me / think of what was. William Dickey. **SP-DickW** *Fr.* In The Dreaming. **SP-DickW**

Thinking of the Lost World. Randall Jarrell. **CP-JarrR; SP-JarrR**

Thinking of you, and all that was, and all. Christina Georgina Rossetti. *Fr.* Monna Innominata. **CP-RosC2**

Thinking of you asleep on a / bed on a pillow, on a. Place. Robert Creeley. **CP-CreeR**

Thinking of you, of your letters. For Anne, at a Little Distance. John Haines. **SP-HainJ**

Thinking of you, where first we met. Reversing. Robert Pack. **SP-PackR**

Thinking Rock. Kenneth Patchen. **CP-PatcK**

Thinking that I would find you. Flight. Anne Sexton. **CP-SextA**

Thinking Thought. Charles Kenneth Williams. **SP-WillC**

Think'st thou I saw thy beauteous eyes. To Caroline. Byron. **CP-Byron**

Think'st thou that this love can stand. Ametas and Thestylis Making Hay-Ropes. Andrew Marvell. **CP-MarvA**

Think'st thou to seduce me then with words that have no meaning? Thomas Campion. **CP-CampT**

Thinness. James Schuyler. **CP-SchuJ**

Third Book, The. Archibald MacLeish. *Fr.* Conquistador. **CP-MacLA**

Third Child: June Eleven, Nineteen Sixty Two. Peter Meinke. **SP-MeinP**

Third Degree. Langston Hughes. **SP-HughL**

Third Elegy. The Fear of Form. Muriel Rukeyser. **CP-RukeM**

Third Epistle. Donald Davie. *Fr.* Six Epistles to Eva Hesse. **CP-DavDo**

Third Epistle to J. Lapraik. Robert Burns. **CP-BurnR**

Third Kissing-Gate, The. Thomas Hardy. **CP-HardT**

Third Letter to Jimin in Manchuria. James Liddy. **CP-LiddJ**

Third Limick. Ogden Nash. **CP-NashO**

Third Mile. James McAuley. *Fr.* Ten-Mile Run. **SP-McAuJ**

Third night after wedding, The. The Newlywed's Cuisine. Wang Chien, *tr. fr.* Chinese by William Carlos Williams *with* David Rafael Wang. **CP-WilW2**

3rd November 1976. Roy Fisher. **SP-FishR**

Third Psalm. Anne Sexton. **NALW** *Fr.* O Ye Tongues. **SP-SextA**

Third Snowfall. Marilyn Hacker. **SP-HackM**

Third Song, The. Thomas Carew. **CP-CareT** *Fr.* Carew's Masque. **CP-CareT**

Third Song. Sir Philip Sidney. **PoEL-1** *Fr.* Astrophil and Stella. **SP-SidnP**

Third Song of Huitzilopochtli. David Herbert Lawrence. **CP-LawrD**

Third Thing, The. David Herbert Lawrence. **CP-LawrD**

Third Universe. Diane Wakoski. *Fr.* The Universes. **SP-WakoD**

Third Use of the Penis, The. Barton Sutter. **SP-SuttB**

Third Version, The. Hayden Carruth. *Fr.* The Mythology of Dark and Light. **CP-CarHL**

Third Voice, The. "Lewis Carroll." *Fr.* The Three Voices. **CP-CarrL**

Third-week moon reaches its light over my father's farm, The. Late Moon. Robert Bly. **SP-BlyR**

Third Wish, The. Leonard Nathan. **SP-NathL**

Third with silence in a tent. Caravan of Silence. Richard Eberhart. **CP-EberR**

Third World Calling. Lawrence Ferlinghetti. **SP-FerlL**

Thirst. Charles Kenneth Williams. **SP-WillC**

Thirst Song. Denise Levertov. **CP-LeveD**

Thirsting Tantalus doth catch at stream[e]s that from him flee, The. 2.13. Horace, *tr.* by Sir Walter Ralegh. **CP-RaleW** *Fr.* Satires.

Thirteen as twelve my Murray always took. *parody of* George Gordon, Lord Byron. Rudyard Kipling. **CP-KiplR** *Fr.* The Muse among the Motors.

XIII. "In That proud port, which her so goodly graceth." Edmund Spenser. **Son** *Fr.* Amoretti. **CP-Spens**

13 Pictures. David Herbert Lawrence. **CP-LawrD**

Thirteen Sonnets. Michael Hartnett.

   "I have been stone, dust of space, sea and sphere." **SP-HarMi**

   "I saw magic on a green country road." **SP-HarMi**

13,000 People. David Herbert Lawrence. *Fr.* Songs I Learnt at School. **CP-LawrD**

Thirteen Ways of Looking at a Blackbird. Wallace Stevens. **CP-StevW**

Thirteen Years. Martin Edmunds. **SP-EdmuM**

Thirteen years / Or haply less, I might have seen, when first. William Wordsworth. **OxAEP-2** *Fr.* Books. *Fr.* The Prelude; Growth of a Poet's Mind [1805 vers.]. **CP-WorW3**

Thirteens (Black), The. Maya Angelou. **SP-AngeM**

Thirteens (White), The. Maya Angelou. **SP-AngeM**

Thirteenth Book, The. Archibald MacLeish. *Fr.* Conquistador. **CP-MacLA**

Thirteenth Labor of Hercules, The. Ogden Nash. *Fr.* Fables Bullfinch Forgot. **CP-NashO**

Thirties. And / A spectre, The. George Oppen. *Fr.* Blood from the Stone. **CP-OppeG**

Thirtieth Anniversary Report of the Class of '41. Howard Nemerov. **CP-NemeH**

30th Birthday. Alice Notley. **SP-NotlA**

Thirtieth inst., too soon the thirtieth ult, The. Canto XXI. Louis MacNeice. *Fr.* Autumn Sequel. **CP-MacNL**

Thirty-Eight (Addressed to Mrs. H----Y). Charlotte Smith. **CP-SmitC**

Thirty Five Mescals in Cuautla. Malcolm Lowry. *Fr.* The Cantinas. **CP-LowrM**

35 Seconds. Charles Bukowski. **SP-BukC2**

XXXIV. "Like as a ship, that through the ocean wide." Edmund Spenser. **NAEL-1; OBSC; PoE** *Fr.* Amoretti. **CP-Spens**

34th Street Song. Grace Paley. **CP-PaleG**

39,000 Feet. William Matthews. **SP-MattW**

Thirty-Ninth Psalm, Adapted, The. Donald Davie. **CP-DavDo**

Thirty Rings. Leonard Nathan. **SP-NathL**

37 Haiku. John Ashbery. **SP-AshbJ**

XXXVII. "What guile [or guyle] is this, that those her golden tresses." Edmund Spenser. **NAEL-1; NoP; OBSC; PAI; Son; TrGrPo** *Fr.* Amoretti. **CP-Spens**

Thirty-some years ago, hitchhiking. Memory of Wilmington. Galway Kinnell. **SP-KinnG**

Thirty striped rumps in a circle with tails dangling. Ringling Brothers, Barnum and Bailey. Mona Van Duyn. **SP-VanDM**

Thirty today? Cheer up, my lad! Lines to Be Scribbled on Somebody Else's Thirtieth Milestone. Ogden Nash. **CP-NashO**

Thirty-two Greeks are dipping their feet in the creek. Near Keokuk. Carl Sandburg. **CP-SandC**

Thirty-two years since, up against the sun. Zermatt: To the Matterhorn. Thomas Hardy. **CP-HardT**

Thirty-two years to go. A Century Dying. Pablo Neruda, *tr. fr. Spanish by* Ben Belitt. **SP-NeruP**

Thirty yards apart, they face. Too Tenuous. Hayden Carruth. **CP-CarHS**

Thirty years after. A Second Attempt. Thomas Hardy. **CP-HardT**

Thirty years unremembered. Abbeyforde. Donald Davie. **CP-DavDo**

Thirtyish, Irish, red-nosed carpenter, The. And the Scream. Stephen Berg. **SP-BergS**

This. Archie Randolph Ammons. **SP-AmmoA**

This. Charles Bukowski. **SP-BukC2**

This / forest pool / A so. Edward Estlin Cummings. **CP-CummE**

This / is / not / more / snow / to / fall. A Valentine. Louis Zukofsky. **CP-ZukLS**

This / is mine, and I can hold it. Edna St. Vincent Millay. **CP-MillE**

This / is what happens when the. Dear Friend. Charles Bukowski. **SP-BukC2**

This. Charles Olson. **CP-OlsoC**

This admirable gadget, when it is. Gyroscope. Howard Nemerov. **CP-NemeH**

This Advent moon shines cold and clear. Advent. Christina Georgina Rossetti. **CP-RosC1**

This after-sunset is a sight for seeing. He Prefers Her Earthly. Thomas Hardy. **CP-HardT**

This afternoon, discomfortable dread. The Possessed. John Berryman. **CP-BerrJ**

This afternoon it rains as never before; and I. Down to the Dregs. César Vallejo, *tr. fr. Spanish by* James Wright. **CP-WrigJ**

This afternoon, let me. Whether There Is Enjoyment in Bitterness. Thomas Merton. **CP-MertT**

This air & life of Italy. Italy. George Meredith. **CP-MerG2**

This all begins on a November day. Hayden Carruth. **CP-CarHS** *Fr.* The Bloomingdale Papers.

This ancient hag. Mexican Market Woman. Langston Hughes. **SP-HughL**

This ancient house so notable. A Country Mansion. Robert Ranke Graves. **CP-GravR**

This, and the Next World. Robert Herrick. **CP-HerrR**

This Antrim Air in Summer. John Hewitt. **CP-HewiJ**

This apartment full of books could crack open. Adrienne Rich. *Fr.* Twenty-one Love Poems. **SP-RicA1; SP-RicA2**

This 'appened in a battle to a batt'ry of the corps. Snarleyow. Rudyard Kipling. **CP-KiplR**

This April some swelltoad begins again. Spring Song. Dabney Stuart. **SP-StuaD**

This augurs well; both in their soft beds. The Promised Ballad. Robert Ranke Graves. **CP-GravR**

This August evening I've been driving. Transcendental Etude. Adrienne Rich. **SP-RicA1; SP-RicA2**

This August heat, this momentary breeze. Nature Poem. Charles Tomlinson. **CP-TomlC**

This Axiom I have often heard. Love. Robert Herrick. **CP-HerrR**

This Band, which bound thy yellow hair. To a Lady. Byron. **CP-Byron**

This Bauble was preferred of Bees. Emily Dickinson. **CP-DickE**

This be the meed, that thy Song creates a thousandfold Echo! Tribute to Wordsworth. Samuel Taylor Coleridge. **CP-ColeS**

This Be the Verse. Philip Larkin. **CP-LarkP**

This beast that rends me in the sight of all. Edna St. Vincent Millay. **CP-MillE**

This Beast, This Angel. Adrienne Rich. **CP-RicAE**

This beautiful ditty / is, for a change, about the city. The City. Ogden Nash. **CP-NashO**

This beauty that I see. Poem. James Schuyler. **CP-SchuJ**

This being a minimum security facility, it feels more like being on a reservation than in a touchable cage. Visiting Day. Al Young. **CP-YounA**

This biplane is the shape of human flight. The Wrights' Biplane. Robert Frost. **WeW** *Fr.* Ten Mills. **CP-FrosR**

This bird was happy once in the high trees. Boethius, *tr. fr. Latin*. **MLL,** *tr. by* Helen Waddell; *Fr.* Consolation of Philosophy, The ("De Consolacione Philosophie"). **CP-ChauG**

This blear-eyed sun. The Wastrel. Daniel Gerard Hoffman. **SP-HoffD**

This blue-washed, old, thatched summerhouse. The Old Summerhouse. Walter de la Mare. **CP-DeLaW**

This boat is of satō-wood, and its gunwhales are cut magnolia. *ad. fr.* Rihaku (Li T'ai Po). Ezra Pound. **SP-PounE**

This boat that we just built is just fine. Homemade Boat. Shel Silverstein. **SP-SilS2**

This body, tapped of every drop of breath. Ambergris. Stanley Jasspon Kunitz. **CP-KuniS**

This body that has fastened. The Wanderer. Daniel Gerard Hoffman. **SP-HoffD**

This book, when I am dead, will be. Journal. Edna St. Vincent Millay. **CP-MillE**

This book will live; it hath a genius: this. On the Honoured Poems of His Honoured Friend, Sir John Beaumont, Baronet. Ben Jonson. **CP-JonsB**

This Boy. The Beatles. **CP-Beatl**

This brand of soap has the same smell as once in the big. Soap Suds. Louis MacNeice. **CP-MacNL**

This Bread I Break. Dylan Thomas. **CP-ThomD**

This breath which now alternate burns. Our Future Lot. Walt Whitman. **CP-WhitW**

This bright morning, the. Whitelash of Air Rapids. Archie Randolph Ammons. **SP-AmmoA**

This Broken Bell. Pablo Neruda, *tr. fr. Spanish* by Ben Belitt. **SP-NeruP**

This bug carries spots on his back. Bug Spots. Carl Sandburg. **CP-SandC**

This burning behind my eyes as I open a door. Defeated. Robert Bly. **SP-BlyR**

This burning flight of summer. Red Trees in the Wind. John Haines. **SP-HainJ**

This business of evil / Like brokers the weevil. Malcolm Lowry. **CP-LowrM**

This cabin, Mary, in my sight appears. Inscription for an Hermitage. William Cowper. **CP-CowpW**

This calcined idiocy, the fool. The Stigmata of Fact. Kenneth Rexroth. **CP-RexKL** *Fr.* The Homestead Called Damascus.

This calls for a toast. She hates. Jane Seagrim's Party. Leonard Nathan. **SP-NathL**

This candle-wax is shaping to a shroud. Standing by the Mantlepiece. Thomas Hardy. **CP-HardT**

This cap, that so stately appears. Gratitude. William Cowper. **CP-CowpW**

This Cave Is Dark. Sir Philip Sidney. **SiPSBD** *Fr.* How Is My Sun. **SP-SidnP** *Fr.* Arcadia.

This celestial seascape, with white herons got up as angels. Seascape. Elizabeth Bishop. **CP-BishE**

This cell we keep unlocked. Green Room. Michael Hartnett. **SP-HarMi**

This century, an iron bell of joy, has scarcely rung. The Years As Catches. Robert Duncan. **SP-DuncR**

This Chasm, Sweet, upon my life. Emily Dickinson. **CP-DickE**

This Chauntecleer stood hye up-on his toos. Geoffrey Chaucer. **FiP** *Fr.* The Nun's Priest's Tale. **FHYEP; NAEL-1; NAWM-1; NoP; OAEL-1; TrGrPo** *Fr.* The Canterbury Tales. **CP-ChauG**

This child, shovelling away. The Tree. Charles Tomlinson. **CP-TomlC**

This cigarette is extremely long. Edward Estlin Cummings. **CP-CummE**

This city is all light, as if a king. Tashkent Blossoms, 1944. Stephen Berg. **SP-BergS**

This clonic earth. Serena II. Samuel Beckett. **CP-BeckS**

This Cold. Stephen Berg. **SP-BergS**

This cold weather. For Nineteenth-Century Burials. Sir John Betjeman. **CP-BetjJ**

This comes after silence. Was it something I said. Wendell Berry. *Fr.* The Country of Marriage. **CP-BerrW**

This Compost. Walt Whitman. **CP-WhitW**

This concord tempers then the elements. Boethius, *tr. fr. Latin*. **MLL,** *tr. by* Helen Waddell; *Fr.* Consolation of Philosophy, The ("De Consolacione Philosophie"). **CP-ChauG**

This Configuration. John Ashbery. **SP-AshbJ**

This Consciousness that is aware. Emily Dickinson. **CP-DickE**

This coral's shape echoes the hand. Coral. Derek Walcott. **CP-WalcD**

This country invades me. Poem. Jim Carroll. **SP-CarrJ**

This country least, but every inhabited country. Praise Life. Robinson Jeffers. **CP-JefR2**

This country parson with the corncob pipe. W.R.R. John Hewitt. **CP-HewiJ**

This country's air is cleansing to the heart. This Antrim Air in Summer. John Hewitt. **CP-HewiJ**

This court, supreme in blindness and in hate. June 19, 1953. Edwin Rolfe. **CP-RolfE**

This creature fills its mouth with venum. The Cobra. Ogden Nash. **CP-NashO**

This creature kneeling / dusted with snow, its teeth. November. Margaret Atwood. **SP-AtwM1**

This cross-tree here. Robert Herrick. **CP-HerrR**

This Crusty Fragment. Marsden Hartley. **CP-HartM**

This crystal sphere. Sometimes It Turns Dry and the Leaves Fall before They Are Beautiful. William Carlos Williams. **CP-WilW2**

This Dark Apartment. James Schuyler. **CP-SchuJ**

This darksome burn, horseback brown. Inversnaid. Gerard Manley Hopkins. **CP-HopkG**

This darksome burn, horseback brown. Inversnaid. Gerard Manley Hopkins. **CP-HopkG**

This Day. Charles Kenneth Williams. **CP-WillC**

This day among the faithful plac'd. On the Christening of a Friend's Child. Samuel Taylor Coleridge. **CP-ColeS**

This day, dear Bec, is thy nativity. Bec's Birthday. Jonathan Swift. **CP-SwifJ**

This day feels put together hastily. New Year's Day. Audre Lorde. **SP-LordA**

This day is Yours Great Charles! and in this War. To the King, upon His Taking of Leicester. Robert Herrick. **CP-HerrR**

This day lies under glass. Burning Dawn. Hayden Carruth. **CP-CarHS**

This day my Julia thou must make. The Bride-Cake. Robert Herrick. **CP-HerrR**

This Day, O Soul. Walt Whitman. **CP-WhitW**

This day our daily. . . . Jenny Joseph. *Fr.* Life and Turgid Times of A. Citizen. **SP-JoseJ**

This day that would tell us what we are. Sunday. John Updike. **CP-UpdiJ**

This day (the year I dare not tell). Corinna. Jonathan Swift. **CP-SwifJ**

This Day This World. Stanley Jasspon Kunitz. **CP-KuniS**

This day throw open all your houses, and forever. The Ointment. Thomas Merton. **CP-MertT**

This day, Time winds th' exhausted chain. Sketch. New Year's Day. To Mrs. Dunlop. Robert Burns. **CP-BurnR**

This day, two hundred years ago. A Song of Harvest. John Greenleaf Whittier. **CP-WhitJ**

This day, whate'er the fates decree. Stella's Birthday ([March 13,] 1727). Jonathan Swift. **CP-SwifJ**

This day winding down now. Author's Prologue. Dylan Thomas. **CP-ThomD**

This day writhes with what? The lecturer. The Ultimate Poem Is Abstract. Wallace Stevens. **CP-StevW**

This dead march is thin. Aside to a Children's Tale. Roy Fisher. **SP-FishR**

This Decoration. Hayden Carruth. **CP-CarHS**

This dinner is too rich for you, Paul. Another Day. The Children Are All Eating. Muriel Rukeyser. **CP-RukeM**

This dirty—little—Heart. Emily Dickinson. **CP-DickE**

This disc, stelliferous. Sand Dollar. John Updike. **CP-UpdiJ**

This ditty is a string of lies. Rudyard Kipling. *See* Study of an Elevation, in Indian Ink.

This do here, by the window? The steak's not bad. Just a snack for lunch. Jenny Joseph. *Fr.* Life and Turgid Times of A. Citizen. **SP-JoseJ**

This docile one inter. Emily Dickinson. **CP-DickE**

This doll upon the topmost bough. The Doll Upon the Topmost Bough. Nicholas Vachel Lindsay. *Fr.* This Section Is a Christmas Tree. **CP-LindV**

This door you might not open, and you did. Bluebeard. Edna St. Vincent Millay. **CP-MillE**

This dream budded bright with leaves round the edges. Dream with Clam-Diggers. Sylvia Plath. **CP-PlatS**

This dream of burnt ivory. Charles Henri Ford. **SP-FordC** *Fr.* Secret Haiku.

This dream the world is having about itself. Vocation. William Stafford. **SP-StafW**

This dun-coloured island, dry and coarse as a cinder. Mykonos. John Hewitt. **CP-HewiJ**

This Dusky Faith. Edna St. Vincent Millay. **CP-MillE**

This Dust, and its Feature. Emily Dickinson. **CP-DickE**

This Dust Was Once the Man. Walt Whitman. *Fr.* Memories of President Lincoln. **CP-WhitW**

This dust was Timas; and they say. The Dust of Timas. Sappho. **AWP** *Fr.* Variations of Greek Themes. **CP-RobiE**

This Early Day. Kenneth Patchen. **CP-PatcK**

This Earth the king said. Return. George Oppen. **CP-OppeG**

This Easter, Arthur Winslow, less than dead. Death from Cancer. Robert Lowell. **SP-LoweR** *Fr.* In Memory of Arthur Winslow.

This effervescing gentleman who despises a secret. Hafiz, *tr. by* Ralph Waldo Emerson. **CP-EmerR** *Fr.* Odes.

This eightieth year of thine sits crowned in light. To Carlyle. George Meredith. **CP-MerG2**

This Element. Erica Jong. **SP-JongE**

This elemental force. Genesis. Theodore Roethke. **CP-RoetT**

This empty street, this sky to blandness scoured. Triple Time. Philip Larkin. **CP-LarkP**

This ends: entering the show of silence. Night Has Been as Beautiful as Virginia. Kenneth Patchen. **CP-PatcK**

This Englishwoman. Stevie Smith. **CP-SmitS**

This evangelist / buttons with his big gollywog voice. Edward Estlin Cummings. **CP-CummE**

This evening, each hour, it grows earlier. Same Story. Pablo Neruda, *tr. fr. Spanish by* Ben Belitt. **SP-NeruP**

This evening, motherly summer moves in the pond. Mayday on Holderness. Ted Hughes. **SP-HughT**

This evening the cuckoo and the corncrake. Seamus Heaney. **IPY** *Fr.* Glanmore Sonnets. **SP-HeanS**

This evening Venus signs alone. Nocturne. Malcolm Lowry. **CP-LowrM**

This ev'ning, Delia, you and I. William Cowper. **CP-CowpW**

This face you got. Phizzog. Carl Sandburg. **CP-SandC**

This faint resemblance of thy charms. To Mary on Receiving Her Picture. Byron. **CP-Byron**

This fair parcel of summer's. Song. Theodore Roethke. **CP-RoetT**

This fall I'm rooting for contraction! Neutrinos. Robert Pack. **SP-PackR**

This Fall, 1933. Louis Zukofsky. *Fr.* 29 Songs. **CP-ZukLS**

This fall, we left your Grandma's. Reconstructions. William DeWitt Snodgrass. **SP-SnodW**

This fall you will taste carrots. Digging In. Marge Piercy. **SP-PierM**

This far south such crippling. Aurora Borealis. Rita Dove. **SP-DoveR**

This fear is no longer dear. You are not going to America and. Edward Estlin Cummings. **CP-CummE**

This fell when dinner-time was done. The Fall of Jock Gillespie. Rudyard Kipling. **CP-KiplR**

This fever doubtless comes in punishment. Blanket Charge. Robert Ranke Graves. **CP-GravR**

This Fevers Me. Richard Eberhart. **CP-EberR**

This field-grass brushed our legs. In the Field. Richard Wilbur. **CP-WilbR**

This figure, that thou here seest put. To the Reader. Ben Jonson. **CP-JonsB**

This fire moves. Upward, upward. The Fiction. Gilbert Sorrentino. **SP-SorrG**

This fireglow is a red womb. Birth Night. David Herbert Lawrence. **CP-LawrD**

This fleur-de-lis. A Formal Design. William Carlos Williams. **CP-WilW2**

This Florida: 1924. William Carlos Williams. **CP-WilW1**

This flower is repeated. Windflower Leaf. Carl Sandburg. **CP-SandC**

This Fog. Brendan Galvin. **SP-GalvB**

This—For the Moon—Yes? Carl Sandburg. **CP-SandC**

This Form of Life Needs Sex. Allen Ginsberg. **CP-GinsA**

This Fresshe Flour. Geoffrey Chaucer. **SeCePo** *Fr.* The Legend of Good Women. **CP-ChauG**

This gentleman the charming duck. A Trueblue Gentleman. Kenneth Patchen. **CP-PatcK**

This girl borrowed no dim light of a star. Eager Youths to a Dead Girl. Allen Tate. **CP-TateA**

This girl child speaks five words. Seventeen Months. Carl Sandburg. **CP-SandC**

This girl was sweeter than the song of swans. De Erotio Puella. Robert Louis Stevenson. **CP-StevR**

This girlchild was born as usual. Barbie Doll. Marge Piercy. **SP-PierM**

This gloomy northern day. Robert Louis Stevenson. **CP-StevR**

This glorious oversleeping half through Sunday. Mother and Father 2. Robert Lowell. **SP-LoweR**

This golden head has wit in it. I live. George Meredith. **NOBVV** *Fr.* Modern Love. **CP-MerG1**

This golden vengeance is one of those red. Sword. Marilyn Hacker. **SP-HackM**

This graveyard with its umbrella pines. An Island Cemetery. Wystan Hugh Auden. **CP-AudeW**

This great Grandmother of all creatures bred. Mutability Claims to Rule the World. Edmund Spenser. **NoSic** *Fr.* The Faerie Queene. **CP-Spens**

This great oppressing Ninus dead, and gone. Semiramis. Anne Bradstreet. **KTR** *Fr.* The Four[e] Monarchies. **CP-BradA**

This great purple butterfly. Another Song of a Fool. William Butler Yeats. **CP-YeatW**

This green is the green of live moss. A Phoebe's Nest. William DeWitt Snodgrass. **SP-SnodW**

This guy / he's got a crazy eye. Hawley's Leaving Town. Charles Bukowski. **SP-BukC1**

This Gypsy bodice of old coins. Old Jewelry. William DeWitt Snodgrass. **SP-SnodW**

This handful of grass, brown, says little. This quarter-mile field of it. Memoranda. Carl Sandburg. **CP-SandC**

This handless clock stares blindly from its tower. A Clock in the Square. Adrienne Rich. **CP-RicAE**

This happened one before when I came to year door no reply. No Reply. The Beatles. **CP-Beatl**

This happy place with all delights abounds. James Thomson *and* David Mallet. **UV** *Fr.* On Beauty [*or*Beauety]. **CP-ThomJ**

This harpie with dry red curls. Red Dust. Philip Levine. **SP-LeviP**

This has nothing / to do with. The Conjugation of the Paramecium. Muriel Rukeyser. **CP-RukeM**

This has to be for my school-chum Billy Greaves. Shropshire. Donald Davie. **CP-DavDo**

This having learnt, thou hast attained the summe. John Milton. **SCV** *Fr.* Book XII. *Fr.* Paradise Lost. **CP-MiltJ**

This head a rest of stone pain. A Dinner Menu a Burnt Offering. James Liddy. *Fr.* Glass after Oblivion. **CP-LiddJ**

This head meant to be massive and therefore. At the Synod in St Patrick's. Donald Davie. **CP-DavDo**

This heap of ashes was a learned girl. La Speakerine de Putney. Stevie Smith. **CP-SmitS**

This heart that broke so long. Emily Dickinson. **CP-DickE**

This Height a ministering Angel might select. View from the Top of Black Comb. William Wordsworth. **CP-WorW1**

This Hermit good lives in that wood. Samuel Taylor Coleridge. **Poetr** *Fr.* The Rime of the Ancient Mariner. **CP-ColeS**

This high summer we love will pour its light. Adrienne Rich. **SP-RicA1** *Fr.* Contradictions: Tracking Poems.

This holy House of God. A Letter to My Friends. Thomas Merton. **CP-MertT**

This Holy Month. Robert Ranke Graves. **CP-GravR**

This honest wife, challenged at dusk. With Her Lips Only. Robert Ranke Graves. **CP-GravR**

This horrible but superb painting. The Parable of the Blind. William Carlos Williams. **CP-WilW2; LCAP; SAmP** *Fr.* Pictures from Brueghel. **CP-WilW2**

This hour is best, darkening. Hayden Carruth. *Fr.* Michigan Water: a Few Riffs before Dawn. **CP-CarHL**

This house built tall, half burnt and raised again. The House on the Hill. John Hewitt. **CP-HewiJ**

This house has been far out at sea all night. Wind. Ted Hughes. **SP-HughT**

This house is a wreck said the children. The Sad Children's Song. Grace Paley. **CP-PaleG**

This House, This Country. Muriel Rukeyser. **CP-RukeM**

This house well fenced with alder, sycamore. September Lull. John Hewitt. **CP-HewiJ**

This house where Love a little while abode. Variations on a Theme. Countee Cullen. **CP-CullC**

This hushed surface where the doves parade. Paul Valéry, *tr. fr. French by* Delmore Schwartz. **SP-SchwD** *Fr.* The Graveyard by the Sea.

This I do, being mad. Siege. Edna St. Vincent Millay. **CP-MillE**

This I had from Kalupso. Canto 102. Ezra Pound. *Fr.* Cantos. **CP-PoCan**

This I saw when the rites were done. Rudyard Kipling. **CP-KiplR** *Fr.* The Naulahka.

This I write, mix ink with tears. Basil Bunting, *after the Persian of* Sadi. **CP-BuntB**

This, if Japanese, / Would represent grey boulders. Thyme Flowering among Rocks. Richard Wilbur. **CP-WilbR**

This Ile tell ye by the way. Charmes. Robert Herrick. **CP-HerrR**

This illuminated address / To that noble animal we all love the best. Welcome Home Oh Our Beloved Hartebeeste. Malcolm Lowry. **CP-LowrM**

This image was drawn by an untaught hand. On the Engraver of His Likeness. John Milton, *tr. fr. Latin and Greek by* John T. Shawcross. **CP-MiltJ**

This impartial dog's nose. The Passport Officer. Basil Bunting. **CP-BuntB**

This institution, / perhaps one should say enterprise. Marriage. Marianne Craig Moore. **CP-MoorM**

This is a baffling and forbidding world of disreputable international shakedowns. Down the Mousehole, and What Science Missed There. Ogden Nash. **CP-NashO**

This is a Blossom of the Brain. Emily Dickinson. **CP-DickE**

This is a brightsome blaze you've lit, good friend, to-night! The Wood Fire. Thomas Hardy. **CP-HardT**

This is a circling of itself and you. Preface to a Love Poem. Derek Mahon. **SP-MahoD**

This is a country where there are no mountains. Morning on the St. John's. Jane Cooper. **SP-CoopJ**

This is a dark woman at a telephone. Judith. Muriel Rukeyser. **CP-RukeM**

This is a day to celebrate can-openers. The Cast Off. Marge Piercy. **SP-PierM**

This is a difficult time. Alkor/Mizar. Siv Cedering Fox. *Fr.* Seven Letters to Zakarias. **SP-CedeS**

This is a good book? Yes? This—For the Moon—Yes? Carl Sandburg. **CP-SandC**

This is a high and sprawling wooden flat. Marilyn Hacker. **SP-HackM** *Fr.* Separations.

This is a hill that holds the church up. The Burning Graves at Netherton. Roy Fisher. **SP-FishR**

This is a land in which you never were. To One Not There. Countee Cullen. **CP-CullC**

This is a lung disease. Silicate dust makes it. The Disease. Muriel Rukeyser. **CP-RukeM**

This is a mistake, / these arms and legs. Margaret Atwood. **SP-AtwM1**

This Is a Photograph of Me. Margaret Atwood. **SP-AtwM1**

This is a poem for Tom. The Snowman. Barton Sutter. **SP-SuttB**

This is a poem for you, Ann. Impromptu. Meadow House. Hayden Carruth. **CP-CarHS**

This Is a Poem I Wrote at Night, Before the Dawn. Delmore Schwartz. **SP-SchwD**

This is a poem like a suitcase. Wedding Preparations in the Country. David St. John. **SP-StJoD**

This is a poem to my son Peter. Peter Meinke. **SP-MeinP**

This is a rope of stars tied to my wrist. Childhood's Body. Charles Wright. **SP-WrigC**

This is a rubbish of human rind. Edward Estlin Cummings. **CP-CummE**

This Is a Sin. Charles Kenneth Williams. **CP-WillC**

This is a slice of the oldest. Tree. Daniel Gerard Hoffman. **SP-HoffD**

This is a song for the genius child. Genius Child. Langston Hughes. **SP-HughL**

This is a song to celebrate banks. Bankers Are Just Like Anybody Else, Except Richer. Ogden Nash. **CP-NashO**

This is a song to the white-armed one. The Fairy Bridal Hymn. Nicholas Vachel Lindsay. **CP-LindV**

This is a spray the Bird clung to. Misconceptions. Robert Browning. **CP-BroR1**

This is a stern Winter. Emily Dickinson. **SP-DickE**

This is a story handed down. Creation Myth. Wendell Berry. **CP-BerrW**

This is a story. You don't have to think about it, it's make-believe. Near the Haunted Castle. Charles Kenneth Williams. **CP-WillC; SP-WillC**

This is a symbol of beauty (you continue). Hilda Doolittle. **NALW** *Fr.* Tribute to the Angels.

This is a threat. Threat. Leonard Cohen. **CP-CoheL**

This is a town of rumours. For eleven days. Chilliwack. Malcolm Lowry. **CP-LowrM**

This is a very sad ballad. My Dear, How Ever Did You Think Up This Delicious Salad? Ogden Nash. **CP-NashO**

This is a wild land, country of my choice. Rocky Acres. Robert Ranke Graves. **CP-GravR**

This Is about Death. Allen Ginsberg. **CP-GinsA**

This is about the stillness in moving things. Howard Nemerov. *Fr.* Runes. **CP-NemeH**

This is about the women of that country. Grace Paley. **CP-PaleG** (That Country.) **CP-PaleG**

This is after all vacation. All that. Louis Zukofsky. **CP-ZukLS**

This is all you go with. Out. Margaret Atwood. **SP-AtwM2**

This is already old. When you find these pages. Attic Poem. Lewis Turco. **SP-TurcL**

This is an age of elegy in our poetry. Out of a Fever: For Robert Lowell (Sept. 13, 1977). John Clellon Holmes. **SP-HolmJ**

This is an architecture for the odd. Wystan Hugh Auden. *Fr.* The Quest. **CP-AudeW**

This is an empty house; not a stick. North of Alliance. Ted Kooser. **SP-KoosT**

This is an energy crisis. Divorce Work. Anne Waldman. **SP-WaldA**

This is an image which put enemies to flight. In Effigiem Oliveri Cromwell [On a Portrait of Oliver Cromwell]. Andrew Marvell, *tr. fr. Latin by* William A. McQueen *and* Kiffin A. Rockwell. **CP-MarvA**

This is before electricity. Game after Supper. Margaret Atwood. **SP-AtwM1**

This is before I'd read Nietzsche. Before Kant or Kierkegaard, even before Whitman and Yeats. The Gas Station. Charles Kenneth Williams. **CP-WillC; SP-WillC**

This is bitter enough: the pallid water. By the Pond. Roy Fisher. *Fr.* City. **SP-FishR**

This is but a fragment. Emily Dickinson. **SP-DickE**

This is common: two ancient buses careening. Santiago: la Avenida Pedro de Valdivia. Stephen Dobyns. **SP-DobyS**

This Is Disgraceful and Abominable. Stevie Smith. **CP-SmitS**

This is for the left-handed mothers. Letter from Persephone. Margaret Atwood. **SP-AtwM2**

This Is for You. Leonard Cohen. **CP-CoheL**

This is for you, Carla, and your quick. Letter for One in Russia. Edwin Rolfe. **CP-RolfE**

This is for your body hidden in words. Forage Sestina. Marilyn Hacker. **SP-HackM**

This is fresh meat right mr nixon? In the Heart of the Beast. Charles Kenneth Williams. **CP-WillC**

This is going to be about smoke. Muriel Rukeyser. **CP-RukeM**

This is he, who, felled by foes. Worship. Ralph Waldo Emerson. **CP-EmerR**

This is his gift. Projector II. Hilda Doolittle. **CP-DoolH**

This is Honor's holly day. Mary Sidney, Countess of Montgomery Wroth. *Fr.* Part 2. *Fr.* Urania. **CP-WrotM**

This is how come I am drowned. Drowning (II). Grace Paley. **CP-PaleG**

This is how I came to be loved. Cables To Rage Or I've Been Talking On This Street Corner. . . . Audre Lorde. **SP-LordA**

This is how it feels to do something you are afraid of. Tear Gas. Adrienne Rich. **CP-RicAE; SP-RicA2**

This is how the wind shifts. The Wind Shifts. Wallace Stevens. **CP-StevW**

This is how to / This is with imperatives. Thomas Merton. *Fr.* Cables to the Ace. **CP-MertT**

This is, indeed, neither the time nor the place. A Toast to Death. Robert Ranke Graves. **CP-GravR**

This is just one more. Eclogue at Nash's Grove. James Wright. **CP-WrigJ**

This Is Just to Say. William Carlos Williams. **CP-WilW1**

This is King Charles his day. Speak it, thou tower. To the King. On His Birthday. An Epigram Anniversary. Novem[ber] 19, 1632. Ben Jonson. **CP-JonsB**

This is like a place. Snowy Night. John Haines. **SP-HainJ**

This is Mr. Woolley, Mrs. Dixon. The Introduction. Ogden Nash. **CP-NashO**

This is my comfort, when she's most unkind. On Fortune. Robert Herrick. **CP-HerrR**

This is my country. If my people came. An Ulsterman. John Hewitt. **CP-HewiJ**

This is my deck I unwrap, and this is the card for me. The Queen of Pentacles. Marge Piercy. *Fr.* Laying Down the Tower. **SP-PierM**

This is my father's gray blanket. Inheritance. Charles Simic. **SP-SimiC**

This Is My Forest. Jim Morrison. **SP-MorrJ**

This is my island. Thirty years ago. Epitaph for John McCutcheon. Archibald MacLeish. **CP-MacLA**

This is my letter to the World. Emily Dickinson. **CP-DickE**

This Is My Own, My Native Tongue. Ogden Nash. **CP-NashO**

This is my piano. Chopin Bukowski. Charles Bukowski. **SP-BukC1**

This is my play's [*or* playes] last scene, here heavens appoint. John Donne. **EBEV; FaBoVe; JCP; LoBV; MeLP; MePo; NIP; OAEP; OBS; OxBoCh; PAI; SeCP; Son; TEP** *Fr.* Divine Meditations. **CP-DonnJ** *Fr.* Holy Sonnets. **CP-DonnJ**

This is my real face. The Clown. Siv Cedering Fox. **SP-CedeS**

This Is My Voice. Leonard Cohen. **CP-CoheL**

This is newness: every little tawdry. New Year on Dartmoor. Sylvia Plath. **CP-PlatS**

This Is No Dream, This Is My Life. Dabney Stuart. **SP-StuaD**

This Is No Land of Constable and Clare. John Hewitt. **CP-HewiJ**

This is no mail order bride, nor a lyrical impulse. An Interlude at the Grand Hotel. Dabney Stuart. **SP-StuaD**

This is no rune nor riddle. Hilda Doolittle. **InPS** *Fr.* Tribute to the Angels. **CP-DoolH**

("This is no rune nor symbol.") **NALW**

This is no rune nor symbol. Hilda Doolittle. *See* This is no rune nor riddle.

This is no time for celebration. There Is No Time. "Lou Reed." **SP-ReedL**

This Is Not a Letter. Kay Boyle. **CP-BoylK**

This is not a pipe. Ceci n'est pas une Pipe. Charles Tomlinson. **CP-TomlC**

This is not my home. How did I get so far from water? It must. Strayed Crab. Elizabeth Bishop. *Fr.* Rainy Season; Sub-Tropics. **CP-BishE**

This is not something that can be renounced. Margaret Atwood. *Fr.* Circe / Mud Poems. **SP-AtwM1**

This is not the event. This. On a Mexican Straw Christ. Charles Tomlinson. **CP-TomlC**

This is not the place I would like to start. Logos. Miller Williams. **SP-WillM**

This is not the way I am. Biography in the First Person. Stephen Dunn. **SP-DunnS**

This is not to be acknowledged thru usual channels. Romance. Al Young. **CP-YounA**

This is not what I meant. Whitsun. Sylvia Plath. **CP-PlatS**

This is our lot if we live so long and labour unto the end. The Old Men. Rudyard Kipling. **CP-KiplR**

This is our perfect silver maple's day. Sonnet. Hayden Carruth. **CP-CarHS** *Fr.* Sonnets.

This is ours by natural, not by civil, right. The Uncut Diamond. Robert Ranke Graves. **CP-GravR**

This Is Pioneer Weather. William Carlos Williams. **CP-WilW2**

This is plum season, the nights. Late August. Margaret Atwood. **SP-AtwM1**

This is Puglia and cruel. The sun is mean. April in Cerignola. Richard Hugo. **CP-HugoR**

This Is Simple. Pablo Neruda, *tr. fr. Spanish by* Ben Belitt. **SP-NeruP**

This is that other place, north of the last. The Master of the Winter Landscape. Leonard Nathan. **SP-NathL**

This is the animal that never existed. *tr. fr. the German of* Rilke. Randall Jarrell. **CP-JarrR**

This is the arsenal. From floor to ceiling. The Arsenal at Springfield. Henry Wadsworth Longfellow. **SP-LongH**

This is the ash-pit of the lily-fire. Geoffrey Hill. *Fr.* Tenebrae. **CP-HillG**

This is the ballad of Boh Da Thone. Rudyard Kipling. *See* The Ballad of Boh Da Thone.

This is the black day when. The Dark Morning. Thomas Merton. **CP-MertT**

This is the cheap motel where. Where They Come to Wait for the Body: A Ghost Story. Robert Penn Warren. *Fr.* Penological Study: Southern Exposure. **SP-WarrR**

This is the chief felicity of life. Euripides, *tr. by* Samuel Johnson. **CP-JohnS** *Fr.* Medea. **CP-JefR3**, *tr. by* Robinson Jeffers;

This is the creature I am! Iron Horse. Allen Ginsberg. **CP-GinsA**

This is the cripples' hour on Seventh Avenue. Muriel Rukeyser. **CP-RukeM**

(Seventh Avenue.) **CP-RukeM**

This is the Cross! First Crusades, The! Kenneth Patchen. **CP-PatcK**

This is the crystal verb. The Verb. Louise McNeill. **SP-McNeL**

This is the day His hour of life draws near. Allen Tate. **NAAL-2; Son** *Fr.* Sonnets at Christmas. **CP-TateA**

This is the day, this is the day! Judgment Day. Ogden Nash. **CP-NashO**

This is the day, which down the void abysm. Percy Bysshe Shelley. **FHYEP** *Fr.* Prometheus Unbound. **CP-ShelP**

This is the debt I pay. The Debt. Paul Laurence Dunbar. **CP-DunbP**

This is the desk I sit at. That Day. Anne Sexton. **CP-SextA**

This is the dirty laundry poem. The Dirty Laundry Poem. Erica Jong. **SP-JongE**

This is the dragon's country, and these his own streams. Dragon Country: To Jacob Boehme. Robert Penn Warren. **SP-WarrR**

This is the dream-journal, knowing the earth slips under. Otherworld. Muriel Rukeyser. **CP-RukeM**

This is the easy time, there is nothing doing. Wintering. Sylvia Plath. **CP-PlatS**

This is the ebb of birdsong. Only now. July. John Hewitt. **CP-HewiJ**

This is the end, beautiful friend. The End. Jim Morrison. **SP-MorrJ**

This is the end but since it is the end. Malcolm Lowry. *Fr.* The Comedian. **CP-LowrM**

This is the end of my life in art. End of My Life in Art. Leonard Cohen. **CP-CoheL**

This is the end whereto men toiled. *parody of* Alfred, Lord Tennyson. Rudyard Kipling. **CP-KiplR** *Fr.* The Muse among the Motors.

This is the face behind my face. You see. A Self-Portrait: David. Charles Tomlinson. **CP-TomlC**

This is the feast of heav'nly wine. Welcome to the Table. William Cowper. *Fr.* Olney Hymns. **CP-CowpW**

This is the female form. Walt Whitman. **ErPo** *Fr.* I sing the body electric. **CP-WhitW**

This is the field where the battle did not happen. At the Un-National Monument along the Canadian Border. William Stafford. **SP-StafW**

This is the final resting place of engines. Silver Star. Richard Hugo. **CP-HugoR**

This is the first soft snow. First Snow. May Sarton. **SP-SartM**

This Is the First Thing. Philip Larkin. **CP-LarkP**

This is the forest primeval. The murmuring pines and the hemlocks. Henry Wadsworth Longfellow. **APN-1; UV** *Fr.* A Tale of Acadie. **MeMAP** *Fr.* Evangeline, a Tale of Acadie. **SP-LongH**

This is the forest primeval. The murmuring pines and the hemlocks. A Tale of Acadie. Henry Wadsworth Longfellow. **MeMAP** *Fr.* Evangeline, a Tale of Acadie. **SP-LongH**

This is the gap. Gap. Leonard Nathan. **SP-NathL**

This is the garden:colours come and go. Edward Estlin Cummings. **CP-CummE**

This is the grass your feet are planted on. Rural Reflections. Adrienne Rich. **CP-RicAE; SP-RicA2**

This is the greatest thing in North America. The Greatest Thing in North America. Delmore Schwartz. **SP-SchwD**

This is the height of Justice, that to doe. Like Pattern, Like People. Robert Herrick. **CP-HerrR**

"This is the hour," said Santa Claus. Santa and the Reindeer. Shel Silverstein. **SP-SilS2**

This is the house of Bedlam. Visits to St. Elizabeths. Elizabeth Bishop. **CP-BishE**

This is the house the poet built. The House the Poet Built. William DeWitt Snodgrass. **SP-SnodW**

This is the key to it. The Breast. Anne Sexton. **CP-SextA**

This is the lair of the landlady. The Landlady. Margaret Atwood. **SP-AtwM1**

This is the lamp where he first read Whitman. Monody on the Death of a Platonist Bank Clerk. Sir John Betjeman. **CP-BetjJ**

This is the land of gods in exile. Sonora for Sale. Richard Shelton. **SP-ShelR**

This—is the land—the Sunset washes. Emily Dickinson. **CP-DickE**

This is the last day of the last week. Last Day. Margaret Atwood. **SP-AtwM2**

This is the last day of the world. On the river docks. Downwards. Charles Kenneth Williams. **CP-WillC; SP-WillC**

This is the last of all, then, this is the last! Monologue of a Mother. David Herbert Lawrence. **CP-LawrD**

This is the last prayer in the book. No Heaven. David St. John. **SP-StJoD**

This is the last; the very, very last! Last Love-Word. Thomas Hardy. **CP-HardT**

This Is the Life. Louis MacNeice. **CP-MacNL**

This is the life of a Congressman. The Disease: After-Effects. Muriel Rukeyser. **CP-RukeM**

This is the light of the mind, cold and planetary. The Moon and the Yew Tree. Sylvia Plath. **CP-PlatS**

This is the long tunnel of wanting you. The Long Tunnel of Wanting You. Erica Jong. **SP-JongE**

This is *The Making of America in Five Panels.* Empire Builders. Archibald MacLeish. **CP-MacLA**

This is the man who classified the bits. Intellectual Detachment. Allen Tate. **CP-TateA**

This is the maneater's skull. Ted Hughes. **SP-HughT** *Fr.* Gaudete.

This is the midnight—let no star. The Storm Cone. Rudyard Kipling. **CP-KiplR**

This is the month, and this the happy morn. John Milton. **FaBoCh** *Fr.* On the Morning of Christs Nativity. **CP-MiltJ**

This is the Month, and this the happy morn. On the Morning of Christs Nativity. John Milton. **CP-MiltJ**

This is the most audacious landscape. The gangster's. Alloy. Muriel Rukeyser. **CP-RukeM**

This is the mouth-filling song of the race that was run by a Boomer. Rudyard Kipling. **CP-KiplR** *Fr.* The Sing-Song of Old Man Kangaroo. *Fr.* Just-So Stories.

This is the needle that we give. Magda Goebbels ("This is the needle that we give"). William DeWitt Snodgrass. **SP-SnodW**

This is the night mail crossing the border. The Night Mail. Wystan Hugh Auden. **CP-AudeW**

This is the night my ship comes in. Johnny Appleseed's Ship Comes In. Nicholas Vachel Lindsay. **CP-LindV**

This is the night the false Saint Jason. Saint Jason. Thomas Merton. **CP-MertT; SP-MertT**

This is the nightmare you now have frequently. No Name. Margaret Atwood. **SP-AtwM2**

This is the one and only. Metaphysics. Allen Ginsberg. **CP-GinsA**

This is the one song everyone. Siren Song. Margaret Atwood. **HAP; NIP; PoA; WeW** *Fr.* Songs of the Transformed. **SP-AtwM1**

This is the only poem. The Only Poem. Leonard Cohen. **CP-CoheL**

This is the order of the music of the morning. In Which a Racing Auto Comes from the East. Nicholas Vachel Lindsay. *Fr.* The Santa-Fé Trail (A Humoresque). **CP-LindV**

This is the other story. There are three. Shirland Road. Marilyn Hacker. **SP-HackM**

This is the outstretched, tentative toe. Hand Me Down My Old School Sliding Pads, or, There's a Hint of Strawberry Leaves in the Air. Ogden Nash. **CP-NashO**

This is the penance: a recurring dream. The Penance. Leonard Nathan. **SP-NathL**

This is the place. Notes towards a Poem That Can Never Be Written. Margaret Atwood. **SP-AtwM2**

This is the place, Craven, the end of our way. Eclogue from Iceland. Louis MacNeice. **CP-MacNL**

This is the place for you if you love quiet. Punchard. Wystan Hugh Auden. **CP-AudWJ**

This is the place it starts—. Corner Tree. Louise McNeill. **SP-McNeL**

This is the place they hoped before. Emily Dickinson. **CP-DickE**

This is the place where Man has laid his hand. The Old Lead-mine. Wystan Hugh Auden. **CP-AudWJ**

This is the place where peace grows. Millpond. Lewis Turco. **SP-TurcL**

This is the place where she lay her head. The Bed. "Lou Reed." **SP-ReedL**

This is the prettiest [or Prittiest] motion. To a Lady That Desired Me I Would Bear My Part with Her in a Song. Richard Lovelace. **CP-LoveR**

This is the reason why Rustum Beg. Rudyard Kipling. *See* A Legend of the Foreign Office.

This is the road to Somewhere. To Somewhere. Leonard Nathan. **SP-NathL**

This is the sadness of the sea. The Sadness of the Sea. William Carlos Williams. **CP-WilW1**

This is the sea then, once. Anchorage. Margaret Atwood. **SP-AtwM2**

This is the sea, then, this great abeyance. Berck-Plage. Sylvia Plath. **CP-PlatS**

This is the season I think most of death. John Hewitt. *Fr.* October Sonnets. **CP-HewiJ**

This is the season of the thistledown. Seeding Time. John Hewitt. **CP-HewiJ**

This is the second day without anyone. Cross Fire. Joseph Ceravolo. **SP-CeraJ**

This is the secret: these hearts. Margaret Atwood. *Fr.* Two-Headed Poems. **SP-AtwM2**

This is the sin against the Holy Ghost. The Unpardonable Sin. Nicholas Vachel Lindsay. **CP-LindV**

This is the sixth winter. Season of Death. Edwin Rolfe. **CP-RolfE**

This is the song / The spice-tree sings. The Spice-Tree. Nicholas Vachel Lindsay. **CP-LindV**

This is the song I rested with. Mammy Hums. Carl Sandburg. **CP-SandC**

This is the sonnet I wanted to write yesterday. Sonnet: Sin. Hayden Carruth. **CP-CarHS** *Fr.* Sonnets.

This is the sorrowful story. The Legends of Evil. Rudyard Kipling. **CP-KiplR**

This is the spot:—how mildly does the sun. Travelling. William Wordsworth. **CP-WorW1**

This is the Spring Symphony. Schumann. The Spring Symphony. Charles Tomlinson. **CP-TomlC**

This is the State above the Law. A Death-Bed. Rudyard Kipling. **CP-KiplR**

This is the story. The Point. Charles Simic. **SP-SimiC**

This is the story a man told me. A Wife Comes Back. Thomas Hardy. **CP-HardT**

This is the story of a dream. The Dream. Lewis Turco. **SP-TurcL**

This is the story of a happy boy. A Happy Boy. John Hewitt. **CP-HewiJ**

This is the story of fire without flames. Charles Henri Ford. **SP-FordC** *Fr.* Seven Poems.

This is the Strait of Messina. Fata Morgana. Siv Cedering Fox. **SP-CedeS**

This is the street I inhabit. Destruction. Alun Lewis. **CP-LewiA**

This is the tale of the man. Ticonderoga: A Legend of the West Highlands. Robert Louis Stevenson. **CP-StevR**

This is the tale of the Tiger Tree. Nicholas Vachel Lindsay. *Fr.* The Tale of the Tiger Tree. **CP-LindV**

This is the time. The Orchard. William Carlos Williams. **CP-WilW2**

This is the time of day when we in the Men's Ward. Five O'Clock Shadow. Sir John Betjeman. **CP-BetjJ**

This is the time of year. The Armadillo. Elizabeth Bishop. **CP-BishE**

This is the time of year. Horned Purple. William Carlos Williams. **CP-WilW1**

This is the time, when most divine to hear. Religious Musings. Samuel Taylor Coleridge. **CP-ColeS**

This is the Track. Wilfred Owen. **CP-OwenW**

This is the vase, Here. Edward Estlin Cummings. **CP-CummE**

This is the village where the funeral. Stranger. Allen Tate. **CP-TateA**

This is the way it goes, the tide. In the Estuary. Charles Tomlinson. **CP-TomlC**

This is the way the road bent then, wide and sullen. Medicine Bow. Richard Hugo. **CP-HugoR**

This is the weather the cuckoo likes. Weathers [or Weather]. Thomas Hardy. **CP-HardT**

This is the white king's palace: snowflakes flounce. The Snow. Hayden Carruth. **CP-CarHS**

This is the wind, the wind in a field of corn. Wind. James Fenton. **SP-FentJ**

This is the wind's eye. Wendell Berry. *Fr.* Window Poems. **CP-BerrW**

This is the winter of the hardest year. Kenneth Rexroth. **CP-RexKL; SP-RexrK** *Fr.* A Prolegomenon to a Theodicy.

This is the witching hour of noon. Dance Unmacabre. Ogden Nash. **CP-NashO**

This is the word our lips caress, our teeth bite. Place-Rituals. Muriel Rukeyser. **CP-RukeM**

This is the world. Celestial Globe. Howard Nemerov. **CP-NemeH**

This is the World that opens and shuts. Emily Dickinson. *See* Is this the Hope that opens and shuts.

This is the world we wanted. Gretel in Darkness. Louise Glück. **SP-GlücL**

This is the year the old ones. September 1961. Denise Levertov. **CP-LeveD**

This is thy hour O Soul, thy free flight into the wordless. A Clear Midnight. Walt Whitman. **CP-WhitW**

This is thy province, this thy wonderous way. John Dryden. **EPCY** *Fr.* MacFlecknoe; or, A Satire [or Satyr] upon the True-Blue [or -Blew] Protestant Poet T. S.

This is to-day, a golden summer's day. To an Ingrate. Paul Laurence Dunbar. **CP-DunbP**

This is to say we remember. Not that remembering saves us. For Victor Jara. Miller Williams. **SP-WillM**

This Is War. Leonard Cohen. **CP-CoheL**

This is what, / at last, it is. Charles Kenneth Williams. **CP-WillC; SP-WillC**

This is what lit the hunters of smoke and the paths of the forest. Muriel Rukeyser. **CP-RukeM**

This is what the man said. Agitato Ma Non Troppo. John Crowe Ransom. *Fr.* Sixteen Poems in Eight Pairings. **SP-RansJ**

This is what those rabbis said. Wisdom of the Talmud. Leonard Nathan. **SP-NathL**

This is what you changed me to. Pig Song. Margaret Atwood. **NoP** *Fr.* Songs of the Transformed. **SP-AtwM1**

This is where the day went slack. Centuries near Spinnazola. Richard Hugo. **CP-HugoR**

This is where the game gets dirty. Roy Fisher. **SP-FishR** *Fr.* Handsworth Liberties.

This is where the serpent lives, the bodiless. Wallace Stevens. **CMoP; PoE** *Fr.* The Auroras of Autumn. **CP-StevW**

This is where those who hate monuments. Ness. Richard Hugo. **CP-HugoR**

This is winter, this is night, small love. By Candlelight. Sylvia Plath. **CP-PlatS**

This is your own who patiently. For Busha. John Hewitt. **CP-HewiJ**

This Italian square. Dancers at the Moy. Paul Muldoon. **SP-MuldP**

This kid got so dirty. Primer. Charles Simic. **SP-SimiC**

This knowledge so innocently it goes this sin. From Now On. Charles Kenneth Williams. **CP-WillC**

This labour passed, by Bridewell all descend. Alexander Pope. **FHYEP** *Fr.* High on a gorgeous seat, that far out-shone. *Fr.* The Dunciad. **CP-PopeA**

This lad, when but a child of six. Ariel. Walter de la Mare. **CP-DeLaW**

This Lady Rides a Languid Dromedary toward Her Dear-God. Marsden Hartley. *Fr.* Boston Portrait Projections. **CP-HartM**

This lady was danger, this. H. D. Donald Davie. **CP-DavDo**

This Lady's short, that Mistresse she is tall. Short and Long Both Likes. Robert Herrick. **CP-HerrR**

This Land of Rainbows spanning glens whose walls. Composed in the Glen of Loch Etive. William Wordsworth. **CP-WorW2**

This land will not always be foreign. The Winds of Orisha. Audre Lorde. **SP-LordA**

This last estate of greed has been reclaimed. Reclamation at Coloma. Richard Hugo. **CP-HugoR**

This late afternoon of April 1964 the despotic old eagle. Celebrating Giacometti. René Char. *tr. fr. French by* Thomas Merton. **CP-MertT**

This Late in the Century. Stephen Dunn. **SP-DunnS**

This latent mine—these unlaunch'd voices—passionate powers. A Font of Type. Walt Whitman. **CP-WhitW**

This Lawn, a Carpet All Alive. William Wordsworth. **CP-WorW2**

This legendary house, this dear enchanted tomb. Monticello. May Sarton. **SP-SartM**

This Life. Stephen Dobyns. **SP-DobyS**

This Life. Rita Dove. **SP-DoveR**

This life is deep and dense. Remora. James Merrill. **SP-MerrJ**

This Life Is Full of Numbness. Christina Georgina Rossetti. **Son** *Fr.* Later Life: A Double Sonnet of Sonnets. **CP-RosC2**

This light is loss backward; delight by hurt and by bias gained. March Twilight. Louise Bogan. **CP-BogaL**

This Lime-Tree Bower My Prison. Samuel Taylor Coleridge. **CP-ColeS**

This little / pair had a little scare. Edward Estlin Cummings. **CP-CummE**

This little bride & groom are. Edward Estlin Cummings. **CP-CummE; SP-CummE**

This Little City. Marsden Hartley. **CP-HartM**

This little house / No smaller than the world. Kathleen Jessie Raine. **SP-RainK**

This little huge / -eyed per-. Edward Estlin Cummings. **CP-CummE**

This little lightweight manacle whereby. Omega. John Updike. **CP-UpdiJ**

This little vault, this narrow room. Thomas Carew. **CP-CareT**

(Another [Epitaph on Lady Mary Villiers] ("This little vault, this narrow room").) **CP-CareT**

This Living Hand, Now Warm and Capable. John Keats. **CP-KeatJ**

This Living in Small Place. Marsden Hartley. **CP-HartM**

This lobster's not a lobster but the telephone. Salvador. Paul Muldoon. *Fr.* 7, Middagh Street. **SP-MuldP**

This lonely figure of not much fun. Absent-Minded Professor. Howard Nemerov. **ELU** *Fr.* Epigrams: "Wasp, climbing the window pane." **CP-NemeH**

This loud morning / sensed a small cry in. Third World Calling. Lawrence Ferlinghetti. **SP-FerlL**

This love of nature, that allures to take. George Meredith. **CP-MerG2**

This love of ours, you of my heart, is no light thing. Reverie. Edward Estlin Cummings, *tr. from Sophocles'* Electra. **CP-CummE**

This love puts all humanity from me. Thomas Hardy. **TOF** *Fr.* She, to Him. **CP-HardT**

This love will see me dead. Geoffrey Hill. *Fr.* The Pentecost Castle. **CP-HillG**

This Loved One. Wystan Hugh Auden. **CP-AudeW**

This lovely flower fell to seed. For My Grandmother. Countee Cullen. **CP-CullC** *Fr.* Four Epitaphs.

This lump of earth has left his estate. Tennyson. *Fr.* Maud [A Monodrama]. **CP-TennA**

"Catch not my breath, O clamorous heart." **NAEL-2**

This Lunar Beauty. Wystan Hugh Auden. **CP-AudeW**

This magic land of sun stars. It's India. Al Young. **CP-YounA**

This makes of you your statue. Cyril Connolly. Stephen Spender. **CP-SpenS**

This man / is tall and slim. Tango-ing. Diane Wakoski. **SP-WakoD**

This man escaped the dirty fates. Flyer's Fall. Wallace Stevens. **CP-StevW**

This man in his own country prayed we know not to what Powers. Hindu Sepoy in France. Rudyard Kipling. *Fr.* Epitaphs of the War [1914–1918]. **CP-KiplR**

This man is o so. Item. Edward Estlin Cummings. **CP-CummE**

This man knew out the secret ways of love. Of Jacopo del Sellaio. Ezra Pound. **SP-PounE**

This man makes a pseudonym. The Fearful. Sylvia Plath. **CP-PlatS**

This man, my mother said, with pony-cart. Isaac McKeown. John Hewitt. **CP-HewiJ**

This man, this poet, said. A Spark of Laurel. Stanley Jasspon Kunitz. **CP-KuniS**

This man was generous not because he wanted to see himself as generous. Convergence of the Many. René Char, *tr. fr. French by* Thomas Merton. **CP-MertT**

This Man Was Your Brother. Kenneth Patchen. **CP-PatcK**

This man's heart / is true to his. Edward Estlin Cummings. **CP-CummE**

This Man's Weakness Is Straw. Charles Olson. **CP-OlsoC**

This map defines your home. The names. Old Map of Uhlerstown. Richard Hugo. **CP-HugoR**

This marching season crested in July. The Eleventh Night. John Hewitt. **CP-HewiJ**

This Marriage, *see also* Commentary—This Marriage *and* Commentary Two—This Marriage. Leonard Cohen. **CP-CoheL**

This marriage is locked. *see also* This Marriage *and* Commentary Two—This Marriage. Leonard Cohen. **CP-CoheL**

This mayden bright Cecilie, as hir lif seith. The Second Nun's Tale. Geoffrey Chaucer. *Fr.* The Canterbury Tales. **CP-ChauG**

This Me—that walks and works—must die. Emily Dickinson. **CP-DickE**

This meal-white snow. Snow. Walter de la Mare. **CP-DeLaW**

This melodious / prison: crowds. Eastern European Eclogues. Rita Dove. **SP-DoveR**

This Merit hath the worst. Emily Dickinson. **CP-DickE**

This message hastens lest we both go down. Allen Tate. *Fr.* Sonnets of the Blood. **CP-TateA**

This might be nature—twenty stories high. New York 1962: Fragment. Robert Lowell. **SP-LoweR**

This milky sky of a dragging afternoon. Hokusai on the Trent. Charles Tomlinson. **CP-TomlC**

This Millimeter. Marsden Hartley. **CP-HartM**

This mind made war. Edward Estlin Cummings. **CP-CummE; SP-CummE**

This modest Stone, what few vain Marbles can. Epitaph on Mr. Elijah Fenton, at Easthamstead in Berks, 1730. Alexander Pope. **CP-PopeA**

This Mohammedan colonel from the Caucasus yells with his voice and. Mohammed Bek Hadjetlache. Carl Sandburg. **CP-SandC**

This moiety war. Sir John Suckling. *Fr.* Brennoralt. **CP-SuckJ**

This moment / 26th Sept / snowdrops. Chronological. Hayden Carruth. *Fr.* Poetical Abstracts. **CP-CarHS**

This Moment Yearning and Thoughtful. Walt Whitman. **CP-WhitW**

This month, / even the rain. El Niño. Martin Edmunds. **SP-EdmuM**

This month you carried me late and heavy. Crescent Moon Like a Canoe. Marge Piercy. **SP-PierM**

This monumental sculpture a / compound of many parts has been. Afternoon Evening and Night in the Courtyard of the Museum of Modern Art. William Dickey. **SP-DickW**

This morn the god of wit and joke. The First of April. Jonathan Swift. **CP-SwifJ**

This morning / My beloved rose, before I did. James Wright. *Fr.* Many of Our Waters: Variations on a Poem by a Black Child. **CP-WrigJ**

This morning. Muriel Rukeyser.
(Waking this Morning.) **CP-RukeM**

This morning / the hawk / rose up. Hawk. Mary Oliver. **SP-OlivM**

This Morning Again It Was in the Dusty Pines. Mary Oliver. **SP-OlivM**

This morning, because the snow swirled deep. Oatmeal Deluxe. Stephen Dobyns. **SP-DobyS**

This morning, between two branches of a tree. The Dependencies. Howard Nemerov. **CP-NemeH**

This morning blue vast clarity of March sky. Birth of Rainbow. Ted Hughes. **SP-HughT**

This morning, flew up the lane. John Crowe Ransom. *See* Lady Lost.

This morning, friends, the blackboard will be black. Lecture. James McAuley. **SP-McAuJ**

This morning Hitler spoke in Danzig, we heard his voice. The Day is a Poem. Robinson Jeffers. **CP-JefR3**

This morning I jumped on my horse. True Story. Shel Silverstein. **SP-SilS2**

This morning I watched. Galway Kinnell. *Fr.* Ruins under the Stars. **SP-KinnG**

This morning is the morning when Mrs. Murphy's treasure chest opens. The Excursion. Or: O Columbus! Thomas McGrath. **SP-McGrT**

This morning the green fists of the peonies are getting ready. Peonies. Mary Oliver. **SP-OlivM**

This morning the wind came, shaking the quince tree. Languedocienne. Marilyn Hacker. **SP-HackM**

This morning there was one McGrath in Aitken County. Afternoon of a McGrath. Thomas McGrath. **SP-McGrT**

This morning, timely rapt [*or* wrapt] with holy fire. On Lucy Countess[e] of Bedford. Ben Jonson. **CP-JonsB**

This morning view / is very plain: thou art. Our Father. James Schuyler. **CP-SchuJ**

This morning, waking. Campanula. Kathleen Jessie Raine. **SP-RainK**

This morning we shall spend a few minutes. Money. Howard Nemerov. **CP-NemeH**

This Mortal Body of a Thousand Days. John Keats. **CP-KeatJ**

This mossy [*or* mossie] bank they pressed [*or* press'd *or* prest]. A Pastoral[l] Dialogue. Thomas Carew. **CP-CareT**

This most afflicts me, that departing hence. John Milton. **PeECV** *Fr.* Book XI. *Fr.* Paradise Lost. **CP-MiltJ**

This moth caught in the room tonight. Lying Awake. William DeWitt Snodgrass. **SP-SnodW**

This motion was of love begot. Ben Jonson. **CP-JonsB** *Fr.* Love Restored.

This movie deals with the epidemic of the way we live now. This Configuration. John Ashbery. **SP-AshbJ**

This must have been before, say, 1840. The Long Bridge. John Hewitt. **CP-HewiJ**

This Narrative. John Hewitt. **CP-HewiJ**

This nation was asylum when we came. Hayden Carruth. *Fr.* The Asylum. **CP-CarHL**

This near-at-hand land breeds pain by measure. Christina Georgina Rossetti. **CP-RosC2**

This Neighborhood. Isabella Gardner. **CP-GardI**

This night has been so strange that it seemed. Presences. William Butler Yeats. **CP-YeatW**

This night is a bitter cry for you. And Winter. Kay Boyle. **CP-BoylK**

This night presents a play, which publick rage. Prologue to Hugh Kelly's *A Word to the Wise.* Samuel Johnson. **CP-JohnS**

This night shall thy soul be required of thee. Scorpion. Stevie Smith. **CP-SmitS**

This night the Moone eclipsed was. Mary Sidney, Countess of Montgomery Wroth. *Fr.* Part 2. *Fr.* Urania. **CP-WrotM**

This night, while sleep begins with heavy wings. Sonnet 38. Sir Philip Sidney. *Fr.* Astrophil and Stella. **SP-SidnP**

This night's colossal quiet, in heaven crowned. Flumen Tenebrarum. Richard Wilbur. **CP-WilbR**

This, no more, doth Callistes recall. George Meredith. *Fr.* The Day of the Daughter of Hades. **CP-MerG1**

This no wonder's of much waight, *sels.* Mary Sidney, Countess of Montgomery Wroth. *Fr.* Part 1. *Fr.* Urania. **CP-WrotM**

This Notebook. James Schuyler. **CP-SchuJ**

This now, this other story makes amends. Jochanan Hakkadosh. Robert Browning. **CP-BroR2**

This nut withering on the shelf. Jenny Joseph. *Fr.* Fables. **SP-JoseJ**

This nutmeg stick of a boy in loose trousers! Notes from a Tunisian Journal. Rita Dove. **SP-DoveR**

This occurred, I swear, one time in a foreign land. Traveler's Tale. David Markson. **CP-MarkD**

This Octopus Exploits Women. James Fenton. **SP-FentJ**

This official bicentennial arts person programing. Bicentennial. John Ciardi. **SP-CiarJ**

This old couple, Nils and Lydia. An Old Photograph. Ted Kooser. **SP-KoosT**

This old man had lavender skin, a handkerchief. River Poem. James Merrill. **SP-MerrJ**

This old man is sly and wise. Homage to John Cowper Powys. Stevie Smith. **CP-SmitS**

This old river town saw the. Chromo. Carl Sandburg. **CP-SandC**

This olde man gan looke in his visage. Geoffrey Chaucer. **OBD** *Fr.* The Pardoner's Tale. **FHYEP; NAEL-1; NAWM-1; NoP; OAEL-1; PoE** *Fr.* The Canterbury Tales. **CP-ChauG**

This one for the telling of sins. And for. Vespers. Donald Davie. *Fr.* Horae Canonicae. **CP-DavDo**

This one request I make to him that sits the clouds above. Love and Debt Alike Troublesome. Sir John Suckling. **CP-SuckJ**

This one teaches. My Comrades. Charles Bukowski. **SP-BukC1**

This open glen's so brimmed with air and light. The Glen of Light. John Hewitt. **CP-HewiJ**

This out of within itself moo. Edward Estlin Cummings. **CP-CummE**

This over-sensuous trapezist. Trapezist's Despair. Marsden Hartley. **CP-HartM**

This Palamon gan knytte his browes tweye. Geoffrey Chaucer. **OBF** *Fr.* The Knight's Tale. *Fr.* The Canterbury Tales. **CP-ChauG**

This Pardoner had hair as yellow as wax. Geoffrey Chaucer. **SCV** *Fr.* The General Prologue. **FHYEP; NAWM-1; OAEL-1; PoE** *Fr.* The Canterbury Tales. **CP-ChauG**

This peace can last no longer than the storm. Rain. Wystan Hugh Auden. **CP-AudWJ**

This pen is where the writing flows in sight. Illustrative Lines. Robert Duncan. **SP-DuncR**

This pencil moves on the page. Sticks and Stones. Dabney Stuart. **SP-StuaD**

This Piece of Eucharist. Marsden Hartley. **CP-HartM**

This pile was raised by Wolsey's impious hands. On the Burning of Whitehall in 1698. Jonathan Swift. **CP-SwifJ**

This pinched face of the moon / all afternoon. September in the Park. William DeWitt Snodgrass. **SP-SnodW**

This place at the beginning of winter flares. Sketch. Stephen Berg. **SP-BergS**

This Place in the Ways. Muriel Rukeyser. **CP-RukeM**

This place is so much. Rain on South-East England. Donald Davie. **CP-DavDo**

This place named you. Tomb Stone. James Dickey. **CP-DickJ**

This Place Rumord to Have Been Sodom. Robert Duncan. **SP-DuncR**

This pleasant tale is like a little copse. Written on a Blank Space at the End of Chaucer's Tale of "The Floure and the Lefe." John Keats. **CP-KeatJ**

This plot of ground. Dedication for a Plot of Ground. William Carlos Williams. **CP-WilW1**

This Poem. Donald Hall. **CP-HallD**

This poem is about being middle class. Being Asked To Define Bourgeois Individuality. William Dickey. **SP-DickW**

This poem is an onion. A Poem for the Governments. Charles Kenneth Williams. **CP-WillC**

This poem is concerned with language on a very plain level. Paradoxes and Oxymorons. John Ashbery. **SP-AshbJ**

This Poem Is for Bear. Gary Snyder. **CP-SnydG** *Fr.* Hunting. *Fr.* Myths and Texts.

This Poem Is for Birds. Gary Snyder. **CP-SnydG** *Fr.* Hunting. *Fr.* Myths and Texts.

This Poem Is for Deer. Gary Snyder. **CP-SnydG** *Fr.* Hunting. *Fr.* Myths and Texts.

This poem is for my wife. Poem in Prose. Archibald MacLeish. **CP-MacLA**

This poem must be done to-day. The Lapse. Paul Laurence Dunbar. **CP-DunbP**

This Poet. Charles Bukowski. **SP-BukC1**

This porthole overlooks a sea. Bendix. John Updike. **CP-UpdiJ**

This Portrait of a Seadove—Dead. Marsden Hartley. **CP-HartM**

This potion is love's portion. This herb. Robert Duncan. **SP-DuncR** *Fr.* The Structure of Rime.

This poverty recognizes. Tenderloin. Thom Gunn. **CP-GunnT**

This private class for one was every day. Who Was C.B. Fry? John Hewitt. **CP-HewiJ**

This queen of prey (now prey to you). A Lady with a Falcon on Her Fist. Richard Lovelace. **CP-LoveR**

This quiet Dust was Gentlemen and Ladies. Emily Dickinson. **CP-DickE**

This quiet morning light. To Mark Anthony in Heaven. William Carlos Williams. **CP-WilW1**

This racer of the watry plain. Catullus. *See* Carmen 4: "My bean-pod boat you see here."

This realm half sky half water. Longitude 170° West, Latitude 35° North. Gary Snyder. **CP-SnydG**

This rich Marble doth enter[r]. An Epitaph on the Marchioness of Winchester. John Milton. **CP-MiltJ**

This Riddle rede or die. The Riddle for Men. George Meredith. **CP-MerG1**

This riot, this obsession, this preoccupation. The Vocation. John Clellon Holmes. **SP-HolmJ**

This river ground to quiet in Sylvana. At the Stilli's Mouth. Richard Hugo. **CP-HugoR**

This road dips and climbs but never bends. The Blond Road. Richard Hugo. **CP-HugoR**

This road is a river, white. Adam in Winter. James Dickey. **CP-DickJ**

This road is not new. Michael Hartnett. **SP-HarMi** *Fr.* A Farewell to English.

This roofer works at night. The Shy Roofer. Gary Gildner. **SP-GildG**

This room has mystery like trance. Kenneth Patchen. *Fr.* Eight Early Poems. **CP-PatcK**

This Room Is Full of Clocks. Isabella Gardner. **CP-GardI**

This ruin now, where moonlight walks alone. Sonnet. Malcolm Lowry. **CP-LowrM**

This rule of manners I will teach my guests. Good Manners at Meat. Robert Herrick. **CP-HerrR**

This same sea, there. Charles Henri Ford. **SP-FordC** *Fr.* Emblems of Arachne.

This saying good-by on the edge of the dark. Good-by and Keep Cold. Robert Frost. **CP-FrosR**

This scarcely uttered they advance, and straight. Virgil, *tr.* by William Wordsworth. **CP-WorW2** *Fr.* The Aeneid [*or* Eneados, *Aeneis*].

This sea will never die, neither will it ever grow old. Middle of the World. David Herbert Lawrence. **CP-LawrD**

This season / Belongs to the creatures. Singing. Daniel Gerard Hoffman. **SP-HoffD**

This Section Is a Christmas Tree. Nicholas Vachel Lindsay. **CP-LindV**
  Doll Upon the Topmost Bough, The.
  In Praise of Gloriana's Remarkable Golden Hair.
  On Receiving One of Gloriana's Letters.
  On Suddenly Receiving a Curl Long Refused.

This seems, in a world where love must take its chances. Mona Van Duyn. **HAP** *Fr.* Footnotes to "The Autobiography of Bertrand Russell." **SP-VanDM**

This shall be thy lullaby. Song to A.A. Emily Brontë. **CP-BronE**

This shawl of hair and sighs. Behold the Woman. Thomas McGrath. **SP-McGrT**

This shining hour is an edifice. Ralph Waldo Emerson. **CP-EmerR**

This should be simple; if one's power were great. Edna St. Vincent Millay. **CP-MillE**

This shuffling fellow, old Tom McAteer. For Any Women Who Pass This House. John Hewitt. **CP-HewiJ**

This Side of the Truth. Dylan Thomas. **CP-ThomD**

This Silence. Daniel Gerard Hoffman. **SP-HoffD**

This silken wreath, which circles in mine arm. Upon a Ribbon [*or* Ribband]. Thomas Carew. **CP-CareT**

This singing / is a kind of dying. The Fury of Guitars and Sopranos. Anne Sexton. *Fr.* The Furies. **CP-SextA**

This single girl is two girls. The Protean Maiden. Thomas Hardy. **CP-HardT**

This, Sir, to them: but unto Majesty. To the King. Sir John Suckling. *Fr.* Aglaura. **CP-SuckJ**

This skinny little dude. Dude in Denver. Al Young. **CP-YounA**

This slow Day moved along. Emily Dickinson. **CP-DickE**

This slow, private man, a paradigm. William J. McClughin. John Hewitt. **CP-HewiJ**

This snake has gone on. A Frozen Stream. Ted Kooser. **SP-KoosT**

This Soft October. James Schuyler. **CP-SchuJ**

This Solitude of Cataracts. Wallace Stevens. **CP-StevW**

This Somonour in his styropes hye stood. The Summoner's Prologue. Geoffrey Chaucer. *Fr.* The Canterbury Tales. **CP-ChauG**

This Song. Hayden Carruth. **CP-CarHS**

This song to the flower of Flaxmans joy. To Mrs Flaxman, 14 September 1800. William Blake. **CP-BlakW**

This South American up here on a Gugg. Interviewed by a Guggenheim Recipient. Charles Bukowski. **SP-BukC2**

This spark now set, retarded, yet forbears. *parody of* John Donne. Rudyard Kipling. **CP-KiplR** *Fr.* The Muse among the Motors.

This sparrow / who comes to sit at my window. The Sparrow. William Carlos Williams. **CP-WilW2**

This spoonful of chocolate tapioca. Thinking of the Lost World. Randall Jarrell. **CP-JarrR; SP-JarrR**

This Spot—at once unfolding sight so fair. Suggested by the View of Lancaster Castle (on the Road from the South). William Wordsworth. *Fr.* Sonnets upon the Punishment of Death. **CP-WorW2**

This spot is loved by all wild things since men. By the Gasworks, Solihull. Wystan Hugh Auden. **CP-AudWJ**

This spring as it comes bursts up in bonfires green. The Enkindled Spring. David Herbert Lawrence. **CP-LawrD**

This Spud's for You. William Matthews. **SP-MattW**
  "I sing of Pedro de Cieza de Leon, one."
  "I sing the canny potato, already buried."
  "Of *solanum tuberosum*, that vagrant vegetable."
  "Thus I do not sing Antoine Augustin."

This started out as a. Jumping Rope. Shel Silverstein. **SP-SilS2**

This statue of Liberty, busy man. The Statue of Liberty. Thomas Hardy. **CP-HardT**

This Stone can tell the storie of my life. Upon the Lady Crew. Robert Herrick. **CP-HerrR**

This story was told to me by another traveller. Margaret Atwood. **NALW** *Fr.* Circe / Mud Poems. **SP-AtwM1**

This strange thing happened to a painter once. Beatrice Signorini. Robert Browning. **CP-BroR2**

This strange thing must have crept. Fork. Charles Simic. **SP-SimiC**

This stranger in my blood, my skin. Tyrant of Syracuse. Archibald MacLeish. **CP-MacLA**

This Street Never Sleeps. Carl Sandburg. **CP-SandC**

This structure of ideas, these ghostly sequences. The Bed of Old John Zeller. Wallace Stevens. **CP-StevW**

This stunted pine whose knotted roots. Alun Lewis. *Fr.* Threnody for a Starry Night. **CP-LewiA**

This Summer and Last. Thomas Hardy. **CP-HardT**

This Summer Day. Kenneth Patchen. **CP-PatcK**

This summer earth. Kenneth Patchen. **CP-PatcK**

This summer, four buntings govern. Indigo Buntings. Peter Meinke. **SP-MeinP**

This summer, most friends out of town. Missoula Softball Tournament. Richard Hugo. **CP-HugoR**

This summer wind, with thee and me. A.G.A. to A.S. Emily Brontë. **CP-BronE**

This Swallows' Empire. Jean Garrigue. **SP-GarrJ**

This Sycamore, oft musical with bees. Inscription for a Fountain on a Heath. Samuel Taylor Coleridge. **CP-ColeS**

"This tabernacle" is a blissful trial. Emily Dickinson. **SP-DickE**

This, That, & the Other. Howard Nemerov. **CP-NemeH**

This that would greet—an hour ago. Emily Dickinson. **CP-DickE**

This the mortared stone. Kenneth Rexroth. **CP-RexKL** *Fr.* A Prolegomenon to a Theodicy.

This the mortared stone. Kenneth Rexroth. *Fr.* This the mortared stone. **CP-RexKL** *Fr.* A Prolegomenon to a Theodicy.
  "This the mortared stone."

This Then—. Charles Bukowski. **SP-BukC1**

This then buddy is the blue routine. My Buddy. Richard Hugo. **CP-HugoR**

This then is our answer under. Louis MacNeice. *Fr.* The Trolls. **CP-MacNL**

This, then, is the grave of my son. The Nettles. Thomas Hardy. **CP-HardT**

This Then My Country. John Hewitt. **CP-HewiJ**

This, then, the river he had to swim. Thomas at the Wheel. Rita Dove. **SP-DoveR**

This they know well: the Goddess yet abides. In Her Praise. Robert Ranke Graves. **CP-GravR**

This thing, that hath a code and not a core. An Object. Ezra Pound. **SP-PounE**

This thing upon me is not death. Old Man, Dead in a Room. Charles Bukowski. **SP-BukC2**

This, this is God's will. The Nun of St. Michan's. James McAuley. **SP-McAuJ**

This, this is he; softly a while. John Milton. **OBS; UnPo** *Fr.* Samson Agonistes. **CP-MiltJ**
  (Samson Fallen.) **OBS**

This ticking is most terrible of all. Thirty Five Mescals in Cuautla. Malcolm Lowry. *Fr.* The Cantinas. **CP-LowrM**

This time has finished me. The Retreat. Charles Bukowski. **SP-BukC1**

This time, I have left my body behind me, crying. Trying to Pray. James Wright. **CP-WrigJ**

This time it happened as he crossed. From the Bridge. Stephen Berg. **SP-BergS**

This time of year a twelvemonth past. Alfred Edward Housman. **CP-HousA**

This time she was able to hear them. The Roses Were Talking. Diane Wakoski. *Fr.* Fifteen Poems for a Lunar Eclipse None of Us Saw. **SP-WakoD**

This time the accordions will cry out—not me, for I'll start laughing. A Square Dance for a Square. Kay Boyle. **CP-BoylK**

This time we were passing into night. For J.A. As Dusk Deepens Canyon. Anne Waldman. **SP-WaldA**

This Tokyo. Gary Snyder. **CP-SnydG**

This told, strange Teras touched her lute, and sung. The Wedding of Alcmane and Mya. George Chapman. **OBSC** *Fr.* Hero and Leander. **CP-MarlC**

This too I love. The Flower. William Carlos Williams. **CP-WilW2**

This town has docks where channel boats come sidling. Arrivals, Departures. Philip Larkin. **CP-LarkP**

This town is haunted by some good deed. Aunt Mabel. William Stafford. **SP-StafW**

This tributary verse receive, my fair. To a Young Lady on Her Birthday. Samuel Johnson. **CP-JohnS**

This Troilus [*or* Troylus], with blisse [*or* Blysse] of that supprysed [*or* supprised]. Geoffrey Chaucer. **EBEV; PoE** *Fr.* Troilus and Criseyde [*or* Criseide]. **CP-ChauG**

This truth came borne with bier and pall. Tennyson. *Fr.* In Memoriam A. H. H. **CP-TennA**

This tuft that thrives on saline nothingness. The Air Plant. Hart Crane. **CP-CranH**

This twilight of two year[e]s, not past nor next. To the Countess of Bedford at New Year's Tide. John Donne. **CP-DonnJ**

This ugly old crone. Age. Walter de la Mare. **CP-DeLaW**

This uncle, Sam, loved any aeroplane. 21st September 1912. John Hewitt. **CP-HewiJ**

This Uninhabited Island. Rudyard Kipling. **CP-KiplR** *Fr.* How the Rhinoceros Got His Skin. *Fr.* Just-So Stories.

This upstate air is open steelwork. Stone Arabia Farm. Brendan Galvin. **SP-GalvB**

This urge, wrestle, resurrection of dry sticks. Cuttings ("This urge, wrestle, resurrection of dry sticks"). Theodore Roethke. **CP-RoetT**

This verse be thine, my friend, nor thou refuse. Epistle to Mr. Jervas, with Dryden's Translation of Fresnoy's *Art of Painting*. Alexander Pope. **CP-PopeA**

This village is so much smoke. Winter Morning of the Village. Leonard Nathan. **SP-NathL**

This Vision Comes. David Markson. **CP-MarkD**

This votive pledge of fond esteem. Stanzas to a Lady, with the Poems of Camoëns. Byron. **CP-Byron**

This warmish night of the thaw. In Memoriam. Hayden Carruth. **CP-CarHS**

This, Warren, is our trouble now. Brief Message. Allen Tate. **CP-TateA**

This was a friendly man I nodded to. Instead of an Elegy. John Hewitt. **CP-HewiJ**

This was a grand passion with him. A Natural Philosopher. Daniel Gerard Hoffman. **SP-HoffD**

This was a Poet—It is That. Emily Dickinson. **CP-DickE**

This was all my light that while. The Giralda. Jean Garrigue. **SP-GarrJ**

This was her dream. A Translation. Charles Olson. **CP-OlsoC**

This was in the White of the Year. Emily Dickinson. **CP-DickE**

This was mine, and I let it slip through my fingers. Some Old Tires. John Ashbery. **SP-AshbJ**

This was Mr. Bleaney's room. He stayed. Mr. Bleaney. Philip Larkin. **CP-LarkP**

This was my dream: I saw a Forest. Bad Dreams III. Robert Browning. **CP-BroR2**

This was my grannie's house, far different. The House at Ballyholme. John Hewitt. **CP-HewiJ**

This was not love but love's true negative. Archibald MacLeish. **CP-MacLA** *Fr.* The Happy Marriage.

This was our first line of defense. It held. Ferniehirst Castle. Richard Hugo. **CP-HugoR**

This was the crucifixion on the mountain. Dylan Thomas. **CMoP** *Fr.* Altarwise by Owl-Light. **CP-ThomD**

This was, the days it lasted, grave suspense. Sanctuary. John Hewitt. **CP-HewiJ**

This was the end and yet, another start. Merlin in the Cave: He Speculates without a Book. Thom Gunn. **CP-GunnT**

This was the end of the battle. Nicholas Vachel Lindsay. *Fr.* The Tale of the Tiger Tree. **CP-LindV**

This was the first day that the leaves. Burning the Leaves. Howard Nemerov. **CP-NemeH**

This was the land's end: the last fingers, knuckled and rheumatic. Finisterre. Sylvia Plath. **CP-PlatS**

This was the last name west on charts. Fort Benton. Richard Hugo. **CP-HugoR**

This was the night that specially we went down. Canto XVII. Louis MacNeice. *Fr.* Autumn Sequel. **CP-MacNL**

This was the pub where I once took that playwright. The Bombed Public House. John Hewitt. **CP-HewiJ**

This was the summit of my views. 2.6. Horace. **SP-SmarC**, *tr. by* Christopher Smart; *Fr.* Satires.

This was the time of their heaviest migration. No Matter What, After All, and That Beautiful Word So. Hayden Carruth. **CP-CarHS**

This was the wedding morn of Priscilla the Puritan Maiden. Henry Wadsworth Longfellow. **TreFS** *Fr.* The Wedding-Day. *Fr.* The Courtship of Miles Standish. **SP-LongH**

This was the woman; what now of the man? George Meredith. **EnVR; OHCV; Son** *Fr.* Modern Love. **CP-MerG1**

This Was Told Me in Confidence. Ogden Nash. **CP-NashO**

This Was Your Place of Birth, This Daytime Palace. Philip Larkin. **CP-LarkP**

This water droplet, charity of the air. The Man Seeking Experience Enquires His Way of a Drop of Water. Ted Hughes. **SP-HughT**

This water started it all, this sullen arm. Bay of Recovery. Richard Hugo. **CP-HugoR**

This wax-mannequin nude, the florist rose. The Florist Rose. Robert Ranke Graves. **CP-GravR**

This way or that way, student, in the sprint. Student Dies in 100 Yard Dash. Howard Nemerov. **CP-NemeH**

This Way Out. Louis MacNeice. **CP-MacNL**

This Way Where November. . . . Hart Crane. **CP-CranH**

This weary body long served kindly use. Epitaph to a Man Not Dead. John Hewitt. **CP-HewiJ**

This week we / didn't meet. I. August Night. James Schuyler. **CP-SchuJ**

This West! this ocean! The bare. Seeing Her Leave. Donald Davie. **CP-DavDo**

This wet morning a seasonal. To Record One Must Be Unwary. Mona Van Duyn. **SP-VanDM**

This wet sack, wavering slackness. Macduff. Charles Tomlinson. **CP-TomlC**

This Wheel's on Fire. "Bob Dylan." **CP-DylaB**

This whole day have I followed in the rocks. Fergus and the Druid. William Butler Yeats. **CP-YeatW**

This wild night, gathering the washing as if it were flowers. From the Roof. Denise Levertov. **CP-LeveD**

This will be answered. The Spanish Lie. Archibald MacLeish. **CP-MacLA**

This will be the last time. Clearly. Doing the House. Richard Hugo. **CP-HugoR**

This wind this / screaming parrot. Hayden Carruth. *Fr.* North Winter. **CP-CarHL**

This wine-press is call'd war on earth. William Blake. **EBEV; EnRP** *Fr.* Milton. **CP-BlakW**

(Wine-Press of Los, The.) **EnRP**

This Winter Day. Maya Angelou. **SP-AngeM**

This winter day in spring I climb the stair. Wet Sunday. Jenny Joseph. **SP-JoseJ**

This winter's revolt of the unbellied trees. Tercets of the Triad. Allen Tate. **CP-TateA**

This, with a face. Item. William Carlos Williams. **CP-WilW1**

This woman cannot live more than one year. Where I? Robinson Jeffers. **CP-JefR2**

This woman! how shall I describe her. Chanson. William Carlos Williams. **CP-WilW2**

This woman is Black. Need: A Chorale for Black Woman Voices. Audre Lorde. **SP-LordA**

This woman light screened through. Woodtime. Tom Clark. **SP-ClarT**

This woman mask that wears her to the bone. Contemporary Portrait. Archibald MacLeish. **CP-MacLA**

This woman with a dead face. A Cold Front. William Carlos Williams. **CP-WilW2**

This wood burns a dark. Dark Wood, Dark Water. Sylvia Plath. **CP-PlatS**

This world is different, belongs to them. Geoffrey Hill. *Fr.* The Mystery of the Charity of Charles Péguy. **CP-HillG**

This world is full of lovely things. Sonnet. Wystan Hugh Auden. **CP-AudWJ**

This World is not Conclusion. Emily Dickinson. **CP-DickE**

This world is tedious. Ralph Waldo Emerson. **CP-EmerR**

This world of ours, before we. Kenneth Rexroth. **SP-RexrK** *Fr.* On Flower Wreath Hill.

This worthy lymytour, this noble Frere. The Friar's Prologue. Geoffrey Chaucer. **PoE** *Fr.* The Canterbury Tales. **CP-ChauG**

This wot all ye whom it concerns. Extempore Verses on Dining with Lord Daer. Robert Burns. **CP-BurnR**

This would not be the war we fought in. See, the foliage. Newsreel. Adrienne Rich. **FaBoWP; HCAP; SP-RicA2** *Fr.* Shooting Script. **CP-RicAE**

This wrecched worldes transmutacioun. Fortune. Geoffrey Chaucer. **CP-ChauG**

This wrestling, as of seamen with a storm. Joseph Conrad. Malcolm Lowry. **CP-LowrM**

This Wretch. Leonard Cohen. **CP-CoheL**

This Year. Charles Olson. **CP-OlsoC**

This year / that Valentine is / late. Louis Zukofsky. **CP-ZukLS**

This year I have sent you. A Christmas Carol for Emanuel Carnevali. Kay Boyle. **CP-BoylK**

This year, last year, one time, ever. Louis MacNeice. *Fr.* Day of Renewal. **CP-MacNL**

This year, maybe, do you think I can graduate? Deferred. Langston Hughes. **SP-HughL**

This year she has changed greatly"—meaning you. Change. Robert Ranke Graves. **CP-GravR**

This year we are making. Dufferin, Simcoe, Grey. Margaret Atwood. **AMV-81** *Fr.* Four Small Elegies. **SP-AtwM2**

This year you gave me. A Glad Day for Laurence Vail. Kay Boyle. **CP-BoylK**

This yearning heart (Love! witness what I say). Love's Sanctuary. Samuel Taylor Coleridge. **CP-ColeS**

This year's jackfruit hang. Charles Henri Ford. **SP-FordC** *Fr.* Secret Haiku.

This you have heard before. Through Bifocals. Donald Davie. **CP-DavDo**

This young question mark man. Edward Estlin Cummings. **CP-CummE**

This youth too long has heard the break. A Tale. Louise Bogan. **CP-BogaL**

This(a up green hugeness who and climbs). Edward Estlin Cummings. **CP-CummE**

Thise olde gentil Brito[u]ns in hir dayes. The Franklin's Prologue. Geoffrey Chaucer. **NAEL-1; OAEL-1** *Fr.* The Canterbury Tales. **CP-ChauG**

This(let's remember)day died again and. Edward Estlin Cummings. **CP-CummE**

This(that / grey)white / (man)horse. Edward Estlin Cummings. **CP-CummE**

Thistle. William Carlos Williams. **CP-WilW1**

Thistles. Ted Hughes. **SP-HughT**

Thither. Samuel Beckett. **CP-BeckS**

Thither as I look I see each result and glory retracing itself and nestling close, always obligated. Savantism. Walt Whitman. **CP-WhitW**

Tho' Artemisia talks, by fits. *in imitation of* the Earl of Dorset. Alexander Pope. **CP-PopeA**

Tho' [or Though] conscience void of all offence. Praise. Christopher Smart. **OxBChV** *Fr.* Hymns for the Amusement of Children. **SP-SmarC**

Tho' day by day old hopes depart. Hopes. Robert Louis Stevenson. **CP-StevR**

Tho' gold and silk their charms unite. To Miss —: On Her Giving the Author a Gold and Silk Net-work Purse. Samuel Johnson. **CP-JohnS**

Tho' [or Though] Grief and Fondness in my Breast rebel. London: A Poem. Samuel Johnson. **CP-JohnS**

Tho' I get home how late—how late. Emily Dickinson. **CP-DickE**

Tho' I my party long have chose. Moderation. Christopher Smart. **NOCV** *Fr.* Hymns for the Amusement of Children. **SP-SmarC**

Tho' I'm no Catholic. The Catholic Bells. William Carlos Williams. **CP-WilW1**

Tho in a sort of summer the hard buds blossom. Technologies. George Oppen. **CP-OppeG**

Tho' much averse, dear Jack, to flicker. Written after a Walk before Supper. Samuel Taylor Coleridge. *Fr.* Poetical Epistles. **CP-ColeS**

Tho' my destiny be Fustian. Emily Dickinson. **CP-DickE**

Tho' rous'd by that dark Vizir Riot rude. Priestley. Samuel Taylor Coleridge. *Fr.* Effusions. **CP-ColeS**

Tho the world. George Oppen. *Fr.* Of Being Numerous. **CP-OppeG**

Tho when as chearelesse night ycovered had. Edmund Spenser. **OAEL-1** *Fr.* The Faerie Queene. **CP-Spens**

Tho' women's minds, like winter winds. Song. Robert Burns. **CP-BurnR**

Thomas at the Wheel. Rita Dove. **SP-DoveR**

Thomas Bewick. Thom Gunn. **CP-GunnT**

Thomas Earp. David Herbert Lawrence. **CP-LawrD**

Thomas Epilogizes. Wystan Hugh Auden. **CP-AudWJ**

Thomas Hardy. Walter de la Mare. **CP-DeLaW**

Thomas Hood. Edwin Arlington Robinson. **CP-RobiE**

Thomas Jefferson had red hair and a violin. Open Letter to the Poet Archibald MacLeish Who Has Forsaken His Massachusetts Farm to Make Propaganda for Freedom. Carl Sandburg. **CP-SandC**

Thomas Lovell Beddoes inquired, "If there were dreams to sell, what would you buy?" I Saw Euterpe Kissing Santa Claus. Ogden Nash. *Fr.* All's Brillig in Tin Pan Alley. **CP-NashO**

Thomas Prologizes. Wystan Hugh Auden. **CP-AudWJ**

Thomas Starr King. John Greenleaf Whittier. **CP-WhitJ**

Thomas, the eldest brother, shipped across. My Brooklyn Uncle. John Hewitt. **CP-HewiJ**

Thomas Tremble new-made me. Inscriptions for a Peal of Eight Bells. Thomas Hardy. **CP-HardT**

Thonga Lament. Thomas Merton. *Fr.* Two Moralities. *Fr.* South. *Fr.* The Geography of Lograire. **CP-MertT**

Thor. Frederick Morgan. **SP-MorgF**

Thoreau, lank ghost, comes back to visit Concord. Walden 1950. Adrienne Rich. **CP-RicAE**

Thorkild's Song. Rudyard Kipling. **CP-KiplR** *Fr.* The Knights of the Joyous Venture. *Fr.* Puck of Pook's Hill.

Thorn, The. Walter de la Mare. **CP-DeLaW**

Thorn, The. William Wordsworth. **CP-WorW1**
"High on a mountain's highest ridge." **Par**

Thorn Apple. Erica Jong. **SP-JongE**

Thorn Forever in the Breast, A. Countee Cullen. **CP-CullC**

Thorns are bleached and brittle, The. Observation Post: Forward Area. Alun Lewis. **CP-LewiA**

Thorsgill. Sir Walter Scott. **SP-ScotW** *Fr.* Rokeby.

Those / various sounds consistently indistinct. Those Various Scalpels. Marianne Craig. Moore. **CP-MoorM**

Those animals that follow us in dream. Xochitepec. Malcolm Lowry. **CP-LowrM**

Those ashes shimmering dully in the fireplace. Housecooling. William Matthews. **SP-MattW**

Those Blind from Birth. Robert Ranke Graves. **CP-GravR**

Those breathing Tokens of your kind regard. Liberty. William Wordsworth. **CP-WorW2**

Those Cambridge generations, Russell's, Keynes'. On Bertrand Russell's "Portraits from Memory." Donald Davie. **CP-DavDo**

Those Cattle smaller than a Bee. Emily Dickinson. **CP-DickE**

Those clarities detached us, gave us form. The Tourist and the Town. Adrienne Rich. **CP-RicAE; SP-RicA2**

Those Coke to Newcastle Blues. Malcolm Lowry. **CP-LowrM**

Those common passions, hopes, and fears, that still. Prologue to the Court. Sir John Suckling. *Fr.* Aglaura. **CP-SuckJ**

Those Dancing Days Are Gone, *fr.* Words for Music Perhaps. William Butler Yeats. **CP-YeatW**

Those days are now. William Wordsworth. **OxAEP-2** *Fr.* Residence in London. *Fr.* The Prelude; Growth of a Poet's Mind [1805 vers.]. **CP-WorW3**

Those dreams that on the silent night intrude. On Dreams. Jonathan Swift. **CP-SwifJ**

Those—dying then. Emily Dickinson. **CP-DickE**

Those ends in War the best contentment bring. Pardons. Robert Herrick. **CP-HerrR**

Those eyes appear to transmit energy. Looks. Thom Gunn. **CP-GunnT**

Those fair—fictitious People. Emily Dickinson. **CP-DickE**

Those famous men of old, the Ogres. Ogres and Pygmies. Robert Ranke Graves. **CP-GravR**

Those fantastic forms, fang-sharp. City without Walls. Wystan Hugh Auden. **CP-AudeW**

Those final Creatures—who they are. Emily Dickinson. **CP-DickE**

Those five or six young guys. Blues. Derek Walcott. **CP-WalcD**

Those flaxen locks, those eyes of blue. To My Son. Byron. **CP-Byron**

Those Garments lasting evermore. Cloaths for Continuance. Robert Herrick. **CP-HerrR**

Those glum, blank-faced, two-, three-story rowhouses in Philly on the fringes of slums. Behind Us. Stephen Berg. **SP-BergS**

Those great rough ranters, Branns. A Simplification. Richard Wilbur. **CP-WilbR**

Those great sweeps of snow that stop suddenly six feet from the house. Snowbanks North of the House. Robert Bly. **SP-BlyR**

Those groans men use. The Mutes. Denise Levertov. **CP-LeveD**

Those grooves in that forehead of sand-coloured flesh. Derek Walcott. **CP-WalcD** *Fr.* Midsummer.

Those had given earliest notice, as the lark. Waldenses. William Wordsworth. *Fr.* Ecclesiastical Sonnets. **CP-WorW2**

Those Horrid Hurdy-Gurdies! "Lewis Carroll." **CP-CarrL**

Those hours, that with gentle work did frame. Sonnet 5. William Shakespeare. **TEP** *Fr.* Sonnets. **CP-ShaWS**

Those hours when happy hours were my estate. Edna St. Vincent Millay. **CP-MillE**

Those ills that mortall men endure. Liberty. Robert Herrick. **CP-HerrR**

Those Images. William Butler Yeats. **CP-YeatW**

Those in whose image I am made. The Ballad of the Scarecrow. Dabney Stuart. **SP-StuaD**

Those incidental charms which first attached. William Wordsworth. **OAEL-2** *Fr.* School-Time. **FHYEP** *Fr.* The Prelude; Growth of a Poet's Mind [1850 vers.]. **CP-WorW3**

Those indians, dreams, &. America As Bullring Arena. Jim Morrison. **SP-MorrJ**

Those Indians who came and didn't stay. Hayden Carruth. *Fr.* Vermont. **CP-CarHL**

Those knights had an eye for strategic location. Duntulm Castle. Richard Hugo. **CP-HugoR**

Those laden lilacs / at the lawn's end. The Lilacs. Richard Wilbur. **CP-WilbR**

Those lights, that plaza—I should know them all. In Time of Carnival. Adrienne Rich. **CP-RicAE**

Those lines on your palm, they can be read. Turn Over Your Hand. William Stafford. **SP-StafW**

Those lines that I before have writ do lie. Sonnet 115. William Shakespeare. *Fr.* Sonnets. **CP-ShaWS**

Those lips that Love's own hand did make. Sonnet 145. William Shakespeare. **Son** *Fr.* Sonnets. **CP-ShaWS**

Those long uneven lines. MCMXIV. Philip Larkin. **CP-LarkP**

Those looks, whose beams be joy, whose motion is delight. Sonnet 77. Sir Philip Sidney. *Fr.* Astrophil and Stella. **SP-SidnP**

Those midland *a*'s. Class. Charles Tomlinson. **CP-TomlC**

Those moments, tasted once and never done. Cornish Cliffs. Sir John Betjeman. **CP-BetjJ**

Those Morning Walks. John Hewitt. **CP-HewiJ**

Those Mythical Silver Pears. Diane Wakoski. **SP-WakoD**

Those not live yet. Emily Dickinson. **CP-DickE**

Those of Us Who Think We Know. Stephen Dunn. **SP-DunnS**

Those old credulities, to nature dear. At Rome.—Regrets.—In Allusion to Niebuhr and Other Modern Historians. William Wordsworth. *Fr.* Memorials of a Tour in Italy, 1837. **CP-WorW2**

Those parts of thee that the world's eye doth view. Sonnet 69. William Shakespeare. *Fr.* Sonnets. **CP-ShaWS**

Those petty [*or* pretty] wrongs that liberty commits. Sonnet 41. William Shakespeare. **InvP; OXAEP-1** *Fr.* Sonnets. **CP-ShaWS**

Those picnics covered with sand. The North Coast. Gary Snyder. **CP-SnydG**

Those piston-driven fingers at the key-. Horowitz. Marsden Hartley. **CP-HartM**

Those plaguy; needling games of ours, where stooks. Osip Emilevich Mandelstam. *Fr.* Octets. **CP-DavDo**

"Those Platonists are a curse," he said. Statistics. William Butler Yeats. **CP-YeatW**

Those possesions short-liv'd are. Possesions. Robert Herrick. **CP-HerrR**

Those profiles, austere in the mine of the craters. The Island (XII). Pablo Neruda, *tr. fr. Spanish by* Ben Belitt. **SP-NeruP** *Fr.* The Separate Rose.

Those rivers run from that land. Song. Robert Creeley. **CP-CreeR**

Those Saints, which God loves best. Temptations. Robert Herrick. **CP-HerrR**

Those scars rooted me. Stigmata stalagmite. The Consolations of Sociobiology. Bill Knott. **SP-KnotB**

Those several times she cleaved my dark. Passage to Worship. Donald Hall. **CP-HallD**

Those sheets, like wretched hulls disgorged to rot. Of Writings Unfinished. David Markson. **CP-MarkD**

Those silver clouds collected round the sun. The Haunted Tree; To———. William Wordsworth. **CP-WorW2**

Those south of us are lavish. Margaret Atwood. *Fr.* Two-Headed Poems. **SP-AtwM2**

Those stars are the fleshed forebears. Fire-Eater. Ted Hughes. **SP-HughT**

Those summer weeks of nineteen twenty-one. Dry Summer, Islandmagee, 1921. John Hewitt. **CP-HewiJ**

Those Swans Remember; A Poem. John Hewitt. **CP-HewiJ**

Those Tapers, which we set upon the grave. Tapers. Robert Herrick. **CP-HerrR**

Those that by bloody force. The Treason Crime. Archibald MacLeish. **CP-MacLA**

Those that can give, open their hands this day. A New Year's Sacrifice: To Lucinda. Thomas Carew. **CP-CareT**

Those that die seem near me. Emily Dickinson. **SP-DickE**

Those that go searching for love. Search for Love. David Herbert Lawrence. **CP-LawrD**

Those that in blood such violent pleasure have. Ben Jonson. **CP-JonsB**

Those thick walls never shake beneath the rumbling wheel. To E.T. Wysta Hugh Auden. **CP-AudWJ**

Those Times. Anne Sexton. **CP-SextA**

Those Upon Whom God Has Labored. Kenneth Patchen. **CP-PatcK**

Those varied dead. The undiscerning sea. Drake's Drum. Geoffrey Hill. *Fr.* Metamorphoses. **CP-HillG**

Those Various Scalpels. Marianne Craig Moore. **CP-MoorM**

Those verses surfaced thirty years ago. Postscript, 1984. John Hewitt. **CP-HewiJ**

Those villages stricken with the melancholia of Sunday. Sabbaths, W.I. Derek Walcott. **CP-WalcD**

Those were the days / And never again. Malcolm Lowry. **CP-LowrM**

Those were the lobsters. September in Kittery. Gilbert Sorrentino. **SP-SorrG**

Those white flecks cropping the ridges of Snowdon. Wales. Derek Walcott. **CP-WalcD**

Those Who Came Short. Robert Ranke Graves. **CP-GravR**

Those who cruise the bars. Icarus. James Liddy. **CP-LiddJ**

Those who dare give nothing. On Giving. Robert Ranke Graves. **CP-GravR**

Those who die young will look forever young. Malcolm Lowry. **CP-LowrM**

Those who favor our plan to alter the river. Plans for Altering the River. Richard Hugo. **CP-HugoR**

Those who have been in the Grave the longest. Emily Dickinson. **CP-DickE**

Those who hold themselves above suicide. Their Heads Bent Toward Each Other Like Flowers. Tess Gallagher. **SP-GallT**

Those who said God is praised. For the New Railway Station in Rome. Richard Wilbur. **CP-WilbR**

Those who say they knew you. Malcolm. Alice Walker. **CP-WalkA**

Those who speak with understanding must hold fast to what is common. Thomas Merton. *Fr.* The Legacy of Herakleitos. **CP-MertT**

Those who straddle foaming sea-horses and ride into the sunrise. Moments of Dawn Riders. Carl Sandburg. **CP-SandC**

Those who went ahead. Paths and Thingscape. Margaret Atwood. **SP-AtwM1**

Those who were far inland. February Floods, 1953. Jenny Joseph. **SP-JoseJ**

Those who will not reason. Wystan Hugh Auden. *Fr.* Shorts [1927–1932] ("Pick a quarrel, go to war"). **CP-AudeW**

Those whom I love avoid all mention of it. North Area. Roy Fisher. *Fr.* City. **SP-FishR**

Those whom nor power, nor lying faith, nor toil. *see also* Otho. Percy Bysshe Shelley. **CP-ShelP**

Those whose faces are turned always to the sun's rising. Lindisfarne. Kathleen Jessie Raine. *Fr.* The Holy Isles. **SP-RainK**

Those whose houses were burned. Beauharnois, Glengarry. Margaret Atwood. *Fr.* Four Small Elegies. **SP-AtwM2**

Those Winter Sundays. Robert Earl Hayden. **CP-HaydR**

Those words were uttered as in pensive mood. William Wordsworth. **CP-WorW1**

Those yawning mornings moored among the pews. The Open Eye. John Hewitt. **CP-HewiJ**

Thou / firsting a hugeness of twi / -light. Edward Estlin Cummings. **CP-CummE**

Thou aged unreluctant earth who dost. Epithalamion. Edward Estlin Cummings. **CP-CummE**

Thou angel face!—like a small exquisite cage. The Cage. Walter de la Mare. **CP-DeLaW**

Thou arrant robber, Death! On the Death of W. C. Paul Laurence Dunbar. **CP-DunbP**

"Thou art a fool," said my head to my heart. Retort. Paul Laurence Dunbar. **CP-DunbP**

Thou art a plant sprung up to wither never. To His Booke. Robert Herrick. **CP-HerrR**

Thou art as tyrannous, so as thou art. Sonnet 131. William Shakespeare. *Fr.* Sonnets. **CP-ShaWS**

Thou art come at length. Sitalkas. Hilda Doolittle. **CP-DoolH**

Thou art fair, and few are fairer. To Sophia [Miss Stacey]. Percy Bysshe Shelley. **CP-ShelP**

Thou Art Fairer Than the Children of Men. Christina Georgina Rossetti. **CP-RosC2**

Thou Art Indeed Just, Lord, If I Contend. Gerard Manley Hopkins. (Justus Quidem Tu Es, Domine.) **CP-HopkG**

Thou Art Like a Flower. Carl Sandburg. **CP-SandC**

Thou art love's victim; and must die. Richard Crashaw. **OBD** *Fr.* A Hymn to the Name and Hono[u]r of the Admirable Saint[e] T[h]eresa. **CP-CrasR**

Thou art my God, sole object of my love. Translation of a Hymn of St. Francis Xavier. Saint Francis Xavier, *tr. by* Alexander Pope. **CP-PopeA**

Thou Art My Lute. Paul Laurence Dunbar. **CP-DunbP**

Thou Art Near at Hand, O Lord. Donald Davie. **CP-DavDo**

Thou Art Not Fair[e], *see also* Beautie without Love Deformitie. Thomas Campion. **CP-CampT**

Thou Art Not False, But Thou Art Fickle. Byron. **CP-Byron**

Thou art not fayer for all thy red and white. *see also* Thou Art Not Fair. Thomas Campion. **CP-CampT**

Thou art not lovelier than lilacs,—no. Edna St. Vincent Millay. **CP-MillE**

Thou art not, Penshurst, built to envious show. To Penshurst. Ben Jonson. **CP-JonsB**

Thou art not so black[,] as my heart. A Jet Ring Sent. John Donne. **CP-DonnJ**

Thou art sad, Castiglione. Scenes from Politian. Edgar Allan Poe. **CP-PoeEd**

Thou art the soul of a summer's day. Song, A. Paul Laurence Dunbar. **CP-DunbP**

Thou art to all lost love the best. To the Willow-Tree. Robert Herrick. **CP-HerrR**

Thou art too hard for me in Love. Love. George Herbert. **CP-HerbG**

Thou bay-crowned living one that oe'r the. Felicia Hemans. Elizabeth Barrett Browning. **CP-BroEB**

Thou bidd'st me mark how swells with rage. Arthur Hugh Clough. **SP-ClouA**

Thou bid'st me come away. To Death. Robert Herrick. **CP-HerrR**

Thou bidst me come; I cannot come; for why. Another. Robert Herrick. **CP-HerrR**

Thou bleedest, my poor Heart! and thy distress. On a Discovery Made Too Late. Samuel Taylor Coleridge. **EnRP; Son** *Fr.* Effusions. **CP-ColeS**

Thou blind fool, Love, what dost thou to mine eyes. Sonnet 137. William Shakespeare. **WeW** *Fr.* Sonnets. **CP-ShaWS**

Thou blind man's mark, thou fool's self-chosen snare, *Wr. considered Sonnet CIX of* Astrophil and Stella. Sir Philip Sidney. **SP-SidnP**

Thou call'st me effeminate, for I love women's joys. Manliness. John Donne. **CP-DonnJ**

Thou call'st me poet, as a term of shame. To My Lord Ignorant. Ben Jonson. **CP-JonsB**

Thou cam'st to cure me (Doctor) of my cold. Upon a Physitian. Robert Herrick. **CP-HerrR**

Thou canst not see him standing by. Foreboding. Walter de la Mare. **CP-DeLaW**

Thou Canst Read Nothing. . . . Hart Crane. **CP-CranH**

Thou cheat'st us Ford, mak'st one seem[e] two by art. Upon Ford's Two Tragedies, "Loves Sacrifice" and "The Broken Heart." Richard Crashaw. **CP-CrasR**

Thou comest! all is said without a word. Sonnet. Elizabeth Barrett Browning. **BWW** *Fr.* Sonnets from the Portuguese. **CP-BroEB**

Thou comest, much wept for: such a breeze. Tennyson. **EBVV; PeECV** *Fr.* In Memoriam A. H. H. **CP-TennA**

Thou comest now impulsive gusty March. March. Wystan Hugh Auden. **CP-AudWJ**

Thou dwellest not, O Lord of all! Hymn for the House of Worship at Georgetown. John Greenleaf Whittier. **CP-WhitJ**

Thou, Earth, calm empire of a happy soul. Percy Bysshe Shelley. **FaBoRV; PeECV** *Fr.* Prometheus Unbound. **CP-ShelP**

Thou fair-hair'd [or fair-haired] angel of the evening. To the Evening Star. William Blake. **CP-BlakW**

Thou famished grave, I will not fill thee yet. Edna St. Vincent Millay. **CP-MillE**

Thou ferse god of armes, Mars the rede. Anelida and Arcite. Geoffrey Chaucer. **CP-ChauG**

Thou flattering mark of friendship kind. To Mrs. C———. Robert Burns. **CP-BurnR**

Thou fool, in thy Phaeton towering. To the Honble Mr. R. M———, of P-nm-re, on His High Phaeton. Robert Burns. **CP-BurnR**

Thou foolish Hafiz! Say, do churls. Friendship. Hafiz, *tr. fr. Persian by* Ralph Waldo Emerson. **CP-EmerR**

Thou, friend, wilt hear all censures; unto thee. Epigram to My Bookseller. Ben Jonson. **CP-JonsB**

Thou gav'st me leave to kiss. Chop-Cherry. Robert Herrick. **CP-HerrR**

Thou gentle Look, that didst my soul beguile. The Gentle Look. Samuel Taylor Coleridge. *Fr.* Effusions. **CP-ColeS**

Thou glorious mirror, where the Almighty's form. Byron. **OxBoS** *Fr.* The Ocean. **PoEL-4** *Fr.* Childe Harold's Pilgrimage. **CP-Byron**

Thou, God, Seest Me. Christina Georgina Rossetti. **CP-RosC2**

Thou great commandress, that dost move. A New Years Gift. To the Queen. Thomas Carew. **CP-CareT**

Thou great offended God of love and kindness. Baccalaureate Hymn. Edna St. Vincent Millay. **CP-MillE,** *ar. by* with music;

Thou had'st the wreath before, now take the Tree. *see also* Upon M. Ben Jonson. Robert Herrick. **CP-HerrR**

Thou hard. I will be blunt: Like widening. Matins. John Berryman. **CP-BerrJ**

Thou hast a lap full of seed. William Blake. **CP-BlakW**

Thou hast begun well, Roe, which stand well too. To Sir Thomas Roe. Ben Jonson. **CP-JonsB**

Thou hast fallen in thine armor. To the Memory of Charles B. Storrs. John Greenleaf Whittier. **CP-WhitJ**

Thou hast left me ever, Jamie. Robert Burns. **CP-BurnR**

Thou hast made many Houses for the Dead. The Bed-Man, or Grave-Maker. Robert Herrick. **CP-HerrR**

Thou hast made me, and shall thy work[e] decay? John Donne. **AnAnS-1; EBEV; EnRePo; FaBoEn; MasP; MeLP; NAEL-1; NOBE; NOCV; NOSC; NoP; OAEP; OBS; OxAEP-1; OxBoCh; PoEL-2; SCGP; SeCP; Son; TEP** *Fr.* Divine Meditations. **CP-DonnJ** *Fr.* Holy Sonnets. **CP-DonnJ**

Thou hast no birds upon thy boughs. The Plane Tree. Wystan Hugh Auden. **CP-AudWJ**

Thou hast no faith of him that hath none. Sir Thomas Wyatt. **CP-WyatT**

Thou hast no lightnings, O thou Just! Divine Justice Amiable. Jeanne Marie Bouvier de la Motte-Guyon, *tr. fr. French by* William Cowper. **CP-CowpW**

Thou hast promis'd, Lord, to be. To God. Robert Herrick. **CP-HerrR**

Thou hast redeem'd us, Will; and future times. To My Friend Will. Davenant, on His Other Poems. Sir John Suckling. **CP-SuckJ**

Thou hast the art on't *Peter*; and canst tell. On St. *Peter* Casting Away His Nets at Our Saviours Call. Richard Crashaw. **CP-CrasR**

Thou hast thy calling to some palace floor. Sonnet. Elizabeth Barrett Browning. **OXAEP-2; Son** *Fr.* Sonnets from the Portuguese. **CP-BroEB**

Thou hearest the nightingale begin the song of spring. William Blake. **EnRP; NOBE; OBNC; PBBP; WiR** *Fr.* Milton. **CP-BlakW**

(Choir of Day, The.) **EnRP**

(Lark's Song, The.) **WiR**

(Vision of Beulah, The ("Thou hearest the nightingale begin the song of spring").) **NOBE**

(Vision of the Lamentation of Beulah, A.) **OBNC**

Thou Heaven of earth! what spells could pall thee then. Percy Bysshe Shelley. *Fr.* Ode to Liberty. **CP-ShelP**

Thou huntress swifter than the Moon! thou terror. Percy Bysshe Shelley. *Fr.* Ode to Liberty. **CP-ShelP**

Thou ill-formed offspring of my feeble brain. The Author to Her Book. Anne Bradstreet. **CP-BradA**

Thou in the fields walk'st out thy supping hours. The Liar. John Donne. **CP-DonnJ**

Thou in whose swordgreat story shine the deeds. Edward Estlin Cummings. **CP-CummE**

Thou indeed, little Swallow. *ad. fr.* Anacreon. Elizabeth Barrett Browning. **CP-BroEB**

Thou issuest from a fissure in the rock. Fragments from the "Christabel" Note-book. William Wordsworth. **CP-WorW1**

Thou Joy'st, Fond Boy. Thomas Campion. **CP-CampT**

Thou Knewest. . . Thou Oughtest Therefore. Christina Georgina Rossetti. **CP-RosC2**

Thou knowest my praise of nature most sincere. William Cowper. **NAEL-1** *Fr.* The Sofa. *Fr.* The Task. **CP-CowpW**

Thou knowest my years entire, my life. Walt Whitman. **TrPWD** *Fr.* Prayer of Columbus. **CP-WhitW**

Thou knowest that toads and snakes and loathly worms. Percy Bysshe Shelley. **PoE** *Fr.* Prometheus Unbound. **CP-ShelP**

Thou know'st, my Julia, that it is thy turn. To Julia, the Flaminica Dialis, or Queen-Priest. Robert Herrick. **CP-HerrR**

Thou large-brained woman and large-hearted man. To George Sand: A Desire. Elizabeth Barrett Browning. **CP-BroEB**

Thou, Liberty, thou art my theme. A Fragment—on Glenriddel's Fox Breaking His Chain. Robert Burns. **CP-BurnR**

Thou Ling'ring Star. Robert Burns.

(Song, A: "Thou lingering Star with lessening ray.") **CP-BurnR**

Thou little kid didst play. The Kid. William Blake. **CP-BlakW**

Thou living light that in thy rainbow hues. Fragment: To the Mind of Man. Percy Bysshe Shelley. **CP-ShelP**

Thou look'st on me and dost fondly think. Address from the Spirit of Cockermouth Castle. William Wordsworth. *Fr.* Poems Composed or Suggested During a Tour, in the Summer of 1833. **CP-WorW2**

Thou lovely Fishermaiden. My Heart. Heinrich Heine, *tr. fr. German by* George Meredith. **CP-MerG2**

Thou magic lyre, whose fascinating sound. Ode on the Marriage of a Friend. William Cowper. **CP-CowpW**

Thou maist be proud and be thou so for me. To a Disdaynefull Fayre. Robert Herrick. **CP-HerrR**

Thou mastering me. The Wreck of the Deutschland. Gerard Manley Hopkins. **CP-HopkG**

Thou mayst of double ignorance boast. On One Ignorant and Arrogant. William Cowper, *fr. the Latin of Owen.* **CP-CowpW**

Thou mighty God of sea and land. Upon My Son Samuel His Going For England. Anne Bradstreet. **CP-BradA**

Thou mighty Lord and master of the Lyre. To Apollo . Robert Herrick. **CP-HerrR**

Thou more than most sweet glove. Ben Jonson. **CP-JonsB** *Fr.* Cynthia's Revels.

Thou Mother with Thy Equal Brood. Walt Whitman. **CP-WhitW**

Thou, of an independent mind. Poetical Inscription, for an Altar to Independence at Kerrouchtry, the Seat of Mr. Heron, Written in Summer 1795. Robert Burns. **CP-BurnR**

Thou Orb Aloft Full-Dazzling. Walt Whitman. **CP-WhitW**

Thou our beloved and light of Earth hast crossed. Epitaph on the Tombstone of James Christopher Wilson. George Meredith. **CP-MerG2**

Thou our Maiden, thou who dwellest in Heaven. Pietá. David Herbert Lawrence. *Fr.* Bits. **CP-LawrD**

Thou Pain, the only guest of loathed constraint. Sir Philip Sidney. **SP-SidnP**

Thou perceivest the flowers put forth their precious odors. The Wild Thyme. William Blake. **WiR** *Fr.* Milton. **CP-BlakW**

Thou pirate nested over Alde! George Meredith. **CP-MerG2**

Thou Power! who hast ruled me through infancy's days. Farewell to the Muse. Byron. **CP-Byron**

Thou promontory dreadfuller than Hatteras. The Sailors. Malcolm Lowry. *Fr.* Songs for Second Childhood. **CP-LowrM**

Thou Reader. Walt Whitman. **CP-WhitW**

Thou ring that shalt my fair girl's finger bind. 2.15. Ovid. **CP-MarlC,** *tr. by* Christopher Marlowe; *Fr.* Elegies.

Thou, run to the dry on this wayside bank. The Empty Purse: A Sermon to our Later Prodigal Son. George Meredith. **CP-MerG1**

Thou sacred Pile! whose turrets rise. Church of San Salvador Seen from the Lake of Lugano. William Wordsworth. *Fr.* Memorials of a Tour of the Continent; 1820. **CP-WorW2**

Thou saidst that I alone thy Heart cou'd move. Catullus. *See* Carmen 72: "There was a time, Lesbia, when."

Thou sail'st with others, in this Argus here. No Shipwrack of Vertue. To a Friend. Robert Herrick. **CP-HerrR**

Thou saist [*or* sayest] Love[']s dart. To Oenone. Robert Herrick. **CP-HerrR**

Thou saist thou lov'st me Sapho; I say no. To Sapho. Robert Herrick. **CP-HerrR**

Thou say'st I'm dull; if edge-lesse so I be. To Perenna ("Thou say'st I'm dull; if edge-lesse so I be"). Robert Herrick. **CP-HerrR**

Thou say'st [*or* saist] my lines are hard. To My Ill Reader. Robert Herrick. **CP-HerrR**

Thou seest me, Lucia, this year droop[e]. Crutches. Robert Herrick. **CP-HerrR**

Thou sent'st to me a True-love-knot; but I. The Jimmall Ring, or True-Love-Knot. Robert Herrick. **CP-HerrR**

Thou shalt have one God only; who. The Latest Decalogue. Arthur Hugh Clough. **SP-ClouA**

Thou shalt make thy house. Ralph Waldo Emerson. **CP-EmerR**

Thou shalt not All die; for while Love's fire shines. Upon Himself. Robert Herrick. **CP-HerrR**

"Thou shalt not covet," said Martin Van Buren, "jail 'em for debt." Canto 37. Ezra Pound. *Fr.* Cantos. **CP-PoCan**

Thou Shalt Not Kill. Kenneth Rexroth. **SP-RexrK**

Thou shalt not laugh in this leaf, Muse, nor they. Satire 5. John Donne. **OBSV** *Fr.* Satires. **CP-DonnJ**

Thou shalt not love mee, neither shall these eyes. Dolus. Thomas Campion. **CP-CampT**

Thou Shepherd that dost Israel keep, *par. by* Milton. Bible, *O.T.* *See* Psalm 80: "Give ear, O Shepherd of Israel. . . ."

Thou sinful Soul, how wilt thou feel. Christmas Canticle. Edna St. Vincent Millay. **CP-MillE**

Thou sleepest fast and I with woeful heart. Sir Thomas Wyatt. **CP-WyatT**

Thou sleepest where the lilies fade. Christina Georgina Rossetti. **CP-RosC3**

Thou snowy farm[e] with thy five tenements! Elinda's [*or* Ellinda's] Glove. Richard Lovelace. **CP-LoveR**

"Thou solitary!" the Blackbird cried. The Riddlers. Walter de la Mare. **CP-DeLaW**

Thou spak'st the word (thy word's a Law). Mark 10; The Blind Cured by the Word of Our Saviour. Bible, *N.T.* **CP-CrasR,** *tr. by* Richard Crashaw; *Fr.* St. Mark.

Thou spectre of terrific mien! Ode to Despair. Charlotte Smith. **CP-SmitC**

Thou splendor of the Father's glory. Splendor Paternae Gloriae. Saint Ambrose, *tr. fr. Latin by* Thomas Merton. **CP-MertT**

Thou standest in the greenwood now. To A.G.A. Emily Brontë. **CP-BronE**

Thou steppest from thy splendour. Song. George Meredith. **CP-MerG2**

Thou still unravished [*or* unravish'd] bride of quietness. Ode on a Grecian Urn. John Keats. **CP-KeatJ**

Thou strainest through the mountain fern. Robert Louis Stevenson. **CP-StevR**

Thou, strange maiden, I can see nought but the glistening. The Witch II. David Herbert Lawrence. **CP-LawrD**

Thou stranger, which for Rome in Rome here seekest. Joachim Du Bellay. **FaBoPP; OBVE** *Fr.* Ruins of Rome. **CP-Spens**

Thou supreme Goddess! by whose power divine. Oedipus Tyrannus; or, Swellfoot the Tyrant. Percy Bysshe Shelley. **CP-ShelP**

Thou telst me, *Barnzy, Dawson* hath a wife. Epigramme. Thomas Campion. *Fr.* Observations in the Art of English Poesie. **CP-CampT**

Thou that at Rome astonished doth behold. Joachim Du Bellay. **FaBoPP** *Fr.* Ruins of Rome. **CP-Spens**

Thou that hast giv'n so much to me. Gratefulness. George Herbert. **CP-HerbG**

Thou, that maks't gain thy end, and wisely well. To My Bookseller. Ben Jonson. **CP-JonsB**

Thou that on sin's wages starvest. Barnfloor and Winepress. Gerard Manley Hopkins. **CP-HopkG**

Thou, that wouldst find the habit of true passion. In Authorem. Ben Jonson. **CP-JonsB**

Thou think'st I flatter, when thy praise I tell. Non Est Mortale Quod Opto. Sir John Suckling. **CP-SuckJ**

Thou, thou that bear'st the sway. An Hymne to Cupid. Robert Herrick. **CP-HerrR**

Thou to me art such a spring. Song. George Meredith. **CP-MerG1**

Thou too art gone, thou loved and lovely one! To Eddleston. Byron. **PeHV** *Fr.* Childe Harold's Pilgrimage. **CP-Byron**

Thou tremblest O my love! thy hand in mine. Song. George Meredith. **CP-MerG2**

Thou trim'st a Prophets Tombe, and dost bequeath. Matthew 23; Yee Build the Sepulchres of the Prophets. Bible, *N.T.* **CP-CrasR,** *tr. by* Richard Crashaw; *Fr.* St. Matthew.

Thou vermin slander, bred in abject minds. Detraction Execrated. Sir John Suckling. **CP-SuckJ**

Thou visitest the earth, and waterest it, *sel., vv. 9–13.* Bible, *O.T. See* Psalm 65: "Praise waiteth for thee, O God, in Sion."

Thou was not born for death, immortal Duck. Malcolm Lowry. **CP-LowrM**

Thou wast all that [*or* that all] to me, love. To One in Paradise. Edgar Allan Poe. **CP-PoeEd**

Thou wast not born for death, immortal Bird! Magic Casements. John Keats. **FaBV** *Fr.* Ode to a Nightingale. **CP-KeatJ**

Thou water turn'st to Wine (faire friend of Life). To Our Lord, upon the Water Made Wine. Richard Crashaw. **CP-CrasR**

Thou well of Kilossa, thy well-chords are of silver. The Well in Africa. David Herbert Lawrence. *Fr.* Bits. **CP-LawrD**

Thou wert not, Cassius, and thou couldst not be. *see also* Fragments Supposed to Be Part of Otho. Percy Bysshe Shelley. **CP-ShelP**

Thou wert the morning star among the living. To Stella. Plato, *tr. fr. Greek by* Shelley. **CP-ShelP**

Thou which art I, ('tis nothing to be so[e]). The Storm[e]. John Donne. **CP-DonnJ**

Thou who art dreary. The End of Time. Christina Georgina Rossetti. **CP-RosC3**

Thou! who behold'st with dewy eye. To Vesper. Charlotte Smith. **CP-SmitC**

Thou who condemnest Jewish hate. Self-Condemnation. George Herbert. **CP-HerbG**

Thou who didst hang upon a barren tree. Long Barren. Christina Georgina Rossetti. **CP-RosC1**

Thou Who didst make and knowest whereof we are / made. Christina Georgina Rossetti. *Fr.* Later Life: A Double Sonnet of Sonnets. **CP-RosC2**

Thou who dost dwell and linger here below. The Water-Course. George Herbert. **CP-HerbG**

Thou Who hast borne all burdens, bear our load. Christina Georgina Rossetti. *Fr.* If Thou Sayest, Behold, We Knew It Not. **CP-RosC2**

Thou who hast slept all night upon the storm. To the Man-of-War Bird. Walt Whitman. **CP-WhitW**

Thou, who in youthful vigour rich, and light. Inscription for a Seat by a Roadside, Half Way up a Steep Hill, Facing the South. William Wordsworth. **CP-WorW1**

Thou who know'st all the sorrows of this earth. The Hour-Glass. Walter de la Mare. **CP-DeLaW**

Thou who shalt stop, where *Thames'* translucent wave. On His Grotto at Twickenham. Alexander Pope. **CP-PopeA**

Thou, who survey'st these walls with curious eye. A Translation of the Latin Epitaph on Sir Thomas Hanmer, Written by Doctor Freind. Samuel Johnson. **CP-JohnS**

Thou, who thy honour as thy God rever'st. Lines Sent to Sir John Whiteford, of Whiteford, Bart. with the Foregoing Poem. Robert Burns. **CP-BurnR**

Thou who wilt not love, do[e] this. Upon Some Women. Robert Herrick. **CP-HerrR**

Thou who with thy long hair. Hafiz, *tr. by* Ralph Waldo Emerson. **CP-EmerR** *Fr.* Odes.

Thou whom chance may hither lead. Written in Friar's Carse Hermitage on the Banks of Nith—June—1788. Robert Burns. **CP-BurnR**

Thou whom I love, for whom I died. Take Care Of Him. Christina Georgina Rossetti. **CP-RosC2**

Thou! whom Prosperity has always led. To a Querulous Acquaintance. Charlotte Smith. **CP-SmitC**

Thou, whom the former precepts have. Superliminare. George Herbert. **CP-HerbG**

Thou, whom these eyes saw never,—say friends true. Lines for the Tomb of Levi Lincoln Thaxter. Robert Browning. **CP-BroR2**

Thou, whose diviner soul hath caused [*or* caus'd] thee now. To Mr. Tilman after he Had Taken Orders. John Donne. **CP-DonnJ**

Thou, whose exterior semblance doth belie. William Wordsworth. *Fr.* Ode: Intimations of Immortality [from Recollections of Early Childhood]. **CP-WorW1**

Thou whose spell can raise the dead. Saul. Byron. **CP-Byron**

Thou, whose sweet youth and early hopes enhance. Perirrhanterium. George Herbert. **CP-HerbG**

Thou, whose sweet youth and early hopes inhance. The Church-Porch. George Herbert. **CP-HerbG**

Thou wilt remember. Thou art not more dear. Robert Browning. **OAEL-2** *Fr.* Pauline [*or* Pauline; A Fragment of a Confession]. **CP-BroR1**

Thou wouldst be loved?—then let thy heart. To F—S S. O—D. Edgar Allan Poe. **CP-PoeEd**

Thou writes in Prose, how sweet all Virgins be. Upon Pearch. Robert Herrick. **CP-HerrR**

Though a wise man all pressures can sustaine. Vertue Is Sensible of Suffering. Robert Herrick. **CP-HerrR**

Though all the Dead were all forgot. Memories. Rudyard Kipling. **CP-KiplR**

Though alone, you know just over the hill. In Your Big Dream. Richard Hugo. **CP-HugoR**

Though authors are a dreadful clan. I Missed His Book, but I Read His Name. John Updike. **CP-UpdiJ**

Though aware of our rank and alert to obey orders. Ode. Wystan Hugh Auden. **CP-AudeW**

Though beauty be the mark of praise. Elegy, An. Ben Jonson. **CP-JonsB**

Though better men may fear that trumpet's warning. We Meet at the Judgement and I Fear It Not. Nicholas Vachel Lindsay. *Fr.* Two Easter Stanzas. **CP-LindV**

Though between sullen hills. Shad-Time. Richard Wilbur. **CP-WilbR**

Though but a simple shelter. Emily Dickinson. **SP-DickE**

Though by well-warding many blowes w'ave past. The Last Stroke Strike Sure. Robert Herrick. **CP-HerrR**

Though clasp'd and cradled in his nurse's arms. William Cowper. **PoEL-3** *Fr.* Hope. **CP-CowpW**

Though Clock, / To tell how night drawes hence, I've none. His Grange, or Private Wealth. Robert Herrick. **CP-HerrR**

Though countless as the Grains of Sand. Boethius, *tr. by* Samuel Johnson. **CP-JohnS; OBVE** *Fr.* Consolation of Philosophy, The ("De Consolacione Philosophie"). **CP-ChauG**

Though cruel Fate should bid us part. The Northern Lass. Robert Burns. **CP-BurnR**

Though cruel seas like mountains fill the bay. Apple Island. Robert Ranke Graves. **CP-GravR**

Though deep indifference should drowse. Robert Louis Stevenson. **CP-StevR**

Though determined Nature can. Wystan Hugh Auden. *Fr.* Ten Songs. **CP-AudeW**

Though Dry, Not Dry. Donald Davie. **CP-DavDo**

Though dusty wits dare scorn astrology. Sonnet 26. Sir Philip Sidney. **OAEL-1; Son** *Fr.* Astrophil and Stella. **SP-SidnP**

Though elderly poets profess to be inveterate. Louis MacNeice. *Fr.* Memoranda to Horace. **CP-MacNL**

Though far from joy, my sorrowes are as far. At. to Thomas Campion *and* to Philip Rosseter. **CP-CampT**

Though fast youth's glorious fable flies. Lone Founts. Herman Melville. **SP-MelvH**

Though fickle fortune has deceiv'd me. Robert Burns. **CP-BurnR**

Though flowers have perished at the touch. St. Martin's Summer. John Greenleaf Whittier. **CP-WhitJ**

Though for your sake I would not have you now. John Brown. Edwin Arlington Robinson. **CP-RobiE**

Though Frankinsense the *Deities* require. A Meane in Our Meanes. Robert Herrick. **CP-HerrR**

Though from without no foes at all we feare. Cloathes, Are Conspirators. Robert Herrick. **CP-HerrR**

Though frost and snow locked [*or* lock'd] from mine eyes. To Saxham. Thomas Carew. **CP-CareT**

Though Glasgow-born, a youngster in Belfast. My Father's Voice. John Hewitt. **CP-HewiJ**

Though good things answer many good intents. Crosses. Robert Herrick. **CP-HerrR**

Though, happy muse, thou know my Digby well. An Epigram to My Muse, the Lady Digby, on Her Husband, Sir Kenelm Digby. Ben Jonson. **CP-JonsB**

Though haunches of whales. Snowstorms in the Midwest. James Wright. **CP-WrigJ**

Though He Can't Know Death, He Must Study Dying. Wendell Berry. *Fr.* The Handing Down. **CP-BerrW**

Though he plays the goat. My Neighbours Two Brothers. James Liddy. **CP-LiddJ**

Though he that ever kind and true. Verses Written in 1872. Robert Louis Stevenson. **CP-StevR**

Though her eye seek other forms. Ralph Waldo Emerson. **CP-EmerR**

Though hourely comforts from the Gods we see. Miseries. Robert Herrick. **CP-HerrR**

Though I, alas! a prisoner be. Jonathan Swift. *Fr.* Riddles. **CP-SwifJ**

Though I am faithful to my loves lived through. Unknown Fair Faces. George Meredith. **CP-MerG1**

Though I am not the first in English terms. To France. Countee Cullen. **CP-CullC**

Though I am young, and cannot tell. Ben Jonson. **CP-JonsB** *Fr.* The Sad Shepherd.

Though I at the time, had no one. More Love to His Life. Alice Walker. **CP-WalkA**

Though I be dead, and buried, yet I have. To the Countess of Bedford. John Donne. **CP-DonnJ**

Though I beheld at first with blank surprise. To a Painter. William Wordsworth. **CP-WorW2**

Though I cannot give thee fires. A Short Hymne to Larr. Robert Herrick. **CP-HerrR**

Though I cannot your cruelty constrain. Sir Thomas Wyatt. **CP-WyatT**

Though I Had Much More To Say. Kenneth Patchen. **CP-PatcK**

Though I Have More. Malcolm Lowry. **CP-LowrM**

Though I have touched her flesh of moons. Modern Craft. Hart Crane. **CP-CranH**

Though I have watched so many mourners weep. The Hope of the Resurrection. Nicholas Vachel Lindsay. *Fr.* Two Easter Stanzas. **CP-LindV**

Though I must live here, and by force. To My Mistress[e] in My Absence. Thomas Carew. **CP-CareT**

Though I myself be bridled of my mind. Sir Thomas Wyatt. **CP-WyatT**

Though I waste watches framing words to fetter. Revulsion. Thomas Hardy. **CP-HardT**

Though if an eye that's downward cast. Tennyson. *Fr.* In Memoriam A. H. H. **CP-TennA**

Though in a little while. The First Autumn. May Sarton. **SP-SartM**

Though it may seem rude. Ballad. Ben Jonson. **CP-JonsB** *Fr.* The Masque of Augurs.

Though Italy and King's are far away. Wystan Hugh Auden. *Fr.* Sonnets from China. **CP-AudeW**

Though jealous March, in marble skies. The City's Spring. Thomas Merton. **CP-MertT**

Though joy attend Thee orient at the birth. To the Planet Venus, an Evening Star. William Wordsworth. **CP-WorW2**

Though joy is better than sorrow, joy is not great. Joy. Robinson Jeffers. **CP-JefR1**

Though leaves are many, the root is one. The Coming of Wisdom with Time. William Butler Yeats. **CP-YeatW**

Though less for love than for the deep. Song for Young Lovers in a City. Edna St. Vincent Millay. **CP-MillE**

Though loath to grieve. Ode, Inscribed to W. H. Channing. Ralph Waldo Emerson. **CP-EmerR**

Though logic-choppers rule the town. Tom O'Roughley. William Butler Yeats. **CP-YeatW**

Though long it be, yeeres may repay the debt. Long Lookt for Comes at Last. Robert Herrick. **CP-HerrR**

Though love be gained only by truth in love. Love Gifts. Robert Ranke Graves. **CP-GravR**

Though love expels the ugly past. Freehold. Robert Ranke Graves. **CP-GravR**

Though love repine, and reason chafe. Sacrifice. Ralph Waldo Emerson. **OtMeF** *Fr.* Quatrains. **CP-EmerR**

Though loves languish and sour. Prospect. Louis MacNeice. **CP-MacNL**

Though lumber was scarce, we found it. The Courtship. James Dickey. **CP-DickJ**

Though many live by logic. He'll to the Moors. Michael Hartnett. **SP-HarMi**

Though many suns have risen and set. To May. William Wordsworth. **CP-WorW2**

Though men may clamor "Why delay?" New Jerusalem 2. John Hewitt. **CP-HewiJ**

Though mild clear weather. There Will Be No Peace. Wystan Hugh Auden. **CP-AudeW**

Though most of them aren't much to write about. The Beautiful Bowel Movement. John Updike. **CP-UpdiJ**

Though most that know me dare, I think, affirm. To My Dear Sister, the Author of these Poems. *Unknown, poem signed* "I, W." **CP-BradA**

Though narrow be that old Man's cares, and near. William Wordsworth. **CP-WorW1**

Though nature weigh our talents, and dispense. Conversation. William Cowper. **CP-CowpW**

Though neither thou doost keepe the Keyes of State. In Honour of the Author by *Tho: Campion* Doctor in Physicke. To the Reader. Thomas Campion. **CP-CampT**

Though no high-hung bells or din. The Silver Jubilee. Gerard Manley Hopkins. **CP-HopkG**

Though no shyer than the others while her pitch is being checked she beams out at the audience. The Prodigy. Charles Kenneth Williams. **SP-WillC**

Though not for common praise of him. Sainte-Nitouche. Edwin Arlington Robinson. **CP-RobiE**

Though now but marble are the marble urns. Postscript. Hart Crane. **CP-CranH**

Though now 'tis neither May nor June. [With Some Poems Sent to a Gentlewoman. II]. Richard Crashaw. **CP-CrasR**

Though nurtured like the sailing moon. First Love. William Butler Yeats. *Fr.* A Man Young and Old. **CP-YeatW**

Though oars are breaking the breathless gaze. A Poem for Someone Killed in Spain. Randall Jarrell. **CP-JarrR**

Though of the sort there be that feign. Sir Thomas Wyatt. **CP-WyatT**

Though once a puppy, and though Fop by name. Epitaph on Fop. William Cowper. **CP-CowpW**

Though once true lovers. *Song:* Though Once True Lovers. Robert Ranke Graves. **CP-GravR**

Though only his shadow / stalks me, I know. My Faithful Lover. Phoebe Hesketh. **SP-HeskP**

Though out of sight now, and as 'twere not the least to us. Paradox. Thomas Hardy. **CP-HardT**

Though painters say Italian light does well. Going to Italy. Donald Davie. **CP-DavDo**

Though Pulpits and the Desk May Fail. William Wordsworth. **CP-WorW2**

Though ready enough with beak and spurs. Cock in Pullet's Feathers. Robert Ranke Graves. **CP-GravR**

Though ready in my chair I do not write. Interruption. Thom Gunn. *Fr.* Transients and Residents. **CP-GunnT**

Though searching damps and many an envious flaw. The Last Supper, by Leonardo da Vinci, in the Refectory of the Convent of Maria della Grazia—Milan. William Wordsworth. *Fr.* Memorials of a Tour of the Continent; 1820. **CP-WorW2**

Though some do grudge to see me joy. Sir Thomas Wyatt. **CP-WyatT**

Though somewhat large, exuberant, and truculent. Byron. **OAEL-2** *Fr.* Canto the Ninth. *Fr.* Don Juan. **CP-Byron**

Though tangled and twisted the course of true love. Rudyard Kipling. *See* The Post That Fitted.

Though the air is full of singing. The Silence. Wendell Berry. **CP-BerrW**

Though the Bold Wings of Poesy Affect. William Wordsworth. **CP-WorW2**

Though the Clerk of the Weather insist. Pebbles. Herman Melville. **SP-MelvH**

Though the crocuses poke up their heads in the usual places. Vernal Sentiment. Theodore Roethke. **CP-RoetT**

Though the day of my destiny's over. Stanzas to Augusta. Byron. **CP-Byron**

Though the Earth Be Removed. Bible, *O.T. See* Psalm 46: "God is our refuge and strength. . . ."

Though the great song return no more. The Nineteenth Century and After. William Butler Yeats. **CP-YeatW**

Though the great Waters sleep. Emily Dickinson. **CP-DickE**

Though the grey year scatter these deathy leaves. These Deathy Leaves. Allen Tate. **CP-TateA**

Though the little clouds ran southward still, the quiet autumnal. Autumn Evening. Robinson Jeffers. **CP-JefR1**

Though the moon beaming matronly and bland. To Lucia at Birth. Robert Ranke Graves. **CP-GravR**

Though the phonograph got melted and the radio. It Doesn't Matter. Jim Carroll. **SP-CarrJ**

Though the practice of chasity confers magical powers. Max Ernst. Charles Henri Ford. *Fr.* Four Elegies. **SP-FordC**

Though the road lead nowhere. A Song of Degrees. Howard Nemerov. **CP-NemeH**

Though the sick beast infect us, we are fraught. Edwin Arlington Robinson. *Fr.* Octaves. **CP-RobiE**

Though the torrents from their fountains. Song for the Wandering Jew. William Wordsworth. **CP-WorW2**

Though the unseen may vanish, though insight fails. A Plain Song for Comadre. Richard Wilbur. **CP-WilbR**

Though the winds be dank. The Meadow Lark. Paul Laurence Dunbar. **CP-DunbP**

Though there are always doctors who advise. The Risk. Robert Ranke Graves. **CP-GravR**

Though there are wild dogs. Orpheus and Eurydice. Geoffrey Hill. **CP-HillG**

Though this the [*or* thy] port and I thy servant true. Sir Thomas Wyatt. **CP-WyatT**

Though thou beest all that Active Love. Another, to God. Robert Herrick. **CP-HerrR**

Though thou hast passed thy summer standing, stay. Epithalamion: or, a Song. Ben Jonson. **CP-JonsB**

Though thou walk through the Valley of the Shadow of Death. Emily Dickinson. **SP-DickE**

Though thou well dost wish me ill. Na Audiart. Ezra Pound. **SP-PounE**

Though thy rafters are grown rotten. Wystan Hugh Auden. **CP-AudWJ**

Though time be blocked in coloured squares. Art's Duped Riddle. John Hewitt. **CP-HewiJ**

Though Time now tears apart. At Parting. Wystan Hugh Auden. **CP-AudWJ**

Though to give timely warning and deter. William Wordsworth. *Fr.* Sonnets upon the Punishment of Death. **CP-WorW2**

Though to my feathers in the wet. The Three Beggars. William Butler Yeats. **CP-YeatW**

Though to the vilest things beneath the moon. Arthur Hugh Clough. *Fr.* Blank Misgivings of a Creature Moving About in Worlds Not Realized. **SP-ClouA**

Though Truth and Falsehood be. John Donne. *See* Satire 3: "Kind pity [*or* Kinde pitty] chokes my spleen[e]; brave scorn forbids."

Though truths in manhood darkly join. Tennyson. **OAEL-2** *Fr.* In Memoriam A. H. H. **CP-TennA**

Though Tuesday, 11 A.M., the shops are locked. In Your Fugitive Dream. Richard Hugo. **CP-HugoR**

Though unseen Poets, many and many a time. On My Songs. Wilfred Owen. **CP-OwenW**

Though veiled in spires of myrtle wreath. Song. Samuel Taylor Coleridge. **CP-ColeS**

Though we are all a little bit disappointed this year there won't be any fireworks. Malcolm Lowry. **CP-LowrM**

Though we are but *sea* birds. Malcolm Lowry. **CP-LowrM**

Though we are each unknown to ourself. Emily Dickinson. **SP-DickE**

Though we may never be seen alive again. Lost in Ladispoli. Miller Williams. **SP-WillM**

Though you are in your shining days. The Lover Pleads with His Friend for Old Friends. William Butler Yeats. **CP-YeatW**

Though You Are Young [*or* Yoong]. Thomas Campion. **CP-CampT**

Though you are young [*or* yoong] and I am old. Though You Are Young [*or* Yoong]. Thomas Campion. **CP-CampT**

hough you breed men to better tree and root. Admonition to Science. John Hewitt. **CP-HewiJ**

hough you complain of me. A Man to a Woman. William Carlos Williams. **CP-WilW1**

hough you, Diana-like, have liv'd still chaste. Lutea Allison. Sir John Suckling. **CP-SuckJ**

hough you forsake me, yet alas permit. Sonnet 6. Mary Sidney, Countess of Montgomery Wroth. *Fr.* Lindamira's Complaint. *Fr.* Part 1. *Fr.* Urania. **CP-WrotM**

hough you know it anyhow. Tin Wedding Whistle. Ogden Nash. **CP-NashO**

hough your blind arrow, shot in time of need. A Blind Arrow. Robert Ranke Graves. **CP-GravR**

hough your professions, ages and conditions. Love and Night. Robert Ranke Graves. **CP-GravR**

hough your sorrows not. Edward Estlin Cummings. **CP-CummE**

hough your strangenesse frets my hart. Thomas Campion. **CP-CampT**

hough you're gone away this morning. You Like Me Too Much. George Harrison. **CP-Beatl**

hought: ("As I sit with others at a great feast, suddenly while the music is playing"). Walt Whitman. **CP-WhitW**

hought, A. Samuel Taylor Coleridge. **CP-ColeS**

hought, A. David Herbert Lawrence. **CP-LawrD**

hought. Howard Nemerov. **CP-NemeH**

hought: ("Of persons arrived at high positions, ceremonies, wealth, scholarships, and the like"). Walt Whitman. **CP-WhitW**

hought, A. Robert Louis Stevenson. **CP-StevR**

hought ("Of Equality. . . "). Walt Whitman. **CP-WhitW**

Thought ("Of Justice—as if Justice could be any thing but the same ample law, expounded by natural judges and saviors"). Walt Whitman. **CP-WhitW**

Thought ("Of obedience, faith, adhesiveness"). Walt Whitman. **CP-WhitW**

Thought ay like a flower upon mine heart, A. Pain in Pleasure. Elizabeth Barrett Browning. **CP-BroEB**

Thought beneath so slight a film, The. Emily Dickinson. **CP-DickE**

Thought does not crush to stone. The Adamant. Theodore Roethke. **CP-RoetT**

Thought for a Lonely Death-Bed, A. Elizabeth Barrett Browning. **CP-BroEB**

Thought-Fox, The. Ted Hughes. **SP-HughT**

Thought from Propertius, A. William Butler Yeats. **CP-YeatW**

Thought I Was Dying. Daniel Gerard Hoffman. **SP-HoffD**

Thought in Two Moods, A. Thomas Hardy. **CP-HardT**

Thought is false happiness: the idea. Crude Foyer. Wallace Stevens. **CP-StevW**

Thought is seldom itself. Thought. Howard Nemerov. **CP-NemeH**

Thought Is Superior. Stevie Smith. **CP-SmitS**

Thought is surrounded by a halo. Tom Clark. *Fr.* Suite. **SP-ClarT**

Thought may well be ever ranging. Arthur Hugh Clough. **SP-ClouA**

Thought[s] of a Briton on the Subjugation of Switzerland. William Wordsworth. **CP-WorW1**

Thought of Columbus, A. Walt Whitman. **CP-WhitW**

Thought of Something Else, The. Wendell Berry. **CP-BerrW**

Thought of Trees, The. Howard Nemerov. **CP-NemeH**

Thought of writing came to me today, The. Wystan Hugh Auden. **NOBL** *Fr.* Letter to Lord Byron. **CP-AudeW**

Thought Revolved, A. Wallace Stevens. **CP-StevW**

Thought went up my mind today, A. Emily Dickinson. **CP-DickE**

Thought While Drowning (Acapulco), [*similar to* Thoughts While Drowning: But Try to Eliminate the Argument.] Malcolm Lowry. **CP-LowrM** *Fr.* The Lighthouse Invites the Storm. **CP-LowrM**

Thought, with good cause thou lik'st so well the night. Sonnet 96. Sir Philip Sidney. *Fr.* Astrophil and Stella. **SP-SidnP**

Thoughtful Lover, The. William Carlos Williams. **CP-WilW2**

Thoughtful of you, I was / anticipating change in. Rain (2) ("Thoughtful of you, I was / anticipating change in"). Robert Creeley. **CP-CreeR**

Thoughts: ("Of public opinion"). Walt Whitman. **CP-WhitW**

Thoughts ("Of ownership—as if one fit to own things could not at pleasure enter upon all, and incorporate them into himself or herself"). Walt Whitman. **CP-WhitW**

Thoughts ("Of these years I sing"). Walt Whitman. **CP-WhitW**

Thoughts about the Christian Doctrine of Eternal Hell. Stevie Smith. **CP-SmitS**

Thoughts about the Person from Porlock. Stevie Smith. **CP-SmitS**

Thoughts at Midnight. Thomas Hardy. **CP-HardT**

Thoughts During an Air Raid. Stephen Spender. **CP-SpenS**

Thoughts for a Speech of Lucifer, in the Tragedy of "Cain." Byron. **CP-Byron**

Thoughts from Sophocles. Thomas Hardy. **CP-HardT**

Thoughts from Underground. Margaret Atwood. **SP-AtwM1**

Thoughts in a Zoo. Countee Cullen. **CP-CullC**

Thoughts of a Young Girl. John Ashbery. **SP-AshbJ**

Thoughts of Phena. Thomas Hardy. **CP-HardT**

Thoughts of the Time. Charles Olson. **CP-OlsoC**

Thoughts on a Breath. Allen Ginsberg. **CP-GinsA**

Thoughts on Looking at a Samuel Palmer Etching at the Tate. Gary Snyder. **CP-SnydG**

Thoughts on Looking into a Thicket. John Ciardi. **SP-CiarJ**

Thoughts on "The Diary of a Nobody." Sir John Betjeman. **CP-BetjJ**

Thoughts on the Seasons. William Wordsworth. **CP-WorW2**

Thoughts on Unpacking. Thom Gunn. **CP-GunnT**

Thoughts—I: Visages. Walt Whitman. **CP-WhitW**

Thoughts Sitting Breathing. Allen Ginsberg. **CP-GinsA**

Thoughts—6: "Of What I Write." Walt Whitman. **CP-WhitW**

Thoughts Suggested by a College Examination. Byron. **CP-Byron**

Thoughts Suggested the Day Following, on the Banks of Nith, near the Poet's Residence. William Wordsworth. **CP-WorW1**

Thoughts, suggestions, aspirations, pictures. L of G. Walt Whitman. **CP-WhitW**

Thoughts Thought after a Bridge Party. Ogden Nash. **CP-NashO**

Thoughts Thought on an Avenue. Ogden Nash. **CP-NashO**

Thoughts Thought While Waiting for a Pronouncement from a Doctor, an Editor, a Big Executive, the Department of Internal Revenue or Any Other Momentous Pronouncer. Ogden Nash. **CP-NashO**

Thoughts to a Concerto of Telemann. Lawrence Ferlinghetti. **SP-FerlL**

Thoughts to Be Erased from My Destiny. Malcolm Lowry. **CP-LowrM**

Thoughts While Driving Home. John Updike. **CP-UpdiJ**

Thoughts While Drowning: But Try to Eliminate the Argument. Malcolm Lowry. **CP-LowrM**

Thou's welcome, Wean! Mischanter fa' me. A Poet's Welcome to His Love-Begotten Daughter [the First Instance that Entitled Him to the Venerable Appellation of Father]. Robert Burns. **CP-BurnR**

Thousand and fifty-one waves, A. Numbers. Stevie Smith. **CP-SmitS**

Thousand and Second Night, The. James Merrill. **SP-MerrJ**

Thousand dangers of ruin has the street of love. Hafiz, *tr. by* Ralph Waldo Emerson. **CP-EmerR** *Fr.* Odes.

Thousand doors ago, A. Young. Anne Sexton. **CP-SextA**

Thousand-hooded one sleeps quietly his big toe in his mouth, The. The Illness. Charles Henri Ford. **SP-FordC**

Thousand minstrels woke within me. Monadnoc. Ralph Waldo Emerson. **CP-EmerR**

Thousand perfect men and women appear, A. Offerings. Walt Whitman. **CP-WhitW**

Thousand pieces or how a thousand, A. Cantico. James Liddy. **CP-LiddJ**

Thousand questions rise to my lips, A. Emily Dickinson. **SP-DickE**

Thousand sounds of happiness, A. Emily Brontë. **CP-BronE**

Thousand sunsets behind tramcar wires in open skies of Warsaw, A. The Moments Return. Allen Ginsberg. **CP-GinsA**

Thousand times ten thousand times, A. The Journey Starts Swiftly. Nicholas Vachel Lindsay. *Fr.* The Tree of Laughing Bells or The Wings of the Morning. **CP-LindV**

Thousand times you've seen that scene, A. Country Burying (1919). Robert Penn Warren. **SP-WarrR**

Thousand years the Earth cried, "Where art thou?", A. Percy Bysshe Shelley. *Fr.* Ode to Liberty. **CP-ShelP**

Thousands each day passe by, which wee. Once Seen, and No More. Robert Herrick. **CP-HerrR**

Thousands of Days. Muriel Rukeyser. **CP-RukeM**

Thousands of sheep, soft-footed, black-nosed sheep—one by one going. Sheep. Carl Sandburg. **CP-SandC**

Thousands of years passed. John Haines. *Fr.* The Traveler. **SP-HainJ**

Thousandth Man, The. Rudyard Kipling. **CP-KiplR**

Thousandth Poem for Dylan Thomas, The. John Ciardi. **SP-CiarJ**

Thracian, The. Vincent Bourne, *tr. fr. Latin by* William Cowper. **CP-CowpW**

Thracian parents, at his birth. The Thracian. Vincent Bourne, *tr. fr. Latin by* William Cowper. **CP-CowpW**

Thrasher in the Willow by the Lake, The. Robert Pack. **SP-PackR**

Thread. Stephen Berg. **SP-BergS**

Thread, The. Denise Levertov. **CP-LeveD**

Thread. Patti Smith. **SP-SmitP**

Thread of Life, The. Christina Georgina Rossetti. **CP-RosC2** "Irresponsive silence of the land, The." **NOBE; OBEV; OBNC; TrGrPo** (Aloof.) **OBEV; TrGrPo** "Therefore myself is that one only thing." "Thus am I mine own prison. Everything."

Thread of silver marks along the sand, A. The Lost Continent. Jenny Joseph. **SP-JoseJ**

Thread was snapped too soon, A. Beyond the Dark Cedars. Kenneth Patchen. **CP-PatcK**

Threads our hands in blindness spin, The. Overruled. John Greenleaf Whittier. **CP-WhitJ**

Threads: Rosa Luxemburg from Prison. Jane Cooper. **SP-CoopJ**
Breslau, November-December 1917.
Breslau, Spring 1918.
Wronke, Spring 1917.

Threat. Leonard Cohen. **CP-CoheL**

Threatened. Alice Walker. **CP-WalkA**

Threatened by abundance, the ranchers. Killing the Calves. Robert Earl Hayden. **CP-HaydR**

Threats come which no submission may assuage. Dissolution of the Monasteries. William Wordsworth. *Fr.* Ecclesiastical Sonnets. **CP-WorW2**

Three / crimson / mongrels / bait. Another Ashtray. Louis Zukofsky. **CP-ZukLS**

Three, The. James Dickey. **CP-DickJ**

Three. Thom Gunn. **CP-GunnT**

3 A.M. John Updike. **CP-UpdiJ**

3 A. M. in a War Year. Mona Van Duyn. **SP-VanDM**

Three Acts from a Play. James McAuley. **SP-McAuJ**
"For one season, much laughter: we learned to take."
"Her womanhood collected into a pale."
"She opened the lower button of her blouse."

Three, almost, now into the ass's years. John Berryman. *Fr.* Sonnets to Chris. **CP-BerrJ**

Three a.m.—a far bell. December. Gary Snyder. **InPS** *Fr.* Six Years. **CP-SnydG**

Three A.M. and Then Five. John Ciardi. **SP-CiarJ**

3 A.M. Kitchen: My Father Talking. Tess Gallagher. **SP-GallT**

3 A.M. The Girl with the Honey Colored Hair. William Carlos Williams. **CP-WilW2**

Three Angels. "Bob Dylan." **CP-DylaB**

Three angels came to the red red clay. From the Coptic. Stevie Smith. **CP-SmitS**

Three astonished sunflowers / gaze at me over the wall. Clown Flowers. Phoebe Hesketh. **SP-HeskP**

Three Badgers, The. "Lewis Carroll." **CP-CarrL** *Fr.* Sylvie and Bruno.

Three Balls. Carl Sandburg. **CP-SandC**

Three Baroque Meditations. Geoffrey Hill. **CP-HillG**
"Anguish bloated by the replete scream."
Dead Bride, The. **TW**
"Do words make up the majesty."

Three Beggars, The. William Butler Yeats. **CP-YeatW**

Three Bells, The. John Greenleaf Whittier. **CP-WhitJ**

Three Beyond. Donald Davie. **CP-DavDo**

Three Bills. Randall Jarrell. **CP-JarrR**

Three Black Women. Muriel Rukeyser. **CP-RukeM**

Three blank walls, a barred window with no view. The Philosopher. Robert Ranke Graves. **CP-GravR**

Three boats headed Northeast, moored. Waiting To Lean to the Master's Command. Richard Eberhart. **CP-EberR**

Three boys, American, in dungarees. February 22. John Updike. **CP-UpdiJ**

Three Bushes, The. William Butler Yeats. **CP-YeatW**

Three captains went to Indian wars. The Casterbridge Captains. Thomas Hardy. **CP-HardT**

Three centuries now are gone. Rose. Walter de la Mare. **CP-DeLaW**

Three Ceremonial Poems. Roy Fisher.
"Absolute / Pity / Advancing." **SP-FishR**
"Metallic sheath / derelict, that resounds." **SP-FishR**
"Oh yellow head." **SP-FishR**

Three chairs— / one for solitude, two for company. From Walden. Phoebe Hesketh. **SP-HeskP**

Three cheers for lusty winter. Parody of Alfred Austin. George Meredith. **CP-MerG2**

Three Cherry Trees, The. Walter de la Mare. **CP-DeLaW**

Three Children. "Lewis Carroll." **CP-CarrL**

Three children dancing around an orange tree. Coins and Coffins under My Bed. Diane Wakoski. **SP-WakoD**

Three Children Looking Over the Edge of the World. Frederick Morgan. **SP-MorgF**

Three Chores. James Merrill. **SP-MerrJ**

Three coke bottles of your Uncle Sal's. Summer School. Brendan Galvin. **SP-GalvB**

Three college sophs, and three pert templars came. Alexander Pope. **FHYEP** *Fr.* High on a gorgeous seat, that far out-shone. *Fr.* The Dunciad. **CP-PopeA**

Three Cottage Girls, The. William Wordsworth. **HBV 1-2** *Fr.* Memorials of a Tour of the Continent; 1820. **CP-WorW2**

Three damsels in the queen's chamber. Algernon Charles Swinburne. **SP-SwinA**
(Christmas Carol, A.) **SP-SwinA**

Three-day-long rain from the east, A. The Dark Day. William Carlos Williams. **CP-WilW1**

Three days for an answer I have waited. Another Reply by the Dean. Jonathan Swift. **CP-SwifJ**

Three Days of Forest, a River, Free. Rita Dove. **SP-DoveR**

Three days of waiting in the islands. The Assault Convoy. Alun Lewis. **CP-LewiA**

Three-Decker, The. Rudyard Kipling. **CP-KiplR**

Three Deer One Coyote Running in the Snow. Gary Snyder. **CP-SnydG**

Three Desk Objects. Margaret Atwood. **SP-AtwM1**

Three Dimensions, The. Ralph Waldo Emerson. **CP-EmerR**

Three Eagles and the Sleepy Lion, The. George Meredith. **CP-MerG2**

Three Elegiac Poems. Wendell Berry. **CP-BerrW**
"He goes free of the earth."
"I stand at the cistern in front of the old barn."
"Let him escape hospital and doctor."

Three endless weeks of sniping all the way. Alun Lewis. *Fr.* Burma Casualty. **CP-LewiA**

Three Enemies, The. Christina Georgina Rossetti. **CP-RosC1**

Three Epigrams. Ernesto Cardenal. *tr. fr. Spanish.*
"Shots were heard last night / Out by the burial ground." **CP-MertT**
"Suddenly in the night the sirens." **CP-MertT**
"We wake up with guns going off." **CP-MertT**

Three Epigrams. Theodore Roethke. **CP-RoetT**
Centaur, The.
Mistake, The. **OBCoV**
Pipling. **OBCoV; TW**

Three Epigrams. Jonathan Swift. **CP-SwifJ**

3 Epiphanies. Anne Waldman. **SP-WaldA**

Three-Faced, The. Robert Ranke Graves. **CP-GravR**

Three faces in a single one. Narcissus in the Desert. Nicolas Calas, *tr. fr. French by* William Carlos Williams. **CP-WilW1**

Three fairies by the Sangamon. Dancing for a Prize. Nicholas Vachel Lindsay. **CP-LindV**

Three Fatal[l] Sisters. Robert Herrick. **CP-HerrR**

Three flies lay sleeping. The Asses' Out-House. Marsden Hartley. **CP-HartM**

Three Floors. Stanley Jasspon Kunitz. **CP-KuniS**

Three-fold terror of love, The; a fallen flare. The Mother of God. William Butler Yeats. **CP-YeatW**

Three for Children. Thom Gunn. **CP-GunnT**
Aquarium, The.
Cannibal.
Seabed, The.

345 W. 15th St. Allen Ginsberg. **CP-GinsA**

Three Fragments for Fishers of Destiny. Carl Sandburg. **CP-SandC**

Three Friends. Chuang Tzu, *tr. fr. Chinese by* Thomas Merton. **CP-MertT**

Three Friends: Outline for a Picture. Marsden Hartley. **CP-HartM**

Three Functions of Irony. Thomas McGrath. **SP-McGrT**

Three Gardens. James Schuyler. **CP-SchuJ**

Three Generations. K'o Chia Tsang, *tr. fr. Chinese by* William Carlos Williams *with* David Rafael Wang. **CP-WilW2**

Three Gentle Shepherds, The. Alexander Pope. **CP-PopeA**

Three Ghosts. Carl Sandburg. **CP-SandC**

Three gifts the dying left me. Hugh Stuart Boyd [Legacies]. Elizabeth Barrett Browning. **CP-BroEB**

Three Gipsies, The. Nikolaus Lenau, *tr. fr. German by* George Meredith. **CP-MerG2**

Three Graces, The. William Carlos Williams. **CP-WilW2**

Three Graves, The, Part 1 and stanzas 1–5 of part 2 sometimes at. to Coleridge. William Wordsworth. **CP-WorW1**
"So gentle Ellen now no more." **ChER**

Three Green Windows. Anne Sexton. **CP-SextA**

Three Gude Fellows Ayont Yon Glen. Robert Burns. **CP-BurnR**

Three gypsies, her skirt, and the tint, The. More than Flesh to Fathom. Edwin Rolfe. **CP-RolfE**

3 Happy Little Ducks. Malcolm Lowry. **CP-LowrM**

Three Hermits, The. William Butler Yeats. **CP-YeatW**

Three Hills Look Different in the Moonshine. Carl Sandburg. **CP-SandC**

Three Horatian Odes. John Hewitt. **CP-HewiJ**
"Already autumn silently / has come to sky and field and tree."
"Since June was hot on head and hand."
"You mid the corn not yet asleep."
Three hours chain-smoking words. In the Evening. Adrienne Rich. **CP-RicAE; SP-RicA2**
3 hours into the afternoon of March 9th. Jim Carroll. Fr. Birthday Poem. **SP-CarrJ**
Three human skulls had been tossed into an alley. The Skulls. Frederick Morgan. **SP-MorgF**
Three hundred thousand opaque years. Let There Be Colored Light. Robert Pack. **SP-PackR**
3 in 1. Robert Creeley. **CP-CreeR**
Three Kids. Richard Eberhart. **CP-EberR**
Three kids running down the meadow. Three Kids. Richard Eberhart. **CP-EberR**
Three Kinds of Pleasures. Robert Bly. **SP-BlyR**
Three Ladies, The. Robert Creeley. **CP-CreeR**
Three little children / On the wide wide earth. Christina Georgina Rossetti. **CP-RosC2**
Three Little Dog-Gone Mice. Malcolm Lowry. **CP-LowrM**
Three little maidens weary of the rail. To Three Puzzled Little Girls, from the Author. "Lewis Carroll." **CP-CarrL**
Three Little Maids. "Lewis Carroll." **CP-CarrL**
Three lives hung on two. A motioning of fingers. As with a Simple Gesture of the Fingers. Gilbert Sorrentino. **SP-SorrG**
Three Locked Hoops. Robert Ranke Graves. **CP-GravR**
Three Locutions Des Pierrots. Hart Crane. **CP-CranH**
"Ah! the divine infatuation."
"Ah! without the moon, what white nights."
"Your eyes, those pools with soft rushes."
Three lost lights are blest by priests. Secular Signs. Thomas Merton. **CP-MertT**
Three lovely sisters working were. Parcæ, The; or, Three Dainty Destinies: The Armilet. Robert Herrick. **CP-HerrR**
Three Loving Men. Marsden Hartley. **CP-HartM**
Three Maidens, The. George Meredith. **CP-MerG1**
Three Marching Songs. William Butler Yeats. **CP-YeatW**
Three Meditations. Denise Levertov. **CP-LeveD**
Three men in a Lurgan pub by chance. In a Lurgan Pub. John Hewitt. **CP-HewiJ**
Three Michaelmas daisies. Basil Bunting. **CP-BuntB**
Three Moments. Christina Georgina Rossetti. **CP-RosC3**
Three Monuments, The. William Butler Yeats. **CP-YeatW**
Three Moral Discoveries. Donald Davie. **CP-DavDo**
Three Movements, The. Donald Hall. **CP-HallD**
Three Movements. William Butler Yeats. **CP-YeatW**
Three Nahuatl Poems. William Carlos Williams. **CP-WilW2**
Three Nuns. Christina Georgina Rossetti. **CP-RosC3**
Three Occasional Poems. Wystan Hugh Auden. **CP-AudeW**
"Let both our Common Rooms combine to cheer."
Metalogue to The Magic Flute.
To T. S. Eliot on His Sixtieth Birthday.
Three Odes of Horace. Horace, tr. fr. Latin by Louis MacNeice. **CP-MacNL**
Aequam Memento.
Carpe Diem.
Solvitur Acris Hiems.
Three of Cups, The. Marge Piercy. Fr. Laying Down the Tower. **SP-PierM**
Three of Swords. Diane Wakoski. **SP-WakoD**
Three of us afloat in the meadow by the swing. Pirate Story. Robert Louis Stevenson. **CP-StevR**
Three old hermits took the air. The Three Hermits. William Butler Yeats. **CP-YeatW**
Three oranges on a blue plate. Song of the Drowned Boy. Stephen Dobyns. **SP-DobyS**
Three-Part Song, A. Rudyard Kipling. **CP-KiplR** Fr. Dymchurch Flit. Fr. Puck of Pook's Hill.
Three-Penny Opera, The. Frank O'Hara. **SP-OharF**
Three people come where no people belong any more. Abandoned Ranch, Big Bend. Hayden Carruth. **CP-CarHS**
Three persons are here, of whom the first. Hayden Carruth. Fr. The Sleeping Beauty. **CP-CarHL**
Three picture-drawn people stepped out of their frames. Family Portraits. Thomas Hardy. **CP-HardT**
Three Pieces on the Smoke of Autumn. Carl Sandburg. **CP-SandC**

Three pillows, end on end, rolled on a daybed. Robert Lowell. **SP-LoweR** Fr. Mexico.
Three Plum Buns. Christina Georgina Rossetti. **CP-RosC2**
Three Poems About Mark Twain. Nicholas Vachel Lindsay. **CP-LindV**
Mark Twain and Joan of Arc.
Raft, The.
When the Mississippi Flowed in Indiana. **CMoP**
Three Poems by Phillipe Jaccotet. Philippe Jaccottet, tr. fr. French by Derek Mahon. **SP-MahoD**
Ignorance.
Voice, The.
Words in the Air.
Three Poems For A Twenty-Fifth Anniversary. Richard Shelton. **SP-ShelR**
Building.
Grandfathering.
Housecleaning.
Three Poems for James Wright. Mary Oliver. **SP-OlivM**
Three Poems for Joanne. Gary Snyder. **CP-SnydG**
Three Poems for the New Year. Charles Wright.
"All day at the window seat." **SP-WrigC**
(Three Poems for the New Year [3].) **SP-WrigC**
"How strange it is to awake." **SP-WrigC**
(Three Poems for the New Year [2].) **SP-WrigC**
"I have nothing to say about the way the sky tilts." **SP-WrigC**
(Three Poems for the New Year [1].) **SP-WrigC**
Three Poems of Departure. Charles Wright. **SP-WrigC**
"Meadow surrounds us on three sides, The."
"Sitting again on the front porch of the first cabin."
"28 August and first frost."
Three Poems of Incarnation. Kathleen Jessie Raine. **SP-RainK**
"At the day's end I found."
"Child in a little boat."
"Who stands at my door in the storm and rain."
Three Poems on Illusion. Kathleen Jessie Raine. **SP-RainK**
Exile.
Instrument, The.
Mirage, The.
Three Poems with Yevtushenko. James Dickey. **CP-DickJ**
Three Postcards from the Monastery. Thomas Merton. **CP-MertT; SP-MertT**
Three Posthumous Poems. Wystan Hugh Auden. **CP-AudeW**
Aubade: "At break of dawn."
Glad.
Minnelied.
Three Praises. Margaret Atwood. **SP-AtwM2**
Three prisoners—the biggest black. O My Name It Is Sam Hall. Randall Jarrell. **CP-JarrR**
Three Quatrains. Edwin Arlington Robinson. **CP-RobiE**
3 Quatrains. Gilbert Sorrentino. **SP-SorrG**
Three red foxes on my head, come down. False Youth: Autumn: Clothes of the Age. James Dickey. **CP-DickJ**
Three Rings or Five rings. Isabella Gardner. **CP-GardI**
Three Rioters, The. Geoffrey Chaucer. **EBNV** Fr. The Pardoner's Tale. **FHYEP; NAEL-1; NAWM-1; NoP; OAEL-1; PoE** Fr. The Canterbury Tales. **CP-ChauG**
Three rompers run together, hand in hand. To ———. Wilfred Owen. **CP-OwenW**
Three sang of love together: one with lips. A Triad. Christina Georgina Rossetti. **CP-RosC1**
Three Seasons. Christina Georgina Rossetti. **CP-RosC1**
Three Seasons and a Gorilla. Charles Kenneth Williams. **CP-WillC**
Three Sentences for a Dead Swan. James Wright. **CP-WrigJ**
3 Short Poems. Jim Carroll. **SP-CarrJ**
Cinco de Mayo.
Compassion.
Poem: "Some trust the wolf."
Three Shrines. Carl Sandburg. **CP-SandC**
Three shrines a woman has for a man. Three Shrines. Carl Sandburg. **CP-SandC**
Three sides, / four. The Box. Robert Creeley. **CP-CreeR**
Three Sides of a Coin. Muriel Rukeyser. **CP-RukeM**
Three Singers to Young Blood, The. George Meredith. **CP-MerG1**
Three Singers, The. Alfonso Cortes, tr. fr. Spanish by Thomas Merton. **CP-MertT**
Three Sisters—and the youngest. Reflections. Walter de la Mare. **CP-DeLaW**

Three sisters at breakfast were feeding the cat. "Lewis Carroll." *Fr.* Puzzles. *Fr.* Puzzles from Wonderland. **CP-CarrL**

Three sixteen seventy. Hayden Carruth. *Fr.* North Winter. **CP-CarHL**

Three Slants at New York. Carl Sandburg. **CP-SandC**

Three Songs. Louise Bogan. **CP-BogaL**

Three Songs. Hayden Carruth. **CP-CarHS**

Three Songs. Hart Crane. **NAAL-2** *Fr.* The Bridge. **CP-CranH**
National Winter Garden. **ErPo; InPS; LiTM; NAAL-2; OxBA**
Southern Cross.
Virginia.

Three Songs. Thom Gunn.
Baby Song. **CP-GunnT**
Hitching into Frisco. **CP-GunnT**
Sparrow. **CP-GunnT**

Three Songs for the Lute. Robert Ranke Graves. **CP-GravR**
Hedges Freaked With Snow. **OxBTC**
In Her Only Way. **OxBSP**
Truth Is Poor Physic.

Three Songs from "The Lamp and the Bell." Edna St. Vincent Millay. **CP-MillE**

Three Songs of Shattering. Edna St. Vincent Millay. **CP-MillE**

Three Songs to the One Burden. William Butler Yeats. **CP-YeatW**

Three Sonnets. William Carlos Williams. **CP-WilW2**

Three Sonnets for the Eyes. Elizabeth Bishop. **CP-BishE**
"They all kept looking at each other's eyes."
"Thy senses are too different to please me."
Tidal Basin.

Three sounds of peace and rich increase. Triad. John Hewitt. **CP-HewiJ**

III. "Soverayne beauty which I doo admire, The." Edmund Spenser. **PoEL-1** *Fr.* Amoretti. **CP-Spens**

Three spirits came to me. April. Ezra Pound. **SP-PounE**

Three Spring Notations on Bipeds. Carl Sandburg. **CP-SandC**

Three Stages. Christina Georgina Rossetti. **CP-RosC3**
"I thought to deal the death-stroke at a blow."
"My happy happy dream is finished with."
Pause of Thought, A. **CP-RosC1; CoGr; FaBoEn; NOBE; OBNC**

3 Stances. William Carlos Williams. **CP-WilW2**

Three Stanzas From Goethe. James Wright. **CP-WrigJ**

Three Steps to the Graveyard. James Wright. **CP-WrigJ**

Three stood listening to a fresh access, The. Snow. Robert Frost. **CP-FrosR**

Three Stops to Ten Sleep. Richard Hugo. **CP-HugoR**

Three Strangers, The. Walter de la Mare. **CP-DeLaW**

Three Students went over the Rhine one day. *see also* "From the German of Uhland," tr. James Weldon Johnson. Ludwig Uhland, *tr. fr. German by* George Meredith. **CP-MerG2**

Three Sunsets. "Lewis Carroll." **CP-CarrL**

Three swans broke the water with a splash, The. Flight. John Hewitt. **CP-HewiJ**

Three tailors of Tooley Street wrote: We, the People. Three Ghosts. Carl Sandburg. **CP-SandC**

Three Tall Men, The. Thomas Hardy. **CP-HardT**

Three Taverns, The. Edwin Arlington Robinson. **CP-RobiE**

Three Things, *fr.* Words for Music Perhaps. William Butler Yeats. **CP-YeatW**

Three things make earth unquiet. A Servant When He Reigneth. Rudyard Kipling. **CP-KiplR**

Three things that men might scorn. Triad. John Hewitt. **CP-HewiJ**

Three thing[e]s there be[e] that prosper up apace. Sir Walter Ra[u]le[i]gh to His Son[ne]. Sir Walter Ralegh. **CP-RaleW**

Three Things to Remember. William Blake. *See* A Robin Redbreast in a cage.

3:30 A.M. Conversation. Charles Bukowski. **SP-BukC2**

3,489 friendly people. Reflections in Sleepy Eye. Allen Ginsberg. **CP-GinsA**

Three thousand years ago. Stanley Jasspon Kunitz. *Fr.* Signs and Portents. **CP-KuniS**

Three Times In Love. Robert Ranke Graves. **CP-GravR**

Three times—we parted—Breath—and I. Emily Dickinson. **CP-DickE**

Three traveling clocks. Ernest Hemingway. **CP-HemiE**

3/23/66. James Schuyler. **CP-SchuJ**

Three Undated Fragments. John Keats. **CP-KeatJ**
"I am as brisk." **CBNP**
"O grant that like to Peter I." **CBNP; ChIV-2**
(O Grant.) **ChIV-2**
"They weren fully glad of their gude hap."

Three Valentines. Elizabeth Bishop. **CP-BishE**

"Love is feathered like a bird."
"Love with his gilded bow and crystal arrows."
"Now a conundrum Love propounds."

Three Valentines to the Wide World. Mona Van Duyn. **SP-VanDM**

Three Views of a Mother. John Ciardi. **SP-CiarJ**

Three Violins. Carl Sandburg. **CP-SandC**

Three violins are trying their hearts. Three Violins. Carl Sandburg. **CP-SandC**

Three Virgins at the break of day. The Golden Net. William Blake. **CP-BlakW**

Three Voices. Stephen Berg. **SP-BergS**

Three Voices, The. "Lewis Carroll." **CP-CarrL**
First Voice, The.
Second Voice, The.
Third Voice, The.

Three Wagnerian Lyrics. Charles Tomlinson. **CP-TomlC**
Good Friday.
Liebestod.
Potion, The.

Three walls aound the town of Tela when I came. Ashurnatsirpal III. Carl Sandburg. **CP-SandC**

Three wealthy sisters swore they'd never part. Edward Estlin Cummings. **CP-CummE**

Three weeks ago I went back. One for the Rose. Philip Levine. **SP-LeviP**

Three weeks ago they came, leaping over. March Winds. Wystan Hugh Auden. **CP-AudWJ**

Three Weeks passed since I had seen Her. Emily Dickinson. **CP-DickE**

Three Who Died. Edwin Rolfe. **CP-RolfE**

Three wide / Funnels raked aft, and the masts slanted, The. George Oppen. **CP-OppeG**

Three Women. Sylvia Plath. **CP-PlatS**
"I see her in my sleep, my red, terrible girl." **TV**

Three Words Only. Robert Ranke Graves. **CP-GravR**

Three years ago, one last time, you forgot. The Last Time. William DeWitt Snodgrass. **SP-SnodW**

Three years I lolled in that country of the girls. Off Point Lotus. Stanley Jasspon Kunitz. **CP-KuniS**

Three years, now, the curve of Elizabeth Bridge. Over Elizabeth Bridge: a Circumvention. Charles Tomlinson. **CP-TomlC**

Three years she grew in sun and shower. William Wordsworth. **FiP; GN; GTBS; GTBS-6; GTBS-P; HAP; HBVY; LoBV; NoP; OAEP; OBRV; PoEL-4; SeCeV; TreFS** *Fr.* Lucy. **CP-WorW1**
(Education of Nature, The.) **GTBS; GTBS-6; GTBS-P**

Three years too late, I'm scholarshipped. Back. Rita Dove. *Fr.* A Suite for Augustus. **SP-DoveR**

Three Years Waiting. Robert Ranke Graves. **CP-GravR**

Three yellow slaves were set to swing. The Daughter of Herodias. Robert Louis Stevenson. **CP-StevR**

Three Young Tenneseans / Whom snobs called plebeians. Fourth Limick. Ogden Nash. **CP-NashO**

Three young women in white dresses. The Disappearance of Oilcloth. Gilbert Sorrentino. **SP-SorrG**

Threefold obstacle The center rock, A. The Brook. Hayden Carruth. *Fr.* Contra Mortem. **CP-CarHL**

Threes. Carl Sandburg. **CP-SandC**

Threnody: "Christian coin, The." William Carlos Williams. **CP-WilW2**

Threnody: "South-wind brings, The." Ralph Waldo Emerson. **CP-EmerR**
"Was there no star that could be sent." **IMW**

Threnody for a Brown Girl. Countee Cullen. **CP-CullC**

Threnody for a Starry Night. Alun Lewis. **CP-LewiA**
"Boy who climbed the creaking stairs, The."
"Lovers who among the grasses."
"Now only beggars still go singing."
"Polish girls singing, in the wind's soughing."
"Socrates on the frozen lake."
"Sweet Mother Church, beleaguered on the hill."
"This stunted pine whose knotted roots."
"White brain crossing, The."
"White frost; intricate bare branches."

Threnody for Old Orchards. Louise McNeill. **SP-McNeL**

Thresher, The. John Hewitt. **CP-HewiJ**

Thresher Duck could o'er the Queen prevail, The. On Stephen Duck, the Thresher, and Favourite Poet. Jonathan Swift. **CP-SwifJ**

Thresher now has stopeed its racket, "Tho." Hands Are Paid. Robert Penn Warren. *Fr.* Boy's Will, Joyful Labor without Pay, and Harvest Home (1918). **SP-WarrR**

Threshing, The. John Hewitt. **CP-HewiJ**

Threshing from left to right, whose. Flame. Charles Tomlinson. **CP-TomlC**

Threshold, The. Rudyard Kipling. **CP-KiplR**

Threshold. Denise Levertov. **CP-LeveD**

Threshold. Howard Nemerov. **CP-NemeH**

Thrice, and above, blest (my soul's [or soules] half[e]) art thou. Country Life: To His Brother, M. Tho. Herrick. Robert Herrick. **CP-HerrR**

Thrice happie Roses, so much grac't, to have. Upon the Roses in Julias Bosome. Robert Herrick. **CP-HerrR**

Thrice happy they whose world is spanned. Verse with Allusions. Theodore Roethke. **CP-RoetT**

Thrice he came. Malacoda. Samuel Beckett. **CP-BeckS**

Thrice, or I moved to sack, I saw you: how. John Berryman. *Fr.* Sonnets to Chris. **CP-BerrJ**

Thrice Toss[e] These Oaken Ashes in the Air [or Ayre]. Thomas Campion. **CP-CampT**

Thrice welcome from the Land of Flowers. A Greeting. John Greenleaf Whittier. **CP-WhitJ**

Thrice welcome to thy sisters of the East. To Delaware. John Greenleaf Whittier. **CP-WhitJ**

Thrice, with a prophet's voice and prophet's power. To Mr. Congreve. Jonathan Swift. **CP-SwifJ**

Thrifty Lover, The. Marge Piercy. **SP-PierM**

Thrill came slowly like a Boon for, The. Emily Dickinson. **CP-DickE**

Thrive gentle plant! and weave a bow'r. On a Plant of Virgin's Bower. William Cowper. **CP-CowpW**

Thriving against facades the ignorant sea. Ode on the Loss of the Titanic. Geoffrey Hill. *Fr.* Of Commerce and Society: Variations on a Theme. **CP-HillG**

Thro' burden and heat of the day. Christina Georgina Rossetti. **CP-RosC2**

Thro' him, the chief, begot by Nun. Conversion of St. Paul. Christopher Smart. *Fr.* Hymns and Spiritual Songs for the Fasts and Festivals of the Church of England. **SP-SmarC**

Thro' the vales to my love! A Bride Song. Christina Georgina Rossetti. **CP-RosC1**

Throe upon the features, A. Emily Dickinson. **CP-DickE**

Throned in the Sun's descending car. A Cento Made By Wordsworth. William Wordsworth. **CP-WorW2**

Thrones, Powers, Dominions, Peoples, Kings. Our Fathers Also. Rudyard Kipling. **CP-KiplR**

Throng like shadowy caresses on the horizon. The Great Sadnesses. Kenneth Patchen. **CP-PatcK**

Through a Dark Wood. Robert Ranke Graves. **CP-GravR**

Through a drain grating, something. The Key. Adrienne Rich. **CP-RicAE**

Through a glass greenly men as trees walking. The Park. Louis MacNeice. **CP-MacNL**

Through a great lion's head clouded by mange. Mass Man. Derek Walcott. **CP-WalcD**

Through a hospital window. *after Henrikas Radauskas*. Randall Jarrell. **CP-JarrR**

Through a place in the roof the sun came down. Patience: In the Mill. James Dickey. **CP-DickJ**

Through a wide window all Somerset might look in. Under a Skylight. Donald Davie. **CP-DavDo**

Through all the cowering world, crouching, shrinking. Song. Edwin Rolfe. **CP-RolfE**

Through all the night. To His Angrie God. Robert Herrick. **CP-HerrR**

Through all the pleasant meadow-side. The Hayloft. Robert Louis Stevenson. **CP-StevR**

Through all the town the busy triflers swarm. Phaedrus, *tr. by* Samuel Johnson. **CP-JohnS** *Fr.* Fabulae.

Through Alpine meadows soft-suffused. Stanzas from the Grande Chartreuse. Matthew Arnold. **SP-ArnoM**

Through and through the inspired leaves. The Book-Worms. Robert Burns. **CP-BurnR**

Through Bifocals. Donald Davie. **CP-DavDo**

Through Binoculars. Charles Tomlinson. **CP-TomlC**

Through centuries he lived in poverty. The Good Man Has No Shape. Wallace Stevens. **CP-StevW**

Through Closed Eyes. Charles Tomlinson. **CP-TomlC**

Through cloudless skies, in silvery sheen. Stanzas. Byron. **CP-Byron**

Through Cumbrian wilds, in many a mountain cove. William Wordsworth. **CP-WorW1**

Through elm, buckeye, thorn. Wendell Berry. *Fr.* The Clearing. **CP-BerrW**

Through every precinct of the wintry city. The Flight into Egypt. Thomas Merton. **CP-MertT; SP-MertT**

Through evolutions of the seed. Motion of Wish. Stanley Jasspon Kunitz. **CP-KuniS**

Through fen and farmland walking. Song for a Summer's Day. Sylvia Plath. **CP-PlatS**

Through floods and flames to your retreat. On His Approaching Visit to Hayley. William Cowper. **CP-CowpW**

Through frost-thick weather. Vanity Fair. Sylvia Plath. **CP-PlatS**

Through Glass. Stephen Berg. **SP-BergS**

Through grass again I am bound to the Lord. On a Protestant Mystic. James Liddy. **CP-LiddJ**

Through Gripus Grounds let rich Pactolus roll. Boethius, *tr. by* Samuel Johnson. **CP-JohnS** *Fr.* Consolation of Philosophy, The ("De Consolacione Philosophie"). **CP-ChauG**

Through heat and cold, and shower and sun. The Drovers. John Greenleaf Whittier. **CP-WhitJ**

Through heaving heather, fallen stones. A Stone Age Figure Far Below. Derek Mahon. **SP-MahoD**

Through him (The Diamond). Charles Henri Ford. **SP-FordC** *Fr.* Secret Haiku.

Through his eye searching far. The Portrait. John Gould Fletcher. **SP-FletJ**

Through intricate motions ran. Stream and Sun at Glendalough. William Butler Yeats. **CP-YeatW**

Through lane it lay—through bramble. Emily Dickinson. **CP-DickE**

Through learned and laborious years. The Outlaws. Rudyard Kipling. **CP-KiplR**

Through life's dull road, so dim and dirty. Byron. **CP-Byron**

Through light green haze, a rolling sea. Milan Cathedral. Herman Melville. **SP-MelvH**

Through mud, fouled nuts, black grime. Removing the Plate of the Pump on the Hydraulic System of the Backhoe. Gary Snyder. **CP-SnydG**

Through my hemlocks and the spruce beyond. An Aspect of the Air. John Ciardi. **SP-CiarJ**

Through my window and across the lawn. Endegeeste. Howard Nemerov. **CP-NemeH**

Through Nightmare. Robert Ranke Graves. **CP-GravR**

Through portal and through peristyle. No Word. Stanley Jasspon Kunitz. **CP-KuniS**

Through portico of my elegant house you stalk. Conversation among the Ruins. Sylvia Plath. **CP-PlatS**

Through purblind night the wiper. The Wiper. Louis MacNeice. **CP-MacNL**

Through rain falling on us no faster. Goodbye to Serpents. James Dickey. **CP-DickJ**

Through scant pride to be so put out! Geoffrey Hill. *Fr.* Metamorphoses. **CP-HillG**

Through shattered galleries, 'mid roofless halls. Composed among the Ruins of a Castle in North Wales. William Wordsworth. **CP-WorW2**

Through slats of our half-open shutters. May 1, 1974. Frederick Morgan. **SP-MorgF**

Through slits in the plantain leaf. Banks of a Stream Where Creatures Bathe. James Merrill. **SP-MerrJ**

Through snowy woods and shady. Seen by the Waits. Thomas Hardy. **CP-HardT**

Through storms you reach them and from storms are free. The Enviable Isles. Herman Melville. **SP-MelvH**

Through the ample open door of the peaceful country barn. A Farm Picture. Walt Whitman. **CP-WhitW**

Through the black, rushing smoke-bursts. Song of Callicles, The. Matthew Arnold. **ChTr; FaBoRV; FiP; LoBV; NOBE; OAEL-2; OBEV; OBVV; WiR** *Fr.* Empedocles on Etna. **SP-ArnoM**

Through the bound cable strands, the arching path. Atlantis. Hart Crane. **HoFi; LiTM; MoPo; NYP; NePA; TwAmPo** *Fr.* The Bridge. **CP-CranH**

Through the Dark Sod—as Education. Emily Dickinson. **CP-DickE**

Through the dimness, curtains drawn, eyes closed. Verse for Urania. James Merrill. **SP-MerrJ**

Through the fading years a town had fallen together on the side. The Discovery of Honey. John Yau. **SP-YauJo**

Through the fog / The gulls. Poem. Thomas McGrath. **SP-McGrT**

Through the forest across the fair hills away. The Primavera. Hayden Carruth. *Fr.* Contra Mortem. **CP-CarHL**

Through the gate, where nowhere and night begin. At the Airport. Howard Nemerov. **CP-NemeH**

Through the great sinful streets of Naples as I past. Easter Day. Naples, 1849. Arthur Hugh Clough. **SP-ClouA**

Through the green forest softly without a sound. Edna St. Vincent Millay. **CP-MillE**

Through the half-open door of the hut. The Extermination Camp. Stanley Jasspon Kunitz. *Fr.* Around Pastor Bonhoeffer. **CP-KuniS**

Through the high window, upright rectangle of distance. A Problem in Spatial Composition. Robert Penn Warren. **SP-WarrR**

Through the hot, pounding rhythm of the waltz. Lines to a Young Lady on Her Having Very Nearly Won a Vögel. Ernest Hemingway. **CP-HemiE**

Through the hours of yesternight. Emily Brontë. **CP-BronE**

Through the Inner City to the Suburbs. Maya Angelou. **SP-AngeM**

Through the long hall the shuttered windows shed. The Panorama. John Greenleaf Whittier. **CP-WhitJ**

Through the Looking-Glass. Wystan Hugh Auden. **CP-AudeW**

Through the Looking-Glass. "Lewis Carroll."

　Acrostic: A boat, beneath a sunny sky. **CP-CarrL**

　Dedication: "Child of the pure unclouded brow." **CP-CarrL**

　"I'll tell thee everything I can." **CP-CarrL**

　(White Knight's Ballad, The.) **CP-CarrL**

　"In winter, when the fields are white." **CP-CarrL**

　(Humpty Dumpty's Recitation.) **CP-CarrL**

　Jabberwocky. **CP-CarrL**

　Red Queen's Lullaby, The. **CP-CarrL**

　"To the Looking-Glass world it was Alice that said." **CP-CarrL**

　(Welcome Queen Alice.) **CP-CarrL**

　Walrus and the Carpenter, The. **CP-CarrL**

　White Queen's Riddle, The. **CP-CarrL**

Through the Metidja to Abd-el-Kadr. Robert Browning. **CP-BroR1**

Through the midlands of Ireland I journeyed by diesel. A Lament for Moira McCavendish. Sir John Betjeman. **CP-BetjJ**

Through the needle's eye. The Heaven of the Poor. Richard Shelton. **SP-ShelR**

Through the Nursery Window. William DeWitt Snodgrass. **SP-SnodW**

Through the Parklands, through the Parklands. The Parklands. Stevie Smith. **CP-SmitS**

Through the Plagues of Egyp' we was chasin' Arabi. The Jacket. Rudyard Kipling. **CP-KiplR**

Through the rain's dissolute footsteps. The Choice of Flowers. Steve Griffiths. **SP-GrifS**

Through the sea's crust of prisms looking up. Sea Burial. John Ciardi. **SP-CiarJ**

Through the shine, through the rain. Twilight Song. Edwin Arlington Robinson. **CP-RobiE**

Through the Smoke Hole. Gary Snyder. **CP-SnydG**

Through the soft evening air enwinding all. Italian Music in Dakota. Walt Whitman. **CP-WhitW**

Through the strait-gate of passion. Paradise Re-entered. David Herbert Lawrence. **CP-LawrD**

Through the strait pass of suffering. Emily Dickinson. **CP-DickE**

Through the streets of Marblehead. The Landmarks. John Greenleaf Whittier. **CP-WhitJ**

Through the tasteless minute efficient room. Edward Estlin Cummings. **CP-CummE**

Through the thin hill fog. Leonard Nathan. **SP-NathL**　*Fr.* To Be Read to Yourself in a Public Place, July 4, 1976.

Through the town-making stones I step lightly. Antipolis. James Dickey. **CP-DickJ**

Through the trees, with the moon underfoot. The Call. James Dickey. **CoPo; NePoEA-2**　*Fr.* The Owl King. **CP-DickJ**

Through the trembling blue the golden porpoise plunged. Valediction. Alun Lewis. **CP-LewiA**

Through the water-eye of night. With the Huntress. George Meredith. **CP-MerG1**

Through the weeks of deep snow. Wendell Berry. **CP-BerrW**

　(Another Descent.) **CP-BerrW**

Through the western window full fell moonlight. Walk by Moonlight in Small Town. Robert Penn Warren. *Fr.* Man in Moonlight. **SP-WarrR**

Through the white chiffon that covered her. Dancer at Kozani's. Richard Hugo. **CP-HugoR**

Through the wide, grey loft window. A Village Life. Derek Walcott. **CP-WalcD**

Through the window I can see then. Dtran of Return. Richard Shelton. **SP-ShelR**

Through the years. *Luftpost* (For Levy). Chuck Miller. **SP-MillC**

Through this forest / burned and sparse, the tines. Margaret Atwood. *Fr.* Circe / Mud Poems. **SP-AtwM1**

Through those old Grounds of memory. Emily Dickinson. **CP-DickE**

Through those trees you traced a loud white roof. Eighteen Days in a Tuscan World. Richard Hugo. **CP-HugoR**

Through throats where many rivers meet, the curlews cry. In the White Giant's Thigh. Dylan Thomas. **CP-ThomD**

Through thy battlements, Newstead, the hollow winds whistle. On Leaving Newstead Abbey. Byron. **CP-Byron**

Through Thy clear spaces, Lord, of old. Invocation. John Greenleaf Whittier. **CP-WhitJ**

Through thy submitting all, to blow[e]s. John Donne. *Fr.* A Litany. **CP-DonnJ**

Through torrid entrances, past icy poles. To Shakespeare. Hart Crane. **CP-CranH**

Through vaults of pain. A Wasted Illness. Thomas Hardy. **CP-HardT**

Through weeds and thorns, and matted underwood. The Picture. Samuel Taylor Coleridge. **CP-ColeS**

Through what extremes of passion. Hymn to Love Ended. William Carlos Williams. **CP-WilW1**

Through what transports of Patience. Emily Dickinson. **CP-DickE**

Through winter-time we call on spring. The Wheel. William Butler Yeats. **CP-YeatW**

Through woods, Mme Une Telle, a trifle ill. Autumn Chapter in a Novel. Thom Gunn. **CP-GunnT**

Throughout black winter the red haws withstood. Mayflower. Sylvia Plath. **CP-PlatS**

Throughout the field I find no grain. Winter in Durnover Field. Thomas Hardy. **CP-HardT**

Throughout the storm and party. Storm. Alice Walker. **CP-WalkA**

Throughout the world, if it were sought. Sir Thomas Wyatt. **CP-WyatT**

Throw away thy rod. Discipline. George Herbert. **CP-HerbG**

Throw Matches at the Sun! Anne Waldman. **SP-WaldA**

Throw my ticket out the window. Tonight I'll Be Staying Here with You. "Bob Dylan." **CP-DylaB**

Throw Roses. Carl Sandburg. **CP-SandC**

Throw roses on the sea where the dead went down. Throw Roses. Carl Sandburg. **CP-SandC**

Throw sand dollars and they sail alive. Near Kalalock. Richard Hugo. **CP-HugoR**

Throwbacks. Carl Sandburg. **CP-SandC**

Throwing a careless pebble in the lake. Archibald MacLeish. **CP-MacLA** *Fr.* The Happy Marriage.

Throwing a Tree. Thomas Hardy. **CP-HardT**

Throwing away the Mail. Wendell Berry. **CP-BerrW**

Throwing Out the Flowers. Gwendolyn Brooks. *Fr.* Notes from the Childhood and the Girlhood. **SP-BrooG**

Throwing the Apple. Richard Eberhart. **CP-EberR**

Throwing Yourself Away. Richard Eberhart. **CP-EberR**

Thrown a, A / -way It. Edward Estlin Cummings. **CP-CummE**

Thrown Away. Rudyard Kipling. *Fr.* Plain Tales from the Hills. "And some are sulky, while some will plunge." **CP-KiplR**

Thru the 12 Houses of Heaven. Canto 113. Luis Cabalquinto. *Fr.* Cantos. **CP-PoCan**

Thrush. Paul Muldoon. **SP-MuldP**

Thrush, because I'd been wrong, A. On Having Mis-identified a Wild Flower. Richard Wilbur. **CP-WilbR**

Thrush in February, The. George Meredith. **CP-MerG1**

Thrush in the Gaelic Islands, The. Archibald MacLeish. **CP-MacLA**

Thrush in the syringa sings, A. Basil Bunting. **CP-BuntB**

Thrush Song at Dawn. Richard Eberhart. **CP-EberR**

T,h;r:u;s,h;e:s / are / silent / now. Edward Estlin Cummings. **CP-CummE**

Thrushes. Ted Hughes. **SP-HughT**

Thrushes sing as the sun is going, The. Proud Songsters. Thomas Hardy. **CP-HardT**

Thrusting its armoury of hot delight. Descartes and the Stove. Charles Tomlinson. **CP-TomlC**

Thud of the brass cannon. October Dory Race. Brendan Galvin. **SP-GalvB**

Thudding was inaudible, The. Across the Board. Ernest Hemingway. **CP-HemiE**

Thugs of clumsy mutter shove upward leaving fat. Noise. Edward Estlin Cummings. **CP-CummE**

Thule. Walter de la Mare. **CP-DeLaW**

Thumb, loose tooth of a horse. Bestiary for the Fingers of My Right Hand. Charles Simic. **SP-SimiC**

Thumbs. Shel Silverstein. **SP-SilS2**

Thump. Thump. The door / which never is knocked upon but cries. The Door. Robert Creeley. **CP-CreeR**

Thumping old tunes give a voice to its whereabouts. Fairground. Wystan Hugh Auden. **CP-AudeW**

Thunder. Elizabeth Bishop. **CP-BishE**

Thunder by the Musician. Wallace Stevens. **CP-StevW**

Thunder in the hills. Clay County. Etheridge Knight. *Fr.* Missouri Haiku. **SP-KnigE**

Thunder in Tuscany. Charles Tomlinson. **CP-TomlC**

Thunder is all it is, and yet. Spring Thunder. Adrienne Rich. **CP-RicAE**

Thunder of the Rain God. A House in Taos. Langston Hughes. **SP-HughL**

Thunder over the Nursery. Ogden Nash. **CP-NashO**

Thunder Storm, A. William Cowper. **CP-CowpW**

Thunderbolt strikes the ocean, The. The Birth of Venus. Randall Jarrell. **CP-JarrR**

Thundercloud fills meadows with heavenly beauty, The. Basil Bunting, *after* Manuchehri. **CP-BuntB**

Thundercloud hung on the mantel of our summer, A. Waterloo. Robert Lowell. **SP-LoweR**

Thunderhead. Archibald MacLeish. **CP-MacLA**

Thunderlight on the split logs: big raindrops. Seamus Heaney. **IPY** *Fr.* Glanmore Sonnets. **SP-HeanS**

Thunderstorm in South Dakota. Kay Boyle. **CP-BoylK**

Thunderstorm in the Ozarks. John Gould Fletcher. **SP-FletJ**

Thunderstorm in Town, A. Thomas Hardy. **CP-HardT**

Thurber, they have come, the secret bearers. Elegy for James Thurber. Thomas Merton. **CP-MertT; SP-MertT**

Thurman Dreaming in Right Field. Paul Zimmer. **SP-ZimmP**

Thurman's Slumping Blues. Paul Zimmer. **SP-ZimmP**

Thursday. Edna St. Vincent Millay. **CP-MillE**

Thursday. James Schuyler. **CP-SchuJ**

Thursday. William Carlos Williams. **CP-WilW1**

Thursday, the eighth of August, four o'clock. Marilyn Hacker. *Fr.* The Regent's Park Sonnets. **SP-HackM**

Thursdays Are Sacred. James Liddy. **CP-LiddJ**

Thurso's Landing. Robinson Jeffers. **CP-JefR2**

Thus. Charles Simic. **SP-SimiC**

Thus Adam himself lamented loud. John Milton. **OAEL-1** *Fr.* Book X. **FHYEP** *Fr.* Paradise Lost. **CP-MiltJ**

Thus all things lead to Charity, secured. Congratulation. William Wordsworth. *Fr.* Ecclesiastical Sonnets. **CP-WorW2**

Thus am I mine own prison. Everything. Christina Georgina Rossetti. *Fr.* The Thread of Life. **CP-RosC2**

Thus been they parted, Arthur on his way. The Cave of Despair. Edmund Spenser. **OBNV** *Fr.* The Faerie Queene. **CP-Spens**

Thus began / Outrage from lifeless things; but Discord first. John Milton. **NAEL-1** *Fr.* Book X. **FHYEP** *Fr.* Paradise Lost. **CP-MiltJ**

Thus being entered, they behold around. Edmund Spenser. **OAEL-1** *Fr.* The Faerie Queene. **CP-Spens**

Thus Belial with words clothed in reason's garb. John Milton. **FaBoPV** *Fr.* Book II. **FHYEP; NAEL-1; OxAEP-1** *Fr.* Paradise Lost. **CP-MiltJ**

Thus can my love excuse the slow offense. Sonnet 51. William Shakespeare. *Fr.* Sonnets. **CP-ShaWS**

Thus critics, of less judgment than caprice. Alexander Pope. **OAEL-1** *Fr.* An Essay on Criticism. **CP-PopeA**

Thus crosslegged on round pillow sat in Teton Space. Mind Breaths. Allen Ginsberg. **CP-GinsA**

Thus did you strive to vouchsafe James to Heaven. On the Same ["Thus did you strive to vouchsafe James to Heaven"]. John Milton, *tr. fr. Latin by* John T. Shawcross. **CP-MiltJ**

Thus ebbs and flows the current of her sorrow. Lucrece's Death. William Shakespeare. **NoSic** *Fr.* The Rape of Lucrece. **CP-ShaWS**

Thus ere another noon they emerged from the shades. The Lakes of the Atchafalaya. Henry Wadsworth Longfellow. **PoEL-5** *Fr.* It was the month of May. Far down the Beautiful River. *Fr.* Part the Second. *Fr.* Evangeline, a Tale of Acadie. **SP-LongH**

Thus Eve to Adam. John Milton. **FaBV** *Fr.* Book IV. **OAEL-1** *Fr.* Paradise Lost. **CP-MiltJ**

Thus far my scanty brain hath built the rhyme. To a Friend [Charles Lamb] Together with an Unfinished Poem. Samuel Taylor Coleridge. *Fr.* Effusions. **CP-ColeS**

Thus far, O Friend! have we, though leaving much. School-Time. William Wordsworth. **FHYEP** *Fr.* The Prelude; Growth of a Poet's Mind [1850 vers.]. **CP-WorW3**

Thus far, O Friend! have we, though leaving much. School-Time. William Wordsworth. *Fr.* The Prelude; Growth of a Poet's Mind [1805 vers.]. **CP-WorW3**

Thus Far So Nobly Advanced. Kenneth Patchen. **CP-PatcK**

Thus far, to March, into the dangerous year. The Dangerous Year. John Berryman. **CP-BerrJ**

Thus, for a season, they fought it fair. Rudyard Kipling. **CP-KiplR** *Fr.* The Rescue of Pluffles. *Fr.* Plain Tales from the Hills.

Thus for a while he stood, and mused by the shore of the ocean. Priscilla. Henry Wadsworth Longfellow. **TreFS** *Fr.* The Courtship of Miles Standish. **SP-LongH**

Thus God the Heav'n created, thus the Earth. John Milton. **PeECV** *Fr.* Book VII. *Fr.* Paradise Lost. **CP-MiltJ**

Thus have I back again[e] to thy bright name. An Apology [*or* Apologie] for the Foregoing Hymn[e]. Richard Crashaw. **CP-CrasR**

Thus having passed all peril, I was come. Happy Isle. Edmund Spenser. **OBSC** *Fr.* The Faerie Queene. **CP-Spens**

Thus having said, forthwith on her way went quick-footed Iris. Achilles over the Trench. Homer, *tr. by* George Meredith. **CP-MerG2** *Fr.* The Iliad.

Thus *Hector*, great in Arms, contends in vain. Homer. *Fr.* The Episode of Sarpedon. **CP-PopeA** *Fr.* The Iliad.

Thus Her Tale. Walter de la Mare. **CP-DeLaW**

Thus I / Pass [*or* Passe] by. Upon His Departure Hence. Robert Herrick. **CP-HerrR**

"Thus I bestride the railing, leg o'er leg." Robert Browning. **EBVVPR**, *sect.* IV; *Fr.* Red Cotton Night-Cap Country. **CP-BroR2**

Thus I do not sing Antoine Augustin. William Matthews. *Fr.* This Spud's for You. **SP-MattW**

Thus I Resolve. Thomas Campion. **CP-CampT**

Thus I resolve, and time hath taught me so. Thus I Resolve. Thomas Campion. **CP-CampT**

Thus I wrote in London, musing on my betters. Robert Browning. **CP-BroR2**

Thus in alternate uproar and sad peace. John Keats. **FHYEP** *Fr.* Hyperion; a Fragment. **CP-KeatJ**

Thus is his cheek the map of days outworn. Sonnet 68. William Shakespeare. **OBSC; SCGP** *Fr.* Sonnets. **CP-ShaWS**

Thus is the storm abated by the craft. Wars of York and Lancaster. William Wordsworth. *Fr.* Ecclesiastical Sonnets. **CP-WorW2**

Thus Lays of Minstrels—may they be the last! -. Byron. **EPCY** *Fr.* English Bards and Scotch Reviewers. **CP-Byron**

Thus man by his own strength to Heaven would soar. John Dryden. **NOCV; WGRP** *Fr.* Religio Laici. **SP-DrydJ**

Thus piteously Love closed what he begat. George Meredith. **EBEV; EnLoPo; EnVR; FaBoEn; GTBS-6; GTBS-P; HAP; HBV; LoBV; NBM; NOBE; NOBVV; NoP; OAEL-2; OAEP; OBNC; OHCV; OXAEP-2; PoE; PoEL-5; SCGP; SeCePo; SeCeV; Son; TFi; TrGrPo; TreFT; WHA** *Fr.* Modern Love. **CP-MerG1**

(Dusty Answer, A.) **SeCePo**

Thus safely low, my friend, thou canst not fall. To the Reverend Patrick Murdoch. James Thomson *and* David Mallet. **CP-ThomJ**

Thus said The Lord in the Vault above the Cherubim. The Last Chantey. Rudyard Kipling. **CP-KiplR**

Thus saying, from her husband's hand her hand. The Fall. John Milton. **PoEL-3** *Fr.* Book IX. **FHYEP; NAEL-1; NAWM-1; NoP; OAEL-1** *Fr.* Paradise Lost. **CP-MiltJ**

Thus saying, from her side the fatal Key. John Milton. **EBEV** *Fr.* Book II. **FHYEP; NAEL-1; OxAEP-1** *Fr.* Paradise Lost. **CP-MiltJ**

Thus saying rose / The monarch, and prevented all reply. Occupations of Hell. John Milton. **NOSC** *Fr.* Book II. **FHYEP; NAEL-1; OxAEP-1** *Fr.* Paradise Lost. **CP-MiltJ**

Thus says the prophet of the Turk. The Love of the World Reproved. William Cowper. **CP-CowpW**

Thus she had lain. Africa. Maya Angelou. **SP-AngeM**

Thus should have been our travels. Over 2000 Illustrations and a Complete Concordance. Elizabeth Bishop. **CP-BishE**

Thus spoke the Goddess of the fearles eye. Greece. James Thomson. *Fr.* Liberty. **CP-ThomJ**

Thus spoke to my Lady, the knight full of care. The Grand Question Debated. Jonathan Swift. **CP-SwifJ**

Thus talking hand in hand alone they pass'd. John Milton. **EBEV** *Fr.* Book IV. **OAEL-1** *Fr.* Paradise Lost. **CP-MiltJ**

Thus the book of the mandates. Canto 24. Ezra Pound. *Fr.* Cantos. **CP-PoCan**

Thus the Mayne Glideth. Robert Browning. **OBEV** *Fr.* Paracelsus. **CP-BroR1**

Thus they in Heav'n, above the starry Sphear. John Milton. **EBEV** *Fr.* Book III. *Fr.* Paradise Lost. **CP-MiltJ**

Thus they in lowliest plight repentant stood. Book XI. John Milton. *Fr.* Paradise Lost. **CP-MiltJ**

Thus to be lost and thus to sink and die. To Constantia, Singing. Percy Bysshe Shelley. **CP-ShelP**

Thus Tophet look'd; so grinned the brawling fiend. Thomas Gray. *See* Tophet.

Thus was Italy mov'd—nor did the chief. Virgil, *tr. by* William Cowper. **CP-CowpW** *Fr.* The Aeneid [*or* Eneados, Aeneis].

Thus was this place, / A happy rural seat of various view. John Milton. **PeECV**, *ll.* 246–275; **FaBoEn** *Fr.* Book IV. **OAEL-1** *Fr.* Paradise Lost. **CP-MiltJ**

(Eden.) **FaBoEn**, *ll.* 246–268.

Thus were my sympathies enlarged, and thus. William Wordsworth. **EnRP** *Fr.* School-Time. **FHYEP** *Fr.* The Prelude; Growth of a Poet's Mind [1850 vers.]. **CP-WorW3**

Thus will despair. The Succubus. Robert Ranke Graves. **CP-GravR**

THWPRVNCL. Thomas Merton. *Fr.* A Selection of Concrete Poems. **CP-MertT**

Thy absence overflows the rose. Old Song. Hart Crane. **CP-CranH**

Thy azure robe, I did behold. Julia's Petticoat. Robert Herrick. **CP-HerrR**

Thy beauty hangs around thee like. Fragment: Beauty's Halo. Percy Bysshe Shelley. **CP-ShelP**

Thy bosom is endeared with all hearts. Sonnet 31. William Shakespeare. **NOBE; OBEV; OBSC; PoEL-2** *Fr.* Sonnets. **CP-ShaWS**

Thy Brother's Blood Crieth. Christina Georgina Rossetti. *Fr.* The German-French Campaign, 1870–1871. **CP-RosC1**

Thy cheek is pale with thought, but not from woe. Sonnet, to the Same. Byron. **CP-Byron**

Thy converse drew us with delight. Tennyson. *Fr.* In Memoriam A. H. H. **CP-TennA**

Thy copp's, too, nam'd of Gamage, thou hast there. Ben Jonson. **FM** *Fr.* To Penshurst. **CP-JonsB**

Thy country, Wilberforce, with just disdain. William Cowper. **CP-CowpW** (Sonnet to Wilberforce.) **CP-CowpW**

Thy country's curse is on thee, darkest crest. To the Lord Chancellor. Percy Bysshe Shelley. **CP-ShelP**

Thy Cross cruciferous doth flower in all. A Bundle of Myrrh Is My Well-Beloved unto Me. Christina Georgina Rossetti. **CP-RosC2**

Thy Days Are Done. Byron. **CP-Byron**

Thy dewy looks sink in my breast. Stanza, Written at Bracknell. Percy Bysshe Shelley. **CP-ShelP**

Thy eagle-sighted prophets too. The Prophets. John Donne. *Fr.* A Litany. **CP-DonnJ**

Thy elder care shall from thy careful face, *speech of the Delphic Oracle.* Sir Philip Sidney. **SP-SidnP** *Fr.* Arcadia.

Thy error, Frémont, simply was to act. To John C. Frémont. John Greenleaf Whittier. **CP-WhitJ**

Thy face is a still white house of holy things. Edward Estlin Cummings. **CP-CummE**

Thy face is far from this our war. To the True Romance. Rudyard Kipling. **CP-KiplR**

Thy fainting spouse, yet still Thy spouse. Christina Georgina Rossetti. **CP-RosC2**

Thy father all from thee, by his last will. Disinherited. John Donne. **CP-DonnJ**

Thy fingers make early flowers of. Edward Estlin Cummings. **CP-CummE; SP-CummE**

Thy flattering picture, Phryne, is like thee. Phryne. John Donne. **CP-DonnJ**

Thy foes to hunt, thy enviers to strike down. To the Shah, from Hafiz. Hafiz, *tr. fr. Persian* by Ralph Waldo Emerson. **CP-EmerR**

Thy forests, Windsor! and thy green retreats. Alexander Pope. **NOEC; OXAEP-1** *Fr.* Windsor-Forest [*or* Windsor Forest]. **CP-PopeA**

Thy former coming was to cure. Christs Twofold Coming. Robert Herrick. **CP-HerrR**

Thy Friend and Thy Father's Friend Forget Not. Christina Georgina Rossetti. **CP-RosC2**

Thy friend, whom thy deserts to thee enchain[e]. To Mr. C.B. John Donne. **CP-DonnJ**

Thy Friendship oft has made my heart to ache [*or* ake]. To Hayley [*or* To H[ayley]]. William Blake. **CP-BlakW**

Thy functions are ethereal. On the Power of Sound. William Wordsworth. **CP-WorW2**

Thy gift, thy tables, are within my brain. Sonnet 122. William Shakespeare. *Fr.* Sonnets. **CP-ShaWS**

Thy glass will show thee how thy beauties wear. Sonnet 77. William Shakespeare. **EnRePo; HeIP; QFR** *Fr.* Sonnets. **CP-ShaWS**

Thy Gleeman Who Flattered Thee. Charles Olson. **CP-OlsoC**

Thy God was making hast into thy roofe. Matthew 8; I Am Not Worthy that Thou Should'st Come Under my Roofe. Bible, *N.T.* **CP-CrasR**, *tr. by* Richard Crashaw; *Fr.* St. Matthew.

Thy gracious ear, O Lord, encline, *par. by* Milton. Bible, *O.T. See* Psalm 86: "Bow down thine ear, O Lord, hear me."

Thy greatest knew thee, Mother Earth; unsoured. The Spirit of Shakespeare. George Meredith. **CP-MerG1**

Thy Guardians are asleep. E.G. to M.R. Emily Brontë. **CP-BronE**

Thy hands are washt, but o the waters spilt. To Pontius Washing His Hands. Richard Crashaw. **CP-CrasR**

Thy husband—poor, poor Heart!—is dead. The Slow Nature. Thomas Hardy. **CP-HardT**

Thy husband to a banquet goes with me. 1.4. Ovid. **CP-MarlC**, *tr. by* Christopher Marlowe; *Fr.* Elegies.

Thy kisses dost thou bid me count. Catullus. *See* Carmen 7: "Curious to learn / how may kiss- / es of your lips."

Thy Land to favour graciously, *par. by* Milton. Bible, *O.T. See* Psalm 85: "Lord, thou hast been favourable unto thy land."

Thy lilies drink the dew, / Thy lambs the rill, and I will drink them too. Christina Georgina Rossetti. **CP-RosC2**

Thy little footsteps on the sands. To William Shelley ("Thy little footsteps on the sands"). Percy Bysshe Shelley. **CP-ShelP**

Thy look of love has power to calm. To Harriet ("Thy look of love has power to calm"). Percy Bysshe Shelley. **CP-ShelP**

Thy Love Is One Thou'st Not Yet Known. Jean Garrigue. **SP-GarrJ**

Thy lovely saints do bring Thee love, / Incense and joy and gold. The Ransomed of the Lord. Christina Georgina Rossetti. **CP-RosC2**

Thy mansion is the Christian's heart. The House of Prayer. William Cowper. **ChIV-2** *Fr.* Olney Hymns. **CP-CowpW**

Thy Name, O Christ, as incense streaming forth. Christina Georgina Rossetti. **CP-RosC2**

Thy pious hand planting fraternal bayes. To His Noble Friend Capt. Dudley Lovelace, upon His Edition of His Brother's Poems. Symon Ognell. *Fr.* Elegies, 1660. **CP-LoveR**

Thy poems Hafiz shame the rose leaves. Hafiz, *tr.* by Ralph Waldo Emerson. **CP-EmerR** *Fr.* Odes.

Thy praise or dispraise is to me alike. To Fool, or Knave. Ben Jonson. **CP-JonsB**

Thy promise was to love me best. Sir Thomas Wyatt. **CP-WyatT**

Thy quiet house / The crozier's curve runs in the wall. Canto 110. Ezra Pound. *Fr.* Cantos. **CP-PoCan**

Thy reliques, ROWE, to this fair Urn we trust. Epitaph Intended for Mr. Rowe, in Westminster Abbey. Alexander Pope. **CP-PopeA**

Thy sacred academe [*or* Academie] above. The Doctors. John Donne. *Fr.* A Litany. **CP-DonnJ**

Thy senses are too different to please me. Elizabeth Bishop. *Fr.* Three Sonnets for the Eyes. **CP-BishE**

Thy servant I am. The Unfulfilling Brightnesses. Kenneth Patchen. **CP-PatcK**

Thy servant is in irons. The Prisoner. Raissa Maritain, *tr. fr.* French by Thomas Merton. **CP-MertT**

Thy Servant Will Go and Fight with This Philistine. Christina Georgina Rossetti. **CP-RosC2**

Thy shadow, Earth, from Pole to Central Sea. At a Lunar Eclipse. Thomas Hardy. **CP-HardT**

Thy sins [*or* sinnes] and hairs [*or* haires] may no man equal[l] call. A Licentious Person. John Donne. **CP-DonnJ**

Thy songs O Hafiz. Hafiz, *tr.* by Ralph Waldo Emerson. **CP-EmerR** *Fr.* Odes.

Thy sooty godhead I desire. To Vulcan. Robert Herrick. **CP-HerrR**

Thy soul / Grown delicate with satieties. Ezra Pound. **SP-PounE** (Imerro.) **SP-PounE**

Thy soul shall find itself alone. Spirits of the Dead. Edgar Allan Poe. **CP-PoeEd**

Thy spirit ere our fatal loss. Tennyson. *Fr.* In Memoriam A. H. H. **CP-TennA**

Thy sting sufficeth, Death. If Heidegger first. Sonnet. Hayden Carruth. **CP-CarHS** *Fr.* Sonnets.

Thy summer voice, Musketaquit. Two Rivers. Ralph Waldo Emerson. **CP-EmerR**

Thy sun is near meridian height. Written in the Gaaldine Prison Caves to A.G.A. Emily Brontë. **CP-BronE**

Thy sword within the scabbard keep. Momus' Song to Mars. John Dryden. **OxBSP** *Fr.* The Secular Masque. **SP-DrydJ**

Thy time is thee to wend. Interludium. Hart Crane. **CP-CranH**

Thy tones are silver melted into sound. To a Lady Playing the Harp. Paul Laurence Dunbar. **CP-DunbP**

Thy trivial harp will never please. Ralph Waldo Emerson. **AA; OxBA** *Fr.* Merlin. **CP-EmerR**

Thy verse is "sad" enough, no doubt. To the Author of a Sonnet Beginning " 'Sad Is My Verse,' You Say, 'And Yet No Tear.' " Byron. **CP-Byron**

Thy voice is heard through rolling drums. Tennyson. **TrGrPo** *Fr.* The Princess. **CP-TennA**

Thy voice is on the rolling air. Tennyson. **EBVV; EBVVPR; FHYEP; HeIP; NoP; OAEL-2; PeHV** *Fr.* In Memoriam A. H. H. **CP-TennA**

Thy Will Be Done. John Greenleaf Whittier. **CP-WhitJ**

Thy wisdom speaks in me, and bids me dare. Percy Bysshe Shelley. **OAEL-2** *Fr.* Epipsychidion. **CP-ShelP**

Thyestes. Donald Davie. **CP-DavDo**

Thyestes. Louis MacNeice. **CP-MacNL**

Thyestes. Seneca, *tr. fr.* Latin.

Second Chorus from Seneca's Tragedy "Thyestes", The. **CP-MarvA**

Thylacine, long thought to be extinct, The. Popular Revivals 1956. John Updike. **CP-UpdiJ**

Thyme. Louis Zukofsky. **CP-ZukLS**

Thyme Flowering among Rocks. Richard Wilbur. **CP-WilbR**

Thyme, tufa, sage, anemone. Frank Templeton Prince. *Fr.* Apollo and the Sibyl. **CP-PrinF**

Thyrsis. Matthew Arnold. **SP-ArnoM**

"How changed is here each spot man makes or fills!" **FaBoPP**

"What though the music of thy rustic flute." **EPCY**

Thyrsis, the music of that murm'ring spring. Winter, the Fourth Pastoral, or Daphne. Alexander Pope. *Fr.* Pastorals. **CP-PopeA**

Thyrsis, when we parted, swore. Song. Thomas Gray. **CP-GrayT**

Ti do l'addio, / Amico mio. Se Fossi Andata a Hastings. Christina Georgina Rossetti. *Fr.* Il Rosseggiar Dell'Oriente Canzoniere. **CP-RosC3**

Tibbie Dunbar. Robert Burns. **CP-BurnR**

Tibbie Fowler. Robert Burns. **CP-BurnR**

Tibby I hae seen the day. Song. Robert Burns. **CP-BurnR**

Tiberio was kind according to the guard. Tiberio's Cliff. Richard Hugo. **CP-HugoR**

Tiberio's Cliff. Richard Hugo. **CP-HugoR**

Tiberius on Capri. Robert Penn Warren. **SP-WarrR**

"All is nothing, nothing all." **NOBA**

"There once, on that goat island, I." **NOBA**

Tibud Maclay. Thomas Merton. *Fr.* East. *Fr.* The Geography of Lograire. **CP-MertT**

Tibullus, whom I love and praise. 1.4. Horace. **SP-SmarC,** *tr. by* Christopher Smart; *Fr.* Epistles.

Tibur is beautiful, too, and the orchard slopes, and the Anio. Claude to Eustace. Arthur Hugh Clough. **GTBS-6** *Fr.* Amours de Voyage. **SP-ClouA**

Tribute to the Renowned Harteebeeste, A. Malcolm Lowry. **CP-LowrM**

Tick. Lewis Turco. **SP-TurcL**

Tick of time that stones the heads of kings, A. Blues for the Old Revolutionary Woman. Thomas McGrath. **SP-McGrT**

Ticker tapes roll down my sides, The. Along the Road. Mona Van Duyn. **SP-VanDM**

Ticket to Ride. The Beatles. **CP-Beatl**

Ticonderoga: A Legend of the West Highlands. Robert Louis Stevenson. **CP-StevR**

Tidal Basin. Elizabeth Bishop. *Fr.* Three Sonnets for the Eyes. **CP-BishE**

Tide, The. John Gould Fletcher. *Fr.* Sand and Spray: A Sea-Symphony. **SP-FletJ**

Tide, The. Denise Levertov. **CP-LeveD**

Tide comes in, and out goes tide—, The. In Robin Hood Cove. Marsden Hartley. **CP-HartM**

Tide goes down, uncovering its gifts, The. The Promise. Charles Tomlinson. **CP-TomlC**

Tide goes up and down in the creek, The. Phenomena. John Updike. **CP-UpdiJ**

Tide is slack in equipoise, The. Motifs. Alun Lewis. **CP-LewiA**

Tide makes music, The. The Tide. John Gould Fletcher. *Fr.* Sand and Spray: A Sea-Symphony. **SP-FletJ**

Tide of Storms. John Gould Fletcher. *Fr.* Sand and Spray: A Sea-Symphony. **SP-FletJ**

Tide, the number 9 and creation, The. A Discrete Gloss. Charles Olson. **CP-OlsoC**

Tides. Jenny Joseph. **SP-JoseJ**

Tie the Strings to my Life, My Lord. Emily Dickinson. **CP-DickE**

Ties. Dabney Stuart. **SP-StuaD**

Tiger [*or* Tyger][!], The. William Blake. **CP-BlakW** *Fr.* Songs of Experience.

Tiger, The. Robert Creeley. **CP-CreeR**

Tiger came, A. Afternoon. Charles Olson. **CP-OlsoC**

Tiger in the tiger-pit, The. Lines for an Old Man. Thomas Stearns Eliot. **CP-ElioT**

Tiger kills hungry. The machine-guns, The. Tiger-Psalm. Ted Hughes. **SP-HughT**

Tiger of Camden Town, The. Alun Lewis. **CP-LewiA**

Tiger on Parade, The. Nicholas Vachel Lindsay. **CP-LindV**

Tiger-Psalm. Ted Hughes. **SP-HughT**

Tiger Skull. Charles Tomlinson. **CP-TomlC**

Tiger-Tiger. Rudyard Kipling. *Fr.* The Second Jungle Book.

"What of the hunting, hunter bold?" **CP-KiplR**

Tiger! Tiger! [*or* Tyger! Tyger!] burning bright. The Tiger [*or* Tyger][!]. William Blake. **CP-BlakW** *Fr.* Songs of Experience.

Tiger was his prototype, The. Tippoo's Tiger. Marianne Craig Moore. **CP-MoorM**

Tight around my waist the knot. Ten Feet of Rope. Stephen Dobyns. **SP-DobyS**

Tight Connection to My Heart (Has Anybody Seen My Love). "Bob Dylan." **CP-DylaB**

Tight Hat. Shel Silverstein. **SP-SilS2**

Tight-socketed in space, they watch. Ponte Veneziano. Charles Tomlinson. **CP-TomlC**

Tightly-folded bud. Born Yesterday. Philip Larkin. **CP-LarkP**

Tightness and the nilness round that space, The. From the Frontier of Writing. Seamus Heaney. **SP-HeanS**

Tilemaker's Hill Fresco, The. Laurence Lieberman. **SP-LiebL**

Tiles of the swimming pool are azure, The. Lines Written in the Euganean Hills. Charles Tomlinson. **CP-TomlC**

Till all sweet gums and juices flow. The Prince's Progress. Christina Georgina Rossetti. **CP-RosC1**

Till Death—is narrow Loving. Emily Dickinson. **CP-DickE**

Till I have peace with thee, war other men. Love's War. John Donne. *Fr.* Elegies. **CP-DonnJ**

Till I shall come again, let this suffice. A Panegyric to Sir Lewis Pemberton. Robert Herrick. **CP-HerrR**

Till it has loved—no man or woman. Emily Dickinson. **SP-DickE**

Till now the doubtful dusk reveal'd. Tennyson. **GTBS-6; GTBS-P** *Fr.* By night we lingered [*or* linger'd] on the lawn. **EBVV; EnVR; FHYEP; HAP; LoBV; NoP; OAEL-2; OBNC; PeECV; PoEL-5; TOF** *Fr.* In Memoriam A. H. H. **CP-TennA**

Till the blue grass turn yellow. Canto 99. Ezra Pound. *Fr.* Cantos. **CP-PoCan**

Till the Wind Gets Right. Paul Laurence Dunbar. **CP-DunbP**

Till thinking had worn out my enterprise. Spring Mountain Climb. Richard Eberhart. **CP-EberR**

Till Tomorrow. Christina Georgina Rossetti. **CP-RosC2**

Till twelve years' [*or* yeres'] age, how Christ His childhood spent. Christ[e]'s Childhood[e]. Robert Southwell. **CP-SoutR**

Tillie. Gertrude Stein. **CP-SteiG**

Tillie Sage (1). Louise McNeill. **SP-McNeL**

Tillie Sage (2). Louise McNeill. **SP-McNeL**

Tillie Sage (3). Louise McNeill. **SP-McNeL**

Tilt. Gilbert Sorrentino. **SP-SorrG**

Tilter, the most may admire thee, though not I. To Sir Annual Tilter. Ben Jonson. **CP-JonsB**

Tilth. Robert Ranke Graves. **CP-GravR**

Tilting toward the hill with vacant frames. Banished. Daniel Gerard Hoffman. **SP-HoffD**

Tim and the Fables. Jonathan Swift. **CP-SwifJ**

Tim Murphy's gon' walkin' wid Maggie O'Neill. Circumstances Alter Cases. Paul Laurence Dunbar. **CP-DunbP**

Timber. John Hewitt. **CP-HewiJ**

Timber Boom. Louise McNeill. **SP-McNeL**

Timber floats in the water. The trees. The Ex-Poet. Malcolm Lowry. **CP-LowrM**

Timber Moon. Carl Sandburg. **CP-SandC**

Timber Wings. Carl Sandburg. **CP-SandC**

Time / all beliefs or loved things, A. A Silk Ascot for the Terrorist. Gilbert Sorrentino. **SP-SorrG**

Time. Tom Clark. **SP-ClarT**

Time, The. Robert Creeley. **CP-CreeR**

Time. Robert Creeley. **CP-CreeR**

Time. Robert Creeley. **CP-CreeR**

Time. Robert Ranke Graves. **CP-GravR**

Time. George Herbert. **CP-HerbG**

Time. George Meredith. **CP-MerG2**

Time. George Meredith. **CP-MerG2**

Time. James Merrill. **SP-MerrJ**

Time. Percy Bysshe Shelley. **CP-ShelP**

Time all of a sudden tightens the tether. Preface to the Past. Ogden Nash. **CP-NashO**

Time and again, time and again I tie. The Edge. Louise Glück. **SP-GlücL**

Time and Love, I. William Shakespeare. *See* Sonnet 64: "When I have seen by Time's fell hand defac'd."

Time and Love, II. William Shakespeare. *See* Sonnet 65: "Since brass, nor stone, nor earth, nor boundless sea."

Time and Sentiment. George Meredith. **CP-MerG1**

Time and Space decreed his lot. *parody of* Ralph Waldo Emerson. Rudyard Kipling. **CP-KiplR** *Fr.* The Muse among the Motors.

Time and Space Were Only Their Disguises. Philip Larkin. **CP-LarkP**

Time and the Thing-in-Itself in a Textbook. Randall Jarrell. **CP-JarrR**

Time as Hypnosis. Robert Penn Warren. **SP-WarrR**

Time breaks the barrier. Hilda Doolittle. **AnAn** *Fr.* Sigil. **CP-DoolH**

Time buzzes in the ear. Somewhere. Home Thoughts. Lewis Turco. **SP-TurcL**

Time came, at last, when only two things had meaning, The. Words Found on a Cave's Wall. Edwin Rolfe. **CP-RolfE**

Time Cannot Be Worn. . . . Hart Crane. **CP-CranH**

Time cannot break the bird's wing from the bird. To a Young Poet. Edna St. Vincent Millay. **CP-MillE**

Time Capsule. William Stafford. **SP-StafW**

Time comes spirit weakens and goes blank apartments shuffled through and forgotten. The Names. Allen Ginsberg. **CP-GinsA**

Time comes to go deeper, The. As I Lay Dying. Charles Bukowski. **SP-BukC2**

Time created out of clay. Eve in the Dawn. Archibald MacLeish. *Fr.* Songs for Eve. **CP-MacLA**

Time does go on. Emily Dickinson. **CP-DickE**

Time does not bring relief; you all have lied. Edna St. Vincent Millay. **CP-MillE**

Time drawes neere. Song: Time Drawes Neere. Anne Waldman. **SP-WaldA**

Time draws near the birth of Christ, The. Tennyson. **EBVV; EBVVPR; FHYEP; FaBoRV; NOCV; OAEL-2; SoSe** *Fr.* In Memoriam A. H. H. **CP-TennA**

Time draws near the birth of Christ, The. Tennyson. **EBVV; OAEL-2; SBVL** *Fr.* In Memoriam A. H. H. **CP-TennA**

Time drops in decay. The Moods. William Butler Yeats. **CP-YeatW**

Time entered the stuffed court, slowly swearing, *same poetry begins* Pijijiapan. Malcolm Lowry. *Fr.* Songs for Second Childhood. **CP-LowrM**

Time entered the stuffed court, slowly swearing. Pijijiapan. Malcolm Lowry. *Fr.* The Lighthouse Invites the Storm. **CP-LowrM**

Time Exposures. Muriel Rukeyser. **PoA** *Fr.* Night-Music. **CP-RukeM**

Time feels so vast that were it not. Emily Dickinson. **CP-DickE**

Time flies, hope flags, life plies a wearied wing. Christina Georgina Rossetti. *Fr.* Monna Innominata. **CP-RosC2**

Time for a Smoke. Louis MacNeice. **CP-MacNL**

Time for a toting up of concessions. Let's Call This. Gilbert Sorrentino. **SP-SorrG**

Time for rain! for your long hot dry autumn. Piano di Sorrento. Robert Browning. **FaBoPP; SeCePo** *Fr.* The Englishman in Italy. **CP-BroR1**

Time for the wood, the clay. Kept. Louise Bogan. **CP-BogaL**

Time grows dim. Time that was so long. For Mr. Death Who Stands with His Door Open. Anne Sexton. **CP-SextA**

Time has been, when yet the muse was young, The. Byron. **FHYEP** *Fr.* English Bards and Scotch Reviewers. **CP-Byron**

Time has come to call a halt, The. Elizabeth Bishop. *Fr.* Songs for a Colored Singer. **CP-BishE**

Time has gone by, The. Never Born. Carl Sandburg. **CP-SandC**

Time heals, you said. For a New Year. Jenny Joseph. **SP-JoseJ**

Time Hinder Not Me; His Arms Reach Here and There. Muriel Rukeyser. **CP-RukeM**

Time in the seed that grief put down, return. Anniversary. Howard Nemerov. **CP-NemeH**

Time is, The. Anger. Robert Creeley. **CP-CreeR**

Time is a child playing draughts. Thomas Merton. *Fr.* The Legacy of Herakleitos. **CP-MertT**

Time is at an end, The. Ox-Bow. Donald Davie. **CP-DavDo**

Time is Berkeley. The Imitation Dance. Al Young. **CP-YounA**

Time is expressed / in the heart. True Music. Patti Smith. **SP-SmitP**

Time is hunger, space is cold. Great Prayer. Alfonso Cortes, *tr. fr. Spanish by* Thomas Merton. **CP-MertT**

Time is not gone. Why the Face of a Clock is not Truly a Circle. Archibald MacLeish. **CP-MacLA**

Time is not remote when I, The. Jonathan Swift. **EBEV; Mes; NOBE; NOBL; NOIV; OBEC; OXAEP-1; PeLV** *Fr.* Verses on the Death of Dr. Swift, D.S.P.D. **CP-SwifJ**

(On the Death of Dean Swift.) **OXAEP-1**

Time Is Our House. Louise McNeill. **SP-McNeL**

Time is short and full. Emily Dickinson. **SP-DickE**

"Time" is some sort of hindsight. Robert Creeley. **CP-CreeR**

Time is the Bound of things, where e're we go. Death Ends All Woe. Robert Herrick. **CP-HerrR**

Time is the sweet cheat that unhinged. The Pharoahs Sacrifice Themselves before Her. Tom Clark. **SP-ClarT**

Time is the sweet cheat that unhinged. Retro. Tom Clark. **SP-ClarT**

Time Lapse with Tulips. Tess Gallagher. **SP-GallT**

Time lengthening, in the lengthening seemeth long. Christina Georgina Rossetti. **CP-RosC2**

Time like an ever-rolling stream. And Our Eternal Home. Donald Davie. **CP-DavDo**

Time Long Past. Percy Bysshe Shelley. **CP-ShelP**

Time Marches On. Ogden Nash. **CP-NashO**

Time mocks but I would mock it. A Way Out. Richard Eberhart. **CP-EberR**

Time, never wand'ring from his annual round. John Milton. *See* Elegy 5: On the Coming of Spring.

Time: 1978. Charles Kenneth Williams. **SP-WillC**

Time: 1976. Charles Kenneth Williams. **SP-WillC**

Time of Bees, A. Mona Van Duyn. **SP-VanDM**

Time of Burning, The. May Sarton. **SRLS** *Fr.* The Invocation to Kali. **SP-SartM**

Time of day: a dim dream, probably. The Yards of Sarajevo. Richard Hugo. **CP-HugoR**

Time of destruction. Of the most rigid powers of ascendance, A. Not Yet. Muriel Rukeyser. **CP-RukeM**

Time of Disturbance. Robinson Jeffers. **CP-JefR3**

Time of finks and nobles, A. Muriel Rukeyser. **CP-RukeM**

Time of gifts has come again, The. The Pressed Gentian. John Greenleaf Whittier. **CP-WhitJ**

Time of school drags by with waiting, The. *ad. fr. the German of* Rilke. Randall Jarrell. **CP-JarrR**

Time of the brown gold comes softly, The. Brown Gold. Carl Sandburg. **CP-SandC**

Time of the Missile. George Oppen. **CP-OppeG**

Time of Waiting, A. Robert Ranke Graves. **CP-GravR**

Time of Waiting, The. Christina Georgina Rossetti. **CP-RosC3**

Time of year comes, The. Saturnalia. Thom Gunn. **CP-GunnT**

Time of year has grown indifferent, The. The Man Whose Pharynx Was Bad. Wallace Stevens. **CP-StevW**

Time! on whose arbitrary wing. To Time. Byron. **CP-Byron**

Time only cause of my unrest. Song 5. Mary Sidney, Countess of Montgomery Wroth. *Fr.* Pamphilia to Amphilanthus. **CP-WrotM**

Time opens in a flower of bells. The Hyacinth. Kathleen Jessie Raine. **SP-RainK**

Time Out. Robert Frost. **CP-FrosR**

Time Passes. Walter de la Mare. **CP-DeLaW**

Time Passes. Richard Eberhart. **CP-EberR**

Time Passes Slowly. "Bob Dylan." **CP-DylaB**

Time passeth away with its pleasure and pain. Christina Georgina Rossetti. **CP-RosC2**

Time Passing, Beloved. Donald Davie. **CP-DavDo**

Time-piece, The. William Cowper. *Fr.* The Task. **CP-CowpW**

Effeminate Englishmen. **EBEvV; ECEV**

   (England.) **FiP**

"Oh for a lodge in some vast wilderness." **EnRP; NOEC; OAEP**

   (Against Slavery.) **NOEC**

Poetic Pains. **FiP; PP**

Time present and time past. Burnt Norton. Thomas Stearns Eliot. **CMoP; LiTM; MoAB; MoAmPo; NAAL-2; PoE** *Fr.* Four Quartets. **CP-ElioT**

Time running beneath the pillow wakes. Disintegration. Philip Larkin. **CP-LarkP**

Time says hush. The Gong of Time. Carl Sandburg. **CP-SandC**

Time seems not short: / If so I call to mind. Christina Georgina Rossetti. **CP-RosC2**

Time shall come, when free as seas or wind, The. Progress. Alexander Pope. **ECEV** *Fr.* Windsor-Forest [*or* Windsor Forest]. **CP-PopeA**

Time Spans. Archie Randolph Ammons. **SP-AmmoA**

Time swings her burning hands. Stanley Jasspon Kunitz. *Fr.* The Way Down. **CP-KuniS**

Time swings her burning hands. Stanley Jasspon Kunitz. *Fr.* The Way Down. **CP-KuniS**

Time telescoped. My mother in two years. The Scattering. John Hewitt. **CP-HewiJ**

Time, that is pleased to lengthen out the day. Edna St. Vincent Millay. **CP-MillE**

Time, that leads the fatall round. Thomas Campion. *Fr.* Lord Hay's Mask.

Time, that renews the tissues of this frame. Sonnet. Edna St. Vincent Millay. **CP-MillE**

Time the Bridegroom stayes from hence, The. Mora Sponsi, the Stay of the Bridegroome. Robert Herrick. **CP-HerrR**

Time the Hangman. William Carlos Williams. **CP-WilW1**

Time there was—as one may guess, A. Before Life and After. Thomas Hardy. **CP-HardT**

Time to Believe!, A. Kenneth Patchen. **CP-PatcK**

Time to Come. Walt Whitman. **CP-WhitW**

Time to go. Robert Creeley. **CP-CreeR**

Time to grow old. Birthday. Robinson Jeffers. **CP-JefR3**

"Time to put off the world and go somewhere." Beggar to Beggar Cried. William Butler Yeats. **CP-YeatW**

Time to Remember Sangster. Richard Hugo. **CP-HugoR**

Time to Rise. Robert Louis Stevenson. **CP-StevR**

Time to split now you & me. Lovesong of O. O. Gabugah. Al Young. **CP-YounA**

Time to Talk, A. Robert Frost. **CP-FrosR**

Time to Tickle a Lizard, The. The Lizard. Theodore Roethke. **CP-RoetT**

Time to Tinker 'Roun'! Paul Laurence Dunbar. **CP-DunbP**

Time was away and somewhere else. Meeting Point. Louis MacNeice. **CP-MacNL**

Time was, ere yet in these degenerate days. Byron. **EPCY; FHYEP** *Fr.* English Bards and Scotch Reviewers. **CP-Byron**

Time was late and the wet yellow woods, The. Gerard Manley Hopkins. *Fr.* Fragments. **CP-HopkG**

Time was. Time is. Time shall be. Solo for Saturday Night Guitar. Carl Sandburg. **CP-SandC**

Time was upon / The wing, to flie away. Upon Time. Robert Herrick. **CP-HerrR**

Time was when his half million drew. Bewick Finzer. Edwin Arlington Robinson. **CP-RobiE**

Time was when I was free as air. On a Goldfinch Starved to Death in His Cage. William Cowper. **CP-CowpW**

Time will come, The. Love after Love. Derek Walcott. **CP-WalcD**

Time will say nothing but I told you so. If I Could Tell You. Wystan Hugh Auden. **CP-AudeW**

Time will wash / away. This. Archie Randolph Ammons. **SP-AmmoA**

Time Works Like Acid. Jim Morrison. **SP-MorrJ**

Time you tell us is the century and the day, The. In the Fullness of Time. Charles Tomlinson. **CP-TomlC**

Time you won your town the race, The. To an Athlete Dying Young. Alfred Edward Housman. **CP-HousA**

Time,be kind;herself and i. Edward Estlin Cummings. **CP-CummE**

Timeless / ly this / (merely and whose). Edward Estlin Cummings. **CP-CummE**

Timeless Meeting. Robert Ranke Graves. **CP-GravR**

Timelessness of Desire. Roy Fisher. **SP-FishR**

Timeo. Isabella Gardner. **CP-GardI**

Times. Stephen Berg. **SP-BergS**

Times are nightfall, look, their light grows less, The. Gerard Manley Hopkins. **CP-HopkG**

Times Are Tidy, The. Sylvia Plath. **CP-PlatS**

Times Change, Damaged. Jim Morrison. **SP-MorrJ**

Time's Fool. John Updike. **CP-UpdiJ**

Time's Glory. William Shakespeare. **ChTr** *Fr.* The Rape of Lucrece. **CP-ShaWS**

Times [*or* Tymes] Go[e] By Turn[e]s. Robert Southwell. *See* The Loppèd tree in time may grow again [*or* againe *or* agayne].

Times have changed, there is not left to us, The. Allen Tate. *See* The Times have changed. Why do you make a fuss.

Times have changed. Why do you make a fuss, The. Allen Tate. *Fr.* Sonnets of the Blood. **CP-TateA**

("Times have changed, there is not left to us, The.") **PoA**

Times is mighty stirrin' 'mong de people up ouah way, De. How Lucy Backslid. Paul Laurence Dunbar. **CP-DunbP**

Time's Revenges. Robert Browning. **CP-BroR1**

Time's sea hath been five years at its slow ebb. To ——. John Keats. **CP-KeatJ**

Times-Square-Shoeshine-Composition. Maya Angelou. **SP-AngeM**

Times Table, The. Robert Frost. **CP-FrosR**

Times They Are A-Changin', The. "Bob Dylan." **CP-DylaB**

Time's wily Chargers will not wait. Emily Dickinson. **CP-DickE**

Times Worsen, The. Randall Jarrell. **CP-JarrR**

Timeshare. Dabney Stuart. **SP-StuaD**

Timesweep. Carl Sandburg. **CP-SandC**
"Among the shapes and shadow-shapes."
"Deep roots moving in lush soil to send a silver-gray beech tree."
"Earth is a forgotten cinder, The."
"I have been woven among meshes of long ropes."
"I have said to the elephant and the flea, 'Each of us makes his life'."
"I was born in the morning of the world."
"In the heave of the hankering sea."
"Pink nipples of the earth in springtime, The."
"Since death is there in the light of the sun, in the song of the."
"There is only one horse on the earth."
"These wheels within wheels."
"Wind carves sand into shapes, The."

Timetable for a Town. Jenny Joseph. **SP-JoseJ**

Timing. Archie Randolph Ammons. **SP-AmmoA**

Timing Her. Thomas Hardy. **CP-HardT**

Timoleon. Herman Melville. **SP-MelvH**

Timon's Villa. Alexander Pope. *See* At Timon's villa let us pass a day.

Timorous Hind, The. Samuel Taylor Coleridge. **CP-ColeS**

Tin bucket, A. Sketch for a Portrait of Henry Ford. William Carlos Williams. **CP-WilW2**

Tin Fish. Rudyard Kipling. **CP-KiplR**

Tin-roofed shack by the railroad, The. Two Guitar Pieces. Philip Larkin. **CP-LarkP**

Tin Wedding Whistle. Ogden Nash. **CP-NashO**

Tinder, The. Thomas Carew. **CP-CareT**

Tingling Back, The. Karl Shapiro. **SP-ShapK**

Tiniest ones are the mightiest, The. Emily Dickinson. **SP-DickE**

Tinker, The. William Wordsworth. **CP-WorW1**

Tinker Camp, The. Richard Hugo. **CP-HugoR**

Tinker Jack and the Tidy Wives. Sylvia Plath. **CP-PlatS**

Tinker out of Bedford, A. The Holy War. Rudyard Kipling. **CP-KiplR**

Tinker sat beside his driftwood fire, The. The Tinker's Answer. John Hewitt. **CP-HewiJ**

Tinker's Answer, The. John Hewitt. **CP-HewiJ**

Tinkers Song, The. Robert Herrick. **CP-HerrR**

Tinkling treble, / Rolling bass. Dream Boogie: Variation. Langston Hughes. **SP-HughL**

Tinsel glitter, and the specious mein, The. Phaedrus, *tr. by* Samuel Johnson. **CP-JohnS** *Fr.* Fabulae.

Tinsel in February, tinsel in August. Pieces. Wallace Stevens. **CP-StevW**

Tint I cannot take—is best, The. Emily Dickinson. **CP-DickE**

Tiny creature moves, A. The Milk Bottle. Galway Kinnell. **SP-KinnG**

Tiny Energies. Gary Snyder. **CP-SnydG**

Tiny fingers outspread. A Failure. David Herbert Lawrence. **CP-LawrD**

Tiny fish enjoy themselves, The. Little Fish. David Herbert Lawrence. **CP-LawrD**

Tiny green birds skate over the surface of the room. Saturday Night in the Parthenon. Kenneth Patchen. **CP-PatcK**

Tiny immortal streams are on the move. Thaw. Philip Larkin. **CP-LarkP**

Tiny Montgomery. "Bob Dylan." **CP-DylaB**

Tiny moon as small and white as a single jasmine flower, A. A White Blossom. David Herbert Lawrence. **CP-LawrD**

Tiny orange-wing-tipped butterfly. Bixby Canyon Ocean Path Word Breeze. Allen Ginsberg. **CP-GinsA**

Tiny Place, A. Robert Creeley. **CP-CreeR**

Tiny Self-Portrait. Al Young. **CP-YounA**

Tiphead. John Hewitt. **CP-HewiJ**

Tippoo's Tiger. Marianne Craig Moore. **CP-MoorM**

Tips of celery. The Farm. Robert Creeley. **CP-CreeR**

Tips of the fronds become swollen, The. James Liddy. *Fr.* Shore. **CP-LiddJ**

Tir'd with vain hopes, and with complaints as vain. For Sir W. Trumbull. Alexander Pope. **CP-PopeA**

Tire, The. Tom Clark. **SP-ClarT**

Tired agnostic longs for prayer, The. The Agnostic. Edna St. Vincent Millay. **CP-MillE**

Tired banana & an empty mind, A. Dante's Tomb. John Berryman. **CP-BerrJ**

Tired boy dreams of rabbits, The. Interval. John Hewitt. **CP-HewiJ**

Tired Cupid, The. Walter de la Mare. **CP-DeLaW**

Tired now both mind and body, bearings loose. North-West Passage: An Old Man Dying. John Hewitt. **CP-HewiJ**

Tired of a landscape known too well when young. Story. Philip Larkin. **CP-LarkP**

Tired of the old descriptions of the world. The Latest Freed Man. Wallace Stevens. **CP-StevW**

Tired With All These. William Shakespeare. *See* Sonnet 66: "Tired [*or* Tyr'd, *or* Tir'd] with all these, for restful death I cry."

Tired [*or* Tyr'd, *or* Tir'd] with all these, for restful death I cry. Sonnet 66. William Shakespeare. **AWP; CBCK; CTC; CoGr; EBEV; FaBoPV; FaFP; GTBS; GTBS-6; GTBS-P; HAP; ImPo; InPS; LiTB; NOBE; NoSic; OAEL-1; OBSC; OXAEP-1; PoEL-2; SeCeV; TFi; TrGrPo; WHA; WeW** *Fr.* Sonnets. **CP-ShaWS**

Tires slowly came to a rubbery stop, The. The Gazing Grain. John Ashbery. **SP-AshbJ**

Tiriel. William Blake. **CP-BlakW**

Tirocinium; or, A Review of Schools. William Cowper. **CP-CowpW**
"Father, who designs his babe a priest, The." **OBSV**
"To you, then, tenants of life's middle state." **OBSV**
"Would you your son should be a sot or dunce." **OBSV**

'Tis a fine deceit. Hayden Carruth. **CP-CarHS** *Fr.* The Bloomingdale Papers.

'Tis a known principle in War. The Eyes. Robert Herrick. **CP-HerrR**

'Tis a May morning. Meditation on a Holiday. Thomas Hardy. **CP-HardT**

'Tis a melancholy song / And it will not keep you long. Miss Jones. "Lewis Carroll." **CP-CarrL**

'Tis a record in heaven. You, that were. Eptiaph on Katherine, Lady Ogle. Ben Jonson. **CP-JonsB**

Tis a strange Place, this Limbo! not a Place. Limbo. Samuel Taylor Coleridge. **CP-ColeS**

'Tis an old deserted homestead. The Old Homestead. Paul Laurence Dunbar. **CP-DunbP**

'Tis Anguish grander than Delight. Emily Dickinson. **CP-DickE**

'Tis better to be vile than vile esteem'd. Sonnet 121. William Shakespeare. **InvP; NoSic; OAEL-1; OXAEP-1; PoEL-2; SCGP** *Fr.* Sonnets. **CP-ShaWS**

Tis but a dog-like madness in bad Kings. Cruelty. Robert Herrick. **CP-HerrR**

'Tis Christmas weather, and a country house. George Meredith. **NAEL-2; NOBVV** *Fr.* Modern Love. **CP-MerG1**

'Tis customary as we part. Emily Dickinson. **CP-DickE**

'Tis Cypher lies beneath this crust. On an Insignificant. Samuel Taylor Coleridge. **CP-ColeS**

'Tis done! Dread Winter spreads his latest glooms. James Thomson. **OxAEP-1** *Fr.* Winter. *Fr.* The Seasons. **CP-ThomJ**

'Tis done:—I tow'r to that degree. *see also* Horace, *Odes* III, 30. Christopher Smart. **SP-SmarC**

'Tis early dark. The lamps are lit. Autumnal. John Hewitt. **CP-HewiJ**

'Tis easier to pity those when dead. Emily Dickinson. **CP-DickE**

'Tis eight o'clock,—a clear March night. The Idiot Boy. William Wordsworth. **CP-WorW1**

'Tis Evanoe's. The House of Splendour. Ezra Pound. **SP-PounE**

'Tis evening now, the sun descends. Emily Brontë. **CP-BronE**

'Tis evening, the black snail has got on his track. Evening. John Clare. **SP-ClarJ**

'Tis Ev'ning, my Sweet. To Electra. Robert Herrick. **CP-HerrR**

'Tis fine to play. A Boy's Summer Song. Paul Laurence Dunbar. **CP-DunbP**

'Tis five years since, "An end," said I. Alfred Edward Housman. **CP-HousA**

'Tis Folly all—let me no more be told. The Nativity. Jeanne Marie Bouvier de la Motte-Guyon, *tr. fr. French by* William Cowper. **CP-CowpW**

'Tis forty to one. On Lord Carteret's Arms. Jonathan Swift. **CP-SwifJ**

'Tis Friendship's pledge, my young, fair FRIEND. To Chloris. Robert Burns. **CP-BurnR**

'Tis gone—with old belief and dream. The Wishing-Gate Destroyed. William Wordsworth. **CP-WorW2**

'Tis good—the looking back on Grief. Emily Dickinson. **CP-DickE**

'Tis good to keep hinderward eyes. George Meredith. **CP-MerG2**

'Tis grown almost a danger to speak true. Epistle. To Katharine, Lady Aubigny. Ben Jonson. **CP-JonsB**

'Tis hard on Bagshot Heath to try. Ode to Sleep. Samuel Taylor Coleridge. **CP-ColeS**

'Tis hard to finde God, but to comprehend. God Not To Be Comprehended. Robert Herrick. **CP-HerrR**

'Tis hard to say, if greater want of skill. An Essay on Criticism. Alexander Pope. **CP-PopeA**

'Tis hard to say, if greater want of skill. Alexander Pope. **OAEL-1,** *ll.* 1–266; *Fr.* An Essay on Criticism. **CP-PopeA**

'Tis He Whose Yester-Evening's High Disdain. William Wordsworth. **CP-WorW2**

'Tis held that sorrow makes us wise. Tennyson. *Fr.* In Memoriam A. H. H. **CP-TennA**

'Tis Heresie in others: In your face. Upon a Scarre in a Virgins Face. Robert Herrick. **CP-HerrR**

'Tis I have seen the coming man. George Meredith. **CP-MerG2**

'Tis in the spirit that attire. Elegance. Christopher Smart. **NOCV** *Fr.* Hymns for the Amusement of Children. **SP-SmarC**

'Tis just beyond mid-August. The summer has run mockingly away, as usual. Sometimes When Lovers Lie Quietly Together, Unexpectedly One of Them Will Feel the Other's Pulse. Hayden Carruth. **CP-CarHS**

Tis know, at least it should be, that throughout. Byron. **NOBRP** *Fr.* Beppo; a Venetian Story. **CP-Byron**

'Tis known, at least it should be, that throughout. Beppo; a Venetian Story. Byron. **CP-Byron**

'Tis liberty to serve one Lord; but he. Slavery. Robert Herrick. **CP-HerrR**

'Tis little—I could care for Pearls. Emily Dickinson. **CP-DickE**

'Tis lost, to trust a tomb with such a guest. A Funeral Elegy. John Donne. *Fr.* Anatomy [*or* Anatomie] of the World, An[: The First Anniversary]. **CP-DonnJ**

'Tis midnight in the skies, my dear. George Meredith. **CP-MerG2**

'Tis midnight now—athwart the murky air. Fragment. Percy Bysshe Shelley. *Fr.* Posthumous Fragments of Margaret Nicholson. **CP-ShelP**

'Tis moonlight, summer moonlight. Emily Brontë. **CP-BronE**

Tis morning' and the sun with ruddy orb. William Cowper. **LAuP; NOEC; PoEL-3** *Fr.* The Winter Morning Walk. *Fr.* The Task. **CP-CowpW** (Frosty Morning, A.) **NOEC**

'Tis morning; and the sun, with ruddy orb. The Winter Morning Walk. William Cowper. *Fr.* The Task. **CP-CowpW**

Tis much among the filthy to be clean. Meane, The. Robert Herrick. **CP-HerrR**

'Tis murk upon the hills, but scarce a drop is flung. Windy Haymaking. George Meredith. **CP-MerG2**

'Tis mute, the word they went to hear on high Dodona mountain. The Oracles. Alfred Edward Housman. **CP-HousA**

'Tis my first night beneath the Sun. Emily Dickinson. **CP-DickE**

'Tis my happiness below. Welcome Cross. William Cowper. *Fr.* Olney Hymns. **CP-CowpW**

'Tis never or but seldom[e] known[e]. Power and Peace. Robert Herrick. **CP-HerrR**

Tis no discomfort in the world to fall. Comfort In Calamity. Robert Herrick. **CP-HerrR**

'Tis not a thousand Bullocks thies. Cheerfulnesse in Charitie: or, The Sweet Sacrifice. Robert Herrick. **CP-HerrR**

'Tis not ev'ry day that I. Not Every Day Fit for Verse. Robert Herrick. **CP-HerrR**

'Tis not for the unfeeling, the falsely refined. The Farmer of Tilsbury Vale. William Wordsworth. **CP-WorW1**

Tis not from cheap thanks thinly to repay. To the Genius of Mr. John Hall. Richard Lovelace. **CP-LoveR**

'Tis not greatness they require. Sweetnesse in Sacrifice. Robert Herrick. **CP-HerrR**

'Tis not my voice now speaks; but as a bird. Nocturne. Walter de la Mare. **CP-DeLaW**

'Tis not that Dying hurts us so. Emily Dickinson. **CP-DickE**

'Tis not that I design to rob. An Epistle to Robert Lloyd, Esq. William Cowper. **CP-CowpW**

'Tis not the food, but the content. Content, Not Cates. Robert Herrick. **CP-HerrR**

'Tis not the lily-brow I prize. Song, ex improviso. Samuel Taylor Coleridge. **CP-ColeS**

'Tis not the swaying frame we miss. Emily Dickinson. **CP-DickE**

'Tis not the Walls, or purple, that defends. True Safety. Robert Herrick. **CP-HerrR**

'Tis not too late to build our young land right. To Reformers in Despair. Nicholas Vachel Lindsay. **CP-LindV**

Tis now dead night, and not a light on earth. To the Most Sacred Queen Anne. Thomas Campion. **CP-CampT**

'Tis now, since I sat[e] down before. Sir John Suckling. **CP-SuckJ** (Siege, The.) **CP-SuckJ**

'Tis One by One—the Father counts. Emily Dickinson. **CP-DickE**

'Tis Opposites—entice. Emily Dickinson. **CP-DickE**

'Tis pleasant to wander along on the sand. An Evening Walk by the Sea-Side. Charlotte Smith. **CP-SmitC**

'Tis raging noon; and vertical, the sun. James Thomson. **EBEV; OAEL-1** *Fr.* Summer. *Fr.* The Seasons. **CP-ThomJ**

Tis rumour'd, *Budgell* on a time. To Eustace Budgell, Esq., on His Translation of the Characters of Theophrastus. Alexander Pope. **CP-PopeA**

'Tis said, as Cupid danced [*or* danc't] among. How Roses Came Red. Robert Herrick. **CP-HerrR**

'Tis said, fantastic ocean doth unfold. Fish-Women.—On Landing at Calais. William Wordsworth. *Fr.* Memorials of a Tour of the Continent; 1820. **CP-WorW2**

'Tis said that some have died for love. William Wordsworth. **CP-WorW1**

'Tis said that to the brow of yon fair hill. A Tradition of Oker Hill in Darley Dale, Derbyshire. William Wordsworth. **CP-WorW2**

'Tis said the Honorable Henry Clay. On the Great Conciliator: Now Honored in the Old Dominion. Allen Tate. *Fr.* Historical Epitaphs. **CP-TateA**

'Tis Seasons since the Dimpled War. Emily Dickinson. **CP-DickE**

'Tis so appalling—it exhilirates. Emily Dickinson. **CP-DickE**

'Tis so much joy! 'Tis so much joy! Emily Dickinson. **CP-DickE**

'Tis spent—this burning day of June! The Waggoner. William Wordsworth. **CP-WorW1**

'Tis spent—this burning day of June! The Waggoner. William Wordsworth. **CP-WorW1**

'Tis spring; come out to ramble. The Lent Lily. Alfred Edward Housman. **CP-HousA**

'Tis still observ'd, that Fame ne'er sings. Fame. Robert Herrick. **CP-HerrR**

'Tis still observ'd, those men most valiant are. More Modest, More Manly. Robert Herrick. **CP-HerrR**

'Tis strange, perchance you'll think, that she, that died. Prologue to the Court. Sir John Suckling. *Fr.* The Fifth Act of Aglaura As Presented to the Court. *Fr.* Aglaura. **CP-SuckJ**

'Tis strange, the Miser should his Cares employ. Epistle IV, to Richard Boyle, Earl of Burlington. Alexander Pope. **CP-PopeA**

'Tis strange, what different thoughts inspire. Desire and Possession. Jonathan Swift. **CP-SwifJ**

'Tis Sunrise—Little Maid—Hast Thou. Emily Dickinson. **CP-DickE**

'Tis sweet to him, who all the week. Home-Sick. Samuel Taylor Coleridge. **CP-ColeS**

'Tis sweet to see the evening star appear. Byron. **MeMBP** *Fr.* Canto the First. **EnRP; NAEL-2; NoP; OAEL-2; PoE** *Fr.* Don Juan. **CP-Byron**

'Tis ten years since. Ten Years Since. Thomas Hardy. **CP-HardT**

'Tis the Chyrurgions praise, and height of Art. Lenitie. Robert Herrick. **CP-HerrR**

Tis [*or* 'Tis] the middle of the night by the castle clock. Christabel. Samuel Taylor Coleridge. **CP-ColeS**

'Tis the terror of tempest. The rags of the sail. A Vision of the Sea. Percy Bysshe Shelley. **CP-ShelP**

'Tis the voice of the Lobster: I heard him declare. Alice's Recitation. "Lewis Carroll." **CP-CarrL** *Fr.* Alice's Adventures in Wonderland.

'Tis the Witching Time [*or* Hour] of Night. John Keats. **CP-KeatJ**

'Tis the year's [*or* years] midnight, and it is the day's [*or* dayes]. A Nocturnal[l] upon Saint Lucy's [*or* S. Lucies] Day, Being the Shortest Day. John Donne. **CP-DonnJ**

'Tis thus the holy Scripture ends. Truth. Christopher Smart. *Fr.* Hymns for the Amusement of Children. **SP-SmarC**

'Tis thus with people in an open boat. Byron. **FaBoPV** *Fr.* Canto the Second. *Fr.* Don Juan. **CP-Byron**

'Tis time, I think, by Wenlock town. Alfred Edward Housman. **CP-HousA**

'Tis told by one whom stormy waters threw. William Wordsworth. **ImOP** *Fr.* Cambridge and the Alps. *Fr.* The Prelude; Growth of a Poet's Mind [1850 vers.]. **CP-WorW3**

'Tis true, dear[e] Ben, thy just chastizing [*or* chastising] hand. To Ben Jonson. Thomas Carew. **CP-CareT**

'Tis true, Idoloclastes Satyrane! A Tombless Epitaph. Samuel Taylor Coleridge. **CP-ColeS**

'Tis true, I'm broke! Vows, oaths, and all I had. Elegy [*or* Elegie], An. Ben Jonson. **CP-JonsB**

'Tis true, my Lord, I gave my word. The Seventh Epistle of the First Book of Horace Imitated. Alexander Pope. **CP-PopeA**

'Tis true that he is dead: but yet to choose. An Elegy upon the Death of My Lord Francis Villiers. Andrew Marvell. **CP-MarvA**

Tis true the beauteous Starre. A Paradox. Richard Lovelace. **CP-LoveR**

'Tis true the wisdom that my mind exacts. My Theme: Continued. George Meredith. **CP-MerG1**

'Tis true—then why should I repine. In Sickness. Jonathan Swift. **CP-SwifJ**

'Tis true—They shut me in the Cold. Emily Dickinson. **CP-DickE**

'Tis true, 'tis day, what though it be? Break[e] of Day. John Donne. **CP-DonnJ**

'Tis well, begone! your errand is perform'd. Agrippina. Thomas Gray. **CP-GrayT**

'Tis well, 'tis something; we may stand. Tennyson. **EBVV** *Fr.* In Memoriam A. H. H. **CP-TennA**

'Tis whiter than an Indian Pipe. Emily Dickinson. **CP-DickE**

Tis worse then barbarous cruelty to show. Pitie to the Prostrate. Robert Herrick. **CP-HerrR**

'Tis wretched in earnest to live like a mope. 3.12. Horace. **SP-SmarC,** *tr.* by Christopher Smart; *Fr.* Odes.

'Tis writ on Paradise's gate. Hafiz, *tr.* by Ralph Waldo Emerson. **CP-EmerR** *Fr.* Odes.

'Tis you, I think? Back from your week's work, Steve? One Who Married above Him. Thomas Hardy. **CP-HardT**

Titan! to whose immortal eyes. Prometheus. Byron. **CP-Byron**

Titanic called at Cherbourg at dusk, The. Lusty Advice of a Fortune-Teller. Malcolm Lowry. **CP-LowrM**

Tithe [*or* Tythe]: To the Bride, The. Robert Herrick. **CP-HerrR**

Tithonus. Derek Mahon. **SP-MahoD**

Tithonus. Tennyson. **CP-TennA**

Title, The. William Carlos Williams. **CP-WilW2**

Title divine—is mine! Emily Dickinson. **CP-DickE**

Title of Poet, The. Robert Ranke Graves. **CP-GravR**

Titmouse. Walter de la Mare. **CP-DeLaW**

Titmouse, The. Ralph Waldo Emerson. **CP-EmerR**

Tizdal my beautiful one. Nodding. Stevie Smith. **CP-SmitS**

T.M. Charles Bukowski. **SP-BukC1**

To ——: "Bowers whereat, in dreams, I see, The." Edgar Allan Poe. **CP-PoeEd**

To ——: "But once I dared to lift my eyes." Byron. **CP-Byron**

To ——: "Fair Nature's priestesses! to whom." John Greenleaf Whittier. **CP-WhitJ**

To —— / For her this rhyme is penned, whose luminous eyes. A Valentine. Edgar Allan Poe. **CP-PoeEd**

To ——: "Happy the feeling from the bosom thrown." William Wordsworth. *See* Happy the feeling from the bosom thrown.

To ——: "I fear thy kisses, gentle maiden." Percy Bysshe Shelley. *See* I fear thy kisses, gentle maiden.

To ——: "I heed not that my earthly lot." Edgar Allan Poe. **CP-PoeEd**

To ——: "I knew thee strong and quiet like the hills." Robert Louis Stevenson. **CP-StevR**

To ——: "I saw thee on thy bridal day." Edgar Allan Poe. **CP-PoeEd**

To ——: "If these brief Records, by the Muses' art." William Wordsworth. **CP-WorW2**

To ——: "Let other bards of angels sing." William Wordsworth. **CP-WorW2**

To ——: "Look at the fate of summer flowers." William Wordsworth. **CP-WorW2**

To ——: "Maiden! with the fair brown tresses." John Greenleaf Whittier. **CP-WhitJ**

To ——: "Music, when soft voices die." Percy Bysshe Shelley. **CP-ShelP**

To ——: "Not long ago, the writer of these lines." Edgar Allan Poe. **CP-PoeEd**

To ——: "O dearer far than light and life are dear." William Wordsworth. **CP-WorW2**

To ——: "Oh! there are spirits of the air." Percy Bysshe Shelley. **CP-ShelP**

To ——: "Oh! well I know your subtle Sex." Byron. **CP-Byron**

To ——: "One word is too often profaned." Percy Bysshe Shelley. *See* One word is too often profaned.

To ——: "Three rompers run together, hand in hand." Wilfred Owen. **CP-OwenW**

To ——: "Time's sea hath been five years at its slow ebb." John Keats. **CP-KeatJ**

To ——: "When passion's trance is overpast." Percy Bysshe Shelley. **CP-ShelP**

To ——: "Yet look on me—take not thine eyes away." Percy Bysshe Shelley. **CP-ShelP**

To ——: "Had I a man's fair form, then might my sighs." John Keats. **CP-KeatJ**

To—— / The Ring is on my hand. Bridal Ballad. Edgar Allan Poe. **CP-PoeEd**

To ——: " 'Wait, prithee, wait!' this answer Lesbia threw." William Wordsworth. **CP-WorW2**

To —, in Her Seventieth Year. William Wordsworth. **CP-WorW2**

To [Mary Frogley]. John Keats. **CP-KeatJ**

To — Upon the Birth of Her First-Born Child, March, 1833. William Wordsworth. **CP-WorW2**

To —. With the Following Poem, *preface to* The Palace of Art. Tennyson. **CP-TennA**

To—, on Her First Ascent to the Summit of Helvellyn. William Wordsworth. **CP-WorW2**

To / spin / a rapture / high. 8 Words. Marsden Hartley. **CP-HartM**

To. William Carlos Williams. **CP-WilW1**

To a Bad Poet. Donald Davie. **CP-DavDo**

To a Beautiful Quaker. Byron. **CP-Byron**

To a Bed of Tulips. Robert Herrick. **CP-HerrR**

To a bell in Lincoln Cathedral. An Oriental Visitor. Donald Davie. **CP-DavDo**

To a Box Turtle. John Updike. **CP-UpdiJ**

To a Bridegroom. Thomas Hardy. **CP-HardT**

To a Brother in the Mystery. Donald Davie. **CP-DavDo**

To a Brown Girl. Countee Cullen. **CP-CullC**

To a Butterfly. James Merrill. **SP-MerrJ**

To a Butterfly. William Wordsworth.

    "I've watched you now a full half-hour." **CP-WorW1**

    "Stay near me—do not take thy flight!" **CP-WorW1**

To a Butterfly in a Window. Charlotte Smith. **CP-SmitC**

To a Calvinist in Bali. Edna St. Vincent Millay. **CP-MillE**

To a Cape Ann Schooner. John Greenleaf Whittier. **CP-WhitJ**

To a Captious Critic. Paul Laurence Dunbar. **CP-DunbP**

To a Certain Cantatrice. Walt Whitman. **CP-WhitW**

To a Certain Civilian. Walt Whitman. **CP-WhitW**

To a Certain Friend. David Herbert Lawrence. **CP-LawrD**

To a Chameleon. Marianne Craig Moore. **CP-MoorM**

To a Child [Written in Her Album]. William Wordsworth. **CP-WorW2**

To a Child. William DeWitt Snodgrass. **SP-SnodW**

To a Child Dancing in the Wind. William Butler Yeats. **CP-YeatW**

To a Child in Calcutta. Galway Kinnell. **SP-KinnG**

To a Child in Tears. Wystan Hugh Auden. **CP-AudWJ**

To a Child Trapped in a Barber Shop. Philip Levine. **SP-LeviP**

To a Chinese Woman. William Carlos Williams. **CP-WilW2**

To a Common Prostitute. Walt Whitman. **CP-WhitW**

To a Communist. Louis MacNeice. **CP-MacNL**

To a Comrade in Arms. Alun Lewis. **CP-LewiA**

To a Comrade in Flanders. Wilfred Owen. **CP-OwenW**

To a Contemporary Bunkshooter. Carl Sandburg. **CP-SandC**

To a Critic. Samuel Taylor Coleridge. **CP-ColeS**

To a Daughter with Artistic Talent. Peter Meinke. **SP-MeinP**

To a Dead Drunk. James Wright. **CP-WrigJ**

To a Dead Flame. John Updike. **CP-UpdiJ**

To a Dead Friend. Paul Laurence Dunbar. **CP-DunbP**

To a Dead Graduate Student. Thom Gunn. **CP-GunnT**

To a Dead Journalist. William Carlos Williams. **CP-WilW1**

To a Dead Man. Carl Sandburg. **CP-SandC**

To a Dead Vole. Stevie Smith. **CP-SmitS**

To a Defeated Savior. James Wright. **CP-WrigJ**

To a Disdaynefull Fayre. Robert Herrick. **CP-HerrR**

To a Dog Injured in the Street. William Carlos Williams. **CP-WilW2**

To a Face in a Crowd. Robert Penn Warren. **SP-WarrR**

To a Fellow Student. Leonard Cohen. **CP-CoheL**

To a Field-mouse. Wystan Hugh Auden. **CP-AudWJ**

To a Fish Head Found on the Beach Near Málaga. Philip Levine. **SP-LeviP**

To a Foil'd European Revolutionaire. Walt Whitman. **CP-WhitW**

To a Freedom Fighter. Maya Angelou. **SP-AngeM**

To a Friend. Matthew Arnold. **SP-ArnoM**

To a Friend("Looke in my Book, and herein see"). Robert Herrick. **CP-HerrR**

To a Friend. Ben Jonson. **CP-JonsB**

To a Friend. Howard Nemerov. **CP-NemeH**

To a Friend. Charlotte Smith. **CP-SmitC**

To a Friend. John Greenleaf Whittier. **CP-WhitJ**

To a Friend. William Carlos Williams. **CP-WilW1**

To a Friend. William Wordsworth. *Fr.* Poems Composed or Suggested During a Tour, in the Summer of 1833. **CP-WorW2**

To a Friend, an Epigram of Him. Ben Jonson. **CP-JonsB**

To a Friend and Fellow Poet. "Hugh MacDiarmid." **SP-MacDH**

To a Friend Concerning Several Ladies. William Carlos Williams. **CP-WilW1**

To a Friend Estranged from Me. Edna St. Vincent Millay. **CP-MillE**

To a Friend, in Answer to a Melancholy Letter. Samuel Taylor Coleridge. *Fr.* Poetical Epistles. **CP-ColeS**

To a Friend in Distress. William Cowper, *tr. fr. the Latin of Owen.* **CP-CowpW**

To a Friend in Love with the Wrong Man Again. Stephen Dunn. **SP-DunnS**

To a Friend in Time of Trouble. Thom Gunn. **CP-GunnT**

To a Friend Lost. George Meredith. **CP-MerG1**

To a Friend on His Marriage. Frank Templeton Prince. **CP-PrinF**

To a Friend Parting. Robert Penn Warren. **SP-WarrR**

To a Friend [Charles Lamb] Together with an Unfinished Poem. Samuel Taylor Coleridge. *Fr.* Effusions. **CP-ColeS**

To a Friend Who Had Been Much Abused in Many Inveterate Libels. Jonathan Swift. **CP-SwifJ**

To a Friend [Charles Lamb] Who Had Declared His Intention of Writing No More Poetry. Samuel Taylor Coleridge. **CP-ColeS**

To a Friend Who Sent Me Some Roses. John Keats. **CP-KeatJ**

To a Friend Whose Work Has Come to Nothing. William Butler Yeats. **CP-YeatW**

To a Friend Whose Work Has Come to Triumph. Anne Sexton. **CP-SextA**

To a Friendly Dun. James Wright. **CP-WrigJ**

To a Fugitive. James Wright. **CP-WrigJ; SP-SchwD**

To A Gardener. Robert Louis Stevenson. **CP-StevR**

To a Gentleman, "To W. Wordsworth," *another vers. of this poem, appears on facing pages.* Samuel Taylor Coleridge. *See* Friend of the wise! and teacher of the good!

To a Gentleman Who Had Sent Him a News-Paper, and Offered to Continue It Free of Expense. Robert Burns. **CP-BurnR**

To a Gentlewoman Objecting to Him His Grey Hairs. Robert Herrick. **CP-HerrR**

To a Gentlewoman on Just Dealing. Robert Herrick. **CP-HerrR**

To a Geranium Which Flowered during the Winter. Charlotte Smith. **CP-SmitC**

To a Giraffe. Marianne Craig Moore. **CP-MoorM**

To a Girl Who Knew What Side Her Bread Was Buttered On. Audre Lorde. **SP-LordA**

To a Golden-Haired Girl in a Louisiana Town. Nicholas Vachel Lindsay. **CP-LindV**

To a Good man of most dear memory. Written after the Death of Charles Lamb. William Wordsworth. **CP-WorW2**

To a Granddaughter on One of Her Suggestions for a Christmas Present. Frank Templeton Prince. **CP-PrinF**

To a Green-Chafer, on a White Rose. Charlotte Smith. **CP-SmitC**

To a Haggis. Robert Burns. **CP-BurnR**

To a Historian. Walt Whitman. **CP-WhitW**

To a Hostess Saying Goodnight. James Wright. **CP-WrigJ**

To a Husband. Maya Angelou. **SP-AngeM**

To a Jilted Lover. Sylvia Plath. **CP-PlatS**

To a Knot of Ungenerous Critics. Byron. **CP-Byron**

To A. L.; Persuasions [*or* Perswasions] to Love. Thomas Carew. **CP-CareT**

To a Lady ["Star that beams on Anna's breast, The"]. William Cowper. **CP-CowpW**

To a Lady. Byron. **CP-Byron**

To a Lady. Byron. **CP-Byron**

To a Lady. Byron. **CP-Byron**

To a Lady. Samuel Taylor Coleridge. **CP-ColeS**

To a Lady. Samuel Taylor Coleridge. **CP-ColeS**

To a Lady. Thomas Hardy. **CP-HardT**

To a Lady. Jonathan Swift. **CP-SwifJ**

To a Lady. William Wordsworth. **CP-WorW2**

To a Lady, a Part of Her. David Markson. **CP-MarkD**

To a Lady in a Train. Stevie Smith. **CP-SmitS**

To a Lady, Not Yet Enjoyed by Her Husband. Thomas Carew. **CP-CareT**

To a Lady Passing Time Better Left Unpassed. Ogden Nash. **CP-NashO**

To a Lady, Persuading Her to a Car, *parody of* Ben Jonson. Rudyard Kipling. **CP-KiplR** *Fr.* The Muse among the Motors.

To a Lady Playing and Singing in the Morning. Thomas Hardy. **CP-HardT**

To a Lady Playing the Harp. Paul Laurence Dunbar. **CP-DunbP**

To a Lady, That Desired I Would Love Her. Thomas Carew. **CP-CareT**

To a Lady That Desired Me I Would Bear My Part with Her in a Song. Richard Lovelace. **CP-LoveR**

To a Lady That Forbade to Love before Company. Sir John Suckling. **CP-SuckJ**

To a Lady Who Presented to the Author a Lock of Hair Braided with His Own, and Appointed a Night in December to Meet Him in the Garden. Byron. **CP-Byron**

To a Lady with Child that Asked [*or* Ask'd] an Old Shirt. Richard Lovelace. **CP-LoveR**

To a Lady with the Temple of Fame. Alexander Pope. **CP-PopeA**

To a Little Girl, One Year Old, in a Ruined Fortress. Robert Penn Warren. **SP-WarrR**

Child Next Door, The.

Colder Fire. **LiTM**

Flower, The.

Gull's Cry.

Sirocco.

To a Locomotive in Winter. Walt Whitman. **CP-WhitW**

To a look in my son's eyes. Address. William Carlos Williams. **CP-WilW2**

To a Louse [On Seeing One on a Lady's Bonnet at Church]. Robert Burns. **CP-BurnR**

To a Love-Feast we both invited are. The Parasceve, or Preparation. Robert Herrick. **CP-HerrR**

To a Lovely Lady Gone to Theory. John Ciardi. **SP-CiarJ**

To a lovely mirtle bound. William Blake. *See* In a Myrtle [*or* Mirtle] Shade.

To a Lovely Old Bitch. William Carlos Williams. **CP-WilW2**

To a Maid. Robert Herrick. **CP-HerrR**

To a Man. Maya Angelou. **SP-AngeM**

To a man and his wife. Ballad. William Carlos Williams. **CP-WilW2**

To a Man Dying on His Feet. William Carlos Williams. **CP-WilW2**

To a Man Going Blind. John Haines. **SP-HainJ**

To a Man on His Horse. Frank Templeton Prince. **CP-PrinF**

To a Mayd. Robert Herrick. **CP-HerrR**

To a mere. The Frozen Lake. Stevie Smith. **CP-SmitS**

To a Mexican Pig-Bank. William Carlos Williams. **CP-WilW1**

To a Mexican Poet Who Has Forsaken Drink. David Markson. **CP-MarkD**

To a Modern Irish Poet. John Hewitt. **CP-HewiJ**

To a Moth Seen in Winter. Robert Frost. **CP-FrosR**

To a Motherless Child. Thomas Hardy. **CP-HardT**

To a Mountain Daisy [On Turning One Down, with the Plough, in April—1786]. Robert Burns. **CP-BurnR**

To a Mouse [On Turning Her Up in Her Nest, with the Plough, November, 1785]. Robert Burns. **CP-BurnR**

To a Mouse says a Miser my dear Mr Mouse. Lucilius. *See* Asclepiades the Miser was horrified.

To a Musician. Edna St. Vincent Millay. **CP-MillE**

To a Nightingale. George Meredith. **CP-MerG1**

To a Nightingale. George Meredith. **CP-MerG2**

To a Nightingale. Charlotte Smith. **CP-SmitC**

To a Novice ("Avoid three kinds of Master"). Thomas Merton. *Fr.* Readings from Ibn Abbad. **CP-MertT**

To a Novice ("Be a son of this instant"). Thomas Merton. *Fr.* Readings from Ibn Abbad. **CP-MertT**

To a Novice ("Fool is one, The"). Thomas Merton. *Fr.* Readings from Ibn Abbad. **CP-MertT**

To a Painter. Robert Burns. *See* Dear——, I'll gie ye some advice.

To a Painter ("All praise the Likeness by thy skill portrayed"). William Wordsworth. **CP-WorW2**

To a Painter ("Though I beheld at first with blank surprise"). William Wordsworth. **CP-WorW2**

To a place of ruined stone we brought you, and sea-reaches. Sirocco. Robert Penn Warren. *Fr.* To a Little Girl, One Year Old, in a Ruined Fortress. **SP-WarrR**

To a Poet. Frank O'Hara. **SP-OharF**

To a Poet and a Lady. Paul Laurence Dunbar. **CP-DunbP**

To a Poet that Died Young. Edna St. Vincent Millay. **CP-MillE.**

To a Poet Who Read in Gloucester Before the Cape Ann Historical Literary and Scientific Society. Charles Olson. **CP-OlsoC**

To a Poet, Who Would Have Me Praise Certain Bad Poets, Imitators of His and Mine. William Butler Yeats. **CP-YeatW**

To a Poetess. Jim Carroll. **SP-CarrJ**

To a Poetical Trio in the City of Gotham. John Greenleaf Whittier. **CP-WhitJ**

To a Poor Old Woman. William Carlos Williams. **CP-WilW1**

To a President. Walt Whitman. **CP-WhitW**

To a Prize Bird. Marianne Craig Moore. **CP-MoorM**

To a Prodigal Old Maid. Allen Tate. **CP-TateA**

To a Proud Old Woman Watching the Tearing Down of the Hurricane Shed. Kay Boyle. **CP-BoylK**

To a Pupil. Walt Whitman. **CP-WhitW**

To a Querulous Acquaintance. Charlotte Smith. **CP-SmitC**

To a Romantic. Allen Tate. **CP-TateA**

To a Romantic Novelist. Allen Tate. **CP-TateA**

To a Scholar in the Stacks. Howard Nemerov. **CP-NemeH**

To a Sea-Cliff. Thomas Hardy. **CP-HardT**

To a Severe Nun. Thomas Merton. **CP-MertT; SP-MertT**

To a Sexton. William Wordsworth. **CP-WorW2**

To a Shade. William Butler Yeats. **CP-YeatW**

To a Siberian Woodsman. Wendell Berry. **CP-BerrW**

"And I am here in Kentucky in the place I have made myself."

"I have thought of you stepping out of your doorway at dawn, your son in your tracks."

"I sit in the shade of the trees of the land I was born in."

"In the thought of you I imagine myself free of the weapons and the official hates that I have borne on my back like a hump."

"There is no government so worthy as your son who fishes with you in silence beside the forest pool."

"Who has invented our enmity? Who has prescribed us."

"You lean at ease in your warm house at night after supper."

To a Sky-Lark. William Wordsworth. **CP-WorW1**

"Up with me! up with me into the clouds!" **FPL; HBV 1-2; TTTS**

To a Skylark. George Meredith. **CP-MerG1**

To a Skylark. Percy Bysshe Shelley. **CP-ShelP**

To a Skylark ("Ethereal minstrel! pilgrim of the sky"). William Wordsworth. **CP-WorW2**

To a Slave Named Job. Stanley Jasspon Kunitz. *Fr.* Words for the Unknown Makers: A Garland of Commemorative Verses. **CP-KuniS**

To a Small Buddha. Wystan Hugh Auden. **CP-AudWJ**

To a Snail. Marianne Craig Moore. **CP-MoorM**

To a Snake. Edna St. Vincent Millay. **CP-MillE**

To a Snow-Drop. William Wordsworth. **CP-WorW2**

To a Solitary Disciple. William Carlos Williams. **CP-WilW1**

To a Southern Statesman. John Greenleaf Whittier. **CP-WhitJ**

To a Sparrow. William Carlos Williams. **CP-WilW2**

To a Squirrel at Kyle-na-no. William Butler Yeats. **CP-YeatW**

To a Star. Percy Bysshe Shelley. **CP-ShelP**

To a Steam Roller. Marianne Craig Moore. **CP-MoorM**

To a Stranger. Walt Whitman. **CP-WhitW**

To a Suitor. Maya Angelou. **SP-AngeM**

To a Teacher of French. Donald Davie. **CP-DavDo**

To a Terrorist. Stephen Dunn. **SP-DunnS**

To a Thinker. Robert Frost. **CP-FrosR**

To a Toadstool. Wystan Hugh Auden. **CP-AudWJ**

To a Tragic Poetess. Ernest Hemingway. **CP-HemiE**

To a Transatlantic Mirror. Erica Jong. **SP-JongE**

To a Tree. Elizabeth Bishop. **CP-BishE**

To a Tree in London. Thomas Hardy. **CP-HardT**

To a Troubled Friend. James Wright. **CP-WrigJ**

To a Vain Lady. Byron. **CP-Byron**

To a Very Slow Air. Philip Larkin. **CP-LarkP**

To a Violet Found on All Saints' Day. Paul Laurence Dunbar. **CP-DunbP**

To a Waterbed. John Updike. **CP-UpdiJ**

To a Waterfowl. Donald Hall. **CP-HallD**

To a Weak Gamester in Poetry. Ben Jonson. **CP-JonsB**

To a Wealthy Man Who Promised a Second Subscription to the Dublin Municipal Gallery if It Were Proved the People Wanted Pictures. William Butler Yeats. **CP-YeatW**

To a Well-Named Dwelling. Thomas Hardy. **CP-HardT**

To a Western Boy. Walt Whitman. **CP-WhitW**

To a Woman. John Berryman. **CP-BerrJ**

To a Woman Seen Once. William Carlos Williams. **CP-WilW2**

To a woman that I knew. Her Eyes. John Crowe Ransom. **SP-RansJ**

To a Wood Thrush. William Carlos Williams. **CP-WilW1**

To a Woodpecker. William Carlos Williams. **CP-WilW2**

To a Wreath of Snow. Emily Brontë. **CP-BronE**

To a Young Artist. Robinson Jeffers. **CP-JefR1**

To a Young Ass. Samuel Taylor Coleridge. **EnRP; OBEC; OxAEP-2** *Fr.* Effusions. **CP-ColeS**

To a Young Beauty. William Butler Yeats. **CP-YeatW**

To a Young Friend. Samuel Taylor Coleridge. **CP-ColeS**

"And haply, bason'd in some unsunn'd cleft." **ChER**

To a Young Friend. William Cowper. **CP-CowpW**

To a Young Girl. Edna St. Vincent Millay. **CP-MillE**

To a Young Girl. William Butler Yeats. **CP-YeatW**

To a Young Lady. Samuel Taylor Coleridge. **CP-ColeS**

To a Young Lady, *Miss Jessy L——, Dumfries; with Books which the Bard Presented Her.* Robert Burns. **CP-BurnR**

To a Young Lady on Her Birthday. Samuel Johnson. **CP-JohnS**

To a Young Lady [Miss Lavinia Poole] on Her Recovery from a Fever. Samuel Taylor Coleridge. **CP-ColeS**

To a Young Lady Who Had Been Reproached for Taking Long Walks in the Country. William Wordsworth. **CP-WorW1**

To a Young Lady Who Sent Me a Laurel Crown. John Keats. **CP-KeatJ**

To a Young Lady Who Stole a Pen. William Cowper. **CP-CowpW**

To a Young Man Entering the World. Charlotte Smith. **CP-SmitC**

To a Young Poet. Edna St. Vincent Millay. **CP-MillE**

To a Young Wretch. Robert Frost. **CP-FrosR**

To a Youth. Robert Louis Stevenson. **CP-StevR**

To a Youthful Friend. Byron. **CP-Byron**

To abate what swells. Basil Bunting. **CP-BuntB**

To account for this, but it cannot be. Malcolm Lowry. **CP-LowrM**

To achieve knowledge, salting away Faust's stock—. Jenny Joseph. *Fr.* Fables. **SP-JoseJ**

To actually see an actual marine monster. Dragons Are Too Seldom. Ogden Nash. **CP-NashO**

To A.D., Unreasonable, Distrustful of Her Own Beauty. Thomas Carew. **CP-CareT**

To A.G.A. Emily Brontë. **CP-BronE**

To ahead and talk about him because he makes you doubt. Property of Jesus. "Bob Dylan." **CP-DylaB**

To Ailsa Rock. John Keats. **CP-KeatJ**

To Alchemists. Ben Jonson. **CP-JonsB**

To Alex. Smith, the "Glasgow Poet," on His Sonnet to "Fame." George Meredith. **CP-MerG2**

To Alfonso Cortes. Thomas Merton. **CP-MertT**

To Alfred. James Thomson *and* David Mallet. **CP-ThomJ** *Fr.* Alfred: A Masque.

To Alfred Tennyson, My Grandson. Tennyson. **CP-TennA**

To Alice Dunbar. Paul Laurence Dunbar. **CP-DunbP**

To Alison Cunningham. Robert Louis Stevenson. **CP-StevR**

To All Angels and Saints. George Herbert. **CP-HerbG**

To all except anguish. Emily Dickinson. **SP-DickE**

To All Gentleness. William Carlos Williams. **CP-WilW2**

To all our wounds, here, whatsoe're they be. Christ. Robert Herrick. **CP-HerrR**

To all that love the far and blue. Robert Louis Stevenson. **CP-StevR**

To All, to Whom I Write. Ben Jonson. **CP-JonsB**

To all to whom this little book may come. Preface, A. Rudyard Kipling. **CP-KiplR** *Fr.* Land and Sea Tales.

To all who carve their love on a picnic table. Open Letter from a Constant Reader. Mona Van Duyn. **SP-VanDM**

To All Young Men That Love. Robert Herrick. **CP-HerrR**

To allow himself to be properly held. The Man Who Closed Shop. Stephen Dunn. **SP-DunnS**

To Alphonso Ferrabosco, on His Book. Ben Jonson. **CP-JonsB**

To Althea, from Prison. Richard Lovelace. **CP-LoveR**

To A.M. George Meredith. **CP-MerG2**

To Amanda ("Come, dear Amanda, quit the town"). James Thomson *and* David Mallet. **CP-ThomJ**

To Amanda ("Unless with my Amanda blest"). James Thomson. **CP-ThomJ**

To Amarantha, That She Would Dishevel[l] Her Hair[e]. Richard Lovelace. **CP-LoveR**

To America. Kay Boyle. **CP-BoylK**

To an Actress. Thomas Hardy. **CP-HardT**

To an all-time, now-time, no-time. New Morning—and the Years Are Ours. Marsden Hartley. **CP-HartM**

To an American Classicist. Donald Davie. **CP-DavDo**

To an American Poet Just Dead. Richard Wilbur. **CP-WilbR**

To an American Publisher. Stevie Smith. **CP-SmitS**

To an Amiable Girl. Charlotte Smith. **CP-SmitC**

To an Ancient. Robert Frost. **CP-FrosR**

To an Artist, to Take Heart. Louise Bogan. **CP-BogaL**

To an Athlete Dying Young. Alfred Edward Housman. **CP-HousA**

To an Autocrat. Diane Wakoski. **SP-WakoD**

To an Elder Poet. William Carlos Williams. **CP-WilW1**

To an Emigrant, Country is idle. Emily Dickinson. **SP-DickE**

To an honest knight if the lucky break befall. Kingdom Come. John Crowe Ransom. *Fr.* Two Gentlemen in Bonds. **SP-RansJ**

To an Imposter of Rosalind. Thomas Hardy. **CP-HardT**

To an Infant. Samuel Taylor Coleridge. *Fr.* Effusions. **CP-ColeS**

To an Ingrate. Paul Laurence Dunbar. **CP-DunbP**

To an Island Princess. Robert Louis Stevenson. **CP-StevR**

To an Isle in the Water. William Butler Yeats. **CP-YeatW**

To an Oak at Newstead. Byron. **CP-Byron**

To an Old Gipsy. Johann N. Vogl, *tr. fr. German by* George Meredith. **CP-MerG2**

To an Old Jaundiced Woman. William Carlos Williams. **CP-WilW1**

To an Old Philosopher in Rome. Wallace Stevens. **CP-StevW**

To an Old Poet in Peru. Allen Ginsberg. **CP-GinsA**

To an old soare a long cure must goe on. Great Maladies, Long Medicines. Robert Herrick. **CP-HerrR**

To an Unborn Pauper Child. Thomas Hardy. **CP-HardT**

To an unfamiliar house once more these feet have wandered. The Unfamiliar House. John Gould Fletcher. **SP-FletJ**

To an Unfortunate Woman at the Theatre. Samuel Taylor Coleridge. **CP-ColeS**

To an Unfortunate Woman Whom the Author Had Known in the Days of Her Innocence. Samuel Taylor Coleridge. **CP-ColeS**

To an Unknown Poet. Countee Cullen. **CP-CullC**

To an Usherette. John Updike. **CP-UpdiJ**

To And. Robert Creeley. **CP-CreeR**

To Andrew Lang. Robert Louis Stevenson. **CP-StevR**

To Anne. Byron. **CP-Byron**

To Anne Bodham. William Cowper. **CP-CowpW**

To Anthea ("Ah my Anthea! must my heart still break?"). Robert Herrick. **CP-HerrR**

To Anthea ("Anthea I am going hence"). Robert Herrick. **CP-HerrR**

To Anthea ("Come Anthea, know thou this"). Robert Herrick. **CP-HerrR**

To Anthea: ("If, deare Anthea, my hard fate it be"). Robert Herrick. **CP-HerrR**

To Anthea: ("Lets call for Hymen if agreed thou art"). Robert Herrick. **CP-HerrR**

To Anthea: ("Now is the time, when all the lights wax dim"). Robert Herrick. **CP-HerrR**

To Anthea: ("Sick is Anthea, sickly is the spring"). Robert Herrick. **CP-HerrR**

To Anthea Lying in Bed. Robert Herrick. **CP-HerrR**

To Anthea, Who May Command Him Anything. Robert Herrick. **CP-HerrR**

To Antonius Julus, the Son of Mark Antony, of the Triumvirate. Horace. *See* 4.2: Praise of Pindar, The ("Pindarum quisquis studet aemulari").

To Any Dweller in Lewis Street. John Hewitt. **CP-HewiJ**

To Any Reader. Robert Louis Stevenson. **CP-StevR**

To Apollo ("Thou mighty lord and master of the Lyre"). Robert Herrick. **CP-HerrR**

To Apollo ("Phoebus! when that I a Verse"). Robert Herrick. **CP-HerrR**

To appease the Gods; or public thanks to yield. Processions Suggested on a Sabbath Morning in the Vale of Chamouny. William Wordsworth. *Fr.* Memorials of a Tour of the Continent; 1820. **CP-WorW2**

To Aristius Fuscus, *see also* Translations of Horace: Odes 1.22 ("Integer vitae"). Horace. *See* NPTITLE/1.22: Translations of Horace ("Integer vitae").

To arrive / unexpectedly / from nowhere. Small Action Poem. Charles Tomlinson. **CP-TomlC**

To Artemis. Hayden Carruth. **CP-CarHS**

To Artina. Langston Hughes. **SP-HughL**

To A.S., 1830. Emily Brontë. **CP-BronE**

To ask the hard question is simple. Question, The. Wystan Hugh Auden. **CP-AudeW**

To Asra. Samuel Taylor Coleridge. **CP-ColeS**

To attempt to speak of what has been. Emily Dickinson. **SP-DickE**

To Auden on His Fiftieth. Richard Eberhart. **CP-EberR**

To Aunt Rose. Allen Ginsberg. **CP-GinsA**

To Auntie. Robert Louis Stevenson. **CP-StevR**

To Autumn. William Blake. **CP-BlakW**

To Autumn. Louise Glück. **SP-GlücL**

To Autumn. John Keats. **CP-KeatJ**

To Avis Keene. John Greenleaf Whittier. **CP-WhitJ**

To Babylon's proud waters brought. Bible, O.T. *See* Psalm 137: "By the rivers of Babylon. . . ."

To Bacchus, a Canticle. Robert Herrick. **CP-HerrR**

To barren heath, bleak moor, and quaking fen. The Brownie's Cell. William Wordsworth. **CP-WorW2**

To B.C. Sir John Suckling. **CP-SuckJ**

To be a Bell and Flower too. Emily Dickinson. **SP-DickE**

To be a child named after a star. Rijl. Tess Gallagher. **SP-GallT**

To be a giant and keep quiet about it. Trees. Howard Nemerov. **CP-NemeH**

To be a Jew in the twentieth century. Muriel Rukeyser. **NALW; TrJP** *Fr.* Letter to the Front. **CP-RukeM**

To be able. To an Elder Poet. William Carlos Williams. **CP-WilW1**

To be able to forget is to be able to yield. Forget. David Herbert Lawrence. **CP-LawrD**

To be adored by a proud Paladin. The Beggar Maid and King Cophetua. Robert Ranke Graves. **CP-GravR**

To be against to resist everything. Chuck Miller. **SP-MillC**

To be alive—is Power. Emily Dickinson. **CP-DickE**

To Be Alone. Jim Morrison. **SP-MorrJ**

To be alone, and not to be lonely. The Poet Dreams and Resolves. Michael Hartnett. *Fr.* Notes on My Contemporaries. **SP-HarMi**

To Be Alone with You. "Bob Dylan." **SP-DylaB**

To be an ape in little of the mountain-making mother. On Building with Stone. Robinson Jeffers. **CP-JefR1**

To be an aristocrat of the sun. Aristocracy of the Sun. David Herbert Lawrence. **CP-LawrD**

To Be at All. Walt Whitman. **CP-WhitW**

To be at home on its native ground. Wendell Berry. *Fr.* Elegy: "To be at home on its native ground." **CP-BerrW**

To be, be thine. Arthur Hugh Clough. **SP-ClouA**

To be beautiful is to somehow keep. Wanda Being Beautiful. Paul Zimmer. **SP-ZimmP**

To be born famous, as your father's son. Troublesome Fame. Robert Ranke Graves. **CP-GravR**

To Be Called A Bear. Robert Ranke Graves. **CP-GravR**

To be carried back to the shrine some dawn. Stone from Delphi. Seamus Heaney. **SP-HeanS** *Fr.* Shelf Life.

To Be Carved on a Stone at Thoor Ballylee. William Butler Yeats. **CP-YeatW**

To be certain we were to meet our Lost. Emily Dickinson. **SP-DickE**

To Be Charmed. Kenneth Patchen. **CP-PatcK**

To Be Closely Written on a Small Piece of Paper Which Folded into a Tight Lozenge Will Fit Any Girl's Locket. William Carlos Williams. **CP-WilW1**

To be constant through a lifetime. The Trip to Huntsville. Donald Davie. **CP-DavDo**

To be dancer / of my own dismay. Dancing. Robert Creeley. **CP-CreeR**

To Be Dead. Randall Jarrell. **CP-JarrR**

To Be Done in Winter. James Dickey. **CP-DickJ**

To Be Engraved on the Skull of a Cormorant. Charles Tomlinson. **CP-TomlC**

To Be Filed for Reference. Rudyard Kipling. *Fr.* Plain Tales from the Hills.
  By the Hoof of the Wild Goat. **CP-KiplR**

To be forgot by thee. Emily Dickinson. **CP-DickE**

To-Be-Forgotten, The. Thomas Hardy. **CP-HardT**

To Be Holy, Be Wholly Your Own. Kenneth Patchen. **CP-PatcK**

To be homeless is a pride. A Jealous Man. Robert Ranke Graves. **CP-GravR**

To be human is more than to be divine. Emily Dickinson. **SP-DickE**

To be humble before other men is degrading, I am humble before no man. Tender Reverence. David Herbert Lawrence. **CP-LawrD**

To Be Hungry Is to Be Great. William Carlos Williams. **CP-WilW1**

To be idiomatic in a vacuum. Poem. Frank O'Hara. **SP-OharF**

To Be in Love. Gwendolyn Brooks. **SP-BrooG**

To Be in Love. Robert Ranke Graves. **CP-GravR**

To be in love is like going out- / side to see what kind of day. The Business. Robert Creeley. **CP-CreeR**

To be lost for good to the gay self-esteem. As When the Mystic. Robert Ranke Graves. **CP-GravR**

To be male, always. Eros. Louise Glück. *Fr.* Dedication to Hunger. **SP-GlücL**

To Be Merry. Robert Herrick. **CP-HerrR**

To be moved comes of want, tho[ugh] want be complete. 1892-1941. Louis Zukofsky. **CP-ZukLS**

To be near her is to be near the furnace. Fire Walker. Robert Ranke Graves. **CP-GravR**

To Be of Use. Marge Piercy. **SP-PierM**

To be old and to be young. Stanley Jasspon Kunitz. *Fr.* The Lincoln Relics. **CP-KuniS**

To be or not to be! That is the question. Byron. **OBCoV** *Fr.* Canto the Ninth. *Fr.* Don Juan. **CP-Byron**

To Be Poets. Robert Ranke Graves. **CP-GravR**

To be possessed by her is to possess—. Possessed. Robert Ranke Graves. **CP-GravR**

To Be Read to Yourself in a Public Place, July 4, 1976. Leonard Nathan.
  "I write you out of fear." **SP-NathL**
  "If you start in loneliness." **SP-NathL**
  "It's a brand new morning." **SP-NathL**
  "On the sink of the Golden Motel washroom." **SP-NathL**
  "There's too much to consecrate." **SP-NathL**
  "Through the thin hill fog." **SP-NathL**

To Be Recited to Flossie on Her Birthday. William Carlos Williams. **CP-WilW2**

To be redeem'd the world's Redeemer brought. The Presentation. Robert Southwell. **CP-SoutR**

To be remember'd thus is fame. Answer to Stanzas Addressed to Lady Hesketh. William Cowper. **CP-CowpW**

To be sane in a mad time. Wendell Berry. *Fr.* The Mad Farmer Manifesto: the First Amendment. **CP-BerrW**

To be singular under plural circumstances. Emily Dickinson. **SP-DickE**

To be so cold and yet not old. Eulenspiegelei. Stevie Smith. **CP-SmitS**

To Be Somebody. Langston Hughes. **SP-HughL**

To Be Sung on the Water. Louise Bogan. **CP-BogaL**

To Be Superior. David Herbert Lawrence. **CP-LawrD**

To be the father of the fatherless. Sonnet to the Prince Regent. Byron. **CP-Byron**

To be the only woman alive in a vast hive of death. The Undead. Robert Ranke Graves. **CP-GravR**

To Be Used in an Address Delivered at the Unveiling of a Plaque Commemorating "George A. Birmingham." John Hewitt. **CP-HewiJ**

To be warm, build an igloo. Spiritual Life. William Matthews. **SP-MattW**

To be well loved. The Hazel Grove. Robert Ranke Graves. **CP-GravR**

To be wise the dull brain so earnestly throbs. Hafiz, *tr. by* Ralph Waldo Emerson. **CP-EmerR** *Fr.* Odes.

To Be Written on the Mirror in Whitewash. Elizabeth Bishop. **CP-BishE**

To Beachey, 1912. Carl Sandburg. **CP-SandC**

To bear an ivy leaf, in one's mind. Poem for My Sister Nora, at the Reading. James Liddy. **CP-LiddJ**

To Beat the Child Was Bad Enough. Maya Angelou. **SP-AngeM**

To become the face of space. Arizona Highway. Charles Tomlinson. **CP-TomlC**

To Bed. Rita Dove. **SP-DoveR**

To bed, to bed: a storm is brewing. The Window Pane. Robert Ranke Graves. **CP-GravR**

To begin a walk / To make an air / Of knowing where to go. Prologue: Why I Have a Wet Footprint on Top of My Mind. Thomas Merton. *Fr.* North. *Fr.* The Geography of Lograire. **CP-MertT**

To begin with he was undoubtedly in love. Frank Templeton Prince. *Fr.* Afterword on Rupert Brooke. **CP-PrinF**

To begin with photographs of summer: lakes. Separations. Stephen Dobyns. **SP-DobyS**

To begin with there are / No wild swans at Norfolk. The Wild Swans at Norfolk. Hayden Carruth. **CP-CarHS**

To Beguile and Betray. Robert Ranke Graves. **CP-GravR**

To believe in a world of beauty: O. Shapes of Winter. Gilbert Sorrentino. **SP-SorrG**

To believe is above all to be in love. Frank Templeton Prince. *Fr.* Drypoints of the Hasidim. **CP-PrinF**

To Belinda on the Rape of the Lock, *see also* Rape of the Lock, The. Alexander Pope. **CP-PopeA**

To Belong to Allah. Thomas Merton. *Fr.* Readings from Ibn Abbad. **CP-MertT**

To Belshazzar. Byron. **CP-Byron**

To Ben Jonson. Thomas Carew. **CP-CareT**

To Benjamin Rudyerd. Ben Jonson. **CP-JonsB**

To Bettine. Elizabeth Barrett Browning. **CP-BroEB**

To Betty the Grisette. Jonathan Swift. **CP-SwifJ**

To Bhain Campbell. John Berryman. **CP-BerrJ**

To Biancha. Robert Herrick. **CP-HerrR**

To Biancha, to Blesse Him. Robert Herrick. **CP-HerrR**

To blase the rising of this glorious sunne. The Epiphanye. Robert Southwell. **CP-SoutR**

To Blossoms. Robert Herrick. **CP-HerrR**

To Bobbie. Robert Creeley. **CP-CreeR**

To Booker T. Washington. Paul Laurence Dunbar. **CP-DunbP**

To B.R. Haydon. William Wordsworth. **CP-WorW2**

To B.R. Haydon, On Seeing His Picture of Napoleon Buonaparte on the Island of St Helena. William Wordsworth. **CP-WorW2**

To B.R. Haydon, with a Sonnet Written on Seeing the Elgin Marbles. John Keats. **CP-KeatJ**

To Brain-Hardy. Ben Jonson. **CP-JonsB**

To Bread and Water none is poore. No Want Where There's Little. Robert Herrick. **CP-HerrR**

To break so vast a Heart. Emily Dickinson. **CP-DickE**

To break the pentameter, Pound's first heave. To a Bad Poet. Donald Davie. **CP-DavDo**

To Bring the Dead to Life. Robert Ranke Graves. **CP-GravR**

To Brooklyn Bridge. Hart Crane. **AP; AiP; AmPP; BLPL; CABA; CMoP; ChIV-1; ClHu; CoBMV; CrMA; EyDe; FaBoEn; HAP; HeIP; HoFi; ImPo; InPS; LiTA; LiTM; MeMAP; MoAB; MoAMPo; MoPo; NOBA; NYP; NePA; NoAM; NoP; OxBA; PoE; PoPl; PrIm; SeCeV; TAP; TFi; TRP; WeW** *Fr.* The Bridge. **CP-CranH**
  (Poem: To Brooklyn Bridge.) **AmFP; AmPP; CMoP; HAP; HeIP; NoAM; NoP; TAP; WeW**

To Buddha. Nicholas Vachel Lindsay. *Fr.* Poems Speaking of Buddha, Prince Siddartha. **CP-LindV**

To bug: an act of intelligence. To Try to Get Down One Citizen as Against Another. Charles Olson. **CP-OlsoC**

To build a window on the west. Leningrad. John Updike. *Fr.* Postcards from Soviet Cities. **CP-UpdiJ**

To C——. Marsden Hartley. **CP-HartM**

To C. T. George Oppen. **CP-OppeG**

To call our sight Vision. I Am Not a Camera. Wystan Hugh Auden. **CP-AudeW**

To. Campiani Epigramma de Instituto Authoris, *accompanied by Eng. translation.* Thomas Campion. **CP-CampT**

To Captain G——, on Being Asked Why I Was Not to Be of the Party with Him and His Brother K-nm-re at Syme's. Robert Burns. **CP-BurnR**

To Captain Hungry. Ben Jonson. **CP-JonsB**

To Captain Riddell. Robert Burns. **CP-BurnR**

To Cardinal Manning. George Meredith. **CP-MerG1**

To Carlyle. George Meredith. **CP-MerG2**

To Carnations. Robert Herrick. **CP-HerrR**

To Caroline ("Oh when shall the grave hide for ever my sorrow?"). Byron. **CP-Byron**

To Caroline ("Think'st thou I saw thy beauteous eyes"). Byron. **CP-Byron**

To Caroline ("When I hear you express an affection so warm"). Byron. **CP-Byron**

To Caroline ("You say you love, and yet your eye"). Byron. **CP-Byron**

To Carrey Clavel. Thomas Hardy. **CP-HardT**

To Carry the Child. Stevie Smith. **CP-SmitS**

To catch the meaning out of the air. Hardening into Print. Richard Eberhart. **CP-EberR**

To cause accord or to ag[g]re[e]. Sir Thomas Wyatt. **CP-WyatT**

To Cedars. Robert Herrick. **CP-HerrR**

To celebrate the culture would have been foreign to me. The Anglo-Welshman and his friends. Steve Griffiths. **SP-GrifS**

To celebrate your brief life. To the Ghost of Marjorie Kinnan Rawlings. William Carlos Williams. **CP-WilW2**

To Celia. Catullus. *See* Carmen 5: "Lesbia / live with me."

To Celia, upon Love's Ubiquity. Thomas Carew. **CP-CareT**

To Censorious Courtling. Ben Jonson. **CP-JonsB**

To Certain Critics. Countee Cullen. **CP-CullC**

To Certain English Poets. Donald Davie. **CP-DavDo**

To Certain Journeymen. Carl Sandburg. **CP-SandC**

To C.F.H. Thomas Hardy. **CP-HardT**

To Charles Baxter. Robert Louis Stevenson. **CP-StevR**

To Charles Baxter. Robert Louis Stevenson. **CP-StevR**

To Charles Cowden Clarke. John Keats. **CP-KeatJ**

    "Oft have you seen a swan superbly frowning." **PBBP**

To Charles Ford, Esq. on His Birthday. Jonathan Swift. **CP-SwifJ**

To Charles Sumner. John Greenleaf Whittier. **CP-WhitJ**

To Charlie. Stephen Berg. **SP-BergS**

To Chatterton. John Keats. **CP-KeatJ**

To Cherry-Blossomes. Robert Herrick. **CP-HerrR**

To Children. George Meredith. **CP-MerG1**

To Chink Whose Trade Is Soldiering. Ernest Hemingway. **CP-HemiE**

To Chloe, Courting Her for His Friend. Richard Lovelace. **CP-LoveR**

To Chloes breast young Cupid slily stole. William Blake. **CP-BlakW**

To Chloris. Robert Burns. **CP-BurnR**

To Chloris. Robert Burns. **CP-BurnR**

To Christ. Robert Herrick. **CP-HerrR**

To Christ Our Lord. Galway Kinnell. **SP-KinnG**

To Christina. John Milton, *tr. fr. Latin by* William Cowper. **CP-CowpW**

To Christopher Marlowe. Charles Henri Ford. **SP-FordC**

To Cipriano, in the Wind. Philip Levine. **SP-LeviP**

To claim, at a dead party, to have spotted a grackle. *with music.* Richard Wilbur. **CP-WilbR**

To Clarinda. Robert Burns. **CP-BurnR**

To Clarinda. David Herbert Lawrence. **CP-LawrD**

To cleanse his eyes, *Tom Brock* makes much adoe. Upon Brock. Robert Herrick. **CP-HerrR**

To Clement Edmonds, on His *Caesar's Commentaries* Observed, and Translated. Ben Jonson. **CP-JonsB**

To climb the belltower. The Crystal Cage. Stanley Jasspon Kunitz. **CP-KuniS**

To climb the intricate heights. Calliope. Hilda Doolittle. **CP-DoolH**

To Clio, Muse of History. Howard Nemerov. **CP-NemeH**

To Close. William Carlos Williams. **CP-WilW2**

To clothe the fiery thought. Poet. Ralph Waldo Emerson. **OxBA; OxBSP; PCP; Spl** *Fr.* Quatrains. **CP-EmerR**

To Coleridge in Sicily. William Wordsworth. **OBNC** *Fr.* Residence in France and French Revolution. *Fr.* The Prelude; Growth of a Poet's Mind [1805 vers.]. **CP-WorW3**

To Colonel Charles. George Meredith. **CP-MerG1**

To Colonel Richard Lovelace, on the Publishing of His Ingenious Poems. Joseph Hall. *Fr.* Commendatory Poems. **CP-LoveR**

To come back from the sweet South, to the North. Italia, Io Ti Saluto! Christina Georgina Rossetti. **CP-RosC2**

To come from Heaven is casual. Emily Dickinson. **SP-DickE**

To Come of Age. Robert Ranke Graves. **CP-GravR**

To come out ready capitalized, with outlines. Roy Fisher. **SP-FishR** *Fr.* The Open Poem and the Closed Poem.

To come to the look in the sacrificer's eyes. Dura. Charles Olson. **CP-OlsoC**

To come to the river. The Resolve. Denise Levertov. **CP-LeveD**

To come unto our own. Emily Dickinson. **SP-DickE**

To conclude, I announce what comes after me. So Long! Walt Whitman. **CP-WhitW**

To congratulate the Redeemed is perhaps superfluous. Emily Dickinson. **SP-DickE**

To Conquer Variety. Hart Crane. **CP-CranH**

To conquer'd men, some comfort 'tis to fall. Some Comfort in Calamity. Robert Herrick. **CP-HerrR**

To Constantia. Percy Bysshe Shelley. **CP-ShelP**

To Constantia, Singing. Percy Bysshe Shelley. **CP-ShelP**

To consummate / the inconsummate, and make of it. "To Work Is to Contradict Contradications, to Do Violence to Natural Violence. . . ." Robert Creeley. **CP-CreeR**

To Cordelia M———. William Wordsworth. *Fr.* Poems Composed or Suggested During a Tour, in the Summer of 1833. **CP-WorW2**

To Courtling. Ben Jonson. **CP-JonsB**

To Crazy Christian. Ernest Hemingway. **CP-HemiE**

To Critic[k]s. Robert Herrick. **CP-HerrR**

To cross a ferry that is no longer there. Crossing Brooklyn Ferry. Charles Tomlinson. **CP-TomlC**

To Crown[e] It. Robert Herrick. **CP-HerrR**

To Crystallization. John Updike. *Fr.* Seven Odes to Seven Natural Processes. **CP-UpdiJ**

To Cupid. Robert Herrick. **CP-HerrR**

To curse the chilled insistence of the dawn. Edwin Arlington Robinson. *Fr.* Octaves. **CP-RobiE**

To D———. Byron. **CP-Byron**

To D———, Dead by Her Own Hand. Howard Nemerov. **CP-NemeH**

To Daddy. Robert Lowell. **SP-LoweR**

To Daffodils [*or* Daffadills]. Robert Herrick. **CP-HerrR**

To Daisies, Not to Shut So Soon[e]. Robert Herrick. **CP-HerrR**

To Dan. Paul Laurence Dunbar. **CP-DunbP**

To Daphne and Virginia. William Carlos Williams. **CP-WilW2**

To Daughters: To Study History. Thomas Merton. *Fr.* Cables to the Ace. **CP-MertT**

To Daunton Me. Robert Burns. **CP-BurnR**

To David, about His Education. Howard Nemerov. **CP-NemeH**

To-day a rude brief recitative. Song for All Seas, All Ships. Walt Whitman. **CP-WhitW**

To-day, across our fathers' graves. The Veterans. Rudyard Kipling. **CP-KiplR**

To-day and Thee. Walt Whitman. **CP-WhitW**

To-day, from each and all, a breath of prayer—a pulse of thought. Abraham Lincoln, Born Feb. 12, 1809. Walt Whitman. **CP-WhitW**

To-day the plant by Williams set. A Spiritual Manifestation. John Greenleaf Whittier. **CP-WhitJ**

To-day, the social consciousness is mutilated. Fear of Society Is the Root of All Evil. David Herbert Lawrence. **CP-LawrD**

To-day, This Insect. Dylan Thomas. **CP-ThomD**

To-day was a beautiful day, the sky was a brilliant. Louis MacNeice. **CP-MacNL** *Fr.* Autumn Journal. **CP-MacNL**

To-day, with bending head and eyes, thou, too, Columbia. The Dead Emperor. Walt Whitman. **CP-WhitW**

To Dean-bourn, a Rude River in Devon, by Which Sometimes He Lived. Robert Herrick. **CP-HerrR**

To Dean Inge Lecturing on Origen. Stevie Smith. **CP-SmitS**

To Dean Swift. Jonathan Swift. **CP-SwifJ**

To Death. Robert Herrick. **CP-HerrR**

To Death. Robinson Jeffers. **CP-JefR3**

To Death. Percy Bysshe Shelley. **CP-ShelP**

To define the sea. Sea Change. Charles Tomlinson. **CP-TomlC**

To Delaware. John Greenleaf Whittier. **CP-WhitJ**

To Delia. William Cowper. **CP-CowpW**

To Delmore Schwartz. Robert Lowell. **SP-LoweR**

To Demosthenis. *Unknown, tr. fr. Greek by* William Cowper. **CP-CowpW**

To Dependence. Charlotte Smith. **CP-SmitC**

To Dewes. A Song. Robert Herrick. **CP-HerrR**

To Dianeme ("Dear, though to part it be a hell"). Robert Herrick. **CP-HerrR**

To Dianeme ("Give me one kiss"). Robert Herrick. **CP-HerrR**

To Dianeme ("I co'd but see thee"). Robert Herrick. **CP-HerrR**

To Dianeme ("Show me thy feet; show me thy legs, thy thighs"). Robert Herrick. **CP-HerrR**

To Dianeme ("Sweet, be not proud of those two eyes"). Robert Herrick. **CP-HerrR**

To Dianeme; a Ceremonie in Glocester. Robert Herrick. **CP-HerrR**

To die be given us, or attain! Resignation. Matthew Arnold. **SP-ArnoM**

To die before it feared to die. Emily Dickinson. **SP-DickE**

To Die before One Wakes Must Be Glad. Alice Walker. **CP-WalkA**

To Die in Milltown. Richard Hugo. **CP-HugoR**

To die—takes just a little while. Emily Dickinson. **SP-DickE**

To die unwrinkled near a breath of fire. The Agony Among the Crowd. Nicolas Calas, *tr. fr. French by* William Carlos Williams. **CP-WilW2**

To die with a forlorn hope, but soon to be raised. The Survivor. Robert Ranke Graves. **CP-GravR**

To die—without the Dying. Emily Dickinson. **CP-DickE**

To dig at Luxor, to peer. Hayden Carruth. **CP-CarHS** *Fr.* The Bloomingdale Papers.

To disappear enhances. Emily Dickinson. **CP-DickE**

To dispense, with justice; or, to dispense. Geoffrey Hill. *Fr.* The Mystery of the Charity of Charles Péguy. **CP-HillG**

To distinctly English writers in England. "Hugh MacDiarmid." **SP-MacDH** *Fr.* England Is Our Enemy.

To Dives (William Beckford). A Fragment. Byron. **CP-Byron**

To divulge itself is Sorrow's Right. Emily Dickinson. **SP-DickE**

To do a magnanimous thing. Emily Dickinson. **CP-DickE**

To Do More Than Hair. Siv Cedering Fox. **SP-CedeS**

To Doctor Alabaster. Robert Herrick. **CP-HerrR**

To Dr. Austin. William Cowper. **CP-CowpW**

To Dr. Blacklock. Robert Burns. **CP-BurnR**

To Dr. Darwin. William Cowper. **CP-CowpW**

To Dr. Delany, on the Libels Writ against Him. Jonathan Swift. **CP-SwifJ**

To Doctor Empiric[k]. Ben Jonson. **CP-JonsB**

To Dr. Hake. Robert Louis Stevenson. **CP-StevR**

To Dr. Helsham. Jonathan Swift. **CP-SwifJ**

To Doctor John Brown. Robert Louis Stevenson. **CP-StevR**

To Dr. John MacKenzie. Robert Burns. **CP-BurnR**

To Dr. Jonathan Swift. Alexander Pope. **OxAEP-1,** *book* I, *ll.* 1–330; **CBNP** *Fr.* The Dunciad. **CP-PopeA**
    ("Books and the Man I sing, the first who brings.") **CBNP,** *book* I, *ll.* 1–84, *first edition vers.*;
    "Here she beholds the chaos dark and deep." **FHYEP**

To Dr Maxwell, on Miss Jessy Staig's Recovery. Robert Burns. **CP-BurnR**

To Dr. Parry of Bath, with Some Botanic Drawings Which Had Been Made Some Years. Charlotte Smith. **CP-SmitC**

To Dr. Sheridan. Jonathan Swift. **CP-SwifJ**

To Dorothy Wellesley. William Butler Yeats. **CP-YeatW**

To Dr. F. B. on His Book of Chess[e]. Richard Lovelace. **CP-LoveR**

To Dr. James Newton Matthews, Mason, Ill. Paul Laurence Dunbar. **CP-DunbP**

To draw no envy (Shakespeare) on thy name. To the Memory of My Beloved, the Author Mr [*or* Master] William Shakespeare[: And What He Hath Left Us]. Ben Jonson. **CP-JonsB**

To drink in moderation, and to smoke. Party Knee. John Updike. **CP-UpdiJ**

To drive Paul out of any lumber camp. Paul's Wife. Robert Frost. **CP-FrosR**

To Dwell Together in Unity. Bible, *O.T. See* Psalm 133: "Behold, how good and how pleasant it is."

To E———. Byron. **CP-Byron**

To E. C. S. John Greenleaf Whittier. **CP-WhitJ**

To E. Fitzgerald. Tennyson. **CP-TennA**

To E. H. K. Paul Laurence Dunbar. **CP-DunbP**

To E. of D. with Six Holy Sonnets. John Donne. **CP-DonnJ**

To E. T.: 1917. Walter de la Mare. **CP-DeLaW**

To Earl Stanhope. Samuel Taylor Coleridge. *Fr.* Effusions. **CP-ColeS**

To earn it by disdaining it. Emily Dickinson. **CP-DickE**

To Earth. Hart Crane. **CP-CranH**

To Earthward. Robert Frost. **CP-FrosR**

To Ed Sissman. John Updike. **CP-UpdiJ**

To Eddleston. Byron. **PeHV** *Fr.* Childe Harold's Pilgrimage. **CP-Byron**

To Edward Alleyn. Ben Jonson. **CP-JonsB**

To Edward FitzGerald. Robert Browning. **CP-BroR2**

To Edward Noel Long, Esq. Byron. **CP-Byron**

To Edward Thomas. Alun Lewis. **CP-LewiA**

To Edward Williams. Percy Bysshe Shelley. **CP-ShelP**

To Ee Is Human. Ogden Nash. **CP-NashO**

To E.L., on His Travels in Greece. Tennyson. **CP-TennA**

To Electra ("Tis Ev'ning, my Sweet"). Robert Herrick. **CP-HerrR**

To Electra ("I'll [*or* Ile] come to thee in all those shapes"). Robert Herrick. **CP-HerrR**

To Electra ("Let not thy Tomb-stone"). Robert Herrick. **CP-HerrR**

To Electra. Love Looks for Love. Robert Herrick. **CP-HerrR**

To Elinor Wylie. Edna St. Vincent Millay. **CP-MillE**

To Eliza. Byron. **CP-Byron**

To Eliza Plucking Laurel in Mr Pope's Gardens. Samuel Johnson. **CP-JohnS**

To Elizabeth, Countess of Rutland. Ben Jonson. **CP-JonsB**

To Ellen. Catullus. *See* Carmen 48: "Iuventius, / were I allowed."

To Ellen, at the South. Ralph Waldo Emerson. **CP-EmerR**

To Ellinda, That Lately I Have Not Written. Richard Lovelace. **CP-LoveR**

To Ellinda. Upon His Late Recovery. Richard Lovelace. **CP-LoveR**

To Elsie. William Carlos Williams. **CP-WilW1**

To Emilia Viviani. Percy Bysshe Shelley. **CP-ShelP**

To Emily Dickinson. Hart Crane. **CP-CranH**

To Emma. Byron. **CP-Byron**

To Emma. John Keats. **CP-KeatJ**

To Empty the Mind. Charles Olson. **CP-OlsoC**

To enact the evil or the good, waking, we say. A Bad Dream. Kathleen Jessie Raine. **SP-RainK**

To end all carols, darling. Carol. Louis MacNeice. **CP-MacNL**

To end up alone. Poem for My 43rd Birthday. Charles Bukowski. **SP-BukC2**

To Endymion. Countee Cullen. **CP-CullC**

To English Connoisseurs. William Blake. **CP-BlakW**

To Englishmen. John Greenleaf Whittier. **CP-WhitJ**

To Enjoy the Time. Robert Herrick. **CP-HerrR**

To enrich the earth I have sowed clover and grass. Enriching the Earth. Wendell Berry. **CP-BerrW**

To Enter That Rhythm Where the Self Is Lost. Muriel Rukeyser. **CP-RukeM**

To Enterprise. William Wordsworth. **CP-WorW2**

To Eros. Wilfred Owen. **CP-OwenW**

To Esmé, Lord Aubigny. Ben Jonson. **CP-JonsB**

To E.T. Wystan Hugh Auden. **CP-AudWJ**

To E.T. Robert Frost. **CP-FrosR**

To Ethelinda. Christopher Smart. **SP-SmarC**

To Eustace Budgell, Esq., on His Translation of the Characters of Theophrastus. Alexander Pope. **CP-PopeA**

To Eva. Ralph Waldo Emerson. **CP-EmerR**

To Eva Descending the Stair. Sylvia Plath. **CP-PlatS**

To Evan. Richard Eberhart. **CP-EberR**

To Evaporation. John Updike. *Fr.* Seven Odes to Seven Natural Processes. **CP-UpdiJ**

To Eve, Man's Dream of Wifehood as Described by Milton. Nicholas Vachel Lindsay. **CP-LindV**

To every creature / Adam gave its name. Ralph Waldo Emerson. **CP-EmerR**

To every ducal palace / When days were old and slow. A Wembley Lad. Sir John Betjeman. **CP-BetjJ**

To every Form of being is assigned. Discourse of the Wanderer and an Evening Visit to the Lake. William Wordsworth. *Fr.* The Excursion. **CP-WorW2**

To every Form of being is assigned. William Wordsworth. **EnRP** *Fr.* Discourse of the Wanderer and an Evening Visit to the Lake. *Fr.* The Excursion. **CP-WorW2**

To Every Seed His Own Body. Christina Georgina Rossetti. **CP-RosC2**

To Evoke Posterity. Robert Ranke Graves. **CP-GravR**

To F———. Edgar Allan Poe. **CP-PoeEd**

To F—S S. O—D. Edgar Allan Poe. **CP-PoeEd**

To fail (transitive and intransitive). Success Story. Philip Larkin. **CP-LarkP**

To Failure. Philip Larkin. **CP-LarkP**

To Fancy. Charlotte Smith. **CP-SmitC**

To Faneuil Hall. John Greenleaf Whittier. **CP-WhitJ**

To Fanny. John Keats. **CP-KeatJ**

To farther this, Achitophel unites. The Malcontents. John Dryden. **OBS** *Fr.* Absalom and Achitophel, Pt. I. **SP-DrydJ**

To feel and speak the astonishing beauty of things — earth, stone and. The Beauty of Things. Robinson Jeffers. **CP-JefR3**

To feel at my heels the smooth stones. James McAuley. *Fr.* The Autobiography of the Impotent Man. **SP-McAuJ**

To Fetch me Wine my *Lucia* went. The Broken Christall. Robert Herrick. **CP-HerrR**

To fight aloud, is very brave. Emily Dickinson. **CP-DickE**

To fight history as it carries us. Phyllis Wounded. Marge Piercy. **SP-PierM**

To fill a Gap. Emily Dickinson. **CP-DickE**

To find a garden-tulip growing. The Ages of Oath. Robert Ranke Graves. **CP-GravR**

To find it, mold it, plant its density. The Cell. Edwin Rolfe. **CP-RolfE**

To find that Tree of Life, whose Fruits did feed. To the King, To Cure the Evill. Robert Herrick. **CP-HerrR**

To find the Western path. Morning. William Blake. **CP-BlakW**

To Find[e] God. Robert Herrick. **CP-HerrR**

To Fine Grand. Ben Jonson. **CP-JonsB**

To Fine Lady Would-Be. Ben Jonson. **CP-JonsB**

To Fire. Gary Snyder. **CP-SnydG**

To F.J.S. Robert Louis Stevenson. **CP-StevR**

To F[laxman] ("I mock thee not"). William Blake. **CP-BlakW**

To F[laxman] ("You call me mad"). William Blake. **CP-BlakW**

To flee from memory. Emily Dickinson. **CP-DickE**

To fleece the Fleece from golden sheep. The Scales of the Eyes. Howard Nemerov. **CP-NemeH**

To Fletcher Reviv'd. Richard Lovelace. **CP-LoveR**

To flex in the upper airs. Utterings. Donald Davie. **CP-DavDo**

To fling my arms wide. Dream Variation[s]. Langston Hughes. **SP-HughL**

To Flood Stage Again. James Wright. **CP-WrigJ**

To Florence. Byron. **CP-Byron**

To Florida. Louise Glück. **SP-GlücL**

To Flossie. William Carlos Williams. **CP-WilW2**

To Flowers. Robert Herrick. **CP-HerrR**

To Flowers from Italy in Winter. Thomas Hardy. **CP-HardT**

To Flush, My Dog. Elizabeth Barrett Browning. **CP-BroEB**

To follow the hard sunlight on the northern harbor. Muriel Rukeyser. **CP-RukeM**

To Fool, or Knave. Ben Jonson. **CP-JonsB**

To Ford Madox Ford in Heaven. William Carlos Williams. **CP-WilW2**

To Foreign Lands. Walt Whitman. **CP-WhitW**

To forget you would be impossible. Emily Dickinson. **SP-DickE**

To forgive Enemies H[ayley] does pretend. William Blake. **CP-BlakW**

To form a just and finished piece. Directions for a Birthday Song. Jonathan Swift. **CP-SwifJ**

To Fortitude. Charlotte Smith. **CP-SmitC**

To Fortune. Samuel Taylor Coleridge. **CP-ColeS**

To Fortune. Robert Herrick. **CP-HerrR**

To Fortune. James Thomson. *See* For ever, Fortune, wilt thou prove.

To Fragmentation. John Updike. *Fr.* Seven Odes to Seven Natural Processes. **CP-UpdiJ**

To France ("I have a dream. . ."). Countee Cullen. **CP-CullC**

To France ("Though I am not the first. . ."). Countee Cullen. **CP-CullC**

To Francis Beaumont. Ben Jonson. **CP-JonsB**

To Frank O'Hara. James Schuyler. **CP-SchuJ**

To Frantz Fanon. Adrienne Rich. **CP-RicAE**

To Fredrika Bremer. John Greenleaf Whittier. **CP-WhitJ**

To freight cars in the air. William Carlos Williams. **InPK** *Fr.* The Descent of Winter. **CP-WilW1**

To Friend-Tree of Counted Days. René Char, *tr. fr. French by* William Carlos Williams. **CP-WilW2**

To friends at home, the lone, the admired, the lost. Robert Louis Stevenson. **CP-StevR**

To Friends, for Good Health. Louis Zukofsky. **CP-ZukLS**

To Friendship. Charlotte Smith. **CP-SmitC**

To fulfill the will of a powerless friend. Emily Dickinson. **SP-DickE**

To G. G. John Greenleaf Whittier. **CP-WhitJ**

To Gary Snyder. Wendell Berry. **CP-BerrW**

To gather flowers Sappha went. The Apron of Flowers. Robert Herrick. **CP-HerrR**

To George B. Cheever. John Greenleaf Whittier. **CP-WhitJ**

To George, Earl Delawarr. Byron. **CP-Byron**

To George Felton Mathew. John Keats. **CP-KeatJ**

To George Sand: A Desire. Elizabeth Barrett Browning. **CP-BroEB**

To George Sand: A Recognition. Elizabeth Barrett Browning. **CP-BroEB**

To Georgiana Augusta Wylie. John Keats. **CP-KeatJ**

To Gerhardt, There, among Europe's Things of Which He Has Written Us in His "Brief an Creely und Olson." Charles Olson. **CP-OlsoC; SP-OlsoC**

To get betimes in Boston town I rose this morning early. Boston Ballad, A [or A Boston Ballad 1854]. Walt Whitman. **CP-WhitW**

To get into it / As it lies. Shirt. Charles Simic. **SP-SimiC**

To get past harping on the laws of Nature. Osip Emilevich Mandelstam. *Fr.* Octets. **CP-DavDo**

To Get the Final Lilt of Songs. Walt Whitman. **CP-WhitW**

To get thine ends, lay bashfulnesse aside. No Bashfulnesse in Begging. Robert Herrick. **CP-HerrR**

To get west you go east. Philip Levine. **SP-LeviP** *Fr.* A Poem with No Ending.

To Giacomo Leopardi in the Sky. Charles Wright. **SP-WrigC**

To give you back this wave. The Wave. Adrienne Rich. **SP-RicA2**

To Gloriana. Nicholas Vachel Lindsay. **CP-LindV**

To Go By Singing. Wendell Berry. **CP-BerrW**

To go by the asters. Luxury. Denise Levertov. **CP-LeveD**

To go in no direction. In No Direction. Robert Ranke Graves. **CP-GravR**

To go in the dark with a light is to know the light. To Know the Dark. Wendell Berry. **CP-BerrW**

To go low, to be as nothing, to die. Howard Nemerov. *Fr.* Runes. **CP-NemeH**

To go to the edge is to discover. Brazil. John Updike. **CP-UpdiJ**

To God. William Blake. **CP-BlakW**

To God ("Come to me God; but do not come"). Robert Herrick. **CP-HerrR**

To God ("Do with me, God! as Thou didst deal with John"). Robert Herrick. **CP-HerrR**

To God ("God gives not onely corne"). Robert Herrick. **CP-HerrR**

To God ("God is all-sufferance here"). Robert Herrick. **CP-HerrR**

To God ("God! to my little meale and oyle"). Robert Herrick. **CP-HerrR**

To God ("God's undivided, One in Persons Three"). Robert Herrick. **CP-HerrR**

To God ("God, who me gives a will"). Robert Herrick. **CP-HerrR**

To God ("I'le come, I'le creep"). Robert Herrick. **CP-HerrR**

To God ("If any thing delight me for to print"). Robert Herrick. **CP-HerrR**

To God ("If I have plaid the Truant"). Robert Herrick. **CP-HerrR**

To God ("Lord, I am like to mistletoe"). Robert Herrick. **CP-HerrR**

To God ("Make, make me Thine"). Robert Herrick. **CP-HerrR**

To God ("Pardon me God"). Robert Herrick. **CP-HerrR**

To God ("Thou hast promis'd, Lord, to be"). Robert Herrick. **CP-HerrR**

To God ("With golden Censers. . . "). Robert Herrick. **CP-HerrR**

To God ("Work is done, The"). Robert Herrick. **CP-HerrR**

To God: an Anthem, Sung in the Chapel at White-Hall, Before the King. Robert Herrick. **CP-HerrR**

To God, His Gift. Robert Herrick. **CP-HerrR**

To God, His Good Will. Robert Herrick. **CP-HerrR**

To God, in Time of Plundering. Robert Herrick. **CP-HerrR**

To God, on His Sickness[e]. Robert Herrick. **CP-HerrR**

To God our strength sing loud, and clear, *par. by* Milton. Bible, *O.T. See* Psalm 81: "Sing aloud unto God our strength."

To God: to illuminate all men. Beginning with Skid Road. PsalmIII. Allen Ginsberg. **CP-GinsA**

To Goethe: a Complaint. Wystan Hugh Auden. *Fr.* Shorts I ("Watch upon my wrist, The"). **CP-AudeW**

To Good Guys Dead. Ernest Hemingway. **CP-HemiE**

To Gottfried Benn. Frank O'Hara. **SP-OharF**

To Graham and Anna: from the Arctic Gate. Letter to Graham and Anna. Louis MacNeice. **CP-MacNL**

To grass, or leaf, or fruit, or wall. The Snail. Vincent Bourne, *tr. fr. Latin by* William Cowper. **CP-CowpW**

To Gravina. William Cowper. **CP-CowpW**

To Greet a Letter-Carrier. William Carlos Williams. **CP-WilW1**

To grip through the ground with your feet. An Old Colonial Imperialist. Howard Nemerov. **CP-NemeH**

To Groom Idiot. Ben Jonson. **CP-JonsB**

To Groves. Robert Herrick. **CP-HerrR**

To H. C.[, Six Years Old]. William Wordsworth. **CP-WorW1**

To H. M. Howard Nemerov. **CP-NemeH**

To hang our head, ostensibly. Emily Dickinson. **CP-DickE**

To Harriet ("Harriet! To see such Circumspection"). Byron. **CP-Byron**

To Harriet ("It is not blasphemy to hope that Heaven"). Percy Bysshe Shelley. **CP-ShelP**

To Harriet Monroe. Richard Eberhart. **CP-EberR**

To Harriet ("Thy look of love has power to calm"). Percy Bysshe Shelley. **CP-ShelP**

To Harriot all accomplish'd fair. Ode to Lady Harriot. Christopher Smart. **SP-SmarC**

To Harvey, Who Traced the Circulation. James Wright. **CP-WrigJ**

To have attained an endless, timeless meeting. Timeless Meeting. Robert Ranke Graves. **CP-GravR**

To have been Diogenes. Why not? Or de Sade. Sonnet. Hayden Carruth. **CP-CarHS** *Fr.* Sonnets.

To have been the missing Hero. Emily Dickinson. **SP-DickE**

To have come among you, rocks–. Soliloquy in Dogtown, Cape Ann. Marsden Hartley. **CP-HartM**

To have done it thirty years. Work. Paul Zimmer. **SP-ZimmP**

To Have Done Nothing. William Carlos Williams. **CP-WilW1**

To have had such Daughters is sanctity. Emily Dickinson. **SP-DickE**

To have intricacies of lakes and forests. Sibelius in Silence. Michael Hartnett. **SP-HarMi**

To have it, sweetheart, is to know you have it. She to Him. Robert Ranke Graves. **CP-GravR**

To have known him, to have loved him. Monody. Herman Melville. **SP-MelvH**

To have met you and loved you and not to have stayed. Love without Frontiers. Phoebe Hesketh. **SP-HeskP**

To have seen, to have held you. Willows Coming into Leaf. Martin Edmunds. **SP-EdmuM**

To have written then, when you writ, seemed to me. To the Countess of Bedford. John Donne. **CP-DonnJ**

To have your face left overnight. Mask. Carl Sandburg. **CP-SandC**

To Hayley. William Cowper. **CP-CowpW**

To Hayley [or To H[ayley]]. William Blake. **CP-BlakW**

To H.C. Marsden Hartley. **CP-HartM**

To H.C. Bunner. Robert Louis Stevenson. **CP-StevR**

To Health. *Unknown, tr. fr. Greek by* William Cowper. **CP-CowpW**

To hear an Oriole sing. Emily Dickinson. **CP-DickE**

To Heaven. Robert Herrick. **CP-HerrR**

To Heaven. Ben Jonson. **CP-JonsB**

To Hedli: ("Acting Younger"). Louis MacNeice. **CP-MacNL**

To Hedli: ("Because the Velet"). Louis MacNeice. **CP-MacNL**

To Helen: ("Helen, thy beauty is to me"). Edgar Allan Poe. **CP-PoeEd**

To Helen: ("I saw thee once—once only—years ago"). Edgar Allan Poe. **CP-PoeEd**

To Helen. Paul Valéry, *tr. fr. French by* Delmore Schwartz. **SP-SchwD**

To Helen Keller. Donald Davie. **CP-DavDo**

To Hell wi' Happiness! "Hugh MacDiarmid." **SP-MacDH**

To Hell with It. Frank O'Hara. **SP-OharF**

To hell with metric—I have read the lore of the ages. With Vengeance Like a Tiger Crawls. Charles Bukowski. **SP-BukC2**

To help our Bleaker Parts. Emily Dickinson. **CP-DickE**

To Henry Crabbe Robinson. William Wordsworth. *Fr.* Memorials of a Tour in Italy, 1837. **CP-WorW2**

To Henry James. Robert Louis Stevenson. **CP-StevR**

To Her. Paul Laurence Dunbar. **CP-DunbP**

To Her Again, She Burning in a Fever. Thomas Carew. *See* Now she burn[e]s as well as I.

To her derided Home. Emily Dickinson. **CP-DickE**

To Her Father, with Some Verses. Anne Bradstreet. **CP-BradA**

To her, for I must still regard her. Dedicatory Poem. Robert Louis Stevenson. **CP-StevR**

To Her I Love. James Thomson. **CP-ThomJ**

To Her in Absence; a Ship. Thomas Carew. **CP-CareT**

To Her Most Honored Father Thomas Dudley, Esquire, These Humbly Presented. Anne Bradstreet. **CP-BradA**

To her, to *be* her, that her hurt and wrong be mine. Hayden Carruth. *Fr.* The Sleeping Beauty. **CP-CarHL**

To Herr Toller, Who Hanged Himself. Malcolm Lowry. **CP-LowrM**

To H.F. Brown. Robert Louis Stevenson. **CP-StevR**

To H.F. Brown. Robert Louis Stevenson. **CP-StevR**

To him after long anguish. Renaissance. Hayden Carruth. **CP-CarHS**

To Him That Was Crucified. Walt Whitman. **CP-WhitW**

To him the window broken in the church. Reconsidering the Madman. Richard Hugo. **CP-HugoR**

To him to whom Events and Omens. Emily Dickinson. **SP-DickE**

To Him Who bade the Heavens abide, yet cease not from their motion. The Supports. Rudyard Kipling. **CP-KiplR** *Fr.* Debits and Credits.

To him who ever thought with love of me. Gerard Manley Hopkins. **CP-HopkG**

To him who fought for liberty. The Secret of the Burning Stars. Pablo Antonio Cuadra, *tr. fr. Spanish by* Thomas Merton. **CP-MertT**

To him, who longs unto his CHRIST to go. Coming to Christ. Robert Herrick. **CP-HerrR**

To Himself. Catullus. *See* Carmen 8: "Break off / fallen Catullus."

To His Angrie God. Robert Herrick. **CP-HerrR**

To His Book[e] ("Have I not blest thee? Then go forth; nor fear"). Robert Herrick. **CP-HerrR**

To His Book[e] ("If hap it must, that I must see thee lye"). Robert Herrick. **CP-HerrR**

To His Book[e] ("Make haste away, and let one be"). Robert Herrick. **CP-HerrR**

To His Book ("Before the Press scarce one co'd see"). Robert Herrick. **CP-HerrR**

To His Booke ("Be bold my Booke, nor be abasht, or feare"). Robert Herrick. **CP-HerrR**

To His Booke ("Come thou not neere those men, who are like Bread"). Robert Herrick. **CP-HerrR**

To His Booke ("Goe thou forth my booke, though late"). Robert Herrick. **CP-HerrR**

To His Booke ("Like to a Bride, come forth my Book, at last"). Robert Herrick. **CP-HerrR**

To his Booke ("Take mine advise, and go not neere"). Robert Herrick. **CP-HerrR**

To His Booke ("Thou art a plant sprung up to wither never"). Robert Herrick. **CP-HerrR**

To His Booke ("While thou didst keep thy candor undefil'd"). Robert Herrick. **CP-HerrR**

To His Brother in Law Master John Wingfield. Robert Herrick. **CP-HerrR**

To His Brother Nicolas Herrick. Robert Herrick. **CP-HerrR**

To His Children in Darkness. James Dickey. **CP-DickJ**

To His Closet-Gods. Robert Herrick. **CP-HerrR**

To His Conscience. Robert Herrick. **CP-HerrR**

To His Coy Mistress. Andrew Marvell. **CP-MarvA**

To His Cynical Mistress. Thom Gunn. **CP-GunnT**

To His Deare Brother Colonel F.L. Richard Lovelace. **CP-LoveR**

To his deare Valentine, Mistresse Margaret Falconbrige. Robert Herrick. **CP-HerrR**

To His Deere God. Robert Herrick. **CP-HerrR**

To His Dying Brother, Master William Herrick. Robert Herrick. **CP-HerrR**

To His Ever-Loving God. Robert Herrick. **CP-HerrR**

To his Faithfull Friend, Master John Crofts, Cup-bearer to the King. Robert Herrick. **CP-HerrR**

To His False Mistress. Catullus. *See* Carmen 72: "There was a time, Lesbia, when."

To His False Mistress. Catullus. *See* Carmen 92: "Lesbia loads me night & day with her curses."

To His False Mistris. Robert Herrick. **CP-HerrR**

To His Father. John Milton. *See* To My Father.

To his Friend, Master J. Jincks. Robert Herrick. **CP-HerrR**

To His Friend, on the Untunable Times. Robert Herrick. **CP-HerrR**

To His Friend the Author upon His *Richard*. Ben Jonson. **CP-JonsB**

To His Friend to Avoid Contention of Words. Robert Herrick. **CP-HerrR**

To His Girles. Robert Herrick. **CP-HerrR**

To his Girles who Would Have Him Sportfull. Robert Herrick. **CP-HerrR**

To His Grace the Archbishop of Dublin. Jonathan Swift. **CP-SwifJ**

To His Heart, Bidding It Have No Fear. William Butler Yeats. **CP-YeatW**

To His Honour'd Friend, Sir Thomas Heale. Robert Herrick. **CP-HerrR**

To His Honoured and Ingenious Friend Col. Richard Lovelace, on His Lucasta. Thomas Rawlins. *Fr.* Commendatory Poems. **CP-LoveR**

To His Honoured and Most Ingenious Friend, Mr. Charles Cotton. Robert Herrick. **CP-HerrR**

To His Honoured Friend, M. John Weare, Councellour. Robert Herrick. **CP-HerrR**

To His Honoured Friend, Sir John Mynts. Robert Herrick. **CP-HerrR**

To His Honoured Kinsman, Sir Richard Stone. Robert Herrick. **CP-HerrR**

To His Honoured Kinsman Sir William Soame. Robert Herrick. **CP-HerrR**

To His Host, Who Has Asked Him To Stay Longer. James McAuley. **SP-McAuJ**

To his house the bodiless. Sculptor. Sylvia Plath. **CP-PlatS**

To His Household Gods. Robert Herrick. **CP-HerrR**

To His Jealous Mistress. Thomas Carew. **CP-CareT**

To His Kinsman, Master Thomas Herrick, Who Desired to Be in His Book. Robert Herrick. **CP-HerrR**

To His Kinsman, Sir Tho. Soame. Robert Herrick. **CP-HerrR**

To His Kinsman, Mrs. Penelope Wheeler. Robert Herrick. **CP-HerrR**

To His Kinswoman, Mistresse Susanna Herrick. Robert Herrick. **CP-HerrR**

To His Lady, Then Mrs Cary. Ben Jonson. **CP-JonsB**

To His Learned Friend M. Jo. Harmar, Phisitian to to Colledge of Westminster. Robert Herrick. **CP-HerrR**

To His Love ("Shall I compare thee to a summer's day?"). William Shakespeare. *See* Sonnet 18: "Shall I compare thee to a summer's day?"

To His Love ("When in the chronicle of wasted time"). William Shakespeare. *See* Sonnet 106: "When in the chronicle of wasted time."

To His Lovely Mistresses. Robert Herrick. **CP-HerrR**

To His Maid Prew. Robert Herrick. **CP-HerrR**

To His Mistress. Thomas Carew. **CP-CareT**

To His Mistress[e]. Robert Herrick. **CP-HerrR**

To His Mistress [or Mistris] Confined. James Shirley. **CP-CareT**

To His Mistress Desiring to Travel with Him as His Page. John Donne. *See* On His Mistress [or Mistris].

To His Mistress Going to Bed. John Donne. **BoLoP; FaBoBl; JCP; NoSic; OAEL-1; PoE; TEP; UnTE** *Fr.* Elegies. **CP-DonnJ**

(Elegie: Going to Bed.) **EnRePo; MePo; OxBM**

(Elegy XIX. To His Mistris Going to Bed.) **NoP**

(To His Mistris Going to Bed.) **CBLP; ErPo; OXAEP-1; SeCP**

To His Mistress Objecting to Him Neither Toying or Talking. Robert Herrick. **CP-HerrR**

To His Mistress Retiring in Affection. Thomas Carew. **CP-CareT**

To His Mistresses. Robert Herrick. **CP-HerrR**

To His Mistresses. Robert Herrick. **CP-HerrR**

To His Mistris Going to Bed. John Donne. *See* To His Mistress Going to Bed.

To His Much and Worthily Esteemed Friend the Author. Ben Jonson. **CP-JonsB**

To His Much Honoured Friend Mr. Richard Lovelace, on His Poems. Sir Benjamin Rudyerd. *Fr.* Commendatory Poems. **CP-LoveR**

To His Much Honoured the Lord Lepington upon His Translation of Malvezzi, His "Romulus" and "Tarquin." Sir John Suckling. **CP-SuckJ**

To His Muse ("Whither, mad maiden, wilt thou roame?"). Robert Herrick. **CP-HerrR**

To His Muse. Robert Herrick. **CP-HerrR**

To His Muse: ("Were I to give thee *Baptime*, I wo'd chuse"). Robert Herrick. **CP-HerrR**

To His Muse, Another to the Same. Robert Herrick. **CP-HerrR**

To His Nephew, to Be Prosperous in His Art of Painting. Robert Herrick. **CP-HerrR**

To His Noble Friend Capt. Dudley Lovelace, upon His Edition of His Brother's Poems. Symon Ognell. *Fr.* Elegies, 1660. **CP-LoveR**

To His Noble Friend Mr. Richard Lovelace upon His Poems. Andrew Marvell. *Fr.* Commendatory Poems. **CP-LoveR**

To His Noble Friend, Mr Richard Lovelace, upon His Poems. Andrew Marvell. **CP-MarvA**

To His Paternall Countrey. Robert Herrick. **CP-HerrR**

To His Peculiar Friend M. Jo: Wicks. Robert Herrick. **CP-HerrR**

To His Peculiar Friend Master Thomas Shapcott, Lawyer. Robert Herrick. **CP-HerrR**

To His Peculiar Friend Sir Edward Fish, Knight Baronet. Robert Herrick. **CP-HerrR**

To His Rival. Sir John Suckling. **CP-SuckJ**

To His Royal Highness the Prince of Wales. James Thomson. **CP-ThomJ**

To His Savior [*or* Saviour]. The New Years [*or* yeers] Gift. Robert Herrick. **CP-HerrR**

To His Saviour. Robert Herrick. **CP-HerrR**

To His Saviour, a Child; a Present, by a Child. Robert Herrick. **CP-HerrR**

To His Saviours Sepulcher: His Devotion. Robert Herrick. **CP-HerrR**

To His Servant. Horace. *See* 1.38: Simplicity.

To his simplicity. Emily Dickinson. **CP-DickE**

To his Singular Friend, William Lithgow. *Unknown, sometimes at. to* Sir Walter Ralegh. **CP-RaleW**

To His Sister in Law, M. Susanna Herrick. Robert Herrick. **CP-HerrR**

To His Skeleton. Richard Wilbur. **CP-WilbR**

To his sweet Lute *Apollo* sung the motions of the Spheares. Thomas Campion. **CP-CampT**

To His Sweet Saviour. Robert Herrick. **CP-HerrR**

To His Tomb-Maker. Robert Herrick. **CP-HerrR**

To His Valentine, on S. Valentines Day. Robert Herrick. **CP-HerrR**

To His Verses. Robert Herrick. **CP-HerrR**

To His Watch. Gerard Manley Hopkins. **CP-HopkG**

To His Wife. Geoffrey Hill. *Fr.* The Songbook of Sebastian Arrurruz. **CP-HillG**

To His Worthy Friend Doctor Witty upon His Translation of the "Popular Errors", *see also* Dignissimo Suo Amico Doctori Witty. Andrew Marvell. **CP-MarvA**

To His Worthy Friend, M. Arthur Bartly. Robert Herrick. **CP-HerrR**

To his Worthy Friend M. John Hall, Student of Grayes-Inne. Robert Herrick. **CP-HerrR**

To Worthy Friend, M. Tho. Falconbirge. Robert Herrick. **CP-HerrR**

To His Worthy Kinsmen, Mr. Stephen Soame. Robert Herrick. **CP-HerrR**

To hold a damaged sparrow. With No Experience in Such Matters. Stephen Dunn. **SP-DunnS**

To hold secure the province of Pure Art. Edna St. Vincent Millay. **CP-MillE**

To Homer. John Keats. **CP-KeatJ**

To Hook the Reader, You, John Murray. Byron. **CP-Byron**

To Hope. John Keats. **CP-KeatJ**

To Hope. Charlotte Smith. **CP-SmitC**

To Hornet. Ben Jonson. **CP-JonsB**

To house the Hag, you must doe this. Another to Bring in the Witch. Robert Herrick. **CP-HerrR**

To humble yourself before a radio on a Sunday. Ode (To Joseph Lesueur) on the Arrow That Flieth by Day. Frank O'Hara. **SP-OharF**

To Hunt. William Blake. **CP-BlakW**

To hurt the Negro and avoid the Jew. University. Karl Shapiro. **SP-ShapK**

To Ianthe. Byron. *Fr.* Childe Harold's Pilgrimage. **CP-Byron**

(Dedication: To Ianthe.) **FaBoEn; OBNC**

To Ianthe. Percy Bysshe Shelley. **CP-ShelP**

To I.F. William Wordsworth. **CP-WorW2**

To Imagination. Emily Brontë. *See* When weary with the long day's care.

To imagine it, to believe it, bring to mind all. Placet Experiri. Mona Van Duyn. **SP-VanDM**

To Impress the Girl Next Door. Ron Koertge. **SP-KoerR**

To indicate is to / turn off   in a world. Data. Joseph Ceravolo. **SP-CeraJ**

To Inez Milholland. Edna St. Vincent Millay. **CP-MillE**

To Inigo, Marquess Would Be, a Corollary. Ben Jonson. **CP-JonsB**

To insist that what is true is good, no matter, no matter. George Oppen. **APSN** *Fr.* Route. **CP-OppeG**

To interrupt His Yellow Plan. Emily Dickinson. **CP-DickE**

To Ireland. Percy Bysshe Shelley. **CP-ShelP**

To Ireland in the Coming Times. William Butler Yeats. **CP-YeatW**

To Isherwood Dying. Thom Gunn. **CP-GunnT**

To Ishtar. Richard Wilbur. **CP-WilbR**

To Ivor Gurney. Charles Tomlinson. **CP-TomlC**

To J. H. Reynolds, Esq. John Keats. **CP-KeatJ**

Epistle to John Hamilton Reynolds. **OBNC**

"O that our dreamings all, of sleep or wake." **OAEL-2**

To J. P. John Greenleaf Whittier. **CP-WhitJ**

To J. Q. Paul Laurence Dunbar. **CP-DunbP**

To J. S. [James Spedding]. Tennyson. **CP-TennA**

To J. S****. Robert Burns. *See* Dear Smith [*or* S****], the sleest, paukie thief.

To J. W. Ralph Waldo Emerson. **CP-EmerR**

To James Boswell in London. Erica Jong. **SP-JongE**

To James Rice. John Keats. **CP-KeatJ**

To James T. Fields. John Greenleaf Whittier. **CP-WhitJ**

To James Whitcomb Riley. Rudyard Kipling. **CP-KiplR**

To Jane Addams at the Hague. Nicholas Vachel Lindsay. **CP-LindV**

Speak Now for Peace.

Tolstoi is Plowing Yet.

To Jane; and in Imitation of Coleridge. Frank O'Hara. **SP-OharF**

To Jane: The Invitation. Percy Bysshe Shelley. *See* Best and brightest, come away!

To Jane: The Keen Stars Were Twinkling. Percy Bysshe Shelley. *See* The Keen stars were twinkling.

To Jane: The Recollection. Percy Bysshe Shelley. **CP-ShelP**

"We wandered to the pine forest." **CH**

To Janus. Jonathan Swift. **CP-SwifJ**

To Jealousie. Robert Herrick. **CP-HerrR**

To Jenny came a gentle youth. The Dance at the Phoenix. Thomas Hardy. **CP-HardT**

To Jesus on His Birthday. Edna St. Vincent Millay. **CP-MillE**

To Jesus, the Crown of my Hope. Longing To Be with Christ. William Cowper. **CP-CowpW**

To J.M. George Meredith. **CP-MerG1**

To Joanna. William Wordsworth. **CP-WorW1**

To John C. Frémont. John Greenleaf Whittier. **CP-WhitJ**

To John Donne ("Donne, the delight of Phoebus, and each Muse"). Ben Jonson. **CP-JonsB**

To John Donne ("Who shall doubt, Donne, where I a poet be"). Ben Jonson. **CP-JonsB**

To John Flaxman, 12 September 1800. William Blake. **CP-BlakW**

To John Johnson. William Cowper. **CP-CowpW**

To John Keats, Poet, at Springtime. Countee Cullen. **CP-CullC**

To John Kennedy. Robert Burns. **CP-BurnR**

To John Milton. *Unknown. Fr.* Complimentary Pieces to Milton. **CP-CowpW**

To John Rouse. John Milton, *tr. fr. Latin by* John T. Shawcross. **CP-MiltJ**

("My two-fold book! single in show.") **CP-CowpW**, *tr. by* William Cowper;

(Ode to Rouse.) **CP-CowpW**, *tr. by* William Cowper;

To John Syme. Robert Burns. **CP-BurnR**

"No more of your guests, be they titled or not."

"O had the malt thy strength of mind."

To John's bro, the sheriff, we lay a kind word in passing. Canto 64. Ezra Pound. *Fr.* Cantos. **CP-PoCan**

To join [*or* joyn] with them, who here confer. His Offering, with the Rest, at the Sepulcher. Robert Herrick. **CP-HerrR**

To Jos: Lo: Bishop of Exeter. Robert Herrick. **CP-HerrR**

To Juan at the Winter Solstice. Robert Ranke Graves. **CP-GravR**

To judge by what they wore on weekdays. Missing Persons. Miller Williams. **SP-WillM**

To Judith Asleep. John Ciardi. **SP-CiarJ**

To Judith, Taking Leave. Adrienne Rich. **CP-RicAE; SP-RicA2**

To Julia ("Offer thy gift"). Robert Herrick. **CP-HerrR**

To Julia ("Help me, Julia, for to pray"). Robert Herrick. **CP-HerrR**

To Julia ("Holy waters hither bring"). Robert Herrick. **CP-HerrR**

To Julia ("I am zeellesse, prethee pray"). Robert Herrick. **CP-HerrR**

To Julia ("Julia, when thy Herrick dies"). Robert Herrick. **CP-HerrR**

To Julia ("Permit me, Julia, now to goe away"). Robert Herrick. **CP-HerrR**

To Julia ("Saints-bell calls; and *Julia*, I must read, The"). Robert Herrick. **CP-HerrR**

To Julia: ("How rich and pleasing thou, my Julia, art"). Robert Herrick. **CP-HerrR**

To Julia, in Her Dawn, or Day-breake. Robert Herrick. **CP-HerrR**

To Julia in the Temple. Robert Herrick. **CP-HerrR**

To Julia, the Flaminica Dialis, or Queen-Priest. Robert Herrick. **CP-HerrR**

To justify God's ways to man. Just You Wait! Donald Davie. **CP-DavDo**

To Juvencius. Catullus. *See* Carmen 48: "Iuventius, / were I allowed."

To K. M. Walter de la Mare. *See* We sat and talked. It was June, and the summer light.

To Kalakaua. Robert Louis Stevenson. **CP-StevR**

To K. de M. Robert Louis Stevenson. **CP-StevR**

To Kathleen. Edna St. Vincent Millay. **CP-MillE**

To Keep a True Lent. Robert Herrick. **CP-HerrR**

To keep an eye on fables of the moon. Fables of the Moon. Richard Eberhart. **CP-EberR**

To Keep Each Other Warm. Jenny Joseph. **SP-JoseJ**

To keep the lamp alive. Dependance. William Cowper. *Fr.* Olney Hymns. **CP-CowpW**

To keep the one you want. Lovers. Stephen Dunn. **SP-DunnS** *Fr.* Sympathetic Magic.

To keep the weakness secret. To deny it and break through. Muriel Rukeyser. **CP-RukeM**

To keep themselves young—Is that why people have children? Louis MacNeice. *Fr.* The Stygian Banks. **CP-MacNL**

To Kelly Miller, Jr. Paul Laurence Dunbar. **CP-DunbP**

To Kenya Tribesmen, the Turkana. Richard Eberhart. **CP-EberR**

To Kill in War Is Not Murder. Robinson Jeffers. **CP-JefR3**

To K[ing] Charles and Q[ueen] Mary, for the Loss of Their First-Born. An Epigram Consolatory. 1629. Ben Jonson. **CP-JonsB**

To King James ("How, best of kings, dost thou a scepter bear[e]!"). Ben Jonson. **CP-JonsB**

To King James ("That we the loss might know, and thou our love"). Ben Jonson. **CP-JonsB**

To King James ("Who would not be thy subject, James, t'obey"). Ben Jonson. **CP-JonsB**

To kneel before some saintly shrine. A Summer Pilgrimage. John Greenleaf Whittier. **CP-WhitJ**

To kneeling Worshippers no earthly floor. Forms of Prayer at Sea. William Wordsworth. *Fr.* Ecclesiastical Sonnets. **CP-WorW2**

To know expanse I read thin books. Keen to Leaky Flowers. Richard Hugo. **CP-HugoR**

To Know in Reverie the Only Phenomenology of the Absolute. Hayden Carruth. **CP-CarHS**

To know just how He suffered—would be dear. Emily Dickinson. **CP-DickE**

To know our destiny is to know the horror. Bweteen Hyssop and Axe. Robert Ranke Graves. **CP-GravR**

To Know Silence Perfectly. Carl Sandburg. **CP-SandC**

To know that there is shelter. Emily Dickinson. **SP-DickE**

To Know the Dark. Wendell Berry. **CP-BerrW**

To know the histories / to know good from evil. Canto 89. Ezra Pound. *Fr.* Cantos. **CP-PoCan**

To know the inhabiting reasons. For the Rebuilding of a House. Wendell Berry. **CP-BerrW**

To know, to esteem, to love,—and then to part. To Two Sisters. Samuel Taylor Coleridge. **CP-ColeS**

To know you better as you flee. Emily Dickinson. **SP-DickE**

To Kosciusko. John Keats. **CP-KeatJ**

To L. Manlius Torquatus. Horace. *See* 4.7: "Snow dissolvd no more is seen, The" ("Diffugere nives").

To Lady Austen. William Cowper. **CP-CowpW**

To Lady Beaumont. William Wordsworth. **CP-WorW1**

To Lady Firebrace. Samuel Johnson. **CP-JohnS**

To Lady Jane. Nicholas Vachel Lindsay. **CP-LindV**

To Lalla, Reading My Verses Topsy-Turvy. Christina Georgina Rossetti. **CP-RosC3**

To Landrum Guy, Beginning to Write at Sixty. James Dickey. **CP-DickJ**

To Larr [or Lar]. Robert Herrick. **CP-HerrR**

To Laurels. Robert Herrick. **CP-HerrR**

To lay the logarithmic spiral on. Figures of Thought. Howard Nemerov. **CP-NemeH**

To lay the soul that loves him low. God Hides His People. Jeanne Marie Bouvier de la Motte-Guyon, *tr. fr. French by* William Cowper. **CP-CowpW**

To lead a better life. Here, There and Everywhere. The Beatles. **CP-Beatl**

To learn the Transport by the Pain. Emily Dickinson. **CP-DickE**

To learn those powers, I surrendered. James McAuley. **SP-McAuJ** *Fr.* Cheiron.

To leave the earth was my wish, and no will stayed my rising. A Temple. Kenneth Patchen. **CP-PatcK**

To Leigh Hunt, Esq. John Keats. **CP-KeatJ**

To Leonora Singing at Rome. John Milton. *See* To the Same ["Another Leonora captured the poet Torquato"].

To Leonora Singing in Rome. John Milton, *tr. fr. Latin by* John T. Shawcross. **CP-MiltJ**

To Lesbia. Byron. **CP-Byron**

To Lesbia. Catullus. *See* Carmen 5: "Lesbia / live with me."

To Lesbia. Catullus. *See* Carmen 7: "Curious to learn / how may kiss- / es of your lips."

To Lesbia. Catullus. *See* Carmen 85: "I hate and I love. And if you ask me how."

To Let Go Or to Hold on—? David Herbert Lawrence. **CP-LawrD**

To Lettice, My Sister, *sl. diff. vers.* David Herbert Lawrence. *See* Brother and Sister.

To Li Po. Tu Fu, *tr. fr. Chinese by* William Carlos Williams *with* David Rafael Wang. **CP-WilW2**

To Liberty. Hart Crane. **CP-CranH**

To lie far off, in bed with a foul cough. A Shift of Scene. Robert Ranke Graves. **CP-GravR**

To Life. Thomas Hardy. **CP-HardT**

To Like, to Love. Anne Sexton. **CP-SextA**

To Lindsay. Allen Ginsberg. **CP-GinsA**

To Listen. Charles Kenneth Williams. **SP-WillC**

To Live Freely. Robert Herrick. **CP-HerrR**

To live illusionless, in the abandoned mine. Double Monologue. Adrienne Rich. **CP-RicAE**

To live lasts always, but to love. Emily Dickinson. **SP-DickE**

To Live Merrily, and To Trust to Good Verses. Robert Herrick. **CP-HerrR**

To live on charm, one must be courteous. She Bitches About Boys. Marilyn Hacker. **SP-HackM**

To live, to lie awake. Incipience. Adrienne Rich. **SP-RicA2**

To Lizbie Browne. Thomas Hardy. **CP-HardT**

To lodge your harvest in the lion's mouth. The Garden of Disorder. Charles Henri Ford. **SP-FordC**

To Londoners. Donald Davie. **CP-DavDo**

To loose the button, is no lesse. Laxare Fibulam. Robert Herrick. **CP-HerrR**

To loosen with all ten fingers held wide and limber. Moss-Gathering. Theodore Roethke. **CP-RoetT**

To Lord Byron. John Keats. **CP-KeatJ**

To Lord Harley, since Earl of Oxford, on His Marriage. Jonathan Swift. **CP-SwifJ**

To Lord Palmerston. George Meredith. **CP-MerG2**

To Lord Thurlow. Byron. **CP-Byron**

To lose one's faith—surpass. Emily Dickinson. **CP-DickE**

To Lose the Earth. Anne Sexton. **CP-SextA**

To lose thee—sweeter than to gain. Emily Dickinson. **CP-DickE**

To Louisa in the Lane. Thomas Hardy. **CP-HardT**

To Louise. Paul Laurence Dunbar. **CP-DunbP**

To Love. Robert Herrick. **CP-HerrR**

To love a man wholly. Warning. Alice Walker. **CP-WalkA**

To Love and to Remember. Christina Georgina Rossetti. **Son** *Fr.* Later Life: A Double Sonnet of Sonnets. **CP-RosC2**

To love love and not its meaning. The Rape of the Swan. Archibald MacLeish. **CP-MacLA**

To love, one must slay. Hilda Doolittle. **CP-DoolH** *Fr.* Electra-Orestes.

To love one woman, or to sit. Woman and Tree. Robert Ranke Graves. **CP-GravR**

To love or pity is easy, if pity, if love. Blessing. John Hewitt. **CP-HewiJ**

To love thee Year by Year. Emily Dickinson. **CP-DickE**

To love you truly. Song: To Become Each Other. Robert Ranke Graves. **CP-GravR**

To Lu Chi. Howard Nemerov. **CP-NemeH**

To Lucasta ("I laugh and sing, but cannot tell"). Richard Lovelace. **CP-LoveR**

To Lucasta ("Like to the sentinel [*or* Sent'nel] stars, I watch all night"). Richard Lovelace. **CP-LoveR**

To Lucasta, About That War. John Ciardi. **SP-CiarJ**

To Lucasta, from Prison. Richard Lovelace. **CP-LoveR**

To Lucasta. Ode Lyrick. Richard Lovelace. **CP-LoveR**

To Lucasta, [on] Going beyond the Seas. Richard Lovelace. **CP-LoveR**

To Lucasta, [on] Going to the War[re]s. Richard Lovelace. **CP-LoveR**

To Lucca Giordano. William Wordsworth. **CP-WorW2**

To Lucia at Birth. Robert Ranke Graves. **CP-GravR**

To Lucy, Countess of Bedford. Ben Jonson. **CP-JonsB**

To Lucy, Countess[e] of Bedford, with Mr. Donnes Satire's [*or* Satyres]. Ben Jonson. **CP-JonsB**

To Lucy Larcom. John Greenleaf Whittier. **CP-WhitJ**

To Lyce, an Elderly Lady. Samuel Johnson. **CP-JohnS**

To Lydia Maria Child. John Greenleaf Whittier. **CP-WhitJ**

To M————. Byron. **CP-Byron**

To M. A. B. "Lewis Carroll." **CP-CarrL**

To M. H. William Wordsworth. **CP-WorW1**

To M. L. S——. Edgar Allan Poe. **CP-PoeEd**

To Madame du Châtelet. Voltaire, *tr. fr.* French by Richard Wilbur. **CP-WilbR**

To Madame Garschine. Robert Louis Stevenson. **CP-StevR**

To make a final conquest of all me. The Fair Singer. Andrew Marvell. **CP-MarvA**

To make a headway against the tide. The Voyage. Richard Eberhart. **CP-EberR**

To make a prairie it takes a clover and one bee. Emily Dickinson. **CP-DickE**

To make an end of all this strife. Sir Thomas Wyatt. **CP-WyatT**

To make even Heaven more heavenly. Emily Dickinson. **SP-DickE**

To make it glad with a goodly crop. An Answer. Christina Georgina Rossetti. **CP-RosC3**

To make One's Toilette—after Death. Emily Dickinson. **CP-DickE**

To make peace (borso / with the others,—or not too. The Cantos. Robert Creeley. **CP-CreeR**

To make Routine a Stimulus. Emily Dickinson. **CP-DickE**

To make the deerskin shirt for her husband. Abenaki Poem. Frederick Morgan. **SP-MorgF**

To make the doubt clear, that no woman's true. The Expostulation. John Donne. *Fr.* Elegies. **CP-DonnJ**

To make them moved, you should start from lightning. Dance of Words. Robert Ranke Graves. **CP-GravR**

To Manso. John Milton. *See* Manso.

To Manuel Altolaguirre. Stephen Spender. **CP-SpenS**

To many men strange fates are given. From the Greek. Stevie Smith. **CP-SmitS**

To Marcus. Robert Louis Stevenson. **CP-StevR**

To Marcus T. Cicero. Catullus. *See* Carmen 49: "Silver-tongued among the sons of Rome."

To Marguerite—Continued. Matthew Arnold. **SP-ArnoM** *Fr.* Switzerland.

To Maria. Robert Burns. **CP-BurnR**

To Maria Gisborne in England, from Italy. Percy Bysshe Shelley. **NOBE** *Fr.* Letter to Maria Gisborne. **CP-ShelP**

To Marina. Kenneth Koch. **SP-KochK**

To Marion. Byron. **CP-Byron**

To Mark Anthony in Heaven. William Carlos Williams. **CP-WilW1**

To Market. Charles Kenneth Williams. **CP-WillC**

To Mary————. Percy Bysshe Shelley. **CP-ShelP**

To Mary. William Cowper. **CP-CowpW**

To Mary. Louis MacNeice. **CP-MacNL**

To Mary, *Dedication to* The Revolt of Islam. Percy Bysshe Shelley. **EnRP** *Fr.* The Revolt of Islam. **CP-ShelP**

To Mary Boyle. Tennyson. **CP-TennA**

To Mary Church Terrell. Paul Laurence Dunbar. **CP-DunbP**

To Mary, Lady Wroth ("How well, fair crown of your fair sex, might he"). Ben Jonson. **CP-JonsB**

To Mary, Lady Wroth ("Madam, had all antiquity been lost"). Ben Jonson. **CP-JonsB**

To Mary on Receiving Her Picture. Byron. **CP-Byron**

To Mary Pridham. Samuel Taylor Coleridge. **CP-ColeS**

To Mary Rossetti. Christina Georgina Rossetti. **CP-RosC3**

To Mary Russell Mitford. Elizabeth Barrett Browning. **CP-BroEB**

To Mary Shelley ("My dearest Mary, wherefore hast thou gone"). Percy Bysshe Shelley. **CP-ShelP**

To Mary Shelley ("World is dreary, The / And I'm weary"). Percy Bysshe Shelley. **CP-ShelP**

To Mary, Who Died in This Opinion. Percy Bysshe Shelley. **CP-ShelP**

To Mary Wollstonecraft Godwin. Percy Bysshe Shelley. **CP-ShelP**

To Marygolds. Robert Herrick. **CP-HerrR**

To Massachusetts. John Greenleaf Whittier. **CP-WhitJ**

To Master Andrew Lang. Robert Louis Stevenson. **CP-StevR**

To M. Denham, on His Prospective Poem. Robert Herrick. **CP-HerrR**

To M. Henry Lawes, the Excellent Composer[,] of his Lyrics. Robert Herrick. **CP-HerrR**

To Master John Burges. Ben Jonson. **CP-JonsB**

To M. Kellam. Robert Herrick. **CP-HerrR**

To M. Laurence Swetnaham. Robert Herrick. **CP-HerrR**

To M. Leonard Willan His Peculiar Friend. Robert Herrick. **CP-HerrR**

To Master W. Montague. Thomas Carew. **CP-CareT**

To Matilda Betham from a Stranger. Samuel Taylor Coleridge. **CP-ColeS**

To May. William Wordsworth. **CP-WorW2**

To me, fair[e] Friend, you never can be old. Sonnet 104. William Shakespeare. **EIL; EnRePo; FPL; FaBoEn; GBL; GTBS; GTBS-6; GTBS-P; HeIP; NoSic; OBEV; OBSC; OXAEP-1; PeHV; Prf; SCGP** *Fr.* Sonnets. **CP-ShaWS**

To me, like hauntings of a vagrant breath. To E. H. K. Paul Laurence Dunbar. **CP-DunbP**

To me my Julia lately sent. The Pomander Bracelet. Robert Herrick. **CP-HerrR**

To me, one silly task is like another. Cassandra. Louise Bogan. **CP-BogaL**

To me the groaning of world-worshippers. Edwin Arlington Robinson. *Fr.* Octaves. **CP-RobiE**

To me this world's a dreary blank. Song. Percy Bysshe Shelley. *Fr.* Original Poetry by Victor and Cazire. **CP-ShelP**

To Meadows [*or* Meddowes]. Robert Herrick. **CP-HerrR**

To Meet, or Otherwise. Thomas Hardy. **CP-HardT**

To Melancholy. Written on the Banks of the Arun, October 1785. Charlotte Smith. **CP-SmitC**

To Melpomene. William Wordsworth. **CP-WorW1**

To Memory. George Oppen. **CP-OppeG**

To mend each tattered Faith. Emily Dickinson. **CP-DickE**

To Meng Hao-Jan. Li Po, *tr. fr.* Chinese by William Carlos Williams *with* David Rafael Wang. **CP-WilW2**

To Mercy, Pity, Peace, and Love. Divine Image, The. William Blake. **BoTP; CoGr; EBCP; EnRP; FHYEP; FaBoEn; HoFi; LAuP; LO; MeMBP; NAEL-2; NOBE; NOBRP; NOEC; NoP; OAEL-2; OAEP; OBEC; OBNC; OxBoCh; PFP; PPP; PeECV; PoE; PoEL-4; TEP; TRV; WGRP** *Fr.* Songs of Innocence. **CP-BlakW**

To merge his shadow with the moonlit earth. The Snowy Owl. Robert Pack. **SP-PackR**

To Mesdames Zassetsky and Garschine. Robert Louis Stevenson. **CP-StevR**

To Mexico! To Mexico! Down the dovegray highway, past Atomic City. Ready to Roll. Allen Ginsberg. **CP-GinsA**

To Military Progress. Marianne Craig Moore. **CP-MoorM**

To Mime. Ben Jonson. **CP-JonsB**

To Minnie. Robert Louis Stevenson. **CP-StevR**

To Minnie (With a Hand-Glass). Robert Louis Stevenson. **CP-StevR**

To Miss —: On Her Giving the Author a Gold and Silk Net-work Purse. Samuel Johnson. **CP-JohnS**

To Miss —: On Her Playing upon the Harpsichord. Samuel Johnson. **CP-JohnS**

To Miss Ainslie, in Church. Robert Burns. *See* Fair maid, you need not take the hint.

To Miss C—on Being Desired To Attempt Writing a Comedy. Charlotte Smith. **CP-SmitC**

To Miss Cornish. Robert Louis Stevenson. **CP-StevR**

To Miss Creuzé. William Cowper. **CP-CowpW**

To Miss C********, a Very Young Lady. Robert Burns. **CP-BurnR**

To Miss Ferrier. Robert Burns. **CP-BurnR**

To Miss Graham of Fintray. Robert Burns. **CP-BurnR**

To Miss — — [Harriet Grove] from Miss — — [Elizabeth Shelley]. Percy Bysshe Shelley. *Fr.* Original Poetry by Victor and Cazire. **CP-ShelP**

To Miss Hickman Playing on the Spinet. Samuel Johnson. **CP-JohnS**

To Miss Isabella Macleod. Robert Burns. **CP-BurnR**

To Miss L——. Robert Burns. **CP-BurnR**

To Miss Macartney. William Cowper. **CP-CowpW**

To Miss Mary Britton. Paul Laurence Dunbar. **CP-DunbP**

To Miss Rawlinson. Robert Louis Stevenson. **CP-StevR**

To Miss Unger. Robert Browning. **CP-BroR2**

To Mr. B. B. John Donne. **CP-DonnJ**

To Mr Ben Jonson in His Journey, by Mr Craven. Ben Jonson. **CP-JonsB**

To Mr. C.B. John Donne. **CP-DonnJ**

To Mr. Congreve. Jonathan Swift. **CP-SwifJ**

To Mr. Davenant for Absence. Sir John Suckling. *See* Wonder not if I stay not here.

To Mr. Delany. Jonathan Swift. **CP-SwifJ**

To Mr E. G. John Donne. **CP-DonnJ**

To Mr. E——— on His Translation of and Commentaries on Martial. Robert Burns. *See* O tuou whom Poetry [*or* Poesy] abhors.

To Mr Gavin Hamilton, Mauchline. Robert Burns. **CP-BurnR**

To Mr. Gay. Jonathan Swift. **CP-SwifJ**

To Mr. Gay, Congratulating Pope on Finishing His House and Gardens. Alexander Pope. **CP-PopeA**

To Mr. Graham of Fintry, On Being Appointed to My Excise Division. Robert Burns. **CP-BurnR**

To Mr. Harley's Surgeon. Jonathan Swift. **CP-SwifJ**

To Mr. Hayley, on Receiving Some Elegant Lines from Him. Charlotte Smith. **CP-SmitC**

To Mr I. L. ("Blessed [or Blesst] are your north parts, for all this long time"). John Donne. **CP-DonnJ**

To Mr I. L. ("Of that short roll of friends writ in my heart"). John Donne. **CP-DonnJ**

To Mr John Burges. Ben Jonson. **CP-JonsB**

To Mr. John Kennedy. Robert Burns. **CP-BurnR**

To Mr. John Milton of London. *Unknown. Fr.* Complimentary Pieces to Milton. **CP-CowpW**

To Mr. John Moore, Author of the Celebrated Worm-Powder. Alexander Pope. **CP-PopeA**

To Mr. John Taylor. Robert Burns. *See* With Pegasus upon a day.

To Mr Jonson upon these Verses. Ben Jonson. **CP-JonsB**

To Mr Joshua Sylvester. Ben Jonson. **CP-JonsB**

To Mr. McMurdo, with a Pound of Lundiefoot Snuff. Robert Burns. **CP-BurnR**

To Mr. Newton. William Cowper. **CP-CowpW**

To Mr. Newton [on His Return from Ramsgate]. William Cowper. **CP-CowpW**

To Mr. Pye. Samuel Taylor Coleridge. **CP-ColeS**

To Mr. R. W. ("If, as mine is, thy life a slumber be"). John Donne. **CP-DonnJ**

To Mr. R. W. ("Kindly I envy thy song's [or songs] perfection"). John Donne. **CP-DonnJ**

To Mr. R. W. ("Muse not that by thy mind thy body is led"). John Donne. **CP-DonnJ**

To Mr. R. W. ("Zealously my Muse doth salute all thee"). John Donne. **CP-DonnJ**

To Mr. Roland Woodward ("Like one who in [or who'in] her third widowhood [or widdowhood] doth profess[e]"). John Donne. **CP-DonnJ**

To Mr S. B. John Donne. **CP-DonnJ**

To Mr. S. McKenzie. Robert Burns. **CP-BurnR**

To Mr. Sheridan, upon His Verse, Written in Circles. Jonathan Swift. **CP-SwifJ**

To Mr. T. W. ("All hail, sweet poet, more full of more strong fire"). John Donne. **CP-DonnJ**

To Mr. T. W. ("At once, from hence, my lines and I depart"). John Donne. **CP-DonnJ**

To Mr. T. W. ("Haste thee harsh verse as fast as thy lame measure"). John Donne. **CP-DonnJ**

To Mr. T. W. ("Pregnant again with th' old twins hope, and fear"). John Donne. **CP-DonnJ**

To Mr. Thomas Southern, on His Birth-Day, 1742. Alexander Pope. **CP-PopeA**

To Mr. Thomson. Aaron Hill. **CP-ThomJ**

To Mr. Thomson. Douglas Malloch. **CP-ThomJ**

To Mr. Thomson, on his Blooming Winter. *Unknown, signed* Mira. **CP-ThomJ**

To Mr. Tilman after He Had Taken Orders. John Donne. **CP-DonnJ**

To Mrs. ****. Charlotte Smith. **CP-SmitC**

To Mrs Alice Sutcliffe, on Her Divine *Meditations*. Ben Jonson. **CP-JonsB**

To Mrs Ann Flaxman. William Blake. **CP-BlakW**

To Mrs Butts. William Blake. **CP-BlakW**

To Mrs. C———. Robert Burns. **CP-BurnR**

To Mrs. Dacosta. Christopher Smart. **SP-SmarC**

To Mrs Flaxman, 14 September 1800. William Blake. **CP-BlakW**

To Mrs. G. Charlotte Smith. **CP-SmitC**

To Mrs. Houghton of Bormount. Jonathan Swift. **CP-SwifJ**

To Mistress Katherine Bradshaw, the Lovely, That Crowned Him with Laurel. Robert Herrick. **CP-HerrR**

To Mistress Katherine Neville, on Her Green Sickness. Thomas Carew. **CP-CareT**

To Mrs. King. William Cowper. **CP-CowpW**

To Mrs. M. B. on Her Birth-Day. Alexander Pope. **CP-PopeA**

To Mrs. M. H. John Donne. **CP-DonnJ**

To [Mrs. M. R.] Councel Concerning Her Choise. Richard Crashaw. *See* Dear, heavn-designing [or heavn-designed] soul!

To Mrs. MacMarland. Robert Louis Stevenson. **CP-StevR**

To Mrs. Magdalen Herbert: of St. Mary Magdalen. John Donne. **CP-DonnJ**

To Mrs. Newton. William Cowper. **CP-CowpW**

To Mrs Phillip Sidney. Ben Jonson. **CP-JonsB**

To Mrs. Reynolds's Cat. John Keats. *See* Cat! who hast passed [or pass'd] thy grand climacteric.

To Mrs Thrale [on Her Thirty-fifth Birthday]. Samuel Johnson. **CP-JohnS**

To Mrs. Throckmorton. William Cowper. **CP-CowpW**

To Mrs. Will H. Low. Robert Louis Stevenson. **CP-StevR**

To Mistresse Amie Potter. Robert Herrick. **CP-HerrR**

To Mistresse Dorothy Parsons. Robert Herrick. **CP-HerrR**

To Mistresse Mary Willand. Robert Herrick. **CP-HerrR**

To Mitzi Mayfair. A Toast to Floyd Collins. Miller Williams. **SP-WillM**

To Momus. Robert Herrick. **CP-HerrR**

To moralize the state, they drag out a man. The Morning's News. Wendell Berry. **CP-BerrW**

To Morning. William Blake. **CP-BlakW**

To-morrow. Macedonius. *Fr.* Variations of Greek Themes. **CP-RobiE**

To-Morrow. Percy Bysshe Shelley. **CP-ShelP**

To-morrow I am going. George Meredith. **CP-MerG2**

To-morrow? Then your one word left is always now the same. To-morrow. Macedonius. *Fr.* Variations of Greek Themes. **CP-RobiE**

To-morrow we're starting for Florence. Arthur Hugh Clough. **EBVVPR,** *canto* 2, 15; *Fr.* Amours de Voyage. **SP-ClouA**

To mortall men great loads alloted be. Poverty the Greatest Pack. Robert Herrick. **CP-HerrR**

To Mother Maryanne. Robert Louis Stevenson. **CP-StevR**

To Motorists, *parody of* Robert Herrick. Rudyard Kipling. **CP-KiplR** *Fr.* The Muse among the Motors.

To mournful ditties, Clio, change thy note. A Quibbling Elegy on the Worshipful Judge Boat. Jonathan Swift. **CP-SwifJ**

To move time back to where it was before I blundered. February 10, One Year Too Late. Charles Olson. **CP-OlsoC**

To M.S.G. ("When I dream that you love me, you'll surely forgive"). Byron. **CP-Byron**

To M.S.G. ("Whene'er I view those lips of thine"). Byron. **CP-Byron**

To multiply the Harbors. Emily Dickinson. **SP-DickE**

To Music. Robert Herrick. **CP-HerrR**

To Music: A Song. Robert Herrick. **CP-HerrR**

To Music Bent Is My Retired Mind. Thomas Campion. **CP-CampT** ("To Musicke bent is my retyred minde.") **CP-CampT**

To Music, to Becalm a Sweet-sick Youth. Robert Herrick. **CP-HerrR**

To Music, to Becalm His Fever. Robert Herrick. **CP-HerrR** "Charm me asleep, and melt me so." **UnS**

To Musicke bent is my retyred minde. Thomas Campion. *See* To Music Bent Is My Retired Mind.

To My Baby Paul. Louis Zukofsky. **CP-ZukLS**

To my best Brother on his Poems, called Lucasta. Francis Lovelace. *Fr.* Commendatory Poems. **CP-LoveR**

To My Book. Ben Jonson. **CP-JonsB**

To My Bookseller. Ben Jonson. **CP-JonsB**

To My Brother George. John Keats. **CP-KeatJ**

To My Brother George. John Keats. **CP-KeatJ**

To My Brother: Killed: Hammont Wood: October, 1918. Louise Bogan. **CP-BogaL**

To My Brother Poet, Seeking Peace. Erica Jong. **SP-JongE**

To My Brothers. John Keats. **CP-KeatJ**

To My Child-Friend. "Lewis Carroll." **CP-CarrL**

To My Children, Fearing for Them. Wendell Berry. **CP-BerrW**

To My Chosen Friend the Learnèd Translator of Lucan, Thomas May, Esquire. Ben Jonson. **CP-JonsB**

To My Contemporaries. Edwin Rolfe. **CP-RolfE**

To My Cousin (C.R.) Marrying My Lady (A.) Thomas Carew. **CP-CareT**

To My Daughter. Gary Gildner. **SP-GildG**

To My Daughter. Stephen Spender. **CP-SpenS**

To My Daughter the Junkie on a Train. Audre Lorde. **SP-LordA**

To My Dear and Loving Husband. Anne Bradstreet. **CP-BradA**

To My Dear Friend Mr Congreve [on His Comedy Called "The Double-Dealer"]. John Dryden. **SP-DrydJ**

To my Dear Friend Mr. E.R. Richard Lovelace. **CP-LoveR**

To My Dear Sister, the Author of these Poems. *Unknown, poem signed* "I, W." **CP-BradA**

To My Dear Son, and Right-Learnèd Friend, Master Joseph Rutter. Ben Jonson. **CP-JonsB**

To My Deare Brother, Colonel Richard Lovelace. Dudley Posthume Lovelace. *Fr.* Commendatory Poems. **CP-LoveR**

To My Dearest Cousin, on Her Removal of us from Silver End, to Weston. William Cowper. **CP-CowpW**

To My Dearest Sister M. Mercie Herrick. Robert Herrick. **CP-HerrR**

To My Father. John Haines. **SP-HainJ**

To My Father. John Milton, *tr. fr. Latin by* John T. Shawcross. **CP-MiltJ** ("Oh that Pieria's spring would thro' my breast.") **CP-CowpW,** *tr. by* William Cowper;

(To His Father.) **CP-CowpW**

To My Father. Robert Louis Stevenson. **CP-StevR**

To My Father's Violin. Thomas Hardy. **CP-HardT**

To My Fior-Di-Lisa. Christina Georgina Rossetti. **CP-RosC3**

To My Friend. Wilfred Owen. **CP-OwenW**

To My Friend Butts I Write. William Blake.

(To Thomas Butts, 2 October 1800.) **CP-BlakW**

To My Friend Elizabeth. Christina Georgina Rossetti. **CP-RosC3**

To My Friend Ezra Pound. William Carlos Williams. **CP-WilW2**

To my Friend G.N. from Wrest. Thomas Carew. **CP-CareT**

To My Friend on the Death of His Sister. John Greenleaf Whittier. **CP-WhitJ**

To My Friend the Late Beatrice Hastings. "Hugh MacDiarmid." **SP-MacDH**

To My Friend, Will. Davenant. Thomas Carew. **CP-CareT**

To My Friend Will. Davenant, on His Other Poems. Sir John Suckling. **CP-SuckJ**

To My Friend Will. Davenant, upon His Poem of "Madagascar." Sir John Suckling. **CP-SuckJ**

To My Friends. Stephen Berg. **SP-BergS**

To My God in His Sickness. Philip Levine. **SP-LeviP**

To My Godson, on His Christening. Mona Van Duyn. **SP-VanDM**

To My Greek. James Merrill. **SP-MerrJ**

To My Honourable Friend, Sr. Thomas Mounson, *Knight and Baronet.* Thomas Campion. **CP-CampT**

To My Honoured Friend, Master Thomas May, Upon His Comedy *The Heir.* Thomas Carew. **CP-CareT**

To My Honoured [*or* Honour'd] Kinsman, John Driden [of Chesterton in the County of Huntingdon, Esquire. John Dryden. **SP-DrydJ**

"No porter guards the passage of your door." **EBEV**

To My Ill Reader. Robert Herrick. **CP-HerrR**

To My Inconstant Mistress [*or* Mistris]. Thomas Carew. **CP-CareT**

To My Lady E.C. at Her Going Out of England. Sir John Suckling. **CP-SuckJ**

To My Least Favorite Reviewer. Howard Nemerov. **CP-NemeH**

To My Lord Fairfax. Andrew Marvell. **NOSC** *Fr.* Upon Appleton House [To My Lord Fairfax]. **CP-MarvA**

To My Lord Ignorant. Ben Jonson. **CP-JonsB**

To My L[ord] the King, on the Christening His Second Son James. Ben Jonson. **CP-JonsB**

To My Lyre. Charlotte Smith. **CP-SmitC**

To My Mere English Censurer. Ben Jonson. **CP-JonsB**

To My Mirtle. William Blake. **CP-BlakW**

To my mishap, alas, I find. Sir Thomas Wyatt. **CP-WyatT**

To My Mistress [*or* Mistris], I Burning in Love. Thomas Carew. **CP-CareT**

To My Mistress[e] in My Absence. Thomas Carew. **CP-CareT**

To My Mistress Sitting by a River's Side; an Eddy. Thomas Carew. **CP-CareT**

To My Mother. Walter de la Mare. **CP-DeLaW**

To My Mother. Edgar Allan Poe. **CP-PoeEd**

To My Mother. Robert Louis Stevenson. **CP-StevR**

To My Mother on Her Birthday. Christina Georgina Rossetti. **CP-RosC3**

To My Much Honoured Friend, Henry, Lord Carey of Leppington, Upon His Translation of Malvezzi. Thomas Carew. **CP-CareT**

To My Much Loved Friend, Richard Lovelace Esq. John Jephson. *Fr.* Commendatory Poems. **CP-LoveR**

To My Muse. Ben Jonson. **CP-JonsB**

To My Name-Child. Robert Louis Stevenson. **CP-StevR**

To My Noble and Most Ingenious Friend, Col. Richard Lovelace, upon His Lucasta. John Pinchbacke. *Fr.* Commendatory Poems. **CP-LoveR**

To My Noble Kinsman T.S. Esq. Richard Lovelace. *See* What means this stately tablature.

To My Old Faithful Servant: And (by His Continued Virtue) My Loving Friend: The Author of this Work, M[r] Rich[ard] Brome. Ben Jonson. **CP-JonsB**

To My Old Familiars. Robert Louis Stevenson. **CP-StevR**

To My Old Schoolmaster. John Greenleaf Whittier. **CP-WhitJ**

To My Other Self. Richard Shelton. **SP-ShelR**

To My Pupil. "Lewis Carroll." **CP-CarrL**

To my quick ear the Leaves—conferred. Emily Dickinson. **CP-DickE**

To my revenge and to her desperate fears. The Bubble; a Song. Robert Herrick. **CP-HerrR**

To My Rival. Thomas Carew. **CP-CareT**

To My Sister. Frank Templeton Prince. **CP-PrinF**

To My Sister. Theodore Roethke. **CP-RoetT**

To My Sister. John Greenleaf Whittier. **CP-WhitJ**

To My Sister. William Wordsworth. **CP-WorW1**

To my small Hearth His fire came. Emily Dickinson. **CP-DickE**

To My Son. Byron. **CP-Byron**

To My Successor. George Herbert. **CP-HerbG**

To My Truely Valiant, Learned Friend, Who in His Booke Resolv'd the Art Gladiatory into the Mathematick's. Richard Lovelace. **CP-LoveR**

To My Truly-Beloved Friend, Mr Browne: on His Pastorals. Ben Jonson. **CP-JonsB**

To My Valentines. Louis Zukofsky. **CP-ZukLS**

To my wash-stand. Louis Zukofsky. *Fr.* 29 Songs. **CP-ZukLS**

To My Wife. Philip Larkin. **CP-LarkP**

To My Wife. Robert Louis Stevenson. **CP-StevR**

To My Worthy and Honoured Friend, Mr George Chapman, on His Translation of Hesiod's *Works and Days.* Ben Jonson. **CP-JonsB**

To My Worthy Friend, Master Davenant Upon His Excellent Play, *The Just Italian.* Thomas Carew. **CP-CareT**

To My Worthy Friend, Master Edward Filmer, on His Work Published. Ben Jonson. **CP-JonsB**

To My Worthy Friend Master George Sands [*or* Sandys], on His Translation of the Psalms. Thomas Carew. **CP-CareT**

To My Worthy Friend Mr. Peter Lely [*or* Lilly]. Richard Lovelace. **CP-LoveR**

To My Worthy Friend, Mr. John Mounson, Sonne and Heyre to Sir Thomas Mounson, Knight and Baronet. Thomas Campion. **CP-CampT**

To My Worthy Friend, Mr. T.B. One of the People Called Quakers. Christopher Smart. **SP-SmarC**

To Myra. James Thomson. **CP-ThomJ**

To Myrrha Hard-Hearted. Robert Herrick. **CP-HerrR**

To Myrto About Herself. Robert Ranke Graves. **CP-GravR**

To Nancy F[laxman]. William Blake. **CP-BlakW**

To Naso. Catullus. *See* Carmen 112: "Naso! an elevated personage."

To Natty Bumppo. Thom Gunn. **CP-GunnT**

To Nature. Samuel Taylor Coleridge. **CP-ColeS**

To Night. Percy Bysshe Shelley. **CP-ShelP**

To Night. Charlotte Smith. **CP-SmitC**

To-night, a first movement, a pulse. Act of Union. Seamus Heaney. **SP-HeanS**

To-night at Seven-thirty. Wystan Hugh Auden. *Fr.* Thanksgiving for a Habitat. **CP-AudeW**

To-night, God knows what thing shall tide. Rudyard Kipling. **CP-KiplR** *Fr.* False Dawn. *Fr.* Plain Tales from the Hills.

To-night is so coarse with chocolate. Ode. Louis MacNeice. **CP-MacNL**

To-night we strive to read, as we may best. Prologue. Henry Wadsworth Longfellow. *Fr.* John Endicott. **SP-LongH**

To-night when a full storm surrounds the house. Wystan Hugh Auden. **CP-AudWJ**

To Nobodaddy. William Blake. **CP-BlakW**

To note precisely all I know. On the Welsh Mountains. Alun Lewis. **CP-LewiA**

To N.V. de G.S. Robert Louis Stevenson. **CP-StevR**

To Oblivion. Charlotte Smith. **CP-SmitC**

To Oenone ("Sweet Oenone, doe but say"). Robert Herrick. **CP-HerrR**

To Oenone ("Thou saist Love's dart"). Robert Herrick. **CP-HerrR**

To Oenone ("What conscience, say, is it in thee"). Robert Herrick. **CP-HerrR**

To offer brave assistance. Emily Dickinson. **CP-DickE**

To Ogmian Hercules. Robert Ranke Graves. **CP-GravR**

To Old Age. Walt Whitman. **CP-WhitW**

To Old-End Gatherer. Ben Jonson. **CP-JonsB**

To Oliver Wendell Holmes. John Greenleaf Whittier. **CP-WhitJ**

To One denied to drink. Emily Dickinson. **CP-DickE**

To one fair Lady out of Court. The Challenge: A Court Ballad. Alexander Pope. **CP-PopeA**

To One in Paradise. Edgar Allan Poe. **CP-PoeEd**

To One Not There. Countee Cullen. **CP-CullC**

To One Shortly to Die. Walt Whitman. **CP-WhitW**

To One that Desired Me Not to Name Him. Ben Jonson. **CP-JonsB**

To One That Desired to Know My Mistress [*or* Mistris]. Thomas Carew. **CP-CareT**

To One Who Has Been Long in City Pent. John Keats. **CP-KeatJ**

To One Who Might Have Borne a Message. Edna St. Vincent Millay. **CP-MillE**

To One Who Published in Print. Samuel Taylor Coleridge. **CP-ColeS**

To One Who, When I Praised My Mistress' Beauty, Said I Was Blind. Thomas Carew. **CP-CareT**

To one whose state is raised over all, *speech by the Suitor.* Sir Philip Sidney. **SP-SidnP** *Fr.* The Lady of May.

To Others than You. Dylan Thomas. **CP-ThomD**

To Ottilie. Robert Louis Stevenson. **CP-StevR**

To Our Lord, upon the Water Made Wine. Richard Crashaw. **CP-CrasR**

To our senses, the elements are four. The Four. David Herbert Lawrence. **CP-LawrD**

To our theme. The man who has stood on the Acropolis. Byron. **InPS; OBSV** *Fr.* Canto the Eleventh. **NOBRP** *Fr.* Don Juan. **CP-Byron**

To Outer Nature. Thomas Hardy. **CP-HardT**

To own a Susan of my own. Emily Dickinson. **CP-DickE**

To own the Art within the Soul. Emily Dickinson. **CP-DickE**

To Oxford. Gerard Manley Hopkins. **CP-HopkG**

To Oxford. Gerard Manley Hopkins. **CP-HopkG**

To P.A. Labouchère Esq. George Meredith. **CP-MerG2**

To Pablo Neruda. Erica Jong. **SP-JongE**

To paint the Fiend, *Pink* would the Devill see. Upon Pink an Ill-Fac'd Painter. Robert Herrick. **CP-HerrR**

To paint thy worth, if rightly I did know it. A Poem Sent Me by Sir William Burlase. Ben Jonson. **CP-JonsB**

To Pansies. Robert Herrick. **CP-HerrR**

To part is painful; nay, to bid adieu. The Ancient Mansion. George Crabbe. **SP-CrabG** *Fr.* Posthumous Tales.

To Partridge Merrithew. Marsden Hartley. **CP-HartM**

To Pasolini. David St. John. **SP-StJoD**

  Art of Argument, the Argument of Art, The.

  At Italo's.

  Hotel of Ash.

  Love for the Dragon.

  1984.

  Ostia.

  Una Vita Violenta (1955).

  Winter Sun.

To pass through pain and not know it. A Wave. John Ashbery. **SP-AshbJ**

To pay my Love to thee, and pay it so. To the Memory of My Worthy Friend, Coll. Richard Lovelace. Charles Cotton. *Fr.* Elegies, 1660. **CP-LoveR**

To Peace. James Thomson *and* David Mallet. **CP-ThomJ** *Fr.* Alfred: A Masque.

To Pennsylvania. John Greenleaf Whittier. **CP-WhitJ**

To Penshurst. Ben Jonson. **CP-JonsB**

  "Thy copp's, too, nam'd of Gamage, thou hast there." **FM**

To people these lands with civil men. In a Brooklyn Park. Charles Tomlinson. **CP-TomlC**

To Perenna ("I a Dirge will pen for thee"). Robert Herrick. **CP-HerrR**

To Perenna ("When I thy parts runne o're, I can't espie"). Robert Herrick. **CP-HerrR**

To Perenna: ("How long, *Perenna*, wilt thou see"). Robert Herrick. **CP-HerrR**

To Perenna, A Mistresse ("Deare Perenna, prethee come"). Robert Herrick. **CP-HerrR**

To Perenna ("Thou say'st I'm dull; if edge-lesse so I be"). Robert Herrick. **CP-HerrR**

To Perilla. Robert Herrick. **CP-HerrR**

To Person Guilty ("Guilty, be wise; and though thou know'st the crimes"). Ben Jonson. **CP-JonsB**

To Person Guilty ("Guilty, because I bad you late be wise"). Ben Jonson. **CP-JonsB**

To Pertinax Cob. Ben Jonson. **CP-JonsB**

To Peter on holy problems. Listen, Saints. Thomas Merton. **CP-MertT**

To Peter Stuart. Robert Burns. **CP-BurnR**

To Pfrimmer. Paul Laurence Dunbar. **CP-DunbP**

To Phyllis to Love and Live with Him. Robert Herrick. **CP-HerrR**

To pile like Thunder to its close. Emily Dickinson. **CP-DickE**

To Pino. David Herbert Lawrence. **CP-LawrD**

To Piraeus. John Hewitt. **CP-HewiJ**

To Pius IX. John Greenleaf Whittier. **CP-WhitJ**

To P.L., 1916–1937. Philip Levine. **SP-LeviP**

To play Segovia / upon waking. Fear and Trembling. Jim Carroll. **SP-CarrJ**

To Playwright. Ben Jonson. **CP-JonsB**

To Plimmer, Verandah and Cello. George Meredith. **CP-MerG2**

To pluck down mine, Poll sets up new wits still. On Court-Parrot. Ben Jonson. **CP-JonsB**

To P.O. Allen Ginsberg. **CP-GinsA**

To Poe: Over the Planet, Air Albany–Baltimore. Allen Ginsberg. **CP-GinsA**

To Poets' Worksheets in the Air-Conditioned Vault of a Library. Mona Van Duyn. **SP-VanDM**

To Pontius Washing His Blood-Stained Hands. Richard Crashaw. **CP-CrasR**

To Pontius Washing His Hands. Richard Crashaw. **CP-CrasR**

To popularize the mule, its neat exterior. The Labors of Hercules. Marianne Craig Moore. **CP-MoorM**

To Portapovitch. Hart Crane. **CP-CranH**

To Posterity. Samuel Johnson. **CP-JohnS**

To Posterity. Louis MacNeice. **CP-MacNL**

To Posthumus. Horace. *See* 2.14: "Ah, Postumus, fleet-footed are the years!"

To praise men as good, and take them for such. Charity in Thought. Samuel Taylor Coleridge. **CP-ColeS**

To praise thy Author, Soul, do not forget. Psalm CIV Paraphrased. James Thomson. **CP-ThomJ**

To praise thy life, or waile thy worthie death. An Epitaph upon the Right Honourable Sir Phillip Sidney, Knight: Lord Governor of Flushing. Edmund Spenser. *Fr.* Astrophel. **CP-Spens**

To praise thy life[,] or wail[e] thy worthy[orwoorthie] death. Sir Walter Ralegh. **CP-RaleW**

  (Epitaph upon the Right Hono[u]rable Sir Philip Sidney Knight, Lord Governor of Flushing, An.) **CP-RaleW**

To preach of peace and brotherhood. Long Ago, Far Away. "Bob Dylan." **CP-DylaB**

To prefer the nest in the linden. Hope. Randall Jarrell. **CP-JarrR**

To Priapus. Robert Louis Stevenson. **CP-StevR**

To Primroses Filled with Morning Dew. Robert Herrick. **CP-HerrR**

To Prince Charles upon his coming to Exeter. Robert Herrick. **CP-HerrR**

To Princess Kaiulani. Robert Louis Stevenson. **CP-StevR**

To print our poems the propulsive cause. Fame Makes Us Forward. Robert Herrick. **CP-HerrR**

To Prowl the Plagiary. Ben Jonson. **CP-JonsB**

To public notice, with reluctance strong. Lines Written on a Blank Leaf in a Copy of the Author's Poem "The Excursion", upon Hearing of the Death of the Late Vicar of Kendal. William Wordsworth. **CP-WorW2**

To Puente Curvo on the Maldonado Spit in Uruguay. Pablo Neruda, *tr. fr. Spanish by* Ben Belitt. **SP-NeruP**

To Pull into Oneself as into a Locked Room. Stephen Dobyns. **SP-DobyS**

To purify their wine some people bleed. Epigram. William Cowper. **CP-CowpW**

To Put It Simply. Robert Ranke Graves. **CP-GravR**

To Put One Brick upon Another. Philip Larkin. **CP-LarkP**

To put out the word, whore, thou dost me woo. To a Friend. Ben Jonson. **CP-JonsB**

To put this World down, like a Bundle. Emily Dickinson. **CP-DickE**

To Quilca. Jonathan Swift. **CP-SwifJ**

To Quinbus Flestrin the Man-Mountain, a Lilliputian Ode. Alexander Pope. **CP-PopeA**

To Quintius. Catullus. *See* Carmen 82: "My eyes in your pledge, Quintius."

To R. B. Gerard Manley Hopkins. **CP-HopkG**

To rail or jest, ye know I use it not. Sir Thomas Wyatt. **CP-WyatT**

To raise an iron tree. A Calder. Karl Shapiro. **SP-ShapK**

To Ramona. "Bob Dylan." **CP-DylaB**

To re-insert it in. The Right Lads. Donald Davie. **CP-DavDo**

To read my book[e], the virgin shy [*or* shie]. Martial, *tr. fr. Latin by* Robert Herrick. **CP-HerrR**

To rebel is suitable philosophical tactics. Sonnet. Hayden Carruth. **CP-CarHS** *Fr.* Sonnets.

To rebel. So I have saved my life, not once. Sonnet. Hayden Carruth. **CP-CarHS** *Fr.* Sonnets.

To Record One Must Be Unwary. Mona Van Duyn. **SP-VanDM**

To Reformers in Despair. Nicholas Vachel Lindsay. **CP-LindV**

To Regain the Day Again. Nicolas Calas, *tr. fr. French by* William Carlos Williams. **CP-WilW2**

To Renton of Lamerton. Robert Burns. **CP-BurnR**

To rest the weary nurse has gone. Isobel's Child. Elizabeth Barrett Browning. **CP-BroEB**

To Return to the Trees. Derek Walcott. **CP-WalcD**

To Rhea. Ralph Waldo Emerson. **CP-EmerR**

To R.H.H. with Daphne. George Meredith. **CP-MerG2**

To Rich Givers. Walt Whitman. **CP-WhitW**

To Richard Brinsley Sheridan, Esq. Samuel Taylor Coleridge. *Fr.* Effusions. **CP-ColeS**

To rid your barn of rats. Rats. Daniel Gerard Hoffman. **SP-HoffD**

To Riddel, much-lamented man. On Robert Riddel. Robert Burns. **CP-BurnR**

To Rilke. Alun Lewis. **CP-LewiA**

To rise you bid me with the lark. By One of the Old School Who Was Bid to Follow Mr. Browning's Flights. Gerard Manley Hopkins. *Fr.* Seven Epigrams. **CP-HopkG**

To Robbers furious, and to Lovers tame. Samuel Johnson, *after the Latin of* Joachim du Bellay. **CP-JohnS**

(Translation of Du Bellay's *Epigram on a Dog*.) **CP-JohnS**

To Robert, Earl of Salisbury ("What need hast thou of me, or of my muse"). Ben Jonson. **CP-JonsB**

To Robert, Earl of Salisbury ("Who can consider thy right courses run"). Ben Jonson. **CP-JonsB**

To R***** G***** of F*****, Esq. Robert Burns. **CP-BurnR**

On Critics. **IHNG**

   (Second Epistle to Robert Graham.) **DBV**

To Robt. Graham of Fintry Esqr, with a Request for an Excise Division. Robert Burns. **CP-BurnR**

To Robert Southey. Samuel Taylor Coleridge. **CP-ColeS**

To Robert Telford Hewitt. John Hewitt. **CP-HewiJ**

To Robin Redbreast. Robert Herrick. **CP-HerrR**

To Robin Redbreast. George Meredith. **CP-MerG1**

To Romance. Byron. **CP-Byron**

To Romney. William Cowper. **CP-CowpW**

To Ronge. John Greenleaf Whittier. **CP-WhitJ**

To Rosabelle. Robert Louis Stevenson. **CP-StevR**

To Rosamounde. Geoffrey Chaucer. **CP-ChauG**

To Rosemary and Baies. Robert Herrick. **CP-HerrR**

To Roses in Julia's Bosome. Robert Herrick. **CP-HerrR**

To Rotha Q—. William Wordsworth. **CP-WorW2**

To rub it out, make it less virulent. Oleum Misericordiae. John Ashbery. **SP-AshbJ**

To Rufus. Catullus. *See* Carmen 69: "Do not wonder when the wench declines."

To Ruin. Robert Burns. **CP-BurnR**

To S. M. Edna St. Vincent Millay. **CP-MillE**

To S. R. Crockett. Robert Louis Stevenson. **CP-StevR**

To S. V. B.—June 15, 1940. Edna St. Vincent Millay. **CP-MillE**

To safeguard man from wrongs, there nothing must. Distrust. Robert Herrick. **CP-HerrR**

To Salzilli, a Roman Poet, Being Ill. John Milton, *tr. fr. Latin by* John T. Shawcross. **CP-CowpW; CP-MiltJ**

   ("My halting Muse, that dragg'st by choice along.") **CP-CowpW,** *tr. by* William Cowper;

To Samuel E. Sewall and Harriet W. Sewall. John Greenleaf Whittier. **CP-WhitJ**

To Sapho ("Sapho, I will chuse to go"). Robert Herrick. **CP-HerrR**

To Sapho ("Thou saist thou lov'st me Sapho; I say no"). Robert Herrick. **CP-HerrR**

To Sappho. Robert Herrick. **CP-HerrR**

To save your world, you asked this man to die. Epitaph for the Unknown Soldier. Wystan Hugh Auden. **FaBoCo** *Fr.* Shorts [1948–1957] ("At peace under this mandarin, sleep, Lucina"). **CP-AudeW**

To Saxham. Thomas Carew. **CP-CareT**

To say great words of kings and life. The Kings Are Gone. Charles Bukowski. **SP-BukC2**

To Say If You Love Someone. Kenneth Patchen. **CP-PatcK**

To say it once held daisies and bluebells. The Broken Bowl. James Merrill. **SP-MerrJ**

To say *We were right* is not boastful. Brigadas Internacionales. Edwin Rolfe. **CP-RolfE**

To S.C. Robert Louis Stevenson. **CP-StevR**

To School! Stevie Smith. **CP-SmitS**

To search for what belongs where it is. Wendell Berry. *Fr.* Letter. **CP-BerrW**

To see a woman long oppressed by fear. Sonnet. Hayden Carruth. **CP-CarHS** *Fr.* Sonnets.

To see a World in a Grain of Sand. Auguries of Innocence. William Blake. **CP-BlakW**

To see a World in a Grain of Sand. William Blake. **EnlH; HoFi; ImOP; InPK; NTP; TRV; TreFS,** *ll.* 1–4; *Fr.* Auguries of Innocence. **CP-BlakW**

To see both blended in one flood. Upon the Infant Martyrs. Richard Crashaw. **CP-CrasR**

To see clearly, not to be deceived. The Private Eye. Howard Nemerov. **CP-NemeH**

To see her is a Picture. Emily Dickinson. **CP-DickE**

To see is perhaps never quite the sorcery. Emily Dickinson. **SP-DickE**

To see the film you buy a ticket. Roy Fisher. **SP-FishR** *Fr.* The Six Deliberate Acts.

To See the Heron. Charles Tomlinson. **CP-TomlC**

To see the infinite pity of this place. To Mother Maryanne. Robert Louis Stevenson. **CP-StevR**

To see the intolerant toss of her silken head. Lines on a Young Girl. Alun Lewis. **CP-LewiA**

To see the mother, naturing Nature, stand. Discouragement. Thomas Hardy. **CP-HardT**

To see the rich autumnal tints depart. Arthur Hugh Clough. *Fr.* Seven Sonnets. **SP-ClouA**

To see the Summer Sky. Emily Dickinson. **CP-DickE**

To see the world the way a painter must. Conversing with Paradise. Howard Nemerov. **CP-NemeH**

To seek each where where man doth live. Sir Thomas Wyatt. **CP-WyatT**

To seek of God more then we well can find. Sobriety in Search. Robert Herrick. **CP-HerrR**

To Seem the Stranger. Gerard Manley Hopkins. *See* To seem the stranger lies my lot, my life.

To seem the stranger lies my lot, my life. Gerard Manley Hopkins. **CP-HopkG**

   (To Seem the Stranger.) **CP-HopkG**

To seize, to seize. Our Lady's Winter Words. Theodore Roethke. **CP-RoetT**

To sell me an old hound dog they'd tricked out to look like a. Yesterday They Tried. Kenneth Patchen. **CP-PatcK**

To separate myself from space. Eve's Now-I-Lay-Me. Archibald MacLeish. *Fr.* Songs for Eve. **CP-MacLA**

To Seraphina. James Thomson. **CP-ThomJ**

To serve a wench if any think it shame. 2.17. Ovid. **CP-MarlC,** *tr. by* Christopher Marlowe; *Fr.* Elegies.

To S.H. William Wordsworth. **CP-WorW2**

To Shakespeare. Hart Crane. **CP-CranH**

To Shakespeare. Thomas Hardy. **CP-HardT**

To Sickness. Ben Jonson. **CP-JonsB**

To silence I open the inertia of fluid. Dirty Souls. Alfonso Cortes, *tr. fr. Spanish by* Thomas Merton. **CP-MertT**

To Silvia ("Pardon my trespasse"). Robert Herrick. **CP-HerrR**

To Silvia ("I am holy, while I stand"). Robert Herrick. **CP-HerrR**

To Silvia ("No more my Silvia, do I mean to pray"). Robert Herrick. **CP-HerrR**

To Silvia to Wed. Robert Herrick. **CP-HerrR**

To Simplicity. Samuel Taylor Coleridge. *Fr.* Sonnets Attempted in the Manner of Contemporary Writers. **CP-ColeS**

To Sincerity. Thomas Hardy. **CP-HardT**

To sing of wars, of captain[e]s, and of kings. Prologue. Anne Bradstreet. **CP-BradA**

To Sir Annual Tilter. Ben Jonson. **CP-JonsB**

To Sir Clipsebie Crew ("Since to th'Country first I came"). Robert Herrick. **CP-HerrR**

To Sir Clipseby Crew ("Give me wine, and give me meate"). Robert Herrick. **CP-HerrR**

To Sir Cod. Ben Jonson. **CP-JonsB**

To Sir Edward Herbert. Ben Jonson. **CP-JonsB**

To Sir Edward Herbert[,] at Juliers [*or* Julyers]. John Donne. **CP-DonnJ**

To Sir George Parrie, Doctor of the Civill Law. Robert Herrick. **CP-HerrR**

To Sir Godfrey Kneller, on His Painting for Me the Statues of Apollo, Venus and Hercules. Alexander Pope. **CP-PopeA**

To Sir Henry Cary. Ben Jonson. **CP-JonsB**

To Sir Henry Goodyer ("Who makes the past, a pattern for next year"). John Donne. **CP-DonnJ**

To Sir Henry Goodyere. Ben Jonson. **CP-JonsB**

To Sir Henry Nevil. Ben Jonson. **CP-JonsB**

To Sir Henry [*or* Henrie] Savile [upon His Translation of Tacitus]. Ben Jonson. **CP-JonsB**

To Sir Henry Wotton ("Here's no more news, than virtue, I may as well"). John Donne. **CP-DonnJ**

To Sir Henry Wotton ("Sir, more than kisses, letters mingle souls"). John Donne. **CP-DonnJ**

To Sir Henry Wotton, at His Going Ambassador to Venice. John Donne. **CP-DonnJ**

To Sir Horace Vere. Ben Jonson. **CP-JonsB**

To Sir John Berkeley, Governour of Exeter. Robert Herrick. **CP-HerrR**

To Sir John Fenn. William Cowper. **CP-CowpW**

To Sir John Radcliffe. Ben Jonson. **CP-JonsB**

To Sir Joshua Reynolds. William Cowper. **CP-CowpW**

To Sir Luckless Woo-All. Ben Jonson. **CP-JonsB**

To Sir Ra[l]ph Shelton. Ben Jonson. **CP-JonsB**

To Sir Robert Wroth. Ben Jonson. **CP-JonsB**

To Sir Thomas Overbury. Ben Jonson. **CP-JonsB**

To Sir Thomas Roe. Ben Jonson. **CP-JonsB**

To Sir William Jephson. Ben Jonson. **CP-JonsB**

To Sir William Uvedale. Ben Jonson. **CP-JonsB**

To sit by graves of freshest green, and watch. The Cemetery. Richard Eberhart. *Fr.* Burr Oaks. **CP-EberR**

To sit on a chair, to eat from a table. Scherzo. Randall Jarrell. **CP-JarrR**

To sit on History in an easy chair. Outside the Crowd. George Meredith. **CP-MerG2**

To Sleep. Robert Ranke Graves. **CP-GravR**

To Sleep. John Keats. **CP-KeatJ**

To Sleep. Sir Philip Sidney. *See* Sonnet 39: "Come sleep, O sleep, the certain knot of peace."

To Sleep. Charlotte Smith. **CP-SmitC**

To Sleep ("Flock of sheep that leisurely pass by, A"). William Wordsworth. **CP-WorW1**

To Sleep ("Fond words have oft been spoken to thee, sleep!"). William Wordsworth. **CP-WorW1**

To Sleep I give my powers away. Tennyson. **EnVR** *Fr.* In Memoriam A. H. H. **CP-TennA**

To Sleep ("O gentle Sleep! do they belong to thee"). William Wordsworth. **CP-WorW1**

Tō So-kin of Rakuyō, ancient friend, Chancellor of Gen. *fr. the Chinese of* Li Po (701-62). Li Po. **SP-PounE**

To Soar in Freedom and in Fullness of Power. Walt Whitman. **CP-WhitW**

To solve the recent brutal bombings. His Last Case. Frederick Morgan. **SP-MorgF**

To Some I Have Talked with by the Fire. William Butler Yeats. **CP-YeatW**

To some it's a jewel in the belt of Alma Mater. Poet in Residence. Karl Shapiro. **SP-ShapK**

To Some Ladies. John Keats. **CP-KeatJ**

To Somewhere. Leonard Nathan. **SP-NathL**

To Sons: Not to Be Numb. Thomas Merton. *Fr.* Cables to the Ace. **CP-MertT**

To Sophia [Miss Stacey]. Percy Bysshe Shelley. **CP-ShelP**

To Speak. Denise Levertov. **CP-LeveD**

To speak in a flat voice. Speak. James Wright. **CP-WrigJ**

To Speak of My Influences. Jean Garrigue. **SP-GarrJ**

To speak of sorrow. To Speak. Denise Levertov. **CP-LeveD**

To speak of this hot day: the flaming fields. Moondial. Jean Garrigue. **SP-GarrJ**

To Speak of Woe That Is in Marriage. Robert Lowell. **SP-LoweR**

To speak quietly at such a distance, to speak. Chocorua to Its Neighbor. Wallace Stevens. **CP-StevW**

To speak the prime word and vanish. Light Journal. Charles Wright. **SP-WrigC**

To spend unsolaced years of pain. Arthur Hugh Clough. **SP-ClouA**

To Spring. William Blake. **CP-BlakW**

To Spring. Charlotte Smith. **CP-SmitC**

To spring impetuously in air and remain. To Be in Love. Robert Ranke Graves. **CP-GravR**

To Springs and Fountains. Robert Herrick. **CP-HerrR**

To stand on common ground. A Common Ground. Denise Levertov. **CP-LeveD**

To stand on the long field in fall. A Harvest Home. Howard Nemerov. **CP-NemeH**

To stand up straight and tread the turning mill. Alfred Edward Housman. **CP-HousA**

To stand(alone)in some. Edward Estlin Cummings. **CP-CummE**

To stare at the ocean in winter. Atlantic City. Stephen Dunn. **SP-DunnS**

To start the world of old. It Is Almost the Year Two Thousand. Robert Frost. **CP-FrosR**

To start with, it looked abstract. Roma I. Charles Wright. **SP-WrigC**

To start,to hesitate;to stop. Edward Estlin Cummings. **CP-CummE; SP-CummE**

To Statecraft Embalmed. Marianne Craig Moore. **CP-MoorM**

To stay / bright as. Providence. Archie Randolph Ammons. **SP-AmmoA**

To Stella. Plato, *tr. fr. Greek by* Shelley. **CP-ShelP**

To Stella. Sir Philip Sidney. *See* Doubt you to whom my Muse these notes intendeth [*or* entendeth].

To Stella. Jonathan Swift. **CP-SwifJ**

To Stella on Her Birthday, Written AD 1721–2. Jonathan Swift. **CP-SwifJ**

To Stella, Visiting Me in My Sickness. Jonathan Swift. **CP-SwifJ**

To Stella, Who Collected and Transcribed His Poems. Jonathan Swift. **CP-SwifJ**

To step out of a bedroom. Fetch. Lewis Turco. **SP-TurcL**

To step out sporting such a topper. Dostoievsky Warns W. D. about Wearing Raskolnikov's Hat. William DeWitt Snodgrass. **SP-SnodW**

To step over the low wall that divides. To the Sea. Philip Larkin. **CP-LarkP**

To S[tothar]d. William Blake. **CP-BlakW**

To such a gap as this our love has come. John Hewitt. *Fr.* Sonnets for Roberta (1954). **CP-HewiJ**

To such of one body as one mind. A Junction. Louis Zukofsky. *Fr.* 29 Songs. **CP-ZukLS**

To Summer. William Blake. **CP-BlakW**

To sup with thee thou didst me home invite. The Invitation. Robert Herrick. **CP-HerrR**

To Susan, Countess of Montgomery. Ben Jonson. **CP-JonsB**

To Sycamores. Robert Herrick. **CP-HerrR**

To Sydney. Robert Louis Stevenson. **CP-StevR**

To Symon Gray. Robert Burns. **CP-BurnR**

"Dear Cimon Gray, / The other day."

"Dulness, with redoubted sway."

"Symon Gray."

To T. H., a Lady Resembling My Mistress. Thomas Carew. **CP-CareT**

To T. S. Eliot on His Sixtieth Birthday. Wystan Hugh Auden. *Fr.* Three Occasional Poems. **CP-AudeW**

To taint th'attentive mind she tries. 3.7. Horace. **CP-JohnS,** *tr. by* Samuel Johnson; *Fr.* Odes.

To Tanya at Christmas. Wendell Berry. **CP-BerrW**

To Tell and Be Told. Robert Ranke Graves. **CP-GravR**

To tell the Beauty would decrease. Emily Dickinson. **CP-DickE**

To tell the Saviour all my wants. The Hidden Life. William Cowper. *Fr.* Olney Hymns. **CP-CowpW**

To tell you the truth, the shoe pinched. Cinderella's Story. Mona Van Duyn. **SP-VanDM**

To Terraughty, on His Birth-Day. Robert Burns. **CP-BurnR**

To Thaliarchus ("Behold yon mountains"). 1.9. Horace. *Fr.* Odes.

To the Accuser Who Is the God of This World. William Blake. *See* Epilogue: "Truly my Satan thou art but a dunce."

To the aged, trembling, illiterate woman yesterday. Sonnet. Hayden Carruth. **CP-CarHS** *Fr.* Sonnets.

To the Airport. Adrienne Rich. **CP-RicAE**

To the Algae. Charles Olson. **CP-OlsoC**

To the August Fallen. James Wright. **CP-WrigJ**

To the Author. Ben Jonson. **CP-JonsB**

To the Author of a Sonnet Beginning " 'Sad Is My Verse,' You Say, 'And Yet No Tear.' " Byron. **CP-Byron**

To the Author of Poems. Samuel Taylor Coleridge. *Fr.* Poetical Epistles. **CP-ColeS**

To the Author of "The Robbers." Samuel Taylor Coleridge. *Fr.* Effusions. **CP-ColeS**

To the Author's Portrait. William Wordsworth. **CP-WorW2**

To the Autumnal Moon. Samuel Taylor Coleridge. *Fr.* Effusions. **CP-ColeS**

To the Babylonians. Howard Nemerov. **CP-NemeH**

To the Beautiful Miss Eliza J———n, on Her Principles of Liberty and Equality. Robert Burns. **CP-BurnR**

To the Being We Are. Stephen Berg. **SP-BergS**

To the belfry, one by one, went the ringers from the sun. Rhyme of the Duchess May. Elizabeth Barrett Browning. **CP-BroEB**

To the Bitter Sweet-heart: a Dream. Wilfred Owen. **CP-OwenW**

To the Bleeding Hearts Association of American Novelists. Howard Nemerov. **CP-NemeH**

To the Bluebell. Emily Brontë. **CP-BronE**

To the bob-white's call. The Red Lily. William Carlos Williams. **CP-WilW1**

To the Body. Allen Ginsberg. **CP-GinsA**

To the Boys in Freshman History (Thermopylae, 480 B.C.) Louise McNeill. **SP-McNeL**

To the bridge of love. Juan Ramón Jiménez. *Fr.* Ten Short Poems. **CP-WrigJ**

To the bright east she flies. Emily Dickinson. **CP-DickE**

To the chief Chanters. God Saves the King. Donald Davie. **CP-DavDo**

To the Children. Robinson Jeffers. *Fr.* The Broken Balance. **CP-JefR1**

To the Christian Reader of "Short Rules of Good Life." Robert Southwell. **CP-SoutR**

To the Christians. William Blake. *See* I give you the end of a golden string.

To the City of Bombay. Rudyard Kipling. **CP-KiplR**

To the Clock. Ralph Waldo Emerson. **CP-EmerR**

To the Cloud Juggler. Hart Crane. **CP-CranH**

To the Clouds. William Wordsworth. **CP-WorW1**

To the cold, dark grave they go. An Easter Ode. Paul Laurence Dunbar. **CP-DunbP**

To the Comic Spirit. George Meredith. **CP-MerG1**

To the Commissioners of Northern Lights. Robert Louis Stevenson. **CP-StevR**

To the Companions. Rudyard Kipling. **CP-KiplR** *Fr.* Debits and Credits.

To the Countess of A—. Written on the Anniversary of Her Marriage. Charlotte Smith. **CP-SmitC**

To the Countess of Anglesey. Thomas Carew. **CP-CareT**

To the Countess of Bedford ("Honour is so sublime perfection"). John Donne. **CP-DonnJ**

To the Countess of Bedford ("Madam, / Reason is Our Soul's Left Hand, Faith Her Right"). John Donne. **CP-DonnJ**

To the Countess of Bedford ("Madam, / You have refined me, and to worthiest things"). John Donne. **CP-DonnJ**

To the Countess of Bedford ("Though I be dead, and buried, yet I have"). John Donne. **CP-DonnJ**

To the Countess of Bedford ("To have written then, when you writ, seemed to me"). John Donne. **CP-DonnJ**

To the Countess of Bedford at New Year's Tide. John Donne. **CP-DonnJ**

To the Countess of Blessington. Byron. **CP-Byron**

To the Countess of Huntingdon ("Madam, / Man to God's image, Eve, to man's was made"). John Donne. **CP-DonnJ**

To the Countess of Huntingdon ("That unripe side of earth, that heavy clime"). John Donne. **CP-DonnJ**

To the Countess of Salisbury. John Donne. **CP-DonnJ**

To the Cuckoo. William Wordsworth. **CP-WorW1**

To the Cuckoo. William Wordsworth. **CP-WorW2**

To the Daisy ("Bright Flower! whose home is everywhere"). William Wordsworth. **CP-WorW1**

To the Daisy ("In youth from rock to rock I went"). William Wordsworth. **CP-WorW1**

To the Daisy ("Sweet Flower! belike one day to have"). William Wordsworth. **CP-WorW1**

To the Dead Owner of a Gym. Thom Gunn. **CP-GunnT**

To the Dean. William Carlos Williams. **CP-WilW2**

To the Detracter. Robert Herrick. **CP-HerrR**

To the Dog Belvoir. Stevie Smith. **CP-SmitS**

To the dry island's dead centre. Monastary, Tourliani, Mykonos. John Hewitt. **CP-HewiJ**

To the Duke of Dorset. Byron. **CP-Byron**

To the Earl of Burlington Asking Who Writ the Libels against Him. Alexander Pope. **CP-PopeA**

To the Earl of Clare. Byron. **CP-Byron**

To the Earl of Egremont. Charlotte Smith. **CP-SmitC**

To the Earl of Lonsdale. William Wordsworth. *Fr.* Poems Composed or Suggested During a Tour, in the Summer of 1833. **CP-WorW2**

To the Earl of Oxford, Late Lord Treasurer. Jonathan Swift. **CP-SwifJ**

To the Earl of Peterborough. Jonathan Swift. **CP-SwifJ**

To the Earle of Westmorland. Robert Herrick. **CP-HerrR**

To the East and to the West. Walt Whitman. **CP-WhitW**

To the Eastern Shore. Paul Laurence Dunbar. **CP-DunbP**

To the Empress Josephine's Statue. Hart Crane. **CP-CranH**

To the End. Christina Georgina Rossetti. **CP-RosC3**

To the Etruscan Poets. Richard Wilbur. **CP-WilbR**

To the Evening Star. William Blake. **CP-BlakW**

To the Evening Star. Samuel Taylor Coleridge. **CP-ColeS**

To the Evening Star: Central Minnesota. James Wright. **CP-WrigJ**

To the Evening Star over Grasmere Water. William Wordsworth. **CP-WorW1**

To the faithful Absence is condensed presence. Emily Dickinson. **SP-DickE**

To the farthest star of all. The Indian Girl Tells the Hero Where to Go to Get the Laughing Bell. Nicholas Vachel Lindsay. *Fr.* The Tree of Laughing Bells or The Wings of the Morning. **CP-LindV**

To the fateless ones. The Fateless Ones. Kathleen Jessie Raine. **SP-RainK**

To the Fever, Not To Trouble Julia. Robert Herrick. **CP-HerrR**

To the Field Mice. Richard Eberhart. **CP-EberR**

To the Film Industry in Crisis. Frank O'Hara. **SP-OharF**

To the Fire-Fly of Jamaica, Seen in a Collection. Charlotte Smith. **CP-SmitC**

To the Flamingos. Boy in the Roman Zoo. Archibald MacLeish. **CP-MacLA**

To the galleys, thief, and sweat your soul out. Thief. Robert Ranke Graves. **CP-GravR**

To the Garden the World. Walt Whitman. **CP-WhitW**

To the Generous Reader. Robert Herrick. **CP-HerrR**

To the Genius of His House. Robert Herrick. **CP-HerrR**

To the Genius of Mr. John Hall. Richard Lovelace. **CP-LoveR**

To the Gentlemen of the Press. With a Capital P. Louis Zukofsky. *Fr.* Michtam. **CP-ZukLS**

To the Ghost of John Milton. Carl Sandburg. **CP-SandC**

To the Ghost of Marjorie Kinnan Rawlings. William Carlos Williams. **CP-WilW2**

To the Ghost of Martial. Ben Jonson. **CP-JonsB**

To the Girl Who Lives In a Tree. Audre Lorde. **SP-LordA**

To the God of all sure mercies let my blessing rise to-day. Cassandra Southwick. John Greenleaf Whittier. **CP-WhitJ**

To the God of Fond Desire. James Thomson. *See* One day the god of fond desire.

To the God Who reigns on high. Hymn. Christina Georgina Rossetti. **CP-RosC3**

To the Goddess. Erica Jong. **SP-JongE**

To the Goddess of Botany. Charlotte Smith. **CP-SmitC**

To the Governor & Legislature of Massachusetts. Howard Nemerov. **CP-NemeH**

To the Great Metropolis. Arthur Hugh Clough. **SP-ClouA**

To the grey rock below the silent park, in grey light. The Confession. James McAuley. **SP-McAuJ**

To the grove, the meadow, the well. Pietro Metastasio, *tr. fr. Italian by* William Wordsworth. **CP-WorW1**

To the Halibut. William Cowper. *See* Where hast thou floated, in what seas pursued.

To the Handsome Mistresse Grace Potter. Robert Herrick. **CP-HerrR**

To the Harbormaster. Frank O'Hara. **SP-OharF**

To the heart of youth the world is a highwayside. Youth and Love II. Robert Louis Stevenson. **CP-StevR**

To the Heavens above us. An Astrologer's Song. Rudyard Kipling. **CP-KiplR**

To the High and Noble Prince, George, Duke, Marquesse, and Earle of Buckingham. Robert Herrick. **CP-HerrR**

To the High-Flyers. Johann Gabriel Seidl, *tr. fr. German by* George Meredith. **CP-MerG2**

To the Highland Girl of Inversneyde. William Wordsworth. **CP-WorW1**

To the Holy Spirit. Wendell Berry. **CP-BerrW**

To the Honble Mr. R. M———, of P-nm-re, on His High Phaeton. Robert Burns. **CP-BurnR**

To the honorable Senate and House. Belinda's Petition. Rita Dove. **SP-DoveR**

To the Honorable, Valiant, and Ingenious Colonel Richard Lovelace, on His Exquisite Poems. Francis Lenton. *Fr.* Commendatory Poems. **CP-LoveR**

To the Honourable Mr. Erskine. Samuel Taylor Coleridge. *Fr.* Effusions. **CP-ColeS**

To the Hon. Mrs. George Lamb. Byron. **CP-Byron**

To the Honoured, Master Endimion Porter. Robert Herrick. **CP-HerrR**

To the Horned God. Erica Jong. **SP-JongE**

To the House. Robinson Jeffers. **CP-JefR1**

To the house on the grassy hill. The Presence. Denise Levertov. **CP-LeveD**

To the Immaculate Virgin, on a Winter Night. Thomas Merton. **CP-MertT**

To the Immortal[l] Memory [*or* Memorie] and Friendship of That Noble Pair[e], Sir Lucius Cary and Sir H. [*or* Henry] Morison. Ben Jonson. **CP-JonsB**

   It Is Not Growing Like a Tree. **ChTr; HeIP; ImPo; LiTB**

   (Noble Nature, The.) **ArNa; GN; GTBS; GTBS-6; GTBS-P; PFP**

   (Oak and Lily.) **TrGrPo**

   (Part of an Ode, A.) **OBEV**

To the Indians Who Died in Africa. Thomas Stearns Eliot. **CP-ElioT**

To the Infant Martyrs. Richard Crashaw. **CP-CrasR**

To the Insect of the Gossamer. Charlotte Smith. **CP-SmitC**

To the Invisible Moon. Charlotte Smith. **CP-SmitC**

To the Jewish People. Kenneth Patchen. **CP-PatcK**

To the Judge of Right and Wrong. The Choice. Rudyard Kipling. **CP-KiplR**

To the King ("If when these Lyricks (Cesar) You shall heare"). Robert Herrick. **CP-HerrR**

To the King. Robert Herrick. **CP-HerrR**

To the King. Sir John Suckling. *Fr.* Aglaura. **CP-SuckJ**

To the King and Queene, upon Their Unhappy Distances. Robert Herrick. **CP-HerrR**

To the King, at His Entrance into Saxham: By Master John Crofts. Thomas Carew. **CP-CareT**

To the King. On His Birthday. An Epigram Anniversary. Novem[ber] 19, 1632. Ben Jonson. **CP-JonsB**

To the King, To Cure the Evill. Robert Herrick. **CP-HerrR**

To the King, upon His Com[m]ing with His Army into the West. Robert Herrick. **CP-HerrR**

To the King, upon His Taking of Leicester. Robert Herrick. **CP-HerrR**

To the King, upon His Welcome to Hampton-Court. Robert Herrick. **CP-HerrR**

To the laboratory then I went. What little. Fragment. John Ciardi. **SP-CiarJ**

To the Lacedemonians. Allen Tate. **CP-TateA**

To the Ladies Who Saw Me Crowned. John Keats. **CP-KeatJ**

To the Lady Bedford. John Donne. **CP-DonnJ**

To the Lady Crew, Upon the Death of her Child. Robert Herrick. **CP-HerrR**

To the Lady E.B. and the Hon. Miss P. William Wordsworth. **CP-WorW2**

To the Lady Elizabeth Queen of Bohemia. George Herbert. **CP-HerbG**

To the Lady Fleming on Seeing the Foundation Preparing for the Erection of Rydal Chapel, Westmoreland. William Wordsworth. **CP-WorW2**

To the Lady Mary Lowther. William Wordsworth. **CP-WorW2**

To the Lady Mary Villars, Governesse to the Princesse Henretta. Robert Herrick. **CP-HerrR**

To the Ladyes. Robert Herrick. **CP-HerrR**

To the Lark. Robert Herrick. **CP-HerrR**

To the Learnèd Critic. Ben Jonson. **CP-JonsB**

To the Leaven'd Soil They Trod. Walt Whitman. **CP-WhitW**

To the legion of the lost ones, to the cohort of the damned. Gentlemen-Rankers. Rudyard Kipling. **CP-KiplR**

To the Liberal Magistrates. James Liddy. **CP-LiddJ**

To the Little Spinners. Robert Herrick. **CP-HerrR**

To the Living. May Sarton. "How faint the horn sounds in the mountain passes." **SP-SartM**

To the London Reader, on the Odcombian Writer, Polytopian Thomas the Traveller. Ben Jonson. **CP-JonsB**

To the Looking-Glass world it was Alice that said. "Lewis Carroll." **CP-CarrL** *Fr.* Through the Looking-Glass. (Welcome Queen Alice.) **CP-CarrL**

To the Lord Chancellor. Percy Bysshe Shelley. **CP-ShelP**

To the Lord Hopton, on His Fight in Cornwall. Robert Herrick. **CP-HerrR**

To the Lords of Convention'—The horses went by. Louis MacNeice. *Fr.* Notes for a Biography. **CP-MacNL**

To the lore of no manner of men. The Burning Book [or the Contented Metaphysician]. Edwin Arlington Robinson. **CP-RobiE**

To the Loud Wind. Donald Hall. **CP-HallD**

To the Mad Poets. Richard Eberhart. **CP-EberR**

To the Maid of Orleans. Edna St. Vincent Millay. **CP-MillE**

To the Maids to Walke Abroad. Robert Herrick. **CP-HerrR**

To the man-in-the-street who, I'm sorry to say. Wystan Hugh Auden. **FiBHP; PoPl** *Fr.* Shorts [1939–1947] ("Motionless, deep in his mind, lies the past the poet's forgotten"). **CP-AudeW**

To the Man in the Yellow Terry. Alice Walker. **CP-WalkA**

To the Man-of-War Bird. Walt Whitman. **CP-WhitW**

To the Man Who Watches Spiders. Siv Cedering Fox. **SP-CedeS**

To the man with his jaw shot away, blood-badged. Protagonists. Richard Eberhart. **CP-EberR**

To the Mannequins. Howard Nemerov. **CP-NemeH**

To the Marquis of Dufferin and Ava. Tennyson. **CP-TennA**

To the meeting despair of eyes in the street, offer. The Uncreating Chaos (Double Portrait in a Mirror). Stephen Spender. **CP-SpenS**

To the Memory of Bernard Berenson. James Liddy. **CP-LiddJ**

To the Memory of Charles B. Storrs. John Greenleaf Whittier. **CP-WhitJ**

To the Memory of James Connolly. John Hewitt. **CP-HewiJ**

To the Memory of John Wheelwright. Howard Nemerov. **CP-NemeH**

To the Memory of Mary Young. Paul Laurence Dunbar. **CP-DunbP**

To the Memory of Mr Oldham. John Dryden. **SP-DrydJ**

To the Memory of My Beloved, the Author Mr [*or* Master] William Shakespeare[: And What He Hath Left Us]. Ben Jonson. **CP-JonsB** "I, therefore, will begin. Soul of the age!" **FaBoEH; NOBE** "Sweet Swan of Avon! what a sight it were." **ChTr**

To the Memory of My Dear and Ever Honored Father Thomas Dudley Esq. Who Deceased July 31, 1653, and of His Age 77. Anne Bradstreet. **CP-BradA**

To the Memory of My Dear Daughter in Law, Mrs. Mercy Bradstreet. Anne Bradstreet. **CP-BradA**

To the Memory of My Worthy Friend, Coll. Richard Lovelace. Charles Cotton. *Fr.* Elegies, 1660. **CP-LoveR**

To the Memory of Raisley Calvert. William Wordsworth. **CP-WorW1**

To the Memory of Sir Isaac Newton. James Thomson. **CP-ThomJ**

To the Memory of Sylvia Plath: A Personal Note. James Liddy. **CP-LiddJ**

To the Memory of That Most Honoured Lady Jane, Eldest Daughter to Cuthbert, Lord Ogle: and Countess of Shrewsbury. Ben Jonson. **CP-JonsB**

To the Memory of the Unfortunate Miss Burns 1791. Robert Burns. **CP-BurnR**

To the Memory of Thomas Shipley. John Greenleaf Whittier. **CP-WhitJ**

To the Memory of Wyndham Lewis. Roy Fisher. **SP-FishR**

To the Men of Kent (October, 1803). William Wordsworth. **CP-WorW1**

To the Merry Men of France. George Meredith. **CP-MerG2**

To the Miami. Paul Laurence Dunbar. **CP-DunbP**

To the mizen, the main, & the fore. Ralph Waldo Emerson. **CP-EmerR**

To the Moon. Thomas Hardy. **CP-HardT**

To the Moon. Percy Bysshe Shelley. **CP-ShelP**

To the Moon. Charlotte Smith. **CP-SmitC**

To the Moon (Composed by the Seaside,—on the Coast of Cumberland). William Wordsworth. **CP-WorW2**

To the Moon (Rydal). William Wordsworth. **CP-WorW2**

To the Moonbeam. Percy Bysshe Shelley. **CP-ShelP**

To the Morning. Satisfaction for Sleepe. Richard Crashaw. **CP-CrasR**

To the Morning Star. Written Near the Sea. Charlotte Smith. **CP-SmitC**

To the Most Accomplisht Gentleman, Master Edward Norgate, Clark of the Signet to His Majesty. Robert Herrick. **CP-HerrR**

To the Most Accomplisht Gentleman Master Michael Oulsworth. Robert Herrick. **CP-HerrR**

To the Most Comely and Proper M. Elizabeth Finch. Robert Herrick. **CP-HerrR**

To the Most Disconsolate Great Brittaine. Thomas Campion. **CP-CampT**

To the Most Fair and Lovely Mistress Anne Soame, Now Lady Abdie. Robert Herrick. **CP-HerrR**

To the Most High and Mighty Prince Charles. Thomas Campion. **CP-CampT**

To the Most Illustrious and Mighty Fredericke the Fift, Count Palantine of the Rhein. Thomas Campion. **CP-CampT**

To the Most Illustrious and Most Hopefull Prince, Charles, Prince of Wales. Robert Herrick. **CP-HerrR**

To the Most Learned, Wise, and Arch-Antiquary, M. John Selden. Robert Herrick. **CP-HerrR**

To the Most Noble, and above His Titles, Robert, Earl of Somerset. Ben Jonson. **CP-JonsB**

To the Most Princely and Vertuous the Lady Elizabeth. Thomas Campion. **CP-CampT**

To the Most Puisant and Gratious James King of Great Britaine. Thomas Campion. *Fr.* Lord Hay's Mask.

To The Most Sacred King James. Thomas Campion. **CP-CampT**

To the Most Sacred Queen Anne. Thomas Campion. **CP-CampT**

To the Most Virtuous Mistress Pot, Who Many Times Entertained Him. Robert Herrick. **CP-HerrR**

To the much-tossed Ulysses, never done. Ulysses. Robert Ranke Graves. **CP-GravR**

To the Mulberry-Tree. Charlotte Smith. **CP-SmitC**

To the Muse. Denise Levertov. **CP-LeveD**

To the Muse. Charlotte Smith. **CP-SmitC**

To the Muse. Robert Louis Stevenson. **CP-StevR**

To the Muse. James Wright. **CP-WrigJ**

To the Muses. William Blake. **CP-BlakW**

To the Naiad of the Arun. Charlotte Smith. **CP-SmitC**

To the Name above Every Name, the Name of Jesus, a Hymn. Richard Crashaw. **CP-CrasR**

To the Nameless One. Marsden Hartley. **CP-HartM**

To the National Endowment for the Arts. Jim Carroll. **SP-CarrJ**

To the New World. Randall Jarrell. **CP-JarrR**

To the New World. Randall Jarrell. **CP-JarrR**

To the New Year [For the Countess of Carlisle]. Thomas Carew. **CP-CareT**

To the Nieuport Scout. Geoffrey Hill. **CP-HillG**

To the Nightingale. Samuel Taylor Coleridge. *Fr.* Effusions. **CP-ColeS**

To the Nightingale. William Cowper. **CP-CowpW**

To the Nightingale. James Thomson. **CP-ThomJ**

To the Nightingale, and Robin-Red-Brest. Robert Herrick. **CP-HerrR**

To the Nile. John Keats. **CP-KeatJ**

To the Nile. Percy Bysshe Shelley. **CP-ShelP**

To the North. May Sarton. **SP-SartM**

To the north, on bright days you may be seen. Freya. Frederick Morgan. **SP-MorgF**

To the Not Impossible Him. Edna St. Vincent Millay. **CP-MillE**

To the Nuptial Bowre. John Milton. **OxBM** *Fr.* Book VIII. *Fr.* Paradise Lost. **CP-MiltJ**

To the Ocean. Byron. *See* Roll on, thou deep and dark blue ocean—roll!

To the ocean now I fly. John Milton. **NOBE; NOSC; OBEV; OBS; OXAEP-1; TrGrPo** *Fr.* Comus; a Masque Presented at Ludlow Castle. (Farewell of the Attendant Spirit.) **TrGrPo** (Spirit Epiloguizes, The.) **NOBE** (Spirit's Epilogue, The.) **NOSC**

To the Ohio. James Wright. *Fr.* Many of Our Waters: Variations on a Poem by a Black Child. **CP-WrigJ**

To the old, long life and treasure. Ben Jonson. **CP-JonsB** *Fr.* The Gypsies Metamorphosed.

To the One in the Gray Coat. Robert Creeley. **CP-CreeR**

To the One of Fictive Music. Wallace Stevens. **CP-StevW**

To the Outer World. William Carlos Williams. **CP-WilW1**

To the Painter. Thomas Carew. **CP-CareT**

To the Painter, To Draw Him a Picture. Robert Herrick. **CP-HerrR**

To the Parliament. Ben Jonson. **CP-JonsB**

To the Passenger. Robert Herrick. **CP-HerrR**

To the Patron of Poets, M. End: Porter. Robert Herrick. **CP-HerrR**

To the Pay Toilet. Marge Piercy. **SP-PierM**

To the Peacock of France. Marianne Craig Moore. **CP-MoorM**

To the Pending Year. Walt Whitman. **CP-WhitW**

To the Pennsylvanians. William Wordsworth. **CP-WorW2**

To the People of Dresden. John Hewitt. **CP-HewiJ**

To the place called of the Red Land. The Seventh Book. Archibald MacLeish. *Fr.* Conquistador. **CP-MacLA**

To the Planet Venus. William Wordsworth. **CP-WorW2**

To the Planet Venus, an Evening Star. William Wordsworth. **CP-WorW2**

To the poet as a basement quilt, but perhaps. Or in My Throat. John Ashbery. **SP-AshbJ**

To the Poet, John Dyer. William Wordsworth. **CP-WorW1**

To the Poets. Howard Nemerov. **CP-NemeH**

To the Poets in New York. James Wright. **CP-WrigJ**

To the Poets: To Make Much of Life. George Oppen. **CP-OppeG**

To the poor (aux pauvres) crime alone (le crime seul) opens. Statue of Liberty. Karl Shapiro. **SP-ShapK**

To the Praise of the Dead, and the Anatomy. John Donne. *Fr.* Anatomy [*or* Anatomie] of the World, An[: The First Anniversary]. **CP-DonnJ**

To the Public. Louis MacNeice. **CP-MacNL**

To the Punks of Dawlish. Allen Ginsberg. **CP-GinsA**

To the Queen. William Blake. *See* Dedication of the Illustrations to Blair's "Grave."

To the Queen. Tennyson. **CP-TennA**

To the Queen. Tennyson. *Fr.* Idylls of the King. **CP-TennA**

To the Queen, an Apologie for the Length of the Following Panegyricke. Richard Crashaw. **CP-CrasR**

To the Queen of My Heart. Percy Bysshe Shelley. **CP-ShelP**

To the Queen, Upon her Numerous Progeny, a Panegyricke, *sl. diff. vers.* Richard Crashaw. *See* Upon the Duke of *Yorke* his Birth a Panegyricke.

To the Queene. Robert Herrick. **CP-HerrR**

To the Queen's Majesty. Richard Crashaw. **CP-CrasR**

To the Reader. Charles Baudelaire, *tr. fr.* French by Stanley Kunitz. **CP-KuniS**

To the Reader. Thomas Campion. **CP-CampT**

To the Reader ("Pray thee, take care, that tak'st my book[e] in hand"). Ben Jonson. **CP-JonsB**

To the Reader ("This figure, that thou here seest put"). Ben Jonson. **CP-JonsB**

To the Reader. Denise Levertov. **CP-LeveD**

To the Reader at Parting. Walt Whitman. **CP-WhitW**

To the Reader of Master William Davenant's Play [*The Wits*]. Thomas Carew. **CP-CareT**

To the Reformers of England. John Greenleaf Whittier. **CP-WhitJ**

To the Republicans of North America. Percy Bysshe Shelley. **CP-ShelP**

To the Rev. W. J. Hort. Samuel Taylor Coleridge. **CP-ColeS**

To the Rev. Christopher Wordsworth, D.D., Master of Harrow School. William Wordsworth. **CP-WorW2**

To the Rev. Dr Wordsworth (with the Sonnets to the River Duddon, and Other Poems in This Collection, 1820). William Wordsworth. *Fr.* The River Duddon [A Series of Sonnets]. **CP-WorW2**

To the Rev. F. D. Maurice. Tennyson. **CP-TennA**

   At Farringford. **FaBoPP**

To the Rev. George Coleridge. Samuel Taylor Coleridge. **CP-ColeS**

To the Rev. John McMath, Inclosing a Copy of *Holy Willie's Prayer*, Which He Had Requested. Robert Burns. **CP-BurnR**

To the Rev. Mr. Newton. William Cowper. **CP-CowpW**

To the Rev. Mr. Powell. Christopher Smart. **SP-SmarC**

To the Reverend Patrick Murdoch. James Thomson *and* David Mallet. **CP-ThomJ**

To the Reverend Shade of His Religious Father. Robert Herrick. **CP-HerrR**

To the Rev. [*or* Reverend] W. L. Bowles. Samuel Taylor Coleridge. **EnRP; Son** *Fr.* Effusions. **CP-ColeS**

To the Rev. William Bull. William Cowper. **CP-CowpW**

To the Richest Treasury. The Dedication to Anne Lovelace. Richard Lovelace. **CP-LoveR**

To the Right Gratious Prince, Lodwick, Duke of Richmond and Lenox. Robert Herrick. **CP-HerrR**

To the Right Hon. the Lord Chancellor (Bacon). George Herbert. **CP-HerbG**

To the Right Honourable, Both in Birth and Vertue, Francis, Earle of Cumberland. Thomas Campion. **CP-CampT**

To the Right Honourable Edward Earle of Dorset. Robert Herrick. **CP-HerrR**

To the Right Hon[oura]ble Hierome, L[ord] Weston. An Ode Gratulatory for His Return from His Embassy. 1632. Ben Jonson. **CP-JonsB**

To the Right Honourable Mildmay, Earl of Westmorland. Robert Herrick. **CP-HerrR**

To the Right Honourable, Philip, Earle of Pembroke, and Montgomerie. Robert Herrick. **CP-HerrR**

To the Right Honourable, the Lord High Treasurer of England. An Epistle Mendicant. 1631. Ben Jonson. **CP-JonsB**

To the Right Honourable, the Lord Treasurer of England. An Epigram. Ben Jonson. **CP-JonsB**

To the Right, Noble, and Vertuous, Henry Lord Clifford, Sonne and Heyre to the Right Honourable, Francis, Earle of Cumberland. Thomas Campion. **CP-CampT**

To the Right Noble and Vertuous Theophilus Howard, Lorde of Walden, Sonne and Heire to the Right Honorable the Earle of Suffolke. Thomas Campion. *Fr.* Lord Hay's Mask.

To the Right Noble Tom, Tell-Troth of His Travels, the Coriat of Odcombe, and His Book Now Going to Travel. Ben Jonson. **CP-JonsB**

To the Right Person. Robert Frost. **CP-FrosR**

To the Right Vertuous, and Honorable, the Lord and Lady Hayes. Thomas Campion. *Fr.* Lord Hay's Mask.

To the Right Worshipfull, My Singular Good Frend, Master Gabriell Harvey, Doctor of the Lawes. Edmund Spenser. **NoSic** *Fr.* Commendatory Sonnets. **CP-Spens**

To the River——— Edgar Allan Poe. **CP-PoeEd**

To the River Arun. Charlotte Smith. **CP-SmitC**

To the River Arun. Charlotte Smith. **CP-SmitC**

To the River Derwent. William Wordsworth. *Fr.* Poems Composed or Suggested During a Tour, in the Summer of 1833. **CP-WorW2**

To the River Duddon: After-Thought. William Wordsworth. *See* I thought of Thee, my partner and my guide.

To the River Greta, near Keswick. William Wordsworth. *Fr.* Poems Composed or Suggested During a Tour, in the Summer of 1833. **CP-WorW2**

To the Road. Paul Laurence Dunbar. **CP-DunbP**

To the Roaring Wind. Wallace Stevens. **CP-StevW**

To the Rock that Will Be a Cornerstone of the House. Robinson Jeffers. **CP-JefR1**

To the Romantic Traditionists. Allen Tate. **CP-TateA**

To the Rose; a Song. Robert Herrick. **CP-HerrR**

To the Rose upon the Rood of Time. William Butler Yeats. **CP-YeatW**

To the Royal Academy. William Blake. **CP-BlakW**

To the Rulers. Howard Nemerov. **CP-NemeH**

To the sagging wharf. A Summer's Dream. Elizabeth Bishop. **CP-BishE**

To the Same [John Lapraik]. Robert Burns. *See* Second Epistle to John Lapraik.

To the Same [Alphonso Ferrabosco]. Ben Jonson. **CP-JonsB**

To the Same [Benjamin Rudyerd] ("If I would wish, for truth, and not for show"). Ben Jonson. **CP-JonsB**

To the Same [Benjamin Rudyerd] ("Writing thyself, or judging others' writ"). Ben Jonson. **CP-JonsB**

To the Same [Celia]. Ben Jonson. **CP-JonsB** *Fr.* Volpone.

To the Same [Robert, Earl of Salisbury] [Upon the Accension of the Treasurership to Him]. Ben Jonson. **CP-JonsB**

To the Same [Sir Henry Goodyere]. Ben Jonson. **CP-JonsB**

To the Same [Sir John Roe]. Ben Jonson. **CP-JonsB**

To the Same [Sir Luckless Woo-All]. Ben Jonson. **CP-JonsB**

To the Same [Sir Thomas Roe]. Ben Jonson. **CP-JonsB**

To the Same ["Another Leonora captured the poet Torquato"]. John Milton, *tr. fr. Latin* by John T. Shawcross. **CP-MiltJ**

  ("Another Leonora once inspir'd.") **CP-CowpW**, *tr. by* William Cowper;

  (To Leonora Singing at Rome.) **CP-CowpW**, *tr. by* William Cowper;

To the Same ["Why, credulous Naples, do you vaunt your clear-voiced Siren"]. John Milton, *tr. fr. Latin* by John T. Shawcross. **CP-CowpW; CP-MiltJ**

  ("Naples, too credulous, ah! boast no more.") **CP-CowpW**, *tr. by* William Cowper;

To the Same. Byron. **CP-Byron**

To the Same. James Thomson. **CP-ThomJ**

To the Same Ayre in English, Thus, *A la Chabot.* Unknown, *tr. fr.* French by Richard Lovelace. **CP-LoveR**

To the Same Flower [The Small Celandine]. William Wordsworth. **CP-WorW1**

To the Same Flower [The Daisy]. William Wordsworth. *See* With little here to do or see.

To the Same, on the Author Being Threatened with His Resentment. Robert Burns. *Fr.* Epigrams on Lord Galloway. **CP-BurnR**

To the Same; on the Same. Ben Jonson. **CP-JonsB**

To the Same Place. Stephen Berg. **SP-BergS** *Fr.* For My Father.

To the Same Sir Cod. Ben Jonson. **CP-JonsB**

To the Scholars of Harvard. John Crowe Ransom. *See* When Sarah Pierrepont let her spirit rage.

To the Sea. Philip Larkin. **CP-LarkP**

To the Secret Poets of Kansas. Jim Carroll. **SP-CarrJ**

To the serenissimo Dno (pronounced Domino). Canto 43. Ezra Pound. *Fr.* Cantos. **CP-PoCan**

To the Shade of Burns. Charlotte Smith. **CP-SmitC**

To the Shade of Po Chü-I. William Carlos Williams. **CP-WilW1**

To the Shah, from Enweri ("From thy worth and weight the stars gravitate"). "Anvari", *tr. fr. Persian by* Ralph Waldo Emerson. **CP-EmerR**

To the Shah, from Enweri ("Not in their houses stand the stars"). "Anvari", *tr. fr. Persian by* Ralph Waldo Emerson. **CP-EmerR**

To the Shah, from Hafiz. Hafiz, *tr. fr. Persian by* Ralph Waldo Emerson. **CP-EmerR**

To the She-Bear: *The 1st Song.* Charles Olson. **CP-OlsoC**

To the Sighing Strephon. Byron. **CP-Byron**

To the Small Celandine. William Wordsworth. **CP-WorW1**

To the Snow-Drop. Charlotte Smith. **CP-SmitC**

To the Sons of Burns, after Visiting the Grave of Their Father. William Wordsworth. **CP-WorW1**

To the Sour[e] Reader. Robert Herrick. **CP-HerrR**

To the South. Paul Laurence Dunbar. **CP-DunbP**

To the South Downs. Charlotte Smith. **CP-SmitC**

To the Spade of a Friend (An Agriculturist). William Wordsworth. **CP-WorW1**

To the States. Walt Whitman. **CP-WhitW**

To the States, To Identify the 16th, 17th, or 18th Presidentiad. Walt Whitman. **CP-WhitW**

To the staunch Dust. Emily Dickinson. **CP-DickE**

To the Stone-Cutters. Robinson Jeffers. **CP-JefR1**

To the Stormy Petrel. Robert Louis Stevenson. **CP-StevR**

To the Story-Tellers. Robinson Jeffers. **CP-JefR3**

To the Sun. Kathleen Jessie Raine. **SP-RainK**

    "Ancestral sun, do you remember us."

    "How address you, greatest of givers."

    "Not that light is holy, but that the holy is the light—."

    "Sun, great giver of all that is."

To the Sun. Charlotte Smith. **CP-SmitC**

To the Sun-set Breeze. Walt Whitman. **CP-WhitW**

To the (Supposed) Patron. Geoffrey Hill. **CP-HillG**

To the Supreme Being. Michelangelo Buonarroti. *See* The Prayers I make will then be sweet indeed.

To the Swallow. Euenus, *tr. fr. Greek by* William Cowper. **CP-CowpW**

To the Swimmer. Countee Cullen. **CP-CullC**

To the Teumessian Vixen. Robert Ranke Graves. **CP-GravR**

To the Thawing Wind. Robert Frost. **CP-FrosR**

To the Thin and Elegant Woman Who Resides Inside of Alix Nelson. Diane Wakoski. **SP-WakoD**

To the Thirty-Ninth Congress. John Greenleaf Whittier. **CP-WhitJ**

To the Three for Whom the Book. Countee Cullen. **CP-CullC**

To the Torrent at the Devil's Bridge, North Wales, 1824. William Wordsworth. **CP-WorW2**

To the Translator of Lucan [*or* Lucan's Pharsalia, 1614]. Sir Walter Ralegh. **CP-RaleW**

To the True Romance. Rudyard Kipling. **CP-KiplR**

To the Tune of an Ancient Song. Kenneth Patchen. **CP-PatcK**

To the Tune of the Coventry Carol. Stevie Smith. **CP-SmitS**

To the Unknown Goddess. Rudyard Kipling. **CP-KiplR**

To the Unseeable Animal. Wendell Berry. **CP-BerrW**

To the Utilitarians. William Wordsworth. **CP-WorW2**

To the vast, shy light. Hovenweep. Kenneth Patchen. **CP-PatcK**

To the vigilance of my exertions a lax pause. Words from Edmund Burke. Frank Templeton Prince. **CP-PrinF**

To [the] Virgins, to Make Much of Time. Robert Herrick. **CP-HerrR**

To the Water Nymphs, Drinking at the Fountain. Robert Herrick. **CP-HerrR**

To the Weaver's Gin Ye Go. Robert Burns. **CP-BurnR**

To the Western Wind. Robert Herrick. **CP-HerrR**

To the Wife of a Sick Friend. Edna St. Vincent Millay. **CP-MillE**

To the Willow-Tree. Robert Herrick. **CP-HerrR**

To the Winds. Charlotte Smith. **CP-SmitC**

To the winds give our banner! St. John. John Greenleaf Whittier. **CP-WhitJ**

To the wonders of the Peak. A Song of the Moon. Ben Jonson. **CP-JonsB**

To the World [A Farewell for a Gentlewoman, Virtuous and Noble]. Ben Jonson. **CP-JonsB**

To the World. Thomas Campion. **CP-CampT**

To the Worthy Author. Thomas Campion. **CP-CampT**

To the Worthy Author M[r] John Fletcher. Ben Jonson. **CP-JonsB**

To the Worthy Author on *The Husband.* Ben Jonson. **CP-JonsB**

To the Yew and Cypress to Grace His Funeral. Robert Herrick. **CP-HerrR**

To the Young Artist. Samuel Taylor Coleridge. **CP-ColeS**

To the young boy standing in front of the large glass tanks, each. John Yau. **SP-YauJo** *Fr.* Carp and Goldfish.

To Thee, dear God of Mercy, both appeal. At the Close. George Meredith. **CP-MerG1**

To Thee, Lord, my cry I send. Bible, *O.T. See* Psalm 28: "Unto thee will I cry, O Lord my rock."

To thee, my way in epigrams seems new. To My Mere English Censurer. Ben Jonson. **CP-JonsB**

To Thee Old Cause. Walt Whitman. **CP-WhitW**

To thee, sweet Fop, these lines I send. Bounce to Fop. Alexander Pope. **CP-SwifJ**

To thee these first fruits of my growing death. Our Lord in His Circumcision to His Father. Richard Crashaw. **CP-CrasR**

To Thee whose eye all Nature owns. Chorus of the Pities. Thomas Hardy. **CP-HardT** *Fr.* The Dynasts.

To their apartment deep. Emily Dickinson. **CP-DickE**

To their Excellencies the Lords Justices of Ireland. Mrs. Harris's Petition. Jonathan Swift. **CP-SwifJ**

To their grey heights they rise. Canna's Basalt Crags. Kathleen Jessie Raine. **SP-RainK**

To them that knew her, there is vital flame. The Lady C. M. George Meredith. **CP-MerG1**

To them who crossed the flood. Inscription. Herman Melville. **SP-MelvH**

To these, whom death again did wed. Richard Crashaw. **CP-CrasR** (Epitaph upon a Young Married Couple, An.) **CP-CrasR**

To Thine Own Self. Edwin Rolfe. **CP-RolfE**

To things we are ghosts, soft shapes. The Furniture. John Updike. **CP-UpdiJ**

To Think of the Life of a Man. Wendell Berry. **CP-BerrW**

To Think of Time. Walt Whitman. **CP-WhitW**

To think that men of former days. Arthur Hugh Clough. **SP-ClouA**

To think that this meaningless thing was ever a rose. Summer Is Ended. Christina Georgina Rossetti. **CP-RosC2**

To think to know the country and not know. A Hillside Thaw. Robert Frost. **CP-FrosR**

To thirst and find no fill—to wail and wander. Fragment: Igniculus Desiderii. Percy Bysshe Shelley. **CP-ShelP**

To this bridge the pale river and flickers away in images of blue. Summer, the Sacramento. Muriel Rukeyser. **CP-RukeM**

To this sad shrine, whoe'er thou art! draw near. Epitaph on the Hon. Simon Harcourt. Alexander Pope. **CP-PopeA**

To this *white Temple* of my *Heroes*, here. To His Honoured Kinsman, Sir Richard Stone. Robert Herrick. **CP-HerrR**

To this World she returned. Emily Dickinson. **CP-DickE**

To Thom Gunn in Los Altos, California. Donald Davie. **CP-DavDo**

To Thomas Atkins. Rudyard Kipling. **CP-KiplR**

To Thomas Butts, 16 August 1803. William Blake. *See* O Why Was I Born With a Different Face?

To Thomas Butts, 2 October 1800. William Blake. *See* To My Friend Butts I Write.

To Thomas Butts, 22 November 1802. William Blake. *See* With Happiness Stretched [*or* stretched] across the Hills.

To Thomas Clarkson, on the Final Passing of the Bill for the Abolition of the Slave Trade. March, 1807. William Wordsworth. **CP-WorW1**

To Thomas, Earl of Suffolk. Ben Jonson. **CP-JonsB**

To Thomas, Lord Chancellor. Ben Jonson. **CP-JonsB**

To Thomas Palmer [on His Book "The Sprite of Trees and Herbs"]. Ben Jonson. **CP-JonsB**

To Thomas Sheridan. Jonathan Swift. **CP-SwifJ**

To Thoreau on Rereading Walden. Isabella Gardner. **CP-GardI**

To those who are isolate. The Failed Spirit. Stevie Smith. **CP-SmitS**

To those who can estimate silence. Emily Dickinson. **SP-DickE**

To Those Who Fear To Join Us. Edwin Rolfe. **CP-RolfE**

To those who know the Lord I speak. Seeking the Beloved. William Cowper. *Fr.* Olney Hymns. **CP-CowpW**

To those who speak to the many deaf ears attend. Triad. Kathleen Jessie Raine. **SP-RainK**

To Those Who've Fail'd. Walt Whitman. **CP-WhitW**

To Those Without Pity. Edna St. Vincent Millay. **CP-MillE**

To Three Puzzled Little Girls, from the Author. "Lewis Carroll." **CP-CarrL**

To throw away the key and walk away. Wystan Hugh Auden. **CMoP; CP-AudWJ; MoBrPo** *Fr.* Paid on Both Sides. **CP-AudeW**
(Chorus: "To throw away the key and walk away.") **MoBrPo**
(Walking Tour, The.) **CMoP**

To throw yourself away. Throwing Yourself Away. Richard Eberhart. **CP-EberR**

To thy bright beams I turn my swimming eyes. By the Same. To the North Star. Charlotte Smith. **CP-SmitC**

To thy lover. *ad.fr. the Italian of* Ceba. Richard Crashaw. **CP-CrasR**

To Thyrza. Byron. **CP-Byron**

To Time. Byron. **CP-Byron**

To Time it never seems that he is brave. I Could Give All to Time. Robert Frost. **CP-FrosR**

To Tirzah. William Blake. **CP-BlakW** *Fr.* Songs of Experience.

To Toss the Troubled Night Long. David Herbert Lawrence. **CP-LawrD**

To Toussaint L'Ouverture. William Wordsworth. **CP-WorW1**

To tragedy I have no addiction. Emancipation of Mr. Poplin, or, Skoal to the Skimmerless. Ogden Nash. **CP-NashO**

To tragic verse while thou Achilles train'st. 2.18. Ovid. **CP-MarlC,** *tr. by* Christopher Marlowe; *Fr.* Elegies.

To Tranquillity. Charlotte Smith. **CP-SmitC**

To Transcend the Cat. Leonard Nathan. **SP-NathL**

To transmute crime to wisdom, & to stem. Ralph Waldo Emerson. **CP-EmerR**

To travel and feel. Linear. Roy Fisher. **SP-FishR**

To True Soldiers. Ben Jonson. **CP-JonsB**

To Try to Get Down One Citizen as Against Another. Charles Olson. **CP-OlsoC**

To try to speak, and miss the way. Emily Dickinson. **CP-DickE**

To Turn Back. John Haines. **SP-HainJ**

To Two Sisters. Samuel Taylor Coleridge. **CP-ColeS**

To Ulster then, my region, now I turn. The Glittering Sod. John Hewitt. *Fr.* Freehold. **CP-HewiJ**

To Ulysses. Tennyson. **CP-TennA**

To understand / each other: anything. Their Attitudes Differ. Margaret Atwood. **SP-AtwM1**

To understand the strength of those dark forces. In Praise Of. Edwin Rolfe. **CP-RolfE**

To undertake is to achieve. Emily Dickinson. **CP-DickE**

To Unwin. William Cowper. **CP-CowpW**

To urge, my loved Alphonso, that bold fame. To Alphonso Ferrabosco, on His Book. Ben Jonson. **CP-JonsB**

To Varus. Catullus. *See* Carmen 22: "I must, Varus, tell you."

To venerate the simple days. Emily Dickinson. **CP-DickE**

To Venetian Artists. William Blake. **CP-BlakW**

To Vera Thompson. John Haines. **SP-HainJ**

To Vesper. Charlotte Smith. **CP-SmitC**

To Victor Hugo of My Crow Pluto. Marianne Craig Moore. **CP-MoorM**

To Violets. Robert Herrick. **CP-HerrR**

To Virgil [*or* Vergil]. Tennyson. **CP-TennA**

To Virgins. Robert Herrick. **CP-HerrR**

To Vulcan. Robert Herrick. **CP-HerrR**

To W. S*****n, Ochiltree. Robert Burns. *See* I gat your letter, winsome Willie.

To W. Wordsworth. Samuel Taylor Coleridge. **CP-ColeS**

To wait an Hour—is long. Emily Dickinson. **CP-DickE**

To wake, and hear a cock. Dawn. Philip Larkin. **CP-LarkP**

To wake the soul by tender strokes of art. Prologue to Mr. Addison's *Tragedy of Cato.* Alexander Pope. **CP-PopeA**

To Waken an Old Lady. William Carlos Williams. **CP-WilW1**

To Wales once more, though not on holiday now. Canto XX. Louis MacNeice. *Fr.* Autumn Sequel. **CP-MacNL**

To Walk on Hills. Robert Ranke Graves. **CP-GravR**

To walk on hills is to employ legs. To Walk on Hills. Robert Ranke Graves. **CP-GravR**

To Walter de la Mare. Thomas Stearns Eliot. **CP-ElioT**

To Wang Wei. Meng Hao Jan, *tr. fr. Chinese by* William Carlos Williams *with* David Rafael Wang. **CP-WilW2**

To Warren Hastings. William Cowper. **CP-CowpW**

To watch the storms, and hear the sky. To Lady Austen. William Cowper. **CP-CowpW**

To watch water, to watch running water. Howard Nemerov. *Fr.* Runes. **CP-NemeH**

To W.E. Henley. Robert Louis Stevenson. **CP-StevR**

To W.E. Henley. Robert Louis Stevenson. **CP-StevR**

To wear the arctic fox. Marianne Craig Moore. **CP-MoorM**
(Arctic Ox (or Goat), The.) **CP-MoorM**

To wear those old moccasins with the backs. Bright Nightgown. Gilbert Sorrentino. **SP-SorrG**

To weary hearts, to mourning homes. The Angel of Patience. John Greenleaf Whittier. **CP-WhitJ**

To wed good blood to bad blood to alleviate. The Fathers. Charles Olson. **CP-OlsoC**

To welcome multitudes—the miracles of deeds. Credo. Edwin Rolfe. **CP-RolfE**

To weld the nation in a name of dread. George Meredith. *Fr.* Napoléon. **CP-MerG1**

To wet your eye withouten tear. Sir Thomas Wyatt. **CP-WyatT**

To what a cumbersome unwieldiness[e]. Love's Diet. John Donne. **CP-DonnJ**

To what end serve the promises. *see also* Desdain ("A quoy servent tant d'artifices"). Sir John Suckling. **CP-SuckJ**

To what good, in the alleys of the lilacs. Last Looks at the Lilacs. Wallace Stevens. **CP-StevW**

To What Listens. Wendell Berry. **CP-BerrW**

To what purpose, April, do you return again? Spring. Edna St. Vincent Millay. **CP-MillE**

To What Purpose Is This Waste? Christina Georgina Rossetti. **CP-RosC3**

To What Serves Mortal Beauty? Gerard Manley Hopkins. **CP-HopkG**

To what shall I compare her. Robert Louis Stevenson. **CP-StevR**

To which as to a Reservoir. Emily Dickinson. **SP-DickE**

To whom a glass full of red wine. Hafiz, *tr. by* Ralph Waldo Emerson. **CP-EmerR** *Fr.* Odes.

To whom does the raggedy condor. Pablo Neruda, *tr. fr. Spanish by* Ben Belitt. **SP-NeruP** *Fr.* Question Book.

To whom I owe the leaping delight. A Dedication to My Wife. Thomas Stearns Eliot. **CP-ElioT**

To Whom It May Concern. Kenneth Patchen. **CP-PatcK**

To whom our Saviour calmly thus reply'd. True and False Glory. John Milton. **LiTB; OBS** *Fr.* Book III. *Fr.* Paradise Regained [*or* Regain'd]. **CP-MiltJ**

To whom should I present this. Carmen 1. Catullus. *Fr.* Carmina. **CP-Catul**

To whom should I sue to ease my pain? Sir Thomas Wyatt. **CP-WyatT**

To whom the Father, without Cloud, serene. John Milton. **PeECV** *Fr.* Book XI. *Fr.* Paradise Lost. **CP-MiltJ**

To whom the fiend with fear abasht repli'd. John Milton. **PeECV** *Fr.* Book IV. *Fr.* Paradise Regained [*or* Regain'd]. **CP-MiltJ**

To whom the house of Montagu. Edna St. Vincent Millay. **CP-MillE**

To Whom the Mornings stand for Nights. Emily Dickinson. **CP-DickE**

To whom the Tempter impudent replied. John Milton. **ChIV-2** *Fr.* Book IV. *Fr.* Paradise Regained [*or* Regain'd]. **CP-MiltJ**

To whom the wingèd hierarch replied. Ascent of Species. John Milton. **NOSC** *Fr.* Book V. *Fr.* Paradise Lost. **CP-MiltJ**

To whom thus also th' Angel last repli'd. John Milton. **FiP; OxAEP-1; PeECV** *Fr.* Book XII. *Fr.* Paradise Lost. **CP-MiltJ**
(Paradise Lost.) **FiP**

To whom thus Michael. Justly thou abhorr'st. John Milton. **FaBoPV** *Fr.* Book XII. *Fr.* Paradise Lost. **CP-MiltJ**

To whom thus Michael. Those whom last thou saw'st. John Milton. *Fr.* Book XI. *Fr.* Paradise Lost. **CP-MiltJ**

To whom with healing words Adam replied. Uncloistered Virtue. John Milton. **NOSC** *Fr.* Book IX. **FHYEP; NAEL-1; NAWM-1; NoP; OAEL-1** *Fr.* Paradise Lost. **CP-MiltJ**

To Will Davies. Ernest Hemingway. **CP-HemiE**

To Will H. Low. Robert Louis Stevenson. **CP-StevR**

To William Camden. Ben Jonson. **CP-JonsB**

To William Carlos Williams. Richard Eberhart. **CP-EberR**

To William Carlos Williams. Galway Kinnell. **SP-KinnG**

To William Creech. Robert Burns. **CP-BurnR**

To William, Earl[e] of Pembroke. Ben Jonson. **CP-JonsB**

To William F. Bradbury. Edward Estlin Cummings. **CP-CummE**

To William Godwin. Samuel Taylor Coleridge. **CP-ColeS**

To William H. Seward. John Greenleaf Whittier. **CP-WhitJ**

To William Hayley, Esq.: In Reply to His Solicitation to Write with Him in a Literary Work. William Cowper. **CP-CowpW**

To William Lloyd Garrison. John Greenleaf Whittier. **CP-WhitJ**

To William, Lord Mounteagle. Ben Jonson. **CP-JonsB**

To William Roe ("Roe (and my joy to name) th'art now, to go"). Ben Jonson. **CP-JonsB**

To William Roe ("When Nature bids us leave to live, 'tis late"). Ben Jonson. **CP-JonsB**

To William Shelley ("Billows on the beach are leaping around it, The"). Percy Bysshe Shelley. **CP-ShelP**

To William Shelley ("My lost William, thou in whom"). Percy Bysshe Shelley. **CP-ShelP**

To William Shelley ("Thy little footsteps on the sands"). Percy Bysshe Shelley. **CP-ShelP**

To William Stewart. Robert Burns. **CP-BurnR**

To Willie and Henrietta. Robert Louis Stevenson. **CP-StevR**

To win the battle of life you have to plan strategical as well as tactical. Caesar Knifed Again, or, Culture Biz Gets Hep, Boffs Profs. Ogden Nash. **CP-NashO**

To win the love of women one should first discover. The Art of Love. Kenneth Koch. **SP-KochK**

To win the love of women one should first discover. Kenneth Koch. **NNaP** *Fr.* The Art of Love. **SP-KochK**

To Wine. Louise Bogan. **CP-BogaL**

To Winter. William Blake. **CP-BlakW**

To wish and want and not obtain. Sir Thomas Wyatt. **CP-WyatT**

To Wish Myself Courage. William Carlos Williams. **CP-WilW1**

To Woman. Byron. **CP-Byron**

To Women. Richard Hugo. **CP-HugoR**

To Women, as Far as I'm Concerned. David Herbert Lawrence. **CP-LawrD**

To Women, to Hide Their Teeth, if They Be Rotten or Rusty. Robert Herrick. **CP-HerrR**

To Wordsworth. Percy Bysshe Shelley. **CP-ShelP**

To work a wonder, God would have her shown. Virgin Mary, The. Robert Herrick. **CP-HerrR**

"To Work Is to Contradict Contradications, to Do Violence to Natural Violence. . . ." Robert Creeley. **CP-CreeR**

To work it out even a thought better. At the Well. Robert Ranke Graves. **CP-GravR**

To work—To Beaconsfield. A suburban train. Canto III. Louis MacNeice. *Fr.* Autumn Sequel. **CP-MacNL**

To work. To my own office, my own job. Canto IV. Louis MacNeice. **FaBCIP** *Fr.* Autumn Sequel. **CP-MacNL**

To write a poem, perfect physical condition. The Art of Poetry. Kenneth Koch. **SP-KochK**

To write a snow poem you must ignore the snow. Snow Poem. Richard Hugo. **CP-HugoR**

To write a verse or two, is all the praise. Praise (1). George Herbert. **CP-HerbG**

To write down all I contain at this moment. The Moment. Kathleen Jessie Raine. **SP-RainK**

To write one book in five years. Portrait. Carl Sandburg. **CP-SandC**

To Write One Song, I Said. Philip Larkin. **CP-LarkP**

To X. (With Ephemeral Kisses). Erica Jong. **SP-JongE**

To You. Kenneth Koch. **SP-KochK**

To You. Richard Shelton. **SP-ShelR**

To You ("Let us twain walk aside from the rest"). Walt Whitman. **CP-WhitW**

To You ("Stranger, if you passing meet me and desire to speak to me, why should you not speak to me?"). Walt Whitman. **CP-WhitW**

To You ("Whoever you are, I fear you are walking the walks of dreams"). Walt Whitman. **CP-WhitW**

To you, Fletcher, from my dark house asleep. The One Dull Thing You Did Was to Die, Fletcher. John Ciardi. **SP-CiarJ**

To you, let snow and roses. Robert Louis Stevenson. **CP-StevR**

To you [*or* yow], my purse [*or* purs], and to non [*or* no *or* noon] other wight. Geoffrey Chaucer. **CP-ChauG**

(Complaint of Chaucer to His Purse, The.) **CP-ChauG**

To you, Sir, this summons I've sent. Extempore—To Mr. Gavin Hamilton. Robert Burns. **CP-BurnR**

To you, so affluently mystical. M.T.—a Relative in Certain Aspects of Metaphysical Divination. Marsden Hartley. **CP-HartM**

To you that sit with Sorrow like chained slaves. Edwin Arlington Robinson. *Fr.* Octaves. **CP-RobiE**

To you, then, tenants of life's middle state. William Cowper. **OBSV** *Fr.* Tirocinium; or, A Review of Schools. **CP-CowpW**

To you, whose virtues I must own. To Mr. Delany. Jonathan Swift. **CP-SwifJ**

To Youth. Robert Herrick. **CP-HerrR**

To Yvor Winters, 1955. Thom Gunn. **CP-GunnT**

Toad and Spyder, The. Richard Lovelace. **CP-LoveR**

Toad, can die of Light, A. Emily Dickinson. **CP-DickE**

Toad the power mower caught, A. The Death of a Toad. Richard Wilbur. **CP-WilbR**

Toadeater, The, *see also* The Toad-Eater ("What of earls with whom you have supt"). Robert Burns. *See* No more of your titled acquaintance boast.

Toads. Philip Larkin. **CP-LarkP**

Toads in the Greenhouse. Gary Gildner. **SP-GildG**

Toads Revisited. Philip Larkin. **CP-LarkP**

Toadstool comes up in a night, A. Christina Georgina Rossetti. **CP-RosC2**

Toast, A ("As quid pro quo for your enchanting verses"). Wystan Hugh Auden. *Fr.* Eleven Occasional Poems. **CP-AudeW**

Toast, A ("What on earth does one say at a Gaudy"). Wystan Hugh Auden. *Fr.* Eleven Occasional Poems. **CP-AudeW**

Toast, A. Robert Burns. **CP-BurnR**

Toast, A. Louis MacNeice. **CP-MacNL**

Toast. Leonard Nathan. **SP-NathL**

Toast to Death, A. Robert Ranke Graves. **CP-GravR**

Toast to Floyd Collins, A. Miller Williams. **SP-WillM**

Tobacco Shed, The. Lewis Turco. **SP-TurcL**

Tobacconist of Eighth Street, The. Richard Eberhart. **CP-EberR**

Tobroken ben the statutz hye in hevene. Lenvoy de Chaucer a Scogan. Geoffrey Chaucer. **CP-ChauG**

"Toby's" in Cos Cob—faded mirrors, a smoked-wood bar. High Society. Daniel Gerard Hoffman. **SP-HoffD**

Toccata of Galuppi's, A. Robert Browning. **CP-BroR1**

Toccata's sails were up and set. Going Backward Going Forward. Richard Eberhart. **CP-EberR**

Today. Allen Ginsberg. **CP-GinsA**

Today. David Herbert Lawrence. **CP-LawrD**

Today / let us think. Roy Fisher. **SP-FishR** *Fr.* The Six Deliberate Acts.

Today. Frank O'Hara. **SP-OharF**

Today. James Schuyler. **SP-SchuJ**

Today: / This leafy apple-tree, gray. Kathleen Jessie Raine. **SP-RainK**

Today a fine old face has gone under the soil. Highland Graveyard. Kathleen Jessie Raine. *Fr.* Eileann Chanaidh. **SP-RainK**

Today a hockey player died in. Next Door. Jim Carroll. **SP-CarrJ**

Today above the gull's call. Aubade. Louise Glück. **SP-GlücL**

Today as I / Looked up at the sky's great face. Kathleen Jessie Raine. **SP-RainK**

Today as the news from Selma and Saigon. Monet's "Waterlilies." Robert Earl Hayden. **CP-HaydR**

Today, autumn. The Fire of Despair Has Been Our Savior. Robert Bly. **SP-BlyR**

Today clouds come to visit. October Window. Al Young. **CP-YounA**

Today, dear friend, this grey day. A Confidence. William Carlos Williams. **CP-WilW1**

Today For Me. Christina Georgina Rossetti. *Fr.* The German-French Campaign, 1870–1871. **CP-RosC1**

Today he's wearing his vinyl shoes. The Salesman. Ted Kooser. **SP-KoosT**

Today How Many Hours. Pablo Neruda, *tr. fr. Spanish by* Ben Belitt. **SP-NeruP**

Today I am at home. A Few Sirens. Alice Walker. **CP-WalkA**

Today I am walking alone in a bare place. Late November in a Field. James Wright. **CP-WrigJ**

Today I asked Aileen. Destruction of Grief. Muriel Rukeyser. **CP-RukeM**

Today I met Von Clausewitz. The Great Men of Former Times. Thomas Merton. **CP-MertT**

Today I read how Japanese fishermen. Having Lost All Capacity. Stephen Dunn. **SP-DunnS**

Today, I remembered Getty, the old man. Getty. Richard Hugo. **CP-HugoR**

Today I saw a picture of the cancer cells. The Cancer Cells. Richard Eberhart. **CP-EberR**

Today I saw a woman wrapped in rags. At the Slackening of the Tide. James Wright. **CP-WrigJ**

Today I Was So Happy, So I Made this Poem. James Wright. **CP-WrigJ**

Today I will let the old boat stand. Waiting. Carl Sandburg. **CP-SandC**

Today I wished without mercy. All Day the Light Is Clear. Tess Gallagher. **SP-GallT**

Today, if a man does something pretentious and deliberate. Shows. David Herbert Lawrence. **CP-LawrD**

Today in the field I saw. Sacred Objects. Louise Glück. *Fr.* Dedication to Hunger. **SP-GlücL**

Today is a black feather and a six. Lunes. Martin Edmunds. **SP-EdmuM**

Today is almost over. Randall Jarrell. **CP-JarrR**

Today is it? Is it today? I shudder. John Berryman. *Fr.* Sonnets to Chris. **CP-BerrJ**

Today is one of those grey days sadder than a day of rain. Letter to Jeffrey Gustavson. Martin Edmunds. **SP-EdmuM**

Today is our sixteenth anniversary. Chicken Unlimited. Peter Meinke. **SP-MeinP**

Today is the day they shipped. Loving the Killer. Anne Sexton. **CP-SextA**

Today is the peace of this mist. The Pitcher of Milk. John Haines. **SP-HainJ**

Today is Wednesday. Miller Williams. **SP-WillM**

Today Isn't Everything. Pablo Neruda, *tr. fr. Spanish by* Ben Belitt. **SP-NeruP**

Today, it's the obsidian. Walking to Work. Ted Kooser. **SP-KoosT**

Today, lonely for my father, I saw. My Father's Wedding. Robert Bly. **SP-BlyR**

Today my poems seem / only the spells I muttered. Hayden Carruth. **CP-CarHS** *Fr.* The Clay Hill Anthology.

Today old Janus opens the new year. A New Year's Gift Sung to King Charles. 1635. Ben Jonson. **CP-JonsB**

Today on the lip of a bowl in the backyard. The Caterpillar. Miller Williams. **SP-WillM**

Today or this noon. Emily Dickinson. **CP-DickE**

Today our thoughts, flower, leaf and stem. A Rhyme for Christmas Morning. John Hewitt. **CP-HewiJ**

Today out of the window. The Trembling of the Veil. Allen Ginsberg. **CP-GinsA**

Today, should you let fall a glass it would. Tramontana at Lerici. Charles Tomlinson. **CP-TomlC**

Today small waves are rippling, crystal clear, upon the pebbles. The Birth of Venus. William Carlos Williams. **CP-WilW2**

Today, society has sanctified. En Masse. David Herbert Lawrence. **CP-LawrD**

Today space is terrific. Wine of Lovers. James Liddy. **CP-LiddJ**

Today the circus poster. The Bells. Anne Sexton. **CP-SextA**

Today the longest day and the people have gone. Midsummer. Derek Mahon. **SP-MahoD**

Today the misty hills are filled with water. Glendun on a Wet July Day. John Hewitt. **CP-HewiJ**

Today, the pastures have dressed in their best grasses. Morning Song. Stephen Dobyns. **SP-DobyS**

Today the room is filled with tomorrows. Jim Carroll. *Fr.* Morning. **SP-CarrJ**

Today the snow is drifting. Snow. Philip Levine. **SP-LeviP**

Today the sunlight is the paint on lead soldiers. Toyland. Roy Fisher. **SP-FishR**

Today there is another marriage. A Wedding on Cape Rosier. Richard Eberhart. **CP-EberR**

Today They Are Roasting Rocky Norse. Gary Gildner. **SP-GildG**

Today they cut down the oak. Stump. Donald Hall. **CP-HallD**

Today they invent. Portents. Thomas McGrath. **SP-McGrT**

Today was a day of cold spring showers. April. Howard Nemerov. *Fr.* Epigrams: "Wasp, climbing the window pane." **CP-NemeH**

Today we carted home the last brown sheaf. Load. John Hewitt. **CP-HewiJ**

Today we move in jade and cease with garnet. Sonnet: To Time. Sylvia Plath. **CP-PlatS**

Today we saw a tiger. The Tiger. Robert Creeley. **CP-CreeR**

Today, when I woke up, I asked myself. Winter Morning. Louise Glück. **SP-GlücL**

Today, you threaten to leave me. The Lie. Maya Angelou. **SP-AngeM**

Today you told me. To an Autocrat. Diane Wakoski. **SP-WakoD**

Today you wear your ribbon red to symbolise your brotherhood. Song for May Day. John Hewitt. **CP-HewiJ**

Today's Burden. Christina Georgina Rossetti. **CP-RosC2**

Today's confident light / squanders the roses. Inside. Pablo Neruda, *tr. fr. Spanish by* Ben Belitt. **SP-NeruP**

Today's your natal day. To My Mother on Her Birthday. Christina Georgina Rossetti. **CP-RosC3**

Tod's Amendment. Rudyard Kipling. *Fr.* Plain Tales from the Hills. "World hath set its heavy yoke, The." **CP-KiplR**

Together. Rudyard Kipling. **CP-KiplR**

Together, keeping in line, slow as if hypnotised. Convoy. Louis MacNeice. **CP-MacNL**

Together once, but never more / While Time and Death run out their runs. Christina Georgina Rossetti. *Fr.* They Put Their Trust in Thee, and Were Not Confounded. **CP-RosC2**

Together, passing by / The dead gull on the heath. Yes and No. Wystan Hugh Auden. **CP-AudWJ**

Together, trustfully, through a dark wood. Through a Dark Wood. Robert Ranke Graves. **CP-GravR**

Together with my dead body shall they arise. Easter Tuesday. Christina Georgina Rossetti. **CP-RosC2**

Toil. Charles Kenneth Williams. **CP-WillC; SP-WillC**

Toil and grow rich. The Witch. William Butler Yeats. **CP-YeatW**

Toilet, The. Alexander Pope. *See* And now, unveiled, the toilet stands displayed.

Tōji. Gary Snyder. **CP-SnydG**

Token, A. Robert Creeley. **CP-CreeR**

Token, The. Frank Templeton Prince. **CP-PrinF**

Token of friendship true and tried. The Relic. John Greenleaf Whittier. **CP-WhitJ**

Toland's Invitation to Dismal to Dine with the Calves' Head Club. Jonathan Swift. **CP-SwifJ**

Told. Philip Levine. **SP-LeviP**

Told me that I shouldn't have books like that. He. Ron Koertge. **SP-KoerR**

Toledo shines out like no other city. A Statement for El Greco and William Carlos Williams. Kay Boyle. **CP-BoylK**

Tolerable Wisdom, A. Derek Mahon. **SP-MahoD**

Tolerance. Thomas Hardy. **CP-HardT**

Tolerance. David Herbert Lawrence. **CP-LawrD**

Toll, bell, toll. For hope is flying / Sighing from the earthbound soul. Christina Georgina Rossetti. **CP-RosC2**

Toll for the brave! On the Loss of the *Royal George*. William Cowper. **CP-CowpW**

Toll of the Roads, The. Stevie Smith. **CP-SmitS**

Tollhouse, The. Lewis Turco. **SP-TurcL**

Tolling Bell. Robert Ranke Graves. **CP-GravR**

Tollund Man, The. Seamus Heaney. **SP-HeanS**

Tolstoi is Plowing Yet. Nicholas Vachel Lindsay. *Fr.* To Jane Addams at the Hague. **CP-LindV**

Tolstoy. William Carlos Williams. **CP-WilW2**

Tom. James Schuyler. **CP-SchuJ**

Tom and Dick had equal fame. Tom Mullinex and Dick. Jonathan Swift. **CP-SwifJ**

Tom at Cruachan, *fr.* Words for Music Perhaps. William Butler Yeats. **CP-YeatW**

Tom Ball's Barn. Ted Kooser. **SP-KoosT**

Tom Blinks his Nose is full of wheales, and these. Upon Blinks. Robert Herrick. **CP-HerrR**

Tom Deadlight. Herman Melville. **SP-MelvH**

Tom-Dobbin. Thom Gunn. **CP-GunnT**

 "He grins, he plunges into orgy. It moves about."

 "Hot in his mind, Tom watches Dobbin fuck."

 "Light is in the pupil."

 "Mammal is with her young. She is unique, The."

 "Ruthlessly gentle, gently ruthless we move."

Tom dreamed he was visiting. Tom's Dream. James Schuyler. **CP-SchuJ**

Tom Fool at Jamaica. Marianne Craig Moore. **CP-MoorM**

Tom, for a goose you keep but base quills. Sheridan, a Goose. Jonathan Swift. **CP-SwifJ**

Tom—garlanded with squat and surly steel. Tom's Garland: Upon the Unemployed. Gerard Manley Hopkins. **CP-HopkG**

Tom Grumblod's bridge has balusters set diagonally. The Other Cambridge. John Berryman. **CP-BerrJ**

Tom left his seabag behind and this uke. Stoker Tom's Ukulele. Malcolm Lowry. **CP-LowrM**

Tom May's Death. Andrew Marvell. **CP-MarvA**

Tom Mullinex and Dick. Jonathan Swift. **CP-SwifJ**

Tom Noddy's body speaks, not so his mind. The Dilemma. Robert Ranke Graves. **CP-GravR**

Tom O'Roughley. William Butler Yeats. **CP-YeatW**

Tom Raban. William Cowper. **CP-CowpW**

Tom Rich. Phoebe Hesketh. **SP-HeskP**

Tom Rich, the gardener, / has a strawberry mark on his face. Tom Rich. Phoebe Hesketh. **SP-HeskP**

Tom shifts the Trenchers; yet he never can. Upon Trencherman. Robert Herrick. **CP-HerrR**

Tom the Lunatic, *fr.* Words for Music Perhaps. William Butler Yeats. **CP-YeatW**

Tom-tom, c'est moi. The blue guitar. Wallace Stevens. **CMoP** *Fr.* The Man with the Blue Guitar. **CP-StevW**

Tom, Tom, the Piper's Son. John Crowe Ransom. *Fr.* Sixteen Poems in Eight Pairings. **SP-RansJ**

Tomatoes. Stephen Dobyns. **SP-DobyS**

Tomb Cover of Imam Riza. *Unknown, tr. fr. Persian by* Thomas Merton. **CP-MertT**

Tomb of a millionaire. Graceland. Carl Sandburg. **CP-SandC**

Tomb of Akr Caar, The. Ezra Pound. **SP-PounE**

Tomb of Arminius! render up thy dead. Percy Bysshe Shelley. *Fr.* Ode to Liberty. **CP-ShelP**

Tomb of Stéphane Mallarmé, The. Charles Simic. **SP-SimiC**

Tomb Stone. James Dickey. **CP-DickJ**

Tombless Epitaph, A. Samuel Taylor Coleridge. **CP-ColeS**

Tombstone Blues. "Bob Dylan." **CP-DylaB**

Tombstone Told When She Died, The. Dylan Thomas. **CP-ThomD**

Tome-Thoughts, from the *Times*. John Updike. **CP-UpdiJ**

Tomlinson. Rudyard Kipling. **CP-KiplR**

Tommies in the Train. David Herbert Lawrence. **CP-LawrD**

Tommy. Rudyard Kipling. **CP-KiplR**

Tommy is three and when he's bad. Red Roses. Anne Sexton. **CP-SextA**

"Tommy" you was when it began. The Service Man. Rudyard Kipling. **CP-KiplR**

Tommy's Pond. John Ciardi. **SP-CiarJ**

Tomorrow. Donald Hall. **CP-HallD**

Tomorrow. Langston Hughes. **SP-HughL**

Tomorrow. Charles Olson. **CP-OlsoC**

Tomorrow. Kenneth Patchen. **CP-PatcK**

Tomorrow. James Schuyler. **CP-SchuJ**

Tomorrow being Monday—. Marsden Hartley. **CP-HartM**

Tomorrow Is a Long Time. "Bob Dylan." **CP-DylaB**

Tomorrow is St. Valentine's: / tomorrow I'll think about. February 13, 1975. James Schuyler. **CP-SchuJ**

Tomorrow, Julia, I betimes must rise. The Perfume. Robert Herrick. **CP-HerrR**

Tomorrow let loveless, let lover tomorrow make love. The Vigil of Venus. *Unknown, tr. fr. Latin by* Allen Tate. **CP-TateA**

Tomorrow meet you? O not tomorrow. Gerard Manley Hopkins. **CP-HopkG**

Tomorrow Morning. Robert Penn Warren. *Fr.* Penological Study: Southern Exposure. **SP-WarrR**

Tomorrow morning at four, the women will be herded. Announcement. Richard Hugo. **CP-HugoR**

Tomorrow Never Knows. The Beatles. **CP-Beatl**

Tomorrow Night, *also stands as sl. diff. separate poem* Picadilly Circus at Night. David Herbert Lawrence. *Fr.* Night Songs. **CP-LawrD**

Tomorrow, Partly Cloudy. Ogden Nash. **CP-NashO**

"Tomorrow"—whose location. Emily Dickinson. **CP-DickE**

Tomorrow with his notes a man will come. Dissertation I. John Hewitt. **CP-HewiJ**

Tomorrow's Envy of Today. Robert Ranke Graves. **CP-GravR**

Tomorrow's Song. Gary Snyder. **CP-SnydG**

Tom's a-Cold. Stephen Spender. **CP-SpenS**

Tom's Angel. Walter de la Mare. **CP-DeLaW**

Tom's Attempt to Seduce Big Brother Steve. James Schuyler. **CP-SchuJ**

Tom's Dream. James Schuyler. **CP-SchuJ**

Tom's Garland: Upon the Unemployed. Gerard Manley Hopkins. **CP-HopkG**

Tone Poem, A. John Ashbery. **SP-AshbJ**

Tones of voice are petty, The. Tom Clark. *Fr.* Suite. **SP-ClarT**

Tongue that serves in courtroom is alien metal, The. For James Schevill. Kay Boyle. **CP-BoylK**

Tongue there is wags, down in the dark wood O, A. John Berryman. *Fr.* Sonnets to Chris. **CP-BerrJ**

Tongue—to tell Him I am true!, A. Emily Dickinson. **CP-DickE**

Tonguless crocodile / Meets eyeless tiger darted. Charles Henri Ford. **SP-FordC** *Fr.* Emblems of Arachne.

Tonight. Charles Bukowski. **SP-BukC1**

Tonight / when you spread your pallet. Accident. Maya Angelou. **SP-AngeM**

Tonight at the end of a long. The New Road. Richard Shelton. **SP-ShelR**

Tonight beside this hearth the farmer sat. The Ceilidhe. John Hewitt. **CP-HewiJ**

Tonight, grave sir, both my poor[e] house and I. Inviting a Friend to Supper. Ben Jonson, *after* Martial. **CP-JonsB**

Tonight I let loose the weasel of my body. Roughhousing. Stephen Dobyns. **SP-DobyS**

Tonight I watch my father's hair. Two Postures beside a Fire. James Wright. **CP-WrigJ**

Tonight I'll Be Staying Here with You. "Bob Dylan." **CP-DylaB**

Tonight in Philadelphia, I saw you, Li Po. For the Ghost of Li Po. Stephen Berg. **SP-BergS**

Tonight it is the wine (or not the wine). Excuse. Alice Walker. **CP-WalkA**

Tonight, nothing is long enough—. The Tunnel. Robert Creeley. **CP-CreeR**

Tonight, on the deck, the lights. Two Stories. Charles Wright. **SP-WrigC**

Tonight she is making her way. Living Near the Rehabilitation Home. Ted Kooser. **SP-KoosT**

Tonight the blessèd state, that long repose. De Quincey in Later Life. Derek Mahon. **SP-MahoD**

Tonight the moon is round golden entire. It. Edward Estlin Cummings. **CP-CummE**

Tonight the toll booth men are. Coming Home, Garden State Parkway. Stephen Dunn. **SP-DunnS**

Tonight the waves march. Moonlight Night: Carmel. Langston Hughes. **SP-HughL**

To-night the Winds Begin. Tennyson. **BiP; EBVV; FaBoEn; GTBS-6; GTBS-P; ImPo; LiTB; NOBE; OAEL-2; OBNC; PeECV; PoEL-5** *Fr.* In Memoriam A. H. H. **CP-TennA**

Tonight the woods are darkened. The Hazel Leaf. Robert Penn Warren. *Fr.* Dark Woods. **SP-WarrR**

Tonight the Woods Are Darkened. Robert Penn Warren. *Fr.* Dark Woods. **SP-WarrR**

Tonight, their simple church grown glamorous. Songs of Praise. Derek Mahon. **SP-MahoD**

Tonight there are only the winter stars. Dezembrum. Wallace Stevens. **CP-StevW**

Tonight There Is a Showing of Champion Lights. Thomas Merton. **CP-MertT**

Tonight this anguish hurts my hands. Bequest. Alun Lewis. **CP-LewiA**

Tonight ungathered let us leave. Tennyson. **EBVV; FHYEP; OAEL-2** *Fr.* In Memoriam A. H. H. **CP-TennA**

Tonight we are driving past Lac Qui Parle toward Boston. Driving toward Boston I Run across One of Robert Bly's Old Poems. Thomas McGrath. **SP-McGrT**

Tonight we dine without the Master. Philip Larkin. **FaBoDD** *Fr.* Livings. **CP-LarkP**

Tonight we feel the muffled peal. Uffington. Sir John Betjeman. **CP-BetjJ**

Tonight with the full green moon. Penance. James McAuley. **SP-McAuJ**

Tonite all is well. . . What a. Allen Ginsberg. **CP-GinsA**

Tonite I got hi in the window of my apartment. I Beg You Come Back & Be Cheerful. Allen Ginsberg. **CP-GinsA**

Tonite I walked out of my red apartment door on East tenth street's. Mugging. Allen Ginsberg. **CP-GinsA**

Tonite I walked out of my red apartment door on East tenth street's dusk. Allen Ginsberg. **HCAP** *Fr.* Mugging. **CP-GinsA**

Tonnage of instinctive / Wisdom in tinsel. Elephants. Louis MacNeice. *Fr.* Circus. **CP-MacNL**

Tony. Richard Hugo. **CP-HugoR**

Too Anxious for Rivers. Robert Frost. **CP-FrosR**

Too big & too intelligent. Elegy for a Whale. Erica Jong. **SP-JongE**

Too Busy. Paul Laurence Dunbar. *See* The Lord had a job for me, but I had so much to do.

Too calm to beg for pity yet too strained. Gaza. Jane Cooper. **SP-CoopJ**

Too cold almost for hope of Spring. St. Valentine's Day 1881. Christina Georgina Rossetti. **CP-RosC3**

Too cold for joy, too cold for woe. George Meredith. **CP-MerG2**

Too cold is this. Emily Dickinson. **CP-DickE**

Too Dear, Too Vague. Wystan Hugh Auden. **CP-AudeW**

Too far away, O love, I know. Drunk. David Herbert Lawrence. **CP-LawrD**

Too fevered to insist. The Invisible Trouble. Leonard Cohen. **CP-CoheL**

Too few the mornings be. Emily Dickinson. **CP-DickE**

Too fierce the candlelight; your gentle voice. A Measure of Casualness. Robert Ranke Graves. **CP-GravR**

Too frail for combat, he stands [or stood]. Aircraft. Rita Dove. **SP-DoveR**

Too frail to keep the lofty vow. Thoughts Suggested the Day Following, on the Banks of Nith, near the Poet's Residence. William Wordsworth. **CP-WorW1**

Too good to be true—a city that empties. Rio de Janeiro. John Updike. **CP-UpdiJ**

Too happy Time dissolves itself. Emily Dickinson. **CP-DickE**

Too large in feature for a world of cuties. Louis MacNeice. *Fr.* The Kingdom. **CP-MacNL**

Too Late. Robert Browning. **CP-BroR1**

Too Late. Charles Bukowski. **SP-BukC3**

Too late / Hard fish / Too late to be morning. It Is Morning. Joseph Ceravolo. **SP-CeraJ**

Too Late? Henry Wadsworth Longfellow. *See* It Is Too Late.

Too Late. Christina Georgina Rossetti. *See* Bride Song.

Too late, alas! the song. Rudyard Kipling. *See* The Plea of the Simla Dancers.

Too late for love, too late for joy. Bride Song. Christina Georgina Rossetti. **OBEV; OBVV; OtMeF; WPE** *Fr.* The Prince's Progress. **CP-RosC1**

Too late for the westend sunset. Moonlighters. Laurence Lieberman. **SP-LiebL**

Too late the anxious fire came. Ralph Waldo Emerson. **CP-EmerR**

Too late, too late! I did not know my fairness. A Beauty's Soliloquy during Her Honeymoon. Thomas Hardy. **CP-HardT**

Too-Late Words to My Father. John Clellon Holmes. **SP-HolmJ**

Too little / has been said. The Door. Charles Tomlinson. **CP-TomlC**

Too little way the House must lie. Emily Dickinson. **CP-DickE**

Too many beautiful women lie alone in bed. INTERIOR: *The Man Turns the Sheet for the Musician* (Dutch). Jenny Joseph. *Fr.* Altarpiece (A Meditation on Lust, Desire and Love). **SP-JoseJ**

Too many curds on the meat, too many dark cloth caps. Constant. Louis MacNeice. **CP-MacNL**

Too many, Lord, abuse thy grace. Abuse of the Gospel. William Cowper. *Fr.* Olney Hymns. **CP-CowpW**

Too many teeth / In this city. Fear of Dreaming. Jim Carroll. **SP-CarrJ**

Too much. The Crunch. Charles Bukowski. **SP-BukC1**

Too Much. Marianne Craig Moore. **CMoP** *Fr.* The Jerboa. **CP-MoorM**

Too much industry. Allen Ginsberg. **EaPr** *Fr.* Ruhr-Gebiet. **CP-GinsA**

Too much industry. Ruhr-Gebiet. Allen Ginsberg. **CP-GinsA**

Too Much of Nothing. "Bob Dylan." **CP-DylaB**

Too much you mint me that cheating counterfeit. Aloof in Gaiety. David Herbert Lawrence. **CP-LawrD**

Too old for love and still to love! The Wild Old Wicked Man. Archibald MacLeish. **CP-MacLA**

Too pale! Too changed! Flowers to the House. Kenneth Patchen. **CP-PatcK**

Too peremptory a Courtship for Earth. Emily Dickinson. **SP-DickE**

Too poor for a bribe, and too proud to importune. Sketch of His Own Character. Thomas Gray. **CP-GrayT**

Too proud to die; broken and blind he died. Elegy. Dylan Thomas. **CP-ThomD**

Too scanty 'twas to die for you. Emily Dickinson. **CP-DickE**

Too soon, too soon, a man will come. Two Horses Playing in the Orchard. James Wright. **CP-WrigJ**

Too soon you wearied of our tears. Darling Daughter of Babylon. Nicholas Vachel Lindsay. **CP-LindV**

Too Tenuous. Hayden Carruth. **CP-CarHS**

Too tight, it is running over. Fence Wire. James Dickey. **CP-DickJ**

Too tired to sleep I switch a picture on. Late Show. Miller Williams. **SP-WillM**

Took my leave (last) five times before the end. In Memoriam (1914–1953). John Berryman. **CP-BerrJ**

Tools. Barton Sutter. **SP-SuttB**

"As a boy my father preached to trees."

"Motto above my table says, The."

"My dad's old man was a carpenter."

Toomai of the Elephants. Rudyard Kipling. *Fr.* The Jungle Book.

"I will remember what I was. I am sick of rope and chain." **CP-KiplR**

Shiv and the Grasshopper. **CP-KiplR**

Toome Road, The. Seamus Heaney. **SP-HeanS**

Tooth-Ache Cured by a Kiss, The. Thomas Carew. **CP-CareT**

Tooth upon Our Peace, A. Emily Dickinson. **CP-DickE**

Toothache Man. John Updike. **CP-UpdiJ**

Tooting down the Gran Via. Madrid, May, 1977. Mona Van Duyn. **SP-VanDM**

Top of the mountain, The. Thinking. Robert Creeley. **CP-CreeR**

Top of the Park, Hillis. Top of the World. Overlooking Yale. Richard Hugo. **CP-HugoR**

Top of the ridge is a cornfield, The. Cornfield Ridge and Stream. Carl Sandburg. **CP-SandC**

Top the burning funnel house with watchman's eyes. Queens Tunnel. Thomas Merton. *Fr.* North. *Fr.* The Geography of Lograire. **CP-MertT**

Top-turfy gimp fiery oes eyes. Queen Anne's Lace. Louis Zukofsky. **CP-ZukLS**

Topaz of the Sixties, The. Marsden Hartley. **CP-HartM**

Tophet. Thomas Gray. **CP-GrayT**

("Thus Tophet look'd; so grinned the brawling fiend.") **CP-GrayT**

Topics. James Merrill. **SP-MerrJ**

Caesarion.

Casual Wear. **NIP**

Popular Demand.

Topless. Stephen Dobyns. **SP-DobyS**

Topographical Map. Richard Hugo. **CP-HugoR**

Topography of History, The. Thomas McGrath. **SP-McGrT**

Tops. Philip Larkin. **CP-LarkP**

Tops heel and yaw. Tops. Philip Larkin. **CP-LarkP**

Tops of the midnight trees move helter-skelter. Window. Robert Lowell. **SP-LoweR**

Topsfield Fair. John Updike. **CP-UpdiJ**

Topsy: Part 2. Al Young. **CP-YounA**

Tor House. Robinson Jeffers. **CP-JefR1**

Torcello. John Hewitt. **CP-HewiJ**

Torch, The. Walt Whitman. **CP-WhitW**

Torch and Crown, 1968, *English Vers. of* Antorcha y Corona, 1968. Robert Ranke Graves. **CP-GravR**

Torch-Bearers' Race, The. Robinson Jeffers. **CP-JefR1**

Torches in the windy corridors, The. Huon of Bordeaux. Robert Duncan. **SP-DuncR**

Tormented with incessant pains. To Stella. Jonathan Swift. **CP-SwifJ**

Torn boughs trailing o'er the tusks aslant, The. Rudyard Kipling. **CP-KiplR**

Torn Canvas. Jim Carroll. **SP-CarrJ**

Torn Down from Glory Daily. Anne Sexton. **CP-SextA**

Torn from the dream-life, torn from the life-dream. Midnight Outcry. Robert Penn Warren. **SP-WarrR**

Torn hillside with its crooked hands, The. A Description of Some Confederate Soldiers. Randall Jarrell. **CP-JarrR**

Torn into light, you woke wriggling. How Much Earth. Philip Levine. **SP-LeviP**

Torn Letter, The. Thomas Hardy. **CP-HardT**

Torn-up newspaper, The. A Perfectly Free Association. Randall Jarrell. **CP-JarrR**

Torn wings of flame are wafting down the sky. The Fall of Day. David Herbert Lawrence. **CP-LawrD**

Tornado Warning. Karl Shapiro. **SP-ShapK**

Torpor and sloth, torpor and sloth. Procrastination Is All of the Time. Ogden Nash. **CP-NashO**

Torquato Tasso rests within this tomb. Gabriello Chiabrera, *tr. fr. Italian by* William Wordsworth. **CP-WorW1**

Torquemada. Stevie Smith. **CP-SmitS**

Torrent, The. Edwin Arlington Robinson. **CP-RobiE**

Torrent that rushes down. Song from *Puck Fair*. Muriel Rukeyser. **CP-RukeM**

Torso, The. Robert Duncan. **SP-DuncR** *Fr.* Passages.

Tortoise, The. Ogden Nash. **CP-NashO**

Tortoise Family Connections. David Herbert Lawrence. **CP-LawrD**

Tortoise Gallantry. David Herbert Lawrence. **CP-LawrD**

Tortoise-Shell. David Herbert Lawrence. **CP-LawrD**

Tortoise Shout. David Herbert Lawrence. **CP-LawrD**

Torture. Margaret Atwood. **SP-AtwM2**

Torture. Alice Walker. **CP-WalkA**

Torture me not with this or that or this. Hilda Doolittle. *Fr.* Epigrams. **CP-DoolH**

Torture scene developed under a glass bell, The. Heirloom. Leonard Cohen. **CP-CoheL**

Tortured, The. May Sarton. **SP-SartM**

Tortures of hell are stern, their fires burn fiercely, The. Malcolm Lowry. *Fr.* Songs for Second Childhood. **CP-LowrM**

Toss, for John Cage, A. Charles Olson. **CP-OlsoC**

Tossed [*or* Toss'd] in a troubled sea of griefs, I float. To Her in Absence; a Ship. Thomas Carew. **CP-CareT**

Tossing and Turning. John Updike. **CP-UpdiJ**

Tossing loneliness of many nights, The. Legende. Hart Crane. **CP-CranH**

Tossing spray of Cocheco's fall, The. How the Women Went from Dover. John Greenleaf Whittier. **CP-WhitJ**

Tosts as snakes or as the mortall *Henbane*. Epigramme. Thomas Campion. *Fr.* Observations in the Art of English Poesie. **CP-CampT**

Total Incandescence. Al Young. **CP-YounA**

Total Influence of Outcome of the Matter: The Sun, The. Marge Piercy. *See* The Sun.

Total Parts of a World, The. Robert Creeley. **CP-CreeR**

Total stranger one black day, A. Edward Estlin Cummings. **CP-CummE**

Totally abashed and smiling. St. Paul and All That. Frank O'Hara. **SP-OharF**

Totem, The. Rudyard Kipling. **CP-KiplR**

Totem. Sylvia Plath. **CP-PlatS**

Totem, The. Gilbert Sorrentino. **SP-SorrG**

Toting It Up. Stephen Dobyns. **SP-DobyS**

Tou Wan Speaks to Her Husband Liu Sheng. Rita Dove. **SP-DoveR**

Toucan, The. Ogden Nash. *Fr.* The Astigmatic Naturalist. **CP-NashO**

Toucan, The. Shel Silverstein. **SP-SilS2**

Toucan's profile is prognathous, The. The Toucan. Ogden Nash. *Fr.* The Astigmatic Naturalist. **CP-NashO**

Touch. Thom Gunn. **CP-GunnT**

Touch. Erica Jong. **SP-JongE**

Touch. David Herbert Lawrence. **CP-LawrD**

Touch, The. Frederick Morgan. **SP-MorgF**

Touch, The. Anne Sexton. **CP-SextA**

Touch-and-Go. Sylvia Plath. **CP-PlatS**

Touch and Go. Stevie Smith. **CP-SmitS**

Touch but thy lyre, my Harry, and I hear. To M. Henry Lawes, the Excellent Composer[,] of his Lyrics. Robert Herrick. **CP-HerrR**

Touch Comes. David Herbert Lawrence. **CP-LawrD**

Touch gently / with the tips of their. Saleswomen in Bakery Shops. Mona Van Duyn. **SP-VanDM**

Touch it: it won't shrink like an eyeball. A Life. Sylvia Plath. **CP-PlatS**

Touch lightly Nature's sweet Guitar. Emily Dickinson. **CP-DickE**

Touch me not forget me not, touch me forget me. Children's Games. Louis MacNeice. **CP-MacNL**

Touch My Shut Lips. Robert Ranke Graves. **CP-GravR**

Touch of flame—the illuminating fire—the loftiest look at last, The. Old Age's Lambent Peaks. Walt Whitman. **CP-WhitW**

Touch of Spring. John Updike. **CP-UpdiJ**

Touch of Things, The. John Hewitt. **CP-HewiJ**

Touch of vocal flattery. Drowse Murmurs. Allen Ginsberg. **CP-GinsA**

Touched by fire, / Holding the light in my hand. Prometheus. Richard Eberhart. **CP-EberR**

Touched with the sin of false play, in his punk. On Captain Hazard the Cheater. Ben Jonson. **CP-JonsB**

Touching. Archie Randolph Ammons. **SP-AmmoA**

Touching "Never." Christina Georgina Rossetti. **CP-RosC2**

Touching you i say(it being Spring). Edward Estlin Cummings. **CP-CummE**

Touchy old gent from Cohasset, A. John Updike. *Fr.* Two Limericks after Lear.

Tough fire and water, you can't just have clouds. Attention: First Lady of the Festival. James Liddy. **CP-LiddJ**

Tough Mama. "Bob Dylan." **CP-DylaB**

Tour, The, *parody of* George Gordon, Lord Byron. Rudyard Kipling. **CP-KiplR** *Fr.* The Muse among the Motors.

Tour, The. Sylvia Plath. **CP-PlatS**

Tour 5. Robert Earl Hayden. **CP-HaydR**

Tourist and the Town, The. Adrienne Rich. **CP-RicAE; SP-RicA2**

Tourist Death. Archibald MacLeish. **CP-MacLA**

Tourist Eye. George Oppen. **CP-OppeG**

"Down-town / Swarms. Surely the oldest city."

"Heart pounds / To be among them, the buildings, The."

"Lights that blaze and promise, The."

"Rectangular, rearing / Black windows into daylight: the sound."

"Solitary are obsessed, The."

Tourists. David Herbert Lawrence. **CP-LawrD**

Tourists at Ensenada. Thomas McGrath. **SP-McGrT**

Tourists in summer, looking at the view. The Sand Man. Thom Gunn. **CP-GunnT**

Tousled Pillow. Robert Ranke Graves. **CP-GravR**

Toussaint L'Ouverture. John Greenleaf Whittier. **CP-WhitJ**

Toussaint, the most unhappy man of men! To Toussaint L'Ouverture. William Wordsworth. **CP-WorW1**

Tout Entouré de Mon Regard. Charles Tomlinson. **CP-TomlC**

Tow generations bridge or part us. *Song:* The Queen of Time. Robert Ranke Graves. **CP-GravR**

Tow Head on his skateboard. Skateboard. Thom Gunn. **CP-GunnT**

Toward a better world I contribute my modest smidgin. The Squab. Ogden Nash. *Fr.* Nature-Walks, or, Not to Mention a Dopping of Sheldrakes. **CP-NashO**

Toward a Definition of Marriage. Mona Van Duyn. **SP-VanDM**

Toward An Organic Philosophy. Kenneth Rexroth. **SP-RexrK**

Toward August's end. Calendar. John Updike. **CP-UpdiJ**

Toward Climax. Gary Snyder. **CP-SnydG**

Toward countries that ripen the mustard. Runaway Sun. Pablo Neruda, *tr. fr. Spanish by* Ben Belitt. **SP-NeruP**

Toward evening, sky's aqua. Nara Park: Twilight Deer Feeding. Laurence Lieberman. **SP-LiebL**

Toward Many Glaciers. John Haines. *Fr.* News from the Glacier. **SP-HainJ**

Toward sun, the sun flared suddenly red. Summer Storm (Circa 1916), and God's Grace. Robert Penn Warren. **SP-WarrR**

Toward the End of Winter. Gilbert Sorrentino. **SP-SorrG**

Toward the Piraeus. Hilda Doolittle. **CP-DoolH**

Toward the sea turning my troubled eye. Edmund Spenser. **ChTr** *Fr.* Visions of the World's Vanity [*or* Vanitie]. **CP-Spens**

(Huge Leviathian, The.) **ChTr**

Toward the Verrazano. Stephen Dunn. **SP-DunnS**

Toward world's end, through the bare. The Magi. Louise Glück. **SP-GlücL**

Towards Autumn. Marilyn Hacker. **SP-HackM**

Towards Break of Day. William Butler Yeats. **CP-YeatW**

Towards nightfall when the wind. Winter Mask. Allen Tate. **CP-TateA**

Towards sending of Ellsworth. Canto 63. Ezra Pound. *Fr.* Cantos. **CP-PoCan**

Towards the altar sober-paced I went. John Keats. **TOF** *Fr.* The Fall of Hyperion. **CP-KeatJ**

Towards the end he sailed into an extraordinary mildness. Herman Melville. Wystan Hugh Auden. **CP-AudeW**

Towards the Noel that morte saison. Villonaud for This Yule. Ezra Pound. **SP-PounE**

Towards the North Star. John Gould Fletcher. **SP-FletJ**

Towards the sun, towards the south-west. Eagle in New Mexico. David Herbert Lawrence. **CP-LawrD**

Towards the sun, towards the south-west. David Herbert Lawrence. **RB** *Fr.* Eagle in New Mexico. **CP-LawrD**

Tower, The. John Gould Fletcher. **SP-FletJ**

Tower, The. Randall Jarrell. **CP-JarrR**

Tower, The. William Butler Yeats. **CP-YeatW**

"Now shall I make my soul." **OBD**

Tower beyond Tragedy, The. Robinson Jeffers. **CP-JefR1**

Tower in tiers of architraves, The. Pisa's Leaning Tower. Herman Melville. **SP-MelvH**

Tower is broken, the house, The. La Torre. Charles Olson. **CP-OlsoC**

Tower of Babel. Thomas Merton. **CP-MertT**

Tower of Babel—A Morality, The. Thomas Merton. **CP-MertT**

City of God, The.

Legend of the Tower, The.

Tower of Famine, The. Percy Bysshe Shelley. **CP-ShelP**

Tower of Love, The. Robert Ranke Graves. **CP-GravR**

Tower of Song, The. Leonard Cohen. **CP-CoheL**

Tower of the Spirit, The. Chuang Tzu, *tr. fr. Chinese by* Thomas Merton. **CP-MertT**

Tower Struck by Lightning Reversed; the Overturning of the Tower, The. Marge Piercy. *Fr.* Laying Down the Tower. **SP-PierM**

Tower there is, where six Maidens do dwell, A. The Six Maidens. Alexander Pope. **CP-PopeA**

Towering wall divides your house from mine, A. The Wall. Robert Ranke Graves. **CP-GravR**

Towers that generations did combine, The. Van Buren. Ralph Waldo Emerson. **CP-EmerR**

Towery city and branchy between towers. Duns Scotus's Oxford. Gerard Manley Hopkins. **CP-HopkG**

Town, The. Charles Olson. **CP-OlsoC**

Town Clerk's Views, The. Sir John Betjeman. **CP-BetjJ**

Town does not exist, The. The Starry Night. Anne Sexton. **CP-SextA**

Town Down the River, The. Edwin Arlington Robinson. **CP-RobiE**

Town Dump, The. Howard Nemerov. **CP-NemeH**

Town Eclogue, A. Jonathan Swift. **CP-SwifJ**

Town grows fiercer with heat!, The. Labour Battalion. David Herbert Lawrence. **CP-LawrD**

Town has opened to the sun, The. Bombardment. David Herbert Lawrence. **CP-LawrD**

Town I was born in holds no memories, The. "Bob Dylan." *Fr.* 11 Outlined Epitaphs. **CP-DylaB**

Town in 1917. David Herbert Lawrence. **CP-LawrD**

Town of American Visions, The. Nicholas Vachel Lindsay. **CP-LindV**

Town of Hill, The. Donald Hall. **CP-HallD**

Town of Schwytz, The. William Wordsworth. *Fr.* Memorials of a Tour of the Continent; 1820. **CP-WorW2**

Town or poem, I don't care how it looks. Old woman. White Center. Richard Hugo. **CP-HugoR**

Town, the churchyard, and the setting sun, The. On Visiting the Tomb of Burns. John Keats. **CP-KeatJ**

Town was famous then, though few recall, The. David's Folly. Daniel Gerard Hoffman. **SP-HoffD**

Town was nameless because it could, The. The Listener. Stephen Dunn. **SP-DunnS**

Townend, 1976. Donald Davie. **CP-DavDo**

Townland of Peace. John Hewitt. *Fr.* Freehold. **CP-HewiJ**

Towns We Know and Leave Behind, the Rivers We Carry with Us, The. Richard Hugo. **CP-HugoR**

Townsfolk, The. Lewis Turco. **SP-TurcL**

Townspeople peer out their windows, The. *Envoi:* The Wind Carol. Lewis Turco. **SM** *Fr.* Bordello. **SP-TurcL**

Townspeople, those Dr. Williams loved and despised, The. Fourth. Hayden Carruth. **CP-CarHS**

Tow'r of brass, whose doors were barr'd, A. 3.16. Horace. **SP-SmarC**, *tr.* by Christopher Smart; *Fr.* Odes.

Toy, The. Roy Fisher. **SP-FishR**

Toy Bone, The. Donald Hall. **CP-HallD**

Toy Factory. Charles Simic. **SP-SimiC**

Toy Trucks and Fried Rice. John Yau. **SP-YauJo**

Toyland. Roy Fisher. **SP-FishR**

Toys and rose The zoo body zigzags. How Spring Comes. Alice Notley. **SP-NotlA**

Trace, The. Roy Fisher. **SP-FishR**

Traces of pink Bergdorf light. Invisible Sleep. Jim Carroll. **SP-CarrJ**

Track. Richard Eberhart. **CP-EberR**

Track across the desert runs vague toward the north star and then more firmly, The. The Dead Men's Child. Robinson Jeffers. **CP-JefR1**

Track cuts west. Slant roof, sun-catcher, The. Muriel Rukeyser. **CP-RukeM**

Track of moonlight on a quiet lake, A. In Peace. John Greenleaf Whittier. **CP-WhitJ**

Track of the Master Builder, The. Marge Piercy. **SP-PierM**

Tracking through this. Love ("Tracking through this"). Robert Creeley. **CP-CreeR**

Trackless and lost between piss colored walls. His Wife at Bellevue. Marilyn Hacker. **SP-HackM** *Fr.* The Navigators.

Tracks of rain and light linger in. Romance Moderne. William Carlos Williams. **CP-WilW1**

Tracks of the snowshoe rabbit across the. Hayden Carruth. *Fr.* North Winter. **CP-CarHL**

Tract. William Carlos Williams. **CP-WilW1**

Tractatus. Derek Mahon. **SP-MahoD**

Traction Engine, The. Wystan Hugh Auden. **CP-AudWJ**

Tractor. Ted Hughes. **SP-HughT**

Tractor stands frozen—an agony, The. Tractor. Ted Hughes. **SP-HughT**

Trade, The. Rudyard Kipling. **CP-KiplR**

Trade, The. Gary Snyder. **CP-SnydG**

Trade-wind jingles the rings in the nets around the racks by the docks on Indian River. Indian River. Wallace Stevens. **CP-StevW**

Trader, The. Frederick Morgan. **SP-MorgF**

Trader I am to the African shore, A. Sweet Meat Has Sour Sauce. William Cowper. **CP-CowpW**

Trades scant aware is plentiful. Zebrina etc. Louis Zukofsky. **CP-ZukLS**

Trading Post, The. Lewis Turco. **SP-TurcL**

Tradition. John Dryden. **OBS** *Fr.* Religio Laici. **SP-DrydJ**

Tradition. William Wordsworth. *Fr.* The River Duddon [A Series of Sonnets]. **CP-WorW2**

Tradition of Oker Hill in Darley Dale, Derbyshire, A. William Wordsworth. **CP-WorW2**

Traditional Tune. Muriel Rukeyser. **CP-RukeM**

Traditionalist, The. Robert Ranke Graves. **CP-GravR**

Traditon, be thou mute! Oblivion, throw. In the Sound of Mull. William Wordsworth. **CP-WorW2**

Trafalgar Day. George Meredith. **CP-MerG2**

Traffic. Jim Carroll. **SP-CarrJ**

Traffic. Donald Hall. **CP-HallD**

Traffic Light. Shel Silverstein. **SP-SilS2**

Traffic Signals. Charles Bukowski. **SP-BukC1**

Traffic, the lion, the sophisticate. The Lion. William Carlos Williams. **CP-WilW2**

Traffic, to speak from knowledge but begun. To the Great Metropolis. Arthur Hugh Clough. **SP-ClouA**

Trafficker. Carl Sandburg. **CP-SandC**

Tragedian to Tragedienne. Thomas Hardy. **CP-HardT**

Tragedy. David Herbert Lawrence. **CP-LawrD**

Tragedy has no curtain. Renewal. Alun Lewis. **CP-LewiA**

Tragedy of that moment, The. That Moment. Thomas Hardy. **CP-HardT**

Tragedy seems to me a loud noise. Tragedy. David Herbert Lawrence. **CP-LawrD**

Tragic Detail. William Carlos Williams. **CP-WilW2**

Tragic man stares at the sun, The. Cloud Seeding. Howard Nemerov. **CP-NemeH**

Trail of Admiral Keppel, The. William Cowper. **CP-CowpW**

Trailed and lagging grass, a pin-point island, A. Logic. Charles Tomlinson. **CP-TomlC**

Trailing Arbutus, The. John Greenleaf Whittier. **CP-WhitJ**

Trailing Clouds, *also stands as separate poem* A Baby Asleep after Pain. David Herbert Lawrence. *Fr.* Baby-Movements. **CP-LawrD**

Trail's high up on the ridge, no one goes down, The. Love-Children. Robinson Jeffers. **CP-JefR1**

Trails of light all start, The. In the Wall. Roy Fisher. **SP-FishR**

Trails of troubles, / Roads of battles. Paths of Victory. "Bob Dylan." **CP-DylaB**

Train, The. David Herbert Lawrence. **CP-LawrD**

Train A-Travelin'. "Bob Dylan." **CP-DylaB**

Train at Night, A. David Herbert Lawrence. **CP-LawrD**

Train at Pershore station was waiting that Sunday night, The. Pershore Station, or a Liverish Journey First Class. Sir John Betjeman. **CP-BetjJ**

Train carries me swiftly by, yet, The. Landscape, Without Color. Charles Olson. **CP-OlsoC**

Train draws forth from the station-yard, The. Love the Monopolist. Thomas Hardy. **CP-HardT**

Train, in running across the weald, has fallen into a steadier stroke, The. Red Moon-Rise. David Herbert Lawrence. **CP-LawrD**

Train is moving, The. The Leave Train. Phoebe Hesketh. **SP-HeskP**

Train of gay and clouded days, A. Life. Ralph Waldo Emerson. **CP-EmerR**

Train Rising Out of the Sea. John Ashbery. **SP-AshbJ**

Train-Signal. Louis Zukofsky. *Fr.* 29 Songs. **CP-ZukLS**

Train sits airtight, The. Dresden to Chesapeake Bay. Jim Carroll. **SP-CarrJ**

Train slows down, The. Arrival and Departure. Archibald MacLeish. **CP-MacLA**

Train Stops at Healy Fork, The. John Haines. **SP-HainJ**

Train to Dublin. Louis MacNeice. **CP-MacNL**

Train Tune. Louise Bogan. **CP-BogaL**

Train went through a burial gate, A. Emily Dickinson. **CP-DickE**

Training. Wilfred Owen. **CP-OwenW**

Training for Kid Aztec. Charles Bukowski. **SP-BukC3**

Trains came threading quietly through my dozing childhood. Trains in the Distance. Louis MacNeice. **CP-MacNL**

Trains in the Distance. Louis MacNeice. **CP-MacNL**

Trains pass and the trains pass, chains of lighted windows, The. A Contact. Louis MacNeice. **CP-MacNL**

Traitor, The. Leonard Cohen. **CP-CoheL**

Traitor. Phoebe Hesketh. **SP-HeskP**

Traitoring *words*, tearing my thought across. John Berryman. *See* Nowhere.

Traitors. David Herbert Lawrence. **CP-LawrD**

Traitors tho' plumed & steel equipped. Ralph Waldo Emerson. **CP-EmerR**

Trajectory of the Traveling Susan. Marge Piercy. **SP-PierM**

Trala Trala Trala La-le-la. William Carlos Williams. **CP-WilW2**

Tramontana at Lerici. Charles Tomlinson. **CP-TomlC**

Tramp, The. John Clare. **SP-ClarJ**

Tramp sailed grimly on her track, The. The Glory of the Sea. Malcolm Lowry. **CP-LowrM**

Tramp thawing out, A. The Sun Bathers. William Carlos Williams. **CP-WilW1**

Tramp's Refusal, The. Nicholas Vachel Lindsay. **CP-LindV**

Trampwoman's Tragedy, A. Thomas Hardy. **CP-HardT**

Trance. Hilda Doolittle. **CP-DoolH**

Trance. Paul Muldoon. **SP-MuldP**

Trance, The. Stephen Spender. **CP-SpenS**

Tranced, The. Theodore Roethke. **CP-RoetT**

Tranquility a manner. Roy Fisher. **SP-FishR** *Fr.* Handsworth Liberties.

Tranquility at length, when autumn comes. Edna St. Vincent Millay. **CP-MillE**

Tranquility! the sovereign aim wert thou. Suggested by the Foregoing [Monument of Mrs Howard]. William Wordsworth. *Fr.* Poems Composed or Suggested During a Tour, in the Summer of 1833. **CP-WorW2**

Tranquillity! thou better name. Ode to Tranquillity. Samuel Taylor Coleridge. **CP-ColeS**

Transcendence of God, The. John Milton. **OBS** *Fr.* Samson Agonistes. **CP-MiltJ**

Transcendental Etude. Adrienne Rich. **SP-RicA1; SP-RicA2**

Transcendentalism: A Poem in Twelve Books. Robert Browning. **CP-BroR1**

Transcontinent. Donald Hall. **CP-HallD**

Transcript, The. Gilbert Sorrentino. **SP-SorrG**

Transcription of Organ Music. Allen Ginsberg. **CP-GinsA**

Transcriptions from the "Anacreontea." Robert Browning. **CP-BroR2**

Transducer. Archie Randolph Ammons. **SP-AmmoA**

Transfer. Archie Randolph Ammons. **SP-AmmoA**

Transfer, The. Richard Eberhart. **CP-EberR**

Transfiguration, The. Robert Herrick. **CP-HerrR**

Transfigured Bird. James Merrill. **SP-MerrJ**

Transformation. Richard Eberhart. **CP-EberR**

Transformation and Disfiguration. Charles Bukowski. **SP-BukC3**

Transformation: For the Sacred Heart, The. Thomas Merton. **CP-MertT**

Transformations. Thomas Hardy. **CP-HardT**

Transformations. Stanley Jasspon Kunitz. **CP-KuniS**

Transformations. David Herbert Lawrence. **CP-LawrD**

Transformed in show, but more transformed in mind, *speech of Cleophila.* Sir Philip Sidney. **SP-SidnP** *Fr.* Arcadia.

Transgress, The. Muriel Rukeyser. **CP-RukeM**

Transgression of the wicked saith within my heart, The. Psalm 36. Bible, O.T. *Fr.* Psalms.

Transient Barracks. Randall Jarrell. **CP-JarrR; SP-JarrR**

Transient tar-paper shack, The. Carl Sandburg. *Fr.* The People, Yes. **CP-SandC**

Transients and Residents. Thom Gunn. **CP-GunnT**

　　Crosswords.

　　Crystal.

　　Falstaff.

　　Interruption.

Transit. John Berryman. **CP-BerrJ**

Transit. Adrienne Rich. **SP-RicA1; SP-RicA2**

Transit. Richard Wilbur. **CP-WilbR**

Transitional. William Carlos Williams. **CP-WilW1**

Translate into Latin for my Epitaph. James Liddy. **CP-LiddJ**

Translate this into higher math. The Physics of Loneliness. Al Young. **CP-YounA**

Translated from Ronsard. Pierre de Ronsard. *See* Nature withheld Cassandra in the skies.

Translating the Birds. Charles Tomlinson. **CP-TomlC**

Translation. Jenny Joseph. *Fr.* Derivations. **SP-JoseJ**

Translation, A. Rudyard Kipling. **CP-KiplR**

Translation. Howard Nemerov. **CP-NemeH**

Translation, A. Charles Olson. **CP-OlsoC**

Translation. William Carlos Williams. **CP-WilW2**

Translation, The. Louis Zukofsky. **CP-ZukLS**

Translation from a Pantomime Version of Benserade's *Ballet de Cassandre.* Samuel Johnson. *See* I Am Cassander Come Down From The Sky.

Translation from Anacreon. Byron. **CP-Byron**

Translation from Catullus ("Equal to Jove that youth must be"). Catullus. *See* Carmen 51: "Godlike the man who."

Translation from Catullus ("Ye Cupids, droop each little head"). Catullus. *See* Carmen 3: "Who loves beauty / vel her statues."

Translation from Horace, *Fr. the Latin of Horace.* Byron. **CP-Byron**

Translation from Pindar's Seventh Olympian, Epode III. Robert Browning. **CP-BroR2**

Translation from the Medea of Euripides, *Fr. the Greek of Euripides.* Byron. **CP-Byron**

Translation from Vittorelli. Jacopo Vittorelli. *See* Of two fair virgins, modest, though admired.

Translation of a Celebrated Greek Song, *after the Greek of* Callistratus. William Wordsworth. **CP-WorW1**

Translation of a Distich on the Duke of Modena. Samuel Johnson. *See* If at your coming princes disappear.

Translation of a Greek Ode on Astronomy. Samuel Taylor Coleridge. **CP-ColeS**

Translation of a Hymn of St. Francis Xavier. Saint Francis Xavier, *tr. by* Alexander Pope. **CP-PopeA**

Translation of a Passage in Ottfried's Metrical Paraphrase of the Gospel. Samuel Taylor Coleridge. **CP-ColeS**

Translation of a Simile in Paradise Lost. John Milton, *tr. fr. English by* William Cowper. **CP-CowpW**

Translation of Addison's Pugmaiogeranomachia; The Battle of the Pygmies and Cranes. Samuel Johnson, *tr. from the Latin of Joseph Addison.* **CP-JohnS**

Translation of Anacreon's *Dove* (Ode ix). Samuel Johnson. *See* Lovely courier of the sky.

Translation of Benserade's Verses *À Son Lit.* Samuel Johnson. *See* In bed we laugh, in bed we cry.

Translation of Dryden's Poem on Milton. John Dryden, *tr. fr. English by* William Cowper. **CP-CowpW**

Translation of Du Bellay's *Epigram on a Dog.* Samuel Johnson. *See* To Robbers furious, and to Lovers tame.

Translation of Epitaph to Northcot. William Cowper, *tr. fr. the Latin of Morley Unwin.* **CP-CowpW**

Translation of Horace "Epode the 2d" ("Beatus Ille"). Horace, *tr. by* Samuel Johnson. **CP-JohnS** *Fr.* Epodes.

Translation of Horace: Epode xi. Horace, *tr. by* Samuel Johnson. **CP-JohnS** *Fr.* Epodes.

Translation of Horace *Odes* IV vii ("Diffugere nives"). Horace. *See* 4.7: "Snow dissolvd no more is seen, The" ("Diffugere nives").

Translation of Lines in Baretti's *Easy Phraseology.* Samuel Johnson. **CP-JohnS**

Translation of Part of the Dialogue Between Hector and Andromach; from the Sixth Book of Homer's *Iliad* (VI 390–502). Homer, *tr. by* Samuel Johnson. **CP-JohnS** *Fr.* The Iliad.

Translation of Prior's Chloe and Euphelia. Matthew Prior, *tr. fr. English by* William Cowper. **CP-CowpW**

Translation of the Beginning of *Rio Verde.* Samuel Johnson. **CP-JohnS**

Translation of the Bible. William Wordsworth. *Fr.* Ecclesiastical Sonnets. **CP-WorW2**

Translation of the Epitaph on Virgil and Tibullus, *Fr. the Latin of Domitius Marsus.* Byron. **CP-Byron**

Translation of the Famous Greek War Song *Deute Paides Tov Ellenon.* Byron. **CP-Byron**

Translation of the Latin Epitaph on Sir Thomas Hanmer, Written by Doctor Freind, A. Samuel Johnson. **CP-JohnS**

Translation of the Romaic Song *Mpeno mes to periboli, Horaiotate Haide, k. t. l.* Byron. **CP-Byron**

Translation of Verses to Lloyd. William Cowper, *ad. fr. the Latin of Vincent Bourne.* **CP-CowpW**

Translation of Virgil: Pastoral V. Virgil, *tr. by* Samuel Johnson. **CP-JohnS** *Fr.* Pastorals.

Translation of Virgil: Pastoral I. Virgil, *tr. by* Samuel Johnson. **CP-JohnS** *Fr.* Pastorals.

Translation of Virgil's Georgic IV. 511–15. Virgil, *tr. by* William Wordsworth. **CP-WorW2** *Fr.* Georgics.

Translations. Adrienne Rich. **SP-RicA2**

Translations from Metastasio ("Grown old in courts, thou art not surely done"). Pietro Metastasio, *tr. by* Samuel Johnson. **CP-JohnS** *Fr.* Adriano in Syria.

Translations from Metastasio ("Would you hope to gain my heart"). Pietro Metastasio, *tr. by* Samuel Johnson. **CP-JohnS** *Fr.* La Clemenza di Tito.

Translations from the Esquimaux: There Are Seasons. Ernest Hemingway. **CP-HemiE**

Translations from the *Medea* of Euripedes ("Err shall they not, who resolute explore"). Euripides, *tr. by* Samuel Johnson. **CP-JohnS** *Fr.* Medea. **CP-JefR3,** *tr. by* Robinson Jeffers;

Translations from the *Medea* of Euripedes ("The rites deriv'd from ancient days"). Euripides, *tr. by* Samuel Johnson. **CP-JohnS** *Fr.* Medea. **CP-JefR3,** *tr. by* Robinson Jeffers;

Translations from the Spanish. William Carlos Williams. **CP-WilW1**

Translations of Roy's Verses on Skaters. Samuel Johnson. **CP-JohnS**

Translations of the Divine. Jim Morrison. **SP-MorrJ**

Translator, The. Alexander Pope. **CP-PopeA**

Translators. Patti Smith. **SP-SmitP**

Translators' Party, The. Daniel Gerard Hoffman. **SP-HoffD**

Translucent Mechanics, The. George Oppen. **NNaP** *Fr.* Some San Francisco Poems. **CP-OppeG**

Translyvania's Greek Revival Chapel. The Graduate. Robert Lowell. **SP-LoweR**

Transmigration. Brendan Galvin. **SP-GalvB**

Transmission, The. Leonard Cohen. **SP-CoheL**

Transplanting. Theodore Roethke. **CP-RoetT**

Transport one cannot contain, A. Emily Dickinson. **CP-DickE**

Transport or Slaves From Maryland to Mississippi, The. Rita Dove. **SP-DoveR**

Transport's mighty price is. Emily Dickinson. **SP-DickE**

Transpositions. Walt Whitman. **CP-WhitW**

Transubstantiation. William Wordsworth. *Fr.* Ecclesiastical Sonnets. **CP-WorW2**

Transvestite, The. Siv Cedering Fox. **SP-CedeS**

Transvestite. Laurence Lieberman. **SP-LiebL**

Trap, The. Robert Creeley. **CP-CreeR**

Trap, The. Robinson Jeffers. **CP-JefR2**

Trap, The. Nicholas Vachel Lindsay. **CP-LindV**

Trap, of a Player turn'd a Priest now is. Upon Trap. Robert Herrick. **CP-HerrR**

Trapeze artists we / Our only net our humanity. The Overbold. Jenny Joseph. **SP-JoseJ**

Trapezists. Louis MacNeice. **VoGa** *Fr.* Circus. **CP-MacNL**

Trapezist's Despair. Marsden Hartley. **CP-HartM**

Trapped. Charles Bukowski. **SP-BukC1**

Trapped. Charles Bukowski. **SP-BukC1**

Trapped, blinded, led; and in the end betrayed. The Minotaur. Muriel Rukeyser. **CP-RukeM**

Trapped in a dismal marsh, he told his troops. All Except Hannibal. Robert Ranke Graves. **CP-GravR**

Trappers. Charles Kenneth Williams. **CP-WillC**

Trappist Abbey: Matins, The. Thomas Merton. **CP-MertT; SP-MertT**

Trappist Cemetery—Gethsemani, The. Thomas Merton. **CP-MertT; SP-MertT**

Trappists, Working. Thomas Merton. **CP-MertT; SP-MertT**

Trash. Charles Kenneth Williams. **CP-WillC**

Trash Book, The. James Schuyler. **CP-SchuJ**

Trattoria in the porto, A. John Lennon in the Porto Santo Stefano. Lawrence Ferlinghetti. **SP-FerlL**

Traulus. Jonathan Swift. **CP-SwifJ**

Traumerai. Philip Larkin. **CP-LarkP**

Travail of Passion, The. William Butler Yeats. **CP-YeatW**

Travel. Leonard Cohen. **CP-CoheL**

Travel. Edna St. Vincent Millay. **CP-MillE**

Travel. Robert Louis Stevenson. **CP-StevR**

Travel Is Over. David Herbert Lawrence. **CP-LawrD**

Travel Poem. Ernest Hemingway. **CP-HemiE**

Travel why to Nature. Emily Dickinson. **SP-DickE**

Traveler, The. Maya Angelou. **SP-AngeM**

Traveler, The. John Haines. **SP-HainJ**
  "Among the quiet people of the frost."
  "Lamp full of shadows burned, A."
  "Thousands of years passed."
  "We were away for a long time."

Traveler, The. Randall Jarrell. **CP-JarrR**

Traveler. Grace Paley. **CP-PaleG**

Traveler and Old Sorrel. Louise McNeill. **SP-McNeL**

Travelers. Charles Kenneth Williams. **SP-WillC**

Traveler's Rest. Ogden Nash. **CP-NashO**

Traveler's Tale. David Markson. **CP-MarkD**

Traveling. Stephen Dunn. **SP-DunnS** *Fr.* Sympathetic Magic.

Traveling at Home. Wendell Berry. **CP-BerrW**

Traveling at thirty thousand feet, we see. Night Flight. Mary Oliver. **SP-OlivM**

Traveling through Fog. Robert Earl Hayden. **CP-HaydR**

Traveling through the Dark. William Stafford. **SP-StafW**

Traveller, The. John Berryman. **CP-BerrJ**

Traveller, The. Robert Creeley. **CP-CreeR**

Traveller, The. Kathleen Jessie Raine. **SP-RainK**

Traveller, The. Allen Tate. **CP-TateA**

Traveller Born, A. Hart Crane. **CP-CranH**

Traveller-Heart, The. Nicholas Vachel Lindsay. **CP-LindV**

Traveller on the skirt of Sarum's Plain, A. Guilt and Sorrow; or Incidents upon Salisbury Plain. William Wordsworth. **CP-WorW1**

Traveller on the skirt of Sarum's Plain, A. Salisbury Plain and Stonehenge. William Wordsworth. **FaBoPP** *Fr.* Guilt and Sorrow; or Incidents upon Salisbury Plain. **CP-WorW1**

Traveller! on thy journey toiling. The Fountain. John Greenleaf Whittier. **CP-WhitJ**

Traveller, stay / On your long way. Inn Song. Wystan Hugh Auden. **CP-AudWJ**

Traveller through Infinity, The, *after* J. P. F. Richter. Samuel Taylor Coleridge. **CP-ColeS**

Travelling. Charles Simic. **SP-SimiC**

Travelling. William Wordsworth. **CP-WorW1**

Travelling alone through Europe. Somewhere. John Updike. **CP-UpdiJ**

Travelling in the Family. Carlos Drummond de Andrade, *tr. fr. Portuguese* by Elizabeth Bishop. **CP-BishE**

Travelling in trains of time, succession and causality. The Halt. Kathleen Jessie Raine. **SP-RainK**

Travelling lady stay a while. Winter Lady. Leonard Cohen. **CP-CoheL**

Travelling many nations, many seas. Catullus. *See* Carmen 101: "Journeying over many seas and through many countries."

Travelling Slaughterhouse. Charles Simic. **SP-SimiC**

Travelling South. John Berryman. **CP-BerrJ**

Travelling to the Capital. Gary Snyder. **CP-SnydG**

Travelogue. George Oppen. **CP-OppeG**

Travelogue for Exiles. Karl Shapiro. **SP-ShapK**

Travels. Denise Levertov. **CP-LeveD**

Travels with a Donkey. Robert Louis Stevenson.
  Country of the Camisards, The. **CP-StevR**

Travesties of the world. Roy Fisher. **SP-FishR** *Fr.* Handsworth Liberties.

Trav'ller, regret not me; for thou shalt find. On a Good Man. *Unknown, tr. fr. Greek* by William Cowper. **CP-CowpW**

Tray. Robert Browning. **CP-BroR2**

Tray-Carrier of Laurels, Liam Miller. James Liddy. **CP-LiddJ**

Treacherous wind pipes a lewd song, The. Hafiz, *tr.* by Ralph Waldo Emerson. **CP-EmerR** *Fr.* Odes.

Treachery. Walter de la Mare. **CP-DeLaW**

Tread back—and back, the lewd and lay. 3.1. Horace. **CP-HopkG** *Fr.* Odes.

Tread, Sirs, as lightly as ye can. Upon an Old Man a Residenciarie. Robert Herrick. **CP-HerrR**

Tread softly! all the earth is holy ground. Christina Georgina Rossetti. *Fr.* Later Life: A Double Sonnet of Sonnets. **CP-RosC2**

Treason. Robert Herrick. **CP-HerrR**

Treason Crime, The. Archibald MacLeish. **CP-MacLA**

Treason of an accent, The, vers. 1. Emily Dickinson. **CP-DickE**

Treason of an Accent, The, vers. 2. Emily Dickinson. **CP-DickE**

Treasure, The. Robinson Jeffers. **CP-JefR1**

Treasure and the Law, The. Rudyard Kipling. *Fr.* Puck of Pook's Hill. Song of the Fifth River. **CP-KiplR**

Treasure found one entring at death's gate, A. Ausonius, *tr. fr. Latin by* Richard Lovelace. **CP-LoveR**

Treasure House, The. Roy Fisher. **SP-FishR** *Fr.* Inscriptions for Bluebeard's Castle.

Treasure Hunt. Robert Penn Warren. **SP-WarrR**

Treasure plies a feather, / Pleasure spreadeth wings. Lay Up for Yourselves Treasures in Heaven. Christina Georgina Rossetti. **CP-RosC2**

Treat me nice, Miss Mandy Jane. A Plea. Paul Laurence Dunbar. **CP-DunbP**

Treatment, The. Charles Olson. **CP-OlsoC**

Trebetherick. Sir John Betjeman. **CP-BetjJ**

Treblinka. Martin Edmunds. **SP-EdmuM**

Tree, The. John Haines. **SP-HainJ**

Tree, The. Thomas Hardy. **CP-HardT**

Tree. Daniel Gerard Hoffman. **SP-HoffD**

Tree, The. Randall Jarrell. **CP-JarrR**

Tree, The. Frederick Morgan. **SP-MorgF**

Tree, The. Ezra Pound. **SP-PounE**

Tree, The. Adrienne Rich. **CP-RicAE**

Tree. Muriel Rukeyser. **CP-RukeM**

Tree, The. Charles Tomlinson. **CP-TomlC**

Tree, The. Charles Tomlinson. **CP-TomlC**

Tree. Charles Tomlinson. **CP-TomlC**

Tree. William Carlos Williams. **CP-WilW1**

Tree and Sky. William Carlos Williams. **CP-WilW1**

Tree and the Chaff, The. Bible, *O.T. See* Psalm 1: "Blessed is the man that walketh. . . ."

Tree and the Cloud, The. Donald Hall. **CP-HallD**

Tree and the Lady, The. Thomas Hardy. **CP-HardT**

Tree at My Window. Robert Frost. **CP-FrosR**

Tree before my eyes bloomed into flame, The. The Captain's Song. John Berryman. **CP-BerrJ**

Tree burial, you tell me, that's. Blue Dwarfs. Margaret Atwood. **SP-AtwM2**

Tree Ceremonies. Edna St. Vincent Millay. **CP-MillE**

Tree House, The. Louise Glück. **SP-GlücL**

Tree House. Shel Silverstein. **SP-SilS2**

Tree hulks in the living-, A. Margaret Atwood. *Fr.* Solstice Poem. **SP-AtwM2**

Tree in Pamela's Garden, The. Edwin Arlington Robinson. **CP-RobiE**

Tree is stiff, the branch, The. Tree. William Carlos Williams. **CP-WilW1**

Tree lay down, The. The Hurricane. William Carlos Williams. **CP-WilW2**

Tree-leaves labour up and down. Nobody Comes. Thomas Hardy. **CP-HardT**

Tree of Faith its bare, dry boughs must shed, The. Adjustment. John Greenleaf Whittier. **CP-WhitJ**

Tree of Guilt, The. Louis MacNeice. **CP-MacNL**

Tree of Guilt, The. Karl Shapiro. *Fr.* Adam and Eve. **SP-ShapK**

Tree of Laughing Bells or The Wings of the Morning, The. Nicholas Vachel Lindsay. **CP-LindV**
  He Climbs the Hill Where the Tree Grows.
  He Gives What He Won to the Indian Girl.
  He Nears the Goal.
  He Receives the Bells.
  He Starts on the Return Journey.
  How the Wings Were Made.
  Indian Girl Tells the Hero Where to Go to Get the Laughing Bell, The.
  Indian Girl Who Made Them, The.
  Journey Starts Swiftly, The.

Tree of Liberty, The. Robert Burns. **CP-BurnR**

Tree of my life. The Tree. John Haines. **SP-HainJ**

Tree of Mystery, The. Samuel Taylor Coleridge. **CP-ColeS**

Tree of night is spangled with a thousand stars, The. Kathleen Jessie Raine. Fr. The Hollow Hill. **SP-RainK**

Tree of rivers flowing through our lives, A. Muriel Rukeyser. **CP-RukeM**

Tree of rivers seen and forgotten, The. Muriel Rukeyser. **CP-RukeM**

Tree Party. Louis MacNeice. **CP-MacNL**

Tree Song, A. Rudyard Kipling. Fr. Weland's Sword. Fr. Puck of Pook's Hill.

Tree Swallows. Richard Eberhart. **CP-EberR**

Tree that bears—, A. Marsden Hartley. **CP-HartM**

Tree that Became a House, The. John Haines. **SP-HainJ**

Tree that lingers at the window is just sixteen, The. What Parents Do Not Yet Know. Kay Boyle. **CP-BoylK**

Tree, the Bird, The. Theodore Roethke. **CP-RoetT**

Tree tempest with a crash of wood, The. On a Tree Fallen across the Road. Robert Frost. **CP-FrosR**

Tree Trimming. John Ciardi. **SP-CiarJ**

Tree wanderer! Wheat rider! Wind! The Linden Trees. Archibald MacLeish. **CP-MacLA**

Trees / breathing / air. Up in the Air. Robert Creeley. **CP-CreeR**

Trees, The. Hayden Carruth. Fr. Contra Mortem. **CP-CarHL**

Trees. Robert Creeley. **CP-CreeR**

Trees. Robert Creeley. **CP-CreeR**

Trees, The. Philip Larkin. **CP-LarkP**

Trees. Howard Nemerov. **CP-NemeH**

Trees, The. Adrienne Rich. **CP-RicAE; SP-RicA1; SP-RicA2**

Trees / were in(give). Edward Estlin Cummings. **CP-CummE**

Trees, The. William Carlos Williams. **CP-WilW1**

Trees. William Carlos Williams. **CP-WilW1**

Trees along this city street, The. City Trees. Edna St. Vincent Millay. **CP-MillE**

Trees and Cattle. James Dickey. **CP-DickJ**

Trees are afraid to put forth buds, The. A Backward Spring. Thomas Hardy. **CP-HardT**

Trees are coming into leaf, The. The Trees. Philip Larkin. **CP-LarkP**

Trees are flowering, The. Japonica. Louise Glück. **SP-GlücL**

Trees are in their autumn beauty, The. The Wild Swans at Coole. William Butler Yeats. **CP-YeatW**

Trees are never the same, The. The Return. Thomas McGrath. **SP-McGrT**

Trees are undressing, and fling in many places, The. Last Week in October. Thomas Hardy. **CP-HardT**

Trees are unusual, unapproachable. My eyes. Notes towards a Video of Avondale House. James Liddy. **CP-LiddJ**

Trees at Night. Charles Simic. **SP-SimiC**

Trees—being trees, The. The Trees. William Carlos Williams. **CP-WilW1**

Trees bend down along the stream, The. A Lazy Day. Paul Laurence Dunbar. **CP-DunbP**

Trees by their yield. Gerard Manley Hopkins. **CP-HopkG**

Trees' Counselling, The. Christina Georgina Rossetti. **CP-RosC3**

Trees Eat Sunshine. John Updike. **CP-UpdiJ**

Trees fret fitfully and twist, The. On the Way. Thomas Hardy. **CP-HardT**

Trees have now hid at the edge of the hurst, The. The Forest Boy. Charlotte Smith. **CP-SmitC**

Trees in groves / Kine in droves. Saadi. Ralph Waldo Emerson. **CP-EmerR**

Trees in Spring, The. Randall Jarrell. **CP-JarrR**

Trees in the Garden. David Herbert Lawrence. **CP-LawrD**

Trees in trouble because of autumn, The. Reality of Peace, 1916. David Herbert Lawrence. **CP-LawrD**

Trees inside are moving out into the forest, The. The Trees. Adrienne Rich. **CP-RicAE; SP-RicA1; SP-RicA2**

Trees is bendin' in de sto'm, De. A Plantation Melody. Paul Laurence Dunbar. **CP-DunbP**

Trees, just trees. The Woman Distorts, with Hunger. Marsden Hartley. **CP-HartM**

Trees lash, warp. Spring Tornado. Archie Randolph Ammons. **SP-AmmoA**

Tree's leaves may be ever so good, A. Leaves Compared with Flowers. Robert Frost. **CP-FrosR**

Trees, like great jade elephants, The. John Gould Fletcher. **SP-FletJ** Fr. Irradiations.

Trees like Tassels—hit—and swung, The. Emily Dickinson. **CP-DickE**

Trees Listening to Bach. James Merrill. **SP-MerrJ**

Trees on the hospital lawn, The. University Hospital, Boston. Mary Oliver. **SP-OlivM**

Trees rise from the darkness of the world, The. In the Ward: The Sacred Wood. Randall Jarrell. **CP-JarrR**

Trees rise taller and taller, lifted, The. Corot. David Herbert Lawrence. **CP-LawrD**

Trees stand like figures in a theatre, The. Landscape, Prophet and Wild-dog. Thomas Merton. **SP-MertT** Fr. Figures for an Apocalypse. **CP-MertT**

Trees, the naked trees. Hayden Carruth. **CP-CarHS** Fr. The Clay Hill Anthology.

Trees were oaks and pines, The. Local Time. Stephen Dunn. **SP-DunnS**

Trees were plucked like iron bars, The. Jumbo. Wallace Stevens. **CP-StevW**

Trees with white perfumed. Charles Henri Ford. **SP-FordC** Fr. Emblems of Arachne.

Trees won't talk; but we've got instruments, The. Progress Report. Leonard Nathan. **SP-NathL**

Treetops are shuddering. Jane Cooper. Fr. The Weather of Six Mornings. **SP-CoopJ**

Tregardock. Sir John Betjeman. **CP-BetjJ**

Trellis of clean men and painted steel, A. To the Memory of Wyndham Lewis. Roy Fisher. **SP-FishR**

Tremble, Kings despised of man! Stanza from a Translation of the Marseillaise Hymn. Percy Bysshe Shelley. **CP-ShelP**

Tremble no more to hear my voice! A Word from the Cannon's Mouth. George Meredith. **CP-MerG2**

Tremble, thou earth, at the Presence of the Lord. The Earth Shall Tremble at the Look of Him. Christina Georgina Rossetti. **CP-RosC2**

'Tremble, thou earth! th' anointed poet said. On the Power of the Supreme Being. Christopher Smart. **SP-SmarC**

Trembling / with delight— / mind takes forms. Soup. Robert Creeley. **CP-CreeR**

Trembling before Thee we fall down to adore Thee. Epiphanytide. Christina Georgina Rossetti. **CP-RosC2**

Trembling of the Veil, The. Allen Ginsberg. **CP-GinsA**

Trench Warfare. Charles Bukowski. **SP-BukC1**

Trepidation of the Druids. William Wordsworth. **Son** Fr. Ecclesiastical Sonnets. **CP-WorW2**

Tres tria, sed longe distantia sæcula, vates. Translation of Dryden's Poem on Milton. John Dryden, tr. fr. English by William Cowper. **CP-CowpW**

Trespass. Robert Frost. **CP-FrosR**

Trespass of my rustic Love, The. Emily Dickinson. **SP-DickE**

Tresses, The. Thomas Hardy. **CP-HardT**

Trestle, The. Lewis Turco. **SP-TurcL**

Tretitoli, Where the Bomb Group Was. Richard Hugo. **CP-HugoR**

Trevenen. Donald Davie. **CP-DavDo**

Treviso, the Pescheria. Donald Davie. **CP-DavDo**

Triad ("Three sounds of peace and rich increase"). John Hewitt. **CP-HewiJ**

Triad ("Three things that men may scorn"). John Hewitt. **CP-HewiJ**

Triad. Robinson Jeffers. **CP-JefR2**

Triad. Kathleen Jessie Raine. **SP-RainK**

Triad, A. Christina Georgina Rossetti. **CP-RosC1**

Triad, The. William Wordsworth. **CP-WorW2**

Triad of British Evils, A. George Meredith. **CP-MerG2**

Trial, The. John Berryman. **CP-BerrJ**

Trial, The. Henry Wadsworth Longfellow. **PAH** Fr. Act IV. Fr. Giles Corey of the Salem Farms. **SP-LongH**

Trial and Death, a Double Feature. Howard Nemerov. **CP-NemeH**

Trial as a Stimulus. Emily Dickinson. **SP-DickE**

Trial by Existence, The. Robert Frost. **CP-FrosR**

Trial of Innocence. Robert Ranke Graves. **CP-GravR**

Trial of Man, The. Sylvia Plath. **CP-PlatS**

Trial of the Dead Cleopatra in Her Beautiful and Wonderful Tomb, The. Nicholas Vachel Lindsay. **CP-LindV**

She Becomes a Goddess.

She Becomes a Soul, Flowering Toward Egyptian Resurrection, B.C. 29.

She Is Lifted with the Old Gods into the Western Sky.

Trial Run, A. Robert Frost. **CP-FrosR**

Trial Runs. Seamus Heaney. **SP-HeanS**

Triangle for Green Men. Richard Hugo. **CP-HugoR**

Triangular Field, The. Stephen Dobyns. **SP-DobyS**

Tribal Memories. Robert Duncan. **SP-DuncR** Fr. Passages.

Tribe of Templars, Play'rs, Apothecaries, The. The Second Satire of the First Book of Horace Imitated. Alexander Pope. **CP-PopeA**

Tribes of Limbo, travellers report, The. Limbo Culture. Wystan Hugh Auden. **CP-AudeW**

Tribes of Rakala, The. Kenneth Patchen. **CP-PatcK**

Tribunes, The. John Hewitt. **CP-HewiJ**

Tributary Stream. William Wordsworth. Fr. The River Duddon [A Series of Sonnets]. **CP-WorW2**

Tribute. Countee Cullen. **CP-CullC**

Tribute, The. Hilda Doolittle. **CP-DoolH**

Tribute. Al Young. **CP-YounA**

Tribute to Neruda the Poet Collector of Seashells. William Carlos Williams. **CP-WilW2**

Tribute to the Angels. Hilda Doolittle. **CP-DoolH**
  "Ah (you say), this is Holy Wisdom." **NALW; NoAM**
  "And the point in the spectrum." **NALW**
  "And yet in some very subtle way." **NALW**
  "Bitter, bitter jewel." **NALW**
  "But nearer than Guardian Angel." **NALW**
  "Every hour, every moment." **NALW; NoAM**
  "Hermes Trismegistus." **NALW**
  "I can not invent it." **NALW**
  "I had been thinking of Gabriel." **NALW**
  "I John saw. I testify." **NALW**
  "Invisible, indivisible Spirit." **BoWoP**
  "Not in our time, O Lord." **NOBA**
  "Now polish the crucible.". **NALW**
  "O swiftly, re-light the flame." **NALW**
  "O yes—you understand, I say." **NALW**
  "Of the no need." **NALW**
  "One of us said, how odd." **NALW**
  "She carried a book, either to imply." **NALW**
  "So she must have been pleased with us." **NALW**
  "Some call that deep-deep bell." **NALW**
  "Swiftly re-light the flame." **NALW**
  "This is a symbol of beauty (you continue)." **NALW**
  "This is no rune nor riddle." **InPS**
    ("This is no rune nor symbol.") **NALW**
  "We have seen her/ the world over." **CRP; NALW; Poetr; VGW**
  " 'What is the jewel colour?'." **NALW**
  "Your walls do not fall, he said." **NALW**
Tribute to the Memory of the Same Dog. William Wordsworth. **CP-WorW1**
Tribute to the Painters. William Carlos Williams. **CP-WilW2**
Tribute to Wordsworth. Samuel Taylor Coleridge. **CP-ColeS**
Tricentennial: 1980. David Markson. **CP-MarkD**
Trick / without anyone's, The. Geography of the Near Past. Al Young. **CP-YounA**
Trick is, to live your days, The. Advice to My Son. Peter Meinke. **SP-MeinP**
Trick of finding what you didn't lose, The. Edward Estlin Cummings. **CP-CummE**
Trick to Dull Our Bleeding, A. Charles Bukowski. **SP-BukC2**
Tricked by Eternity the Heart. Archibald MacLeish. **CP-MacLA**
Trickle Drops. Walt Whitman. **CP-WhitW**
Tricks With Mirrors. Margaret Atwood. **SP-AtwM1**
Tricodon of Bruges, a Flemish. Annals. John Ciardi. **SP-CiarJ**
Tricycle, The. John Hewitt. **CP-HewiJ**
Tried always and Condemned by thee. Emily Dickinson. **CP-DickE**
Trigg having turn'd his sute, he struts in state. Upon Trigg. Robert Herrick. **CP-HerrR**
Trigger. Archie Randolph Ammons. **SP-AmmoA**
Trigorin. Stephen Spender. **CP-SpenS**
Trillion moons the thimbleberries: coral, A. Prayer from the Wicket Gate for Forty One Doors for Forty Two. Malcolm Lowry. **CP-LowrM**
Trillium. Robert Pack. **SP-PackR**
Trilogy for X. Louis MacNeice. **CP-MacNL**
  "And love hung still as crystal over the bed." **CIP; GBL; MoBrPo**
    (And Love Hung Still.) **MoBrPo**
  "March gave clear days."
  "When clerks and navvies fondle." **BoLoP; EnLoPo; ErPo**
    (For X.) **BoLoP; EnLoPo**
Trim the lamp; polish the lens; draw, one by one, rare. Geoffrey Hill. **FaBoMo** *Fr.* Mercian Hymns. **CP-HillG**
Trimountain. Ralph Waldo Emerson. **CP-EmerR**
Trinacria. Basil Bunting. **CP-BuntB**
Trinacria. Charles Olson. **CP-OlsoC**
Trinc: Praises II. Thomas McGrath. **SP-McGrT**
Trinitas. John Greenleaf Whittier. **CP-WhitJ**
Trinity Churchyard. Muriel Rukeyser. **CP-RukeM**
Trinity Place. Carl Sandburg. **CP-SandC**
Trinity Sunday. George Herbert. **CP-HerbG**
Trinity Sunday. George Herbert. **CP-HerbG**
Trinity Sunday. Christina Georgina Rossetti. **CP-RosC2**
Trinity Sunday. Christopher Smart. *Fr.* Hymns and Spiritual Songs for the Fasts and Festivals of the Church of England. **SP-SmarC**

Trio of instruments you love the notes, A. Battery. Anne Waldman. **SP-WaldA**
Trio of Love Songs. Sylvia Plath. **CP-PlatS**
Trio of Triolets, A. Gerard Manley Hopkins. **CP-HopkG**
  Child is Father to the Man, The. **FaBoCo; NOBVV; NTP** (Triolet.) **NOBL**
  Cockle's Antibilious Pills.
  Legetai Ti Khainon.
Triolet: "Bad die old, The." Isabella Gardner. **CP-GardI**
Triolet. Gerard Manley Hopkins. *See* The Child is Father to the Man.
Triolet: "Perfectly clear liquid like water, A." Anne Waldman. **SP-WaldA**
Trip, A. Daniel Gerard Hoffman. **SP-HoffD**
Trip. James Schuyler. **CP-SchuJ**
Trip on the Staten Island Ferry, A. Audre Lorde. **SP-LordA**
Trip to Huntsville, The. Donald Davie. **CP-DavDo**
Triple Bronze. Robert Frost. **CP-FrosR**
Triple Fool, The. John Donne. **CP-DonnJ**
Triple Time. Philip Larkin. **CP-LarkP**
Triplet. Archie Randolph Ammons. **SP-AmmoA**
Triplex. Hilda Doolittle. **CP-DoolH**
Trippers. Wystan Hugh Auden. **CP-AudWJ**
Trippers and askers surround me. Walt Whitman. **EnlH; UnPo** *Fr.* Song of Myself. **CP-WhitW**
Tripping down. Jenny Joseph. *Fr.* Life and Turgid Times of A. Citizen. **SP-JoseJ**
Triptych. Richard Eberhart. **CP-EberR**
Triptych. Seamus Heaney. **SP-HeanS**
  After a Killing.
  At the Water's Edge.
  Sibyl.
Triptych for the Living. William Everson.
  Wise, The. **SP-EverW**
Tristan. Edna St. Vincent Millay. **CP-MillE**
Tristan: The Lay of the Goatleaf. John Hewitt.
  "We too have gone down little roads in spring." **CP-HewiJ**
Triste Corbiére. Lawrence Ferlinghetti. **SP-FerlL**
Tristi Tu, Memini. Gerard Manley Hopkins. *Fr.* Elegiacs. **CP-HopkG**
Tristia. Stanley Jasspon Kunitz. **CP-KuniS**
Tristia: 1891–1938. Geoffrey Hill. *Fr.* Four Poems Regarding the Endurance of Poets. **CP-HillG**
Tristium. Ovid, *tr. fr. Latin.*
  "Gainst Fate no counsell can prevaile." **CP-RaleW**
Tristram and Iseult. Matthew Arnold.
  Iseult of Brittany. **SP-ArnoM**
Tristram's Song. Tennyson. **FaBoRV** *Fr.* The Last Tournament. *Fr.* Idylls of the King. **CP-TennA**
Tritemius of Herbipolis, one day. The Gift of Tritemius. John Greenleaf Whittier. **CP-WhitJ**
Triumph. David Herbert Lawrence. **CP-LawrD**
Triumph—may be of several kinds. Emily Dickinson. **CP-DickE**
Triumph now with Joy and mirth. Thomas Campion. *Fr.* Lord Hay's Mask.
Triumph of Achilles, The. Louise Glück. **SP-GlücL**
Triumph of Charis, The. Ben Jonson. *See* Her Triumph.
Triumph of Death, The. William Shakespeare. *See* Sonnet 71: "No longer mourn for me when I am dead."
Triumph of Dullness [or Dulness], The. Alexander Pope. *See* The Reign of Chaos.
Triumph of Dullness, The. Alexander Pope. **NOEC** *Fr.* Yet, yet a moment, one dim ray of light. **NAEL-1; OAEL-1; PoEL-3** *Fr.* The Dunciad. **CP-PopeA**
Triumph of Education, The. Howard Nemerov. **CP-NemeH**
Triumph of Heavenly Love Desired, The. Jeanne Marie Bouvier de la Motte-Guyon, *tr. fr. French by* William Cowper. **CP-CowpW**
Triumph of Life, The. Percy Bysshe Shelley. **CP-ShelP**
Triumph of the Machine, The. David Herbert Lawrence. **CP-LawrD**
Triumph of the Postmodern. Lawrence Ferlinghetti. **SP-FerlL**
Triumph of the Shell, The. Archibald MacLeish. **CP-MacLA**
Triumph of Time, The. Algernon Charles Swinburne. **SP-SwinA**
Triumph of Vice, The. Alexander Pope. *See* Virtue may choose the high or low degree.
Triumphal March. Thomas Stearns Eliot. **OBWP; WaaP** *Fr.* Coriolan. **CP-ElioT**
Triumphal March. Thomas McGrath. **SP-McGrT**
Triumphs of Owen, The. Thomas Gray. **CP-GrayT**
Triumphs of Philamore and Amoret, The. Richard Lovelace. **CP-LoveR**
Troades. Euripides.
  Aurora and Tithonus. **CP-BroEB**, *tr. by* Elizabeth Barrett Browning;

Troades. Seneca, *tr. fr. Latin by* the Earl of Rochester.
　"Insulting chance ne'er call'd with louder voice." **CP-JohnS**

Trŏchēe trĭps frŏm lōng tŏ shōrt. Metrical Feet. Samuel Taylor Coleridge. **CP-ColeS**

Trogger, The. Robert Burns. **CP-BurnR**

Troilus. Charles Olson. **CP-OlsoC**

Troilus and Cresida. William Wordsworth. **CP-WorW1**

Troilus and Cressida. John Dryden.
　"Can Life be a blessing." **SP-DrydJ**
　(Song: "Can life be a blessing.") **SP-DrydJ**

Troilus and Criseyde [*or* Criseide]. Geoffrey Chaucer. **CP-ChauG**
　At the Gate. **SeCePo**
　Complaint of Troilus, The. **NOBE; OBEV**
　Go, Little Book ("Go, litel book, go litel myn tragedy"). **OAEL-1; OxBM; ViBoPo**
　(Chaucer's Wishes for his 'Troilus'.) **EPCY**
　(Envoy, The.) **FiP**
　"If no love is, O God, what fele I so." **AWP; FF; OAEL-1**
　(Song of Troylus, The.) **AWP**
　"In May, that moder is of monthes glade." **EnVB**
　Love Unfeigned. **LO; NOBE; OBEV; OxBM**
　Sorrow of Troilus, The. **PoEL-1**
　"Swich fyn hath, lo, this Troilus for love!" **NOCV**
　"This Troilus [*or* Troylus], with blisse [*or* Blysse] of that supprysed [*or* supprised]." **EBEV; PoE**
　"Whan they unto the paleys were yoemen." **PoE**
　Wooing of Criseide, The, III. **PoEL-1**

Trolley-cars / are my inland waters. The Twist. Charles Olson. **SP-OlsoC** *Fr.* The Maximus Poems.

Trolley has stopped long since, The. The Dump. Donald Hall. **CP-HallD**

Trolling for Blues. Richard Wilbur. **CP-WilbR**

Trolls, The. Louis MacNeice. **CP-MacNL**
　"Death has a look of finality."
　"In the misty night humming to themselves like morons."
　"Than which not any could be found other."
　"Than which not any. Time."
　"This then is our answer under."

Troll's Courtship. Louis MacNeice. **CP-MacNL**

Troll's Nosegay, The. Robert Ranke Graves. **CP-GravR**

Trompe L'Oeil. Stanley Jasspon Kunitz. *Fr.* Words for the Unknown Makers: A Garland of Commemorative Verses. **CP-KuniS**

Troop will be impatient; let us hie, The. Borderers, The. A Tragedy. William Wordsworth. **CP-WorW1**

Troopin'. Rudyard Kipling. **CP-KiplR**

Troopin', troopin', troopin' to the sea. Troopin'. Rudyard Kipling. **CP-KiplR**

Troops, The. Charles Bukowski. **SP-BukC3**

Troopship in the Tropics, A. Alun Lewis. **CP-LewiA**

Trophies. Muriel Rukeyser. **CP-RukeM**

Trophies of Peace. Herman Melville. **SP-MelvH**

Tropic. David Herbert Lawrence. **CP-LawrD**

Tropic, indeed, a memory. Emily Dickinson. **SP-DickE**

Tropic Rain. Robert Louis Stevenson. **CP-StevR**

Tropic Zone. Derek Walcott. **CP-WalcD** *Fr.* Midsummer.

Tropical Beetles. John Updike. **CP-UpdiJ**

Tropics. Thomas Merton. **CP-MertT; SP-MertT**

Tropics vanish, and meseems that I, The. Robert Louis Stevenson. **CP-StevR**

Trosachs, The. William Wordsworth. **CP-WorW2**

Trossachs, The. Alexandre Dumas. **SP-ScotW** *Fr.* The Lady of the Pearls.

Trossachs, The. Sir Walter Scott. **SP-ScotW** *Fr.* The Lady of the Lake.

Troth, Tom, I must confess I much admire. Upon T.C. Having the Pox. Sir John Suckling. **CP-SuckJ**

Troth with the Dead. David Herbert Lawrence. **CP-LawrD**

Troths. Carl Sandburg. **CP-SandC**

Troubadour Removed, A. Richard Hugo. **CP-HugoR**

Trouble. "Bob Dylan." **CP-DylaB**

Trouble. James Wright. **CP-WrigJ**

Trouble, A / archaically fettered. It Is a Living Coral. William Carlos Williams. **CP-WilW1**

Trouble about those that set up to be moral judges, The. Censors. David Herbert Lawrence. **CP-LawrD**

Trouble coming, on a Saturday or a Monday. Roy Fisher. **SP-FishR** *Fr.* Diversions.

Trouble in de Kitchen. Paul Laurence Dunbar. **CP-DunbP**

Trouble in Mind. "Bob Dylan." **CP-DylaB**

Trouble in Paradise. Gilbert Sorrentino. **SP-SorrG**

Trouble in the city, trouble in the farm. Trouble. "Bob Dylan." **CP-DylaB**

Trouble is there's, The. The Connection. Charles Olson. **CP-OlsoC**

Trouble, not of clouds, or weeping rain, A. On the Departure of Sir Walter Scott from Abbotsford, for Naples. William Wordsworth. **CP-WorW2**

Trouble with a kitten is, The. The Kitten. Ogden Nash. **CP-NashO**

Trouble with me is that whether I get love or not, The. On the Roof. Charles Kenneth Williams. **CP-WillC**

Trouble with the Times, The. Thomas McGrath. **SP-McGrT**

Trouble with tragedy is the fuss it makes, The. Nicolas-Sébastien Roch Chamfort, *tr. fr. French by* Samuel Beckett. **CP-BeckS**

Trouble with Women Is Men, The. Ogden Nash. **CP-NashO**

Troubled long with warring notions. Near the Spring of the Hermitage. William Wordsworth. *Fr.* Inscriptions Supposed to Be Found in and near a Hermit's Cell; 1818. **CP-WorW2**

Troubled that you are not, as they say. George Oppen. **APSN** *Fr.* Route. **CP-OppeG**

Troubled Woman. Langston Hughes. **SP-HughL**

Troubles, 1922, The. John Hewitt. **CP-HewiJ**

Troubles of Charles the First. William Wordsworth. *Fr.* Ecclesiastical Sonnets. **CP-WorW2**

Troubleshooting. William Stafford. **SP-StafW**

Troublesome Fame. Robert Ranke Graves. **CP-GravR**

Troublesome Reign, The. Geoffrey Hill. **CP-HillG**

Troubling are masks . the faces of friends, my face. John Berryman. *Fr.* Sonnets to Chris. **CP-BerrJ**

Troughs of Sea. Robert Ranke Graves. **CP-GravR**

Trout. Richard Hugo. **CP-HugoR**

Trout Kill on the Sacramento. Tom Clark. **SP-ClarT**

Trout Map, The. Allen Tate. **CP-TateA**

Trouvée. Elizabeth Bishop. **CP-BishE**

Troy Depicted. William Shakespeare. **OBSC** *Fr.* The Rape of Lucrece. **CP-ShaWS**

Truant. Phoebe Hesketh. **SP-HeskP**

Truant Dove from Pilpay, The. Charlotte Smith. **CP-SmitC**

Truants. Roy Fisher. **SP-FishR** *Fr.* Interiors with Various Figures.

Truce. Charles Bukowski. **SP-BukC3**

Truce. Walter de la Mare. **CP-DeLaW**

Truce. Paul Muldoon. **SP-MuldP**

Truce between the Sexes, The. Erica Jong. **SP-JongE**

Truce for a Moment. Edna St. Vincent Millay. **CP-MillE**

Truce in Love Intreated. Thomas Carew. **CP-CareT**

Truce of Piscataqua, The. John Greenleaf Whittier. **CP-WhitJ**

Truce of the Bear, The. Rudyard Kipling. **CP-KiplR**

Truck-Garden Market-Day. Edna St. Vincent Millay. **CP-MillE**

Truck gears grinding up Marin. Aubade. Tom Clark. **SP-ClarT**

Truck put me off on Fell. Hitching into Frisco. Thom Gunn. **CP-GunnT** *Fr.* Three Songs.

Truck Stop: Minnesota. Stephen Dunn. **SP-DunnS**

Trucker, A. Thom Gunn. **CP-GunnT**

Trucks and station wagons, VWs, old Chevys, Pintos. Traffic. Donald Hall. **CP-HallD**

Trudge, Body! Robert Ranke Graves. **CP-GravR**

Trudging to Eden, looking backward. Emily Dickinson. **CP-DickE**

True / poet who could live and die. Cummings. Archibald MacLeish. **CP-MacLA**

True Account of Talking to Judy Holiday, October 13, A. Alice Notley. **SP-NotlA**

True Account of Talking to the Sun at Fire Island, A. Frank O'Hara. **SP-OharF**

True and False Comforts. William Cowper. *Fr.* Olney Hymns. **CP-CowpW**

True and False Glory. John Milton. **LiTB; OBS** *Fr.* Book III. *Fr.* Paradise Regained [*or* Regain'd]. **CP-MiltJ**

True Beauty, The. Thomas Carew. **GTBS; GTBS-6; GTBS-P** *Fr.* Disdain Returned. **CP-CareT**
　(Disdain Returned.) **PFP**

True Believer. Allen Tate. **CP-TateA**

True Brahmin, in the morning meadows wet. Gardener. Ralph Waldo Emerson. **OxBA** *Fr.* Quatrains. **CP-EmerR**

True Confessional, *See also* Mock Confessional. Lawrence Ferlinghetti. **SP-FerlL**

True Conquerors. Walt Whitman. **CP-WhitW**

True Democracy. David Herbert Lawrence. **CP-LawrD**

True ease in writing comes from art, not chance. Alexander Pope. **InPK; TrGrPo,** *ll.* 362–383; *Fr.* An Essay on Criticism. **CP-PopeA**

True Encounter, The. Edna St. Vincent Millay. **CP-MillE**

True Evil. Robert Ranke Graves. **CP-GravR**

True faith discovered was, The. Wisdom. William Butler Yeats. **CP-YeatW**

True Friendship. Robert Herrick. **CP-HerrR**

True genius, but true woman! dost deny. To George Sand: A Recognition. Elizabeth Barrett Browning. **CP-BroEB**

True harvests no mere intent may reap. The Necessity of Faith. Wendell Berry. **CP-BerrW**

True-hearted was he, the sad swain o' the Yarrow. Jessie—A New Scots Song. Robert Burns. **CP-BurnR**

True History of Bernál Díaz. Archibald MacLeish. *Fr.* Conquistador. **CP-MacLA**

True, I happen. So. Hayden Carruth. **CP-CarHS** *Fr.* The Clay Hill Anthology.

True it is that Ambrosio Salinero. Gabriello Chiabrera, *tr. fr. Italian by* William Wordsworth. **CP-WorW1**

True Joy. Robert Ranke Graves. **CP-GravR**

True Love. William Shakespeare. *See* Sonnet 116: "Let me not to the marriage of true minds."

True Love at Last. David Herbert Lawrence. **CP-LawrD**

True Love in this differs from gold and clay. Percy Bysshe Shelley. **FHYEP; OBNC** *Fr.* Epipsychidion. **CP-ShelP**

True Love is founded in rocks of Remembrance. Love and Law. Nicholas Vachel Lindsay. **CP-LindV**

True Love Leaves No Traces, *see also* As the Mist Leaves No Scar. Leonard Cohen. **CP-CoheL**

True Love Tends to Forget. "Bob Dylan." **CP-DylaB**

True Lover, The. Alfred Edward Housman. **CP-HousA**

True lovers in each happening of their hearts. Edward Estlin Cummings. **CP-CummE; SP-CummE**

True Magic. Robert Ranke Graves. **CP-GravR**

True Man, The. Chuang Tzu, *tr. fr. Chinese by* Thomas Merton. **CP-MertT**

True mirth resides not in the smiling skin. Mirth. Robert Herrick. **CP-HerrR**

True Music. Patti Smith. **SP-SmitP**

True Nature of Time, The. Robert Penn Warren. **SP-WarrR**
Enclave, The.
Faring, The.

True Night. Gary Snyder. **CP-SnydG**

True Numbers. Charles Olson. **CP-OlsoC**

True or False. Catullus. *See* Carmen 75: "Reason blinded by sin, Lesbia."

True Pleasures. William Cowper. **CP-CowpW** *Fr.* Olney Hymns. **CP-CowpW**

True rev'rence is (as Cassiodore doth prove). Reverence. Robert Herrick. **CP-HerrR**

True Safety. Robert Herrick. **CP-HerrR**

True Smith of Tieveragh, The. John Hewitt. **CP-HewiJ**

True Stories. Margaret Atwood. **SP-AtwM2**

True Story, A. Christina Georgina Rossetti. **CP-RosC3**

True Story. Shel Silverstein. **SP-SilS2**

True Story of Being at the Pool. Anne Waldman. **SP-WaldA**

True, the time, to one who does not love farce. A Little Scraping. Robinson Jeffers. **CP-JefR2**

True, the walls fell. In Our Town. Hilda Doolittle. **CP-DoolH**

True to your self, and sheets, you'll have me swear. To a Gentlewoman on Just Dealing. Robert Herrick. **CP-HerrR**

True Tyrant or the Spirit of Duty Rebuked, The. Stevie Smith. **CP-SmitS**

True wit is Nature to advantage dressed. Alexander Pope. **HAP** *Fr.* An Essay on Criticism. **CP-PopeA**

True word of eternity is spoken only in the spirit of that man who is himself a wilderness, The, *ad. from* Eckhart *and* Ruysbroeck. Thomas Merton. *Fr.* Cables to the Ace. **CP-MertT**

Trueblue Gentleman, A. Kenneth Patchen. **CP-PatcK**

Truest Poetry Is the Most Feigning, The [or, Ars Poetica for Hard Times]. Wystan Hugh Auden. **CP-AudeW**

Truggin a Footman was; but now, growne lame. Upon Truggin. Robert Herrick. **CP-HerrR**

Truisms, The. Louis MacNeice. **CP-MacNL**

Truly God is good to Israel. Psalm 73. Bible, *O.T. Fr.* Psalms. **CP-Psal**

Truly my Satan thou art but a dunce. Epilogue. William Blake. **FHYEP; HAP; ImPo; NoP; OAEL-2; OBNC; OxBSP; PeECV; PoE; SCGP; TrGrPo; WeW** *Fr.* The Gates of Paradise.

Truly my soul waiteth upon God. Psalm 62. Bible, *O.T. Fr.* Psalms. **CP-Psal**

Truly our fathers had the gout. Wystan Hugh Auden. **CP-AudWJ**

Truly poore Night thou wellcome art to mee. Sonnet 15. Mary Sidney, Countess of Montgomery Wroth. *Fr.* Pamphilia to Amphilanthus. **CP-WrotM**

Truly the Light Is Sweet. Christina Georgina Rossetti. **CP-RosC2**

Truly ye come of The Blood; slower to bless than to ban. England's Answer. Rudyard Kipling. **CP-KiplR**

Trumpan. Richard Hugo. **CP-HugoR**

Trumpet and drum, the old soldier said. The Old Soldiers' Home. Howard Nemerov. **CP-NemeH**

Trumpet pealed thro' France. Then Italy. The Massacre of Perugia. Christina Georgina Rossetti. **CP-RosC3**

Trumpet Player. Langston Hughes. **SP-HughL**

Trumpeters / from the Comandancia militar. Valle de Oaxaca. Charles Tomlinson. **CP-TomlC**

Trumpets. Georg Trakl, *tr. fr. German by* James Wright. **CP-WrigJ**

Trumpets. A valley opens and beyond. Drums in Scotland. Richard Hugo. **CP-HugoR**

Trumpet's loud clangor, The. Fife and Drum. John Dryden. **GN** *Fr.* A Song for St Cecilia's Day [1687]. **SP-DrydJ**

Trumpet's voice, loud and authoritative, The. Reasons for Attendance. Philip Larkin. **CP-LarkP**

Truncated Bird, The. Richard Eberhart. **CP-EberR**

Trundled from / the strangeness of the sea. The Sea-Elephant. William Carlos Williams. **CP-WilW1**

Truro Bear, The. Mary Oliver. **SP-OlivM**

Trust. David Herbert Lawrence. **CP-LawrD**

Trust. John Greenleaf Whittier. **CP-WhitJ**

Trust adjusts her "Peradventure." Emily Dickinson. **CP-DickE**

Trust in the Lord: So shalt thou dwell, vv. 1–7, par. by Charles Frederic Sheldon. Bible, *O.T. See* Psalm 37: "Fret not thyself because of evildoers."

Trust in the Unexpected. Emily Dickinson. **CP-DickE**

Trust me, I have not earned your dear rebuke. Christina Georgina Rossetti. *Fr.* Monna Innominata. **CP-RosC2**

Trust me Ladies, I will do. To the Ladyes. Robert Herrick. **CP-HerrR**

Trust me, the meed of praise, dealt thriftily. In a Letter to the Same [C. P.]. William Cowper. **CP-CowpW**

"Trust only to thyself"; the maxim's sound. The Lark's Nest. Charlotte Smith. **CP-SmitC**

Trust Yourself. "Bob Dylan." **CP-DylaB**

Trusting God. Bible, *O.T. See* Psalm 23: "Lord is my shepherd, I shall not want, The."

Trusting the first warm day of spring. The Early Butterfly. Charlotte Smith. **CP-SmitC**

Trusting the happy flower. Emily Dickinson. **SP-DickE**

Trusty as the stars. Emily Dickinson. **CP-DickE**

Trusty, dusky, vivid, true. My Wife. Robert Louis Stevenson. **CP-StevR**

Truth ("Truth is best found out by the time, and eyes"). Robert Herrick. **CP-HerrR**

Truth. Gwendolyn Brooks. **SP-BrooG** *Fr.* The Womanhood.

Truth. Geoffrey Chaucer. *See* Fle[e] fro[m] the pres[s] [or prees] and dwelle with soothfastnesse [or soth[e]fastnesse].

Truth, The. Alfonso Cortes, *tr. fr. Spanish by* Thomas Merton. **CP-MertT**

Truth. William Cowper. **CP-CowpW**
"Man on the dubious waves of error toss'd." **NOCV**

Truth. John Donne. *See* Satire 3: "Kind pity [or Kinde pitty] chokes my spleen[e]; brave scorn forbids."

Truth, The. Richard Eberhart. **CP-EberR**

Truth, The. Randall Jarrell. **CP-JarrR**

Truth. Howard Nemerov. **CP-NemeH**

Truth. Christopher Smart. *Fr.* Hymns for the Amusement of Children. **SP-SmarC**

Truth also is the pursuit of it. Leviathan. George Oppen. **CP-OppeG**

Truth and Divine Love Rejected by the World. Jeanne Marie Bouvier de la Motte-Guyon, *tr. fr. French by* William Cowper. **CP-CowpW**

Truth and Error. Robert Herrick. **CP-HerrR**

Truth and Falsehood. Robert Herrick. **CP-HerrR**

Truth by her own simplicity is known. Truth and Falsehood. Robert Herrick. **CP-HerrR**

Truth Game. Phoebe Hesketh. **SP-HeskP**

Truth in platonic ornaments bedeck'd. Boethius, *tr. by* Samuel Johnson. **CP-JohnS** *Fr.* Consolation of Philosophy, The ("De Consolacione Philosophie"). **CP-ChauG**

Truth in Poetry. George Crabbe. **SP-CrabG** *Fr.* The Village. (Rural Life.) **SP-CrabG**

Truth is a golden thread seen here and there. Arthur Hugh Clough. **SP-ClouA**

Truth—is as old as God. Emily Dickinson. **CP-DickE**

Truth is best found out by the time, and eyes. Truth . Robert Herrick. **CP-HerrR**

Truth is eternal, and the son of heaven. Ode to Dr. William Sancroft. Jonathan Swift. **CP-SwifJ**

Truth Is Poor Physic. Robert Ranke Graves. *Fr.* Three Songs for the Lute. **CP-GravR**

Truth—is stirless, The. Emily Dickinson. **CP-DickE**

Truth is that there comes a time, The. Sad Strains of a Gay Waltz. Wallace Stevens. **CP-StevW**

Truth is the trial of itself. From *The Touchstone of Truth.* Ben Jonson. **CP-JonsB**

Truth Like the Belly of a Woman Turning, The. Gary Snyder. **CP-SnydG**

Truth-loving Persians do not dwell upon. The Persian Version. Robert Ranke Graves. **CP-GravR**

Truth of my prologue is this: Down with sleazy romanticists!, The. The Men (II). Pablo Neruda, *tr. fr. Spanish by* Ben Belitt. **SP-NeruP** *Fr.* The Separate Rose.

Truth of the Matter, The. John Gould Fletcher. **SP-FletJ**

Truth of the Matter, The. Howard Nemerov. **CP-NemeH**

Truth, so far, in my book; the truth which draws. Elizabeth Barrett Browning. WGRP *Fr.* Aurora Leigh. **CP-BroEB**

Truth, sprung from heaven, shall shine. Thomas Campion. *Fr.* The Ayres that Were Sung and Played, at *Brougham Castle* in *Westmerland*, in the Kings Entertainment. **CP-CampT**

Truth the Dead Know, The. Anne Sexton. **CP-SextA**

Truthful Song, The. Rudyard Kipling. **CP-KiplR**

Try and trust Roger, was the word, but now. To the Right Noble Tom, Tell-Troth of His Travels, the Coriat of Odcombe, and His Book Now Going to Travel. Ben Jonson. **CP-JonsB**

Try as he will, no man breaks wholly loose. The Virginity. Rudyard Kipling. **CP-KiplR**

Try It Suns. and Hols.; It's Closed Then. Ogden Nash. **CP-NashO**

Try the might the Muse affords. Ralph Waldo Emerson. **CP-EmerR**

Try to be yourself, they told the child. Polonius Passing Through a Stage. Howard Nemerov. **CP-NemeH**

Try to see it my way. We Can Work It Out. The Beatles. **CP-Beatl**

Trying. Miller Williams. **SP-WillM**

Trying to chop mother down is like. She Went to Stay. Robert Creeley. **CP-CreeR**

Trying to Dream Up an Answer. Barton Sutter. **SP-SuttB**

Trying to enter each other. Marge Piercy. *Fr.* Doing It Differently. **SP-PierM**

Trying to explain it to them. Esquimos Have No Word for "War," The. Mary Oliver. **SP-OlivM**

Trying to Feel Something. John Ciardi. **SP-CiarJ**

Trying to find a way to say something that would make it. Ten Songs. John Yau. **SP-YauJo**

Trying to Flatter Twelve Mile River. Brendan Galvin. **SP-GalvB**

Trying to Get Even. Charles Bukowski. **SP-BukC1**

Trying to get "our men / back" and "our ship". The Province. Robert Creeley. **CP-CreeR**

Trying to Hold It All Together. Richard Eberhart. **CP-EberR**

Trying to open locked doors with a sword, threading. Sojourn in the Whale. Marianne Craig Moore. **CP-MoorM**

Trying to Pray. James Wright. **CP-WrigJ**

Trying to read in Nature's book. In Nine Sleep Valley. James Merrill. **SP-MerrJ**

Trying to read the news, after your visit. The Winged Heart. Robert Ranke Graves. **CP-GravR**

Trying to Reconcile. Robert Pack. **SP-PackR**

Trying to Remember. Miller Williams. **SP-WillM**

Trying to remember you. Grief. Stephen Dobyns. **SP-DobyS**

Trying to Separate. Robert Pack. **SP-PackR**

Trying to Talk with a Man. Adrienne Rich. **SP-RicA1; SP-RicA2**

Trying to tell you how. When We Dead Awaken. Adrienne Rich. **SP-RicA2**

Trying to Tell You Something. Robert Penn Warren. **SP-WarrR**

Trying to think of. The Rocks. Robert Creeley. **CP-CreeR**

Trying to understand myself, I fetch. Obiter Dicta. Donald Davie. **CP-DavDo**

Trying to understand the words. Bird-Language. Wystan Hugh Auden. **CP-AudeW**

Trying to Understand Violence. Jenny Joseph. **SP-JoseJ**

Tryst. Archie Randolph Ammons. **SP-AmmoA**

Tryst, The. Walter de la Mare. **CP-DeLaW**

Tryst, The. Walter de la Mare. **CP-DeLaW**

Tryst, The. Paul Laurence Dunbar. **CP-DunbP**

Tryst. John Hewitt. **CP-HewiJ**

Tsar, who knew you? Who. Hayden Carruth. **CP-CarHS** *Fr.* The Clay Hill Anthology.

Tsokadze O Altitudo. John Updike. **CP-UpdiJ**

Tu Catherina, mei solatrix unica luctus. Ad sanctam catherinam, virginem et martyrem. Robert Southwell. **CP-SoutR**

Tu scendi dalle stelle, O Re del Cielo. Christina Georgina Rossetti. **CP-RosC3**

Tu tacitas nosti lacrimas, tu saucia cernis. Jesus. Marye. Robert Southwell. **CP-SoutR**

Tubes. Donald Hall. **CP-HallD**

Tubes from the brain. Dylan. David Markson. **CP-MarkD**

Tübingen—Hamburg Schlafwagen. Allen Ginsberg. **CP-GinsA**

Tubs of. . . / memory. Roof Garden. James Schuyler. **CP-SchuJ**

Tuck, Demitroïa, / Ariadne, and Froyja. George Meredith. **CP-MerG2**

Tuck, my treasure! Tuck, my pleasure! George Meredith. **CP-MerG2**

Tuck, sweet charmer, tell me why. George Meredith. **CP-MerG2**

Tuck, thou graceless sinner!—. George Meredith. **CP-MerG2**

Tuck! Tuck! Once you would flatter me. George Meredith. **CP-MerG2**

Tucking in yellow curls, she poises, set. The Diver. Leonard Nathan. **SP-NathL**

Tudor indeed is gone and every rose. Ezra Pound. *See* Canto 80: "Ain' committed no federal crime."

Tuesday and Friday. Hero Sandwiches. Charles Tomlinson. **CP-TomlC**

Tuesday in Holy Week. Christina Georgina Rossetti. **CP-RosC2**

Tuesdays all his kids would be out. No Trespassing. Al Young. **CP-YounA**

Tuft of Flowers, The. Robert Frost. **CP-FrosR**

Tuft of Kelp, The. Herman Melville. **SP-MelvH**

Tuft of Primroses, The. William Wordsworth. **CP-WorW1**

Tufts lies on a drumlin, a pocket of till. The Highest Place in Town. John Ciardi. **SP-CiarJ**

Tugs of Hull, The. George Oppen. **CP-OppeG**

Tulip. Louis Zukofsky. **CP-ZukLS**

Tulip Bed, The. William Carlos Williams. **CP-WilW1**

Tulips, The. Denise Levertov. **CP-LeveD**

Tulips. Sylvia Plath. **CP-PlatS**

Tulips are too excitable, it is winter here, The. Tulips. Sylvia Plath. **CP-PlatS**

Tully to thee Rome's eloquent Sole Heir. Catullus. *See* Carmen 49: "Silver-tongued among the sons of Rome."

Tulsa. John Updike. **CP-UpdiJ**

Tumble me down, and I will sit. To Fortune. Robert Herrick. **CP-HerrR**

Tumblers of the rapids go white, go green, The. Carl Sandburg. *Fr.* The People, Yes. **CP-SandC**

Tumbling-hair / picker of buttercups. Edward Estlin Cummings. **CP-CummE**

Tumbling Spore, The. John Hewitt. **CP-HewiJ**

Tumult and turmoil, trouble and toil. Peace I Leave wth You. Christina Georgina Rossetti. **CP-RosC2**

Tumult in the heart, The. Conversation. Elizabeth Bishop. *Fr.* Four Poems. **CP-BishE**

Tumultuously void of a clean scheme. Edwin Arlington Robinson. *Fr.* Octaves. **CP-RobiE**

Tundra, The. John Haines. **SP-HainJ**

Tundra is a living, The. The Tundra. John Haines. **SP-HainJ**

Tundra, the distant marches. And wind veering, clatter of steely grasses. Terra. Hayden Carruth. *Fr.* Journey to a Known Place. **CP-CarHL**

Tune. Al Young. **CP-YounA**

Tune beyond us as we are, A. Wallace Stevens. **CMoP** *Fr.* The Man with the Blue Guitar. **CP-StevW**

Tune for an Ill-Tempered Clavichord. Ogden Nash. **CP-NashO**

Tune for Festive Dances in the Nineteen Sixties, A. Thomas Merton. **CP-MertT**

Tune, in American Type. John Updike. **CP-UpdiJ**

Tune in to a raga. Assassination Raga. Lawrence Ferlinghetti. **SP-FerlL**

Tune Me, O Lord, into One Harmony. Christina Georgina Rossetti. **CP-RosC2**

Tune thy chearefull voyce to mine. A Dialogue Sung the First Night. Thomas Campion. *Fr.* The Ayres that Were Sung and Played, at *Brougham Castle* in *Westmerland*, in the Kings Entertainment. **CP-CampT**

Tune thy music[ke] to thy heart [*or* hart]. Heart's Music. Thomas Campion. **CP-CampT**

Tunisian Nostalgia. Lawrence Ferlinghetti. **SP-FerlL**

Tunnel, The. Hart Crane. **CMoP; HoFi; MAT; MoAB; MoAmPo; OxBA** *Fr.* The Bridge. **CP-CranH**

Tunnel, The. Robert Creeley. **CP-CreeR**

Tunnel, The. John Haines. **SP-HainJ**

Tunnel, The. Phoebe Hesketh. **SP-HeskP**

Tunnel, The. Muriel Rukeyser. **CP-RukeM**

Tunneling through the earth. Dreams. Robert Creeley. **CP-CreeR**

Tunstall Forest. Donald Davie. **CP-DavDo**

Turban, The. John Hewitt. **CP-HewiJ**

Turbaned Race are poured in thickening swarms, The. Crusades. William Wordsworth. *Fr.* Ecclesiastical Sonnets. **CP-WorW2**

Turf-Carrier [*or* Turf Carrier] on Aranmore. John Hewitt. **CP-HewiJ**

Turf-Stacks. Louis MacNeice. *See* Among These Turf-Stacks.

Turkey, The. Ogden Nash. **CP-NashO**

Turkey-Cock. David Herbert Lawrence. **CP-LawrD**

Turkey in the Straw. William Carlos Williams. **CP-WilW2**

Turkey vulture, / a shy bird ungainly on the ground, The. The Best Defense is Offensive. Marge Piercy. **SP-PierM**

Turkeys. John Clare.
    "Turkeys wade the close to catch the bees." **SP-ClarJ**

Turkeys wade the close to catch bees, The. Turkeys. John Clare.

Turkeys wade the close to catch the bees. John Clare. **SP-ClarJ** *Fr.* Turkeys.

Turn, The. Robert Creeley. **CP-CreeR**

Turn, The. Frederick Morgan. **SP-MorgF**

Turn again, Higginson / thrice Mayor of London! Public House Drunk. Sir John Betjeman. **CP-BetjJ**

Turn again, thou fair Eliza. Fair Eliza. Robert Burns. **CP-BurnR**

Turn again, Whittington. Riding the surf. Louis MacNeice. *Fr.* Day of Renewal. **CP-MacNL**

"And so for all of us. Bits and pieces." **NAs**

Turn back in thought to when a little town. Pro Tanto Quid Retribuamas. John Hewitt. **CP-HewiJ**

Turn back. Turn, young lady dear. The Robber Bridegroom. Allen Tate. **CP-TateA**

Turn Back, You Wanton Flyer. Thomas Campion.
    (Turne Backe You Wanton Flier.) **CP-CampT**

Turn from that girl. I Shall Laugh Purely. Robinson Jeffers. **CP-JefR3**

Turn him, and see his threads; look if he be. Ben Jonson. **OBF** *Fr.* An Epistle to Master Arth[ur] Squib. **CP-JonsB**

Turn me on your knees. C'mon Jack. Allen Ginsberg. **CP-GinsA**

Turn now and rise. Charles Olson. **CP-OlsoC**

Turn, now, tired mind, unto your rest. Forests. Walter de la Mare. **CP-DeLaW**

Turn O Libertad. Walt Whitman. **CP-WhitW**

Turn of head, that searching light, A. Brother and Sister. Walter de la Mare. **CP-DeLaW**

Turn of the Head, A. Denise Levertov. **CP-LeveD**

Turn of the Moon. Robert Ranke Graves. **CP-GravR**

Turn of the Wheel. Carl Sandburg. **CP-SandC**

Turn of the wheel, I thrust, A. The Twelve-Spoked Wheel Flashing. Marge Piercy. **SP-PierM**

Turn off the boob-tube, take an ulcer pill. Early Morning Walk to Work. James McAuley. **SP-McAuJ**

Turn off the tap, Mahavveray, it's too cold here. Mahavveray. Louis MacNeice. **CP-MacNL**

Turn off your mind, relax And float down stream. Tomorrow Never Knows. The Beatles. **CP-Beatl**

Turn on my tongue, O Spanish verse; confirm. Ewigkeit. Jorge Luis Borges, *tr. fr. Spanish by* Richard Wilbur. **CP-WilbR**

Turn on the prudent Ant, thy heedless eyes. Samuel Johnson. **CP-JohnS** (Ant, The.) **CP-JohnS**

Turn out all the lights. Tanck's Song About Earl Hines. Hayden Carruth. **CP-CarHS** *Fr.* Songs About What Comes Down: The Complete Works of Mr. Septic Tanck.

Turn out the light, turn over, shut your eyes. City, City! Randall Jarrell. **CP-JarrR**

Turn out the lights around the statues. When in the Course of Human Events. Kenneth Patchen. **CP-PatcK**

Turn Over Your Hand. William Stafford. **SP-StafW**

Turn Right Next Corner. Wichita Vortex Sutra. Allen Ginsberg. **CP-GinsA**

Turn toward the holocaust, it approaches. A Discipline. Wendell Berry. **CP-BerrW**

Turn we next to the dead. Matthew Arnold. **SP-ArnoM** *Fr.* Haworth Churchyard.

Turnabout. Charles Bukowski. **SP-BukC1**

Turne all thy thoughts to eyes. Thomas Campion. **CP-CampT**

Turne Backe You Wanton Flier. Thomas Campion. *See* Turn Back, You Wanton Flyer.

Turned Down. David Herbert Lawrence. **CP-LawrD**

Turned from the "eau-forte." Mauberly (1920). Ezra Pound. *Fr.* Hugh Selwyn Mauberley. (Life and Contacts). **SP-PounE**

Turned from the "eau-forte." Ezra Pound. *Fr.* Mauberly (1920). *Fr.* Hugh Selwyn Mauberley. (Life and Contacts). **SP-PounE**

Turner. Kenneth Patchen. **CP-PatcK**

Turner's Seas. Kathleen Jessie Raine. **SP-RainK**

Turning. Archie Randolph Ammons. **SP-AmmoA**

Turning, The. John Haines. **SP-HainJ**
    "Bear loped before me, A."
    "I keep a fire and tell a story."

Turning / one wants it all—. Change. Robert Creeley. **CP-CreeR**

Turning. Adrienne Rich.
    "Whatever you are that has tracked us this far." **SP-RicA1**

Turning always in my mind toward you. Wendell Berry. *Fr.* Letter. **CP-BerrW**

Turning and turning in the widening gyre. The Second Coming. William Butler Yeats. **CP-YeatW**

Turning at every few thigh-straining pushes. Climber. Steve Griffiths. **SP-GrifS**

Turning Away. James Dickey. **CP-DickJ**

Turning clumsily into the embrace. One Incident of Many. William Dickey. **SP-DickW**

Turning Fifty. Stephen Dunn. **SP-DunnS**

Turning of the Babies in the Bed, The. Paul Laurence Dunbar. **CP-DunbP**

Turning the Wheel. Adrienne Rich. **SP-RicA2**
    Apparition.
    Burden Baskets.
    Hohokam.
    Location.
    Mary Jane Colter, 1904.
    Particularity.
    "Road to the great canyon always feels, The." **SP-RicA1; SP-RicA2**
    (Turning the Wheel.) **SP-RicA2**
    Self-hatred.

Turning the Wheel. Adrienne Rich. *See* The Road to the great canyon always feels.

Turnip-Hoer, The. Thomas Hardy. **CP-HardT**

Turnip Vendor, The. Samuel Johnson.
    (Burlesque Translation of Lines from Lope de Vega's *Arcadia*.) **CP-JohnS**
    ("If the Man who Turneps cries.") **CP-JohnS**

Turnpike, The. Louise McNeill. **SP-McNeL**

Turns in a Worm's Lane. Ogden Nash. **CP-NashO**

Turnstone turned rover, A. Upon Learning That a Bird Exists Called the Turnstone. John Updike. **CP-UpdiJ**

Turntables. Dabney Stuart. **SP-StuaD**

Turquoise sea off Grottamare. Grottamare. Lawrence Ferlinghetti. **SP-FerlL**

Turtle, The. Chuang Tzu, *tr. fr. Chinese by* Thomas Merton. **CP-MertT**

Turtle, The. Frederick Morgan. **SP-MorgF**

Turtle, The. Mary Oliver. **SP-OlivM**

Turtle, The. William Carlos Williams. **CP-WilW2**

Turtle Dove, The. Geoffrey Hill. **CP-HillG**

Turtle Dove, The. Geoffrey Hill. **CP-HillG**

Turtle Goddess. The Film. Denise Levertov. **CP-LeveD**

Turtle in swamp. Ralph Waldo Emerson. **CP-EmerR**

Turtle Lake. Richard Hugo. **CP-HugoR**

Turtle lives 'twixt plated decks, The. The . Ogden Nash. **CP-NashO**

Turtle Soup. "Lewis Carroll." *See* Beautiful Soup, so rich and green.

Turtles on the ledges of July, The. Concord River. Adrienne Rich. **CP-RicAE**

Tuscan Brutus, The. Donald Davie. **CP-DavDo**

Tuscan cypresses / What is it? Cypresses. David Herbert Lawrence. **CP-LawrD**

Tuscan Life. Elizabeth Barrett Browning. **FaBoPP** *Fr.* Aurora Leigh. **CP-BroEB**

Tuscan Morning. Donald Davie. **CP-DavDo**

Tuskegee Song. Paul Laurence Dunbar. **CP-DunbP**

Tuskegee, thou pride of the swift growing South. Tuskegee Song. Paul Laurence Dunbar. **CP-DunbP**

Tutored Child, The. Stanley Jasspon Kunitz. **CP-KuniS**

Tutorial. Ted Hughes. *Fr.* Boom. **SP-HughT**

Tutti Colori Quality of Light, The. Al Young. **CP-YounA**

Tutting, he wrenched at a snarled root of dead crab-apple. Geoffrey Hill. *Fr.* Mercian Hymns. **CP-HillG**

TV. Howard Nemerov. **CP-NemeH**

Tw / oo / ld / o / nce upo / n. Edward Estlin Cummings. **CP-CummE**

Twa bonny [*or* bony] lads were Sandy and Jockie. Robert Burns. **CP-BurnR**
    (Sandy and Jockie.) **CP-BurnR**

Twa Dogs, The. Robert Burns. **CP-BurnR**
    Luath. **GDP**

"'Twas in that place o' Scotland's isle." **OBF**

Twangs & Little Twists. Archie Randolph Ammons. **SP-AmmoA**

'Twas a blith Prince exchang'd five hundred Crowns. On Sanazar's Being Honoured. Richard Lovelace. **CP-LoveR**

'Twas a long journey lay before us. 1.5. Horace, *tr. by* William Cowper. **CP-CowpW** *Fr.* Satires.

'Twas a long Parting—but the time. Emily Dickinson. **CP-DickE**

'Twas a saying in use with the great Mr. Lowndes. Very Original Poem, Written with Even a Greater Endeavour than Ordinary after Intelligibility, and Hitherto Only Published on the First Leaf of the Author's Son's Account-Book. Robert Browning. **CP-BroR2**

'Twas at the royal feast, for Persia won. Alexander's Feast; or, The Power of Music [*or* Musique]. John Dryden. **SP-DrydJ**

'Twas awkward, but it fitted me. Emily Dickinson. **CP-DickE**

'Twas Bedford Special Assize, one daft Midsummer's Day. Ned Bratts. Robert Browning. **CP-BroR2**

'Twas brillig, and the slithy toves. Jabberwocky. "Lewis Carroll." **CP-CarrL** *Fr.* Through the Looking-Glass.

'Twas but a single Rose. Upon a Virgin Kissing a Rose. Robert Herrick. **CP-HerrR**

'Twas Cesars saying: Kings no lesse conquerers are. Counsell. Robert Herrick. **CP-HerrR**

'Twas comfort in her Dying Room. Emily Dickinson. **CP-DickE**

'Twas Crisis—All the length had passed. Emily Dickinson. **CP-DickE**

'Twas dead of the night, when I sat in my dwelling. *for diff. vers., see* Fragment, or The Triumph of Conscience. Percy Bysshe Shelley. *Fr.* Poems from St. Irvyne, or, The Rosicrucian. **CP-ShelP**

'Twas dead of the night when I sate in my dwelling. *for diff. vers., see* Victoria. Percy Bysshe Shelley. *Fr.* Original Poetry by Victor and Cazire. **CP-ShelP**

'Twas down in Mississippi not so long ago. The Death of Emmett Till. "Bob Dylan." **CP-DylaB**

'Twas ev'n, the dewy fields were green. Song. On Miss W. A. Robert Burns. **CP-BurnR**

'Twas fighting for his Life he was. Emily Dickinson. **CP-DickE**

'Twas Fultah Fisher's boarding-house. The Ballad of Fisher's Boardinghouse. Rudyard Kipling. **CP-KiplR**

'Twas Goethe taught us all / By diagnosis. Burlesque for Palgrave on the Pronunciation of "Metamorphosis." Robert Browning. **CP-BroR2**

'Twas here my summer paused. Emily Dickinson. **CP-DickE**

'Twas in a glimmering starlight. George Meredith. **CP-MerG2**

'Twas in a tavern that with old age stooped. Falstaff. Walter de la Mare. **CP-DeLaW**

'Twas in another lifetime, one of toil and blood. Shelter from the Storm. "Bob Dylan." **CP-DylaB**

'Twas in that place o' Scotland's isle. Robert Burns. **OBF** *Fr.* The Twa Dogs. **CP-BurnR**

'Twas in the glad season. The Morning Dream. William Cowper. **CP-CowpW**

'Twas in the seventeen hunder year. Johnie B———'s Lament. Robert Burns. **CP-BurnR** *Fr.* The Heron Ballads, 1795.

Twas in the springtime of the year. Ballad. Malcolm Lowry. **CP-LowrM**

'Twas just at gnat and cobweb-time. The Rift. Thomas Hardy. **CP-HardT**

'Twas just this time, last year, I died. Emily Dickinson. **CP-DickE**

'Twas later when the summer went. Emily Dickinson. **CP-DickE**

'Twas like a Maelstrom, with a notch. Emily Dickinson. **CP-DickE**

'Twas Love—not me. Emily Dickinson. **CP-DickE**

'Twas my last waking thought, how it could be. The Two Founts. Samuel Taylor Coleridge. **CP-ColeS**

'Twas my one Glory. Emily Dickinson. **CP-DickE**

'Twas my purpose, on a day. A Figurative Description of the Procedure of Divine Love. Jeanne Marie Bouvier de la Motte-Guyon, *tr. fr. French by* William Cowper. **CP-CowpW**

'Twas na her bonie blue e'e was my ruin. Song. Robert Burns. **CP-BurnR**

'Twas night; her comrades gathered all. Geraldine. Emily Brontë. **CP-BronE**

'Twas noontide of summer. Evening Star. Edgar Allan Poe. **CP-PoeEd**

'Twas not a mist, nor was it quite a cloud. Samuel Taylor Coleridge. *Fr.* Some Fragments, Mainly from Manuscripts of 1797–8. **CP-ColeS**

'Twas not for some calm blessing to receive. Her Muffe. Richard Lovelace. **CP-LoveR**

'Twas not Lov's Dart. A Hymne to Sir Clipseby Crew. Robert Herrick. **CP-HerrR**

Twas not while England's sword unsheathed. The American Rebellion. Rudyard Kipling. **CP-KiplR**

'Twas now the hour when Night had driven. *Fr. the Greek of* Anacreon. Byron. **CP-Byron**

'Twas on a Holy Thursday, their innocent faces clean. Holy Thursday. William Blake. **CH; EnRP; FHYEP; HBV; HoFi; InPS; LAuP; MeMBP; NAEL-2; NAWM-2; NOBE; NOBRP; NOEC; NoP; OAEL-2; OAEP; OBEC; OFD; PeECV; PoE; SCV; TEP; TFi; TrCP** *Fr.* Songs of Innocence. **CP-BlakW**

'Twas on a lofty vase's side. Ode on the Death of a Favourite [*or* Favorite] Cat, Drowned in a Tub [*or* Bowl] of Gold Fishes. Thomas Gray. **CP-GrayT**

'Twas on a Monday morning. Charlie He's My Darling. Robert Burns. **CP-BurnR**

'Twas on a summer's day—the sixth of June. Byron. **PPP** *Fr.* Canto the First. **EnRP; NAEL-2; NoP; OAEL-2; PoE** *Fr.* Don Juan. **CP-Byron**

Twas on a sunny summer day. An Incident. Arthur Hugh Clough. **SP-ClouA**

'Twas one of the charmëd days. The Heart of All the Scene. Ralph Waldo Emerson. **AA** *Fr.* Woodnotes I ("For this present, hard"). **CP-EmerR**

'Twas one of those dark, cloudy days. Emily Brontë. **CP-BronE**

'Twas past ane o'clock in a cauld frosty morning. Cauld Frosty Morning. Robert Burns. **CP-BurnR**

'Twas said, long since, by various moral sages. Prologue to *What is She?* A Comedy, in Five Acts. Charlotte Smith. **CP-SmitC** *Fr.* What is She?

'Twas said, long since, by various moral sages. What is She? Charlotte Smith.

'Twas such a little little boat. Emily Dickinson. **CP-DickE**

'Twas summer, and the sun had mounted high. *see also* The Ruined Cottage. William Wordsworth. **EnRP** *Fr.* The Excursion. **CP-WorW2**

'Twas sweet to know it only possible. Samuel Taylor Coleridge. *Fr.* Some Fragments, Mainly from Manuscripts of 1797–8. **CP-ColeS**

'Twas the apple that in Eden. The Unlucky Apple. Paul Laurence Dunbar. **CP-DunbP**

'Twas the first day of the springtime. Snowman. Shel Silverstein. **SP-SilS2**

'Twas the old—road—through pain. Emily Dickinson. **CP-DickE**

'Twas the voice of the sweet dove. The Old Sweet Dove of Wiveton. Stevie Smith. **CP-SmitS**

'Twas the voice of the Wanderer, I heard her exclaim. The Wanderer. Stevie Smith. **CP-SmitS**

'Twas three an' thirty year ago. The Rivals. Paul Laurence Dunbar. **CP-DunbP**

'Twas to greet the new rector I called here. The Old Neighbour and the New. Thomas Hardy. **CP-HardT**

'Twas warm—at first—like Us. Emily Dickinson. **CP-DickE**

'Twas where the birch and sounding thong are plyed. A Tale. Robert Burns. **CP-BurnR**

'Twas yesterday, at early dawn. M.G. For The U.S. Emily Brontë. **CP-BronE**

'Twas yesterday such a black-dye-day. George Meredith. **CP-MerG2**

Tweedledee and Tweedledoom. Ogden Nash. **CP-NashO**

Twelfe Night, or King and Queene. Robert Herrick. **CP-HerrR**

Twelfth Book, The. Archibald MacLeish. *Fr.* Conquistador. **CP-MacLA**

Twelfth Morning; or What You Will. Elizabeth Bishop. **CP-BishE**

Twelfth Night. Louis MacNeice. **CP-MacNL**

Twelfth of July, The. John Hewitt. **CP-HewiJ**

Twell de Night Is Pas'. Paul Laurence Dunbar. **CP-DunbP**

Twelve, The. Wystan Hugh Auden. *Fr.* Six Commissioned Texts. **CP-AudeW**

Twelve, The. Allen Tate. **CP-TateA**

Twelve arrows, and a bow, and spear. Song. George Meredith. **CP-MerG2**

Twelve Articles. Jonathan Swift. **CP-SwifJ**

Twelve Dancing Princesses, The. Anne Sexton. **CP-SextA**

12:18 A.M. Charles Bukowski. **SP-BukC1**

Twelve Études for Voice and Kazoo. Gilbert Sorrentino. **SP-SorrG**
    Girl at Sixteen with Lightning.
    Huge Man in Tight Pants.
    Impromptu Solo on a Balcony.
    In Which There is Nothing Up the Sleeve.
    Jaime Valerosa y Borracho Consults His Journal.
    Le Bateau d'Amour Descried on the Briny.
    Man in Old Blue Suit at the Plaza.
    Solitary Man Discovered in a Field of Daisies.
    Some Sap Sings a Poor Pantoum.
    Ultima Despedida del Principe Poniatowski de Su Familia.
    Waltz of the Empty Roadhouse.
    Woman Irritable because of Her Menses.

Twelve Hours Out of New York After Twenty-Five Days at Sea. Gary Snyder. **CP-SnydG**

Twelve Line Poem. William Carlos Williams. **CP-WilW2**

Twelve o'clock. / Along the reaches of the street. Rhapsody on a Windy Night. Thomas Stearns Eliot. **CP-ElioT**

12 O'Clock News. Elizabeth Bishop. **CP-BishE**

Twelve people, most of us strangers, stand in a room. Eating the Pig. Donald Hall. **CP-HallD**

Twelve Poems from *The Keeper of the Flocks*. Fernando Pessoa, *tr. fr. Portuguese by* Thomas Merton. **CP-MertT**

"Bus has gone by, The."

"I do not bother with rhymes."

"If I sometimes say that flowers smile."

"If people insist on my having."

"Last evening a city man."

"Lightly, lightly, so lightly."

"My gaze is clear as a sunflower."

" 'Mystery of things'—where is it found?, The."

"Poor flowers in geometric beds."

"Rather the flying bird, leaving no trace."

"Tagus is finer than the creek, The."

"What we see of things is the things themselves."

Twelve Seasons. Donald Hall. **CP-HallD**

12. 6. 71. Louise Glück. **SP-GlücL**

Twelve smoky gates flame with mass-demonstrations. Thomas Merton. *Fr.* Cables to the Ace. **CP-MertT**

Twelve snails went walking after night. The Haughty Snail-King. Nicholas Vachel Lindsay. **CP-LindV**

Twelve Songs. Wystan Hugh Auden. **CP-AudeW**

"At last the secret is out, as it always must come in the end."

Autumn Song.

"Dear, though the night is gone."

"Fish in the unruffled lakes." **BoLoP; CBLP; CMoP; ChMP; MoAB; MoBrPo; MoP**

"Let a florid music praise."

"O lurcher-loving collier, black as night."

"O the valley in the summer where I and my John." **PIP**

(Johnny.) **PIP**

Roman Wall Blues. **DTC; FaBoEH; NTP**

"Some say that love's a little boy." **PAW**

Song of the Beggars. **PeLV**

"Stop all the clocks, cut off the telephone." **MoBrPo; OPOU; RB**

(Song: "Stop all the clocks, cut off the telephone.") **MoBrPo; OPOU**

"Underneath an abject willow."

Twelve-Spoked Wheel Flashing, The. Marge Piercy. **SP-PierM**

Twelve-Thousand-Day Honeymoon, The. Anne Sexton. **CP-SextA**

Twelve years ago I came here. The Burn. Galway Kinnell. **SP-KinnG**

Twelve years to the day. Anniversary. Rita Dove. **SP-DoveR**

Twentieth Century, The. Daniel Gerard Hoffman. **SP-HoffD**

20th Street Spring. Grace Paley. **CP-PaleG**

Twentieth year is well-nigh past, The. To Mary. William Cowper. **CP-CowpW**

Twenty Bridges from Tower to Kew. The River's Tale. Rudyard Kipling. **CP-KiplR**

28. Philip Levine. **SP-LeviP**

28 August and first frost. Charles Wright. *Fr.* Three Poems of Departure. **SP-WrigC**

Twenty-eight naked young women bathed by the shore. A Dream of Whitman Paraphrased, Recognized and Made More Vivid by Renoir. Delmore Schwartz. **SP-SchwD**

Twenty-eight years before on the living room couch he'd stared at me, I said. Don't Grow Old. Allen Ginsberg. **CP-GinsA**

Twenty-eight young men crossing by the shore. Walt Whitman. **HAP; LPA; NoP; SAmP** *Fr.* Song of Myself. **CP-WhitW**

21st Century Man. Richard Eberhart. **CP-EberR**

21st September 1912. John Hewitt. **CP-HewiJ**

2500 years Before Proust. Time. Tom Clark. **SP-ClarT**

24:IV:40075, 3:30 PM, N. of Coaldale, Nevada, a Glimpse through a Break in the Storm of the Summit of the White Mountains. O Mother Gaia. Gary Snyder. **CP-SnydG**

Twenty-four Years. Dylan Thomas. **CP-ThomD**

Twenty men crossing a bridge. Metaphors of a Magnifico. Wallace Stevens. **CP-StevW**

Twenty men stand watching the muckers. Muckers. Carl Sandburg. **CP-SandC**

20 minutes later. Charles Bukowski. **NGP** *Fr.* Horsemeat. **SP-BukC3**

29 Poems. Louis Zukofsky. **CP-ZukLS**

"And looking to where shone Orion."

"And to paradise which is a port."

"Ask of the sun."

Aubade, 1925.

"Blue light is the night harbor-slip." **PoE**

"Buoy—no, how."

"Cactus rose-mauve and gray, twin overturned."

"Cars once steel and green, now old." **VGW**

(Cars Once Steel and Green, Now Old.) **VGW**

"Close your eyes."

"Cocktails / and signs of."

During the Passaic Strike of 1926.

"Dying away as of trees, A."

Ferry.

"How many / Times round."

"Like the oceans, or the leaves of fine Southern."

Memory of V. I. Ulianov.

"Millennium of sun—."

"Not much more than being." **PoE**

"O sleep, the sky goes down behind the poplars."

"Only water—."

"Passing tall."

"Run on, you still dead to the sound of a name." **CP-ZukLS**

Song Theme.

"Stubbing the cloud-fields—the searchlight, high." **CP-ZukLS**

"Tall and singularly dark you pass among the breakers—."

Tam Cari Capitis.

Two Dedications: D.R.

Two Dedications: Tibor Serly.

"We are crossing the bridge now."

29 Songs. Louis Zukofsky. **CP-ZukLS**

Arizona.

"Checkers, checkmate and checkerboard."

"Crickets' / thickets / light, / delight."

"Do not leave me."

"Ears beringed with fuzz."

"Happier, happier, now."

—"Her Soil's Birth."

Home for Aged Bomb Throwers—U.S.S.R.

Imitation.

Immature Pebbles.

"Immediate Aim, The."

"In Arizona / (how many years in the mountains)." **TRP**

(In Arizona.) **TRP**

"In that this happening." **CP-BuntB**

(*incl. Latin tr. by* Basil Bunting.) **CP-BuntB**

It's a Gay Li-ife.

Junction, A.

Madison, Wis., Remembering the Bloom of Monticello (1931).

"Mirror oval sabres   playing, The."

N.Y.

No One Inn.

Prop. LXI.

"Sand: For the cigarette finished, The."

"Snows' night's winds on the window rattling."

Song—3/4 time.

"Specifically, a writer of music."

This Fall, 1933.

"To my wash-stand."

Train-Signal.

"Whatever makes this happening."

"Who endure days like this."

Twenty-one Love Poems. Adrienne Rich. **SP-RicA1; SP-RicA2**

"Across a city from you, I'm with you." **PeHV**

"Can it be growing colder when I begin." **NAAL-2**

"Dark lintels, the blue and foreign stones, The." **NALW; NoAM**

"Every peak is a crater. This is the law of volcanoes." **NAAL-2; NALW; NoAM**

Floating Poem, Unnumbered, The. **NALW; NoAM**

"I can see myself years back at Sunion."

"I come home from you through the early light of spring." **BoWoP**

"I wake up in your bed. I know I have been dreaming." **NAAL-2; NoAM; TRP; UnAS; VBLP**

"If I lay on that beach with you."

"It was your vision of the pilot."

"No one's fated or doomed to love anyone."

"Rain on the West Side Highway." **NAAL-2**

"Rules break like a thermometer, The."

"Since we're not young, weeks have to do time." **UnAS; VBLP**

"Sleeping, turning in turn like planets." **PeHV; TRP**

"That conversation we were always on the edge." **BoWoP; NoAM**

"This apartment full of books could crack open."

"What kind of beast would turn its life into words?"

"Wherever in this city, screens flicker." **PeHV**

"Your dog, tranquil and innocent, dozes through."

"Your silence today is a pond where drowned things live."

"Your small hands, precisely equal to my own." **PoE; TRP**

Twenty or more big cloth roses, pale rose or scarlet. Christmas Tree. Robert Lowell. **SP-LoweR**

XXVII. "Fair proud, now tell me, why should fair be proud." Edmund Spenser. **Son** *Fr.* Amoretti. **CP-Spens**

XXVI. "Sweet is the rose, but grows upon a brere." Edmund Spenser. **EIl.** *Fr.* Amoretti. **CP-Spens**

Twenty-some years ago, I read Graham Stuart Thomas's. Horse-Chestnut Trees and Roses. James Schuyler. **CP-SchuJ**

Twenty sparrows / on. Breakfast. William Carlos Williams. **CP-WilW1**

Twenty-third Psalm, The. George Herbert. **CP-HerbG**

23rd Street Runs into Heaven. Kenneth Patchen. **CP-PatcK**

Twenty Three Point Prospectus for Small College in the Badlands. Thomas Merton. **CP-MertT**

Twenty-two degrees below zero. Hayden Carruth. *Fr.* North Winter. **CP-CarHL**

Twenty-two mud-daubed figures battling together on a. The Punt. Ernest Hemingway. **CP-HemiE**

XXII. "This holy season, fit to fast and pray." Edmund Spenser. **PoE** *Fr.* Amoretti. **CP-Spens**

22,000 Dollars in 3 Months. Charles Bukowski. **SP-BukC2**

22,000 feet over Hazed square Vegetable planet Floor. Going to Chicago. Allen Ginsberg. **CP-GinsA**

Twenty Years. Walt Whitman. **CP-WhitW**

Twenty Years Ago. David Herbert Lawrence. **CP-LawrD**

Twentyseven bums give a prostitute the once. Edward Estlin Cummings. **CP-CummE**

'Twere sweet to have a comrade here. Dream of the City Shopwoman. Thomas Hardy. **CP-HardT**

'Twere time that I died too, now she is dead. Elegy on My Muse. Ben Jonson. **GoBC** *Fr.* Eupheme. **CP-JonsB**

Twi- / is -Light bird. Edward Estlin Cummings. **CP-CummE**

Twice. Christina Georgina Rossetti. **CP-RosC1**

Twice a week / then / every morning. She Used to Water the Plants. Siv Cedering Fox. **SP-CedeS**

Twice a week the winter thorough. Alfred Edward Housman. **CP-HousA**

Twice had Summer her fair Verdure. Emily Dickinson. **CP-DickE**

Twice has *Pudica* been a Bride, and led. Upon a Lady Faire, but Fruitlesse. Robert Herrick. **CP-HerrR**

Twice having seen your shingled heads adorable. Evening on Lesbos. Edna St. Vincent Millay. **CP-MillE**

Twice I'd tried / to pass the / bastard outside. Arroyo Hondo. Charles Tomlinson. **CP-TomlC**

Twice in the past two weeks I think I met. The Couple. Robert Lowell. **SP-LoweR**

Twice Lovely. Walter de la Mare. **CP-DeLaW**

Twice More. Charles Kenneth Williams. **CP-WillC**

Twice, now, I've gone back there, like a part-time ghost. Return to Marsh Street. Thomas McGrath. **SP-McGrT**

Twice Of The Same Fever. Robert Ranke Graves. **CP-GravR**

Twice one summer. Look Back. Gary Snyder. **CP-SnydG**

Twice or thrice had I loved thee. Air[e] and Angels. John Donne. **CP-DonnJ**

Twice ten years old not fully told. Upon a Fit of Sickness, Anno 1632. Anne Bradstreet. **CP-BradA**

Twice this Christmas Day you tried. Amplitude. Tess Gallagher. **SP-GallT**

Twice you have been around the world. The One Who Was Different. Randall Jarrell. **CP-JarrR**

Twicknam [or Twickenham] Garden. John Donne. **CP-DonnJ**

Twig sprouteth, / The moth outeth, The. Are Ye Not Much Better Than They? Christina Georgina Rossetti. **CP-RosC2**

Twigs of the birch imprint the December sky, The. The Prospect. Thomas Hardy. **CP-HardT**

Twilight. Walter de la Mare. **CP-DeLaW**

Twilight. Paul Laurence Dunbar. **CP-DunbP**

Twilight ("Twilight is no other thing [we say], The"). Robert Herrick. **CP-HerrR**

Twilight ("Twilight, no other thing is, Poets say"). Robert Herrick. **CP-HerrR**

Twilight. Stanley Jasspon Kunitz. **CP-KuniS**

Twilight. David Herbert Lawrence. **CP-LawrD**

Twilight. David Herbert Lawrence. **CP-LawrD**

Twilight. David Herbert Lawrence. **CP-LawrD**

Twilight. Walt Whitman. **CP-WhitW**

Twilight and little mountain. Lackawanna Twilight. Carl Sandburg. **CP-SandC**

Twilight approaches, with its last brief spot-lit. All That Is. Richard Wilbur. **CP-WilbR**

Twilight Calm. Christina Georgina Rossetti. **CP-RosC1**

Twilight Comes. Hayden Carruth. **CP-CarHS**

Twilight drivels down the mountain There below. The Village. Hayden Carruth. *Fr.* Contra Mortem. **CP-CarHL**

Twilight falls; I soften the dusting feathers, The. Sappho. James Wright. **CP-WrigJ**

Twilight is long fingers and black hair, The. Long Fingers. Allen Tate. **CP-TateA**

Twilight is no other thing (we say), The. Twilight. Robert Herrick. **CP-HerrR**

Twilight leaned mirrored in a pool. The Old Angler. Walter de la Mare. **CP-DeLaW**

Twilight Music. George Meredith. **CP-MerG1**

Twilight Night. Christina Georgina Rossetti. **CP-RosC1**

Twilight, no other thing is, Poets say. Twilight. Robert Herrick. **CP-HerrR**

Twilight, old friend, has come back to the lower orchard. Vesper Journal. Charles Wright. **SP-WrigC**

Twilight on the frozen lake. Never Say Goodbye. "Bob Dylan." **CP-DylaB**

Twilight on the Waste Lands. Donald Davie. **CP-DavDo**

Twilight Song. Edwin Arlington Robinson. **CP-RobiE**

Twilight Song, A. Walt Whitman. **CP-WhitW**

Twilight stifled the valley wearily. Lityerses. Allen Tate. **CP-TateA**

Twilight was a going of the gods: the air. Under the Moon's Reign. Charles Tomlinson. **CP-TomlC**

Twilights. James Wright. **CP-WrigJ**

Twin, The. Robert Pack. **SP-PackR**

Twin Falls, The. James Dickey. **CP-DickJ**

Twin of Sleep, The. Robert Ranke Graves. **CP-GravR**

Twin Snakes. Leonard Nathan. **SP-NathL**

Twin spheres full of fur and noise. Poem. Frank O'Hara. **SP-OharF**

Twin stars of light! whose blended rays. Hymn to Love and Life. Charlotte Smith. **CP-SmitC**

Twin streaks twice higher than cumulus. Vapor Trails. Gary Snyder. **CP-SnydG**

Twined together and, as is customary. Never Such Love. Robert Ranke Graves. **CP-GravR**

Twinkle, twinkle, little bat! "Lewis Carroll." **CP-CarrL** *Fr.* Alice's Adventures in Wonderland.

(Mad Hatter's Song, The.) **CP-CarrL**

Twinkletoes in the ballroom. Light Music. Derek Mahon. **SP-MahoD**

Twinkling lamps stream up the hill, The. California. Wystan Hugh Auden. **CP-AudWJ**

Twins, The. Robert Browning. **CP-BroR1**

Twins. Charles Bukowski. **SP-BukC1**

Twins. Jane Cooper. **SP-CoopJ**

Twins. Robert Ranke Graves. **CP-GravR**

Twins. William Matthews. **SP-MattW**

Twins, The. Karl Shapiro. **SP-ShapK**

Twins, The. Mona Van Duyn. **SP-VanDM**

Twirling your blue skirts, travelling the sward. Blue Girls. John Crowe Ransom. **SP-RansJ**

Twirls on the tips of a carnation. The Oriental Ballerina. Rita Dove. **SP-DoveR**

Twist, The. Charles Olson. **SP-OlsoC** *Fr.* The Maximus Poems.

Twist along the spine begins the form, A. A Spiral Shell. Howard Nemerov. *Fr.* Epigrams: "Wasp, climbing the window pane." **CP-NemeH**

Twist me a crown of wind-flowers. Christina Georgina Rossetti. **CP-RosC2**

Twist ye, twine ye! even so. The Spindle Song. Sir Walter Scott. **SP-ScotW**

Twist your fingers, cheery. New Song for Indiana Ophelias. Carl Sandburg. **CP-SandC**

Twisted Heart, The. John Hewitt. **CP-HewiJ**

Twisted rhombs ceased their clamour of accompaniment, The. Ezra Pound. **MeMAP** *Fr.* Homage to Sextus Propertius. **SP-PounE**

Twister to Magnum. Citizen CB. Al Young. **CP-YounA**

'Twixt a smile and a tear. Twilight. Paul Laurence Dunbar. **CP-DunbP**

'Twixt dream and wake we wandered on. The Encounter. Walter de la Mare. **CP-DeLaW**

'Twixt Kings and Subjects ther's this mighty odds. The Difference Betwixt King and Subjects. Robert Herrick. **CP-HerrR**

'Twixt Kings and Tyrants there's this difference known. Kings and Tyrants. Robert Herrick. **CP-HerrR**

'Twixt my house and thy house the pathway is broad. The Houses. Rudyard Kipling. **CP-KiplR**

'Twixt "Perphaps" and "May be." "Lewis Carroll." *Fr.* Solutions. *Fr.* Puzzles from Wonderland. **CP-CarrL**

'Twixt Truth and Errour, there's this difference known. Truth and Error. Robert Herrick. **CP-HerrR**

Two. Robert Creeley. **CP-CreeR**

Two. Robert Creeley. **CP-CreeR**

Two. Frederick Morgan. *Fr.* Eight Triolets. **SP-MorgF**

Two. Carl Sandburg. **CP-SandC**

Two. James Schuyler. **CP-SchuJ**

Two Acrostics: Round the wondrous globe / Maidens, if a maid you meet. "Lewis Carroll." **CP-CarrL**

2 a.m. / December, and still no moon. Late Moon. Philip Levine. **SP-LeviP**

Two A.M. Al Young. **CP-YounA**

Two Amsterdams. Lawrence Ferlinghetti. **SP-FerlL**

Two and a half years later the interpreter. Frank Templeton Prince. *Fr.* Afterword on Rupert Brooke. **CP-PrinF**

Two and One Are a Problem. Ogden Nash. **CP-NashO**

Two Angels, The. John Greenleaf Whittier. **CP-WhitJ**

Two angels among the throng of angels. A Vision. Denise Levertov. **CP-LeveD**

Two April Mornings, The. William Wordsworth. **CP-WorW1**

Two Armies. Stephen Spender.
("Deep as the winter plain, two armies.") **CP-SpenS**
(Two Armies.) **CP-SpenS**

Two Aspects of April. William Carlos Williams. **CP-WilW1**

Two at Norfolk. Wallace Stevens. **CP-StevW**

Two athletes / Are dancing in the cathedral. Spring Images. James Wright. **CP-WrigJ**

Two Beggars: A Reminiscence. Frank Templeton Prince. **CP-PrinF**

Two beings were drifting. The Destined Pair. Thomas Hardy. **CP-HardT**

Two bells   six bells   two bells   six bells. Night Bells. Carl Sandburg. **CP-SandC**

Two big red fists pawing the air. The Tackle. Ernest Hemingway. **CP-HemiE**

Two birds are perched in the midnight tree. Poem of the Self. Frederick Morgan. **SP-MorgF**

Two Blackbirds, The. George Meredith. **CP-MerG1**

Two blue glasses of neat. Living in the Moment. Marilyn Hacker. **SP-HackM**

Two boats parked / and posing in. White Boat, Blue Boat. James Schuyler. **CP-SchuJ**

Two boats with nets lying off the sea-beach, quite still. A Paumanok Picture. Walt Whitman. **CP-WhitW**

Two bodies in the river. Frederick Morgan. *Fr.* The River. **SP-MorgF**

Two Boxes. Shel Silverstein. **SP-SilS2**

Two Boys Went Into a Dream Diner. Allen Ginsberg. **CP-GinsA**

Two bres's, 'n' 'gongo 'brella. Little Cannibal's Bedtimesong. Kenneth Patchen. **CP-PatcK**

Two bricklayers are setting the walls. The Bricklayer's Lunch Hour. Allen Ginsberg. **CP-GinsA**

Two British Airmen. Thomas Merton. **CP-MertT**

Two Brothers, The. "Lewis Carroll." **CP-CarrL**

Two brothers, Oakes and Oliver. Two Gardens in Linndale. Edwin Arlington Robinson. **CP-RobiE**

Two Brothers went a journey hand in hand. Creed. George Meredith. **CP-MerG2**

Two bubbles found they had rainbows on their curves. Bubbles. Carl Sandburg. **CP-SandC**

Two Butterflies went out at Noon. Emily Dickinson. **CP-DickE**

Two, by themselves, each other, love and fear. Pyramus and Thisbe. John Donne. **CP-DonnJ**

Two Camels. Robert Browning. **CP-BroR2**

Two Campers in Cloud Country. Sylvia Plath. **CP-PlatS**

Two Canadian Memorials. Rudyard Kipling. *Fr.* Epitaphs of the War [1914–1918]. **CP-KiplR**

Two centuries ago Linnaeus said "nose frightful, tears / pitiful" of you. The Sloth. Isabella Gardner. **CP-GardI**

Two Children, The. Emily Brontë. **CP-BronE**
(A.E. And R.C.) **CP-BronE**

Two Children, The. Emily Brontë. **CP-BronE**
(A.E. and R.C.) **CP-BronE**
A.E. **NBM**
R.C.

Two children bow their heads. The Puzzle. Howard Nemerov. **CP-NemeH**

Two children, dressed in court costume. An Old Picture. Howard Nemerov. **CP-NemeH**

Two Chorale-Preludes: On Melodies by Paul Celan. Geoffrey Hill. **CP-HillG**

Two Chorus's to the Tragedy of Brutus. Alexander Pope. **CP-PopeA**
Chorus of Athenians.
Chorus of Youths and Virgins.

Two Christmas-Cards. Robinson Jeffers. **CP-JefR3**

Two Christs were at Golgotha. Early Lynching. Carl Sandburg. **CP-SandC**

Two Cities. Marilyn Hacker. **SP-HackM**

Two Climbs. Wystan Hugh Auden. **CP-AudeW**

Two college sophs of Cambridge growth. Cassinus and Peter. Jonathan Swift. **CP-SwifJ**

Two Conceits. Allen Tate. **CP-TateA**

Two cops who are really famous actors. In Your Dream after Falling in Love. Richard Hugo. **CP-HugoR**

Two crows, criss-crossing, carom. All Hallows' Eve in Kansas. Gary Gildner. **SP-GildG**

Two Crucial Generations. Robert Ranke Graves. **CP-GravR**

Two cups / a given grace. A Given Grace. Charles Tomlinson. **CP-TomlC**

Two dayes now in that sea he sayled has. Guyon's Voyage to the Bower of Bliss. Edmund Spenser. **NoSic** *Fr.* The Faerie Queene. **CP-Spens**

Two dayes now in that sea he sayled has. Edmund Spenser. **OxBoS** *Fr.* Guyon's Voyage to the Bower of Bliss. **NoSic** *Fr.* The Faerie Queene. **CP-Spens**

Two days ago with dancing glancing hair. My Friend. Christina Georgina Rossetti. **CP-RosC1**

Two days later I'm on the train. Sea Huns. Brendan Galvin. **SP-GalvB**

Two days of listening to a police radio. Connections. Stephen Dobyns. **SP-DoveR**

Two days with one eye. Revelation. John Updike. **CP-UpdiJ**

Two Dedications. Donald Davie. **CP-DavDo**
Barnsley Cricket Club.
Wide France.

Two Dedications: D.R. Louis Zukofsky. *Fr.* 29 Poems. **CP-ZukLS**

Two Dedications: Tibor Serly. Louis Zukofsky. *Fr.* 29 Poems. **CP-ZukLS**

Two Deliberate Exercises. William Carlos Williams. **CP-WilW2**

Two Desert Fathers. Thomas Merton. **CP-MertT**

Two Devills at one blow thou hast laid flat. Luke 11; Upon the Dumbe Devill Cast Out, and the Slanderous Jewes Put to Silence. Bible, *N.T.* **CP-CrasR**, *tr. by* Richard Crashaw; *Fr.* St. Luke.

Two dimensions. Diptych divided by a house wall seen end-on. Colour Supplement Pages. Roy Fisher. **SP-FishR**

Two Disciplines. Robert Ranke Graves. **CP-GravR**

Two dogs / wait for the crumbs. Quarai. Charles Tomlinson. **CP-TomlC**

Two Dogs Have I. Ogden Nash. **CP-NashO**

Two doves upon the selfsame branch. Song. Christina Georgina Rossetti. **CP-RosC1**

Two Dreams. Allen Ginsberg. **CP-GinsA**

Two Drowned at the Gateway. Marsden Hartley. **CP-HartM**

Two Easter Stanzas. Nicholas Vachel Lindsay. **CP-LindV**
Hope of the Resurrection, The.
We Meet at the Judgement and I Fear It Not.

Two Egrets. John Ciardi. **SP-CiarJ**

Two Egyptian Portrait Masks. Robert Earl Hayden. **CP-HaydR**

2 8 3 2 5 6 7 4 5 4 9. Pablo Neruda, *tr. fr. Spanish by* Ben Belitt. **SP-NeruP**

Two Elizabeths, The. John Greenleaf Whittier. **CP-WhitJ**

Two Epigrams on Byron's *Cain*. William Wordsworth. **CP-WorW2**

Two evils, monstrous either one apart. Winter Remembered. John Crowe Ransom. **SP-RansJ**

Two executioners stalk along over the knolls, The. Throwing a Tree. Thomas Hardy. **CP-HardT**

Two eyes, two hands—. Gemini. Robert Creeley. **CP-CreeR**

Two-faced Janus, god of Time. To Janus. Jonathan Swift. **CP-SwifJ**

Two Fawns That Didn't See the Light This Spring. Gary Snyder. **CP-SnydG**

Two Figures in Dense Violet Night. Wallace Stevens. **CP-StevW**

Two Fires, The. Margaret Atwood. **SP-AtwM1**

Two Fish. Carl Sandburg. **CP-SandC**

Two fishes swimming in the sea. Laughing Blue Steel. Carl Sandburg. **CP-SandC**

Two flower-enfolding crystal vases she. Grace and Love. George Meredith. **CP-MerG1**

Two-Fold. David Herbert Lawrence. **CP-LawrD**

Two-fold gift in this my volume lies, A. Phaedrus, tr. by Samuel Johnson. **CP-JohnS** *Fr.* Fabulae.

Two for History. Kenneth Patchen. **CP-PatcK**

Birthday. Dabney Stuart. **SP-StuaD**

Two Formal Elegies. Geoffrey Hill. **CP-HillG**

Two forms move among the dead, high sleep. The Owl in the Sarcophagus. Wallace Stevens. **CP-StevW**

Two Foscari, The. Byron. **CP-Byron**

Swimming. **GN**

Two Founts, The. Samuel Taylor Coleridge. **CP-ColeS**

Two Fragments. Stephen Berg. **SP-BergS**

Two Fragments on Sleep. David Herbert Lawrence. **CP-LawrD**

"Ah life, God, Law, whatever name you have."

"Is not the wondrous sense of being flung."

Two friends who met here and embraced are gone. Wystan Hugh Auden. *Fr.* The Quest. **CP-AudeW**

Two from Ireland. Donald Davie. **CP-DavDo**

1977, Near Mullingar.

1969, Ireland of the Bombers.

Two frozen claws / In two frozen minutes. Malcolm Lowry. **CP-LowrM**

Two full generations. *Song:*Seven Fresh Years. Robert Ranke Graves. **CP-GravR**

Two Gardens in Linndale. Edwin Arlington Robinson. **CP-RobiE**

Two gazed into a pool, he gazed and saw. An Echo from Willowwood. Christina Georgina Rossetti. **CP-RosC3**

Two Gentlemen in Bonds. John Crowe Ransom. **SP-RansJ**

Bad News.

Epithalamion of a Peach.

Fait Accompli.

In Bed Not Dead.

Injured Sire.

Kingdom Come.

L'etat C'est Moi.

Misanthrope.

Pink and Pale.

Primer for Statesmen.

Rain.

Thinking, Drinking.

Two Gentlemen Scholars. John Crowe Ransom. *Fr.* Sixteen Poems in Eight Pairings. **SP-RansJ**

Two Ghosts Together. Kenneth Patchen. **CP-PatcK**

Two Girls. Howard Nemerov. **CP-NemeH**

Two girls discover. The Secret. Denise Levertov. **CP-LeveD**

Two girls one blond one latin with fixed hair. Girls Fighting, Broadway. Karl Shapiro. **SP-ShapK**

Two girls there are: within the house. Two Sisters of Persephone. Sylvia Plath. **CP-PlatS**

Two Goes into Two Once, If You Can Get It There. Ogden Nash. **CP-NashO**

Two grades above me, though two inches shorter. First Love. Robert Lowell. **SP-LoweR**

Two Graves in a Day. Richard Hugo. **CP-HugoR**

Two great elms. Hills beyond them. The Silo. Lewis Turco. **SP-TurcL**

Two grey herons flying. Marsden Hartley. **CP-HartM**

Two Guitar Pieces. Philip Larkin. **CP-LarkP**

Two Hands. Anne Sexton. **CP-SextA**

Two hands lie still, the hairy and the white. Love for a Hand. Karl Shapiro. **SP-ShapK**

Two Hangovers. James Wright. **CP-WrigJ**

"I slouch in bed."

I Try to Waken and Greet the World Once Again.

Two-Headed Poems. Margaret Atwood. **SP-AtwM2**

"Despite us / there is only one universe, the sun."

"If I were a foreigner, as you say."

"Investigator is here, The."

"Is this what we wanted."

"Our leader / is a man of water."

"Surely in your language."

"This is the secret: these hearts."

"Those south of us are lavish."

"We think of you as one."

"Well, we felt / we were almost getting somewhere."

"You can't live here without breathing."

Two Hearts. Anne Waldman. **SP-WaldA**

Two heavy trestles, and a board. My Table. William Butler Yeats. **CP-YeatW; LiTB** *Fr.* Meditations in Time of Civil War. **CP-YeatW**

Two homecomings link my life. Homecomings. Pablo Neruda, tr. fr. *Spanish by* Ben Belitt. **SP-NeruP**

Two Hoppers. John Updike. **CP-UpdiJ**

Two horses / white. Beyond the Broken House. Marsden Hartley. **CP-HartM**

Two horses in yellow light. August. Adrienne Rich. **SP-RicA2**

Two Horses Playing in the Orchard. James Wright. **CP-WrigJ**

Two Hours. John Ciardi. **SP-CiarJ**

Two hours after midnight she was in her proper position. The Run-In. Alun Lewis. **CP-LewiA**

Two hours I've walked. Haiku. Etheridge Knight. **SP-KnigE**

Two Houses, The. Thomas Hardy. **CP-HardT**

Two hummingbirds as evanescent as. Vision. Richard Eberhart. **CP-EberR**

Two Humpties. Carl Sandburg. **CP-SandC**

Two hundred and seven paces. Basil Bunting. **CP-BuntB**

200,000 rhododendron blossoms I estimate. Spring Notes from Robin Hill. Hayden Carruth. **CP-CarHS**

225 Pounds. Charles Bukowski. **SP-BukC1**

Two Illuminations, The. Muriel Rukeyser. **CP-RukeM**

Two Illustrations That the World Is What You Make of It. Wallace Stevens. **CP-StevW**

Two Immortals. Gary Snyder. **CP-SnydG**

Two in August. John Crowe Ransom. **SP-RansJ**

Two in the afternoon. The restlessness. Long Summers. Robert Lowell. **SP-LoweR**

Two in the Campagna. Robert Browning. **CP-BroR1**

Two infants vis-à-vis. Bleecker Street. Jean Garrigue. **SP-GarrJ**

Two instruments belong unto our God. The Staffe and Rod. Robert Herrick. **CP-HerrR**

Two Invocations of Death. Kathleen Jessie Raine. **SP-RainK**

"Death, I repent." **MoAB; OxBTC**

(Invocation of Death.) **MoAB**

"From a place I came." **OxBTC**

Two Invocations of the Virgin, I. Geoffrey Chaucer. **ACP** *Fr.* The Second Nun's Prologue. *Fr.* The Canterbury Tales. **CP-ChauG**

Two Invocations of the Virgin, II. Geoffrey Chaucer. **ACP** *Fr.* The Prioress's Prologue. *Fr.* The Canterbury Tales. **CP-ChauG**

Two Irish Saints. John Hewitt. **CP-HewiJ**

Colmcille.

Saint Patrick.

Two Items. Carl Sandburg. **CP-SandC**

Two ivory women by a milky sea. The Bathers. Hart Crane. **CP-CranH**

Two Kinds of Deliverance. Mary Oliver. **SP-OlivM**

Two Kinds of Song. John Yau. **SP-YauJo**

Two Kings, The. William Butler Yeats. **CP-YeatW**

Two Kings and No-Form. Chuang Tzu, tr. fr. *Chinese by* Thomas Merton. **CP-MertT**

Two Kopjes. Rudyard Kipling. **CP-KiplR**

Two ladies walked on the soft green grass. A Dream of Comparison. Stevie Smith. **CP-SmitS**

2 lbs bananas. A Dance for Li Po. Al Young. **CP-YounA**

Two Leading Lights. Robert Frost. **CP-FrosR**

Two Legends: for Greece. Alun Lewis. **CP-LewiA**

Defeat.

Victory.

Two Lengths has every Day. Emily Dickinson. **CP-DickE**

Two Limericks after Lear. John Updike.

(Two Limericks for the Elderly.) **CP-UpdiJ**

"There was an old poop from Poughkeepsie."

"Touchy old gent from Cohasset, A."

Two Limericks for the Elderly. John Updike. *See* Two Limericks after Lear.

Two Lips. Thomas Hardy. **CP-HardT**

Two Little Boots. Paul Laurence Dunbar. **CP-DunbP**

Two little girls near London dwell. Double Acrostic: Two little girls near London dwell. "Lewis Carroll." **CP-CarrL**

Two little girls, one fair, one dark. The Lost Children. Randall Jarrell. **CP-JarrR; SP-JarrR**

Two Little Songs. Stephen Berg. **SP-BergS**

2 little whos / (he and she). Edward Estlin Cummings. **CP-CummE**

Two Look at Two. Robert Frost. **CP-FrosR**

Two Lovely Ones. Marsden Hartley. **CP-HartM**

Two Lovers and a Beachcomber by the Real Sea. Sylvia Plath. **CP-PlatS**

Two Loves. Richard Eberhart. **CP-EberR**

Two Loves, The. John Greenleaf Whittier. **CP-WhitJ**

Two Loves I Have. William Shakespeare. *See* Sonnet 144: "Two loves I have of comfort and despair."

Two loves I have of comfort and despair, *sl. diff. vers. also in* The Passionate Pilgrim. Sonnet 144. William Shakespeare. **CABA; EBEV; HelP; InvP; LoBV; NAEL-1; NIP; OAEL-1; OAEP; PFP; PeHV; PoEL-2; Son** *Fr.* Sonnets. **CP-ShaWS**

Two loves I have, of comfort and despair, *sl. diff. vers. also in* Sonnets. *Various Authors.* **CP-ShaWS** *Fr.* The Passionate Pilgrim. **CP-ShaWS**

Two Lyrics from Kilroy's Carnival: A Masque. Delmore Schwartz. **SP-SchwD**

  Aria. **ErPo**

  Song: "Under the yellow sea."

Two Masks, The. George Meredith. **CP-MerG1**

Two Meditations on Guanajuato. John Yau.

  "I do not imagine anyone I know, including myself, would like to." **SP-YauJo**

  "Postcards are fragments of an encyclopedia; and typical of one an- / nouncing." **SP-YauJo**

Two Memories. "Hugh MacDiarmid." **SP-MacDH**

Two Men, The. Thomas Hardy. **CP-HardT**

Two Men. Ron Koertge. **SP-KoerR**

Two Men. Edwin Arlington Robinson. **CP-RobiE**

Two men came out of Shannon's, having known. A Song at Shannon's. Edwin Arlington Robinson. **CP-RobiE**

Two men sat by a stone in what dim place. Night and the City. John Berryman. **CP-BerrJ**

Two men talking business, The. Business Men. Louis MacNeice. *Fr.* Entered in the Minutes. **CP-MacNL**

Two men walk along the edge of a country road. Under the Green Ceiling. Stephen Dobyns. **SP-DobyS**

Two minutes long it pitches through some bar. Elvis Presley. Thom Gunn. **CP-GunnT**

Two Minute's Silence. Ted Hughes. *Fr.* Scapegoats and Rabies. **SP-HughT**

Two Mites, two drops (yet all her house and land). The Widow[e]'s Mites. Richard Crashaw. **CP-CrasR**

Two Months. Rudyard Kipling. **CP-KiplR**

Two Moon Fantasies. Carl Sandburg. **CP-SandC**

Two Moralities. Thomas Merton. *Fr.* South. *Fr.* The Geography of Lograire. **CP-MertT**

  Hare's Message.

  Thonga Lament.

Two morning stars, Venus and Jupiter. New Year's Dawn, 1947. Robinson Jeffers. **CP-JefR3**

Two Mothers lifting prayers unto one God. War. George Meredith. **CP-MerG2**

Two murderous thugs / Sledge at each other. Uphill. James McAuley. *Fr.* Ten-Mile Run. **SP-McAuJ**

Two Neighbors. Carl Sandburg. **CP-SandC**

Two neighbours furiously dispute. The Cause Won. Vincent Bourne, *tr. fr. Latin by* William Cowper. **CP-CowpW**

Two never-ever-will-be lovers each. Mathematics of Encounter. Isabella Gardner. **CP-GardI**

Two noble knights, whom true desire and zeal. A Speech Presented unto King James at a Tilting in the Behalf of the Two Noble Brothers S[ir] Robert and S[ir] Henry Rich, Now Earls of Warwick and Holland. Ben Jonson. **CP-JonsB**

Two Nocturns. Carl Sandburg. **CP-SandC**

Two Norwegian firemen, friends in the same watch, stand looking up at the ship. For Nordahl Grieg Ship's Fireman. Malcolm Lowry. **CP-LowrM**

Two nudists of Dover. Third Limick. Ogden Nash. **CP-NashO**

Two nymphs, both nearly of an age. The Judgment of the Poets. William Cowper. **CP-CowpW**

Two of a thousand things, are disallow'd. Two Things Odious. Robert Herrick. **CP-HerrR**

Two, of course there are two. Death & Co. Sylvia Plath. **CP-PlatS**

Two of far nobler shape erect and tall. John Milton. **PeECV,** *ll.* 288–299; **TreFS,** *ll.* 288–324; *Fr.* Book IV. **OAEL-1** *Fr.* Paradise Lost. **CP-MiltJ**

Two of Us. The Beatles. **CP-BeatI**

Two Old Crows. Nicholas Vachel Lindsay. **CP-LindV**

Two old dancing shoes my grandfather. Genius. Philip Levine. **SP-LeviP**

Two old guys behind me were talking, The. Charles Bukowski. *Fr.* Horsemeat. **SP-BukC3**

Two old men / meet at the lunch. Speeches. Donald Hall. **CP-HallD**

Two old, simple problems ever intertwined, The. Life and Death. Walt Whitman. **CP-WhitW**

Two omens seems propitious to my fame. To Sir John Fenn. William Cowper. **CP-CowpW**

Two on the stairs in a house where they had loved. In a Dark House. Muriel Rukeyser. **CP-RukeM**

Two or three lines across; the black ones, down. Crayon House. Muriel Rukeyser. **CP-RukeM**

Two or Three, or a Receipt to Make a Cuckold. Alexander Pope. **CP-PopeA**

Two or Three Posies. John Keats. **CP-KeatJ**

Two or three things in the past. Dancer. Langston Hughes. **SP-HughL**

Two Organs. John Berryman. **CP-BerrJ**

2 Outside, As Bones Break in My Kitchen. Charles Bukowski. **SP-BukC2**

Two Pair. Howard Nemerov. **CP-NemeH**

Two pale women cried, The. A Parting-Scene. Thomas Hardy. **CP-HardT**

Two Palm Trees, The. Miguel Hernández, *tr. fr. Spanish by* Thomas Merton. **CP-MertT**

Two Parents, The. "Hugh MacDiarmid." **SP-MacDH**

Two-part book rejoicing in single garb. To John Rouse. John Milton, *tr. fr. Latin by* John T. Shawcross. **CP-MiltJ**

Two Parted. Christina Georgina Rossetti. **CP-RosC3**

Two parts of us successively command. The Hand and Tongue. Robert Herrick. **CP-HerrR**

Two Pendants: For the Ears. William Carlos Williams. **CP-WilW2**

Two people can be. Charles Henri Ford. **SP-FordC** *Fr.* Secret Haiku.

Two people in a room, speaking harshly. Novella. Adrienne Rich. **CP-RicAE; SP-RicA2**

Two people saying goodbye / but not saying it. At the *Gare Bruxelles-Midi.* Lawrence Ferlinghetti. **SP-FerlL**

Two people wakened suddenly by an earthquake. The Earthquake. Jane Cooper. **SP-CoopJ**

Two Performing Elephants. David Herbert Lawrence. **CP-LawrD**

Two philosophers a thousand years from now met in a grotto secretly. In Cape Code with Conrad Aiken. Malcolm Lowry. **CP-LowrM**

Two Photographs. Basil Bunting. **CP-BuntB**

Two plantations Greatgrandmother brought, The. John Berryman. *Fr.* Sonnets to Chris. **CP-BerrJ**

Two Poems. "Nikolai Nikolaevich Morshen", *tr. fr. Russian by* Richard Wilbur. **CP-WilbR**

  "Nights rolled upon the river's face."

  "Star in the sky. How many words and tears, A."

Two Poems. Howard Nemerov. **CP-NemeH**

Two Poems. Charles Olson. *Fr.* West. **CP-OlsoC**

  "Men are only known in memory."

  "Pedens, who re-walked the trails, hobbyists, The."

Two Poems. Adrienne Rich. **CP-RicAE**

Two Poems about President Harding. James Wright. **CP-WrigJ**

Two Poems about Suddenly and a Rose. Robert Penn Warren. **SP-WarrR**

  Dawn.

  Intuition.

Two Poems for a Poet. Kay Boyle. **CP-BoylK**

  After New York—May Seventeenth.

  April Thirtieth 1960.

Two Poems for Black Relocation Centers. Etheridge Knight. Poem for Black Relocation Centers, A. **SP-KnigE**

Two Poems for Christmas, 1937. Hilda Doolittle. **CP-DoolH**

  Star by Day.

  Wooden Animal.

Two Poems for Sub-Zero Times. Mona Van Duyn. **SP-VanDM**

  "Who says the world is mud? For the fifth day."

  "Winter has stiffened the ground, the birds are gone."

Two Poems from the War. Archibald MacLeish. **CP-MacLA**

Two Poems of Flight Sleep. James Dickey. **CP-DickJ**

Two Poems of Going Home. James Dickey. **CP-DickJ**

Two Poems of the Military. James Dickey. **CP-DickJ**

Two Poems on the Passing of an Empire. Derek Walcott. **CP-WalcD**

  "Heron flies across the morning marsh and brakes, A."

  "In the small coffin of his house, the pensioner."

Two Poems on titles proposed by Octavio and Marie José Paz. Charles Tomlinson. **CP-TomlC**

  La Promenade de Protée.

  Le Rendez-Vous des Paysages.

Two Poems to a Dead Woman. Frederick Morgan. **SP-MorgF**

  "Lady, the strange malignancy."

  "Whitish dawn had just appeared, The."

Two Poems to Rachel Daniel. "Lewis Carroll." **CP-CarrL**

For *The Garland of Rachel.*

"Oh pudgy podgy pup! / Why *did* they wake you up?"

Two Poems, with Birds. Mona Van Duyn. **SP-VanDM**

Two Poets of Croisic, The. Robert Browning. **CP-BroR2**

Two poets, (poets by report). To Dr. Darwin. William Cowper. **CP-CowpW**

Two Portraits of Sex. Philip Larkin. **CP-LarkP**

Two Postures beside a Fire. James Wright. **CP-WrigJ**

Two powder'd coxcombs wait at your command. Lines with Two Cockscombs. William Cowper. **CP-CowpW**

Two Priests, The. Archibald MacLeish. **CP-MacLA**

2 Propositions and 3 Proof. Charles Olson. **CP-OlsoC**

Two Pursuits. Christina Georgina Rossetti. **CP-RosC3**

Two Quatrains. Edwin Arlington Robinson. **CP-RobiE**

"As eons of incalculable strife."

"We shriek to live, but no man ever lives."

Two Quatrains for First Frost. Richard Wilbur. **CP-WilbR**

Two Rabbins, The. John Greenleaf Whittier. **CP-WhitJ**

Two Races. Rudyard Kipling. **CP-KiplR**

Two Riddles. Charles Simic. **SP-SimiC**

Two Riddles from Aldhelm. Richard Wilbur. **CP-WilbR**

Two Rivers. Ralph Waldo Emerson. **CP-EmerR**

Two Rivulets. Walt Whitman. **CP-WhitW**

Two roads diverged in a yellow wood. The Road Not Taken. Robert Frost. **CP-FrosR**

Two Romance Poems. George Oppen. **CP-OppeG**

Two Romantic Pieces. Hayden Carruth. **CP-CarHS**

Two Rosalinds, The. Thomas Hardy. **CP-HardT**

Two Rossettis (Brothers They), The. Christina Georgina Rossetti. **CP-RosC1**

Two Round Spaces on the Tombstone, The. Samuel Taylor Coleridge. **CP-ColeS**

Two Saints. John Ciardi. **SP-CiarJ**

Two Sapphics. Isabella Gardner. **CP-GardI**

Two Sayings, The. Elizabeth Barrett Browning. **CP-BroEB**

Two Scavengers in a Truck, Two Beautiful People in a Mercedes. Lawrence Ferlinghetti. **SP-FerlL**

Two Scenes. John Ashbery. **SP-AshbJ**

Two Seasons. Galway Kinnell. **SP-KinnG**

Two Serenades. Thomas Hardy. **CP-HardT**

2 shes / both not quite / young perfectly. Edward Estlin Cummings. **CP-CummE**

Two-Sided Man, The. Rudyard Kipling. **CP-KiplR** *Fr.* Kim.

Two Sides to an Outside: Meditation from Empson. Howard Nemerov. **CP-NemeH**

Two Sisters of Persephone. Sylvia Plath. **CP-PlatS**

Two Sketches. Elizabeth Barrett Browning. **CP-BroEB**

Two Soldiers, The. Thomas Hardy. **CP-HardT**

Two Songs. Wystan Hugh Auden. **CP-AudeW**

Song of the Devil.

Song of the Ogres. **RHPC**

Two Songs. Paul Laurence Dunbar. **CP-DunbP**

Two Songs. Derek Mahon. **SP-MahoD**

Two Songs. Adrienne Rich. **CP-RicAE; SP-RicA2**

"Sex, as they harshly call it." **NIP; NOBA; TAP**

"That 'old last act'! / And yet sometimes." **NIP; NOBA; TAP**

Two Songs at the Marriage of the Lord Fauconberg and the Lady Mary Cromwell. Andrew Marvell. **CP-MarvA**

First Song.

Second Song.

Two Songs for a Boss Named Mr. Longwell. Ogden Nash. **CP-NashO**

Two Songs from a Play. William Butler Yeats. **CP-YeatW**, *sect.* 1-2; *Fr.* The Resurrection.

Two Songs from *Sweeny Agonistes.* Thomas Stearns Eliot. **UnPo** *Fr.* Sweeney Agonistes. **CP-ElioT**

Song by Klipstein and Krumpacker.

Song by Wauchope and Horsfall.

"You'll be my little seven stone missionary!"

Two Songs from "The Hunted Revolutionaries." Thomas McGrath. **SP-McGrT**

Two Songs in a Stanza of Beddoes'. Richard Wilbur. **CP-WilbR**

Two Songs of a Fool. William Butler Yeats. **CP-YeatW**

Two Songs Rewritten for the Tune's Sake. William Butler Yeats. **CP-YeatW**

Two Sonnets. Allen Ginsberg. **CP-GinsA**

Two Sonnets. John Hewitt. **CP-HewiJ**

He Suggests a Solution.

Little Bourgeois is Upset, The.

Two Sonnets. Edwin Arlington Robinson. **CP-RobiE**

"Just as I wonder at the twofold screen."

"Never until our souls are strong enough."

Two Sonnets on Fame. John Keats.

"Fame, like a wayward girl, will still be coy." **CP-KeatJ**

(On Fame ("Fame, like a wayward girl, will still be coy").) **CP-KeatJ**

"How fever'd is the man who cannot look." **CP-KeatJ**

(On Fame ("How fever'd is the man who cannot look").) **CP-KeatJ**

Two Sonnets on the Free State of Censorship Bill. John Hewitt. **CP-HewiJ**

"Grim Dean, who sleeps within his pulpit's shade."

"Oh, ban the books and save the children's lives."

Two Sonnets Whose Titles Came to Me Simultaneously. John Updike. **CP-UpdiJ**

Dying Phobiac Takes His Fears with Him, The.

No More Access to Her Underpants.

Two Sons. Anne Sexton. **CP-SextA**

Two sons are gone. Later Still. Philip Levine. **SP-LeviP**

Two souls move here, and mine (a third) must move. The Harbinger to the Progress. John Donne. *Fr.* Of the Progres[se] of the Soule; the Second Anniversarie. **CP-DonnJ**

Two Sounds When We Sit by the Ocean. Robert Bly. **SP-BlyR**

Two Spanish cowhands from Monterey. Local Legend. Robinson Jeffers. **CP-JefR3**

Two Spectres Haunt Me. John Hewitt. **CP-HewiJ**

Two Spirits[: An Allegory], The. Percy Bysshe Shelley. **CP-ShelP**

Two Spring Charms. James Wright. **CP-WrigJ**

Two stand / admiring morning. The Meeting. Charles Tomlinson. *Fr.* In Winter Woods. **CP-TomlC**

Two States of Prayer. Thomas Merton. **CP-MertT**

Two statesmen met by moonlight. What the Moon Saw. Nicholas Vachel Lindsay. **CP-LindV**

Two Stories. Charles Wright. **SP-WrigC**

Two Strangers Breakfast. Carl Sandburg. **CP-SandC**

Two streams came from a different source, The. Malcolm Lowry. **CP-LowrM**

Two strings, one pierced cry. Variation on Pain. Rita Dove. **SP-DoveR**

Two Studies in Idealism: Short Survey of American and Human History. Robert Penn Warren. **SP-WarrR**

Bear Track Plantation: Shortly after Shiloh.

Harvard '61: Battle Fatigue.

Two summers since, I saw at Lammas Fair. Phoebe Dawson. George Crabbe. **SP-CrabG** *Fr.* The Parish Register.

Two Swede families live downstairs and an Irish policeman upstairs, and. House. Carl Sandburg. **CP-SandC**

Two swimmers wrestled on the spar. Emily Dickinson. **CP-DickE**

2 takes from *Love in Los Angeles.* Al Young. **CP-YounA**

Two Tales of Liadoff. Wallace Stevens. **CP-StevW**

Two taxi drivers stopped for a red light. Madison and 42nd. Carl Sandburg. **CP-SandC**

Two that could not have lived their single lives. Two in August. John Crowe Ransom. **SP-RansJ**

Two Thieves. "Lewis Carroll." **CP-CarrL**

Two Thieves, The; or, the Last Stage of Avarice. William Wordsworth. **CP-WorW1**

Two thigh hills hold us at the fork. Song of the Tangle. Gary Snyder. **CP-SnydG**

Two things a man's built for, killing and you-know-what. Bear Track Plantation: Shortly after Shiloh. Robert Penn Warren. *Fr.* Two Studies in Idealism: Short Survey of American and Human History. **SP-WarrR**

Two things do make society to stand. Society. Robert Herrick. **CP-HerrR**

Two things hast thou made known to half the nation. To One Who Published in Print. Samuel Taylor Coleridge. **CP-ColeS**

Two things I have never understood: first, the difference between. Will You Have Your Tedium Rare or Medium? Ogden Nash. **CP-NashO**

Two Things Odious. Robert Herrick. **CP-HerrR**

Two Things of Opposite Natures Seem to Depend. Wallace Stevens. **MeMAP** *Fr.* It Must Change. *Fr.* Notes toward a Supreme Fiction. **CP-StevW**

Two things thou shalt not long for, if thou love a mind serene. From Ibn Jemin. Ibn-i-Yamin, *tr. fr. Persian by* Ralph Waldo Emerson. **CP-EmerR**

Two Thoughts of Death. Countee Cullen. **CP-CullC**

Two Thoughts of Death. Christina Georgina Rossetti. **CP-RosC3**

2433, First Home, Last House in Missoula. Richard Hugo. **CP-HugoR**

Two Times ("Image / docteur"). Robert Creeley. **CP-CreeR**

Two Times ("It takes so long to look down"). Robert Creeley. **CP-CreeR**

Two Tramps in Mud Time. Robert Frost. **CP-FrosR**

Two Travellers perishing in Snow. Emily Dickinson. **CP-DickE**

Two Trees, The. Archibald MacLeish. **CP-MacLA**

Two Trees, The. William Butler Yeats. **CP-YeatW**

Two trees outside my window stood. Prayer for Sun. Phoebe Hesketh. **SP-HeskP**

Two Triolets. Wystan Hugh Auden. **CP-AudWJ**

Two trunks like bodies, bodies like twined trunks. Philemon and Baucis. Thom Gunn. **CP-GunnT**

Two Twilights for William Carlos Williams. Kay Boyle. **CP-BoylK**

Two Variations. Denise Levertov. **CP-LeveD**

Two Versions of the Same Poem. Wallace Stevens. **CP-StevW**

Two Vietnam Poems: (1966). Bill Knott. **SP-KnotB**

Two Views of a Cadaver Room. Sylvia Plath. **CP-PlatS**

Two Views of a Philosopher. Howard Nemerov. **CP-NemeH**

Two Views of Two Ghost Towns. Charles Tomlinson. **CP-TomlC**

Two Views of Withens. Sylvia Plath. **CP-PlatS**

Two Villages. Grace Paley. **CP-PaleG**

Two virtues ride, by stallion, by nag. The Death of Myth-making. Sylvia Plath. **CP-PlatS**

Two Voices. Edna St. Vincent Millay. **CP-MillE**

Two Voices, The. Tennyson. **CP-TennA**

Two voices / took turns using my eyes. The Double Voice. Margaret Atwood. **SP-AtwM1**

Two voices are there; one is of the sea. Thought[s] of a Briton on the Subjugation of Switzerland. William Wordsworth. **CP-WorW1**

Two Voices in a Meadow. Richard Wilbur. **CP-WilbR**

Two Walls. Robert Lowell. **SP-LoweR**

Two Ways of Living and Dying. David Herbert Lawrence. **CP-LawrD**

Two Ways of Looking in a Mirror. Robert Creeley. **CP-CreeR**

Two Ways of Love. Marsden Hartley. **CP-HartM**

Two ways only / For the weary lover. Nahoa Urn, for a Woman. Pablo Antonio Cuadra, tr. fr. Spanish by Thomas Merton. **CP-MertT**

Two wedded Hearts, if e'er were such. Wedded Love. Samuel Taylor Coleridge. **CP-ColeS**

Two wedded lovers watched the rising moon. Song. George Meredith. **CP-MerG1**

Two well-assorted travellers use. Love and Thought. Ralph Waldo Emerson. **CP-EmerR**

Two went to pray? o rather say. Two Went Up into the Temple To Pray. Richard Crashaw. **CP-CrasR**

Two Went Up into the Temple To Pray. Richard Crashaw. **CP-CrasR**

Two—were immortal twice. Emily Dickinson. **CP-DickE**

Two were silent in a sunless church, The. Her Dilemma. Thomas Hardy. **CP-HardT**

Two Who Crossed a Line (She Crosses). Countee Cullen. **CP-CullC**

Two Who Crossed a Line. Countee Cullen. **CP-CullC**

Two Widows in Tashkent. Donald Davie. **CP-DavDo**

Two Witches. Robert Frost. **CP-FrosR**

    Pauper Witch of Grafton, The.

    Witch of Coös, The. **InPS; LiTM; MeMAP; MoAB; MoP; NOBA; NoAM; PoE**

Two Witches, The. Robert Ranke Graves. **CP-GravR**

Two Wives, The. Thomas Hardy. **CP-HardT**

Two Wives. David Herbert Lawrence. **CP-LawrD**

Two Women. James Dickey. **CP-DickJ**

Two Women. Carl Sandburg. **CP-SandC**

Two Women and Their Fathers. Carl Sandburg. **CP-SandC**

Two women: one as good as bread. Ruby and Amethyst. Robert Ranke Graves. **CP-GravR**

Two women sit at a table by a window. Light breaks. After Twenty Years. Adrienne Rich. **SP-RicA2**

Two women stroll among the orange-trees. The Mirror. Robert Duncan. **SP-DuncR**

Two Women Talking. Archibald MacLeish. **CP-MacLA**

Two wooden tubs of blue hydrangeas stand at the foot of the stone steps. Banal Sojourn. Wallace Stevens. **CP-StevW**

Two workmen were carrying a sheet of asbestos. Christo's. Paul Muldoon. **SP-MuldP**

Two worlds are asleep, are sleeping, now, The. An Old Man Asleep. Wallace Stevens. **CP-StevW**

Two W.P.A. men. A Portrait of the Times. William Carlos Williams. **CP-WilW2**

Two Years. Muriel Rukeyser. **CP-RukeM**

Two years high by the world wide. The Gone-Tomorrow. Louis MacNeice. Fr. A Hand of Snapshots. **CP-MacNL**

Two-Years' Idyll, A. Thomas Hardy. **CP-HardT**

Two Years Later. William Butler Yeats. **CP-YeatW**

Two years we spent. The Woods. Derek Mahon. **SP-MahoD**

Twofold. David Herbert Lawrence. **CP-LawrD**

'Twould ease—a Butterfly. Emily Dickinson. **CP-DickE**

Tŷ Newydd. Steve Griffiths. **SP-GrifS**

Tyl it was noon, they stoden for to se. At the Gate. Geoffrey Chaucer. **SeCePo** Fr. Troilus and Criseyde [or Criseide]. **CP-ChauG**

Tylor believed it important; he put it down; he asks us to read it, to look. Carl Sandburg. Fr. The People, Yes. **CP-SandC**

Tynwald Hill. William Wordsworth. Fr. Poems Composed or Suggested During a Tour, in the Summer of 1833. **CP-WorW2**

Type of the antique Rome! Rich reliquary. The Coliseum. Edgar Allan Poe. **CP-PoeEd**

Type of two mighty continents!—combining. Kossuth. John Greenleaf Whittier. **CP-WhitJ**

Types and Symbols of Eternity. William Wordsworth. **CBCK** Fr. Cambridge and the Alps. Fr. The Prelude; Growth of a Poet's Mind [1850 vers.]. **CP-WorW3**

Typhoid and smallpox. Charles Henri Ford. **SP-FordC** Fr. Secret Haiku.

Typical Affair, A. Allen Ginsberg. **CP-GinsA**

Typical Optical. John Updike. **CP-UpdiJ**

Tyr. Frederick Morgan. **SP-MorgF**

Tyrannic Love. John Dryden.

    Epilogue to Tyrannic[k] Love. **SP-DrydJ**

Tyranny of method! the outrageous smile. Third Elegy. The Fear of Form. Muriel Rukeyser. **CP-RukeM**

Tyranny of your car—so far resembles. John Berryman. Fr. Sonnets to Chris. **CP-BerrJ**

Tyrant of Syracuse. Archibald MacLeish. **CP-MacLA**

Tyrant passed, and friendlier was his eye, The. Solon. George Meredith. **CP-MerG1**

Tyrant, why swel'st [or swell'st] thou thus, par. by Countess of Pembroke, Mary Sidney Herbert. Bible, O.T. See Psalm 52: "Why boastest thou thyself in mischief. . . ."

Tyson & Jo, Tyson & Jo. Death Ballad. John Berryman. **CP-BerrJ**

Tywater. Richard Wilbur. **CP-WilbR**

U

U. S. 1946 King's X. Robert Frost. **CP-FrosR**

Ubique. Rudyard Kipling. **CP-KiplR**

Ubiquity of the Need for Love, The. Ron Koertge. **SP-KoerR**

Uccello-delle rose e del dolore. Luscious and Sorrowful. Christina Georgina Rossetti. Fr. Il Rosseggiar Dell'Oriente Canzoniere. **CP-RosC3**

Udai Chand lay sick to death. The Last Suttee. Rudyard Kipling. **CP-KiplR**

Udite, si dolgono mesti fringuelli. Christina Georgina Rossetti. **CP-RosC3**

Uffington. Sir John Betjeman. **CP-BetjJ**

Ugh! the planet screams. Morning. Allen Ginsberg. **CP-GinsA**

Ugly, evil, dying. The old soft lines. Hayden Carruth. Fr. Paragraphs. **CP-CarHS**

Ugly in My Own Eyes. Leonard Cohen. **CP-CoheL**

Ugly look, close to tears, on a man's face. Skew Lines. Denise Levertov. **CP-LeveD**

Ugly Secret, The. Robert Ranke Graves. **CP-GravR**

Ugly Sister. Philip Larkin. **CP-LarkP**

Ugly woman clutched, The. In Sisterly Fashion. William Carlos Williams. **CP-WilW2**

Ugly women loud in public. Or Another Place. Richard Hugo. **CP-HugoR**

Ugolino. Dante Alighieri, tr. by Shelley. **CP-ShelP** Fr. Inferno. Fr. Divina Commedia.

Uig Registrar. Richard Hugo. **CP-HugoR**

Ukelele once in pawn I saw, a. Malcolm Lowry. Fr. The Moon in Scandinavia. **CP-LowrM**

Ukiyo-E. Siv Cedering Fox. **SP-CedeS**

Ulalume [or Ulalume—a Ballad]. Edgar Allan Poe. **CP-PoeEd**

Ulcerated tooth keeps me awake, there is. Letters from a Father. Mona Van Duyn. **SP-VanDM**

Ulster. Rudyard Kipling. **CP-KiplR**

Ulster Landowner's Song, An. John Hewitt. **CP-HewiJ**

Ulster Names. John Hewitt. **CP-HewiJ**

Ulster Winter (1942). John Hewitt. **CP-HewiJ**

Ulsterman, An. John Hewitt. **CP-HewiJ**

Ulsterman. John Hewitt. **CP-HewiJ**

Ulsterman in England Remembers, An. John Hewitt. **CP-HewiJ**

Ultima Despedida del Principe Poniatowski de Su Familia. Gilbert Sorrentino. Fr. Twelve Études for Voice and Kazoo. **SP-SorrG**

Ultimate Act, The. Adrienne Rich. **CP-RicAE**

Ultimate Poem Is Abstract, The. Wallace Stevens. **CP-StevW**

Ultimate Problems. William Stafford. **SP-StafW**

Ultimate Reality. David Herbert Lawrence. **CP-LawrD**

Ultimate Song. Richard Eberhart. **CP-EberR**

Ultimately. Ernest Hemingway. **CP-HemiE**

Ultimately the air. From Disaster. George Oppen. **CP-OppeG**

Ultimatum. Countee Cullen. **CP-CullC**

Ultimatum. Langston Hughes. **SP-HughL**

Ultimatum. Philip Larkin. **CP-LarkP**

Ultimatum. Philip Larkin. **FL** *Fr.* Poetry of Departures. **CP-LarkP**

Ultimus Heroum: or, To the Most Learned, and to the Right Honourable, Henry, Marquesse of Dorchester. Robert Herrick. **CP-HerrR**

Uluru Wild Fig Song. Gary Snyder. **CP-SnydG**

Ulvade Texas to Nashville Tennessee. Picker. Miller Williams. **SP-WillM**

Ulysses. Robert Ranke Graves. **CP-GravR**

Ulysses. Tennyson. **CP-TennA**

Ulysses, much-experienced man. To Ulysses. Tennyson. **CP-TennA**

Umber was painting of a lion [*or* Lyon] fierce. Upon Umber: Epigram. Robert Herrick. **CP-HerrR**

Umbra, *acc. by English translation.* Thomas Campion. **CP-CampT**

Umbra. Alexander Pope. **CP-PopeA**

Umbrageous cedars murmuring symphonies. Hamlet. Walter de la Mare. **CP-DeLaW**

Umbrella, The. Donald Hall. **CP-HallD**

Umpire. Dabney Stuart. **SP-StuaD**

Un / der fog / 's / touch. Edward Estlin Cummings. **CP-CummE**

Un Morceau en Forme de Poire. Diane Wakoski. **SP-WakoD**

Un Recuerdo—Hermano—Hart Crane R.I.P. Marsden Hartley. **CP-HartM**

    Afterlude.

    "And, should it be left like this."

    Spirits Are Organized Men.

    Tear Is an Intellectual Thing, A.

    Whole Creation Groans to Be Delivered, The.

Una. Ralph Waldo Emerson. **CP-EmerR**

Una Vita Violenta (1955). David St. John. *Fr.* To Pasolini. **SP-StJoD**

Unable are the Loved to die. Emily Dickinson. **CP-DickE**

Unable to bear. Middle Aged Lovers, I. Erica Jong. **SP-JongE**

Unable to bear the falsehoods. The Demon Lover. Erica Jong. **SP-JongE**

Unable to begin / At the beginning, the fortunate, *sl. diff. vers. in* Of Being Numerous. George Oppen. *Fr.* A Language of New York. **CP-OppeG**

Unable to begin / At the beginning, the fortunate. George Oppen. *Fr.* Of Being Numerous. **CP-OppeG**

Unable to sleep. The Family Tree. Laurence Lieberman. **SP-LiebL**

Unable to sleep, or pray, I stand. Ice Storm. Robert Earl Hayden. **CP-HaydR**

Unaccustomed ripeness in the wood; An. Elizabeth. Robert Lowell. **SP-LoweR**

Unanswered by Request. Ogden Nash. **CP-NashO**

Unanswering Correspondences, The. Kenneth Patchen. **CP-PatcK**

Unappeasable Host, The. William Butler Yeats. **CP-YeatW**

Unbar the door, since thou the Opener art. Omar Khayyám, *tr. fr. Persian by* Ralph Waldo Emerson. **CP-EmerR**

Un(bee)mo / vi / n(in)g. Edward Estlin Cummings. **CP-CummE**

Unbelievable as an antique ritual. A Ceremony By the Sea. Richard Eberhart. **CP-EberR**

Unbelievable doom tacked onto the words, An. The Lecture on Time and Space. Gilbert Sorrentino. **SP-SorrG**

Unbeliever, The. Elizabeth Bishop. **CP-BishE**

Unbiassed at least he was when he arrived on his mission. Partition. Wystan Hugh Auden. **CP-AudeW**

Unblinding, The. Laurence Lieberman. **SP-LiebL**

Unboastful Bard! whose verse concise yet clear. To the Author of Poems. Samuel Taylor Coleridge. *Fr.* Poetical Epistles. **CP-ColeS**

Unborn, The. Thomas Hardy. **CP-HardT**

Unborn Child, An. Derek Mahon. **SP-MahoD**

Unborn Song. Muriel Rukeyser. **CP-RukeM**

Unburying the Birch. Robert Pack. **SP-PackR**

Uncalendared Love. Robert Ranke Graves. **CP-GravR**

Uncertain lease—develops lustre. Emily Dickinson. **CP-DickE**

Uncertain of the Crime. Paul Éluard, *tr. fr. French by* William Carlos Williams. **CP-WilW2**

Uncertainty. William Wordsworth. *Fr.* Ecclesiastical Sonnets. **CP-WorW2**

Uncertainty in Love. Samuel Taylor Coleridge. **CP-ColeS**

Unchangeable, The. William Shakespeare. *See* Sonnet 109: "O [*or* Oh], never say that I was false of heart."

Unchanged within, to see all changed without. Duty Surviving Self-Love. Samuel Taylor Coleridge. **CP-ColeS**

Unchanging, The. Walter de la Mare. **CP-DeLaW**

Unchill'd I handle stinging snow. Fragments. Gerard Manley Hopkins. **CP-HopkG**

Unchosen, The. Daniel Gerard Hoffman. **SP-HoffD**

Uncle. Philip Levine. **SP-LeviP**

Uncle Adler. Ted Kooser. **SP-KoosT**

Uncle Ananias. Edwin Arlington Robinson. **CP-RobiE**

Uncle Dick and Aunt Bertha. John Hewitt. **CP-HewiJ**

Uncle George at the Home. Gary Gildner. **SP-GildG**

Uncle George says, "My brain is eighty-two and free." Uncle George at the Home. Gary Gildner. **SP-GildG**

Uncle Henry. Wystan Hugh Auden. **CP-AudeW**

Uncle Jim. Countee Cullen. **CP-CullC**

Uncle Jim. Peter Meinke. **SP-MeinP**

Uncle Joe. Peter Meinke. **SP-MeinP**

Uncle John, he makes me tired. A Confidence. Paul Laurence Dunbar. **CP-DunbP**

Uncle Sam. Kenneth Rexroth. **SP-RexrK** *Fr.* A Bestiary. **SP-RexrK**

Uncle Sam and Aunt Edie. John Hewitt. **CP-HewiJ**

Uncle Sam in the White House. Diane Wakoski. **SP-WakoD**

Uncle Sam with a knife at his throat. Thomas Merton. *Fr.* Cables to the Ace. **CP-MertT**

Uncle Speaks in the Drawing Room, The. Adrienne Rich. **CP-RicAE; SP-RicA1**

Uncle Tom. Langston Hughes. **SP-HughL**

Uncle Torquemada. Torquemada. Stevie Smith. **CP-SmitS**

Uncle Will, the Gardener. Stephen Berg. **SP-BergS**

Unclean Start, The. Leonard Cohen. **CP-CoheL**

Unclench Yourself. Marge Piercy. **SP-PierM**

Uncloistered Virtue. John Milton. **NOSC** *Fr.* Book IX. **FHYEP; NAEL-1; NAWM-1; NoP; OAEL-1** *Fr.* Paradise Lost. **CP-MiltJ**

Unclouded seas of bluebells have ebbed and passed, The. Campions. David Herbert Lawrence. **CP-LawrD**

Uncreating Chaos (Double Portrait in a Mirror), The. Stephen Spender. **CP-SpenS**

Unctuous Platitudes. John Ashbery. **SP-AshbJ**

Uncut Diamond, The. Robert Ranke Graves. **CP-GravR**

Undazzled, keen, / love sits. Charles Olson. **CP-OlsoC**

Undead, The. Robert Ranke Graves. **CP-GravR**

Undead, The. Richard Wilbur. **CP-WilbR**

Undead, The. Charles Kenneth Williams. **CP-WillC**

Undenominational. Sir John Betjeman. **CP-BetjJ**

Under. Carl Sandburg. **CP-SandC**

Under a daisied bank. The Milkmaid. Thomas Hardy. **CP-HardT**

Under a Hat Rim. Carl Sandburg. **CP-SandC**

Under a lawne, than skyes more cleare. Upon Roses. Robert Herrick. **CP-HerrR**

Under a low sky. Silence. William Carlos Williams. **CP-WilW2**

Under a prairie fog moon. Pearl Horizons. Carl Sandburg. **CP-SandC**

Under a priceless sun. B.W.I. John Updike. **CP-UpdiJ**

Under a red face, black velvet shyness. Chicago Morning. Ted Berrigan. **SP-BerrT**

Under a sky the color of pea soup. The Seven of Pentacles. Marge Piercy. **CrSp** *Fr.* Laying Down the Tower. **SP-PierM**

Under a Skylight. Donald Davie. **CP-DavDo**

Under a Splendid Chestnut Tree. Philip Larkin. **CP-LarkP**

Under a spreading chestnut tree. The Village Blacksmith. Henry Wadsworth Longfellow. **SP-LongH**

Under a Telephone Pole. Carl Sandburg. **CP-SandC**

Under a Tree. Kenneth Patchen. **CP-PatcK**

Under a Tree. Richard Wilbur. **CP-WilbR**

Under an elm tree where the river reaches. Archibald MacLeish. **CP-MacLA** *Fr.* The Happy Marriage.

Under an overwashed, stiff, gray. In the Missouri Ozarks. Mona Van Duyn. **SP-VanDM**

Under an undermined, and shot-bruised wall. Fall of a Wall. John Donne. **CP-DonnJ**

Under bare Ben Bulben's head. William Butler Yeats. **FaBoRV; WeW** *Fr.* Under Ben Bulben. **CP-YeatW**

Under Ben Bulben. William Butler Yeats. **CP-YeatW**

    "Cast a cold eye." **FaBoEE**

    "Irish poets, learn your trade." **OXAEP-2**

    "Under bare Ben Bulben's head." **FaBoRV; WeW**

Under black oak beams which seemed original. The Blue Lias Inn. John Hewitt. **CP-HewiJ**

Under boughs of breathing May. Song. George Meredith. **CP-MerG1**

Under cerulean, amid her backyard's knobby rhubarb squats. My Cousin in April. Louise Glück. **SP-GlücL**

Under Cygnus. Richard Wilbur. **CP-WilbR**

Under dead leaves Tanya finds a tortoise. Berry Territory. Gary Snyder. **CP-SnydG**

Under dense fir boughs. The Bower. Richard Eberhart. **CP-EberR**

Under each starry leafless tree. Alun Lewis. *Fr.* Songs for the Night. **CP-LewiA**

Under every green tree, sex. Charles Olson. **CP-OlsoC**

Under great heat we're searching. Near Garmsley Camp. Roy Fisher. **SP-FishR**

Under High-Stoy Hill. Thomas Hardy. **CP-HardT**

Under his helmet, up against his pack. Asleep. Wilfred Owen. **CP-OwenW**

Under his view the wind. The View. Howard Nemerov. **CP-NemeH**

Under its hangar the afternoon. The Beautiful Aeroplane. Charles Tomlinson. **CP-TomlC**

Under Libra: Weights and Measures. James Merrill. **SP-MerrJ**

Under my bowels, yellow with smoke. The Other. Anne Sexton. **CP-SextA**

Under my elbow. In my elbow. Sun. Diane Wakoski. **SP-WakoD**

Under my window-ledge the waters race. Coole Park and Ballylee, 1931. William Butler Yeats. **CP-YeatW**

Under my windows, between the road and the sea-cliff, bitter wild grass. Robinson Jeffers. *Fr.* The Broken Balance. **CP-JefR1**

Under Mynydd-y-Tŵr. Steve Griffiths. **SP-GrifS**

Under new management, Your Majesty. John Berryman. *Fr.* Eleven Addresses to the Lord. **CP-BerrJ**

Under no hanging heaven-rooted tree. Stony Limits. "Hugh MacDiarmid." **SP-MacDH**

Under orders to shoot the spy, I discharged. Imaginary Universes. Allen Ginsberg. **CP-GinsA**

Under our stillness fled the same low hooves. The Racetrack. Jane Cooper. *Fr.* Acceptances. **SP-CoopJ**

Under pure skies of April blue I stood. The Cherry Trees. Walter de la Mare. **CP-DeLaW**

Under St Paul's. Donald Davie. **CP-DavDo**

Under sand clay. Dig, wait. Basil Bunting. **CP-BuntB**

Under Saturn. William Butler Yeats. **CP-YeatW**

Under silver wing. Crossing Nation. Allen Ginsberg. **CP-GinsA**

Under Sirius. Wystan Hugh Auden. **CP-AudeW**

Under Stars. Tess Gallagher. **SP-GallT**

Under Taurus. Louise Glück. **SP-GlücL**

Under that benign calm eye that sees. The Dream. Charles Tomlinson. **CP-TomlC**

Under that summer asphalt, under vistas. The Capital. Adrienne Rich. **CP-RicAE**

Under the arbor. 1949. Frederick Morgan. **SP-MorgF**

Under the bamboo. Snow as Tambo. Swarts as Bones. Thomas Stearns Eliot. *Fr.* Two Songs from *Sweeny Agonistes*. **UnPo** *Fr.* Sweeney Agonistes. **CP-ElioT**

Under the Bell Jar. Howard Nemerov. **CP-NemeH**

Under the Black Oaks. Stephen Dunn. **SP-DunnS**

Under the blue-grey twilight, heaped. Twilight. David Herbert Lawrence. **CP-LawrD**

Under the bluffs of Oroville, blue cloud September skies. Beginning of a Poem of These States. Allen Ginsberg. **CP-GinsA**

Under the blunt pine / In the winter sun. Elias—Variations on a Theme. Thomas Merton. **CP-MertT**

Under the Bridge. Charles Tomlinson. **CP-TomlC**

Under the bronze crown. A Baroque Wall-Fountain in the Villa Sciarra. Richard Wilbur. **CP-WilbR**

Under the Capitol Dome. Carl Sandburg. **CP-SandC**

Under the cedar tree. Court-Martial. Robert Penn Warren. **SP-WarrR**

Under the cliff, green powdered in from the open. Exchanges. James Dickey. **CP-DickJ**

Under the cobbled bridge the white swans float. Swans on the River Ayr. Mary Oliver. **SP-OlivM**

Under the concrete benches. Weed Puller. Theodore Roethke. **CP-RoetT**

Under the day's crust a half-eaten child. The Pied Piper. John Ashbery. **SP-AshbJ**

Under the eglantine / The fretful concubine. Anything Is Beautiful If You Say It Is. Wallace Stevens. **CP-StevW**

Under the enormous pier-shadow. The River Down Home. James Wright. **CP-WrigJ**

Under the ever-moving, mighty dreams. Whales. Kathleen Jessie Raine. **SP-RainK**

Under the eyes. Hustings, The ("Under the eyes"). Charles Olson. **CP-OlsoC**

Under the familiar weight. New Year Letter. Wystan Hugh Auden. **CP-AudeW**

Under the Floor. Ogden Nash. **CP-NashO**

Under the French horns of a November afternoon. A Man in Blue. James Schuyler. **CP-SchuJ**

Under the full moon strange birds. Kenneth Rexroth. **CP-RexKL** *Fr.* The Heart's Garden, the Garden's Heart.

Under the glassy Christmas tree. The Family. Donald Hall. **CP-HallD**

Under the Great Comedian's tomb the crowd. Parnell's Funeral. William Butler Yeats. **CP-YeatW**

Under the great hill sloping bare. The King's Missive. John Greenleaf Whittier. **CP-WhitJ**

Under the Green Ceiling. Stephen Dobyns. **SP-DobyS**

Under the green leaf hangs a little pouch. The Fig. May Sarton. **SP-SartM**

Under the green ledge. Kenneth Patchen. **CP-PatcK**

Under the green umbrellas. A View of the Terrace. Adrienne Rich. **CP-RicAE**

Under the Grind. Marge Piercy. **SP-PierM**

Under the ground, on a Saturday afternoon in winter. Variation on a Theme by T. W. Rolleston. Sir John Betjeman. **CP-BetjJ**

Under the half moon. Kenneth Rexroth. **SP-RexrK** *Fr.* The Silver Swan.

Under the Hanger. James Schuyler. **CP-SchuJ**

Under the Harvest Moon. Carl Sandburg. **CP-SandC**

Under the hill a winter twilight. Hayden Carruth. *Fr.* North Winter. **CP-CarHL**

Under the hive-like dome the stooping haunted readers. The British Museum Reading Room. Louis MacNeice. **CP-MacNL**

Under the humming *continuo*. James McAuley. **SP-McAuJ** *Fr.* Vivaldi in Venice.

Under the hundred lamps whose flare. The Mail-train, Crewe. Wystan Hugh Auden. **CP-AudWJ**

Under the ivy bush / One sits sighing. Christina Georgina Rossetti. **CP-RosC2**

Under the lamp your hands do not seem red. Inquest. William DeWitt Snodgrass. **SP-SnodW**

Under the lamp's exhausted glare. At Parting. Wystan Hugh Auden. **CP-AudWJ**

Under the Light, yet under. Emily Dickinson. **CP-DickE**

Under the long dark boughs, like jewels red. Cherry Robbers. David Herbert Lawrence. **CP-LawrD**

Under the maples at moonrise. In Moonlight, Somewhere, They Are Singing. Robert Penn Warren. **SP-WarrR**

Under the Maud Moon. Galway Kinnell. **SP-KinnG**

Under the Mirabeau Bridge there flows the Seine. Mirabeau Bridge. Guillaume Apollinaire, *tr. fr. French by* Richard Wilbur. **CP-WilbR**

Under the Moon. William Butler Yeats. **CP-YeatW**

Under the moon my brother's body lay. Antigone. Howard Nemerov. **CP-NemeH**

Under the Moon's Reign. Charles Tomlinson. **CP-TomlC**

Under the Mountain. Louis MacNeice. **CP-MacNL**

Under the muscled limbs. A Spanish Providence. Steve Griffiths. **SP-GrifS**

Under the night window. The Attic. Derek Mahon. **SP-MahoD**

Under the Oak. David Herbert Lawrence. **CP-LawrD**

Under the olive trees. Basil Bunting. *Fr.* Villon. **CP-BuntB**

Under the olive trees, from the ground. The Coward. Stephen Spender. **CP-SpenS**

Under the Olives. Robert Ranke Graves. **CP-GravR**

Under the orchid, blooming as it bloomed. The Subway from New Britain to the Bronx. Randall Jarrell. **CP-JarrR**

Under the pie crust. Howard Nemerov. *Fr.* Seven Macabre Songs. **CP-NemeH**

Under the pink quilted covers. The Fortress. Anne Sexton. **CP-SextA**

Under the pond, among rocks. The Dragonfly. Howard Nemerov. **CP-NemeH**

Under the Pot. Robert Ranke Graves. **CP-GravR**

Under the rock on the trail. Arabian Ballad. Johann Wolfgang von Goethe, *tr. fr. German by* Ralph Waldo Emerson. **CP-EmerR**

Under the Round Tower. William Butler Yeats. **CP-YeatW**

Under the rush of caravans on the Holyhead road. Llantysilio, Overgrown. Steve Griffiths. **SP-GrifS**

Under the rustling elms his separate path. The Student. Dabney Stuart. **SP-StuaD**

Under the separated leaves of shade. A Man Meets a Woman in the Street. Randall Jarrell. **CP-JarrR; SP-JarrR**

Under the shadow of a cloud, the light. Lines on Leaving Appledore. John Greenleaf Whittier. **CP-WhitJ**

Under the shadow of a stately Pile. At Florence. William Wordsworth. **VLP** *Fr.* Memorials of a Tour in Italy, 1837. **CP-WorW2**

Under the shuddering eyelid. Maudgalyâyana Saw Hell. Gary Snyder. **CP-SnydG** *Fr.* Burning. *Fr.* Myths and Texts.

Under the Skin of It. Gary Snyder. **CP-SnydG**

Under the star and beech-shade braiding. Lullaby: A Motion Like Sleep. Robert Penn Warren. **SP-WarrR**

Under the strained. Pietà. Louise Glück. **SP-GlücL**

Under the stretched skin of the houses. Ciudadela, 1991. Steve Griffiths. **SP-GrifS**

Under the Sunlamp. John Updike. *Fr.* Living with a Wife. **CP-UpdiJ**

Under the surface of flux and of fear there is an underground movement. Louis MacNeice. **LiTM** *Fr.* The Kingdom. **CP-MacNL**

Under the tall black sky you look out of your body. Endless. Muriel Rukeyser. **CP-RukeM**

Under the terrible north-light north-sea. Lakes of Värmland. James Dickey. **CP-DickJ**

Under the thick beams of that swirly smoking light. The Examination. William DeWitt Snodgrass. **SP-SnodW**

Under the thin hoop of gold. George Meredith. *Fr.* The Nuptials of Attila. **CP-MerG1**

Under the thunder-dark, the cicadas resound. Dark Summer. Louise Bogan. **CP-BogaL**

Under the too white marmoreal Lincoln Memorial. The March 1. Robert Lowell. **SP-LoweR**

Under the trees. Running Water Music. Gary Snyder. **CP-SnydG**

Under the trimmed willows, where brown children. Trumpets. Georg Trakl, tr. fr. German by James Wright. **CP-WrigJ**

Under the Viaduct, 1932. Rita Dove. **SP-DoveR**

Under the water tower at the edge of town. To the Evening Star: Central Minnesota. James Wright. **CP-WrigJ**

Under the Waterfall. Thomas Hardy. **CP-HardT**

Under the wave it is altogether still. The Return of Aphrodite. May Sarton. **SP-SartM**

Under the wide and starry sky. Requiem. Robert Louis Stevenson. **CP-StevR**

Under the wide and starry sky. Stevenson. Ernest Hemingway. **CP-HemiE**

Under the Window: Ouro Prêto. Elizabeth Bishop. **CP-BishE**

Under the World There's a Lot of Ass, a Lot of Cunt. Allen Ginsberg. **CP-GinsA**

Under the yellow sea. Song. Delmore Schwartz. *Fr.* Two Lyrics from Kilroy's Carnival: A Masque. **SP-SchwD**

Under their great hats the women walk. Enthusiasm for Hats. Howard Nemerov. **CP-NemeH**

Under these hills too high and bare. Kathleen Jessie Raine. **SP-RainK**

Under this Marble, or under this Sill. *see also* Epitaph for One Who Would Not Be Buried in Westminster Abbey ("Heroes, and Kings! your distance keep"). Alexander Pope. **CP-PopeA**

Under this rain-wind the sombre magnificence of the coast. Solstice. Robinson Jeffers. **CP-JefR2**

Under this stone lie Dicky and Dolly. An Elegy on Dicky and Dolly. Jonathan Swift. **CP-SwifJ**

Under this stone there lieth at rest. An Epitaph of Sir Thomas Gravener, [Knight]. Sir Thomas Wyatt. **CP-WyatT**

Under thy shadow may I lurk a while. Richard Crashaw. **CP-CrasR** (Acts 5; Sicke Implore St. Peter's Shadow, The.) **CP-CrasR**

Under what spell are we debased. The Call. George Meredith. **CP-MerG2**

Under Which Lyre, a Reactionary Tract for the Times. Wystan Hugh Auden. **CP-AudeW**

Under Willows. Christina Georgina Rossetti. **CP-RosC3**

Under Wrong Trees. . . or Freeing the Colonial Peoples. Stevie Smith. **CP-SmitS**

Under yonder beech-tree single on the green-sward, *Longer vers. (1878).* Love in the Valley. George Meredith. **CP-MerG1**

Under yonder beech-tree standing on the green-sward, *Shorter vers. (1851).* George Meredith. *See* Love in the Valley.

Under your illkempt yellow roses. Delia Rexroth. Kenneth Rexroth. **SP-RexrK**

Under your Milky Way. Return of the Goddess [Artemis]. Robert Ranke Graves. **CP-GravR**

Undercliff Evening. Richard Eberhart. **CP-EberR**

Underground, The. Seamus Heaney. **SP-HeanS**

Underground, The. Thomas McGrath. **SP-McGrT**

Underground grower, blind and a common brown, An. Potato. Richard Wilbur. **CP-WilbR**

Underground Stream, The. James Dickey. **CP-DickJ**

Underground System. Edna St. Vincent Millay. **CP-MillE**

Underground the Darkness Is the Light. Hayden Carruth. **CP-CarHS**

Undermining of the Defense Economy, The. James Wright. **CP-WrigJ**

Underneath. David Herbert Lawrence. **CP-LawrD**

Underneath an abject willow. Wystan Hugh Auden. *Fr.* Twelve Songs. **CP-AudeW**

Underneath an old oak tree. The Raven. Samuel Taylor Coleridge. **CP-ColeS**

Underneath my lids another eye has opened. From the Prison House. Adrienne Rich. **SP-RicA2**

Underneath My Window. Sir Philip Sidney. *See* Eleventh Song.

Underneath the autumn sky. The Veteran. Paul Laurence Dunbar. **CP-DunbP**

Underneath the Bottle. "Lou Reed." **SP-ReedL**

Underneath the broad hat is the face of the Ambassador. The Ambassador. Stevie Smith. **CP-SmitS**

Underneath the growing grass. The Bourne. Christina Georgina Rossetti. **CP-RosC1**

Underneath the ice. Saffron. Stevie Smith. **CP-SmitS**

Underneath the leaves of life. The Riddle. Wystan Hugh Auden. **CP-AudeW**

Underneath the tangled tree. Voices about the Princess Anemone. Stevie Smith. **CP-SmitS**

Underneath the tree on some. Like They Say. Robert Creeley. **CP-CreeR**

Undersea. Archie Randolph Ammons. **SP-AmmoA**

Undersea Fragment in Colons. James Dickey. **CP-DickJ**

Undersea Poem. Edwin Rolfe. **CP-RolfE**

Undersong, The. Ralph Waldo Emerson. **AA** *Fr.* Woodnotes II ("As sunbeams stream through liberal space"). **CP-EmerR**

Understand me please there's no man underneath there's. Twice More. Charles Kenneth Williams. **CP-WillC**

Understand that they were sitting just inside the door. The State of the Nation. Kenneth Patchen. **CP-PatcK**

Understand That This Is a Dream. Allen Ginsberg. **CP-GinsA**

Understanding, The. Leonard Nathan. **SP-NathL**

Understanding the logic of. Logic. Marsden Hartley. **CP-HartM**

Understanding's copper coin, The. Hafiz, tr. by Ralph Waldo Emerson. **CP-EmerR** *Fr.* Odes.

Understandings in Blue. Carl Sandburg. **CP-SandC**

Undertaker, who was with the local minister, The. Fall. John Updike. **CP-UpdiJ**

Undertakers, The. Rudyard Kipling. *Fr.* The Second Jungle Book. Ripple Song, A. **CP-KiplR** "When ye say to Tabaqui, 'My Brother!' when ye call the Hyena to meat." **CP-KiplR**

Undertakers, hearse drivers, grave diggers. To Certain Journeymen. Carl Sandburg. **CP-SandC**

Undertaker's Horse, The. Rudyard Kipling. **CP-KiplR**

Undertaking, The. John Donne. **CP-DonnJ**

Undertaking, The. Louise Glück. **SP-GlücL**

Undertaking in New Jersey, The. George Oppen. **CP-OppeG**

Undertow is strong tonight, my love, The. Integration. Phoebe Hesketh. **SP-HeskP**

Underwater Autumn. Richard Hugo. **CP-HugoR**

Underwater eyes, an eel's. An Otter. Ted Hughes. **SP-HughT**

Underwater, I could still hear music. Growing Deaf. Peter Meinke. **SP-MeinP**

Underwear. Lawrence Ferlinghetti. **SP-FerlL**

Undesirable you may have been, untouchable. September Song. Geoffrey Hill. **CP-HillG**

Undine. Christina Georgina Rossetti. **CP-RosC3**

Undo time's work. R[2]. Charles Olson. **CP-OlsoC**

Undone or done up with love. Carmen 100. Catullus. *Fr.* Carmina. **CP-Catul**

Undue Significance a starving man attaches. Emily Dickinson. **CP-DickE**

Undying love to buy. *fr.* Words for Music Perhaps. William Butler Yeats. **CP-YeatW**

Une Présence Absolue. Hayden Carruth. **CP-CarHS**

Uneasiness in Fall. Robert Bly. *See* The Fall has come, clear as the eyes of chickens.

Unemployed. Stephen Spender. **CP-SpenS**

Unemployed / Without a stake in the country, The. Carl Sandburg. *Fr.* The People, Yes. **CP-SandC**

Unexpected interest made him flush, The. Episode of Hands. Hart Crane. **CP-CranH**

Unexplorer, The. Edna St. Vincent Millay. **CP-MillE**

Unexpress'd, The. Walt Whitman. **CP-WhitW**

Unexpressed. Paul Laurence Dunbar. **CP-DunbP**

Unextinguished, The. Theodore Roethke. **CP-RoetT**

Unfallen Love. John Milton. *See* Their Wedded Love.

Unfamiliar House, The. John Gould Fletcher. **SP-FletJ**

Unfathomable sea, and time, and tears, The. To N.V. de G.S. Robert Louis Stevenson. **CP-StevR**

Unfathomable Sea! whose waves are years. Time. Percy Bysshe Shelley. **CP-ShelP**

Unfathomed deep, unfetter'd waste. Ocean. John Greenleaf Whittier. **CP-WhitJ**

Unfelt, unheard, unseen. Lines. John Keats. **CP-KeatJ**

Unfinished. David Markson. **CP-MarkD**

Unfinished Double Sonnet. Stephen Berg. **SP-BergS**

Unfinished Dream, The. Walter de la Mare. **CP-DeLaW**

Unfinished History. Archibald MacLeish. **CP-MacLA**

Unfinished Poem. Philip Larkin. **CP-LarkP**

Unfinished (raw) hero—un-, The. Charles Olson. **CP-OlsoC**

Unfinished Rendering of "When Icicles Hang by the Wall." Gerard Manley Hopkins. *Fr.* Songs from Shakespeare, in Latin and Greek. **CP-HopkG**

"Unfinished," The. Frank O'Hara. **SP-OharF**

Unfold! Unfold! Theodore Roethke. **CP-RoetT**

Unfolded Out of the Folds. Walt Whitman. **CP-WhitW**

Unforeseen. Walter de la Mare. **CP-DeLaW**

Unforgiven, The. Edwin Arlington Robinson. **CP-RobiE**

Unforgotten. Christina Georgina Rossetti. **CP-RosC3**

Unforgotten I, The ("In dreams, unhappy, I behold you stand"). Robert Louis Stevenson. **CP-StevR**

Unforgotten II, The ("She rested by the Broken Brook"). Robert Louis Stevenson. **CP-StevR**

Unformed volcanic earth, a female thing, The. Robinson Jeffers. **CP-JefR3**

Unfortunate Lover, The. Andrew Marvell. **CP-MarvA**

Unfrocked Priest, The. William Carlos Williams. **CP-WilW1**

Unfulfilled to Observation. Emily Dickinson. **CP-DickE**

Unfulfilling Brightnesses, The. Kenneth Patchen. **CP-PatcK**

Unfunny uncles who insist. Exchanging Hats. Elizabeth Bishop. **CP-BishE**

Ungainly grounded, how do you bear it, two. Albatross. Martin Edmunds. **SP-EdmuM**

Ungar and Rolfe. Herman Melville. **SP-MelvH** *Fr.* Clarel: A Poem and Pilgrimage in the Holy Land.

Ungrateful Country, if thou e'er forget. Obligations of Civil to Religious Liberty. William Wordsworth. *Fr.* Ecclesiastical Sonnets. **CP-WorW2**

Ungratefulness. George Herbert. **CP-HerbG**

Unhappy about some far off things. The Stars Go Over the Lonely Ocean. Robinson Jeffers. **CP-JefR3**

Unhappy country what wings you have. Even here. Eagle Valor, Chicken Mind. Robinson Jeffers. **CP-JefR3**

Unhappy Dives! in an evil hour. To Dives (William Beckford). A Fragment. Byron. **CP-Byron**

Unhappy exile, whom his fates confine, The. Charlotte Smith. **CP-SmitC**

Unhappy Lot of all that shine in Courts. Samuel Johnson. **CP-JohnS** *Fr.* Irene.

Unhappy people in a happy world, An. Wallace Stevens. **CMoP; PoE** *Fr.* The Auroras of Autumn. **CP-StevW**

Unhappy poets of a sunken prime! The Point of Taste. George Meredith. **CP-MerG1**

Unhappy sight, and hath she vanished by. Sonnet 105. Sir Philip Sidney. *Fr.* Astrophil and Stella. **SP-SidnP**

Unhappy Souls. David Herbert Lawrence. **CP-LawrD**

Unhappy summer you. This Summer and Last. Thomas Hardy. **CP-HardT**

Unhappy time why have you built up your house. Air-Raid Rehearsals. Robinson Jeffers. **CP-JefR2**

Unhappy wit, like most mistaken things. Alexander Pope. **EPCY** *Fr.* An Essay on Criticism. **CP-PopeA**

Unhappy youth betrayd by Fate. Against the Love of Great Ones. Richard Lovelace. **CP-LoveR**

Unharvested. Robert Frost. **CP-FrosR**

Unheard Melodies. Walter de la Mare. **CP-DeLaW**

Unheard, omnivorous, The. Air. Derek Walcott. **CP-WalcD**

Uni eqo mallem placuisse docto, *accompanied by English translation.* Thomas Campion. *Fr.* Description of a Maske: Presented in the Banqueting Roome at *Whitehall*, on Saint Stephens Night Last, at the Marriage of the Right Honourable the Earle of *Somerset:* and the Right Noble the Lady FRANCES *Howard.* **CP-CampT**

Unicorn. Phoebe Hesketh. **SP-HeskP**

Unicorn, The, *tr. fr. the German of* Rilke. Randall Jarrell. **CP-JarrR**

Unicorn. Kenneth Rexroth. **SP-RexrK** *Fr.* A Bestiary. **SP-RexrK**

Unicorn, The. Shel Silverstein. **SP-SilS2**

Unicorn and the White Doe. Robert Ranke Graves. **CP-GravR**

Unicorn is supposed, The. Unicorn. Kenneth Rexroth. **SP-RexrK** *Fr.* A Bestiary. **SP-RexrK**

Unicorn with burning heart. Unicorn and the White Doe. Robert Ranke Graves. **CP-GravR**

Unidentified Flying Object. Robert Earl Hayden. **CP-HaydR**

Uniformly over the whole countryside. On What Planet. Kenneth Rexroth. **SP-RexrK**

Unimaginable beings— / Our own dead friends, the dead. The Harrow. Donald Davie. **CP-DavDo**

Unintentional Paint. Carl Sandburg. **CP-SandC**

Union in Disseverance. George Meredith. **CP-MerG1**

Union Pier Michigan. We called it Shapiro. That Was Then. Isabella Gardner. **CP-GardI**

Union Sundown. "Bob Dylan." **CP-DylaB**

Unison, A. William Carlos Williams. **CP-WilW2**

Unit Assignment. Edwin Rolfe. **CP-RolfE**

Unit, like Death, for Whom? Emily Dickinson. **CP-DickE**

Unit Meeting. Edwin Rolfe. **CP-RolfE**

United Dames of America. Wallace Stevens. **CP-StevW**

United 555. Richard Eberhart. **CP-EberR**

United Front, The. William Carlos Williams. **CP-WilW2**

United Nations Hymn. Wystan Hugh Auden. *Fr.* Six Commissioned Texts. **CP-AudeW**

United States, The. Kay Boyle. **CP-BoylK**

United States, The. William Carlos Williams. **CP-WilW2**

United States to Old World Critics, The. Walt Whitman. **CP-WhitW**

Unity. Ralph Waldo Emerson. **CP-EmerR**

Unity with Nature. Samuel Taylor Coleridge. **CP-ColeS**

Universal Prayer [Deo Opt. Max.], The. Alexander Pope. **CP-PopeA**

Universality of things, The. The Eyeglasses. William Carlos Williams. **CP-WilW1**

Universe, The. Walter de la Mare. **CP-DeLaW**

Universe expands and contracts like a great heart, The. The Great Explosion. Robinson Jeffers. **CP-JefR3**

Universe Flows, The. David Herbert Lawrence. **CP-LawrD**

Universe is but the Thing of things, The. Accidentally on Purpose. Robert Frost. **CP-FrosR**

Universe of course is infinite, The. Two Sides to an Outside: Meditation from Empson. Howard Nemerov. **CP-NemeH**

Universe-Solitude. Paul Éluard, *tr. fr. French by* Samuel Beckett. **CP-BeckS**

Universes, The. Diane Wakoski. **SP-WakoD**

    Fifth Universe.

    First Universe.

    Fourth Universe.

    Second Universe.

    Third Universe.

University. Karl Shapiro. **SP-ShapK**

University Hospital, Boston. Mary Oliver. **SP-OlivM**

University of the South, The. Donald Davie. **CP-DavDo**

Unjeweled in black as ever comedienne. Words for Maria. James Merrill. **SP-MerrJ**

Unjust decrees, that do at once exact. Song. Sir John Suckling. **CP-SuckJ**

Unkempt and furtive the wind crawls. Before. Wystan Hugh Auden. **CP-AudWJ**

Unkept Good Fridays. Thomas Hardy. **CP-HardT**

Unkind Poem, An. Charles Bukowski. **SP-BukC1**

Unkindly May, An. Thomas Hardy. **CP-HardT**

Unkindness. George Herbert. **CP-HerbG**

Unknowable? Perhaps Not Altogether. John Berryman. **CP-BerrJ**

Unknowing. Thomas Hardy. **CP-HardT**

Unknown, The. Denise Levertov. **CP-LeveD**

Unknown, The. William Carlos Williams. **CP-WilW2**

Unknown Citizen, The. Wystan Hugh Auden. **CP-AudeW**

Unknown Fair Faces. George Meredith. **CP-MerG1**

Unknown Female Corpse. Rudyard Kipling. **PoWW** *Fr.* Epitaphs of the War [1914–1918]. **CP-KiplR**

Unknown Girl in the Maternity Ward. Anne Sexton. **CP-SextA**

Unknown is the largest need, The. Emily Dickinson. **SP-DickE**

Unknown Soldier, The. Alun Lewis. **CP-LewiA**

Unknown War, The. Carl Sandburg. **CP-SandC**

Unlearning to Not Speak. Marge Piercy. **SP-PierM**

Unless the soul, to vice a thrall. Boethius, *tr. by* Samuel Johnson. **CP-JohnS** *Fr.* Consolation of Philosophy, The ("De Consolacione Philosophie"). **CP-ChauG**

Unless this is the shelf of whatever happens? John Ashbery. **SP-AshbJ** *Fr.* Fantasia on "The Nut-Brown Maid."

Unless to Peter's Chair the viewless wind. Papal Dominion. William Wordsworth. *Fr.* Ecclesiastical Sonnets. **CP-WorW2**

Unless with my Amanda blest. To Amanda. James Thomson. **CP-ThomJ**

Unless you can muse in a crowd all day. Elizabeth Barrett Browning. **PFP** *Fr.* A Woman's Shortcomings. **CP-BroEB**

Unless you come of the gipsy stock. Gipsy Vans. Rudyard Kipling. **CP-KiplR** *Fr.* Debits and Credits.

Unlesse there were consent twixt hell and heaven. *At.* to Thomas Campion *and to* Philip Rosseter. **CP-CampT**

Unlike are we, unlike, O princely heart! Sonnet. Elizabeth Barrett Browning. **BWW; EnVR; HBV; OAEP; OBEV; OBVV; OXAEP-2; TrGrPo** *Fr.* Sonnets from the Portuguese. **CP-BroEB**

Unlike Joubert. James Schuyler. **CP-SchuJ**

Unlike the heroes of each ancient race. Byron. **NOBRP** *Fr.* O'er the glad waters of the dark blue sea. *Fr.* The Corsair. **CP-Byron**

Unlike the moon. James Liddy. **CP-LiddJ**

Unlike the neat dénouement in the popular novel. Mystery II. Edwin Rolfe. **CP-RolfE**

Unlike the ribald, whose licentious jest. Lucan, *tr.* by Samuel Johnson. **CP-JohnS** *Fr.* Ad Pisonem.

Unload me, brother. I have brought a few. September. Christina Georgina Rossetti. *Fr.* The Months: A Pageant. **CP-RosC2**

Unlocking the bathroom; / handing over the keys of the house. Defeathered. Phoebe Hesketh. **SP-HeskP**

Unlooked-For Season, The. Jenny Joseph. **SP-JoseJ**

Unloved, The. Kathleen Jessie Raine. **SP-RainK**

Unlovely you called yourself. Tam Cari Capitis. Louis Zukofsky. *Fr.* 29 Poems. **CP-ZukLS**

Unlove's the heavenless hell and homeless home. Edward Estlin Cummings. **CP-CummE**

Unluckily for a Death. Dylan Thomas. **CP-ThomD**

Unlucky Apple, The. Paul Laurence Dunbar. **CP-DunbP**

Unlucky the hero born. The Times Are Tidy. Sylvia Plath. **CP-PlatS**

Unmarried, near-sighted, rather deaf. The Maker. Wystan Hugh Auden. **CP-AudeW**

Unmeasured Tempo. Maya Angelou. **SP-AngeM**

Unmetalled Road. Steve Griffiths. **SP-GrifS**

Unmindful of the roses, / Unmindful of the thorns. One Sea-Side Grave. Christina Georgina Rossetti. **CP-RosC2**

"Unmitigated England" / Came swinging down the line. Great Central Railway, Sheffield Victoria to Banbury. Sir John Betjeman. **CP-BetjJ**

Unmoving vault / receives their movement, The. At Wells: Polyphony. Charles Tomlinson. **CP-TomlC**

Unmuzzle the broad joke. Hymeneal. Catullus. **PeHV,** *tr.* by James Michie; *Fr.* Carmen 61: "Hill (breeder) of Helicon." **CP-ZukLS; OxBM** *Fr.* Carmina. **CP-Catul**

Unnamable God, you are fathomless. Bible, *O.T. See* Psalm 104: "Bless the Lord, O my soul. . . ."

Unnamed Lands. Walt Whitman. **CP-WhitW**

Unnamed Spell, The. Robert Ranke Graves. **CP-GravR**

Unnatural History of Peru, The. Kenneth Patchen. **CP-PatcK**

Unnatural Love. Allen Tate. **CP-TateA**

Unnatural Unselection. Hayden Carruth. **CP-CarHS**

Unnecessary Dread, The. John Hewitt. **CP-HewiJ**

Unnoted as the setting of a star. Mulford. John Greenleaf Whittier. **CP-WhitJ**

Unnoticed woman from whose kind large flesh. Edward Estlin Cummings. **CP-CummE**

Unnumbered suppliants crowd preferment's gate. Samuel Johnson. **OBSV** *Fr.* The Vanity of Human Wishes [The Tenth Satire of Juvenal Imitated]. **CP-JohnS**

Unobtrusive trampships gather, The. Southend at Dusk. Alun Lewis. **CP-LewiA**

Unoccupied Zone, The. Louis Aragon, *tr. fr. French by* Louis MacNeice. **CP-MacNL**

Unpacking in the raw new rooms, I clear. Thoughts on Unpacking. Thom Gunn. **CP-GunnT**

Unpardonable Sin, The. Nicholas Vachel Lindsay. **CP-LindV**

Unpenned Poem, The. Robert Ranke Graves. **CP-GravR**

Unperishing youth! / Thou leapest from forth. *ad. fr. the German of* Stolberg. Samuel Taylor Coleridge. **CP-ColeS**

Unplanted Primrose, The. Thomas Hardy. **CP-HardT**

Unplayed idea returned to haunt you, Yukio Mishima, The. Mishima. Charles Henri Ford. *Fr.* Four Elegies. **SP-FordC**

Unpopular, Lonely and Loving. Stevie Smith. **CP-SmitS**

Unposted Letter. Robert Ranke Graves. **CP-GravR**

Unpredictable but Providential. Wystan Hugh Auden. **CP-AudeW**

Unprofitably pleasing, and unsound. Sonnet 11. Mary Sidney, Countess of Montgomery Wroth. *Fr.* A Crowne of Sonetts Dedicated to Love. *Fr.* Pamphilia to Amphilanthus. **CP-WrotM**

Unpurged images of day recede, The. Byzantium. William Butler Yeats. **CP-YeatW**

Unquiet Childhood here by special grace. The Infant M— M—. William Wordsworth. **CP-WorW2**

Unquiet griefe search farder, in my hart. Sonnet. Mary Sidney, Countess of Montgomery Wroth. *Fr.* Part 1. *Fr.* Urania. **CP-WrotM**

Unquiet Ones, The. Stanley Jasspon Kunitz. **CP-KuniS**

Unraveling a rope. The Rope's End. Howard Nemerov. **CP-NemeH**

Unrealized. Thomas Hardy. **CP-HardT**

Unregarding. Walter de la Mare. **CP-DeLaW**

Unremitting Voice of Nightly Streams, The. William Wordsworth. **CP-WorW2**

Unrequited. Erica Jong. **SP-JongE**

Unresponsbile / people versus / serious. The News. Robert Creeley. **CP-CreeR**

Unreturning, The. Wilfred Owen. **CP-OwenW**

Unreturning Hosts, The. Kenneth Patchen. **CP-PatcK**

Unrhymed, unrhythmical, the chatter goes. At the Party. Wystan Hugh Auden. **CP-AudeW**

Unripe harvest there hath none to reap it. A Castle-Builder's World. Christina Georgina Rossetti. **CP-RosC2**

Unrisen splendour of the brightest sun. Fragment. Percy Bysshe Shelley. **CP-ShelP**

Unsaid Word, An. Adrienne Rich. **CP-RicAE; RicA1; SP-RicA2**

Unscientific Postscript. Howard Nemerov. **CP-NemeH**

Unseasonable man, statue of ice. Eclogue 1613. December 26. John Donne. **CP-DonnJ**

Unseen Buds. Walt Whitman. **CP-WhitW**

Unseen Playmate, The. Robert Louis Stevenson. **CP-StevR**

Unseene, unknowne, I here alone complaine. Mary Sidney, Countess of Montgomery Wroth. *Fr.* Part 1. *Fr.* Urania. **CP-WrotM**

Unselfish Husband, The. Ogden Nash. **CP-NashO**

Unser Vater. Stevie Smith. **CP-SmitS**

Unsettled again and hearing Russian spoken. Hearing Russian Spoken. Donald Davie. **CP-DavDo**

Unsettled Motorcyclist's Vision of His Death, The. Thom Gunn. **CP-GunnT**

Unshaven, gaping-jawed, with muffled brain. My Father's Death in Hospital. John Hewitt. **CP-HewiJ**

Unsleeping principle of delight that, The. Interjection #8: Or, Sometimes, Night. Robert Penn Warren. **SP-WarrR**

Unsnack your snood, madanna, for the stars. Late Hymn from the Myrrh-Mountain. Wallace Stevens. **CP-StevW**

Unsounded. Adrienne Rich. **CP-RicAE**

Unspotted lambs to follow the one Lamb. Christina Georgina Rossetti. **CP-RosC2**

Unstable as water, thou shalt not excel. Howard Nemerov. *Fr.* Runes. **CP-NemeH**

Unstable dream[e] [*or* dreme], according [*or* accordyng] to the place. Sir Thomas Wyatt. **CP-WyatT**

Unstamped Letter in Our Rural Letter Box, An. Robert Frost. **CP-FrosR**

Unsteady Yellow. Tess Gallagher. **SP-GallT**

Unstill Universe. Lucio Piccolo, *tr. fr. Italian by* Charles Tomlinson. **CP-TomlC**

Unsung Heroes, The. Paul Laurence Dunbar. **CP-DunbP**

Unsupported by reason's enigma. Scheherazade. John Ashbery. **SP-AshbJ**

Untenable Situation, An. Pablo Neruda, *tr. fr. Spanish by* Ben Belitt. **SP-NeruP**

Unthrifty loveliness, why dost thou spend. Sonnet 4. William Shakespeare. *Fr.* Sonnets. **CP-ShaWS**

Until and i heard. Edward Estlin Cummings. **CP-CummE**

Until I asked her to please stop doing it and was astonished to find that she not only could. My Mother's Lips. Charles Kenneth Williams. **CP-WillC; SP-WillC**

Until I stand on the January platform. Muriel Rukeyser. **CP-RukeM**

Until the Day Break. Christina Georgina Rossetti. **CP-RosC2**

Until the Desert knows. Emily Dickinson. **CP-DickE**

Until the Sea Is Dead. David St. John. **SP-StJoD**

Until thy feet have trod the Road. The Comforters. Rudyard Kipling. **CP-KiplR**

Until tonight they were separate specialities. A Story for Rose on the Midnight Flight to Boston. Anne Sexton. **CP-SextA**

Until We Both. Robert Ranke Graves. **CP-GravR**

Untilted. John Ashbery. **SP-AshbJ**

Untimely. Rudyard Kipling. **CP-KiplR** *Fr.* Debits and Credits.

Untitled. John Clare. **SP-ClarJ** *Fr.* The Badger grunting on his woodland track.

Untitled. Jenny Joseph. **SP-JoseJ**

Untitled. Alice Notley. **SP-NotlA**

Untitled Poem. Ussin Kerim, *tr. fr. Bulgarian by* William Matthews. **SP-MattW**

Unto a broken heart. Emily Dickinson. **CP-DickE**

Unto blest Melancholy's house one happy day. The Son of Melancholy. Walter de la Mare. **CP-DeLaW**

Unto like Story—Trouble has incited me. Emily Dickinson. **CP-DickE**

"Unto me?" I do not know you. Emily Dickinson. **CP-DickE**

Unto my Books—so good to turn. Emily Dickinson. **CP-DickE**

Unto no body my woman saith she had rather a wife be. Catullus. *See* Carmen 70: "Lesbia says she'ld rather marry me."

Unto Pastillus ranke Gorgonius came. Upon Gorgonius. Robert Herrick. **CP-HerrR**

Unto that love must we through fire attain. The Hueless Love. George Meredith. **CP-MerG1**

Unto the caitiff wretch whom long affliction holdeth, *speech of Philisides.* Sir Philip Sidney. **SP-SidnP** *Fr.* Arcadia.

Unto the Whole—how add? Emily Dickinson. **CP-DickE**

Unto thee i / burn incense. Edward Estlin Cummings. **CP-CummE**

Unto thee lift I up mine eyes, O thou that dwellest in the heavens. Psalm 123. Bible, *O.T. Fr.* Psalms. **CP-Psal**

Unto thee, O God, do we give thanks. Psalm 75. Bible, *O.T. Fr.* Psalms. **CP-Psal**

Unto thee, O Lord, do I lift up my soul. Psalm 25. Bible, *O.T. Fr.* Psalms. **CP-Psal**

Unto thee will I cry, O Lord my rock. Psalm 28. Bible, *O.T. Fr.* Psalms. **CP-Psal**

Unto this place when as the Elfin Knight. The Hill of the Graces. Edmund Spenser. **NOBE** *Fr.* The Faerie Queene. **CP-Spens**

Unto whose use the pregnant suns are poised. Rudyard Kipling. **CP-KiplR** *Fr.* Kim.

Untold Want, The. Walt Whitman. **CP-WhitW**

Untouched ones, the, The. Charles Henri Ford. **SP-FordC** *Fr.* Emblems of Arachne.

Untouched through all severity of cold. Filial Piety. William Wordsworth. **CP-WorW2**

Untoward Occurance at Embassy Poetry Reading. Marilyn Hacker. **SP-HackM**

Untrampled Footsteps. Jim Morrison. **SP-MorrJ**

Untruth is become the mode. Hafiz, *tr. by* Ralph Waldo Emerson. **CP-EmerR** *Fr.* Odes.

Unused tent, The. The Attic Which Is Desire. William Carlos Williams. **CP-WilW1**

Unusual Precautions. John Ashbery. **SP-AshbJ**

Unwandering, I can move. For Robert Bhain Campbell. James Dickey. **CP-DickJ**

Unwanted 1943 Chappaqua Flashback. John Clellon Holmes. **SP-HolmJ**

Unwarmed by any sunset light. The World Transformed. John Greenleaf Whittier. **AA** *Fr.* Snow-Bound [*or* Snow-Bound; a Winter Idyl]. **CP-WhitJ**

Unwarned, catch into this. The Eagle's Mile. James Dickey. **CP-DickJ**

Unwashed, unbedded. / He has fine bones and a. Charles Henri Ford. **SP-FordC** *Fr.* Secret Haiku.

Unwashed, unshat. Iceland Revisited. Wystan Hugh Auden. **CP-AudeW**

Unwatched [*or* unwatch'd], the garden bough shall sway. Tennyson. **EBVV; ELP; FHYEP; FaBoPP; GTBS-6; GTBS-7; OBNC; PeECV; PoEL-5; PoPle; SCV; SeCeV** *Fr.* In Memoriam A. H. H. **CP-TennA** (Somersby, Lincolnshire; after Leaving the Refectory.) **FaBoPP**

Unwillingly Miranda wakes. A Lady Thinks She Is Thirty. Ogden Nash. **CP-NashO**

Unwin, I should but ill repay. To Unwin. William Cowper. **CP-CowpW**

Unwinged Ones, The. Ogden Nash. **CP-NashO**

Unwithered Garland, The. Stanley Jasspon Kunitz. **CP-KuniS**

Unworn long gown, meant for dances, The. Disposal. William DeWitt Snodgrass. **SP-SnodW**

Unworthy of her Breast. Emily Dickinson. **CP-DickE**

Unworthy porter, bound in chains full sore. 1.6. Ovid. **CP-MarlC,** *tr. by* Christopher Marlowe; *Fr.* Elegies.

Unwritten Chapters. Steve Griffiths. **SP-GrifS**

Unyielding in the pride of his defiance. The Flying Dutchman. Edwin Arlington Robinson. **CP-RobiE**

Up. James Schuyler. **CP-SchuJ**

Up a heavy wooded hill. Christmas Tree. Richard Eberhart. **CP-EberR**

Up among the stucco pears, the iron vines. Dirge for a Town in France. Thomas Merton. **CP-MertT; SP-MertT**

Up and be doing, all who have a hand. A Call to National Service. Thomas Hardy. **CP-HardT**

Up and Down. James Merrill. **SP-MerrJ**

Up and down / she walks, listless. The Rose. Robert Creeley. **CP-CreeR**

Up and Down. Stevie Smith. **CP-SmitS**

Up and down / what falls. They Say. Robert Creeley. **CP-CreeR**

Up and down and up and down. The Fuel Vendor. John Gould Fletcher. *Fr.* Arizona Poems. **SP-FletJ**

Up and down stairs of the inner ear. Pentecost. Donald Davie. **CP-DavDo**

Up and down the small streets, in which. The Widows. Donald Hall. **CP-HallD**

Up and down the village streets. The Prophecy of Samuel Sewall. John Greenleaf Whittier. **CP-WhitJ**

Up and Warn A' Willie. Robert Burns. **CP-BurnR**

Up at a Villa—Down in the City. Robert Browning. **CP-BroR1**

Up at dawn. 7.IV.64. Gary Snyder. **CP-SnydG**

Up at La Serra. Charles Tomlinson. **CP-TomlC**

Up Balls Pond Road the turkey's. The Doors of the Year, Well Done. Steve Griffiths. **SP-GrifS**

Up-Beat. Langston Hughes. **SP-HughL**

Up beyond sense and praise. Little Fanfare for Felix Magowan. James Merrill. **SP-MerrJ**

Up, black, striped and damasked like the chasuble. The Skunk. Seamus Heaney. **SP-HeanS**

Up came the young Centaur-colts from the plains they were fathered in. The Centaurs. Rudyard Kipling. **CP-KiplR** *Fr.* Debits and Credits.

"Up, down, good, bad," said. Tubes. Donald Hall. **CP-HallD**

Up from many a sheeted valley. The Margrave's Birthnight. Herman Melville. **SP-MelvH**

Up from oysters. The Fish That Walked. Anne Sexton. **CP-SextA**

Up from South Jersey and the low persistent. Toward the Verrazano. Stephen Dunn. **SP-DunnS**

Up from the bronze, I saw. Roman Fountain. Louise Bogan. **CP-BogaL**

Up from the Egg; the Confessions of a Nuthatch Avoider. Ogden Nash. **CP-NashO**

Up from the meadows rich with corn. Barbara Frietchie. John Greenleaf Whittier. **CP-WhitJ**

Up from the sea the wild north wind is blowing. The Wind of March. John Greenleaf Whittier. **CP-WhitJ**

Up from the street and the crowds that went. Her Eyes. Edwin Arlington Robinson. **CP-RobiE**

Up from the valley. Now and Then. James Schuyler. **CP-SchuJ**

Up from the Wheelbarrow. Ogden Nash. **CP-NashO**

Up He Goes! David Herbert Lawrence. **CP-LawrD**

Up here among the gull cries. Magnolia Shoals. Sylvia Plath. **CP-PlatS**

Up here we don't plant trees sometimes we take them down. For My Friend Who Planted a Tree for His Daughter Jane. Grace Paley. **CP-PaleG**

Up I rose, my lads, an' i heard yer. Up He Goes! David Herbert Lawrence. **CP-LawrD**

Up in dirt alley / eat korean food. March. Gary Snyder. *Fr.* Six Years. **CP-SnydG**

Up in Here. Tom Clark. **SP-ClarT**

Up in northern California. The Little Girls. Charles Bukowski. **SP-BukC1**

Up in the air / among the Iroquois': no. Above Manhattan. Charles Tomlinson. **CP-TomlC**

Up in the Air. Robert Creeley. **CP-CreeR**

Up in the high. Song. David Herbert Lawrence. **CP-LawrD**

Up in the Morning Early. Robert Burns. **CP-BurnR**

Up in the second balcony. Burlesque. Muriel Rukeyser. **CP-RukeM**

Up in the sky the star is waiting. Randall Jarrell. **CP-JarrR**

Up in this warm, solid house of yours. East Boston. Al Young. **CP-YounA**

Up into the cherry-tree. Foreign Lands. Robert Louis Stevenson. **CP-StevR**

Up into the silence the green. Edward Estlin Cummings. **CP-CummE**

Up, Jack. Richard Wilbur. **CP-WilbR**

Up, laggards of Freedom!—our free flag is cast. A Song for the Time. John Greenleaf Whittier. **CP-WhitJ**

Up Life's Hill with my little Bundle. Emily Dickinson. **CP-DickE**

Up, my drowsing eyes! / Up, my sinking heart! Vigil of all Saints. Christina Georgina Rossetti. **CP-RosC2**

Up north here, in my own country, and free-. Long Summers. Robert Lowell. **SP-LoweR**

Up on the hillside a long row of larches. Grey Symphony. John Gould Fletcher. **SP-FletJ**

Up on the white veranda. Black Diamond Bay. "Bob Dylan" *and* Jacques Levy. **CP-DylaB**

Up past the burnt hills. Distance and the crowd. Muriel Rukeyser. **CP-RukeM**

Up public joy, remember. An Ode, or Song, by All the Muses. Ben Jonson. **CP-JonsB**

Up Rising. Robert Duncan. **SP-DuncR** *Fr.* Passages.

Up rose the moon in glory. Despair. Christina Georgina Rossetti. **CP-RosC3**

Up Tail[e]s All. Robert Herrick. **CP-HerrR**

Up the ash tree climbs the ivy. Upper Lambourne. Sir John Betjeman. **CP-BetjJ**

Up the block, all you kids. Louie the Barber. Lewis Turco. **SP-TurcL**

Up the chasm-walls of my bleeding heart. The Hive. Hart Crane. **CP-CranH**

Up the damp gravelled drive as the laurels dripped. The Portrait. John Hewitt. **CP-HewiJ**

Up the Dark Valley. Thomas McGrath. **SP-McGrT**

Up the hillside, down the glen. Texas. John Greenleaf Whittier. **CP-WhitJ**

Up the old hill to the old house again. The Long Race. Edwin Arlington Robinson. **CP-RobiE**

Up the reputable walks of old established trees. The Campus on the Hill. William DeWitt Snodgrass. **SP-SnodW**

Up the steep brae the ill-matched horses climb. The Ploughman. John Hewitt. **CP-HewiJ**

Up the streets of Aberdeen. Barclay of Ury. John Greenleaf Whittier. **CP-WhitJ**

Up There. Wystan Hugh Auden. **OxBTC** *Fr.* Thanksgiving for a Habitat. **CP-AudeW**

Up Thy Hill of Sorrows / Thou all alone. Good Friday Morning. Christina Georgina Rossetti. **CP-RosC2**

Up, Timothy, up with your staff and away! The Childless Father. William Wordsworth. **CP-WorW1**

Up to battle! Sons of Suli. Song to the Suliotes. Byron. **CP-Byron**

Up to Me. "Bob Dylan." **CP-DylaB**

Up to the throne of God is borne. The Labourer's Noon-Day Hymn. William Wordsworth. **CP-WorW2**

Up up and away! Hiway Poesy: L.A.–Albuquerque–Texas–Witchita. Allen Ginsberg. **CP-GinsA**

Up, up, lad, time's a-wastin', press the ignition. Ms. Found in a Quagmire. Ogden Nash. **CP-NashO**

Up, up, my drowsie [or drowsy] Soul[e], where thy new ear[e]. Our Companie in the Next World. John Donne. **OBS** *Fr.* The Second Anniversary [or Anniversarie]. **ESCV; SeCP** *Fr.* Of the Progres[se] of the Soule; the Second Anniversarie. **CP-DonnJ**

Up! Up! my Friend, and quit your books. The Tables Turned. William Wordsworth. **CP-WorW1**

Up, up, up—next step of the staircase. Fust and His Friends. Robert Browning. **CP-BroR2**

Up, up! ye dames, ye [or dames and ye] lasses gay! Samuel Taylor Coleridge. **CP-ColeS** *Fr.* Zapolya.

(Hunting Song.) **CP-ColeS**

Up wi' the carls of Dysart. Hey Ca' thro'. Robert Burns. **CP-BurnR**

Up winding stair, / here, where, in what theater lost? Logic and The Magic Flute. Marianne Craig Moore. **CP-MoorM**

Up with me! up with me into the clouds! To a Sky-Lark. William Wordsworth. **CP-WorW1**

Up with me! up with me into the clouds! William Wordsworth. **FPL; HBV 1-2; TTTS** *Fr.* To a Sky-Lark. **CP-WorW1**

Up with the jolly Bird of Light. Amarantha. A Pastoral. Richard Lovelace. **CP-LoveR**

Up with the Quintill, that the Rout. The Quintell. Robert Herrick. **CP-HerrR**

Up with the sun, the breeze arose. An English Breeze. Robert Louis Stevenson. **CP-StevR**

Up Your Yellow River. Charles Bukowski. **SP-BukC1**

Up, youths and virgins, up, and praise. Epithalamion. Ben Jonson. **CP-JonsB** *Fr.* The Haddington Masque.

Upbraiding, An. Thomas Hardy. **CP-HardT**

Upcountry. Adrienne Rich. **SP-RicA1; SP-RicA2**

Update. Stephen Dunn. **SP-DunnS**

Upended, it crouches on broken limbs. Poem. Charles Tomlinson. **CP-TomlC**

Uphill. James McAuley. *Fr.* Ten-Mile Run. **SP-McAuJ**

Uphill [or Up-Hill]. Christina Georgina Rossetti. **CP-RosC1**

Upland flocks grew starved and thinned, The. The Lambs of Grasmere, 1860. Christina Georgina Rossetti. **CP-RosC1**

Upland Shepherd, as reclined he lies, The. The Sea View. Charlotte Smith. **CP-SmitC**

Uplands in May. Carl Sandburg. **CP-SandC**

Uplifted and waved till immobilized. Elephants. Marianne Craig Moore. **CP-MoorM**

Upon a bank, easeless with knobs of gold. Gloria Mundi. Walter de la Mare. **CP-DeLaW**

Upon a Black Twist, Rounding the Arm of the Countess of Carlisle. Robert Herrick. **CP-HerrR**

Upon a Bleare-Ey'd Woman. Robert Herrick. **CP-HerrR**

Upon a Cheap Laundresse: Epigram. Robert Herrick. **CP-HerrR**

Upon a Cherrystone Sent to the Tip of the Lady Jemmonia Walgraves Eare. Robert Herrick. **CP-HerrR**

Upon a Child. Robert Herrick. *See* Here a pretty baby lies.

Upon a Child. An Epitaph. Robert Herrick. **CP-HerrR**

Upon a Child That Died [or Dyed]. Robert Herrick. **CP-HerrR**

Upon a Comely, and Curious Maide. Robert Herrick. **CP-HerrR**

Upon a Crooked Maid. Robert Herrick. **CP-HerrR**

Upon a Day when the Dog-star. The Toad and Spyder. Richard Lovelace. **CP-LoveR**

Upon a Delaying Lady. Robert Herrick. **CP-HerrR**

Upon a Dying Lady. William Butler Yeats. **CP-YeatW**

Upon a Fit of Sickness, Anno 1632. Anne Bradstreet. **CP-BradA**

Upon a Flie. Robert Herrick. **CP-HerrR**

Upon a Free Maid, with a Foule Breath. Robert Herrick. **CP-HerrR**

Upon a Gentlewoman with a Sweet Voice. Robert Herrick. **CP-HerrR**

Upon a Grave. Stevie Smith. **CP-SmitS**

Upon a Hoarse Singer. Robert Herrick. **CP-HerrR**

Upon a holy thursday their innocent faces clean. William Blake. **CP-BlakW** *Fr.* An Island in the Moon.

Upon a House Shaken by the Land Agitation. William Butler Yeats. **CP-YeatW**

Upon a Lady Faire, but Fruitlesse. Robert Herrick. **CP-HerrR**

Upon a Lady That Dyed in Child-Bed, and Left a Daughter behind Her. Robert Herrick. **CP-HerrR**

Upon a Lilac Sea. Emily Dickinson. **CP-DickE**

Upon a Maid ("Gone she is a long, long way"). Robert Herrick. **CP-HerrR**

Upon a Maid[e]. Robert Herrick. **CP-HerrR**

Upon a Maid That Died [or Dyed] the Day She Was Married [or Marryed]. Meleager, tr. fr. Greek by Robert Herrick. **CP-HerrR**

Upon a Maide ("Hence a blessed soule is fled"). Robert Herrick. **CP-HerrR**

Upon a Moebius strip. The Moebius Strip. Charles Olson. **CP-OlsoC**

Upon a Mole in Celia's Bosom. Thomas Carew. **CP-CareT**

Upon a noon I pilgrimed through. Her Immortality. Thomas Hardy. **CP-HardT**

Upon a Painted Gentlewoman. Robert Herrick. **CP-HerrR**

Upon a peak in Darien. The Sage of Darien. Ogden Nash. **CP-NashO**

Upon a Physitian. Robert Herrick. **CP-HerrR**

Upon a poet's page I wrote. Her Initials. Thomas Hardy. **CP-HardT**

Upon a Portrait. William Wordsworth. **CP-WorW2**

Upon a Ribbon [or Ribband]. Thomas Carew. **CP-CareT**

Upon a rock yet uncreate. Ralph Waldo Emerson. **CP-EmerR**

Upon a Sabbath-day it fell. The Eve of St. Mark. John Keats. **CP-KeatJ**

Upon a Scarre in a Virgins Face. Robert Herrick. **CP-HerrR**

Upon a simmer Sunday morn. The Holy Fair. Robert Burns. **CP-BurnR**

Upon a Sowre-Breath Lady. Robert Herrick. **CP-HerrR**

Upon a time, before the faery broods. John Keats. **NOBRP** *Fr.* Lamia. **CP-KeatJ**

Upon a time, before the faery broods. Lamia. John Keats. **CP-KeatJ**

Upon a Venerable Rival. William Cowper. **CP-CowpW**

Upon a Virgin. Robert Herrick. **CP-HerrR**

Upon a Virgin Kissing a Rose. Robert Herrick. **CP-HerrR**

Upon a Wife That Dyed Mad with Jealousie. Robert Herrick. **CP-HerrR**

Upon a Young Mother of Many Children. Robert Herrick. **CP-HerrR**

Upon Adam Peapes. Robert Herrick. **CP-HerrR**

Upon A.M. Sir John Suckling. **CP-SuckJ**

Upon an Eunuch: A Poet. Andrew Marvell, tr. fr. Latin by William A. McQueen and Kiffin A. Rockwell. **CP-MarvA**

Upon an hill a bright flame I did see. Joachim Du Bellay. *Fr.* The Visions of Bellay. **CP-Spens**

Upon an Old Man a Residenciarie. Robert Herrick. **CP-HerrR**

Upon an Old Woman. Robert Herrick. **CP-HerrR**

Upon Apennine Slope. Arthur Hugh Clough. *See* Ah, That I Were Far Away.

Upon Appleton House [To My Lord Fairfax]. Andrew Marvell. **CP-MarvA**

After Floods on the Wharfe. **FaBoPP**

"And now to the abyss I pass." **OAEL-1**

Carrying Their Coracles. **ChTr**

"From that blest bed the hero came." **JCP**

Garden of Appleton House, The ("When in the east the morning ray"). **NOBE**

Hewel, or Woodpecker, The. **ChTr**

Kingfisher, The. **ChTr; PB**

"Oh thou, that dear and happy isle." **OxBoLi**

"See how the flowers, as at parade." **OBEV; TrGrPo**

(Garden, A.) **OBEV**

"Then, to conclude these pleasant acts." **CBNP**

To My Lord Fairfax. **NOSC**

"When first the eye this forest sees." **PBBP**

Upon Batt. Robert Herrick. **CP-HerrR**

Upon Ben Jo[h]nson. Robert Herrick. **CP-HerrR**

Upon Bice. Robert Herrick. **CP-HerrR**

Upon Bishop Andrewes's [or Andrewes His] Picture before His Sermons. Richard Crashaw. **CP-CrasR**

("See here a Shadow from that setting Sunne.") **CP-CrasR**

Upon Blanch: ("Blanch swears her Husband's lovely; when a scald"). Robert Herrick. **CP-HerrR**

Upon Blanch. Robert Herrick. **CP-HerrR**

Upon Blinks. Robert Herrick. **CP-HerrR**

Upon Blisse. Robert Herrick. **CP-HerrR**

Upon Boreman. Epig. Robert Herrick. **CP-HerrR**

Upon Bran. Robert Herrick. **CP-HerrR**

Upon Bridget. Robert Herrick. **CP-HerrR**

Upon Brock. Robert Herrick. **CP-HerrR**

Upon Buggins. Robert Herrick. **CP-HerrR**

Upon Bunce: Epigram. Robert Herrick. **CP-HerrR**

Upon Bungie. Robert Herrick. **CP-HerrR**

Upon Burr. Robert Herrick. **CP-HerrR**

Upon Candlemasse Day. Robert Herrick. **CP-HerrR**

Upon Case. Robert Herrick. **CP-HerrR**

Upon Center a Spectacle-Maker with a Flat Nose. Robert Herrick. **CP-HerrR**

Upon Chub. Robert Herrick. **CP-HerrR**

Upon Clunn. Robert Herrick. **CP-HerrR**

Upon Cob. Robert Herrick. **CP-HerrR**

Upon Cock. Robert Herrick. **CP-HerrR**

Upon Comely a Good Speaker but an Ill Singer. Robert Herrick. **CP-HerrR**

Upon Concluded Lives. Emily Dickinson. **CP-DickE**

Upon Coone. Robert Herrick. **CP-HerrR**

Upon Crab. Robert Herrick. **CP-HerrR**

Upon Craw. Robert Herrick. **CP-HerrR**

Upon Croot. Robert Herrick. **CP-HerrR**

Upon Cuffe. Epig. Robert Herrick. **CP-HerrR**

Upon Cupid ("As lately I a Garland bound"). Robert Herrick. **CP-HerrR**

Upon Cupid ("Love, like a beggar, came to me"). Robert Herrick. **CP-HerrR**

Upon Cupid ("Love, like a Gypsie, lately come"). Robert Herrick. **CP-HerrR**

Upon Cupid ("Old wives have often told, how they"). Robert Herrick. **CP-HerrR**

Upon Cuts. Robert Herrick. **CP-HerrR**

Upon Deb. Robert Herrick. **CP-HerrR**

Upon Dol. Robert Herrick. **CP-HerrR**

Upon Doll. Robert Herrick. **CP-HerrR**

Upon Dundrige. Robert Herrick. **CP-HerrR**

Upon Eeles. Robert Herrick. **CP-HerrR**

Upon Electra. Robert Herrick. **CP-HerrR**

Upon Electra's Teares. Robert Herrick. **CP-HerrR**

Upon Faunus. Robert Herrick. **CP-HerrR**

Upon First Reading the Immortal Literature of the World—. Charles Bukowski. **SP-BukC3**

Upon Flimsey: Epigram. Robert Herrick. **CP-HerrR**

Upon Flood, Or a Thankfull Man. Robert Herrick. **CP-HerrR**

Upon Fone a School-master. Epigram. Robert Herrick. **CP-HerrR**

Upon Ford's Two Tragedies, "Loves Sacrifice" and "The Broken Heart." Richard Crashaw. **CP-CrasR**

Upon Four Dismal Stories in the Doctor's Letter. Jonathan Swift. **CP-SwifJ**

Upon Franck: ("Franck wo'd go scoure her teeth; and setting to't"). Robert Herrick. **CP-HerrR**

Upon Franck. Robert Herrick. **CP-HerrR**

Upon Gander. Robert Herrick. **CP-HerrR**

Upon Glasco. Epig. Robert Herrick. **CP-HerrR**

Upon Glass: Epigram. Robert Herrick. **CP-HerrR**

Upon God ("God is all fore-part; for, we never see"). Robert Herrick. **CP-HerrR**

Upon God ("God is not only said to be"). Robert Herrick. **CP-HerrR**

Upon God ("God when He takes my goods and chattels hence"). Robert Herrick. **CP-HerrR**

Upon Gorgonius. Robert Herrick. **CP-HerrR**

Upon Greedy. Robert Herrick. **CP-HerrR**

Upon Groynes. Robert Herrick. **CP-HerrR**

Upon Grubs. Robert Herrick. **CP-HerrR**

Upon Grudgings. Robert Herrick. **CP-HerrR**

Upon Gryll. Robert Herrick. **CP-HerrR**

Upon Gubbs. Robert Herrick. **CP-HerrR**

Upon Guesse. Robert Herrick. **CP-HerrR**

Upon Gut. Robert Herrick. **CP-HerrR**

Upon Hanch a Schoolmaster. Robert Herrick. **CP-HerrR**

Upon Happiness. James Thomson. **CP-ThomD**

Upon Her Almes. Robert Herrick. **CP-HerrR**

Upon Her Blush. Robert Herrick. **CP-HerrR**

Upon her breast her hands and hair. Caught in a Net. Nicholas Vachel Lindsay. **CP-LindV**

Upon her cheekes she wept, and from those showers. Upon Electra's Teares. Robert Herrick. **CP-HerrR**

Upon Her Eyes. Robert Herrick. **CP-HerrR**

Upon Her Feet. Robert Herrick. **CP-HerrR**

Upon her plodding palfrey. Ballad of a Wilful Woman. David Herbert Lawrence. **CP-LawrD**

Upon her soothing breast. Emily Brontë. **CP-BronE**

Upon Her Voice. Robert Herrick. **CP-HerrR**

Upon Her Weeping. Robert Herrick. **CP-HerrR**

Upon Himself ("Mop-eyed I am, as some have said"). Robert Herrick. **CP-HerrR**

Upon Himself: ("I dislikt but even now"). Robert Herrick. **CP-HerrR**

Upon Himself: ("Th'art hence removing, (like a Shepherds Tents)"). Robert Herrick. **CP-HerrR**

Upon Himself: ("Thou shalt not All die"). Robert Herrick. **CP-HerrR**

Upon Himselfe ("I lately fri'd, but now behold"). Robert Herrick. **CP-HerrR**

Upon Himselfe ("I am Sive-like, and can hold"). Robert Herrick. **CP-HerrR**

Upon Himselfe ("I co'd never love indeed"). Robert Herrick. **CP-HerrR**

Upon Himselfe Being Buried. Robert Herrick. **CP-HerrR**

Upon Himself ("Come, leave this loathed Country-life, and then"). Robert Herrick. **CP-HerrR**

Upon His Departure Hence. Robert Herrick. **CP-HerrR**

Upon His Eye-Sight Failing Him. Robert Herrick. **CP-HerrR**

Upon His Gray Haires. Robert Herrick. **CP-HerrR**

Upon His Julia. Robert Herrick. **CP-HerrR**

Upon his Kinswoman Mrs. M. S. Robert Herrick. **CP-HerrR**

Upon His Kinswoman Mistresse Bridget Herrick. Robert Herrick. **CP-HerrR**

Upon His Kinswoman Mistris Elizabeth Herrick. Robert Herrick. **CP-HerrR**

Upon his Saddle sprung a Bird. Emily Dickinson. **CP-DickE**

Upon His Sister-in-Law, Mistress Elizabeth Herrick. Robert Herrick. **CP-HerrR**

Upon His Spaniel[l] Tracie [or Tracy]. Robert Herrick. **CP-HerrR**

Upon His Verses. Robert Herrick. **CP-HerrR**

Upon Hog. Robert Herrick. **CP-HerrR**

Upon Horne. Robert Herrick. **CP-HerrR**

Upon Huncks: Epigram. Robert Herrick. **CP-HerrR**

Upon Irene. Robert Herrick. **CP-HerrR**

Upon Jack and Jill: Epigram. Robert Herrick. **CP-HerrR**

Upon Jollies Wife. Robert Herrick. **CP-HerrR**

Upon Jolly and Jilly. Robert Herrick. **CP-HerrR**

Upon Jone and Jane. Robert Herrick. **CP-HerrR**

Upon Judith. Robert Herrick. **CP-HerrR**

Upon Julia['s] Washing Herself in the River. Robert Herrick. **CP-HerrR**

Upon Julia's Breasts. Robert Herrick. **CP-HerrR**

Upon Julia's Clothes. Robert Herrick. **CP-HerrR**

Upon Julia's Fall. Robert Herrick. **CP-HerrR**

Upon Julia's Haire, Bundled up in a Golden Net. Robert Herrick. **CP-HerrR**

Upon Julia's Haire Fill'd with Dew. Robert Herrick. See Dew Sat on Julia's Hair.

Upon Julia's Recovery. Robert Herrick. **CP-HerrR**

Upon Julia's Ribband. Robert Herrick. **CP-HerrR**

Upon Julia's Sweat. Robert Herrick. **CP-HerrR**

Upon Julia's Unlacing Her Self. Robert Herrick. **CP-HerrR**

Upon Julia's Voice. Robert Herrick. **CP-HerrR**

Upon Kings. Robert Herrick. **CP-HerrR**

Upon Lazarus His Teares. Richard Crashaw. **CP-CrasR**

Upon Learning That a Bird Exists Called the Turnstone. John Updike. **CP-UpdiJ**

Upon Learning That a Town Exists in Virginia Called Upperville. John Updike. **CP-UpdiJ**

Upon Leech. Robert Herrick. **CP-HerrR**

Upon Letcher: Epigram. Robert Herrick. **CP-HerrR**

Upon Linnit. Robert Herrick. **CP-HerrR**

Upon L.M. Weeping. Sir John Suckling. **CP-SuckJ**

Upon Loach. Robert Herrick. **CP-HerrR**

Upon Looking into Sylvia Plath's *Letters Home*. John Updike. **CP-UpdiJ**

Upon Love ("Christall Violl Cupid brought, A"). Robert Herrick. **CP-HerrR**

Upon Love ("I held Love's head while it did ake"). Robert Herrick. **CP-HerrR**

Upon Love ("In a Dreame, Love bad me go"). Robert Herrick. **CP-HerrR**

Upon Love ("Love is a circle"). Robert Herrick. **CP-HerrR**

Upon Love ("Love, I have broke"). Robert Herrick. **CP-HerrR**

Upon Love ("Some salve to every sore, we may apply"). Robert Herrick. **CP-HerrR**

Upon Love: ("I plaid with Love, as with the fire"). Robert Herrick. **CP-HerrR**

Upon Love: ("Love scorch'd my finger, but did spare"). Robert Herrick. **CP-HerrR**

Upon Love: ("Love's a thing, (as I do heare)"). Robert Herrick. **CP-HerrR**

Upon Love, by Way of Question and Answer. Robert Herrick. **CP-HerrR**

Upon Love ("Love brought me to a silent Grove"). Robert Herrick. **CP-HerrR**

Upon Lucia. Robert Herrick. **CP-HerrR**

Upon Lucia Dabled in the Deaw. Robert Herrick. **CP-HerrR**

Upon Lucie. Robert Herrick. **CP-HerrR**

Upon Luggs. Robert Herrick. **CP-HerrR**

Upon Lulls. Robert Herrick. **CP-HerrR**

Upon Lungs. Robert Herrick. **CP-HerrR**

Upon Lupes. Robert Herrick. **CP-HerrR**

Upon Luske. Robert Herrick. **CP-HerrR**

Upon Madam Ursly. Robert Herrick. **CP-HerrR**

Upon Magot a Frequenter of Ordinaries. Robert Herrick. **CP-HerrR**

Upon Man. Robert Herrick. **CP-HerrR**

Upon M. Ben Jo[h]nson: Epigram. Robert Herrick. **CP-HerrR**

Upon Master Fletchers Incomparable Playes. Robert Herrick. **CP-HerrR**

Upon Master W. Montague, His Return from Travel. Thomas Carew. *See* Lead the black bull to slaughter, with the boar.

Upon M. William Lawes, the Rare Musitian. Robert Herrick. **CP-HerrR**

Upon Mease. Robert Herrick. **CP-HerrR**

Upon Meeting Don L. Lee, in a Dream. Rita Dove. **SP-DoveR**

Upon Megg. Robert Herrick. **CP-HerrR**

Upon Mr. Thomas Coryat's Crudities. John Donne. *Fr.* Satires. **CP-DonnJ**

Upon Mrs. Anne Bradstreet, Her Poems, Etc. John Rogers. **CP-BradA**

Upon Mistress Elizabeth Wheeler under the Name of Amarillis. Robert Herrick. **CP-HerrR**

Upon Mistresse Susanna Southwell, Her Cheeks. Robert Herrick. **CP-HerrR**

Upon Much-More. Robert Herrick. **CP-HerrR**

Upon Mudge. Robert Herrick. **CP-HerrR**

Upon mutability—if it were possible. But you don't. Ovid, Old Buddy, I Would Discourse with You a While. Hayden Carruth. **CP-CarHS**

Upon My Daughter Hannah Wiggin her Recovery from a Dangerous Fever. Anne Bradstreet. **CP-BradA**

Upon My Dear and Loving Husband His Going into England. Anne Bradstreet. **CP-BradA**

Upon My Lady Carlisle's Walking in Hampton Court Garden. Sir John Suckling. **CP-SuckJ**

Upon My Life, Sir Nevis, I Am Piqued. John Keats. **CP-KeatJ**

Upon My Lord Brohall's Wedding. Sir John Suckling. **CP-SuckJ**

Upon My Lord Chief Justice's Election of My Lady Anne Wentworth [*or* A.W.] for His Mistress. Thomas Carew. **CP-CareT**

Upon My Son Samuel His Going For England. Anne Bradstreet. **CP-BradA**

Upon my throat your kisses blur their man. Meditation of My Lady of Sorrows. Kenneth Patchen. **CP-PatcK**

Upon Nis. Robert Herrick. **CP-HerrR**

Upon Nodes. Robert Herrick. **CP-HerrR**

Upon One-Ey'd Broomsted. Robert Herrick. **CP-HerrR**

Upon One Lillie, Who Marryed with a Maid Call'd Rose. Robert Herrick. **CP-HerrR**

Upon One Who Said She Was Alwayes Young. Robert Herrick. **CP-HerrR**

Upon Our Saviour's Tomb[e] Wherein Never Man Was Laid. Richard Crashaw. *See* How life and death in Thee.

Upon Pagget. Robert Herrick. **CP-HerrR**

Upon Parrat. Robert Herrick. **CP-HerrR**

Upon Parson Beanes. Robert Herrick. **CP-HerrR**

Upon Parting. Robert Herrick. **CP-HerrR**

Upon Paske a Draper. Robert Herrick. **CP-HerrR**

Upon Patrick a Footman. Robert Herrick. **CP-HerrR**

Upon Paul. Robert Herrick. **CP-HerrR**

Upon Pearch. Robert Herrick. **CP-HerrR**

Upon Peason. Robert Herrick. **CP-HerrR**

Upon Pennie. Robert Herrick. **CP-HerrR**

Upon Perusing the "Epistle [To Sir George Howland Beaumont]" Thirty Years after Its Composition. William Wordsworth. **CP-WorW2**

Upon Pievish. Robert Herrick. **CP-HerrR**

Upon Pimpe. Robert Herrick. **CP-HerrR**

Upon Pink an Ill-Fac'd Painter. Robert Herrick. **CP-HerrR**

Upon Prickles. Robert Herrick. **CP-HerrR**

Upon Prig ("Prig now drinks Water, who before drank Beere"). Robert Herrick. **CP-HerrR**

Upon Prigg ("Prigg, when he comes to houses, oft doth use"). Robert Herrick. **CP-HerrR**

Upon Prudence Baldwin Her Sickness[e]. Robert Herrick. **CP-HerrR**

Upon Prue [*or* Prew], His Maid. Robert Herrick. **CP-HerrR**

Upon Punchin. Robert Herrick. **CP-HerrR**

Upon Pusse and her Prentice. Robert Herrick. **CP-HerrR**

Upon Ralph ("Ralph pares his nayles"). Robert Herrick. **CP-HerrR**

Upon Ralph. Robert Herrick. **CP-HerrR**

Upon Raspe. Robert Herrick. **CP-HerrR**

Upon Reape. Robert Herrick. **CP-HerrR**

Upon Reflection. Lawrence Ferlinghetti. **SP-FerlL**

Upon Rook: Epigram. Robert Herrick. **CP-HerrR**

Upon Roots. Robert Herrick. **CP-HerrR**

Upon Roses. Robert Herrick. **CP-HerrR**

Upon Rumpe. Robert Herrick. **CP-HerrR**

Upon Rush. Robert Herrick. **CP-HerrR**

Upon Sapho. Robert Herrick. **CP-HerrR**

Upon Sapho, Sweetly Playing, and Sweetly Singing. Robert Herrick. **CP-HerrR**

Upon Scobble [Epigram]. Robert Herrick. **CP-HerrR**

Upon seeing a Coloured Drawing of the Bird of Paradise in an Album. William Wordsworth. **CP-WorW2**

Upon Shark. Robert Herrick. **CP-HerrR**

Upon Shaving Off One's Beard. John Updike. **CP-UpdiJ**

Upon Shift. Robert Herrick. **CP-HerrR**

Upon Shopter. Robert Herrick. **CP-HerrR**

Upon Showbread [*or* Shewbread]: Epigram. Robert Herrick. **CP-HerrR**

Upon Sibb. Robert Herrick. **CP-HerrR**

Upon Sibilla. Robert Herrick. **CP-HerrR**

Upon Silvia, a Mistresse. Robert Herrick. **CP-HerrR**

Upon Sir John Lawrence's Bringing Water over the Hills [to My L. Middlesex His House at Witten]. Sir John Suckling. **CP-SuckJ**

Upon Skinns. Robert Herrick. **CP-HerrR**

Upon Skoles. Robert Herrick. **CP-HerrR**

Upon Skrew. Robert Herrick. **CP-HerrR**

Upon Skurffe. Robert Herrick. **CP-HerrR**

Upon Slouch. Robert Herrick. **CP-HerrR**

Upon Smeaton. Robert Herrick. **CP-HerrR**

Upon Snare, an Usurer. Robert Herrick. **CP-HerrR**

Upon Sneape. Robert Herrick. **CP-HerrR**

Upon Some Alterations in My Mistress, after My Departure into France. Thomas Carew. **CP-CareT**

Upon Some Distemper of Body. Anne Bradstreet. **CP-BradA**

Upon Some Women. Robert Herrick. **CP-HerrR**

Upon Spalt. Robert Herrick. **CP-HerrR**

Upon Spenke. Robert Herrick. **CP-HerrR**

Upon Spokes. Robert Herrick. **CP-HerrR**

Upon Spunge. Robert Herrick. **CP-HerrR**

Upon Spur. Robert Herrick. **CP-HerrR**

Upon Strut. Robert Herrick. **CP-HerrR**

Upon Sudds, a Laundress[e]. Robert Herrick. **CP-HerrR**

Upon Taking Hold. Robert Duncan. **SP-DuncR**

Upon Tap. Robert Herrick. **CP-HerrR**

Upon T.C. Having the Pox. Sir John Suckling. **CP-SuckJ**

Upon Teage. Robert Herrick. **CP-HerrR**

Upon Teares. Robert Herrick. **CP-HerrR**

Upon that night, when fairies light. Halloween. Robert Burns. **CP-BurnR**

Upon the Annunciation and Passion Falling upon One Day. 1608. John Donne. **CP-DonnJ**

Upon the Asse That Bore Our Saviour. Richard Crashaw. **CP-CrasR**

Upon the Author. *Unknown, poem signed* "C. B." **CP-BradA**

Upon the Author. By a Known Friend. Benjamin Woodbridge. **CP-BradA**

Upon the birth of the Princesse Elizabeth. Richard Crashaw. **CP-CrasR**

Upon the Bishop of Lincolne's Imprisonment. Robert Herrick. **CP-HerrR**

Upon the Black Spots Worn, by My Lady D.E. Sir John Suckling. **CP-SuckJ**

Upon the Book and Picture of the Seraphical Saint Teresa. Richard Crashaw. *See* O thou undaunted daughter of desires!

Upon the Circumcision. John Milton. **CP-MiltJ**

Upon the Curtain[e] of Lucasta's Picture [It Was Thus Wrought]. Richard Lovelace. **CP-LoveR**

Upon the dead grass. March Is a Light. William Carlos Williams. **CP-WilW1**

Upon the Death of a Freind. Richard Crashaw. **CP-CrasR**

Upon the Death of a Gentleman. Richard Crashaw. **CP-CrasR**

Upon the Death of His Sparrow; an Elegie. Robert Herrick. **CP-HerrR**

Upon the Death of Mister Herrys. Richard Crashaw. **CP-CrasR**

Upon the Death of the Lord Hastings. Andrew Marvell. **CP-MarvA**

Upon the Death of the Most Desired Mister Herrys. Richard Crashaw. **CP-CrasR**

Upon the decks they take beef tea. Passage Steamer. Louis MacNeice. **CP-MacNL**

Upon the Duke of *Yorke* his Birth a Panegyricke. Richard Crashaw. **CP-CrasR**

Upon the Eastern Shore of Windermere. On Windermere; Bowness Bay and Belle Isle. William Wordsworth. **FaBoPP** *Fr.* School-Time. *Fr.* The Prelude; Growth of a Poet's Mind [1805 vers.]. **CP-WorW3**

Upon the Ensuing Treatises [of Mr. Shelford]. Richard Crashaw. **CP-CrasR**

Upon the Faire Ethiopian Sent to a Gentlewoman. Richard Crashaw. **CP-CrasR**

Upon the fallen. In the 'Sconset Bus. William Carlos Williams. **CP-WilW1**

Upon the Feast of St Simon and St Jude. Samuel Johnson. **CP-JohnS**

Upon the First Sight of My Lady Seymour. Sir John Suckling. **CP-SuckJ**

Upon the gallows hung a wretch. Emily Dickinson. **CP-DickE**

Upon the Gunpowder Treason ("Grow plumpe, leane Death"). Richard Crashaw. **CP-CrasR**

Upon the Gunpowder Treason ("Reach me a quill"). Richard Crashaw. **CP-CrasR**

Upon the Hill and Grove at Bilbrough. Andrew Marvell. **CP-MarvA**

Upon the Horrid Plot Discovered by Harlequin the Bishop of Rochester's French Dog. Jonathan Swift. **CP-SwifJ**

Upon the Image of Death. Robert Southwell. **CP-SoutR**

"Before my face the picture hangs." **NoSic; OBD**

Upon the Infant Martyrs. Richard Crashaw. **CP-CrasR**

Upon the Kings Coronation ("Sound forth, cælestiall Organs, lett heavens quire"). Richard Crashaw. **CP-CrasR**

Upon the Kings Coronation ("Strange Metamorphosis! It was but now"). Richard Crashaw. **CP-CrasR**

Upon the King's Sickness. Thomas Carew. **CP-CareT**

Upon the Lady Crew. Robert Herrick. **CP-HerrR**

Upon the Last Day of His Forty-Ninth Year. John Updike. **CP-UpdiJ**

Upon the Late General Fast. March, 1832. William Wordsworth. **CP-WorW2**

Upon the Lonely Moor. "Lewis Carroll." **CP-CarrL**

Upon the Losse of His Finger. Robert Herrick. **CP-HerrR**

Upon the Loss[e] of His Mistresses. Robert Herrick. **CP-HerrR**

Upon the mountain of the young. I Heard a Hermit Speak. Adrienne Rich. **CP-RicAE**

Upon the mountain's Edge all lightly resting. Samuel Taylor Coleridge. *See* A Sunset.

Upon the Much Lamented, Mr. J. Warr. Robert Herrick. **CP-HerrR**

Upon the Nipples of Julia's Breast. Robert Herrick. **CP-HerrR**

Upon the Posthume and Precious Poems of the Nobly Extracted Gentleman Mr. R.L. James Howell. *Fr.* Elegies, 1660. **CP-LoveR**

Upon the Powder Day. Richard Crashaw. **CP-CrasR**

Upon the rivers of Babylon, there we sat and wept. Bible, *O.T. See* Psalm 137: "By the rivers of Babylon. . . ."

Upon the room's / silence,i will sew. Edward Estlin Cummings. **CP-CummE**

Upon the Roses in Julia's Bosome. Robert Herrick. **CP-HerrR**

Upon the Same. Ausonius, *tr. fr. Latin by* Richard Crashaw. **CP-CrasR**

Upon the Same. Robert Herrick. **CP-HerrR**

Upon the Same Event, *see also* On a Celebrated Event in Ancient History. William Wordsworth. **CP-WorW1**

Upon the Sepulchre of our Lord. Richard Crashaw. **CP-CrasR**

Upon the Sickness of E.S. Thomas Carew. **CP-CareT**

Upon the Sight of a Beautiful Picture. William Wordsworth. **CP-WorW1**

Upon the Sight of the Portrait of a Female Friend. William Wordsworth. **CP-WorW2**

Upon the South Sea Project. Jonathan Swift. **CP-SwifJ**

Upon the table in their bowl. The Disputants. William Carlos Williams. **CP-WilW1**

Upon the Thornes Taken Downe from Our Lords Head Bloody. Richard Crashaw. **CP-CrasR**

Upon the Translation of the Psalms by Sir Philip Sidney, and the Countess of Pembroke His Sister. John Donne. **CP-DonnJ**

Upon the Troublesome Times. Robert Herrick. **CP-HerrR**

Upon the wall a face. Projected Slide of an Unknown Soldier. Margaret Atwood. **SP-AtwMI**

Upon the water in the boat. Arthur Hugh Clough. **SP-ClouA**

Upon this age, that never speaks its mind. Edna St. Vincent Millay. **CP-MillE**

Upon This Beach. Louis MacNeice. **CP-MacNL**

Upon this leafy bush. The Linnet. Walter de la Mare. **CP-DeLaW**

Upon this line between adventure. Between Adventure. Wystan Hugh Auden. **CP-AudeW**

Upon this marble bust that is not I. To Inez Milholland. Edna St. Vincent Millay. **CP-MillE**

Upon this primrose hill. The Primrose[, Being at Montgomery Castle, upon the Hill, on Which It Is Situate]. John Donne. **CP-DonnJ**

Upon this scene, this show. Red Jacket (from Aloft). Walt Whitman. **CP-WhitW**

Upon those lips, those placid lips, I look. Upon the Sight of the Portrait of a Female Friend. William Wordsworth. **CP-WorW2**

Upon Time. Robert Herrick. **CP-HerrR**

Upon Tooly. Robert Herrick. **CP-HerrR**

Upon Trap. Robert Herrick. **CP-HerrR**

Upon Trencherman. Robert Herrick. **CP-HerrR**

Upon Trigg. Robert Herrick. **CP-HerrR**

Upon Truggin. Robert Herrick. **CP-HerrR**

Upon Tubbs. Robert Herrick. **CP-HerrR**

Upon Tuck. Robert Herrick. **CP-HerrR**

Upon Two Greene Apricockes Sent to Cowley by Sir Crashaw. Richard Crashaw. **CP-CrasR**

Upon Two Sisters. Sir John Suckling. **CP-SuckJ**

Upon Umber: Epigram. Robert Herrick. **CP-HerrR**

Upon Urles. Robert Herrick. **CP-HerrR**

Upon Ursley. Robert Herrick. **CP-HerrR**

Upon Venus Putting on Mars His Armes. Leonidas of Alexandria, *tr. fr. Classical Greek by* Richard Crashaw. **CP-CrasR**

Upon Vinegar. Robert Herrick. **CP-HerrR**

Upon waking a nerve complains in the. A Fortification. Margaret Atwood. **SP-AtwM1**

Upon Woman and Mary. Robert Herrick. **CP-HerrR**

Upon Wrinkles. Robert Herrick. **CP-HerrR**

Upon Your Leaving. Etheridge Knight. **SP-KnigE**

Upon Zelot. Robert Herrick. **CP-HerrR**

Upper Birch-Leaves, The. Thomas Hardy. **CP-HardT**

Upper Broadway. Adrienne Rich. **SP-RicA2**

Upper corner—probably, The. Roy Fisher. **SP-FishR** *Fr.* Mystery Poems.

Upper Lambourne. Sir John Betjeman. **CP-BetjJ**

Upper slopes are busy with the cricket. Elegy on the Dust. Thom Gunn. **NoAM** *Fr.* Misanthropos. **CP-GunnT**

Upper Voight's, to All the Cutthroat There. Richard Hugo. **CP-HugoR**

Uprising. Stephen Dobyns. **SP-DobyS**

Uproot that burning tree of lightning struck veins. A Few Ashes for Sunday Morning. Marge Piercy. **SP-PierM**

Uprooted, The. David Herbert Lawrence. **CP-LawrD**

Uprose the King of Men with speed. The Descent of Odin. Thomas Gray. **CP-GrayT**

Uprose, uprose, the stony fields uprose. The Tree, the Bird. Theodore Roethke. **CP-RoetT**

Upshore from the cloud. By a Lake in Minnesota. James Wright. **CP-WrigJ**

Upshot, The. Archie Randolph Ammons. **SP-AmmoA**

Upstairs. Carl Sandburg. **CP-SandC**

Upstairs. Shel Silverstein. **SP-SilS2**

Upstairs there is a bed. The House. Lewis Turco. **SP-TurcL**

Upstairs to my downstairs. All the While. John Updike. *Fr.* Living with a Wife. **CP-UpdiJ**

Upstate. Derek Walcott. **CP-WalcD**

Upstream. Carl Sandburg. **CP-SandC**

Uptown. Allen Ginsberg. **CP-GinsA**

Upward into the dome of brilliance, limping. Ignis. Hayden Carruth. *Fr.* Journey to a Known Place. **CP-CarHL**

Upward Moon and the Downward Moon, The. Robert Bly. **SP-BlyR**

Upward through the dark, this. Hayden Carruth. *Fr.* The Sleeping Beauty. **CP-CarHL**

Ur Burial. Richard Eberhart. **CP-EberR**

Urania, *see also* Pamphilia to Amphilanthus. Mary Sidney, Countess of Montgomery Wroth. **CP-WrotM**

Part 1.

"Adieu sweet Sun."

"As these drops fall: so Hope drops now on me."

"Beare part with me most straight and pleasant Tree."

("Bear part with me most straight and pleasant tree.") **WPE**

(Morea's Sonnet.) **WPE**

"Blame me not dearest, though grieved for your sake."

"Cruell Remembrance alas now be still."

"Deare Love, alas, how have I wronged thee."

"Deare, though unconstant, these I send to you."

Dialogue: Sheapherd, and Sheapherdess.

"Did I boast of liberty?"

"Drowne not in your cruell teares."

"*Egypts* Pyramids inclose their Kings."

"Faithfull lovers keepe from hence."

"Fond aged man, why doe you on me gaze."

"From a long way, and Pilgrimage for Love."

"From victory in love I now am come."

"Have I lost my liberty."

"Heart drops distilling like a new cut-vine."

"Here all alone in silence might I mourne."

"How doe ·I find my soules extreamest anguish."

"I, who doe feele the highest part of griefe."

"If a clear [*or* cleere] fountain[e] still keeping a sad course." **WPE**

(Duke's Song, The.) **WPE**

"Infernall Spirits listen to my moanes."

"Joy you say the Heavens in motion trie, The."

Lindamira's Complaint.

Sonnet: "O Memory [*or* Memorie], could I but loose thee now." **BWW; WPE**

("Leave me vaine Hope, too long thou hast possesst.") **BWW**

Sonnet 1: "Deare eyes farewell, my Sunne once, now my end."

Sonnet 2: "O deadly rancour to a constant heart."

Sonnet 3: "Surgeon I would aske, but 'tis too late."

Sonnet 5: "Leave me vain Hope, too long thou hast posses[s]t." **BWW**

Sonnet 6: "Though you forsake me, yet alas permit."

Sonnet 7: "Some doe, perhaps, both wrong my love, and care."

"Loss[e] my molester at last patient be." **WPE**

(Pamphilia's Sonnet.) **WPE**

"Love among the clouds did hover."

"Love farewell I now discover."

"Love growne proud with victory."

"Love peruse me, seeke, and finde."

"My thoughts thou hast supported without rest."

"O! that I might but now as senceles bee."

"Pray thee *Diana* tell mee, is it ill."

"Rise, rise from sluggishness, fly fast my Deere."

"Sheapherd who noe care did take, A."

Song: "Gon is my joy while heere I mourne."

Song: "Love what art thou? A vaine thought."

Song: "Who can blame mee if I love?"

Sonnet: "Unquiet griefe search farder, in my hart."

"Stay mine eyes, these floods of teares."

"Sunne hath no long journey now to goe, The."

"Sweete solitarines, joy to those hearts."

"Teares some times flow from mirth, as well as sorrow."

"That which to some their wishes ends present."

"This no wonder's of much waight."

"Unseene, unknowne, I here alone complaine."

"When I with trembling aske if you love still."

"Why doe you so much wish for raine, when I."

"You powers divine of love-commanding eyes."

"You pure and holy fire."

"You, who ending never saw."

Part 2.

"Beehold this sacred fire."

"Come deere, lett's waulke into this spring."

"Come lusty gamesters of the sea."

"Fierce love, alas yett lett mee rest."

"Had I loved butt att that rate."

"Honor now injoye the day."

"Love butt a phantesie light, and vaine."

"Love lett mee live, ore lett mee dye."

"Lying upon the beach."

"Most deere, more hapy soverainsing harts."

"Most hapy memory bee ever blest."

"Returne my thoughts, why fly you soe?"

"Stay holy fires."

"This is Honor's holly day."

"This night the Moone eclipsed was."

"Was I to blame to trust."

"Were ever eyes of such devinitie."

"Why doe you thus torment my poorest hart?"

Urania speaks with darkened brow. Tennyson. **OAEL-2** *Fr.* In Memoriam A. H. H. **CP-TennA**

Uranus. Arthur Hugh Clough. **SP-ClouA**

Urashima, the fisher boy, was abroad on the sea. The Third Version. Hayden Carruth. *Fr.* The Mythology of Dark and Light. **CP-CarHL**

Urban Convalescence, An. James Merrill. **SP-MerrJ**

Urban Hunting Scenes. Dabney Stuart. **SP-StuaD**

Urban Renewal. Ron Koertge. **SP-KoerR**

Urchin, The. Robinson Jeffers. **CP-JefR3**

Urged by Ambition, who with subtlest skill. Influence Abused. William Wordsworth. *Fr.* Ecclesiastical Sonnets. **CP-WorW2**

Urged by your needs and my desire. Trial of Innocence. Robert Ranke Graves. **CP-GravR**

Urgencies. Stephen Dunn. **SP-DunnS**

Urgent letter that I try to write, The. Night Letter. Stanley Jasspon Kunitz. **CP-KuniS**

Urging Her of a Promise. Ben Jonson. *Fr.* A Celebration of Charis in Ten Lyric[k] Pieces [*or* Peeces]. **CP-JonsB**

Uriel. Ralph Waldo Emerson. **CP-EmerR**

Uriel to his charge. Now Came Still Evening On. John Milton. **FaBoRV** *Fr.* Book IV. **OAEL-1** *Fr.* Paradise Lost. **CP-MiltJ**

Urizen's Curse upon His Children. William Blake. **TW** *Fr.* Vala; or The Four Zoas. **CP-BlakW**

Urles had the Gout so, that he co'd not stand. Upon Urles. Robert Herrick. **CP-HerrR**

Urlicht. Charles Tomlinson. **CP-TomlC**

Urn with a Political Profile. Pablo Antonio Cuadra, *tr. fr. Spanish by* Thomas Merton. **CP-MertT**

Ursley, she thinks those Velvet Patches grace. Upon Ursley. Robert Herrick. **CP-HerrR**

Ursula, in a garden, found / A bed of radishes. Cy Est Pourtraicte, Madame Ste Ursule, et Les Unze Mille Vierges. Wallace Stevens. **CP-StevW**

Us. Anne Sexton. **CP-SextA**

Us. Shel Silverstein. **SP-SilS2**

Us. Stephen Spender. **CP-SpenS**

Us if therefore must forget ourselves. Edward Estlin Cummings. **CP-CummE**

USA slowly lost its mandate, The. Tomorrow's Song. Gary Snyder. **CP-SnydG**

Use of Books, The. Thomas McGrath. **SP-McGrT**

Use will in man new grace reveal. Ralph Waldo Emerson. **CP-EmerR**

Use your numbered line / To describe constellations. Solemn Music. Thomas Merton. *Fr.* Cables to the Ace. **CP-MertT**

"Used Handkerchiefs 5[dc]." James Schuyler. **CP-SchuJ**

Used to climb trees that were. He. Ron Koertge. **SP-KoerR**

Used to do most everything himself. He. Ron Koertge. **SP-KoerR**

Used to identify with my father first making me want to be a. The Problem of Identity. Al Young. **CP-YounA**

Used to stumble, go down, bounce. Tanck's Song About Fear of Falling. Hayden Carruth. **CP-CarHS** *Fr.* Songs About What Comes Down: The Complete Works of Mr. Septic Tanck.

Used Up. Thomas McGrath. **SP-McGrT**

Useless, The. Chuang Tzu, *tr. fr. Chinese by* Thomas Merton. **CP-MertT**

Useless Tree, The. Chuang Tzu, *tr. fr. Chinese by* Thomas Merton. **CP-MertT**

Useless Words. Carl Sandburg. **CP-SandC**

Uses. Anne Sexton. **CP-SextA**

Uses of Poetry. Lawrence Ferlinghetti. **SP-FerlL**

Uses of Poetry, The. William Carlos Williams. **CP-WilW1**

Uses of the Lost Poets. Thomas McGrath. **SP-McGrT**

Usk. Thomas Stearns Eliot. **FaBoCh; NOCV; PeECV** *Fr.* Landscapes. **CP-ElioT**

Usual hazards seem to be worse this fall, The. Santana. Laurence Lieberman. **SP-LiebL**

Usual Prayer, A. John Berryman. **CP-BerrJ**

Usurers of Heaven, The. William Carlos Williams. **CP-WilW2**

Usurper. Richard Eberhart. **CP-EberR**

Ut Queant. Paul the Deacon, *tr. fr. Latin by* Thomas Merton. **CP-MertT**

Ut Quid Iubes, Pusiole. Godeschalk. *Fr.* Four Medieval Latin Poems. **CP-MacNL**

Ute Mountain. Charles Tomlinson. **CP-TomlC**

Utensil. Archie Randolph Ammons. **SP-AmmoA**

Utilitarian View of the Monitor's Fight, A. Herman Melville. **SP-MelvH**

Utopian Journey, A. Randall Jarrell. **CP-JarrR**

Utter indifference to your welfare, Caesar. Carmen 93. Catullus. *Fr.* Carmina. **CP-Catul**

Utter Rim, The. Robert Ranke Graves. **CP-GravR**

Utter the song, O my soul! the flight and return of Mohammed. Mahomet. Samuel Taylor Coleridge. **CP-ColeS**

Utterance. John Greenleaf Whittier. **CP-WhitJ**

Uttered by whom, or how inspired—designed. On Approaching the Staub-Bach, Lauterbrunnen. William Wordsworth. *Fr.* Memorials of a Tour of the Continent; 1820. **CP-WorW2**

Uttering idle words from a reprobate mind. Dead Man, Dead Man. "Bob Dylan." **CP-DylaB**

Utterings. Donald Davie. **CP-DavDo**

Utterly and amusingly I am pash. Edward Estlin Cummings. **CP-CummE**

Uvedale, thou piece of the first times, a man. To Sir William Uvedale. Ben Jonson. **CP-JonsB**

Uxorem Crispinus habet; tamen indigus unam. *acc. by English translation.* Thomas Campion. **CP-CampT**

V

V. Stevie Smith. **CP-SmitS**

V. B. Nimble, V. B. Quick. John Updike. **CP-UpdiJ**

V. B. Wigglesworth wakes at noon. V. B. Nimble, V. B. Quick. John Updike. **CP-UpdiJ**

V—Is for Victory as You Can Plainly See. Marsden Hartley. **CP-HartM**

V-J Day. John Ciardi. **SP-CiarJ**

V-Letter. Karl Shapiro. **SP-ShapK**

Vacancy in the Park. Wallace Stevens. **CP-StevW**

Vacant Day, The. Walter de la Mare. **CP-DeLaW**

Vacant Lot, The. Gwendolyn Brooks. **NAAL-2; NOBA; NoAM** *Fr.* A Street in Bronzeville. **SP-BrooG**

Vacant lot has long been vacant, The. Anthropomorphism Reversed. Jenny Joseph. **SP-JoseJ**

Vacant lots are occupied, the woods, The. Shillington. John Updike. **CP-UpdiJ**

Vacant Possession, A. James Fenton. **SP-FentJ**

Vacant shuttles / Weave the wind. I have no ghosts. Thomas Stearns Eliot. **UV** *Fr.* Gerontion. **CP-ElioT**

Vacation. Jim Carroll. **SP-CarrJ**

Vacation Trip. William Stafford. **SP-StafW**

Vacation? Well, our children took our love apart. Any Time. William Stafford. **SP-StafW**

Vachel, the stars are out. To Lindsay. Allen Ginsberg. **CP-GinsA**

Vacillation. William Butler Yeats. **CP-YeatW**

"Must we part, Von Hügel, though much alike." **OBMV**

"My fiftieth year had come and gone." **RaBo**

Vacuum, The. Howard Nemerov. **CP-NemeH**

V.A.D. (Mediterranean). Rudyard Kipling. *Fr.* Epitaphs of the War [1914–1918]. **CP-KiplR**

Vagabond, The. Robert Louis Stevenson. **CP-StevR**

Vagabonds. Langston Hughes. **SP-HughL**

Vagg Hollow. Thomas Hardy. **CP-HardT**

Vagrant visitor erstwhile, The. Essex. Sir John Betjeman. **CP-BetjJ**

Vagrants. Paul Laurence Dunbar. **CP-DunbP**

Vagrant's Song. Thomas Hardy. **CP-HardT**

Vague clamor attendant upon fame, A. In Which There is Nothing Up the Sleeve. Gilbert Sorrentino. *Fr.* Twelve Études for Voice and Kazoo. **SP-SorrG**

Vague mist hanging 'round half the pages, A. Apparitions. Walt Whitman. **CP-WhitW**

Vague pearl, a wan pearl, A. Spells and Incantation (a Fragment). Wilfred Owen. **CP-OwenW**

Vague sea thuds against the marble cliffs, The. Time. Robert Ranke Graves. **CP-GravR**

Vaguely I hear the purple roar of the torn-down Third Avenue El. You Are Gorgeous and I'm Coming. Frank O'Hara. **SP-OharF**

Vaile, love, mine eyes, O hide from me. Thomas Campion. **CP-CampT**

Vaile thou thine eyes a while my Deare. The Eclipse. Robert Herrick. **CP-HerrR**

Vain against him were hostile blows. Ralph Waldo Emerson. **CP-EmerR**

Vain and Careless. Robert Ranke Graves. **CP-GravR**

Vain Bards! I can discover all. Song of Taliesin. Taliesin, Ralph Waldo Emerson's *ad. of English tr., fr. the Welsh of* Taliesin, *by* David William Nash. **CP-EmerR**

Vain Finding. Walter de la Mare. **CP-DeLaW**

Vain Gratuities. Edwin Arlington Robinson. **CP-RobiE**

Vain is the wish to try rhyming it, writing it! The History of an Hour. Thomas Hardy. **CP-HardT**

Vain man runs headlong, to caprice resign'd. Juvenal, *tr. by* Samuel Johnson. **CP-JohnS** *Fr.* Satires.

Vain Men, Whose Follies. Thomas Campion. **CP-CampT**

Vain Painter why dost strive my face to draw. Ausonius, *tr. fr. Latin by* Richard Lovelace. **CP-LoveR**

Vain, proud, rebellious Prince, thy treacherous hair. Absalom. Walter de la Mare. **CP-DeLaW**

Vain Questioning. Walter de la Mare. **CP-DeLaW**

Vain Shadow, A. Christina Georgina Rossetti. **CP-RosC2**

Vain surety of man's mind so near to death. Marlowe. Robert Lowell. **SP-LoweR**

Vaine men, whose follies make a God of Love. Vain Men, Whose Follies. Thomas Campion. **CP-CampT**

Vainly the Tyrian Purple bright. Boethius, *tr. by* Samuel Johnson. **CP-JohnS** *Fr.* Consolation of Philosophy, The ("De Consolacione Philosophie"). **CP-ChauG**

Vala, Night the Ninth Being the Last Judgment. William Blake. **OAEL-2** *Fr.* Vala; or The Four Zoas. **CP-BlakW**

Vala; or The Four Zoas. William Blake. **CP-BlakW**

Enion Replies from the Caverns of the Grave. **OBNC**

Enitharmon Revives with Los. **OBNC**

(Enitharmon's Song.) **ChTr**

It Is Not So with Me. **SeCePo**

Lamentation of Enion, The. **OBNC**

Night VIII (The Eternal Man). **PoE**

Price of Experience, The. **EnRP; Prf**

(Night II (Enion's Lament).) **PoE**

Song of Enitharmon. **OAEL-2**

Urizen's Curse upon His Children. **TW**

Vala, Night the Ninth Being the Last Judgment. **OAEL-2**

Vale of Esthwaite, The. William Wordsworth. **CP-WorW1**

Vale of Tear[e]s, A. Robert Southwell. **CP-SoutR**

Vale of the Merrimac, The. John Greenleaf Whittier. **CP-WhitJ**

Vale there is, enwrapped [or enwrapt] with dreadful[l] shades, A. A Vale of Tear[e]s. Robert Southwell. **CP-SoutR**

Valediction: "I Who Witnessed the Nail's Desire." Richard Shelton. **SP-ShelR**

Valediction ("Through the trembling blue. . ."). Alun Lewis. **CP-LewiA**

Valediction, A. William DeWitt Snodgrass. **SP-SnodW**

Valediction: "Their verdure dare not show. . . their verdure dare not show." Louis MacNeice. **CP-MacNL**

Valediction, A: "God be with thee, my beloved,—God be with thee!" Elizabeth Barrett Browning. **CP-BroEB**

Valediction, A: Forbidding Mourning. John Donne. **CP-DonnJ**

Valediction, A: Of My Name in the Window. John Donne. **CP-DonnJ**

Valediction, A: Of the Book. John Donne. **CP-DonnJ**

Valediction, A: Of Weeping. John Donne. **CP-DonnJ**

Valediction Forbidding Mourning, A. Adrienne Rich. **CP-RicAE; SP-RicA1; SP-RicA2**

Valediction Lines to My WEA Students. John Hewitt. **CP-HewiJ**

Valediction, The: "Farewell, false hearts! whose best affections fail." William Cowper. **CP-CowpW**

Valediction to the River Duddon. William Wordsworth. *See* I thought of Thee, my partner and my guide.

Valedictory Poem. Ralph Waldo Emerson. **CP-EmerR**

Valedictory Sonnet. William Wordsworth. **CP-WorW2**

Valedictory Sonnet to the River Duddon. William Wordsworth. *See* I thought of Thee, my partner and my guide.

Valenciennes. Thomas Hardy. **CP-HardT**

Valentine, A. "Lewis Carroll." **CP-CarrL**

Valentine. Hayden Carruth. **CP-CarHS**

Valentine. Ernest Hemingway. **CP-HemiE**

Valentine. Edna St. Vincent Millay. **CP-MillE**

Valentine, A. Edgar Allan Poe. **CP-PoeEd**

Valentine, A. Louis Zukofsky. **CP-ZukLS**

Valentine, 1882, A. Christina Georgina Rossetti. *See* My blessed mother dozing in her chair.

Valentine, 1877, A. Christina Georgina Rossetti. **CP-RosC3**

Valentine for Harry Crosby, A. Kay Boyle. **CP-BoylK**

Valentine Gift, A. Charles Bukowski. **SP-BukC3**

Valentines from C.G.R. Christina Georgina Rossetti. **CP-RosC3**

Valentine's Night. David Herbert Lawrence. **CP-LawrD**

Valiant Love. Richard Lovelace. **CP-LoveR**

Valle de Oaxaca. Charles Tomlinson. **CP-TomlC**

Vallejo writing about. What They Want. Charles Bukowski. **SP-BukC1**

Valley Candle. Wallace Stevens. **CP-StevW**

Valley holds its shadow, The. Wendell Berry. *Fr.* The Strait. **CP-BerrW**

Valley of Morning. Donald Hall. **CP-HallD**

Valley of the Black Pig, The. William Butler Yeats. **CP-YeatW**

Valley of the Shadow, The. Edwin Arlington Robinson. **CP-RobiE**

Valley of the Shadow of Death, The. "Lewis Carroll." **CP-CarrL**

Valley of the Shadow of Death, The. William Cowper. *Fr.* Olney Hymns. **CP-CowpW**

Valley of Unrest, The. Edgar Allan Poe. **CP-PoeEd**

Valley rings with mirth and joy, The. Idle Shepherd-Boys, The; or, Dungeon-Ghyll Force. A Pastoral. William Wordsworth. **CP-WorW1**

Valley-sleeper, the Children, the Snakes, and the Giant, The. Kenneth Patchen. **CP-PatcK**

Valley Song (Sunset Swept"). Carl Sandburg. **CP-SandC**

Valley Song ("Your eyes"). Carl Sandburg. **CP-SandC**

Valley was swept with a blue broom to the west, The. Santa Fe Sketches. Carl Sandburg. **CP-SandC**

Valley Where I Don't Belong, A. Marge Piercy. **SP-PierM**

Valleys are not aware. Rock Has Not Learned. Ted Hughes. **SP-HughT**

Valleys crack and burn, the exhausted plains, The. The Mahratta Ghats. Alun Lewis. **CP-LewiA**

Valley's Singing Day, The. Robert Frost. **CP-FrosR**

Vallombrosa—I longed in thy shadiest wood. At Vallombrosa. William Wordsworth. *Fr.* Memorials of a Tour in Italy, 1837. **CP-WorW2**

Vallombrosa! I longed in thy shadiest wood. Stanzas Composed in the Simplon Pass. William Wordsworth. *Fr.* Memorials of a Tour of the Continent; 1820. **CP-WorW2**

Valor in the dark. Emily Dickinson. **SP-DickE**

Valour and Innocence. The Queen's Men. Rudyard Kipling. **CP-KiplR**

Valse, The. Paul Laurence Dunbar. **CP-DunbP**

Valuable. Stevie Smith. **CP-SmitS**

Valuation. John Greenleaf Whittier. **CP-WhitJ**

Value of Gold, The. Thom Gunn. **CP-GunnT**

Values. John Hewitt. **CP-HewiJ**

Values are split, summer, the fierce. The Pause. William Carlos Williams. **CP-WilW2**

Values in Use. Marianne Craig Moore. **CP-MoorM**

Vampire, The. Rudyard Kipling. **CP-KiplR**

Vampirine Fair, The. Thomas Hardy. **CP-HardT**

Van Black, an Old Farmer in His Dell. Richard Eberhart. **CP-EberR**

Van Buren. Ralph Waldo Emerson. **CP-EmerR**

Van der Lubbe. Stephen Spender. **CP-SpenS**

Van Gogh. Charles Tomlinson. **CP-TomlC**

Van Gogh: "The Starry Night." William DeWitt Snodgrass. **SP-SnodW**

Van Gogh's old pensioner. On a Report That in Some Rest Homes Residents Who Are Depressed Will be Charged at a Higher Rate. Frank Templeton Prince. **CP-PrinF**

Van Winkle. Hart Crane. **AmPP; FaBV; MoAB; MoAmPo** *Fr.* Powhatan's Daughter. *Fr.* The Bridge. **CP-CranH**

Vanbrug's House. Jonathan Swift. **CP-SwifJ**

Vancouver. Donald Davie. **CP-DavDo**

Vancouver is a place of fears. Noble City Full of Pigeons or Everyone a Hypocrite Including Me. Malcolm Lowry. **CP-LowrM**

Vane on Hughley steeple, The. Hughley Steeple. Alfred Edward Housman. **CP-HousA**

Vane, young in yeares, but in sage counsell old. John Milton. **CP-MiltJ** (Sonnet 17: "Vane, young in yeares, but in sage counsell old.") **CP-MiltJ**

Vanguard of liberty, ye Men of Kent. To the Men of Kent (October, 1803). William Wordsworth. **CP-WorW1**

Vanish, vanish hence, confusion. Thomas Campion. *Fr.* Description of a Maske: Presented in the Banqueting Roome at *Whitehall*, on Saint Stephens Night Last, at the Marriage of the Right Honourable the Earle of *Somerset:* and the Right Noble the Lady FRANCES *Howard.* **CP-CampT**

Vanished house that for an hour I knew, A. Souvenir. Edwin Arlington Robinson. **CP-RobiE**

Vanishers, The. John Greenleaf Whittier. **CP-WhitJ**

Vanishing, The. "Lewis Carroll." **OXAEP-2** *Fr.* The Hunting of the Snark. **CP-CarrL**

Vanishing Institution, A. Kenneth Patchen. **CP-PatcK**

Vanishing Point, The. Miller Williams. **SP-WillM**

Vanishing Red, The. Robert Frost. **CP-FrosR**

Vanishings, The. Stephen Dunn. **SP-DunnS**

Vanities. Elizabeth Barrett Browning. **CP-BroEB**

Vanity. Stephen Dobyns. **SP-DobyS**

Vanity. Robert Ranke Graves. **CP-GravR**

Vanity Fair. Sylvia Plath. **CP-PlatS**

Vanity! hog-vanity, ape-lust. Vespers. John Berryman. **CP-BerrJ**

Vanity (like a belly / dancer's romance): just. Apple Uppfle. Robert Creeley. **CP-CreeR**

Vanity of All Worldly Things, The. Anne Bradstreet. **CP-BradA**

Vanity of Human Wishes [The Tenth Satire of Juvenal Imitated], The. Samuel Johnson. **CP-JohnS**

"Let Observation with extensive View." **UV**

Life's Last Scene. **OBEC; SeCePo**

On Gold. **IHNG**

"On what foundation stands the warrior's pride." **NOBE; OBWP** (Charles XII of Sweden.) **NOBE**

Power of Prayer, The. **NOBE**

"Unnumbered suppliants crowd preferment's gate." **OBSV**

"When first the college rolls receive his name." **FaBoEn; NOBE; OBEC; OBSV; SeCePo** (Scholar's Life, The.) **FaBoEn; NOBE; OBEC; SeCePo**

Vanity of the Bright Boys, The. John Crowe Ransom. *Fr.* Sixteen Poems in Eight Pairings. **SP-RansJ**

Vanity of the World. William Cowper. *Fr.* Olney Hymns. **CP-CowpW**

Vanity of Vanities. Christina Georgina Rossetti. **CP-RosC1**

Vanity of Vanities. Christina Georgina Rossetti. **CP-RosC2**

Vanity of vanities, the Preacher saith. The One Certainty. Christina Georgina Rossetti. **CP-RosC1**

Vanity of Wealth, The. Samuel Johnson. **CP-JohnS**

Vanity [*or* Vanitie] (1). George Herbert. **CP-HerbG**

Vanity, saith the preacher, vanity! The Bishop Orders His Tomb at Saint Praxed's Church. Robert Browning. **CP-BroR1**

Vanity (2). George Herbert. **CP-HerbG**

Vanity, vanity, all is vanity. Ha! Original Sin! Ogden Nash. **CP-NashO**

Vanquished Knight, The. Robert Louis Stevenson. **CP-StevR**

Vantage, The. Frederick Morgan. **SP-MorgF**

Vantage Point, The. Robert Frost. **CP-FrosR**

Vapid Transit. Gilbert Sorrentino. **SP-SorrG**

Vapor Trail Reflected in the Frog Pond. Galway Kinnell. **SP-KinnG**

Vapor Trails. Gary Snyder. **SP-SnydG**

Vaporish closeness of this two-month fog, The. 1930's. Robert Lowell. **SP-LoweR**

Variables of Green. Robert Ranke Graves. **CP-GravR**

Variant. John Ashbery. **SP-AshbJ**

Variant, The. Charles Simic. **SP-SimiC**

Variant on a Scrap of Conversation. Charles Tomlinson. **CP-TomlC**

Variation, A. Robert Creeley. **CP-CreeR**

Variation of the Song of the Moon. Percy Bysshe Shelley. *Fr.* Prometheus Unbound. **CP-ShelP**

Variation on a Sentence. Louise Bogan. **CP-BogaL**

Variation on a Theme by Newbolt. Sir John Betjeman. **CP-BetjJ**

Variation on a Theme by T. W. Rolleston. Sir John Betjeman. **CP-BetjJ**

Variation on Gaining a Son. Rita Dove. **SP-DoveR**

Variation on Guilt. Rita Dove. **SP-DoveR**

Variation on Heraclitus. Louis MacNeice. **CP-MacNL**

Variation on Lines of Landor, A. Robert Browning. **CP-BroR2**

Variation on Pain. Rita Dove. **SP-DoveR**

Variation on Paz. Charles Tomlinson. **CP-TomlC**

Variation on the Word *Sleep*. Margaret Atwood. **SP-AtwM2**

Variation on "To Say to Go to Sleep," A, *tr. fr. the German of* Rilke. Randall Jarrell. **CP-JarrR**

Variations. Robert Creeley. **CP-CreeR**

Variations. Randall Jarrell. **CP-JarrR**

Variations, Calypso and Fugue on a Theme of Ella Wheeler Wilcox. John Ashbery. **SP-AshbJ**

Variations Done for Gerald Van de Wiele. Charles Olson. **CP-OlsoC; SP-OlsoC**

Variations of Greek Themes. *Various Authors, tr. fr. Greek by* E. A. Robinson. **CP-RobiE**

Aretemias.

Doricha. **AWP; FaBoEE; OBVE**

Dust of Timas, The. **AWP**

Eutychides. **OBAL**

Happy Man, A. **AWP**

Inscription by the Sea, An. **AWP; ChTr; ELU; FaBoEE**

Lais to Aphrodite. **FaBoEE**
Mighty Runner, A. **MeMAP; OBAL; SD**
Old Story, The. **AWP**
Raven, The. **AWP; FaBoEE; OBAL**
To-morrow.
Variations on a Summer Day. Wallace Stevens. **CP-StevW**
Variations on a Theme. Countee Cullen. **CP-CullC**
Variations on a Theme. John Hewitt. **CP-HewiJ**
Variations on a Theme. Carl Sandburg. **CP-SandC**
Variations on a Theme by William Carlos Williams. Kenneth Koch. **SP-KochK**
Variations on Corpse and Mirror. John Yau. **SP-YauJo**
Variations on Corpse and Mirror (Second Set). John Yau. **SP-YauJo**
Variations on Pasternak's "Mein Liebchen, Was Willst Du Noch Mehr?" Frank O'Hara. **SP-OharF**
Variations: The Air Is Sweetest That a Thistle Guards. James Merrill. **SP-MerrJ**
Variations 2. Gilbert Sorrentino. **SP-SorrG**
Variations 3. Gilbert Sorrentino. **SP-SorrG**
Varick Street. Elizabeth Bishop. **CP-BishE**
Varied colours are a fitful heap, The. The Year's Sheddings. George Meredith. **CP-MerG1**
Variegated flowers, nuts, cockle-shells. The Necklace. Robert Ranke Graves. **CP-GravR**
Variety. John Donne. *Fr.* Elegies. **CP-DonnJ**
Various ills ordain'd to man by fate, The. Ovid, *tr. by* Samuel Johnson. **CP-JohnS** *Fr.* Metamorphoses.
Various Protestations From Various People. Etheridge Knight. **SP-KnigE**
'Varsity Students' Rag, The. Sir John Betjeman. **CP-BetjJ**
Varus old crony had me visit his love. Catullus. *See* Carmen 10: "Alfenus Varus / buttonholes me."
Varus, whom I chanced to meet. Catullus. *See* Carmen 10: "Alfenus Varus / buttonholes me."
Vas en Afrique! Back to Africa! the butcher we used to patronize in the Rue Cadet market. Racists. Charles Kenneth Williams. **SP-WillC**
Vasectomy. William Matthews. **SP-MattW**
Vast and grey, the sky. The Desolate Field. William Carlos Williams. **CP-WilW1**
Vast Confusion, A. Lawrence Ferlinghetti. **SP-FerlL**
Vast rose of July. Marsden Hartley. **CP-HartM**
Vast, tremulous. I Sent Thee Late. Louis Zukofsky. **CP-ZukLS**
Vast unmapped badlands spread without a road. The Lone Ranger. Donald Hall. **CP-HallD**
Vastest earthly Day, The. Emily Dickinson. **CP-DickE**
Vastness and Indifference of the World, The. Richard Eberhart. **CP-EberR**
Vastness was a silver dropper. The Mystical Forest. Marsden Hartley. **CP-HartM**
Vaudeville Dancer. Carl Sandburg. **CP-SandC**
Vaudois, The. William Wordsworth. *Fr.* Ecclesiastical Sonnets. **CP-WorW2**
Vaudois Teacher, The. John Greenleaf Whittier. **CP-WhitJ**
Vaudracour and Julia. William Wordsworth. **CP-WorW1**
Vault on the opal carpet of the sun. To Portapovitch. Hart Crane. **CP-CranH**
Vaunting Oak. John Crowe Ransom. **SP-RansJ**
("He is a tower unleaning. But how he'll break.") **SP-RansJ**
Vayne loves, avaunt! infamous is your pleasure. Love's Gardyne Greife. Robert Southwell. **CP-SoutR**
Veal and mushrooms, wine, a too pungent salad. Joint. James Schuyler. **CP-SchuJ**
Veer-Voices: Two Sisters under Crows. James Dickey. **CP-DickJ**
Vegetable King, The. James Dickey. **CP-DickJ**
Vegetables please us with their modes and virtues, The. Praises. Thomas McGrath. **SP-McGrT**
Vegetarians, The. John Ashbery. **SP-AshbJ**
Vegetation. Kathleen Jessie Raine. **SP-RainK**
Vehicle: Absence. Charles Kenneth Williams. **SP-WillC**
Vehicle: Conscience. Charles Kenneth Williams. **SP-WillC**
Vehicle: Violence. Charles Kenneth Williams. **SP-WillC**
Veil, A. Leonard Cohen. **CP-CoheL**
Veil, The. Walter de la Mare. **CP-DeLaW**
Veil of Light, The. Samuel Taylor Coleridge. **CP-ColeS**
Veil of Spirit, The. Samuel Taylor Coleridge. **CP-ColeS**
Veil them, cover them, wall them round. Rudyard Kipling. **CP-KiplR** *Fr.* Letting in the Jungle. *Fr.* The Second Jungle Book.
Veil upon veil. Natura Naturans. Kathleen Jessie Raine. **SP-RainK**
Veiled in night's cloak a silent moment came. At the Meeting of the Days. John Gould Fletcher. **SP-FletJ**

Veils of clarity. Metric Figure. William Carlos Williams. **CP-WilW1**
Veins of other Flowers, The. Emily Dickinson. **CP-DickE**
Veins that stand on the back of my sunburned hand, The. Grace Paley. **CP-PaleG**
Velocity of Cows, The. Stephen Dobyns. **SP-DobyS**
Velocity with which they write—, The. Movie Actors Scribbling Letters Very Fast in Crucial Scenes. Jean Garrigue. **SP-GarrJ**
Velvet Rocks. Richard Eberhart. **CP-EberR**
Velvet Roses. James Schuyler. **CP-SchuJ**
Veneris Venefica Agrestis. Lucio Piccolo, *tr. fr. Italian by* Charles Tomlinson. **CP-TomlC**
Venetian; all thy Colouring is no more. William Blake. **CP-BlakW**
Venetian Blind. Thom Gunn. **CP-GunnT**
Venetian Blind, The. Randall Jarrell. **CP-JarrR**
Venez vite / Avec moi. Come. Stevie Smith. **CP-SmitS**
Venga Amicizia e sia la benvenuta. Amicizia: Sirocchia Son D'Amor. Christina Georgina Rossetti. *Fr.* Il Rosseggiar Dell'Oriente Canzoniere. **CP-RosC3**
Vengeance Is Mine. David Herbert Lawrence. **CP-LawrD**
Vengeance Is Mine, Saith the Lord. Donald Davie. **CP-DavDo**
Vengeance is Sweet. Paul Laurence Dunbar. **CP-DunbP**
Vengeance of Apollo, The. Homer, *tr. by* George Meredith. **CP-MerG2** *Fr.* The Iliad.
Vengeful across the cold November moors. The Pity of the Leaves. Edwin Arlington Robinson. **CP-RobiE**
Veni. Arthur Hugh Clough. **SP-ClouA**
Veni Coronaberis. Geoffrey Hill. **CP-HillG**
Veni, Deus. Old ideas, like stairs. Prelude in Darkness. James McAuley. **SP-McAuJ**
Veni Redemptor, but not in our time. Geoffrey Hill. *Fr.* Tenebrae. **CP-HillG**
Venice. Byron. **CP-Byron**
Venice. Herman Melville. **SP-MelvH**
Venice. Charles Tomlinson. **CP-TomlC**
Venice, November, 1966. Erica Jong. **SP-JongE**
Venice, 182–. John Berryman. **CP-BerrJ**
Venice portrait: he, The. The Humanist. Geoffrey Hill. **CP-HillG**
Venom. James Dickey. **CP-DickJ**
Venomous thorns that are so sharp and keen. Sir Thomas Wyatt. **CP-WyatT**
Vento gentil che verso il mezzodi. Nostre Voluntà Quieti Virtù di Carità. Christina Georgina Rossetti. *Fr.* Il Rosseggiar Dell'Oriente Canzoniere. **CP-RosC3**
Ventricles of his heart burst, The. O Bitter Madrigal. Marsden Hartley. **CP-HartM**
Venus, again[e] thou mov'st a war[re]. 4.1. Horace, *tr. by* Ben Jonson. **CP-JonsB** *Fr.* Odes.
Venus and Adonis. William Shakespeare. **CP-ShaWS**
Venus and the Ark. Anne Sexton. **CP-SextA**
Venus de Milo didn't have one, at least no pussy, The. Cunts. John Updike. **CP-UpdiJ**
Venus glows in the east. Work to Do Toward Town. Gary Snyder. **CP-SnydG**
Venus in Furs. "Lou Reed." **SP-ReedL**
Venus, in sport, to please therewith her dear. Sir Thomas Wyatt. **CP-WyatT**
Venus Over the Desert. William Carlos Williams. **CP-WilW2**
Venus seems my Mouse, A. My Mouse. Christina Georgina Rossetti. **CP-RosC3**
Venus unto the Gods a sure did move. Mary Sidney, Countess of Montgomery Wroth. *Fr.* Pamphilia to Amphilanthus. **CP-WrotM**
Venus When Young Choosing Death. Stevie Smith. **CP-SmitS**
Venus Will Now Say a Few Words. Wystan Hugh Auden. **CP-AudeW**
Venus, with young Adonis sitting by her. Bartholomew Griffin. **CP-ShaWS** *Fr.* The Passionate Pilgrim. **CP-ShaWS**
Venus's Looking-Glass. Christina Georgina Rossetti. **CP-RosC1**
Venus's Looking-glass. Louis Zukofsky. **CP-ZukLS**
Ver anni Lunaeque fuit, pars verna diei. *acc. by English translation.* Thomas Campion. **CP-CampT**
Veracruz. Robert Earl Hayden. **AmNP** *Fr.* An Inference of Mexico. **CP-HaydR**
Verae ut supersint nuptiae, *accompanied by English translation.* Thomas Campion. *Fr.* Description of a Maske: Presented in the Banqueting Roome at *Whitehall*, on Saint Stephens Night Last, at the Marriage of the Right Honourable the Earle of *Somerset:* and the Right Noble the Lady FRANCES *Howard.* **CP-CampT**
Verandah. Derek Walcott. **CP-WalcD**
Verandahs, where the pages of the sea. Another Life. Derek Walcott. **CP-WalcD**

Veraniolus, / first of friends. Carmen 9. Catullus. *Fr. Carmina.* **CP-Catul**

Veranius, my dear friend, the friend worth. Catullus. *See* Carmen 9: "Veraniolus, / first of friends."

Veranius of all my beloved friends. Catullus. *See* Carmen 9: "Veraniolus, / first of friends."

Verb, The. Louise McNeill. **SP-McNeL**

Verba volant; verum: quid enim velocius illis?, *acc. by English translation.* Thomas Campion. **CP-CampT**

Verbalist of Summer, The. Richard Eberhart. **CP-EberR**

Verbatim from Boileau. Alexander Pope. **CP-PopeA**

Verborum satis est; oneri sunt plura libello. *?acc. by English translation.* Thomas Campion. **CP-CampT**

Verdicts, The. Rudyard Kipling. **CP-KiplR**

Verdun. Robert Lowell. **SP-LoweR**

Verily it snows. Emily Dickinson. **SP-DickE**

Veritable night, The. Rigamarole. William Carlos Williams. **CP-WilW1**

Verlaine. Edwin Arlington Robinson. **CP-RobiE**

Verlaine's Innocents. Gilbert Sorrentino. **SP-SorrG**

Vermeer. Howard Nemerov. **CP-NemeH**

Vermont. Hayden Carruth. **CP-CarHL**
　"I don't say you can't find him in New Hampshire."
　"I'm from Connecticut. But please, not Stamford."
　"It's French, of course—our name. And I must think."
　"Republicans? We've got a few. In fact."
　"Those Indians who came and didn't stay."
　"Well, I've said that Robert Frost had curiosity."
　"West Bolton is due north of Bolton, East."

Vermont. John Updike. **CP-UpdiJ**

Vermont Diary, A. James Schuyler. **CP-SchuJ**

Vermont Idyll. Richard Eberhart. **CP-EberR**

Verna diu saevas sensurunt pascua nubes. Inundatio Oxoniana. Gerard Manley Hopkins. **CP-HopkG**

Vernal Ode. William Wordsworth. **CP-WorW2**

Vernal Sentiment. Theodore Roethke. **CP-RoetT**

Verona, Ohio / right 3 miles. Jaunt. Louis Zukofsky. **CP-ZukLS**

Veronica's Napkin. William Butler Yeats. **CP-YeatW**

Vers Libre. John Hewitt. **CP-HewiJ**

Versailles. Adrienne Rich. **CP-RicAE**

Verse, a breeze [']mid blossoms straying. Youth and Age. Samuel Taylor Coleridge. **CP-ColeS**

Verse and Fame. John Donne. **FaBoRV** *Fr.* Anatomy [*or* Anatomie] of the World, An[: The First Anniversary]. **CP-DonnJ**
incl. Latin tr. by Basil Bunting. Louis Zukofsky. *See* In that this happening.

Verse Composed and Repeated by *Burns*, to the Master of the House, on Taking Leave at a Place in the Highlands, Where He Had Been Hospitably Entertained, A. Robert Burns. **CP-BurnR**

Verse for Urania. James Merrill. **SP-MerrJ**

Verse from Defensio Secunda. John Milton, *tr. fr. Latin by* John T. Shawcross. **CP-MiltJ**

Verse from Pro Populo Anglicano Defensio. John Milton, *tr. fr. Latin by* John T. Shawcross. **CP-MiltJ**

Verse from the Advertisement to Blake's Exhibition of Paintings, 1809. William Blake. **CP-BlakW**

Verse hath a middle nature; heaven keepes soules. Verse and Fame. John Donne. **FaBoRV** *Fr.* Anatomy [*or* Anatomie] of the World, An[: The First Anniversary]. **CP-DonnJ**

Verse hath a middle nature: heaven keeps souls. John Donne. *See* The First Anniversary [*or* Anniversarie].

Verse with Allusions. Theodore Roethke. **CP-RoetT**

Verses. Robert Herrick. **CP-HerrR**

Verses: "I am a keeper of the law." Robert Burns. **CP-BurnR**

Verses: "I confirm'd a woman can." Sir John Suckling. **CP-SuckJ**

Verses Addressed to Amanda. James Thomson. **CP-ThomJ**

Verses Addressed to J. Horne Tooke and the Company Who Met on 28 June 1796 to Celebrate His Poll at the Westminster Election. Samuel Taylor Coleridge. **CP-ColeS**

Verses for a Centennial. Archibald MacLeish. **CP-MacLA**

Verses Found in a Summer-House at Hales-Owen. Byron. **CP-Byron**

Verses from Quilica. Jonathan Swift. **CP-SwifJ**
　Blessings of a Country Life, The.
　"Eat like a Turk."
　Plagues of a Country Life.

Verses from the Shepherd's Hymn. Richard Crashaw. *See* Shepherd's Hymn, The ("We saw Thee in Thy balmy nest").

Verses Intended to Be Written below a Noble Earl's Picture. Robert Burns. **CP-BurnR**

Verses Intended to Have Been Prefixed to the Novel of Emmeline, but Then Suppressed. Charlotte Smith. **CP-SmitC**

Verses Left by Mr. Pope, on His Lying in the Same Bed which Wilmot, the Celebrated Earl of Rochester, Slept in, at Adderbury, then Belonging to the Duke of Argyle, July 9th, 1739. Alexander Pope. **CP-PopeA**

Verses Left in a Window of Dublin Castle. Jonathan Swift. **CP-SwifJ**

Verses Made for the Women Who Cry Apples, etc. Jonathan Swift. **CP-SwifJ**
　Apples. **AnIV; NCEP; OnYI**
　Asparagus.
　Herrings. **AnIV; NCEP; OnYI**
　Onyons. **BIrV; FaBoUs**
　(Onions.) **CP-SwifJ**
　Oranges.
　Oysters.

Verses Modelled on Pope. Samuel Johnson. *See* While Many a Merry Tale.

Verses Occasioned by an &c. at the End of Mr. D'Urfy's Name in the Title to One of His Plays. Alexander Pope. **CP-PopeA**

Verses Occasioned by the Sudden Drying Up of St. Patrick's Well near Trinity College, Dublin. Jonathan Swift. **CP-SwifJ**

Verses on a Cat. Percy Bysshe Shelley. **CP-ShelP**

Verses on Games. Rudyard Kipling. **CP-KiplR**
　APRIL (*Rowing*).
　AUGUST (*Coaching*).
　DECEMBER (*Skating*).
　FEBRUARY (*Coursing*).
　JANUARY (*Hunting*).
　JULY (*Archery*).
　JUNE (*Cricket*).
　MARCH (*Racing*).
　MAY (*Fishing*).
　NOVEMBER (*Boxing*).
　(Boxing.) **OtMeF**
　OCTOBER (*Golf*).
　SEPTEMBER (*Shooting*).

Verses on I Know Not What. Jonathan Swift. **CP-SwifJ**

Verses on Receiving a Flower from his Mistress. James Thomson. **CP-ThomJ**

Verses, on the death of [Henrietta O'Neill], written in September, 1794. Charlotte Smith. **CP-SmitC**

Verses on the Death of Dr. Swift, D.S.P.D. Jonathan Swift. **CP-SwifJ**
　"Behold the fatal day arrive!" **PeLV; SCV**
　"Doctors tender of their fame, The." **NOBL**
　"Here shift the scene, to represent." **OBD**
　"My female friends, whose tender hearts." **NOBL; SeCePo**
　"Now Curll his shop from rubbish drains." **PeLV**
　"Perhaps I may allow, the Dean." **EPCY; FaBoEn; NOBE; PeLV**
　"Suppose me dead; and then suppose." **LoBV; NOBE; NOEC; OxBoLi; PeLV; PoEL-3; TEP**
　"Time is not remote when I, The." **EBEV; Mes; NOBE; NOBL; NOIV; OBEC; OXAEP-1; PeLV**
　(On the Death of Dean Swift.) **OXAEP-1**

Verses on the Death of His Mother. Samuel Johnson. **CP-JohnS**

Verses on the Revival of the Order of the Bath. Jonathan Swift. **CP-SwifJ**

Verses on the Upright Judge. Jonathan Swift. **CP-SwifJ**

Verses Said to Be Written on the Union. Jonathan Swift. **CP-SwifJ**

Verses Spoken Extempore by Dean Swift on His Curate's Complaint of Hard Duty. Jonathan Swift. **CP-SwifJ**

Verses Supposed to Have Been Written in the New Forest, in Early Spring. Charlotte Smith. **CP-SmitC**

Verses to Amanda. In Imitation of Tibullus. James Thomson. **CP-ThomJ**

Verses to Be Placed under the Picture of England's Arch-Poet: Containing a Compleat Catalogue of His Works. Alexander Pope. **CP-PopeA**

Verses to be Prefix'd before Bernard Lintot's New Miscellany. Alexander Pope. **CP-PopeA**

Verses Trivocular. Samuel Taylor Coleridge. **CP-ColeS**

Verses Turned in Aid of a Public Subscription (1952) Towards the Restoration of the Church of St. Katherine Chiselhampton, Oxon. Sir John Betjeman. **CP-BetjJ**

Verses Written at Bath on Finding the Heel of a Shoe. William Cowper. **CP-CowpW**

Verses Written for Student Antidraft Registration Rally 1980. Allen Ginsberg. **CP-GinsA**

Verses Written in 1872. Robert Louis Stevenson. **CP-StevR**

Verses Written on a Window of the Inn at Carron. Robert Burns. **CP-BurnR**

Verses Wrote in a Lady's Ivory Table-Book. Jonathan Swift. **CP-SwifJ**

Verses you sent on the bottling your wine, The. Dr. Swift's Answer to Dr. Sheridan. Jonathan Swift. **CP-SwifJ**

Versi. Christina Georgina Rossetti. **CP-RosC3**

Versicles on Sign-Posts. Robert Burns. **CP-BurnR**

"He looked / Just as your Sign-post lions do."

"Head pure, sinless quite of brain or soul, A." **FaBoEE**

"His face with smile eternal drest."

"Patient Stupidity / So, heavy, passive to the tempest's shocks."

Version. Robert Frost. **CP-FrosR**

Version of Ossian's Address to the Sun, A. Byron. **CP-Byron**

Version of the First Psalm, for the Use of a Young Lady, A, *see also* Psalm 1. Alexander Pope. **CP-PopeA**

Version of the Phoenix Story, A. Jenny Joseph. **SP-JoseJ**

Vertigo. Adrienne Rich. **CP-RicAE**

Vertue. Robert Herrick. **CP-HerrR**

Vertue Best United. Robert Herrick. **CP-HerrR**

Vertue Is Sensible of Suffering. Robert Herrick. **CP-HerrR**

Vertue the Best Monument. *Unknown, sometimes at. to* Sir Walter Ralegh. **CP-RaleW**

Vertumnus and Pomona. Ovid, *tr. by* Alexander Pope. **CP-PopeA** *Fr.* Metamorphoses.

Vervain. . . basil. . . orison. Incantation. Walter de la Mare. **CP-DeLaW**

Very. Charles Bukowski. **SP-BukC2**

Very bitter were the sorrows. *after* Ferdinand Gregorovius. Randall Jarrell. **CP-JarrR**

Very Brave. Jim Morrison. **SP-MorrJ**

Very cool that bed must be. There Remaineth Therefore a Rest. Christina Georgina Rossetti. **CP-RosC3**

Very dark and clear with an onshore wind. Malcolm Lowry. **CP-LowrM**

Very Dove, A. Allen Ginsberg. **CP-GinsA**

Very felicitous eye, A. Delightful Evening. Wallace Stevens. **CP-StevW**

Very Funny, Very Funny. Ogden Nash. **CP-NashO**

Very Languor, The. Marsden Hartley. **CP-HartM**

"Very last time I ever was here, The," he said. Jubilate. Thomas Hardy. **CP-HardT**

Very Many People. Rudyard Kipling. **CP-KiplR**

Very Mournful Ballad, A. Byron. **CP-Byron**

Very Old, The. Ted Kooser. **SP-KoosT**

Very old are the woods. All That's Past. Walter de la Mare. **CP-DeLaW**

Very Old Song, A. "William Laird." **CP-HerrR**

Very old woman / Lives in yon house, A. Alone. Walter de la Mare. **CP-DeLaW**

Very Original Poem, Written with Even a Greater Endeavour than Ordinary after Intelligibility, and Hitherto Only Published on the First Leaf of the Author's Son's Account-Book. Robert Browning. **CP-BroR2**

Very proud / he barely asked directions. The Black Prince. Alice Walker. **CP-WalkA**

Very reverend Dean Smedley, The. Dean Smedley Gone to Seek His Fortune. Jonathan Swift. **CP-SwifJ**

Very rocks were novel in their mass, The. The Adventure. Frederick Morgan. **SP-MorgF**

Very Small Casualty, A. Phoebe Hesketh. **SP-HeskP**

Very Tree. Stanley Jasspon Kunitz. **CP-KuniS**

Very Unclubbable Man, The. Ogden Nash. **CP-NashO**

Very Very Important. Carl Sandburg. **CP-SandC**

Very West-of-Wessex girl, A. The West-of-Wessex Girl. Thomas Hardy. **CP-HardT**

Vesper Hymn for Tuesday and June, after the Visit of Henry Wells. Marsden Hartley. **CP-HartM**

Vesper Journal. Charles Wright. **SP-WrigC**

Vesper out there, you vain knees can sure get up: Vesper, Olympus. Catullus. *See* Carmen 62: "Gather young men as the twilight gathers."

Vespers. Wystan Hugh Auden. **FaBoMo** *Fr.* Horae Canonicae. **CP-AudeW**

Vespers. John Berryman. **CP-BerrJ**

Vespers. Donald Davie. *Fr.* Horae Canonicae. **CP-DavDo**

Vessel blatting, A. Measure. Charles Olson. **CP-OlsoC**

Vessels. James Dickey. **CP-DickJ**

Vessels of heavenly medicine! may the breeze. Sonnet: On Launching Some Bottles Filled with Knowledge into the Bristol Channel. Percy Bysshe Shelley. **CP-ShelP**

Vessels thrown awry by strong gusts. Basil Bunting. **CP-BuntB**

Vesta. John Greenleaf Whittier. **CP-WhitJ**

Vestal, The. Alexander Pope. **ACP** *Fr.* Eloisa to Abelard. **CP-PopeA** (Life of a Nun.) **ECEV**

Vested Priest before the Altar stands, The. The Marriage Ceremony. William Wordsworth. *Fr.* Ecclesiastical Sonnets. **CP-WorW2**

Vestiges. Basil Bunting. **CP-BuntB**

"Jengiz to Chang Chun: China."

"Salt grass silent of hooves, the lake stinks."

Veteran, The. Paul Laurence Dunbar. **CP-DunbP**

Veteran Sirens. Edwin Arlington Robinson. **CP-RobiE**

Veterans, The. Rudyard Kipling. **CP-KiplR**

Veterans of Foreign Wars. Gilbert Sorrentino. **SP-SorrG**

Vetran tilesmith, The. The Tilemaker's Hill Fresco. Laurence Lieberman. **SP-LiebL**

Vex'd elm-heads are pale with the view, The. A Windy Day in Summer. Gerard Manley Hopkins. **CP-HopkG**

Vexilla Regis, *Ad. from the Medieval* Hymnus de Passione Domini. Richard Crashaw. **CP-CrasR**

Vezelay. Daniel Gerard Hoffman. **SP-HoffD**

Via appia. James Dickey. **CP-DickJ**

Via Crucis. Herman Melville. **SP-MelvH** *Fr.* Clarel: A Poem and Pilgrimage in the Holy Land.

Via Portello. Donald Davie. **CP-DavDo**

"Via Portello," I wrote. The Hardness of Light. Donald Davie. **CP-DavDo**

Vibennius & son, renowned. Carmen 33. Catullus. *Fr.* Carmina. **CP-Catul**

Vibration. John Updike. **CP-UpdiJ**

Vibration of Justice. David Herbert Lawrence. **CP-LawrD**

Vicar, The. George Crabbe. **SP-CrabG** *Fr.* The Borough.

"But let applause be dealt in all we may." **OBNC**

Vicar's Son. David Herbert Lawrence. *Fr.* Bits. **CP-LawrD**

Vices. Robinson Jeffers. **CP-JefR1**

Vicious Circle. "Lou Reed." **SP-ReedL**

Vicious tight curl, The. Who Goes There? Gilbert Sorrentino. **SP-SorrG**

Vicious winter finally yields, The. William DeWitt Snodgrass. **MoLi; NePoEA; SM** *Fr.* Heart's Needle. **SP-SnodW**

Viciousness in the kitchen! Lesbos. Sylvia Plath. **CP-PlatS**

Vicissitudes Experienced in the Christian Life, The. Jeanne Marie Bouvier de la Motte-Guyon, *tr. fr. French by* William Cowper. **CP-CowpW**

Vicissitudes of the Creator. Archibald MacLeish. **CP-MacLA**

Vickery's Mountain. Edwin Arlington Robinson. **CP-RobiE**

Vicovicovicovicovico. Thomas Merton. *Fr.* A Selection of Concrete Poems. **CP-MertT**

Victim, The. Thom Gunn. **CP-GunnT**

Victim not of an accident. A Proposal for Recycling Wastes. Marge Piercy. **SP-PierM**

Victims. John Haines. **SP-HainJ**

Victims, a Play for the Home, The. Muriel Rukeyser. **CP-RukeM**

Victor. Wystan Hugh Auden. **CP-AudeW**

Victor, The. Daniel Gerard Hoffman. **SP-HoffD**

Victor Dog, The. James Merrill. **SP-MerrJ**

Victor was a little baby. Victor. Wystan Hugh Auden. **CP-AudeW**

Victoria, *for diff. vers., see* Fragment, or The Triumph of Conscience. Percy Bysshe Shelley. *Fr.* Poems from St. Irvyne, or, The Rosicrucian. **CP-ShelP**

Victorian Rehearsal, A. Thomas Hardy. **CP-HardT**

Victorian Steps Out, A. John Hewitt. **CP-HewiJ**

Victoria's Tears. Elizabeth Barrett Browning. **CP-BroEB**

Victors, The. Denise Levertov. **CP-LeveD**

Victory. James Dickey. **CP-DickJ**

Victory. Alun Lewis. *Fr.* Two Legends: for Greece. **CP-LewiA**

Victory, The. Thomas Merton. **CP-MertT**

Victory comes late. Emily Dickinson. **CP-DickE**

Vida, Mykonos. John Hewitt. **CP-HewiJ**

Video Violence. "Lou Reed." **SP-ReedL**

Vieil aller / vieux arrêts. Samuel Beckett. **CP-BeckS**

Vienna the Volk iss very lustig. Lustspiel. William Carlos Williams. **CP-WilW2**

Vietnam Addenda. Audre Lorde. **SP-LordA**

Vietnam Memorial. Karl Shapiro. **SP-ShapK**

View, The. Philip Larkin. **CP-LarkP**

View, The. Howard Nemerov. **CP-NemeH**

View, A. James Schuyler. **CP-SchuJ**

View, The. Charles Tomlinson. **CP-TomlC**

View, A. Mona Van Duyn. **SP-VanDM**

View. William Carlos Williams. **CP-WilW1**

View Across the Roman Campagna. Elizabeth Barrett Browning. **CP-BroEB**

View by Color Photography on a Commercial Calendar. William Carlos Williams. **CP-WilW2**

View from an Attic Window, The. Howard Nemerov. **CP-NemeH**

View from an Empty Chair. Tess Gallagher. **SP-GallT**

View from Cortona, A. Richard Hugo. **CP-HugoR**

View from Pisgah, The. Howard Nemerov. **CP-NemeH**

View from Rosehill Cemetery: Vicksburg. Alice Walker. **CP-WalkA**

View from the Top of Black Comb. William Wordsworth. **CP-WorW1**

View is fine from fifty, The. The View. Philip Larkin. **CP-LarkP**

View it, by day, from the back. Movie House. John Updike. **CP-UpdiJ**

View Mee, Lord. Thomas Campion. **CP-CampT**

View of a Lake. William Carlos Williams. **CP-WilW1**

View of a Pig. Ted Hughes. **SP-HughT**

View of Fujiyama after the War, A. James Dickey. **CP-DickJ**

View of Merton College, A. Adrienne Rich. **CP-RicAE**

View of the Capitol from the Library of Congress. Elizabeth Bishop. **CP-BishE**

View of the Terrace, A. Adrienne Rich. **CP-RicAE**

View of winter trees. Jersey Lyric. William Carlos Williams. **CP-WilW2**

Viewing the Body. William DeWitt Snodgrass. **SP-SnodW**

Viewless and invisible Consequence, The. Fragment. Percy Bysshe Shelley. **CP-ShelP**

Views of Myself. John Berryman. **CP-BerrJ**

Vigil. Walter de la Mare. **CP-DeLaW**

Vigil. John Hewitt. **CP-HewiJ**

Vigil. James McAuley. *Fr.* Requiem. **SP-McAuJ**

Vigil / taking over hours and losing them. Roy Fisher. **SP-FishR** *Fr.* New Diversions.

Vigil. Allen Tate. *Fr.* The Progress of Œnia. **CP-TateA**

Vigil Forget. Malcolm Lowry. *Fr.* The Roar of the Sea and the Darkness. **CP-LowrM**

Vigil: He Lies Awake in the Barracks Room, Fearful She Will Not Come, The. Alun Lewis. *Fr.* War Wedding. **CP-LewiA**

Vigil of all Saints. Christina Georgina Rossetti. **CP-RosC2**

Vigil of Corpus Christi, The. Thom Gunn. **CP-GunnT**

Vigil of St. Bartholomew. Christina Georgina Rossetti. **CP-RosC2**

Vigil of St. Peter. Christina Georgina Rossetti. **CP-RosC2**

Vigil of the Annunciation. Christina Georgina Rossetti. **CP-RosC2**

Vigil of the Presentation. Christina Georgina Rossetti. **CP-RosC2**

Vigil of Venus, The. *Unknown, tr. fr. Latin by* Allen Tate. **CP-TateA** (Pervigilium Veneris.) **CP-TateA**

Vigil: She Tarries, Far-Off, in a Strange Anguish, The. Alun Lewis. *Fr.* War Wedding. **CP-LewiA**

Vigil Strange I Kept on the Field One Night. Walt Whitman. **CP-WhitW**

Vigilance. Lewis Turco. **SP-TurcL**

Vignette. John Clellon Holmes. **SP-HolmJ**

Vigo County. Etheridge Knight. *Fr.* Indiana Haiku—2. **SP-KnigE**

Vigor and majesty of the air, The. Light From Above. Richard Eberhart. **CP-EberR**

Viking Dublin: Trial Pieces. Seamus Heaney. **SP-HeanS**

Villa Adriana. Adrienne Rich. **CP-RicAE; SP-RicA2**

Villa-Fàmes, August 1986. Steve Griffiths. **SP-GrifS**

Villa—I would be brief, yet say—. Marsden Hartley. *Fr.* Several Pieces for Jose Garcia Villa. **CP-HartM**

Village, The. Hayden Carruth. *Fr.* Contra Mortem. **CP-CarHL**

Village, The. George Crabbe.

    Truth in Poetry. **SP-CrabG**

    (Rural Life.) **SP-CrabG**

Village Blacksmith, The. Henry Wadsworth Longfellow. **SP-LongH**

Village Funeral: Maharashtra. Alun Lewis. **CP-LewiA**

Village Improvement Parade, The. Nicholas Vachel Lindsay. **CP-LindV**

Village in East Anglia, A. Donald Hall. **CP-HallD**

Village in Late Summer. Carl Sandburg. **CP-SandC**

Village Inn, The. Sir John Betjeman. **CP-BetjJ**

Village is growing fertile, The. Holi. Alun Lewis. **CP-LewiA**

Village Life, A. Derek Walcott. **CP-WalcD**

Village Minstrel, The. John Clare. **CP-ClarT**

Village Tale, A. May Sarton. **SP-SartM**

Village Tudda, The. Kenneth Patchen. **CP-PatcK**

Villager. Richard Hugo. **CP-HugoR**

Villagers and Death, The. Robert Ranke Graves. **CP-GravR**

Villagers who gather round. Spiel of [the] Three Mountebanks. John Crowe Ransom. **SP-RansJ**

Villain shows his indiscretion. Curtain. Paul Laurence Dunbar. **CP-DunbP**

Villains. Stevie Smith. **CP-SmitS**

Villains and fools, The. To a Granddaughter on One of Her Suggestions for a Christmas Present. Frank Templeton Prince. **CP-PrinF**

Villaknell. Malcolm Lowry. **CP-LowrM**

Villanelle: "Christ is walking in your blood today." Richard Eberhart. **CP-EberR**

Villanelle: "Every day our bodies seperate." Marilyn Hacker. **SP-HackM**

Villanelle, an Interview on Morale. Malcolm Lowry. **CP-LowrM**

Villanelle for Pamela. Robert Pack. **SP-PackR**

Villanelle: Late Summer. Marilyn Hacker. **SP-HackM**

Villanelle of Change. Edwin Arlington Robinson. **CP-RobiE**

Villanelle of the Suicide's Mother. Charles Kenneth Williams. **SP-WillC**

Villanelle: The Psychological Hour. Ezra Pound. **SP-PounE**

Villers. Alexander Pope. *See* The Duke of Buckingham.

Villian at the Gallows tree, The. A Pitiful Case. William Blake. **CP-BlakW**

Villon. Basil Bunting. **CP-BuntB**

    "He whom we anatomized."

    "Let his days be few and let."

    "Under the olive trees."

Villonaud for This Yule. Ezra Pound. **SP-PounE**

Vince Viet Cong! The testimony of walls. Tarquinia. Charles Tomlinson. **CP-TomlC**

Vincent. Edwin Rolfe. **CP-RolfE**

Vindication of Jovan Babic, The. Donald Davie. **CP-DavDo**

Vindictives, The. Robert Frost. **CP-FrosR**

Vine, The. Robert Herrick. **CP-HerrR**

Vine, The. Phoebe Hesketh. **SP-HeskP**

Vine, The. Thomas Merton. **CP-MertT**

Vine and Clarel. Herman Melville. **SP-MelvH** *Fr.* Clarel: A Poem and Pilgrimage in the Holy Land.

Vinegar is no other I define. Upon Vinegar. Robert Herrick. **CP-HerrR**

Vines. Louis Zukofsky. **CP-ZukLS**

Vines tougher than wrists. Forcing House. Theodore Roethke. **CP-RoetT**

Vines with Their. Kenneth Patchen. **CP-PatcK**

Vineyard, The. Rudyard Kipling. **CP-KiplR** *Fr.* Debits and Credits.

Vingt-et-un. Louis MacNeice. *Fr.* Indoor Sports. **CP-MacNL**

Vintage to the Dungeon, The. Richard Lovelace. **CP-LoveR**

Viol lace each stilled note. Violet. Louis Zukofsky. **CP-ZukLS**

Violas are moaning, a harpsichord chiming. James McAuley. **SP-McAuJ** *Fr.* Vivaldi in Venice.

Violence. Allen Ginsberg. **CP-GinsA**

Violence. Adrienne Rich. **CP-RicAE**

Violence in the dream, violation of body and spirit; torment, mutiliation, butchery, debasement. The Crime. Charles Kenneth Williams. **SP-WillC**

Violence threatens you no longer. The Cliff Edge. Robert Ranke Graves. **CP-GravR**

Violent darkness claims us all, The. Two Songs from "The Hunted Revolutionaries." Thomas McGrath. **SP-McGrT**

Violent Hand, The. Stevie Smith. **CP-SmitS**

Violent order is disorder, A; and. Connoisseur of Chaos. Wallace Stevens. **CP-StevW**

Violent Pastoral. James Merrill. **SP-MerrJ**

Violent Space, The. Etheridge Knight. **SP-KnigE**

Violently asleep in the old house. The Blue Ghazals. Adrienne Rich. **CP-RicAE; SP-RicA2**

Violet. Louis Zukofsky. **CP-ZukLS**

Violet and Jasper. Richard Wilbur. **CP-WilbR**

Violet at Ninety. Phoebe Hesketh. **SP-HeskP**

Violet Grape—and Shadowy Myrtle Leaf. Marsden Hartley. **CP-HartM**

Violet hush: and sunbursts, A. Heather and Calendulas. James Schuyler. **CP-SchuJ**

Violets. David Herbert Lawrence. **CP-LawrD**

Violets. George Meredith. **CP-MerG1**

Violets. Charlotte Smith. **CP-SmitC**

Violets are by my side, The. Emily Dickinson. **SP-DickE**

Violets for the Dead. David Herbert Lawrence. **CP-LawrD**

Violinist's shadow vanishes, The. Cadenza. Ted Hughes. **SP-HughT**

Violins tended to shriek, The. Triumph of the Postmodern. Lawrence Ferlinghetti. **SP-FerlL**

Viper-Man. Donald Davie. **CP-DavDo**

Vir I–XII. James Liddy. **CP-LiddJ**

    Vir.

    Vir II.

    Vir III.

    Vir IV.

    Vir V.

    Vir VI.

    Vir VII.

    Vir VIII.

    Vir IX.

    Vir X.

    Vir XI.

    Vir XII.

Vire will wind in other shadows. Saint-Lô. Samuel Beckett. **CP-BeckS**

Virgils Gnat. Edmund Spenser. **CP-Spens**

Virgin, The. Richard Eberhart. **CP-EberR**

Virgin, The. William Wordsworth. **GoBC** *Fr.* Ecclesiastical Sonnets. **CP-WorW2**

(Sonnet to the Virgin.) **ISi**

Virgin and Martyr. Howard Nemerov. **CP-NemeH**

Virgin Carrying a Lantern, The. Wallace Stevens. **CP-StevW**

Virgin in a Tree. Sylvia Plath. **CP-PlatS**

Virgin Marie was (as I have read), The. Virgin Mary, The. Robert Herrick. **CP-HerrR**

Virgin Mary, The. John Donne. *Fr.* A Litany. **CP-DonnJ**

Virgin Mary, The ("To work a wonder, God would have her shown"). Robert Herrick. **CP-HerrR**

Virgin Mary, The ("Virgin Marie was [as I have read], The"). Robert Herrick. **CP-HerrR**

Virgin Mary to Christ on the Crosse, The. Robert Southwell. **CP-SoutR**

Virgin Mary to the Child Jesus, The. Elizabeth Barrett Browning. **CP-BroEB**

Virgin Mirror. Robert Ranke Graves. **CP-GravR**

Virgin Mother, The. David Herbert Lawrence. **CP-LawrD**

Virgin-Mother stood at distance (there), The. Observation. Robert Herrick. **CP-HerrR**

Virgin Mother walked barefoot, The. Begotten of the Spleen. Charles Simic. **SP-SimiC**

Virgin-Mountain, wearing like a Queen, The. Illustration; the Jung-Frau and the Fall of the Rhine near Schaffhausen. William Wordsworth. *Fr.* Ecclesiastical Sonnets. **CP-WorW2**

Virgin Youth. David Herbert Lawrence. **CP-LawrD**

Virginal, A. Ezra Pound. **SP-PounE**

Virginia. Hart Crane. *Fr.* Three Songs. **NAAL-2** *Fr.* The Bridge. **CP-CranH**

Virginia. Thomas Stearns Eliot. **InPK** *Fr.* Landscapes. **CP-ElioT**

Virginia Britannia. Marianne Craig Moore. **CP-MoorM**

Virginia Reel, A. Paul Laurence Dunbar. **CP-DunbP**

Virginia Reel. Charles Wright. **SP-WrigC**

Virginia—the West. Walt Whitman. **CP-WhitW**

Virginia Woolf. James Schuyler. **CP-SchuJ**

Virginia Woolf Gathers Mushrooms. William Dickey. **SP-DickW**

Virginity, The. Rudyard Kipling. **CP-KiplR**

Virgins, The. John Donne. *Fr.* A Litany. **CP-DonnJ**

Virgin's Cradle-Hymn, The, *tr. from anonymous Latin print.* Samuel Taylor Coleridge. **CP-ColeS**

Virgins promis'd when I died [ordy'd]. An Epitaph upon a Child. Robert Herrick. **CP-HerrR**

Virgins, time-past, known were these. How Primroses Came Green. Robert Herrick. **CP-HerrR**

Virgo. Malcolm Lowry. **CP-LowrM**

Viridian and gamboge and vermilion. Song of the Man Forsaken and Obsessed. John Berryman. **CP-BerrJ**

Virtue [*or* Vertue]. George Herbert. **CP-HerbG**

Virtue. Walter de la Mare. **CP-DeLaW**

Virtue. Kenneth Patchen. **CP-PatcK**

Virtue. William Carlos Williams. **CP-WilW1**

Virtue, alas, now let me take some rest. Sonnet 4. Sir Philip Sidney. *Fr.* Astrophil and Stella. **SP-SidnP**

Virtue, beauty, and speech, did strike, wound, charm, *speech of Philoclea.* Sir Philip Sidney. **SP-SidnP** *Fr.* Arcadia.

Virtue concealed within our breast. Part of the Ninth Ode of the Fourth Book of Horace. Jonathan Swift. **CP-SwifJ**

Virtue in that—. —"Her Soil's Birth." Louis Zukofsky. *Fr.* 29 Songs. **CP-ZukLS**

Virtue may choose the high or low degree. Alexander Pope. **NOBE; OBSV** *Fr.* Epilogue to the Satires, in Two Dialogues. **CP-PopeA**

(Triumph of Vice, The.) **NOBE; OBSV**

Virtue runs before the Muse. Loss and Gain. Ralph Waldo Emerson. **CP-EmerR**

Virtue, the greatest of all monarchies. Ode to the Honourable Sir William Temple. Jonathan Swift. **CP-SwifJ**

Virtues and Woes alike too great for man. With Fielding's *Amelia.* Samuel Taylor Coleridge. **CP-ColeS**

Virtues of Sid Hamet the Magician's Rod, The. Jonathan Swift. **CP-SwifJ**

Virtuoso, The. Stevie Smith. **CP-SmitS**

Virtuoso Literature for Two and Four Hands. Diane Wakoski. **SP-WakoD**

Virtuous Agent, The. William Carlos Williams. **CP-WilW2**

Virtuous girl wakes in the arms of her husband, The. Morning. Louise Glück. **SP-GlücL**

Virus, The. Robert Ranke Graves. **CP-GravR**

Virus and its hash of knobby aches, A. Plane Ticket. Robert Lowell. **SP-LoweR**

Viscous air, wheres' ere she fly, The. The Kingfisher. Andrew Marvell. **ChTr; PB** *Fr.* Upon Appleton House [To My Lord Fairfax]. **CP-MarvA**

Visible, invisible. A Jellyfish. Marianne Craig Moore. **CP-MoorM**

Visible the Untrue, The. Hart Crane. **CP-CranH**

Vision. Wystan Hugh Auden. **CP-AudWJ**

Vision, A. Wendell Berry. *Fr.* Work Song. **CP-BerrW**

Vision, The. Robert Burns. **CP-BurnR**

Duan First.

"Sun had clos'd the winter-day, The." **BSV**

"Sun had clos'd the winter-day, The." **OxBS**

Duan Second.

Vision. Edward Estlin Cummings. **CP-CummE**

Vision. Richard Eberhart. **CP-EberR**

Vision. John Gould Fletcher. **SP-FletJ** *Fr.* The Ghosts of an Old House.

Vision, The. ("Methought I Saw"). Robert Herrick. **CP-HerrR**

Vision, The. ("Sitting Alone"). Robert Herrick. **CP-HerrR**

Vision. Phoebe Hesketh. **SP-HeskP**

Vision, A. Denise Levertov. **CP-LeveD**

Vision. Peter Meinke. **SP-MeinP**

Vision, A. John Updike. **CP-UpdiJ**

Vision, A. William Butler Yeats.

All Souls' Night. **CP-YeatW**

Vision and Prayer. Dylan Thomas. **CP-ThomD**

Vision and Prayer. Miller Williams. **SP-WillM**

Vision Beatific. Allen Tate. **CP-TateA**

Vision by Sweetwater. John Crowe Ransom. **SP-RansJ**

Vision: Circa 1880, A. Robert Penn Warren. *Fr.* Mortmain. **SP-WarrR**

Vision is locked in stone. The Lion and the Rose. May Sarton. **SP-SartM**

Vision like quanta shooting off any which way. Memory. Richard Eberhart. **CP-EberR**

Vision must have severity. Wendell Berry. *Fr.* The Clearing. **CP-BerrW**

Vision 1948. Allen Ginsberg. **CP-GinsA**

Vision of Belshazzar, The. Byron. **CP-Byron**

Vision of Ben Jonson, on the Muses of His Friend M. Drayton, The. Ben Jonson. **CP-JonsB**

Vision of Beulah, The ("There is a place where contrarieties are equally true"). William Blake. **OAEL-2** *Fr.* Milton. **CP-BlakW**

Vision of Beulah, The ("Thou hearest the nightingale begin the song of spring"). William Blake. *See* Thou hearest the nightingale begin the song of spring.

Vision of Christ that thou dost see, The. William Blake. **ChIV-2** *Fr.* The Everlasting Gospel. **CP-BlakW**

Vision of Delight, The. Ben Jonson.

"Break, Fant'sy, from thy cave of cloud." **CP-JonsB**

Vision of Echard, The. John Greenleaf Whittier. **CP-WhitJ**

Vision of Felicity, The. William Everson. **SP-EverW** *Fr.* The Rose of Solitude.

Vision of Immortal Life has been fulfilled, The. Emily Dickinson. **SP-DickE**

Vision of Judgment, The. Byron. **CP-Byron**

"At length with jostling, elbowing, and the aid." **OBRV; OBSV**

George III. **TW**

George the Third. **FiP**

(George III.) **TW**

"He said—(I only give the heads)—he said." **EPCY**

"Saint Peter sat by the celestial gate." **FHYEP; OBSV; OXAEP-2; OxBoLi**

(Vision of Judgment, The.) **OXAEP-2**

Vision of Judgment, The. Byron. *See* Saint Peter sat by the celestial gate.

Vision of Labor, A: 1931. William Carlos Williams. **CP-WilW2**

Vision of Poets, A. Elizabeth Barrett Browning. **CP-BroEB**

Vision of Scotland, A. "Hugh MacDiarmid." **SP-MacDH**

Vision of Sin, The. Tennyson. **CP-TennA**

Song at the Ruin'd Inn. **PoEL-5**

Vision of the City from a Window. Gilbert Sorrentino. **SP-SorrG**

Vision of the Garden, A. James Merrill. **SP-MerrJ**

Vision of the Graces, The. Edmund Spenser. **NoSic** *Fr.* The Faerie Queene. **CP-Spens**

Vision of the Lamentation of Beulah, A. William Blake. *See* Thou hearest the nightingale begin the song of spring.

Vision of the Mermaids, A. Gerard Manley Hopkins. **CP-HopkG**

"Rowing, I reach'd a rock—the sea was low." **ChTr**

Vision of the Sea, A. Percy Bysshe Shelley. **CP-ShelP**

Vision of the Shepherds, The, *sels.* Wystan Hugh Auden. *Fr.* For the Time Being; a Christmas Oratorio. **CP-AudeW**

Vision of Three Angels Viewing the Progress of Socialism. Thomas McGrath. **SP-McGrT**

Vision reaches the ground. Wendell Berry. *Fr.* The Clearing. **CP-BerrW**

Vision Test, The. Mona Van Duyn. **SP-VanDM**

Vision through Timothy. Richard Eberhart. **CP-EberR**

Vision to Electra, The. Robert Herrick. **CP-HerrR**

Vision under the October Mountain: A Love Poem. Robert Penn Warren. **SP-WarrR**

Vision upon This Concei[p]t of the Faerie [*or* Faery] Queen[e], A. Sir Walter Ralegh. **CP-RaleW** *Fr.* Commendatory Verses to Edmund Spenser's Fairy Queen.

Visionary, The, *see also* Julian M. and A.G. Rochelle *and* The Prisoner. Emily Brontë. **CP-BronE**

Visionary, The. Walter de la Mare. **CP-DeLaW**

Visionary and not believed. The Frozen City. Howard Nemerov. **CP-NemeH**

Visionary Hope, The. Samuel Taylor Coleridge. **CP-ColeS**

Visionary Picnic, The. William Matthews. **SP-MattW**

Visions of Bellay, The. Joachim Du Bellay, *tr. fr. French by* Edmund Spenser. **CP-Spens**
  "At length, even at the time when Morpheus."
  "Hard by a rivers side a virgin faire."
  "I saw a river swift, whose fomy billowes."
  "I saw a spring out of a rocke forth rayle."
  "I saw a wolfe under a rockie cave."
  "I saw raysde up on yvorie pillours tall."
  "I saw the bird that can the sun endure." **Son**
  "It was the time, when rest, soft sliding downe." **AWP; Son**
  "Long having deeply gron'd these visions sad."
  "Much richer then that vessell seem'd to bee."
  "On high hills top I saw a stately frame."
  "Then all astoined with this mighty ghoast."
  "Then did a sharped spyre of diamond bright."
  "Then was the faire Dodonian tree far seene."
  "Upon an hill a bright flame I did see."

Visions of flame fanned out from cigarette. The Dying Phobiac Takes His Fears with Him. John Updike. *Fr.* Two Sonnets Whose Titles Came to Me Simultaneously. **CP-UpdiJ**

Visions of Johanna. "Bob Dylan." **CP-DylaB**

Visions of Mackenzie King, The. John Updike. **CP-UpdiJ**

Visions of Petrarch, The. Petrarch, *tr. fr. Italian by* Edmund Spenser. **CP-Spens**
  "After, at sea a tall ship did appeare."
  "At last, so faire a ladie did I spie."
  "Being one day at my window all alone."
  "I saw a phoenix in the wood alone." **ChTr**
  "Then heavenly branches did I see arise."
  "When I behold this tickle trustles state."
  "Within this wood, out of a rocke did rise."

Visions of the Daughters of Albion. William Blake. **CP-BlakW**
  Desire and Jealousy. **ECEV**
  "Infancy! fearless, lustful, happy, nestling for delight." **OXAEP-2**
  Take Thy Bliss, O Man. **EnRP**

Visions of the World's Vanity [*or* Vanitie]. Edmund Spenser. **CP-Spens**
  "Beside the fruitfull shore of muddie Nile."
  "Hideous dragon, dreadfull to behold, A."
  "High on a hill a goodly cedar grewe."
  "In summers day, when Phœbus fairly shone."
  "Kingly bird, that beares Joves thunder-clap, The."
  "Looking far foorth into the ocean wide."
  "Mighty lyon, lord of all the wood, A."
  "One day, whiles that my daylie cares did sleepe."
  "Soone after this I saw an elephant."
  "Toward the sea turning my troubled eye." **ChTr**
  (Huge Leviathan, The.) **ChTr**
  "What time the Romaine Empire bore the raine."
  "When these sad sights were overpast and gone."

Visit, A. Wystan Hugh Auden. **CP-AudWJ**

Visit, The. Stephen Berg. **SP-BergS**

Visit, The. Ralph Waldo Emerson. **CP-EmerR**

Visit, The. Ogden Nash. **CP-NashO**

Visit. Tu Fu, *tr. fr. Chinese by* William Carlos Williams *with* David Rafael Wang. **CP-WilW2**

Visit, The. William Carlos Williams. **CP-WilW2**

Visit From Dr. Fell, A. Ogden Nash. **CP-NashO**

Visit from the Sea, A. Robert Louis Stevenson. **CP-StevR**

Visit of the Gods, The, *ad. fr. the German of* Schiller. Samuel Taylor Coleridge. **CP-ColeS**

Visit to Castletown House, A. Michael Hartnett. **SP-HarMi**

Visit to Croom, 1745, A. Michael Hartnett. **SP-HarMi**

Visit to Mab, The. Nicholas Vachel Lindsay. **CP-LindV**

Visit to Rouen. Louis MacNeice. **CP-MacNL**

Visit to the Asylum, A. Edna St. Vincent Millay. **CP-MillE**

Visit to Toronto, with Companions. Margaret Atwood. **SP-AtwM1**

Visitant. Seamus Heaney. **SP-HeanS**

Visitant, The. Theodore Roethke. **CP-RoetT**

Visitation, The. Robert Ranke Graves. **CP-GravR**

Visitation, A. Daniel Gerard Hoffman. **SP-HoffD**

Visitation, The. Robert Southwell. **CP-SoutR**

Visitation of the Sick. William Wordsworth. *Fr.* Ecclesiastical Sonnets. **CP-WorW2**

Visitations. Louis MacNeice. **CP-MacNL**
  "And the Lord was not in the whirlwind." **EaLo**
  (And the Lord Was Not in the Whirlwind.) **EaLo**
  "Gull hundreds of miles below him, The."
  "Man woman and child."
  "Merman under the Plough, The."
  "Never so lithe in the green dingle."
  "When the indefinable / Moment apprises."
  "When the stranger came out of the night."

Visiting. Jenny Joseph. *Fr.* Life and Turgid Times of A. Citizen. **SP-JoseJ**

Visiting a Dead Man on a Summer Day. Marge Piercy. **SP-PierM**

Visiting Belfast at the end of June. Belfast on a Sunday Afternoon. Donald Davie. **CP-DavDo**

Visiting Day. Al Young. **CP-YounA**

Visiting Mountains. Ted Kooser. **SP-KoosT**

Visiting the Farallones. Robert Bly. **SP-BlyR**

Visiting the Stone. Stephen Berg. **SP-BergS**

Visiting the Wreck: An Able Seaman Explains. Malcolm Lowry. **CP-LowrM**

Visitor, The. Siv Cedering Fox. **SP-CedeS**

Visitor, The. Paul Laurence Dunbar. **CP-DunbP**

Visitor, The. Li Po, *tr. fr. Chinese by* William Carlos Williams *with* David Rafael Wang. **CP-WilW2**

Visitor, A. Mary Oliver. **SP-OlivM**

Visitor, The. Barton Sutter. **SP-SuttB**

Visitor. Lewis Turco. **SP-TurcL**

Visitor in Marl, A. Emily Dickinson. **CP-DickE**

Visitor, you've come and you've gone while I was. Visitor. Lewis Turco. **SP-TurcL**

Visitors Laugh at Locksmiths or, Hospital Doors Haven't Got Locks Anyhow. Ogden Nash. **CP-NashO**

Visits to St. Elizabeths. Elizabeth Bishop. **CP-BishE**

Visor'd. Walt Whitman. **CP-WhitW**

Vistas. Louis MacNeice. **CP-MacNL**

Vistas of richness and reward. The cedar. Geoffrey Hill. *Fr.* The Mystery of the Charity of Charles Péguy. **CP-HillG**

Vita Nuova. Stanley Jasspon Kunitz. **CP-KuniS**

Vita venit, vitae cum votis obvius ito. In renovationem votorum, festis natalis domini. Robert Southwell. **CP-SoutR**

Vital Choice, The. George Meredith. **CP-MerG1**

Vital Imperatives for Chester. Thomas Merton. *Fr.* Cables to the Ace. **CP-MertT**

Vital spark of heavenly [*or* heav'nly] flame! Alexander Pope, *par. fr. the Latin of* Emperor Hadrian. **CP-PopeA**
  (Ode: The Dying Christian to His Soul.) **CP-PopeA**

Vital Statistics. Robert Penn Warren. *Fr.* Homage to Theodore Dreiser. **SP-WarrR**

Vitality. David Herbert Lawrence. **CP-LawrD**

Vittoria Concluding the Opera of "Camilla." George Meredith. **CP-MerG2**

Vittoria's *Italia* Song. George Meredith. **CP-MerG2**

Viva La Resistènza. Richard Hugo. **CP-HugoR**

Vivaldi in Venice. James McAuley.
  "Arched corridors. Bare white walls." **SP-McAuJ**
  "Under the humming *continuo*." **SP-McAuJ**
  "Violas are moaning, a harpsichord chiming." **SP-McAuJ**

Vivamos, Mea Lesbia, atque Amemus. Catullus. *See* Carmen 5: "Lesbia / live with me."

Vivat. Frank Templeton Prince. **CP-PrinF**

Vive morte ma seule saison. Samuel Beckett. **CP-BeckS**

Vivid in our immortal Group. Emily Dickinson. **SP-DickE**

Vivid to the myopic are the blue. The Blue Eye. James Merrill. **SP-MerrJ**

Vividly gloomy, with bright darkling glows. Purple. Wilfred Owen. **CP-OwenW**

Vivien's Song. Tennyson. **OAEL-2** *Fr.* Balin and Balan. *Fr.* Idylls of the King. **CP-TennA**

Vivien's Song. Tennyson. *See* In Love, If Love Be Love.

Vocalism. Walt Whitman. **CP-WhitW**

Vocation, The. John Clellon Holmes. **SP-HolmJ**

Vocation. William Stafford. **SP-StafW**

Vocations. Geoffrey Hill. *Fr.* An Apology for the Revival of Christian Architecture in England. **CP-HillG**

Vodka-weary / I scowl at the bar. At the Lion's Head. David Markson. **CP-MarkD**

Voice, A. Margaret Atwood. **SP-AtwM1**

Voice, The. Stephen Berg. **SP-BergS**

Voice, The. Walter de la Mare. **CP-DeLaW**

Voice, The. Thomas Hardy. **CP-HardT**

Voice, The. Philippe Jaccottet. *Fr.* Three Poems by Phillipe Jaccottet. **SP-MahoD**

Voice, The. Philip Levine. **SP-LeviP**

Voice, The. Theodore Roethke. **CP-RoetT**

Voice and Violl, The. Robert Herrick. **CP-HerrR**

Voice by the cedar tree, A. Tennyson. *Fr.* Maud [A Monodrama]. **CP-TennA**

Voice came loudly round the corner, The. Going to Sylvie's. Jenny Joseph. *Fr.* Life and Turgid Times of A. Citizen. **SP-JoseJ**

Voice disguiser with membrane of a spider's egg-case, A. James Fenton. *Fr.* Exempla. **SP-FentJ**

Voice flew out of the river as morning flew, A. Song. Muriel Rukeyser. **CP-RukeM**

Voice from Death, A. Walt Whitman. **CP-WhitW**

Voice from heartless vacuum. Afterlude. Marsden Hartley. *Fr.* Un Recuerdo—Hermano—Hart Crane R.I.P. **CP-HartM**

Voice, from long-expecting thousands sent, A. Acquittal of the Bishops. William Wordsworth. *Fr.* Ecclesiastical Sonnets. **CP-WorW2**

Voice from the other country, A. A Voice. Margaret Atwood. **SP-AtwM1**

Voice from the Side of Etna, The; or, the Mad Monk, *longer and sl. diff. vers.* Samuel Taylor Coleridge. *See* The Mad Monk.

Voice from the Tomb (1). Stevie Smith. **CP-SmitS**

Voice from the Tomb (2). Stevie Smith. **CP-SmitS**

Voice from the Tomb (3). Stevie Smith. **CP-SmitS**

Voice from the Tomb (4). Stevie Smith. **CP-SmitS**

Voice from the Tomb (5). Stevie Smith. **CP-SmitS**

Voice from the World, A. Gerard Manley Hopkins. **CP-HopkG**

Voice from under the Table, A. Richard Wilbur. **CP-WilbR**

Voice grows thicker. Drunkard. Langston Hughes. **SP-HughL**

Voice of a people suffering long. The Jubilee Singers. John Greenleaf Whittier. **CP-WhitJ**

Voice of Age, The. Edwin Arlington Robinson. **CP-RobiE**

Voice of America. Miller Williams. **SP-WillM**

Voice of Jesus I. Rush singing, The. Poem Beginning "The." Louis Zukofsky. **CP-ZukLS**

Voice of one across the water, high. For R.S. Thomas. John Hewitt. **CP-HewiJ**

Voice of resigned subsidence, A. Calling Infinity. Tom Clark. **SP-ClarT**

Voice of Rock, The. Allen Ginsberg. **CP-GinsA**

Voice of St. Francis of Assisi, The. Nicholas Vachel Lindsay. **CP-LindV**

Voice of song from distant lands shall call, The. The King of Sweden. William Wordsworth. **CP-WorW1**

Voice of the Ancient Bard, The. William Blake. **CP-BlakW** *Fr.* Songs of Experience.

Voice of the Banjo, The. Paul Laurence Dunbar. **CP-DunbP**

Voice of the Devil, The. William Blake. **NU** *Fr.* The Marriage of Heaven and Hell. **CP-BlakW**

("All Bibles or sacred codes have been the causes of the following Errors:.")

Voice of the Dharma, The. Regarding Wave. Gary Snyder. **CP-SnydG**

Voice of the Earthquake, The. Nicholas Vachel Lindsay. *Fr.* Golden Whales of California. **CP-LindV**

Voice of the Holy Spirit, making known. The Word. John Greenleaf Whittier. **CP-WhitJ**

Voice of the last cricket, The. Splinter. Carl Sandburg. **CP-SandC**

Voice of the Man Impatient with Visions and Utopias, The. Nicholas Vachel Lindsay. *Fr.* An Argument. **CP-LindV**

Voice of the Moon, The. Richard Shelton. **SP-ShelR**

Voice of the Rain, The. Walt Whitman. **CP-WhitW**

Voice of the Thorn, The. Thomas Hardy. **CP-HardT**

Voice of the Woodthrush, Played at Half Speed, The. Daniel Gerard Hoffman. **SP-HoffD**

Voice of Things, The. Thomas Hardy. **CP-HardT**

Voice said: "Follow, follow;" and I rose, A. Two Pursuits. Christina Georgina Rossetti. **CP-RosC3**

Voice said, "Hurl her down!,"The. The Lovely Shall Be Choosers. Robert Frost. **CP-FrosR**

Voice said, Look me in the stars, A. A Question. Robert Frost. **CP-FrosR**

Voice spoke in the night, A. Frederick Morgan. *Fr.* The River. **SP-MorgF**

Voice that stands for Floods to me, The. Emily Dickinson. **CP-DickE**

Voice Ways. Robert Frost. **CP-FrosR**

Voices. Walter de la Mare. **CP-DeLaW**

Voices. Muriel Rukeyser. **CP-RukeM**

Voices, The. John Greenleaf Whittier. **CP-WhitJ**

Voices about the Princess Anemone. Stevie Smith. **CP-SmitS**

Voices against England in the Night. Stevie Smith. **CP-SmitS**

Voices at the Window. Sir Philip Sidney. *See* Eleventh Song.

Voices from above and from beneath, / Voices of creation near and far. And There Was No More Sea. Christina Georgina Rossetti. **CP-RosC2**

Voices from the Other World. James Merrill. **SP-MerrJ**

Voices from Things Growing in a Churchyard. Thomas Hardy. **CP-HardT**

Voices of Waking. Muriel Rukeyser. **CP-RukeM**

Voices on the Wind. John Gould Fletcher. **SP-FletJ**

Voices to voices, lip to lip. Edward Estlin Cummings. **CP-CummE; SP-CummE**

Void in Law. Elizabeth Barrett Browning. **CP-BroEB**

Voided by too many hopes betrayed, too many. Hayden Carruth. *Fr.* The Sleeping Beauty. **CP-CarHL**

Voiture! whose gentle Papers so refin'd. Lines Prefixed to John Davies' Translation of Voiture's Letters, 1657. Richard Lovelace. **CP-LoveR**

Voix Glauque. Lawrence Ferlinghetti. **SP-FerlL**

Vol de nuit: It's that French. Night Flight. Marge Piercy. **SP-PierM**

Vola, preghiera, e digli. Chiesa E Signore. Christina Georgina Rossetti. **CP-RosC3**

Volant Tribe of Bards on Earth Are Found, A. William Wordsworth. **CP-WorW2**

Volcanic Venus. David Herbert Lawrence. **CP-LawrD**

Volcano. Derek Walcott. **CP-WalcD**

Volcano in Kyushu, A. Gary Snyder. **CP-SnydG**

Volcano is dark and suddenly thunder, The. Malcolm Lowry. **CP-LowrM**

Volcanoes be in Sicily. Emily Dickinson. **CP-DickE**

Volgo la faccia verso l'oriente. Finestra Mia Orientale. Christina Georgina Rossetti. *Fr.* Il Rosseggiar Dell'Oriente Canzoniere. **CP-RosC3**

Volpone. Ben Jonson.

   "Fools, they are the only nation." **CP-JonsB**

   "Had old Hippocrates, or Galen." **CP-JonsB**

   Song. To Celia: ("Come my Celia, let us prove"). **CP-JonsB**

   To the Same [Celia]. **CP-JonsB**

   "You that would last long, list to my song." **CP-JonsB**

Voltaire at Ferney. Wystan Hugh Auden. **CP-AudeW**

Voluble Wheel Chair, The. Ogden Nash. **CP-NashO**

Voluntaries. Ralph Waldo Emerson. **CP-EmerR**

   In an Age of Fops and Toys. **FPL; LiTA; PoLF**

   Duty. **FaFP; GN; HBV 1-2; HBVY; TRV; TreF; TreFS; YaD**

Voluntary. Robert Louis Stevenson. **CP-StevR**

Volunteer, The. John Hewitt. **CP-HewiJ**

Volunteer, The. John Hewitt. **CP-HewiJ**

Voluptuousness torturer of bodies. Prayers of a Pagan. James Liddy. **CP-LiddJ**

Volusian sheets / shit-shotten Annals. Carmen 36. Catullus. *Fr.* Carmina. **CP-Catul**

Von Masoch met the Count de Sade. The Encounter. Robert Ranke Graves. **CP-GravR**

Voortrekker, The. Rudyard Kipling. **CP-KiplR**

Voraciousness of that only gaze, The. Emily Dickinson. **SP-DickE**

Voracities and Verities Sometimes Are Interacting. Marianne Craig Moore. **CP-MoorM**

Vos dum stertitis ore sic supino. While You Here Do Snoring Lie. Gerard Manley Hopkins. *Fr.* Songs from Shakespeare, in Latin and Greek. **CP-HopkG**

Votaries of Both Sexes Cry First to Venus. Stevie Smith. **CP-SmitS**

Votum. William Cowper. **CP-CowpW**

Vow, A. Allen Ginsberg. **CP-GinsA**

Vow, The. Robert Ranke Graves. **CP-GravR**

Vow, The. David Markson. **CP-MarkD**

Vow. John Updike. **CP-UpdiJ**

Vow of Washington, The. John Greenleaf Whittier. **CP-WhitJ**

Vow to Mars, A. Robert Herrick. **CP-HerrR**

Vow to Minerva, A. Robert Herrick. **CP-HerrR**

Vow to Venus, A. Robert Herrick. **CP-HerrR**

Vowels, The. John Gould Fletcher. **SP-FletJ**

Vowels plowed into other: opened ground. Seamus Heaney. NoP *Fr.* Glanmore Sonnets. **SP-HeanS**

Vows. Daniel Gerard Hoffman. **SP-HoffD**

Vox Humana. Thom Gunn. **CP-GunnT**

Voyage, A. Wystan Hugh Auden. **CP-AudeW**

  Hong Kong.

  Macao. **MeMAP**

  Major Port, A.

  Ship, The.

  Sphinx, The.

  Whither?

Voyage, The. Richard Eberhart. **CP-EberR**

Voyage. Archibald MacLeish. **CP-MacLA**

Voyage Autour de Mes Cartes Postales. James Schuyler. **CP-SchuJ**

Voyage en Provence. Archibald MacLeish. **CP-MacLA**

Voyage of Kevin O'Riordine, The. Malcolm Lowry. **CP-LowrM**

Voyage of the Jettie. John Greenleaf Whittier. **CP-WhitJ**

Voyage of the Needle, The. James Dickey. **CP-DickJ**

Voyage of the "Ophir," The. George Meredith. **CP-MerG2**

Voyage on the Thames, The. Alexander Pope. *See* Not with more glories, in th'ethereal plain.

Voyage through the Low Countries, A. Two Amsterdams. Lawrence Ferlinghetti. **SP-FerlL**

Voyage to Arran, The. Sir Walter Scott. **SP-ScotW** *Fr.* The Lord of the Isles.

Voyage to Cytherea, A. James Liddy. **CP-LiddJ**

Voyage to the Moon. Archibald MacLeish. **CP-MacLA**

Voyage West. Archibald MacLeish. **CP-MacLA**

Voyager returned, but much perplexed, The. Who Did Not Die in Vain. Howard Nemerov. **CP-NemeH**

Voyages. Hart Crane. **CP-CranH**

  "Above the fresh ruffles of the surf." **AmPP; CABA; MOS; MoP; NAAL-2; OxBA; PoE; VGW**

  "—And yet this great wink of eternity." **AmPP; CoBMV; DTC; GGP; HAP; ImPo; LiTM; MOS; MoAB; MoAmPo; MoPo; MoVE; NePA; OxBA; PPP; PPoe; PoE; RaBo; TRP; TwAmPo; UnPo; VGW**

  "Infinite consanguinity it bears." **MoPo; MoVE; OxBA**

  "Meticulous, past midnight in clear rime." **NAAL-2; PoE**

  "Where icy and bright dungeons lift." **CABA; HAP; MoAB; MoAmPo; MoVE; SeCeV; TwAmPo; UnPo**

  "Whose counted smile of hours and days, suppose."

Voyages always beginning, always ending, The. Departure of the Ships. Howard Nemerov. **CP-NemeH**

Voyeur, The. Mona Van Duyn. **SP-VanDM**

Voznesensky's "Silent Tingling." Allen Ginsberg. **CP-GinsA**

V.R. 1819–1901. Thomas Hardy. **CP-HardT**

Vucceria. James Fenton. **CP-FentJ**

Vuillard: "The Mother and Sister of the Artist." William DeWitt Snodgrass. **SP-SnodW**

Vulcan. George Oppen. **CP-OppeG**

Vulcan begat me. Minerva me taught. Sir Thomas Wyatt. **CP-WyatT**

Vulcan is up there, hammering. Making Repairs. James McAuley. **SP-McAuJ**

Vulture, The. Samuel Beckett. **CP-BeckS** *Fr.* Echo's Bones.

Vulture. Robinson Jeffers. **CP-JefR3**

Vulture. Kenneth Rexroth. **NNaP; SP-RexrK** *Fr.* A Bestiary. **SP-RexrK**

Vulture Peak: Gridhakuta Hill. Allen Ginsberg. **CP-GinsA**

Vulture stabs his beak into the sun, The. *Vigil: He Lies Awake in the Barracks Room, Fearful She Will Not Come, The.* Alun Lewis. *Fr.* War Wedding. **CP-LewiA**

Vultures. Margaret Atwood. **SP-AtwM2**

Vultures. Mary Oliver. **SP-OlivM**

Vultures at the zoo, The. Rain or Shine. Charles Bukowski. **SP-BukC1**

Vultures hover wheel and hover, The. Day of the Dead (Tehuantepec). Robert Earl Hayden. *Fr.* An Inference of Mexico. **CP-HaydR**

VW needs serious transmission work, The. January. Al Young. **CP-YounA**

Vying. Donald Davie. **CP-DavDo**

W

W. Louis Zukofsky. *Fr.* Chloride of Lime and Charcoal. **CP-ZukLS**

W. D. Attempts to Save Cock Robin. William DeWitt Snodgrass. **SP-SnodW**

W. D. Attempts to Swallow the Symbol ' ' ' ' ' ' ' ' ' ' ' ' ' ' ' . William DeWitt Snodgrass. **SP-SnodW**

W. D. Creates a Device for Escaping. William DeWitt Snodgrass. **SP-SnodW**

W. D. Disguised as Cock Robin and Hidden Deep in Crimson. William DeWitt Snodgrass. **SP-SnodW**

W. D., Don't Fear That Animal. William DeWitt Snodgrass. **SP-SnodW**

W. D. Is Concerned About the Character Assassination of Cock Robin. William DeWitt Snodgrass. **SP-SnodW**

W. D. Lifts Ten Times the Weight of His Own Body. William DeWitt Snodgrass. **SP-SnodW**

W. D. Meets Mr. Evil while Removing the Record of Bartok and Replacing It with a Recent Recording by the Everly Brothers in Order to Create a Mood Conducive to Searching for Cock Robin. William DeWitt Snodgrass. **SP-SnodW**

W. D. Sits in Kafka's Chair and Is Interrogated Concerning the Assumed Death of Cock Robin. William DeWitt Snodgrass. **SP-SnodW**

W. D. Tries to Warn Cock Robin. William DeWitt Snodgrass. **SP-SnodW**

W. H. Auden & Mantan Moreland. Al Young. **CP-YounA**

W. S. *Eheu!.* Samuel Taylor Coleridge. **CP-ColeS**

W. S. Landor. Marianne Craig Moore. **CP-MoorM**

Waddling / madam star, The. Edward Estlin Cummings. **CP-CummE**

Wade / through black jade. The Fish. Marianne Craig Moore. **CP-MoorM**

Wader, / Watcher by water. William Everson. *Fr.* In the Fictive Wish. **SP-EverW**

Wadin' in de Crick. Paul Laurence Dunbar. **CP-DunbP**

Wading at Wellfleet. Elizabeth Bishop. **CP-BishE**

Wadsworth Moor. Ted Hughes. **SP-HughT**

Wae Is My Heart. Robert Burns. **CP-BurnR**

Wae worth thy pow'r, thou cursed leaf! Lines Written on a Bank-Note. Robert Burns. **CP-BurnR**

Wage-Slaves, The. Rudyard Kipling. **CP-KiplR**

Wager, The. George Crabbe. **SP-CrabG** *Fr.* Tales.

Wages. Robert Herrick. **CP-HerrR**

Wages. David Herbert Lawrence. **CP-LawrD**

Wagging their hoary heads, glaring through their bright spectacles. Miching Mallecho. Robinson Jeffers. **CP-JefR3**

Waggoner, The. William Wordsworth. **CP-WorW1**

Waggoner, The. William Wordsworth. **CP-WorW1**

  Cumberland Water Authority. **FaBoDD**

Wagner gave six concerts: five. Impromptu on Richard Wagner. Robert Browning. **CP-BroR2**

Wagon stopped before the house, A; she heard. Edna St. Vincent Millay. *Fr.* Sonnets from an Ungrafted Tree. **CP-MillE**

Wagon Wheel Gap is a place I never saw. Localities. Carl Sandburg. **CP-SandC**

Wagons went on west; the people fared, The. The Burning Mountain. John Gould Fletcher. **SP-FletJ**

Wagtail, The. Theodore Roethke. **CP-RoetT**

Wagtail and Baby. Thomas Hardy. **CP-HardT**

Wagtail splutters in the stream, A. Elegy. Wystan Hugh Auden. **CP-AudWJ**

Wail of Prometheus Bound, The. Aeschylus. **WGRP** *Fr.* Prometheus Bound. **CP-BroEB**

Wail of the newborn, cry of the dying. Idol. Robert Earl Hayden. *Fr.* An Inference of Mexico. **CP-HaydR**

Wain upon the northern steep, The. Astronomy. Alfred Edward Housman. **CP-HousA**

Wait. Galway Kinnell. **SP-KinnG**

Wait. The Beatles. **CP-Beatl**

Wait. / Wait. / Wait. The Murder of Two Men by a Young Kid Wearing Lemon-colored Gloves. Kenneth Patchen. **CP-PatcK**

Wait for Me. Robert Creeley. **CP-CreeR**

Wait, for now. Wait. Galway Kinnell. **SP-KinnG**

"Wait. Let me think a minute," you said. The Wit. Elizabeth Bishop. **CP-BishE**

Wait Mister. Which way is home? Music Swims Back to Me. Anne Sexton. **CP-SextA**

"Wait, prithee, wait!" this answer Lesbia threw. To ———: " 'Wait, prithee, wait!' this answer Lesbia threw." William Wordsworth. **CP-WorW2**

Wait; the great horned owls. Owls. William DeWitt Snodgrass. **SP-SnodW**

Wait till the Majesty of Death. Emily Dickinson. **CP-DickE**

Waiters / 'gliding' / with the accuracy. Ship's Waiters. Charles Tomlinson. **CP-TomlC**

Waiting. Jane Cooper. **SP-CoopJ**

Waiting. Robert Creeley. **CP-CreeR**

Waiting. Walter de la Mare. **CP-DeLaW**

Waiting. Paul Laurence Dunbar. **CP-DunbP**

Waiting. Robert Frost. **CP-FrosR**

Waiting. Phoebe Hesketh. **SP-HeskP**

Waiting. Ron Koertge. **SP-KoerR**

Waiting. Carl Sandburg. **CP-SandC**

Waiting, The. John Greenleaf Whittier. **CP-WhitJ**

Waiting. William Carlos Williams. **CP-WilW1**

Waiting Both. Thomas Hardy. **CP-HardT**

Waiting Can Be Pretty Lousy. Kenneth Patchen. **CP-PatcK**

Waiting for a bus. Peace. Robert Creeley. **CP-CreeR**

Waiting for Breakfast, While She Brushed Her Hair. Philip Larkin. **CP-LarkP**

Waiting for her in some small park. Justin. Thom Gunn. **CP-GunnT**

Waiting for Icarus. Muriel Rukeyser. **CP-RukeM**

Waiting for the Chariot. Carl Sandburg. **CP-SandC**

Waiting for the Miracle. Leonard Cohen. **CP-CoheL**

Waiting for the Paper to be Delivered. Miller Williams. **SP-WillM**

Waiting for the signal to change. Season's Greetings. Leonard Nathan. **SP-NathL**

Waiting for when the sun an hour or less. In Santa Maria del Popolo. Thom Gunn. **CP-GunnT**

Waiting Head, The. Anne Sexton. **CP-SextA**

Waiting in Line. William Stafford. **SP-StafW**

Waiting on the Corners. Donald Hall. **CP-HallD**

Waiting Room Only. Leonard Nathan. **SP-NathL**

Waiting Rooms. Howard Nemerov. **CP-NemeH**

Waiting Rooms. John Updike. **CP-DickE**
  Boston Lying-In.
  Mass. Mental Health.

Waiting Soul, The. William Cowper. *Fr.* Olney Hymns. **CP-CowpW**

Waiting To Lean to the Master's Command. Richard Eberhart. **CP-EberR**

Waiting to leave all day I hear the words. The Gates. Muriel Rukeyser. **CP-RukeM**

Waiting with Two Members of a Motorcycle Gang for My Child to Be Born. Stephen Dunn. **SP-DunnS**

Waitress. Thom Gunn. **CP-GunnT**

Waitress. Karl Shapiro. **SP-ShapK**

Waitress looks at my face, The. Truck Stop: Minnesota. Stephen Dunn. **SP-DunnS**

Wake. Rita Dove. *Fr.* A Suite for Augustus. **SP-DoveR**

Wake, The. Robert Herrick. **CP-HerrR**

Wake, The. John Hewitt. **CP-HewiJ**

Wake. Langston Hughes. **SP-HughL**

Wake, A. Jim Morrison. **SP-MorrJ**

Wake / Shake dreams from your hair, A. A Wake. Jim Morrison. **SP-MorrJ**

Wake, friend, from forth thy lethargy: the drum. An Epistle to a Friend, to Persuade Him to the Wars. Ben Jonson. **CP-JonsB**

Wake not for the world-heard thunder. Alfred Edward Housman. **CP-HousA**

Wake, now my love, awake; for it is time. Edmund Spenser. **GBL** *Fr.* Epithalamion: "Ye learned sisters, which have oftentimes." **CP-Spens**

Wake! Our mirth begins to die. Ben Jonson. **CP-JonsB** *Fr.* The Poetaster.

Wake, sisters, wake! the day-star shines. Hymn of the Dunkers. John Greenleaf Whittier. **CP-WhitJ**

Wake the serpent not—lest he. Fragment. Percy Bysshe Shelley. **CP-ShelP**

Wake: the silver dusk returning. Reveille. Alfred Edward Housman. **CP-HousA**

Wake up high up. Things To Do in New York (City). Ted Berrigan. **SP-BerrT**

Wake, yes, wake (the Irish have a grimmer meaning). Poem on Getting up Early in the Morning (or Even Late in the Morning), When One is Old. Kay Boyle. **CP-BoylK**

Waken, lords and ladies gay. Hunting Song. Sir Walter Scott. **SP-ScotW**

Wakening at noon I smelled airplanes and hay. A Sonnet for Jane Freilicher. Frank O'Hara. **SP-OharF**

Wakening is forbidden. What the Green Tree Said. Archibald MacLeish. *Fr.* Songs for Eve. **CP-MacLA**

Wakening with the window over fields. Poem. Charles Tomlinson. **CP-TomlC**

Wakes that boats make, The. The Ways. Louis Zukofsky. **CP-ZukLS**

Wakes wet; is promptly toileted. The One-Year-Old. John Updike. **CP-UpdiJ**

Waking. Archie Randolph Ammons. **SP-AmmoA**

Waking. Stephen Dobyns. **SP-DobyS**

Waking, A. Daniel Gerard Hoffman. **SP-HoffD**

Waking / I was eating pears! The Fruit. William Carlos Williams. **CP-WilW2**

Waking. Jenny Joseph. *Fr.* Life and Turgid Times of A. Citizen. **SP-JoseJ**

Waking. Archibald MacLeish. **CP-MacLA**

Waking, The. Theodore Roethke. **CP-RoetT**

Waking, The. Theodore Roethke. **CP-RoetT**

Waking Alone. Anne Sexton. **CP-SextA**

Waking alone in a multitude of loves when morning's light. On the Marriage of a Virgin. Dylan Thomas. **CP-ThomD**

Waking an Angel. Philip Levine. **SP-LeviP**

Waking at Dusk from a Nap. William Matthews. **SP-MattW**

Waking Dream, A. Thom Gunn. **CP-GunnT**

Waking Early Sunday Morning. Robert Lowell. **SP-LoweR**

Waking Father, The. Paul Muldoon. **SP-MuldP**

Waking from a winter's sleep. For Mrs. Jones. Chuck Miller. **SP-MillC**

Waking from Sleep. Robert Bly. **SP-BlyR**

Waking half-drunk in a strange pad. North Beach Alba. Gary Snyder. **CP-SnydG**

Waking, he found himself in a train, andante. Slow Movement. Louis MacNeice. **CP-MacNL**

Waking, he stared raptly at her face. Think It Over. "Lou Reed." **SP-ReedL**

Waking, I Always Waked You Awake. Jean Garrigue. **SP-GarrJ**

Waking, I look at you sleeping beside me. Waking. Stephen Dobyns. **SP-DobyS**

Waking in a Newly Built House. Thom Gunn. **CP-GunnT**

Waking in New York. Allen Ginsberg. **CP-GinsA**

Waking in the Blue. Robert Lowell. **SP-LoweR**

Waking in the Dark. Adrienne Rich. **SP-RicA1; SP-RicA2**

Waking in Winter. Sylvia Plath. **CP-PlatS**

Waking into Sleep. Kenneth Patchen. **CP-PatcK**

Waking Jed. Charles Kenneth Williams. **CP-WillC; SP-WillC**

Waking on the Seventh Day of Creation. The Sabbath. Wystan Hugh Auden. **CP-AudeW**

Waking one morning / we cannot find. New Animals. Donald Hall. **CP-HallD**

Waking outside his Babylonian binge. The Thousandth Poem for Dylan Thomas. John Ciardi. **SP-CiarJ**

Waking thickheaded by crow's light. Continuum. Adrienne Rich. **CP-RicAE**

Waking this Morning. Muriel Rukeyser. *See* This Morning.

Waking to My Name. Robert Pack. **SP-PackR**

Waking to silence. Goodbye. Philip Levine. **SP-LeviP**

Waking Up in Santa Cruz at Sea. Al Young. **CP-YounA**

Waking was laughing then. Grammar Lesson. Stanley Jasspon Kunitz. **CP-KuniS**

Waking wassails of wistful welcome. Malcolm Lowry. **CP-LowrM**

Waldeinsamkeit. Ralph Waldo Emerson. **CP-EmerR**

Walden 1950. Adrienne Rich. **CP-RicAE**

Waldenses. William Wordsworth. *Fr.* Ecclesiastical Sonnets. **CP-WorW2**

Waldo Jeffers had reached his limit. The Gift. "Lou Reed." **SP-ReedL**

Wales. Derek Walcott. **CP-WalcD**

Wales Visitation. Allen Ginsberg. **CP-GinsA**

Walgh-Vogel, The. Richard Wilbur. **CP-WilbR**

Walk, The. Wystan Hugh Auden. **CP-AudWJ**

Walk, The. Thomas Hardy. **CP-HardT**

Walk, The. James Schuyler. **CP-SchuJ**

Walk, A. Gary Snyder. **CP-SnydG**

Walk, The. Derek Walcott. **CP-WalcD**

Walk After Dark, A. Wystan Hugh Auden. **CP-AudeW**

Walk by Moonlight in Small Town. Robert Penn Warren. *Fr.* Man in Moonlight. **SP-WarrR**

Walk by the Charles, A. Adrienne Rich. **CP-RicAE; SP-RicA2**

Walk by the Water, A. Charlotte Smith. **CP-SmitC**

Walk high on the bridge of Estador. The Bridge of Estador. Hart Crane. **CP-CranH**

Walk in Canada. Malcolm Lowry. **CP-LowrM**

Walk in Late Summer, A. Theodore Roethke. **CP-RoetT**

Walk in the Shrubbery, A. Charlotte Smith. **CP-SmitC**

Walk in the woods at the hour when the fuddled sun. Jenny Joseph. **SP-JoseJ** *Fr.* The Building Site.

Walk in this faithless grass with studious tread. Cold Pastoral. Allen Tate. **CP-TateA**

Walk on the delicate parts. A Foot-Note. William Carlos Williams. **CP-WilW1**

Walk on the Wild Side. "Lou Reed." **SP-ReedL**

Walk out if it doesn't feel right. Walk Out in the Rain. "Bob Dylan" *and* Helena Springs. **CP-DylaB**

Walk Out in the Rain. "Bob Dylan" *and* Helena Springs. **CP-DylaB**

Walk quietly around in. Ars Poetica. Donald Davie. **CP-DavDo**

Walk right in / sit right down. Things To Do in Anne's Room. Ted Berrigan. **SP-BerrT**

Walk softly on my grave. An Address. William Carlos Williams. **CP-WilW2**

Walk the night-scented streets. Lighted Windows (For Judy). Chuck Miller. **SP-MillC**

"Walk the plank" says Pirate Jim. Pirate Captain Jim. Shel Silverstein. **SP-SilS2**

Walk through, minding the nettles. Roy Fisher. **SP-FishR** *Fr.* Diversions.

Walk through the fern but do not tear the root. Warning. Louise McNeill. **SP-McNeL**

Walk through the Notebooks, A. Denise Levertov. **CP-LeveD**

Walk Warily. David Herbert Lawrence. **CP-LawrD**

Walk with Tom Jefferson, A. Philip Levine. **SP-LeviP**

Walked in the basement all winter. For exercise. He. Ron Koertge. **SP-KoerR**

"Walked into State. . . ." Tom Clark. **SP-ClarT**

Walker. Alice Walker. **CP-WalkA**

Walker dead now— / Urge to words. For Walker Evans. John Clellon Holmes. **SP-HolmJ**

Walkin' Down the Line. "Bob Dylan." **CP-DylaB**

Walking. Robert Creeley. **CP-CreeR**

Walking about the emptied house I. A Measured Tread. Donald Davie. **CP-DavDo**

Walking again along these well-loved paths. Walking Back. Phoebe Hesketh. **SP-HeskP**

Walking along a street in a neighborhood. Housing. Grace Paley. **CP-PaleG**

Walking along in this not quite prose way. Near. William Stafford. **SP-StafW**

Walking along the tow-path. Diptera. John Hewitt. **CP-HewiJ**

Walking among the antlered oaks. All Hallows. Phoebe Hesketh. **SP-HeskP**

Walking around in the park. Toads Revisited. Philip Larkin. **CP-LarkP**

Walking at dusk often. Roy Fisher. **SP-FishR** *Fr.* Glenthorne Poems.

Walking at night on asphalt campus. Death News. Allen Ginsberg. **CP-GinsA**

Walking Away. Phoebe Hesketh. **SP-HeskP**

Walking away means. Purifying the Language of the Tribe. William Stafford. **SP-StafW**

Walking Back. Phoebe Hesketh. **SP-HeskP**

Walking back to the farm from the depot. The Table. Donald Hall. **CP-HallD**

Walking Beside a Creek. Ted Kooser. **SP-KoosT**

Walking beside the wall towards the stream. Roy Fisher. *Fr.* Five Morning Poems from a Picture by Manet. **SP-FishR**

Walking by lakeshore, feet in slush, it rains. Four Auguries. Margaret Atwood. **SP-AtwM1**

Walking by map, I chose unwonted ground. On the Hall at Stowey. Charles Tomlinson. **CP-TomlC**

Walking by the edge of the woods across the crest of the hill. Dead Dog (For Goo). Chuck Miller. **SP-MillC**

Walking down / backward, wall. A Tiny Place. Robert Creeley. **CP-CreeR**

Walking down a / walk, a stone. Pay. Robert Creeley. **CP-CreeR**

Walking down 3rd Avenue / in the 50s on a June morning. Sweet Charity. John Clellon Holmes. **SP-HolmJ**

Walking Down Westgate in the Fall. Howard Nemerov. **CP-NemeH**

Walking Home at Night. Allen Ginsberg. **CP-GinsA**

Walking home through the tall. Missoula in a Dusty Light. John Haines. **SP-HainJ**

Walking in February. Thin Ice. Gary Snyder. **CP-SnydG**

Walking in Paris. Anne Sexton. **CP-SextA**

Walking in the dry winter woods. The Stallion. Barton Sutter. **SP-SuttB**

Walking in the flat Oxfordshire fields. Subjected Earth. Robinson Jeffers. **CP-JefR2**

Walking in the warmest afternoon. The Stoat. John Hewitt. **CP-HewiJ**

Walking into Love. Marge Piercy. **SP-PierM**

Behold: A Relationship.

Difference of Ages.

Little Scandal, A.

Meditation in My Favorite Position.

What Feeling Is This?

Words Are Said, the Love Is Made, The.

Walking Man of Rodin, The. Carl Sandburg. **CP-SandC**

Walking north toward the point, I come on a dead seal. The Dead Seal [near McClure's Beach]. Robert Bly. **SP-BlyR**

Walking on the River Ice. Wendell Berry. **CP-BerrW**

Walking on this springy grass. First Universe. Diane Wakoski. *Fr.* The Universes. **SP-WakoD**

Walking on Water. James Dickey. **CP-DickJ**

Walking one day in the park in winter. In the Park. Stevie Smith. **CP-SmitS**

Walking Past Paul Blackburn's Apt. on 7th St. Diane Wakoski. **SP-WakoD**

Walking Praed Street. Richard Hugo. **CP-HugoR**

Walking, remembering. Precision. Diane Wakoski. **SP-WakoD**

Walking Swiftly. Robert Bly. **SP-BlyR**

Walking swiftly with a dreadful duchess. Infelice. Stevie Smith. **CP-SmitS**

Walking the Dog. Robert Creeley. **CP-CreeR**

Walking the Dog: A Diatribe. Mona Van Duyn. **SP-VanDM**

Walking the Fire Line. James Dickey. **CP-DickJ**

Walking the Marshland. Stephen Dunn. **SP-DunnS**

Walking the prairies—sky so vast. Flood Light. William Matthews. *Fr.* Flood. **SP-MattW**

Walking this field I remember. The Premonition. Theodore Roethke. **CP-RoetT**

Walking through the Upper East Side. Erica Jong. **SP-JongE**

Walking to Bells. Charles Tomlinson. **CP-TomlC**

Walking to Sleep. Richard Wilbur. **CP-WilbR**

Walking to the edge with a cup of coffee. The Edge in the Morning. James Schuyler. *Fr.* The Cenotaph. **CP-SchuJ**

Walking to Work. Ted Kooser. **SP-KoosT**

Walking to Work. Frank O'Hara. **SP-OharF**

Walking today beneath the bankrupt trees. November Wood. John Hewitt. **CP-HewiJ**

Walking Tour, The. Wystan Hugh Auden. *See* To throw away the key and walk away.

Walking up from the barn to the house. Mara. Robinson Jeffers. **CP-JefR3**

Walking with a virgin heart. The Hills of May. Robert Ranke Graves. **CP-GravR**

Walking with God. William Cowper. **ECEV; EnRP; FiP; NOCV; NOEC; PeECV; PoEL-3; SCGP; TEP; TOF** *Fr.* Olney Hymns. **CP-CowpW**

Walking with you and another lady. A Dream of Jealousy. Seamus Heaney. **SP-HeanS**

Walks. Wystan Hugh Auden. **CP-AudeW**

Walks all night through the streets. The Age of Desire. Richard Shelton. *Fr.* The Seven Ages of Man. **SP-ShelR**

Walks in Rome. Frank Templeton Prince. **CP-PrinF**

"Mine old dear enemy."

"My last morning and so, here."

"Painter's face—if, The."

"Sun floats in sublime, The."

Wall, A. Robert Creeley. **CP-CreeR**

Wall, The. Robert Ranke Graves. **CP-GravR**

Wall, The. Louis MacNeice. **CP-MacNL**

Wall / one's up against, The. Robert Creeley. **CP-CreeR**

Wall, The. Anne Sexton. **CP-SextA**

Wall, A. Charles Simic. **SP-SimiC**

Wall, a bastion, A. St Luke. David Herbert Lawrence. **CP-LawrD**

Wall and Cloud. James Dickey. **CP-DickJ**

Wall, as I watched, came neck-high, The. The Girl. William Carlos Williams. **CP-WilW2**

Wall is of brick. The buildings, The. The College. Lewis Turco. **SP-TurcL**

Wall ritual. These. Charles Henri Ford. **SP-FordC** *Fr.* Emblems of Arachne.

Wall Shadows. Carl Sandburg. **CP-SandC**

Wallabout Martyrs, The. Walt Whitman. **CP-WhitW**

Wallace Stevens, what's he done? A Rouse for Stevens. Theodore Roethke. **CP-RoetT**

Walled hilltop, islanded in sea-mist. Erice, Western Sicily. John Hewitt. **CP-HewiJ**

Walled In. Phoebe Hesketh. **SP-HeskP**

Wallflower. "Bob Dylan." **CP-DylaB**

Wallflower. Anne Sexton. **CP-SextA**

Wallful of quoted passages from his work, The. Nabokov's Blues. William Matthews. **SP-MattW**

Wallowing in this bloody sty. The Drunken Fisherman. Robert Lowell. **SP-LoweR**

Walls, The. Charles Bukowski. **SP-BukC3**

Walls. Robert Creeley. **CP-CreeR**

Walls are of rough plank, The. The Ice House. Lewis Turco. **SP-TurcL**

Walls constituting our / access to the property—, The. Way. Robert Creeley. **CP-CreeR**

Walls Do Not Fall, The. Hilda Doolittle. **CP-DoolH**

"Incident here and there, An." **OBWP**

"O heart, small urn." **LLLT,** sect. 28;

"Sirius: / what mystery is this?" **PBWP**

"We have seen how the most amiable." **BoWoP; PBWP**

Walls, except that they stretch through China. Variations on Pasternak's "Mein Liebchen, Was Willst Du Noch Mehr?" Frank O'Hara. **SP-OharF**

Walls, from its looted stones, defend. At the Hill Fort. Charles Tomlinson. **CP-TomlC**

Walls have been shaded for so many years, The. The Soldier Walks under the Trees of the University. Randall Jarrell. **CP-JarrR**

Walls, mounds, enclosing corrugations. The Castle. Robert Ranke Graves. **CP-GravR**

Walls of Red Wing. "Bob Dylan." **CP-DylaB**

Walls of remorse are steep, there is no belay, The. Malcolm Lowry. Fr. The Moon in Scandinavia. **CP-LowrM**

Walls of this hotel are paper-thin, The. Paper-Thin Hotel. Leonard Cohen. **CP-CoheL**

Walls To Put Up, Walls To Take Down. Stephen Dobyns. **SP-DobyS**

Walls were painted blue so long ago, you think. Cantina Iannini. Richard Hugo. **CP-HugoR**

Walls widened, and were the horizon's rim, The. She Is Lifted with the Old Gods into the Western Sky. Nicholas Vachel Lindsay. Fr. The Trial of the Dead Cleopatra in Her Beautiful and Wonderful Tomb. **CP-LindV**

Walnut. Robert Pack. **SP-PackR**

Walpole talks of "a man and his price." Rudyard Kipling. See Public Waste.

Walrus and the Carpenter, The. "Lewis Carroll." **CP-CarrL** Fr. Through the Looking-Glass.

Walrus stretches forth a wrinkled hand, The. The Kingfisher's Boxing Gloves. James Fenton. **SP-FentJ**

Walt, my old classmates who write poems. Crossing Walt Whitman Bridge. Daniel Gerard Hoffman. **SP-HoffD**

Walt Whitman. Walt Whitman. **BiP; NoAM** Fr. Song of Myself. **CP-WhitW**

Walt Whitman, a kosmos, of Manhattan the son. Walt Whitman. **NoP; SAmP; SCV** Fr. Song of Myself. **CP-WhitW**

Walter Armistead. James Dickey. **CP-DickJ**

Walter Rawley [or Ralegh or Rawely] of the Middle Temple, in Commendation of the Steel[e] Glass[e]. Sir Walter Ralegh. See Sweet [or Swete] were the sauce would please e[a]ch kind of tast[e].

Walter Scott. James Schuyler. **CP-SchuJ**

Walton's Book of Lives. William Wordsworth. Fr. Ecclesiastical Sonnets. **CP-WorW2**

Waltz, The. Byron. **CP-Byron**

"Endearing Waltz!—to thy more melting tune." **DIP**

"Muse of the many-twinkling feet! whose charms." **OBSV**

"Muse of the many-twinkling feet! whose charms." **DIP**

"Seductive Waltz!—though on thy native shore." **DIP**

"Such was the time when Waltz might best maintain." **DIP**

Waltz for Accordion. Isabella Gardner. Fr. Saloon Suite. **CP-GardI**

Waltz of the Empty Roadhouse. Gilbert Sorrentino. Fr. Twelve Études for Voice and Kazoo. **SP-SorrG**

Waltzer in the House, The. Stanley Jasspon Kunitz. **CP-KuniS**

Waltzing Matilda. Alice Notley. **SP-NotlA**

Waltzing Matilda whipped out her wallet. Street Hassle: Waltzing Matilda. "Lou Reed." **SP-ReedL**

Wan / Swan. The Bereaved Swan. Stevie Smith. **CP-SmitS**

Wan Heralds of the Sun and Summer gale! Snowdrops. Charlotte Smith. **CP-SmitC**

Wan leafs shak, atour us like the snaw, The. Farewell to Dostoevski. "Hugh MacDiarmid." **NAEL-2** Fr. A Drunk Man Looks at the Thistle. **SP-MacDH**

Wand, The. Robert Ranke Graves. **CP-GravR**

Wand of gold from the reaper's moon, A. George Meredith. **CP-MerG2**

Wanda and the Fish. Paul Zimmer. **SP-ZimmP**

Wanda and Zimmer. Paul Zimmer. **SP-ZimmP**

Wanda Being Beautiful. Paul Zimmer. **SP-ZimmP**

Wanda is gone and I sweat like concrete. Cecil Sliding Away from the Memory of Wanda. Paul Zimmer. **SP-ZimmP**

Wanda, my pussy willow, cupcake. Wanda and Zimmer. Paul Zimmer. **SP-ZimmP**

Wanda was having an ugly night. Lester Tells of the End of the Summer. Paul Zimmer. **SP-ZimmP**

Wander, spirit?—I!. Which Way? Walter de la Mare. **CP-DeLaW**

Wanderer, The. Wystan Hugh Auden. **CP-AudeW**

Wanderer, The. Thomas Hardy. **CP-HardT**

Wanderer, The. Daniel Gerard Hoffman. **SP-HoffD**

Wanderer, The. Stevie Smith. **CP-SmitS**

Wanderer: A Rococo Study, The. **CP-WilW1**

Wanderer, The. see also The Ruined Cottage. William Wordsworth. **EnRP** Fr. The Excursion. **CP-WorW2**

"Supine the Wanderer lay." **NOBRP**

Wanderer Recalls the Past, The. **OBNC**

Wanderer in our skies. Voyage to the Moon. Archibald MacLeish. **CP-MacLA**

Wanderer moon / smiling a. Summer Song. William Carlos Williams. **CP-WilW1**

Wanderer Recalls the Past, The. William Wordsworth. **OBNC** Fr. The Wanderer. **EnRP** Fr. The Excursion. **CP-WorW2**

Wanderer! that stoop'st so low, and com'st so near. To the Moon (Composed by the Seaside,—on the Coast of Cumberland). William Wordsworth. **CP-WorW2**

Wanderer, The: A Rococo Study. William Carlos Williams. **CP-WilW1**

Wanderers, The. Robert Browning. **OBEV** Fr. Paracelsus. **CP-BroR1**

Wanderers, The. Walter de la Mare. **CP-DeLaW**

Wanderers of the Pale Wood. Kenneth Patchen. **CP-PatcK**

"And forth from that shadow of a shadow."

"And then a bird that was like a great pale wolf flying down."

"And then it was that the Bridegroom beheld the Bride wraith- / like."

"And they walked in the ancient wonder of the morning light."

"Animals of the morning wood watching in silence as, The."

"But the Beast of the Wood came as a smiling man."

"For here indeed was the unassailable kingdom of the heart itself."

"Listen / Listen / O what is that sound."

"O out of that feast in the blond wood of the morning."

"O sorrow it is."

"Then at last the Lovers began to speak together."

"Then did the wind move sunful fingers through her hair."

Wandering among the chimneys. The Gentle Negress. William Carlos Williams. **CP-WilW2**

Wandering at Morn. Walt Whitman. **CP-WhitW**

Wandering Burgess, The. "Lewis Carroll." **CP-CarrL**

Wandering Cosmos, The. David Herbert Lawrence. **CP-LawrD**

Wandering gadling in the summer tide, The. Sir Thomas Wyatt. **CP-WyatT**

Wandering, in autumn, the woods of boyhood. Gold Glade. Robert Penn Warren. **SP-WarrR**

Wandering in the country roads in winter. For Barbara. Chuck Miller. **SP-MillC**

Wandering Jew, The. Edwin Arlington Robinson. **CP-RobiE**

Wandering Jew's Soliloquy, The. Percy Bysshe Shelley. **CP-ShelP**

Wandering Outlaw, The. Byron. **FiP** Fr. Childe Harold's Pilgrimage. **CP-Byron**

Wandering oversea dreamer. Prayer after World War. Carl Sandburg. **CP-SandC**

Wandering through cold streets tangled like old string. Brussels in Winter. Wystan Hugh Auden. **CP-AudeW**

Wandering Willie. George Meredith. **CP-MerG2**

Inspiration of the Great West Wind, The.

Last Wandering of Poor Willie, The.

Willie's Dirge on Little Marian.

Wanderings of Cain, The. Samuel Taylor Coleridge. **CP-ColeS**

Wanderings of Oisin, The. William Butler Yeats. **CP-YeatW**

Old Man Stirs the Fire to a Blaze, An. **RB**

"We galloped over the glossy sea." **SeCePo**

Wanderings of the Tribe, The. Alí Chumacero, tr. fr. Spanish by William Carlos Williams. **CP-WilW2**

Waning Crescent Moon, The. Richard Shelton. Fr. Five Lies About the Moon. **SP-ShelR**

Waning Moon, The. Percy Bysshe Shelley. **CP-ShelP**

Waning moon looks upward; this grey night, The. Nostalgia. David Herbert Lawrence. **CP-LawrD**

Wansfell! This Household Has a Favoured Lot. William Wordsworth. **CP-WorW2**

Want. Robert Herrick. **CP-HerrR**

Want. Robert Herrick. **CP-HerrR**

Want is a softer Wax, that takes thereon. Want. Robert Herrick. **CP-HerrR**

Want of Peace, The. Wendell Berry. **CP-BerrW**

Want to trade me, do you, mistah? Oh, well, now, I reckon not. Dat Ol' Mare o' Mine. Paul Laurence Dunbar. **CP-DunbP**

Wanta / spendsix / dollars Kid. Edward Estlin Cummings. **CP-CummE**

Wantage Bells. Sir John Betjeman. **CP-BetjJ**

Wanted Man. "Bob Dylan." **CP-DylaB**

Wanting is—what? Robert Browning. **CP-BroR2**

Wanting the Impossible. Carl Sandburg. **CP-SandC**

Wanting throat crown narcissus proves. Snowflake. Louis Zukofsky. **CP-ZukLS**

Wanting to Be Heavier. Stephen Berg. **SP-BergS**

Wanting to Die. Anne Sexton. **CP-SextA**

Wanting to get away. Roy Fisher. **SP-FishR** *Fr.* New Diversions.

Wanting to Get Closer. Stephen Dunn. **SP-DunnS**

Wanting to make music. Not the Blood a Dreamer Kissed from My Mouth. Diane Wakoski. *Fr.* Fifteen Poems for a Lunar Eclipse None of Us Saw. **SP-WakoD**

Wanting to save their fortunes for. The Usurers of Heaven. William Carlos Williams. **CP-WilW2**

Wanting You. Robert Creeley. **CP-CreeR**

Wanton and lascivious eye. A. The Eye. Robert Herrick. **CP-HerrR**

Wanton troopers riding by, The. The Nymph Complaining for the Death of Her Faun [*or* Fawn]. Andrew Marvell. **CP-MarvA**

Wanton Wenches doe not bring. To His Girles. Robert Herrick. **CP-HerrR**

Wanton's charms, however bright, The. To Seraphina. James Thomson. **CP-ThomJ**

Wantons we are; and though our words be such. Poets. Robert Herrick. **CP-HerrR**

Wants. Philip Larkin. **CP-LarkP**

Wap and rowe, wap and row. The Reel o' Stumpie. Robert Burns. **CP-BurnR**

Wapiti, The. Ogden Nash. **CP-NashO**

War. Charles Henri Ford. **SP-FordC**

War, A. Randall Jarrell. **CP-JarrR; SP-JarrR**

War. George Meredith. **CP-MerG2**

War. Percy Bysshe Shelley. *Fr.* Posthumous Fragments of Margaret Nicholson. **CP-ShelP**

War. Richard Shelton. **SP-ShelR**

War. Charles Kenneth Williams. **SP-WillC**

War against the Trees, The. Stanley Jasspon Kunitz. **CP-KuniS**

War and Silence. Robert Bly. **SP-BlyR**

War-Baby. David Herbert Lawrence. **CP-LawrD**

War broke: and now the Winter of the world. 1914. Wilfred Owen. **CP-OwenW**

War Comes into my Room, The. Muriel Rukeyser. **CP-RukeM**

War ends, and he's returning. A Wife and Another. Thomas Hardy. **CP-HardT**

War games are over, The. We'll to the Woods No More, the Laurels Are Cut Down. May Sarton. **SP-SartM**

War God, The. Stephen Spender. **CP-SpenS**

War Guilt. Edwin Rolfe. **CP-RolfE**

War-Guilt Trials. Robinson Jeffers. **CP-JefR3**

War Heroes. Louis MacNeice. *Fr.* Out of the Picture. **CP-MacNL**

War in the Garden. Brendan Galvin. **SP-GalvB**

War is a fevered god. Telesila. Hilda Doolittle. **CP-DoolH**

War is far away, sweet, The. The Sea Coming Indoors. Marilyn Hacker. **SP-HackM**

War Is the Statesman's Game. Percy Bysshe Shelley. **FF; PPON** *Fr.* Queen Mab. **CP-ShelP**

War of your great beauty is in all the skies, The. At Dawn. William Carlos Williams. **CP-WilW1**

War on the Mind in a Time of Love. Charles Olson. **CP-OlsoC**

War Profit Litany. Allen Ginsberg. **CP-GinsA**

War Resisters' Song. Thomas McGrath. **SP-McGrT**

War shook the land where Levi dwelt. The Field of Glory. Edwin Arlington Robinson. **CP-RobiE**

War Song [to Englishmen], A. William Blake. **CP-BlakW**

War, the Destroyer. William Carlos Williams. **CP-WilW2**

War-Token, The. Henry Wadsworth Longfellow. **PAH** *Fr.* John Alden. *Fr.* The Courtship of Miles Standish. **SP-LongH**

War was not strife, The. The Late War. David Herbert Lawrence. **CP-LawrD**

War Wedding. Alun Lewis. **CP-LewiA**
   He Gives Her Botticelli's Birth of Venus as a Wedding Gift.
   Marriage Bed, The.
   She Comes To Him in the Night.
   She Remains.
   She Wakes Early, While He Still Sleeps.
   They Part at Daybreak, Returning Their Inevitable Ways.
   Vigil: He Lies Awake in the Barracks Room, Fearful She Will Not Come, The.

Vigil: She Tarries, Far-Off, in a Strange Anguish, The.

War-Wife of Catknoll, The. Thomas Hardy. **CP-HardT**

War with England. "Hugh MacDiarmid."
   "I was better with the sounds of the sea." **SP-MacDH**

War Wound, The. James Dickey. **CP-DickJ**

Warble for Lilac-Time. Walt Whitman. **CP-WhitW**

Warble me now for joy of lilac-time (returning in reminiscence). Warble for Lilac-Time. Walt Whitman. **CP-WhitW**

Ward F4. Phoebe Hesketh. **SP-HeskP**

Ward in the States, A. Randall Jarrell. **CP-JarrR; SP-JarrR**

Ward is barred with moonlight, The. A Ward in the States. Randall Jarrell. **CP-JarrR; SP-JarrR**

Ward of the Law!—dread Shadow of a King! On the Death of His Majesty (George the Third). William Wordsworth. **CP-WorW2**

Warden, The. Stevie Smith. **CP-SmitS**

Warden Said to Me the Other Day, The. Etheridge Knight. **SP-KnigE**

Warden's Charm, The. "Lewis Carroll." **CP-CarrL** *Fr.* Sylvie and Bruno.

Wardrobe towers above the table lamp, The. Madness. Allen Tate. **CP-TateA**

Wards, The. Muriel Rukeyser. **CP-RukeM**

Warehouse Chute, The. Dabney Stuart. **SP-StuaD**

Waring. Robert Browning. **CP-BroR1**

Warm air throbbing with locust songs. Summer Song. Edward Estlin Cummings. **CP-CummE**

Warm are the still and lucky miles. Wystan Hugh Auden. *Fr.* Ten Songs. **CP-AudeW**

Warm day in December, A. Wendell Berry. *Fr.* Window Poems. **CP-BerrW**

Warm Day in Winter, A. Paul Laurence Dunbar. **CP-DunbP**

Warm flute on the cold snow. Nine Variations in a Chinese Winter Setting. Charles Tomlinson. **CP-TomlC**

Warm gale, a dose of spring—revert to the pores. Catullus. *See* Carmen 46: "Now spring bursts."

"Warm hands, cold heart," they say; and vice-versa. Hot Hands. Donald Davie. **CP-DavDo**

Warm in her Hand these accents lie. Emily Dickinson. **CP-DickE**

Warm in the pool the wasted man. Slow Dialogue between Pain and Roosevelt. Muriel Rukeyser. **CP-RukeM**

Warm in the underbough of dark. Witches Waken the Natural World in Spring. James Wright. **CP-WrigJ**

Warm Mountain Poem for Matt Liban. James Liddy. **CP-LiddJ**

Warm rains / wash away winter's. The Hermaphroditic Telephones. William Carlos Williams. **CP-WilW1**

Warm ripe days. The sun floods the ridge with color. Tom Clark. *Fr.* Suite. **SP-ClarT**

Warm spring day. . . the end of March, A. Pioneer. John Hewitt. **CP-HewiJ**

Warm sun is failing, the bleak wind is wailing, The. Autumn: A Dirge. Percy Bysshe Shelley. **CP-ShelP**

Warm sun. Perhaps these yellow wild-flowers have the minds of little girls. Thomas Merton. *Fr.* Cables to the Ace. **CP-MertT**

Warm sun, quiet air. Election Day. William Carlos Williams. **CP-WilW2**

Warm yellowy-green / In the blue serene. The Upper Birch-Leaves. Thomas Hardy. **CP-HardT**

Warm'd by the summer sun's meridian ray. Upon Happiness. James Thomson. **CP-ThomD**

Warmed over pine-cones. Fairy Song. Randall Jarrell. **CP-JarrR**

Warmth. Joseph Ceravolo. **SP-CeraJ**

Warmth. Brendan Galvin. **SP-GalvB**

Warmth / is the way. Looking Out. Robert Creeley. **CP-CreeR**

Warmth. Barton Sutter. **SP-SuttB**

Warmth of cows, The. A Carol. Donald Hall. **CP-HallD**

Warned to avoid / any fruit without peel or rind. The Skateboard Throne: an Ode to Citizen Amputees. Laurence Lieberman. **SP-LiebL**

Warning. Leonard Cohen. **CP-CoheL**

Warning, The. Robert Creeley. **CP-CreeR**

Warning, *See also* Hughes's Warning: Augmented. Langston Hughes. **SP-HughL**

Warning. Jenny Joseph. **SP-JoseJ**

Warning, The. Henry Wadsworth Longfellow. **SP-LongH**

Warning. Louise McNeill. **SP-McNeL**

Warning, The. George Meredith. **CP-MerG2**

Warning, A. Grace Paley. **CP-PaleG**

Warning. Shel Silverstein. **SP-SilS2**

Warning. Alice Walker. **CP-WalkA**

Warning, The. William Wordsworth. **CP-WorW2**

Warning and Reply. Emily Brontë. *See* In the earth, the earth, thou shalt be laid.

Warning: Augmented, *See also Hughes's* Warning. Langston Hughes. **SP-HughL**

Warning: Children at Play. Howard Nemerov. **CP-NemeH**

Warning from False Cape Horn. Malcolm Lowry. **CP-LowrM**

Warning to Children. Robert Ranke Graves. **CP-GravR**

Warning to My Readers, A. Wendell Berry. **CP-BerrW**

Warning to the Man in Receiving at Sears, A. Diane Wakoski. **SP-WakoD**

Warning to Wives, A. Ogden Nash. **CP-NashO**

Warped this perhapsy. Edward Estlin Cummings. **CP-CummE**

Warrant for Pablo Neruda, A. Thomas McGrath. **SP-McGrT**

Warre. Robert Herrick. **CP-HerrR**

Warren G. Harding invented the word "normalcy." Qualm. John Ashbery. **SP-AshbJ**

Warrioe Who Went With a Crowd, my sand-painter grandfather. Navajo Setting the Record Straight. John Berryman. **CP-BerrJ**

Warrior is afraid, The. Verses Written for Student Antidraft Registration Rally 1980. Allen Ginsberg. **CP-GinsA**

Warriors and chiefs! should the shaft or the sword. Song of Saul before His Last Battle. Byron. **CP-Byron**

Warriors of the North, The. Ted Hughes. **SP-HughT**

Warrior's Prayer, The. Paul Laurence Dunbar. **CP-DunbP**

Wars, The. Pablo Neruda, *tr. fr. Spanish by* Ben Belitt. **SP-NeruP**

Wars. Carl Sandburg. **CP-SandC**

Wars of York and Lancaster. William Wordsworth. *Fr.* Ecclesiastical Sonnets. **CP-WorW2**

Wars that are just? A simpler question: In the event. George Oppen. **APSN** *Fr.* Route. **CP-OppeG**

Wars worse than civil on Thessalian plains. Lucan, *tr. by* Christopher Marlowe. **CP-MarlC** *Fr.* Pharsalia.

Wart, The. Robert Penn Warren. **SP-WarrR**

Warwickshire. Donald Davie. **CP-DavDo**

Wary of lightning, / we dodge the thundercloud's blue-black. Skin-Flying into the Storm Center. Laurence Lieberman. **SP-LiebL**

Wary of time O it seizes the soul tonight. Easter Eve 1945. Muriel Rukeyser. **CP-RukeM**

Was. Robert Creeley. **CP-CreeR**

Was 'a barbaric yawp'. Ned Skinner. Paul Muldoon. **SP-MuldP**

Was a Man. John Ciardi. **SP-CiarJ**

Was always old, so when I saw her at the nursing. My Grandmother. Ron Koertge. **SP-KoerR**

Was enabled to ride. A Matchstick-Viewed-without-Regard-to-Its-Outer-Surface. Kenneth Patchen. **CP-PatcK**

Was Ever a Dream a Drum? Carl Sandburg. **CP-SandC**

Was Galahad hired, / Artemis laid? Folkways. Isabella Gardner. **CP-GardI**

Was He Married? Stevie Smith. **CP-SmitS**

Was he preaching or writing poetry or talking through his hat? He was. Carl Sandburg. *Fr.* The People, Yes. **CP-SandC**

Was I angry with Hayley who used me so ill. William Blake. **CP-BlakW**

Was I clever enough? Was I charming? Thoughts While Driving Home. John Updike. **CP-UpdiJ**

Was I never yet of your love grieved. Sir Thomas Wyatt. **CP-WyatT**

Was I to blame to trust. Mary Sidney, Countess of Montgomery Wroth. *Fr.* Part 2. *Fr.* Urania. **CP-WrotM**

Was I too glib about eternal things. The Sequel. Theodore Roethke. **CP-RoetT**

Was It. James Schuyler. **CP-SchuJ**

Was it a blast to the balls dear brother. A Black Poet Leaps to His Death. Etheridge Knight. **SP-KnigE**

Was it a chance that made her pause. Guesses. Christina Georgina Rossetti. **CP-RosC3**

Was it a dream, or was it memory? The Festivals. Robert Duncan. **SP-DuncR**

Was it an animal was it a bird? The Lovepet. Ted Hughes. **SP-HughT**

Was it for this. William Wordsworth. **RB** *Fr.* Introduction—Childhood and School-Time. *Fr.* The Prelude; Growth of a Poet's Mind [1805 vers.]. **CP-WorW3**

Was it for this I uttered prayers. Grown-up. Edna St. Vincent Millay. **CP-MillE**

Was it greed for possession of these salty crags. James McAuley. **SP-McAuJ** *Fr.* Map.

Was it, I wondered, some freak. Hertfordshire. Donald Davie. **CP-DavDo**

Was It Not Curious? Stevie Smith. **CP-SmitS**

Was it the double of my dream. Towards Break of Day. William Butler Yeats. **CP-YeatW**

Was it the proud full sail of his great verse. Sonnet 86. William Shakespeare. **InvP; NoSic; OAEL-1; OAEP; OXAEP-1; SCGP; Son; TEP** *Fr.* Sonnets. **CP-ShaWS**

Was it the sound a blue spruce makes. The Fort. Lewis Turco. **SP-TurcL**

Was it to disenchant, and to undo. Aix-la-Chapelle. William Wordsworth. *Fr.* Memorials of a Tour of the Continent; 1820. **CP-WorW2**

Was it we who stumbled. Another Border. Daniel Gerard Hoffman. **SP-HoffD**

Was it wind off the dumps. Summer Home. Seamus Heaney. **SP-HeanS**

Was it wise to count the ranks of teeth. George Meredith. **CP-MerG2**

Was it with the fields of green. Emily Brontë. **CP-BronE**

Was it worms, having once bitten. A Pear like a Potato. John Updike. **CP-UpdiJ**

Was it worth keeping the Halt open. Dilton Marsh Halt. Sir John Betjeman. **CP-BetjJ**

Was Jesus Chaste? or did he. William Blake. **ChIV-2** *Fr.* The Everlasting Gospel. **CP-BlakW**

Was Jesus Humble? or did he. William Blake. **ChIV-2** *Fr.* The Everlasting Gospel. **CP-BlakW**

Was looking for work at 47 and the owner of a. He. Ron Koertge. **SP-KoerR**

Was my bones[. As I gave them]. What She Wanted. Ron Koertge. **SP-KoerR**

Was never called Wild Bill. He. Ron Koertge. **SP-KoerR**

Was never form and never face. Beauty. Ralph Waldo Emerson. **CP-EmerR**

Was Not the Lost Dauphin. Robert Penn Warren. *Fr.* Audubon. **SP-WarrR**

"Was not" was all the Statement. Emily Dickinson. **CP-DickE**

Was pain within you then—a grinning thing. Dostoyevsky. Kenneth Patchen. **CP-PatcK**

Was innocent? Too beautiful for that. Hayden Carruth. *Fr.* The Sleeping Beauty. **CP-CarHL**

Was she so chaste? She Rebukes Hippolyta. Hilda Doolittle. **CP-DoolH**

Was sitting here, drinking a glass of. Not All That Bad. Charles Bukowski. **SP-BukC3**

Was taken out of school after. He. Ron Koertge. **SP-KoerR**

Was the aim frustrated by force or guile. Malham Cove. William Wordsworth. **CP-WorW2**

Was the Word and the Word was just. Thinking Friday Night with a Gothic Storm Going About Final Causes and Logos and Mitzi Mayfair. Miller Williams. **SP-WillM**

Was there a garden or was the garden a dream? Adam Cast Forth. Richard Eberhart. **CP-EberR**

Was There a Time. Dylan Thomas. **CP-ThomD**

Was there designer sackcloth. Cantico Per Lo Tuo Amore II. James Liddy. **CP-LiddJ**

Was there ever a cause too lost. Hannibal. Robert Frost. **CP-FrosR**

Was there no star that could be sent. Ralph Waldo Emerson. **IMW** *Fr.* Threnody: "South-wind brings, The." **CP-EmerR**

Was thirty when we met. I was. Pandora's Box, An Ode. Ted Berrigan. **SP-BerrT**

Was this going to sell the beer. Chips. Steve Griffiths. **SP-GrifS**

Was This the Face. Christopher Marlowe. **EBEV; EBEvV; GBL; HeIP; LPA; NIP; TrGrPo; TreF** *Fr.* Doctor Faustus. **CP-JefR2**

(Face of Helen, The.) **FaBV**

(Helen.) **BLPL; FaFP; ImPo; LiTB; WHA**

(Helen of Troy.) **F**

Was this the face that launched a thousand ships? Was This the Face. Christopher Marlowe. **BLPL; EBEV; EBEvV; FF; FaBV; FaFP; GBL; HeIP; ImPo; LPA; LiTB; NIP; TrGrPo; TreF; WHA** *Fr.* Doctor Faustus. **CP-JefR2**

Was Thy Wrath against the Sea? Christina Georgina Rossetti. **CP-RosC2**

Was very kind. When she regained. The Raper from Passenack. William Carlos Williams. **CP-WilW1**

Was Yahweh chosen by the chosen people? Sonnet. Hayden Carruth. **CP-CarHS** *Fr.* Sonnets.

Was yesterday. I went out in the yard. August First, 1974. James Schuyler. **CP-SchuJ**

Was your's a daddy. Question. David Herbert Lawrence. **CP-LawrD**

Wash. John Updike. **CP-UpdiJ**

Wash clean the Vessell, lest ye soure. Sincerity. Robert Herrick. **CP-HerrR**

Wash me on home, mama. Gary Snyder. **CP-SnydG** *Fr.* Burning. *Fr.* Myths and Texts.

Wash of cold river. Hilda Doolittle. **CP-DoolH**

Wash, the plunge / down, The. The Sea. Robert Creeley. **CP-CreeR**

Wash your hands, or else the fire. Another to the Maids. Robert Herrick. **CP-HerrR**

Washback of the waters, swirl of time. Sea-Ruck. Richard Eberhart. **CP-EberR**

Washed into the doorway. The Guest. Wendell Berry. **CP-BerrW**

Washer Womans Song, The. William Blake. **CP-BlakW**

Washerwoman. Carl Sandburg. **CP-SandC**

Washerwoman is a member of the Salvation Army, The. Washerwoman. Carl Sandburg. **CP-SandC**

Washing. Randall Jarrell. **CP-JarrR**

Washing hangs upon the line, A. Elizabeth Bishop. **FaBoVe; FaBoWP** *Fr.* Songs for a Colored Singer. **CP-BishE**

Washing hangs upon the line, A. Songs for a Colored Singer. Elizabeth Bishop. **CP-BishE**

Washing is jerked from shade into the sun, The. Jenny Joseph. *Fr.* Fables. **SP-JoseJ**

Washing Kai in the sauna. The Bath. Gary Snyder. **CP-SnydG**

Washing Socks. Leonard Nathan. **SP-NathL**

Washing the Corpse, *tr. from the German of* Rilke. Randall Jarrell. **CP-JarrR**

Washing Your Feet. John Ciardi. **SP-CiarJ**

Washington. John Updike. **CP-UpdiJ**

Washington Cathedral. Karl Shapiro. **SP-ShapK**

Washington in Love. John Berryman. **CP-BerrJ**

Washington Monument by Night. Carl Sandburg. **CP-SandC**

Washington: Tourist View. John Updike. **CP-UpdiJ**

Washington's Monument, February, 1885. Walt Whitman. **CP-WhitW**

Washoe, believe me, humans are much worse. The Human Pile. Robert Pack. **CP-PackR**

Wasn't perfect, a few chips and holes. The Shell. Peter Meinke. **SP-MeinP**

Wasp, The. Ogden Nash. **CP-NashO**

Wasp, climbing the window pane. Invocation. Howard Nemerov. *Fr.* Epigrams: "Wasp, climbing the window pane." **CP-NemeH**

Wasp skims nearby up the bright warm air, A. John Berryman. *Fr.* Sonnets to Chris. **CP-BerrJ**

WASP Woman Visits a Black Junkie in Prison, A. Etheridge Knight. **SP-KnigE**

Waspish. Robert Frost. **BoAnP** *Fr.* Ten Mills. **CP-FrosR**

Wassail for the New Year, A. George Meredith. **CP-MerG2**

Wassail the trees, that they may bear. Robert Herrick. **PChr** *Fr.* Ceremonies for Christmas[se]. **CP-HerrR**

Wassaile, The. Robert Herrick. **CP-HerrR**

Wassaile the Trees, that they may beare. Another. Robert Herrick. **CP-HerrR**

Waste. Wystan Hugh Auden. **CP-AudWJ**

Waste Carpet, The. William Matthews. **SP-MattW**

Waste Land, The. Thomas Stearns Eliot. **CP-ElioT**

    Death by Water. **OBVE**

    Game of Chess, A. **SCV**

    "When Lil's husband got demobbed, I said." **NAs**

    "When lovely woman stoops to folly and." **UV**

Wasted Illness, A. Thomas Hardy. **CP-HardT**

Wasted sleepy corpse, The. Village Funeral: Maharashtra. Alun Lewis. **CP-LewiA**

Wasted, wasted minutes that couldn't be worse. While Someone Telephones. Elizabeth Bishop. **NMP** *Fr.* Four Poems. **CP-BishE**

Waster, The. Rudyard Kipling. **CP-KiplR**

Wasting money & running to the store. Blues in December. Al Young. **CP-YounA**

Wastrel, The. Daniel Gerard Hoffman. **SP-HoffD**

Watch, The. Robert Ranke Graves. **CP-GravR**

Watch, The. Robert Herrick. **CP-HerrR**

Watch a wild turkey come in to land. Birds, Like Thoughts. John Ciardi. **SP-CiarJ**

Watch, and be firm! for soul-subduing vice. Temptations from Roman Refinements. William Wordsworth. *Fr.* Ecclesiastical Sonnets. **CP-WorW2**

Watch any day his nonchalant pauses, see. Wystan Hugh Auden. **CP-AudeW**

    (Free One, A.) **CP-AudeW**

Watch, I warn you. Watching Song. Frank Templeton Prince. **CP-PrinF**

Watch out for power. Admonitions to a Special Person. Anne Sexton. **CP-SextA**

Watch out for this peeled doorlight! In the Rain and the Sun. Thomas Merton. **CP-MertT; SP-MertT**

Watch people stop by bodies in funeral homes. On the Symbolic Consideration of Hands and the Significance of Death. Miller Williams. **SP-WillM**

Watch Repair. Charles Simic. **SP-SimiC**

Watch the Lights Fade. Robinson Jeffers. **CP-JefR3**

Watch upon my wrist, The. Parable. Wystan Hugh Auden. **FaBoCo** *Fr.* Shorts I ("Watch upon my wrist, The"). **CP-AudeW**

Watch with me, men, women, and children dear. Christina Georgina Rossetti. *Fr.* Old and New Year Ditties. **CP-RosC1**

Watch yet a while, / Weep till that day shall dawn when thou shalt smile. The Day Is At Hand. Christina Georgina Rossetti. **CP-RosC1**

Watched and sleeping all the sodden afternoon. Fear in the Afternoon. John Clellon Holmes. **SP-HolmJ**

Watched clock never moves, they said, A. The Slow Starter. Louis MacNeice. **CP-MacNL**

Watched Example Never Boils, A. Ogden Nash. **CP-NashO**

Watcher, The. Robert Bly. **SP-BlyR**

Watcher, The. Kenneth Patchen. **CP-PatcK**

Watchers, The. Wystan Hugh Auden. **CP-AudeW**

Watchers, The. John Hewitt. **CP-HewiJ**

Watchers. Robert Pack. **SP-PackR**

Watchers, The. Christina Georgina Rossetti. **CP-RosC3**

Watchers, The. Muriel Rukeyser. **CP-RukeM**

Watchers, The. John Greenleaf Whittier. **CP-WhitJ**

Watcher's Regret, A. Thomas Hardy. **CP-HardT**

Watchful. Stevie Smith. **CP-SmitS**

Watching. Marsden Hartley. **CP-HartM**

Watching. Christopher Smart. *Fr.* Hymns for the Amusement of Children. **SP-SmarC**

Watching a child watching a witch. Jenny Joseph. **AIW** *Fr.* Derivations. **SP-JoseJ**

Watching a tv show. The Sword. Charles Bukowski. **SP-BukC3**

Watching, among the rifled branches, for the sun, our hero. Poem. Thomas Merton. **CP-MertT; SP-MertT**

Watching baseball. Baseball Canto. Lawrence Ferlinghetti. **SP-FerlL**

Watching Football on TV. Howard Nemerov. **CP-NemeH**

Watching hands transplanting. Transplanting. Theodore Roethke. **CP-RoetT**

Watching Morning In. John Clellon Holmes. **SP-HolmJ**

Watching my paralytic friend. The Figurehead. Karl Shapiro. **SP-ShapK**

Watching Neighbors' Children. Kenneth Patchen. **CP-PatcK**

Watching Song. Frank Templeton Prince. **CP-PrinF**

Watching the Fire. John Haines. **SP-HainJ**

Watching the Jet Planes Dive. William Stafford. **SP-StafW**

Watching the mistlines flow slowly in. Mistlines. Charles Tomlinson. **CP-TomlC**

Watching the River Flow. "Bob Dylan." **CP-DylaB**

Watching the shied core. As Bad as a Mile. Philip Larkin. **CP-LarkP**

Watching the stream come spilling over its ledge. Silver Creek Falls. William Dickey. **SP-DickW**

Watching the White Image, electric moon, white mist drifting over woods. In a Moonlit Hermit's Cabin. Allen Ginsberg. **CP-GinsA**

Watching the world from my peeled doorlight. Poem in the Rain and the Sun. Thomas Merton. **CP-MertT**

Watching this dawn's mnemonic of old dawning. Sestina in a Cantina. Malcolm Lowry. **CP-LowrM**

Watching two surfers walk toward the tide. The Moment. Charles Tomlinson. **CP-TomlC**

Watching unto God in the Night-Season. Jeanne Marie Bouvier de la Motte-Guyon, *tr. fr. French by* William Cowper. **CP-CowpW**

Watching what an ant would find to do when. Ploughing. Wystan Hugh Auden. **CP-AudWJ**

Watching winter drop its white punctuations. Watching. Marsden Hartley. **CP-HartM**

Watching You. James Schuyler. **CP-SchuJ**

Watching you in the mirror I wonder. The Mirror. Louise Glück. **SP-GlücL**

Watching you sleep. Watching You. James Schuyler. **CP-SchuJ**

Watchmaker God. Robert Lowell. **SP-LoweR**

Watchman, What of the First First Lady? Ogden Nash. **CP-NashO**

Water, The. Hayden Carruth. *Fr.* Contra Mortem. **CP-CarHL**

Water, The. Hayden Carruth. *Fr.* Mother. **CP-CarHL**

Water. Robert Creeley. **CP-CreeR**

Water. Ralph Waldo Emerson. **CP-EmerR**

Water. Philip Larkin. **CP-LarkP**

Water. Robert Lowell. **SP-LoweR**

Water / neither knows / who drinks. Down Home. Robert Creeley. **CP-CreeR**

Water. Kathleen Jessie Raine. **SP-RainK**

Water. Anne Sexton. **CP-SextA**

Water. Gary Snyder. **CP-SnydG**

Water! / Star! / and somewhere near now nodding. Lao Tsze. Kenneth Patchen. **CP-PatcK**

Water / waiting far / off to the. The. Robert Creeley. **CP-CreeR**

Water. Diane Wakoski. *Fr.* Fifteen Poems for a Lunar Eclipse None of Us Saw. **SP-WakoD**

Water and windmills, greenness, Islets green. The Netherlands. Samuel Taylor Coleridge. **CP-ColeS**

Water Ballad. Samuel Taylor Coleridge. **CP-ColeS**

Water bumps and bounces white. Gooseprairie. Richard Hugo. **CP-HugoR**

Water calmly flowing, / Sun-light deeply glowing. Earth and Heaven. Christina Georgina Rossetti. **CP-RosC3**

Water, cold, and sweet, and pure. Xenophanes. Louis Zukofsky. **CP-ZukLS**

Water-Course, The. George Herbert. **CP-HerbG**

Water drips, / a fissure of leaking. Water (2). Robert Creeley. **CP-CreeR**

Water Fowl. William Wordsworth. **CP-WorW1**

Water from the Rock. Marsden Hartley. **CP-HartM**

Water-Front Streets. Langston Hughes. **SP-HughL**

water-grass under had never waved, the. The Rain Guitar. James Dickey. **CP-DickJ**

Water-hammer, the history of ice, The. Muriel Rukeyser. **CP-RukeM**

Water: How Weather Feels the Cotton Hotels. Joseph Ceravolo. **SP-CeraJ**

Water in a bottle, The. Kenneth Rexroth. **CP-RexKL** *Fr.* The Heart's Garden, the Garden's Heart.

Water in the millrace, through a sluice of stone. Winter Landscape, with Rooks. Sylvia Plath. **CP-PlatS**

Water is always the same. Kenneth Rexroth. **CP-RexKL** *Fr.* The Heart's Garden, the Garden's Heart.

Water is beginning, is end, is pure, is pure gift. Louis MacNeice. *Fr.* Our Sister Water. **CP-MacNL**

Water is deeper than the land, The. Emily Dickinson. **SP-DickE**

Water is H2O, hydrogen two parts, oxygen one. The Third Thing. David Herbert Lawrence. **CP-LawrD**

Water is heavy silver over stone. What Any Lover Learns. Archibald MacLeish. **CP-MacLA**

Water, is taught by thirst. Emily Dickinson. **CP-DickE**

Water-Lilies. Edward Estlin Cummings. **CP-CummE**

Water-lilies in myriads rocked on the slight undulations. On the Atchafalaya. Henry Wadsworth Longfellow. **AA** *Fr.* It was the month of May. Far down the Beautiful River. *Fr.* Part the Second. *Fr.* Evangeline, a Tale of Acadie. **SP-LongH**

Water makes many Beds. Emily Dickinson. **CP-DickE**

Water Music. Robert Creeley. **CP-CreeR**

Water Music. Alun Lewis. **CP-LewiA**

Water Music. "Hugh MacDiarmid."
  "Archin' here and arrachin there." **SP-MacDH**
  ("Wheesht, wheesht, Joyce, and let me hear.") **SP-MacDH**

Water Night. Muriel Rukeyser. **CP-RukeM**

Water of Life. "Hugh MacDiarmid." **SP-MacDH**

Water-poet lay down with flowers above, The. A Room in Rome. Karl Shapiro. **SP-ShapK**

Water Snake. Mary Oliver. **SP-OlivM**

Water Spirit's Song, The. Christina Georgina Rossetti. **CP-RosC3**

Water still flows. Illegitimate Things. William Carlos Williams. **CP-WilW2**

Water taps running, the sun part out. February. Gary Snyder. *Fr.* Six Years. **CP-SnydG**

Water turns / a long way down over the raw stone, The The. You Are Happy. Margaret Atwood. **SP-AtwM1**

Water (2). Robert Creeley. **CP-CreeR**

Water understands / Civilization well, The. Water. Ralph Waldo Emerson. **CP-EmerR**

Water Walker. Richard Wilbur. **CP-WilbR**

Water wanted to live. How Water Began to Play. Ted Hughes. **SP-HughT**

"Water" was her answer and I fell instantly and I knew self-destructively in love with her. The Game. Charles Kenneth Williams. **SP-WillC**

Water, water I desire. The Scar[e]-Fire. Robert Herrick. **CP-HerrR**

Water, Water I espie. His Misery in a Mistresse. Robert Herrick. **CP-HerrR**

Water, wind-impelled, advancing, The. Marine. Charles Tomlinson. **CP-TomlC**

Watercolor of Grantchester Meadows. Sylvia Plath. **CP-PlatS**

Watercolour, The. John Hewitt. **CP-HewiJ**

Watered-Down Love. "Bob Dylan." **CP-DylaB**

Waterfall, The. Mary Oliver. **SP-OlivM**

Waterfall. Robert Pack. **SP-PackR**

Waterfall and the Eglantine, The. William Wordsworth. **CP-WorW1**

Waterfall at Powerscourt, The. Donald Davie. **CP-DavDo**

Waterfront for Allan Ross MacDougall, A. Kay Boyle. **CP-BoylK**

Watergaw, The. "Hugh MacDiarmid." **SP-MacDH**

Watering-Place Lady Inventoried, A. Thomas Hardy. **CP-HardT**

Watering the Horse. Robert Bly. **SP-BlyR**

Waterlily Fire. Muriel Rukeyser. **CP-RukeM**

Waterloo. Byron. *See* There was a sound of revelry by night.

Waterloo. Robert Lowell. **SP-LoweR**

Watermelons. Charles Simic. **SP-SimiC**

Waters. Donald Hall. **CP-HallD**

Waters, The. William Matthews. *Fr.* Flood. **SP-MattW**

Waters, The. Richard Wilbur. **CP-WilbR**

Waters are flashing, The. The Fugitives. Percy Bysshe Shelley. **CP-ShelP**

Waters are loose: from Judith and the Larb. Schoolcraft's Diary Written on the Missouri: 1830. Robert Bly. **SP-BlyR**

Waters by this music. James Liddy. *Fr.* Sandhills. **CP-LiddJ**

Waters chased him as he fled, The. Emily Dickinson. **CP-DickE**

Waters come welling into this valley. After the Storm. Charles Tomlinson. **CP-TomlC**

Waters deep, the waters dark, The. Casting. Howard Nemerov. **CP-NemeH**

Water's Fine, I'm Fine, The. Dabney Stuart. **SP-StuaD**

Waters I'm going to go walking beside, The. The New Mystic. Al Young. **CP-YounA**

Waters saw thee, O God, The. Bible, *O.T. See* Psalm 77: "I cried unto God with my voice. . . ."

Watertowers, The. Wystan Hugh Auden. *See* Who stands, the crux left of the watershed.

Watsonville after the Quake. Al Young. **CP-YounA**

Watteau. Derek Walcott. **CP-WalcD** *Fr.* Midsummer.

Waukrife Minnie, A. Robert Burns. **CP-BurnR**

Wave, A. John Ashbery. **SP-AshbJ**

Wave, The. Elizabeth Bishop. **CP-BishE**

Wave, The. Adrienne Rich. **SP-RicA2**

Wave. Patti Smith. **SP-SmitP**

Wave. Gary Snyder. **CP-SnydG**

Wave in the round of the port-hole. Party on Shipboard. George Oppen. **CP-OppeG**

Wave is breaking on the shore, The. The New Year. John Greenleaf Whittier. **CP-WhitJ**

Wave of an awful torrent, thronging down. The Past and Coming Year. John Greenleaf Whittier. **CP-WhitJ**

Wave of sorrow. Island. Langston Hughes. **SP-HughL**

Wave of the Nineties, The. James Liddy. *Fr.* Glass after Oblivion. **CP-LiddJ**

Wave sucks back and with the last of water, The. On Being Idolized. Robert Frost. **CP-FrosR**

Wave them / Flap white wings and yellow pinions. Fire. David Herbert Lawrence. **CP-LawrD**

Wave withdrawing, The. "Dover Beach"—a Note to That Poem. Archibald MacLeish. **CP-MacLA**

Wavelength. David St. John. **SP-StJoD**

Waves are pressing up with force, The. George Meredith. **CP-MerG2**

Waves of Fear. "Lou Reed." **SP-ReedL**

Waves of their purposefulness go flooding through me, The. The Covenanters. "Hugh MacDiarmid." **SP-MacDH**

Waves on the Normandy coast jump heavily toward us, The. Normandy Beach. Miller Williams. **SP-WillM**

Waves policed the sand to call. Beachthieves. Richard Hugo. **CP-HugoR**

Waves pumping at you, The. Mercury Clouds. Jim Carroll. **SP-CarrJ**

Waves rush up, pause, and drag pebbles back around. Two Sounds When We Sit by the Ocean. Robert Bly. **SP-BlyR**

Waving Adieu, Adieu, Adieu. Wallace Stevens. **CP-StevW**

Waving and Waving Goodbye. Charles Bukowski. **SP-BukC1**

Waving Good-Bye. Leonard Nathan. **SP-NathL**

Waving goodbye, from your banked hospital bed. Ted Hughes. **SP-HughT** *Fr.* Gaudete.

Waving slowly before me, pushed into the dark. Sickness. David Herbert Lawrence. **CP-LawrD**

Waxwings gather along thin phonewire:. Interlude, with Alter Ego. James McAuley. **SP-McAuJ** *Fr.* Meditations of Afternoon.

Way, The. Robert Creeley. **CP-CreeR**

Way. Robert Creeley. **CP-CreeR**

Way, The. Robert Herrick. **CP-HerrR**

Way, The. Frederick Morgan. **SP-MorgF**

Way a crow, The. Dust of Snow. Robert Frost. **CP-FrosR**

Way a Ghost Behaves, The. Richard Hugo. **CP-HugoR**

Way a Ghost Dissolves, The. Richard Hugo. **CP-HugoR**

Way a man sits, The. How Relaxed. Jim Carroll. **SP-CarrJ**

Way a tired Chippewa woman, The. Hush. David St. John. **SP-StJoD**

Way a word does when, The. One Way. Howard Nemerov. **CP-NemeH**

Way at night these piping peepers, The. The Peepers in Our Meadow. Archibald MacLeish. **CP-MacLA**

Way Back, The. Leonard Cohen. **CP-CoheL**

Way Back, The. Alun Lewis. **CP-LewiA**

Way boxers postulate a feeling to label that with which they overcome the body's vile fears, The. Vehicle: Violence. Charles Kenneth Williams. **SP-WillC**

Way Down, The. Stanley Jasspon Kunitz. **CP-KuniS**

"Time swings her burning hands."

"Time swings her burning hands."

"When the magician died, I wept."

Way Down South in Dixie. Song for a Dark Girl. Langston Hughes. **SP-HughL**

Way enchased with glass and beads, A. The Temple. Robert Herrick. **CP-HerrR**

Way eyes turn, The. A New Yorker. James Schuyler. **CP-SchuJ**

Way He Went, The. Daniel Gerard Hoffman. **SP-HoffD**

Way, her father dead a day ago, the child goes in his closet, finds herself inside his closet, The. Vehicle: Absence. Charles Kenneth Williams. **SP-WillC**

Way Hope builds his House, The. Emily Dickinson. **CP-DickE**

Way I go is by a mere, The. Swan's Nest. John Hewitt. **CP-HewiJ**

Way I read a Letter's—this, The. Emily Dickinson. **CP-DickE**

Way In, The. Charles Tomlinson. **CP-TomlC**

Way in a Crowd. Robert Herrick. **CP-HerrR**

Way in is to pause and look again, look back, The. Frank Templeton Prince. *Fr.* Afterword on Rupert Brooke. **CP-PrinF**

Way It Goes or the Proper Use of Leisure Time, The. Stephen Dobyns. **SP-DobyS**

Way It Is, The. Daniel Gerard Hoffman. **SP-HoffD**

Way It Is, The. Charles Simic. **SP-SimiC**

Way MacLane died, they set, The. The Place of Value. Howard Nemerov. **CP-NemeH**

Way men live is a lie, The. Kenneth Patchen. **CP-PatcK**

Way of a World, The. Charles Tomlinson. **CP-TomlC**

Way of Life, A. Howard Nemerov. **CP-NemeH**

Way of love is unlimited, The. Hafiz, *tr. by* Ralph Waldo Emerson. **CP-EmerR** *Fr.* Odes.

Way of man has no wisdom, but the way of God has, The. Thomas Merton. *Fr.* The Legacy of Herakleitos. **CP-MertT**

Way of many ways: a god, A. Doctor Faustus. Geoffrey Hill. **CP-HillG**

Way of Pain, The. Wendell Berry. **CP-BerrW**

Way of the Conventicle of the Trees, The. Hayden Carruth. **CP-CarHS**

Way of the World, The. Christina Georgina Rossetti. **CP-RosC3**

Way of the World, The. Carl Sandburg. **CP-SandC**

Way on high burned white beneath the sun, The. Defeat. Walter de la Mare. **CP-DeLaW**

Way our American wildflowers hover, The. The Fleckings. John Updike. **CP-UpdiJ**

Way Out, A. Richard Eberhart. **CP-EberR**

Way Out, The. David Herbert Lawrence. **CP-LawrD**

Way out they are riding, it is an old. The Herd. Robert Creeley. **CP-CreeR**

Way some of us played cards and some drank, The. Every Tub. William Matthews. **SP-MattW**

Way someone stays home, that's all, stays in the house, in the room, just stays, The. The Race of the Flood. Charles Kenneth Williams. **CP-WillC**

Way spring comes this time, with a soft, The. Zalmoxis. Howard Nemerov. **CP-NemeH**

Way-Station. Archibald MacLeish. **CP-MacLA**

Way the light, The. Near Old Fort Pike on the Des Moines River. Chuck Miller. **SP-MillC**

Way the world came swinging around my ears, The. The Perennial Answer. Adrienne Rich. **CP-RicAE; SP-RicA2**

Way the world is not, The. Sonnet. Bill Knott. **SP-KnotB**

Way these days she dresses with more attention to go out to pass the afternoon alone, The. The Mirror. Charles Kenneth Williams. **SP-WillC**

Way this willow traps, The. Willow, Wishbone, Warblers. Brendan Galvin. **SP-GalvB**

Way through the Woods, The. Rudyard Kipling. **CP-KiplR**

Way T'ings Come, De. Paul Laurence Dunbar. **CP-DunbP**

Way to hump a cow is not, The. Edward Estlin Cummings. **CP-CummE**

Way to know the Bobolink, The. Emily Dickinson. **CP-DickE**

Way to Love God, A. Robert Penn Warren. **SP-WarrR**

Way to Make a Living, A. James Wright. **CP-WrigJ**

Way to School, The. John Hewitt. **CP-HewiJ**

Way to the boiler was dark, The. The Return. Theodore Roethke. **NAAL-2** *Fr.* The Lost Son. **CP-RoetT**

Way we get under cars and in, The. Just Right. Charles Kenneth Williams. **CP-WillC**

Way We Live, The. John Haines. **SP-HainJ**

Way West, Underground, The. Gary Snyder. **CP-SnydG**

Ways. Alun Lewis. **CP-LewiA**

Ways, The. Louis Zukofsky. **CP-ZukLS**

Ways about it. In fact, that only scratches the surface; for—well. There Are Two. Kenneth Patchen. **CP-PatcK**

Ways and Means. Richard Eberhart. **CP-EberR**

Ways and the Peoples, The. Randall Jarrell. **CP-JarrR**

Ways of Day. Robert Penn Warren. **SP-WarrR**

Ways of God to Men, The. John Milton. **OBS** *Fr.* Samson Agonistes. **CP-MiltJ**

Ways of Keys, The. Stephen Dobyns. **SP-DobyS**

Ways of man with a maid be strange, yet simple and tame, The. Rudyard Kipling. *Fr.* Certain Maxims of Hafiz. **CP-KiplR**

Wdnt let anybody. Telling You True, About My Fantasy Life. Diane Wakoski. **SP-WakoD**

We. Miller Williams. **SP-WillM**

We ain't got nobody. Evolutionary Poem No. 2. Etheridge Knight. **SP-KnigE**

We all go back with flowers. Visiting. Jenny Joseph. *Fr.* Life and Turgid Times of A. Citizen. **SP-JoseJ**

We all have moments with the dust. Emily Dickinson. **SP-DickE**

We all know about death that. In Death, Cannot Reach What Is Most Near. Allen Ginsberg. **CP-GinsA**

We all know too much of loneliness. I used to think. The Meeting. Gilbert Sorrentino. **SP-SorrG**

We All Shall Rest at Last. Walt Whitman. **CP-WhitW**

We all traveled into that big room. How We Did It. Muriel Rukeyser. **CP-RukeM**

We all were watching the quiz on television. A Singular Metamorphosis. Howard Nemerov. **CP-NemeH**

We Alone. Alice Walker. **CP-WalkA**

We already had some gospels, when he fell. Scrolls from the Dead. Daniel Gerard Hoffman. **SP-HoffD**

We always talked about getting it right. Right. William Matthews. **SP-MattW**

We alwus had to herd cattle. Mona Van Duyn. **SP-VanDM**

We and They. Rudyard Kipling. **CP-KiplR** *Fr.* Debits and Credits.

We are a little people, in this island. A Little People. John Hewitt. **CP-HewiJ**

We are a meadow where the bees hum. Bedtime. Denise Levertov. **CP-LeveD**

We are afraid that we have not lived. Calidus Juventa? Allen Tate. **CP-TateA**

We are again / walking in a / straight line—feet. For Betsy and Tom. Robert Creeley. **CP-CreeR**

We are all children to the past. The Memoirs of Glückel of Hameln. Randall Jarrell. **CP-JarrR**

We are all docile Dough-Faces. Song for Certain Congressmen. Walt Whitman. **CP-WhitW**

We are all hustling and dealing. Marge Piercy. *Fr.* Living in the Open. **SP-PierM**

We are all liars, because. Lies About Love. David Herbert Lawrence. **CP-LawrD**

We Are All Vultures. John Yau. **SP-YauJo**

We are always saying / "Good-bye, good-bye!" Saying Good-bye. Thomas Hardy. **CP-HardT**

We are America. The Firebombers. Anne Sexton. **CP-SextA**

We are approaching sleep: the chestnut blossoms in the mind. Awakening. Robert Bly. **SP-BlyR**

We are as clouds that veil the midnight moon. Mutability. Percy Bysshe Shelley. **CP-ShelP**

We are as maidens one and all. Death. Robert Louis Stevenson. **CP-StevR**

We are asleep under mirrors. What do I. Before the War. Marilyn Hacker. **SP-HackM**

We are betrayed by what is false. Within. Anima. Richard Eberhart. **CP-EberR**

We are beyond the ways of the far ships. The Landfall. Thomas Merton. **CP-MertT; SP-MertT**

We are born into life—it is sweet, it is strange. A Rhapsody of Life's Progress. Elizabeth Barrett Browning. **CP-BroEB**

We are born with luck. The Evil Seekers. Anne Sexton. **CP-SextA**

We are budding, Master, budding. The Master and the Leaves. Thomas Hardy. **CP-HardT**

We are careful never to / say "Waterford" or "Cork" or. Irish Glass. John Hewitt. **CP-HewiJ**

We are Coheires with Christ; nor shall His own. Coheires. Robert Herrick. **CP-HerrR**

We are crossing the bridge now. Louis Zukofsky. *Fr.* 29 Poems. **CP-ZukLS**

We are driven to odd attempts; once it would not have occurred to. Adrienne Rich. **HCAP; SP-RicA1; SP-RicA2** *Fr.* Shooting Script. **CP-RicAE**

We are false and evanescent, and aware of our deceit. The False Gods. Edwin Arlington Robinson. **CP-RobiE**

We are fishermen in a flat scene. Water. Anne Sexton. **CP-SextA**

We are flying white air. The most pioneering. Flying, Reflying, Farming. Richard Hugo. **CP-HugoR**

We are free to find our own way. Off the Trail. Gary Snyder. **CP-SnydG**

We Are Getting to the End. Thomas Hardy. **CP-HardT**

We are ghosts on the plains of November. Putting Up Snow Fence. Chuck Miller. **SP-MillC**

We are given a chance. The First Time. Robert Creeley. **CP-CreeR**

We are going away now. Ave atque Vale. Gilbert Sorrentino. **SP-SorrG**

We are going in the water for the rest of the day. Going In. Anne Waldman. **SP-WaldA**

We are going the park. Struggling. Joseph Ceravolo. **SP-CeraJ**

We are happy all the time. Sweet Briars of the Stairways. Nicholas Vachel Lindsay. **CP-LindV**

We are happy in our way of life. Parergon. John Ashbery. **SP-AshbJ**

We are hard on each other. Margaret Atwood. **SP-AtwM1**

We are having wonderful weather. The Language of Postcards. Richard Shelton. **SP-ShelR**

We are here by the ocean. By the Ocean. John Haines. **SP-HainJ**

We are involved in a transpersonified state. Chinese Nightingale. Ted Berrigan. **SP-BerrT**

We are knitting now. Marsden Hartley. *Fr.* Ironies out of St. George's. **CP-HartM**

We are large with pity, slow and awkward. False Country of the Zoo. Jean Garrigue. **SP-GarrJ**

We Are Leaves. James Schuyler. **CP-SchuJ**

We are like doves, well-paired. The Green-Sailed Vessel. Robert Ranke Graves. **CP-GravR**

We are like the masters of a lost dog. Zimmer and the Ghost. Paul Zimmer. **SP-ZimmP**

We are mind! Progress. Peter Meinke. **SP-MeinP**

We are not a large concern, although compared. The Promotion. Miller Williams. **SP-WillM**

We are not born yet, and everything's crystal under our feet. California Dreaming. Charles Wright. **SP-WrigC**

We are not lovers. Man and Wife. Anne Sexton. **CP-SextA**

We are not often alone, we two. The Voice. Walter de la Mare. **CP-DeLaW**

We are not wasted. We are not left out. Welcome to Quetzalcoatl. David Herbert Lawrence. **CP-LawrD**

We Are Not Worthy, Lord. Kenneth Patchen. **CP-PatcK**

We are of those who tremble at Thy word. Christina Georgina Rossetti. **CP-RosC2**

We Are Only Ourselves. Robert Penn Warren. *Fr.* Audubon. **SP-WarrR**

We are others and the earth. From the Distance. Wendell Berry. **CP-BerrW**

We are out on the open road. On the March. David Herbert Lawrence. **CP-LawrD**

We are passing it now. Our boat. Bannerman's Island. Richard Hugo. **CP-HugoR**

We are pleased to present for your listening pleasure. We. Miller Williams. **SP-WillM**

We are pressed, pressed on each other. George Oppen. *Fr.* Of Being Numerous. **CP-OppeG**

We Are Seven. William Wordsworth. **CP-WorW1**
"I met a little cottage Girl." **UV**

We are snatching our jewels from the frost. Emily Dickinson. **SP-DickE**

We are standing— / empedestaled—inside the God's. Daibutsu. Laurence Lieberman. **SP-LiebL**

We are talking about anxiety that comes up. For Phil. Chuck Miller. **SP-MillC**

We are the antlers of that white animal. Afterwards. Muriel Rukeyser. **CP-RukeM**

We are the desperate. Vagabonds. Langston Hughes. **SP-HughL**

We are the hollow men. The Hollow Men. Thomas Stearns Eliot. **CP-ElioT**

We are the little men grown huge with death. From a Play. Alun Lewis. **CP-LewiA**

We are the seas through whom the great fish passed. Neruda, the Wine. Muriel Rukeyser. **CP-RukeM**

We are the smirched. Queen Honor is the spotless. Honor Among Scamps. Nicholas Vachel Lindsay. **CP-LindV**

We are things of dry hours and the involuntary plan. Kitchenette Building. Gwendolyn Brooks. **BPo; FF; FaBoWP; NAAL-2; NoP; PoE; PoNe; Poetr; UnPo** *Fr.* A Street in Bronzeville. **SP-BrooG**

We Are Those People. Robinson Jeffers. **CP-JefR3**

We are three women eating out. Crêpes Flambeau. Tess Gallagher. **SP-GallT**

We are tired of your tiresome imitations of Mayakovsky. Answer to Voznesensky and Evtushenko. Frank O'Hara. **SP-OharF**

We are to tell one man tonight good-bye. Farewell to Miles. John Berryman. **CP-BerrJ**

We are too much on the outside. The Whip. Charles Tomlinson. **CP-TomlC**

We Are Transmitters. David Herbert Lawrence. **CP-LawrD**

We are trying to live. Rough Times. Marge Piercy. **SP-PierM**

We are trying to recollect specific things. Miss and Hit. Gilbert Sorrentino. **SP-SorrG**

We are two acquaintances on a train. Sunday Evening. Adrienne Rich. **CP-RicAE**

We are two countries girded for the war. Foreign Affairs. Stanley Jasspon Kunitz. **CP-KuniS**

We are two lovers of no careless breed. To Be Poets. Robert Ranke Graves. **CP-GravR**

We are very much a part of the boredom. Poem. Jim Carroll. **SP-CarrJ**

We are very slightly changed. A General Summary. Rudyard Kipling. **CP-KiplR**

We are waitresses / or female. To Do More Than Hair. Siv Cedering Fox. **SP-CedeS**

We are warned by slow footsteps. The Second People. Kenneth Patchen. **CP-PatcK**

We are what we are made; each following day. Written in Naples, March, 1833. Ralph Waldo Emerson. **CP-EmerR**

We are what we hear. A well known singer died. Langaig. Richard Hugo. **CP-HugoR**

We are wise in ways which none has preordained. Testament to a Flowering Race. Edwin Rolfe. **CP-RolfE**

We asked for rain. It didn't flash and roar. Our Hold on the Planet. Robert Frost. **CP-FrosR**

We ate with steeps of sky about our shoulders. The Terrace. Richard Wilbur. **CP-WilbR**

We Awoke, Talking. Jim Morrison. **SP-MorrJ**

We be the Gods of the East. Rudyard Kipling. **CP-KiplR** *Fr.* The Naulahka.

We Become New. Marge Piercy. **SP-PierM**

We become the children. Borges Death Mask. Jim Carroll. **SP-CarrJ**

We—Bee and I—live by the quaffing. Emily Dickinson. **CP-DickE**

We being not each other:without love. Edward Estlin Cummings. **CP-CummE**

We believed in highdays then. Yuletide in a Younger World. Thomas Hardy. **CP-HardT**

We bent our backs, the two of us, climbing. Coming Down from the Acropolis. William DeWitt Snodgrass. **SP-SnodW**

We Better Talk This Over. "Bob Dylan." **CP-DylaB**

We bid you welcome to this ancient house. Prologue for an Evening at the Whitefriars. John Hewitt. **CP-HewiJ**

We blame, nay we despise her paines. Out of Time, Out of Tune. Robert Herrick. **CP-HerrR**

We both are mortal; but thou, frailer creature. On a Very Old Glass. Jonathan Swift. **CP-SwifJ**

We boys are privates in our Regiment's ranks. Conclusion of a Compliment to the Captain. Robert Browning. **CP-BroR2**

We breed plants, order seeds from. The Daily Life of the Worker Bee. Marge Piercy. **SP-PierM**

We built a ship upon the stairs. A Good Play. Robert Louis Stevenson. **CP-StevR**

We buried her among the flowers. Song. Christina Georgina Rossetti. **CP-RosC3**

We call them beautiful. Turner's Seas. Kathleen Jessie Raine. **SP-RainK**

We call up the green to hide us. Summer Wish. Louise Bogan. **CP-BogaL**

We called him by his family name, one known. The Actor: Decline and Death. James McAuley. **SP-McAuJ**

We called him—with his three / chins, earnest. Rumour. Charles Tomlinson. **CP-TomlC**

We cam' na here to view your warks. Verses Written on a Window of the Inn at Carron. Robert Burns. **CP-BurnR**

We came by night. Near Hartland. Charles Tomlinson. **CP-TomlC**

We came here to live in a small town. Main Street. Miller Williams. **SP-WillM**

We came into this area quite accidentally. Corps de Plane. Patti Smith. **SP-SmitP**

We came over the moor-top. The Great Carbuncle. Sylvia Plath. **CP-PlatS**

We came then to his time of pain. Wendell Berry. *Fr.* Elegy: "To be at home on its native ground." **CP-BerrW**

We came to visit the cow. Freedom, New Hampshire. Galway Kinnell. **SP-KinnG**

We came where the salmon were so many. That Morning. Ted Hughes. **SP-HughT**

We camp by a stream among rugged stumps. Bride of the Bear. William Everson. **SP-EverW**

We can but follow to the Sun. Emily Dickinson. **CP-DickE**

We can do little for these living dead. The Virus. Robert Ranke Graves. **CP-GravR**

We can endure that He should waste our lands. Indignation of a High-Minded Spaniard 1810. William Wordsworth. **CP-WorW1**

We can look into the stove tonight. Burning Oneself Out. Adrienne Rich. **SP-RicA2**

We can not weather all this gold. Late Spring. Hilda Doolittle. **CP-DoolH**

We Can Work It Out. The Beatles. **CP-Beatl**

We cannot believe for each other. Emily Dickinson. **CP-DickE**

We cannot disinter the girls of nineteen-eight. Frank Templeton Prince. *Fr.* Afterword on Rupert Brooke. **CP-PrinF**

We cannot go to the country. Raleigh Was Right. William Carlos Williams. **CP-WilW2**

We cannot live, except thus mutually. Love. Elizabeth Barrett Browning. **CP-BroEB**

We Can't Be Too Careful. David Herbert Lawrence. **CP-LawrD**

We carried you in our arms. Tears of Rage. "Bob Dylan." **CP-DylaB**

We caught lions copulating on the plains. Lions Copulating. Richard Eberhart. **CP-EberR**

We chanced in passing by that afternoon. The Black Cottage. Robert Frost. **CP-FrosR**

We choose to say goodbye against our will. *with music.* Robert Pack. **SP-PackR**

We Christmas-carolled down the Vale, and up the Vale, and round the Vale. The Rash Bride. Thomas Hardy. **CP-HardT**

We circle the sinkhole. Bottommost. Archie Randolph Ammons. **SP-AmmoA**

We climbed all afternoon. John Haines. *Fr.* News from the Glacier. **SP-HainJ**

We climbed by the old quarries to the wide highland of heath. The Broadstone. Robinson Jeffers. **CP-JefR2**

We climbed out of timber. On the Mountain. John Haines. **SP-HainJ**

We climbed that day. The Glacier. Charles Tomlinson. **CP-TomlC**

We climbed the steep ascent to heaven. The Saddest Day. David Herbert Lawrence. **CP-LawrD**

We climbed to the very top that August day. Castle Rock. Frederick Morgan. **SP-MorgF**

We come for nothing but we read the stones —. Graves at Mukilteo. Richard Hugo. **CP-HugoR**

We come here tourist on a bad sky day. Cataldo Mission. Richard Hugo. **CP-HugoR**

We conquered France, but felt our captive's charms. Alexander Pope. **EPCY** *Fr.* The First Epistle of the Second Book of Horace Imitated. **CP-PopeA**

We consider / precedent to that Shekinah, She. The Maiden. Robert Duncan. **SP-DuncR**

We consider the underlying fallacy of the plaintiff's argument. Plessy vs Ferguson: Theme and Variations. Thomas Merton. **CP-MertT**

"We could try it," / Ralph says to Harold. The Green Door. James Schuyler. **CP-SchuJ**

We couldn't even keep the furnace lit! To Delmore Schwartz. Robert Lowell. **SP-LoweR**

We counted several flames in one small fire. The Tranced. Theodore Roethke. **CP-RoetT**

We counterfeited once for your disport. Actors. Rudyard Kipling. *Fr.* Epitaphs of the War [1914–1918]. **CP-KiplR**

We Cover Thee—Sweet Face. Emily Dickinson. **CP-DickE**

We crammed one compartment and crowded the windows. Away Match: June 1924. John Hewitt. **CP-HewiJ**

We credit most our sight; one eye doth please. The Eyes before the Eares. Robert Herrick. **CP-HerrR**

We cross the prairie as of old. The Kansas Emigrants. John Greenleaf Whittier. **CP-WhitJ**

We cross the Sacramento River at Colusa. River in the Valley. Gary Snyder. **CP-SnydG**

We crossed Champlain to Keeseville with our friends. The Adirondacs. Ralph Waldo Emerson. **CP-EmerR**

We crouched and waited as the day ebbed off. The Watchers. John Hewitt. **CP-HewiJ**

We Cry Out. Leonard Cohen. **CP-CoheL**

We cut the sod. We dug the heavy mould. The Souterrain. John Hewitt. **CP-HewiJ**

We dance round in a ring and suppose. The Secret Sits. Robert Frost. **CP-FrosR**

We descended the first night from Europe riding the ship's sling. Coming Back to America. James Dickey. **CP-DickJ**

We did at last manage to get the eyes. The Colony of the Sun. Kenneth Patchen. **CP-PatcK**

We did not know the first thing about. Thinking about Bill, Dead of AIDS. Miller Williams. **SP-WillM**

We did not know, then, what the wen. Cancer. Lewis Turco. **SP-TurcL**

We didn't know at the time. It was. Long Distance. William Stafford. **SP-StafW**

We die. Great Contemporary Discoveries. Archibald MacLeish. **CP-MacLA**

We die, / Welcoming Bluebeards to our darkening closets. The Detached. Maya Angelou. **SP-AngeM**

We die in different directions. Calm Under Fire. Jim Carroll. **SP-CarrJ**

We Die Together. David Herbert Lawrence. **CP-LawrD**

We dine in a glade concealed in peach petals. In Dream's Wake. Ts'un Hsu Li, *tr. fr. Chinese by* William Carlos Williams *with* David Rafael Wang. **CP-WilW2**

We do not bargain for delight; vitality. Ark: Angelus: Anvil. Kenneth Patchen. **CP-PatcK**

We do not curse thee, Waterloo! Ode from the French. Byron. **CP-Byron**

WE do not go—we stay—. There Are No Names. Marsden Hartley. **CP-HartM**

We do not know / If there be fairies now. Belief. Wystan Hugh Auden. **CP-AudWJ**

We do not know the time we lose. Emily Dickinson. **CP-DickE**

We do not play on Graves. Emily Dickinson. **CP-DickE**

We do not realize what we want. Letter to a Lost Friend. Richard Shelton. **SP-ShelR**

We do not see them come. Scala Coeli. Kathleen Jessie Raine. **SP-RainK**

We don't bother nobody. Wendell Berry. *Fr.* The Clearing. **CP-BerrW**

We don't cry—Tim and I. Emily Dickinson. **CP-DickE**

We dont drive so long distances are out. No More Doors Tonight. Al Young. **CP-YounA**

We don't exist unless we are deeply and sensually in touch. Non-Existence. David Herbert Lawrence. **CP-LawrD**

We don't give a shit about all this. *see also* Working Man, A. Leonard Cohen. **CP-CoheL**

We don't have to know. Star by Day. Hilda Doolittle. *Fr.* Two Poems for Christmas, 1937. **CP-DoolH**

We don't know how lovely the elements are. The Elements. David Herbert Lawrence. **CP-LawrD**

We don't need a face in the picture to know. Hands. Wystan Hugh Auden. **CP-AudeW**

We Don't Need to Leave Yet, Do We? Or, Yes We Do. Ogden Nash. **CP-NashO**

We don't speak the same language. The Understanding. Leonard Nathan. **SP-NathL**

We don't want to fight. On Benjamin Disraeli. Robert Browning. **CP-BroR2**

We dream—it is good we are dreaming. Emily Dickinson. **CP-DickE**

We drive between lakes just turning green. Driving through Minnesota during the Hanoi Bombings. Robert Bly. **SP-BlyR**

We drove long straggling fields of the Model County. 1949: Child Redmond to Dark Wexford Came. James Liddy. **CP-LiddJ**

We drove through October, Grandmother pointing at cows. The River Styx, Ohio. Mary Oliver. **SP-OlivM**

We dust the walls. Aus Einem April. Frank O'Hara. **SP-OharF**

We each play our roles. Charles Henri Ford. **SP-FordC** *Fr.* Emblems of Arachne.

We eat this body and remain ourselves. Air without Incense. Adrienne Rich. **CP-RicAE**

We enter this evening as we enter a quartet. Evening Music. May Sarton. **SP-SartM**

We entered silence / before the clock struck. Suspension. Audre Lorde. **SP-LordA**

We feel and see with different hearts and eyes. Christina Georgina Rossetti. *Fr.* Later Life: A Double Sonnet of Sonnets. **CP-RosC2**

We feel my dear. Billets Doux for the Harteebeeste. Malcolm Lowry. **CP-LowrM**

We Field-Women. Thomas Hardy. **CP-HardT**

We fight for hours, through dinner, through the endless evening, who even knows now what about. Peace. Charles Kenneth Williams. **SP-WillC**

We find ourselves at the exact place. Strangers. Richard Shelton. **SP-ShelR**

We find your soft utopias as white. The Voice of the Man Impatient with Visions and Utopias. Nicholas Vachel Lindsay. *Fr.* An Argument. **CP-LindV**

We finished clearing the last. Above Pate Valley. Gary Snyder. **CP-SnydG**

We flung against their gods. After Troy. Hilda Doolittle. **CP-DoolH**

We fly through a night of stars. Spiritual Explorations. Stephen Spender. **CP-SpenS**

We forget sometimes that no matter what. Convivio. William Carlos Williams. **CP-WilW2**

We found the sea in pieces at Pendeen. Cornwall, Touring. Richard Hugo. **CP-HugoR**

We Free Singers Be. Etheridge Knight. **SP-KnigE**

We galloped over the glossy sea. William Butler Yeats. **SeCePo** *Fr.* The Wanderings of Oisin. **CP-YeatW**

We gathered in the joiner's rock-floored shop. Fame. John Hewitt. **CP-HewiJ**

We gathered praties in the upper field. Gathering Praties. John Hewitt. **CP-HewiJ**

We gaze—nor grieve to think that we must die. Upon a Portrait. William Wordsworth. **CP-WorW2**

We get into camp after. The Great Nebula of Andromeda. Kenneth Rexroth. **SP-RexrK** *Fr.* The Lights in the Sky are Stars.

We get no good/ By being ungenerous. Reading. Elizabeth Barrett Browning. **GN** *Fr.* Aurora Leigh. **CP-BroEB**

We give the world to understand. Drapier's Hill. Jonathan Swift. **CP-SwifJ**

We give thy natal day to hope. Our Country. John Greenleaf Whittier. **CP-WhitJ**

We give to chivalry a separate age. Chivalry. George Meredith. **CP-MerG2**

We giving all gained all. Two Canadian Memorials. Rudyard Kipling. *Fr.* Epitaphs of the War [1914–1918]. **CP-KiplR**

We go by detachments to the strange Home. Emily Dickinson. **SP-DickE**

We go no more to Calverly's. Calverly's. Edwin Arlington Robinson. **CP-RobiE**

We go out of our way to get home. Advice. Ted Kooser. **SP-KoosT**

We go out together into the staring town. Kenneth Patchen. **SP-PatcK**

We go sailing on your breasts. Gentle as the Lamb of God Made into Mad Cutlets. Chuck Miller. **SP-MillC**

We got lucky not too long ago. Growing Up. Jim Carroll. **SP-CarrJ**

We got on a train and went somewhere else. Ernest Hemingway. **CP-HemiE** *Fr.* The Soul of Spain with McAlmon and Bird the Publishers.

We got ourselves up. Fishing at Forty. Barton Sutter. **SP-SuttB**

We got rid of the big people. Before This. Charles Kenneth Williams. **CP-WillC**

We gotta story, we gotta story. Three Little Dog-Gone Mice. Malcolm Lowry. **CP-LowrM**

We grant they're thine, those beauties all. Extempore—On Being Shown a Beautiful County Seat Belonging to the Same [Maxwell of Cardoness]. Robert Burns. **CP-BurnR**

We grow accustomed to the Dark. Emily Dickinson. **CP-DickE**

We had a female Passenger who came. September 1, 1802. William Wordsworth. **CP-WorW1**

We had a motorbike all through the war. A Motorbike. Ted Hughes. **SP-HughT**

We had been wandering for many days. The Bridal of Pennacook. John Greenleaf Whittier. **CP-WhitJ**

We had codes. Scraps. Louise Glück. **SP-GlücL**

We had come from being kind. What Happened in the Camps. Kenneth Patchen. **CP-PatcK**

We had done naught of service. Sweetheart Winter. Nicholas Vachel Lindsay. *Fr.* Sweethearts of the Year. **CP-LindV**

We had no petnames, no diminutives for you. Mary Gravely Jones. Adrienne Rich. **MDDM** *Fr.* Grandmothers. **SP-RicA2**

We had not expected it, the whole street. Red Hook: December. George Oppen. **CP-OppeG**

We had our chance Pilate. Racist Poem. Bill Knott. **SP-KnotB**

We had our cricket team, our football team. On Dunmore's Waste. John Hewitt. **CP-HewiJ**

We had ridden three days Eugenie and I. Who Shot Eugenie? Stevie Smith. **CP-SmitS**

We had to get him off, the dirty elf—. The Squatter on Company Land. Richard Hugo. **CP-HugoR**

We had to take the world as it was given. Ideal Landscape. Adrienne Rich. **CP-RicAE; SP-RicA2**

We hadn't eaten in two days. we were entirely intoxicated. Hymn. Patti Smith. **SP-SmitP**

We hadn't met for six or seven years. The Reference. John Hewitt. **CP-HewiJ**

We hardly ever see the moon any more. Avenue A. Frank O'Hara. **SP-OharF**

We hate the Victorians so much. The Deadly Victorians. David Herbert Lawrence. **CP-LawrD**

We Have a Beautiful Mother. Alice Walker. **CP-WalkA**

We have a lawn of moss. For Doreen. A Voice from the Garden. Donald Davie. **CP-DavDo**

We Have a Map of the World. Alice Walker. **CP-WalkA**

We have a song for the death in her body. Ballad, A. Robert Creeley. **CP-CreeR**

We have acquaintances. Frederick Morgan. *Fr.* Blue Hill Poems. **SP-MorgF**

We have all been in rooms. Adultery. James Dickey. **CP-DickJ**

We have another Viceroy now,—those days are dead and done. Rudyard Kipling. *See* Delilah.

We have been here quite a while. Dialogue. Carl Sandburg. **CP-SandC**

We have been shown. Six Variations. Denise Levertov. **CP-LeveD**

We have been underground too long. Song of the Worms. Margaret Atwood. *Fr.* Songs of the Transformed. **SP-AtwM1**

We have bit no forbidden apple. Renascence. David Herbert Lawrence. **CP-LawrD**

We have broken bread. Marsden Hartley. **CP-HartM**

"We have brought you," they said, "a map of the country." Have a Good Time. Wystan Hugh Auden. **CP-AudeW**

We have come back to the cold North. To the North. May Sarton. **SP-SartM**

We have cried in our despair. When Helen Lived. William Butler Yeats. **CP-YeatW**

We have decided to accept the actual. O reilly? Evils of the City. Gilbert Sorrentino. **SP-SorrG**

We have found a certain heavy kind of wolf. The Research Team in the Mountains. William Stafford. **SP-StafW**

We have gone out in boats upon the sea at night. Passage over Water. Robert Duncan. **SP-DuncR**

We Have Gone Through Great Rooms Together. Carl Sandburg. **CP-SandC**

We Have Gone Too Far. David Herbert Lawrence. **CP-LawrD**

We have gone too far; we do not know how to stop: impetus. Edna St. Vincent Millay. **CP-MillE**

We have got to come together. Coming from the Heart (The Road Is Long). "Bob Dylan" *and* Helena Springs. **CP-DylaB**

We have heard of Quintia's beauty. To me she is tall, slender. Carmen 86. Catullus. *Fr.* Carmina. **CP-Catul**

We have heard of the undimmed air. Icarium Mare. Richard Wilbur. **CP-WilbR**

We have heard with our ears, O God. Psalm 44. Bible, *O.T. Fr.* Psalms. **CP-Psal**

We have lashed oars on the thatch. Brecht in Svendborg. Derek Mahon. **SP-MahoD**

We have loved each other in this time twenty years. Unfinished History. Archibald MacLeish. **CP-MacLA**

We Have Loved of Yore. Robert Louis Stevenson. **CP-StevR**

We have met in the cafés of two countries / Vayo. Rendezvous. Kay Boyle. **CP-BoylK**

We have met late—it is too late to meet. A Denial. Elizabeth Barrett Browning. **CP-BroEB**

We have never quite starved, thanks to some God or other. The Cretan Woman. Robinson Jeffers. **CP-JefR3**

We have no father and no mother. Thank You. Stevie Smith. **CP-SmitS**

We have no heart for the fishing—we have no hand for the oar. The Dykes. Rudyard Kipling. **CP-KiplR**

We have no history. Ballad for Americans. Charles Olson. **CP-OlsoC**

We have no prairies. Bogland. Seamus Heaney. **SP-HeanS**

We have no statutes here. Emily Dickinson. **SP-DickE**

We have not passed into a doleful City. Greenock. William Wordsworth. *Fr.* Poems Composed or Suggested During a Tour, in the Summer of 1833. **CP-WorW2**

We have now set forth, in our imperfect way. Epilogue. Thomas Hardy. **CP-HardT** *Fr.* The Dynasts.

We have now won two world-wars; neither of which concerned us; we. So Many Blood-Lakes. Robinson Jeffers. **CP-JefR3**

We have opened the door. The Dead Feast of the Kol-Folk. John Greenleaf Whittier. **CP-WhitJ**

We have reached the end of pastime, for always. End of Play. Robert Ranke Graves. **CP-GravR**

We have seen a house in the sleeping town. Death of the Horses by Fire. Tess Gallagher. **SP-GallT**

We have seen her/ the world over. Hilda Doolittle. **CRP; NALW; Poetr; VGW** *Fr.* Tribute to the Angels. **CP-DoolH**

We have seen how dignity can be torn. A Hard Death. May Sarton. **SP-SartM**

We have seen how the most amiable. Hilda Doolittle. **BoWoP; PBWP** *Fr.* The Walls Do Not Fall. **CP-DoolH**

We have seen mighty men ballooning high. The Warning. George Meredith. **CP-MerG2**

We Have Seen Thee, O Love. Algernon Charles Swinburne. **SP-SwinA** *Fr.* Atalanta in Calydon.

We have served our day. Journalists. Rudyard Kipling. *Fr.* Epitaphs of the War [1914–1918]. **CP-KiplR**

We have shut the doors behind us, and the velvet flowers of night. Hyde Park at Night, before the War. David Herbert Lawrence. **CP-LawrD**

We have shut the doors behind us, and the velvet flowers of night. *also stands as sl. diff., shorter, separate poem* Hyde Park at Night before the War. David Herbert Lawrence. *Fr.* Night Songs. **CP-LawrD**

We have slept too long. 'Tis time now to awaken. May Day Song. Edwin Rolfe. **CP-RolfE**

We have struck the regions wherein we are keel or reef. Zone. Louise Bogan. **CP-BogaL**

We have the looks you want. Purists Will Object. John Ashbery. **SP-AshbJ**

We have the picture of you in mind. The Three Graces. William Carlos Williams. **CP-WilW2**

We have the waking of an eye. In the Dry. George Meredith. **CP-MerG2**

We have wintered the death of the old, cold year. The Coming of May. Edward Estlin Cummings. **CP-CummE**

We have written. The Genius. William Carlos Williams. **CP-WilW2**

We have written to Giulia, saying. Gemona-del-Friuli, 1961–1976. Donald Davie. **CP-DavDo**

We hear nothing these days. Margaret Atwood. **SP-AtwM1**

We heard a rumor, ran to swell the crowd. A Case of Mistaken Identity. John Hewitt. **CP-HewiJ**

We heard of that king & his building. Events in a Rustic Mirror. George Meredith. **CP-MerG2**

We heard the corncrake's call from close at hand. First Corncrake. John Hewitt. **CP-HewiJ**

We held a meeting in Eureka. The Arts Council Meets in Eureka. Gary Snyder. **CP-SnydG**

We here renounce our Saxon blood. Nicholas Vachel Lindsay. *Fr.* Our Mother Pocahontas. **CP-LindV**

We Hesitate. John Ashbery. **SP-AshbJ**

We hit like a hoof. Hands. Archibald MacLeish. **CP-MacLA**

We hold these truths to be self-evident. Decoy. John Ashbery. **SP-AshbJ**

We Hold These Truths to Be Self-Evident. Kenneth Patchen. **CP-PatcK**

We humans / do not freeze often. After St. John of the Cross. Jim Carroll. **SP-CarrJ**

We hunted the mad bastard. As It Should Be. Derek Mahon. **SP-MahoD**

We hurry back to resume our awaited commissions. The Men (XIX). Pablo Neruda, *tr. fr. Spanish by* Ben Belitt. **SP-NeruP** *Fr.* The Separate Rose.

We idle, circling the wide hilltop courtyard of Fort Charlotte. The Dungeon Amorist. Laurence Lieberman. **SP-LiebL**

We in all lights are coming. Dark Ones. James Dickey. **CP-DickJ**

We in our season like progress and inventions. Parallel Invention. Muriel Rukeyser. **CP-RukeM**

We in the Fields. William Everson. **SP-EverW**

We in this summer have lived to see our final refuge broken. August, 1940. John Gould Fletcher. **SP-FletJ**

We introduce ourselves. Emily Dickinson. **CP-DickE**

We Irish pride ourselves as patriots. Ireland. John Hewitt. **CP-HewiJ**

We is gathahed hyeah, my brothahs. An Ante-Bellum Sermon. Paul Laurence Dunbar. **CP-DunbP**

We join the animals. Heroic Sculpture. Frank O'Hara. **SP-OharF**

We Kiss'd Again with Tears. Tennyson. *See* As through the land at eve we went.

We kissed at the barrier; and passing through. On the Departure Platform. Thomas Hardy. **CP-HardT**

We knew. / Anne to come. New. Gertrude Stein. **CP-SteiG**

We knew how to order. Just the dash. Gay Chaps at the Bar. Gwendolyn Brooks. **SP-BrooG**

We knew it was not a valid thing. A Poor Man and a Lady. Thomas Hardy. **CP-HardT**

We knew not that we were to live. Emily Dickinson. **CP-DickE**

We knew thee of old. Rudyard Kipling. **CP-KiplR** (Greek National Anthem, The.) **CP-KiplR**

We know not a voice of that River, / If vocal or silent it be. Whitsun Monday. Christina Georgina Rossetti. **CP-RosC2**

We know not when, we know not where. Christina Georgina Rossetti. **CP-RosC2**

We know that hereabouts. Wonders of Obligation. Roy Fisher. **SP-FishR**

We know the cities by their stones. A Postcard from Berlin. Derek Mahon. **SP-MahoD**

We know the Rocket's upward whizz. The Bonfires. Rudyard Kipling. **CP-KiplR**

We know the story. The children. Remembering the Children of Auschwitz. Thomas McGrath. **SP-McGrT**

We know those tales of gods in hot pursuit. Under a Tree. Richard Wilbur. **CP-WilbR**

We, knowing the family history. Wystan Hugh Auden. **CP-AudWJ**

We lack nothing / But the milieu. Milieux. Charles Tomlinson. *Fr.* Antecedents. **CP-TomlC**

We lack the courage to be where we are. Edwin Arlington Robinson. *Fr.* Octaves. **CP-RobiE**

We lack, yet cannot fix upon the lack. Christina Georgina Rossetti. *Fr.* Later Life: A Double Sonnet of Sonnets. **CP-RosC2**

We last of Yugo-Slav. Well-Found Poem. Donald Davie. **CP-DavDo**

We laugh, we frown, our fingers twitch. Ageless Reason. Robert Ranke Graves. **CP-GravR**

We laughed when he sat down at the piano. "You've Tried the World, Try Jesus." Robert Creeley. **CP-CreeR**

We lay beneath the alder tree. What Must. Archibald MacLeish. **CP-MacLA**

We lay red roses on his grave. Paul Laurence Dunbar. Robert Earl Hayden. **CP-HaydR**

We lay together on the beach. On the Beach. John Gould Fletcher. **SP-FletJ**

We lean'd beneath the purple vine. Rhine-Land. George Meredith. **CP-MerG2**

We learn a method by the absence of. Dead of Night. Jenny Joseph. **SP-JoseJ**

We learn from Horace, Homer sometimes sleep. Byron. **EPCY** *Fr.* Canto the Third. *Fr.* Don Juan. **CP-Byron**

We learn in the Retreating. Emily Dickinson. **CP-DickE**

We Learned. Erica Jong. **SP-JongE**

We learned the Whole of Love. Emily Dickinson. **CP-DickE**

We leave the well-beloved place. Tennyson. **EBVV; FHYEP; PoEL-5** *Fr.* In Memoriam A. H. H. **CP-TennA**

We leave them all quite easily. Black-Ass Poem After Talking to Pamela Churchill. Ernest Hemingway. **CP-HemiE**

We Leave You Pleasure. Kenneth Patchen. **CP-PatcK**

We left the River seven days ago. Gary Gildner. *Fr.* Letters from Vicksburg. **SP-GildG**

We left the western island to live among strangers. The Search. John Hewitt. **CP-HewiJ**

We lent to Alexander the strength of Hercules. Parade-Song of the Camp Animals. Rudyard Kipling. **CP-KiplR** *Fr.* Her Majesty's Servants. *Fr.* The Jungle Book.

We lie like the gods. Perfect Love Casteth Out Everything. Randall Jarrell. **CP-JarrR**

We lie together in the grass. The Sun on Your Shoulder. John Haines. **SP-HainJ**

We like a Hairbreadth 'scape. Emily Dickinson. **CP-DickE**

We like March, vers. of 1872; see also *We like March—his shoes are Purple*. Emily Dickinson. **CP-DickE**

We like March—his shoes are Purple, vers. of 1878; see also *We like March*. Emily Dickinson. **CP-DickE**

We liked its name: those ones, feminine plural. Celles. Marilyn Hacker. **SP-HackM**

We likened one man to a ship adrift. Malcolm Lowry. *Fr.* The Roar of the Sea and the Darkness. **CP-LowrM**

We live by Faith; but Faith is not the slave. Requirement. John Greenleaf Whittier. **CP-WhitJ**

We live by love, but not by love alone. Oysters and Hermits. Donald Hall. **CP-HallD**

We live in this flat blue basin. Invitation. William Carlos Williams. **CP-WilW1**

We live only once. Carl Sandburg. *Fr.* The People, Yes. **CP-SandC**

We live to see. Gerard Manley Hopkins. *Fr.* Fragments. **CP-HopkG**

We lived beneath the mat, / Warm and snug and fat. Mouse's Tale, The. "Lewis Carroll." **CP-CarrL**

We lived deep in a land of optative moods. From the Canton of Expectation. Seamus Heaney. **SP-HeanS**

We lived in province snow range. O Heart Uncovered. Joseph Ceravolo. **SP-CeraJ**

We look for her that sunlike stood. France. George Meredith. **CP-MerG1**

We look for her that sunlike stood. George Meredith. *Fr.* France. **CP-MerG1**

We looked at Matthew's child, our granddaughter. Grandparents. Stephen Spender. **CP-SpenS**

We looked at the hawthorn with the helpless joy. The Trees in Spring. Randall Jarrell. **CP-JarrR**

We looked for the tide, for the full river. Severnside. Charles Tomlinson. **CP-TomlC**

We looked, we loved, and therewith instantly. Pure Death. Robert Ranke Graves. **CP-GravR**

We lose—because we win. Emily Dickinson. **CP-DickE**

We Love, But Cannot Live. David Markson. **CP-MarkD**

We love each other very dearly. Edward Estlin Cummings. **CP-CummE**

We love Paris. The Migration of Cities. Thomas McGrath. **SP-McGrT**

We love the venerable house. Hymn Sung at the Second Church, Boston, at the Ordination of Rev. Chandler Robbins. Ralph Waldo Emerson. **CP-EmerR**

We Love This Body. Robert Bly. **SP-BlyR**

We love to think of Alan Gaylord. A Clerihew for Alan Gaylord. Richard Eberhart. **CP-EberR**

We Lying by Seasand. Dylan Thomas. **CP-ThomD**

We made all possible preparations. Let History Be My Judge. Wystan Hugh Auden. **CP-AudeW**

We made love on a winter afternoon. Winter Poem. Frederick Morgan. **SP-MorgF**

We made strong poems for each other. Neighbors. Audre Lorde. **SP-LordA**

We made them. Best Friends. Erica Jong. **SP-JongE**

We make our meek adjustments. Chaplinesque. Hart Crane. **CP-CranH**

We Make Our Vows Together with All Beings. Gary Snyder. **CP-SnydG**

We make ourselves a place apart. Revelation. Robert Frost. **CP-FrosR**

We may not always rate. The Laws Can Say. Louis Zukofsky. **CP-ZukLS**

We may not climb the heavenly steeps. John Greenleaf Whittier. **BLRP; WBLP,** *ll.* 17–64; *Fr.* Our Master. **CP-WhitJ**

We may well ask now: "Where are the lilacs?" Yes. . . . Lament for Pablo Neruda. Thomas McGrath. **SP-McGrT**

We Meet at the Judgement and I Fear It Not. Nicholas Vachel Lindsay. *Fr.* Two Easter Stanzas. **CP-LindV**

We meet by courtesy of Jack Kerouac. Thursdays Are Sacred. James Liddy. **CP-LiddJ**

We meet, eating, smoking. William Dickey. **SP-DickW** *Fr.* In The Dreaming. **SP-DickW**

We meet in an evil land. Rudyard Kipling. **CP-KiplR** *Fr.* The Naulahka.

We meet in joy, tho' we part in sorrow. Martyrs' Song. Christina Georgina Rossetti. **CP-RosC1**

We meet no Stranger. Emily Dickinson. **SP-DickE**

We meet not as we parted. Lines. Percy Bysshe Shelley. **CP-ShelP**

We merit all we suffer, and by far. Sufferings. Robert Herrick. **CP-HerrR**

We met as Sparks—Diverging Flints. Emily Dickinson. **CP-DickE**

We met, hand to hand. Twilight Night. Christina Georgina Rossetti. **CP-RosC1**

We met in a crowded auditorium, agreed to rendezvous on a train. Spin, Spell, Spill. John Yau. **SP-YauJo**

We met the British in the dead of winter. Meeting the British. Paul Muldoon. **SP-MuldP**

We miss a Kinsman more. Emily Dickinson. **CP-DickE**

We miss Her, not because We see. Emily Dickinson. **CP-DickE**

We miss you,jack—tactfully you(with one cocked). Edward Estlin Cummings. **CP-CummE**

We more than others have the perfect right. Song of the Moderns. John Gould Fletcher. **SP-FletJ**

We move already thru a low-pitched heaven. Palm Drive Palo Alto. Al Young. **CP-YounA**

We move as dragons in the lethargy. The Albigenses. Robert Duncan. **SP-DuncR**

We move thru rooms & down the middle of freeways. Dancing All Alone. Al Young. **CP-YounA**

We moved down the valley. The Forms of Knowledge. Kenneth Patchen. **CP-PatcK**

We moved with pensive paces. The Noble Lady's Tale. Thomas Hardy. **CP-HardT**

We must admire her perfect aim. The Colder the Air. Elizabeth Bishop. **CP-BishE**

We must anticipate the dawn one day. The Roe Deer. Charles Tomlinson. **CP-TomlC**

We must be careful what we say. Emily Dickinson. **SP-DickE**

We must be less than Death. Emily Dickinson. **SP-DickE**

We Must Be Polite. Carl Sandburg. **CP-SandC**

We Must Be Slow. Kenneth Patchen. **CP-PatcK**

We must be slow and delicate; return. My Generation Reading the Newspapers. Kenneth Patchen. **CP-PatcK**

We must be the only ones. After the Flood, We. Margaret Atwood. **SP-AtwM1**

We must bring no Twilight. Emily Dickinson. **SP-DickE**

We must dream inwards, and we must dream. Variation on Paz. Charles Tomlinson. **CP-TomlC**

We must go back and find a trail on the ground. Watching the Jet Planes Dive. William Stafford. **SP-StafW**

We must not honor a girl of Minnie's kind. Moments of Minnie. John Crowe Ransom. **SP-RansJ**

We must observe the amenities. James Schuyler. *Fr.* Four Poems. **CP-SchuJ**

We must remember cleanly why we fought. Postscript to a War. Edwin Rolfe. **CP-RolfE**

We must say it all, and as clearly. Each One, Pull One. Alice Walker. **CP-WalkA**

We must sit down. Councils. Marge Piercy. **SP-PierM**

We must work. Resolve. Archie Randolph Ammons. **SP-AmmoA**

We must work & play and John Jacob Niles. The Home Ballad. John Berryman. **CP-BerrJ**

We Mutually Pledge to Each Other. Kenneth Patchen. **CP-PatcK**

We need a private bush. Somehow. Marge Piercy. **SP-PierM**

We need some rallying point round which. George Meredith. **CP-MerG2**

We needs must love the highest when we see it. The Friend. Stevie Smith. **CP-SmitS**

We Never Close. Dabney Stuart. **SP-StuaD**

"We never dreamed he'd be so bad", said thrall. In Bed Not Dead. John Crowe Ransom. *Fr.* Two Gentlemen in Bonds. **SP-RansJ**

We never know how high we are. Emily Dickinson. **CP-DickE**

We never know we go when we are going. Emily Dickinson. **CP-DickE**

We never know what we have lost, or what we have found. We Are Only Ourselves. Robert Penn Warren. *Fr.* Audubon. **SP-WarrR**

We never made it. Time and time again. Derbyshire. Donald Davie. **CP-DavDo**

We never rode out so. A Byron-Shelley Conversation. Frank Templeton Prince. **CP-PrinF**

We never sang together. On the Tune Called the Old-Hundred-and-Fourth. Thomas Hardy. **CP-HardT**

We never see him now, except at dinner. Robert Lowell. **SP-LoweR**

We never would have loved had love not struck. Under the Olives. Robert Ranke Graves. **CP-GravR**

We now, held in captivity. Rudyard Kipling. **CP-KiplR**

We now lament not, but congratulate. John Donne. **NOSC** *Fr.* The Second Anniversary [*or* Anniversarie]. **ESCV; SeCP** *Fr.* Of the Progres[se] of the Soule; the Second Anniversarie. **CP-DonnJ**

We on that morning, working, faced south and east where the sun was in winter at rising. The Rain on That Morning. William Everson. **SP-EverW**

We open infant eyes. Dear Friends and Gentle Hearts. Countee Cullen. **CP-CullC**

We ought, I think, to say in civil terms: You be damned. Canto 42. Ezra Pound. *Fr.* Cantos. **CP-PoCan**

We outgrow love like other things. Emily Dickinson. **CP-DickE**

We overstate the ills of life, and take. Exaggeration. Elizabeth Barrett Browning. **CP-BroEB**

We pace each other for a long time. Iva's Pantoum. Marilyn Hacker. **SP-HackM**

We park and stare. A full sky of the stars. The Death of the Sheriff. Robert Lowell. **SP-LoweR**

We parted where the old gas-lamp still burned. Afterthoughts. Edwin Arlington Robinson. **CP-RobiE**

We passed the ice of pain. The Moment. Theodore Roethke. **CP-RoetT**

We passed where flag and flower. Middle-Age Enthusiasms. Thomas Hardy. **CP-HardT**

We pattern our Heaven. Earthworm. John Updike. **CP-UpdiJ**

We pile the brush high. Wendell Berry. *Fr.* The Clearing. **CP-BerrW**

We piled in the car. After World War II. Gary Gildner. **SP-GildG**

We play at Paste. Emily Dickinson. **CP-DickE**

We pledged our hearts, my love and I. The Exchange. Samuel Taylor Coleridge. **CP-ColeS**

We Poets in Our Youth. William Wordsworth. **FaBoRV** *Fr.* Resolution and Independence. **CP-WorW1**

We praise not now the poet's art. Bryant on His Birthday. John Greenleaf Whittier. **CP-WhitJ**

We pray 'gainst Warre, yet we enjoy no Peace. Things of Choice, Long a Comming. Robert Herrick. **CP-HerrR**

We pray—to Heaven. Emily Dickinson. **CP-DickE**

We prayed not, yet she came to us. Sweetheart Summer. Nicholas Vachel Lindsay. *Fr.* Sweethearts of the Year. **CP-LindV**

We pressed our faces. The Train Stops at Healy Fork. John Haines. **SP-HainJ**

We pulled for you when the wind was against us and the sails were low. Song of the Galley-Slaves. Rudyard Kipling. **CP-KiplR**

We put a prop beneath the sagging bough. The Wild Cherry. Malcolm Lowry. **CP-LowrM**

We quarreled / Alone I. Grace Paley. **CP-PaleG**

We quit that road of sad homes long ago. Listen, Ripley. Richard Hugo. **CP-HugoR**

We ran across the meadow scabbed with cow-dung, past. Geoffrey Hill. **HAP** *Fr.* Mercian Hymns. **CP-HillG**

We ranging down this lower track. Tennyson. *Fr.* In Memoriam A. H. H. **CP-TennA**

We reach for destinies beyond. Beyond What. Alice Walker. **CP-WalkA**

We reach the utmost limit of the earth. Prometheus Bound. Aeschylus, *tr. fr. Greek by* Elizabeth Barrett Browning. **CP-BroEB**

We reached the sea in early afternoon. Day Trip to Donegal. Derek Mahon. **SP-MahoD**

We read and hear about you every day. To the Rulers. Howard Nemerov. **CP-NemeH**

We read how Faunus, he the sheapherds God. Upon Faunus. Robert Herrick. **CP-HerrR**

We read in a tremendous Book. Emily Dickinson. **SP-DickE**

We read of kings and gods that kindly took. A Cruel Mistress. Thomas Carew. **CP-CareT**

We read the words but know them not. Emily Dickinson. **SP-DickE**

We Real Cool. Gwendolyn Brooks. **SP-BrooG**

We rebuilt our childhood, leaf by leaf. Call of the North. Phoebe Hesketh. **SP-HeskP**

We reckon Cooke our best chemist alive. Research and Development: Classified. Robert Ranke Graves. **CP-GravR**

We regretted the rain. Japanese Prints. May Sarton. **SP-SartM**

We remind her we love her. Emily Dickinson. **SP-DickE**

We reserve the right to refuse to anyone, pal. Memory of the Hospitality of American Barmen. Malcolm Lowry. *Fr.* The Cantinas. **CP-LowrM**

We resolve to think of ourselves. A Testament. Robert Creeley. **CP-CreeR**

We ripple aspen the way we move out. At the Cabin. Richard Hugo. **CP-HugoR**

We Rise on Sun Beams and Fall in the Night. Allen Ginsberg. **CP-GinsA**

"We rode out the depression on technique." How gratifying, how rare. "Sure," Said Benny Goodman. Hayden Carruth. **CP-CarHS**

We rolled apart on the forest floor. Existence Before Essence. Hayden Carruth. **CP-CarHS**

"We," said my young radical neighbor, smashing my window. Encounter. John Ciardi. **SP-CiarJ**

We said our goodbyes. The Night Before. The Beatles. **CP-Beatl**

We sail out of season into an oyster-gray wind. Crossing the Atlantic. Anne Sexton. **CP-SextA**

We sang plenty of songs then. A Poem to Read in August. Gilbert Sorrentino. **SP-SorrG**

We Sat. Wystan Hugh Auden. **CP-AudWJ**

We sat across the table. The Friend. Marge Piercy. **SP-PierM**

We sat and talked. It was June, and the summer light. Walter de la Mare. **CP-DeLaW**

(To K. M.) **CP-DeLaW**

We Sat at the Window. Thomas Hardy. **CP-HardT**

We sat beneath the humming pines. George Meredith. **CP-MerG2**

We sat by the shore. Philip Levine. **SP-LeviP** *Fr.* A Poem with No Ending.

We sat in the room. Outside the Casement. Thomas Hardy. **CP-HardT**

We sat in the shaded lamplight. We Sat. Wystan Hugh Auden. **CP-AudWJ**

We Sat Smoking at a Table. . . . May Sarton. **SP-SartM**

We sat together at one summer's end. Adam's Curse. William Butler Yeats. **CP-YeatW**

We sat together, last May-day, and talked. Within the Gate. John Greenleaf Whittier. **CP-WhitJ**

We sat under an old thorn-tree. Summer and Spring. William Butler Yeats. *Fr.* A Man Young and Old. **CP-YeatW**

We sat with the banqueting-party. At a Fashionable Dinner. Thomas Hardy. **CP-HardT**

We sat within the farm-house old. The Fire of Drift-Wood. Henry Wadsworth Longfellow. **SP-LongH**

We sate down and wept by the waters. By the Rivers of Babylon We Sat Down and Wept. Byron. **CP-Byron**

We sauntered amidst miracles. Ralph Waldo Emerson. **CP-EmerR**

We Saw Beyond Our Seeming. Maya Angelou. **SP-AngeM**

We saw, but surely, in the motley crowd. Cave of Staffa. William Wordsworth. **VLP** *Fr.* Poems Composed or Suggested During a Tour, in the Summer of 1833. **CP-WorW2**

We saw him first stretching for blackberries. The Brothers. John Hewitt. **CP-HewiJ**

We saw him in his powered wheelchair. Poem for Zen Hofman. Richard Hugo. **CP-HugoR**

We saw leaves go to glory. November. Robert Frost. **CP-FrosR**

We saw nothing but change in all the ways we went. Nothing But Change. Richard Eberhart. **CP-EberR**

"We saw reindeer / browsing," a friend who'd been in Lapland, said. Rigorists. Marianne Craig Moore. **CP-MoorM**

We saw the slow tides go and come. A Sea Dream. John Greenleaf Whittier. **CP-WhitJ**

We saw the star of knowledge. James Liddy. *Fr.* A Munster Song of Love and War. **CP-LiddJ**

We Saw the Swallows. George Meredith. *See* We saw the swallows gathering in the sky.

We saw the swallows gathering in the sky. George Meredith. **ELP; EnLoPo; FaBoEn; GTBS-6; GTBS-P; Mes; NOBE; NOBVV; OAEL-2; OBNC; SeCeV; WHA** *Fr.* Modern Love. **CP-MerG1**

(We Saw the Swallows.) **ELP**

We saw Thee in Thy balmy nest. Shepherd's Hymn, The . Richard Crashaw. **ACP; OBEV; TrGrPo** *Fr.* In the Holy Nativity of Our Lord God.

We saw this beautiful confection in the window. The Feast. Jenny Joseph. **SP-JoseJ**

We say that some are mad. In fact. A Little Poem. Miller Williams. **SP-WillM**

We Say We Shall Not Meet. Thomas Hardy. **CP-HardT**

We scatter in booths. Evening at Axel's. James Liddy. **CP-LiddJ**

We search the world for truth; we cull. The Book Our Mothers Read. John Greenleaf Whittier. **BLRP; PoToHe** *Fr.* Miriam. **CP-WhitJ**

We see—Comparatively. Emily Dickinson. **CP-DickE**

We see in authors, too stiff to recant. John Donne. *See* Poor soul, in this thy flesh what dost thou know?

We see not, know not; all our way. Thy Will Be Done. John Greenleaf Whittier. **CP-WhitJ**

We See Seals. Boats Go By. James Schuyler. *Fr.* The Cenotaph. **CP-SchuJ**

We see the farther in the far. George Meredith. **CP-MerG2**

We See the Spring Breaking across Rough Stone. Philip Larkin. **CP-LarkP**

We see us as we truly behave. Two Scenes. John Ashbery. **SP-AshbJ**

We see you as we see a face. Katharine. Robert Louis Stevenson. **CP-StevR**

We send the Wave to find the Wave. Emily Dickinson. **CP-DickE**

We set great wreaths of brightness on the graves of the passionate. Song for Dead Children. Muriel Rukeyser. **CP-RukeM**

We shall break out. Meteorologist, September. Donald Davie. **CP-DavDo**

We shall come tomorrow morning, who were not to have her love. Emily Hardcastle, Spinster. John Crowe Ransom. **SP-RansJ**

We shall find the Cube of the Rainbow. Emily Dickinson. **CP-DickE**

We shall never be one mummy only. From the French (2). Stevie Smith. **CP-SmitS**

We shall not always plant while others reap. From the Dark Tower. Countee Cullen. **CP-CullC**

We shall not cease from exploration. Thomas Stearns Eliot. **ImOP** *Fr.* Little Gidding. **FaBoMo; FaBoPV; FaBoTw; GTBS-6; GTBS-P; MoP; NAEL-2; NAWM-2; NOBA; NOBE; NoAM; OAEL-2; OXAEP-2; OxBTC; PeECV; PrIm; TAP; TFi** *Fr.* Four Quartets. **CP-ElioT**

We shall see her no more. The Rejected Member's Wife. Thomas Hardy. **CP-HardT**

We shall watch its final plunge from afar. The Ship. Edwin Rolfe. **CP-RolfE**

We shopped for dresses which were always wrong. Fourteen. Marilyn Hacker. **SP-HackM**

We should be hidden from their eyes. His Memories. William Butler Yeats. *Fr.* A Man Young and Old. **CP-YeatW**

We should not mind so small a flower. Emily Dickinson. **CP-DickE**

We should think / we can get. Fortitude. Archie Randolph Ammons. **SP-AmmoA**

We shriek to live, but no man ever lives. Edwin Arlington Robinson. *Fr.* Two Quatrains. **CP-RobiE**

We shun because we prize her Face. Emily Dickinson. **CP-DickE**

We shun it ere it comes. Emily Dickinson. **CP-DickE**

We sit at a sidewalk table. The Firebreathers at the Café Deux Magots. Miller Williams. **SP-WillM**

We sit indoors and talk of the cold outside. There Are Roughly Zones. Robert Frost. **CP-FrosR**

We Sit Unhackled Drunk and Mad to Edit, *sl. diff. vers.* Malcolm Lowry. *See* Notions of freedom are tied up with drink.

We six pile in, the engine churning ink. Nigger Song: An Odyssey. Rita Dove. **SP-DoveR**

We slapped the smirking mother. The Learners. Mona Van Duyn. **SP-VanDM**

We slipped and slithered down the thick-timbered hill. The Descent. John Hewitt. **CP-HewiJ**

We smile at astrological hopes. For the Conjunction of Two Planets. Adrienne Rich. **CP-RicAE; SP-RicA2**

We snicked the latch where one was dead. The Wake. John Hewitt. **CP-HewiJ**

We sow the glebe, we reap the corn. Human Life's Mystery. Elizabeth Barrett Browning. **CP-BroEB**

We speak the verses out of Mark. Maundy Thursday's Candles. Donald Hall. **CP-HallD**

We spend our lives in learning pilotage. The Wisdom of Eld. George Meredith. **CP-MerG1**

We spend our swift years learning how to read. The Lettered Snow. John Hewitt. **CP-HewiJ**

We spray the fields and scatter. Harvest Hymn. Sir John Betjeman. **CP-BetjJ**

We spurred our parents to the kiss. Children of Darkness. Robert Ranke Graves. **CP-GravR**

We squat upon the beach of love. Lawrence Ferlinghetti. **SP-FerlL**

We stand in line all morning long to see it. The Most Expensive Picture in the World. Howard Nemerov. **CP-NemeH**

We started our house midway through the Cultural Revolution. Building. Gary Snyder. **CP-SnydG**

We started to walk but it was wading-slow. Eel. Muriel Rukeyser. **CP-RukeM**

We stayed the night in the pathless gorge of Ventana Creek, up th east. Oh, Lovely Rock. Robinson Jeffers. **CP-JefR2**

We still go about our lives. A Winter Light. John Haines. **SP-HainJ**

We still remain we. The New Eternity. Robert Ranke Graves. **CP-GravR**

We stood and pondered on the stones. Ossian's Grave, Lubitavish, County Antrim. John Hewitt. **CP-HewiJ**

We stood around the raw new-planted garden. Divining Water. Muriel Rukeyser. **CP-RukeM**

We stood at the back door. And the Trains Go On. Philip Levine. **SP-LeviP**

We stood by a pond that winter day. Neutral Tones. Thomas Hardy. **CP-HardT**

We stood by the library. It was an August night. Dedication, A. William Stafford. **SP-StafW**

We stood in the garden alone. George Meredith. **CP-MerG2**

We stood on a height. Wendell Berry. *Fr.* Elegy: "To be at home on its native ground." **CP-BerrW**

We stood there nude embracing while the sculptor. The Sculpture. Bill Knott. **CP-KnotB**

We stood together, side by side, rooted. Iron Palace. Robert Ranke Graves. **CP-GravR**

We stopped at her hut. The Ballad of Ballymote. Tess Gallagher. **SP-GallT**

We strike camp on that portion of road completed. Corduroy Road. Rita Dove. **SP-DoveR**

We stripped in the first warm spring night. Belle Isle, 1949. Philip Levine. **SP-LeviP**

We surfed out of the alley. Genghis Chan: Private Eye III. John Yau. **SP-YauJo**

We swallow the odors of Southern cities. A Georgia Song. Maya Angelou. **SP-AngeM**

We tack into the lagoon. East with Malinowski. Thomas Merton. *Fr.* East. *Fr.* The Geography of Lograire. **CP-MertT**

We talk about this film. Iron Mike. Charles Bukowski. **SP-BukC1**

We talk of taxes, and I call you friend. Edna St. Vincent Millay. **CP-MillE**

We talked as Girls do. Emily Dickinson. **CP-DickE**

We talked of things but all the time we wanted each other. And What with the Blunders. Kenneth Patchen. **CP-PatcK**

We talked with each other about each other. Emily Dickinson. **CP-DickE**

We talked [*or* talk'd] with open heart, and tongue. The Fountain. William Wordsworth. **CP-WorW1**

"We thank thee Oh Father" for these strange Minds. Emily Dickinson. **SP-DickE**

We that have done and thought. Spilt Milk. William Butler Yeats. **CP-YeatW**

We, the old children, are now old again. The Borrowed Ones. Tess Gallagher. **SP-GallT**

We think of you as one. Margaret Atwood. *Fr.* Two-Headed Poems. **SP-AtwM2**

We thirst at first—'tis Nature's Act. Emily Dickinson. **CP-DickE**

We thought the château was safe. The men were gone. Hayden Carruth. *Fr.* The Sleeping Beauty. **CP-CarHL**

We thought to be proud. Nicholas Vachel Lindsay. *Fr.* The Master of the Dance. **CP-LindV**

We thought we did so well to leave the house. Go Back to Square One. Jenny Joseph. **SP-JoseJ**

We thought we owned the apple. Opportunity. Leonard Nathan. **SP-NathL**

We thought we ranked above the chance of ill. The Covenant. Rudyard Kipling. **CP-KiplR**

We thought we'd try the new saloons. Nordeast. Barton Sutter. **SP-SuttB**

We three are on the cedar-shadowed lawn. George Meredith. **NOBVV** *Fr.* Modern Love. **CP-MerG1**

We thrill too strangely at the master's touch. Edwin Arlington Robinson. *Fr.* Octaves. **CP-RobiE**

We to your story, game and smugness, do add. Tomorrow. Kenneth Patchen. **CP-PatcK**

We told of him as one who should have soared. Discovery. Edwin Arlington Robinson. **CP-RobiE**

We Too Had Known Golden Hours. Wystan Hugh Auden. **CP-AudeW**

We too have gone down little roads in spring. John Hewitt. **CP-HewiJ** *Fr.* Tristan: The Lay of the Goatleaf.

We too, we too, descending once again. Archibald MacLeish. **CP-MacLA** (Silent Slain, The.) **CP-MacLA**

We took a room at the Westbury. Frederick Morgan. **SP-MorgF**

We tossed our beer cans down among the rocks. The Fishermen. James Wright. **CP-WrigJ**

We touch them at the raw turns. The Melancholy of Storm Windows. John Updike. **CP-UpdiJ**

We transients, we deadbeats: we blunder about. The Men (IV). Pablo Neruda, *tr. fr. Spanish by* Ben Belitt. **SP-NeruP** *Fr.* The Separate Rose.

We travel through Dublin's wide streets bearing. Patrick Kavanagh's Dublin. James Liddy. **CP-LiddJ**

We travelled in the print of olden wars. The Country of the Camisards. Robert Louis Stevenson. **CP-StevR** *Fr.* Travels with a Donkey.

We trenched, we trumpeted and drummed. Valenciennes. Thomas Hardy. **CP-HardT**

We Trust not to the multitude in Warre. Multitude. Robert Herrick. **CP-HerrR**

We turn not older with years. Emily Dickinson. **SP-DickE**

We turn off. To Bed. Rita Dove. **SP-DoveR**

We turn off the bedroom light. Nightshade. Siv Cedering Fox. **SP-CedeS**

We turned and waved, arms raised above our load. No Map Available. Jenny Joseph. **SP-JoseJ**

We twin cherubs above the Mercy Seat. Sun-Face and Moon-Face. Robert Ranke Graves. **CP-GravR**

We Two. Hilda Doolittle. **CP-DoolH**

We two are last in Hell: what may we fear[e]. Barley-Break; or, Last in Hell. Robert Herrick. **CP-HerrR**

We Two Boys Together Clinging. Walt Whitman. **CP-WhitW**

We, two elementals, woman and man. The Meeting. Robert Ranke Graves. **CP-GravR**

We Two, How Long We Were Fool'd. Walt Whitman. **CP-WhitW**

We two kept house, the Past and I. The Ghost of the Past. Thomas Hardy. **CP-HardT**

We two stood simply friend-like side by side. Inapprehensiveness. Robert Browning. **CP-BroR2**

We uncommiserate pass into the night. Robert Louis Stevenson. **CP-StevR**

We used to go to Froom-hill Barrow. Seeing the Moon Rise. Thomas Hardy. **CP-HardT**

We used to picnic where the thrift. Trebetherick. Sir John Betjeman. **CP-BetjJ**

We used to see him, then a shambling lad. The Free Foot. John Hewitt. **CP-HewiJ**

We used to strike sparks. Living Happily Ever After. Erica Jong. **SP-JongE**

We vainly wrestle with the blind belief. Robert Frost. **CP-FrosR**

We violets white and blue. George Meredith. **CP-MerG2**

We voted 'em in, and we'll vote 'em out! Flapper Vote. David Herbert Lawrence. **CP-LawrD**

We wait beneath the furnace-blast. Ein Feste Burg Ist Unser Gott. John Greenleaf Whittier. **CP-WhitJ**

We waited for the sun. In the Garden. Thomas Hardy. **CP-HardT**

We wake and watch the sun make bright. Another Sunday Morning. Derek Mahon. **SP-MahoD**

We wake up with guns going off. Ernesto Cardenal, *tr. by* Thomas Merton. **CP-MertT** *Fr.* Three Epigrams.

We Walk. James Schuyler. **CP-SchuJ**

We walk in the cedar groves. Margaret Atwood. *Fr.* Circe / Mud Poems. **SP-AtwM1**

We walk up Madison. It is the end. On Madison. Charles Tomlinson. **CP-TomlC**

We walked [*or* walk'd] along, while bright and red. The Two April Mornings. William Wordsworth. **CP-WorW1**

We walked beside the sea. A Sea-side walk. Elizabeth Barrett Browning. **CP-BroEB**

We walked through the afternoon's diminishing arches until we. Bare Sheets I. John Yau. **SP-YauJo**

We walked under cliffs where the Upward and Downward are. Fifth Dimension. Kenneth Patchen. **CP-PatcK**

We walked where Victor Jove was shrined awhile. Rome: On the Palatine. Thomas Hardy. **CP-HardT**

We wandered diligently and widely. Mountain Lovers. Robert Ranke Graves. **CP-GravR**

We wandered to the pine forest. Percy Bysshe Shelley. **CH** *Fr.* To Jane: The Recollection. **CP-ShelP**

We watch the heavy-odoured beast. Port of Call: Brazil. Alun Lewis. **CP-LewiA**

We watch through the shop-front while. Blackie, the Electric Rembrandt. Thom Gunn. **CP-GunnT**

We watched the selfsame scene on that long drive. Alike and Unlike. Thomas Hardy. **CP-HardT**

We, we children, why our lives are circumscribed, circumferential. Unusual Precautions. John Ashbery. **SP-AshbJ**

We wear our sober Dresses when we die. Emily Dickinson. **CP-DickE**

We Wear the Mask. Paul Laurence Dunbar. **CP-DunbP**

We went a day's excursion to the stream. Best Times. Thomas Hardy. **CP-HardT**

We went our Christmas rounds once more. The Paphian Ball. Thomas Hardy. **CP-HardT**

We went there on the train. *They had big barges that they towed.* Protocols. Randall Jarrell. **CP-JarrR**

We went through the hedge. Midnight Special. Gilbert Sorrentino. **SP-SorrG**

We went to church, by custom, not compelled. Going to Church. John Hewitt. **CP-HewiJ**

We went to sleep as if it were a country. Emily Dickinson. **SP-DickE**

We went to the moon those empty Sundays. The Sandbanks. Richard Hugo. **CP-HugoR**

We went to the park. Some Objects of Wood and Stone. Margaret Atwood. **SP-AtwM1**

We went where we had often been when young. A Seaside Town. John Hewitt. **CP-HewiJ**

We were a band of kids willing to learn something. The Queer Client and the Forest-Inn. Kenneth Patchen. **CP-PatcK**

We were a noisy crew; the sun in heaven. Fishing. William Wordsworth. **SD** *Fr.* Introduction—Childhood and School-Time. **EnRP; FHYEP** *Fr.* The Prelude; Growth of a Poet's Mind [1850 vers.]. **CP-WorW3**

We were all one heart and one race. The Declaration of London. Rudyard Kipling. **CP-KiplR**

We were apart; yet, day by day. Isolation: To Marguerite. Matthew Arnold. **SP-ArnoM** *Fr.* Switzerland.

We were at the faculty dining table. Father in a Dream. Robert Lowell. **SP-LoweR**

We were away for a long time. John Haines. *Fr.* The Traveler. **SP-HainJ**

We were bound on the wheel of an endless conversation. Adrienne Rich. **SP-RicA1; SP-RicA2** *Fr.* Shooting Script. **CP-RicAE**

We were chosen, we were chosen. Song for My Assassin. Leonard Cohen. **CP-CoheL**

We were driving the river road. Looking across the River. William Stafford. **SP-StafW**

We were entwined in red rings. Kin. Maya Angelou. **SP-AngeM**

We were hiding / Somewhere in the Alps. Alpine. George Oppen. **CP-OppeG**

We were in bed and. 225 Pounds. Charles Bukowski. **SP-BukC1**

We were in Rome not far from the Piazza di Spagna. The Restoration of the Pictures. Raissa Maritain, *tr. in French by* Thomas Merton. **CP-MertT**

We were interested in ways of being. Kenneth Rexroth. **CP-RexKL; SP-RexrK** *Fr.* A Prolegomenon to a Theodicy.

We were not ever of their feline race. Frightened Men. Robert Ranke Graves. **CP-GravR**

We were on the pier, you desiring. Under Taurus. Louise Glück. **SP-GlücL**

We were set once. When it rained, each man. Starting Back. Richard Hugo. **CP-HugoR**

We were sitting outside. Cascade. John Yau. **SP-YauJo**

We were starving. A Sweaty Day in August. Charles Bukowski. **SP-BukC3**

We were surprised by Mi-Carême's obtruding. Mi-Carême. Daniel Gerard Hoffman. **SP-HoffD**

We were taken from the ore-bed and the mine. The Secret of the Machines. Rudyard Kipling. **CP-KiplR**

We were talking about the space between us. Within You Without You. George Harrison. **CP-Beatl**

We were taught the very same things: respect for the church. The Men (IX). Pablo Neruda, *tr. fr. Spanish by* Ben Belitt. **SP-NeruP** *Fr.* The Separate Rose.

We were the fore-runners of an army. The Journey. Alun Lewis. **CP-LewiA**

We were together since the War began. A Servant. Rudyard Kipling. **PeFWW** *Fr.* Epitaphs of the War [1914–1918]. **CP-KiplR**

We were two lovers; let me lie by her. Bifurcation. Robert Browning. **CP-BroR2**

We were very tired, we were very merry. Recuerdo. Edna St. Vincent Millay. **CP-MillE**

We were walking from one end of the island to the other. She told. Return of Ulysses II. John Yau. **SP-YauJo**

We were walking through the bees. The Calm. Tess Gallagher. **SP-GallT**

We were with you, of course. The Connecticut River in Flood. Brendan Galvin. **SP-GalvB**

We western fellow students salute with Calypso anthems. Western Fellow Students Salute with Calypso Anthems the Movie Career of Robert Lax. Thomas Merton. **CP-MertT**

We which were Ovid's five books now are three. 1.1. Ovid. **CP-MarlC**, *tr. by* Christopher Marlowe; *Fr.* Elegies.

We who are old, old and gay. A Faery Song. William Butler Yeats. **CP-YeatW**

We who confide our dreams. Furnished Rooms. Marsden Hartley. **CP-HartM**

We who have lived too long among your wicked children. Pilgrims' Song. Thomas Merton. **CP-MertT**

We who have seen Italia in the throes. The Centenary of Garibaldi. George Meredith. **CP-MerG2**

We who have so much. Strawman. "Lou Reed." **SP-ReedL**

We who prayed and wept. Wendell Berry. **CP-BerrW** (We Who Prayed and Wept.) **CP-BerrW**

We Who Prayed and Wept. Wendell Berry. *See* We who prayed and wept.

We, who remember the Faith, the grey-headed ones. Anglo-Catholic Congresses. Sir John Betjeman. **CP-BetjJ**

We who survived the war and took to wife. Thirtieth Anniversary Report of the Class of '41. Howard Nemerov. **CP-NemeH**

We will be equal, we say, new man and new woman. Marge Piercy. *Fr.* Doing It Differently. **SP-PierM**

We will have nothing. Tilt. Gilbert Sorrentino. **SP-SorrG**

We will have to go away, said the girls in the circus. The Circus. Kenneth Koch. **SP-KochK**

We will see no more. Requiem. Wendell Berry. **CP-BerrW**

We Will Taste the Islands and the Sea. Charles Bukowski. **SP-BukC1**

We will weep / yet not weep together. Kisses Forgotten. Carl Sandburg. **CP-SandC**

We will write a / simple epic of. June 6, 1970. Robert Creeley. **CP-CreeR**

We wish like the glass. Hafiz, *tr. by* Ralph Waldo Emerson. **CP-EmerR** *Fr.* Odes.

We with our Fair pitched among the feathery clover. The Individualist Speaks. Louis MacNeice. **CP-MacNL**

We wondered what might change. The Survivors. William DeWitt Snodgrass. **SP-SnodW**

We wondered what our walk should mean. Peace Walk. William Stafford. **SP-StafW**

We work here together. The Pine Planters. Thomas Hardy. **CP-HardT**

We would climb the highest dune. With Kit, Age Seven, at the Beach. William Stafford. **SP-StafW**

We would do nought but good. Hafiz, *tr. by* Ralph Waldo Emerson. **CP-EmerR** *Fr.* Odes.

We Would Refer You to Our Service Department, If We Had One. Ogden Nash. **CP-NashO**

We would'nt mind the sun, dear. Emily Dickinson. **SP-DickE**

Weak after long fasting, felt a slow. Comanches. Daniel Gerard Hoffman. **SP-HoffD**

Weak and irresolute is man. Human Frailty. William Cowper. **CP-CowpW**

Weak is the assurance that weak flesh reposeth. By Her That Is Most Assured to Her Self. Edmund Spenser. **EnRePo** *Fr.* Amoretti. **CP-Spens**

Weak is the will of Man, his judgement blind. William Wordsworth. **CP-WorW1**

Weak Mind in the Mountains, A. Wallace Stevens. **CP-StevW**

Weak Monk, The. Stevie Smith. **CP-SmitS**

Weaker and weaker, the sunlight falls. Lebensweisheitspielerei. Wallace Stevens. **CP-StevW**

Weakest Thing, The. Elizabeth Barrett Browning. **CP-BroEB**

Weald is good, the Downs are best, The. The Run of the Downs. Rudyard Kipling. **CP-KiplR**

Wealth. Ralph Waldo Emerson. **CP-EmerR**

Wealth. David Herbert Lawrence. **CP-LawrD**

Wealth and dominion fade into the mass. Fragment: Amor Aeternus. Percy Bysshe Shelley. **CP-ShelP**

Wean Poem. Gary Gildner. **SP-GildG**

Weaned from life and torn away. Emily Brontë. **CP-BronE**

Weaned from moon. Aubade. Daniel Gerard Hoffman. **SP-HoffD**

Weapon, The. "Hugh MacDiarmid." **SP-MacDH**

Weapon shapely, naked, wan. The Broad-Ax. Walt Whitman. **MoAmPo** Fr. Song of the Broad-Axe [or Broad-Ax]. **CP-WhitW**

Weapon shapely, naked, wan. Song of the Broad-Axe [or Broad-Ax]. Walt Whitman. **CP-WhitW**

Weaponed Woman. Gwendolyn Brooks. Fr. A Catch of Shy Fish. **SP-BrooG**

Wear the Gown, and wear the Hat. On Hearing Miss Thrale Deliberate about Her Hat. Samuel Johnson. **CP-JohnS**

Wear the weight of equinoctial evening. September 21. Adrienne Rich. **CP-RicAE**

Wearied of sinning, wearied of repentance. For Thine Own Sake, O My God. Christina Georgina Rossetti. **CP-RosC2**

Wearied Pilgrim, I have wandred here, A. On Himself ("Wearied Pilgrim, I have wandered here, A"). Robert Herrick. **CP-HerrR**

Wearied with saying grace and prayer. Dan Jackson's Reply. Jonathan Swift. **CP-SwifJ**

Wearing away / wears. Pebble's Story. Archie Randolph Ammons. **SP-AmmoA**

Wearing of the Green, The. Donald Davie. **CP-DavDo**

Weary and weak,—accept my weariness. I Will Arise. Christina Georgina Rossetti. **CP-RosC2**

Weary Blues, The. Langston Hughes. **SP-HughL**

Weary fa' you, Duncan Gray. Duncan Gray ["Weary fa' you, Duncan Gray"]. Robert Burns. **CP-BurnR**

Weary in Well-Doing. Christina Georgina Rossetti. **CP-RosC1**

Weary novice thumbed his beads, The. The Novice. John Hewitt. **CP-HewiJ**

Weary of jangling noises never stilled. The Story of Ida. John Greenleaf Whittier. **CP-WhitJ**

Weary of myself, and sick of asking. Self-Dependence. Matthew Arnold. **SP-ArnoM**

Weary psalmist paused, The. Song for Abraham Klein. Leonard Cohen. **CP-CoheL**

Weary Pund o' Tow, The. Robert Burns. **CP-BurnR**

Weary Rory dawdles on the path. The Picture of Little Rory in a Municipal Park. Robert Penn Warren. **SP-WarrR**

Weary traveller who tired sought, The. Sonnet 10. Mary Sidney, Countess of Montgomery Wroth. Fr. Pamphilia to Amphilanthus. **CP-WrotM**

Weary Walker, The. Thomas Hardy. **CP-HardT**

Weary with toil, I haste me to my bed. Sonnet 27. William Shakespeare. **HeIP; NoSic; OBSC; PIP; SCGP** Fr. Sonnets. **CP-ShaWS**

Weary with travel, hungry and afraid. Egyptian Night. John Hewitt. **CP-HewiJ**

Weasel Snout. William Carlos Williams. **CP-WilW1**

Weather. Kay Boyle. **CP-BoylK**

Weathers [or Weather]. Thomas Hardy. **CP-HardT**

Weather in the drawing-room, The. Ceremony and Vision. John Berryman. **CP-BerrJ**

Weather is changing. The mountainous temperate climate, The. Late August. Marilyn Hacker. **SP-HackM**

Weather is like Africa, The. Emily Dickinson. **SP-DickE**

Weather is mild, The. Charles Henri Ford. **SP-FordC** Fr. Emblems of Arachne.

Weather is sharp, The. Music in a Snowy Street. Thomas Hardy. **CP-HardT**

Weather is so very mild, The. A Watched Example Never Boils. Ogden Nash. **CP-NashO**

Weather of flashes, fragments, A. In October. Charles Tomlinson. **CP-TomlC**

Weather of living in an island, The. Emigrant, to the Receding Shore. Donald Davie. **CP-DavDo**

Weather of Olympus, The. Robert Ranke Graves. **CP-GravR**

Weather of Six Mornings, The. Jane Cooper. **SP-CoopJ**
　"All is closed in."
　"If the weather breaks."
　"Rest. / A violin bow, a breeze."
　"Sunlight lies along my table."
　"Treetops are shuddering."
　"Yesterday a letter / spoke of our parting."

Weather of the World, The. Howard Nemerov. **CP-NemeH**

Weather of this winter night, my dream-wife, The. James Merrill. See Childlessness.

Weather of this winter night, my mistress, The. Childlessness. James Merrill. **SP-MerrJ**

Weather releases him from the tyranny of rooms. Weatherman. Charles Tomlinson. **CP-TomlC**

Weather Report. Charles Bukowski. **SP-BukC1**

Weather Report. William Stafford. **SP-StafW**

Weather the frost, stir. Rose-hips. Charles Tomlinson. **CP-TomlC**

Weather wept, and all the trees bent down, The. The Shimmer of Evil. Theodore Roethke. **CP-RoetT**

Weathercock on the Cathedral of Quito, The. Jorge Carrera Andrade, tr. fr. Spanish by Thomas Merton. **CP-MertT**

Weathercocks, The. Charles Tomlinson. **CP-TomlC**

Weathering. Archie Randolph Ammons. **SP-AmmoA**

Weathering. Martin Edmunds. **SP-EdmuM**

Weathering Out. Rita Dove. **SP-DoveR**

Weatherman. Charles Tomlinson. **CP-TomlC**

Weather's at its coldest these, The. Bus Stop. Alice Notley. **SP-NotlA**

Weather's changes are the private rites, The. Walking Down Westgate in the Fall. Howard Nemerov. **CP-NemeH**

Weave a Circle Round Me Thrice. Brendan Galvin. **SP-GalvB**

Weave In, My Hardy Life. Walt Whitman. **CP-WhitW**

Weaver, The. John Haines. **SP-HainJ**

Weazened Irrefutable unastonished. Edward Estlin Cummings. **CP-CummE**

Web, The. Robert Earl Hayden. **CP-HaydR**

Web One Weaves of Italy, The. Marianne Craig Moore. **CP-MoorM**

Webbe. Roy Fisher. **SP-FishR** Fr. Five Pilgrims in the Prologue to the Canterbury Tales.

Webs. Carl Sandburg. **CP-SandC**

Webs of misery spread in the brain. Kenneth Rexroth. **CP-RexKL** Fr. The Phoenix and the Tortoise.

Webs of misery spread in the brain. Kenneth Rexroth. **SP-RexrK** Fr. Webs of misery spread in the brain. **CP-RexKL** Fr. The Phoenix and the Tortoise.

　"Webs of misery spread in the brain." **SP-RexrK**

Webster. Ralph Waldo Emerson. See Why did all manly gifts in Webster fail?

Webster was much possessed by death. Whispers of Immortality. Thomas Stearns Eliot. **CP-ElioT**

We'd found an old Boche dug-out, and he knew. The Sentry. Wilfred Owen. **CP-OwenW**

We'd had any number of joints and some. Trying to Get Even. Charles Bukowski. **SP-BukC1**

We'd loved, we two, some while. The Fight on Durnover Moor. Thomas Hardy. **CP-HardT**

We'd rather have the iceberg than the ship. The Imaginary Iceberg. Elizabeth Bishop. **CP-BishE**

Wedded Love. Samuel Taylor Coleridge. **CP-ColeS**
　("Builder left one narrow rent, The.") **CP-ColeS**

Wedded Love. John Milton. See Their Wedded Love.

Wedding, The. James Dickey. **CP-DickJ**

Wedding, The. Richard Eberhart. **CP-EberR**

Wedding, The. Robert Ranke Graves. **CP-GravR**

Wedding Day. Seamus Heaney. **SP-HeanS**

Wedding-Day, The. Henry Wadsworth Longfellow. Fr. The Courtship of Miles Standish. **SP-LongH**
　"This was the wedding morn of Priscilla the Puritan Maiden." **TreFS**

Wedding-Dress, The. Jim Morrison. **SP-MorrJ**

Wedding Morn. David Herbert Lawrence. **CP-LawrD**

Wedding Morning, The. Thomas Hardy. **CP-HardT**

Wedding Night, The. Anne Sexton. **CP-SextA**

Wedding of Alcmane and Mya, The. George Chapman. **OBSC** Fr. Hero and Leander. **CP-MarlC**

Wedding of the Rose and the Lotus, The. Nicholas Vachel Lindsay. **CP-LindV**

Wedding on Cape Rosier, A. Richard Eberhart. **CP-EberR**

Wedding Party. Donald Hall. **CP-HallD**

Wedding Photograph. Steve Griffiths. **SP-GrifS**

Wedding Photograph, The. Stevie Smith. **CP-SmitS**

Wedding Postponed. Carl Sandburg. **CP-SandC**

Wedding Preparations in the Country. David St. John. **SP-StJoD**

Wedding Present, The. John Hewitt. **CP-HewiJ**

Wedding Presents. Muriel Rukeyser. **CP-RukeM**

Wedding Ring Dance, The. Anne Sexton. **CP-SextA**

Wedding Song. "Bob Dylan." **CP-DylaB**

Wedding Toast, A. Richard Wilbur. **CP-WilbR**

Wedding-Wind. Philip Larkin. **CP-LarkP**

Wedged in by earthworks. Merely to Know. Adrienne Rich. **CP-RicAE; SP-RicA2**

Wedlock. David Herbert Lawrence. **CP-LawrD**

Wedlock, The. Anne Sexton. **CP-SextA**

Wednesday. Philip Levine. **SP-LeviP**

Wednesday in Holy Week. Christina Georgina Rossetti. **CP-RosC2**

Wednesday Matinee. Ogden Nash. **CP-NashO**

Wednesday morning at five o'clock as the day begins. She's Leaving Home. The Beatles. **CP-Beatl**

Wednesday nights. Original Sin. Miller Williams. **SP-WillM**

Wee, modest, crimson-tipped flow'r. To a Mountain Daisy [On Turning One Down, with the Plough, in April—1786]. Robert Burns. **CP-BurnR**

Wee people / dwelling / between serene. Edward Estlin Cummings. **CP-CummE**

Wee, sleeket [or sleekit], cow'rin' [or cowran], tim'rous beastie. To a Mouse [On Turning Her Up in Her Nest, with the Plough, November, 1785]. Robert Burns. **CP-BurnR**

Wee wee husband, / Give me some money. Christina Georgina Rossetti. **CP-RosC2**

Wee Willie Gray. Robert Burns. **CP-BurnR**

Weed, The. Elizabeth Bishop. **CP-BishE**

Weed from Catholic Europe, it took root, A. Macao. Wystan Hugh Auden. **MeMAP** *Fr.* A Voyage. **CP-AudeW**

Weed Garden, The. Lewis Turco. **SP-TurcL**

Weed, moss-weed. Sea Iris. Hilda Doolittle. **CP-DoolH**

Weed Puller. Theodore Roethke. **CP-RoetT**

Weeding the garden, Clayfeld sprained his finger. Clayfeld Renews His Vow to Evelyn. Robert Pack. **SP-PackR**

Weeds. James Dickey. **CP-DickJ**

Weeds. Edna St. Vincent Millay. **CP-MillE**

Weeds. Carl Sandburg. **CP-SandC**

Weeds. Louis Zukofsky. **CP-ZukLS**

Week, A. Thomas Hardy. **CP-HardT**

Week is dealt out like a hand, The. Hope. Randall Jarrell. **CP-JarrR**

Week That Was, The. John Ciardi. **SP-CiarJ**

Week the nuclear protesters stormed the gates, The. Birth Report. Stephen Dobyns. **SP-DobyS**

Week to Christmas, A. Louis MacNeice. **TIRV** *Fr.* Nelson stands on a black pillar. *Fr.* Autumn Journal. **CP-MacNL**

Weekend Away. John Clellon Holmes. **SP-HolmJ**

Weekend Bathers. Kenneth Patchen. **CP-PatcK**

Weekend Glory. Maya Angelou. **SP-AngeM**

Weekly I am murdering. Suicide. Al Young. **CP-YounA**

Weeknight Service. David Herbert Lawrence. **CP-LawrD**

Weeks go by. I shelve them, The. Firstborn. Louise Glück. **SP-GlücL**

Weeks hitting the road, one fasting in the bathtub. Returning Turtle. Robert Lowell. **SP-LoweR**

Weeks of blizzard over, The. Wystan Hugh Auden. **CP-AudWJ**

Weeks of wild delirium past. Rosina. Emily Brontë. **CP-BronE**

Weep, and weep long, but do not weep for me. To a Troubled Friend. James Wright. **CP-WrigJ**

Weep balm and myrrh, you sweet Arabian trees. Stanzas from Saint Peter's Complaint. Robert Southwell. **ACP** *Fr.* Saint Peter's Complaint. **CP-SoutR**

Weep, daughter of a royal line. Lines to a Lady Weeping. Byron. **CP-Byron**

Weep him dead and mourn as you may. Keen. Edna St. Vincent Millay. **CP-MillE**

Weep no more but pity me. Postscript. Wystan Hugh Auden. *Fr.* The Sea and the Mirror. **CP-AudeW**

Weep no more, thou weary one. The Irrevocable. Walter de la Mare. **CP-DeLaW**

Weep no more, woful shepherds weep no more. John Milton. **FaBoRV** *Fr.* Lycidas. **CP-MiltJ**

Weep not, belovèd Friends! nor let the air. Gabriello Chiabrera, *tr. fr. Italian* by William Wordsworth. **CP-WorW1**

Weep not, my dear, for I shall go. Parting, Celia Weeps. Thomas Carew. **CP-CareT**

Weep not, nor backward turn your beams. A Lover, upon an Accident Necessitating His Departure, Consults with Reason. Thomas Carew. **CP-CareT**

Weep not sweet child, for now thy tears. To a Child in Tears. Wystan Hugh Auden. **CP-AudWJ**

Weep not, you who love her. Threnody for a Brown Girl. Countee Cullen. **CP-CullC**

Weep, weep, little day. Original Sin. Thomas Merton. *Fr.* Cables to the Ace. **CP-MertT**

Weep [or Weepe] with me, all you that read. Epitaph on S.P. [Salomon or Salathiel Pavy], a Child of Q[ueen] El[izabeth's] Chapel. Ben Jonson. **CP-JonsB**

Weep yet a while / Weep till that day shall dawn when thou shalt smile. The Heart Knoweth Its Own Bitterness. Christina Georgina Rossetti. **CP-RosC3**

Weepe for the dead, for they have lost this light. On Himselfe . Robert Herrick. **CP-HerrR**

Weepe, living thinges, of life the mother dyes. The Death of our Ladie. Robert Southwell. **CP-SoutR**

Weeper, The. Richard Crashaw. **CP-CrasR**

Weeper in Jalisco. Charles Tomlinson. **CP-TomlC**

Weepies, The. Paul Muldoon. **SP-MuldP**

Weeping, *in imitation of* Cowley. Alexander Pope. **CP-PopeA**

Weeping Burgher, The. Wallace Stevens. **CP-StevW**

Weeping Cherry, The. Robert Herrick. **CP-HerrR**

Weeping oaks grieve, chestnuts raise. Basil Bunting. **CP-BuntB**

Weeping Pleiads wester, The. Alfred Edward Housman. **CP-HousA**

Weeping Saviour, The. Elizabeth Barrett Browning. **CP-BroEB**

Weeping, standing still—then going out again into the garden. Last Letter. Louise Glück. *Fr.* Marathon. **SP-GlücL**

Wehlener Sonnenuhr Auslese 1959. William Matthews. **SP-MattW**

Weigh all my faults and follies righteously. Christina Georgina Rossetti. **CP-RosC2**

Weigh me the fire; or canst thou find. To Find[e] God. Robert Herrick. **CP-HerrR**

Weight. Archie Randolph Ammons. **SP-AmmoA**

Weight him down, O side-stars, with the great weightings of the end. Madame La Fleurie. Wallace Stevens. **CP-StevW**

Weight of awe, not easy to be borne, A. The Monument Commonly Called Long Meg and Her Daughters, near the River Eden. William Wordsworth. *Fr.* Poems Composed or Suggested During a Tour, in the Summer of 1833. **CP-WorW2**

Weight of the world, The. Song. Allen Ginsberg. **CP-GinsA**

Weight with Needles on the pounds, A. Emily Dickinson. **CP-DickE**

Weights, the secret. The Mathematical Secret, and the Apron. Charles Olson. **CP-OlsoC**

Weird bait-headed mongrels. Curses & Invocations. Jim Morrison. **SP-MorrJ**

Weland's Sword. Rudyard Kipling. *Fr.* Puck of Pook's Hill. Tree Song, A. **CP-KiplR**

Welcome. Stephen Dunn. **SP-DunnS**

Welcome. Thomas Merton. **CP-MertT**

Welcome Address. Paul Laurence Dunbar. **CP-DunbP**

Welcome all that [or who] lead or follow. Over the Door at the Entrance into the Apollo. Ben Jonson. **CP-JonsB**

Welcome Back, Mr. Knight: Love of My Life. Etheridge Knight. **SP-KnigE**

Welcome, Brazilian brother—thy ample place is ready. A Christmas Greeting. Walt Whitman. **CP-WhitW**

We[e]lcome! but yet no entrance, till we bless[e]. The Entertainment, or Porch-Verse, at the Marriage of Mr. Henry Northleigh [or Hen. Northly] and the Most Witty Mrs. Lettice Yard. Robert Herrick. **CP-HerrR**

Welcome Cross. William Cowper. *Fr.* Olney Hymns. **CP-CowpW**

Welcome dear feast of Lent: who loves not thee. Lent. George Herbert. **CP-HerbG**

Welcome Death. David Herbert Lawrence. **CP-LawrD**

Welcome, deep WILEY! from the sylvan dells. Prologue to Wiley on November 17, 1941. Randall Jarrell. **CP-JarrR**

Welcome, eccentric life, / Attracted to my star. By Lamplight. Stanley Jasspon Kunitz. **CP-KuniS**

Welcome! Enter! This is the Inn at the Cross Roads. Hospital. Walter de la Mare. **CP-DeLaW**

Welcome from War. Muriel Rukeyser. **CP-RukeM**

Welcome, Great Cesar, welcome now you are. To the King, upon His Welcome to Hampton-Court. Robert Herrick. **CP-HerrR**

Welcome Home. Thomas Hardy. **CP-HardT**

Welcome home again, brave seaman! with thy thoughtful brow and gray. The Branded Hand. John Greenleaf Whittier. **CP-WhitJ**

Welcome Home Oh Gladsome Springhorned Beloved and Famed Harteebeeste. Malcolm Lowry. **CP-LowrM**

Welcome Home Oh Harteebeeste. Malcolm Lowry. **CP-LowrM**

Welcome Home oh Harteebeeste beloved who doth with thy. Malcolm Lowry. **CP-LowrM**

Welcome Home oh Harteebeeste mio. Malcolm Lowry. **CP-LowrM**

Welcome Home—Oh Most Beloved Harteebeeste. Malcolm Lowry. **CP-LowrM**

Welcome Home Oh Most Loved and Famed Harteebeeste. Malcolm Lowry. **CP-LowrM**

Welcome Home Oh Our Beloved Harteebeeste. Malcolm Lowry. **CP-LowrM**

Welcome Home Oh Our Most Beloved Harteebeeste. Malcolm Lowry. **CP-LowrM**

Welcome Home, Oh Our Sweetest Harteebeeste Beloved. Malcolm Lowry. **CP-LowrM**

Welcome Home, Oh Sweetest Harteebeeste. Malcolm Lowry. **CP-LowrM**

Welcome Home Oh Sweetest Harteebeeste with Quadruple Devotion from All the Little Animals. Malcolm Lowry. **CP-LowrM**

Welcome Home Our Own. Malcolm Lowry. **CP-LowrM**

WELCOME HOME YE LADS OF THE EIGHTH ARMY. Trial Runs. Seamus Heaney. **SP-HeanS**

Welcome is the word. The Lords Welcome, sung before the Kings Good-night. Thomas Campion. *Fr.* The Ayres that Were Sung and Played, at *Brougham Castle* in *Westmerland,* in the Kings Entertainment. **CP-CampT**

Welcome Joy, and Welcome Sorrow. John Keats. **CP-KeatJ**

Welcome, maids of honor. To Violets. Robert Herrick. **CP-HerrR**

Welcome me, if you will. For James Dean. Frank O'Hara. **SP-OharF**

Welcome Morning. Anne Sexton. **CP-SextA**

Welcome, most welcome to our Vow[e]s and us. To the King, upon His Com[m]ing with His Army into the West. Robert Herrick. **CP-HerrR**

Welcome my Griefe, my Joy; how deare's. John 16; Verily I Say unto You, Yee Shall Weep and Lament. Bible, *N.T.* **CP-CrasR,** *tr.* by Richard Crashaw; *Fr.* St. John.

Welcome Queen Alice. "Lewis Carroll." *See* To the Looking-Glass world it was Alice that said.

Welcome stranger to this place. Song 1st By a Shepherd. William Blake. **CP-BlakW**

Welcome, Summer. Geoffrey Chaucer. *See* Now Welcom[e], Somer [*or* Summer].

Welcome sweet and sacred cheer. The Banquet. George Herbert. **CP-HerbG**

Welcome the Wrath. Stanley Jasspon Kunitz. **CP-KuniS**

Welcome, thrice welcome to thy native Place! Mary Gulliver to Capt. Lemuel Gulliver. John Gay *and* Alexander Pope. **CP-PopeA**

Welcome to Lowell, A. John Greenleaf Whittier. **CP-WhitJ**

Welcome to Quetzalcoatl. David Herbert Lawrence. **CP-LawrD**

Welcome to Sack, The. Robert Herrick. **CP-HerrR**

Welcome to the American Night. Jim Morrison. **SP-MorrJ**

Welcome to the Table. William Cowper. *Fr.* Olney Hymns. **CP-CowpW**

Welcome to These Lines. Leonard Cohen. **CP-CoheL**

Welcome to this book of slaves. Aquarian Age. Leonard Cohen. **CP-CoheL**

Welcome to this flowrie place. Thomas Campion. *Fr.* A Relation of the Late Royall Entertainment Given by the Right Honourable the Lord Knowles, at *Cawsome*-House neere *Redding:* to Our Most *Gracious Queene, Queene* ANNE, *in her* Progresse toward the *Bathe,* upon *the Seven and Eight and Twentie Dayes of Aprill.* **CP-CampT**

Welcome to this my college [*or* colledge], and though late. To His Kinsman, Master Thomas Herrick, Who Desired to Be in His Book. Robert Herrick. **CP-HerrR**

Welcome, welcome, King of guests. The Kings Good-night. Thomas Campion. *Fr.* The Ayres that Were Sung and Played, at *Brougham Castle* in *Westmerland,* in the Kings Entertainment. **CP-CampT**

Welcome, welcome, little star! White Dwarf. John Updike. **CP-UpdiJ**

Welcome, welcome, mortal wight. Sir John Suckling. *Fr.* The Goblins. **CP-SuckJ**

Welcome What Comes. Robert Herrick. **CP-HerrR**

Well, The. John Gould Fletcher. **SP-FletJ** *Fr.* The Ghosts of an Old House.

Well. / He was a poet. Well. Alice Walker. **CP-WalkA**

Well, / it is better. Ode on Necrophilia. Frank O'Hara. **SP-OharF**

Well / it's interesting what does go on. A Minor Impulse to Complain. Charles Bukowski. **SP-BukC2**

Well, The. Denise Levertov. **CP-LeveD**

Well, / now some eat to forget and some drink to forget and some. Now. Charles Bukowski. **SP-BukC3**

Well. Charles Olson. **CP-OlsoC**

Well, The. Adrienne Rich. **CP-RicAE**

Well, The. Charles Tomlinson. **CP-TomlC**

Well. Alice Walker. **CP-WalkA**

Well and wisely said the Greek. Pericles. Ralph Waldo Emerson. *Fr.* Quatrains. **CP-EmerR**

Well anyway even tho. Some Spice for Jack Spicer. Al Young. **CP-YounA**

Well, are you the lover or the loved? Are You the Lover or Loved? Al Young. **CP-YounA**

Well, as Kavanagh said, we have lived. Singing School. Seamus Heaney. **SP-HeanS**

We'll be confined and free. Roads end fast. A Map of Skye. Richard Hugo. **CP-HugoR**

Well, beat on, beat on. Hayden Carruth. **CP-CarHS** *Fr.* The Clay Hill Anthology.

Well-Beloved, The. Thomas Hardy. **CP-HardT**

Well, Bokardo, here we are. Bokardo. Edwin Arlington Robinson. **CP-RobiE**

Well, but the saw-edged maple-leaf can suffer. Osip Emilevich Mandelstam. *Fr.* Octets. **CP-DavDo**

Well, death's been here. Live. Anne Sexton. **CP-SextA**

Well Dennis O'Grady. Thom Gunn. **CP-GunnT**

We'll die / soon enough. Robert Creeley. **CP-CreeR**

Well died the world, that we might live to see. To the Praise of the Dead, and the Anatomy. John Donne. *Fr.* Anatomy [*or* Anatomie] of the World, An[: The First Anniversary]. **CP-DonnJ**

Well Disciplined Bargeman, The. William Carlos Williams. **CP-WilW2**

Well Dressed Man with a Beard, The. Wallace Stevens. **CP-StevW**

Well, early in the mornin'. Pledging My Time. "Bob Dylan." **CP-DylaB**

Well, everyone wants to know, of course, that's. Septic Tanck. Hayden Carruth. **CP-CarHS**

Well-Found Poem. Donald Davie. **CP-DavDo**

Well, Frankie Lee and Judas Priest. The Ballad of Frankie Lee and Judas Priest. "Bob Dylan." **CP-DylaB**

Well God is / love. Calypsos. William Carlos Williams. **CP-WilW2**

Well hast thou spoken—and yet not taught. My Comforter. Emily Brontë. **CP-BronE**

We'll have beds full of delicate scents. The Death of Lovers. James Liddy. **CP-LiddJ**

We'll have the sun now. Confidence. Marsden Hartley. **CP-HartM**

Well have yon Railway Labourers to THIS ground. At Furness Abbey. William Wordsworth. **CP-WorW2**

Well, he was drunk. That much was clear. Archibald MacLeish. **CP-MacLA** *Fr.* The Happy Marriage.

Well-Head, The. Robert Louis Stevenson. **CP-StevR**

Well, heart's muse, lover, mistress of palaces. Mercenary Muse. David St. John. **SP-StJoD**

Well here again that don't apply. Thomas Stearns Eliot. **FaBoVe** *Fr.* Sweeney Agonistes. **CP-ElioT**

Well, here I am thirty-eight. Not George Washington's, Not Abraham Lincoln's, but Mine. Ogden Nash. **CP-NashO**

We'll Hide the Couper behint the Door. Robert Burns. **CP-BurnR**

Well House, The. Robert Penn Warren. **SP-WarrR**

Well Hung. "Hugh MacDiarmid." **SP-MacDH**

Well, I ain't a-gonna grieve no more, no more. Ain't Gonna Grieve. "Bob Dylan." **CP-DylaB**

Well, I ain't got my childhood. Guess I'm Doin' Fine. "Bob Dylan." **CP-DylaB**

Well I can see you now. Bob Visits Friends. Grace Paley. **CP-PaleG**

Well, I had to move fast. Tight Connection to My Heart (Has Anybody Seen My Love). "Bob Dylan." **CP-DylaB**

Well I have and in fact. On Being Asked to Write a Poem Against the War in Vietnam. Hayden Carruth. **CP-CarHS**

Well, I have given. Nomads. Dabney Stuart. **SP-StuaD**

"Well, I have had a happy life," said Hazlitt. The Boyg, Peer Gynt, the One Only One. Randall Jarrell. **CP-JarrR**

Well, I have lost you; and I lost you fairly. Edna St. Vincent Millay. **CP-MillE**

Well, I just got into town about an hour ago. L.A. Woman. Jim Morrison. **SP-MorrJ**

Well, I may now receive, and die: my sin. Satire 4. John Donne. **OBSV** *Fr.* Satires. **CP-DonnJ**

Well I remember the pigeons in the sunny arbour. The Pigeons. Edna St. Vincent Millay. **CP-MillE**

Well, I ride on a mailtrain, baby. It Takes a Lot to Laugh, It Takes a Train to Cry. "Bob Dylan." **CP-DylaB**

Well, I see you got your brand new leopard-skin pill-box hat. Leopard-Skin Pill-Box Hat. "Bob Dylan." **CP-DylaB**

Well, I still have a train ticket valid. The Poor Washed Up by Chicago Winter. James Wright. **CP-WrigJ**

Well, I thought that the rain would cool things down. Seeing the Real You at Last. "Bob Dylan." **CP-DylaB**

Well, I took me a woman late last night. I Shall Be Free. "Bob Dylan." **CP-DylaB**

Well, I was feelin' sad and feelin' blue. Talkin' John Birch Paranoid Blues. "Bob Dylan." **CP-DylaB**

Well, I woke up in the morning. On the Road Again. "Bob Dylan." **CP-DylaB**

Well I'd rather see you dead, little girl than to be with another man. Run for Your Life. The Beatles. **CP-Beatl**

Well, if a King's a lion, at the least. Alexander Pope. **ECEV; OBSV** *Fr.* The First Epistle of the First Book of Horace Imitated. **CP-PopeA** (Profiteers.) **ECEV**

Well; if ever I saw such another man since my mother bound my head. Mary the Cook-Maid's Letter to Dr. Sheridan. Jonathan Swift. **CP-SwifJ**

Well if he treats me like a young girl still. Ms. Lot. Muriel Rukeyser. **CP-RukeM**

Well, if I had to do it all over again. All Over You. "Bob Dylan." **CP-DylaB**

Well, if it be my time to quit the stage. Satire IV of Dr. John Donne, Versified. Alexander Pope. **CP-PopeA**

Well! If the Bard was weather-wise, who made. Dejection; an Ode. Samuel Taylor Coleridge. **CP-ColeS**

Well! if the Bard was weatherwise, who made. Letter to Sara Hutchinson. Samuel Taylor Coleridge. **CP-ColeS**

Well, if you wilt, then, ask me. A Philosophical Fantasy. Thomas Hardy. **CP-HardT**

Well, if you're travelin' in the north country fair. Girl of the North Country. "Bob Dylan." **CP-DylaB**

Well, I'm hangin' on to a solid rock. Solid Rock. "Bob Dylan." **CP-DylaB**

Well, I'm pressing on. Pressing On. "Bob Dylan." **CP-DylaB**

Well, I'm standin' on the highway. Standing on the Highway. "Bob Dylan." **CP-DylaB**

Well, I'm walkin' down the highway. Down the Highway. "Bob Dylan." **CP-DylaB**

Well, I'm walkin' down the line. Walkin' Down the Line. "Bob Dylan." **CP-DylaB**

Well in Africa, The. David Herbert Lawrence. *Fr.* Bits. **CP-LawrD**

Well in the Desert, The. John Gould Fletcher. *Fr.* Arizona Poems. **SP-FletJ**

Well-Intentioned Consul, The. John Hewitt. **CP-HewiJ**

Well is not used now, The. The Well. John Gould Fletcher. **SP-FletJ** *Fr.* The Ghosts of an Old House.

Well, it's all up from Florida at the start of the spring. Dusty Old Fairgrounds. "Bob Dylan." **CP-DylaB**

Well, it's still the loveliest meadow in all Vermont. My Meadow. Hayden Carruth. **CP-CarHS**

Well, I've already had two beers. Please, Mrs. Henry. "Bob Dylan." **CP-DylaB**

Well, I've said that Robert Frost had curiosity. Hayden Carruth. *Fr.* Vermont. **CP-CarHL**

Well, Jim says that the couplet at the end. Sonnet. Hayden Carruth. **CP-CarHS** *Fr.* Sonnets.

Well, life has been a baffled vehicle. Weaponed Woman. Gwendolyn Brooks. *Fr.* A Catch of Shy Fish. **SP-BrooG**

Well, Lizzie Anderson! seventeen men—and. To a Friend. William Carlos Williams. **CP-WilW1**

Well may I weene, faire ladies, all this while. Edmund Spenser. **OAEL-1** *Fr.* The Faerie Queene. **CP-Spens**

Well may my Book come forth like Publique Day. To the Most Illustrious and Most Hopefull Prince, Charles, Prince of Wales. Robert Herrick. **CP-HerrR**

Well may the continental eagles scream. To Lord Palmerston. George Meredith. **CP-MerG2**

Well mayst thou halt—and gaze with brightening eye! Admonition. William Wordsworth. **CP-WorW1**

Well meaning readers! you that come as friends [*or* freinds]. The Flaming Heart. Richard Crashaw. **CP-CrasR**

We'll meet in Madrid. Once We Meant It. Thomas McGrath. **SP-McGrT**

Well, mind, here we have. Promenade. William Carlos Williams. **CP-WilW1**

Well, my friend, you prefer jurisprudence to contemplation! Letter to a Sufi Who Has Abandoned Sufism to Study Law. Thomas Merton. *Fr.* Readings from Ibn Abbad. **CP-MertT**

Well, my shoes, they come from Singapore. Union Sundown. "Bob Dylan." **CP-DylaB**

Well, narrower draw the circle round. Douglas's Ride. Emily Brontë. **CP-BronE**

Well-nigh the voyage now is overpast. Michelangelo Buonarroti, *tr. fr. Italian by* William Wordsworth. **CP-WorW1**

We'll not begin again to love. Song to Aurore. Thomas Hardy. **CP-HardT**

Well, now he's decided to be happy. Prince Rupert's Drop. Gilbert Sorrentino. **SP-SorrG**

Well, nuncle, this plainly won't do. Floral Decorations for Bananas. Wallace Stevens. **CP-StevW**

Well of Loch Maree, The. John Greenleaf Whittier. **CP-WhitJ**

Well of Lycopolis, The. Basil Bunting. **CP-BuntB**
  "Infamous poetry, abject love."
  "May my libation of flat beer stood overnight."
  "Slinking by the jug-and-bottle."
  "Stuck in the mud they are saying: 'We were sad'."

Well, Old Flame, the fire's out. Static. Barton Sutter. **SP-SuttB**

Well-Ordered Life, The. Miller Williams. **SP-WillM**

We'll pass without the parting. Emily Dickinson. **CP-DickE**

Well past first blush and rife with thigh. Anne-on-Avon. David Markson. **CP-MarkD**

Well *Peter* dost thou wield thy active sword. On Saint Peter Cutting of Malchus His Eare. Richard Crashaw. **CP-CrasR**

Well Rising, The. William Stafford. **SP-StafW**

Well sang the Bard who called the grave, in strains. The Earl of Breadalbane's Ruined Mansion, and Family Burial-Place, near Killin. William Wordsworth. **CP-WorW2**

We'll see what we'll see. Carl Sandburg. *Fr.* The People, Yes. **CP-SandC**

Well, shadow'd landskip, fare ye well. Sir John Suckling. *See* Farewell to Love.

Well, she told me I had an aura. "What?" I said. Sonnet. Hayden Carruth. **CP-CarHS**

Well she walked out of my life. Her young breasts. Marjorie. Gilbert Sorrentino. **SP-SorrG**

Well she was just seventeen. I Saw Her Standing There. The Beatles. **CP-Beatl**

Well, so that is that. Now we must dismantle the tree. Wystan Hugh Auden. **LiTA; MeMAP; MoAB; MoBrPo; OAEL-2; OBCP** *Fr.* The Flight into Egypt. **CP-AudeW** *Fr.* For the Time Being; a Christmas Oratorio. **CP-AudeW**
  (After Christmas.) **MoAB; MoBrPo**
  (Narrator.) **MeMAP**

Well, so youve gone & overdone it again. Herrick Hospital, Fifth Floor. Al Young. **CP-YounA**

Well, some may hate, and some may scorn. Stanzas to———. Emily Brontë. **CP-BronE**

Well, son, I'll tell you. Mother to Son. Langston Hughes. **SP-HughL**

Well speed they mission, bold Iconoclast! The Men of Old. John Greenleaf Whittier. **CP-WhitJ**

We'll stay until ice begins. Styro. Jim Carroll. **SP-CarrJ**

Well-tam'd Heart, A. Specifications for a Perfect Lover. Richard Crashaw. **CBCK** *Fr.* Wishes. To His (Supposed) Mistresse. **CP-CrasR**

Well, that big dumb blonde. Million Dollar Bash. "Bob Dylan." **CP-DylaB**

Well, that old big fat man. Mona Van Duyn. **SP-VanDM**

Well, that was Saturday, day before Easter. Mona Van Duyn. **SP-VanDM**

Well, the brilliance is gone. Paraphrase from Notebooks. Howard Nemerov. **CP-NemeH**

Well, the clock says it's time to close—now. Soul Kitchen. Jim Morrison. **SP-MorrJ**

Well, the comic book and me, just us, we caught the bus. Yea! Heavy and a Bottle of Bread. "Bob Dylan." **CP-DylaB**

Well, the grass is a pleasant thing. Latesummer Blues. Kenneth Patchen. **CP-PatcK**

Well, the las' time I saw my mother. Con/tin/u/way/shun Blues. Etheridge Knight. **SP-KnigE**

Well, the Lone Ranger and Tonto. Bob Dylan's Blues. "Bob Dylan." **CP-DylaB**

Well, the neighborhood bully, he's just one man. Neighborhood Bully. "Bob Dylan." **CP-DylaB**

Well, the pressure's down, the boss ain't here. Sweetheart Like You. "Bob Dylan." **CP-DylaB**

Well, the rainman comes with his magic wand. I Wanna Be Your Lover. "Bob Dylan." **CP-DylaB**

Well, the redwin's a public charge! Over. Malcolm Lowry. *Fr.* The Canadian Turned Back at the Border. **CP-LowrM**

Well then, a man has got to stop somewhere. Tale. Howard Nemerov. **CP-NemeH**

Well then, poor G——— lies under ground! Epitaph. Alexander Pope. **CP-PopeA**

Well then, the promised [or promis'd] hour is come at last. To My Dear Friend Mr Congreve [on His Comedy Called "The Double-Dealer"]. John Dryden. **SP-DrydJ**

Well, there you have your seasons, prodigy! Derek Walcott. **PBCV** *Fr.* Another Life. **CP-WalcD**

Well, they are gone, and here must I remain. This Lime-Tree Bower My Prison. Samuel Taylor Coleridge. **CP-ColeS**

Well, they loaded him with armor and left him. Childe Horvald to the Dark Tower Came. John Ciardi. **SP-CiarJ**

Well, they rocked him with road-apples. Not a Movie. Langston Hughes. **SP-HughL**

Well, they'll stone ya when you're trying to be so good. Rainy Day Women # 12 & 35. "Bob Dylan." **CP-DylaB**

Well, things / be / pretty bad now, Mother. Report to the Mother. Etheridge Knight. **SP-KnigE**

Well! Thou Art Happy. Byron. **CP-Byron**

Well, though it seems. Liddell and Scott. Thomas Hardy. **CP-HardT**

Well thought! who would not rather hear. To James T. Fields. John Greenleaf Whittier. **CP-WhitJ**

Well, 'tis as Bickerstaff had guessed. Elegy On the Supposed Death of Mr. Partridge, the Almanac Maker. Jonathan Swift. **CP-SwifJ**

Well-to-Do Invalid, A. Randall Jarrell. **CP-JarrR**

Well, to the matter then, there's grown of late. Old England. Anne Bradstreet. **KTR** *Fr.* A Dialogue between Old England and New. **CP-BradA**

We'll to the woods no more. Alfred Edward Housman. **CP-HousA**

We'll to the Woods No More, the Laurels Are Cut Down. May Sarton. **SP-SartM**

Well upon the Brook, The. Emily Dickinson. **CP-DickE**

We'll walk the woods no more. Robert Louis Stevenson. *Fr.* Rondels. **CP-StevR**

Well was dry beside the door, The. Going for Water. Robert Frost. **CP-FrosR**

Well Water. Randall Jarrell. **CP-JarrR; SP-JarrR**

Well, we felt / we were almost getting somewhere. Margaret Atwood. *Fr.* Two-Headed Poems. **SP-AtwM2**

Well, well,—Heaven bless you all from day to day! Arthur Hugh Clough. *Fr.* Blank Misgivings of a Creature Moving About in Worlds Not Realized. **SP-ClouA**

Well, well, little poet! For a Critic Who Tries to Write Poems. Thomas McGrath. **SP-McGrT**

Well, well, well, so this is summer, isn't that *mirabile dictu*. September Is Summer, Too. Ogden Nash. **CP-NashO**

Well, what shall I do today? On Waking to the Third Rainy Morning of a Long Week End. Ogden Nash. **CP-NashO**

Well, World, you have kept faith with me. He Never Expected Much. Thomas Hardy. **CP-HardT**

Well worthy to be magnified are they. Aspects of Christianity in America— the Pilgrim Fathers. William Wordsworth. **AiP; PAH** *Fr.* Ecclesiastical Sonnets. **CP-WorW2**

Well, ya better mail one to M.S. or she'll prob. What to Do with Contributor's Copies? Charles Bukowski. **SP-BukC2**

Well you can tell ev'rybody. Tiny Montgomery. "Bob Dylan." **CP-DylaB**

Well, you shall have that song which Leonard wrote. The Golden Year. Tennyson. **CP-TennA**

Well, you should see Polythene Pam. Polythene Pam. The Beatles. **CP-Beatl**

Well, your clock is gonna stop. I'd Hate to Be You on That Dreadful Day. "Bob Dylan." **CP-DylaB**

Well, your railroad gate, you know I just can't jump it. Absolutely Sweet Marie. "Bob Dylan." **CP-DylaB**

Well, Zimmer, old reeking cricket. Zimmer Warns Himself with Vivid Images Against Old Age. Paul Zimmer. **SP-ZimmP**

Well/Well/Not-At-All. Hart Crane. **CP-CranH**

Wellfleet: The House. Richard Wilbur. **CP-WilbR**

Well)here's looking at ourselves. Edward Estlin Cummings. **CP-CummE**

Wells. Donald Hall. **CP-HallD**

Wells of shadow by the stream. Roy Fisher. *Fr.* Five Morning Poems from a Picture by Manet. **SP-FishR**

Wellsian Futures. David Herbert Lawrence. **CP-LawrD**

Welsh Incident. Robert Ranke Graves. **CP-GravR**

Welsh Marches, The. Alfred Edward Housman. **CP-HousA**

Welsh Night, A. Alun Lewis. **CP-LewiA**

Weltschmertz. Paul Laurence Dunbar. **CP-DunbP**

Wembley Lad, A. Sir John Betjeman. **CP-BetjJ**

W'en daih's chillun in de house. The Old Front Gate. Paul Laurence Dunbar. **CP-DunbP**

W'en de clouds is hangin' heavy in de sky. My Sweet Brown Gal. Paul Laurence Dunbar. **CP-DunbP**

W'en de colo'ed ban'. comes ma'chin' down de street. The Colored Band. Paul Laurence Dunbar. **CP-DunbP**

W'en de evenin' shadders. The Boogah Man. Paul Laurence Dunbar. **CP-DunbP**

W'en de snow's a-fallin'. A Grievance. Paul Laurence Dunbar. **CP-DunbP**

W'en I git up in de mo'nin' an' de clouds is big an' black. Fishing. Paul Laurence Dunbar. **CP-DunbP**

W'en I Gits Home. Paul Laurence Dunbar. **CP-DunbP**

W'en us fellers stomp around, makin' lots o' noise. When a Feller's Itchin' to be Spanked. Paul Laurence Dunbar. **CP-DunbP**

W'en you full o' worry. Advice. Paul Laurence Dunbar. **CP-DunbP**

Wendigo, The. Ogden Nash. **CP-NashO**

Wendy out her black eyes on me. Sweeping Wendy: Study in Fugue. Carl Sandburg. **CP-SandC**

Went to See the Gypsy. "Bob Dylan." **CP-DylaB**

Went up a year this evening! Emily Dickinson. **CP-DickE**

Went up the steep stone hill, thinking. Squaw Lilies: Some Notes. Margaret Atwood. **SP-AtwM2**

Went weeping, little bones. But where? I Cry, Love! Love! Theodore Roethke. **CP-RoetT**

Went with us to the beach. A Blue Towel. James Schuyler. **CP-SchuJ**

Went you to conquer? and have so much lost. H. W. in Hibernia Belligeranti. John Donne. **CP-DonnJ**

Wept to say it. George C. Tilyou Smiles. Gilbert Sorrentino. **SP-SorrG**

Wepyng and waylyng, care and oother sorwe. The Merchant's Prologue. Geoffrey Chaucer. *Fr.* The Canterbury Tales. **CP-ChauG**

We're all Americans, except the Doc. A Mad Negro Soldier Confined at Munich. Robert Lowell. **SP-LoweR**

We're both in Greenville, but a state apart. Letter from Goose Creek: April. Marilyn Hacker. **SP-HackM**

Were *Death* an *evil*, would *I* let thee *live?*. Thoughts for a Speech of Lucifer, in the Tragedy of "Cain." Byron. **CP-Byron**

Were disappearing left and right, so the police. Old People. Ron Koertge. **SP-KoerR**

Were ever eyes of such devinitie. Mary Sidney, Countess of Montgomery Wroth. *Fr.* Part 2. *Fr.* Urania. **CP-WrotM**

We're foot—slog—slog—slog—sloggin' over Africa. Boots. Rudyard Kipling. **CP-KiplR**

Were half the power that fills the world with terror. A Message of Peace. Henry Wadsworth Longfellow. **WBLP** *Fr.* The Arsenal at Springfield. **SP-LongH**

Were I in Trouble. Robert Frost. **OxBSP** *Fr.* Five Nocturnes. **CP-FrosR**

Were I myself more blithe. Song. Robert Creeley. **CP-CreeR**

Were I to cut my hand. The Dangerous Gift. Robert Ranke Graves. **CP-GravR**

Were I to give thee *Baptime*, I wo'd chuse. To His Muse. Robert Herrick. **CP-HerrR**

Were I to take an iron gun. Facts. "Lewis Carroll." **CP-CarrL**

Were I with you or you with me. Arthur Hugh Clough. **SP-ClouA**

We're in the Great Place, Fable Place, Beulah, Man wedded to Earth, Planet of green Grass. Falling Asleep in America. Allen Ginsberg. **CP-GinsA**

Were it but Me that gained the Height. Emily Dickinson. **CP-DickE**

Were it indeed an accident of birth. Blemish. Paul Muldoon. **SP-MuldP**

Were it that you so shun me 'cause you wish. A Forsaken Lady to Her False Servant. Richard Lovelace. **CP-LoveR**

Were it to be the last. Emily Dickinson. **CP-DickE**

Were made were not for lament for sore melodious grief were not. A Landscape for Wyn Henderson. Kay Boyle. **CP-BoylK**

We're marchin' on relief over Injia's sunny plains. Route Marchin'. Rudyard Kipling. **CP-KiplR**

"We're married," said Eddie. The Newlyweds. John Updike. **CP-UpdiJ**

Were men of such importance as they deem. George Meredith. **CP-MerG2**

Were My Bosom As False As Thou Deem'st It to Be. Byron. **CP-Byron**

Were My Heart as Some Men's Are. Thomas Campion. **CP-CampT**

Were nature mortal lady. Emily Dickinson. **CP-DickE**

We're not so old in the Army List. The Irish Guards. Rudyard Kipling. **CP-KiplR**

We're out here, our feet in the soil, our heads craned up at the sky. Charles Wright. *Fr.* Homage to Paul Cézanne. **SP-WrigC**

We're related—you and I. Brothers. Langston Hughes. **SP-HughL**

We're Sergeant Pepper's Lonely Hearts Club Band. Sgt. Pepper's Lonely Hearts Club Band (Reprise). The Beatles. **CP-Beatl**

Were the Velocity of Affection. Emily Dickinson. **SP-DickE**

Were there, below, a spot of holy ground. Descriptive Sketches Taken During a Pedestrian Tour among the Alps. William Wordsworth. **CP-WorW1**

Were there no rain there would be little noise. The Code. John Updike. **CP-UpdiJ**

Were there not a Matter known. Passion. Robert Herrick. **CP-HerrR**

Were there too many revolving mirrors? Air Circus. Carl Sandburg. **CP-SandC**

Were they shepherds, who sat all day. The Death Of A.G.A. Emily Brontë. **CP-BronE**

Were they that named you, prophets? Did they see. To Susan, Countess of Montgomery. Ben Jonson. **CP-JonsB**

Were we not then, before we were. The Dice. Frank Templeton Prince. **CP-PrinF**

Were we now to fall. The Mechanic. Robert Creeley. **CP-CreeR**

Were worn down. The Teeth of These Mountains. Richard Shelton. **SP-ShelR**

Were you born as I was, beautiful witch? For Lucy, on Her Birthday. Miller Williams. **SP-WillM**

Were you born of a lioness in the Libyan Mountains. Catullus. *See* Carmen 60: "Hard. Hard. As she-cat whelped in desert mountains."

Were you but lying cold and dead. He Wishes His Beloved Were Dead. William Butler Yeats. **CP-YeatW**

Were you to break the vow we swore together. A Court of Love. Robert Ranke Graves. **CP-GravR**

Wereman, The. Margaret Atwood. **SP-AtwM1**

Were't aught to me I bore the canopy. Sonnet 125. William Shakespeare. NoSic *Fr.* Sonnets. **CP-ShaWS**

Werewind. Lewis Turco. **SP-TurcL**

Werewolf Movies. Margaret Atwood. **SP-AtwM2**

Werner; or, The Inheritance. Byron. **CP-Byron**

Wert Thou but ill—that I might show thee. Emily Dickinson. **CP-DickE**

Wery and weet, as beste is in the reyn. Bedroom Farce. Geoffrey Chaucer. FaBoDD *Fr.* The Reeve's Tale. *Fr.* The Canterbury Tales. **CP-ChauG**

Wessex Guidebook. Louis MacNeice. **CP-MacNL**

Wessex Heights. Thomas Hardy. **CP-HardT**

West, The. Alfred Edward Housman. **CP-HousA**

West. Louis MacNeice. *Fr.* Sleeping Winds. **CP-MacNL**

West. Thomas Merton. *Fr.* The Geography of Lograire. **CP-MertT**
  At This Precise Moment of History.
  Day Six O'Hare Telephane.
  Ghost Dance.
  Ghost Dance: Prologue.

West. Charles Olson. **CP-OlsoC**
  As of Bozeman.
  Two Poems.
    "Men are only known in memory."
    "Pedens, who re-walked the trails, hobbyists, The."
  West 4 and 5.
  West 6.

West. George Oppen. **CP-OppeG**

West and away the wheels of darkness roll. Revolution. Alfred Edward Housman. **CP-HousA**

West Bolton is due north of Bolton, East. Hayden Carruth. *Fr.* Vermont. **CP-CarHL**

West Branch Ponds, Kokadjo, Maine. Mona Van Duyn. **SP-VanDM**

West cheek to rose. Marsden Hartley. **CP-HartM**

West Country Song. Edna St. Vincent Millay. **CP-MillE**

West 4 and 5. Charles Olson. *Fr.* West. **CP-OlsoC**

West Gloucester. Charles Olson. **SP-OlsoC** *Fr.* The Maximus Poems.

West Laithe. Ted Hughes. **SP-HughT**

West Marginal Way. Richard Hugo. **CP-HugoR**

West of Childhood. Isabella Gardner. **CP-GardI**

West of Eden. Tom Clark. **SP-ClarT**

West of Logan Pass, where. John Haines. *Fr.* News from the Glacier. **SP-HainJ**

West of Omaha the freshly plowed fields. Spring Plowing. Ted Kooser. **SP-KoosT**

West-of-Wessex Girl, The. Thomas Hardy. **CP-HardT**

West pink, The. The Intended Angle of Vision Is from My Kitchen. Charles Olson. **CP-OlsoC**

West Pitch at the Falls. Marsden Hartley. **CP-HartM**

West-running Brook. Robert Frost. **CP-FrosR**

West 6. Charles Olson. *Fr.* West. **CP-OlsoC**

West Texas. Langston Hughes. **SP-HughL**

West Virginia. Louise McNeill. **SP-McNeL**

West Virginia. Muriel Rukeyser. **CP-RukeM**

West Virginia's Auburn. Donald Davie. **CP-DavDo**

West was getting out of gold, The. Looking for a Sunset Bird in Winter. Robert Frost. **CP-FrosR**

West Wind. Kenneth Koch. **SP-KochK**

West Window. Ted Kooser. **SP-KoosT**

West window is a panel of marching onions, The. Panels. Carl Sandburg. **CP-SandC**

Westering. Seamus Heaney. **SP-HeanS**

Western Air boat bouncing. Over Laramie. Allen Ginsberg. **CP-GinsA**

Western Approaches, The. Howard Nemerov. **CP-NemeH**

Western Ballad, A. Allen Ginsberg. **CP-GinsA**

Western clouds a deepening gloom display, The. William Wordsworth. **CP-WorW1**

Western Fellow Students Salute with Calypso Anthems the Movie Career of Robert Lax. Thomas Merton. **CP-MertT**

Western Landscape. Louis MacNeice. **CP-MacNL**

Western Music. Diane Wakoski. *Fr.* Fifteen Poems for a Lunar Eclipse None of Us Saw. **SP-WakoD**

Western Ocean, The. Malcolm Lowry. **CP-LowrM**

Western waves of ebbing day, The. The Trossachs. Alexandre Dumas. **SP-ScotW** *Fr.* The Lady of the Pearls.

Western waves of ebbing day, The. The Trossachs. Sir Walter Scott. **SP-ScotW** *Fr.* The Lady of the Lake.

Westgate-on-Sea. Sir John Betjeman. **CP-BetjJ**

Westminster Abbey. Alun Lewis. **CP-LewiA**

Westmoreland Girl, The. William Wordsworth. **CP-WorW2**

Westmorland. Donald Davie. **CP-DavDo**

Westphalian Song. *Unknown, tr. fr. German by* Samuel Taylor Coleridge. **CP-ColeS**

Westport. Galway Kinnell. **SP-KinnG**

Westward from Sète / As I went long before. Word of Mouth. Muriel Rukeyser. **CP-RukeM**

Westward Mother-mountains drift Pacific, green-sloped canyons vaster than Mexico City. Past Silver Durango Over Mexic Sierra-Wrinkles. Allen Ginsberg. **CP-GinsA**

Westward on the high-hilled plains. Alfred Edward Housman. **CP-HousA**

"Westward the course of empire takes its way." Welcome Address. Paul Laurence Dunbar. **CP-DunbP**

Wet / the tide out. March Here. James Schuyler. **CP-SchuJ**

Wet almond-trees, in the rain. Bare Almond-Trees. David Herbert Lawrence. **CP-LawrD**

Wet August, A. Thomas Hardy. **CP-HardT**

Wet Casements. John Ashbery. **SP-AshbJ**

Wet dawn inks are doing their blue dissolve, The. Winter Trees. Sylvia Plath. **CP-PlatS**

Wet fire / it turns out. Hayden Carruth. *Fr.* North Winter. **CP-CarHL**

Wet Hair: If Now His Mother Should Come. Robert Penn Warren. **NoAM** *Fr.* Penological Study: Southern Exposure. **SP-WarrR**

Wet heat drifts through the afternoon. Ann Arbor Variations. Frank O'Hara. **SP-OharF**

Wet leaves along the threshold of the mid-day. Love Rockets. Jim Carroll. **SP-CarrJ**

Wet Litany, The. Rudyard Kipling. **CP-KiplR**

Wet Night, A. Thomas Hardy. **CP-HardT**

Wet roads between black hedges, and a sky. East Antrim Winter. John Hewitt. **CP-HewiJ**

Wet streets in Liverpool. Poem. Malcolm Lowry. **CP-LowrM**

Wet Sunday. Jenny Joseph. **SP-JoseJ**

Wet Time, A. Wendell Berry. **CP-BerrW**

Wetness of that street, the light, The. A Place. Robert Creeley. **CP-CreeR**

We)under)over,the thing of floating Of. Edward Estlin Cummings. **CP-CummE**

We've all been off some little while—some one place, some another. The Old High School and the New. Paul Laurence Dunbar. **CP-DunbP**

We've always been unlucky with our tramps. The Knife. John Hewitt. **CP-HewiJ**

We've beej you, baby. Because the countryside here. To My Godson, on His Christening. Mona Van Duyn. **SP-VanDM**

We've covered enough ground since that awkward day. Wystan Hugh Auden. *Fr.* Shorts I ("Watch upon my wrist, The"). **CP-AudeW**

We've drunk to the Queen—God bless her! The Native-Born. Rudyard Kipling. **CP-KiplR**

We've fought with many men acrost the seas. Fuzzy-Wuzzy. Rudyard Kipling. **CP-KiplR**

We've got a change of government. Change of Government. David Herbert Lawrence. **CP-LawrD**

We've got the cholera in camp—it's worse than forty fights. Cholera Camp. Rudyard Kipling. **CP-KiplR**

We've learned in hard ways when we have to go. To His Host, Who Has Asked Him To Stay Longer. James McAuley. **SP-McAuJ**

We've made a child. Audre Lorde. *See* And What About the Children.

We've made a great mess of love. The Mess of Love. David Herbert Lawrence. **CP-LawrD**

We've our business to attend Day's duties. Bending the Bow. Robert Duncan. **SP-DuncR**

We've plodded through a weird and weary time. Metamorphosis. Edward Estlin Cummings. **CP-CummE**

We've rode and fought and ate and drunk as rations come to hand. The Parting of the Columns. Rudyard Kipling. **CP-KiplR**

We've seen that worried face upon the box. Prime Minister. John Hewitt. **CP-HewiJ**

We've sent our little Cupids all ashore. The Second Voyage. Rudyard Kipling. **CP-KiplR**

We've taken the dog out for his walk. To a Child. William DeWitt Snodgrass. **SP-SnodW**

We've walked the grounds. The Monastery at Vršac. Charles Wright. **SP-WrigC**

Wha, in a brulzie, will first cry a parley? Bannocks o' Bear-Meal. Robert Burns. **CP-BurnR**

Wha Is That at My Bower-Door? Robert Burns. **CP-BurnR**

Wha kens on whatna Bethlehems. The Innumerable Christ. "Hugh MacDiarmid." **SP-MacDH**

Wha looks on water and's no' affected yet. Water of Life. "Hugh MacDiarmid." **SP-MacDH**

Wha will buy my Troggin. Buy Braw Troggin. An Excellent New Song. Robert Burns. **CP-BurnR** *Fr.* The Heron Ballads, 1795.

Whale, The. John Donne. **ChTr** *Fr.* The Progress[e] of the Soul[e]. **CP-DonnJ**

Whale, The. Theodore Roethke. **CP-RoetT**

Whale. Anne Sexton. **CP-SextA**

Whale butting through scarps of moving marble, The. Explorations. Louis MacNeice. **CP-MacNL**

Whale in the Blue Washing Machine, The. John Haines. **SP-HainJ**

Whale Knot, The. Roy Fisher. **SP-FishR**

Whale Poem. Frederick Morgan. **SP-MorgF**

Whalen, curious vulture. A Sinecure for P. Whalen. Gary Snyder. **CP-SnydG**

Whaler's Wife, The. Thomas Hardy. **CP-HardT**

Whales. Kathleen Jessie Raine. **SP-RainK**

Whales are singing, The. Cetus, a Letter from Jonah. Siv Cedering Fox. **SP-CedeS**

Whales have calves / Cats have kittens. The Guppy. Ogden Nash. **CP-NashO**

Wha'll M-w Me Now. Robert Burns. **CP-BurnR**

Wham will we send to London town. The Heron Ballads, 1795.

Whan ended was my tale of Melibee. The Prologue of the Monk's Tale. Geoffrey Chaucer. *Fr.* The Canterbury Tales. **CP-ChauG**

Whan ended was the lyf of Seinte Cecile. The Canon's Yeoman's Prologue. Geoffrey Chaucer. *Fr.* The Canterbury Tales. **CP-ChauG**

Whan folk hadde laughen at this nyce cas. The Reeve's Prologue. Geoffrey Chaucer. *Fr.* The Canterbury Tales. **CP-ChauG**

Whan Phebus dwelled heere in this erthe adoun. The Manciple's Tale. Geoffrey Chaucer. *Fr.* The Canterbury Tales. **CP-ChauG**

Whan said [or seyd orseyde] was al this miracle, every man. Prologue to Sir Thopas. Geoffrey Chaucer. **NAEL-1; Par** *Fr.* The Canterbury Tales. **CP-ChauG**

Whan that Aprille [or April, or Aprill] with his[e] shoures [or showres] sote [orsoote]. Geoffrey Chaucer. **ChTr; TRP,** *ll.* 1–18; **TrGrPo,** *ll.* 1–18, *incl. mod. vers. by* Louis Untermeyer; **PPP,** *ll.* 1–271; **FiP,** *ll.* 1–34; **CTC,** *ll.* 1–37; **SCV,** *ll.* 1–42, *incl. mod. vers. by* Nevill Coghill; **EBEvV,** *ll.* 1–78; **PrIm** *Fr.* The General Prologue. **FHYEP; NAWM-1; OAEL-1; PoE** *Fr.* The Canterbury Tales. **CP-ChauG**

(When April with Its Sweet Showers.) **PrIm,** *ll.* 1–18;

("When April with its sweet showers.") **TFi,** *ll.* 1–42, *mod. vers. by* William Harmon.

("When in April the sweet showers fall.") **TEP,** *ll.* 1–34, *mod. vers. by* Nevill Coghill.

("When the sweet showers of April fall and shoot.") **SCV,** *ll.* 1–42, *mod. vers. by* Nevill Coghill.

("When the sweet showers of April follow March.") **TrGrPo,** *ll.* 1–18, *mod. vers. by* Louis Untermeyer.

Whan that Aprille [or April or Aprill] with his[e] shoures [or showres] sote [or soote]. The General Prologue. Geoffrey Chaucer. **FHYEP; OAEL-1; PoE** *Fr.* The Canterbury Tales. **CP-ChauG**

Whan that the Knight [or Knyght] had[de] thus his tale yto[o]ld. The Miller's Prologue. Geoffrey Chaucer. **NAEL-1; OAEL-1** *Fr.* The Canterbury Tales. **CP-ChauG**

Whan they unto the paleys were yoemen. Geoffrey Chaucer. **PoE** *Fr.* Troilus and Criseyde [or Criseide]. **CP-ChauG**

Whare are you gaun, my bony lass. A Waukrife Minnie. Robert Burns. **CP-BurnR**

Whare hae ye been sae braw, lad! Killiecrankie. Robert Burns. **CP-BurnR**

Whare live ye my bonie lass. My Collier Laddie. Robert Burns. **CP-BurnR**

Wharf of singleness. Dock Song Crazy. Al Young. **CP-YounA**

What? Walter de la Mare. **CP-DeLaW**

What / do you think it is. Robert Creeley. **CP-CreeR**

What. Stephen Dunn. **SP-DunnS**

What / has happened. Here. Robert Creeley. **CP-CreeR**

What? Langston Hughes. **SP-HughL**

What? Christina Georgina Rossetti. **CP-RosC3**

What. James Schuyler. **CP-SchuJ**

What / singular upright flourishing. Numbers. Robert Creeley. **CP-CreeR**

What / the sun touches. The Treasure House. Roy Fisher. **SP-FishR** *Fr.* Inscriptions for Bluebeard's Castle.

What a Day. Shel Silverstein. **SP-SilS2**

What a dream of a landscape! Landscape with Figures. Howard Nemerov. **CP-NemeH**

What a fair and happy place. The Columbian's Song. Walt Whitman. **CP-WhitW**

What a girl called "the dailiness of life." Well Water. Randall Jarrell. **CP-JarrR; SP-JarrR**

What a grand time was the war! World War II. Langston Hughes. **SP-HughL**

What a Hazard a Letter is! Emily Dickinson. **SP-DickE**

What a hot day it is! for. A Terrestrial Cuckoo. Frank O'Hara. **SP-OharF**

What a hulking bore it must be for you! An Enzyme Poem for Suzanne. Paul Zimmer. **SP-ZimmP**

What a message! what a picture! A Postcard from John Ashbery. Frank O'Hara. **SP-OharF**

What a pity that Bela Bartok. Basil Bunting. **CP-BuntB**

What a pity, when a man looks at himself in the glass. Man's Image. David Herbert Lawrence. **CP-LawrD**

What a pretty tale you told me. Robert Browning. **CP-BroR2**

What a proud dreamhorse pulling(smoothloomingly)through. Edward Estlin Cummings. **CP-CummE; SP-CummE**

What a scurvy mind. The Observer. William Carlos Williams. **CP-WilW2**

What a sound his. Charles Kenneth Williams. **CP-WillC**

What a team. He Has Beaten about the Bush Long Enough. William Carlos Williams. **CP-WilW2**

What a thrill. Cut. Sylvia Plath. **CP-PlatS**

What a traffick amongst limbs and loins. The Picture. Charles Olson. **CP-OlsoC**

What a walk. First mile uphill. The road. Sneosdal. Richard Hugo. **CP-HugoR**

What a way to spend the golden years, Tomasito! Poem—Unfinished Poem. Thomas McGrath. **SP-McGrT**

What a wild room / We enter, when the gloom. A Man-Made World. Stephen Spender. **CP-SpenS**

What a Wonder Among the Instruments Is the Walloping Tramboone! Hayden Carruth. **CP-CarHS**

"What a wonderful thing has come to pass." One of the Crowd on the Shore Tells How It Was. Miller Williams. **SP-WillM**

What a word and I thought it would be. Alone. Richard Shelton. **SP-ShelR**

What about all this writing? Young Love. William Carlos Williams. **CP-WilW1**

What about measure, I learnt. Peri Poietikes. Louis Zukofsky. **CP-ZukLS**

What Adam Said. Archibald MacLeish. *Fr.* Songs for Eve. **CP-MacLA**

What Ails My Fern? James Schuyler. **CP-SchuJ**

What ails Thee? David Herbert Lawrence. **CP-LawrD**

What ails you now, ye lousy b———h. Robert Burns' Answer [to Epistle from a Taylor]. Robert Burns. **CP-BurnR**

What aim had they, the Pair of Monks, in size. At the Eremite or Upper Convent of Camaldoli. William Wordsworth. *Fr.* Memorials of a Tour in Italy, 1837. **CP-WorW2**

What! alive and so bold, O Earth! Lines Written on Hearing the News of the Death of Napoleon. Percy Bysshe Shelley. **CP-ShelP**

What all the books of ages paint, I have. Ralph Waldo Emerson. **CP-EmerR**

What Almost Every Woman Knows Sooner or Later. Ogden Nash. **CP-NashO**

What Am I After All. Walt Whitman. **CP-WhitW**

What am I dreaming of? Charles Henri Ford. **SP-FordC** *Fr.* Secret Haiku.

What am I? Nosing here, turning leaves over. Wodwo. Ted Hughes. **SP-HughT**

What, Amicus, constitutes mastery? The Master at a Mediterranean Port. Howard Nemerov. **CP-NemeH**

What ancestor of mine in wet Wales or wild Scotland. Patronymic. Robinson Jeffers. **CP-JefR3**

What, and how great, the Virtue and the Art. The Second Satire of the Second Book of Horace Imitated. Alexander Pope. **CP-PopeA**

What anger in my hard-won bones. Spring People. Audre Lorde. **SP-LordA**

What animals dream of I do not know. The Interpretation of Dreams. William Matthews. **SP-MattW**

What Any Lover Learns. Archibald MacLeish. **CP-MacLA**

What Appears to Be Yours. Frank O'Hara. **SP-OharF**

What are all the flowers. Ralph Waldo Emerson. **CP-EmerR**

What are Cities For? Robinson Jeffers. **CP-JefR2**

What are days for? Days. Philip Larkin. **CP-LarkP**

What Are Heavy? Christina Georgina Rossetti. **CP-RosC2**

What are his machines. New England Capitalist. Ralph Waldo Emerson. **CP-EmerR**

What are our patches, tatters, raggs, and rents. Raggs. Robert Herrick. **CP-HerrR**

What are ruins to us. At Lindos. May Sarton. **SP-SartM**

"What are the bugles blowin' for?" said Files-on-Parade. Danny Deever. Rudyard Kipling. **CP-KiplR**

What Are the Gods? David Herbert Lawrence. **CP-LawrD**

What are the hills of Ross-shire like? The Ross-shire Hills. "Hugh MacDiarmid." **SP-MacDH**

What are the islands to me. The Islands. Hilda Doolittle. **CP-DoolH**

What are the major men? All men are brave. Paisant Chronicle. Wallace Stevens. **CP-StevW**

What are the marks of the enemy? / He has no wit. Thomas Merton. **CP-MertT**

What are the signs of life? the breath, the pulse. For a Song of the Languagers. Robert Duncan. **SP-DuncR**

What are the springs of sleep? What is the motion. Causerie. Allen Tate. **CP-TateA**

What are the things that make life bright? To J. Q. Paul Laurence Dunbar. **CP-DunbP**

What Are the Wild Waves Saying? David Herbert Lawrence. **CP-LawrD**

What, are there gods? herself she hath forswore. 3.3. Ovid. **CP-MarlC,** *tr.* by Christopher Marlowe; *Fr.* Elegies.

What are these elations I have. The Descent of Winter. William Carlos Williams. **CP-WilW1**

What are these lovely ones, yea, what are these? Christina Georgina Rossetti. **CP-RosC2**

What are these songs. Louis Zukofsky. **CP-ZukLS**

What are these very desolate ones. So It Ends. Kenneth Patchen. **CP-PatcK**

What are those of the known but to ascend and enter the Unknown? Portals. Walt Whitman. **CP-WhitW**

What are to me those honours or renown. Last Words on Greece. Byron. **CP-Byron**

What are we first? First, animals; and next. George Meredith. **GBL; HAP; NBM; NoP; OAEP; PoEL-5** *Fr.* Modern Love. **CP-MerG1**

What are we having for dinner tonight? Ballad. Edwin Rolfe. **CP-RolfE**

What are we set on earth for? Say, to toil. Work. Elizabeth Barrett Browning. **CP-BroEB**

What are we to do with this hour of the evening. Staying. Miller Williams. **SP-WillM**

What Are Years? Marianne Craig Moore. **CP-MoorM**

What are you able to build with your blocks? Block City. Robert Louis Stevenson. **CP-StevR**

What *are* you, apple! There are men. Still Life. George Oppen. **CP-OppeG**

What are you doing, dear Ingelo, a deserter to the northern zone. A Letter to Doctor Ingelo. Andrew Marvell, *tr. fr. Latin by* William A. McQueen *and* Kiffin A. Rockwell. **CP-MarvA**

What are you doing outside my walls. The New Dawn's Business. Thomas Hardy. **CP-HardT**

What are you doing today, brother? Poem Written after Reading Certain Poets Sired by the English School and Bitched by the C.P. Kenneth Patchen. **CP-PatcK**

What are you doing up, my cat. Intruding. Marge Piercy. **SP-PierM**

What are you doing with all those paper. She Said. Charles Bukowski. **SP-BukC3**

What are you hiding under your hump? Pablo Neruda, *tr. fr. Spanish by* Ben Belitt. **SP-NeruP** *Fr.* Question Book.

What are you looking for. On a Shell-strewn Beach. Kathleen Jessie Raine. **SP-RainK**

What! are you still asleep in bed. Early Morning Bathing. Wystan Hugh Auden. **CP-AudWJ**

What are you still, still thinking. The Moth-Signal. Thomas Hardy. **CP-HardT**

What armies ride November clouds. These Years a Winter. Thomas Merton. **CP-MertT**

What art and anti-art to lead us by the sharpness. Semite. George Oppen. **CP-OppeG**

What art thou, frost? and whence are thy keen stores. James Thomson. **OxBS** *Fr.* Winter. *Fr.* The Seasons. **CP-ThomJ**

What art thou, Presumptuous, who profanest. Fragment: The False Laurel and the True. Percy Bysshe Shelley. **CP-ShelP**

"What art thou thinking of," said the Mother. Mother and Child. Christina Georgina Rossetti. **CP-RosC3**

What aspect bore the Man who roved or fled. William Wordsworth. *Fr.* The River Duddon [A Series of Sonnets]. **CP-WorW2**

What avails it me. Ralph Waldo Emerson. **CP-EmerR**

What awful pageants crowd the evening sky! Written September 1791, During a Remarkable Thunder Storm, in which the Moon Was Perfectly Clear, While the Tempest Gathered in Various Directions Near the Earth. Charlotte Smith. **CP-SmitC**

What awful pérspective! while from our sight. Same, The [Inside of King's College Chapel, Cambridge]. William Wordsworth. *Fr.* Ecclesiastical Sonnets. **CP-WorW2**

What bannered pardon slapping on the mast. For One Who Did Not March. John Hewitt. **CP-HewiJ**

What be those crowned forms high over the sacred fountain? Parnassus. Tennyson. **CP-TennA**

What beast in wilderness or cultured field. Archbishop Chichely to Henry V. William Wordsworth. *Fr.* Ecclesiastical Sonnets. **CP-WorW2**

What beast of chase hath broken from the cover? Echo, upon the Gemmi. William Wordsworth. *Fr.* Memorials of a Tour of the Continent; 1820. **CP-WorW2**

What beauty would have lovely styled. Epitaph, An. Ben Jonson. **CP-JonsB**

What beckoning [or beck'ning] ghost, along the moonlight shade. Elegy to the Memory of an Unfortunate Lady. Alexander Pope. **CP-PopeA**

What began as death's avenue. At Père Lachaise. Mona Van Duyn. **SP-VanDM**

What being in rank-old nature should earlier have that breath been. Gerard Manley Hopkins. **CP-HopkG**

What Best I See in Thee. Walt Whitman. **CP-WhitW**

What bile must rise within his throat. Daily Reviewer-Haupt. David Markson. **CP-MarkD**

What body can be ploughed. Chanson un Peu Naïve. Louise Bogan. **CP-BogaL**

What boots it on the Gods to call? A Recantation. Rudyard Kipling. **CP-KiplR**

What boots it, thy virtue. Tact. Ralph Waldo Emerson. **CP-EmerR**

What bright soft thing is this? The Tear[e]. Richard Crashaw. **CP-CrasR**

What can a man do that a beast cannot. In Shame and Humiliation. James Wright. **CP-WrigJ**

What can a young lassie, what shall a young lassie. Robert Burns. **CP-BurnR**

What Can I Do for You? "Bob Dylan." **CP-DylaB**

"What can I do for you?" she asked gently. Wild Cyclamen. Robert Ranke Graves. **CP-GravR**

What can I do in Poetry. The Departure of the Good Daemon. Robert Herrick. **CP-HerrR**

What Can I Do to Drive Away. John Keats. **CP-KeatJ**

What can I do with this bayonet? Bayonet. Anne Sexton. **CP-SextA**

What can I give Him. My Gift. Christina Georgina Rossetti. **FaPON; PChr; SiSoSe** *Fr.* Christmas Carol, A: "In the bleak mid-winter." **CP-RosC1**

What can I give thee back, O liberal. Sonnet. Elizabeth Barrett Browning. **BWW; HBV 1-2; OBVV; OXAEP-2** *Fr.* Sonnets from the Portuguese. **CP-BroEB**

What Can I Tell My Bones? Theodore Roethke. **AmPP; NOBA** *Fr.* Meditations of an Old Woman. **CP-RoetT**

What can I tell you, future ones. Kathleen Jessie Raine. *Fr.* Testimony. **SP-RainK**

What can I tell you of the past. To the Boys in Freshman History (Thermopylae, 480 B.C.) Louise McNeill. **SP-McNeL**

What can it mean to endure. Pablo Neruda, *tr. fr. Spanish by* Ben Belitt. **SP-NeruP** *Fr.* Question Book.

What can lambkins do. A Chill. Christina Georgina Rossetti. **CP-RosC1**

What can my Kellam drink his Sack. To M. Kellam. Robert Herrick. **CP-HerrR**

What can occur / invests the weather, also. To Bobbie. Robert Creeley. **CP-CreeR**

What can purge my heart. Song for Billie Holiday. Langston Hughes. **SP-HughL**

What can the cause be, when the king hath [*or* K. have] given. An Epigram. To the Household. 1630. Ben Jonson. **CP-JonsB**

What can the spirit believe? The Young Girl. Theodore Roethke. **CP-RoetT**

What can the white man say to the black woman? Right to Life, The: What Can the White Man Say to the Black Woman? Alice Walker. **CP-WalkA**

What can to you this music wakes my years. John Berryman. *Fr.* Sonnets to Chris. **CP-BerrJ**

What Can We Not Ask? Robert Ranke Graves. **CP-GravR**

What can we say of the night? Far Rockaway Night Till Morning. Carl Sandburg. **CP-SandC**

What can you say about Pennsylvania. Returning Native. John Updike. **CP-UpdiJ**

What care I if good God be. Egocentric. Stevie Smith. **CP-SmitS**

What care I, so they stand the same. Merops. Ralph Waldo Emerson. **CP-EmerR**

What care the Dead, for Chanticleer. Emily Dickinson. **CP-DickE**

What catches the eye the quick hand reaches toward. Consciousness. Robinson Jeffers. **CP-JefR1**

What cave are you in, hiding, rained on? A Man Writes to a Part of Himself. Robert Bly. **SP-BlyR**

What charming peals are these. To My Worthy Friend, Master Edward Filmer, on His Work Published. Ben Jonson. **CP-JonsB**

What cheer, O Ren Jaldain? Down in the Lone Valley. Kenneth Patchen. **CP-PatcK**

What chores these churls do put upon the great. Edna St. Vincent Millay. **CP-MillE**

What coarse god / Was the gear-box in the rain. Ovid in Tomis. Derek Mahon. **SP-MahoD**

What comes here? Splenetic. Catnap, with Nightmare. James McAuley. **SP-McAuJ** *Fr.* Meditations of Afternoon.

What common language to unravel? Paterson: The Falls. William Carlos Williams. **CP-WilW2**

What connects me to this moon. Chemistry. Al Young. **CP-YounA**

What conscience, say, is it in thee. To Oenone. Robert Herrick. **CP-HerrR**

What could / they give me I. They. Robert Creeley. **CP-CreeR**

What could be more endearing, on a long, too quiet, lonely evening in an unfamiliar house. Time: 1978. Charles Kenneth Williams. **SP-WillC**

What could she say to the fantastic foolybear. Lawrence Ferlinghetti. **SP-FerlL**

What creeps in is the awareness of death. At a Friend's Birthday Party in the Garden at Night. Stephen Berg. **SP-BergS**

What crowd is this in Catknoll Street. The War-Wife of Catknoll. Thomas Hardy. **CP-HardT**

What crowd is this? what have we here! we must not pass it by. Star-Gazers. William Wordsworth. **CP-WorW1**

What crowd is this? what have we here! we must not pass it by. William Wordsworth. **Poetr** *Fr.* Star-Gazers. **CP-WorW1**

What cry of peach blossoms. Peach Blossoms. Carl Sandburg. **CP-SandC**

What Curious Dresses All Men Wear. Delmore Schwartz. **SP-SchwD**

What curious things we said. Intra Sepulchrum. Thomas Hardy. **CP-HardT**

What dark and terrible shadow is swaying in the wind?. Easter at Christmas. Alun Lewis. **CP-LewiA**

What Day Is. Robert Penn Warren. **SP-WarrR**

What day was that which, all sad haps to bring. 3.11. Ovid. **CP-MarlC**, *tr. by* Christopher Marlowe; *Fr.* Elegies.

What death is worse than this? Sir Thomas Wyatt. **CP-WyatT**

What death means is not this. Canticle. Wendell Berry. **CP-BerrW**

What demented malice, my silly Ravidus. Catullus. *See* Carmen 40: "Whatever could have possessed you."

What demon lurked among those olive-trees. The Tower of Love. Robert Ranke Graves. **CP-GravR**

What did he do except lie. Banneker. Rita Dove. **SP-DoveR**

What did Hiamovi, the red man, Chief of. Carl Sandburg. *Fr.* The People, Yes. **CP-SandC**

What did I come for? To see. John Haines. *Fr.* Homestead. **SP-HainJ**

What Did I Dream? Robert Ranke Graves. **CP-GravR**

What did I eat when I ate apple? Eve Answers the Burdock. Archibald MacLeish. *Fr.* Songs for Eve. **CP-MacLA**

What did I see when first I went to Greece? Greek Orthodox. Sir John Betjeman. **CP-BetjJ**

What did I think, a storm clutching a clarinet. The Blues. William Matthews. **SP-MattW**

What Did It mean? Thomas Hardy. **CP-HardT**

What did she see on the train? James McAuley. **SP-McAuJ** *Fr.* Witness.

What did that old philosopher say? Lovable Babblers. Carl Sandburg. **CP-SandC**

What did the caterpillars do. Incubus. Daniel Gerard Hoffman. **SP-HoffD**

What did the day bring? Letter from a Coward to a Hero. Robert Penn Warren. **SP-WarrR**

What Did the Man Do with the Clouds? Charles Kenneth Williams. **CP-WillC**

What did They do since I saw Them? Emily Dickinson. **CP-DickE**

What did you do? Cannot you let me know? Reluctant Confession. Thomas Hardy. **CP-HardT**

What did you do for the holiday? Eclogue between the Motherless. Louis MacNeice. **CP-MacNL**

What did you do last summer? 8/22/38–8/22/68. Gary Gildner. **SP-GildG**

What Did You Say? Robert Ranke Graves. **CP-GravR**

What did you say? Which? Walter de la Mare. **CP-DeLaW**

What did you say to me. The Bird. Robert Creeley. **CP-CreeR**

What did you see, Cromarty, by the house. Seeing. Archibald MacLeish. **CP-MacLA**

What did you think, restless one? Talking To Grandpa Eastman. Barton Sutter. **SP-SuttB**

What dire offence from am'rous causes springs. Alexander Pope. **EBNV; NOEC; Poetr** *Fr.* The Rape of the Lock[, an Heroi-Comical Poem]. **CP-PopeA**

What dire offence from am'rous causes springs. *see also* To Belinda on the Rape of the Lock. Alexander Pope. **CP-PopeA**

What Do I Care? David Herbert Lawrence. **CP-LawrD**

What do I care. Pursuit. Hilda Doolittle. **CP-DoolH**

What do I catch upon the night-wind, husband? A Sound in the Night. Thomas Hardy. **CP-HardT**

What Do I Give You? Muriel Rukeyser. **CP-RukeM**

What do I remember of my visit to Ravenna? Firstly. Ravenna. Louis MacNeice. **CP-MacNL**

What do I want in these rooms papered with visions of money? Paterson. Allen Ginsberg. **CP-GinsA**

What do the stars do / Up in the sky. Christina Georgina Rossetti. **CP-RosC2**

"What do they look like," he said. The Birds of Paradise Being Very Plain Birds. Diane Wakoski. **SP-WakoD**

What do they sing, the last birds. Last Songs. Galway Kinnell. **SP-KinnG**

What do they think has happened, the old fools. The Old Fools. Philip Larkin. **CP-LarkP**

What do we see / In the perfect thing? Is our seeing. Images of Perfection. Charles Tomlinson. **CP-TomlC**

What Do We See? Muriel Rukeyser. **CP-RukeM**

What do you / want, love. To be. Song. Robert Creeley. **CP-CreeR**

What do you do when you've wedded a girl all legal and lawful. Aside to Husbands. Ogden Nash. **CP-NashO**

What do you know about it? the Architect said. The Controversy. William Carlos Williams. **CP-WilW2**

What do you know of America? I asked a little Russian schoolgirl. Muriel Rukeyser. **CP-RukeM**

What do you look for down there. The Absent-Minded Are Always to Blame. Adrienne Rich. **CP-RicAE**

"What do you make so fair and bright?" The Cloak, the Boat, and the Shoes. William Butler Yeats. **CP-YeatW**

What do you really know? I asked, phrasing the question. Problems of Knowledge. Daniel Gerard Hoffman. **SP-HoffD**

What do you remember thinking back. Ever Since. Archibald MacLeish. **CP-MacLA**

What do you say to the mother. The Ring of Irony. Diane Wakoski. **SP-WakoD**

What do you see in that time-touched stone. In the British Museum. Thomas Hardy. **CP-HardT**

What do you see in Vagg Hollow. Vagg Hollow. Thomas Hardy. **CP-HardT**

What do you so regret, my lady. The Lady of Forebodings. Thomas Hardy. **CP-HardT**

What do you teach me / Mama my cow? Thomas Merton. *Fr.* Cables to the Ace. **CP-MertT**

What do you think of us in fuzzy endeavor. Garbageman: the Man with the Orderly Mind. Gwendolyn Brooks. **CAPP** *Fr.* A Catch of Shy Fish. **SP-BrooG**

What do you want / To tell while the world. The Speech at Soli. George Oppen. **CP-OppeG**

What do you write? Muriel Rukeyser. **CP-RukeM**

What doating bigot to his faults so blind. 1.1. Horace, *tr. by* Samuel Johnson. **CP-JohnS** *Fr.* Satires.

What does he think about. The Bootblack. Charles Tomlinson. **CP-TomlC**

What does it matter? you ask. What Ovid Taught Me. Alice Walker. **CP-WalkA**

What does it mean? Lord knows; least of all I. An Apology for Using the Word "Heart" in Too Many Poems. Hayden Carruth. **CP-CarHS**

What does little Ernest croon. Edward Estlin Cummings. **CP-CummE**

What does not change / is the will to change. The Kingfishers. Charles Olson. **CP-OlsoC; SP-OlsoC**

What Does She See When She Shuts Her Eyes. Gertrude Stein. **CP-SteiG**

What Does She Want? David Herbert Lawrence. **CP-LawrD**

What Does the Bee Do? Christina Georgina Rossetti. **CP-RosC2**

What does the donkey bray about? Christina Georgina Rossetti. **CP-RosC2**

What does the hangman think about. The Hangman at Home. Carl Sandburg. **CP-SandC**

What does the horse give you. Horse. Louise Glück. **SP-GlücL**

What Does the Novice Soldier Think. Edwin Rolfe. **CP-RolfE**

What does the song hope for? And his moved hands. Orpheus. Wystan Hugh Auden. **CP-AudeW**

What does the storm say? What the trees wish. The Ways and the Peoples. Randall Jarrell. **CP-JarrR**

What does this day bestow? Kathleen Jessie Raine. **SP-RainK**

What does this wind say, plunging upon the land. Hayden Carruth. *Fr.* The Asylum. **CP-CarHL**

What doest thou here, Elijah? The Ghost of Abel. William Blake. **CP-BlakW**

What dost thou here far from thy native place? Banquo. Walter de la Mare. **CP-DeLaW**

What dost thou in that mansion fair. On Seeing the Beautiful County-Seat of Lord G———. Robert Burns. *Fr.* Epigrams on Lord Galloway. **CP-BurnR**

What doth this noise of thoughts within my heart. The Family [*or* Familie]. George Herbert. **CP-HerbG**

What doubt'st thou hand? sad Cato 'tis to kill. Pentadius, *tr. fr. Latin by* Richard Lovelace. **CP-LoveR**

What dreams we have and how they fly. Dreams. Paul Laurence Dunbar. **CP-DunbP**

What dreams you must have had last night. The Dream. Randall Jarrell. **CP-JarrR**

What Ducks Require. John Crowe Ransom. **SP-RansJ**

What ends / Is that. George Oppen. *Fr.* Image of the Engine. **CP-OppeG**

What Eve Said. Archibald MacLeish. *Fr.* Songs for Eve. **CP-MacLA**

What Eve Sang. Archibald MacLeish. *Fr.* Songs for Eve. **CP-MacLA**

What ever happened to. 3 Epiphanies. Anne Waldman. **SP-WaldA**

What ever men for Loyalty pretend. Distrust. Robert Herrick. **CP-HerrR**

What ever story of their crueltie. On the Still Surviving Markes of Our Saviours Wounds. Richard Crashaw. **CP-CrasR**

What explanation is given for the phosphorus light. Ukiyo-E. Siv Cedering Fox. **SP-CedeS**

What face, in the water. Lament. William Carlos Williams. **CP-WilW2**

What faire pompe have I spide of glittering Ladies. Thomas Campion. *See* What Fair[e] Pomp[e].

What Fair[e] Pomp[e]. Thomas Campion.

  (Canto Secundo.) **CP-CampT**

  ("What faire pompe have I spide of glittering Ladies.") **CP-CampT**

What fate decreed, Time now ha's made us see. To Prince Charles upon his coming to Exeter. Robert Herrick. **CP-HerrR**

What Fears, what Terrors does thy Gift create! On a Lady's Presenting a Sprig of Myrtle to a Gentleman. Samuel Johnson. **CP-JohnS**

What features, form, mien, manners, with a mind. The Neapolitan John Baptist Manso. *Unknown. Fr.* Complimentary Pieces to Milton. **CP-CowpW**

What Feeling Is This? Marge Piercy. *Fr.* Walking into Love. **SP-PierM**

What field of all the civil wars. Andrew Marvell. **FaBoEH** *Fr.* An Horatian Ode upon Cromwell's Return from Ireland. **CP-MarvA**

What Fifty Said. Robert Frost. **CP-FrosR**

What fire feeds on is mostly air, but I dwell. House Burning Down. James McAuley. **SP-McAuJ**

What flecks the outer gray beyond. The Dead Ship of Harpswell. John Greenleaf Whittier. **CP-WhitJ**

What flies forever and rests never? The Wind. So say Senegalese. Maybe. Riddles and Whims. Carl Sandburg. **CP-SandC**

What flowing central forces, say. Ralph Waldo Emerson. **CP-EmerR**

What fool would feel. Naked. William Carlos Williams. **CP-WilW1**

What forced labor / for Hitler in Hell? Pablo Neruda, *tr. fr. Spanish by* Ben Belitt. **SP-NeruP** *Fr.* Question Book.

What freedom's not some under's mere above. Edward Estlin Cummings. **CP-CummE; SP-CummE**

What from this barren being do we reap? Byron. **FHYEP** *Fr.* Canto the Fourth. *Fr.* Childe Harold's Pilgrimage. **CP-Byron**

What from this barren being do we reap? Byron. **NOBRP** *Fr.* Canto the Fourth. *Fr.* Childe Harold's Pilgrimage. **CP-Byron**

What from this barren being do we reap. Ralph Waldo Emerson. **CP-EmerR**

What, Gelliús, of the man. Carmen 88. Catullus. *Fr.* Carmina. **CP-Catul**

What General has a good army in himself, has a good army. Leaflets. Walt Whitman. **CP-WhitW**

What generations could have dreamed. Pedestrian. George Oppen. **CP-OppeG**

What gentle echoes. Massachusetts. Robert Creeley. **CP-CreeR**

What gentle ghost, besprent with April dew. An Elegy [*or* Elegie] on the Lady Jane Pawlet [*or* Paulet], [Marchioness of Winton]. Ben Jonson. **CP-JonsB**

What Ghosts Can Say. Adrienne Rich. **CP-RicAE**

What ghosts of cuckoo-spit and dew. Louis MacNeice. **CP-MacNL** *Fr.* Jigsaws. **CP-MacNL**

What girl but, having gathered flowers. Humility. Robert Browning. **CP-BroR2**

What Gives. Richard Eberhart. **CP-EberR**

What gives it power makes it change its mind. The Beautiful Lawn Sprinkler. Howard Nemerov. **CP-NemeH**

What glories would we? Motions of the soul? The Renewal. Theodore Roethke. **CP-RoetT**

What glory for a boy of ten. Robert Louis Stevenson. *Fr.* The Family. **CP-StevR**

What God gives, and what we take. Robert Herrick. **CP-HerrR** (Graces for Children.) **CP-HerrR**

What God Is. Robert Herrick. **CP-HerrR**

What God is like to him I serve? Anne Bradstreet. **CP-BradA**

What God, what Genius did the Pencil move. To Sir Godfrey Kneller, on His Painting for Me the Statues of Apollo, Venus and Hercules. Alexander Pope. **CP-PopeA**

What Goes On? The Beatles. **CP-Beatl**

What goes on in the pauses. Torture. Margaret Atwood. **SP-AtwM2**

What golden splendent star is this so bright. In Praise of the Author, Mistress Anne Bradstreet, Virtue's True and Lively Pattern. *Unknown, poem signed* "N. H." **CP-BradA**

What good did your blood do you. Dedicated to Robert McAlmon. Kay Boyle. **CP-BoylK**

What good is it compromising myself. Grass. Joseph Ceravolo. **SP-CeraJ**

What Good Shall My Life Do Me? ("Have dead men"). Christina Georgina Rossetti. **CP-RosC2**

What Good Shall My Life Do Me? ("No hope"). Christina Georgina Rossetti. **CP-RosC3**

What Got him was Noth. Edward Estlin Cummings. **CP-CummE**

What Grandpa Mouse Said. Nicholas Vachel Lindsay. **CP-LindV**

What great genius invented the waiting room? Waiting Rooms. Howard Nemerov. **CP-NemeH**

What Greece, when learning flourished [*or* flourish'd], only [*or* onle] knew. Prologue to the University of Oxford, 1673. John Dryden. **SP-DrydJ**

What grouchy war-tanks intend to shred. He Cut His Finger on Eternity. Charles Henri Ford. **SP-FordC**

What Had to Go. Charles Olson. **CP-OlsoC**

What hand may wreathe thy natal crown. For *The Garland of Rachel.* "Lewis Carroll." *Fr.* Two Poems to Rachel Daniel. **CP-CarrL**

What Happened. Rudyard Kipling. **CP-KiplR**

What Happened. Diane Wakoski. **SP-WakoD**

What Happened. Robert Penn Warren. *Fr.* Tale of Time. **SP-WarrR**

What Happened Here Before. Gary Snyder. **CP-SnydG**

What Happened in the Camps. Kenneth Patchen. **CP-PatcK**

What happened there, it was not much. The Well House. Robert Penn Warren. **SP-WarrR**

What happened to her. Time. Robert Creeley. **CP-CreeR**

What happens / to the leaves after. Roses, Late Summer. Mary Oliver. **SP-OlivM**

What happens afterwards, none need enquire. Conjunction. Robert Ranke Graves. **CP-GravR**

What happens is, the kind of snow that sweeps. For a Lost Child. William Stafford. **SP-StafW**

What happens to a dream deferred? Harlem. Langston Hughes. **SP-HughL** *Fr.* Lenox Avenue Mural.

What happens when the juice of the sun. Sunjuice. Erica Jong. **SP-JongE**

What happy appellations these. The Squid. Ogden Nash. *Fr.* Nature-Walks, or, Not to Mention a Dopping of Sheldrakes. **CP-NashO**

What hard work it takes. Charles Henri Ford. *Fr.* Epigrams. **SP-FordC**

What harts content can he finde. *At. to* Thomas Campion *and to* Philip Rosseter. **CP-CampT**

What Harvest Half So Sweet Is. Thomas Campion. **CP-CampT** "Dove alone expresses, The." **PBBP**

What has happened? Grace Paley. **CP-PaleG**

What has happened here will do. Boundary. Adrienne Rich. **CP-RicAE**

What has happened in the world? Volcanic Venus. David Herbert Lawrence. **CP-LawrD**

What has happened to the young men of Eng.? Eng. Stevie Smith. **CP-SmitS**

What has killed mankind—for the bulk of mankind is dead—is lies. Poison. David Herbert Lawrence. **CP-LawrD**

What hast thou, O my soul, with pardise? Blandula, Tenella, Vagula. Ezra Pound. **SP-PounE**

What Hath God Wrought! Christina Georgina Rossetti. **CP-RosC2**

"What have I earned for all that work," I said. The People. William Butler Yeats. **CP-YeatW**

What Have I Learned. Gary Snyder. **CP-SnydG**

What have I saved out of a morning? Moon Riders. Carl Sandburg. **CP-SandC**

What, have I thus betrayed my liberty? Sonnet 47. Sir Philip Sidney. **GBL; NAEL-1; NIP; NoP; PoEL-1; TrGrPo** *Fr.* Astrophil and Stella. **SP-SidnP**

What have I to regret. Kathleen Jessie Raine. **SP-RainK**

What have I to say to you? A Love Song: First Version, 1915. William Carlos Williams. **CP-WilW1**

What have they done to our dollar, darling. On the Recently Minted Hundred-Cent Piece. John Updike. **CP-UpdiJ**

What Have They Done to You? David Herbert Lawrence. **CP-LawrD**

What have they done to you, all-conquering love? Observations of P. Ovidus Naso on the Incidence of Sex in the Contemporary Novel. Archibald MacLeish. **CP-MacLA**

What Have We All—a Soliloquy of Essences. Marsden Hartley. **CP-HartM**

What have we done this winter to deserve. Fly. John Updike. **CP-UpdiJ**

What have *we* ever done to bear this grudge. The Plea of the Simla Dancers. Rudyard Kipling. **CP-KiplR**

What Have You Brought Home from the Wars? Muriel Rukeyser. **CP-RukeM**

What Have You Got of Your Own. Al Young. **CP-YounA**

What have you left for us to say to you? Letter to the Old Men. Kenneth Patchen. **CP-PatcK**

What have you looked at, Moon. To the Moon. Thomas Hardy. **CP-HardT**

What he holds to / is a cross. The Women. Robert Creeley. **CP-CreeR**

What, he on whom our voices unanimously ran. The Pope and the Net. Robert Browning. **CP-BroR2**

What He[e] Suffered. Ben Jonson. *Fr.* A Celebration of Charis in Ten Lyric[k] Pieces [*or* Peeces]. **CP-JonsB**

What He—who, 'mid the kindred throng. Effusion in the Pleasure-Ground on the Banks of the Bran, Near Dunkeld. William Wordsworth. **CP-WorW2**

What heartbeats, lisping like a lizard in a broken cistern. Ode to the Present Century. Thomas Merton. **CP-MertT**

What heaven-entreated [*or* heaven-besiegèd *or* heav'n-beseiged] heart is this? Richard Crashaw. **CP-CrasR**

(Letter to the Countess of Denbigh.) **CP-CrasR**

What Heavenly Smiles! O Lady Mine. William Wordsworth. **CP-WorW2**

What helps it woman to be free from war. 2.14. Ovid. **CP-MarlC,** *tr. by* Christopher Marlowe; *Fr.* Elegies.

What knew we hope for, we shall once inherit. Faith. Robert Herrick. **CP-HerrR**

What hill can ever hold us? Cats and a Cock. Muriel Rukeyser. **CP-RukeM**

What holds the floor up, Father. Taking Sides. Dabney Stuart. **SP-StuaD**

What hope is here for modern rhyme. Tennyson. **EnVR; MeMBP; PP** *Fr.* In Memoriam A. H. H. **CP-TennA**

What hurrying human tides, or day or night! Broadway. Walt Whitman. **CP-WhitW**

What I am is not important, whether I live or die. Children in Exile. James Fenton. **SP-FentJ**

What I am learning to give you is my death. Wendell Berry. *Fr.* The Country of Marriage. **CP-BerrW**

What I am not, and what I fain would be. An Epistle to Master Arth[ur] Squib. Ben Jonson. **CP-JonsB**

What I am now is the cock. What Must I Do To Be Lost? Charles Kenneth Williams. **CP-WillC**

What I am saying now was said before. Sonnet. Countee Cullen. **CP-CullC**

What I can do—I will. Emily Dickinson. **CP-DickE**

What I did I did. Letter to Her. Robert Bly. **SP-BlyR**

What I did not say the other day to you for today. Or a Valentine. Louis Zukofsky. **CP-ZukLS**

What, I disturb thee at thy morning-meal. Cherries. Robert Browning. **CP-BroR2**

What I Expected. Stephen Spender. **CP-SpenS**

What I fancy, I approve. No Loathsomnesse in Love. Robert Herrick. **CP-HerrR**

What i feel when i'm playing guitar. High on Rebellion. Patti Smith. **SP-SmitP**

What I Know About Life. Ogden Nash. **CP-NashO**

What I lost was not a part of this. Old Poet with Distant Admirers. Geoffrey Hill. *Fr.* Soliloquies. **CP-HillG**

What I love best in all the world. Robert Browning. **FaBoPP; OBTV** *Fr.* De Gustibus. **CP-BroR1**

(Italy of the South.) **FaBoPP**

What I miss most is / that live. Fire of Myself. Joseph Ceravolo. **SP-CeraJ**

What I saw in his head. The Friend. Robert Creeley. **CP-CreeR**

What I See. Muriel Rukeyser. **CP-RukeM**

What I see not, I better see. Emily Dickinson. **CP-DickE**

What I think I am looking for is a place. Sometimes. John Yau. **SP-YauJo**

What I took in my hand. Song Robert Creeley. **CP-CreeR**

What I used to regard as a glory shut in my face. Life. Juan Ramón Jiménez. *Fr.* Ten Short Poems. **CP-WrigJ**

What I want in heart. But of Life? Kenneth Patchen. **CP-PatcK**

What I Want to Say. Mona Van Duyn. **SP-VanDM**

What I Wanted to Say. Stephen Berg. **SP-BergS**

What I was would not work. Encounter in the Cage Country. James Dickey. **CP-DickJ**

What, I wonder, were we hurrying to. Leaving Church Early. John Updike. **CP-UpdiJ**

What I'd Like to Do. Allen Ginsberg. **CP-GinsA**

What I'd like to know is. Kenneth Patchen. **CP-PatcK**

What I'd really like to do tonight. Mrs. Barton Sutter. **SP-SuttB**

What idiocy could transform the moon, that old sea-overgrown. Not the Moon. Margaret Atwood. **SP-AtwM2**

What If a Day [or a Month or a Year]. Thomas Campion. **CP-CampT**

What if a much of a which of a wind. Edward Estlin Cummings. **CP-CummE; SP-CummE**

What if his glance is bold and free. To a Brown Girl. Countee Cullen. **CP-CullC**

What if I bade you leave. Those Images. William Butler Yeats. **CP-YeatW**

What if I say I shall not wait! Emily Dickinson. **CP-DickE**

What if it should turn out eternity. A Steeple on the House. Robert Frost. **CP-FrosR**

What if our numbers barely could defy. William Wordsworth. **CP-WorW1**

What if Prince Paris, after taking thought. Judgement of Paris. Robert Ranke Graves. **CP-GravR**

What If Some Little Paine the Passage Have. Edmund Spenser. **CH; EtS** *Fr.* The Faerie Queene. **CP-Spens**

What if the ethical gunmen isolated evil. How Humble We Were before This. Charles Kenneth Williams. **CP-WillC**

What if the foot, ordain'd the dust to tread. Alexander Pope. **FaBoPV** *Fr.* An Essay on Man. **CP-PopeA**

What if the poet in a moment of terror. The Helmet of Goliath. Robert Duncan. **SP-DuncR**

What if the psychologians, those grand old frauds. Sonnet. Hayden Carruth. **CP-CarHS** *Fr.* Sonnets.

What if the revolution comes and I'm in it and my job. The Rabbit Fights for His Life the Leopard Eats Lunch. Charles Kenneth Williams. **CP-WillC**

What if the wild confinement were empty. The City after Noon. Thomas Merton. **CP-MertT**

What if the wind do howl without. Right's Security. Paul Laurence Dunbar. **CP-DunbP**

What if the world's corruption nears. The Ultimate Act. Adrienne Rich. **CP-RicAE**

What if this present were the world's last night? John Donne. **EBEV; HeIP; ImPo; InPS; JCP; LiTB; MeLP; NAEL-1; NOCV; NOSC; OAEP; OBS; OxAEP-1; PeECV; PoE; SeCeV; Son; TEP** *Fr.* Divine Meditations. **CP-DonnJ** *Fr.* Holy Sonnets. **CP-DonnJ**

What if to edge of dream. Owl, The. Walter de la Mare. **CP-DeLaW**

What I'm about to say should have been said. Waving Good-Bye. Leonard Nathan. **SP-NathL**

What I'm Doing Here. Leonard Cohen. **CP-CoheL**

What I'm trying to say is that if an experience is. Around the Fire. Ted Berrigan. **SP-BerrT**

What impression God and reason. The Fifth of November. Christopher Smart. *Fr.* Hymns and Spiritual Songs for the Fasts and Festivals of the Church of England. **SP-SmarC**

What indeed is Earth but a Nest. Emily Dickinson. **SP-DickE**

What Inn is this. Emily Dickinson. **CP-DickE**

What intense colloquy with the self. Gilbert Sorrentino. **SP-SorrG**

What is / a / voyage / ? Edward Estlin Cummings. **CP-CummE**

What is a day, what is a year of vain delight and pleasure? *Unknown.* ("What is a day, what is a yeere.") **CP-CampT**

What is a day, what is a yeere. *Unknown. See* What is a day, what is a year of vain delight and pleasure?

What is a Jew in solitude? Yom Kippur 1984. Adrienne Rich. **SP-RicA1**

What is a judge? A judge is a seated torso and head sworn before God. Carl Sandburg. *Fr.* The People, Yes. **CP-SandC**

What is a kiss[e]? Why this, as some approve. A Kiss[e]. Robert Herrick. **CP-HerrR**

What Is a Man to Do? David Herbert Lawrence. **CP-LawrD**

What is a man worth? Buyers and Sellers. Carl Sandburg. **CP-SandC**

What Is a Person? Phoebe Hesketh. **SP-HeskP**

What Is a Saint. Leonard Cohen. **CP-CoheL**

What is a What Not. What Nots? Hart Crane. **CP-CranH**

What is a woman that you forsake her. Harp Song of the Dane Women. Rudyard Kipling. **CP-KiplR** *Fr.* The Knights of the Joyous Venture. *Fr.* Puck of Pook's Hill.

What is Africa to me. Heritage. Countee Cullen. **CP-CullC**

What Is and Is Not. Charles Kenneth Williams. **CP-WillC**

What is around me is. Mother Country. Anne Waldman. **SP-WaldA**

What is beyond reproof / Is done in this building. Thomas Merton. **CP-MertT**

What Is Bibbidi-Bobbidi-Boo in Sanskrit? Ogden Nash. **CP-NashO**

What is death, I ask. Hurry Up Please It's Time. Anne Sexton. **CP-SextA**

What Is God? Phoebe Hesketh. **SP-HeskP**

What is God, we shall never know! The Song of Don Ramon. David Herbert Lawrence. **CP-LawrD**

What is good for a bootless bene? Force of Prayer, The; or, The Founding of Bolton Priory; A Tradition. William Wordsworth. **CP-WorW1**

What is green in me. Stepping Westward. Denise Levertov. **CP-LeveD**

What is hard to hide? the Fire! Confession. Johann Wolfgang von Goethe, *tr. fr.* German by George Meredith. **CP-MerG2**

What Is He? David Herbert Lawrence. **CP-LawrD**

What is he buzzing in my ears? Confessions. Robert Browning. **CP-BroR1**

What is he saying? What is the Madman saying. And If You Don't See What You Want, Ask for It. Edwin Rolfe. **CP-RolfE**

What is he staring at, that waif. Recollections. Ussin Kerim, *tr. fr. Bulgarian* by William Matthews. **SP-MattW**

What is heaven? 'tis a country. Heaven. Christina Georgina Rossetti. **CP-RosC3**

What is important about Tarzan is muscles, he is. You White Cunning Devils. William Dickey. **SP-DickW**

What is it all for, this poetry. August 22, 1939. Kenneth Rexroth. **SP-RexrK**

What is it, child, you ask of me? Ut Quid Iubes, Pusiole. Godeschalk. *Fr.* Four Medieval Latin Poems. **CP-MacNL**

What is it for / this form of saying, truce. Ars Poetica. Charles Tomlinson. **CP-TomlC**

What is it, Gwen, my girl? why do you hover and haunt me? Fragment. Gerard Manley Hopkins. **CP-HopkG**

What is it I most want in all the world? To Tell and Be Told. Robert Ranke Graves. **CP-GravR**

What is it, it does not. Margaret Atwood. **SP-AtwM1**

What is it Jesus saith unto the soul? Christina Georgina Rossetti. **CP-RosC2**

What is it like to have just one shirt. The Likeness. Leonard Nathan. **SP-NathL**

What is it men in women do require? William Blake. **ErPo; FaBoEE; GBL; MeMBP; NoP; OAEL-2; OxBM** *Fr.* Several Questions Answered. **CP-BlakW**

(Question Answered, The [*or* A].) **ErPo; FaBoEE; GBL; MeMBP; NoP; OxBM**

What is it that all men possess, among themselves conversing? Thomas Campion. **CP-CampT**

What is it that goes round and round the house. The Riddle. Louis MacNeice. **CP-MacNL**

What is it that sings when the other voices are silent? The Voice. Philippe Jaccottet. *Fr.* Three Poems by Phillipe Jaccottet. **SP-MahoD**

What is it that tells my soul the Sun is setting? William Wordsworth. **CP-WorW1**

What is it to grow old? Growing Old. Matthew Arnold. **SP-ArnoM**

What is it to look into a human eye. Name-Day Night. Charles Olson. **CP-OlsoC**

What is it to sail. Ralph Waldo Emerson. **CP-EmerR**

What is it we want: not battleships. Pick Up the Evening Paper. Kenneth Patchen. **CP-PatcK**

What is it you're mumbling, old Father, my Dad? By the Exeter River. Donald Hall. **CP-HallD**

What Is Life? Samuel Taylor Coleridge. **CP-ColeS**

What is Life? John Haines. **SP-HainJ**

What is life? Life is stepping down a step or sitting in a chair. You and Me and P.B. Shelley. Ogden Nash. **CP-NashO**

What is life that we should love it. Present and Future. Christina Georgina Rossetti. **CP-RosC3**

What is love—. Robert Creeley. **CP-CreeR**

What is Love? Robert Ranke Graves. **CP-GravR**

What Is Man? Bible, *O.T. See* Psalm 8: "O Lord our Lord, how excellent. . . ."

What is man that you should weigh. Levity. Donald Davie. **CP-DavDo**

What Is Man Without an Income. David Herbert Lawrence. **CP-LawrD**

What is meant by a "true man"? The True Man. Chuang Tzu, *tr. fr. Chinese* by Thomas Merton. **CP-MertT**

What is more gentle than a wind in summer? Sleep and Poetry. John Keats. **CP-KeatJ**

What is more odious than all. Disguised as Humpty-Dumpty, W. D. Practices Tumbling. William DeWitt Snodgrass. **SP-SnodW**

What is most like a bee in May? "Lewis Carroll." *Fr.* Puzzles. *Fr.* Puzzles from Wonderland. **CP-CarrL**

What is named. The Need for Dictionaries II. Thomas McGrath. **SP-McGrT**

What is nightfall. Prelude. Al Young. **CP-YounA**

What is our innocence. What Are Years? Marianne Craig Moore. **CP-MoorM**

What is our life? a play of passion. Sir Walter Ralegh. **CP-RaleW** (On the Life of Man.) **CP-RaleW**

What is—"Paradise." Emily Dickinson. **CP-DickE**

What is past is here, as we. Gilbert Sorrentino. **SP-SorrG**

What Is Pink? Christina Georgina Rossetti. **CP-RosC2**

What Is Poetry. John Ashbery. **SP-AshbJ**

WHAT IS PRUDERY? / 'Tis a Beldam. Answer to the Following Question of Mrs. Howe. Alexander Pope. **CP-PopeA**

What is reality? Self in 1958. Anne Sexton. **CP-SextA**

What is required of us is the recognition of the frontiers. Geography of this Time. Archibald MacLeish. **CP-MacLA**

What Is Sacrament. Marsden Hartley. **CP-HartM**

What is She? Charlotte Smith.

　　Epilogue [A] to *What Is She?*. **CP-SmitC**

　　Epilogue [B] to *What Is She?*. **CP-SmitC**

　　Epilogue [C] to *What Is She?*. **CP-SmitC**

　　Prologue to *What is She? A Comedy, in Five Acts.* **CP-SmitC**

"What is she[?]"—Aye, there's the important question. Epilogue [A] to *What Is She?*. Charlotte Smith. **CP-SmitC** *Fr.* What is She?

What is she, while I live?—. The Other. Theodore Roethke. **CP-RoetT**

What Is She Writing? Perhaps It Will Be Good. Stevie Smith. **CP-SmitS**

What is so strange about a tree alone in an open field? Hunting Pheasants in a Cornfield. Robert Bly. **SP-BlyR**

What is sometimes called a / tongue of flame. Autumn. Grace Paley. **CP-PaleG**

What is strictly fiercely and wholly dies. Edward Estlin Cummings. **CP-CummE**

"What is that flower?" we asked right away. What a sight! Postcards from Cape Split. Mona Van Duyn. **SP-VanDM**

What is that smoke that ever still. Emily Brontë. **CP-BronE**

What Is That to Thee? Follow Thou Me. Christina Georgina Rossetti. **CP-RosC2**

What Is the Beautiful? Kenneth Patchen. **CP-PatcK**

What Is the beginning? Love. What the course? Love still. Christina Georgina Rossetti. **CP-RosC2**

What Is the Blues? Al Young. **CP-YounA**

What is the boy now, who has lost his ball. The Ball Poem. John Berryman. **CP-BerrJ**

What is the division between good intention. Short Rides. Stephen Dobyns. **SP-DobyS**

What is the end of fame? 'Tis but to fill. Byron. **OBCoV** *Fr.* Canto the First. **EnRP; NAEL-2; NoP; OAEL-2; PoE** *Fr.* Don Juan. **CP-Byron**

What is the face, the fairest face, till Care. To Madame Garschine. Robert Louis Stevenson. **CP-StevR**

What is the form is the gro- / tesquerie—the accident. The Place. Robert Creeley. **CP-CreeR**

What is the heavy, hot hand. Loss. David Herbert Lawrence. **CP-LawrD**

"What is the jewel colour?" Hilda Doolittle. **NALW** *Fr.* Tribute to the Angels. **CP-DoolH**

What is the metre of the dictionary? Dylan Thomas. **CMoP; FaBoMo** *Fr.* Altarwise by Owl-Light. **CP-ThomD**

What is the moral? Who rides may read. The Winners. Rudyard Kipling. **CP-KiplR** *Fr.* The Story of the Gadsbys.

What is the name of King Ringang's daughter? Beauty Rohtraut. Eduard Friedrich Mörike, tr. fr. German by George Meredith. **CP-MerG1**

What is the noise that shakes the night. Christmas in the Elgin Room. Thomas Hardy. **CP-HardT**

What is the point. Songless. Alice Walker. **CP-WalkA**

What is the reason Coone so dully smels? Upon Coone. Robert Herrick. **CP-HerrR**

What is the skill of this waking? Heard the singing. For Kayle Boyle. Muriel Rukeyser. **CP-RukeM**

What is the song the children sing. A Counting-Out Song. Rudyard Kipling. **CP-KiplR** *Fr.* Land and Sea Tales.

What is the task that to the Muse belongs? Lines on Marlefield. James Thomson. **CP-ThomJ**

What Is the Time?; or, St. Hugh of Lincoln. Stevie Smith. **CP-SmitS**

What is the use of being sagacious. Sagacity. Richard Eberhart. **CP-EberR**

What is the world, O soldiers? Napoleon. Walter de la Mare. **CP-DeLaW**

What is there for us two. Fifty-Fifty. Carl Sandburg. **CP-SandC**

What is there in my heart that you should sue. Lachrimae Amantis. Geoffrey Hill. **GTBS-6; NOCV** *Fr.* Lachrimae; or Seven Tears Figured in Seven Passionate Pavans. **CP-HillG**

What is there in the universal Earth. To the Ladies Who Saw Me Crowned. John Keats. **CP-KeatJ**

What is there in the vale of life. Love Abused. William Cowper. **CP-CowpW**

What is there which so approaches an art form in its stubborn patience, its devotion to technique. Resentment. Charles Kenneth Williams. **SP-WillC**

What is this above thy head, / O Man? Christina Georgina Rossetti. **CP-RosC2**

What is this, behind this veil, is it ugly, is it beautiful? A Birthday Present. Sylvia Plath. **CP-PlatS**

What is this creature who must sweat all day. A Riddle the Sphinx Forgot. Howard Nemerov. **CP-NemeH**

What is this flesh and blood compounded of. Allen Tate. *Fr.* Sonnets of the Blood. **CP-TateA**

What is this strange and uncouth thing? The Cross[e]. George Herbert. **CP-HerbG**

What is this whiteness on the fields? Grace Paley. **CP-PaleG**

What is thy mouth to me? Edward Estlin Cummings. **CP-CummE**

What is to be born already fidgets in the stem. A Christmas Card, After the Assassinations. Mona Van Duyn. **SP-VanDM**

What is to be understood. Gilbert Sorrentino. **SP-SorrG**

What is truth? says Pilate. Louis MacNeice. **CP-MacNL**

What is war. War, the Destroyer. William Carlos Williams. **CP-WilW2**

What is Worthless? Robinson Jeffers. **CP-JefR3**

What is your substance, whereof are you made. Sonnet 53. William Shakespeare. **CTC; EBEV; EIL; EnRePo; FaFP; ImPo; LiTB; MasP; NoSic; OAEL-1; OAEP; OBEV; OBSC; OXAEP-1; PeHV; SCGP** *Fr.* Sonnets. **CP-ShaWS**

What islands known, what passages discovered. Ship's Log. Archibald MacLeish. **CP-MacLA**

What is't, fine Grand, makes thee my friendship fly. To Fine Grand. Ben Jonson. **CP-JonsB**

What is't that wasts a Prince? example showes. Flatterie. Robert Herrick. **CP-HerrR**

What it is, the literal size / incorporates. The Riddle. Robert Creeley. **CP-CreeR**

What It Was Like. Charles Tomlinson. *Fr.* Four Kantian Lyrics. **CP-TomlC**

What it was struck the terror into me? Imperante Augusto Natus Est. Robert Browning. **CP-BroR2**

What itch of contrdiction bids me find. Conacre. John Hewitt. **CP-HewiJ**

What Joy to Live. Robert Southwell. **CP-SoutR**

What just excuse had agèd Time. Ben Jonson. **CP-JonsB** *Fr.* Love Freed from Ignorance and Folly.

What, keep love in *perspective?*—that old lie. In Perspective. Robert Ranke Graves. **CP-GravR**

What Kind of a Guy Was He? Howard Nemerov. **CP-NemeH**

What kind of beast would turn its life into words? Adrienne Rich. *Fr.* Twenty-one Love Poems. **SP-RicA1; SP-RicA2**

What Kind of Mistress[e] He Would Have. Robert Herrick. **CP-HerrR**

What kind of people / Are these? Some stammer. Love Poem in Twos and Threes. Robert Bly. **SP-BlyR**

What kind of woman goes searching and searching? Searching / Not Searching. Muriel Rukeyser. **CP-RukeM**

What know we of the Blest above. Scene on the Lake of Brientz. William Wordsworth. *Fr.* Memorials of a Tour of the Continent; 1820. **CP-WorW2**

What laid, I said. Rhyme. Louise Bogan. **CP-BogaL**

What large, dark hands are those at the window. Love on the Farm. David Herbert Lawrence. **CP-LawrD**

What lasts is what you start with. A Journal of Southern Rivers. Charles Wright. **SP-WrigC**

What length of verse can serve brave *Mopsa*'s good to show?, *speech of Alethes.* Sir Philip Sidney. **SP-SidnP** *Fr.* Arcadia.

What life is better—stone and stone? Northwest Retrospective: Mark Tobey. Richard Hugo. **CP-HugoR**

What lifts the ocean into clouds. To Evaporation. John Updike. *Fr.* Seven Odes to Seven Natural Processes. **CP-UpdiJ**

What light painted. Secret. James McAuley. *Fr.* Requiem. **SP-McAuJ**

What light will, in your eyes, like an archangel. Holy Communion: the City. Thomas Merton. **CP-MertT**

What lightning / strikes. Time Spans. Archie Randolph Ammons. **SP-AmmoA**

What links are ours with orbs that are. Meditation under Stars. George Meredith. **CP-MerG1**

What lips my lips have kissed, and where, and why. Edna St. Vincent Millay. **CP-MillE**

What Little Happened There. John Hewitt. **CP-HewiJ**

What lively lad most pleasured me. *fr.* A Woman Young and Old. William Butler Yeats. **CP-YeatW**

What lovelier forms things wear. Hafiz, tr. by Ralph Waldo Emerson. **CP-EmerR** *Fr.* Odes.

What lovelier home could gentle Fancy choose? Between Namur and Liege. William Wordsworth. *Fr.* Memorials of a Tour of the Continent; 1820. **CP-WorW2**

What lovely things / Thy hand hath made. The Scribe. Walter de la Mare. **CP-DeLaW**

What made that mirth last night? the neighbours say. Upon Bran. Robert Herrick. **CP-HerrR**

What made the place a landscape of despair. Claus von Stauffenberg. Thom Gunn. **CP-GunnT**

What Magic Drum? William Butler Yeats. **CP-YeatW**

What makes it hard to understand. George Meredith. **CP-MerG2**

What makes my bed seem hard seeing it is soft? 1.2. Ovid. **CP-MarlC**, *tr.* by Christopher Marlowe; *Fr.* Elegies.

What makes one man go mad makes. Veterans of Foreign Wars. Gilbert Sorrentino. **SP-SorrG**

What makes people unsatisfied. Courage. David Herbert Lawrence. **CP-LawrD**

What man could do. The Crowded Countries of the Bomb. George Oppen. **CP-OppeG**

What Man could esteem, or what Woman could love. Epitaph on R. Muir. Robert Burns. **CP-BurnR**

What man could stomach the sight. Carmen 29. Catullus. *Fr.* Carmina. **CP-Catul**

What man is he, that boasts of fleshly might. Edmund Spenser. **FHYEP** *Fr.* The Faerie Queene. **CP-Spens**

What man is he that yearneth. Sophocles, tr. by A. E. Housman. **CP-HousA** *Fr.* Oedipus at Colonus.

What man may learn, what man may do. Robert Louis Stevenson. **CP-StevR**

What man so wise, what earthly wit so ware. Edmund Spenser. **FHYEP** *Fr.* The Faerie Queene. **CP-Spens**

What man will now take liberal arts in hand. 3.7. Ovid. **CP-MarlC**, *tr.* by Christopher Marlowe; *Fr.* Elegies.

What marching men of Buffalo. Nicholas Vachel Lindsay. *Fr.* Niagara. **CP-LindV**

What? Mars his sword? faire Cytherea say. Upon Venus Putting on Mars His Armes. Leonidas of Alexandria, *tr. fr. Classical Greek by* Richard Crashaw. **CP-CrasR**

What Mary is when she a little smiles. Dante Alighieri. **CP-ShelP**, *tr.* by Percy Bysshe Shelley; *Fr.* La Vita Nuova.

What matter for thick armchairs and fine shelves for books? Jim Carroll. **SP-CarrJ**

What matter that you understood no word! Ribh in Ecstasy. William Butler Yeats. **CP-YeatW**

What Matter the Pangs of a Husband and Father. Byron. **CP-Byron**

What Matters. David Herbert Lawrence. **CP-LawrD**

What matters that I stormed and swore? For an Anarchist. Countee Cullen. **CP-CullC**

What may the woman labour to confess? George Meredith. *Fr.* Modern Love. **CP-MerG1**

What may we chant, O thou within this tomb? Outlines for a Tomb. Walt Whitman. **CP-WhitW**

What may words say, or what may words not say. Sonnet 35. Sir Philip Sidney. *Fr.* Astrophil and Stella. **SP-SidnP**

What meanes this folly, now to brave it so. Thomas Campion. **CP-CampT**

What means this stately tablature. Richard Lovelace. **CP-LoveR**

(To My Noble Kinsman T.S. Esq.) **CP-LoveR**

What means [*or* meaneth *or* menethe] this when I lie [*or* lye] alone. Sir Thomas Wyatt. **CP-WyatT**

What means you apparition in the sky. A Pastoral Betwixt David, Thirsis, and the Angel Gabriel, upon the Birth of our Saviour. James Thomson. **CP-ThomJ**

What men gain fairly—that they should possess. Fragment. Percy Bysshe Shelley. **CP-ShelP**

What merriment has taen the whigs. The German Lairdie. Robert Burns. **CP-BurnR**

What message from imagined Paradise. Kathleen Jessie Raine. **SP-RainK**

What mighty princes poets are! those things. To My Friend Will. Davenant, upon His Poem of "Madagascar." Sir John Suckling. **CP-SuckJ**

What mind lying open to my mind. On a Cold Night. Frank Templeton Prince. **CP-PrinF**

What Miracles the News is! Emily Dickinson. **SP-DickE**

What mischief cleaves to unsubdued regret. Composed by the Sea-Shore. William Wordsworth. **CP-WorW2**

What mist hath dimd that glorious face? what seas of griefe my sun doth tosse? The Virgin Mary to Christ on the Crosse. Robert Southwell. **CP-SoutR**

What more is there to love than I have loved? Montrachet-le-Jardin. Wallace Stevens. **CP-StevW**

What more is there to say in a pome? Election Night Pome. Al Young. **CP-YounA**

What mournful stave, what bellow shakes the grove? Basil Bunting. *Fr.* Attis: Or, Something Missing. **CP-BuntB**

What Must. Archibald MacLeish. **CP-MacLA**

What must a man do to be at home in the world? The Silence. Wendell Berry. **CP-BerrW**

What Must I Do To Be Lost? Charles Kenneth Williams. **CP-WillC**

What My Child Learns of the Sea. Audre Lorde. **SP-LordA**

What! my friend! you're surely daft. Glee. George Meredith. **CP-MerG2**

What my hand follows on your body. Beneath My Hand and Eye the Distant Hills, Your Body. Gary Snyder. **CP-SnydG**

What mystery pervades a well! Emily Dickinson. **CP-DickE**

What name could. Stormy. William Carlos Williams. **CP-WilW2**

What name do I have for you? Just Walking Around. John Ashbery. **SP-AshbJ**

What nature, alas! has denied. The Winter Nosegay. William Cowper. **CP-CowpW**

What need has man of heavenly things. Two Triolets. Wystan Hugh Auden. **CP-AudWJ**

What need hast thou of me, or of my muse. To Robert, Earl of Salisbury. Ben Jonson. **CP-JonsB**

What need of clamorous bells, or ribands gay. Composed on the Eve of the Marriage of a Friend in the Vale of Grasmere, 1812. William Wordsworth. **CP-WorW1**

What need? This strange desire for something which desire. The Roses of Life. Kenneth Patchen. **CP-PatcK**

What need we marry Women, when. Women Uselesse. Robert Herrick. **CP-HerrR**

What need you, being come to sense. September 1913. William Butler Yeats. **CP-YeatW**

What needest thou?—a few brief hours of rest. Vain Questioning. Walter de la Mare. **CP-DeLaW**

What needeth these threnning words and wasted wind? Sir Thomas Wyatt. **CP-WyatT**

What needs complaints. Comfort to a Youth That Had Lost His Love. Robert Herrick. **CP-HerrR**

What needs my *Shakespear[e]* for his honour'd [*or* honoured *or* honored] Bones. On Shakespear[e]. John Milton. **CP-MiltJ**

What needs this din about the town o' Lon'on. Scots Prologue, For Mrs. Sutherland's Benefit Night, Spoken at the Theatre Dumfries. Robert Burns. **CP-BurnR**

What never is but only is to be. The Indifference of the Heavens. Samuel Taylor Coleridge. **CP-ColeS**

What never was no, & still will be. Ralph Waldo Emerson. **CP-EmerR**

What new element before us unborn in nature? Is there a new thing under the Sun? Plutonian Ode. Allen Ginsberg. **CP-GinsA**

What News, What News? Queen Orraca. Byron. **CP-Byron**

What! no more favours? Not a ribbon more. To a Lady That Forbade to Love before Company. Sir John Suckling. **CP-SuckJ**

What, No Oysters? Ogden Nash. **CP-NashO**

What no, Perdy [*or* Perdie *or* perdie][!] ye may be sure[!]. Sir Thomas Wyatt. **CP-WyatT**

What, No Sheep? Ogden Nash. **CP-NashO**

What not to do for him. Accomplishment. Tess Gallagher. **SP-GallT**

What nothing earthly gives, or can destroy. The Soul's Calm Sunshine. Alexander Pope. **FaBoRV** *Fr.* An Essay on Man. **CP-PopeA**

What Nots? Hart Crane. **CP-CranH**

What now / what now dumb nigger damn near dead. Another Poem for Me (after Recovering from an O.D.) Etheridge Knight. **SP-KnigE**

What now do the waves say. Foreign Shore, Old Woman, Slaughter of Octopus. Robert Penn Warren. **SP-WarrR**

What, now, in the eighties! Smoking Pot on the Bus. Thom Gunn. **CP-GunnT**

What now, O Man! thou dost, or mean'st to do. For a Market-Clock. Samuel Taylor Coleridge. **CP-ColeS**

What now we like, anon we disapprove. Change Gives Content. Robert Herrick. **CP-HerrR**

What Odd Expedients. Robinson Jeffers. **CP-JefR3**

What of It? Robinson Jeffers. **CP-JefR3**

What of the Day? John Greenleaf Whittier. **CP-WhitJ**

What of the diary. Lost in the Stars. Gilbert Sorrentino. **SP-SorrG**

What of the faith and fire within us. Men Who March Away. Thomas Hardy. **CP-HardT**

What of the hunting, hunter bold? Rudyard Kipling. **CP-KiplR** *Fr.* Tiger-Tiger. *Fr.* The Second Jungle Book.

What of the Night? Stanley Jasspon Kunitz. **CP-KuniS**

"One summer, like a stone."

"What wakes me now."

What of the structure of Rime? I said. Robert Duncan. **SP-DuncR** *Fr.* The Structure of Rime.

What of this man? No striding Amos sent. Richard Jefferies. Wystan Hugh Auden. **CP-AudWJ**

What offspring other men have got. Upon His Verses. Robert Herrick. **CP-HerrR**

What on earth does one say at a Gaudy. Toast, A. Wystan Hugh Auden. *Fr.* Eleven Occasional Poems. **CP-AudeW**

What other men do with other women. Geoffrey Hill. *Fr.* The Songbook of Sebastian Arrurruz. **CP-HillG**

What other oaths are wanted now? Carl Sandburg. *Fr.* The People, Yes. **CP-SandC**

What others have cheapnesse seene, and ease. To His Brother Nicolas Herrick. Robert Herrick. **CP-HerrR**

What over and which under. Edward Estlin Cummings. **CP-CummE**

What Ovid Taught Me. Alice Walker. **CP-WalkA**

What pain, to wake and miss you! Quite Forsaken. David Herbert Lawrence. **CP-LawrD**

What Parents Do Not Yet Know. Kay Boyle. **CP-BoylK**

What passing-bells for these who die as cattle? Anthem for Doomed Youth. Wilfred Owen. **CP-OwenW**

What Patron could I chuse, great *Lord*, but you? To the Right Honourable, Both in Birth and Vertue, Francis, Earle of Cumberland. Thomas Campion. **CP-CampT**

What Place Is Besieged? Walt Whitman. **CP-WhitW**

What place is this? / All's strange to me, and I. Heresy. Walter de la Mare. **CP-DeLaW**

What place is this. At the Centre. Thom Gunn. **CP-GunnT**

What Plagues, what Tortures are in store for thee. Samuel Johnson. **CP-JohnS** *Fr.* Irene.

What pleasanter task for All Fools' Day than going over all the. Raven, Don't Stay Away from My Door—A Chant for April First. Ogden Nash. **CP-NashO**

What pleased him more. The Days of Yore. Stevie Smith. **CP-SmitS**

What pleasure can a bannish'd creature have. Sonnet 38. Mary Sidney, Countess of Montgomery Wroth. *Fr.* Pamphilia to Amphilanthus. **CP-WrotM**

What pleasure in such vehement commotion. Boethius, *tr. fr. Latin.* **MLL,** *tr. by* Helen Waddell; *Fr.* Consolation of Philosophy, The ("De Consolacione Philosophie"). **CP-ChauG**

What portents, from what distant region, ride. On the Ice Islands Seen Floating in the German Ocean. William Cowper. **CP-CowpW**

What potions have I drunk of Siren tears. Sonnet 119. William Shakespeare. **OXAEP-1; WHA** *Fr.* Sonnets. **CP-ShaWS**

What Quetzalcoatl Saw in Mexico. David Herbert Lawrence. **CP-LawrD**

What race is mine, unnatural to earth. Time Is Our House. Louise McNeill. **SP-McNeL**

What rage is this? What furo[u]r of what kind [*or* kynd]? Sir Thomas Wyatt. **CP-WyatT**

What rattles in the dark? The blinds at Brewster? In Limbo. Richard Wilbur. **CP-WilbR**

What rich joke does. Natural Question. John Updike. **CP-UpdiJ**

What Riddle Asked the Sphinx. Archibald MacLeish. **CP-MacLA**

What rider spurs him from the darkening east. Edna St. Vincent Millay. **CP-MillE**

What Sappho Would Have Said Had Her Leap Cured Instead of Killing Her. Christina Georgina Rossetti. **CP-RosC3**

What Savage Blossom. Edna St. Vincent Millay. **CP-MillE**

What savage world is this when folk to live. Minotaur. John Hewitt. **CP-HewiJ**

"What say I?"—not a syllable further in prose. Fragment of an Epistle to Thomas Moore. Byron. **CP-Byron**

What say you, critic, now you have become. Camelus Saltat. George Meredith. **CP-MerG1**

What says the wind to the waving trees? The Secret. Paul Laurence Dunbar. **CP-DunbP**

What scenes appear where-e'er I turn my view. Eloisa. Alexander Pope. SeCePo *Fr.* Eloisa to Abelard. **CP-PopeA**

What seas what shores what grey rocks and what islands. Marina. Thomas Stearns Eliot. **CP-ElioT**

What seems a soul where Love's outside the porch. Response to a Translation by Longfellow. Robert Browning. **CP-BroR2**

What Semiramis Said. Nicholas Vachel Lindsay. **CP-LindV**

What shakes the eye but the invisible? The Decision. Theodore Roethke. **CP-RoetT**

What shall a poor girl do. Cappadocian Song. Hayden Carruth. **CP-CarHS**

What shall I bring you? The Colour. Thomas Hardy. **CP-HardT**

What Shall I Do for the Land that Bred Me. Gerard Manley Hopkins. **CP-HopkG**

What shall I do now—it whimpers so. Emily Dickinson. **CP-DickE**

What shall I do when the Summer troubles. Emily Dickinson. **CP-DickE**

What shall I do with my friends. Trees. Robert Creeley. **CP-CreeR**

What shall I do with the Verner money? Lydia Verner. Louise McNeill. **SP-McNeL**

What shall I do with this absurdity. The Tower. William Butler Yeats. **CP-YeatW**

What shall I give my children? who are poor. Gwendolyn Brooks. **SP-BrooG** *Fr.* The Children of the Poor. **SP-BrooG**, *sect.* I, *pt.* 1-5; *Fr.* The Womanhood.

What shall I render to thy Name. In Thankful[l] Remembrance for My Dear Husband[']s Safe Arrival[l]. Anne Bradstreet. **CP-BradA**

What shall I say, because talk I must? The Yellow Flower. William Carlos Williams. **CP-WilW2**

What shall I say, dear friends, to whom I owe. Farewell, A. John Greenleaf Whittier. **CP-WhitJ**

What shall I say to Walt Whitman tonight? Centennial For Whitman. Richard Eberhart. **CP-EberR**

What shall I say to you all as you watch me dying? Tillie Sage (3). Louise McNeill. **SP-McNeL**

What shall I wish him? Strength and health. Lines Written in an Album. John Greenleaf Whittier. **CP-WhitJ**

What shall the world do with its children? Romans Angry about the Inner World. Robert Bly. **SP-BlyR**

What shall we add now? He is dead. Died. . . . Elizabeth Barrett Browning. **CP-BroEB**

What shall we do with Margery? Margery. Christina Georgina Rossetti. **CP-RosC3**

What shall we know we don't know. Somebody Died. Robert Creeley. **CP-CreeR**

What shall we say of this curious young man? Lord Mope. Stevie Smith. **CP-SmitS**

What shape can I build of rhythm or melody. Sorrow. John Gould Fletcher. **SP-FletJ**

What she has known, how may our hearts surmise? Studies for an Actress. Jean Garrigue. **SP-GarrJ**

What she made in her body is broken. Poem for J. Wendell Berry. **CP-BerrW**

What she refused him—in the name of love. Love as Lovelessness. Robert Ranke Graves. **CP-GravR**

What She Wanted. Ron Koertge. **SP-KoerR**

What Ship Puzzled at Sea. Walt Whitman. **CP-WhitW**

What should a man do but love excellence. Speech to the Detractors. Archibald MacLeish. **CP-MacLA**

What should be counted was counted. Insomnia. Stephen Dunn. **SP-DunnS**

What should I be but a prophet and a liar. The Singing-Woman from the Wood's Edge. Edna St. Vincent Millay. **CP-MillE**

What should I say. Sir Thomas Wyatt. **CP-WyatT**

What should I say of Henry Miller. To the Dean. William Carlos Williams. **CP-WilW2**

What should I tell them? Richard Wilbur. **CRP** *Fr.* The Mind-Reader. **CP-WilbR**

What should one / wish a child / and that, one's own. The Picture of J. T. in a Prospect of Stone. Charles Tomlinson. **CP-TomlC**

What should the young / man say, because he is buying. The Lover. Robert Creeley. **CP-CreeR**

What should we be without the sexual myth. Men Made Out of Words. Wallace Stevens. **CP-StevW**

What shul these clothes thus manyfold. Proverbs. Geoffrey Chaucer. **CP-ChauG**

What Sigbjørn Said. Malcolm Lowry. **CP-LowrM**

What sight so lured him through the fields he knew. Far-Far-Away. Tennyson. **CP-TennA**

What siren zooming is sounding our coming. The Exiles. Wystan Hugh Auden. **CP-AudeW**

What slender youth bedewed [*or* bedew'd] with liquid odours. 1.5. Horace. **CP-MiltJ** *Fr.* Odes.

What so beyond all madness[e] is the elf. Cupid Far Gone. Richard Lovelace. **CP-LoveR**

What? So Soon! Langston Hughes. **SP-HughL**

What Soft—Cherubic Creatures. Emily Dickinson. **CP-DickE**

What soothes the angry snail? Eine Kleine Snailmusik. May Sarton. **SP-SartM**

What sort of man is coming. The Lady's Second Song. William Butler Yeats. **CP-YeatW**

What sort of message—. The Poet's Message. Roy Fisher. **SP-FishR**

What soul would bargain for a cure that brings. George Meredith. **HBV 1-2** *Fr.* Modern Love. **CP-MerG1**

What sound awakened me, I wonder. The Deserter. Alfred Edward Housman. **CP-HousA**

What sounds are those, Helvellyn, that are heard. Retrospect Love of Nature Leading to Love of Mankind. William Wordsworth. *Fr.* The Prelude; Growth of a Poet's Mind [1850 vers.]. **CP-WorW3**

What sounds are those, Helvellyn, that are heard. William Wordsworth. **EnRP** *Fr.* Retrospect Love of Nature Leading to Love of Mankind. *Fr.* The Prelude; Growth of a Poet's Mind [1850 vers.]. **CP-WorW3**

What sounds are those, Helvellyn, which are heard. Retrospect Love of Nature Leading to Love of Mankind. William Wordsworth. *Fr.* The Prelude; Growth of a Poet's Mind [1805 vers.]. **CP-WorW3**

What sphinx of cement and aluminum bashed open their skulls. Allen Ginsberg. **NeAP; PoCh; SOTW; TAP** *Fr.* Howl. **CP-GinsA**

What Splendid Birthdays. Kenneth Patchen. **CP-PatcK**

What splendour of imperial station man. Milton. George Meredith. **CP-MerG2**

What starts things. What. Stephen Dunn. **SP-DunnS**

What State Street Said to South Carolina, and What South Carolina Said to State Street. John Greenleaf Whittier. **CP-WhitJ**

What strikes the eye hurts, what one hears is a lie. Soviet Souvenir. Ted Berrigan. **SP-BerrT**

What strong allurement draws, what spirit guides. To the Planet Venus. William Wordsworth. **CP-WorW2**

What succour can I hope the Muse will send. To the Morning. Satisfaction for Sleepe. Richard Crashaw. **CP-CrasR**

What suns had to rise and set. Three Desk Objects. Margaret Atwood. **SP-AtwM1**

What sweeter music[k] can we bring. A Christmas Caroll Sung to the King in the Presence at White-Hall. Robert Herrick. **CP-HerrR**

What sweeter Shelter than the Hearts. Emily Dickinson. **SP-DickE**

What syllable are you seeking. To the Roaring Wind. Wallace Stevens. **CP-StevW**

What teares (Deare Prince) can serve to water all. A Songe Made by Sir Walter Rawley. *Unknown, sometimes at. to* Sir Walter Ralegh. **CP-RaleW**

What tenements of clover. Emily Dickinson. **CP-DickE**

What the Bird with the Human Head Knew. Anne Sexton. **CP-SextA**

What the Birds Said. John Greenleaf Whittier. **CP-WhitJ**

What the birds say / is colored. Shade. "Internal and External Forms." Donald Hall. **CP-HallD**

What the blind lost when radio. Miller Williams. **SP-WillM** (After the Revolution for Jesus a Secular Man Prepares His Final Remarks.) **SP-WillM**

What the Brand New Freeway Won't Go By. Richard Hugo. **CP-HugoR**

What the Chairman Told Tom. Basil Bunting. **CP-BuntB**

What the children remember about Uncle Jim. Uncle Jim. Peter Meinke. **SP-MeinP**

What the Clown Said. Nicholas Vachel Lindsay. **CP-LindV**

What the Coal-Heaver Said. Nicholas Vachel Lindsay. **CP-LindV**

What the cosmologist meant by what constitutes. Americans, The ("What the cosmologist meant by what constitutes"). Charles Olson. **CP-OlsoC**

What the Country Man Knows By Heart. Barton Sutter. **SP-SuttB**

What the Country Man Knows By Heart. Barton Sutter. **SP-SuttB**

"He would never say any of this."

"Why he lives there he can't say."

What the Deceased Had to Say about Himself. Nicanor Parra, *tr. fr. Spanish by* Thomas Merton. **CP-MertT**

What the Earth Asked Me. James Wright. **CP-WrigJ**

What the Finger Writes. Alice Walker. **CP-WalkA**

What the Forester Said. Nicholas Vachel Lindsay. **CP-LindV**

What the Gardener Said to Mrs. Trail. Malcolm Lowry. **CP-LowrM**

What the Ghost of the Gambler Said. Nicholas Vachel Lindsay. **CP-LindV**

What the Gray-Winged Fairy Said. Nicholas Vachel Lindsay. **CP-LindV**

What the Grecian Earns. Kenneth Patchen. **CP-PatcK**

What the Green Tree Said. Archibald MacLeish. *Fr.* Songs for Eve. **CP-MacLA**

What the hen does. Classical. Hayden Carruth. *Fr.* Poetical Abstracts. **CP-CarHS**

What the Hyena Said. Nicholas Vachel Lindsay. **CP-LindV**

What the Indians. Control Burn. Gary Snyder. **CP-SnydG**

What the Irish Soldier Said. Malcolm Lowry. **CP-LowrM**

What the Lion Said to the Child. Archibald MacLeish. *Fr.* Songs for Eve. **CP-MacLA**

What the Miner in the Desert Said. Nicholas Vachel Lindsay. **CP-LindV**

What the Moon Saw. Nicholas Vachel Lindsay. **CP-LindV**

What the Motorcycle Said. Mona Van Duyn. **SP-VanDM**

What the night prepares. Until the Sea Is Dead. David St. John. **SP-StJoD**

What the Old Women Say. Archibald MacLeish. **CP-MacLA**

What the Owl Sees. Marge Piercy. **SP-PierM**

What the people learn out of lifting and hauling and waiting and losing. Carl Sandburg. **OBAL** *Fr.* The People, Yes. **CP-SandC**

What the People Said. Rudyard Kipling. **CP-KiplR**

What the picture tells me is itself. Tom Clark. *Fr.* Suite. **SP-ClarT**

What the Rattlesnake Said. Nicholas Vachel Lindsay. **CP-LindV**

What the Recent Survey Has Revealed. James McAuley. **SP-McAuJ**

What the Scarecrow Said. Nicholas Vachel Lindsay. **CP-LindV**

What the Serpent Said to Adam. Archibald MacLeish. **ChIV-1; MeMAP; NePA** *Fr.* Songs for Eve. **CP-MacLA**

What the Sexton Said. Nicholas Vachel Lindsay. **CP-LindV**

What the Snow Man Said. Nicholas Vachel Lindsay. **CP-LindV**

What the Traveller Said at Sunset. John Greenleaf Whittier. **CP-WhitJ**

What the Vine Said to Eve. Archibald MacLeish. *Fr.* Songs for Eve. **CP-MacLA**

What the Voice Said. John Greenleaf Whittier. **CP-WhitJ**

What the warbler must have seen. Glass. Brendan Galvin. **SP-GalvB**

What the Well-Read Patient Is Talking About, or, Look, Ma, What I Got! Ogden Nash. **CP-NashO**

What the White Had to Say. Charles Simic. **SP-SimiC**

What the Wind Said to the Water: What the Water Replied. Archibald MacLeish. *Fr.* Songs for Eve. **CP-MacLA**

What the words, / abstracted, tell. Phone. Robert Creeley. **CP-CreeR**

What Then? William Butler Yeats. **CP-YeatW**

What Then Is Evil? David Herbert Lawrence. **CP-LawrD**

What Then Is Love But Mourning? *At.* to Thomas Campion *and* to Philip Rosseter. **CP-CampT**

  ("What thing is love but mourning?") **CP-CampT**

What then is the new surrealism and just who. Barely Aware of the Insistent Loud Roars. Gilbert Sorrentino. **SP-SorrG**

What There Is. Kenneth Patchen. **CP-PatcK**

What there is as a surround to our figures. Pleasure Island. Wystan Hugh Auden. **CP-AudeW**

What they did. At Eleusis. Hilda Doolittle. **CP-DoolH**

What They Said. Muriel Rukeyser. **CP-RukeM**

What they say on the quay is. On the Quay. Theodore Roethke. **CP-RoetT**

What they undertook to do. Gratitude to the Unknown Instructors. William Butler Yeats. **CP-YeatW**

What They Want. Charles Bukowski. **SP-BukC1**

What They Wanted. Stephen Dunn. **SP-DunnS**

What thing is love but mourning? *At.* to Thomas Campion *and* to Philip Rosseter. *See* What Then Is Love But Mourning?

What thing is that that I both have and lack. Sir Thomas Wyatt. **CP-WyatT**

What thing is this that, built of salt and lime. Fatal Interview. Edna St. Vincent Millay. **CP-MillE**

What things for dream there are when specter-like. Waiting. Robert Frost. **CP-FrosR**

What Think You I Take My Pen in Hand? Walt Whitman. **CP-WhitW**

What thou lovest well remains, *subsel.* Ezra Pound. *See* Canto 81: "Zeus lies in Ceres' bosom."

What Thou Lovest Well Remains American. Richard Hugo. **CP-HugoR**

What though around thee blazes. To Massachusetts. John Greenleaf Whittier. **CP-WhitJ**

What though, for showing truth to flatter'd [*or* flattered] state. Written on the Day That Mr. Leigh Hunt Left Prison. John Keats. **CP-KeatJ**

What though green leaves only witness. Wreath for a Bridal. Sylvia Plath. **CP-PlatS**

What though *Harry* braggs, let him be noble. Epigramme. Thomas Campion. *Fr.* Observations in the Art of English Poesie. **CP-CampT**

What though my harp, and viol[l] be. To God, on His Sickness[e]. Robert Herrick. **CP-HerrR**

What though Reason forged your scheme? A Reasonable Constitution. Herman Melville. **SP-MelvH**

What though the Accused, upon his own appeal. Humanity. William Wordsworth. **CP-WorW2**

What though the chilly wide-mouth'd quacking chorus. Lines to a Comic Author, on an Abusive Review. Samuel Taylor Coleridge. **CP-ColeS**

What Though the Field Be Lost? John Milton. **EaLo** *Fr.* Book I. **FHYEP; NAEL-1; OAEL-1; OxAEP-1** *Fr.* Paradise Lost. **CP-MiltJ** (Satan's Adjuration.) **FaBoEn**

What though the Heaven be lowring now. Hope Well and Have Well: or, Faire after Foule Weather. Robert Herrick. **CP-HerrR**

What though the Italian pencil wrought not here. Effusion in the Presence of the Painted Tower of Tell, at Altorf. William Wordsworth. *Fr.* Memorials of a Tour of the Continent; 1820. **CP-WorW2**

What though the music of thy rustic flute. Matthew Arnold. **EPCY** *Fr.* Thyrsis. **SP-ArnoM**

What though the sea be calme? Trust to the shore. Safety on the Shore. Robert Herrick. **CP-HerrR**

What though, while the wonders of nature exploring. To Some Ladies. John Keats. **CP-KeatJ**

What thoughts could ride or hover in my mind. Strambotti. Frank Templeton Prince. **CP-PrinF**

What thoughts I have of you tonight, Walt Whitman. A Supermarket in California. Allen Ginsberg. **CP-GinsA**

What thousands never knew the road! The Narrow Way. William Cowper. *Fr.* Olney Hymns. **CP-CowpW**

What time are the big people. The Big People. César Vallejo, *tr. fr. Spanish by* James Wright. **CP-WrigJ**

What time I lay these rhymes anear thy feet. To Mary Russell Mitford. Elizabeth Barrett Browning. **CP-BroEB**

What time is it i wonder never mind. Edward Estlin Cummings. **CP-CummE**

What time is it in your bedroom? The Green Bus. Jim Carroll. **SP-CarrJ**

What time is it? Yes. Tailpiece. William Carlos Williams. **CP-WilW2**

What time is it?it is by every star. Edward Estlin Cummings. **CP-CummE**

What time of day is it? After Reading H.D.'s *Hermetic Definitions*. Robert Duncan. **SP-DuncR**

What time the Romaine Empire bore the raine. Edmund Spenser. *Fr.* Visions of the World's Vanity [*or* Vanitie]. **CP-Spens**

What times of sweetnesse this faire day fore-shows. Upon One Lillie, Who Married with a Maid Call'd Rose. Robert Herrick. **CP-HerrR**

What to Do? Christina Georgina Rossetti. **CP-RosC3**

What to do / when the days' heavy heart. Peace. Ted Berrigan. **SP-BerrT**

What to Do until the Doctor Goes or It's Tomorrow Than You Think. Ogden Nash. **CP-NashO**

What to do with a day. The Satisfaction Coal Company. Rita Dove. **SP-DoveR**

What to Do with Contributor's Copies? Charles Bukowski. **SP-BukC2**

What to Think When It Rains Blood. Thomas Merton. **CP-MertT; SP-MertT**

What tongue can her perfections tell. Sir Philip Sidney. **SP-SidnP** *Fr.* Arcadia.

What Tottles Meant. "Lewis Carroll." **CP-CarrL** *Fr.* Sylvie and Bruno Concluded.

What tracks the night made. Thaw. Daniel Gerard Hoffman. **SP-HoffD**

What tree may not the fig be gathered from? Wild Grapes. Robert Frost. **CP-FrosR**

What Troubles I Have Seen in Birdlegged Spring. Thomas Merton. **CP-MertT**

What Twigs We held by. Emily Dickinson. **CP-DickE**

What two brave perils of the private sword. On Sir John Roe. Ben Jonson. **CP-JonsB**

What use is it to slumber here. Emily Brontë. **CP-BronE**

What vaileth [*or* 'vaileth] truth [*or* trouth]? or by it to take pain [*or* payn]? Sir Thomas Wyatt. **CP-WyatT**

What various hindrances we meet. Exhortation to Prayer. William Cowper. **NOCV** *Fr.* Olney Hymns. **CP-CowpW**

What Virginia Said. Charles Tomlinson. **CP-TomlC**

What virtue or what mental grace. Friendship. William Cowper. **CP-CowpW**

What voice did on my spirit fall. Peschiera. Arthur Hugh Clough. **SP-ClouA**

What voice is it that speaks. Frederick Morgan. *Fr.* The Gorge. **SP-MorgF**

What voice is that I hear. Sorcery. Walter de la Mare. **CP-DeLaW**

What waiting in the halls. The Passage. Robert Creeley. **CP-CreeR**

What wakes me now. Stanley Jasspon Kunitz. *Fr.* What of the Night? **CP-KuniS**

What was Ashore, then? Cargoed with Forget. John Berryman. *Fr.* Sonnets to Chris. **CP-BerrJ**

What was he doing, the great god Pan. A Musical Instrument. Elizabeth Barrett Browning. **CP-BroEB**

What was her beauty in our first estate. *with music.* Richard Wilbur. **CP-WilbR**

What *Was* Her Name. John Ciardi. **SP-CiarJ**

What was I looking for today? Looking. William DeWitt Snodgrass. **SP-SnodW**

What was it like, that country house? Country Villa. Jean Garrigue. **SP-GarrJ**

What was it we should strike the road again? Fragments. Gerard Manley Hopkins. **CP-HopkG**

What was it? What was it? Woman as Market. Muriel Rukeyser. **CP-RukeM**

What was left before crumbling. For George (I). Grace Paley. **CP-PaleG**

What was longed for and, once, certain. Randall Jarrell. **CP-JarrR**

What Was Lost. William Butler Yeats. **CP-YeatW**

What was lost is found. The Secret Waters. David Herbert Lawrence. **CP-LawrD**

What was not human. Prayer at Death. Michael Hartnett. **SP-HarMi**

What was she doing when it blew in. The Detective. Sylvia Plath. **CP-PlatS**

What was that story of an older dream. Malcolm Lowry. *Fr.* Peter Gaunt and the Canals. **CP-LowrM**

What was that?—The crack of doom or a sonic boom. Crack! Daniel Gerard Hoffman. **SP-HoffD**

What was the blond child building. The Builder of Houses. Jane Cooper. **SP-CoopJ**

What was the name you called me? Evening Waterfall. Carl Sandburg. **CP-SandC**

What Was the Promise That Smiled from the Maples at Evening? Robert Penn Warren. **SP-WarrR**

What was the shriek that struck Fancy's ear. The Spectral Horseman. Percy Bysshe Shelley. *Fr.* Posthumous Fragments of Margaret Nicholson. **CP-ShelP**

What was't that fell but now. On Gelli-Flowers Begotten. Robert Herrick. **CP-HerrR**

What waste in the labour of Chariot and Steed! On Seeing Some Tourists of the Lakes Pass by Reading; a Practice Very Common. William Wordsworth. **CP-WorW1**

What we are / given. Charles Kenneth Williams. **CP-WillC; SP-WillC**

What we do best is breed. A Christening. Donald Davie. **CP-DavDo**

What we do not know of ourselves. A B Cs (2). Charles Olson. **CP-OlsoC**

What we failed to see. Old Man's Beard. Charles Tomlinson. **CP-TomlC**

What we have been becomes. An Anniversary. Wendell Berry. **CP-BerrW**

What we have, comrades. To Those Who Fear To Join Us. Edwin Rolfe. **CP-RolfE**

What we know to be not possible. Nones. Wystan Hugh Auden. *Fr.* Horae Canonicae. **CP-AudeW**

What we leave behind to sleep. Wendell Berry. *Fr.* From the Crest. **CP-BerrW**

What we need is one of those gods. The Little Shirt. Charles Kenneth Williams. **CP-WillC**

What We Said. William DeWitt Snodgrass. **SP-SnodW**

What we see here in the sand dunes of the white moon alone with. Dunes. Carl Sandburg. **CP-SandC**

What We See Is What We Think. Wallace Stevens. **CP-StevW**

What we see of things is the things themselves. Fernando Pessoa. *Fr.* Twelve Poems from *The Keeper of the Flocks.* **CP-MertT**

What we see we know somewhat. Emily Dickinson. **CP-DickE**

What We Think We Know. Thomas McGrath. **SP-McGrT**

What we were searching for. Tapestry, with Unicorn. Erica Jong. **SP-JongE**

What we, when face to face we see. Arthur Hugh Clough. **SP-ClouA**

What weird rewards the waves wash up. Driftrose. Barton Sutter. **SP-SuttB**

What Were They Like? Denise Levertov. **CP-LeveD**

What were we playing? Was it prisoner's base? Running. Richard Wilbur. **CP-WilbR**

What Were You Thinking Dear Mother? Robert Penn Warren. *Fr.* Tale of Time. **SP-WarrR**

What wholly blameless fun. A Dutch Courtyard. Richard Wilbur. **CP-WilbR**

What will / the shame be. The Shame. Robert Creeley. **CP-CreeR**

What Will Be, Is. Robert Ranke Graves. **CP-GravR**

What will his crimes become, now that her hands. A Long Novel. John Ashbery. **SP-AshbJ**

What Will I Do Gin My Hoggie Die. Robert Burns. **CP-BurnR**

What will it be, O my soul, what will it be. Christina Georgina Rossetti. **CP-RosC3**

What will our reputations be? Poetical Remains. Archibald MacLeish. **CP-MacLA**

What will the Poles think of my hat. Pablo Neruda, *tr. fr. Spanish by* Ben Belitt. **SP-NeruP** *Fr.* Question Book.

What will ye (my poor Orphans) do. To His Verses. Robert Herrick. **CP-HerrR**

What will you do, my brother, my friend. Ballad of the Noble Intentions. Edwin Rolfe. **CP-RolfE**

What will you give me for my pound? Christina Georgina Rossetti. **CP-RosC2**

What winter floods, what showers of spring. Emily Brontë. **CP-BronE**

What Wisdome, Learning, Wit, or Worth. Upon the Much Lamented, Mr. J. Warr. Robert Herrick. **CP-HerrR**

What with hounds and friends and, in the winter. Pushkin. A Didactic Poem. Donald Davie. **CP-DavDo**

What woman hugs her infant there? A Nativity. William Butler Yeats. **CP-YeatW**

What word have you, interpreters, of men. Of Heaven Considered as a Tomb. Wallace Stevens. **CP-StevW**

What word is that that changeth not. Sir Thomas Wyatt. **CP-WyatT**

What words are these have fallen from me? Tennyson. **EBEV** *Fr.* In Memoriam A. H. H. **CP-TennA**

What words can make / seems next to nothing now. Dedication in These Days. Hayden Carruth. **CP-CarHS**

What Words Have Passed. John Milton. **TrCP** *Fr.* Book IX. **FHYEP; NAEL-1; NAWM-1; NoP; OAEL-1** *Fr.* Paradise Lost. **CP-MiltJ**

What would happen / if there were a terrific shortage of goldenrod. Grace Paley. **CP-PaleG**

What would I do without this world faceless incurious, *Author's own English vers. of his* "Que ferais-je sans ce monde sans visage sans questions." Samuel Beckett. **CP-BeckS**

What Would I Give? Christina Georgina Rossetti. **CP-RosC1**

What would I give to see his face? Emily Dickinson. **CP-DickE**

What would it profit you, now as good as dead, if Monday came. Sick Man in the Sun. Pablo Neruda, *tr. fr. Spanish by* Ben Belitt. **SP-NeruP**

What would the world be, once bereft. Wildness. Gerard Manley Hopkins. **EaPr; OtMeF** *Fr.* Inversnaid. **CP-HopkG**

What would this Man? Now upward will he soar. Alexander Pope. **HeIP** *Fr.* An Essay on Man. **CP-PopeA**

What would ye more of me, your slave, require. Sir Thomas Wyatt. **CP-WyatT**

What Would You Do If You Lost It. Allen Ginsberg. **CP-GinsA**

What Would You Fight For? David Herbert Lawrence. **CP-LawrD**

What years of the other times, what centuries. Message from Abroad. Allen Tate. **CP-TateA**

"What, you are stepping westward?"—"Yea." Stepping Westward. William Wordsworth. **CP-WorW1**

What you give me I cheerfully accept. To Rich Givers. Walt Whitman. **CP-WhitW**

What You Have Come To Expect. Stephen Dobyns. **SP-DobyS**

What you have done, Odysseus. Canto 6. Ezra Pound. *Fr.* Cantos. **CP-PoCan**

What, you have never seen a lifeless thing flower. Not Men Alone. Edwin Rolfe. **CP-RolfE**

What you hold. To Be Done in Winter. James Dickey. **CP-DickJ**

What you know of me[Lx] / pale water. Sign. Robert Creeley. **CP-CreeR**

What you love is gone; the worst have got it. Aban Kavost and Ivar Oakeson. Robert Bly. **SP-BlyR**

What you may cluster 'round the knees of space. To the Cloud Juggler. Hart Crane. **CP-CranH**

What you may yank up *readiest* Yank. The Pillar and the Post. Hart Crane. **CP-CranH**

What You Need. William Matthews. **SP-MattW**

What You Need to Be a Writer. Erica Jong. **SP-JongE**

What you see is what you see. A Horse With Greenblue Eyes. Charles Bukowski. **SP-BukC1**

What You Seize Is What You Git. Al Young. **CP-YounA**

What You Should Know to Be a Poet. Gary Snyder. **CP-SnydG**

What You Waited For. Marge Piercy. **SP-PierM**

What you wanted I told you. A Rant. Frank O'Hara. **SP-OharF**

What you wrote to know. The Littleton Whale. Charles Tomlinson. **CP-TomlC**

What You're Doing. The Beatles. **CP-Beatl**

What Zimmer Would Be. Paul Zimmer. **SP-ZimmP**

Whatcha Gonna Do. "Bob Dylan." **CP-DylaB**

Whate'er I be, old England is my dam! The Old Chartist. George Meredith. **CP-MerG1**

Whate'er is Born of Mortal Birth. To Tirzah. William Blake. **CP-BlakW** Fr. Songs of Experience.

Whateer is done to her she cannot know. On the Virginity of the Virgin Mary & Johanna Southcott. William Blake. **CP-BlakW**

Whate'er of praise, and of regret attend. Inscription on a Stone, in the Church-Yard at Boreham. Charlotte Smith. **CP-SmitC**

Whate'er the passion--knowledge, fame, or pelf. Alexander Pope. **FiP; TrGrPo** Fr. An Essay on Man. **CP-PopeA** (Human Folly.) **FiP**

Whate'er your predecessors taught us. A Letter to the Reverend Dr. Sheridan. Jonathan Swift. **CP-SwifJ**

Whatever a man of the sons of men. Les Noyades. Algernon Charles Swinburne. **SP-SwinA**

Whatever awaits us of Doom or Home. Emily Dickinson. **SP-DickE**

Whatever Became of Me. Richard Shelton. **SP-ShelR**

Whatever Becomes of the Living. Al Young. **CP-YounA**

Whatever comes, let's be content withall. Welcome What Comes. Robert Herrick. **CP-HerrR**

Whatever constitutes. The Act of Love. Robert Creeley. **CP-CreeR**

Whatever could have possessed you. Carmen 40. Catullus. Fr. Carmina. **CP-Catul**

Whatever course of Life great Jove allots. Festina Lentè. Samuel Johnson. **CP-JohnS**

Whatever else they say of me. As for Me, I'm a Patriot. David Herbert Lawrence. **CP-LawrD**

Whatever else we learned. Homecoming: Anse La Raye. Derek Walcott. **CP-WalcD**

Whatever else you come to be. For Reuben, at Twelve Months. Miller Williams. **SP-WillM**

Whatever Happened? Philip Larkin. **CP-LarkP**

Whatever happens with us, your body. The Floating Poem, Unnumbered. Adrienne Rich. **NALW; NoAM** Fr. Twenty-one Love Poems. **SP-RicA1; SP-RicA2**

Whatever I have said or sung. Tennyson. Fr. In Memoriam A. H. H. **CP-TennA**

Whatever I have said to praise. Epilogue to Œnia. Allen Tate. Fr. The Progress of Œnia. **CP-TateA**

Whatever is here, it is. Confessions of the Life Artist. Thom Gunn. **CP-GunnT**

Whatever is said to be so. Expecting Silence. Donald Davie. **CP-DavDo**

Whatever is to become of me. The Wind. Robert Creeley. **CP-CreeR**

Whatever it is it is the murmur of evil. Correspondences. James Liddy. **CP-LiddJ**

Whatever it is, it's a passion. Love in America. Marianne Craig Moore. **CP-MoorM**

Whatever it is—she has tried it. Emily Dickinson. **CP-DickE**

Whatever it is that jigs and gleams. Indian Village. Louis MacNeice. **CP-MacNL**

Whatever It Is, Wherever You Are. John Ashbery. **SP-AshbJ**

Whatever it may be whoever it may be. Patna-Benares Express. Allen Ginsberg. **CP-GinsA**

Whatever it was she had so fiercely fought. The Recognition of Eve. Karl Shapiro. **ChIV-1; MoAB** Fr. Adam and Eve. **SP-ShapK**

Whatever it was: the grains of the glacier caked in the boot-cleats. Adrienne Rich. **FaBoWP; HCAP; SP-RicA1; SP-RicA2** Fr. Shooting Script. **CP-RicAE**

Whatever last slump of flesh. Faint Praise. Charles Kenneth Williams. **CP-WillC**

Whatever lifts the body up—muscles. The Body's Hope. Stephen Dobyns. **SP-DobyS**

Whatever makes this happening. Louis Zukofsky. Fr. 29 Songs. **CP-ZukLS**

Whatever Man Makes. David Herbert Lawrence. **CP-LawrD**

Whatever may be going through our heads. Sarabande. Howard Nemerov. **CP-NemeH**

Whatever roams the air is traveling. Phaneron. Muriel Rukeyser. **CP-RukeM**

Whatever roams the air is traveling. Muriel Rukeyser. **CP-RukeM**

Whatever sleeping in the world awakes. Creation of Anguish. Howard Nemerov. **CP-NemeH**

Whatever they promise for money, luck. The Tinker Camp. Richard Hugo. **CP-HugoR**

Whatever we do to a landscape—even to look—damages it. An Extinct Vertebrate. Robinson Jeffers. **CP-JefR3**

Whatever you are that has tracked us this far. Adrienne Rich. **SP-RicA1** Fr. Turning.

Whatever you have to say, leave. These Days. Charles Olson. **CP-OlsoC**

Whatever You Say Say Nothing. Seamus Heaney. **SP-HeanS**

Whatever's lost, it first was won. Elizabeth Barrett Browning. **TrPWD** Fr. De Profundis. **CP-BroEB**

Whatever's merely wilful, / and not miraculous. Edward Estlin Cummings. **CP-CummE**

What's all this hubbub and yelling. Armistice Day, 1918. Robert Ranke Graves. **CP-GravR**

What's bad about all. Luck. Charles Bukowski. **SP-BukC1**

What's become of all the glory and the grandeur of the gold-men and the gunmen. Les Neiges d'Antan. Louis MacNeice. Fr. Out of the Picture. **CP-MacNL**

What's become of Waring. Waring. Robert Browning. **CP-BroR1**

What's Dead? Allen Ginsberg. **CP-GinsA**

What's fame? A fancied life in others' breath. Alexander Pope. **FHYEP** Fr. An Essay on Man. **CP-PopeA**

What's Fame with Men, by Custom of the Nation. To a Lady with the Temple of Fame. Alexander Pope. **CP-PopeA**

What's filling up the mirror? O, it is not I. after Werfel. Robert Lowell. **SP-LoweR**

What's for Dinner. Robert Creeley. **CP-CreeR**

What's Good for the Soul is Good for Sales. Richard Wilbur. **NBLV** Fr. Flippancies. **CP-WilbR**

What's got by Justice is establisht sure. Rapine Brings Ruine. Robert Herrick. **CP-HerrR**

What's greater, Pebble or Pond? Once More, the Round. Theodore Roethke. **CP-RoetT**

What's in a Name? Christina Georgina Rossetti. **CP-RosC2**

What's in a Name? Here's What's in a Name, or, I Wonder What Became of John and Mary. Ogden Nash. **CP-NashO**

What's in a Name? Some Letter I Always Forget. Ogden Nash. **CP-NashO**

What's in a name that's. Petunia. Louis Zukofsky. **CP-ZukLS**

"What's in a park they warn girls out of?" "Queers." Marilyn Hacker. Fr. The Regent's Park Sonnets. **SP-HackM**

What's in the brain that ink may character. Sonnet 108. William Shakespeare. Fr. Sonnets. **CP-ShaWS**

What's In the Sack? Shel Silverstein. **SP-SilS2**

What's in the wind? There is no wind. In the Time of Hesitation. Edwin Rolfe. **CP-RolfE**

What's in this grave is worth your tear. For Myself. Countee Cullen. **CP-CullC**

What's in those pills? / After lunch and I can. What. James Schuyler. **CP-SchuJ**

What's in your mind, my dove, my coney. Wystan Hugh Auden. Fr. Five Songs ("What's in your mind, my dove, my coney"). **CP-AudeW**

What's it like? You take it from me. Capper Kaplinski at the North Side Cue Club. Hayden Carruth. **CP-CarHS**

What's love that's always strong? For Anybody's Martyr's Song. Jean Garrigue. **SP-GarrJ**

What's missing is the eyeballs. "Daddy" Warbucks. Anne Sexton. **CP-SextA**

What's over England? A cloud. What's over France? A flame. The Child Asleep. Muriel Rukeyser. Fr. Night-Music. **CP-RukeM**

What's riches to him. The Peacock. William Butler Yeats. **CP-YeatW**

What's Sane and What Isn't, sl. diff. vers. David Herbert Lawrence. See Bawdy Can Be Sane.

What's sweeter than at the end of a summer's day. Thanksgiving. Kenneth Koch. **SP-KochK**

What's that? / An egg? Whoroscope. Samuel Beckett. **CP-BeckS**

What's That. Anne Sexton. **CP-SextA**

What's that approaching like dust like poverty. Ballad. Charles Simic. **SP-SimiC**

What's that shining in the leaves. Elizabeth Bishop. Fr. Songs for a Colored Singer. **CP-BishE**

What's That Smell in the Kitchen? Marge Piercy. **SP-PierM**

What's that tapping at night: tack, tack. The Three Tall Men. Thomas Hardy. **CP-HardT**

What's that that hirples at my side? Heriot's Ford. Rudyard Kipling. **CP-KiplR** Fr. The Light That Failed.

What's that we see from far? the spring of Day. A Nuptiall Song, or Epithalamie, on Sir Clipseby Crew and His Lady. Robert Herrick. **CP-HerrR**

What's the best life for a man? Robinson Jeffers. **CP-JefR3**

What's the best thing in the world? The Best Thing in the World. Elizabeth Barrett Browning. **CP-BroEB**

What's the good of a man. Glimpses. David Herbert Lawrence. **CP-LawrD**

What's the good of going to Ridgeway. Old Excursions. Thomas Hardy. **CP-HardT**

What's the Matter, Haven't You Got Any Sense of Humor? Ogden Nash. **CP-NashO**

What's the matter with me. Watching the River Flow. "Bob Dylan." **CP-DylaB**

What's the Riddle. Randall Jarrell. **CP-JarrR**

What's the Use. Paul Laurence Dunbar. **CP-DunbP**

What's the Use. Ogden Nash. **CP-NashO**

What's there to praise. The Use of Books. Thomas McGrath. **SP-McGrT**

What's There to Tell? Thomas Hardy. **CP-HardT**

What's this? A dish for fat lips. The Shape of the Fire. Theodore Roethke. **CP-RoetT**

"What's this?" I pondered. Have I slept? Canto VII: Sad Souvenaunce. "Lewis Carroll." *Fr.* Phantasmagoria. **CP-CarrL**

What's this of death, from you who never will die? Edna St. Vincent Millay. **CP-MillE**

What's to Be Done. David Herbert Lawrence. **CP-LawrD**

What's to be said. Robert Creeley. **CP-CreeR**

What's up, today, with our lovers? The Lovers Go Fly a Kite. William DeWitt Snodgrass. **SP-SnodW**

What's Wrong. David Herbert Lawrence. **CP-LawrD**

What's wrong will always be wrong. I've seen him lean. Villager. Richard Hugo. **CP-HugoR**

What's wrong with American literature? Question and Answer. William Carlos Williams. **CP-WilW1**

What's Wrong with Pindar. Charles Olson. **CP-OlsoC**

What's wrong with you-zie? Her-zie. Stevie Smith. **CP-SmitS**

Whatso it be, howso it be, Amen. / Blessed it is, believing, not to see. Christina Georgina Rossetti. *Fr.* They Put Their Trust in Thee, and Were Not Confounded. **CP-RosC2**

Whatsoever Is Right, That Shall Ye Receive, *shorter, very diff. vers.* Christina Georgina Rossetti. *See* The Heart Knoweth Its Own Bitterness.

Whatsoever thing I see. Love Dislikes Nothing. Robert Herrick. **CP-HerrR**

Wheat. Gary Gildner. **SP-GildG**

Wheat-Ear, The. Charlotte Smith. **CP-SmitC**

Wheat sways heavy, oats are airy. August. Christina Georgina Rossetti. *Fr.* The Months: A Pageant. **CP-RosC2**

Wheel, The. Wendell Berry. **CP-BerrW**

Wheel, The. Robert Earl Hayden. **CP-HaydR**

Wheel, The. John Hewitt. **CP-HewiJ**

Wheel, The. William Butler Yeats. **CP-YeatW**

Wheel King, The. Howard Nemerov. **CP-NemeH**

Wheel me gently to the garage, since my car and I must part. *parody of* Adam Lindsay Gordon. Rudyard Kipling. **CP-KiplR** *Fr.* The Muse among the Motors.

Wheel of Being I, The. Hayden Carruth. *Fr.* Contra Mortem. **CP-CarHL**

Wheel of Being II, The. Hayden Carruth. *Fr.* Contra Mortem. **CP-CarHL**

Wheel of Fortune, The. Thom Gunn. **CP-GunnT**

Wheel of Fortune. Richard Hugo. **CP-HugoR**

Wheel of memory, wheel of forgetting, bitter. Cemetery Nights V. Stephen Dobyns. **SP-DobyS**

Wheels and galleries of the control of tears. Muriel Rukeyser. **CP-RukeM**

Wheels, Fireclouds. Leonard Cohen. **CP-CoheL**

Wheesht, Wheesht. "Hugh MacDiarmid." **SP-MacDH**

Wheesht, wheesht, Joyce, and let me hear. "Hugh MacDiarmid." *See* Archin' here and arrachin there.

Whelks. Mary Oliver. **SP-OlivM**

When . a . y and I . told . a . . ie they'd seen a. Puzzle. "Lewis Carroll." **CP-CarrL**

When / (day's amazing murder with). Edward Estlin Cummings. **CP-CummE**

When. James Dickey. **CP-DickJ**

When / from a sidewalk. Edward Estlin Cummings. **CP-CummE**

When. Charles Kenneth Williams. **SP-WillC**

When / you were small, I. Charles Kenneth Williams. **CP-WillC**

When a bar of pure silver or ignot of gold. The Flatting Mill. William Cowper. **CP-CowpW**

When a bird flips his tail in getting his balance on a tree. Many Mansions. David Herbert Lawrence. **CP-LawrD**

When a chile gets to be thirteen. Mystery. Langston Hughes. **SP-HughL**

When a comet passes over the town, whoever sees it knows a corpse. John Yau. **SP-YauJo** *Fr.* Corpse and Mirror II.

When a common noun becomes a Proper One. Capitals. Howard Nemerov. **CP-NemeH**

When a corpse meets a corpse there is a mirror between them. Variations on Corpse and Mirror. John Yau. **SP-YauJo**

When a daffadill [*or* daffodil] I see. Divination by a Daffadill [*or* Daffodil]. Robert Herrick. **CP-HerrR**

When a dark-eyed dawn. Vagrant's Song. Thomas Hardy. **CP-HardT**

When a daughter tries suicide. The Risk. Anne Sexton. **CP-SextA**

When a Feller's Itchin' to be Spanked. Paul Laurence Dunbar. **CP-DunbP**

When a friend calls to me from the road. A Time to Talk. Robert Frost. **CP-FrosR**

When a Hideous Man. Chuang Tzu, *tr. fr. Chinese by* Thomas Merton. **CP-MertT**

When a holy black Suede, the Son of Bob. The Windsor Prophecy. Jonathan Swift. **CP-SwifJ**

When a hundred years had passed nature seemed to man / a clock. Delmore Schwartz. *Fr.* Phoenix Lyrics. **SP-SchwD**

When a live flower, a single name of names. Desert Fringe. Robert Ranke Graves. **CP-GravR**

When a lover clasps his fairest. Fragment. Percy Bysshe Shelley. **CP-ShelP**

When a lover hies abroad. Rudyard Kipling. **CP-KiplR** *Fr.* The Naulahka.

When a Lover is a Beggar. Emily Dickinson. **CP-DickE**

When a magnet is / struck by a hammer. A Simple Experiment. Muriel Rukeyser. **CP-RukeM**

When a man can love no more. Basta! David Herbert Lawrence. **CP-LawrD**

When a man had gone. The Unfrocked Priest. William Carlos Williams. **CP-WilW1**

When a Man has Married a Wife. William Blake. **CP-BlakW**

When a man hath no freedom to fight for at home. Byron. **CP-Byron** (When a Man Hath No More Freedom to Fight for at Home.) **CP-Byron**

When a man he serves the Lord, it makes his life worthwhile. Ain't No Man Righteous, No Not One. "Bob Dylan." **CP-DylaB**

When a man loves the desert. Richard Shelton. *Fr.* Dry Season. **SP-ShelR**

When a man starts out with nothing. Freedom's Plow. Langston Hughes. **SP-HughL**

When a mans Faith is frozen up, as dead. The Lamp. Robert Herrick. **CP-HerrR**

When a mounting skylark sings / In the sunlit summer morn. Christina Georgina Rossetti. **CP-RosC2**

When a night in November. On One Who Lived and Died Where He Was Born. Thomas Hardy. **CP-HardT**

When a sister, born for each strong month-brother. Ad Mariam. Gerard Manley Hopkins. **CP-HopkG**

When a tree falls in a forest. Bedtime Story. Charles Simic. **SP-SimiC**

When a Warlock Dies. Isabella Gardner. **CP-GardI**

When a woman looks up at you with a twist about her eyes. The Made to Order Smile. Paul Laurence Dunbar. **CP-DunbP**

When Abraham Lincoln was shoveled into the tombs. Cool Tombs. Carl Sandburg. **CP-SandC**

When Abraham was bless'd. Circumcision. Christopher Smart. *Fr.* Hymns and Spiritual Songs for the Fasts and Festivals of the Church of England. **SP-SmarC**

When Achilles fought and fell. Randall Jarrell. **CP-JarrR**

When Adam and when Eve left Paradise. Christina Georgina Rossetti. *Fr.* Later Life: A Double Sonnet of Sonnets. **CP-RosC2**

When Adam named the crowding beasts. Name and Number. John Hewitt. **CP-HewiJ**

When Adam walked in Eden young. Alfred Edward Housman. **CP-HousA**

When after many Lustrs thou shalt be. To His Worthy Friend, M. Arthur Bartly. Robert Herrick. **CP-HerrR**

When after the screens of the evening of defeat. Willkie in the *Gulliver.* Muriel Rukeyser. **CP-RukeM**

When Age or Chance has made me blind. Being Once Blind, His Request to Biancha. Robert Herrick. **CP-HerrR**

When aince Aprile has fairly come. Robert Louis Stevenson. **CP-StevR**

When Alexander Pope strolled in the city. Mr. Pope. Allen Tate. **CP-TateA**

When Algebra is done boys. Keep Troth. Basil Bunting. **CP-BuntB**

When all / My waterfall. Her Time. Theodore Roethke. **CP-RoetT**

When all analogies are broken. In the Black Museum. Howard Nemerov. **CP-NemeH**

When all around grew drear and dark. Stanzas to Augusta. Byron. **CP-Byron**

When all Birds els[e] do of their music[k] fail[e]. Money Makes the Mirth. Robert Herrick. **CP-HerrR**

When All Is Done. Paul Laurence Dunbar. **CP-DunbP**

When all is over and you march for home. Spoils. Robert Ranke Graves. **CP-GravR**

When All My Five and Country Senses See. Dylan Thomas. **CP-ThomD**

When all my hours are mine. Preoccupation's Gift. Donald Davie. **CP-DavDo**

When all our apparatus of report. Wystan Hugh Auden. *Fr.* Sonnets from China. **CP-AudeW**

When all the others were away at Mass. Seamus Heaney. **PNI** *Fr.* Clearances. **SP-HeanS**

When all the overwork of life. The Heart Knoweth Its Own Bitterness. Christina Georgina Rossetti. **CP-RosC2**

When all the world would keep a matter hid. The Fabulists. Rudyard Kipling. **CP-KiplR**

When all their blooms the meadows flaunt. May. Ralph Waldo Emerson. **CP-EmerR**

When all things forget color and shape. The Mirror's Mission. Jorge Carrera Andrade, *tr. fr. Spanish by* Thomas Merton. **CP-MertT**

When all turned to altitude. Pablo Neruda, *tr. fr. Spanish by* Ben Belitt. **SP-NeruP** *Fr.* Skystones.

When all within is peace. Song. William Cowper. **CP-CowpW**

When all works that have. The Fool by the Roadside. William Butler Yeats. **CP-YeatW**

When along the pavement. Submergence. David Herbert Lawrence. **CP-LawrD**

When Alpine Vales threw forth a suppliant cry. Persecution of the Scottish Covenanters. William Wordsworth. *Fr.* Ecclesiastical Sonnets. **CP-WorW2**

When amatory poets sing their loves. Canto the Fifth. Byron. *Fr.* Don Juan. **CP-Byron**

When America closes for the night. Promises. Richard Shelton. **SP-ShelR**

When an archer is shooting for nothing. The Need to Win. Chuang Tzu, *tr. fr. Chinese by* Thomas Merton. **CP-MertT**

When an auctioneer's seen with a good-looking boy. Carmen 106. Catullus. *Fr.* Carmina. **CP-Catul**

When an hour is harmonious. The Swinging Bridge. Richard Eberhart. **CP-EberR**

When Anaxagoras says: Even snow is black! Anaxagoras. David Herbert Lawrence. **CP-LawrD**

When ancient girl is garbed in spite. The Smile. Stevie Smith. **CP-SmitS**

When and Why. Robert Ranke Graves. **CP-GravR**

When Angels Came to Zimmer. Paul Zimmer. **SP-ZimmP**

When anger comes to the coast of our desolate country. The Peril. Thomas Merton. **CP-MertT; SP-MertT**

When any mortal(even the most odd). Edward Estlin Cummings. **CP-CummE**

When April with her wild blue eye. The Death of Winter. George Meredith. **CP-MerG1**

When April with its sweet showers. Geoffrey Chaucer. *See* Whan that Aprille [*or* April, *or* Aprill] with his[e] shoures [*or* showres] sote [*orsoote*].

When April with Its Sweet Showers. Geoffrey Chaucer. *See* Whan that Aprille [*or* April, *or* Aprill] with his[e] shoures [*or* showres] sote [*orsoote*].

When as in silks my Julia goes. Upon Julia's Clothes. Robert Herrick. **CP-HerrR**

When as Leander young was drown'd. Leanders Obsequies. Robert Herrick. **CP-HerrR**

When, as the captive of Your own invincible consent. Freedom as Experience. Thomas Merton. **CP-MertT; SP-MertT**

When as thine eye hath chose the dame. *Various Authors.* **CP-ShaWS** *Fr.* The Passionate Pilgrim. **CP-ShaWS**

When as we sat all sad and desolate. Bible, *O.T. See* Psalm 137: "By the rivers of Babylon. . . ."

When asked, I used to say. What Zimmer Would Be. Paul Zimmer. **SP-ZimmP**

When at Collatium this false lord arrived. [Before the Rape]. William Shakespeare. **NoSic** *Fr.* The Rape of Lucrece. **CP-ShaWS**

When at home alone I sit. The Little Land. Robert Louis Stevenson. **CP-StevR**

When at last after long despair, our hopes ring true again. Catullus. *See* Carmen 107: "If ever anyone anywhere, Lesbia, is looking."

When at last he was well enough to take the sun. A Leg in a Plaster Cast. Muriel Rukeyser. **CP-RukeM**

When at the end of *Don Pasquale.* A Seductive Piece of Business. Randall Jarrell. **CP-JarrR**

When August days are hot an' dry. In August. Paul Laurence Dunbar. **CP-DunbP**

When Aulus, the nocturnal thief, made prize. On a Thief. *Unknown, tr. fr. Greek by* William Cowper. **CP-CowpW**

When Aunt Emily died, her husband would not look at her. New England Protestant. Richard Eberhart. *Fr.* Attitudes. **CP-EberR**

When battles were fought / With a chivalrous sense of Should and Ought. Then and Now. Thomas Hardy. **CP-HardT**

When beasts could speak, (the learned say). The Beasts' Confession to the Priest. Jonathan Swift. **CP-SwifJ**

When beauty breaks and falls asunder. Juan's Song. Louise Bogan. **CP-BogaL**

When bells ring, wild rain pelts the river. No Bells to Believe. Richard Hugo. **CP-HugoR**

When Bells stop ringing—Church—begins. Emily Dickinson. **CP-DickE**

When Bishop Berkeley said "there was no matter." Canto the Eleventh. Byron. **NOBRP** *Fr.* Don Juan. **CP-Byron**

When biting *Boreas*, fell and doure. A Winter Night. Robert Burns. **CP-BurnR**

When blackguards and murderers. In Chains. William Carlos Williams. **CP-WilW2**

When blessed Marie [*or* Mary] wip'd her Saviours [*or* Saviour's] feet. Mary [*or* Marie] Magdalene. George Herbert. **CP-HerbG**

When blooming spring. Song. James Thomson. **CP-ThomJ**

When blue moons start to roll around. Real Time. Al Young. **CP-YounA**

When books have all seized up like the books in graveyards. To Posterity. Louis MacNeice. **CP-MacNL**

When Bradbury sang, "The Roast Beef of Old England." Dissent. A Fable. Donald Davie. *Fr.* A Dissentient Voice. **CP-DavDo**

When branches bend in fruitful stupor. Not Even for Brunch. Ogden Nash. **CP-NashO**

When brave chast Arria to her Pætus gave. Martial, *tr. fr. Latin by* Richard Lovelace. **CP-LoveR**

When breathless queens release their panthers. Winter Poem. Kenneth Patchen. **CP-PatcK**

When Britain first, at heaven's command. Rule, Britannia! James Thomson *and* David Mallet. **CP-ThomJ** *Fr.* Alfred: A Masque.

When British Freedom for an happier land. To the Honourable Mr. Erskine. Samuel Taylor Coleridge. *Fr.* Effusions. **CP-ColeS**

When Bryan came to Springfield, and Altgeld gave him greeting. Nicholas Vachel Lindsay. *Fr.* Bryan, Bryan, Bryan, Bryan. **CP-LindV**

When buds of palm do burst and spread. Song: Spring. George Meredith. **CP-MerG1**

When Bunyan swung his whopping axe. Folk Tune. Richard Wilbur. **CP-WilbR**

When by a generous Public's kind acclaim. Prologue. Robert Burns. **CP-BurnR**

When by my solitary hearth I sit. To Hope. John Keats. **CP-KeatJ**

When by the labour of my 'ands. Half-Ballad of Waterval. Rudyard Kipling. **CP-KiplR**

When by thy scorn[e], O murd'ress[e] [*or* murderess], I am dead. The Apparition. John Donne. **CP-DonnJ**

When by Zeus relenting the mandate was revoked. Phoebus with Admetus. George Meredith. **CP-MerG1**

When Byron's eyes were shut in death. Matthew Arnold. **EPCY** *Fr.* Memorial Verses. **SP-ArnoM**

When Caesar Fell. Edna St. Vincent Millay. **CP-MillE**

When chapman [*or* chapmen] billies leave the street. Tam o' Shanter [A Tale]. Robert Burns. **CP-BurnR**

When children are playing alone on the green. The Unseen Playmate. Robert Louis Stevenson. **CP-StevR**

When chill November's surly blast. Man Was Made to Mourn, a Dirge. Robert Burns. **CP-BurnR**

When Chloë flies on silken wings. Chloë's Poem. John Updike. **CP-UpdiJ**

When Christ, by grouth, disclosèd His descent. Josephe's Amazement. Robert Southwell. **CP-SoutR**

When Christ descended into Hell. Christ in Hades. Wystan Hugh Auden. **CP-AudWJ**

When Christ, the seaman, was aboard. Ode to Admiral Sir George Pocock. Christopher Smart. **SP-SmarC**

When Christ went up to Heaven the Apostles stayed. Ascension Day. Christina Georgina Rossetti. **CP-RosC2**

When Christ, with care and pangues of death opprest. Christe's Sleeping Frendes. Robert Southwell. **CP-SoutR**

When Chub brings in his harvest, still he cries. Upon Chub. Robert Herrick. **CP-HerrR**

When citied day with the sonorous homes. Edward Estlin Cummings. **CP-CummE**

When class was in the garden at Greylands. Thomas Merton. **CP-MertT**

When clerks and navvies fondle. Louis MacNeice. **BoLoP; EnLoPo; ErPo** *Fr.* Trilogy for X. **CP-MacNL**

(For X.) **BoLoP; EnLoPo**

When closer than breathing. Walled In. Phoebe Hesketh. **SP-HeskP**

When cockle takes over it's. Cockle. Louis Zukofsky. **CP-ZukLS**

When cold November sits among the reeds like an unlucky fisher. The Regret. Thomas Merton. **CP-MertT; SP-MertT**

When Coldness Wraps This Suffering Clay. Byron. **CP-Byron**

When comes the lighted day for men to read. Hawarden. George Meredith. **CP-MerG1**

When conditions of frost and. Hayden Carruth. *Fr.* North Winter. **CP-CarHL**

When Confucius was visiting the state of Chu. Confucius and the Madman. Chuang Tzu, *tr. fr. Chinese by* Thomas Merton. **CP-MertT**

When Contemplation, like the night calm felt. Books. William Wordsworth. *Fr.* The Prelude; Growth of a Poet's Mind [1850 vers.]. **CP-WorW3**

When Contemplation, like the night-calm felt. William Wordsworth. **OAEL-2** *Fr.* Books. *Fr.* The Prelude; Growth of a Poet's Mind [1850 vers.]. **CP-WorW3**

When Continents expire. Emily Dickinson. **SP-DickE**

When country fiddlers held a convention in. Hell on the Wabash. Carl Sandburg. **CP-SandC**

When Cromwell fought for power, and while he reigned. William Cowper. **EPCY** *Fr.* Table Talk. **CP-CowpW**

When cuckoo calls and I may hear. Gerard Manley Hopkins. *Fr.* Fragments. **CP-HopkG**

When Cupid did his grandsire Jove entreat. On Mrs. Biddy Floyd. Jonathan Swift. **CP-SwifJ**

When daring Blood his rents to have regained. Bludius et Corona [Blood and the Crown]. Andrew Marvell. **CP-MarvA**

When darkness long has veil'd my mind. Peace after a Storm. William Cowper. *Fr.* Olney Hymns. **CP-CowpW**

When darkness narrowed on our anxious days. Valediction Lines to My WEA Students. John Hewitt. **CP-HewiJ**

When days of Beauty deck the earth. Emily Brontë. **CP-BronE**

When de Co'n Pone's Hot. Paul Laurence Dunbar. **CP-DunbP**

When de fiddle gits to singin' out a ol' Vahginny reel. Angelina. Paul Laurence Dunbar. **CP-DunbP**

When Dead. Thomas Hardy. **CP-HardT**

When dear Clarinda, matchless fair. Answer to the Foregoing—Extempore [Clarinda]. Robert Burns. **CP-BurnR**

When, dearest, I but think on [or of] thee. Song. Sir John Suckling *and* Owen Feltham. **CP-SuckJ**

When Death and Hell their right in Herode clayme. Christe's Retorne out of Egipt. Robert Southwell. **CP-SoutR**

When Death Came April Twelve 1945. Carl Sandburg. **CP-SandC**

When Death Comes. Mary Oliver. **SP-OlivM**

When death draws down the blinds in this old house. Reflections in an Old House. Allen Tate. **CP-TateA**

When death shall part us from these kids. A Dialogue between Thyrsis and Dorinda. Andrew Marvell. **CP-MarvA**

When Death was young and bleaching bones were few. Edna St. Vincent Millay. *Fr.* Epitaph for the Race of Man. **CP-MillE**

When death's dark stream I ferry o'er. A Verse Composed and Repeated by Burns, to the Master of the House, on Taking Leave at a Place in the Highlands, Where He Had Been Hospitably Entertained. Robert Burns. **CP-BurnR**

When Denmark's raven soar'd on high. Thorsgill. Sir Walter Scott. **SP-ScotW** *Fr.* Rokeby.

When descends on the Atlantic. Seaweed. Henry Wadsworth Longfellow. **SP-LongH**

When despair for the world grows in me. The Peace of Wild Things. Wendell Berry. **CP-BerrW**

When devils bite. Ralph Waldo Emerson. **CP-EmerR**

When dews fall fast, and rosy day. The Moth. Charlotte Smith. **CP-SmitC**

When Dey 'Listed Colored Soldiers. Paul Laurence Dunbar. **CP-DunbP**

When Diamonds are a Legend. Emily Dickinson. **CP-DickE**

When did I ever deny, though this was fleeting. Edna St. Vincent Millay. **CP-MillE**

When did I first become aware—. Marge Piercy. *Fr.* Women's Laughter. **SP-PierM**

When did you start your tricks. The Mosquito. David Herbert Lawrence. **CP-LawrD**

When Dido feasted first the wandering Trojan knight. Iopas's Song. Sir Thomas Wyatt. **CP-WyatT**

When do poppies bloom I ask myself, stopping again. Charles Olson. **SP-OlsoC** *Fr.* The Maximus Poems.

When doctors with tirades on Tea affright us. Classicality Applied to Tea-Dealing: A Fancy Inspired by Westbourne Grove. Robert Browning. **CP-BroR2**

When does a town become a city? This. Townend, 1976. Donald Davie. **CP-DavDo**

When does the butterfly read. Pablo Neruda, *tr. fr. Spanish by* Ben Belitt. **SP-NeruP** *Fr.* Question Book.

When, doff'd his casque, he felt free air. The Death of Marmion. Sir Walter Scott. **SP-ScotW** *Fr.* Marmion.

When Doris Danced. Richard Eberhart. **CP-EberR**

When down I went to the rust-red quarry. The Wedding. Robert Ranke Graves. **CP-GravR**

When Dragon-fly would fix his wings. The Flower of Mending. Nicholas Vachel Lindsay. **CP-LindV**

When drunk he crawled home on his knees. Poem. Malcolm Lowry. **CP-LowrM**

When Dryden's fool, "unknowing what he sought." Verses Found in a Summer-House at Hales-Owen. Byron. **CP-Byron**

When early morn walks forth in sober grey. Song. William Blake. **CP-BlakW**

When Earth's Last Picture Is Painted. Rudyard Kipling. *See* When Earth's last picture is painted, and the tubes are twisted and dried.

When Earth's last picture is painted, and the tubes are twisted and dried. Rudyard Kipling. **CP-KiplR**

(When Earth's Last Picture Is Painted.) **CP-KiplR**

When Eighty-five was seven month auld. The Mauchline Wedding. Robert Burns. **CP-BurnR**

When energising objects men pursue. Parenthetical Address. Byron. **CP-Byron**

When England did enjoy her halcyon days. An Elegy Upon that Honorable and Reknowned Knight Sir Philip Sydney. Anne Bradstreet. **CP-BradA**

When ere I go, or what so ere befalls. To My Dearest Sister M. Mercie Herrick. Robert Herrick. **CP-HerrR**

When ere my heart, Love's warmth, but entertaines. Against Love. Robert Herrick. **CP-HerrR**

When Etna basks and purrs. Emily Dickinson. **CP-DickE**

When Eve ate the apple / My woes began. The Ineffable. Richard Eberhart. **CP-EberR**

When Eve was cloned from Adam's rib, and stood. Peter Meinke. *Fr.* Mendel's Laws. **SP-MeinP**

When Even The. Leonard Cohen. **CP-CoheL**

When even to withhold. Ensamhet. Chuck Miller. **SP-MillC**

When evening comes to its gentle arias. Robin Hood Cove—Georgetown, Maine. Marsden Hartley. **CP-HartM**

When every one to pleasing pastime hies. Sonnet 23. Mary Sidney, Countess of Montgomery Wroth. **WPE** *Fr.* Pamphilia to Amphilanthus. **CP-WrotM**

When everything was over. Child Poems. Hilda Doolittle. **CP-DoolH**

When everything was over. Dedication. Hilda Doolittle. *Fr.* Child Poems. **CP-DoolH**

When eyeless fish meet her on. The Goddess. Thom Gunn. **CP-GunnT**

When eyes that cast about the heights of heaven. Gerard Manley Hopkins. **CP-HopkG**

When faces called flowers float out of the ground. Edward Estlin Cummings. **CP-CummE; SP-CummE**

When faint and sad o'er Sorrow's desart wild. *1796 vers.* Samuel Taylor Coleridge. **CP-ColeS**

When Faith and Love which parted from thee never. John Milton. **CP-MiltJ**

(Sonnet 14: "When Faith and Love which parted from thee never.") **CP-MiltJ**

When, far and wide, swift as the beams of the moon. Upon the Same Event. William Wordsworth. **CP-WorW1**

When far-spent night persuades each mortal eye. Sonnet 99. Sir Philip Sidney. **CABA; NoSic; OBSC; PoE; Son** *Fr.* Astrophil and Stella. **SP-SidnP**

When feare admits no hope of safety, then. No Danger to Men Desperate. Robert Herrick. **CP-HerrR**

When fears and sorrows me beset. For the Restoration of My Dear Husband from a Burning Ague. Anne Bradstreet. **CP-BradA**

When fierce conflicting passions urge. *Fr. the Greek of Euripides.* Byron. **CP-Byron**

When first by Eden Tree. Song of the Fifth River. Rudyard Kipling. **CP-KiplR** *Fr.* The Treasure and the Law. *Fr.* Puck of Pook's Hill.

When first, descending from the moorlands. Extempore Effusion upon the Death of James Hogg. William Wordsworth. **CP-WorW2**

When first Diana leaves her bed. The Progress of Beauty. Jonathan Swift. **CP-SwifJ**

When first, fair mistress, I did see your face. To B.C. Sir John Suckling. **CP-SuckJ**

When first I came to Stewart Kyle. Fragment, A. Robert Burns. **CP-BurnR**

When first I find those Numbers thou do'st write. To His Learned Friend M. Jo. Harmar, Phisitian to Colledge of Westminster. Robert Herrick. **CP-HerrR**

When first I made. William Wordsworth. **EnRP** *Fr.* Summer Vacation. *Fr.* The Prelude; Growth of a Poet's Mind [1850 vers.]. **CP-WorW3**

When first I made. William Wordsworth. **OBRV** *Fr.* Summer Vacation. *Fr.* The Prelude; Growth of a Poet's Mind [1805 vers.]. **CP-WorW3**

When first I saw our banner wave. Astræa at the Capitol. John Greenleaf Whittier. **CP-WhitJ**

When first mine eyes did view and mark. Sir Thomas Wyatt. **CP-WyatT**

When first my brave Johnie lad came to this town. Cock up Your Beaver. Robert Burns. **CP-BurnR**

When first my lines [*or* verse] of heavenly [*or* heav'nly] joy[e]s made mention. Jordan (2). George Herbert. **CP-HerbG**

When first, my lord, I saw you back your horse. An Epigram. To William, Earl of Newcastle. Ben Jonson. **CP-JonsB**

When first my way to fair I took. Alfred Edward Housman. **CP-HousA**

When first of wise to old Johnson taught. At Cheshire Cheese. Paul Laurence Dunbar. **CP-DunbP**

When first the college rolls receive his name. Samuel Johnson. **FaBoEn; NOBE; OBEC; OBSV; SeCePo** *Fr.* The Vanity of Human Wishes [The Tenth Satire of Juvenal Imitated]. **CP-JohnS**

(Scholar's Life, The.) **FaBoEn; NOBE; OBEC; SeCePo**

When first the eye this forest sees. Andrew Marvell. **PBBP** *Fr.* Upon Appleton House [To My Lord Fairfax]. **CP-MarvA**

When first the peasant, long inclin'd to roam. The Young Author. Samuel Johnson. **CP-JohnS**

When first thou didst entice to thee my heart. Affliction (1). George Herbert. **CP-HerbG**

When first thy sweet and gracious eye. The Glance. George Herbert. **CP-HerbG**

When first we came together. Our Self. Robert Ranke Graves. **CP-GravR**

When First We Faced, and Touching Showed. Philip Larkin. **CP-LarkP**

When first we knew it, gibbet-bare. The Tree of Guilt. Louis MacNeice. **CP-MacNL**

When first you fluttered on this scene. A Hundred Years Since. Thomas Hardy. **CP-HardT**

When fishes set umbrellas up / If the rain-drops run. Christina Georgina Rossetti. **CP-RosC2**

When flowing garments I behold. Leprosie in Cloathes. Robert Herrick. **CP-HerrR**

When foes are o'ercome, we preserve them from slaughter. A Serious Poem upon William Wood. Jonathan Swift. **CP-SwifJ**

When, foot to wheel and back to wind. In the Matter of One Compass. Rudyard Kipling. **CP-KiplR**

When, for the fifteenth year, Tiberius Caesar. St. John Baptist. Thomas Merton. **CP-MertT**

When for the thorns with which I long, too long. The Coronet. Andrew Marvell. **CP-MarvA**

When formerly we thought, Dear. Looking Back. Thomas Hardy. **CP-HardT**

When forty winters shall besiege thy brow. Sonnet 2. William Shakespeare. **BLPL; FF; HeIP; ImPo; LiTB; NoSic; OBSC; SCGP; Son; TEP** *Fr.* Sonnets. **CP-ShaWS**

When France got free Europe 'twixt Fools & Knaves. William Blake. **CP-BlakW**

When Freedom, on her natal day. The Moral Warfare. John Greenleaf Whittier. **CP-WhitJ**

When Fresh, It Was Sweet. William Carlos Williams. **CP-WilW1**

When friendly summer calls again. Summer Schemes. Thomas Hardy. **CP-HardT**

When Friendship or Love our sympathies move. The Tear. Byron. **CP-Byron**

When, from the heart where Sorrow sits. Impromptu, in Reply to a Friend. Byron. **CP-Byron**

When from the opening chambers of the east. The Morning in the Country. James Thomson. **CP-ThomJ**

When from the pallid sky the sun descends. James Thomson. **OAEL-1; OxBS** *Fr.* Winter. *Fr.* The Seasons. **CP-ThomJ**

When from the Vallais we had turned, and clomb. William Wordsworth. **TOF** *Fr.* Cambridge and the Alps. *Fr.* The Prelude; Growth of a Poet's Mind [1850 vers.]. **CP-WorW3**

When from thee, weeping I removed. The Exile's Return. Elizabeth Barrett Browning. **CP-BroEB**

When from your sleepy mind the day's burden. Secret Theatre. Robert Ranke Graves. **CP-GravR**

When fruit-filled Tuscia should a wife give me. 3.12. Ovid. **CP-MarlC**, *tr. by* Christopher Marlowe; *Fr.* Elegies.

When getting my nose in a book. A Study of Reading Habits. Philip Larkin. **CP-LarkP**

When gin is gone and all is over. Country Poem with Little Country. Ernest Hemingway. **CP-HemiE**

When glad vacation time began. The Visit to Mab. Nicholas Vachel Lindsay. **CP-LindV**

When gloaming droops / To the raven's croak. The Captive. Walter de la Mare. **CP-DeLaW**

When God at first made Man. The Pulley. George Herbert. **CP-HerbG**

When god decided to invent. Edward Estlin Cummings. **CP-CummE; SP-CummE**

When god lets my body be. Edward Estlin Cummings. **CP-CummE; SP-CummE**

When God makes a great Man he intends all others to crush him. Arthur Hugh Clough. **OBSV** *Fr.* Amours de Voyage. **SP-ClouA**

When God scooped up a handful of dust. They Ask: Is God, Too, Lonely. Carl Sandburg. **CP-SandC**

When Goethe becomes an Apollo, he becomes a plaster cast. Goethe and Pose. David Herbert Lawrence. **CP-LawrD**

When Golda Meir Was in Africa. Alice Walker. **CP-WalkA**

When Golden Flies Upon My Carcass Come. Richard Eberhart. **CP-EberR**

When great Nature sighs, we hear the winds. The Breath of Nature. Chuang Tzu, *tr. fr. Chinese by* Thomas Merton. **CP-MertT**

When green buds hang in the elm like dust. Alfred Edward Housman. **CP-HousA**

When *Guilford* good our Pilot stood. Fragment, A. Robert Burns. **CP-BurnR**

When H—y finds out what you cannot do. On H[ayle]ys Friendship. William Blake. **CP-BlakW**

When Hagar found the bottle spent. For the Poor. William Cowper. *Fr.* Olney Hymns. **CP-CowpW**

When hair falls off and eyes blur And. Edward Estlin Cummings. **CP-CummE**

When Hamlet had sunk to the moist ground. The Hamlet Father. Richard Eberhart. **CP-EberR**

When Han Kan was summoned. The Master. Frederick Morgan. **SP-MorgF**

When Harry Wylie saw his father's ghost. What Ghosts Can Say. Adrienne Rich. **CP-RicAE**

When Haughty Expectations Prostrate Lie. William Wordsworth. **CP-WorW2**

When have I last looked on. Lines Written in Dejection. William Butler Yeats. **CP-YeatW**

When have the old forgiven us these things. The Twelfth Book. Archibald MacLeish. *Fr.* Conquistador. **CP-MacLA**

When having something to do. Coda: Song. Ted Berrigan. **SP-BerrT**

When he and I. Robert Creeley. **CP-CreeR**

When he began to witness, it was not to a journey. Muriel Rukeyser. **CP-RukeM**

When he brings home a whale. Naughty Boy. Robert Creeley. **CP-CreeR**

When he came to he knew. After the Crash. Louis MacNeice. **CP-MacNL**

When he clambered down from the bus. Hospitality: For E.K. John Hewitt. **CP-HewiJ**

When he considered his linguistic fallacy. Man's Type. Richard Eberhart. **CP-EberR**

When he diagnosed. Rescue Poem. Diane Wakoski. **SP-WakoD**

When he goes out in the morning. The Companions. Wendell Berry. **CP-BerrW**

When he got into bed. Damon & Pythias. Robert Creeley. **CP-CreeR**

When he had carried to term the sacred poem. Aftermath. Howard Nemerov. **CP-NemeH**

When he has finished his address. Memorial Service. John Hewitt. **CP-HewiJ**

When he is dead. Of a Professor. John Hewitt. **CP-HewiJ**

When he is well. Wystan Hugh Auden. *Fr.* Shorts [1927–1932] ("Pick a quarrel, go to war"). **CP-AudeW**

When he kissed my nipple. After Thoughts. Allen Ginsberg. **CP-GinsA**

When he lies in the night away from her. The Jealous Lovers. Donald Hall. **CP-HallD**

When he lit the candles there. The Young Churchwarden. Thomas Hardy. **CP-HardT**

When he protested, not too solemnly. Erasmus. Edwin Arlington Robinson. **CP-RobiE**

When he pushed his bush of black hair off his brow. Sicilian Cyclamens. David Herbert Lawrence. **CP-LawrD**

When He Returns. "Bob Dylan." **CP-DylaB**

When he stands in the judgement place. The Stone Verdict. Seamus Heaney. **SP-HeanS**

When he was a little boy. Protestant Easter. Anne Sexton. **CP-SextA**

When he was here alive, Eileen. Lisette and Eileen. Edwin Arlington Robinson. **CP-RobiE**

When he was small I lay awake at night. Corral. Lewis Turco. **SP-TurcL**

When he was young in Harlem my father. Jim Carroll. **SP-CarrJ**

When he, who is the unforgiven. The Unforgiven. Edwin Arlington Robinson. **CP-RobiE**

When He Would Have His Verses Read. Robert Herrick. **CP-HerrR**

When heat leaves the walls at last. Adrienne Rich. **SP-RicA1** *Fr.* Darklight.

When Helen Lived. William Butler Yeats. **CP-YeatW**

When her need for you dies. In Her Only Way. Robert Ranke Graves. **OxBSP** *Fr.* Three Songs for the Lute. **CP-GravR**

When here with Carthage Rome to conflict came. Near the Lake of Thrasymene. William Wordsworth. *Fr.* Memorials of a Tour in Italy, 1837. **CP-WorW2**

When he's returned I'll tell him———oh. A. J. J. Alfred Edward Housman. **CP-HousA**

When hills give out, the river loses power. Bad Vision at the Skagit. Richard Hugo. **CP-HugoR**

When His Excellency Prince Norodom Chantaraingsey. Dead Soldiers. James Fenton. **SP-FentJ**

When his head has been wired with a hundred electrodes. Brainwaves. Daniel Gerard Hoffman. **SP-HoffD**

When his hour for death had come. Osceola. Walt Whitman. **CP-WhitW**

When Hope but made Tranquillity be felt. Hope and Tranquillity. Samuel Taylor Coleridge. **CP-ColeS**

When Horse and Rider each can trust the other everywhere. Together. Rudyard Kipling. **CP-KiplR**

When Howitzers Began. Hayden Carruth. **CP-CarHS**

When human touch (as monkish books attest). St Catherine of Ledbury. William Wordsworth. **CP-WorW2**

When I a ship see on the Seas. The Way. Robert Herrick. **CP-HerrR**

When I a verse shall make. His Prayer to Ben[.] Jo[h]nson. Robert Herrick. **CP-HerrR**

When I a winsome babe did creep. Pappy Wants a Poppy. Ogden Nash. **CP-NashO**

When I Am a Cup. Hilda Doolittle. **CP-DoolH**

When I am alone I am happy. Waiting. William Carlos Williams. **CP-WilW1**

When I am an old woman I shall wear purple. Warning. Jenny Joseph. **SP-JoseJ**

When I am clothed I am a moral man. Moral Clothing. David Herbert Lawrence. **CP-LawrD**

When I am dead, and Doctors know not why. The Damp[e]. John Donne. **CP-DonnJ**

When I am dead, even then. Then. Muriel Rukeyser. **CP-RukeM**

When I am dead, it will not be. Two Thoughts of Death. Countee Cullen. **CP-CullC**

When I am dead, my dearest. Song. Christina Georgina Rossetti. **CP-RosC1**

When I am feeling depressed and anxious sullen. Poem. Frank O'Hara. **SP-OharF**

When I am going on journeys. Married People Going to Work. Jenny Joseph. **SP-JoseJ**

When I am gone. Ute Mountain. Charles Tomlinson. **CP-TomlC**

When I am grown to man's estate. Robert Louis Stevenson. **CP-StevR** (Looking Forward.)

When i am in boston,i do not speak. Edward Estlin Cummings. **CP-CummE**

When I am in hell or some such place. One Ralph Blossom Soliloquizes. Thomas Hardy. **CP-HardT**

When I am in the purgatory of the unread. Malcolm Lowry. **CP-LowrM**

When I am old. One of These Days. Lawrence Ferlinghetti. **SP-FerlL**

When I am out of sorts with the things. A Patient old cripple. Jenny Joseph. *Fr.* Life and Turgid Times of A. Citizen. **SP-JoseJ**

When I am riding round the ring no longer. Circus-Rider to Ringmaster. Thomas Hardy. **CP-HardT**

When I am sick and tired it is God's will. Who Have a Form of Godliness. Christina Georgina Rossetti. **CP-RosC3**

When I arrived. November. Richard Shelton. **SP-ShelR**

When I asked the very old man. Quotations. George Oppen. **CP-OppeG**

When I attain to utter forth in verse. Insufficiency. Elizabeth Barrett Browning. **CP-BroEB**

When I awoke on the morning. On Reaching the Age of Two Hundred. Donald Hall. **CP-HallD**

When I awoke, the glancing day looked gay. The Promisers. Wilfred Owen. **CP-OwenW**

When I become the land, when they will build. One Forever Alien. Howard Nemerov. **CP-NemeH**

When I beeheld the Image of my deere. Sonnet 4. Mary Sidney, Countess of Montgomery Wroth. *Fr.* Pamphilia to Amphilanthus. **CP-WrotM**

When I beheld the poet blind, yet bold. On Mr Milton's "Paradise Lost." Andrew Marvell. **CP-MarvA**

When I behold a forrest spread. Art above Nature, to Julia. Robert Herrick. **CP-HerrR**

When I behold, by warrant from thy pen. To My Friend, Will. Davenant. Thomas Carew. **CP-CareT**

When I behold the heavens as in their prime. Anne Bradstreet. **PBWP** *Fr.* Contemplations. **CP-BradA**

When I behold Thee, almost slain. His Anthem, to Christ on the Crosse. Robert Herrick. **CP-HerrR**

When I behold this tickle trustles state. Petrarch. *Fr.* The Visions of Petrarch. **CP-Spens**

When I bethinke me on that speech whyleare. Edmund Spenser. **NoSic; OAEL-1; OxBoCh** *Fr.* The Faerie Queene. **CP-Spens**

When I Buy Pictures. Marianne Craig Moore. **CP-MoorM**

When I by thy faire shape did sweare. Sonnet. Richard Lovelace. **CP-LoveR**

When I call you up. You Won't See Me. The Beatles. **CP-Beatl**

When I came back from my last dream, when I. The Alarm. James Wright. **CP-WrigJ**

When I came from my mother's womb. Mars. Howard Nemerov. **CP-NemeH**

When I came here first the lake was full. Meridian. Richard Hugo. **CP-HugoR**

When I came last to Ludlow. Alfred Edward Housman. **CP-HousA**

When I can hold a stone within my hand. Rumination. Richard Eberhart. **CP-EberR**

When I carefully consider the curious habits of dogs. Meditatio. Ezra Pound. **SP-PounE**

When I carry my little son in the cold. Poem. Thomas McGrath. **SP-McGrT**

When I come back. The Last Monarch of the Season. Gary Gildner. **SP-GildG**

When I come in f'm de c'on-fiel' aftah wo'kin ha'd all day. At Candle-Lightin' Time. Paul Laurence Dunbar. **CP-DunbP**

When I come near the red peony flower. At the Time of Peony Blossoming. Robert Bly. **SP-BlyR**

When I consider (Dearest) thou dost stay. To His Kinswoman, Mistresse Susanna Herrick. Robert Herrick. **CP-HerrR**

When I consider everything that grows. Sonnet 15. William Shakespeare. **AWP; BLPL; MasP; NAEL-1; NoSic; OAEP; OBSC; SCGP; Son; TEP; TrGrPo** *Fr.* Sonnets. **CP-ShaWS**

When I consider how my life is spent. Reminiscent Reflection. Ogden Nash. **CP-NashO**

When I consider how my light is spent. John Milton. **CP-MiltJ** (Sonnet 19: "When I consider how my light is spent.") **CP-MiltJ**

When I Consider Life. John Dryden. **FiP** *Fr.* Aureng-Zebe. **SP-DrydJ**

When I consider men of golden talents. So That's Who I Remind Me Of. Ogden Nash. **CP-NashO**

When I consider the children of the middle class. The World as Will and Representation. Hayden Carruth. **CP-CarHS**

When I consider thy heavens, the work of thy fingers. Bible, *O.T.* See Psalm 8: "O Lord our Lord, how excellent. . . ."

When I considered it too closely, when I wore it like an element and smelt it like water. Meditation on Saviors. Robinson Jeffers. **CP-JefR1**

When I contemplate all alone. Tennyson. *Fr.* In Memoriam A. H. H. **CP-TennA**

When I count the seeds. Emily Dickinson. **CP-DickE**

When I cross. The Last River. Galway Kinnell. **SP-KinnG**

When I departed am, ring thou my knell. To the Nightingale, and Robin-Red-Brest. Robert Herrick. **CP-HerrR**

When I did goe from thee, I felt that smart. His Parting from Mistress Dorothy Keneday. Robert Herrick. **CP-HerrR**

When I die, oh lay me low. Sir Eustace Grey. Christina Georgina Rossetti. **CP-RosC3**

When I die there'll be evidence. Naturally. Stephen Dunn. **SP-DunnS**

When I died / the light around me, that. Major Work. Dabney Stuart. **SP-StuaD**

When I died [or dyed] last, and, dear [Deare], I die [or dye]. The Legacy [or Legacie]. John Donne. **CP-DonnJ**

When I died, love, when I died. A Western Ballad. Allen Ginsberg. **CP-GinsA**

When I Do Count the Clock. William Shakespeare. *See* Sonnet 12: "When I do count the clock that tells the time."

When I do count the clock that tells the time. Sonnet 12. William Shakespeare. **AWP; EIL; EnRePo; FaFP; HeIP; InPS; MasP; NAEL-1; NoP; NoSic; OAEL-1; OBSC; SCGP; Son; TEP** *Fr.* Sonnets. **CP-ShaWS**

When I doe see. Mary Sidney, Countess of Montgomery Wroth. *Fr.* Love's Victorie. **CP-WrotM**

When I dream of you this way. Wing and Claw. Jim Carroll. **SP-CarrJ**

When I dream that you love me, you'll surely forgive. To M.S.G. Byron. **CP-Byron**

When I drop four cubes of ice. Sympathy in White Major. Philip Larkin. **CP-LarkP**

When I entertained evil. Evil. Richard Eberhart. **CP-EberR**

When I face north a lost Cree. Returned to Say. William Stafford. **SP-StafW**

When I faded back to pass. Ties. Dabney Stuart. **SP-StuaD**

When I fall asleep. Hands. Siv Cedering Fox. **SP-CedeS**

When I find myself in times of trouble. Let It Be. The Beatles. **CP-Beatl**

When I first reached this country. Thoughts from Underground. Margaret Atwood. **SP-AtwM1**

When I first started out to make what later became known as Hayden's Runaway. Underground the Darkness Is the Light. Hayden Carruth. **CP-CarHS**

When I flew into Russia I said to my friend. Willkie: Words from Russia. Muriel Rukeyser. **SP-RukeM**

When I Get Home. The Beatles. **CP-Beatl**

When I get older losing my hair many years from now. When I'm Sixty Four. The Beatles. **CP-Beatl**

When I get to be a composer. Daybreak in Alabama. Langston Hughes. **SP-HughL**

When I get to the bottom I go back to the top of the slide. Helter Skelter. The Beatles. **CP-Beatl**

When I get up he has been long at work. Willingly. Tess Gallagher. **SP-GallT**

When I go free. The Little Salamander. Walter de la Mare. **CP-DeLaW**

When I go up through the mowing field. A Late Walk. Robert Frost. **CP-FrosR**

When I go West you wear a marshal's star. Cops and Robbers. Donald Hall. **CP-HallD**

When I goe Hence ye Closet-Gods, I feare. To His Closet-Gods. Robert Herrick. **CP-HerrR**

"When I grow up." Grown Up. Hilda Doolittle. *Fr.* Child Poems. **CP-DoolH**

When I had been born eight years I was born again. And When in Scenes of Glory. Miller Williams. **SP-WillM**

When I had read your holy *Meditations*. To Mrs Alice Sutcliffe, on Her Divine *Meditations*. Ben Jonson. **CP-JonsB**

When I had spread it all on linen cloth. The Wife's Tale. Seamus Heaney. **SP-HeanS**

When I have borne in memory what has tamed. William Wordsworth. **CP-WorW1**

When I Have Fears That I May Cease to Be. John Keats. **CP-KeatJ**

When I Have Not Rage. Leonard Cohen. **CP-CoheL**

When I have read your hard and lively words. Sonnet. John Hewitt. **CP-HewiJ**

When I have seen by Time's fell hand defac'd [*or* defaced]. Sonnet 64. William Shakespeare. **AWP; BLPL; CABA; EIL; EnLoPo; EnRePo; FaFP; GTBS; GTBS-6; GTBS-P; HAP; HeIP; ImPo; LO; LiTB; NOBE; NoP; NoSic; OAEL-1; OBSC; OXAEP-1; PPoe; PlP; PoE; PoRA; SCGP; SeCeV; Son** *Fr.* Sonnets. **CP-ShaWS**

When I have seen the Sun emerge. Emily Dickinson. **CP-DickE**

When I have struggled through three hundred years. Ballad of the Scholar's Lament. Edward Estlin Cummings. **CP-CummE**

When i have thought of you somewhat too. Edward Estlin Cummings. **CP-CummE**

When I hear a man spouting about humility, today. Humility Mongers. David Herbert Lawrence. **CP-LawrD**

When I hear somebody complain of being lonely. Lonely, Lonesome, Loney—O! David Herbert Lawrence. **CP-LawrD**

When I hear you express an affection so warm. To Caroline. Byron. **CP-Byron**

When I Heard at the Close of the Day. Walt Whitman. **CP-WhitW**

When I heard Monica's. Cider 5[dc] A Glass. Donald Hall. **CP-HallD**

When I heard R. Dobson Moulton. The Last Man in the Quabbin. Brendan Galvin. **SP-GalvB**

When I Heard the call of the osprey. Ospreys in Cry. Richard Eberhart. **CP-EberR**

When I Heard the Learn'd Astronomer. Walt Whitman. **CP-WhitW**

When I heard the screaming, I ran back through the woods. The Murder. Frederick Morgan. **SP-MorgF**

When I hoked there, I would find. Terminus. Seamus Heaney. **SP-HeanS**

When I hoped I feared. Emily Dickinson. **CP-DickE**

When I hoped, I recollect. Emily Dickinson. **CP-DickE**

When I hug you, you are light as a grasshopper. For Jeriann's Hands. Marge Piercy. **SP-PierM**

When I imagine Delaware. Imagining Delaware. Richard Hugo. **CP-HugoR**

When I know what people think of me. The End. Robert Creeley. **CP-CreeR**

When I landed in the republic of conscience. From the Republic of Conscience. Seamus Heaney. **SP-HeanS**

When I left Ithaca. Family Circle. Leonard Nathan. **SP-NathL**

When I left my father's house. Nothing I Can Lose. Leonard Cohen. **CP-CoheL**

When I left Rome for Lalage's sake. Rimini. Rudyard Kipling. **CP-KiplR** *Fr.* Puck of Pook's Hill.

When I Left the King. Leonard Cohen. **CP-CoheL**

When I lie down to love. Old Dwarf Heart. Anne Sexton. **CP-SextA**

When I lie down to sleep dream the Wishing Well it rings. I Am a Victim of Telephone. Allen Ginsberg. **CP-GinsA**

When I lie where shades of darkness. Fare Well. Walter de la Mare. **CP-DeLaW**

When I lie within my little room. The Circus. Wystan Hugh Auden. **CP-AudWJ**

When I look forth at dawning, pool. Nature's Questioning. Thomas Hardy. **CP-HardT**

When I looked at the tree the bough was still shaking. The Tree. Randall Jarrell. **CP-JarrR**

When I looked up at my love-birds. Her Love-Birds. Thomas Hardy. **CP-HardT**

When I love, (as some have told). A Hymne to the Graces. Robert Herrick. **CP-HerrR**

When I meet the morning beam. The Immortal Part. Alfred Edward Housman. **CP-HousA**

When I meet the skier she is always. Transit. Adrienne Rich. **SP-RicA1; SP-RicA2**

When I must come to you, O my God, I pray. A Prayer to Go to Paradise with the Donkeys. Francis Jammes, *tr. fr. French by* Richard Wilbur. **CP-WilbR**

When I no longer have your heart. Walker. Alice Walker. **CP-WalkA**

When I of Villars doe but heare the name. To the Lady Mary Villars, Governesse to the Princesse Henretta. Robert Herrick. **CP-HerrR**

When I opened your book. The Double Rainbow. Charles Tomlinson. **CP-TomlC**

When I Paint My Masterpiece. "Bob Dylan." **CP-DylaB**

When I peered out, he had nine nights to spare. Drugs Alcohol Little Sister. John Berryman. **CP-BerrJ**

When I Peruse the Conquer'd Fame. Walt Whitman. **CP-WhitW**

When I pictured you. Ollie, Answer Me. Stephen Berg. **SP-BergS**

When I play on my fiddle in Dooney. The Fiddler of Dooney. William Butler Yeats. **CP-YeatW**

When I, poor Lais, with my crown. Lais to Aphrodite. Plato. **FaBoEE** *Fr.* Variations of Greek Themes. **CP-RobiE**

When I put her out, once, by the garbage pail. The Geranium. Theodore Roethke. **CP-RoetT**

When I reached his place. It Was All Very Tidy. Robert Ranke Graves. **CP-GravR**

When I reached the sea. Identities. Paul Muldoon. **SP-MuldP**

When I read poems to the art students. Marilyn Hacker. **SP-HackM** *Fr.* Taking Notice.

When I Read Shakespeare. David Herbert Lawrence. **CP-LawrD**

When I Read the Book. Walt Whitman. **CP-WhitW**

When I recall I could believe you'd go. John Berryman. *Fr.* Sonnets to Chris. **CP-BerrJ**

When I remember bygone days. The Middle. Ogden Nash. **CP-NashO**

When I remember first it rhymed with breath. The Word. Leonard Nathan. **SP-NathL**

When I remember, friend, whom lost I call. To a Friend Lost. George Meredith. **CP-MerG1**

When I Remember the Advent. Delmore Schwartz. **SP-SchwD**

When I returned from lovers' lane. The Kimono. James Merrill. **SP-MerrJ**

When I returned with drinks and nuts my friend. The Friend of the Fourth Decade. James Merrill. **SP-MerrJ**

When I rise up. Wendell Berry. **EaPr** *Fr.* Prayers and Sayings of the Mad Farmer. **CP-BerrW**

When I rode the zebra past your door. Apparitions Are Not Singular Occurrences. Diane Wakoski. **SP-WakoD**

When I rolled three 7's. Situation. Langston Hughes. **SP-HughL**

When I Roved a Young Highlander. Byron. **CP-Byron**

When I saw. William Carlos Williams. **CP-WilW1** *Fr.* Paterson.

When I saw birches in Wasienki Park. Robert Frost in Warsaw. Peter Meinke. **SP-MeinP**

When I saw her straying a little dazed through her untidy house. The Spanish Wife. David Herbert Lawrence. **CP-LawrD**

When I saw that clumsy crow. Night Crow. Theodore Roethke. **CP-RoetT**

When I saw the fox, it was kneeling. The Fox. Charles Tomlinson. **CP-TomlC**

When I saw the grapefruit drying, cherry in each centre lying. Reproof Deserved; or After the Lecture. Sir John Betjeman. **CP-BetjJ**

When I saw the jewelled girdle tied at her waist I thought of. George Meredith. *Fr.* Arabic Poems. **CP-MerG2**

When I say her hair was alive. My Hostess at the Renovated Inn. Dabney Stuart. **SP-StuaD**

When I say, love, it has. 3 Quatrains. Gilbert Sorrentino. **SP-SorrG**

When I search the past for you. Heloise. Ted Berrigan. **SP-BerrT**

When I see a couple of kids. High Windows. Philip Larkin. **CP-LarkP**

When I see a rabbit. Fragment, A. Jim Carroll. **SP-CarrJ**

When I see a Rubens Rembrandt [or] Correggio. William Blake. **CP-BlakW**

When I see a young tree. My Lady Is Compared to a Young Tree. Nicholas Vachel Lindsay. **CP-LindV**

When I see birches bend to left and right. Birches. Robert Frost. **CP-FrosR**

When I see the great cities. City-Life. David Herbert Lawrence. **CP-LawrD**

When I see the ignoble procession. The Ignoble Procession. David Herbert Lawrence. **CP-LawrD**

When I see the room it hurts me. A Musical Incident. Thomas Hardy. **CP-HardT**

When I see workless men I hurry by. Mister Faintheart Middleclass. John Hewitt. **CP-HewiJ**

When I see you in the first light, again. The Mirror. Robert Creeley. **CP-CreeR**

When I see your picture in its frame. As If You Had Never Been. Richard Eberhart. **CP-EberR**

When I Set Out for Lyonnesse. Thomas Hardy. **CP-HardT**

When I shall marry, if I do not find. A Married Woman. Thomas Carew. **CP-CareT**

When I shall sin, pardon my trespasse here. Gods Pardon. Robert Herrick. **CP-HerrR**

When I sit before a paper. After All, What Else Is There to Say? Allen Ginsberg. **CP-GinsA**

When I sold my fake Vermeers to Goering. The Forger. Derek Mahon. **SP-MahoD**

When I sought out the Cottage Hospital. The Ballad. John Hewitt. **CP-HewiJ**

When I speak to you, you stand to attention. Hermann Göring, Former Reichsmarschall. William DeWitt Snodgrass. **SP-SnodW**

When I spread out my hand here today. Sitting by a Bush in Broad Sunlight. Robert Frost. **CP-FrosR**

When I stand in the center of that man's madness. Reflection by a Mailbox. Stanley Jasspon Kunitz. **CP-KuniS**

When I take your hand. Sometimes. Thomas McGrath. **SP-McGrT**

When I tell you to read page 256. Page 256. Stephen Berg. **SP-BergS**

When I, the easy one, was hurt. Emily Dickinson. John Hewitt. **CP-HewiJ**

When I Think about Myself. Maya Angelou. **SP-AngeM**

When I think of death. Bop Lyrics. Allen Ginsberg. **CP-GinsA**

When I think of death I see. Wendell Berry. *Fr.* From the Crest. **CP-BerrW**

When I think of him, midnight. One Soldier. Muriel Rukeyser. **CP-RukeM**

When I think of it now I still see just how ugly and dirty the. Iowa. Stephen Berg. **SP-BergS**

When I think of my fear. The Unblinding. Laurence Lieberman. **SP-LiebL**

When I Think of Myself Dead. Charles Bukowski. **SP-BukC1**

When I think of the liberation of Palestine. Israel. Karl Shapiro. **SP-ShapK**

When I think of the little children learning. The Cairn. Edna St. Vincent Millay. **CP-MillE**

When I think of you. Christmas Syllabics for a Wife. Donald Davie. **CP-DavDo**

When I think that Wanda doesn't love me. Christian Fearing the Sky. Paul Zimmer. **SP-ZimmP**

When I through all my many poems look. To the Most Virtuous Mistress Pot, Who Many Times Entertained Him. Robert Herrick. **CP-HerrR**

When I throw back my head and howl. The Life with a Hole in It. Philip Larkin. **CP-LarkP**

When I thy parts runne o're, I can't espie. To Perenna. Robert Herrick. **CP-HerrR**

When I thy singing next shall heare. *see also* Upon Julia's Voice. Robert Herrick. **CP-HerrR**

When I too long have looked upon your face. Edna St. Vincent Millay. **CP-MillE**

When I took a job teaching in Massachusetts. To the Governor & Legislature of Massachusetts. Howard Nemerov. **CP-NemeH**

When I visited Fort Robinson. Fort Robinson. Ted Kooser. **SP-KoosT**

When I wake, I hear sheep eating apple peels just. Walking Swiftly. Robert Bly. **SP-BlyR**

When I wake in the night. The Voice of the Moon. Richard Shelton. **SP-ShelR**

When I wake next / to you, those moments. Places. Robert Creeley. **CP-CreeR**

When I wake up early in the morning. I'm Only Sleeping. The Beatles. **CP-Beatl**

When I walked roseless tracks and wide. Before Knowledge. Thomas Hardy. **CP-HardT**

When I was a boy, a relative. A Way to Make a Living. James Wright. **CP-WrigJ**

When I was a boy here. Horses. Wendell Berry. **CP-BerrW**

When I was a boy, I used to go to bed. The Remorse for Time. Howard Nemerov. **CP-NemeH**

When I was a callant, born far hence. Inkidoo and the Queen of Babel. Robert Ranke Graves. **CP-GravR**

When I was a child. Autobiographia Literaria. Frank O'Hara. **SP-OharF**

When I was a child. The Witch's Life. Anne Sexton. **CP-SextA**

When I was a child and we lived at home. Over the Mountain. Louise McNeill. **SP-McNeL**

When I was a child, I thought. Best Society. Philip Larkin. **CP-LarkP**

When I was a chile we used to play. Children's Rhymes. Langston Hughes. **SP-HughL**

When I was a Curragh stableboy. James McAuley. **SP-McAuJ** *Fr.* Cheiron.

When I was a girl in Los Angeles we'd go gleaning. Gleaning. Randall Jarrell. **CP-JarrR; SP-JarrR**

When I was a King and a Mason—a Master proven and skilled. The Palace. Rudyard Kipling. **CP-KiplR**

When I was a mailman. The Famous Writer. Charles Bukowski. **SP-BukC3**

When I was a windy boy and a bit. Lament. Dylan Thomas. **CP-ThomD**

When I was a young boy in Brooklyn going to public school. My Old Man. "Lou Reed." **SP-ReedL**

When I was about eight, I once stabbed somebody, another kid, a little girl. Blades. Charles Kenneth Williams. **CP-WillC; SP-WillC**

When I Was Alive. Alice Notley. **SP-NotlA**

When I was back there in seminary school. The Soft Parade. Jim Morrison. **SP-MorrJ**

When I was born. The Day's Ration. Ralph Waldo Emerson. **CP-EmerR**

When I was born, my mother taped my ears. Youth's Progress. John Updike. **CP-UpdiJ**

When I was born, one of the crooked. Seven-Sided Poem. Carlos Drummond de Andrade, *tr. fr. Portuguese by* Elizabeth Bishop. **CP-BishE**

When I was born the row began. Birthright. Louis MacNeice. **CP-MacNL**

When I was but a boy. Epstein, Spare That Yule Log! Ogden Nash. **CP-NashO**

When I was changed from a feeble cosmopolite. Serpent. Robert Lowell. **SP-LoweR**

When I was dead, my spirit turned. At Home. Christina Georgina Rossetti. **CP-RosC1**

When I was down beside the sea. At the Seaside [or Sea-Side]. Robert Louis Stevenson. **CP-StevR**

When I was dying. Love Song. Dabney Stuart. **SP-StuaD**

When I was eleven and they. Twins. William Matthews. **SP-MattW**

When I was employed at Cooperative Fashions, in spite of the. Hell is Graduated. Max Jacob, *tr. fr. French by* Elizabeth Bishop. **CP-BishE**

When I was first born. Let Me Be. Philip Levine. **SP-LeviP**

When I was forced from Stella ever dear. Sonnet 87. Sir Philip Sidney. **NAEL-1** *Fr.* Astrophil and Stella. **SP-SidnP**

When I was four my father went to Scotland. The Truth. Randall Jarrell. **CP-JarrR**

When I Was Home Last Christmas. Randall Jarrell. **CP-JarrR; SP-JarrR**

When I Was in Trouble I Called upon the Lord. Christina Georgina Rossetti. **CP-RosC2**

When I was just a youngster. Your Lead, Partner, I Hope We've Read the Same Book. Ogden Nash. **CP-NashO**

When I was just as far as I could walk. The Telephone. Robert Frost. **CP-FrosR**

When I was known as Aphrodite, men. Milady Reflects. John Updike. **CP-UpdiJ**

When I was little and he was riled. The Midnight Snack. James Merrill. *Fr.* Five Old Favorites. **SP-MerrJ**

When I was nine years old, in 1889. John L. Sullivan, the Strong Boy of Boston. Nicholas Vachel Lindsay. **CP-LindV**

When I was one-and-twenty. Alfred Edward Housman. **CP-HousA**

When I was out in the Nyasaland Missions. A Clever Strategem: Or, How to Handle Mystics. Thomas Merton. *Fr.* South. *Fr.* The Geography of Lograire. **CP-MertT**

When I was Saul, and sat among the cloaks. St. Paul. Thomas Merton. **CP-MertT; SP-MertT**

When I was seventeen or so. Eheu! Fugaces, or, What a Difference a Lot of Days Make. Ogden Nash. **CP-NashO**

When I was sick and lay a-bed. The Land of Counterpane. Robert Louis Stevenson. **CP-StevR**

When I was sleeping this morning one of my feet. The Last. Charles Kenneth Williams. **CP-WillC**

When I was small, a Woman died. Emily Dickinson. **CP-DickE**

When I was told, as Delta children were. Ruby Tells All. Miller Williams. **SP-WillM**

When I was twelve, I happened to guess the winning horse. Kentucky Derby Day, Belfast, Maine. Stephen Dobyns. **SP-DobyS**

When I was we'd visit my aunt's friend. A Night with Lions. Randall Jarrell. *Fr.* The Lost World. **CP-JarrR; SP-JarrR**

When I was young and shiny as an apple in the good Lord's garden. Love Poem 1990. Peter Meinke. **SP-MeinP**

When I was young I believed in intellectual conversation. In the Men's Room(s). Marge Piercy. **SP-PierM**

When I was young I broke all drinking records. Malcolm Lowry. **CP-LowrM**

When I was young I longed for Love. Vengeance is Sweet. Paul Laurence Dunbar. **CP-DunbP**

When I was young, I used to. Men. Maya Angelou. **SP-AngeM**

When I was young in school in Switzerland, about the time of the Boer. End of the World. Robinson Jeffers. **CP-JefR3**

When I was young, just starting at our game. To My Least Favorite Reviewer. Howard Nemerov. **CP-NemeH**

When I was young my teachers were the old. What Fifty Said. Robert Frost. **CP-FrosR**

When I was young, the mildew on my soul. The Days Like Smitten Cymbals of Brass. Malcolm Lowry. **CP-LowrM**

When I was young, we dwelt in a vale. In a Vale. Robert Frost. **CP-FrosR**

When I was younger. Pastoral. William Carlos Williams. **CP-WilW1**

When I watch the living meet. Alfred Edward Housman. **CP-HousA**

When I weekly knew. Quid Hic Agis? Thomas Hardy. **CP-HardT**

When I went into my room, at mid-morning. Man and Bat. David Herbert Lawrence. **CP-LawrD**

When I went looking for you. The Second Version. Hayden Carruth. *Fr.* The Mythology of Dark and Light. **CP-CarHL**

When I went out to kill myself, I caught. Saint Judas. James Wright. **CP-WrigJ**

When I went there first. Three Steps to the Graveyard. James Wright. **CP-WrigJ**

When I Went to the Circus. David Herbert Lawrence. **CP-LawrD**

When I Went to the Film. David Herbert Lawrence. **CP-LawrD**

When I went to the scientific doctor. The Scientific Doctor. David Herbert Lawrence. **CP-LawrD**

When I wish I was rich, then I know I am ill. Riches. David Herbert Lawrence. **CP-LawrD**

When I with trembling aske if you love still. Mary Sidney, Countess of Montgomery Wroth. *Fr.* Part 1. *Fr.* Urania. **CP-WrotM**

When I woke. Dylan Thomas. **CP-ThomD**

When I woke, a new snow had fallen. Robert Bly. *Fr.* Six Winter Privacy Poems. **SP-BlyR**

When I woke, the lake-lights were quivering on the wall. Coming Awake. David Herbert Lawrence. **CP-LawrD**

When I woke up this morning. The Lost Love. Randall Jarrell. **CP-JarrR**

When I woke up to the snow. Kathleen Jessie Raine. **SP-RainK**

When I would image her features. George Meredith. **CP-MerG1**

When I would know thee Goodyere, my thought looks. To the Same [Sir Henry Goodyere]. Ben Jonson. **CP-JonsB**

When I would muse in boyhood. Alfred Edward Housman. **CP-HousA**

When I write I am no longer I alone. Catalogue of I. Edwin Rolfe. **CP-RolfE**

When I write poems, I need to be near grass that no one else sees. Grass from Two Years. Robert Bly. **SP-BlyR**

When I Wrote a Little. Hayden Carruth. **CP-CarHS**

When I wrote of the women in their dances and wildness. The Poem as Mask. Muriel Rukeyser. **CP-RukeM**

When I wrote the abstract of Heaven. An Evaluation Under a Pine Tree, Lying On Pine Needles. Richard Eberhart. **CP-EberR**

When if ever life is sweet. St. Elizabeth of Hungary. Christina Georgina Rossetti. **CP-RosC3**

When I'm no longer young. The Carpenter's Song. Stephen Dunn. **SP-DunnS**

When I'm Sixty Four. The Beatles. **CP-Beatl**

When I'm walking beside her. Every Little Thing. John Lennon *and* Paul McCartney. **CP-Beatl**

When in a thousand swarms, the Summer o'er. Written for the Benefit of a Distressed Player, Detained at Brighthelmstone for Debt, November 1792. Charlotte Smith. **CP-SmitC**

When in April the sweet showers fall. Geoffrey Chaucer. *See* Whan that Aprille [*or* April, *or* Aprill] with his[e] shoures [*or* showres] sote [*orsoote*].

When, in Disgrace. William Shakespeare. *See* Sonnet 29: "When, in disgrace with fortune and men's eyes."

When, in disgrace with Fortune and men's eyes. Sonnet 29. William Shakespeare. AWP; CTC; EBEV; EIL; FaBV; FaBoEn; FaBoRV; FaPoB; GBL; GTBS; GTBS-6; GTBS-P; HAP; HBV; HeIL; HeIP; ImPo; InPK; InPS; InvP; LiTB; LoBV; MasP; NAEL-1; NOBE; NoP; NoSic; OAEL-1; OAEP; OBEV; OBSC; OPOP; OPOU; OXAEP-1; PFP; PeHV; PoEL-2; PoPl; Poetr; SCGP; Son; TFi; WeW *Fr.* Sonnets. **CP-ShaWS**

When in eternity the light. Hafiz, *tr.* by Ralph Waldo Emerson. **CP-EmerR** *Fr.* Odes.

When in from Delos came the gold. The White Lights. Edwin Arlington Robinson. **CP-RobiE**

When in Rome. . . . Isabella Gardner. **CP-GardI**

When in still air and still in summertime. Threshold. Howard Nemerov. **CP-NemeH**

When in that gold. Listening to Foxhounds. James Dickey. **CP-DickJ**

When in the Antique age of bow and spear. On the Same Occasion [on Seeing the Foundation Preparing for the Erection of Rydal Chapel]. William Wordsworth. **CP-WorW2**

When in the brazen leaves of Fame. On the Duke of Buckingham. Thomas Carew. **CP-CareT**

When in the chronicle of wasted time. Sonnet 106. William Shakespeare. AWP; BLPL; CTC; EBEvV; EIL; EnLoPo; EnRePo; FaBV; FaBoCh; FiP; GTBS; GTBS-6; GTBS-P; ImPo; LiTB; NAEL-1; NOBE; NoP; NoSic; OBEV; OBSC; OXAEP-1; PoRA; SCGP; Son; TEP; TrGrPo *Fr.* Sonnets. **CP-ShaWS**

When in the Course of Human Events. Kenneth Patchen. **CP-PatcK**

When, in the dark, the frost cracks on the window. The Winter's Night. Thomas Merton. **CP-MertT; SP-MertT**

When, in the darkness of his dream. Legendary Progress. Thomas McGrath. **SP-McGrT**

When in the down I sink my head. Tennyson. *Fr.* In Memoriam A. H. H. **CP-TennA**

When in the east the morning ray. Garden of Appleton House, The ("When in the east the morning ray"). Andrew Marvell. NOBE *Fr.* Upon Appleton House [To My Lord Fairfax]. **CP-MarvA**

When in the morning I rose to depart, my love came to say farewell. The Last Minute. David Herbert Lawrence. *Fr.* Bits. **CP-LawrD**

When in the Soul of the Serene Disciple. Thomas Merton. **CP-MertT; SP-MertT**

When in their ignorance and haste the skies must fall. Spring Storm. Thomas Merton. **CP-MertT; SP-MertT**

When in your middle years. Halley's Comet. Kenneth Rexroth. **SP-RexrK** *Fr.* The Lights in the Sky are Stars.

When into the night the yellow light is roused like dust above the towns. Piccadilly Circus at Night. David Herbert Lawrence. **CP-LawrD**

When into the night the yellow light is roused like dust above the towns. *also stands as sl. diff. separate poem* Picadilly Circus at Night. David Herbert Lawrence. *Fr.* Night Songs. **CP-LawrD**

When is a man not a man? The Gentleman. David Herbert Lawrence. **CP-LawrD**

When is winter spring? Home for Aged Bomb Throwers—U.S.S.R. Louis Zukofsky. *Fr.* 29 Songs. **CP-ZukLS**

When Israel Came Forth out of Egypt, sl. diff. vers. Bible, O.T. *See* Psalm 114: "When Israel went out of Egypt."

When Israel came from Egypt's coast. Bible, O.T. *See* Psalm 114: "When Israel went out of Egypt."

When Israel came out of Egypt, par. by David Rosenberg. Bible, O.T. *See* Psalm 114: "When Israel went out of Egypt."

When Israel Came Out of Egypt. Arthur Hugh Clough. **SP-ClouA**

When Israel, of the Lord beloved [*or* belov'd]. Rebecca's Hymn. Sir Walter Scott. **SP-ScotW** *Fr.* Ivanhoe.

When Israel out of Egypt came. Alfred Edward Housman. **CP-HousA**

When Israel went out of Egypt. Psalm 114. Bible, O.T. TrJP *Fr.* Psalms. **CP-Psal**

When Israel's Daughters mourn'd their past Offences. Epigram in a Maid of Honour's Prayer-Book. Alexander Pope. **CP-PopeA**

When Israel's ruler on the royal bed. Hymn to the Supreme Being. Christopher Smart. **SP-SmarC**

When it comes down turning. Snow. Adrienne Rich. **CP-RicAE**

When it comes to lamentations. A Different Drum. Leonard Cohen. **CP-CoheL**

When it comes to the calling of names. Man and Wife. Gilbert Sorrentino. **SP-SorrG**

When it is cold it stinks, and not till then. Samuel Beckett's Dublin. Donald Davie. **CP-DavDo**

When it is finally ours, this freedom, this liberty, this beautiful. Frederick Douglass. Robert Earl Hayden. **CP-HaydR**

When It Is Over. Edna St. Vincent Millay. **CP-MillE**

When it is sensation time at the home. A Song: Sensation Time at the Home. Thomas Merton. **CP-MertT**

When it is spring, / When the huge bulls roam in their pens. Spring: Monastery Farm. Thomas Merton. **CP-MertT**

When it rained and rained. Frederick Morgan. **SP-MorgF**

When it snowed hard, cars failed. Bystanders. William Matthews. **SP-MattW**

When it was day, we heard the panes of windows. Song, A. Thomas Merton. **CP-MertT**

When it was found a fault. The Scythian Charioteers. Donald Davie. **CP-DavDo**

When Jane was absent Edgar's eye. Ralph Waldo Emerson. **CP-EmerR**

When Januar' wind war blawing cauld. Robert Burns. **CP-BurnR**

(Bonie Lass Made the Bed to Me, The.) **CP-BurnR**

When jessie's fever went up god got farther away so he could see better. The Next to the Last Poem about God. Charles Kenneth Williams. **CP-WillC**

When Jesus commanded us to love our neighbor. Commandments. David Herbert Lawrence. **CP-LawrD**

When Jesus' friend had ceased to be. The Weeping Saviour. Elizabeth Barrett Browning. **CP-BroEB**

When Jesus got my broken back for Christmas, Juniors. Carol, A. Thomas Merton. **CP-MertT**

When Jesus walked into the wilderness. Jesus Walking. Anne Sexton. **CP-SextA**

When Jill complain[e]s to Jack for want of meat[e]. Upon Jack and Jill: Epigram. Robert Herrick. **CP-HerrR**

When John moved out Grandmother could foresee. My Grandmother's Restlessness. John Hewitt. **CP-HewiJ**

When Jove, in anger to the sons of Earth. The Origin of Flattery. Charlotte Smith. **CP-SmitC**

When Julia blushes, she do's show. Upon Her Blush. Robert Herrick. **CP-HerrR**

When Julia chid, I stood as mute the while. Teares are Tongues. Robert Herrick. **CP-HerrR**

When Julius Fabricius, Sub-Prefect of the Weald. The Land. Rudyard Kipling. **CP-KiplR**

When Kai is born. Not Leaving the House. Gary Snyder. **CP-SnydG**

When Katie walks, this simple pair accompany her side. Emily Dickinson. **CP-DickE**

When Klopstock England defied. William Blake. **CP-BlakW**

When Knowledge Went North. Chuang Tzu, tr. fr. Chinese by Thomas Merton. **CP-MertT**

When L———lles thought fit from this world to depart. On Captn. L———lles. Robert Burns. **CP-BurnR**

When labor is light and the morning is fair. Riding to Town. Paul Laurence Dunbar. **CP-DunbP**

When lads were home from labour. Fancy's Knell. Alfred Edward Housman. **CP-HousA**

When last before her people's face her own fair face she bent. Crowned and Wedded. Elizabeth Barrett Browning. **CP-BroEB**

When last I saw thee, I did not[t] thee see. Sonnet 21. Mary Sidney, Countess of Montgomery Wroth. Fr. Pamphilia to Amphilanthus. **CP-WrotM**

When late (grave Palmer) these thy graffs [or grafts] and flowers. To Thomas Palmer [on His Book "The Sprite of Trees and Herbs"]. Ben Jonson. **CP-JonsB**

When, lately Stella's form display'd. Stella in Mourning. Samuel Johnson. **CP-JohnS**

When latest Autumn spreads her evening veil. To Melancholy. Written on the Banks of the Arun, October 1785. Charlotte Smith. **CP-SmitC**

When Laura smiles her sight revives both night and day. At. to Thomas Campion and to Philip Rosseter. **CP-CampT**

When Lawes full power have to sway, we see. Lawes. Robert Herrick. **CP-HerrR**

When Lawyers strive to heal a breach. The Sergeant's Song. Thomas Hardy. **CP-HardT**

When Lazarus left his charnel-cave. Tennyson. **EBVV; FHYEP; OAEL-2; PeECV; TOF** Fr. In Memoriam A. H. H. **CP-TennA**

When Learning's Triumph o'er her barb'rous [or barbarous] Foes. Prologue Spoken by Mr[.] Garrick at the Opening of the Theatre in Drury Lane, 1747. Samuel Johnson. **CP-JohnS**

When Libra, Solidus, Denarius. [dP] S. D. Robert Ranke Graves. **CP-GravR**

When life is quite through with. Edward Estlin Cummings. **CP-CummE**

When life, love, poems. With Warm Regards to Miss Moore and Mr. Ransom. Mona Van Duyn. **SP-VanDM**

When, Like a Running Grave. Dylan Thomas. **CP-ThomD**

When Lilacs Last in the Dooryard Bloom'd. Walt Whitman. **OFD,** sect. 1, 2, and 6; **AP; APN-1; AWP; AmPP; BiP; CABA; CBCWP; FPL; FaBoEn; HAP; HBV; LiTA; LoBV; MasP; MeMAP; MoAmPo; NAAL-1; NAAL-3; NiP; NOBA; NoP; OxBA; PAI; PAL; PPP; PPoe; PoEL-5; PoRA; SAmP; SeCeV; TAP; TFi; TrGrPo; TreF** Fr. Memories of President Lincoln. **CP-WhitW**

"Come lovely and soothing death." **DL; SCV**

(Carol of Death, The.) **DL**

"In the swamp in secluded recesses." **RFM**

When Lil's husband got demobbed, I said. Thomas Stearns Eliot. **NAs** Fr. The Waste Land. **CP-ElioT**

When little boys grown [or grow] patient at last, weary. Death of Little Boys. Allen Tate. **CP-TateA**

When Little Claus meets Big Claus in the road. Pride. Wystan Hugh Auden. **CP-AudWJ**

When little more than boy in age. William Cowper, tr. fr. the Latin of Owen. **CP-CowpW**

When Loie Fuller's Chinese dancers enwound. William Butler Yeats. **DIP** Fr. Nineteen Hundred and Nineteen. **CP-YeatW**

When long sequester'd from his throne. On the Queens's Visit to London. William Cowper. **CP-CowpW**

When looking at that picture, all the past. Dedicated to Dear Nana Clarke. Edward Estlin Cummings. **CP-CummE**

When, looking on the present face of things. October, 1803 ("When, looking on the present face of things"). William Wordsworth. **CP-WorW1**

When loons laugh he does not. Barton Sutter. Fr. Deathwatch. **SP-SuttB** Fr. The Complaints of Poverty.

When Lord Byron wrote so glowingly of the isles of Greece. Chloe and the Roué. Ogden Nash. Fr. Fables Bullfinch Forgot. **CP-NashO**

When loud by landside streamlets gush. Spring Carol. Robert Louis Stevenson. **CP-StevR**

When Love at first did move. Ben Jonson. **CP-JonsB** Fr. The Masque of Beauty.

When love is a shimmering curtain. On Diverse Deviations. Maya Angelou. **SP-AngeM**

When love is for- / bidden, it / is the most! Now Then. Robert Creeley. **CP-CreeR**

When Love Is Not. Robert Ranke Graves. **CP-GravR**

When Love, puffed up with rage of high disdain. Sir Philip Sidney. **SP-SidnP**

When Love was born of heavenly line. The Birth of Love. William Wordsworth. **CP-WorW1**

When love with unconfinèd wings. To Althea, from Prison. Richard Lovelace. **CP-LoveR**

When love would strike th' offending fair. in imitation of Waller. Alexander Pope. **CP-PopeA**

When lovely woman stoops to folly and. Thomas Stearns Eliot. **UV** Fr. The Waste Land. **CP-ElioT**

When Lowell let me audit his writing course I left New York. Lowell: Self-Portrait. Stephen Berg. **SP-BergS**

When Lucifer was undefiled. The Last Song of Lucifer. Nicholas Vachel Lindsay. **CP-LindV**

When lyart leaves bestrow the yird. Robert Burns. Fr. The Jolly Beggars. **CP-BurnR**

When lyart leaves bestrow the yird. The Jolly Beggars. Robert Burns. **CP-BurnR**

When M-r-ne, deceased, to the devil went down. On J-hn M-r-ne, Laird of L-gg-n. Robert Burns. **CP-BurnR**

When mack smacked phyllis on the snout. Adhuc sub Judice Lis. Edward Estlin Cummings. **CP-CummE**

When Maggie once to Oxford came. Maggie's Visit to Oxford. "Lewis Carroll." **CP-CarrL**

When maguey gives way to pine. April 1937 In the Oaxaca Train. Malcolm Lowry. **CP-LowrM** Fr. The Lighthouse Invites the Storm. **CP-LowrM**

When Malindy Sings. Paul Laurence Dunbar. **CP-DunbP**

When Man Enters Woman. Anne Sexton. **CP-SextA**

When Man, expell'd from Eden's bowers. To a Lady. Byron. **CP-Byron**

When Man is gone and only gods remain. Edna St. Vincent Millay. *Fr.* Epitaph for the Race of Man. **CP-MillE**

When man is punisht, he is plagued still. The Will the Cause of Woe. Robert Herrick. **CP-HerrR**

When Mary cam over the Border. Bonie Mary. Robert Burns. **CP-BurnR**

When maukin bucks at early f—s. Ode to Spring. Robert Burns. **CP-BurnR**

When May is painting with her colours gay. Fragment: May the Limner. Percy Bysshe Shelley. **CP-ShelP**

When melancholy Autumn comes to Wembley. Harrow-on-the-Hill. Sir John Betjeman. **CP-BetjJ**

When Memory is full. Emily Dickinson. **CP-DickE**

When men a dangerous disease did 'scape. To Doctor Empiric[k]. Ben Jonson. **CP-JonsB**

When men are made in bottles. Wellsian Futures. David Herbert Lawrence. **CP-LawrD**

When Men Got to the Summit. Ted Hughes. **SP-HughT**

When men lie down for ever / and names their tombstones take. Grief. John Hewitt. **CP-HewiJ**

When men see Han-Shan. Gary Snyder. **CP-SnydG**

When men think they are like gods. Men Like Gods. David Herbert Lawrence. **CP-LawrD**

When men turn mob. Music and Drum. Archibald MacLeish. **CP-MacLA**

When Mercury and Love and Death. Emasculation. David Herbert Lawrence. **CP-LawrD**

When mid-autumn's moan shook the night-time. The Mother Mourns. Thomas Hardy. **CP-HardT**

When midnight comes a host of dogs and men. Badger. John Clare. **SP-ClarJ**

When midnight mists are creeping. Dreamland. "Lewis Carroll." **CP-CarrL**

When midnight occupied the porches of the Poet's reason. The Holy Child's Song. Thomas Merton. **CP-MertT**

When milder autumn summer's heat succeeds. Alexander Pope. **PBBP; SeCePo** *Fr.* Windsor-Forest [*or* Windsor Forest]. **CP-PopeA**

(Field notes.) **SeCePo**

When Mill first came to court, the unprofiting fool. On Mill, My Lady's Woman. Ben Jonson. **CP-JonsB**

When Miriam Tazewell heard the tempest bursting. Miriam Tazewell. John Crowe Ransom. **SP-RansJ**

When Mr. Apollinax visited the United States. Mr. Apollinax. Thomas Stearns Eliot. **CP-ElioT**

When Mrs. Welch's chimney smokes. Jonathan Swift. **CP-SwifJ**

When M'Liss went away from the old home. M'Liss and Louie. Carl Sandburg. **CP-SandC**

When moiling seems at cease. According to the Mighty Working. Thomas Hardy. **CP-HardT**

When Moses in Horeb struck the rock. On Certain Wits. Howard Nemerov. **CP-NemeH**

When most I wink, then do mine eyes best see. Sonnet 43. William Shakespeare. *Fr.* Sonnets. **CP-ShaWS**

When Most Men Die. David Herbert Lawrence. **CP-LawrD**

When Mother Clud had rose from play. The History of Vanbrug's House. Jonathan Swift. **CP-SwifJ**

When Mother died. The Routine Things Around the House. Stephen Dunn. **SP-DunnS**

When mountain rocks and leafy trees. Nature's Lineaments. Robert Ranke Graves. **CP-GravR**

When muckers pimps and tratesmen. Edward Estlin Cummings. **CP-CummE**

When music sounds, gone is the earth I know. Music. Walter de la Mare. **CP-DeLaW**

When my arms wrap you round I press. He Remembers Forgotten Beauty. William Butler Yeats. **CP-YeatW**

When my body leaves me. Gone Away. Denise Levertov. **CP-LeveD**

When my breast labours with oppressive care. A Paraphrase on the Latter Part of the Sixth Chapter of St. Matthew's. James Thomson. **CP-ThomJ**

When my contemporaries were driving. A Private Man on Public Men. Thomas Hardy. **CP-HardT**

When my date's done, and my gray age must die. To the Earle of Westmerland. Robert Herrick. **CP-HerrR**

When my dears die, the festival-colored brightness. Gwendolyn Brooks. **SP-BrooG** *Fr.* The Children of the Poor. **SP-BrooG,** sect. I, pt. 1-5; *Fr.* The Womanhood.

When my devotions could not pierce. Denial[l]. George Herbert. **CP-HerbG**

When my dreams showed signs. North American Time. Adrienne Rich. **SP-RicA1; SP-RicA2**

When my father had been dead a week. White Apples. Donald Hall. **CP-HallD**

When my good angel guides me to the place. Sonnet 60. Sir Philip Sidney. *Fr.* Astrophil and Stella. **SP-SidnP**

When my grandfather came to live with us. Orchard Country. John Hewitt. **CP-HewiJ**

When my grave is broke up again[e]. The Relic. John Donne. **CP-DonnJ**

When my hair was first trimmed across my forehead. Long Banister Lane. Li Po, tr. fr. Chinese by William Carlos Williams with David Rafael Wang. **CP-WilW2**

When My Heart Is Vexed, I Will Complain ("O Lord how can Thou say. . ."). Christina Georgina Rossetti. **CP-RosC1**

When My Heart Is Vexed I Will Complain ("Fields are white to harvest, look and see, The"). Christina Georgina Rossetti. **CP-RosC2**

When my life his pillar has raised to heaven. Sapphics. Edward Estlin Cummings. **CP-CummE**

When my little son leaps in my sight. George Meredith. **CP-MerG2**

When my love came home to me. In the Lane. Christina Georgina Rossetti. **CP-RosC3**

When my love comes to see me it's. Edward Estlin Cummings. **CP-CummE**

When my love swears [*or* sweares] that she is made of truth, *sl. diff. vers. also in* The Passionate Pilgrim. Sonnet 138. William Shakespeare. **AWP; BiP; CABA; EBEV; HeIP; NAEL-1; NoP; NoSic; OAEL-1; OAEP; OXAEP-1; PAI; PPP; PlP; PoEL-2; Poetr; SoSe; TEP; TrGrPo** *Fr.* Sonnets. **CP-ShaWS**

When my love swears that she is made of truth, *sl. diff. vers. also in* Sonnets. *Various Authors.* **CP-ShaWS** *Fr.* The Passionate Pilgrim. **CP-ShaWS**

When my lover touches me, what I feel in my body. Song of Obstacles. Louise Glück. *Fr.* Marathon. **SP-GlücL**

When my madness comes. Soliloquy. James McAuley. **SP-McAuJ**

When my mother died I was very young. Chimney Sweeper, The. William Blake. **CH; EnRP; FF; FHYEP; FaBoPV; HeIP; HoFi; InPK; LAuP; NAEL-2; NAWM-2; NOEC; OAEL-2; OXAEP-2; OxBChV; PAI; PPP; PPoe; PoE; Poetr; SCGP; SaC; SoSe; TEP; TFi** *Fr.* Songs of Innocence. **CP-BlakW**

When my off'ring next I make. The Frankincense. Robert Herrick. **CP-HerrR**

When my sensational moments are no more. Edward Estlin Cummings. **CP-CummE**

When my soul was raging, a flock of birds which whir up. Quail. Charles Olson. **CP-OlsoC**

When my Uncle came to visit us. Wouldn't You Be after a Jaunt of 964,000,000,000,000 Million Miles? Kenneth Patchen. **CP-PatcK**

When my wife's sister's husband came to die. John Hewitt. *Fr.* October Sonnets. **CP-HewiJ**

When my wiser brother. Daniel Gerard Hoffman. **SP-HoffD**

When my young lady has grown great and staid. To Rosabelle. Robert Louis Stevenson. **CP-StevR**

When Nations grow Old. The Arts grow Cold. William Blake. **CP-BlakW**

When Nature bids us leave to live, 'tis late. To William Roe. Ben Jonson. **CP-JonsB**

When Nature her great Masterpiece designed. To Robt. Graham of Fintry Esqr, with a Request for an Excise Division. Robert Burns. **CP-BurnR**

When Nature made her chief work, Stella's eyes. Sonnet 7. Sir Philip Sidney. **CABA; NAEL-1; NIP; Son** *Fr.* Astrophil and Stella. **SP-SidnP**

When nature once in lustful hot undress. *see also tr. by* Roy Campbell, "Of old when Nature, in her verve defiant." Charles Baudelaire, *tr. fr. French by* Karl Shapiro. **SP-ShapK**

When Nellie, my old pussy. A Theory of Prosody. Philip Levine. **SP-LeviP**

When night believes itself alone. Five Women Bathing in Moonlight. Richard Wilbur. **CP-WilbR**

When night comes black. The Shrike. Sylvia Plath. **CP-PlatS**

When night comes down upon the Chesapeake. Night on the Chesapeake. Paul Laurence Dunbar. **CP-DunbP**

When night falls / dead drum / in honor of night. Thomas Merton. *Fr.* The Early Legend. **CP-MertT**

When Night is almost done. Emily Dickinson. **CP-DickE**

When night moved through the air. A Poem for Dylan Thomas. Al Young. **CP-YounA**

When night slinks, like a puma, down the sky. Street Lamps. Philip Larkin. **CP-LarkP**

When night was lifting. At Waking. Thomas Hardy. **CP-HardT**

When night's [*or* nights] black mantle could most darkes prove. Sonnet 1. Mary Sidney, Countess of Montgomery Wroth. **Son** *Fr.* Pamphilia to Amphilanthus. **CP-WrotM**

When no one listens. Stranger. Thomas Merton. **CP-MertT**

When noon-time comes the whistle blows. Nuptials. Allen Tate. **CP-TateA**

When nuts behind the hazel-leaf. Song: Autumn. George Meredith. **CP-MerG1**

When Oats Were Reaped. Thomas Hardy. **CP-HardT**

When ocean-clouds over inland hills. Misgivings. Herman Melville. **SP-MelvH**

When o'er the Aegean vast he sails. 2.16. Horace. **SP-SmarC**, *tr. by* Christopher Smart; *Fr.* Odes.

When o'er the hill the eastern star. The Lea-Rig. Robert Burns. **CP-BurnR**

When oer the world the son of genius rose. Poem on Eloquence by R. W. Emerson. Ralph Waldo Emerson. **CP-EmerR**

When of tender mind and body. The Bridge of Lodi. Thomas Hardy. **CP-HardT**

When of your eyes one smile entirely brings down. Edward Estlin Cummings. **CP-CummE**

When old Grimes died, he left a son. Young Grimes. Walt Whitman. **CP-WhitW**

When old women say, it smells of snow. Northern Exposure. Charles Simic. **SP-SimiC**

When 'Omer Smote 'Is Bloomin' Lyre. Rudyard Kipling. **CP-KiplR**

When on Euphrates' banks we sate. Bible, *O.T. See* Psalm 137: "By the rivers of Babylon. . . ."

When on fair Celia I did spy. The Mistake. Thomas Carew. **CP-CareT**

When on My Bed the Moonlight Falls. Tennyson. **LoBV; MeMBP; NoP; OAEL-2; PeECV; SCGP; SeCePo; SeCeV** *Fr.* In Memoriam A. H. H. **CP-TennA**

When on my day of life the night is falling. At Last. John Greenleaf Whittier. **CP-WhitJ**

When on my faithful charger. Song. George Meredith. **CP-MerG2**

When on some balmy-breathing night of Spring. The Glow-Worm. Charlotte Smith. **CP-SmitC**

When on the altar of my hand. In the Person of a Lady To Her Inconstant Servant. Thomas Carew. **CP-CareT**

When on the banks of winter trees strip bare. Values. John Hewitt. **CP-HewiJ**

When on the cliffs we met, by chance. Recognition. Robert Ranke Graves. **CP-GravR**

When on the coral-red steps of old brownstones. Summer: West Side. John Updike. **CP-UpdiJ**

When on the primal peaceful blank profound. Uranus. Arthur Hugh Clough. **SP-ClouA**

When on the sandy shore I sit. Size and Tears. "Lewis Carroll." **CP-CarrL**

When, on your dangerous mission gone. Confidential Instructions. Stanley Jasspon Kunitz. **CP-KuniS**

When once the sin has fully acted been. Sin Seen. Robert Herrick. **CP-HerrR**

When once the Soule has lost her way. The Soule. Robert Herrick. **CP-HerrR**

When Once the Twilight Locks No Longer. Dylan Thomas. **CP-ThomD**

When One Age Goes with It Suddenly Its Errors Evaporate. Charles Olson. **CP-OlsoC**

When One has given up One's life. Emily Dickinson. **CP-DickE**

When one is lonely (and You. Minnelied. Wystan Hugh Auden. *Fr.* Three Posthumous Poems. **CP-AudeW**

When one is past, another care we have. Sorrows Succeed. Robert Herrick. **CP-HerrR**

When one of my oldest and dearest friends died and another friend called to console me. The Call. Charles Kenneth Williams. **SP-WillC**

When one of our citizens dies, his corpse is placed in his chariot. John Yau. **SP-YauJo** *Fr.* Corpse and Mirror I.

When one of our citizens dies, his head is cut off and placed inside. John Yau. **SP-YauJo** *Fr.* Corpse and Mirror I.

When one that you and I had all but sworn. Edwin Arlington Robinson. *Fr.* Octaves. **CP-RobiE**

When open trucks with German prisoners in them. Wiedersehen. Miller Williams. **SP-WillM**

When other Ladies to the Groves go down. Epigram. Alexander Pope. **CP-PopeA**

When others gain much by the present cast. Gain and Gettings. Robert Herrick. **CP-HerrR**

When our brother Fire was having his dog's day. Brother Fire. Louis MacNeice. **CP-MacNL**

When our hands touched, my darling, suddenly I heard. A Sentimental Delusion. Mona Van Duyn. **SP-VanDM**

When our privacy starts over again. Early Spring Between Madison and Bellingham. Robert Bly. **SP-BlyR**

When our two souls stand up erect and strong. Sonnet. Elizabeth Barrett Browning. **BWW; BoWoP; EnVR; GGP; NAEL-2; NALW; NOBE; OBEV; PFP; TrGrPo; VBLP; WPE** *Fr.* Sonnets from the Portuguese. **CP-BroEB**

When out of bed my love doth spring. Upon Electra. Robert Herrick. **CP-HerrR**

When over the flowery, sharp pasture's. Flowers by the Sea. William Carlos Williams. **CP-WilW1**

When overwhelmed to know. Emily Dickinson. **SP-DickE**

When Owen Roe. Commodore Barry. Donald Davie. **CP-DavDo**

When painfully athwart my brain. The Play-Ground. Walt Whitman. **CP-WhitW**

When pale famine fed on thee. To the Most Disconsolate Great Brittaine. Thomas Campion. **CP-CampT**

When panting sighs the bosom fill. Arthur Hugh Clough. **SP-ClouA**

When Parnell's Irish in the House. Wilfred Owen's Photographs. Ted Hughes. **SP-HughT**

When parsing warmths of dusk construe. Edward Estlin Cummings. **CP-CummE**

When passion's trance is overpast. To ———. Percy Bysshe Shelley. **CP-ShelP**

When pavements were blown up, exposing wires. Epilogue to a Human Drama. Stephen Spender. **CP-SpenS**

When people are born. People. Miller Williams. **SP-WillM**

When people are dead and peaceless. Dead People. David Herbert Lawrence. **CP-LawrD**

When people aren't asking questions. More About People. Ogden Nash. **CP-NashO**

When people bandy about bright sayings they like to attribute. There Were Giants in Those Days or Maybe There Weren't. Ogden Nash. **CP-NashO**

When people tell me French is difficult, I show my dimple. What Is Bibbidi-Bobbidi-Boo in Sanskrit? Ogden Nash. **CP-NashO**

When Peter Jackson Preached in the Old Church. Nicholas Vachel Lindsay. **CP-LindV**

When Philoctetes in the Lemnian Isle. William Wordsworth. **CP-WorW2**

When Phoebus was am'rous, and long' to be rude. Apollo and Daphne. Christopher Smart. **SP-SmarC**

When Phyllis sighs and from her eyes. Response. Paul Laurence Dunbar. **CP-DunbP**

When Pimpes feet sweat (as they doe often use). Upon Pimpe. Robert Herrick. **CP-HerrR**

When pimps out of loneliness cry. Sliver of Sermon. Langston Hughes. **SP-HughL**

When plans were announced to tear down. Condo Moon. John Updike. **CP-UpdiJ**

When Polly's reddening hand. Three Chores. James Merrill. **SP-MerrJ**

When poor Rossetti lost his wife. Dante Gabriel. David Markson. **CP-MarkD**

When Portia her dear I Lord's sad fate did hear. Martial, *tr. fr. Latin by* Richard Lovelace. **CP-LoveR**

When pre-pubescent I felt. A Thanksgiving. Wystan Hugh Auden. **CP-AudeW**

When Princes and Prelates and het-headed zealots. Why Should Na Poor Folk Mowe. Robert Burns. **CP-BurnR**

When psalms surprise me with their music. Psalm, A. Thomas Merton. **CP-MertT; SP-MertT**

When Queen Djenira slumbers through. Queen Djenira. Walter de la Mare. **CP-DeLaW**

When rain, (sings light) rain has devoured my house. Song. Thomas Merton. **CP-MertT**

When rain whom fear. Edward Estlin Cummings. **CP-CummE**

When recently, at the same time against the King and the British lords. On the Gunpowder Plot. John Milton, *tr. fr. Latin by* John T. Shawcross. **CP-MiltJ**

When reeds are dead and a straw to thatch the marshes. The Death of Autumn. Edna St. Vincent Millay. **CP-MillE**

When rites and melodies begin. Wystan Hugh Auden. **NePA; OAEL-2** *Fr.* Five Songs ("Deftly, admiral, cast your fly"). **CP-AudeW**

(Proof, The.) **NePA; OAEL-2**

When Romans gambled in the clash of lancelight. The Sponge Full of Vinegar. Thomas Merton. **CP-MertT**

When, Rome, I read thee in thy mighty pair. To My Chosen Friend the Learnèd Translator of Lucan, Thomas May, Esquire. Ben Jonson. **CP-JonsB**

When Rome was rotten-ripe to her fall. The Pirates in England. Rudyard Kipling. **CP-KiplR**

When Roses cease to bloom, Sir. Emily Dickinson. **CP-DickE**

When rosy May comes in wi' flowers. The Gardener wi' His Paddle—or, The Gardener's March. Robert Burns. **CP-BurnR**

When rosy plumelets tuft the larch. Tennyson. **FHYEP; FaBoEn; OBNC** *Fr.* In Memoriam A. H. H. **CP-TennA**

When Ruth was left half desolate. Ruth [or, The Influences of Nature]. William Wordsworth. **CP-WorW1**

When sages speak of the freedom of the will. Philosophy. Howard Nemerov. **CP-NemeH**

When Sam'l Sings. Paul Laurence Dunbar. **CP-DunbP**

When Samson set my brush afire. Fox-Hunting. Rudyard Kipling. **CP-KiplR**

When Samson went in unto Delilah. Samson. Frederick Morgan. **SP-MorgF**

When Sarah Pierrepont let her spirit rage. John Crowe Ransom. **SP-RansJ** (To the Scholars of Harvard.) **SP-RansJ**

When Sarah wrote Peter how she slept. Sarah's Letter to Peter. Carl Sandburg. **CP-SandC**

When Satan Fell. David Herbert Lawrence. **CP-LawrD**

When science starts to be interpretive. Self-Protection. David Herbert Lawrence. **CP-LawrD**

When senselessness has pounded you around on the ropes. In Celebration of Surviving. Chuck Miller. **SP-MillC**

When senses, which thy so[u]ldiers are. John Donne. *Fr.* A Litany. **CP-DonnJ**

When serpents bargain for the right to squirm. Edward Estlin Cummings. **CP-CummE; SP-CummE**

When Severn's Sweeping Flood Had Overthrown. William Wordsworth. **CP-WorW2**

When shadows climb. Landscape With A Woman. Richard Shelton. **SP-ShelR**

When shall I behold again the cold limbed bare breasted. Return. Archibald MacLeish. **CP-MacLA**

When shall I see the half-moon sink again. End of Another Home Holiday. David Herbert Lawrence. **CP-LawrD**

When shall that fuel fed fire grown fatter. A Humane Materialist at the Burning of a Heretic. Stevie Smith. **CP-SmitS**

When shall we learn, what should be clear as day. Canzone. Wystan Hugh Auden. **CP-AudeW**

When She Cam Ben She Bobbed. Robert Burns. **CP-BurnR**

When she came on, you couldn't keep your seat. He Hears That His Beloved Has Become Engaged. Philip Larkin. **CP-LarkP**

When she came suddenly in. The Door. Robert Ranke Graves. **CP-GravR**

When she died she became a wind. Werewind. Lewis Turco. **SP-TurcL**

When she had her stroke the china dogs. Louis MacNeice. **CP-MacNL** *Fr.* The Kingdom. **CP-MacNL**

When she laughs there is a glitter as of morning before me. George Meredith. *Fr.* Arabic Poems. **CP-MerG2**

When she left she took everything—her hair. A Suite of Imitations Written After Reading Translations of Poems by Li He And Li Shang-yin. John Yau. **SP-YauJo**

When she married years ago. The Italian Garden. William Carlos Williams. **CP-WilW2**

When she rises in the morning. Gloire de Dijon. David Herbert Lawrence. **CP-LawrD**

When she rises in the morning, *also stands as sl. diff. separate poem* Gloire de Dijon. David Herbert Lawrence. *Fr.* All of Roses. **CP-LawrD**

When she said, / "Don't waste your words, they're just lies." Fourth Time Around. "Bob Dylan." **CP-DylaB**

When she speaks it is like coming onto a grave. Gray Eyes. Tess Gallagher. **SP-GallT**

When she took the whiskey sours out. The Servant of Stars. Leonard Nathan. **SP-NathL**

When she was born the wind was north. Marina—. Malcolm Lowry. **CP-LowrM**

When she was drunk. Gus Sees Wanda Drinking. Paul Zimmer. **SP-ZimmP**

When she was young she wanted. Grace Paley. *Fr.* Stanzas: Old Age and the Conventions of Retirement Have Driven My Friends from the Work They Love. **CP-PaleG**

When she was young she wanted. Stanzas: Old Age and the Conventions of Retirement Have Driven My Friends from the Work They Love. Grace Paley. **CP-PaleG**

When sick of life and all the world. I Will Lift Up Mine Eyes unto the Hills. Christina Georgina Rossetti. **CP-RosC2; CP-RosC3**

When silly Sol in winter roisters. Song of the Open Fireplace. John Updike. **CP-UpdiJ**

When silver Snow decks Susan's clothes. Blind-Man's Buff. William Blake. **CP-BlakW**

When silver snow decks Sylvio's cloaths [or clothes]. Song 3rd By an Old Shepherd. William Blake. **CP-BlakW**

When simple *Macer*, now of high renown. Macer: A Character. Alexander Pope. **CP-PopeA**

When singing songs of scariness. The Worst. Shel Silverstein. **SP-SilS2**

When Sir Gawain was led to his bridal-bed. The Song of Courtesy. George Meredith. **CP-MerG1**

When Sir Harry asked Government Agent Nicol "who that woman" was. And a Few More Cargo Songs. Thomas Merton. *Fr.* East. *Fr.* The Geography of Lograire. **CP-MertT**

When Sir [or Sr] Joshua Reynolds died. William Blake. **CP-BlakW**

When slow Disease, with all her host of pains. Childish Recollections. Byron. **CP-Byron**

When slow from pensive twilight's latest gleams. William Wordsworth. **CP-WorW1**

When smoke stood up from Ludlow. Alfred Edward Housman. **CP-HousA**

When snow like sheep lay in the fold. In Memory of Jane Fraser [or Frazer]. Geoffrey Hill. **CP-HillG**

When snows begin to fill the park. The Seasonless. James Wright. **CP-WrigJ**

When soft September brings again. Arthur Hugh Clough. **SP-ClouA**

When soft winds and sunny skies. Fragment. Percy Bysshe Shelley. **CP-ShelP**

When some amazonian indians for whom. Hayden Carruth. *Fr.* North Winter. **CP-CarHL**

When some beloved voice that was to you. Substitution. Elizabeth Barrett Browning. **CP-BroEB**

When some beloveds, 'neath whose eyelids lay. Bereavement. Elizabeth Barrett Browning. **CP-BroEB**

When some brisk youth, the tenant of a stall. Byron. **PF** *Fr.* English Bards and Scotch Reviewers. **CP-Byron**

When some proud son of man returns to earth. Inscription on the Monument of a Newfoundland Dog. Byron. **CP-Byron**

When some shall say, Faire once my Silvia was. Upon Silvia, a Mistresse. Robert Herrick. **CP-HerrR**

When some were happy as the grass was green. A Baptist Childhood. Donald Davie. *Fr.* A Dissentient Voice. **CP-DavDo**

When someone leans in and says, "Koohurch?" Pronouncing My Name. Ron Koertge. **SP-KoerR**

When sorrow (using mine own fire's might). Sonnet 108. Sir Philip Sidney. *Fr.* Astrophil and Stella. **SP-SidnP**

When sorrows had begirt me round. For Deliverance from a Fever. Anne Bradstreet. **CP-BradA**

When, soul in soul reflected. Unknowing. Thomas Hardy. **CP-HardT**

When speaking of people and their beliefs I wear my belief on my sleeve. Seeing Eye to Eye Is Believing. Ogden Nash. **CP-NashO**

When sperm leaves us. For Fathers of Girls. Stephen Dunn. **SP-DunnS**

When spring-time flushes the desert grass. The Ballad of the King's Jest. Rudyard Kipling. **CP-KiplR**

When Statesmen gravely say, "We must be realistic." Wystan Hugh Auden. **FaBoCo; OBCoV; PV** *Fr.* Shorts [1939–1947] ("Motionless, deep in his mind, lies the past the poet's forgotten"). **CP-AudeW**

(Statesmen.) **OBCoV**

When, staunchly entering port. The Beauty of the Ship. Walt Whitman. **CP-WhitW**

When Stella strikes the tuneful String. To Miss —: On Her Playing upon the Harpsichord. Samuel Johnson. **CP-JohnS**

When storms arise. Hymn. Paul Laurence Dunbar. **CP-DunbP**

When stormy day is cold & gray. George Meredith. **CP-MerG2**

When strife is a thing of two. Strife. David Herbert Lawrence. **CP-LawrD**

When Structure Fails Rhyme Attempts to Come to the Rescue. William Carlos Williams. **CP-WilW2**

When success exalts thy lot. Ralph Waldo Emerson. **CP-EmerR**

When Sue Wears Red. Langston Hughes. **SP-HughL**

When summer came, we locked up our lives and fled. The Gentle Snorer. Mona Van Duyn. **SP-VanDM**

When summer heat has drowsed the day. Memory. Walter de la Mare. **CP-DeLaW**

When summer shone / Its sweetest on. The Faithful Swallow. Thomas Hardy. **CP-HardT**

When summer time has come, and all. In Summer Time. Paul Laurence Dunbar. **CP-DunbP**

When summer's end is nighing. Alfred Edward Housman. **CP-HousA**

When sun, light handed, sows this Indian water. Aubade: Lake Erie. Thomas Merton. **CP-MertT; SP-MertT**

When sunset, a brass gong. The Saddhu of Couva. Derek Walcott. **CP-WalcD**

When Susan's work was done, she'd [or she would] sit. Old Susan. Walter de la Mare. **CP-DeLaW**

When Tartine turned 20, her Papa. Tartine's Banishment. Laurence Lieberman. **SP-LiebL**

When that day comes, whose evening sayes I'm gone. His Sailing from Julia. Robert Herrick. **CP-HerrR**

When that dead-certainty appals my thought. Death, from a Distance. Jorge Guillén, *tr. fr. Spanish by* Richard Wilbur. **CP-WilbR**

When that I call unto my mind. Sir Thomas Wyatt. **CP-WyatT**

When that jackbooted choreography. Marilyn Hacker. **SP-HackM** *Fr.* Taking Notice.

When that prime heroine of our nation, Alice. Alice. Robert Ranke Graves. **CP-GravR**

When that rich soul [*or* soule] which to her heaven is gone. The First Anniversary [*or* Anniversarie]. John Donne. **AnAnS-1; MasP; SeCV-1** *Fr.* Anatomy [*or* Anatomie] of the World, An[: The First Anniversary]. **CP-DonnJ**

When that with meat and drink they had fulfilled. *parody of* John Milton. Rudyard Kipling. **CP-KiplR** *Fr.* The Muse among the Motors.

When the air was damp. The Tresses. Thomas Hardy. **CP-HardT**

When the albums of this century's intermingling. Island Sun. John Updike. **CP-UpdiJ**

When the alcoholic passed the crucial point. Point of No Return. Robert Ranke Graves. **CP-GravR**

When the 'arf-made recruity goes out to the East. The Young British Soldier. Rudyard Kipling. **CP-KiplR**

When the Astronomer stops seeking. Emily Dickinson. **CP-DickE**

When the autumn roses. Song-Day in Autumn. David Herbert Lawrence. **CP-LawrD**

When the badger glimmered away. The Badgers. Seamus Heaney. **SP-HeanS**

When the bare feet of the baby beat across the grass, *sl. diff. vers.* David Herbert Lawrence. *See* Baby Running Barefoot.

When the bee lands the. Transfer. Archie Randolph Ammons. **SP-AmmoA**

When the bees are humming in the honeysuckle vine. Love's Seasons. Paul Laurence Dunbar. **CP-DunbP**

When the Bell Rings in the Steeple. John Hewitt. **CP-HewiJ**

When the bells justle in the tower. Alfred Edward Housman. **CP-HousA**

When the Berry Bush Dies I'll Swim Down the Green River with My Hair on Fire. Charles Bukowski. **SP-BukC2**

When the birds are singing in the bushes. Evening Bird Song. Richard Eberhart. **CP-EberR**

When the black snake. The Black Snake. Mary Oliver. **SP-OlivM**

When the blackberries hang. August. Mary Oliver. **SP-OlivM**

When the blest seed of *Terah's* faithfull Son. A Paraphrase on Psalm 114. John Milton. **CP-MiltJ**

When the boys came home, everything stopped. The Bird Frau. Rita Dove. **SP-DoveR**

When the bright lamp is carried in. North-West Passage. Robert Louis Stevenson. **CP-StevR**

When the British warrior queen. Boadicea: An Ode. William Cowper. **CP-CowpW**

When the cabin port-holes are dark and green. Rudyard Kipling. **CP-KiplR** *Fr.* How the Whale Got his Throat. *Fr.* Just-So Stories.

When the car at night. Insight. Mona Van Duyn. **SP-VanDM**

When the car spun from the road and your neck broke. Death and the Sun. Derek Mahon. **SP-MahoD**

When the cataract dries up, my dear. A Note. William Carlos Williams. **CP-WilW2**

When the Century Dragged. Robert Penn Warren. **MoAmPo** *Fr.* Infant Boy at Midcentury. **SP-WarrR**

When the charge of election bribery was brought against an Illinois. Implications. Carl Sandburg. **CP-SandC**

When the children of Israel, when the noble tribes of Jacob. Psalm 114. John Milton, *tr. fr. Greek by* John T. Shawcross. **CP-MiltJ**

When the clock-tick fades. The Sound of Time. Charles Tomlinson. **CP-TomlC**

When the cloud shut down on the morning shine. The Occultation. Thomas Hardy. **CP-HardT**

When the clouds' swoln bosoms echo back the shouts of the many and strong. Thomas Hardy. **BrPo; CMoP; ChIV-1; LiTM; NoAM; OxBTC; VLP** *Fr.* In Tenebris. **CP-HardT**

When the colossus of the will's dominion. Villa Adriana. Adrienne Rich. **CP-RicAE; SP-RicA2**

When the colossuses multiplied, / walked upright into their own. The Island (VII). Pablo Neruda, *tr. fr. Spanish by* Ben Belitt. **SP-NeruP** *Fr.* The Separate Rose.

When the coolie blew. Charles Henri Ford. **SP-FordC** *Fr.* Emblems of Arachne.

When the corn stands yellow in September. Harvest. Carl Sandburg. **CP-SandC**

When the corn's all cut and the bright stalks shine. Corn-Stalk Fiddle, The. Paul Laurence Dunbar. **CP-DunbP**

When the cows come home the milk is coming. Christina Georgina Rossetti. **CP-RosC2**

When the crickets. Louis Zukofsky. **CP-ZukLS**

When the crow. Crow Ride. Archie Randolph Ammons. **SP-AmmoA**

When the crows fly away. My Love. Richard Shelton. **SP-ShelR**

When the cuckoo, the cow, and the coffe-plant chipped the. Him with His Tail in His Mouth. David Herbert Lawrence. **CP-LawrD**

When the dark dawn humped off to die. A Little Girl on Her Way to School. James Wright. **CP-WrigJ**

When the darkened Fifties dip to the North. Song of the Wise Children. Rudyard Kipling. **CP-KiplR**

When the days grow teeth at last and games. A Letter to the Young Men. Kenneth Patchen. **CP-PatcK**

When the Dead Arise. Stanley Jasspon Kunitz. **CP-KuniS**

When the Deadly Nightshade flowers. Deadly Nightshade. Erica Jong. **SP-JongE**

When the departing sun resigns. An Ode on a Lady Leaving Her Place of Abode; Almost Impromptu. Samuel Johnson. **CP-JohnS**

When the devil brings him. How to Name Your Familiar. Erica Jong. **SP-JongE**

When the Devil Was Sick Could He Prove It? Ogden Nash. **CP-NashO**

When the difference is not a name. Incident of Cherries and Peaches. Diane Wakoski. **SP-WakoD**

When the dim light, at Lauds, comes strike her window. Aubade—the Annunciation. Thomas Merton. **CP-MertT**

When the drums begin to beat. The Juggler's Song. Rudyard Kipling. **CP-KiplR** *Fr.* Kim.

When the Dumb Speak. Robert Bly. **SP-BlyR**

When the eagle soared clear through a dawn distilling of emerald. Crow and the Birds. Ted Hughes. **SP-HughT**

When the earth was sick and the skies were grey. Rudyard Kipling. **CP-KiplR** *Fr.* The Other Man. *Fr.* Plain Tales from the Hills.

When the elephant's-ear in the park. Tea. Wallace Stevens. **CP-StevW**

When the eleventh hour / Unbars the burning west. The Fall of Night. Thomas Merton. **CP-MertT**

When the exposed spirit, busy in daytime. Time Exposures. Muriel Rukeyser. **PoA** *Fr.* Night-Music. **CP-RukeM**

When the eye hardly sees. Long Looked For. Christina Georgina Rossetti. **CP-RosC3**

When the eye of day is shut. Alfred Edward Housman. **CP-HousA**

When the fight was over. The Victor. Daniel Gerard Hoffman. **SP-HoffD**

When the first signs go on. Ernesto Cardenal, *tr. by* Thomas Merton. **CP-MertT** *Fr.* Gethsemani, KY.

When the first white flakes. The Romantic. John Hewitt. **CP-HewiJ**

When the flaming lute-thronged angelic door is wide. The Travail of Passion. William Butler Yeats. **CP-YeatW**

When the flood of gelid extasy has done. This Living in Small Place. Marsden Hartley. **CP-HartM**

When the flush of a new-born sun fell first on Eden's green and gold. The Conundrum of the Workshops. Rudyard Kipling. **CP-KiplR**

When the Flyin' Scot. Uncle Henry. Wystan Hugh Auden. **CP-AudeW**

When the fog dropped swiftly. Café Vue des Alpes. Peter Meinke. **SP-MeinP**

When the foot opens like a cup. Matin Pour Matta. Charles Henri Ford. **SP-FordC**

When the footbridge washes away. The Roadway. Adrienne Rich. **CP-RicAE**

When the forehead drains. Ah. Archie Randolph Ammons. **SP-AmmoA**

When the full fields begin to smell of sunrise. The Trappist Abbey: Matins. Thomas Merton. **CP-MertT; SP-MertT**

When the Full-Grown Poet Came. Walt Whitman. **CP-WhitW**

When the Glass of My Body Broke. Anne Sexton. **CP-SextA**

When the gnats dance at evening. Gnat-Psalm. Ted Hughes. **SP-HughT**

When the God of Merrie Love. Thomas Campion. **CP-CampT**

When the gods who once ruled over the. Withdrawal. Tom Clark. **SP-ClarT**

When the golden day is done. Night and Day. Robert Louis Stevenson. **CP-StevR**

When the grass was closely mown. The Dumb Soldier. Robert Louis Stevenson. **CP-StevR**

When the Great Ark. Rudyard Kipling. **CP-KiplR**

When the great bell / Booms over the Portland stone urn, and. City. Sir John Betjeman. **CP-BetjJ**

When the great Kings return to clay. The Burial. Rudyard Kipling. **CP-KiplR**

When the great nothingness was everything. Mystery of the Abstract. Richard Eberhart. **CP-EberR**

When the great ship ran madly towards the rocks. Gorgon Mask. Robert Ranke Graves. **CP-GravR**

When the green army battled and drove North. Semi-Centennial. John Crowe Ransom. *Fr.* Sixteen Poems in Eight Pairings. **SP-RansJ**

When the green army drove the black one North. Birthday of an Aging Seer. John Crowe Ransom. *Fr.* Sixteen Poems in Eight Pairings. **SP-RansJ**

When the Green Woods Laugh. William Blake. **CH; EnRP; GoJo; HoFi; LAuP; NBLV; OxBChV; PoSC; SUS; SoPo; TiPo** *Fr.* Songs of Innocence. **CP-BlakW**

(Laughing Song.) **BoTP; FHYEP; NAEL-2**

When the grey geese heard the Fool's tread. The Flight. Rudyard Kipling. **CP-KiplR**

When the grey stranger shows up in your dream. Nightmare. Howard Nemerov. **CP-NemeH**

When the half-body dies its frightful death. Resurrection of the Right Side. Muriel Rukeyser. **CP-RukeM**

When the hamlet hailed a birth. Mad Judy. Thomas Hardy. **CP-HardT**

When the Harteebeeste is on the horse. With Sweetest Love from All the Little Animals As from 2 Old Friends. Malcolm Lowry. **CP-LowrM**

When the Head of Bran / Was firm on British shoulders. The Head of Bran the Blest. George Meredith. **CP-MerG1**

When the hermit made an end. Tennyson. *PeVV Fr.* The Holy Grail. *Fr.* Idylls of the King. **CP-TennA**

When the hero of the threshold enters our lives and our houses. Hero Speech. Muriel Rukeyser. **CP-RukeM**

When the heroes came back from the ten-years' war. War Heroes. Louis MacNeice. *Fr.* Out of the Picture. **CP-MacNL**

When the Himalayan peasant meets the he-bear in his pride. The Female of the Species. Rudyard Kipling. **CP-KiplR**

When the historical process breaks down and armies organize with. The Age of Anxiety. Wystan Hugh Auden. **CP-AudeW**

When the hounds of spring are on winter's traces. The Hounds of Spring. Algernon Charles Swinburne. **SP-SwinA** *Fr.* Atalanta in Calydon.

When the ice starts to shiver. On Edges. Adrienne Rich. **CP-RicAE; SP-RicA1; SP-RicA2**

When the immense drugged universe explodes. Ecstasy of Chaos. Robert Ranke Graves. **CP-GravR**

When the indefinable / Moment apprises. Louis MacNeice. *Fr.* Visitations. **CP-MacNL**

When the inmate stirs, the birds retire discreetly. A Bird-Scene at a Rural Dwelling. Thomas Hardy. **CP-HardT**

When the Journey Was Intended to the City, *parody of* John Milton. Rudyard Kipling. **CP-KiplR** *Fr.* The Muse among the Motors.

When the June bugs were a-circlin'. The Inexpressible. Ernest Hemingway. **CP-HemiE**

When the jury files in to deliver a verdict after weeks of direct and cross. Lawyer. Carl Sandburg. **CP-SandC**

When the King found that his money was nearly all, *sels.* "Lewis Carroll." *Fr.* Puzzles. *Fr.* Puzzles from Wonderland. **CP-CarrL**

When the King sat down to the feast and the golden lid revealed. Thyestes. Louis MacNeice. **CP-MacNL**

When the kitchen is lit by lilacs. Familial. William Matthews. **SP-MattW**

When the knight had finished, no one, young or old. Geoffrey Chaucer. *See* The Miller's Prologue.

When the lad for longing sighs. Alfred Edward Housman. **CP-HousA**

When the lamp glowed. Bye-Child. Seamus Heaney. **SP-HeanS**

When the lamp is shattered [*or* shatter'd]. Lines. Percy Bysshe Shelley. **CP-ShelP**

When the last mirage. Red Fountain. John Yau. **SP-YauJo**

When the last sunshine of expiring day. Monody on the Death of the Right Hon. R. B. Sheridan. Byron. **CP-Byron**

When the lieutenant of the Guardia de Asalto. On the Murder of Lieutenant José Del Castillo by the Falangist Bravo Martinez, July 12, 1936. Philip Levine. **SP-LeviP**

When the Light Falls. Stanley Jasspon Kunitz. **CP-KuniS**

When the light spine of a society. For the Spanish Poet Miguel Hernandez. Thomas Merton. **CP-MertT**

When the light was shutting down on you. Reading Aloud. Tess Gallagher. **SP-GallT**

When the lithe moonlight silently. Nocturne. Edward Estlin Cummings. **CP-CummE**

When the little girl was told that the sun someday. The Saving Way. Hayden Carruth. **CP-CarHS**

When the Lord brought back those that returned to Zion. Bible, *O.T. See* Psalm 126: "When the Lord turned again the captivity of Zion. . . ."

When the Lord turned again the captivity of Zion, we were like them that dream. Psalm 126. Bible, *O.T. Fr.* Psalms. **CP-Psal**

When the lovely bride and groom came out onto the grand front steps. A Report on a Happening in Washington Square San Francisco. Lawrence Ferlinghetti. **SP-FerlL**

When the magician died, I wept. Stanley Jasspon Kunitz. *Fr.* The Way Down. **CP-KuniS**

When the maiden leaves off teasing. Gallant's Song. Thomas Hardy. **CP-HardT**

When the man in the plane is a man I could shoot him on sight. The Illegal Heart. Malcolm Lowry. **CP-LowrM**

When the man is busy. Revolution Is One Form of Social Change. Audre Lorde. **SP-LordA**

When the Master was calling the roll. Anseo. Paul Muldoon. **SP-MuldP**

When the Medina Luminous Division marched into. The Commanders. Tom Clark. **SP-ClarT**

When the Mississippi Flowed in Indiana. Nicholas Vachel Lindsay. **CMoP** *Fr.* Three Poems About Mark Twain. **CP-LindV**

When the moon falls on a man's blood. Moon Memory. David Herbert Lawrence. **CP-LawrD**

When the moon rises. Out Here. Richard Shelton. **SP-ShelR**

When the moon was a hammock of gold. Moon Hammock. Carl Sandburg. **CP-SandC**

When the morning was waking over the war. Among Those Killed in the Dawn Raid Was a Man Aged a Hundred. Dylan Thomas. **CP-ThomD**

When the mouse died at night. The Mouse. Jean Garrigue. **SP-GarrJ**

When the movie ends and the lights come on, the audience is puzzled. John Yau. **SP-YauJo** *Fr.* Corpse and Mirror III.

When the movie ends, the lights come on. The audience is puzzled. John Yau. **SP-YauJo** *Fr.* Corpse and Mirror III.

When the Music's Over. Jim Morrison. **SP-MorrJ**

When the new frogs in their exuberant arrivals. On Returning to a Lake in Spring. Richard Eberhart. **SP-EberR**

When the Night Comes Falling from the Sky. "Bob Dylan." **CP-DylaB**

When the Night Puts Twenty Veils. Philip Larkin. **CP-LarkP**

When the nightingale to his mate. Alba ("When the nightingale to his mate"). Ezra Pound. **SP-PounE** *Fr.* Langue d'Oc.

When the night's coming and the last light falls. The Ancestors. Allen Tate. **CP-TateA**

When the north and the east crawled with armed tribes toward mindless wars. At the Birth of an Age. Robinson Jeffers. **CP-JefR2**

When the odds are long. When You Say That, Smile! or All Right Then, Don't Smile. Ogden Nash. **CP-NashO**

When the Old Man Smokes. Paul Laurence Dunbar. **CP-DunbP**

When the old mirror crashed in the ruined mansion. The Reprieve. Frederick Morgan. **SP-MorgF**

When the old servant reveals she is the mother. A Night at the Opera. Charles Tomlinson. **CP-TomlC**

When the people knew you. Lonely Particular. Alice Walker. **CP-WalkA**

When the pistol muzzle oozing blue vapour. That Moment. Ted Hughes. **SP-HughT** *Fr.* Crow.

When the planes come in all night, and the lights reach, wavering. The Learners. Randall Jarrell. **CP-JarrR**

When the Present has latched its postern behind my tremulous stay. Afterwards. Thomas Hardy. **CP-HardT**

When the proficient poison of pure sleep. Edward Estlin Cummings. **CP-CummE**

When the proud fleet that bears the red-cross flag. William Wordsworth. **FaBoPV** *Fr.* Residence in France and French Revolution. *Fr.* The Prelude; Growth of a Poet's Mind [1850 vers.]. **CP-WorW3**

When the Pulitzers showered on some dope. Words for Hart Crane. Robert Lowell. **SP-LoweR**

When the rain is over / I go to the woods. Dreams. Mary Oliver. **SP-OlivM**

When the rain stops. Midnight. Robert Creeley. **CP-CreeR**

When the rattlesnake bit, I lay. The Poisoned Man. James Dickey. **CP-DickJ**

When the raving tuskèd boar. Defeat. Alun Lewis. *Fr.* Two Legends: for Greece. **CP-LewiA**

When the reaper's task was ended, and the summer wearing late. The Swan Song of Parson Avery. John Greenleaf Whittier. **CP-WhitJ**

When the red pond fills fish appear. Ayers Rock / Uluru Song. Allen Ginsberg. **CP-GinsA**

When the Retarded Swim. Gary Gildner. **SP-GildG**

When the Revolution Came. Stephen Dunn. **SP-DunnS**

When the Ripe Fruit Falls. David Herbert Lawrence. **CP-LawrD**

When the road forked. Richard Shelton. *Fr.* Angel and the Anchorite. **SP-ShelR**

When the roads first came. The Hard Road. Louise McNeill. **SP-McNeL**

When the robust and Brass-bound Man commissioned first for sea. Poseidon's Law. Rudyard Kipling. **CP-KiplR**

When the Romantic Ego had begun to fester. A Letter to W.H. Auden. Daniel Gerard Hoffman. **SP-HoffD**

When the rose is faded. Walter de la Mare. **CP-DeLaW**

When the runner's whistle lights the last miles of darkness. Soldier [T. P.]. Randall Jarrell. **CP-JarrR**

When the Russian Tanks Roll Westward. Philip Larkin. **CP-LarkP**

When the Saints Come Marching In. Audre Lorde. **SP-LordA**

When the scale were sucking. Toads in the Greenhouse. Gary Gildner. **SP-GildG**

When the Scientists Told Me of the Expanding Universe. Louise McNeill. **SP-McNeL**

When the scrapers of the. Many Hats. Carl Sandburg. **CP-SandC**

When the sea is everywhere. North Atlantic. Carl Sandburg. **CP-SandC**

When the sea pours out under the bridge. Froth. Richard Eberhart. **CP-EberR**

When the seaswell takes me in. Oblique Frontier. Marsden Hartley. **CP-HartM**

When the serpent emerged, earth-bowel brown. A Horrible Religious Error. Ted Hughes. **SP-HughT**

When the shining boughs are bare. Song: The Wren. George Meredith. **CP-MerG2**

When the Ship Comes In. "Bob Dylan." **CP-DylaB**

When the Shoe Fits. Chuang Tzu, *tr. fr. Chinese* by Thomas Merton. **CP-MertT**

When the sky stopped glowering and glazed hailstones. A Felled Tree. Daniel Gerard Hoffman. **SP-HoffD**

When the snow falls the flakes. The Dance. William Carlos Williams. **CP-WilW2**

When the soft hand of sleep had closed the latch. Ode: 1814. William Wordsworth. **CP-WorW2**

When the soprano sang. Broken Hearted Soprano. Carl Sandburg. **CP-SandC**

When the soul is mad. The Desperate. Alun Lewis. **CP-LewiA**

When the sound of forest leaves is like the sleep-talk. Vessels. James Dickey. **CP-DickJ**

When the South sang like a nightingale. George Meredith. *Fr.* The Young Princess. **CP-MerG1**

When the Sparrow Flies. Stevie Smith. **CP-SmitS**

When the spent day begins to frail. Edward Estlin Cummings. **CP-CummE**

When the spent sun throws up its rays on cloud. Acceptance. Robert Frost. **CP-FrosR**

When the spring comes round, and a certain day. Joys of Memory. Thomas Hardy. **CP-HardT**

When the stern god. Mythic Fragment. Louise Glück. **SP-GlücL**

When the still sea conspires an armor. Horse Latitudes. Jim Morrison. **SP-MorrJ**

When the stones burst into flame. Kenneth Patchen. **CP-PatcK**

When the stranger came out of the night. Louis MacNeice. *Fr.* Visitations. **CP-MacNL**

When the streetcar stalled on Joy Road. On the Birth of Good & Evil During the Long Winter of '28. Philip Levine. **SP-LeviP**

When the stuffed prophets quarrel, when the sawdust comes. Roosevelt. Nicholas Vachel Lindsay. **CP-LindV**

When the substitute asked my eighth-grade daughter. The Substitute. Stephen Dunn. **SP-DunnS**

When the Summer fields are mown. Aftermath. Henry Wadsworth Longfellow. **SP-LongH**

When the sun comes after rain. Robert Louis Stevenson. **CP-StevR**

When the sun gets low, in winter. Human Things. Howard Nemerov. **CP-NemeH**

When the sun goes in a shadow flies over. Sun, Aeroplane, Lovers. Malcolm Lowry. **CP-LowrM**

When the sun shouts and people abound. Summer Holiday. Robinson Jeffers. **CP-JefR1**

When the sun was winter high. Winter Day. John Hewitt. **CP-HewiJ**

When the surf licking with its tongues. Indian Point. Marsden Hartley. **CP-HartM**

When the swans turned my sister into a swan. The Black Swan. Randall Jarrell. **CP-JarrR; SP-JarrR**

When the sweet showers of April fall and shoot. Geoffrey Chaucer. *See* Whan that Aprille [*or* April, *or* Aprill] with his[e] shoures [*or* showres] sote [*orsoote*].

When the sweet showers of April follow March. Geoffrey Chaucer. *See* Whan that Aprille [*or* April, *or* Aprill] with his[e] shoures [*or* showres] sote [*orsoote*].

When the sword of sixty comes nigh his head. Basil Bunting, *after the Persian of* Firdausi. **CP-BuntB**

When the synchrotron was being built. Almagest, Last Letter to Zakarias. Siv Cedering Fox. **SP-CedeS**

When the tall puffy. Donald Hall. **CP-HallD**

(Old Timer's Day.) **CP-HallD**

When the third summer freed us from restraint. William Wordsworth. **OAEL-2** *Fr.* Cambridge and the Alps. *Fr.* The Prelude; Growth of a Poet's Mind [1850 vers.]. **CP-WorW3**

When the thorn on the down. The Voice of the Thorn. Thomas Hardy. **CP-HardT**

When the thunder stalks the sky. Summer Serenade. Ogden Nash. **CP-NashO**

When the tide was out. A Ship Burning and a Comet All in One Day. Richard Eberhart. **CP-EberR**

When the time has arrived. Trala Trala Trala La-le-la. William Carlos Williams. **CP-WilW2**

When the torch is taken / And the room is dark. Seneca. Thomas Merton. **CP-MertT**

When the train whistles, it wants to say. The See-er of Cities. Randall Jarrell. **CP-JarrR**

When the tree-sparrows with no sound through the pearl-pale air. Edna St. Vincent Millay. **CP-MillE**

When the trees do laugh with our merry wit. Song 2nd By a Young Shepherd. William Blake. **CP-BlakW**

When the true things meet us at the place we reach, they are all. Muriel Rukeyser. **CP-RukeM**

When the two fish spoke. Two Fish. Carl Sandburg. **CP-SandC**

When the vain triumph of the imperial lord. Condolatory Address. Byron. **CP-Byron**

When the voices of children are heard on the green / And laughing is heard on the hill. Nurse's Song. William Blake. **AWP; BLPL; CH; EnRP; FHYEP; FaBoBe; FaPON; HBV; HBVY; HoFi; LAuP; NAEL-2; OBEC; OxBChV; PeLV; SCGP** *Fr.* Songs of Innocence. **CP-BlakW**

When the voices of children are heard on the green / And whisperings [*or* whisprings] are in the dale. Nurse's Song. William Blake. **CP-BlakW** *Fr.* Songs of Experience.

When the walls were red. The Ageing House. Thomas Hardy. **CP-HardT**

When the war is over the bones of the lonely dead. The Monkey's Paw. Peter Meinke. **SP-MeinP**

When the warl's couped soon' [*or* roun'] as a peerie. Moonstruck. "Hugh MacDiarmid." **NeBP** *Fr.* Au Clair de la Lune. **SP-MacDH**

When the warnings. To My Other Self. Richard Shelton. **SP-ShelR**

When the wasting embers redden the chimney-breast. Night in the Old Home. Thomas Hardy. **CP-HardT**

When the waters' countenance. The Wet Litany. Rudyard Kipling. **CP-KiplR**

When the Waters were dried an' the Earth did appear. Sappers. Rudyard Kipling. **CP-KiplR**

When the white feet of the baby beat across the grass. Baby Running Barefoot. David Herbert Lawrence. **CP-LawrD**

When the white feet of the baby beat across the grass. *also stands as sl. diff. and separate poem* A Baby Running Barefoot. David Herbert Lawrence. *Fr.* Baby-Movements. **CP-LawrD**

When the white fog burns off. The Depths. Denise Levertov. **CP-LeveD**

When the white stars talk together like sisters. A Christmas Card. Thomas Merton. **CP-MertT**

When the wild strawberry leaves turn. Grace Paley. **CP-PaleG**

When the Wind. Stevie Smith. **CP-SmitS**

When the wind blows her veil. Birdcage Walk. David Herbert Lawrence. **CP-LawrD**

When the wind works against us in the dark. Storm Fear. Robert Frost. **CP-FrosR**

When the windows of the West Side clash like cymbals in the setting sunlight. Hymn of Not Much Praise for New York City. Thomas Merton. **CP-MertT**

When the winter sky, snow-ominous, crowds in. First Snow in the Glens. John Hewitt. **CP-HewiJ**

When the wooden sea guard. Breakwater. Dabney Stuart. **SP-StuaD**

When the world is frozen. Ice Fishing. Siv Cedering Fox. **SP-CedeS**

When the world takes over for us. Lear. William Carlos Williams. **CP-WilW2**

When the Year Grows Old. Edna St. Vincent Millay. **CP-MillE**

When the young man reaches his full height. Muriel Rukeyser. **CP-RukeM**

When them old hooters had plenty eating material. Hayden Carruth. *Fr.* The Sleeping Beauty. **CP-CarHL**

When there are so many we shall have to mourn. In Memory of Sigmund Freud. Wystan Hugh Auden. **CP-AudeW**

When there was air, when you could. Remembering. William Stafford. **SP-StafW**

When there were no depths. I Weep, Fountain of Jazer. Charles Olson. **CP-OlsoC**

When these, and such, their voices have employed. To His Friend the Author upon His *Richard*. Ben Jonson. **CP-JonsB**

When these graven lines you see. A Happy Man. Carphyllides. **AWP** *Fr.* Variations of Greek Themes. **CP-RobiE**

When these sad sights were overpast and gone. Edmund Spenser. *Fr.* Visions of the World's Vanity [*or* Vanitie]. **CP-Spens**

When these two butterflies flutter upward toward the blue-white agatine sky. Rhopaloceral. Hayden Carruth. *Fr.* Poetical Abstracts. **CP-CarHS**

When these were past, thus gan the Titanesse. Mutability. Edmund Spenser. **PoEL-1** *Fr.* The Faerie Queene. **CP-Spens**

When Theseus in the labyrinth. Victory. Alun Lewis. *Fr.* Two Legends: for Greece. **CP-LewiA**

When Theseus went down. Ariadne and the Minotaur. Charles Tomlinson. **CP-TomlC**

When they came for Him in the garden, did they know? In the Garden. "Bob Dylan." **CP-DylaB**

When they came near. The Names. Robert Creeley. **CP-CreeR**

When they come back—if Blossoms do. Emily Dickinson. **CP-DickE**

When they did greet me Father, sudden Awe. Sonnet on Receiving a Letter Informing Me of the Birth of a Son. Samuel Taylor Coleridge. **CP-ColeS**

When they have completed its re-edification. South Parks Road. James Fenton. *Fr.* Exempla. **SP-FentJ**

When they killed my mother it made me nervous. The State. Randall Jarrell. **CP-JarrR**

When they mow the fields, I see the world reformed. 7/16/68: ii. Adrienne Rich. **CP-RicAE** *Fr.* Ghazals: Homage to Ghalib. **SP-RicA2**

When they plan a freeway thru a city. The End of Krim's Pad. Richard Hugo. **CP-HugoR**

When they put him in rompers the habits. The Habits. Louis MacNeice. **CP-MacNL**

When they said *Carrickfergus* I could hear. The Singer's House. Seamus Heaney. **SP-HeanS**

When they torture your mother. Torture. Alice Walker. **CP-WalkA**

When they turn the sun. Yellow. Anne Sexton. **CP-SextA**

When They Were Come unto the Faery's Court. John Keats. **CP-KeatJ**

When they're decent about women, they're frightful about. What Do We See? Muriel Rukeyser. **CP-RukeM**

When thin-strewn memory I look through. Miss Loo. Walter de la Mare. **CP-DeLaW**

When things are creatures and the creatures speak. Eagles. Daniel Gerard Hoffman. **SP-HoffD**

When things began to happen to our favorite spot. To T. S. Eliot on His Sixtieth Birthday. Wystan Hugh Auden. *Fr.* Three Occasional Poems. **CP-AudeW**

When things get very bad, they pass beyond tragedy. At Last. David Herbert Lawrence. **CP-LawrD**

When This American Woman. Leonard Cohen. **CP-CoheL**

When This Clangor in the Brain. Adrienne Rich. **CP-RicAE**

When this fly lived, she used to play. A Fly That Flew into My Mistress'[s] Eye. Thomas Carew. **CP-CareT**

When this grave's mould is broken up again. Instructions for the World Librarian. John Clellon Holmes. **SP-HolmJ**

When this hand is gone to earth. Artifact. Muriel Rukeyser. **CP-RukeM**

When this is the thing you put on. Armor. James Dickey. **CP-DickJ**

When this yokel comes maundering. The Plot against the Giant. Wallace Stevens. **CP-StevW**

When Thomas set this tablet here. For Richmond's Garden Wall. Robert Louis Stevenson. **CP-StevR**

When those of us who seem. Marriages. Philip Larkin. **CP-LarkP**

When those who can never again forgive themselves. Muriel Rukeyser. *Fr.* Night-Music. **CP-RukeM**

When thou art dead,dead,and far from the splendid sin. Edward Estlin Cummings. **CP-CummE**

When thou art little as I am, mother. Karma. Walter de la Mare. **CP-DeLaW**

When thou do'st play, and sweetly sing. Upon Sapho, Sweetly Playing, and Sweetly Singing. Robert Herrick. **CP-HerrR**

When thou goest through the Waters. Emily Dickinson. **SP-DickE**

When thou hast taken thy last applause,and when. Edward Estlin Cummings. **CP-CummE**

When Thou Must Home. Thomas Campion. **CP-CampT**

When thou must home to shades of underground [*or* under ground]. When Thou Must Home. Thomas Campion. **CP-CampT**

When thou, poor[e] excommunicate. To My Inconstant Mistress [*or* Mistris]. Thomas Carew. **CP-CareT**

When thou shalt be dispos'd to set me light. Sonnet 88. William Shakespeare. **OXAEP-1** *Fr.* Sonnets. **CP-ShaWS**

When thou sittest moping. Ralph Waldo Emerson. **CP-EmerR**

When thou to my true-love [*or* true love] com'st. Westphalian Song. Unknown, tr. fr. German by Samuel Taylor Coleridge. **CP-ColeS**

When Thou wast taken, Lord, I oft have read. His Words to Christ, Going to the Cross. Robert Herrick. **CP-HerrR**

When Thurlow This Damn'd Nonsense Sent. Byron. **CP-Byron**

When thy great soul was freed from mortal chains. His Descendents. William Wordsworth. *Fr.* Ecclesiastical Sonnets. **CP-WorW2**

When thy soul / Is filled with a just image fear not thou. Ralph Waldo Emerson. **CP-EmerR**

When time delicately is sponging sum after. Edward Estlin Cummings. **CP-CummE**

When Time, or soon or late, shall bring. Euthanasia. Byron. **CP-Byron**

When time was young, and the world in infancy. The Four[e] Monarchies. Anne Bradstreet. **CP-BradA**

When times are troubled, then forbeare; but speak. Speake in Season. Robert Herrick. **CP-HerrR**

When to a House I come, and see. Leprosie in Houses. Robert Herrick. **CP-HerrR**

When, to disarm suspicious minds at lunch. A Household. Wystan Hugh Auden. **CP-AudeW**

When to Her Lute. At. to Thomas Campion *and to* Philip Rosseter. **CP-CampT**

When to my melancholy. Revivals. Denise Levertov. **CP-LeveD**

When to sweet music my lady is dancing. The Valse. Paul Laurence Dunbar. **CP-DunbP**

When, to the attractions of the busy world. William Wordsworth. **CP-WorW1**

When to the inward darkness of my mind. Twilight. Walter de la Mare. **CP-DeLaW**

When to the sessions of sweet silent thought. Sonnet 30. William Shakespeare. **AWP; ArLo; BiP; CABA; CTC; ClHu; EBEV; EBEvV; EiL; EnRePo; FF; FPL; FaBV; FaBoEn; FaBoRV; FaFP; FaPoB; GBL; GTBS; GTBS-6; GTBS-P; HAP; HBV; HeIP; ImPo; InPS; LiTB; LoBV; MasP; NAEL-1; NOBE; NoP; NoSic; OAEL-1; OAEP; OBEV; OBSC; OXAEP-1; PAI; PPP; PoE; PoEL-2; PoLF; PoPle; PoRA; PrIm; SCGP; SeCeV; TEP; TFi; TRV; TrGrPo; TreFS; WHA** *Fr.* Sonnets. **CP-ShaWS**

When, to their airy hall, my fathers' voice. Fragment, A. Byron. **CP-Byron**

When to thy Porch I come, and (ravisht) see. To the Honoured, Master Endimion Porter. Robert Herrick. **CP-HerrR**

When Toller died, the roses at his bier. May 22nd 1939. Edwin Rolfe. **CP-RolfE**

When, towards the summer's close. The Yellow-Hammer. Thomas Hardy. **CP-HardT**

When true love broke my heart in half. The Surly One. Theodore Roethke. **CP-RoetT**

When twilight comes, before it gets too late. Evening Walk in France. May Sarton. **SP-SartM**

When twilight darkens, and one by one. Evening. Walter de la Mare. **CP-DeLaW**

When two suns do appear, *speech of Basilius*. Sir Philip Sidney. **SP-SidnP** *Fr.* Arcadia.

When two times two was three. The Chicken Without a Head. Charles Simic. **SP-SimiC**

When Ulysses braved the wine-dark sea. Making the Move. Paul Muldoon. **SP-MuldP**

When unexpected sun beat day-long down. Summer Park. John Hewitt. **CP-HewiJ**

When unity, having found its way throughout. Roundel. Archie Randolph Ammons. **SP-AmmoA**

When unto nights of autumn do complain. Edward Estlin Cummings. **CP-CummE**

When up aloft / I fly and fly. The Robin. Thomas Hardy. **CP-HardT**

When Vice triumphant holds her sov'reign sway. Byron. **FHYEP** *Fr.* English Bards and Scotch Reviewers. **CP-Byron**

When Victor Emanuel the King. The Sword of Castruccio Castracani. Elizabeth Barrett Browning. **CP-BroEB**

When Walking. Stevie Smith. **CP-SmitS**

When was it long ago the murmurings began. Carl Sandburg. *Fr.* The People, Yes. **CP-SandC**

When was it that we swore to love for ever? The Rose. Robert Ranke Graves. **CP-GravR**

When was the last time. Sun Tan at Dusk. James Wright. **CP-WrigJ**

When was there contract better driven by Fate? On the Union. Ben Jonson. **CP-JonsB**

When Watchful came to me he said. Watchful. Stevie Smith. **CP-SmitS**

When water turns ice does it remember. Metamorphosis. Carl Sandburg. **CP-SandC**

When we are going toward someone we say. Simple-Song. Marge Piercy. **SP-PierM**

When we are old and these rejoicing veins. Edna St. Vincent Millay. **CP-MillE**

When we are satisfied or get what we want. Mermaid. Stephen Dobyns. **SP-DobyS**

When we as strangers sought. At an Inn. Thomas Hardy. **CP-HardT**

When we came out of the wood. The Attack. David Herbert Lawrence. **CP-LawrD**

When we came up the Gorge that Sunday. Hôtel de la Truite. Peter Meinke. **SP-MeinP**

When we can all so excellently give. Sonnet. Edwin Arlington Robinson. **CP-RobiE**

When we climbed the slopes of the cutting. The Railway Children. Seamus Heaney. **SP-HeanS**

When we consider what this life we lead. Christina Georgina Rossetti. *Fr.* Later Life: A Double Sonnet of Sonnets. **CP-RosC2**

When We Dead Awaken. Adrienne Rich. **SP-RicA2**

When we do give, Alphonso, to the light. To the Same [Alphonso Ferrabosco]. Ben Jonson. **CP-JonsB**

When we finally tracked him down, the old man (not really all that very old, we thought). Rungs. Charles Kenneth Williams. **SP-WillC**

When we first met and loved, I did not build. Sonnet. Elizabeth Barrett Browning. *Fr.* Sonnets from the Portuguese. **CP-BroEB**

When we [first] moved here, pulled. An Oregon Message. William Stafford. **SP-StafW**

When we 'gainst Satan stoutly fight, the more. Satan. Robert Herrick. **CP-HerrR**

When we get back, the wagon will be gone. The Refusal. James Wright. **CP-WrigJ**

When we get out of the glass bottles of our ego. David Herbert Lawrence. **CP-LawrD**

(Escape.) **CP-LawrD**

When we have / played with. Merchandise. Archie Randolph Ammons. **SP-AmmoA**

When we have ceased to care. Emily Dickinson. **CP-DickE**

When we have thrown off this old suit. The Question Whither. George Meredith. **CP-MerG1**

When we lay where Budmouth Beach is. Budmouth Dears. Thomas Hardy. **CP-HardT** *Fr.* The Dynasts.

When we locked up the house at night. Locked Out. Robert Frost. **CP-FrosR**

When we look at things in the light of Tao. Great and Small. Chuang Tzu, *tr. fr.* Chinese by Thomas Merton. **CP-MertT**

When We Look Up. Denise Levertov. **BTR** *Fr.* During the Eichmann Trial. **CP-LeveD**

When we mesh badly, with scraping and squeaking. Marge Piercy. *Fr.* Doing It Differently. **SP-PierM**

When we met. The Awakening. Alice Walker. **CP-WalkA**

When we, our weary limbs to rest. Bible, *O.T. See* Psalm 137: "By the rivers of Babylon. . . ."

When we sailed homewards burning embers. The Odyssey. Alun Lewis. **CP-LewiA**

When we sat his mother on her tail, he mouthed her teat. Ted Hughes. **OBD** *Fr.* The Sheep has stopped crying. *Fr.* Sheep. **SP-HughT**

When we say fresh eggs we mean fresh. Carl Sandburg. *Fr.* The People, Yes. **CP-SandC**

When We Say Goodbye. Thomas McGrath. **SP-McGrT**

When we shall hear no more the cradle-songs. Edwin Arlington Robinson. *Fr.* Octaves. **CP-RobiE**

When we spurt off. Moving. William Matthews. **SP-MattW**

When we stand on the tops of Things. Emily Dickinson. **CP-DickE**

When we start breaking up in the wet darkness. Consolations of Philosophy. Derek Mahon. **SP-MahoD**

When we stop where you lived, the house. Disappearances in the Guarded Sector. Tess Gallagher. **SP-GallT**

When we stormed the city Sirk in the mountains. From a Forgotten Book. Frederick Morgan. **SP-MorgF**

When we that wore the myrtle wear the dust. Edna St. Vincent Millay. **CP-MillE**

When we thought him near. Gone Away. Phoebe Hesketh. **SP-HeskP**

When We Two Parted. Byron. **CP-Byron**

When We Were Children. Louis MacNeice. **CP-MacNL**

When we were children said. Jemez. Charles Tomlinson. **CP-TomlC**

When we were half asleep we thought it seemed. The Rookery. Wystan Hugh Auden. **CP-AudWJ**

When We Were Here Together. Kenneth Patchen. **CP-PatcK**

When We with Sappho. Kenneth Rexroth. **SP-RexrK**

When Wearily We Shrink Away. Thomas Hardy. **CP-HardT**

When weary with the long day's care. Emily Brontë. **CP-BronE**

(To Imagination.) **CP-BronE**

When weather shouted at us: vagabond. Graves at Coupeville. Richard Hugo. **CP-HugoR**

When welcome slumber sets my spirit free. Charlotte Smith. **CP-SmitC**

When well we speak, & nothing do that's good. The Chewing [of] the Cud. Robert Herrick. **CP-HerrR**

When we've been divorced for a while, and you get. After Yeats, After Ronsard, *Pace* Hopkins. James McAuley. **SP-McAuJ**

When what hugs stopping earth than silent is. Edward Estlin Cummings. **CP-CummE**

When what is lov'd, is Present, love doth spring. Presence and Absence. Robert Herrick. **CP-HerrR**

When, when, and whenever death closes our eyelids. Ezra Pound. **MeMAP; MoAB; OBMV; PoA** *Fr.* Homage to Sextus Propertius. **SP-PounE**

When white people speak of being uptight. The Dancer. Al Young. **CP-YounA**

When wickedness is broken as a tree / Paradise comes to light, ah holy land! Christina Georgina Rossetti. **CP-RosC2**

When wild War's deadly blast was blawn. Robert Burns. **CP-BurnR**

When will the bell ring and end this weariness. *also stands as sl. diff. separate poem,* Last Lesson of the Afternoon, *and incl. in* The Schoolmaster [B]. David Herbert Lawrence. *Fr.* The Schoolmaster [A]. **CP-LawrD**

When will the bell ring, and end this weariness? *also stands as sl. diff. separate poem,* Last Lesson of the Afternoon, *and incl. in* The Schoolmaster [A]. David Herbert Lawrence. *Fr.* The Schoolmaster [B]. **CP-LawrD**

When will the bell ring, and end this weariness? Last Lesson of the Afternoon. David Herbert Lawrence. **CP-LawrD**

When will the day bring its pleasure? Until the Day Break. Christina Georgina Rossetti. **CP-RosC2**

When Will was at home in his palace of zinc. George Meredith. **CP-MerG2**

When will you ever, Peace, wild wooddove, shy wings shut. Peace. Gerard Manley Hopkins. **CP-HopkG**

When will you learn, my self, to be. The Leaf and the Tree. Edna St. Vincent Millay. **CP-MillE**

When Willie Crosby died I thought too much. Survival in Missouri. John Ciardi. **SP-CiarJ**

When Wilt Thou Teach the People? David Herbert Lawrence. **CP-LawrD**

When wilt thou wake, O Mother, wake and see. The Sleep-Worker. Thomas Hardy. **CP-HardT**

When wind and winter turn our vineyard. The Vine. Thomas Merton. **CP-MertT**

When Winds and Seas do rage. The Goodnesse of His God. Robert Herrick. **CP-HerrR**

When winds that move not its calm surface sweep. Moschus, *tr. fr. Greek by* Shelley. **CP-ShelP**

(From the Greek of Moschus.) **CP-ShelP**

When winter comes. The White Hotel. Richard Shelton. **SP-ShelR**

When winter covering all the ground. When Winter Darkening All Around. Paul Laurence Dunbar. **CP-DunbP**

When Winter Darkening All Around. Paul Laurence Dunbar. **CP-DunbP**

When winter's glaze is lifted from the greens. The Sometime Sportsman Greets the Spring. John Updike. **CP-UpdiJ**

When wise Lord Berkeley first came here. The Discovery. Jonathan Swift. **CP-SwifJ**

When wise Ulysses from his native Coast. Argus. Alexander Pope. **CP-PopeA**

When wit and genius meet their doom. *see also* On the Burning of Lord Mansfield's Library. William Cowper. **CP-CowpW**

When wit, and learning are so hardly set. To Mr Ben Jonson in His Journey, by Mr Craven. Ben Jonson. **CP-JonsB**

When, with a pain he desires to explain to his servitors, Baby. The Nurses. Rudyard Kipling. **CP-KiplR** *Fr.* Land and Sea Tales.

When with day's woes night haunts wake-weary eyes. A Prayer. Walter de la Mare. **CP-DeLaW**

When with his hunting dog I see a cloud. Canto 82. Ezra Pound. *Fr.* Cantos. **CP-PoCan**

When with the Virgin morning thou dost rise. Matins [*or* Mattens], *or* Morning Prayer. Robert Herrick. **CP-HerrR**

When women stop carrying. A Beginning. Charles Bukowski. **SP-BukC3**

When words we want, Love teacheth to endite. Writing. Robert Herrick. **CP-HerrR**

When workless men walk down the street. The Simple-Minded Christian. John Hewitt. **CP-HewiJ**

When, wounded by her anger at some trifle. The Pearl. Robert Ranke Graves. **CP-GravR**

When wrath & terror changed Jove's regal port. Ralph Waldo Emerson. **CP-EmerR**

When Yankee soldiers reach the barricade. Mark Twain and Joan of Arc. Nicholas Vachel Lindsay. *Fr.* Three Poems About Mark Twain. **CP-LindV**

When ye say to Tabaqui, "My Brother!" when ye call the Hyena to meat. Rudyard Kipling. **CP-KiplR** *Fr.* The Undertakers. *Fr.* The Second Jungle Book.

When ye stood up in the house. The Fourfold Aspect. Elizabeth Barrett Browning. **CP-BroEB**

When yer head gets twisted and yer mind grows numb. Last Thoughts on Woody Guthrie. "Bob Dylan." **CP-DylaB**

When you and I on the Palos Verdes cliff. Shane O'Neill's Cairn. Robinson Jeffers. **CP-JefR2**

When you and I were all. Randall Jarrell. **CP-JarrR**

When you and I were young, the days. Retrospection. Paul Laurence Dunbar. **CP-DunbP**

When you and my true lover meet. The Lady's Third Song. William Butler Yeats. **CP-YeatW**

When you appeared it was as if. Happenstance. Rita Dove. **SP-DoveR**

When you are come by ways emptied of light. Art. Allen Tate. **CP-TateA**

When you are dead and the frosty iron of laughter. Vigil. Allen Tate. *Fr.* The Progress of Œnia. **CP-TateA**

When you are dead, and your disturbing eyes. Edna St. Vincent Millay. **CP-MillE**

When you are Mistresse of the song. To the Queen, an Apologie for the Length of the Following Panegyricke. Richard Crashaw. **CP-CrasR**

When You Are Old. William Butler Yeats, *after the French of* Pierre de Ronsard. **CP-YeatW**

When you are old and beautiful. At Majority. Adrienne Rich. **CP-RicAE**

When you are old as I now am. Serpent's Tail. Robert Ranke Graves. **CP-GravR**

When you are picked up dead. To Chink Whose Trade Is Soldiering. Ernest Hemingway. **CP-HemiE**

When you are silent,shining host by guest. Edward Estlin Cummings. **CP-CummE**

When you are very old, by candleglow. Pour Hélène. Pierre de Ronsard, *tr. fr. French by* John Hewitt. **CP-HewiJ**

When you ask for Cockle's Pills. Cockle's Antibilious Pills. Gerard Manley Hopkins. *Fr.* A Trio of Triolets. **CP-HopkG**

When you began your story all its words. To a Scholar in the Stacks. Howard Nemerov. **CP-NemeH**

When you break a mirror, you must count up the pieces to see if. John Yau. **SP-YauJo** *Fr.* Corpse and Mirror II.

When you came and you talked and you read with your. To William Carlos Williams. Galway Kinnell. **SP-KinnG**

When you came, it was as if I saw you. The Evening News. Gilbert Sorrentino. **SP-SorrG**

When you can no longer / eat. Attentiveness. Alice Walker. **CP-WalkA**

When you climb up to the middle classes. Climbing Up. David Herbert Lawrence. **CP-LawrD**

When you close your eyes. Charles Henri Ford. **SP-FordC** *Fr.* Secret Haiku.

When you come / Every evening. An Exchange of Gifts. May Sarton. **SP-SartM**

When you come, as you soon must, to the streets of our city. Advice to a Prophet. Richard Wilbur. **CP-WilbR**

When you come to London Town. London Stone. Rudyard Kipling. **CP-KiplR**

When You Come to Me. Maya Angelou. **SP-AngeM**

When you do say hello I am never sure. Progress Report. Audre Lorde. **SP-LordA**

When you find a gold stone know. Gold Stone. Richard Hugo. **CP-HugoR**

When you first arrived in Kirchstetten, trains had. Lines to Dr Walter Birk On His Retiring from General Practice. Wystan Hugh Auden. *Fr.* Eleven Occasional Poems. **CP-AudeW**

When you first introduced me to your nurse. A Well-to-Do Invalid. Randall Jarrell. **CP-JarrR**

When You Gonna Wake Up? "Bob Dylan." **CP-DylaB**

When you ground the lenses and the moons swam free. The Emancipators. Randall Jarrell. **CP-JarrR**

When you happened to sprain your wrist or ankle. Glanders. Paul Muldoon. **SP-MuldP**

When you have nothing more to say, just drive. The Peninsula. Seamus Heaney. **SP-HeanS**

When you have shoved aside the scribbled worksheet. Osip Emilevich Mandelstam. *Fr.* Octets. **CP-DavDo**

When you hear it languishing. The Oxford Voice. David Herbert Lawrence. **CP-LawrD**

When you hear me singing. Rat Song. Margaret Atwood. **NIP** *Fr.* Songs of the Transformed. **SP-AtwM1**

When you hefted them you knew at once. The Boat-Builder's Caulking Irons. John Hewitt. **CP-HewiJ**

When you hobble, tattered through the square. Pizzeria S. Biagio. Richard Hugo. **CP-HugoR**

When you imagine trumpet-faced musicians. Homage to Literature. Muriel Rukeyser. **CP-RukeM**

When you kissed me it was as if. Pencil Sketch of Self & Other. Jane Cooper. **SP-CoopJ**

When you live in your car. Chuck Miller. **SP-MillC**

When you look at a picture you always can see. William Blake. **CP-BlakW**

When you look at nothing. Margaret Atwood. *Fr.* Circe / Mud Poems. **SP-AtwM1**

When you look down from the airplane you see lines. Field and Forest. Randall Jarrell. **CP-JarrR; SP-JarrR**

When you paced forth, to await maternity. At a Bridal. Thomas Hardy. **CP-HardT**

When you plunged. The Otter. Seamus Heaney. **SP-HeanS**

When You Point Your Finger. Alfonso Cortes, *tr. fr. Spanish by* Thomas Merton. **CP-MertT**

When you put on that inmost ring. The Felled Elm and She. Thomas Hardy. **CP-HardT**

When you rang at Dick Mid's Place. Edward Estlin Cummings. **CP-CummE**

When you reach home tonight you will see. Does the Wild Rose? Robert Penn Warren. **SP-WarrR**

When you remember me, my child. Mississippi Winter II. Alice Walker. **CP-WalkA**

When you rest your hands. Narcissus Blues. William Matthews. **SP-MattW**

When you roll along admiring the view. The Voluble Wheel Chair. Ogden Nash. **CP-NashO**

When you said "accidental" / I thought it was that you were formal. Je Vois dans le Hasard Tous les Biens Que J'espere. Robert Creeley. **CP-CreeR**

When you said it wasn't my fault. Explanation. Leonard Nathan. **SP-NathL**

When You Say That, Smile! or All Right Then, Don't Smile. Ogden Nash. **CP-NashO**

When you see me sitting quietly. On Aging. Maya Angelou. **SP-AngeM**

When you see them. Take Time Out. Maya Angelou. **SP-AngeM**

When you shall arrive. Paul. William Carlos Williams. **CP-WilW2**

When you shall see me in the toils of Time. Thomas Hardy. **OxBTC** *Fr.* She, to Him. **CP-HardT**

When you sleep and know it not. The Song of the Grey Dog. David Herbert Lawrence. **CP-LawrD**

When you slowly emerged from the den of Time. A Plaint to Man. Thomas Hardy. **CP-HardT**

When you speak about ice, do you mean live ice. About Ice. Malcolm Lowry. **CP-LowrM**

When You Speak to Me. Tess Gallagher. **SP-GallT**

When you spit from the twenty-sixth floor. My Hobby. Shel Silverstein. **SP-SilS2**

When you stop to consider. Derek Mahon. **SP-MahoD**
(Dream Days.) **SP-MahoD**

When you stumble suddenly. The Embrace. Leonard Cohen. **CP-CoheL**

When you, that at this moment are to me. Edna St. Vincent Millay. **CP-MillE**

When you the sun-burnt pilgrim see. Good Counsel to a Young Maid. Thomas Carew. **CP-CareT**

When you think strong enough, you get something. The Six. James Dickey. **CP-DickJ**

When You Throw Amber into the Well of the Moon. Diane Wakoski. **SP-WakoD**

When you told me that he was in jail. Marilyn Hacker. **SP-HackM** *Fr.* The Navigators.

When you turn the corner. Final Curve. Langston Hughes. **SP-HughL**

When you walked in with your suitcase, leaving. Rosy. Louise Glück. **SP-GlücL**

When you went away it was morning. Edward Estlin Cummings. **CP-CummE**

When you went, how was it you carried with you. Grey Evening. David Herbert Lawrence. **CP-LawrD**

When you were explaining America, Robert, you did not. Pastor Errante. Donald Davie. **CP-DavDo**

When you were starving, you waited—how long? Malcolm Lowry. *Fr.* The Cantinas. **CP-LowrM**

When young I scribbled, boasting, on my wall. The Summing-up. Stanley Jasspon Kunitz. **CP-KuniS**

When, young, I slept in a cold bed. The Dream Range. Thomas McGrath. **SP-McGrT**

When your bones turn. Transmigration. Brendan Galvin. **SP-GalvB**

When your fingers squeeze the bulb. Girl at Play. Dabney Stuart. **SP-StuaD**

When your honest redskin toma. Edward Estlin Cummings. **CP-CummE**

When your loud axe's echo on the ponds, at early morning. St. Alberic. Thomas Merton. **CP-MertT; SP-MertT**

When your mother sends back all your invitations. Queen Jane Approximately. "Bob Dylan." **CP-DylaB**

When your soft welcomings were said. On a Discovered Curl of Hair. Thomas Hardy. **CP-HardT**

When your sperm enters me, it is altered. Adrienne Rich. **CP-RicAE**

When your widow had left the graveside. The Ritual of Memories. Tess Gallagher. **SP-GallT**

When you're growing up in a small town. Small Town. "Lou Reed." **SP-ReedL**

When you're lost in the rain in Juarez. Just Like Tom Thumb's Blues. "Bob Dylan." **CP-DylaB**

When you're ready to sell your diamonds. Commercial Variations. Frank O'Hara. **SP-OharF**

When Youth his faery reign began. The Sigh. Samuel Taylor Coleridge. *Fr.* Effusions. **CP-ColeS**

When you've shouted "Rule Britania," when you've sung "God Save the Queen." The Absent-Minded Beggar. Rudyard Kipling. **CP-KiplR**

When/Then. Adrienne Rich. **SP-RicA2**

Whenas in jeans today she goes. Julia Now. David Markson. **CP-MarkD**

Whenas we sat in Babylon. Bible, *O.T.* *See* Psalm 137: "By the rivers of Babylon. . . ."

Whence are ye, vague desires. Arthur Hugh Clough. **SP-ClouA**

Whence comes solace?—Not from seeing. On a Fine Morning. Thomas Hardy. **CP-HardT**

Whence comes that small continuous silence. Swallows Flown. Walter de la Mare. **CP-DeLaW**

Whence comest thou, Gehazi. Gehazi. Rudyard Kipling. **CP-KiplR**

Whence deathless *Kit-Cat* took its Name. Epigram on the Toasts of the Kit-Cat Club, Anno 1716. Alexander Pope. **CP-PopeA**

Whence did all that fury come? A Stick of Incense. William Butler Yeats. **CP-YeatW**

Whence from these gray. Lines to Be Read at the Casting of Scott FitzGerald's Balls into the Sea from Eden Roc (Antibes, Alpes Maritimes). Ernest Hemingway. **CP-HemiE**

Whence Had They Come? William Butler Yeats. **CP-YeatW**

Whence is it, that amaz'd I hear. To the Nightingale. William Cowper. **CP-CowpW**

Whence that low voice?—A whisper from the heart. William Wordsworth. *Fr.* The River Duddon [A Series of Sonnets]. **CP-WorW2**

Whence the brooch of burning gold. The Brooch of Lorn. Sir Walter Scott. **SP-ScotW** *Fr.* The Lord of the Isles.

Whence thou returnst, and whither wentst, I know. Leave Taking. John Milton. **FaBoEn** *Fr.* Book XII. *Fr.* Paradise Lost. **CP-MiltJ**

Whene'er I view those lips of thine. To M.S.G. Byron. **CP-Byron**

Whene'er the mist, that stands 'twixt God and thee. Reason. Samuel Taylor Coleridge. **CP-ColeS**

Whene'er this Stone, now hid beneath the Lake. To Posterity. Samuel Johnson. **CP-JohnS**

Whenever Auntie moves around. Auntie's Skirts. Robert Louis Stevenson. **CP-StevR**

Whenever I am got under my gravestone. Soliloquy. Ted Hughes. **SP-HughT**

Whenever I behold an asp. The Asp. Ogden Nash. **CP-NashO**

Whenever I do not create. Beast. Alice Walker. **CP-WalkA**

Whenever I go by there nowadays. The Tavern. Edwin Arlington Robinson. **CP-RobiE**

Whenever I happen to see you. Ugly in My Own Eyes. Leonard Cohen. **CP-CoheL**

Whenever I have an appointment to see the assistant. A Poem for Benn's Graduation from High School. John Ciardi. **SP-CiarJ**

Whenever I plunge my arm, like this. Under the Waterfall. Thomas Hardy. **CP-HardT**

Whenever I return. Recapitulation. Phoebe Hesketh. **SP-HeskP**

Whenever I See Beauty I See Death. Richard Eberhart. **CP-EberR**

Whenever I see for the first time. Wystan Hugh Auden. **CP-AudWJ**

Whenever I talk of my art. Resolutions. Donald Davie. **CP-DavDo**

Whenever I want you around yeh. All I've Got to Do. John Lennon *and* Paul McCartney. **CP-Beatl**

Whenever it rains the four fingers. A Letter From My Good Hand. Gary Gildner. **SP-GildG**

Whenever I've been one, I've known the end. Moralists. Stephen Dunn. **SP-DunnS**

Whenever poets want to give you the idea that something is par-. Don't Cry, Darling, It's Blood All Right. Ogden Nash. **CP-NashO**

Whenever Richard Cory went down town. Richard Cory. Edwin Arlington Robinson. **CP-RobiE**

Whenever Richard Gallup is dissevered. Poem in the Traditional Manner. Ted Berrigan. **SP-BerrT** *Fr.* The Sonnets.

Whenever the landlord and landlady get. Buffalo Bill. Charles Bukowski. **SP-BukC2**

Whenever the moon and stars are set. Windy Nights. Robert Louis Stevenson. **CP-StevR**

Whenever you are thought, the mind. Few and Simple. Wystan Hugh Auden. **CP-AudeW**

Whenever you dress me dolls, mammy. The Dolls. Thomas Hardy. **CP-HardT**

Whenever you wake, you will find journeying. Voices of Waking. Muriel Rukeyser. **CP-RukeM**

Where. Wendell Berry. **CP-BerrW**

Where? Walter de la Mare. **CP-DeLaW**

Where / if it's not too much to ask. Carmen 55. Catullus. *Fr.* Carmina. **CP-Catul**

Where a faint light shines alone. The Dark House. Edwin Arlington Robinson. **CP-RobiE**

—Where a heavy. A Bastard Peace. William Carlos Williams. **CP-WilW1**

Where a Poet's From. Archibald MacLeish. **CP-MacLA**

Where a river roars in rapids. Our Guardian Angels and Their Children. Nicholas Vachel Lindsay. **CP-LindV**

Where aerial gunnery was, you think at first a cadaver. Gila Bend. James Dickey. **CP-DickJ**

Where all is black. Nature and Man. George Meredith. **CP-MerG2**

Where aloneness fiercely. Fragment, A. Alun Lewis. **CP-LewiA**

Where and to whom. Two Sons. Anne Sexton. **CP-SextA**

Where are all thy beauties now, all hearts enchaining? [*or* harts enchayning?]. Thomas Campion. **CP-CampT**

Where are my pretty ones! My Pretty Animals. Kenneth Patchen. **CP-PatcK**

Where are the horses of the sun? The Charioteer of Delphi. James Merrill. **SP-MerrJ**

Where are the joys I have met in the morning. Fair Jenny. Robert Burns. **CP-BurnR**

Where are the merchants and the money-lenders. Death. Thomas Merton. **CP-MertT**

Where are the poems? Why do I now write none? At the Gate. Robert Ranke Graves. **CP-GravR**

Where are the Red Men? Watching the Fire. John Haines. **SP-HainJ**

Where are the rose-colored cities. Gilbert Sorrentino. **SP-SorrG**

Where are the songs I used to know. The Key-Note. Christina Georgina Rossetti. **CP-RosC2**

Where are the women who, *entre deux guerres*. Ballad of Ladies Lost and Found. Marilyn Hacker. **SP-HackM**

Where are they going. Home Home Home. Lawrence Ferlinghetti. **SP-FerlL**

Where are they, not those young men, not those. The Lost Romans. Muriel Rukeyser. **CP-RukeM**

Where are they now, those wanton Boys? Sequel to *Beggars* Composed Many Years After. William Wordsworth. **CP-WorW2**

Where Are Those High and Haunting Skies. Richard Eberhart. **CP-EberR**

Where are those honours, Ida! once you own. On a Change of Masters at a Great Public School. Byron. **CP-Byron**

Where are we. Bahamas. George Oppen. **CP-OppeG**

Where are we going? where are we going. Song of Slaves in the Desert. John Greenleaf Whittier. **CP-WhitJ**

Where are you, Bianca Capello, beautiful child. Bianca. Frederick Morgan. **SP-MorgF**

Where are you damn'd? Christopher Marlowe. **OBD** *Fr.* Doctor Faustus. **CP-JefR2**

Where Are You Going? Stevie Smith. **CP-SmitS**

Where are you going to-night, to-night. John Evereldown. Edwin Arlington Robinson. **CP-RobiE**

Where are you now—. The Face of the Precipice is Black with Lovers. Thomas McGrath. **SP-McGrT**

Where Are You Tonight? (Journey through Dark Heat). "Bob Dylan." **CP-DylaB**

Where are your monuments, your battles, martyrs? The Sea is History. Derek Walcott. **CP-WalcD**

Where art thou / Thou beautiful dream. Ralph Waldo Emerson. **CP-EmerR**

Where art thou, beloved To-morrow? To-Morrow. Percy Bysshe Shelley. **CP-ShelP**

Where art thou friend, whom I shall never see. Gerard Manley Hopkins. **CP-HopkG**

Where art thou, genius? I should use. An Ode to James, Earl of Desmond. Ben Jonson. **CP-JonsB**

Where art thou, Muse, that thou forget'st so long. Sonnet 100. William Shakespeare. **OBSC** *Fr.* Sonnets. **CP-ShaWS**

Where art thou, my beloved Son. The Affliction of Margaret—. William Wordsworth. **CP-WorW1**

Where art thou Sol, while thus the blind-fold Day. On a Foule Morning, Being Then to Take a Journey. Richard Crashaw. **CP-CrasR**

Where be the noisy followers of the game. After Landing—The Valley of Dover, Nover, 1820. William Wordsworth. *Fr.* Memorials of a Tour of the Continent; 1820. **CP-WorW2**

Where be the temples which in Britain's Isle. Artegal and Elidure. William Wordsworth. **CP-WorW2**

Where be those roses gone, which sweetened so our eyes? Sonnet 102. Sir Philip Sidney. *Fr.* Astrophil and Stella. **SP-SidnP**

Where Be You [or Ye] Going, You [or Ye] Devon Maid? John Keats. **CP-KeatJ**

Where beams the sun the brightest. To A.S., 1830. Emily Brontë. **CP-BronE**

Where bells no more affright the morn. Emily Dickinson. **CP-DickE**

Where Blackmoor was, the road that led. Geographical Knowledge. Thomas Hardy. **CP-HardT**

Where braving angry Winter's storms. Robert Burns. **CP-BurnR**

Where Buildings Congregate. Edwin Rolfe. **CP-RolfE**

Where, but here / would you. The Matachines. Charles Tomlinson. **CP-TomlC**

Where can I shit. The Old Dog's Song. Grace Paley. **CP-PaleG**

Where can the heart be hidden in the ground. Edna St. Vincent Millay. **CP-MillE**

Where Cart rins rowin to the sea. The Gallant Weaver. Robert Burns. **CP-BurnR**

Where ceaseless Spring her garland twines. Kinsman. John Greenleaf Whittier. **CP-WhitJ**

Where cliffs arise by winter crown'd. The Peasant of the Alps. Charlotte Smith. **CP-SmitC**

Where, Corinth, charm incarnate, are your shrines? Antipater of Sidon. Hilda Doolittle. **CP-DoolH**

Where Depths Are Surfaces. Donald Davie. **CP-DavDo**

Where Did That One Go to, 'Erbert. Malcolm Lowry. **CP-LowrM**

Where did the storm come from? No warning. How to Use a Storm. Richard Hugo. **CP-HugoR**

Where did we stop? In dead summer, that is. A Kindness. William Dickey. **SP-DickW**

Where did your words go. To Cipriano, in the Wind. Philip Levine. **SP-LeviP**

Where didst thou find, young Bard, thy sounding lyre? Sonnet. John Keats. **CP-KeatJ**

Where dips the rocky highland. The Stolen Child. William Butler Yeats. **CP-YeatW**

Where do all the failed fathers. Failed Fathers. Lewis Turco. **SP-TurcL**

Where do I begin. . . on the heels of Rimbaud. Desire (Liner Notes). "Bob Dylan." **CP-DylaB**

Where do the roads go—. The Roads. Louise McNeill. **SP-McNeL**

Where do the roots go? The Pit. Theodore Roethke. **NAAL-2** *Fr.* The Lost Son. **CP-RoetT**

Where do these / invisible seeds. The Advantage. Charles Olson. **CP-OlsoC**

Where do they come from? Those whom we so much dread. They. Wystan Hugh Auden. **CP-AudeW**

Where do they travel to. Stone Walls. Wystan Hugh Auden. **CP-AudWJ**

Where do we go from here? I Wonder. Charles Henri Ford. **SP-FordC**

Where do you come from? The land of Epigram. Malcolm Lowry. *Fr.* Songs for Second Childhood. **CP-LowrM**

Where do you think, serpent. The Bagatelles the Madrigals. Wallace Stevens. **CP-StevW**

Where does a dead man go?—The dead man dies. Edwin Arlington Robinson. *Fr.* Octaves. **CP-RobiE**

Where does Cinderella sleep? Parvenu. Nicholas Vachel Lindsay. **CP-LindV**

Where does the rain come from? Ordinary Poem. Diane Wakoski. **SP-WakoD**

Where does the sadness come from? The great Seychellesan tortoise that heaved its. Cross My Heart and Hope to Die, It Was the Very Same Song Exactly. Hayden Carruth. **CP-CarHS**

Where does this journey look which the watcher upon the quay. Whither? Wystan Hugh Auden. *Fr.* A Voyage. **CP-AudeW**

Where dost [or do'st] thou careless[e] lie. An Ode. To Himself. Ben Jonson. **CP-JonsB**

Where Dream Begins. May Sarton. **SP-SartM**

Where droop the little ivy shoots. In a Churchyard. James Schuyler. **CP-SchuJ**

Where dust gritty as. Paul Valéry Stood on the Cliff and Confronted the Furious Energies of Nature. Robert Penn Warren. **SP-WarrR**

Where earth is, is also. A Detail. Gilbert Sorrentino. **SP-SorrG**

Where ends our chancel in a vaulted space. The Vicar. George Crabbe. **SP-CrabG** *Fr.* The Borough.

Where ever Nodes do's in the Summer come. Upon Nodes. Robert Herrick. **CP-HerrR**

Where every bird is bold to go. Emily Dickinson. **CP-DickE**

Where every female delights to give her maiden to her husband. Male & Female Loves in Beulah. William Blake. **OBNC** *Fr.* Jerusalem; The Emanation of the Giant Albion. **CP-BlakW**

Where Every Prospect. Kenneth Patchen. **CP-PatcK**

Where faces are hueless, where eyelids are dewless. Requiem. George Meredith. **CP-MerG1**

Where far in forest I am laid. A Riddle. Richard Wilbur. **CP-WilbR**

Where five old graves lay circled on a hill. The Graveyard. Jane Cooper. **NePoEA-2** *Fr.* Acceptances. **SP-CoopJ**

Where giant wordlings interrupt the stuttering machine-gun wit. Descriptions of Imaginary Poetries. Robert Duncan. **SP-DuncR**

Where Go the Boats? Robert Louis Stevenson. **CP-StevR**

Where God is merry, there write down my fears. Gods Mirth, Mans Mourning. Robert Herrick. **CP-HerrR**

Where grac'd with many a classic spoil. Absence. Samuel Taylor Coleridge. **CP-ColeS**

Where gray walks slope through shadows shaped like lace. Duet, with Muffled Brake Drums. John Updike. **CP-UpdiJ**

Where had her sweetness gone? Quarrel in Old Age. William Butler Yeats. **CP-YeatW**

Where had I heard this wind before. Bereft. Robert Frost. **CP-FrosR**

Where has he of race divine. Chorus of Satyrs, Driving Their Goats. Euripides. **AWP** *Fr.* The Cyclops. **CP-ShelP**

Where has Maid Quiet gone to. Maid Quiet. William Butler Yeats. **CP-YeatW**

Where has tenderness gone, he asked the mirror. *also appears independently of Cantinas in* CP-LOWRY. Malcolm Lowry. **FaBoTw; OxBTC** *Fr.* The Cantinas. **CP-LowrM**

Where has tenderness gone, he asked the mirror. Of the Francia. Malcolm Lowry. *Fr.* The Lighthouse Invites the Storm. **CP-LowrM**

Where hast thou floated, in what seas pursued. William Cowper. **CP-CowpW**

(To the Halibut.) **CP-CowpW**

Where have I "heard" a silence before. The Glen of Silence. "Hugh MacDiarmid." **SP-MacDH**

Where have I lost my way among money and horses? The Lament of a New England Mother. Richard Eberhart. **CP-EberR**

Where have these hands been. Musician. Louise Bogan. **CP-BogaL**

Where have these strangers come from. Blood Deeper than Night. Lewis Turco. **SP-TurcL**

Where have you been this while away. The Widow's Party. Rudyard Kipling. **CP-KiplR**

Where Helen Lies, *see also* Helen of Kirconnell. Robert Burns. **CP-BurnR**

Where history was. Sightseers. Howard Nemerov. **CP-NemeH**

Where holy ground begins, unhallowed ends. A Parsonage in Oxfordshire. William Wordsworth. **CP-WorW2**

Where Humber pours his rich commercial stream. A Tale, Founded on a Fact. William Cowper. **CP-CowpW**

Where hundreds of frogs. West Branch Ponds, Kokadjo, Maine. Mona Van Duyn. **SP-VanDM**

Where I? Robinson Jeffers. **CP-JefR2**

Where I could think of no thoroughfare. Were I in Trouble. Robert Frost. **OxBSP** *Fr.* Five Nocturnes. **CP-FrosR**

Where I grew up, I used to see. The Rabbi. Robert Earl Hayden. **CP-HaydR**

Where I have lost, I softer tread. Emily Dickinson. **CP-DickE**

Where I Live in This Honorable House of the Laurel Tree. Anne Sexton. **CP-SextA**

Where I spat in the harbor the oranges were bobbing. The Metamorphoses. Randall Jarrell. **CP-JarrR**

Where icy and bright dungeons lift. Hart Crane. **CABA; HAP; MoAB; MoAmPo; MoVE; SeCeV; TwAmPo; UnPo** *Fr.* Voyages. **CP-CranH**

Where in the new fruit. A Morning Poem for Michael. Al Young. **CP-YounA**

Where Innocent Bright-Eyed Daisies Are. Christina Georgina Rossetti. **CP-RosC2**

Where is Alex, keeper of horses? Alex. Mary Oliver. **SP-OlivM**

Where is David?. . . Oh God's people. In Which Roosevelt Is Compared to Saul. Nicholas Vachel Lindsay. **CP-LindV**

Where is he now, in his soiled shirt reeking of garlic. For Pao-Chin, a Boatman on the Yellow Sea. Edna St. Vincent Millay. **CP-MillE**

Where is he taking us. Eros. Hilda Doolittle. **CP-DoolH**

Where is he, that giddy sprite. William Wordsworth. **PBBP** *Fr.* The Kitten and [the] Falling Leaves. **CP-WorW1**

Where is love when love is not? When Love Is Not. Robert Ranke Graves. **CP-GravR**

Where is McKinley, that respectable McKinley. Nicholas Vachel Lindsay. *Fr.* Bryan, Bryan, Bryan, Bryan. **CP-LindV**

Where is my cat, my rake. Bad Times Song. Jean Garrigue. **SP-GarrJ**

Where is my love— / In silence and shadow she lies. Where? Walter de la Mare. **CP-DeLaW**

Where is my love! I cried. Ballad of Love. Edward Estlin Cummings. **CP-CummE**

Where is Skrymir? Giant Skrymir? Ralph Waldo Emerson. **CP-EmerR**

Where Is Tao? Chuang Tzu, *tr. fr. Chinese* by Thomas Merton. **CP-MertT**

Where is that holy fire, which verse is said. Sappho to Philaenis. John Donne. **FaBoBl** *Fr.* Elegies. **CP-DonnJ**

Where is that sugar, Hammond. Early Evening Quarrel. Langston Hughes. **SP-HughL**

Where is that woman of the west. The Woman Who Went East. Thomas Hardy. **CP-HardT**

Where is the albatross at home? The Bird, in Soliloquizing Voices a Woman's Wish. Marsden Hartley. **CP-HartM**

Where is the Black Beast? The Black Beast. Ted Hughes. **SP-HughT**

Where is the child that I was. Pablo Neruda, *tr. fr. Spanish* by Ben Belitt. **SP-NeruP** *Fr.* Question Book.

Where is the finely drunk? Is the great drunkard? The Last Man in the Dôme Malcolm Lowry. *Fr.* The Cantinas. **CP-LowrM**

Where is the grave of Sir Arthur O'Kellyn? The Knight's Tomb. Samuel Taylor Coleridge. **CP-ColeS**

Where is the Jack that built the house. Château Jackson. Louis MacNeice. **CP-MacNL**

Where is the Jim Crow section. Merry-Go-Round. Langston Hughes. **SP-HughL**

Where is the marvelous thief. Dirge for the Proud World. Thomas Merton. **CP-MertT**

Where is the nightingale. Hilda Doolittle. **MoAmPo,** *sect.* 2; *Fr.* Songs from Cyprus. **CP-DoolH**

Where is the prisoner? The Two Foscari. Byron. **CP-Byron**

Where Is the Real Non-Resistant? Nicholas Vachel Lindsay. **CP-LindV**

Where is the restaurant cat? The Grand Canyon. Jean Garrigue. **SP-GarrJ**

Where is the simple myth we used to have? Jane Cooper. *Fr.* After the Bomb Tests. **SP-CoopJ**

Where is the sky hurrying to. Coeur Simple. Stevie Smith. **CP-SmitS**

Where is the truth to indulge my heart. Seven Years. Robert Ranke Graves. **CP-GravR**

"Where is the world!" cries Young at eighty. Byron. **FaBoPV** *Fr.* Canto the Eleventh. **NOBRP** *Fr.* Don Juan. **CP-Byron**

Where is this stupendous stranger. The Nativity of Our Lord and Saviour Jesus Christ. Christopher Smart. **EBEV; HAP; LAuP; LoBV; NAs; NOBE; NOCV; NOEC; PoEL-3; SBVL; SCGP; WeW** *Fr.* Hymns and Spiritual Songs for the Fasts and Festivals of the Church of England. **SP-SmarC**

Where Is Thy Victory? Walter de la Mare. **CP-DeLaW**

Where it says snow. Errata. Charles Simic. **SP-SimiC**

Where It Was at Back Then. Anne Sexton. **CP-SextA**

Where Jennie Used to Swim. Richard Hugo. **CP-HugoR**

Where Knock Is Open Wide. Theodore Roethke. **CP-RoetT**

Where lately harboured many a famous whore. On the New Hot-House. Ben Jonson. **CP-JonsB**

Where lies the land to which the ship would go? Arthur Hugh Clough. **SP-ClouA** *Fr.* Songs in Absence.

(Mari Magno II.) **SP-ClouA**

Where lies the Land to which yon Ship must go? William Wordsworth. **CP-WorW1**

Where Lies the Truth? Has Man in Wisdom's Creed. William Wordsworth. **CP-WorW2**

Where, like a pillow on a bed. The Ecstasy. John Donne. **CP-DonnJ**

Where limestone water cleft a time-worn ledge. The Flame. Louise McNeill. **SP-McNeL**

Where long and deeply hath been fixed the root. William Wordsworth. *Fr.* Ecclesiastical Sonnets. **CP-WorW2**

Where love begins, there dead thy first desire. Another. Robert Herrick. **CP-HerrR**

Where love is, there comes sorrow / Today or else tomorrow. Christina Georgina Rossetti. **CP-RosC2**

Where man's profane and tainting hand. Fragment of a Sonnet: Farewell to North Devon. Percy Bysshe Shelley. **CP-ShelP**

Where might there be a refuge for me. Tell Me, Tell Me. Marianne Craig Moore. **CP-MoorM**

Where Mission Creek Runs Hard for Joy. Richard Hugo. **CP-HugoR**

Where my imaginary line. Beech. Robert Frost. **CP-FrosR**

Where my stag-antlered love moves. Kenneth Patchen. **CP-PatcK**

Where Neither Rust Nor Moth Doth Corrupt. Christina Georgina Rossetti. **CP-RosC2**

Where never tempest heaveth, / Nor sorrow grieveth. Christina Georgina Rossetti. **CP-RosC2**

Where no question possibly remains—someone crying, someone dead—blame asks: whose fault? Blame. Charles Kenneth Williams. **SP-WillC**

Where Nostrand crosses Flatlands Avenue. Flatbush. Peter Meinke. **SP-MeinP**

Where now has our young Adam. Nocturne. John Crowe Ransom. **SP-RansJ**

Where now the huts are empty. What the Ghost of the Gambler Said. Nicholas Vachel Lindsay. **CP-LindV**

Where O America are you. After Dead Souls. Allen Ginsberg. **CP-GinsA**

Where o where is the message which today. Hafiz, *tr. by* Ralph Waldo Emerson. **CP-EmerR** *Fr.* Odes.

Where once I loved my flesh. The Progress of the Soul. Thomas McGrath. **SP-McGrT**

Where once the Dove and Olive-Bough. Cumberland Water Authority. William Wordsworth. **FaBoDD** *Fr.* The Waggoner. **CP-WorW1**

Where Once the Waters of Your Face. Dylan Thomas. **CP-ThomD**

Where once we danced, where once we sang. An Ancient to Ancients. Thomas Hardy. **CP-HardT**

Where one mountain sits on top of another. Navajo Song. Richard Shelton. **SP-ShelR**

Where others love, and praise my Verses; still. To the Detracter. Robert Herrick. **CP-HerrR**

Where, over heathen doom-rings and gray stones of the Horg. King Volmer and Elsie. John Greenleaf Whittier. **CP-WhitJ**

Where Pleasures rule a Kingdome, never there. Pleasures Pernicious. Robert Herrick. **CP-HerrR**

Where Purples Now the Fig. Robert Penn Warren. **SP-WarrR**

Where Roses would not dare to go. Emily Dickinson. **CP-DickE**

Where run your colts at pasture? White Horses. Rudyard Kipling. **CP-KiplR**

Where sanity is. God. David Herbert Lawrence. **CP-LawrD**

Where sea breaks inland, claiming the Quinalt. Tahola. Richard Hugo. **CP-HugoR**

Where sea meets land. Njord. Frederick Morgan. **SP-MorgF**

Where shall I find a white rose blowing? Christina Georgina Rossetti. **CP-RosC2**

Where shall I find you. Sub Terra. William Carlos Williams. **CP-WilW1**

Where shall I have at mine own will. Sir Thomas Wyatt. **CP-WyatT**

Where shall I refuge seeke, if you refuse mee? Thomas Campion. **CP-CampT**

Where shall the lover rest. Fitz-Eustace's Song. Sir Walter Scott. **SP-ScotW** *Fr.* Marmion.

Where shall we go? The Hounded Lovers. William Carlos Williams. **CP-WilW2**

Where She Her Sacred Bower Adorns. Thomas Campion. **CP-CampT**

("Where shee her sacred bowre adornes.") **CP-CampT**

Where she lived the close remained the best. The Way a Ghost Dissolves. Richard Hugo. **CP-HugoR**

Where she was burned the early market. Visit to Rouen. Louis MacNeice. **CP-MacNL**

Where shee her sacred bowre adornes. Thomas Campion. *See* Where She Her Sacred Bower Adorns.

Where Ships of Purple—gently toss. Emily Dickinson. **CP-DickE**

Where should he seek, to go away. The Mark. Louise Bogan. **CP-BogaL**

Where should we go. Marsden Hartley. *Fr.* Ironies out of St. George's. **CP-HartM**

Where sunless rivers weep. Dream Land. Christina Georgina Rossetti. **CP-RosC1**

Where the bells peal far at sea. The Mirror Speaks. Robert Louis Stevenson. **CP-StevR**

Where the cedar leaf divides the sky. Passage. Hart Crane. **CP-CranH**

Where the child's eyes glaze with memory where the man's glaze. The Nothing II. Hayden Carruth. *Fr.* Contra Mortem. **CP-CarHL**

Where the cities end, the. Transcontinent. Donald Hall. **CP-HallD**

Where the city's ceaseless crowd moves on the livelong day. Sparkles from the Wheel. Walt Whitman. **CP-WhitW**

Where the Danube and Sava Rivers Meet. Al Young. **CP-YounA**

Where the East wind is brewed fresh and fresh every morning. The North Sea Patrol. Rudyard Kipling. **CP-KiplR**

Where the flickering river loiters. A Man at Play on the River. David Herbert Lawrence. **CP-LawrD**

Where the fungus broad & red. Ralph Waldo Emerson. **CP-EmerR**

Where the Great Lake's sunny smiles. The Grave by the Lake. John Greenleaf Whittier. **CP-WhitJ**

Where the green leaves exclude the summer beam. Petrarch, *tr.* by Charlotte Smith. **CP-SmitC** *Fr.* Sonnets to Laura.

Where the Hayfields Were. Archibald MacLeish. **CP-MacLA**

Where the hillside stream unearths itself. Confluence. Charles Tomlinson. **CP-TomlC**

Where the House Was. Richard Hugo. **CP-HugoR**

Where the lane from the highway swerves the first drops fell. John Berryman. *Fr.* Sonnets to Chris. **CP-BerrJ**

Where the living with effort go. The White Ship. Geoffrey Hill. **CP-HillG**

Where the lizard ran to its little prey. The Range in the Desert. Randall Jarrell. **CP-JarrR**

Where the minnows trace. Narcissus. David Herbert Lawrence. **CP-LawrD**

Where the mothers. Wadsworth Moor. Ted Hughes. **SP-HughT**

Where the mountain river flows. West Virginia. Louise McNeill. **SP-McNeL**

Where the path closed / down and over. Egrets. Mary Oliver. **SP-OlivM**

Where the Picnic Was. Thomas Hardy. **CP-HardT**

Where the quiet-coloured [or colored] end of evening smiles. Love among the Ruins. Robert Browning. **CP-BroR1**

Where the Rainbow Ends. Robert Lowell. **SP-LoweR**

Where the ranch-house disappeared its garden. Under the Bridge. Charles Tomlinson. **CP-TomlC**

Where the remote Bermudas ride. Bermudas. Andrew Marvell. **CP-MarvA**

Where the road came, no longer bearing men. The Supplanting. Wendell Berry. **CP-BerrW**

Where the road divides. The Poplars. Roy Fisher. *Fr.* City. **SP-FishR**

Where the sally tree went pale in every breeze. Field Work. Seamus Heaney. **SP-HeanS**

Where the Sidewalk Ends. Shel Silverstein. **SP-SilS2**

Where the Slow Fig's Purple Sloth. Robert Penn Warren. **SP-WarrR**

Where the slow river. Leda. Hilda Doolittle. **CP-DoolH**

Where the snow bank leans. Hayden Carruth. *Fr.* North Winter. **CP-CarHL**

Where the sober-coloured cultivator smiles. A Tale of Two Cities. Rudyard Kipling. **CP-KiplR**

Where the three magenta. Man in Black. Sylvia Plath. **CP-PlatS**

Where the Treasure is. Emily Dickinson. **SP-DickE**

Where the trees rise like cliffs, proud and blue-tinted in the distance. Guards. David Herbert Lawrence. **CP-LawrD**

Where the wheel of light is turned. Archibald MacLeish. **CP-MacLA**

(Pole Star.) **CP-MacLA**

Where the white bridge rears up its stamping arches. In Memory of the Spanish Poet Federico Garcia Lorca. Thomas Merton. **CP-MertT; SP-MertT**

Where the wild woods and pathless forests frown. Charlotte Smith. **CP-SmitC**

Where the wings of a sunny Dome expand. America. Herman Melville. **SP-MelvH**

Where Their Worm Dieth Not, and the Fire Is Not Quenched. Christina Georgina Rossetti. **CP-RosC2**

Where then shall hope and fear their objects find? An Additional Poem. John Ashbery. **SP-AshbJ**

Where then shall Hope and Fear their objects find? The Power of Prayer. Samuel Johnson. **NOBE** *Fr.* The Vanity of Human Wishes [The Tenth Satire of Juvenal Imitated]. **CP-JohnS**

Where there is personal liking we go. The Hero. Marianne Craig Moore. **CP-MoorM** *Fr.* Part of a Novel, Part of a Poem, Part of a Play.

Where there was nothing. Widdop. Ted Hughes. **SP-HughT**

Where there were angels I saw no one. Witt. Patti Smith. **SP-SmitP**

Where There's a Will, There's Velleity. Ogden Nash. **CP-NashO**

Where They Come to Wait for the Body: A Ghost Story. Robert Penn Warren. *Fr.* Penological Study: Southern Exposure. **SP-WarrR**

Where They Lived. Thomas Hardy. **CP-HardT**

Where Thou art—that—is Home. Emily Dickinson. **CP-DickE**

Where thou dwellest, in what Grove. The Birds. William Blake. **CP-BlakW**

Where three eagles cross in the sky. Cabin Site Christmas Island, N.S. Martin Edmunds. **SP-EdmuM**

Where Three Roads Joined. Thomas Hardy. **CP-HardT**

Where thy broad branches brave the bitter North. Apostrophe to an Old Tree. Charlotte Smith. **CP-SmitC**

Where Time the measure of his hours. The Star of Bethlehem. John Greenleaf Whittier. **CP-WhitJ**

Where towers are crushed, and unforbidden weeds. The Pillar of Trajan. William Wordsworth. *Fr.* Memorials of a Tour in Italy, 1837. **CP-WorW2**

Where true Love burns Desire is Love's pure flame. Desire. Samuel Taylor Coleridge. **CP-ColeS**

Where, twining subtile fears with hope. Andrew Marvell. **OBD** *Fr.* An Horatian Ode upon Cromwell's Return from Ireland. **CP-MarvA**

Where two boots labored yesterday across the. Hayden Carruth. *Fr.* North Winter. **CP-CarHL**

Where Two O'clock Came From. Kenneth Patchen. **CP-PatcK**

Where two or three were flung together, or fifty. The March 2. Robert Lowell. **SP-LoweR**

Where wardes are weake and foes encountring, strong. Scorne Not the Leaste. Robert Southwell. **CP-SoutR**

Where waterfalls in shining folds. Italian Garden. May Sarton. **SP-SartM**

Where We Are. Stephen Dobyns. **SP-DobyS**

Where we are there must. Robert Creeley. **CP-CreeR**

Where We Belong, A Duet. Maya Angelou. **SP-AngeM**

Where We Crashed. Richard Hugo. **CP-HugoR**

Where we made the fire. Where the Picnic Was. Thomas Hardy. **CP-HardT**

Where we owe so much it defies Money. Emily Dickinson. **SP-DickE**

Where we went in the boat was a long bay. The Mediterranean. Allen Tate. **CP-TateA**

Where were the greenhouses going. Big Wind. Theodore Roethke. **CP-RoetT**

Where were they headed, the one winged birds. The Cripples. Richard Hugo. **CP-HugoR**

Where were ye all? and where wert thou? Emily Brontë. **CP-BronE**

Where were ye, nymphs, when the remorseless deep. The Dog—An Idyllium. William Wordsworth. **CP-WorW1**

Where were you last night? I watched at the gate. Last Night. Christina Georgina Rossetti. **CP-RosC3**

Where, west of the sun, our loved remembered home? Iona. Kathleen Jessie Raine. *Fr.* The Holy Isles. **SP-RainK**

Where where where. The Gypsy Wife. Leonard Cohen. **CP-CoheL**

Where wildered anemones hay-lei moony. Grape-Hyacinth. Louis Zukofsky. **CP-ZukLS**

Where will they stop, those breathing powers. Devotional Incitements. William Wordsworth. **CP-WorW2**

Where will you be tonight? Past Lisbon, flying. Muriel Rukeyser. **CP-RukeM**

Where wilt thou lead me? Speak. Archibald MacLeish. *Fr.* Hamlet of A. Macleish. **CP-MacLA**

Where yon crenellated mansion on the hill surmounts the pines. A Literary Discovery. Sir John Betjeman. **CP-BetjJ**

Where yonder villa hogs the sea. Delectable Duchy. Sir John Betjeman. **CP-BetjJ**

Where you are. Ancient Wisdom Speaks. Hilda Doolittle. **CP-DoolH**

Where you are rigidly anchored. Landfall, Grenada. Derek Walcott. **CP-WalcD**

Where you dream of water. For an Anniversary. Robert Creeley. **CP-CreeR**

Whereas at morning in a jeweled crown. Edna St. Vincent Millay. **CP-MillE**

Whereas by dark really released,the modern. Edward Estlin Cummings. **CP-CummE**

Whereas the man who hits. The Carnival. Robert Creeley. **CP-CreeR**

Whereat—the King unthroned, the God. Actfive. Archibald MacLeish. **CP-MacLA**

Where'er I find the Good, the True, the Fair. The Philosophical Trinity. Samuel Taylor Coleridge. **CP-ColeS**

Where'er we tread 'tis haunted, holy ground. Byron. **GrIP** *Fr.* Childe Harold's Pilgrimage. **CP-Byron**

Where'er you find the cooling western breeze. Alexander Pope. **OBCoV** *Fr.* An Essay on Criticism. **CP-PopeA**

Wherefore and how I am certain, I can hardly tell; but it [or is so]. Arthur Hugh Clough. **EBVVPR,** *canto* 2, 13; *Fr.* Amours de Voyage. **SP-ClouA**

Wherefore do thy sad numbers flow. Grief Engrossed. Thomas Carew. **CP-CareT**

Wherefore doth vaine Antiquitie so vaunt. Edmund Spenser. *Fr.* Commendatory Sonnets. **CP-Spens**

Wherefore should man or thoughtless boy. The Hedge-Hog Seen in a Frequented Path. Charlotte Smith. **CP-SmitC**

Wherein are words sublime or noble? What. Karenge Ya Marenge. Countee Cullen. **CP-CullC**

Wherein is Moscow's dignity. The Men. William Carlos Williams. **CP-WilW1**

Wherein war is expressed. Babelfield. Patti Smith. **SP-SmitP**

Wherelings whenlings / (daughters of if but offspring of hopefear). Edward Estlin Cummings. **CP-CummE**

Whereof memory of man runneth not to the contrary. Canto 67. Ezra Pound. *Fr.* Cantos. **CP-PoCan**

Where's Agnes? Elizabeth Barrett Browning. **CP-BroEB**

Where's he born? Where a Poet's From. Archibald MacLeish. **CP-MacLA**

Where's Jack Was / General Was. Edward Estlin Cummings. **CP-CummE**

Where's Madge then / Madge and her men? Edward Estlin Cummings. **CP-CummE**

Where's the lamp that Hero lit. A Song of Travel. Rudyard Kipling. **CP-KiplR**

Where's the need of singing now? Momus. Edwin Arlington Robinson. **CP-RobiE**

Where's the Poet? Show Him! Show Him. John Keats. **CP-KeatJ**

Where's this barn's house? It never had a house. The Old Barn at the Bottom of the Fogs. Robert Frost. **CP-FrosR**

Wheresoe'er I turn my View. Lines on Thomas Warton's Poems. Samuel Johnson. **CP-JohnS**

Whereto shall we liken this Blessed Mary Virgin. Feast of the Annunciation. Christina Georgina Rossetti. **CP-RosC2**

Whereupon i seize a train and suddenly i am in Paris toward night, in Mai. The Rain Is a Handsome Animal. Edward Estlin Cummings. **CP-CummE**

Wherever. Daniel Gerard Hoffman. **SP-HoffD**

Wherever. Muriel Rukeyser. **CP-RukeM**

Wherever he may be, whether on sea or land. The Lid. John Gould Fletcher. **SP-FletJ**

Wherever I am, and whatever I do. Song. John Dryden. **SP-DrydJ** *Fr.* The Conquest of Granada.

Wherever I surface I reinvent. April Interval. Marilyn Hacker. **SP-HackM**

Wherever I walked I went green among young growing. Trinity Churchyard. Muriel Rukeyser. **CP-RukeM**

Wherever in this city, screens flicker. Adrienne Rich. **PeHV** *Fr.* Twenty-one Love Poems. **SP-RicA1; SP-RicA2**

Wherever shadow falls wherever the drowning. The Being. Hayden Carruth. **PoA** *Fr.* Contra Mortem. **CP-CarHL**

Wherever the dead are, there they are and. Creation. Kenneth Patchen. **CP-PatcK**

Wherever we may be. Song: Wherever We May Be. Robert Ranke Graves. **CP-GravR**

Wherupon I told, / That once in the stillness of a summer's moon. William Wordsworth. **PoEL-4** *Fr.* Books. *Fr.* The Prelude; Growth of a Poet's Mind [1850 vers.]. **CP-WorW3**

Whether all towns and all who live in them. Tasker Norcross. Edwin Arlington Robinson. **CP-RobiE**

Whether, as the intensity of seeing increases, one's distance. George Oppen. *Fr.* Of Being Numerous. **CP-OppeG**

Whether awaken'd from unquiet rest. To the Sun. Charlotte Smith. **CP-SmitC**

Whether away my sweetest deerest? Thomas Campion. **CP-CampT**

Whether before have been. Archibald MacLeish. *Fr.* Hamlet of A. Macleish. **CP-MacLA**

Whether conditioned by God or their neural structure, still. Wystan Hugh Auden. *Fr.* Shorts [1939–1947] ("Motionless, deep in his mind, lies the past the poet's forgotten"). **CP-AudeW**

Whether he will go on singing. Orpheus (2). Margaret Atwood. **SP-AtwM2**

Whether I was my selfe, or else did see. The School or Perl of Putney, the Mistress of All Singular Manners, Mistresse Portman. Robert Herrick. **CP-HerrR**

Whether it is a speaker, taut on a platform. Metaphor to Action. Muriel Rukeyser. **CP-RukeM**

Whether it is possible to become lost. How To Tell One Country from Another. Margaret Atwood. **SP-AtwM2**

Whether it was your way of walking. Your Private Way. Robert Ranke Graves. **CP-GravR**

Whether my bark went down at sea. Emily Dickinson. **CP-DickE**

Whether my day is day for you. The Ladder. Kenneth Patchen. **CP-PatcK**

Whether on Ida's shady brow. To the Muses. William Blake. **CP-BlakW**

Whether one walks around the hill, or over. There Was Glass and There Are Stars. Randall Jarrell. **CP-JarrR**

Whether or Not. David Herbert Lawrence. **CP-LawrD**

Whether sooner or later. Later or Sooner. Richard Eberhart. **CP-EberR**

Whether sunshine, snow or rain. Timber. John Hewitt. **CP-HewiJ**

Whether that soul which now comes up to you. Hymn to the Saints, and to Marquis Hamilton[, An]. John Donne. **CP-DonnJ**

Whether the bees have thoughts, we cannot say. The Long Waters. Theodore Roethke. **NYBP** *Fr.* North American Sequence. **CP-RoetT**

Whether the moorings are invisible. Conversation. John Berryman. **CP-BerrJ**

Whether the rain comes down. Reverie and Invocation. William Carlos Williams. **CP-WilW2**

Whether the sensitive plant, or that. Percy Bysshe Shelley. **OAEL-2** *Fr.* The Sensitive Plant. **CP-ShelP**

Whether the State can loose and bind. MacDonough's Song. Rudyard Kipling. **CP-KiplR**

Whether the Turkish new moon minded be. Sonnet 30. Sir Philip Sidney. **NoSic; PoE** *Fr.* Astrophil and Stella. **SP-SidnP**

Whether There Is Enjoyment in Bitterness. Thomas Merton. **CP-MertT**

Whether There Is Sorrow in the Demons. John Berryman. **CP-BerrJ**

Whether they have forgotten. Emily Dickinson. **CP-DickE**

Whether thus hasts my little booke so fast? The Writer to his Booke. Thomas Campion. *Fr.* Observations in the Art of English Poesie. **CP-CampT**

Whether to sally and see thee, girl of my dreams. To Meet, or Otherwise. Thomas Hardy. **CP-HardT**

Whether to *use* time, or to *kill* time, either. Moment. Robert Creeley. **CP-CreeR**

Whether to wend through straight streets strictly. *parody of early English aliterative verse.* Rudyard Kipling. **CP-KiplR** *Fr.* The Muse among the Motors.

Whether upon the garden seat. To Any Reader. Robert Louis Stevenson. **CP-StevR**

Whether we come, in last imaginings. The Companion. Daniel Gerard Hoffman. **SP-HoffD**

Whether we fall asleep under the moon. Sleep. John Haines. **SP-HainJ**

Whether we fight with rifles or carry knives. Marching Song of the Children of Darkness. Edwin Rolfe. **CP-RolfE**

Whether we like it, or don't. Poem for a Class Re-Union. Robert Louis Stevenson. **CP-StevR**

Whether you say it, think it, know it. Ted Hughes. **NoAM** *Fr.* Stations. **SP-HughT**

Which? Robert Browning. **CP-BroR2**

Which? Walter de la Mare. **CP-DeLaW**

Which act is / Violence. George Oppen. *Fr.* A Language of New York. **CP-OppeG**

Which ain't much barn at that, maybe twenty head. Hayden Carruth. *Fr.* The Sleeping Beauty. **CP-CarHL**

Which are beauties sweetest dress. William Blake. *See* Soft deceit & idleness.

Which being so, which beauties being evanescent but also recurrent. Louis MacNeice. *Fr.* Donegal Triptych. **CP-MacNL**

Which cannot be begun, however, until you meet somebody. Kenneth Koch. *Fr.* The Art of Love. **SP-KochK**

Which eye's his eye? The Gentleman of Shalott. Elizabeth Bishop. **CP-BishE**

Which is best? Heaven. Emily Dickinson. **CP-DickE**

Which is like a stock room anyway. In an Automotive Store. Charles Olson. **CP-OlsoC**

Which is ours, which is ourselves. George Oppen. *Fr.* Of Being Numerous. **CP-OppeG**

Which is the best—the Moon or the Crescent? Emily Dickinson. **CP-DickE**

Which is the day I have decided to understand. Today is Wednesday. Miller Williams. **SP-WillM**

Which is the very. Edward Estlin Cummings. **CP-CummE**

Which is the weakest thing of all. The Weakest Thing. Elizabeth Barrett Browning. **CP-BroEB**

Which is worse the lieutenant raising his rifle. Poor Hope. Charles Kenneth Williams. **CP-WillC**

Which is you, old two-in-one? What the Serpent Said to Adam. Archibald MacLeish. **ChIV-1; MeMAP; NePA** *Fr.* Songs for Eve. **CP-MacLA**

Which it / was, form, The. Robert Creeley. **CP-CreeR**

Which misses most. Emily Dickinson. **CP-DickE**

Which of the fairest three. Apollo to the Graces. John Keats. **CP-KeatJ**

Which of thy names I take, not only bears. To Sir Horace Vere. Ben Jonson. **CP-JonsB**

Which ones / Of the eager faces, garlic or iris. The Woman in the Valley. Ted Hughes. **SP-HughT**

Which reminds me. Some Picnic. Charles Bukowski. **SP-BukC1**

Which should I better like of, day, or night. Sonnet 18. Mary Sidney, Countess of Montgomery Wroth. *Fr.* Pamphilia to Amphilanthus. **CP-WrotM**

Which still is much. Here in this mountain village. Louis MacNeice. *Fr.* The Island. **CP-MacNL**

Which things being so, as we said when we studied. Louis MacNeice. *Fr.* Autumn Journal. **CP-MacNL**

"I ought to be glad." **OBCoV**

Which Way? Walter de la Mare. **CP-DeLaW**

Which way and whence the lightning flew. Ben Jonson. **CP-JonsB** *Fr.* The Masque of Augurs.

Which way I fly is Hell; my self am Hell. John Milton. **TW** *Fr.* Book IV. **OAEL-1** *Fr.* Paradise Lost. **CP-MiltJ**

Whichever way you turn. The Mexican Girls. Charles Bukowski. **SP-BukC2**

Whiffletree. Carl Sandburg. **CP-SandC**

Whiffs of the Ohio River at Cinncinnati. Carl Sandburg. **CP-SandC**

Whil virgin Spring, by Eden's flood. Address to the Shade of Thomson. Robert Burns. **CP-ThomJ**

While a late thaw began in the boarded eaves. Knut Hamsun in Old Age. Derek Mahon. **SP-MahoD**

While a once world slips from. Edward Estlin Cummings. **CP-CummE**

While Anna's Peers and Early Playmates Tread. William Wordsworth. **CP-WorW2**

While any two are talking, one. Small Garden Near a Field. Tess Gallagher. **SP-GallT**

While Asters— / On the Hill. Emily Dickinson. **CP-DickE**

While at her bedroom window once. The Keys of Morning. Walter de la Mare. **CP-DeLaW**

While at the stook the shearers cow'r. To the Rev. John McMath, Inclosing a Copy of *Holy Willie's Prayer*, Which He Had Requested. Robert Burns. **CP-BurnR**

While Beams of Orient Light Shoot Wide and High. William Wordsworth. **CP-WorW2**

While Beast instructs his fair, and innocent wife. On Sir Voluptuous Beast. Ben Jonson. **CP-JonsB**

While behind All, Firm and Erect. Walt Whitman. **CP-WhitW**

While briers an' woodbines budding green. Robert Burns. **CP-BurnR** (Epistle to J. L*****k, an Old Scotch Bard.) **CP-BurnR**

While Celia's tears make sorrow bright. *in imitation of* Cowley. Alexander Pope. **CP-PopeA**

While Christ lay dead the widowed world / Wore willow green for hope undone. Our Church Palms are Budding Willow Twigs. Christina Georgina Rossetti. **CP-RosC2**

While dancing rests, fit place to musicke graunting. Thomas Campion. *Fr.* Description of a Maske: Presented in the Banqueting Roome at *Whitehall*, on Saint Stephens Night Last, at the Marriage of the Right Honourable the Earle of *Somerset:* and the Right Noble the Lady FRANCES *Howard.* **CP-CampT**

While deep in love with one another. Pride of Progeny. Robert Ranke Graves. **CP-GravR**

While Drawing in a Churchyard. Thomas Hardy. **CP-HardT**

While Europe's eye is fixed on mighty things. The Rights of Woman—Spoken by Miss Fontenelle on Her Benefit Night. Robert Burns. **CP-BurnR**

While everyone else is laughing & drinking. Carmen 12. Catullus. *Fr.* Carmina. **CP-Catul**

While everything external / dies away in the far off. As the Human Village Prepares for Its Fate. Tom Clark. **SP-ClarT**

While faith forecasts millenial years. The Age of the Antonines. Herman Melville. **SP-MelvH**

While Fate permits us, let's be merry. To Enjoy the Time. Robert Herrick. **CP-HerrR**

While favour fed my hope, delight with hope was brought. Fifth Song. Sir Philip Sidney. *Fr.* Astrophil and Stella. **SP-SidnP**

While fishing in the blue lagoon. The Silver Fish. Shel Silverstein. **SP-SilS2**

While flowing rivers yield a blameless sport. Written upon a Blank Leaf in "The Compleat Angler." William Wordsworth. **CP-WorW2**

While friends defected, you stayed and were sure. Vocations. Geoffrey Hill. *Fr.* An Apology for the Revival of Christian Architecture in England. **CP-HillG**

While from the purpling east departs. Ode Composed on May Morning. William Wordsworth. **CP-WorW2**

While he looks into the eyes of women. Bran. Paul Muldoon. **SP-MuldP**

While he was here with breath and bone. The Casual Acquaintance. Thomas Hardy. **CP-HardT**

While I beside her stood austere. I Dreamt My Love A-Dying Lay. Daniel Gerard Hoffman. **SP-HoffD**

While I, from that reed-throated whisperer. William Butler Yeats. **CP-YeatW**

While I sit at the door. Eve. Christina Georgina Rossetti. **CP-RosC1**

While I stood here, in the open, lost in myself. Milkweed. James Wright. **CP-WrigJ**

While I stood listening, discreetly dumb. Growth of "Lorraine," The. Edwin Arlington Robinson. **CP-RobiE**

While I turned in a warm cocoon. A New Birth. Daniel Gerard Hoffman. **SP-HoffD**

While I was / Sitting on the porch, involved in air. Learning from Nature. Richard Eberhart. **CP-EberR**

While I was building neat. It Is Dangerous to Read Newspapers. Margaret Atwood. **SP-AtwM1**

While I watch the Christmas blaze. The Reminder. Thomas Hardy. **CP-HardT**

While I wrought out these fitful Danaan dreams. To Some I Have Talked with by the Fire. William Butler Yeats. **CP-YeatW**

While in heroic numbers some relate. A Pastoral Entertainment. James Thomson. **CP-ThomJ**

While intently on ourselves we look. In the Sap. George Meredith. **CP-MerG2**

While it is alive. Emily Dickinson. **CP-DickE**

While Janet eyes the Lanthorn's Magic. George Meredith. **CP-MerG2**

While labouring thousands ply their task. Veni. Arthur Hugh Clough. **SP-ClouA**

While larks with little wing. Phillis the Fair. Robert Burns. **CP-BurnR**

While leanest beasts in pastures feed. Supreme Fortune Falls Soonest. Robert Herrick. **CP-HerrR**

While Love Is Unfashionable. Alice Walker. **CP-WalkA**

While, Lydia, I was lov'd of thee. 3.9. Horace. **CP-HerrR,** *tr. by* Robert Herrick; *Fr.* Odes.

While lying on a beach, he remembers the photographs he once saw. Halfway to China. John Yau. **SP-YauJo**

While Many a Merry Tale. Samuel Johnson. (Verses Modelled on Pope.) **CP-JohnS**

While Marquis De Sade had himself buggered. East European Cooking. Charles Simic. **SP-SimiC**

While maudlin Whigs deplored [*or* deplor'd] their Cato's Fate. On a Lady Who P-ssed [*or* P———st] at the Tragedy of Cato. Alexander Pope. **CP-PopeA**

While Merlin paced the Cornish sands. The Egyptian Maid; or, The Romance of the Water Lilly. William Wordsworth. **CP-WorW2**

While My Guitar Gently Weeps. George Harrison. **CP-Beatl**

While my wife at my side lies slumbering, and the wars are long over. The Artilleryman's Vision. Walt Whitman. **CP-WhitW**

While my young cheek retains its healthful hues. Sonnet to William Linley. Samuel Taylor Coleridge. **CP-ColeS**

While Nature mocks her truth with mimic shows. George Meredith. **CP-MerG2**

While new-ca'd kye rowte at the stake. Second Epistle to John Lapraik. Robert Burns. **CP-BurnR**

While not a leaf seems faded; while the fields. William Wordsworth. **CP-WorW2** (September, 1815.) **CP-WorW2**

While Not the Past Forgetting. Walt Whitman. **CP-WhitW**

While now at poise the wings of shade. Mortmain Reappears. Herman Melville. **SP-MelvH** *Fr.* Clarel: A Poem and Pilgrimage in the Holy Land.

While now, to serve the pilgrim train. Vine and Clarel. Herman Melville. **SP-MelvH** *Fr.* Clarel: A Poem and Pilgrimage in the Holy Land.

While others go to Church. Emily Dickinson. **SP-DickE**

While people live the life. Two Ways of Living and Dying. David Herbert Lawrence. **CP-LawrD**

While poring Antiquarians search the ground. Roman Antiquities Discovered at Bishopstone, Hereforshire. William Wordsworth. **CP-WorW2**

While Prose-work and rhymes. Ballad, A. Robert Burns. **CP-BurnR**

While Psyche wept upon the rock forsaken. *verse tr. fr.* Metamorphoses *by* Apuleius. Elizabeth Barrett Browning. **CP-BroEB**

While rain, with eve in partnership. Beyond the Last Lamp. Thomas Hardy. **CP-HardT**

While rashly her womb's burden she casts out. 2.13. Ovid. **CP-MarlC,** *tr. by* Christopher Marlowe; *Fr.* Elegies.

While Red set sail on a junkboat. Rojo. Tom Clark. **SP-ClarT**

While riding on a train goin' west. Bob Dylan's Dream. "Bob Dylan." **CP-DylaB**

While roses are so red. Beauty Is Vain. Christina Georgina Rossetti. **CP-RosC1**

While roses bloomed along the plain. Elyas Yusof Nezami Ganjavi, *tr. fr.* Persian *by* Ralph Waldo Emerson. **CP-EmerR**

While secret-leaguing nations frown around. To His Royal Highness the Prince of Wales. James Thomson. **CP-ThomJ**

While she sits. Young Woman at a Window. William Carlos Williams. **CP-WilW1**

While ships / guided by his beacon glide. The Keeper. Bill Knott. **SP-KnotB**

While sitting home one warm night, I hear the burglars fiddling. Moving Day. Ron Koertge. **SP-KoerR**

While snow fell carelessly. The Crack. Denise Levertov. **CP-LeveD**

While Someone Telephones. Elizabeth Bishop. **NMP** *Fr.* Four Poems. **CP-BishE**

While, Stella, to your lasting praise. To Stella on Her Birthday, Written AD 1721–2. Jonathan Swift. **CP-SwifJ**

While sun and sea—and I, and I. The Island. Randall Jarrell. **CP-JarrR**

While that my soul repairs to her devotion. Church Monuments. George Herbert. **CP-HerbG**

While the carrots sang arias into the holy earth. The Passion of the Mad Rabbit. Anne Sexton. **CP-SextA**

While the far farewell music thins and fails. Departure. Thomas Hardy. **CP-HardT**

While the frozen armies trembled. The Home Front. Derek Mahon. **FaBCIP** *Fr.* Autobiographies. **SP-MahoD**

While the house was away. The Taker. Anne Sexton. **CP-SextA**

While the hum and the hurry. Under a Hat Rim. Carl Sandburg. **CP-SandC**

While the inimitable roof of the Louvre rises. Inscribenda Luparae [To Be Written on the Louvre]. Andrew Marvell, *tr. fr. Latin by* William A. McQueen *and* Kiffin A. Rockwell. **CP-MarvA**

While the milder Fates consent. A Lyric to Mirth. Robert Herrick. **CP-HerrR**

While the Poor gather round, till the end of time. Countess' Pillar. William Wordsworth. **CP-WorW2**

While the snaffle holds or the long-neck stings. Rudyard Kipling. **CP-KiplR** *Fr.* The Broken-Link Handicap. *Fr.* Plain Tales from the Hills.

While the south rains, the north. Sled Burial, Dream Ceremony. James Dickey. **CP-DickJ**

While the summer's growth kept me. The Heron. Wendell Berry. **CP-BerrW**

While the train waited for an hour in Troy. Home for the Holidays. Howard Nemerov. **CP-NemeH**

While thirteen moons saw smoothly run. William Cowper. **CP-CowpW**

While this America settles in the mould of its vulgarity, heavily thickening to empire. Shine, Perishing Republic. Robinson Jeffers. **CP-JefR1**

While thou didst keep thy candor undefil'd. To His Booke. Robert Herrick. **CP-HerrR**

While three hundred Americans died in flight. John Finley. Richard Eberhart. **CP-EberR**

While thus from theme to theme the Historian passed. The Churchyard among the Mountains (Continued). William Wordsworth. *Fr.* The Excursion. **CP-WorW2**

While thus he spake, th'Angelic Squadron bright. John Milton. **SCV** *Fr.* Book IV. **OAEL-1** *Fr.* Paradise Lost. **CP-MiltJ**

While thus I wander, cheerless and unblest. Written on Passing by Moon-Light through a Village, While the Ground Was Covered with Snow. Charlotte Smith. **CP-SmitC**

While thus I wander'd, step by step led on. William Wordsworth. **OxAEP-1** *Fr.* Summer Vacation. *Fr.* The Prelude; Growth of a Poet's Mind [1805 vers.]. **CP-WorW3**

While virgin Spring, By Eden's flood. Address, to the Shade of Thomson, on Crowning His Bust, at *Ednam, Roxburgh-shire*, with Bays. Robert Burns. **CP-BurnR**

While we are drilled in error, we are lost. Edwin Arlington Robinson. *Fr.* Octaves. **CP-RobiE**

While we sail and laugh, joke and fight, comes death. In Memoriam; Ingvald Bjorndal and His Comrade. Malcolm Lowry. **CP-LowrM**

While we sleep. The Tide. Denise Levertov. **CP-LeveD**

While we slumber and sleep / The sun leaps up from the deep. A Song of Flight. Christina Georgina Rossetti. **CP-RosC2**

While we talk we hear across the town. The Young Man, Thinking of the Old. Wendell Berry. *Fr.* The Handing Down. **CP-BerrW**

While we were fearing it, it came. Emily Dickinson. **CP-DickE**

While we were sleeping. Ice. Siv Cedering Fox. **SP-CedeS**

While we who wished to help stood helplessly by. A Grave. James Schuyler. **CP-SchuJ**

While winds frae off Ben-Lomond blaw. Epistle to Davie, a Brother Poet. Robert Burns. **CP-BurnR**

While with the public, you, my Lord, lament. A Poem to the Memory of the Righ Honourable the Lord Talbot. James Thomson. **CP-ThomJ**

While yet Rolfe's foot in stirrup stood. Inscription, The. Herman Melville. **SP-MelvH** *Fr.* Clarel: A Poem and Pilgrimage in the Holy Land.

While you, great Patron of Mankind! sustain. The First Epistle of the Second Book of Horace Imitated. Alexander Pope. **CP-PopeA**

While You Here Do Snoring Lie. Gerard Manley Hopkins. *Fr.* Songs from Shakespeare, in Latin and Greek. **CP-HopkG**

While you read / the sleepmoth begins. The Cat. William Matthews. **SP-MattW**

While you stood talking at the counter, cutting. Sonnet. Hayden Carruth. **CP-CarHS** *Fr.* Sonnets.

While you were promised to me. Song: The Promise. Robert Ranke Graves. **CP-GravR**

While your widow clatters water into a kettle. Father-in-Law. Derek Mahon. **SP-MahoD**

While you're a white-hot youth, emit the rays. The Star System. Richard Wilbur. **NBLV** *Fr.* Flippancies. **CP-WilbR**

Whiles I admire, thy first and second wayes. To his Singular Friend, William Lithgow. *Unknown, sometimes at. to* Sir Walter Ralegh. **CP-RaleW**

Whiles someone did chant this lovely lay, The. Edmund Spenser. **EIL; FF; OBVE** *Fr.* The Faerie Queene. **CP-Spens**

(Gather the Rose.) **EIL**

(Song of Bliss.) **FF**

Whilom, as antique stories tellen us. Edmund Spenser. **EPCY** *Fr.* The Faerie Queene. **CP-Spens**

Whilom, as olde stories tellen us. The Knight's Tale. Geoffrey Chaucer. *Fr.* The Canterbury Tales. **CP-ChauG**

Whilom ther was dwellynge in Lumbardye. *see also* January and May, or the Merchant's Tale, *mod. vers. by* Alexander Pope. Geoffrey Chaucer. *Fr.* The Canterbury Tales. **CP-ChauG**

Whilom ther was dwellynge in my contree. The Friar's Tale. Geoffrey Chaucer. **PoE** *Fr.* The Canterbury Tales. **CP-ChauG**

Whilst I alone did call upon thy aid. Sonnet 79. William Shakespeare. *Fr.* Sonnets. **CP-ShaWS**

Whilst I disdain the populace. Ibn-i-Yamin, *tr. fr. Persian by* Ralph Waldo Emerson. **CP-EmerR**

Whilst in an Amber-shade the Ant doth feast. Martial, *tr. fr. Latin by* Richard Lovelace. **CP-LoveR**

Whilst, Lydia, I was loved of thee. 3.9. Horace. **CP-JonsB**, *tr. by* Ben Jonson; *Fr.* Odes.

Whilst on Septimius' panting Breast. Catullus. *See* Carmen 45: "Phyllis Corydon clutched to him."

Whilst pale Anxiety, corrosive Care. On the Prospect of Establishing a Pantisocracy in America. Samuel Taylor Coleridge. **CP-ColeS**

Whilst thus the darlings of the gods. The Third Song. Thomas Carew. **CP-CareT** *Fr.* Carew's Masque. **CP-CareT**

Whil[']st thy weighed judgments [*or* weigh'd judgements], Egerton, I hear[e]. To Thomas, Lord Chancellor. Ben Jonson. **CP-JonsB**

Whilst yet to prove. Farewell to Love. John Donne. **CP-DonnJ**

Whilst you three merry poets traffic. On Dan Jackson's Picture. Jonathan Swift. **CP-SwifJ**

Whim of Time, the general arbiter, A. In 1929. Stephen Spender. **CP-SpenS**

Whimper of Sympathy. George Meredith. **CP-MerG1**

Whimsicality is a thing in itself. Triptych. Richard Eberhart. **CP-EberR**

Whip, The. Robert Creeley. **CP-CreeR**

Whip, The. Edwin Arlington Robinson. **CP-RobiE**

Whip, The. Charles Tomlinson. **CP-TomlC**

Whip-Poor-Will. Donald Hall. **CP-HallD**

Whip-Poor-Will and Katy-Did. Paul Laurence Dunbar. **CP-DunbP**

Whiplash. William Matthews. **SP-MattW**

Whipper-In, The. Thomas Hardy. **CP-HardT**

Whippersnappers. Ron Koertge. **SP-KoerR**

Whipping, The. Robert Earl Hayden. **CP-HaydR**

Whipping the face. Europe, with all her winds. The Jetty. Dover. Muriel Rukeyser. **CP-RukeM**

Whippoorwill this / moonday into. Edward Estlin Cummings. **CP-CummE**

Whips. Robert Herrick. **CP-HerrR**

Whirl Is King. Brendan Galvin. **SP-GalvB**

Whirl up, sea. Oread. Hilda Doolittle. **CP-DoolH**

Whirl, whorl, or wharve! the world. Reel. John Updike. **CP-UpdiJ**

Whirled dust, world dust. Falling Leaves. Kathleen Jessie Raine. **SP-RainK**

Whirls. Carl Sandburg. **CP-SandC**

Whirlwind in the fields, A. Interference. Archie Randolph Ammons. **SP-AmmoA**

Whirlwind lifts, The. Hollows. Archie Randolph Ammons. **SP-AmmoA**

WHISKE / WHI SK. Thomas Merton. *Fr.* A Selection of Concrete Poems. **CP-MertT**

Whiskey-colored sun, The. Skimpy Day at the Solstice. Marge Piercy. **SP-PierM**

Whiskey on your breath, The. My Papa's Waltz. Theodore Roethke. **CP-RoetT**

Whiskey Priest Recites His Holy Office, The. James McAuley. **SP-McAuJ** *Fr.* The Exile's Recurring Nightmare.

Whisper, The. Denise Levertov. **CP-LeveD**

Whisper, dry and insane, A. John Haines. *Fr.* Cicada. **SP-HainJ**

Whisper echoes, A. Frederick Morgan. *Fr.* Moments. **SP-MorgF**

Whispered at the Church-Opening. Thomas Hardy. **CP-HardT**

Whispers collect there, the bad news. Beneath the Sidewalk. Stephen Dunn. **SP-DunnS**

Whispers in the Next Room. Charles Simic. **SP-SimiC**

Whispers of Heavenly Death. Walt Whitman. **CP-WhitW**

Whispers of Immortality. Thomas Stearns Eliot. **CP-ElioT**

Whispers of maroon came on the little river. Maroon with Silver Frost. Carl Sandburg. **CP-SandC**

Whistle. A Ballad, The. Robert Burns. **CP-BurnR**

Whistle Aloud, Too Weedy Wren. Wallace Stevens. **LiTA** *Fr.* It Must Give Pleasure. *Fr.* Notes toward a Supreme Fiction. **CP-StevW**

Whistle Buoy. Tom Clark. **SP-ClarT**

Whistle o'er the Lave o't. Robert Burns. **CP-BurnR**

Whistling Sam. Paul Laurence Dunbar. **CP-DunbP**

Whit Monday. John Hewitt. **CP-HewiJ**

Whit Monday. Louis MacNeice. **CP-MacNL**

White. James Schuyler. **CP-SchuJ**

White. Charles Simic. **SP-SimiC**

White, a shingled path. Icos. Charles Tomlinson. **CP-TomlC**

White almonds of a statue stare, The. From This Far. Derek Walcott. **CP-WalcD**

White & blue my breathing lady leans. "Venice, 182—." John Berryman. **CP-BerrJ**

White and silky neck with light brown curls. Butcher's. Jenny Joseph. *Fr.* Life and Turgid Times of A. Citizen. **SP-JoseJ**

White and the River. Siv Cedering Fox. **SP-CedeS**

White and yellow were the flowers. Arabella. Stevie Smith. **CP-SmitS**

White Apples. Donald Hall. **CP-HallD**

White as an Indian Pipe. Emily Dickinson. **CP-DickE**

White as squid among the roseate prawns. Mountains, Fall on Us. Michael Hartnett. **SP-HarMi**

White as the snow on mountaintop. Lament of a Graying Woman. Wen Chun Cho, *tr. fr. Chinese by* William Carlos Williams *with* David Rafael Wang. **CP-WilW2**

White as Zenobias teeth, the which the Girles. The Candor of Julias Teeth. Robert Herrick. **CP-HerrR**

White Ash. Carl Sandburg. **CP-SandC**

White bark writhed and sputtered like a fish, The. Edna St. Vincent Millay. *Fr.* Sonnets from an Ungrafted Tree. **CP-MillE**

White barns this morning match the trees. Iowa. John Updike. **CP-UpdiJ**

White Bear, with smoking mouth, embraces, The. Goose. Ted Hughes. **SP-HughT**

White Begonia. Louis Zukofsky. **CP-ZukLS**

White Birds, The. William Butler Yeats. **CP-YeatW**

White Blossom, A. David Herbert Lawrence. **CP-LawrD**

White Boat, Blue Boat. James Schuyler. **CP-SchuJ**

White bone found. Bone Dreams. Seamus Heaney. **SP-HeanS**

White bone in the yellow flats of sun. The Columns of the Parthenon. Donald Hall. **CP-HallD**

White brain crossing, The. Alun Lewis. *Fr.* Threnody for a Starry Night. **CP-LewiA**

White butterfly, A. The Graceful Bastion. William Carlos Williams. **CP-WilW2**

White Center. Richard Hugo. **CP-HugoR**

White chocolate jar full of petals, The. Chez Jane. Frank O'Hara. **SP-OharF**

White City, A. James Schuyler. **CP-SchuJ**

White cloud bearing to me the darkness of my mind, The. Wall and Cloud. James Dickey. **CP-DickJ**

White Cloud, White Blossom. Roy Fisher. **SP-FishR**

White clouds, red leaves flying. Frederick Morgan. *Fr.* Moments. **SP-MorgF**

White clouds, whose shadows haunt the deep. Summer by the Lakeside. John Greenleaf Whittier. **CP-WhitJ**

White coats / White aprons. Interne at Provident. Langston Hughes. **SP-HughL**

White Cockade, The. Robert Burns. **CP-BurnR**

White cock's tail, The / Tosses in the wind. Ploughing on Sunday. Wallace Stevens. **CP-StevW**

White Collar. Stephen Dunn. **SP-DunnS**

White-collar man blue-collar / Man I am a no-collar man. Solitary Life. Thomas Merton. **CP-MertT**

White day, black river. The Predicter of Famine. William Carlos Williams. **CP-WilW2**

White decorators interested in Art. Marilyn Hacker. **SP-HackM**

(Nights of 1964-1966: The Old Reliable.) **SP-HackM**

White Doe of Rylstone, The; or, The Fate of the Nortons. William Wordsworth. **CP-WorW1**

"In trellised shed with clustering roses gay." **EPCY**

White dory, face down, its rusted keel staining, A. Tropic Zone. Derek Walcott. **CP-WalcD** *Fr.* Midsummer.

White dove cooeth in her downy nest, The. Whitsun Eve. Christina Georgina Rossetti. **CP-RosC3**

White Dwarf. John Updike. **CP-UpdiJ**

White Eyes. Anne Waldman. **SP-WaldA**

White Feather. John Berryman. **CP-BerrJ**

White Fish in Reeds. Joseph Ceravolo. **SP-CeraJ**

White Flowers. Mary Oliver. **SP-OlivM**

White fog lifting & falling on mountain-brow. Wales Visitation. Allen Ginsberg. **CP-GinsA**

"White folks is white," says Uncle Jim. Uncle Jim. Countee Cullen. **CP-CullC**

White. From the / Under arm of T. George Oppen. **CP-OppeG**

White frost; intricate bare branches. Alun Lewis. *Fr.* Threnody for a Starry Night. **CP-LewiA**

White girl lay on the grass, A. Mythological Introduction. Philip Larkin. **CP-LarkP**

White girls lift their heads like trees, The. Song for Our Lady of Cobre. Thomas Merton. **CP-MertT; SP-MertT**

White Goddess, The. Robert Ranke Graves. **CP-GravR**

White goose by palm tree, palm ragged, among stones the white oleander. Gull's Cry. Robert Penn Warren. *Fr.* To a Little Girl, One Year Old, in a Ruined Fortress. **SP-WarrR**

White gown transparent on her. Exotica. Frederick Morgan. **SP-MorgF**

White guardians of the universe of sleep. Edward Estlin Cummings. **CP-CummE**

White gulls blow from the Rockies like Norway. Malcolm Lowry. *Fr.* The Canadian Turned Back at the Border. **CP-LowrM**

White-Haired Girl. Archibald MacLeish. **CP-MacLA**

White Hands. Carl Sandburg. **CP-SandC**

White haze over Manhattan's towers. Swirls of Black Dust on Avenue D. Allen Ginsberg. **CP-GinsA**

White hen sitting / On white eggs three, A. Christina Georgina Rossetti. **CP-RosC2**

White Horse, The. David Herbert Lawrence. **CP-LawrD**

White Horse. Charles Olson. **CP-OlsoC**

White Horses. Rudyard Kipling. **CP-KiplR**

White Hotel, The. Richard Shelton. **SP-ShelR**

White house is silent, The. Arriving in the Country Again. James Wright. **CP-WrigJ**

White houses bank the hill. The Rooftop. Thom Gunn. **CP-GunnT**

White in the moon the long road lies. Alfred Edward Housman. **CP-HousA**

White Innocence, that now liest spread. To Mistress Katherine Neville, on Her Green Sickness. Thomas Carew. **CP-CareT**

White Iris, The. Philip Levine. **SP-LeviP**

White is right, / Yellow mellow. Argument. Langston Hughes. **SP-HughL**

White Island: or Place of the Blest, The. Robert Herrick. **CP-HerrR**

White Knight's Ballad, The. "Lewis Carroll." *See* I'll tell thee everything I can.

White leaf trailing the water light. Vacation. Jim Carroll. **SP-CarrJ**

White Lemons. Gilbert Sorrentino. **SP-SorrG**

White light is artificial, and hygienic as heaven, The. The Surgeon at 2 A.M. Sylvia Plath. **CP-PlatS**

White Lights, The. Edwin Arlington Robinson. **CP-RobiE**

White light's wet glaze on asphalt city floor. Studying the Signs. Allen Ginsberg. **CP-GinsA**

White lions are roaring on the water. Kenneth Patchen. **CP-PatcK**

White-maned, wide-throated, the heavy-shouldered children of the wind leap at the sea-cliff. Granite and Cypress. Robinson Jeffers. **CP-JefR1**

White Man's Burden, The. Rudyard Kipling. **CP-KiplR**

White marble pillars in the Rector's courtyard. Eroica. Allen Ginsberg. **CP-GinsA**

White mares lashed to the sulky carriages. In Ohio. James Wright. **CP-WrigJ**

White Moon comes in on a baby face. Baby Face. Carl Sandburg. **CP-SandC**

White moon takes the sea away from the sea. Rose of the Sea. Juan Ramón Jiménez. *Fr.* Ten Short Poems. **CP-WrigJ**

White morning flows into the mirror. The Parting: II. Adrienne Rich. **CP-RicAE; SP-RicA2**

White moth to the closing vine, The. The Gipsy Trail. Rudyard Kipling. **CP-KiplR**

White Negress, The. Karl Shapiro. **SP-ShapK**

White Night. Kadya Molodovsky, *tr. fr. Yiddish by* Adrienne Rich. **CP-RicAE; SP-RicA2**

White Night. Mary Oliver. **SP-OlivM**

White Night. Adrienne Rich. **SP-RicA2**

White night roared with a huge north-wind, The. Ballade. Edward Estlin Cummings. **CP-CummE**

White Nights, 1938. Martin Edmunds. **SP-EdmuM**

White, O white face. Prayer. Hilda Doolittle. **CP-DoolH**

White of her Colonial, The. Archibald MacLeish. **CP-MacLA** *Fr.* The Happy Marriage.

White Owl Flies Into and Out of the Field. Mary Oliver. **SP-OlivM**

White paint splotches on blue head bandanas. Painting the North San Juan School. Gary Snyder. **CP-SnydG**

White Phosphorus. Alice Notley. **SP-NotlA**

White Pig. Stephen Dobyns. **SP-DobyS**

White Pines, Felled 1984. Richard Eberhart. **CP-EberR**

White Queen's Riddle, The. "Lewis Carroll." **CP-CarrL** *Fr.* Through the Looking-Glass.

White rolling battlements on rumbling lead. Louis MacNeice. *Fr.* Notes for a Biography. **CP-MacNL**

White Rose. Hilda Doolittle. **CP-DoolH**

White Rose. César Vallejo, *tr. fr. Spanish by* James Wright. **CP-WrigJ**

White rose my soul, The. Dedication. Edward Estlin Cummings. **CP-CummE**

White rose your sea shell. December. William Carlos Williams. **CP-WilW2**

White Roses. John Ashbery. **SP-AshbJ**

White roses shatter, overblown. Providence 1. John Hewitt. **CP-HewiJ**

White roses, tiny and old, flare among thorns. Old Roses. Donald Hall. **CP-HallD**

White Seal, The. Rudyard Kipling. *Fr.* The Jungle Book. Lukannon. **CP-KiplR**

"Oh! hush thee, my baby, the night is behind us." **CP-KiplR**

"You mustn't swim till you're six weeks old." **CP-KiplR**

White Ship, The. Geoffrey Hill. **CP-HillG**

White ship disappears. Blood Bridge. Jim Carroll. **SP-CarrJ**

White Shoulders. Carl Sandburg. **CP-SandC**

White-sided flowers are thrusting up on the hillside. Hawaii Dantesca. Charles Wright. **SP-WrigC**

White Skirt, The. Stephen Dobyns. **SP-DobyS**

White sky, over the hemlocks bowed with snow. The Buck in the Snow. Edna St. Vincent Millay. **CP-MillE**

White Snake, The. Anne Sexton. **CP-SextA**

White spire, / Its peak encircled, A. The Shell. Charles Tomlinson. **CP-TomlC**

White spot of a Flicker, The. Tiny Energies. Gary Snyder. **CP-SnydG**

White Stag, The. Ezra Pound. **SP-PounE**

White stars scattering / Pale rain of spray-drops. The Gulls. John Gould Fletcher. *Fr.* Sand and Spray: A Sea-Symphony. **SP-FletJ**

White suffused with red. The Crimson Cyclamen. William Carlos Williams. **CP-WilW1**

White sun, The. Late November. Archie Randolph Ammons. **SP-AmmoA**

White sunlight and the dripping oars! Frank Templeton Prince. *Fr.* Apollo and the Sibyl. **CP-PrinF**

White sunshine on sweating skulls. Anti-Vietnam War Peace Mobilization. Allen Ginsberg. **CP-GinsA**

White Symphony. John Gould Fletcher. **SP-FletJ**

White-Tailed Hornet, The. Robert Frost. **CP-FrosR**

White, the silent stars, The. Poem: 1939. Thomas Merton. **CP-MertT**

White, these villages. White. In Connecticut. Charles Tomlinson. **CP-TomlC**

White Thighs. Stephen Dobyns. **SP-DobyS**

White though ye be, yet, lillies, know. How Lillies Came White. Robert Herrick. **CP-HerrR**

White Thought, The. Stevie Smith. **CP-SmitS**

White Thought in a White Shade, A. James Liddy. **CP-LiddJ**

White-throat beyond my window. In the Pitch of Night. Daniel Gerard Hoffman. **SP-HoffD**

White Tintoretto clouds beneath my naked feet. The Strand. Louis MacNeice. **CP-MacNL**

White toga'd God of the gold sandals. Two Saints. John Ciardi. **SP-CiarJ**

White Troops Had Their Orders but the Negroes Looked Like Men. Gwendolyn Brooks. **SP-BrooG**

White trumpet flower along the river, The. Sister Beach, Sister Garden. James Liddy. **CP-LiddJ**

White Van, The. Charles Tomlinson. **CP-TomlC**

White villa sat at the lip of rock, The. The Lemons. David St. John. **SP-StJoD**

White violet, The. Sea Violet. Hilda Doolittle. **CP-DoolH**

White walls of this airy house assume, The. A Flower-Arranging Summer. May Sarton. **SP-SartM**

White-washed monastery where we sat, The. October in Hyde Park. Derek Mahon. **SP-MahoD**

White water now in the snowflake's prison. Howard Nemerov. *Fr.* Runes. **CP-NemeH**

White water, white water, feather of a form. Howard Nemerov. *Fr.* Runes. **CP-NemeH**

White, white in that dawnlight, the world was exploding, white. Time as Hypnosis. Robert Penn Warren. **SP-WarrR**

White, white, luminous but. Fog. Robert Penn Warren. **SP-WarrR**

White winter sun struck its stroke on the bridge, The. The Thing Unplanned. Thomas Hardy. **CP-HardT**

White Witchcraft. Robert Browning. **CP-BroR2**

White with daisies and red with sorrel. Weeds. Edna St. Vincent Millay. **CP-MillE**

White World. Hilda Doolittle. **CP-DoolH**

Whitelash of Air Rapids. Archie Randolph Ammons. **SP-AmmoA**

Whitelight. Carl Sandburg. **CP-SandC**

Whitely, while benzine / Rinsings from the moon. Lachrymae Christi. Hart Crane. **CP-CranH**

Whiteness. Stephen Dunn. **SP-DunnS**

Whiteness being what I remember. Whiteness I Remember. Sylvia Plath. **CP-PlatS**

Whiteness I Remember. Sylvia Plath. **CP-PlatS**

Whiteness most white. Ah, to be clean again. They Shall Be as White as Snow. Christina Georgina Rossetti. **CP-RosC2**

Whiteness near and far, The. From a Notebook. James Merrill. **SP-MerrJ**

Whiteness of moonlight builds a house that is not there. Kathleen Jessie Raine. *Fr.* The Hollow Hill. **SP-RainK**

Whiter / than the crust. The Wind Sleepers. Hilda Doolittle. **CP-DoolH**

Whiter bone: / the sea-voice, A. Sea Poem. Charles Tomlinson. **CP-TomlC**

Whiteskinned boy, halfdrowned, A. Episodes for a Panel. James McAuley. **SP-McAuJ** *Fr.* Studies for a Self-Portrait at Forty.

Whitewashed room, roof, The. To P.O. Allen Ginsberg. **CP-GinsA**

Whitewashed Wall, The. Thomas Hardy. **CP-HardT**

Whither? Wystan Hugh Auden. *Fr.* A Voyage. **CP-AudeW**

Whither are all her false oathes blowne. To His False Mistris. Robert Herrick. **CP-HerrR**

Whither away delight? The Glimpse. George Herbert. **CP-HerbG**

Whither dost thou whorry me. To Bacchus, a Canticle. Robert Herrick. **CP-HerrR**

Whither, mad maiden, wilt thou roame? To His Muse. Robert Herrick. **CP-HerrR**

Whither, O, whither art thou fled. The Search. George Herbert. **CP-HerbG**

Whither? Say, whither shall I fly. The Frozen Zone; or, Julia Disdainful. Robert Herrick. **CP-HerrR**

Whither the Tribes Go Up, Even the Tribes of the Lord. Christina Georgina Rossetti. **CP-RosC2**

Whither thus hastes my little book so fast? Thomas Campion. *See* The Writer to his Booke.

Whitish dawn had just appeared, The. Frederick Morgan. *Fr.* Two Poems to a Dead Woman. **SP-MorgF**

Whitman. John Gould Fletcher. **SP-FletJ**

Whitman: "April 19, 1864." George Oppen. *Fr.* Of Being Numerous. **CP-OppeG**

Whitman in Black. Ted Berrigan. **SP-BerrT**

Whitman took the cars. Empathy and New Year. James Schuyler. **CP-SchuJ**

Whitshed's Motto on His Coach. Jonathan Swift. **CP-SwifJ**

Whitsun. Sylvia Plath. **CP-PlatS**

Whitsun Canticle, A. Thomas Merton. **CP-MertT**

Whitsun Day. Christina Georgina Rossetti. **CP-RosC2**

Whitsun Eve. Christina Georgina Rossetti. **CP-RosC2**

Whitsun Eve. Christina Georgina Rossetti. **CP-RosC3**

Whitsun Monday. Christina Georgina Rossetti. **CP-RosC2**

Whitsun Tuesday. Christina Georgina Rossetti. **CP-RosC2**

Whitsun Weddings, The. Philip Larkin. **CP-LarkP**

Whitsunday. George Herbert. **CP-HerbG**

Whitsunday. Christopher Smart. *Fr.* Hymns and Spiritual Songs for the Fasts and Festivals of the Church of England. **SP-SmarC**

Whitsunday in Kirchstetten. Wystan Hugh Auden. **CP-AudeW**

Whittier. Paul Laurence Dunbar. **CP-DunbP**

Whittled chrystal: fissured, The. Head Hewn with an Axe. Charles Tomlinson. **CP-TomlC**

Who / am I—. Intervals. Robert Creeley. **CP-CreeR**

Who? Walter de la Mare. **CP-DeLaW**

Who. Allen Ginsberg. **CP-GinsA**

Who. Charles Olson. **CP-OlsoC**

Who. Shel Silverstein. **SP-SilS2**

Who / threw the silver dollar up into the tree? Edward Estlin Cummings. **CP-CummE**

Who? Alice Walker. **CP-WalkA**

Who / was that who. Zukofsky. Gilbert Sorrentino. **SP-SorrG**

Who abdicated Ambush. Emily Dickinson. **CP-DickE**

Who after his transgression doth repent. Penitence. Robert Herrick. **CP-HerrR**

Who after this would commit his thoughts to babbling paper. Illustrissimo Viro Domino Lanceloto Josepho de Maniban Grammatomanti [To That Renowned Man Lord Lancelot Joseph de Maniban Graphologist]. Andrew Marvell, tr. fr. Latin by William A. McQueen and Kiffin A. Rockwell. **CP-MarvA**

Who Am I? Carl Sandburg. **CP-SandC**

Who am I chasing—underwater—in my life? The Spearing. Laurence Lieberman. **SP-LiebL**

Who am I? Saliva. Milarepa Taste. Allen Ginsberg. **CP-GinsA**

Who am I, who. Self. Kathleen Jessie Raine. **SP-RainK**

Who am I worthless that You spent such pains. A Prayer for the Self. John Berryman. **PPP** Fr. Eleven Addresses to the Lord. **CP-BerrJ**

Who appreciates the fingers cramped. Politely like Snakes in the Oats. Richard Hugo. **CP-HugoR**

Who are the rulers of Ind—to whom shall we bow the knee? Rudyard Kipling. Fr. Certain Maxims of Hafiz. **CP-KiplR**

Who Are These Coming to the Sacrifice? Geoffrey Hill. Fr. An Apology for the Revival of Christian Architecture in England. **CP-HillG**

Who are these coming to the sacrifice? John Keats. Fr. Ode on a Grecian Urn. **CP-KeatJ**

Who are these horsemen here riding and roaming over our forest trails? The Horsemen. Louise McNeill. **SP-McNeL**

Who are these men tramping the roads. The Great Depression. Louise McNeill. **SP-McNeL**

Who are these people at the bridge to meet me? They are the villagers. The Bee Meeting. Sylvia Plath. **CP-PlatS**

Who are these small determined figures. Imaginary Landscapes. Erica Jong. **SP-JongE**

Who are these strange faces in Mexico? What Quetzalcoatl Saw in Mexico. David Herbert Lawrence. **CP-LawrD**

Who are these? Why sit they here in twilight? Mental Cases. Wilfred Owen. **CP-OwenW**

Who are these women and offices. College Under Water. Anne Waldman. **SP-WaldA**

Who are we now, who are we ever. The Jack of Hearts. Lawrence Ferlinghetti. **SP-FerlL**

Who are we, S.S. The Poem For a Certain Lady on Her 33rd Birthday. Etheridge Knight. **SP-KnigE**

"Who are we waiting for?" "Soup burnt?" ". . . Eight." The Feckless Dinner Party. Walter de la Mare. **CP-DeLaW**

Who are you / calling me in the dusk. A Moose Calling. John Haines. **SP-HainJ**

Who are you dusky woman, so ancient hardly human. Ethiopia Saluting the Colors. Walt Whitman. **CP-WhitW**

Who are you, little i. Edward Estlin Cummings. **CP-CummE**

Who/ Are you/ Who is born. Vision and Prayer. Dylan Thomas. **CP-ThomD**

Who art thou that comest with a stedfast face. I Have Fought a Good Fight. Christina Georgiana Rossetti. **CP-RosC3**

Who(at / her nons- / elf). Edward Estlin Cummings. **CP-CummE**

Who Be Kind To. Allen Ginsberg. **CP-GinsA**

Who beckons the green ivy up. The Miracle. Walter de la Mare. **CP-DeLaW**

Who before dying demands not rebirth. Edward Estlin Cummings. **CP-CummE**

Who begs to die for feare of humane need. Need. Robert Herrick. **CP-HerrR**

Who but hails the sight with pleasure. Hint from the Mountains for Certain Political Pretenders. William Wordsworth. **CP-WorW2**

Who but Is Pleased to Watch the Moon on High. William Wordsworth. **CP-WorW2**

Who but the Goddess? All that is. To Memory. George Oppen. **CP-OppeG**

Who But the Lord? Langston Hughes. **SP-HughL**

Who by Fire? Leonard Cohen. **CP-CoheL**

Who call her Mother and who calls her Wife. M. M. George Meredith. **CP-MerG1**

"Who called?" I said, and the words. Echo. Walter de la Mare. **CP-DeLaW**

Who Called Love Conquering. Philip Larkin. **CP-LarkP**

Who Called That Robin a Piccolo Player? Ogden Nash. **CP-NashO**

Who calleth?—Thy Father calleth. The Master Is Come, and Calleth for Thee. Christina Georgina Rossetti. **CP-RosC1**

Who calls her two-faced? Faces, she has three. The Three-Faced. Robert Ranke Graves. **CP-GravR**

Who can believe with common sense. Epigram on Fasting. Jonathan Swift. **CP-SwifJ**

Who can blame mee if I love? Song. Mary Sidney, Countess of Montgomery Wroth. Fr. Part 1. Fr. Urania. **CP-WrotM**

Who can consider thy right courses run. To Robert, Earl of Salisbury. Ben Jonson. **CP-JonsB**

Who can ever praise enough. The Price. Wystan Hugh Auden. **CP-AudeW**

Who can go beyond the first four words? see also My Wife and I. Leonard Cohen. **CP-CoheL**

Who can kick a football. Who. Shel Silverstein. **SP-SilS2**

Who can know more deeply than I your loneliness there? Fragment. Hayden Carruth. **CP-CarHS**

Who can make a poem of the depths of weariness. Carl Sandburg. Fr. The People, Yes. **CP-SandC**

Who can persuade the sea. Pablo Neruda, tr. fr. Spanish by Ben Belitt. **SP-NeruP** Fr. Question Book.

Who can pick up the weight of Britain. Imago. Wallace Stevens. **CP-StevW**

"Who can speak the crimes of rhyming?" Clown's Song. John Gould Fletcher. **SP-FletJ**

Who can surrender to Christ, dividing his best with the stranger. Where Is the Real Non-Resistant? Nicholas Vachel Lindsay. **CP-LindV**

Who can tell who was born of what? Doorstep, Lightning, Waif-Dreaming. James Dickey. **CP-DickJ**

Who can think of the sun costuming clouds. A Fading of the Sun. Wallace Stevens. **CP-StevW**

Who cares for earthly bread tho' white? Christina Georgina Rossetti. **CP-RosC2**

Who Cares, Long as It's B-Flat. Hayden Carruth. **CP-CarHS**

Who challenged my soldier mother? A Catechism. William Stafford. **SP-StafW**

Who chides the tears that weep so dear a head? 1.24. Horace. **CP-CummE,** tr. by E. E. Cummings; Fr. Odes.

Who comes to-night? We ope the doors in vain. Henry James. Robert Louis Stevenson. **CP-StevW**

Who comes—with rapture greeted, and caressed. Charles the Second. William Wordsworth. Fr. Ecclesiastical Sonnets. **CP-WorW2**

Who compares a poem. Hafiz, tr. by Ralph Waldo Emerson. **CP-EmerR** Fr. Odes.

Who could be ill in March. Emily Dickinson. **SP-DickE**

Who could be motherless. Emily Dickinson. **SP-DickE**

Who could believe an ant in theory? Credibility. John Ciardi. **SP-CiarJ**

Who could have figured, when the harnesses improved. The Wide Prospect. Randall Jarrell. **CP-JarrR**

Who could have thought that men and women could feel. Old Paintings on Italian Walls. Kathleen Jessie Raine. **SP-RainK**

Who could possibly approve of Metternich. Pseudo-Questions. Wystan Hugh Auden. **CP-AudeW**

Who Court obtain within Himself. Emily Dickinson. **CP-DickE**

Who cries all art is a fraud & Genius a trick. William Blake. See Blakes apology for His Catalogue.

Who dares affirm this is no pious age. An Epilogue to a Play for the Benefit of the Weavers in Ireland. Jonathan Swift. **CP-SwifJ**

Who dares deny, that all first fruits are due. To K[ing] Charles and Q[ueen] Mary, for the Loss of Their First-Born. An Epigram Consolatory. 1629. Ben Jonson. **CP-JonsB**

Who dat knockin' at de do'? Encouragement. Paul Laurence Dunbar. **CP-DunbP**

Who decided what is useful in its beauty. Looking at Quilts. Marge Piercy. **SP-PierM**

Who dedicates himself to the glass. Hafiz, tr. by Ralph Waldo Emerson. **CP-EmerR** Fr. Odes.

Who Did Not Die in Vain. Howard Nemerov. **CP-NemeH**

Who Did Which? or Who Indeed? Ogden Nash. **CP-NashO**

Who died nails, key-rings. Deaths. Derek Mahon. **SP-MahoD**

Who do I want to tell it. Poem. Alice Notley. **SP-NotlA**

Who do you think stands watching. Everlasting Flowers. David Herbert Lawrence. **CP-LawrD**

Who does not blush when charged with selfish views? Against Interested Love. William Cowper. **CP-CowpW**

Who does not sit in the seat of the scoffer. Blessed Is the Man. Marianne Craig Moore. **CP-MoorM**

Who does the mountain belong to anyway? As Wordsworth. The Mountain. Stephen Dobyns. **SP-DobyS**

Who dreamed [or dream'd] that beauty passes like a dream? The Rose of the World. William Butler Yeats. **CP-YeatW**

Who dreams these isles. Nameless Islets. Kathleen Jessie Raine. *Fr.* Eileann Chanaidh. **SP-RainK**

Who Edmonds, reads thy book, and doth not see. To the Same; on the Same. Ben Jonson. **CP-JonsB**

Who else, in God's name, comes out in these woods? Friends of the Family, or Bowling a Sticky Cricket. Robert Penn Warren. *Fr.* Ballad of a Sweet Dream of Peace. **SP-WarrR**

Who endure days like this. Louis Zukofsky. *Fr.* 29 Songs. **CP-ZukLS**

Who enters this / kingdom. And. Laughing. Robert Creeley. **CP-CreeR**

Who even dead, yet hath his mind entire! Canto 47. Ezra Pound. **CMoP; PoE; SP-PounE; VGW** *Fr.* Cantos. **CP-PoCan**

Who Ever Loved, That Loved Not at First Sight? Christopher Marlowe. *See* It lies not in our power to love, or hate.

Who ever saw me / cutting stalks, threshing chaff from the wheat? Negative Hands. Pablo Neruda, *tr. fr. Spanish by* Ben Belitt. **SP-NeruP**

Who ever suffered as I from separation? Hafiz, *tr. by* Ralph Waldo Emerson. **CP-EmerR** *Fr.* Odes.

Who extols a wilderness? Love Defended. Christina Georgina Rossetti. **CP-RosC3**

Who fancied what a pretty sight. William Wordsworth. **CP-WorW1**

Who fights behind a shield. Trinacria. Charles Olson. **CP-OlsoC**

Who for their living lived. The Unnatural History of Peru. Kenneth Patchen. **CP-PatcK**

Who for those ages ever without some blood. John Berryman. *Fr.* Sonnets to Chris. **CP-BerrJ**

Who formes a Godhead out of Gold or Stone. Devotion Makes the Deity. Robert Herrick. **CP-HerrR**

Who gave me grassy Lawns for miry ways. To My Dearest Cousin, on Her Removal of us from Silver End, to Weston. William Cowper. **CP-CowpW**

Who gave thee, O Beauty. Ralph Waldo Emerson. **PoEL-4** *Fr.* Ode to Beauty. **CP-EmerR**

Who gave thee, O Beauty. Ode to Beauty. Ralph Waldo Emerson. **CP-EmerR**

Who gave thy cheek the mixed tint. Hafiz, *tr. by* Ralph Waldo Emerson. **CP-EmerR** *Fr.* Odes.

Who gave us flowers? Purple Anemones. David Herbert Lawrence. **CP-LawrD**

Who Giants know, with lesser Men. Emily Dickinson. **CP-DickE**

Who gives and hides the giving hand. Giving and Taking. John Greenleaf Whittier. **CP-WhitJ**

Who gives him the Bath? The New Knighthood. Rudyard Kipling. **CP-KiplR**

Who goes There? Gilbert Sorrentino. **SP-SorrG**

Who goes there? hankering, gross, mystical, nude. Walt Whitman. **TrGrPo** *Fr.* Song of Myself. **CP-WhitW**

Who goes to dine must take his Feast. Emily Dickinson. **CP-DickE**

Who Goes with Fergus? William Butler Yeats. **CP-YeatW**

Who has gone farthest? for I would go farther. Excelsior. Walt Whitman. **CP-WhitW**

Who has hold of Juliet's nipples. Aubade. Frederick Morgan. *Fr.* Enigmas. **SP-MorgF**

Who has invented our enmity? Who has prescribed us. Wendell Berry. *Fr.* To a Siberian Woodsman. **CP-BerrW**

Who has not been. Who? Alice Walker. **CP-WalkA**

Who has not been exiled. Ovid. Siv Cedering Fox. **SP-CedeS**

Who has not found the Heaven—below. Emily Dickinson. **CP-DickE**

Who has not seen Brancusi's White Negress? The White Negress. Karl Shapiro. **SP-ShapK**

Who Has Seen the Wind? Christina Georgina Rossetti. **CP-RosC2**

Who has sounded or again shalt sound. Rembrandt—Rouault—Piero. Marsden Hartley. **CP-HartM**

Who has told you what discoveries. Basics. James Dickey. **CP-DickJ**

Who hasn't been frustrated. A Plea for Mercy. William Carlos Williams. **CP-WilW2**

Who hath desired the Sea?—the sight of salt water unbounded. The Sea and the Hills. Rudyard Kipling. **CP-KiplR**

Who Hath Despised the Day of Small Things? Christina Georgina Rossetti. **CP-RosC2**

Who Hath Given Man Speech? Algernon Charles Swinburne. **SP-SwinA** *Fr.* Atalanta in Calydon.

Who hath he[a]rd of such[e] cruelty before. Sir Thomas Wyatt. **CP-WyatT**

Who hath not glow'd above the page where fame. Address Intended to be Recited at the Caledonian Meeting. Byron. **CP-Byron**

Who Have a Form of Godliness. Christina Georgina Rossetti. **CP-RosC3**

Who have been lonely once. Careless Love. Stanley Jasspon Kunitz. **CP-KuniS**

Who he was, remained an open question. A Question of Identity. Stephen Spender. **CP-SpenS**

Who hears of Helen's Tower, may dream perchance. Helen's Tower. Robert Browning. **CP-BroR2**

Who hears that whistle blowing? The Little Black Train. Kenneth Patchen. **CP-PatcK**

Who hears the humming. Breath. Philip Levine. **SP-LeviP**

Who hock in toss regret. Hyacinth. Louis Zukofsky. **CP-ZukLS**

Who holds the flag while I hole out in three ? Though I Have More. Malcolm Lowry. **CP-LowrM**

Who hurt you so. Edna St. Vincent Millay. **CP-MillE**

Who I was & what I wanted & what I did & what happened. The Cure. Anne Waldman. **SP-WaldA**

Who in One Lifetime. Muriel Rukeyser. **CP-RukeM**

Who, in the dark, has cast the harbor-chain? Putting to Sea. Louise Bogan. **CP-BogaL**

Who in the Hell is Tom Jones? Charles Bukowski. **SP-BukC1**

Who in the Realm to-day lays down dear life for the sake of a land more dear? Dead King, The [Edward VII; 1910]. Rudyard Kipling. **CP-KiplR**

Who includes diversity and is Nature. Kosmos. Walt Whitman. **CP-WhitW**

Who is a white / woman / and. For Mary Ellen McAnally. Etheridge Knight. **SP-KnigE**

Who Is at My Window. Denise Levertov. **CP-LeveD**

Who is director of this movie. Hallucinogenic Halleluuuu. Al Young. **CP-YounA**

Who is ever quite without his landscape. Detective Story. Wystan Hugh Auden. **CP-AudeW**

Who is he? Despair. Anne Sexton. **CP-SextA**

Who is it beside me, who is here beside me, in the hollow hill? In the Hill at Newgrange. Robinson Jeffers. **CP-JefR2**

Who is it calling by the darkened river. Voices. Walter de la Mare. **CP-DeLaW**

Who is it seeks my Pillow Nights. Emily Dickinson. **CP-DickE**

Who is it that says most? which can say more. Sonnet 134. William Shakespeare. *Fr.* Sonnets. **CP-ShaWs**

Who Is It That This Dark Night. Sir Philip Sidney. *See* Eleventh Song.

Who is it that this dark[e] night. Eleventh Song. Sir Philip Sidney. **EIL; EnRePo; NAEL-1; NOBE; NoSic; OBEV; OBSC; OxAEP-1; PoE; PoEL-1; PoPle; SCGP; SeCePo; TEP** *Fr.* Astrophil and Stella. **SP-SidnP**

Who is my father in this world, in this house. The Irish Cliffs of Moher. Wallace Stevens. **CP-StevW**

Who Is Now Reading This? Walt Whitman. **CP-WhitW**

Who is she, coming along the street, turning the heads. David St. John. **SP-StJoD**

Who is that blue / Dark, dreamer dreaming / Of me? To Harvey, Who Traced the Circulation. James Wright. **CP-WrigJ**

Who is that boy making his slow way among. Blue Like the Heavens. Gary Gildner. **SP-GildG**

Who is that man with the handshake? Don't you know. The Satirist. Louis MacNeice. **CP-MacNL**

Who is that well-dressed handsome man? The Man With Two New Suits. Ogden Nash. **CP-NashO**

Who is the East? Emily Dickinson. **CP-DickE**

Who is the happy warrior? Who is he. Character of the Happy Warrior. William Wordsworth. **CP-WorW1**

Who is the honest man? Constancy. George Herbert. **CP-HerbG**

Who is the man that stands against this bridge. For Danton. Charles Tomlinson. **CP-TomlC**

Who Is the Same, Which at My Window Peepes? Edmund Spenser. **NAs** *Fr.* Epithalamion: "Ye learned sisters, which have oftentimes." **CP-Spens**

Who is the shroudy stranger of the night. Please Open the Window and Let Me In. Allen Ginsberg. **CP-GinsA**

Who is the ugly one slump-slopping down the street? Psychological Profile. Robert Penn Warren. *Fr.* Homage to Theodore Dreiser. **SP-WarrR**

Who is there. Choros Translations. Euripides, *tr. fr. Greek by* Hilda Doolittle ("H.D."). **CP-DoolH** *Fr.* Bacchae.

Who is this / dai / nty mademoiselle. Edward Estlin Cummings. **CP-CummE**

Who is this that comes in splendour, coming from the blazing East? The Airy Christ. Stevie Smith. **CP-SmitS**

Who is this that cometh up not alone. Christina Georgina Rossetti. **CP-RosC2**

Who Is This Who Howls and Mutters? Stevie Smith. **CP-SmitS**

Who is unhappiest, the villain or. Munich. Edwin Rolfe. **CP-RolfE**

Who it is who sits. The Babe. Charles Olson. **CP-OlsoC**

Who keeps his ceaselessly attentive eye. After God. Daniel Gerard Hoffman. **SP-HoffD**

Who keeps the owl's breath? Whose eyes desire? Elegy. David St. John. **SP-StJoD**

Who Kill'd John Keats? Byron. **CP-Byron**

Who killed Cock Robin? Coroner's Inquest. William DeWitt Snodgrass. **SP-SnodW**

Who Killed Davey Moore? "Bob Dylan." **CP-DylaB**

Who Killed Lawless Lean? Stevie Smith. **CP-SmitS**

Who knocks? I, who was beautiful. The Ghost. Walter de la Mare. **CP-DeLaW**

Who Knows? Nicholas Vachel Lindsay. **CP-LindV**

Who knows? God knows: and what He knows / Is well and best. Take No Thought for The Morrow. Christina Georgina Rossetti. **CP-RosC2**

Who knows how deep the Heart is. Emily Dickinson. **SP-DickE**

Who knows how long I've loved you. I Will. The Beatles. **CP-Beatl**

Who knows how the Wag-tail woos? The Wagtail. Theodore Roethke. **CP-RoetT**

Who knows if the moon's. Edward Estlin Cummings. **CP-CummE; SP-CummE**

Who knows the heart of the Christian? How does he reason? Hadramauti. Rudyard Kipling. **CP-KiplR** Fr. Plain Tales from the Hills.

Who knows the people, the migratory harvest hands and berry pickers. Carl Sandburg. Fr. The People, Yes. **CP-SandC**

Who knows this or that? Ralph Waldo Emerson. **CP-EmerR**

Who knows what I know. Night's Nothings Again. Carl Sandburg. **CP-SandC**

Who knows where our hearts go. Emily Dickinson. **SP-DickE**

Who knows where you go. The Odds. Al Young. **CP-YounA**

Who knows yon star that blinks at us. Nebula. John Hewitt. **CP-HewiJ**

Who leads a happy life. The Tinker. William Wordsworth. **CP-WorW1**

Who Learns My Lesson Complete. Walt Whitman. **CP-WhitW**

Who lies with his milk-white maiden. Song of Praise. Countee Cullen. **CP-CullC**

Who list his wealth and ease retain. Sir Thomas Wyatt. **CP-WyatT**

Who list the Romane greatnes forth to figure. Joachim Du Bellay. **OBVE** Fr. Ruins of Rome. **CP-Spens**

Who listens, when in the concert-hall. Kathleen Jessie Raine. **SP-RainK**

Who live under the shadow of a war. Shadow of War. Stephen Spender. **CP-SpenS**

Who lived at the top end of our street. The Retired Colonel. Ted Hughes. **SP-HughT**

Who lives in love, loves lest to live. Life's Death, Love's Life. Robert Southwell. **CP-SoutR**

Who lives in the biggest, whitest house in town? Beautiful Funerals. James Schuyler. **CP-SchuJ**

Who lives o on Helicon hill. Catullus. See Carmen 61: "Hill (breeder) of Helicon."

Who lives where beggars rarely speed. My Mary. John Clare. **CP-MacNL**

Who long for rest, who look for pleasure. Penmaen Pool. Gerard Manley Hopkins. **CP-HopkG**

Who, looking backward from his manhood's prime. The Reward. John Greenleaf Whittier. **CP-WhitJ**

Who loved more? William Carlos Williams. William Carlos Williams. Robert Lowell. **SP-LoweR**

Who loves beauty / veil her statues. Carmen 3. Catullus. Fr. Carmina. **CP-Catul**

Who loves his friend with his heart of hearts. Sadi, tr. fr. Persian by Ralph Waldo Emerson. **CP-EmerR**

Who loves me here and has my love. Daphne. Gerard Manley Hopkins. **CP-HopkG**

Who loves not Knowledge? Who shall rail. Tennyson. Fr. In Memoriam A. H. H. **CP-TennA**

Who loves to peer up at the morning sun. On "The Story of Rimini." John Keats. **CP-KeatJ**

Who loves you most. Emily Dickinson. **SP-DickE**

Who made Paul Bunyan, who gave him birth as a myth, who joked him. Carl Sandburg. Fr. The People, Yes. **CP-SandC**

Who made the world? The Summer Day. Mary Oliver. **SP-OlivM**

Who made this suicide pact of love? Malcolm Lowry. **CP-LowrM**

Who made you come and find the door to there? William Dickey. **SP-DickW** Fr. Part Song, With Concert of Recorders. **SP-DickW**

Who makes the past, a pattern for next year. To Sir Henry Goodyer. John Donne. **CP-DonnJ**

Who Maketh the Grass to Grow, greatly abr. Bible, O.T. See Psalm 147: "Praise ye the Lord: for it is good. . . ."

Who may do most, do's least: The bravest will. The More Mighty, the More Merciful. Robert Herrick. **CP-HerrR**

Who may tell the tale. Tailpiece. Samuel Beckett. **CP-BeckS**

Who may withstand them. Death. Lewis Turco. **SP-TurcL**

Who "meddled" with the costly Hearts. Emily Dickinson. **SP-DickE**

Who murmurs, hither, hither: who. With the Persuader. George Meredith. **CP-MerG1**

Who needs their names? Another genus built. Wystan Hugh Auden. Fr. Sonnets from China. **CP-AudeW**

Who never lost, are unprepared. Emily Dickinson. **CP-DickE**

Who never wanted—maddest Joy. Emily Dickinson. **CP-DickE**

Who now calls on thee, Nevil, is a muse. To Sir Henry Nevil. Ben Jonson. **CP-JonsB**

Who now does follow the foule Blatant Beast. Edmund Spenser. **OAEL-1** Fr. The Faerie Queene. **CP-Spens**

Who, now, put dreams into thy slumbering mind? The Death-Dream. Walter de la Mare. **CP-DeLaW**

Who now read Thomson or Collins? Surrey. Donald Davie. **CP-DavDo**

Who now reads Cowley? if he pleases yet. Alexander Pope. **EPCY** Fr. The First Epistle of the Second Book of Horace Imitated. **CP-PopeA**

Who now remembers Almack's balls. Reminiscences of a Dancing Man. Thomas Hardy. **CP-HardT**

Who, now, seeing Her so. Et in Arcadia Ego. Wystan Hugh Auden. **CP-AudeW**

Who, now, when evening darkens the water and the stream is dull. To a Musician. Edna St. Vincent Millay. **CP-MillE**

Who now will praise the Wizard in the street. The Wizard in the Street. Nicholas Vachel Lindsay. **CP-LindV**

Who occupies this House? Emily Dickinson. **CP-DickE**

Who of us is not mad. Reading Nijinsky's Diary. Al Young. **CP-YounA**

Who often found their way to pleasant meadows. Elegy for Minor Poets. Louis MacNeice. **CP-MacNL**

Who on your breast pillows his head now. A Lost Jewel. Robert Ranke Graves. **CP-GravR**

Who owns these scrawny little feet? Death. Examination at the Womb-Door. Ted Hughes. **SP-HughT**

Who plants an Olive, but to eate the Oile? Recompence. Robert Herrick. **CP-HerrR**

Who plots, then, the lines. Le Fou. Robert Creeley. **CP-CreeR**

Who ponders National events shall find. In Allusion to Various Recent Histories and Notices of the French Revolution, Continued. William Wordsworth. **CP-WorW2**

Who prop, thou ask'st, in these bad days, my mind? To a Friend. Matthew Arnold. **SP-ArnoM**

Who put up that cage? Money, Politics, Love, and Glory. Carl Sandburg. **CP-SandC**

Who puts off shift. My Naked Aunt. Archibald MacLeish. **CP-MacLA**

Who, railing, drives the Lazar from his door. Biting of Beggars. Robert Herrick. **CP-HerrR**

Who rashly strove thy Image to portray? Upon seeing a Coloured Drawing of the Bird of Paradise in an Album. William Wordsworth. **CP-WorW2**

Who read a chapter when they rise. Charms and Knots. George Herbert. **CP-HerbG**

Who read'st this Book, that I have writ. To Momus. Robert Herrick. **CP-HerrR**

Who recalls the twilight and the rangèd tents in order. Dirge of Dead Sisters. Rudyard Kipling. **CP-KiplR**

Who Reigns? Percy Bysshe Shelley. **SeCePo** Fr. Prometheus Unbound. **CP-ShelP**

Who released to Salmasius his "hundred." Verse from Pro Populo Anglicano Defensio. John Milton, tr. fr. Latin by John T. Shawcross. **CP-MiltJ**

Who remembers him also, he thinks. For a Friend. Robert Creeley. **CP-CreeR**

Who remembers the Great Flood? The scope. Cheville. "Hugh MacDiarmid." **SP-MacDH**

Who represents my body in Pentagon? Who spends. Pentagon Exorcism. Allen Ginsberg. **CP-GinsA**

Who rises on the banks of Seine. Ode. William Wordsworth. **CP-WorW2**

Who royally bedded. Hafiz, tr. by Ralph Waldo Emerson. **CP-EmerR** Fr. Odes.

Who rules the duller earth, the wind-swolne streames. 3.4. Horace. **CP-RaleW**, tr. by Sir Walter Ralegh; Fr. Odes.

Who Runs America? Allen Ginsberg. **CP-GinsA**

Who Said It Was Simple. Audre Lorde. **SP-LordA**

Who said you were bred. Eve's Rebuke to Her Child. Archibald MacLeish. Fr. Songs for Eve. **CP-MacLA**

Who saith our times nor have, nor can. Ode Allegoric. Ben Jonson. **CP-JonsB**

Who saw no Sunrise cannot say. Emily Dickinson. **CP-DickE**

Who saw the hid beginnings. Ralph Waldo Emerson. **CP-EmerR**

Who says I shall not straighten till I bend. Under Cygnus. Richard Wilbur. **CP-WilbR**

Who says my hea't ain't true to you? Protest. Paul Laurence Dunbar. **CP-DunbP**

Who says, she is in danger. Song. George Meredith. **CP-MerG2**

Who say[e]s that fictions onl[e]y and false hair. George Herbert. **CP-HerbG**

(Jordan (1).) **CP-HerbG**

Who says that Giles and Joan at discord be? On Giles and Joan. Ben Jonson. **CP-JonsB**

Who says the world is mud? For the fifth day. Mona Van Duyn. *Fr.* Two Poems for Sub-Zero Times. **SP-VanDM**

Who scans time heals forgets to add. Traitor. Phoebe Hesketh. **SP-HeskP**

Who scans the bright machinery of the skies. Carmen 66. Catullus. *Fr.* Carmina. **CP-Catul**

Who scatters tares shall reap no wheat. Rogationtide. Christina Georgina Rossetti. **CP-RosC2**

Who shall bridle the winds, in their seven directions. Winter Afternoon. Thomas Merton. **CP-MertT**

Who shall decide, when Doctors disagree. Epistle III, to Allen Lord Bathurst. Alexander Pope. **CP-PopeA**

Who Shall Deliver Me? Christina Georgina Rossetti. **CP-RosC1**

Who Shall Doubt. George Oppen. **CP-OppeG**

Who shall doubt, Donne, where [or whe'er] I a poet be[e]. To John Donne. Ben Jonson. **CP-JonsB**

Who shall my wandering thoughts steady & fix. Christina Georgina Rossetti. **CP-RosC3**

Who shall speak for the people? Carl Sandburg. **OxBA** *Fr.* The People, Yes. **CP-SandC**

Who shall speak for the people? Carl Sandburg. *Fr.* The People, Yes. **CP-SandC**

Who shall tell the lady's grief. On the Death of a Cat. Christina Georgina Rossetti. **CP-RosC3**

Who shall tell what did befall. Wealth. Ralph Waldo Emerson. **CP-EmerR**

Who shall we send to fetch him away. The Choosers. Stevie Smith. **CP-SmitS**

Who sharpens every dull. Edward Estlin Cummings. **CP-CummE**

Who shook thy roundness in his finger's cup? Michael Angelo. David Herbert Lawrence. **CP-LawrD**

Who Shot Eugenie? Stevie Smith. **CP-SmitS**

Who showed me. To Flossie. William Carlos Williams. **CP-WilW2**

Who sits with the King in His Throne? Not a slave but a Bride. Christina Georgina Rossetti. **CP-RosC2**

Who slays the Spanish sun. Charles Olson. **CP-OlsoC**

Who so wil seeke by right deserts t'attaine. Edmund Spenser. *Fr.* Commendatory Sonnets. **CP-Spens**

Who Spilled the Salt? Isabella Gardner. **CP-GardI**

Who standeth at the gate?—A woman old. Behold, I stand at the door and knock. Christina Georgina Rossetti. **CP-RosC3**

Who stands at my door in the storm and rain. Kathleen Jessie Raine. *Fr.* Three Poems of Incarnation. **SP-RainK**

Who stands on that cliff, like a figure of stone. Mogg Megone. John Greenleaf Whittier. **CP-WhitJ**

Who stands, the crux left of the watershed. Wystan Hugh Auden. **CP-AudWJ; CP-AudeW**

(Watertowers, The.) **CP-AudeW**

Who swerves from innocence, who mkes divorce. William Wordsworth. *Fr.* The River Duddon [A Series of Sonnets]. **CP-WorW2**

Who takes thy volume to his virtuous hand. To His Much and Worthily Esteemed Friend the Author. Ben Jonson. **CP-JonsB**

Who talks of Plato's spindle. *fr.* Words for Music Perhaps. William Butler Yeats. **CP-YeatW**

Who Taught Caddies to Count? or A Burnt Golfer Fears the Child. Ogden Nash. **CP-NashO**

Who teaches child that snivelling guilt. Eve to the Storm of Thunder. Archibald MacLeish. *Fr.* Songs for Eve. **CP-MacLA**

Who telleth a tale of unspeaking death? Percy Bysshe Shelley. **OBD** *Fr.* On Death. **CP-ShelP**

Who that can feel the gentleness of Death. The Gentleness of Death. George Meredith. **CP-MerG2**

Who, then, was Cestius. Rome: At the Pyramid of Cestius near the Graves of Shelley and Keats. Thomas Hardy. **CP-HardT**

Who thought in high midsummer. Boethius, *tr. fr. Latin.* **MLL**, *tr. by* Helen Waddell; *Fr.* Consolation of Philosophy, The ("De Consolacione Philosophie"). **CP-ChauG**

Who to the North, or South, doth set. Observation. Robert Herrick. **CP-HerrR**

Who told my mother of my shame. Sister Maude. Christina Georgina Rossetti. **CP-RosC1**

Who tracks this author's, or translator's pen. On the Author, Work, and Translator. Ben Jonson. **CP-JonsB**

Who travels [or travels] by the wearie wandring way. Edmund Spenser. **OBD; OXAEP-1** *Fr.* The Faerie Queene. **CP-Spens**

Who travels by the weary wandering way. Despair. Edmund Spenser. **SeCePo** *Fr.* The Faerie Queene. **CP-Spens**

Who Understands Who Anyhow? Ogden Nash. **CP-NashO**

Who used to lie with his love. Pastoral—1954. Edwin Rolfe. **CP-RolfE**

Who violates the Customes, hurts the Health. Lawes. Robert Herrick. **CP-HerrR**

Who, Virtue, can thy power forget. Ben Jonson. **CP-JonsB** *Fr.* The Masque of Queens.

Who Wakes. May Sarton. **SP-SartM**

Who walks on white feet turned. For a Lady of Whom I Speak. Charles Olson. **CP-OlsoC**

Who Walks There? Kenneth Patchen. **CP-PatcK**

Who wants a pancake. Pancake? Shel Silverstein. **SP-SilS2**

Who wants action. A Promise. Charles Olson. **CP-OlsoC**

Who wants my jellyfish? The Jellyfish. Ogden Nash. **CP-NashO**

Who was born January first. A Birthday Book. Gertrude Stein. **CP-SteiG**

Who was born too soon? I will tell you who was born too soon. All, All Are Gone, the Old Familiar Quotations. Ogden Nash. **CP-NashO**

Who Was C.B. Fry? John Hewitt. **CP-HewiJ**

Who was it came. Daniel Gerard Hoffman. **SP-HoffD**

Who was that antique Chinese crook who put over his revolution and. Carl Sandburg. *Fr.* The People, Yes. **CP-SandC**

Who was that early sodbuster in Kansas? He leaned at the gatepost and. Carl Sandburg. *Fr.* The People, Yes. **CP-SandC**

Who was the great devil who, we are told, was judged worthy beyond others in the veneration of all? The Idol of Sarapis. Clement of Alexandria, *tr. by* Thomas Merton. **CP-MertT** *Fr.* Diatribe Against the Old Gods.

Who was the last English king. School. William Matthews. **SP-MattW**

Who weeps for strangers? Many wept. Elegiac Stanzas Composed in the Churchyard of Grasmere. William Wordsworth. **CP-WorW1**

Who were so dark of heart they might not speak. Edward Estlin Cummings. **CP-CummE**

Who were "the Father and the Son." Emily Dickinson. **CP-DickE**

Who were the twain that trod this track. A Jog-Trot Pair. Thomas Hardy. **CP-HardT**

Who were those editors picking the most. Carl Sandburg. *Fr.* The People, Yes. **CP-SandC**

Who whispered, souls have shapes? My Sisters. Stanley Jasspon Kunitz. **CP-KuniS**

Who Whistled for the Wind, That It Should Break. Philip Larkin. **CP-LarkP**

Who, who will be the next man to entrust his girl to a friend? Ezra Pound. **FaBoMo** *Fr.* Homage to Sextus Propertius. **SP-PounE**

Who will be masters of our land tomorrow? The Nine. Edwin Rolfe. **CP-RolfE**

Who will believe my verse in time to come. Sonnet 17. William Shakespeare. **OBSC** *Fr.* Sonnets. **CP-ShaWS**

Who will cure the nation's ill? Wystan Hugh Auden. *Fr.* Shorts [1939–1947] ("Motionless, deep in his mind, lies the past the poet's forgotten"). **CP-AudeW**

Who Will Endure. Wystan Hugh Auden.

(No Change of Place.) **CP-AudeW**

Who will go drive with Fergus now. Who Goes with Fergus? William Butler Yeats. **CP-YeatW**

Who will in fairest book of Nature know. Sonnet 71. Sir Philip Sidney. **CABA; InPS; NAEL-1; NoP; NoSic; OAEL-1; PoE; Poetr** *Fr.* Astrophil and Stella. **SP-SidnP**

Who will laugh / in coldest glee. Frederick Morgan. *Fr.* Death Mother. **SP-MorgF**

Who will, may hear Sordello's story told. Sordello. Robert Browning. **CP-BroR1**

Who will ne tried to-day? Act IV. Henry Wadsworth Longfellow. *Fr.* Giles Corey of the Salem Farms. **SP-LongH**

Who will not honour Noble Numbers, when. Verses. Robert Herrick. **CP-HerrR**

Who will remember / that past it past. Pentagram. Gilbert Sorrentino. **SP-SorrG**

Who will take away. Spell Against Sorrow. Kathleen Jessie Raine. **SP-RainK**

Who Will Take Over the Universe? Allen Ginsberg. **CP-GinsA**

Who will wed the Dowager's youngest daughter. Romance of a Youngest Daughter. John Crowe Ransom. **SP-RansJ**

Who with a little cannot be content. *see also* Poverty and Riches. Robert Herrick. **CP-HerrR**

Who with thy leaves shall wipe (at need). Robert Herrick. **CP-HerrR**

Who would have ever thought. Sir Thomas Wyatt. **CP-WyatT**

Who would have thought. An Old Likeness. Thomas Hardy. **CP-HardT**

Who would here sojourn for an outstreched spell. Thoughts from Sophocles. Thomas Hardy. **CP-HardT**

Who would love you. The Happy Man. Robert Creeley. **CP-CreeR**

Who would not be thy subject, James, t'obey. To King James. Ben Jonson. **CP-JonsB**

Who would not laugh, if Lawrence, hired to grace. Hints from Horace. Byron. **CP-Byron**

Who would think, herein to look. Robert Louis Stevenson. **CP-StevR**

Who would wish back the Saints upon our rough. Christina Georgina Rossetti. **CP-RosC2**

Whoa ah Whoa ah / I got a whole lot of things to tell her when I get home. When I Get Home. The Beatles. **CP-Beatl**

Whoa, hillbilly, you've got me where you want me. Chanson Pour Billie. Charles Henri Ford. **SP-FordC**

Who'd be likely to forget. Shaking the President's Hand. Daniel Gerard Hoffman. **SP-HoffD**

Who'd go out there. There. Daniel Gerard Hoffman. **SP-HoffD**

Whoe doesn't love / roses, and who. Hummingbird Pauses at the Trumpet Vine. Mary Oliver. **SP-OlivM**

Whoe'er he be that sojourns here. Epigram. Robert Burns. **CP-BurnR**

Who'er thou art, O reader, know. On Wee Johnie. Robert Burns. **CP-BurnR**

Whoe're thou art whom this fair statue charms. On the Statue of *Cleopatra*, Made into a Fountain by *Leo* the Tenth. Baldassare, Count of Novilara Castiglione, *tr. fr. Latin by* Alexander Pope. **CP-PopeA**

Whoever [*or* Who ever] comes to shroud me, do not harm[e]. The Funeral[l]. John Donne. **CP-DonnJ**

Whoever despises the clitoris despises the penis. The Speed of Darkness. Muriel Rukeyser. **CP-RukeM**

Whoever dies—dies for the love. Marsden Hartley. **CP-HartM**

Whoever disenchants. Emily Dickinson. **CP-DickE**

Whoever [*or* Who ever] guesses, thinks, or dream[e]s he know[e]s. The Curse. John Donne. **CP-DonnJ**

Whoever has drowned and awhile entered. True Joy. Robert Ranke Graves. **CP-GravR**

Whoever hath her wish, thou hast thy Will. Sonnet 135. William Shakespeare. **NAEL-1; OAEL-1** *Fr.* Sonnets. **CP-ShaWS**

Whoever he be, would write a story at. To the London Reader, on the Odcombian Writer, Polytopian Thomas the Traveller. Ben Jonson. **CP-JonsB**

Whoever is able will pursue the plainly. The Giant's Ring. Robinson Jeffers. **CP-JefR2**

Whoever lives beside a mountain knows. Burden. Richard Eberhart. **CP-EberR**

Whoever lives true life, will love true love. The Sweetness of England. Elizabeth Barrett Browning. **OXAEP-2** *Fr.* Aurora Leigh. **CP-BroEB**

Whoever loves, if he do not propose. Love's Progress. John Donne. **LiTB; OAEL-1** *Fr.* Elegies. **CP-DonnJ**

Whoever made this piece began. Trompe L'oeil. Stanley Jasspon Kunitz. *Fr.* Words for the Unknown Makers: A Garland of Commemorative Verses. **CP-KuniS**

Whoever pleaseth to inquire. On the Little House by the Churchyard of Castleknock. Jonathan Swift. **CP-SwifJ**

Whoever spoke first would lose something. After the Argument. Stephen Dunn. **SP-DunnS**

Whoever swings an ax. Ax. Charles Simic. **SP-SimiC**

Whoever vies with Pindar's strain. Horace. *See* 4.2: Praise of Pindar, The ("Pindarum quisquis studet aemulari").

Whoever wants to make it. Paradise of Squares. Nicanor Parra, *tr. fr. Spanish by* Thomas Merton. **CP-MertT**

Whoever was the cause your tears were shed. Upon L.M. Weeping. Sir John Suckling. **CP-SuckJ**

Whoever with the compasses of his eyes. Waitress. Karl Shapiro. **SP-ShapK**

Whoever You Are Holding Me Now in Hand. Walt Whitman. **CP-WhitW**

Whoever you are, I fear you are walking the walks of dreams. To You. Walt Whitman. **CP-WhitW**

Whoever you are, this poem is clearly about you. Clearly about You. Robert Penn Warren. **SP-WarrR**

Who(is?are)who. Edward Estlin Cummings. **CP-CummE**

Whole / Weight of / Everything, The. For Creely's Ear. Allen Ginsberg. **CP-GinsA**

Whole blear world, The. Sunset. Allen Ginsberg. **CP-GinsA**

Whole countryside deployed on the hills of heather, an army with, The. Shooting Season. Robinson Jeffers. **CP-JefR2**

Whole Creation Groans to Be Delivered, the. Marsden Hartley. *Fr.* Un Recuerdo—Hermano—Hart Crane R.I.P. **CP-HartM**

Whole day long, under the walking sun, The. The Sleeping Giant. Donald Hall. **CP-HallD**

Whole day thro', in contempt and pity, The. Robert Louis Stevenson. **CP-StevR**

Whole Duty of Children. Robert Louis Stevenson. **CP-StevR**

Whole family weeping. Charles Henri Ford. **SP-FordC** *Fr.* Emblems of Arachne.

Whole Gulfs—of Red—and Fleets—of Red. Emily Dickinson. **CP-DickE**

Whole Head Is Sick, and the Whole Heart Faint, The. Christina Georgina Rossetti. **CP-RosC3**

Whole hillside is scribbled on, but men, The. The Old Mine. Wystan Hugh Auden. **CP-AudWJ**

Whole Love. Robert Ranke Graves. **CP-GravR**

Whole lower panel of the chain-link fence girdling my old grammar school playground, The. Soon. Charles Kenneth Williams. **CP-WillC**

Whole man has no corners. He curves and curves, The. Corners. Laurence Lieberman. **SP-LiebL**

Whole new town of them, *dislocados* from the war. Dislocado. Chuck Miller. **SP-MillC**

Whole night in form the whorl on earth. Pamphylian. Louis Zukofsky. **CP-ZukLS**

Whole of appearance is a toy, The. For this. The Dove in the Belly. Wallace Stevens. **CP-StevW**

Whole of creation shall come to his funeral, The. Absolutely Vernal. Charles Olson. **CP-OlsoC**

Whole of it came not at once, The. Emily Dickinson. **CP-DickE**

Whole Point, The. Erica Jong. **SP-JongE**

Whole process is a lie, The. The Ivy Crown. William Carlos Williams. **CP-WilW2**

Whole rich process of twined opposites, The. To a Dead Graduate Student. Thom Gunn. **CP-GunnT**

Whole section of the city I live in has been urban renewed, some of it torn down, A. Bread. Charles Kenneth Williams. **CP-WillC; SP-WillC**

Whole towns shut down. The Late Snow & Lumber Strike of the Summer of Fifty-four. Gary Snyder. **CP-SnydG**

Whole white world is ours, The. White World. Hilda Doolittle. **CP-DoolH**

Whole World, The. Charles Olson. **CP-OlsoC**

Whole World Coal, The. Gilbert Sorrentino. **SP-SorrG**

Whole world here, leavened with madness, swells, The. Ben Jonson. **JCP** *Fr.* An Epistle to a Friend, to Persuade Him to the Wars. **CP-JonsB**

Whole world is flat, The. Another Language. Erica Jong. **SP-JongE**

Whole world on a raft! A King is here, The. The Raft. Nicholas Vachel Lindsay. *Fr.* Three Poems About Mark Twain. **CP-LindV**

Whole world seated / at table, The. Sitting Down. Pablo Neruda, *tr. fr. Spanish by* Ben Belitt. **SP-NeruP**

Whole World's in a Terrible Chassis, The. Isabella Gardner. **CP-GardI**

Wholeness. Chuang Tzu, *tr. fr. Chinese by* Thomas Merton. **CP-MertT**

Who'll that be. Kenneth Patchen. **CP-PatcK**

Wholly absorbed / into my own conduits to. Charles Olson. **SP-OlsoC** *Fr.* The Maximus Poems.

Wholly from idiosyncratic reasons, my feet. Narcissus Unbound. William Dickey. **SP-DickW**

Whom are you carrying. João Cabral de Melo Neto. **CP-BishE** *Fr.* The Death and Life of a Severino.

Whom bomb? Hūm Bom! Allen Ginsberg. **CP-GinsA**

Whom can I ask / what I meant to achieve in this world? Pablo Neruda, *tr. fr. Spanish by* Ben Belitt. **SP-NeruP** *Fr.* Question Book.

Whom can we love in all these little wars? Meteors. Jane Cooper. **SP-CoopJ**

Whom do I give my neat little volume. Catullus. *See* Carmen 1: "To whom should I present this."

Whom do you love, she said, when you look out. Archibald MacLeish. **CP-MacLA** *Fr.* The Happy Marriage.

Whom I ask for no gift. Michael Hartnett. **SP-HarMi**

Whom I have trusted to no end (Rufus). Carmen 77. Catullus. *Fr.* Carmina. **CP-Catul**

Whom I saw in a Dream Push Baby N. To the Dog Belvoir. Stevie Smith. **CP-SmitS**

Whom impious Rome had just marked out for her curses. On the Same ["Whom impious Rome had just marked out for her curses"]. John Milton, *tr. fr. Latin by* John T. Shawcross. **CP-MiltJ**

Whom seek you here, sweet Mistress Fell? Mistress Fell. Walter de la Mare. **CP-DeLaW**

Whom sho'd I feare to write to, if I can. To Jos: Lo: Bishop of Exeter. Robert Herrick. **CP-HerrR**

Whom the gods love, die young. Old Men. David Herbert Lawrence. **CP-LawrD**

Whom the Lord Loveth He Chasteneth. Christina Georgina Rossetti. **CP-RosC2**

Whom the untaught Shepherds call. Songs of the Pixies. Samuel Taylor Coleridge. **CP-ColeS**

Whom thus answer'd th' Arch Fiend now undisguis'd. Satan's Guile. John Milton. **LiTB; OBS** *Fr.* Book I. *Fr.* Paradise Regained [*or* Regain'd]. **CP-MiltJ**

Whom undone David upto the dire van sent. John Berryman. *Fr.* Sonnets to Chris. **CP-BerrJ**

Whore has her knowledge, The. Choose One From Among Them. Richard Shelton. **SP-ShelR**

Whoroscope. Samuel Beckett. **CP-BeckS**

Who's gonna throw that minstrel boy a coin? Minstrel Boy. "Bob Dylan." **CP-DylaB**

Who's in the Next Room? Thomas Hardy. **CP-HardT**

Who's most afraid of death?thou. Edward Estlin Cummings. **CP-CummE**

Who's she, / that one in your arms. The Interrogation of the Man of Many Hearts. Anne Sexton. **CP-SextA**

Who's that? Walter de la Mare. **CP-DeLaW**

Who's that guy on the glass? Conversation with the Kid. Patti Smith. **SP-SmitP**

Who's to tell the night heron. Summer Solstice. Daniel Gerard Hoffman. **SP-HoffD**

Who's Who. Wystan Hugh Auden. **CP-AudeW**

Whose are the little beds, I asked. Emily Dickinson. **CP-DickE**

Whose are these(wraith a clinging with a wraith). Edward Estlin Cummings. **CP-CummE**

Whose braggart 'scutcheon, whose complaisant crest. Gerard Manley Hopkins. *Fr.* Fragments. **CP-HopkG**

Whose cheek is this? Emily Dickinson. **CP-DickE**

Whose child is this they bring. The Christening. Thomas Hardy. **CP-HardT**

Whose counted smile of hours and days, suppose. Hart Crane. *Fr.* Voyages. **CP-CranH**

Whose freedom is by suff'rance, and at will. William Cowper. **EnRP** *Fr.* The Winter Morning Walk. *Fr.* The Task. **CP-CowpW**

Whose head befringed with bescattered tresses. The Descripcion; of a Woman. Robert Herrick. **CP-HerrR**

"Whose heart" "might be lost?" "Whose mask is this?" "Who has a mask." White Phosphorus. Alice Notley. **SP-NotlA**

Whose hoax to put up with, outstare, protest patience. Catullus. *See* Carmen 29: "What man could stomach the sight."

Whose is my pain, if I reject it. Pain Is an Eagle Clinging to Your Name. Pablo Antonio Cuadra, *tr. fr. Spanish by* Thomas Merton. **CP-MertT**

Whose is that noble dauntless brow? Verses Intended to Be Written below a Noble Earl's Picture. Robert Burns. **CP-BurnR**

Whose is the body you. The Garden. Roy Fisher. **SP-FishR** *Fr.* Inscriptions for Bluebeard's Castle.

Whose is the love that gleaming through the world. Queen Mab. Percy Bysshe Shelley. **CP-ShelP**

Whose little lady is you, chile. Possession. Paul Laurence Dunbar. **CP-DunbP**

Whose minds like horse or ox. The Learned Men. Archibald MacLeish. **CP-MacLA**

Whose Pink career may have a close. Emily Dickinson. **CP-DickE**

Whose senses in so ill consort their step-dame Nature lays. Seventh Song. Sir Philip Sidney. *Fr.* Astrophil and Stella. **SP-SidnP**

Whose west walls take the sunset like a blow. The House. James Merrill. **SP-MerrJ**

Whose wood this is I think I know. Now He Knows All There Is to Know: Now He Is Acquainted With the Day and Night. Delmore Schwartz. **SP-SchwD**

Whose woods these are I think I know. Stopping by Woods on a Snowy Evening. Robert Frost. **CP-FrosR**

Whose work could this be, Chapman, to refine. To My Worthy and Honoured Friend, Mr George Chapman, on His Translation of Hesiod's *Works and Days.* Ben Jonson. **CP-JonsB**

Whoso alas is young. Ralph Waldo Emerson. **CP-EmerR**

Whoso for hours or lengthy days. Eunice. Thomas Hardy. **CP-HardT**

Whoso hath anguish is not dead in sin. Subject To Like Passions as We Are. Christina Georgina Rossetti. **CP-RosC2**

Whoso hears a chiming for Christmas at the nighest. Christina Georgina Rossetti. *Fr.* Christmas Carols. **CP-RosC2**

Whoso list to haunt could do worse than to. The Domestic Life of Ghosts. Tom Clark. **SP-ClarT**

Whoso list to hunt, I know where is an hind. Sir Thomas Wyatt. **CP-WyatT**

Whoso walks in solitude. Ralph Waldo Emerson. **OBVV** *Fr.* Woodnotes II ("As sunbeams stream through liberal space"). **CP-EmerR**

Whut dat you whisperin' keepin' f'om me? The News. Paul Laurence Dunbar. **CP-DunbP**

"Whut do you spose thet thing is," Oi said. "Whut?" Sonnet. Hayden Carruth. **CP-CarHS**

Whut time 'd dat clock strike? At Night. Paul Laurence Dunbar. **CP-DunbP**

Whut you say, dah? huh, uh! chile. A Cabin Tale. Paul Laurence Dunbar. **CP-DunbP**

W.H.W., Jr. Edward Estlin Cummings. **CP-CummE**

Why—? David Herbert Lawrence. **CP-LawrD**

Why / do the / fingers. Edward Estlin Cummings. **CP-CummE**

Why / don't / be / sil / ly. Edward Estlin Cummings. **CP-CummE**

Why. Richard Eberhart. **CP-EberR**

Why. "Hugh MacDiarmid." **SP-MacDH**

Why? Christina Georgina Rossetti. **CP-RosC2**

Why a Hush Should Not Be Rushed. Al Young. **CP-YounA**

Why am I / the laggard, as if. Same. Robert Creeley. **CP-CreeR**

Why am I loth to leave this earthly scene? Stanzas on the Same Occasion [in the Prospect of Death]. Robert Burns. **CP-BurnR**

Why am I not myself these many days. An Evangelist's Wife. Edwin Arlington Robinson. **CP-RobiE**

Why am I sad? / It is autumn. And Fall. Phoebe Hesketh. **SP-HeskP**

Why am I so angry at Kissinger? Tübingen–Hamburg Schlafwagen. Allen Ginsberg. **CP-GinsA**

Why Are the Clergy. . . ? Stevie Smith. **CP-SmitS**

Why are the public buildings so high? How come you don't know? Wystan Hugh Auden. **FaBoCo** *Fr.* Shorts [1939–1947] ("Motionless, deep in his mind, lies the past the poet's forgotten"). **CP-AudeW**

Why are the stamps adorned with kings and presidents? Power to the People. Howard Nemerov. **CP-NemeH**

Why are these pipples taking their hets off? ? Edward Estlin Cummings. **CP-CummE**

Why are we frightened of the word for love? Language Teaching: Naming. Jenny Joseph. **SP-JoseJ**

Why Are We Here? Stephen Berg. **SP-BergS**

Why are we[e] by all creatures waited on? John Donne. **CABA; JCP; NOCV; OBS; PoE; PoEL-2; TrCP** *Fr.* Divine Meditations. **CP-DonnJ** *Fr.* Holy Sonnets. **CP-DonnJ**

Why are women so energetic? Energetic Women. David Herbert Lawrence. **CP-LawrD**

Why are you so bent down before your time. The Old Workman. Thomas Hardy. **CP-HardT**

Why are your eyes as big as saucers—big as saucers? Man in the Street. Robert Penn Warren. **SP-WarrR**

Why Art Thou Silent [Is Thy Love a Plant]. William Wordsworth. **CP-WorW2**

Why art thou silent and invisible. To Nobodaddy. William Blake. **CP-BlakW**

Why ask to know the date—the clime? Emily Brontë. **CP-BronE**

Why ask to know what date, what clime? Emily Brontë. **CP-BronE**

Why Be at Pains? Thomas Hardy. **CP-HardT**

"Why?" Because all I haply can and do. Why I Am a Liberal. Robert Browning. **CP-BroR2**

Why Birch Trees Are White. Barton Sutter. **SP-SuttB**

Why boastest thou thyself in mischief, O mighty man? Psalm 52. Bible, *O.T. Fr.* Psalms. **CP-Psal**

Why Brownlee Left. Paul Muldoon. **SP-MuldP**

Why, by an ingrained habit, deviate. With the Grain. Donald Davie. **CP-DavDo**

Why call the miser miserable? as. Byron. **UnPo** *Fr.* Canto the Twelfth. *Fr.* Don Juan. **CP-Byron**

Why can I never when I think about it. For My Mother in Her First Illness, from a Window Overlooking Notre Dame. Jane Cooper. **SP-CoopJ**

Why cannot the one good. The War God. Stephen Spender. **CP-SpenS**

Why can't, Chris, why shouldn't *they* fall in love? John Berryman. *Fr.* Sonnets to Chris. **CP-BerrJ**

Why cast ye back along the Gallic shore. On Being Stranded near the Harbour of Boulogne. William Wordsworth. *Fr.* Memorials of a Tour of the Continent; 1820. **CP-WorW2**

Why complain, brothers, to you, my writing. Sonnet. Hayden Carruth. **CP-CarHS** *Fr.* Sonnets.

Why covet what eye cannot see. Out Of Bounds. Walter de la Mare. **CP-DeLaW**

Why, credulous Naples, do you vaunt your clear-voiced Siren. To the Same ["Why, credulous Naples, do you vaunt your clear-voiced Siren"]. John Milton, *tr. fr. Latin by* John T. Shawcross. **CP-MiltJ**

Why deck with flow'rs these humble mounds? Memorial Day. Paul Laurence Dunbar. **CP-DunbP**

Why did all manly gifts in Webster fail? Ralph Waldo Emerson. **CP-EmerR**

(Webster.) **CP-EmerR**

Why did baby die, / Making Father sigh. Christina Georgina Rossetti. **CP-RosC2**

Why did he write to her. One Parting. Carl Sandburg. **CP-SandC**

Why Did I Dream of You Last Night? Philip Larkin. **CP-LarkP**

Why Did I Laugh Tonight? John Keats. **CP-KeatJ**

Why did I print upon myself the names. *tr. fr. the German of* Rilke. Randall Jarrell. **CP-JarrR**

Why Did I Sketch. Thomas Hardy. **CP-HardT**

Why did [*or* do] I write? what sin to me unknown. Alexander Pope. **ChTr; EBEV; EPCY; FiP; TOF** *Fr.* Epistle to Dr. Arbuthnot. **CP-PopeA**

Why did Massenet compose *Thaïs?.* Greetings from the Chateau. James Schuyler. **CP-SchuJ**

Why did the children. Carl Sandburg. **OBAL; PBMP** *Fr.* The People, Yes. **CP-SandC**

Why did the woman want to kill one dog? A Village Tale. May Sarton. **SP-SartM**

Why Did What Was When. John Yau. **SP-YauJo**

Why did you flutter in vain hope, poor bird. The Cage. Walter de la Mare. **CP-DeLaW**

Why did you give no hint that night. The Going. Thomas Hardy. **CP-HardT**

Why did you go. Edward Estlin Cummings. **CP-CummE**

Why did you kiss the girl who cried. What the Earth Asked Me. James Wright. **CP-WrigJ**

Why didn't you say you was promised, Rose-Ann. Rose-Ann. Thomas Hardy. **CP-HardT**

Why didst thou promise such a beauteous day. Sonnet 34. William Shakespeare. **HeIP; OBSC; OXAEP-1** *Fr.* Sonnets. **CP-ShaWS**

Why, disease, dost thou molest. To Sickness. Ben Jonson. **CP-JonsB**

Why Do I? Thomas Hardy. **CP-HardT**

Why Do I. Stevie Smith. **CP-SmitS**

Why do I deny manna to another? Sather Gate Illumination. Allen Ginsberg. **CP-GinsA**

Why do I go on doing these things? Why Do I? Thomas Hardy. **CP-HardT**

Why do I hate that lone green dell? Emily Brontë. **CP-BronE**

Why do I imagine the death of Mandelstam. Preparing for Exile. Derek Walcott. **CP-WalcD**

Why do I languish thus, drooping and dull. Dulness[e]. George Herbert. **CP-HerbG**

Why do I live among the green mountains? Poet's Laughter. Archibald MacLeish. **CP-MacLA**

"Why do I love" You, Sir? Emily Dickinson. **CP-DickE**

Why do I see these empty boats, sailing on airy seas? The Empty Boats. Nicholas Vachel Lindsay. **CP-LindV**

Why do I write today? Apology. William Carlos Williams. **CP-WilW1**

Why do so many fat people go to Disney World. The Magic Kingdom. Peter Meinke. **SP-MeinP**

Why do the Gentiles tumult, and the Nations, *par.* by Milton. Bible, *O.T. See* Psalm 2: "Why do the heathen rage."

Why do the heathen rage. Psalm 2. Bible, *O.T.* **NAAL-1; NAAL-3** *Fr.* Psalms. **CP-Psal**

Why do they make boys out of meat? Boy Made of Meat, The; A Poem for Children. William DeWitt Snodgrass. **SP-SnodW**

Why do they ring that bell. The Signal. Archibald MacLeish. **CP-MacLA**

Why—do they shut Me out of Heaven? Emily Dickinson. **CP-DickE**

Why do we labor at the poem. Reasons for Music. Archibald MacLeish. **CP-MacLA**

Why do we waste so much time in arguing? Sushi. Paul Muldoon. **SP-MuldP**

Why do[e] ye weep, sweet babes? To Primroses Filled with Morning Dew. Robert Herrick. **CP-HerrR**

"Why do you." Poem for Molly's Fortieth Birthday. Erica Jong. **SP-JongE**

Why do you dig like long-clawed scavengers. Verlaine. Edwin Arlington Robinson. **CP-RobiE**

Why do you fly from the drowned shores of Galilee. The Quickening of St. John the Baptist. Thomas Merton. **CP-MertT**

Why do you follow me? Daphne. Edna St. Vincent Millay. **CP-MillE**

Why do you go about looking for me, mother? Mourning. David Herbert Lawrence. *Fr.* Bits. **CP-LawrD**

Why do you harbour that great cheval-glass. The Cheval-Glass. Thomas Hardy. **CP-HardT**

Why do you listen, trees? The Farm. Archibald MacLeish. **CP-MacLA**

Why do you play such dreary music. Radio. Frank O'Hara. **SP-OharF**

Why Do You Rage? Stevie Smith. **CP-SmitS**

Why do you seek the sun. The Queen of Bubbles. Nicholas Vachel Lindsay. **CP-LindV**

Why do you sit, o pale thin man. Penance. Thomas Hardy. **CP-HardT**

Why do you spurt and sprottle. Rabbit Snared in the Night. David Herbert Lawrence. **CP-LawrD**

Why do you stand by the window. The Window. Leonard Cohen. **CP-CoheL**

Why do you stand in the dripping rye. The Woman in the Rye. Thomas Hardy. **CP-HardT**

Why do you stay there in the wood? The Hunter. Kenneth Patchen. **CP-PatcK**

Why do you talk so much. For Robert Frost. Galway Kinnell. **SP-KinnG**

Why do you weep there, O sweet lady. Memorial Brass, The: 186–. Thomas Hardy. **CP-HardT**

Why doe not all fresh maids appeare. Upon the Death of His Sparrow; an Elegie. Robert Herrick. **CP-HerrR**

Why doe you so much wish for raine, when I, *sels.* Mary Sidney, Countess of Montgomery Wroth. *Fr.* Part 1. *Fr.* Urania. **CP-WrotM**

Why doe you thus torment my poorest hart? Mary Sidney, Countess of Montgomery Wroth. *Fr.* Part 2. *Fr.* Urania. **CP-WrotM**

Why does she turn in that soft shy way. The Whitewashed Wall. Thomas Hardy. **CP-HardT**

Why Does She Weep? David Herbert Lawrence. **CP-LawrD**

Why does the raven cry aloud and no eye pities her? The Lamentation of Enion. William Blake. **OBNC** *Fr.* Vala; or The Four Zoas. **CP-BlakW**

Why does the sea burn? Why do the hills cry? Zaydee. Philip Levine. **SP-LeviP**

Why does the sea moan evermore? By the Sea. Christina Georgina Rossetti. **CP-RosC1**

Why does the thin grey strand. Sorrow. David Herbert Lawrence. **CP-LawrD**

Why don't people leave off being lovable. Elemental. David Herbert Lawrence. **CP-LawrD**

Why Don't We Do It in the Road. The Beatles. **CP-Beatl**

Why don't you like the wild cry of the madmen. Old Dichotomy: Choosing Sides. Richard Eberhart. **CP-EberR**

Why Don't You Try. Leonard Cohen. **CP-CoheL**

Why don't you write you never. Dear Reader. Peter Meinke. **SP-MeinP**

Why dost thou dally, Death, and tarry on the way? Come, Death (1). Stevie Smith. **CP-SmitS**

Why dost thou haste away, *speech of Basilius.* Sir Philip Sidney. **SP-SidnP** *Fr.* Arcadia.

Why dost thou persecute me, Saul of Tarsus? Act II. Henry Wadsworth Longfellow. *Fr.* John Endicott. **SP-LongH**

Why dost thou sound, my dear[e] Aurelian. In Answer of an Elegiacal[l] Letter, Upon the Death of the King of Sweden [from Aurelian Townsend, Inviting Me to Write on That Subject]. Thomas Carew. **CP-CareT**

Why dost thou tear me? Had I done thee hurt? Hayden Carruth. *Fr.* The Sleeping Beauty. **CP-CarHL**

Why do'st thou wound, & break my heart? His Covenant or Protestation to Julia. Robert Herrick. **CP-HerrR**

Why dost Thou wound my wounds, o Thou that passest by. Luke 10; And a Certaine Priest Comming that Way Looked on Him and Passed by. Bible, *N.T.* **CP-CrasR,** *tr. by* Richard Crashaw; *Fr.* St. Luke.

Why droopst thou, *Trefeild?* Will *Hurst* the Banker. Epigramme. Thomas Campion. *Fr.* Observations in the Art of English Poesie. **CP-CampT**

Why East Wind Chills. Dylan Thomas. **CP-ThomD**

Why Else but to Forestall This Hour. Adrienne Rich. **CP-RicAE**

Why extremely do we observe more of. Sonnet. Hayden Carruth. **CP-CarHS** *Fr.* Sonnets.

Why Fades a Dream? Paul Laurence Dunbar. **CP-DunbP**

Why fear to die. Ralph Waldo Emerson. **CP-EmerR**

Why Flowers Change Color. Robert Herrick. **CP-HerrR**

Why from this her and him. Edward Estlin Cummings. **CP-CummE**

Why gird at Lollius if he care. *after* Horace, Book 5, Ode 13. Rudyard Kipling. **CP-KiplR**

Why go the east road now? By Henstridge Cross at the Year's End. Thomas Hardy. **CP-HardT**

Why go to Saint-Juliot? What's Juliot to me? A Dream or No. Thomas Hardy. **CP-HardT**

Why God Permits Evil: For Answers to This Question of Interest to Many Write Bible Answers Dept. E-7. Miller Williams. **SP-WillM**

Why Golf is Art and Art is Golf. OCTOBER (*Golf*). Rudyard Kipling. *Fr.* Verses on Games. **CP-KiplR**

Why has Spring one syllable less. What's in a Name? Christina Georgina Rossetti. **CP-RosC2**

Why hath the rose faded and fallen, yet these eyes have not seen. Awake! Walter de la Mare. **CP-DeLaW**

Why have such scores of lovely, gifted girls. A Slice of Wedding Cake. Robert Ranke Graves. **CP-GravR**

Why Have You Sought? Hilda Doolittle. **CP-DoolH**

Why he lives there he can't say. Barton Sutter. *Fr.* What the Country Man Knows By Heart. **SP-SuttB**

Why he lives there he can't say. What the Country Man Knows By Heart. Barton Sutter. **SP-SuttB**

Why hold that poets are so sensitive? To the Public. Louis MacNeice. **CP-MacNL**

Why honor the new men. Ralph Waldo Emerson. **CP-EmerR**

Why, how now dapper black. The Beau's Reply to the Five Ladies' Answer. Jonathan Swift. **CP-SwifJ**

Why, how now, saucy Tom. Bowles and Campbell. Byron. **CP-Byron**

Why I Am a Liberal. Robert Browning. **CP-BroR2**

Why I Am Not a Painter. Frank O'Hara. **SP-OharF**

Why I Didn't Notice It. William Matthews. **SP-MattW**

Why I Never Went into Politics. Richard Shelton. **SP-ShelR**

Why, I saw you with the sexton, outside the church-door. She Saw Him, She Said. Thomas Hardy. **CP-HardT**

Why I Think of Dumar Sadly. Richard Hugo. **CP-HugoR**

Why I tie [*or* tye] about thy wrist. The Bracelet; to Julia. Robert Herrick. **CP-HerrR**

Why I Turned Vegetarian. Rita Dove. **SP-DoveR**

Why I Voted the Socialist Ticket. Nicholas Vachel Lindsay. **CP-LindV**

Why I Write Not of Love. Ben Jonson. **CP-JonsB**

Why if it be so, for the dismal morn. Gerard Manley Hopkins. **CP-HopkG**

Why in my heart, O Grief. The Disguise. Walter de la Mare. **CP-DeLaW**

Why Is God Love, Jack? Allen Ginsberg. **CP-GinsA**

Why is it modern poets are ignored. Martial, *tr.* by William Matthews. **SP-MattW** *Fr.* Epigrams.

Why is it Nobleness makes us ashamed. Emily Dickinson. **SP-DickE**

Why is it said thou canst not live. Love. Percy Bysshe Shelley. **CP-ShelP**

Why is it that whenever I talk with the duchess. Complaint. Richard Wilbur. **CP-WilbR**

"Why is my District death-rate low?" Rudyard Kipling. *See* Municipal.

Why is my verse so barren of new pride. Sonnet 76. William Shakespeare. **EBEV; InvP; NoSic; OXAEP-1; PP** *Fr.* Sonnets. **CP-ShaWS**

Why is the child so pale. Louise. Stevie Smith. **CP-SmitS**

Why is the face in the water a woman? Because. Hayden Carruth. *Fr.* The Sleeping Beauty. **CP-CarHL**

Why is the universe mysterious? Questions. Howard Nemerov. **CP-NemeH**

Why is the word pretty so underrated? Pretty. Stevie Smith. **CP-SmitS**

Why listen, even the water is sobbing for something. The Maid's Thought. Robinson Jeffers. **CP-JefR1**

Why Log Truck Drivers Rise Earlier than Students of Zen. Gary Snyder. **CP-SnydG**

Why, Madam, will ye longer weep. To the Lady Crew, Upon the Death of her Child. Robert Herrick. **CP-HerrR**

Why make it doubt—it hurts it so. Emily Dickinson. **CP-DickE**

Why make so much of fragmentary blue. Fragmentary Blue. Robert Frost. **CP-FrosR**

Why marry ogre. Marriage Counsel. John Updike. **CP-UpdiJ**

Why me? Pili's Wall. Philip Levine. **SP-LeviP**

Why, Minstrel, These Untuneful Murmurings. William Wordsworth. **CP-WorW2**

Why must itself up every of a park. Edward Estlin Cummings. **CP-CummE**

Why My Mother Likes Liberace. Diane Wakoski. **SP-WakoD**

Why nag at the ideas of Hercules, Don Don? New England Verses. Wallace Stevens. **CP-StevW**

Why need I say, Louisa dear! To a Young Lady [Miss Lavinia Poole] on Her Recovery from a Fever. Samuel Taylor Coleridge. **CP-ColeS**

Why not merely the despaired of. Cascando. Samuel Beckett. **CP-BeckS**

Why not ride / with pleasure. Some Afternoon. Robert Creeley. **CP-CreeR**

Why now, in God's name, is the robe de nuit. You Never Knew Her Either, Though You Thought You Did. Robert Penn Warren. *Fr.* Ballad of a Sweet Dream of Peace. **SP-WarrR**

Why, now it has happened. Louis MacNeice. *Fr.* The Closing Album. **CP-MacNL**

Why of the sheep do you not learn peace? An Answer to the Parson. William Blake. **CP-BlakW**

Why of the Weather, The. Robert Ranke Graves. **CP-GravR**

Why, on her way to the oracle of Love. The Tree of Guilt. Karl Shapiro. *Fr.* Adam and Eve. **SP-ShapK**

Why, Pigot, complain of this damsel's disdain. Reply to Some Verses of J.M.B. Pigot, Esq., on the Cruelty of His Mistress. Byron. **CP-Byron**

Why presumes thy pride on that, that must so private be. Thomas Campion. **CP-CampT**

Why reclining, interrogating? why myself and all drowsing? To the States, To Identify the 16th, 17th, or 18th Presidentiad. Walt Whitman. **CP-WhitW**

Why repeat? I heard you the first time. Carl Sandburg. **OBAL** *Fr.* The People, Yes. **CP-SandC**

Why rouse from thy long winter sleep? A Queen Wasp. Walter de la Mare. **CP-DeLaW**

Why Sapri Will Never Be Italian. Richard Hugo. **CP-HugoR**

Why say "death"? Death is neither harsh nor kind. The Presence. Robert Ranke Graves. **CP-GravR**

Why say to them. Robert Creeley. **CP-CreeR**

Why seek to alter people, why not leave them alone? The Mills of God. David Herbert Lawrence. **CP-LawrD**

Why seraphim like lutanists arranged. Evening without Angels. Wallace Stevens. **CP-StevW**

Why, Sergeant, stray on the Ivel Way. San Sebastian. Thomas Hardy. **CP-HardT**

Why shall I keep the old name? Blacklisted. Carl Sandburg. **CP-SandC**

Why She Moved House. Thomas Hardy. **CP-HardT**

Why sho'd we covet much, when as we know. Not to Covet Much Where Little is the Charge. Robert Herrick. **CP-HerrR**

Why should any man try to find the distance to the moon by guessing. Carl Sandburg. *Fr.* The People, Yes. **CP-SandC**

Why should dull Art, which is wise Nature's ape. A Divine Love. Thomas Carew. **CP-CareT**

Why should I be bound to thee. To My Mirtle. William Blake. **CP-BlakW**

Why should I be wondering. Hummingbird Woman. Carl Sandburg. **CP-SandC**

Why should I blame her that she filled my days. No Second Troy. William Butler Yeats. **CP-YeatW**

Why should I call Thee Lord, Who art my God? After Communion. Christina Georgina Rossetti. **CP-RosC1**

Why should I care about drooling age. Beside Oneself. Malcolm Lowry. **CP-LowrM**

Why Should I Care for the Men of Thames? William Blake. (Thames.) **CP-BlakW**

Why should I discipline myself to verse. Against the Tricks of Time. Basil Bunting. **CP-BuntB**

Why should I keep holiday. Compensation. Ralph Waldo Emerson. **CP-EmerR**

Why should I let him shave the hairs from me? The Small Room. Roy Fisher. **SP-FishR** *Fr.* Interiors with Various Figures.

Why should I let the toad work. Toads. Philip Larkin. **CP-LarkP**

Why should I live. Ralph Waldo Emerson. **CP-EmerR**

Why should I seek for love or study it? Ribh Considers Christian Love Insufficient. William Butler Yeats. **CP-YeatW**

Why should I strike you with my name. Geoffrey Hill. *Fr.* Psalms of Assize. **CP-HillG**

Why should I, who know the cost so well. The Sale. William Carlos Williams. **CP-WilW2**

Why should I wish to hold in this low sphere. By the Same. Just before His Death. Charlotte Smith. **CP-SmitC**

Why should it be *my* loneliness. Tell Me. Langston Hughes. **SP-HughL**

Why should it stir me, when, each face intent. Carol Singers. John Hewitt. **CP-HewiJ**

Why should my anxious breast repine. L'Amitié Est L'Amour Sans Ailes. Byron. **CP-Byron**

Why Should Na Poor Folk Mowe. Robert Burns. **CP-BurnR**

Why should the Enthusiast, journeying through this Isle. William Wordsworth. *Fr.* Poems Composed or Suggested During a Tour, in the Summer of 1833. **CP-WorW2**

Why should their foolish bands, their hopeless hearses. Gerard Manley Hopkins. **CP-HopkG**

Why should this flower delay so long. The Last Chrysanthemum. Thomas Hardy. **CP-HardT**

Why should we defer our joys? Dule of a Dewsbury Matron. Donald Davie. **CP-DavDo**

Why should we hurry—why indeed? Emily Dickinson. **CP-DickE**

Why should we weep or mourn, Angelic boy. Sonnet. William Wordsworth. **CP-WorW2**

Why should you [*or* shouldst thou] swear I am forsworn. The Scrutiny [*or* Scrutinie]. Richard Lovelace. **CP-LoveR**

Why Sleeps the future, as a snake enrolled. Conclusion. William Wordsworth. *Fr.* Ecclesiastical Sonnets. **CP-WorW2**

Why so often, silent one. The Musing Maiden. Thomas Hardy. **CP-HardT**

Why so pale and wan, fond lover? Sir John Suckling. **AWP; AnAnS-2; BeJo; BoLoP; CABA; CaPo; ClHu; EBEvV; ELP; EnLoPo; EvOK; FPL; FaBV; FaFP; GTBS; GTBS-6; GTBS-P; HAP; HBV; HeIP; HoPM; InPS; JCP; LoBV; MePo; NAEL-1; NBLV; NIP; NOBE;**

OBEV; OBS; OPOP; OtMeF; OxAEP-1; PAI; PBMP; PIP; PoE; PoEL-3; PoPl; PoRA; PrIm; SeCP; SeCV-1; SeCePo; TEP; TFi; TrGrPo; TreFS; UnPo　*Fr.* Aglaura.　**CP-SuckJ**

(Encouragements to a Lover.)　**FaFP; GTBS; GTBS-6; GTBS-P; PBMP**

(Song: "Why so pale and wan, fond lover?")　**AnAnS-2; BeJo; BoLoP; CABA; CaPo; ClHu; EBEvV; EnLoPo; HBV; HeIP; InPS; JCP; LoBV; MePo; NAEL-1; NBLV; NIP; OPOP; OxAEP-1; PAI; PIP; PoEL-3; PoPl; PrIm; SeCP; SeCV-1; TFi**

Why so slowly do you move. The Delaying Bride. Robert Herrick. **CP-HerrR**

Why Some Look up to Planets and Heroes. Thomas Merton. **CP-MertT; SP-MertT**

Why speak of memory and death. Two Views of Two Ghost Towns. Charles Tomlinson. **CP-TomlC**

Why speak of the use / of poetry? Poetry. Hayden Carruth. **CP-CarHS**　*Fr.* The Clay Hill Anthology.

Why stand we gazing on the sparkling Brine. By the Sea-Shore, Isle of Man. William Wordsworth.　*Fr.* Poems Composed or Suggested During a Tour, in the Summer of 1833. **CP-WorW2**

Why standest thou afar off, O Lord? Psalm 10. Bible, O.T.　*Fr.* Psalms. **CP-Psal**

Why stirs, with sad alarm, the heart. Farewell Song. Paul Laurence Dunbar. **CP-DunbP**

Why talk of cities. Marsden Hartley. **CP-HartM**

Why that wild poet came to me to damn me. Lycambes Talks to John. Allen Tate. **CP-TateA**

Why the Face of a Clock is not Truly a Circle. Archibald MacLeish. **CP-MacLA**

Why the full heart is speechless. Emily Dickinson. **SP-DickE**

Why the Heart Has Dreams Is Why the Mind Goes Mad. Jean Garrigue. **SP-GarrJ**

Why the Postman Has to Ring Twice, or, Yellow Envelope, Where Have You Gone? Ogden Nash. **CP-NashO**

Why the Soup Tastes Like the *Daily News*. Marge Piercy. **SP-PierM**

Why the Telephone Wires Dip and the Poles Are Cracked and Crooked. John Updike. **CP-UpdiJ**

Why the Thief ingredient accompanies all Sweetness. Emily Dickinson. **SP-DickE**

Why, then, if love is all there is need to give. The Argument. Walter de la Mare. **CP-DeLaW**

Why, then, weep not. This Dusky Faith. Edna St. Vincent Millay. **CP-MillE**

Why then, why there. Elegy for J.F.K. Wystan Hugh Auden.　*Fr.* Eleven Occasional Poems. **CP-AudeW**

Why They Stopped Singing. Roy Fisher. **SP-FishR**

Why this day you're going so much wind? Eileen. Richard Hugo. **CP-HugoR**

Why this Flower is now call'd so. How the Wall-Flower Came First, and Why So Called. Robert Herrick. **CP-HerrR**

Why this man gelded Martial[l] I muse. Raderus. John Donne. **CP-DonnJ**

Why this preoccupation, soul, with Death. Sonnet Dialogue. Countee Cullen. **CP-CullC**

Why Time Spins Fast. Robert Browning. **FaBoDD**　*Fr.* Rabbi Ben Ezra. **CP-BroR1**

Why, Tityrus! But you've forgotten me. Build Soil. Robert Frost. **CP-FrosR**

Why urge the long, unequal fight. The Voices. John Greenleaf Whittier. **CP-WhitJ**

Why wait for Death to mow? Body and Soul. Hilda Doolittle. **CP-DoolH**

Why Wait for Death. Robert Frost. **CP-FrosR**

Why walkes Nick Flimsey like a Male-content? Upon Flimsey: Epigram. Robert Herrick. **CP-HerrR**

Why want to go afar. An Expostulation. Thomas Hardy. **CP-HardT**

Why was Cupid a Boy. William Blake. **CP-BlakW**

Why was it Bavaria? The house in the forest. To Know in Reverie the Only Phenomenology of the Absolute. Hayden Carruth. **CP-CarHS**

Why was it that the thunder voice of Fate. Robert Gould Shaw. Paul Laurence Dunbar. **CP-DunbP**

Why was it that you gave us no warning. Elegy. Wystan Hugh Auden. **CP-AudWJ**

Why was the passenger pigeon exterminated? Hayden Carruth.　*Fr.* Paragraphs. **CP-CarHS**

Why We Are Going Back to Paradise Island. Marilyn Hacker. **SP-HackM**

Why We Are Truly a Nation. William Matthews. **SP-MattW**

Why, we puzzle, / does Viola choose. Girard, Girard. Laurence Lieberman. **SP-LiebL**

Why weep ye by the tide, ladie? Jock of Hazeldean. Sir Walter Scott. **SP-ScotW**

Why weeps the muse for England? What appears. Expostulation. William Cowper. **CP-CowpW**

Why were you born when the snow was falling? Dirge, A. Christina Georgina Rossetti. **CP-RosC1**

Why—what men were they that beneath the moon. Archibald MacLeish.　*Fr.* Hamlet of A. Macleish. **CP-MacLA**

Why, who makes much of a miracle? Miracles. Walt Whitman. **CP-WhitW**

Why why / How many winds make wonderful. Edward Estlin Cummings. **CP-CummE**

Why, why tell thy lover. Fragment. Robert Burns. **CP-BurnR**

Why will you vex me with. To His Skeleton. Richard Wilbur. **CP-WilbR**

Why, William, on that old grey [or gray] stone. Expostulation and Reply. William Wordsworth. **CP-WorW1**

Why wilt thou take my heart? It fawnlike flies. The Hunter. Walter de la Mare. **CP-DeLaW**

Why wore th'Egyptians Jewells in the Eare? Eare-rings. Robert Herrick. **CP-HerrR**

Why, ye tenants of the lake. On Scaring Some Waterfowl in Loch Turit, a Wild Scene among the Hills of Oughtertyre. Robert Burns. **CP-BurnR**

Why yet, my noble hearts, they cannot say. A Speech According to Horace. Ben Jonson. **CP-JonsB**

Why you need to have one. A Secret Life. Stephen Dunn. **SP-DunnS**

Whylom [*or* Whilom] ther was dwellyng[e] at Oxenford[e]. The Miller's [*or* Milleres] Tale. Geoffrey Chaucer. **FaBoBl; NAEL-1; OAEL-1; OxBoLi; PeLV**　*Fr.* The Canterbury Tales. **CP-ChauG**

Why'n't you bring me. To Greet a Letter-Carrier. William Carlos Williams. **CP-WilW1**

Wichita Vortex Sutra. Allen Ginsberg. **CP-GinsA**

Wicked and corrupt. Evangelie, or, The Figure of Literary Corruption, Seeking Glory Not Truth. Stevie Smith. **CP-SmitS**

Wicked man is bad enough on earth, A. John Lackland. George Meredith. **CP-MerG1**

Wicked Messenger, The. "Bob Dylan." **CP-DylaB**

Wicker Basket, A. Robert Creeley. **CP-CreeR**

Wicliffe. William Wordsworth.　*Fr.* Ecclesiastical Sonnets. **CP-WorW2**

Wide Awake, Full of Love. William Carlos Williams. **CP-WilW2**

Wide cathedral aisles are lone, The. Emily Brontë. **CP-BronE**

Wide France. Donald Davie.　*Fr.* Two Dedications. **CP-DavDo**

Wide Prospect, The. Randall Jarrell. **CP-JarrR**

Wide river flowed outside our door, A. Non-communicant. Jenny Joseph. **SP-JoseJ**

Wide though the interrupt be that divides us, runers and counters. The Aliens. Wystan Hugh Auden. **CP-AudeW**

Wide, wide in the rose's side. Kenneth Patchen. **CP-PatcK**

Wide, Wide World, The. Rudyard Kipling. **OtMeF**　*Fr.* In the Neolithic Age. **CP-KiplR**

Widener Library, Reading Room. John Updike. **CP-UpdiJ**

Widest prairies have electric fences, The. Wires. Philip Larkin. **CP-LarkP**

Widow, The. Walter de la Mare. **CP-DeLaW**

Widow, A. Ted Kooser. **SP-KoosT**

Widow. Sylvia Plath. **CP-PlatS**

Widow, The. Dabney Stuart. **SP-StuaD**

Widow, The. Miller Williams. **SP-WillM**

Widow at "Whaleroad's End," The. Brendan Galvin. **SP-GalvB**

Widow at Windsor, The. Rudyard Kipling. **CP-KiplR**

Widow Betrothed, The. Thomas Hardy. **CP-HardT**

Widow Bird, A. Percy Bysshe Shelley.　*See* A Widow bird sate mourning for her love.

Widow bird sate mourning for her love, A. Percy Bysshe Shelley. **BoTP; CH; CoGr; ELP; FaBoEn; FaPON; GTBS; GTBS-6; GTBS-P; LO; LoBV; MeMBP; NOBE; OBNC; OxBSP; PoEL-4**　*Fr.* Charles the First. **CP-ShelP**

(Song, A: "Widow bird sate mourning for her love, A.") **MeMBP; NOBE; OBNC; OxBSP; PoEL-4**

(Widow Bird, A.) **BoTP; CH; FaPON**

Widow has burned her book, The. Richard Shelton.　*Fr.* The Stone Garden. **SP-ShelR**

Widow kept a favourite cat, A. A Fable of the Widow and Her Cat. Jonathan Swift. **CP-SwifJ**

Widow Lester, The. Ted Kooser. **SP-KoosT**

Widow of Naim, The. Thomas Merton. **CP-MertT**

Widow on Windmere Side, The. William Wordsworth. **CP-WorW2**

Widow returns to the house, The. Mourners. James McAuley.　*Fr.* Requiem. **SP-McAuJ**

Widow rises, A. In the Social Security Office. Gary Gildner. **SP-GildG**

Widow Woman. Langston Hughes. **SP-HughL**

Widower. Donald Davie. **CP-DavDo**

Widower, The. Rudyard Kipling. **CP-KiplR**

Widowers. Donald Davie. **CP-DavDo**

Widower's Monologue. Alí Chumacero, *tr. fr. Spanish by* William Carlos Williams. **CP-WilW2**

Widower's Winter. Bill Knott. **SP-KnotB**

Widowhood. Phoebe Hesketh. **SP-HeskP**

Widowhood. Leonard Nathan. **SP-NathL**

Widowhood or The Home-Coming of Lady Ross. Stevie Smith. **CP-SmitS**

Widows, The. Donald Hall. **CP-HallD**

Widow's Lament in Springtime, The. William Carlos Williams. **CP-WilW1**

Widow[e]'s Mites, The. Richard Crashaw. **CP-CrasR**

Widow's Party, The. Rudyard Kipling. **CP-KiplR**

Widow's Song, The, *tr. fr. the German of* Rilke. Randall Jarrell. **CP-JarrR**

Widow's Tears [*or* Widdowes Teares]: or, Dirge of Dorcas, The. Robert Herrick. **CP-HerrR**

Widow's Yard, The. Isabella Gardner. **CP-GardI**

Wiedersehen. Miller Williams. **SP-WillM**

Wife, The. Robert Creeley. **CP-CreeR**

Wife. Louise McNeill. **SP-McNeL**

Wife. Barton Sutter. **SP-SuttB**

Wife and Another, A. Thomas Hardy. **CP-HardT**

Wife—at Daybreak I shall be, A. Emily Dickinson. **CP-DickE**

Wife being absent, I could find. Rosalind. George Meredith. **CP-MerG2**

Wife Comes Back, A. Thomas Hardy. **CP-HardT**

Wife did she live, yet virgin did she die. Our Ladye's Spousalls. Robert Southwell. **CP-SoutR**

Wife in London, A. Thomas Hardy. **CP-HardT**

Wife of Bath, The, *see also* Wife of Bath's Tale, The. Geoffrey Chaucer. **CP-PopeA** *Fr.* The Canterbury Tales. **CP-ChauG**

   "If poor (you say) she drains her husband's purse." **OBSV**

Wife of Bath's Prologue, The. Geoffrey Chaucer. **FHYEP; NAEL-1; OAEL-1,** *ll.* 1–862 *complete*; *Fr.* The Canterbury Tales. **CP-ChauG**

   "Experience, though noon auctoritee." **OxBoLi; PeLV**

   "If there were no authority on earth." **OxBM**

   "My fifth housebonde, god his soule blesse!" **FiP**

   "Tell me to what conclusion or in aid." **OxBM**

Wife of Bath's Tale, The, *See also* Wife of Bath, The *mod. vers. by* Alexander Pope. Geoffrey Chaucer. **FHYEP; NAEL-1; OAEL-1** *Fr.* The Canterbury Tales. **CP-ChauG**

Wife of Manoah to Her Husband, The. John Greenleaf Whittier. **CP-WhitJ**

Wife of the Friend of those I most revere. To Mrs Butts. William Blake. **CP-BlakW**

Wife sits all afternoon, The. Richard Shelton. *Fr.* The Stone Garden. **SP-ShelR**

Wife Talks to Herself, A. Stephen Berg. **SP-BergS**

Wife: there was nothing wrong with our dreams. A Bird in the Hand: Two Solos. Richard Shelton. **SP-ShelR**

Wife to Husband. Christina Georgina Rossetti. **CP-RosC1**

Wife Waits, A. Thomas Hardy. *Fr.* At Casterbridge Fair. **CP-HardT**

Wifebeater, The. Anne Sexton. **CP-SextA**

Wife's Tale, The. Seamus Heaney. **SP-HeanS**

Wiffie! I'm *sure* that something *is* the matter. Prologue. "Lewis Carroll." **CP-CarrL**

Wigging in, wigging out: / when I stop to think. Trip. James Schuyler. **CP-SchuJ**

Wigs and Beards. Robert Ranke Graves. **CP-GravR**

Wild, The. Wendell Berry. **CP-BerrW**

Wild air, world-mothering air. The Blessed Virgin Compared to the Air We Breathe. Gerard Manley Hopkins. **CP-HopkG**

Wild Apple Trees. Brendan Galvin. **SP-GalvB**

Wild beast falling sick, A. Truth Is Poor Physic. Robert Ranke Graves. *Fr.* Three Songs for the Lute. **CP-GravR**

Wild bird, whose warble, liquid sweet. Tennyson. **NoP; PBBP** *Fr.* In Memoriam A. H. H. **CP-TennA**

Wild Birds, The. Randall Jarrell. **CP-JarrR**

Wild blackberries I gathered that morning, The. Near Things. Leonard Nathan. **SP-NathL**

Wild Blue sky abreast of Winds, A. Emily Dickinson. **CP-DickE**

Wild Boar. Shel Silverstein. **SP-SilS2**

Wild Boar Clough. Donald Davie. **CP-DavDo**

Wild-cat, gnat and I. Edna St. Vincent Millay. **CP-MillE**

Wild cherries ripen, black and fat, The. Fall. Wendell Berry. **CP-BerrW**

Wild Cherry, The. Malcolm Lowry. **CP-LowrM**

Wild Common, The. David Herbert Lawrence. **CP-LawrD**

Wild curlew whistle I offer my death to. James Liddy. *Fr.* Birds. **CP-LiddJ**

Wild Cyclamen. Robert Ranke Graves. **CP-GravR**

Wild Dog, The. Stevie Smith. **CP-SmitS**

Wild Dreams of a New Beginning. Lawrence Ferlinghetti. **SP-FerlL**

Wild Duck, The. Ted Hughes. **SP-HughT**

Wild-duck swam in the gold-fish pond, The. Malcolm Lowry. **CP-LowrM**

Wild Duck's Nest, The. William Wordsworth. **CP-WorW2**

Wild Ducks, People and Distances. Wallace Stevens. **CP-StevW**

Wild Edge, The. Gary Snyder. **CP-SnydG**

Wild Eggs. James Schuyler. **CP-SchuJ**

Wild Flowers. Charlotte Smith. **CP-SmitC**

Wild Flower's Song, The. William Blake. **CP-BlakW**

Wild Garden, The. Alexander Pope. **PrIm** *Fr.* Awake, my St. John! leave all meaner things. **NAEL-1; NoP; OAEP; PoEL-3** *Fr.* An Essay on Man. **CP-PopeA**

Wild Gazelle, The. Byron. **CP-Byron**

Wild Geese, The. Wendell Berry. **CP-BerrW**

Wild Geese. Mary Oliver. **SP-OlivM**

Wild geese waking in the March wind. Withdrawal Letter. Jim Carroll. **SP-CarrJ**

Wild Geranium. Louis Zukofsky. **CP-ZukLS**

Wild Grapes. Robert Frost. **CP-FrosR**

Wild grass in spate in a rainy wind. Louis MacNeice. *Fr.* Country Week-End. **CP-MacNL**

Wild Honey Pie. The Beatles. **CP-Beatl**

Wild Honeysuckle. Louis Zukofsky. **CP-ZukLS**

Wild Jackass, The. Ogden Nash. **CP-NashO**

Wild Life and Tamed Life. Richard Eberhart. **CP-EberR**

Wild Life Cameo, Early Morn. Lawrence Ferlinghetti. **SP-FerlL**

Wild Life Studies. James Fenton.

   Wild Ones[, The]. **SP-FentJ**

Wild Nights—Wild Nights! Emily Dickinson. **CP-DickE**

Wild Oats. Philip Larkin. **CP-LarkP**

Wild Old Wicked Man, The. Archibald MacLeish. **CP-MacLA**

Wild Old Wicked Man, The. William Butler Yeats. **CP-YeatW**

Wild Ones[, The]. James Fenton. **SP-FentJ** *Fr.* Wild Life Studies.

Wild Orchard. William Carlos Williams. **CP-WilW1**

Wild Orphan. Allen Ginsberg. **CP-GinsA**

Wild, pale, and wonder-stricken, even as one. Ginevra. Percy Bysshe Shelley. **CP-ShelP**

Wild patience has taken me this far, A. Integrity. Adrienne Rich. **SP-RicA1; SP-RicA2**

Wild Provoke of the Endurance Sky. Joseph Ceravolo. **SP-CeraJ**

Wild red-wing black-, The. The Red-Wing Blackbird. William Carlos Williams. **CP-WilW2**

Wild Redbreast! hadst thou at Jemima's lip. In the Woods of Rydal. William Wordsworth. **CP-WorW2**

Wild Rose, The. George Meredith. **CP-MerG2**

Wild Rose and the Snowdrop, The. George Meredith. **CP-MerG1**

Wild Shakespeare. James Thomson. **EPCY** *Fr.* Summer. *Fr.* The Seasons. **CP-ThomJ**

Wild Sky, The. Adrienne Rich. **CP-RicAE**

Wild Swans. Edna St. Vincent Millay. **CP-MillE**

Wild Swans at Coole, The. William Butler Yeats. **CP-YeatW**

Wild Swans at Norfolk, The. Hayden Carruth. **SP-CarrH**

Wild Swans of Inverane, The. Richard Eberhart. **CP-EberR**

Wild Things in Captivity. David Herbert Lawrence. **CP-LawrD**

Wild Thyme, The. William Blake. **WiR** *Fr.* Milton. **CP-BlakW**

Wild time *liveforever* horsethyme ice. Liveforever. Louis Zukofsky. **CP-ZukLS**

Wild trees have bought me. Song. Audre Lorde. **SP-LordA**

Wild Turkeys in Paradise. Robert Pack. **SP-PackR**

Wild warblers are warbling in the jungle, The. Meditation Celestial & Terrestrial. Wallace Stevens. **CP-StevW**

Wild Whore Laughs, The. Jim Morrison. **SP-MorrJ**

Wild, wild the storm, and the sea high running. Patrolling Barnegat. Walt Whitman. **CP-WhitW**

Wild winds weep, The. Mad Song. William Blake. **CP-BlakW**

Wild with ego, wild with world-blame. Interjection #5: Solipsism and Theology. Robert Penn Warren. **SP-WarrR**

Wild(at our first)beasts uttered human words. Edward Estlin Cummings. **CP-CummE**

Wilderness, The. Kathleen Jessie Raine. **SP-RainK**

Wilderness, The. Edwin Arlington Robinson. **CP-RobiE**

Wilderness. Carl Sandburg. **CP-SandC**

Wilderness Starts towards Him, A. Wendell Berry. *Fr.* The Handing Down. **CP-BerrW**

Wildflower, The. William Carlos Williams. **CP-WilW1**

Wildflowers withering with the same death. Mountain: One from Bryant. Muriel Rukeyser. **CP-RukeM**

Wilding little stubble flower, A. George Meredith. **CP-MerG2**

Wildly bound the bells this morning. The Tarrying Bridegroom. Thomas Hardy. **CP-HardT**

Wildly dissimilar. Scribe. Hilda Doolittle. **CP-DoolH**

Wildly he wandered on. Percy Bysshe Shelley. **TOF** *Fr.* Alastor; or, The Spirit of Solitude. **CP-ShelP**

Wildly he wandered on. William Wordsworth. **TOF** *Fr.* Summer Vacation. *Fr.* The Prelude; Growth of a Poet's Mind [1850 vers.]. **CP-WorW3**

Wildly round our woodland quarters. The Lumbermen. John Greenleaf Whittier. **CP-WhitJ**

Wildness. Gerard Manley Hopkins. **EaPr; OtMeF** *Fr.* Inversnaid. **CP-HopkG**

Wildness of nature is in Florida. Opposition. Richard Eberhart. **CP-EberR**

Wildness sleeps upon the mountain. The Fisher Cat. Richard Eberhart. **CP-EberR**

WIldrose. Robert Lowell. **SP-LoweR**

Wilds horrid and dark with o'ershadowing trees. Scenes Favourable to Meditation. Jeanne Marie Bouvier de la Motte-Guyon, *tr. fr. French by* William Cowper. **CP-CowpW**

Wildwest. Archibald MacLeish. **CP-MacLA**

Wilfred Owen's Photographs. Ted Hughes. **SP-HughT**

Wilful-Missing. Rudyard Kipling. **CP-KiplR**

Will, The. John Donne. **CP-DonnJ**

Will. John Hewitt. **CP-HewiJ**

Will, The. James Merrill. **SP-MerrJ**

Will. Tennyson. **CP-TennA**

Will. Alice Walker. **CP-WalkA**

Will a narrow lane / Save Cain? Thomas Merton. *Fr.* South. *Fr.* The Geography of Lograire. **CP-MertT**

Will Consider Situation. Ogden Nash. **CP-NashO**

Will Dallas grow, or wither? Fear Not. Gary Snyder. **CP-SnydG**

Will Ever? Stevie Smith. **CP-SmitS**

Will Faulkner, Will Faulkner. The Ballad of the Corn-Cob and the Lie. Archibald MacLeish. **CP-MacLA**

Will forbids; the heart has flown, The. I Am Not Resigned. Phoebe Hesketh. **SP-HeskP**

Will i ever forget that precarious moment? Edward Estlin Cummings. **CP-CummE**

Will I have some mo' dat pie? Reluctance. Paul Laurence Dunbar. **CP-DunbP**

Will is always near, dear, The. Emily Dickinson. **SP-DickE**

Will it be one of those. Viper-Man. Donald Davie. **CP-DavDo**

Will it last? he says. The Snowflake Which Is Now and Hence Forever. Archibald MacLeish. **CP-MacLA**

Will it never be possible. A Portrait in Greys. William Carlos Williams. **CP-WilW1**

Will Makes the Work, or Consent Makes the Cure, The. Robert Herrick. **CP-HerrR**

Will Man Ever Face Fact and Not Feel Flat? Stevie Smith. **CP-SmitS**

Will no one say hush! to thee. Poor Bit of a Wench! David Herbert Lawrence. **CP-LawrD**

Will Not Come Back. Robert Lowell. **SP-LoweR**

Will not some dozen sacks of rags. Marianne Moore. William Carlos Williams. **CP-WilW1**

Will o' the Wisp. George Meredith. **CP-MerG1**

Will of the Lord Be Done, The. Christina Georgina Rossetti. **CP-RosC2**

Will of the weed to startle, The. Charles Henri Ford. *Fr.* Epigrams. **SP-FordC**

Will out of the kindness of their hearts a few philosophers tell me. Edward Estlin Cummings. **CP-CummE**

Will people accept them? Tenzone. Ezra Pound. **SP-PounE** *Fr.* Contemporania.

Will Somers. Lewis Turco. *Fr.* Bordello. **SP-TurcL**

'Will sprawl, now that the heat of day is best. Caliban upon Setebos; or, Natural Theology in the Island. Robert Browning. **CP-BroR1**

Will suddenly trees leap up from winter and will. Edward Estlin Cummings. **CP-CummE**

Will: termite mothers. Charles Olson. **CP-OlsoC**

Will the blight end the chestnut? Evil Tendencies Cancel. Robert Frost. *Fr.* Ten Mills. **CP-FrosR**

Will the Cause of Woe, The. Robert Herrick. **CP-HerrR**

Will the day be bright or cloudy? Emily Brontë. **CP-BronE**

Will: the rat. Charles Olson. **CP-OlsoC**

Will there really be a "morning"? Emily Dickinson. ("Will there really be a 'Morning'?") **CP-DickE**

Will there really be a "Morning"? Emily Dickinson. *See* Will there really be a "morning"?

Will These Hands Ne'er Be Clean? Christina Georgina Rossetti. **CP-RosC3**

Will they gape for the husks that ye proffer. Rudyard Kipling. **CP-KiplR** *Fr.* The Naulahka.

Will they occur. Brasilia. Sylvia Plath. **CP-PlatS**

Will To, The. Charles Olson. **CP-OlsoC**

Will To Be Working, A. Robert Herrick. **CP-HerrR**

Will to Change, The. Adrienne Rich. **CP-RicAE**

Will used a broken pen, must have broken many. The Broken Pen. Richard Eberhart. **CP-EberR**

Will we be raised from the dead. Hasta la Victoria Siempre. Chuck Miller. **SP-MillC**

Will we make it to 2000? Young and the Old, the. Richard Eberhart. **CP-EberR**

Will we speak to each other. The Answer. Robert Creeley. **CP-CreeR**

Will Whistle. George Meredith. **CP-MerG2**

Will ye go to the Highlands Leezie Lindsay. Leezie Lindsay. Robert Burns. **CP-BurnR**

Will ye go to the Indies, my Mary. Song. Robert Burns. **CP-BurnR**

Will ye heare, what I can say. Upon His Julia. Robert Herrick. **CP-HerrR**

Will ye see what wonders love hath wrought? Sir Thomas Wyatt. **CP-WyatT**

Will you be there? my yearning heart has cried. Christina Georgina Rossetti. **CP-RosC3**

Will you be well will you be well. More Grammar for a Sentence. Gertrude Stein. **CP-SteiG**

Will you conquer my heart with your beauty, my soul going out from afar? To the Unknown Goddess. Rudyard Kipling. **CP-KiplR**

Will you give yourself airs. Her face the Book of—Love Delights in—Praises. Louis Zukofsky. **CP-ZukLS**

Will you glimmer on the sea? Moonrise. Hilda Doolittle. **CP-DoolH**

Will You Have Your Tedium Rare or Medium? Ogden Nash. **CP-NashO**

Will you hear my story also. Donald. Robert Browning. **CP-BroR2**

Will you please rush down and see. To Close. William Carlos Williams. **CP-WilW2**

Will you seek afar off? you surely come back at last. Walt Whitman. **ChIV-1** *Fr.* A Song for Occupations. **CP-WhitW**

Will you still lament and rayse. Parkinsons Shade to the House of Mr. Pallauicine Taking His Death Ill. Robert Herrick. **CP-HerrR**

Will you teach a. Edward Estlin Cummings. **CP-CummE**

Will you turn a deaf ear. The Questioner Who Sits So Sly. Wystan Hugh Auden. **CP-AudeW**

"Will you walk a little faster?" said a [*or* the] whiting to a [*or* the] snail. "Lewis Carroll." **CP-CarrL** *Fr.* Alice's Adventures in Wonderland. (Mock Turtle's Song, The.) **CP-CarrL**

Will you write in a new book. Request. Richard Eberhart. **CP-EberR**

Willful Homing. Robert Frost. **CP-FrosR**

William Adams Delano. Archibald MacLeish. **CP-MacLA**

William Blake. Allen Tate. **CP-TateA**

William Bond. William Blake. **CP-BlakW**

William Carlos Williams. Robert Lowell. **SP-LoweR**

William Carlos Williams Alive! Louis Zukofsky. *Fr.* Songs of Degrees. **CP-ZukLS**

William Carlos Williams Reading His Poems. Stephen Berg. **SP-BergS**

William Conor RHA, 1881–1968. John Hewitt. **CP-HewiJ**

William Cowper Esqre. William Blake. *See* The Only man that eer I knew.

William Dewy, Tranter Reuben, Farmer Ledlow late at plough. Friends Beyond. Thomas Hardy. **CP-HardT**

William does thy frigid soul. Ralph Waldo Emerson. **CP-EmerR**

William Forster. John Greenleaf Whittier. **CP-WhitJ**

William Francis Bartlett. John Greenleaf Whittier. **CP-WhitJ**

William is away, and I am minding. Caroline Herschel (1750–1848). Siv Cedering Fox. *Fr.* Letters from the Astronomers. **SP-CedeS**

William J. McClughin. John Hewitt. **CP-HewiJ**

William Lisle Bowles. Byron. **OBNC** *Fr.* English Bards and Scotch Reviewers. **CP-Byron**

William, my teacher, my friend! dear William and dear Dorothea! Hexameters. Samuel Taylor Coleridge. **CP-ColeS**

William Rufus and the Jew. Ralph Waldo Emerson. **CP-EmerR**

William Shakespeare to Mrs Anne, Regular Servant to the Rev. Mr Precentor of York. Thomas Gray. **CP-GrayT**

William the Norman was brave in the field. The Succession of Kings. Christina Georgina Rossetti. **CP-RosC3**

William the Third. William Wordsworth. *Fr.* Ecclesiastical Sonnets. **CP-WorW2**

William was once a bashful youth. Of Himself. William Cowper. **CP-CowpW**

William Zanzinger killed poor Hattie Carroll. The Lonesome Death of Hattie Carroll. "Bob Dylan." **CP-DylaB**

Williams Avenue Zionist Church, The. Russia. William Carlos Williams. **CP-WilW2**

Willie. Maya Angelou. **SP-AngeM**

Willie Brew'd [or Brewed] a Peck o' Maut. Robert Burns. **CP-BurnR**

Willie Francis and the Electric Chair. Charles Olson. **CP-OlsoC**

Willie Henderson, Massachusetts-born, painted and dreamed in Chicago. Scripture. Carl Sandburg. **CP-SandC**

Willie was a man without fame. Willie. Maya Angelou. **SP-AngeM**

Willie Wastle dwalt [or dwalls] on Tweed. Sic a Wife as Willie Had. Robert Burns. **CP-BurnR**

Willie's Dirge on Little Marian. George Meredith. Fr. Wandering Willie. **CP-MerG2**

Willing pitifully to bewitch. Edward Estlin Cummings. **CP-CummE**

Willing Prisoner to His Mistress, The. Thomas Carew. See Let fools great Cupid's yoke disdain.

Willing to die, / you give up. Poem. Wendell Berry. **CP-BerrW**

Willingly. Tess Gallagher. **SP-GallT**

Willis, I didn't want you here today:. The Self-Seeker. Robert Frost. **CP-FrosR**

Willkie in the Gulliver. Muriel Rukeyser. **CP-RukeM**

Willkie—Stopless Falling through Air. Muriel Rukeyser. **CP-RukeM**

Willkie: Words from Russia. Muriel Rukeyser. **CP-RukeM**

Willock, 82 my pal Thomas. 82 X 48. Laurence Lieberman. **SP-LiebL**

Willow, The. Walter de la Mare. **CP-DeLaW**

Willow. James Merrill. **SP-MerrJ**

Willow Garland, The. Robert Herrick. **CP-HerrR**

Willow Pattern. John Hewitt. **CP-HewiJ**

Willow Poem. William Carlos Williams. **CP-WilW1**

Willow-Tree, The. "Lewis Carroll." **CP-CarrL**

Willow, Wishbone, Warblers. Brendan Galvin. **SP-GalvB**

Willows carried a slow sound, The. Repose of Rivers. Hart Crane. **CP-CranH**

Willows Coming into Leaf. Martin Edmunds. **SP-EdmuM**

Willows of Massachusetts, The. Denise Levertov. **CP-LeveD**

Willowware Cup. James Merrill. **SP-MerrJ**

Will's at the dance in the Club-room below. A Wife Waits. Thomas Hardy. Fr. At Casterbridge Fair. **CP-HardT**

Wills of the Wisp, The, ad. fr. the German of Stolberg. Samuel Taylor Coleridge. **CP-ColeS**

Willy Lyons. James Wright. **CP-WrigJ**

Willy Wet-Leg. David Herbert Lawrence. **CP-LawrD**

Wilson. John Greenleaf Whittier. **CP-WhitJ**

Wilson and Pilcer and Snack stood before the zoo elephant. Elephants Are Different to Different People. Carl Sandburg. **CP-SandC**

Wilson in Hell. Robinson Jeffers. **CP-JefR3**

Wilt thou be my Dearie. Robert Burns. **CP-BurnR**

Wilt thou forget the happy hours. The Past. Percy Bysshe Shelley. **CP-ShelP**

Wilt thou forgive that sin where I begun. A Hymn to God the Father. John Donne. **CP-DonnJ**

Wilt thou forsake me who in life's bright May. To the Muse. Charlotte Smith. **CP-SmitC**

Wilt thou life's best elixir drain? Fayzi, tr. fr. Persian by Ralph Waldo Emerson. **CP-EmerR**

Wilt thou love God, as he thee? [or thee!] then digest. John Donne. **JCP; OBS; TrCP** Fr. Divine Meditations. **CP-DonnJ** Fr. Holy Sonnets. **CP-DonnJ**

Wilt thou my true Friend be? True Friendship. Robert Herrick. **CP-HerrR**

Wilt thou never come again. The Phantom. Walter de la Mare. **CP-DeLaW**

Wilt thou seal up the avenues of ill? Suum Cuique. Ralph Waldo Emerson. **APN-1** Fr. Quatrains. **CP-EmerR**

Wilt thou then serve the Philistines with that gift. John Milton. **EBEV** Fr. Samson Agonistes. **CP-MiltJ**

Wiltshire. Donald Davie. **CP-DavDo**

Win' a-blowin' gentle so de san' lay low. A Florida Night. Paul Laurence Dunbar. **CP-DunbP**

Win' is blowin' wahmah, De. A Christmas Folksong. Paul Laurence Dunbar. **CP-DunbP**

Win' is hollahin' "Daih you," De. A Little Christmas Basket. Paul Laurence Dunbar. **CP-DunbP**

Winander Lake. William Wordsworth. See There Was a Boy.

Wincing in a Los Angeles future glare. West of Eden. Tom Clark. **SP-ClarT**

Wind, The. Robert Creeley. **CP-CreeR**

Wind. James Fenton. **SP-FentJ**

Wind. Ted Hughes. **SP-HughT**

Wind, The. Chuck Miller. **SP-MillC**

Wind. Kathleen Jessie Raine. **SP-RainK**

Wind, The. Robert Louis Stevenson. **SP-StevR**

Wind. Charles Tomlinson. **CP-TomlC**

Wind. John Updike. **CP-UpdiJ**

Wind. Robert Penn Warren. **SP-WarrR**

Wind, and all the midges in the air. A View of Fujiyama after the War. James Dickey. **CP-DickJ**

Wind & sea are as playmates. George Meredith. **CP-MerG2**

Wind and the Rain, The. Robert Frost. **CP-FrosR**

Wind and the Sea, The. Paul Laurence Dunbar. **CP-DunbP**

Wind and the whirling of white mists. Voices on the Wind. John Gould Fletcher. **SP-FletJ**

Wind and Tree. Paul Muldoon. **SP-MuldP**

Wind and Window Flower. Robert Frost. **CP-FrosR**

Wind arrow, wind rose, the wind currents in air. Muriel Rukeyser. **CP-RukeM**

Wind at Dog Lake whispered "stranger" "stranger", The. Turtle Lake. Richard Hugo. **CP-HugoR**

Wind at Night, The. Roy Fisher. Fr. City. **SP-FishR**

Wind at Penistone, The. Donald Davie. **CP-DavDo**

Wind-bags, The. "Hugh MacDiarmid." **SP-MacDH**

Wind begun to knead the Grass, The, First Version. Emily Dickinson. **CP-DickE**

Wind begun to rock the Grass, The, Second version. Emily Dickinson. See The Wind begun to knead the Grass.

Wind billowing out the seat of my britches, The. Child on Top of a Greenhouse. Theodore Roethke. **CP-RoetT**

Wind blew all my wedding-day, The. Wedding-Wind. Philip Larkin. **CP-LarkP**

Wind blew harsh down Thompson Street, The. 1928. Frederick Morgan. Fr. Eight Triolets. **SP-MorgF**

Wind blew hollow frae the hills, The. Lament for James, Earl of Glencairn. Robert Burns. **CP-BurnR**

Wind blew shrill and smart, The. Robert Louis Stevenson. **CP-StevR**

Wind Blew Words, The. Thomas Hardy. **CP-HardT**

Wind Bloweth Where It Listeth, The. Countee Cullen. **CP-CullC**

Wind blows, The. Peace. Alun Lewis. **CP-LewiA**

Wind blows a piece of paper to my feet, The. At the Crossroads. Bill Knott. **SP-KnotB**

Wind blows. The corn leans. The corn leaves go rustling. The march, The. Ripe Corn. Carl Sandburg. **CP-SandC**

Wind came across the corn laughing, The. Corn Prattlings. Carl Sandburg. **CP-SandC**

Wind Carol, The. Lewis Turco. See Envoi: The Wind Carol.

Wind carves sand into shapes, The. Carl Sandburg. Fr. Timesweep. **CP-SandC**

Wind Chimes. Stephen Dobyns. **SP-DobyS**

Wind-claps of soot and snow. Barnsley, 1966. Donald Davie. **CP-DavDo**

Wind comes from the north, The. Suspense. David Herbert Lawrence. **CP-LawrD**

Wind created by his fall, The. Lucifer. Howard Nemerov. Fr. Dialectical Songs. **CP-NemeH**

Wind deserted the pond this morning. The day. Birthday. Richard Hugo. **CP-HugoR**

Wind didn't come from the Orchard—today, The. Emily Dickinson. **CP-DickE**

Wind drew off, The. Emily Dickinson. **CP-DickE**

Wind felt for the breastbone, A. First Meeting. Wystan Hugh Auden. **CP-AudWJ**

Wind Flashes the Grass, A. Ted Hughes. **SP-HughT**

Wind. Flower. Pretty village. For the Mother of My Mother's Mother. Kenneth Patchen. **CP-PatcK**

Wind from off the sea says nothing new, The. The Marrow. Theodore Roethke. **CP-RoetT**

Wind from the frozen lake. The Past. Frederick Morgan. **SP-MorgF**

Wind from the mountains is closing my doors, The. Putting It All Away. Stephen Dobyns. **SP-DobyS**

Wind goes over it. You see, The. An Insufficiency of Earth. Charles Tomlinson. Fr. Four Kantian Lyrics. **CP-TomlC**

Wind had hidden his head in a pit in the sand, The. South. Louis MacNeice. Fr. Sleeping Winds. **CP-MacNL**

Wind-haired, mufflered. Exile. Derek Walcott. **CP-WalcD**

Wind has been blowing from the Sahara, The. A Meteorology. Jenny Joseph. **SP-JoseJ**

Wind has blown the rain away and blown, A. Edward Estlin Cummings. **CP-CummE**

Wind has such a rainy sound, The. Christina Georgina Rossetti. **CP-RosC2**

Wind has swept from the wide atmosphere, The. A Summer Evening Churchyard. Percy Bysshe Shelley. **CP-ShelP**

Wind Horses. Carl Sandburg. **CP-SandC**

Wind, I hear it sighing, The. Emily Brontë. **CP-BronE**

Wind I know blows dirt, A. A Conditioned Air. Donald Davie. **CP-DavDo**

Wind in a Jar. Stephen Dunn. **SP-DunnS**

Wind in the ash-tree sounds like surf on the shore at Truro, The. Memory of Cape Cod. Edna St. Vincent Millay. **CP-MillE**

Wind in the corn leaves among the naked stalks, The. Carl Sandburg. *Fr.* The People, Yes. **CP-SandC**

Wind in the fleece of ivy. The Gorge. Charles Tomlinson. **CP-TomlC**

Wind in the pines, a dark, damp, Novemb'ring wind. Hayden Carruth. *Fr.* The Sleeping Beauty. **CP-CarHL**

Wind in the Street. Thom Gunn. **CP-GunnT**

Wind in the Tree, The. Frank Templeton Prince. **CP-PrinF**

Wind Increases, The. William Carlos Williams. **CP-WilW1**

Wind is a Lady with, The. Edward Estlin Cummings. **CP-CummE**

Wind is a stealth of memory. Footsteps fall. Hayden Carruth. *Fr.* The Asylum. **CP-CarHL**

Wind is blowing, A. The book being written. The Novel. Denise Levertov. **CP-LeveD**

Wind Is Blowing West, The. Joseph Ceravolo. **SP-CeraJ**

Wind is east but the hot weather continues, The. American Letter. Archibald MacLeish. **CP-MacLA**

Wind is East, the wind is West, The. A Stave of Roving Tim. George Meredith. **CP-MerG1**

Wind is 95. It still pours from the east, The. Bear Paw. Richard Hugo. **CP-HugoR**

Wind is now thy organist;—a clank, The. Composed in Roslin Chapel, During a Storm. William Wordsworth. **CP-WorW2**

Wind is out in its rage tonight, The. The Fisher Child's Lullaby. Paul Laurence Dunbar. **CP-DunbP**

Wind is ruffling the tawny pelt, A. A Far Cry from Africa. Derek Walcott. **CP-WalcD**

Wind is the breath of it. Charles Henri Ford. *Fr.* Epigrams. **SP-FordC**

Wind is the Wall of the Year. Marge Piercy. **SP-PierM**

Wind is without there and howls in the trees, The. Robert Louis Stevenson. **CP-StevR**

Wind lay still on the deck of Brandan's ship, The. West. Louis MacNeice. *Fr.* Sleeping Winds. **CP-MacNL**

Wind may blaw the lee-lang way, The. To Mesdames Zassetsky and Garschine. Robert Louis Stevenson. **CP-StevR**

Wind meets me at Penistone, The. The Wind at Penistone. Donald Davie. **CP-DavDo**

Wind might blow a lotus petal, A. History. William Carlos Williams. **CP-WilW1**

Wind mills churn on Windy City's. Written on Hotel Napkin: Chicago Futures. Allen Ginsberg. **CP-GinsA**

Wind of January, The. Christina Georgina Rossetti. **YeAr** *Fr.* A Year's Windfalls. **CP-RosC1**

Wind of March, The. John Greenleaf Whittier. **CP-WhitJ**

Wind of the night, wind of the long cool shadows. The Night Wind. John Gould Fletcher. *Fr.* Sand and Spray: A Sea-Symphony. **SP-FletJ**

Wind of the sea, / O where. Sea-Choros. Euripides, *tr. by* Hilda Doolittle ("H.D."). *Fr.* Hecuba. **CP-DoolH**

Wind of the Village. William Carlos Williams. **CP-WilW1**

Wind on Crow Hill was her darling, The. Emily Brontë. Ted Hughes. **SP-HughT**

Wind on the Lyre. George Meredith. **CP-MerG1**

Wind on the Way, The. Carl Sandburg. **CP-SandC**

Wind played, The. Still Frame. Archie Randolph Ammons. **SP-AmmoA**

Wind rests its cheek upon the ground and feels the cool damp, The. Hymn to Life. James Schuyler. **CP-SchuJ**

Wind rocks / the porch chairs. Calling. Archie Randolph Ammons. **SP-AmmoA**

Wind rocks the car. / We sit parked by the river. Like This Together. Adrienne Rich. **CP-RicAE; SP-RicA1; SP-RicA2**

Wind-sacked beast, The. The Leaf Eater. Dabney Stuart. **SP-StuaD**

Wind scatters the fragrance of the willows over the shop. In the Wineshop of Chinling. Li Po, *tr. fr. Chinese by* William Carlos Williams *with* David Rafael Wang. **CP-WilW2**

Wind-scraped headland, a sludgy, dishwater sea, A. Derek Walcott. **CP-WalcD** *Fr.* Midsummer.

Wind scruffing it, the bay, The. Green and White. Wendell Berry. **CP-BerrW**

Wind Secrets. Diane Wakoski. **SP-WakoD**

Wind shall lull us yet, The. From the Antique. Christina Georgina Rossetti. **CP-RosC3**

Wind Shifts, The. Wallace Stevens. **CP-StevW**

Wind sidles up to, The. Meeting the Opposition. Archie Randolph Ammons. **SP-AmmoA**

Wind sighing, crying, singing in the pines. Who knows. Hayden Carruth. *Fr.* The Sleeping Beauty. **CP-CarHL**

Wind Sings Welcome in Early Spring, The. Carl Sandburg. **CP-SandC**

Wind, sink to rest in the heather. Emily Brontë. **CP-BronE**

Wind slams across the tops. Heptonstall Cemetery. Ted Hughes. **SP-HughT**

Wind Sleepers, The. Hilda Doolittle. **CP-DoolH**

Wind Song. Carl Sandburg. **CP-SandC**

Wind sounds only in opposing straits, The. Finite and Infinite. Elizabeth Barrett Browning. **CP-BroEB**

Wind Sprang Up at Four o'Clock, The. Thomas Stearns Eliot. **CP-ElioT**

Wind stops, the wind begins, The. Sand Scribblings. Carl Sandburg. **CP-SandC**

Wind-Struck Music, The. Robinson Jeffers. **CP-JefR2**

Wind sways the pines, A. Dirge in Woods. George Meredith. **CP-MerG1**

Wind—tapped like a tired Man, The. Emily Dickinson. **CP-DickE**

Wind tears up the sun, The. Poem. James Schuyler. **CP-SchuJ**

Wind, that beats the mountain, blows, The. To J. S. [James Spedding]. Tennyson. **CP-TennA**

Wind that blew the clouds away so silently, The. Frost. Wystan Hugh Auden. **CP-AudWJ**

Wind that blows these words to you, The. Beyond Howth Head. Derek Mahon. **SP-MahoD**

Wind, that passes by so fleet, The. Gerard Manley Hopkins. *Fr.* Fragments. **CP-HopkG**

Wind that rose, A. Emily Dickinson. **CP-DickE**

Wind, the Rascal, The. David Herbert Lawrence. **CP-LawrD**

Wind, the season-climate mixer. Clear and Colder. Robert Frost. **CP-FrosR**

Wind thrashes the maple seed-pods, The. John Ashbery. **SP-AshbJ** *Fr.* The Skaters.

Wind told the little leaves to hurry, The. The Chase. Paul Laurence Dunbar. **CP-DunbP**

Wind took off with the sunset, The. The Egg-Shell. Rudyard Kipling. **CP-KiplR**

Wind took up the Northern Things, The. Emily Dickinson. **CP-DickE**

Wind, transparent, cannot displace, The. Antigua. John Updike. **CP-UpdiJ**

Wind-wafted from the sunset, o'er the swell. The Isle's Enchantress. Robert Browning. **CP-BroR2**

Wind warningly tugged, The. At the Consecration. Steve Griffiths. *Fr.* Hymns and Backward Glances. **SP-GrifS**

Wind was curled in a ball asleep in a tree, The. North. Louis MacNeice. *Fr.* Sleeping Winds. **CP-MacNL**

Wind was rough which tore, The. Emily Brontë. **CP-BronE**

Wind was slumped on a charpoy in the bazaar, The. East. Louis MacNeice. *Fr.* Sleeping Winds. **CP-MacNL**

Wind, wave, and bark, bear Euthukles and me. Aristophanes' Apology. Robert Browning. **CP-BroR2**

Wind wore me north, London I left a year, The. London. Randall Jarrell. **CP-JarrR**

Wind World. William Stafford. **SP-StafW**

Wind your thread. The Rocking Woman. William Carlos Williams. **CP-WilW2**

Windflower. Louis Zukofsky. **CP-ZukLS**

Windflower Leaf. Carl Sandburg. **CP-SandC**

Windhover, The. Gerard Manley Hopkins. **CP-HopkG**

Winding grain. Old Rotting Tree Trunk Down. Gary Snyder. **CP-SnydG**

Winding Up. Derek Walcott. **CP-WalcD**

Winding way the serpent takes, The. Norembega. John Greenleaf Whittier. **CP-WhitJ**

Windmills, The. John Gould Fletcher. *Fr.* Arizona Poems. **SP-FletJ**

Windmills, like great sunflowers of steel, The. The Windmills. John Gould Fletcher. *Fr.* Arizona Poems. **SP-FletJ**

Window, The. Leonard Cohen. **CP-CoheL**

Window, The. Leonard Cohen. **CP-CoheL**

Window, The. Robert Creeley. **CP-CreeR**

Window, The. Robert Creeley. **CP-CreeR**

Window, The. Walter de la Mare. **CP-DeLaW**

Window, The. Stephen Dobyns. **SP-DobyS**

Window, A. Denise Levertov. **CP-LeveD**

Window. Robert Lowell. **SP-LoweR**

Window, The. Louis MacNeice. **CP-MacNL**

"How, yes how? In this mirrored maze—."

"How, yes how! To achieve in a world of flux and bonfires."

"Neck of an hour-glass on its side—."

Window. Carl Sandburg. **CP-SandC**

Window / the icicle / the gleaming moon, The. Hayden Carruth. *Fr.* North Winter. **CP-CarHL**

Window, a wide pane in the bare, The. Waking in a Newly Built House. Thom Gunn. **CP-GunnT**

Window bars are spider webs, The. Hall Five. Hayden Carruth. **CP-CarHS** *Fr.* The Bloomingdale Papers.

Window Cleaner to Nude Manikin. Marsden Hartley. **CP-HartM**

Window grows fragile, The. Wendell Berry. *Fr.* Window Poems. **CP-BerrW**

Window has forty, The. Wendell Berry. *Fr.* Window Poems. **CP-BerrW**

Window here is hung in the west wall, The. Evening: A Studio in Rome. Miller Williams. **SP-WillM**

Window in Cherry Valley, A. Jim Carroll. **SP-CarrJ**

Window of the Woman Burning, The. Marge Piercy. **SP-PierM**

Window Pane, The. Robert Ranke Graves. **CP-GravR**

Window Poems. Wendell Berry. **CP-BerrW**

"Bloodroot is white, The."

"Country where he lives, The."

"Foliage has dropped, The."

"For a night and a day."

"He has known a tunnel."

"He stood on the ground."

"His love returns / and walks among the trees."

"His mind gone from the window."

"How fine / to have a long-legged house."

"In the early morning dark."

"In the heron's eye."

"Longest night is past, The."

"Look in / and see him looking out."

"Now that April with sweet rain."

"Outside the window."

"Peace. May he waken."

"Rising, the river."

"River is rising, The."

"Sometimes he thinks the earth."

"Still sleeping, he heard."

"Sycamore gathers / out of the sky, white, The."

"There is a sort of vertical."

"This is the wind's eye."

"Warm day in December, A."

"Window grows fragile, The."

"Window has forty, The."

"Window. Window. / The wind's eye."

Window screen, The. Sunday Rain. John Updike. **CP-UpdiJ**

Window showed a willow in the west, The. Elegy in a Firelit Room. James Wright. **CP-WrigJ**

Window Sill, The. Robert Ranke Graves. **CP-GravR**

Window was made of ice with bears lumbering across it, The. Bad Dream. Louis MacNeice. **CP-MacNL**

Window Washer. Charles Simic. **SP-SimiC**

Window Washer—Avenue C. Marsden Hartley. **CP-HartM**

Window. Window. / The wind's eye. Wendell Berry. *Fr.* Window Poems. **CP-BerrW**

. . . window. . . winter. . . . Poem. Delmore Schwartz. **SP-SchwD**

Windowglass, warmed plush, a sneeze. Flèche d'Or. James Merrill. **SP-MerrJ**

Windows, The. George Herbert. **CP-HerbG**

Windows. Randall Jarrell. **CP-JarrR; SP-JarrR**

Windows flash in Taunton town, The. Monmouth. George Meredith. **CP-MerG2**

Windows from a Machine Shop. Malcolm Lowry. **CP-LowrM**

Windows go orange in the slowly. Edward Estlin Cummings. **CP-CummE**

Windows reflect the fuscous clouds. Serenade. John Yau. **SP-YauJo**

Windows wide through day and night, The. Last Days at Teddington. Thom Gunn. **CP-GunnT**

Windowscape. Louis MacNeice. **CP-MacNL**

Winds. Wystan Hugh Auden. *Fr.* Bucolics. **CP-AudeW**

Winds. Kathleen Jessie Raine. **SP-RainK**

Winds / which blew my daughter, The. Charles Olson. **CP-OlsoC**

Winds, The. William Carlos Williams. **CP-WilW1** *Fr.* A Folded Skyscraper.

Wind's an old man, The. In an Old Apple Orchard. Ted Kooser. **SP-KoosT**

Winds are cold, the days are dark, The. Ralph Waldo Emerson. **CP-EmerR**

Winds blow the open grasy places bleak. Atmosphere. Robert Frost. **CP-FrosR**

Winds from Cook's Strait cannot blow. Trevenen. Donald Davie. **CP-DavDo**

Winds of Another Sphere. Edwin Rolfe. **CP-RolfE**

Winds of hatred blow, The. Lull. Theodore Roethke. **CP-RoetT**

Winds of Orisha, The. Audre Lorde. **SP-LordA**

Winds of the World, give answer! They are whimpering to and fro. The English Flag. Rudyard Kipling. **CP-KiplR**

Winds on the stems make them creak like manmade things. Stalin. Robert Lowell. **SP-LoweR**

Winds out of the west land blow, The. Alfred Edward Housman. **CP-HousA**

Wind's Prophecy, The. Thomas Hardy. **CP-HardT**

Winds sing to us where we lie, The. Let Them Rejoice in Their Beds. Christina Georgina Rossetti. **CP-RosC3**

Winds; words of the wind; rumor of great walls pierced. Hayden Carruth. **SM** *Fr.* The Asylum. **CP-CarHL**

Windshield, The. Charles Tomlinson. **CP-TomlC**

Windsor-Forest [or Windsor Forest]. Alexander Pope. **CP-PopeA**

"Groves of Eden, vanished now so long, The." **OAEL-1**

"Here hills and vales, the woodland and the plain." **ECEV**

"Here too, 'tis sung, of old Diana stray'd." **OXAEP-1**

Hunt, The. **NIP**

Progress. **ECEV**

"See! from the brake the whirring Pheasant springs." **ECEV; FHYEP; FM; PoEL-3**

(Hunting and Fishing.) **ECEV**

"Thy forests, Windsor! and thy green retreats." **NOEC; OXAEP-1**

"When milder autumn summer's heat succeeds." **PBBP; SeCePo**

(Field Sports.) **SeCePo**

Windsor Poetics. Byron. **CP-Byron**

Windsor Prophecy, The. Jonathan Swift. **CP-SwifJ**

Windy City, The. Carl Sandburg. **CP-SandC**

Windy Day in Summer, A. Gerard Manley Hopkins. **CP-HopkG**

Windy evening of autumn. On the Banks of the Sumida. John Gould Fletcher. **SP-FletJ**

Windy gentlement wreathing a long verandah. Prometheus in Straits. John Crowe Ransom. **SP-RansJ**

Windy Haymaking. George Meredith. **CP-MerG2**

Windy hunks of light, not prop wash, bend. Tretitoli, Where the Bomb Group Was. Richard Hugo. **CP-HugoR**

Windy Night. Charles Bukowski. **SP-BukC3**

Windy Nights. Robert Louis Stevenson. **CP-StevR**

Windy shell singing upon the shore, A. To What Purpose Is This Waste? Christina Georgina Rossetti. **CP-RosC3**

Wine and a bobwhite / And the afternoon sun. O Sweet Irrational Worship. Thomas Merton. **CP-MertT; SP-MertT**

Wine and oil gleaming within their heads. Double Ode. Muriel Rukeyser. **CP-RukeM**

Wine Bowl. Hilda Doolittle. **CP-DoolH**

Wine comes in at the mouth. A Drinking Song. William Butler Yeats. **CP-YeatW**

Wine from These Grapes. Edna St. Vincent Millay. **CP-MillE**

Wine-maiden / Of the jazz-tuned night. Midnight Dancer. Langston Hughes. **SP-HughL**

Wine makes the dirtiest hovel into. The Poison. James Liddy. **CP-LiddJ**

Wine Menagerie, The. Hart Crane. **CP-CranH**

Wine-O. Langston Hughes. **SP-HughL**

Wine of Cyprus. Elizabeth Barrett Browning. **CP-BroEB**

Wine of Lovers. James Liddy. **CP-LiddJ**

Wine of the grey sky. Idyl. William Carlos Williams. **CP-WilW1**

Wine-Press of Los, The. William Blake. *See* This wine-press is call'd war on earth.

Wine resembles the Lord Jesus. Hafiz, *tr. by* Ralph Waldo Emerson. **CP-EmerR** *Fr.* Odes.

Wing. Patti Smith. **SP-SmitP**

Wing / torn out of stone. Emblem. Roy Fisher. **SP-FishR**

Wing and Claw. Jim Carroll. **SP-CarrJ**

Wing fin and wrist bend wishfully. The Compleat Anglers. Isabella Gardner. **CP-GardI**

Wing Wong,uninterred at twice. Edward Estlin Cummings. **CP-CummE**

Wingaersheek Beach. Marsden Hartley. **CP-HartM**

Wingèd Goddess—clothed in vesture wrought, A. After Visiting the Field of Waterloo. William Wordsworth. *Fr.* Memorials of a Tour of the Continent; 1820. **CP-WorW2**

Winged Hats, The. Rudyard Kipling. *Fr.* Puck of Pook's Hill.
    Pict Song, A. **CP-KiplR**

Winged Heart, The. Robert Ranke Graves. **CP-GravR**

Winged Rock. Robinson Jeffers. **CP-JefR2**

Wingèd shadow with the self within, The. Plane. Howard Nemerov. **CP-NemeH**

Winged spark doth soar about, A. Emily Dickinson. **CP-DickE**

Wingfoot Lake. Rita Dove. **SP-DoveR**

Wings. Bible, *O.T.* *See* Psalm 55: "Give ear to my prayer, O God."

Wings, The. Denise Levertov. **CP-LeveD**

Wings filmed, the threads of knowledge thicken. The Jam Trap. Charles Tomlinson. **CP-TomlC**

Wings lacking a trunk, The. The Idea of Flying. Donald Hall. **CP-HallD**

Wings Lifted over the Black Pit. Allen Ginsberg. **CP-GinsA**

Wings of Time are black and white, The. Compensation. Ralph Waldo Emerson. **CP-EmerR**

Wings outstretched, a horned owl. Signatures. Daniel Gerard Hoffman. **SP-HoffD**

Wings rise, the shrubs flutter. He Bathes in the Morning. Frank Templeton Prince. *Fr.* Chaka. **CP-PrinF**

Wingtip. Carl Sandburg. **CP-SandC**

Winked too much and were afraid of snakes. The Monkeys. Marianne Craig Moore. **CP-MoorM**

Winking drop on the lens. Roy Fisher. **SP-FishR** *Fr.* The Open Poem and the Closed Poem.

Winnah, The! pure as snow. The Aftermath. William Carlos Williams. **CP-WilW2**

Winners, The. Rudyard Kipling. **CP-KiplR** *Fr.* The Story of the Gadsbys.

Winnie Mandela We Love You. Alice Walker. **CP-WalkA**

Wino. Ted Hughes. *Fr.* Boom. **SP-HughT**

Winsome Woman, A. Thomas Hardy. **CP-HardT**

Wintah, summah, snow er shine. Song. Paul Laurence Dunbar. **CP-DunbP**

Wintah time hit comin'. The Plantation Child's Lullaby. Paul Laurence Dunbar. **CP-DunbP**

Winter,— / Summer's rainbow-mantle of colour fades. From the Japanese, II. John Gould Fletcher. **SP-FletJ**

Winter. Charles Bukowski. **SP-BukC1**

Winter, / damn, / again. Charles Kenneth Williams. **CP-WillC**

Winter. ("Green Mistletoe!"). Walter de la Mare. **CP-DeLaW**

Winter. ("Clouded with Snow"). Walter de la Mare. **CP-DeLaW**

Winter / form across the road tumult of a schoolyard. Chuck Miller. **SP-MillC**

Winter. Philip Larkin. **CP-LarkP**

Winter. Pablo Neruda, *tr. fr. Spanish by* Ben Belitt. **SP-NeruP**

Winter. Mary Oliver. **SP-OlivM**

Winter. Adrienne Rich. **CP-RicAE**

Winter. Richard Shelton. **SP-ShelR**

Winter. Edmund Spenser. **GN** *Fr.* The Faerie Queene. **CP-Spens**

Winter. Robert Louis Stevenson. **CP-StevR**

Winter. James Thomson. *Fr.* The Seasons. **CP-ThomJ**
    "As thus the snows arise, and foul and fierce." **ECEV; SeCePo**
    (Winter Tragedy, A.) **ECEV**
    "Drooping, the labourer-ox." **FM**
    "Fowls of heaven, The." **PBBP**
    "Keener tempests come, The: and fuming dun." **EBEV; EnRP; NoP**
    "Now, when the cheerless empire of the sky." **OxBA**
    "See, Winter comes, to rule the varied year." **NOEC; TEP**
    "'Tis done! Dread Winter spreads his latest glooms." **OxAEP-1**
    "What art thou, frost? and whence are thy keen stores." **OxBS**
    "When from the pallid sky the sun descends." **OAEL-1; OxBS**
    Winter Night, A. **NOBE**

Winter. Charles Tomlinson. **CP-TomlC**

Winter. William Carlos Williams. **CP-WilW1**

Winter, a Dirge. Robert Burns. **CP-BurnR**

Winter After, The. Charles Olson. **CP-OlsoC**

Winter Afternoon. Wystan Hugh Auden. **CP-AudWJ**

Winter Afternoon. Thomas Merton. **CP-MertT**

Winter Afternoon. Grace Paley. **CP-PaleG**

Winter at the Inn. Kenneth Patchen. **CP-PatcK**

Winter Bells. Wallace Stevens. **CP-StevW**

Winter birds have come, The. An Elm Tree. William DeWitt Snodgrass. **SP-SnodW**

Winter Carol. May Sarton. **SP-SartM**

Winter comes but once a year but it lasts for most of it. Summergreen for President. Ogden Nash. **CP-NashO**

Winter Comes to a Lot of Places in August. Charles Bukowski. **SP-BukC2**

Winter crisp and the brittleness of snow. Words for Love. Ted Berrigan. **SP-BerrT**

Winter Daffodils. Phoebe Hesketh. **SP-HeskP**

Winter Dawn. David Herbert Lawrence. **CP-LawrD**

Winter Dawn. Chuck Miller. **SP-MillC**

Winter Day. John Hewitt. **CP-HewiJ**

Winter Day. John Hewitt. **CP-HewiJ**

Winter Day (Coal Country). Louise McNeill. **SP-McNeL**

Winter Day in Ohio, A. James Wright. **CP-WrigJ**

Winter deepening, the hay all in, The. Sonnet. Richard Wilbur. **CP-WilbR**

Winter Dusk. Walter de la Mare. **CP-DeLaW**

Winter Eden, A. Robert Frost. **CP-FrosR**

Winter Encounters. Charles Tomlinson. **CP-TomlC**

Winter Evening. John Clare. **SP-ClarJ**

Winter Evening, The. William Cowper. *Fr.* The Task. **CP-CowpW**
    Arrival of the Mail. **ECEV**
    (Post-Boy, The.) **FiP**
    "Come evening once again, season of peace." **NAEL-1**
    "Just when our drawing-rooms begin to blaze." **NOEC**
    Reading the Newspaper. **ECEV**
    (Hissing Urn, The.) **FaBoDD**
    "Thee too, enamoured of the life I loved." **EPCY**

Winter evening settles down, The. Thomas Stearns Eliot. **MoShBr; OPOU** *Fr.* Preludes (I–IV). **CP-ElioT**

Winter Exercise. Howard Nemerov. **CP-NemeH**

Winter Fable, A. Kay Boyle. **CP-BoylK**

Winter Fires. David St. John. **SP-StJoD**

Winter garden in an alder swamp, A. A Winter Eden. Robert Frost. **CP-FrosR**

Winter Gold. Carl Sandburg. **CP-SandC**

Winter had spoiled his Georgia. Uncle Will, the Gardener. Stephen Berg. **SP-BergS**

Winter has a joy for me. I Will Praise the Lord at All Times. William Cowper. *Fr.* Olney Hymns. **CP-CowpW**

Winter has spent this snow. M.B. William Carlos Williams. **CP-WilW1**

Winter has stiffened the ground, the birds are gone. Mona Van Duyn. *Fr.* Two Poems for Sub-Zero Times. **SP-VanDM**

Winter Heavens. George Meredith. **CP-MerG1**

Winter in Durnover Field. Thomas Hardy. **CP-HardT**

Winter in Muscovy. Lewis Turco. **SP-TurcL**

Winter in the Boulevard. David Herbert Lawrence. **CP-LawrD**

Winter in the Country. Mary Oliver. **SP-OlivM**

Winter in the country, Southampton, pale horse. Frank O'Hara. Ted Berrigan. **SP-BerrT**

Winter Is Another Country. Archibald MacLeish. **CP-MacLA**

Winter is cold-hearted. Summer. Christina Georgina Rossetti. **CP-RosC1**

Winter is fallen early. The Children of Stare. Walter de la Mare. **CP-DeLaW**

Winter is for Eskimos a castle of content. The Man of Autumn. Richard Eberhart. *Fr.* The Seasons. **CP-EberR**

Winter is good—his Hoar Delights. Emily Dickinson. **CP-DickE**

Winter is long in this climate. March. William Carlos Williams. **CP-WilW1**

Winter is white on turf and tree. The Seasons of Her Year. Thomas Hardy. **CP-HardT**

Winter It Is Past, The. Robert Burns. **CP-BurnR**

Winter Kill. Richard Eberhart. **CP-EberR**

Winter Lady. Leonard Cohen. **CP-CoheL**

Winter landscape hangs in balance now, The. Prologue to Spring. Sylvia Plath. **CP-PlatS**

Winter Landscape Near Ely, A. Donald Davie. **CP-DavDo**

Winter Landscape, with Rooks. Sylvia Plath. **CP-PlatS**

Winter Landscapes. Donald Davie. **CP-DavDo**

Winter Leaves. Al Young. **CP-YounA**

Winter Light, A. John Haines. **SP-HainJ**

Winter Lightning, The. Howard Nemerov. **CP-NemeH**

Winter-Lull. David Herbert Lawrence. **CP-LawrD**

Winter Mask. Allen Tate. **CP-TateA**

Winter Milk. Carl Sandburg. **CP-SandC**

Winter Moon. Langston Hughes. **SP-HughL**

Winter moon / You have sailed into the morning with me. Moon in the morning. Jenny Joseph. *Fr.* Life and Turgid Times of A. Citizen. **SP-JoseJ**

Winter Morning. Louise Glück. **SP-GlücL**

Winter morning, and the sea, A. The Rain Glass. John Haines. **SP-HainJ**

Winter Morning of the Village. Leonard Nathan. **SP-NathL**

Winter Morning Walk, The. William Cowper. *Fr.* The Task. **CP-CowpW**

"'Tis morning' and the sun with ruddy orb." LAuP; NOEC; PoEL-3 (Frosty Morning, A.) NOEC

"Whose freedom is by suff'rance, and at will." **EnRP**

Winter: My Secret. Christina Georgina Rossetti. **CP-RosC1**

Winter News. John Haines. **SP-HainJ**

Winter Night, A. Robert Burns. **CP-BurnR**

Winter Night. Edna St. Vincent Millay. **CP-MillE**

Winter Night. Charles Simic. **SP-SimiC**

Winter Night, The. Charlotte Smith. **CP-SmitC**

Winter Night, A. James Thomson. NOBE *Fr.* Winter. *Fr.* The Seasons. **CP-ThomJ**

Winter Night, A. Georg Trakl, *tr. fr. German by* James Wright. **CP-WrigJ**

Winter Night. John Greenleaf Whittier. TrGrPo *Fr.* Snow-Bound [*or* Snow-Bound; a Winter Idyl]. **CP-WhitJ**

Winter Night in Woodland. Thomas Hardy. **CP-HardT**

Winter-night now well-nigh worn away, The. The Salad. William Cowper, *ad. fr. Virgil's tr. of Parthenius.* **CP-CowpW**

Winter Night Poem for Mary. Wendell Berry. **CP-BerrW**

Winter night requires our constant attention, The. The Vision of the Shepherds. Wystan Hugh Auden. *Fr.* For the Time Being; a Christmas Oratorio. **CP-AudeW**

Winter Nightfall. Wendell Berry. **CP-BerrW**

Winter nights / old age slumber. Leonardo. Anne Waldman. **SP-WaldA**

Winter Nocturne. Philip Larkin. **CP-LarkP**

Winter Nosegay, The. William Cowper. **CP-CowpW**

Winter Ocean. John Updike. **CP-UpdiJ**

Winter Ode. Diane Wakoski. **SP-WakoD**

Winter owl banked just in time to pass, The. Questioning Faces. Robert Frost. **CP-FrosR**

Winter Oysters. Brendan Galvin. **SP-GalvB**

Winter Palace, The. Philip Larkin. **CP-LarkP**

Winter Paradise. Kathleen Jessie Raine. **SP-RainK**

Winter Park. John Hewitt. **CP-HewiJ**

Winter-Piece. Charles Tomlinson. **CP-TomlC**

Winter-Piece to a Friend Away, A. John Berryman. **CP-BerrJ**

Winter Ploughing. William Everson. **SP-EverW**

Winter Poem. Robert Bly. **SP-BlyR**

Winter Poem. Frederick Morgan. **SP-MorgF**

Winter Poem. Kenneth Patchen. **CP-PatcK**

Winter Poem for Tony Weinburger Written on the Occasion of Feeling Very Happy, A. Diane Wakoski. **SP-WakoD**

Winter Quiet. William Carlos Williams. **CP-WilW1**

Winter Rain, The. Wendell Berry. **CP-BerrW**

Winter Rain. Christina Georgina Rossetti. **CP-RosC1**

Winter Remembered. John Crowe Ransom. **SP-RansJ**

Winter Roads. Thomas McGrath. **SP-McGrT**

Winter Roses. John Greenleaf Whittier. **CP-WhitJ**

Winter Runner, The. Brendan Galvin. **SP-GalvB**

Winter Sanctuaries. Archie Randolph Ammons. **SP-AmmoA**

Winter Scene. Archie Randolph Ammons. **SP-AmmoA**

Winter Seascape. Sir John Betjeman. **CP-BetjJ**

Winter Ship, A. Sylvia Plath. **CP-PlatS**

Winter Sky, A. Galway Kinnell. **SP-KinnG**

Winter Solstice. Charles Olson. **CP-OlsoC**

Winter Solstice. Kathleen Jessie Raine. **SP-RainK**

Winter Solstice scarce is past, The. Ode to the Missel Thrush. Charlotte Smith. **CP-SmitC**

Winter-Song. Paul Laurence Dunbar. **CP-DunbP**

Winter Song. Wilfred Owen. **CP-OwenW**

Winter Spring. Richard Wilbur. **CP-WilbR**

Winter Sun. David St. John. *Fr.* To Pasolini. **SP-StJoD**

Winter Sunset. William Carlos Williams. **CP-WilW1**

Winter Swan. Louise Bogan. **CP-BogaL**

Winter Talent, A. Donald Davie. **CP-DavDo**

Winter, that coils in the thickets now. Deciduous Branch. Stanley Jasspon Kunitz. **CP-KuniS**

Winter, that is a fireless room. Girl's Song. Louise Bogan. **CP-BogaL**

Winter, the Fourth Pastoral, or Daphne. Alexander Pope. *Fr.* Pastorals. **CP-PopeA**

Winter Time [*or* Winter-Time]. Robert Louis Stevenson. **CP-StevR**

Winter to Spring: the west wind melts the frozen rancour. Solvitur Acris Hiems. Horace. *Fr.* Three Odes of Horace. **CP-MacNL**

Winter Tragedy, A. James Thomson. *See* As thus the snows arise, and foul and fierce.

Winter Trees. Sylvia Plath. **CP-PlatS**

Winter Trees. William Carlos Williams. **CP-WilW1**

Winter Trout. James Dickey. **CP-DickJ**

Winter Tuesday, the city pouring fire, A. Coming Home, *Detroit,* 1968. Philip Levine. **SP-LeviP**

Winter twilight. She comes out of the lab-. Frame. Adrienne Rich. **SP-RicA2**

Winter under cultivation. Emily Dickinson. **CP-DickE**

Winter Walk at Noon, The. William Cowper. *Fr.* The Task. **CP-CowpW**

"Groans of nature in this nether world, The." NoP

"Lord of all, himself through all diffused, The." OAEL-1

"Night was winter in his roughest mood, The." EnRP; FHYEP; TEP

"No noise is here, or none that hinders thought." PBBP

Winter Weather. Carl Sandburg. **CP-SandC**

Winter will bar the swimmer soon. Swimming Chenango Lake. Charles Tomlinson. **CP-TomlC**

Winter will be feasts and fires in the shut houses. Fall in Corrales. Richard Wilbur. **CP-WilbR**

Winter wind is loud and wild, The. I.M. to I.G. Emily Brontë. **CP-BronE**

Winter winter winter. Winter Ode. Diane Wakoski. **SP-WakoD**

Winter with the Gulf Stream. Gerard Manley Hopkins. **CP-HopkG**

Winter Words. Philip Levine. **SP-LeviP**

Wintering. Sylvia Plath. **CP-PlatS**

Winterlong, off La Manche, wind leaning. Gray stones of the gray. Flaubert in Egypt. Robert Penn Warren. **SP-WarrR**

Winterlude. "Bob Dylan." **CP-DylaB**

Winter's Age. Jim Carroll. **SP-CarrJ**

Winter's Approach. Paul Laurence Dunbar. **CP-DunbP**

Winters are so short, The. Emily Dickinson. **CP-DickE**

Winters close, springs open, no child stirs, The. John Berryman. NAAL-2; NAs *Fr.* Homage to Mistress Bradstreet. **CP-BerrJ**

Winter's Day, A. Paul Laurence Dunbar. **CP-DunbP**

Winter's Evening, A. William Wordsworth. **CP-WorW1**

Winter's Ghost Plagues Them. Edwin Rolfe. **CP-RolfE**

Winters know / Easily to shed the snow. Nature 1. Ralph Waldo Emerson. **CP-EmerR**

Winter's latest snowflake is the snowdrop flower. 1886, St. Valentine's Day. Christina Georgina Rossetti. **CP-RosC3**

Winter's Night, The. Thomas Merton. **CP-MertT; SP-MertT**

Winter's Tale, The, *after Henrikas Radauskas.* Randall Jarrell. **CP-JarrR**

Winter's Tale, The. Randall Jarrell. **CP-JarrR**

Winter's Tale, A. David Herbert Lawrence. **CP-LawrD**

Winter's Tale, A. Sylvia Plath. **CP-PlatS**

Winter's Tale, A. Dylan Thomas. **CP-ThomD**

Winter's Tale, by a Wife, A. Mona Van Duyn. **SP-VanDM**

Winter's tale is told in, A. Hayden Carruth. *Fr.* North Winter. **CP-CarHL**

Winter's Talents. Donald Davie. **CP-DavDo**

Winter's wake: week after week the sopping northwesters. Reaper. William Everson. **SP-EverW**

Winter's Walk, The. Samuel Johnson. **CP-JohnS**

Wintertime nighs. Thomas Hardy. NoAM; OAEL-2; SCGP *Fr.* In Tenebris. **CP-HardT**

Wintertime nighs. In Tenebris. Thomas Hardy. **CP-HardT**

Winthrop Mackworth Redivivus. Sir John Betjeman. **CP-BetjJ**

Wintry boughs against a wintry sky; / Yet the sky is partly blue. There Is a Budding Morrow in Midnight. Christina Georgina Rossetti. **CP-RosC2**

Wintry haw is burning out of season, The. The Haw Lantern. Seamus Heaney. **SP-HeanS**

Wintry Sonnet, A. Christina Georgina Rossetti. **CP-RosC2**

Wintry West extends his blast, The. Winter, a Dirge. Robert Burns. **CP-BurnR**

Wiper, The. Louis MacNeice. **CP-MacNL**

Wire. Louis Zukofsky. **CP-ZukLS**

Wire Brier. Louise McNeill. **SP-McNeL**

Wire cage flues / on / the roofs. Wire. Louis Zukofsky. **CP-ZukLS**

Wire fence is tall, The. The Penal Farm. Etheridge Knight. *Fr.* Indiana Haiku—2. **SP-KnigE**

Wired up at the ankles and one wrist. Heart Test with an Echo Chamber. Margaret Atwood. **SP-AtwM2**

Wires. Philip Larkin. **CP-LarkP**

Wiring. Archie Randolph Ammons. **SP-AmmoA**

Wisdom. William Cowper. ChIV-1 *Fr.* Olney Hymns. **CP-CowpW**

Wisdom. Robert Creeley. **CP-CreeR**

Wisdom. Thomas Merton. **CP-MertT; SP-MertT**

Wisdom. William Butler Yeats. **CP-YeatW**

Wisdom and Science—honor'd Powers! Robert Burns. *Fr.* Annotations in Verse. **CP-BurnR**

Wisdom and Spirit of the universe! Influence of Natural Objects [in Calling Forth and Strengthening the Imagination in Boyhood and Early Youth]. William Wordsworth. **AWP; CP-WorW1; OBRV** *Fr.* Introduction—Childhood and School-Time. **EnRP; FHYEP** *Fr.* The Prelude; Growth of a Poet's Mind [1850 vers.]. **CP-WorW3**

Wisdom and Spirit of the universe! William Wordsworth. **NOBE** *Fr.* Introduction—Childhood and School-Time. *Fr.* The Prelude; Growth of a Poet's Mind [1805 vers.]. **CP-WorW3**

Wisdom Cometh with the Years. Countee Cullen. **CP-CullC**

Wisdom is one thing: it is to know the thought by which all things are steered through all things. Thomas Merton. *Fr.* The Legacy of Herakleitos. **CP-MertT**

Wisdom, Madam, of your private life, The. An Epigram. To the Honoured——, Countess of——. Ben Jonson. **CP-JonsB**

Wisdom of Eld, The. George Meredith. **CP-MerG1**

Wisdom of Insecurity, The. Richard Eberhart. **CP-EberR**

Wisdom of the Talmud. Leonard Nathan. **SP-NathL**

Wisdom Unapplied. Elizabeth Barrett Browning. **CP-BroEB**

Wise, The. Countee Cullen. **CP-CullC**

Wise, The. William Everson. **SP-EverW** *Fr.* Triptych for the Living.

Wise, and many-headed bench, that sits, The. To the Worthy Author M[r] John Fletcher. Ben Jonson. **CP-JonsB**

Wise are ye, O ancient woods! Woods. Ralph Waldo Emerson. **CP-EmerR**

Wise Brothers, The. Edwin Arlington Robinson. **CP-RobiE**

Wise child is born, The. Hayden Carruth. **CP-CarHS** *Fr.* The Clay Hill Anthology.

Wise do send their hearts before them to, The. Christina Georgina Rossetti. *Fr.* Later Life: A Double Sonnet of Sonnets. **CP-RosC2**

Wise emblem of our politic[k] world. The Snail [*or* Snayl]. Richard Lovelace. **CP-LoveR**

Wise house, and / man to know it. For a Bus on Its Side and the Man Inside It. Robert Creeley. **CP-CreeR**

Wise little twilight disappearing in the sky. Third Letter to Jimin in Manchuria. James Liddy. **CP-LiddJ**

WISE•MAN•ALWAYS•KNOWS•HE•MAY, A. HEINRICH•HIMMLER•FORMER•REICHSFUEHRER•SS—29•APRIL•1945•. William DeWitt Snodgrass. **SP-SnodW**

Wise Men in Their Bad Hours. Robinson Jeffers. **CP-JefR1**

Wise men patience never want. Thomas Campion. **CP-CampT**

Wise pretend to make it clear, The. The Answer to Dr. Delany. Jonathan Swift. **CP-SwifJ**

Wise Rochefoucauld a maxim writ. The Life and Genuine Character of Dr Swift. Jonathan Swift. **CP-SwifJ**

Wise Rochefoucauld a maxim writ. *From* The Life and Character of Dean Swift. Jonathan Swift. **NOBL** *Fr.* The Life and Genuine Character of Dr Swift. **CP-SwifJ**

Wiseman wary lives, yet most secure, A. Epigramme. Thomas Campion. *Fr.* Observations in the Art of English Poesie. **CP-CampT**

Wisest man is an ape compared to God. Thomas Merton. *Fr.* The Legacy of Herakleitos. **CP-MertT**

Wisest of sparrows that sparrow which sitteth alone. Christina Georgina Rossetti. **CP-RosC2**

(Yea, the Sparrow Hath Found Her an House.) **CP-RosC2**

Wisest scholar of the wight most wise, The. Sonnet 25. Sir Philip Sidney. **NoP; OAEL-1** *Fr.* Astrophil and Stella. **SP-SidnP**

Wish, A. Samuel Taylor Coleridge. **CP-ColeS**

Wish, A. Robert Creeley. **CP-CreeR**

Wish. Roy Fisher. **SP-FishR**

Wish, A. Louis Zukofsky. *Fr.* Songs of Degrees. **CP-ZukLS**

Wish for a Young Wife. Theodore Roethke. **CP-RoetT**

Wish for Dreamful Sleep, A. Samuel Taylor Coleridge. **CP-ColeS**

Wish for something moral like a wound, A. Something. Stephen Dunn. **SP-DunnS**

Wish for Unconsciousness, A. Thomas Hardy. **CP-HardT**

Wish: Metamorphosis to Heraldic Emblem. Margaret Atwood. **SP-AtwM1**

Wish of To-day, The. John Greenleaf Whittier. **CP-WhitJ**

Wish, that of the living whole, The. Tennyson. **EBVV; EBVVPR; EnVR; FHYEP; HAP; NoP; OAEL-2; OBNC; TOF** *Fr.* In Memoriam A. H. H. **CP-TennA**

Wish to Be Believed, The. Mona Van Duyn. **SP-VanDM**

Wish to Be Generous, The. Wendell Berry. **CP-BerrW**

Wish to Comply, A. Robert Frost. **CP-FrosR**

Wish we could talk today. Remembering Williams. Charles Tomlinson. **CP-TomlC**

Wishbone, The. Paul Muldoon. **SP-MuldP**

Wishes left on your lips. Wistful. Carl Sandburg. **CP-SandC**

Wishes on this child's mouth, The. Helga. Carl Sandburg. **CP-SandC**

Wishes: Sonnet. Christina Georgina Rossetti. **CP-RosC3**

Wishes. To His (Supposed) Mistresse. Richard Crashaw. **CP-CrasR** Specifications for a Perfect Lover. **CBCK**

Wishfully I look and languish. Robert Burns. *See* The Bonnie [*or* Bonny] Wee Thing.

Wishing Bridge, The. John Greenleaf Whittier. **CP-WhitJ**

Wishing-Caps, The. Rudyard Kipling. **CP-KiplR** *Fr.* Kim.

Wishing-Gate, The. William Wordsworth. **CP-WorW2**

Wishing-Gate Destroyed, The. William Wordsworth. **CP-WorW2**

Wishing He Had a Theory in Key West. Peter Meinke. **SP-MeinP** *Fr.* Lines from Key West.

Wishing Tree, The. Seamus Heaney. **SP-HeanS**

Wisp & meteor nightly falling. Ralph Waldo Emerson. **CP-EmerR**

Wistful. Carl Sandburg. **CP-SandC**

Wistful, / they speak of / satis- / faction, love. The People. Robert Creeley. **CP-CreeR**

Wistful Lady, The. Thomas Hardy. **CP-HardT**

Wit, The. Elizabeth Bishop. **CP-BishE**

Wit in a prologue poets justly may. Prologue. Sir John Suckling. *Fr.* The Goblins. **CP-SuckJ**

Wit in fools has something shocking. Long after Chamfort. Nicolas-Sébastien Roch Chamfort, *tr. fr. French by* Samuel Beckett. **CP-BeckS**

Wit Punisht, Prospers Most. Robert Herrick. **CP-HerrR**

Wit, weight, or wealth there was not. An Experience. Thomas Hardy. **CP-HardT**

Witch, The. John Hewitt. **CP-HewiJ**

Witch, The. William Butler Yeats. **CP-YeatW**

Witch Doctor. Robert Earl Hayden. **CP-HaydR**

Witch-elms that counterchange the floor. Tennyson. **EBVV; OBNC** *Fr.* In Memoriam A. H. H. **CP-TennA**

Witch I, The. David Herbert Lawrence. **CP-LawrD**

Witch II, The. David Herbert Lawrence. **CP-LawrD**

Witch of Atlas, The. Percy Bysshe Shelley. **CP-ShelP** "And whilst the outer lake beneath the lash." **PBBP**

Witch of Coös, The. Robert Frost. **InPS; LiTM; MeMAP; MoAB; MoP; NOBA; NoAM; PoE** *Fr.* Two Witches. **CP-FrosR**

Witch of Wenham, The. John Greenleaf Whittier. **CP-WhitJ**

Witch that came (the withered hag), The. Provide, Provide. Robert Frost. **CP-FrosR**

Witch Tree. Barton Sutter. **SP-SuttB**

Witch-Wife. Edna St. Vincent Millay. **CP-MillE**

Witch-woman, / tall, slender. Figure of the Witch. Erica Jong. **SP-JongE**

Witchcraft by a Picture. John Donne. **CP-DonnJ**

Witchcraft has not a Pedigree. Emily Dickinson. **CP-DickE**

Witchcraft was hung, in History. Emily Dickinson. **CP-DickE**

Witches. Ted Hughes. **SP-HughT**

Witches' Charms, The. Ben Jonson. *Fr.* The Masque of Queens. Charm[e]. **CP-JonsB**

Witches Waken the Natural World in Spring. James Wright. **CP-WrigJ**

Witch's Life, The. Anne Sexton. **CP-SextA**

With a Bouquet of Twelve Roses. Nicholas Vachel Lindsay. *Fr.* Poems Speaking of Buddha, Prince Siddartha. **CP-LindV**

With a Capital P. Louis Zukofsky. *Fr.* Michtam. **CP-ZukLS**

With a clatter, the sea pushes. Misrule, Towyn, 1990. Steve Griffiths. **SP-GrifS**

With a cold and wintry noon-light. At Washington. John Greenleaf Whittier. **CP-WhitJ**

With a dry eye, she. For Sappho, Back. Charles Olson. **CP-OlsoC; SP-OlsoC**

With a fair boy a Cryer we behold. Catullus, *tr. fr. Latin by* Richard Lovelace. **CP-LoveR**

With a Gift of Rings. Robert Ranke Graves. **CP-GravR**

With a glass of / boiled water. Deaths. Denise Levertov. **CP-LeveD**

With a glory of winter sunshine. The Poet and the Children. John Greenleaf Whittier. **CP-WhitJ**

With a Great Goodmorning Kiss and Luck and Love to Our Beloved Harteeste from All the Little Animals. Malcolm Lowry. **CP-LowrM**

With a Guitar, to Jane. Percy Bysshe Shelley. **CP-ShelP**

With a half-glance upon the sky. A Character. Tennyson. **CP-TennA**

With a lantern that wouldn't burn. The Draft Horse. Robert Frost. **CP-FrosR**

With a Little Book of Pottery. John Hewitt. **CP-HewiJ**

With a Little Help from My Friends. The Beatles. **CP-Beatl**

With a pale green curly. The Love of Lettuce. Marge Piercy. **SP-PierM**

With a pert moustache and a ready candid smile. The Mixer. Louis MacNeice. **CP-MacNL**

With a Photograph to Zell, Now Bound for Spain. Hart Crane. **CP-CranH**

With a Picture Sent to a Friend. Richard Crashaw. **CP-CrasR**

With a quick / jump he caught. Hello. Robert Creeley. **CP-CreeR**

With a Rose, to Brunhilde. Nicholas Vachel Lindsay. **CP-LindV**

With a Small Present. William Wordsworth. **CP-WorW2**

With a southwest wind blowing late August. The Wedding. Richard Eberhart. **CP-EberR**

With a sudden shock. Perceive. Gilbert Sorrentino. **SP-SorrG**

With a tiny bird whistle. An Evening with the Master. Charles Simic. **SP-SimiC**

With a Valentine (the 12 February). Louis Zukofsky. *Fr.* Songs of Degrees. **CP-ZukLS**

With a Valentine (the 14 February). Louis Zukofsky. *Fr.* Songs of Degrees. **CP-ZukLS**

With a Wave of Her Old Hand. Kathleen Jessie Raine. **SP-RainK**

With a "weed" among men or horses verily this is the best. Rudyard Kipling. *Fr.* Certain Maxims of Hafiz. **CP-KiplR**

With a whirl of thought oppressed. Jonathan Swift. **CP-SwifJ** (On the Day of Judgement.) **CP-SwifJ**

With a Wife. Gertrude Stein. **CP-SteiG**

With a withered bird hand. Old Lady in the Park. Marsden Hartley. **CP-HartM**

With Age Wisdom. Archibald MacLeish. **CP-MacLA**

With Akhmatova at the Black Gates. Stephen Berg. **SP-BergS**

With Alfred and St. Louis he doth win. The Emperor Frederick of Our Time. George Meredith. **CP-MerG1**

With all a woman's virtues but the pox. Alexander Pope. **OBSV** *Fr.* The First Satire of the Second Book of Horace [Imitated]. **CP-PopeA**

With all a woman's virtues but the pox. Alexander Pope. **OBSV** *Fr.* The Second Satire of the Second Book of Horace Imitated. **CP-PopeA**

With all its sinful doings, I must say. Italy. Byron. **NOBE; OBRV; PlP; SeCePo** *Fr.* Beppo; a Venetian Story. **CP-Byron**

With all my questions. The God-Monger. Anne Sexton. **CP-SextA**

With all the powres my poor heart hath. *ad. fr. the medieval* Rhythmus ad Sacram Eucharistiam. Richard Crashaw. **CP-CrasR**

With all these loads of injuries opprest. John Dryden. **EBEV** *Fr.* Absalom and Achitophel, Pt. I. **SP-DrydJ**

With all this clamour for progress. Homage to Clichés. Louis MacNeice. **CP-MacNL**

With all those I love. From a Long Way Out of Pah-Gatzin-Kay. Thomas McGrath. **SP-McGrT**

With All Thy Gifts. Walt Whitman. **CP-WhitW**

With an elaborate veil. Special Effects. Charles Henri Ford. **SP-FordC**

With Anna at Camaldoli. Richard Hugo. **CP-HugoR**

With Anne at the Peabody. Brendan Galvin. **SP-GalvB**

With Annie gone. For Anne. Leonard Cohen. **CP-CoheL**

With Antecedents. Walt Whitman. **CP-WhitW**

With anyone to death, comes so far short. Robert Frost. **OBF** *Fr.* Home Burial. **CP-FrosR** (Temperament.) **OBF**

With banners furled, and [or the] clarions mute. The Night-March. Herman Melville. **SP-MelvH**

With beams December planets dart. S.H. Ralph Waldo Emerson. *Fr.* Quatrains. **CP-EmerR**

With beasts and gods, above, the wall is bright. Children Selecting Books in a Library. Randall Jarrell. **CP-JarrR; SP-JarrR**

With beauty, with pleasure surrounded, to languish. Amatory Lines. Thomas Gray. **CP-GrayT**

With B.E.F. June 10. Dear Wife. The Letter. Wilfred Owen. **CP-OwenW**

With bells for hooves in sounding streets. Lawrence Ferlinghetti. **SP-FerlL**

With Bernard de Mandeville. Robert Browning. **CP-BroR2**

With big breasts. The Girl. William Carlos Williams. **CP-WilW1**

With blackest moss the flower-pots [or flowerpots]. Mariana. Tennyson. **CP-TennA**

With blameless carriage, I lived [or liv'd] here. An Epitaph upon a Sober Matron. Robert Herrick. **CP-HerrR**

With breathing as(faithfully)her lownecked. Liz. Edward Estlin Cummings. *Fr.* Five Americans. **CP-CummE**

With Bruce and Ronald bides the tale. Loch Coruisk. Sir Walter Scott. **SP-ScotW** *Fr.* The Lord of the Isles.

With Buck still tied to the log, on comes the light. Double Feature. Theodore Roethke. **CP-RoetT**

With careful steps to keep his balance up. Braggart. John Clare. **SP-ClarJ**

With caws and chirrupings, the woods. Duddingstone. Robert Louis Stevenson. **CP-StevR**

With Chance on first, and Evers on third. The Opening Game. Ernest Hemingway. **CP-HemiE**

With changeful sound life beats upon the ear. Silence. Walter de la Mare. **CP-DeLaW**

With Charles Avison, *with music*. Robert Browning. **CP-BroR2**

With Christopher Smart. Robert Browning. **CP-BroR2**

With cicada's nymphal skin. The Largess. Richard Eberhart. **CP-EberR**

With clearer light, Cross of the South, shine forth. Freedom in Brazil. John Greenleaf Whittier. **CP-WhitJ**

With closer clutch for that which remains. Emily Dickinson. **SP-DickE**

With conscience cocked to listen for the thunder. Luther. Wystan Hugh Auden. **CP-AudeW**

With conscious eyes not yet sincere enough. Edwin Arlington Robinson. *Fr.* Octaves. **CP-RobiE**

With copious eulogy in prose or rhyme. Elegiac Musings in the Grounds of Coleorton Hall, the Seat of the Late Sir G.H. Beaumont, BART. William Wordsworth. **CP-WorW2**

With Dad gone, Mom and I worked. Adolescence—III. Rita Dove. **SP-DoveR**

With Daniel Bartoli. Robert Browning. **CP-BroR2**

With Dearest Love Enfolded and Enclosed from *All* the Litle Animals. Malcolm Lowry. **CP-LowrM**

With Dearest Morning Love and Kisses. Malcolm Lowry. **CP-LowrM**

With Devotion Entire from All Your Little Animals We Thought Fit to Revive the Following Ditty. Malcolm Lowry. **CP-LowrM**

With dog and catalpa, panicles. She Who Hits at Will. Charles Olson. **CP-OlsoC**

With Donne, whose muse on dromedary trots. On Donne's Poetry. Samuel Taylor Coleridge. **CP-ColeS**

With Drake in the Tropics. Rudyard Kipling. **CP-KiplR**

With each recurrence of this glorious morn. Composed in One of the Valleys of Westmoreland, on Easter Sunday. William Wordsworth. **CP-WorW2**

With E.M.F. on 28th December 1965. John Hewitt. **CP-HewiJ**

With equal largesse spends the sun. Equality. John Hewitt. **CP-HewiJ**

With Esop's lion, Burns says, sore I feel. Robert Burns. *Fr.* Lines on Stirling. **CP-BurnR**

With favour and fortune fastidiously blessed [or blest]. The Character of Sir Robert Walpole. Jonathan Swift. **CP-SwifJ**

With Fielding's *Amelia*. Samuel Taylor Coleridge. **CP-ColeS**

With fifty years between you and your well-kept wedding vow. The Golden Wedding of Longwood. John Greenleaf Whittier. **CP-WhitJ**

With fire to the eastward and fire to the west. Potherbs (Of the Edible Wild Plants My Granny Taught Me). Louise McNeill. **SP-McNeL**

With focus sharp as Flemish-painted face. Dome of Sunday, The [or A]. Karl Shapiro. **SP-ShapK**

With folk for tea, there in the dining room. Folk for Tea. John Hewitt. **CP-HewiJ**

With Francis Furini. Robert Browning. **CP-BroR2**

With Frank and George at Lexington. James Schuyler. **CP-SchuJ**

With frost again the thought is clear and wise. Frost. John Hewitt. **CP-HewiJ**

With George Bubb Dodington. Robert Browning. **CP-BroR2**

With Gerard de Lairesse. Robert Browning. **CP-BroR2**

With ginger hair dragged over. Art Student. Stephen Spender. **CP-SpenS**

With Glaze of Tears. Jean Garrigue. **SP-GarrJ**

With glinting pince-nez and a trimmed moustache. My Father. John Hewitt. **CP-HewiJ**

With God on Our Side. "Bob Dylan." **CP-DylaB**

With golden Censers, and with Incense, here. To God. Robert Herrick. **CP-HerrR**

With gravel glued together for arms and legs. The Hermit. Diane Wakoski. **SP-WakoD**

With Great Love Oh Beloved Harteebeeste from El Leon. Malcolm Lowry. **CP-LowrM**

With great satisfaction I take. What the Deceased Had to Say about Himself. Nicanor Parra, *tr. fr. Spanish by* Thomas Merton. **CP-MertT**

With great speed I set the young man free. Thomas Merton. *Fr.* The Early Legend. **CP-MertT**

With half a heart I wander here. In the States. Robert Louis Stevenson. **CP-StevR**

With half an eye. The Answer to Delany's Riddle. Jonathan Swift. **CP-SwifJ**

With hands in pocket hid and buttoned up. The Clown. John Clare. **SP-ClarJ**

With Happiness Stretched [or stretched] across the Hills. William Blake. (To Thomas Butts, 22 November 1802.) **CP-BlakW**

With haste, with the haggard color. The Woman on the Stair. Archibald MacLeish. **CP-MacLA**

With heads like chessmen, bishop or queen. Another Cold May. Louis MacNeice. **CP-MacNL**

With heavy doleful clamour, hour on hour, and day on day. The Groundswell. John Gould Fletcher. *Fr.* Sand and Spray: A Sea-Symphony. **SP-FletJ**

With heedless feet on fires you go. 2.1. Horace. **CP-JohnS**, *tr. by* Samuel Johnson; *Fr.* Odes.

With her latest roses happily encumbered. Eunice. Sir John Betjeman. **CP-BetjJ**

With Her Lips Only. Robert Ranke Graves. **CP-GravR**

With him ther[e] was his son[e], a young [*or* yong *or* youthful] Squier [*or* Squyer *or* Squire]. Seven Pilgrims: A Squire [*or* Squyer]. Geoffrey Chaucer. **TrGrPo** *Fr.* The General Prologue. **FHYEP; NAWM-1; OAEL-1; PoE** *Fr.* The Canterbury Tales. **CP-ChauG**

With his head full of Shakespearean tempests. Venice, November, 1966. Erica Jong. **SP-JongE**

With his kind[e] mother who partakes thy woe. Temple. John Donne. *Fr.* La Corona. **ChIV-2; ESCV; OBS; Son** *Fr.* Holy Sonnets. **CP-DonnJ**

With His Mouth Full of Food. Shel Silverstein. **SP-SilS2**

With his shopping cart, his bags of booty and his wine, I'd always found him inoffensive. Harm. Charles Kenneth Williams. **SP-WillC**

With holy earnest eyes enshrined. St. Thérèse. George Meredith. **CP-MerG2**

With horns and [with] hounds, I waken the day. Diana's Hunting-Song. John Dryden. **NOBE; SeCePo** *Fr.* The Secular Masque. **SP-DrydJ**

With houses hung that slanted and remote. Montesano Unvisited. Richard Hugo. **CP-HugoR**

With how sad steps, O Moon, thou climb'st the skies. Sonnet 31. Sir Philip Sidney. **AWP; BoLoP; BoNaP; CH; ChTr; EiL; EnLoPo; EnRePo; FaBoEn; GBL; HAP; HBV; HeIL; HeIP; InPK; InPS; InvP; MAT; MOON; NAEL-1; NOBE; NoP; NoSic; OAEP; OBEV; OBSC; OXAEP-1; PBMP; PPP; PPoe; PoE; PoEL-1; PoRA; SCGP; SeCeV; Son; TEP; TFi; TRP; TrGrPo; WHA; WeW** *Fr.* Astrophil and Stella. **SP-SidnP**

With how sad steps, O Moon, thou climb'st the sky, *After a sonnet by Sir Philip Sidney,* Astrophil and Stella XXXI. William Wordsworth. **CP-WorW1**

With huge impatience, he inly swelt. The House of Busyrane. Edmund Spenser. **NoSic** *Fr.* The Faerie Queene. **CP-Spens**

With huge jowls that wobble with sad o. The Sorrow. Charles Kenneth Williams. **CP-WillC**

With hungry old eyes. Consequences. Steve Griffiths. **SP-GrifS**

With Husky-Haughty Lips, O Sea! Walt Whitman. **CP-WhitW**

With Ignorance. Charles Kenneth Williams. **CP-WillC; SP-WillC**

With infinite feather-poultices. With Sweetest Love from All the Little Animals to Their Beloved Harteebeeste. Malcolm Lowry. **CP-LowrM**

With innocent wide penguin eyes, three. Bird-witted. Marianne Craig Moore. **CP-MoorM**

With its baby rivers and little towns, each with its abbey or its cathedral. England. Marianne Craig Moore. **CP-MoorM**

With its burden of dreams. Sleep. James Schuyler. **CP-SchuJ**

With its cloud of skirmishers in advance. An Army Corps on the March. Walt Whitman. **CP-WhitW**

With Janice. Kenneth Koch. **SP-KochK**

With joy my heart. Songs of Sleep. Alun Lewis. **CP-LewiA**

With joy she showed the traveller Macy's. 34th Street Song. Grace Paley. **CP-PaleG**

With Kathy in Wisdom. Richard Hugo. **CP-HugoR**

With Kit, Age Seven, at the Beach. William Stafford. **SP-StafW**

With Leopards for Playmates, the beautiful Child. Emily Dickinson. **SP-DickE**

With Life and Death I walked when Love appeared. Hymn to Colour. George Meredith. **CP-MerG1**

With little food to spare. Waterfall. Robert Pack. **SP-PackR**

With little here to do or see. William Wordsworth. **CP-WorW1**
(To the Same Flower [The Daisy].) **CP-WorW1**

With love exceeding a simple love of the things. Melampus. George Meredith. **CP-MerG1**

With many a pause and oft reverted eye. Lines Composed While Climbing the Left Ascent of Brockley Coomb, in the County of Somerset, May, 1795. Samuel Taylor Coleridge. *Fr.* Effusions. **CP-ColeS**

With me retire and leave the pomp of courts. Virgil, *tr. by* Samuel Johnson. **CP-JohnS** *Fr.* Eclogues.

With me, so you call me man. Mo Ghrá Thú. Michael Hartnett. **PeIV** *Fr.* Anatomy of a Cliché. **SP-HarMi**

With me this is normal. Every Evening in Axel's. James Liddy. **CP-LiddJ**

With Melissa on the Shore. Richard Hugo. **CP-HugoR**

With Mercy for the Greedy. Anne Sexton. **CP-SextA**

With Midsummer Devotion from All the Little Animals to Their Beloved Harteebeeste. Malcolm Lowry. **CP-LowrM**

With music strong I come, with my cornets and my drums. Walt Whitman. **TrGrPo** *Fr.* Song of Myself. **CP-WhitW**

With musing-deep, astonish'd stare. Duan Second. Robert Burns. *Fr.* The Vision. **CP-BurnR**

With my hat on backwards. One More Time. Richard Shelton. **SP-ShelR**

With my looks I am bound to look simple or fast I would rather look simple. Magna Est Veritas. Stevie Smith. **CP-SmitS**

With my whole body I taste these peaches. A Dish of Peaches in Russia. Wallace Stevens. **CP-StevW**

With No Experience in Such Matters. Stephen Dunn. **SP-DunnS**

With no language. A Fan Sketched with Silver Egrets. David St. John. **SP-StJoD**

With no poetic ardour fir'd. Verses Left by Mr. Pope, on His Lying in the Same Bed which Wilmot, the Celebrated Earl of Rochester, Slept in, at Adderbury, then Belonging to the Duke of Argyle, July 9th, 1739. Alexander Pope. **CP-PopeA**

With no rich viands overcharg'd, I send. John Milton. *See* Elegy 6: To Charles Deodati.

With noble and strange devices Man hath spanned. The Bridge. Walter de la Mare. **CP-DeLaW**

With oh such peculiar branching and over-reaching of wire. St. Saviour's, Aberdeen Park, Highbury, London, N. Sir John Betjeman. **CP-BetjJ**

With oil that streaks streets a magic color. Ballade of Poisons. Allen Ginsberg. **CP-GinsA**

With one black shadow at its feet. Mariana in the South. Tennyson. **CP-TennA**

With one consuming roar along the shingle. Felixstowe, or, The Last of Her Order. Sir John Betjeman. **CP-BetjJ**

With only his dim lantern. Charles Simic. *See* Charon's Cosmology.

With orange sashes, flanked by shining blades. The Twelfth of July. John Hewitt. **CP-HewiJ**

With pale green hopes and the gay colors flying. Parthenia. Allen Tate. **CP-TateA**

With Pantheist energy of will. Venice. Herman Melville. **SP-MelvH**

With paste of almonds Syb her hands doth scour[e]. Upon Sibilla. Robert Herrick. **CP-HerrR**

With Pegasus upon a day. Robert Burns. **CP-BurnR**
(To Mr. John Taylor.) **CP-BurnR**

With Pinions of Disdain. Emily Dickinson. **CP-DickE**

With prayer-plant eyes annually winter-leggy. Zinnia. Louis Zukofsky. **CP-ZukLS**

With prune-dark eyes, thick lips, jostling each other. Refugees. Louis MacNeice. **CP-MacNL**

With quiet step and careful breath. The Owl. John Hewitt. **CP-HewiJ**

With reeds and bird-lime from the desert air. On a Fowler. Isidorus, *tr. fr. Greek by* William Cowper. **CP-CowpW**

With Ripley at the Grave of Albert Parenteau. Richard Hugo. **CP-HugoR**

With rolled umbrella, little bowler hat. Bradford Millionaire. John Hewitt. **CP-HewiJ**

With rotund word and bloated epithet. Cold Warrior: Anzac Day, 1946. John Hewitt. **CP-HewiJ**

With rue my heart is laden. Alfred Edward Housman. **CP-HousA**

With sacrifice before the rising morn. Laodamia. William Wordsworth. **CP-WorW2**

With saddest music all day long. Melancholetta. "Lewis Carroll." **CP-CarrL**

With sagest craft Arachne worked. A Garden Idyl. George Meredith. **CP-MerG1**

With Scindia to Delhi. Rudyard Kipling. **CP-KiplR**

With seed the sowers scatter. Alfred Edward Housman. **CP-HousA**

With serving still. Sir Thomas Wyatt. **CP-WyatT**

With sharp lights winking. Thinking Back Toward Christmas: A Statement for the Virgin. William Carlos Williams. **CP-WilW2**

With Ships the sea was sprinkled far and nigh. William Wordsworth. **CP-WorW1**

With shrewd snout the hedgehog. The Hedgehog: For R. John Hewitt. **CP-HewiJ**

With sick and famished [*or* famisht] eyes. Longing. George Herbert. **CP-HerbG**

With sleep-crowned eyes I / see the morning sunlight. Sleep-Gummed Eyes. James Schuyler. **CP-SchuJ**

With sleepless toil on land and wave. Force and His Master. George Meredith. **CP-MerG2**

WITH solicitude / that mirrored turbationem. Canto 86. Ezra Pound. *Fr.* Cantos. **CP-PoCan**

With sombre mien, the Evening Grey. Farewell to Arcady. Paul Laurence Dunbar. **CP-DunbP**

[With Some Poems Sent to a Gentlewoman. I]. Richard Crashaw. **CP-CrasR**

[With Some Poems Sent to a Gentlewoman. II]. Richard Crashaw. **CP-CrasR**

With sorrow that the Joy is past. Emily Dickinson. **SP-DickE**

With splendour of a silver day. Night of Frost in May. George Meredith. **CP-MerG1**

With spotles mindes now mount we to the tree. Thomas Campion. *Fr.* Lord Hay's Mask.

With stammering lips and insufficient sound. The Soul's Expression. Elizabeth Barrett Browning. **CP-BroEB**

With Stars. Tess Gallagher. **SP-GallT**

With stars past troughs to sounds. Train-Signal. Louis Zukofsky. *Fr.* 29 Songs. **CP-ZukLS**

With subtle poise he grips his tray. Atlantic City Waiter. Countee Cullen. **CP-CullC**

With such compelling cause to grieve. Tennyson. **EBVV** *Fr.* In Memoriam A. H. H. **CP-TennA**

With summer over, all unparalleled. Failed Image. John Hewitt. **CP-HewiJ**

With Sweet Devotion and True from All the Little Animals. Malcolm Lowry. **CP-LowrM**

With Sweet Sweet Love from All Your Amused Little Animals. Malcolm Lowry. **CP-LowrM**

With Sweetest Devotion from *All* the Little Animals to Their Most Beloved Harteebeeste. Malcolm Lowry. **CP-LowrM**

With Sweetest Love and Sunday Anthems or Sweetest Goodnight from All the Little Animals. Malcolm Lowry. **CP-LowrM**

With Sweetest Love and Welcome from All the Little Animals. Malcolm Lowry. **CP-LowrM**

With Sweetest Love from All the Little Animals As from 2 Old Friends. Malcolm Lowry. **CP-LowrM**

With Sweetest Love from All the Little Animals to Their Beloved Harteebeeste. Malcolm Lowry. **CP-LowrM**

With sweetest milk and sugar first. The Nymph and Her Fawn. Andrew Marvell. **BoTP; FaBoCh** *Fr.* The Nymph Complaining for the Death of Her Faun [*or* Fawn]. **CP-MarvA**

With Sweetest Morning Love to Their Beloved Harteebeeste. Malcolm Lowry. **CP-LowrM**

With sweetest protective dotings. Welcome Home Oh Gladsome Springhorned Beloved and Famed Harteebeeste. Malcolm Lowry. **CP-LowrM**

With sweetness unabated. Emily Dickinson. **CP-DickE**

With tall and silent trees to guard its mounts. On Combe Bottom: Surrey. George Meredith. **CP-MerG2**

With Tewksbury and Barnet heath. Battle of Stone River, Tennessee. Herman Melville. **SP-MelvH**

With that delight the royal captiv[e]'s brought. The Lady A. L., My Asylum [in a Great Extremity]. Richard Lovelace. **CP-LoveR**

With that he stripped him to the ivory skin. Amorous Neptune. Christopher Marlowe. **NOBE** *Fr.* Hero and Leander. **CP-MarlC**

With that I saw two swans of goodly hue. Edmund Spenser. **PBBP** *Fr.* Prothalamion. **CP-Spens**

With the actual the illusory. Orford. Donald Davie. **CP-DavDo**

With the blue-dark dome old-starred at night, green boat-lights purring over water. Galilee Shore. Allen Ginsberg. **CP-GinsA**

With the boys busy. Philomena Andronico. William Carlos Williams. **CP-WilW2**

With the effect almost of carving the hillside. Donald Davie. *See* For an Age of Plastics. [Plymouth].

With the effect as of carving, almost, the hillside. For an Age of Plastics. [Plymouth]. Donald Davie. **CP-DavDo**

With the fall of the first leaf that winds rend. Of Margaret. John Crowe Ransom. *Fr.* Sixteen Poems in Eight Pairings. **SP-RansJ**

With the fierce rage of winter deep suffused. A Winter Night. James Thomson. **NOBE** *Fr.* Winter. *Fr.* The Seasons. **CP-ThomJ**

With the first gray light of dawn. John Yau. *See* Broken Off by the Music.

With the frenzy of an old snake shedding its skin. Derek Walcott. **CP-WalcD** *Fr.* Midsummer.

With the fury of cinders, with the despair of dusty. A Warrant for Pablo Neruda. Thomas McGrath. **SP-McGrT**

With the Gift of a Lion's Claw. Robert Ranke Graves. **CP-GravR**

With the Grain. Donald Davie. **CP-DavDo**

With the green lamp of the spirit. Into the Glacier. John Haines. **SP-HainJ**

With the help of three dwarfs from a nearby world. I Suddenly Became Conscious That This Thing Was Looking at Me Intently. Kenneth Patchen. **CP-PatcK**

With the Herring Fishers. "Hugh MacDiarmid." **SP-MacDH**

With the Huntress. George Meredith. **CP-MerG1**

With the idea of water still in mind. After Returning from Camden Harbor. Robert Pack. **SP-PackR**

With the key of the secret he marches faster. Ralph Waldo Emerson. **CP-EmerR**

With the Lark. Paul Laurence Dunbar. **CP-DunbP**

With the motion of angels, out of. Skiers. Robert Penn Warren. **SP-WarrR**

With the old kindness, the old distinguished grace. Upon a Dying Lady. William Butler Yeats. **CP-YeatW**

With the pale horse. The Poet As Equestrian. Richard Shelton. **SP-ShelR**

With the Persuader. George Meredith. **CP-MerG1**

With the roar of the gas my heart gives a shout. Suicide on Junction Road Station after Abstention from Evening Communion in North London. Sir John Betjeman. **CP-BetjJ**

With the same heart, I said, I'll answer thee. Sonnet. Elizabeth Barrett Browning. *Fr.* Sonnets from the Portuguese. **CP-BroEB**

With the spring flowers I likewise am. The Bird, the Bird, the Bird. Robert Creeley. **CP-CreeR**

With the stampeding hiss and scurry of green lemmings. Derek Walcott. **CP-WalcD** *Fr.* Midsummer.

With the storm moved on the next town. Centipede. Rita Dove. **SP-DoveR**

With the sun half way down the tall pines. River Water Music. Richard Eberhart. **CP-EberR**

With the toys of your nape. Poem. Bill Knott. **SP-KnotB**

With the World in My Blood Stream. Thomas Merton. **CP-MertT**

With thee conversing I forget all time. John Milton. **ArLo; ChTr; FaBoEn; GBL; TrGrPo; TreFS; UV; WiR** *Fr.* Book IV. **OAEL-1** *Fr.* Paradise Lost. **CP-MiltJ**

(Eve Speaks to Adam.) **ArLo; ChTr**

(Eve to Adam.) **FaBoEn; TrGrPo**

With thee—in the Desert. Emily Dickinson. **CP-DickE**

With their backs to the sea two fiddlers stand. At the Aquatic Sports. Thomas Hardy. **CP-HardT**

With their money they bought ignorance. Killers. Alice Walker. **CP-WalkA**

With their respective lions. Sea Unicorns and Land Unicorns. Marianne Craig Moore. **CP-MoorM**

With their throb and yearn, their sad. Exeunt the Viols. Rita Dove. **SP-DoveR**

With them there rode a lustie Engineere. *parody of* Geoffrey Chaucer. Rudyard Kipling. **CP-KiplR** *Fr.* The Muse among the Motors.

With these folk gone, next door was tenanted. The Irish Dimension. John Hewitt. **CP-HewiJ**

With these moody negations / I said goodbye to the mirrors. Conditions. Pablo Neruda, *tr. fr. Spanish by* Ben Belitt. **SP-NeruP**

With this body worship her. Cross-Legged, the Spider and the Web. Charles Olson. **CP-OlsoC; SP-OlsoC**

With this Chanoun I dwelt have seven yeer. The Canon's Yeoman's Tale. Geoffrey Chaucer. *Fr.* The Canterbury Tales. **CP-ChauG**

With this you trim it. Do it right and it'll fly. Two Poems of Flight Sleep. James Dickey. **CP-DickJ**

With those that bred, with those that loosed the strife. General Joubert. Rudyard Kipling. **CP-KiplR**

With thy small stock, why art [*or* are] thou vent'ring [*or* venturing] still. To a Weak Gamester in Poetry. Ben Jonson. **CP-JonsB**

With trees backing them. A Photo of Miners. Brendan Galvin. **SP-GalvR**

With trembling fingers did we weave. Tennyson. **EBVV; FHYEP; OAEL-2** *Fr.* In Memoriam A. H. H. **CP-TennA**

With troubled heart and trembling hand I write. In Memory of My Dear Grandchild Anne Bradstreet. Anne Bradstreet. **CP-BradA**

With two spurs or one; no great matter which. The Cantab. Vincent Bourne, *tr. fr. Latin by* William Cowper. **CP-CowpW**

With two strange fires of equal heat possessed [*or* possest]. Sir Philip Sidney. **SP-SidnP** *Fr.* Arcadia.

With two white roses on her breasts. A Brown Girl Dead. Countee Cullen. **CP-CullC**

With us there rade a Maister-Cook that came. *parody of* Chaucer. Rudyard Kipling. **CP-KiplR** *Fr.* Land and Sea Tales.

With *Usura*. Canto 45. Ezra Pound. **CMoP; LiTM; MeMAP; MoPo; NAAL-2; NOBA; NePA; PoE; SP-PounE; TW** *Fr.* Cantos. **CP-PoCan**

With Vengeance Like a Tiger Crawls. Charles Bukowski. **SP-BukC2**

With Warm Regards to Miss Moore and Mr. Ransom. Mona Van Duyn. **SP-VanDM**

With warning hand I mark Time's rapid flight. Inscriptions. John Greenleaf Whittier. **CP-WhitJ**

With weary steps I loiter on. Tennyson. *Fr.* In Memoriam A. H. H. **CP-TennA**

With what conviction the young man spoke. Wystan Hugh Auden. **PV** *Fr.* Shorts [1939–1947] ("Motionless, deep in his mind, lies the past the poet's forgotten"). **CP-AudeW**

With what fond ignorance we came. The Land We Did Not Know. Jean Garrigue. **SP-GarrJ**

With what I got out. Charles Olson. **CP-OlsoC**

With what joy / I left home to deposit one thousand, one hundred and nineteen. Middle Age Poem. Grace Paley. **CP-PaleG**

With what panache, he said. The Lions. Robert Earl Hayden. **CP-HaydR**

With what sharp checks I in myself am shent. Sonnet 18. Sir Philip Sidney. **NAEL-1; NoSic** *Fr.* Astrophil and Stella. **SP-SidnP**

With what thou gavest me, O Master. Equipment. Paul Laurence Dunbar. **CP-DunbP**

With white frost gone. Strumpet Song. Sylvia Plath. **CP-PlatS**

With wisdom far beyond her years. How Mary Grew. John Greenleaf Whittier. **CP-WhitJ**

With wisdomes eyes had but blind fortune seene. Epizeuxis, the Underlay, or Coocko-spel. Sir Walter Ralegh. *Fr.* The Arte of English Poesie. **CP-RaleW**

With women like Marie no holds are barred. The Hung Wu Vase. Robert Ranke Graves. **CP-GravR**

With wood from a hundred-year-old tree. The Five Enemies. Chuang Tzu, *tr. fr.* Chinese by Thomas Merton. **CP-MertT**

With Words. Diane Wakoski. **SP-WakoD**

With you for mast and sail and flag. The Narrow Sea. Robert Ranke Graves. **CP-GravR**

With you it is still the middle of the night. The Lag. Adrienne Rich. **CP-RicAE**

With you, pray not without you, trapped on the edge of the world. Louis MacNeice. *Fr.* Flowers in the Interval. **CP-MacNL**

With you to Bideford. The Admiral to His Lady. Donald Davie. **CP-DavDo**

With your assistance, departed citizens. Certain Dead. John Haines. **SP-HainJ**

With your mercury mouth in the missionary times. Sad-Eyed Lady of the Lowlands. "Bob Dylan." **CP-DylaB**

Withal a meagre [*or* meager] man was Aaron Stark. Aaron Stark. Edwin Arlington Robinson. **CP-RobiE**

Withdrawal. Tom Clark. **SP-ClarT**

Withdrawal Letter. Jim Carroll. **SP-CarrJ**

Withdrawal of the Fuel of Rapture, The. Emily Dickinson. **SP-DickE**

Withdrawing water would be thus discreet. Tidal Basin. Elizabeth Bishop. *Fr.* Three Sonnets for the Eyes. **CP-BishE**

Withdrawn from the Object-World. Lines for Elizabeth Mayer. Wystan Hugh Auden. *Fr.* Eleven Occasional Poems. **CP-AudeW**

Withdrawn to a third your size, and frowning doubts. Angling. Robert Lowell. **SP-LoweR**

Wither'd with yeeres, and bed-rid *Mumma* lyes. Upon a Bleare-Ey'd Woman. Robert Herrick. **CP-HerrR**

Withered rushes made a flame, The. The Well-Head. Robert Louis Stevenson. **CP-StevR**

Withered silence filled my chest of sorrow, A. Debt. Allen Tate. **CP-TateA**

Withering and keen the winter comes. January: A Winters Day. John Clare. **SP-ClarJ** *Fr.* The Shepherd's [*or* Shepheards] Calendar.

Withering of the Boughs, The. William Butler Yeats. **CP-YeatW**

Within— / The beaten pride. Uncle Tom. Langston Hughes. **SP-HughL**

Within a churchyard, on a recent grave. The Caged Goldfinch. Thomas Hardy. **CP-HardT**

Within a hollow elm, whose scanty shade. The Dictatorial Owl. Charlotte Smith. **CP-SmitC**

Within a London garret high. The Garret. Paul Laurence Dunbar. **CP-DunbP**

Within a low wall falling away. Jewish Graveyards, Italy. Philip Levine. **SP-LeviP**

Within a park's area vast. The Jay in Masquerade. Charlotte Smith. **CP-SmitC**

Within a Quad. John Updike. **CP-UpdiJ**

Within a shadowland of trees. Reflections in a Forest. Wystan Hugh Auden. **CP-AudeW**

Within a Temple of the Toes. Phantasy. George Meredith. **CP-MerG1**

Within her gilded cage confined. The Contrast; the Parrot and the Wren. William Wordsworth. **CP-WorW2**

Within King's College Chapel, Cambridge. William Wordsworth. *See* Inside of King's College Chapel, Cambridge.

Within my breast I never thought it gain. Sir Thomas Wyatt. **CP-WyatT**

Within my Garden, rides a Bird. Emily Dickinson. **CP-DickE**

Within my mind two spirits strayed. The Wanderers. Walter de la Mare. **CP-DeLaW**

Within my reach! Emily Dickinson. **CP-DickE**

Within our happy Castle there dwelt One. Stanzas Written in My Pocket-Copy of Thomson's "Castle of Indolence." William Wordsworth. **CP-WorW1**

Within Reason. Robert Ranke Graves. **CP-GravR**

Within that little Hive. Emily Dickinson. **CP-DickE**

Within that parsonage / There is a personage. An Impoverished Irish Peer. Sir John Betjeman. **CP-BetjJ**

Within the circles of our lives. Song (4). Wendell Berry. **CP-BerrW**

Within the city of the burning cloud. Open the Gates. Stanley Jasspon Kunitz. **CP-KuniS**

Within the cloister blissful of thy sides. Two Invocations of the Virgin, I. Geoffrey Chaucer. **ACP** *Fr.* The Second Nun's Prologue. *Fr.* The Canterbury Tales. **CP-ChauG**

Within the Dream You Said. Philip Larkin. **CP-LarkP**

Within the Gate. John Greenleaf Whittier. **CP-WhitJ**

Within the grated dungeon of the eye. Among the Gods. Stanley Jasspon Kunitz. **CP-KuniS**

Within the limestone mantle of the shelf. Limits. Howard Nemerov. **CP-NemeH**

Within, the little house was dark with hate. The Little House. John Hewitt. **CP-HewiJ**

Within the mind strong fancies work. The Pass of Kirkstone. William Wordsworth. **CP-WorW2**

Within the surface of Time's fleeting river. Percy Bysshe Shelley. *Fr.* Ode to Liberty. **CP-ShelP**

Within the town of Buffalo. Nicholas Vachel Lindsay. *Fr.* Niagara. **CP-LindV**

Within the Veil. Christina Georgina Rossetti. **CP-RosC3**

Within the well-house through whose lattice fell. The Scythe. John Gould Fletcher. **SP-FletJ**

Within the wires of the post, unloading the cans of garbage. Prisoners. Randall Jarrell. **CP-JarrR**

Within these circling Hollies Woodbine-clad. *ad. fr.* "Die Vögel" *by* Friedrich von Hagedorn. Samuel Taylor Coleridge. **CP-ColeS**

Within these dusky woods. Keeper's Wood. Frank Templeton Prince. **CP-PrinF**

Within these gates all opening begins. Wystan Hugh Auden. *Fr.* The Quest. **CP-AudeW**

Within this sober frame expect. Upon Appleton House [To My Lord Fairfax]. Andrew Marvell. **CP-MarvA**

Within this wood, out of a rocke did rise. Petrarch. *Fr.* The Visions of Petrarch. **CP-Spens**

Within those walls, and near that house of glass. Epigram on School Days. Robert Browning. **CP-BroR2**

Within thy Grave! Emily Dickinson. **CP-DickE**

Within You Without You. George Harrison. **CP-Beatl**

Within your delight I'm warm, exquisite, take pride. Dialogue Between the Self & the Soul. Anne Waldman. **SP-WaldA**

Within,a coldly echoing floor:a terror. Death's Chimney. Edward Estlin Cummings. **CP-CummE**

Without. Gary Snyder. **CP-SnydG**

Without a Counterpart. Thom Gunn. **CP-GunnT**

Without a smile—Without a Throe. Emily Dickinson. **CP-DickE**

Without a stone to mark the spot. To Thyrza. Byron. **CP-Byron**

Without any necessity to name it or anything. Depressionism. Bill Knott. **SP-KnotB**

Without arms or charm of culture. The Twelve. Wystan Hugh Auden. *Fr.* Six Commissioned Texts. **CP-AudeW**

Without bed or board. Sweeney's Lament on Alisa Craig. Seamus Heaney. **SP-HeanS**

Without Benefit of Clergy. Rudyard Kipling. *Fr.* Life's Handicap. "Before my Spring I garnered Autumn's gain." **CP-KiplR**

Without Ceremony. Thomas Hardy. **CP-HardT**

Without Commercials. Alice Walker. **CP-WalkA**

Without considering whether they were fit. Elizabeth Barrett Browning. **PFP** *Fr.* Aurora Leigh. **CP-BroEB**

Without drowsy dust the wet, the brave. Dear Anima, Show These Words. James Liddy. **CP-LiddJ**

Without excess no galaxies. Civilities of Lamplight. Charles Tomlinson. **CP-TomlC**

Without expectation. Summer Oracle. Audre Lorde. **SP-LordA**

Without going out of my door. The Inner Light. George Harrison. **CP-Beat1**

Without Location. Roy Fisher. **SP-FishR**

Without me, the world became what it was what it always is. Homage to the Afterlife. Stephen Berg. **SP-BergS**

Without meaning to, they watch him play. *tr. fr. the German of* Rilke. Randall Jarrell. **CP-JarrR**

Without my meaning nothing, nothing means. Howard Nemerov. *Fr.* Quaerendo Invenietis. **CP-NemeH**

Without my melancholia I am lonely. After the Shrink. Alice Walker. **CP-WalkA**

Without, Not within Her. Thomas Hardy. **CP-HardT**

Without Notice Beforehand. Carl Sandburg. **CP-SandC**

Without noticing the fire descending into the. John Yau. **SP-YauJo** *Fr.* Scenes from the Life of Boullee.

Without other cost than breath. The Quality of Heaven. William Carlos Williams. **CP-WilW2**

Without Parachutes. Erica Jong. **SP-JongE**

Without saddle, without stirrup. The Sweetheart of the Csikos. Johann N. Vogl, *tr. fr.* German by George Meredith. **CP-MerG2**

Without shedding of blood there is no remission of sin. Shedding of Blood. David Herbert Lawrence. **CP-LawrD**

Without sleep, without dreaming. Sleeplessness. Jim Carroll. **SP-CarrJ**

Without spectators there is no spectacle. Daring to Be the Same. Tom Clark. **SP-ClarT**

Without the Cane and the Derby. Carl Sandburg. **CP-SandC**

Without the daily chores of the people. Carl Sandburg. *Fr.* The People, Yes. **CP-SandC**

Without the grand old British Museum. Serena I. Samuel Beckett. **CP-BeckS**

Without the mercy of / your eyes your. Edward Estlin Cummings. **CP-CummE**

Without the Season of Structure, Modes Lie Like Gods Thrown Down, Helpless Before the Newness Upsets Genesis When the Young Men Pour In. Charles Olson. **CP-OlsoC**

Without this—there is nought. Emily Dickinson. **CP-DickE**

Without your laws directing us. The Dead King. Robert Pack. **SP-PackR**

Witley Court. James Schuyler. **CP-SchuJ**

Witness. Donald Davie. **CP-DavDo**

Witness. James McAuley.

   "Had I been at that scene." **SP-McAuJ**

   "She felt, as she left the station." **SP-McAuJ**

   "What did she see on the train?" **SP-McAuJ**

Witness at Leipzig. Edwin Rolfe. **CP-RolfE**

Witness now this trust! the rain. Possessions. Hart Crane. **CP-CranH**

Witness thou / The dear companion of my lonely walk. Fragment. William Wordsworth. **CP-WorW1**

Witness, would you. Keller Gegen Dom. William Carlos Williams. **CP-WilW1**

Witnesses, The. Wystan Hugh Auden. **CP-AudeW**

Witnesses. Daniel Gerard Hoffman. **SP-HoffD**

Witnesses, The. Charles Tomlinson. **CP-TomlC**

Wit's an unruly engine, wildly striking. George Herbert. **OBF** *Fr.* The Church-Porch. **CP-HerbG**

Wit's End. Ted Hughes. *Fr.* Scapegoats and Rabies. **SP-HughT**

Witt. Patti Smith. **SP-SmitP**

Wives in the Sere. Thomas Hardy. **CP-HardT**

Wives of the black-sailed seminarians, The. 20th Street Spring. Grace Paley. **CP-PaleG**

Wives on day-coaches traveling with a baby. Good-bye, Wendover; Good-bye, Mountain Home. Randall Jarrell. **CP-JarrR**

Wizard in the Street, The. Nicholas Vachel Lindsay. **CP-LindV**

Wizard Pink Wick Deodorizer is capped, The. Mass. Ave., Cambridge, Mass. James Schuyler. *Fr.* Four Poems. **CP-SchuJ**

Wizard touch of Merlin's gone, The. Pendragon. John Hewitt. **CP-HewiJ**

Wizard Wind, The. Nicholas Vachel Lindsay. **CP-LindV**

Wizened elf woman. Baby & the Gypsy. Anne Waldman. **SP-WaldA**

Wm. Brazier. Robert Ranke Graves. **CP-GravR**

Wm. Yates, colored. Sick African. William Carlos Williams. **CP-WilW1**

Wo is me woe's me when I think. Michelangelo Buonarroti, *tr. fr. Italian by* Ralph Waldo Emerson. **CP-EmerR**

Wo'd I see Lawn, clear as the Heaven, and thin? The Lawne. Robert Herrick. **CP-HerrR**

Wo'd I wooe, and wo'd I winne. To Biancha, to Blesse Him. Robert Herrick. **CP-HerrR**

Wo'd ye oyle of Blossoms get? Upon Julia's Sweat. Robert Herrick. **CP-HerrR**

Wodwo. Ted Hughes. **SP-HughT**

Woe, A. Daniel Gerard Hoffman. **SP-HoffD**

Woe. David Herbert Lawrence. **CP-LawrD**

Woe alas my guilty hand. William Blake. *See* Little Fly.

Woe for the day; Regina's pride. Emily Brontë. **CP-BronE**

Woe for the young who say that life is long. The Whole Head Is Sick, and the Whole Heart Faint. Christina Georgina Rossetti. **CP-RosC3**

Woe, having made with many fights his own. Sonnet 57. Sir Philip Sidney. *Fr.* Astrophil and Stella. **SP-SidnP**

Woe, he went galloping into the war. Rosny. Robert Browning. **CP-BroR2**

Woe is me! an old man said. The Last *Complaint*. Christina Georgina Rossetti. **CP-RosC3**

Woe to the Crown that doth the Cowl obey! Danish Conquests. William Wordsworth. *Fr.* Ecclesiastical Sonnets. **CP-WorW2**

Woe to you, Prelates! rioting in ease. Corruptions of the Higher Clergy. William Wordsworth. *Fr.* Ecclesiastical Sonnets. **CP-WorW2**

Woe unto Thee! Donald Davie. **CP-DavDo**

Woe, woe to them, who (by a ball of strife). To the King and Queene, upon Their Unhappy Distances. Robert Herrick. **CP-HerrR**

Woke up one morning with a stone tied to his. A Man like a Curtain. Ron Koertge. **SP-KoerR**

Woken, I lay in the arms of my own warmth and listened. First Things First. Wystan Hugh Auden. **CP-AudeW**

Wolf, A. Paul Éluard, *tr. fr. French by* William Carlos Williams. **CP-WilW2**

Wolf, A. Paul Éluard, *tr. fr. French by* William Carlos Williams. **CP-WilW2**

Wolf. Kenneth Rexroth. **NNaP; SP-RexrK** *Fr.* A Bestiary. **SP-RexrK**

"Wolf!" cried my cunning heart. The True Encounter. Edna St. Vincent Millay. **CP-MillE**

Wolf-cub at even lay hid in the corn, The. Rudyard Kipling. **CP-KiplR** *Fr.* The Light That Failed.

Wolf Knife. Donald Hall. **CP-HallD**

Wolf Moon. Mary Oliver. **SP-OlivM**

Wolf of winter, The. Kenneth Patchen. **CP-PatcK**

Wolf Pack, The. Robert Pack. **SP-PackR**

Wolf, wolf, cried the boy in the fable. Malcolm Lowry. *Fr.* The Moon in Scandinavia. **CP-LowrM**

Wolfe demanded during dying. Emily Dickinson. **CP-DickE**

Wolfe Tone. Seamus Heaney. **SP-HeanS**

Wolves. John Haines. **SP-HainJ**

Wolves. Louis MacNeice. **CP-MacNL**

Wolves, The. Allen Tate. **CP-TateA**

Wolves howling against the lips of. Heifetz—On the Air, Bell Telephone Program. Marsden Hartley. **CP-HartM**

Wolves in the Zoo. Howard Nemerov. **CP-NemeH**

Woman, The. Hayden Carruth. *Fr.* Contra Mortem. **CP-CarHL**

Woman, The. Robert Creeley. **CP-CreeR**

Woman, The. Robert Creeley. **CP-CreeR**

Woman. Randall Jarrell. **CP-JarrR**

Woman. John Milton. **OBS** *Fr.* Samson Agonistes. **CP-MiltJ**

Woman / of bronze / unhappy, A. Edward Estlin Cummings. **CP-CummE**

Woman, A. John Greenleaf Whittier. **CP-WhitJ**

Woman, A / who loves a woman. Rapunzel. Anne Sexton. **CP-SextA**

Woman across the lane, The. Roy Fisher. **SP-FishR** *Fr.* Diversions.

Woman and child running / in a field A man planted. Mother-Right. Adrienne Rich. **SP-RicA2**

Woman and Emblems. Muriel Rukeyser. **CP-RukeM**

Woman and Leopard. David St. John. **SP-StJoD**

Woman and the Wife, The. Edwin Arlington Robinson. **CP-RobiE**

Woman and Tree. Robert Ranke Graves. **CP-GravR**

Woman as Market. Muriel Rukeyser. **CP-RukeM**

Woman at the checkstand, The. How Much Can It Hurt? Philip Levine. **SP-LeviP**

Woman at the Washington Zoo, The. Randall Jarrell. **CP-JarrR; SP-JarrR**

Woman Bewildered, The. Robert Bly. **SP-BlyR**

Woman, by my mother much admired, A. My Naming. John Hewitt. **CP-HewiJ**

Woman dancing with hair. The Window of the Woman Burning. Marge Piercy. **SP-PierM**

Woman Dead in Her Forties, A. Adrienne Rich. **SP-RicA2**

Woman Distorts, with Hunger, The. Marsden Hartley. **CP-HartM**

Woman dreamed / In that *jacal*, a jungle hut, and awoke. Primitive. George Oppen. **CP-OppeG**

Woman Driving, A. Thomas Hardy. **CP-HardT**

Woman-Enough. Tess Gallagher. **SP-GallT**

Woman Enough. Erica Jong. **SP-JongE**

Woman every night, A. Universe-Solitude. Paul Éluard, *tr. fr. French by* Samuel Beckett. **CP-BeckS**

Woman! experience might have told me. To Woman. Byron. **CP-Byron**

Woman exposed as rock, A. Aphrodite. Louise Glück. **SP-GlücL**

Woman fears for man, he goes. Abel's Bride. Denise Levertov. **CP-LeveD**

Woman for whom the great gods might strive! A. The Chosen. Thomas Hardy. **CP-HardT**

Woman had done hin wrong, The. Without the Cane and the Derby. Carl Sandburg. **CP-SandC**

Woman has given me strength and affluence, A. Manifesto. David Herbert Lawrence. **CP-LawrD**

Woman he thought liked him enough, The. Surprise. Leonard Nathan. **SP-NathL**

Woman-hearted Confessor prepares, The. The Norman Conquest. William Wordsworth. *Fr.* Ecclesiastical Sonnets. **CP-WorW2**

Woman Homer Sung, A. William Butler Yeats. **CP-YeatW**

Woman I have never seen before, A. Transit. Richard Wilbur. **CP-WilbR**

Woman I Met, The. Thomas Hardy. **CP-HardT**

Woman in blue, The. Diamonds in the Mine. Leonard Cohen. **CP-CoheL**

Woman in Front of a Bank, A. William Carlos Williams. **CP-WilW2**

Woman in my class wrote that she is sick, A. Desire. Stephen Dobyns. **SP-DobyS**

Woman in Sunshine, The. Wallace Stevens. **CP-StevW**

Woman in the Ordinary, The. Marge Piercy. **SP-PierM**

Woman in the Rye, The. Thomas Hardy. **CP-HardT**

Woman in the shape of a monster, A. Planetarium. Adrienne Rich. **CP-RicAE; SP-RicA1; SP-RicA2**

Woman in the spiked device, The. A Women's Issue. Margaret Atwood. **SP-AtwM2**

Woman in the Valley, The. Ted Hughes. **SP-HughT**

Woman in the Window. Jim Morrison. **SP-MorrJ**

Woman invented fire and called it, A. Grace Paley. **CP-PaleG**

Woman Irritable because of her Menses. Gilbert Sorrentino. *Fr.* Twelve Études for Voice and Kazoo. **SP-SorrG**

Woman is not a pear tree, A. Right to Life. Marge Piercy. **SP-PierM**

Woman Is Not a Potted Plant, A. Alice Walker. **CP-WalkA**

Woman is perfected, The. Edge. Sylvia Plath. **CP-PlatS**

Woman is reading a poem on the street, A. The Hug. Tess Gallagher. **SP-GallT**

Woman Looking at a Vase of Flowers. Wallace Stevens. **CP-StevW**

Woman Makes Peace with Her Faulty Heart, The. Margaret Atwood. **SP-AtwM2**

Woman Me. Maya Angelou. **SP-AngeM**

"Woman," men say of him, and women, "Man." To Be Dead. Randall Jarrell. **CP-JarrR**

Woman Mourned by Daughters, A. Adrienne Rich. **CP-RicAE; SP-RicA2**

Woman much missed, how you call to me, call to me. The Voice. Thomas Hardy. **CP-HardT**

Woman named Tomorrow, The. Four Preludes on Playthings of the Wind. Carl Sandburg. **CP-SandC**

"Woman never agreed to it! A" said my knowing friend to me. The Elopement. Thomas Hardy. **CP-HardT**

Woman of Greece. Robert Ranke Graves. **CP-GravR**

Woman on Edgehill Road, The. Stephen Dunn. **SP-DunnS**

Woman on the fourth floor said You slut! don't you knock on my, The. On the Fourth Floor. Grace Paley. **CP-PaleG**

Woman on the Porch, The. Miller Williams. **SP-WillM**

Woman on the Road. John Haines. **SP-HainJ**

Woman on the Stair, The. Archibald MacLeish. **CP-MacLA**

Woman Poet and Man Poet. Robert Ranke Graves. **CP-GravR**

Woman power / is / Black power. NOW. Audre Lorde. **SP-LordA**

Woman Pulls the Wires. Ogden Nash. **CP-NashO**

Woman rapped my door tonight and stood, A. The Little Bourgeois is Upset. John Hewitt. *Fr.* Two Sonnets. **CP-HewiJ**

Woman riding the two mares of her thighs. The Steamboat Whistle. Archibald MacLeish. **CP-MacLA**

Woman rises naked from the bed, A. Mnemosyne: The Empty Room. James McAuley. **SP-McAuJ**

Woman said: / Is there any point in reducing, The. Nachtmusik. David Markson. **CP-MarkD**

Woman sails, man must row. Sail and Oar. Robert Ranke Graves. **CP-GravR**

Woman scaly & a Man all Hairy, A. William Blake. **CP-BlakW**

Woman singeth at her spinning-wheel, The. Work and Contemplation. Elizabeth Barrett Browning. **CP-BroEB**

Woman Sings a Song for a Soldier Come Home, A. Wallace Stevens. **CP-StevW**

Woman Skating. Margaret Atwood. **SP-AtwM1**

Woman smells like fresh-plowed ground, A. Could She See the Whole Real World with Her Ghost Breast Eyes Shut under a Blouse Lid? Gary Snyder. **CP-SnydG**

Woman standing in the doorway, A. Evening Song. Langston Hughes. **SP-HughL**

Woman! the Power who left His throne on high. Thanksgiving after Childbirth. William Wordsworth. *Fr.* Ecclesiastical Sonnets. **CP-WorW2**

Woman Thing, The. Audre Lorde. **SP-LordA**

Woman to the man, The. Welcome from War. Muriel Rukeyser. **CP-RukeM**

Woman told a man, A. Up Your Yellow River. Charles Bukowski. **SP-BukC1**

Woman travels to Brazil for plastic, A. Tomatoes. Stephen Dobyns. **SP-DobyS**

Woman Unconscious, A. Ted Hughes. **SP-HughT**

Woman Waiting. Mona Van Duyn. **SP-VanDM**

Woman Waits for Me, A. Walt Whitman. **CP-WhitW**

Woman waking behind grimed blinds slatted across a courtyard, A. Adrienne Rich. **SP-RicA1** *Fr.* Shooting Script. **CP-RicAE**

Woman Walking. William Carlos Williams. **CP-WilW1**

Woman walks by and I look at her and know that her existence is, A. Notations from a Muddled Indolence. Charles Bukowski. **SP-BukC2**

Woman was made for man's delight. A Helpmeet For Him. Christina Georgina Rossetti. **CP-RosC2**

Woman was playing, A. At the Piano. Thomas Hardy. **CP-HardT**

Woman watching / her daughter watching, A. Appalachia. Martin Edmunds. **SP-EdmuM**

Woman! When I Behold Thee Flippant, Vain. John Keats. **CP-KeatJ**

Woman Who Could Not Live With Her Faulty Heart, The. Margaret Atwood. **SP-AtwM2**

Woman, who had cried out, "O thou, The". Robert Penn Warren. *Fr.* Saul at Gilboa. **SP-WarrR**

Woman who has grown old, The. The Crows. Louise Bogan. **CP-BogaL**

Woman who is waiting for the evening draws, The. The Window. Stephen Dobyns. **SP-DobyS**

Woman who kicked out the back window, The. The Great Doubters of History. Stephen Dobyns. **SP-DobyS**

Woman who lived, A. The Moon. Donald Hall. **CP-HallD**

Woman who packs up the kitchen, The. A Little Litany for Moving Day. Barton Sutter. **SP-SuttB**

Woman Who Raised Goats, The. Tess Gallagher. **SP-GallT**

Woman Who Went East, The. Thomas Hardy. **CP-HardT**

Woman who writes feels too much, A. The Black Art. Anne Sexton. **CP-SextA**

Woman whose face / is a blurred map of roots. To Vera Thompson. John Haines. **SP-HainJ**

Woman with a Past. Carl Sandburg. **CP-SandC**

Woman with Five Hearts, The. Stephen Dunn. **SP-DunnS**

Woman with Girdle. Anne Sexton. **CP-SextA**

Woman with her forests, moons, flowers, waters. At Best, Poets. Robert Ranke Graves. **CP-GravR**

Woman Work. Maya Angelou. **SP-AngeM**

Womanhood, The, *sels.* Gwendolyn Brooks.

   Ballad of the Light-Eyed Little Girl, The. **SP-BrooG**

   Beverly Hills, Chicago. **SP-BrooG**

   Children of the Poor, The. **SP-BrooG**, *sect.* I, *pt.* 1-5;

      "And shall I prime my children, pray, to pray?"

      "First fight. Then fiddle. Ply the slipping string."

      "People who have no children can be hard."

      "What shall I give my children? who are poor."

      "When my dears die, the festival-colored brightness."

   I Love Those Little Booths at Benvenuti's. **SP-BrooG**

   Life for My Child is Simple, and Is Good. **SP-BrooG**

   "Light and diplomatic bird, A." **SP-BrooG**

   "Men of careful turns, haters of forks in the road." **SP-BrooG**

   "One wants a Teller in a time like this." **SP-BrooG**

   "People protest in sprawling lightless ways." **SP-BrooG**

   Rites for Cousin Vit, The. **SP-BrooG**

   Truth. **SP-BrooG**

Womanly Noblesse. Geoffrey Chaucer. **CP-ChauG**

Woman's breasts, A. St. Valentine. William Carlos Williams. **CP-WilW2**

Woman's Constancy. John Donne. **CP-DonnJ**

Woman's Decision, A. Leonard Cohen. **CP-CoheL**

Woman's face with Nature's own hand painted, A. Sonnet 20. William Shakespeare. **ErPo; HeIP; InvP; MasP; NAEL-1; NoSic; OAEL-1; OXAEP-1; PeHV** *Fr.* Sonnets. **CP-ShaWS**

Woman's Fancy, A. Thomas Hardy. **CP-HardT**

Woman's friendship! God whom I trust in, A. A Satirical Shrub. Ben Jonson. **CP-JonsB**

Woman's Genitals, The. Hayden Carruth. *Fr.* Contra Mortem. **CP-CarHL**

Woman's Last Word, A. Robert Browning. **CP-BroR1**

Woman's Nipples Is the Rose of the World, A. Charles Olson. **CP-OlsoC**

Woman's sho' a cur'ous critter. The Turning of the Babies in the Bed. Paul Laurence Dunbar. **CP-DunbP**

Woman's Shortcomings, A. Elizabeth Barrett Browning. **CP-BroEB**

"Unless you can muse in a crowd all day." **PFP**

Woman's Tongue. Laurence Lieberman. **SP-LiebL**

Woman's Trust, A. Thomas Hardy. **CP-HardT**

Woman's Voice. Jim Morrison. **SP-MorrJ**

Womb can / remind you of mosquitoes, The. The Green Lake Is Awake. Joseph Ceravolo. **SP-CeraJ**

Womb, The / Rattles its pod, the moon. Childless Woman. Sylvia Plath. **CP-PlatS**

Wombat, The. Ogden Nash. **CP-NashO**

Wombwell on Strike. Donald Davie. **CP-DavDo**

Women. Louise Bogan. **CP-BogaL**

Women, The. Robert Creeley. **CP-CreeR**

Women. Adrienne Rich. **CP-RicAE; SP-RicA2**

Women. Alice Walker. **GOA; WPOW** *Fr.* In These Dissenting Times. **CP-WalkA**

Women / who build nations. The Seventh Sign. Audre Lorde. **SP-LordA**

Women, although they're so goodly make it. Deniall in Women No Disheartning to Men. Robert Herrick. **CP-HerrR**

Women and Masks. Gábor Devecseri, *tr. fr. Hungarian by* Robert Graves. **CP-GravR**

Women and poets see the truth arrive. Muriel Rukeyser. *Fr.* Letter to the Front. **CP-RukeM**

Women and Roses. Robert Browning. **CP-BroR1**

Women are dancing around a fire. A Message Hidden in an Empty Wine Bottle that I Threw into a Gully of Maple Trees One Night at an Indecent Hour. James Wright. **CP-WrigJ**

Women are lost in the void. The Closet. Gilbert Sorrentino. **SP-SorrG**

Women at Point Sur, The. Robinson Jeffers. **CP-JefR1**

Women at Streatham Hill. Jenny Joseph. **SP-JoseJ**

Women ben full of ragerie, *in imitation of* Chaucer. Alexander Pope. **CP-PopeA**

Women don't know how to love. Me. Charles Bukowski. **SP-BukC1**

Women don't want wistful. Women Want Fighters for Their Lovers. David Herbert Lawrence. **CP-LawrD**

Women drowse through mornings, nurturing life. Women in A.M. John Clellon Holmes. **SP-HolmJ**

Women have loved before as I love now. Edna St. Vincent Millay. **CP-MillE**

Women have no wilderness in them. Women. Louise Bogan. **CP-BogaL**

Women in A.M. John Clellon Holmes. **SP-HolmJ**

Women in anger, it seems, become theatrical. Sonnet. Hayden Carruth. **CP-CarHS** *Fr.* Sonnets.

Women in their marble glory still, The. Klimt and Schiele Confront the Cunt. John Updike. **CP-UpdiJ**

Women leave the funeral procession, The. At Nightfall. Siv Cedering Fox. **SP-CedeS**

Women let the tide go out, The. Grace Paley. **CP-PaleG**

Women like new brooms. Hayden Carruth. **CP-CarHS** *Fr.* The Clay Hill Anthology.

"Women of Color" Have Rarely Had the Opportunity to Write about Their Love Affairs. Alice Walker. **CP-WalkA**

Women of night life amid the lights. It Is Much. Carl Sandburg. **CP-SandC**

Women of Samos are lost in love for me. Ibycus of Samos. Robert Ranke Graves. **CP-GravR**

Women of the city where I was forgotten, The. François Villon Forgotten. Carl Sandburg. **CP-SandC**

Women of Trachis. Sophocles, *tr. fr. Greek by* Ezra Pound.

"PHOEBUS, Phoebus, ere thou slay." **SP-PounE**

Women on a Bus. Randall Jarrell. **CP-JarrR**

Women sit or move to and fro, some old, some young. Beautiful Women. Walt Whitman. **CP-WhitW**

Women swarm in Tauentsienstrasse. Basil Bunting. *Fr.* Aus Dem Zweiten Reich. **CP-BuntB**

Women Uselesse. Robert Herrick. **CP-HerrR**

Women Want Fighters for Their Lovers. David Herbert Lawrence. **CP-LawrD**

Women Washing Their Hair. Carl Sandburg. **CP-SandC**

Women who heard / Pipsissewa. Saying Her Name. Brendan Galvin. **SP-GalvB**

Women who were turned inside-out. Love. Gary Snyder. **CP-SnydG**

Women with hats like the rear ends of pink ducks. To a Waterfowl. Donald Hall. **CP-HallD**

Women your age have decided. Suzy. William Carlos Williams. **CP-WilW2**

Women's House of Detention. David Markson. **CP-MarkD**

Women's Issue, A. Margaret Atwood. **SP-AtwM2**

Women's Laughter. Marge Piercy. **SP-PierM**

"My friend, on the deck we sit."

"When did I first become aware—."

"Years ago I had a friend."

Women's Prison: El Salvador / The Ballad of Visiting Day, The. Grace Paley. **CP-PaleG**

Women's Tug of War at Lough Arrow. Tess Gallagher. **SP-GallT**

Wonder / And pain / And terror. Juliet. Langston Hughes. **SP-HughL**

Wonder. Maya Angelou. **SP-AngeM**

Wonder. Langston Hughes. **SP-HughL**

Wonder, The. Rudyard Kipling. *Fr.* Epitaphs of the War [1914–1918]. **CP-KiplR**

Wonder / once / whence / mulier. The Translation. Louis Zukofsky. **CP-ZukLS**

Wonder as of old things. Uplands in May. Carl Sandburg. **CP-SandC**

Wonder Bar / Wishing Well. Neon Signs. Langston Hughes. **SP-HughL**

Wonder if / you're gross. Miss. Archie Randolph Ammons. **SP-AmmoA**

Wonder—is not precisely Knowing. Emily Dickinson. **CP-DickE**

Wonder not if I stay not here. Sir John Suckling. **CP-SuckJ**

(To Mr. Davenant for Absence.) **CP-SuckJ**

Wonder not much, if thus amaz'd I look. Upon the First Sight of My Lady Seymour. Sir John Suckling. **CP-SuckJ**

Wonder not, though I am blind. To One Who, When I Praised My Mistress' Beauty, Said I Was Blind. Thomas Carew. **CP-CareT**

Wonder of light is your familiar tale, The. Sonnet to Beauty. Allen Tate. **CP-TateA**

Wondered why the building was so small. Chuck Miller. **SP-MillC**

Wonderful bears that walked my room all night. Bears. Adrienne Rich. **CP-RicAE; SP-RicA2**

Wonderful creatures! And Thus with All Praise. William Carlos Williams. **CP-WilW1**

Wonderful freshness, air, A. Light from Canada. James Schuyler. **CP-SchuJ**

Wonderful love / Beautiful love. With Sweetest Love and Sunday Anthems or Sweetest Goodnight from All the Little Animals. Malcolm Lowry. **CP-LowrM**

Wonderful Musician, The. Anne Sexton. **CP-SextA**

Wonderful Spiritual Women. David Herbert Lawrence. **CP-LawrD**

Wonderful thoughtful women who make such good companions to a man, The. Wonderful Spiritual Women. David Herbert Lawrence. **CP-LawrD**

Wonderful time—the War, A. Green Memory. Langston Hughes. **SP-HughL**

Wonderful World. James Schuyler. **CP-SchuJ**

Wondering long, how I could harmless see. Love's Burning-Glass. Sir John Suckling. **CP-SuckJ**

Wonders are many and none is more wonderful than man. Glengormley. Derek Mahon. **SP-MahoD**

Wonders of Obligation. Roy Fisher. **SP-FishR**

Wonders of the World. Richard Shelton. **SP-ShelR**

Wondrous the Gods, more wondrous are the Men. William Blake. **CP-BlakW**

(Imitation of Pope A Compliment to the Ladies.) **CP-BlakW**

Won't forget / his nervous. Clemente (1934-1972). Tom Clark. **SP-ClarT**

Won't It Be Strange—? David Herbert Lawrence. **CP-LawrD**

Won't our life be a tunnel. Pablo Neruda, *tr. fr. Spanish by* Ben Belitt. **SP-NeruP** *Fr.* Question Book.

Won't You? Shel Silverstein. **SP-SilS2**

Woo me now & you'll win me. Song. George Meredith. **CP-MerG2**

Wood, A. Richard Wilbur. **CP-WilbR**

Wood, an Insect. Jonathan Swift. **CP-SwifJ**

Wood Dove at Sandy Spring, The. Archibald MacLeish. **CP-MacLA**

Wood-doves are singing along the Perkiomen, The. Thinking of a Relation between the Images of Metaphors. Wallace Stevens. **CP-StevW**

Wood Fire, The. Thomas Hardy. **CP-HardT**

Wood Giant, The. John Greenleaf Whittier. **CP-WhitJ**

Wood lark whistles. Hogs carry straw. Under the Hanger. James Schuyler. **CP-SchuJ**

Wood-Pile, The. Robert Frost. **CP-FrosR**

Wood Road, The. Edna St. Vincent Millay. **CP-MillE**

Wood Song. Alun Lewis. **CP-LewiA**

Wood-sorrel lady's-sorrel 3-hearts tow ox. Oxalis. Louis Zukofsky. **CP-ZukLS**

Wood, swollen with mushrooms, The. The Circle. Jean Garrigue. **SP-GarrJ**

Wood was rather old and dark, The. Little Boy Lost. Stevie Smith. **CP-SmitS**

Wood Weasel, The. Marianne Craig Moore. **CP-MoorM**

Woodcarver, The. Chuang Tzu, *tr. fr. Chinese by* Thomas Merton. **CP-MertT**

Woodcock rises, The. Ornithology. Siv Cedering Fox. **SP-CedeS**

Woodcut. Thomas McGrath. **SP-McGrT**

Woodcutting on Lost Mountain. Tess Gallagher. **SP-GallT**

Wooden Animal. Hilda Doolittle. *Fr.* Two Poems for Christmas, 1937. **CP-DoolH**

Wooden Buildings. John Ashbery. **SP-AshbJ**

Wooden Darning Egg, A. John Updike. **CP-UpdiJ**

Wooden Spring. Muriel Rukeyser. **CP-RukeM**

Woodenbridge Golf Club. James Liddy. **CP-LiddJ**

Woodland Peace. George Meredith. **CP-MerG1**

Woodlark, The. Gerard Manley Hopkins. **CP-HopkG**

Woodman, The. Robert Louis Stevenson. **CP-StevR**

Woodman and Echo. George Meredith. **CP-MerG1**

Woodman and the Nightingale, The. Percy Bysshe Shelley. **CP-ShelP**

Woodman whose rough heart was out of tune, A. The Woodman and the Nightingale. Percy Bysshe Shelley. **CP-ShelP**

Woodnotes I ("For this present, hard"). Ralph Waldo Emerson. **CP-EmerR**

   Heart of All the Scene, The. **AA**

   "In unplowed Maine he sought the lumberers' gang." **MeMAP; TAP**

Woodnotes II ("As sunbeams stream through liberal space"). Ralph Waldo Emerson. **CP-EmerR**

   "All the forms are fugitive." **WGRP**

   "As the sunbeams stream through liberal space." **OHIP**

   Mighty Heart, The. **AA**

   "Once again the pine-tree sung." **APN-1**

   Undersong, The. **AA**

   "Whoso walks in solitude." **OBVV**

Woodpecker, The. William Carlos Williams. **CP-WilW2**

Woodpigeons at Raheny. Donald Davie. **CP-DavDo**

Woodrow Wilson. Robinson Jeffers. **CP-JefR1**

Woods. Wystan Hugh Auden. *Fr.* Bucolics. **CP-AudeW**

Woods. Wendell Berry. **CP-BerrW**

Woods. Ralph Waldo Emerson. **CP-EmerR**

Woods. Louis MacNeice. **CP-MacNL**

Woods, The. Derek Mahon. **SP-MahoD**

Woods are dark, tempt not its ways!, The. The Boy's Death. Ludwig Uhland, *tr. fr. German by* George Meredith. **CP-MerG2**

Woods are down, The. Lady Fitzwilliam. James Liddy. *Fr.* His Resplendent Neighbours. **CP-LiddJ**

Woods are full of men with umbrellas, The. Rain Song. Stephen Dobyns. **SP-DobyS**

Woods are preparing to wait out winter, The. The View. Charles Tomlinson. **CP-TomlC**

Woods decay, the woods decay and fall, The. Tithonus. Tennyson. **CP-TennA**

Woods in one half of my binocular vision, The. Dusk in the Woods. Chuck Miller. **SP-MillC**

Woods in Rain. Wystan Hugh Auden. **CP-AudWJ**

Woods in Spring. Gerard Manley Hopkins. **CP-HopkG**

Woods is shining this morning, The. Grace. Wendell Berry. **CP-BerrW**

Woods of Arcady are dead, The. The Song of the Happy Shepherd. William Butler Yeats. **CP-YeatW**

Woods of Westermain, The. George Meredith. **CP-MerG1**

   "Enter these enchanted woods."

   "Here the snake across your path."

   "Open hither, open hence."

   "You must love the light so well."

Woods were black and crimson, The. Sweetheart Autumn. Nicholas Vachel Lindsay. *Fr.* Sweethearts of the Year. **CP-LindV**

Woods were still. No breath of air, The. The Dreamer. Walter de la Mare. **CP-DeLaW**

Woods, you need not frown on me. Emily Brontë. **CP-BronE**

Woodsmen blow their horns, and close the day, The. The Fair in the Woods. Thom Gunn. **CP-GunnT**

Woodsmoke. Brendan Galvin. **SP-GalvB**

Woodsmoke and a distant loudspeaker. Yaddo: The Grand Manor. Sylvia Plath. **CP-PlatS**

Woodsmoke at 70. Hayden Carruth. **CP-CarHS**

Woodsprites / & deer arrive. Summoning the Muse to a New House. Erica Jong. **SP-JongE**

Woodthrush, The. William Carlos Williams. **CP-WilW2**

Woodtime. Tom Clark. **SP-ClarT**

Woodwind light / rollever breast sounds, The. Water: How Weather Feels the Cotton Hotels. Joseph Ceravolo. **SP-CeraJ**

Woody Guthrie was my last idol. "Bob Dylan." *Fr.* 11 Outlined Epitaphs. **CP-DylaB**

Wooe her, and win her, he that can. Song, The. Thomas Campion. *Fr.* The Lords Mask[e].

Wooing, The. Paul Laurence Dunbar. **CP-DunbP**

Wooing of Criseide, The, III. Geoffrey Chaucer. **PoEL-1** *Fr.* Troilus and Criseyde [*or* Criseide]. **CP-ChauG**

Wool white horses and their heads sag and roll. Sky Talk. Carl Sandburg. **CP-SandC**

Woolen socks, woolen socks! Shinking Song. Ogden Nash. **CP-NashO**

Woolly-cheeked wink flasher. Gray, Intermittently Blue, Eyed Hero. James Schuyler. **CP-SchuJ**

Woolly dog, A. From the Italian. Stevie Smith. **CP-SmitS**

Woolworth's. Donald Hall. **CP-HallD**

Woot ye nat where ther stant a litel toun. The Manciple's Prologue. Geoffrey Chaucer. *Fr.* The Canterbury Tales. **CP-ChauG**

Worcestershire. Donald Davie. **CP-DavDo**

Word, The. Robert Ranke Graves. **CP-GravR**

Word, The. John Hewitt. **CP-HewiJ**

Word, The. The Beatles. **CP-Beatl**

Word, The. Leonard Nathan. **SP-NathL**

Word, The. Stevie Smith. **CP-SmitS**

Word. Stephen Spender. **CP-SpenS**

Word, The. John Greenleaf Whittier. **CP-WhitJ**

Word—a Responsory, The. Thomas Merton. **CP-MertT**

Word about Winter, A. Ogden Nash. **CP-NashO**

Word and Its Meaning, A. Marsden Hartley. **CP-HartM**

Word Arrangements for Pictures by Morris Graves. Marsden Hartley. **CP-HartM**

   Eagle of the Inner Eye.

   Little Bird Alone.

   Little Known Bird of the Inner Eye.

Word Basket Woman. Gary Snyder. **CP-SnydG**

Word bites like a fish, The. Word. Stephen Spender. **CP-SpenS**

Word came down to Dives in Torment where he lay, The. The Peace of Dives. Rudyard Kipling. **CP-KiplR**

Word, defining, muzzles, The; the drawn line. Poems, Potatoes. Sylvia Plath. **CP-PlatS**

Word dropped careless on a Page, A. Emily Dickinson. **CP-DickE**

Word for the Dumb, A. Christina Georgina Rossetti. **CP-RosC3**

Word for the Hour, A. John Greenleaf Whittier. **CP-WhitJ**

Word for Today is "panoptic," which the goddamn, The. Sonnet. Hayden Carruth. **CP-CarHS** *Fr.* Sonnets.

Word forms / on the left: you must, The. A B Cs. Charles Olson. **CP-OlsoC**

Word from the Cannon's Mouth, A. George Meredith. **CP-MerG2**

Word From the Piazza del Limbo, A. Isabella Gardner. **CP-GardI**

Word has been abroad, is back, with a tanned look, The. Annunciations. Geoffrey Hill. **CP-HillG**

Word I spoke in anger, The. The Quarrel. Stanley Jasspon Kunitz. **CP-KuniS**

Word in Edgeways, A. Charles Tomlinson. **CP-TomlC**

Word in the bread feeds me, The. Rune. Muriel Rukeyser. **CP-RukeM**

Word in the hand is the sound in the eye is the sight in the, The. Writing as Writing. Robert Duncan. **SP-DuncR**

Word is dead, A. Emily Dickinson. **CP-DickE**

Word is his shepherd, The. Ps/alm 23 Revisited. Patti Smith. **SP-SmitP**

Word is unspoken, The. The Word. Robert Ranke Graves. **CP-GravR**

Word is writ that he who runs may read, The. Booker T. Washington. Paul Laurence Dunbar. **CP-DunbP**

Word Made Flesh. Kathleen Jessie Raine. **SP-RainK**

Word made Flesh is seldom, A. Emily Dickinson. **CP-DickE**

Word of a snail on the plate of a leaf, The? The Couriers. Sylvia Plath. **CP-PlatS**

WORD of endless adoration. New Year. Christopher Smart. *Fr.* Hymns and Spiritual Songs for the Fasts and Festivals of the Church of England. **SP-SmarC**

Word of Mouth. Muriel Rukeyser. **CP-RukeM**

Word of the Lord by night, The. Boston Hymn. Ralph Waldo Emerson. **CP-EmerR**

Word of the Lord came unto me, saying, The. Chorus from "The Rock." Thomas Stearns Eliot. **LiTB** *Fr.* Choruses from "The Rock." **CP-ElioT**

Word on the Quick and Modern Poem-Makers, A. Charles Bukowski. **SP-BukC2**

Word on Wind, A. Ogden Nash. **CP-NashO**

Word over all, beautiful as the sky. Reconciliation. Walt Whitman. **CP-WhitW**

Word sticks in the wind's throat, A. Apology. Richard Wilbur. **CP-WilbR**

Word that burned into a page, The. The Ideal and the Real. Richard Eberhart. **CP-EberR**

Word traps catch big bears in silence. Winter Kill. Richard Eberhart. **CP-EberR**

Word unearths the hidden dream, A. Undersea Poem. Edwin Rolfe. **CP-RolfE**

WORD, Was, Is, Will, BE, The. Genesis 11. Etheridge Knight. **SP-KnigE**

Word whose breath is the world-circling atmosphere. Word Made Flesh. Kathleen Jessie Raine. **SP-RainK**

Word with José Rodríguez-Feo. Wallace Stevens. **CP-StevW**

Word with You, A. Elizabeth Bishop. **CP-BishE**

Wordes of the Host [*or* Hooste] to the Phisicien and the Pardoner, The, *see* Introduction to the Pardoner's Prologue and Tale. Geoffrey Chaucer. *See* Introduction to the Pardoner's Tale.

Words. Wystan Hugh Auden. **CP-AudeW**

Words. Wystan Hugh Auden. *See* Base words are uttered only by the base.

Words. Robert Creeley. **CP-CreeR**

Words. Richard Eberhart. **CP-EberR**

Words. Thom Gunn. **CP-GunnT**

Words. Phoebe Hesketh. **SP-HeskP**

Words. Daniel Gerard Hoffman. **SP-HoffD**

Words. Philip Levine. **SP-LeviP**

Words. Robert Lowell. **SP-LoweR**

Words. Sylvia Plath. **CP-PlatS**

Words. Anne Sexton. **CP-SextA**

Words. Miller Williams. **SP-WillM**

Words. William Butler Yeats. **CP-YeatW**

Words and Music. Samuel Beckett.
  Song: "Age is when to a man." **CP-BeckS**

Words are a beautiful music, The. Water Music. Robert Creeley. **CP-CreeR**

Words are flying out like endless rain into a paper cup. Across the Universe. John Lennon *and* Paul McCartney. **CP-Beatl**

Words are like leaves; and where they most abound. The Art of Poetry. Alexander Pope. **ECEV** *Fr.* An Essay on Criticism. **CP-PopeA**

Words Are Said, the Love Is Made, The. Marge Piercy. *Fr.* Walking into Love. **SP-PierM**

Words as plain as hen-birds' wings. Modesties. Philip Larkin. **CP-LarkP**

Words beget Anger: Anger brings forth blowes. To His Friend to Avoid Contention of Words. Robert Herrick. **CP-HerrR**

Words cannot be wholly transparent. And that is the. George Oppen. **APSN** *Fr.* Route. **CP-OppeG**

Words cannot utter / Christ His returning. Easter Day. Christina Georgina Rossetti. **CP-RosC2**

Words Continue Their Journey, The. Margaret Atwood. **SP-AtwM2**

Words fail me. The ocean traveling stone. The Inlet. Louise Glück. **SP-GlücL**

Words for a Nursery. Sylvia Plath. **CP-PlatS**

Words for a Trumpet Chorale Celebrating the Autumn. Delmore Schwartz. **SP-SchwD**

Words for Dr. Williams. Daniel Gerard Hoffman. **SP-HoffD**

Words for Hart Crane. Robert Lowell. **SP-LoweR**

Words for Love. Ted Berrigan. **SP-BerrT**

Words for Maria. James Merrill. **SP-MerrJ**

Words for Muffin, a Guinea Pig. Robert Lowell. **SP-LoweR**

Words for Some Ash. Thom Gunn. **CP-GunnT**

Words for the Madrigalist. Charles Tomlinson. **CP-TomlC**

Words for the Unknown Makers: A Garland of Commemorative Verses. Stanley Jasspon Kunitz. **CP-KuniS**
  Blessing of Women, A.
  Girl with Sampler.
  Sacred to the Memory.

To a Slave Named Job.

Trompe L'oeil.

Words for the Wind. Theodore Roethke. **CP-RoetT**

Words Found on a Cave's Wall. Edwin Rolfe. **CP-RolfE**

Words from Babylon. Jim Carroll. **SP-CarrJ**

Words from Edmund Burke. Frank Templeton Prince. **CP-PrinF**

Words from the mirror softly pass. The Lament of the Looking-Glass. Thomas Hardy. **CP-HardT**

Words have been said, well polished by use. After the Burial. Wystan Hugh Auden. **CP-AudWJ**

Words Heard, by Accident, over the Phone. Sylvia Plath. **CP-PlatS**

Words, idle words, are what people's social life contains a goodly store of. I'll Write Their Number Down When We Get Home. Ogden Nash. **CP-NashO**

Words in a Certain Appropriate Mode. Hayden Carruth. **CP-CarHS**

Words in the Air. Philippe Jaccottet. *Fr.* Three Poems by Phillipe Jaccottet. **SP-MahoD**

Words in the Mourning Time. Robert Earl Hayden. **CP-HaydR**
  "For King, for Robert Kennedy." **CNA**

Words in Time. Archibald MacLeish. **CP-MacLA**

Words Lying Idle, The. William Carlos Williams. **CP-WilW2**

Words move, music moves. Thomas Stearns Eliot. **UnS** *Fr.* Burnt Norton. **CMoP; LiTM; MoAB; MoAmPo; NAAL-2; PoE** *Fr.* Four Quartets. **CP-ElioT**

Words of the Preacher, The. Stanley Jasspon Kunitz. **CP-KuniS**

Words on a Grave. Malcolm Lowry. **CP-LowrM**

Words Rising. Robert Bly. **SP-BlyR**

Words that I have written, The. Poppies of the Red Year. John Gould Fletcher. **SP-FletJ**

Words the happy say, The. Emily Dickinson. **CP-DickE**

Words, the Words, the Words, The. William Carlos Williams. **CP-WilW2**

Words to be Spoken. Archibald MacLeish. **CP-MacLA**

Words we might else have been compelled to say. Lines to the Memory of James Dow. Robert Browning. **CP-BroR2**

Words words like steel. Itch, Come and Gone. Charles Bukowski. **SP-BukC2**

Words Written Near a Candle. Tess Gallagher. **SP-GallT**

Words you said grow faint, The. Faithless. Walter de la Mare. **CP-DeLaW**

Wordsworth. John Greenleaf Whittier. **CP-WhitJ**

Wordsworth Reading Chaucer. William Wordsworth. **EPCY** *Fr.* Residence at Cambridge. *Fr.* The Prelude; Growth of a Poet's Mind [1850 vers.]. **CP-WorW3**

Wordsworth Skates on Esthwaite Water. William Wordsworth. **FaBoPP** *Fr.* Introduction—Childhood and School-Time. *Fr.* The Prelude; Growth of a Poet's Mind [1805 vers.]. **CP-WorW3**

Wordsworth upon Helvellyn! Let the cloud. On a Portrait of Wordsworth by B. R. Haydon. Elizabeth Barrett Browning. **CP-BroEB**

Wordsworth's Grave. Matthew Arnold. **FaBoPP** *Fr.* Memorial Verses. **SP-ArnoM**

Wordsworth's Old Age. Phoebe Hesketh. **SP-HeskP**

Work. Elizabeth Barrett Browning. **CP-BroEB**

Work? / I don't have to work. Necessity. Langston Hughes. **SP-HughL**

Work. David Herbert Lawrence. **CP-LawrD**

Work, The. Barton Sutter. **SP-SuttB**

Work. Robert Penn Warren. **SaC** *Fr.* Boy's Will, Joyful Labor without Pay, and Harvest Home (1918). **SP-WarrR**

Work. Charles Kenneth Williams. **SP-WillC**

Work. Paul Zimmer. **SP-ZimmP**

Work and Contemplation. Elizabeth Barrett Browning. **CP-BroEB**

Work Drafts. Robert Ranke Graves. **CP-GravR**

Work for my living? Would to God I could. The Ex-Serviceman. John Hewitt. **SP-HewiJ**

Work, for the Day Is Coming. Muriel Rukeyser. **CP-RukeM**

Work Gangs. Carl Sandburg. **CP-SandC**

Work in the loss of mass, The. Muriel Rukeyser. **CP-RukeM**

Work is a bleak redeemer. Emily Dickinson. **SP-DickE**

Work is done; now let my Lawrell be, The. To God. Robert Herrick. **CP-HerrR**

Work[e] is done: young men, and maidens set, The. On Himselfe. Robert Herrick. **CP-HerrR**

Work is heavy, The. I see. To the Shade of Po Chü-I. William Carlos Williams. **CP-WilW1**

Work of Artifice, A. Marge Piercy. **SP-PierM**

Work of Creation, The. David Herbert Lawrence. **CP-LawrD**

Work of Happiness, The. May Sarton. **SP-SartM**

Work of Her that went, The. Emily Dickinson. **CP-DickE**

Work on in the faith. John Clellon Holmes. **SP-HolmJ**

Work-Room. Robert Ranke Graves. **CP-GravR**

Work Song. Wendell Berry. **CP-BerrW**
  Beginning, A.
  Lineage, A.
  Vision, A.

Work Song. Patti Smith. **SP-SmitP**

Work-table, litter, books and standing lamp. Night Sweat. Robert Lowell. **SP-LoweR**

Work to Do Toward Town. Gary Snyder. **CP-SnydG**

Work, which no one asked me to do, The. The Work. Barton Sutter. **SP-SuttB**

Work without Hope. Samuel Taylor Coleridge. **CP-ColeS**

Workable fancy. Old petulant, A. Geoffrey Hill. *Fr.* The Songbook of Sebastian Arrurruz. **CP-HillG**

Workbox, The. Thomas Hardy. **CP-HardT**

Work'd into sudden rage by wintry show'rs. Homer, *tr. by* Samuel Johnson. **CP-JohnS** *Fr.* The Iliad.

Worker, The. Ernest Hemingway. **CP-HemiE**

Workers. Stephen Dunn. **SP-DunnS**

Worker's Creed, A. Stephen Dunn. **SP-DunnS**

Workers of Spain have themselves become the Cid Campeador, The. Major Road Ahead. "Hugh MacDiarmid." **SP-MacDH** *Fr.* The Battle Continues.

Workers Rose on May Day or Postcript to Karl Marx, The. Audre Lorde. **SP-LordA**

Working Girls. Carl Sandburg. **CP-SandC**

Working girls in the morning are going to work, The. Working Girls. Carl Sandburg. **CP-SandC**

Working Man, A, *see also* Commentary—A Working Man. Leonard Cohen. **CP-CoheL**

Working Man, The. David Herbert Lawrence. **CP-LawrD**

Working on the '58 Willys Pickup. Gary Snyder. **CP-SnydG**

Working Outdoors in Winter. John Updike. **CP-UpdiJ**

Workingman with hand so hairy-sturdy. Edward Estlin Cummings. **CP-CummE**

Workingmen believed / He busted trusts. Roosevelt. Ernest Hemingway. **CP-HemiE**

Workman. George Oppen. **CP-OppeG**

Works of ancient bards divine, The. Retaliation. William Cowper, *tr. fr. the Latin of Owen.* **CP-CowpW**

Worky Shallows. Archie Randolph Ammons. **SP-AmmoA**

World / arranged in zones, A. Roy Fisher. **SP-FishR** *Fr.* Diversions.

World, The. Robert Creeley. **CP-CreeR**

World, The. George Herbert. **CP-HerbG**

World: / Image on water, waves. Kathleen Jessie Raine. **SP-RainK**

World, The. Kathleen Jessie Raine. **SP-RainK**

World, The. Christina Georgina Rossetti. **CP-RosC1**

World / you know as / one piece after, The. Sunset. Robert Creeley. **CP-CreeR**

World and the Child, The. James Merrill. **SP-MerrJ**

World around her like a shadow, A. O Western Wind. George Oppen. **CP-OppeG**

World as Brueghel Imagined It, The. Howard Nemerov. **CP-NemeH**

World as Meditation, The. Wallace Stevens. **CP-StevW**

World as we reach stretches, The. Upon Taking Hold. Robert Duncan. **SP-DuncR**

World as Will and Representation, The. Hayden Carruth. **CP-CarHS**

World at his feet. A Carpet Not Bought. James Merrill. **SP-MerrJ**

World atop Maine and our heads is north, The. My Heavenly Shiner (Elizabeth). Robert Lowell. **SP-LoweR**

World autumn, The. Louis Zukofsky. **CP-ZukLS**

World begins again!, The. The Birds. William Carlos Williams. **CP-WilW1**

World below the Brine, The. Walt Whitman. **CP-WhitW**

World Breaking Apart. Louise Glück. **SP-GlücL**

World Comes Galloping: A True Story, The. Robert Penn Warren. *Fr.* Mexico Is a Foreign Country: Four Studies in Naturalism. **SP-WarrR**

World Contracted to a Recognizable Image, The. William Carlos Williams. **CP-WilW2**

World discerns it selfe, while I the world behold, The. Ovid, *tr. by* Sir Walter Ralegh. **CP-RaleW** *Fr.* Metamorphoses.

World-famous golden-thighed Pythagoras. A Line of Verse of Yeats. Richard Eberhart. **CP-EberR**

World—feels Dusty, The. Emily Dickinson. **CP-DickE**

World forsaken, all its busy cares, The. At the Convent of Camaldoli, Continued. William Wordsworth. *Fr.* Memorials of a Tour in Italy, 1837. **CP-WorW2**

World full of successful people's, A. Darlings. Charles Bukowski. **SP-BukC3**

World goes none the lamer, The. Alfred Edward Housman. **CP-HousA**

World has finally worn him, The. He Is in the Habit of the World. Wendell Berry. *Fr.* The Handing Down. **CP-BerrW**

World has many seas, Mediterranean, Atlantic, but here is the shore of the one ocean, The. Contrast. Robinson Jeffers. **CP-JefR1**

World hath set its heavy yoke, The. Rudyard Kipling. **CP-KiplR** *Fr.* Tod's Amendment. *Fr.* Plain Tales from the Hills.

World I did not wish to enter, A. A Necessitarian's Epitaph. Thomas Hardy. **CP-HardT**

World in a / plastic octa- / gon from a. Kiki. Robert Creeley. **CP-CreeR**

World is a beautiful place, The. Lawrence Ferlinghetti. **SP-FerlL**

World is a bride superbly dressed, The. Hafiz, *tr. by* Ralph Waldo Emerson. **CP-EmerR** *Fr.* Odes.

World Is a Bundle of Hay, The. Byron. **CP-Byron**

World is a painted memory, where coloured shapes, The. Dreams Old and Nascent: Nascent. David Herbert Lawrence. **CP-LawrD**

World Is a Parable, The. Robert Penn Warren. **SP-WarrR**

World Is a Round Earthenware Plate, The. Pablo Antonio Cuadra, *tr. fr. Spanish by* Thomas Merton. **CP-MertT**

World is a snob, and the man who wins, The. For the Man Who Fails. Paul Laurence Dunbar. **CP-DunbP**

World is an invention of the spirit the spirit, The. Revisionist Poem—Octavio Paz. Thomas McGrath. **SP-McGrT**

World is but a sorry scene, The. Crucifixion of Our Blessed Lord. Christopher Smart. **ChIV-2** *Fr.* Hymns and Spiritual Songs for the Fasts and Festivals of the Church of England. **SP-SmarC**

World is charged with the grandeur of God, The. God's Grandeur. Gerard Manley Hopkins. **CP-HopkG**

World is come upon me, I used to keep it a long way off, The. The Deserter. Stevie Smith. **CP-SmitS**

World is composed of a pair of, The. Kenneth Rexroth. **SP-RexrK** *Fr.* The Double Hellas. **CP-RexKL** *Fr.* The Homestead Called Damascus.

World is dreary, The / And I'm weary. To Mary Shelley ("World is dreary, The / And I'm weary"). Percy Bysshe Shelley. **CP-ShelP**

World is everything that is the case, The. Brief Lives. Donald Hall. **CP-HallD**

World is everything that is the case, The. Tractatus. Derek Mahon. **SP-MahoD**

World is full of colored, The. Song. Alice Walker. **CP-WalkA**

World is full of different fates, The. George Meredith. **CP-MerG2**

World is full of loss; bring, wind, my love, The. Song. Muriel Rukeyser. **CP-RukeM**

World is full of mostly invisible things, The. To David, about His Education. Howard Nemerov. **CP-NemeH**

World is kaleidoscopic, ever changing, The. Stopping a Kaleidoscope. Richard Eberhart. **CP-EberR**

World is moving, moving still, towards further democracy, The. Future Relationships. David Herbert Lawrence. **CP-LawrD**

World is my dream, says the wise child, The. Solipsism. Karl Shapiro. **SP-ShapK**

World is now our dwelling-place, The. *see also* To William Shelley ("Billows on the beach are leaping around it, The"). Percy Bysshe Shelley. **CP-ShelP**

World is so full of a number of things, The. Happy Thought. Robert Louis Stevenson. **CP-StevR**

World is, The / not with us enough. O Taste and See. Denise Levertov. **CP-LeveD**

World is too much with us; late and soon, The. William Wordsworth. **CP-WorW1**

World is treating me bad, The. Misery. The Beatles. **CP-Beatl**

World is very big, and we, The. Edward Estlin Cummings. **CP-CummE**

World is young, the world is well, The. George Meredith. **CP-MerG2**

World made penniless by that departure. Emily Dickinson. **CP-DickE**

World Narrowed to a Point, The. William Carlos Williams. **CP-WilW2**

World of change & loss, a world of death, A. February 14. 1883. Christina Georgina Rossetti. **CP-RosC3**

World of Dreams, The. George Crabbe. **SP-CrabG**

World of ghosts moves closer every hour, The. Lines Written on Reading Dostoievski. Malcolm Lowry. *Fr.* The Roar of the Sea and the Darkness. **CP-LowrM**

World of God has turned its two stone faces, The. To a Brother in the Mystery. Donald Davie. **CP-DavDo**

World of Purple Light, The. Frederick Morgan. **SP-MorgF**

World of the Perfect Tear, The. Thomas McGrath. **SP-McGrT**

World of Words, The. "Hugh MacDiarmid."
"Ah, Joyce, this is our task." **SP-MacDH**

World orecome, victorious Cæsar, The. Of Cato. Pentadius, *tr. fr. Latin by* Richard Lovelace. **CP-LoveR**

World Outside, The. Denise Levertov. **CP-LeveD**

World outside is dark; my fire burns low, The. The Passing of the Year. Edward Estlin Cummings. **CP-CummE**

World-Passport Visa. Marsden Hartley. **CP-HartM**

World pours in / on wings of song, The. Mary's Fancy. Robert Creeley. **CP-CreeR**

World shall now no longer mourne, nor vex, The. John Needler. *Fr.* Commendatory Poems. **CP-LoveR**

World-Soul, The. Ralph Waldo Emerson. **CP-EmerR**

World speeding toward / Bottle green starlight chaos. Desert Wars. Tom Clark. **SP-ClarT**

World—stands—solemner—to me, The. Emily Dickinson. **CP-DickE**

World Take Good Notice. Walt Whitman. **CP-WhitW**

World-Telegram. John Berryman. **CP-BerrJ**

World; The Lovers; Falling Stars, The. Thomas McGrath. **SP-McGrT**

World Tour. Kay Boyle. **CP-BoylK**

World Transformed, The. John Greenleaf Whittier. **AA** *Fr.* Snow-Bound [*or* Snow-Bound; a Winter Idyl]. **CP-WhitJ**

World values books, and thinks that in so doing, The. Duke Hwan and the Wheelwright. Chuang Tzu, *tr. fr. Chinese by* Thomas Merton. **CP-MertT**

World vibrates, my sleepless nights, The. Vibration. John Updike. **CP-UpdiJ**

World War. Richard Eberhart. **CP-EberR**

World War II. Langston Hughes. **SP-HughL**

World War II. The Troops. Charles Bukowski. **SP-BukC3**

World was made by someone else, The. Creator. Archibald MacLeish. **CP-MacLA**

World,—what a world, ah me! / Mouldy, worm-eaten, grey. A Vain Shadow. Christina Georgina Rossetti. **CP-RosC2**

World Whose Sun Retreats Before the Brave, A. Kenneth Patchen. **CP-PatcK**

World Will Little Note, The. Kenneth Patchen. **CP-PatcK**

World within World. Peter Meinke. **SP-MeinP**

"World without Objects Is a Sensible Emptiness, A." Richard Wilbur. **CP-WilbR**

World without Peculiarity. Wallace Stevens. **CP-StevW**

World, World—. George Oppen. **CP-OppeG**

World world world world / I sit in my room. Europe! Europe! Allen Ginsberg. **CP-GinsA**

World world world world / and the face grave. Enueg II. Samuel Beckett. **CP-BeckS**

Worldly Failure. Richard Eberhart. **CP-EberR**

World's / not wanton, The. Implosions. Adrienne Rich. **CP-RicAE; SP-RicA1; SP-RicA2**

Worlds. Richard Wilbur. **CP-WilbR**

World's a mirror. Break it and you die!, The. Charles Henri Ford. *Fr.* Epigrams. **SP-FordC**

World's Advance, The. George Meredith. **CP-MerG1**

World's as the world is; the nations rearm and prepare to change; the, The. Night Without Sleep. Robinson Jeffers. **CP-JefR2**

World's best is water; in the megrims of parched. Louis MacNeice. *Fr.* Our Sister Water. **CP-MacNL**

World's Bliss. Alice Notley. **SP-NotlA**

World's Convention, The. John Greenleaf Whittier. **CP-WhitJ**

World's Fair. John Berryman. **CP-BerrJ**

World's Great Age, The. Percy Bysshe Shelley. *See* The World's great age begins anew.

World's great age begins anew, The. Percy Bysshe Shelley. **AWP; ChTr; EBEV; EnRP; FiP; HAP; HeIP; ImPo; MeMBP; NAEL-2; NOBE; NoP; OAEL-2; OBEV; PoE; PoEL-4; SeCePo; TEP; TrGrPo** *Fr.* Hellas. **CP-ShelP**

(Chorus from "Hellas.") **AWP**

(Chorus: "World's great age begins anew, The.") **EBEV; HAP; NOBE; NoP; OAEL-2; PoEL-4**

(Final Chorus.) **SeCePo**

(Hellas.) **ChTr; OBEV**

(New World, A.) **TrGrPo**

(World's Great Age, The.) **ImPo; MeMBP**

World's Greatest Tricycle-Rider, The. Charles Kenneth Williams. **CP-WillC; SP-WillC**

World's Harmonies, The. Christina Georgina Rossetti. **CP-RosC3**

World's just mad enough to have been made, The. Creation Myth on a Moebius Band. Howard Nemerov. **CP-NemeH**

World's light shines; shine as it will, The. But Men loved Darkness[e] Rather Than [*or* Then] Light. Richard Crashaw. **CP-CrasR**

Worlds light shines; shine as it will, The. John 3; But Men Loved Darknesse Rather than Light. Bible, *N.T.* **CP-CrasR,** *tr. by* Richard Crashaw; *Fr.* St. John.

Worlds on Worlds. Percy Bysshe Shelley. *See* Worlds on worlds are rolling ever.

Worlds on worlds are rolling ever. Percy Bysshe Shelley. **EnRP; HeIP; NAEL-2; NoP; TEP** *Fr.* Hellas. **CP-ShelP**

(Chorus: "Worlds on worlds are rolling ever.") **NAEL-2**

(Worlds on Worlds.) **HeIP**

World's one song is passing, The. Wendell Berry. *Fr.* The Strait. **CP-BerrW**

World's reflected smoothly in our eyes, The. News of a Marriage. Steve Griffiths. **SP-GrifS**

World's Wanderers, The. Percy Bysshe Shelley. **CP-ShelP**

World's Way, The. William Shakespeare. *See* Sonnet 66: "Tired [*or* Tyr'd, *or* Tir'd] with all these, for restful death I cry."

World's Wonders, The. Robinson Jeffers. **CP-JefR3**

Worm / In an otherwise, A. Interlude. Charles Simic. **SP-SimiC**

Worm artist, The. The Earth Worm. Denise Levertov. **CP-LeveD**

Worm beneath the grass, The. Frederick Morgan. *Fr.* Blue Hill Poems. **SP-MorgF**

Worm Either Way. David Herbert Lawrence. **CP-LawrD**

Worm Turns, The. David Herbert Lawrence. **CP-LawrD**

Worms and the Wind. Carl Sandburg. **CP-SandC**

Worms at Heaven's Gate, The. Wallace Stevens. **CP-StevW**

Worms would rather be worms. Worms and the Wind. Carl Sandburg. **CP-SandC**

Worn on the. Kenneth Patchen. **CP-PatcK**

Worn Out. Paul Laurence Dunbar. **CP-DunbP**

Worn plush of the seat chafes your bare legs, The. What You Have Come To Expect. Stephen Dobyns. **SP-DobyS**

Worrier, The. Stephen Dunn. **SP-DunnS**

Worry at night how I can fence the pasture—. Pasture Line Fence. Louise McNeill. **SP-McNeL**

Worry hedges my days. On Not Deserving. Donald Davie. **CP-DavDo**

Worrying About You All the Time. Paul Zimmer. **SP-ZimmP**

Worrying Fruit. Christina Georgina Rossetti. *See* Morning and evening.

"Worse than the sunflower," she had said. The Ecclesiast. John Ashbery. **SP-AshbJ**

Worse things could happen, life is insecure. First Things. Robert Lowell. **SP-LoweR**

Worsening Situation. John Ashbery. **SP-AshbJ**

Worship. Ralph Waldo Emerson. **CP-EmerR**

Worship. David Herbert Lawrence. **CP-LawrD**

Worship. John Greenleaf Whittier. **CP-WhitJ**

Worship God. Christina Georgina Rossetti. **CP-RosC2**

Worship of Nature, The. John Greenleaf Whittier. **CP-WhitJ**

Worship this world of watercolor mood. April Aubade. Sylvia Plath. **CP-PlatS**

Worshipping same / they squirm and they spawn. Edward Estlin Cummings. **CP-CummE**

Worst, The. Shel Silverstein. **SP-SilS2**

Worst and the Best, The. Charles Bukowski. **SP-BukC1**

Worst conspired, their differences sunk, The. The Court Revolt. Thom Gunn. **CP-GunnT**

Worst has happened: nothing ever was worse, The. A Hangover—Reading Rilke, Schnitzler or Someone. Malcolm Lowry. **CP-LowrM**

Worst is over; the people, The. Flash Flood. William DeWitt Snodgrass. **SP-SnodW**

Worst of It, The. Robert Browning. **CP-BroR1**

Worst of it is, The. Modern Problems. David Herbert Lawrence. **CP-LawrD**

Worst of the younger generation, those Latter-Day sinners, The. Latter-Day Sinners. David Herbert Lawrence. **CP-LawrD**

Worst side of it all, The. White Roses. John Ashbery. **SP-AshbJ**

Worst Sinner, Jonathan Edwards' God, The. Robert Lowell. **SP-LoweR**

Worth no more than a man's hard pride. Question Is, Who Is Afraid of What, The? Kenneth Patchen. **CP-PatcK**

Worthlessness of Earthly things, The. Emily Dickinson. **CP-DickE**

Worthy art Thou, O Lord of praise! Deliverance from a Fit of Fainting. Anne Bradstreet. **CP-BradA**

Wot makes the soldier's 'eart to penk, wot makes 'im to perspire! Oonts. Rudyard Kipling. **CP-KiplR**

Would a man 'scape the rod? Ben Karshook's Wisdom. Robert Browning. **CP-BroR2**

Would any one the true cause find. Out of the Italian. Ammianus Marcellinus, *tr. fr. Italian by* Richard Crashaw. **CP-CrasR**

Would-Be Merman, The. Nicholas Vachel Lindsay. **CP-LindV**

Would come down, would ever come down. James Fenton. *Fr.* A German Requiem. **SP-FentJ**

Would God, my Burges, I could think. To Mr John Burges. Ben Jonson. **CP-JonsB**

Would he might come. La Gretchen de Nos Jours (I). Stevie Smith. **CP-SmitS**

Would I could cast a sail on the water. The Collarbone [*or* Collar-Bone] of a Hare. William Butler Yeats. **CP-YeatW**

Would I might rouse the Lincoln in you all. Lincoln. Nicholas Vachel Lindsay. **OHIP** *Fr.* Litany of the Heroes. **CP-LindV**

Would it had been the man of our wish! In the Room of the Bride-Elect. Thomas Hardy. **InPK** *Fr.* Satires of Circumstance in Fifteen Glimpses. **CP-HardT**

Would it were anything but merely voice! King and No King. William Butler Yeats. **CP-YeatW**

Would it were I had been false, not you! The Worst of It. Robert Browning. **CP-BroR1**

Would my Delia know if I love, let her take. The Symptoms of Love. William Cowper. **CP-CowpW**

Would that I were a turnip white. Christina Georgina Rossetti. **CP-RosC3**

"Would that I'd not drawn breath here!" some one said. In Time of Wars and Tumults. Thomas Hardy. **CP-HardT**

Would that our scrupulous Sires had dared to leave. Regrets. William Wordsworth. *Fr.* Ecclesiastical Sonnets. **CP-WorW2**

Would that the structure brave, the manifold music I build. Abt Vogler. Robert Browning. **CP-BroR1**

Would that young Amenophis Fourth returned. Litany of the Heroes. Nicholas Vachel Lindsay. **CP-LindV**

Would we were blind with Milton, and we sang. Invocation for "The Map of the Universe." Nicholas Vachel Lindsay. **CP-LindV**

Would—would that there were. In a Library. Walter de la Mare. **CP-DeLaW**

Would [*or* Wo'd] ye[e] have fresh cheese and cream? Fresh Cheese and Cream. Robert Herrick. **CP-HerrR**

Would you believe, when you this monsieur see. On English Monsieur. Ben Jonson. **CP-JonsB**

Would you buy a flow-wer? Tenpence each for a flow-wer. Subscription. Jenny Joseph. *Fr.* Life and Turgid Times of A. Citizen. **SP-JoseJ**

Would you care to explain. Something to Say. Robert Ranke Graves. **CP-GravR**

Would You Go to the House by the True Gate. Byron. **CP-Byron**

Would you have me peel an orange and. The Swans Walk My Brain in April It Rains. Charles Bukowski. **SP-BukC2**

Would You Hear of an Old-Time [*or* Old-Fashioned] Sea fight? Walt Whitman. **SAmP**, *sect.* XXXV; **ImGa**, *sect.* XXXV–XXXVI; *Fr.* Song of Myself. **CP-WhitW**

(Battle of the *Bonhomme Richard* and the *Serapis*.) **MOS**; **RB**; **UnPo**, *sect.* XXXV-XXXVI.

(Old-Time Sea-Fight, An.) **OnMSP**

Would you hope to gain my heart. Translations from Metastasio. Pietro Metastasio, *tr. by* Samuel Johnson. **CP-JohnS** *Fr.* La Clemenza di Tito.

Would you know what joy is hid. Ralph Waldo Emerson. **CP-EmerR**

Would you know what's soft? I dare. James Shirley. **CP-CareT**

Would you like summer? Taste of ours. Emily Dickinson. **CP-DickE**

Would you like to buy a dog with a tail at either end? Double-Tail Dog. Shel Silverstein. **SP-SilS2**

Would you like to hear. The Battle. Shel Silverstein. **SP-SilS2**

Would you like to throw a stone at me? Peach. David Herbert Lawrence. **CP-LawrD**

Would you not like a broomstick? As for me. Johann Wolfgang von Goethe, *tr. by* Shelley. **CP-ShelP** *Fr.* Faust.

Would you rise in the church, be stupid and dull. Advice to a Parson. Jonathan Swift. **CP-SwifJ**

Would you your son should be a sot or dunce. William Cowper. **OBSV** *Fr.* Tirocinium; or, A Review of Schools. **CP-CowpW**

Wouldn't You Be after a Jaunt of 964,000,000,000,000 Million Miles? Kenneth Patchen. **CP-PatcK**

Wouldst thou be free? I think it not, indeed;. In Maximum. Robert Louis Stevenson. **CP-StevR**

Wouldst thou be gathered to Christ's chosen flock. Inscription on a Rock at Rydal Mount. William Wordsworth. **CP-WorW2**

Wouldst thou be taught, when sleep has taken flight. The Cuckoo-Clock. William Wordsworth. **CP-WorW2**

Wouldst thou give me a heavy jewelled crown. Christina Georgina Rossetti. **CP-RosC3**

Wouldst thou grace this land with song? Words for Dr. Williams. Daniel Gerard Hoffman. **SP-HoffD**

Wouldst thou hear, what man can say. Epitaph on Elizabeth, L. H. Ben Jonson. **CP-JonsB**

Would'st thou then happy be. Self to self. Walter de la Mare. **CP-DeLaW**

Would'st thou then have *me* tempt the comic scene. To Miss C—on Being Desired To Attempt Writing a Comedy. Charlotte Smith. **CP-SmitC**

Wouldst thou to some stedfast Seat. Boethius, *tr. by* Samuel Johnson. **CP-JohnS** *Fr.* Consolation of Philosophy, The ("De Consolacione Philosophie"). **CP-ChauG**

Wound, The. Louise Glück. **SP-GlücL**

Wound, The. Thom Gunn. **CP-GunnT**

Wound, The. Thomas Hardy. **CP-HardT**

Wound-Dresser, The. Walt Whitman. **CP-WhitW**

Wound is open, The. Grandfather, Your Wound. Anne Sexton. **CP-SextA**

Wound kills that does not bleed, The. A Woman Sings a Song for a Soldier Come Home. Wallace Stevens. **CP-StevW**

Wounded Bat, The. Malcolm Lowry. **CP-LowrM**

(Note, A.) **CP-LowrM**

Wounded Cupid, The. Robert Herrick. **CP-HerrR**

Wounded Deer—leaps highest, A. Emily Dickinson. **CP-DickE**

Wounded football hero / Is nominated to share / In the human condition, The. Thomas Merton. *Fr.* Cables to the Ace. **CP-MertT**

Wounded Heart, The. Robert Herrick. **CP-HerrR**

Wounded I sing, tormented I indite. Joseph's Coat. George Herbert. **CP-HerbG**

Wounded Otter, The. Michael Hartnett. **SP-HarMi**

Wounded Person, The. Walt Whitman. **PoNe** *Fr.* Song of Myself. **CP-WhitW**

Wounded voice over the telephone, A. Malcolm Lowry. *Fr.* The Comedian. **CP-LowrM**

Wow, but your letter made me vauntie! To Dr. Blacklock. Robert Burns. **CP-BurnR**

W.R. Rodgers. John Hewitt. **CP-HewiJ**

Wraith, The. Paul Laurence Dunbar. **CP-DunbP**

Wraith. Edna St. Vincent Millay. **CP-MillE**

Wrapped in a yielding air, beside. As He Is. Wystan Hugh Auden. **CP-AudeW**

Wrapped in the dark-red mantle of warm memories. After All Saints' Day. David Herbert Lawrence. **CP-LawrD**

Wrapped in the night's diseases. Encirclement. Alun Lewis. **CP-LewiA**

Wrathful East of smoke and iron, The. Ode to the Setting Sun. Allen Ginsberg. **CP-GinsA**

We drink in the mountains while the flowers bloom. Drinking Together. Li Po, *tr. fr. Chinese by* William Carlos Williams *with* David Rafael Wang. **CP-WilW2**

Wreath, The. Robert Ranke Graves. **CP-GravR**

Wreath, A. George Herbert. **CP-HerbG**

Wreath for a Bridal. Sylvia Plath. **CP-PlatS**

Wreath is plaited wicker: the green varnish, The. The Place of Death. Randall Jarrell. **CP-JarrR**

Wreath of banquet overnight lay withered on the neck, The. With Scindia to Delhi. Rudyard Kipling. **CP-KiplR**

Wreath of Women. Muriel Rukeyser. **CP-RukeM**

Wreathe no more lilies in my hair. The Summer Is Ended. Christina Georgina Rossetti. **CP-RosC3**

Wreathed garland of deserved praise, A. A Wreath. George Herbert. **CP-HerbG**

Wreaths. Geoffrey Hill. **CP-HillG**

Wreaths, / the bloom faded of red stains, The. Murder. Steve Griffiths. **SP-GrifS**

Wreck, The. Walter de la Mare. **CP-DeLaW**

Wreck, The. John Gould Fletcher. *Fr.* Sand and Spray: A Sea-Symphony. **SP-FletJ**

Wreck of Rivermouth, The. John Greenleaf Whittier. **CP-WhitJ**

Wreck of the Circus Train, The. Hayden Carruth. **CP-CarHS**

Wreck of the Deutschland, The. Gerard Manley Hopkins. **CP-HopkG**

"On Saturday sailed from Bremen." **SeCePo**

"Sister, a sister calling." **FaBoVe**

Wreck of the *Hesperus*, The. Henry Wadsworth Longfellow. **SP-LongH**

Wreck of the *Swan*, The. "Hugh MacDiarmid." **SP-MacDH**

Wreckage, The. Donald Hall. **CP-HallD**

Wreckage of Europe or the birth of Africa, The. To Lose the Earth. Anne Sexton. **CP-SextA**

Wreckage of the Pagoda Moons. Laurence Lieberman. **SP-LiebL**

Wrecks dissolve above us; their dust drops down from afar, The. The Deep-Sea Cables. Rudyard Kipling. **CP-KiplR**

Wren and Barry, Rennie and Mylne and Dance. Under St Paul's. Donald Davie. **CP-DavDo**

Wren-song in trellis: a light ecstasy of butterflies courting. Light Poem. Theodore Roethke. **CP-RoetT**

Wrens and robins in the hedge. Christina Georgina Rossetti. **CP-RosC2**

Wrens have troubles like us. The house of a wren will not run itself, The. People of the Eaves, I Wish You Good Morning. Carl Sandburg. **CP-SandC**

Wren's Nest, The. Robert Burns. **CP-BurnR**

Wren's Nest, A. William Wordsworth. **CP-WorW2**

Wressley of the Foreign Office. Rudyard Kipling. *Fr.* Plain Tales from the Hills.
Tarrant Moss. **CP-KiplR**

Wrested from Mirrors. Nicolas Calas, *tr. fr. French by* William Carlos Williams. **CP-WilW2**

Wrestler, The. Roy Fisher. **SP-FishR** *Fr.* Interiors with Various Figures.

Wrestlers on the Vase, The. Charles Tomlinson. **CP-TomlC**

Wrestling. Thom Gunn. **CP-GunnT**

Wrestling with iambics in the stormy wood. Bright as the Pleiades Upon the Soul. Malcolm Lowry. **CP-LowrM**

Wretch that often has deceiv'd, The. Phaedrus, *tr. by* Samuel Johnson. **CP-JohnS** *Fr.* Fabulae.

Wretched and foolish jealousy [*or* jealousie]. Against Jealousy [*or* Jealousie]. Ben Jonson. **CP-JonsB**

Wretched Asse the Æneids did destroy, A. The Asse Eating the Ænieds. Quintus Catulus, *tr. fr. Latin by* Richard Lovelace. **CP-LoveR**

Wretched Catullus, play the fool no more. Catullus. *See* Carmen 8: "Break off / fallen Catullus."

Wretched of the earth, The. I Arrive in Madrid. Al Young. **CP-YounA**

Wretched Woman. Stevie Smith. **CP-SmitS**

Wrights' Biplane, The. Robert Frost. **WeW** *Fr.* Ten Mills. **CP-FrosR**

Wrinkled ostler, grim and thin! Song at the Ruin'd Inn. Tennyson. **PoEL-5** *Fr.* The Vision of Sin. **CP-TennA**

Wrinkles no more are, or no lesse. Upon Wrinkles. Robert Herrick. **CP-HerrR**

Wrists web rythms / And the poke. Of an Evening Pulling Off a Little Experience (with the english language). Hart Crane. **CP-CranH**

Writ, The. Charles Olson. **CP-OlsoC**

Write. Diane Wakoski. *Fr.* Fifteen Poems for a Lunar Eclipse None of Us Saw. **SP-WakoD**

Write a giggly ode about. Citizen. Robert Creeley. **CP-CreeR**

Write a prayer to a computer? Thomas Merton. *Fr.* Cables to the Ace. **CP-MertT**

Write to Sardis, saith the Lord. Sardis. William Cowper. **ChIV-2** *Fr.* Olney Hymns. **CP-CowpW**

Write your wishes. Corn Hut Talk. Carl Sandburg. **CP-SandC**

Writer, A. Philip Larkin. **CP-LarkP**

Writer, The. Muriel Rukeyser. **CP-RukeM**

Writer, The. Richard Wilbur. **CP-WilbR**

Writer-in-Residence. William Matthews. **SP-MattW**

Writer to his Booke, The. Thomas Campion. **OAEP** *Fr.* Observations in the Art of English Poesie. **CP-CampT**

("Whither thus hastes my little book so fast?") **OAEP**

Writer was wrong. You can go home again, The. Ashville. Richard Hugo. **CP-HugoR**

Writer's Lament. David Markson. **CP-MarkD**

Writer's Prologue to a Play in Verse. William Carlos Williams. **CP-WilW2**

Writhe and / gape of tortured. Edward Estlin Cummings. **CP-CummE**

Writhing vines were her only apparel. Virtue. Kenneth Patchen. **CP-PatcK**

Writing. Robert Herrick. **CP-HerrR**

Writing. Howard Nemerov. **CP-NemeH**

Writing as Writing. Robert Duncan. **CP-DuncR**

Writing Class. Stephen Berg. **SP-BergS**

Writing Is a State of Trance. Charles Bukowski. **SP-BukC3**

Writing is brief and fleeting. Emily Dickinson. **SP-DickE**

Writing Machine, The. Dabney Stuart. **SP-StuaD**

Writing on Sand. Charles Tomlinson. **CP-TomlC**

Writing Poetry. Isabella Gardner. **CP-GardI**

Writing the Atheneum talk, I wonder. John Clellon Holmes. **SP-HolmJ**

Writing the Great American Poem in Key West. Peter Meinke. **SP-MeinP** *Fr.* Lines from Key West.

Writing thyself, or judging others' writ. To the Same [Benjamin Rudyerd]. Ben Jonson. **CP-JonsB**

Writings of the Mystics, The. Charles Simic. **SP-SimiC**

Written after a Walk before Supper. Samuel Taylor Coleridge. *Fr.* Poetical Epistles. **CP-ColeS**

Written after Leaving Her at New Burns. William Cowper. **CP-CowpW**

Written after Reading an Item in the Paper about a Young Lady Who Went Mad upon Forsaking Her Lover. He Is Here Assumed to Speak. Kenneth Patchen. **CP-PatcK**

Written after Swimming from Sestos to Abydos. Byron. **CP-Byron**

Written after the Death of Charles Lamb. William Wordsworth. **CP-WorW2**

Written at Bignor Park in Sussex, in August, 1799. Charlotte Smith. **CP-SmitC**

Written at Bristol in the Summer of 1794. Charlotte Smith. **CP-SmitC**

Written at Exmouth, Midsummer, 1795. Charlotte Smith. **CP-SmitC**

Written at Penshurst, in Autumn 1788. Charlotte Smith. **CP-SmitC**

Written at Shurton Bars, near Bridgewater, September 1795, in Answer to a Letter from Bristol. Samuel Taylor Coleridge. *Fr.* Poetical Epistles. **CP-ColeS**

Written at the Close of Spring. Charlotte Smith. *See* The Garlands fade that Spring so lately wove.

Written at the Request of Sir George Beaumont, BART., and in His Name, for an Urn, Placed by Him at the Termination of a Newly-Planted Avenue, in the Same Grounds, *see also* Inscription in the Grounds of Coleorton, the Seat of Sir George Beaumont, BART., Leicestershire *and* Inscription in a Garden of the Same. William Wordsworth. **CP-WorW1**

Written at the Same Place, on Seeing a Seaman Return Who Had Been Imprisoned at Rochfort. Charlotte Smith. **CP-SmitC**

Written at Weymouth in Winter. Charlotte Smith. **CP-SmitC**

Written by Maggie B———. Maggie B———. "Lewis Carroll." **CP-CarrL**

Written for a Musician. Nicholas Vachel Lindsay. **CP-LindV**

Written for the Benefit of a Distressed Player, Detained at Brighthelmstone for Debt, November 1792. Charlotte Smith. **CP-SmitC**

Written in a Blank Leaf of MacPherson's *Ossian*. William Wordsworth. *Fr.* Poems Composed or Suggested During a Tour, in the Summer of 1833. **CP-WorW2**

Written in a Copy of Swift's Poems, for Wayne Burns. James Wright. **CP-WrigJ**

Written in a Grotto. William Wordsworth. **CP-WorW1**

Written in a Quarrel. William Cowper. **CP-CowpW**

Written in a Tempestuous Night, on the Coast of Sussex. Charlotte Smith. **CP-SmitC** *Fr.* Montalbert.

Written in a Volume of Goethe. Ralph Waldo Emerson. **CP-EmerR**

Written in a Year When Many of My People Died, *sels.* Nicholas Vachel Lindsay. *Fr.* Alexander Campbell. **CP-LindV**

Written in Aspin Castle. Emily Brontë. **CP-BronE**

Written in Disgust of Vulgar Superstition. John Keats. **CP-KeatJ**

Written in Early Youth, the Time an Autumnal Evening. Samuel Taylor Coleridge. *Fr.* Effusions. **CP-ColeS**

Written in Farm Wood, South Downs, in May 1784. Charlotte Smith. **CP-SmitC**

Written in Friar's Carse Hermitage on the Banks of Nith—June—1788. Robert Burns. **CP-BurnR**

Written in Germany on One of the Coldest Days of the Century. William Wordsworth. **CP-WorW1**

Written in "Letters to an Italian Nun and an English Gentleman: by J.J. Rousseau: Founded on Facts." Byron. **CP-Byron**

Written in London, September, 1802. William Wordsworth. **CP-WorW1**

Written in March [While Resting on the Bridge at the Foot of Brother's Water]. William Wordsworth. **CP-WorW1**

Written in Mrs Field's Album opposite a Pen-and-Ink Sketch in the Manner of a Rembrandt Etching Done by Edmund Field. William Wordsworth. **CP-WorW2**

Written in Naples, March, 1833. Ralph Waldo Emerson. **CP-EmerR**

Written in October. Charlotte Smith. **CP-SmitC**

Written in Sickness. Ralph Waldo Emerson. **CP-EmerR**

Written in the Church-yard at Middleton in Sussex. Charlotte Smith. *See* Pressed by the Moon, Mute Arbitress of Tides.

Written in the Gaaldine Prison Caves to A.G.A. Emily Brontë. **CP-BronE**

Written in the Strangers' Book at "The Station," Opposite Bowness. William Wordsworth. **CP-WorW2**

Written in Very Early Youth. William Wordsworth. **CP-WorW1**

Written near a Port on a Dark Evening. Charlotte Smith. **CP-SmitC**

Written Next to a Blue Flower. Pablo Antonio Cuadra, *tr. fr. Spanish by* Thomas Merton. **CP-MertT**

Written on a Blank Space at the End of Chaucer's Tale of "The Floure and the Lefe." John Keats. **CP-KeatJ**

Written on Hotel Napkin: Chicago Futures. Allen Ginsberg. **CP-GinsA**

Written on Passing by Moon-Light through a Village, While the Ground Was Covered with Snow. Charlotte Smith. **CP-SmitC**

Written on Returning to the P. of I. on the 10th of January, 1827. Emily Brontë. **CP-BronE**

Written on the Day That Mr. Leigh Hunt Left Prison. John Keats. **CP-KeatJ**

Written on the Sea Shore.—October, 1784. Charlotte Smith. **CP-SmitC**

Written September 1791, During a Remarkable Thunder Storm, in which the Moon Was Perfectly Clear, While the Tempest Gathered in Various Directions Near the Earth. Charlotte Smith. **CP-SmitC**

Written to Music. Kenneth Rexroth.
    Married Blues. **SP-RexrK**

Written under the Picture of the Celebrated Miss Burns. Robert Burns. **CP-BurnR**

Written upon a Blank Leaf in "The Compleat Angler." William Wordsworth. **CP-WorW2**

Written with a Pencil over the Chimney-Piece, in the Parlour of the Inn at Kenmore, Taymouth. Robert Burns. **CP-BurnR**

Written with a Pencil, Standing by the Fall of Fyers, near Loch-Ness. Robert Burns. **CP-BurnR**

Written with a Pencil upon a Stone in the Wall of the House (an Out-House), on the Island at Grasmere. William Wordsworth. **CP-WorW1**

Written with a Slate Pencil on a Stone, on the Side of the Mountain of Black Comb. William Wordsworth. **CP-WorW1**

Written with a Slate Pencil upon a Stone, the Largest of a Heap Lying near a Deserted Quarry, upon One of the Islands at Rydal. William Wordsworth. **CP-WorW1**

Wrong. William Matthews. **SP-MattW**

Wrong Door, The. William Carlos Williams. **CP-WilW2**

Wrong has a twisty look like wrung misprinted. Ritornello. Charles Tomlinson. **CP-TomlC**

Wrong Kind of Insurance, The. John Ashbery. **SP-AshbJ**

Wrong look into heavy stone, A. Tapestry and Sail. James Dickey. **CP-DickJ**

Wrong Man, The. Leonard Cohen. **CP-CoheL**

Wrong Number. Charles Bukowski. **SP-BukC2**

Wrong Side, The. Frederick Morgan. **SP-MorgF**

Wrong Time, The. Roy Fisher. *Fr.* Interiors with Various Figures.

Wrong Train. Ted Berrigan. **SP-BerrT**

Wrong'd, yet not daring to expresse my paine. Virgils Gnat. Edmund Spenser. **CP-Spens**

Wrongs if neglected, vanish in short time. Anger. Robert Herrick. **CP-HerrR**

Wronke, Spring 1917. Jane Cooper. *Fr.* Threads: Rosa Luxemburg from Prison. **SP-CoopJ**

Wrote on the Blank Leaf of a Copy of My First Edition, Which I Sent to an Old Sweetheart, Then Married. Robert Burns. **CP-BurnR**

Wrote This Last Night. Allen Ginsberg. **CP-GinsA**

Wrote two letters while rain. Marge Piercy. *Fr.* The Homely War. **SP-PierM**

Wrought by the odd desire for permanence. This Swallows' Empire. Jean Garrigue. **SP-GarrJ**

W.R.R. John Hewitt. **CP-HewiJ**

Wundiwundiwundiwundiwundiwundi. Thomas Merton. *Fr.* A Selection of Concrete Poems. **CP-MertT**

Wuthering Heights. Sylvia Plath. **CP-PlatS**

WW I. Miller Williams. **SP-WillM**

Wyatt, with no insurance on his own head. "Himself let him unknown contain." Tom Clark. **SP-ClarT**

Wyeth's Mild Cans. Richard Wilbur. **CP-WilbR**

Wykehamist, The. Sir John Betjeman. **CP-BetjJ**

Wyndham! 'tis not thy blood, tho' pure it runs. To the Earl of Egremont. Charlotte Smith. **CP-SmitC**

Wystan. Paul Muldoon. *Fr.* 7, Middagh Street. **SP-MuldP**

Wystan Auden. James Schuyler. **CP-SchuJ**

"X." Louis Zukofsky. **CP-ZukLS**

X

X marks the spot. A postcard from home. Jenny Joseph. *Fr.* Derivations. **SP-JoseJ**

X-Ray Waiting Room in the Hospital, The. Randall Jarrell. **CP-JarrR**

X to the Nth. Charles Olson. **CP-OlsoC**

X, whom society's most mild command. The Nonconformist. Donald Davie. **CP-DavDo**

Xenophanes. Ralph Waldo Emerson. **CP-EmerR**

Xenophanes. Louis Zukofsky. **CP-ZukLS**

Xenophanes, the Monist of Colophon. Thomas Hardy. **CP-HardT**

Xmas. Robert Creeley. **CP-CreeR**

Xmas. Gary Gildner. **SP-GildG**

Xmas Gift. Allen Ginsberg. **CP-GinsA**
    (Xmas Gift.) **CP-ColeS**

Xmas Poem: Bolinas. Robert Creeley. **CP-CreeR**

Xoanon. Lewis Turco. **SP-TurcL**

Xochipilli, the Flower Giver. Ce Xochitl: The Sign of Flowers. Thomas Merton. *Fr.* South. *Fr.* The Geography of Lograire. **CP-MertT**

Xochitepec. Malcolm Lowry. **CP-LowrM**

Xylophone of the Spine, The. Erica Jong. **SP-JongE**

Y

Y. Patti Smith. **SP-SmitP**

Y is a WELL KNOWN ATHELETE'S BRIDE. Edward Estlin Cummings. **CP-CummE**

Y is the covenant. Y. Patti Smith. **SP-SmitP**

Y mae'n llewyn yma'n llon. Cywydd. Gerard Manley Hopkins. **CP-HopkG**

Yacht, The. Catullus. *See* Carmen 4: "My bean-pod boat you see here."

Yacht for Sale. Archibald MacLeish. **CP-MacLA**

Yachts, The. William Carlos Williams. **CP-WilW1**

Yaddo: The Grand Manor. Sylvia Plath. **CP-PlatS**

Yadwigha, on a Red Couch, among Lilies. Sylvia Plath. **CP-PlatS**

Yadwigha, the literalists once wondered how you. Yadwigha, on a Red Couch, among Lilies. Sylvia Plath. **CP-PlatS**

Yahoo's Overthrow, The. Jonathan Swift. **CP-SwifJ**

Yak, The. Theodore Roethke. **CP-RoetT**

Yakka-hoola-hikki-doola. Well/Well/Not-At-All. Hart Crane. **CP-CranH**

Yan tan tethera pethera pimp. Basil Bunting. **CP-BuntB**

Yankee Doodle. Nicholas Vachel Lindsay. **CP-LindV**

Yankee Girl, The. John Greenleaf Whittier. **CP-WhitJ**

Yánnina. James Merrill. **SP-MerrJ**

Yard has sopped into its green-grizzled self its new year whiteness, The. In January. James Schuyler. **CP-SchuJ**

Yard Journal. Charles Wright. **SP-WrigC**

Yardley Oak. William Cowper. **CP-CowpW**

Yards of Sarajevo, The. Richard Hugo. **CP-HugoR**

Yarrow. Louis Zukofsky. **CP-ZukLS**

Yarrow Revisited. William Wordsworth. **CP-WorW2**

Yarrow Unvisited [1803]. William Wordsworth. **CP-WorW1**

Yarrow Visited [September, 1814]. William Wordsworth. **CP-WorW2**

Yase: September. Gary Snyder. **CP-SnydG**

Yaupon. Louis Zukofsky. **CP-ZukLS**

Y'ave laught enough (sweet) vary now your Text. Laugh and Lie Downe. Robert Herrick. **CP-HerrR**

Yawn, A. Christina Georgina Rossetti. **CP-RosC3**

Yawning, sunned concave, A. The Sheep-Boy. Thomas Hardy. **CP-HardT**

YCVS and the Ulster Division, The. John Hewitt. **CP-HewiJ**

Ye Appennines! with all your fertile vales. Musings near Aquapendente April, 1837. William Wordsworth. *Fr.* Memorials of a Tour in Italy, 1837. **CP-WorW2**

Ye Are Come unto Mount Sion. Christina Georgina Rossetti. **CP-RosC2**

Ye banks, and braes, and streams around. Highland Mary. Robert Burns. **CP-BurnR**

Ye banks and braes o' Bonnie Doon, *see also* "Ye flowery banks o' bonie Doon." Robert Burns. **CP-BurnR**
    (Banks O' Doon, The.) **CP-BurnR**

Ye beauties! O how great the sun. On a Bed of Guernsey Lilies. Christopher Smart. **SP-SmarC**

Ye blessed Creatures, I have heard the call. William Wordsworth. *Fr.* Ode: Intimations of Immortality [from Recollections of Early Childhood]. **CP-WorW1**

Ye blind, ye deaf, ye mute! Ho, here's healing! Lines for a Hospital. Countee Cullen. **CP-CullC**

Ye blooming train who give despair or joy. An Epilogue to *The Distrest Mother*. Samuel Johnson. **CP-JohnS**

Ye brood of conscience—Spectres! that frequent. William Wordsworth. *Fr.* Sonnets upon the Punishment of Death. **CP-WorW2**

Ye Capete Knyghte. "Lewis Carroll." **CP-CarrL**

Ye Clouds! that far above me float and pause. France; an Ode. Samuel Taylor Coleridge. **CP-ColeS**

Ye copses wild, where April bids arise. The Sleeping Woodman. Written in April 1790. Charlotte Smith. **CP-SmitC**

Ye Cupids, droop each little head. Catullus. *See* Carmen 3: "Who loves beauty / vel her statues."

Ye dainty nymphs, that in this blessed brook. Elisa ("Ye dainty nymphs, that in this blessed brook"). Edmund Spenser. **NOBE; OBSC** *Fr.* Aprill.

NAEL-1; OBEV; OBSC; PoEL-1 *Fr.* The Shepheardes [*or* Shepeards *or* Shepherd's] Calender. **CP-Spens**

Ye distant spires, ye antique towers. Ode on a Distant Prospect of Eton College. Thomas Gray. **CP-GrayT**

Ye Dorian woods and waves, lament aloud,—. *see also translations by* Chapman ("Ye mountain valleys. . .") *and* Wordsworth ("Ah me! the lowliest children. . . "). Moschus, *tr. fr. Greek by* Shelley. **CP-ShelP**

Ye elms that wave on Malvern Hill. Malvern Hill. Herman Melville. **SP-MelvH**

Ye fabled Muses, I your aid disclaim. On the Death of his Mother. James Thomson. **CP-ThomJ**

Ye Fattale Cheyse. "Lewis Carroll." **CP-CarrL**

Ye flags of Piccadilly, / Where I posted up and down. Arthur Hugh Clough. **SP-ClouA**

Ye flaming Powers, and winged Warrio[u]rs bright. Upon the Circumcision. John Milton. **CP-MiltJ**

Ye flowery banks o' bonie Doon, *see also* "Ye banks and braes o' bonie Doon." Robert Burns. **CP-BurnR**

(Banks o' Doon, The: "Ye flowery banks o' bonie Doon.") **CP-BurnR**

Ye gallants bright I red you right. Beware o' Bonie Ann. Robert Burns. **CP-BurnR**

Ye gentle visitations of calm thought. Fragment. Percy Bysshe Shelley. **CP-ShelP**

Ye glitt'ring Train! whom Lace and Velvet bless. Samuel Johnson. **CP-JohnS** *Fr.* Irene.

Ye [*or* you] goat-herd gods, [that love the grassy mountains]. Sir Philip Sidney. **SP-SidnP** *Fr.* Arcadia.

Ye gods that have a home beyond the world. The Chorus of Old Men in "Ægeus." Edwin Arlington Robinson. **CP-RobiE**

Ye hasten to the grave! What seek ye there. Sonnet. Percy Bysshe Shelley. **CP-ShelP**

Ye have been fresh and green. To Meadows [*or* Meddowes]. Robert Herrick. **CP-HerrR**

Ye Have Forgotten the Exhortation. Christina Georgina Rossetti. **CP-RosC3**

Ye have Grace. Ralph Waldo Emerson. **CP-EmerR**

Ye heavenly spirites, whose ashie cinders lie. Ruins of Rome. Joachim Du Bellay, *tr. fr.* French *by* Edmund Spenser. **CP-Spens**

Ye intelligences, turning the third sphere. The Banquaet. Dante Alighieri, *tr. fr. Italian by* Howard Nemerov. **CP-NemeH** *Fr.* Convito.

Ye Irish Lords, ye *knights* an' *squires*. The Author's Earnest Cry and Prayer, to the Right Honorable and Honorable, the Scotch Representatives in the House of Commons. Robert Burns. **CP-BurnR**

Ye Jacobites By Name. Robert Burns. **CP-BurnR**

Ye jovial boys who love the joys. The Fornicator. A New Song. Robert Burns. **CP-BurnR**

Ye juster Powers of Love and Fate. Invocation, The. Sir John Suckling. **CP-SuckJ**

Ye kings, in wisdom, sense and power, supreme. Imitation of Juvenal — Satire VIII. William Wordsworth. **CP-WorW1**

Ye know my heart, my lady dear. Sir Thomas Wyatt. **CP-WyatT**

Ye learned sisters, which have oftentimes. Epithalamion. Edmund Spenser. **CP-Spens**

Ye Lime-trees, ranged before this hallowed Urn. *see also* Inscription in the Grounds of Coleorton, the Seat of Sir George Beaumont, BART., Leicestershire *and* Inscription in a Garden of the Same. William Wordsworth. **CP-WorW1**

Ye Linnets, let us try, beneath this grove. God Neither Known Nor Loved by the World. Jeanne Marie Bouvier de la Motte-Guyon, *tr. fr.* French *by* William Cowper. **CP-CowpW**

Ye living lamps, by whose dear light. The Mower to the Glow-Worms [*or* Glowworms *or* Glo-Worms]. Andrew Marvell. **CP-MarvA**

Ye living powers enclosed in stately shrine, *speech of Philoclea.* Sir Philip Sidney. **SP-SidnP** *Fr.* Arcadia.

Ye Lords and Commons, Men of Wit. Sandys's Ghost, or a Proper New Ballad on the New Ovid's Metamorphosis as it Was Intended to Be. Alexander Pope. **CP-PopeA**

Ye maggots, feed on Willie's brains. Robert Burns. **CP-BurnR**

(Epitaph for William Nicol.) **CP-BurnR**

Ye may simper, blush, and smile. To Cherry-Blossomes. Robert Herrick. **CP-HerrR**

Ye men of wit and wealth, why all this sneering. Lines *Written on a Window, at the King's Arms Tavern, Dumfries.* Robert Burns. **CP-BurnR**

Ye motions of delight, that through the fields. William Wordsworth. **OBNC** *Fr.* Imagination, How Impaired and Restored. *Fr.* The Prelude; Growth of a Poet's Mind [1805 vers.]. **CP-WorW3**

Ye noble Lords who bravely fight. George Meredith. **CP-MerG2**

Ye nymphs! if e'er your eyes were red. William Cowper. **CP-CowpW**

(On Mrs. Throckmorton's Bulfinch.) **CP-CowpW**

Ye nymphs of Himera (for ye have shed). John Milton. *See* Damon's Epitaph.

Ye Nymphs of Solyma! begin the song. Messiah [a Sacred Eclogue, in Imitation of Virgil's Pollio]. Alexander Pope. **CP-PopeA**

Ye nymphs whom starry rays invest. To Lyce, an Elderly Lady. Samuel Johnson. **CP-JohnS**

Ye old mule, that thin[c]k your self so fair [*or* fayre]. Sir Thomas Wyatt. **CP-WyatT**

Ye paltry [*or* paultry] underlings of state. On the Irish Club. Jonathan Swift. **CP-SwifJ**

Ye patriot Crouds, who burn for *England's* Fame. A New Prologue Spoken at the Representation of *Comus.* Samuel Johnson. **CP-JohnS**

Ye poets ragged and forlorn. Advice to the Grub Street Verse-Writers. Jonathan Swift. **CP-SwifJ**

Ye pow'rs who make mankind your care. Malcolm Lowry. **CP-LowrM**

Ye sacred Nurseries of blooming Youth! Oxford, May 30, 1820. William Wordsworth. **CP-WorW2**

Ye scenes of my childhood, whose loved recollection. On a Distant View of the Village and School of Harrow on the Hill. Byron. **CP-Byron**

Ye shades, where sacred truth is sought. Chorus of Athenians. Alexander Pope. *Fr.* Two Chorus's to the Tragedy of Brutus. **CP-PopeA**

Ye shadowy Beings, that have rights and claims. Cave of Staffa. William Wordsworth. **VLP** *Fr.* Poems Composed or Suggested During a Tour, in the Summer of 1833. **CP-WorW2**

Ye[e] silent shades, whose each tree here. To Groves. Robert Herrick. **CP-HerrR**

Ye sister pow'rs, who o'er the sacred groves. John Milton. *See* On the Platonic Idea as Aristotle Understood It.

Ye sons of earth prepare the plough. The Sower. William Cowper. **ChIV-2; SaC** *Fr.* Olney Hymns. **CP-CowpW**

Ye sons of old Killie, assembled by Willie. The Sons of Old Killie. Robert Burns. **CP-BurnR**

Ye souls unus'd to lofty verse. The Nose. Samuel Taylor Coleridge. **CP-ColeS**

Ye Storms, resound the praises of your King! On the Same Occasion. William Wordsworth. **CP-WorW2**

Ye That Fear Him, Both Small and Great. Christina Georgina Rossetti. **CP-RosC2**

Ye that nourish hopes of fame! The Teaching of the Blows of Fortune. George Meredith. **CP-MerG2**

Ye, too, must fly before a chasing hand. Saints. William Wordsworth. *Fr.* Ecclesiastical Sonnets. **CP-WorW2**

Ye towers sublime! deserted now and drear! Written at Penshurst, in Autumn 1788. Charlotte Smith. **CP-SmitC**

Ye Trees! whose slender roots entwine. Among the Ruins of a Convent in the Apennines. William Wordsworth. *Fr.* Memorials of a Tour in Italy, 1837. **CP-WorW2**

Ye true "Loyal Natives", attend to my song. Extempore [on the *Loyal Natives'* Verses]. Robert Burns. **CP-BurnR**

Ye vagrant Winds! yon clouds that bear. To the Winds. Charlotte Smith. **CP-SmitC**

Ye vales and hills whose beauty hither drew. Inscription for a Monument in Crosshwaite Curch, in the Vale of Keswick. William Wordsworth. **CP-WorW2**

Ye vales and woods! fair scenes of happier hours. Petrarch, *tr. by* Charlotte Smith. **CP-SmitC** *Fr.* Sonnets to Laura.

Ye vig'rous swains! while youth ferments your blood. The Hunt. Alexander Pope. **NIP** *Fr.* Windsor-Forest [*or* Windsor Forest]. **CP-PopeA**

Ye who intelligent the Third Heaven move. The First Canzone of the Convito. Dante Alighieri, *tr. fr. Italian by* Shelley. **CP-ShelP**

Ye, who with buoyant spirits blessed. Inscription for a Seat by the Pathway Side Ascending to Windy Brow. William Wordsworth. **CP-WorW1**

Ye wild-eyed Muses, sing the Twins of Jove. Hymn to Castor and Pollux. *Unknown.* **CP-ShelP** *Fr.* Homeric Hymns.

Ye wise, instruct me to endure. On Censure. Jonathan Swift. **CP-SwifJ**

Ye wise philosophers! explain. Upon the South Sea Project. Jonathan Swift. **CP-SwifJ**

Yea, as I sit here, crutched, and cricked, and bent. Panthera. Thomas Hardy. **CP-HardT**

Yea, blessed and holy is he that hath part in the First / Resurrection! Christina Georgina Rossetti. **CP-RosC2**

Yea! Heavy and a Bottle of Bread. "Bob Dylan." **CP-DylaB**

Yea, I Have a Goodly Heritage. Christina Georgina Rossetti. **CP-RosC5**

Yea, I have put thee from me utterly. Dictum. Countee Cullen. **CP-CullC**

Yea, if Thou wilt, Thou canst put up Thy sword. Christina Georgina Rossetti. **CP-RosC2**

Yea, my King. Robert Browning. **WGRP** *Fr.* Saul. **CP-BroR1**

Yea, the Sparrow Hath Found Her an House. Christina Georgina Rossetti. *See* Wisest of sparrows that sparrow which sitteth alone.

Yea, though a Kafir die, to him is remitted Jehannum. Rudyard Kipling. *Fr.* Certain Maxims of Hafiz. **CP-KiplR**

Year, The. Carl Sandburg. **CP-SandC**

Year Afterwards, A. Christina Georgina Rossetti. **CP-RosC3**

Year ago you swore, fond she!, A. Endorsement to the Deed of Separation, in the April of 1816. Byron. **CP-Byron**

Year by year these old ladies had saved. Louis MacNeice. *Fr.* As In Their Time. **CP-MacNL**

Year dulls toward its eaves-dripping end, The. Late Subterfuge. Robert Penn Warren. **SP-WarrR**

Year: 452. The Place: the southern, The. An Encounter. Wystan Hugh Auden. **CP-AudeW**

Year had flown, and o'er the sea away, A. Iseult of Brittany. Matthew Arnold. **SP-ArnoM** *Fr.* Tristram and Iseult.

Year has cast its cloak away, The. Rondeau. Charles, Duc d'Orléans, *tr. fr. French by* Richard Wilbur. **CP-WilbR**

Year has passed, A. A Fleet of Deer. Patti Smith. **SP-SmitP**

Year in its cold beginning, The. Gift-Poem ("Year in its cold beginning"). Muriel Rukeyser. **CP-RukeM**

Year Is a Great Circle or the Year Is a Great Mistake, The. Charles Olson. **CP-OlsoC**

Year is boarding, The. New Year's Eve. Richard Shelton. **SP-ShelR**

Year it didn't rain we waited, The. The Farmer's Testimony. Richard Shelton. **SP-ShelR**

Year of Grace and My Great-Grandfather. John Hewitt. **CP-HewiJ**

Year of griefs being through, they had to merge, The. A Blank. Thom Gunn. **CP-GunnT**

Year of Meteors (1859–60). Walt Whitman. **CP-WhitW**

Year of the Child, The. Robert Earl Hayden. **CP-HaydR**

Year or two, and grey Euripides, A. Baccalaureate. Archibald MacLeish. **CP-MacLA**

Year passes behind me, A. Speech of the Mother, from "The Middle of the Air." Muriel Rukeyser. **CP-RukeM**

Year runs through her phases; rain and sun, The. To W.E. Henley. Robert Louis Stevenson. **CP-StevR**

Year stood at its equinox, The. Christina Georgina Rossetti. **CP-RosC1** (Farm Walk, A.) **CP-RosC1**

Year That Trembled and Reel'd beneath Me. Walt Whitman. **CP-WhitW**

Year the head / went out into a, The. 1971. Robert Creeley. **CP-CreeR**

Year this truck was made, The. Working on the '58 Willys Pickup. Gary Snyder. **CP-SnydG**

Year turns. The wolf takes back her tit, The. Saturnalia. Louise Glück. **SP-GlücL**

Year was river-throated, with the stare of legend, The. Mother Garden's Round. Muriel Rukeyser. **CP-RukeM**

Yearling buck, shot through the lungs, The. Spikehorn. William Everson. **SP-EverW**

Yearly Distress, The. William Cowper. **CP-CowpW**

Yearly, with tent and rifle, our careless white men go. The Truce of the Bear. Rudyard Kipling. **CP-KiplR**

Years. Sylvia Plath. **CP-PlatS**

Years, The. Gary Snyder. **CP-SnydG**

Years after surviving. Word Basket Woman. Gary Snyder. **CP-SnydG**

Years after the neighbors. A Kind of Glory. Richard Shelton. **SP-ShelR**

Years ago I had a friend. Marge Piercy. *Fr.* Women's Laughter. **SP-PierM**

Years ago I lost. The Unquiet Ones. Stanley Jasspon Kunitz. **CP-KuniS**

Years ago I sat in this garden. The Politics of This Book. Leonard Cohen. **CP-CoheL**

Years ago my father read to me. John Haines. *Fr.* Roadways. **SP-HainJ**

Years ago, when I was rotten with virtue. Loveliness. Stephen Dunn. **SP-DunnS**

Years are but half a score, The. On the Big Horn. John Greenleaf Whittier. **CP-WhitJ**

Years are many since his hand, The. William Forster. John Greenleaf Whittier. **CP-WhitJ**

Years are many since, in youth and hope, The. Miriam. John Greenleaf Whittier. **CP-WhitJ**

Years As Catches, The. Robert Duncan. **SP-DuncR**

Year's at the spring, The. Robert Browning. **ArNa; BLPA; BLPL; BoTP; CoGr; EBCP; EBEvV; FHYEP; FaBV; FaBoBe; FaFP; FaPON; GoJo; HBV; HBVY; ImPo; LiTB; NTCP; OBEV; OBVV; OHIP; PAI; PDV; PoPl; PoToHe; SoSe; TEP; TFi; TRV; TrCP; TrGrPo; TreF; UnPo; WGRP; YeAr** *Fr.* Pippa Passes. **CP-BroR1**

(Pippa's Song.) **BLPL; BoTP; CoGr; EBCP; FaFP; FaPON; GoJo; ImPo; LiTB; NTCP; OBEV; OBVV; OHIP; PDV; TEP; TRV; TrCP; TreF; UnPo**

(Song: "Year's at the Spring, The.") **EBEvV; FHYEP; HBV; HBVY;**

PoPl; SoSe; TFi; TrGrPo

Year's Awakening, The. Thomas Hardy. **CP-HardT**

Years back, I hitched to Jamaica husband He makin' good. Tartine, Strumming Her Opera. Laurence Lieberman. **SP-LiebL**

Years before action when the wish alone. Course. Muriel Rukeyser. **CP-RukeM**

Year's doors open, The. January First. Octavio Paz, *tr. fr. Spanish by* Elizabeth Bishop. **CP-BishE**

Year's End. John Clellon Holmes. **SP-HolmJ**

Year's End. Ted Kooser. **SP-KoosT**

Year's End. Richard Wilbur. **CP-WilbR**

Years gone by in Chicago once. Algeria. Hayden Carruth. **CP-CarHS**

Years Had Worn Their Season's Belt, The. George Meredith. **CP-MerG2**

Years have gathered grayly, The. In a Eweleaze near Weatherbury. Thomas Hardy. **CP-HardT**

Years have gone. It is spring, The. Andrée Rexroth. Kenneth Rexroth. **SP-RexrK**

Years in the bottom scum. Mayflies. Brendan Galvin. **SP-GalvB**

Years later / I fall back in. The Robbie's Dance. Al Young. **CP-YounA**

Years later, I find the old grammar, yellowed. Night. Fox-Fire: 1956. Robert Penn Warren. *Fr.* Mortmain. **SP-WarrR**

Years. Many years. Friends laugh, including. Essay on Love. Hayden Carruth. **CP-CarHS**

Years of my life were odd that now are even, The. The Guilty Man. Stanley Jasspon Kunitz. **CP-KuniS**

Years of the Dog. Archibald MacLeish. **CP-MacLA**

Years of the Modern. Walt Whitman. **CP-WhitW**

Year's run out, The. Timing. Archie Randolph Ammons. **SP-AmmoA**

Years seem to tumble, The. The Years. Gary Snyder. **CP-SnydG**

Year's Sheddings, The. George Meredith. **CP-MerG2**

Years since (but names to me before). The Singer. John Greenleaf Whittier. **CP-WhitJ**

Years spin quicker since that day I stood, The. In Recollection of Drumcliffe, September 1948. John Hewitt. **CP-HewiJ**

Year's Spinning, A. Elizabeth Barrett Browning. **CP-BroEB**

Years standing round in a ring, The. Malcolm Lowry. **CP-LowrM**

Years that did not count—Civilians in the towns, The. Hiatus. Louis MacNeice. **CP-MacNL**

Years that since we met have flown, The. An Autograph. John Greenleaf Whittier. **CP-WhitJ**

Year's Windfalls, A. Christina Georgina Rossetti. **CP-RosC1**

Wind of January, The. **YeAr**

Yeats Died Saturday in France. Delmore Schwartz. **SP-SchwD**

Yee happy floods! that now must passe. Lucasta, Taking the Waters at Tunbridge. Richard Lovelace. **CP-LoveR**

Yee pretty Huswives, wo'd ye know. To the Little Spinners. Robert Herrick. **CP-HerrR**

Yell'ham-Wood's Story. Thomas Hardy. **CP-HardT**

Yellow. Robert Creeley. **CP-CreeR**

Yellow. Anne Sexton. **CP-SextA**

Yellow Afternoon. Wallace Stevens. **CP-StevW**

Yellow and pale as ripened corn. Lines for a Painting by Leighton. Robert Browning. **CP-BroR2**

Yellow Cab. Charles Bukowski. **SP-BukC1**

Yellow Chimney, The. William Carlos Williams. **CP-WilW2**

Yellow dust on a bumble. Troths. Carl Sandburg. **CP-SandC**

Yellow Emperor went wandering, The. The Lost Pearl. Chuang Tzu, *tr. fr. Chinese by* Thomas Merton. **CP-MertT**

Yellow Evening Star. Carl Sandburg. **CP-SandC**

Yellow fingers / lift a match to. Match. Donald Hall. **CP-HallD**

Yellow flower / (Light and spirit), A. Song for Nobody. Thomas Merton. **CP-MertT; SP-MertT**

Yellow Flower, The. William Carlos Williams. **CP-WilW2**

Yellow Flowers. James Schuyler. **CP-SchuJ**

Yellow-Hammer, The. Thomas Hardy. **CP-HardT**

Yellow leaf, from the darkness, A. Brooding Grief. David Herbert Lawrence. **CP-LawrD**

Yellow leaves speak early November's heart on the river. Prairie Woodland. Carl Sandburg. **CP-SandC**

Yellow-lit Budweiser signs over oaken bars. Uptown. Allen Ginsberg. **CP-GinsA**

Yellow of the Mask, The. Charles Olson. **CP-OlsoC**

Yellow Pitcher Plant. Thom Gunn. **CP-GunnT**

Yellow ramtilla stiffens in the noon. Alun Lewis. *Fr.* Indian Day. **CP-LewiA**

Yellow scarf runs through his fingers, A. Courtship, Diligence. Rita Dove. **SP-DoveR**

Yellow Season, The. William Carlos Williams. **CP-WilW2**

Yellow Stones—Sea of Majestic Doves. Kenneth Patchen. **CP-PatcK**

Yellow Submarine. The Beatles. **CP-Beatl**

Yellow sun steps over the mountain-top, The. A Bad Beginning. David Herbert Lawrence. **CP-LawrD**

Yellow Tree Peony, The. William Carlos Williams. **CP-WilW2**

Yellow, yellow, yellow, yellow! Primrose. William Carlos Williams. **CP-WilW1**

Yeou taught men to break branches. Canto 53. Ezra Pound. **SP-PounE** *Fr.* Cantos. **CP-PoCan**

Yer Blues. The Beatles. **CP-Beatl**

Yerevan. John Updike. *Fr.* Postcards from Soviet Cities. **CP-UpdiJ**

Yes – we excel in arts and arms. A Story of a Cock and a Bull. Christopher Smart. **SP-SmarC**

Yes. / It's May 20th and the leaves. Leaves That Talk. Anne Sexton. **CP-SextA**

Yes, / of old wire hangers that remain in the closet. Three of Swords. Diane Wakoski. **SP-WakoD**

Yes, a long cool vindt is pacing over the plains and beside it Captain. Captain Bada. Frank O'Hara. **SP-OharF**

Yes. After all my arguments with myself. Sonnet. Hayden Carruth. **CP-CarHS** *Fr.* Sonnets.

Yes! all is past—swift time has fled away. Fragment. Percy Bysshe Shelley. *Fr.* Posthumous Fragments of Margaret Nicholson. **CP-ShelP**

Yes, always now / He follows me. The Robin. Wystan Hugh Auden. **CP-AudWJ**

Yes and It's Hopeless. Allen Ginsberg. **CP-GinsA**

Yes and No. Wystan Hugh Auden. **CP-AudWJ**

Yes and No. Ogden Nash. **CP-NashO**

Yes and when the warm unseasonable weather. Memory Green. Archibald MacLeish. **CP-MacLA**

Yes at first you / go down smooth as. Margaret Atwood. **SP-AtwM1**

Yes. Autumn. The leaves yellow and red. The Answer. Stephen Berg. **SP-BergS**

Yes brothers you invented jazz. Tribute. Al Young. **CP-YounA**

Yes but even / 4 or(&). Edward Estlin Cummings. **CP-CummE**

Yes but your sweetness. Echo. Robert Creeley. **CP-CreeR**

Yes, call me by my pet-name! let me hear. Sonnet. Elizabeth Barrett Browning. *Fr.* Sonnets from the Portuguese. **CP-BroEB**

Yes, clients report it the tidiest way. Rumor Unverified Stop Can You Confirm Stop. Robert Penn Warren. *Fr.* Ballad of a Sweet Dream of Peace. **SP-WarrR**

Yes, contumelious fair, you scorn. The Author Apologizes to a Lady, for His Being a Little Man. Christopher Smart. **SP-SmarC**

—Yes for a time they held as well. Gerard Manley Hopkins. **CP-HopkG**

Yes, friend, I own these tales of Arabia. Tales of Arabia. Robert Louis Stevenson. **CP-StevR**

Yes, holy be thy resting place. Emily Brontë. **CP-BronE**

Yes! hope may with my strong desire keep pace. Michelangelo Buonarroti, *tr. fr.* Italian by William Wordsworth. **CP-WorW1**

Yes, I am a thief of thoughts. "Bob Dylan." *Fr.* 11 Outlined Epitaphs. **CP-DylaB**

"Yes," I answered you last night. Lady's "Yes," The. Elizabeth Barrett Browning. **CP-BroEB**

Yes, I beheld th' Athenian Queen. On Receiving from the Right Hon. the Lady Frances Shirley a Standish and Two Pens. Alexander Pope. **CP-PopeA**

Yes, I being / the terrible puppet of my dreams, shall. The Visible the Untrue. Hart Crane. **CP-CranH**

Yes, I have lied, and so must walk my way. Arthur Hugh Clough. *Fr.* Blank Misgivings of a Creature Moving About in Worlds Not Realized. **SP-ClouA**

Yes, I have seen their eyes. In peaceful gardens. Eighth Elegy. Children's Elegy. Muriel Rukeyser. **CP-RukeM**

Yes, I have walked in California. A Short Walk along the Coast. Nicholas Vachel Lindsay. *Fr.* Golden Whales of California. **CP-LindV**

Yes, I have written. Albert Einstein (1879–1955). Siv Cedering Fox. *Fr.* Letters from the Astronomers. **SP-CedeS**

Yes, I know. February 17th. Anne Sexton. **CP-SextA**

Yes, I Know. Stevie Smith. **CP-SmitS**

Yes, I know—Yes. Marsden Hartley. **CP-HartM**

Yes, I loved him all to well. Eva. Christina Georgina Rossetti. **CP-RosC3**

Yes, I only got here on my own. On My Own. Philip Levine. **SP-LeviP**

Yes: I perceive it's to your Love. The Letter's Triumph. Thomas Hardy. **CP-HardT**

Yes, I promise I will spread my sails to leave you. Personal Odyssey. James Liddy. **CP-LiddJ**

Yes, I remember, and still remember wailing. Robert Louis Stevenson. **CP-StevR**

Yes, I too could face death and not shrink. Christina Georgina Rossetti. **CP-RosC3**

Yes, I was only sidesman here when last. Bristol and Clifton. Sir John Betjeman. **CP-BetjJ**

Yes, if the intensities of hope and fear. The Liturgy. William Wordsworth. *Fr.* Ecclesiastical Sonnets. **CP-WorW2**

Yes I'm glad. The Leadbelly Song. Al Young. **CP-YounA**

Yes I'm lonely wanna die. Yer Blues. The Beatles. **CP-Beatl**

Yes, I'm the lady he wrote the sonnets to. Long View from the Suburbs. Jane Cooper. **SP-CoopJ**

Yes: [or Yes!] in the sea of life enisled. To Marguerite—Continued. Matthew Arnold. **SP-ArnoM** *Fr.* Switzerland.

Yes is a pleasant country. Edward Estlin Cummings. **CP-CummE; SP-CummE**

Yes It Is. The Beatles. **CP-Beatl**

Yes, it is there, the city full of music. It Is There. Muriel Rukeyser. **CP-RukeM**

Yes, it was Bedford Park the vision came from. Narcissus. Sir John Betjeman. **CP-BetjJ**

Yes, it was the mountain Echo. William Wordsworth. **CP-WorW1**

Yes it was the prince's kiss. Fable. Muriel Rukeyser. **CP-RukeM**

Yes, it's slow, docked of amours. Basil Bunting, *after the Latin of* Horace. **CP-BuntB**

Yes, let them gather! Summon forth. The World's Convention. John Greenleaf Whittier. **CP-WhitJ**

Yes, my ha't 's ez ha'd ez stone. A Coquette Conquered. Paul Laurence Dunbar. **CP-DunbP**

Yes! my Lesbia! let us prove. Catullus. *See* Carmen 5: "Lesbia / live with me."

Yes, noble old Warrior! this heart has beat high. *ad. fr. German of* Stolberg. Samuel Taylor Coleridge. **CP-ColeS**

Yes, our election's past, and we've been free. The Election. George Crabbe. **SP-CrabG** *Fr.* The Borough.

Yes, pile the marble o'er him! It is well. Leggett's Monument. John Greenleaf Whittier. **CP-WhitJ**

Yes, rub some soap upon your feet! A Hike on the Downs. Sir John Betjeman. **CP-BetjJ**

"Yes," said the sister with the little pinched face. The Drunkard's Funeral. Nicholas Vachel Lindsay. **CP-LindV**

Yes, self-obsession fills our daily clothes. John Updike. *Fr.* Spanish Sonnets. **CP-UpdiJ**

Yes; since she knows not need. Rake-hell Muses. Thomas Hardy. **CP-HardT**

Yes; such it was. A Two-Years' Idyll. Thomas Hardy. **CP-HardT**

Yes; thank my stars! as early as I knew. Satire II of Dr. John Donne, Versified. Alexander Pope. **CP-PopeA**

Yes, that was a Sunless bad Friday. Reply of the County of Surrey to the Poet's Pathetic Address in Dispraise of Jean. George Meredith. **CP-MerG2**

Yes, the Dead Speak to Us. Carl Sandburg. **CP-SandC**

Yes, the gal I got. Hero Blues. "Bob Dylan." **CP-DylaB**

Yes, the Secret Mind Whispers. Al Young. **CP-YounA**

Yes the simplicity of my life. Dancing. Al Young. **CP-YounA**

"Yes, the Town Clerk will see you." In I went. The Town Clerk's Views. Sir John Betjeman. **CP-BetjJ**

Yes, then, always, as the rain, a star. The Billion Freedoms. Kenneth Patchen. **CP-PatcK**

Yes, there is one thing braver than all flowers. Immortal. William Carlos Williams. **CP-WilW1**

Yes, these are the dog-days, Fortunatus. Under Sirius. Wystan Hugh Auden. **CP-AudeW**

Yes, they are alive and can have those colors. A Blessing in Disguise. John Ashbery. **SP-AshbJ**

Yes, they remember you. William Dickey. **SP-DickW** *Fr.* At Your Old House. **SP-DickW**

Yes, theyll let you play. A Poem for Players. Al Young. **CP-YounA**

Yes, this family portrait. Family Portrait. Carlos Drummond de Andrade, *tr. fr. Portuguese by* Elizabeth Bishop. **CP-BishE**

Yes, this is how it was to have been born. Upon Looking into Sylvia Plath's Letters Home. John Updike. **CP-UpdiJ**

Yes, this is the place. He Revisits the Spot. Wystan Hugh Auden. **CP-AudWJ**

Yes! Thou Art Fair, Yet Be Not Moved. William Wordsworth. **CP-WorW2**

Yes, though He well may tremble at the sound. Conclusion. William Wordsworth. *Fr.* Sonnets upon the Punishment of Death. **CP-WorW2**

Yes, wave your magic. Charles Henri Ford. **SP-FordC** *Fr.* Emblems of Arachne.

Yes, we are fighting at last, it appears. This morning, as usual. Claude to Eustace. Arthur Hugh Clough. **EBVV; OXAEP-2; PeVV** *Fr.* Amours de Voyage. **SP-ClouA**

Yes, we have liv'd—one pang, and then we part! Epitaph on Dr. Francis Atterbury, Bishop of Rochester, Who Died in Exile at Paris, 1732; a Dialogue. Alexander Pope. **CP-PopeA**

Yes, we were looking at each other. Looking at Each Other. Muriel Rukeyser. **CP-RukeM**

Yes, we'll pic-nic in the woods. George Meredith. **CP-MerG2**

Yes; we'll wed, my little fay. The Conformers. Thomas Hardy. **CP-HardT**

Yes! we've our Borough-vices, and I know. The Poor and Their Dwellings. George Crabbe. **SP-CrabG** *Fr.* The Borough.

Yes. Why do we áll, séeing of a soldier, bless him? bléss. The Soldier. Gerard Manley Hopkins. **CP-HopkG**

Yes! wisdom shines in all his mien. R. C. Dallas. Byron. **CP-Byron**

Yes, yes, and there is even a photograph. Meditation on a News Item. John Updike. **CP-UpdiJ**

Yes; yes; I am old. In me appears. The Aged Newspaper Soliloquizes. Thomas Hardy. **CP-HardT**

Yes, yes! that boon, life's richest treat. The Improvisatore. Samuel Taylor Coleridge. **CP-ColeS**

Yes, you despise the man to Books confin'd. Epistle I, to Sir Richard Temple, Lord Cobham. Alexander Pope. **CP-PopeA**

Yes, you have it; I can see. Partnership. Edwin Arlington Robinson. **CP-RobiE**

Yes; your up-dated modern page. The Jubilee of a Magazine. Thomas Hardy. **CP-HardT**

Yesterday. The Beatles. **CP-Beatl**

Yesterday a letter / spoke of our parting. Jane Cooper. *Fr.* The Weather of Six Mornings. **SP-CoopJ**

Yesterday all my troubles seemed so far away. Yesterday. The Beatles. **CP-Beatl**

Yesterday and Tomorrow. Paul Laurence Dunbar. **CP-DunbP**

Yesterday doth never smile. Nun's Aspiration. Ralph Waldo Emerson. **CP-EmerR**

Yesterday I felt this ode. Ode to Laziness. Pablo Neruda, *tr. fr. Spanish by* William Carlos Williams. **CP-WilW2**

Yesterday I held your hand. Yesterday and Tomorrow. Paul Laurence Dunbar. **CP-DunbP**

Yesterday I saw a face. The Horse of Desire. Robert Bly. **SP-BlyR**

Yesterday I wanted to. For Love. Robert Creeley. **CP-CreeR**

Yesterday I was told. Byron vs. DiMaggio. Peter Meinke. **SP-MeinP**

Yesterday, in a big market, I made seven thousand dollars. Back through the Looking Glass to This Side. John Ciardi. **SP-CiarJ**

Yesterday, in the night. Marsden Hartley. **CP-HartM**

Yesterday is History. Emily Dickinson. **CP-DickE**

Yesterday, Licinius, what a day it was. Catullus. *See* Carmen 50: "Other day we spent, The."

Yesterday Mrs. Friar phoned. "Mr. Ciardi." Suburban. John Ciardi. **SP-CiarJ**

Yesterday morning enormous the moon hung low on the ocean. Their Beauty Has More Meaning. Robinson Jeffers. **CP-JefR3**

Yesterday the fields were only grey with scattered snow. A Winter's Tale. David Herbert Lawrence. **CP-LawrD**

Yesterday They Tried. Kenneth Patchen. **CP-PatcK**

Yesterday, Today, and Forever. Emily Dickinson. **SP-DickE**

Yesterday you past / into your lips. . . your hips. Poem. Jim Carroll. **SP-CarrJ**

Yesterday's sundown was very beautiful—I know it is out of fashion to. The Ocean's Tribute. Robinson Jeffers. **CP-JefR3**

Yesternight, *also stands as sl. diff., shorter, separate poem* Hyde Park at Night before the War. David Herbert Lawrence. *Fr.* Night Songs. **CP-LawrD**

Yestreen I had a pint o' wine. Robert Burns. **CP-BurnR**

(Song: "Yestreen I had a pint o' wine.") **CP-BurnR**

Yet / Ere the season died a-cold. Ezra Pound. *See* Canto 81: "Zeus lies in Ceres' bosom."

Yet A Little While ("Heavan is not far, tho' far the sky"). Christina Georgina Rossetti. **CP-RosC2**

Yet a Little While ("I dreamed and did not seek: today I seek"). Christina Georgina Rossetti. **CP-RosC3**

Yet a Little While ("These days are long before I die"). Christina Georgina Rossetti. *See* Heaven Is Not Far.

Yet all comes out of this, that one door. Hafiz, *tr. by* Ralph Waldo Emerson. **CP-EmerR** *Fr.* Odes.

Yet are they here the same unbroken knot. Gypsies. William Wordsworth. **CP-WorW1**

Yet at the last, ere our spearmen had found him. Rudyard Kipling. **CP-KiplR** *Fr.* The Light That Failed.

Yet Cloe [*or* Chloe] sure was form'd without a Spot—. Alexander Pope. **AWP; ErPo; NOBE; OBSV** *Fr.* Epistle [II,] to a Lady[: Of the Characters of Women]. **CP-PopeA**

(Cloe [*or* Chloe].) **AWP; NOBE; OBSV**

Yet Dish. Gertrude Stein. **CP-SteiG**

Yet Do I Marvel. Countee Cullen. **CP-CullC**

Yet earth was very good in days of old, / And earth is lovely still. Sexagesima. Christina Georgina Rossetti. **CP-RosC2**

Yet from the antique heights or deeps of what. Front Door Soliloquy. Robert Ranke Graves. **CP-GravR**

Yet from those days three sights delighted me. The Tricycle. John Hewitt. **CP-HewiJ**

Yet Gentle Will the Griffin Be. Nicholas Vachel Lindsay. **CP-LindV** *Fr.* Poems about the Moon.

Yet had I not much. That I Had Had Courage When Young. Hayden Carruth. **CP-CarHS**

Yet Ha'e I Silence Left. "Hugh MacDiarmid." **NAEL-2** *Fr.* A Drunk Man Looks at the Thistle. **SP-MacDH**

Yet if some voice that man could trust. Tennyson. **OAEL-2** *Fr.* In Memoriam A. H. H. **CP-TennA**

Yet, if we look more closely, we shall find. Alexander Pope. **FiP** *Fr.* An Essay on Criticism. **CP-PopeA**

Yet in an hour to come, disdainful dust. Edna St. Vincent Millay. **CP-MillE**

Yet in spite / Of pleasure won, and knowledge not withheld. William Wordsworth. **PoEL-4** *Fr.* Summer Vacation. *Fr.* The Prelude; Growth of a Poet's Mind [1850 vers.]. **CP-WorW3**

Yet in the end, defeated too, worn out and ready to fall. The Oak-Leaves. Edna St. Vincent Millay. **CP-MillE**

Yet it was plain she struggled, and that salt. George Meredith. **EnVR** *Fr.* Modern Love. **CP-MerG1**

Yet let me flap this bug with gilded wings. Alexander Pope. **ECEV** *Fr.* Epistle to Dr. Arbuthnot. **CP-PopeA**

Yet look on me—take not thine eyes away. To ———. Percy Bysshe Shelley. **CP-ShelP**

Yet, love, mere love, is beautiful indeed. Sonnet. Elizabeth Barrett Browning. **BWW; CTC; HBV; OHCV; OXAEP-2; VLP** *Fr.* Sonnets from the Portuguese. **CP-BroEB**

Yet many a Novice of the cloistral shade. Continued [Dissolution of the Monasteries]. William Wordsworth. *Fr.* Ecclesiastical Sonnets. **CP-WorW2**

Yet men and beasts, astronomers will tell. The Element Fire Boasts of the Constellations. Anne Bradstreet. **CBCK** *Fr.* The Four Elements. **CP-BradA**

Yet more,—round many a Convent's blazing fire. Monastic Voluptuousness. William Wordsworth. *Fr.* Ecclesiastical Sonnets. **CP-WorW2**

Yet, O stricken heart, remember, O remember. In Memoriam F. A. S. Robert Louis Stevenson. **CP-StevR**

Yet once again do I behold the forms. William Wordsworth. **CP-WorW1**

(Fragment: "Yet once again.") **CP-WorW1**

Yet once again, ye banks and bowery nooks. July's Farewell. Arthur Hugh Clough. **SP-ClouA**

Yet once more, O ye Laurels, and once more. Lycidas. John Milton. **CP-MiltJ**

Yet pity for a horse o'er-driven. Tennyson. *Fr.* In Memoriam A. H. H. **CP-TennA**

Yet see (may as I do) a confect of my cure—a dolor. Catullus. *See* Carmen 65: "Although entangled in prolonged grief."

Yet shall my soule in silence still, *par. by* Countess of Pembroke, Mary Sidney Herbert. Bible, *O.T. See* Psalm 62: "Truly my soul waiteth upon God."

Yet sighs, dear sighs, indeed true friends you are. Sonnet 95. Sir Philip Sidney. *Fr.* Astrophil and Stella. **SP-SidnP**

Yet sometimes to the sorrow stricken. Ralph Waldo Emerson. **CP-EmerR**

Yet though thou fetch thy pedegree so farre, *ad. fr. Latin of* Juvenal. Sir Walter Ralegh. **CP-RaleW**

Yet to the wondrous St. Peter's, and yet to the solemn Rotonda. Ah, That I Were Far Away. Arthur Hugh Clough. **FaBoPP; OBNC** *Fr.* Amours de Voyage. **SP-ClouA**

Yet Truth is keenly sought for, and the wind. Latitudinarianism. William Wordsworth. *Fr.* Ecclesiastical Sonnets. **CP-WorW2**

Yet Unsayable, The. Robert Ranke Graves. **CP-GravR**

Yet we are safely at this port of call. Alun Lewis. *Fr.* Letter From the Cape. **CP-LewiA**

Yet what is this? the spring returns. George Meredith. **CP-MerG2**

Yet when I sawe my selfe to you was true. Ploche, or the Doubler. Sir Walter Ralegh. *Fr.* The Arte of English Poesie. **CP-RaleW**

Yet womanhood you reverence. The Lady and the Painter. Robert Browning. **SP-BroR2**

Yet, yet a moment, one dim ray of light. Alexander Pope. **NAEL-1; OAEL-1; PoEL-3** *Fr.* The Dunciad. **CP-PopeA**

   Carnations and Butterflies. **NOEC**

   Certain Type of Scientist Speaks, A. **ECEV**

   "More had she spoke, but yawn'd—All nature nods." **FHYEP**

   "Next, bidding all draw near on bended knees." **ECEV; OBSV**

    (Idle Pursuits.) **ECEV,** book IV, ll. 565–604;

   "Oh (cry'd the Goddess) for some pedant Reign!" **FaBoEH**

   Reign of Chaos, The. **EBEV; FaBoPV; SCV**

    (Chaos.) **LoBV**

    (Reign of Chaos, The.) **FiP**

    (Triumph of Dullness [or Dulness], The.) **NOBE; NoP**

   "She comes! she comes! the sable throne behold." **ECEV**

   Triumph of Dullness, The. **NOEC**

   Young Traveller Is Presented to the Goddess Dulness, A. **NOEC**

Yet, yet, Biscayans! we must meet our Foes. Feelings of a Noble Biscayan at One of Those Funerals 1810. William Wordsworth. **CP-WorW1**

Yet, Yet Ye Downcast Hours. Walt Whitman. **CP-WhitW**

Yett is ther hope: Then Love butt play thy part. Sonnet 3. Mary Sidney, Countess of Montgomery Wroth. *Fr.* Pamphilia to Amphilanthus. **CP-WrotM**

Yeux Glauques. Ezra Pound. **MoAmPo** *Fr.* Hugh Selwyn Mauberley. (Life and Contacts). **SP-PounE**

Yevtushenko, Voznesensky and I. A Dream. Charles Tomlinson. **CP-TomlC**

Yew Tree Guest House. Phoebe Hesketh. **SP-HeskP**

Yew-Tree on the Downs, The. David Herbert Lawrence. **CP-LawrD**

Yew-Trees. William Wordsworth. **CP-WorW1**

Yew's black fingers wag, The. Little Fugue. Sylvia Plath. **CP-PlatS**

Yggdrasill. Paul Muldoon. **SP-MuldP**

YgUDuh / ydoan / yunnuhstan. Edward Estlin Cummings. **CP-CummE**

Yield all, my love; but be withal as coy. Upon A.M. Sir John Suckling. **CP-SuckJ**

Yielding the Initiative. Marsden Hartley. **CP-HartM**

Yillow, yillow, yillow. Metamorphosis. Wallace Stevens. **CP-StevW**

Yipiyuk, The. Shel Silverstein. **SP-SilS2**

Yippee! she is shooting in the harbor! he is jumping. Blocks. Frank O'Hara. **SP-OharF**

Yoke of Tyranny, The. Sir Philip Sidney. *See* Sonnet 47: "What, have I thus betrayed my liberty?"

Yoko. Thom Gunn. **CP-GunnT**

Yom Kippur 1984. Adrienne Rich. **SP-RicA1**

Yon flakes that fret the eastern sky. Alfred Edward Housman. **CP-HousA**

Yon upland slope which hides the sun. Pastoral 2. George Meredith. *Fr.* Pastorals. **CP-MerG1**

Yon wild, mossy mountains sae lofty and wide. Robert Burns. **CP-BurnR**

Yonder. Richard Eberhart. **CP-EberR**

Yonder beyond all hopes of access. The Gorge. Robert Ranke Graves. **CP-GravR**

Yonder, by the eastward sea. Landscape: Beast. Thomas Merton. **SP-MertT** *Fr.* Figures for an Apocalypse. **CP-MertT**

Yonder deadfromtheneckup graduate of a. Edward Estlin Cummings. **CP-CummE**

Yonder see the morning blink. Alfred Edward Housman. **CP-HousA**

"Yonder," they told him, "things are not the same." By No Means Native. Adrienne Rich. **CP-RicAE**

Yonder's the man with his life in his hand. Atkins. George Meredith. **CP-MerG2**

Yong man called Melibeus, myghty and riche, A. The Tale of Melibee. Geoffrey Chaucer. *Fr.* The Canterbury Tales. **CP-ChauG**

YONG TCHING / his fourth son, to honour his forebears. Canto 61. Ezra Pound. *Fr.* Cantos. **CP-PoCan**

Yonnondio. Walt Whitman. **CP-WhitW**

Yorick is dead. Boy Hamlet walks forlorn. Epitaph for John Bunny, Motion-Picture Comedian. Nicholas Vachel Lindsay. *Fr.* Epitaphs for Two Players. **CP-LindV**

Yorkshire. Donald Davie. **CP-DavDo**

Yorkshire Pudding. Ogden Nash. *Fr.* Table Talk. **CP-NashO**

Yorktown. John Greenleaf Whittier. **CP-WhitJ**

You. Wystan Hugh Auden. **CP-AudeW**

You. Stephen Berg. **SP-BergS**

You. Charles Bukowski. **SP-BukC1**

You. Robert Creeley. **CP-CreeR**

You / in win / ter who sit. Edward Estlin Cummings. **CP-CummE**

You. David Herbert Lawrence. **CP-LawrD**

You. Kenneth Rexroth. **HoPM** *Fr.* A Bestiary. **SP-RexrK**

You a gentleman and I up from the grime—. December 24 and George McBride Is Dead. Richard Hugo. **CP-HugoR**

You Ain't Goin' Nowhere. "Bob Dylan." **CP-DylaB**

You: air-driven reft from the tuber-bitten soil. Adrienne Rich. **SP-RicA1** *Fr.* Contradictions: Tracking Poems.

You All Know the Story of the Other Woman. Anne Sexton. **CP-SextA**

You all your Youth observd the Golden Rule. To S[tothar]d. William Blake. **CP-BlakW**

You Also, Gaius Valerius Catullus. Archibald MacLeish. **CP-MacLA**

You always are making a god of your spouse. To Mrs. Houghton of Bormount. Jonathan Swift. **CP-SwifJ**

You always read about it. Cinderella. Anne Sexton. **CP-SextA**

You, Amos? But you're dead now. Hayden Carruth. *Fr.* The Sleeping Beauty. **CP-CarHL**

You & I out of all dreaming. It Sounds It. Anne Waldman. **SP-WaldA**

You and I think about it: who pays. The Bottom Line. Richard Shelton. **SP-ShelR**

You and Me and P.B. Shelley. Ogden Nash. **CP-NashO**

You & Rimbaud. I Believe in You. Charles Olson. **CP-OlsoC**

You, Andrew Marvell. Archibald MacLeish. **CP-MacLA**

You Angel You. "Bob Dylan." **CP-DylaB**

You announce that you are beautiful. Martial, *tr. by* William Matthews. **SP-MattW** *Fr.* Epigrams.

You approach me carrying a book. Superballs. Tom Clark. **SP-ClarT**

You Are. Etheridge Knight. **SP-KnigE**

You are a cousin of mine. The Seamless Garment. "Hugh MacDiarmid." **SP-MacDH**

You are a dead man. Your Death. Leonard Cohen. **CP-CoheL**

You are a friend then, as I make it out. Ben Jonson Entertains a Man from Stratford. Edwin Arlington Robinson. **CP-RobiE**

You are a lord, an earl[e], nay more, a man. To the Right Honourable Mildmay, Earl of Westmorland. Robert Herrick. **CP-HerrR**

You are a pond mirroring. In the Tub. John Updike. *Fr.* Living with a Wife. **CP-UpdiJ**

You are a roast beef I have purchased. Buying the Whore. Anne Sexton. **CP-SextA**

You are a sunrise. To a Golden-Haired Girl in a Louisiana Town. Nicholas Vachel Lindsay. **CP-LindV**

You are a tulip seen today. A Meditation for His Mistress[e]. Robert Herrick. **CP-HerrR**

You are a typical American woman. Fertile. William Carlos Williams. **CP-WilW2**

You are a wild look—out of an egg. Ted Hughes. **NoAM,** *sect.* 4; *Fr.* Stations. **SP-HughT**

You are alone on a desert. Hot blasting sand. In Your Hot Dream. Richard Hugo. **CP-HugoR**

You are already. Touch. Thom Gunn. **CP-GunnT**

You are always / with me. Words. Robert Creeley. **CP-CreeR**

You are an opening in me. Marge Piercy. *Fr.* Doing It Differently. **SP-PierM**

You are as faithless as a Carthaginian. A Satire on an Inconstant Lover. Jonathan Swift. **CP-SwifJ**

You are as gold. Song. Hilda Doolittle. **CP-DoolH**

You are beside me like a wall; I touch you with my fingers and. Adrienne Rich. **SP-RicA2** *Fr.* Shooting Script. **CP-RicAE**

You are clear. Garden. Hilda Doolittle. **CP-DoolH**

You are deceiv'd; I sooner may dull fair. Ode. Richard Lovelace. **CP-LoveR**

You are esconced in your vain folly. Crossing Lady-Stanley, Here, 1868. Steve Griffiths. **SP-GrifS**

You are ever / in my thoughts. Roxy. James Schuyler. **CP-SchuJ**

You are falling asleep and I sit looking at you. After Dark. Adrienne Rich. **CP-RicAE; SP-RicA1; SP-RicA2**

You are fishing a lake but so far no fish. In Your Blue Dream. Richard Hugo. **CP-HugoR**

You are fishing but have walked away from your rod. In Your Wild Dream. Richard Hugo. **CP-HugoR**

You are forever April. Song. William Carlos Williams. **CP-WilW2**

You are going to be pleasantly surprised by this. Miami You Are About to Be Surprised. Thomas Merton. *Fr.* South. *Fr.* The Geography of Lograire. **CP-MertT**

You are going to fall in love. James Liddy. *Fr.* A Munster Song of Love and War. **CP-LiddJ**

You Are Gorgeous and I'm Coming. Frank O'Hara. **SP-OharF**

You Are Happy. Margaret Atwood. **SP-AtwM1**

You are here now. The Sleeping Fury. Louise Bogan. **CP-BogaL**

"You are large, Father Graham," the young fan opined. The Jolly Greene Giant. John Updike. **CP-UpdiJ**

You are like born at the end of the year. Born in December. Muriel Rukeyser. **CP-RukeM**

You are like the snow only. Edward Estlin Cummings. **CP-CummE**

You are lovely as a river. A Flowing River. William Carlos Williams. **CP-WilW2**

You are made of almost nothing. The Dragonfly. Louise Bogan. **CP-BogaL**

You are most illustrious. Emily Dickinson. **SP-DickE**

You Are My Heart's Bouquet. Gilbert Sorrentino. **SP-SorrG**

You are near me. The night. Passion for the Sky. Joseph Ceravolo. **SP-CeraJ**

You are not going to,dear. You are not going to and. Edward Estlin Cummings. **CP-CummE**

You are not here! the quaint witch Memory sees. To Maria Gisborne in England, from Italy. Percy Bysshe Shelley. **NOBE** *Fr.* Letter to Maria Gisborne. **CP-ShelP**

You are not looking at all well, my dear. The Doctor. Stevie Smith. **CP-SmitS**

"You are not pregnant," said the man. All the Little Animals. Muriel Rukeyser. **CP-RukeM**

You are not random picked. I tell you you. Lofty in the Palais de Danse. Thom Gunn. **CP-GunnT**

You are not that Daphne. Changes. John Haines. **SP-HainJ**

You are not the first man to have the shakes. Comfort. Malcolm Lowry. **CP-LowrM**

You are not to trouble yourself. For Joanne in Poland. Al Young. **CP-YounA**

You are now / In London, that great sea. Percy Bysshe Shelley. **ChER; EBEV; OBRV** *Fr.* Letter to Maria Gisborne. **CP-ShelP**

"You Are Old, Father William," the young man said. Father William. "Lewis Carroll." **CP-CarrL** *Fr.* Alice's Adventures in Wonderland.

"You are old," said the youth, "and your jaws are too weak." "Lewis Carroll." **OxBM** *Fr.* Father William. **CP-CarrL** *Fr.* Alice's Adventures in Wonderland.

You are only one of many. One of Many. Stevie Smith. **CP-SmitS**

You are parceled out over the post office. The De Carlo Lots. Anne Waldman. **SP-WaldA**

You are sick and old, and there is a closing in. Sick Man Looks at Flowers. Gwendolyn Brooks. *Fr.* A Catch of Shy Fish. **SP-BrooG**

You are sick, that's sure—they say. Robert Browning. **CP-BroR2**

You are so interested in yourself. To a Certain Friend. David Herbert Lawrence. **CP-LawrD**

You are talking to a man named Buss. You knew Buss. In Your Dream on the Eve of Success. Richard Hugo. **CP-HugoR**

You Are That Frail. . . . Hart Crane. **CP-CranH**

You are "the best of cut-throats:"—do not start. Byron. **FaBoEH; IHNG** *Fr.* Canto the Ninth. *Fr.* Don Juan. **CP-Byron**

(On Wellington ("You are 'the best of cut-throats' ").) **IHNG**

You are the cause of this destruction, Lesbia. Catullus. *See* Carmen 75: "Reason blinded by sin, Lesbia."

You are the children of Eve by the apple. The Serpent's Cradle Song. Archibald MacLeish. *Fr.* Songs for Eve. **CP-MacLA**

You are the dark song / of the morning. Rage. Mary Oliver. **SP-OlivM**

You are the dreamer who dreams the world, and yet. Hayden Carruth. *Fr.* The Sleeping Beauty. **CP-CarHL**

You are the far / far figure straying there. Seascape for an Engraver. Kay Boyle. **CP-BoylK**

You are the first muse who came to stay. The Muse Who Came to Stay. Erica Jong. **SP-JongE**

You are the last. George Oppen. *Fr.* Of Being Numerous. **CP-OppeG**

You are the mask I was given. Face. Richard Shelton. **SP-ShelR**

You are the one man. For a Friend. Robert Creeley. **CP-CreeR**

You are the scorched columns, the green nave which struck thirteen times. For an American. Kay Boyle. **CP-BoylK**

You are the sun / in reverse, all energy. Margaret Atwood. **SP-AtwM1**

You are tired, / (I think). Edward Estlin Cummings. **CP-CummE**

You are to me, love, half family half tree. She. Charles Olson. **CP-OlsoC**

You are traveling to play basketball. Your team's. In Your Young Dream. Richard Hugo. **CP-HugoR**

You are walking / down the corridor. A man. Pornographic Poem. Marilyn Hacker. **SP-HackM**

You are walking in the grounds. A Belated Birthday Poem. James Schuyler. **CP-SchuJ**

You are white clean through. Heimdall. Frederick Morgan. **SP-MorgF**

You are younger than I am, you are. Girl and Horse, 1928. Margaret Atwood. **SP-AtwM1**

You arrived arthritic for the cure. Hot Springs. Richard Hugo. **CP-HugoR**

You Ask for a "Volume of Nonsense." Byron. **CP-Byron**

You ask for love but what you want is healing. Twins. Jane Cooper. **SP-CoopJ**

You ask me, brothers, why I flinch. Time Marches On. Ogden Nash. **CP-NashO**

You ask me how I write. This is how I write. I Bury My Girlfriend. Leonard Cohen. **CP-CoheL**

You ask me questions. Poetry, the Unpredictable. Diane Wakoski. *Fr.* Fifteen Poems for a Lunar Eclipse None of Us Saw. **SP-WakoD**

You ask me what is Genius?' 'tis that. George Meredith. **CP-MerG2**

You ask me why I bear such rage in heart. Antéros. Gérard de Nerval, *tr. fr. French by* Richard Wilbur. **CP-WilbR**

You ask what I have found, and far and wide I go. The Curse of Cromwell. William Butler Yeats. **CP-YeatW**

You ask why can't Clarissa hold her tongue. Gerard Manley Hopkins. *Fr.* Seven Epigrams. **CP-HopkG**

You ask why I am sad to-day. Weltschmertz. Paul Laurence Dunbar. **CP-DunbP**

You Ask Why Sometimes I Say Stop. Marge Piercy. **SP-PierM**

You asked me if I wrote now? Emily Dickinson. **SP-DickE**

You asked me to come:it was raining a little. Edward Estlin Cummings. **CP-CummE**

You ask[e] me what I do[e], and how I live? His Answer to a Friend. Robert Herrick. **CP-HerrR**

You bear the mark of what you are. Frederick Morgan. *Fr.* Meditations for Autumn. **SP-MorgF**

You beastly child, I wish you had miscarried. Lightly Bound. Stevie Smith. **CP-SmitS**

You beat your Pate, and fancy Wit will come. Another [Epigram]. Alexander Pope. **CP-PopeA**

You beauty, O you beauty! Invocation to the Moon. David Herbert Lawrence. **CP-LawrD**

You been down to the bottom with a bad man, babe. Baby, Stop Crying. "Bob Dylan." **CP-DylaB**

You Begin. Margaret Atwood. **SP-AtwM2**

You being in love. Edward Estlin Cummings. **CP-CummE**

You believed in a world that has never come. In Memory. Jean Garrigue. **SP-GarrJ**

You *Bellenden, Griffin*, and little *Lepell*. Alexander Pope. *Fr.* Epigrams Occasion'd by an Invitation to Court. **CP-PopeA**

You bet it would've made a tender movie! Sweet Sixteen Lines. Al Young. **CP-YounA**

You Bet Travel Is Broadening. Ogden Nash. **CP-NashO**

You better sure shall live, not evermore, *tr. of* Horace, *Odes, 2.10.* Sir Philip Sidney. **SP-SidnP**

You bid me hold my peace. Worn Out. Paul Laurence Dunbar. **CP-DunbP**

You bid me write t' amuse the tedious hours. 5.12. Ovid, *tr. by* William Cowper. **CP-CowpW** *Fr.* Elegies.

You big sun. Sun with Hands for Rays. Diane Wakoski. *Fr.* Fifteen Poems for a Lunar Eclipse None of Us Saw. **SP-WakoD**

You blame me that I ran away? Arcades Ambo. Robert Browning. **CP-BroR2**

You blessed shades, which give mee silent rest. Sonnet 30. Mary Sidney, Countess of Montgomery Wroth. **KTR** *Fr.* Pamphilia to Amphilanthus. **CP-WrotM**

You blessed starrs which doe heavns glory show. Sonnet 41. Mary Sidney, Countess of Montgomery Wroth. *Fr.* Pamphilia to Amphilanthus. **CP-WrotM**

You borrow through dusty labyrinths of time. The Whole World's in a Terrible Chassis. Isabella Gardner. **CP-GardI**

You breathe / through your mouth. Cold Faces. Jim Carroll. **SP-CarrJ**

You bring me good news from the clinic. Face Lift. Sylvia Plath. **CP-PlatS**

You bring me Ocean Star a dreaming Song. This Summer Day. Kenneth Patchen. **CP-PatcK**

You bring the hawthorn and laburnum back. Peace Pact. John Hewitt. **CP-HewiJ**

You, browed maiden, your eyes' bright pictures have caught me. The Witch I. David Herbert Lawrence. **CP-LawrD**

You built your house. Building. Richard Shelton. *Fr.* Three Poems For A Twenty-Fifth Anniversary. **SP-ShelR**

You call: / guarded voices. O. Janis Joplin's Dead: Long Live Pearl. James Schuyler. **CP-SchuJ**

You call it, "Love lies bleeding,"—so you may. Love Lies Bleeding. William Wordsworth. **CP-WorW2**

You call me Mad tis Folly to do so. To F[laxman]. William Blake. **CP-BlakW**

You call me sane, insane—I tell you men. The Murderess. Louise Glück. **SP-GlücL**

You call yourself a man. Mary, Pity Women! Rudyard Kipling. **CP-KiplR**

You called yourself a dishwater blond. What You Waited For. Marge Piercy. **SP-PierM**

You came / to be / in the Month of Malcolm. Circling the Daughter. Etheridge Knight. **SP-KnigE**

You came as sleep, warily. Frederick Morgan. *Fr.* Death Mother. **SP-MorgF**

You Came By on Bamboo Stilts, Playing Horse. . . . James Liddy. **CP-LiddJ**

You came from the Aztecs. Aztec. Carl Sandburg. **CP-SandC**

You came to see me that day and. That Day. Archie Randolph Ammons. **SP-AmmoA**

You came to the side of the bed. The Encounter. Louise Glück. *Fr.* Marathon. **SP-GlücL**

You came with a cello in one hand. The Left-Handed Cellist. Rita Dove. **SP-DoveR**

You can / die for it— / an idea. Sunrise. Mary Oliver. **SP-OlivM**

You can always spot them, even from high up. From Altitude, the Diamonds. Richard Hugo. **CP-HugoR**

You can appreciate. Soaker. Archie Randolph Ammons. **SP-AmmoA**

You Can Be a Republican, I'm a Genocrat. Ogden Nash. **CP-NashO**

You can beat me, beat me! beat me, said the demon who stood. Patience of an Angel. Max Jacob, *tr. fr. French by* Elizabeth Bishop. **CP-BishE**

You can count on anything, but you can't count on impulse. Impulse. David Herbert Lawrence. **CP-LawrD**

You can drum on immense drums. Carl Sandburg. *Fr.* The People, Yes. **CP-SandC**

You Can Have It. Philip Levine. **SP-LeviP**

You can hurry the pictures toward you but. The Lamp. Charles Olson. **CP-OlsoC; SP-OlsoC**

You can join the others now. First Goodbye. Louise Glück. *Fr.* Marathon. **SP-GlücL**

You can just about keep pace with his. His Steps. Daniel Gerard Hoffman. **SP-HoffD**

You can scarcely grant me now. As a Less than Robber. Robert Ranke Graves. **CP-GravR**

You can see them from the road: go far and deep. Charleston Plantations. May Sarton. **SP-SartM**

You Can Start the Poetry Now, Or: News from Crazy Horse. Thomas McGrath. **SP-McGrT**

You cannot make Remembrance grow. Emily Dickinson. **CP-DickE**

You cannot, must not, Orpheus, look back, my soul. Malcolm Lowry. *Fr.* The Roar of the Sea and the Darkness. **CP-LowrM**

You cannot put a big load in a small bag. Symphony for a Sea Bird. Chuang Tzu, *tr. fr. Chinese by* Thomas Merton. **CP-MertT**

You cannot put a Fire out. Emily Dickinson. **CP-DickE**

You cannot take itself. Emily Dickinson. **CP-DickE**

You can't / tell what's. Cold Rheum. Archie Randolph Ammons. **SP-AmmoA**

You can't come in! (*Knock, knock*) The store is closed! A Masque of Mercy. Robert Frost. **CP-FrosR**

You can't come with us. Another Day (You can't come). Muriel Rukeyser. **CP-RukeM**

You can't depend on your family. Busload of Faith. "Lou Reed." **SP-ReedL**

You Can't Do That. The Beatles. **CP-Beatl**

You can't grip years, Postume. Basil Bunting, *after the Latin of* Horace. **CP-BuntB**

You can't live here without breathing. Margaret Atwood. *Fr.* Two-Headed Poems. **SP-AtwM2**

You can't make it. Sour Milk. Diane Wakoski. **SP-WakoD**

You can't remember, giving a day. Dreams. James Schuyler. **CP-SchuJ**

You can't say it that way any more. And "Ut Pictura Poesis" Is Her Name. John Ashbery. **SP-AshbJ**

You can't take me with a look. Red Sun. Joseph Ceravolo. **SP-CeraJ**

You can't weep like them, can't pound the rail. Docking at Palermo. Richard Hugo. **CP-HugoR**

You cast me from your filthy womb. Frederick Morgan. *Fr.* Death Mother. **SP-MorgF**

You celebrate with kisses the good fortune. Mankind and Ocean. Robert Ranke Graves. **CP-GravR**

You, Charidemus, who my cradle swung. In Charidemum. Robert Louis Stevenson. **CP-StevR**

You charmed [*or* charm'd] me not with that fair face. Song. John Dryden. **SP-DrydJ** *Fr.* An Evening's Love.

You chose a lion to be your lover—. Lion Lover. Robert Ranke Graves. **CP-GravR**

You, Chris, *contrite* I never thought to see. John Berryman. *Fr.* Sonnets to Chris. **CP-BerrJ**

You climb three "golden steps." Always Another Viewpoint. Kenneth Patchen. **CP-PatcK**

You coasted along / to larger houses, gadgets, more machines. The Coasters. John Hewitt. **CP-HewiJ**

You come along. . . tearing your shirt. . . yelling about Jesus. To a Contemporary Bunkshooter. Carl Sandburg. **CP-SandC**

You come blonde visiting through the black air. John Berryman. *Fr.* Sonnets to Chris. **CP-BerrJ**

You come down to a time. Myth & Ritual. Howard Nemerov. **CP-NemeH**

You come from poets, kings, bankrupts, preachers. For My Son. Muriel Rukeyser. **CP-RukeM**

You come in late, wiping your lips. The Other. Sylvia Plath. **CP-PlatS**

You come to fetch me from my work tonight. Putting in the Seed. Robert Frost. **CP-FrosR**

You come to Spain but do not remain. Anna Veronica. Ernest Hemingway. **CP-HemiE** *Fr.* The Soul of Spain with McAlmon and Bird the Publishers.

You Communists and Republicans! The Approaching Hour. William Carlos Williams. **CP-WilW2**

You constituted Time. Emily Dickinson. **CP-DickE**

You could be sitting now in a carrel. A Late Aubade. Richard Wilbur. **CP-WilbR**

You could be the beginning of treated birds. To a Lovely Lady Gone to Theory. John Ciardi. **SP-CiarJ**

You could go on / talking to an imaginary. Wisdom. Robert Creeley. **CP-CreeR**

You could love here, not the lovely goat. The Milltown Union Bar. Richard Hugo. **CP-HugoR**

You could pick one up, any one. Flood Plain. William Matthews. *Fr.* Flood. **SP-MattW**

You could see it way out crawling slow. Storm in Acquafredda. Richard Hugo. **CP-HugoR**

You could sit there with the stains on your shoes. Robert Frost. **OBD** *Fr.* Home Burial. **CP-FrosR**

You could then, my heart, wit, eye, mean in proposing love our aim. Catullus. *See* Carmen 109: "Joy of my life! you tell me this."

You couldn't have heard about it there—. A Letter From Aunt Belle. Ted Kooser. **SP-KoosT**

You couldn't pack a Broadwood half a mile. The Song of the Banjo. Rudyard Kipling. **CP-KiplR**

You crash over the trees. Storm. Hilda Doolittle. **CP-DoolH**

You cried. You cried. Stanley Jasspon Kunitz. *Fr.* Journal for My Daughter. **CP-KuniS**

You cross the ramp, its sure suspension. Still Moment at Dun Laoghaire. Tess Gallagher. **SP-GallT**

You cry, waking from a nightmare. Little Sleep's-Head Sprouting Hair in the Moonlight. Galway Kinnell. **SP-KinnG**

You curve in dandelion wine and in. Upper Voight's, to All the Cutthroat There. Richard Hugo. **CP-HugoR**

You dance just under the highest billow of the big top. You Dance Up There. Vasil Sotirov, *tr. fr. Bulgarian by* William Matthews. **SP-MattW**

You Dance Up There. Vasil Sotirov, *tr. fr. Bulgarian by* William Matthews. **SP-MattW**

You did it / it was you who started the countdown. Margaret Atwood. **SP-AtwM1**

You did not clock the turning of the leaves. Return. Audre Lorde. **SP-LordA**

You did not come. A Broken Appointment. Thomas Hardy. **CP-HardT**

You did not come to Rome to dream. Rafael Alberti, *tr. by* Thomas Merton. **CP-MertT** *Fr.* Roman Nocturnes.

You did not come to the Paris. A Complaint for Mary and Marcel. Kay Boyle. **CP-BoylK**

You did not see wood blackened by rot, or rust-emblazoned iron. To a Proud Old Woman Watching the Tearing Down of the Hurricane Shed. Kay Boyle. **CP-BoylK**

You did not walk with me. The Walk. Thomas Hardy. **CP-HardT**

You died. And because you were Greek they gave you. None. Hayden Carruth. **CP-CarHS**

You died, and made but little of it! After the Death of a Friend. Thomas Hardy. **CP-HardT**

You died nine years ago today. *with music.* Frederick Morgan. **SP-MorgF**

You do not always know what I am feeling. For Grace, after a Party. Frank O'Hara. **SP-OharF**

You do not come dramatically, with dragons. To Failure. Philip Larkin. **CP-LarkP**

You do not do, you do not do. Daddy. Sylvia Plath. **CP-PlatS**

You do not have to be good. Wild Geese. Mary Oliver. **SP-OlivM**

You Do Not Have to Love Me. Leonard Cohen. **CP-CoheL**

You do not know my pride. A Kind of Scorn. Nicholas Vachel Lindsay. **CP-LindV**

You do what you must—this world and then the next—one world at a. Carl Sandburg. *Fr.* The People, Yes. **CP-SandC**

You, Doctor Martin. Anne Sexton. **CP-SextA**

You dont believe I wont attempt to make ye. William Blake. **CP-BlakW**

You don't find it for yourself. Someone takes you. The Rainbow Grocery. William Dickey. **SP-DickW**

You Don't Know What Love Is. Al Young. **CP-YounA**

You don't look at all well, quite loin de l'être in fact. Loin de l'Être. Stevie Smith. **CP-SmitS**

You don't need to study any ponderous tome. I Know You'll Like Them. Ogden Nash. **CP-NashO**

You don't realize how much I need you. I Need You. George Harrison. **CP-Beatl**

You don't say / it is no / answer—you. Little Time—and Place. Robert Creeley. **CP-CreeR**

"You dream," he said, "because of the child". The Dream. Stephen Spender. **CP-SpenS**

You drink a bitter draught. To a Freedom Fighter. Maya Angelou. **SP-AngeM**

You drive a hard-nosed, ungelded bargain. Poem for a Painter Bent on Suicide. Kay Boyle. **CP-BoylK**

You drive, the road aims for a mountain. A View. Mona Van Duyn. **SP-VanDM**

You drowsed my senses by your misty kings. To a Modern Irish Poet. John Hewitt. **CP-HewiJ**

You drunken / tottering. The Drunkard. William Carlos Williams. **CP-WilW1**

You dwell within a lovely bower. To a Green-Chafer, on a White Rose. Charlotte Smith. **CP-SmitC**

You dweller in the dark cabin. Hymn from a Watermelon Pavilion. Wallace Stevens. **CP-StevW**

You dynamiting the structure of our loves. Theory of Flight. Muriel Rukeyser. **CP-RukeM**

You endless torments that my rest opress. Sonnet 11. Mary Sidney, Countess of Montgomery Wroth. *Fr.* Pamphilia to Amphilanthus. **CP-WrotM**

You enter a room—Indians, Iraqis. The Party. Stephen Dobyns. **SP-DobyS**

You entered my sleep. I Dream of Leslie. Kenneth Rexroth. **SP-RexrK**

You exquisite chunk of mud. K. McB. William Carlos Williams. **CP-WilW1**

You Eyes, you large and all-inquiring Eyes. For Arvia. Edwin Arlington Robinson. **CP-RobiE**

You feel the hollowness of being excluded. Chuck Miller. **SP-MillC**

You Felons on Trial in Courts. Walt Whitman. **CP-WhitW**

You Fit into Me. Margaret Atwood. (NOTL.) **SP-AtwM1**

You flung your taunt across the wave. To Englishmen. John Greenleaf Whittier. **CP-WhitJ**

You fucking whore, I thought that you were really interested. *see also* Commentary—The News You Really Hate. Leonard Cohen. **CP-CoheL**

You gave, but will not give again. To a Wealthy Man Who Promised a Second Subscription to the Dublin Municipal Gallery if It Were Proved the People Wanted Pictures. William Butler Yeats. **CP-YeatW**

You gave me the child. Letter to My Lover after Seven Years. Erica Jong. **SP-JongE**

You gave yourself to death but never to me. Malcolm Lowry. *Fr.* The Comedian. **CP-LowrM**

You gentlemen, by dint of long seclusion. Byron. **EPCY** *Fr.* Dedication: "Bob Southey! You're a poet--poet-laureate." **CTC; EnRP; OAEL-2; OBSV** *Fr.* Don Juan. **CP-Byron**

You get right down into the physical world. Drawing. Al Young. **CP-YounA**

You get the blues in twos. Memo #43. Etheridge Knight. **SP-KnigE**

You give no hint how shy you really are, so thoroughly your warm and welcoming temperament masks. Fifteen. Charles Kenneth Williams. **SP-WillC**

You give quite a party, old Cocky. Punch Rubicundus. Thom Gunn. **CP-GunnT**

You give your cheeks a rosy stain. Lucianus, *tr. fr. Greek by* William Cowper. **CP-CowpW**

(On a Similar Character.) **CP-CowpW**

You go / And you are glad. Envoi No. 2. Wystan Hugh Auden. **CP-AudWJ**

You go / Now you are glad. Envoi. Wystan Hugh Auden. **CP-AudWJ**

You go away for a trip, either business or pleasure. The Name Is Too Familiar. Ogden Nash. **CP-NashO**

You go by bushes with dog-roses, through long grass. Frank Templeton Prince. *Fr.* Afterword on Rupert Brooke. **CP-PrinF**

You go down shade to the river, where naked men sit on flat brown rocks, to watch the ferry, in the sun. Elephant. David Herbert Lawrence. **CP-LawrD**

You go for these wenches, she said. Pacific Telephone. Charles Bukowski. **SP-BukC1**

You go into a store and select half-a-dozen shirts and charge them. The Friendly Touch. Ogden Nash. **CP-NashO**

You, God. William Everson. **SP-EverW**

You, going along the path. Cyclops. Margaret Atwood. **SP-AtwM1**

You goodly pines, which still with brave ascent, *speech of Musidorus/*XIT/*. Sir Philip Sidney. **SP-SidnP** *Fr.* Arcadia.

You got a lotta nerve. Positively 4th Street. "Bob Dylan." **CP-DylaB**

You grow / in your cocoon of sleep. And So. William Matthews. **SP-MattW**

You gulp your breakfast and glance at the clock. Everybody Eats Too Much Anyhow. Ogden Nash. **CP-NashO**

You had everything to rattle the men who wrote. Margaret Fuller Drowned. Robert Lowell. **SP-LoweR**

You had *your* crowd. Good Time Girl. Charles Bukowski. **SP-BukC3**

You had your own reasons for getting. New Personal Poem. Ted Berrigan. **SP-BerrT**

You hand me a cup of water. It Breaks. Marge Piercy. **SP-PierM**

You hang at dawn, they said. The Hostage. Stevie Smith. **CP-SmitS**

You happy blessed eyes. Song 6. Mary Sidney, Countess of Montgomery Wroth. *Fr.* Pamphilia to Amphilanthus. **CP-WrotM**

You, Hart Crane. Charles Olson. **CP-OlsoC**

You Hated Spain. Ted Hughes. **SP-HughT**

You have / taken. Poem for a Little Boy on the Buddha's Birthday. Diane Wakoski. **SP-WakoD**

You have a big hammer. Thor. Frederick Morgan. **SP-MorgF**

You have ask'd for a verse—the request. To the Countess of Blessington. Byron. **CP-Byron**

You have beaten me with swords. Ariadne. Hilda Doolittle. **CP-DoolH**

You have been far, and I. To Marcus. Robert Louis Stevenson. **CP-StevR**

You have been living now for a long time and there is nothing you do not know. Sortes Vergilianae. John Ashbery. **SP-AshbJ**

You have beheld a smiling Rose. The Lilly in a Christal. Robert Herrick. **CP-HerrR**

You have betrayed me, Eros. The Reproach. Louise Glück. **SP-GlücL**

You have broken the path of the dragonfly. Pearls. Rita Dove. **SP-DoveR**

You have closed your eyes. Stanley Jasspon Kunitz. *Fr.* Meditations on Death. **CP-KuniS**

You have come back to us windblown. The Failed Suicide. Ted Kooser. **SP-KoosT**

You have come between me and the terrifying presence. Love Song. William Carlos Williams. **CP-WilW1**

You have come your way, I have come my way. Fronleichnam. David Herbert Lawrence. **CP-LawrD**

You have denied hard fact, or never tried. Epitaph on a Philosopher the Reports of Whose Death Have Been Grossly Minimized. Howard Nemerov. **CP-NemeH**

You have entered, you have turned and closed the door. The Arrival. Roy Fisher. **SP-FishR** *Fr.* Interiors with Various Figures.

You have experienced Sanctity. Emily Dickinson. **SP-DickE**

You have given everything to me. What Can I Do for You? "Bob Dylan." **CP-DylaB**

You have heard "A Spanish Lady." The Armenian Lady's Love. William Wordsworth. **CP-WorW2**

You have heard nothing; of course I know you can have heard / nothing. Arthur Hugh Clough. **EBVVPR,** *canto* 5, 11; *Fr.* Amours de Voyage. **SP-ClouA**

You have lived long but over-lonely. Advent of Summer. Robert Ranke Graves. **CP-GravR**

You have loved forty women, but you have only one thumb. Personality. Carl Sandburg. **CP-SandC**

You have many wrinkles. Pocoangelini 38. Lewis Turco. **SP-TurcL**

You Have More Freedom in a House. Ogden Nash. **CP-NashO**

You Have No Form. Leonard Cohen. **CP-CoheL**

You have no word for soldiers to enjoy. Looking. Gwendolyn Brooks. **SP-BrooG**

You have nor face nor hands. Robert Creeley. **CP-CreeR**

You have not heard my love's dark throat. A Song of Praise. Countee Cullen. **CP-CullC**

You have noticed the curious increasing exasperation. Nerves. Robinson Jeffers. **CP-JefR3**

You have now fallen three times in love. Three Times In Love. Robert Ranke Graves. **CP-GravR**

You have only to wait, they will find you. Messengers. Louise Glück. **SP-GlücL**

You Have Pissed Your Life. William Carlos Williams. **CP-WilW1**

You have put your two hands upon me, and your mouth. Betrothed. Louise Bogan. **CP-BogaL**

You have replaced Beethoven. Sometimes Even My Knees Smile. Diane Wakoski. **SP-WakoD**

You have seen a plough. Lines. Charles Tomlinson. **CP-TomlC**

You have seen better days, dear? So have I. Prince Hohenstiel-Schwangau, Saviour of Society. Robert Browning. **CP-BroR1**

You have seen faces of dead men uncovered. Something Still Lives. Edwin Rolfe. **CP-RolfE**

You have Sir said it well but I have if. Aeneas at New York. Allen Tate. **CP-TateA**

You have so much to give they said. He who remains. Richard Shelton. **SP-ShelR**

You have spoken the answer. The Answer. Carl Sandburg. **CP-SandC**

You have stood on a quayside in the flat grey morning. The Lost Sea. Jenny Joseph. **SP-JoseJ**

You have such a way of talking of Him! Gothic Candor. William Carlos Williams. **CP-WilW2**

You Have Sweetened Your Word. Leonard Cohen. **CP-CoheL**

You Have the Lovers. Leonard Cohen. **CP-CoheL**

You have to smile. Northern Fields (For Carol). Chuck Miller. **SP-MillC**

You have used a word. And When Freedom Is Achieved. Kenneth Patchen. **CP-PatcK**

You have wandered widely through your own mind. Within Reason. Robert Ranke Graves. **CP-GravR**

You have your hat and coat on and she says she will be right down. The Evening Out. Ogden Nash. **CP-NashO**

You haven't / fucked for months now. Robert Creeley. **CP-CreeR**

You having turned from me. 12. 6. 71. Louise Glück. **SP-GlücL**

You hear a woman say: I love my husband dearly. Emotional Lies. David Herbert Lawrence. **CP-LawrD**

You hear my step. To His Children in Darkness. James Dickey. **CP-DickJ**

You hear that heroic big land music? Poem. Alice Notley. **SP-NotlA**

You hear the call. Jim Carroll. *Fr.* The Runners. **SP-CarrJ**

You hear the gurgling of the bull. The Ladies and the Pigeons. Marsden Hartley. **CP-HartM**

You hear the long roll of the plunging ground. A Prayer in My Sickness. James Wright. **CP-WrigJ**

You, Helen, who see the stars. The Appeal. David Herbert Lawrence. **CP-LawrD**

You, hiding there in your words. The Book. Adrienne Rich. **CP-RicAE; SP-RicA2**

You hitch a ride with a cyclist. You sit in back. In Your Racing Dream. Richard Hugo. **CP-HugoR**

You hitched a thousand miles. August on Sourdough, a Visit from Dick Brewer. Gary Snyder. **CP-SnydG**

You hold the negative up. Split: 1962. Stephen Dunn. **SP-DunnS**

You hold your eager head. To a Romantic. Allen Tate. **CP-TateA**

You hunted me with all the pack. The Quarry. Walter de la Mare. **CP-DeLaW**

You idiot! What makes you think decay will. Basil Bunting. **CP-BuntB**

You, if you were sensible. Under the Oak. David Herbert Lawrence. **CP-LawrD**

You in a tallness slenderly, as a lone. Sonnet. Hayden Carruth. **CP-CarHS** *Fr.* Sonnets.

You in the flesh and here. Bad Dreams II. Robert Browning. **CP-BroR2**

You in your stone home where the sycamore. John Berryman. *Fr.* Sonnets to Chris. **CP-BerrJ**

You intend no doubt. Gift. Alice Walker. **CP-WalkA**

You, invincibly yourself. Apology. Adrienne Rich. **CP-RicAE**

You invite me to a banquet in your honor. Envy. Stephen Dobyns. **SP-DobyS**

You jump right out of your skin. The Moon Up Close in Winter by the Telescope. Al Young. **CP-YounA**

You just maturing youth! You male or female! Poem of Remembrances for a Girl or a Boy of These States. Walt Whitman. **CP-WhitW**

You keep the cold from the body, the cold from the mind. A Tolerable Wisdom. Derek Mahon. **SP-MahoD**

You kin talk about yer anthems. The Ol' Tunes. Paul Laurence Dunbar. **CP-DunbP**

You know / if a blind boy. James Wright. *Fr.* Many of Our Waters: Variations on a Poem by a Black Child. **CP-WrigJ**

You know / it was very good. The Miracle is the Shortest Time. Charles Bukowski. **SP-BukC3**

You know being swallowed the thrill of. Dream of a Strange One. James Liddy. **CP-LiddJ**

You know da Vinci's painting of. A Name Day. James Schuyler. **CP-SchuJ**

You know if you break my heart I'll go. I'll Be Back. The Beatles. **CP-Beatl**

You know in the muddy pond the fish is there. Trying to Remember. Miller Williams. **SP-WillM**

You know it's hard for me. Little Sister. "Lou Reed." **SP-ReedL**

You Know My Name (Look up the Number). The Beatles. **CP-Beatl**

You know, or you don't know, that great Bacon saith. Byron. **NOBL** *Fr.* Canto the Fourteenth. *Fr.* Don Juan. **CP-Byron**

"You know," she said, "you were at." Sexpot. Charles Bukowski. **SP-BukC1**

You know that Portrait in the Moon. Emily Dickinson. **CP-DickE**

You know the way to Arcady. To H.C. Bunner. Robert Louis Stevenson. **CP-StevR**

You know there is not much. To a Friend Concerning Several Ladies. William Carlos Williams. **CP-WilW1**

You know, there's two ol' maids layin' in the bed. Get Your Rocks Off! "Bob Dylan." **CP-DylaB**

You know those windless summer evenings, swollen to stasis. Cicadas. Richard Wilbur. **CP-WilbR**

You know, verse. Charles Olson. **CP-OlsoC**

You know we French stormed [*or* storm'd] Ratisbon. Incident of the French Camp. Robert Browning. **CP-BroR1**

You know what? Hayden Carruth. *Fr.* The Sleeping Beauty. **CP-CarHL**

You know what it is to be born alone. Baby Tortoise. David Herbert Lawrence. **CP-LawrD**

You know what it's like Sundays to. Rubber Rats. Stephen Berg. **SP-BergS**

You Know Who I Am. Leonard Cohen. **CP-CoheL**

You know you made me cry. Not a Second Time. The Beatles. **CP-Beatl**

You know your name. The Summoning. Bill Knott. **SP-KnotB**

You know you've come back home again. American Time. Al Young. **CP-YounA**

You lament your lot at the bottom of an abyss. Consolations for Double Bass. Charles Tomlinson. **CP-TomlC**

You lay in bed depressed, passive as butter. Marge Piercy. *Fr.* Doing It Differently. **SP-PierM**

You lay in the nest of your real death. Elizabeth Gone. Anne Sexton. **CP-SextA**

You lay there on that couch as if in effigy. Hayden Carruth. *Fr.* The Sleeping Beauty. **CP-CarHL**

You lean at ease in your warm house at night after supper. Wendell Berry. *Fr.* To a Siberian Woodsman. **CP-BerrW**

You learn the names of trees. Dream Report. John Yau. **SP-YauJo**

You learned Lear's *Nonsense Rhymes* by heart, not rote. A Plea to Boys and Girls. Robert Ranke Graves. **CP-GravR**

You leave / nobody else. Basil Bunting. **CP-BuntB**

You leave us: you will see the Rhine. Tennyson. *Fr.* In Memoriam A. H. H. **CP-TennA**

You led me through cactus. Guilt. Richard Shelton. **SP-ShelR**

You left me—Sire—two Legacies. Emily Dickinson. **CP-DickE**

You let down, from arched. Family Affairs. Maya Angelou. **SP-AngeM**

You lie and I concur. You "give." Martial, *tr.* by William Matthews. **SP-MattW** *Fr.* Epigrams.

You lie packed. Self-Portrait 1. William Carlos Williams. **CP-WilW1**

You lie there, Anna. Grave by a Holm-Oak. Stevie Smith. **CP-SmitS**

You lied to your mother, you told her you didn't do it. Opusthirteen. Hayden Carruth. **CP-CarHS**

You like it under the trees in autumn. The Motive for Metaphor. Wallace Stevens. **CP-StevW**

You Like Me Too Much. George Harrison. **CP-Beatl**

'You like my flowers?' That woke me suddenly. Flowers and Stationmaster. Wystan Hugh Auden. **CP-AudWJ**

You like not that French novel? Tell me why. George Meredith. **EnVR; NOBVV** *Fr.* Modern Love. **CP-MerG1**

You like the state of West Virginia very much, do you not? Statement: Philippa Allen. Muriel Rukeyser. **CP-RukeM**

You like to hear about gold. The Vindictives. Robert Frost. **CP-FrosR**

You Lingering Sparse Leaves of Me. Walt Whitman. **CP-WhitW**

You Live like a God. Leonard Cohen. **CP-CoheL**

You lived and moved among the best society. Wystan Hugh Auden. **OBSV** *Fr.* Letter to Lord Byron. **CP-AudeW**

You lived before Ian Gibson. Churros. James Liddy. **CP-LiddJ**

You lived out of town where the land. Harry Orchard. Richard Shelton. **SP-ShelR**

You look at me with children. Johann. Alice Walker. **CP-WalkA**

"You look like a widdower, " she said. In a London Flat. Thomas Hardy. **CP-HardT**

You look, my Joseph, I should something say. To My Dear Son, and Right-Learnèd Friend, Master Joseph Rutter. Ben Jonson. **CP-JonsB**

You look out and you see people. Song. Robert Creeley. **CP-CreeR**

You looked so tempting in the pew. Robert Louis Stevenson. **CP-StevR**

You looked up and said. Genghis Chan: Private Eye V. John Yau. **SP-YauJo**

You love all, you say. May's Love. Elizabeth Barrett Browning. **CP-BroEB**

You, love, and I. Counting the Beats. Robert Ranke Graves. **CP-GravR**

You love me strangely, and in strangeness. Strangeness. Robert Ranke Graves. **CP-GravR**

You love me—you are sure. Emily Dickinson. **CP-DickE**

You love the Lord—you cannot see. Emily Dickinson. **CP-DickE**

You loved me not at all, but let it go. Edna St. Vincent Millay. **CP-MillE**

You loved the daughter of Don Manrique? The Night-Scene. Samuel Taylor Coleridge. **CP-ColeS**

You made algebra: his tastes in food. Marilyn Hacker. **SP-HackM** *Fr.* The Navigators.

You made healing as you wanted us to make bread and poems. Mendings. Muriel Rukeyser. **CP-RukeM**

You make me dizzy with lust. The Examination. James McAuley. **SP-McAuJ**

"You make me sick!" this, with rancor, vehemence, disgust—again, "You hear me? Sick!." Kin. Charles Kenneth Williams. **SP-WillC**

You May All Go Home Now. Kenneth Patchen. **CP-PatcK**

You may be an ambassador to England or France. Gotta Serve Somebody. "Bob Dylan." **CP-DylaB**

You may be right: "How can I dare to feel?" Rejoinder to a Critic. Donald Davie. **CP-DavDo**

You may have all things from me, save my breath. Fifteenth Farewell. Louise Bogan. **CP-BogaL**

You may have met a man—quite young. So Various. Thomas Hardy. **CP-HardT**

You may have seen, in road or street. The Calf. Thomas Hardy. **CP-HardT**

You may never understand. A Double-Ended Dory. Brendan Galvin. **SP-GalvB**

You may praise this bloody awful world. The Communist. Malcolm Lowry. **CP-LowrM**

You may say this is no poem. May 1943. Hilda Doolittle. **CP-DoolH**

You may smell the breath of the gods in the common roses. Cabbage-Roses. David Herbert Lawrence. **CP-LawrD**

You may talk o' gin and [or an'] beer. Gunga Din. Rudyard Kipling. **CP-KiplR**

You may vow Ile not forgett. His Mistris to Him at His Farwell. Robert Herrick. **CP-HerrR**

You may walk among fuchsias unloud. Vision Beatific. Allen Tate. **CP-TateA**

You may wonder why I'm not describing the landscape for you. Margaret Atwood. *Fr.* Circe / Mud Poems. **SP-AtwM1**

You may write me down in history. Still I Rise. Maya Angelou. **SP-AngeM**

You mid the corn not yet asleep. John Hewitt. *Fr.* Three Horatian Odes. **CP-HewiJ**

You might as well haul up. Epitaph for Fire and Flower. Sylvia Plath. **CP-PlatS**

You might come here Sunday on a whim. Degrees of Gray in Philipsburg. Richard Hugo. **CP-HugoR**

You might die anywhere. You will die in Ayr. Ayr. Richard Hugo. **CP-HugoR**

You Might Get in Trouble. Allen Ginsberg. **CP-GinsA**

You might not know I remembered you. Emily Dickinson. **SP-DickE**

You might not know this old tree by its bark. A Black Birch in Winter. Richard Wilbur. **CP-WilbR**

You mince, you start. The Young Cat and the Chrysanthemums. William Carlos Williams. **CP-WilW1**

You mocked me that hot day at Carcassonne. Dear Jool, I Miss You in Saint-Saturnin. Marilyn Hacker. **SP-HackM**

You, Morningtide Star, now are steady-eyed, over the east. Lying Awake. Thomas Hardy. **CP-HardT**

You most sophisticated most beautiful angel. The Litany of Satan. James Liddy. **CP-LiddJ**

You must agree that Rubens was a Fool. To English Connoisseurs. William Blake. **CP-BlakW**

You must be / nearly lost to. Poetry to the Rescue. Archie Randolph Ammons. **SP-AmmoA**

You Must Confront. Jim Morrison. **SP-MorrJ**

You must fly your 35 missions again. In Your War Dream. Richard Hugo. **CP-HugoR**

You must fuse mind and wit with all the senses. Sense of Truth. David Herbert Lawrence. **CP-LawrD**

You Must Have Some Idea Where They've Gone. Kenneth Patchen. **CP-PatcK**

You must leave now, take what you need, you think will last. It's All Over Now, Baby Blue. "Bob Dylan." **CP-DylaB**

You must live through the time when everything hurts. The Double Shame. Stephen Spender. **CP-SpenS**

You must love the light so well. George Meredith. *Fr.* The Woods of Westermain. **CP-MerG1**

You must never unlock the cedar closet. The Music Room. Isabella Gardner. **CP-GardI**

You must not call me Maggie, you must not call me Dear. Maggie a Lady. Christina Georgina Rossetti. **CP-RosC1**

You must not change your life plan over. Moira. Tom Clark. **SP-ClarT**

You Must Remember. John Yau. **SP-YauJo**

You must thank / yo dookey don't stank. What You Seize Is What You Git. Al Young. **CP-YounA**

You mustn't groom an Arab with a file. *parody.* Rudyard Kipling. **CP-KiplR** *Fr.* The Muse among the Motors.

You mustn't swim till you're six weeks old. Rudyard Kipling. **CP-KiplR** *Fr.* The White Seal. *Fr.* The Jungle Book.

You, my friends, and you strangers, all of you. The Sheep in the Ruins. Archibald MacLeish. **CP-MacLA**

You, my photographer, you, most aware. Poem. Delmore Schwartz. **SP-SchwD**

You need an empty burlap. Safari. Daniel Gerard Hoffman. **SP-HoffD**

You need call no psychiatrist. Moral Assessment. Robert Penn Warren. *Fr.* Homage to Theodore Dreiser. **SP-WarrR**

You need not see what someone is doing. Sext. Wystan Hugh Auden. *Fr.* Horae Canonicae. **CP-AudeW**

You need the untranslatable ice to watch. Appendix to the Anniad. Gwendolyn Brooks. **SP-BrooG**

You never come back. Mill-Doors. Carl Sandburg. **CP-SandC**

You Never Give Me Your Money. The Beatles. **CP-Beatl**

You never heard of me, I dare. Voice from the Tomb (5). Stevie Smith. **CP-SmitS**

You Never Knew Her Either, Though You Thought You Did. Robert Penn Warren. *Fr.* Ballad of a Sweet Dream of Peace. **SP-WarrR**

You never painted this picture, Vincent. Letter to Vincent. Phoebe Hesketh. **SP-HeskP**

You no / tice / nobod / y wants. Edward Estlin Cummings. **CP-CummE**

You on the Tower. Thomas Hardy. **CP-HardT**

You, once a belle in Shreveport. Snapshots of a Daughter-in-Law. Adrienne Rich. **CP-RicAE; SP-RicA1; SP-RicA2**

You open to me. Middle Aged Lovers, II. Erica Jong. **SP-JongE**

You ought to have seen what I saw on my way. Blueberries. Robert Frost. **CP-FrosR**

You out there, so secret. Poem. Thomas McGrath. **SP-McGrT**

You peculiar pink stinks been crowdin'. A Message from the Assistant Chief of the Fly People. Kenneth Patchen. **CP-PatcK**

You people are dead. Estais Muertos. César Vallejo, *tr. fr. Spanish by* Thomas Merton. **CP-MertT**

You pick one up along the shore. Shells. Howard Nemerov. **CP-NemeH**

You pillars of light mournful and beautiful. The Island (XVII). Pablo Neruda, *tr. fr. Spanish by* Ben Belitt. **SP-NeruP** *Fr.* The Separate Rose.

You pleasant floury meade. Mary Sidney, Countess of Montgomery Wroth. *Fr.* Love's Victorie. **CP-WrotM**

You powers divine of love-commanding eyes. Mary Sidney, Countess of Montgomery Wroth. *Fr.* Part 1. *Fr.* Urania. **CP-WrotM**

You prepare for one sorrow. Oddjob, a Bull Terrier. Derek Walcott. **CP-WalcD**

You promise me when certain things are done. The Prospect. Adrienne Rich. **CP-RicAE**

You promised to send me some violets. Did you forget? Letter from Town: The Almond-Tree. David Herbert Lawrence. **CP-LawrD**

You pure and holy fire. Mary Sidney, Countess of Montgomery Wroth. *Fr.* Part 1. *Fr.* Urania. **CP-WrotM**

You pursue the matter. The Conversation. Thom Gunn. **CP-GunnT**

You put on my clothes. The Recognition. Wendell Berry. **CP-BerrW**

You rang me up this morning from Marseilles. Marilyn Hacker. *Fr.* The Regent's Park Sonnets. **SP-HackM**

You read the clicking keys as gibberish. Analogue. Howard Nemerov. **CP-NemeH**

You read the New York Times. Alfred Corning Clark. Robert Lowell. **SP-LoweR**

You, Reader, need no prologue. Do you think these Horatian Odes are all about you? Thomas Merton. *Fr.* Cables to the Ace. **CP-MertT**

You, reading over my shoulder, peering beneath. The Reader over My Shoulder. Robert Ranke Graves. **CP-GravR**

You recognize it like. Dolly. Thom Gunn. **CP-GunnT**

You refuse to own / yourself, you permit. Margaret Atwood. **SP-AtwM1**

You reject the rainbow. A Dream of Hell. Robert Ranke Graves. **CP-GravR**

You remember down at Florence our Cascine. The Dance. Elizabeth Barrett Browning. **CP-BroEB**

You remember, I suppose. To Ottilie. Robert Louis Stevenson. **CP-StevR**

You remember Rossignano. Hyphens. Donald Davie. **CP-DavDo**

You remember that village where the border ran. The Boundary Commission. Paul Muldoon. **SP-MuldP**

You remember the name was Jensen. She seemed old. What Thou Lovest Well Remains American. Richard Hugo. **CP-HugoR**

You rest unpleasantly. Jormungand. Frederick Morgan. **SP-MorgF**

You rise from your sleep. John Haines. *Fr.* Daphne. **SP-HainJ**

You rise like a mountain over the white building. Quarrel with a Cloud. Richard Eberhart. **CP-EberR**

You rose from our embrace and the small light spread. Sonnet. Hayden Carruth. **CP-CarHS** *Fr.* Sonnets.

You ruffled black blossom. Turkey-Cock. David Herbert Lawrence. **CP-LawrD**

You said Is / there anything which. Edward Estlin Cummings. **CP-CummE**

You said that I "was Great"—one Day. Emily Dickinson. **CP-DickE**

You said, that October. December at Yase. Gary Snyder. *Fr.* Four Poems for Robin. **CP-SnydG**

You said the anger would come back. Again and Again and Again. Anne Sexton. **CP-SextA**

You said the world has no identity. Conversation at Midnight with Oscar Williams. Isabella Gardner. **CP-GardI**

You said you got to go home & feed your pussycat. Pussy Blues. Allen Ginsberg. **CP-GinsA**

You said you would kill it this morning. Pheasant. Sylvia Plath. **CP-PlatS**

You sailed in sky-high, with your speech askew. John Berryman. *Fr.* Sonnets to Chris. **CP-BerrJ**

You sat in the tub. The Swimmer. Louise Glück. **SP-GlücL**

You saw the sunlight ripen upon the wall. Grace in the Fore Street. Donald Davie. **CP-DavDo**

You say / This is all. Out There. Anne Waldman. **SP-WaldA**

You say, as I have often given tongue. To a Poet, Who Would Have Me Praise Certain Bad Poets, Imitators of His and Mine. William Butler Yeats. **CP-YeatW**

You say, but with no touch of scorn. Tennyson. **NOCV; WGRP** *Fr.* In Memoriam A. H. H. **CP-TennA**

(Doubt.) **WGRP**

You say Hello and part of what you spend. Entropy. Miller Williams. **SP-WillM**

You say I love not, 'cause I do not play. To His Mistress Objecting to Him Neither Toying or Talking. Robert Herrick. **CP-HerrR**

You say I must write *another* book? But I've just written this one. To an American Publisher. Stevie Smith. **CP-SmitS**

You say I O.K.ed. Madam and the Phone Bill. Langston Hughes. **SP-HughL**

You say it's your birthday. Birthday. John Lennon *and* Paul McCartney. **CP-Beatl**

You say love is this, love is that. Memory of April. William Carlos Williams. **CP-WilW1**

You say, O Sage, when weather-checked. The Child and the Sage. Thomas Hardy. **CP-HardT**

You say reserve & modesty he has. On Stothard. William Blake. **CP-BlakW**

You say: "Since life is cruel enough at best." Edna St. Vincent Millay. **CP-MillE**

You say their Pictures well Painted be. William Blake. **CP-BlakW**

You say, to me-wards your affection's strong. Love Me Little, Love Me Long. Robert Herrick. **CP-HerrR**

You say y'are sweet; how sho'd we know. On a Perfum'd Lady. Robert Herrick. **CP-HerrR**

You say y'are young; but when your Teeth are told. Upon One Who Said She Was Alwayes Young. Robert Herrick. **CP-HerrR**

You say yes. Hello Goodbye. The Beatles. **CP-Beatl**

You say you know what's up, what's what, what is or isn't true. Coup de Grace. Anne Waldman. **SP-WaldA**

You say you love, and yet your eye. To Caroline. Byron. **CP-Byron**

You say you love; but with a voice. Stanzas. John Keats. **CP-KeatJ**

You say you love me. Most Likely You Go Your Way (and I'll Go Mine). "Bob Dylan." **CP-DylaB**

You say, you love me; that I thus must prove. To a Maid. Robert Herrick. **CP-HerrR**

You say you will love me if I have to go. Things We Said Today. The Beatles. **CP-Beatl**

You say you'l kiss me, and I thanke you for it. Upon a Free Maid, with a Foule Breath. Robert Herrick. **CP-HerrR**

You scarcely need my tardy thanks. My Namesake. John Greenleaf Whittier. **CP-WhitJ**

You sea! I resign myself to you also—I guess what you mean. Walt Whitman. OxBoS *Fr.* Song of Myself. **CP-WhitW**

You see a man / trying to think. Ghost of a Chance. Adrienne Rich. **CP-RicAE; SP-RicA1; SP-RicA2**

You see all those words thick on endless shelves. Chrysanth. Jenny Joseph. *Fr.* Life and Turgid Times of A. Citizen. **SP-JoseJ**

You see before you an icing of skin. The Root Canal. Marge Piercy. **SP-PierM**

You see I cannot see—your lifetime. Emily Dickinson. **CP-DickE**

You see I have been here a long time now. Man in a Bar. Jenny Joseph. **SP-JoseJ**

You see me alone tonight. I Have Had to Learn to Live with My Face. Diane Wakoski. **SP-WakoD**

You see the jerked. Robert Creeley. **CP-CreeR**

You see them everywhere, the grinning martyrs. Orthodontia. John Updike. **CP-UpdiJ**

You see them vanish in their speeding cars. Fugue. Howard Nemerov. **CP-NemeH**

You see these halted days of March as a fixed season. Spring. Kay Boyle. **CP-BoylK**

You see, they have no judgment. The Drowned Children. Louise Glück. **SP-GlücL**

You see this dog. It was but yesterday. Flush or Faunus. Elizabeth Barrett Browning. **CP-BroEB**

You see this gentle streame, that glides. Proof to No Purpose. Robert Herrick. **CP-HerrR**

You see those mothers squabbling there? In the Cemetery. Thomas Hardy. **InPK; Son** *Fr.* Satires of Circumstance in Fifteen Glimpses. **CP-HardT**

You see we keep a jealous Heart. Emily Dickinson. **SP-DickE**

You seem to cast, my vent'rous book. 1.20. Horace. **SP-SmarC,** *tr. by* Christopher Smart; *Fr.* Epistles.

You send me your poems. The Conspiracy. Robert Creeley. **CP-CreeR**

You senses, never still, but shrill as children. The Holy Sacrament of the Altar. Thomas Merton. **CP-MertT**

You shadow and flame. Valentine's Night. David Herbert Lawrence. **CP-LawrD**

You shall above all things be glad and young. Edward Estlin Cummings. **CP-CummE; SP-CummE**

You shall be, my dear. Well Hung. "Hugh MacDiarmid." **SP-MacDH**

You Shall Have Homes. Carl Sandburg. **CP-SandC**

You shall have peace with night and sleep. Peace, Night, Sleep. Carl Sandburg. **CP-SandC**

You shall hear how Hiawatha. Hiawatha's Fasting. Henry Wadsworth Longfellow. **SP-LongH** *Fr.* The Song of Hiawatha.

You shall not be overbold. The Titmouse. Ralph Waldo Emerson. **CP-EmerR**

You shall not love me for what daily spends. Ralph Waldo Emerson. **CP-EmerR**

You shall sing my songs, O earth. Edward Estlin Cummings. **CP-CummE**

You shift / into lonely music. Savage Bubbles. Jim Carroll. **SP-CarrJ**

You shook the liquid amber tree. A Poem for Arthur. Kay Boyle. **CP-BoylK**

You should be gone in winter, that Nature mourn. John Berryman. *Fr.* Sonnets to Chris. **CP-BerrJ**

You should hammer on him to clean. Son. Al Young. **CP-YounA**

You should have heard the old men cry. The One Who Stayed. Shel Silverstein. **SP-SilS2**

You should have known. The moon. Song without Forgiveness. David St. John. **SP-StJoD**

You shouldn't have gone off the pill without. Trying to Reconcile. Robert Pack. **SP-PackR**

You show me the poems of some woman. Translations. Adrienne Rich. **SP-RicA2**

You sing, and the gift of State's applause. To a Poet and a Lady. Paul Laurence Dunbar. **CP-DunbP**

You sing in my lap. Lines. Dabney Stuart. **SP-StuaD**

You sit as I do. The Place between Us. Stephen Dobyns. **SP-DobyS**

You sit beside the bed. Bedside. Margaret Atwood. **SP-AtwM2**

You sit here on solid sand banks trying to figure. Daybreak. James Dickey. **CP-DickJ**

You sit on the couch. I've Seen Too Many Glazed-Eyed Bums Sitting under a Bridge Drinking Cheap Wine. Charles Bukowski. **SP-BukC1**

You sit talking in all earnestness to a woman. Drawing-Room. David Herbert Lawrence. **CP-LawrD**

You sit there because I like to look at you. Another Day (You sit there). Muriel Rukeyser. **CP-RukeM**

You sit to have waves rush to your open hands. To a Poetess. Jim Carroll. **SP-CarrJ**

You slapped my face. Short Poem. William Carlos Williams. **CP-WilW2**

You sleep in a room with bluegreen curtains. In the Wake of Home. Adrienne Rich. **SP-RicA1; SP-RicA2**

You sleep in the darkness. For My Husband. Erica Jong. **SP-JongE**

You sleep too well—too far away. To E. T.: 1917. Walter de la Mare. **CP-DeLaW**

You sleeping I bend to cover. Night-Pieces: For a Child. Adrienne Rich. **CP-RicAE; SP-RicA2**

"You slut," he flung at her. Blue Maroons. Carl Sandburg. **CP-SandC**

You smile upon your friend to-day. Alfred Edward Housman. **CP-HousA**

You Smoke a Cigarette. Charles Bukowski. **SP-BukC2**

You sold a slave just yesterday. Martial, tr. by William Matthews. **SP-MattW** *Fr.* Epigrams.

You—Spanish-speaking. Hayden Carruth. **CP-CarHS** *Fr.* The Clay Hill Anthology.

You speak of the collective. Marge Piercy. *Fr.* A Shadow Play For Guilt. **SP-PierM**

You speak to me. Sign Language. "Bob Dylan." **CP-DylaB**

You splice together two broomsticks, then reef. Sonnet at Easter. Howard Nemerov. **CP-NemeH**

You spoke of "Hope" surpassing "Home." Emily Dickinson. **SP-DickE**

You spoke of spring and summer. Of the Seasons. May Sarton. **SP-SartM**

You squeeze me in your arms the while your eyes. Love and Suspicion. John Gould Fletcher. **SP-FletJ**

You stand as rocks stand. Portland, 1968. Louise Glück. **SP-GlückL**

You stand at the door / bright as an icon. Margaret Atwood. *Fr.* Circe / Mud Poems. **SP-AtwM1**

You stand before the dark / Wet night of leaves. To Alfonso Cortes. Thomas Merton. **CP-MertT**

You stand in isolation like the first bloom. Peter Meinke. **SP-MeinP**

You stand in my mind. Tending. Dabney Stuart. **SP-StuaD**

You stand near the window as lights wink. 23rd Street Runs into Heaven. Kenneth Patchen. **CP-PatcK**

You stand thinking of great principles. Great Principles Are Thrown Down by Time. Richard Eberhart. **CP-EberR**

You stand waiting. You listen. Vigilance. Lewis Turco. **SP-TurcL**

You stared out of the window at [or on] the emptiness. To Manuel Altolaguirre. Stephen Spender. **CP-SpenS**

You start it all. You are lovely. To Women. Richard Hugo. **CP-HugoR**

You start with your own body. How to Be Happy: Another Memo to Myself. Stephen Dunn. **SP-DunnS**

You still carry. Brother. Richard Shelton. **SP-ShelR**

You stir, or is it the first birds. Night Fishing. Daniel Gerard Hoffman. **SP-HoffD**

You stood up in a dream. One. Stephen Berg. **SP-BergS**

You stop to rest, far up, you teeter. Ted Hughes. *Fr.* Skylarks. **SP-HughT**

You strolled in the open, leisurely and alone. To the Poets in New York. James Wright. **CP-WrigJ**

You strop my anger, especially. To the Pay Toilet. Marge Piercy. **SP-PierM**

You suddenly squeak breathlessly like a sqeezed rubber toy. The Last Trump. Isabella Gardner. **CP-GardI**

You suit me well, for you can make me laugh. To a Prize Bird. Marianne Craig Moore. **CP-MoorM**

You sullen pig of a man. Libertad! Igualdad! Fraternidad! William Carlos Williams. **CP-WilW1**

You take me to the restaurant where one. The Catch. Erica Jong. **SP-JongE**

You take me to the woods. Pomegranates. Siv Cedering Fox. **SP-CedeS**

You take my hand and. Margaret Atwood. **SP-AtwM1**

You talk constantly. Like a Woman in the Kitchen. Siv Cedering Fox. **SP-CedeS**

You talk like / they don't kick. Comment on Curb. Langston Hughes. **SP-HughL** *Fr.* Lenox Avenue Mural.

You Taught Me. Thomas McGrath. **SP-McGrT**

You taught me language and my profit on't. Thomas Merton. *Fr.* Cables to the Ace. **CP-MertT**

You taught me Waiting with Myself. Emily Dickinson. **CP-DickE**

You tell lies thinkin' I can't see. I'm Down. The Beatles. **CP-Beatl**

You tell me about politics. "Bob Dylan." *Fr.* Some Other Kinds of Songs. **CP-DylaB**

You tell me every man has a soul to save? Souls to Save. David Herbert Lawrence. **CP-LawrD**

You tell me I am wrong. Pomegranate. David Herbert Lawrence. **CP-LawrD**

You tell me that I love myself. Flattery. William Carlos Williams. **CP-WilW2**

You tell me that silence. Gift. Leonard Cohen. **CP-CoheL**

You tell me that the world is fair, in spite. A Fair World Tho' a Fallen. Christina Georgina Rossetti. **CP-RosC3**

You tell me that you've got everything you want. And Your Bird Can Sing. John Lennon *and* Paul McCartney. **CP-Beatl**

You tell these young spratasses around here. Pa McCabe. Hayden Carruth. **CP-CarHS**

You, that are much a fisher in the pool. To Master Andrew Lang. Robert Louis Stevenson. **CP-StevR**

You that are she and you, that's double she. To the Lady Bedford. John Donne. **CP-DonnJ**

You that are sprung of northern stock. To a Calvinist in Bali. Edna St. Vincent Millay. **CP-MillE**

You that can aptly mix your joyes with cries. An Elegie. Princesse Katherine. Richard Lovelace. **CP-LoveR**

You, that decipher out the fate. Mourning. Andrew Marvell. **CP-MarvA**

You that do search for every purling spring. Sonnet 15. Sir Philip Sidney. **NAEL-1; NoSic; OAEL-1; OBSC; OXAEP-1; Son** *Fr.* Astrophil and Stella. **SP-SidnP**

You that in love find[e] luck[e] and [h]abunda[u]nce. Sir Thomas Wyatt. **CP-WyatT**

You that in vain would front the coming order. The Old King's New Jester. Edwin Arlington Robinson. **CP-RobiE**

You that Jehovah's servants are, *par. by* Countess of Pembroke, Mary Sidney Herbert. Bible, *O.T. See* Psalm 134: "Behold, bless ye the Lord, all ye servants of the Lord."

You that shall live awhile before / Old Time tyr's, and is no more. On the Death of Mrs. Elizabeth Filmer. Richard Lovelace. **CP-LoveR**

You that think Love can convey. Celia Singing. Thomas Carew. **CP-CareT**

You that will a wonder know. In Praise of His Mistress. Thomas Carew. **CP-CareT**

You that with allegory's curious frame. Sonnet 28. Sir Philip Sidney. **InPK; NoSic; OAEL-1** *Fr.* Astrophil and Stella. **SP-SidnP**

You that would bite the whole pie and. Vengeance Is Mine, Saith the Lord. Donald Davie. **CP-DavDo**

You that would last long, list to my song. Ben Jonson. **CP-JonsB** *Fr.* Volpone.

You the very old, I have come. Waiting in Line. William Stafford. **SP-StafW**

You, the woman; I, the man; this, the world. The Character of Love Seen as a Search for the Lost. Kenneth Patchen. **CP-PatcK**

You then. Your eyes hooded, shrewd a little. Hayden Carruth. *Fr.* The Sleeping Beauty. **CP-CarHL**

You think a life can end? For the Anniversary of my Mother's Death. Archibald MacLeish. **CP-MacLA**

You think a wooden animal. Wooden Animal. Hilda Doolittle. *Fr.* Two Poems for Christmas, 1937. **CP-DoolH**

You think Fuseli is not a Great Painter. I'm glad. To Hunt. William Blake. **CP-BlakW**

You think I am your servant but you are wrong. Table Talk. Derek Mahon. **SP-MahoD**

You Think I Don't Know. Jim Morrison. **SP-MorrJ**

You think in the circle. Robert Creeley. **CP-CreeR**

You think it horrible that lust and rage. The Spur. William Butler Yeats. **CP-YeatW**

You Think They Are Permanent But They Pass. Richard Eberhart. **CP-EberR**

You think we don't have messages in Kentucky? Here is one I got by hounds, on the day of a blizzard. Message to Be Inscribed on Mark Van Doren's Hamilton Medal. Thomas Merton. **CP-MertT**

You think you are a man shaking the hands of that dog. Malcolm Lowry. **CP-LowrM**

You think you are safe at last. Margaret Atwood. *Fr.* Circe / Mud Poems. **SP-AtwM1**

You thought it heartless. Of Grief. May Sarton. **SP-SartM**

You thought my heart too far diseased. Tennyson. *Fr.* In Memoriam A. H. H. **CP-TennA**

"You thought we knew," she said, "but we were wrong." The Woman and the Wife. Edwin Arlington Robinson. **CP-RobiE**

You three:—my wife. Louis Zukofsky. **CP-ZukLS**

You tiny flames of blue. Alpine Violets. John Gould Fletcher. **SP-FletJ**

You told me, I remember, glory, built. Table Talk. William Cowper. **CP-CowpW**

You told me resurrection in images of roots. The Loan. Muriel Rukeyser. **CP-RukeM**

You told me: they all went in and saw the glass. Junk-Heap at Murano. Muriel Rukeyser. **CP-RukeM**

You too if you work hard enough. Ponce de León: A Morning Walk. Al Young. **CP-YounA**

You, too, my mother, read my rhymes. To My Mother. Robert Louis Stevenson. **CP-StevR**

You too will cool, though from your distance light. Howard Nemerov. *Fr.* Four Sonnets. **CP-NemeH**

You took it in / at a glance: the March. The Windshield. Charles Tomlinson. **CP-TomlC**

You tore out your own right eye, father. Odin. Frederick Morgan. **SP-MorgF**

You Tore Your Shirt. Leonard Cohen. **CP-CoheL**

You tossed a blanket from the bed. Thomas Stearns Eliot. *Fr.* Preludes (I–IV). **CP-ElioT**

You tourist composed upon that fence. The Baler. Hayden Carruth. **CP-CarHS**

You try to fix your mind upon his death. For W——— Who Commanded Well. Howard Nemerov. **CP-NemeH**

You turn into a plant on the coasts of time. A Man from Ecuador beneath the Eiffel Tower. Jorge Carrera Andrade, *tr. fr. Spanish by* Thomas Merton. **CP-MertT**

You turn on your pillow. It Is God that Moves in Your Heart. Al Young. **CP-YounA**

You turn your back on them no more. Cherry Saplings. William DeWitt Snodgrass. **SP-SnodW**

You turn your back, you turn your back. To Carrey Clavel. Thomas Hardy. **CP-HardT**

You understand both Adolphe and Fabrice. Birthday Poem. Thom Gunn. **CP-GunnT**

You understand the colors on the hillside have faded. Crucifixion. Hayden Carruth. **CP-CarHS**

You use your mind. To Military Progress. Marianne Craig Moore. **CP-MoorM**

You used to wear dungarees & blue workshirt. Brooklyn College Brain. Allen Ginsberg. **CP-GinsA**

You (V) (after Holderlin). Tom Clark. **SP-ClarT**

You ventured occasionally. To His Wife. Geoffrey Hill. *Fr.* The Songbook of Sebastian Arrurruz. **CP-HillG**

You vines wreathe sands printless. Vines. Louis Zukofsky. **CP-ZukLS**

You wake, all windows blind—embattled sprays. Winter-Piece. Charles Tomlinson. **CP-TomlC**

You wake me. Kenneth Rexroth. **SP-RexrK** *Fr.* Love Poems of Marichiko.

You wake slowly without abruptness. Late September. Chuck Miller. **SP-MillC**

You wake tired, in the cabin light has filled. To a Friend in Time of Trouble. Thom Gunn. **CP-GunnT**

You walk down the road. Letting Go. Richard Shelton. **SP-ShelR**

You walk into the room. Ballad of a Thin Man. "Bob Dylan." **CP-DylaB**

You walked in front of me. Orpheus (1). Margaret Atwood. **SP-AtwM2**

You walked the length of Italy. Catherine of Siena. Rita Dove. **SP-DoveR**

You want to go back. Margaret Atwood. **SP-AtwM1**

You watch the night for images of death. According to His Seasons. Howard Nemerov. **CP-NemeH**

You watched them at work. Surgery. Richard Shelton. **SP-ShelR**

You watchers on the wall. Geoffrey Hill. *Fr.* The Pentecost Castle. **CP-HillG**

You waves, though you dance at my feet like children at play. The Meditation of the Old Fisherman. William Butler Yeats. **CP-YeatW**

You weep whole heartedly—your shining tears. Stolen Jewel. Robert Ranke Graves. **CP-GravR**

You Went to Work. Leonard Cohen. **CP-CoheL**

You were a child and I your veteran. Child with Veteran. Robert Ranke Graves. **CP-GravR**

You were born in the Spring. To Mary Rossetti. Christina Georgina Rossetti. **CP-RosC3**

You were both quiet, looking out over the water. Swans. Louise Glück. **SP-GlücL**

You were by my side, though I could not see you. The Prohibition. Robert Ranke Graves. **CP-GravR**

You were forever finding some new play. The Exposed Nest. Robert Frost. **CP-FrosR**

You were here at his young beginning. End of the Year 1912. Thomas Hardy. **CP-HardT**

You were here on earth, in cities. Sad Dust Glories. Allen Ginsberg. **CP-GinsA**

You were in hell fire? had been all your life?, *incl. in* Pijijiapan. Malcolm Lowry. *Fr.* The Comedian. **CP-LowrM**

You were sleeping? That's the time you're. Possession. Daniel Gerard Hoffman. **SP-HoffD**

You were the last to love America; too grim. Letter to Those Who Are About to Die. Kenneth Patchen. **CP-PatcK**

You were the promise at dawn. Is This What You Wanted. Leonard Cohen. **CP-CoheL**

You Were the Sort that Men Forget. Thomas Hardy. **CP-HardT**

You were to leave and being all but gone. Departure. Charles Tomlinson. **CP-TomlC**

You were too beautiful to go on living. Balder. Frederick Morgan. **SP-MorgF**

You were unreasonably kind. S. Dead. Marge Piercy. **SP-PierM**

You Were Wearing. Kenneth Koch. **SP-KochK**

You were wrong about the way it happens. Instructions to a Medium, to be Transmitted to the Shade of W.B. Yeats, the Latter Having Responded in a Séance Held on 13 June 1965, Its Hundredth Birthday. Daniel Gerard Hoffman. **SP-HoffD**

"You! What d'you mean by this?" I rapped. Inspection. Wilfred Owen. **CP-OwenW**

You which could grin three smiles into a dead. Edward Estlin Cummings. **CP-CummE**

You White Cunning Devils. William Dickey. **SP-DickW**

You who are bent, and bald, and blind. The Wanderings of Oisin. William Butler Yeats. **CP-YeatW**

You who are so mighty. Appeal. William Carlos Williams. **CP-WilW1**

You who celebrate bygones. To a Historian. Walt Whitman. **CP-WhitW**

You who come after us. Only the Red Fox, Only the Crow. Charles Olson. **CP-OlsoC**

You who, conspicuous with your shining mace, were accustomed. Elegy 2. John Milton, *tr. fr. Latin by* John T. Shawcross. **CP-MiltJ**

You, who contain augmented tears, explosions. To the Empress Josephine's Statue. Hart Crane. **CP-CranH**

You who desired so much—in vain to ask. To Emily Dickinson. Hart Crane. **CP-CranH**

You, who ending never saw. Mary Sidney, Countess of Montgomery Wroth. *Fr.* Part 1. *Fr.* Urania. **CP-WrotM**

You who flutter and quiver. Vision. John Gould Fletcher. **SP-FletJ** *Fr.* The Ghosts of an Old House.

You who follow Henry Thoreau. A Fish is the Flower of Water. Charles Olson. **CP-OlsoC**

You who go out on schedule. Two Variations. Denise Levertov. **CP-LeveD**

You who had the sense. Invitation. William Carlos Williams. **CP-WilW1**

You Who Have Done. Marsden Hartley. **CP-HartM**

You, who have power over. To the Nameless One. Marsden Hartley. **CP-HartM**

You who have spoken words in the earth. Reproach to Dead Poets. Archibald MacLeish. **CP-MacLA**

You who in water move as one. You Who Swim. John Updike. **CP-UpdiJ**

You who looked on passed ages as a glass. Christina Georgina Rossetti. **CP-RosC3**

You who outlive us, you, our mortal brothers. Ballade. François Villon, *tr. fr. French by* Isabella Gardner. **CP-GardI**

You Who Pour Mercy into Hell. Leonard Cohen. **CP-CoheL**

You Who Question Souls. Leonard Cohen. **CP-CoheL**

You Who Swim. John Updike. **CP-UpdiJ**

You who think I find words for everything. Adrienne Rich. **SP-RicA1** *Fr.* Contradictions: Tracking Poems.

You who were made for this music. Louis Zukofsky. **CP-ZukLS**

You? Why you're. A Fond Farewell. William Carlos Williams. **CP-WilW2**

You will be aware of an absence, presently. For a Fatherless Son. Sylvia Plath. **CP-PlatS**

You will be standing alone. Instructions to a Sentry. John Haines. **SP-HainJ**

You will be walking some night. Do Not Be Ashamed. Wendell Berry. **CP-BerrW**

You will come one day in a waver of love. Dream Girl. Carl Sandburg. **CP-SandC**

You will drive out over edges. Sea Engraving—Style of 1880. Marsden Hartley. **CP-HartM**

You will like their upstairs. A Reunion. James Schuyler. **CP-SchuJ**

You will never be here. Robert Creeley. **CP-CreeR**

You will not forswear the bargainings. Quality of Mercy. Allen Tate. **CP-TateA**

You will not haunt the rue Vavin. To S. V. B.—June 15, 1940. Edna St. Vincent Millay. **CP-MillE**

You will of course remember the night. Sing a Song of Singapore. Al Young. **CP-YounA**

You will read the official histories—true, no doubt. Brightness of Distance. Robert Penn Warren. *Fr.* Infant Boy at Midcentury. **SP-WarrR**

You will remember the tourist's jawbone. Genghis Chan: Private Eye VII. John Yau. **SP-YauJo**

You will remember, when the bombs. Paris—Christmas 1938. Edwin Rolfe. **CP-RolfE**

You will search, babe. I'll Keep It with Mine. "Bob Dylan." **CP-DylaB**

You will see Coleridge, he who sits obscure. Percy Bysshe Shelley. **EPCY** *Fr.* Letter to Maria Gisborne. **CP-ShelP**

You will see this big-jawed man walking up and down. The Explorer on Main Street. Richard Eberhart. **CP-EberR**

You, with my enemy, strolling down my street. Basil Bunting, *after* Manuchehri. **CP-BuntB**

You, with the lamp and pick, what is your labor. Stoic (Circa 1907). Louise McNeill. **SP-McNeL**

You with your wings like spatulas. Gull. Anne Sexton. **CP-SextA**

You woke me, rising—this in Paris once. Et Tu In Arcadia Vixisti. John Hewitt. **CP-HewiJ**

You won not verses, Madam, you won me. Epistle. To My Lady Covell. Ben Jonson. **CP-JonsB**

You wonder, Lupus, who's the best schoolmaster. Martial, *tr. by* William Matthews. **SP-MattW** *Fr.* Epigrams.

You wonder who this is! And, why I name. On the Town's Honest Man. Ben Jonson. **CP-JonsB**

You wonder Who this Thing has writ. To the Earl of Burlington Asking Who Writ the Libels against Him. Alexander Pope. **CP-PopeA**

You won't become a *gourmet* cook. Lines Written in the Fannie Farmer Cookbook. Elizabeth Bishop. **CP-BishE**

You Won't See Me. The Beatles. **CP-Beatl**

You wore the same quite correct clothing. Amitites. Ezra Pound. **SP-PounE**

You worry that I will leave you. Owning Everything. Leonard Cohen. **CP-CoheL**

You would have said. The Woman on the Porch. Miller Williams. **SP-WillM**

You would not think the room. Eight Observations on the Nature of Eternity. Charles Tomlinson. **CP-TomlC**

You would not want too reserved a speaker—. Some Shadows. William Stafford. **SP-StafW**

You would think the fury of aerial bombardment. The Fury of Aerial Bombardment. Richard Eberhart. **CP-EberR**

You would think with so much going on outside. The Studio. Derek Mahon. **SP-MahoD**

You wouldn't / walk alone. That's. But. Robert Creeley. **CP-CreeR**

You, yellow climber. Saturday. Marsden Hartley. **CP-HartM**

You, you are all unloving, loveless, you. The Sea. David Herbert Lawrence. **CP-LawrD**

You, you, there you go again. Moonlessness. Al Young. **CP-YounA**

You Zimmer! Whimpering, heavy, mumbling, lewd. Leaves of Zimmer. Paul Zimmer. **SP-ZimmP**

You'd be surprised how much, at. Bamberg. Randall Jarrell. **CP-JarrR**

You'd hardly notice at first how everything. James McAuley. **SP-McAuJ** *Fr.* Studies for a Self-Portrait at Forty.

You'd look right with a wolf from Tambov. An Arrow in the Wall. Andrei Voznesensky, *tr. fr. Russian by* Richard Wilbur. **CP-WilbR**

You'd never have thought the Queen was Helen's sister—Troy's burning-flower from Sparta, the beautiful sea-flower. The Tower beyond Tragedy. Robinson Jeffers. **CP-JefR1**

Youful / larger / of smallish). Edward Estlin Cummings. **CP-CummE**

You'll be / coming home alone on the AA. Prayer for my Daughter. Marilyn Hacker. **SP-HackM**

You'll be my little seven stone missionary! Thomas Stearns Eliot. *Fr.* Two Songs from *Sweeny Agonistes*. **UnPo** *Fr.* Sweeney Agonistes. **CP-ElioT**

"You'll be wanting a woman," Cavanaugh said with a laugh. The Trader. Frederick Morgan. **SP-MorgF**

You'll be wonderin' whut's de reason. Expectation. Paul Laurence Dunbar. **CP-DunbP**

You'll find—it when you try to die. Emily Dickinson. **CP-DickE**

You'll go on, talking away. Hilda Doolittle. **AnAn** *Fr.* Sigil. **CP-DoolH**

You'll know Her—by Her Foot. Emily Dickinson. **CP-DickE**

You'll know it—as you know 'tis Noon. Emily Dickinson. **CP-DickE**

You'll never know how much I really love you. Do You Want to Know a Secret? John Lennon *and* Paul McCartney. **CP-Beatl**

You'll not forget these rocks and what I told you? Dialogue on the Headland. Robert Ranke Graves. **CP-GravR**

You'll take back your Grand-duke? An August Voice. Elizabeth Barrett Browning. **CP-BroEB**

You'll wait a long, long time for anything much. On Looking Up by Chance at the Constellations. Robert Frost. **CP-FrosR**

Young / man sitting, The. Edward Estlin Cummings. **CP-CummE**

Young. Anne Sexton. **CP-SextA**

Young Abdul scorched in fire of a desert sun. True Believer. Allen Tate. **CP-TateA**

Young and Simple though I Am. Thomas Campion. **CP-CampT**

Young and souple was I, when I lap the dyke. Broom Besoms ["Young and souple was I, when I lap the dyke"]. Robert Burns. **CP-BurnR**

Young and the Old, the. Richard Eberhart. **CP-EberR**

Young and Their Moral Guardians, The. David Herbert Lawrence. **CP-LawrD**

Young and willing to learn (but what?) he was the boy. Razzmatazz. Gilbert Sorrentino. **SP-SorrG**

Young Are Not Greedy, The. David Herbert Lawrence. **CP-LawrD**

Young Are Not Mean in Material Things, The. David Herbert Lawrence. **CP-LawrD**

Young Author, The. Samuel Johnson. **CP-JohnS**

Young Birch, A. Robert Frost. **CP-FrosR**

Young body, light, A. To Beat the Child Was Bad Enough. Maya Angelou. **SP-AngeM**

Young boys play in pairs. Indianapolis War Memorial. Etheridge Knight. *Fr.* Indiana Haiku—2. **SP-KnigE**

Young British Soldier, The. Rudyard Kipling. **CP-KiplR**

Young broke ribs and thighs, holding, The. James McAuley. **SP-McAuJ** *Fr.* Cheiron.

Young Bullfrogs. Carl Sandburg. **CP-SandC**

Young Calidore is paddling o'er the lake. Calidore. A Fragment. John Keats. **CP-KeatJ**

Young captain of a crazy bark! The Last Contention. George Meredith. **CP-MerG1**

Young Cat and the Chrysanthemums, The. William Carlos Williams. **CP-WilW1**

Young child, Christ, is straight and wise, The. Child. Carl Sandburg. **CP-SandC**

Young Churchwarden, The. Thomas Hardy. **CP-HardT**

Young cock in his plebe strut, A. Come Morning. John Ciardi. **SP-CiarJ**

Young Cordwainer, The. Robert Ranke Graves. **CP-GravR**

Young Dead Soldiers, The. Archibald MacLeish. **SP-MacLA**

Young Death. Christina Georgina Rossetti. **CP-RosC3**

Young doctor dreamed of revolution, The. Poetry As Continuity. Jane Cooper. **SP-CoopJ**

Young dog runs and leaps, The. A Toss, for John Cage. Charles Olson. **CP-OlsoC**

Young elm that must be cut, The. Living While It May. Denise Levertov. **CP-LeveD**

Young England—What Is Then Become of Old. William Wordsworth. **CP-WorW2**

Young Fathers. David Herbert Lawrence. **CP-LawrD**

Young Fellow Named Crane, A. Malcolm Lowry. **CP-LowrM**

Young flowers were whispering in melody. Song. Edgar Allan Poe. **NOBA** *Fr.* Al Aaraaf. **CP-PoeEd**

Young Gal's Blues. Langston Hughes. **SP-HughL**

Young, gentle, and candid lover that I am. Sonnet 6. John Milton, *tr. fr. Italian by* John T. Shawcross. **CP-MiltJ**

Young German poked his head, The. The Rare Gist. William Carlos Williams. **CP-WilW2**

Young Girl, A. Walter de la Mare. **CP-DeLaW**

Young Girl, The. Theodore Roethke. **CP-RoetT**

Young girl cousined them, whose character was, A. Thinking, Drinking. John Crowe Ransom. *Fr.* Two Gentlemen in Bonds. **SP-RansJ**

Young girl found me at the track, The. On Being Recognized. Charles Bukowski. **SP-BukC3**

Young girl jogging in mittens and skimpy gym shorts through a freezing rainstorm up our block, The. Fat. Charles Kenneth Williams. **SP-WillC**

Young Girl of the Mississippi Valley, The. Muriel Rukeyser. **CP-RukeM**

Young girl slacks the leash and lingers while, The. In a Suburban Avenue. John Hewitt. **CP-HewiJ**

Young girls alone are lovely. Young Womanhood. John Hewitt. **CP-HewiJ**

Young girls look up, The. The Young Watch Us. Donald Hall. **CP-HallD**

Young girls wear flowers, / Young brides a flowery wreath. The Flowers Appear on the Earth. Christina Georgina Rossetti. **CP-RosC2**

Young Glass-Stainer, The. Thomas Hardy. **CP-HardT**

Young Greek, Killed In The Wars, A. Richard Eberhart. **CP-EberR**

Young Grimes. Walt Whitman. **CP-WhitW**

Young, having risen early, had gone, The. The Guardians. Geoffrey Hill. **CP-HillG**

Young Highland Rover, The. Robert Burns. **CP-BurnR**

Young Housewife, The. William Carlos Williams. **CP-WilW1**

Young Hunter, The. Richard Eberhart. **CP-EberR**

Young I was, but [*or* who] now am old. On Himselfe. Robert Herrick. **CP-HerrR**

Young is the blood that yonder. Alfred Edward Housman. **CP-HousA**

Young Jockey was the blythest lad. Robert Burns. **CP-BurnR**

Young Juan wandered by the glassy brooks. Byron. **OBCoV,** *canto* 1, *stanzas* 90–96; *Fr.* Canto the First. **EnRP; NAEL-2; NoP; OAEL-2; PoE** *Fr.* Don Juan. **CP-Byron**

Young knight, what ever that dost armes professe. Edmund Spenser. **FHYEP** *Fr.* The Faerie Queene. **CP-Spens**

Young lass, A. Spring Song. Li Po, *tr. fr. Chinese by* William Carlos Williams *with* David Rafael Wang. **CP-WilW1**

Young Laundryman, The. William Carlos Williams. **CP-WilW1**

Young Love. Andrew Marvell. **CP-MarvA**

Young Love. William Carlos Williams. **CP-WilW1**

Young Love lies sleeping. Dream-Love. Christina Georgina Rossetti. **CP-RosC1**

Young m / oon:be kind to olde. Edward Estlin Cummings. **CP-CummE**

Young Mage, The. Louise Bogan. **CP-BogaL**

Young man, alone, on the high bridge over the Tagus, A. The High Bridge above the Tagus River at Toledo. William Carlos Williams. **CP-WilW2**

Young man cannot answer. Is this life?, The. Canto XVI. Louis MacNeice. *Fr.* Autumn Sequel. **CP-MacNL**

Young man carrying a battered straw suit-case, A. Such Counsels You Gave to Me. Robinson Jeffers. **CP-JefR2**

Young Man From Oaxaca, The. Malcolm Lowry. **CP-LowrM**

Young man said to me, A. Ultimate Reality. David Herbert Lawrence. **CP-LawrD**

Young man seated at his table, A. The Lack of Repose. Wallace Stevens. **CP-StevW**

Young man, the world's outside that door. An Interview. Howard Nemerov. **CP-NemeH**

Young Man, Thinking of the Old, The. Wendell Berry. *Fr.* The Handing Down. **CP-BerrW**

Young man with the guitar, testing new riffs, The. Song: The Young Man with the Guitar, Testing. Hayden Carruth. **CP-CarHS**

Young Man's Epigram on Existence, A. Thomas Hardy. **CP-HardT**

Young Man's Exhortation, A. Thomas Hardy. **CP-HardT**

Young man's numinous eye is like the sun, The. Death of Alexander. Robert Lowell. **SP-LoweR**

Young Man's Song, *fr.* Words for Music Perhaps. William Butler Yeats. **CP-YeatW**

Young Matrons Dancing. John Updike. **CP-UpdiJ**

Young Men, The. Muriel Rukeyser. **CP-RukeM**

Young Men at the Manor. Rudyard Kipling. *Fr.* Puck of Pook's Hill. Sir Richard's Song. **CP-KiplR**

Young Men Aye Were Fickle Found Since Summer Trees Were Leafy. Christina Georgina Rossetti. **CP-RosC3**

Young men go walking in the woods. The Pediment of Appearance. Wallace Stevens. **CP-StevW**

Young men, having no real joy in life and no hope in the future. Young Fathers. David Herbert Lawrence. **CP-LawrD**

Young men late in the night. The Witnesses. Wystan Hugh Auden. **CP-AudeW**

Young mouth laughs at a gift, A. Her Words. Theodore Roethke. **CP-RoetT**

Young Night Thought. Robert Louis Stevenson. **CP-StevR**

Young Oak! when I planted thee deep in the ground. To an Oak at Newstead. Byron. **CP-Byron**

Young of the mole, The. Moles. Ted Kooser. **SP-KoosT**

Young-ones gathered in from hill and dale, The. Confirmation. William Wordsworth. *Fr.* Ecclesiastical Sonnets. **CP-WorW2**

Young or old / What was I but a story told. Kathleen Jessie Raine. **SP-RainK**

Young Owls. Brendan Galvin. **SP-GalvB**

Young Peggy blooms our bonniest lass. A Song. On Miss P——— K———. Robert Burns. **CP-BurnR**

Young Person came out of the mists, A. Wystan Hugh Auden. *Fr.* Shorts [1948–1957] ("At peace under this mandarin, sleep, Lucina"). **CP-AudeW**

Young Poet, A. Frank O'Hara. **SP-OharF**

Young Princess, The. George Meredith. **CP-MerG1**
 "Lord Dusiote sprang from priest and squire."
 "Lords of the Court they sighed heart-sick, The."
 "Soft night–wind went laden to death, The."
 "When the South sang like a nightingale."

Young Queen, The. Elizabeth Barrett Browning. **CP-BroEB**

Young Queen, The. Rudyard Kipling. **CP-KiplR**

Young queen Nature, ever sweet and fair, The. Nature and Art. Paul Laurence Dunbar. **CP-DunbP**

Young question of *What it is for* stays always, The. Frank Templeton Prince. *Fr.* Afterword on Rupert Brooke. **CP-PrinF**

Young Rabbits. John Clare. **SP-ClarJ**

Young Reynard. George Meredith. **CP-MerG1**

Young rice plants are just being. Kenneth Rexroth. **CP-RexKL** *Fr.* The Heart's Garden, the Garden's Heart.

Young Sailor. Langston Hughes. **SP-HughL**

Young Sea. Carl Sandburg. **CP-SandC**

Young Sibyl, The. Robert Ranke Graves. **CP-GravR**

Young Soldier with Bloody Spurs, The. David Herbert Lawrence. **CP-LawrD**

Young Son, The. John Ashbery. **SP-AshbJ**

Young Sycamore. William Carlos Williams. **CP-WilW1**

Young thing in spring green slippers, stockings, A. Whiffs of the Ohio River at Cinncinnati. Carl Sandburg. **CP-SandC**

Young to-day are born prisoners, The. Poor Young Things. David Herbert Lawrence. **CP-LawrD**

Young Traveller Is Presented to the Goddess Dulness, A. Alexander Pope. **NOEC** *Fr.* Yet, yet a moment, one dim ray of light. **NAEL-1; OAEL-1; PoEL-3** *Fr.* The Dunciad. **CP-PopeA**

Young unmarried man, with a good name, A. Byron. **NOBL** *Fr.* Canto the Twelfth. *Fr.* Don Juan. **CP-Byron**

Young Usurper, The. George Meredith. **CP-MerG1**

Young Want to Be Just, The. David Herbert Lawrence. **CP-LawrD**

Young Watch Us, The. Donald Hall. **CP-HallD**

Young Wife, A. David Herbert Lawrence. **CP-LawrD**

Young Woman. Robert Creeley. **CP-CreeR**

Young Woman. Howard Nemerov. **CP-NemeH**

Young Woman at a Window. William Carlos Williams. **CP-WilW1**

Young Woman at a Window. William Carlos Williams. **CP-WilW1**

Young Womanhood. John Hewitt. **CP-HewiJ**

Young Woman's Song. John Berryman. **CP-BerrJ**

Young Wordsworth's London, The. William Wordsworth. **FaBoPP** *Fr.* Residence in London. *Fr.* The Prelude; Growth of a Poet's Mind [1805 vers.]. **CP-WorW3**

Younger Sister, Going Swimming. Margaret Atwood. **SP-AtwM1**

Youngest of them, Richard, had a wife, The. Uncle Dick and Aunt Bertha. John Hewitt. **CP-HewiJ**

Your anger charms me. Hyacinth. Hilda Doolittle. **CP-DoolH**

Your ashes will not stir, even on this high ground. In Carrowdore Churchyard. Derek Mahon. **SP-MahoD**

Your average tourist: Fifty. 2.3. Casual Wear. James Merrill. **NIP** *Fr.* Topics. **SP-MerrJ**

Your Basic Black Poet. Al Young. **CP-YounA**

Your beauty is a thunder. Black Ode. Maya Angelou. **SP-AngeM**

Your beauty once the profit of your scorn. Howard Nemerov. *Fr.* Four Sonnets. **CP-NemeH**

Your beauty, which I lost sight of once. Love Song. Denise Levertov. **CP-LeveD**

Your billet, Sir, I grant receipt. To Renton of Lamerton. Robert Burns. **CP-BurnR**

Your birthday comes to tell me this. Edward Estlin Cummings. **CP-CummE**

Your Birthday in Wisconsin You Are 140. John Berryman. **CP-BerrJ**

Your blonde hair / is the way I live—. Promise. Leonard Cohen. **CP-CoheL**

Your body may be a sack. *see also* Steps for a Dancer. Howard Nemerov. **CP-NemeH**

Your bony head, Jazbo, O dock walloper. Singing Nigger. Carl Sandburg. **CP-SandC**

Your bow swept over a string, and a long low note quivered to the air. Jan Kubelik. Carl Sandburg. **CP-SandC**

Your breasts / sliced-off The scars. A Woman Dead in Her Forties. Adrienne Rich. **SP-RicA2**

Your breasts are like. When Even The. Leonard Cohen. **CP-CoheL**

Your breath is sweet. One More Cup of Coffee (Valley Below). "Bob Dylan." **CP-DylaB**

Your brother has a falcon. Christina Georgina Rossetti. **CP-RosC2**

Your brother is dead. Dreaming with a Friend. Stephen Berg. **SP-BergS**

Your brother will trim my hedges! Eavesdropper. Sylvia Plath. **CP-PlatS**

Your Catullus is depressed, Cornificus. Catullus. *See* Carmen 38: "Angst, / ennui & angst."

Your claims to immortality were two. To an Ancient. Robert Frost. **CP-FrosR**

Your clear eye is the one absolutely beautiful thing. Child. Sylvia Plath. **CP-PlatS**

Your coming is a symptom of Summer. Emily Dickinson. **SP-DickE**

Your cottage, Furius, sheltered. Carmen 26. Catullus. *Fr.* Carmina. **CP-Catul**

Your cup of instant coffee by the bed. Crosswords. Thom Gunn. *Fr.* Transients and Residents. **CP-GunnT**

Your Dailiness. Alice Notley. **SP-NotlA**

Your daisies have come. The Break Away. Anne Sexton. **CP-SextA**

Your dark eyes will never need to understand. Picture of a Black Child with a White Doll. Thomas Merton. **CP-MertT**

Your Daughter. Jim Carroll. **SP-CarrJ**

Your daughters / Zeus, provider. Zeus-Provider. Hilda Doolittle. **CP-DoolH** *Fr.* Temple of the Sun.

Your day breaks, your mind aches. For No One. John Lennon *and* Paul McCartney. **CP-Beatl**

Your Death. Leonard Cohen. **CP-CoheL**

Your death, dear Lady, was quite cold. Elegy for Eugenesis. Allen Tate. **CP-TateA**

Your dog, tranquil and innocent, dozes through. Adrienne Rich. *Fr.* Twenty-one Love Poems. **SP-RicA1; SP-RicA2**

Your dream: / At first its name is Heliopolis. Hayden Carruth. *Fr.* The Sleeping Beauty. **CP-CarHL**

Your dream: / Her name was Hestia, sister of God. Hayden Carruth. *Fr.* The Sleeping Beauty. **CP-CarHL**

Your dream: / His name is Heraclitus, and he is huge. Hayden Carruth. *Fr.* The Sleeping Beauty. **CP-CarHL**

Your dream: / His name was Hannibal, i.e., by Baal's. Hayden Carruth. *Fr.* The Sleeping Beauty. **CP-CarHL**

Your dream: / His name was Harlequin. He wore the mask. Hayden Carruth. *Fr.* The Sleeping Beauty. **CP-CarHL**

Your dream: / His name was Heathcliff, and he was clearly. Hayden Carruth. *Fr.* The Sleeping Beauty. **CP-CarHL**

Your dream: / His name was Hegel, a dear sweet man. Hayden Carruth. *Fr.* The Sleeping Beauty. **CP-CarHL**

Your dream: / His name was Hendryk Hudson. And oh, the glory! Hayden Carruth. *Fr.* The Sleeping Beauty. **CP-CarHL**

Your dream: / His name was Hermann, tender, quiet. Hayden Carruth. *Fr.* The Sleeping Beauty. **CP-CarHL**

Your dream: / His name was Hermes, and he was all to all. Hayden Carruth. *Fr.* The Sleeping Beauty. **CP-CarHL**

Your dream: / His name was Hero, and his other name. Hayden Carruth. *Fr.* The Sleeping Beauty. **CP-CarHL**

Your dream: / His name was Herod. No? How close. Hayden Carruth. *Fr.* The Sleeping Beauty. **CP-CarHL**

Your dream: / His name was Hesiod, a darkish man. Hayden Carruth. *Fr.* The Sleeping Beauty. **CP-CarHL**

Your dream: / His name was Hilarity but he never laughed. Hayden Carruth. *Fr.* The Sleeping Beauty. **CP-CarHL**

Your dream: / His name was Hitler and he lived over. Hayden Carruth. *Fr.* The Sleeping Beauty. **CP-CarHL**

Your dream: / His name was Hölderlin. Ah, name, name! Hayden Carruth. *Fr.* The Sleeping Beauty. **CP-CarHL**

Your dream: / His name was Homer. He was blind. Hayden Carruth. *Fr.* The Sleeping Beauty. **CP-CarHL**

Your dream: / His name was Husband, his title Herr. Hayden Carruth. *Fr.* The Sleeping Beauty. **CP-CarHL**

Your dream: / His name was unheard of, very strange. Hayden Carruth. *Fr.* The Sleeping Beauty. **CP-CarHL**

Your dream: / Its name apparently is Honeywell. Hayden Carruth. *Fr.* The Sleeping Beauty. **CP-CarHL**

Your dream: / Its peculiar name is Hydrogen Bomb. Hayden Carruth. *Fr.* The Sleeping Beauty. **CP-CarHL**

Your dream: / The letters HIV appear. Hayden Carruth. *Fr.* The Sleeping Beauty. **CP-CarHL**

Your dream is Hamlet again. Hayden Carruth. *Fr.* The Sleeping Beauty. **CP-CarHL**

Your dust will be upon the wind. What the Sexton Said. Nicholas Vachel Lindsay. **CP-LindV**

Your duty is to cling. Moralizing Overheard in a Forest. Jean Garrigue. **SP-GarrJ**

Your dying was a difficult enterprise. Lament. Thom Gunn. **CP-GunnT**

Your electric hair's beautiful gold as Blake's Glad Day boy. To the Punks of Dawlish. Allen Ginsberg. **CP-GinsA**

Your enchantment / enchants me, stretched. Poem. James Schuyler. **CP-SchuJ**

Your eye-light wanes with an ail of care. Every Artemisia. Thomas Hardy. **CP-HardT**

Your even two will slay me suddenly. *mod. vers.* Geoffrey Chaucer. **ACP; BoLoP; EnVB; NAEL-1; SCGP; TrGrPo** *Fr.* Merciles[s] Beaute [*or* Beautée *or* Beauty]. **CP-ChauG**

Your Eyes. Leonard Cohen. **CP-CoheL**

Your eyes and the valley are memories. Valley Song. Carl Sandburg. **CP-SandC**

Your eyes are widely open flowers. Mysteries. Alice Walker. **CP-WalkA**

Your eyes change. Definitions of Old Age. Archibald MacLeish. **CP-MacLA**

Your eyes of draiad speak. Your Eyes. Charles Olson. **CP-OlsoC**

"Your eyes that once were never weary of mine." Ephemera. William Butler Yeats. **CP-YeatW**

Your eyes, those pools with soft rushes. Hart Crane. *Fr.* Three Locutions Des Pierrots. **CP-CranH**

Your face Your tongue Your wit. In the Grace of Wit, of Tongue and Face. Sir Walter Ralegh. **CP-RaleW**

Your face is like a chamber where a king. Edna St. Vincent Millay. **CP-MillE**

Your Face on the Dog's Neck. Anne Sexton. **CP-SextA**

Your face scrapes my sleep tonight. Letter to be Disguised as a Gas Bill. Marge Piercy. **SP-PierM**

Your face, voice, name will tell. For Any Irishman. John Hewitt. **CP-HewiJ**

Your faire lookes urge my desire. Thomas Campion. *See* Be Wise, and Fly Not.

Your Fair[e] Look[e]s Inflame [My Desire]. Thomas Campion. **CP-CampT**

Your famous city stood, plucked out of time. To the People of Dresden. John Hewitt. **CP-HewiJ**

Your Fearful Symmetries. Isabella Gardner. **CP-GardI**

Your feigned indifference hardly hides your love. Atropos to Ophelia. Alun Lewis. **CP-LewiA**

Your fine white hand is Heaven's gift. The Merciful Hand. Nicholas Vachel Lindsay. **CP-LindV**

Your fingers can dart. A Gesture. James McAuley. **SP-McAuJ**

Your first dog was a Pekinese. Stanley Jasspon Kunitz. *Fr.* Journal for My Daughter. **CP-KuniS**

Your fleshed body, sickle. Margaret Atwood. *Fr.* Circe / Mud Poems. **SP-AtwM1**

Your friends come fondly to your living room. Birthday Card for a Psychiatrist. Mona Van Duyn. **SP-VanDM**

Your friendship much can make me blest. Interpolation. Robert Burns. **CP-BurnR**

Your frosty hands. The Cats' Month. William Carlos Williams. **CP-WilW1**

Your ghost will walk, you lover of trees. Robert Browning. **PIP** *Fr.* De Gustibus. **CP-BroR1**

Your ghost will walk, you lover of trees. De Gustibus. Robert Browning. **CP-BroR1**

Your gift of life was idleness. Kathleen Jessie Raine. **SP-RainK**

Your gift to me was a gray stone cast upon a wild shore, traced over. Soliloquy Upon Love. Kathleen Jessie Raine. **SP-RainK**

Your Gifts are from the Sky. Emily Dickinson. **SP-DickE**

Your gold cloud, towering far above me. Gold Cloud. Robert Ranke Graves. **CP-GravR**

Your grandad worked the signals. Northern Metres. Donald Davie. **CP-DavDo**

Your Granny's had pneumonia, a bad cold. Asleep. Daniel Gerard Hoffman. **SP-HoffD**

Your great mistake is to disregard the satire. The Mute Phenomena. Derek Mahon. **SP-MahoD**

Your grieving moonlight face looks down. Reproach. Robert Ranke Graves. **CP-GravR**

Your hand in mine, we walk out. A Sword in a Cloud of Light. Kenneth Rexroth. **SP-RexrK** *Fr.* The Lights in the Sky are Stars.

Your hand trailed over the hammock's side. Ode to Joy. Daniel Gerard Hoffman. **SP-HoffD**

Your hands / Lumpish roots of earth cunning. Now You Have to Push. Ted Hughes. **SP-HughT**

Your hands / make Pallas wonder. Myrtle Bough. Hilda Doolittle. **CP-DoolH**

Your hands are like two mirrors which press. Winter's Age. Jim Carroll. **SP-CarrJ**

Your hands easy. Remembrance. Maya Angelou. **SP-AngeM**

Your hay it is mowed, and your corn is reaped. Harvest Home. John Dryden. **SP-DrydJ** *Fr.* King Arthur.

Your health, Master Willow. Contrive me a bat. Tree Party. Louis MacNeice. **CP-MacNL**

Your heart was handed over. Foxgloves. Carl Sandburg. **CP-SandC**

Your homecoming will be my homecoming. Edward Estlin Cummings. **CP-CummE**

Your honest heart of duty, Worden. In the Turret. Herman Melville. **SP-MelvH**

Your hooves have stamped at the black margin of the wood. On a Picture of a Black Centaur by Edmund Dulac. William Butler Yeats. **CP-YeatW**

Your Horoscope. Charles Henri Ford. **SP-FordC**

Your Ibsen volumes, violet-spined. Juvenilia. Adrienne Rich. **CP-RicAE; SP-RicA2**

Your insomniac sorrow settles. Alba. Al Young. **CP-YounA**

Your jar of Virginny. Poor Honest Men. Rudyard Kipling. **CP-KiplR**

Your Labours are performed, your Bye-works too. To Ogmian Hercules. Robert Ranke Graves. **CP-GravR**

Your lashes leave me naked in the square. Barren. Audre Lorde. **SP-LordA**

Your Last Drive. Thomas Hardy. **CP-HardT**

Your Lead, Partner, I Hope We've Read the Same Book. Ogden Nash. **CP-NashO**

"Your leg must go. Okay?" the surgeon said. Alun Lewis. *Fr.* Burma Casualty. **CP-LewiA**

Your Letter. Adrienne Rich. **CP-RicAE**

Your letter came.—Glutted the earth & cold. A Winter-Piece to a Friend Away. John Berryman. **CP-BerrJ**

Your letter describes / what you see from your window. You chose. Letter to an English Poet. Donald Hall. **CP-HallD**

Your lists of victims dear. Becoming Somebody Else. Charles Kenneth Williams. **CP-WillC**

Your little mental gallantries. Emily Dickinson. **SP-DickE**

Your little voice / Over the wires came leaping. Edward Estlin Cummings. **CP-CummE**

Your looks so often cast. Sir Thomas Wyatt. **CP-WyatT**

Your love and pity doth the impression fill. Sonnet 112. William Shakespeare. *Fr.* Sonnets. **CP-ShaWS**

Your love to me was like an unread book. Bright Bindings. Countee Cullen. **CP-CullC**

Your lovely hands. William Carlos Williams. **CP-WilW1** *Fr.* Paterson.

Your low birth puts you beneath me. Carl Sandburg. *Fr.* The People, Yes. **CP-SandC**

Your lungs fill & spread themselves. Flying Inside Your Own Body. Margaret Atwood. **SP-AtwM2**

Your midriff sags toward your knees. Woman with Girdle. Anne Sexton. **CP-SextA**

Your mind and you are our Sargasso Sea. Portrait d'une Femme. Ezra Pound. **SP-PounE**

Your mind was wrought in cosmic solitude. John Milton. Allen Tate. **CP-TateA**

Your mission, in any disputed area, is to find. Diplomacy: The Father. William DeWitt Snodgrass. **SP-SnodW**

Your mistress [or mistris], that you follow whores, still taxeth you. A Self[e] Accuser. John Donne. **CP-DonnJ**

Your Momma kissed the chaffeur. The Thirteens (White). Maya Angelou. **SP-AngeM**

Your Momma took to shouting. The Thirteens (Black). Maya Angelou. **SP-AngeM**

Your most recent acquisition, Flavius. Carmen 6. Catullus. *Fr.* Carmina. **CP-Catul**

Your Mother Should Know. The Beatles. **CP-Beatl**

Your mother, whom the mirror-world has claimed. The Tutored Child. Stanley Jasspon Kunitz. **CP-KuniS**

Your name includes the shadow flight of birds. Kenneth Patchen. *Fr.* Eight Early Poems. **CP-PatcK**

Your name scrawled on a bit of paper moves me. What the Finger Writes. Alice Walker. **CP-WalkA**

Your News and review, Sir, I've read through and through, Sir. To Captain Riddell. Robert Burns. **CP-BurnR**

Your Nipples. Siv Cedering Fox. **SP-CedeS**

Your nurse could only speak Italian. Sailing Home from Rapallo. Robert Lowell. **SP-LoweR**

Your pain still hangs in air. Memory Unsettled. Thom Gunn. **CP-GunnT**

Your pardon, my friend, if my rhymes did offend. To the Sighing Strephon. Byron. **CP-Byron**

Your passion was ever plural, apart. To Thoreau on Rereading Walden. Isabella Gardner. **CP-GardI**

Your patience, Sirs. The Devil took me up. Rudyard Kipling. **CP-KiplR** *Fr.* The Naulahka.

Your peal of ten ring over then this town. On Hearing the Full Peal of Ten Bells from Christ Church, Swindon, Wilts. Sir John Betjeman. **CP-BetjJ**

Your pen needs but a ruffle. On Receiving One of Gloriana's Letters. Nicholas Vachel Lindsay. *Fr.* This Section Is a Christmas Tree. **CP-LindV**

Your pencil will do particles and waves—. Drawing Lessons. Howard Nemerov. **CP-NemeH**

Your perch is the branch. To a Sparrow. William Carlos Williams. **CP-WilW2**

Your picture smiles as first it smiled. The Amulet. Ralph Waldo Emerson. **CP-EmerR**

Your Pleasure in my Cemetery. James Liddy. *Fr.* Glass after Oblivion. **CP-LiddJ**

Your Poem must eternal be. To Mr. Pye. Samuel Taylor Coleridge. **CP-ColeS**

"Your poems about the girls will still be around." Tonight. Charles Bukowski. **SP-BukC1**

Your presence like a benison to me. To Her. Paul Laurence Dunbar. **CP-DunbP**

Your Private Way. Robert Ranke Graves. **CP-GravR**

Your relentless Music. Emily Dickinson. **SP-DickE**

Your Riches—taught me—Poverty. Emily Dickinson. **CP-DickE**

Your sentences cast print and paper to the winds. The Jews among the Nations. Kay Boyle. **CP-BoylK**

Your shining—where?—rays my wide room with gold. John Berryman. *Fr.* Sonnets to Chris. **CP-BerrJ**

Your shoulder stiffens to my kiss. The Evolution of the Dragon. Wystan Hugh Auden. **CP-AudWJ**

Your silence against my shoulder. Tanck's Song About Silence. Hayden Carruth. **CP-CarHS** *Fr.* Songs About What Comes Down: The Complete Works of Mr. Septic Tanck.

Your silence today is a pond where drowned things live. Adrienne Rich. *Fr.* Twenty-one Love Poems. **SP-RicA1; SP-RicA2**

Your skin like dawn. Passing Time. Maya Angelou. **SP-AngeM**

Your small embattled eyes dispute a face. On Looking in the Looking Glass. Isabella Gardner. **CP-GardI**

Your small hands, precisely equal to my own. Adrienne Rich. **PoE; TRP** *Fr.* Twenty-one Love Poems. **SP-RicA1; SP-RicA2**

Your smile, delicate. Woman Me. Maya Angelou. **SP-AngeM**

Your smiling, or the hope, the thought of it. A Simile for Her Smile. Richard Wilbur. **CP-WilbR**

Your son presses against me. The Apple Trees. Louise Glück. **SP-GlücL**

Your song where you lie long dead on the shore of a Spanish river. Segre Song. Muriel Rukeyser. **CP-RukeM**

Your Soul Shines. Alice Walker. **CP-WalkA**

Your special witness, as I recollect. Selina, Countess of Huntingdon. Donald Davie. **CP-DavDo**

Your spoken words are roses fine and sweet. Roses and Pearls. Paul Laurence Dunbar. **CP-DunbP**

Your stature is modelled. The Contest. Hilda Doolittle. **CP-DoolH**

Your sudden laugh restored felicity. The Laugh. Robert Ranke Graves. **CP-GravR**

Your summerhouse of underdone meat is still standing, boy. Message for Rimbaud. Charles Henri Ford. **SP-FordC**

Your sweetness of soul was a mystery to me. Hattie Rice Rich. Adrienne Rich. *Fr.* Grandmothers. **SP-RicA2**

Your thighs are appletrees. Portrait of a Lady. William Carlos Williams. **CP-WilW1**

Your thoughts don't have words every day. Emily Dickinson. **CP-DickE**

Your thoughts make shape like snow; in one night only. To a Communist. Louis MacNeice. **CP-MacNL**

Your tits are rosy in the dawn. Alba. Robert Creeley. **CP-CreeR**

Your tongue thrums and moves. Kenneth Rexroth. **SP-RexrK** *Fr.* Love Poems of Marichiko.

Your toothbrush won't remember your mouth. And Then. Miller Williams. **SP-WillM**

Your trail runs to the westward. To James Whitcomb Riley. Rudyard Kipling. **CP-KiplR**

Your train leaves at eleven-forty-five and it is now but eleven. Dr. Fell and Points West. Ogden Nash. **CP-NashO**

Your tree—your oak. Ted Hughes. **SP-HughT** *Fr.* Gaudete.

Your tribe. white car. a whole spectrum of whites. Judith Revisited. Patti Smith. **SP-SmitP**

Your troubles shrink not, though I feel them less. A Confession to a Friend in Trouble. Thomas Hardy. **CP-HardT**

Your turn, Grass of confusion. Stanley Jasspon Kunitz. *Fr.* Journal for My Daughter. **CP-KuniS**

Your unbruised eyes over the hurt mouth. The Suzy Q. John Clellon Holmes. **SP-HolmJ**

Your verses were commended, as 'tis true. To Mr Jonson upon these Verses. Ben Jonson. **CP-JonsB**

Your voice always whacked me right on the funny bone. Burying Blues for Janis. Marge Piercy. **SP-PierM**

Your voice at times a fist. To a Husband. Maya Angelou. **SP-AngeM**

Your voice comes to me, George, on the winter night. Questions. Hayden Carruth. **CP-CarHS**

Your voice, with clear location of June days. June Light. Richard Wilbur. **CP-WilbR**

Your walls do not fall, he said. Hilda Doolittle. **NALW** *Fr.* Tribute to the Angels. **CP-DoolH**

Your western heads here cast on money. A Coin. Carl Sandburg. **CP-SandC**

Your white shoulders. White Shoulders. Carl Sandburg. **CP-SandC**

Your whitelight flashes the frost tonight. Whitelight. Carl Sandburg. **CP-SandC**

"Your wife," the doctor said. Mr. and Mrs. Billings. Donald Hall. **CP-HallD**

Your windfall at fifteen   your Steinway grand. Solfeggietto. Adrienne Rich. **SP-RicA1**

"Your wish came true". Robert Creeley. **CP-CreeR**

Your words my friend (right healthful caustics) blame. Sonnet 21. Sir Philip Sidney. **CABA; NAEL-1; NoSic; PoE; TEP** *Fr.* Astrophil and Stella. **SP-SidnP**

You're. Sylvia Plath. **CP-PlatS**

You're. James Schuyler. **CP-SchuJ**

You're a beast, she said. You. Charles Bukowski. **SP-BukC1**

You're a Big Girl Now. "Bob Dylan." **CP-DylaB**

You're a long way off becoming a saint. Wystan Hugh Auden. *Fr.* Shorts [1927–1932] ("Pick a quarrel, go to war"). **CP-AudeW**

You're caught in a vicious circle. Vicious Circle. "Lou Reed." **SP-ReedL**

You're displeased / maybe I should just stop. A Fire of Unknown Origin. Patti Smith. **SP-SmitP**

You're Going to Lose That Girl. The Beatles. **CP-Beatl**

You're Gonna Make Me Lonesome When You Go. "Bob Dylan." **CP-DylaB**

You're growing up / and rain sort of remains. Little Ode on St. Anne's Day. Jim Carroll. **SP-CarrJ**

You're hot to trot? Well then I'm not. Martial, *tr. by* William Matthews. **SP-MattW** *Fr.* Epigrams.

You're my friend: / I was the man the Duke spoke to. The Flight of the Duchess. Robert Browning. **CP-BroR1**

You're my friend: / I was the man the Duke spoke to. The Flight of the Duchess. Robert Browning. **CP-BroR1**

You're not asleep? A Masque of Reason. Robert Frost. **CP-FrosR**

You're not going yet? I must; I have to work. This Way Out. Louis MacNeice. **CP-MacNL**

You're Not Supposed to Be Here. Leonard Cohen. **CP-CoheL**

You're right—"the way is narrow." Emily Dickinson. **CP-DickE**

You're sleeping with your hands. Every Day. Tom Clark. **SP-ClarT**

You're sucking / for a bruise. Harry. Robert Creeley. **CP-CreeR**

You're the can and I'm the salmon. A Dialogue between Soul and Body. Randall Jarrell. **CP-JarrR**

You're the invention. Cut Worm. Roy Fisher. **SP-FishR**

You're too late. The Blues. Byron. **CP-Byron**

You're two, that's great. Charles Kenneth Williams. **CP-WillC**

You're welcome to Despots, Dumourier. Address to General Dumourier. Robert Burns. **CP-BurnR**

You're Welcome, Willie Stewart. Robert Burns. **CP-BurnR**

You're wondering if I'm lonely. Song. Adrienne Rich. **SP-RicA2**

Your Eyes. Charles Olson. **CP-OlsoC**

Yours. Charles Kenneth Williams. **CP-WillC; SP-WillC**

Yours, Barbara, was a literal way of death. And Thou No Breath at All? Isabella Gardner. **CP-GardI**

Yours is the music for no instrument. Edward Estlin Cummings. **CP-CummE**

Yours is the shame and sorrow, *sl. diff. vers.* David Herbert Lawrence. *See* Last Words to Miriam.

Yours is the sullen sorrow. Last Words to Miriam. David Herbert Lawrence. **CP-LawrD**

Yours Next. Louis MacNeice. **CP-MacNL**

Yours this moment I unseal. Extempore Reply to an Invitation. Robert Burns. **CP-BurnR**

Yours Truly. Leonard Nathan. **SP-NathL**

Yours was the original freak-out: Samuel Beckett's. To Helen Keller. Donald Davie. **CP-DavDo**

Yourself, myself and our togetherness. Three Locked Hoops. Robert Ranke Graves. **CP-GravR**

Yourself walked in the room tonight. Away. Robert Creeley. **CP-CreeR**

Youth. Robert Browning. *See* Oh, the wild joys of living! the leaping from rock up to rock.

Youth. James Wright. **CP-WrigJ**

Youth and Age. Samuel Taylor Coleridge. **CP-ColeS**

Youth, and Age. Robert Herrick. **CP-HerrR**

Youth and Age. Frank Templeton Prince. **CP-PrinF**

Youth and Age. William Shakespeare. *See* Crabbed age and youth cannot live together.

Youth and Age. William Butler Yeats. **CP-YeatW**

Youth and Age on Beaulieu River, Hants. Sir John Betjeman. **CP-BetjJ**

Youth and Art. Robert Browning. **CP-BroR1**

Youth and Beauty. William Carlos Williams. **CP-WilW1**

Youth and Love I ("Once only by the garden gate"). Robert Louis Stevenson. **CP-StevR**

Youth and Love II ("To the heart of youth the world is a highwayside"). Robert Louis Stevenson. **CP-StevR**

Youth at Eve had drunk his fill, The. The Lady of the Ladle. "Lewis Carroll." **CP-CarrL**

Youth, Day, Old Age and Night. Walt Whitman. **CP-WhitW**

Youth eminent from his country and his virtues, A. To Mr. John Milton of London. *Unknown.* *Fr.* Complimentary Pieces to Milton. **CP-CowpW**

Youth from the capital rides by the east of the city, The. The Youth on Horseback. Li Po, *tr. fr. Chinese by* William Carlos Williams *with* David Rafael Wang. **CP-WilW2**

Youth gone, and beauty gone if ever there. Christina Georgina Rossetti. **GBL; OBNC; Son** *Fr.* Monna Innominata. **CP-RosC2**

Youth in Age. George Meredith. **CP-MerG2**

Youth in Memory. George Meredith. **CP-MerG1**

Youth is the ruggedest burden that can score. The Septuagenarian. Robert Ranke Graves. **CP-GravR**

Youth is the time when hearts are large. On the Slain Collegians. Herman Melville. **SP-MelvH**

Youth, large, lusty, loving—youth full of grace, force, fascination. Youth, Day, Old Age and Night. Walt Whitman. **CP-WhitW**

Youth, like Indian Summer. Emily Dickinson. **SP-DickE**

Youth Mowing, A. David Herbert Lawrence. **CP-LawrD**

Youth, Nature, and Relenting Jove. Byron. **CP-Byron**

Youth now flees on feathered foot. To Will H. Low. Robert Louis Stevenson. **CP-StevR**

Youth of delight, come hither. The Voice of the Ancient Bard. William Blake. **CP-BlakW** *Fr.* Songs of Experience.

Youth of Nature. Matthew Arnold. **SP-ArnoM**

Youth of Nature: Wordsworth's Country, The. **FaBoPP**

Youth of Nature: Wordsworth's Country, The. Matthew Arnold. **FaBoPP** *Fr.* The Youth of Nature. **SP-ArnoM**

Youth on Horseback, The. Li Po, *tr. fr. Chinese by* William Carlos Williams *with* David Rafael Wang. **CP-WilW2**

Youth played in the blear hotel, The. Edwin Booth. Nicholas Vachel Lindsay. *Fr.* Epitaphs for Two Players. **CP-LindV**

Youth Sings a Song of Rosebuds. Countee Cullen. **CP-CullC**

Youth that trafficked long with Death. The Expert. Rudyard Kipling. **CP-KiplR**

Youth too certain of his power to wade, A. Isle of Man. William Wordsworth. *Fr.* Poems Composed or Suggested During a Tour, in the Summer of 1833. **CP-WorW2**

Youth walks up to the white horse, to put its halter on, The. The White Horse. David Herbert Lawrence. **CP-LawrD**

Youth went faring up and down, A. The Wooing. Paul Laurence Dunbar. **CP-DunbP**

Youth Who Carried a Light, The. Thomas Hardy. **CP-HardT**

Youth who scarce had seen his twentieth year, A. The Character of Wallenstein. Samuel Taylor Coleridge. **CP-ColeS** *Fr.* The Death of Wallenstein.

Youthful Poet's Unspoke Response to a Woman Talking Too Loudly in His Favorite Bookstore, The. David Markson. **CP-MarkD**

Youthful Quest, The. George Meredith. **CP-MerG1**

Youth's Progress. John Updike. **CP-UpdiJ**

You've come! O how flustered and anxious I've been. Basil Bunting, *after the Persian of* Sadi. **CP-BuntB**

You've dressed yourself so white for it! And you poise. A Saying of Farewell. James Dickey. **CP-DickJ**

You've got another love / and I know it. Poor Girl. Maya Angelou. **SP-AngeM**

"You've got to cross that lonesome valley" and. The Handshake, the Entrance. John Berryman. **CP-BerrJ**

You've got to fuck a great many women. How to Be a Great Writer. Charles Bukowski. **SP-BukC1**

You've Got to Hide Your Love Away. The Beatles. **CP-Beatl**

You've gotten in through the transom. To a Child Trapped in a Barber Shop. Philip Levine. **SP-LeviP**

You've kept your word and come to visit me. Leviathan. Robert Pack. **SP-PackR**

You've lost your religion, the Rabbi said. Debate with the Rabbi. Howard Nemerov. **CP-NemeH**

You've made it clear, Charles Darwin, why. Grandeur. Robert Pack. **SP-PackR**

You've mastered the bleak art of Changes. James McAuley. *Fr.* Aor Against the Ingrate Who Abused Our Hospitality. **SP-McAuJ**

You've only just heard? Paid on Both Sides. Wystan Hugh Auden. **CP-AudeW**

You've seen a strawberry. Nevertheless. Marianne Craig Moore. **CP-MoorM**

You've seen Balloons set—Haven't You? Emily Dickinson. **CP-DickE**

You've seen how it works. Evolution. Leonard Nathan. **SP-NathL**

You've seen it perhaps in the wrong setting. The Photograph in the Hallway. Stephen Dunn. **SP-DunnS**

You've swallowed a wool sock, and you've got. The Cold. Barton Sutter. **SP-SuttB**

You've taken my blues and gone. Note on Commercial Theatre. Langston Hughes. **SP-HughL**

You've toughed it out pretty well, old Body, done. Robert Penn Warren. **SP-WarrR**

(Interjection #7: Remarks of Soul to Body.) **SP-WarrR**

"You've Tried the World, Try Jesus." Robert Creeley. **CP-CreeR**

Yr element. Water. Diane Wakoski. *Fr.* Fifteen Poems for a Lunar Eclipse None of Us Saw. **SP-WakoD**

Ytte wes a mirke an dreiry cave. Ye Fattale Cheyse. "Lewis Carroll." **CP-CarrL**

Yüan Chên Variations. Frank Templeton Prince. **CP-PrinF**

"Eight times the autumn weather."

"His old fame is dumb."

"I can be more solitary."

"I think of waking / In the country inn."

Yuletide in a Younger World. Thomas Hardy. **CP-HardT**

Yum yum the stars are out. Rape. Patti Smith. **SP-SmitP**

Yup, our disgraces are. Asymptotes. Charles Olson. **CP-OlsoC**

Yvonne stood there silently / the roar of the plane still in her ears. Malcolm Lowry. **CP-LowrM**

Z

Za Ki Tan Ke Parlay Lot. Audre Lorde. **SP-LordA**

Zaccheus he / Did climb the tree. Sycamore. Robert Frost. **CP-FrosR**

Zaddik, you showed me. A Letter to William Kinter of Muhlenberg. Denise Levertov. **CP-LeveD**

Zakarias, day follows day. Dubhe. Siv Cedering Fox. *Fr.* Seven Letters to Zakarias. **SP-CedeS**

Zakarias, I know I have not yet begun. Megrez. Siv Cedering Fox. *Fr.* Seven Letters to Zakarias. **SP-CedeS**

Zakarias, it is right that I address you. Phekda. Siv Cedering Fox. *Fr.* Seven Letters to Zakarias. **SP-CedeS**

Zakarias, sometimes I wonder in which direction. Alioth. Siv Cedering Fox. *Fr.* Seven Letters to Zakarias. **SP-CedeS**

Zakarias, there are still Finlands. Alkaid. Siv Cedering Fox. *Fr.* Seven Letters to Zakarias. **SP-CedeS**

Zalmoxis. Howard Nemerov. **CP-NemeH**

Zander on God. Howard Nemerov. **CP-NemeH**

Zapolya. Samuel Taylor Coleridge.

Glycine's Song.

(Song: "Sunny shaft did I behold, A.") **CP-ColeS**

"Up, up! ye dames, ye [*or* dames and ye] lasses gay!" **CP-ColeS**

(Hunting Song.) **CP-ColeS**

Zara. ("I dreamed") Christina Georgina Rossetti. **CP-RosC3**

Zara. ("Now the pain") Christina Georgina Rossetti. **CP-RosC3**

Zara. ("Pale sad face") Christina Georgina Rossetti. **CP-RosC3**

Zaydee. Philip Levine. **SP-LeviP**

Zeal Required in Love. Robert Herrick. **CP-HerrR**

Zealously my Muse doth salute all thee. To Mr. R. W. John Donne. **CP-DonnJ**

Zebra-striped pillow. The restlessness. John Yau. **SP-YauJo** *Fr.* Scenes from the Life of Boullee.

Zebrina etc. Louis Zukofsky. **CP-ZukLS**

Zei Gesund. Isabella Gardner. **CP-GardI**

Zen & the Art of Poetry. Erica Jong. **SP-JongE**

Zenith. Jenny Joseph. **SP-JoseJ**

Zenith and After, The. Ron Koertge. **SP-KoerR**

Zeno. Randall Jarrell. **CP-JarrR**

Zéphyrine Drouhin / lines out her. Like Lorraine Ellison. James Schuyler. **CP-SchuJ**

Zeppelin Factory, The. Rita Dove. **SP-DoveR**

Zeppelin Nights. David Herbert Lawrence. *Fr.* Bits. **CP-LawrD**

Zermatt: To the Matterhorn. Thomas Hardy. **CP-HardT**

Zero. Tess Gallagher. **SP-GallT**

Zero, a nothing, A. Armies of the Plain. George Oppen. **CP-OppeG**

Zero burped by, A. Figuring. Charles Simic. **SP-SimiC**

Zeroes—taught us—Phosphorus, The. Emily Dickinson. **CP-DickE**

Zeus' Couchmate,—who of mortals knows not me. Herakles. Robert Browning. **CP-BroR2**

Zeus Is Dead. Clement of Alexandria, *tr. by* Thomas Merton. **CP-MertT** *Fr.* Diatribe Against the Old Gods.

Zeus is snake no longer, nor swan, nor eagle. Zeus Is Dead. Clement of Alexandria, *tr. by* Thomas Merton. **CP-MertT** *Fr.* Diatribe Against the Old Gods.

Zeus lies in Ceres' bosom. Canto 81. Ezra Pound. **FaBoMo; MoAB; MoP; NAAL-2; NOBA; NoAM; VGW** *Fr.* Cantos. **CP-PoCan**

Zeus over Redeye. Robert Earl Hayden. **CP-HaydR**

Zeus-Provider. Hilda Doolittle. **CP-DoolH** *Fr.* Temple of the Sun.

Zeus was once overheard to shout at Hera. The Weather of Olympus. Robert Ranke Graves. **CP-GravR**

Zimmer and the Ghost. Paul Zimmer. **SP-ZimmP**

Zimmer at the Diggings. Paul Zimmer. **SP-ZimmP**

Zimmer Directs Himself Home from the Diggings. Paul Zimmer. **SP-ZimmP**

Zimmer Drunk and Alone, Dreaming of Old Football Games. Paul Zimmer. **SP-ZimmP**

Zimmer Envying Elephants. Paul Zimmer. **SP-ZimmP**

Zimmer Fearing Anemia. Paul Zimmer. **SP-ZimmP**

Zimmer Finds Imbellis in the Ancient Graves. Paul Zimmer. **SP-ZimmP**

Zimmer Guilty of the Burnt Girl. Paul Zimmer. **SP-ZimmP**

Zimmer Imagines Heaven. Paul Zimmer. **SP-ZimmP**

Zimmer in Grade School. Paul Zimmer. **SP-ZimmP**

Zimmer Loathing the Gentry. Paul Zimmer. **SP-ZimmP**

Zimmer Remembering Wanda. Paul Zimmer. **SP-ZimmP**

Zimmer the Drugstore Cowboy. Paul Zimmer. **SP-ZimmP**

Zimmer Warns Himself with Vivid Images Against Old Age. Paul Zimmer. **SP-ZimmP**

Zimmer with Lester Under the Moon. Paul Zimmer. **SP-ZimmP**

Zimmer, you are getting sloppy. Zimmer Directs Himself Home from the Diggings. Paul Zimmer. **SP-ZimmP**

Zimmer's Head Thudding against the Blackboard. Paul Zimmer. **SP-ZimmP**

Zimmer's Last Gig. Paul Zimmer. **SP-ZimmP**

Zimmer's Love Poem After A Hard Dream. Paul Zimmer. **SP-ZimmP**

Zimmershire Lad, A. Paul Zimmer. **SP-ZimmP**

Zimri: "In the first rank of These did Zimri stand." John Dryden. *See* In the first rank of these did Zimri stand.

Zimri: "Numerous host of dreaming saints succeed." John Dryden. *See* Zimri: The Duke of Buckingham.

Zimri: "Some of their chiefs were princes of the land." John Dryden. *See* Some of their chiefs were princes of the land.

Zimri: The Duke of Buckingham. John Dryden. **NOBE; OBSV** *Fr.* Absalom and Achitophel, Pt. I. **SP-DrydJ**

(Zimri: "Numerous host of dreaming saints succeed.") **AWP; SeCePo**

Zinc roofs in the moonlight, The. Ernesto Cardenal, *tr. by* Thomas Merton. **CP-MertT** *Fr.* Gethsemani, KY.

Zinnia. Louis Zukofsky. **CP-ZukLS**

Zinnias. Robert Earl Hayden. **CP-HaydR**

Zinnias you look so much like Gentiles. Louis Zukofsky. *Fr.* There when the water was not potable. *Fr.* Chloride of Lime and Charcoal. **CP-ZukLS**

Zion. Donald Davie. **CP-DavDo**

Zion. Rudyard Kipling. **CP-KiplR**

Zion Said. Christina Georgina Rossetti. **CP-RosC3**

Zip! Donald Davie. **CP-DavDo**

ZIP Code Ode. John Updike. *See* aMERICA, you caTNip bIN.

Zmyrna, my own Cinna, nine harvests passed making his hymn. Catullus. *See* Carmen 95: "Nine harvests & nine winters since its inception."

Zodiac, The. Donald Davie. **CP-DavDo**

Zodiac, The. James Dickey. **CP-DickJ**

"Tenderness, ache on me, and lay your neck." **TAP**

Zola. Edwin Arlington Robinson. **CP-RobiE**

Zombie. Lewis Turco. **SP-TurcL**

Zone. Guillaume Apollinaire, *tr. fr. French.* **CP-BeckS**, *tr. by* Samuel Beckett;

Zone. Louise Bogan. **CP-BogaL**

Zoo, The. Stevie Smith. **CP-SmitS**

Zoo, The. Gilbert Sorrentino. **SP-SorrG**

Zoo Bats. John Updike. **CP-UpdiJ**

Zoo Keeper's Wife. Sylvia Plath. **CP-PlatS**

Zoraster long ago / Said poetry presents us. Kenneth Rexroth. **CP-RexKL** *Fr.* The Dragon and the Unicorn.

"Boswell: Sir, what is the chief." **SP-RexrK**

Zorro Man, A. Maya Angelou. **SP-AngeM**

Zucca, The. Percy Bysshe Shelley. **CP-ShelP**

Zukofsky. Gilbert Sorrentino. **SP-SorrG**

Zulu Girl, The. George Oppen. **CP-OppeG**

Zulus Live in Land without a Square. John Updike. **CP-UpdiJ**

Zumer Is Icumen In. Paul Zimmer. **SP-ZimmP**

AUTHOR INDEX

Translated poems are listed here under the names of their translators, under the sub-heading Translations, Coauthored Poems, *etc. Exceptions are Catullus and Pablo Neruda, whose translated poems are listed under their own names. Pseudonymous names are enclosed in quotation marks.*

A

Ammons, Archie Randolph (b. 1926)
After Yesterday.
Ah.
Anxiety.
Around Here.
Attention.
Bay Bank.
Blue Skies.
Bottommost.
Bride.
Bulletin.
Calling.
Camels.
Capture.
Catch.
Celestial Dealings.
Chasm.
Circling Splinters.
Clarifications.
Cleavage.
Close Relations.
Cold Rheum.
Coming Right Up.
Coming To.
Communication.
Correction.
Course Work.
Cousins.
Coward.
Cracking a Few Hundred Million Years.
Crinkling Trails.
Crow Ride.
De l on one, The.
Deaf Zone.
Digging Wonder.
Double Exposure.
Down Low.
Enough.
Equilibrations.
Exotic.
Figuring Belief.
Filling in the Dots.
For Doyle Fosso.
For Louise and Tom Gossett.
Fortitude.
Gardening.
Glacials.
Glass Globe.
Glass Speciality.
Grisly Grit.
Grove's Way.
Holding On.
Hollows.
Hype.
I Went Back.
Imaginary Number.
Immediacy.
Immoderation.
Increment.
Interference.
Juice.
Kingpin.
Late Look.
Late November.
Layabout.
Leaning Up.

Likely Story.
Lofty.
Lost and Found.
Mark, The.
Market Adviser.
Mediation.
Meeting the Opposition.
Merchandise.
Milepost.
Mirrorment.
Miss.
Modality.
Natives.
Nearing Equinox.
Negligence These Days.
Night Chill.
Night Post.
North Street.
Oblivion's Room.
One Thing and Another.
Orchard.
Over and Done With.
Pebble's Story.
Pedagogy Agog.
Permanence.
Photosynthesis.
Planet Actions.
Poem: "In a high wind the."
Poetry to the Rescue.
Precious Weak Fields.
Preexistence.
Progress Report.
Providence.
Quit That.
Rainy Morning.
Reading.
Recording.
Recovery.
Reflective.
Release.
Reorganization.
Resolve.
Resurrections.
Roundel.
Salute.
Scarecrow.
Scour, The.
Second Party.
Self.
Settlement.
Shading Flight In.
Sitting Down, Looking Up.
Sizing.
Small Song.
Snow Roost.
Soaker.
Songlet.
Soul's Seas.
Spaceship.
Spring Clearing.
Spring Tornado.
Spruce Woods.
Squall Ball.
Still Frame.
Stills.
Stoning Stone.
Substantial Planes.
Success Story.

Swoggled.
Teleology.
That Day.
Their Sex Life.
Theory Center.
This.
Time Spans.
Timing.
Touching.
Transducer.
Transfer.
Trigger.
Triplet.
Tryst.
Turning.
Twangs & Little Twists.
Undersea.
Upshot, The.
Utensil.
Waking.
Weathering.
Weight.
Whitelash of Air Rapids.
Winter Sanctuaries.
Winter Scene.
Wiring.
Worky Shallows.

Angelou, Maya (b. 1928)
Accident.
Africa.
After.
Ain't That Bad.
Alone.
America.
Amoebaean for Daddy.
Arrival.
Artful Pose.
Avec Merci, Mother.
Awaking in New York.
Black Ode.
Brief Innocence.
Bump d'Bump.
Caged Bird.
California Prodigal.
Call Letters: Mrs. V.B.
Calling of Names, The.
Changes.
Chicken-Licken.
Child Dead in Old Seas.
Come. And Be My Baby.
Communication I.
Communication II.
Conceit, A.
Contemporary Announcement.
Country Lover.
Detached, The.
Elegy: "I lay down in my grave."
Faces.
Family Affairs.
For Us, Who Dare Not Dare.
Gamut, The.
Georgia Song, A.
Good Woman Feeling Bad, A.
Greyday.
Harlem Hopscotch.
Health-Food Diner, The.
Here's to Adhering.

How I Can Lie to You.
I Almost Remember.
Impeccable Conception.
In a Time.
In Retrospect.
Insomniac.
John J.
Junkie Monkey Reel.
Just for a Time.
Just Like Job.
Kin.
Kind of Love, Some Say, A.
Lady Luncheon Club.
Last Decision, The.
Late October.
Lesson, The.
Let's Majeste.
Letter to an Aspiring Junkie.
Lie, The.
Life Doesn't Frighten Me.
Little Girl Speakings.
Lord, in My Heart.
Martial Choreograph.
Memory, The.
Men.
Miss Scarlet, Mr. Rhett and other Latter-Day
    Saints.
Momma Welfare Roll.
Mothering Blackness, The.
Mourning Grace.
My Arkansas.
My Guilt.
My Life Has Turned to Blue.
No Loser, No Weeper.
No No No No.
Now Long Ago.
On a Bright Day, Next Week.
On Aging.
On Diverse Deviations.
On Reaching Forty.
On Working White Liberals.
One More Round.
Passing Time.
Phenomenal Woman.
Pickin Em Up and Layin Em Down.
Plagued Journey, A.
Poor Girl.
Prelude to a Parting.
Prescience.
Prisoner.
Pusher, The.
Recovery.
Refusal.
Remembering.
Remembrance.
Request.
Reverses.
Riot: 60's.
Senses of Insecurity.
Sepia Fashion Show.
Shaker, Why Don't You Sing?
Singer Will Not Sing, The.
Slave Coffle.
Song for the Old Ones.
Sounds Like Pearls.
Southeast Arkanasia.
Starvation.
Still I Rise.
Take Time Out.
Tears.
Telephone, The.
Thank You, Lord.
They Went Home.
Thirteens (Black), The.
Thirteens (White), The.
This Winter Day.
Through the Inner City to the Suburbs.
Times-Square-Shoeshine-Composition.
To a Freedom Fighter.
To a Husband.
To a Man.
To a Suitor.
To Beat the Child Was Bad Enough.
Traveler, The.
Unmeasured Tempo.
We Saw Beyond Our Seeming.
Weekend Glory.

When I Think about Myself.
When You Come to Me.
Where We Belong, A Duet.
Willie.
Woman Me.
Woman Work.
Wonder.
Zorro Man, A.

Antoninus, Brother *see* Everson, William
Arnold, Matthew (1822–88)
At Some Lone Alehouse.
Buried Life, The.
But the majestic river floated on.
Dover Beach.
Empedocles on Etna.
Farewell, A: "My horse's feet beside the
    lake."
Forsaken Merman, The.
Growing Old.
Haworth Churchyard *sels.*
In Harmony with Nature.
In Utrumque Paratus.
Iseult of Brittany.
Isolation: To Marguerite.
Life and Thought.
Meeting.
Memorial Verses.
Quiet Work.
Requiescat.
Resignation.
Scholar-Gipsy, The.
Self-Dependence.
Shakespeare.
Sick King in Bokhara, The.
Sohrab and Rustum *sels.*
Song of Callicles, The ("Through the black,
    rushing smoke-burst").
Stanzas from the Grande Chartreuse.
Stanzas in Memory of the Author of
    "Obermann."
Summer Night, A.
Switzerland *sels.*
Thyrsis.
To a Friend.
To Marguerite—Continued.
Tristram and Iseult *sels.*
Turn we next to the dead.
Wordsworth's Grave.
Youth of Nature, The.
Youth of Nature: Wordsworth's Country,
    The.

Ashbery, John (b. 1927)
Absence of a Noble Presence, The.
Additional Poem, An.
And I'd Love You to Be in It.
And Others, Vaguer Presences.
And "Ut Pictura Poesis" Is Her Name.
And You Know.
Another Chain Letter.
As One Put Drunk into the Packet-Boat.
As We Know.
As You Came from the Holy Land.
At North Farm.
At the Inn.
Bird's-Eye View of the Tool and Die Co.
Blessing in Disguise, A.
Blue Sonata.
Boy, A.
Bungalows, The.
Business Personals.
Chateau Hardware, The.
Clepsydra.
Couple in the Next Room, The.
Crazy Weather.
Daffy Duck in Hollywood.
Darlene's Hospital.
Decoy.
Ecclesiast, The.
Errors.
Fantasia on "The Nut-Brown Maid" *sels.*
Farm Implements and Rutabagas in a
    Landscape.
Faust.
Flowering Death.
For John Clare.
Forties Flick.
Friends.

Frontispiece.
Gazing Grain, The.
Glazunoviana.
Grand Galop.
Grapevine, The.
Haunted Landscape.
He.
Here Everything Is Still Floating.
Hollywood Everything, A.
Hop o' My Thumb.
Houseboat Days.
How Much Longer Will I Be Able to Inhabit
    the Divine Sepulcher.
Ice-Cream Wars, The.
If the Birds Knew.
Illustration.
Instruction Manual, The.
Into the Dusk-Charged Air.
It Was Raining in the capital.
Ivory Tower, The.
Just Walking Around.
Lament upon the Waters, The.
Landscape (After Baudelaire).
Last Month.
Last World, A.
Late Echo.
Le Livre Est sur la Table.
Leasing of September, The.
Litany *sels.*
Litany.
Lonedale Operator, The.
Long Novel, A.
Love Poem, A.
Many Wagons Ago.
Märchenbilder.
Mixed Feelings.
More Pleasant Adventures.
My Erotic Double.
New Realism, The *sels.*
Old heavens, you used to tweak above us.
Oleum Misericordiae.
On the Towpath.
Ongoing Story, The.
Or in My Throat.
Other Cindy, The.
Other Tradition, The.
Otherwise.
Our Youth.
Painter, The.
Paradoxes and Oxymorons.
Parergon.
Picture of Little J. A. in a Prospect of
    Flowers, The.
Pied Piper, The.
Plainness in Diversity.
Plural of "Jack-in-the-Box,"The.
Popular Songs.
Punishing the Myth.
Purists Will Object.
Pursuit of Happiness, The.
Pyrography.
Qualm.
Recent Past, The.
Rivers and Mountains.
Saying It to Keep It from Happening.
Scheherazade.
Self-Portrait in a Convex Mirror.
Silhouette.
Skaters, The *sels.*
Some certified nut.
Some Old Tires.
Some Trees.
Some Words.
Something Similar.
Song: "Song tells us of our old way of
    living, The."
Songs We Know Best, The.
Sonnet: "Each servant stamps the reader with
    a look."
Soonest Mended.
Sortes Vergilianae.
Spring Day.
Street Musicians.
Summer.
Syringa.
System, The.
Tapestry.

Task, The.
Thank You for Not Cooperating.
Their Day.
There was calm rapture in the way she
　spoke.
37 Haiku.
This Configuration.
Thoughts of a Young Girl.
Tone Poem, A.
Train Rising Out of the Sea.
Two Scenes.
Unctuous Platitudes.
Unless this is the shelf of whatever happens?
Untilted.
Unusual Precautions.
Variant.
Variations, Calypso and Fugue on a Theme
　of Ella Wheeler Wilcox.
Vegetarians, The.
Wave, A.
We Hesitate.
Wet Casements.
What Is Poetry.
Whatever It Is, Wherever You Are.
White Roses.
Wind thrashes the maple seed-pods, The.
Wooden Buildings.
Worsening Situation.
Wrong Kind of Insurance, The.
Young Son, The.

Atwood, Margaret (b. 1939)
After all you are quite.
After Heraclitus.
After the agony in the guest / bedroom, you
　lying by the.
After the Flood, We.
Against Still Life.
Aging Female Poet on Laundry Day.
Aging Female Poet Reads Little Magazines.
Aging Female Poet Sits on the Balcony.
All Bread.
Alternate Thoughts from Underground.
Anchorage.
Animals in That Country, The.
Another Elegy.
At first I was given centuries.
At the Tourist Centre in Boston.
Axiom.
Backdrop Addresses Cowboy.
Bad Mouth.
Beauharnois.
Beauharnois, Glengarry.
Bedside.
Beyond truth, / tenacity: of those.
Blue Dwarfs.
Boat, A.
Book of Ancestors.
Buffalo in Compound: Alberta.
Bull Song.
Bus along St Clair: December, A.
Bus to Alliston, Ontario, The.
Carrying Food Home in Winter.
Charivari.
Christmas Carols.
Circe / Mud Poems.
Circle Game, The.
City Planners, The.
Comic Books vs. History.
Conversation, A.
Corpse Song.
Crow Song.
Cyclops.
Daguerreotype Taken in Old Age.
Death of a Young Son by Drowning.
Deaths of the Other Children, The.
Departure from the Bush.
Digging.
Disembarking at Quebec.
Double Voice, The.
Dream 1: the Bush Garden.
Dream 2: Brian the Still-Hunter.
Dream 3: Night Bear Which Frightened
　Cattle.
Dreams of the Animals.
Dufferin, Simcoe, Grey.
Eating Fire.
Eating Snake.

1837 War in Retrospect.
Elegy for the Giant Tortoises.
Eurydice.
Eventual Proteus.
Explorers, The.
First Neighbours.
Fishing for Eel Totems.
Five Poems for Dolls.
Five Poems for Grandmothers.
Flying Inside Your Own Body.
Fortification, A.
Foundling, A.
Four Auguries.
Four Small Elegies.
Further Arrivals.
Galiano Coast: Four Entrances.
Game after Supper.
Georgia Beach.
Girl and Horse, 1928.
Habitation.
Head against White.
Heart Test with an Echo Chamber.
Hesitations Outside the Door.
Highest Altitude.
How To Tell One Country from Another.
I am sitting on the / edge of the impartial.
I can't tell you my name.
I look up, you are standing.
I see you fugitive, stumbling across the
　prarie.
Immigrants, The.
Interlunar.
Is / Not.
It Is Dangerous to Read Newspapers.
Journey to the Interior.
Keep.
Landcrab I.
Landcrab II.
Landlady, The.
Last Day.
Late August.
Later in Belleville: Career.
Letter from Persephone.
Looking in a Mirror.
Lying here, everything in me.
Machine. Gun. Nest.
Marrying the Hangman.
Marsh, Hawk.
Metempsychosis.
Midwinter, Presolstice.
Migration: C.P.R.
More and More.
Morning, A.
Mothers.
Mushrooms.
My beautiful wooden leader.
Newsreel: Man and Firing Squad.
Night Poem.
Nightshade on the Way to School.
No Name.
Not the Moon.
Notes towards a Poem That Can Never Be
　Written.
Nothing.
November.
Orpheus (1).
Orpheus (2).
Out.
Owl Song.
Paper Bag, A.
Paths and Thingscape.
Pig Song.
Place: Fragments, A.
Planters, The.
Porcupine Meditation.
Porcupine Tree.
Postcard.
Pre-Amphibian.
Precognition.
Procedures for Underground.
Progressive Insanities of a Pioneer.
Projected Slide of an Unknown Soldier.
Psalm to Snake.
Quattrocento.
Rat Song.
Red Shirt, A.
Reincarnation of Captain Cook, The.

Rest, The.
Resurrection.
Robber Bridegroom, The.
Roominghouse, Winter.
Settlers, The.
She.
She Considers Evading Him.
Siren Song.
Small Cabin, The.
Snake Woman.
Solipsism While Dying.
Solstice Poem.
Some Objects of Wood and Stone.
Song of the Fox.
Song of the Hen's Head.
Song of the Worms.
Songs of the Transformed.
Soul, Geologically, A.
Speeches for Dr Frankenstein.
Spring again, can I stand it.
Squaw Lilies: Some Notes.
Sunday Drive, A.
Sunset II.
Their Attitudes Differ.
There Is Only One of Everything.
They Are Hostile Nations.
They Eat Out.
They were all inaccurate.
This is a mistake, / these arms and legs.
This Is a Photograph of Me.
Thoughts from Underground.
Three Desk Objects.
Three Praises.
Torture.
Tricks With Mirrors.
True Stories.
Two Fires, The.
Two-Headed Poems.
Variation on the Word *Sleep*.
Visit to Toronto, with Companions.
Voice, A.
Vultures.
We are hard on each other.
We hear nothing these days.
Wereman, The.
Werewolf Movies.
What is it, it does not.
Wish: Metamorphosis to Heraldic Emblem.
Woman Makes Peace with Her Faulty Heart,
　The.
Woman Skating.
Woman Who Could Not Live With Her
　Faulty Heart, The.
Women's Issue, A.
Words Continue Their Journey, The.
Yes at first you / go down smooth as.
You Are Happy.
You are the sun / in reverse, all energy.
You Begin.
You did it / it was you who started the
　countdown.
You fit into me.
You refuse to own / yourself, you permit.
You take my hand and.
You want to go back.
Younger Sister, Going Swimming.

Auden, Wystan Hugh (1907–73)
A. E. Housman.
Academic Graffiti.
Address to the Beasts.
Adolescence.
Advent.
After.
After Reading a Child's Guide to Modern
　Physics.
After Reading Keats' Ode.
After the Burial.
After the Storm.
Age of Anxiety, The.
Aliens, The.
Allendale.
Alone.
Alston Moor.
Amor Loci.
Amor Vincit Omnia.
Annunciation, The.
Another Time.

Anthem for St. Cecilia's Day.
Anthem: "Let us praise our Maker, with true passion extol Him."
Appletreewick.
April.
April in a Town.
Archaeology.
Art of Healing, The.
Arthur's Quoit, Dyffryn.
As He Is.
As I Walked Out One Evening.
Ascension Day, 1964.
At last, down in the lane.
At Parting.
At the Grave of Henry James.
At the Maison Lyons.
At the Manger.
At the Party.
Atlantis.
Aubade: "At break of dawn."
Aubade: "Beckoned anew to a World."
August 1968.
Autumn.
Autumn Evening.
Autumn Song.
Aware.
Bach and the Lady.
Bad Night, A.
Ballad: "He offered her his paucity."
Ballad of Barnaby, The.
Bank Holiday.
Bathtub Thoughts.
Bawbee.
Because sap fell away.
Before.
Belief.
Below me Ticknall lay but in the light.
Bestiaries Are Out.
Between Adventure.
Bird-Language.
Blessed Event.
Blind Lead the Blind, The.
Bonfires, The.
Bride in the 30's, A.
Brussels in Winter.
Bucolics.
Buzzards.
By the Fire.
By the Gasworks, Solihull.
Caliban to the Audience.
California.
Calypso.
Canal, Froghall, The.
Candles Gutter Low, The.
Canzone: "When shall we learn, what should be clear as day."
Capital, The.
Carter's Funeral, The.
Casino.
Cat, The.
Cattivo Tempo.
Cave of Making, The.
Cave of Nakedness, The.
Change of Air, A.
Chimaeras, The.
Chloe to Daphnis in Hyde Park.
Christ in Hades.
Christmas Eve.
Cinders.
Circe.
Circus, The.
City without Walls.
Clocks cannot tell our time of day.
Colonel to be shot at dawn, The.
Coming of Love, The.
Common Life, The.
Compline.
Composer, The.
Consequences.
Consider.
Contra Blake.
Contrast, A.
Control of the passes was, he saw, the key.
Council, The.
Crocus stars the border, The.
Crowing of the cock, The.
Curse, A.

Daily Bread.
Dame Kind.
Damming Stream.
Danse Macabre.
Dark Fiddler, The.
Dark Years, The.
Dawn.
Day-dreams of a Tourist.
Death's Echo.
Decoys, The.
Deemed this an outpost, I.
Detective Story.
Dethroned.
Dew steams off the thatches, The.
Diaspora.
Dichtung und Wahrheit.
Doggerel by a Senior Citizen.
Domesday Song.
Dover.
Down There.
Dragon-fly, The.
Dream, A.
Duet, The.
Dying House, The.
Early Morning.
Early Morning Bathing.
Earth's Praises.
Easter Monday.
Easy Knowledge.
Ebes Anthos Apollumenon.
Economics.
Edward Lear.
Elegy for J.F.K.
Elegy: "Liebe Frau Emma."
Elegy: "Wagtail splutters in the stream, A."
Elegy: "Why was it that you gave us no warning."
Eleven Occasional Poems.
Encomium Balnei.
Encounter.
Encounter, An.
Engine House, The.
Envoi: "From the red chimneys smoke climbs slow and straight."
Envoi No. 2.
Envoi: "Take up your load and go, lad."
Envoi: "You go / Now you are glad."
Epigoni, The.
Episode, An.
Epistle to a Godson.
Epitaph for the Unknown Soldier.
Epitaph on a Tyrant.
Epithalamium: "All folk-tales mean by ending."
Et in Arcadia Ego.
Eulogy.
Everest.
Evolution of the Dragon, The.
Exiles, The.
Extract.
Fairground.
Fall of Rome, The.
Family Ghosts.
Farglow.
February Dawn, A.
Felo de se.
Few and Simple.
Finis.
First Meeting.
First Things First.
Five Songs ("Deftly, admiral, cast your fly").
Five Songs ("What's in your mind, my dove, my coney").
Fleet Visit.
Flight into Egypt, The.
Flowers and Stationmaster.
For Friends Only.
For the Time Being; a Christmas Oratorio
    sels.
For the Time Being; a Christmas Oratorio.
Forty Years On.
Four sat on in the bare room, The.
Free One, A.
Friday's Child.
Friendship.
From the very first coming down.
Frost.

Gare du Midi.
Garrison, The.
Geography of the House, The.
Gipsy Girl, The.
Glad.
Golden Age, The.
Good-Bye to the Mezzogiorno.
Grow thin by walking and go inland.
Grub First, Then Ethics.
Half Way.
Hammerfest.
Hands.
Happy Ending.
Happy Tree, The.
Have a Good Time.
He Revisits the Spot.
Healthy Spot, A.
Heard and Seen.
Heavy Date.
Helen.
Hell.
Herman Melville.
Hidden Lane, The.
Hidden Law, The.
His Excellency.
History of Science, The.
History of Truth, The.
Hodge Looks toward London.
Homage to Clio.
Hong Kong.
Horae Canonicae.
Horatians, The.
Household, A.
Houses rolled into the sun, The.
Humpty Dumpty.
Hunting Season.
I Am Not a Camera.
I chose this lean country.
Iceland Revisited.
If I Could Tell You.
In a Country Churchyard.
In a Train.
In Due Season.
In Memoriam L. K.-A. 1950–1952.
In Memory of Ernst Toller.
In Memory of Sigmund Freud.
In Memory of W. B. Yeats.
In Praise of Limestone.
In Schrafft's.
In Sickness and in Health.
In the Nursery.
In Transit.
Inn Song.
Insignificant Elephants.
Ischia.
Island Cemetery, An.
Islands.
James Honeyman.
Job.
Josef Weinheber.
Journey to Iceland.
Joy.
J.S. Bach.
Kairos and Logos.
Lady[,] Weeping at the Crossroads.
Lakes.
Landscape.
Last Bus, Saturday Night.
Last of the Old Year, The.
Last Time, The.
Lauds.
Law like Love.
Lead's the Best.
Leap Before You Look.
Legend.
Lesson, The.
Let History Be My Judge.
Letter, The.
Letter to Lord Byron.
Light strives with darkness, right with wrong.
Like a Vocation.
Like other men, when I go past.
Limbo Culture.
Lines for Elizabeth Mayer.
Lines to Dr Walter Birk On His Retiring from General Practice.
Loneliness.

Lost.
Lost Secret, The.
Love Feast, The.
Lovers' Lane.
Lullaby: "Din of work is subdued, The."
Lullaby: "Lay your sleeping head, my love."
Luther.
Macao.
Mail-train, Crewe, The.
Major Port, A.
Maker, The.
Makers of History.
Man of La Mancha sels.
Managers, The.
Many Happy Returns.
March.
March Song.
March Winds.
Marginalia.
Maria Hat Geholfen.
Massacre of the Innocents, The.
May.
Maze, The.
Meditation of Simeon, The.
Megalopsych, The.
Meiosis.
Memento Creatoris Tui.
Memorial for the City.
Merax & Mullin.
Metalogue to The Magic Flute.
Metaphor.
Mill (Hempstead), The.
Mill, The.
Mind to body spoke the whole night through, The.
Miner's Wife, The.
Minnelied.
Miss Gee.
Missing.
Misunderstanding, A.
Model, The.
Moment, A.
Montaigne.
Moon Landing.
Moralities.
More Loving One, The.
Mosaic for Marianne Moore, A.
Motherhood.
Mountains.
Mundus et Infans.
Musée des Beaux Arts.
Music Is International.
My Lady of the Wood.
Narcissus.
Natural Linguistics.
Never Stronger.
New Year Greeting, A.
New Year Letter.
Night Mail, The.
Nightfall.
1929.
No Change of Place.
No, not from this life, not from this life is any.
No, Plato, No.
No trenchant parting this.
Nocturne: "Appearing unannounced, the moon."
Nocturne: "Do squamous and squiggling fish."
Nones.
Nor was that final, for about that time.
North, The.
Not in Baedeker.
Novelist, The.
November at Weybourne.
Now from far eastern wolds, the bay.
Numbers and Faces.
Nursery Rhyme.
O What Is That Sound [Which So Thrills the Ear].
Objects.
Ode: "Though aware of our rank and alert to obey orders."
Ode to Gaea.
Ode to Terminus.
Ode to the Diencephalon.

Ode to the Medieval Poets.
Often the man, alone shut, shall consider.
Old Colliery, The.
Old Lead-mine, The.
Old Man's Road, The.
Old Mine, The.
Old People's Home.
On a Greek Tomb Relief.
On Receiving a Christmas Card.
On Seeing Some Dutch Pictures.
On Sunday Walks.
On the Circuit.
On the frontier at dawn getting down.
On This Island.
One Circumlocution.
Orpheus.
Our Bias.
Our Hunting Fathers.
Out of sight assuredly, not out of mind.
Owl, The.
Oxford.
Paid on Both Sides sels.
Paid on Both Sides.
Parable.
Pardon.
Partition.
Paysage Moralisé.
Permanent Way, A.
Photograph of a Boy in Costume, The.
Plains.
Plane Tree, The.
Pleasure Island.
Ploughing.
Portrait.
Posthumous Letter to Gilbert White.
Postscript.
Prayer.
Precious Five.
Preface: "Aged catch their breath, The."
Price, The.
Pride.
Prime.
Profile.
Progress.
Progress?
Prologue at Sixty.
Prologue: The Birth of Architecture.
Prophets, The.
Prospero to Ariel.
Pseudo-Questions.
Pumping Engine, Cashwell, The.
Punchard.
Quest, The.
Question, The: "All of us believe."
Question, The ("To ask the hard question is simple").
Questioner Who Sits So Sly, The.
Quique Amavit.
Rain.
Rainy Afternoon, A.
Recitative by Death.
Reflections in a Forest.
Reminder, A.
Richard Jefferies.
Riddle, The.
Rimbaud.
River Profile.
Road's Your Place, The.
Robin, The.
Rois Fainéants.
Roman Wall Blues.
Rookery, The.
Rookhope (Weardale, Summer 1922).
Runner.
Sabbath, The.
Sawmill, The.
Say Yes!
Schoolchildren.
Sea and the Mirror, The.
Secondary Epic.
Secret Agent, The.
Secrets.
September.
Sext.
Shield of Achilles, The.
Ship, The.
Shock, A.

Short Ode to a Philologist, A.
Short Ode to the Cuckoo.
Shorts I ("Watch upon my wrist, The").
Shorts II [1958–1971] ("Poet's hope: to be, A").
Shorts [1927–1932] ("Pick a quarrel, go to war").
Shorts [1939–1947] ("Motionless, deep in his mind, lies the past the poet's forgotten").
Shorts [1948–1957] ("At peace under this mandarin, sleep, Lucina").
Shorts [1972–1973] ("None of us are as young").
Since.
Since the Autumn day.
Six Commissioned Texts.
Skyreholme Mill.
Smelt and Tasted.
So I must go my way.
Some say that handsome raider still at large.
Song: "Crocus stars the border, The."
Song: "I have a little book."
Song: "Merriest cuckoo / Which haunted us in May, The."
Song of the Beggars.
Song of the Devil.
Song of the Ogres.
Song: "Past all your knowing."
Song: "Relation seemed ordained for us."
Song, The: "So large a morning[,] so itself[,] to lean."
Sonnet: "April is here but when will Easter come?"
Sonnet I: "There was desolate silence on the world."
Sonnet II: "It matters not that we shall cease to be."
Sonnet: "This world is full of lovely things."
Sonnets from China.
Sower, The.
Speech.
Sphinx, The.
Spring unsettles sleeping partnerships, The.
Spring will come, The.
Stark bewölkt.
Stone Walls.
Streams.
Summer Night, A.
Summer quickens grass, The.
Summons, The.
Sunday Morning.
Sunken Lane, The.
Sunshine.
Supporting Cast, Sotto Voce, The.
Suppose they met, the inevitable procedure.
Symmetries & Asymmetries.
T the Great.
Tale, A.
Talking to Dogs.
Talking to Mice.
Talking to Myself.
Taller To-day.
Taller to-day, we remember similar evenings.
Tarn, The.
Tea-time in November.
Temptation of St. Joseph, The.
Ten Songs.
Terce.
Thank You, Fog.
Thanksgiving, A.
Thanksgiving for a Habitat.
Their Lonely Betters.
There is so much that I can share with you.
There Will Be No Peace.
They.
This Loved One.
This Lunar Beauty.
Thomas Epilogizes.
Thomas Prologizes.
Though thy rafters are grown rotten.
Three Occasional Poems.
Three Posthumous Poems.
Through the Looking-Glass.
To a Child in Tears.
To a Field-mouse.
To a Small Buddha.
To a Toadstool.

To E.T.
To Goethe: a Complaint.
To-night at Seven-thirty.
To-night when a full storm surrounds the house.
To T. S. Eliot on His Sixtieth Birthday.
To throw away the key and walk away.
Toast, A ("As quid pro quo for your enchanting verses").
Toast, A ("What on earth does one say at a Gaudy").
Too Dear, Too Vague.
Traction Engine, The.
Trippers.
Truest Poetry Is the Most Feigning, The [or, Ars Poetica for Hard Times].
Truly our fathers had the gout.
Twelve Songs.
Twelve, The.
Two Climbs.
Two Songs.
Two Triolets.
Uncle Henry.
Under Sirius.
Under Which Lyre, a Reactionary Tract for the Times.
United Nations Hymn.
Unknown Citizen, The.
Unpredictable but Providential.
Up There.
Venus Will Now Say a Few Words.
Vespers.
Victor.
Vision.
Vision of the Shepherds, The.
Visit, A.
Voltaire at Ferney.
Voyage, A.
Walk After Dark, A.
Walk, The.
Walks.
Wanderer, The.
Waste.
Watchers, The.
Watertowers, The.
We, knowing the family history.
We Sat.
We Too Had Known Golden Hours.
Weeks of blizzard over, The.
Whenever I see for the first time.
Whither?
Whitsunday in Kirchstetten.
Who stands, the crux left of the watershed.
Who's Who.
Winds.
Winter Afternoon.
Witnesses, The.
Woods.
Woods in Rain.
Words.
Yes and No.
You.
Translations, Coauthored Poems, etc.:
Suicide.

B

"B. V." see Thomson, James
Basualto, Neftalí Ricardo Reyes see Neruda, Pablo
Beatles, The: John Lennon (1940–1980), George Harrison (b. 1943), Paul McCartney (b. 1942), *and* **Richard Starkey ("Ringo Starr") (b. 1940)**
Across the Universe.
All I've Got to Do.
All My Loving.
All Together Now.
All You Need Is Love.
And I Love Her.
And Your Bird Can Sing.
Another Girl.
Any Time at All.
Ask Me Why.
Baby You're a Rich Man.
Baby's in Black.

Back in the USSR.
Ballad of John and Yoko, The.
Because.
Being for the Benefit of Mr. Kite.
Birthday.
Blackbird.
Blue Jay Way.
Can't Buy Me Love.
Carry That Weight.
Come Together.
Continuing Story of Bungalow Bill, The.
Cry Baby Cry.
Day in the Life, A.
Day Tripper.
Dear Prudence.
Dig a Pony.
Dig It.
Do You Want to Know a Secret?
Doctor Robert.
Don't Bother Me.
Don't Let Me Down.
Don't Pass Me By.
Drive My Car.
Eight Days a Week.
Eleanor Rigby.
End, The.
Every Little Thing.
Everybody's Got Something to Hide Except Me and My Monkey.
Fixing a Hole.
Fool on the Hill, The.
For No One.
For You Blue.
From Me to You.
Get Back.
Getting Better.
Girl.
Glass Onion.
Golden Slumbers.
Good Day Sunshine.
Good Morning Good Morning.
Goodnight.
Got to Get You into My Life.
Happiness Is a Warm Gun.
Hard Day's Night, A.
Hello Goodbye.
Help!
Helter Skelter.
Her Majesty.
Here Comes the Sun.
Here, There and Everywhere.
Hey Bulldog.
Hey Jude.
Hold Me Tight.
Honey Pie.
I Am the Walrus.
I Call Your Name.
I Don't Want to Spoil the Party.
I Feel Fine.
I Me Mine.
I Need You.
I Saw Her Standing There.
I Should Have Known Better.
I Wanna Be Your Man.
I Want to Hold Your Hand.
I Want to Tell You.
I Want You.
I Will.
If I Fell.
If I Needed Someone.
I'll Be Back.
I'll Cry Instead.
I'll Follow the Sun.
I'll Get You.
I'm a Loser.
I'm Down.
I'm Happy Just to Dance with You.
I'm Looking Through You.
I'm Only Sleeping.
I'm So Tired.
In My Life.
Inner Light, The.
It Won't Be Long.
It's All Too Much.
It's Only Love.
I've Got a Feeling.
I've Just Seen a Face.

Julia.
Lady Madonna.
Let It Be.
Little Child.
Long and Winding Road, The.
Long Long Long.
Love Me Do.
Love You To.
Lovely Rita.
Lucy in the Sky with Diamonds.
Magical Mystery Tour.
Martha My Dear.
Maxwell's Silver Hammer.
Mean Mr. Mustard.
Michelle.
Misery.
Mother Nature's Son.
Night Before, The.
No Reply.
Norwegian Wood.
Not a Second Time.
Nowhere Man.
Ob-La-Di Ob-La-Da.
Octopus's Garden.
Oh! Darling.
Old Brown Shoe.
One after 909.
Only a Northern Song.
Paperback Writer.
Penny Lane.
Piggies.
Please Please Me.
Polythene Pam.
P.S. I Love You.
Rain.
Revolution.
Rocky Raccoon.
Run for Your Life.
Savoy Truffle.
Sgt. Pepper's Lonely Hearts Club Band.
Sgt. Pepper's Lonely Hearts Club Band (Reprise).
Sexy Sadie.
She Came in Through the Bathroom Window.
She Loves You.
She Said She Said.
She's a Woman.
She's Leaving Home.
Something.
Strawberry Fields Forever.
Sun King.
Taxman.
Tell Me What You See.
Tell Me Why.
Thank You Girl.
There's a Place.
Things We Said Today.
Think For Yourself.
This Boy.
Ticket to Ride.
Tomorrow Never Knows.
Two of Us.
Wait.
We Can Work It Out.
What Goes On?
What You're Doing.
When I Get Home.
When I'm Sixty Four.
While My Guitar Gently Weeps.
Why Don't We Do It in the Road.
Wild Honey Pie.
With a Little Help from My Friends.
Within You Without You.
Word, The.
Yellow Submarine.
Yer Blues.
Yes It Is.
Yesterday.
You Can't Do That.
You Know My Name (Look up the Number).
You Like Me Too Much.
You Never Give Me Your Money.
You Won't See Me.
Your Mother Should Know.
You're Going to Lose That Girl.
You've Got to Hide Your Love Away.

Translations, Coauthored Poems, etc.:
Maggie Mae.

Beckett, Samuel (1906–89)
À elle l'acte calme.
À l'instant de s'entendre dire.
À peine à bien mené.
Ainsi a-t-on beau.
Alba.
Arènes de Lutèce.
Ascension.
Asylum under my tread all this day.
Bois seul.
Bon bon il est un pays.
Cascando.
Ce qu'a de pis.
Ce qu'ont les yeux.
Chaque jour envie.
Da Tagte Es.
D'abord / à plat sur du dur.
De pied ferme.
Dieppe.
Dortmunder.
D'où / la voix qui dit.
Dread Nay.
Echo's Bones *sels.*
Écoute-les / s'ajouter.
Elles viennent.
En face.
Enueg II.
Enueg I.
Être là sans mâchoires sans dents.
Fin fond du néant.
Fleuves et océans.
Flux cause.
Fous qui disiez.
Gnome.
Home Olga.
Hors crâne seul dedans.
I would like my love to die.
Imagine si ceci.
Je suis ce cours de sable qui glisse.
Je voudrais que mon amour meure.
Jusque dans la caverne ciel et sol.
La Mouche.
La nuit venue où l'âme allait.
Lueurs lisières.
Malacoda.
Mort de A.D.
Morte parmi.
Mots survivants.
Musique de l'indifférence.
My way is in the sand flowing.
Ne manquez pas à Stuttgart.
Ne manquez pas à Tanger.
Noire soeur.
Nuit qui fais tant.
Ooftish.
Pas à pas.
Pas davantage.
Plus loin un autre commémore.
Que ferais-je sans ce monde sans visage sans
    questions.
Rentrer / À la nuit.
Rêve / sans fin.
Rien nul / n'aura été.
Roundelay: "On all that strand."
Rue de Vaugirard.
Saint-Lô.
Samedi répit.
Sanies I.
Sanies II.
Serena I.
Serena II.
Serena III.
Silence tel que ce qui fut.
Sitôt sorti de l'ermitage.
Something There.
Somme toute / tout compte fait.
Son ombre une nuit.
Song: "Age is when to a man."
Tailpiece.
They come.
Thither.
Vieil aller / vieux arrêts.
Vive morte ma seule saison.
Vulture, The.

What would I do without this world faceless
    incurious.
Whoroscope.
Words and Music *sels.*
Translations, Coauthored Poems, etc.:
Ask of all-healing, all consoling thought.
Better on your arse than on your feet.
Confections.
Hope is a knave befools us evermore.
How hollow heart and full.
Lady Love.
Live and clean forget from day to day.
Long after Chamfort.
Out of Sight in the Direction of My Body.
Scarcely Disfigured.
Scene.
Second Nature.
Sleep till death.
Trouble with tragedy is the fuss it makes,
    The.
Universe-Solitude.
Zone.

"Bell, Ellis" *see* Brontë, Emily Jane
Berg, Stephen (b. 1934)
And the Scream.
Answer, The.
At a Friend's Birthday Party in the Garden at
    Night.
At the Door.
Bandage.
Behind Us.
Between Us.
Both.
Bread.
Brothers.
Cherries.
Coat, The.
Crutches.
Daughters, The.
Day, A.
Desnos Reading the Palms of Men on Their
    Way to the Gas Chambers.
Don't Forget.
Dreaming with a Friend.
Driving Out Again at Night.
Dust.
Eating Outside.
Endings.
First Cold.
Following It.
For My Father *sels.*
For the Ghost of Li Po.
Fragment, 1959.
From the Bridge.
God, A.
Good.
Gooseberries.
Gratitude.
Heartache.
Holes, The.
Homage to the Afterlife.
In Blue Light.
In Death I Know Well Enough All Things
    End in Emptiness.
In It.
In the Evening.
In Washington Square.
Iowa.
It Is.
Kiss, The.
Lament: "My mother wants to be burned, she
    told me."
Last Elegy.
Last Meeting.
Leaves.
Lightbulb.
Lowell: Self-Portrait.
Memory.
Milk.
Mother Political.
Music.
New Year's.
1911.
1945.
1914.
1909.
1922.

No Word.
Not That.
Nothingness.
Oblivion.
Ollie, Answer Me.
On the Steps.
On This Side of the River.
One.
Page 256.
People Trying to Love.
Prayer: "Nobody understands so let the
    Rabbi."
Red Weed.
Remembering and Forgetting.
Rocks, The.
Roses.
Rubber Rats.
Sad Invective.
Self-Portrait at Six.
Shoeshine.
Sister Ann.
Sketch.
Soul, The.
Sticks.
Summer Twilight.
Sunday Afternoon.
Talking.
Tashkent Blossoms, 1944.
This Cold.
Thread.
Three Voices.
Through Glass.
Times.
To Charlie.
To My Friends.
To the Being We Are.
To the Same Place.
Two Fragments.
Two Little Songs.
Uncle Will, the Gardener.
Unfinished Double Sonnet.
Visit, The.
Visiting the Stone.
Voice, The.
Wanting to Be Heavier.
What I Wanted to Say.
Why Are We Here?
Wife Talks to Herself, A.
William Carlos Williams Reading His Poems.
With Akhmatova at the Black Gates.
Writing Class.
You.
Translations, Coauthored Poems, etc.:
Alone.

Berrigan, Ted (1934–83)
Academy of the future is opening its doors,
    The.
After Peire Vidal, & Myself.
American Express.
Ann Arbor Song.
Around the Fire.
Banging around in a cigarette she isn't "in
    love."
Banging around in a cigarette she isn't "in
    love" / She murmurs of signs to her
    fingers.
Bean Spasms.
Bulbs burn phosphorescent, white, The.
Certain Slant of Sunlight, A.
Chicago English Afternoon.
Chicago Morning.
Chinese Nightingale.
Clarity! clarity! a semblance of motion,
    omniscience. / There is no such thing as a
    breakdown.
Coda: Song.
Cranston Near the City Line.
Crystal.
DEAR CHRIS / It is 3:17 a.m. in New York
    city, yes, it is.
Dear Margie, hello. It is 5:15 a.m.
Dear Ron: hello. Your name is now a
    household name.
Dear Ron: Keats was a baiter of bears etc.
Dinner at George & Katie Schneeman's.
Each tree stands alone in stillness.

Epithalamion: "Pussy put her paw into the pail of paint."
February Air.
Final Sonnet, A.
For You.
44th Birthday Evening, at Harris's.
Frank O'Hara.
Grace to be born and live as variously as possible.
Harum-scarum haze on the Pollock streets / Where Snow White sleeps among the silent dwarfs.
Heloise.
His piercing pince-nez. Some dim frieze.
How strange to be gone in a minute / Bearden is dead Gallup is dead Margie is dead.
I Heard Brew Moore Say, One Day.
I like to beat people up.
In Anselm Hollo's Poems.
In Joe Brainard's collage its white arrow.
In my paintings for they are present.
In the 51st State.
Into the closed air of the slow.
It is a human universe: & I.
It is night. You are asleep. And beautiful tears.
It was summer. We were there. And THERE WAS NO.
It's Important.
Lady.
Last Poem.
Lines for Lauren Owen.
Lord, it is time. Summer was very great.
Many Happy Returns.
Mountains of twine and.
Musick strides through these poems.
My dream a drink with Lonnie Johnson we discuss the code.
New Personal Poem.
Old-Fashioned Air.
On the 15th day of November in the year of the motorcar.
On the green a white boy goes / We may read about all those radio waves.
Orange Clock, An.
Pandora's Box, An Ode.
Paul Blackburn.
Peace.
Penn Station.
People Who Died.
Personal Poem #9.
Poem in the Modern Manner.
Poem in the Traditional Manner.
Poem: "Of morning, Iowa City, blue."
Poem upon the page is as massive as, The.
Red Shift.
Sandy's Sunday Best.
Scorpio.
Seurat and Juan Gris combine this season.
She.
She (Not to be confused with she, a girl).
Sleep half sleep half silence and with reasons.
So Going Around Cities.
Something Amazing Just Happened.
Sonnets, The *sels*.
Soviet Souvenir.
Stronger than alcohol, more great than song.
Summer so histrionic, marvelous dirty days.
Sweeter than sour apples flesh to boys.
Tambourine Life.
Things To Do in Anne's Room.
Things To Do in New York (City).
Things to Do in Providence.
Whitman in Black.
Words for Love.
Wrong Train.

Berry, Wendell (b. 1934)
Adze, The.
Against the War in Vietnam.
Air and Fire.
Anger against Beasts.
Anniversary, An.
Another Descent.
April Woods: Morning.
Architecture, An.

Aristocracy, The.
Arrival, The.
At a Country Funeral.
Autumn Burning, An.
Awake at Night.
Before Dark.
Beginning, A.
Below.
Bird Killer, The.
Birth (Near Port William), The.
Boone.
Breaking.
Broken Ground, The.
Canticle.
Clear Days, The.
Clearing, The.
Cold Pane, The.
Cold, The.
Companions, The.
Contrariness of the Mad Farmer, The.
Conversation, The.
Country of Marriage, The.
Creation Myth.
Current, The.
Dance, A.
Dance, The.
Dark with power.
Design of a House, The.
Desolation.
Discipline, A.
Do Not Be Ashamed.
Dream, The.
Earth and Fire.
Elegy: "All day our eyes could find no resting place."
Elegy: "To be at home on its native ground."
Enriching the Earth.
Envoy: "Love, all day there has been at the edge of my mind."
Except.
Fall.
Falling Asleep.
Familiar, The.
Farmer among the Tombs, The.
Farmer and the Sea, The.
Farmer, Speaking of Monuments, The.
Fear of Darkness, The.
Fear of Love, The.
February 2, 1968.
Fern, The.
Finches, The.
First, The.
For the Future.
For the Hog Killing.
For the Rebuilding of a House.
Forty Years.
Freedom of Loving, The.
From the Crest.
From the Distance.
Gathering, The.
Gift of Gravity, The.
Goods.
Grace.
Grandmother, The.
Green and White.
Grief.
Guest, The.
Handing Down, The.
He Has Lived through Another Night.
He Is in the Habit of the World.
He Looks out the Window at the Town.
He Takes His Time.
Heaviness of His Wisdom, The.
Her First Calf.
Heron, The.
Hidden Singer, The.
History.
Homecoming, A.
Horses.
In Memory: Stuart Egnal.
In Rain.
In This World.
Independence Day.
July, 1773.
Kentucky River Junction.
Law That Marries All Things, The.
Letter.

Light, The.
Lilies, The.
Lineage, A.
Long Hunter, The.
Mad Farmer in the City, The.
Mad Farmer Manifesto: the First Amendment, The.
Mad Farmer Revolution, The.
Mad Farmer's Love Song, The.
Man Born to Farming, The.
Man Walking and Singing, A.
Manifesto: the Mad Farmer Liberation Front.
March Snow.
March 22, 1968.
Marriage.
Marriage, an Elegy, A.
May Song.
Meadow, The.
Meditation in the Spring Rain.
Meeting, A.
Morning's News, The.
Music, A.
My Great-Grandfather's Slaves.
Necessity of Faith, The.
New House, The.
New Roof, The.
Observance.
October 10.
Old Elm Tree by the River, The.
Old Man Is Older in History than in Time, The.
On the Hill Late at Night.
Our Children, Coming of Age.
Passing the Strait.
Peace of Wild Things, The.
Plan, The.
Planting Crocuses.
Planting Trees.
Poem for J.
Poem of Thanks, A.
Poem: "Willing to die, / you give up."
Porch over the River, The.
Praise.
Praise, A.
Prayer after Eating.
Prayers and Sayings of the Mad Farmer.
Purification, A.
Rain.
Recognition, The.
Requiem: "We will see no more."
Returning.
Ripening.
Rising.
River Bridged and Forgot, The.
Satisfactions of the Mad Farmer, The.
Seeds, The.
September 2, 1969.
Setting Out.
Seventeen Years.
Silence, The.
Sleep.
Slip, The.
Snake, The.
Song (1).
Song (2).
Song (3).
Song (4).
Song: "I tell my love in rhyme."
Song in a Year of Catastrophe.
Song Sparrow Singing in the Fall, A.
Sorrel Filly, The.
Sowing.
Sparrow.
Springs, The.
Standing Ground, A.
Star, The.
Stay Home.
Stones, The.
Strait, The.
Supplanting, The.
Sycamore, The.
Testament.
Thief, The.
Though He Can't Know Death, He Must Study Dying.
Thought of Something Else, The.
Three Elegiac Poems.

Throwing away the Mail.
To a Siberian Woodsman.
To Gary Snyder.
To Go By Singing.
To Know the Dark.
To My Children, Fearing for Them.
To Tanya at Christmas.
To the Holy Spirit.
To the Unseeable Animal.
To Think of the Life of a Man.
To What Listens.
Traveling at Home.
Vision, A.
Walking on the River Ice.
Want of Peace, The.
Warning to My Readers, A.
Way of Pain, The.
We Who Prayed and Wept.
Wet Time, A.
Wheel, The.
Where.
Wild Geese, The.
Wild, The.
Wilderness Starts towards Him, A.
Window Poems.
Winter Night Poem for Mary.
Winter Nightfall.
Winter Rain, The.
Wish to Be Generous, The.
Woods.
Work Song.
Young Man, Thinking of the Old, The.

Berryman, John (1914–72)
American Lights, Seen from Off Abroad.
Amos.
Ancestor.
Animal Trainer, The.
Antitheses.
Apparition, The.
At Chinese Checkers.
Away.
Back.
Ball Poem, The.
Beethoven Triumphant.
Black Book, The *sels.*
Boston Common.
Cadenza on Garnette.
Canto Amor.
Captain's Song, The.
Caravan.
Ceremony and Vision.
Certainty Before Lunch.
Cloud and Flame.
Communist.
Compline.
Conversation.
Crisis.
Curse, The.
Damn You, Jim D., You Woke Me Up.
Damned.
Dangerous Year, The.
Dante's Tomb.
Death Ballad.
Defensio in Extremis.
Desire Is a World by Night.
Desires of Men and Women.
Despair.
Disciple, The.
Dispossessed, The.
Down & Back.
Drugs Alcohol Little Sister.
Drunks.
Ecce Homo.
Eleven Addresses to the Lord.
Enemies of the Angels, The.
Epilogue: "He died in December. He must
   descend."
Facts & Issues, The.
Fare Well.
Farewell to Miles.
First Night at Sea.
Form, The.
Formal Elegy.
Freshman Blues.
Friendless.
Gislebertus' Eve.
Grandfather, sleepless in a room upstairs.

Handshake, the Entrance, The.
Have a Genuine American Horror-&-Mist on
   the Rocks.
He Resigns.
Heaven.
Hell Poem, The.
Hello.
Henry by Night.
Her & It.
Heroes, The.
Homage to Mistress Bradstreet.
Home Ballad, The.
How Do You Do, Dr Berryman, Sir?
Huddle of Need, A.
I Know.
Images of Elspeth.
In & Out.
In Memoriam (1914–1953).
Interstitial Office.
King David Dances.
Lauds.
Letter to His Brother.
Lightning, The.
Lines to Mr Frost.
London.
Long Home, The.
Lover & child, a little sing.
Luftmenschen dream, the men who live on
   air.
Matins.
Meditation.
Meeting.
Message.
Minnesota Thanksgiving.
Monkhood.
Moon and the Night and the Men, The.
My Special Fate.
Mysteries, The.
Narcissus Moving.
Navajo Setting the Record Straight.
New Year's Eve.
Night and the City.
Nineteen Thirty-Eight.
No.
Nones.
Not to Live.
Note to Wang Wei.
Nowhere.
Of Suicide.
Old Man Goes South Again Alone.
Olympus.
On the London Train.
1 September 1939.
Opus Dei.
Other Cambridge, The.
Overseas Prayer.
Pacifist's Song, The.
Parting as Descent.
Poem for Bhain, A.
Poet's Final Instructions, The.
Point of Age, A.
Possessed, The.
Prayer After All, A.
Prayer for the Self, A.
Prayer of the Middle-Aged Man, The.
Prime.
Professor's Song, A.
Purgatory.
Recovery.
Relations.
River Rouge, 1932.
Rock-Study with Wanderer.
Sanctuary.
Scholars at the Orchid Pavilion.
Scots Poem.
Search, The.
Sext.
Shirley & Auden.
Somber Prayer.
Song from "Cleopatra."
Song of the Bridegroom, The.
Song of the Demented Priest, The.
Song of the Man Forsaken and Obsessed.
Song of the Tortured Girl, The.
Song of the Young Hawaiian, The.
Sonnets to Chris.
Spinning Heart, The.

Statue, The.
Surviving Love.
Sympathy, a Welcome, A.
Tampa Stomp.
Tea.
Terce.
Thanksgiving: Detroit.
They Have.
To a Woman.
To Bhain Campbell.
Transit.
Traveller, The.
Travelling South.
Trial, The.
Two Organs.
Unknowable? Perhaps Not Altogether.
Usual Prayer, A.
Venice, 182.
Vespers.
Views of Myself.
Washington in Love.
Whether There Is Sorrow in the Demons.
White Feather.
Winter-Piece to a Friend Away, A.
World-Telegram.
World's Fair.
Young Woman's Song.
Your Birthday in Wisconsin You Are 140.

Betjeman, Sir John (1906–84)
Agricultural Caress.
Aldershot Crematorium.
Anglo-Catholic Congresses.
Archaeological Picnic, The.
Arrest of Oscar Wilde at the Cadogan Hotel,
   The.
Autumn 1964.
Back from Australia.
Ballad of the Investiture 1969, A.
Bay in Anglesey, A.
Beaumaris, December 21, 1963.
Before Invasion, 1940.
Before the Anæsthetic; or, A Real Fright.
Beside the Seaside.
Blackfriars.
Bristol.
Bristol and Clifton.
Business Girls.
By the Ninth Green, St. Enodoc.
Calvinistic Evensong.
Camberley.
Caprice.
Cheltenham.
Child Ill, A.
Christmas.
Church of England Thoughts Occasioned by
   Hearing the Bells of Magdalen Tower from
   the Botanic Garden, Oxford on St. Mary
   Magdalen's Day.
City.
City, The.
Clash went the Billiard Balls.
Cockney Amorist, The.
Commander, The.
Cornish Cliffs.
Costa Blanca, The.
Cottage Hospital, The.
County.
Cricket Master.
Croydon.
Dear Old Village, The.
Death in Leamington.
Death of King George V.
Delectable Duchy.
Devonshire Street W.1.
Diary of a Church Mouse.
Dilton Marsh Halt.
Distant View of a Provincial Town.
Dorset.
East Anglian Bathe.
Edwardian Sunday, Broomhill, Sheffield, An.
Eighteenth-Century Calvinistic Hymn, An.
Essex.
Eunice.
Exchange of Livings.
Executive.
Exeter.
False Security.

Felixstowe, or, The Last of Her Order.
Five O'Clock Shadow.
Flight from Bootle, The.
For Nineteenth-Century Burials.
For Patrick, Aetat: LXX.
14 November, 1973.
From the Great Western.
Fruit.
Good-bye.
Great Central Railway, Sheffield Victoria to
    Banbury.
Greek Orthodox.
Greenaway.
Group Life: Letchworth.
Harrow-on-the-Hill.
Harvest Hymn.
Heart of Thomas Hardy, The.
Hearts Together.
Henley-on-Thames.
Hertfordshire.
Hike on the Downs, A.
Holy Trinity, Sloane Street.
Hon. Sec., The.
House of Rest.
How to Get On in Society.
Hunter Trials.
Huxley Hall.
Hymn: "Church's Restoration, The."
I.M. Walter Ramsden, Ob. March 26, 1947,
    Pembroke College, Oxford.
Impoverished Irish Peer, An.
In a Bath Teashop.
In Memoriam: A. C., R. J. O., K. S.
In Memory of Basil, Marquess of Dufferin
    and Ava.
In Memory of George Whitby, Architect.
In the Public Gardens.
In Westminster Abbey.
In Willesden Churchyard.
Incident in the Early Life of Ebenezer Jones,
    Poet, 1828, An.
Indoor Games near Newbury.
Inevitable.
Inexpensive Progress.
Inland Waterway.
Invasion Exercise on the Poultry Farm.
Ireland with Emily.
Ireland's Own; or the Burial of Thomas
    Moore.
Irish Unionist's Farewell to Greta Hellstrom
    in 1922, The.
Lake District.
Lament for Moira McCavendish, A.
Last Laugh, The.
Late-flowering Lust.
Lenten Thoughts of a High Anglican.
Licorice Fields at Pontefract, The.
Lincolnshire Church, A.
Lincolnshire Tale, A.
Lines Written to Martyn Skinner Before His
    Departure from Oxfordshire in Search of
    Quiet—1961.
Literary Discovery, A.
Loneliness.
Longfellow's Visit to Venice.
Lord Cozens Hardy.
Love in a Valley.
Manor House, Hale, Near Liverpool, The.
Margate, 1940.
Matlock Bath.
May-Day Song for North Oxford.
Meditation on a Constable Picture.
Meditation on the A30.
Metropolitan Railway, The.
Middlesex.
Mind's Journey to Diss, A.
Monody on the Death of a Platonist Bank
    Clerk.
Monody on the Death of Aldersgate Street
    Station.
Mortality.
Myfanwy.
Myfanwy at Oxford.
Narcissus.
Newest Bath Guide, The.
Norfolk.
North Coast Recollections.

NW5 and N6.
Old Friends sels.
Old Friends.
Old Liberals, The.
Olney Hymns.
Olympic Girl, The.
On a Painting by Julius Olsson R.A.
On a Portrait of a Deaf Man.
On an Old-Fashioned Water-Colour of
    Oxford.
On Hearing the Full Peal of Ten Bells from
    Christ Church, Swindon, Wilts.
On Leaving Wantage 1972.
On Seeing an Old Poet in the Café Royal.
Original Sin on the Sussex Coast.
Our Padre.
Oxford: Sudden Illness at the Bus-stop.
Parliament Hill Fields.
Perp. Revival i' the North.
Pershore Station, or a Liverish Journey First
    Class.
Planster's Vision, The.
Potpourri from a Surrey Garden.
Preface to "High and Low."
Public House Drunk.
Reproof Deserved; or After the Lecture.
Russell Flint, A.
Saint Cadoc.
Sandemanian Meeting-House in Highbury
    Quadrant, The.
Seaside Golf.
Senex.
Shattered Image.
Shropshire Lad, A.
Sir John Piers.
Slough.
Small Towns of Ireland, The.
South London Sketch, 1844.
South London Sketch, 1944.
St. Barnabas, Oxford.
St. Saviour's, Aberdeen Park, Highbury,
    London, N.
Station Syren.
Subaltern's Love-Song, A.
Suicide on Junction Road Station after
    Abstention from Evening Communion in
    North London.
Sunday Afternoon Service in St. Enodoc
    Church, Cornwall.
Sunday Morning, King's Cambridge.
Thoughts on "The Diary of a Nobody."
Town Clerk's Views, The.
Trebetherick.
Tregardock.
Uffington.
Undenominational.
Upper Lambourne.
Variation on a Theme by Newbolt.
Variation on a Theme by T. W. Rolleston.
'Varsity Students' Rag, The.
Verses Turned in Aid of a Public
    Subscription (1952) Towards the
    Restoration of the Church of St. Katherine
    Chiselhampton, Oxon.
Village Inn, The.
Wantage Bells.
Wembley Lad, A.
Westgate-on-Sea.
Winter Seascape.
Winthrop Mackworth Redivivus.
Wykehamist, The.
Youth and Age on Beaulieu River, Hants.

Bishop, Elizabeth (1911–79)
Anaphora.
Argument.
Armadillo, The.
Arrival at Santos.
At the Fishhouses.
Behind Stowe.
Bight, The.
Brazil, January 1, 1502.
Britannia Rules the Waves.
Burglar of Babylon, The.
Cape Breton.
Casabianca.
Chemin de Fer.
Cirque d'Hiver.

Cold Spring, A.
Colder the Air, The.
Conversation.
Cootchie.
Crusoe in England.
Electrical Storm.
End of March, The.
Exchanging Hats.
Faustina, or Rock Roses.
Filling Station.
First Death in Nova Scotia.
Fish, The.
Five Flights Up.
Flood, The.
Florida.
For C.W.B.
Four Poems.
From the Country to the City.
From Trollope's Journal.
Gentleman of Shalott, The.
Giant Snail.
Giant Toad.
Going to the Bakery.
Hanging of the Mouse, The.
House Guest.
Hymn to the Virgin.
Imaginary Iceberg, The.
Imber Nocturnus.
In the Waiting Room.
Insomnia.
Invitation to Miss Marianne Moore.
Jerónimo's House.
Large Bad Picture.
Late Air.
Letter to N. Y.
Lines Written in the Fannie Farmer
    Cookbook.
Little Exercise.
Love Lies Sleeping.
Lullaby for the Cat.
Man-Moth, The.
Manners.
Manuelzinho.
Map, The.
Miracle for Breakfast, A.
Monument, The.
Moose, The.
Mountain, The.
Night City.
North Haven.
Norther—Key West, A.
O Breath.
One Art.
Over 2000 Illustrations and a Complete
    Concordance.
Paris, 7 A.M.
Pink Dog.
Pleasure Seas.
Poem: "About the size of an old-style dollar
    bill."
Prodigal, The.
Quai d'Orléans.
Questions of Travel.
Rain Towards Morning.
Rainy Season; Sub-Tropics.
Reprimand, The.
Riverman, The.
Roosters.
Sandpiper.
Santarém.
Seascape.
Sestina: "September rain falls on the house."
Shampoo, The.
Sleeping on the Ceiling.
Sleeping Standing Up.
Some Dreams They Forgot.
Song for the Rainy Season.
Song: "Summer is over upon the sea."
Songs for a Colored Singer.
Sonnet: "Caught—the bubble."
Sonnet: "I am in need of music that would
    flow."
Squatter's Children.
Strayed Crab.
Summer's Dream, A.
Sunday at Key West.
Sunday, 4 A.M.

Thank-You Note.
Three Sonnets for the Eyes.
Three Valentines.
Thunder.
Tidal Basin.
To a Tree.
To Be Written on the Mirror in Whitewash.
Trouvée.
Twelfth Morning; or What You Will.
12 O'Clock News.
Unbeliever, The.
Under the Window: Ouro Prêto.
Varick Street.
View of the Capitol from the Library of Congress.
Visits to St. Elizabeths.
Wading at Wellfleet.
Wave, The.
Weed, The.
While Someone Telephones.
Wit, The.
Word with You, A.
Translations, Coauthored Poems, etc.:
All the heaven and earth.
Along Galeana Street.
Banks.
Brazilian Tragedy.
Cemetery of Childhood.
Death and Life of a Severino, The *sels.*
Don't Kill Yourself.
Elegy for Maria Alves.
Family Portrait.
Four Sambas.
Grove, The.
Hell is Graduated.
In the Middle of the Road.
Infancy.
January First.
Key of Water, The.
My Last Poem.
My name is Severino.
Objects & Apparitions.
Patience of an Angel.
Rainbow.
Seven-Sided Poem.
Sonnet of Intimacy.
Table, The.
Travelling in the Family.
Whom are you carrying.

Blake, William (1757–1827)
Advice of the Popes Who Succeeded the Age of Rafael.
Ah said Sipsop, I only wish Jack [*Hunter*] Tearguts had.
Ah, Sun-Flower [*or* Ah! Sun-Flower].
All Pictures thats Panted with sense & with Thought.
All Religions Are One.
America; a Prophecy.
Ancient Proverb, An.
And Did Those Feet in Ancient Time.
And his legs carried it like a long fork.
And in Melodious Accents I.
Angel That Presided o'er My Birth, The.
Angel, The.
Anger & Wrath my bosom rends.
Another [Epitaph]: "Here lies John Trot, the Friend of all mankind."
Another [Epitaph]: "I was buried near this Dike."
Answer to the Parson, An.
Are not the joys of morning sweeter.
Argument, The.
Around the Springs of Gray my wild root weaves.
Auguries of Innocence.
Beneath the white thorn lovely May.
Birds, The.
Blakes apology for His Catalogue.
Blind-Man's Buff.
Blossom, The.
Book of Ahania, The.
Book of Los, The.
Book of Thel, The.
Book of Urizen [*or* First Book of Urizen], The.

Call that the Public Voice which is their Error.
Can there be anything more mean.
Caverns of the Grave Ive seen, The.
Chimney Sweeper, The ("A little black thing among the snow").
Chimney Sweeper, The ("When my mother died I was very young").
Chorus: "Let the Priests of the Raven of dawn, no longer in deadly black."
Christian Forbearance.
Clod and [*or* &] the Pebble, The.
Cosway Frazer & Baldwin of Egypts Lake.
Cradle Song, A: "Sleep, sleep, beauty bright."
Cradle Song, A: "Sweet dreams, form a shade."
Cripple every step Drudges & labours, The.
Cr[omek] loves artists as he loves his Meat.
Cromek Speaks.
Crowned king, A.
Crystal Cabinet, The.
Cunning sures & the Aim at yours, The.
Day.
Desire and Jealousy.
Divine Image, The ("To Mercy, Pity, Peace, and Love").
Door of Death is made of Gold, The.
Door of Death, The.
Dream, A.
Each Man is in His Spectres power.
Earth's Answer.
Echoing [*or* Ecchoing] Green, The.
Empire Is No More.
English Encouragement of Art Cromeks Opinions Put Into Rhyme.
Enion Replies from the Caverns of the Grave.
Enitharmon Revives with Los.
Epilogue: "Truly my Satan thou art but a dunce."
Epitaph, An: "Come knock your heads against this stone."
Errors of a Wise Man make your Rule, The.
Eternity ("He who binds [*or* bends] to himself a joy").
Ethinthus, Queen of Waters.
Europe; A Prophecy.
Everlasting Gospel, The.
Fair Elenor.
Fairy skipd [*or* leapt] upon my knee, A.
Fairy, The.
Fayette beside King Lewis stood.
Fields from Islington to Marybone, The.
Florentine Ingratitude.
Fly, The.
Fox, the owl, the spider, and the mole, The.
French Revolution, The.
From Cratetos.
Garden of Love, The.
Ghost of Abel, The.
Give pensions to the Learned Pig.
Gnomic Verses.
Golden Net, The.
Great Men & Fools do often me Inspire.
Great Things [Are Done].
Grey Monk, The.
Grown old in Love from Seven till Seven times Seven.
Gwin, King of Norway.
He is a Cock would.
Hear then the pride & knowledge of a Sailor.
Hebrew Nation did not write it, The.
Her whole life is an Epigram smack smooth & neatly pend.
Hes a Blockhead who wants a proof of what he Cant Percieve.
Holy Thursday ("Is this a holy thing to see").
Holy Thursday (" 'Twas on a Holy Thursday, their innocent faces clean").
How came pride in Man.
How to Know Love from Deceit.
Human Abstract, The.
Human Image, The.
I am no Homers Hero You all know.
I asked a thief to steal me a peach.
I asked [*or* askd] my Dear Friend, Orator Prigg.

I feard the fury [*or* roughness] of my wind.
I found them blind, I taught them how to see.
I give you the end of a golden string.
I heard an Angel singing.
I laid me down upon a bank.
I rose up at the dawn of day.
I Rubens am a Statesman & a Saint.
I saw a chapel all of gold.
I say this evening [*we'd*] we'll all get drunk.
I told my love I told my love.
I wander tho each dirty street.
I will tell you what Joseph of Arimathea.
If I eer Grow to a Mans Estate.
If it is True What the Prophets write.
If Men will act like a maid smiling over a Churn.
If you play a Game of Chance know before you begin.
If you trap the moment before its ripe.
Imitation of Pope   A Compliment to the Ladies.
Imitation of Spen[s]er, An.
Immortal, The.
In a Myrtle [*or* Mirtle] Shade.
In a wife I would desire.
In Deadly Fear.
In Seed Time Learn.
In the moon as Phebus stood over his oriental Gardening.
Infant Joy.
Infant Sorrow.
Introduction: "Hear the voice of the Bard!"
Island in the Moon, An *sels.*
It Is Not So with Me.
Jerusalem; The Emanation of the Giant Albion *sels.*
Jerusalem; The Emanation of the Giant Albion.
Kid, The.
King Edward the Third.
Lacedemonian Instruction.
Lamb, The.
Lamentation of Enion, The.
Land of Dreams, The.
Let the Brothels of Paris be opened.
Lily, The.
Little Black Boy, The.
Little Boy Found, The.
Little Boy Lost, A ("Nought loves another as itself").
Little Boy Lost, The ("Father, father, where are you going?").
Little Fly.
Little Girl Found, The.
Little Girl Lost, A.
Little Girl Lost, The.
Little Vagabond, The.
London ("I wander through each chartered street").
Long John Brown & Little Mary Bell.
[*Look Flaxman & Stothard do*] old acquaintance well.
Louis XVI.
Mad Song.
Madman I have been calld Fool they call thee.
Male & Female Loves in Beulah.
Marriage of Heaven and Hell, The.
Mary.
Memorable Fancy, A ("Angel came to me and said").
Memorable Fancy, A ("As I was walking among the fires of hell").
Memorable Fancy, A ("I was in a printing house in Hell & I saw the method in").
Memorable Fancy, A ("Once I saw a Devil in a flame of fire").
Memorable Fancy, A ("Prophets Isaiah and Ezekiel dined with me, and, The").
Mental Traveller, The.
Merlins Prophecy.
Milton.
Mr Cromek to Mr Stothard.
Mr Stothard to Mr Cromek.
Mock On, Mock On, Voltaire, Rousseau.
Monk, The.

Morning.
Motto to the Songs of Innocence & of Experience.
Mutual forgiveness of each vice.
My Pretty Rose Tree.
My Spectre around Me Night and Day.
My title as an Genius thus is provd.
Nail his neck to the cross nail it with a nail.
Never seek [or pain] to tell thy love.
Night.
Night VIII (The Eternal Man).
No real Style of Colouring ever appears.
NOTL.
Now Art has lost its mental Charms.
Nurse's Song ("When the voices of children are heard on the green / And laughing is heard on the hill").
Nurse's Song ("When the voices of children are heard on the green / And whisperings [ot whisprings] are in the dale").
O dear Mother outline of knowledge most sage.
O I say you Joe.
O lapwing, thou fliest around the heath.
O Reader behold the Philosophers Grave.
Of H[ayley]s birth this was the happy lot.
Old maid early eer I knew, An.
On Another's Sorrow.
On Flaxman and Stothard.
On H[ayley] the Pick Thank.
On H[ayle]ys Friendship.
On Stothard.
On the Great Encouragement Given By English Nobility & Gentry to Correggio Rubens Rembrandt Reynolds Gainsborough Catalani Ducrowe & Dilbury Doodle.
On the Venetian Painter.
On the Virginity of the Virgin Mary & Johanna Southcott.
Opposition Is True Friendship.
Pair of Stays to mend the Shape, A.
Petty sneaking Knave I knew, A.
Phebe drest like beauties Queen.
P[hillips] loved me, not as he loved his Friends.
Piping Down the Valleys Wild.
Pitiful Case, A.
Poison Tree, A.
Pretty Epigram for [Those] the Entertainment of Those Who [Pay] Have Paid Great Sums in the Venetian & Flemish Ooze, A.
Price of Experience, The.
Pride of the Peacock, The.
Prologue, Intended for a Dramatic Piece of King Edward the Fourth.
Prologue to King John.
Prophecy, A.
Proverbs of Hell.
Rafael Sublime Majestic Graceful Wise.
Reason and Imagination.
Reveal the dragon thro' the human; coursing swift as fire.
Riches.
School Boy, The.
Secrets of the Earth, The.
Several Questions Answered.
Shepherd, The.
Sick Rose, The.
Silent Silent Night.
Since all the Riches of this World
Sir Jo[s]hua praised Rubens with a Smile.
Sir Joshua Praises Michael Angelo.
Smile, The.
Soft Snow.
Some look. to see the sweet Outlines.
Some Men created for destruction come.
Some people admire the work of a Fool.
Song 1st By a Shepherd.
Song: "Fresh from the dewy hill, the merry year."
Song: "How sweet I roamed [or roam'd] from field to field."
Song: "I love the jocund dance."
Song: "Love and harmony combine."
Song: "Memory, hither come."
Song: "My silks and fine array."
Song of Enitharmon.

Song of Liberty, A.
Song of Los, The.
Song 2nd By a Young Shepherd.
Song 3rd By an Old Shepherd.
Song: "When early morn walks forth in sober grey."
Songs of Experience
Songs of Innocence.
Spring.
S[tothard] in Childhood on the Nursery floor.
Sussex Men are Noted Fools, The.
Swelld limbs with no outline that you can descry.
Take Thy Bliss, O Man.
Terror in the house does roar.
Thames.
Thel.
Thel's Motto.
Then the Cynic sung.
There Is No Natural Religion.
These are the Idiots chiefest arts.
Thou hast a lap full of seed.
Tiger [or Tyger][!], The.
Tiriel.
To Autumn.
To Chloes breast young Cupid slily stole.
To English Connoisseurs.
To F[laxman].
To Flaxman.
To forgive Enemies H[ayley] does pretend.
To God.
To Hayley [or To H[ayley]].
To Hunt.
To John Flaxman, 12 September 1800.
To Mrs Ann Flaxman.
To Mrs Butts.
To Mrs Flaxman, 14 September 1800.
To Morning.
To My Mirtle.
To Nancy F[laxman].
To Nobodaddy.
To Spring.
To S[tothar]d.
To Summer.
To the Evening Star.
To the Muses.
To the Royal Academy.
To Thomas Butts, 16 August 1803.
To Thomas Butts, 2 October 1800.
To Thomas Butts, 22 November 1802.
To Tirzah.
To Venetian Artists.
To Winter.
Upon a holy thursday their innocent faces clean.
Urizen's Curse upon His Children.
Vala, Night the Ninth Being the Last Judgment.
Vala; or The Four Zoas.
Venetian; all thy Colouring is no more.
Verse from the Advertisement to Blake's Exhibition of Paintings, 1809.
Vision of Beulah, The ("There is a place where contrarieties are equally true").
Visions of the Daughters of Albion.
Voice of the Ancient Bard, The.
Voice of the Devil, The.
War Song [to Englishmen], A.
Was I angry with Hayley who used me so ill.
Washer Womans Song, The.
When a Man has Married a Wife.
When France got free Europe 'twixt Fools & Knaves.
When I see a Rubens Rembrandt [or] Correggio.
When Klopstock England defied.
When Nations grow Old. The Arts grow Cold.
When Sir [or Sr] Joshua Reynolds died.
When the Green Woods Laugh.
When you look at a picture you always can see.
Why was Cupid a Boy.
Wild Flower's Song, The.
Wild Thyme, The.
William Bond.

William Cowper Esqre.
Woman scaly & a Man all Hairy, A.
You dont believe I wont attempt to make ye.
You say their Pictures well Painted be.

Bly, Robert (b. 1926)
Aban Kavost and Ivar Oakeson.
After Drinking All Night with a Friend, We Go Out in a Boat at Dawn to See Who Can Write the Best Poem.
After Long Busyness.
After Working.
Ant Mansion, The.
Ants.
As the Asian War Begins.
Asian Peace Offers Rejected without Publication.
At a March against the Vietnam War.
At Midocean.
At the Time of Peony Blossoming.
August Rain.
Awakening.
Bouquet of Ten Roses, A.
Calm Day at Drake's Bay.
Caterpillar, A.
Chinese Tomb Guardians.
Christmas Eve Service at Midnight at St. Michael's.
Conversation, A.
Conversation with a Holy Woman Not Seen for Many Years.
Cornpicker Poem.
Counting Small-boned Bodies.
Crazy Carlson's Meadow.
Cry Going Out over Pastures, The.
Danger of Loss, The.
Dawn in Threshing Time.
Dead Seal [near McClure's Beach], The.
December 23, 1926.
Defeated.
Digging Worms.
Dream of a Brother, A.
Dream of Retarded Children, A.
Dream of What Is Missing, A.
Dream on the Night of First Snow, A.
Dried Sturgeon, The.
Driving through Minnesota during the Hanoi Bombings.
Driving toward the Lac Qui Parle River.
Early Spring Between Madison and Bellingham.
Empty Place, An.
Evening When the Full Moon Rose as the Sun Set, An.
Executive's Death, The.
Falling Asleep.
Ferns.
Fifty Males Sitting Together.
Finding the Father.
Fire of Despair Has Been Our Savior, The.
For My Son Noah, Ten Years Old.
Four Seasons in American Woods sels.
Four Ways of Knowledge.
Getting Up Late.
Glimpse of the Waterer.
Good Silence, The.
Grass from Two Years.
Hatred of Men with Black Hair.
Hawk, The.
Hockey Poem, The.
Hollow Tree, A.
Home in Dark Grass, A.
Horse of Desire, The.
Hunting Pheasants in a Cornfield.
In Mourning for Betrayal.
In Rainy September.
In the Month of May.
Indigo Bunting, The.
Johnson's Cabinet Watched by Ants.
July Morning.
Kennedy's Inauguration.
Kneeling Down to Look [or Peer] into a Culvert.
Late Moon.
Letter to Her.
Listening to Bach.
Listening to the Köln Concert.
Loon's Cry, The.

Love Poem in Twos and Threes.
Man and a Woman Sit Near Each Other.
Man Locked Inside the Oak, The.
Man Writes to a Part of Himself, A.
Meditation on Philosophy, A.
My Father's Wedding.
Near the Giant's House.
Night.
Night Frogs.
Night of First Snow.
November Day at McClure's Beach.
Old Boards.
On a Ferry across Chesapeake Bay.
On Meditation.
Opening the Door of a Barn I Thought Was
    Empty on New Year's Eve.
Orchard Keeper, The.
Origin of the Praise of God, The.
"Out of the Rolling Ocean, the Crowd . . ."
Out Picking up Corn.
Pilgrim Fish Heads.
Poem in Three Parts.
Praise for All Dancers.
Prodigal Son, The.
Reading in Fall Rain.
Romans Angry about the Inner World.
Schoolcraft's Diary Written on the Missouri:
    1830.
Sitting on Some Rocks in Shaw Cove.
Six Winter Privacy Poems.
Snow Geese.
Snowbanks North of the House.
Snowfall in the Afternoon.
Solitude Late at Night in the Woods.
Spring has come; I look up and see.
Starfish, The.
Surprised by Evening.
Teeth Mother Naked at Last, The.
Three Kinds of Pleasures.
Two Sounds When We Sit by the Ocean.
Uneasiness in Fall.
Upward Moon and the Downward Moon,
    The.
Visiting the Farallones.
Waking from Sleep.
Walking Swiftly.
War and Silence.
Watcher, The.
Watering the Horse.
We Love This Body.
When the Dumb Speak.
Winter Poem.
Woman Bewildered, The.
Words Rising.

Bogan, Louise (1897–1970)
Ad Castitatem.
Alchemist, The.
Animal, Vegetable and Mineral.
At a Party.
Baroque Comment.
Betrothed.
Cartography.
Cassandra.
Changed Woman, The.
Chanson un Peu Naïve.
Come, Break with Time.
Come, Sleep.
Crossed Apple, The.
Crows, The.
Cupola, The.
Daemon, The.
Dark Summer.
Didactic Piece.
Division.
Dragonfly, The.
Dream, The.
Drum, The.
Evening in the Sanitarium.
Evening-Star.
Exhortation.
Feuer-Nacht.
Fiend's Weather.
Fifteenth Farewell.
For a Marriage.
Frightened Man, The.
From Heine.
Girl's Song.

Heard by a Girl.
Henceforth, from the Mind.
Homunculus.
Hypocrite Swift.
I Saw Eternity.
If We Take All Gold.
Italian Morning.
Juan's Song.
July Dawn.
Kept.
Knowledge.
Last Hill in a Vista.
Late.
M., Singing.
Man Alone.
March Twilight.
Mark, The.
Medusa.
Meeting, The.
Memory.
Men Loved Wholly beyond Wisdom.
Morning.
Musician.
My Voice Not Being Proud.
Night.
Old Countryside.
Packet of Letters.
Poem in Prose.
Portrait.
Putting to Sea.
Question in a Field.
Rhyme.
Roman Fountain.
Romantic, The.
St. Christopher.
Second Song.
Several Voices Out of a Cloud.
Short Summary.
Simple Autumnal.
Single Sonnet.
Sleeping Fury, The.
Solitary Observation Brought Back from a
    Sojourn in Hell.
Song for a Lyre.
Song for a Slight Voice.
Song for the Last Act.
Song: "It is not now I learn."
Sonnet: "Dark, underground, is furnished with
    the bone."
Sonnet: "Since you would claim the sources
    of my thought."
Sorcerer's Daughter, The.
Spirit's Song.
Stanza: "No longer burn the hands that
    seized."
Statue and Birds.
Sub Contra.
Summer Wish.
Tale, A.
Tears in Sleep.
Three Songs.
To an Artist, to Take Heart.
To Be Sung on the Water.
To My Brother: Killed: Hammont Wood:
    October, 1918.
To Wine.
Train Tune.
Variation on a Sentence.
Winter Swan.
Women.
Young Mage, The.
Zone.
Translations, Coauthored Poems, etc.:
Kapuzinerberg (Salzburg).

"Boyd, Nancy" see Millay, Edna St. Vincent
Boyle, Kay (1903–93)
Advice to the Old.
After New York—May Seventeenth.
After the Earth Quaked.
American Citizen.
And Winter.
Angels for Djuna Barnes.
April Thirtieth 1960.
Artist Speaks..the Woman Answers, The.
Battlefield, The.
Branded for Slaughter.
Career.

Carnival 1927.
Christmas Carol for Emanuel Carnevali, A.
Cloak for a Man Who Has No Heed for
    Winter, A.
Comeallye for Robert Carlton Brown, A.
Communication to Nancy Cunard, A.
Complaint for Mary and Marcel, A.
Confession to Eugene Jolas, A.
Crow, The.
December 1989.
Dedicated to Robert McAlmon.
Dedicated to *Terre des Hommes.*
Dialogue of Birds for Howard Nemerov, A.
Dreams Dreamed.
Evening Grass, The.
For an American.
For James Baldwin.
For James Schevill.
For Marianne Moore's Birthday.
Funeral in Hungary.
Glad Day for Laurence Vail, A.
Hunt.
In Defense of Homosexuality.
Jews among the Nations, The.
Landscape for Wyn Henderson, A.
Lesson in Anatomy, A.
Letter to Archibald Craig, A.
Letter to Francis Picabia, A.
Lost Dogs of Phnom Penh, The.
Mothers.
New Emigration, The.
Night Letter, A.
O This Is Not Spring.
October 1954.
Ode to a Maintenance Man and His Family.
On Taking up Residence in Virginia.
On the Death of My Student, the Poet
    Serafin.
Only Bird That Sang, The.
Painter Speaks—the Woman Answers, The.
People's Cry, The.
Poem about Black Power, A.
Poem about the Jews, A.
Poem for a Painter Bent on Suicide.
Poem for a Painter Who Drinks Wine.
Poem for Arthur, A.
Poem for February First 1975, A.
Poem for Samuel Beckett, A.
Poem for the Students of Greece, A.
Poem for the Teesto Diné of Arizona, A.
Poem for Vida Hadjebi Tabrizi, A.
Poem in One Sentence, A.
Poem of Gratitude, A.
Poem of Love, A.
Poem on Getting up Early in the Morning (or
    Even Late in the Morning), When One is
    Old.
Poets.
Print from a Lucite Block.
Rendezvous.
Seascape for an Engraver.
Short Poem in Color, A.
Spring.
Square Dance for a Square, A.
Statement for El Greco and William Carlos
    Williams, A.
Stones of a Seventeenth Century Village,
    The.
Testament for My Students, 1968–1969.
This Is Not a Letter.
Thunderstorm in South Dakota.
To a Proud Old Woman Watching the
    Tearing Down of the Hurricane Shed.
To America.
Two Poems for a Poet.
Two Twilights for William Carlos Williams.
United States, The.
Valentine for Harry Crosby, A.
Waterfront for Allan Ross MacDougall, A.
Weather.
What Parents Do Not Yet Know.
Winter Fable, A.
World Tour.

Bradstreet, Anne (c.1612–1672)
see Letter to Her Husband, Absent upon
    Public[k] Employment, A.

see Letter to Her Husband, Absent upon
  Public[k] Employment, A.
As spring the winter doth succeed.
As weary pilgrim, now at rest.
Author to Her Book, The.
Before the Birth of One of Her Children.
Contemplations.
David's Lamentation for Saul and Jonathan.
Deliverance from a Fit of Fainting.
Dialogue between Old England and New, A.
Elegy Upon that Honorable and Reknowned
  Knight Sir Philip Sydney, An.
Element Fire Boasts of the Constellations,
  The.
Epitaph on my Dear and Ever Honored
  Mother Mrs. Dorothy Dudley.
Flesh and the Spirit, The.
For Deliverance from a Fever.
For the Restoration of My Dear Husband
  from a Burning Ague.
Four Elements, The.
Four[e] Monarchies, The.
Four Seasons of the Year, The.
From Another Sore Fit.
Here Follow[es] Some Verses upon the
  Burning of Our House [July 10th, 1966.
  Copied Out of a Loose Paper].
In Honor of Du Bartas, 1641.
In Honour of That High and Mighty Princess
  Queen Elizabeth of Happy Memory.
In Memory of My Dear Grandchild Anne
  Bradstreet.
In Memory of My Dear Grandchild Elizabeth
  Bradstreet Who Deceased August, 1665,
  Being a Year and a Half Old.
In My Solitary Hours in My Dear Husband
  His Absence.
In Reference to Her Children, 23 June, 1659
  [*or* 1656].
In Thankful Acknowledgement for the Letters
  I Received from My Husband Out Of
  England.
In Thankful[l] Remembrance for My Dear
  Husband[']s Safe Arrival[l].
Letter to Her Husband, Absent upon
  Public[k] Employment, A.
My soul, rejoice thou in thy God.
My thankful heart with glorying tongue.
New England.
Occasional Meditations: "By night, when
  others soundly slept."
Of the Four Ages of Man.
Of the Four Humors in Man's Constitution.
Old England.
On My Dear Grandchild Simon Bradstreet,
  [Who Died on 16TH November, 1669,
  Being But A Month And One Day Old].
On My Son's Return Out of England.
Prologue: "To sing of wars, of captain[e]s,
  and of kings."
Semiramis.
To Her Father, with Some Verses.
To Her Most Honored Father Thomas
  Dudley, Esquire, These Humbly Presented.
To My Dear and Loving Husband.
To the Memory of My Dear and Ever
  Honored Father Thomas Dudley Esq. Who
  Deceased July 31, 1653, and of His Age
  77.
To the Memory of My Dear Daughter in
  Law, Mrs. Mercy Bradstreet.
Upon a Fit of Sickness, Anno 1632.
Upon My Daughter Hannah Wiggin her
  Recovery from a Dangerous Fever.
Upon My Dear and Loving Husband His
  Going into England.
Upon My Son Samuel His Going For
  England.
Upon Some Distemper of Body.
Vanity of All Worldly Things, The.
What God is like to him I serve?
Translations, Coauthored Poems, etc.:
Anagram, An.
Another ("*Artes bred neat An*").
Another to Mrs. Anne Bradstreet, Author of
  this Poem.

Funeral Elegy Upon that Pattern and Patron
  of Virtue, A.
I cannot wonder at Apollo now.
In Praise of the Author, Mistress Anne
  Bradstreet, Virtue's True and Lively
  Pattern.
Mercury showed Apollo Bartas' book.
To My Dear Sister, the Author of these
  Poems.
Upon Mrs. Anne Bradstreet, Her Poems, Etc.
Upon the Author.
Upon the Author. By a Known Friend.

Brontë, Emily Jane ("Ellis Bell") (1818–48)
A.A.A.
A.E.
A.E. And R.C.
A.G.A. to A.E.
A.G.A. to A.S.
Alcona, in its changing mood.
All day I've toiled, but not with pain.
All hushed and still within the house.
Alone I sat; the summer day.
And first an hour of mournful musing.
And like myself lone, wholly lone.
And now the house-dog stretched once more.
Anticipation.
A.S. to G.S.
At such a time, in such a spot.
Awaking morning laughs from heaven.
Away, away, resign me now.
Aye, there it is! It wakes to-night.
Battle had passed from the height, The.
Blue bell is the sweetest flower, The.
But the hearts that once adored me.
Castle Wood.
Cold, clear, and blue, the morning heaven.
Coldly, bleakly, drearily.
Come hither, child—who gifted thee.
Come, walk with me.
Companions, all day long we've stood.
Darkness was overtraced on every face.
Day Dream, A.
Death.
Death Of A.G.A., The.
Deep, deep down in the silent grave.
D.G.C. to J.A.
Douglas's Ride.
E.G. to M.R.
Enough of Thought, Philosopher.
Evening sun was sinking down, The.
E.W. to A.G.A.
F. de Samara to A. G. A.
Fair sinks the summer evening now.
Fall, leaves, fall; die, flowers, away.
Far, far away is mirth withdrawn.
Farewell To Alexandria, A.
From a D— W— in the N. C.
From a Dungeon Wall in the Southern
  College.
From our evening fireside now.
Geraldine.
Gleneden's Dream.
H.A. and A.S.
Had there been falsehood in my breast.
Harp of wild and dream-like strain.
Heaven's glory shone where he was laid.
Here, with my knee upon thy stone.
High waving heather, 'neath stormy blasts
  bending.
His land may burst the galling chain.
Hope.
How Clear She Shines!
How golden bright from earth and heaven.
How long will you remain? The midnight
  hour.
How loud the storm sounds round the Hall!
How still, how happy! These [*or* Those] are
  words.
I am the only being whose doom.
I gazed upon the cloudless moon.
I gazed within thine earnest eyes.
I know not how it falls on me.
I paused on the threshold, I turned to the
  sky.
I saw thee, child, one summer's day.
I see around me tombstones grey.
I would have touched the heavenly key.

Iernë's eyes were glazed and dim.
If grief for grief can touch thee.
I'll come when thou art saddest.
I'm happiest when most away.
I'm standing in the forest now.
I.M. to I.G.
In dungeons dark I cannot sing.
Inspiring music's thrilling sound, The.
It is not pride, it is not shame.
It is too late to call thee now.
It was night, and on the mountains.
It will not shine again.
It's over now; I've known it all.
I've been wandering in the greenwoods.
Julian M. and A.G. Rochelle.
Lady, in your Palace Hall.
Lady to Her Guitar, The.
Last Words.
Lines by Claudia.
Lines: "Far away is the land of rest."
Lines: "I die; but when the grave shall
  press."
Lines: "Soft unclouded blue of air, The."
Little while, a little while, A.
Lonely at her window sitting.
Long Neglect Has Worn Away.
Loud without the wind roaring.
Love and Friendship.
M. Douglas to E.R. Gleneden.
M.A. Written on the Dungeon Wall.
May flowers are opening.
Methinks this heart should rest awhile.
M.G. For The U.S.
Mild the mist upon the hill.
Month after month, year after year.
My Comforter.
Night is darkening round me, The.
Night of storms has passed, The.
Night was dark, yet winter breathed, The.
Night Wind, The.
No coward soul is mine.
None but one beheld him dying.
None of my kindred now can tell.
Not a vapour had stained the breezeless blue.
Not many years but long enough to see.
Now trust a heart that trusts in you.
O come again; what chains withhold.
O come with me, thus ran the song.
O Dream, where art thou now?
O evening, why is thy light so sad?
O God of heaven! the dream of horror.
O hinder me by no delay.
O mother, I am not regretting.
O wander not so far away!
Old church tower and garden wall, The.
Old Hall of Elbë, ruined, lonely now.
Old Stoic, The.
On the Fall of Zalona.
Only some spires of bright green grass.
Organ swells, the trumpets sound, The.
Plead for Me.
Prisoner, The.
R. Alcona to J. Brenzaida.
R.C.
Redbreast, Early in the morning.
Remembrance.
Rodric Lesley. 1830.
Rosina.
Self-Interrogation.
Shall Earth no more inspire thee.
She dried her tears, and they did smile.
Shed no tears o'er that tomb.
Sleep brings no joy to me.
Song by Julius Angora.
Song By Julius Brenzaida To G.S.
Song: "King Julius left the south country."
Song: "Linnet in the rocky dells, The."
Song: "O between distress and pleasure."
Song to A.A.
Stanzas: "I'll not weep that thou art going to
  leave me."
Stanzas: "Often rebuked, yet always back
  returning."
Stanzas to———.
Starry night shall tidings bring, The.
Stars.
Start not! upon the minister wall.

Still as she looked the iron clouds.
Still beside that dreary water.
Strong I stand, though I have borne.
Sudden chasm of ghastly light, A.
Sun Has Set, The.
Sympathy.
Tell me, tell me, smiling child.
That dreary lake, that midnight sky.
That wind, I used to hear it swelling.
There are two trees in a lonely field.
There let thy bleeding branch atone.
There shines the moon, at noon of night.
There swept adown that dreary glen.
There was a time when my cheek burned.
Thousand sounds of happiness, A.
Through the hours of yesternight.
'Tis evening now, the sun descends.
'Tis moonlight, summer moonlight.
To a Wreath of Snow.
To A.G.A.
To A.S., 1830.
To Imagination.
To the Bluebell.
'Twas one of those dark, cloudy days.
Two Children, The.
Upon her soothing breast.
Visionary, The.
Warning and Reply.
Was it with the fields of green.
Weaned from life and torn away.
What is that smoke that ever still.
What use is it to slumber here.
What winter floods, what showers of spring.
When days of Beauty deck the earth.
Where were ye all? and where wert thou?
Why ask to know the date—the clime?
Why ask to know what date, what clime?
Why do I hate that lone green dell?
Wide cathedral aisles are lone, The.
Will the day be bright or cloudy?
Wind, I hear it sighing, The.
Wind, sink to rest in the heather.
Wind was rough which tore, The.
Woe for the day; Regina's pride.
Woods, you need not frown on me.
Written in Aspin Castle.
Written in the Gaaldine Prison Caves to
   A.G.A.
Written on Returning to the P. of I. on the
   10th of January, 1827.
Yes, holy be thy resting place.

Brooks, Gwendolyn (b. 1917)
And shall I prime my children, pray, to pray?
Anniad, The.
Appendix to the Anniad.
Ballad of Chocolate Mabbie, The.
Ballad of Rudolph Reed, The.
Ballad of the Late Annie, The.
Ballad of the Light-Eyed Little Girl, The.
Bean Eaters, The.
Beverly Hills, Chicago.
Big Bessie Throws Her Son into the Street.
Bronzeville Man with a Belt in the Back.
Bronzeville Mother Loiters in Mississippi.
   Meanwhile, a Mississippi Mother Burns
   Bacon, A.
Bronzeville Woman in a Red Hat.
Catch of Shy Fish, A.
Chicago Defender Sends a Man to Little
   Rock, The.
Children of the Poor, The.
Crazy Woman, The.
Do Not Be Afraid of No.
Empty Woman, The.
First fight. Then fiddle. Ply the slipping
   string.
Firstly Inclined to Take What It Is Told.
Garbageman: the Man with the Orderly
   Mind.
Gay Chaps at the Bar.
God Works in a Mysterious Way.
Hunchback Girl: She Thinks of Heaven.
I Love Those Little Booths at Benvenuti's.
In Emanuel's Nightmare: Another Coming of
   Christ.
In Honor of David Anderson Brooks, My
   Father.

Independent Man, The.
Jessie Mitchell's Mother.
Kitchenette Building.
Langston Hughes.
Last Quatrain of the Ballad of Emmett Till,
   The.
Life for My Child is Simple, and Is Good.
Light and diplomatic bird, A.
Looking.
Love Note I: Surely.
Love Note II: Flags.
Lovely Love, A.
Lovers of the Poor, The.
Man of the Middle Class, A.
Men of careful turns, haters of forks in the
   road.
Mentors.
Mother, The.
Mrs. Small.
My Dreams, My Works, Must Wait Till after
   Hell.
My Little 'Bout-Town Gal Has Gone.
Negro Hero.
Notes from the Childhood and the Girlhood.
Of De Witt Williams on His Way to Lincoln
   Cemetery.
Of Robert Frost.
Old Mary.
Old People Working (Garden, Car).
Old Relative.
Old Tennis Player.
One wants a Teller in a time like this.
Parents: People Like Our Marriage Maxie
   and Andrew, The.
Penitent Considers Another Coming of Mary,
   A.
People protest in sprawling lightless ways.
People who have no children can be hard.
Piano after War.
Preacher: Ruminates Behind the Sermon, The.
Progress, The.
Pygmies Are Pygmies Still, Though Percht
   on Alps.
Riders to the Blood-Red Wrath.
Rites for Cousin Vit, The.
Sadie and Maud.
Sick Man Looks at Flowers.
Song in the Front Yard, A.
Southeast Corner.
Spaulding and Francois.
Still Do I Keep My Look, My Identity. . . .
Street in Bronzeville, A.
Strong Men, Riding Horses.
Sunday Chicken.
Sundays of Satin-Legs Smith, The.
Sunset of the City, A.
Surrealist and Omega, A.
Throwing Out the Flowers.
To Be in Love.
Truth.
Vacant Lot, The.
We Real Cool.
Weaponed Woman.
What shall I give my children? who are poor.
When my dears die, the festival-colored
   brightness.
White Troops Had Their Orders but the
   Negroes Looked Like Men.
Womanhood, The *sels.*

Brother Antoninus *see* Everson, William

Browning, Elizabeth Barrett (1806–61)
Adequacy.
Amy's Cruelty.
Apprehension, An.
August Voice, An.
Aurora Leigh.
Bereavement.
Bertha in the Lane.
Best Thing in the World, The.
Bianca among the Nightingales.
Calls on the Heart.
Casa Guidi Windows.
Catarina to Camoens.
Change Upon Change.
Cheerfulness Taught by Reason.
Child Asleep, A.
Child's Grave at Florence, A.

Child's Thought of God, A.
Christmas Gifts.
Claim, The.
Comfort.
Confessions.
Consolation.
Convinced by Sorrow.
Court Lady, A.
Cowper's Grave.
Crowned and Buried.
Crowned and Wedded.
Cry of the Children, The.
Cry of the Human, The.
Dance, The.
De Profundis.
Dead Pan, The.
Dead Rose, A.
Denial, A.
Deserted Garden, The.
Died.
Discontent.
Drama of Exile, A.
Earth and Her Praisers.
Exaggeration.
Exile's Return, The.
False Step, A.
Felicia Hemans.
Finite and Infinite.
First News from Villafranca.
Flower in a Letter, A.
Flush or Faunus.
Forced Recruit, The.
Fourfold Aspect, The.
Futurity.
Garibaldi.
Grief.
Heaven and Earth.
Hector in the Garden.
Hiram Powers' "Greek Slave."
House of Clouds, The.
Hugh Stuart Boyd [His Blindness].
Hugh Stuart Boyd [His Death, 1848].
Hugh Stuart Boyd [Legacies].
Human Life's Mystery.
Insufficiency.
Irreparableness.
Island, An.
Isobel's Child.
Italy and the World.
King Victor Emanuel Entering Florence,
   April, 1860.
King's Gift, The.
L. E. L.'s Last Question.
Lady Geraldine's Courtship.
Lady's "Yes," The.
Last Translation, The.
Lay of the Brown Rosary, The.
Lay of the Early Rose, A.
Lessons from the Gorse.
Life.
Life and Love.
Little Friend, The.
Little Mattie.
Look, The.
Lord Walter's Wife.
Lost Bower, The.
Love.
Loved Once.
Man and Nature.
Man's Requirements, A.
Marriage of Psyche and Cupid.
Mask, The.
May's Love.
Meaning of the Look, The.
Measure, The.
Mediator, The.
Memory and Hope.
Mercury Carries Psyche to Olympus.
Mother and Poet.
Mountaineer and Poet.
Mourning Mother, The.
Musical Instrument, A.
My Doves.
My Heart and I.
My Kate.
Napoleon III in Italy.
Nature's Remorses.

Night and the Merry Man.
North and the South, The.
Ode to the Swallow.
Olives and Mountains.
On a Portrait of Wordsworth by B. R. Haydon.
Only a Curl.
Pain in Pleasure.
Parting Lovers.
Past and Future.
Patience Taught by Nature.
Perplexed Music.
Pet-Name, The.
Poet and the Bird, The.
Poet, The.
Poet's Vow, The.
Portrait, A.
Prisoner, The.
Proof and Disproof.
Prospect, The.
Psyche and Cerberus.
Psyche and Pan.
Psyche and Proserpine.
Psyche and Venus.
Psyche Gazing on Cupid.
Psyche Propitiating Ceres.
Psyche Wafted by Zephyrus.
Pyche and the Eagle.
Question and Answer.
Reading.
Reed, A.
Rhapsody of Life's Progress, A.
Rhyme of the Duchess May.
Romance of the Ganges, A.
Romance of the Swan's Nest, The.
Romaunt of Margret, The.
Romaunt of the Page, The.
Runaway Slave at Pilgrim's Point, The.
Sabbath Morning at Sea, A.
Sea-Mew, The.
Sea-side walk, A.
Seraph and Poet, The.
Seraphim, The.
Since Without Thee We Do No Good.
Sleep, The.
Sleeping and Watching.
Song against Singing, A.
Song for the Ragged Schools of London, A.
Sonnet: "Accuse me not, beseech thee, that I wear."
Sonnet: "And therefore if to love can be desert."
Sonnet: "And wilt thou have me fashion into speech."
Sonnet: "And yet, because thou overcomest so."
Sonnet: "Because thou hast the power and own'st the grace."
Sonnet: "Beloved, my beloved, when I think."
Sonnet: "Beloved, thou hast brought me many flowers."
Sonnet: "But only three in all God's universe."
Sonnet: "Can it be right to give what I can give."
Sonnet: "Face of all the world is changed, I think, The."
Sonnet: "First time he kissed me, he but only kissed."
Sonnet "First time that the sun rose on thine oath, The."
Sonnet: "Go from me. Yet I feel that I shall stand."
Sonnet: "Heavy heart, Beloved, have I borne, A."
Sonnet: "How do I love thee? Let me count the ways."
Sonnet: "I lift my heavy heart up solemnly."
Sonnet: "I lived with visions for my company."
Sonnet: "I never gave a lock hair away."
Sonnet: "I see thine image through my tears tonight."
Sonnet: "I thank all who have loved me in their hearts."

Sonnet: "I think of thee! My thoughts do twine and bud."
Sonnet: "I thought once how Theocritus had sung."
Sonnet: "If I leave all for thee, wilt thou exchange."
Sonnet: "If thou must love me, let it be for nought."
Sonnet: "Indeed this very love which is my boast."
Sonnet: "Is it indeed so? If I lay here dead."
Sonnet: "Let the world's sharpness, like a clasping knife."
Sonnet: "My future will not copy fair my past."
Sonnet: "My letters! All dead paper, mute and white."
Sonnet: "My own Beloved, who hast lifted me."
Sonnet: "My poet, thou canst touch on all the notes."
Sonnet: "Oh, yes! they love through all this world of ours."
Sonnet: "Pardon, oh, pardon, that my soul should make."
Sonnet: "Say over again, and yet once over again."
Sonnet: "Soul's Rialto hath its merchandise, The."
Sonnet: "Thou comest! all is said without a word."
Sonnet: "Thou hast thy calling to some palace floor."
Sonnet: "Unlike are we, unlike, O princely heart!"
Sonnet: "What can I give thee back, O liberal."
Sonnet: "When our two souls stand up erect and strong."
Sonnet: "When we first met and loved, I did not build."
Sonnet: "With the same heart, I said, I'l answer thee."
Sonnet: "Yes, call me by my pet-name! let me hear."
Sonnet: "Yet, love, mere love, is beautiful indeed."
Sonnets from the Portuguese.
Soul's Expression, The.
Soul's Travelling, The.
Sounds.
Stanzas: "I may sing; but minstrel's singing."
Student, The.
Substitution.
Summing Up in Italy.
Supplication for Love, A.
Sweetness of England, The.
Sword of Castruccio Castracani, The.
Tale of Villafranca, A.
Tears.
That Day.
Thought for a Lonely Death-Bed, A.
To Bettine.
To Flush, My Dog.
To George Sand: A Desire.
To George Sand: A Recognition.
To Mary Russell Mitford.
Tuscan Life.
Two Sayings, The.
Two Sketches.
Valediction, A: "God be with thee, my beloved,—God be with thee!"
Vanities.
Victoria's Tears.
View Across the Roman Campagna.
Virgin Mary to the Child Jesus, The.
Vision of Poets, A.
Void in Law.
Weakest Thing, The.
Weeping Saviour, The.
Where's Agnes?
Wine of Cyprus.
Wisdom Unapplied.
Woman's Shortcomings, A.
Work.
Work and Contemplation.
Year's Spinning, A.

Young Queen, The.
Translations, Coauthored Poems, etc.:
Aurora and Tithonus.
Bacchus and Ariadne.
Complaint of Annelida to False Arcite, The.
Cyclops, The.
Daughters of Pandarus, The.
Dionysiaca *sels.*
Hector and Andromache.
How Bacchus Comforts Ariadne.
Iliad, The *sels.*
Lament for Adonis.
Odyssey *sels.*
Prometheus Bound.
Queen Annelida and False Arcite.
So the storms bore the daughters of Pandarus out into thrall.
Song of the Rose.
Theogony *sels.*
Troades *sels.*
Wail of Prometheus Bound, The.

Browning, Robert (1812–89)
Abt Vogler.
Adam, Lilith, and Eve.
Aeschylus' Soliloquy.
After.
Among the Rocks.
Amphibian.
Andrea del Sarto.
Another Way of Love.
Any Wife to Any Husband.
Apollo and the Fates.
Apparent Failure.
Appearances.
Arcades Ambo.
Aristophanes' Apology.
Artemis Prologizes.
At the "Mermaid."
Awakening of Man, The.
Bad Dreams I.
Bad Dreams II.
Bad Dreams III.
Bad Dreams IV.
Balaustion's Adventure.
Bean-Feast, The.
Bean-Stripe: also, Apple-Eating, A.
Beatrice Signorini.
Before.
Belief and Unbelief.
Ben Karshook's Wisdom.
Bifurcation.
Bishop Blougram's Apology.
Bishop Orders His Tomb at Saint Praxed's Church, The.
Blind man to the maiden said, The.
Boot and Saddle.
Boy and the Angel, The.
Burlesque for Palgrave on the Pronunciation of "Metamorphosis."
By the Fire-Side.
Caliban upon Setebos; or, Natural Theology in the Island.
Camel-Driver, A.
Cardinal and the Dog, The.
Cavalier Tunes.
Cenciaja.
Cherries.
Childe Roland to the Dark Tower Came.
Christmas-Eve.
Classicality Applied to Tea-Dealing: A Fancy Inspired by Westbourne Grove.
Cleon.
Clive.
Conclusion of a Compliment to the Captain.
Conclusion of a Sonnet on "Keely's Discovery."
Confessional, The.
Confessions.
Count Gismond.
Cristina.
Cristina and Monaldeschi.
Dance of Death, The.
De Gustibus.
Deaf and Dumb.
Death in the Desert, A.
Delivery to the Secular Arm, The: A Scene

During the Existence of the Spanish Inquisition at Antwerp, 1570.
Development.
Dialogue between Father and Daughter.
Dîs Aliter Visum; or, Le Byron de Nos Jours.
Doctor———.
Dogma Triumphant, The.
Donald.
Dubiety.
Eagle, The.
Earth Breaks Up.
Earth's Immortalities.
Easter-Day.
Echetlos.
Englishman in Italy, The.
Epigram on School Days.
Epilogue: "At the midnight in the silence of the sleep-time."
Epilogue: "Oh, Love—no, Love! All the noise below, Love."
Epilogue: "On the first of the Feast of Feasts."
Epilogue: "Poets pour us wine, The."
Epistle Containing the Strange Medical Experience of Karshish, the Arab Physician, An.
Epps.
Eurydice to Orpheus.
Evelyn Hope.
Face, A.
Fame.
Family, The.
Fears and Scruples.
Fever.
Fifine at the Fair.
Filippo Baldinucci on the Privilege of Burial.
First-Born of Egypt, The.
Flight of the Duchess, The.
Flower's Name, The.
Flute-Music, with an Accompaniment.
Folkestone Limerick.
Forest Thought, A.
Forgiveness, A.
Founder of the Feast, The.
Fra Lippo Lippi.
Fust and His Friends.
Garden Fancies.
Gerousios Oinos.
Glove, The.
Gold Hair.
Goldoni.
Good, to forgive.
Grammarian's Funeral, A.
Greece.
Guardian-Angel, The.
Halbert and Hob.
Helen's Tower.
Herakles.
Heretic's Tragedy, The.
Hervé Riel.
Holy-Cross Day.
Home-Thoughts, from Abroad.
Home-Thoughts, from the Sea.
House.
Householder, The.
How It Strikes a Contemporary.
How They Brought the Good News from Ghent to Aix.
Humility.
Imperante Augusto Natus Est.
Impromptu Lines to Greet Marie Bancroft.
Impromptu on Hearing a Sermon by the Rev. T. R—Pronounced "Heavy."
Impromptu on Richard Wagner.
In a Balcony.
In a Gondola.
In a Year.
In the Doorway.
In Three Days.
Inapprehensiveness.
Incident of the French Camp.
Inn Album, The.
Inscription for a Sketch.
Instans Tyrannus.
Isle's Enchantress, The.
Italian in England, The.

Ivàn Ivànovitch.
Ixion.
James Lee's Wife.
Jochanan Hakkadosh.
Johannes Agricola in Meditation.
La Saisiaz.
Laboratory, The [Ancien Régime].
Lady and the Painter, The.
Last Poem.
Last Ride Together, The.
Life in a Love.
Light Woman, A.
Likeness, A.
Lines for a Gift.
Lines for a Painting by Leighton.
Lines for the Jubilee Window.
Lines for the Tomb of Levi Lincoln Thaxter.
Lines on Swinburne.
Lines to the Memory of James Dow.
Lost Leader, The.
Lost Mistress, The.
Love.
Love among the Ruins.
Love in a Life.
Lovers' Quarrel, A.
Madness.
Magical Nature.
Martin Relph.
Mary Wollstonecraft and Fuseli.
Master Hugues of Saxe-Gotha.
May and Death.
Meeting at Night.
Melon-Seller, The.
Memorabilia.
Mesmerism.
Mettle and Metal.
Mihrab Shah.
Misconceptions.
Mr Sludge, "The Medium."
"Moses" of Michael Angelo, The.
Muckle-Mouth Meg.
Muléykeh.
My Last Duchess [Ferrara].
My Star.
Names, The.
Nationality in Drinks.
Natural Magic.
Ned Bratts.
Never the Time and the Place.
Numpholeptos.
Of Pacchiarotto, and How He Worked in Distemper.
Oh Love, Love, thou that from the eyes diffusest.
Old Pictures in Florence.
On Benjamin Disraeli.
On Correggio.
On Ignaz Moscheles.
On Singers.
One Way of Love.
One Word More.
Pambo.
Pan and Luna.
Paracelsus.
Parting at Morning.
Patriot, The [An Old Story].
Pauline [or Pauline; A Fragment of a Confession].
Pearl, a Girl, A.
Phases of the Moon.
Pheidippides.
Piano di Sorrento.
Pictor Ignotus.
Pied Piper of Hamelin, The.
Pietro of Abano.
Pillar at Sebzevar, A.
Pippa Passes.
Pisgah-Sights. I.
Pisgah-Sights. II.
Plot-Culture.
Poetics.
Ponte dell' Angelo, Venice.
Pope and the Net, The.
Popularity.
Porphyria's Lover.
Pretty Woman, A.

Prince Hohenstiel-Schwangau, Saviour of Society.
Prologue: "O the old wall here! How I could pass."
Prologue: "Poet's age is sad: for why?, The."
Prologue: "Pray, Reader, have you eaten ortolans."
Prospice.
Protus.
Rabbi Ben Ezra.
Rawdon Brown.
Red Cotton Night-Cap Country.
Reflections on Reading a Life of Dickens.
Rephan.
Replies to Challenges to Rhyme.
Respectability.
Response to a Translation by Longfellow.
Reverie.
Rhyme for a Child Viewing a Naked Venus in a Painting of "The Judgement of Paris."
Rhyme on Edward Burne-Jones.
Rhyming Exercises.
Rosny.
Round Robin, A.
Rudel to the Lady of Tripoli.
Saint Martin's Summer.
Saul.
Serenade at the Villa, A.
Service.
Shah Abbas.
She was fifteen—had great eyes.
Shop.
Sibrandus Schafnaburgensis.
Sipping grog one day at sea.
Soliloquy of the Spanish Cloister.
Solomon and Balkis.
Song: "Give her but a least excuse to love me!"
Song: "Nay but you, who do not love her."
Sonnet: "Eyes, calm beside thee, (Lady couldst thou know!)."
Sordello.
Speculative.
Spoils of Youth, The.
Statue and the Bust, The.
Such a starved bank of moss.
Suggestion for a Telegraphic Birthday Greeting.
Summum Bonum.
Sun, The.
Terse Verse.
Through the Metidja to Abd-el-Kadr.
Thus I wrote in London, musing on my betters.
Thus the Mayne Glideth.
Time's Revenges.
To Edward FitzGerald.
To Miss Unger.
Toccata of Galuppi's, A.
Too Late.
Transcendentalism: A Poem in Twelve Books.
Transcriptions from the "Anacreontea."
Translation from Pindar's Seventh Olympian, Epode III.
Tray.
Twins, The.
Two Camels.
Two in the Campagna.
Two Poets of Croisic, The.
Up at a Villa—Down in the City.
Variation on Lines of Landor, A.
Very Original Poem, Written with Even a Greater Endeavour than Ordinary after Intelligibility, and Hitherto Only Published on the First Leaf of the Author's Son's Account-Book.
Wanderers, The.
Wanting is—what?
Waring.
What a pretty tale you told me.
Which?
White Witchcraft.
Why I Am a Liberal.
Why Time Spins Fast.
With Bernard de Mandeville.
With Charles Avison.

With Christopher Smart.
With Daniel Bartoli.
With Francis Furini.
With George Bubb Dodington.
With Gerard de Lairesse.
Woman's Last Word, A.
Women and Roses.
Worst of It, The.
You are sick, that's sure—they say.
Youth and Art.

Bukowski, Charles (1920–94)
$$$$$$.
About Cranes.
About My Very Tortured Friend, Peter.
About Pain.
After the Reading.
Ah.
All I Know.
All the Casualties.
Almost Made Up Poem, An.
Alone with Everybody.
American Express, Athens, Greece.
Another Bed.
Anthony.
Ants, The.
Art, An.
Artist.
Artists.
As Crazy As I Ever Was.
As I Lay Dying.
Ashes.
Ass But No Class.
Bad Action.
Beach Trip.
Beast, The.
Beauti-ful.
Beautiful Young Girl Walking Past the
    Graveyard—, The.
Bedpans.
Beds, Toilets, You and Me—.
Bee, The.
Beer.
Bee's 5th.
Beginning, A.
Best Way to Get Famous Is to Run Away,
    The.
Big Bastard with a Sword.
Big John of Echo Park.
Big Max.
Blackbirds Are Rough Today, The.
Blue Cheese and Chili Peppers.
Brave Bull.
Bravo.
Breakout.
Bring Down the Beams.
Buffalo Bill.
Change of Habit, A.
Chicago.
Chopin Bukowski.
Christmas Eve, Alone.
Clean Old Man.
Cockroach.
Cold Plums.
Communion.
Condition, The.
Conversation in a Cheap Room.
Conversation on Morality, Eternity and
    Copulation, A.
Counsel.
Countryside.
Coupons.
Cows in Art Class.
Crunch, The.
Dagwood and Blondie.
Dark Shades.
Darlings.
Day I Kicked Away a Bankroll, The.
Day the Epileptic Spoke, The.
Dead Now.
Dear Friend.
Dear Pa and Ma.
Death Wants More Death.
Defeat.
Destroying Beauty.
Dog.
Dogs.
Dogs, The.

Dogs of Egypt, The.
Don't Touch the Girls.
Doom and Siesta Time.
Dow Jones: Down.
Drill, The.
Eat.
Eat Your Heart Out.
Eaten by Butterflies.
Eating My Senior Citizen's Dinner at the
    Sizzler.
86'd.
Empire of Coins, An.
End of a Short Affair, The.
End, The.
Escape, The.
Eulogy to a Hell of a Dame—.
Everything.
Experience.
Face While Shaving.
Fall Out.
Famous Writer, The.
Farewell, Foolish Objects.
Farewell Thing While Breathing, A.
Fear.
56 Year Old Poem, A.
Fleg.
For Al—.
462-0614.
4:30 A.M.
Fragile!
Freedom: The Unmolested Eagle of Myself.
Friendly Advice to a Lot of Young Men.
Frozen Food Section.
Fuck.
Funny.
Genius of the Crowd, The.
Gentleman and the Bastard, The.
Gift, The.
Ginsberg?
Girl on the Bus Stop Bench, The.
Girls.
Girls at the Green Hotel, The.
Girls Coming Home.
Girls From Nowhere.
Girls in Pantyhose.
Gloomy Lady.
Gold Pocket Watch, A.
Goldfish.
Good Life, The.
Good Loser, The.
Good One, A.
Good Time Girl.
Goodbye.
Greek, The.
Green.
Guru.
Gypsies Near Del Mar, The.
Hangover and Sick Leave.
Hawley's Leaving Town.
Hello, Willie Shoemaker.
Here I Am.
Hey, Ezra, Listen to This.
High-Rise of the New World, The.
History of a Tough Motherfucker, The.
Hog.
Horse on Fire.
Horse With Greenblue Eyes, A.
Horsemeat.
How Come You're Not Unlisted?
How Do They Get Your Number?
How I Got Started.
How to Be a Great Writer.
Huge Ear Rings.
Hustle, The.
I Am Visited by an Editor and a Poet.
I Am with the Roots of Flowers.
I Cannot Stand Tears.
I Don't Need a Bedsheet with Slits for Eyes
    to Kill You In.
I Fall into It Without Trying.
I Have Lived in England.
I Have Shit Stains in My Underwear Too.
I Kneel.
I Made a Mistake.
I Wait in the White Rain.
I Was Born to Hustle Roses Down the
    Avenues of the Dead.

I Write This Upon the Last Drink's Hammer.
I'm Getting Back to Where I Was.
Imagination and Reality.
Imbecile Night.
In a Neighborhood of Murder.
Insane Always Loved Me, The.
Insomnia.
Interviewed by a Guggenheim Recipient.
Iron Mike.
Itch, Come and Gone.
It's Not Who Lived Here.
It's Nothing to Laugh About.
It's the Way You Play the Game.
I've Seen Too Many Glazed-Eyed Bums
    Sitting under a Bridge Drinking Cheap
    Wine.
Jack-Knife.
Japanese Wife, The.
John Dillinger Marches On.
Junkies.
Killer, A.
Kind of Lecture on a Dull Day When There
    Isn't Even a Fly Around to Kill, A.
Kings Are Gone, The.
Krutz.
Lady Poet, The.
Last Generation, The.
Layover.
Letter from the North.
Liberty.
Light Brown.
Like a Flower in the Rain.
Literary Life, The.
Little Girls, The.
Little Tigers Everywhere.
Longshot.
Look:, The.
Loser, The.
Love.
Love Is a Dog from Hell.
Love Is a Piece of Paper Torn to Bits.
Love Poem, A.
Lovely Couple, A.
Luck.
Macho Man.
Madness.
Making It.
Man with the Hot Nose, The.
Me.
Meek Have Inherited, The.
Melancholia.
Mercy, Wherever You Are, Come Running in
    to Me and Grab Me in Your Good Arms—.
Mexican Girls, The.
Millionaire, The.
Minor Impulse to Complain, A.
Miracle is the Shortest Time, The.
Moaning and Groaning.
Monday Beach, Cold Day.
Most, The.
Mother and Son.
My Comrades.
My Friend.
My Groupie.
My Old Man.
Naked at 92 Degrees.
New Place, The.
Nice Place, A.
Nice Try.
Night I Fucked My Alarm Clock, The.
Night on a Visa Card.
Night They Took Whitey, The.
9 Rings.
99 to One.
Not All That Bad.
Not Quite So Soon.
Not To Worry.
Notations from a Muddled Indolence.
Note to the Boys in the Back Room, A.
Note Upon the Love Letters of Beethoven.
Nothing Subtle.
Now.
Now, If You Were Teaching Creative
    Writing, He Asked, What Would You Tell
    Them?
Numb Your Ass and Your Brain and Your
    Heart—.

O, We Are the Outcasts.
Object Lesson.
Oh, Yes.
Old Buddy, An.
Old Gang, The.
Old Man, Dead in a Room.
On a Night You Don't Sleep.
On and Off the Road.
On Being Recognized.
On Being 20.
On Going Back to the Street after Viewing an Art Show.
On Seeing an Old Civil War Painting with My Love.
On the Continent.
On the Failure of a Poet.
One for Old Snaggle-Tooth.
One for the Old Boy.
One for the Shoeshine Man.
One Hundred and Ninety-Nine Pounds of Clay Leaning Forward.
103 Degrees.
One Night Stand.
One of the Hottest.
One to the Breastplate.
Our Curious Position.
Out of the Blue.
Overhead Mirrors.
Pace is the Essence.
Pacific Telephone.
Pansies.
Parts of an Opera, Parts of a Guitar, Part of Nowhere.
Patriot of Life, A.
Photographs.
Place Didn't Look Bad, The.
Plate Glass Window, A.
Playing It Out.
Poem for Liz.
Poem for My 43rd Birthday.
Poem to a Most Affectionate Lady.
Practice.
Prayer in Bad Weather.
Price, The.
Private First Class.
Problems About the Other Woman.
Professors, The.
Promenade.
Promise, The.
Puzzle, The.
Quiet Clean Girls in Gingham Dresses..
Rain or Shine.
Rat Rises, A.
Red Up and Down.
Regard Me.
Report Upon the Consumption of Myself, A.
Reprieve and Admixture.
Result.
Retreat, The.
Reunion.
Rose, Rose.
Sad-Eyed Mules of Men.
Sad Poem, A.
Sandra.
Sardines in Striped Dresses.
Saying Goodbye to Love.
Scarlet.
Seahorse.
2nd Novel, The.
Sex.
Sex and/or Love.
Sexpot.
She Came Out of the Bathroom With Her Flaming Red Hair and Said—.
She Said.
Shit Time.
Sickness, The.
Simplicity of Everything in Viet Nam, The.
Singing Is Fire.
Sitting in a Sandwich Joint.
6 A.M.
6 Foot Goddess, The.
60 Yard Pass.
Skaters, The.
Sky Sign.
Sleep.
Social.

Soirée.
Some of My Readers.
Some Picnic.
Somebody Always Breaking My Dainty Solitude..
Something.
Soul.
Space Creatures.
Spain Sits Like a Hidden Flower in My Coffeepot.
Sparks.
Spider, The.
Star, The.
Stethoscope Case, A.
Stolen.
Strange Moment, A.
Strangest Sight You Ever Did See—, The.
Suggestion for an Arrangement.
Suicide.
Sun Wields Mercy, The.
Sundays Kill More Men Than Bombs.
Swans Walk My Brain in April It Rains, The.
Sweater.
Sweaty Day in August, A.
Sweet Music.
Sword, The.
Take It.
Talking to My Mailbox..
10 Lions and the End of the World.
Terminology.
Texan.
Thank God for Alleys.
There Once Was a Woman Who Put Her Head into an Oven.
Thermometer.
35 Seconds.
This.
This Poet.
This Then—.
3:30 A.M. Conversation.
T.M.
Tonight.
Too Late.
Traffic Signals.
Training for Kid Aztec.
Transformation and Disfiguration.
Trapped.
Trench Warfare.
Trick to Dull Our Bleeding, A.
Troops, The.
Truce.
Trying to Get Even.
Turnabout.
12:18 A.M.
22,000 Dollars in 3 Months.
Twins.
225 Pounds.
2 Outside, As Bones Break in My Kitchen.
Unkind Poem, An.
Up Your Yellow River.
Upon First Reading the Immortal Literature of the World—.
Valentine Gift, A.
Very.
Walls, The.
Waving and Waving Goodbye.
We Will Taste the Islands and the Sea.
Weather Report.
What They Want.
What to Do with Contributor's Copies?
When I Think of Myself Dead.
When the Berry Bush Dies I'll Swim Down the Green River with My Hair on Fire.
Who in the Hell is Tom Jones?
Windy Night.
Winter.
Winter Comes to a Lot of Places in August.
With Vengeance Like a Tiger Crawls.
Word on the Quick and Modern Poem-Makers, A.
Worst and the Best, The.
Writing Is a State of Trance.
Wrong Number.
Yellow Cab.
You.
You Smoke a Cigarette.

Bunting, Basil (1900–1985)
After the grimaces of capitulation.
Against the Tricks of Time.
All the cants they peddle.
All the teeth ever I had are worn down and fallen out.
Amru'l Qais and Labīd and Akhtal and blind A'sha and Qais.
Arles, an arles for my hiring, An.
As appleblossom to crocus.
As to my heart, that may as well be forgotten.
At Briggflatts Meetinghouse.
Attis: Or, Something Missing.
Aus Dem Zweiten Reich.
Baudelaire in Cythera.
Birthday Greeting.
Briggflatts [An Autobiography].
Came to me— / Who?
Carmencita's tawny paps.
Chomei at Toyama.
Chorus of Furies.
Complaint of the Morpethshire Farmer, The.
Coryphée gravefooted precise, dance to the gracious music.
Darling of Gods and Men, beneath the gliding stars.
Day being Whitsun we had pigeon for dinner, The.
Dear be still! Time's start of us lengthens slowly.
Duke Valentine had been in Lombardy with the King.
Empty vast days built in the waste memory seem a jail for.
Envoi to the Reader.
Farewell ye sequent graces.
Flat land lies under water, The.
Fruits breaking the branches.
Gertie Gitana's hymn to waltzing.
Gin the Goodwife Stint.
Ginger, who are you going with?
Hi, tent-boy, get that tent down.
Hymn to Alias Thor.
I am agog for foam. Tumultuous come.
I'm the worse for drink again, it's.
Isn't it poetical, a chap's mind in the dumps?
Keep Troth.
Last night without sight of you my brain was ablaze.
Let them remember Samangan, the bridge and tower.
Like a fawn you dodge me, Molly.
Loud intolerant bells (the shrinking nightflower closes).
Many well-known people have been packed away in cemeteries.
Mesh cast for mackerel.
Molten pool, incandescent spilth of.
Muzzle and jowl and beastly brow.
Narciss, my numerous cancellations prefer.
Night is hard by. I am vexed and bothered by sleep.
Night swallowed the sun as.
Not to thank dogwood nor.
Nothing / substance utters or time.
Now that sea's over that island.
Now we've no hope of going back.
O everlastingly self-deluded!
O, it is godlike to sit selfpossessed.
On highest summits dawn comes soonest.
On the Fly-Leaf of Pound's Cantos.
Once, so they say, pinetrees seeded on Pelion's peak swam.
Orotava Road, The.
Passport Officer, The.
Pious Cat, The.
Please stop gushing about his pink.
Poor soul! Softy, whisperer.
Reading X's Collected Works.
Search under every veil.
See! Their verses are laid.
Shall I sulk because my love has a double heart?
Snow's on the fellside, look! How deep.
Soil sandy and the plow light, neither, The.
Song for Rustam, A.

Song of the Ackworth Clock, The.
Southwind, tell her what.
Spoils, The.
Stones trip Coquet burn.
Such syllables flicker out of grass.
That filly couldn't carry a rider nor.
That volatile poet called Jonathan.
These tracings from a world that's dead.
They Say Etna.
This I write, mix ink with tears.
Three Michaelmas daisies.
Thrush in the syringa sings, A.
Thundercloud fills meadows with heavenly beauty, The.
To abate what swells.
Trinacria.
Two hundred and seven paces.
Two Photographs.
Under sand clay. Dig, wait.
Vessels thrown awry by strong gusts.
Vestiges.
Villon.
Weeping oaks grieve, chestnuts raise.
Well of Lycopolis, The.
What a pity that Bela Bartok.
What the Chairman Told Tom.
When the sword of sixty comes nigh his head.
Yan tan tethera pethera pimp.
Yes, it's slow, docked of amours.
You can't grip years, Postume.
You idiot! What makes you think decay will.
You leave / nobody else.
You, with my enemy, strolling down my street.
You've come! O how flustered and anxious I've been.
Translations, Coauthored Poems, etc.:
Faridun watched the road.
Faridun's Sons *sels.*
Light of my eyes, there *is* something to be said.
29 Songs *sels.*
incl. Latin *tr. by* Basil Bunting.
Burns, Robert (1759–96)
Act Sederunt of the Session—A Scots Ballad.
Adam A———'s Prayer.
Address of Beelzebub.
Address to Edinburgh.
Address to General Dumourier.
Address to the Deil.
Address, to the Shade of Thomson, on Crowning His Bust, at *Ednam, Roxburgh-shire,* with Bays.
Address to the Tooth-Ache.
Address to the Unco Guid, or the Rigidly Righteous.
Address to the Woodlark.
After Dinner.
Afton Water.
Allan Water.
Altered from an Old English Song.
Amang the trees, where humming bees.
And I'll kiss thee yet, yet.
Annotations in Verse.
Another [Epigram on Said Occasion].
Answer, The [To the Guidwife of Wauchope-House].
Answer to an Invitation.
Answer to the Foregoing—Extempore [Clarinda].
As I was a wand'ring ae midsummer e'enin.
As I Went Out Ae May Morning.
At Brownhill Inn.
At Roslin Inn.
At Whigham's Inn, Sanquar.
Auld Farmer's New-Year-Morning Salutation to His Auld Mare, Maggie, on Giving Her the Accustomed Ripp of Corn to Hansel in the New-Year, The.
Auld Man's Mare's Dead, The.
Auld Man's Winter Thought, The.
Auld Rob Morris.
Author's Earnest Cry and Prayer, to the Right Honorable and Honorable, the Scotch Representatives in the House of Commons, The.

Awa Whigs Awa.
Ay Waukin O.
Ballad, A: "There was a lass and she was fair."
Ballad, A: "While Prose-work and rhymes."
Banks O' Doon, The.
Banks o' Doon, The: "Ye flowery banks o' bonie Doon."
Banks of Cree.
Banks of Nith, The.
Banks of the Devon, The.
Bannocks o' Bear-Meal.
Bard's Epitaph, A.
Battle of Sherra-Moor, The.
Before Dinner.
Bess[y] and Her Spinning-Wheel.
Beware o' Bonie Ann.
Birks of Aberfeldy, The [Composed on the Spot].
Birth-Day Ode. December 31st 1787, A.
Blue-Eyed Lassie, The.
Bob o' Dumblane, The.
Bonie Bell.
Bonie Dundee.
Bonie Lad That's Far Awa, The.
Bonie Laddie, Highland Laddie.
Bonie Lass Made the Bed to Me, The.
Bonie Mary.
Bonnie Peg.
Bonnie [or Bonny] Wee Thing, The.
Book-Worms, The.
Braes o' Ballochmyle, The.
Brigs of Ayr, a Poem. Inscribed to J. B*********, Esq; Ayr, The.
Broom Besoms ["I maun hae a wife, whatsoe'er she be"].
Broom Besoms ["Young and souple was I, when I lap the dyke"].
Brose and Butter.
Burns Grace at Kirkudbright.
Buy Braw Troggin. An Excellent New Song.
Ca' the Ewes [or Yowes] [to the Knowes].
Ca' the Yowes [to the Knowes].
Caledonia.
Calf, The.
Campbells Are Comin, The.
Can Ye Labor Lea.
Can You Leave Me Thus, My Katy.
Captain's Lady, The.
Cardin o't, The.
Cares o' love are sweeter far, The.
Carl an the King Come.
Castle Gordon—*Intended to Be Sung to Morag.*
Cauld Frosty Morning.
Cauld Is the E'enin Blast.
Charlie He's My Darling.
Clarinda.
Cock up Your Beaver.
Come rede me, dame, come tell me, dame.
Comin[g] thro' [or through] the Rye.
Cotter's Saturday Night [Inscribed to Robert Aiken [or R. A****], Esq.], The.
Country Lassie.
Craigieburn-Wood—A Song.
Dainty Davie.
Dean of Faculty—a New Ballad, The.
Death and Doctor Hornbook [A True Story].
Death and Dying Words of Poor Mailie, the Author's Only Pet Yowe, an Unco Mournfu' Tale, The.
Dedication to G**** H******* Esq., A.
De'il's [or Deil's] Awa wi' th' [or the] Exciseman, The.
Delia.
Despondency, an Ode.
Deuks Dang o'er My Daddie, The.
Down the Burn Davie.
Dream, A.
Duan First.
Duan Second.
Dumfires Volunteers, The.
Dumfries Epigrams.
Duncan Davison.
Duncan Gray.
Duncan Gray ["Weary fa' you, Duncan Gray"].

Dusty Miller.
Election: A New Song, The.
Elegy on Captain Matthew Henderson [or Capt. M——— H———] [A *Gentleman* Who Held the Patent for His Honours Immediately from Almighty God!].
Elegy on Mister William Cruikshank A. M.
Elegy on Peg Nicholson.
Elegy on the Death of Robert Ruisseaux.
Elegy on the Year 1788.
English Song.
Epigram on Capt. Francis Grose, the Celebrated Antiquary.
Epigram on Doctor Babington.
Epigram on James Baillie Swan.
Epigram on Rough Roads.
Epigram on Said Occasion.
Epigram: "Whoe'er he be that sojourns here."
Epigrams on Lord Galloway.
Epistle to a Young Friend.
Epistle to Captn Willm Logan at Park.
Epistle to Davie, a Brother Poet.
Epistle to Hugh Parker.
Epistle to J. L*****k, an Old Scotch Bard.
Epistle to J. R******, Enclosing Some Poems.
Epistle to John Goldie in Kilmarnock, Author of, the Gospel Recovered.
Epistle to Mr Tytler of Woodhouselee, Author of a Defence of Mary Queen of Scots.
Epistle to Robt. Graham Esq: of Fintry on the Election for the Dumfries String of Boroughs, Anno 1790.
Epitaph Extempore, on a Person Nicknamed the Marquis, Who Desired Burns to Write One on Him.
Epitaph for H——— L———, Esq., of L———.
Epitaph for J. H. Writer in Ayr.
Epitaph for William Nicol.
Epitaph. Here Lies Robert Fergusson, Poet.
Epitaph: "Lo worms enjoy the seat of bliss."
Epitaph on a Henpecked Country Squire.
Epitaph on a Wag in Mauchline.
Epitaph on D——— C———.
Epitaph on Holy Willie.
Epitaph on J-hn B-shby.
Epitaph on John Dove [Innkeeper, Mauchline].
Epitaph on Mr. Burton.
Epitaph on My Own Friend, and My Father's Friend, Wm Muir in Tarbolton Miln.
Epitaph on R. Muir.
Eppie McNab.
Extemporaneous Effusion on Being Appointed to the Excise, An.
Extempore.
Extempore Epistle to Mr. McAdam of Craigengillian, (Wrote in Nanse Tinnock's, Mauchline) in Answer to an Obliging Letter He Sent in the Commencement of My Poetic Career.
Extempore, in the Court of S———.
Extempore—On Being Shown a Beautiful County Seat Belonging to the Same [Maxwell of Cardoness].
Extempore—on Some Commemorations of Thomson.
Extempore Reply to an Invitation.
Extempore—To Mr. Gavin Hamilton.
Extempore Verses on Dining with Lord Daer.
Extempore [on the *Loyal Natives'* Verses].
Fair Eliza.
Fair Jenny.
Farewell, The: "Farewell, old Scotia's bleak domains."
Farewell. To the Brethren of St. James' Lodge, Tarbolton, The.
Fête Champetre, The.
First Psalm, The.
First Six Verses of the Ninetieth Psalm, The.
Five Carlins—A Ballad—Tune, Chevy Chase, The.
For G. H. Esq.
For R. A. Esq.
For the Author's Father.

For the Sake o' Somebody.
Fornicator. A New Song, The.
Frae the friends and Land I love.
Fragment, A: "Green grow the rashes, O; / Green grow the rashes, O; / The lasses they hae wimble bores."
Fragment, A: "One night as I did wander."
Fragment, A: "When first I came to Stewart Kyle."
Fragment, A: "When *Guilford* good our Pilot stood."
Fragment: "Altho' my bed were in yon muir."
Fragment—Epistle from Esopus to Maria.
Fragment: "Her flowing locks, the raven's wing."
Fragment: "Now health forsakes that angel face."
Fragment—on Glenriddel's Fox Breaking His Chain, A.
Fragment, Which Was Meant for the Beginning of an Elegy on the Late Miss Burnet of Monboddo, A.
Fragment: "Why, why tell thy lover."
Galla Water.
Gallant Weaver, The.
Galloway Tam.
Gardener wi' His Paddle—or, The Gardener's March, The.
German Lairdie, The.
Gie the Lass her Fairin'.
Gloomy December.
Godly Girzie.
Grace after Dinner.
Grace after Meat.
Grace before Dinner, Extempore, A.
Graces———at the Globe Tavern.
Green Grow the Rashes [*or* Rushes] [A Fragment].
Green Sleeves [and Tartan Ties].
Grim Grizzle.
Gude Wallace.
Gudeen to You Kimmer.
Had I the Wyte She Bade Me.
Halloween.
Henpeck'd Husband, The.
Here Awa' There Awa ["Here awa', there awa' wandering, Willie"].
Here's, a bottle and an honest friend.
Here's a Health to Ane I Lo'e Dear.
Here's a Health to Them That's Awa'.
Here's His Health in Water.
Here's to Thy Health My Bonie Lass.
Heron Ballads, 1795, The *sels.*
Hey Ca' thro'.
Hey for a Lass wi' a Tocher.
Hey Tuti Tatey.
Highland Balou, The.
Highland Laddie.
Highland Lassie O.
Highland Mary.
Highland Widow's Lament, The.
Holy Fair, The.
Holy Tulzie, The.
Holy Willie's Prayer.
How lang and dreary is the night.
Hue and Cry of John Lewars, The.
Hughie Graham.
Humble Petition of Bruar Water to the Noble Duke of Athole, The.
Hunting Song.
I do confess thou art sae fair.
I dream'd I lay where flowers were springing.
I Hae a Wife o' My Ain.
I Look to the North.
I Love My Jean.
I Love My Love in Secret.
I Once Was a Maid.
I'll Ay[e] Ca' in by Yon Town.
Ill-fated Genius! Heaven-taught Fergusson.
I'll Mak You Be Fain to Follow Me.
I'm Owre [*or* O'er] Young to Marry Yet.
Impomptu, on Mrs. W. Riddell's Birthday, 4th Novr. 1793.
Inscription on a Goblet.
Interpolation.

Inventory, The.
It is na, Jean, thy bonie face.
It Was A' for Our Rightfu' King.
Jamie Come Try Me.
Jeremiah 15th Ch. 10 V.
Jessie—A New Scots Song.
Jockey Fou and Jenny Fain.
Jockey's Ta'en the Parting Kiss.
John Anderson, My Jo.
John Barleycorn [a Ballad].
John Come Kiss Me Now.
Johnie B———'s Lament.
Johnie Blunt.
Johnie Cope.
Jolly Gauger, The.
Jumpin John.
Keekin' Glass, The.
Kellyburnbraes.
Ken ye ought o' Captain Grose?
Ken Ye What Meg o' the Mill Has Gotten.
Killiecrankie.
Kirk of Scotland's Garland—a New Song, The.
Laddies by the banks o' Nith, The.
Lady Onlie.
Lament for James, Earl of Glencairn.
Lament. Occasioned by the Unfortunate Issue of a Friend's Amour, The.
Lament of Mary Queen of Scots on the Approach of Spring.
Lass of Ecclefechan, The.
Lassie Lie near Me.
Lassie wi' the Lintwhite Locks.
Lazy Mist, The.
Lea-Rig, The.
Leezie Lindsay.
Let Me in This Ae Night.
Letter to J———s T———t, Gl—nc———r.
Libel Summons.
Lines Addressed to Mr. John Ranken.
Lines: "He who of R--k-n sang, lies stiff and dead."
Lines on Stirling.
Lines Sent to Sir John Whiteford, of Whiteford, Bart. with the Foregoing Poem.
Lines Written in the Kirk of Lamington.
Lines Written on a Bank-Note.
Lines *Written on a Window, at the King's Arms Tavern, Dumfries.*
Lines *Written on the Windows of the Globe Tavern, Dumfries.*
Lord Galloway.
Lord Gregory.
Lord Ronald My Son.
Louis, What Reck I by Thee.
Lovely Davies.
Lovely Lass o' Inverness, The.
Lovely Polly Stewart.
Lover's Morning Salute to His Mistress, The.
Luath.
Lying at a Reverend Friend's House One Night, the Author Left the Following *Verses* in the Room Where He Slept.
Man Was Made to Mourn, a Dirge.
Man's Inhumanity to Man.
Mary Morison.
Mauchline Wedding, The.
[On] Maxwell of Cardoness.
McPherson's Farewell.
Merry Hae I Been Teethin a Heckle.
Monody on Maria.
Mother's Lament for the Loss of Her Only Son, A.
Muirland Meg.
Musing on the roaring ocean.
My Bonie Laddie's Young but He's Growin Yet.
My Bonnie [*or* Bony] Mary.
My Collier Laddie.
My Eppie.
My Harry was a gallant gay.
My Heart's in the Highlands.
My Lady's Gown There's Gairs upon't.
My Love She's But a Lassie Yet.
My Nannie's Awa'.
My Peggy's Face.
My Tocher's the Jewel.

My Wife's a Wanton Wee Thing.
My Wife's a Winsome Wee Thing.
Nature's Law.
New Psalm for the Chapel of Kilmarnock, on the Thanksgiving-Day for His Majesty's Recovery, A.
Night was still, and o'er the hill, The.
Nithsdale's Welcome Hame.
Northern Lass, The.
O An Ye Were Dead Gudeman.
O Ay My Wife She Dang Me.
O Dear Minny What Shall I Do?
O, for Ane-and-Twenty Tam.
O Gin My Love Were Yon Red Rose.
O gude ale comes and gude ale goes.
O ken ye what Meg o' the mill has gotten.
O Kenmure's on and awa, Willie.
O Lay Thy Loof in Mine Lass.
O leave novels, ye Mauchline belles.
O Mally's Meek, Mally's Sweet.
O May Thy Morn.
O once I loved [*or* lov'd] a bonie lass.
O raging Fortune's withering blast.
O saw ye bonny Lesley.
O Saw Ye My Maggie.
O Steer Her Up and Had Her Gaun.
O That I Had Ne'er Been Married.
O were I on Parnassus hill.
O Were My Love Yon Lilac[k] Fair.
O [*or* Oh] Wert Thou in the Cauld Blast.
Occasional Address, Spoken by Miss Fontenell, on Her Bnefit-Night, Decr. 4th. 1793.—Written by Mr Burns.
Ode, Sacred to the Memory of Mrs. ——— of ———.
Ode to Spring.
Ode to the Departed Regency-Bill—1789.
Ode [for General Washington's Birthday].
O'er the Water to Charlie.
On a Bank of Flowers.
On a Celebrated Ruling Elder.
On a Dog of Lord Eglinton's.
On a Noisy Polemic.
On a Schoolmaster in Cleish Parish, Fifeshire.
On a Scotch Bard Gone to the West Indies.
On an Innkeeper in Tarbolton.
On an Old Acquaintance Who Seemed to Pass the Bard without Notice.
On Andrew Turner.
On Being Asked Why God Had Made Miss D——— So Little and Mrs A——— So Big.
On Captn. L———lles.
On Capt. W——— R-dd-ck of C-rb——ton.
On Chloris Requesting Me to Give Her a Spray of a Sloe-Thorn in Full Blossom.
On Commissary Goldie's Brains.
On Critics.
On Fergusson.
On Gabriel Richardson.
On Jas. Grieve, Laird of Boghead, Tarbolton.
On Jessy Lewars.
On J-hn M-r-ne, Laird of L-gg-n.
On John McMurdo.
On Johnson's Opinion of Hampden.
On Lord Galloway.
On Marriage.
On Miss J. Scott, of Ayr.
On Mr. Burke by an Opponent and a Friend to Mr. Hastings.
On Mr. James Gracie.
On Mr. Pitt's [*or* Pit's] Hair-Powder Tax.
On Reading, in a Newspaper, the Death of J——— McL———, Esq. Brother to a Young Lady, a Particular Friend of the Author's.
On Robert Riddel.
On Scaring Some Waterfowl in Loch Turit, a Wild Scene among the Hills of Oughtertyre.
On Seeing a Wounded Hare Limp by Me, Which a Fellow Had Just Shot At.
On Seeing Miss Fontenelle in a Favourite Character.
On Seeing Mrs. Kemble in Yarico.

On Seeing the Beautiful County-Seat of Lord G——.
On Seeing the Royal Palace at Stirling in Ruins.
On Tam the Chapman.
On the Birth of a Posthumous Child, Born in Peculiar Circumstances of Family Distress.
On the Death of Echo, a Lap-Dog.
On the Death of Sir J. Hunter Blair.
On the Death of the Late Lord President Dundas.
On the Duchess of Gordon's Reel Dancing.
On the Late Captain Grose's Peregrinations thro' Scotland, Collecting the Antiquities of That King.
On the Seas and Far Away.
On W. R——, Esq.
On Wee Johnie.
On William Graham [or W—— Gr-h-m], Esq., of Mossknowe [or M-sskn-w].
On Willie Chalmers.
Open the Door to Me, Oh!
Orananaoig, or, the Song of Death.
Ordination, The.
Passion's Cry.
Patriarch, The.
Penitential Thought, in the Hour of Remorse—Intended for a Tragedy, A.
Phillis the Fair.
Pinned to Mrs R——'s Carriage.
Ploughman, The.
Poem: "Friend o' the Poet, tired and leal."
Poem on Life.
Poetical Inscription, for an Altar to Independence at Kerrouchtry, the Seat of Mr. Heron, Written in Summer 1795.
Poor Mailie's Elegy.
Posie, The.
Postscript [To W. S*****n, Ochiltree].
Prayer, in the Prospect of Death, A.
Prayer, under the Pressure of Violent Anguish, A.
Primrose, The.
Prologue: "No song nor dance I bring from yon great city."
Prologue: "When by a generous Public's kind acclaim."
Rantin' Dog, the Daddie o't, The.
Rantin Laddie, The.
Rattlin, Roarin Willie.
Raving winds around her blowing.
Red, Red Rose, A.
Reel o' Stumpie, The.
Remorse.
Reply to Robert Riddell.
Revision for Clarinda.
Rights of Woman—Spoken by Miss Fontenelle on Her Benefit Night, The.
Robert Bruce's March to Bannockburn.
Robert Burns' Answer [to Epistle from a Taylor].
Robin Shure in Hairst.
Ronalds of the Bennals, The.
Rosebud, The.
Rowin 't in Her Apron, The.
Rusticity's ungainly form.
Sae Far Awa.
Sandy and Jockie.
Saw Ye My Phely (Quasi Dicat, Phillis).
Scotch Drink.
Scotch Song.
Scotish Ballad.
Scotish Song.
Scots Ballad.
Scots Prologue, For Mrs. Sutherland's Benefit Night, Spoken at the Theatre Dumfries.
Scroggam.
Second Epistle to Davie.
Seventh of November, The.
She Says She Lo'es Me Best of A'.
Shepherd's Wife, The.
She's fair and fause that causes my smart.
Sic a Wife as Willie Had.
Sketch.
Sketch for an Elegy.
Sketch. Inscribed to the Rt. Hon. Ch. J. Fox Esq.

Sketch. New Year's Day. To Mrs. Dunlop.
Slave's Lament, The.
Solemn League and Covenant, The.
Song: " 'Twas na her bonie blue e'e was my ruin."
Song, A: "Thou lingering Star with lessening ray."
Song: "Adown winding Nith I did wander."
Song: "Ae fond kiss, and then we sever."
Song, Altered from an Old English One.
Song: "Anna, thy charms my bosom fire."
Song: "As I cam down by yon castle wa' ."
Song: "As I stood by yon roofless tower."
Song: "Behind yon hills where Lugar flows."
Song: "Behold the hour, the boat arrive."
Song: "Blythe hae I been on yon hill."
Song.—Composed at Auchtertyre on Miss Euphemia Murray of Lentrose.
Song, Composed in August.
Song: "Contented wi' little, and cantie wi' mair."
Song: "Farewell, thou stream that winding flows."
Song—For A' That and A' That.
Song: "From thee, ELIZA, I must go."
Song: "Full well thou knowest I love thee dear."
Song: "Gloomy night is gath'ring fast, The."
Song: "Had I a cave on some wild, distant shore."
Song: "I murder hate by field or flood."
Song: "I'll tell you a tale of a wife."
Song: "In Mauchline there dwells six proper young Belles."
Song.—In the Character of a Ruined Farmer.
Song: "It was upon a Lammas night."
Song: "Let not Woman e'er complain."
Song: "Mark yonder pomp of costly fashion."
Song: "My father was a farmer upon the Carrick border O."
Song: "My girl she's airy, she's buxom and gay."
Song: "No Churchman am I for to rail and to write."
Song: "O, Logan, sweetly didst thou glide."
Song: "O Philly, happy be that day."
Song: "O poortith cauld, and restless love."
Song: "O this is no my ain lassie."
Song: "O wat ye wha's in yon town."
Song: "O wat ye what that lo'es me."
Song: "O whistle, and I'll come to ye, my lad."
Song: "On Cessnock banks a lassie dwells."
Song—(On Chloris Being Ill).
Song. On Miss P—— K——, A.
Song. On Miss W. A.
Song: "Sensibility how charming."
Song: "Small birds rejoice in the green leaves returning, The."
Song: "Their groves o' sweet myrtle let Foreign Lands reckon."
Song: "Tho' women's minds, like winter winds."
Song: "Tibby I hae seen the day."
Song: "Will ye go to the Indies, my Mary."
Song: "Yestreen I had a pint o' wine."
Sonnet—On Hearing a Thrush Sing on a Morning Walk in January.
Sonnet on the Death of Robert Riddel, Esq. of Glen Riddel, April 1794.
Sonnet upon Sonnets, A.
Sons of Old Killie, The.
Stanzas on the Same Occasion [in the Prospect of Death].
Stay, my Charmer, can you leave me.
Strathallan's Lament.
Such a Parcel of Rogues in a Nation.
Sutors o' Selkirk.
Sweet fa's the eve on Craigieburn.
Sweetest May.
Tale, A.
Tam Glen.
Tam o' Shanter [A Tale].
Tam Samson's Elegy.
Tarbolton Lasses, The.
Taylor fell thro' the bed, thimble an' a', The.
Taylor, The.

Then Guidwife Count the Lawin.
Theniel Menzies' Bony Mary.
There Grows a Bonie Brier-Bush.
There Was a Bonie Lass.
There was a lad was born in Kyle.
There was twa wives, and twa witty wives.
There'll Never Be Peace Till Jamie Comes Hame.
There's a youth in this city, it were a great pity.
There's News Lasses News.
Thine am I, my Chloris fair.
Third Epistle to J. Lapraik.
Thou hast left me ever, Jamie.
Though fickle fortune has deceiv'd me.
Three Gude Fellows Ayont Yon Glen.
Tibbie Dunbar.
Tibbie Fowler.
To a Gentleman Who Had Sent Him a News-Paper, and Offered to Continue It Free of Expense.
To a Haggis.
To a Louse [On Seeing One on a Lady's Bonnet at Church].
To a Mountain Daisy [On Turning One Down, with the Plough, in April—1786].
To a Mouse [On Turning Her Up in Her Nest, with the Plough, November, 1785].
To a Painter.
To a Young Lady, Miss Jessy L——, Dumfries; with Books which the Bard Presented Her.
To Alexander Cunningham.
To Alexander Findlater.
To Captain G——, on Being Asked Why I Was Not to Be of the Party with Him and His Brother K-nm-re at Syme's.
To Captain Riddell.
To Chloris.
To Clarinda.
To Daunton Me.
To Dr. Blacklock.
To Dr. John MacKenzie.
To Dr Maxwell, on Miss Jessy Staig's Recovery.
To J. S****.
To John Kennedy.
To John Syme.
To Maria.
To Miss Ainslie, in Chuch.
To Miss C********, a Very Young Lady.
To Miss Ferrier.
To Miss Graham of Fintray.
To Miss Isabella Macleod.
To Miss L——.
To Mr. E—— on His Translation of and Commentaries on Martial.
To Mr Gavin Hamilton, Mauchline.
To Mr. Graham of Fintry, On Being Appointed to My Excise Division.
To Mr. John Kennedy.
To Mr. John Taylor.
To Mr. McMurdo, with a Pound of Lundiefoot Snuff.
To Mr. S. McKenzie.
To Mrs. C——.
To Peter Stuart.
To R***** G***** of F*****, Esq.
To Renton of Lamerton.
To Robt. Graham of Fintry Esqr, with a Request for an Excise Division.
To Ruin.
To Symon Gray.
To Terraughty, on His Birth-Day.
To the Beautiful Miss Eliza J——n, on Her Principles of Liberty and Equality.
To the Honble Mr. R. M——, of P-nm-re, on His High Phaeton.
To the Memory of the Unfortunate Miss Burns 1791.
To the Rev. John McMath, Inclosing a Copy of Holy Willie's Prayer, Which He Had Requested.
To the Same, on the Author Being Threatened with His Resentment.
To the Weaver's Gin Ye Go.
To W. S*****n, Ochiltree.

To William Creech.
To William Stewart.
Toadeater, The.
Toast, A.
Tree of Liberty, The.
Trogger, The.
Twa Dogs, The.
Up and Warn A' Willie.
Up in the Morning Early.
Verse Composed and Repeated by *Burns*, to the Master of the House, on Taking Leave at a Place in the Highlands, Where He Had Been Hospitably Entertained, A.
Verses: "I am a keeper of the law."
Verses Intended to Be Written below a Noble Earl's Picture.
Verses Written on a Window of the Inn at Carron.
Versicles on Sign-Posts.
Vision, The.
Wae Is My Heart.
Waukrife Minnie, A.
Weary Pund o' Tow, The.
Wee Willie Gray.
We'll Hide the Couper behint the Door.
Wha Is That at My Bower-Door?
Wha'll M-w Me Now.
Wham will we send to London town.
What can a young lassie, what shall a young lassie.
What Will I Do Gin My Hoggie Die.
When lyart leaves bestrow the yird.
When She Cam Ben She Bobbed.
When wild War's deadly blast was blawn.
Where braving angry Winter's storms.
Where Helen Lies.
While new-ca'd kye rowte at the stake.
Whistle. A Ballad, The.
Whistle o'er the Lave o't.
White Cockade, The.
Why Should Na Poor Folk Mowe.
Willie Brew'd [*or* Brewed] a Peck o' Maut.
Wilt thou be my Dearie.
Winter, a Dirge.
Winter It Is Past, The.
Winter Night, A.
Wren's Nest, The.
Written in Friar's Carse Hermitage on the Banks of Nith—June—1788.
Written under the Picture of the Celebrated Miss Burns.
Written with a Pencil over the Chimney-Piece, in the Parlour of the Inn at Kenmore, Taymouth.
Written with a Pencil, Standing by the Fall of Fyers, near Loch-Ness.
Wrote on the Blank Leaf of a Copy of My First Edition, Which I Sent to an Old Sweetheart, Then Married.
Ye Jacobites By Name.
Yon wild, mossy mountains sae lofty and wide.
Young Highland Rover, The.
Young Jockey was the blythest lad.
You're Welcome, Willie Stewart.
Translations, Coauthored Poems, etc.:
Geordie [An Old Ballad].
Tam Lin.

Byron, George Gordon Noel Byron, 6th Baron (1788–1824)
Address.
Address Intended to Be Recited at the Caledonian Meeting.
Adieu, The.
Age of Bronze, The.
All Is Vanity, Saith the Preacher.
And Dost Thou Ask the Reason of My Sadness?
And Thou Art Dead, as Young and Fair.
And Wilt Thou Weep When I Am Low?
Another Simple Ballat.
Answer to ——'s Professions of Affection.
Answer to a Beautiful Poem, Entitled "The Common Lot."
Answer to Some Elegant Verses.
Answer to the Foregoing, Addressed to Miss——.

Aristomenes.
As the Liberty Lads o'er the Sea.
At Thirty Years.
Away, Away, Ye Notes of Woe!
Ballad: "Of all the twice ten thousand bards."
Beppo; a Venetian Story.
Blues, The.
Bowles and Campbell.
Brave Champions! Go On with the Farce.
Braziers, It Seems, Are Preparing to Pass, The.
Bride of Abydos, The.
Bright Be the Place of Thy Soul!
By the Rivers of Babylon We Sat Down and Wept.
Cain: A Mystery.
Canto the First.
Canto the Second.
Canto the Third.
Canto the Fourth.
Canto the Fifth.
Canto the Sixth.
Canto the Seventh.
Canto the Ninth.
Canto the Eleventh.
Canto the Twelfth.
Canto the Thirteenth.
Canto the Fourteenth.
Canto the Fifteenth.
Chain I Gave, The.
Childe Harold's Farewell to England.
Childe Harold's Pilgrimage.
Childish Recollections.
Churchill's Grave.
Condolatory Address.
Conquest, The.
Cornelian, The.
Corsair, The.
Curse of Minerva, The.
Damaetas.
Darkness.
Dear Doctor, I Have Read Your Play.
Death of Haidée, The.
Dedication: "Bob Southey! You're a poet—poet-laureate."
Deformed Transformed, The.
Destruction of Sennacherib, The.
Devil's Drive, The.
Don Juan.
Donna Julia.
Dream, The.
Duel, The.
Dying Gladiator, The.
E Nihilo Nihil.
Egotism. A Letter to J.T. Becher.
Elegiac Stanzas on the Death of Sir Peter Parker, Bart.
Elegy: "Behold the blessings of a lucky lot!"
Elegy on Newstead Abbey.
Endorsement to the Deed of Separation, in the April of 1816.
English Bards and Scotch Reviewers.
Epigram on an Old Lady Who Had Some Curious Notions Respecting the Soul.
Epigrams: "Oh, Castlereagh! thou art a patriot now."
Epilogue: "There's something in a stupid ass."
Episode of Nisus and Euryalus, The.
Epistle to a Friend.
Epistle to Augusta.
Epitaph for Joseph Blacket.
Epitaph on a Friend.
Epitaph on John Adams, of Southwell.
Euthanasia.
Evening.
Fame.
Fare Thee Well.
Farewell! If Ever Fondest Prayer.
Farewell Petition to J.C.H., Esq.
Farewell to Malta.
Farewell to the Muse.
Fill the Goblet.
First Kiss of Love, The.
For Orford and for Waldegrave.

Fragment, A: "Could I remount the river of my years."
Fragment, A: "When, to their airy hall, my fathers' voice."
Fragment from the "Monk of Athos."
Fragment: "I would to heaven that I were so much clay."
Fragment of an Epistle to Thomas Moore.
Fragment Written Shortly after the Marriage of Miss Chaworth.
From Anacreon ("I wish to tune my quivering lyre").
From Anacreon ("'Twas now the hour when Night had driven").
From the French.
From the Prometheus Vinctus of Aeschylus.
George the Third.
Giaour, The.
Girl of Cadiz, The.
God Maddens Him Whom 'T Is His Will to Lose.
Good Plays Are Scarce.
Granta—A Medley.
Growing Old.
Gulbeyaz.
Haidee.
Haidée and Don Juan.
Harp the Monarch Minstrel Swept, The.
Heaven and Earth.
Here's a Happy New Year! But with Reason.
Here's to Her Who Long.
Herod's Lament for Mariamne.
Hints from Horace.
Hock and Soda Water.
I Read the "Christabel."
I Saw Thee Weep.
I Would I Were a Careless Child.
Ich Dien.
If for Silver, or for Gold.
If Sometimes in the Haunts of Men.
If That High World.
Imitation of Tibullus.
Impromptu.
Impromptu, in Reply to a Friend.
In the Valley of Waters.
In This Beloved Marble View.
Inscription on the Monument of a Newfoundland Dog.
Irish Avatar, The.
Island, The.
It Is the Hush of Night.
Italy.
Jephtha's Daughter.
Journal in Cephalonia.
Juan and Haidée.
Juan in England.
Julian [A Fragment].
La Revanche.
Lachin y Gair.
Lake Leman ("Clear, placid Leman! thy contrasted lake").
Lament of Tasso, The.
L'Amitié Est L'Amour Sans Ailes.
Lara.
Last Words on Greece.
Lines Addressed to a Young Lady.
Lines: "Dear Becher, you tell me to mix with mankind."
Lines Inscribed upon a Cup Formed from a Skull.
Lines on Hearing That Lady Byron Was Ill.
Lines to a Lady Weeping.
Lines to Mr Hodgson.
Lines Written beneath a Picture.
Lines Written beneath an Elm in the Churchyard of Harrow.
Lines Written in an Album, at Malta.
Lines Written in the Travellers' Book at Orchomenus.
Lines Written on a Blank Leaf of the "Pleasures of Memory."
Love and Death.
Love and Gold.
Love's Last Adieu.
Lucietta. A Fragment.
Maid of Athens, Ere We Part.
Manfred: A Dramatic Poem.

Marino Faliero, Doge of Venice.
Martial, Lib. I. Epig. I.
Mazeppa.
Monody on the Death of the Right Hon. R. B. Sheridan.
My Boat Is on the Shore.
My Days of Love Are Over.
My Dear Mr. Murray.
My Soul Is Dark.
Napoleon's Farewell.
Napoleon's Snuff-Box.
New Song to the Tune of "Whare Hae Ye Been a' Day, My Boy Tammy O? Courting O' a Young Thing, Just Come Frae Her Mammie O?"
New Vicar of Bray, The.
Newstead Abbey.
No Infant Sotheby, Whose Dauntless Head.
Occasional Prologue Delivered Previous to the Performance of "The Wheel of Fortune" at a Private Theatre, An.
Ocean, The.
Ode from the French.
Ode on Venice.
Ode to a Lady Whose Lover Was Killed by a Ball, Which at the Same Time Shivered a Portrait next His Heart.
Ode to Napoleon Buonaparte.
Ode to the Framers of the Frame Bill, An.
Oh factious viper! whose envenom'd tooth.
Oh How I Wish That an Embargo.
Oh! Snatch'd Away in Beauty's Bloom.
Oh! Weep for Those.
Oh You, Who in All Names Can Tickle the Town.
On a Change of Masters at a Great Public School.
On a Cornelian Heart Which Was Broken.
On a Distant View of the Village and School of Harrow on the Hill.
On a Royal Visit to the Vaults.
On Being Asked What Was the "Origin of Love."
On Finding a Fan.
On Jordan's Banks.
On Leaving Newstead Abbey.
On Parting.
On Revisiting Harrow.
On Sam Rogers.
On the Birth of John William Rizzo Hoppner.
On the Day of the Destruction of Jerusalem by Titus.
On the Death of a Young Lady.
On the Eyes of Miss A——— H———.
On the Quotation "And My True Faith Can Alter Never, Though Thou Art Gone Perhaps Forever."
On the Star of "The Legion of Honour."
On This Day I Complete My Thirty-sixth Year.
Once Fairly Set Out on His Party of Pleasure.
One Struggle More, and I Am Free.
Oscar of Alva.
Ossian's Address to the Sun in "Carthon."
Parenthetical Address.
Parisina.
Pignus Amoris.
Poet and the World, The.
Poetical Commandments.
Prayer of Nature, The.
Prisoner of Chillon, The.
Prometheus.
Prophecy of Dante, The.
Queries to Casuists.
R. C. Dallas.
Remember Him Whom Passion's Power.
Remember Thee! Remember Thee!
Remembrance.
Remind Me Not, Remind Me Not.
Reply to Some Verses of J.M.B. Pigot, Esq., on the Cruelty of His Mistress.
Rome by Metella's Tomb.
Sardanapalus.
Saul.
She Walks in Beauty.

Siege of Corinth, The.
Sketch, A.
So We'll Go No More a Roving.
So[,] We'll Go No More a-Roving.
Soliloquy of a Bard in the Country.
Song: "Breeze of the night in gentler sighs."
Song of Saul before His Last Battle.
Song to the Suliotes.
Sonnet on Chillon.
Sonnet on the Nuptials of the Marquis Antonio Cavalli with the Countess Clelia Rasponi of Ravenna.
Sonnet, to Genevra.
Sonnet to Lake Leman.
Sonnet to the Prince Regent.
Sonnet, to the Same.
Southey and Wordsworth.
Spell Is Broke, the Charm is Flown, The.
Spirit Pass'd Before Me, A.
Stanzas: "Chill and mirk is the nightly blast."
Stanzas: "Could Love for ever."
Stanzas for Music ("There be none of Beauty's daughters").
Stanzas for Music ("There's not a joy the world can give like that it takes away").
Stanzas for Music ("They say that Hope").
Stanzas: "I heard thy fate without a tear."
Stanzas: "Oh!—my lonely—lonely—lonely Pillow!"
Stanzas: "Through cloudless skies, in silvery sheen."
Stanzas to a Lady on Leaving England.
Stanzas to a Lady, with the Poems of Camoëns.
Stanzas to Augusta.
Stanzas to Jessy.
Stanzas to the Po.
Stanzas Written on the Road between Florence and Pisa.
Strahan, Tonson, Lintot of the Times.
Substitute for an Epitaph.
Sun of the Sleepless!
Sunset over the Aegean.
Swimming.
Tear, The.
There Was a Time, I Need Not Name.
Thou Art Not False, But Thou Art Fickle.
Thoughts for a Speech of Lucifer, in the Tragedy of "Cain."
Thoughts Suggested by a College Examination.
Through Life's Dull Road, So Dim and Dirty.
Thy Days Are Done.
To ———: "But once I dared to lift my eyes."
To ———: "Oh! well I know your subtle Sex."
To a Beautiful Quaker.
To a Knot of Ungenerous Critics.
To a Lady.
To a Lady Who Presented to the Author a Lock of Hair Braided with His Own, and Appointed a Night in December to Meet Him in the Garden.
To a Vain Lady.
To a Youthful Friend.
To an Oak at Newstead.
To Anne.
To Belshazzar.
To Caroline ("Oh when shall the grave hide for ever my sorrow?").
To Caroline ("Think'st thou I saw thy beauteous eyes").
To Caroline ("When I hear you express an affection so warm").
To Caroline ("You say you love, and yet your eye").
To D———.
To Dives (William Beckford). A Fragment.
To E———.
To Eddleston.
To Edward Noel Long, Esq.
To Eliza.
To Emma.
To Florence.
To George, Earl Delawarr.

To Harriet ("Harriet! To see such Circumspection").
To Hook the Reader, You, John Murray.
To Ianthe.
To Lesbia.
To Lord Thurlow.
To M———.
To Marion.
To Mary on Receiving Her Picture.
To M.S.G. ("When I dream that you love me, you'll surely forgive").
To M.S.G. ("Whene'er I view those lips of thine").
To My Son.
To Romance.
To the Author of a Sonnet Beginning " 'Sad Is My Verse,' You Say, 'And Yet No Tear'."
To the Countess of Blessington.
To the Duke of Dorset.
To the Earl of Clare.
To the Hon. Mrs. George Lamb.
To the Same.
To the Sighing Strephon.
To Thyrza.
To Time.
To Woman.
Translation from Anacreon.
Translation from Horace.
Translation from the Medea of Euripides.
Translation of the Epitaph on Virgil and Tibullus.
Translation of the Famous Greek War Song Deute Paides Tov Ellenon.
Translation of the Romaic Song Mpeno mes to periboli, oraiotate chaede, k. t. l.
Two Foscari, The.
Venice.
Verses Found in a Summer-House at Hales-Owen.
Version of Ossian's Address to the Sun, A.
Very Mournful Ballad, A.
Vision of Belshazzar, The.
Vision of Judgment, The.
Waltz, The.
Wandering Outlaw, The.
Well! Thou Art Happy.
Were My Bosom As False As Thou Deem'st It to Be.
Werner; or, The Inheritance.
What Matter the Pangs of a Husband and Father.
What News, What News? Queen Orraca.
When a Man Hath No More Freedom to Fight for at Home.
When Coldness Wraps This Suffering Clay.
When I Roved a Young Highlander.
When Thurlow This Damn'd Nonsense Sent.
When We Two Parted.
Who Kill'd John Keats?
Wild Gazelle, The.
William Lisle Bowles.
Windsor Poetics.
World Is a Bundle of Hay, The.
Would You Go to the House by the True Gate.
Written after Swimming from Sestos to Abydos.
Written in "Letters to an Italian Nun and an English Gentleman: by J.J. Rousseau: Founded on Facts."
You Ask for a "Volume of Nonsense."
Youth, Nature, and Relenting Jove.
Translations, Coauthored Poems, etc.:
Adrian's Address to His Soul When Dying.
Carmina sels.
Divina Commedia sels.
Francesca of Rimini.
Hadrian's Address to His Soul When Dying sels.
Morgante Maggiore, The.
Oh! might I kiss those eyes of fire.
Prophecy.
Translation from Catullus ("Equal to Jove that youth must be").
Translation from Catullus ("Ye Cupids, droop each little head").

Translation from Vittorelli.

C

Campion, Thomas (1567–1620)
Ad Amorem.
Ad ampliss. totius Angliae Cancellarium, Fr. Ba.
Ad Cambricum.
Ad Carolum Fitz Geofridum.
Ad Caspiam.
Ad Castricum.
Ad Chloen.
Ad Ed. Mychelburnum.
Ad Ed. Spencerum.
Ad Ge. Chapmannum.
Ad Graios.
Ad Guil. Camdenum.
Ad Invictissimum Serenissimumque Iacobum *Magnae Britanniae Regem.*
Ad Io. Davisium.
Ad Io. Dolundum.
Ad Leam.
Ad Librum.
Ad Lucium.
Ad Melleam.
Ad Nashum.
Ad nobiliss. virum Gul. Percium.
Ad Rob. Caraeum Equitem Auratum Nobilissimum.
Ad Rusticum.
Ad Thamesin.
Ad Tho. Munsonium, equitem Auratum et Baronetum.
Another Dialogue, To Be Sung at the Same Time.
Are you what your faire lookes expresse?
As by the streames of *Babilon.*
As on a day Sabina fell asleepe.
Author of light, revive my dying spright.
Awake, Awake! [Thou Heavy Sprite].
Awake, thou spring of speaking grace, mute rest becomes not thee.
Ayres that Were Sung and Played, at *Brougham Castle* in *Westmerland*, in the Kings Entertainment, The *sels.*
Ayres that Were Sung and Played, at *Brougham Castle* in *Westmerland*, in the Kings Entertainment, The.
Ballad, A: "Dido was the Carthage Queene."
Bar Not the Door.
Be thou then my beauty named.
Be Wise, and Fly Not.
Beautie Without Love Deformitie.
Beauty, Since You So Much Desire.
Bravely deckt, come forth, bright day.
Breake now my heart and dye! Oh no, she may relent.
Canto Primo.
Canto Secundo.
Canto Tertio.
Canto Quarto.
Canto Quinto.
Come away, arm'd with loves delights.
Come, Cheerful Day!
Come Let Us Sound With Melodie.
Come, you pretty false-eyed wanton [or false-ey'd wanton].
Could my heart more tongues imploy.
Could my poore hart whole worlds of toungs employ.
Dance, The.
De Catullo et Martiale.
De Epigrammate.
De Fran. Draco.
De horologio portabili.
De obitu Phil. Sydnaei equitis aurati generosissimi.
De Regis reditu e Scotia.
Dear If I with Guile.
Description of a Maske: Presented in the Banqueting Roome at *Whitehall*, on Saint Stephens Night Last, at the Marriage of the Right Honourable the Earle of *Somerset:* and the Right Noble the Lady FRANCES *Howard.*

Dialogue Sung the First Night, A.
Dolus.
Eiusdem ad Authorem.
Elegeia I (1595).
Elegia I (1619).
Elegie upon the Untimely Death of Prince *Henry*, An.
Elegye, An: "Constant to none, but ever false to me."
English *Sapphick*, The.
Epigram, An: "Merlin, the great King Arthur being slaine."
Epigram: "None then should through thy beawty, Lawra, pine."
Epigramma: "Haeredem (ut spes est) pariet nova nupta Scot Anglum."
Epigramma: "Quid tu te numeris immisces? anne medentem."
Epigramme: "All in sattin Oteny will be suited."
Epigramme: "All wonders Barnzy speakes, all grosely faind."
Epigramme: "Arthure brooks only those that brooke not him."
Epigramme: "At all thou frankly throwst, while, Frank, thy wife."
Epigramme: "Barnzy stiffly vowes that hees no Cuckold."
Epigramme: "Buffe loves fat vians, fat ale, fat all things."
Epigramme: "Cease, fond wretch, to love, so oft deluded."
Epigramme: "Drue feasts no Puritans; the churles, he saith."
Epigramme: "Drue gives thee money, yet thou thankst not him."
Epigramme: "His late losse the Wiveless Higs in order."
Epigramme: "If fancy can not erre which vertue guides."
Epigramme: "Kate can fancy only berdles husbands."
Epigramme: "Lockly spits apace, the rhewme he cals it."
Epigramme: "Phoebe all the rights Elisa claymeth."
Epigramme: "Smith, by sute divorst, the knowne adultres."
Epigramme: "Thou telst me, Barnzy, Dawson hath a wife."
Epigramme: "Tosts as snakes or as the mortall Henbane."
Epigramme: "What though Harry braggs, let him be noble."
Epigramme: "Why droopst thou, Trefeild? Will Hurst the Banker."
Epigramme: "Wiseman wary lives, yet most secure, A."
Ev'ry Dame affects good fame, what ere her doings be.
Fain Would I Wed.
Faine would I my love disclose.
Faire If You Expect Admiring.
Farewell Song, The.
Fire, fire, fire, fire!
Fire that must flame is with apt fuell fed.
First Love.
Follow Thy Fair Sun[ne] [Unhappy Shadow].
Follow Your Saint [Follow with Accents Sweet].
Full Song, A.
Good men, shew, if you can tell.
Heart's Music.
Her fayre inflaming eyes.
Her rosie cheekes, her ever smiling eyes.
Hide not, sweetest Love, a sight so pleasing.
How eas'ly wert thou chained.
Hymne in Praise of Neptune, A.
I Care Not for These Ladies.
I must complain, yet doe enjoy my Love.
If any hath the heart to kill.
If Love loves truth, then women doe not love.
If thou longst so much to learne (sweet boy) what 'tis to love.
Illustrissimo, Potentissimoque Principi,

Frederico Quinto, Rheni Comiti Palatino, Duci Bavariae, &c.
In Barnum.
In Bretonem.
In Cambrum.
In Crispinum.
In eosdem.
In Honour of the Author by *Tho: Campion* Doctor in Physicke. To the Reader.
In Laurentiam.
In Ligonem.
In Lycium et Clytham.
In Melleam.
In Morachum.
In Nervam.
In obitum Gual. Devoreux fratris clariss. Comitus Essexiae.
In Obitum Hen. Mag. Brit. Principis.
In obitum Iacobi Huissii.
In Pandarum.
In Sannium.
In se.
Incipit Thomas Campianus Medicine Doctor. In Peragrantissimi, Itinerosissimi, *Montiscandentissimique Peditis, Thomae Coryati,* viginti-hebdomadarium *Diarium, sex pedibus gradiens,* partim vero claudicans, Encomiasticon.
It Fell on a Summer's [*or* Sommers] Day [*or* Daie].
Jacke and *Jone,* they thinke no ill.
Kind Are Her Answers.
Kings Good-night, The.
Lamentation, A.
Leave prolonging thy distresse.
Lift up to heav'n, sad wretch, thy heavy spright.
Lighten, heavy hart, thy spright.
Loe, when backe mine eye.
Lords Welcome, sung before the Kings Good-night, The.
Love Me or Not.
Man of Life Upright, The.
Maydes are simple, some men say.
Mistris [*or* Mistress] Since You So Much Desire.
Most sweet and pleasing are thy wayes, O God.
My Life's Delight.
My Love Hath Vowd.
Never love unlesse you can.
Now let her change and spare not.
Now Winter Nights Enlarge.
O deare, that I with thee might live.
O griefe, O spight, to see poore Vertue scorn'd.
O Love, where are thy Shafts, thy Quiver, and thy Bow?
O never to be moved.
O what unhop't for sweet supply!
Observations in the Art of English Poesie *sels.*
Observations in the Art of English Poesie. Of this Ensuing Discourse.
Oft have I sigh'd for him that heares me not.
Out of My Soul's Depth.
Peaceful Western Wind, The.
Peacefull westerne winde the wintrye stormes hath calmde, The.
Pin'd I am, and like to die.
Relation of the Late Royall Entertainment Given by the Right Honourable the Lord *Knowles,* at *Cawsome*-House neere *Redding:* to Our Most *Gracious Queene,* Queene ANNE, *in her* Progresse toward the *Bathe,* upon *the Seven and Eight and Twentie Dayes of Aprill,* A.
Respect my faith, regard my service past.
Rose-cheekt Lawra, come.
Secret Love or Two I Must Confess[e], A.
See Where She Flies.
Seek the Lord.
Shadowes before the shining sunne do vanish.
Shal I come, if I swim? wide are the waves, you see.
Shall I Come, Sweet Love.

Shall I then hope when faith is fled?
Since she, ev'n shee, for whom I liv'd.
Sing a song of joy.
So many loves have I neglected.
So Quicke, So Hot, So Mad is Thy Fond Sute.
So sweet is thy discourse to me.
Some can flatter, some can faine.
Song, A: "Come away; bring thy golden theft."
Song: "Now hath Flora rob'd [or robbed] her bowers."
Song: "Shadowes darkning our intents, The."
Song, The: "Wooe her, and win her, he that can."
Spyres Curten, The.
Stars Dance, The.
Tarry sweete love.
There Is a Garden in Her Face.
There Is None, O None but You.
Think'st thou to seduce me then with words that have no meaning?
Thou Joy'st, Fond Boy.
Though You Are Young [or Yoong].
Though your strangenesse frets my hart.
Thrice Toss[e] These Oaken Ashes in the Air [or Ayre].
To. Campiani Epigramma de Instituto Authoris.
To his sweet Lute *Apollo* sung the motions of the Spheares.
To Music Bent Is My Retired Mind.
To My Honourable Friend, Sr. Thomas Mounson, *Knight and Baronet.*
To My Worthy Friend, Mr. John Mounson, Sonne and Heyre to Sir Thomas Mounson, Knight and Baronet.
To the Most Disconsolate Great Brittaine.
To the Most High and Mighty Prince Charles.
To the Most Illustrious and Mighty Fredericke the Fift, Count Palatine of the Rhein.
To the Most Princely and Vertuous the Lady Elizabeth.
To the Most Puisant and Gratious James King of Great Britaine.
To The Most Sacred King James.
To the Most Sacred Queen Anne.
To the Reader.
To the Right Honourable, Both in Birth and Vertue, Francis, Earle of Cumberland.
To the Right, Noble, and Vertuous, Henry Lord Clifford, Sonne and Heyre to the Right Honourable, Francis, Earle of Cumberland.
To the Right Noble and Vertuous Theophilus Howard, Lorde of Walden, Sonne and Heire to the Right Honorable the Earle of Suffolke.
To the Right Vertuous, and Honorable, the Lord and Lady Hayes.
To the World.
To the Worthy Author.
Turne all thy thoughts to eyes.
Turne Backe You Wanton Flier.
Umbra.
Vaile, love, mine eyes, O hide from me.
Vain Men, Whose Follies.
Verba volant; verum: quid enim velocius illis?
View Mee, Lord.
Were My Heart as Some Men's Are.
What Harvest Half So Sweet Is.
What If a Day [or a Month or a Year].
What is it that all men possesse, among themselves conversing?
What meanes this folly, now to brave it so.
When the God of Merrie Love.
When Thou Must Home.
Where are all thy beauties now, all hearts enchaining? [or harts enchayning?].
Where shall I refuge seeke, if you refuse mee?
Where She Her Sacred Bower Adorns.
Whether away my sweetest deerest?

Why presumes thy pride on that, that must so private be.
Wise men patience never want.
Writer to his Booke, The.
Young and Simple though I Am.
Your Fair[e] Look[e]s Inflame [My Desire].
Translations, Coauthored Poems, etc.:
And would you faine the reason know.
And Would You See My Mistress' Face?
Art Thou That She.
Aye me, that love should natures workes accuse!
Carmina *sels.*
Do Not, Oh, Do Not Prize.
Harden now thy tyred hart, with more than flinty rage.
If I hope, I pine; if I feare, I faint and die.
If I urge my kinde desires.
If she forsake me, I must die.
Kinde in unkindnesse, when will you relent.
Let him that will be free and keep his hart from care.
Long have mine eies gaz'd with delight.
My Dearest Mistress.
My Sweetest Lesbia [Let Us Live and Love].
No grave for woe, yet earth my watrie teares devoures.
Reprove not love, though fondly thou hast lost.
Shall then a traiterous kis or a smile.
Sweete, come againe.
Though far from joy, my sorrowes are as far.
Unlesse there were consent twixt hell and heaven.
What harts content can he finde.
What is a day, what is a yeere.
What Then Is Love But Mourning?
When Laura smiles her sight revives both night and day.

Carew, Thomas (1594?–1640?)
Another [Epitaph on Lady Mary Villiers] ("This little vault, this narrow room").
Another [Epitaph on the Lady Mary Villiers] ("Purest soul that e'er was sent, The").
Another [On the Duke of Buckingham].
Boldness[e] in Love.
Can we not force from widowed poetry.
Carew's Masque *sels.*
Carew's Masque.
Carver. To His Mistress, The.
Celia Bleeding, to the Surgeon.
Celia Singing ("You that think Love can convey").
Celia Singing ("Hark, how my Celia, with the choice").
Coelum Britannicum.
Comparison, The.
Complement, The.
Conquest by Flight.
Cruel Mistress, A.
Dart, The.
Deposition from Love, A.
Disdain Returned.
Divine Love, A.
Divine Mistress, A.
Elegy on the La: Pen: Sent to My Mistress Out of France, An.
Epitaph on the Lady Mary Villiers.
Epitaph on the Lady S.: Wife of Sir W.S.
Eternity of Love Protested.
Fancy, A.
Feminine Honour.
First of Jealousy. Dialogue, The.
First Song, The.
Fly That Flew into My Mistress'[s] Eye, A.
For a Picture Where a Queen Laments over the Tomb of a Slain Knight.
Four Songs, by Way of Chorus To a Play.
Fourth Song, The.
Good Counsel to a Young Maid ("When you the sun-burnt pilgrim see").
Grief Engrossed.
Hymeneall[l] Dialogue, An.
Hymneal Song, on the Nuptials of the Lady Ann Wentworth and the Lord Lovelace.
In Answer of an Elegiacal[l] Letter, Upon the Death of the King of Sweden [from

Aurelian Townsend, Inviting Me to Write on That Subject].
In Praise of His Mistress.
In the Person of a Lady To Her Inconstant Servant.
Incommunicability of Love.
Ingrateful[l] Beauty Threatened.
Lady, Rescued from Death by a Knight, Who in the Instant Leaves Her, Complains Thus, A.
Looking-Glass, A.
Lover, in the Disguise of an Amazon, Is Dearly Beloved of His Mistress, A.
Lover, upon an Accident Necessitating His Departure, Consults with Reason, A.
Love's Courtship.
Love's Force.
Maria Wentworth.
Married Woman, A.
Mediocrity in Love Rejected.
Mistake, The.
Mr. Carew to His Friend.
My Mistress Commanding Me to Return Her Letters.
New Year's Gift. To the King, A.
New Years Gift. To the Queen, A.
New Year's Sacrifice: To Lucinda, A.
Obsequies to the Lady Anne Hay.
On a Damask[e] Rose, Sticking upon a Lady's Breast.
On Mistress N.
On Sight of a Gentlewoman's Face in the Water.
On the Death of Donne.
On the Duke of Buckingham.
On the Marriage of T. K. and C. C.: The Morning Stormy.
Parting, Celia Weeps.
Pastoral[l] Dialogue, A.
Persuasions to Enjoy.
Prayer to the Wind, A.
Protestation [A Sonnet], The.
Rapture, A.
Red and White Roses.
Second Rapture, The.
Second Song, The.
Secrecy [or Secresie] Protested.
Separation of Lovers.
Song, [A]: "Ask[e] me no more where Jove bestows."
Song: Beautiful Mistress, A.
Song: Murdering Beauty.
Spring, The.
Third Song, The.
Tinder, The.
To A. L.; Persuasions [or Perswasions] to Love.
To a Lady, Not Yet Enjoyed by Her Husband.
To a Lady, That Desired I Would Love Her.
To A.D., Unreasonable, Distrustful of Her Own Beauty.
To Ben Jonson.
To Celia, upon Love's Ubiquity.
To Her Again, She Burning in a Fever.
To Her in Absence; a Ship.
To His Jealous Mistress.
To His Mistress.
To His Mistress Retiring in Affection.
To Master W. Montague.
To Mistress Katherine Neville, on Her Green Sickness.
To My Cousin (C.R.) Marrying My Lady (A.).
To my Friend G.N. from Wrest.
To My Friend, Will. Davenant.
To My Honoured Friend, Master Thomas May, Upon His Comedy *The Heir.*
To My Inconstant Mistress [or Mistris].
To My Mistress [or Mistris], I Burning in Love.
To My Mistress[e] in My Absence.
To My Mistress Sitting by a River's Side; an Eddy.
To My Much Honoured Friend, Henry, Lord Carey of Leppington, Upon His Translation of Malvezzi.

To My Rival.
To My Worthy Friend, Master Davenant
   Upon His Excellent Play, *The Just Italian.*
To My Worthy Friend Master George Sands
   [*or* Sandys], on His Translation of the
   Psalms.
To One That Desired to Know My Mistress
   [*or* Mistris].
To One Who, When I Praised My Mistress'
   Beauty, Said I Was Blind.
To Saxham.
To T. H., a Lady Resembling My Mistress.
To the Countess of Anglesey.
To the King, at His Entrance into Saxham:
   By Master John Crofts.
To the New Year [For the Countess of
   Carlisle].
To the Painter.
To the Reader of Master William Davenant's
   Play [*The Wits*].
Tooth-Ache Cured by a Kiss, The.
Truce in Love Intreated.
True Beauty, The.
Upon a Mole in Celia's Bosom.
Upon a Ribbon [*or* Ribband].
Upon Master W. Montague, His Return from
   Travel.
Upon My Lord Chief Justice's Election of
   My Lady Anne Wentworth [*or* A.W.] for
   His Mistress.
Upon Some Alterations in My Mistress, after
   My Departure into France.
Upon the King's Sickness.
Upon the Sickness of E.S.
Willing Prisoner to His Mistress, The.
Translations, Coauthored Poems, etc.:
Eyes of a Blind Man.
Guiltless Inconstant, The.
Hue and Cry, The.
Lips and Eyes.
Methodus Amandi.
On His Mistress[e] Going to Sea.
To His Mistress [*or* Mistris] Confined.

Carroll, Jim (b. 1951)
Ad Man's Daughter, The.
After St. John of the Cross.
Apple at Dawn, An.
At eighteen years of age.
August.
Back Home.
Back to the streets always, ravaged and wet.
Birth and Death of the Sun, The.
Birthday Poem.
Blood Bridge.
Blue Pill, The.
Blue Poles.
Borges Death Mask.
Burning of Bustin's Island, The.
California Poem.
Calm Under Fire.
Caves, The.
Chelsea May.
Child Growing Up with the Sun, A.
Chop Chop.
Cinco de Mayo.
Coda.
Cold Faces.
Compassion.
Cosmopolitan Sense, The.
Cough Syrup.
Crossed Wires.
Dead Salamander's Song.
Desert Casino, The.
Distances, The.
Dog Crunch.
Dresden to Chesapeake Bay.
Dueling the Monkey.
Early Morning Crucifixion, An.
El Hombre del Ombre.
Epiphany.
Eugene, Orgeon.
Evening News.
Fear and Trembling.
Fear of Dreaming.
For Elizabeth.
For Ezra Pound.
For John Donne.

For Robert Smithson.
For Sue's Birthday.
For Your Birthday.
Fragment, A: "When I see a rabbit."
Fragment: Little N.Y. Ode.
Gliding.
Green Bus, The.
Growing Up.
Here I walked with a memory of workers in
   midtown.
Heroes.
Highway Report.
How Relaxed.
I Am Not Kurt Schwitters.
I am trying to abide by the clues.
I drank cough syrup in alcoves.
I have walked these streets so often I could.
I rest with the dogs across the feathers of
   birds.
I stored daylight in secret attics.
I watched a street gang heading.
In Four Seasons.
In midtown again the way you stop.
In the Deep Green Vase.
In the Gears.
In the Valley.
In This Room Particularly.
In Time, AIDS.
Inauguration Day.
Invisible Sleep.
It Doesn't Matter.
It seems I have misplaced the directions for
   childhood.
Jet Fizzle.
Judging the Pageant.
Leaving N.Y.C.
Like a rabid goat, this obsession.
Little Ode on St. Anne's Day.
Living at the Movies.
Loft, The.
Love Poem: "I see myself, sad now, as in a
   mirror."
Love Poem (Later).
Love Rockets.
Love Story.
M. Verdoux, The Wife Killer.
Marked by a more distant sky, I hold.
Maybe I'm Amazed.
Mercury Clouds.
Micky.
Midnight.
Morning.
Moss under your fingernails it feeds, The.
Music Television.
My body has been perforated.
My Debt.
My needs were few and pure.
Narrows, The.
New Death, The.
New Year 1970.
Next Door.
Night Outing, A.
Nightclubbing.
Noiselessly, the world has begun to defect.
Not surprisingly / I lost track of the seasons.
On Susan's Birthday.
On the Rush.
On Tour.
One Flight Up.
Other Garden, The.
Our Desires.
Painting by Flashlight.
Paregoric Babies.
Poem: "I snatch a grape from her breast."
Poem: "It's sad this vision required."
Poem: "My footsteps in the shallow."
Poem on My Son's Birthday.
Poem: "People down / The hallway who,
   The."
Poem: "Some trust the wolf."
Poem: "Tea is boiling, The."
Poem: "This country invades me."
Poem: "We are very much a part of the
   boredom."
Poem: "Yesterday you past / into your lips..
   your hips."
Post-Modernism.

Praying Mantis.
Prell.
Prologue: "Starting with little in mind."
Runners, The.
Saint Theresa.
Savage Bubbles.
Sea Battle.
Seltzer.
Short Reminder, A.
Silver Mirrors.
Sleeplessness.
Some detectives in worn suits slide at my
   door.
Song: "In minute gestures / that jet wetly
   slight."
Song: "It goes, it / Goes."
Styro.
Sure.
Tenth Try, The.
Thick veins on the back of my forearm.
Things That Fly.
3 Short Poems.
To a Poetess.
To the National Endowment for the Arts.
To the Secret Poets of Kansas.
Torn Canvas.
Traffic.
Vacation.
What matter for thick armchairs and fine
   shelves for books?
When he was young in Harlem my father.
Window in Cherry Valley, A.
Wing and Claw.
Winter's Age.
Withdrawal Letter.
Words from Babylon.
Your Daughter.

**"Carroll, Lewis" (Charles Lutwidge Dodgson)
(1832–98)**
Acrostic: A boat, beneath a sunny sky.
Acrostic: "Are you deaf, Father William?"
Acrostic: Around my lonely hearth, to-night.
Acrostic: Dreams, that elude the Waker's
   frenzied grasp—.
Acrostic: Is all our Life, then, but a dream.
Acrostic: Little maidens, when you look.
Acrostic: Love-lighted eyes, that will not
   start.
Acrostic: Maiden, though thy heart may
   quail.
Acrostic: Maidens! if you love the tale.
After Three Days.
Alice's Adventures in Wonderland *sels.*
Alice's Recitation.
As It Fell upon a Day.
Atalanta in Camden-Town.
Bachanalian Ode, A.
Baker's Tale, The.
Beatrice.
Bruno's Song.
Canto I: The Trystyng.
Canto II: Hys Fyve Rules.
Canto III: Scarmoges.
Canto IV: Hys Nouryture.
Canto V: Byckerment.
Canto VI: Dyscomfyture.
Canto VII: Sad Souvenaunce.
Christmas Greetings.
Coronach.
Dedication.
Dedication: "All in the golden afternoon."
Dedication: "Child of the pure unclouded
   brow."
Deserted Parks, The.
Double Acrostic: I sing a place wherein
   agree.
Double Acrostic: Two little girls near London
   dwell.
Dreamland.
Duchess's Lullaby, The.
Echoes.
Elections to the Hebdomadal Council, The.
Evidence Read at the Trial of the Knave of
   Hearts.
Examination Statute.
Faces in the Fire.
Facts.

Fame's Penny-Trumpet.
Father William.
First Voice, The.
Fit the Fifth: The Beaver's Lesson.
Fit the Fourth: The Hunting.
Fit the Seventh: The Banker's Fate.
Fit the Sixth: The Barrister's Dream.
For *The Garland of Rachel.*
Four Riddles.
Game of Fives, A.
Hiawatha's Photographing.
Horrors.
How doth the little crocodile.
Humpty Dumpty's Recitation.
Hunting of the Snark, The.
Jabberwocky.
King-Fisher [*or* King-Fisher's] Song, The.
Lady Muriel's Song.
Lady of the Ladle, The.
Lang Coortin', The.
Lays of Mystery, Imagination, and Humour,
    No. 1: The Palace of Humbug.
Lays of Sorrow, No. 1.
Lays of Sorrow, No. 2.
Lesson in Latin, A.
Limerick, A.
Little Man That Had a Little Gun, The.
Love among the Roses.
Lyceum, The.
Mad Gardener's Song, The.
Mad Hatter's Song, The.
Madrigal: "He shouts amain, he shouts
    again."
Maggie B———.
Maggie's Visit to Oxford.
Majesty of Justice, The.
Matilda Jane.
Melancholetta.
Melodies.
Miss Jones.
Misunderstandings.
Mock Turtle's Song, The: "Beneath the
    waters of the sea."
Mouse's Tale, The ("Fury said...").
Mouse's Tale, The: "We lived beneath the
    mat."
My Fairy.
My Fancy.
New Belfry of Christ Church, Oxford, The.
Nursery Darling, A.
Ode To Damon.
Only a Woman's Hair.
Path of Roses, The.
Peter and Paul.
Phantasmagoria.
Photography Extraordinary.
Pig-Tale, The.
Poeta Fit, Non Nascitur.
Prologue: "Ladies and Gentlemen seems stiff
    and cold."
Prologue to "La Guida Di Bragia."
Prologue: "Wiffie! I'm *sure* that something *is*
    the matter."
Puck Lost and Found.
Punctuality.
Puzzle.
Puzzles.
Puzzles from Wonderland.
Red Queen's Lullaby, The.
Rhyme? and Reason?
Riddle, A.
Rules and Regulations.
Sailor's Wife, The.
Second Voice, The.
She's All My Fancy Painted Him.
Size and Tears.
Solitude.
Solutions.
Song of Love, A.
Stolen Waters.
Sylvie and Bruno *sels.*
Sylvie and Bruno Concluded *sels.*
Tèma con Variazioni.
Third Voice, The.
Those Horrid Hurdy-Gurdies!
Three Badgers, The.
Three Children.

Three Little Maids.
Three Sunsets.
Three Voices, The.
Through the Looking-Glass *sels.*
To M. A. B.
To My Child-Friend.
To My Pupil.
To Three Puzzled Little Girls, from the
    Author.
Turtle Soup.
Two Acrostics: Round the wondrous globe /
    Maidens, if a maid you meet.
Two Brothers, The.
Two Poems to Rachel Daniel.
Two Thieves.
Upon the Lonely Moor.
Valentine, A.
Valley of the Shadow of Death, The.
Vanishing, The.
Walrus and the Carpenter, The.
Wandering Burgess, The.
Warden's Charm, The.
Welcome Queen Alice.
What Tottles Meant.
White Knight's Ballad, The.
White Queen's Riddle, The.
Willow-Tree, The.
Ye Capete Knyghte.
Ye Fattale Cheyse.

Carruth, Hayden (b. 1921)
Abandoned Ranch, Big Bend.
Adolf Eichmann.
Æolian.
Aer.
Afterword: What the Poet Had Written.
Again on dark looms.
Against the wall he / gropes like ivy, you
    pray, I.
Algeria.
Alive.
All my life that's been / the watchword:
    Resist! Resist!
All Things.
Almanach du Printemps Vivarois.
Always this special / secret feeling, the
    failure.
Am I wrong? The roads.
Anent Socrates, or Somebody.
Anima.
Anxious View of a Tree.
Apology for Using the Word "Heart" in Too
    Many Poems, An.
Aqua.
Assignment.
Asylum, The.
August.
August First.
August 14, 1961.
Aw, Dylan, have you left us? Have you
    gone?
Backyard in California, A.
Baler, The.
Bearer, The.
Bears at Raspberry Time.
Because in the heart / of darkness I could not
    see.
Being, The.
Being as Memory, The.
Being as Moment, The.
Being as Prevision, The.
Billie Holiday.
Birds of Vietnam, The.
Birth of Venus, The.
Bitcheries of Madison Avenue, The.
Block.
Bloomingdale Papers, The *sels.*
Book, The.
Bouquet in Dog Time.
Brook, The.
Buddhist Painter Prepares to Paint, The.
Burning Dawn.
Cappadocian Song.
Capper Kaplinski at the North Side Cue
    Club.
Carnations.
Cave Painting.
Chase in Spring, The.

Chicory.
Child, The.
Child's Being, The.
Chronological.
Classical.
Clay Hill Anthology, The *sels.*
Coarse leaf, alder leaf.
Coming Down to the Desert at Lordsburg,
    N.M.
Coming of Snow, The.
Comparative Iconography.
Concerning Necessity.
Continuo.
Contra Mortem.
Cows at Night, The.
Cowshed Blues, The.
Cross My Heart and Hope to Die, It Was the
    Very Same Song Exactly.
Crow's Mark.
Crucifixion.
Dawn. Hoar on the grass.
Death, The.
December now. Winter deepens and darkens.
    Stars.
Dedication in These Days.
Diagnosis is / Anxiety psychoneurosis, The.
Ducks, waking at sea.
"Ecstasy is the / disaster of pleasure": this.
Ecstasy, The.
Ekstase, Alptraum, Schlaf in einem Nest von
    Flammen.
Electroshock. Bang—.
Emergency Haying.
Emptiness—you know.
Essay.
Essay on Death.
Essay on Love.
Essay on Marriage.
Essay on Stone.
Eternal City.
Eternity Blues.
Études de Plusiers Paysages de l'Âme.
Event, The.
Event Itself, The.
Excellence requires / leaf-rakers to sweep one
    spot.
Excursus of Reassurance in Begonia Time,
    An.
Existence Before Essence.
Existing Pool, The.
Expatiation on the Combining of Weathers at
    Thirty-Seventh and Indiana Where the
    Southern More or Less Crosses the Dog,
    An.
Expectantly and fearfully I sing.
Fact of the Matter, The.
Fall, The.
Family Reunion.
Far-removed Mountain Men, The.
Fat Lady, The.
Fathers die, but sons.
Fifth Version, The.
Final Version, The.
First Version, The.
For Papa.
For thon demgeorne dreorigne oft.
For your love given.
Forward! You must. Keep.
Fourth.
Fourth Version, The.
Fragment: "Who can know more deeply than
    I your loneliness there?"
Freedom and Discipline.
French Hill.
Godhulivela.
Gods.
Great Death, The.
Green Mountain Idyl.
Hall Five.
Hard journey—yes, A.
Have you ever seen.
He: Life is an old / casino in the park. I.
Her Dream.
Hey, Basho, you there!
His Dream.
Ho-Hum Again.
Homage to John Lyly and Frankie Newton.

Homecoming.
Horologikos.
How Lewisburg, Pa., Escaped the Avenging Angel.
How To.
I Could Take.
I Know, I Remember, But How Can I Help You.
I know there is a country where we go.
I live where Frost lived.
I Tell You For Several Years of My Madness I Heard the Voice of Lilith Singing in the Trees of Chicago.
Ideas hit life like / planks hitting water. Some skim.
If It Were Not for You.
Ignis.
Imagine bird bones.
Impossible Indispensability of the Ars Poetica, The.
In deep winter the sea roams.
In Memoriam.
In Russia.
In the hot high summer I came.
In Tobey Woods.
Incident of May.
Incorrigible Dirigible, The.
Insomniac Sleeps Well for Once and, The.
Introspectional.
"I've Never Seen Such a Real Hard Time Before": Three-Part Invention.
John Dryden.
Johnny Spain's White Heifer.
Journey to a Known Place.
Joy and Agony of Improvisation, The.
Lady.
Lana.
Language of Flowers, Etc., The.
Last year of youth, The.
Leaf from Mr. Dyer's Woods, A.
Leaves, The.
Let my snow-tracks lead.
Letter to Maxine Sullivan.
Light in the Locust Tree.
Line, The.
Lines Written in an Asylum.
Listen.
Little Death, The.
Little Fire in the Woods, The.
Little Old Funky Homeric Blues for Herm, A.
Living Alone.
Loneliness[: An Outburst of Hexasyllables].
Look, a cypress tree.
Loon on Forrester's Pond, The.
Lost.
Mansion burned. Maids, The.
Marge.
Marshall Washer.
Marvin McCabe.
Master, Grieved with Age, The.
Meadow House.
Meditation in the Presence of "Ostrich Walk."
Metaphysical.
Michigan Water: a Few Riffs before Dawn.
Mild Winter.
Missing the Bo in the Henhouse.
Mix the Ingredients.
Moon, The.
Moonset.
Mother.
Mother, The.
Mountain, The.
Mountain Cabin, The.
Mountain Fastness, The.
Mouse, The.
Museum Piece.
My Father's Face.
My Hut.
My Meadow.
Mythology of Dark and Light, The.
Names.
Naming for Love.
New Hartford.
New Orleans.
Niobe, your tears.

No, I was wrecked here.
No Matter What, After All, and That Beautiful Word So.
No Supervening Thought of Grace.
None.
North Winter.
Not Transhistorical Death, or at Least Not Quite.
Notes from Robin Hill Cottage.
Nothing I, The.
Nothing II, The.
November: Indian Summer.
November Jeans Song.
October. Twilight / flutters like cloth of silver.
Of Brook and Stone.
Of course make love not.
Of Distress Being Humiliated by the Classical Chinese Poets.
Oldest Killed Lake in North America, The.
On a Certain Engagement South of Seoul.
On Being Asked to Write a Poem Against the War in Vietnam.
On Canann Mountain Meadow.
Once and Again.
Once More.
Once on a night in spring.
One ant turns backward.
Ontological Episode of the Asylum.
Opusthirteen.
Out of the garden.
Over and over.
Ovid, Old Buddy, I Would Discourse with You a While.
Pa McCabe.
Paragraphs.
Parting up / down from / one on the shore, two egrets—.
Phantasmagoria, The.
Phone.
Poet, The.
Poetical Abstracts.
Point, The.
Post-Impressionist Susurration for the First of November, 1983, A.
Pray You Young Woman.
President's Speech, The.
Primavera, The.
Purana, Meaning Once Upon a Time.
Questions.
Ravine, The.
Ray.
Re-Acquaintance.
Reflexive.
Regarding Chainsaws.
Renaissance.
Return to Love.
Reversions, always.
Rhopaloceral.
Rimrock, Where It Is.
R.M.D.
Rule of the majority is / strictly enforced in all matters, The.
Rummage.
Sam and Poll Go Back to the City.
Sanskrit root word, The.
Saving Way, The.
Second Version, The.
Septic Tanck.
Sex.
Shadow sprang out, The.
Shake, Well Before Using.
She lay like a book.
Ship, The.
Shirt, britches, paper.
Sigh, you seven seas.
Silence.
Simple.
Sleeping Beauty, The.
Smallish Son, The.
Snow, The.
Sociology of Toyotas and Jade Chrysanthemums, The.
Sometimes When Lovers Lie QuietlyTogether, Unexpectedly One of Them Will Feel the Other's Pulse.
Son, The.

Song: Luxury.
Song of the Two Crows.
Song: So Often, So Long I Have Thought.
Song: So Why Does This Dead Carnation.
Song: "Summer burns on the edges of day."
Song: The Famous Vision of America.
Song: The Old, Old Man.
Song: The Young Man with the Guitar, Testing.
Songs About What Comes Down: The Complete Works of Mr. Septic Tank *sels.*
Sonnet: "All revolutions in modern times have led."
Sonnet: "At the hospital where I had the echocardiagram."
Sonnet: "The Bo was three when we slugged through Arizona."
Sonnet: "But still, still.. / In stillness mystery calls."
Sonnet: "Cindy, I've used my writing all my life."
Sonnet: "Cindy, the secret's out. Yes, you're addict-."
Sonnet: "Dearest, I never knew such loving. There."
Sonnet: "Fear of falling is why the old men walk."
Sonnet: "Freedom in love? It has been questioned. Think."
Sonnet: "From our very high window at the Sheraton."
Sonnet: "Honey, darling, baby..but no endearments."
Sonnet: "How is it, tell me, that this new self can be—."
Sonnet: "The hubbub of the Hall of Languages, our Babel."
Sonnet: "I think continually of the differences."
Sonnet: "I want to do a complaint now. Which is to say."
Sonnet: "If I die today, which statistically speaking."
Sonnet: "If you see a child that shivers when it hears."
Sonnet: "In the mind of the kiss occurs a thought so rich."
Sonnet: "It's said by the thoughtful masters that to know death."
Sonnet: "Key-reist, I am fed and sick unto death with this."
Sonnet: "Last night, I don't know if from habit or intent."
Sonnet: "Like the magnificent stationary animal it is."
Sonnet: "The loving mind in this death-haunted body."
Sonnet: "Most brainy woman, the sexuality of your thought."
Sonnet: "Must genius always struggle, always exaggerate."
Sonnet: "O Jesus, thou who sittest up there on the right."
Sonnet: "Persistent is the thought for me of that."
Sonnet: "Poor little book, *The Sleeping Beauty* died."
Sonnet: Sin.
Sonnet: The Recollected Actual Voices of Romanticism.
Sonnet: "This is our perfect silver maple's day."
Sonnet: "Thy sting sufficeth, Death. If Heidegger first."
Sonnet: "To have been Diogenes. Why not? Or de Sade."
Sonnet: "To rebel is suitable philosophical tactics."
Sonnet: "To rebel. So I have saved my life, not once."
Sonnet: "To see a woman long oppressed by fear."
Sonnet: "To the aged, trembling, illiterate woman yesterday."
Sonnet: "Was Yahweh chosen by the chosen people?"

Sonnet: "Well, Jim says that the couplet at the end."
Sonnet: "Well, she told me I had an aura. 'What?' I said."
Sonnet: "What if the psychologians, those grand old frauds."
Sonnet: "While you stood talking at the counter, cutting."
Sonnet: " 'Whut do you spose thet thing is,' Oi said. 'Whut?' "
Sonnet: "Why complain, brothers, to you, my writing."
Sonnet: "Why extremely do we observe more of."
Sonnet: "Women in anger, it seems, become theatrical."
Sonnet: "The Word for Today is 'panoptic,' which the goddamn."
Sonnet: "Yes. After all my arguments with myself."
Sonnet: "You in a tallness slenderly, as a lone."
Sonnet: "You rose from our embrace and the small light spread."
Sonnets *sels.*
Sorrow Song, The.
Sound of Snow, The.
Sparrows.
Speaking for Them.
Spring 1967.
Spring Notes from Robin Hill.
Steeple bush, hardhack.
Stepping Backward.
Stone, The.
Summer, The.
Summer's Early End at Hudson's Bay.
Sun, The.
"Sure," Said Benny Goodman.
Survival as Tao, Beginning at 5:00 A.M.
Tabula Rasa.
Tanck's Brag.
Tanck's Epilogue.
Tanck's Prolegomenon.
Tanck's Song About Brains.
Tanck's Song About Dying Young.
Tanck's Song About Earl Hines.
Tanck's Song About Fear of Falling.
Tanck's Song About His Birthday.
Tanck's Song About His Unicameral Mind.
Tanck's Song About November.
Tanck's Song About Pride.
Tanck's Song About Silence.
Tanck's Song About Survival.
Tanck's Song About the Jinx.
Tanck's Song About the Transportation Business.
Tanck's Song About the Younger Generation.
Tanck's Song About Women.
Tanck's Song About Youth and Age.
Terra.
That I Had Had Courage When Young.
Thaw.
Thaw, The.
There! Whitman's skull—.
Therefore to us, time's / final lesson: be content.
They Accuse Me of Not Talking.
They gave me in trust.
Third Version, The.
This all begins on a November day.
This Decoration.
This Song.
Three Songs.
'Tis a fine deceit.
To Artemis.
To dig at Luxor, to peer.
To Know in Reverie the Only Phenomenology of the Absolute.
Today my poems seem / only the spells I muttered.
Too Tenuous.
Trees, The.
Trees, the naked trees.
True, I happen. So.
Tsar, who knew you? Who.
Twilight Comes.
Two Romantic Pieces.

Underground the Darkness Is the Light.
Une Présence Absolue.
Unnatural Unselection.
Valentine.
Vermont.
Village, The.
Water, The.
Way of the Conventicle of the Trees, The.
Well, beat on, beat on.
What a Wonder Among the Instruments Is the Walloping Tramboone!
Wheel of Being I, The.
Wheel of Being II, The.
When Howitzers Began.
When I Wrote a Little.
Who Cares, Long as It's B-Flat.
Why speak of the use / of poetry? Poetry.
Wild Swans at Norfolk, The.
Wise child is born, The.
Woman, The.
Woman's Genitals, The.
Women like new brooms.
Woodsmoke at 70.
Words in a Certain Appropriate Mode.
World as Will and Representation, The.
Wreck of the Circus Train, The.
You—Spanish-speaking.
Translations, Coauthored Poems, etc.:
Afternoon of a Faun.

Catullus (Gaius [*or* Caius] Valerius Catullus)
(87–c.54 B.C.)
Carmen 1: "To whom should I present this."
Carmen 2: "Lesbia's sparrow! / Lesbia's plaything!"
Carmen 3: "Who loves beauty / veil her statues."
Carmen 4: "My bean-pod boat you see here."
Carmen 5: "Lesbia / live with me."
Carmen 6: "Your most recent acquisition, Flavius."
Carmen 7: "Curious to learn / how may kiss- / es of your lips."
Carmen 8: "Break off / fallen Catullus."
Carmen 9: "Veraniolus, / first of friends."
Carmen 10: "Alfenus Varus / buttonholes me."
Carmen 11: "Furius, Aurelius, friends of my youth."
Carmen 12: "While everyone else is laughing & drinking."
Carmen 13: "I shall expect / you in to dine."
Carmen 14: "If, my irrepressible Calvus, I didn't."
Carmen 15: "*My love & I* are yours to command."
Carmen 16: "Pedicabo et irrumabo."
Carmen 17: "Cologna Veneta - / where the good folk."
Carmen 18: "I dedicate, I consecrate this grove to thee."
Carmen 21: "Impresario of neediness."
Carmen 22: "I must, Varus, tell you."
Carmen 23: "Friend Furius, / 'who has no slaves & no money'."
Carmen 24: "Best sprig of the clan."
Carmen 25: "From Thallus the pederast."
Carmen 26: "Your cottage, Furius, sheltered."
Carmen 27: "Falernian, / old Falernian!"
Carmen 28: "In Piso's suite / are empty pockets."
Carmen 29: "What man could stomach the sight."
Carmen 30: "Alfenus from Cremona / forsakes the friendship of friends."
Carmen 31: "Apple of islands, Sirmio, & bright peninsulas, set."
Carmen 32: "Call me to you / at siesta."
Carmen 33: "Vibennius & son, renowned."
Carmen 34: "Moving in her radiant care."
Carmen 35: "Fetch, papyrus, / our soft-measured poet."
Carmen 36: "Volusian sheets / shit-shotten Annals."
Carmen 37: "Nine posts, five doors, up the Clivus."
Carmen 38: "Angst, / ennui & angst."

Carmen 39: "Because he has bright white teech, Eg- / natius whips out a."
Carmen 40: "Whatever could have possessed you."
Carmen 41: "Formianus's whore, / long-nosed."
Carmen 42: "From the quarters of the compass."
Carmen 43: "O elegant whore!"
Carmen 44: "It depends who's talking if you're a 'Sabine'."
Carmen 45: "Phyllis Corydon clutched to him."
Carmen 46: "Now spring bursts."
Carmen 47: "Lucius Calpurnius Piso Caesoninus."
Carmen 48: "Iuventius, / were I allowed."
Carmen 49: "Silver-tongued among the sons of Rome."
Carmen 50: "Other day we spent, The."
Carmen 51: "Godlike the man who."
Carmen 52: "Drop dead, Catullus, lie right down & die."
Carmen 53: "I laughed. Calvus. I laughed today."
Carmen 54: "If not by all that his friends boast."
Carmen 55: "Where / if it's not too much to ask."
Carmen 56: "Matter for mirth, Cato, & a smile, A."
Carmen 57: "*Caesar Mamurraque!* / A peerless pair of brazen buggers."
Carmen 058: "Lesbia, our Lesbia, the same old Lesbia."
Carmen 59: "Menenius' wife, / a red-headed cat from Bologna."
Carmen 60: "Hard. Hard. As she-cat whelped in desert mountains."
Carmen 61: "Hill (breeder) of Helicon."
Carmen 62: "Gather young men as the twilight gathers."
Carmen 63: "Plunging towards Phrygia over violent water."
Carmen 64: "In old days / driving through soft waters."
Carmen 65: "Although entangled in prolonged grief."
Carmen 66: "Who scans the bright machinery of the skies."
Carmen 67: "Sweet entrance to a husband's pleasure."
Carmen 68: "Borne down by bitter misfortune."
Carmen 69: "Do not wonder when the wench declines."
Carmen 70: "Lesbia says she'ld rather marry me."
Carmen 71: "If ever anyone / was deservedly plagued by a goat under his armpits."
Carmen 72: "There was a time, Lesbia, when."
Carmen 73: "Cancel, Catullus, the expectancies of friendship."
Carmen 74: "Gellius, / hearing his uncle anathematise the mere mention."
Carmen 75: "Reason blinded by sin, Lesbia."
Carmen 76: "If evocations of past kindness shed."
Carmen 77: "Whom I have trusted to no end (Rufus)."
Carmen 78: "Gallus's brothers possess / one, the most attractive of wives."
Carmen 79: "They nickname Lesbia's brother 'pulcher'."
Carmen 80: "How is it, Gellius."
Carmen 81: "Surely, Iuventius, one of this throng in Rome."
Carmen 82: "My eyes in your pledge, Quintius."
Carmen 83: "Lesbia is extraordinarily vindictive."
Carmen 84: "'*H*advantageous' breathes Arrius heavily."
Carmen 85: "I hate and I love. And if you ask me how."

Carmen 86: "We have heard of Quintia's beauty. To me she is tall, slender."
Carmen 87: "No woman loved, in truth, Lesbia."
Carmen 88: "What, Gellius, of the man."
Carmen 89: "Gellius is thin. / So?"
Carmen 90: "Let there stem (Gellius)."
Carmen 91: "In this hopeless & wasting love of mine."
Carmen 92: "Lesbia loads me night & day with her curses."
Carmen 93: "Utter indifference to your welfare, Caesar."
Carmen 94: "Stuffing, O'Toole naturally stuffs with his tool."
Carmen 95: "Nine harvests & nine winters since its inception."
Carmen 96: "If, Calvus, effects of grief."
Carmen 97: "As God is my witness where is the difference between."
Carmen 98: "Same can be said of you, Victius, The."
Carmen 99: "Purloining while you played in honeyed youth."
Carmen 100: "Undone or done up with love."
Carmen 101: "Journeying over many seas and through many countries."
Carmen 102: "If, Cornelius, we entrust our secrets."
Carmen 103: "Either give me my hundred pounds back, Silo."
Carmen 104: "Do you really believe I could blacken my life."
Carmen 105: "O'Toole / attempting an entry of the *mons Parnassus.*"
Carmen 106: "When an auctioneer's seen with a good-looking boy."
Carmen 107: "If ever anyone anywhere, Lesbia, is looking."
Carmen 108: "If, by general consent, it should be decided."
Carmen 109: "Joy of my life! you tell me this."
Carmen 110: "Men always praise an honest whore."
Carmen 111: "In constancy content with one man, there."
Carmen 112: "Naso! an elevated personage."
Carmen 113: "In The Year of Pompey's First Consulate, Cinna."
Carmen 114: "O'Toole is generally accounted."
Carmen 115: "O'Toole is the proud master of."
Carmen 116: "Conscientiously bringing my mind to bear on this problem."
Carmina.
Hymeneal.

Cedering Fox, Siv see Fox, Siv Cedering

Ceravolo, Joseph (1934–88)
Autumn Break.
Autumn-Time, Wind and the Planet Pluto.
Book of Wild Flowers, The.
Caught in the Swamp.
Chains of Mountains.
Contrast.
Cool Breeze.
Cross Fire.
Dangers of the Journey to the Happy Land.
Data.
Don't Break It.
Down.
Drunken Winter.
Dusk.
Fill and Illumined.
Fire of Myself.
Floating Gardens.
Fly.
Grass.
Green Lake Is Awake, The.
Grow.
Happiness in the Trees.
Heart Feels the Water.
Ho Ho Ho Caribou.
I Like to Collapse.
In My Crib.
Indian Suffering.

It Is Morning.
Lighthouse.
May.
Migratory Noon.
Note from St. Francis.
O gong of wept / O unviolet.
O Heart Uncovered.
Ocean.
Pain Songs.
Passion for the Sky.
Passivation.
Pregnant, I Come.
Red Sun.
Risk.
Route.
Sea Level.
Song of Autumn, A.
Soul in Migration.
Spring.
Spring in This World of Poor Mutts.
Star Song.
Struggling.
Warmth.
Water: How Weather Feels the Cotton Hotels.
White Fish in Reeds.
Wild Provoke of the Endurance Sky.
Wind Is Blowing West, The.

Chaucer, Geoffrey (1340?–1400)
ABC, An.
Against Women Unconstant [or A Ballade against Woman Inconstant].
Anelida and Arcite.
At the Gate.
Balade of Complaint, A.
Bedroom Farce.
Book of the Duchesse, The.
Canon's Yeoman's Prologue, The.
Canon's Yeoman's Tale, The.
Canterbury Tales, The.
Chaucer's Retraction.
Chaucer's Wordes unto Adam, his Owne Scriveyn.
Clerk's Prologue, The.
Clerk's Tale, The.
Complaint of Chaucer to His Purse, The.
Complaint of Mars, The.
Complaint of Troilus, The.
Complaint of Venus, The.
Complaint unto His Lady, A.
Complaint unto Pity, The.
Complaynt d'Amours.
Controlling the Tongue.
Cook's Prologue, The.
Cook's Tale, The.
Death and the Three Revellers.
Dream, The.
Epilogue to the Man of Laws' Tale, The.
Epilogue to the Merchant's Tale.
Epilogue to the Nun's Priest's Tale.
Former Age, The.
Fortune.
Franklin's Prologue, The.
Franklin's Tale, The.
Friar's Prologue, The.
Friar's Tale, The.
General Prologue, The.
Gentilesse.
Go, Little Book ("Go, litel book, go litel myn tragedy").
House of Fame, The.
Introduction to the Franklin's Prologue and Tale.
Introduction to the Man of Law's Tale.
Introduction to the Pardoner's Tale.
Introduction to the Parson's Tale, The.
Introduction to the Squire's Tale.
January and May, or the Merchant's Tale.
Knight's Tale, The.
Lak of Stedfastnesse.
Legend of Good Women, The.
Lenvoy de Chaucer a Bukton.
Love Unfeigned.
Man of Law's Tale, The.
Maniple's Prologue, The.
Maniple's Tale—A Modernization, The.
Maniple's Tale, The.

Merchant's Prologue, The.
Merchant's Tale, The.
Mercile[s] Beaute [or Beautée or Beauty].
Merciless Beauty.
Miller's Prologue, The.
Miller's [or Milleres] Tale, The.
Monk's Tale, The.
Now Welcom[e], Somer [or Summer].
Nun's Priest's Tale, The.
Pardoner's Prologue, The.
Pardoner's Tale, The.
Parlement of Foules, The.
Parson's Prologue, The.
Parson's Tale, The.
Patient Griselda.
Physician's Tale, The.
Prioress' Tale—A Modernization, The.
Prioress's Prologue, The.
Prioress's Tale, The.
Prologue of the Monk's Tale, The.
Prologue of the Nun's Priest's Tale, The.
Prologue of the Prioress's Tale.
Prologue to Sir Thopas.
Proverbs: "What shul these clothes thus manyfold."
Reeve's Prologue, The.
Reeve's Tale, The.
Second Nun's Prologue, The.
Second Nun's Tale, The.
Seven Pilgrims: A Miller.
Seven Pilgrims: A Squire [or Squyer].
Shipman, The ("Parson him answered, 'Benedicite!,' The").
Shipman, The ("Shipman was ther, woning fer by weste, A").
Shipman's Tale, The.
Sir Thopas.
Sorrow of Troilus, The.
Squire's Tale, The.
Summoner's Prologue, The.
Summoner's Tale, The.
Tale of Melibee, The.
This Fresshe Flour.
Three Rioters, The.
To Rosamounde.
Troilus and Criseyde [or Criseide].
Truth.
Two Invocations of the Virgin, I.
Two Invocations of the Virgin, II.
Wife of Bath, The.
Wife of Bath's Prologue, The.
Wife of Bath's Tale, The.
Womanly Noblesse.
Wooing of Criseide, The, III.
Translations, Coauthored Poems, etc.:
Consolation of Philosophy, The ("De Consolacione Philosophie").
Garden of Amour, The.
Happy Too Much.
Heu Quam Precipiti.
Huc omnes pariter.
New Year's Eve.
Romance [or Romaunt] of the Rose, The.

Ciardi, John (1916–86)
Addio.
After Sunday Dinner We Uncles Snooze.
Alec.
Annals.
Apartment with a View, An.
Apology for Not Invoking the Muse, An.
Aspect of the Air, An.
At First Flower of the Easy Day.
Aunt Mary.
Baboon and the State, The.
Back through the Looking Glass to This Side.
Bashing the Babies.
Bedlam Revisited.
Bees and Morning Glories.
Being Called.
Benefits of an Education, The.
Between.
Bicentennial.
Bird in Whatever Name, The.
Birds, Like Thoughts.
Birthday.
Blue Movie.

Box Comes Home, A.
Boy.
Bridal Photo, 1906.
Cal Coolidge and the Co.
Catalpa, The.
Censorship.
Childe Horvald to the Dark Tower Came.
Citation on Retirement.
Come Morning.
Conversation with Leonardo, A.
Craft.
Crate of Sterling Loving Cups, A.
Credibility.
Daemons.
Dialogue with Outer Space.
Differences.
Divorced, Husband Demolishes Home.
Driving across the American Desert and
   Thinking of the Sahara.
Elegy Just in Case.
Elegy: "My father was born with a spade in
   his hand and traded it."
11:02 A.M. The Bird Disappeared.
Encounter.
Epilogue: The Burial of the Last Elder.
Epithalamium at St. Michael's Cemetary.
Evil Eye, The.
Exit Line.
Faces.
Fast As You Can Count to Ten.
Feasts.
Five-Year Step, A.
For Instance.
For Myra out of the Album.
Fragment of a Bas Relief.
Fragment: "To the laboratory then I went.
   What little."
Gift, The.
Goodnight.
Graph, The.
Gulls Land and Cease to Be.
Highest Place in Town, The.
In Place of a Curse.
In the Hole.
Invasion of Sleep Walkers, The.
Island Galaxy, An.
It Took Four Flowerboats to Convoy My
   Father's Black.
January 1.
Joshua on Eighth Avenue.
Keeping.
Knothole in Spent Time, A.
Knowing Bitches.
Lamb, The.
Lung Fish, The.
Machine.
Magus, A.
Measurements.
Memo: Preliminary Draft of a Prayer to God
   the Father.
Memory of the Sad Chair, A.
Men Marry What They Need.
Minus One.
Morning: I Know Perfectly How in a Minute
   You Will Stretch and Smile.
Most Like an Arch This Marriage.
My Tribe.
Naples.
No White Bird Sings.
October 18: Boston.
On a Photo of Sgt. Ciardi a Year Later.
On Flunking a Nice Boy out of School.
On Passion as a Literary Tradition.
On the Orthodoxy and Creed of My Power
   Mower.
On the Patio.
On Wet Iota.
One Dull Thing You Did Was to Die,
   Fletcher, The.
One Jay at a Time.
One Morning.
Poem for Benn's Graduation from High
   School, A.
Poems from Italy.
Prayer to the Mountain, A.
Prologue: Letter to an Indolent Norn.
Requisitioning.

River, The.
Romancing with Our Beasts.
Saturday, March 6.
Scene Twelve: Take Seven.
Sea Burial.
Sea Marshes in Winter.
Selectivity.
Shaft, The.
Size of Song, The.
Song for an Allegorical Play.
Sorrow of Obedience, The.
S.P.Q.R. A Letter from Rome.
Suburban.
Survival in Missouri.
Talking Myself to Sleep at One More Hilton.
Temptation.
Tenzone.
Thanks to a Botanist, A.
Thoughts on Looking into a Thicket.
Thousandth Poem for Dylan Thomas, The.
Three A.M. and Then Five.
Three Views of a Mother.
To a Lovely Lady Gone to Theory.
To Judith Asleep.
To Lucasta, About That War.
Tommy's Pond.
Tree Trimming.
Trying to Feel Something.
Two Egrets.
Two Hours.
Two Saints.
V-J Day.
Was a Man.
Washing Your Feet.
Week That Was, The.
What Was Her Name.

Clare, John (1793–1864)
August.
Badger ("When midnight comes a host of
   dogs and men").
Ballad: "Summer morning is risen."
Bean Field, The.
Braggart.
Child Harold sels.
Clown, The.
Don Juan sels.
Dying Child, The.
Evening.
February: A Thaw.
Gipsies: "Gipsies seek wide sheltering woods
   again, The."
Gipsies: "Snow falls deep; the forest lies
   alone, The."
Grasshoppers.
Hedgehog, The.
I Am.
Impromptu on Winter.
January: A Winters Day.
Lout, The: "For Sunday's play he never
   makes excuse."
Lout, The: "No sort of learning ever hurts his
   head."
Love and Solitude.
Marten.
Merry Maid.
Mole-Catcher, The.
My Mary
Old Man, The.
"Poets are born"—and so are whores—the
   trade is.
Scandal.
Shepherd's [or Shepheards] Calendar, The
   sels.
Song: "Dying gales of sweet even."
Song: "I peeled bits of straw and I got
   switches too."
Song: "Say What Is Love—To Live In
   Vain."
Sonnet: "I love to see the summer beaming
   forth."
Tramp, The.
Turkeys sels.
Turkeys.
Untitled.
Winter Evening.
Young Rabbits.
Translations, Coauthored Poems, etc.:

Parish: A Satire, The.
Village Minstrel, The.
Clark, Tom (b. 1941)
Ace of Destiny.
After the Fire—The Woman.
Afternoons.
Ah—There.
Air.
Ancestors.
Angel's Choice.
Antiquarian.
As the Human Village Prepares for Its
   Fate.
Aubade: "Truck gears grinding up Marin."
Autorotation without Gravity.
Baby Book Fate Dream.
Baseball and Classicism.
Bathed.
"Because They Are Desiring.."
"Before Dawn.."
Birds.
Blue Dress.
Calling Infinity.
Change.
Clemente (1934-1972).
Color of Stepped on Gum, The.
Commanders, The.
Coral.
Crisis on the Savannah.
Crows.
Culebra Cascabel.
Daring to Be the Same.
Dark Continent.
Day Detail—Low Light of Afternoon.
De Ira Dei.
Desert Wars.
Diary of Desert War.
Difference, A.
Domestic Life of Ghosts, The.
Door Gunner to the Moment, (A Shau Valley
   1968), The.
Door to the Forest, The.
Easter Sunday.
Egypt, Everything.
Energy of the Pre-World as a Bungee Cable
   Jumper.
"enforced lapse .., The."
Eos.
Eternity.
Every Day.
Fate.
Fate Spinners in Time-Editing Studio,
   Eternity Blvd., 2 A.M.
Fireflies.
"First cold winter twilights.."
Forty Days.
Garland of Red, A.
Gift of Tongue.
Greeks, The.
"Himself let him unknown contain."
Human Life.
I Was Born to Speak Your Name.
I'm on an Island.
"In the Bond Scandals.."
In the Dark Mountains, Brilliant.
"In This River.."
Lake, The.
Last Poem (after Robert Desnos), The.
Life Notes.
"Like Musical Instruments.."
Love (after La Rochefoucauld).
Lyric, The: "Suffering / lament, sorrow and
   wild."
Magic Arrival No. 7.
Milky Turqoise Cloud.
Millennial Icon.
Mist Sleeve Flight.
Moira.
Moirai, The.
Moira's Messages.
Momentum.
Moodsville.
Motion, 1953.
"My heart in pieces."
My Hypertrophic Devotion.
Narcissism.
Night Patrol.

Nimble Rays of Day Bring Oxygen to Her Blood.
1968.
Nodding.
Now She Dwells Here.
October.
On Marine Silence Street.
One.
Or.
Out of Darkness I Came.
Personal Angel Glimpsed.
Pharoahs Sacrifice Themselves before Her, The.
Pillow.
"Point is Fixed..., A."
Radio.
Realism.
Retro.
Rojo.
Sedge.
Silence of the Lambs, The.
Sky.
Sleepwalker.
Sleepwalker's Fate.
Sleepwalker's Way.
Slow Life.
Somnambulism.
Song of the Drowned Ghost in the Pool's, The.
Sounding Chinese at Inspiration Point.
Spiritual.
Statue.
Suite.
"sun shoots high..", The.
Superballs.
Terminator Too.
Theatre.
Theory of the Universe, A.
Things About You.
Time.
Tire, The.
Trout Kill on the Sacremento.
Up in Here.
"Walked into State.."
West of Eden.
Whistle Buoy.
Withdrawal.
Woodtime.
You (V) (after Holderlin).

Clough, Arthur Hugh (1819–61)
About what sort of thing.
Adam and Eve.
Ah, That I Were Far Away.
Ah, what is love, our love, she said.
Alcaics.
Alteram Partem.
Amours de Voyage.
As, at a railway junction, men.
As one who shoots an arrow overhead.
Assuredly a lively scene.
Away, haunt not thou me.
Because a Lady chose to say.
Bethesda: A Sequel.
Blank Misgivings of a Creature Moving About in Worlds Not Realized.
But that from slow dissolving pomps of dawn.
Claude to Eustace.
Claude to Eustace: "Ah, Let Me Look."
Claude to Eustace—from Bellagio.
Claude to Eustace: "I am in love.."
Claude to Eustace: "Juxtaposition is great."
Claude to Eustace: "No, the Christian faith, as at any rate I understood it."
Claude to Eustace: "Shall we come out of it all.."
Claude to Eustace: "There are two different kinds, I believe, og human attraction."
Claude to Eustace: "These are the facts."
Claude to Eustace: "Tibur is beautiful, too, and the orchard slopes, and the Anio."
Claude to Eustace: "Yes, we are fighting at last, it appears. This morning, as usual."
Clergyman's Second Tale, The.
Come home, come home! and where an home hath he.

Come pleasant thoughts; sweet thoughts, at will.
Currente Calamo.
Dance on, dance on, we see, we see.
Dipsychus [and the Spirit] sels.
Do duty feeling nought and truth believe.
Duty—that's to say, complying.
Easter Day II.
Easter Day. Naples, 1849.
Effusions of a School-Patriarch, The.
Enough, small Room,—though all too true.
Epi-Strauss-ium.
From far and near / He drew the scattered ciphers.
From the contamination / Of laudation.
From thy far sources 'mid mountains airily climbing.
Georgina Trevellyn to Luisa: "At last dearest Louisa, I take my pen to address you."
Georgina Trevellyn to Luisa: "Dearest Louisa, Enquire if you please.."
Go foolish thoughts, and join the throng.
He sate, no stiller stands a rock.
Here have I been these one and twenty years.
Homo Sum, Nihil Humani—.
How in all wonder Columbus got over.
Human spirits saw I on a day, The.
Hymnos Aymnos.
I dreamed a dream: I dreamt that I espied.
I watched them from the window, thy children at their play.
If help there is not, but the Muse.
If to write, rewrite, and write again.
In controversial foul impureness.
In Stratis Viarum I.
In Stratis Viarum II.
In Stratis Viarum III.
In Stratis Viarum IV.
Incident, An.
Irritability unnatural.
It fortifies my soul to know.
July's Farewell.
Juxtaposition.
Latest Decalogue, The.
Light words they were, and lightly, falsely said.
Like one that in a dream would fain arise.
Look you, my simple friend, 'tis one of those.
Mari Magno sels.
Mari Magno I.
Mari Magno II.
Mary Trevellyn to Miss Roper.
My wind is turned to bitter north.
Natura Naturans.
Nay draw not yet the cork, my friend.
O happy they whose hearts receive.
O Heaven, and thou most loving family.
O Qui Me—!
O stream, descending to the sea.
O Theos Meta Sou.
O'Brien, most disconsolate of Men.
Oh, ask not what is love, she said.
Oh, I have done those things that my Soul fears.
Old things need not be therefore true.
Peschiera.
Qua Cursum Ventus.
Qui Laborat, Orat.
Resignation—to Faustus.
Rome ("Rome disappoints me much").
Sa Majestá Très Chrétienne.
Say not the struggle nought [or naught] availeth.
Sectantem levia nervi deficiunt.
See! the faint green tinge from the western sky has.
Seven Sonnets.
Songs in Absence sels.
Sweet streamlet bason! at thy side.
That out of sight is out of mind.
That there are powers above us I admit.
"There is no God," the wicked saith.
These vulgar ways that round me be.
Thesis and Antithesis.
Thou bidd'st me mark how swells with rage.
Thought may well be ever ranging.

To be, be thine.
To spend unsolaced years of pain.
To the Great Metropolis.
To think that men of former days.
Truth is a golden thread seen here and there.
Upon the water in the boat.
Uranus.
Veni.
Were I with you or you with me.
What we, when face to face we see.
When Israel Came Out of Egypt.
When panting sighs the bosom fill.
When soft September brings again.
Whence are ye, vague desires.
Ye flags of Piccadilly, / Where I posted up and down.

"Clout, Colin" see Spenser, Edmund

Cohen, Leonard (b. 1934)
Ain't No Cure for Love.
All My Life.
All Right, Edith.
All There Is to Know about Adolph Eichmann.
Altar, The.
Angelica.
Another Family.
Another Room.
Anthem: "Birds they sang, The."
Any System.
Aquarian Age.
As the Mist Leaves No Scar.
Asthmatic, The.
Avalanche.
Ballad of the Absent Mare.
Be with Me.
Beetle, The.
Believe Me, Edith.
Beneath My Hands.
Beside My Son.
Big World, The.
Bird on the Wire.
Blessed Are You.
Café, The.
Came So Far for Beauty.
Captain, The.
Change, The.
Chelsea Hotel.
Cherry Orchards.
Closing Time.
Coming Back to You.
Commentary—A Working Man.
Commentary—Another Room.
Commentary—Beside My Son.
Commentary—Death to This Book.
Commentary—Final Examination.
Commentary—How to Speak Poetry.
Commentary—Hurry to Your Dinner.
Commentary—It's Probably Spring.
Commentary—My Wife and I.
Commentary—She Has Given Me the Bullet.
Commentary—The Altar.
Commentary—The Asthmatic.
Commentary—The Beetle.
Commentary—The Café.
Commentary—The Change.
Commentary—The News You Really Hate.
Commentary—This Marriage.
Commentary II—This Marriage.
Cross Didn't Fall on Me, A.
Cuckold's Song, The.
Dance Me to the End of Love.
Dark at Four O'Clock.
Days of Kindness.
Death of a Lady's Man.
Death to This Book.
Deep Happiness, A.
Democracy.
Diamonds in the Mine.
Different Drum, A.
Disguises.
Don't Go Home with Your Hard-on.
Dove, The.
Drawer's Condition on November 28, 1961, The.
Dream, The.
Embrace, The.
End of My Life in Art.

Escape, The.
Etiquette.
Event, The.
Every Pebble.
Everybody Knows.
Failure of a Secular Life, The.
Famous Blue Raincoat.
Far from the Soil.
Field Commander Cohen.
Final Examination.
Fingerprints.
First We Take Manhattan.
Flowers That I Left in the Ground, The.
Fly, The.
For Anne.
For E. J. P.
Fragment from a Journal.
French and English.
Friend, When You Speak.
Front Lawn.
Future Night, A.
Future, The.
Gift.
Good Fight, The.
Great Feast in Quebec, A.
Guests, The.
Gypsy Wife, The.
Hallelujah.
Heirloom.
Hey, That's No Way to Say Goodbye.
Hitler.
Holy Is Your Name.
How to Speak Poetry.
Hurry to Your Dinner.
Hydra 1960.
I Am Dying.
I Am Punished.
I Bury My Girlfriend.
I Can't Forget.
I Decided.
I Draw Aside the Curtain.
I Had It for a Moment.
I Have Not Lingered in European
　Monasteries.
I Have Two Bars of Soap.
I Heard My Soul Singing.
I Knelt Beside a Stream.
I Left a Woman.
I Left a Woman Waiting.
I Like the Way You Opposed Me.
I Long to Hold Some Lady.
I Lost My Way.
I Perceived the Outline of Your Breasts.
I See You on a Greek Mattress.
I Stopped to Listen.
I Tried to Leave You.
I Try to Keep in Touch.
I Wanted to Be a Doctor.
I Wonder How Many People in This City.
I'd Like to Read.
If It Be Your Will.
I'm Your Man.
In the Eyes of Men.
Invisible Tonight.
Invisible Trouble, The.
Is This What You Wanted.
Isaiah.
Israel.
It Is All Around Me.
It Is to You I Turn.
It Uses Us!
see also Commentary—It's Probably Spring.
Joan of Arc.
Killers, The.
Kite Is a Victim, A.
Lady Midnight.
Letter.
Light as the Breeze.
Lists, The.
Love Is a Fire.
Lovers.
Magic Is Alive.
Marita.
Marvellous Woman, A.
Master Song.
Memories.
Montreal.

Morning Song.
Morocco.
Music Crept by Us, The.
My Greed.
My Honour.
My Lady Can Sleep.
My Room.
My Teacher.
My Wife and I.
News You Really Hate, The.
Next One, The.
Night Comes On, The.
1967.
Not Going Back.
Not Knowing Where to Go.
Nothing I Can Lose.
O Wife Unmasked.
On Hearing a Name Long Unspoken.
On Seeing Kabir's Poems on Her Dressing
　Table.
One.
One Night I Burned.
One of These Days.
One of Us Cannot Be Wrong.
Only Poem, The.
Opium and Hitler.
Our Lady of Solitude.
Owning Everything.
Paper-Thin Hotel.
Paris Models.
Peace.
Person Who Eats Meat, A.
Petitions.
Photograph, The.
Poem: "I heard of a man."
Poems Don't Love Us Any More, The.
Politics of This Book, The.
Portrait of a Girl.
Prayer for Messiah.
Price of This Book, The.
Promise.
Purest of Occasions.
Queen Victoria and Me.
Reason I Write, The.
Rebellion, The.
Road to Larissa, The.
Rose, The.
Roshi.
Roshi Again.
Seems So Long Ago, Nancy.
She Has Given Me the Bullet.
Singer Must Die, A.
Sisters of Mercy.
Sit Down, Master.
Sky.
Slowly I Married Her.
Snow Is Falling.
So Long, Marianne.
Song for Abraham Klein.
Song for My Assassin.
Song: "I almost went to bed."
Song to Make Me Still.
Stay.
Story of Isaac.
Stranger Song, The.
Streetcars.
Style.
Summer Haiku.
Suzanne [Takes You Down].
Take this Longing.
Take This Waltz (After Lorca).
Teachers.
There Are No Traitors.
There are Some Men.
There Is a War.
These Heroics.
This Is for You.
This Is My Voice.
This Is War.
This Marriage.
This Wretch.
Threat.
To a Fellow Student.
Tower of Song, The.
Traitor, The.
Transmission, The.
Travel.

True Love Leaves No Traces.
Ugly in My Own Eyes.
Unclean Start, The.
Veil, A.
Waiting for the Miracle.
Warning.
Way Back, The.
We Cry Out.
Welcome to These Lines.
What I'm Doing Here.
What Is a Saint.
Wheels, Fireclouds.
When Even The.
When I Have Not Rage.
When I Left the King.
When This American Woman.
Who by Fire?
Why Don't You Try.
Window, The.
Winter Lady.
Woman's Decision, A.
Working Man, A.
Wrong Man, The.
You Do Not Have to Love Me.
You Have No Form.
You Have Sweetened Your Word.
You Have the Lovers.
You Know Who I Am.
You Live like a God.
You Tore Your Shirt.
You Went to Work.
You Who Pour Mercy into Hell.
You Who Question Souls.
Your Death.
Your Eyes.
You're Not Supposed to Be Here.

Coleridge, Samuel Taylor (1772–1834)
Absence.
Ad Lyram.
Ad Vilmum Axiologum.
Addressed to a Young Man of Fortune.
Alice Du Clos.
All Seasons Shall Be Sweet.
Alla Sua Amica.
Angel Visitant, An.
Answer to a Child's Question.
Anthem for the Children of Christ's Hospital.
Apologia pro Vita Sua.
Ballad of the Dark Ladié, The.
Barberry-Tree, The.
Bitter Reflection, A.
Blossoming of the Solitary Date-Tree, The.
Body Imaging Soul.
British Stripling's War-Song, The.
Burke.
Catullian Hendecasyllables.
Character, A.
Character of Wallenstein, The.
Charity in Thought.
Child's Evening Prayer, A.
Christabel.
Christabel and Geraldine.
Christmas Carol, A: "Shepherds went their
　hasty way, The."
Cologne.
Complaint of Ninathóma, The.
Constancy to an Ideal Object.
Day-Dream, A ("My eyes make pictures,
　when they are shut").
Day-Dream, The ("If thou wert here, these
　tears were tears of light").
Death of Wallenstein, The sels.
Death Wish, A.
Dejection; an Ode.
Delinquent Travellers, The.
Desire.
Despair.
Destiny of Nations, The.
Destruction of the Bastile.
Devil's Thoughts, The.
Devonshire Road, A.
Domestic Peace.
Drinking versus Thinking.
Dungeon, The.
Duty Surviving Self-Love.
Eagle and the Tortoise, The.
Effusions.

Elegy Imitated from One of Akenside's Blank-Verse Inscriptions.
Encinctured with a twine of leaves.
Eolian Harp, The.
Epitaph on an Infant.
Epitaph: "Stop, Christian passer-by!—Stop, child of God."
Epitaphium Testamentarium.
Eros aei lalethros hetairos.
Exchange, The.
Exile, An.
Faith, Hope, and Charity.
Fancy in Nubibus.
Farewell to Love.
Fears in Solitude.
Fire, Famine, and Slaughter.
First Advent of Love.
For a Market-Clock.
Forbearance.
Foster-Mother's Tale, The.
Fragment: "O'er the raised earth the gales of evening sigh."
France; an Ode.
Frost at Midnight.
Garden of Boccaccio, The.
Genevieve.
Gentle Look, The.
Good Great Man, The.
Happy Home, The.
Happy Husband, The.
He Prayeth Best.
He Prayeth Well.
Her Thoughts.
Hexameters.
Home-Sick.
Homeless.
Homeric Hexameter, The.
Hope and Time.
Hope and Tranquillity.
Hour When We Shall Meet Again, The.
Human Life; on the Denial of Immortality.
Humility the Mother of Charity.
Hunting Song.
Hymn before Sunrise, in the Vale of Chamouni.
Hymn to the Earth.
Imitated from Ossian.
Imitated from the Welch.
Improvisatore, The.
In the Touch of This Bosom There Worketh a Spell.
Indifference of the Heavens, The.
Inscription for a Fountain on a Heath.
Invocation, An: "Hear, sweet spirit, hear the spell."
Inward Light.
Israel's Lament.
Keepsake, The.
Kiss, The.
Kisses.
Knight's Tomb, The.
Koskiusko.
Kubla Khan; or, A Vision in a Dream.
La Fayette.
Letter to Sara Hutchinson.
Lewti.
Life.
Life in Death.
Limbo.
Lines Composed in a Concert-Room.
Lines Composed While Climbing the Left Ascent of Brockley Coomb, in the County of Somerset, May, 1795.
Lines in the Manner of Spenser.
Lines on a Friend.
Lines on a Portrait of a Lady.
Lines Suggested by the Last Words of Berengarius.
Lines to a Beautiful Spring in a Village.
Lines to a Comic Author, on an Abusive Review.
Lines to Thomas Poole.
Lines Written at the King's Arms, Ross, Formerly the House of the "Man of Ross."
Lines Written in the Album at Elbingerode, in the Har[t]z Forest.
Looking Down on Nether Stowey.

Looking Seaward.
Loss.
Love.
Love and Friendship Opposite.
Love, Hope, and Patience in Education.
Lover's Complaint to His Mistress, A.
Love's Apparition and Evanishment.
Love's Burial-Place.
Love's Sanctuary.
Lunar Entrancement.
Mad Monk, The.
Mahomet.
Mathematical Problem, A.
Melancholy.
Metrical Feet.
Mighty Fountain, A.
Mrs. Siddons.
Monody on the Death of Chatterton.
Moon and the Waves, The.
My Baptismal Birthday [or Birth-Day].
Names.
Ne Plus Ultra.
Netherlands, The.
Night-Mare Death in Life, The.
Night-Scene, The.
Nightingale, The.
Nightingales.
Nose, The.
Not at Home.
O My Mother Isle!
O My Mother Isle! ("Not yet enslaved, not wholly vile").
Ode in the Manner of Anacreon, An.
Ode on the Departing Year.
Ode on the Ottery and Tiverton Church Music.
Ode to Georgiana, Duchess of Devonshire.
Ode to Sleep.
Ode to the Rain, An.
Ode to Tranquillity.
Old Man of the Alps, The.
On a Cataract.
On a Discovery Made Too Late.
On a Late Connubial Rupture in High Life.
On a Ruined House in a Romantic Country.
On a Volunteer Singer.
On an Infant Which Died before Baptism.
On an Insignificant.
On Donne's First Poem.
On Donne's Poetry.
On My Joyful Departure from the Same City.
On Observing a Blossom on the First of February 1796.
On Receiving an Account That His Only Sister's Death Was Inevitable.
On Revisiting the Sea-Shore, after Long Absence.
On Seeing a Youth Affectionately Welcomed by a Sister.
On the Christening of a Friend's Child.
On the Prospect of Establishing a Pantisocracy in America.
Outcast, The.
Ovidian Elegiac Metre, The.
Pains of Sleep, The.
Pang More Sharp Than All, The.
Pantisocracy.
Parliamentary Oscillators.
Perspiration: A Travelling Eclogue.
Phantom.
Phantom or Fact?
Philosophical Trinity, The.
Picture, The.
Pitt.
Pity.
Poetical Epistles.
Presence of Love, The.
Priestley.
Psyche.
Raven, The.
Reason.
Reason for Love's Blindness.
Recantation.
Recollections of Love.
Reflections on Having Left a Place of Retirement.
Religious Musings.

Remorse *sels.*
Reproof and Reply, The.
Rime of the Ancient Mariner, The.
Rose, The.
Sancti Dominici Pallium.
Scars Remaining, The.
Self-Knowledge.
Separation from Asra.
Sigh, The.
Silent City, A.
Silver Thimble, The.
Snow-Drop, The.
Soliloquy on the Full Moon, She Being in a Mad Passion, A.
Some Fragments, Mainly from Manuscripts of 1797–8.
Something Childish, but Very Natural.
Song, ex improviso.
Song: "Sunny shaft did I behold, A."
Song: "Though veiled in spires of myrtle wreath."
Songs of the Pixies.
Sonnet Composed on a Journey Homeward; the Author Having Received Intelligence of the Birth of a Son, 20 September 1796.
Sonnet on Quitting Christ's Hospital.
Sonnet on Receiving a Letter Informing Me of the Birth of a Son.
Sonnet to a Friend Who Asked[,] How I Felt When the Nurse First Presented My Infant to Me.
Sonnet to the River Otter.
Sonnet to William Linley.
Sonnet [to Charles Lloyd].
Sonnets Attempted in the Manner of Contemporary Writers.
Stanger Minstrel, A.
Suicide's Argument, The.
Sunset, A.
Superstition.
Tell's Birth-Place.
This Lime-Tree Bower My Prison.
Thought, A.
Timorous Hind, The.
To a Critic.
To a Friend, in Answer to a Melancholy Letter.
To a Friend [Charles Lamb] Together with an Unfinished Poem.
To a Friend [Charles Lamb] Who Had Declared His Intention of Writing No More Poetry.
To a Gentleman.
To a Lady.
To a Young Ass.
To a Young Friend.
To a Young Lady.
To a Young Lady [Miss Lavinia Poole] on Her Recovery from a Fever.
To an Infant.
To an Unfortunate Woman at the Theatre.
To an Unfortunate Woman Whom the Author Had Known in the Days of Her Innocence.
To Asra.
To Earl Stanhope.
To Fortune.
To Mary Pridham.
To Matilda Betham from a Stranger.
To Mr. Pye.
To Nature.
To One Who Published in Print.
To Richard Brinsley Sheridan, Esq.
To Robert Southey.
To Simplicity.
To the Author of Poems.
To the Author of "The Robbers."
To the Autumnal Moon.
To the Evening Star.
To the Honourable Mr. Erskine.
To the Nightingale.
To the Rev. W. J. Hort.
To the Rev. George Coleridge.
To the Rev. [or Reverend] W. L. Bowles.
To the Young Artist.
To Two Sisters.
To W. Wordsworth.
To William Godwin.

Tombless Epitaph, A.
Translation of a Greek Ode on Astronomy.
Translation of a Passage in Ottfried's
   Metrical Paraphrase of the Gospel.
Traveller through Infinity, The.
Tree of Mystery, The.
Tribute to Wordsworth.
Two Founts, The.
Two Round Spaces on the Tombstone, The.
Uncertainty in Love.
Unity with Nature.
Veil of Light, The.
Veil of Spirit, The.
Verses Addressed to J. Horne Tooke and the
   Company Who Met on 28 June 1796 to
   Celebrate His Poll at the Westminster
   Election.
Verses Trivocular.
Virgin's Cradle-Hymn, The.
Visionary Hope, The.
Visit of the Gods, The.
W. H. *Eheu!*
Wanderings of Cain, The.
Water Ballad.
Wedded Love.
What Is Life?
Wills of the Wisp, The.
Wish, A.
Wish for Dreamful Sleep, A.
With Fielding's *Amelia.*
Work without Hope.
Written after a Walk before Supper.
Written at Shurton Bars, near Bridgewater,
   September 1795, in Answer to a Letter
   from Bristol.
Written in Early Youth, the Time an
   Autumnal Evening.
Youth and Age.
Zapolya *sels.*
Translations, Coauthored Poems, etc.:
Xmas Gift.
Mignon's Song.
Mythology in an Age of Reason.
Piccolomini, The *sels.*
Three Graves, The.
Westphalian Song.

Cooper, Jane (b. 1924)
Acceptances.
After Fever.
After the Bomb Tests.
All These Dreams.
Back.
Bermuda.
Blind Girl.
Blue Anchor, The.
Breslau, November-December 1917.
Breslau, Spring 1918.
Builder of Houses, The.
Circle, a Square, a Triangle and a Ripple of
   Water, A.
Coda.
Conversation by the Body's Light.
Dispossessions.
Door, The.
Earthquake, The.
El Sueño de la Razón.
Eve.
Faithful, The.
Feathers.
Flashboat, The.
Flute Song.
For a Boy Born in Wartime.
For My Mother in Her First Illness, from a
   Window Overlooking Notre Dame.
Gaza.
Graveyard, The.
Holding Out.
Hunger Moon.
In a Room with Picassos.
In Silence Where We Breathe.
In the House of the Dying.
In the Last Few Moments Came the Old
   German Cleaning Woman.
Inheritances.
Jittoku, Buddhist Mystic—15th Century.
Knowledge That Comes through Experience,
   The.

Leaving Water Hyacinths.
Letters.
Little Vesper, A.
Long View from the Suburbs.
March.
Messages.
Meteors.
Middle Age.
Mission with the Night, A.
Morning on the St. John's.
My Young Mother.
Nightmare of the Suburbs, A.
No More Elegies.
Obligations.
Pencil Sketch of Self & Other.
Poetry As Continuity.
Praise.
Racetrack, The.
Rent.
Rock Climbing.
Roman Dream.
Song: "Here I am yours, and here, and here."
Souvenirs.
Suicide Note.
Sundial, The.
Things.
Threads: Rosa Luxemburg from Prison.
Twins.
Waiting.
Weather of Six Mornings, The.
Wronke, Spring 1917.

Cowper, William (1731–1800)
Abuse of the Gospel.
Address to the Mob, An.
Afflictions Sanctified by the Word.
Against Interested Love.
Ah brother Poet! send me of your shade.
Alexander Selkirk.
Annus Memorabilis, 1789.
Another.
Another Version.
Another [Addressed to a Young Lady].
Answer to Stanzas Addressed to Lady
   Hesketh.
Anti-Thelyphthora.
Apology, An.
Attempt at the Manner of Waller, An.
Away goes Sussex William with his pack.
Beau's Reply.
Bee and the Pine-Apple, The.
Bid adieu, my sad heart, bid adieu to thy
   peace.
Boadicea: An Ode.
Card, A.
Castaway, The.
Catharina.
Catharina, the Second Part.
Charity.
Christian, The.
Cock-Fighters Garland.
Colubriad, The.
Comparison, A.
Contentment.
Contrite Heart, The.
Conversation.
Covenant, The.
Delia, th' unkindest girl on earth.
Dependance.
Distressed Travellers, The.
Dog and the Water-Lily, The.
Doves, The.
Ease.
Effeminate Englishmen.
Ephraim Repenting.
Epigram is but a feeble thing, An.
Epigram on the Refusal of the University of
   Oxford to Subscribe to His Translation of
   Homer.
Epigram: "To purify their wine some people
   bleed."
Epigrams on His Garden Shed.
Epistle to a Protestant Lady in France, An.
Epistle to Hill.
Epistle to Lady Austen.
Epistle to Robert Lloyd, Esq., An.
Epitaph, An: "Here lies one, who never
   drew."

Epitaph on a Free but Tame Redbreast.
Epitaph on a Hare.
Epitaph on Dr. Johnson.
Epitaph on Fop.
Epitaph on Mr. Chester.
Epitaph on Mrs. Higgins.
Epitaphium Alterum.
Exhortation to Prayer.
Expostulation.
Fable, A: "Raven, while with glossy breast,
   A."
Faithful Friend, The.
Flatting Mill, The.
For the Poor.
Four Ages, The.
Fragment: "He came to him in the extasy of
   pray'r."
Friendship.
Future Peace and Glory of the Church, The.
Garden, The.
God Made the Country.
Grace and Providence.
Gratitude.
Grief of an Heir, The.
Happy Change, The.
Hatred of Sin.
Heart Healed and Changed by Mercy, The.
Heroism.
Heu! Quam Remotus.
Hidden Life, The.
Hope.
Hope, like the short-liv'd ray that gleams
   awhile.
House of Prayer, The.
How blest the youth whom Fate ordains.
How to Grow Cucumbers.
Human Frailty.
Hymn for the Sunday School at Olney.
I Will Praise the Lord at All Times.
Impromptu ["If John marries Mary, and Mary
   alone"].
Impromptu ["So I have seen the maids in
   vain"].
In a Letter to C.P.
In a Letter to the Same [C. P.].
In Memory of John Thorton.
In Seditionem Horrendum.
Inscription for a Bust of Homer.
Inscription for a Moss-House.
Inscription for a Stone.
Inscription for an Hermitage.
Inscription for the Tomb of Hamilton.
It is a maxim of much weight.
Jehovah-Jesus.
Jehovah-Jireh.
Jehovah-Nissi.
Jehovah Our Righteousness.
Jehovah-Rophi.
Jehovah-Shalom.
Jehovah-Shammah.
Jesus Hasting to Suffer.
John Gilpin.
Joy and Peace in Believing.
Judgment of the Poets, The.
Let Banister now lend his aid.
Letter in Verse.
Light and Glory of the World, The.
Light Shining out of Darkness.
Lily and the Rose, The.
Lines after the Manner of Homer.
Lines for a Memorial of Ashley Cowper.
Lines on Receiving His Mother's Picture.
Lines with Two Cockscombs.
Lines Written During a Period of Insanity.
Lines Written for Miss Patty More.
Lines Written in the Monthly Review.
Lines Written upon a Window-Shutter at
   Weston.
Lively Hope, and Gracious Fear.
Living and a Dead Faith, A.
London Suburbs.
Longing To Be with Christ.
Looking Upwards in a Storm.
Lord Will Happiness Divine, The.
Love Abused.
Love Constraining to Obedience.
Love of the World Reproved, The.

Lovest Thou Me?
Methinnks I see thee decently array'd.
Modern Patriot, The.
Moralizer Corrected, The.
Morning Dream, The.
Mortals around your destin'd heads.
Motto on the King's Clock.
Mourning and Longing.
Mutual Forbearance.
My former hopes are fled.
My pens are all spilt, and my ink-glass is dry.
My Soul Thirsteth for God.
Narrow Way, The.
Needless Alarm, The.
Negro's Complaint, The.
New Convert, The.
Nightingale and Glow-Worm, The.
Not of Works.
O Lord I Will Praise Thee.
O Lord, my best desire fulfil.
Ode on *Sir Charles Grandison.*
Ode on the Marriage of a Friend.
Ode: Secundum Artem, An.
Ode to Apollo.
Ode to Peace.
Of Himself.
Old-Testament Gospel.
Olney Hymns *sels.*
Olney Hymns.
On a Goldfinch Starved to Death in His Cage.
On a Letter of Miss Fanshawe.
On a Mischievous Bull.
On a Mistake in His Translation of Homer.
On a Plant of Virgin's Bower.
On a Review Condemning Thelyphthora.
On a Similar Occasion for the Year 1788.
On a Similar Occasion for the Year 1789.
On a Similar Occasion for the Year 1790.
On a Similar Occasion for the Year 1792.
On a Similar Occasion for the Year 1793.
On a Spaniel Called Beau Killing a Young Bird.
On Flaxman's Penelope.
On Hayley's Portrait.
On Her Endeavoring to Conceal Her Grief at Parting.
On His Approaching Visit to Hayley.
On His Majesty's Sea Bathing.
On His Portrait.
On Loyalty.
On Madan's Answer to Newton.
On Mrs. Montagu's Feather-Hangings.
On Mrs. Throckmorton's Bulfinch.
On One Ignorant and Arrogant.
On Opening a Place for Social Prayer.
On Receiving Hayley's Picture.
On Receiving Heyne's Virgil.
On the Author of Letters on Literature.
On the Biographia Britannica.
On the Burning of Lord Mansfield's Library.
On the Death of a Minister.
On the Death of Russell.
On the Engraver of His Pourtrait.
On the High Price of Fish.
On the Ice Islands Seen Floating in the German Ocean.
On the Loss of the *Royal George.*
On the Promotion of Thurlow.
On the Queens's Visit to London.
On the Receipt of My Mother's Picture out of Norfolk [the Gift of My Cousin Ann Bodham].
On the Same.
On the Shortness of Life.
On Thurlow.
One parson, one poet, one belman, one crier.
Pairing Time Anticipated.
Peace after a Storm.
Philosopher and the King, The.
Pine-Apple and the Bee, The.
Pity for Poor Africans.
Pleading for and with Youth.
Poet, the Oyster, and Sensitive Plant, The.
Poetic Pains.
Poet's New-Year's Gift, The.

Poplar Field, The.
Praise for Faith.
Praise for the Fountain Opened.
Prayer for a Blessing.
Prayer for Children.
Prayer for Patience.
Progress of Error, The.
Prudent Simplicity.
Reading the Newspaper.
Reflection on the Foregoing Ode.
Report of an Adjudged Case.
Retaliation.
Retired Cat, The.
Retirement.
Riddle: "I am just two and two, I am warm, I am cold."
Rose, The.
R.S.S.
R.S.S. Written in a Fit of Illness.
Salad, The.
Sardis.
See Where the Thames, the Purest Stream.
Seeking the Beloved.
Self-Acquaintance.
Shining Light, The.
Shrubbery, The.
Sofa, The.
Song, A: "On the green margin of the brook."
Song, A: "Sparkling eye, the mantling cheek."
Song: "No more shall hapless Celia's ears."
Song of Mercy and Judgment, A.
Song on Peace.
Song: "When all within is peace."
Sonnet Addressed to Mr. Phillips, A.
Sonnet to Henry Cowper.
Sonnet to Mrs. Unwin.
Sonnet to Wilberforce.
Sower, The.
Stanzas on Milton's Remains.
Stanzas Printed on Bills of Mortality 1787–1790, 1792, 1793.
Submission.
Sunset and Sunrise.
Sweet Meat Has Sour Sauce.
Symptoms of Love, The.
Table Talk.
Tale, A: "In Scotland's realm, where trees are few."
Tale, Founded on a Fact, A.
Task, The.
Temptation.
Thanks for a Gift of Pheasants.
This ev'ning, Delia, you and I.
Thunder Storm, A.
Time-piece, The.
Tirocinium; or, A Review of Schools.
To a Friend in Distress.
To a Lady ["Star that beams on Anna's breast, The"].
To a Young Friend.
To a Young Lady Who Stole a Pen.
To Anne Bodham.
To Delia.
To Dr. Austin.
To Dr. Darwin.
To Gravina.
To Hayley.
To John Johnson.
To Lady Austen.
To Mary.
To Miss Creuzé.
To Miss Macartney.
To Mr. Newton.
To Mrs. King.
To Mrs. Newton.
To Mrs. Throckmorton.
To Mr. Newton [on His Return from Ramsgate].
To My Dearest Cousin, on Her Removal of us from Silver End, to Weston.
To Romney.
To Sir John Fenn.
To Sir Joshua Reynolds.
To the Halibut.
To the Nightingale.

To the Rev. Mr. Newton.
To the Rev. William Bull.
To Unwin.
To Warren Hastings.
To William Hayley, Esq.: In Reply to His Solicitation to Write with Him in a Literary Work.
Tom Raban.
Trail of Admiral Keppel, The.
Translation of Epitaph to Northcot.
Translation of Verses to Lloyd.
True and False Comforts.
True Pleasures.
Truth.
Upon a Venerable Rival.
Valediction, The: "Farewell, false hearts! whose best affections fail."
Valley of the Shadow of Death, The.
Vanity of the World.
Verses Written at Bath on Finding the Heel of a Shoe.
Votum.
Waiting Soul, The.
Walking with God.
Welcome Cross.
Welcome to the Table.
When little more than boy in age.
Winter Evening, The.
Winter Morning Walk, The.
Winter Nosegay, The.
Winter Walk at Noon, The.
Wisdom.
Written after Leaving Her at New Burns.
Written in a Quarrel.
Yardley Oak.
Yearly Distress, The.
Translations, Coauthored Poems, etc.:
1.5: "'Twas a long journey lay before us."
1.9: "Saunt'ring along the street one day."
1.38: Simplicity.
2.10: "Receive, dear friend, the truths I teach" ("Rectius vives").
5.12: "You bid me write t' amuse the tedious hours."
Acquiescence of Pure Love, The.
Aeneid [*or* Eneados, *Aeneis*], The *sels.*
Ænigma, An.
Another Translation of the Same Ode.
Another ["Art thou some individual of a kind"].
Another ["At three-score winters' end I died"].
Another ["Miser, traversing his house, A"].
Another ["Painter, this likeness is too strong"].
Another ["Take to thy bosom, gentle earth, a swain"].
Aspirations of the Soul after God.
Avarus et Plutus.
By Callimachus.
By Heraclides.
By Moschus.
By Palladas.
By Philemon.
Cantab, The.
Canzone: "Scoffing, amorous maidens and young men."
Cause Won, The.
Child of God Longing To See Him Beloved, A.
Complimentary Pieces to Milton.
Cottager and His Landlord, The.
Cricket, The.
Denner's Old Woman.
Divine Justice Amiable.
Divine Love Endures No Rival.
Ease is the weary merchant's pray'r.
Elegies *sels.*
Elegy 1: To Charles Diodati.
Elegy 2: On the Death of the Beadle of Cambridge University.
Elegy 3: On the Death of the Bishop of Winchester.
Elegy 4: To Thomas Young.
Elegy 5: On the Coming of Spring.
Elegy 6: To Charles Deodati.

Elegy 7: "Not yet did I know your laws, enticing Amathusia."
Entire Surrender, The.
Epigram, An: "Meles and Mincio, both your urns depress."
Epigram of Homer, An.
Epitaph, An: "My name—my country—what are they to thee."
Familiarity Dangerous.
Figurative Description of the Procedure of Divine Love, A.
From Julianus.
From Menander.
Glory to God Alone.
Glow-worm, The.
God Hides His People.
God Neither Known Nor Loved by the World.
Gratitude and Love to God.
Happy Solitude—Unhappy Men.
Innocent Thief, The.
Invitation to the Redbreast.
Jackdaw, The.
Joy in Martyrdom.
Joy of the Cross, The.
Lepus Multis Amicus.
Living Water.
Love Faithful in the Absence of the Beloved.
Love Increased by Suffering.
Love of God the End of Life, The.
Love Pure and Fervent.
Manual, A.
Maze, The.
Nativity, The.
Nature Unimpaired by Time.
Neapolitan John Baptist Manso, The.
Necessity of Self-Abasement.
No Sorrow Peculiar to the Sufferer.
Ode, An: "Exalt me, Clio, to the skies."
Ode on the Death of a Lady.
Odes sels.
On a Bath.
On a Battered Beauty.
On a Fowler.
On a Good Man.
On a Miser.
On a Similar Character.
On a Thief.
On a True Friend.
On an Infant.
On an Old Woman.
On an Ugly Fellow.
On Envy.
On Female Inconstancy.
On Flatterers.
On Hermocratia.
On Invalids.
On Late-acquired Wealth or Riches.
On Miltiades.
On Niobe.
On Pallas Bathing.
On Pedigree.
On the Astrologers.
On the Death of Damon.
On the Death of the Bishop of Ely.
On the Death of the Vice-Chancellor, a Physician.
On the Grasshopper.
On the Inventor of Guns.
On the Picture of a Sleeping Child.
On the Platonic Idea as Aristotle Understood It.
On the Reed.
see also Watching unto God in the Night-Season.
Papilio et Limax.
Parrot, The.
Perfect Sacrifice, The.
Philosophus et Phasiani.
Psalms sels.
Reciprocal Kindness the Primary Law of Nature.
Repose in God.
Satires sels.
Scenes Favourable to Meditation.

Secrets of Divine Love Are To Be Kept, The.
See'st thou yon mountains laden with deep snow.
Self-Diffidence.
Self-Love and Truth Incompatible.
Silk Worm, The.
Simile Latinised, A.
Simple Trust.
Snail, The.
Sonnet 2: "Charming lady, she whose beautiful name honors."
Sonnet 3: "As on a rugged mountain at the darkening of evening."
Sonnet 4: "Diodati, and I will say it to you with wonder."
Sonnet 5: "In truth your fair eyes, my lady."
Sonnet 6: "Young, gentle, and candid lover that I am."
Soul That Loves God Finds Him Every Where, The.
Sparrows Self-Domesticated.
Strada's Nightingale.
Such were the trophies, that, in earlier days.
Swallow, The.
Tears of a Painter, The.
Testimony of Divine Adoption, The.
Thracian, The.
Thus was Italy mov'd—nor did the chief.
To Babylon's proud waters brought.
To Christina.
To Demosthenis.
To Health.
To His Father.
To John Milton.
To Leonora Singing at Rome.
To Manso.
To Mr. John Milton of London.
To Salzilli, a Roman Poet, Being Ill.
To the Same ["Why, credulous Naples, do you vaunt your clear-voiced Siren"].
To the Swallow.
Translation of a Simile in Paradise Lost.
Translation of Dryden's Poem on Milton.
Translation of Prior's Chloe and Euphelia.
Triumph of Heavenly Love Desired, The.
Truth and Divine Love Rejected by the World.
Vicissitudes Experienced in the Christian Life, The.
Watching unto God in the Night-Season.

Crabbe, George (1754–1832)
Alms-House and Trustees, The.
Ancient Mansion, The.
Arrival of the Players, The.
Borough, The sels.
Condemned Felon, The.
Contented Peasant, The.
Edward Shore.
Election, The.
Ellen.
Frank Courtship, The.
Frenzy.
Lady Barbara; or, The Ghost.
Mother, The.
On Receiving from a Lady a Present of a Ring.
Parish Register, The sels.
Phoebe Dawson.
Poor and Their Dwellings, The.
Posthumous Tales sels.
Richard's Youth.
Rural Life.
Ruth.
Sea: A Summer and Winter View, The.
Sir Eustace Grey.
Smugglers and Poachers.
Tales sels.
Tales of the Hall sels.
Truth in Poetry.
Vicar, The.
Village, The sels.
Wager, The.
World of Dreams, The.

Crane, Hart (1899–1932)
After Jonah.
Air Plant, The.

Alert Pillow..., The.
All This..
America's Plutonic Ecstasies.
And Bees of Paradise.
Annunciations.
At Melville's Tomb.
Atlantis.
Ave Maria.
Bacardi Spreads the Eagle's Wing.
Bathers, The.
Black Tambourine.
Bridge, The.
Bridge of Estador, The.
Broken Tower, The.
By Nilus Once I Knew.
C 33.
Cape Hatteras.
Carmen de Boheme.
Chaplinesque.
Circumstance, The.
Cutty Sark.
Dance, The.
Dust Now Is..
Echoes.
Emblems of Conduct.
Enrich My Resignation.
Episode of Hands.
Eternity.
Euclid Avenue.
Exile.
Fear.
Fernery, The.
For the Marriage of Faustus and Helen.
Forgetfulness.
Garden Abstract.
Great Western Plains, The.
Harbor Dawn, The.
Havana Rose.
Her Eyes Had..
Hieroglyphic.
Hive, The.
Hurricane, The.
I Have That Sure Enclitic.
I Rob My Breast.
Idiot, The.
Imperator Victus.
In a Court.
In Shadow.
Indiana.
Interior.
Interludium.
Island Quarry.
Key West.
Lachrymae Christi.
Legend.
Legende.
Mango Tree, The.
March.
Masters, The.
Meditation.
Medusa.
Mermen, The.
Modern Craft.
Moment Fugue.
Moth That Made God Blind, The.
My Grandmother's Love Letters.
Name for All, A.
National Winter Garden.
North Labrador.
O Carib Isle!
O Moon, Thou Cool..
October-November.
Of an Evening Pulling Off a Little Experience (with the english language).
Old Song.
Paraphrase.
Passage.
Pastorale.
Persuasion, A.
Pillar and the Post, The.
Porphyro in Akron.
Possessions.
Postscript.
Postscript, A.
Powhatan's Daughter.
Praise for an Urn.
Purgatorio.

Quaker Hill.
Recitative.
Repose of Rivers.
River, The.
Royal Palm.
Sad Indian, The.
Sea Raised Up..., The.
Shall I Subsume..
So Dream Thy Sails..
Song for Happy Feast Days, A.
Sonnet: "Ere elfish Night shall sift another
　day."
Southern Cross.
Stark Major.
Sunday Morning Apples.
Supplication to the Muses on a Trying Day.
Tenderness and Resolution.
There Are the Local..
They Were There..
This Way Where November..
Thou Canst Read Nothing..
Three Locutions Des Pierrots.
Three Songs.
Time Cannot Be Worn..
To Brooklyn Bridge.
To Conquer Variety.
To Earth.
To Emily Dickinson.
To Liberty.
To Portapovitch.
To Shakespeare.
To the Cloud Juggler.
To the Empress Josephine's Statue.
Traveller Born, A.
Tunnel, The.
Van Winkle.
Virginia.
Visible the Untrue, The.
Voyages.
Well/Well/Not-At-All.
What Nots?
Wine Menagerie, The.
With a Photograph to Zell, Now Bound for
　Spain.
You Are That Frail..

Crashaw, Richard (1613?–1649)
Act 5; Sicke Implore St. Peter's Shadow,
　The.
Acts 8; On the Baptized Æthiopian.
Acts 21; I Am Ready Not Onely To Be
　Bound but To Dye.
Adoro Te. The Hymn of Saint Thomas in
　Adoration of the Blessed Sacrament.
Alexias.
Another on [Mr. Herrys].
Apology [or Apologie] for the Foregoing
　Hymn[e], An.
Authors Motto, The.
But Men loved Darkness[e] Rather Than [or
　Then] Light.
But Now They Have Seen, and Hated.
C[h]aritas Nimia; or, The Dear[e] Bargain.
Christs Victory.
Come we shepheards whose blest sight.
Compline.
Death's Lecture.
Description of a Religious House and
　Condition of Life.
Easter Day.
Elegie on the Death of Doctor Porter, An.
Elegy upon the Death of Mr. Stanninow
　Fellow of Queenes Colledge.
Epitaph upon a Young Married Couple, An.
Epitaph. Upon Doctor Brooke, An.
Epitaph upon Mr. Ashton, a Conformable
　Citizen, An.
Epithalamium: "Come virgin Tapers of pure
　waxe."
Evensong.
Flaming Heart, The.
For the Hour of Prime.
Howres for the Hours of Matines, The.
Hymn for New Year's Day.
Hymn in the Assumption.
Hymn in the Glorious Epiphanie.
Hymn to Sainte Teresa, A.

Hymn to the Name and Hono[u]r of the
　Admirable Saint[e] T[h]eresa, A.
Hymne of the Nativity, Sung by the
　Shepheards, A.
I Am the Doore.
In Amorem Divinum.
In Cicatrices Domini Jesu.
It Is Better To Go into Heaven with One
　Eye.
Lauda Sion Salvatorem.
Letter to the Countess of Denbigh.
Love's Horoscope.
[Mr. Herrys,] His Epitaph.
Music[k]'s Duel[l].
O Gloriosa Domina.
Ode on a Prayer-Book.
On a Foule Morning, Being Then to Take a
　Journey.
On Marriage.
On Mr. G. Herberts Booke, The Temple.
On Our Crucified Lord Naked, and Bloody.
On St. *Peter* Casting Away His Nets at Our
　Saviours Call.
On Saint Peter Cutting of Malchus His Eare.
On Taking Physicke.
On the Bleeding Wounds of Our Crucified
　Lord.
On the Blessed Virgins Bashfulnesse.
On the Frontispiece of Isaacsons Chronologie
　Explained.
On the Gunpowder-Treason.
On the Miracle of Loaves.
On the Miracle of Multiplied [or Multiplyed]
　Loaves.
On the Still Surviving Markes of Our
　Saviours Wounds.
On the Water of Our Lord's Baptism[e].
On the Wounds of Our Crucified Lord.
Our Lord in His Circumcision to His Father.
Out of Euphormio.
Out of *Grotius* his Tragedy of *Christes*
　Sufferinges.
Out of the Italian; a Song.
Prayer, A.
Psalmus 1.
Recommendation, The.
Samson to His De[ora]lilah.
Sancta Maria Dolorum.
Shepherds' Hymn, The.
Shepherd's Hymn, The ("We saw Thee in
　Thy balmy nest").
Specifications for a Perfect Lover.
Tear[e], The.
To [Mrs. M. R.] Councel Concerning Her
　Choise.
To Our Lord, upon the Water Made Wine.
To Pontius Washing His Blood-Stained
　Hands.
To Pontius Washing His Hands.
To the Infant Martyrs.
To the Morning. Satisfaction for Sleepe.
To the Name above Every Name, the Name
　of Jesus, a Hymn.
To the Queen, an Apologie for the Length of
　the Following Panegyricke.
To the Queen, Upon her Numerous Progeny,
　a Panegyricke.
To the Queen's Majesty.
Two Went Up into the Temple To Pray.
Upon Bishop Andrewes's [or Andrewes His]
　Picture before His Sermons.
Upon Ford's Two Tragedies, "Loves
　Sacrifice" and "The Broken Heart."
Upon Lazarus His Teares.
Upon Our Saviour's Tomb[e] Wherein Never
　Man Was Laid.
Upon the Asse That Bore Our Saviour.
Upon the birth of the Princesse Elizabeth.
Upon the Death of a Freind.
Upon the Death of a Gentleman.
Upon the Death of Mister Herrys.
Upon the Death of the Most Desired Mister
　Herrys.
Upon the Ensuing Treatises [of Mr.
　Shelford].
Upon the Faire Ethiopian Sent to a
　Gentlewoman.

Upon the Gunpowder Treason ("Grow
　plumpe, leane Death").
Upon the Gunpowder Treason ("Reach me a
　quill").
Upon the Infant Martyrs.
Upon the Kings Coronation ("Sound forth,
　cælestiall Organs, lett heavens quire").
Upon the Kings Coronation ("Strange
　Metamorphosis! It was but now").
Upon the Powder Day.
Upon the Sepulchre of our Lord.
Upon the Thornes Taken Downe from Our
　Lords Head Bloody.
Upon Two Greene Apricockes Sent to
　Cowley by Sir Crashaw.
Vexilla Regis.
Weeper, The.
Widow[e]'s Mites, The.
Wishes. To His (Supposed) Mistresse.
With a Picture Sent to a Friend.
[With Some Poems Sent to a Gentlewoman.
　I].
[With Some Poems Sent to a Gentlewoman.
　II].
Translations, Coauthored Poems, etc.:
Beginning of Heliodorus, The.
Dies Irae.
Georgics *sels.*
Happy me! o happy sheepe!
John 3; But Men Loved Darknesse Rather
　than Light.
John 15; Upon Our Lords Last Comfortable
　Discourse with His Disciples.
John 16; Verily I Say unto You, Yee Shall
　Weep and Lament.
Luke 2; Quærit Jesum Suum Maria.
Luke 7; She Began To Wash His Feet with
　Teares and Wipe Them with the Haires of
　Her Head.
Luke 10; And a Certaine Priest Comming
　that Way Looked on Him and Passed by.
Luke 11; Blessed Be the Paps Which Thou
　Hast Sucked.
Luke 11; Upon the Dumbe Devill Cast Out,
　and the Slanderous Jewes Put to Silence.
Luke 15; On the Prodigall.
Luke 16; Dives *Asking a Drop.*
Mark 4; Why Are Yee Afraid, O Yee of
　Little Faith?
Mark 7; The Dumbe Healed, and the People
　Enjoyed Silence.
Mark 10; The Blind Cured by the Word of
　Our Saviour.
Mark 12; (Give to Cæsar———) (And to
　God———).
Matthew 8; I Am Not Worthy that Thou
　Should'st Come Under my Roofe.
Matthew 16:25; Whosoever Shall Loose His
　Life.
Matthew 22; Neither Durst Any Man from
　that Day Aske Him Any More Questions.
Matthew 23; Yee Build the Sepulchres of the
　Prophets.
Matthew 27; And He Answered Them
　Nothing.
Matthew 28; Come See the Place where the
　Lord Lay.
Mistress, The *sels.*
Odes *sels.*
On Hope.
On Nanus Mounted on an Ant.
On the proud banks of great Euphrates'
　flood.
Out of Catullus.
Out of Horace.
Out of Martiall.
Out of Petronius.
Out of the Greeke Cupid's Cryer.
Out of the Italain.
Out of the Italian.
Out of Virgil, in the Praise of the Spring.
Psalms *sels.*
Sospetto d'Herode.
St. John *sels.*
St. Luke *sels.*
St. Mark *sels.*
St. Matthew *sels.*

Strage degli innocenti, La *sels.*
Upon the Same.
Upon Venus Putting on Mars His Armes.

Creeley, Robert (b. 1926)
A.
Act of Love, The.
After Lorca.
After Mallarmé.
Again.
Agh—man / thinks.
Air: "Cat Bird Singing."
Air: "The Love of a Woman."
Alba.
Alice.
All around / the town.
All That Is Lovely in Men.
All the fantasies that.
All this flesh, meat.
America.
And.
Anger.
Animal, The.
Answer, The.
Anywhere.
Apology, The.
Apple Uppfle.
As Now It Would Be Snow.
As real as thinking.
As We Sit.
As You Come.
Awakening, The.
Away.
B——.
Backwards.
Ball Game, The.
Ballad, A: "We have a song for the death in
    her body."
Ballad of the Despairing Husband.
Bed, The.
Berlin: First Night & Early Morning.
Billfold.
Bird, The.
Bird, the Bird, the Bird, The.
Birds, The.
Birthday, A.
Blesséd water, blesséd man..
Blue.
Bobbie.
"Bolinas and Me.."
Box, The.
Boy, the.
Bringing you back here—.
Broken Back Blues.
Business, The.
But.
But You.
Can feel it in the pushing.
Canada.
Cantos, The.
Canzone: "As would any sound make."
Car / moving / the hill / down, The.
Car, The.
Carnival, The.
Chance, The.
Change.
Changes, The.
Chanson.
Characteristically.
Charm, The.
Chasing the Bird.
Chicago.
Christmas: May 10, 1970.
Circle.
Circle, The.
Citizen.
City, The.
Colors.
Comfort.
Conspiracy, The.
Continuing forward with a trembling.
Could write of fucking—.
Counterpoint, A.
Crisis, The.
Crow, The.
Curse.
Damon & Pythias.
Dancing.

Day comes and goes, The.
Day was gathered on waking, The.
Days and Days.
Days in the train, a.
Days later—neither having.
Dead in the year—.
Dear Dorothy.
Death of / one is, The.
Death of Venus, The.
Delight dances.
"Dicky the Stick"—.
Diction.
Dimensions.
Disappointment, The.
Dishonest Mailmen, The.
Distance.
Divisions.
"Do You Think.."
Don't Sign Anything.
Door, The.
Down Home.
Dream, The.
Dreams.
Dreary, heavy / accumulation.
Drums, The.
Dying.
Ear, The.
Easter.
Echo.
Echo Of.
Echoes.
Edge, The.
End of the Day, The.
End, The.
Enough.
Entre Nous.
Envoi: "Particulars they want."
Epic Expands, The.
Epigraph: "Lot's wife, / married to chance."
Eros.
Europeans, The.
Every Day.
Eye, The.
Fall.
Falling.
Falling downhill—.
Family, The.
Fancy.
Fantasies / indulged, great.
Farm, The.
Festival, The.
Figures, The.
"Fine China".
Finger, The.
Fire.
Fire, The.
First / time is / the first, The.
First Time, The.
Flesh.
Flesh's / signals.
Flower, The.
Flowers.
Folk Song, A: "Hitch up honey for the /
    market race all."
"Follow the Drinking Gourd.."
For a Bus on Its Side and the Man Inside It.
For a Friend.
For a Screaming Lady.
For Allen.
For an Anniversary.
For Anybody.
For Arthur Okamura.
For Benny and Sabina.
For Betsy and Tom.
For Chuck Hinman.
For days neglected.
For Ebbe.
For Fear.
For Friendship.
For Helen.
For Irving.
For Joel.
For Leslie.
For Lewis, to Say It.
For Love.
For Marisol.
For Martin.

For My Mother: Genevieve Jules Creeley.
For No Clear Reason.
For Rainer Gerhardt.
"For Some Weeks.."
For Somebody's Marriage.
For the Graduation.
For the Graduation: Bolinas, 1972.
For the New Year.
For Tom.
For Walter Chappell.
For W.C.W. ("Pleasure of the wit sustains,
    The").
For W.C.W. ("Rhyme is after, The").
For You.
Form of Adaptation, A.
Form of Women, A.
Forms' passage as.
Four.
Fragment, A: "On the street I am met with
    constant hostility."
Fragments: "Decorous, and forbearing further
    correction."
Friend, The.
Friends, The.
From Pico & the Women: A Life.
Funny.
Gangster.
Gemini.
Gesture, The.
Get it anyway.
Gift of Great Value, A.
Gift, The.
Going.
Going to Bed.
Goodbye.
Greendoon's Song.
Guido, i' vorrei che tu e Lapo ed io.
Hands, The.
Happy love, this.
Happy Man, The.
Harry.
Hart Crane.
Hart Crane 2.
Having to— / what do I think.
Heaven.
Hélas.
Hello.
Herd, The.
Here.
Here Again.
Hero.
Hero, The.
Heroes.
Hey.
Hi There!
Hill, The.
Hole, The.
Home.
House, The.
How that fact of.
How wise age is—.
Hunger.
I.
I Am Held by My Fear of Death.
I cannot see you.
I can't / for this variance.
I don't hate you lately.
"I Keep to Myself Such Measures."
I Know a Man.
I want to fuck you.
I was never so upset.
Ice Cream.
If You.
Illness, An.
Immoral Proposition, The.
In a Boat Shed.
In an Act of Pity.
In London.
In secret / the out's in—.
In the / mouth—a.
In the Fall.
In the house of.
Indians.
Innocence, The.
Insistent / this yearning / toward.
Intervals.
Interview, The.

Invitation, The.
Invoice, The.
Irish.
Irishman's Lament on the Approaching
    Winter, An.
It Is at Times.
It is funny—strange—to see the young.
Jack's Blues.
Je Vois dans le Hasard Tous les Biens Que
    J'espere.
Joke, The.
Joy.
Juggler's Thought.
June 6, 1970.
Just Friends.
Kate's.
Kick / of the foot against..., The.
Kid.
Kid, The.
Kids walking beach.
Kiki.
Kind of Act Of, The.
Kitchen.
Knokke.
Kore.
La Noche.
Lady Bird.
Lady in Black.
Language, The.
Last sweet night, The.
Late Comer, The.
Laughing.
Le Fou.
Let something else be / the question—.
Letter, The.
Like a man committed to searching.
Like They Say.
Lion and the Dog, The.
Listless, / the heat rises—.
Little Time—and Place.
Littleton, N.H.
Look.
Looking for a way.
Looking Out.
Loop, A.
Los Guitaristas.
Love— / let it / Out, / open up.
Love Comes Quietly.
Love ("Not enough. The question: what is").
Love ("Thing comes / of itself, The").
Love ("Tracking through this").
Lover, The.
Love's faint trace..
Man, The.
Marriage, A.
Mary's Fancy.
Massachusetts.
Master of All.
Measure, The.
Mechanic, The.
Medallion.
Memory, The.
Men in my life were, The.
Menu, The.
Message, The.
Messengers, The.
Method, A.
Method of Actuality, The.
Midnight.
Mind's Heart.
Mirror, The.
Mobile Homes.
Moment.
Moon, The.
Mountains in the Desert, The.
Mouths Nuzz.
My Love.
Name, The.
Names.
Names, The.
Nathaniel Hawthorne.
Naughty Boy.
Neither sadness nor desire.
New Year's.
News, The.
Night.
Night in NYC.

Night Sky, A.
1971.
No.
No clouds out the window.
Not Again.
Not Now.
Note read re / letter of Lawrence's.
Now Then.
Now there is.
Numbers.
NYC—.
Obscene Poem, An.
Of Years.
Oh, Love.
Oh Mabel.
"Oh My Love.."
Oh No.
Old Song.
On Acid.
On Vacation.
One Day.
One thing / done, the.
One Way.
One/the Sun/ / Moon/one.
Operation, The.
Out.
Out of Sight.
Pacing as with some consequent.
Paradox, The.
Passage, The.
Pattern, The.
Pay.
Peace.
Pedigree, The.
Penitent, The.
People.
People, The.
People without their own scene.
Person.
Persons.
Phone.
Photo.
Picnic, The.
Picture, A.
Piece, A.
Pieces.
Pieces of cake crumbling.
Place.
Place, A.
Place, The.
Places.
Plan Is the Body, The.
Plan, The.
Please.
Pleasures of pain.
Poem, A: "If the water forms."
Poem for Beginners.
Poem for Bob Leed.
Poem for D. H. Lawrence.
Pool, The.
Post Cards.
Prejudice, The.
Pretension's.
Problem, The.
Province, The.
Pryaer, A.
Puritan Ethos, The.
Question, The.
Quick-Step.
Quick talk / their speech—.
Rain, The.
Rain ("Things one sees through").
Rain (2) ("Thoughtful of you, I was /
    anticipating change in").
Re C—.
Reason, A.
Rescue, The.
Return.
Revelation, The.
Rhyme, The.
Rhythm, The.
Riddle, The.
Rippling eyelids.
Rites, The.
Roads.
Rocks, The.
Rose, The.

Saints, The.
Same.
Sanine to Leda.
Saturday Afternoon.
Sea.
Sea, The.
Sentence, The.
Shame, The.
She Went to Stay.
Shot.
Sick.
Sight, A.
Sign.
Sign Board, The.
Sing Song.
Sitting Here.
Sitting up to fill pages.
Situation of feeling increasingly.
Skeleton, The.
Sleep.
Slow slowing—.
Smell of gum wrappers as of Saturday
    afternoon at movies.
Smell of stale air, The.
Smells, / sounds.
Smoke.
Snow, The.
So Big.
So-called poet of love, The.
So sweet / the body.
So tired.
Some Afternoon.
Some Echoes.
Some nights, a fearful.
Some Place.
Somebody Died.
Something.
Something for Easter.
Somewhere.
Song: "What I took in my hand."
Song, A: "I had wanted a quiet testament."
Song: "God give you pardon from gratitue."
Song: "Grit / of things, The."
Song: "How simply / for another."
Song: "I wouldn't / embarrass you."
Song, The: "It still makes sense."
Song: "Those rivers run from that land."
Song: "Were I myself more blithe."
Song: "What do you / want, love. To be."
Song: "You look out and you see people."
Sopa.
Sound.
Sounds.
Soup.
Souvenir, The.
Spring.
Statue, The.
Step, A.
Still.
Still Life Or.
Stomping with Catullus.
Story, The.
Such strangeness of mind I know.
Sunset.
Surf: An Elegy, The.
Surgeons.
Sweet, sad / nostalgia—.
Swinging Down Central.
Tally, A.
Teachings, The.
Temper, The.
Testament, A.
Than I.
Thank You.
That day / in an oak tree—.
The.
"There.."
There.
There Is.
There is a space / of trees—.
They.
They Say.
They (2).
Think.
Thinking.
3 in 1.
Three Ladies, The.

Tiger, The.
Time.
"Time" is some sort of hindsight.
Time, The.
Time to go.
Tiny Place, A.
To And.
To Bobbie.
To the One in the Gray Coat.
"To Work Is to Contradict Contradictions, to Do Violence to Natural Violence.."
Token, A.
Total Parts of a World, The.
Trap, The.
Traveller, The.
Trees.
Tunnel, The.
Turn, The.
Two.
Two Times ("Image / docteur").
Two Times ("It takes so long to look down").
Two Ways of Looking in a Mirror.
Up in the Air.
Variation, A.
Variations.
Wait for Me.
Waiting.
Walking.
Walking the Dog.
Wall / one's up against, The.
Wall, A.
Walls.
Wanting You.
Warning, The.
Was.
Water.
Water Music.
Water (2).
Way.
Way, The.
We'll die / soon enough.
What / do you think it is.
What is love—.
What's for Dinner.
What's to be said.
When he and I.
Where we are there must.
Which it / was, form, The.
Whip, The.
Why say to them.
Wicker Basket, A.
Wife, The.
Wind, The.
Window, The.
Wisdom.
Wish, A.
Woman, The.
Women, The.
Words.
World, The.
Xmas.
Xmas Poem: Bolinas.
Yellow.
You.
You have nor face nor hands.
You haven't / fucked for months now.
You see the jerked.
You think in the circle.
You will never be here.
Young Woman.
"Your wish came true."
"You've Tried the World, Try Jesus."

Cullen, Countee (1903–46)
Advice to a Beauty.
After a Visit.
Any Human to Another.
Apostrophe to the Land.
At a Parting.
At the Wailing Wall in Jerusalem.
Atlantic City Waiter.
Ballad of the Brown Girl, The.
Black Christ, The.
Black Magdalens.
Black Majesty.
Bright Bindings.
Brown Boy to Brown Girl.

Brown Girl Dead, A.
Christus Natus Est.
Colored Blues Singer.
Colors.
Cor Cordium.
Counter Mood.
Dear Friends and Gentle Hearts.
Dictum.
Epilogue: "Lily, being white not red, The."
Epitaph: "She leans across a golden table."
Foolish Heart, The.
For a Lady I Know.
For a Mouthy Woman.
For a Pessimist.
For a Poet.
For an Anarchist.
For an Atheist.
For an Evolutionist and His Opponent.
For Daughters of Magdalen.
For Helen Keller.
For John Keats, Apostle of Beauty.
For Joseph Conrad.
For My Grandmother.
For Myself.
For Paul Laurence Dunbar.
Four Epitaphs sels.
From the Dark Tower.
Fruit of the Flower.
Ghosts.
Harsh World That Lashest Me.
Heritage.
Hunger.
I Have a Rendezvous with Life.
If You Should Go.
In Spite of Death.
Incident.
Judas Iscariot.
Karenge Ya Marenge.
La Belle, La Douce, La Grande.
Lament: "Now let all lovely things embark."
Life's Rendezvous.
Lines for a Hospital.
Lines to My Father.
Litany of the Dark People, The.
Little Sonnet to Little Friends.
Love Tree, The.
Love's Way.
Magnets.
Medusa.
Minutely Hurt.
Mood.
More Than a Fool's Song.
Negro Mother's Lullaby, A.
Night Rain.
Not Sacco and Vanzetti.
Nothing Endures.
One Day We Played a Game.
Only the Polished Skeleton.
Pagan Prayer.
Pity the Deep in Love.
Poet, The.
Protest.
Proud Heart, The.
Requiescam.
Saturday's Child.
Scottsboro, Too, Is Worth Its Song.
Self Criticism.
She of the Dancing Feet Sings.
Shroud of Color, The.
Simon the Cyrenian Speaks.
Singing in the Rain.
Song in Spite of Myself.
Song of Praise.
Song of Praise, A.
Song of Sour Grapes, A.
Sonnet Dialogue.
Sonnet: "I have not loved you in the noblest way'".
Sonnet: "I know now how a man whose blood is hot."
Sonnet: "Some for a little while do love, and some for long."
Sonnet: "These are no wind-blown rumors, soft say-sos."
Sonnet: "What I am saying now was said before."
Spring Reminiscence.

Street Called Crooked, The.
Tableau.
That Bright Chimeric Beast.
Therefore, Adieu.
Thorn Forever in the Breast, A.
Thoughts in a Zoo.
Threnody for a Brown Girl.
To a Brown Girl.
To an Unknown Poet.
To Certain Critics.
To Endymion.
To France.
To John Keats, Poet, at Springtime.
To One Not There.
To the Swimmer.
To the Three for Whom the Book.
Tribute.
Two Thoughts of Death.
Two Who Croseed a Line (She Crosses).
Two Who Crossed a Line.
Ultimatum.
Uncle Jim.
Variations on a Theme.
Wind Bloweth Where It Listeth, The.
Wisdom Cometh with the Years.
Wise, The.
Yet Do I Marvel.
Youth Sings a Song of Rosebuds.
Translations, Coauthored Poems, etc.:
Cat, The.
Cats.
Death to the Poor.

Cummings, Edward Estlin (1894–1962)
A- / float on some.
A / mong crum / bling people(a).
Above a between-the-acts prattling of.
Adhuc sub Judice Lis.
After all white horses are in bed.
After five / times the poem.
After-Glow.
After screamgroa / ning.ish:ly.
After Seeing French Funeral.
After your poppied hair inaugurates.
Air, / be / comes / or.
All ignorance toboggans into know.
All in green went my love riding.
All nearness pauses,while a star can grow.
All stars are(and not one star only)love.
All which isn't singing is mere talking.
All worlds have halfsight,seeing either with.
Allbutnotquitemost.
Along the brittle treacherous bright streets.
Along the justexisting road to Roupy.
Always before your voice my soul.
Am was. are leaves few this. is these a or.
American critic ad 1935.
Amiable putrescence carpenters, An.
Among / these / red pieces of.
Ance)dance / -ing millions all.
A(ncient)a / weigh / tless.
&(all during the / dropsin).
And i imagine.
&-moon-He-be-hind-a-mills.
& sun & / sil / e / nce.
And this day it was Spring..us.
And what were roses.   Perfume?for i do.
An(fragrance)Of / (Begins) / millions.
Annie died the other day.
Any man is wonderful.
Anyone lived in a pretty how town.
Applaws) / "fell / ow."
"April" / this letter's dated.
Ardensteil-henarub-izabeth) / this noN.
As / we lie side by side.
As any(men's) hells having wrestled with).
As freedom is a breakfastfood.
As if as / if a mys.
As is the sea marvelous.
As Joe Gould says in.
As one who(having written).
As that named Fred.
As usual i did not find him in cafes,the more dissolute atmosphere.
At dusk / just when.
At just 5 a / m i hear eng.
At the ferocious phenomenon of 5 o'clock i find myself gently decompos.

At the head of this street a gasping organ is waving moth-eaten.
Autumn is:that between there and here.
Awful darkness of the town, The.
B / eLl / s? / bE.
B / et / wee / n no / w dis.
Babylon slim / -ness of / evenslicing.
Ballad of an Intellectual.
Ballad of Love.
Ballad of the Scholar's Lament.
Ballade: "Does something lie who'd rather stand."
Ballade of Soul.
Ballade: "White night roared with a huge north-wind, The."
Be of love(a little).
Be unto love as rain is unto colour;create.
Beautiful / is the / unmea.
Because / an obstreperous grin minutely floats.
Because / you go away i give roses who.
Because i love you)last night.
Because it's / Spring / thingS.
Because you take life in your stride(instead.
Bed is not very big, The.
Before the fragile gradual throne of night.
Being / twelve / who hast merely.
Being to timelessness as it's to time.
Being(just a little).
Belgium.
Between green / mountains.
Between nose-red gross.
Between the breasts / of bestial.
Beware beware beware / because because because.
Beyond the brittle towns asleep.
Beyond the stolid iron pond.
Bigness of cannon, The.
Birds(/ here,inven / ting air).
Birds meet above the new Moon.
!blac / k / agains / t.
Blossoming are people / nimbler than Really.
Blue the triangular why.
Blue woman with sticking out breasts hanging, A.
Both eaching come ghostlike.
Boy and the Man, The.
Boys i mean are not refined, The.
Breathe with me this fear.
BrIght / bRight s??? big / (soft).
Bud(spiggy nuvduh fienus).
Buffalo Bill's / defunct / who used to.
Buncha hardboil guys frum duh A.C. fulla.
"But / he" i / staring / into winter twi.
But also dying / (as well as).
But being not amazing:without love.
But granted that it's nothing paradoxically enough beyond mere personal.
But if a living dance upon dead minds.
But if i should say.
But mr can you maybe listen there's.
But observe;although / once is never the beginning of.
But the other / day i was passing a certain.
But   turning   a corner   ,i.
"but why should" / the / greatest.
Buy me an ounce and i'll sell you a pound.
By god i want above fourteenth.
By little accurate saints thickly which tread.
Cambridge ladies who live in furnished souls, The.
Candles and / Here Comes a glass box.
Chas sing does(who).
Chaucer.
Chérie / the very,picturesque,last Day.
Chilly,murky night, A.
Christ but they're few.
Ci-gît l Foetus(unborn to not die).
Cleopatra built / like a smooth arrow or.
Clown's smirk in the skull of a baboon, A.
Come a little further—why be afraid.
Come from his gal's.
Come nothing to my comparable soul.
Come(all your mischief- / hatchers hatch).
Comedian stands on a corner,the sky is, The.
Come,gaze with me upon this dome.
Coming of May, The.

Conceive a man,should he have anything.
Connotation of infinity, A.
Consider O / woman this / my body.
Cont)- / in / this / crazily.
Conversation with my friend is particularly.
"Could that"i marveled"be / you?"
Crazy jay blue) / demon laughshriek.
Cri / C / k / et / in.
Cruelly,love / walk the autumn long.
Curtains part) / the peacockappareled.
D-re-A-mi-N-gl-Y / leaves / (sEe).
Darling!because my blood can sing.
Dawn / and now.begins / feeling.
Dead every enormous piece.
Death is more than.
Death(having lost)put on his universe.
Death's Chimney.
Dedicated to Dear Nana Clarke.
Dedication: "White rose my soul, The."
Denied night's face / have shadowless they?
Devil crept in eden wood.
Dick Mid's large bluish face without eyebrows.
Dim / i / nu / tiv / e this park is e.
Dirty colours of her kiss have just, The.
Dive for dreams / or a slogan may topple you.
Do. / omful / relaxing.
Do you remember when the fluttering dusk.
Does yesterday's perfection seem not quite.
Doll's boy's asleep / under a stile.
Dominic has / a doll wired.
Don't cries to please my.
Don't get me wrong oblivion.
Doveglion.
Dress was a suspicious madder,importing the cruelty of roses, The.
Dying is fine)but Death.
E / cco the uglies / t.
Eagle, The.
Early Summer Sketch.
Earth like a tipsy.
Ecco a letter starting "dearest we."
"Economic secu / rity" is a cu.
Emperor / sleeps in a palace of porphyry, The.
Emptied.hills.listen.
Enter no(silence is the blood whose flesh).
Enters give / whose lost is his found.
Epithalamion: "Thou aged unreluctant earth who dost."
Ev erythingex Cept: / that / 's what she's.
Even a pencil has fear to.
Even if all desires things moments be.
Every one of the red roses opened.
Everybody happy? / WE-WE-WE.
Except in your / honour.
Exit a band of unkindness exit.
F / eeble a blu / r of cr.
F is for foetus(a).
Fabulous against   ,a,fathoming jelly.
Fair ladies tall lovers / riding are through the.
Faithfully tinying at twilight voice.
Fame Speaks.
Fea / therr / ain / :dreamin.
Fearlessandbosomy / this / grand:gal.
Finis.
Fire stop thief help murder save the world.
First Jock he / was kilt a handsome.
First of All My Dreams, The.
First president to be loved by his, The.
First robin the; / you say something.
First she like a piece of ill-oiled.
5 / derbies-with-men-in-them smoke Helmar.
Five Americans.
Fl / a / tt / ene / d d.
Float / ing / ly) / i / (in Khoury's warm).
Floatfloafloflf / lloloa.
Flotsam and jetsam / are gentlemen poeds.
Football with white eyebrows the, A.
For any ruffian of the sky.
For him alone life's worse than worst.
For prodigal read generous.
Fragrant sag of fruit distinctly grouped, A.
Fran.
From spiralling ecstatically this.
From the cognoscenti.

FULL SPEED ASTERN).
G / ra / D / ua / lLy &.
"Gay" is the captivating cognomen of a Young Woman of cambridge,mass.
Gee i like to think of dead it means nearer because deeper firmer.
Gert.
Girl's Ring, A.
Glazed mind layed in a, A).
Glory is fallen out of, The.
God.
God gloats upon Her stunning flesh. Upon.
God pity me whom(god distinctly has).
God,Thine the hand that doth extend.
—GON splashes-sink.
Goo-dmore-ning(en / ter)nize-aday(most).
Goodby Betty,don't remember me.
Go(perpe)go / (tu)to(al).
Gr, a / eyhaire / d(m).
Granted the all / saving our young kiss only.
Great, A / man / is / gone.
Great advantage of being alive, The.
Great Dante stands in Florence, looking down.
Greedy the people, The.
GrEEn's d / an / cing on hollow was.
Grin without a / face(a look), A.
Guilt is the cause of more disauders.
Hair your a brook.
Handsome and clever and he went cruising.
Hanged / if n / y in a real hot spell.
Harder perhaps than a newengland bed.
Hate blows a bubble of despair into.
He as o, A / ld as who stag.
He does not have to feel because he thinks.
Helen.
Hello is what a mirror says.
Helves surling out of eakspeasies per(reel)hapsingly.
Her / flesh / Came / at.
Her careful distinct sex whose sharp lips comb.
Here is little Effie's Head.
Here is the ocean,this is moonlight:say.
Here pasture ends— / this girl and boy.
Here's a little mouse)and.
Here's s / omething round(& so).
Here's to opening and upward,to leaf and to sap.
Hills / like poets put on, The.
Hills chime with thrush.
Hips lOOsest OOping shoulders blonde& pastoral hair,strong.
Hist   whist / little ghostthings.
Hokku.
Home means that / when the certainly.
Honour corruption villainy holiness.
!Hope / faith! / !life / love!
Hours rise up putting off stars and it is, The.
How / ses humble.
How / tinily / of / squir(two be).
How dark and single,where he ends,the earth.
How generous is that himself the sun.
How many moments must(amazing each).
How this uncouth enchanted.
Humanity i love you.
Humble one(gifted with / illimitable joy).
Hush) / noones / are coming.
I / (meet)t(touch).
I / never / guessed any / thing(even a).
I am a beggar always.
I am a little church(no great cathedral).
I am going to utter a tree,Noboby.
I am so glad and very.
I carry your heart with me(i carry it in).
I go to this window.
I have found what you are like.
I have looked upon thee—and I have loved thee.
I have loved,let us see if that's all.
I have seen her a stealthily frail.
I like / to think that on.
I like my body when it is with your.
I love you / for your little,startled,thoughtless ways.
I love you much(most beautiful darling).
I met a man under the moon.

I remark that this beach has been used too.   much Too.   originally.
I say no world.
I shall imagine life.
I sing of Olaf glad and big.
I spoke to thee.
I thank You God for most this amazing.
"I think you like."
I walked the boulevard.
I was considering how.
I was sitting in mcsorly's.   outside it was New York and beauti- / fully snowing.
I will be / M o ving in the Street of her.
I will cultivate within.
I will wade out.
I'd think "wonder / if" if.
If.
If a cheerfulest Elephantangelchild should sit.
If being mortised with a dream.
If everything happens that can't be done.
If i / or anybody don't.
If i believe / in death be sure.
If i have made,my lady,intricate.
If i love You.
If i should sleep with a lady called death.
If in beginning twilight of winter will stand.
If learned darkness from our searched world.
If night's mostness(and whom did merely day / close).
If seventy were young / and death uncommon.
If the / green / opens.
If the Lovestar grows most big.
If there are any heavens my mother will(all by herself)have.
If up's the word;and a world grows greener.
If within tonight's erect.
If you and i awakening.
If you can't eat you got to.
If you like my poems let them.
If(among / silent skies).
If(touched by love's own secret)we,like homing.
If(you are i why certainly).
IKEY(GOLDBERG)'S WORTH I'M.
I'll tell you a dream i had once i was away up in the sky Blue,everything.
I'm / asking / you dear to.
I'm very fond of.
(Im)c-a-t(mo).
Impossibly / motivated by midnight.
In / Spring comes(no- / one).
In a middle of a room.
IN) all those who got.
In front of your house i.
In hammamet did camping queers et al).
In Healey's Palace I was sitting.
In heavenly realms of hellas dwelt.
In Just- / spring   when the world is mud-.
In making Marjorie god hurried.
In spite of everything.
In the rain- / darkness,   the sunset.
In time of daffodils(who know.
In time's a noble mercy of proportion.
Infinite jukethrob smoke & swallow to dis.
Innerly / UningstrolL / (stamens & pistil).
Insu nli gh t / o / verand.
Inthe,exquisite; / morning   sure   lyHer eye s exactly sit,ata little roundtable.
Into a truly / curving form.
Into the smiting / sky tense.
Into the strenuous briefness.
Irreproachable ladies firmly lewd.
Is / it / because there struts a distinct silver lady.
Is there a flower(whom).
It is at moments after i have dreamed.
It is funny,you will be dead some day.
It is so long since my heart has been with yours.
It is winter a moon in the afternoon.
It may not always be so; and i say.
It really must / be Nice,never to.
It started when Bill's chip let on to.
It was a goodly co.
Item.
Item:is / Clumsily with of.

It)It will it.
It's / so damn sweet when Anybody.
It's jolly / odd what pops into.
It's just like a coffin's.
It's over a(see just).
I've come to ask you if there isn't a.
Ivory performing rose, The.
Jack's white horse(up).
Jake hates / all the girls(the).
Jehovah buried,Satan dead.
Jimmie's got a goil.
Joyful your complete fearless and pure love.
Joys faces friends / feet terrors fate.
Kike is the most dangerous, A.
Kind) / YM&WC / (of sort of).
"Kitty." sixteen,5'1[mM],white,prostitute.
Kumrads die because they're told).
L(a / le / af / fa / ll / s).
Ladies and gentlemen this little girl.
Lady / i pray to what is unimaginable.
Lady of Silence.
Lady will you come with me into.
Lady you have written me a letter.
Lady,i will touch you with my mind.
Lady,since your footstep.
Laughing to find / Anyone's blind.
Lean candles hunger in.
Leastlessly / out / of this.
Let it go—the.
Let us lie here in the disturbing grass.
Let us suspect,chérie,this not very big.
(Let us tremble)a personal radiance sits.
Let's live suddenly without thinking.
Let's start a magazine.
Let's,from some loud unworld's most rightful wrong.
Life / shuts &)opens the world.
Life boosts herself rapidly at me.
Life hurl my.
Life is more true than reason will deceive.
Light cursed falling in a singular block.
Light Out), A.
Light's lives lurch / a once world quickly from rises.
Like a, A / grey / rock wanderin.
Like a little bear twilight.
Like most godhouses this particular house.
Lily has a rose.
Lis / -ten / you know what i mean when.
Listen / beloved / i dreamed.
(Listen) / this a dog barks and.
Listen my children and you.
Little horse is newlY, The.
Little joe gould has lost his teeth and doesn't know where.
Little ladies more / than dead exactly dance.
Little man / (in a hurry).
Little tree / little silent Christmas tree.
Lively and loathesome moe's respectably dead.
Liz.
Logeorge / lo / wellifitisn't eddy   how's the boy.
Long ago,between a dream and a dream.
Longing.
Look / my fingers,which.
Look at this) / a 75 done.
Lord John Unalive(having a fortune of fifteengrand).
Love is a guess / that deepens.
Love is a place.
Love is a spring at which.
Love is more thicker than forget.
Love is the every only god.
Love our so right.
Love was—entire excellently steep.
Love's absence is illusion,alias time.
Love's function is to fabricate unknownness.
Love's the i guess most only verb that lives.
Lucky means finding / Holes where.
Luminous tendril of celestial wish.
Maggie and milly and molly and may.
Maker of many mouths.
Mame.
Man who had fallen among thieves, A.
Marianne Moore.
Marj.

Mary green / cheerful & generous.
May i be gay.
May i feel said he.
May my heart always be open to little.
Maybe god / is a child.
Me Up at Does.
,Mean- / hum / a)now / (nit.
Meet mr universe(who clean).
Memorabilia.
Memory believes / fragrance of a town(whose).
Metamorphosis.
Mi(dreamlike)st / makes / big each dim.
Might these be thrushes climbing through almost(do they).
Mighty guest of merely me.
Mind is its own beautiful prisoner, The.
Mind's(/ I never you never), The.
Mist.
Mr. smith / is reading / his letter.
Mr u will not be missed.
Mr youse needn't be so spry.
Mrs / and mr across the way are kind of.
Moan / (is) / ing / the she of the.
Moon falls through the autumn   Behind prisons she grins, The.
Moon-in-the-Trees, / The old canoe awaits you.
Moon is hiding in, The.
Moon-lit snow is falling like strange candy into the big eyes of the, The.
Moon looked into my window, The.
Moon over gai.
MOOn Over tOwns mOOn.
Morsel miraculous and meaningless.
Mortals) / climbi / ng i / nto eachness begi.
Most(people / simply / can't).
Mouse)Won / derfully is.
Move / deeply,rain / (dream hugely)wish.
Much i cannot) / tear up the world:& toss.
Murderfully in midmost o.c.an.
Music.
Must being shall.
My darling since / you and.
My deathly body's deadly lady.
My eyes are fond of the east side.
My father moved through dooms of love.
My girl's tall with hard long eyes.
My humorous ghost precisely will.
My lady is an ivory garden.
My little heart is so wonderfully sorry.
My love / thy hair is one kingdom.
My love is building a building.
My mind is.
My naked lady framed.
My Prayer.
My smallheaded pearshaped.
My sonnet is A light goes on in.
My specialty is living said.
My strength becoming wistful in a glib.
My sweet old etcetera.
My uncle / Daniel fought in the civil.
My youthful lady will have other lovers.
My(his from daughter's mother's zero mind).
Myself,walking in Dragon st.
N / ot eth / eold almos.
N / OthI / n / g can / s / urPas / s.
N / Umb a / stree / t's wintr.
Nearer:breath of my breath:take not thy tingling.
Neither awake / (there's your general).
Neither could say / (it comes so slow).
Never could anyone / who simply lives to die.
Newly / cued / motif smites truly to beautifully.
Newlys of silence.
Next to of course god america i.
Night.
Night shall eat these girls and boys.
Nine birds(rising / through a gold moment)climb.
Nite) / thatthis / crou / ched.
No man,if men are gods;but if gods must.
No time ago / or else a life.
Nobody could / in superhuman flights.
Nobody loses all the time.

Nobody loved this.
Nobody wears a yellow.
Nocturne: "When the lithe moonlight
   silently."
Noise.
Nonsun blob a / cold to.
Noone and a star stand,am to am.
Noone" autumnal this great lady's gaze.
Nor woman / (just as it be).
Noster was a ship of swank, The.
Not time's how(anchored in what
   mountaining roots).
Nothing false and possible is love.
Nothing is more exactly terrible than.
"Nothing" the unjust man complained.
Nothing whichful about / thick big this.
Notice the convulsed orange inch of moon.
Nouns to nouns / wan / wan.
N(o)w / the / how / dis(appeared
   cleverly)world.
Now air is air and thing is thing:no bliss.
Now all the fingers of this tree(darling)have.
Now comes the good rain farmers pray
   for(and.
Now dis "daughter" uv eve(who aint
   precisely slim)sim.
Now does our world descend.
Now i lay(with everywhere around).
Now is a ship / which captain am.
Now that fierce few.
Now that,more nearest even than your fate.
Now two old ladies sit peacefully knitting.
Now what were motionless move(exists no).
Now winging selves sing sweetly, while
   ghosts(there).
Now(more near ourselves than we).
Numb(and / that was).
Nw / O / h / S / LoW.
O / nly this / darkness(in).
O / sure)but / nobody unders(no).
O / the round / little man we.
O by the by / has anybody seen.
O Distinct / Lady of my unkempt adoration.
O It's Nice To Get Up In,the slipshod
   mucous kiss.
O my wholly unwise and definite.
O pr / gress verily thou art m.
O purple finch / please tell me why.
! / o(rounD)moon,how.
O sweet spontaneous.
O the sun comes up-up-up in the opening.
O Thou to whom the musical white spring.
O to be in finland.
oDE: "O / the sweet & aged people."
Of all the blessings which to man.
Of all things under our.
Of an it ignoblest he, The.
Of Ever-Ever Land i speak.
Of evident invisibles / exquisite the hovering.
Of my / soul a street is.
Of Nicolette.
Of this sunset(which is so).
Of this wilting wall the colour drub.
Off a pane)the.
Ohld song / you Know.
Oil tel duh woil doi sez.
Old age sticks / up Keep.
Old mr ly / fresh from a fu.
On littlest this / the of twig three.
On souls robbed of their birth-right's better
   part.
On the Madam's best april the.
Once like a spark.
Once White & Gold / daisy in the dust.
"Ondumonde" / (first than caref.
One / t / hi / s / snowflake.
(One!) twisti-twisti barber.
One April dusk the.
One day a nigger.
(One fine day) / let's take the train.
One nonsufficiently inunderstood.
One slipslouch twi / tterstamp.
One winter afternoon / (at the magical hour).
One(Floatingly)arrive / (silent)one by(alive).
One's not half two. It's two are halves of
   one.
Only as what(out of a flophouse)floats.

Open green those / (dear).
Open his head,baby.
Open your heart: / i'll give you a treasure.
Opening of the chambers close.
Or who and who.
Other guineahen, The.
Our Flag.
Our touching hearts slenderly comprehend.
Out of a supermetamathical subpreincestures.
Out of midsummer's blazing most not night.
Out of more find than seeks.
Out of night's almosT Floats a colour(in).
Out of the bigg / est the knownun.
Out of the lie of no.
Out of the mountain of his soul comes.
Out of the pants which cover me.
Over us if(as what dusk becomes).
Painted wind has sprung, A.
Paper Palace, The.
Paris;this April sunset completely utters.
Paris,thou art not.
Passing of the Year, The.
People who, The.
Peopleshaped toomany-ness far too, A.
Perfectly a year,we watched Together les
   enfants jumping and.
Perhaps it is to feel strike.
Perhaps it was Myself sits down in this
   chair. There were two chairs,in fact.
Perished have safe small.
Phonograph may(if it likes)be prophe, The.
Phonograph's voice like a keen spider
   skipping, The.
Picasso / you give us Things.
Pieces(in darker / than small is dirtiest).
Pity his how illimitable plight.
Pity This Busy Monster, Manunkind.
Plant Magic dust / expect hope doubt.
Plato told / him:he couldn't.
Poem her belly marched through me as, The.
Poem, or Beauty Hurts Mr. Vinal.
POEM(or "the divine right of majorities, that
   illegitimate offspring of the divine right of
   kings" Homer Lea).
Poets yeggs and thirsties.
Politician, A.
Ponder,darling,these busted statues.
Poor But TerFLY / went(flesh is grass).
Porky & porkie.
Possibly thrice we glimpsed.
Pound pound pound / on thy cold grey
   corona oh P.
Precisely as unbig a why as i'm.
Pretty a day, A.
Proud of his scientific attitude.
Puella Mea.
Purer than purest pure.
Put off your faces,Death:for day is over.
Q:dwo / we know of anything which can.
?
Quick i the death of thing.
R-P-O-P-H-E-S-S-A-G-R.
Rain Is a Handsome Animal, The.
Rain or hail / sam done.
Rainsweet / s / tillnes / s.
Raise the shade.
Reason let others give and realness bring.
Red Front, The.
Red-rag and pink-flag.
Remarked Robinson Jefferson.
Reverie.
Right here the other night something.
Ringed / with monstrous / a doomed.
River of Mist, The.
Riverly is a flower.
Rose / is dying the, The.
Rosetree,rosetree / —you're a song to
   see:whose.
Round a so moon could dream(i sus).
Round face near the top of the stairs, A.
S(/ these out of in).
Salesman is an it that stinks excuse, A.
Sapphics.
Says ol man no body.
Season 'tis,my lovely lambs, The.
Seeker of truth / follow no path.
16 heures / l'Etoile.

Semi-Spring.
Sentinel robins two / guard me and you.
Serene immediate silliest and whose.
S.F.D.
Sh estiffl / ystrut sal.
She being Brand.
She had that softness which is falsity.
She sits dropping on a caret of clenched
   arms.
She,straddling my lap.
Should far this from mankind's unmysteries.
Should this fool die.
Silence / .is / a / looking.
Silent unday by silently not night.
Silently if,out of not knowable.
Silently little blue elephant shyly(he was
   terri), The.
Since feeling is first.
Sitting in a tree-.
Six / are in a room's dark around).
Skating.
Skies may be blue;yes.
Skinny voice / of the leatherfaced, The.
Sky / was   can dy / lu   mi, The.
Sky a silver, The.
Slightly before the middle of Congressman
   Pudd.
SNO / a white idea(Listen).
SNOW / cru / is / ingw Hi.
Snow means that / life is a black cannonadin.
Snow)says!Says / over un / graves.
So isn't small one littlest why.
So little he is.
So many selves(so many fiends and gods).
So shy shy shy(and with a).
So standing.our eyes filled with the wind,and
   the.
So you're hunting for ann well i'm looking
   for will.
Softly from its still lair in Plympton Street.
Some ask praise of their fellows.
Somebody knew Lincoln somebody Xerxes.
Sometime,perhaps in Paris we will.
Sometimes / in)Spring a someone will
   lie(glued).
Sometimes i am alive because with.
Somewhere I have never travelled,gladly
   beyond.
Song: "But we've the may / (for you are in
   love)."
Sonnet entitled how to run the world).
Sonnet: "For that I have forgot the world
   these days."
Sonnet: "I dreamed I was among the
   conquerors."
Sonnet: "Long since, the flicker brushed with
   shameless wing."
Sonnet: "No sunset, but a grey, great,
   struggling sky."
Sonnet: "Rain-drop on the eyelids of the
   earth, A."
Space being(don't forget to
   remember)Curved.
Speaking of love(of).
Spirit colossal / (& daunted by always).
Spoke joe to jack.
Spring has been exquisite and the, The.
Spring is like a perhaps hand.
Spring omnipotent goddess thou dost.
Spring!may— / everywhere's here.
Spring(side / walks are)is.
Squints a blond / job at her.
S.T.
Stand with your lover on the ending earth.
Stinging / gold swarms.
S.ti:rst;hiso,nce;ma:n.
Structure,miraculous challenge,devout am.
Summer is over / —it's no use demanding.
Summer Silence.
Summer Song.
Sunlight was over.
Sunset.
Sunset)edges become swiftly.
Suppose / Life is an old man carrying
   flowers on his head.
Supposing i dreamed this).

Surely / Cued / motif smites truly to Beautifully, The.
Sweet spring is your.
Swi(/ across!gold's / rouNdly.
Swim so now million many worlds in each.
(Swooning)a pillar of youngly.
Ta / ppin / g / toe / hip.
Take for example this.
T.A.M.
Taxis toot whirl people moving perhaps laugh into the slowly.
Tell me not how electricity or.
Than(by yon sunset's wintry glow).
Thanksgiving (1956).
That famous fatheads find that each.
That melancholy / fellow'll play / his handorgan.
That which we who're alive in spite of mirrors.
The / nimble / heat / had.
The / sky / was / can dy lu.
The(/ Wistfully / dead seem generous)don't.
Thee will i praise between those rivers whose.
Them which despair.
The(oo)is / lOOk / (aliv / e)e / yes.
There are possibly 2 1/2 or impossibly 3.
There are 6 doors.
There are so many tictoc.
There is a / moon sole.
There is a here and.
These children singing in stone a.
These from my mother's greatgrandmother's rosebush white.
These people socalled were not given hearts.
These(whom;pretends / blue nothing).
Thethe / the pink / Tartskids with.
They have hung the sky with arrows.
Theys sO alive.
Thing most new complete fragile intense, A.
Thing no is(of).
Think of it:not so long ago.
This / forest pool / A so.
This cigarette is extremely long.
This evangelist / buttons with his big gollywog voice.
This fear is no longer dear. You are not going to America and.
This is a rubbish of human rind.
This is the garden:clours come and go.
This little / pair had a little scare.
This little bride & groom are.
This little huge / -eyed per-.
This man's heart / is true to his.
This mind made war.
This out of within itself moo.
This young question mark man.
This(a up green hugeness who and climbs).
This(let's remember)day died again and.
This(that / grey)white / (man)horse.
Thou / firsting a hugeness of twi / -light.
Thou in whose swordgreat story shine the deeds.
Though your sorrows not.
Three wealthy sisters swore they'd never part.
Through the tasteless minute efficient room.
Thrown a, A / -way It.
T,h;r;u;s,h;e:s / are / silent / now.
Thy face is a still white house of holy things.
Thy fingers make early flowers of.
Time,be kind;herself and i.
Timeless / ly this / (merely and whose).
To stand(alone)in some.
To start,to hesitate;to stop.
To William F. Bradbury.
Tonight the moon is round golden entire. It.
Total stranger one black day, A.
Touching you i say(it being Spring).
Trees / were in(give).
Trick of finding what you didn't lose, The.
True lovers in each happening of their hearts.
Tumbling-hair / picker of buttercups.
Tw / oo / ld / o / nce upo / n.
Twentyseven bums give a prostitute the once.
Twi- / is -Light bird.

2 little whos / (he and she).
2 shes / both not quite / young perfectly.
Un / der fog / 's / touch.
Un(bee)mo / vi / n(in)g.
Unlove's the heavenless hell and homeless home.
Unnoticed woman from whose kind large flesh.
Until and i heard.
Unto thee i / burn incense.
Up into the silence the green.
Upon the room's / silence,i will sew.
Us if therefore must forget ourselves.
Utterly and amusingly I am pash.
Vision.
Voices to voices, lip to lip.
Waddling / madam star, The.
Wanta / spendsix / dollars Kid.
Warped this perhapsy.
Water-Lilies.
Way to hump a cow is not, The.
We being not each other:without love.
We love each other very dearly.
We miss you,jack—tactfully you(with one cocked).
Weazened Irrefutable unastonished.
Wee people / dwelling / between serene.
Well)here's looking at ourselves.
We)under)over,the thing of floating Of.
What a proud dreamhorse pulling(smoothloomingly)through.
What does little Ernest croon.
What freedom's not some under's mere above.
What Got him was Noth.
What if a much of a which of a wind.
What is / a / voyage / ?
What is strictly fiercely and wholly dies.
What is thy mouth to me?
What over and which under.
What time is it i wonder never mind.
What time is it?it is by every star.
Whatever's merely wilful, / and not miraculous.
When / (day's amazing murder with).
When / from a sidewalk.
When any mortal(even the most odd).
When cited day with the sonorous homes.
When faces called flowers float out of the ground.
When god decided to invent.
When god lets my body be.
When hair falls off and eyes blur And.
When i am in boston,i do not speak.
When i have thought of you somewhat too.
When life is quite through with.
When muckers pimps and tratesmen.
When my love comes to see me it's.
When my sensational moments are no more.
When of your eyes one smile entirely brings down.
When parsing warmths of dusk construe.
When rain whom fear.
When serpents bargain for the right to squirm.
When the proficient poison of pure sleep.
When the spent day begins to frail.
When thou art dead,dead,and far from the splendid sin.
When thou hast taken thy last applause,and when.
When time delicately is sponging sum after.
When unto nights of autumn do complain.
When what hugs stopping earth than silent is.
When you are silent,shining host by guest.
When you rang at Dick Mid's Place.
When you went away it was morning.
When your honest redskin toma.
Whereas by dark really released,the modern.
Wherelings whenlings / (daughters of if but offspring of hopefear).
Where's Jack Was / General Was.
Where's Madge then / Madge and her men?
Which is the very.
While a once world slips from.
Whippoorwill this / moonday into.
White guardians of the universe of sleep.

Who / threw the silver dollar up into the tree?
Who are you,little i.
Who(at / her nons- / elf).
Who before dying demands not rebirth.
Who is this / dai / nty mademoiselle.
Who knows if the moon's.
Who sharpens every dull.
Who were so dark of heart they might not speak.
Who(is?are)who.
Who's most afraid of death?thou.
Whose are these(wraith a clinging with a wraith).
W.H.W., Jr.
Why / do the / fingers.
Why / don't / he / sil / ly.
Why did you go.
Why from this her and him.
Why must itself up every of a park.
Why why / How many winds make wonderful.
Wild(at our first)beasts uttered human words.
Will i ever forget that precarious moment?
Will out of the kindness of their hearts a few philosophers tell me.
Will suddenly trees leap up from winter and will.
Will you teach a.
Willing pitifully to bewitch.
Wind has blown the rain away and blown, A.
Wind is a Lady with, The.
Windows go orange in the slowly.
Wing Wong,uninterred at twice.
Without the mercy of / your eyes your.
Woman / of bronze / unhappy, A.
Workingman with hand so hairy-sturdy.
World is very big, and we, The.
Worshipping same / they squirm and they spawn.
Writhe and / gape of tortured.
Y is a WELL KNOWN ATHLETE'S BRIDE.
Yes but even / 4 or(&).
Yes is a pleasant country.
YgUDuh / ydoan / yunnuhstan.
Yonder deadfromtheneckup graduate of a.
You / in win / ter who sit.
You are like the snow only.
You are not going to,dear. You are not going to and.
You are tired, / (I think).
You asked me to come:it was raining a little.
You being in love.
You no / tice / nobod / y wants.
You said Is / there anything which.
You shall above all things be glad and young.
You shall sing my songs, O earth.
You which could grin three smiles into a dead.
Youful / larger / of smallish).
Young / man sitting, The.
Young m / oon:be kind to olde.
Your birthday comes to tell me this.
Your homecoming will be my homecoming.
Your little voice / Over the wires came leaping.
Yours is the music for no instrument.
Translations, Coauthored Poems, etc.:
1.4: "Fetters of winter are shattered,shatter, The."
1.24: "Who chides the tears that weep so dear a head?"
2.14: "Ah, Postumus, fleet-footed are the years!"
4.6: "O, blessed of the gods."
4.7: "Farewell,runaway snows! For the meadow is green,and the tree stands."
Odes *sels.*

D

"D., H." *see* Doolittle, Hilda
Davie, Donald (1922–95)
  Abbeyforde.
  Across the Bay.

Admiral to His Lady, The.
Advent.
After an Accident.
After the Calamitous Convoy (July 1942).
After the Match.
Against Confidences.
Agave in the West.
Alzheimer's Disease.
Amazonian.
Among Artisans' Houses.
And Our Eternal Home.
Anglican Lady, An.
Apparition, An.
Ars Poetica.
Articulacy. Hints from the Koran.
Artifex in Extremis.
At Knaresborough.
At the Café Parnasse.
At the Cradle of Genius.
At the Synod in St Patrick's.
Attar of Roses.
Aubade: "I wish for you that when you
    wake."
Autumn Imagined.
Back of Affluence.
Baptist Childhood, A.
Barnsley and District.
Barnsley Cricket Club.
Barnsley, 1966.
Battered Wife, The.
Battlefield, A.
Bedfordshire.
Behind the North Wind.
Being Angry with God.
Belfast on a Sunday Afternoon.
Benedictus.
Bent, The.
Berkshire.
Black Hoyden.
Blank of the Wall, The.
Bolyai, the Geometer.
Bougainville.
Bowing the Head.
Brantôme.
Break, The.
Bride of Reason, The.
Brilliance.
Buckinghamshire.
By the Road to Upper Midhope.
Cambridgeshire.
Cannibals.
Catullus on Friendship.
Cherry Ripe.
Cheshire.
Christening, A.
Christian Hero, A.
Christmas Syllabics for a Wife.
Chrysanthemums.
Church Militant.
Church of Ireland.
Cold Spring in Essex.
Comforter, The.
Commodore Barry.
Compline.
Conditioned Air, A.
Cornwall.
Corrib: An Emblem.
County Durham.
Creature David, The.
Creon's Muse.
Cumberland.
Curtains!
Cypress Avenue, The.
Dancing Measures.
David Dancing.
Death in the West, A.
Death of a Painter.
Death of a Voice.
Demi-Exile. Howth.
Democrats.
Departed, The.
Depravity: Two Sermons.
Derbyshire.
Derbyshire Turf.
Devil on Ice.
Devonshire.
Dissent. A Fable.

Dissentient Voice, A.
Dorset.
Dream Forest.
Dublin Georgian.
Dublin Georgian (2).
Dudwood.
Dule of a Dewsbury Matron.
Eden.
Eight Years After.
Elect, The.
Emigrant, to the Receding Shore.
England.
English Revenant, An.
Epistle. To Enrique Caracciolo Trejo.
Equestrian Sestina.
Essex.
Evangelist, The.
Evening on the Boyne.
Except the Lord Build the House.
Expecting Silence.
Ezra Pound in Pisa.
Fare Thee Well.
Father, the Cavalier.
Feeders, The.
Felicity's Fourth Order.
Fifth Epistle.
First Epistle.
For an Age of Plastics. [Plymouth].
For Doreen. A Voice from the Garden.
Fountain of Arethusa, The.
Fountain of Cyanë, The.
Fountain, The.
Fourth Epistle.
From the New World.
Frontenac.
G. M. B.
Garden Party, The.
Gardens No Emblems.
Garland for Ivor Gurney, A.
Garland for Ronsard, A.
Gathered Church, A.
Gemona-del-Friuli, 1961–1976.
Gloucestershire.
God of Details, The.
God Saves the King.
Going to Italy.
Grace in the Fore Street.
Grazia Deledda, Young.
Green River.
Gripping Serial.
Grudging Respect.
H. D.
Hampshire.
Hardness of Light, The.
Harrow, The.
Having No Ear.
Hawkshead and Dachau in a Christmas Glass.
Hearing Russian Spoken.
Heart Beats.
Heigh-ho on a Winter Afternoon.
Helena Morley.
Herefordshire.
Hermes and Mr Shaw.
Hertfordshire.
Hill Field, The.
His Themes.
Homage to George Whitefield.
Homage to John L. Stephens.
Homage to William Cowper.
Horae Canonicae.
Hornet.
Hot Hands.
House-martin.
Housekeeping.
Humanly Speaking.
Huntingdonshire.
Hyphens.
Hypochondriac Logic.
I Have Said, Ye Are Gods.
Idyll: "As a horn of the high moon veers in
    clear skies over Main Street."
If I Take the Wings of the Morning.
In California.
In Chopin's Garden.
In the Stopping Train.
Inditing a Good Matter.
Intervals in a Busy Life.

Iowa.
Ironist, The.
Jacob's Ladder.
January.
Jesuits in North America, The.
July, 1964.
Just You Wait!
Kent.
Killala.
Kingship.
Lady Cochrane.
Lancashire.
Lasalle.
Late Anniversary, A.
Leicestershire.
Letter to Curtis Bradford, A.
Levity.
Life Encompassed.
Life of Service, The.
Lily at Noon, A.
Limited Achievement.
Lincolnshire.
Liverpool Epistle, A.
Livingshayes.
Looking Out from Ferrara.
Love and the Times.
Love-Poems: for Mairi MacInnes.
Low Lands.
Machineries of Shame.
Mamertinus on Rhetoric, A.D. 291.
Mandelstam, on Dante.
Mandelstam's Hope for the Best.
Master & Man.
Measured Tread, A.
Meeting of Cultures, A.
Mens Sana in Corpore Sano.
Metals.
Meteorologist, September.
Method. For Ronald Gaskell.
Middlesex.
Mr Sharp in Florence.
Monmouthshire.
Montcalm.
Morning.
Mother.
Mushroom Gatherers, The.
Mustered into the Avant-Garde.
My Father's Honour.
Nashville Mornings.
New Year Wishes for the English.
New York in August.
1945.
Nineteen-Seventeen.
1977, Near Mullingar.
1969, Ireland of the Bombers.
No Epitaph.
Nonconformist, The.
Nones.
Norfolk.
North & South.
North Dublin.
North Sea, in a Snowstorm, The.
North Sea, The.
Northamptonshire.
Northern Metres.
Northumberland.
Nosegay, The.
Nottinghamshire.
Oak Openings.
Obiter Dicta.
On a Proposed Celebration of Ezra Pound.
On Bertrand Russell's "Portraits from
    Memory."
On Generous Lines.
On Not Deserving.
On Sutton Strand.
Or, Solitude.
Ordinary God.
Orford.
Oriental Visitor, An.
Orpheus.
Our Lady.
Out of East Anglia.
Owl Minerva, The.
Ox-Bow.
Oxfordshire.
Pacer in the Fresco. John the Baptist, The.

Pastor Errante.
Penelope.
Pentecost.
Pietà.
Pilate.
Poem as Abstract.
Poet Redeemed & Dead.
Pontiac.
Porec.
Portland.
Portrait of the Artist as a Farmyard Fowl.
Preoccupation's Gift.
Prime.
Priory of St Saviour, Glendalough, The.
Prolific Spell, The.
Pushkin. A Didactic Poem.
Put Not Your Trust in Princes.
Rain on South-East England.
Recollections of George Oppen in a Letter to
  an English Friend.
Red Rock of Utah.
Reflections on Deafness.
Rejoinder to a Critic.
Remembering the 'Thirties.
Reminded of Bougainville.
Resolutions.
Revenge for Love.
Revulsion.
Right Lads, The.
Right Wing Sympathies.
Rodez.
Rousseau in His Day.
Rutland.
Samuel Beckett's Dublin.
Savannah.
Saw I Never the Righteous Forsaken.
Screech-Owl.
"Sculpture" of Rhyme, The.
Sculptures in Hungary.
Scythian Charioteers, The.
Second Epistle.
Seeing Her Leave.
Selina, Countess of Huntingdon.
Seur, near Blois.
Sext.
Short Run to Camborne.
Shropshire.
Siloam.
Sing unto the Lord a New Song.
Six Epistles to Eva Hesse.
Sixth Epistle.
Skelpick.
So Make Them Melt as the Dishouséd Snail.
Some Future Moon.
Some Shires Revisited.
Somerset.
Sorting the Personae.
Sounds of a Devon Village.
Spring Song, A.
Staffordshire.
Standings.
Stratford on Avon.
Strathnaver.
Suffolk.
Summer Lightning.
Sunburst.
Sunday Morning.
Surrey.
Sussex.
Sylvae.
Terce.
Thanks to Industrial Essex.
Their Rectitude Their Beauty.
They, to Me.
Third Epistle.
Thirty-Ninth Psalm, Adapted, The.
Thou Art Near at Hand, O Lord.
Though Dry, Not Dry.
Three Beyond.
Three Moral Discoveries.
Through Bifocals.
Thyestes.
Time Passing, Beloved.
To a Bad Poet.
To a Brother in the Mystery.
To a Teacher of French.
To an American Classicist.

To Certain English Poets.
To Helen Keller.
To Londoners.
To Thom Gunn in Los Altos, California.
Townend, 1976.
Trevenen.
Treviso, the Pescheria.
Trip to Huntsville, The.
Tunstall Forest.
Tuscan Brutus, The.
Tuscan Morning.
Twilight on the Waste Lands.
Two Dedications.
Two from Ireland.
Two Widows in Tashkent.
Under a Skylight.
Under St Paul's.
University of the South, The.
Utterings.
Vancouver.
Vengeance Is Mine, Saith the Lord.
Vespers.
Via Portello.
Vindication of Jovan Babic, The.
Viper-Man.
Vying.
Warwickshire.
Waterfall at Powerscourt, The.
Wearing of the Green, The.
Well-Found Poem.
West Virginia's Auburn.
Westmorland.
Where Depths Are Surfaces.
Wide France.
Widower.
Widowers.
Wild Boar Clough.
Wiltshire.
Wind at Penistone, The.
Winter Landscape Near Ely, A.
Winter Landscapes.
Winter Talent, A.
Winter's Talents.
With the Grain.
Witness.
Woe unto Thee!
Wombwell on Strike.
Woodpigeons at Raheny.
Worcestershire.
Yorkshire.
Zion.
Zip!
Zodiac, The.
Translations, Coauthored Poems, etc.:
House, The.
Octets.

De la Mare, Walter ("Walter Ramal") (1873–
1956)
Abandoned Church, An.
Absalom.
Adieu.
Age.
Alexander.
All That's Past.
Alone.
Anatomy.
April.
April Moon.
Arabia.
Argument, The.
Ariel.
Assignation, The.
At Ease.
Autumn.
Awake!
Away.
Ballad of Christmas, A.
Banquo.
Be angry now no more!
Before Dawn.
Bells, The.
Beneath a motionless yew.
Betrayal.
Beware!
Bindweed, The.
Birthnight: To F., The.
Bitter Waters.

Blind Boy, The.
Bottle, The.
Break of Morning.
Breughel's Winter.
Bridge, The.
Bright Life.
Brother and Sister.
Cage, The.
Captive, The.
Catechism, The.
Cherry Trees, The.
Child Asleep, A.
Children of Stare, The.
Clavichord.
Clear Eyes.
Comfort.
Corner Stone, The.
Courage.
Crazed.
Daisy, The.
Dark Château, The.
Dawn.
Death-Dream, The.
Decoy, The.
Defeat.
Disguise, The.
Dove, The.
Dream, A.
Dreamer, The.
Dreams.
Drugged.
Dry August Burned.
Dust to Dust.
Dwelling-Place, The.
Echo.
Empty House, The.
Encounter, The.
England.
English Downs.
Episodes.
Epitaph, An: "Here lies a most beatiful lady."
Epitaph, An: "Last, Stone, a little yet."
Estranged.
Euphrasy.
Even In The Grave.
Evening.
Exile.
Exile, The.
Eyes.
Faint Music.
Fairy in Winter, The.
Faithless.
Falstaff.
Familiar, The.
Fare Well.
Fat Woman, The.
Fear.
Feckless Dinner Party, The.
Fleeting, The.
Flight, The.
Flotsam.
Flower, The.
Fog.
Fool's Song, The.
For All the Grief.
Foreboding.
Forests.
Forgiveness.
Futility.
Galliass, The.
Ghost, The.
Glance, The.
Glimpse, The.
Gloria Mundi.
Gold.
Goliath.
Good-bye.
Good Company.
Hamlet.
Happy Encounter, The.
Hare, A.
Haunted.
Hawthorn Hath a Deathly Smell, The.
Here Sleeps.
Heresy.
Homesick.
Hospital.

Hour-Glass, The.
How Blind!
How Sleep the Brave.
Humanity.
Hunter, The.
I Sit Alone.
Iago.
Idleness.
Image, The.
Imagination's Pride, The.
Imogen.
Imp Within, The.
In a Library.
In Disgrace.
In the Dock.
In the Garden.
In Vain.
Incantation.
Interlude, An.
Invocation: "Burning fire shakes in the night,
  The."
Irrevocable, The.
Isaac Meek.
Jenny Wren.
Journey, The.
Juliet's Nurse.
Karma.
Keep Innocency.
Keys of Morning, The.
Last Arrow, The.
Last Chapter, The.
Last Coachload, The.
Life.
Linnet, The.
Listeners, The.
Little Salamander, The.
Looking Glass, The.
Lucy.
Macbeth.
Maerchen.
Making a fire.
Marionettes, The.
Market-Place, The.
Martha.
Martins: September.
Massacre, The.
Memory.
Mercutio.
Mermaids, The.
Miracle, The.
Mirage.
Miss Loo.
Mist.
Mistress Fell.
Mrs. Grundy.
Moment, The.
Monologue, The.
Moonlight.
Moth, The.
Motley.
Mountains, The.
Mourn'st Thou Now?
Music.
Music Unheard.
Myself.
Napoleon.
Never More, Sailor.
Never-To-Be.
News.
Night.
Nocturne: "'Tis not my voice now speaks;
  but as a bird."
Nod.
Noon and Night Flower.
Not Only.
Not that way.
O Childish Mind!
Of a Son.
Oh, Why?
Old Angler, The.
Old Ben.
Old Men, The.
Old Summerhouse, The.
Old Susan.
Omen, The.
On the Esplanade.
One in the Public Gallery.

Ophelia.
Out Of Bounds.
Outskirts, The.
Owl, The ("Door-Bell...").
Owl, The ("What If To Edge Of Dream").
Peace.
Peeping Tom.
Phantom, The.
Pollie.
Polonius.
Portrait, A.
Pot Of Musk, A.
Prayer, A.
Quarry, The.
Queen Djenira.
Queen Wasp, A.
Quiet.
Quiet Enemy, The.
Rachel.
Railway Junction, The.
Reawakening, The.
Reconciliation.
Reflections.
Remembrance.
Remonstrance, The.
Reserved.
Revenant, The.
Reverie.
Riddle, A.
Riddlers, The.
Robin, A.
Rooks In October.
Rose.
Rose in Candlelight, A.
Rose in Water, A.
Round, The.
Sallie's Musical Box.
Satire, The.
Scarecrow, The.
Scribe, The.
Sea-Magic.
Self to self.
Shade, The.
Shadow.
Sign, A.
Silence.
Sleep.
Sleeper, The.
Slum Child, The.
Snow.
Snowdrop, The.
Snowflake, The.
Snowing.
Solitude.
Son of Melancholy, The.
Sorcery.
Sotto Voce.
Spark, The.
Spectre, The.
Speech.
Spirit of Air, The.
Strange Spirit, The.
Stranger, The.
Stratagem, The.
Suicide, The.
Sunday, A.
Sunk Lyonesse.
Sunken Garden, The.
Sunrise.
Swallows Flown.
Taciturn, The.
Tailor, The.
There Blooms No Bud in May.
They Told Me.
Thomas Hardy.
Thorn, The.
Three Cherry Trees, The.
Three Strangers, The.
Thule.
Thus Her Tale.
Time Passes.
Tired Cupid, The.
Titmouse.
To E. T.: 1917.
To K. M.
To My Mother.
Tom's Angel.

Treachery.
Truce.
Tryst, The.
Twice Lovely.
Twilight.
Unchanging, The.
Unfinished Dream, The.
Unforeseen.
Unheard Melodies.
Universe, The.
Unregarding.
Vacant Day, The.
Vain Finding.
Vain Questioning.
Veil, The.
Vigil.
Virtue.
Visionary, The.
Voice, The.
Voices.
Waiting.
Wanderers, The.
What?
When the rose is faded.
Where?
Where Is Thy Victory?
Which?
Which Way?
Who?
Who's that?
Widow, The.
Willow, The.
Window, The.
Winter.
Winter Dusk.
Wreck, The.
Young Girl, A.

Dickey, James (b. 1923)
Adam in Winter.
Adultery.
Angel of the Maze, The.
Angina.
Antipolis.
Apollo.
Approaching Prayer.
Armor.
At Darien Bridge.
At the Home for Unwed Mothers.
Attempted Departure.
Autumn.
Awaiting the Swimmer.
Ax God:Sea Pursuit, The.
Baggage King, The.
Basics.
Bee, The.
Beholders, The.
Being, The.
Between Two Prisoners.
Birth, A.
Birthday Dream, The.
Blood.
Blowgun and Rattlesnake.
Bread.
Breath.
Buckdancer's Choice.
Bums, on Waking.
By Canoe through the Fir Forest.
Call, The.
Cancer Match, The.
Celebration, The.
Change, The.
Chenille.
Cherrylog Road.
Circuit.
Coming Back to America.
Common Grave, The.
Courtship, The.
Craters.
Dark Ones.
Daughter.
Daybreak.
Deborah as Scion.
Deer among Cattle.
Diabetes.
Dog Sleeping on My Feet, A.
Doorstep, Lightning, Waif-Dreaming.
Dover: Believing in Kings.

Dream Flood, The.
Drifting.
Drinking from a Helmet.
Driver, The.
Drowning with Others.
Dusk of Horses, The.
Dust.
Eagles.
Eagle's Mile, The.
Enclosure, The.
Encounter in the Cage Country.
Escape, The.
Exchanges.
Expanses.
Eye-Beaters, The.
Faces Seen Once.
Facing Africa.
Falling.
False Youth: Autumn: Clothes of the Age.
False Youth: Two Seasons.
Farmers.
Fathers and Sons.
Fence Wire.
Fiend, The.
Firebombing, The.
Flash, The.
Fog Envelops the Animals.
Folk Singer of the Thirties, A.
For a Time and Place.
For Richard Wilbur.
For Robert Bhain Campbell.
For the Death of Vince Lombardi.
For the Last Wolverine.
For the Nightly Ascent of the Hunter Orion
   over a Forest Clearing.
For the Running of the New York City
   Marathon.
Form.
Fox Blood.
From Time.
Gamecock.
Gila Bend.
Goodbye to Serpents.
Head-Aim, The.
Heads.
Heaven of Animals, The.
Hedge Life.
Horses and Prisoners.
Hospital Window, The.
Hunting Civil War Relics at Nimblewill
   Creek.
Ice Skin, The.
Immortals.
In the Child's Night.
In the Lupanar at Pompeii.
In the Marble Quarry.
In the Mountain Tent.
In the Pocket.
In the Tree House at Night.
Inside the River.
Into the Stone.
Island, The.
Jewel, The.
Judas.
Knock.
Kudzu.
Lakes of Värmland.
Lazarus to the Assembled.
Leap, The.
Letter, A.
Liberator Explodes, The.
Lifeguard, The.
Listening to Foxhounds.
Little More, The.
Lord in the Air, the.
Low Voice, Out Loud.
Madness.
Magus, The.
Mangham.
Mary Sheffield.
Math.
May Day Sermon to the Women of Gilmer
   County, Georgia, by a Woman Preacher
   Leaving the Baptist Church.
Meadow Bridge.
Mercy.
Messages.

Mexican Valley.
Moon Flock.
Morning, A.
Movement of Fish, The.
Nameless.
Near Darien.
Night Bird.
Night Pool, The.
Obstructions.
Olympian, The.
On the Coosawattee.
On the Hill below the Lighthouse.
One, The.
Other, The.
Owl King, The.
Paestum.
Patience: In the Mill.
Performance, The.
Pine.
Place of the Skull, The.
Poem: "For having left the birds that left
   me."
Poem: "O death, so dear to me."
Poisoned Man, The.
Power and Light.
Purgation ("Before and after the eye, grasses
   go over the long fields").
Purgation ("Beyond the eye, grasses go over
   the long fields").
Pursuit from Under.
Rafters, The.
Rain Guitar, The.
Reading *Genesis* to a Blind Child.
Reincarnation (I) ["Still, passed through the
   spokes of an old wheel, on and around"].
Reincarnation (II).
Remnant Water.
Rib, The.
Root-light, or the Lawyer's Daughter.
Salt Marsh, The.
Saying of Farewell, A.
Scarred Girl, The.
Scratch, The.
Screened Porch in the Country, A.
Seeking the Chosen.
Shark's Parlor, The.
Sheep Child, The.
Six, The.
Slave Quarters.
Sled Burial, Dream Ceremony.
Sleepers.
Sleeping Out at Easter.
Small Song.
Snakebite.
Snow on a Southern State.
Snow Thickets.
Spring-Shock.
Springer Mountain.
Springhouse, Menses, Held Apple, House and
   Beyond.
Sprinter at Forty, The.
String, The.
Summons, The.
Sun.
Sustainment.
Tapestry and Sail.
Them, Crying.
Three Poems with Yevtushenko.
Three, The.
To Be Done in Winter.
To His Children in Darkness.
To Landrum Guy, Beginning to Write at
   Sixty.
Tomb Stone.
Trees and Cattle.
Turning Away.
Twin Falls, The.
Two Poems of Flight Sleep.
Two Poems of Going Home.
Two Poems of the Military.
Two Women.
Underground Stream, The.
Undersea Fragment in Colons.
Veer-Voices: Two Sisters under Crows.
Vegetable King, The.
Venom.

Vessels.
Via appia.
Victory.
View of Fujiyama after the War, A.
Voyage of the Needle, The.
Walking on Water.
Walking the Fire Line.
Wall and Cloud.
Walter Armistead.
War Wound, The.
Wedding, The.
Weeds.
When.
Winter Trout.
Zodiac, The.

Dickey, William (b. 1928)
Afternoon Evening and Night in the
   Courtyard of the Museum of Modern Art.
Alligators and Paris and North America.
And he lies dead—.
And I, who lay so warm and quiet there—.
Androids.
Anniversary, The.
At Maganosc / in the stone bedroom.
At Your Old House *sels*.
At Your Old House.
Avalanche.
Being Asked To Define Bourgeois
   Individuality.
Chickens in San Francisco.
Come, Doctor, we must fly someotherwhere.
Confidence.
Coyote's Song.
Die Älte Frau, Die Älte Marschallin.
Do they remember me?
Doctor, I did not see that you were there.
Dog Under False Pretences.
Dolls Play at Hansel and Gretel, The.
Elegy Before the Time.
Ezekiel's Rabbit.
Face-Paintings of the Caduveo Indians.
For Every Last Batch When the Next One
   Comes Along.
For we have gone a curious way from there.
Fred and the Holy Grail.
Fretful and sick, you ask.
Fretful and sick, you long.
Gambling at Reno.
G.F. Died 1954, Aged 27.
Here, in the summer city.
Here There Are Three of Us Driving South
   in This Expensive Car.
Heroine, The.
His Death from Cancer.
History of the Moon, The.
I did not know you when you came in there.
If forgiveness comes / it will be gradual.
In The Dreaming *sels*.
In The Dreaming.
In the dreaming / we walk throug the streets
   of Oxford.
Joy.
Kindness, A.
Lady of Shalott, Her Mirror Broken, The.
Læestrygonians, The.
Life Moving More Rapidly Than Hands Can
   Manage.
Love among the Manichees.
Making Love.
Memoranda.
More Under Saturn.
Narcissus Unbound.
Nevertheless, sleep / And as your eyes close.
New Place, The.
No, the night has gone.
One Incident of Many.
Part Song, With Concert of Recorders.
Performances.
Post-Therapy Room.
Pruned Roses, The.
Rainbow Grocery, The.
Sagittarius, Scorpio Rising.
Self Prepares for an Unwilling Journey, The.
Silver Creek Falls.
Stella Dallas.
Therefore.
Things Kept.

Thinking of me / think of what was.
Virginia Woolf Gathers Mushrooms.
We meet, eating, smoking.
Who made you come and find the door to
    there?
Yes, they remember you.
You White Cunning Devils.

Dickinson, Emily (1830–86)
Above Oblivion's Tide there is a Pier.
Abraham to kill him.
Absence disembodies—so does Death.
Absent Place—an April Day.
Abstinence from Melody.
Accept my timid happiness.
Acts of Light which beautified, The.
Admirations—and Contempts—of time, The.
Adrift! A little boat adrift!
Adulation is inexpensive.
Advance is Life's condition.
Affection is like bread.
Affection wants you to know it is here.
Afraid! Of whom am I afraid?
After a brief unconsciousness.
After a hundred years.
After all Birds have been investigated and
    laid aside.
After great pain, a formal feeling comes.
After the great intrusion of Death.
After the Sun comes out.
Again—his voice is at the door.
Ah! dainty—dainty Death!
Ah, Moon—and Star!
Ah, Necromancy Sweet!
Ah, Teneriffe!
Air has no Residence, no Neighbor.
Air is soft as Italy, The.
All but Death can be Adjusted.
All Circumstances are the Frame.
All forgot for recollecting.
All I may, if small.
All men for Honor hardest work.
All overgrown by cunning moss.
All that I do.
All the letters I can write.
All these my banners be.
All things swept sole away.
All this and more, though is there more?
All we secure of Beauty.
Alone and in a Circumstance.
Alone, I cannot be.
Alter! When the Hills do.
Altered look about the hills, An.
Although I put away his life.
Always begins.
Always Mine!
Am told that fasting gives to food.
Amalgams are abundant.
Amazing human [or Human] heart [or Heart].
Ambition found him.
Amherst Heart is plain and whole, The.
Ample make this Bed.
Anatomical dishabille.
And I, consign myself to you.
And this of all my Hopes.
And with what body do they come?
Angel begins in the morning, The.
Angels, in the early morning.
Angle of a Landscape, The.
Anguish sometimes gives a cause.
Answer July.
Antiquated Grace, An.
Antiquated Tree, An.
Apology for Her.
Apparently with no surprise.
"Arcturus" is his other name.
Are Friends Delight or Pain?
Area— / no test of depth.
Arrows enamored of his Heart.
Art thou the thing I wanted?
Artists wrestled here!
As by the dead we love to sit.
As Children bid the Guest "Good Night."
As far from pity, as complaint.
As from the earth the light Balloon.
As Frost is best conceived.
As if I asked a common Alms.
As if some little Arctic flower.

As if the Sea should part.
As imperceptibly as Grief.
As old as Woe.
As One does Sickness over.
As plan for Noon and plan for Night.
As Sleigh Bells seem in summer.
As subtle as tomorrow.
As Summer into Autumn slips.
As the Starved Maelstrom lap the Navies.
As Watchers hang upon the East.
As we pass Houses musing slow.
As we take nature, without permission.
As willing lid o'er weary eye.
Ascension has.
Ashes denote that Fire was.
Astounding subjects are the only ones, The.
At Half past Three, a single Bird.
At last, to be identified!
At least—to pray—is left—is left.
At leisure is the Soul.
Atmospheric acquaintance, The.
Auctioneer of Parting, The.
Audacity of Bliss, said Jacob to the Angel.
Aurora is the effort.
Austin is a Poet, Austin writes a psalm.
Autumn is among us.
Autumn—overlooked my Knitting.
Awake ye muses nine, sing me a strain
    divine.
Away from Home are some and I.
Awful Tempest mashed the air, An.
Awkward as the homely are.
Baby's flight will embellish History.
Back from the cordial Grave I drag thee.
Baffled for just a day or two.
Banish Air from Air.
Bat is dun, with wrinkled Wings, The.
Battle fought between the Soul, The.
Be gentle with it—Coax it.
Be Mine the Doom.
Beauty be not caused—It Is.
Beauty crowds me till I die.
Beauty is often timidity.
Because He loves Her.
Because I could not stop for Death.
Because my Brook is fluent.
Because that you are going.
Because the Bee may blameless hum.
Because 'twas Riches I could own.
Bee his burnished Carriage, A.
Bee! I'm expecting you!
Bee is not afraid of me, The.
Bees are Black, with Gilt Surcingles.
Before He comes we weigh the Time!
Before I got my eye put out.
Before the ice is in the pools.
Before you thought of Spring.
Beggar at the Door for Fame, The.
Beggar Lad—dies early, The.
Behind Me—dips Eternity.
Behold this little Bane.
Believing that we are to have no Face.
Belshazzar had a Letter.
Bereaved of all, I went abroad.
Bereavement in their death to feel.
Besides the autumn poets sing.
Besides this May.
Best Gains—must have the Losses' Test.
Best Things dwell out of Sight.
Best Witchcraft is Geometry.
Betrothed to Righteousness might be.
Better—than Music! For I—who heard it.
Between My Country—and the Others.
Between the form of Life and Life.
Bible is an antique Volume, The.
Bind me—I still can sing.
Biography first convinces us.
Bird came down the Walk, A.
Bird did prance—the Bee did play, The.
Bird her punctual music brings, The.
Bird must sing to earn the Crumb, The.
Bird would be a soundless thing, The.
Birds are very bold this Morning, The.
Birds begun at Four o'clock, The.
Birds reported from the South, The.
Birthday of but a single pang.
Black Berry—wears a Thorn in his side, The.

Blazing in Gold and quenching in Purple.
Bless God, he went as soldiers.
Bliss is the plaything of the child.
Blood is more showy (gaudy) than the
    Breath, The.
Bloom—is Result—to meet a Flower.
Bloom upon the Mountain—stated.
Blossom perhaps is an introduction, A.
Blossoms will run away.
Blunder is an estimate, The.
Bobolink is gone, The.
Body grows without, The.
Bone that has no Marrow, The.
Book is only the Heart's Portrait, A.
Bound—a trouble.
Brain—is wider than the Sky, The.
Brain, within its Groove, The.
Bring me the sunset in a cup.
Brother of Ingots—Ah Peru.
Brother of Ophir.
Brow is that of Deity, The.
Bulbs are in the sod, The.
Burdock—clawed my Gown, A.
Business enough indeed.
Bustle in a House, The.
Busy missing you.
But little Carmine hath her face.
Butterfly in honored Dust, The.
Butterfly obtains, The.
Butterfly upon the Sky, The.
Butterfly's Assumption Gown, The.
Butterfly's Numidian Gown, The.
By a departing light.
By a flower—By a letter.
By Chivalries as tiny.
By homely gift and hindered Words.
By my Window have I for Scenery.
By such and such an offering.
Cages do not suit the Swiss.
Candor—my tepid friend.
Cap of Lead across the sky, A.
Career of flowers differs from ours, The.
Changelessness / is Nature's change.
Charm invests a face, A.
Chemical conviction, The.
Cherishing that is speechless, The.
Child's faith is new, The.
Chilly Peace infests the Grass, A.
Choose Flowers that have no Fang, Dear.
Circumference thou Bride of Awe.
Civilization—spurns—the Leopard!
Climbing to reach the costly Hearts.
Clock stopped, A.
Clock strikes one that just struck two, The.
Cloud withdrew from the Sky, A.
Clouds their Backs together laid, The.
Clover's simple Flame, The.
Cocoon above! Cocoon below!
Coffin—is a small Domain, A.
Color, Caste, Denomination.
Color of the Grave is Green, The.
Come show thy Durham Breast.
Come slowly—Eden!
Competitions of the sky, The.
Complacency! My Father!
Conferring with myself.
Confirming All who analyze.
Conjecturing a Climate.
Conscious am I in my Chamber.
Consciousness is the only home.
Consulting summer's clock.
Consummation is the hurry of fools.
Contained in this short Life.
Cosmopolites without a plea.
Could Hope inspect her Basis.
Could I but ride indefinite.
Could—I do more—for Thee.
Could I—then—shut the door.
Could I visit the Beds.
Could live—did live.
Could mortal lip divine.
Could that sweet Darkness where they dwell.
Could you tell me how to grow.
Count not that far that can be had.
Counterfeit—a Plated Person, A.
Court is far away, The.
Crickets sang, The.

Crisis is a Hair.
Crisis is sweet and yet the Heart.
Crumbling elms and evergreens, The.
Crumbling is not an instant's Act.
Curious Cloud surprised the Sky, A.
Daisy follows soft the Sun, The.
Dandelion's pallid tube, The.
Danger is not at first.
Dare you see a Soul at the White Heat?
Darting fear, a pomp, a tear, A.
Dawn and Dew my Bearers be.
Day came slow—till Five o'clock, The.
Day grew small, surrounded tight, The.
Day! Help! Help! Another Day!, A
Day she goes, The.
Day that I was crowned, The.
Day undressed—Herself, The.
Days that we can spare, The.
Dear arrears of tenderness.
Dear friend, can you walk.
Dear March, Come in.
Dear Mr. Bowles found out too late.
Death blow is a Life blow to Some, A.
Death cannot plunder half so fast.
Death goes far around.
Death has only to touch a trifle.
Death is a Dialogue between.
Death is like the insect.
Death is perhaps an intimate friend.
Death is potential to that Man.
Death is the supple Suitor.
Death leaves Us homesick, who behind.
Death obtains the Rose.
Death sets a Thing significant.
Death warrants are supposed to be.
Death's Waylaying not the sharpest.
Declaiming Waters none may dread.
Deed knocks first at Thought, A.
Definition of Beauty is, The.
Defrauded I a Butterfly.
Delayed till she had ceased to know.
Delight—becomes pictorial.
Delight has no Competitor.
Delight is as the flight.
Delight's Despair at setting.
Denial—is the only fact.
Departed—to the Judgment.
Deprived of other Banquet.
Despair's advantage is achieved.
Devil, had he fidelity, The.
Devotion should always wear a fence.
Dew—is the Freshet in the Grass.
Dew suffices itself, A.
Diamond on the Hand, A.
Did life's penurious length.
Did Our Best Moment last.
Did she suffer—except to leave you?
Did the Harebell loose her girdle.
Did We abolish Frost.
Did we disobey Him?
Did you ever stand in a Cavern's Mouth.
Difference between Despair, The.
Dimple in the Tomb, A.
Distance—is not the Realm of Fox.
Distance that the dead have gone, The.
Distrustful of the Gentian.
Ditch is dear to the Drunken man, The.
Do Peolpe moulder equally
Doctor calls it "revenge of the nerves," The.
Dominion lasts until obtained.
Don't put up my Thread and Needle.
Doom is the House without the Door.
Doom of Fruit without the Bloom, A.
Doomed—regard the Sunrise, The.
Door just opened on a street, A.
Doubt if it be Us, A.
Doubt Me! My Dim Companion!
Down Time's quaint stream.
Drab Habitation of Whom?
Drama's Vitallest Expression is the Common
    Day.
Dreams are the subtle Dower.
Dreams—are well—but Waking's better.
Drop fell on the Apple Tree, A.
Drop, that wrestles in the Sea, The.
Dropped into the Ether Acre.
Drowning is not so pitiful.

Drunkard cannot meet a Cork, A.
Dust behind I strove to join, The.
Dust is the only Secret.
Dust like the Mosquito, The.
Duties of the Wind are few, The.
Dying at my music!
Dying! Dying in the night!
Dying is a wild Night.
Dying need but little, Dear, The.
Dying Tiger—moaned for Drink, A.
Dying! To be afraid of thee.
Each Life Converges to some Centre.
Each Scar I'll keep for Him.
Each Second is the last.
Each that we lose takes part of us.
Earth has many keys, The.
Earth would not seem homelike without.
Eat the bit of cake in your garden.
Ecstasy to guess, The.
Eden is that old-fashioned House.
Element of Elegy, The.
Elijah's Wagon knew no thill.
Elizabeth told Essex.
Elysium is as far as to.
Embarrassment of one another.
Emerson's intimacy with his "Bee."
Empty my Heart, of Thee.
Endanger it, and the Demand.
Ended, ere it begun.
Endow the Living—with the Tears.
Enough is so vast a sweetness.
Escape is such a thankful Word.
Escaping backward to perceive.
Essential oils—are wrung.
Estranged from Beauty, none can be.
Eternity may imitate.
Event was directly behind Him, The.
Everywhere of Silver, An.
Except the Heaven had come so near.
Except the smaller size.
Except to Heaven, she is nought.
Exhiliration is the Breeze.
Exhiliration—is within.
Expanse cannot be lost.
Expectation—is Contentment.
Experience is the Angled Road.
Experiment escorts us last.
Experiment to me.
Expulsion from Eden grows indistinct.
Extol thee—could I? Then I will.
Exultation is the going.
Face devoid of love or grace, A.
Face I carry with me—last, The.
Face in evanescence lain, The.
Face we choose to miss, The.
Fact that Earth is Heaven, The.
Facts by our side are never sudden.
Faded Boy—in sallow Clothes, A.
Fairer through Fading—as the Day.
Fairest Home I ever knew, The.
"Faith" is a fine invention.
Faith—is the Pierless Bridge.
Faithful "I am sorry", A.
"Faithful to the end" Amended.
Falsehood of Thee could I suppose.
Fame is a bee.
Fame is a fickle food.
Fame is the one that does not stay.
Fame is the tint that Scholars leave.
Fame of Myself, to justify.
Fame's Boys and Girls, who never die.
Far from Love the Heavenly Father.
Farthest Thunder that I heard, The.
Fascinating chill that music leaves, The.
Fate slew Him, but He did not drop.
Fear—like Dying, dilates trust.
Feather from the Whippoorwill, A.
Feet of people walking home, The.
Ferocious as a Bee without a wing.
Few, yet enough.
Fidelity never flickers.
Field of Stubble, lying sere, A.
Finding is the first Act.
Fingers of the Light, The.
Finite life, little statue.
Finite—to fail, but infinite to Venture.
First Day that I was a Life, The.

First Day's Night had come, The.
First Mute Coming, A.
First We knew of Him was Death, The.
Fitter to see Him, I may be.
Flake the Wind exasperate, The.
Floss won't save you from an Abyss.
Flower keeps it's appointment.
Flower must not blame the Bee, The.
Flower will not trouble her, it has so small a
    Foot, A.
Flowers—Well—if anybody.
Follow wise Orion.
Footlights cannot improve the grave.
For Death—or rather.
For each ecstatic instant.
For every Bird a Nest.
For largest Woman's Heart I knew.
For the comprehension of Suffering.
For this—accepted Breath.
Forbidden Fruit a flavor has.
Forever at His side to walk.
Forever honored be the Tree.
Forever—is composed of Nows.
Forget! The lady with the Amulet.
Forgive me if I come too much.
Fortitude incarnate.
Four Trees—upon a solitary Acre.
Frequently the woods are pink.
Friend Anguish reveals is, The.
Friend is a / solemnity, A.
Friends are nations in themselves.
Frigid and sweet Her parting Face.
From all the Jails the Boys and Girls.
From Blank to Blank.
From Cocoon forth a Butterfly.
From his slim Palace in the Dust.
From Us She wandered now a Year.
Frost of Death was on the Pane, The.
Frost was never seen, The.
Full fed Rose on meals of Tint, A.
Funny—to be a Century.
Further in Summer than the Birds.
Future—never spoke, The.
Fuzzy fellow, without feet, A.
Garlands for Queens, may be.
Gathered into the Earth.
Genius is the ignition of affection.
Gentian has a parched Corolla, The.
Gentian weaves her fringes, The.
Gethsemene and Cana.
Gift of neither Heaven nor Earth, The.
Give little Anguish.
Given in Marriage unto Thee.
Glass was the Street—in tinsel Peril.
Gleam of an heroic Act, The.
Glee—The great storm is over.
Glory is that bright tragic thing.
Glowing is her Bonnet.
Go not too near a House of Rose.
Go slow, my soul, to feed thyself.
"Go tell it." What a Message.
Go thy great way!
Go traveling with us!
God gave a Loaf to every Bird.
God is a distant—stately Lover.
God is indeed a jealous God.
God made a little Gentian.
God made no act without a cause.
God permits industrious Angels.
God seems much more friendly.
Going from a world we know, The.
Going to Heaven!
Going—to—Her!
Going to Him! Happy letter!
Good Morning—Midnight.
Good night, because we must.
Good Night! Which put the Candle out?
Good times are always mutual.
Good to hide, and hear 'em hunt!
Good Will of a Flower, The.
Grace—Myself—might not obtain, The.
Grapes were big and fresh, The.
Grass so little has to do, The.
Gratitude—is not the mention.
Gratitude is the timid wealth.
Grave my little cottage is, The.
Great Caesar! Condescend.

Great Hope fell, A.
Great Hungers feed themselves.
Great Streets of silence led away.
Grief is a Mouse.
Grief of wonder at her fate.
Growth of Man—like Growth of Nature.
Guest am I to have.
Guest is gold and crimson, The.
Had I a pleasure you had not.
Had I known that the first was the last.
Had I not seen the Sun.
Had I not This, or This, I said.
Had I presumed to hope.
Had this one Day not been.
Had we known the Ton she bore.
Had we less to say to those we love.
Had we our senses.
Had you an Hour unengrossed.
Hallowing of Pain, The.
"Happiness" without a cause, The.
Happy lip—breaks sudden, A.
Harm of Years is on him, The.
Has All.
Have any like Myself.
Have you got a Brook in your little heart.
He ate and drank the precious Words.
He forgo—and I—remembered.
He fought like those Who've nought to lose.
He found my Being—set it up.
He fumbles at your Soul.
He gave away his Life.
He has had his Future.
He is alive, this morning.
He lived the Life of Ambush.
He outstripped Time with but a Bout.
He parts Himself—like Leaves.
He preached upon "Breadth" till it argued
    him narrow.
He put the Belt around my life.
He scanned it—staggered.
He strained my faith.
He that is robbed and smiles.
He told a homely tale.
He touched me, so I live to know.
He was my host—he was my guest.
He was weak, and I was strong—then.
He went by sleep that drowsy route.
He who in Himself believes.
Healed Heart shows its shallow scar, The.
Heart asks Pleasure—first, The.
Heart has many Doors, The.
Heart has narrow Banks, The.
Heart is the Capital of the Mind, The.
Heart is the only workman, The.
Heart, not so heavy as mine.
Heart wants what it wants.
Heart! We [or Heart, we] will forget him!
Hearts in Amherst ache tonight, The.
Hearts that never lean, must fall, The.
"Heaven" has different Signs—to me.
Heaven is but a little way.
Heaven is so far of the Mind.
"Heaven"—is what I cannot reach!
Heaven vests for Each, The.
Heaven will not be as good as Earth.
"Heavenly Father"—take to thee.
Her breast is fit for pearls.
Her dying feels to me.
Her face was in a bed of hair.
Her final Summer was it.
Her Grace is all she has.
Her—"last Poems."
Her little Parasol to lift.
Her Losses make our Gains ashamed.
Her reluctances are sweeter.
Her smile was shaped like other smiles.
Her sovereign People.
Her spirit rose to such a height.
Her Sweet turn to leave the Homestead.
Her sweet Weight on my Heart a Night.
Her thot's tho' they are older.
Here, where the Daisies fit my Head.
Hereafter, I will pick no Rose.
Herein a Blossom lies.
High from the earth I heard a bird.
Hills erect their Purple Heads, The.
Hills in Purple syllables, The.

Himmaleh was known to stoop, The.
His Bill an Auger is.
His Bill is clasped—his Eye forsook.
His Cheek is his Biographer.
His Feet are shod with Gauze.
His Heart was darker then the starless night.
His Life was so shy and his tastes so
    unknown.
His little Hearse like Figure.
His Mansion in the Pool.
His Mind like Fabrics of the East.
His mind of man, a secret makes.
His oriental heresies.
His voice decrepit was with Joy.
Hollows round His eager Eyes, The.
Home is the riddle of the wise.
Home itself is far from home.
Honest Tear, An.
Honey you went so far to seek, The.
Hope is a strange invention.
Hope is a subtle Glutton.
"Hope" is the thing with feathers.
Hour for books, those enthralling friends, An.
Hour is a Sea, An.
Hours have Wings.
House upon the Height, A.
"Houses"—so the wise men tell me.
How brittle are the Piers.
How can we thank each other.
How dare the robins sing.
How destitute is he.
How far is it to Heaven?
How firm Eternity must look.
How fits his Umber Coat.
How fleet—how indiscreet an one.
How fortunate the Grave.
How good his Lava Bed.
How happy I was if I could forget.
How happy is the little Stone.
How Human Nature dotes.
How know it from a Summer's Day?
How lonesome the Wind must feel Nights.
How lonesome to be an Article!
How luscious is the dripping.
How many Flowers fail in Wood.
How many schemes may die.
How many times these low feet staggered.
How much of Source escapes with thee.
How much the present moment means.
How near this suffering Summer.
How News must feel when travelling.
How noteless Men, and Pleiads, stand.
How precious Thought and Speech are!
How ruthless are the gentle.
How sick—to wait—in any place—but thine.
How slow the Wind.
How small the furniture of bliss!
How soft a Caterpillar steps.
How soft this Prison is.
How spacious must be the Heart.
How still the Bells in Steeples stand.
How strange that Nature does not knock.
How sweet that he rose in the morning.
How sweet the "Life that now is."
How the old Mountains drip with Sunset.
How the Waters closed above Him.
How to repair my shattered ranks.
How vast is the chastisement of Beauty.
How well I knew Her not.
However you stem Nature.
Humming Birds and Orioles, The.
I always ran Home to Awe when a child.
I am afraid to own a Body.
I am alive—I guess.
I am ashamed—I hide.
I am bringing a little Granite Book.
I am glad you are in the open Air.
I am sorry you need Health.
I am speechlessly grateful for a friend.
I am studying music now with the jays.
I am sure I feel as Noah did.
I asked no other thing.
I bet with every Wind that blew.
I breathed enough to take the Trick.
I bring an unaccustomed wine.
I Came to buy a smile—today.
I can wade Grief.

I cannot be ashamed.
I cannot buy it—'tis not sold.
I cannot conjecture a form of space.
I cannot dance upon my Toes.
I cannot depict a friend to my mind.
I cannot live with You.
I cannot meet the Spring unmoved.
I cannot see my soul but know 'tis there.
I cannot tell how Eternity seems.
I cannot want it more.
I cant tell how it is.
I can't tell you—but you feel it.
I cautious, scanned my little life.
I confess that I love him.
I could bring You Jewels—had I a mind to.
I could die—to know.
I could not drink it, Sweet.
I could not prove the Years had feet.
I could not weigh myself, Myself.
I could suffice for Him, I knew.
I cried at Pity—not at Pain.
I cross till I am weary.
I did not reach Thee.
I died for Beauty—but was scarce.
I dreaded that first Robin, so.
I dream about father every night.
I dwell in Possibility.
I envy seas—whereon He rides.
I fear a Man of frugal Speech.
I fear we think too lightly of.
I fear you have much happiness.
I felt a Cleaving in my Mind.
I felt a Funeral, in my Brain.
I felt my life with both my hands.
I fit for them.
I found the words to every thought.
I gained it so.
I gave myself to Him.
I got so I could take his name.
I groped for him before I knew.
I had a daily Bliss.
I had a guinea golden.
I had been hungry, all the Years.
I had hoped to express more.
I had no Cause to be awake.
I had no time to Hate.
I had not minded—Walls.
I had some things that I called mine.
I had the Glory—that will do.
I have a Bird in spring.
I have a King, who does not speak.
I have felt like a troubled Top.
I have long been a Lunatic on Bulbs.
I have never seen "Volcanoes."
I have no Life but this.
I have seen one Bird and part of another.
I have the friend who loves me.
I haven't told my garden yet.
I heard a fly buzz—when I died.
I heard, as if I had no Ear.
I held a Jewel in my fingers.
I hesitate which word to take.
I hide myself within my flower.
I hope that you are well.
I hope you are joyful frequently.
I hope you may not go.
I hope you may sometime be.
I hope your rambles have been sweet.
I keep my pledge.
I knew a Bird that would sing as firm.
I knew that I had gained.
I know a place where Summer strives.
I know but little of Little Ones.
I know lives, I could miss.
I know not how to thank you.
I know of people in the Grave.
I know some lonely Houses off the Road.
I know Suspense, it steps so terse.
I know that He exists.
I know where Wells grow—Droughtless
    Wells.
I learned—at least—what Home could be.
I lift the lid to my box of Phantoms.
I like a look of Agony.
I like to see it lap the Miles.
I live with Him—I see His face.
I lived on Dread.

I lost a World—the other day!
I made slow Riches but my Gain.
I make His Crescent fill or lack.
I many times thought Peace had come.
I meant to find Her when I came.
I meant to have but modest needs.
I measure every Grief I meet.
I met a King this afternoon!
I never felt at Home—Below.
I never hear that one is dead.
I never hear the word "escape."
I never knew a broken Heart.
I never lost as much but twice.
I never saw a Moor.
I never told the buried gold.
I notice where Death has been introduced.
I noticed People disappeared.
I often passed the village.
I often wish I was a grass.
I often wonder how.
I pay—in Satin Cash.
I play at Riches—to appease.
I prayed, at first, a little Girl.
I raise only robins on my farm.
I read my sentence—steadily.
I reason, Earth is short.
I reckon—when I count at all.
I remember the leaves were falling.
I remember your coming as serious
    sweetness.
I robbed the Woods.
I rose—because He sank.
I saw no Way. The Heavens were stitched.
I saw that the Flake was on it.
I saw the Jays this Morning.
I saw the wind within her.
I see thee better—in the Dark.
I see thee clearer for the Grave.
I send Two Sunsets.
I send you a decrepit flower.
I shall keep singing!
I shall know why—when Time is over.
I shall not murmur if at last.
I shall watch your passage from Crutch to
    Cane.
I should have been too glad, I see.
I should not dare to be so sad.
I should not dare to leave my friend.
I showed her Heights she never saw.
I sing to use the Waiting.
I sometimes drop it, for a Quick.
I started Early—Took my Dog.
I stepped from Plank to Plank.
I stole them from a Bee.
I sued the News—yet feared—the News.
I suppose the time will come.
I taste a liquor never brewed.
I tend my flowers for thee.
I think I was enchanted.
I think it sad to have a friend.
I think just how my shape will rise.
I think that the Root of the Wind is Water.
I think the Hemlock likes to stand.
I think the longest Hour of all.
I think to Live—may be a Bliss.
I thought that being a Poem one's self.
I thought that nature was enough.
I thought the Train would never come.
I thought to shun the Loneliness.
I thought your approbation Fame.
I tie my Hat—I crease my Shawl.
I took my Power in my Hand.
I took one Draught of Life.
I tried to think a lonelier Thing.
I trust this sweet May Morning.
I trust you may have the dearest summer.
"I want"—it pleaded—All its life.
I was a Phoebe—nothing more.
I was the slightest in the House.
I was with you in all the loneliness.
I watched her face to see which way.
I watched the Moon around the House.
I weave for the Lamp of Evening.
I went to Heaven.
I went to thank Her.
I wish I might say one liquid word.
I wish one could be sure the suffering.

I work to drive the awe away.
I worked for chaff and earning Wheat.
I would distil a cup.
I would not paint—a picture.
I write in the midst of Sweet-Peas.
I Years had been from Home.
Icebergs italicize the Sea.
I'd rather recollect a setting.
Ideals are the Fairy Oil.
If all the griefs I am to have.
If any sink, assure that this, now standing.
If anybody's friend be dead.
If Blame be my side—forfeit Me.
If ever the lid gets off my head.
If He dissolve—then—there is nothing—
    more.
If He were living—dare I ask.
If I can stop one Heart from breaking.
If I could bribe them by a Rose.
If I could tell how glad I was.
If I may have it, when it's dead.
If I should cease to bring a Rose.
If I should die.
If I shouldn't be alive.
If I'm lost—now.
If it had no pencil.
If my Bark sink.
If Nature smiles—the Mother must.
If pain for peace prepares.
If recollecting were forgetting.
If roses had not faded.
If she had been the Mistletoe.
If the anguish of others helped one with
    one's own.
If the foolish, call them "flowers."
If the future is mighty as the past.
If this is "fading."
If those I loved were lost.
If What we could—were what we would.
If wrecked upon the Shoal of Thought.
If you were coming in the Fall.
If your Nerve, deny you.
Ignominy to receive, The.
Ignorance a Sunset, An.
I'll clutch—and clutch.
I'll send the feather from my Hat!
I'll tell you how the Sun rose.
I'm ceded—I've stopped being Theirs.
I'm Nobody! Who are you?
I'm saying every day.
I'm sorry for the Dead—Today.
I'm the little "Heart's Ease"!
I'm "wife"—I've finished that.
Image of Light, Adieu.
Immortal is an ample word.
Immortality of Flowers, The.
Immortality she gave, The.
Immured in Heaven!
Impossibility, like Wine.
In a World too full of Beauty for Peace.
In Ebon Box, when years have flown.
In falling Timbers buried.
In lands I never saw—they say.
In many and reportless places.
In rags mysterious as these.
In snow thou comest.
In this place of shafts, I hope.
In this short Life.
In thy long Paradise of Light.
In Winter in my Room.
Incarcerate me in yourself.
Incidents of love, The.
Inconceivably solemn!
Incredible never surprises us, The.
Incredible the Lodging.
Inferential Knowledge, The.
Infinite a sudden Guest, The.
"Infinite Beauty"—of which you speak, The.
Interview is acres.
Intrusiveness of flowers.
Inundation of the Spring, The.
Is Bliss then, such Abyss.
Is Heaven a Physician?
Is his sweet wife too faint to remember.
Is Immortality a bane.
Is is too late to touch you, Dear?
Is is true, dear Sue?

Is it a joyous expanse of Year.
Is it Intellect that the Patriot means.
Is not an absent friend as mysterious.
Is not the distinction of Affection.
Is this the Hope that opens and shuts.
It always felt to me—a wrong.
It bloomed and dropt, a Single Noon.
It came at last but prompter Death.
It came his turn to beg.
It can't be "Summer"!
It ceased to hurt me, though so slow.
It comforts the Criminal little to know.
It consoles the happy Sorrow of Autumn.
It did not surprise me.
It don't sound so terrible—quite—as it did.
It dropped so low—in my Regard.
It feels a shame to be Alive.
It is a lonesome Glee.
It is a Suffering, to have a sea.
It is an honorable Thought.
It is Anguish I long conceal from you.
It is dead. Find it.
It is delicate that each Mind is itself.
It is easier to look behind at a pain.
It is easy to work when the soul is at play.
It is of Realms unratified.
It is solemn to remember.
It is still as distinct as Paradise.
It is the Meek that Valor wear.
It is very wrong that you were ill.
It knew no lapse, nor Diminution.
It knew no Medicine.
It makes no difference abroad.
It may have been she came to show you.
It might be lonelier.
It must have been as if he had come.
It perished with beautiful reluctance.
It rises—passes—on our South.
It sifts from Leaden Sieves.
It sounded as if the Streets were running.
It stills, incites, infatuates.
It stole along so stealthy.
It struck me—every Day.
It tossed—and tossed.
It troubled me as once I was.
It was a Grave, yet bore no Stone.
It was a quiet seeming Day.
It was a quiet way.
It was given to me by the Gods.
It was much—that far and ill.
It was not Death, for I stood up.
It was not Saint—it was too large.
It was so delicious to see you.
It was too late for Man.
It will be Summer—eventually.
It would have starved a Gnat.
It would never be Common—more—I said.
It would not know if it were spurned.
It's all I have to bring today.
It's coming—the postponeless Creature.
It's easy to invent a Life.
It's evening and the orchestra of winds.
It's fragrant news, to know they pine.
Its Hour with itself.
It's like the Light.
Its little Ether Hood.
It's such a little thing to weep.
It's thoughts—and just One Heart.
I've dropped my Brain—My Soul is numb.
I've got an arrow here.
I've heard an Organ talk, sometimes.
I've known a Heaven, like a Tent.
I've none to tell me to but Thee.
I've nothing else—to bring, You know.
I've seen a Dying Eye.
Jay his Castanet has struck, The.
Jennie—my Jennie Humphrey.
Jesus! thy Crucifix.
Joy that has no stem nor core, The.
Joy to have merited the Pain.
Joy we most revere, The.
Judge is like the Owl, The.
Judgment is justest.
Juggler's Hat her Country is, The.
Just as He spoke it from his Hands.
Just lost, when I was saved!
Just Once! Oh least Request!

Just so—Jesus—raps.
Kill your Balm—and its Odors bless you.
Knock with tremor.
Knows how to forget!
Labor might fatigue.
Lad of Athens, faithful be.
Lady feeds Her little Bird, The.
Lady red amid the Hill, A.
Lain in Nature—so suffice us.
Lamp burns sure—within, The.
Landscapes reverence the Frost.
Lane of Yellow led the eye, A.
Largest Fire ever known, The.
Lassitudes of Contemplation, The.
Last Night that She lived, The.
Last of Summer is Delight, The.
Lay this Laurel on the One.
Least Bee that brew.
Least Rivers—docile to some sea.
Left in immortal Youth.
Lest any doubt that we are glad that they
     were born Today.
Lest they should come—is all my fear.
Lest this be Heaven indeed.
Let down the Bars, Oh Death.
Let me not mar that perfect Dream.
Let me not thirst with this Hock at my Lip.
Let my first Knowing be of thee.
Let the phantom love that enrolls the
     sparrow.
Let Us play Yesterday.
"Lethe" in my flower.
Letter always seemed to me, A.
Letter is a joy of Earth, A.
Life, and Death, and Giants.
Life is death we're lengthy at.
Life is so strong a vision.
Life is the finest secret.
Life—is what we make it.
Life that tied too tight escapes, The.
Life we have is very great, The.
Lifetime is for two.
Lift it—with the Feathers.
Light exists in Spring, A.
Light is sufficient to itself.
Lightly stepped a yellow star.
Lightning is a yellow Fork, The.
Lightning playeth—all the while, The.
Like a Memoir of the Sun.
Like Brooms of Steel.
Like Eyes that looked on Wastes.
Like Flowers, that heard the news of Dews.
Like her the Saints retire.
Like Men and Women Shadows walk.
Like Mighty Foot Lights—burned the Red.
Like Rain it sounded till it curved.
Like Some Old fashioned Miracle.
Like Time's insidious wrinkle.
Like Trains of Cars on Tracks of Plush.
Lilac is an ancient shrub, The.
Little bread, a crust, a crumb, A.
Little Dog that wags his tail, A.
Little East of Jordan, A.
Little garden within, The.
Little Madness in the Spring, A.
Little overflowing word, The.
Little package of Ceylon, The.
Little poem we will write unto our Cousin
     John, A.
Little Road—not made of Man, A.
Little sentences I began, The.
Little Snow was here and there, A.
Lives he in any other world.
Loneliness One dare not sound, The.
Lonesome for they know not What, The.
Long—long Sleep—a famous—Sleep, A.
Long sigh of the Frog, The.
Long Years apart can make no.
Longest day that God appoints, The.
Longing is like the Seed.
Look back on Time, with kindly eyes.
Look of thee, what is it like, The.
Loss of something ever felt I, A.
Love a Life can show Below, The.
Love can do all but raise the Dead.
Love is done when Love's begun.
Love—; is anterior to life.

Love—is that later Thing than Death.
Love is that one perfect labor.
Love of God may be taught, The.
Love reckons by itself—alone.
Love—thou art high.
Love which comes without aspect, The.
Lovely Face to sit by, A.
Lovely flowers embarrass me, The.
Love's stricken "why."
Loving the Blest without Abode.
Low at my problem bending.
Low at the knee that bore her once.
Luck is not chance.
Luxury to apprehend, The.
Magic, as it electrifies.
Make me a picture of the sun.
Malay took the Pearl, The.
Mama never forgets her birds.
Man may make a Remark, A.
Manner of its Death, The.
Many a phrase has the English language.
Many an angel, with its needle.
Many can boast a hollyhock.
Many cross the Rhine.
March is the Month of Expectation.
Martyr Poets—did not tell, The.
Maturity only enhances mystery.
Me, change! Me, alter!
Me—come! My dazzled face.
Me from Myself—to banish.
Me prove it now—Whoever doubt.
Meeting by Accident.
Meeting is well worth parting.
Memory is a strange Bell.
Memory is the Sherry Flower.
Merchant of the Picturesque, The.
Midsummer, was it, when They died.
Mien to move a Queen, A.
Mighty dying of my Father, The.
Mind is so near itself, The.
Mind lives on the Heart, The.
Mine—by the Right of the White Election!
Mine Enemy is growing old.
Mine there is no Man would own, A.
Minor Toys of the Year are alike, The.
Missing All—prevented Me, The.
Mob within the heart, The.
Months have ends—the Years—a knot, The.
Moon is distant from the Sea, The.
Moon upon her fluent Route, The.
Moon was but a Chin of Gold, The.
More Life—went out—when He went.
More than the Grave is closed to me.
Morning after Woe, The.
Morning is due to all.
Morning—is the place for Dew.
"Morning"—means "Milking"—to the
     Farmer.
Morning that comes but once.
Morning without you is a dwindled Dawn.
Morns are meeker than they were, The.
Morns like these—we parted.
Most important population, The.
Most of our Moments.
Most pathetic thing I do, The.
Most she touched me by her muteness.
Most triumphant Bird I ever knew or met,
     The.
Moth the hue of this, A.
"Mother," to me, is so sacred a Name.
Mother's dying almost stunned my spirit.
Mountain sat upon the Plain, The.
Mountains grow—unnoticed, The.
Mountains stood in Haze, The.
Much madness is divinest sense.
Mud is very deep, The.
Murmur in the Trees—to note, A.
Murmur of a Bee, The.
Murmuring of Bees, has ceased, The.
Mushroom is the Elf of Plants, The.
Musicians wrestle everywhere.
Must be a Woe.
Must I lose the Friend that saved my Life.
Mute thy Coronation.
My best Acquaintances are those.
My Cocoon tightens—Colors tease.
My country need not change her gown.

My Country, 'tis of thee.
My Eye is fuller than my vase.
My Faith is larger than the Hills.
My family of Apparitions.
My first well Day—since many ill.
My flowers are near and foreign.
My friend attacks my friend!
My friend must be a Bird.
My Garden—like the Beach.
My God—He sees thee.
My Heart ran so to thee.
My Heart upon a little Plate.
My life closed twice before its close.
My Life had stood—a Loaded Gun.
My life has been too simple and stern.
My little Balm might be o'erlooked.
My Maker—let me be.
My nosegays are for Captives.
My period had come for Prayer.
My Portion is Defeat—today.
My Reward for Being, was This.
My River runs to thee.
My Season's furthest Flower.
My Soul—accused me—And I quailed.
My Triumph lasted till the Drums.
My Wars are laid away in Books.
My wheel is in the dark!
My Worthiness is all my Doubt.
Myself can read the Telegrams.
Myself was formed—a Carpenter.
Mysteries of human nature, The.
Name—of it—is "Autumn", The.
Narrow Fellow in the Grass, A.
Nature affects to be sedate.
Nature and God—I neither knew.
Nature assigns the Sun.
Nature can do no more.
Nature gives her love.
Nature is a Haunted House.
Nature is our eldest mother.
"Nature" is what we see.
Nature must be too young to feel.
Nature rarer uses Yellow.
Nature, seems it to myself.
Nature—sometimes sears a Sapling.
Nature—the Gentlest Mother is.
Nature's faithful Blossoms.
Nearest Dream recedes—unrealized, The.
Nearness to Tremendousness, A.
Neither fearing Extinction.
Neither in Heaven nor Earth.
Never for Society.
New feet within my garden go.
Night is my favorite Day.
Night—there lay the Days between, A.
Night was wide, and furnished scant, The.
Night's capacity varies.
No Autumn's intercepting Chill.
No Bobolink—reverse His Singing.
No Brigadier throughout the Year.
No Crowd that has occurred.
No event of Wind or Bird.
No heart that broke but further went.
No ladder needs the bird but skies.
No Life can pompless pass away.
No Man can compass a Despair.
No man saw awe, nor to his house.
No matter—now—Sweet.
No matter where the Saints abide.
No Notice gave She, but a Change.
No Other can reduce.
No Passenger was known to flee.
No Prisoner be.
No Rack can torture me.
No Romance sold unto.
No Rose, yet felt myself a'bloom.
Nobody knows this little Rose.
None can experience stint.
None who saw it ever told it.
Noon—is the Hinge of Day.
Nor Mountain hinder Me.
Not a flake assaults my birds.
Not all die early, dying young.
Not all of life to live, is it.
Not any higher stands the Grave.
Not any more to be lacked.
Not any sunny tone.

Not at Home to Callers.
Not in this World to see his face.
Not knowing when the Dawn will come.
Not One by Heaven defrauded stay.
Not probable—The barest Chance.
Not "Revelation" 'tis, that waits.
Not seeing, still we know.
Not Sickness stains the Brave.
Not so the infinite Relations—Below.
Not that he goes—we love him more.
Not to discover weakness is.
Not what the stars have done.
Not what We did, shall be the test.
Not with a Club, the Heart is broken.
Nothing in her Life became her.
Nothing inclusive of a human Heart.
Notice that is called the Spring, The.
November always seemed to me.
Now I knew I lost her.
Now I lay thee down to Sleep.
Now the Grass is Glass.
Obtaining but our own Extent.
Of all the Souls that stand create.
Of all the Sounds despatched abroad.
Of Being is a Bird.
Of Bronze—and Blaze.
Of Brussels—it was not.
Of Consciousness, her awful Mate.
Of Course—I prayed.
Of Death I try to think like this.
Of Glory not a Beam is left.
Of God we ask one favor.
Of Life to own.
Of Nature I shall have enough.
Of nearness to her sundered Things.
Of Paradise' existence.
Of Paul and Silas it is said.
Of Silken Speech and Specious Shoe.
Of so divine a Loss.
Of the Heart that goes in, and closes the Door.
Of their peculiar light.
Of this is Day composed.
Of Tolling Bell I ask the cause?
Of Tribulation, these are They.
Of whom so dear.
Of Yellow was the outer Sky.
Oh Future! thou secreted peace.
Oh give it Motion—deck it sweet.
Oh, honey of an hour.
Oh Matchless Earth—We underrate.
Oh Shadow on the Grass.
Oh Sumptuous moment.
Oh there is much to speak of.
Oh what a Grace is this.
On a Columnar Self.
On my volcano grows the Grass.
On such a night, or such a night.
On that dear Frame the Years had worn.
On that specific Pillow.
On the World you colored.
On this long storm the Rainbow rose.
On this wondrous sea.
Once more, my now bewildered Dove.
One and One—are One.
One Anguish—in a Crowd.
One Blessing had I than the rest.
One crown that no one seeks.
One Crucifixion is recorded—only.
One Day is there of the Series.
One dignity delays for all.
One Joy of so much anguish.
One Life of so much Consequence!
One need not be a Chamber—to be Haunted.
One of the ones that Midas touched.
One Sister have I in our house.
One thing of it we borrow.
One who could repeat the Summer day, The.
One Year ago—jots what?
Ones that disappeared are back, The.
Only a Shrine, but Mine.
Only Balmless Wound, The.
Only Ghost I ever saw, The.
Only God—detect the Sorrow.
Only Love can wound.
Only News I know, The.

Open the Door, open the Door.
Opening and the Close, The.
Opinion is a flitting thing.
Organ is moaning, The.
Our journey had advanced.
Our little Kinsmen—after Rain.
Our little secrets slink away.
Our lives are Swiss.
Our man has mown today.
Our own possessions—though our own.
Our share of night to bear.
Ourselves we do inter with sweet derision.
Ourselves were wed one summer—dear.
Out of sight? What of that?
Outer—from the Inner, The.
Over and over, like a Tune.
Over the fence.
Overtakelessness of those, The.
Pain—expands the Time.
Pain—has an Element of Blank.
Pain has but one Acquaintance.
Pang is more conspicuous in Spring, A.
Papa above!
Paradise is of the option.
Paradise is that old mansion.
Parasol is the umbrella's daughter, The.
Parents of Beauty, The.
Partake as doth the Bee.
Parting is one of the exactions.
Parting with Thee reluctantly.
Pass to thy Rendezvous of Light.
Past is not a package, The.
Past is such a curious Creature, The.
Patience—has a quiet Outer.
Pattern of the sun, The.
Peace is a fiction of our Faith.
Pedigree of Honey, The.
Perception of an object costs.
Perhaps I asked too large.
Perhaps the dear, grieved Heart.
Perhaps they do not go so far.
Perhaps you smile at me.
Perhaps you think me stooping.
Perhaps you'd like to buy a flower.
Peril as a Possession.
Picture of the pretty Home, The.
Pigmy seraphs—gone astray.
Pile of Years is not so high, The.
Pink—small—and punctual.
Pit—but Heaven over it, A.
Plants went into camp last night, The.
Plated Life—diversified, A.
Please rest the Life so many own.
Poets light but Lamps, The.
Poor little Heart!
Poor torn heart, a tattered heart, A.
Popular Heart is a Cannon first, The.
Port of Peace has many Coves, The.
Portraits are to daily faces.
Power is a familiar growth.
Power to be true to You, The.
Power to fly is sweet, The.
Praise it—'tis dead.
Prank of the Heart at play on the Heart, The.
Prayer is the little implement.
Precious—moldering pleasure—'tis, A.
Precious to Me—She still shall be.
Presentiment—is that long Shadow—on the Lawn.
Presumption has it's Affliction.
Pretty boarders are leaving the trees, The.
Pretty Rain from those sweet Eaves, The.
Prison gets to be a friend, A.
Products of my Farm are these, The.
Promise is firmer than a Hope, A.
Promise This, When You be Dying.
Prompt—executive Bird is the Jay, A.
Props assist the House, The.
Proud of my broken heart, since thou didst break it.
Province of the Saved, The.
Prudence is a tedious one.
Publication—is the Auction.
Pungent atom in the Air, The.
Purple—/ Color of a Queen, is this, The.
Purple—is fashionable twice.
Pursuing you in your transitions.

Put up my lute!
Quicker deceit dies, The.
Quite empty, quite at rest.
Rainbow never tells me, The.
Rat is the concisest Tenant, The.
Rat surrendered here, A.
Rather arid delight.
Ravenousness of fondness, The.
Read—Sweet—how others—strove.
Rearrange a "Wife's" affection!
Recollect the Face of me.
Red—Blaze—is the Morning, The.
Red Leaves take the Green Leaves place, The.
"Red Sea," indeed! Talk not to me.
Rehearsal to Ourselves.
"Remember me" implored the Thief!
Remembrance has a Rear and Front.
Remorse—is Memory—awake.
Remove—from Accident of Loss.
Renunciation—is a piercing Virtue.
Reportless Subjects, to the Quick.
Rests at Night.
Reticent volcano keeps, The.
Reverse cannot befall.
Revolution is the Pod.
Ribbons of the Year.
Riddle we can guess, The.
Right to perish might be thought, The.
Risk is the Hair that holds the Tun.
Risks of Immortality, The.
Road to Paradise is plain, The.
Road was lit with Moon and star, The.
Robbed by Death—but that was easy.
Robin for the Crumb, The.
Robin is a Gabriel, The.
Robin is the One, The.
Robin's my Criterion for Tune, The.
"Robins?" They are writing now, The.
Rose did caper on her cheek, The.
Route of Evanescence, A.
Saddest noise, the sweetest noise, The.
Safe Despair it is that raves.
Safe in their Alabaster Chambers.
Said Death to Passion.
Sailor cannot see the North, The.
Sang from the Heart, Sire.
Satisfaction—is the Agent.
Saucer holds a Cup, A.
Save me from the idolatry.
Savior! I've no one else to tell.
Savior must have been, The.
Savior's only signature, The.
Scatter a fragrant flower.
Science—so the Savants say, A.
Science will not trust us.
Sea said "Come" to the Brook, The.
Secret told, A.
"Secrets" is a daily word.
Sepal, petal, and a thorn, A.
September's Baccalaureate.
Seraphic shame generosity causes, The.
Service without Hope, The.
Severer Service of myself.
Sexton! My Master's sleeping here.
Shade upon the mind there passes, A.
Shady friend—for Torrid days, A.
Shall I take thee, the Poet said.
Shame is the shawl of Pink.
She bore it till the simple veins.
She could not live upon the Past.
She dealt her pretty words like Blades.
She died at play./ Gambolled away.
She died—this was the way she died.
She dwelleth in the Ground.
She hideth Her the last.
She is the Lane to the Indes.
She laid her docile Crescent down.
She lay as if at play.
She rose as high as His Occasion.
She rose to His Requirement—dropt.
She sights a Bird—she chuckles.
She slept beneath a tree.
She sped as Petals of a Rose.
She staked her Feathers—Gained an Arc.
She sweeps with many-colored Brooms.
She talked of you before she went.

She went as quiet as the Dew.
Shells from the Coast mistaking.
She's happy, with a new Content.
Should you but fail at—Sea.
Show is not the Show, The.
Show me Eternity, and I will show you
   Memory.
Sic transit gloria mundi.
Sickness of this World it most occasions, A.
Silence is all we dread.
Silence' oblation to the Ear.
Single clover Plank, A.
Single Screw of Flesh, A.
Sister of Ophir.
Size circumscribes—it has no room.
Skies can't keep their secret!, The.
Sky is low—the Clouds are mean, The.
Slash of Blue, A.
Sleep is supposed to be.
Slips of the last rose of summer, The.
Sloop of Amber slips away, A.
Small weight is obnoxious, A.
Smiling back from Coronation.
Smouldering embers blush, The.
Snow beneath whose chilly softness.
Snow flakes / I counted till they danced so.
Snow that never drifts, The.
So bashful when I spied her!
So delicate a diffidence.
So from the mould/ Scarlet and Gold.
So gay a Flower.
So give me back to Death.
So glad we are—a Stranger'd deem.
So has a Daisy vanished.
So I pull my Stockings off.
So large my Will/ The little that I may.
So much of Heaven has gone from Earth.
So much Summer.
So proud she was to die.
So set its Sun in Thee.
So the Eyes accost—and sunder.
So valiant is the intimacy.
So well that I can live without.
Society for me my misery.
Soft as the massacre of Suns.
Soft Sea washed around the House, A.
Soil of Flint, if steady tilled.
Solemn thing—it was—I said, A.
Solemn thing within the Soul, A.
Some Arrows slay but whom they strike.
Some Days retired from the rest.
Some keep the Sabbath going to Church.
Some one prepared this mighty show.
Some Rainbow—coming from the Fair!
Some say goodnight—at night.
Some such Butterfly be seen.
Some things that fly there be.
Some time is longer than the rest.
Some, too fragile for winter winds.
Some we see no more, Tenements of
   Wonder.
Some—Work for Immortality.
Some Wretched creature, savior take.
Somehow myself survived the Night.
Something in a summer's Day, A.
Sometimes with the Heart.
Somewhat, to hope for.
Somewhere upon the general Earth.
Sorrow almost resents love.
Sorrow, benighted with Fathoms.
Soto! Explore thyself!
Soul has Bandaged moments, The.
Soul must go by Death alone, The.
Soul selects her own Society, The.
Soul should always stand ajar, The.
Soul, take thy risk.
Soul that hath a Guest, The.
Soul unto itself, The.
Soul, Wilt thou toss again?
Soul's distinct connection, The.
Soul's Superior instants, The.
South Wind—has a pathos, A.
South Winds jostle them.
Sown in dishonor!
Sparrow took a Slice of Twig, A.
Speculate with all our might.
"Speech"—is a prank of Parliament.

Speech is one symptom of Affection.
Spell cannot be tattered, A.
Spider as an Artist, The.
Spider holds a Silver Ball, The.
Spider sewed at Night, A.
Spirit is the Conscious Ear, The.
Spirit lasts, but in what mode, The.
Split the Lark—and you'll find the Music.
Spring, and not a Blue Bird.
Spring comes on the World.
Spring is a happiness so beautiful.
Spring is the Period.
Spring's first conviction is a wealth.
Spry Arms of the Wind, The.
Spurn the temerity.
Stagnant pleasure like a Pool, A.
Stars are old, that stood for me, The.
Stem of a departed Flower, The.
Step lightly on this narrow spot.
Still as the Profile of a Tree.
Still own thee—still thou art.
Still—Volcano—Life, A.
Stimulus, beyond the Grave, The.
Stimulus of Loss, The.
Strong Draughts of Their Refreshing Minds.
Struck, was I, not yet by Lightning.
Suburbs of a Secret, The.
Success is counted sweetest.
Success is dust, but an aim.
Such are the inlets of the mind.
Such is the Force of Happiness.
Summer begins to have the look.
Summer day on which you came, The.
Summer for thee, grant I may be.
Summer has been wide and deep, The.
Summer has two Beginnings.
Summer is shorter than any one.
Summer laid her simple Hat.
Summer that we did not prize, The.
Summer—we all have seen.
Summers of bloom—and months of frost.
Sun and Fog contested, The.
Sun and Moon must make their haste, The.
Sun in reining to the West, The.
Sun is one—and on the Tare, The.
Sun—just touched the Morning, The.
Sun kept setting—setting—still, The.
Sun kept stooping—stooping—low!, The.
Sun retired to a cloud, The.
Sun went down—no Man looked on, The.
Sunrise runs for Both, The.
Sunset at Night—is natural.
Sunset stopped on Cottages, The.
Sunset that screens, reveals.
Superfluous were the Sun.
Superiority to Fate.
Surgeons must be very careful.
Surprise is like a thrilling—pungent.
Suspense—is Hostiler than Death.
Sweet Acclamation of Death divulges it, The.
Sweet and soft as summer, Darlings.
Sweet hours have perished here.
Sweet is it as Life.
Sweet is the swamp with its secrets.
Sweet Land of Liberty.
Sweet Mountains—Ye tell Me no lie.
Sweet Pirate of the heart.
Sweet—safe—Houses.
Sweet Skepticism of the Heart.
Sweet, to have had them lost.
Sweet toil for smitten hands.
Sweet—You forgot—but I remembered.
Sweetest Heresay received, The.
Sweetest way I think of you, The.
Sweets of Pillage, can be known, The.
Symptom of the Gale, The.
Take all away.
Take all away from me, but leave me
   Ecstasy.
Take Your Heaven further on.
Taken from men—this morning.
Taking up the fair Ideal.
Talk not to me of Summer Trees.
Talk with prudence to a Beggar.
Teach Him—When He makes the names.
Tell all the Truth but tell it slant.
Tell as a Marksman—were forgotten.

Tenderness has not a Date.
Test of Love—is Death, The.
Than Heaven more remote.
Thank God there is a world.
Thank her dear power for having come.
"Thank you" ebbs between us.
Thank you in my heart obstructs, The.
That a pansy is transitive.
That after Horror—that 'twas us.
That Bareheaded life under the grass.
That bleeding beginning that every mourner
   knows.
That Distance was between Us.
That first Day, when you praised Me, Sweet.
That I did always love.
That is solemn we have ended.
That it is true, Master.
That it will never come again.
That Love is all there is.
That must be a silver bell.
That odd old man is dead a year.
That Possession fairest lies.
That sacred Closet when you sweep.
That she forgot me was the least.
That short—potential stir.
That Sorrow dare to touch the Loved.
That Such have died enable Us.
That sweet Physician, an approaching spring.
That the Divine has been human.
That this should feel the need of Death.
That we are permanent.
That you return to us alive.
That your loved Confederate and yourself.
Their Barricade against the Sky.
Their dappled importunity.
Their Height in Heaven comforts not.
Themself are all I have.
Then will I not repine.
There are Sweets of Pathos.
There are two Mays.
There are two Ripenings—one—of sight.
There came a Day at Summer's full.
There came a Wind like a Bugle.
There comes a warning like a spy.
There comes an hour when begging stops.
There is a finished feeling.
There is a flower that Bees prefer.
There is a June when Corn is cut.
There is a Languor of the Life.
There is a morn by men unseen.
There is a pain—so utter.
There is a Shame of Nobleness.
There is a solitude of space.
There is a strength in proving that it can be
   borne.
There is a tall—pale snow storm.
There is a word/ Which bears a sword.
There is a Zone whose even Years.
There is an arid Pleasure.
There is another Loneliness.
There is another sky.
There is no first, or last, in Forever.
There is no Frigate like a Book.
There is no Silence in the Earth—so silent.
There is not so much Life as talk of Life.
There is nothing sweeter than Honor, but
   Love.
There lurked a dread that you had gone.
There seems a spectral power.
There's a certain Slant of light.
There's been a Death, in the Opposite House.
There's something quieter than sleep.
There's the Battle of Burgoyne.
These are the days that Reindeer love.
These are the days when Birds come back—.
These are the Nights that Beetles love.
These are the Signs to Nature's Inns.
These brief imperfect meetings.
These Fevered Days—to take them to the
   Forest.
These held their Wick above the West.
These Indian-Summer Days.
These—saw Visions.
These Strangers, in a foreign World.
These tested Our Horizon.
They ask but our Delight.
They called me to the Window, for.

They dropped like Flakes.
They have a little Odor—that to me.
"They have not chosen me," he said.
They leave us with the Infinite.
They might not need me—yet they might.
They put Us far apart.
They say that absence conquers.
They say that "Time assuages."
They shut me up in Prose.
They talk as slow as Legends grow.
They won't frown always—some sweet Day.
Things of which we want the proof, The.
Things that never can come back, are several,
  The.
Things we thought that we should do, The.
Think of that great courageous place.
This Bauble was preferred of Bees.
This Chasm, Sweet, upon my life.
This Consciousness that is aware.
This dirty—little—Heart.
This docile one inter.
This Dust, and its Feature.
This heart that broke so long.
This is a Blossom of the Brain.
This is a stern Winter.
This is but a fragment.
This is my letter to the World.
This—is the land—the Sunset washes.
This is the place they hoped before.
This Me—that walks and works—must die.
This Merit hath the worst.
This quiet Dust was Gentlemen and Ladies.
This slow Day moved along.
"This tabernacle" is a blissful trial.
This that would greet—an hour ago.
This was a Poet—It is That.
This was in the White of the Year.
This World is not Conclusion.
Tho' I get home how late—how late.
Tho' my destiny be Fustian.
Those Cattle smaller than a Bee.
Those—dying then.
Those fair—fictitious People.
Those final Creatures—who they are.
Those not live yet.
Those that die seem near me.
Those who have been in the Grave the
  longest.
Though but a simple shelter.
Though the great Waters sleep.
Though thou walk through the Valley of the
  Shadow of Death.
Though we are each unknown to ourself.
Thought beneath so slight a film, The.
Thought went up my mind today, A.
Thousand questions rise to my lips, A.
Three times—we parted—Breath—and I.
Three Weeks passed since I had seen Her.
Thrill came slowly like a Boon for, The.
Throe upon the features, A.
Through lane it lay—through bramble.
Through the Dark Sod—as Education.
Through the strait pass of suffering.
Through those old Grounds of memory.
Through what transports of Patience.
Tie the Strings to my Life, My Lord.
Till Death—is narrow Loving.
Till it has loved—no man or woman.
Time does go on.
Time feels so vast that were it not.
Time is short and full.
Time's wily Chargers will not wait.
Tiniest ones are the mightiest, The.
Tint I cannot take—is best, The.
'Tis Anguish grander than Delight.
'Tis customary as we part.
'Tis easier to pity those when dead.
'Tis good—the looking back on Grief.
'Tis little—I could care for Pearls.
'Tis my first night beneath the Sun.
'Tis not that Dying hurts us so.
'Tis not the swaying frame we miss.
'Tis One by One—the Father counts.
'Tis Opposites—entice.
'Tis Seasons since the Dimpled War.
'Tis so appalling—it exhilirates.
'Tis so much joy! 'Tis so much joy!

'Tis Sunrise—Little Maid—Hast Thou.
'Tis true—They shut me in the Cold.
'Tis whiter than an Indian Pipe.
Title divine—is mine!
To all except anguish.
To an Emigrant, Country is idle.
To attempt to speak of what has been.
To be a Bell and Flower too.
To be alive—is Power.
To be certain we were to meet our Lost.
To be forgot by thee.
To be human is more than to be divine.
To be singular under plural circumstances.
To break so vast a Heart.
To come from Heaven is casual.
To come unto our own.
To congratulate the Redeemed is perhaps
  superfluous.
To die—without the Dying.
To die before it feared to die.
To die—takes just a little while.
To disappear enhances.
To divulge itself is Sorrow's Right.
To do a magnanimous thing.
To earn it by disdaining it.
To fight aloud, is very brave.
To fill a Gap.
To flee from memory.
To forget you would be impossible.
To fulfill the will of a powerless friend.
To hang our head, ostensibly.
To have been the missing Hero.
To have had such Daughters is sanctity.
To hear an Oriole sing.
To help our Bleaker Parts.
To her derided Home.
To him to whom Events and Omens.
To his simplicity.
To interrupt His Yellow Plan.
To know just how He suffered—would be
  dear.
To know that there is shelter.
To know you better as you flee.
To learn the Transport by the Pain.
To live lasts always, but to love.
To lose one's faith—surpass.
To lose thee—sweeter than to gain.
To love thee Year by Year.
To make a prairie it takes a clover and one
  bee.
To make even Heaven more heavenly.
To make One's Toilette—after Death.
To make Routine a Stimulus.
To mend each tattered Faith.
To multiply the Harbors.
To my quick ear the Leaves—conferred.
To my small Hearth His fire came.
To offer brave assistance.
To One denied to drink.
To own a Susan of my own.
To own the Art within the Soul.
To pile like Thunder to its close.
To put this World down, like a Bundle.
To see her is a Picture.
To see is perhaps never quite the sorcery.
To see the Summer Sky.
To tell the Beauty would decrease.
To the bright east she flies.
To the faithful Absence is condensed
  presence.
To the staunch Dust.
To their apartment deep.
To this World she returned.
To those who can estimate silence.
To try to speak, and miss the way.
To undertake is to achieve.
To venerate the simple days.
To wait an Hour—is long.
To which as to a Reservoir.
To Whom the Mornings stand for Nights.
Toad, can die of Light, A.
Today or this noon.
"Tomorrow"—whose location.
Tongue—to tell Him I am true!, A.
Too cold is this.
Too few the mornings be.
Too happy Time dissolves itself.

Too little way the House must lie.
Too peremptory a Courtship for Earth.
Too scanty 'twas to die for you.
Tooth upon Our Peace, A.
Touch lightly Nature's sweet Guitar.
Train went through a burial gate, A.
Transport one cannot contain, A.
Transport's mighty price is.
Travel why to Nature.
Treason of an Accent, The.
Treason of an accent, The.
Trees like Tassels—hit—and swung, The.
Trespass of my rustic Love, The.
Trial as a Stimulus.
Tried always and Condemned by thee.
Triumph—may be of several kinds.
Tropic, indeed, a memory.
Trudging to Eden, looking backward.
Trust adjusts her "Peradventure."
Trust in the Unexpected.
Trusting the happy flower.
Trusty as the stars.
Truth—is as old as God.
Truth—is stirless, The.
'Twas a long Parting—but the time.
'Twas awkward, but it fitted me.
'Twas comfort in her Dying Room.
'Twas Crisis—All the length had passed.
'Twas fighting for his Life he was.
'Twas here my summer paused.
'Twas just this time, last year, I died.
'Twas later when the summer went.
'Twas like a Maelstrom, with a notch.
'Twas Love—not me.
'Twas my one Glory.
'Twas such a little little boat.
'Twas the old—road—through pain.
'Twas warm—at first—like Us.
Twice had Summer her fair Verdure.
Two Butterflies went out at Noon.
Two Lengths has every Day.
Two swimmers wrestled on the spar.
Two Travellers perishing in Snow.
Two—were immortal twice.
'Twould ease—a Butterfly.
Unable are the Loved to die.
Uncertain lease—develops lustre.
Under the Light, yet under.
Undue Significance a starving man attaches.
Unfulfilled to Observation.
Unit, like Death, for Whom?
Unknown is the largest need, The.
Until the Desert knows.
Unto a broken heart.
Unto like Story—Trouble has incited me.
"Unto me?" I do not know you.
Unto my Books—so good to turn.
Unto the Whole—how add?
Unworthy of her Breast.
Up Life's Hill with my little Bundle.
Upon a Lilac Sea.
Upon Concluded Lives.
Upon his Saddle sprung a Bird.
Upon the gallows hung a wretch.
Valor in the dark.
Vastest earthly Day, The.
Veins of other Flowers, The.
Verily it snows.
Victory comes late.
Violets are by my side, The.
Vision of Immortal Life has been fulfilled,
  The.
Visitor in Marl, A.
Vivid in our immortal Group.
Voice that stands for Floods to me, The.
Volcanoes be in Sicily.
Voraciousness of that only gaze, The.
Wait till the Majesty of Death.
Warm in her Hand these accents lie.
"Was not" was all the Statement.
Water is deeper than the land, The.
Water, is taught by thirst.
Water makes many Beds.
Waters chased him as he fled, The.
Way Hope builds his House, The.
Way I read a Letter's—this, The.
Way to know the Bobolink, The.

We all have moments with the dust.
We are snatching our jewels from the frost.
We—Bee and I—live by the quaffing.
We can but follow to the Sun.
We cannot believe for each other.
We Cover Thee—Sweet Face.
We do not know the time we lose.
We do not play on Graves.
We don't cry—Tim and I.
We dream—it is good we are dreaming.
We go by detachments to the strange Home.
We grow accustomed to the Dark.
We have no statutes here.
We introduce ourselves.
We knew not that we were to live.
We learn in the Retreating.
We learned the Whole of Love.
We like a Hairbreadth 'scape.
We like March.
We like March—his shoes are Purple.
We lose—because we win.
We meet no Stranger.
We met as Sparks—Diverging Flints.
We miss a Kinsman more.
We miss Her, not because We see.
We must be careful what we say.
We must be less than Death.
We must bring no Twilight.
We never know how high we are.
We never know we go when we are going.
We outgrow love like other things.
We play at Paste.
We pray—to Heaven.
We read in a tremendous Book.
We read the words but know them not.
We remind her we love her.
We see—Comparatively.
We send the Wave to find the Wave.
We shall find the Cube of the Rainbow.
We should not mind so small a flower.
We shun because we prize her Face.
We shun it ere it comes.
We talked as Girls do.
We talked with each other about each other.
"We thank thee Oh Father" for these strange
    Minds.
We thirst at first—'tis Nature's Act.
We turn not older with years.
We wear our sober Dresses when we die.
We went to sleep as if it were a country.
We would'nt mind the sun, dear.
Weather is like Africa, The.
Weight with Needles on the pounds, A.
We'll pass without the parting.
Well upon the Brook, The.
Went up a year this evening!
Were it but Me that gained the Height.
Were it to be the last.
Were nature mortal lady.
Were the Velocity of Affection.
Wert Thou but ill—that I might show thee.
What a Hazard a Letter is!
What care the Dead, for Chanticleer.
What did They do since I saw Them?
What I can do—I will.
What I see not, I better see.
What if I say I shall not wait!
What indeed is Earth but a Nest.
What Inn is this.
What is—"Paradise."
What Miracles the News is!
What mystery pervades a well!
What shall I do now—it whimpers so.
What shall I do when the Summer troubles.
What Soft—Cherubic Creatures.
What sweeter Shelter than the Hearts.
What tenements of clover.
What Twigs We held by.
What we see we know somewhat.
What would I give to see his face?
Whatever awaits us of Doom or Home.
Whatever it is—she has tried it.
When a Lover is a Beggar.
When Bells stop ringing—Church—begins.
When Continents expire.
When Diamonds are a Legend.
When Etna basks and purrs.

When I count the seeds.
When I have seen the Sun emerge.
When I hoped I feared.
When I hoped, I recollect.
When I was small, a Woman died.
When Katie walks, this simple pair
    accompany her side.
When Memory is full.
When Night is almost done.
When One has given up One's life.
When overwhelmed to know.
When Roses cease to bloom, Sir.
When the Astronomer stops seeking.
When they come back—if Blossoms do.
When thou goest through the Waters.
When we have ceased to care.
When we stand on the tops of Things.
Where bells no more affright the morn.
Where every bird is bold to go.
Where I have lost, I softer tread.
Where Roses would not dare to go.
Where Ships of Purple—gently toss.
Where the Treasure is.
Where Thou art—that—is Home.
Where we owe so much it defies Money.
Whether my bark went down at sea.
Whether they have forgotten.
Which is best? Heaven.
Which is the best—the Moon or the
    Crescent?
Which misses most.
While Asters—/ On the Hill.
While it is alive.
While others go to Church.
While we were fearing it, it came.
White as an Indian Pipe.
Who abdicated Ambush.
Who could be ill in March.
Who could be motherless.
Who Court obtain within Himself.
Who Giants know, with lesser Men.
Who goes to dine must take his Feast.
Who has not found the Heaven—below.
Who is it seeks my Pillow Nights.
Who is the East?
Who knows how deep the Heart is.
Who knows where our hearts go.
Who loves you most.
Who "meddled" with the costly Hearts.
Who never lost, are unprepared.
Who never wanted—maddest Joy.
Who occupies this House?
Who saw no Sunrise cannot say.
Who were "the Father and the Son."
Whoever disenchants.
Whole Gulfs—of Red—and Fleets—of Red.
Whole of it came not at once, The.
Whose are the little beds, I asked.
Whose cheek is this?
Whose Pink career may have a close.
"Why do I love" You, Sir?
Why—do they shut Me out of Heaven?
Why is it Nobleness makes us ashamed.
Why make it doubt—it hurts it so.
Why should we hurry—why indeed?
Why the full heart is speechless.
Why the Thief ingredient accompanies all
    Sweetness.
Wife—at Daybreak I shall be, A.
Wild Blue sky abreast of Winds, A.
Wild Nights—Wild Nights!
Will is always near, dear, The.
Will there really be a "Morning?"
Wind begun to knead the Grass, The.
Wind didn't come from the Orchard—today,
    The.
Wind drew off, The.
Wind—tapped like a tired Man, The.
Wind that rose, A.
Wind took up the Northern Things, The.
Winged spark doth soar about, A.
Winter is good—his Hoar Delights.
Winter under cultivation.
Winters are so short, The.
Witchcraft has not a Pedigree.
Witchcraft was hung, in History.
With closer clutch for that which remains.

With Leopards for Playmates, the beautiful
    Child.
With Pinions of Disdain.
With sorrow that the Joy is past.
With sweetness unabated.
With thee—in the Desert.
Withdrawal of the Fuel of Rapture, The.
Within my Garden, rides a Bird.
Within my reach!
Within that little Hive.
Within thy Grave!
Without a smile—Without a Throe.
Without this—there is nought.
Wolfe demanded during dying.
Wonder—is not precisely Knowing.
Word dropped careless on a Page, A.
Word is dead, A.
Word made Flesh is seldom, A.
Words the happy say, The.
Work is a bleak redeemer.
Work of Her that went, The.
World—feels Dusty, The.
World made penniless by that departure.
World—stands—solemner—to me, The.
Worthlessness of Earthly things, The.
Would you like summer? Taste of ours.
Wounded Deer—leaps highest, A.
Writing is brief and fleeting.
Yesterday is History.
Yesterday, Today, and Forever.
You are most illustrious.
You asked me if I wrote now?
You cannot make Remembrance grow.
You cannot put a Fire out.
You cannot take itself.
You constituted Time.
You have experienced Sanctity.
You know that Portrait in the Moon.
You left me—Sire—two Legacies.
You love me—you are sure.
You love the Lord—you cannot see.
You might not know I remembered you.
You said that I "was Great"—one Day.
You see I cannot see—your lifetime.
You see we keep a jealous Heart.
You spoke of "Hope" surpassing "Home."
You taught me Waiting with Myself.
You'll find—it when you try to die.
You'll know Her—by Her Foot.
You'll know it—as you know 'tis Noon.
Your coming is a symptom of Summer.
Your Gifts are from the Sky.
Your little mental gallantries.
Your relentless Music.
Your Riches—taught me—Poverty.
Your thoughts don't have words every day.
You're right—"the way is narrow."
Youth, like Indian Summer.
You've seen Balloons set—Haven't You?
Zeroes—taught us—Phosphorus, The.
Translations, Coauthored Poems, etc.:
    Boston Lying-In.
    Mass. Mental Health.
    Sun is gay or stark, The.
    Waiting Rooms.

Dobyns, Stephen (b. 1941)
    Absence.
    After the War With the Eskimos.
    Anger.
    Beauty.
    Belly, The.
    Birth Report.
    Black Dog, Red Dog.
    Bleeder.
    Body of Romulus, The.
    Body's Curse, The.
    Body's Hope, The.
    Body's Journey, The.
    Body's Strength, The.
    Body's Weight, The.
    Bowlers Anonymous.
    Bravado.
    Card Game, The.
    Careers.
    Cemetery Nights.
    Cemetery Nights II.
    Cemetery Nights IV.

Cemetery Nights V.
Cézanne and the Love of Color.
Cézanne and Zola.
Cézanne's Ambition.
Cézanne's Doubts.
Cézanne's Love of Poetry.
Cézanne's Outrageousness.
Clouds.
Community, The.
Confession.
Contingencies.
Conviviality of Cows, The.
Counterparts.
Covetousness.
Crossroads.
Cuidadores de Autos.
Dancing in Vacationland.
Day the World Ends, The.
Dead Baby.
Delicate, Plummeting Bodies, The.
Desire.
Envy.
Explaining the Nature of Evidence.
Eyelids.
Faces.
Fatal Kisses.
Favorite Iraqi Soldier.
Fear.
Footstep.
Fragments.
Freight Cars.
Frenchie.
Funny.
Gardener, The.
Geese.
General and the Tango Singer, The.
General Matthei Drives Home through
    Santiago.
Getting Up.
Giver of Gifts, The.
Gluttony.
Gottéron Landscape.
Grandfather Poem, The.
Great Doubters of History, The.
Greedy Child, The.
Grief.
Guitar Lesson, The.
Gun, The.
Hidden Within the Sleeves of Those Dark
    Robes.
How Could You Ever Be Fine.
How It Was at the End.
How To Like It.
In a Row.
In the Hospital.
Inappropriate Gestures.
Invisibles, The.
It's Like This.
Japanese Girl with Red Table.
Katia Reading.
Kentucky Derby Day, Belfast, Maine.
Leaving the Bar and Low Life at Closing, I
    Unsuccessfully Pursue Sainthood.
Letter Beginning with the First Line of Your
    Letter.
Living Room, The.
Long Story.
Marsyas, Midas and the Barber.
Men with Long Faces, The.
Mermaid.
Morning Song.
Mountain, The.
Music One Looks Back On, The.
Name-Burning.
Night Swimmer.
Nihilist, The.
No Map.
Noise the Hairless Make, The.
Noses.
Oatmeal Deluxe.
Orpheus.
Pablo Neruda.
Party, The.
Passing the Word.
Pastel Dresses.
Place between Us, The.
Place in Maine, A.

Putting It All Away.
Querencia.
Rain Song.
Receivers of the World's Attention.
Red Geraniums.
Refusing the Necessary.
Room, The.
Rootless.
Roughhousing.
Santaigo: In Praise of Community.
Santaigo: Five Men in the Street: Number
    One.
Santaigo: Five Men in the Street: Number
    Two.
Santaigo: Forestal Park.
Santaigo: la Avenida Pedro de Valdivia.
Santaigo: Market Day in Winter.
Seeing Off a Friend.
Separate Time, A.
Separations.
Shaving.
Short Rides.
Silence.
Six Poems on Moving.
Slipping Away.
Sloth.
Somewhere It Still Moves.
Song for Making the Birds Come.
Song of Four Dancers.
Song of the Drowned Boy.
Song of the Wrong Response.
Spiritual Chickens.
Spite.
Spleen.
Spring Rain.
Street, The.
Streetlight.
Sweat.
Syracuse Nights.
Ten Feet of Rope.
Tenderly.
Theseus Within the Labyrinth.
This Life.
To Pull into Oneself as into a Locked Room.
Tomatoes.
Topless.
Toting It Up.
Triangular Field, The.
Under the Green Ceiling.
Uprising.
Vanity.
Velocity of Cows, The.
Waking.
Walls To Put Up, Walls To Take Down.
Way It Goes or the Proper Use of Leisure
    Time, The.
Ways of Keys, The.
What You Have Come To Expect.
Where We Are.
White Pig.
White Skirt, The.
White Thighs.
Wind Chimes.
Window, The.

Dodgson, Charles Lutwidge *see* "Carroll, Lewis"
Donne, John (1572–1631)
    Air[e] and Angels.
    Anagram, The.
    Anatomy [or Anatomie] of the World, An[:
        The First Anniversary].
    Angels, The.
    Anniversary [or Anniversarie], The.
    Annunciation.
    Antiquary.
    Apostles, The.
    Apparition, The.
    Ascension [or Ascention].
    Autumnal[l], The.
    Bait[e], The.
    Blossom [or Blossome], The.
    Bracelet, The.
    Break[e] of Day.
    Broken Heart, The.
    Burnt Ship, A.
    Cales and Guiana.
    Calm[e], The.
    Canonization, The.

Change.
Community.
Comparison, The.
Computation, The.
Confessors, The.
Confined Love.
Contemplation of Our State in Our Deathbed.
Cross, The.
Crucifying.
Curse, The.
Damp[e], The.
Dark Churches.
Disinherited.
Dissolution, The.
Divine Meditations.
Doctors, The.
Doth not a Tenarif[e], or Higher Hill.
Dream, The.
Dream[e], The.
Eclogue 1613. December 26.
Ecstasy, The.
Elegies.
Elegy on Mistress Boulstred.
Elegy on the L. C.
Elegy on the Lady Markham.
Elegy upon the Death of Mistress Boulstred,
    An.
Elegy upon the Untimely Death of the
    Incomparable Prince Henry.
Epitaph on Himself.
Epithalamion, An, or Marriage Song on the
    Lady Elizabeth and Count Palatine Being
    Married on St. Valentine's Day.
Epithalamion Made at Lincoln's Inn [or
    Lincolnes Inne].
Expiration, The.
Expostulation, The.
Fall of a Wall.
Farewell to Love.
Father, The.
Fever, A.
First Anniversary [or Anniversarie], The.
Flea, The.
Funeral Elegy, A.
Funeral[l], The.
Good Friday [or Goodfriday], 1613. Riding
    Westward.
Good Morrow, The.
H. W. in Hibernia Belligeranti.
Harbinger to the Progress, The.
Hero and Leander.
His Parting from Her.
His Picture.
Holy Ghost, The.
Holy Sonnets *sels.*
Holy Sonnets.
Hymn [or Hymne] to Christ, at the Author's
    Last Going into Germany, A.
Hymn[e] to God My God, In My Sickness[e].
Hymn to God the Father, A.
Hymn to the Saints, and to Marquis
    Hamilton[, An].
I Can Love Both Fair and Brown.
Indifferent, The.
Jealousy.
Jet Ring Sent, A.
Julia.
Klockius.
La Corona.
Lame Beggar, A.
Lamentations of Jeremy, for the Most Part
    According to Tremeullius.
Lecture upon the Shadow, A.
Legacy [or Legacie], The.
Letter to the Lady Carey, and Mistress Essex
    Rich, from Amiens, A.
Letter Written by Sir H. G. and J. D. alternis
    vicibus, A.
Liar, The.
Licentious Person, A.
Litany, A.
Lovers' Infiniteness[e].
Love's Alchemy [or Alchemie].
Love's Deity [or Deitie].
Love's Diet.
Love's Exchange.
Love's Growth.

Love's Progress.
Love's Usury.
Love's War.
Manliness.
Martyrs, The.
Mercurius Gallo-Belgicus.
Message, The.
Nativity [or Nativitie].
Negative Love.
Niobe.
Nocturnal[l] upon Saint Lucy's [or S. Lucies] Day, Being the Shortest Day, A.
Obscure Writer, An.
Obsequies to the Lord Harrington, Brother to the Lady Lucy, Countess of Bedford.
Of the Progres[se] of the Soule; the Second Anniversarie.
On His Mistress [or Mistris].
Our Companie in the Next World.
Paradox, The.
Patriarchs, The.
Perfume, The.
Phryne.
Primrose[, Being at Montgomery Castle, upon the Hill, on Which It Is Situate], The.
Progress[e] of the Soul[e], The.
Prohibition, The.
Prophets, The.
Pyramus and Thisbe.
Raderus.
Ralphius.
Relic, The.
Resurrection.
Resurrection, Imperfect.
Sappho to Philaenis.
Satire 1: "Away thou fondling motley humourist."
Satire 2: "Sir: though (I thank God for it) I do hate."
Satire 3: "Kind pity [or Kinde pitty] chokes my spleen[e]; brave scorn forbids."
Satire 4: "Well, I may now receive, and die: my sin."
Satire 5: "Thou shalt not laugh in this leaf, Muse, nor they."
Satires.
Second Anniversary [or Anniversarie], The.
Self Love.
Self[e] Accuser, A.
Sir John Wingfield.
Son, The.
Song: "Go, and catch a falling star."
Song: "Sweetest Love, I Do Not Go."
Sonnet. The Token.
Storm at Sea, A.
Storm[e], The.
Sun[ne] Rising, The.
Tale of a Citizen and His Wife, A.
Temple.
To E. of D. with Six Holy Sonnets.
To His Mistress Going to Bed.
To Mr. B. B.
To Mr E. G.
To Mr I. L. ("Blessed [or Blesst] are your north parts, for all this long time").
To Mr I. L. ("Of that short roll of friends writ in my heart").
To Mr. R. W. ("If, as mine is, thy life a slumber be").
To Mr. R. W. ("Kindly I envy thy song's [or songs] perfection").
To Mr. R. W. ("Muse not that by thy mind thy body is led").
To Mr. R. W. ("Zealously my Muse doth salute all thee").
To Mr. Roland Woodward ("Like one who in [or who'in] her third widowhood [or widdowhood] doth profess[e]").
To Mr S. B.
To Mr. C.B.
To Mr. T. W. ("All hail, sweet poet, more full of more strong fire").
To Mr. T. W. ("At once, from hence, my lines and I depart").
To Mr. T. W. ("Haste thee harsh verse as fast as thy lame measure").

To Mr. T. W. ("Pregnant again with th' old twins hope, and fear").
To Mr. Tilman after He Had Taken Orders.
To Mrs. M. H.
To Mrs. Magdalen Herbert: of St. Mary Magdalen.
To Sir Edward Herbert[,] at Juliers [or Julyers].
To Sir Henry Goodyer ("Who makes the past, a pattern for next year").
To Sir Henry Wotton, at His Going Ambassador to Venice.
To Sir Henry Wotton ("Here's no more news, than virtue, I may as well").
To Sir Henry Wotton ("Sir, more than kisses, letters mingle souls").
To the Countess of Bedford at New Year's Tide.
To the Countess of Bedford ("Honour is so sublime perfection").
To the Countess of Bedford ("Madam, / Reason is Our Soul's Left Hand, Faith Her Right").
To the Countess of Bedford ("Madam, / You have refined me, and to worthiest things").
To the Countess of Bedford ("Though I be dead, and buried, yet I have").
To the Countess of Bedford ("To have written then, when you writ, seemed to me").
To the Countess of Huntingdon ("Madam, / Man to God's image, Eve, to man's was made").
To the Countess of Huntingdon ("That unripe side of earth, that heavy clime").
To the Countess of Salisbury.
To the Lady Bedford.
To the Praise of the Dead, and the Anatomy.
Triple Fool, The.
Twicknam [or Twickenham] Garden.
Undertaking, The.
Upon Mr. Thomas Coryat's Crudities.
Upon the Annunciation and Passion Falling upon One Day. 1608.
Upon the Translation of the Psalms by Sir Philip Sidney, and the Countess of Pembroke His Sister.
Valediction, A: Forbidding Mourning.
Valediction, A: Of My Name in the Window.
Valediction, A: Of the Book.
Valediction, A: Of Weeping.
Variety.
Verse and Fame.
Virgin Mary, The.
Virgins, The.
Whale, The.
Will, The.
Witchcraft by a Picture.
Woman's Constancy.

Doolittle, Hilda ("H. D.") (1886–1961)
Acon.
Adonis.
After Troy.
All Mountains.
Ancient Wisdom Speaks.
Antipater of Sidon.
Archer.
Ariadne.
At Baia.
At Croton.
At Eleusis.
At Ithaca.
Birds in Snow.
Body and Soul.
Calliope.
Calypso.
Cassandra.
Centaur Song.
Chance.
Chance Meeting.
Charioteer.
Child Poems.
Choros Sequence.
Christmas 1944.
Circe.
Cities.
Cliff Temple, The.

Contest, The.
Cuckoo Song.
Dancer, The.
Dead Priestess Speaks, A.
Dedication: "When everything was over."
Delphi.
Demeter.
Dodona.
Dream.
Ecce Sponsus.
Egypt.
Electra-Orestes *sels.*
Envy.
Epigram: "Golden one is gone from the banquets, The."
Epigrams.
Epitaph: "So I may say."
Erige Cor Tuum ad Me in Caelum.
Eros.
Eurydice.
Evadne.
Evening.
Flowering of the Rod, The.
Flute Song.
For Bryher and Perdita.
Fragment Thirty six: "I know not what to do."
Fragment Forty: "Keep love and he wings."
Fragment Forty one: "Am I blind alas."
Fragment 113: "Not honey, / not the plunder of the bee."
Garden.
Gift.
Gift, The.
God, The.
Grown Up.
Halcyon.
He marked the pattern of the sky.
Helen.
Heliodora.
Helios.
Helios and Athene.
Helmsman, The.
Hermes of the Ways.
Hermonax.
Hippolytus Temporizes.
Holy Satyr.
Huntress.
Hyacinth.
Hymen.
I Said.
If You Will Let Me Sing.
If Your Eyes Had Been Blue.
In Our Town.
In the Rain.
Islands, The.
Lais.
Late Spring.
Leda.
Let Zeus Record.
Lethe.
Look-out, The.
Loss.
Lovers may come and go.
Magician [Master].
Master, The.
May 1943.
Mid-day.
Moonrise.
Myrtle Bough.
Mysteries, The.
Never let it be said.
Night.
No.
No one knows, / the heart of a child.
Nossis.
Orchard.
Oread.
Orestes Theme.
Orion Dead.
Other Sea-Cities.
Pear Tree.
Phaedra.
Poet, The.
Pool, The.
Prayer: "White, O white face."
Priest.

Prisoners.
Projector.
Projector II.
Psyche.
Pursuit.
Pygmalion.
R.A.F.
Red Roses for Bronze.
Saturn.
Scribe.
Sea Gods.
Sea Heroes.
Sea Iris.
Sea Lily.
Sea Poppies.
Sea Rose.
Sea Violet.
She Contrasts with Herself Hippolyta.
She is dead.
She Rebukes Hippolyta.
Sheltered Garden.
Shepherd, The.
Shrine, The.
Sigil.
Simaetha.
Sitalkas.
Socratic.
Song: "You are as gold."
Songs from Cyprus.
Star by Day.
Storm.
Telesila.
Temple of the Sun *sels.*
Thetis.
To love, one must slay.
Toward the Piraeus.
Trance.
Tribute, The.
Tribute to the Angels.
Triplex.
Two Poems for Christmas, 1937.
Walls Do Not Fall, The.
Wash of cold river.
We Two.
When I Am a Cup.
White Rose.
White World.
Why Have You Sought?
Wind Sleepers, The.
Wine Bowl.
Wooden Animal.
Zeus-Provider.
Translations, Coauthored Poems, etc.:
And Pergamos, / City of the Phrygians.
Bacchae *sels.*
Birds from Parnassus, / swift.
Burnished-head / By burnished-head.
Choros Translations.
Chorus of the Women of Chalkis.
Chorus of Troizenian Women.
Crowd of the Greek force, The.
Daemon initiate, spirit.
Hecuba.
Hippolytus *sels.*
Ion *sels.*
Iphigenia [*or* Iphigeneia] in Aulis *sels.*
It is not for me, the day.
Lift my head, help me up.
Men you strike.
Muse, / tell me of this man of wit.
No more, O my spirit.
Now sing, O slight girls.
O for wings.
O Spirit, / spark by spark.
Odyssey *sels.*
Paris came to Ida.
Sea-Choros.

Dove, Rita (b. 1952)
Abduction, The.
Adolescence—I.
Adolescence—II.
Adolescence—III.
Agosta the Winged Man and Rasha the Black
  Dove.
Aircraft.
Anniversary.
Anti-Father.

Ants of Argos, The.
At the German Writers Conference in
  Munich.
Augustus Observes the Sunset.
Aurora Borealis.
Back.
Banneker.
Beauty and the Beast.
Belinda's Petition.
Bird Frau, The.
Boast, The.
Boccaccio: The Plague Years.
Catherine of Alexandria.
Catherine of Siena.
Centipede.
Champagne.
Charm, The.
Cholera.
Company.
Compendium.
Copper Beech, The.
Corduroy Road.
Courtship.
Courtship, Diligence.
D. C.
David Walker (1785–1830).
Daystar.
Definition in the Face of Unnamed Fury.
Delft.
Dusting.
Early Morning on the Tel Aviv-Haifa
  Freeway.
Eastern European Eclogues.
Event, The.
Exeunt the Viols.
Father out Walking on the Lawn, A.
Fiammetta Breaks Her Peace.
First Kiss.
Fish in the Stone, The.
Five Elephants.
Flirtation.
For Kazuko.
Geometry.
Gospel.
Grape Sherbet.
Great Uncle Beefheart.
Happenstance.
Headdress.
Hill Has Something to Say, The.
Hill of Beans, A.
His Shirt.
House on Bishop Street, The.
House Slave, The.
Ike.
In the Bulrush.
In the Old Neighborhood.
Jiving.
Kadava Kumbis Devise a Way to Marry for
  Love, The.
Kentucky, 1833.
Left-Handed Cellist, The.
Lightnin' Blues.
Lines Muttered in Sleep.
Magic.
Motherhood.
My Father's Telescope.
Nestor's Bathtub.
Nexus.
Nigger Song: An Odyssey.
Night Watch.
Nightmare.
1963.
Notes from a Tunisian Journal.
Nothing Down.
November for Beginners.
Ö.
Obedience.
One Volume Missing.
Oriental Ballerina, The.
Pamela.
Parsley.
Pearls.
Pithos.
Planning the Perfect Evening.
Pomade.
Primer for the Nuclear Age.
Promises.

Reading Hölderlin on the Patio with the Aid
  of a Dictionary.
Receiving the Stigmata.
Recovery.
Refrain.
Roast Possum.
Robert Schumann, Or: Musical Genius
  Begins with Affliction.
Roses.
Sahara Bus Trip, The.
Sailor in Africa, The.
Satisfaction Coal Company, The.
Secret Garden, The.
Shakespeare Say.
Sightseeing.
Slave's Critique of Practical Reason, The.
Small Town.
Snow King, The.
Someone's Blood.
Son, The.
Song. Summer.
Spy.
Straw Hat.
Stroke, The.
Suite for Augustus, A.
Sunday Greens.
Sunday Night at Grandfather's.
Taking in Wash.
Teach Us to Number Our Days.
Then Came Flowers.
This Life.
Thomas at the Wheel.
Three Days of Forest, a River, Free.
To Bed.
Tou Wan Speaks to Her Husband Liu Sheng.
Transport or Slaves From Maryland to
  Mississippi, The.
Under the Viaduct, 1932.
Upon Meeting Don L. Lee, in a Dream.
Variation on Gaining a Son.
Variation on Guilt.
Variation on Pain.
Wake.
Weathering Out.
Why I Turned Vegetarian.
Wingfoot Lake.
Zeppelin Factory, The.
Translations, Coauthored Poems, etc.:
Connections.

Dryden, John (1631–1700)
Absalom and Achitophel, Pt. I.
Achitophel: The Earl of Shaftsbury.
Albion and Albanius *sels.*
Alexander's Feast; or, The Power of Music
  [*or* Musique].
All, All of a Piece Throughout.
All human things are subject to decay.
Almighty crowd, thou shorten'st all dispute.
Annus Mirabilis *sels.*
Aureng-Zebe.
Cheerful soldiers, with new stores supplied,
  The.
Conquest of Granada, The *sels.*
Diana's Hunting-Song.
Disdain Punished.
Don Sebastian *sels.*
Epilogue to the Second Part of *The Conquest
  of Granada.*
Epilogue to the University of Oxford, 1674.
Epilogue to *Tyrannic[k] Love.*
Evening's Love, An *sels.*
Fife and Drum.
Hind and the Panther, The *sels.*
Indian Emperor, The *sels.*
King Arthur *sels.*
Lady's Song, The.
Malcontents, The.
Medal [*or* Medall], The *sels.*
Momus' Song to Mars.
Popish Plot, The.
Priestcraft and Private Judgement.
Prologue: "Our author by experience finds it
  true."
Prologue to *Don Sebastian.*
Prologue to *The Spanish Friar.*
Prologue to *The Tempest* [*or The Enchanted
  Island*].

Prologue to the University of Oxford, 1673.
Prologue to the University of Oxford, 1674.
Religio Laici.
Scriptures, The.
Secret Love; or, The Maiden Queen *sels.*
Secular Masque, The.
Song: "Ah fading joy, how quickly art thou past!"
Song by Comus and Three Peasants, A.
Song: "Can life be a blessing."
Song: "Fair, sweet and young, receive a prize."
Song: "Fairest isle, all isles excelling."
Song: "Farewell fair Arminda, my joy and my grief."
Song: "Farewell ungrateful[l] traitor [*or* traytor]."
Song for St Cecilia's Day [1687], A.
Song: "Go tell Amynta, gentle swain."
Song: "How happy the lover."
Song: "I feed a flame within, which so torments me."
Song of the River Thames, A.
Song to a Fair Young Lady, Going Out of the Town in the Spring.
Song: "Wherever I am, and whatever I do."
Song: "You charmed me not with that fair face."
Spanish Friar [*or* Fryar], The *sels.*
Swallow, privileged above the rest, The.
Sylvae *sels.*
Theodore and Honoria, From [Fables Ancient and Modern from] Boccace.
To My Dear Friend Mr Congreve [on His Comedy Called "The Double-Dealer"].
To My Honoured [*or* Honour'd] Kinsman, John Driden [of Chesterton in the County of Huntingdon, Esquire].
To the Memory of Mr Oldham.
Tradition.
Troilus and Cressida *sels.*
Tyrannic Love *sels.*
When I Consider Life.
Zimri: The Duke of Buckingham.
Translations, Coauthored Poems, etc.:
   Absalom and Achitophel, Pt. II *sels.*
   Doeg, though without knowing how or why.

Dunbar, Paul Laurence (1872–1906)
Absence.
Accountability.
Advice.
After a Visit.
After Many Days.
After the Quarrel.
After While.
Alexander Crummel—Dead.
Alice.
Anchored.
Angelina.
Ante-Bellum Sermon, An.
Appreciation.
At Candle-Lightin' Time.
At Cheshire Cheese.
At Loafing-Holt.
At Night.
At Sunset Time.
At the Tavern.
Awakening, The.
Back-Log Song, A.
Ballad: "I know my love is true."
Ballad: "By Mystic's banks I held my dream."
Banjo Song, A.
Barrier, The.
Behind the Arras.
Bein' Back Home.
Beyond the Years.
Black Samson of Brandywine.
Blue.
Bohemian, The.
Boogah Man, The.
Booker T. Washington.
Border Ballad, A.
Boy's Summer Song, A.
Breaking the Charm.
Bridal Measure, A.
By Rugged Ways.

By the Stream.
Cabin Tale, A.
Capture, The.
Career, A.
Change, The.
Change Has Come, The.
Changing Time.
Chappie, A.
Charity.
Chase, The.
Choice, A.
Chrismus Is A-Comin'.
Chrismus on the Plantation.
Christmas.
Christmas Carol: "Ring out, ye bells!"
Christmas Folksong, A.
Christmas in the Heart.
"Chronic Kicker," The.
Circumstances Alter Cases.
Colored Band, The.
Colored Soldiers, The.
Columbian Ode.
Come and Kiss Me Sweet and Twenty.
Common Things.
Communion.
Companion's Progress, A.
Comparison.
Compensation.
Comrade.
Concert, The.
Confessional.
Confidence, A.
Confirmation.
Conquerors, The.
Conscience and Remorse.
Content.
Coquette Conquered, A.
Corn-Song, A.
Corn-Stalk Fiddle, The.
Crisis, The.
Critters' Dance, De.
Crumb, a Crumb, and a Little Seed, A.
Curiosity.
Curtain.
Dance, The.
Dat Ol' Mare o' Mine.
Dawn.
Day.
Deacon Jones' Grievance.
Dead.
Death.
Death of the First Born, The.
Death Song, [A].
Debt, The.
Delinquent, The.
Dely.
Deserted Plantation, The.
Despair.
Differences.
Dilettante, The: A Modern Type.
Dinah Kneading Dough.
Diplomacy.
Dirge for a Soldier.
Dirge: "Place this bunch of mignonette."
Disappointed.
Discovered.
Discovery, The.
Distinction.
Disturber, The.
Douglass.
Dove, The.
Dream Song I.
Dream Song II.
Dreamer, The.
Dreamin' Town.
Dreams.
Drizzle.
Drowsy Day, A.
Easter Ode, An.
Easy-Goin' Feller, An.
Emancipation.
Encouraged.
Encouragement.
End of the Chapter, The.
Equipment.
Ere Sleep Comes Down to Soothe the Weary Eyes.

Evening.
Expectation.
Faith.
Farewell Song.
Farewell to Arcady.
Farm Child's Lullaby, The.
Fisher Child's Lullaby, The.
Fishing.
Florida Night, A.
Foolin' wid de Seasons.
For the Man Who Fails.
For Theodore Roosevelt.
Forest Greeting, The.
Forever.
Fount of Tears, The.
Frederick Douglass.
Frolic, A.
From the Porch at Runnymede.
Fulfilment.
Garret, The.
God Reigns.
Goin' Back.
Goin' Home.
Golden Day, A.
Good-Night.
Gourd, The.
Grievance, A.
Growin' Gray.
Harriet Beecher Stowe.
Haunted Oak, The.
He Had His Dream.
Her Thought and His.
Home Longings.
Hope.
How Lucy Backslid.
How Shall I Woo Thee.
Howdy, Honey, Howdy!
Hunting Song.
Hymn, A: "Lead gently, Lord, and slow."
Hymn: "O li'l lamb out in de col'."
Hymn: "When storms arise."
If.
If I Could But Forget.
In a English Garden.
In August.
In May.
In Summer.
In Summer Time.
In the Morning.
In the Tents of Akbar.
Inspiration.
Invitation to Love.
Ione.
Itching Heels.
Jack Frost at Bedtime.
James Whitcomb Riley.
Jealous.
Jilted.
Joggin' Erlong.
John Boyle O'Reilly.
Johnny Speaks.
Just Whistle a Bit.
Justice.
Keep A-Pluggin' Away.
Keep a Song Up on de Way.
Kidnaped.
King is Dead, The.
Knight, The.
Lager Beer.
Land o' Used to Be, The.
Lapse, The.
Lawyers' Ways, The.
Lazy Day, A.
Lesson, The.
Letter, A.
Life.
Life's Tragedy.
Light, The.
Light was on the golden sands, The.
Li'l' Gal.
Lily of the Valley, The.
Limitations.
Lincoln.
Little Brown Baby.
Little Christmas Basket, A.
Little Lucy Landman.
Liza May.

Lonesome.
Long Ago.
'Long To'ds Night.
Longing.
Looking-Glass, The.
Lost Dream, A.
Love.
Love and Grief.
Love Despoiled.
Love Is a Star.
Love is the light of the world, my dear.
Love Letter, A.
Love Song, A: "Ah, love, my love is like a cry in the night."
Love-Song: "If Death should claim me for her own to-day."
Lover and the Moon, The.
Lover's Lane.
Love's Apotheosis.
Love's Castle.
Love's Chastening.
Love's Draft.
Love's Humility.
Love's Phases.
Love's Pictures.
Love's Seasons.
Lullaby: "Bedtime's come fu' little boys."
Lullaby: "Kiver up yo' haid, my little lady."
Lyric, A: "My lady love lives far away."
Made to Order Smile, The.
Madrigal, A: "Dream days of fond delight and hours."
Mare Rubrum.
Master-Player, The.
Masters, The.
Matter of Locality, A.
Meadow Lark, The.
Melancholia.
Memorial Day.
Memory of Martha, The.
Merry Autumn.
Misapprehension.
Misty Day, A.
Monk's Walk, The.
Morning.
Morning Song of Love.
Mortality.
Murdered Lover, The.
Musical, A.
My Best Girl.
My Corn-Cob Pipe.
My dear love died last night.
My Lady of Castle Grand.
My Little March Girl.
My Love Irene.
My Sort o' Man.
My Sweet Brown Gal.
Mystery, The.
Mystic Sea, The.
Nature and Art.
Negro Love Song, A.
News, The.
Night.
Night, Dim Night.
Night of Love.
Night on the Chesapeake.
Noddin' by de Fire.
Noon.
Nora: A Serenade.
Not They Who Soar!
Nutting Song.
October.
Ode for Memorial Day.
Ode to Ethiopia.
Oh little fledgling out of the nest.
Ol' Tunes, The.
Old.
Old Apple-Tree, The.
Old Cabin, The.
Old Front Gate, The.
Old High School and the New, The.
Old Homestead, The.
Old Memory, An.
Old Story, The.
On a Clean Book.
On the Death of W. C.
On the Dedication of Dorothy Hall.

On the River.
On the Road.
On the Sea Wall.
One Life.
Opportunity.
Our Martyred Soldiers.
Over the Hills.
Paradox, The.
Parted.
Party, The.
Passage, The.
Passion and Love.
Path, The.
Phantom Kiss, The.
Philosophy.
Photograph, The.
Phyllis.
Place Where the Rainbow Ends, The.
Plantation Child's Lullaby, The.
Plantation Melody, A.
Plantation Portrait, A.
Plea, A.
Poet, The.
Poet and His Song, The.
Poet and the Baby, The.
Pool, The.
Poor Withered Rose.
Possession.
Possum.
Possum Trot.
Prayer, A: "O lord, the hard-won miles."
Precedent.
Preference, A.
Premonition.
Preparation.
Prometheus.
Promise.
Protest.
Puttin' the Baby Away.
Question, A.
Quilting, The.
Rain-Songs.
Real Question, The.
Religion.
Reluctance.
Remembered.
Resignation.
Response.
Retort.
Retrospection.
Riding to Town.
Right to Die, The.
Right's Security.
Rising of the Storm, The.
Rivals, The.
River of Ruin, The.
Roadway, A.
Robert Gould Shaw.
Roses.
Roses and Pearls.
Sailor's Song, A.
Sand-Man, The.
Scamp.
Sea speaks to me of you, The.
Secret, The.
Seedling, The.
She Gave Me a Rose.
She Told Her Beads.
Ships That Pass in the Night.
Signs of the Times.
Silence.
Sling Along.
Slow through the Dark.
Snowin'.
Soliloquy of a Turkey.
Song, A: "On a summer's day as I sat by a stream."
Song, A: "Thou art the soul of a summer's day."
Song: "De bee hit sip some honey f'om de matermony vine."
Song: "My heart to thy heart."
Song of Summer.
Song, The: "My soul, lost in the music's mist."
Song: "Wintah, summah, snow er shine."
Songs.

Sonnet; "Emblem of blasted hope and lost desire."
Sparrow, The.
Speakin' at de Cou't-House.
Speakin' o' Christmas.
Spellin'-Bee, The.
Spiritual, A.
Spring Fever.
Spring Song.
Spring Wooing, A.
Starry Night, A.
Stirrup Cup, The.
Suitor, The.
Sum, The.
Summer in the South.
Summer Night, A.
Summer Pastoral, A.
Summer's Night, A.
Sunset.
Suppose.
Sympathy.
Temptation.
Thanksgiving Poem, A.
Then and Now.
Theology.
There are brilliant heights of sorrow.
Thou Art My Lute.
Till the Wind Gets Right.
Time to Tinker 'Roun'!
To a Captious Critic.
To a Dead Friend.
To a Lady Playing the Harp.
To a Poet and a Lady.
To a Violet Found on All Saints' Day.
To Alice Dunbar.
To an Ingrate.
To Booker T. Washington.
To Dan.
To Dr. James Newton Matthews, Mason, Ill.
To E. H. K.
To Her.
To J. Q.
To Kelly Miller, Jr.
To Louise.
To Mary Church Terrell.
To Miss Mary Britton.
To Pfrimmer.
To the Eastern Shore.
To the Memory of Mary Young.
To the Miami.
To the Road.
To the South.
Too Busy.
Trouble in de Kitchen.
Tryst, The.
Turning of the Babies in the Bed, The.
Tuskegee Song.
Twell de Night Is Pas'.
Twilight.
Two Little Boots.
Two Songs.
Unexpressed.
Unlucky Apple, The.
Unsung Heroes, The.
Vagrants.
Valse, The.
Vengeance is Sweet.
Veteran, The.
Virginia Reel, A.
Visitor, The.
Voice of the Banjo, The.
Wadin' in de Crick.
Waiting.
Warm Day in Winter, A.
Warrior's Prayer, The.
Way T'ings Come, De.
We Wear the Mask.
Welcome Address.
Weltschmertz.
W'en I Gits Home.
What's the Use.
When a Feller's Itchin' to be Spanked.
When All Is Done.
When de Co'n Pone's Hot.
When Dey 'Listed Colored Soldiers.
When Malindy Sings.
When Sam'l Sings.

When the Old Man Smokes.
When Winter Darkening All Around.
Whip-Poor-Will and Katy-Did.
[Whistling Sam]
Whittier.
Why Fades a Dream?
Wind and the Sea, The.
Winter-Song.
Winter's Approach.
Winter's Day, A.
With the Lark.
Wooing, The.
Worn Out.
Wraith, The.
Yesterday and Tomorrow.

Duncan, Robert (b. 1919)
Achilles' Song.
Adoration of the Virgin, The.
After a Long Illness.
After Reading H.D.'s *Hermetic Definitions*.
Albigenses, The.
Among my friends love is a great sorrow.
Architecture, The.
Back to the figure.
Ballad of the Enamord Image, The.
Banners, The.
Before the Judgment.
Beginning of Writing, The.
Bending the Bow.
Best of ways. That there be a law the Earth
  gives and the Mountain.
Book of Resemblances, A.
Bring It Up from the Dark.
Circulations of the Song.
Concert, The.
Dante Études *sels*.
Descriptions of Imaginary Poetries.
Dreamers, The.
Erecting beyond the boundaries of all
  government.
Everything Speaks to Me.
Festivals, The.
Fire, The.
First Invention on the Theme of the Adam.
For a Muse Meant.
For a Song of the Languagers.
Four Songs the Night Nurse Sang.
Helmet of Goliath, The.
Household, The.
Human Communion. Traces, The.
Huon of Bordeaux.
I Am a Most Fleshly Man.
I ask the unyielding Sentence that shows
  Itself forth in the language.
Illustrative Lines.
Imagining in Writing.
In Blood's Domaine.
In Waking.
Kingdom of Jerusalem, The.
Maiden, The.
Master of Rime told me, You must learn to
  lose heart, The.
Mirror, The.
My Mother Would Be a Falconress.
Nel Mezzo del Cammin di Nostra Vita.
O Outrider! / when you come to the
  threshold of the stars.
Often I Am Permitted to Return to a
  Meadow.
Old women came from their caves to close
  the too many doors, The.
Passage over Water.
Passages *sels*.
Poem Beginning with a Line by Pindar, A.
Poem in Stretching, A.
Poetry, a Natural Thing.
Poetry Disarranged.
Reaper, The.
Roots and Branches.
Salvages: An Evening Place.
Sentinels, The.
Song of the Borderguard, The.
Source.
Stage Directions.
Structure of Rime, The *sels*.
There are memories everywhere then.
  Rememberd, we go out, as in.

This Place Rumord to Have Been Sodom.
This potion is love's portion. This herb.
Torso, The.
Tribal Memories.
Up Rising.
Upon Taking Hold.
What of the structure of Rime? I said.
Writing as Writing.
Years As Catches, The.

Dunn, Stephen (b. 1939)
About the Elk and the Coyotes That Killed
  Her Calf.
After Losses.
After the Argument.
Afterlife.
All That We Have.
Almost Everyone.
American Film, An.
Amidst the Faltering.
As It Moves.
At the Smithville Methodist Church.
Atlantic City.
Bad Angels, The.
Beautiful Women.
Because We Are Not Taken Seriously.
Belly Dancer at the Hotel Jerome.
Beneath the Sidewalk.
Between Angels.
Beyond Hammonton.
Biography in the First Person.
Briefcases.
Bringing It Down.
Building in Nova Scotia.
Carpenter's Song, The.
Checklist.
Chipping Away at Death.
Clarities, The.
Cleanliness.
Coming Home, Garden State Parkway.
Competition.
Corners.
Dancing with God.
Danse Manhattanique.
Day and Night Handball.
Decorum.
Desire.
Dinner, The.
Each from Different Heights.
Eggs.
Emptiness.
Essay on Sanity.
Essay on the Personal.
Fable of the Water Merchants.
Fairy Tale.
For Fathers of Girls.
From the Manifesto of the Selfish.
Good Life, A.
Guardian Angel, The.
Halves.
Happiness.
Hard Work 1956.
Having Lost All Capacity.
Here and There.
He/She.
His Music.
Homage to the Divers.
Honesty.
How to Be Happy: Another Memo to Myself.
I Come Home Wanting to Touch Everyone.
In a Dream of Horses.
In the House.
In the 20th Century.
Insomnia.
Instead of You.
Introduction to the 20th Century.
Kindness.
Landscape, The.
Landscape at the End of the Century.
Legacy.
Letter About Myself to You.
Letter Home.
Letting the Puma Go.
Listener, The.
Local Time.
Loneliness.
Long Term.
Loveliness.

Lovers.
Loves.
Man Who Closed Shop, The.
Man Who Never Loses His Balance, The.
Meditation on Two Themes.
Midnight.
Mon Semblable.
Moralists.
My Brother's Work.
Naturally.
Night Truths.
Not the Occult.
Nova Scotia.
Observer, The.
On Hearing the Airlines Will Use a
  Psychological Profile to Catch Potential
  Skyjackers.
One Side of the Story.
Ordinary Days.
Parable of the Fictionist.
Petty Thing, A.
Photograph Album, The.
Photograph in the Hallway, The.
Primer for Swimming at Black Point, A.
Privilege.
Regardless.
Response to a Letter from France.
Resurrection, The.
Return, The.
Romance, A.
Room and the World, The.
Round Trip.
Routine Things Around the House, The.
Secret Life, A.
Sister.
Smiles.
Snow Leopard, The.
Snowmass Cycle, The.
Some Things I Wanted to Say to You.
Something.
Something Like Happiness.
Split: 1962.
Substitute, The.
Sudden Light and the Trees, The.
Sweetness.
Sympathetic Magic *sels*.
Teacher Answering Young Radicals.
Temporarily.
Tenderness.
That Saturday Without a Car.
This Late in the Century.
Those of Us Who Think We Know.
To a Friend in Love with the Wrong Man
  Again.
To a Terrorist.
Toward the Verrazano.
Traveling.
Truck Stop: Minnesota.
Turning Fifty.
Under the Black Oaks.
Update.
Urgencies.
Vanishings, The.
Waiting with Two Members of a Motorcycle
  Gang for My Child to Be Born.
Walking the Marshland.
Wanting to Get Closer.
Welcome.
What.
What They Wanted.
When the Revolution Came.
White Collar.
Whiteness.
Wind in a Jar.
With No Experience in Such Matters.
Woman on Edgehill Road, The.
Woman with Five Hearts, The.
Workers.
Worker's Creed, A.
Worrier, The.

"Dylan, Bob" (Robert Zimmerman) (b. 1941)
Abandoned Love.
Absolutely Sweet Marie.
Advice for Geraldine on Her Miscellaneous
  Birthday.
Ain't Gonna Grieve.
Ain't No Man Righteous, No Not One.

All Along the Watchtower.
All I Really Want to Do.
All Over You.
Alternatives to College.
Apple Suckling Tree.
Are You Ready?
As I Went Out One Morning.
Baby, I'm in the Mood for You.
Baby, Stop Crying.
Ballad for a Friend.
Ballad in Plain D.
Ballad of a Thin Man.
Ballad of Donald White.
Ballad of Frankie Lee and Judas Priest, The.
Ballad of Hollis Brown.
Billy.
Black Crow Blues.
Blowin' in the Wind.
Bob Dylan's Blues.
Bob Dylan's Dream.
Bob Dylan's New Orleans Rag.
Bob Dylan's 115th Dream.
Boots of Spanish Leather.
Bringing It All Back Home.
Buckets of Rain.
California.
Can You Please Crawl Out Your Window?
Caribbean Wind.
Changing of the Guards.
Chimes of Freedom.
Clean-Cut Kid.
Clothes Line.
Corrina, Corrina.
Country Pie.
Covenant Woman.
Dark Eyes.
Day of the Locusts.
Dead Man, Dead Man.
Dear Landlord.
Death of Emmett Till, The.
Denise.
Desire (Liner Notes).
Desolation Row.
Dirge: "I hate myself for lovin' you and the
   weakness that it showed."
Do Right to Me Baby (Do Unto Others).
Don't Fall Apart on Me Tonight.
Don't Think Twice, It's All Right.
Don't Ya Tell Henry.
Down Along the Cove.
Down in the Flood.
Down the Highway.
Drifter's Escape.
Dusty Old Fairgrounds.
11 Outlined Epitaphs.
Emotionally Yours.
Eternal Circle.
Every Grain of Sand.
Farewell Angelina.
Farewell: "Oh it's fare thee well my darlin'
   true."
Father of Night.
Forever Young.
Fourth Time Around.
From a Buick 6.
Gates of Eden.
George Jackson.
Get Your Rocks Off!
Girl of the North Country.
Goin' to Acapulco.
Going, Going, Gone.
Golden Loom.
Gonna Change My Way of Thinking.
Gotta Serve Somebody.
Groom's Still Waiting at the Altar, The.
Guess I'm Doin' Fine.
Gypsy Lou.
Hard Rain's A-Gonna Fall, A.
Hard Times in New York Town.
Hazel.
Heart of Mine.
Hero Blues.
Highway 61 Revisited.
Highway 61 Revisited (liner Notes).
Honey, Just Allow Me One More Chance.
I Am a Lonesome Hobo.
I and I.

I Believe in You.
I Don't Believe You (She Acts Like We
   Never Have Met).
I Dreamed I Saw St. Augstine.
I Pity the Poor Immigrant.
I Shall Be Free.
I Shall Be Free No. 10.
I Shall Be Released.
I Threw It All Away.
I Wanna Be Your Lover.
I Want You.
I'd Hate to Be You on That Dreadful Day.
Idiot Wind.
If Dogs Run Free.
If Not for You.
If You Gotta Go, Go Now.
If You See Her, Say Hello.
I'll Be Your Baby Tonight.
I'll Keep It with Mine.
I'll Remember You.
In the Garden.
In the Summertime.
Is Your Love in Vain?
It Ain't Me, Babe.
It Takes a Lot to Laugh, It Takes a Train to
   Cry.
It's All Over Now, Baby Blue.
It's Alright, Ma (I'm Only Bleeding).
Joan Baez in Concert, Part 2.
John Brown.
John Wesley Harding.
John Wesley Harding (Liner Notes).
Jokerman.
Just Like a Woman.
Just Like Tom Thumb's Blues.
Knockin' on Heavin's Door.
Last Thoughts on Woody Guthrie.
Lay Down Your Weary Tune.
Lay, Lady, Lay.
Legionnaire's Disease.
Lenny Bruce.
Leopard-Skin Pill-Box Hat.
Let Me Die in My Footsteps.
Let's Keep It Between Us.
License to Kill.
Like a Rolling Stone.
Lily, Rosemary, and the Jack of Hearts.
Living the Blues.
Lo and Behold!
Lonesome Death of Hattie Carroll, The.
Long Ago, Far Away.
Long-Distance Operator.
Long Time Gone.
Love Is Just a Four-Letter Word.
Love Minus Zero/No Limit.
Maggie's Farm.
Mama, You Been on My Mind.
Man Gave Names to All the Animals.
Man in Me, The.
Man of Peace.
Man on the Street.
Masters of War.
Meet Me in the Morning.
Million Dollar Bash.
Minstrel Boy.
Mr. Tambourine Man.
Mixed Up Confusion.
Most Likely You Go Your Way (and I'll Go
   Mine).
Motorpsycho Nightmare.
My Back Pages.
My Life in a Stolen Moment.
Need a Woman.
Neighborhood Bully.
Never Gonna Be the Same Again.
Never Say Goodbye.
New Morning.
New Pony.
No Time to Think.
Nobody 'Cept You.
North Country Blues.
Nothing Was Delivered.
Obviously Five Believers.
Odds and Ends.
Off the Top of My Head.
On a Night Like This.
On the Road Again.

One More Cup of Coffee (Valley Below).
One More Night.
One More Weekend.
One of Us Must Know (Sooner or Later).
One Too Many Mornings.
Only a Hobo.
Only a Pawn in Their Game.
Open the Door, Homer.
Outlaw Blues.
Oxford Town.
Paths of Victory.
Peggy Day.
Percy's Song.
Playboys and Playgirls.
Please, Mrs. Henry.
Pledging My Time.
Poor Boy Blues.
Positively 4th Street.
Precious Angel.
Pressing On.
Property of Jesus.
Queen Jane Approximately.
Quinn the Eskimo.
Quit Your Low Down Ways.
Rainy Day Women # 12 & 35.
Rambling, Gambling Willie.
Restless Farewell.
Romance in Durango.
Sad-Eyed Lady of the Lowlands.
Sara.
Saved.
Saving Grace.
Seeing the Real You at Last.
Señor (Tales of Yankee Power).
Seven Curses.
Seven Days.
She Belongs to Me.
Shelter from the Storm.
She's Your Lover Now.
Shot of Love.
Sign Language.
Sign on the Cross.
Sign on the Window.
Silent Weekend.
Simple Twist of Fate.
Sitting on a Barbed-Wire Fence.
Slow Train.
Solid Rock.
Some Other Kinds of Songs.
Something There Is About You.
Something's Burning, Baby.
Song to Woody.
Spanish Harlem Incident.
Standing on the Highway.
Stuck Inside of Mobile with the Memphis
   Blues Again.
Subterranean Homesick Blues.
Sweetheart Like You.
Talkin' John Birch Paranoid Blues.
Talkin' World War III Blues.
Talking Bear Mountain Picnic Massacre
   Blues.
Talking New York.
Tangled Up in Blue.
Tears of Rage.
Tell Me, Momma.
Tell Me That It Isn't True.
Temporary Like Achilles.
This Wheel's on Fire.
Three Angels.
Tight Connection to My Heart (Has Anybody
   Seen My Love).
Time Passes Slowly.
Times They Are A-Changin', The.
Tiny Montgomery.
To Be Alone with You.
To Ramona.
Tombstone Blues.
Tomorrow Is a Long Time.
Tonight I'll Be Staying Here with You.
Too Much of Nothing.
Tough Mama.
Train A-Travelin'.
Trouble.
Trouble in Mind.
True Love Tends to Forget.
Trust Yourself.

Union Sundown.
Up to Me.
Visions of Johanna.
Walkin' Down the Line.
Wallflower.
Walls of Red Wing.
Wanted Man.
Watching the River Flow.
Watered-Down Love.
We Better Talk This Over.
Wedding Song.
Went to See the Gypsy.
What Can I Do for You?
Whatcha Gonna Do.
When He Returns.
When I Paint My Masterpiece.
When the Night Comes Falling from the Sky.
When the Ship Comes In.
When You Gonna Wake Up?
Where Are You Tonight? (Journey through
    Dark Heat).
Who Killed Davey Moore?
Wicked Messenger, The.
Winterlude.
With God on Our Side.
Yea! Heavy and a Bottle of Bread.
You Ain't Goin' Nowhere.
You Angel You.
You're a Big Girl Now.
You're Gonna Make Me Lonesome When
    You Go.
Translations, Coauthored Poems, etc.:
Black Diamond Bay.
Catfish.
Coming from the Heart (The Road Is Long).
Hurricane.
I'd Have You Any Time.
If I Don't Be There by Morning.
Isis.
Joey.
Love You Too Much.
Money Blues.
Mozambique.
Oh, Sister.
Rita May.
Walk Out in the Rain.

E

Eberhart, Richard (b. 1904)

Adam Cast Forth.
Address to you.
Aesthetics after War.
Airman Considers His Power, An.
Am I My Neighbor's Keeper.
American Hakluyt.
Analogue of Unity in Multeity.
Angels, The.
Anima.
Anxiety I Felt in Guanajuato, The.
Apple Buds.
As If You Had Never Been.
Assassin, The.
At Night.
At The Canoe Club.
At the End of the War.
Attic, The.
Attitudes.
Austere Poem.
Autumnal.
Ball Game.
Barn, The.
Bath Room, The.
Bells of a Chinese Temple, The.
Big Rock.
Birth and Death.
Birth of the Spirit, The.
Blessed Are the Angels in Heaven.
Bones of Coleridge, The.
Book of Nature, The.
Bower, The.
Breathless, The.
Broken Pen, The.
Broken Wing Theory.
Brotherhood of Men.
Burden.

Burr Oaks.
By the Stream.
Cage, The.
Cancer Cells, The.
Caravan of Silence.
Cemetery, The.
Centennial For Whitman.
Ceremonial.
Ceremony By the Sea, A.
Child, The.
Christmas Tree.
Clam Diggers and Diggers of Sea Worms,
    The.
Clerihew for Alan Gaylord, A.
Coast of Maine.
Commas in Wintertime.
Commitment, A.
Concord Cats.
Configuration.
Cousin Florence.
Cover Me Over.
Critic With His Pained Eye, The.
Dam Neck, Virginia.
Day-Bed, The.
Dead Skunk.
Death in the Mines.
Deep Fishing.
Despair.
Difficulty of Ideas, The.
Dream, A.
Dream, The.
Dream Journey of the Head and Heart.
Dry Rot, The.
Edgar Lee Masters.
Emblem.
Emerson's Concord.
Emily Dickinson.
Enigma, The.
Equivalence of Gnats and Mice.
Evaluation Under a Pine Tree, Lying On Pine
    Needles, An.
Evening Bird Song.
Evil.
Examination of Psyche: Thoughts of Home.
Experience Evoked.
Explorer on Main Street, The.
Extremity.
Fables of the Moon.
Face, Ocean.
Fantasy of a Small Idea.
Fisher Cat, The.
Flag, The.
Flow of Thought.
Flux.
For a Lamb.
Forgotten Rock, The.
Formative Mastership.
Forms of the Human.
Fortune's Mist.
Four Exposures.
Four Lakes' Days.
Fragment of New York, 1929.
Froth.
Full of Joy Do Not Know; They Need Not,
    The.
Fury of Aerial Bombardment, The.
Garden God, The.
Gesture, The.
Giantess, The.
Gnat on My Paper.
Gnats.
Go to the Shine That's on a Tree.
Goal of Intellectual Man, The.
God and Man.
Gods of Washington, D.C., The.
Going.
Going Backward Going Forward.
Going to Maine.
Grave Piece.
Great Praises.
Great Principles Are Thrown Down by Time.
Groundhog, The.
Groundhog Revisiting, The.
Grove, The.
Gulled.
Half-bent Man.
Hamlet Father, The.

Hand, The.
Hand and the Shadow, The.
Hard Structure of the World, The.
Hardening into Print.
Hardy Perennial.
Harvard Stadium.
Hatred of the Old River.
Haystack, The.
Height of Man, The.
Hill Dream of Youth, Thirty Years Later.
Homage to the North.
Hoot Owls.
Hop-Toad, The.
Hornets by the Sill.
Horse Chestnut Tree, The.
How It Is.
Human Being is a Lonely Creature, The.
Humanist, The.
I Walked Out to the Graveyard to See the
    Dead.
I Walked over the Grave of Henry James.
I Went to See Irving Babbitt.
I Will Not Dare to Ask One Question.
Ichetucknee.
Ideal and the Real, The.
Ides of March, The.
If I Could Only Live at the Pitch That Is
    near Madness.
Illusion of Eternity, The.
Imagining How It Would Be to Be Dead.
In a Hard Intellectual Light.
In after Time.
In Prisons of Established Craze.
In the Garden.
Inchiquin Lake, Penobscot Bay.
Incidence of Flight.
Incomparable Light, The.
Indian Pipe.
Ineffable, The.
Instruments.
Irish Catholic.
Ives.
John Finley.
John Ledyard.
Jungle, The.
Kaire.
Key West.
Killer, The.
Kinaesthesia.
La Crosse at Ninety Miles an Hour.
Lament of a New England Mother, The.
Laocoön.
Largess, The.
Later or Sooner.
Learning from Nature.
Legend of Viable Women, A.
Let the Tight Lizard on the Wall.
Life and Death.
Life as Visionary Spirit.
Light From Above.
Light, Time, Dark.
Line of Verse of Yeats, A.
Lions Copulating.
Listing.
Long Swing, The.
Long Term Suffering.
Looking At The Stars.
Looking at the Stars.
Looking Head On.
Loon Call, A.
Lorca.
Loss.
Lost, The.
Lost Children, The.
Love among The Ruins.
Love Poem, A: "I am the lightness that I
    know."
Lucubration.
Lyric Absolute, The.
Maine Roustabout, A.
Mais L'Amour Infini Me Montera Dans
    L'Ame.
Man and Nature.
Man of Autumn, The.
Man of Summer, The.
Man Who Was Blown Down by the Wind,
    A.

Man's Greed and Envy Are So Great.
Man's Type.
Marrakech.
Matador.
May Evening.
Maze.
Meaningless Poem.
Meditation, A.
Meditation Two.
Mediterranean Song.
Memory.
Mind and Nature.
Mistaken Identity.
Moment of Equilibrium among the Islands.
Moment of Vision, The.
My Bones Flew Apart.
My Brains Are Slipping in the Fields of
    Eros.
My Golden and My Fierce Assays.
Mystery of the Abstract.
Mystical Beast in the Shadows, The.
Mysticism Has Not the Patience To Wait for
    God's Revelation.
Necessity.
New England Bachelor, A.
New England Protestant.
New Hampshire, February.
News.
Nexus.
1934.
Noble Man, The.
Nostalgia for Edith Sitwell.
Nothing But Change.
Now Is The Air Made of Chiming Balls.
O Wild Chaos!
Oak, The.
Ode to Silence.
Ode to the Chinese Paper Snake.
Oedipus.
Off Spectacle Island.
Old Dichotomy: Choosing Sides.
Old Fashioned American Business Man, An.
Old Question.
Old Tom.
Old Tree by the Penobscot.
On a Squirrel Crossing the Road in Autumn,
    in New England.
On Returning to a Lake in Spring.
On Seeing an Egyptian Mummy in Berlin,
    1932.
On Shooting Particles beyond the World.
On the Fragility of Mind.
On the Subtle Man.
Once More, O Ye.
Only in the Dream.
Opposition.
Opulence.
Orchard.
Orchard, The.
Ospreys in Cry.
Parker River, The.
Passage, The.
Pasture, The.
Perception as a Guided Missile.
Placation of Reality.
Place, The.
Play, The.
Poem as Trajectory, The.
Poet, The.
Poetry and Games.
Portrait of Rilke.
Project, The.
Prometheus.
Propositions.
Protagonists.
Pull of Memory, The.
Quanta.
Quarrel with a Cloud.
Question Mark.
R. G. E.
Rape of the Cataract, The.
Reading Room, The New York Public
    Library.
Reality.
Recapitulation, The.
Recognition.
Recollection of Childhood.

Redemption.
Refrains.
Request.
Request for Offering.
Retrospective Forelook.
Return, The.
Return of Odysseus, The.
Rifkin Movement.
River Water Music.
Ruby Daggett.
Rumination.
Sacrifice, The.
Sagacity.
Sailing to Buck's Harbor.
Sainte Anne De Beaupré.
Salem.
Sanders Theater.
Santa Claus in Oaxaca.
Scarf of June, The.
Scouring, The.
Sea Burial from the Cruiser *Reve*.
Sea-Hawk.
Sea-Ruck.
Sea Storm.
Seals, Terns, Time.
Seasons, The.
Secret Heart, The.
Seeing is Deceiving.
Sestina: "I die, no matter what I do I die."
Ship Burning and a Comet All in One Day,
    A.
Skier and the Mountain, The.
Slow Boat Ride.
Snow Cascades.
Snowfall, A.
Snowy Owl.
Solace.
Soldier Rejects His Times Addressing His
    Contemporaries, A.
Sometimes the Longing for Death.
Somewhere Else.
Soul.
Soul Longs to Return Whence It Came, The.
Sphinx.
Spider, The.
Spite Fence.
Spring Man.
Spring Mountain Climb.
Standards, The.
Statue of Liberty.
Stealth and Subtleties of Growth.
Stopping a Kaleidoscope.
Suicide Note.
Suite in Prison.
Summer Landscape.
Sunday in October.
Supreme Authority of the Imagination, The.
Swallows Return, The.
Swinging Bridge, The.
Testament, A.
Testimony.
There Is an Evil in the Air.
This Fevers Me.
Three Kids.
Throwing the Apple.
Throwing Yourself Away.
Thrush Song at Dawn.
Time Passes.
To Auden on His Fiftieth.
To Evan.
To Harriet Monroe.
To Kenya Tribesmen, the Turkana.
To the Field Mice.
To the Mad Poets.
To William Carlos Williams.
Tobacconist of Eighth Street, The.
Track.
Transfer, The.
Transformation.
Tree Swallows.
Triptych.
Truncated Bird, The.
Truth, The.
Trying to Hold It All Together.
21st Century Man.
Two Loves.
Ultimate Song.

Undercliff Evening.
United 555.
Ur Burial.
Usurper.
Van Black, an Old Farmer in His Dell.
Vastness and Indifference of the World, The.
Velvet Rocks.
Verbalist of Summer, The.
Vermont Idyll.
Villanelle: "Christ is walking in your blood
    today."
Virgin, The.
Vision.
Vision through Timothy.
Voyage, The.
Waiting To Lean to the Master's Command.
Way Out, A.
Ways and Means.
Wedding, The.
Wedding on Cape Rosier, A.
What Gives.
When Doris Danced.
When Golden Flies Upon My Carcass Come.
Whenever I See Beauty I See Death.
Where Are Those High and Haunting Skies.
White Pines, Felled 1984.
Why.
Wild Life and Tamed Life.
Wild Swans of Inverane, The.
Winter Kill.
Wisdom of Insecurity, The.
Words.
World War.
Worldly Failure.
Yonder.
You Think They Are Permanent But They
    Pass.
Young and the Old, the.
Young Greek, Killed In The Wars, A.
Young Hunter, The.
Translations, Coauthored Poems, etc.:
New Entrepreneurial Plan.

Edmunds, Martin (b. 1955)
Albatross.
Appalachia.
Back Home.
Bella Roma.
Black Bull, The.
Cabin Site Christmas Island, N.S.
Chromo.
December Frost.
December 27, 1988.
Doña Sebastiana.
Egypt.
El Niño.
El Santuario de Chimayó.
Farewell: "Farewell, my love, goodbye."
Fever.
Fire, The.
Gaea.
Going Out to Look at the Year's First
    Blossoms.
High Road to Taos, The.
Highlands 1966, The.
Hill Village, A.
I Have Tried to Find You.
In Memoriam: Robert Fitzgerald.
Jonathan Lazarus Wright, 1702–1729.
Lancaster Street.
Landing in Cairo.
Letter to Jeffrey Gustavson.
Like A Green Branch.
Lunes.
Monday.
Moon.
Morada La Muerte, The.
My Love Has Been.
Nocturne.
November.
One for the Road.
One Look at the Creation.
Passion Week Monday after Palm Sunday.
Stone.
Taos.
Thirteen Years.
Treblinka.
Weathering.

White Nights, 1938.
Willows Coming into Leaf.

Eliot, Thomas Stearns (1888–1965)
And Would It Have Been Worth It?
Animula.
Ash Wednesday [or Ash-Wednesday].
Aunt Helen.
Boston Evening Transcript, The.
Burbank with a Baedeker: Beistein with a
  Cigar.
Burnt Norton.
Cape Ann.
Chorus from "The Rock."
Choruses from "The Rock."
Conversation Galante.
Cooking Egg, A.
Coriolan.
Cousin Nancy.
Cultivation of Christmas Trees, The.
Dans le Restauramt.
Death by Water.
Dedication to My Wife, A.
Defense of the Islands.
Difficulties of a Statesman.
Dry Salvages, The.
East Coker.
Eyes That Last I Saw in Tears.
Five-Finger Exercises.
Four Quartets.
Fragment of an Agon.
Game of Chess, A.
Gerontion.
Hippopotamus, The.
Hollow Men, The.
Hysteria.
Journey of the Magi.
La Figlia Che Piange.
Landscapes.
Le Directeur.
Lines for an Old Man.
Lines for Cuscuscaraway and Mirza Murad
  Ali Beg.
Lines to a Duck in a Park.
Lines to a Persian Cat.
Lines to a Yorkshire Terrier.
Lines to Ralph Hodgson Esqre.
Little Gidding.
Love Song of J. Alfred Prufrock, The.
Lune de Miel.
Marina.
Mélange Adultère de Tout.
Mr. Apollinax.
Mr. Eliot's Sunday Morning Service.
Morning at the Window.
New Hampshire.
Note on War Poetry, A.
Portrait of a Lady.
Preludes (I–IV).
Rannoch, by Glencoe.
Rhapsody on a Windy Night.
Song by Klipstein and Krumpacker.
Song by Wauchope and Horsfall.
Song for Simeon, A.
Sweeney Agonistes.
Sweeney among the Nightingales.
Sweeney Erect.
To the Indians Who Died in Africa.
To Walter de la Mare.
Triumphal March.
Two Songs from *Sweeny Agonistes*.
Usk.
Virginia.
Waste Land, The.
Whispers of Immortality.
Wind Sprang Up at Four o'Clock, The.

Emerson, Ralph Waldo (1803–82)
A. H.
'ΑΔΑΚΡΥΝ ΝΕΜΟΝΤΑΙ ΑΙΩΝΑ.
Adirondacs, The.
Ah! not to me these dreams belong.
Ah strange strange strange.
All day the waves assailed the rock.
All that thy virgin soul can ask be thine.
All the great & good.
All things rehearse.
Alone in Rome! Why Rome is lonely too.
Alphonso of Castile.

Always day & night.
Amulet, The.
Ancient drop of feudal blood, An.
Ancient lady who dwelt in Rome, An.
And as the light divided the dark.
And do I waste my time.
And Ellen, when the greybeard years.
And he like me is not too proud.
And hungry Debt beseiged my door.
And man of wit & mark.
And rival Coxcombs with enamored stare.
And the best gift of God.
And though he dearly prized the bards of
  fame.
And when I am entombed in my place.
Apology, The.
April.
April and May.
Archangel Hope / Looks to the azure cope,
  The.
Around the man who seeks a noble end.
Art.
Artist.
As I walked in the woods.
As the drop feeds its fated flower.
Asmodaean feat be mine, The.
Astræa.
At last the poet spoke.
At Plymouth in the friendly crowd.
At Sea, September 1833.
Atom displaces all atoms beside, The.
Atom from atom yawns as far.
Awed I behold once more.
Bacchus.
Bard or dunce is blest, but hard.
Be of good cheer, brave spirit; steadfastly.
Beauty.
Bended to fops who bent to him.
Berrying.
Best of life is presence of a muse, The.
Bird was gone   the ghastly trees, The.
Blackbird's song the blackbird's song, The.
Blight.
Bluebeard. Let the gentle wife prepare.
Bohemian Hymn, The.
Borrow Urania's subtile wings.
Borrowing from the French.
Boston.
Boston Hymn.
Botanist.
Brahma.
Brave Empedocles defying fools, The.
Brother, no decrepitude.
Burn your literary verses.
But as this fugitive sunlight.
But God will keep his promise yet.
But if thou do thy best.
But Nature whistled with all her winds.
But never yet the man was found.
But O to see his solar eyes.
By art, by music, overthrilled.
By kinds I keep my kinds in check.
By the unacknowledged tie.
Casella.
Character.
Chartist's Complaint, The.
Chladni strewed on glass the sand.
Civil world will much forgive, The.
Climacteric.
Cloud upon cloud / Clouds after rain.
Cloud upon cloud / The world is seeming.
Coil of space the cones of light, The.
Coin the daydawn into lines.
Comfort with a purring cat.
Compensation ("Why should I keep
  holiday").
Compensation ("Wings of Time are black and
  white, The").
Comrade of the snow & wind.
Comrade or the book is good, The.
Coral worm beneath the sea, The.
Crowning hour when bodies vie with souls,
  The.
Culture.
Cup of life is not so shallow, The.
Cupido.
Dæmonic and the Celestial Love, The.

Dangerous gift & grace is mine, A.
Dark Flower of Cheshire garden.
Days.
Days pass over me, The.
Day's Ration, The.
Dear are the pleasant memories.
Dear brother, would you know the life.
Dear Ellen, many a golden year.
Dervish whined to *Said*, The.
Dirge: "Knows he who tills this lonely field."
Discontented Poet: A Masque, The.
Divine Inviters! I accept.
Do that which you can do.
Dost thou not hear me Ellen.
Dull uncertain brain, A.
Dust unto dust! and shall no more be said.
Duty.
Each and All.
Earth, The.
Easy to match what others do.
Elizabeth Hoar.
Enough is done highminded friend go sleep.
Eros.
Etienne de la Boéce.
Eve roved in Paradise, I've heard.
Ever the Rock of Ages melts.
Excelsior.
Experience.
Fable: "Mountain and the squirrel, The."
Fame.
Far seen the river glides below.
Fate ("Deep in the man sits fast his fate").
Fate ("Her planted eye to-day controls").
Fate ("That you are fair or wise is vain").
Few are free / All might be.
Fine presentiments controlled him.
For deathless powers to verse belong.
For every god.
For fifteen winter days.
For Genius made his cabin wide.
For joy & beauty planted it.
For Lucifer, that old athlete.
For Lyra yet shall be the pole.
For Nature true & like in every place.
For that a man is a mark.
For what need I of book or priest.
Forbearance.
Forbore the ant hill, shunned to tread.
Forerunners.
Forester.
Freedom.
Friends to me are frozen wine.
Friendship ("Ruddy drop of manly blood,
  A").
From a far mountain creeping down.
From Alcuin.
From Frodmer's Drama "The Friends."
From high to higher forces.
From Nature's beginning.
From the stores of eldest Matter.
Future, The.
Gardener.
Genial spark the poet felt, The.
Gentle Spring has charmed the earth.
Give All to Love.
Γν&ohgr;θι Σεαυτον.
Go boldly forth, and feast on being's
  banquet.
Go if thou wilt ambrosial Flower.
Go into the garden.
Go out into Nature and plant trees.
God only knew how Saadi dined.
God The Lord save Massachusetts.
Gods walk in the breath of the woods, The.
Good-bye.
Good Charles the springs adorer.
Grace.
Guy.
Hafiz.
Hamatreya.
Hard is it to persuade the public mind of its
  plain duty & true interest.
Harp, The.
Have ye seen the caterpillar.
He could condense cerulean ether.
He lives not who can refuse me.
He loved to watch & wake.

He must have / Droll fancies sometimes cross his quiet thoughts.
He walked the streets of great New York.
He whom God had thus preferred.
Hearst thou, sweet spirit, thou hast heard before.
Heart of All the Scene, The.
Heartily heartily / Nothing be false.
Heartily heartily sing.
Heavy blue chain, The.
Heri, Cras, Hodie.
Hermione.
Heroism.
His instant thought the Poet spoke.
History *sels.*
History & prophecy are alike.
Hold of the Maker, not the made.
Holidays.
Honor bright o muse.
Horoscope.
House, The.
How drearily in College hall.
Humble-Bee, The.
Husband has the nearest acres, The.
Hush!
Hymn[:] Sung at the Completion of the Concord Monument, April 19, 1836.
Hymn Sung at the Second Church, Boston, at the Ordination of Rev. Chandler Robbins.
I am alone. Sad is my solitude.
I am an exile from my home; heavily.
I am not black in my mind.
I am owner of the sphere.
I call her beautiful;—she says.
I cannot find a place so lonely.
I care not whither I may go.
I grieve that better souls than mine.
I have an arrow that can find its mark.
I have found a nobler love.
I have no brothers & no peers.
I have supped with the gods tonight.
I know the appointed hour.
I leave the book, I leave the wine.
I left my dreamy page & sallied forth.
I live among ideal men.
I love thy music, mellow bell.
I must not borrow light.
I never knew but one.
I rake no coffined clay, nor publish wide.
I sat upon the ground.
I spread my gorgeous sail.
I to my garden went.
I use the knife.
I wear no badge; no tinsel star.
I will not hesitate to speak the word.
I will not live out of me.
Idealism.
If bright the sun, he tarries.
If curses be the wage of love.
If he go apart.
If thy body pine.
If wishes would carry me over the land.
Illusions like the tints of pearl.
In an Age of Fops and Toys.
In dreamy woods, what forms abound.
In Memoriam.
In my garden three ways meet.
In the deep heart of man a poet dwells.
In this sour world, o summerwind.
In Walden wood the chickadee.
Initial, Dæmonic, and Celestial Love.
Inscription on a Well in Memory of the Martyrs of the War.
Inspired we must forget our books.
Intellect / Gravely broods apart on joy.
Intellect.
Is Jove immortal / So is Cerberus at his portal.
Is the pace of nature slow?
It takes a philosopher or fool.
I've found the dainty malice out.
James Russell Lowell.
Kind & holy were the words.
King. If farmers make my land secure.
Know he who tills this lonely field.
Land was all electric, The.
Leave me, Fear! thy throbs are base.

Let not conceited sages laugh aloud.
Letters ("Every day brings...").
Letters ("My tongue is prone to lose the way").
Life.
Life is great / Men are small.
Like vaulters in the circus round.
Lines on the Death of Miss M. B. Farnham.
Lobster-car, boat, or fishbasket.
Look danger in the eye it vanishes.
Loss and Gain.
Love / Asks nought his brother cannot give.
Love.
Love and Thought.
Lover's Petition.
Low December vault in June be up-lifted high.
Maia.
Maiden Speech of the Æolian Harp.
Manners.
Mask thy wisdom with delight.
May.
May-Day.
Memory.
Merlin.
Merlin's Song.
Merops.
Mighty Heart, The.
Miracle, The.
Mithridates.
Monadnoc.
More sweet than my refrain.
Motto to "Circles."
Motto to "Considerations by the Way."
Motto to "Fate."
Motto to "Gifts."
Motto to "Illusions."
Motto to "Intellect."
Motto to "Nature" ("Rounded world is fair to see, The").
Motto to "Nature" ("Subtle chain of countless rings, A").
Motto to "New England Reformers."
Motto to "Nominalist and Realist."
Motto to "Power."
Motto to "The Poet."
Mottoes to "History."
Muse / Can at pleasure use, The.
Musketaquid.
My days roll by me like a train of dreams.
My Garden.
My Thoughts.
Nature.
Nature 1 ("Winters know / Easily to shed the snow").
Nature 2 ("She is gamesome and good").
Nature ("Day by day for her darlings to her much she added more").
Nature in Leasts.
Nature saith / I am not infinite.
Nature says, / These craggy hills that front the dawn.
Nature will not lose.
Natures web star broidered.
Nemesis.
New England Capitalist.
No fate, save by the victim's fault, is low.
No song so tuneful, quoth the fox.
None spares another yet it pleases me.
Northman.
No. 13 Hymn Written in Concord Sept. 1814.
Nun's Aspiration.
O Boston city lecture-hearing.
O sun! take off thy hood of clouds.
O what are heroes prophets men.
O What have I to do.
O what is Heaven but the fellowship.
October woods, wherein.
Ode, Inscribed to W. H. Channing.
Ode Sung in the Town Hall.
Ode to Beauty.
Oil & Wine, / Sparkling gems, & rich attire.
Old Age.
On a raisin stone.
On bravely through the sunshine & the showers.
On that night the poet went.

On the chamber, on the stairs.
On the Death of Mr. John Haskins.
On thee has God conferred.
Once the priest / Lived in an age.
One hand washes the other.
One night he dreamed of a palace fair.
Orator.
Original—"Apropos."
Painting and Sculpture.
Pair of crystal eyes will lead me, A.
Pale Genius roves alone.
Panoply of Paradise is mine.
Papas Blondine / Grew tall & wise.
Park, The.
Parks & ponds are good by day.
Past, The.
Patch of meadow & upland, A.
Patient Pan / Drunken with nectar, The.
Pedants all / They would be original.
Perhaps thy lot in life is higher.
Pericles.
Philosophers are lined with eyes within.
Pilgrims, The.
Poem on Eloquence by R. W. Emerson.
Poem, Spoken Before the ΦBK Society, August, 1834.
Poet ("Ever the poet *from* the land").
Poet ("To clothe the fiery thought").
Poet is at home, A.
Poet of poets / Is Time, the distiller.
Poets are colorpots.
Politics.
Pour the wine! pour the wine!
Power.
Problem, The.
Proteus.
Prudence.
Puff of air or dry or damp, A.
Put in, drive home the sightless wedges.
Quatrains.
Queen rejoices in her peers, A.
Quoth Saadi, when I stood before.
Rex.
Rhodora, The [On Being Asked Whence Is the Flower].
Romany Girl, The.
Roomy Eternity / Casts her schemes rarely.
Rubies.
Rules to men made evident, The.
S. H.
S. R.
Saadi.
Saadi held the Muse in awe.
Saadi loved the new & old.
Sacrifice.
Samson stark at Dagon's knee.
Scholar is a ball thats spent.
Score of airy miles will smooth, A.
Sea reflects the rosy sky, The.
Sea-Shore.
Seashore.
Secret that should not be blown, The.
See how Romance adheres.
See yonder leafless trees against the sky.
Seemed, tho' the soft sheen all enchants.
Seemed to me—never maid.
Seyd planted where the deluge ploughed.
Shakspeare.
Shall the Muse sing for thousands & not sing.
She had wealth of mornings in her year.
She never comes to me.
She paints with white & red the moors.
She walked in flowers around my field.
Shout to the Sheperds, A.
Shun passion, fold the hands of thrift.
Silence.
Simple people each with basket or tool, The.
Since the devil hopping on.
Skeptic, The.
Snow-Storm, The.
Softens the air so cold & rude.
Solar insect on the wing.
Solution.
Song: "Shout for those whose course is done."
Song of Nature.

South Wind.
Sparrow is rich in her nest, THe.
Sphinx, The.
Spices in the plants that run.
Spirits of the wise, sit on the clouds, The.
Spiritual Laws.
Spring.
Star seer Copernicus / Only could earn a
    curse.
Stout Sparta shrined the god of Laughter.
Such another peerless queen.
Sun athwart the cloud thought it no sin, The.
Sun is the sole inconsumable fire, The.
Sunshine was he.
Sursum Corda.
Suum Cuique ("Rain has spoiled the farmer's
    day, The").
Suum Cuique ("Wilt thou seal up the avenues
    of ill?").
Tact.
Teach me I am forgotten by the dead.
Teach me your mood, O patient stars!
Tell me maiden dost thou use.
Tell men what they knew before.
Terminus ("For thought & not praise").
Terminus ("It is time to be old").
Test, The.
Thank the gods thy governors.
Thanks to those who go & come.
That each should in his house abide.
That wandering fire to me appears.
There are beggars in Iran and Araby.
There is in all the sons of men.
There is no evil but can speak.
Thermometer.
These trees like tho'ts that to visions congeal.
Thine Eyes Still Shined.
Things oft miscalling, as the hen-.
Think how the gods receive thy prayer.
This shining hour is an edifice.
This world is tedious.
Thou shalt make thy house.
Though thy eye seek other forms.
Three Dimensions, The.
Threnody: "South-wind brings, The."
Titmouse, The.
To Ellen, at the South.
To Eva.
To every creature / Adam gave its name.
To J. W.
To Rhea.
To the Clock.
To the mizen, the main, & the fore.
To transmute crime to wisdom, & to stem.
Too late the anxious fire came.
Traitors tho' plumed & steel equipped.
Trimountain.
Try the might the Muse affords.
Turtle in swamp.
Two Rivers.
Una.
Undersong, The.
Unity.
Upon a rock yet uncreate.
Uriel.
Use will in man new grace reveal.
Vain against him were hostile blows.
Valedictory Poem.
Van Buren.
Visit, The.
Voluntaries.
Waldeinsamkeit.
Water.
We sauntered amidst miracles.
Wealth.
Webster.
What all the books of ages paint, I have.
What are all the flowers.
What avails it me.
What flowing central forces, say.
What from this barren being do we reap.
What is it to sail.
What never was no, & still will be.
When devils bite.
When Jane was absent Edgar's eye.
When success exalts thy lot.
When thou sittest moping.

When thy soul / Is filled with a just image
    fear not thou.
When wrath & terror changed Jove's regal
    port.
Where art thou / Thou beautiful dream.
Where is Skrymir? Giant Skrymir?
Where the fungus broad & red.
Who knows this or that?
Who saw the hid beginnings.
Whoso alas is young.
Why fear to die.
Why honor the new men.
Why should I live.
William does thy frigid soul.
William Rufus and the Jew.
Winds are cold, the days are dark, The.
Wisp & meteor nightly falling.
With the key of the secret he marches faster.
Woodnotes I ("For this present, hard").
Woodnotes II ("As sunbeams stream through
    liberal space").
Woods.
World-Soul, The.
Worship.
Would you know what joy is hid.
Written in a Volume of Goethe.
Written in Naples, March, 1833.
Written in Sickness.
Xenophanes.
Ye have Grace.
Yet sometimes to the sorrow stricken.
You shall not love me for what daily spends.
Translations, Coauthored Poems, etc.:
Ah, could I hide me in my song.
Alas, Alas, that I am betrayed.
Alas! till now I had not known.
All day the rain.
And had Hafiz.
And since round lines are drawn.
Arabian Ballad.
Art thou wise, four things resign.
Blame not mine thou hoarse preacher.
Body and Soul.
Boy bring the bowl full of wine.
Bring wine release me.
Builder of heaven, The.
By breath of beds of roses drawn.
Chemist of love, The.
Color, taste, and smell, smaragdus, sugar, and
    musk.
Come let us strew roses.
Come!—the palace of heaven rests on aëry
    pillars.
Dante's Vita Nuova.
Dearest, where thy shadow falls.
Desire no bread, forsake the guest hall of the
    earth.
Drink, hear my counsel, my son, that the
    world fret thee not.
Drink till the turbans are all unbound.
Drink wine, and the heaven.
Early after the night long revel.
Epitaph: "Bethink, poor heart, what bitter
    kind of jest."
Eternal Watcher, who doth wake, The.
Exile, The.
Fair fall thy soft heart!
Fit for the Pleiads' azure chord.
Flute, The.
For his constant dwelling place has Hafiz.
For pearls, plunge in the sea.
For two rewards, & nought beside.
Fortune and Hope! I've made my port.
Free thyself from wo.
Friend is he, who, hunted as a foe, A.
Friendship ("Thou foolish Hafiz! Say, do
    churls").
From "Bird Conversations."
From Hafiz.
From Ibn Jemin.
From Omar Chiam.
From the Persian of Hafiz.
Ghaselle.
Good is what goes on the road of Nature.
Had I the world for my enemy.
Hafiz since on the world.
Hafiz thou art from Eternity.

Has thine enemy slandered thy house.
He who has a thousand friends has not a
    friend to spare.
Hear what the glass will tell thee.
High heart, O Hafiz! though not thine.
His learning truly lifted Hafiz to Heaven.
I am: what I am.
I batter the wheel of heaven.
I have no hoarded treasure.
I know this perilous love-lane.
I never went out of my country.
I read on the porch of a palace bold.
I said to the East wind.
I shall go from my sickbed to heaven.
I will be drunk and down with wine.
If my darling should depart.
If thy darling favor thee.
In bounding youth the night & train.
In Senahar, my first born sleeps.
In the kingdom of Poesy Hafiz waves like a
    banner.
In thy holiday of life.
It is certain that who his mind.
Knowst thou the luck the friends face to see.
Lament not, o Hafiz, the distribution.
Last Farewell, The.
Lo! where from Heaven's high roof.
Loose the knots of the heart; never think on
    thy fate.
Many our needs, yet we spare prayers.
Ninefold table of Heaven, The.
No physician has a balsam for my wo.
Novice, hear me what I say.
Now tells the flower.
O follow the sonnet's flight.
O friend blame not Hafiz.
O Hafiz, give me thought.
O Hafiz! speak not of thy need.
Odes *sels.*
O'er the garden water goes the wind alone.
Oft have I said, I say it once more.
On earth's wide thoroughfares below.
On prince or bride no diamond stone.
On two days it steads not to run from thy
    grave.
Only three things lengthen life.
Our Shah's counsel is the efflux.
Out of the East, and out of the West, no man
    understands me.
Pain of love's a better fate, The.
Phoenix, The.
Plunge in yon angry waves.
Power of a beautiful face lifts me to heaven,
    The.
Prince the ball of heaven should.
Principle of all things; entrails made.
Reach me wine No counsel weakens the
    conclusion of the lot.
Red rose blooms, The.
Roguish wind and I, The.
Ruler after word & thought.
Salve Senescentem.
Secretly to love & to drink, what is it? tis a
    dissolute day's work.
See & hear the fraud, the malice of the
    change of fortune.
See how the roses burn!
Shah Sandschar, whose lowest slave.
Should I shed my tears.
Since you set no worth on the heart.
So long as there's a trace.
Song of Seyd [*or* Seid] Nimetollah of
    Kuhistan.
Song of Taliesin.
Sonnet of Michel Angelo Buonaroti.
Soul, The.
Spare thou neither time nor blood for thy
    friend.
Stand up, that we may sacrifice the soul.
Stately bride is the shining world, A.
Sweet, sweet, is sleep,—Ah! sweeter, to be
    stone.
Take my heart in thy hand, O beautiful boy
    of Schiraz!
Teach your child to earn his meal.
There resides in the grieving.
They say, through patience, chalk.

They strew in the path of kings and czars.
This effervescing gentleman who despises a
    secret.
Thou who with thy long hair.
Thousand dangers of ruin has the street of
    love.
Thy poems Hafiz shame the rose leaves.
Thy songs O Hafiz.
'Tis writ on Paradise's gate.
To be wise the dull brain so earnestly throbs.
To the Shah, from Enweri ("From thy worth
    and weight the stars gravitate").
To the Shah, from Enweri ("Not in their
    houses stand the stars").
To the Shah, from Hafiz.
To whom a glass full of red wine.
Treacherous wind pipes a lewd song, The.
Unbar the door, since thou the Opener art.
Understanding's copper coin, The.
Untruth is become the mode.
Way of love is unlimited, The.
We wish like the glass.
We would do nought but good.
What lovelier forms things wear.
When in eternity the light.
Where o where is the message which today.
While roses bloomed along the plain.
Whilst I disdain the populace.
Who compares a poem.
Who dedicates himself to the glass.
Who ever suffered as I from separation?
Who gave thy cheek the mixed tint.
Who loves his friend with his heart of hearts.
Who royally bedded.
Wilt thou life's best elixir drain?
Wine resembles the Lord Jesus.
Wo is me woe's me when I think.
World is a bride superbly dressed, The.
Yet all comes out of this, that one door.

Everson, William (Brother Antoninus) (b. 1912)
And then that humming.
Annul in Me My Manhood.
Answer, The.
Attila.
August.
Bard.
Black Hills, The.
Blood of the Poet, The.
Blowing of the Seed, The *sels.*
Bride of the Bear.
Burning Book, The.
Canticle for the Feast of the Most Precious
    Blood, 1954, A.
Canticle of the Rose, The.
Canticle to the Christ in the Holy Eucharist,
    A.
Canticle to the Waterbirds, A.
Challenge, The.
Chronicle of Division *sels.*
Cross Tore a Hole, The *sels.*
Cutting the Firebreak.
Danse Macabre.
Dark Waters.
Dusk, The.
Eastward the armies.
Encounter, The.
Falling of the Grain, The *sels.*
Frost Lay White on California, A.
God Germed in Raw Granite.
Hare: An Earlier Episode, The.
High Embrace, The.
I Am Long Weaned.
If you were to try to say.
In All These Acts.
In the Breach.
In the Fictive Wish.
In the Ripeness of the Weed.
Kingfisher Flat.
Kiss of the Cross, The.
Lava Bed.
Muscat Pruning.
Narrows of Birth, The.
October Tragedy.
Of such touch given.
Orion.
Out of the Ash.
Passion Week.

Poet Is Dead, The.
Raging of the Rose, The.
Raid, The.
Rain on That Morning, The.
Rattlesnake August.
Reaper.
Residual Years, The.
River-Root: A Syzygy *sels.*
River-Root: as even under high drifts, those
    fierce wind-grappled cuts of the Rockies.
Rose of Solitude, The *sels.*
Rose of Solitude, The.
Scout, The.
Screed of the Flesh, The.
Sea: / And in its flaw the sprung silence.
Sixty Five.
Song the Body Dreamed in the Spirit's Mad
    Behest, The.
South Coast, The.
Spikehorn.
Spotfire.
Steelhead.
Stone Face Falls.
Storm-Surge.
Tendril in the Mesh.
Triptych for the Living *sels.*
Vision of Felicity, The.
We in the Fields.
Winter Ploughing.
Wise, The.
You, God.

F

Fenton, James (b. 1949)
Cambodia.
Children in Exile.
Chosun.
Dead Soldiers.
Doctor Gliedschirm, skin specialist, surgeries
    14–16 hours or by appointment.
Exempla.
Fruit-Grower in War-time (and Some of His
    Enemies), The.
German Requiem, A *sels.*
German Requiem, A.
God, A Poem.
Killer Snails, The.
Kingfisher's Boxing Gloves, The.
Letter to John Fuller.
Lines for Translation into Any Language.
Lollipops of the Pomeranian Baroque.
Lullaby for a Summer Recess.
Nest of Vampires.
Nothing.
Pitt-Rivers Museum, Oxford, The.
Prison Island.
Skip, The.
Song That Sounds like This, The.
South Parks Road.
Staffordshire Murderer, A.
Tauler.
Terminal Moraine, A.
This Octopus Exploits Women.
Vacant Possession, A.
Vucceria.
Wild Life Studies *sels.*
Wild Ones[, The].
Wind.
Translations, Coauthored Poems, etc.:
In a Notebook.

Ferlinghetti, Lawrence (b. 1919)
Adieu À Charlot.
Along the Appian Way / children are
    playing.
And she "like a young year."
Ascending over Ohio.
Assassination Raga.
Astonished Heart, The.
At midnight on the next balcony.
At the *Gare Bruxelles-Midi.*
Autobiography.
Away above a harborful.
Baja Beatitudes.
Baja Revisited.
Baseball Canto.

Belated Palinode for Dylan Thomas.
Buddha in the Woodpile, A.
Café Notre Dame.
Canti Romani *sels.*
Canticle of Jack Kerouac, The.
Carrara, Looking Seaward.
Cat, The.
Come lie with me and be my love.
Constantly risking absurdity.
Cro-Magnons.
Dark Portrait, A.
Deep Chess.
Deflowering.
Director of Alienation.
Dog.
Don't let that horse.
Dove sta amore / Where lies love.
Elegy on the Death of Kenneth Patchen, An.
Elegy to Dispel Gloom, An.
Endless Life.
Euphoria.
Expressionist History of German
    Expressionism.
Firenze, a Lifetime Later.
General Song of Humanity, The.
Goya & the Sleep of Reason.
Grottamare.
He with the Beating Wings.
Heap of Broken Images, A.
Heaven / was only half as far that night.
Hidden Door.
Hilarious God.
History of the World: a TV Docu-Drama.
Home Home Home.
I am waiting for my case to come up.
I Genitori Perduti.
I have not lain with beauty all my life.
Imaginary Happening, London, An.
In Golden Gate Park that day.
In Goya's greatest scenes we seem to see.
In hintertime Praxiteles.
In Paris in a loud dark winter.
In woods where many rivers run.
It was a face which darkness could kill.
Jack of Hearts, The.
John Lennon in the Porto Santo Stefano.
Just as I used to say.
Ladakh Buddhess Biker.
Late Impressionist Dream.
Light, The.
Living Theatre, The.
L'Occupation Obsédée.
London / crossfigured / creeping with trams.
Lost Parents.
Love Nut, The.
Making Love in Poetry.
Man Who Rode Away, The.
Matisse at the Modern, Magritte at the Met.
Mock Confessional.
Morlaix: Into the Future with Neil Young.
Moscow in the Wilderness, Segovia in the
    Snow.
Mouth of truth, The.
New York—Albany.
Olbers' Paradox.
Old Italians Dying, The.
Old Sailors, The.
One of These Days.
Oral Messages *sels.*
Overpopulation.
Painter's Dream, The.
Paris Transformations.
Pennycandystore beyond the El, The.
People Getting Divorced.
Photo of Emily, The.
Plan du Centre de Paris à Vol D'Oiseau.
Plough of Time, The.
Poem for Old Walt.
Poet as Fisherman.
Poet's eye obscenely seeing, The.
Populist Manifesto.
Pound at Spoleto.
Queens Cemetery, Setting Sun.
Reading Apollinaire by the Rogue River.
Reading Yeats I do not think.
Rebels, The.

Report on a Happening in Washington Square San Francisco, A.
Retired Ballerinas, Central Park West.
Returning to Paris with Pissarro.
River Still To Be Found, A.
Roman Morn.
Rough Song of Animals Dying.
Sailing thru the straits of Demos.
San Jose Symphony Reception.
Sandinista Avioncitos.
Sarolla's women in their picture hats.
Sea and Ourselves at Cape Ann, The.
Sea Is Calm Tonight, The.
See / it was like this when.
Sherman's March Reglitterized.
Short Story on a Painting of Gustav Klimt.
Sometime during eternity / some guys show up.
Spirit of the Crusades.
Sueño Real.
Sweet and various the woodlark.
That fellow on the boattrain who insisted.
They were putting up the statue.
Third World Calling.
Thoughts to a Concerto of Telemann.
Triste Corbiére.
Triumph of the Postmodern.
True Confessional.
Tunisian Nostalgia.
Two Amsterdams.
Two Scavengers in a Truck, Two Beautiful People in a Mercedes.
Underwear.
Upon Reflection.
Uses of Poetry.
Vast Confusion, A.
Voix Glauque.
We squat upon the beach of love.
What could she say to the fantastic foolybear.
Wild Dreams of a New Beginning.
Wild Life Cameo, Early Morn.
With bells for hooves in sounding streets.
World is a beautiful place, The.

Firbank, Louis see "Reed, Lou"

Fisher, Roy (b. 1930)
Absolute / Pity / Advancing.
After Working.
Also.
Armoury, The.
Arrival, The.
Artists, Providers, Places to Go.
As He Came near Death.
Aside to a Children's Tale.
At No Distance.
At Once.
At sunset over the water.
At the end of the familiar.
Barnardine's Reply.
Billiard Table, The.
Blood-red and blue glass.
Built for quoting in a tight corner.
Burning Graves at Netherton, The.
Burnt year. Trick riders blunder about the concrete, A.
Butterton Ford.
By the Pond.
Castle, The.
Cat's glinting face as it stared, The.
Chirico.
City.
Civic water / with lilies and flies.
Colour Supplement Pages.
Commuter.
Continuity.
Convalescent / to get along the shop fronts.
Cook.
Corner.
Correspondence.
Counterfeit bucolic scene, A.
Critics Can Bleed.
Crooked-angle wings.
Crumpled clothes come slowly off.
Cut Worm.
Dark on Dark.
Dawn birds at noon.
Debt for Tomorrow, A.
Dirty Dozen, The.

Discovering the Form.
Diversions *sels.*
Doctor Meinière—.
Don't Ask.
Downpour that subdued everybody and, The.
Duchamp and Man Ray.
Dusk.
Dyere.
Eight or nine yards.
Elohim Creating Adam, The.
Emblem.
Emptying his bowel.
Entertainment of War, The.
Epitaph: Lorine Niedecker.
Everything cast in iron.
Experimenting.
Eye ascending / is gone up, The.
Falling away, A.
Five Morning Poems from a Picture by Manet.
Five Pilgrims in the Prologue to the Canterbury Tales *sels.*
For Realism.
Foyer, The.
Freedoms / out of contrivance.
From an English Sensibility.
From here to there—.
From the 'Town Guide.'
From the wrecked byre.
Garden, The.
Glenthorne Poems *sels.*
Gone down / from the upper air.
Grammar for Doctrine, A.
Grey weather beating across the upland.
Half hearing, half in a veil, to lope.
Half reconciled, half healed: but.
Handsworth Liberties *sels.*
He is going to the woman.
Here comes the modulation.
Hill behind the Town, The.
Hills lie thick, The.
Hit the bottom and spread out.
Home Pianist's Companion, The.
Hospital in Winter, The.
How he come to be wearing that suit.
I have slept shallow a long while.
I saw what there was to write and I wrote it.
I work in my garden.
Idea of defence, The.
If I declare *Peace.*
If I Didn't.
In a dull hour thinking of the swan.
In long shapes over the channel's.
In the Black Country.
In the evening the smoke blows far away.
In the Wall.
In Touch.
Inscriptions for Bluebeard's Castle *sels.*
Instruments of Torture, The.
Interiors with Various Figures *sels.*
Intruder, The.
Irish cheekbones and close-set eyes.
Irreversible.
It Is Writing.
Just beside my track through the dark.
Kites are the best sort of gods, The.
Klonk! The smoker's trick.
Knight.
Lake of Tears, The.
Lampshade, The.
Land, The.
Last Door, The.
Lazily into the curve.
Leaden August with the life gone out of it.
Least, The.
Leaving July.
Lesson in Composition, The.
Linear.
Lullaby and Exhortation for the Unwilling Hero.
Magritte Imitated Himself.
Making of the Book, The.
Masterpieces in my sleep. A suppressed.
Matrix *sels.*
Memorial Fountain, The.
Metallic sheath / derelict, that resounds.
Metamorphoses *sels.*

Mild blight, a sterility, A.
Mounted on all four walls, the neat.
Mouth-Talk.
Mystery Poems *sels.*
Nation, The.
Near Garmsley Camp.
Necessaries.
New Diversions *sels.*
News for the Ear.
No dark in the body.
North Area.
Occasional Poem 7.1.72.
Ocean-lights go flashing.
Of the Empirical Self and for Me.
Oh yellow head.
On the Neglect of Figure Composition *sels.*
On the Open Side.
107 Poems.
Only Image, The.
Only target / is the eyeball, The.
Open— / and away.
Open Poem and the Closed Poem, The *sels.*
Out in the early morning, by empty roads.
Out to one side.
Outlines / start to appear.
Paraphrases.
Park, The.
Passing Newbridge-on-Wye.
Passive Partner, The.
Periodicity: the crack.
Pete Brown's Old Eggs Still Hatch.
Pilgrim disposition—, The.
Poem not a Picture, A.
Poem: "Small / poem / the unit of feeling, The."
Poem to Be Watched, A.
Poet's Message, The.
Poplars, The.
Portcullis, The.
Prelude: "Hundreds upon hundreds of years of Lapiths."
Provision.
Quarry Hills.
Real things move.
Red and the Black, The.
Red beans to soak.
Releases.
Religious garden.
Report on August.
Riding out of the built-up.
Roused from a double.
Rudiments.
Rules and Ranges for Ian Tyson.
Running Changes, The.
Rust. Limewash. The iron tyres.
Self-Portraits and Their Mirrors.
Sets.
Seven Attempted Moves.
She sleeps, in the day, in the silence.
Shines coldly away.
Ship's Orchestra, The.
Sign, The.
Simple Location.
Six Deliberate Acts, The *sels.*
Sketch for the First Exhibition of the New Heroic Art.
Sky, the Sea, The.
Sliding the tongue-leaved.
Sloping and tapering away.
Small Room, The.
So, the water gate.
Some Loss.
Something has to happen here.
Staffordshire Red.
Starting to Make a Tree.
Steam Crane, The.
Steep turn down, A.
Stopped Frames and Set-Pieces.
Straight into the sea fog.
Studies *sels.*
Style.
Sugar flowers.
Sun Hacks, The.
Suppose—.
Supposed Dancer, The.
Tall place, The.
Tapicer.

Then some calm and formal portrait.
There is a place of cypress fingers.
There's a belief to fix. It feels strong.
There's a time, finally.
Thin smoke, A.
Thing About Joe Sullivan, The.
3rd November 1976.
This is where the game gets dirty.
Three Ceremonial Poems *sels.*
Timelessness of Desire.
To come out ready capitalized, with outlines.
To see the film you buy a ticket.
To the Memory of Wyndham Lewis.
Today / let us think.
Toy, The.
Toyland.
Trace, The.
Tranquility a manner.
Travesties of the world.
Treasure House, The.
Trouble coming, on a Saturday or a Monday.
Truants.
Upper corner—probably, The.
Vigil / taking over hours and losing them.
Walk through, minding the nettles.
Walking at dusk often.
Wanting to get away.
Webbe.
Whale Knot, The.
White Cloud, White Blossom.
Why They Stopped Singing.
Wind at Night, The.
Winking drop on the lens.
Wish.
Without Location.
Woman across the lane, The.
Wonders of Obligation.
World / arranged in zones, A.
Wrestler, The.
Wrong Time, The.

Fletcher, John Gould (1886–1950)
Alpine Violets.
America.
And at these words there rose against the ark.
And God, looking out upon earth, said, "Lo, it is time / To create mankind."
Arizona Poems.
As Adam, clutching earth, lay stunned within the darkness.
As I wandered over the city through the night.
Aster Flower, The.
At the Meeting of the Days.
August, 1940.
Back Stairs, The.
Bedroom.
Birth of Christ, The.
Black Rock, The.
Blessing of the Worms, The.
Blue Symphony.
Branches of Adam *sels.*
Buddha and Christ.
Burning Mountain, The.
Cain and Abel in the meantime had grown.
Calendar in the Attic, The.
Calm, The.
City Lights.
Cliff-dwelling.
Clipper-Ships.
Clown's Song.
Court Lady Standing under Cherry Tree.
Crucifixion of the Skyscraper.
Crucifixion, The.
Dahlias, The.
Discontent.
Dogwood.
Down the Mississippi.
Elegy in a Civil War Cemetery.
Elegy on a Nordic White Protestant.
Elegy on an Empty Skyscraper.
Elegy on London.
Elegy on Tintern Abbey.
Empty Days, The.
End of Job, The.
England Again.

Epilogue: "By the glare of the guttering torch."
Evening Clouds, The.
Father's Thought of His Daughter, The.
Flickering of incessant rain.
Flood Symphony, The.
Fourfold is made the divine nature of man.
Fragments of Eternity.
From Portofino Point.
From the Chinese.
From the Japanese, "I"
From the Japanese, "II"
From the Japanese, "III"
From the Japanese, "IV"
From the Japanese, "V"
From the Japanese, "VI"
Fuel Vendor, The.
Gale, The.
Ghosts of an Old House, The *sels.*
Golden Demon, The.
Grandfather's Grave.
Green Symphony.
Grey Symphony.
Groundswell, The.
Gulf Stream.
Gulls, The.
Hard Sayings.
Hour of Peace, The.
Houses of the city no longer hum and play, The.
In the Garden of Dreams.
In the still evening of the sixth long day.
Invocation to Evening.
Irradiations *sels.*
Isle Iranim.
Jade Elegy, The.
Journey Day.
Joy.
Lake Shore at Night.
Last Frontier, The.
Last Judgment, The.
Levite and the Samaritan, The.
Lid, The.
Life.
Lincoln.
Lines Written at Taormina, Sicily.
Love and Suspicion.
Marriage.
Memory: The Walk on the Beach.
Mexican Quarter.
Midsummer Dawn at Sea.
Midwinter Sunset.
Morning is clean and blue and the wind blows up the clouds, The.
My stiff-spread arms / Break into sudden gesture.
New Beatitudes, The.
Night lay upon the ocean like a sword.
Night of Stars.
Night Song.
Night Wind, The.
1921.
November Days.
Now it was noonday, fortieth of the flood.
Now it was the ninth morning and the unseen God.
Oiran and Her Kamuso, An.
Old Nursery.
Old South, The.
On Mesa Verde.
On My Father's Hundredth Birthday.
On the Banks of the Sumida.
On the Beach.
On the Verandah.
Out of the waves they clomb, plant, insect, fish, and bird.
Over the roof-tops race the shadows of clouds.
Parables of Antichrist, The *sels.*
Parables of Christ, The *sels.*
Passing of the South, The.
Poppies of the Red Year.
Portrait, The.
Prayer of the Antichrist, The.
Prelude: "Before the beginning of things."
Procession, The.
Rain in the Desert.

Requiem for a Twentieth-Century Outlaw.
Reunion.
Sailboats.
Sand and Spray: A Sea-Symphony *sels.*
Sands, The.
Saturday Night: Horses Going to Pasture.
Scene from a Drama.
Scythe, The.
Sea-Sounding Bells.
Sea-Violins.
Sharaku Dreams.
Six long days was the unseen God in labour with the earth.
Snow at Sea.
Song of Natchez Under the Hill, The.
Song of the Moderns.
Sorrow.
Spattering of the rain upon pale terraces, The.
Stars, The.
Steamers.
Symphony of Snow.
Then the archangels all together abandoned the black menacing sky.
There was a pool that rippled in the silence of the north.
They buried Abel at sunset in the red wet earth.
Thunderstorm in the Ozarks.
Tide of Storms.
Tide, The.
Towards the North Star.
Tower, The.
Trees, like great jade elephants, The.
Truth of the Matter, The.
Unfamiliar House, The.
Vision.
Voices on the Wind.
Vowels, The.
Well in the Desert, The.
Well, The.
White Symphony.
Whitman.
Windmills, The.
Wreck, The.

Ford, Charles Henri (b. 1913)
ABC's.
Activity without / Attachment. One link with the.
After the drama.
Afternoon with André Breton, An.
And no night visitors.
And take your time.
And the first owl of.
And the Path of Least.
Astride the chiffonier of post-oral conductions.
Baby on the way!
Baby's in Jail; the Animal Day Plays Alone.
Bad Habit, The.
Bala Krishna's voice.
Ballad for Baudelaire.
Beautiful new / Character may enter the, A.
Bedraggled rose, The.
Before his father.
Being nor whim nor.
Black dog in a, A.
Break up conventional.
Brought in tame from the.
Butterfly and the Bull, The.
Candy Darling.
Chakora bird / Like a partridge. It is said, The.
Chanson Pour Billie.
Chinaberries / Change from green to yellow. In, The.
Clouds covered it, The.
Comedy of Belief.
Consider the sound.
Convalescence, The.
Crows in the fog, dogs.
Curse for the War Machine, A.
Dampness in the air.
Day has twenty-four hours, The.
Death's-head moth, A.
Dew falls but the, The.
Dicty Glide in Central Park Menagerie.
Dreaming of walking.

Eagle carries / Off a single sheep. Carry, An.
Emblems of Arachne *sels.*
Epigrams.
Face of the Earth, The.
First owl of the evening.
Flag of Ecstasy.
For Djuna Barnes.
Forms and flowers.
Fortune's Wheel. In the.
Four Elegies.
Garden flooded with.
Garden of Disorder, The.
He Cut His Finger on Eternity.
He has a luminous.
Heartfelt installations. / Beginnings are
benevolent.
He's out on the loggia.
Human kites, fantastic.
I am Mantra.
I do put art before.
I felt my forefinger.
I thought I heard Indra's.
I Wonder.
I'd like to linger.
Illness, The.
I'm attached, and he's.
Impossibility of Dying in Your Arms Does
Not Sadden Me, The.
In a dream you had.
In my hair he's put.
In struggling to get.
In the maze of the.
In the playpen of.
In the tentacles.
Indra; my house; the.
Indra needs a haircut.
Invisible envelopes, / A standstill afternoon.
Is he a blood relation of yours.
It Seems You Never Were.
Jeweled Bat, The.
Juggernaut chanting.
Krishna climbs up there.
Large bead on the.
Like a wild bird he.
Little boys, faces smeared.
Masks without faces.
Matin Pour Matta.
Max Ernst.
Message for Rimbaud.
Mishima.
Modesty, chastity.
Mount Stavros sits on.
Neurotic demon, / Trying to convince
himself.
No beings but.
Not locking onto.
Nubian in / Tangerine, carrying a, A.
O.
Oh, a patch of green.
On a high branch two.
Only one destiny.
Owlet pulls / Pieces of meat from between
the, The.
Peaks of pleasure, peaks.
Place in which to, A.
Plaint.
Poem for Paul Eluard.
Poverty is always / Imaginary. The.
Pre-puberty boys.
Prevalence of the.
Prison Life.
Ram wears a cowboy.
Real dreams. More real than.
Realization / Of fantasy, yes. This, A.
Rise to capture the.
Roots.
St.-John Perse.
Secret Haiku *sels.*
Seeking out corpses.
Seis Hermanos.
Serenade to Leonor.
Seven Poems *sels.*
Sharp eyes, hoodlum skin.
Shaven heads, rubber.
Small black goat with, A.
Soldiers walk around.
Soleil d'automne. Do.

Some flowers come up.
Some flowers wickedly.
Someone made up my eyes.
Sorer the joints, The.
Special Effects.
Standing on the garden.
That first and last word.
Theatre of winter, The.
There's a howling stray.
There's No Place to Sleep in This Bed,
Tanguy.
There's that praying.
These days of small but.
They need no other.
This dream of burnt ivory.
This is the story of fire without flames.
This same sea, there.
This year's jackfruit hang.
Through him (The Diamond).
To Christopher Marlowe.
Tonguless crocodile / Meets eyeless tiger
darted.
Trees with white perfumed.
Two people can be.
Typhoid and smallpox.
Untouched ones, the, The.
Unwashed, unbedded. / He has fine bones
and a.
Wall ritual. These.
War.
We each play our roles.
Weather is mild, The.
What am I dreaming of?
When the coolie blew.
When you close your eyes.
Whole family weeping.
Yes, wave your magic.
Your Horoscope.

Fox, Siv Cedering (b. 1939)
Acrobat, The.
Albert Einstein (1879–1955).
Alioth.
Alkaid.
Alkor/Mizar.
Almagest, Last Letter to Zakarias.
Aloe.
Angel of Death, The.
April Fool.
At Nightfall.
At the Edge of the Suburbs.
Beasts Have Entered, The.
Blanc de Blanc.
Blue Dress, The.
Caroline Herschel (1750–1848).
Cetus, a Letter from Jonah.
Child Called *Morte*, A.
Clown, The.
Cup of Cold Water.
Dead Women.
Dog Days.
Dubhe.
Dwarfs, The.
Exposing Fox and Artifice.
Fata Morgana.
Figure Eights.
Finding the Andromeda Nebula.
Five Stanzas for My Two Brothers.
Galileo Galilei (1564–1642).
Grandmother.
Guillermo's Wedding.
Hands.
Help Me with the Buttons.
Horses, The.
Ice.
Ice Fishing.
If He Had Not Had Two Hands Tattooed on
His Chest.
In Search of a Love Poem.
In the Land of Shinar.
In the Planetarium.
Islanders.
Johannes Kepler (1571–1630).
Juggler, The.
Lemons, Limes.
Letter from the Snake Woman.
Letter to Peter Wilkins.
Letters from the Astronomers.

Letters from the Island.
Like a Woman in the Kitchen.
Lyre, The.
Megrez.
Merak.
Miss Pimberton Of.
Mother Is.
Mother Was a Good.
My Father's Face.
My Father's Oldest Sister.
Nail of the Index Finger, The.
Names and Travelers of the Milky Way.
Nicholas Copernicus (1473–1543).
Night and Day.
Nightshade.
Offering.
On Some Such Morning.
On the Other Side of Uji Bridge.
On This Shore.
Onna-E, Pictures of Women.
Ornithology.
Ovid.
Peaches.
Peregrine Falcon.
Phekda.
Poem for My Mother.
Pomegranates.
Raccoon, A.
Rescue.
River and Light.
Roads in That Town Have No Name, The.
Say It Has Been Snowing.
Sentence, A.
Servants of the Emperor, The.
Seven Letters to Zakarias.
She Used to Water the Plants.
Shipbuilder, The.
Shunga.
Story of Toile, The.
Sunflowers.
Susanna.
To Do More Than Hair.
To the Man Who Watches Spiders.
Transvestite, The.
Ukiyo-E.
Visitor, The.
White and the River.
Your Nipples.

Frost, Robert (1874–1963)
A-Wishing Well.
Acceptance.
Accidentally on Purpose.
Acquainted with the Night.
After Apple-picking.
Afterflakes.
Aim Was Song, The.
All Revelation.
America Is Hard to See.
Answer, An.
Any Size We Please.
Armful, The.
Assurance.
Astrometaphysical.
At Woodward's Gardens.
Atmosphere.
Auspex.
Away!
Axe-Helve, The.
Bad Island, The—Easter.
Bear, The.
Bearer of Evil Tidings, The.
Beech.
Bereft.
Beyond Words.
Birches.
Birthplace, The.
Black Cottage, The.
Blue-Butterfly Day.
Blue Ribbon at Amesbury, A.
Blueberries.
Boeotian.
Bond and Free.
Bonfire, The.
Boundless Moment, A.
Bravado.
Broken Drought, The.
Brook in the City, A.

Brown's Descent; or, The Willy-Nilly.
Build Soil.
Bursting Rapture.
But God's Own Descent.
But outer Space.
Cabin in the Clearing, A.
Canis Major.
Carpe Diem.
Case for Jefferson, A.
Census-Taker, The.
Christmas Trees.
Clear and Colder.
Cliff Dwelling, A.
Closed for Good.
Cloud Shadow, A.
Cocoon, The.
Code, The.
Come In.
Concept Self-Conceived, A.
Considerable Speck, A.
Courage to Be New, The.
Cow in Apple Time, The.
Death of the Hired Man, The.
Demiurge's Laugh, The.
Departmental.
Desert Places.
Design.
Devotion.
Directive.
Discovery of the Madeiras, The.
Does No One at All Ever Feel This Way in
     the Least?
Door in the Dark, The.
Draft Horse, The.
Dream Pang, A.
Drumlin Woodchuck, A.
Dust in the Eyes.
Dust of Snow.
Egg and the Machine, The.
Empty Threat, An.
Encounter, An.
Ends.
Equalizer, An.
Escapist—Never.
Etherealizing.
Evening in a Sugar Orchard.
Evil Tendencies Cancel.
Exposed Nest, The.
Fear of God, The.
Fear of Man, The.
Fear, The.
Figure in the Doorway, The.
Fire and Ice.
Fireflies in the Garden.
Five Nocturnes.
Flood, The.
Flower Boat, The.
Flower-Gathering.
For John F. Kennedy; His Inauguration.
For Once, Then, Something.
Forgive, O Lord, my little jokes on Thee.
Fountain, a Bottle, a Donkey's Ears and
     Some Books, A.
Four-room shack aspiring high.
Fragmentary Blue.
Freedom of the Moon, The.
From Iron.
From Plane to Plane.
Gathering Leaves.
Generations of Men, The.
Ghost House.
Gift Outright, The.
Girl's Garden, A.
Going for Water.
Gold Hesperidee, The.
Good-by and Keep Cold.
Good Hours.
Grindstone, The.
Gum-Gatherer, The.
Haec Fabula Docet.
Hannibal.
Happiness Makes Up in Height for What It
     Lacks in Length.
Hardship of Accounting, The.
Hill Wife, The.
Hillside Thaw, A.
Home Burial.

House Fear.
Housekeeper, The.
How Hard It Is to Keep from Being King
     When It's in You and in the Situation.
Hundred Collars, A.
Hyla Brook.
I Could Give All to Time.
I Will Sing You One-O.
Immigrants.
Importer, An.
Impulse, The.
In a Disused Graveyard.
In a Glass of Cider.
In a Poem.
In a Vale.
In Divés' Dive.
In Hardwood Groves.
In Neglect.
In the Home Stretch.
In the Long Night.
In Time of Cloudburst.
In winter in the woods alone
Ingenuities of Debt, The.
Innate Helium.
Into My Own.
Investment, The.
Iota Subscript.
Iris by Night.
It Bids Pretty Fair.
It Is Almost the Year Two Thousand.
It takes all sorts of in- and outdoor schooling
Kitchen Chimney, The.
Kitty Hawk.
Last Mowing, The.
Last Word of a Bluebird, The.
Late Walk, A.
Leaf-Treader, A.
Leaves Compared with Flowers.
Lesson for Today, The.
Line-Gang, The.
Line-Storm Song, A.
Lines Written in Dejection on the Eve of
     Great Success.
Literate Farmer and the Planet Venus, The.
Locked Out.
Lockless Door, The.
Lodged.
Lone Striker, A.
Loneliness.
Looking for a Sunset Bird in Winter.
Loose Mountain, A.
Lost Follower, The.
Lost in Heaven.
Love and a Question.
Lovely Shall Be Choosers, The.
Lucretius versus the Lake Poets.
Maple.
Masque of Mercy, A.
Masque of Reason, A.
Master Speed, The.
Meeting and Passing.
Mending Wall.
Middleness of the Road, The.
Milky Way Is a Cowpath, The.
Minor Bird, A.
Misgiving.
Missive Missile, A.
Mood Apart, A.
Moon Compasses.
Most of It, The.
Mountain, The.
Mowing.
My Butterfly.
My November Guest.
Nature Note, A.
Need of Being Versed in Country Things,
     The.
Neither Out Far nor In Deep.
Never Again Would Birds' Song Be the
     Same.
Never Naught Song, A.
New Hampshire.
Night Light, The.
No Holy Wars for Them.
Not All There.
Not of School Age.
Not Quite Social.

Not to Keep.
Nothing Gold Can Stay.
November.
Now Close the Windows.
Objection to Being Stepped On, The.
October.
Of the Stones of the Place.
Oft-Repeated Dream, The.
Old Barn at the Bottom of the Fogs, The.
Old Man's Winter Night, An.
On a Bird Singing in its Sleep.
On a Tree Fallen across the Road.
On Being Chosen Poet of Vermont.
On Being Idolized.
On Going Unnoticed.
On Looking Up by Chance at the
     Constellations.
On Making Certain Anything Has Happened.
On Our Sympathy with the Under Dog.
On Taking from the Top to Broaden the
     Base.
On the Heart's Beginning to Cloud the Mind.
Once by the Pacific.
One Guess.
One More Brevity.
One Step Taken Backward.
Onset, The.
Our Doom to Bloom.
Our Hold on the Planet.
Our Singing Strength.
Out, Out —.
Oven Bird, The.
Pan with Us.
Passing Glimpse, A.
Pasture, The.
Patch of Old Snow, A.
Paul's Wife.
Pauper Witch of Grafton, The.
Pea Brush.
Peaceful Shepherd, The.
Peck of Gold, A.
Peril of Hope.
Pertinax.
Place for a Third.
Planners, The.
Plowmen.
Pod of the Milkweed.
Prayer in Spring, A.
Precaution.
Provide, Provide.
Putting in the Seed.
Quandary.
Quest of the Purple-Fringed, The.
Question, A.
Questioning Faces.
Rabbit Hunter, The.
Range-finding.
Record Stride, A.
Reflex, A.
Reluctance.
Revelation.
Riders.
Road Not Taken, The.
Roadside Stand, A.
Rogers Group, A.
Rose Family, The.
Rose Pogonias.
Runaway, The.
Sand Dunes.
Secret Sits, The.
Self-Seeker, The.
Semi-Revolution, A.
Serious Step Taken Lightly, A.
Servant to Servants, A.
Silken Tent, The.
Sitting by a Bush in Broad Sunlight.
Skeptic.
Smile, The.
Snow.
Soldier, A.
Some Science Fiction.
Something for Hope.
Sound of Trees, The.
Span of Life, The.
Spring Pools.
Star in a Stoneboat, A.
Stars.

Steeple on the House, A.
Stopping by Woods on a Snowy Evening.
Storm Fear.
Strong Are Saying Nothing, The.
Subverted Flower, The.
Sycamore.
Take Something Like a Star.
Telephone, The.
Ten Mills.
Thatch, The.
There Are Roughly Zones.
They Were Welcome to Their Belief.
Time Out.
Time to Talk, A.
Times Table, The.
To a Moth Seen in Winter.
To a Thinker.
To a Young Wretch.
To an Ancient.
To Earthward.
To E.T.
To the Right Person.
To the Thawing Wind.
Too Anxious for Rivers.
Tree at My Window.
Trespass.
Trial by Existence, The.
Trial Run, A.
Triple Bronze.
Tuft of Flowers, The.
Two Leading Lights.
Two Look at Two.
Two Tramps in Mud Time.
Two Witches.
Unharvested.
Unstamped Letter in Our Rural Letter Box,
    An.
U. S. 1946 King's X.
Valley's Singing Day, The.
Vanishing Red, The.
Vantage Point, The.
Version.
Vindictives, The.
Voice Ways.
Waiting.
Waspish.
We vainly wrestle with the blind belief.
Were I in Trouble.
West-running Brook.
What Fifty Said.
White-Tailed Hornet, The.
Why Wait for Science.
Wild Grapes.
Willful Homing.
Wind and the Rain, The.
Wind and Window Flower.
Winter Eden, A.
Wish to Comply, A.
Witch of Coös, The.
Wood-Pile, The.
Wrights' Biplane, The.
Young Birch, A.

G

Gallagher, Tess (b. 1943)
Accomplishment.
All Day the Light Is Clear.
Amplitude.
As If It Happened.
Backdrop With Lovers, 1931.
Ballad of Ballymote, The.
Beginning to Say No.
Bird-Window-Flying.
Black Money.
Black Silk.
Boat Ride.
Bonfire.
Borrowed Ones, The.
Breasts.
Calm, The.
Candle, Lamp & Firefly.
Clearing.
Coats, The.
Coming Home.
Conversation with a Fireman from Brooklyn.

Corona.
Cougar Meat.
Cows, a Vision.
Crêpes Flambeau.
Croce e Delizia al Cor.
Death of the Horses by Fire.
Devotion: That It Flow; That There Be
    Concentration.
Dim House, Bright Face.
Disappearances in the Guarded Sector.
Each Bird Walking.
Even Now You Are Leaving.
Ever After.
Four Dancers at an Irish Wedding.
From Dread in the Eyes of Horses.
Gray Eyes.
Hands of the Blindman, The.
Harmless Streets.
His Shining Helmet; Its Horsehair Crest.
Horse in the Drugstore, The.
Hug, The.
I Save Your Coat, But You Lose It Later.
If Blood Were Not as Powerful as It Is.
If Poetry Were Not a Morality.
In Maceio.
Instructions to the Double.
Into the Known.
Kidnap[p]er.
Linoleum.
Love Poem to Be Read to an Illiterate
    Friend.
Meeting, The.
Message for the Sinecurist.
My Mother Remembers That She Was
    Beautiful.
Not There.
On Your Own.
Open Fire Near a Shed.
Photograph of a Lighthouse Through Fog.
Poem in Translation, A.
Present.
Reading Aloud.
Redwing.
Refusing Silence.
Rhododendrons.
Rijl.
Ritual of Memories, The.
Same Kiss After Many Years, The.
Second Language.
Simple Sonatina.
Small Garden Near a Field.
Snowheart.
Some Painful Butterflies Pass Through.
Some with Wings, Some with Manes.
Stepping Outside.
Still Moment at Dun Laoghaire.
Story of a Citizen, The.
Sudden Journey.
Sugar.
Survival of a Heart.
Tableau Vivant.
That Kind of Thing.
Their Heads Bent Toward Each Other Like
    Flowers.
3 A.M. Kitchen: My Father Talking.
Time Lapse with Tulips.
Under Stars.
Unsteady Yellow.
View from an Empty Chair.
When You Speak to Me.
Willingly.
With Stars.
Woman-Enough.
Woman Who Raised Goats, The.
Women's Tug of War at Lough Arrow.
Woodcutting on Lost Mountain.
Words Written Near a Candle.
Zero.

Galvin, Brendan (b. 1938)
After Midnight.
Apple Trees, The.
Assembling a Street.
Backtalk.
Bats, The.
Carrowkeel.
Chickadee.
Connecticut River in Flood, The.

Defending the Provinces.
Dog Love.
Donegal.
Double-Ended Dory, A.
1847.
Fall Squashes.
Fear of *Gray's Anatomy*.
Fear of the Waldorf Cafeteria.
Field of Inheritance, The.
First Night of Fall, The.
Fog Township.
For a Little Girl of Pompeii.
Glass.
Grackles, The.
Great Blue.
Great Horned Owls.
Green Evening, A.
Hearing Irish Spoken.
Holy Well, A.
In Egg Time.
In Ireland I Remebered the Foxes of Truro,
    Massachusetts.
Inventing Ballygalvin.
Kale Soup.
Knot Hole Gang, The.
Last Man in the Quabbin, The.
Last Open-Air Concert, The.
Light from Fundy.
Listening by a Woodpile, Night of Moon
    after Snow.
Long Pond Summer.
Lying to Fall Warblers.
Mayflies.
Mockingbird, The.
My Grandmother Steals Her Last Trout.
Needsong.
Night Ways.
October Dory Race.
Old Clothes, The.
Old Map of Barnstable County.
Old Trip by Dream Train, The.
Old Woman Telling Another Version.
Old Woodsroads.
Photo of Miners, A.
Pitch Pines.
Pollen.
Running.
Rural Mailboxes.
Saying Her Name.
Sea Fogs at the Chequammitt Inn.
Sea Huns.
Seals in the Inner Harbor.
Sengekontacket.
Stealing the Christmas Greens.
Stone Arabia Farm.
Summer School.
Tar.
Tautog.
This Fog.
Transmigration.
Trying to Flatter Twelve Mile River.
War in the Garden.
Warmth.
Weave a Circle Round Me Thrice.
Whirl Is King.
Widow at "Whaleroad's End," The.
Wild Apple Trees.
Willow, Wishbone, Warblers.
Winter Oysters.
Winter Runner, The.
With Anne at the Peabody.
Woodsmoke.
Young Owls.

Gardner, Isabella (1915–81)
Abraham and Isaac.
Accomplices, The.
And Thou No Breath at All?
Are Poets Ball Players?
At a Summer Hotel.
At the Zoo.
Autumn: Early Morning.
Baldur Was Beautiful Too.
Bronchitis at the Chelsea—or Salud Raul.
Cadenza.
Canzonetta.
Card Island or Cod Island?
Children Are Game.

Cock-a-Hoop.
Cockchafer.
Collage of Echoes.
Compleat Anglers, The.
Convalescence in Summer 1949.
Conversation at Midnight with Oscar
    Williams.
Cowardice.
Daughter.
Disenchanted, The.
Eros in May at MacDowell.
Fall in Massachusetts.
Feminine Ending or, Abandoned, She Died.
Fixing the Clock.
Fly in Amber.
Folkways.
Fright among the Runes.
Gimboling.
Grocery Bouquet, The.
Homo Gratia Artis.
In Memory of Lemuel Ayers, Scene
    Designer, Dead of Cancer in His Fortieth
    Year.
In the Museum.
Incantate the Cockatrice.
It Rained Last Night.
Jig for Harmonica.
Knowing.
Last Trump, The.
Letter from Slough Pond.
Lines to a Seagreen Lover.
Little Rock Arkansas 1957.
Loud Song, Mother, A.
Man of Faith, The.
Masked Shrew, The.
Mathematics of Encounter.
Mea Culpa.
Milkman, The.
Minotaur, The.
Moth Happened, The.
Music Room, The.
Nightmare.
Nor Good Red Herring.
Not At All What One Is Used To.
Nursery Rhyme No. 1.
Nursery Rhyme No. 2.
Of Conscience.
Of Flesh and Bone.
Of Mercy.
On Looking in the Looking Glass.
One Sunday in 1966.
Only Relic, The.
Panic Vine, The.
Part of the Darkness.
Prospero's Isle.
Reveille for a Rockinghorse Poet.
Roundelay: "Blood-red bird with one green
    eye, A."
Saloon Suite.
Salt.
Searchlight, The.
Sloth, The.
Sonnet for My Acquaintances.
Southwest of True North.
Spendthrift.
Summer Evening.
Summer Remembered.
Summers Ago.
Tango for Zither.
Telephone, The.
That Common Moth.
That "Craning of the Neck."
That Princeling.
That Was Then.
This Neighborhood.
This Room Is Full of Clocks.
Three Rings or Five rings.
Timeo.
To Thoreau on Rereading Walden.
Triolet: "Bad die old, The."
Two Sapphics.
Waltz for Accordion.
West of Childhood.
When a Warlock Dies.
When in Rome..
Who Spilled the Salt?
Whole World's in a Terrible Chassis, The.

Widow's Yard, The.
Word From the Piazza del Limbo, A.
Writing Poetry.
Your Fearful Symmetries.
Zei Gesund.
Translations, Coauthored Poems, etc.:
    Ballade: "Lady of Heaven, Queen of nature."
    Ballade: "You who outlive us, you, our
        mortal brothers."
    Feeling of Time.
    Jean Sans Terre The Chest of Drawers.
    Jean Sans Terre Wraps Himself in a Red
        Coat.

"Gardons, S. S." *see* Snodgrass, William DeWitt
Garrigue, Jean (1914–72)
    Address to the Migrations.
    After Reading "The Country of the Pointed
        Firs."
    Again, Again.
    Amsterdam Letter.
    Attempting to Persuade You to Go for a
        Walk in the Public Gardens.
    Bad Times Song.
    Beaucaire.
    Beheld in Naples.
    Bleecker Street.
    Brook, The.
    Catch What You Can.
    Circle, The.
    Civilization Constantly Worrying about Itself
        as It Goes on Doing What It Is Worrying
        About That It Is Doing, A.
    Clovers, The.
    Cortège for Colette.
    Country Villa.
    Cracked Looking Glass.
    Demon Came to Me, A.
    Doggerel of a Diehard Who Sleeps in a Nest
        of Newspapers.
    Enemy of Those Who Are Enemies of Sleep.
    Epitaph for My Cat.
    False Country of the Zoo.
    Figure for J.V. Meer, A.
    Flux of Autumn, The.
    For an Orchard Tree.
    For Anybody's Martyr's Song.
    For J.
    For Such a Bird He Had No Convenient
        Cage.
    For the Fountains and Fountaineers of Villa
        d'Este.
    Forest.
    From Venice Was That Afternoon.
    Giralda, The.
    Grand Canyon, The.
    Gravepiece.
    Grenoble Café.
    Grief Was to Go Out, Away.
    Homage to Ghosts.
    Improvisation upon the Theme of the Lady
        and the Unicorn, An.
    In Memory.
    Incantatory Poem.
    Invitation to a Hay.
    Invocation to Old Windylocks.
    Iowa City Zoo.
    Land We Did Not Know, The.
    Last Letter to the Scholar.
    Lead in the Water.
    Maimed Grasshopper Speaks Up, The.
    Mask and Knife, The.
    Moondial.
    Moralizing Overheard in a Forest.
    Motifs from the Dark Wood.
    Mourning, A.
    Mouse, The.
    Movie Actors Scribbling Letters Very Fast in
        Crucial Scenes.
    My Frantic Heart.
    Note to La Fontaine, A.
    On Going by Train to White River Junction,
        Vt.
    One for the Roses.
    Only the Irresistible Abides.
    Pays Perdu.
    Poem: "I saw the mountains in a rose-fire
        light."

Primer of Plato.
Rain Song.
Requiem: "In the sudden white silence, where
    are you?"
Resistance Meeting: Boston Common.
Shore.
Smoke Shop Owner's Daughter, The.
Song for "Buvez les Vins du Postillion"—
    Advt.
Song in Sligo.
Song: "O beautiful, my relic bone."
Spring Song II.
Stranger, The.
Strike of the Night, The.
Studies for an Actress.
Suite.
There Is a Dark River.
This Swallows' Empire.
Thy Love Is One Thou'st Not Yet Known.
To Speak of My Influences.
Waking, I Always Waked You Awake.
Why the Heart Has Dreams Is Why the Mind
    Goes Mad.
With Glaze of Tears.

Gildner, Gary (b. 1938)
    After World War II.
    All Hallows' Eve in Kansas.
    Always in Late Summer Now, in the City.
    Around the Horn.
    Around the Kitchen Table.
    Blue Like the Heavens.
    Burn-Out.
    Day Before Thanksgiving, a Call Comes to
        Me Concerning Insulation, The.
    Digging for Indians.
    Edward.
    Eeny, Meeny, Miney, Mo, Miss Beech.
    8/22/38–8/22/68.
    Farm, The.
    Field Mouse at My Fishing Hole, A.
    First Practice.
    For Judy.
    4th Base.
    Geisha.
    Girl in the Red Convertible, The.
    Harold Fogel Could Be Anywhere.
    Heart Attack.
    High-Class Bananas, The.
    House on Buder Street, The.
    Ice Shanties.
    In the Beginning.
    In the Social Security Office.
    Is My Heart Really Big As My Fist?
    It's Spring, Lover.
    Jabón.
    Johann Gaertner (1793–1887).
    Kneeling in the Snow.
    Last Articles.
    Last Monarch of the Season, The.
    Letter From My Good Hand, A.
    Letter to a Substitute Teacher.
    Letters from Vicksburg.
    Life & Death in Skokie.
    Life of the Wolf, The.
    Man and the Goshawk, The.
    Mark Only One Circle.
    Meeting My Best Friend from the Eighth
        Grade.
    Meeting the Reincarnation Analyst.
    Memory, A.
    My Coed Wife.
    My Father after Work.
    My Mother Writes..
    Nails.
    Old Farm in Northern Michigan.
    Page Turner, The.
    Passion Play.
    Poem: "My daughter and I lie in the snow."
    Poem with Levels of Meaning.
    Poems.
    Porch, The.
    Prayer for My Father.
    Runner, The.
    Rustling a Hog.
    Shy Roofer, The.
    Statistics.
    Szostak.

That Summer.
They Have Turned the Church Where I Ate
    God.
To My Daughter.
Toads in the Greenhouse.
Today They Are Roasting Rocky Norse.
Uncle George at the Home.
Wean Poem.
Wheat.
When the Retarded Swim.
Xmas.

Ginsberg, Allen (b. 1926)
Aether.
After All, What Else Is There to Say?
After Dead Souls.
After Thoughts.
After Whitman & Reznikoff.
After Yeats.
Afternoon Seattle.
America.
American Change.
Angkor Wat.
Anti-Vietnam War Peace Mobilization.
Archetype Poem, The.
Asphodel, An.
At Apollinaire's Grave.
Atypical Affair, An.
Auto Poesy: On the Lam from Bloomington.
Autumn Gold: New England Fall.
Ayers Rock / Uluru Song.
Back on Times Square, Dreaming of Times
    Square.
Ballade of Poisons.
Battleship Newsreel.
Bayonne Entering NYC.
Bayonne Turnpike to Tuscarora.
Beginning of a Poem of These States.
Big Beat.
Birdbrain.
Bixby Canyon.
Bixby Canyon Ocean Path Word Breeze.
Blame the Thought, Cling to the Bummer.
Blessed Be the Muses.
Blue Angel, The.
Bop Lyrics.
Bricklayer's Lunch Hour, The.
Brooklyn College Brain.
Cabin in the Rockies.
Café in Warsaw.
Capitol Air.
Car Crash.
Carmel Valley.
Cézanne's Ports.
Chances "R."
Change: *Kyoto-Tokyo Express*, The.
Chicago to Salt Lake by Air.
City Midnight Junk Strains.
Cleveland, the Flats.
C'mon Jack.
Come All Ye Brave Boys.
Complaint of the Skeleton to Time.
Consulting I Ching Smoking Pot Listening to
    the Fugs Sing Blake.
Contest of Bards.
Continuation of a Long Poem of These
    States.
Crash.
Crazy Spiritual, A.
Crossing Nation.
Dakar Doldrums.
Death News.
Death on All Fronts.
Death to Van Gogh's Ear!
December 31, 1978.
Defending the Faith.
Describe: The Rain on Dasaswamedh Ghat.
Desolation.
Do We Understand Each Other?
Done, Finished with the Biggest Cock.
Don't Grow Old.
Dream, A.
Dream Record: June 8, 1955.
"Drive All Blames into One."
Drowse Murmurs.
Easter Sunday.
Eastern Ballad, An.
Ecologue.

Ego Confession.
Elegy Che Guevara.
Elegy for Neal Cassady.
End, The.
Epigram on a Painting of Golgotha.
Eroica.
Europe! Europe!
Eye Altering Alters All, The.
Falling Asleep in America.
Father Death Blues.
Father Guru.
Fie My Fum.
Flash Back.
Flying Elegy.
Footnote to Howl.
For Creely's Ear.
Four Haiku.
Fourth Floor, Dawn, Up All Night Writing
    Letters.
Fragment 1956.
Fragment: The Names II.
Friday the Thirteenth.
Funny Death.
Further Proposal, A.
Fyodor.
Galilee Shore.
Garden State.
Ghost May Come, A.
Going to Chicago.
Gospel Noble Truths.
Graffiti 12th Cubicle Men's Room Syracuse
    Airport.
Grant Park: August 28, 1968.
Green Automobile, The.
Green Valentine Blues.
Gregory Corso's Story.
Grim Skeleton.
Growing Old Again.
G.S. Reading Poesy at Princeton.
Guru.
Guru Om.
Hadda Be Playing on the Jukebox.
Haunting Poe's Baltimore.
Havana 1953.
Have You Seen This Movie?
Heat.
Hiway Poesy: L.A.–Albuquerque–Texas–
    Witchita.
Holy Ghost on the Nod over the Body of
    Bliss.
Homework.
Hospital Window.
How Come He Got Canned at the Ribbon
    Factory.
Howl.
HūMLOWDOTBom!
Hymmnn.
Hymn: "No hyacinthine imagination can
    express this clock of meat bleakly pining."
I Am a Victim of Telephone.
I attempted to concentrate.
I Beg You Come Back & Be Cheerful.
I feel as if I am at a dead.
I Have Increased Power.
I Lay Love on My Knee.
I learned a world from each.
I made love to myself.
Ignu.
Imaginary Rose in a Book, An.
Imaginary Universes.
In a Moonlit Hermit's Cabin.
In Back of the Real.
In Death, Cannot Reach What Is Most Near.
In Memoriam: William Cannastra, 1922–
    1950.
In Society.
In the Baggage Room at Greyhound.
Independence Day.
Iron Horse.
Jaweh and Allah Battle.
Journal Night Thoughts.
Junk Mail.
Kaddish.
Kansas City to Saint Louis.
Kiss Ass.
Kral Majales.
Lack Love.

Land O'Lakes, Wisc.
Land O'Lakes, Wisconsin: Vajrayana
    Seminary.
Las Vegas: Verses Improvised for El Dorado
    H.S. Newspaper.
Last Night in Calcutta.
Laughing Gas.
Lion for Real, The.
Long Live the Spiderweb.
Love Forgiven.
Love Letter.
Love Poem on Theme by Whitman.
Love Replied.
Love Returned.
Lover's Garden, A.
Lysergic Acid.
Mad Gleam, A.
Magic Psalm.
Malest Cornifici Tuo Catullo.
Manhattan May Day Midnight.
Manhattan Thirties Flash.
Manifesto.
Man's Glory.
Many Loves.
Marijuana Notation.
Maybe Love.
Meaningless Institution, A.
Memory Gardens.
Mescaline.
Message.
Message II.
Metaphysics.
Methedrine Vision in Hollywood, A.
Milarepa Taste.
Mind Breaths.
Moments Return, The.
Morning.
Mugging.
My Alba.
My Sad Self.
Nagasaki Days.
Names, The.
Neruda's "Que dispierte el leñador."
News Bulletin.
Night-Apple, The.
Night Gleam.
Northwest Passage.
Nov. 23, 1963: Alone.
Ode: My 24th Year.
Ode to Failure.
Ode to the Setting Sun.
Old Pond.
Old Village before I Die, The.
On Burroughs' Work.
On Illness.
On Neal's Ashes.
On Neruda's Death.
On Reading William Blake's "The Sick
    Rose."
Open Window on Chicago, An.
Over Denver Again.
Over Kansas.
Over Laramie.
Past Silver Durango Over Mexic Sierra-
    Wrinkles.
Paterson.
Patna-Benares Express.
Pentagon Exorcism.
Pertussin.
Please Master.
Please Open the Window and Let
    Me In.
Plutonian Ode.
Poem on America, A.
Poem Rocket.
Portland Coliseum.
Prophecy, A.
Psalm I.
Psalm II: "Ah, still Lord, ah sweet Divinity."
Psalm III: "To God: to illuminate all men.
    Beginning with Skid Road."
Psalm IV.
Punk Rock Your My Big Crybaby.
Pussy Blues.
Rain-Wet Asphalt Heat, Garbage Curbed
    Cans Overflowing.
Reading French Poetry.

Ready to Roll.
Reflections at Lake Louise.
Reflections in Sleepy Eye.
Refrain.
Reply, The.
Returning North of Vortex.
Returning to the Country for a Brief Visit.
Rising Over Night-Blackened Detroit Streets.
Rolling Thunder Stones.
Ruhr-Gebiet.
Sad Dust Glories.
Sakyamuni Coming Out from the Mountain.
Sather Gate Illumination.
Scribble.
Seabattle of Salamis Took Place off Perama.
September on Jessore Road.
S.F. Southward.
Shrouded Stranger, The.
Sickness Blues.
Siesta in Xbalba.
Smoke Rolling Down Street.
Some Love.
Sometime Jailhouse Blues.
Song: "Weight of the world, The."
Sonora Desert-Edge.
Spring Fashions.
Squeal.
Stanzas: Written at Night in Radio City.
Stool Pigeon Blues.
Stotras to Kali Destroyer of Illusions.
Strange New Cottage in Berkeley, A.
Studying the Signs.
Sunflower Sutra.
Sunset.
Sunset S.S. Azemour.
Supermarket in California, A.
Sweet Boy, Gimme Yr Ass.
Sweet Levinsky.
Swirls of Black Dust on Avenue D.
Tears.
Television Was a Baby Crawling toward That
    Deathchamber.
Terms in Which I Think of Reality, The.
Tethnakin D'oligo Pideuis Fainom Alaia.
Teton Village.
These States: Into L.A.
These States: to Miami Presidential
    Convention.
This Form of Life Needs Sex.
This Is about Death.
Thoughts on a Breath.
Thoughts Sitting Breathing.
345 W. 15th St.
To an Old Poet in Peru.
To Aunt Rose.
To Lindsay.
To P.O.
To Poe: Over the Planet, Air Albany–
    Baltimore.
To the Body.
To the Punks of Dawlish.
Today.
Tonite all is well. . .What a.
Transcription of Organ Music.
Trembling of the Veil, The.
Tübingen–Hamburg Schlafwagen.
Two Boys Went Into a Dream Diner.
Two Dreams.
Two Sonnets.
Typical Affair, A.
Under the World There's a Lot of Ass, a Lot
    of Cunt.
Understand That This Is a Dream.
Uptown.
Verses Written for Student Antidraft
    Registration Rally 1980.
Very Dove, A.
Violence.
Vision 1948.
Voice of Rock, The.
Vow, A.
Voznesensky's "Silent Tingling."
Vulture Peak: Gridhakuta Hill.
Waking in New York.
Wales Visitation.
Walking Home at Night.
War Profit Litany.

We Rise on Sun Beams and Fall in the
    Night.
Western Ballad, A.
What I'd Like to Do.
What Would You Do If You Lost It.
What's Dead?
Who.
Who Be Kind To.
Who Runs America?
Who Will Take Over the Universe?
Why Is God Love, Jack?
Wichita Vortex Sutra.
Wild Orphan.
Wings Lifted over the Black Pit.
Written on Hotel Napkin: Chicago Futures.
Wrote This Last Night.
Xmas Gift.
Yes and It's Hopeless.
You Might Get in Trouble.
Translations, Coauthored Poems, etc.:
Pull My Daisy.

Glück, Louise (b. 1943)
Abishag.
Adult Grief.
All Hallows.
Aphrodite.
Apple Trees, The.
Archipelago.
Aubade: "Today above the gull's call."
Autumnal.
Baskets.
Beginning, The.
Brennende Liebe.
Bridal Piece.
Brooding Likeness.
Cell, The.
Chicago Train, The.
Cottonmouth Country.
Cripple in the Subway, The.
Day Without Night.
Dedication to Hunger.
Departure.
Descending Figure.
Deviation, The.
Dream of Mourning, The.
Drowned Children, The.
Early December in Croton-on-Hudson.
Easter Season.
Edge, The.
Egg, The.
Elms.
Embrace, The.
Encounter, The.
End of the World, The.
Epithalamium: "There were others; their
    bodies."
Eros.
Exile.
Fire, The.
First Goodbye.
Firstborn.
Flowering Plum.
For Jane Myers.
For My Father.
For My Mother.
Fortress, The.
From the Japanese.
From the Suburbs.
Game, The.
Garden, The.
Gemini.
Gift, The.
Grandmother.
Grandmother in the Garden.
Gratitude.
Gretel in Darkness.
Happiness.
Hawk's Shadow.
Here Are My Black Clothes.
Hesitate to Call.
Horse.
Hyacinth.
Illuminations.
Inlet, The.
Islander, The.
Japonica.
Jeanne d'Arc.

La Force.
Labor Day.
Lady in the Single, The.
Lamentations.
Last Letter.
Late Snow.
Legend.
Letter from our Man in Blossomtime.
Letter from Provence.
Letters, The.
Liberation.
Love Poem.
Magi, The.
Marathon *sels.*
Marathon.
Memo from the Cave.
Meridian.
Messengers.
Metamorphosis.
Mirror, The.
Mock Orange.
Morning.
Mountain, The.
Murderess, The.
My Cousin in April.
My Life Before Dawn.
My Neighbor in the Mirror.
Mythic Fragment.
Nativity Poem.
Night.
Night Piece.
Night Song.
Northwood Path.
Nurse's Song.
Palais des Arts.
Parable, A.
Phenomenal Survivals of Death in Nantucket.
Pictures of the People in the War.
Pietà.
Poem: "In the early evening, as now, a man
    is bending."
Pomegranate.
Pond, The.
Porcelain Bowl.
Portland, 1968.
Portrait.
Portrait of the Queen in Tears.
Racer's Widow, The.
Reproach, The.
Return, The.
Returning a Lost Child.
Rosy.
Sacred Objects.
Saturnalia.
School Children, The.
Scraps.
Seated Figure.
Seconds.
Shad-Blow Tree, The.
Silverpoint.
Slave Ship, The.
Solstice.
Song of Invisible Boundaries.
Song of Obstacles.
Song of the River.
Still Life.
Summer.
Swans.
Swimmer, The.
Tango.
Thanksgiving.
To Autumn.
To Florida.
Tree House, The.
Triumph of Achilles, The.
12. 6. 71.
Under Taurus.
Undertaking, The.
Winter Morning.
World Breaking Apart.
Wound, The.

Graves, Robert Ranke (1895–1985)
Above the Edge of Doom.
Absent Crusader.
Accomplice, The.
Acrobats.
Advent of Summer.

Advice from a Mother.
Advocates.
After the Flood.
Against Witchcraft.
Age Gap.
Ageless Reason.
Ages of Oath, The.
Alice.
All Except Hannibal.
All I Tell You From My Heart.
Allie.
Always.
Ambience.
Ambrosia of Dionysus and Semele, The.
Ample Garden, The.
Ancestors.
Angry Samson.
Antorcha Y Corona, 1968.
Any Honest Housewife.
Apollo of the Physiologists.
Apple Island.
Apples and Water.
Ark, The.
Armistice Day, 1918.
Around the Mountain.
Arrears of Moonlight.
Arrow on the Vane.
Arrow Shots.
As a Less than Robber.
As All Must End.
As When the Mystic.
At Best, Poets.
At First Sight.
At the Gate.
At the Well.
Awakening, The.
Bank Account.
Bards, The.
Batxóca.
Beach, The.
Beatrice and Dante.
Beauty in Trouble.
Beds of Grainne and Diarmuid, The.
Beggar Maid and King Cophetua, The.
Between Moon and Moon.
Between Trains.
Beware, Madam!
Bird of Paradise.
Birth of a Goddess.
Birth of Angels.
Bites and Kisses.
Black.
Black Goddess, The.
Blackening Sky.
Blanket Charge.
Blessed Sun.
Blind Arrow, A.
Blue-Fly, The.
Bower-Bird.
Bracelet, A.
Breakfast Table.
Brief Reunion.
Broken Compact.
Broken Girth, The.
Broken Neck.
Brother.
Bweteen Hyssop and Axe.
Call It a Good Marriage.
Carol of Patience.
Casse-Noisette.
Castle, The.
Cat-Goddesses.
Certain Mercies.
Change.
Charm for Sound Sleeping, A.
Child with Veteran.
Children of Darkness.
Chink, The.
Christmas Robin, The.
Circus Ring.
Cliff and Wave.
Cliff Edge, The.
Climate of Thought, The.
Cloak, The.
Cock in Pullet's Feathers.
Colophon.
Colours of Night, The.

Compact.
Complaint and Reply.
Confess, Marpessa.
Conjunction.
Consortium of Stones.
Cool Web, The.
Coronation Murder, The.
Coronet of Moonlight.
Counting the Beats.
Country Mansion, A.
Court of Love, A.
Crab-Tree, The.
Crane, The.
Crucibles of Love.
Cry Faugh!
Crystal, The.
Cuirassiers of the Frontier, The.
Cure, The.
Dance of Words.
Dancing Flame.
Dangerous Gift, The.
Dans un Seul Lit.
Darien.
Dawn Bombardment.
Dazzle of Darkness.
De Arte Poetica.
Dead Hand.
Death by Drums.
Death Grapple, The.
Death Room, The.
Deed of Gift.
Deliverance.
Depth of Love.
Descent into Hell.
Desert Fringe.
Despite and Still.
Devil's Advice to Story-Tellers, The.
Dialogue on the Headland.
Dilemma, The.
Discarded Love Poem, The.
Door, The.
Double Bass.
Down.
Down, Wanton, Down!
Dream of Frances Speedwell, A.
Dream of Hell, A.
Dream Recalled on Waking.
Dreaming Children.
Druid Love.
Earlier Lovers.
East Wind, An.
Ecstasy of Chaos.
1805.
Elsewhere.
Encounter, The.
End of Play.
Endless Pavement.
Envoi: "There is no now for us but always."
Eurydice.
Everywhere Is Here.
Expect Nothing.
Face in the Mirror, The.
Fact of the Act.
Falcon Woman, The.
Fallen Tower of Siloam, The.
Fast Bound Together.
Fetter, The.
Field-Postcard, The.
Finding of Love, The.
Fire Walker.
First Love.
Five.
Florist Rose, The.
Flowering Aloe, The.
Flying Crooked.
Food of the Dead.
Fools.
For Ever.
Forbidden Words.
Foreboding, The.
Former Attachment, A.
Fortunate Child.
Fragment: "Are you shaken, are you stirred."
Fragment of a Lost Poem.
Freehold.
Friday Night.
Frightened Men.

Frog and the Golden Ball, The.
From the Embassy.
Front Door Soliloquy.
Frosty Night, A.
Full Moon.
Furious Voyage, The.
Garden, The.
Gardener.
Gateway, The.
Gentleman, The.
Gift of Sight.
Gold and Malachite.
Gold Cloud.
Golden Anchor.
Good Night to the Old Gods.
Gooseflesh Abbey.
Gorge, The.
Gorgon Mask.
Grace Notes.
Gratitude for a Nightmare.
Great-Grandmother, The.
Green Castle, The.
Green-Sailed Vessel, The.
Green Woods of Unrest, The.
Grotesques.
Growing Pains.
H.
Hag-Ridden.
Half-Finished Letter, The.
Halls of Bedlam, The.
Haunted House, The.
Hazel Grove, The.
Hearth, The.
Heaven.
Hedges Freaked With Snow.
Hell.
Henry and Mary.
Her Beauty.
Her Brief Withdrawal.
Hercules at Nemea.
Hero, The.
Hidden Garden, The.
Hills of May, The.
History of the Fall.
Home-Coming, The.
Hooded Flame.
Hoopoe Tells Us How, The.
Horizon.
How It Started.
Hung Wu Vase, The.
I Will Write.
Iago.
Ibycus of Samos.
I'd Die for You.
If No Cuckoo Sings.
Imminent Seventies, The.
Impossible Day, The.
Impossible, The.
In Broken Images.
In Disguise.
In Her Only Way.
In Her Praise.
In No Direction.
In Perspective.
In Procession.
In the Vestry.
In the Wilderness.
In Time.
In Time of Absence.
In Trance At A Distance.
Injuries.
Inkidoo and the Queen of Babel.
Instructions to the Orphic Adept.
Interruption.
Invitation to Bristol.
Iron Palace.
Is Now the Time?
It Was All Very Tidy.
Jealous Man, A.
Joan and Darby.
Joseph and Mary.
Judgement of Paris.
Judges, The.
Jugum Improbum.
Jus Primae Noctis.
Knobs and Levers.
La Mejicana.

To Be Poets.
To Beguile and Betray.
To Bring the Dead to Life.
To Come of Age.
To Evoke Posterity.
To Juan at the Winter Solstice.
To Lucia at Birth.
To Myrto About Herself.
To Ogmian Hercules.
To Put It Simply.
To Sleep.
To Tell and Be Told.
To the Teumessian Vixen.
To Walk on Hills.
Toast to Death, A.
Tolling Bell.
Tomorrow's Envy of Today.
Torch and Crown, 1968.
Touch My Shut Lips.
Tousled Pillow.
Tower of Love, The.
Traditionalist, The.
Trial of Innocence.
Troll's Nosegay, The.
Troublesome Fame.
Troughs of Sea.
Trudge, Body!
True Evil.
True Joy.
True Magic.
Truth Is Poor Physic.
Turn of the Moon.
Twice Of The Same Fever.
Twin of Sleep, The.
Twins.
Two Crucial Generations.
Two Disciplines.
Two Witches, The.
Ugly Secret, The.
Ulysses.
Uncalendared Love.
Uncut Diamond, The.
Undead, The.
Under the Olives.
Under the Pot.
Unicorn and the White Doe.
Unnamed Spell, The.
Unpenned Poem, The.
Unposted Letter.
Until We Both.
Utter Rim, The.
Vain and Careless.
Vanity.
Variables of Green.
Villagers and Death, The.
Virgin Mirror.
Virus, The.
Visitation, The.
Vow, The.
Wall, The.
Wand, The.
Warning to Children.
Watch, The.
Weather of Olympus, The.
Wedding, The.
Welsh Incident.
What Can We Not Ask?
What Did I Dream?
What Did You Say?
What is Love?
What Will Be, Is.
When and Why.
When Love Is Not.
White Goddess, The.
Whole Love.
Why of the Weather, The.
Wigs and Beards.
Wild Cyclamen.
Window Pane, The.
Window Sill, The.
Winged Heart, The.
With a Gift of Rings.
With Her Lips Only.
With the Gift of a Lion's Claw.
Within Reason.
Wm. Brazier.
Woman and Tree.
Woman of Greece.

Woman Poet and Man Poet.
Word, The.
Work Drafts.
Work-Room.
Wreath, The.
Yet Unsayable, The.
Young Cordwainer, The.
Young Sibyl, The.
Your Private Way.
Translations, Coauthored Poems, etc.:
In the Name of Virtue.
P'eng That Was a K'un, The.
Single Fare.
Women and Masks.

Gray, Thomas (1716–71)
Agrippina.
Alliance of Education and Government, The.
Amatory Lines.
Bard, The [A Pindaric Ode].
Caradoc.
Conan.
Concluding Lines of Epitaph on Mrs Mason.
Couplet about Birds.
Death of Hoel, The.
Descent of Odin, The.
Elegy Written in a Country Churchyard.
Epitaph: "Here rests his head upon the lap of earth."
Epitaph on a Child.
Epitaph on Mrs Jane Clarke.
Epitaph on Sir William Williams.
Fatal Sisters, The.
Hymn to Adversity.
Hymn to Ignorance.
Impromptu.
Long Story, A.
Ode for Music.
Ode on a Distant Prospect of Eton College.
Ode on the Death of a Favourite [*or* Favorite] Cat, Drowned in a Tub [*or* Bowl] of Gold Fishes.
Ode on the Pleasure Arising from Vicissitude.
Ode on the Spring.
Pindaric Ode, A.
Progress of Poesy, The.
Sketch of His Own Character.
Song: "Thyrsis, when we parted, swore."
Sonnet [on the Death of Mr. Richard West].
Stanzas to Mr Richard Bentley.
Tophet.
Triumphs of Owen, The.
William Shakespeare to Mrs Anne, Regular Servant to the Rev. Mr Precentor of York.

Grieve, Christopher Murray *see* "MacDiarmid, Hugh"

Griffiths, Steve (b. 1949)
Anglo-Welshman and his friends, The.
At the Consecration.
Belonging.
Cemaes Songs.
Children in a Walled Garden.
Chiming at Trwyn Du, The.
Chips.
Choice of Flowers, The.
Christmas Night.
Ciudadela, 1991.
Climber.
Consequences.
Contact.
Continuity.
Contractions.
Courage.
Courting Prosperity.
Craig-y-Don.
Crossing Lady-Stanley, Here, 1868.
Decision.
Doors of the Year, Well Done, The.
Education.
Elegy for John Tripp.
Everyone Watches the Sunset.
Expectations.
Fathers.
Few Bars Over Again, A.
Fluidity, Charmouth.
For the Irish Sea.
From Waterloo Bridge, Ensuing Dark.

Fruits of Virtue.
Geriatrics.
Getting It Wrong, Again.
Giving Them What For.
Glyndŵr Subdued.
Guardianship.
Guesthouse, The.
Hairdresser, Age 55, Dalston.
Horse's Mouth, The.
Hymns and Backward Glances.
In the Railway Hotel at Cordoba.
Island with Army, Pines and Wind.
Llangefni Market.
Llantysilio, Overgrown.
Mines in Sepia Tint, The.
Misrule, Towyn, 1990.
Murder.
Nearness.
News of a Marriage.
Oil Terminal.
Old Hope.
Optimism.
Out of a Descended Generation.
Patchworks.
Post Imperial.
Refugees.
Rivers Are Running Beneath Us.
Shamanism, Dalston.
Shooting of Levellers, Burford, 1649.
Shrinking Horizon.
Small Substantial Shadow.
Spanish Providence, A.
Still Too Quick to Hold.
Suffering Does for the Character.
Taking Shelter.
Tŷ Newydd.
Under Mynydd-y-Tŵr.
Unmetalled Road.
Unwritten Chapters.
Villa-Famès, August 1986.
Wedding Photograph.

Gunn, Thom (b. 1929)
Adolescence.
Adultery.
All Do Not All Things Well.
All Night, Legs Pointed East.
Allegory of the Wolf Boy, The.
Amorous Debate, An.
Annihilation of Nothing, The.
Another All-Night Party.
Apartment Cats.
Aquarium, The.
Aqueduct.
As Expected.
At an Intersection.
At the Back of the North Wind.
At the Barriers.
At the Centre.
Autobiography.
Autumn Chapter in a Novel.
Baby Song.
Back to Life.
Bally *Power Play.*
Barren Leaves.
Bath House, The.
Beach Head, The.
Beautician, The.
Bed, The.
Before the Carnival.
Behind the Mirror.
Being Born.
Berlin in Ruins.
Birthday Poem.
Black Jackets.
Blackie, the Electric Rembrandt.
Blank, A.
Bone.
Book of the Dead, The.
Breaking Ground.
Bringing to Light.
Bulletin from the Stadium, A.
Byrnies, The.
Cafeteria in Boston.
Cannibal.
Captain in Time of Peace.
Carnal Knowledge.
Cat and the Wind, The.

Cherry Tree, The.
Claus von Stauffenberg.
Clock, The.
Colour Machine, The.
Confessions of the Life Artist.
Considering the Snail.
Conversation of Old Men, The.
Conversation, The.
Cool Stream, The.
Corporal, The.
Corridor, The.
Courage, a Tale.
Court Revolt, The.
Courtesies of the Interregnum.
Crosswords.
Crystal.
Death's Door.
Diagrams.
Differences, The.
Discovery of the Pacific, The.
Dolly.
Donahue's Sister.
Drive to Los Alamos, A.
During an Absence.
Elegy: "I can almost see it."
Elegy on the Dust.
Elvis Presley.
Exercise, The.
Expression.
Fair in the Woods, The.
Falstaff.
Faustus Triumphant.
Feel of Hands, The.
Fennel.
Fever.
First Man, The.
First Meeting with a Possible Mother-in-Law.
Flooded Meadows.
Flying Above California.
For a Birthday.
For Signs.
From an Asian Tent.
From the Highest Camp.
From the Wave.
Garden of the Gods, The.
Geyser, The.
Geysers, The.
Girls Next Door, The.
Goddess, The.
Grasses.
Hampstead; the Horse Chestnut Trees.
Helen's Rape.
Her Pet.
Here Come the Saints.
Hide and Seek.
High Fidelity.
His Rooms in College.
Hitching into Frisco.
Hotblood on Friday.
Hug, The.
Idea of Trust, The.
Improvisation.
In Praise of Cities.
In Santa Maria del Popolo.
In the Tank.
In Time of Plague.
Incident on a Journey.
Inherited Estate, The.
Innocence.
Inside-Outside Game, The.
Interruption.
Invitation, An.
Iron Landscapes (and the Statue of Liberty).
J Car, The.
Jack Straw's Castle.
Jamesian.
Jesus and His Mother.
Julian the Apostate.
June.
Justin.
JVC.
Keats at Highgate.
Kent.
Kind of Ethics, A.
Kiss at Bayreuth, The.
La Prisonnière.

Lament: "Your dying was a difficult
   enterprise."
Last Days at Teddington.
Last Man, The.
Lazarus Not Raised.
Legal Reform.
L'Epreuve.
Lerici.
Life of the Otter, The.
Lights among Redwood.
Lines for a Book.
Lines for My 55th Birthday.
Listening to Jefferson Airplane.
Lofty in the Palais de Danse.
Looking Glass.
Looks.
Loot.
Man With Night Sweats, The.
Mandrakes.
Map of the City, A.
Market at Turk.
Meat.
Memoirs of the World.
Memory Unsettled.
Menace, The.
Merlin in the Cave: He Speculates without a
   Book.
Messenger, The.
Miracle, The.
Mirror for Poets, A.
Misanthropos.
Missing, The.
Modes of Pleasure.
Moly.
Monster, The.
Monterey.
My Sad Captains.
Nasturtium.
Nature of an Action, The.
New York.
Night Piece, The.
Night Taxi.
1975.
No Speech from the Scaffold.
Odysseus on Hermes.
Old Meg.
Old Woman, The.
On the Move.
Outdoor Concert, The.
Outside the Diner.
Painkillers.
Patch Work.
Phaedra in the Farm House.
Philemon and Baucis.
Pierce Street.
Plan of Self-Subjection, A.
Plunge, The.
Punch Rubicundus.
Rastignac at 45.
Readings in French.
Reassurance, The.
Release, The.
Right Possessor, The.
Rites of Passage.
Road Map, The.
Rooftop, The.
Round and Round.
Sacred Heart.
St. Martin and the Beggar.
San Francisco Streets.
Sand Man, The.
Saturnalia.
Seabed, The.
Secret Sharer, The.
Seesaw.
Selves.
Separation, The.
Silver Age, The.
Skateboard.
Sketch of the Great Dejection, A.
Sleep by the Hot Stream.
Slow Waker.
Small Plane in Kansas.
Smoking Pot on the Bus.
Song of a Camera.
Sparrow.
Stealer, The.

Still Life.
Street Song.
Sunlight.
Sweet Things.
Talbot Road.
Tamer and Hawk.
Taylor Street.
Tenderloin.
Terminal.
Thomas Bewick.
Thoughts on Unpacking.
Three.
Three for Children.
Three Songs sels.
To a Dead Graduate Student.
To a Friend in Time of Trouble.
To His Cynical Mistress.
To Isherwood Dying.
To Natty Bumppo.
To the Dead Owner of a Gym.
To Yvor Winters, 1955.
Tom-Dobbin.
Touch.
Transients and Residents.
Trucker, A.
Unsettled Motorcyclist's Vision of His Death,
   The.
Value of Gold, The.
Venetian Blind.
Victim, The.
Vigil of Corpus Christi, The.
Vox Humana.
Waitress.
Waking Dream, A.
Waking in a Newly Built House.
Well Dennis O'Grady.
Wheel of Fortune, The.
Wind in the Street.
Without a Counterpart.
Words.
Words for Some Ash.
Wound, The.
Wrestling.
Yellow Pitcher Plant.
Yoko.

H

"H. D." *see* Doolittle, Hilda
Hacker, Marilyn (b. 1942)
  Across the mud flats and the wide roads,
    over rivers and borders.
  Adult Entertainment.
  After the Revolution.
  Against Silence.
  And I shout at Iva, whine at you. Easily.
  Angry, I speak, and pass the hurt to you.
  April Interval.
  Art of a Novel, The.
  As yoked to her by absence as by prescence.
  Aube Provençale.
  Autumn 1980.
  Azure striation swirls beyond the stones.
  Ballad of Ladies Lost and Found.
  Before the War.
  Between us on our wide bed we cuddle an
    incubus.
  Callers, The.
  Canzone: "Consider the three functions of the
    tongue."
  Celles.
  Chaplet for Judith Landry, A.
  Christmas Crown, A.
  Coda.
  Companion, The.
  Country & Western.
  Country & Western II.
  Crépusule Provençale.
  Culled from the brambled ceiling of my wide
  Days of 1959.
  Days of 1944: Three Friends.
  Dear Jool, I Miss You in Saint-Saturnin.
  Elegy: "Crying from exile, I."
  Elektra on Third Avenue.
  Elevens.
  Exiles.

February of the merely real, A.
Feeling and Form.
Fifteen to Eighteen.
For Elektra.
For Jean Migrenne.
For K.J., Leaving and Coming Back.
Forage Sestina.
Fourteen.
Friend (this is an imaginary letter).
Geographer.
Gerda in the Aerie.
Going Back to the River.
Graffiti from the Gare Saint-Manqué.
Grizzled doorman lets the doctors' wives, The.
Hang-Glider's Daughter, The.
His Wife at Bellevue.
Home, and I've.
I still balk at my preference for rhyme.
I will never be only a Lesbian.
If we talk, we're too tired to make love; if we.
I'll dabble in specifics in my bath.
I'll tell you what I don't want: an affair.
Inheritances.
Iva's Birthday Poem.
Iva's Pantoum.
La Fontaine de Vaucluse sels.
Languedocienne.
Last Time, The.
Late August.
Late August Letter.
Le Travail Rajeunit.
Letter from Goose Creek: April.
Lines Declining a Transatlantic Dinner Invitation.
Little Robber Girl Considers the Wide World, The.
Little Robber Girl Gets On in the Wide World, The.
Living in the Moment.
More circumspect good friend, if by "deceive."
Morning: the phone jangles me from words: you.
Mother.
Mother II.
My child wants dolls, a tutu, that girls' world made.
Navigators, The sels.
Nights of 1964-1966: The Old Reliable.
Nights of 1962: The River Merchant's Wife.
1976.
1973.
No better lost than any other woman.
Orpheus and animus, / drawing back to journeys now.
Pantoum.
Part of a True Story.
Partial Analysis.
Peterborough.
Pornographic Poem.
Prayer for my Daughter.
Presentation Piece.
Regent's Park Sonnets, The.
Rhetoric.
Riposte.
Robber Woman, The.
Rooms in Bloomsbury.
Rune of the Finland Woman.
Satisfied loves eat big breakfasts. I.
Sea Coming Indoors, The.
Separate Lives.
Separations sels.
Sestina: "For a week now our bodies have whispered."
She Bitches About Boys.
She twists scraps of her hair in unshelled snails.
Shirland Road.
Sisterhood.
Somewhere in a Turrent.
Sword.
Taking Notice sels.
Third Snowfall.
This is a high and sprawling wooden flat.
Towards Autumn.

Two Cities.
Untoward Occurance at Embassy Poetry Reading.
Villanelle: "Every day our bodies seperate."
Villanelle: Late Summer.
When I read poems to the art students.
When that jackbooted choreography.
When you told me that he was in jail.
Why We Are Going Back to Paradise Island.
You made algebra: his tastes in food.

Haines, John (b. 1924)
Alive in the World.
And When the Green Man Comes.
Arlington.
At Slim's River.
Blood Lake, The.
Book of the Jungle.
Brand.
By the Ocean.
Calendar, The.
Cauliflower, The.
Certain Dead.
Changes.
Choosing a Stone.
Cicada.
Circles and Squares.
Cranes.
Daphne.
Denali Road.
Deserted Cabin.
Divided, the Man is Dreaming.
Dream of the Lynx.
Dream of the Police, The.
Driving through Oregon (Dec. 1973).
Dürer's Vision.
Dusk of the Revolutionaries.
End of the Street, The.
End of the Summer, The.
Eye in the Rock, The.
Fairbanks Under the Solstice.
Field of the Caribou, The.
Flight, The.
For Anne, at a Little Distance.
For Daphne at Lone Lake.
Foreboding.
Fossil, The.
Ghost Hunter, The.
Goshawk, The.
Guevara.
Harvest.
Head on the Table, The.
Hermitage, The.
Homestead.
Horns.
House of the Injured, The.
Hunger.
If the Owl Calls Again.
In Nature.
In the Middle of America.
Incurable Home, The.
Insects, The.
Instructions to a Sentry.
Into the Glacier.
Invaders, The.
It Must All Be Done Over.
Kitchen, The.
Lake in the Sky, The.
Leaves and Ashes.
Legend of Paper Plates, The.
Lemmings, The.
Listening in October.
Men Against the Sky.
Middle Ages, The.
Mirror, The.
Missoula in a Dusty Light.
Mole, The.
Moose Calling, A.
Moosehead, The.
Mothball Fleet: Benicia, California.
News from the Glacier.
On Banner Dome.
On the Mountain.
On the Road.
Paul Klee.
Pickers.
Pitcher of Milk, The.
Poem About Birch Trees.

Poem for a Cold Journey.
Poem: "Immense sadness / of approaching winter, The."
Poem of the Forgotten.
Prayer to the Snowy Owl.
Rain Glass, The.
Red Trees in the Wind.
Roadways.
Rolling Back.
Ryder.
Skagway.
Sleep.
Snowy Night.
South Wind.
Stone Bear, The.
Stone Harp, The.
Stones.
Sun on Your Shoulder, The.
Sweater of Vladimir Ussachevsky, The.
There Are No Such Trees in Alpine, California.
To a Man Going Blind.
To My Father.
To Turn Back.
To Vera Thompson.
Train Stops at Healy Fork, The.
Traveler, The.
Tree, The.
Tree that Became a House, The.
Tundra, The.
Tunnel, The.
Turning, The.
Victims.
Watching the Fire.
Way We Live, The.
Weaver, The.
Whale in the Blue Washing Machine, The.
What is Life?
Winter Light, A.
Winter News.
Wolves.
Woman on the Road.

Hall, Donald (b. 1928)
Abroad Thoughts from Home.
Acorns.
Adultery At Forty.
Airstrip in Essex, 1960, An.
Alligator Bride, The.
Apples.
At Delphi.
Baseball Players, The.
Beau of the Dead.
"Between the Clock and the Bed."
Black Faced Sheep, The.
Blue Wing, The.
Body Politic, The.
Brief Lives.
By the Exeter River.
Carlotta's Confession.
Carol, A.
Child, The.
Child's Garden, A.
Christ Church Meadows, [Oxford].
Christmas Eve in Whitneyville, 1955.
Cider 5[dc] A Glass.
Clown, The.
Coal Fire, The.
Coffee Cup, The.
Cold Water.
Columns of the Parthenon, The.
Conduct and Work.
Cops and Robbers.
Corner, The.
Dancers.
Day I Was Older, The.
Days, The.
Digging.
Dump, The.
Eating the Pig.
Edward's Anecdote.
Eleanor's Letters.
Elegy for Wesley Wells.
Exile.
Family, The.
Farm, The.
Fathers and Sons.
Fête.

Flies.
For an Exchange of Rings.
Foundations of American Industry, The.
Friend Revisited, A.
Gold.
Grace, A.
Granite and Grass.
Grave The Well, The.
Great Day in the Cows' House.
Green Shelf, The.
Grown-Ups, The.
Henyard Round, The.
High Pasture, The.
Hole, The.
Hut of the man alone, The.
Idea of Flying, The.
Illustration.
Impossible Marriage, The.
In the Kitchen of the Old House.
"Internal and External Forms."
Je Suis une Table.
Jealous Lovers, The.
Kicking the Leaves.
Kill, The.
"King and Queen."
"Kiss, The."
Letter to an English Poet.
Lone Ranger, The.
Long River, The.
Love Is Like Sounds.
Man in the Dead Machine, The.
Maple Syrup.
"Marat's Death."
Match.
Material.
Maundy Thursday's Candles.
Merle Bascom's .22.
Milkers Broken Up.
Mr. and Mrs. Billings.
Mr. Wakeville on Interstate 90.
Moon Clock.
Moon, The.
Mount Kearsarge.
My Friend Felix.
My Son, My Executioner.
Mycenae.
Names of Horses.
New Animals.
New Hampshire.
1934.
No Color Man.
No Deposit.
Nose.
Notes For Nobody.
O Cheese.
"O Flodden Field."
Old Home Week.
Old Houses.
Old Pilot, The.
Old Roses.
Old Timer's Day.
On a Horse Carved in Wood.
On Reaching the Age of Two Hundred.
Our Walk in Yorkshire.
Ox Cart Man.
Oysters and Hermits.
Passage to Worship.
Persistence of 1937.
Photographs of China.
Pictures of Philippa.
Poem, The: "It discovers by night."
Poem With One Fact.
Praise for Death.
President and Poet.
Presidentiad, The.
Raisin, The.
"Reclining Figure."
Red Branch, The.
Religious Articles.
Repeated Shapes, The.
Revolution, The.
Rocker, The.
Scenic View.
"Scream, The."
Sea, The.
Second Stanza, A.
Self-Portrait as a Bear.

September Ode.
Sestina: "Hang it all, Ezra Pound, there is
    only the one sestina."
Set of Seasons, A.
Sew.
Shudder [, The].
Sister by the Pond, A.
Sister on the Tracks, A.
Six Naps in One Day.
Sleeping.
Sleeping Giant, The.
Small Fig Tree, A.
Snow, The.
Some Oddities.
Southwest of Buffalo.
Speeches.
Stone Walls.
Stones.
Stories.
Stump.
Sums.
Sun, The.
Swan.
Table, The.
This Poem.
Three Movements, The.
To a Waterfowl.
To the Loud Wind.
Tomorrow.
Town of Hill, The.
Toy Bone, The.
Traffic.
Transcontinent.
Tree and the Cloud, The.
Tubes.
Twelve Seasons.
Umbrella, The.
Valley of Morning.
Village in East Anglia, A.
Waiting on the Corners.
Waters.
Wedding Party.
Wells.
Whip-Poor-Will.
White Apples.
Widows, The.
Wolf Knife.
Woolworth's.
Wreckage, The.
Young Watch Us, The.

Hardy, Thomas (1840–1928)
Abbey Mason, The.
Aberdeen.
Absolute Explains, The.
According to the Mighty Working.
Aerolite, The.
After a Journey.
After a Romantic Day.
After Reading Psalms XXXIX, XL, etc.
After Schiller.
After the Burial.
After the Club-Dance.
After the Death of a Friend.
After the Fair.
After the Last Breath.
After the Visit.
After the War.
Afternoon Service at Mellstock.
Afterwards.
Aged Newspaper Soliloquizes, The.
Ageing House, The.
Agnosto Theo [To an Unknown God].
A.H., 1855–1912.
Ah, Are You Digging on My Grave?
Alarm, The.
Alike and Unlike.
Amabel.
Ancient to Ancients, An.
And There Was a Great Calm.
Anniversary, An.
Announcement, The.
Any Little Old Song.
Apostrophe to an Old Psalm Tune.
Appeal to America on Behalf of the Belgian
    Destitute, An.
Aquae Sulis.
Architectural Masks.

Aristodemus the Messenian.
As 'Twere To-night.
At a Bridal.
At a Country Fair.
At a Fashionable Dinner.
At a Hasty Wedding.
At a House in Hampstead.
At a Lunar Eclipse.
At a Pause in a Country Dance.
At a Rehearsal of One of J.M.B.'s Plays.
At a Seaside Town in 1869.
At a Watering-Place.
At an Inn.
At Casterbridge Fair.
At Castle Boterel.
At Day-Close in November.
At Lulworth Cove a Century Back.
At Madame Tussaud's in Victorian Years.
At Mayfair Lodgings.
At Middle-Field Gate in February.
At Moonrise and Onwards.
At Rushy-Pond.
At Shag's Heath.
At Tea.
At the Altar-Rail.
At the Aquatic Sports.
At the Dinner-Table.
At the Draper's.
At the Entering of the New Year.
At the Mill.
At the Piano.
At the Railway Station, Upway.
At the Royal Academy.
At the War Office, London.
At the Wicket-Gate.
At the Word "Farewell."
At Waking.
At Wynard's Gap.
August Midnight, An.
Autumn in King's Hintock Park.
Autumn Rain-Scene, An.
Background and the Figure, The.
Backward Spring, A.
Bad Example, The.
Bags of Meat.
Ballad of Love's Skeleton, The.
Ballad-Singer, The.
Ballet, The.
Barthélémon at Vauxhall.
Beauty, The.
Beauty's Soliloquy during Her Honeymoon,
    A.
Bedridden Peasant, The.
Beeny Cliff.
Before and after Summer.
Before Knowledge.
Before Life and After.
Before Marching and After.
Before My Friend Arrived.
Bereft.
Bereft, She Thinks She Dreams.
Best She Could, The.
Best Times.
Between Us Now.
Beyond the Last Lamp.
Bird-Catcher's Boy, The.
Bird-Scene at a Rural Dwelling, A.
Birds at Winter Nightfall.
Blinded Bird, The.
Blow, The.
Boy's Dream, The.
Boys Then and Now.
Bride-Night Fire, The.
Bridge of Lodi, The.
Broken Appointment, A.
Brother, The.
Budmouth Dears.
Bullfinches, The.
Burghers, The.
Burning the Holly.
By Henstridge Cross at the Year's End.
By Her Aunt's Grave.
By the Barrows.
By the Earth's Corpse.
By the Runic Stone.
Bygone Occasion, A.
Caged Goldfinch, The.

Caged Thrush Freed and Home Again, The.
Calf, The.
Call to National Service, A.
Cardinal Bembo's Epitaph on Raphael.
Caricature, The.
Carrier, The.
Casterbridge Captains, The.
Casual Acquaintance, The.
Catching Ballet of the Wedding Clothes, The.
Cathedral Façade at Midnight, A.
Change, The.
Channel Firing.
Chapel-Organist, The.
Cheval-Glass, The.
Child and the Sage, The.
Childhood among the Ferns.
Children and Sir Nameless, The.
Chimes Play "Life's a Bumper!", The.
Chimes, The.
Choirmaster's Burial, The.
Chorus of the Pities.
Chosen, The.
Christening, The.
Christmas Ghost-Story, A.
Christmas in the Elgin Room.
Christmas: 1924.
Christmastide.
Church and the Wedding, The.
Church-Builder, The.
Church Romance, A.
Circular, A.
Circus-Rider to Ringmaster.
Clasped Skeleton, The.
Clock of the Years, The.
Clock-Winder, The.
Collector Cleans His Picture, The.
Colonel's Soliloquy, The.
Colour, The.
Come Not; Yet Come!
Comet at Yell'ham, The.
Coming of the End, The.
Coming Up Oxford Street: Evening.
Commonplace Day, A.
Compassion.
Concerning Agnes.
Concerning His Old Home.
Confession to a Friend in Trouble, A.
Conformers, The.
Conjecture.
Contretemps, The.
Convergence of the Twain, The.
Conversation at Dawn, A.
Copying Architecture in an Old Minster.
Coquette, and After, The.
Coronation, The.
Could I but Will.
Countenance, A.
Country Wedding, The.
Cross-Currents.
Cry of the Homeless.
Curate's Kindness, The.
Curtains Now Are Drawn, The.
Cynic's Epitaph.
Dame of Athelhall, The.
Dance at the Phoenix, The.
Dark-Eyed Gentleman, The.
Darkling Thrush, The.
Daughter Returns, A.
Dawn after the Dance, The.
Days to Recollect.
Dead and the Living One, The.
Dead Bastard, The.
Dead Man Walking, The.
Dead Quire, The.
Dead "Wessex" the Dog to the Household.
Dear, The.
Death-Day Recalled, A.
Death of Regret, The.
Departure.
Destined Pair, The.
Difference, The.
Discouragement.
Discovery, The.
Dissemblers, The.
Ditty: "Beneath a knap where flown."
Division, The.
Dolls, The.

Domicilium.
Donaghadee.
Doom and She.
Drawing Details in an Old Church.
Dream-Follower, The.
Dream Is—Which? The.
Dream of the City Shopwoman.
Dream or No, A.
Dream Question, A.
Drinking Song.
Drizzling Easter Morning, A.
Drummer Hodge.
Duel, The.
Duettist to her Pianoforte, A.
During Wind and Rain.
Dynasts, The sels.
East-End Curate, An.
Echo-Elf Answers, The.
Elopement, The.
Embarcation.
End of the Episode, The.
End of the Year 1912.
Enemy's Portrait, The.
England to Germany in 1914.
Epeisodia.
Epigraph to "The Woodlanders."
Epilogue: "We have now set forth, in our
   imperfect way."
Epitaph for G. K. Chesterton.
Epitaph for George Moore.
Epitaph: "I never cared for Life: Life cared
   for me."
Epitaph on a Pessimist.
Eunice.
Eve of Waterloo, The.
Evelyn G. of Christminster.
Evening in Galilee, An.
Evening Shadows.
Every Artemisia.
Everything Comes.
Exeunt Omnes.
Expectation and Experience.
Experience, An.
Expostulation, An.
Face at the Casement, The.
Faded Face, The.
Fading Rose, The.
Faintheart in a Railway Train.
Faithful Swallow, The.
Faithful Wilson.
Fallow Deer at the Lonely House, The.
Family Portraits.
Farm-Woman's Winter, The.
Farmer Dunman's Funeral.
Felled Elm and She, The.
Fetching Her.
Fiddler, The.
Fight on Durnover Moor, The.
Figure in the Scene, The.
First or Last.
First Sight of Her and After.
Five Students, The.
Flirt's Tragedy, The.
Flower's Tragedy, The.
For Life I Had Never Cared Greatly.
Forbidden Banns, The.
Forgotten Miniature, A.
Former Beauties.
Four Footprints.
Four in the Morning.
Fragment: "At last I entered a long dark
   gallery."
Freed the Fret of Thinking.
Friends Beyond.
From Her in the Country.
From Victor Hugo.
Frozen Greenhouse, The.
Gallant's Song.
Gap in the White, The.
Garden Seat, The.
Genitrix Laesa.
Genoa and the Mediterranean.
Gentleman's Epitaph on Himself and a Lady,
   Who Were Buried Together, A.
Gentleman's Second-Hand Suit, A.
Geographical Knowledge.
George Meredith (1828-1909).

Ghost of the Past, The.
Glimpse, The.
God-Forgotten.
God's Education.
God's Funeral.
Going, The.
Going and Staying.
Going of the Battery, The.
Graveyard of Dead Creeds, The.
Great Things.
Green Slates.
Growth in May.
Had You Wept.
Hap.
Harbour Bridge, The.
Harvest-Supper, The.
Hatband, The.
Haunter, The.
Haunting Fingers.
He Abjures Love.
He Did Not Know Me.
He Fears His Good Fortune.
He Follows Himself.
He Inadvertently Cures His Love-Pains.
He Never Expected Much.
He Prefers Her Earthly.
He Resolves to Say No More.
He Revisits His First School.
He Wonders about Himself.
Head above the Fog, The.
Heiress and Architect.
Henley Regatta.
Her Apotheosis.
Her Confession.
Her Death and After.
Her Definition.
Her Dilemma.
Her Father.
Her Haunting-Ground.
Her Immortality.
Her Initials.
Her Late Husband.
Her Love-Birds.
Her Reproach.
Her Second Husband Hears Her Story.
Her Secret.
Her Song.
Her Temple.
Heredity.
High-School Lawn, The.
His Country.
His Heart.
His Immortality.
His Visitor.
History of an Hour, The.
Homecoming, The.
Honeymoon Time at an Inn.
Horses Aboard.
House of Hospitalities, The.
House of Silence, The.
House with a History, A.
How Great My Grief.
How She Went to Ireland.
Hundred Years Since, A.
Hurried Meeting, A.
Husband's View, The.
I Am the One.
I Found Her Out There.
I Have Lived with Shades.
I Knew a Lady.
I Look in Her Face.
I Look into My Glass.
I Looked Back.
I Looked Up from My Writing.
I Met a Man.
I Need Not Go.
I Rose and Went to Rou'tor Town.
I Rose Up as My Custom Is.
I Said and Sang Her Excellence.
I Said to Love.
I Say, "I'll Seek Her."
I Sometimes Think.
I Thought, My Heart.
I Travel as a Phantom Now.
I Was Not He.
I Was the Midmost.
I Watched a Blackbird.

I Worked No Wile to Meet You.
Ice on the Highway.
If It's Ever Spring Again.
If You Had Known.
Imaginings.
Impercipient, The.
In a Cathedral City.
In a Eweleaze near Weatherbury.
In a Former Resort after Many Years.
In a London Flat.
In a Museum.
In a Waiting-Room.
In a Whispering Gallery.
In a Wood.
In Childbed.
In Church.
In Death Divided.
In Front of the Landscape.
In Her Precincts.
In St. Paul's a While Ago.
In Sherborne Abbey.
In Tenebris.
In the British Museum.
In the Cemetery.
In the Days of Crinoline.
In the Evening.
In the Garden.
In the Marquee.
In the Mind's Eye.
In the Moonlight.
In the Night She Came.
In the Nuptial Chamber.
In the Old Theatre, Fiesole.
In the Restaurant.
In the Room of the Bride-Elect.
In the Servants' Quarters.
In the Seventies.
In the Small Hours.
In the Street.
In the Study.
In the Vaulted Way.
In Time of "The Breaking of Nations."
In Time of Wars and Tumults.
In Vision I Roamed.
In Weatherbury Stocks.
Inconsistent, The.
Inquiry, An.
Inquiry, The.
Inscription, The.
Inscriptions for a Peal of Eight Bells.
Interloper, The.
Intra Sepulchrum.
It Never Looks Like Summer.
Ivy-Wife, The.
January Night, A.
Jezreel.
Jingle on the Times, A.
Jog-Trot Pair, A.
John and Jane.
Joys of Memory.
Jubilate.
Jubilee of a Magazine, The.
Julie-Jane.
June Leaves and Autumn.
Just the Same.
King's Experiment, The.
King's Soliloquy, A.
Kiss, A.
Known Had I.
Lacking Sense, The.
Lady in the Furs, The.
Lady of Forebodings, The.
Lady Vi.
Lament: "How she would have loved."
Lament of the Looking-Glass, The.
Last Chorus.
Last Chrysanthemum, The.
Last Journey, A.
Last Leaf, The.
Last Look round St. Martin's Fair.
Last Love-Word.
Last Performance, The.
Last Signal, The.
Last Time, The.
Last Week in October.
Last Words to a Dumb Friend.
Later Autumn, The.

Lausanne: In Gibbon's Old Garden: 11–12 p.m.
Leader of Fashion, A.
Leaving, A.
Leipzig.
Let Me Believe.
Let Me Enjoy.
Letter's Triumph, The.
Levelled Churchyard, The.
Liddell and Scott.
Life and Death at Sunrise.
Life Laughs Onward.
Light Snow-Fall after Frost, A.
Lines: "Before we part to alien thoughts and aims."
Lines to a Movement in Mozart's E-Flat Symphony.
Little Old Table, The.
Lizard, The.
Lodging-House Fuchsias, The.
Logs on the Hearth.
Lonely Days.
Long Plighted.
Looking Across.
Looking at a Picture on an Anniversary.
Looking Back.
Lorna the Second.
Lost Love.
Lost Pyx, The.
Louie.
Love-Letters, The.
Love the Monopolist.
Love Watches a Window.
Lover to Mistress.
Lying Awake.
Mad Judy.
Maid of Keinton Mandeville, The.
Maiden's Pledge, A.
Man, A.
Man He Killed, The.
Man Was Drawing Near to Me, A.
Man Who Forgot, The.
Man with a Past, The.
Marble-Streeted Town, The.
Marble Tablet, The.
Market-Girl, The.
Masked Face, The.
Master and the Leaves, The.
Meditation on a Holiday.
Meeting with Despair, A.
Memorial Brass, The: 186–.
Memory and I.
Men Who March Away.
Merrymaking in Question, A.
Middle-Age Enthusiasms.
Midnight on Beechen, 187–.
Midnight on the Great Western.
Milestone by the Rabbit-Burrow, The.
Military Appointment, A.
Milkmaid, The.
Minute before Meeting, The.
Misconception.
Mismet.
Missed Train, The.
Mock Wife, The.
Molly Gone.
Moments of Vision.
Mongrel, The.
Month's Calendar, The.
Monument-Maker, The.
Moon Looks In, The.
Moth-Signal, The.
Mother Mourns, The.
Mound, The.
Murmurs in the Gloom.
Music in a Snowy Street.
Musical Box, The.
Musical Incident, A.
Musing Maiden, The.
Mute Opinion.
My Cicely.
My Love's Gone a-Fighting.
My Spirit Will Not Haunt the Mound.
Nature's Questioning.
Near Lanivet, 1872.
Necessitarian's Epitaph, A.
Nettles, The.

Neutral Tones.
New Boots, The.
New Dawn's Business, The.
New Toy, The.
New Year's Eve.
New Year's Eve in War Time, A.
Newcomer's Wife, The.
News for Her Mother.
Night in November, A.
Night in the Old Home.
Night of Questionings, A.
Night of the Dance, The.
Night of Trafalgar, The.
Night-Time in Mid-Fall.
Nightmare, and the Next Thing, A.
1967.
No Bell-Ringing.
No Buyers [or No Buyers: A Street Scene].
Noble Lady's Tale, The.
Nobody Comes.
Not Known.
Not Only I.
Nothing Matters Much.
O I Won't Lead a Homely Life.
Obliterate Tomb, The.
Occultation, The.
Often When Warring.
Old Excursions.
Old Furniture.
Old Gown, The.
Old Likeness, An.
Old Neighbour and the New, The.
Old Workman, The.
On a Discovered Curl of Hair.
On a Fine Morning.
On a Heath.
On a Midsummer Eve.
On an Invitation to the United States.
On Martock Moor.
On One Who Lived and Died Where He Was Born.
On Stinsford Hill at Midnight.
On Sturminster Foot-Bridge.
On the Belgian Expatriation.
On the Death-Bed.
On the Departure Platform.
On the Doorstep.
On the Esplanade.
On the Portrait of a Woman About to Be Hanged.
On the Tune Called the Old-Hundred-and-Fourth.
On the Way.
Once at Swanage.
One Ralph Blossom Soliloquizes.
One We Knew.
One Who Married above Him.
Opportunity, The.
Orphaned Old Maid, The.
Our Old Friend Dualism.
Outside the Casement.
Outside the Window.
Over the Coffin.
Overlooking the River Stour.
Oxen, The.
Pair He Saw Pass, The.
Panthera.
Paphian Ball, The.
Paradox.
Parting-Scene, A.
Passer-By, The.
Pat of Butter, The.
Paths of Former Time.
Paying calls.
Peace-Offering, The.
Peace Peal, The.
Peasant's Confession, The.
Pedestrian, The.
Pedigree, The.
Penance.
Phantom Horsewoman, The.
Philosophical Fantasy, A.
Photograph, The.
Pine Planters, The.
Pink Frock, The.
Pity of It, The.
Place on the Map, The.

Places.
Placid Man's Epitaph, A.
Plaint to Man, A.
Plena Timoris.
Poet, A.
Poet's Thoughts, A.
Poor Man and a Lady, A.
Popular Personage at Home, A.
Postponement.
Practical Woman, A.
Premonitions.
Private Man on Public Men, A.
Problem, The.
Procession of Dead Days, A.
Prologue: "In these stern times of ours, when
    crimson strife."
Prophetess, The.
Prospect, The.
Protean Maiden, The.
Proud Songsters.
Puzzled Game-Birds, The.
Queen Caroline to Her Guests.
Question of Marriage, A.
Quid Hic Agis?
Rain on a Grave.
Rake-hell Muses.
Rambler, The.
Rash Bride, The.
Re-Enactment, The.
Read by Moonlight.
Recalcitrants, The.
Refusal, A.
Regret Not Me.
Rejected Member's Wife, The.
Reluctant Confession.
Reminder, The.
Reminiscences of a Dancing Man.
Respectable Burgher, The.
Retty's Phases.
Revisitation, The.
Revulsion.
Riddle, The.
Rift, The.
Rival, The.
Robin, The.
Roman Gravemounds, The.
Roman Road, The.
Rome: At the Pyramid of Cestius near the
    Graves of Shelley and Keats.
Rome: Building a New Street in the Ancient
    Quarter.
Rome: On the Palatine.
Rome: The Vatican: Sala delle Muse.
Rose-Ann.
Rover Come Home, The.
Royal Sponsors.
Ruined Maid, The.
Sacred to the Memory.
Sacrilege, The.
Sailor's Mother, The.
St. Launce's Revisited.
San Sebastian.
Sapphic Fragment.
Satin Shoes, The.
Satires of Circumstance in Fifteen Glimpses.
Saying Good-bye.
Schreckhorn, The.
Sea Fight, The.
Seasons of Her Year, The.
Second Attempt, A.
Second Night, The.
Second Visit, The.
Seeing the Moon Rise.
Seen by the Waits.
Self-Glamourer, A.
Self-Unconscious.
Self-Unseeing, The.
Selfsame Song, The.
Sergeant's Song, The.
Seven Times, The.
Seventy-four and Twenty.
Sexton at Longpuddle, The.
Shadow on the Stone, The.
She at His Funeral.
She Charged Me.
She Did Not Turn.
She Hears the Storm.

She, I, and They.
She Opened the Door.
She Revisits Alone the Church of Her
    Marriage.
She Saw Him, She Said.
She, to Him.
She Who Saw Not.
She Would Welcome Old Tribulations.
Sheep-Boy, The.
Sheep Fair, A.
Shelley's Skylark.
Shiver, The.
Shortening Days at the Homestead.
Shut Out That Moon.
Sick Battle-God, The.
Side by Side.
Sigh, The.
Sign-Seeker, A.
Signs and Tokens.
Silences.
Sine Prole.
Singer Asleep, A.
Singing Lovers.
Singing Woman, The.
Single Witness, The.
Sitting on the Bridge.
Six Boards, The.
Sleep-Worker, The.
Slow Nature, The.
Snow in the Suburbs.
So, Time.
So Various.
Something Tapped.
Something that Saved Him, The.
Song from Heine.
Song of Hope.
Song of the Soldiers' Wives and Sweethearts.
Song to an Old Burden.
Song to Aurore.
Son's Portrait, The.
Souls of the Slain, The.
Sound in the Night, A.
Spectres That Grieve.
Spell of the Rose, The.
Spellbound Palace, A.
Spot, A.
Spring Call, The.
Squire Hooper.
Standing by the Mantlepiece.
Starlings on the Roof.
Statue of Liberty, The.
Strange House, The.
Stranger's Song, The.
Subalterns, The.
Summer Schemes.
Sun on the Bookcase, The.
Sun on the Letter, The.
Sunday Morning Tragedy, A.
Sundial on a Wet Day, The.
Sun's Last Look on the Country Girl, The.
Sunshade, The.
Superseded, The.
Supplanter, The.
Surview [or Surview: Cogitavi Vias Meas].
Suspense.
Sweet Hussy, The.
Tarrying Bridegroom, The.
Telegram, The.
Temporary the All, The.
Ten Years Since.
Tenant-for-Life, The.
Tess's Lament.
That Kiss in the Dark.
That Moment.
Then and Now.
There Seemed a Strangeness.
They Are Great Trees.
They Would Not Come.
Thing Unplanned, The.
Third Kissing-Gate, The.
This Summer and Last.
Thought in Two Moods, A.
Thoughts at Midnight.
Thoughts from Sophocles.
Thoughts of Phena.
Three Tall Men, The.
Throwing a Tree.

Thunderstorm in Town, A.
Timing Her.
To a Bridegroom.
To a Lady.
To a Lady Playing and Singing in the
    Morning.
To a Motherless Child.
To a Sea-Cliff.
To a Tree in London.
To a Well-Named Dwelling.
To an Actress.
To an Imposter of Rosalind.
To an Unborn Pauper Child.
To-Be-Forgotten, The.
To Carrey Clavel.
To C.F.H.
To Flowers from Italy in Winter.
To Life.
To Lizbie Browne.
To Louisa in the Lane.
To Meet, or Otherwise.
To My Father's Violin.
To Outer Nature.
To Shakespeare.
To Sincerity.
To the Moon.
Tolerance.
Torn Letter, The.
Tragedian to Tragedienne.
Trampwoman's Tragedy, A.
Transformations.
Tree and the Lady, The.
Tree, The.
Tresses, The.
Turnip-Hoer, The.
Two Houses, The.
Two Lips.
Two Men, The.
Two Rosalinds, The.
Two Serenades.
Two Soldiers, The.
Two Wives, The.
Two-Years' Idyll, A.
Unborn, The.
Under High-Stoy Hill.
Under the Waterfall.
Unkept Good Fridays.
Unkindly May, An.
Unknowing.
Unplanted Primrose, The.
Unrealized.
Upbraiding, An.
Upper Birch-Leaves, The.
Vagg Hollow.
Vagrant's Song.
Valenciennes.
Vampirine Fair, The.
Victorian Rehearsal, A.
Voice of the Thorn, The.
Voice of Things, The.
Voice, The.
Voices from Things Growing in a
    Churchyard.
V.R. 1819–1901.
Wagtail and Baby.
Waiting Both.
Walk, The.
Wanderer, The.
War-Wife of Catknoll, The.
Wasted Illness, A.
Watcher's Regret, A.
Watering-Place Lady Inventoried, A.
We Are Getting to the End.
We Field-Women.
We Sat at the Window.
We Say We Shall Not Meet.
Weary Walker, The.
Weathers [or Weather].
Wedding Morning, The.
Week, A.
Welcome Home.
Well-Beloved, The.
Wessex Heights.
West-of-Wessex Girl, The.
Wet August, A.
Wet Night, A.
Whaler's Wife, The.

What Did It mean?
What's There to Tell?
When Dead.
When I Set Out for Lyonnesse.
When Oats Were Reaped.
When Wearily We Shrink Away.
Where the Picnic Was.
Where They Lived.
Where Three Roads Joined.
While Drawing in a Churchyard.
Whipper-In, The.
Whispered at the Church-Opening.
Whitewashed Wall, The.
Who's in the Next Room?
Why Be at Pains?
Why Did I Sketch.
Why Do I?
Why She Moved House.
Widow Betrothed, The.
Wife and Another, A.
Wife Comes Back, A.
Wife in London, A.
Wife Waits, A.
Wind Blew Words, The.
Wind's Prophecy, The.
Winsome Woman, A.
Winter in Durnover Field.
Winter Night in Woodland.
Wish for Unconsciousness, A.
Wistful Lady, The.
Without Ceremony.
Without, Not within Her.
Wives in the Sere.
Woman Driving, A.
Woman I Met, The.
Woman in the Rye, The.
Woman Who Went East, The.
Woman's Fancy, A.
Woman's Trust, A.
Wood Fire, The.
Workbox, The.
Wound, The.
Xenophanes, the Monist of Colophon.
Year's Awakening, The.
Yell'ham-Wood's Story.
Yellow-Hammer, The.
You on the Tower.
You Were the Sort that Men Forget.
Young Churchwarden, The.
Young Glass-Stainer, The.
Young Man's Epigram on Existence, A.
Young Man's Exhortation, A.
Your Last Drive.
Youth Who Carried a Light, The.
Yuletide in a Younger World.
Zermatt: To the Matterhorn.
Translations, Coauthored Poems, etc.:
Carmina *sels.*
Catullus: XXXI.

Harrison, George *see* Beatles, The

Hartley, Marsden (1877–1943)
A. Lincoln—Odd, or Even.
Afterlude.
Albert Ryder—Moonlightist.
Alice Miriam.
American Ikon—Lincoln.
And, if the Popocatapetl.
And Now—September.
Androscoggin.
Any Page of Thomas Mann's.
Are You There, Rose Trumbull?
As the Buck Lay Dead.
Asses' Out-House, The.
At Half Past Anything.
B. is for Bach—.
Back Road Country.
Beautiful rush, The.
Being new inside—so that outside, the
    outside.
Bend of the Androscoggin, The.
Berry House, The.
Beyond the Broken House.
Bird, in Soliloquizing Voices a Woman's
    Wish, The.
Blair Purves: Bluenose Portrait Effect #2.
Blessed Event.
Boston Common—Long Time Ago.

Boston Portrait Projections.
Brown Gulls.
Bulldog on the Roof—Avenue C.
Buttons for Swallows.
Canticle for October.
Cellaphon–a Favorite Word with Picabia.
Chirico—and There are Blue and White.
Chitter of chipmunk.
Chromatism in Red.
Cicada.
City Vignettes.
Cobwebs and Ratholes.
Come, / tired old thing.
Concert.
Confidence.
Corillyn is Dark.
Corniche—Marseille.
Courage for Lost Poems.
Crucifixion of Noel, The.
Cyriaque d'Etremont: Bluenose Portrait Effect
    #1.
Daily Library Visitor.
Day is dark—the night, The.
Diabolo.
Do nothing to injure the living.
Dusty olive trees.
Eagle of the Inner Eye.
Eagle wants no friends, The.
8 Words.
Eilshemius.
Elias Gove—or, The Second Coming.
Encompassed.
Fabian Bell—His Last Visit to Cuernavaca.
Family Album in Red Plush.
Fantasy and phantom—.
Fence Between.
Festival of the Corn, The.
Find the Face.
Fishermen's Last Supper.
Fishmonger.
Five Women.
Flatterers, The.
Flight, The.
For Gaston Lachaise—a Sort of Written
    Frieze.
For the Shut Eye.
Fork of Annie, The.
Fourth Printing.
From a Paris Window—High.
Furnished Rooms.
Geometric Death.
Giant and Saint.
Go Lightly.
Going Man, A.
Gulls at Gloucester.
He Too Wore a Butterfly.
Heifetz—On the Air, Bell Telephone
    Program.
Her Daughter.
Hiccoughs of old ladies.
Holding in reserve.
Hollander's Animal Faith.
Horowitz.
How like the sea / to be.
Ichneumon.
If It Were the Eye.
If We Could.
Immortal Face.
In Robin Hood Cove.
In the Frail Wood.
In Those Exquisite Areas.
Indian Point.
Inner Distance.
Invitation.
Ironies out of St. George's.
Islands in Penobscot Bay.
It is as if at times.
It was to learn that grief is a major.
John Donne in His Shroud.
K. von F.—1914—Arras-Bouquoi.
King Amenemhat III.
Kuzan—First Avenue.
Ladies and the Pigeons, The.
Lapping of waters / thick, upon razorblade.
Laughter of Steel 1.
Laughter of Steel 2.
Lay warm gentle hand upon me.

Les Baux.
"Lewiston Is a Pleasant Place."
Life ahead, life behind—.
Light-Heavy at Prayer.
Light of Night.
Listening to the Music.
Little Bird Alone.
Little Green Snake.
Little Known Bird of the Inner Eye.
Local Boys and Girls Small Town Stuff.
Logic.
Lonely Return to the Lonely, the divine to
    the Divine—Proclus, The.
Look down ever-intimate one.
Lost, Alone, The.
Man the Father, The.
Marianne Moore.
Metaphysic.
Midnight—the City.
Miracle Cary, and His Twelve Loaves—
    Twelve Fishes.
Modigliani's Death Mask.
Mole.
Moralizing.
M.T.—a Relative in Certain Aspects of
    Metaphysical Divination.
Musicologist—Preference, Prokofieff.
Mystic, kneeling / in the forests of Malines,
    The.
Mystical Forest, The.
Nameless Speaks, The.
Nature.
New Morning—and the Years Are Ours.
New Rains.
O Bitter Madrigal.
O lift me—majestic Sire.
O where have I wandered—out.
Oblique Frontier.
October Afternoon.
Old Lady in the Park.
Outcast City on the Kennebec, The.
Passionate Rebuke.
Perhaps Macabre.
Perusing Mallarmé in Maine.
Pilgrimage, and the Game Warden, The.
Pistols for Pleasure—Guitars for Defense.
Plover.
Pot-Luck among the Casuals.
Present to the Sun, A.
Queen Nefertiti–Small Fragment of Nose and
    Mouth Only.
Rapture.
Recognition of Region.
Reflex.
Rembrandt—Rouault—Piero.
Return of the Native.
Richard Rolle.
Robin Hood Cove—Georgetown, Maine.
Royal Love Child, The.
Salutations to a Mouse.
Same Fragment—Second Look.
Saturday.
Sea Engraving—Style of 1880.
Serving the Curve.
Sestets.
Several Pieces for Jose Garcia Villa.
She Sauntered Most Elegantly Down.
Signatures of Multiple Things.
Sister, The.
Soldier on His Knees in the Snow.
Soliloquy in Dogtown, Cape Ann.
Solitude is kind.
Some Moments with Locatelli.
Somewhere, between the coming.
Spinsters.
Spirits Are Organized Men.
Stones to Wind.
Summer Evening.
Summer is done—.
Surprise Package.
Swallows.
Sweet Old Man.
Tear Is an Intellectual Thing, A.
There Are No Names.
There Are No Rocks and Trees.
There Is an Island.
There Is Spit upon the Daisy Stem.

These exquisite mementos.
These miracles of Paris.
These shells are paradox.
These Six or Several Houses.
This Crusty Fragment.
This Lady Rides a Languid Dromedary toward Her Dear-God.
This Little City.
This Living in Small Place.
This Millimeter.
This Piece of Eucharist.
This Portrait of a Seadove—Dead.
Three Friends: Outline for a Picture.
Three Loving Men.
To C——.
To H.C.
To Partridge Merrithew.
To the Nameless One.
Tomorrow being Monday—.
Topaz of the Sixties, The.
Trapezist's Despair.
Tree that bears—, A.
Two Drowned at the Gateway.
Two grey herons flying.
Two Lovely Ones.
Two Ways of Love.
Un Recuerdo—Hermano—Hart Crane R.I.P.
V—Is for Victory as You Can Plainly See.
Vast rose of July.
Very Languor, The.
Vesper Hymn for Tuesday and June, after the Visit of Henry Wells.
Violet Grape—and Shadowy Myrtle Leaf.
Watching.
Water from the Rock.
We have broken bread.
West cheek to rose.
West Pitch at the Falls.
What Have We All—a Soliloquy of Essences.
What Is Sacrament.
Whoever dies—dies for the love.
Whole Creation Groans to Be Delivered, The.
Why talk of cities.
Window Cleaner to Nude Manikin.
Window Washer—Avenue C.
Wingaersheek Beach.
Woman Distorts, with Hunger, The.
Word and Its Meaning, A.
Word Arrangements for Pictures by Morris Graves.
World-Passport Visa.
Yes, I Know—Yes.
Yesterday, in the night.
Yielding the Initiative.
You Who Have Done.

Hartnett, Michael (b. 1941)
Anatomy of a Cliché.
Bereft of Its Great Poets.
Bread.
Death of an Irishwoman.
Falling Out, A.
Farewell to English, A *sels.*
For My Grandmother, Bridget Halpin.
Green Room.
He'll to the Moors.
I have been stone, dust of space, sea and sphere.
I Have Exhausted the Delighted Range.
I Heard Him Whistle.
I saw magic on a green country road.
I say farewell to English verse.
Inchicore Haiku.
Lament for Tadhg Cronin's Children.
Last Vision of Eoghan Rua Ó Súilleabháin, The.
Man Who Wrote Yeats, the Man Who Wrote Mozart, The.
Mo Ghrá Thú.
Mountains, Fall on Us.
Naked Surgeon, The.
No Avail.
Notes on My Contemporaries.
Oatwoman, The.
Old Catechism, The.
Person as Dreamer: We Talk about the Future, The.

Pity the Man Who English Lacks.
Poem for Lara, 10.
Poet as Black Sheep, The.
Poet as Mastercraftsman, The.
Poet Down, The.
Poet Dreams and Resolves, The.
Prayer at Death.
Prisoners.
Retreat of Ita Cagney, The.
Sad Singing in Darkness.
Sibelius in Silence.
Sickroom.
Small Farm, A.
That Actor Kiss.
There Will Be a Talking.
Thirteen Sonnets *sels.*
This road is not new.
Visit to Castletown House, A.
Visit to Croom, 1745, A.
Whom I ask for no gift.
Wounded Otter, The.

Hayden, Robert Earl (1913–80)
Across lunar wastes of wind and snow.
American Journal.
Approximations.
As My Blood Was Drawn.
Astronauts.
Aunt Jemima of the Ocean Waves.
Bahá'u'lláh in the Garden of Ridwan.
Ballad of Nat Turner, The.
Ballad of Remembrance, A.
Ballad of Sue Ellen Westerfield, The.
Beginnings.
Belsen, Day of Liberation.
Bone-Flower Elegy.
Broken Dark, The.
Burly Fading One, The.
Butterfly Piece.
Crispus Attucks.
"Dance the Orange."
Dawnbreaker.
Day of the Dead (Tehuantepec).
Diver, The.
Dogwood Trees, The.
Double Feature.
Dream, The.
El-Hajj Malik El-Shabazz.
Electrical Storm.
Elegies for Paradise Valley.
For a Young Artist.
Frederick Douglass.
Free Fantasia: Tiger Flowers.
From the Corpse Woodpiles, from the Ashes.
Full Moon.
Gulls.
Homage to Paul Robeson.
Homage to the Empress of the Blues.
Ice Storm.
Idol.
Incense of the Lucky Virgin.
Inference of Mexico, An.
Islands, The.
It is beginning oh.
John Brown.
Kid.
Killing the Calves.
Kodachromes of the Island.
La Corrida.
Lear Is Gay.
Letter.
Letter from Phillis Wheatley, A.
Lions, The.
Locus.
Market.
Middle Passage.
Mirages, The.
Monet's "Waterlilies."
Moose Wallow, The.
Mountains.
Mourning Poem for the Queen of Sunday.
"Mystery Boy" Looks for Kin in Nashville.
Names.
Night-Blooming Cereus, The.
Night, Death, Mississippi.
No sun these months. Ice-dark and cold.
O Daedalus, Fly Away Home.
October.

On Lookout Mountain.
Paul Laurence Dunbar.
Peacock Room, The.
Performers, The.
Perseus.
Plague of Starlings, A.
Point, The.
Prisoners, The.
Rabbi, The.
Rag Man, The.
Return, The.
Richard Hunt's "Arachne."
Road in Kentucky, A.
Runagate Runagate.
Smelt Fishing.
Snow.
Snow Lamp, The *sels.*
Sojourner Truth.
Soledad.
Sphinx.
Stars.
Sub Specie Aeternitatis.
Summertime and the Living.
Tattooed Man, The.
Theme and Variation.
Theory of Evil.
Those Winter Sundays.
Tour 5.
Traveling through Fog.
Two Egyptian Portrait Masks.
Unidentified Flying Object.
Veracruz.
Web, The.
Wheel, The.
Whipping, The.
Witch Doctor.
Words in the Mourning Time.
Year of the Child, The.
Zeus over Redeye.
Zinnias.

Heaney, Seamus (b. 1939)
Act of Union.
After a Killing.
Afterwards, An.
Alphabets.
Anahorish.
Artist, An.
At the Water's Edge.
Badgers, The.
Blackberry-Picking.
Bog Oak.
Bog Queen.
Bogland.
Bone Dreams.
Broagh.
Bye-Child.
Casualty.
Chekhov on Sakhalin.
Clearances.
Cleric, The.
Cloistered.
Death of a Naturalist.
Digging.
Disappearing Island, The.
Dream of Jealousy, A.
Drifting Off.
Drink of Water, A.
England's Difficulty.
Field Work.
First Flight, The.
First Kingdom, The.
Follower.
From the Canton of Expectation.
From the Frontier of Writing.
From the Republic of Conscience.
Funeral Rites.
Gifts of Rain.
Glanmore Sonnets.
Granite Chip.
Graubelle Man, The.
Guttural Muse, The.
Hailstones.
Harvest Bow, The.
Haw Lantern, The.
Hazel Stick for Catherine Ann, A.
Hercules and Antaeus.
Holly.

In Illo Tempore.
In Memoriam Francis Ledwidge.
In the Beech.
Incertus.
King of the Ditchbacks, The.
Kite for Michael and Christopher, A.
Limbo.
Making Strange.
Master, The.
Mid-Term Break.
Milk Factory, The.
Mossbawn.
Mossbawn Sunlight.
Mud Vision, The.
Nesting-Ground.
New Song, A.
Night Drive.
North.
Old Smoothing Iron.
On the Road.
Oracle.
Other Side, The.
Otter, The.
Oysters.
Peninsula, The.
Personal Helicon.
Poem: "Love, I shall perfect for you the child."
Punishment.
Railway Children, The.
Relic of Memory.
Requiem for the Croppies.
Sandstone Keepsake.
Scribes, The.
Seed Cutters, The.
Shelf Life sels.
Sibyl.
Singer's House, The.
Singing School.
Skunk, The.
Sloe Gin.
Song: "Rowan like a lip-sticked girl, A."
Spoonbait, The.
Station Island.
Stations of the West, The.
Stone from Delphi.
Stone Verdict, The.
Strand at Lough Beg, The.
Strange Fruit.
Summer Home.
Sweeney Astray.
Sweeney in Connacht.
Sweeney Praises the Trees.
Sweeney Redivivus sels.
Sweeney's Lament on Alisa Craig.
Sweeney's Last Poem.
Terminus.
Thatcher.
Tollund Man, The.
Toome Road, The.
Trial Runs.
Triptych.
Underground, The.
Viking Dublin: Trial Pieces.
Visitant.
Wedding Day.
Westering.
Whatever You Say Say Nothing.
Wife's Tale, The.
Wishing Tree, The.
Wolfe Tone.

Hemingway, Ernest (1899–1961)
Across the Board.
Advice to a Son.
After a while there were no bull fights. What the hell.
Age Demanded, The.
All armies are the same.
Along with Youth.
And everything the author knows.
Arsiero, Asiago, / Half a hundred more.
At night I lay with you.
Battle of Copenhagen, The.
Big Dance on the Hill, The.
Bird of Night.
Black-Ass Poem After Talking to Pamela Churchill.

Blood is thicker than water.
Captives.
Champs d'Honneur.
Chapter Heading.
Country Poem with Little Country.
D'Annunzio.
Dedicated to F. W.
Defense of Luxembourg.
Earnest Liberal's Lament, The.
Estocada stuck well stuck. They run round in circles.
First Poem to Mary in London.
Flat Roofs.
FOR THE HARLOT HAS A HARDLOT.
God is away for the summer.
Grass smooth on the prairies.
How Ballad Writing Affects Our Seniors.
I Like Americans.
I Like Canadians.
I think that I have never trod.
If my Valentine you won't be.
I'm off'n wild wimmen.
In a magazine.
In the rain in the rain in the rain in the rain in Spain.
Inexpressible, The.
Killed Piave—July 8—1918.
Kipling.
Lady Poets With Foot Notes, The.
Lines to a Girl 5 Days After Her 21st Birthday.
Lines to a Young Lady on Her Having Very Nearly Won a Vögel.
Lines to Be Read at the Casting of Scott FitzGerald's Balls into the Sea from Eden Roc (Antibes, Alpes Maritimes).
Little drops of grain alcohol.
Little Mr. Wilson / Wrote a little book.
Mitrailliatrice.
Modern Version of Polonius' Advice, A.
Montparnasse.
Neothomist Poem.
Night comes with soft and drowsy plumes.
Oily Weather.
Oklahoma.
Opening Game, The.
Poem Is By Maera, The.
Poem, 1928.
Poem: "Only man I ever loved, The."
Poem to Mary (Second Poem).
Poem to Miss Mary.
Poetry.
Portrait of a Lady.
Punt, The.
Rail ends do not meet, The.
Riparto d'Assalto.
Road to Avallon, The.
Robert Graves.
Roosevelt.
Safety Man, The.
Schwarzwald.
Sequal.
Ship Translated Being La Paquebot, The.
Shock Troops.
Some day when you are picked up.
Soul of Spain with McAlmon and Bird the Publishers, The sels.
Sport of Kings, The.
Stevenson.
Tackle, The.
There is no night life in Spain. They stay up late but.
There was Ike and Tony and Jaque and me.
They All Made Peace—What Is Peace?
Three traveling clocks.
To a Tragic Poetess.
To Chink Whose Trade Is Soldiering.
To Crazy Christian.
To Good Guys Dead.
To Will Davies.
Translations from the Esquimaux: There Are Seasons.
Travel Poem.
Ultimately.
Valentine.
We got on a train and went somewhere else.
Worker, The.

You come to Spain but do not remain. Anna Veronica.

Herbert, George (1593–1633)
Aaron.
Affliction (1).
Affliction (2).
Affliction (3).
Affliction (4).
Affliction (5).
Agony [or Agonie], The.
Altar, The.
Ana(Mary-Army)gram.
Answer, The.
Antiphon: "Let all the world in ev'ry corner sing / My God and King."
Antiphon (2): "Praised be the God of love."
Artillery [or Artillerie].
Assurance.
Bag, The.
Banquet, The.
Bitter-Sweet.
British Church, The.
Bunch of Grapes, The.
Business.
Call, The.
Charms and Knots.
Christmas.
Church-Floor[e], The.
Church-Lock and Key.
Church Militant, The.
Church Monuments.
Church-Music[k].
Church-Porch, The.
Church-Rents and Schisms.
Clasping of Hands.
Collar, The.
Colossians 3:3.
Complaining.
Confession.
Conscience.
Constancy.
Content.
Cross[e], The.
Dawning, The.
Death.
Decay.
Dedication, The: "Lord, my first fruits present themselves to thee."
Denial[l].
Dialogue, A.
Dialogue-Anthem, A.
Discharge, The.
Discipline.
Divinity.
Doomsday.
Dotage.
Dulness[e].
Easter.
Easter Wings.
Elixir [or Elixer], The.
Employment (1).
Employment (2).
see also To the Lady Elizabeth Queen of Bohemia.
Ephesians 4:30. Grieve not the Holy Spirit, etc.
Evensong.
Evensong [or Even-Song].
Faith.
Family [or Familie], The.
Flower, The.
Foil, The.
Forerunners, The.
Frailty.
Giddiness.
Glance, The.
Glimpse, The.
Good Friday.
Grace.
Gratefulness.
Grief.
Heaven.
Holdfast, The.
Holy Baptism (1).
Holy Baptism (2).
H[oly] Communion, The.
Holy Communion, The.

Holy Scriptures (1), The.
Holy Scriptures (2), The.
Home.
Hope.
Humility.
Invitation, The.
Jesu.
Jews, The.
Jordan (1).
Jordan (2).
Joseph's Coat.
Judgement.
Justice (1).
Justice (2).
Knell, The.
Lent.
L'Envoy.
Life.
Longing.
Love.
Love-Joy.
Love (1).
Love (2).
Love ("Thou art too hard for me in Love").
Love Unknown.
Man.
Man's Medley.
Mary [or Marie] Magdalene.
Matins.
Method, The.
Misery [or Miserie].
Mortification.
Nature.
Obedience.
Odour, The. (2 Corinthians 2).
Offering, An.
Paradise.
Parody [or Parodie], A.
Peace.
Pearl. Matthew 13:45, The.
Perirrhanterium.
Perseverance.
Pilgrimage, The.
Posy [or Posie], The.
Praise (1).
Praise (2).
Praise (3).
Prayer (1): "Prayer the Church's banquet, Angels' age."
Prayer (2).
Priesthood, The.
Providence.
Pulley, The.
Quidditie [or Quiddity], The.
Quip, The.
Redemption.
Repentance.
Reprisal[l], The.
Rose, The.
Sacrifice, The.
Search, The.
Self-Condemnation.
Sepulchre.
Sighs and Groans [or Grones].
Sin: "O that I could a sin once see!"
Sin (1).
Sinner, The.
Sin's Round.
Sion.
Size, The.
Son[ne], The.
Sonnet: "My God, where is that ancient heat towards Thee."
Sonnet: "Sure Lord, there is enough in thee to dry."
Star[re], The.
Storm, The.
Submission.
Sunday.
Superliminare.
Temper (1), The.
Temper (2), The.
Thanksgiving, The.
Time.
To All Angels and Saints.
To My Successor.
To the Lady Elizabeth Queen of Bohemia.

To the Right Hon. the Lord Chancellor (Bacon).
Trinity Sunday.
Twenty-third Psalm, The.
Ungratefulness.
Unkindness.
Vanity (2).
Vanity [or Vanitie] (1).
Virtue [or Vertue].
Water-Course, The.
Whitsunday.
Windows, The.
World, The.
Wreath, A.

Herrick, Robert (1591–1674)
Abels Bloud.
Abstinence.
Accusation.
Adversity ("Adversity hurts none, but onely such").
Adversity ("Love is maintain'd by wealth; when all is spent").
Advice the Best Actor.
Advice to a Maid.
Affliction.
After Autumne, Winter.
Again.
Againe.
Against Love.
Age Unfit for Love.
All Things Decay and Die.
All Things Run Well for the Righteous.
Almes.
Amber Bead, The.
Ambition: ("In man, ambition is the common'st thing").
Ambition ("In wayes to greatnesse, think on this").
Anacreontike.
Anacrontik Verse.
Angells.
Anger.
Another ("Art thou not destin'd? then, with hast, go on").
Another ("As Sun-beames pierce the glasse, and streaming in").
Another ("Bloud of Abel was a thing, The").
Another Charme for Stables.
Another ("God is *Jehovah* cal'd; which name of His").
Another Grace for a Child.
Another ("If ye fear to be affrighted").
Another ("In the morning when ye rise").
Another ("Love he that will; it best likes me").
Another New-Yeeres Gift, or Song for the Circumcision.
Another of God.
Another on Her.
Another on Love ("Love's of it self, too sweet").
Another on the Same.
Another ("Shame of mans face is no more, The").
Another ("Sin is an act so free, that if we shall").
Another ("Sin is the cause of death").
Another ("That there's a God").
Another ("Thou bidst me come; I cannot come; for why").
Another to Bring in the Witch.
Another, to God ("Lord, do not beat me").
Another, to God ("Though thou beest").
Another, to His Saviour.
Another to Neptune.
Another to the Maids.
Another Upon Her.
Another upon Her Weeping.
Another ("Wassaile the Trees, that they may beare").
Another ["Thou had'st the wreath before, now take the Tree"].
Another [To His Booke].
Another("Let the superstitious wife").
Another("Where love begins, there dead thy first desire").
Anthea's Retractation.

Any Way for Wealth.
Apron of Flowers, The.
Argument of His Book, The.
Art above Nature, to Julia.
Ass[e], The.
Bacchanalian Verse, A.
Bachanalian Verse, A.
Bad May Be Better.
Bad Princes Pill Their People.
Bad Season Makes the Poet Sad, The.
Bad Wages for Good Service.
Bag of the Bee, The.
Baptisme.
Barley-Break; or, Last in Hell.
Bashfulnesse.
Bastards.
Beauty.
Bed-Man, or Grave-Maker, The.
Beggar to Mab, the Fairy [or Fairie] Queen, The.
Beggars.
Begger, The.
Beginning, Difficult.
Beginnings and Endings.
Being Once Blind, His Request to Biancha.
Bell-Man, The.
Bellman, The.
Best To Be Merry.
Beucolick, or Discourse of Neatherds, A.
Biting of Beggars.
Blame.
Blame the Reward of Princes.
Bleeding Hand: or, The Sprig of Eglantine Given to a Maid, The.
Body, The.
Bondman, The.
Bracelet of Pearle: To Silvia, The.
Bracelet; to Julia, The.
Bribes and Gifts Get All.
Bride-Cake, The.
Broken Christall, The.
Bubble; a Song, The.
Bucolick betwixt Two: Lacon and Thyrsis, A.
Buriall.
By Use Comes Easinesse.
Calling, and Correcting.
Candor of Julias Teeth, The.
Canticle to Apollo, A.
Captived Bee; or, The Little Filcher, The.
Care a Good Keeper.
Carkanet, The.
Casualties.
Caution, A.
Caution in Councell.
Ceremonies for Candlemasse Day, The.
Ceremonies for Candlemas[se] Eve.
Ceremonies for Christmas[se].
Ceremony upon Candlemas Eve.
Change Common to All.
Change Gives Content.
Changes to Corinna, The.
Charme, or an Allay for Love, A.
Charmes.
Charon and Phylomel, a Dialogue Sung.
Charroll Presented to Dr. Williams Bp. of Lincolne as a Newyears Guift, A.
Cheat of Cupid; or, The Ungentle Guest, The.
Cheerfulnesse in Charitie: or, The Sweet Sacrifice.
Cherrie-Ripe.
Cherry-Pit.
Chewing [of] the Cud, The.
Choose for the Best.
Chop-Cherry.
Christ.
Christian Militant.
Christmas Caroll Sung to the King in the Presence at White-Hall, A.
Christmasse-Eve, Another Ceremonie.
Christs Action.
Christs Birth.
Christs Incarnation.
Christs Part.
Christs Sadnesse.
Christs Suffering.
Christs Twofold Coming.

Christs Words on the Crosse, My God, My God.
Clemency.
Clemency in Kings.
Cloathes, Are Conspirators.
Cloaths for Continuance.
Clothes Do But Cheat and Cozen [or Cousen] Us.
Cloud, The.
Clouds.
Coblers Catch, The.
Cock-Crow.
Coheires.
Comfort In Calamity.
Comfort to a Lady Upon the Death of Her Husband.
Comfort to a Youth That Had Lost His Love.
Comforts in Contentions.
Comforts in Crosses.
Coming of Good Luck, The.
Coming to Christ.
Confession.
Conformitie.
Conformity Is Comely.
Confusion of Face.
Conjuration, to Electra, A.
Connubii Flores, or the Well-Wishes at Weddings.
Consultation.
Content, Not Cates.
Contention.
Corinna's Going a-Maying.
Correction.
Counsell.
Country Life: To His Brother, M. Tho: Herrick.
Country Life, to the Honored Mr. Endymion Porter[, Groome of the Bed-Chamber to His Maj.], The.
Courage Cool'd.
Covetous Still Captives, The.
Credit of the Conquerer, The.
Crosse and Pile.
Crosses.
Crowd and Company, The.
Cruell Maid, The.
Cruelties.
Cruelty.
Cruelty Base in Commanders.
Crutches.
Cunctation in Correction.
Curse. A Song, The.
Custard, The.
Dangers Wait on Kings.
Death Ends All Woe.
Defence for Women, A.
Definition of Beauty, The.
Delay.
Delaying Bride, The.
Delight in Disorder.
Deluge, The.
Deniall in Women No Disheartning to Men.
Departure of the Good Daemon, The.
Descripcion; of a Woman, The.
Devotion Makes the Deity.
Dialogue Betwixt Himselfe and Mistresse Eliza: Wheeler, Under the Name of Amarillis, A.
Diet.
Difference Betwixt King and Subjects, The.
Dirge of Jephthah's Daughter, The.
Dirge upon the Death of the Right Valiant Lord, Bernard Stuart, A.
Discontents in Devon.
Discord Not Disadvantageous.
Disswasions from Idlenesse.
Distance Betters Dignities.
Distrust ("To safeguard man from wrongs, there nothing must").
Distrust ("What ever men for Loyalty pretend").
Divination by a Daffadill [or Daffodil].
Doomes-Day.
Draw, and Drinke.
Draw Gloves.
Dream, The.
Dreame, The.

Dream[e]s.
Duty to Tyrants.
Eare-rings.
Ease.
Eclipse, The.
Eclogue, or Pastorall between Endimion Porter and Lycidas Herrick, An.
Elegy: "Since louely sweete, much like unto a Dewe."
Empires.
End Decreed, An.
End of His Work, The.
End, The.
Entertainment, or Porch-Verse, at the Marriage of Mr. Henry Northleigh [or Hen. Northly] and the Most Witty Mrs. Lettice Yard, The.
Epitaph on a Man who Had a Scold to His Wife.
Epitaph on the Tomb of Sir Edward Giles and His Wife in the South Aisle of Dean Prior Church.
Epitaph upon a Child, An.
Epitaph upon a Sober Matron, An.
Epitaph upon a Virgin, An.
Epithalamy to Sir Thomas Southwell and His Lady, An.
Eternity [or Eternitie].
Eucharist, The.
Evensong.
Event of Things Not in Our Power.
Evill.
Examples, or Like Prince, Like People.
Excesse.
Expenses Exhaust.
Eye, The.
Eyes before the Eares, The.
Eyes, The.
Factions.
Fair[e] Days; or, Dawn[e]s Deceitful[l].
Faire after Foule.
Faire Shewes Deceive.
Fairies, The.
Fairy Temple; or, Oberon's Chapel, The.
Faith.
Faith Four-square.
False Mourning.
Fame.
Fame Makes Us Forward.
Farewell Frost; or, Welcome the Spring.
Farewell, The: "Sweetest Loue since wee must part."
Fast, or Lent, The.
Feare.
Fear[e] Gets Force.
Felicitie Knowes No Fence.
Felicity, Quick of Flight.
Few Fortunate.
First Marrs or Makes, The.
First Work, and Then Wages.
Flatterie.
Foolishnesse.
Fortune.
Fortune Favours.
Four[e] Things Make Us Happy Here.
Frankincense, The.
Free Welcome.
Fresh Cheese and Cream.
Frolic[k], A.
Frozen Heart, The.
Frozen Zone; or, Julia Disdainful, The.
Funeral[l] Rites of the Rose, The.
Gain and Gettings.
Gentlenesse.
Glorie.
Glory.
God, and Lord.
God, and the King.
God ("God (as the learned Damascen write)").
God ("God, in the *holy Tongue*, they call").
God ("God is more here, then in another place").
God Has a Twofold Part.
God Heares Us.
God ("In God there's nothing, but 'tis known to be").

God is One.
God Not To Be Comprehended.
God Sparing in Scourging.
God to Be First Served.
Gods Anger.
Gods Anger without Affection.
Gods Blessing.
Gods Bounty ("God, as He's potent, so He's likewise known").
Gods Bounty ("Gods Bounty, that ebbs lesse and lesse").
Gods Commands.
Gods Descent.
Gods Dwelling.
Gods Gifts Not Soon[e] Granted.
Gods Grace.
Gods Hands.
Gods Keyes.
Gods Mercy.
Gods Mirth, Mans Mourning.
Gods Pardon.
Gods Power.
Gods Presence ("God is all-present to what e'er we do").
Gods Presence ("God's evident, and may be said to be").
Gods Presence ("God's present ev'ry where; but most of all").
Gods Price, and Mans Price.
Gods Providence.
Gods Prt.
Gods Time Must End Our Trouble.
Gold and Frankincense.
Gold, before Goodnesse.
Good, and Bad.
Good Christians.
Good Death, A.
Good Friday: Rex Tragicus; or, Christ Going to His Cross[e].
Good Husband, A.
Good Luck Not Lasting.
Good Manners at Meat.
Good Men Afflicted Most.
Good-Night, or Blessing, The.
Good Precepts, or Counsell.
Goodnesse of His God, The.
Graces for Children.
Great Boast, Small Rost.
Great Grief, Great Glory.
Great Maladies, Long Medicines.
Great Spirits Supervive.
Griefe ("Consider sorroowes how they are aright").
Griefe ("Sorrowes divided amongst many, lesse").
Griefes.
Hag, The ("Hag is astride, The").
Hag[g], The ("Staff[e] is now greased [or greas'd], The").
Hand and Tongue, The.
Happinesse.
Happinesse to Hospitalitie, or a Hearty Wish to Good House-Keeping.
Hardning of Hearts.
Haste Hurtfull.
Head-Ake, The.
Health.
Heart, The.
Heaven.
Hell Fire ("Fire of Hell this strange condition hath, The").
Hell Fire ("One onely fire has Hell; but yet it shall").
Hell ("Hell is no other, but a soundlesse pit").
Hell ("Hell is the place where whipping-cheer abounds").
Her Bed.
Her Legs.
His Age, Dedicated to His Peculiar Friend, Master John Wickes, under the Name of Posthumus.
His Almes.
His Answer to a Friend.
His Answer to a Question.
His Anthem, to Christ on the Crosse.
His Cavalier.

His Change.
His Charge to Julia at His Death.
His Comfort.
His Coming to the Sepulcher.
His Confession.
His Content in the Country.
His Covenant or Protestation to Julia.
His Creed.
His Desire.
His Dream[e].
His Ejaculation to God.
His Embalming to Julia.
His Farewell [or Fare-well] to Sack.
His Grange.
His Grange, or Private Wealth.
His Hope or Sheet-Anchor.
His Lachrimae or Mirth, Turn'd to Mourning.
His Last Request to Julia.
His Letanie, To the Holy Spirit.
His Losse.
His Meditation upon Death.
His Misery in a Mistresse.
His Mistris to Him at His Farwell.
His Offering, with the Rest, at the Sepulcher.
His Own Epitaph.
His Parting from Mistress Dorothy Keneday.
His Petition.
His Poetry His Pillar.
His Power.
His Prayer for Absolution.
His Prayer to Ben[.] Jo[h]nson.
His Protestation to Perilla.
His Recantation.
His Request to Julia.
His Return to London.
His Sailing from Julia.
His Saviour[']s Words, Going to the Cross[e].
His Tears to Thamesis [or Thamasis].
His Weaknesse in Woes.
His Winding-Sheet.
His Wish.
His Wish ("Fat be my Hinde").
His Wish to God.
His Wish to Privacie.
His Words to Christ, Going to the Cross.
Hock-Cart, or Harvest Home, The.
Honours Are Hindrances.
Hony-Combe, The.
Hope Heartens.
Hope Well and Have Well: or, Faire after Foule Weather.
How He Would Drinke His Wine.
How His Soule Came Ensnared.
How Lillies Came White.
How Marigolds Came Yellow.
How Pansies or Hearts-Ease Came First.
How Primroses Came Green.
How Roses Came Red.
How Springs Came First.
How the Wall-Flower Came First, and Why So Called.
How Violets Came Blue.
Humility.
Hunger.
Hymn[e] to Bacchus, A.
Hymne to Bacchus, A.
Hymne to Cupid, An.
Hymne to Juno, An.
Hymne to Love, An.
Hymne to Sir Clipseby Crew, A.
Hymne to the Graces, A.
Hymne, to the Lares, A.
Hymne to the Muses, A ("O! You the Virgins nine!").
Hymne to the Muses, An.
Hymne to Venus, and Cupid, A.
I Call and I Call.
Ill Government.
Impossibilities to His Friend.
In Praise of Women.
In the Dark None Dainty.
Invitation, The.
Jack and Jill.
JEHOVAH.
Jimmall Ring, or True-Love-Knot, The.
Judgement Day, The.
Judgment-Day, The.

Julia's Churching, or Purification.
Julia's Petticoat.
Just Man, A.
King and No King, A.
Kings.
Kings and Tyrants.
Kiss[e], A.
Kisse, The.
Kisses.
Kisses Loathesome.
Kissing and Bussing.
Kissing Usurie.
Knowledge.
Labour.
Lamp, The.
Large Bounds Doe but Bury Us.
Larr's Portion, and the Poets Part.
Lasciviousnesse.
Last Stroke Strike Sure, The.
Laugh and Lie Downe.
Lawes ("When Lawes full power have to sway, we see").
Lawes ("Who violates the Customes, hurts the Health").
Lawne, The.
Laxare Fibulam.
Leanders Obsequies.
Lenitie.
Leprosie in Cloathes.
Leprosie in Houses.
Leven.
Liberty.
Life Is the Body's [or Bodies] Light.
Light Lightly Pleased.
Like Loves His Like.
Like Pattern, Like People.
Lilly in a Christal, The.
Lines Have Their Linings, and Bookes Their Buckram.
Lip Labour.
Lips Tongueless[e].
Little and Loud.
Littlenesse No Cause of Leanesse.
Loading and Unloading.
Long and Lazy [or Lazie].
Long Life.
Long Lookt for Comes at Last.
Losse from the Heat.
Lots to Be Liked.
Love.
Love Dislikes Nothing.
Love Is a Sirrup.
Love Kill'd by Lack.
Love Me Little, Love Me Long.
Love Palpable.
Love Perfumes All Parts.
Love What It Is.
Lovers How They Come and Part.
Love's Play at Push-Pin.
Lyric[k] for Legacies.
Lyric to Mirth, A.
Mad Maid's Song, The.
Maiden-Blush, The.
Maids Nay's Are Nothing.
Manna.
Man's Dying-Place Uncertain.
Martha, Martha.
Matins [or Mattens], or Morning Prayer.
May-Pole, The.
Meane in Our Meanes, A.
Meane, The ("Imparitie doth ever discord bring").
Meane, The ("Tis much among the filthy to be clean").
Meane Things Overcome Mighty.
Meat without Mirth.
Meddow Verse; or, Aniversary to Mistris Bridget Lowman, The.
Meditation for His Mistress[e], A.
Men Mind No State in Sicknesse.
Mercy.
Mercy and Love.
Merits Make the Man.
Mirth.
Miseries.
Mr. Hericke his Daughter's Dowrye.
Mr. Robert Hericke His Farwell unto Poetrie.

Mrs. Eliz. Wheeler, Under the Name of the Lost Shepardesse.
Moderation.
Money Gets the Mastery [or Masterie].
Money Makes the Mirth.
Montes Scripturarum, the Mounts of the Scriptures.
Mora Sponsi, the Stay of the Bridegroome.
More Mighty, the More Merciful, The.
More Modest, More Manly.
More Potent, Lesse Peccant.
Most Words, Lesse Workes.
Mount of the Muses, The.
Multitude.
Need.
Neglect.
Neutrality Loathsome.
Never Too Late to Dye.
New Charon, The.
New-Year's [or New-Yeares] Gift Sent to Sir Simeon Steward, A.
New-Yeeres Gift, or Circumcisions Song, Sung to the King in the Presence at White Hall, The.
New-Yeeres Gift, The.
Night-Piece, to Julia, The.
No Action Hard to Affection.
No Bashfulnesse in Begging.
No Coming to God without Christ.
No Danger to Men Desperate.
No Despight to the Dead.
No Difference in the Dark [or i'th'dark].
No Escaping the Scourging.
No Fault in Women.
No Loathsomnesse in Love.
No Lock against Lechery.
No Luck in Love.
No Man Without Money.
No Paines, No Gaines.
No Shipwrack of Vertue. To a Friend.
No Spouse but a Sister.
No Time in Eternity.
No Want Where There's Little.
None Free from Fault.
None Truly Happy Here.
Nor Buying or Selling.
North and South.
Not Every Day Fit for Verse.
Not to Covet Much Where Little is the Charge.
Not To Love.
Nothing Free-Cost.
Nothing New.
Number of Two, The.
Nuptiall Song, or Epithalamie, on Sir Clipseby Crew and His Lady, A.
Nuptiall Verse to Mistresse Elizabeth Lee, Now Lady Tracie.
Obedience.
Obedience in Subjects.
Oberon's Feast.
Oberon's Palace.
Observation.
Observation ("Jewes, when they built Houses [I have read], The").
Observation ("Virgin-Mother stood at distance [there], The").
Ode for Him, An.
Ode on the Birth of Our Saviour, An.
Ode, or Psalme, to God, An.
Ode to Master Endymion Porter, upon His Brother's Death, An.
Ode to Sir Clipsebie Crew, An.
Of all the good things whatsoe're we do.
Of Love. A Sonnet.
Of Love: ("I do not love, nor can it be").
Of Love ("Ile get me hence").
Of Love ("Instruct me now, what love will do").
Old Wives Prayer, The.
Olive Branch, The.
On a Perfum'd Lady.
On Fortune.
On Gelli-Flowers Begotten.
On Heaven.
On Himself ("Wearied Pilgrim, I have wandered here, A").

On Himselfe ("Aske me, why I do not sing").
On Himselfe: ("Born[e] I was to meet with Age").
On Himselfe ("Here down my wearyed limbs Ile lay").
On Himselfe ("I fear no Earthly Powers").
On Himselfe ("I will no longer kiss").
On Himselfe: ("If that my Fate has now fulfill'd my yeere").
On Himselfe ("Ile sing no more, nor will I longer write").
On Himselfe ("I'll write no more of Love; but now repent").
On Himselfe ("Let me not live, if I not love").
On Himselfe ("Live by thy Muse thou shalt; when others die").
On Himselfe ("Lost to the world").
On Himselfe ("Love-sick I am, and must endure").
On Himselfe ("One Eare tingles; some there be").
On Himselfe ("Some parts may perish; dye thou canst not all").
On Himselfe ("Weep for the dead, for they have lost this light").
On Himselfe ("Work is done: young men, and maidens set, The").
On Himselfe ("Young I was, but [or who] now am old").
On His Booke ("Bound (almost) now of my book I see, The").
On Jone.
On Julia's Breath.
On Julias Lips.
On Julia's Picture.
On Love.
On Love("Love is a kind of warre").
On Love("That love 'twixt men do's ever longest last").
On Poet Prat.
On Tomasin Parsons.
Once Poore, Still Penurious.
Once Seen, and No More.
Orpheus.
Orpheus and Pluto.
Our Owne Sinnes Unseen.
Out of Time, Out of Tune.
Paine and Pleasure.
Paines without Profit.
Painting Sometimes Permitted.
Pain[e] Ends in Pleasure.
Panegyric to Sir Lewis Pemberton, A.
Paradise.
Paranæticall, or Advisive Verse, to His Friend, M. John Wicks.
Parasceve, or Preparation, The.
Parcæ, The; or, Three Dainty Destinies: The Armilet.
Parcell-gil't-Poetry.
Pardon.
Pardons.
Parkinsons Shade to the House of Mr. Pallauicine Taking His Death Ill.
Parliament of Roses to Julia, The.
Parting Verse, Or Charge to His Supposed Wife When He Travelled, The.
Parting Verse, the Feast There Ended, The.
Passion.
Pastorall Sung to the King: Montano, Silvio, and Mirtillo, Shepards, A.
Pastorall Upon the Birth of Prince Charles, A.
Patience in Princes.
Patience, or Comforts in Crosses.
Peace not Permanent.
Penitence.
Penitencie.
Perfume, The.
Persecutions Profitable.
Persecutions Purifie.
Perseverance.
Peter-penny, The.
Physitians.
Pillar of Fame, The.
Primitiæ to Parents, The.

Pitie to the Prostrate.
Pittie, and Punishment.
Plaudite, or End of Life, The.
Pleasures Pernicious.
Plots Not Still Prosperous.
Plunder, The.
Poet Hath Lost His Pipe, The.
Poet Loves a Mistress, but Not to Marry, The.
Poetry Perpetuates the Poet.
Poets.
Poets Good Wishes for the Most Hopefull and Handsome Prince, the Duke of Yorke, The.
Pollicie in Princes.
Pomander Bracelet, The.
Poore Mans Part, The.
Poores Portion, The.
Position in the Hebrew Divinity, A.
Possesions.
Posting to Printing.
Potentates.
Poverty and Riches.
Poverty the Greatest Pack.
Power and Peace.
Power in the People, The.
Pray and Prosper.
Prayer.
Prayers Must Have Poise.
Precepts.
Predestination.
Prescience.
Presence and Absence.
Present Government Grievous.
Present: or, The Bag of the Bee, The.
Present Time But Pleaseth, The.
Prevision, or Provision.
Pride Allowable in Poets.
Primrose, The.
Princes and Favourites.
Prognostick, A.
Proof to No Purpose.
Psalme or Hymne to the Graces, A.
Purgatory.
Purposes.
Putrefaction.
Quintell, The.
Raggs.
Rainbow; or Curious Covenant, The.
Rainbow, The.
Rapine Brings Ruine.
Readinesse.
Recompence.
Recompence, The.
Regression Spoiles Resolution.
Repletion.
Request to the Graces, An.
Rest.
Rest Refreshes.
Resurrection, Possible, and Probable, The.
Resurrection, The.
Revenge.
Reverence.
Reverence to Riches.
Rewards.
Rewards and Punishments.
Riches and Poverty.
Right Hand, The.
Ring Presented to Julia, A.
Roaring.
Rock of Rubies: and The Quarrie of Pearls, The.
Rod, The.
Rosarie, The.
Rose, The.
Rosemarie Branch, The.
Rules for Our Reach.
Sabbaths.
Sacrifice, by Way of Discourse betwixt Himselfe and Julia, The.
Sadness of Things for Sappho's Sickness, The.
Safety on the Shore.
Safety To Look to Ones Selfe.
Saint Distaffs Day, or the Morrow after Twelfth Day.
Salutation.

Satan.
Satisfaction for Sufferings.
Sauce for Sorrowes.
Scar[e]-Fire, The.
School or Perl of Putney, the Mistress of All Singular Manners, Mistresse Portman, The.
Seek[e] and Find[e].
Seest thou those diamonds which she wears.
Shame, No Statist.
Ship-Wrack.
Sho[o]e Tying, The.
Short and Long Both Likes.
Short Hymne to Larr, A.
Short Hymne to Venus, A.
Showre of Blossomes, The.
Showre of Roses, The.
Silence.
Silken Snake, The.
Sin.
Sin and Strife.
Sin Seen.
Sin Severely Punisht.
Sin ("Sin leads the way, but as it goes, it feels").
Sin ("Sin never slew a soule, unlesse there went").
Sin ("Sin no Existence; Nature none it hath").
Sin ("Sin once reacht up to Gods eternall Sphere").
Sin ("There is no evill that we do commit").
Sincerity.
Single Life Most Secure.
Sinners.
Sins Loathed, and Yet Loved.
Slavery.
Smart.
Smell of the Sacrifice, The.
Sobriety in Search.
Society.
Soft Musick.
Some Comfort in Calamity.
Song, A: "Loose no time nor youth but be."
Song: "Burne or drowne me."
Song to the Maskers, A.
Song upon Silvia, A.
Sonnet, A: "Ile dote noe more, nor shall mine eyes."
Sonnet of Perilla, A.
Sorrowes.
Sorrows Succeed.
Soul Is the Salt, The.
Soule, The.
Speake in Season.
Spell, The.
Staffe and Rod, The.
Star-Song; a Carol to the King; Sung at White-Hall, The.
Steam in Sacrifice.
Stool-Ball.
Strength to Support Soveraignty.
Studies to Be Supported.
Succession of the Foure Sweet Months, The.
Suffer Thou that Canst not Shift.
Sufferance.
Sufferings.
Summe, and the Satisfaction, The.
Supreme Fortune Falls Soonest.
Surfeits.
Suspicion Makes Secure.
Suspition upon His Over-much Familiarity with a Gentlewoman, The.
Sweetnesse in Sacrifice.
Tapers.
Teare Sent to Her from Stanes, The.
Teares, and Laughter.
Teares are Tongues.
Teares: ("God from our eyes all teares..").
Teares: ("Our present Teares here (not our present laughter)").
Teares ("Teares most prevaile; with teares too thou mayst move").
Teares: ("Teares of Saints more sweet by farre, The").
Temple, The.
Temporall Goods.

Temptations ("No man is tempted so, but may o'recome").
Temptations ("Temptations hurt not, though they have accesse").
Temptations ("Those Saints, which God loves best").
Ternarie of Littles, upon a Pipkin of Jellie [or Jelly] Sent to a Lady, A.
Thanksgiving.
Thanksgiving to God for His House, A.
Things Mortal Still Mutable.
Things of Choice, Long a Comming.
This, and the Next World.
This cross-tree here.
Three Fatal[l] Sisters.
Tinkers Song, The.
Tithe [or Tythe]: To the Bride, The.
To a Bed of Tulips.
To a Disdaynefull Fayre.
To a Friend("Looke in my Book, and herein see").
To a Gentlewoman Objecting to Him His Grey Hairs.
To a Gentlewoman on Just Dealing.
To a Maid.
To a Mayd.
To All Young Men That Love.
To Anthea: ("Ah my Anthea! must my heart still break?").
To Anthea ("Anthea I am going hence").
To Anthea ("Come Anthea, know thou this").
To Anthea: ("If, deare Anthea, my hard fate it be").
To Anthea: ("Lets call for Hymen if agreed thou art").
To Anthea Lying in Bed.
To Anthea: ("Now is the time, when all the lights wax dim").
To Anthea: ("Sick is Anthea, sickly is the spring").
To Anthea, Who May Command Him Anything.
To Apollo ("Thou mighty lord and master of the Lyre").
To Apollo("Phoebus! when that I a Verse").
To Bacchus, a Canticle.
To Be Merry.
To Biancha.
To Biancha, to Blesse Him.
To Blossoms.
To Carnations.
To Cedars.
To Cherry-Blossomes.
To Christ.
To Critic[k]s.
To Crown[e] It.
To Cupid.
To Daffodils [or Daffadills].
To Daisies, Not to Shut So Soon[e].
To Dean-bourn, a Rude River in Devon, by Which Sometimes He Lived.
To Death.
To Dewes. A Song.
To Dianeme; a Ceremonie in Glocester.
To Dianeme ("Dear, though to part it be a hell").
To Dianeme ("Give me one kiss").
To Dianeme ("I co'd but see thee").
To Dianeme ("Show me thy feet; show me thy legs, thy thighs").
To Dianeme ("Sweet, be not proud of those two eyes").
To Doctor Alabaster.
To Electra.
To Electra ("I'll [or Ile] come to thee in all those shapes").
To Electra. Love Looks for Love.
To Electra ("'Tis Ev'ning, my Sweet").
To Electra("Let not thy Tomb-stone").
To Enjoy the Time.
To Find[e] God.
To Flowers.
To Fortune.
To God: an Anthem, Sung in the Chapel at White-Hall, Before the King.
To God ("Come to me God; but do not come").

To God ("Do with me, God! as Thou didst deal with John").
To God ("God gives not onely corne").
To God ("God is all-sufferance here").
To God ("God! to my little meale and oyle").
To God ("God, who me gives a will").
To God ("God's undivided, One in Persons Three").
To God, His Gift.
To God, His Good Will.
To God ("If any thing delight me for to print").
To God ("If I have plaid the Truant").
To God ("I'le come, I'le creep").
To God, in Time of Plundering.
To God ("Lord, I am like to mistletoe").
To God ("Make, make me Thine").
To God, on His Sickness[e].
To God ("Pardon me God").
To God ("Thou hast promis'd, Lord, to be").
To God ("With golden Censers..").
To God ("Work is done, The").
To Groves.
To Heaven.
To His Angrie God.
To His Book ("Before the Press scarce one co'd see").
To His Book[e]: ("Have I not blest thee? Then go forth; nor fear").
To His Booke ("Be bold my Booke, nor be abasht, or feare").
To His Booke ("Come thou not neere those men, who are like Bread").
To His Booke ("Goe thou forth my booke, though late").
To His Booke ("Like to a Bride, come forth my Book, at last").
To his Booke ("Take mine advise, and go not neere").
To His Booke ("Thou art a plant sprung up to wither never").
To His Booke ("While thou didst keep thy candor undefil'd").
To His Book[e] ("If hap it must, that I must see thee lye").
To His Book[e] ("Make haste away, and let one be").
To His Brother in Law Master John Wingfield.
To His Brother Nicolas Herrick.
To His Closet-Gods.
To His Conscience.
To his deare Valentine, Mistresse Margaret Falconbrige.
To His Deere God.
To His Dying Brother, Master William Herrick.
To His Ever-Loving God.
To his Faithfull Friend, Master John Crofts, Cup-bearer to the King.
To His False Mistris.
To his Friend, Master J. Jincks.
To His Friend, on the Untunable Times.
To His Friend to Avoid Contention of Words.
To His Girles.
To his Girles who Would Have Him Sportfull.
To His Honour'd Friend, Sir Thomas Heale.
To His Honoured and Most Ingenious Friend, Mr. Charles Cotton.
To His Honoured Friend, M. John Weare, Councellour.
To His Honoured Friend, Sir John Mynts.
To His Honoured Kinsman, Sir Richard Stone.
To His Honoured Kinsman Sir William Soame.
To His Household Gods.
To His Kinsman, Master Thomas Herrick, Who Desired to Be in His Book.
To His Kinsman, Sir Tho. Soame.
To His Kinswoman, Mrs. Penelope Wheeler.
To His Kinswoman, Mistresse Susanna Herrick.
To His Learned Friend M. Jo. Harmar, Phisitian to to Colledge of Westminster.

To His Lovely Mistresses.
To His Maid Prew.
To His Mistress Objecting to Him Neither Toying or Talking.
To His Mistresses.
To His Mistress[e].
To His Muse.
To His Muse, Another to the Same.
To His Muse: ("Were I to give thee Baptime, I wo'd chuse").
To His Muse ("Whither, mad maiden, wilt thou roame?").
To His Nephew, to Be Prosperous in His Art of Painting.
To His Paternall Countrey.
To His Peculiar Friend M. Jo: Wicks.
To His Peculiar Friend Master Thomas Shapcott, Lawyer.
To His Peculiar Friend Sir Edward Fish, Knight Baronet.
To His Savior [or Saviour]. The New Years [or yeers] Gift.
To His Saviour.
To His Saviour, a Child; a Present, by a Child.
To His Saviours Sepulcher: His Devotion.
To His Sister in Law, M. Susanna Herrick.
To His Sweet Saviour.
To His Tomb-Maker.
To His Valentine, on S. Valentines Day.
To His Verses.
To His Worthy Friend, M. Arthur Bartly.
To his Worthy Friend M. John Hall, Student of Grayes-Inne.
To Worthy Friend, M. Tho. Falconbirge.
To His Worthy Kinsmen, Mr. Stephen Soame.
To Jealousie.
To Jos: Lo: Bishop of Exeter.
To Julia ("Help me, Julia, for to pray").
To Julia ("Holy waters hither bring").
To Julia: ("How rich and pleasing thou, my Julia, art").
To Julia ("I am zeellesse, prethee pray").
To Julia, in Her Dawn, or Day-breake.
To Julia in the Temple.
To Julia ("Julia, when thy Herrick dies").
To Julia ("Offer thy gift").
To Julia ("Permit me, Julia, now to goe away").
To Julia ("Saints-bell calls; and Julia, I must read, The").
To Julia, the Flaminica Dialis, or Queen-Priest.
To Keep a True Lent.
To Larr [or Lar].
To Laurels.
To Live Freely.
To Live Merrily, and To Trust to Good Verses.
To Love.
To Marygolds.
To M. Denham, on His Prospective Poem.
To M. Henry Lawes, the Excellent Composer[,] of his Lyrics.
To M. Kellam.
To M. Laurence Swetnaham.
To M. Leonard Willan His Peculiar Friend.
To Meadows [or Meddowes].
To Mistresse Katherine Bradshaw, the Lovely, That Crowned Him with Laurel.
To Mistresse Amie Potter.
To Mistresse Dorothy Parsons.
To Mistresse Mary Willand.
To Momus.
To Music.
To Music: A Song.
To Music, to Becalm a Sweet-sick Youth.
To Music, to Becalm His Fever.
To My Dearest Sister M. Mercie Herrick.
To My Ill Reader.
To Myrrha Hard-Hearted.
To Oenone ("Sweet Oenone, doe but say").
To Oenone ("Thou saist Love's dart").
To Oenone ("What conscience, say, is it in thee").
To Pansies.

To Perenna, A Mistresse ("Deare Perenna, prethee come").
To Perenna: ("How long, *Perenna*, wilt thou see").
To Perenna ("I a Dirge will pen for thee").
To Perenna ("Thou say'st I'm dull; if edge-lesse so I be").
To Perenna ("When I thy parts runne o're, I can't espie").
To Perilla.
To Phyllis to Love and Live with Him.
To Primroses Filled with Morning Dew.
To Prince Charles upon his coming to Exeter.
To Robin Redbrest.
To Rosemary and Baies.
To Roses in Julia's Bosome.
To Sapho ("Sapho, I will chuse to go").
To Sapho ("Thou saist thou lov'st me Sapho; I say no").
To Sappho.
To Silvia ("I am holy, while I stand").
To Silvia ("No more my Silvia, do I mean to pray").
To Silvia ("Pardon my trespasse").
To Silvia to Wed.
To Sir Clipsebie Crew ("Since to th'Country first I came").
To Sir Clipseby Crew ("Give me wine, and give me meate").
To Sir George Parrie, Doctor of the Civill Law.
To Sir John Berkeley, Governour of Exeter.
To Springs and Fountains.
To Sycamores.
To the Detracter.
To the Earle of Westmerland.
To the Fever, Not To Trouble Julia.
To the Generous Reader.
To the Genius of His House.
To the Handsome Mistresse Grace Potter.
To the High and Noble Prince, George, Duke, Marquesse, and Earle of Buckingham.
To the Honoured, Master Endimion Porter.
To the King.
To the King and Queene, upon Their Unhappy Distances.
To the King ("If when these Lyricks (Cesar) You shall heare").
To the King, To Cure the Evill.
To the King, upon His Com[m]ing with His Army into the West.
To the King, upon His Taking of Leicester.
To the King, upon His Welcome to Hampton-Court.
To the Lady Crew, Upon the Death of her Child.
To the Lady Mary Villars, Governesse to the Princesse Henretta.
To the Ladyes.
To the Lark.
To the Little Spinners.
To the Lord Hopton, on His Fight in Cornwall.
To the Maids to Walke Abroad.
To the Most Accomplisht Gentleman, Master Edward Norgate, Clark of the Signet to His Majesty.
To the Most Accomplisht Gentleman Master Michael Oulsworth.
To the Most Comely and Proper M. Elizabeth Finch.
To the Most Fair and Lovely Mistress Anne Soame, Now Lady Abdie.
To the Most Illustrious and Most Hopefull Prince, Charles, Prince of Wales.
To the Most Learned, Wise, and Arch-Antiquary, M. John Selden.
To the Most Virtuous Mistress Pot, Who Many Times Entertained Him.
To the Nightingale, and Robin-Red-Brest.
To the Painter, To Draw Him a Picture.
To the Passenger.
To the Patron of Poets, M. End: Porter.
To the Queene.
To the Reverend Shade of His Religious Father.

To the Right Gratious Prince, Lodwick, Duke of Richmond and Lenox.
To the Right Honourable Edward Earle of Dorset.
To the Right Honourable Mildmay, Earl of Westmorland.
To the Right Honourable, Philip, Earle of Pembroke, and Montgomerie.
To the Rose; a Song.
To the Sour[e] Reader.
To [the] Virgins, to Make Much of Time.
To the Water Nymphs, Drinking at the Fountain.
To the Western Wind.
To the Willow-Tree.
To the Yew and Cypress to Grace His Funeral.
To Violets.
To Virgins.
To Vulcan.
To Women, to Hide Their Teeth, if They Be Rotten or Rusty.
To Youth.
Transfiguration, The.
Treason.
True Friendship.
True Safety.
Truth and Error.
Truth and Falsehood.
Truth ("Truth is best found out by the time, and eyes").
Twelfe Night, or King and Queene.
Twilight ("Twilight is no other thing [we say], The").
Twilight ("Twilight, no other thing is, Poets say").
Two Things Odious.
Ultimus Heroum: or, To the Most Learned, and to the Right Honourable, Henry, Marquesse of Dorchester.
Up Tail[e]s All.
Upon a Black Twist, Rounding the Arm of the Countess of Carlisle.
Upon a Bleare-Ey'd Woman.
Upon a Cheap Laundresse: Epigram.
Upon a Cherrystone Sent to the Tip of the Lady Jemmonia Walgraves Eare.
Upon a Child.
Upon a Child. An Epitaph.
Upon a Child That Died [or Dyed].
Upon a Comely, and Curious Maide.
Upon a Crooked Maid.
Upon a Delaying Lady.
Upon a Flie.
Upon a Free Maid, with a Foule Breath.
Upon a Gentlewoman with a Sweet Voice.
Upon a Hoarse Singer.
Upon a Lady Faire, but Fruitlesse.
Upon a Lady That Dyed in Child-Bed, and Left a Daughter behind Her.
Upon a Maid[e].
Upon a Maid ("Gone she is a long, long way").
Upon a Maide ("Hence a blessed soule is fled").
Upon a Painted Gentlewoman.
Upon a Physitian.
Upon a Scarre in a Virgins Face.
Upon a Sowre-Breath Lady.
Upon a Virgin.
Upon a Virgin Kissing a Rose.
Upon a Wife That Dyed Mad with Jealousie.
Upon a Young Mother of Many Children.
Upon Adam Peapes.
Upon an Old Man a Residenciarie.
Upon an Old Woman.
Upon Batt.
Upon Ben Jo[h]nson.
Upon Bice.
Upon Blanch.
Upon Blanch: ("Blanch swears her Husband's lovely; when a scald").
Upon Blinks.
Upon Blisse.
Upon Boreman. Epig.
Upon Bran.
Upon Bridget.

Upon Brock.
Upon Buggins.
Upon Bunce: Epigram.
Upon Bungie.
Upon Burr.
Upon Candlemasse Day.
Upon Case.
Upon Center a Spectacle-Maker with a Flat Nose.
Upon Chub.
Upon Clunn.
Upon Cob.
Upon Cock.
Upon Comely a Good Speaker but an Ill Singer.
Upon Coone.
Upon Crab.
Upon Craw.
Upon Croot.
Upon Cuffe. Epig.
Upon Cupid.
Upon Cupid ("As lately I a Garland bound").
Upon Cupid ("Love, like a Gypsie, lately come").
Upon Cupid ("Old wives have often told, how they").
Upon Cuts.
Upon Deb.
Upon Dol.
Upon Doll.
Upon Dundrige.
Upon Eeles.
Upon Electra.
Upon Electra's Teares.
Upon Faunus.
Upon Flimsey: Epigram.
Upon Flood, Or a Thankfull Man.
Upon Fone a School-master. Epigram.
Upon Franck.
Upon Franck: ("Franck wo'd go scoure her teeth; and setting to't").
Upon Gander.
Upon Glasco. Epig.
Upon Glass: Epigram.
Upon God ("God is all fore-part; for, we never see").
Upon God ("God is not only said to be").
Upon God ("God when He takes my goods and chattels hence").
Upon Gorgonius.
Upon Greedy.
Upon Groynes.
Upon Grubs.
Upon Grudgings.
Upon Gryll.
Upon Gubbs.
Upon Guesse.
Upon Gut.
Upon Hanch a Schoolmaster.
Upon Her Almes.
Upon Her Blush.
Upon Her Eyes.
Upon Her Feet.
Upon Her Voice.
Upon Her Weeping.
Upon Himself: ("I dislikt but even now").
Upon Himself ("Mop-eyed I am, as some have said").
Upon Himself: ("Th'art hence removing, (like a Shepherds Tents)").
Upon Himself ("Thou shalt not All die").
Upon Himselfe Being Buried.
Upon Himselfe ("I am Sive-like, and can hold").
Upon Himselfe ("I co'd never love indeed").
Upon Himselfe ("I lately fri'd, but now behold").
Upon Himself ("Come, leave this loathed Country-life, and then").
Upon His Departure Hence.
Upon His Eye-Sight Failing Him.
Upon His Gray Haires.
Upon His Julia.
Upon his Kinswoman Mrs. M. S.
Upon His Kinswoman Mistresse Bridget Herrick.

Upon His Kinswoman Mistris Elizabeth Herrick.
Upon His Sister-in-Law, Mistress Elizabeth Herrick.
Upon His Spaniel[l] Tracie [or Tracy].
Upon His Verses.
Upon Hog.
Upon Horne.
Upon Huncks: Epigram.
Upon Irene.
Upon Jack and Jill: Epigram.
Upon Jollies Wife.
Upon Jolly and Jilly.
Upon Jone and Jane.
Upon Judith.
Upon Julia['s] Washing Herself in the River.
Upon Julia's Breasts.
Upon Julia's Clothes.
Upon Julia's Fall.
Upon Julia's Haire, Bundled up in a Golden Net.
Upon Julia's Haire Fill'd with Dew.
Upon Julia's Recovery.
Upon Julia's Ribband.
Upon Julia's Sweat.
Upon Julia's Unlacing Her Self.
Upon Julia's Voice.
Upon Kings.
Upon Leech.
Upon Letcher: Epigram.
Upon Linnit.
Upon Loach.
Upon Love, by Way of Question and Answer.
Upon Love ("Christall Violl Cupid brought, A").
Upon Love ("I held Love's head while it did ake").
Upon Love: ("I plaid with Love, as with the fire").
Upon Love ("In a Dreame, Love bad me go").
Upon Love ("Love brought me to a silent Grove").
Upon Love ("Love, I have broke").
Upon Love ("Love is a circle").
Upon Love: ("Love scorch'd my finger, but did spare").
Upon Love: ("Love's a thing, (as I do heare)").
Upon Love ("Some salve to every sore, we may apply").
Upon Lucia.
Upon Lucia Dabled in the Deaw.
Upon Lucie.
Upon Luggs.
Upon Lulls.
Upon Lungs.
Upon Lupes.
Upon Luske.
Upon Madam Ursly.
Upon Magot a Frequenter of Ordinaries.
Upon Man.
Upon M. Ben Jo[h]nson: Epigram.
Upon Master Fletchers Incomparable Playes.
Upon M. William Lawes, the Rare Musitian.
Upon Mease.
Upon Megg.
Upon Mistress Elizabeth Wheeler under the Name of Amarillis.
Upon Mistresse Susanna Southwell, Her Cheeks.
Upon Much-More.
Upon Mudge.
Upon Nis.
Upon Nodes.
Upon One-Ey'd Broomsted.
Upon One Lillie, Who Marryed with a Maid Call'd Rose.
Upon One Who Said She Was Alwayes Young.
Upon Pagget.
Upon Parrat.
Upon Parson Beanes.
Upon Parting.
Upon Paske a Draper.
Upon Patrick a Footman.

Upon Paul.
Upon Pearch.
Upon Peason.
Upon Pennie.
Upon Pievish.
Upon Pimpe.
Upon Pink an Ill-Fac'd Painter.
Upon Prickles.
Upon Prig ("Prig now drinks Water, who before drank Beere").
Upon Prigg ("Prigg, when he comes to houses, oft doth use").
Upon Prudence Baldwin Her Sickness[e].
Upon Prue [or Prew], His Maid.
Upon Punchin.
Upon Pusse and her Prentice.
Upon Ralph.
Upon Ralph ("Ralph pares his nayles").
Upon Raspe.
Upon Reape.
Upon Rook: Epigram.
Upon Roots.
Upon Roses.
Upon Rumpe.
Upon Rush.
Upon Sapho.
Upon Sapho, Sweetly Playing, and Sweetly Singing.
Upon Scobble [Epigram].
Upon Shark.
Upon Shift.
Upon Shopter.
Upon Showbread [or Shewbread]: Epigram.
Upon Sibb.
Upon Sibilla.
Upon Silvia, a Mistresse.
Upon Skinns.
Upon Skoles.
Upon Skrew.
Upon Skurffe.
Upon Slouch.
Upon Smeaton.
Upon Snare, an Usurer.
Upon Sneape.
Upon Some Women.
Upon Spalt.
Upon Spenke.
Upon Spokes.
Upon Spunge.
Upon Spur.
Upon Strut.
Upon Sudds, a Laundress[e].
Upon Tap.
Upon Teage.
Upon Teares.
Upon the Bishop of Lincolne's Imprisonment.
Upon the Death of His Sparrow; an Elegie.
Upon the Lady Crew.
Upon the Losse of His Finger.
Upon the Loss[e] of His Mistresses.
Upon the Much Lamented, Mr. J. Warr.
Upon the Nipples of Julia's Breast.
Upon the Roses in Julia's Bosome.
Upon the Same.
Upon the Troublesome Times.
Upon Time.
Upon Tooly.
Upon Trap.
Upon Trencherman.
Upon Trigg.
Upon Truggin.
Upon Tubbs.
Upon Tuck.
Upon Umber: Epigram.
Upon Urles.
Upon Ursley.
Upon Vinegar.
Upon Woman and Mary.
Upon Wrinkles.
Upon Zelot.
Verses.
Vertue.
Vertue Best United.
Vertue Is Sensible of Suffering.
Vine, The.
Virgin Mary, The ("To work a wonder, God would have her shown").

Virgin Mary, The ("Virgin Marie was [as I have read], The").
Vision, The.
Vision to Electra, The.
Voice and Violl, The.
Vow to Mars, A.
Vow to Minerva, A.
Vow to Venus, A.
Wages.
Wake, The.
Want.
Warre.
Wassaile, The.
Watch, The.
Way in a Crowd.
Way, The.
Weeping Cherry, The.
Welcome to Sack, The.
Welcome What Comes.
What God Is.
What Kind of Mistress[e] He Would Have.
When He Would Have His Verses Read.
Whips.
White Island: or Place of the Blest, The.
Why Flowers Change Color.
Widow's Tears [or Widdowes Teares]: or, Dirge of Dorcas, The.
Will Makes the Work, or Consent Makes the Cure, The.
Will the Cause of Woe, The.
Will To Be Working, A.
Willow Garland, The.
Wit Punisht, Prospers Most.
Women Uselesse.
Wounded Cupid, The.
Wounded Heart, The.
Writing.
Youth, and Age.
Zeal Required in Love.
Translations, Coauthored Poems, etc.:
3.9: Dialogue between Horace and Lydia, A ("Donec gratus eram").
Another [To His Booke].
Odes *sels.*
Upon a Maid That Died [or Dyed] the Day She Was Married [or Marryed].
Very Old Song, A.

Hesketh, Phoebe (b. 1909)

Academic.
After Ecclesiastes.
After Verlaine.
All Hallows.
Analyst.
And Fall.
Animals' Last Words.
At Four A.M.
Autumn at Whitewell.
Betterwear Man, The.
Bleasdale: The Wooden Circle.
Bolton-Le-Moors, 1960.
Boy Drowning.
Brain Child.
Brief Encounter.
Bull Alone.
Buttercup Children, The.
Call of the North.
Cap, The.
Cats.
Changing Colour.
Child's Guide to Philosophy, A.
Christmas Blackmail.
Clown.
Clown Flowers.
Comparison with a Sunflower.
Credo.
Cross.
Days.
Dead Blackbird.
Death of a Gardener.
Defeathered.
Different.
Dilemma.
Edward Thomas.
Emily Dickinson.
Evergreen.
First Day, The.
Fisherman Poet.

Fox, The.
From the Day Room.
From Walden.
Giraffes.
Gone Away.
Gymnasts, The.
He Saved Others..
Heat-Wave.
Horses, The.
House In the Tree.
How to Do It.
I Am.
I Am Not Resigned.
I Cannot Look into the Sun.
I Give Death to a Son.
Imagination.
Imprint.
Integration.
Invitation.
It Was Not I.
Joke, The.
Jolly Good Fellow, A.
Journey.
July 2nd, 1916.
Leave Train, The.
Letter to Vincent.
Limbo.
Love without Frontiers.
Love's Advocate.
Lyric Evening.
Mallard, The.
Mary.
Master Cotton Spinner.
Meths Men, The.
Mill Clock, The.
More than Grass.
Moving Staircase.
My Faithful Lover.
Naked Ostrich.
No Reply at Christmas.
Northern Stone.
On Iona.
Orpheus in the Underground.
Owl.
Paint Box.
Panther and the Antelope, The.
Partridge.
Party, The.
Poem is a Painting, A.
Prayer for Sun.
Preparing to Leave.
Protean Lover.
Recapitulation.
Reclaimed.
Reflections.
Reply to a Philistine.
Retreat.
Return.
Rise.
Rivals, The.
Roots.
St. Luke's Summer.
Sally.
Scapegoat.
Second Childhood.
Shaping Spirit, The.
Single Footprints.
Skeleton Bride.
Snow Leopard.
So Little It Can Take.
Starlings.
Sun Up.
Sundowner.
Survival.
Survivors.
Tom Rich.
Traitor.
Truant.
Truth Game.
Tunnel, The.
Unicorn.
Very Small Casualty, A.
Vine, The.
Violet at Ninety.
Vision.
Waiting.
Walking Away.

Walking Back.
Walled In.
Ward F4.
What Is a Person?
What Is God?
Widowhood.
Winter Daffodils.
Words.
Wordsworth's Old Age.
Yew Tree Guest House.

Hewitt, John (1907–87)
Administration.
Admonition to Science.
Aesthete's Renunciation.
After Reading *Sonnets* by Rev. Charles
  Turner (1864) and *The New Day*, Sonnets
  by Dr T. Gordon Hake (1890).
After the Fire.
Age and Youth.
Agenda.
Agitator.
Agrigento, Sicily.
Alder Stick, The.
Alien Harvest.
Anglo-Irish Accord, The.
Anti-Promethean Ode.
Antrim April.
Any Rich Suburban Church.
Apparition.
April.
April Awake.
Aquarium.
Aristocratic Area.
Arithmetic.
Ars Poetica.
Art and Technology.
Art Room in a City School.
Art's Duped Riddle.
As You Like It.
Ashes in the Wind.
At Shottery, Anne Hathaway's Cottage.
At the Newsagent's.
Atlas.
August 1939.
Aunt Cis and Uncle Tom.
Autumn Gale.
Autumn Valley.
Autumnal.
Awareness of Time.
Away Match: June 1924.
Ballad, The.
Balloons and Wooden Guns.
Bandstand.
Bangor, Spring 1916.
Beastie, The.
Because I Paced My Thought.
Belfastman Abroad Argues with Himself.
Belfastman, The.
Bell, The.
Below the Mournes in May.
Betrayal.
Bifocal in Gaza.
Big Room, The.
Birthday Rhyme for Roberta, A.
Black and White.
Bleeze.
Blessing.
Bloody Brae, The.
Blossomed Thorn, The.
Blue Lias Inn, The.
Boat-Builder's Caulking Irons, The.
Bogside, Derry, 1971.
Bombed Public House, The.
Booleys, The.
B.O.W.
Boy Seen in a Bus Journey.
Bradford Millionaire.
Braes O' Layde, The.
Breach, The.
Breastplate.
Brothers, The.
Brown's Bay, Islandmagee, Spring 1917.
Burnt Post, The.
By Air to Birmingham on a Mid-June
  Evening.
Camaradas Y Compañeros.
Cape Sunion.

Carnations.
Carol Singers.
Carol Singers from the Church, The.
Carson at Six Road Ends.
Case of Mistaken Identity, A.
Ceilidhe, The.
Chant for the Five-Year Plan.
Child, the Chair, the Leaf, The.
Chinese Fluteplayer.
Christmas Eve.
Christmas Rhymers, Ballynure, 1941, The.
City Morning.
Clink of Rhyme, The.
Clogh-Oir: September 1971.
Coasters, The.
Cobweb.
Cold Warrior: Anzac Day, 1946.
Collector's Choice.
College Fence, The.
Colmcille.
Colney Hatch.
Colonial Consequence.
Colony, The.
Colour.
Comment on Verse.
Company.
Compton Wynates, Warwickshire.
Conacre.
Consequences.
Conversations in Hungary, August 1969.
Corncrake.
Corridor.
Country Talk.
Country Walk in March, A.
Country Walk in May, A.
Covenanter's Grave, The.
Crossing, The.
Cultra Manor: The Ulster Folk Museum.
Curfew Tower, The.
Cushkib Fair.
Dedication.
Dedication: "I have a certain skill in phrase."
Dedication of "The Rhyming Weavers."
Defeat.
Delos.
Demagogue.
Descent, The.
Dichotomy.
Difficult Man, A.
Dilemma, The.
Diptera.
Disaster on the Box.
Dissertation I.
Dissertation II.
Distances, The.
Doctor Muses, The.
Doctor's Bag, The.
Domestic Help.
Dommie's Log, A.
Double-Ended Tram, The.
Drift of Petals, The.
Dry Summer, Islandmagee, 1921.
Drypoint.
Dungannon Cattle Market.
Dustcart, The.
Dusty Roads.
Eager Journey.
East Antrim Winter.
Easter Flock.
Easter Tuesday.
Ecce Homo.
Egyptian Night.
E.H.
Eleventh Night, The.
Ellendene.
Emily Dickinson.
Encounter Nineteen Twenty.
Encounter With R.J. Welch, The Antiquary.
End of the World, The.
Epitaph for a Conscript, 1940.
Epitaph for a Gardener.
Epitaph to a Man Not Dead.
Epithalamion: "O who will share with me."
Equality.
Erice, Western Sicily.
Et Tu In Arcadia Vixisti.
Evangelist.

Evening in Spring.
Ex-Serviceman, The.
Executives Third Tier.
Exile.
Expectancy.
Eye for Color, An.
Fables for Stormont.
Faded Leaf: A Chapter of Family History, The.
Failed Image.
Fair Game.
Fairy-Man at Layde, The.
Fairy Thresher, The.
Fame.
Farmer's Second Son, The.
Father Explains, A.
Father's Death, A.
Feathers on Turf.
Filled Stocking, The.
First Corncrake.
First Funeral.
First Honey.
First Letters.
First Pantomime.
First Ride.
First Snow in the Glens.
Flight.
Folk Custom.
Folk for Tea.
Fontanel.
Fool's Cap, The.
Footing Turf.
For a Mild Season.
For a Moment of Darkness over the Nations.
For a September Afternoon of Unexpected Brightness.
For Any Irishman.
For Any Women Who Pass This House.
For Busha.
For Certain Subscribers to the Miners' Fund.
For Deirdre.
For Jean.
For One Who Did Not March.
For R.
For Roberta in the Garden.
For R.S. Thomas.
For Stonecutters.
"Forty-Four Hours" Strike, 1919, The.
Free Foot, The.
Free Mason.
Freehold.
From a Museum Man's Album.
From the Chinese of Wang Li Shi.
From the Tibetan.
Frontier, The.
Frost.
Function.
Gap, The.
Garron Top.
Gathering Praties.
Gentle Bush, The.
Geriatric Ward, The.
Ghosts.
Glen of Light, The.
Glenaan.
Glenarriffe and Parkmore.
Glendun.
Glendun on a Wet July Day.
Glens of Atrim, The.
Glens, The.
Glittering Sod, The.
Gloss, on the Difficulties of Translation.
Going to Church.
Going up to Dublin.
Golden Boy, The.
Grandfather Robinson Dies in 1898.
Great Event, A.
Great Headmaster, A.
Green Shoot, The.
Grey and White.
Grief ("I thought when the grave was sodded").
Grief ("When men lie down for ever / and names their tombstones take").
Habit of Mercy, The.
Halloweve: A Glensman Speaks.
Hand over Hand.

Happy Boy, A.
Happy Man, The.
Hay.
Haymaking in the Low Meadow.
He Suggests a Solution.
Heart of Joy, The.
Hedgehog.
Hedgehog: For R., The.
Hen and the Cock: A Glens Folk Rhyme, The.
Here at the Tide's Turn.
Hesitant Memorial.
Hill-Farm, The.
Hired Lad's Farewell, The.
His Majesty's Inspectors.
Hollyhocks against the Wall, The.
Holy Place, A.
Homestead.
Hospitality: For E.K.
Host.
Hour with E.M.F. at Ninety, An.
House at Ballyholme, The.
House Demolished, A.
House on the Hill, The.
How have I served you? I have let you waste.
Hymn: "Noon in an English county."
I Cannot Make a Song Tonight.
I Go to School.
I Learn About Art.
I Lie Alone.
I Remember.
I Still Had a Friend.
I Talked and Raged and Planned.
I Told My Heart to Rest.
I Turn to Trees.
I Turned My Touch to Campion.
I Write For.
Immortality.
In a Lurgan Pub.
In a Suburban Avenue.
In Memorium: D.H. Lawrence.
In Praise of Elizabeth.
In Recollection of Drumcliffe, September 1948.
In That Fair and Pleasant Land.
In the Lenin Library, Dushanbe.
In the Luxembourg Gardens.
In the Rosses.
In This Year of Grace.
Incident, An.
Instead of an Elegy.
Interim.
Interval.
Ireland.
Irish Dimension, The.
Irish Glass.
Irishman in Coventry, An.
Iron and Stone.
Iron Circle, The.
Iron Pot, The.
Isaac McKeown.
Island Folk Tale, An.
I've Known Her Turn from Bitter Phrase.
Jacob and the Angel.
J.B. Shelton (1876–1958), The Coventry Antiquarian.
Jenny Geddes.
July.
King Concerned, The.
King's Horses, The.
Knife, The.
Labour Victory, A.
Lagan in October, The.
Lake Bled, Slovenia.
Landscape.
"Lass of Richmond Hill", or The Royal Garden Party, The.
Last Call, The.
Last Crusade, The.
Last Summer, For Roberta (1975), The.
Late Spring.
Late Spring, 1912.
Lead Soldiers and Regimental Uniforms.
Leaf.
Leaving for Holiday.
Legend in His Own Lifetime.

Lettered Snow, The.
Lifting, The.
Lilibulero.
Limitations.
Lines for a Dead Alderman.
Lines on the Opening of the Belgrade Theatre.
Lint Pulling, The.
Listener, The.
Little Bourgeois is Upset, The.
Little Death, The.
Little Glen, The.
Little House, The.
Little Lough, The.
Little People, A.
Little Ships.
Living Landscape, The.
Load.
Local Poet, A.
Lonely Heart, The.
Long Bridge, The.
Lonsdale Street.
Lost *Argo*, Islandmagee, Summer 1919.
Lyric: "Chestnut and beech / sycamore and willow."
Lyric: "Let but a thrush begin."
Lyric: "Let this last lyric of a passing day."
Lyric Sonorously Rhymed, The.
MacDonnell's Question.
Mad Applegrower, The.
Magician, The.
Mainland, The.
Man Fish and Bird.
Man from Malabar, The.
Man from the Mountains, The.
March Day.
Mary Hagan, Islandmagee, 1919.
Mary's Lullaby.
Mask, The.
Mass.
Mathematics.
Mauberly's Son: A Summary.
May Alter.
Memorandum for the Moderates.
Memorial Service.
Methodists.
Mid-April.
Middle Infant.
Mile-Long Street, The.
Minister.
Minor Poet's Dilemma, 1940.
Minor Victorian Painter, A.
Minotaur.
Mirror.
Miss Murdoch.
Mist.
Mister Faintheart Middleclass.
Mobile Mollusc, A.
Modelled Head, The.
Monarch, The.
Monastary, Tourliani, Mykonos.
Montelepre.
Moon, The.
Morning Hymn.
Morning Moment.
Mortal Place, The.
Mosaic.
Moscow Moment.
Mother and Son.
Motives.
Mourne Mountains.
Municipal Gallery Revisited, October 1954.
Music Lessons.
My Aunt Sarah and Uncle Joe.
My Brooklyn Uncle.
My Father.
My Father's Death in Hospital.
My Father's Ghost.
My Father's Mother.
My Father's Voice.
My First Reported Words.
My Future Wife.
My Grandfather Dies, 1923.
My Grandmother Robinson.
My Grandmother's Garter.
My Grandmother's Restlessness.
My Great-Grandfather's Refusal.

My Mother.
My Naming.
My Own and Not My Own.
My Parents' Courtship.
My Sister.
My Teachers.
My Uncle.
My Uncle Johnny.
My Uncle Willy.
My Widowed Mother.
Mycenae and Epidaurus.
Mykonos.
Name and Number.
Names We Used, The.
Nebula.
Neglected Lane, The.
Neighbor's Funeral, A.
Neither an Elegy Nor a Manifesto.
Nettles of Offence.
New Jerusalem.
New Jerusalem 1.
New Jerusalem 2.
Nicolai, Courier in Belgrade.
1957–1972.
Nineteen Sixteen, or the Terrible Beauty.
96 Clifton Park Avenue and the Robinsons.
No Comment!
No Cresta Run.
No Second Troy.
North-West Passage: An Old Man Dying.
Northern Spring.
Note on Intellectuals.
Nourish Your Heart.
November Park.
November Wood.
Novice, The.
Now in the Spring.
O Country People.
Ocean, 1940.
October-Born.
October Sonnets.
October's Child.
Of a Professor.
Old Corinth.
Old Men Sitting.
Old Mill-Race, The.
Omens and Auguries.
On a Country Bus Forty Years Ago.
On a January Train Journey.
On Choosing Some Verses for My Sister's
  Cremation.
On Colinward: The Scattering.
On Dunmore's Waste.
On Hearing a Traveller's Tale of the Alps.
On Reading Terence de Vere White on
  Landor.
On Reading Wallace Stevens' *Collected
  Poems* after Many Years.
On the Canal.
On the Choice of a Title.
On the Grand Dublin Canal: Musing on the
  "Two Nations" Theory.
On the Preservation of Work Sheets.
On the Use of Dialect Words.
Once Alien Here.
One I Loved, The.
Open Eye, The.
Ophelia.
Orchard Country.
Orientations.
Ossian's Grave, Lubitavish, County Antrim.
Our Avenue.
Our Sunday School Teacher.
Outside the Creeds.
Overture for an Ulster Literature.
Owl, The.
Paid Quarterly.
Palimpsest.
Palmist, The.
Pangur Ban.
Paper Banners.
Parallels Never Meet.
Paraphrase of Verses by Mayakovsky.
Passion.
Path Ahead, The.
Pavane for a Dead Professor.
Peace Pact.

Pendragon.
Periodicity.
Pet Shop, The.
Peter Peri (1899-1967).
Pioneer.
Ploughman, The.
Poem: "Consider Wordsworth in his withered
  age."
Poem in May.
Poem: "My name is Revolution—let me
  speak."
Poetry, Then.
Poet's Trade, The.
Portrait, The.
Portraits on the Walls.
Portstewart, 1914.
Portstewart, July 1914.
Postscript, 1984.
Practical Mysticism.
Prague, or Novotny, If You Remember Him.
Prelude to an Ode for Barnum.
Prelude to Consternation.
Priest Goes through the Motions of the Play,
  The.
Prime Minister.
Prisoners on the Roof, The.
Pro Tanto Quid Retribuamas.
Prologue for an Evening at the Whitefriars.
Providence 1.
Providence 3.
Providence 2.
Psychometrist's Remarkable Forecast, The.
Raindrop.
Ram's Horn, The.
Rank-and-Filer, The.
Reading.
Real Estate.
Rebel, The.
Reference, The.
Remembering a Conversation: Itzik Manger
  at the PEN Conference, Edinburgh, 1950.
Resource.
Response, The.
Retreaded Rhymes.
Return (1885), The.
Return, The.
Revenant.
Rhyme for Blake, A.
Rhyme for Christmas Morning, A.
Riders, The.
Rite.
Rite, Lubitavish, Glenaan.
River Streets, The.
R.K.
Roll Call.
Roman Fort, The.
Romantic, The.
Rome Sunday[,] June 1960.
Roseblade's Visitants and Mine.
Rotterdam.
R.P.M.
Ruins Answer, The.
Saint Patrick.
St Rosalie: Monte Pellegrino.
St Stephen's Day.
Salute.
Salute to Matthew Arnold.
Sanctuary.
Sap in the Sticks Again.
Sarcophagus.
Scar, The.
Scarlatina.
Scattering, The.
School Upstairs, The.
Scissors For a One-Armed Tailor.
Scottish Interlude.
Search, The.
Seaside Town, A.
Season's End.
Season's Return.
Second Front: Double Summertime, July
  1943.
Seeding Time.
Seedsman, The.
September Lull.
Sheep Fair.
Sheep Skull, The.

Shortened Day, The.
Silver Was the Barbèd Hook.
Simple-Minded Christian, The.
Skypiece.
Song for May Day.
Song of the Shipyard Men, The.
Songs I Sing, The.
Sonnet: "Among the many selves that throng
  my flesh."
Sonnet: "By the sea's edge, on gravel and on
  sand."
Sonnet: "I have no time to worship. I must
  live."
Sonnet: "I think of Glasgow, where
  reluctantly."
Sonnet: "I thought tonight of all the lovers
  gone."
Sonnet in Autumn.
Sonnet: "Our love is full of memorable
  things."
Sonnet: "Since brooding men put beauty in a
  rime."
Sonnet: "There in the lonely quarry where at
  dawn."
Sonnet: "When I have read your hard and
  lively words."
Sonnets for Roberta (1954) *sels.*
Sonnets in October.
Souterrain, The.
Sparrowhawk.
Spectacle of Truth, The.
Splendid Dawn, The.
Spring of the Year.
Spring Restored, The.
S.S.K.
Stallion.
Stoat, The.
Stone.
Storm, The.
Strangers and Neighbors.
Street Names.
Style.
Substance and Shadow.
Suburb.
Suburban Spring in Warwickshire.
Summer Arcady.
Summer Park.
Sunset.
Sunset over Glenaan.
Survival.
Swan.
Swan's Nest.
Swathe Uncut, The.
Teacher's Residence, The.
Teetotal Master.
Terrible Choice, The.
Test, The.
This Antrim Air in Summer.
This Is No Land of Constable and Clare.
This Narrative.
This Then My Country.
Those Morning Walks.
Those Swans Remember; A Poem.
Three Horatian Odes.
Thresher, The.
Threshing, The.
Timber.
Tinker's Answer, The.
Tiphead.
To a Modern Irish Poet.
To Any Dweller in Lewis Street.
To Be Used in an Address Delivered at the
  Unveiling of a Plaque Commemorating
  "George A. Birmingham."
To Piraeus.
To Robert Telford Hewitt.
To the Memory of James Connolly.
To the People of Dresden.
Torcello.
Touch of Things, The.
Townland of Peace.
Triad ("Three sounds of peace and rich
  increase").
Triad ("Three things that men may scorn").
Tribunes, The.
Tricycle, The.
Tristan: The Lay of the Goatleaf *sels.*

Troubles, 1922, The.
True Smith of Tieveragh, The.
Tryst.
Tumbling Spore, The.
Turban, The.
Turf-Carrier [or Turf Carrier] on Aranmore.
Twelfth of July, The.
21st September 1912.
Twisted Heart, The.
Two Irish Saints.
Two Sonnets.
Two Sonnets on the Free State of Censorship
  Bill.
Two Spectres Haunt Me.
Ulster Landowner's Song, An.
Ulster Names.
Ulster Winter (1942).
Ulsterman.
Ulsterman, An.
Ulsterman in England Remembers, An.
Uncle Dick and Aunt Bertha.
Uncle Sam and Aunt Edie.
Unnecessary Dread, The.
Valediction Lines to My WEA Students.
Values.
Variations on a Theme.
Vers Libre.
Victorian Steps Out, A.
Vida, Mykonos.
Vigil.
Volunteer, The.
Wake, The.
Watchers, The.
Watercolour, The.
Way to School, The.
We too have gone down little roads in
  spring.
Wedding Present, The.
Well-Intentioned Consul, The.
What Little Happened There.
Wheel, The.
When the Bell Rings in the Steeple.
Whit Monday.
Who Was C.B. Fry?
Will.
William Conor RHA, 1881–1968.
William J. McClughin.
Willow Pattern.
Winter Day.
Winter Park.
Witch, The.
With a Little Book of Pottery.
With E.M.F. on 28th December 1965.
Word, The.
W.R. Rodgers.
W.R.R.
YCVS and the Ulster Division, The.
Year of Grace and My Great-Grandfather.
Young Womanhood.
Translations, Coauthored Poems, etc.:
Matin sur le Port.
Pour Hélène.

Hill, Geoffrey (b. 1932)
After Cumae.
Annunciations.
Apology for the Revival of Christian
  Architecture in England, An.
Apostles: Versailles, 1919, The.
Asmodeus.
Assisi Fragments, The.
Bibliographers, The.
Bidden Guest, The.
Canaan.
Canticle for Good Friday.
Christmas Trees.
Churchill's Funeral.
Coplas.
Cowan Bridge; At the Site of 'Lowood
  School.'
Cycle.
Damon's Lament for his Clorinda, Yorkshire
  1654.
De Jure Belli ac Pacis.
Dead Bride, The.
Death of Shelley, The.
Distant Fury of Battle, The.
Doctor Faustus.

Domaine Public.
Drake's Drum.
Elegiac Stanzas: On a Visit to Dove Cottage.
Emblem, The.
Eve of St Mark, The.
Fantasia on 'Horbury'; John Bacchus Dykes,
  1859.
Fear, The.
Fidelities.
Florentines.
Four Poems Regarding the Endurance of
  Poets.
From the Latin.
Funeral Music.
Genesis.
God's Little Mountain.
Good Husbandry.
Guardians, The.
Herefordshire Carol, The.
History as Poetry.
Holy Thursday.
Humanist, The.
Hymns to Our Lady of Chartres.
I Had Hope When Violence Was Ceas't.
Idylls of the King.
Imaginative Life, The.
In Memory of Jane Fraser [or Frazer].
In Piam Memoriam.
Lachrimae Amantis.
Lachrimae Antiquae Novae.
Lachrimae Coactae.
Lachrimae; or Seven Tears Figured in Seven
  Passionate Pavans.
Lachrimae Verae.
Laurel Axe, The.
Letter from Armenia, A.
Little Apocalypse; Hölderlin: 1770–1843.
Locust Songs.
Loss and Gain.
Lowlands of Holland, The.
Martyrdom of Saint Sebastian.
Martyrium.
Masque of Blackness, The.
Men Are a Mockery of Angels.
Mercian Hymns.
Merlin.
Metamorphoses.
Mobile, immaculate and austere.
Mystery of the Charity of Charles Péguy,
  The.
Ode on the Loss of the Titanic.
Of Coming-into-Being and Passing-Away.
Of Commerce and Society: Variations on a
  Theme.
Old Poet with Distant Admirers.
Order of Service, An.
Orpheus and Eurydice.
Ovid in the Third Reich.
Pavana Dolorosa.
Pentecost Castle, The.
Picture of a Nativity.
Postures.
Prayer to the Sun, A.
Pre-Raphaelite Notebook, A.
Psalms of Assize.
Quaint Mazes.
Re-birth of Venus, The.
Requiem for the Plantagenet Kings.
Respublica.
Ritornelli.
Scenes with Harlequins.
September Song.
Shiloh Church, 1862: Twenty–Three
  Thousand.
Short History of British India (I), A.
Short History of British India (III), A.
Short History of British India (II), A.
Sobieski's Shield.
Soliloquies.
Solomon's Mines.
Song Contest.
Song from Armenia, A.
Songbook of Sebastian Arrurruz, The.
Sorrel.
Stone Man, The.
Tenebrae.

Terribilis Est Locus Iste; *Gaugin and the
  Pont-Aven School.*
Three Baroque Meditations.
To His Wife.
To the Nieuport Scout.
To the (Supposed) Patron.
Tristia: 1891–1938.
Troublesome Reign, The.
Turtle Dove, The.
Two Chorale-Preludes: On Melodies by Paul
  Celan.
Two Formal Elegies.
Veni Coronaberis.
Vocations.
White Ship, The.
Who Are These Coming to the Sacrifice?
Wreaths.

Hoffman, Daniel Gerard (b. 1923)
After God.
Another Border.
Another Country.
Ants.
Aphrodite.
April, An.
Armada of Thirty Whales, An.
As I Was Going to Saint-Ives.
Asleep.
At Don's Garage.
At Evening.
At Provincetown.
At the Roman Wall, 1956.
Aubade: "Weaned from moon."
Auricle's Oracle.
Awoke into a Dream of Singing.
Banished.
Barn Burnt in Ohio, A.
Battle of Hastings, The.
Blood.
Boar.
Brainwaves.
Breathing Purely.
Burning Bush.
Casualty, A.
Center of Attention, The.
Chosen, The.
City of Satisfactions, The.
Clams, The.
Climbing Katahdin.
Comanches.
Companion, The.
Crack!
Crop-Dusting.
Crossing Walt Whitman Bridge.
Dark of the Moon.
David's Folly.
Dijon.
Dogfish.
Dread, A.
Dreamer, The.
Eagles.
Egg.
Ephemeridae.
Essay on Style.
Evening.
Exploration.
Far-Off Light.
February.
Felled Tree, A.
Finish, The.
First Flight.
Flushing Meadows, 1939.
Folk Tale.
Fontaine-les-Dijon Revisited.
Fortune, A.
Gestures.
Great American Novel, The.
Great Horse Strode without a Rider, The.
Great Owl.
Halflives.
He was the first who had returned.
Her Obedient Servant.
Hermit of Cape Rosier, The.
High Society.
Himself.
His Steps.
Historian, A.
I Am the Sun.

I Dreamt My Love A-Dying Lay.
In Provence.
In That High House.
In the Beginning.
In the Days of Rin-Tin-Tin.
In the Graeco-Roman Room.
In the Pitch of Night.
Incubus.
Instructions to a Medium, to be Transmitted to the Shade of W.B. Yeats, the Latter Having Responded in a Séance Held on 13 June 1965, Its Hundredth Birthday.
Inviolable.
It cannot come because desired.
Jogger.
Keys.
Larks, The.
Last Arrival, The.
Last Lynx.
Letter to W.H. Auden, A.
Letter to William Frohock.
Lines for Jack Clemo.
Lines for Scott Nearing.
Mark Twain, 1909.
Marked Man, A.
Marriage, A.
Meeting, A.
Mi-Carême.
Mother.
Moving among the Creatures.
Natural Philosopher, A.
New Birth, A.
Night Fishing.
1956.
Northern Lights.
O Personages.
Ode to Joy.
Old Bug up There.
Old Reprobate.
On the Extinction of a Species.
On the Industrial Highway.
Open Letter, Returning a Questionnaire Unanswered.
Over the Rim.
Peaceable Kingdom, The.
Poem, The: "Arriving at last."
Possession.
Power.
Princess Casamassima, The.
Print-Out Song.
Problems of Knowledge.
Pursued, The.
Rats.
Reasons.
Reflections.
Resolution.
Runner.
Sacred Fount, The.
Safari.
Saint-Apollinaire.
Scrolls from the Dead.
Seals in Penobscot Bay, The.
Shaking the President's Hand.
Shell.
Shrew.
Sickness.
Signatures.
Singing.
Slick.
Snatches for Charles Ives.
Snow.
Solitary, A.
Sonnet, The: "Sonnet, she told the crowd of bearded, The."
Sounds, The.
Special Train, A.
Stillness, A.
Stone, A.
Stop the Deathwish! Stop It! Stop!
Summer Solstice.
Summerhouse, The.
Tale-Teller, The.
Testament.
That Morning.
That the Pear Delights Me Now.
Thaw.
There.

This Silence.
Thought I Was Dying.
Translators' Party, The.
Tree.
Trip, A.
Twentieth Century, The.
Unchosen, The.
Vezelay.
Victor, The.
Visitation, A.
Voice of the Woodthrush, Played at Half Speed, The.
Vows.
Waking, A.
Wanderer, The.
Wastrel, The.
Way He Went, The.
Way It Is, The.
When my wiser brother.
Wherever.
Who was it came.
Witnesses.
Woe, A.
Words.
Words for Dr. Williams.

Holmes, John Clellon (1926–88)
Bad Turn, A.
Berryman's Dead.
Chinese Poets.
Cold Window.
Death Drag (The Elegist).
Decline of the West.
Dire Coasts.
Doctor Trustus: Man of Good Will.
Dying Lawrence.
Fayetteville Dawn (1).
Fayetteville Dawn (2).
Fear in the Afternoon.
For Walker Evans.
Instructions for the World Librarian.
Lawrence in Taos.
Les Italiennes.
Memoirs of an Imaginary Man, The.
Midnight Oil.
Mouth.
Muse Wooing: A Song.
Night Music.
Northfork October Return.
Obituary for Jan Masaryk.
Old Saybrook House, The.
Out of a Fever: For Robert Lowell (Sept. 13, 1977).
Petition Concerning the Death-Wish.
Premonitory July.
Sade on Calvary.
Samoan Head.
Statements in a Personal Winter.
Storm in the Ozarks.
Survivors, The.
Suzy Q, The.
Sweet Charity.
Too-Late Words to My Father.
Unwanted 1943 Chappaqua Flashback.
Vignette.
Vocation, The.
Watching Morning In.
Weekend Away.
Women in A.M.
Work on in the faith.
Writing the Atheneum talk, I wonder.
Year's End.

Hopkins, Gerard Manley (1844–89)
Ad Episcopum Salopiensem.
Ad Mariam.
Ad Matrem Virginem.
Ad Reverendum Patrem Fratrem Thomam Burke O.P. Collegium S. Beunonis Invisentem.
Alchemist in the City, The.
All as that moth call'd Underwing, alighted.
Andromeda.
Angelus Ad Virginem.
As it fell upon a day.
As kingfishers catch fire, dragonflies draw flame.
Ashboughs.
At the Wedding March.

Barnfloor and Winepress.
Basket broad of woven white rods, A.
Beginning of the End, The.
Bellisle! that is a fabling name, but we.
Binsey Poplars (Felled 1879).
Blessed Virgin Compared to the Air We Breathe, The.
Boughs being pruned, birds preenèd, show more fair.
Brothers.
Bugler's First Communion, The.
But what indeed is ask'd of me?
By Mrs. Hopley.
By One of the Old School Who Was Bid to Follow Mr. Browning's Flights.
Caged Skylark, The.
Candle Indoors, The.
Carrion Comfort.
Castara Victrix.
Cheery Beggar.
Child is Father to the Man, The.
Cockle's Antibilious Pills.
Cold whip-adder unespied, The.
Come Unto These Yellow Sands.
Complaint, A.
Confirmed beauty will not bear a stress.
Continuation of R. Garnett's *Nix*.
Cywydd.
Daphne.
Dark-out Lucifer detesting this, The.
Dawn.
Denis, / Whose motionable, alert, most vaulting wit.
Did Helen steal my love from me?
Distance / Dappled with diminish'd trees.
Duns Scotus's Oxford.
During the eastering of untainted morns.
Earth and heaven, so little known, The.
Easter.
Easter Communion.
Ecquis Binas.
Elegiacs.
Elopement, The.
Epithalamion: "Hark, hearer, hear what I do; lend a thought now, make believe."
Escorial, The.
Felix Randal.
Floris in Italy.
For a Picture of Saint Dorothea.
Fragment of Anything You Like, A.
Fragments.
Fragments on St. Winefred.
From any hedgerow, any copse.
Full Fathom Five.
Furl of fresh-leaved dogrose down, The.
Glimmer'd along the square-cut steep.
God's Grandeur.
Habit of Perfection, The.
Haec te jubent salvere, quod possunt, loca.
Half-way House, The.
Handsome Heart, The.
Harry Ploughman.
He hath abolished the old drouth.
He might be slow and something feckless first.
Heaven-Haven.
Henry Purcell.
Her prime of life—cut down too soon.
—Hill / Heaven and every field, are still.
Hope holds to Christ.
How all is one way wrought!
Hurrahing in Harvest.
"I am like a slip of comet."
I hear a noise of waters drawn away.
I must hunt down the prize.
I wake and feel the fell of dark, not day.
Il Mystico.
In Honour of St. Alphonsus Rodriguez.
In S. Winefridam.
In the staring darkness.
In the Valley of the Elwy.
In Themclam Virginem.
Inundatio Oxoniana.
Inversnaid.
Io.
It was a hard thing to undo this knot.
Jesu Dulcis Memoria.

Justus Quidem Tu Es, Domine.
Lantern Out of Doors, The.
Late I fell in the ecstasy.
Leaden Echo and the Golden Echo, The.
Legetai Ti Khainon.
"Let me be to Thee as the circling bird."
Like Shuttles Fleet the Clouds.
Lines for a Picture of St. Dorothea.
Loss of the Eurydice, The.
Love me as I love thee. O double sweet!
Love Preparing to Fly.
Lover's Stars, The.
Margaret Clitheroe.
May Lines.
May Magnificat, The.
Miror surgentem per puram Oriona noctem.
Miss Story's character! too much you ask.
Modern Poets.
Moonless darkness stands between.
Moonrise June 19 1876.
Morning, Midday, and Evening Sacrifice.
Mothers are doubtless happier for their babes.
My Own Heart.
My prayers must meet a brazen heaven.
Myself unholy, from myself unholy.
New Readings.
Nightingale, The.
"No, they are come; their horn is lifted up."
No worst, there is none. Pitched past pitch of
grief.
Noise of falls I am possessèd by, A.
Nondum.
Not kind! to freeze me with forecast.
Now I am minded to take a pipe in hand.
O Death, Death, He is come.
O Deus, Ego Amo Te.
O what a silence is this wilderness!
O where is it, the wilderness.
Ochenaid Sant Francis Xavier, Apostol Yr
Indiaid.
On a Dunce Who Had Not a Word to Say
for Himself.
On a Poetess.
On One Who Borrowed His Sermons.
On St. Winefred.
On the Portrait of Two Beautiful Young
People.
Or else their cooings came from bays of
trees.
Oratio Patris Condren: O Jesu Vivens in
Maria.
Orpheus With His Lute Made Trees.
Patience, Hard Thing!
Peace.
Peacock's Eye, The.
Penmaen Pool.
Pied Beauty.
Pilate.
Proved Etherege prudish, selfish, hypocrite,
heartless.
Queen's Crowning, The.
Quique haec membra malis vis esse obnoxia
multis.
Rainbow, The.
Repeat That, Repeat.
Ribblesdale.
Richard.
Rosa Mystica.
S. Thomae Aquinatis Rhythmus ad SS.
Sacramentum.
St. Dorothea.
St. Winefred's Well.
Sea and the Skylark, The.
Sea Took Pity, The.
See how Spring opens with disabling cold.
Seven Epigrams.
Shakspere.
She Schools the Flighty Pupils of Her Eyes.
Shepherd's Brow, The.
Silver Jubilee, The.
Silver scarce-call-silver gloss, A.
Soldier, The.
Soliloquy of One of the Spies Left in the
Wilderness, A.
Songs from Shakespeare, in Latin and Greek.
Spelt from Sibyl's Leaves.
Spring.

Spring and Death.
Spring and Fall.
St. Thecla.
Starlight Night, The.
Stars were packed so close that night, The.
Stephen and Barberie.
Strike, churl; hurl, cheerless wind, then;
heltering hail.
Summa.
Summer Malison, The.
Tell Me Where Is Fancy Bred.
That Nature Is a Heraclitean Fire and of the
Comfort of the Resurrection.
Thee, God, I come from, to thee go.
Think of an opening page illuminèd.
Times are nightfall, look, their light grows
less, The.
To him who ever thought with love of me.
To His Watch.
To Oxford.
To R. B.
To Seem the Stranger.
To What Serves Mortal Beauty?
Tomorrow meet you? O not tomorrow.
Tom's Garland: Upon the Unemployed.
Trees by their yield.
Trio of Triolets, A.
Tristi Tu, Memini.
Unfinished Rendering of "When Icicles Hang
by the Wall."
Vision of the Mermaids, A.
Voice from the World, A.
What being in rank-old nature should earlier
have that breath been.
What Shall I Do for the Land that Bred Me.
When eyes that cast about the heights of
heaven.
Where art thou friend, whom I shall never
see.
While You Here Do Snoring Lie.
Why if it be so, for the dismal morn.
Why should their foolish bands, their
hopeless hearses.
Wildness.
Windhover, The.
Windy Day in Summer, A.
Winter with the Gulf Stream.
Woodlark, The.
Woods in Spring.
Wreck of the Deutschland, The.
—Yes for a time they held as well.
Translations, Coauthored Poems, etc.:
Horace: Odi Profanum Volgus Et Arceo.
Horace: Persicos Odi, Puer, Apparatus.
Incomplete Latin Version of "In all things
beautiful" by Robert Bridges.
Milton.
Odes sels.

Housman, Alfred Edward (1859–1936)
A. J. J.
Along the field as we came by.
As I gird on for fighting.
As through the wild green hills of Wyre.
Ask me no more, for fear I should reply.
Astronomy.
Atys.
Be still, my soul, be still; the arms you bear
are brittle.
Because I liked you better.
Bells in tower at evening toll.
Bredon Hill.
Bring, in this timeless grave to throw.
By shores and woods and steeples.
Carpenter's Son, The.
Chestnut casts his flambeaux, and the
flowers, The.
Clunton and Clunbury.
Could man be drunk for ever.
Crossing alone the nighted ferry.
Culprit, The.
Day of Battle, The.
Defeated, The.
Delight it is in youth and May.
Deserter, The.
Diffugere Nives.
Easter Hymn.
Eight O'Clock.

1887.
Epitaph, An: "Stay, if you list, O passer by
the way."
Epitaph on an Army of Mercenaries.
Epithalamium: "He is here, Urania's son."
Fairies break their dances, The.
Fancy's Knell.
Far in a western brookland.
Far known to sea and shore.
Farewell to a name and a number.
Farewell to barn and stack and tree.
Farms of home lie lost in even, The.
First of May, The.
For My Funeral.
For these of old the trader.
From far, from eve and morning.
From the wash the laundress sends.
Give me a land of boughs in leaf.
God's Acre.
Good creatures, do you love your lives.
Grenadier.
Half-moon westers low, my love, The.
Half-way, for one commandment broken.
He looked at me with eyes I thought.
He, standing hushed, a pace or two apart.
He would not stay for me; and who can
wonder?
Hell Gate.
Her strong enchantments failing.
Here are the skies, the planets seven.
Here dead lie we because we did not choose.
Ho, everyone that thirsteth.
How clear, how lovely bright.
Hughley Steeple.
I did not lose my heart in summer's even.
I hoed and trenched and weeded.
I lay me down and slumber.
I promise nothing: friends will part.
I shall not die for you.
I to my perils.
I wake from dreams and turning.
If it chance your eye offend you.
If truth in hearts that perish.
Illic Jacet.
Immortal Part, The.
In midnights of November.
In my own shire, if I was sad.
"In the morning, in the morning."
In valleys green and still.
Into my heart an air that kills.
Is my team ploughing.
Isle of Portland, The.
It is no gift I tender.
It nods and curtseys and recovers.
Lads in their hundreds to Ludlow come in
for the fair, The.
Lancer.
Land of Biscay, The.
Laws of God, the laws of man, The.
Lent Lily, The.
Like mine, the veins of these that slumber.
Loitering with a vacant eye.
Look not in my eyes, for fear.
Loveliest of trees, the cherry now.
March.
Merry Guide, The.
Mill-stream, now that noises cease, The.
"My dreams are of a field afar."
New Mistress, The.
New Year's Eve.
Night is freezing fast, The.
Now dreary dawns the eastern light.
Now hollow fires burn out to black.
Now to her lap the incestuous earth.
Oh fair enough are sky and plain.
Oh is it the jar of nations.
Oh on my breast in days hereafter.
Oh see how thick the goldcup flowers.
Oh stay at home, my lad, and plough.
Oh turn not in from marching.
Oh were he and I together.
Oh, when I was in love with you.
Oh who is that young sinner with the
handcuffs on his wrists?
Olive, The.
On forelands high in heaven.
On moonlit heath and lonesome bank.

On the idle hill of summer.
On Wenlock Edge the wood's in trouble.
On your midnight pallet lying.
Oracles, The.
Others, I am not the first.
Parta Quies.
R. L. S.
Rain, it streams on stone and hillock, The.
Rainy Pleiads wester, The.
Recruit, The.
Reveille.
Revolution.
Sage to the Young Man, The.
Say, lad, have you things to do?
"Shake hands, we shall never be friends, all's over."
Shot? so quick, so clean an ending?
Sigh that heaves the grasses, The.
Sinner's Rue.
Sloe was lost in flower, The.
Smooth between sea and land.
Soldier from the wars returning.
Some can gaze and not be sick.
Spring Morning.
Stars have not dealt me the worst they could do, The.
Stars, I have seen them fall.
Stone, steel, dominions pass.
Street sounds to the soldiers' tread, The.
Tarry, delight, so seldom met.
Tell Me Not Here [It Needs Not Saying].
Terence, This Is Stupid Stuff.
There pass the careless people.
They say my verse is sad: no wonder.
They shall have breath that never were.
Think no more, lad; laugh, be jolly.
This time of year a twelvemonth past.
'Tis five years since, "An end," said I.
'Tis time, I think, by Wenlock town.
To an Athlete Dying Young.
To stand up straight and tread the turning mill.
True Lover, The.
Twice a week the winter thorough.
Wake not for the world-heard thunder.
Weeping Pleiads wester, The.
We'll to the woods no more.
Welsh Marches, The.
West, The.
Westward on the high-hilled plains.
When Adam walked in Eden young.
When first my way to fair I took.
When green buds hang in the elm like dust.
When I came last to Ludlow.
When I was one-and-twenty.
When I watch the living meet.
When I would muse in boyhood.
When Israel out of Egypt came.
When smoke stood up from Ludlow.
When summer's end is nighing.
When the bells justle in the tower.
When the eye of day is shut.
When the lad for longing sighs.
White in the moon the long road lies.
Winds out of the west land blow, The.
With rue my heart is laden.
With seed the sowers scatter.
"World goes none the lamer, The"
Yon flakes that fret the eastern sky.
Yonder see the morning blink.
You smile upon your friend to-day.
Young is the blood that yonder.
Translations, Coauthored Poems, etc.:
Alcestis sels.
In heaven-high musings and many.
Now do our eyes behold.
Oedipus at Colonus sels.
Seven against Thebes, The sels.
What man is he that yearneth.

Hughes, Langston (1902–67)
Advice.
Africa.
Afro-American Fragment.
American Heartbreak.
Angels Wings.
Ardella.
Argument.

As Befits a Man.
As I Grew Older.
Aunt Sue's Stories.
Baby.
Bad Luck Card.
Bad Morning.
Ballad of the Fortune Teller.
Ballad of the Girl Whose Name Is Mud.
Ballad of the Gypsy.
Ballad of the Landlord.
Ballad of the Man Who's Gone.
Bar.
Be-Bop Boys.
Beale Street.
Black Maria.
Black Pierrot, A.
Blue Bayou.
Blue Monday.
Blues at Dawn.
Boogie: 1 A.M.
Border Line.
Bound No'th Blues.
Brothers.
Buddy.
Café: 3 A.M.
Casualty.
Catch.
Children's Rhymes.
Chord.
College Formal: Renaissance Casino.
Comment on Curb.
Consider Me.
Cora.
Corner Meeting.
Could Be.
Croon.
Cross.
Crossing.
Dancer.
Danse Africaine.
Daybreak in Alabama.
Dead in There.
Deferred.
Delinquent.
Demand.
Democracy.
Desert.
Desire.
Dime.
Dive.
Down and Out.
Dream.
Dream Boogie.
Dream Boogie: Variation.
Dream Dust.
Dream Variation[s].
Drum.
Drunkard.
Early Evening Quarrel.
Easy Boogie.
Elevator Boy.
End.
Ennui.
Evening Song.
Evil.
Fact.
Fantasy in Purple.
Feet o' Jesus.
50–50.
Final Curve.
Fire.
Fired.
Flatted Fifths.
Freedom Train.
Freedom's Plow.
Fulfilment.
Garden.
Gauge.
Genius Child.
Georgia Dusk.
Gone Boy.
Good Morning.
Graduation.
Green Memory.
Gypsy Melodies.
Hard Daddy.
Harlem.

Harlem Night Song.
Havana Dreams.
Heaven.
High to Low.
Homecoming.
Hope.
House in Taos, A.
I, Too.
In Explanation of Our Times.
In Time of Silver Rain.
Interne at Provident.
Island.
Jam Session.
Joe Louis.
Joy.
Judgment Day.
Juke Box Love Song.
Juliet.
Kid in the Park.
Kid Sleepy.
Ku Klux.
Lady's Boogie.
Lament over Love.
Late Last Night.
Lenox Avenue Mural sels.
Letter.
Life Is Fine.
Likewise.
Litany: "Gather up / In the arms of your pity."
Little Green Tree.
Little Lyric (of Great Importance).
Little Old Letter.
Live and Let Live.
Long Trip.
Love.
Lover's Return.
Low to High.
Luck.
Lunch in a Jim Crow Car.
Madam and Her Madam.
Madam and Her Might-Have-Been.
Madam and the Census Man.
Madam and the Charity Child.
Madam and the Fortune Teller.
Madam and the Minister.
Madam and the Number Writer.
Madam and the Phone Bill.
Madam and the Rent Man.
Madam and the Wrong Visitor.
Madam's Calling Cards.
Madam's Past History.
Magnolia Flowers.
Mama and Daughter.
March Moon.
Maybe.
Me and the Mule.
Mellow.
Merry-Go-Round.
Mexican Market Woman.
Midnight Dancer.
Midnight Raffle.
Midwinter Blues.
Migrant.
Misery.
Miss Blues'es Child.
Monroe's Blues.
Moonlight Night: Carmel.
Morning After.
Mother to Son.
Motto.
Movies.
Mulatto.
My People.
Mystery.
Natcha.
Necessity.
Negro.
Negro Mother, The.
Negro Speaks of Rivers, The.
Neighbor.
Neon Signs.
New Yorkers.
Night: Four Songs.
Night Funeral in Harlem.
Nightmare Boogie.
No Regrets.

Not a Movie.
Note on Commercial Theatre.
Numbers.
October 16 [: The Raid].
Old Walt.
One.
125th Street.
One-Way Ticket.
Parade.
Passing.
Personal.
Port Town.
Porter.
Prayer: "I ask you this."
Prayer Meeting.
Preference.
Projection.
Puzzled.
Question.
Railroad Avenue.
Refugee in America.
Relief.
Request.
Reverie on the Harlem River.
Roland Hayes Beaten (Georgia: 1942).
Ruby Brown.
S-sss-ss-sh!
Same in Blues.
Sea Calm.
Seascape.
Seashore through Dark Glasses (Atlantic City).
Shame on You.
Share-Croppers.
Shout.
Silhouette.
Sinner.
Sister.
Situation.
Sliver.
Sliver of Sermon.
Snail.
So Long.
Song for a Dark Girl.
Song for Billie Holiday.
South, The.
Southern Mammy Sings.
Spirituals.
Stars.
Still Here.
Stony Lonesome.
Strange Hurt.
Street Song.
Subway Rush Hour.
Suicide's Note.
Summer Evening (Calumet Avenue).
Sun Song.
Sunday by the Combination.
Sunday Morning Prophecy.
Sylvester's Dying Bed.
Tag.
Tambourines.
Tell Me.
Testimonial.
Theme for English B.
Third Degree.
To Artina.
To Be Somebody.
Tomorrow.
Troubled Woman.
Trumpet Player.
Ultimatum.
Uncle Tom.
Up-Beat.
Vagabonds.
Wake.
Warning.
Warning: Augmented.
Water-Front Streets.
Weary Blues, The.
West Texas.
What?
What? So Soon!
When Sue Wears Red.
Who But the Lord?
Widow Woman.
Wine-O.

Winter Moon.
Wonder.
World War II.
Young Gal's Blues.
Young Sailor.

Hughes, Ted (b. 1930)
And Owl.
And the Falcon Came.
And the Phoenix Has Come.
Apple Dumps.
Apple Tragedy.
At the bottom of the Arctic sea, they say.
Bang—a burning, A.
Bar-Toom TV.
Bayonet Charge.
Birth of Rainbow.
Black Beast, The.
Boom.
Bowled Over.
Bride and Groom Lie Hidden for Three Days.
Bull Moses, The.
Cadenza.
Calves harshly parted from their mamas.
Cat and Mouse.
Childish Prank, A.
Cleopatra to the Asp.
Collision with the earth has finally come—.
Coming Down through Somerset.
Contender, The.
Couples Under Cover.
Cranefly in September, A.
Crow *sels*.
Crow and the Birds.
Crow Hill.
Crow's First Lesson.
Crow's Last Stand.
Curlews Lift.
Dawn's Rose.
Dead Farms, Dead Leaves.
Dead, she became space-earth.
Deaf School.
Do Not Pick Up the Telephone.
Dove Came, The.
Dream Time, The.
Eagle.
Earth locked out the light, The.
Earth-Numb.
Egg-Head.
Emily Brontë.
Esther's Tomcat.
Examination at the Womb-Door.
Executioner, The.
Face was necessary—I found face.
Fallgrief's Girlfriends.
Famous Poet.
February 17th.
Fern.
Fire-Eater.
Football at Slack.
For Billy Holt.
Formal Auctioneer, The.
Fourth of July.
Full Moon and Little Frieda.
Gaudete *sels*.
Ghost Crabs.
Gnat-Psalm.
God, A.
Gog.
Goose.
Grass-blade is not without, The.
Green Wolf, The.
Harvest Moon, The.
Haunting, A.
Hawk Roosting.
Heptonstall.
Heptonstall Cemetery.
Heptonstall Old Church.
Her Husband.
Horrible Religious Error, A.
Horses, The.
How Water Began to Play.
Howling of Wolves, The.
I know well / You are not infallible.
I see the oak's bride in the oak's grasp.
I walk / Unwind with activity of legs.
If mouth could open its cliff.

Jaguar, The.
Kafka.
Knight, The.
Kreutzer Sonata.
Life Is Trying to Be Life.
Littleblood.
Lovepet, The.
Lovesong: "He loved her and she loved him."
Man Seeking Experience Enquires His Way of a Drop of Water, The.
March Calf, A.
Martyrdom of Bishop Farrar, The.
Mascot, The.
Mayday on Holderness.
Meeting.
Motorbike, A.
Mount Zion.
Mountains.
New Moon in January.
Night Arrival of Sea-Trout.
Notes for a Little Play.
November.
Now I know I never shall.
Now You Have to Push.
October Dawn.
October Salmon, An.
Once I said lightly.
Otter, An.
Out.
Owl's Song.
Pibroch.
Pike.
Primrose petal's edge, A.
Prometheus on His Crag *sels*.
Prospero and Sycorax.
Rat's Dance, The.
Ravens.
Relic.
Remembrance Day.
Retired Colonel, The.
Risen, The.
Rock Has Not Learned.
Roe-Deer.
Salmon Eggs.
Scapegoats and Rabies.
Second Glance at a Jaguar.
Seven Dungeon Songs *sels*.
Sheep.
Six Young Men.
Skylarks.
Snowdrop.
Soliloquy: "Whenever I am got under my gravestone."
Sometimes it comes, a gloomy flap of lightning.
Song: "O lady, when the tipped cup of the moon blessed you."
Song, The: "Did not want the air."
Speech Out of Shadow.
Stations.
Stealing Trout on a May Morning.
Still-Life.
Stone, The.
Strawberry Hill.
Sunstroke.
Swallow—rebuilding, The.
Swift Comes the Swift, The.
Swifts.
TV Off.
That Moment.
That Morning.
Theology.
This is the maneater's skull.
Thistles.
Thought-Fox, The.
Thrushes.
Tiger-Psalm.
Tractor.
Tutorial.
Two Minute's Silence.
View of a Pig.
Wadsworth Moor.
Warriors of the North, The.
Waving goodbye, from your banked hospital bed.
West Laithe.

When Men Got to the Summit.
Widdop.
Wild Duck, The.
Wilfred Owen's Photographs.
Wind.
Wind Flashes the Grass, A.
Wino.
Witches.
Wit's End.
Wodwo.
Woman in the Valley, The.
Woman Unconscious, A.
You Hated Spain.
Your tree—your oak.

Hugo, Richard (1923–82)
After a Train Trip, One Town Remains.
Again, Kapowsin.
Alki Beach.
Anacortes-Sydney Run, The.
Announcement.
Antiques in Ellettsville.
Antisocial Easter.
Approaching the Castle.
April in Cerignola.
Argo.
Art of Poetry, The.
Ashville.
At Cronkhite.
At Our Best.
At the Cabin.
At the Stilli's Mouth.
Ayr.
Back of Gino's Place.
Bad Eyes Spinning the Rock.
Bad Vision at the Skagit.
Ballad of the Upper Bumping.
Ballpark at Moiese, The.
Bannerman's Island.
Bass.
Bassetti's Lions.
Bay of Recovery.
Bay of Resolve.
Bay of Sad Loss.
Beachthieves.
Bear Paw.
Beaverbank.
Beggar in Sapri.
Belt.
Between the Bridges.
Birthday.
Blond Road, The.
Blue Stone.
Bone Hunting.
Bouquets from Corley.
Braes, The.
Bridge of Sighs, The.
Brief History.
Brown Stone.
Brueghel in the Doria.
Cairn in Loch An Duin, The.
Camas Prairie School.
Cantina Iannini.
Cape Alava.
Cape Nothing.
Carloway Broch.
Carnival Inside, The.
Castel Sant'Angelo.
Cataldo Mission.
Cattails.
Centuries near Spinnazola.
Changes at Meridian.
Changes in Policy at Taholah.
Chapel Further West than Most, A.
Christmas with Shepherds in Brefaro.
Church on Comiaken Hill, The.
Chysauster.
Clachard.
Clearances, The.
Cleggan.
Clouds of Uig, The.
Colors of a Bird, The.
Confederate Graves in Little Rock.
Cornwall, Touring.
Crinan Canal.
Cripples, The.
Culloden.
Dancer at Kozani's.

Death in the Aquarium.
Death of the Kapowsin Tavern.
December 24, Alone.
December 24 and George McBride Is Dead.
Degrees of Gray in Philipsburg.
Digging Is an Art.
Distances.
District in the City, A.
Dixon.
Docking at Palermo.
Dog Lake with Paula.
Doing the House.
Driving Montana.
Druid Stones at Kensaleyre.
Drums in Scotland.
Duntulm Castle.
Duwamish.
Duwamish Head.
Duwamish No. 2.
Dwelling.
Eighteen Days in a Tuscan World.
Eileen.
Elegy: "I expected him to look dead in the
   casket."
End of Krim's Pad, The.
Fairfield.
Farmer, Dying.
Ferniehirst Castle.
Field of wind gave license for defeat, A.
First South and Cambridge.
Flying, Reflying, Farming.
For a Northern Woman.
For Jennifer, 6, on the Teton.
Fort Benton.
Fort Casey, without Guns.
Freaks at Spurgin Road Field, The.
From Altitude, the Diamonds.
From the Rain Forest Down.
G. I. Graves in Tuscany.
Galileo's Chair.
Galleria Umberto I.
George Stubbs at Yale.
Getty.
Ghost in a Field of Mint.
Ghosts at Garnet.
Glen Uig.
Gold Man on the Beckler, The.
Gold Stone.
Good Day for Seeing Your Limitations, A.
Good View from Flagstaff, A.
Goodbye, Iowa.
Gooseprairie.
Graves.
Graves at Coupeville.
Graves at Elkhorn.
Graves at Mukilteo.
Graves in Queens.
Graves in Uig.
Gray Stone.
Green Stone.
Greystone Cottage.
Gull Hardly Explained, The.
Guns at Fort Flagler.
Hawk in Uig.
Helena, Where Homes Go Mad.
Here, but Unable to Answer.
Hideout.
High Grass Prairie.
Hilltop, The.
History of the Sketch, A.
Holy Family.
Hot Springs.
House on 15th S.W., The.
Houses.
Houses Lie, Believe the Lying Sea.
How Meadows Trick You.
How to Use a Storm.
Imagining Delaware.
In Stafford Country.
In Your Bad Dream.
In Your Big Dream.
In Your Blue Dream.
In Your Dream after Falling in Love.
In Your Dream on the Eve of Success.
In Your Fugitive Dream.
In Your Good Dream.
In Your Hot Dream.

In Your Racing Dream.
In Your Small Dream.
In Your War Dream.
In Your Wild Dream.
In Your Young Dream.
Index.
Indian Girl.
Indian Graves at Jocko.
Introduction to the Hoh.
Invasion North.
Iowa Déjà Vu.
Italian Town Abandoned.
Kapowsin.
Keen to Leaky Flowers.
Kennedy Ucciso.
Keokuk.
Kilmuir Cemetery: Stone with Two Skulls
   and No Name.
Kilmuir Cemetery: The Knight in Blue-Green
   Relief.
La Push.
Lady in Kicking Horse Reservoir, The.
Lake Byron, Maybe Gordon Lord.
Landscapes.
Langaig.
Last Day There.
Last Words from Maratea.
Last Words to James Wright.
Late Summer, Drummond.
Leaving the Dream.
Lecture.
Letter to Ammons from Maratea.
Letter to Annick from Boulder.
Letter to Bell from Missoula.
Letter to Birch from Deer Lodge.
Letter to Blessing from Missoula.
Letter to Bly from La Push.
Letter to Gale from Ovando.
Letter to Garber from Skye.
Letter to Gildner from Wallace.
Letter to Goldbarth from Big Fork.
Letter to Haislip from Hot Springs.
Letter to Hanson from Miami.
Letter to Hill from St. Ignatius.
Letter to Kathy from Wisdom.
Letter to Kizer from Seattle.
Letter to Levertov from Butte.
Letter to Libbey from St. Regis.
Letter to Logan from Milltown.
Letter to Mantsch from Havre.
Letter to Matthews from Barton Street Flats.
Letter to Mayo from Missoula.
Letter to Oberg from Pony.
Letter to Peterson from the Pike Place
   Market.
Letter to Reed from Lolo.
Letter to Scanlon from Whitehall.
Letter to Simic from Boulder.
Letter to Sister Madeline from Iowa City.
Letter to Snyder from Montana.
Letter to Stafford from Polson.
Letter to Wagoner from Port Townsend.
Letter to Welch from Browning.
Letter to Wright from Gooseprairie.
Listen, Ripley.
Living Alone.
Lone Cheer from the Stands for a Bitter
   Crane.
Lone Lake, Whidbey.
Making Certain It Goes On.
Map of Montana in Italy, A.
Map of Skye, A.
Map of the Peninsula, A.
Maratea Antica.
Maratea Porto.
Maratea Porto: Saying Good-bye to the
   Vitolos.
Maratea Porto: The Bitter Man.
Maratea Porto: The Dear Postmistress There.
Medicine Bow.
Memoirs.
Mendocino, Like You Said.
Meridian.
Mill at Romesdal.
Milltown Union Bar, The.
Mission in Carmel.
Mission to Linz.

Missoula Softball Tournament.
Montana Ranch Abandoned.
Montesano Unvisited.
Montgomery Hollow.
Morning in Padova.
Museum of Cruel Days.
My Buddy.
Name the Mystery Fin and Win a Doll.
Napoli Again.
Near Kalalock.
Neighbor.
Ness.
Night at the Napi in Browning, A.
Night with Cindy at Heitman's, A.
No Bells to Believe.
North.
Northwest Retrospective: Mark Tobey.
Note from Capri to Richard Ryan on the
    Adriatic Floor.
Note to R. H. from Strongsville.
Spinazzola: *Quella Cantina Là*.
O-Mok-See at Nine Mile.
Ocean on Monday.
Ode to the Trio Fruit Company of Missoula.
Old Map of Uhlerstown.
Old Scene.
On Hearing a New Escalation.
One by Twachtman at the Frye.
One Son North to Naples.
Only Bar in Dixon, The.
Open Country.
Or Another Place.
Orcas in the Eyes.
Other Beaverbank, The.
Other Grave, The.
Ovando.
Overlooking Yale.
Paestum.
Park at Villammare, The.
Phoning from Sweathouse Creek.
Picnic in the Saracen Ruin, The.
Pike Place Market.
Piping to You on Skye from Lewis.
Pishkun.
Pishkun Reservoir.
Pizzeria S. Biagio.
Places and Ways to Live.
Plans for Altering the River.
Plunking the Skagit.
Poem for Zen Hofman.
Point No Point.
Politely like Snakes in the Oats.
Port Townsend.
Port Townsend, 1974.
Prado: Bosch: S. Antonio, The.
Prado: Number 2671, Anonimo Español, The.
Reading at the Old Federal Courts Building,
    St. Paul.
Reclamation at Coloma.
Reconsidering the Madman.
Red Stone.
Remember Graham.
Remote Farm on the Dubrovnik-Sarajevo
    Run.
Repairing the House, the Church, Restoring
    the Music.
Resulting from Magnetic Interference.
Right Madness on Skye, The.
River Now, The.
Road Ends at Tahola.
S. Miniato: One by Aretino.
Sailing Dalmatia.
Sailing from Naples.
St. Clement's: Harris.
St. Ignatius Where the Salish Wail.
St. John's Chapel.
Salt Water Story.
Sandbanks, The.
Saying Goodbye to Mrs. Noraine.
Scene.
Schoolgirl at Seola.
Second Chances.
Semi-Lunatics of Kilmuir, The.
Shark Island.
Silver Star.
1614 Boren.
Skykomish River Running.

Small Oil Left in the House We Rented in
    Boulder, The.
Snapshot of 15th S.W., A.
Snapshot of the Auxiliary, A.
Snapshot of Uig in Montana, A.
Sneosdal.
Snoqualmie.
Snow Poem.
Somersby.
Sound Track Conditional.
South Italy, Remote and Stone.
Spinning the Sava.
Squatter on Company Land, The.
Standing Stones of Callanish, The.
Starting Back.
Storm in Acquafredda.
Sweet Piece from Fontal.
Swimmer at Lake Edward, The.
Tahola.
Taneum Creek.
Three Stops to Ten Sleep.
Tiberio's Cliff.
Time to Remember Sangster.
Tinker Camp, The.
To Die in Milltown.
To Women.
Tony.
Topographical Map.
Towns We Know and Leave Behind, the
    Rivers We Carry with Us, The.
Tretitoli, Where the Bomb Group Was.
Triangle for Green Men.
Troubadour Removed, A.
Trout.
Trumpan.
Turtle Lake.
Two Graves in a Day.
2433, First Home, Last House in Missoula.
Uig Registrar.
Underwater Autumn.
Upper Voight's, to All the Cutthroat There.
View from Cortona, A.
Villager.
Viva La Resistènza.
Walking Praed Street.
Way a Ghost Behaves, The.
Way a Ghost Dissolves, The.
West Marginal Way.
What the Brand New Freeway Won't Go By.
What Thou Lovest Well Remains American.
Wheel of Fortune.
Where Jennie Used to Swim.
Where Mission Creek Runs Hard for Joy.
Where the House Was.
Where We Crashed.
White Center.
Why I Think of Dumar Sadly.
Why Sapri Will Never Be Italian.
With Anna at Camaldoli.
With Kathy in Wisdom.
With Melissa on the Shore.
With Ripley at the Grave of Albert
    Parenteau.
Yards of Sarajevo, The.

J

Jarrell, Randall (1914–65)

Above the waters in their toil.
Absent with Official Leave.
Afterwards.
Aging.
All or None.
And did she dwell in innocence and joy.
Angels at Hamburg, The.
Archangel' Song, The.
Augsburg Adoration, The.
Author to the Reader, The.
Automaton, The.
Bad Music, The.
Bamberg.
Bats.
Because of me, because of you.
Bird of Night, The.
Birth of Venus, The.
Black Swan, The.

Blind Man's Song, The.
Blind Sheep, The.
Boyg, Peer Gynt, the One Only One, The.
Breath of Night, The.
Bronze David of Donatello, The.
Burning the Letters.
Camp in the Prussian Forest, A.
Carnegie Library, Juvenile Division, The.
Charles Dodgson's Song.
Che Farò; Senza Euridice.
Child, The.
Childhood.
Children Selecting Books in a Library.
Children's Arms.
Chipmunk's Day, The.
Christmas Roses, The.
Cinderella.
City, City!
Clock in the Tower of the Church, The.
Come to the Stone.
Conversation with the Devil, A.
Country Life, A.
Country Was, The.
Cow wandering in the bare field, The.
Dead in Melanesia, The.
Dead, The.
Dead Wingman, The.
Death.
Death of the Ball Turret Gunner, The.
Description of Some Confederate Soldiers, A.
Deutsch durch Freud.
Dialogue between Soul and Body, A.
Difficult Resolution, The.
"Do such, wait so," you said; I waited. Did
    you wait?
Dream of Waking, The.
Dream, The.
Dreams.
Dummies.
Eighth Air Force.
Eine Kleine Nachtmusik.
Elementary Scene, The.
Emancipators, The.
End of the Rainbow, The.
English Garden in Austria, An.
Enormous Love, it's no good asking.
Essay on the Human Will, An.
Esthetic Theories: Art as Expression.
Evening.
Evening Star, The.
Face, The.
Faded.
Fairy Song.
Falling in love is never as simple.
Farewell Symphony, The.
Fat, aging, the child clinging to her hand.
Fear.
Field and Forest.
Field Hospital, A.
Fire at the Waxworks, The.
For the Madrid Road.
Forest Murmurs.
Forsaken Girl, The.
Front, A.
Game at Salzburg, A.
Germans Are Lunatics, The.
Ghost, a Real Ghost, A.
Ghost Story, A.
Girl Dreams That She Is Giselle, The.
Girl in a Library, A.
Gleaning.
Good-bye, Wendover; Good-bye, Mountain
    Home.
Great Night, The.
Grown-Up, The.
Gunner.
Hanged man on the gallows, The.
Happy Cat, The.
He.
Head of Wisdom, The.
Hohensalzburg: Fantastic Variations on a
    Theme of Romantic Character.
Hope.
House in the Wood, The.
Hunt in the Black Forest, A.
I loved you, too. There was no use. I had no
    time.

Iceberg, The.
In a Hospital Garden.
In Galleries.
In Montecito.
In Nature There Is Neither Right nor Left nor
   Wrong.
In the Camp There Was One Alive.
In the Ward: The Sacred Wood.
In Those Days.
Indian Market in Mexico, An.
Indian, The.
Island, The.
Islands, The.
Jack.
Jamestown.
January 1938.
Jerome.
Jews at Haifa.
Jonah.
Kirilov on a Skyscraper.
Knight, Death, and the Devil, The.
La Belle au Bois Dormant.
Laboratory, The.
Lady Bates.
Lady on a Balcony, A.
Lament: "All is far."
Lament of the Children of Israel in Rome.
Le Poète Contumace.
Learners, The.
Leave.
Let's love each other for what we are.
Lines, The.
Little Poem, A.
London.
Lonely Man, The.
Loss.
Losses.
Lost Children, The.
Lost Love, The.
Lost World, The.
Lot is vacant still, The.
Love for One Orange, The.
Love, in its separate being.
Lullaby, A: "For wars his life and half a
   world away."
Machine-Gun, The.
Mail Call.
Man.
Man in Majesty.
Man Meets a Woman in the Street, A.
Man with the axe stands profound and
   termless, The.
Märchen, The.
Memoirs of Glückel of Hameln, The.
Metamorphoses, The.
Meteorite, The.
Miller, The.
Mockingbird, The.
Money.
Mother, Said the Child.
Moving.
My aunt kept turnips in a flock.
Nestus Gurley.
New Georgia.
News.
Next Day.
Night before the Night before Christmas,
   The.
Night with Lions, A.
1945: The Death of the Gods.
1914.
1938: Tales from the Vienna Woods.
1938: The Spring Dances.
90 North.
Nollekens.
Northern Snows, The.
November Ghosts, The.
Nursery Rhyme, A.
O My Name It Is Sam Hall.
O weary mariners, here shaded, fed.
Officers' Prison Camp Seen from a Troop-
   Train, An.
Old and the New Masters, The.
Old orchard in the middle of the forest, The.
Old Poems.
Old Song, An.
Olive Garden, The.

On the Railway Platform.
One Who Was Different, The.
Orestes at Tauris.
Orient Express, The.
Over the florid capitals.
Overture: The Hostages.
Owl's Bedtime Story, The.
Perfect Love Casteth Out Everything.
Perfectly Free Association, A.
Picture in the Paper, A.
Pilot from the Carrier, A.
Pilots, Man Your Planes.
Place of Death, The.
Player Piano, The.
Poem for Someone Killed in Spain, A.
Port of Embarkation.
Prayer at Morning, A.
Prince, The.
Princess Wakes in the Wood, The.
Prisoners.
Prologue to Wiley on November 17, 1941.
Protocols.
Quilt-Pattern, A.
Rabbit hurries to the brim of its wood, The.
Randall Jarrell, Office Hours 10-11.
Range in the Desert, The.
Reader, The.
Refugees, The.
Requiem for the Death of a Boy.
Rhapsody on Irish Themes, A.
Rising Sun, The.
Romance of Science, The.
Say Good-bye to Big Daddy.
Scherzo.
School of Summer, The.
Sears Roebuck.
Second Air Force.
Seductive Piece of Business, A.
See-er of Cities, The.
Seele im Raum.
1789–1939.
Sick Child, A.
Sick Nought, The.
Siegfried.
Sign, The.
Skaters, The.
Sleeping Beauty: Variation of the Prince,
   The.
Snow-Leopard, The.
Soldier, The.
Soldier Walks under the Trees of the
   University, The.
Soldier [T. P.].
Song: Not There.
Soul, A.
Sphinx's Riddle to Oedipus, The.
Stalag Luft.
State, The.
Story, A.
Street Has Changed, The.
Street off Sunset, A.
Subway from New Britain to the Bronx, The.
Summer Night, A.
Survivor among Graves, The.
Terms.
There Was Glass and There Are Stars.
Thinking of the Lost World.
Three Bills.
Time and the Thing-in-Itself in a Textbook.
Times Worsen, The.
To Be Dead.
To the New World.
Today is almost over.
Tower, The.
Transient Barracks.
Traveler, The.
Tree, The.
Trees in Spring, The.
Truth, The.
Unicorn, The.
Up in the sky the star is waiting.
Utopian Journey, A.
Variation on "To Say to Go to Sleep," A.
Variations.
Venetian Blind, The.
War, A.
Ward in the States, A.

Washing.
Washing the Corpse.
Ways and the Peoples, The.
Well-to-Do Invalid, A.
Well Water.
What was longed for and, once, certain.
What's the Riddle.
When Achilles fought and fell.
When I Was Home Last Christmas.
When you and I were all.
Wide Prospect, The.
Widow's Song, The.
Wild Birds, The.
Windows.
Winter's Tale, The.
Woman.
Woman at the Washington Zoo, The.
Women on a Bus.
X-Ray Waiting Room in the Hospital, The.
Zeno.

Jeffers, Robinson (1887–1962)
Advice to Pilgrims.
After Lake Leman.
Age in Prospect.
Air-Raid Rehearsals.
All night long the rush and trampling of
   water.
All the Little Hoof-Prints.
Animals.
Animula.
Answer, The.
Ante Mortem.
Antrim.
Apology for Bad Dreams.
Artist, An.
As the eye fails through age or disease.
Ascent to the Sierras.
At the Birth of an Age.
At the Fall of an Age.
At the near approach of a star..huge tides.
Autumn Evening.
Ave Caesar.
Battle.
Be Angry at the Sun.
Beach, The.
Beaks of Eagles, The.
Beautiful Captive, The.
Beauty of Things, The.
Bed by the Window, The.
Bird with the Dark Plumes, The.
Birds.
Birds and Fishes.
Birth and Death.
Birth-Dues.
Birthday.
Birthday (Autobiography).
Bixby's Landing.
Blind Horses.
Blood-Guilt, The.
Bloody Sire, The.
Boats in a Fog.
Bowl of Blood, The.
Broadstone, The.
Broken Balance, The.
Calm and Full the Ocean.
Carmel.
Carmel Point.
Cassandra.
Cawdor.
Clouds of Evening.
Coast-Road, The.
Come Little Birds.
Consciousness.
Contemplation of the Sword.
Continent's End.
Contrast.
Credo.
Cretan Woman, The.
Cruel Falcon, The.
Crumbs or the Loaf.
Curb Science?
Cycle, The.
Dawn.
Day is a Poem, The.
De Rerum Virtute.
Dead Men's Child, The.
Dead to Clemenceau: November 1929, The.

Dear Judas.
Decaying Lambskins.
Deer Lay Down Their Bones, The.
Delusion of Saints.
Diagram.
Distant Rainfall.
Divinely Superfluous Beauty.
Dog in the Sky, The.
Double Axe, The.
Drunken Charlie.
Eagle and hawk with their great claws and hooked heads.
Eagle Valor, Chicken Mind.
Edison.
End of the World.
Epic Stars, The.
Evening Ebb.
Excesses of God, The.
Explosion.
Extinct Vertebrate, An.
Eye, The.
Faith.
Fantasy.
Fawn's Foster-Mother.
Fire.
Fire on the Hills.
Flight of Swans.
Fog.
For fifty thousand years man has been dreaming of powers.
For Una.
Fourth Act.
Gale in April.
George Sterling.
George Sterling's Death.
Ghost.
Ghosts in England.
Giant's Ring, The.
Give Your Heart to the Hawks.
Give Your Wish Light.
Goethe, they say, was a great poet, Pindar, perhaps, was a great poet.
Going to Horse Flats.
Granddaughter.
Granite and Cypress.
Gray Weather.
Great Explosion, The.
Great Men.
Great Sunset, The.
Greater Grandeur.
Hand.
Hands.
Haunted Country.
Heavy and yellow with the clay wrack from the flooded valley.
Hellenistics.
Historical Choice.
Home.
Hooded Night.
Hope is Not for the Wise.
House Dog's Grave, The.
Humanist's Tragedy, The.
Hungerfield.
Hurt Hawks.
I am seventy-four years old and suddenly all my strength.
I have been warned. It is more than thirty years since I wrote.
I have told you in another poem, whether you've read it or not.
I saw a regiment of soldiers shuffling and stumbling.
I Shall Laugh Purely.
I walk on my cliff above the Pacific Ocean and feel the tides.
In the Hill at Newgrange.
Inhumanist, The.
Ink-Sack.
Inquisitors, The.
Inscription for a Gravestone.
Intellectuals.
Invasion.
Iona: the Graves of the Kings.
Irish Headland, An.
It flows out of mystery into mystery: there is no beginning—.
It is a pity the shock-waves.

It nearly cancels my fear of death, my dearest said.
It was good of my father, whom I hated at times.
Joy.
July Fourth by the Ocean.
King of Beasts, The.
Last Conservative, The.
Let Them Alone.
Life from the Lifeless.
Little Scraping, A.
Local Legend.
Love and the Hate, The.
Love-Children.
Love the Wild Swan.
Loving Shepherdess, The.
Low Sky, The.
Machine, The.
Maid's Thought, The.
Mara.
Margrave.
Mathematicians and physics men, The.
Medea.
Meditation on Saviors.
Memoir.
Metamorphosis.
Miching Mallecho.
Moments of Glory.
Monument.
Moon and Five Planets.
Morro Bay.
My Dear Love.
Natural Music.
Nerves.
Neutrals, The.
New Mexican Mountain.
New Year's Dawn, 1947.
New Year's Eve.
Night.
Night Without Sleep.
Nightpiece.
No Resurrection.
Noon.
Northern Heather.
Not Our Good Luck.
Nova.
November Surf.
Now Returned Home.
Ocean.
Ocean's Tribute, The.
October Evening.
October Week-End.
Ode to Hengist and Horsa.
Oh, Lovely Rock.
Old age hath clawed me with his scaly clutch.
Old half blinded hawk—but how can he hunt with only one eye?—, The.
Old Stone-Mason, The.
Old Wolf My Father, The.
On an Anthology of Chinese Poems.
On Building with Stone.
Orca.
Ordinary Newscaster, An.
Original Sin.
Ossian's Grave.
Our eyes by day are good enough: only the birds.
Oysters.
Palinode.
Passenger Pigeons.
Patronymic.
Pearl Harbor.
Pelicans.
People and a Heron.
Phenomena.
Place for No Story, The.
Pleasures.
Point Joe.
Point Pinos and Point Lobos.
Polar ice-caps are melting, the mountain glaciers, The.
Post Mortem.
Practical People.
Praise Life.
Prelude: "I drew solitude over me, on the lone shore."

Prescription of Painful Ends.
Purse-Seine, The.
Quia Absurdum.
Real and Half Real.
Rearmament.
Red Mountain.
Redeemer, A.
Reference to a Passage in Plutarch's Life of Sulla.
Resurrection.
Return.
Roan Stallion.
Rock and Hawk.
Salmon Fishing.
Salvage.
Science.
Second-Best.
Self-Criticism in February.
Seventieth Birthday.
Shakespeare's Grave.
Shane O'Neill's Cairn.
Shears, The.
Shine, Empire.
Shine, Perishing Republic.
Shine, Republic.
Shiva.
Shooting Season.
Sign-Post.
Silent Shepherds, The.
Sinverguenza.
Sirens, The.
Skunks.
So Many Blood-Lakes.
Soliloquy: "August and laurelled have been content to speak".
Solstice.
Soul's Desert, The.
Staggering Back Toward Life.
Stars Go Over the Lonely Ocean, The.
Steelhead, Wild Pig, the Fungus.
Still the Mind Smiles.
Stone Axe, The.
Storm blowing up, rain and dark weather and the roaring wind, The.
Subjected Earth.
Such Counsels You Gave to Me.
Summer Holiday.
Summit Redwood, The.
Tamar.
Teheran.
That Noble Flower.
Thebaid.
Their Beauty Has More Meaning.
Theory of Truth.
There is no God but God; he is all that exists.
There is this infinite energy, the power of God forever working.
Thurso's Landing.
Time of Disturbance.
To a Young Artist.
To Death.
To Kill in War Is Not Murder.
To the Children.
To the House.
To the Rock that Will Be a Cornerstone of the House.
To the Stone-Cutters.
To the Story-Tellers.
Tor House.
Torch-Bearers' Race, The.
Tower beyond Tragedy, The.
Trap, The.
Treasure, The.
Triad.
Two Christmas-Cards.
Unformed volcanic earth, a female thing, The.
Urchin, The.
Vices.
Vulture.
War-Guilt Trials.
Watch the Lights Fade.
We Are Those People.
What are Cities For?
What is Worthless?
What Odd Expedients.

What of It?
What's the best life for a man?
Where I?
Wilson in Hell.
Wind-Struck Music, The.
Winged Rock.
Wise Men in Their Bad Hours.
Women at Point Sur, The.
Woodrow Wilson.
World's Wonders, The.
Translations, Coauthored Poems, etc.:
Doctor Faustus.
Medea.
Translations from the *Medea* of Euripedes ("Err shall they not, who resolute explore").
Translations from the *Medea* of Euripedes ("The rites deriv'd from ancient days").
Was This the Face.

Johnson, Samuel (1709–84)
Aginst the Head which Innocence secures.
Ambition is the Stamp impress'd by Heav'n.
Ant, The.
Art thou too fall'n? ere anger could subside.
Aspasia, yet pursue the sacred Theme.
At my Command yon' Iron Gates unfold.
Aurora Est Musis Amica.
Burlesque Translation of Lines from Lope de Vega's *Arcadia.*
Celestial pow'rs! that piety regard.
Charade on Dr Thomas Barnard.
Epigram on Colley Cibber.
Epilogue to Horace's *Carmen Seculare.*
Epilogue to *The Distrest Mother,* An.
Epitaph on Claudy Phillips, a Musician, An.
Epitaph on William Hogarth, An.
Evening Ode, An.
Extempore Elegy, An.
Festina Lentè.
French Distichs.
Gnothi Seauton (Post Lexicon Anglicanum Auctum et Emendatum).
How Heav'n in Scorn of human Arrogance.
In Rivum a Mola Stoana Lichfeldiæ Diffluentem.
Irene *sels.*
Life's Last Scene.
Lines on Thomas Warton's Poems ("Wheresoe'er I turn my View").
Lines on Thomas Warton's Poems ("Hermit hoar, in solemn cell").
London: A Poem.
New Prologue Spoken at the Representation of *Comus,* A.
Ode, An: "Stern winter now, by spring repress'd."
Ode, De Skia Insula.
Ode on a Lady Leaving Her Place of Abode; Almost Impromptu, An.
Ode on Friendship, An.
On a Daffodil, the First Flower the Author Had Seen That Year.
On a Lady's Presenting a Sprig of Myrtle to a Gentleman.
On Gold.
On Hearing Miss Thrale Deliberate about Her Hat.
On Losing the Power of Speech.
On Seeing a Portrait of Mrs Montagu.
On the Death of Dr [*or* Mr] Robert Levet [a Practiser in Physic].
Parodies of Bishop Percy's *Hermit of Warkworth.*
Parva qudem regio, sed relligione primorum.
Power of Prayer, The.
Prayer: "Summe Deus, cui caeca patent penetralia cordis."
Prologue Spoken by Mr[.] Garrick at the Opening of the Theatre in Drury Lane, 1747.
Prologue to Garrick's *Lethe.*
Prologue to Goldsmith's *The Good Natur'd Man.*
Prologue to Hugh Kelly's *A Word to the Wise.*
Reply to Impromptu Verses by Baretti, A.

Short Song of Congratulation [*or* To a Young Heir], A.
Skia, An Ode on the Isle of Skye.
Song, A: "Not the soft sighs of vernal gales."
Song Composed for Fanny Burney, A.
Sons of *Greece,* The.
Soon fades the rose; once past the fragrant hour.
Stella in Mourning.
To a Young Lady on Her Birthday.
To Eliza Plucking Laurel in Mr Pope's Gardens.
To Lady Firebrace.
To Lyce, an Elderly Lady.
To Miss —: On Her Giving the Author a Gold and Silk Net-work Purse.
To Miss —: On Her Playing upon the Harpsichord.
To Miss Hickman Playing on the Spinet.
To Mrs Thrale [on Her Thirty-fifth Birthday].
To Posterity.
Translation from a Pantomime Version of Benserade's *Ballet de Cassandre.*
Translation of a Distich on the Duke of Modena.
Translation of Addison's Pugmaiogeranomachia; The Battle of the Pygmies and Cranes.
Translation of Anacreon's *Dove* (Ode ix).
Translation of Benserade's Verses *À Son Lit.*
Translation of Du Bellay's *Epigram on a Dog.*
Translation of Lines in Baretti's *Easy Phraseology.*
Translation of the Beginning of *Rio Verde.*
Translation of the Latin Epitaph on Sir Thomas Hanmer, Written by Doctor Freind, A.
Translations of Roy's Verses on Skaters.
Unhappy Lot of all that shine in Courts.
Upon the Feast of St Simon and St Jude.
Vanity of Human Wishes [The Tenth Satire of Juvenal Imitated], The.
Vanity of Wealth, The.
Verses Modelled on Pope.
Verses on the Death of His Mother.
What Plagues, what Tortures are in store for thee.
Winter's Walk, The.
Ye glitt'ring Train! whom Lace and Velvet bless.
Young Author, The.
Translations, Coauthored Poems, etc.:
1.1: "What doating bigot to his faults so blind."
1.24: "I mist my end, and lost my way."
2.1: "Each inly murm'ring at th'unequal meed."
2.1: "In books the various scenes of life he drew."
2.1: "With heedless feet on fires you go."
2.2: "Bold be the critic, zealous to his trust."
2.5: "Maid whom now you court in vain, The."
2.9: Translation of Horace: *Odes* II ix.
2.14: Translation of Horace *Odes* II xiv ("Eheu Fugaces").
2.20: Translation of Horace: *Odes* II xx.
3.2: "Stranger to folly and to fear."
3.7: "To taint th'attentive mind she tries."
3.23: "If rustic Phidyle her prayer renews."
3.24: "He whom the dread of want ensnares."
Ad Pisonem *sels.*
Adriano in Syria *sels.*
Aeneid [*or* Eneados, Aeneis], The *sels.*
All Men throughout the peopled Earth.
Amid the storms of war, with curious eyes.
Amores *sels.*
Art of Love, The *sels.*
At busy hearts in vain love's arrows fly.
Be gone ye blockheads, *Heraclitus* cries.
Beasts of each kind their fellows spare.
Before my closing eyes, dear Cynthia, stand.
Blest was my reign, retiring Cynthia cry'd.
Capricious fortune ever joys.
Chearful sage, when solemn dictatees fail.

Consolation of Philosophy, The ("De Consolacione Philosophie") *sels.*
Eclogues *sels.*
Elegies *sels.*
Epigrams *sels.*
Epistles *sels.*
Epodes *sels.*
Ev'n yet his voice from Hell's dread shades we hear.
Exiles, the proverb says, subsist on hope.
Fabulae *sels.*
Fickle crowd with fortune comes and goes, The.
For healthful indigence in vain they pray.
For not the brave, or wise, or great.
Frail as the leaves that quiver on the sprays.
Gaurus pretends to *Cato's* fame.
Georgics *sels.*
Give me, O Father! to thy throne access.
Happy he whose eyes have view'd.
Hercules Furens *sels.*
Heroides *sels.*
Hippolytus *sels.*
How sweet in sleep to pass the careless hours.
Iliad, The *sels.*
Insulting chance ne'er call'd with louder voice.
La Clemenza di Tito *sels.*
Let *Cæsar* spread his conquests far.
Let those whom folly prompts to sneer.
Man who pants for ample Sway, The.
Man will surely fail who dares delay, The.
Medea *sels.*
Metamorphoses *sels.*
Mind of mortals, in perverseness strong, The.
More safely truth to urge her claim presumes.
No faith of partnership dominion owns.
None dares with impious steel the grove to rend.
Not faster in the summer's ray.
Not him I prize who poorly gains.
Nought from my birth or ancestors I claim.
Now *Dædalus,* behold, by fate assign'd.
O! save ye Gods, omnipotent and kind.
O thou whose pow'r o'er moving worlds presides.
Obscure, unpriz'd, and dark, the magnet lies.
Odes *sels.*
Of mortal Justice if thou scorn the rod.
On life, on morals, be thy thoughts employ'd.
On vent'rous wing in quest of praise I go.
Our bane and physic the same earth bestows.
Pastorals *sels.*
Pharsalia *sels.*
Phœnissae *sels.*
Polish'd with endless toil, my lays.
Prudent Hind intent on Gain, The.
Pythian Odes *sels.*
Remediae Amoris *sels.*
Satires *sels.*
See the wild purchase of the bold and vain.
Succeeding years thy early frame destroy.
Sylvae *sels.*
This is the chief felicity of life.
Though countless as the Grains of Sand.
Through all the town the busy triflers swarm.
Through Gripus Grounds let rich Pactolus roll.
Tinsel glitter, and the specious mein, The.
To Aristius Fuscus.
Translation of Horace "Epode the 2d" ("Beatus Ille").
Translation of Horace: Epode xi.
Translation of Horace *Odes* IV vii ("Diffugere nives").
Translation of Part of the Dialogue Between Hector and Andromach; from the Sixth Book of Homer's *Iliad* (VI 390–502).
Translation of Virgil: Pastoral V.
Translation of Virgil: Pastoral I.
Translations from Metastasio ("Grown old in courts, thou art not surely done").
Translations from Metastasio ("Would you hope to gain my heart").
Translations from the *Medea* of Euripedes

("Err shall they not, who resolute explore").
Translations from the *Medea* of Euripedes ("The rites deriv'd from ancient days").
Translations of Horace ("Integer vitae").
Troades *sels*.
Truth in platonic ornaments bedeck'd.
Two-fold gift in this my volume lies, A.
Unless the soul, to vice a thrall.
Unlike the ribald, whose licentious jest.
Vain man runs headlong, to caprice resign'd.
Vainly the Tyrian Purple bright.
Various ills ordain'd to man by fate, The.
With me retire and leave the pomp of courts.
Work'd into sudden rage by wintry show'rs.
Wouldst thou to some stedfast Seat.
Wretch that often has deceiv'd, The.

Jong, Erica (b. 1941)
After the Earthquake.
Aging.
Alcestis on the Poetry Circuit.
Alphabet Poem: To the Letter I.
Another Language.
Anti-Conception.
Anti-Matter.
Artist as an Old Man, The.
Assuming Our Dominance.
At the Edge of the Body.
At the Museum of Natural History.
Aura.
Autumn Perspective.
Baby-Witch.
Beast, Book, Body.
Becoming a Nun.
Bed of the World, The.
Best Friends.
Birth of the Water Baby, The.
Bitter Herb.
Blood & Honey.
Books.
Buddha in the Womb, The.
By Train from Berlin.
Catch, The.
Cheever's People.
Color of Snow, The.
Commandments, The.
Deadly Nightshade.
Dear Anne Sexton, I.
Dear Anne Sexton, II.
Dear Colette.
Dear Keats.
Dear Marys, Dear Mother, Dear Daughter.
Dearest Man-in-the-Moon.
Death of a Romantic.
Deaths of the Goddesses, The.
Demeter at Dusk.
Demon Lover, The.
Depression in Early Spring.
Dirty Laundry Poem, The.
Divorce.
Doubts before Dreaming.
Driving Me Away.
Eggplant Epithalamion, The.
Egyptology.
Elegy for a Whale.
Empty.
Eveningsong at Bellosguardo.
Evidence, The.
Exam Dream, The.
Figure of the Witch.
Flight to Catalina.
Flying You Home.
For all those who died.
For an Earth-Landing.
For Molly, Concerning God.
For My Husband.
For My Sister, against Narrowness.
Fruits & Vegetables.
Gardener.
Gazing Out, Gazing In.
Good Carpenters.
Heidelberg Landlady, The.
Henbane.
Her Broom, or the Ride of the Witch.
Here Comes.
His Tuning of the Night.
Horse from Hell, The.

House-Hunting in the Bicentennial Year.
How to Name Your Familiar.
I Live in New York.
I Sit at My Desk Alone.
If God is a Dog.
If You Come Back.
Imaginary Landscapes.
Impressionists, The.
In Defense of the English Portrait School.
In My Cauldron under the Full Moon.
In Sylvia Plath Country.
In the Glass-Bottomed Boat.
Insomnia & Poetry.
January in New York.
Jubilate Canis.
Keys, The.
Land of Fuck, The.
Letter to My Lover after Seven Years.
Lives of the Poets: Three Profiles, The.
Living Happily Ever After.
Long Tunnel of Wanting You, The.
Love Magick.
Love Spell: against Endings.
Lullabye for a Dybbuk.
Man under the Bed, The.
Mandrake.
Middle Aged Lovers, I.
Middle Aged Lovers, II.
Monkshood.
Mother.
Muse Who Came to Stay, The.
My Daughter Says.
My death.
My Love Is Too Much.
Nazi Amphitheatre, The.
Near the Black Forest.
New England Winter.
Nota in una Bottiglia.
Nursing You.
Ode to My shoes.
On Reading a Vast Anthology.
On Sending You a Lock of My Hair.
On the Avenue.
Ordinary Miracles.
Other Side of the Page, The.
Pane Caldo.
Paper Cuts.
Parable of the Four-Poster.
People Who Live.
Perfect Poet, The.
Perishable Women.
Poem for Molly's Fortieth Birthday.
Poet Writes in *I*, The.
Poetry Suit, The.
Prisoner, The.
Puzzle, The.
Rain is My Home, The.
Raspberries in My Driveway, The.
Reading, A.
Ritratto.
Sailing Home.
Saturday Market, The.
Self-Portrait in Shoulder Stand.
Seventeen Warnings in Search of a Feminist Poem.
Still Life with Tulips.
Student Revolution.
Summoning the Muse to a New House.
Sunjuice.
Surgery of the Sea, The.
Tapestry, with Unicorn.
There Is Only One Story.
This Element.
Thorn Apple.
To a Transatlantic Mirror.
To James Boswell in London.
To My Brother Poet, Seeking Peace.
To Pablo Neruda.
To the Goddess.
To the Horned God.
To X. (With Ephemeral Kisses).
Touch.
Truce between the Sexes, The.
Unrequited.
Venice, November, 1966.
Walking through the Upper East Side.
We Learned.

What You Need to Be a Writer.
Whole Point, The.
Without Parachutes.
Woman Enough.
Xylophone of the Spine, The.
Zen & the Art of Poetry.

Jonson, Ben (1572–1637)
Against Jealousy [*or* Jealousie].
And Must I Sing? What Subject Shall I Choose?
Another. In Defense of Their Inconstancy [*or* Inconstancie]. A Song.
Another Lady's [*or* Ladyes] Exception, Present at the Hearing.
Another to Him.
Author ad Librum.
Ballad: "Though it may seem rude."
Bartholomew Fair *sels*.
Begging Another, on Colour of Mending the Former.
Ben Jonson's Grace before King James.
Bid all profane away.
Blush, folly, blush: here's none that fears.
Bow both your heads at once, and hearts.
Break, Fant'sy, from thy cave of cloud.
Buzz [*or* buz], quoth the blue fly [*or* flie].
Celebration of Charis in Ten Lyric[k] Pieces [*or* Peeces], A.
Charles Cavendish to His Posterity.
Charm[e], The.
Chloridia *sels*.
Christmas His Masque *sels*.
Claiming [*or* Clayming] a Second Kiss[e] by Desert.
Cocklorel would needs have the devil his guest.
Come forth, come forth, the gentle Spring.
Come, noble nymphs, and do not hide.
Come on, come on! And where you go.
Crown, a crown for Love's bright head, A.
Cynthia's Revels *sels*.
Daughters of the subtle flood.
Dedication of the King's New Cellar. To Bacchus, The.
Dream[e], The.
Elegy, An: "By those bright eyes, at whose immortal fires."
Elegy, An: "Can beauty that did prompt me first to write."
Elegy [*or* Elegie], An: "Let me be what I am, as Virgil cold."
Elegy, An: "Since you must go, and I must bid farewell."
Elegy, An: "That love's a bitter sweet, I ne'er conceive."
Elegy, An: "Though beauty be the mark of praise."
Elegy [*or* Elegie], An: "'Tis true, I'm broke! Vows, oaths, and all I had."
Elegy on My Muse.
Elegy [*or* Elegie] on the Lady Jane Pawlet [*or* Paulet], [Marchioness of Winton], An.
Epicoene; or, The Silent Woman *sels*.
Epigram, An: "That you have seen the pride, beheld the sport."
Epigram on Sir Edward Coke, when He Was Lord Chief Justice of England, An.
Epigram on the Court Pucell, An.
Epigram on the Prince's Birth. 1630, An.
Epigram on William, Lord Burl[eigh], Lo[rd] High Treasurer of England, An.
Epigram. To a Friend and Son.
Epigram. To K[ing] Charles for a[n] Hundred Pounds He Sent Me in My Sickness. 1629, An.
Epigram to My Bookseller.
Epigram to My Jovial Good Friend Mr Robert Dover, on His Great Instauration of His Hunting and Dancing at Cotswold, An.
Epigram to My Muse, the Lady Digby, on Her Husband, Sir Kenelm Digby, An.
Epigram. To our Great and Good K[ing] Charles on his Anniversary Day. 1629, An.
Epigram to the Coucillor That Pleaded and Carried the Cause, An.
Epigram. To the Honoured———, Countess of———, An.

Epigram. To the Household. 1630, An.

Epigram to the Queen, Then Lying In. 1630, An.

Epigram. To the Small-Pox, An.

Epigram. To Thomas Lo[rd] Ellsmere, the Last Term He Sat Chancellor, An.

Epigram. To William, Earl of Newcastle, An.

Epigramma Martialis. Lib. VIII. lxxvii. The Same Translated.

Epistle Answering to One That Asked to Be Sealed of the Tribe of Ben, An.

Epistle to a Friend, An ("Censure not sharply then, but me advise").

Epistle to a Friend, An ("Sir, I am thankful, first, to heaven, for you").

Epistle to a Friend ("They are not, sir, worst owers, that do pay").

Epistle to a Friend, to Persuade Him to the Wars, An.

Epistle to Elizabeth, Countess of Rutland.

Epistle. To Katharine, Lady Aubigny.

Epistle to Master Arth[ur] Squib, An.

Epistle to Master John Selden, An.

Epistle to Mr Arthur Squib.

Epistle. To My Lady Covell.

Epistle to Sir Edward Sackville, now Earl of Dorset, An.

Epitaph, An: "What beauty would have lovely styled."

Epitaph on Elizabeth, L. H.

Epitaph, on Henry L[ord] La-ware. To the Passer-By, An.

Eptiaph on Katherine, Lady Ogle.

Epitaph on Master Philip Gray, An.

Epitaph on Master Vincent Corbet[t], An.

Epitaph on S.P. [Salomon or Salathiel Pavy], a Child of Q[ueen] El[izabeth's] Chapel.

Epithalamion: "Glad time is at his point arrived."

Epithalamion: or, a Song.

Epithalamion: "Up, youths and virgins, up, and praise."

Epode: "Not to know vice at all, and keep[e] true state."

Euclia's Hymn.

Eupheme.

Execration upon Vulcan, An.

Expostulation with Inigo Jones, An.

Eye of looking back were well, An.

Fair friend, 'tis true, your beauties move.

Fairy [or Faery or Faiery] beam[e] upon you, The.

Fit of Rhyme [or Rime] against Rhyme [or Rime], A.

Fools, they are the only nation.

From the famous Peak of Derby.

From The Touchstone of Truth.

Garland [or Ghyrlond] of the Blessèd Virgin Mary [or Marie], The.

Gentle knights, / Know some measure of your nights.

Gentle Love, be not dismayed.

Give end unto thy pastimes, Love.

Gypsies Metamorphosed, The sels.

Had old Hippocrates, or Galen.

Had those that dwell in error foul.

Haddington Masque, The sels.

Have men beheld the graces dance.

Help, help all tongues to celebrate this wonder.

Her Man Described by Her Own[e] Dictamen.

Her Triumph.

Here Follow Certain Other Verses, as Charms to Unlock the Mystery of the Crudities.

His Discourse with Cupid.

His Excuse for Loving.

Horace, of the Art of Poetry.

Hour-Glass [or Houre-Glasse], The.

How He Saw Her.

How young and fresh I am tonight.

Howe'er the brightness may amaze.

Hum drum, sauce for a cony.

Humble Petition of Poor Ben to the Best of Monarchs, Masters, Men, King Charles, The.

Hymn[e] on the Nativity [or Nativitie] of My Saviour, A.

Hymn: "Room, room, make room for the bouncing belly."

Hymn[e] to God the Father, A.

If all these Cupids now were blind.

If I freely may discover.

In Authorem.

In the Person of Womankind [A Song Apologetic].

Inviting a Friend to Supper.

Irish Masque, The sels.

It follows now you are to prove.

It Is Not Growing Like a Tree.

It Was a Beauty That I Saw.

Little Shrub Growing By, A.

Lord Bacon's Birthday.

Love Freed from Ignorance and Folly sels.

Love is blind, and a wanton.

Love Restored sels.

Love's Triumph through Callipolis sels.

Martial. Epigram XLVII, Book X.

Masque of Augurs, The sels.

Masque of Beauty, The sels.

Masque of Blackness, The sels.

Masque of Hymen sels.

Masque of Queens, The sels.

Melt earth to sea, sea flow to air.

Mercury Vindicated sels.

Mind of the Frontispiece to a Book, The.

Mind, The.

Modest, and fair, for fair and good are near.

Musical Strife; in a Pastoral Dialogue, The.

My masters and friends, and good people draw near.

My Picture Left in Scotland.

Nay, nay, / You must not stay.

Neptune's Triumph sels.

New Cry, The.

New Inn, The sels.

New years [or yeares], expect new gifts: sister, your harp[e].

New Year's Gift Sung to King Charles. 1635, A.

News from the New World sels.

Nor do you think that their legs is all.

Nor yet, nor yet, O you in this night blessed.

Now Dian, with her burning face.

Now look and see in yonder throne.

Now, my cunning lady moon.

Now, now begin to set.

Nymph's Passion, A.

O how came Love, that is himself a fire.

O know to end, as to begin.

O, that joy so soon should waste!

O yet how early, and before her time.

Oberon, the Fairy Prince sels.

Ode, An: "Helen, did Homer never see."

Ode, An: "High-spirited friend, / I send not balms, nor corsives to your wound."

Ode Allegoric.

Ode Enthusiastic.

Ode: "If men, and times were now."

Ode, or Song, by All the Muses, An.

Ode to Himself.

Ode. To Himself, An.

Ode to James, Earl of Desmond, An.

Ode. To Sir William Sydney, on His Birthday.

Of Death.

Of Life and Death.

Oh Do Not Wanton with Those Eyes.

On a Robbery.

On Bank the Usurer.

On Bawds and Usurers.

On Captain Hazard the Cheater.

On Cashiered Capt[ain] Surly.

On Cheveril.

On Cheveril the Lawyer.

On Chuff, Banks the Usurer's Kinsman.

On Court-Parrot.

On Court-Worm[e].

On Don Surly.

On English Monsieur.

On Giles and Joan.

On Groin.

On Gut.

On Gypsy.

On Lieutenant Shift.

On Lip the Teacher.

On Lucy Countess[e] of Bedford.

On Margaret Ratcliffe.

On Mill, My Lady's Woman.

On Mongrel Esquire.

On My First Daughter.

On My First Son [or Sonne].

On Old Colt.

On Playwright ("Playwright, by chance, hearing some toys I had writ").

On Playwright ("Playwright convict of public wrongs to men").

On Poet-Ape.

On Reformed Gamester.

On Sir Cod the Perfumed.

On Sir John Roe ("In place of scutcheons, that should deck thy hearse").

On Sir John Roe ("What two brave perils of the private sword").

On Sir Voluptuous Beast.

On Something, That Walks [or Walkes] Somewhere.

On Spies.

On the Author, Work, and Translator.

On the Famous Voyage.

On the Honoured Poems of His Honoured Friend, Sir John Beaumont, Baronet.

On the King's Birthday.

On the Magnetic Lady.

On the New Hot-House.

On the New Motion.

On the Right Honourable and Virtuous Lord Weston, L[ord] High Treasurer of England, upon the Day He Was Made Earl of Portland, 17. Febr. 1632. To the Envious.

On the Same Beast.

On the Town's Honest Man.

On the Union.

Over the Door at the Entrance into the Apollo.

Panegyre, on the Happy Entrance of James, Our Sovreign, to His First High Session of Parliament in This Kingdom, the 19 of March, 1603, A.

Phoenix Analysed, The.

Picture of the Body, The.

Pleasure Reconciled to Virtue sels.

Poem Sent Me by Sir William Burlase, A.

Poetaster, The sels.

Proludium.

Queen and huntress, chaste and fair.

Reverse on the Back Side, The.

Sad Shepherd, The sels.

Satirical Shrub.

Sinner's Sacrifice, The.

Slow, slow, fresh fount, keep time with my salt tears.

So beauty on the waters stood.

So breaks the sun earth's rugged chains.

Soft, subtle fire, thou soul of art.

Solemn rites are well begun, The.

Song, A: "Come, let us here enjoy the shade."

Song of the Moon, A.

Song of Welcome to King Charles, A.

Song. That Women Are But Men's Shadows.

Song. To Celia: ("Come my Celia, let us prove").

Song. To Celia ("Drink to me only with thine eyes").

Sonnet to the Noble Lady, the Lady Mary Wroth, A.

Sound, sound aloud / The welcome of the orient flood.

Speech According to Horace, A.

Speech Presented unto King James at a Tilting in the Behalf of the Two Noble Brothers S[ir] Robert and S[ir] Henry Rich, Now Earls of Warwick and Holland, A.

Stay, view this stone: and, if thou beest not such.

Still to be neat, still to be dressed [or Drest].

Still turn, and imitate the heaven.

Swell me a bowl with lusty wine.

These, these are they.

Think yet how night doth waste.

This motion was of love begot.

Those that in blood such violent pleasure have.

Thou more than most sweet glove.

Though I am young, and cannot tell.

To a Friend.

To a Friend, an Epigram of Him.

To a Weak Gamester in Poetry.

To Alchemists.

To All, to Whom I Write.

To Alphonso Ferrabosco, on His Book.

To Benjamin Rudyerd.

To Brain-Hardy.

To Captain Hungry.

To Censorious Courtling.

To Clement Edmonds, on His *Caesar's Commentaries* Observed, and Translated.

To Courtling.

To Doctor Empiric[k].

To Edward Alleyn.

To Elizabeth, Countess of Rutland.

To Esmé, Lord Aubigny.

To Fine Grand.

To Fine Lady Would-Be.

To Fool, or Knave.

To Francis Beaumont.

To Groom Idiot.

To Heaven.

To His Friend the Author upon His *Richard*.

To His Lady, Then Mrs Cary.

To His Much and Worthily Esteemed Friend the Author.

To Hornet.

To Inigo, Marquess Would Be, a Corollary.

To John Donne ("Donne, the delight of Phoebus, and each Muse").

To John Donne ("Who shall doubt, Donne, where I a poet be").

To K[ing] Charles and Q[ueen] Mary, for the Loss of Their First-Born. An Epigram Consolatory. 1629.

To King James ("How, best of kings, dost thou a scepter bear[e]!").

To King James ("That we the loss might know, and thou our love").

To King James ("Who would not be thy subject, James, I'obey").

To Lucy, Countess of Bedford.

To Lucy, Countess[e] of Bedford, with Mr. Donnes Satire's [*or* Satyres].

To Mary, Lady Wroth ("How well, fair crown of your fair sex, might he").

To Mary, Lady Wroth ("Madam, had all antiquity been lost").

To Master John Burges.

To Mime.

To Mr Ben Jonson in His Journey, by Mr Craven.

To Mr John Burges.

To Mr Jonson upon these Verses.

To Mr Joshua Sylvester.

To Mrs Alice Sutcliffe, on Her Divine *Meditations*.

To Mrs Phillip Sidney.

To My Book.

To My Bookseller.

To My Chosen Friend the Learnèd Translator of Lucan, Thomas May, Esquire.

To My Dear Son, and Right-Learnèd Friend, Master Joseph Rutter.

To My Lord Ignorant.

To My L[ord] the King, on the Christening His Second Son James.

To My Mere English Censurer.

To My Muse.

To My Old Faithful Servant: And (by His Continued Virtue) My Loving Friend: The Author of this Work, Mr Rich[ard] Brome.

To My Truly-Beloved Friend, Mr Browne: on His Pastorals.

To My Worthy and Honoured Friend, Mr George Chapman, on His Translation of Hesiod's *Works and Days*.

To My Worthy Friend, Master Edward Filmer, on His Work Published.

To Old-End Gatherer.

To One that Desired Me Not to Name Him.

To Penshurst.

To Person Guilty ("Guilty, be wise; and though thou know'st the crimes").

To Person Guilty ("Guilty, because I bad you late be wise").

To Pertinax Cob.

To Playwright.

To Prowl the Plagiary.

To Robert, Earl of Salisbury ("What need hast thou of me, or of my muse").

To Robert, Earl of Salisbury ("Who can consider thy right courses run").

To Sickness.

To Sir Annual Tilter.

To Sir Cod.

To Sir Edward Herbert.

To Sir Henry Cary.

To Sir Henry Goodyere.

To Sir Henry Nevil.

To Sir Henry [*or* Henrie] Savile [upon His Translation of Tacitus].

To Sir Horace Vere.

To Sir John Radcliffe.

To Sir Luckless Woo-All.

To Sir Ra[l]ph Shelton.

To Sir Robert Wroth.

To Sir Thomas Overbury.

To Sir Thomas Roe.

To Sir William Jephson.

To Sir William Uvedale.

To Susan, Countess of Montgomery.

To the Author.

To the Ghost of Martial.

To the Immortal[l] Memory [*or* Memorie] and Friendship of That Noble Pair[e], Sir Lucius Cary and Sir H. [*or* Henry] Morison.

To the King. On His Birthday. An Epigram Anniversary. Novem[ber] 19, 1632.

To the Learnèd Critic.

To the London Reader, on the Odcombian Writer, Polytopian Thomas the Traveller.

To the Memory of My Beloved, the Author Mr [*or* Master] William Shakespeare[: And What He Hath Left Us].

To the Memory of That Most Honoured Lady Jane, Eldest Daughter to Cuthbert, Lord Ogle: and Countess of Shrewsbury.

To the Most Noble, and above His Titles, Robert, Earl of Somerset.

To the old, long life and treasure.

To the Parliament.

To the Reader ("Pray thee, take care, that tak'st my book[e] in hand").

To the Reader ("This figure, that thou here seest put").

To the Right Hon[oura]ble Hierome, L[ord] Weston. An Ode Gratulatory for His Return from His Embassy. 1632.

To the Right Honourable, the Lord High Treasurer of England. An Epistle Mendicant. 1631.

To the Right Honourable, the Lord Treasurer of England. An Epigram.

To the Right Noble Tom, Tell-Troth of His Travels, the Coriat of Odcombe, and His Book Now Going to Travel.

To the Same; on the Same.

To the Same Sir Cod.

To the Same [Alphonso Ferrabosco].

To the Same [Benjamin Rudyerd] ("If I would wish, for truth, and not for show").

To the Same [Benjamin Rudyerd] ("Writing thyself, or judging others' writ").

To the Same [Celia].

To the Same [Robert, Earl of Salisbury] [Upon the Accession of the Treasurership to Him].

To the Same [Sir Henry Goodyere].

To the Same [Sir John Roe].

To the Same [Sir Luckless Woo-All].

To the Same [Sir Thomas Roe].

To the World [A Farewell for a Gentlewoman, Virtuous and Noble].

To the Worthy Author M[r] John Fletcher.

To the Worthy Author on *The Husband*.

To Thomas, Earl of Suffolk.

To Thomas, Lord Chancellor.

To Thomas Palmer [on His Book "The Sprite of Trees and Herbs"].

To True Soldiers.

To William Camden.

To William, Earl[e] of Pembroke.

To William, Lord Mounteagle.

To William Roe ("Roe (and my joy to name) th'art now, to go").

To William Roe ("When Nature bids us leave to live, 'tis late").

Urging Her of a Promise.

Vision of Ben Jonson, on the Muses of His Friend M. Drayton, The.

Vision of Delight, The *sels*.

Volpone *sels*.

Wake! Our mirth begins to die.

What He[e] Suffered.

What just excuse had agèd Time.

When Love at first did move.

Which way and whence the lightning flew.

Who, Virtue, can thy power forget.

Why I Write Not of Love.

You that would last long, list to my song.

Translations, Coauthored Poems, etc.:

3.9: To Lydia. Dialogue of Horace and Lydia.

4.1: To Venus.

Epodes *sels*.

Fragmentum Petron. Arbitr. The Same Translated.

Odes *sels*.

Pharsalia *sels*.

Praises of a Country Life, The.

Speech out of Lucan, A.

Joseph, Jenny (b. 1932)

Abstract Study—Circles.

Against the Personality Cult.

ALLEGORY: *Old Man's Fancy* (Poussin).

Altarpiece (A Meditation on Lust, Desire and Love).

Animal Story, An.

Another Old Tale.

Anthropomorphism Reversed.

Back to Base.

Beyond Descartes.

Birthday Poem.

Bound upon a Wheel.

Bride to Groom.

Building Site, The *sels*.

But they could *do* something about that.

Butcher's.

Catch.

CENTERPIECE: *St. Sebastian* (Italian).

Certain Weathers.

Cherry.

Chorale.

Chrysanth.

Cloud.

Cutting Off One's Ears for Someone Else Is Wrong.

Danaë.

Dawn Walkers.

Dead of Night.

Derivations.

Descartes—You There?

Diary.

Dog Body and Cat Mind.

Eurydice to Orpheus.

Even Over the Flat Land.

Exile in Devon, An.

Exorcism.

Fables *sels*.

Fables.

False Postulate.

Feast, The.

February Floods, 1953.

Figure in a Landscape.

First Spring Dawn.

For a New Year.

Genus: Homo.

Geranium.

Getting Up in Winter.

Go Back to Square One.

Goddess of Nature's Diatribe to her People, The.
Going to Sylvie's.
Here Lies Treasure: Here Be Monsters.
High Devil, Deep Pit.
High life.
Homo Sapiens.
If you can't join them beat them.
In Memory of God.
Inland Sea, The.
Instant on the Viaduct, An.
INTERIOR: *The Man Turns the Sheet for the Musician* (Dutch).
Inverts.
Jack and the Beanstalk.
Just a snack for lunch.
Knock Knock.
Lady.
LANDSCAPE: *Jungle Days* (Dutch).
Language Teaching: Naming.
Lazarus.
Letter to comfort a friend.
Life and Turgid Times of A. Citizen.
Little dots.
Living Off Other People—Welfare.
Lost Continent, The.
Lost Hold.
Lost Sea, The.
Love and Justice.
Lure.
Man as Cannibal (PLAIN; BIOLOGY).
Man as Image (MASSIF; CHEMISTRY).
Man as Matter.
Man as Matter (ISLAND; PHYSICS).
Man as Real (CITY; HUMAN).
Man in a Bar.
Married People Going to Work.
Meeting Up.
Meteorology, A.
Mirror, Mirror.
Modern witches 1: crouching.
Modern witches 2: sentinels.
Moon.
Moon in the morning.
Muse.
No Map Available.
Non-communicant.
Not a Rootless Lily.
Not able to resist the spring.
Old Man Going.
On the Embankment.
On the Nature of Scientific Law.
Overbold, The.
Patient old cripple, A.
Persephone Returns.
PROEM: *Against metaphor—but how then?*
Puppet Show, The.
Puppeteer.
Recovered from the Sea.
Reported Missing.
River Rising in India.
Road from Glastonbury, The.
Rose.
Rose in the Afternoon.
Round: "Body of a child lay in the pool, The."
Shadows Coming.
Still Reading Fairy Stories.
Story.
STUDY: *A Lady in her Bedroom* (Bonnard).
Subscription.
Summer Amnesty.
Sun Has Burst the Sky, The.
Sunripe.
There are more accidents in the home than on the roads.
Think of the minute amount a mouse eats.
This day our daily..
Tides.
Timetable for a Town.
To Keep Each Other Warm.
Translation.
Tripping down.
Trying to Understand Violence.
Unlooked-For Season, The.
Untitled.
Version of the Phoenix Story, A.

Visiting.
Waking.
Walk in the woods at the hour when the fuddled sun.
Warning.
Watching a child watching a witch.
Wet Sunday.
Women at Streatham Hill.
X marks the spot. A postcard from home.
Zenith.

K

Keats, John (1795–1821)
Acrostic.
Addressed to Haydon.
After Dark Vapours Have Oppressed Our Plains.
Ah! Ken Ye What I Met the Day.
All Gentle Folks Who Owe a Grudge.
And What Is Love? It Is a Doll Dressed Up.
Apollo to the Graces.
As from the Darkening Gloom a Silver Dove.
Banquet, The.
Blue! 'Tis the Life of Heaven, the Domain.
Bright Star! Would I Were Steadfast as Thou Art.
Bruised Titans, The.
Calidore. A Fragment.
Can Death Be Sleep, When Life Is But a Dream.
Cap and Bells; or, The Jealousies, The.
Character of Charles Brown.
Day Is Gone and All Its Sweets Are Gone, The.
Dream, A.
Dream, after Reading Dante's Episode of Paolo and Francesca, A.
Endymion: Poetic Romance.
Epistle to John Hamilton Reynolds.
Eve of St. Agnes, The.
Eve of St. Mark, The.
Extracts from an Opera.
Faery Bird's Song.
Faery Song.
Fall of Hyperion, The.
Fancy.
Fill for Me a Brimming Bowl.
For There's Bishop's Teign.
Fragment of the "Castle Builder."
Gif Ye Wol Stonden Hardie Wight.
Give Me Women, Wine, and Snuff.
God of the Meridian.
Gripus.
Happy Is England! I Could Be Content.
Hence Burgundy, Claret, and Port.
Hither, Hither, Love.
House of Mourning Written by Mr Scott, The.
How Many Bards Gild the Lapses of Time!
Human Seasons, The.
Hymn to Pan.
Hyperion; a Fragment.
Hyperion and Saturn.
I Cry Your Mercy, Pity, Love—Ay, Love!
I Stood Tip-Toe upon a Little Hill.
If by Dull Rhymes Our English Must be Chained.
Imitation of Spenser.
In After-Time, a Sage of Mickle Lore.
In Drear-nighted December.
Isabella; or, The Pot of Basil.
Keen, Fitful Gusts Are Whispering Here and There.
King Stephen. A Fragment of a Tragedy.
La Belle Dame Sans Merci.
Lamia.
Life Again.
Lines on the Mermaid Tavern.
Lines Rhymed in a Letter Received (by J. H. R[eynolds]) from Oxford.
Lines: "Unfelt, unheard, unseen."
Lines Written in the Highlands after a Visit to Burns's Country.
Lines Written on 29 May / The Anniversary of the Restoration of Charles the 2nd.

Magic Casements.
Minnows.
Nebuchadnezzar's Dream.
O Blush Not So! O Blush Not So!
O! How I Love, on a Fair Summer's Eve.
O Solitude! If I Must With Thee Dwell.
O Thou Whose Face Hath Felt the Winter's Wind.
Ode: "Bards of passion and of mirth."
Ode on a Grecian Urn.
Ode on Indolence.
Ode on Melancholy.
Ode to a Nightingale.
Ode to Apollo.
Ode to May. Fragment.
Ode to Psyche.
Of Late Two Dainties Were before Me Placed.
Old Meg She Was a Gipsy.
On a Leander Gem which Miss Reynolds, My Kind Friend, Gave Me.
On Fame ("Fame, like a wayward girl, will still be coy").
On Fame ("How fever'd is the man who cannot look").
On First Looking into Chapman's Homer.
On Leaving Some Friends at an Early Hour.
On Peace.
On Receiving a Curious Shell, and a Copy of Verses, from the Same Ladies.
On Receiving a Laurel Crown from Leigh Hunt.
On Seeing the Elgin Marbles.
On Sitting Down to Read "King Lear" Once Again.
On the Grasshopper and [the] Cricket.
On the Sea.
On "The Story of Rimini."
On Visiting Staffa.
On Visiting the Tomb of Burns.
Otho the Great.
Over the Hill and Over the Dale.
Pensive They Sit, and Roll Their Languid Eyes.
Poet, The.
Prest her cold finger closer to her lips.
Read Me a Lesson, Muse, and Speak It Loud.
Recollection of the Stone Circle near Keswick, A.
Robin Hood.
See, the Ship in the Bay Is Riding.
Sleep and Poetry.
Sleeping Youth, A.
Song about Myself, A.
Song: "Hush, hush! tread softly! hush, hush my dear."
Song: "I had a dove and the sweet dove died."
Song of Four Faeries.
Song of the Indian Maid ("O' Sorrow...").
Song of the Indian Maid, The ("Beneath my palm-trees, by the riverside").
Song: "Spirit here that reignest!"
Song: "Stay, ruby-breasted warbler, stay."
Sonnet: "Where didst thou find, young Bard, thy sounding lyre?"
Specimen of an Induction to a Poem.
Spenser! A Jealous Honourer of Thine.
Stanzas on Some Skulls in Beauly Abbey, Near Inverness.
Stanzas: "You say you love; but with a voice."
Sweet Peas.
Sweet, Sweet Is the Greeting of Eyes.
Thing of Beauty, A.
Think Not of It, Sweet One, So.
This Living Hand, Now Warm and Capable.
This Mortal Body of a Thousand Days.
Three Undated Fragments.
'Tis the Witching Time[*or* Hour] of Night.
To ———: "Had I a man's fair form, then might my sighs."
To a Friend Who Sent Me Some Roses.
To a Young Lady Who Sent Me a Laurel Crown.
To Ailsa Rock.

To Autumn.
To B.R. Haydon, with a Sonnet Written on
　　Seeing the Elgin Marbles.
To Charles Cowden Clarke.
To Chatterton.
To Emma.
To Fanny.
To George Felton Mathew.
To Georgiana Augusta Wylie.
To Homer.
To Hope.
To J. H. Reynolds, Esq.
To James Rice.
To Kosciusko.
To Leigh Hunt, Esq.
To Lord Byron.
To [Mary Frogley].
To Mrs. Reynolds's Cat.
To My Brother George.
To My Brothers.
To One Who Has Been Long in City Pent.
To Sleep.
To Some Ladies.
To the Ladies Who Saw Me Crowned.
To the Nile.
Two or Three Posies.
Two Sonnets on Fame *sels*.
Upon My Life, Sir Nevis, I Am Piqued.
Welcome Joy, and Welcome Sorrow.
What Can I Do to Drive Away.
When I Have Fears That I May Cease to Be.
When They Were Come unto the Faery's
　　Court.
Where Be You [*or* Ye] Going, You [*or* Ye]
　　Devon Maid?
Where's the Poet? Show Him! Show Him.
Why Did I Laugh Tonight?
Woman! When I Behold Thee Flippant, Vain.
Written in Disgust of Vulgar Superstition.
Written on a Blank Space at the End of
　　Chaucer's Tale of "The Floure and the
　　Lefe."
Written on the Day That Mr. Leigh Hunt
　　Left Prison.
Translations, Coauthored Poems, etc.:
　　On Seeing a Lock of Milton's Hair.
　　To ———: "Time's sea hath been five years
　　　　at its slow ebb."
　　Translated from Ronsard.

Kinnell, Galway (b. 1927)
After Making Love We Hear Footsteps.
Another Night in the Ruins.
Apple Tree, The.
Avenue Bearing the Initial of Christ into the
　　New World, The.
Bear, The.
Blackberry Eating.
Burn, The.
Correspondence School Instructor Says
　　Goodbye to His Poetry Students, The.
Daybreak.
Dead Shall Be Raised Incorruptible, The.
Falls, The.
Feast, The.
Fergus Falling.
First Song.
Flower Herding on Mount Monadnock.
Fly, The.
Flying Home.
For Robert Frost.
Freedom, New Hampshire.
Goodbye.
Gray Heron, The.
Hen Flower, The.
How Many Nights.
Last River, The.
Last Songs.
Lastness.
Little Sleep's-Head Sprouting Hair in the
　　Moonlight.
Meditation Among the Tombs.
Memory of Wilmington.
Middle of the Way.
Milk Bottle, The.
Poem of Night.
Porcupine, The.
River That Is East, The.

Ruins under the Stars.
Saint Francis and the Sow.
Schoolhouse, The.
Still Time, The.
Supper after the Last, The.
There Are Things I Tell to No One.
To a Child in Calcutta.
To Christ Our Lord.
To William Carlos Williams.
Two Seasons.
Under the Maud Moon.
Vapor Trail Reflected in the Frog Pond.
Wait.
Westport.
Winter Sky, A.

Kipling, Rudyard (1865–1936)
Absent-Minded Beggar, The.
Actors.
Advertisement, The.
Akbar's Bridge.
All the world over, nursing their scars.
American, An.
American Rebellion, The.
Anchor Song.
And some are sulky, while some will plunge.
And you may lead a thousand men.
Angutivaun Taina.
Answer, The.
Anvil, The.
Appeal, The.
APRIL (*Rowing*).
Arithmetic on the Frontier.
Army Headquarters.
Arterial.
As the Bell Clinks.
Astrologer's Song, An.
At His Execution.
At the hole where he went in.
AUGUST (*Coaching*).
Ave Imperatrix!
Azrael's Count.
Back to the Army Again.
Ballad of Boh Da Thone, The.
Ballad of East and West, The.
Ballad of Fisher's Boardinghouse, The.
Ballad of Minepit Shaw, The.
Ballad of the "Bolivar", The.
Ballad of the Cars, The.
Ballad of the *Clampherdown*, The.
Ballad of the King's Jest, The.
Ballad of the King's Mercy, The.
Ballad of the Red Earl, The.
Ballade of Burial, A.
Ballade of Jakko Hill, A.
Banquet Night.
Batteries Out of Ammunition.
Beasts Are Very Wise, The.
Beat off in our last fight were we?
Because I sought it far from men.
Bee-Boy's Song, The.
Bees and the Flies, The.
Before a Midnight Breaks in Storm.
Before my Spring I garnered Autumn's gain.
Beginner, The.
Beginnings, The.
Bell Buoy, The.
Bells and Queen Victoria, The.
Belts.
Benfactors, The.
Betrothed, The.
Between the waving tufts of jungle-grass.
Beware the man who's crossed in love.
Big Steamers.
Bill 'Awkins.
"Birds of Prey" March.
Birthright, The.
Blue Roses.
Bobs.
Bombed in London.
Bonfires, The.
Boots.
Bother, The.
Boy Scouts' Patrol Song, A.
Braggart, The.
Bridegroom, The.
Bridge-Guard in the Karroo.

British-Roman Song, A.
Broken Men, The.
Brookland Road.
Brown Bess.
Buddha at Kamakura.
Burden, The.
Burial, The.
Butterflies.
By the Hoof of the Wild Goat.
Cain and Abel.
Camel's hump is an ugly lump, The.
Captive, The.
Carmen Circulare.
Carol, A: "Our Lord Who did the Ox
　　command."
Cells.
Centaurs, The.
Certain Maxims of Hafiz.
Changelings, The.
Chant-Pagan.
Charm, A.
Chartres Windows.
Children, The.
Child's Garden, A.
Chil's Song.
China-going P. & O.'s.
Choice, The.
Cholera Camp.
Christmas in India.
Cities and Thrones and Powers.
City of Brass, The.
City of Sleep, The.
Cleared.
Clerks and the Bells, The.
Coastwise Lights, The.
Code of Morals, A.
Coiner, The.
Cold Iron.
Columns.
Comforters, The.
Common Form.
Consolations of Memory, The.
Contradictions.
Conundrum of the Workshops, The.
Convoy Escort.
Counting-Out Song, A.
Covenant, The.
Coward, The.
Craftsman, The.
Cruisers.
Cry "Murder" in the market-place, and each.
Cuckoo Song.
Curé, The.
Dane-Geld.
Danny Deever.
Dark children of the mere and marsh.
Darzee's Chaunt.
Dawn Wind, The.
Dead King, The [Edward VII; 1910].
Dead Statesman, A.
Death-Bed, A.
Debits and Credits *sels*.
DECEMBER (*Skating*).
Declaration of London, The.
Dedication, A: "And they were stronger
　　hands than mine."
Dedication from "Barrack-Room Ballads."
Deep-Sea Cables, The.
Delilah.
Departure, A.
Derelict, The.
Destroyers, The.
Destroyers in Collision.
Dinah in Heaven.
Dirge of Dead Sisters.
Disciple, The.
Divided Destinies.
Doctors.
Doors were wide, the story saith, The.
Dove of Dacca, The.
Drifter off Tarentum, A.
Dutch in the Medway, The.
Dying Chauffer, The.
Dykes, The.
Earth gave up her dead that tide, The.
'Eathen, The.
Eddi's Service.

Edgehill Fight.
Egg-Shell, The.
En-dor.
England's Answer.
English Flag, The.
English Way, The.
Epitaphs of the War [1914–1918].
Equality of Sacrifice.
Et Dona Ferentes.
Evarra and His Gods.
Ex-Clerk.
Exiles' Line, The.
Expert, The.
Explanation, The.
Explorer, The.
Fabulists, The.
Fairies' Siege, The.
Fall of Jock Gillespie, The.
Farewell and adieu to you, Harwich Ladies.
Fastness.
Favour, The.
FEBRUARY (*Coursing*).
Feet of the Young Men, The.
Female of the Species, The.
FIies, The.
Fires, The.
First Chantey, The.
Flight, The.
Floods, The.
Flowers, The.
Follow Me 'Ome.
For All We Have and Are [1914].
For our white and our excellent nights—for the nights of swift running.
For to Admire.
Ford o' Kabul River.
Four Angels, The.
Four-Feet.
Four Points, The.
Fox-Hunting.
France.
Frankie's Trade.
French Wars, The.
Friends, The.
Fuzzy-Wuzzy.
Galley-Slave, The.
Gallio's Song.
Gehazi.
General Joubert.
General Summary, A.
Gentlemen-Rankers.
Gertrude's Prayer.
Gethsemane.
Giffen's Debt.
Gift of the Sea, The.
Gipsy Trail, The.
Gipsy Vans.
Glories, The.
Glory of the Garden, The.
Go, stalk the red dear o'er the heather.
Gods of the Copybook Headings, The.
Grave Near Cairo, A.
Grave of the Hundred Dead, The.
Great-Heart.
Greek National Anthem, The.
Gunga Din.
Hadramauti.
Half-Ballad of Waterval.
Harp Song of the Dane Women.
He drank strong waters and his speech was coarse.
Helen All Alone.
Heriot's Ford.
Heritage, The.
Hindu Sepoy in France.
His Apologies.
His spots are the joy of the Leopard: his horns are the Buffalo's pride.
Holy War, The.
Hour of the Angel, The.
Houses, The.
Hunting Song of the Seonee Pack.
Hyænas [*or* Hyenas], The.
Hymn before Action.
Hymn of Breaking Strain.
Hymn of the Triumphant Airman.
Hymn to Physical Pain.

I am the Most Wise Baviaan, saying in most wise tones.
"I have a thousand men," said he.
I keep six honest serving-men.
I will remember what I was. I am sick of rope and chain.
Idiot Boy, The.
If.
If I have taken the common clay.
Imperial Rescript, An.
In Springtime.
In the daytime, when she moved about me.
In the Matter of One Compass.
In the Neolithic Age.
Instructor, The.
Inventor, The.
Irish Guards, The.
Islanders, The.
It was not in the open fight.
I've never sailed the Amazon.
Jacket, The.
James I.
Jane's Marriage.
JANUARY (*Hunting*).
Jester, The.
Jobson's Amen.
Journalists.
Jubal and Tubal Cain.
Juggler's Song, The.
JULY (*Archery*).
JUNE (*Cricket*).
Jungle Book, The *sels*.
Junk and the Dhow, The.
Just-So Stories *sels*.
Justice.
Justice's Tale, The.
Kim *sels*.
King, The.
King and the Sea, The.
King Henry VII. And the Shipwrights.
Kingdom, The.
King's Job, The.
King's Pilgrimage, The.
King's Task, The.
Kitchener's School.
La Nuit Blanche.
Ladies, The.
Lady Geraldine's Hardship.
Lament of the Border Cattle Thief, The.
Land, The.
Land and Sea Tales *sels*.
Landau, The.
Lark will make her hymn to God, The.
Last Chantey, The.
Last Department, The.
Last Lap, The.
Last Ode, The.
Last of the Light Brigade, The.
Last Rhyme of True Thomas, The.
Last Suttee, The.
Late Came the God.
Law of the Jungle, The.
Legend of Mirth, The.
Legend of the Foreign Office, A.
Legend of Truth, A.
Legends of Evil, The.
L'Envoi; Departmental Ditties.
'Less you want your toes trod off you'd better get back at once.
Lesson, The.
Lichtenberg.
Life's Handicap *sels*.
Light That Failed, The *sels*.
Liner She's a Lady, The.
Little Blind Fish, thou art marvellous wise!
Lollius.
London Stone.
Long Trail, The.
Look, you have cast out Love! What Gods are these.
Looking Glass, The.
Loot.
Lord Roberts.
Lost Legion, The.
Love Song of Har Dyal, The.
Lovers' Litany, The.
Lowestoft Boat, The.

Lukannon.
M. I.
McAndrew's Hymn.
MacDonough's Song.
Man goes to Man! Cry the challenge though the Jungle!
Man Who Could Write, The.
Mandalay.
MARCH (*Racing*).
Mare's Nest, The.
Marrèd Drives of Windsor, The.
Married Man, The.
Mary Gloster, The.
Mary, Pity Women!
Mary's Son.
Masque of Plenty, The.
Master-Cook, The.
Maxim.
MAY (*Fishing*).
Memories.
Men That Fought at Minden, The.
Merchantmen, The.
Merrow Down.
Mesopotamia.
Mine Sweepers.
Miracles, The.
Moon of Other Days, The.
Moral, The.
Morning Song in the Jungle.
Mother-Lodge, The.
Mother o' Mine.
Mother's Son, The.
Mowgli's Song against People.
Mulholland's Contract.
Municipal.
Muse among the Motors, The *sels*.
My Boy Jack.
My Father's Chair.
My Lady's Law.
My New-Cut Ashlar.
My Rival.
Naaman's Song.
Native-Born, The.
Native Water-Carrier (M.E.F.).
Nativity, A.
Natural Theology.
Naulahka, The *sels*.
Necessitarian, The.
Neighbours.
New Knighthood, The.
Night we felt the earth would move, The.
Non Nobis Domine!
Norman and Saxon.
North Sea Patrol, The.
Not though you die to-night, O Sweet, and wail.
NOVEMBER (*Boxing*).
Now Chil the Kite brings home the night.
Now it is not good for the Christian's health to hustle the Aryan brown.
Nurses, The.
Nursing Sister, The.
Obedient, The.
OCTOBER (*Golf*).
Ode: "So long as memory, valour, and faith endure."
Oh! hush thee, my baby, the night is behind us.
Old Issue, The.
Old Men, The.
Old Mother Laidinwool.
Old Song, An.
Oldest Song, The.
One Viceroy Resigns.
Only Son, An.
Only Son, The.
Oonts.
Open Door, The.
Our Fathers Also.
Our Fathers of Old.
Our Lady of the Sackcloth.
Our Lady of the Snows.
Outlaws, The.
Outsong in the Jungle.
Overland Mail, The.
Pageant of Elizabeth, A.
Pagett, M. P.

Palace, The.
Pan in Vermont.
Parade-Song of the Camp Animals.
Parting of the Columns, The.
Peace of Dives, The.
Pelicans in the Wilderness (A Grave near Halfa).
Penalty, The.
People of the Eastern Ice, they are melting like the snow, The.
Pharaoh and the Sergeant.
Philadelphia.
Pict Song, A.
Piet.
Pilgrim's Way, A.
Pink Dominoes.
Pirates in England, The.
Pit where the buffalo cooled his hide.
Plain Tales from the Hills *sels.*
Playmate, The.
Plea of the Simla Dancers, The.
Pleasant it is for the Little Tin Gods.
Poison of Asps.
Poor Honest Men.
Portent, The.
Poseidon's Law.
Possibilities.
Post That Fitted, The.
Power of the Dog, The.
Prairie, The.
Prayer, The: "My brother kneels, so saith Kabir."
Prayer of Miriam Cohen, The.
Preface, A: "To all to whom this little book may come."
Prelude to "Departmental Ditties."
Press, The.
Private Ortheris's Song.
Pro-Consuls, The.
Prodigal Son, The.
Progress of the Spark, The.
Prophets at Home.
Public Waste.
Puck of Pook's Hill *sels.*
Puck's Song.
Pussy can sit by the fire and sing.
Put forth to watch, unschooled, alone.
Puzzler, The.
Queen's Men, The.
Quest, The.
Question, The.
Rabbi's Song, The.
R.A.F. (Aged Eighteen).
Rahere.
Raped and Revenged.
Rebel, The.
Rebirth.
Recall, The.
Recantation, A.
Recessional.
Rector's Memory, A.
Reeds of Runnymede, The.
Refined Man, The.
Reformers, The.
Return of the Children, The.
Return, The.
Rhodes Memorial, Table Mountain.
Rhyme of the Three Captains, The.
Rhyme of the Three Sealers, The.
Ride with an idle whip, ride with an unused heel.
Rimini.
Rimmon.
Ripple Song, A.
River's Tale, The.
Road Song of the *Bandar-Log.*
Roman Centurion's Song, The.
Romulus and Remus.
Rosicrucian subtleties / In the Orient had rise.
Route Marchin'.
Rowers, The.
Run of the Downs, The.
Runes on Weland's Sword, The.
Runners, The.
Rupaiyat of Omar Kal'vin, The.
Russia to the Pacifists.

Sack of the Gods, The.
Sacrifice of Er-Heb, The.
St. Helena Lullaby, A.
Salonikan Grave.
Samuel Pepys.
Sappers.
Scholars, The.
School Song, A.
Screw-Guns.
Sea and the Hills, The.
Sea-Wife, The.
Second Jungle Book, The *sels.*
Second Voyage, The.
Secret of the Machines, The.
SEPTEMBER (*Shooting*).
Sepulchral.
Sergeant's Weddin', The.
Servant, A.
Servant When He Reigneth, A.
Service Man, The.
Sestina of the Tramp-Royal.
Settler, The.
Seven Watchmen.
Shillin' a Day.
Shiv and the Grasshopper.
Shock.
Shut-Eye Sentry, The.
Sir Richard's Song.
Sky is lead, and our faces are red, The.
Sleepy Sentinel, The.
Smuggler's Song, A.
Snarleyow.
So we loosed a bloomin' volley.
So we settled it all when the storm was done.
Soldier an' Sailor Too.
Soldier, Soldier.
Son, A.
Song at Cock-Crow, A.
Song for the Women, The.
Song in Storm, A.
Song in the Desert, A.
Song of Bananas, A.
Song of Diego Valdez, The.
Song of French Roads, A.
Song of Kabir, A.
Song of Seven Cities, The.
Song of Seventy Horses.
Song of the Banjo, The.
Song of the Cities, The.
Song of the Dead, The.
Song of the Dynamo.
Song of the English, A.
Song of the Fifth River.
Song of the Galley-Slaves.
Song of the Lathes, The.
Song of the Little Hunter, The.
Song of the Men's Side.
Song of the Old Guard, The.
Song of the Red War-Boat.
Song of the Sons, The.
Song of the White Men, A.
Song of the Wise Children.
Song of Travel, A.
Song to Mithras, A.
Sons of Martha, The.
South Africa.
Spies' March, The.
Stellenbosch.
Stone's throw out on either hand, A.
'Stopped in the straight when the race was his own.
Storm Cone, The.
Story of the Gadsbys, The *sels.*
Story of Ung, The.
Story of Uriah, The.
Stranger, The.
Study of an Elevation, in Indian Ink.
Such As in Ships.
Supplication of the Black Aberdeen.
Supports, The.
Survival, The
Sussex.
Tale of Two Cities, A.
Tarrant Moss.
That Day.
Then a pile of heads he laid.

Then we brought the lances down—then the trumpets blew.
There is a tide in the affairs of men.
There is pleasure in the wet, wet clay.
There was a strife 'twixt man and maid.
There was never a queen like Balkis.
There were three friends that buried the fourth.
There's a convict more in the Central Jail.
These are the four that are never content, that have never been filled since the Dews began.
They burnt a corpse upon the sand.
They killed a Child to please the Gods.
Things and the Man.
This I saw when the rites were done.
This is the mouth-filling song of the race that was run by a Boomer.
This Uninhabited Island.
Thorkild's Song.
Thousandth Man, The.
Three-Decker, The.
Three-Part Song, A.
Threshold, The.
Thus, for a season, they fought it fair.
Tin Fish.
To a Lady, Persuading Her to a Car.
To James Whitcomb Riley.
To Motorists.
To-night, God knows what thing shall tide.
To the City of Bombay.
To the Companions.
To the True Romance.
To the Unknown Goddess.
To Thomas Atkins.
Together.
Tomlinson.
Tommy.
Torn boughs trailing o'er the tusks aslant, The.
Totem, The.
Tour, The.
Trade, The.
Translation, A
Tree Song, A.
Troopin'.
Truce of the Bear, The.
Truthful Song, The.
Two Canadian Memorials.
Two Kopjes.
Two Months.
Two Races.
Two-Sided Man, The.
Ubique.
Ulster.
Undertaker's Horse, The.
Unknown Female Corpse.
Untimely.
Unto whose use the pregnant suns are poised.
V.A.D. (Mediterranean).
Vampire, The.
Veil them, cover them, wall them round.
Verdicts, The.
Verses on Games.
Very Many People.
Veterans, The.
Vineyard, The.
Virginity, The.
Voortrekker, The.
Wage-Slaves, The.
Waster, The.
Way through the Woods, The.
We and They.
We be the Gods of the East.
We meet in an evil land.
We now, held in captivity.
Wet Litany, The.
What Happened.
What of the hunting, hunter bold?
What the People Said.
When a lover hies abroad.
When Earth's Last Picture Is Painted.
When 'Omer Smote 'Is Bloomin' Lyre.
When the cabin port-holes are dark and green.
When the earth was sick and the skies were grey.

When the Great Ark.
When the Journey Was Intended to the City.
When ye say to Tabaqui, "My Brother!"
     when ye call the Hyena to meat.
While the snaffle holds or the long-neck
     stings.
White Horses.
White Man's Burden, The.
Wide, Wide World, The.
Widow at Windsor, The.
Widower, The.
Widow's Party, The.
Wilful-Missing.
Will they gape for the husks that ye proffer.
Winners, The.
Wishing-Caps, The.
With Drake in the Tropics.
With Scindia to Delhi.
Wolf-cub at even lay hid in the corn, The.
Wonder, The.
World hath set its heavy yoke, The.
Yet at the last, ere our spearmen had found
     him.
You mustn't swim till you're six weeks old.
Young British Soldier, The.
Young Queen, The.
Your patience, Sirs. The Devil took me up.
Zion.

Knight, Etheridge (1933–91)
And Tell Me Poet, Can Love Exist in
     Slavery?
Another Poem for Me (after Recovering from
     an O.D.).
Apology for Apostasy?
As You Leave Me.
At a VA Hospital in the Middle of the
     United States of America: An Act in a
     Play.
Belly Song.
Birthday Poem.
Black Poet Leaps to His Death, A.
Bones of My Father, The.
Boone County.
Boston 5:00 A.M.—10/74.
Cell Song.
Circling the Daughter.
Clay County.
Con/tin/u/way/shun Blues.
Cop-Out Session.
Crown Hill Cemetary, Indianapolis.
Dark Prophecy: I Sing of Shine.
Eat Helen B Happy (a Found Poem).
Evolutionary Poem No. 1.
Evolutionary Poem No. 2.
Fable: "Once upon a today and yesterday and
     nevermore there were 7 men."
Feeling Fucked Up.
For a Brookline Lady I Love.
For Black Poets Who Think of Suicide.
For Freckle-Faced Gerald.
For Langston Hughes.
For Malcolm, a Year After.
For Mary Ellen McAnally.
Genesis.
Genesis 11.
Green Grass and Yellow Balloons.
Haiku: "Eastern guard tower."
Haiku 1: "Slender Finger of Light, A."
Haiku: "Two hours I've walked."
Harlem.
He Sees Through Stone.
I And Your Eyes.
Idea of Ancestry, The.
Ilu, the Talking Drum.
Indiana Avenue, 1949.
Indiana Haiku.
Indiana Haiku—2.
Indianapolis War Memorial.
Indianapolis Winter, 1973.
It Was a Funky Deal.
Keeping of a Promise, The.
Last Words By "Slick."
Memo #2.
Memo #5.
Memo #9.
Memo #32.
Memo #43.

Missouri Haiku.
Mizzu.
My Life, the Quality of Which.
My Uncle is My Honor and a Guest in My
     House.
No Moon Floods the Memory of that Night.
On Seeing the Black Male as #1 Sex Object
     in America.
On the Birth of a Black / Baby / Boy.
On the Projects Playground.
On the Yard.
On Watching Politicians Perform at Martin
     Luther King's Funeral.
Once on a Night in the Delta: A Report
     From Hell.
Outside St. Louis.
Penal Farm, The.
Poem For a Certain Lady on Her 33rd
     Birthday, The.
Poem for Black Relocation Centers, A.
Poem for Myself (or Blues for a Mississippi
     Black Boy), A.
Poem for the Liberation of Southern Africa.
Poem of Attrition, A.
Poem on the Middle East "Peace Process",
     A.
Poem to Galway Kinnell, A.
Portrait of Mary.
Rehabilitation & Treatment in the Prisons of
     America.
Report to the Mother.
Riverside Park.
Stretching of the Belly, The.
Sun Came, The.
Talking in the Woods with Karl Amorelli.
Television Speaks.
Two Poems for Black Relocation Centers
     sels.
Upon Your Leaving.
Various Protestations From Various People.
Vigo County.
Violent Space, The.
Warden Said to Me the Other Day, The.
WASP Woman Visits a Black Junkie in
     Prison, A.
We Free Singers Be.
Welcome Back, Mr. Knight: Love of My
     Life.
You Are.

Knott, Bill
Ant Dodger.
At the Crossroads.
Beddybye.
Brighton Rock by Graham Greene.
Closet, The.
Consolations of Sociobiology, The.
Death.
Depressionism.
(Face) (Autumn) (En Face).
Fear of Domesticity.
Feeding the Sun.
Funny Poem.
Goodbye.
Juggler to His Audience, The.
Keeper, The.
Lesson.
Mitts and Gloves.
My Mother's List of Names.
Obsolescent and His Deity (Polyptych), An.
Poem: "Beach holds and sifts us through her
     dreaming fingers, The."
Poem (How I Lost My Pen-Name).
(Poem): "Like a room."
Poem (the Starfish One).
Poem: "With the toys of your nape."
Prophet in a Landscape of Immemorial Time.
Racist Poem.
Rigor Vitus.
Ritual.
Sculpture, The.
(Sergey) (Yesenin) Speaking (Isadora)
     (Duncan).
Shorts / Excerpts ("Hope..goosestep").
Shorts / Excerpts ("I keep a TV monitor on
     my chest").
Shorts / Excerpts ("I write these lines to
     cripple the dead").

Shorts / Excerpts ("Night, in whose death did
     your ennui take refuge?").
Shorts / Excerpts ("Other strangers than our
     own may remember").
Shorts / Excerpts ("Our farewells lack the
     plausibility of our departures").
Shorts / Excerpts ("Searching it goes").
Shorts / Excerpts ("Suddenly I understood").
(Sideshow).
Sonnet: "Way the world is not, The."
Summoning, The.
Two Vietnam Poems: (1966).
Widower's Winter.

Koch, Kenneth (b. 1925)
Alive for an Instant.
Art of Love, The.
Art of Poetry, The.
Artist, The.
Aus Einer Kindheit.
Boiling Water, The.
Brassiere Factory, The.
Bricks, The.
Burning Mystery of Anna in 1951, The.
Circus, The.
Collected Poems.
Days and Nights.
Departure from Hydra, The.
Desire for Spring.
Down at the Docks.
Fate.
Fresh Air.
Geography.
Girl and Baby Florist Sidewalk Pram
     Nineteen Seventy Something.
Hearing.
In Bed.
In Love with You.
In the Morning.
Invention of Poetry, The.
Locks.
Lunch.
Ma Provence.
Magic of Numbers, The.
On Beauty.
On the Great Atlantic Rainway.
Our Hearts.
Out and In.
Permanently.
Pleasures of Peace, The.
Poem: "Thing / To do / Is organize / The
     Sea, The."
Railway Stationery, The.
Secret, The.
Simplicity of the Unknown Past, The.
Sleeping with Women.
Some General Instructions.
Spring.
Stones of Time, The.
Summery Weather.
Taking a Walk with You.
Thank You.
Thanksgiving.
To Marina.
To You.
Variations on a Theme by William Carlos
     Williams.
West Wind.
With Janice.
You Were Wearing.

Koertge, Ron (b. 1940)
Burglar, The.
Caboose Factory, The.
Coign of Vantage.
Coming Out.
Day Alvero Pineda Was Killed, The.
Excerpts from God's Secret Diary.
For My Daughter.
Getting the License.
Gretel.
He ("Bought a three-bedroom house in
     1948").
He ("Drove a school bus for the extra
     money").
He ("Gave me 50 dollars for Christmas one
     year").
He ("Gave me his car").

He ("Got drunk once with another cowpuncher").
He ("Had a bay stallion once that the Triple Bar C").
He ("Has a new double-knit suit with slightly flared").
He ("Has never written me a letter himself").
He ("Told me that I shouldn't have books like that").
He ("Used to climb trees that were").
He ("Used to do most everything himself").
He ("Walked in the basement all winter. For exercise").
He ("Was looking for work at forty-seven and the owner of a").
He ("Was never called Wild Bill").
He ("Was taken out of school after").
I Wanted My Name on the Side of a Building I Wanted to Be as Feared as the Word Biopsy.
If Other Students.
In South America on Business He Does Something He Is Ashamed of yet on the Way Home Dreams of It Again and Again.
In the Underground Station.
Jockey, A.
Last-Minute Change of Plans.
Life on the Edge of the Continent.
Loving Ugly.
Man like a Curtain, A.
Mr. Big.
Moving Day.
My Father ("Lies on the same couch that he used to").
My Father ("Once owned a blind horse, a big gray who").
My Father ("Said, 'What the devil!' when he dropped").
My Grandmother.
Night Games.
Old People.
Orientation Week.
Panty Hose.
Primary Considerations.
Pronouncing My Name.
Quiz, The.
Reading at the Local High School.
Royce Newport Money.
Sex Object.
Sidekicks.
Sleep.
Sometimes.
Streetsweeper, The.
Sunday.
"These Students Couldn't Write Their Way out of a Paper Bag"—Anonymous.
To Impress the Girl Next Door.
Two Men.
Ubiquity of the Need for Love, The.
Urban Renewal.
Waiting.
What She Wanted.
Whippersnappers.
Zenith and After, The.

Kooser, Ted (b. 1939)
Abandoned Farmhouse.
Advice.
After My Grandmother's Funeral.
After the Funeral: Cleaning Out the Medicine Cabinet.
Afterlife, The.
At the Bait Stand.
At the Bus Stop Next to the Funeral Home.
At the End of the Weekend.
August.
Beer Bottle.
Birthday.
Blind Always Come as Such a Surprise, The.
Boarding House.
Book Club.
Carrie.
Christmas Eve.
Constellation Orion, The.
Death at the Office, A.
Drive in the Country, A.
Dry Winter Letter to Friends, A.
Empty Place, An.

Failed Suicide, The.
First Snow.
Five P.M.
For a Friend.
Fort Robinson.
Frozen Stream, A.
Furnace.
Geek, The.
Goldfish Floats to the Top of His Life, The.
Grandfather.
Grandfather Cap, The.
Hairnet with Stars, A.
Highway 30.
Hot Night in Wheat Country, A.
Houses at the Edge of Town.
How to Foretell a Change in the Weather.
How to Make Rhubarb Wine.
In a Country Cemetery in Iowa.
In an Old Apple Orchard.
In the Corners of Fields.
In the Kitchen, at Midnight.
Late February.
Late Lights in Minnesota.
Late September.
Leaky Faucet, The.
Letter From Aunt Belle, A.
Living Near the Rehabilitation Home.
Looking for You, Barbara.
Man with the Hearing Aid, The.
Moles.
My Grandfather Dying.
New Year's Day.
North of Alliance.
Notes on the Death of Nels Paulssen, Farmer, at the Ripe Old Age of 93.
Old Photograph, An.
Old Soldiers' Home.
Old Woman, The.
Place in Kansas, A.
Pocket Poem.
Presidential Poem, A.
Red Wing Church, The.
Salesman, The.
Selecting a Reader.
Self-Portrait at Thirty-Nine.
Shooting a Farmhouse.
Sitting All Evening Alone in the Kitchen.
Skeleton in the Closet, The.
Sleeping Cat.
Snow Fence.
So This Is Nebraska.
Soul of Twins, The.
Spring Plowing.
Summer Night, A.
Sunday Morning.
Sure Signs.
Tattooed Lady, The.
There Is Always a Little Wind.
They Had Torn Off My Face at the Office.
Tom Ball's Barn.
Uncle Adler.
Very Old, The.
Visiting Mountains.
Walking Beside a Creek.
Walking to Work.
West Window.
Widow, A.
Widow Lester, The.
Year's End.

Kunitz, Stanley Jasspon (b. 1905)
After the Last Dynasty.
Again! Again!
Ambergris.
Among the Gods.
Approach of Autumn.
Approach to Thebes, The.
Around Pastor Bonhoeffer.
Artist, The.
As Flowers Are.
Benediction.
Between the Acts.
Beyond Reason.
Blessing of Women, A.
Bottom of the Glass, The.
By Lamplight.
Careless Love.
Catch, The.

Change.
Choice of Weapons, A.
Class Will Come to Order, The.
Confidential Instructions.
Crystal Cage, The.
Customs Collector's Report, The.
Dark and the Fair, The.
Daughters of the Horseleech, The.
Death in Moonlight.
Deciduous Branch.
Dragonfly, The.
Eagle.
Economist's Song, The.
End of Summer.
Extermination Camp, The.
Father and Son.
Firesticks.
First Love.
Fitting of the Mask, The.
Flight of Apollo, The.
For Proserpine.
For the Word Is Flesh.
Foreign Affairs.
Game, The.
Geometry of Moods.
Girl with Sampler.
Gladiators, The.
Goose Pond.
Grammar Lesson.
Green Ways.
Guilty Man, The.
Hand-Rolled Cigarettes.
Harsh Judgment, The.
He.
Hemorrhage, The.
Hermetic Poem.
How Long Is the Night?
I Dreamed That I Was Old.
Illumination, The.
Illusionist, The.
In a Strange House.
Indian Summer at Land's End.
Invocation: "Soul of my soul, in the ancestral wood."
Journal for My Daughter.
King of the River.
Knot, The.
Last Picnic, The.
Last Question, The.
Last Words.
Layers, The.
Lincoln Relics, The.
Lovers Relentlessly.
Magic Curtain, The.
Man Upstairs, The.
Master and Mistress.
Me and the Rock.
Meditations on Death.
Mens Creatrix.
Motion of Wish.
Mound Builders, The.
Mulch, The.
My Sisters.
My Surgeons.
Next to Last Things.
Night Letter.
Night-Piece.
No Word.
Off Point Lotus.
Old Clothes Man, The.
Old Cracked Tune, An.
Open the Gates.
Organic Bloom.
Particular Lullaby.
Parting.
Pivot, The.
Plot Against Hitler, The.
Poem: "O Heart: this is a dream I had, or not a dream."
Portrait, The.
Postscript.
Promise Me.
Prophecy on Lethe.
Quarrel, The.
Quinnapoxet.
Reckoning, The.
Reflection by a Mailbox.

Regard of Tangents.
Revolving Meditation.
River Road.
Robin Redbreast.
Route Six.
Rover.
Sacred to the Memory.
Science of the Night, The.
Scourge, The.
Separation, The.
She Wept, She Railed.
Signal from the House, The.
Signs and Portents.
Silence.
Single Vision.
So Intricately Is This World Resolved.
Sotto Voce.
Spark of Laurel, A.
Strange Calendar.
Summer Solstice.
Summing-up, The.
Supper Before Last, The.
System, The.
Testing-Tree, The.
Thief, The.
Thing That Eats the Heart, The.
This Day This World.
Three Floors.
To a Slave Named Job.
Transformations.
Tristia.
Trompe L'Oeil.
Tutored Child, The.
Twilight.
Unquiet Ones, The.
Unwithered Garland, The.
Very Tree.
Vita Nuova.
Waltzer in the House, The.
War against the Trees, The.
Way Down, The.
Welcome the Wrath.
What of the Night?
When the Dead Arise.
When the Light Falls.
Words for the Unknown Makers: A Garland
    of Commemorative Verses.
Words of the Preacher, The.
Translations, Coauthored Poems, etc.:
Bolsheviks.
Boris Pasternak.
Cleopatra.
Dante.
To the Reader.

L

Larkin, Philip (1922–85)
Absences.
Administration.
After-Dinner Remarks.
Afternoons.
Age.
All Catches Alight.
Ambulances.
And Now the Leaves Suddenly Lose
    Strength.
And the Wave Sings Because It Is Moving.
Annus Mirabilis.
Ape Experiment Room.
April Sunday Brings the Snow, An.
Arrival.
Arrivals, Departures.
Arundel Tomb, An.
As a War in Years of Peace.
As Bad as a Mile.
At Grass.
At the Chiming of Light upon Sleep.
At Thirty-One, When Some Are Rich.
Aubade: "I work all day, and get half-drunk
    at night."
Autobiography at an Air-Station.
Autumn.
Autumn Has Caught Us in Our Summer
    Wear.
Best Society.

Born Yesterday.
Bottle Is Drunk Out by One, The.
Breadfruit.
Bridge for the Living.
Broadcast.
Building, The.
By Day, a Lifted Study-Storehouse.
Card-Players, The.
Church Going.
Climbing the Hill within the Deafening
    Wind.
Come Then to Prayers.
Coming.
Coming at Last to Night's Most Thankful
    Springs.
Compline.
Conscript.
Continuing to Live.
Counting.
Cut Grass.
Daily Things We Do, The.
Dance, The.
Dancer, The.
Dawn.
Days.
Dear CHARLES, My Muse, Asleep or Dead.
Deceptions.
Dedicated, The.
Deep Analysis.
Disintegration.
Dockery and Son.
Dublinesque.
Essential Beauty.
Explosion, The.
Faith Healing.
Far Out.
Femmes Damnees.
Fiction and the Reading Public.
First Sight.
For Sidney Bechet.
Forget What Did.
Fragment from May.
Friday Night in the Royal Station.
Gathering Wood.
Going.
Going, Going.
Good for You, Gavin.
Having Grown Up in Shade of Church and
    State.
He Hears That His Beloved Has Become
    Engaged.
Heads in the Women's Ward.
Heaviest of Flowers, the Head.
Here.
High Windows.
Hills in Their Recumbent Postures, The.
Homage to a Government.
Home Is So Sad.
Horns of the Morning, The.
Hospital Visits.
House on the Edge of the Serious Wood,
    The.
How.
How Distant.
How to Sleep.
I Am Washed upon a Rock.
I Dreamed of an Out-Thrust Arm of Land.
I Have Started to Say.
I Put My Mouth.
I Remember, I Remember.
I See a Girl Dragged by the Wrists.
If Grief Could Burn Out.
If Hands Could Free You, Heart.
If My Darling.
Ignorance.
Importance of Elsewhere, The.
In TImes When Nothing Stood.
Is It Now Or For Always.
Kick Up the Fire, and Let the Flames Break
    Loose.
Large Cool Store, The.
Last Will and Testament.
Latest Face.
Letter to a Friend about Girls.
Life with a Hole in It, The.
Lift through the Breaking Day.
Like the Train's Beat.

Lines on a Young Lady's Photograph Album.
Literary World, The.
Little Lives of Earth and Form, The.
Livings.
Local Snivels through the Field, The.
Long Last.
Long Lion Days.
Long Roots Moor Summer to Our Side of
    Earth.
Long Sight in Age.
Love.
Love Again.
Love Songs in Age.
Love, We Must Part Now.
Maiden Name.
Many Famous Feet Have Trod.
March Past, The.
Marriages.
Maturity.
May Weather.
Midsummer Night, 1940.
Midwinter Waking.
Mr. Bleaney.
Modesties.
Money.
Moon Is Full Tonight, The.
Morning at Last: There in the Snow.
Morning Has Spread Again.
Mother, Summer, I.
Mower, The.
Mythological Introduction.
Myxomatosis.
Naturally the Foundation Will Bear Your
    Expenses.
Negative Indicative.
Neurotics.
New Eyes Each Year.
New Year.
Next, Please.
Night-Music.
MCMXIV.
No Road.
None of the Books Have Time.
North Ship, The.
Nothing Significant Was Really Said.
Nothing to Be Said.
Nursery Tale.
Observation.
Old Fools, The.
On Being Twenty-Six.
One Man Walking a Deserted Platform.
Out in the Lane I Pause.
Party Politics.
Past Days of Gales.
Pigeons.
Places, Loved Ones.
Plymouth.
Poem about Oxford.
Poetry of Departures.
Portrait.
Posterity.
Pour Away That Youth.
Reasons for Attendance.
Reference Back.
Sad Steps.
School in August, The.
Schoolmaster.
Scratch on the Scratch Pad.
Self's the Man.
Send No Money.
Seventy Feet Down.
Show Saturday.
Since the Majority of Me.
Sinking Like Sediment through the Day.
Skin.
Slight Relax of Air Where Cold Was, A.
So through that unripe day you bore your
    head.
So You Have Been, Despite Parental Ban.
Solar.
Spirit Wooed, The.
Spring.
Spring Warning.
Stone Church Damaged by a Bomb, A.
Story.
Strangers.
Street Lamps.

Study of Reading Habits, A.
Success Story.
Summer Nocturne.
Sunny Prestatyn.
Sympathy in White Major.
Take One Home for the Kiddies.
Talking in Bed.
Thaw.
There Is No Language of Destruction.
This Be the Verse.
This Is the First Thing.
This Was Your Place of Birth, This Daytime
    Palace.
Time and Space Were Only Their Disguises.
To a Very Slow Air.
To Failure.
To My Wife.
To Put One Brick upon Another.
To the Sea.
To Write One Song, I Said.
Toads.
Toads Revisited.
Tops.
Traumerai.
Trees, The.
Triple Time.
Two Guitar Pieces.
Two Portraits of Sex.
Ugly Sister.
Ultimatum.
Under a Splendid Chestnut Tree.
Unfinished Poem.
View, The.
Waiting for Breakfast, While She Brushed
    Her Hair.
Wants.
Water.
We See the Spring Breaking across Rough
    Stone.
Wedding-Wind.
Whatever Happened?
When First We Faced, and Touching
    Showed.
When the Night Puts Twenty Veils.
When the Russian Tanks Roll Westward.
Whitsun Weddings, The.
Who Called Love Conquering.
Who Whistled for the Wind, That It Should
    Break.
Why Did I Dream of You Last Night?
Wild Oats.
Winter.
Winter Nocturne.
Winter Palace, The.
Wires.
Within the Dream You Said.
Writer, A.

Lawrence, David Herbert (1885–1930)
À La Maniere De D. H. Lawrence.
Absolute Reverence.
Abysmal Immortality.
After All Saints' Day.
After All the Tragedies Are Over.
After Dark.
After Many Days.
After School.
After the Opera.
Afternoon in School / The Last Lesson.
Afternoon / The Last Lesson.
Ah, Muriel!
Ah, with His Blessing Bright on Thy Mouth
    and Thy Brow.
All I Ask.
All-Knowing.
All of Roses.
All Sorts of Gods.
All Souls.
All Souls' Day.
All That We Have Is Life.
Almond Blossom.
Aloof in Gaiety.
Altercation.
Always This Paying.
American Eagle, The.
Amo Sacrum Vulgus.
Anaxagoras.
And Jude the Obscure and His Beloved.

And Oh—That the Man I Am Might Cease
    to Be.
Andraitx—Pomegranate Flowers.
Another Ophelia.
Apostrophe to a Buddhist Monk.
Appeal, The.
Are You Pining?
Argonauts, The.
Aristocracy of the Sun.
As for Me, I'm a Patriot.
As Thyself!
Ass, The.
Assuming the Burden.
Astronomical Changes.
At Last.
At Midnight.
At the Bank in Spain.
At the Cearne.
At the Front.
At the Window.
Attack, The.
Attila.
August Holidays.
Auto-Da-Fé.
Autumn at Taos.
Autumn Rain.
Autumn Sunshine.
Aware.
Baby Asleep after Pain, A.
Baby-Movements.
Baby Running Barefoot.
Baby Songs Ten Months Old.
Baby Tortoise.
Bad Beginning, A.
Ballad of a Wilful Woman.
Ballad of Another Ophelia.
Bare Almond-Trees.
Bare Fig-trees.
Basta!
Bat.
Bathing Resort.
Battle of Life.
Bavarian Gentians.
Be a Demon!
Be It So.
Be Still!
Beautiful Old Age.
Behaviour.
Bei Hennef.
Being Alive.
Belief.
Bells.
Beloved.
Bereavement.
Best of School, The.
Beware, O My Dear Young Men.
Beware the Unhappy Dead!
Beyond the Rockies.
Bibbles.
Birdcage Walk.
Birth Night.
Birthday.
Bits *sels*.
Bits.
Blank.
Blue Jay, The.
Blueness.
Bodiless God.
Body of God, The.
Bombardment.
Boredom, Ennui, Depression.
Both Sides of the Medal.
Boundary Stone, The.
Bourgeois and Bolshevist.
Bowls.
Bread upon the Waters.
Breath of Life, The.
Bride, The.
British Boy, The.
British Sincerity.
British Workman and the Government, The.
Brittannia's Baby.
Broadcasting to the G.B.P.
Brooding Grief.
But I Say unto You: Love One Another.
Butterfly.
Cabbage-Roses.

Call into Death.
Campions.
Can't Be Borne.
Canvassing for the Election.
Casualty.
Censors.
Cerebral Emotions.
Change.
Change of Government.
Change of Life.
Chastity.
Cherry Robbers.
Chief Mystery, The.
Child and the Soldier, The.
Children Singing in School.
Chimaera.
Choice.
Choice of Evils.
Church, The.
City-Life.
Classes.
Climb Down, O Lordly Mind.
Climbing Down.
Climbing Up.
Clydesider.
Cold Blood.
Coldness in Love.
Collier's Wife, The.
Combative Spirit, The.
Come Spring, Come Sorrow.
Coming Awake.
Coming of Quetzalcoatl, The.
Commandments.
Compari.
Conceit.
Conscience.
Conundrums.
Corot.
Correspondence in After Years.
Courage.
Cowardice and Impudence.
Cowards.
Craving for Spring.
Cross, The.
Cry of the Masses.
Cups.
Cypresses.
Daddy-Do-Nothing.
Dark Satanic Mills.
Daughter of the Great Man, The.
Dawn Verse, The.
Dead People.
Deadly Victorians, The.
Death.
Death of Our Era, The.
Death of the Baron, The.
December Night.
Decision, A.
Deeper Than Love.
Deepest Sensuality, The.
Delight of Being Alone.
Demiurge.
Democracy.
Democracy Is Serivce.
Demon Justice.
Departure.
Desire.
Desire Goes Down into the Sea.
Desire Is Dead.
Destiny.
Dies Illa.
Dies Irae.
Difference, The.
Difficult Death.
Disagreeable Advice.
Discipline.
Discord in Childhood.
Dissolute.
Doe at Evening, A.
Dog-Tired.
Dolour of Autumn.
Dominant Woman.
Don Juan.
Don't Look at Me.
Don'ts.
Doors.
Drained Cup, The.

Drama, A.
Drawing-Room.
Dream-Confused.
Dreams Old and Nascent.
Dreams Old and Nascent: Nascent.
Dreams Old and Nascent: Old.
Drill in the Heat.
Drunk.
Dust in the East.
Eagle in New Mexico.
Early Spring.
Editorial Office.
Effort of Love, The.
Ego-Bound.
Ego-Bound Women.
Egoists, The.
Elderly Discontented Women.
Elegy: "Sun immense and rosy, The."
Elemental.
Elements, The.
Elephant.
Elephant Is Slow to Mate, The.
Elephants in the Circus.
Elephants Plodding.
Elixir.
Eloi, Eloi, Lama Sabachthani?
Elysium.
Emasculation.
Embankment at Night, before the War: Charity.
Embankment at Night, before the War: Outcasts.
Emotional Friend, The.
Emotional Lies.
En Masse.
End of Another Home Holiday.
End, The.
End, The Beginning, The.
Endless Anxiety.
Energetic Women.
England in 1929.
English Are So Nice!, The.
Enkindled Spring, The.
Erinnyes.
Erotic.
Escape.
Eve.
Evening.
Evening Land, The.
Everlasting Flowers.
Evil Is Homeless.
Evil World-Soul, The.
Factory Cities, The.
Failure, A.
Fall of Day, The.
Fallen Leaves.
False Democracy and Real.
Fatality.
Fate and the Younger Generation.
Fatigue.
Fear of Society Is the Root of All Evil.
Fellow-Men.
Female Coercion.
Fidelity.
Fight! O My Young Men.
Figs.
Film Passion.
Finding Your Level.
Fire.
Fireflies in the Corn.
First Morning.
First Song of Huitzilopochtli.
Fish.
Flapper.
Flapper Vote.
Flat-Foot's Song.
Flat Suburbs, S.W., in the Morning.
Flowers.
Flowers and Men.
Food of the North.
For a Moment.
For All That.
For the Heroes Are Dipped in Scarlet.
Forecast.
Foreign Sunset.
Forget.
Forsaken and Forlorn.

Forte Dei Marmi.
Four, The.
Free Will.
Fresh Water.
From a College Window.
Fronleichnam.
Frost Flowers.
Full Life.
Furniture.
Future Relationships.
Future Religion.
Future States.
Future War.
Gazelle Calf, The.
Gentleman, The.
Giorno dei Morti.
Gipsy.
Girl in Cairo, The.
Give Me a Sponge.
Give Us Gods.
Give Us the Thebaïd.
Gladness of Death.
Glimpses.
Gloire de Dijon.
Glory.
Glory of Darkness.
God.
God and the Holy Ghost.
God Is Born.
Gods.
Gods, The.
Gods! The Gods!, The.
Goethe and Pose.
Going Back.
Good Husbands Make Unhappy Wives.
Goodnight.
Grapes.
Grasshopper Is a Burden.
Great Newspaper Editor to His Subordinate, The.
Greeks Are Coming!, The.
Green.
Grey Evening.
Grey Nurse, The.
Grief.
Gross, Coarse, Hideous.
Grudge of the Old, The.
Guards.
Guelder Roses.
Gulf, The.
Half-Blind, The.
Hands of God, The.
Hands of the Betrothed, The.
Hard-Boiled Conservatives.
Hark in the Dusk!
Have Done With It.
He-Goat.
Healing.
Heart of Man, The.
Henriette.
Hibiscus and Salvia Flowers.
Hills, The.
Him with His Tail in His Mouth.
History.
Hold Back!
Honeymoon.
Hostile Sun, The.
Houseless Dead, The.
How Beastly the Bourgeois Is.
How can I teach you when your blue.
Huitzilopochtli Gives the Black Blade of Death.
Huitzilopochtli's Watch.
Human Face, The.
Humanity Needs Pruning.
Humiliation.
Humility.
Humility Mongers.
Humming-Bird.
Hyde Park at Night, before the War.
Hymn to Nothingness.
Hymn to Priapus.
I Am in a Novel.
I Am Like a Rose.
I Dare Do All.
I Heard Her Say.
I Know a Noble Englishman.

I Wish I Knew a Woman.
If You Are a Man.
Ignoble Procession, The.
Image-Making Love.
Immoral Man.
Immorality.
Impulse.
In a Boat.
In a Spanish Tram-Car.
In Church.
In Nottingham.
In the Cities.
In the Dark.
In Trouble and Shame.
Inheritance, The.
Initiation Degrees.
Innocent England.
Intimates.
Invocation to the Moon.
Irreverent Thoughts.
It's Either You Fight or You Die.
It's No Good!
Jealousy.
Jesus' Farewell.
Jeune Fille, The.
Jewess and the V.C., The.
Kangaroo.
Keep It Up.
Kill Money.
Kiss, A.
Kisses in the Train.
Kissing and Horrid Strife.
Know-All.
Know Deeply, Know Thyself More Deeply.
Know Thyself.
Know Thyself, and That Thou Art Mortal.
Labour Battalion.
Lady Wife.
Land-Worker.
Last Hours.
Last Lesson of the Afternoon.
Last Minute, The.
Last Words to Miriam.
Last Words to Muriel.
Late at Night.
Late War, The.
Latent Desire, The.
Latter-Day Sinners.
Laughter.
Leave Sex Alone.
Leaves of Grass, Flowers of Grass.
Leda.
Let the Dead Bury Their Dead.
Let There Be Light!
Let Us Be Men.
Let Us Talk, Let Us Laugh.
Letter from Town: On a Grey Morning in March.
Letter from Town: The Almond-Tree.
Liaison.
Liberty's Old Old Story.
Lies.
Lies About Love.
Life and the Human Consciousness.
Lightning.
Like the Green Candles of Malintzi.
Lilies in the Fire.
Listen to the Band!
Listening.
Litany of Grey Nurses.
Little-Boy Brilliant.
Little Fish.
Little Town at Evening, The.
Little Wowser, The.
Living, A.
Living Quetzalcoatl, The.
Lizard.
Loggerheads.
London Mercury.
Loneliness.
Lonely, Lonesome, Loney—O!
Lord of the Morning Star.
Lord Tennyson and Lord Melchett.
Lords of Life Are the Masters of Death, The.
Lord's Prayer.
Loss.
Lotus and Frost.

Love.
Love as an Escape.
Love Comes Late.
Love Message.
Love on the Farm.
Love-Passage, A.
Love Song, A: "Reject me not if I should say to you."
Love Storm.
Love Thy Neighbour.
Lucifer.
Lucky Little Britisher.
Lui et Elle.
Magnificent Democracy.
Maiden's Prayer.
Malade.
Man, A.
Man and Bat.
Man and Machine.
Man at Play on the River, A.
Man Hauling a Wagon.
Man in the Street, The.
Man Is More Than *Homo Sapiens*.
Man of Tyre, The.
Man Reaches a Point.
Man Who Died, A.
Mana of the Sea.
Manifesto.
Many Mansions.
Married in June.
Martyr à la Mode.
Masses and Classes.
Maximus.
Maybe.
Mediterranean in January.
Medlars and Sorb-Apples.
Meeting among the Mountains.
Men and Women.
Men Are Not Bad.
Men in New Mexico.
Men Like Gods.
Mesopotamia.
Mess of Love, The.
Message to Perfidious Soldier.
Metal for Resistance.
Michael Angelo.
Mid-Day Verse, The.
Middle-Class Children.
Middle Classes, The.
Middle of the World.
Mills of God, The.
Minorities in Danger.
Misery.
Mr Squire.
Modern Prayer.
Modern Problems.
Money.
Money-Madness.
Monologue of a Mother.
Moon Memory.
Moon New-Risen.
Moonrise.
Moral Clothing.
Morality.
Morning / Scripture Lesson.
Morning Work.
Mosquito Knows, The.
Mosquito, The.
Moth and Rust.
Mother's Son in Salonika.
Mountain Lion.
Mournful Young Man.
Mourning.
Mowers, The.
Multitudes.
Munitions.
Murder.
Murderous Weapons.
Mutilation.
My Enemy.
My Little Critics.
My Name Is Jesus.
My Native Land.
My Naughty Book.
My Way Is Not Thy Way.
Mystery.
Mystic.

Name the Gods!
Narcissus.
Natural Complexion.
Neither Moth Nor Rust.
Nemesis.
Neptune's Little Affair with Freedom.
New Brooms.
New Heaven and Earth.
New Houses, New Clothes.
New Moon.
New Word, The.
New Year's Eve.
New Year's Night.
Next Morning.
Night.
Night Songs.
No Joy in Life.
No! Mr Lawrence!
No News.
Noble.
Noise of Battle.
Noli Me Tangere.
Non-Existence.
Nonentity.
North Country, The.
Nostalgia.
Nothing to Save.
Nottingham's New University.
November by the Sea.
Now It's Happened.
Nullus.
O! Americans.
O! Start a Revolution.
Obscenity.
Obsequial Ode.
Oh Wonderful Machine!
Old Archangels.
Old Idea of Sacrifice, The.
Old Men.
Old Orchard, The.
Old People.
Old Song.
On and On and On.
On That Day.
On the Balcony.
On the Drum.
On the March.
On the Road.
One Woman to All Women.
Only Man.
Only the Best Matters.
Optimist, The.
Other Women Have Reared in Me.
Our Day Is Over.
Our Moral Age.
Oxford Voice, The.
Painter's Wife, The.
Paltry-Looking People.
Pang of Reminiscence, A.
Paradise Re-entered.
Parliament Hill in the Evening.
Passing-Bell, A.
Passing Visit to Helen.
Pax.
Peace.
Peace and War.
Peach.
Peacock.
Pear-Blossom.
People.
People, The.
People Who Care.
Phoenix.
Piano.
Piano, The.
Piccadilly Circus at Night.
Pietá.
Played-Out Game, A.
Poison.
Police Spies.
Pomegranate.
Poor Bit of a Wench!
Poor Young Things.
Portraits.
Poverty.
Prayer: "Give me the moon at my feet."
Prestige.

Primal Passions, The.
Prisoner at Work in a Turkish Garden.
Prisoners at Work in the Rain.
Proper Pride.
Property and No-Property.
Property Question, The.
Prophet.
Prophet in the Rose Garden, The.
Protestant Churches, The.
Punisher, The.
Purple Anemones.
Puss-Puss!
Question.
Quetzalcoatl Looks Down on Mexico.
Quite Forsaken.
Rabbit Snared in the Night.
Race and Battle.
Rainbow.
Rainbow, The.
Rallying-Point.
Reach Over.
Reading a Letter.
Reading in the Evening.
Real Democracy.
Reality of Peace, 1916.
Rebuked.
Red.
Red Geranium and Godly Mignonette.
Red-Herring.
Red Moon-Rise.
Red Wolf, The.
Refused Friendship.
Relativity.
Release.
Religion.
Reminder.
Renaissance.
Repulsed.
Restlessness.
Resurrection.
Resurrection of the Flesh.
Retort to Jesus.
Retort to Whitman.
Return.
Return of Returns.
Revolutionary, The.
Revolutions as Such!
Riches.
Rise in the World, A.
Risen Lord, The.
River Roses.
Robot-Democracy.
Robot Feelings.
Rondeau of a Conscientious Objector.
Root of Our Evil, The.
Rose and Cabbage.
Rose Is Not a Cabbage, A.
Rose of All the World.
Rose of England, The.
Roses.
Roses on the Breakfast Table.
Ruination.
Running Barefoot.
Saddest Day, The.
St George and the Dragon.
St John.
St Luke.
St Mark.
St Matthew.
Salt.
Salt of the Earth.
Salvation.
Sane and Insane.
Sane Revolution, A.
Sane Universe, The.
Satisfaction.
Scent of Irises.
School on the Outskirts.
Schoolmaster [A], The *sels*.
Schoolmaster [A], The.
Schoolmaster [B], The.
Scientific Doctor, The.
Sea-Bathers.
Sea, The.
Sea, the Sea, The.
Sea-Weed.
Search for Love.

Search for Truth.
Second Song of Huitzilopochtli.
Secret Waters, The.
Seekers.
Self-Conscious People.
Self-Pity.
Self-Protection.
Self-Sacrifice.
Sense of Truth.
Separated.
Service.
Seven Seals.
Sex and Trust.
Sex Isn't Sin.
Sex Won't Work.
Shades.
Shadow of Death, The.
Shadows.
She-Goat.
She Looks Back.
She Said as Well to Me.
She Was a Good Little Wife.
Shedding of Blood.
Ship of Death.
Ship of Death, The.
Ships in Bottles.
Shows.
Sicilian Cyclamens.
Sick.
Sickness.
Side-Step, O Sons of Men!
Sigh No More.
Sighs.
Sight of God, The.
Signs of the Times.
Silence.
Sinners.
Sleep.
Sleep and Waking.
Snake.
Snap-Dragon.
Snowy Day at School, A.
Snowy Day in School, A.
So Let Me Live.
So There!
Softly, Then, Softly.
Solomon's Baby.
Someone Will Enter between the Gates.
Son of the Morning Star.
Song-Day in Autumn.
Song of a Man Who Has Come Through.
Song of a Man Who Is Loved.
Song of a Man Who Is Not Loved.
Song of Death.
Song of Don Ramon, The.
Song of the Dead.
Song of the Grey Dog, The.
Song to the Tune of La Cucaracha.
Song: "Up in the high."
Songs I Learnt at School.
Sorrow.
Souls to Save.
Southern Night.
Space.
Spanish Privilege.
Spanish Wife, The.
Sphinx.
Spilling the Salt.
Spiral Flame.
Spirits Summoned West.
Spiritual Woman, A.
Spray.
Spring Morning.
Stand Up!
Stoic.
Stop It.
Storm in the Black Forest.
Street Lamps.
Strife.
Study.
Submergence.
Suburbs on a Hazy Day.
Sun in Me.
Sun-Men.
Sun-Women.
Sunday Afternoon in Italy.
Sunset.

Sunset Verse, The.
Suspense.
Swan.
Swing Song of a Girl and a Soldier.
Sympathy.
Tabernacle.
Tale Told by an Idiot, A.
Tales.
Talk.
Talk of Faith.
Talk of Loyalty.
Tarantella.
Tarts.
Tease.
Temples.
Tender Reverence.
Terra Incognita.
There Are No Gods.
There Are Too Many People.
There Is No Way Out.
There Is Rain in Me.
There Was a Gay Bird Named Christine.
They Say the Sea Is Loveless.
Thief in the Night.
Things Made by Iron.
Things Men Have Made.
Think—!
Third Song of Huitzilopochtli.
Third Thing, The.
13 Pictures.
13,000 People.
Thomas Earp.
Thought.
To a Certain Friend.
To Be Superior.
To Clarinda.
To Let Go Or to Hold on—?
To Lettice, My Sister.
To Pino.
To Toss the Troubled Night Long.
To Women, as Far as I'm Concerned.
Today.
Tolerance.
Tommies in the Train.
Tomorrow Night.
Tortoise Family Connections.
Tortoise Gallantry.
Tortoise-Shell.
Tortoise Shout.
Touch.
Touch Comes.
Tourists.
Town in 1917.
Tragedy.
Trailing Clouds.
Train at Night, A.
Train, The.
Traitors.
Transformations.
Travel Is Over.
Trees in the Garden.
Triumph.
Triumph of the Machine, The.
Tropic.
Troth with the Dead.
True Democracy.
True Love at Last.
Trust.
Turkey-Cock.
Turned Down.
Twenty Years Ago.
Twilight.
Two-Fold.
Two Fragments on Sleep.
Two Performing Elephants.
Two Ways of Living and Dying.
Two Wives.
Twofold.
Ultimate Reality.
Under the Oak.
Underneath.
Unhappy Souls.
Universe Flows, The.
Up He Goes!
Uprooted, The.
Valentine's Night.
Vengeance Is Mine.

Vibration of Justice.
Vicar's Son.
Violets.
Violets for the Dead.
Virgin Mother, The.
Virgin Youth.
Vitality.
Volcanic Venus.
Wages.
Walk Warily.
Wandering Cosmos, The.
War-Baby.
Way Out, The.
We Are Transmitters.
We Can't Be Too Careful.
We Die Together.
We Have Gone Too Far.
Wealth.
Wedding Morn.
Wedlock.
Weeknight Service.
Welcome Death.
Welcome to Quetzalcoatl.
Well in Africa, The.
Wellsian Futures.
What Ails Thee?
What Are the Gods?
What Are the Wild Waves Saying?
What Do I Care?
What Does She Want?
What Have They Done to You?
What Is a Man to Do?
What Is He?
What Is Man Without an Income.
What Matters.
What Quetzalcoatl Saw in Mexico.
What Then Is Evil?
What Would You Fight For?
Whatever Man Makes.
What's Sane and What Isn't.
What's to Be Done.
What's Wrong.
When I Read Shakespeare.
When I Went to the Circus.
When I Went to the Film.
When Most Men Die.
When Satan Fell.
When the Ripe Fruit Falls.
When Wilt Thou Teach the People?
Whether or Not.
White Blossom, A.
White Horse, The.
Why—?
Why Does She Weep?
Wild Common, The.
Wild Things in Captivity.
Willy Wet-Leg.
Wind, the Rascal, The.
Winter Dawn.
Winter in the Boulevard.
Winter-Lull.
Winter's Tale, A.
Witch I, The.
Witch II, The.
Woe.
Women Want Fighters for Their Lovers.
Wonderful Spiritual Women.
Won't It Be Strange—?
Work.
Work of Creation, The.
Working Man, The.
Worm Either Way.
Worm Turns, The.
Worship.
Yesternight.
Yew-Tree on the Downs, The.
You.
Young and Their Moral Guardians, The.
Young Are Not Greedy, The.
Young Are Not Mean in Material Things, The.
Young Fathers.
Young Soldier with Bloody Spurs, The.
Young Want to Be Just, The.
Young Wife, A.
Youth Mowing, A.
Zeppelin Nights.

Lennon, John see Beatles, The

Levertov, Denise (b. 1923)
Abel's Bride.
About Marriage.
Above the Cave.
Ache of Marriage, The.
Air of November.
Altars in the Street, The.
Annuals.
Another Spring.
As It Happens.
Bedtime.
Breathing, The.
Cat as Cat, The.
Ce bruit da la mer.
City Psalm.
Claritas.
Closed World, The.
Clouds.
Come into Animal Presence.
Coming Fall, The.
Common Ground, A.
Crack, The.
Cure of Souls, A.
Day Begins, A.
Deaths.
Depths, The.
Didactic Poem.
Disclosure, The.
During the Eichmann Trial.
Earth Psalm.
Earth Worm, The.
Else a great Prince in prison lies.
Elves, The.
Eros.
Eros at Temple Stream.
Face to Face.
Figure of Time, A.
Film, The.
Five Poems from Mexico.
For Floss.
Fountain, The.
From the Roof.
Garden Wall, The.
Gone Away.
Grace-Note, The.
Grey Sparrow Addresses the Mind's Ear.
Ground-Mist, The.
Hymn to Eros.
Hypocrite Women.
Illustration [—a Footnote], The.
In Abeyance.
In Memory of Boris Pasternak.
In Mind.
Into the Interior.
Jacob's Ladder, The.
Joy.
Kingdoms of Heaven.
Lamentation, A.
Leaving Forever.
Letter to William Kinter of Muhlenberg, A.
Life at War.
Living.
Living While It May.
Looking-Glass.
Losing Track.
Love Song.
Luxury.
Man, A.
Map of the Western Part of the County of
    Essex in England, A.
March, A.
Matins.
Melody Grundy.
Message.
Message, The.
Music, A.
Mutes, The.
Necessity, The.
Night on Hatchet Cove.
Note to Olga (1966), A.
Novel, The.
Novices, The.
O Taste and See.
October.
Old Adam, The.
Olga Poems.

Our Bodies.
Overheard.
Part, The.
Partial Resemblance.
Perspectives.
Postcards: A Triptych, The.
Prayer, The.
Presence, The.
Psalm Concerning the Castle.
Psalm Praising the Hair of Man's Body, A.
Pulse, The.
Puñal.
Rainwalkers, The.
Remembering.
Resolve, The.
Resting Figure.
Revivals.
Ripple, The.
Runes, The.
Second Didactic Poem.
Secret, The.
Seedtime.
September 1961.
Sequence, A.
Shalom.
Six Variations.
Skew Lines.
Solitude, A.
Son, The.
Song for a Dark Voice.
Song for Ishtar.
Sparks.
Stems.
Stepping Westward.
Stonecarver's Poem, The.
Thirst Song.
Thread, The.
Three Meditations.
Threshold.
Tide, The.
To Speak.
To the Muse.
To the Reader.
Travels.
Tulips, The.
Turn of the Head, A.
Two Variations.
Unknown, The.
Victors, The.
Vision, A.
Walk through the Notebooks, A.
Well, The.
What Were They Like?
When We Look Up.
Whisper, The.
Who Is at My Window.
Willows of Massachusetts, The.
Window, A.
Wings, The.
World Outside, The.

Levine, Philip (b. 1928)
Across the world / in the high mountains of
    the West.
And the Trains Go On.
Angel Butcher.
Animals Are Passing from Our Lives.
Ashes.
Ask the Roses.
At the Fillmore.
Baby Villon.
Belief.
Belle Isle, 1949.
Blasting from Heaven.
Breath.
Buying and Selling.
Cemetery at Academy, California, The.
Children's Crusade, The.
Clouds.
Coming Home, *Detroit*, 1968.
Conductor of Nothing, The.
Detroit Grease Shop Poem.
Dog Poem.
Face, The.
Fist.
For Fran.
Fox, The.
Francisco, I'll Bring You Red Carnations.

Genius.
Gift for a Believer.
Goodbye.
Grandmother in Heaven.
Having Been Asked "What is a Man?" I
    Answer.
Hear Me.
Heaven.
Helmet, The.
Hold Me.
Holding On.
Horse, The.
How many lives were torn apart.
How Much Can It Hurt?
How Much Earth.
I Could Believe.
I reenter a day in a late summer.
I Was Born in Lucerne.
Jewish Graveyards, Italy.
Last Step, The.
Late Answer, A.
Late Moon.
Later Still.
Let Me Be.
Let Me Begin Again.
Letters for the Dead.
L'Homme et La Bête.
Lights I Have Seen Before.
Look.
Lost and Found.
Making It New.
Making Light of It.
Memory of rain falling slowly, The.
Midget, The.
Milkweed.
Miracle, The.
My Poets.
My Son and I.
New Day, A.
New Season.
1933.
Nitrate.
No One Remembers.
Noon.
On a Drawing by Flavio.
On My Own.
On the Birth of Good & Evil During the
    Long Winter of '28.
On the Corner.
On the Edge.
On the Murder of Lieutenant José Del
    Castillo by the Falangist Bravo Martinez,
    July 12, 1936.
One for the Rose.
Ordinary Morning, An.
Pili's Wall.
Planting.
Poem Circling Hamtramck, Michigan, All
    Night in Search of You, The.
Poem of Flight, The.
Poem with No Ending, A *sels.*
Rain Downriver.
Red Dust.
Renaming the Kings.
Roofs.
Salami.
Salts and Oils.
Saturday Sweeping.
7 Years from Somewhere.
Silent in America.
Sleepless Night, A.
Snow.
Sources.
Starlight.
Suit, The.
Sweet Will.
Theory of Prosody, A.
These Streets.
They Feed They Lion.
To a Child Trapped in a Barber Shop.
To a Fish Head Found on the Beach Near
    Málaga.
To Cipriano, in the Wind.
To get west you go east.
To My God in His Sickness.
To P.L., 1916–1937.
Told.

28.
Uncle.
Voice, The.
Waking an Angel.
Walk with Tom Jefferson, A.
We sat by the shore.
Wednesday.
White Iris, The.
Winter Words.
Words.
You Can Have It.
Zaydee.

Lewis, Alun (1915–44)
After Dunkirk.
All Day It Has Rained.
Assault Convoy, The.
Atropos to Ophelia.
Autumn, 1939.
Belief.
Beloved Beware.
Bequest.
Bivouac.
Burma Casualty.
By the Gateway of India: Bombay.
Captivity, The.
Chanson Triste.
Christmas Holiday.
Civil Servant, The.
Compassion.
Corfe Castle.
Country Gentleman, The.
Crucifixion, The.
Dancer, The.
Dawn on the East Coast.
Defeat.
Defeated: for Wales, The.
Departure, The.
Desperate, The.
Destruction.
East, The.
Easter at Christmas.
Encirclement.
Encounter, The.
Fever.
Finale.
Fragment, A: "Where aloneness fiercely."
From a Play.
Goodbye.
Greetings.
He Gives Her Botticelli's Birth of Venus as a
    Wedding Gift.
Holi.
Home Thoughts from Abroad.
Horace at Twenty.
Humanist, The.
In Hospital: Poona (1).
In Hospital: Poona (2).
Indian Day.
Indolence.
Infantry.
Island, The.
Jason and Medea.
Journey, The.
Jungle, The.
Karanje Village.
Lady in Black.
Lament: "Oh Absalom, beloved, what can I
    say?"
Letter From the Cape.
Lines on a Tudor Mansion.
Lines on a Young Girl.
Madman, The.
Mahratta Ghats, The.
Marriage Bed, The.
Merchants Wife, The.
Mid-Winter.
Midnight in India.
Mine Host.
Miniature on a Book of Hours.
Monologue.
Motifs.
Mountain over Aberdare, The.
Observation Post: Forward Area.
Odi et Amo.
Odyssey, The.
Olwen and Taliesin.
On a Bereaved Girl.

On Embarkation.
On Leave: Marriage.
On the Welsh Mountains.
Parable.
Pastorals.
Patrol, The.
Peace.
Peasant Song.
Peasants, The.
Poems from the Chinese.
Poet, The.
Port of Call: Brazil.
Post-Script: for Gweno.
Prelude and Fugue.
Prologue: The Grinder.
Public Gardens, The.
Quest, The.
Raid, The.
Raiders' Dawn.
Renewal.
Rhondda, The.
River Temple: Wai, The.
Run-In, The.
Sacco Writes to His Son.
Sentry, The.
Separation, A.
Shadows.
She Comes To Him in the Night.
She Remains.
She Wakes Early, While He Still Sleeps.
Slug, The.
Soldier, The.
Song: "I lay in sheets of softest linen."
Song: "O have you seen the thorn that
    grows."
Song: "Oh journeyman, Oh journeyman."
Song (On Seeing Dead Bodies Floating Off
    the Cape).
Songs for the Night.
Songs of Sleep.
Sonnet (Aboard a Troopship) to Gweno.
Soubrettes, The.
Southend at Dusk.
Suicide, The.
Swan's Way, The.
Swimmer, The.
They Part at Daybreak, Returning Their
    Inevitable Ways.
Threnody for a Starry Night.
Tiger of Camden Town, The.
To a Comrade in Arms.
To Edward Thomas.
To Rilke.
Troopship in the Tropics, A.
Two Legends: For Greece.
Unknown Soldier, The.
Valediction: "Through the trembling blue the
    golden porpoise plunged."
Victory.
Vigil: He Lies Awake in the Barracks Room,
    Fearful She Will Not Come, The.
Vigil: She Tarries, Far-Off, in a Strange
    Anguish, The.
Village Funeral: Maharashtra.
War Wedding.
Water Music.
Way Back, The.
Ways.
Welsh Night, A.
Westminster Abbey.
Wood Song.

Liddy, James (b. 1934)
After Hal'amová.
After Kraske.
After Life.
Afterword.
Anglos Have Gone, The.
Art Is Not for Grown-ups.
At a Czech Tomb in Tuam.
At castle shadowed mouth of the / Doonbeg.
Attention: First Lady of the Festival.
Bicentennial Words for the Liberal
    Magistrates of 1798.
Birds.
Blue Mountain.
Bright Crown of Freedom, The.
Cantico.

Cantico Per Lo Tuo Amore II.
Cantico Per Lo Tuo Amore III.
Cantico Per Lo Tuo Amore IV.
Cantico Per Lo Tuo Amore V.
Churros.
City Life.
City of Dreadful Knight, The.
Clare De Lughnasa.
Clare, the Butterflies.
Cliffs.
Coolgreany.
Correspondences.
Cottage by the Bridge.
Country Life.
Cracks in the Pavement.
Dear Anima, Show These Words.
Death of Artists, The.
Death of Lovers, The.
Death of Mathmaticians, The.
Death of the Poor.
Deaths and Electrocutions.
Debt, The.
Delphine and Hippolyta.
Dinner Menu a Burnt Offering, A.
Dorcas.
Dream of a Strange One.
Enchanter of Yellow Gold to the Old Friend,
    The.
Epithalamion I–IV: "Along a leafy lonely
    river God-shy-eyed fisher boys."
Eugene Connolly.
Evening at Axel's.
Every Evening in Axel's.
For Jimin in Manchuria II.
From This Distance: The Last Poem of the
    Clare Bards in Praise of the MacDonnells
    of Kilkee.
Glass after Oblivion.
His Refugees.
His Resplendent Neighbours.
History.
Holden.
Holden, a Thought From Abroad.
Homage to Conor Cruise O'Brien.
I Hear the Wife of the Governor of
    Wisconsin Singing.
I. M. George Fitzpatrick.
Icarus.
In a Blue Smoke.
In the Bowling Alley.
Inscribed on the Flyleaf of Richard Shay's
    Copy of Rimbaud's *Illuminations*.
Josie.
Jours-Fixes.
June 16, 1992.
Katherine Young.
Kerouac's Ronsard Dance.
La Muerte de Joselito.
Lady Fitzwilliam.
Lady/Lord in Doorway.
Last Light in Clare's Mind.
Lesbos.
Letter to Eamonn Wall, A.
Letter to Sainte-Beuve.
Litany of Satan, The.
Little Song for Ivy Day, 1991.
Love Songs of Corca Bascinn.
Many Mansions.
Maud Gonne Rode Out on a White Horse to
    Coolgreany.
May Day Song.
Miles.
Miles II.
Miles III.
Mothermas.
Munster Song of Love and War, A.
My Neighbours Two Brothers.
Narcissus and the Young Men.
Necessity of Writing in This Tongue, The.
1949: Child Redmond to Dark Wexford
    Came.
Note.
Notes towards a Video of Avondale House.
Notes towards an Ivy Leaf Video.
On a Protestant Mystic.
Orpheus as a Christian Scientist.
Orpheus in Connaught.

Ossie Esmonde.
Patrick Kavanagh's Dublin.
Personal Odyssey.
Poem for My Sister Nora, at the Reading.
Poison, The.
Prayers of a Pagan.
Price, The.
Proverbs of Corca Bascinn.
Quarter, The.
Reply of the Friend, The.
Republic 1939, The.
Requiem for a Non-Croppy.
Richard, Oremus.
River Video, The.
Roses of Parnell & Mellowes, The.
Saadians, Marble, Tile, and Flower, The.
Saint Orpheus.
Sandhills.
Scott Rautmann, Saturday Night.
Sergeant Valentine Function, at Hollyfort.
Shore.
Sister Beach, Sister Garden.
Slovak Tongue, The.
Song about Sinn Fein for Serena.
Sound of a Moment at Scariff, The.
Swinburne on the Playing Fields.
Taking One's Students to Avondale.
Third Letter to Jimin in Manchuria.
Thursdays Are Sacred.
To the Liberal Magistrates.
To the Memory of Bernard Berenson.
To the Memory of Sylvia Plath: A Personal
    Note.
Translate into Latin for my Epitaph.
Tray-Carrier of Laurels, Liam Miller.
Vir I–XII.
Vir.
Vir II.
Vir III.
Vir IV.
Vir V.
Vir VI.
Vir VII.
Vir VIII.
Vir IX.
Vir X.
Vir XI.
Vir XII.
Voyage to Cytherea, A.
Warm Mountain Poem for Matt Liban.
Wave of the Nineties, The.
White Thought in a White Shade, A.
Wine of Lovers.
Woodenbridge Golf Club.
You Came By on Bamboo Stilts, Playing
    Horse.
Your Pleasure in my Cemetery.

Lieberman, Laurence (b. 1935)
Banana Dwarf, The.
Banana Madonna, The.
Black Lotus of the Links.
Bulwark.
Coral Reef, The.
Corners.
Courtship of the Jersey Lineman.
Creole Mephistopheles, The.
Daibutsu.
Diving Ballet, The.
Dungeon Amorist, The.
82 X 48.
Eros at the World Kite Pageant.
Family Tree, The.
Flamingos of the Soda Lakes.
Flying below Sea Level.
Girard, Girard.
God's Measurements.
Homage to Austin Warren.
House Skin, The.
Increasing Night.
Inside the Gyroscope.
Island Trashfires.
Kimono.
Kofukuji Arsonists, The.
Lobsters in the Brain Coral.
Love, the Barber.
Loves of the Peacocks.
Moonlighters.

Mural of Wakeful Sleep, The.
My Father Dreams of Baseball.
Nara Park: Twilight Deer Feeding.
Organist's Black Carnation, The.
Osprey Suicides, The.
Prayer against the Curse Bomb.
Psychodrama: Tokyo Mime Film.
Queen of the Billiards.
Saltcod Red.
Santana.
Siesta.
Skateboard Throne: an Ode to Citizen
    Amputees, The.
Skin-Flying into the Storm Center.
Skin Song.
Song of the Thrush.
Spearing, The.
Stubby Carrot.
Sunday: My Throat Afire.
Swimming Pool Pastoral.
Tarpon.
Tartine, for All Her Bulk.
Tartine, Strumming Her Opera.
Tartine's Banishment.
Tilemaker's Hill Fresco, The.
Transvestite.
Unblinding, The.
Woman's Tongue.
Wreckage of the Pagoda Moons.

Lindsay, Nicholas Vachel (1879–1931)
Chinese Nightingale, The.
Above the Battle's Front.
Abraham Lincoln Walks at Midnight.
After Reading the Sad Story of the Fall of
    Babylon.
Aladdin and the Jinn.
Alexander Campbell.
Alone in the Wind, on the Prairie.
Amaranth, The.
Angel and the Clown, The.
Apology for the Bottle Volcanic, An.
Argument, An.
At Mass.
Babylon, Babylon, Babylon the Great.
Beggar Speaks, The.
Beggar's Valentine, The.
Being a Seven-Year-Old Boy's Elaborate
    Memory of the Day of His Birth.
Being My Notion, as a Ferocious Small-Boy,
    of My Ancestral Protector.
Being the Dedication of a Morning.
Beyond the Moon.
Billboards and Galleons.
Blacksmith's Serenade, The.
Booker Washington Trilogy, The.
Broncho That Would Not Be Broken, The.
Bryan, Bryan, Bryan, Bryan.
By the Spring at Sunset.
Caught in a Net.
Celestial Circus, The.
Censer-Moon, The.
Chanting of the Whales, The.
City That Will Not Repent, The.
Cold Sunbeams.
Comet of Prophecy, The.
Congo, The.
Cornfields, The.
Crickets on a Strike.
Curse for Kings, A.
Dancing for a Prize.
Dandelion, The.
Dangerous Little Boy Fairies, The.
Daniel.
Darling Daughter of Babylon.
Dirge for a Righteous Kitten, A.
Doctor Mohawk.
Doll Upon the Topmost Bough, The.
Doll's "Arabian Nights," A.
Dream of All the Springfield Writers, The.
Drunkard's Funeral, The.
Drunkards in the Street, The.
Drying Their Wings.
Eagle That Is Forgotten, The.
Eden in Winter.
Edwin Booth.
Empty Boats, The.
Encyclopædia, The.

Epilogue to the Adventures While Preaching
    the Gospel of Beauty.
Epitaph for John Bunny, Motion-Picture
    Comedian.
Epitaphs for Two Players.
Euclid.
Explanation of the Grasshopper, An.
Factory Windows Are Always Broken.
Fairy Bridal Hymn, The.
Fairy from the Apple-Seed, The.
Firemen's Ball, The.
Flower of Mending, The.
Flute of the Lonely, The.
Flying House, and the May Queen Eternal,
    The.
For All Who Ever Sent Lace Valentines.
Foreign Missions in Battle Array.
Galahad, Knight Who Perished.
Gamblers, The.
General William Booth Enters into Heaven.
Genesis.
Ghost of the Buffaloes, The.
Ghosts in Love.
Golden Whales of California.
Gospel of Beauty, A.
Hail to the Sons of Roosevelt.
Hamlet.
Harps in Heaven.
Haughty Snail-King, The.
He Climbs the Hill Where the Tree Grows.
He Gives What He Won to the Indian Girl.
He Nears the Goal.
He Receives the Bells.
He Starts on the Return Journey.
Heart of God.
Hearth Eternal, The.
Here's to the Spirit of Fire.
Honor Among Scamps.
Hope of the Resurrection, The.
How a Little Girl Danced.
How a Little Girl Sang.
How Dulcenia del Toboso Is Like the Left
    Wing of a Bird.
How Johnny Appleseed Walked Alone in the
    Jungles of Heaven.
How Samson Bore Away the Gates of Gaza.
How the Wings Were Made.
I Heard Immanuel Singing.
I Know All This When Gipsy Fiddles Cry.
I Want to Go Wandering.
I Went Down into the Desert.
Illinois Village, The.
In Memory of a Child.
In Memory of My Friend, Joyce Kilmer, Poet
    and Soldier.
In Praise of Gloriana's Remarkable Golden
    Hair.
In Praise of Johnny Appleseed.
In Praise of Songs That Die.
In the Beginning.
In the Immaculate Conception Church.
In Which a Racing Auto Comes from the
    East.
In Which Many Autos Pass Westward.
In Which Roosevelt Is Compared to Saul.
Incense.
Indian Girl Tells the Hero Where to Go to
    Get the Laughing Bell, The.
Indian Girl Who Made Them, The.
Indian Summer Day on the Prairie, An.
Indians Worship Him, but He Hurries On,
    The.
Invocation for "The Map of the Universe."
Jingo and the Minstrel, The.
John Brown.
John L. Sullivan, the Strong Boy of Boston.
Johnny Appleseed Speaks of Great Cities in
    the Future.
Johnny Appleseed Speaks of the
    Appleblossom Amaranth That Will Come
    to This City.
Johnny Appleseed's Hymn to the Sun.
Johnny Appleseed's Old Age.
Johnny Appleseed's Ship Comes In.
Johnny Appleseed's Wife from the Palace of
    Eve.
Johnny Appleseed's Wife of the Mind.

Journey Starts Swiftly, The.
Kalamazoo.
Kallyope Yell, The.
Kansas.
Kind of Scorn, A.
King Arthur's Men Have Come Again.
King of Yellow Butterflies, The.
King Solomon and the Queen of Shiba.
Knight in Disguise, The.
Lame Boy and the Fairy, The.
Last Song of Lucifer, The.
Leaden-Eyed, The.
Life Transcendent.
Lincoln.
Lion, The.
Litany of the Heroes.
Little Turtle, The.
Look You, I'll Go Pray.
Love and Law.
Mae Marsh, Motion Picture Actress.
Mark Twain and Joan of Arc.
Master of the Dance, The.
Merciful Hand, The.
Mid-Morning.
Moon Is a Painter, The.
Moon's the North Wind's Cooky, The.
Mouse That Gnawed the Oak-Tree Down,
    The.
My Fathers Came from Kentucky.
My Lady in Her White Silk Shawl.
My Lady Is Compared to a Young Tree.
Mysterious Cat, The.
Net to Snare the Moonlight, A.
Niagara.
Noon.
North Star Whispers to the Blacksmith's Son,
    The.
Old Horse in the City, The.
On Reading Omar Khayyam.
On Receiving One of Gloriana's Letters.
On Suddenly Receiving a Curl Long Refused.
On the Building of Springfield.
On the Garden Wall.
On the Road to Nowhere.
One Brief Hour of Grown-up Glory on the
    Gulf of Mexico.
Our Guardian Angels and Their Children.
Our Mother Pocahontas.
Over the Appalachian Barricade.
Parvenu.
Path in the Sky, The.
Pearl of Biloxi, The.
Perfect Marriage, The.
Poems about the Moon *sels.*
Poems Speaking of Buddha, Prince Siddartha.
Potatoes' Dance, The.
Prairie Battlements, The.
Prayer to All the Dead Among Mine Own
    People, A.
Preface to "Bob Taylor's Birthday."
Prologue to "Rhymes to be Traded for
    Bread."
Proud Farmer, The.
Queen Mab in the Village.
Queen of Bubbles, The.
Raft, The.
Rhyme About an Electrical Advertising Sign,
    A.
Rhyme for All Zionists, A.
Rhymed Address to All Renegade
    Campbellites, Exhorting Them to Return,
    A.
Rhymer's Reply: Incense and Splendor, The.
Roosevelt.
Rose of Midnight, The.
St. Francis of San Francisco.
Santa-Fé Trail (A Humoresque), The.
Scissors-Grinder, The.
Sea Serpent Chantey, The.
Sense of Humor, A.
Sew the Flags Together.
Shantung[, or The Empire of China is
    Crumbling Down].
She Becomes a Goddess.
She Becomes a Soul, Flowering Toward
    Egyptian Resurrection, B.C. 29.

She Is Lifted with the Old Gods into the
    Western Sky.
Shield of Faith, The.
Short Walk along the Coast, A.
Simon Legree—A Negro Sermon.
Song for Elizabeth, A.
Song in July, A.
Song of the Garden-Toad, The.
Song of the Sturdy Snails, The.
Sorceress!, The.
Soul of a Butterfly, The.
Soul of a Spider, The.
Soul of the City Receives the Gift of the
    Holy Spirit, The.
Speak Now for Peace.
Spice-Tree, The.
Spider and the Ghost of the Fly, The.
Springfield Magical.
Springfield of the Far Future, The.
Star of My Heart.
Statue of Old Andrew Jackson, The.
Storm-Flower, The.
Strength of the Lonely, The.
Sun Says His Prayers, The.
Sunset.
Sunshine.
Sweet Briars of the Stairways.
Sweetheart Autumn.
Sweetheart Spring.
Sweetheart Summer.
Sweetheart Winter.
Sweethearts of the Year.
Tale of the Tiger Tree, The.
This Section Is a Christmas Tree.
Three Poems About Mark Twain.
Tiger on Parade, The.
To a Golden-Haired Girl in a Louisiana
    Town.
To Buddha.
To Eve, Man's Dream of Wifehood as
    Described by Milton.
To Gloriana.
To Jane Addams at the Hague.
To Lady Jane.
To Reformers in Despair.
Tolstoi is Plowing Yet.
Town of American Visions, The.
Tramp's Refusal, The.
Trap, The.
Traveller-Heart, The.
Tree of Laughing Bells or The Wings of the
    Morning, The.
Trial of the Dead Cleopatra in Her Beautiful
    and Wonderful Tomb, The.
Two Easter Stanzas.
Two Old Crows.
Unpardonable Sin, The.
Village Improvement Parade, The.
Visit to Mab, The.
Voice of St. Francis of Assisi, The.
Voice of the Earthquake, The.
Voice of the Man Impatient with Visions and
    Utopias, The.
We Meet at the Judgement and I Fear It Not.
Wedding of the Rose and the Lotus, The.
What Grandpa Mouse Said.
What Semiramis Said.
What the Clown Said.
What the Coal-Heaver Said.
What the Forester Said.
What the Ghost of the Gambler Said.
What the Gray-Winged Fairy Said.
What the Hyena Said.
What the Miner in the Desert Said.
What the Moon Saw.
What the Rattlesnake Said.
What the Scarecrow Said.
What the Sexton Said.
What the Snow Man Said.
When Peter Jackson Preached in the Old
    Church.
When the Mississippi Flowed in Indiana.
Where Is the Real Non-Resistant?
Who Knows?
Why I Voted the Socialist Ticket.
With a Bouquet of Twelve Roses.
With a Rose, to Brunhilde.

Wizard in the Street, The.
Wizard Wind, The.
Would-Be Merman, The.
Written for a Musician.
Written in a Year When Many of My People
    Died.
Yankee Doodle.
Yet Gentle Will the Griffin Be.

Longfellow, Henry Wadsworth (1807–82)
Aftermath.
Arsenal at Springfield, The.
Children's Hour, The.
Courtship of Miles Standish, The.
Cross of Snow, The.
Day Is Done, The.
Embarkation, The.
Evangeline, a Tale of Acadie.
Evangeline in Acadie.
Expedition to Wessagusset, The.
Finding of Gabriel, The.
Fire of Drift-Wood, The.
Giles Corey of the Salem Farms.
Hawthorne.
Hiawatha's Childhood.
Hiawatha's Fasting.
It Is Too Late.
Jewish Cemetery at Newport, The.
John Alden.
John Endicott.
Lakes of the Atchafalaya, The.
Landlord's Tale: Paul Revere's Ride, The.
Life.
Love and Friendship.
Lover's Errand, The.
March of Miles Standish, The.
Message of Peace, A.
Mezzo Cammin.
Miles Standish.
Morituri Salutamus.
My Lost Youth.
Nature.
Occultation of Orion, The.
On the Atchafalaya.
Poet's Tale: The Birds of Killingworth, The.
Priscilla.
Proclamation, The.
Prologue: "Delusions of the days that once
    have been."
Prologue: "To-night we strive to read, as we
    may best."
Psalm of Life, A.
Ropewalk, The.
Sailing of the Mayflower, The.
Seaweed.
Skeleton in Armor [or Armour], The.
Slave Singing at Midnight, The.
Snow-Flakes.
Song of Hiawatha, The *sels.*
Spinning-Wheel, The.
Tale of Acadie, A.
Tales of a Wayside Inn *sels.*
Tell Me Not in Mournful Numbers.
Theologian's Tale: Torquemada, The.
Trial, The.
Village Blacksmith, The.
War-Token, The.
Warning, The.
Wedding-Day, The.
Wreck of the *Hesperus*, The.

Lorde, Audre (1934–92)
Afterimages.
American Cancer Society Or There Is More
    Than One Way to Skin a Coon.
And Don't Think I Won't Be Waiting.
And What About the Children.
As I Grew Up Again.
Ballad from Childhood.
Barren.
Bees, The.
Birthday Memorial to Seventh Street, A.
Black Mother Woman.
Blackstudies.
Bloodbirth.
Bridge Through My Window.
Brown Menace or Poem to the Survival of
    Roaches, The.

Cables To Rage Or I've Been Talking On This Street Corner.
Change of Season.
Coal.
Conclusion.
Conversations in Crisis.
Day They Eulogized Mahalia, The.
Dear Toni Instead of a Letter of Congratulation.
Dozens, The.
Dreams Bite.
Echo.
Equinox.
Evening News, The.
Family Resemblance, A.
Fantasy and Conversation.
Father Son and Holy Ghost.
Father, the Year Has Fallen.
For Each of You.
For My Singing Sister.
Gemini.
Generation.
Generation II.
Good Mirrors are Not Cheap.
Hard Love Rock.
Hard Love Rock II.
Keyfoods.
Love, Maybe.
Love Poem.
Maiden, The.
Martha.
Memorial I.
Memorial II.
Memorial III—from a Phone Booth on Broadway.
Mentor.
Monkeyman.
Movement Song.
Moving out or the End of Cooperative Living.
My Fifth Trip to Washington Ended in Northeast Delaware.
Need: A Chorale for Black Woman Voices.
Neighbors.
New Year's Day.
New York City.
NOW.
Now That I Am Forever with Child.
Oaxaca.
October.
On a Night of the Full Moon.
Oya.
Pirouette.
Poem for a Poet.
Poem for Women in Rage, A.
Progress Report.
Release Time.
Relevant Is Different Points on the Circle.
Return.
Revolution Is One Form of Social Change.
Rites of Passage.
Rooming Houses are Old Women.
Sacrifice.
St. Louis Out of Time.
Separation.
Seventh Sign, The.
Sewerplant Grows In Harlem Or I'm a Stranger Here Myself..
Signs.
Sister, Morning Is a Time for Miracles.
Song for a Thin Sister.
Song: "Wild trees have bought me."
Sowing.
Spring People.
Story Books on a Kitchen Table *sels.*
Suffer the Children.
Summer Oracle.
Suspension.
To a Girl Who Knew What Side Her Bread Was Buttered On.
To My Daughter the Junkie on a Train.
To the Girl Who Lives In a Tree.
Trip on the Staten Island Ferry, A.
Vietnam Addenda.
What My Child Learns of the Sea.
When the Saints Come Marching In.
Who Said It Was Simple.

Winds of Orisha, The.
Woman Thing, The.
Workers Rose on May Day or Postcript to Karl Marx, The.
Za Ki Tan Ke Parlay Lot.

Lovelace, Richard (1618–58)
A La Bourbon.
Advice to My Best Brother, Colonel Francis Lovelace.
Against the Love of Great Ones.
Amarantha. A Pastorall.
Amyntor from beyond the Sea to Alexis.
Amyntor's Grove.
Anniversary on the Hymeneals of My Noble Kinsman, Thomas Stanley, Esquire, An.
Another ("As I beheld a winters evening air").
Another ("I Did believe I was in Heav'n").
Another ("The centaur, siren I forgo").
Answer, The.
Ant, The.
Apostasy of One and But One Lady, The.
Being Treated to Ellinda.
Black Patch on Lucasta's Face, A.
Calling Lucasta from Her Retirement.
Courante Monsieur.
Cupid Far Gone.
Dedication to Anne Lovelace, The.
Dialogue. Lucasta, Alexis.
Dialogue. Lute and Voice, A.
Elegie. On the Death of Mrs. Cassandra Cotton, An.
Elegie. Princesse Katherine, An.
Elinda's [*or* Ellinda's] Glove.
Epilogue, The: "Stubborne Author of the trifle, Crime, The."
Faire Begger, The.
Falcon, The.
Female Glory.
Fly about a Glass[e] of Burnt Claret, A.
Fly Caught in a Cobweb, A.
Fool much bit by fleas put out the light, A.
Forsaken Lady to Her False Servant, A.
Grasse-Hopper, The.
Gratiana Dancing [*or* Dauncing] and [*or* &] Singing.
Guiltlesse Lady Imprisoned; after Penanced, A.
Her Muffe.
Her Reserved Looks.
In Allusion to the French Song.
La Bella Bona Roba.
Lady A. L., My Asylum [in a Great Extremity], The.
Lady with a Falcon on Her Fist, A.
Lines Prefixed to John Davies' Translation of Voiture's Letters, 1657.
Loose Saraband, A: ("Ah me! the little tyrant Theefe!").
Loose Saraband, A: ("Nay, prethee [*or* prithee] dear, draw nigher").
Love Conquer'd.
Love Inthron'd.
Love Made in the First Age[: To Chloris].
Lucasta at the Bath.
Lucasta Laughing.
Lucasta Paying Her Obsequies.
Lucasta, Taking the Waters at Tunbridge.
Lucasta Weeping.
Lucasta's Fan[ne], with a Looking-Glass[e] in It.
Lucasta's World.
Mock Charon, A.
Mock Song, A.
Night.
Ode: "You are deceiv'd; I sooner may dull fair."
Ode to Lucasta: The Rose.
Ode To My Lady H.
On Sanazar's Being Honoured.
On the Best, Last, and Only Remaining Comedy of Mr. Fletcher.
On the Death of Mrs. Elizabeth Filmer.
Orpheus to Beasts.
Orpheus to Woods.
Painture [*or* Peinture].
Paradox, A.

Paris's Second Judgement.
Princesse Löysa drawing.
Prologue to the Scholars, A.
Scrutiny [*or* Scrutinie], The.
Sir Thomas Wortley's Sonnet Answered.
Snail [*or* Snayl], The.
Song: "In mine one [*or* own] monument I lie [*or* lye]."
Song: "Strive not, vain Lover, to be fine."
Sonnet: "Depose your finger of that Ring."
Sonnet: "When I by Thy Faire Shape Did Sweare."
Sonnet. To Generall Goring.
To a Lady That Desired Me I Would Bear My Part in a Song.
To a Lady with Child that Asked [*or* Ask'd] an Old Shirt.
To Althea, from Prison.
To Amarantha, That She Would Dishevel[l] Her Hair[e].
To Chloe, Courting Her for His Friend.
To Dr. F. B. on His Book of Chess[e].
To Ellinda, That Lately I Have Not Written.
To Ellinda. Upon His Late Recovery.
To Fletcher Reviv'd.
To His Deare Brother Colonel F.L.
To Lucasta, from Prison.
To Lucasta ("I laugh and sing, but cannot tell").
To Lucasta ("Like to the sentinel [*or* Sent'nel] stars, I watch all night").
To Lucasta. Ode Lyrick.
To Lucasta, [on] Going beyond the Seas.
To Lucasta, [on] Going to the War[re]s.
To my Dear Friend Mr. E.R.
To My Noble Kinsman T.S. Esq.
To My Truely Valiant, Learned Friend, Who in His Booke Resolv'd the Art Gladiatory into the Mathematick's.
To My Worthy Friend Mr. Peter Lely [*or* Lilly].
To the Genius of Mr. John Hall.
Toad and Spyder, The.
Triumphs of Philamore and Amoret, The.
Upon the Curtain[e] of Lucasta's Picture [It Was Thus Wrought].
Valiant Love.
Vintage to the Dungeon, The, *etc.*
Translations, Coauthored Poems, etc.:
AD EUNDEM.
Another, upon the Poems.
As once I bad good morning to the day.
Ask'd in the Country, what I did, I said.
Asse Eating the Ænieds, The.
Because with bought books, Sir, your study's fraught.
Both lurks and shines hid in an Amber-tear.
By thy fault is my mind brought to that pass.
Carmina *sels.*
Cinna seems poor in show.
Clitophon and Lucippe.
Commendatory Poems.
Cynicks narrow houshold stuffe of Crutch, The.
De Domino Richardo Lovelacio, Armigero & Chiliarcha, Viro Incomparabili.
Dedication To the Right Honorable John Lovelace. The.
Elegie, An: "Me thinks when Kings, Prophets, and Poets dye."
Elegies, 1660.
Exastichon.
Fabullus I will treat you handsomely.
Female Inconstancy.
Hand by which no King but Serjeant dies, The.
Hand of sacred Cato bad to tear, The.
Her jealous Husband an Adultresse gave.
I hate and love, wouldst thou the reason know?
If James the King of wit.
If you are Phœbus Sister Delia, pray.
It is not, y' are deceav'd, it is not blisse.
No one can boast herself so much belov'd.
Of a Drunkard.
Of Cato.
On My Brother.

On the Death of My Dear Brother.
On the Poems.
On the Sicilian strand a hare well wrought.
On the Truly Honourable Coll. Richard Lovelace, Occasioned by the Publication of His Posthume-Poems.
One stabbe could not fierce Cato's Life unty.
Parent and Prince of Heav'n O lead I pray.
Peri Tou Autou.
Quintia is handsome, fair, tall, straight, all these.
Sacred to the Memory of My Late Honoured Friend, Collonell Richard Lovelace.
Sanazar's Hexaflick.
Swain, Hind, Knight; I fed, till'd, did command, A.
Sylo pray pay me my ten Sesterces.
That me alone you lov'd, you once did say.
To Colonel Richard Lovelace, on the Publishing of His Ingenious Poems.
To His Honoured and Ingenious Friend Col. Richard Lovelace, on His Lucasta.
To His Much Honoured Friend Mr. Richard Lovelace, on His Poems.
To His Noble Friend Capt. Dudley Lovelace, upon His Edition of His Brother's Poems.
To His Noble Friend Mr. Richard Lovelace upon His Poems.
To Juvencius.
To Marcus T. Cicero.
To my best Brother on his Poems, called Lucasta.
To My Deare Brother, Colonel Richard Lovelace.
To My Much Loved Friend, Richard Lovelace Esq.
To My Noble and Most Ingenious Friend, Col. Richard Lovelace, upon His Lucasta.
To Quintius.
To Rufus.
To the Honorable, Valiant, and Ingenious Colonel Richard Lovelace, on His Exquisite Poems.
To the Memory of My Worthy Friend, Coll. Richard Lovelace.
To the Same Ayre in English, Thus.
Treasure found one entring at death's gate, A.
Upon the Posthume and Precious Poems of the Nobly Extracted Gentleman Mr. R.L.
Vain Painter why dost strive my face to draw.
What doubt'st thou hand? sad Cato 'tis to kill.
When brave chast Arria to her Pætus gave.
When Portia her dear I Lord's sad fate did hear.
Whilst in an Amber-shade the Ant doth feast.
With a fair boy a Cryer we behold.

Lowell, Robert (1917–77)
Abraham Lincoln.
After the Surprising Conversions.
Alexander.
Alfred Corning Clark.
Angling.
Anne Dick 1. 1936.
Anne Dick 2. 1936.
Artist's Model.
As if we chewed dry twigs and salt grasses.
At the Altar.
At the Indian Killer's Grave.
Attila, Hitler.
Beethoven.
Between the Porch and the Altar.
Beyond the Alps.
Bobby Delano.
Bosworth Field.
Bringing a Turtle Home.
Buenos Aires.
Careless Night.
Central Park.
Charles V by Titian.
Child's Song.
Christmas.
Christmas Tree.
Cicero, the Sacrificial Killing.
Coleridge.

Coleridge and Richard II.
Colloquy in Black Rock.
Commander Lowell.
Couple, The.
Dames du Temps Jadis.
Dante 3. Buonconte.
Das ewig Weibliche.
Death and the Bridge.
Death from Cancer.
Death of Alexander.
Death of Anne Boleyn.
Death of Count Roland.
Death of the Sheriff, The.
Die Gold Orangen.
Difficulties, the impossibilities, The.
Dolphin.
Double Vision.
Draw.
Drinker, The.
Drunken Fisherman, The.
Dunbarton.
During Fever.
Eight Months Later.
Elizabeth.
End of Camp Alamoosook.
Exile's Return, The.
Eye and Tooth.
Fall 1961.
Fall Weekend at *Milgate*.
Fat Man in the Mirror, The.
Father.
Father in a Dream.
Father's Bedroom.
First Love.
First Things.
Fishnet.
Flaw, The.
Flight.
Florence.
Flounder.
For Eugene McCarthy.
For George Santayana.
For Robert Kennedy Nineteen Twenty-Five to Sixty-Eight.
For Sale.
For the Union Dead.
Ford Madox Ford ("Lobbed ball plops, then dribbles to the cup, The").
Fourth of July in Maine.
Foxfur.
Ghost, The.
Graduate, The.
Grandparents.
Growth (Harriet).
Hard Way, The.
Harriet.
Harriet's Dream.
Hawthorne.
Her Dead Brother.
History.
Holy Innocents, The.
Home after Three Months Away.
Ice.
In Memory of Arthur Winslow *sels*.
In the Cage.
In the Mail.
Inauguration Day: January 1953.
It Did.
Ivana.
Joinville and Louis IX.
Jonathan Edwards in Western Massachusetts.
July in Washington.
Late Summer at *Milgate*.
Leaf-Lace Dress.
Left out of vacation.
Like Henry VIII, Mohammed got religion.
Lizard rusty as a leaf rubbed rough.
Long Summer.
Long Summers.
Lost Fish.
Lost Tune, The.
Mad Negro Soldier Confined at Munich, A.
Man and Wife.
Man and Woman.
March 1, The.
March 2, The.
Marcus Cato 234–149 B.C.

Marcus Cato 95–42 B.C.
Margaret Fuller Drowned.
Marlowe.
Mary Stuart.
Mary Winslow.
Memories of West Street and Lepke.
Mermaid.
Mermaid Emerging.
Mexico *sels*.
Middle Age.
Midwinter in Cuernavaca, tall red flowers.
Mills of the Kavanaughs, The.
Mr. Edwards and the Spider.
Mother and Father 1.
Mother and Father 2.
Mother Marie Therese.
Mother, 1972.
Mouth of the Hudson, The.
My Heavenly Shiner (Elizabeth).
My Last Afternoon with Uncle Devereux Winslow.
Myopia: a Night.
Napoleon.
Near the Ocean.
Neo-Classical Urn, The.
New York 1962: Fragment.
Night Sweat.
Nihilist as Hero, The.
1930's.
No artist perhaps, you go beyond their phrases;.
No Hearing.
No Messiah.
Nunc Est Bibendum, Cleopatra's Death.
Obit.
Old Flame, The.
Old snapshot from Venice 1952.
Opposite House, The.
Our Twentieth Wedding Anniversary (Elizabeth).
Outlivers (Harriet and Elizabeth).
Plane Ticket.
Plotted.
Poor child, you were kissed so much you thought you were walked on;.
Public Garden, The.
Quaker Graveyard in Nantucket, The.
Randall Jarrell 1. October 1965.
Randall Jarrell 2.
Randall Jarrell 3.
Reading Myself.
Records.
Rembrandt.
Returning.
Returning Turtle.
Robert Frost.
Robespierre and Mozart as Stage.
Sailing Home from Rapallo.
Saint-Just 1767–93.
Seals.
Searching.
Serpent.
Serpent, The.
Sick.
Sir Thomas More.
Skunk Hour.
Sleepless.
Snake.
Soft Wood.
South of Boston, south of Washington.
Stalin.
Sunrise.
Symptoms.
Tenth Muse.
Terminal Days at Beverly Farms.
Thanksgiving's Over.
These Winds.
Three pillows, end on end, rolled on a daybed.
To Daddy.
To Delmore Schwartz.
To Speak of Woe That Is in Marriage.
Two Walls.
Verdun.
Waking Early Sunday Morning.
Waking in the Blue.
Watchmaker God.

Water.
Waterloo.
We never see him now, except at dinner.
Where the Rainbow Ends.
WIldrose.
Will Not Come Back.
William Carlos Williams.
Window.
Words.
Words for Hart Crane.
Words for Muffin, a Guinea Pig.
Worst Sinner, Jonathan Edwards' God, The.

Lowry, Malcolm (1909–57)
Abacus, The.
About Ice.
After Labour Day.
Afternoon Nocturne.
Alas, there is no still path in my soul.
Alcoholic.
Alternative.
And now I brood on what I think I know.
And now the seagulls feed on the front
    porch.
And partly they deserve dishonest death.
And Samson said if yo' shave ma hair.
And, when you go—much as a meteor.
And Who Is It That With Snow-Freaked
    Antlers Vicariously Musheth.
And who is it through the forest after the.
And yet his suffering got involved with all
    this.
And yet I am of England too; odi et amo.
Another Immorality.
April 1937 In the Oaxaca Train.
Arctic fox / With snow white hocks, The.
Arise, arrogant arsemongers / Come! clashing
    clowns.
As from All the Little Animals.
As to report, / Within his court.
Asperin tree outside told me to say, The.
At the Bar.
Au clair de la lune.
Autopsy on this childhood then reveals, An.
Ballad: "Twas in the springtime of the year."
Beneath the Malebolge lies Hastings street.
Beside Oneself.
Betty and Gerald Noxon.
Billetin.
Billets Doux for the Harteebeeste.
Bird in the Tree, The.
Blepharipappus Glandulosus or White Tidy-
    Tips.
Boatmen swing their lanterns on the
    Caribbean, The.
Born ailing on a hemisphere apart.
Bosun's Song.
Bright as the Pleiades Upon the Soul.
!Bulletin!
Burnt pier: the last passenger: the farewells,
    The.
But we little animaux have gone.
Byzantium: Or Where the Great Life Begins.
Canadian Turned Back at the Border, The.
Canny Castor, Punching Pollux.
Cantinas, The.
Cap and gown instead of a sweatrag, A.
Child may find no words for its sorrow, A.
Chilliwack.
Christ I am tired of fruit in poetry.
Closed Pub, The.
Cold Roast Hamlet Blues, Blubberhouses
    Blues, Ugley Blues.
Comedian, The.
Comfort.
Communal Message.
Communist, The.
Conclusion—Poem, A.
Consider what you have lost by lack of faith.
Consolation.
Contemplation of Dead Reckoning.
Conversations With Goethe.
Cook in the Galley, The.
Correcting Manuscript.
Courage is not standing on the crosstrees.
Crane over seas and forests seeks her home,
    The.
Curse.

Curse, A.
Danish Sailor's Song.
Dark Path.
Days Like Smitten Cymbals of Brass, The.
Dead men tell cryptic tales and this is one.
Deal was here, / Oh love alas, The.
Death of an Oaxaqueñian.
Delirium in Los Angeles.
Delirium in Vera Cruz.
Der Tag.
Deserter.
Devil is a gentleman, The.
Devil was a Gentleman, The.
Doctor Usquebaugh.
Dodder, The.
Doggerel.
Dollarton Bus Stop, The.
Donne He's Regular.
Don't, Have One for the Road.
Draft Board.
Dream of the Departing Soldier.
Dried Up River is like the Soul, A.
Drunkards, The *sels.*
Drunkards, The.
Duck Train—Vocal Arctic Fox-Trot.
Duckturne.
Eels.
El Leon Sends His Greetings.
Elsinore was the battlements of Oaxaca.
Epitaph: "Dear Scipio Sprague / sans plague
    sans blague."
Epitaph on Our Gardener, Dead Near
    Liverpool.
Ex-Poet, The.
Exile's Return.
Eye-Opener.
Faking was three times married to Faking.
Fear ringed by doubt is my eternal moon.
Fiesta.
Fisherman's Return.
For Nordahl Grieg Ship's Fireman.
For Our Sweetharteebeeste on Harteebeeste
    Day.
For *Under the Volcano.*
Foul, or Twenty-Five.
Fragment: "Dead tree that, frozen, utters at
    the top, The."
Fragments from the Duck Anthology to Greet
    Our Beloved Harteebeeste in the Morning
    Watch.
Freighter 1940.
French Pronunciation Simplified for Julian
    Trevelyan.
From Helsinki to Liverpool with Lumber.
From *The Gleanings of a Gadwall.*
From This Acceptance, Sir, We Might
    Proceed.
Fyrbøterer.
Ghosts in New Houses.
Give me a poem / To wring the hearts of
    men.
Give me the money, / Give me the money.
Glaucous Winged Gull, The.
Glory of the Sea, The.
Goldeneye and Goldfish.
Good Luck.
Good Morning to Our Sweetest Harteebeeste!
Got a date with a bottle of / gin.
Half of the harm that is done in this world.
Hangover—Reading Rilke, Schnitzler or
    Someone, A.
Happiest of Harteebeeste Days and Devoted
    Love Eterne.
Happiness.
Happy birthday to you.
Harpies.
Hartebeeste Both Grave and Gay, The.
Harteebeeste Is Here Again, The.
Harteebeeste with flying hoof, The.
Heat Wave.
Here him play / That sinister melody.
Hindu Babe / I love you.
Homoeopathic Blues in J.
Hospitality.
Hostage.
How overjoyed I am to get your letter.
Hunger.

Hypocrite! Oxford Grouper! Yahoo!
I am speeding through the northern lights.
I am very small.
I bet you don't know who I am.
I do not wish to live.
I don't want to criticize war.
I met a man who had got drunk with Christ.
I met the spirit of tragedy in the wood.
I set this down as humble prayer.
I sing the joy of poverty, not such.
I think that I shall never see.
I tried to think of something good.
I wrote: In the dark cavern of our birth.
Illegal Heart, The.
Imprisoned in a Liverpool of self.
In Cape Code with Conrad Aiken.
In Memoriam; Ingvald Bjorndal and His
    Comrade.
In Praise of an Understudy.
In the Oaxaca Train.
Indian Arm.
Injured Choriant or Paeonic.
Iphigenia in Aulis. Agamemnon Speaks'.
Iron Thoughts Sail Out at Evening.
Is there no song that I can sing.
Isle of Man Wildflowers.
I've Said Goodbye to Shanghai.
Jokes Aloft.
Jokes Amidships.
Jokes in the Galley.
Jokes on the Poop.
Joseph Cconrad.
Just a Merry Little Ditty of Welcome for the
    Most Beloved Harteebeeste on Easter
    Sunday.
Just some love and kisses.
Kingfishers in British Columbia.
Kraken, Eagles, in British Columbia.
Ladder, The.
Lament in the Pacific Northwest.
Lament—June 1944.
Lapis dawn is gleaming, A.
Last Man in the Dôme, The.
Letter from Oaxaca to North Africa 1936.
Lighthouse Invites the Storm, The *sels.*
Lighthouse Invites the Storm, The.
Like the black iron steps.
Lines on the Poet Being Informed That His
    Epic About the Philistines Etc. Needed
    Cutting.
Lines Written on Reading Dostoievski.
Little Ditty for This Day to the Beloved
    Harteebeeste, A.
Look Out! The Bloody Bosun.
Love and wisdom have no home.
Love of a Seagull.
Lull.
Lusty Advice of a Fortune-Teller.
Lyrical Morning Poem.
Mackerel shouldn't take, A.
Mad Poem: Wind Blowing Through the
    Shack.
Magic World, The.
Marathon of gulls / a chiming of chickadees,
    A.
Marching down the road to China.
Margeries and the malcolms did, The.
Marina—.
May well befall the common weal.
Memory of the Hospitality of American
    Barmen.
Men With Coats Thrashing.
Midnight denies poursuivant of the dawn.
Minstrel in Labrador, A.
Mr. Lowry's Good Friday under a Real
    Cactus.
Moon in Scandinavia, The.
More Impatience.
Morning Address of Love to the Beloved
    Harteebeeste.
Morning bird is bathing, The.
Morning bird is singing, The.
Morning bird sits mutely, The.
Morning coat is walking, A.
Morning rain is rained, The.
Morning rain is raining / A morning pain is
    paining, The.

Morning rain is raining / The morning leg is paining, The.
Morning rain is sleeting, The.
Morning rain is weeping, The.
Morning sleet is sleeting, The.
Morning sneat is snewing, The.
Morning Song for the Harteebeeste.
Morning song of El Leon.
Morning stove is wheezing, The.
Morning tanker gleameth, The.
My Beloved Harteebeeste.
My hate is as a wind that buffets me.
My love now lies upon his rump.
My two hands broke in two: and they broke me!
Mysterious Hint, A.
Nagging at myself something awful.
Names of Mexican rivers I forgot, The.
Need it be so niggardly of meaning too?
Never in a comedian's life have I laughed till then!
Never seek to tell thy stove.
New Guinea Gardener Bird, The.
No Kraken Shall Be Found Till Sought By Name.
No prayer for the people.
No Time to Stop and Think.
No wonder it feared peace, the knees of years.
No words assess, no pencil knows.
Noble City Full of Pigeons or Everyone a Hypocrite Including Me.
Nocturne: "This evening Venus signs alone."
Not all of us were heroes said my brother wit.
Note.
Note, A.
Note For a Poem.
November, 1937.
Number 8 Fireman.
October Sunset.
Of the Francia.
Oh and / Who is it unforlorn.
Oh gentle Jesus of the hymnal once.
Oh love / Oh Shame, we are late.
Oh, poor Mary Ann / When she got to the top.
Oh Storms / Oh The Seal!
Oh the Harteebeeste is *dear* to us.
Oh the Pyrrus boys are we.
Oh welcome Home /To thy cot by the foam.
Old Blake was warm, he got down to the hub.
Old Freighter in an Old Port.
Old Woman who Buried Cats, The.
On board the Matsue Maru.
On Reading Edmund Wilson's Remarks about Rimbaud.
On Reading Redburn.
On Reading R.L.S.
Only God Knows How.
Only God Knows How III.
Only thing that Jack had, The.
Outside was the roar of the sea and the darkness.
Outward Bound.
Pacific is a feeble symbol of death.
Passing Impatience With a Noble Country, A.
Perhaps for Eridanus.
Personal.
Peter Gaunt and the Canals.
Picture, A.
Pigs—For T.H.
Pijijiapan.
Pilgrim passes through the town by night, A.
Pines write a Chinese poem upon the white-gold sun.
Plagiarist, The.
Platinum sun rising. / Platinum frost on porch.
Playing alone / Drunk and bored.
Plingen plangen auf gefangen.
Poem: "Wet streets in Liverpool."
Poem: "When drunk he crawled home on his knees."
Poem Influenced By John Davenport and Cervantes.

Poem Inspired By Auden and Clare's Snail.
Poem of God's Mercy, A.
Poem On Gold.
Poem to be Placed at the Conclusion of a Long Obscure Passionate and Eloquent Book of Poems.
Poets are Godlike in that they.
Poor Butterfly that stamped.
Port has a sweeter name than Saigon, The.
Port Moody.
"Portly & middleaged" can never.
Prayer: "Give way, you fiends, and give that man some happiness."
Prayer: "I pray that I may form a prayer, oh Lord."
Prayer, A: "God give those drunkards drink who wake at dawn."
Prayer from the Wicket Gate for Forty One Doors for Forty Two.
Prayer: "Oh thou who art not above."
Prelude to Another Drink.
Prelude To Mammon.
Promises made drunk should be kept drunk.
Quarrel, A.
Quartermaster at the Wheel.
Queer Poem.
R. Usher.
Rain Fell Heavily, The.
Reflection to Windward.
Report on Conditions.
Reveille.
Rich man, poor man, beggarman, thief.
Roar of the Sea and the Darkness, The.
Rocksie Ann was a Roxy and she live on Histon, Eng.
S.O.S. Sinking fast by both bow and stern.
Sadness is so much a part of me.
Sailors, The.
Salmon Drowns Eagle.
Save that the optimistic ones are worse.
Schoolboy's Complaint, The.
Scribner's Sons.
Search, The.
Sestina in a Cantina.
Shakespeare's house is safe and sound.
Ship.
Ship is Turning Homeward, The.
Ship stands drawn like a jewelled dagger, A.
Ship will sail again, the watches sing, The.
Simple Seabird's Tribute to Her Harteebeeste, A.
Singing. / The morning bird. / (Humphum!).
Slough of Despond: Or the House of Hope, The.
Some years ago he started to escape.
Song about Madrid, Useful Any Time.
Song for a Marimba.
Song for My Wife.
Song: "Pity the blind and the halt but yet pity."
Songs for Second Childhood.
Sonnet: "This ruin now, where moonlight walks alone."
Soul, The.
Soul's Pentonville, The.
Spark Poetry.
Spiderweb.
Stars have simple paradigms, The.
Still speeding to your heart.
Stoker Tom's Ukulele.
Stowaway, The.
Success is like some horrible disaster.
Sun, Aeroplane, Lovers.
Sun was almost shining, The.
Sunrise.
Sweet Good Night Poem to Our Beloved Hartebeeste from All the Little Animals.
Sweet night / And sleep thin, A.
Tashtego Believed Red.
Ten fifty eight *may* arrive.
That she could cook.
That's What I Mean.
There Is a Metallurgy.
There is a sort of conspiracy about the great.
There is no poetry when you live there.
There was an old Consul called Firmin.

There's something burning, you said, when we were hammering.
They will be ashamed after they are dead.
Thing to know is how to write a verse, The.
Thirty Five Mescals in Cuautla.
This business of evil / Like brokers the weevil.
Those Coke to Newcastle Blues.
Those were the days / And never again.
Those who die young will look forever young.
Thou was not born for death, immortal Duck.
Though I Have More.
Though we are all a little bit disappointed this year there won't be any fireworks.
Though we are but *sea* birds.
Thought While Drowning (Acapulco).
Thoughts to Be Erased from My Destiny.
Thoughts While Drowning: But Try to Eliminate the Argument.
3 Happy Little Ducks.
Three Little Dog-Gone Mice.
Tibute to the Renowned Harteebeeste, A.
To account for this, but it cannot be.
To Herr Toller, Who Hanged Himself.
Two frozen claws / In two frozen minutes.
Two streams came from a different source, The.
Very dark and clear with an onshore wind.
Vigil Forget.
Villaknell.
Villanelle, an Interviewo on Morale.
Virgo.
Visiting the Wreck: An Able Seaman Explains.
Volcano is dark and suddenly thunder, The.
Voyage of Kevin O'Riordine, The.
Waking wassails of wistful welcome.
Walk in Canada.
Warning from False Cape Horn.
We Sit Unhackled Drunk and Mad to Edit.
Welcome Home Oh Gladsome Springhorned Beloved and Famed Harteebeeste.
Welcome Home Oh Harteebeeste.
Welcome Home oh Harteebeeste beloved who doth with thy.
Welcome Home oh Harteebeeste mio.
Welcome Home—Oh Most Beloved Harteebeeste.
Welcome Home Oh Most Loved and Famed Harteebeeste.
Welcome Home Oh Our Beloved Harteebeeste.
Welcome Home Oh Our Most Beloved Harteebeeste.
Welcome Home, Oh Our Sweetest Harteebeeste Beloved.
Welcome Home, Oh Sweetest Harteebeeste.
Welcome Home Oh Sweetest Harteebeeste with Quadruple Devotion from All the Little Animals.
Welcome Home Our Own.
Western Ocean, The.
What Sigbjørn Said.
What the Gardener Said to Mrs. Trail.
What the Irish Soldier Said.
When I am in the purgatory of the unread.
When I was young I broke all drinking records.
Where Did That One Go to, 'Erbert.
Who made this suicide pact of love?
Wild Cherry, The.
Wild-duck swam in the gold-fish pond, The.
Windows from a Machine Shop.
With a Great Goodmorning Kiss and Luck and Love to Our Beloved Harteeste from All the Little Animals.
With Dearest Love Enfolded and Enclosed from *All* the Litle Animals.
With Dearest Morning Love and Kisses.
With Devotion Entire from All Your Little Animals We Thought Fit to Revive the Following Ditty.
With Great Love Oh Beloved Harteebeeste from El Leon.
With Midsummer Devotion from All the

Little Animals to Their Beloved
Harteebeeste.
With Sweet Devotion and True from All the
Little Animals.
With Sweet Sweet Love from All Your
Amused Little Animals.
With Sweetest Devotion from *All* the Little
Animals to Their Most Beloved
Harteebeeste.
With Sweetest Love and Sunday Anthems or
Sweetest Goodnight from All the Little
Animals.
With Sweetest Love and Welcome from All
the Little Animals.
With Sweetest Love from All the Little
Animals As from 2 Old Friends.
With Sweetest Love from All the Little
Animals to Their Beloved Harteebeeste.
With Sweetest Morning Love to Their
Beloved Harteebeeste.
Words on a Grave.
Xochitepec.
Ye pow'rs who make mankind oyour care.
Years standing round in a ring, The.
You think you are a man shaking the hands
of that dog.
Young Fellow Named Crane, A.
Young Man From Oaxaca, The.
Yvonne stood there silently / the roar of the
plane still in her ears.

M

McAuley, James (b. 1935)
Actor: Decline and Death, The.
After the Blizzard *sels.*
After Yeats, After Ronsard, *Pace* Hopkins.
Air of an old song's in my head, The.
"Alle Herrlichkeit Des Menschen."
Allegro Moderato.
Allegro Vivace.
Andante Cantabile.
Aor Against the Bad Reviewer.
Aor Against the Ingrate Who Abused Our
Hospitality.
Aor Against the Philistine Who Destroyed
Lovely Dublin Vistas With His Ugly
Erections, Then Absconded to London.
Aor Against the Termagant from California
Who Confused Instruction With
Indignation.
Aor Against the Warmonger.
Arched corridors. Bare white walls.
Artist, Reclining, The.
Astronomy.
Autobiography of the Impotent Man, The.
Baldungan Castle.
Behind a brightening cloud.
Better the big NOW, singular.
Beyond the crowding spires of pine, the hill.
Blessing.
Caruso.
Catnap, with Nightmare.
Cheiron *sels.*
Cock the right eyebrow: Heredity.
Coming & Going.
Confession, The.
Creed.
Daybreak.
De Mortuis.
Death of Fathers.
Downhill.
Draft Balance Sheet.
Dust-Devils.
Dying Swan, The.
Early Morning Walk to Work.
Episodes for a Panel.
Examination, The.
Exile, *En Famille*, The.
Exile on His Failing Vision, The.
Exile Takes Stock of His Surroundings, The.
Exile's Fifth Symphony, The.
Exile's Recurring Nightmare, The *sels.*
Fifth Mile.
Fire's gone down: burnt pine, The.
First Mile.

For the Humanism Class at Fairchild Airforce
Base, in Place of a Session on the Book of
Job.
Gesture, A.
Glory.
Green Beer *sels.*
Habitations *sels.*
Had I been at that scene.
House Burning Down.
I became a single sinew.
I dream a flag snaps in a cold wind.
I lounge on the warm step, watching the
child.
I planned a little fountain.
In six-inch scale, the Mayo baronies.
In the Red Corner.
In this trance before sleep.
Interlude, with Alter Ego.
Irish Bull, An.
Journey With a Conjuror.
Labor and Tribulation.
Late Afternoon, Running: Close Reasoning,
Listening Closely.
Late Morning Talk.
Leave the hair white, uncombed.
Lecture.
Letter to Richard Hugo From Drumcliff.
Making Repairs.
Map *sels.*
Meditations of Afternoon *sels.*
Memoirs of a Son of Erin.
Mnemosyne: The Empty Room.
Mother, sisters, brother.
Mourners.
Near the Finish.
Ninth Mile.
Noon Apocrypha.
Not a sound. The house could be.
Nun of St. Michan's, The.
On Saint Paddy's Day, the jukebox plays.
Owen at Play.
Papers everywhere—piled onto tables and
shelves—.
Path, The.
Penance.
Photographer's Model, The.
Pool at the Y.
Prelude in Darkness.
Press Conference: King James Version.
Prologue: "Not for me, the crusader cross."
Questions for my Grandfather.
Rage swept them across the Vistula, Danube,
Elbe.
Requiem.
Ritual.
Running in Snow.
Scherzo.
Secret.
She felt, as she left the station.
Short Journeys Before Daybreak.
Signs.
Siren.
Soliloquy.
Spokane Perspective.
Studies for a Self-Portrait at Forty *sels.*
Sunflowers: An Ode *sels.*
Sunset.
Survivors.
Ten-Mile Run.
Tenor Solo on St. Cecilia's Day.
Third Mile.
Three Acts from a Play.
To His Host, Who Has Asked Him To Stay
Longer.
To learn those powers, I surrendered.
Under the humming *continuo.*
Uphill.
Vigil.
Violas are moaning, a harpsichord chiming.
Vivaldi in Venice *sels.*
Was it greed for possession of these salty
crags.
What did she see on the train?
What the Recent Survey Has Revealed.
When I was a Curragh stableboy.
Whiskey Priest Recites His Holy Office, The.
Witness *sels.*

You'd hardly notice at first how everything.
Young broke ribs and thighs, holding, The.
McCartney, Paul *see* Beatles, The
**"MacDiarmid, Hugh" (Christopher Murray
Grieve) (1892–1978)**
Ah, Joyce, this is our task.
Ah, sweetheart, what a pool! Broad, deep,
strong, silent, and sedate!
All dreams of "imperialism" must be
exorcised.
All life's million conflicting interests and
relationships.
And a poetry in which as in a film.
And all this here, everything I write, of
course.
And thus a poetry which fully understands.
Another Epitaph on an Army of Mercenaries.
Archin' here and arrachin there.
Are my poems spoken in the factories and
fields.
As I have often told.
As Lovers Do.
At My Father's Grave.
At the Cenotaph.
Au Clair de la Lune.
Back to the great music, Scottish Gaels. Too
long.
Bagpipe Music.
Battle Continues, The *sels.*
Bonnie Broukit Bairn, The.
Bracken Hills in Autumn.
But shairly, shairly, there maun be.
Caledonian Antisyzygy, The.
Celtic genius—Cornwall, Scotland, Ireland,
Wales—, The.
Cheville.
Come, follow me into the realms of music.
Here is the gate.
Conception.
Cornish Heroic Song for Valda Trevlyn *sels.*
Covenanters, The.
Credo.
Crowdieknowe.
Crystals like Blood.
Dead Liebknecht, The.
Direadh III.
Drunk Man Looks at the Thistle, A.
Dying Earth, The.
Dytiscus.
Eemis-Stane, The.
Empty Vessel.
England Is Our Enemy *sels.*
England's Double Knavery *sels.*
Esplumeoir *sels.*
Everlasting layers / Of ideas, images,
feelings.
Ex Vermibus.
Facing the Chair.
Farewell to Dostoevski.
First Love.
Focherty.
Fool, The.
Frae Anither Window in Thrums *sels.*
Further Passages from The Kind of Poetry I
Want *sels.*
Gairmscoile.
Gin but the oor 'ud chop and set me free.
Glasgow, 1960.
Glass of Pure Water, The.
Glen of Silence, The.
Good-bye Twilight *sels.*
Greatest poets undergo a kind of crisis in
their art, The.
Happy on Heimaey.
Harry Semen.
Here in the hauf licht hoo I've grown!
Here in the hauf licht waitin' till the clock.
His attitude towards woman is the basic
point.
Hokum.
Huntress and Her Dogs, The.
I dream of poems like the bread-knife.
I mind when ny first wife died.
I sing of Cornwall.
I was better with the sounds of the sea.
I'm weary o' the shapes mere chance can
thraw.

In Memoriam James Joyce *sels.*
In the Children's Hospital.
In the Slums of Glasgow.
Innumerable Christ, The.
Island Funeral.
It is possible that a change may come.
John Maclean (1879-1923).
Kind of Poetry I Want, The *sels.*
Last Song, A.
Left-wing poetry represents a rise in the price
   of bread.
Light and Shadow.
Little White Rose, The.
Lo! A Child Is Born.
Lourd on My Hert.
Love-sick Lass, The.
Major Road Ahead.
Man in the Moon, The.
Milk-Wort and Bog Cotton.
Moment in Eternity, A.
Moonstruck.
My Love Is to the Light of Lights.
My Songs Are Kandym in the Waste Land.
O Ease My Spirit.
Ode to All Rebels *sels.*
Of John Davidson.
Of My First Love.
Old Wife in High Spirits.
On a Raised Beach.
On the Ocean Floor.
One loves the temporal, some unique
   manifestation.
One of the Principal Causes of War.
Perfect.
Plaited Like the Generations of Men *sels.*
Poetry and Science.
Poetry full of *cynghanedd,* and hair-trigger
   relationships, A.
Poetry in which all connections will
   constantly render such services, A.
Poetry like a lance at rest, A.
Poetry like the barrel of a gun, A.
Poetry like the character of Indian culture, A.
Poetry like the hope of achieving ere very
   long.
Poetry of such an integration as cannot be
   effected.
Poetry that goes all the way, A.
Poetry that never for a moment forgets, A.
Poetry the quality of which, A.
Ross-shire Hills, The.
Sauchs in the Reuch Heuch Hauch, The.
Scotland.
Scotland Small?
Seamless Garment, The.
Second Hymn to Lenin *sels.*
Servant Girl's Bed.
Skald's Death.
Skeleton of the Future, The.
Snares of Varuna, The *sels.*
So, like him, we cry *"l'honneur des hommes:
   Saint Langage."*
Stony Limits.
That's the condition o't or near.
Think not that I forget a single pang.
To a Friend and Fellow Poet.
To distinctly English writers in England.
To Hell wi' Happiness!
To My Friend the Late Beatrice Hastings.
Two Memories.
Two Parents, The.
Vision of Scotland, A.
War with England, The *sels.*
Water Music *sels.*
Water of Life.
Watergaw, The.
Weapon, The.
Well Hung.
Wheesht, Wheesht.
Wheesht, wheesht, Joyce, and let me hear.
Why.
Wind-bags, The.
With the Herring Fishers.
World of Words, The *sels.*
Wreck of the *Swan,* The.
Yet Ha'e I Silence Left.

McGrath, Thomas (1916–90)
Afternoon of a McGrath.
Against the False Magicians.
Ah.. to the Villages!
All the Dead Soldiers.
Anniversaries.
Another Season.
Ars Poetica: Or: Who Lives in the Ivory
   Tower?
Autumn Song.
Behold the Woman.
Beyond Seattle.
Beyond the Red River.
Black Train, The.
Blues for Jimmy.
Blues for the Old Revolutionary Woman.
Blues for Warren.
Bread of this World; Praises III, The.
Buffalo Coat, The.
Celebration.
Celebration for June 24.
Changeling, The.
Citizen Dreaming, The.
Coal Fire in Winter, A.
Columbus.
Dawn Song.
Death for the Dark Stranger.
Deep South.
Deprivation.
Don't Think You Know My Name!
Dream Range, The.
Dreams of Wild Horses, The.
Driving toward Boston I Run across One of
   Robert Bly's Old Poems.
Drowned Man: Death Between Two Rivers,
   The.
Edge of the River, The.
Emblems of Exile.
Encounter.
End of the Line, The.
End of the World, The.
Enemy, The.
Epitaph: "Again, traveller, you have come a
   long way led by that star."
Everything in Order.
Excursion: Or: O Columbus!, The.
Face of the Precipice is Black with Lovers,
   The.
Fatigue of Objects, The.
Flint and Steel.
For a Critic Who Tries to Write Poems.
Fresco: Departure for an Imperialist War.
From a Long Way Out of Pah-Gatzin-Kay.
Get Out of Town.
Go Ask the Dead.
Gone Away Blues.
Guiffre's Nightmusic.
Heroes of Childhood, The.
History.
In Dream Time.
In Early Autumn.
In Praise of Necessity.
In Sickness Like Sleep.
In the Sleep of Reason.
Incident in the Life of a Prophet, An.
Inheritance, The.
Lament for Pablo Neruda.
Legendary Progress.
Letter for Marian, A.
Little Odyssey of Jason Quint, of Science,
   Doctor, The.
Little Song about Charity, A.
Long Goodbye.
Long Way Outside Yellowstone, A.
Love in a Bus.
Mediterranean.
Memorial.
Migration of Cities, The.
Near Pah-Gotzin-Kay.
Need for Dictionaries II, The.
Need for Stoicism in the Stoa of Attalus,
   The.
News and the Weather, The.
Night Work.
Nocturne Militaire.
Note on the Late Elections, A.
Nuclear Winter.

Ode for the American Dead in Asia.
Offering.
Once We Meant It.
Ordonnance.
Orphan, The.
Parable.
Passages.
People Are So Busy: Or: That's Life!
Perpetual Motion.
Poem: "Down the small and crooked road."
Poem: "How could I have come so far?"
Poem: "In the list of one thousand false
   addresses."
Poem: "Light flares from the tombstones.."
Poem: "Long wound of the summer—, The."
Poem: "My little son comes running with
   open arms!"
Poem: "My little son, laughing, singing.."
Poem: "Through the fog / The gulls."
Poem—Unfinished Poem.
Poem: "When I carry my little son in the
   cold."
Poem: "You out there, so secret."
Poet of the Prison Isle: Ritsos Against the
   Colonels, The.
Political Song for the Year's End.
Portents.
Praises.
Praises IV.
Progress of the Soul, The.
Proletarian in Abstract Light.
Proverbs of the Middle World.
Reading the Names of the Vietnam War
   Dead.
Rediscovery.
Remembering Loves and Deaths.
Remembering the Children of Auschwitz.
Repeated Journey, The.
Residencies.
Restless Night, The.
Return, The.
Return to Marsh Street.
Revisionist Poem: Machado.
Revisionist Poem—Octavio Paz.
Seekers, The.
Something Is Dying Here.
Sometimes.
Such Simple Love.
Theory, A.
Three Functions of Irony.
Topography of History, The.
Tourists at Ensenada.
Trinc: Praises II.
Triumphal March.
Trouble with the Times, The.
Two Songs from "The Hunted
   Revolutionaries."
Underground, The.
Up the Dark Valley.
Use of Books, The.
Used Up.
Uses of the Lost Poets.
Vision of Three Angels Viewing the Progress
   of Socialism.
War Resisters' Song.
Warrant for Pablo Neruda, A.
What We Think We Know.
When We Say Goodbye.
Winter Roads.
Woodcut.
World of the Perfect Tear, The.
World; The Lovers; Falling Stars, The.
You Can Start the Poetry Now, Or: News
   from Crazy Horse.
You Taught Me.

MacLeish, Archibald (1892–1983)
Acknowledgement.
Actfive.
Adam in the Evening.
Adam's Jealousy: Eve's Answer.
Adam's Riddle.
Aeterna Poetae Memoria.
Against Illuminations.
America Was Promises.
American Letter.
Ancestral.
& Forty-Second Street.

And he had used love's dream of love before.
April in November.
Arrival and Departure.
Ars Poetica.
At the Lincoln Memorial.
Autobiography.
Autumn.
Babe's Riddle, The.
Baccalaureate.
Background with Revolutionaries.
Bahamas.
Ballad of the Corn-Cob and the Lie, The.
Beauty is that Medusa's head.
Bed, The.
Before March.
Bernál Díaz' Preface to his Book.
Beside her in the dark the chime.
Black Day, The.
Black Humor.
Boatmen of Santorin, The.
Boy in the Roman Zoo.
Brave New World.
Broken Promise.
Brooks Atkinson.
Burial, The.
Burying Ground by the Ties.
But she was both,—she was both loved and love.
Calypso's Island.
Captivity of the Fly.
Carrion Crow, The.
Carrion Spring, The.
Cat in the Wood, The.
Chartres.
Cinema of a Man.
Colloquy for the States.
Companions.
Conquistador.
Contemporary Portrait.
Conversation in a Belfry.
Conway Burying Ground.
Cook County.
Corporate Entity.
Creator.
Critics on the Lawn.
Crossing.
Cummings.
Danger in the Air, The.
De Votre Bonheur Il ne Reste Que Vos Photos.
Definition of the Frontiers.
Definitions of Old Age.
Dr. Sigmund Freud Discovers the Sea Shell.
"Dover Beach"—a Note to That Poem.
Dozing on the Lawn.
Edwin Muir.
1892—19—.
Eighth Book, The.
Einstein.
Eleven.
Eleventh Book, The.
Empire Builders.
End of the World, The.
Epistle to Be Left in the Earth.
Epistle to Léon-Paul Fargue.
Epitaph for John McCutcheon.
Eplenor.
Eternity, An.
Eve Answers the Burdock.
Eve Explains Everything to the Thrush Who Repeats Everything.
Eve in the Dawn.
Eve Old.
Eve Quiets Her Children.
Eve to the Storm of Thunder.
Ever Since.
Eve's Child.
Eve's Exile.
Eve's First Prophecy.
Eve's Now-I-Lay-Me.
Eve's Rebuke to Her Child.
Eve's Riddle.
Eve's Second Prophecy.
Excavation of Troy.
Ezry.
Fall!, The.

Family Group.
Farm, The.
Fifteenth Book, The.
Fifth Book, The.
First Book, The.
First I will tell you something of these two.
For the Anniversary of my Mother's Death.
Fourteenth Book, The.
Fourth Book, The.
Galán.
Geography of this Time.
German Girls! The German Girls!, The.
Good Man in a Bad Time, A.
Grazing Locomotives.
Great Contemporary Discoveries.
Hamlet of A. Macleish.
Hands.
Happy Marriage, The *sels.*
He had used love or lust or what's between.
He leans against the window-sill.
Hearts' and Flowers'.
Hebrides.
Hemingway.
Here, O wanderer, here is the hill and the harbor.
Hotel Breakfast.
How the River Ninfa Runs through the Ruined Town Beneath the Lime Quarry.
Humid air precipitates, The.
Hurricane.
Hypocrite Auteur.
Immortal Autumn.
Immortal Helix.
In and Come In.
Infinite Reason, The.
Interrogate the Stones.
Invocation to the Social Muse.
Journey Home.
La Foce.
L'An Trentiesme de Mon Eage.
Land's End.
Landscape as a Nude.
Late Abed.
Le Secret Humain.
Le Seul Malheur Est que Je ne Sais pas Lire.
Learned Men, The.
Liberty.
Linden Branch, The.
Linden Trees, The.
Lines for a Prologue.
Lines for an Interment.
Long Hot Summer.
Lost Speakers, The.
Love is the way that lovers never know.
Man!
Man's Work, A.
March.
Mark Van Doren and the Brook.
Mark's Sheep.
Memorial Rain.
Memory Green.
Men.
Men of My Century Loved Mozart.
Midsummer Dawn.
Mistral Over the Graves.
Mother Goose's Garland.
Music and Drum.
My Naked Aunt.
Nat Bacon's Bones.
National Security.
New England Weather.
Night Dream, The.
Night Watch in the City of Boston.
Ninth Book, The.
No doubt he'd once had eyes to see.
No Lamp Has Ever Shown Us Where to Look.
Nocturne: "Earth, still heavy and warm with afternoon, The."
Not Marble nor the Gilded Monuments.
November.
O hide your eyes.
Observations of P. Ovidus Naso on the Incidence of Sex in the Contemporary Novel.
Oil Painting of the Artist as the Artist.
Old Gray Couple (1), The.

Old Gray Couple (2), The.
Old Man to the Lizard, The.
Old Man's Journey.
Old Men in the Leaf Smoke, The.
Out of Sleep Awakened.
Pablo Casals.
Passing her in the day he had but dared.
Peepers in Our Meadow, The.
Pity's Sake.
Poem for the Time of Change.
Poem in Prose.
Poet.
Poetical Remains.
Poet's Laughter.
Pole Star.
Pony Rock.
Population Explosion.
Pot of Earth, The.
Prologue: "And the way goes on in the worn earth."
Psyche with the Candle.
Rainbow at Evening.
Rape of the Swan, The.
Reasons for Music.
Reef Fisher, The.
Renovated Temple, The.
Reply to Mr. Wordsworth.
Reproach to Dead Poets.
Return.
Revenant, The.
Revolution of the Children.
Rue Carpenter.
St. Philip's Church in Antigua.
Salute.
Seafarer.
Second Book, The.
Seeing.
Selene Afterwards.
Sentiments for a Dedication.
Serpent's Cradle Song, The.
Serpent's Riddle, The.
Seventh Book, The.
Shallow Grass, The.
She was herself, not his, not anything.
Sheep in the Ruins, The.
Ship in the Tomb.
Ship of Fools.
Ship's Log.
Signal, The.
Signature for Tempo.
Silent Slain, The.
Sixth Book, The.
Sketch for a Portrait of Mme. G———M———.
Snow Fall, The.
Snowflake Which Is Now and Hence Forever, The.
Some Aspects of Immortality.
Songs for Eve.
Sowing of the Dead Corn, The.
Spanish Lie, The.
Speech to a Crowd.
Speech to the Detractors.
Speech to Those Who Say Comrade.
Spring in These Hills.
Starved Lovers.
State Funeral: March 31, 1969.
Steamboat Whistle, The.
Sunset Piece, The.
Survivor.
Tenth Book, The.
Theory of Poetry.
They Come No More, Those Words, Those Finches.
They say they are one flesh.
Things he had loved because he knew them lost.
Third Book, The.
Thirteenth Book, The.
This was not love but love's true negative.
Throwing a careless pebble in the lake.
Thrush in the Gaelic Islands, The.
Thunderhead.
Tourist Death.
Treason Crime, The.
Tricked by Eternity the Heart.
Triumph of the Shell, The.

True History of Bernál Díaz.
Twelfth Book, The.
Two Poems from the War.
Two Priests, The.
Two Trees, The.
Two Women Talking.
Tyrant of Syracuse.
Under an elm tree where the river reaches.
Unfinished History.
Verses for a Centennial.
Vicissitudes of the Creator.
Voyage.
Voyage en Provence.
Voyage to the Moon.
Voyage West.
Waking.
Way-Station.
Well, he was drunk. That much was clear.
What Adam Said.
What Any Lover Learns.
What Eve Said.
What Eve Sang.
What Must.
What Riddle Asked the Sphinx.
What the Green Tree Said.
What the Lion Said to the Child.
What the Old Women Say.
What the Serpent Said to Adam.
What the Vine Said to Eve.
What the Wind Said to the Water: What the
    Water Replied.
Where a Poet's From.
Where the Hayfields Were.
White-Haired Girl.
White of her Colonial, The.
Whom do you love, she said, when you look
    out.
Why the Face of a Clock is not Truly a
    Circle.
Wild Old Wicked Man, The.
Wildwest.
William Adams Delano.
Winter Is Another Country.
With Age Wisdom.
Woman on the Stair, The.
Wood Dove at Sandy Spring, The.
Words in Time.
Words to be Spoken.
Yacht for Sale.
Years of the Dog.
You Also, Gaius Valerius Catullus.
You, Andrew Marvell.
Young Dead Soldiers, The.

MacNeice, Louis (1907–63)
After the Crash.
Aftermath.
Alcohol.
All Over Again.
Although we say we disbelieve.
Another Cold May.
Apple Blossom.
April Fool.
April Manifesto, An.
Areopagus.
As In Their Time.
Atlantic Tunnel, The.
Aubade for Infants.
Aubade: "Having bitten on life like a sharp
    apple."
August.
Autobiography.
Autolycus.
Autumn Journal *sels.*
Autumn Journal.
Autumn Sequel.
Babel.
Back-Again, The.
Bad Dream.
Bagpipe Music.
Bar-Room Matins.
Barcelona in Wartime.
Bards wha hae for Hellas bled—.
Belfast.
Beni Hasan.
Birmingham.
Birthright.
Blasphemies, The.

Bluebells.
Bottleneck.
Brandy Glass, The.
Breaking Webs.
British Museum Reading Room, The.
Brother Fire.
Budgie.
Burnt Bridge, The.
Business Men.
Candles.
Canto I: "August. Render to Caesar. Speak
    parrot: a gimmick for Poll."
Canto II: "'On the other hand,' said Gavin—
    or could have said."
Canto III: "To work—To Beaconsfield. A
    suburban train."
Canto IV: "To work. To my own office, my
    own job."
CantoV: "Hence these arrears, this filing
    cabinet crammed."
Canto VI: "Everydayness is good; particular-
    dayness."
Canto VII: "Cloud of witnesses. To whom?
    To what?, A."
Canto VIII: "Fair; not to say radiant. The
    Twentyfifth of September."
Canto IX: "Master closed the door. The
    unmodern words, The."
Canto X: "Daily news. And today? There is
    not so much to note."
Canto XI: "Golden guineas filter through the
    mist, The."
Canto XII: "Now to dissolve in port. I take
    the train."
Canto XIII: "Leaving the colleges then and
    their half-remembered."
Canto XIV: "Battle? That is one way of
    looking at the matter, A."
Canto XV: "Been here before? Whether he
    has or no."
Canto XVI: "Young man cannot answer. Is
    this life?, The."
Canto XVII: "This was the night that
    specially we went down."
Canto XVIII: "Lament for the Makers.
    Monday comes; at noon."
Canto XIX: "All out!" the voices cry in the
    Park, "All out!"
Canto XX: "To Wales once more, though not
    on holiday now."
Canto XXI "Thirtieth inst., too soon the
    thirtieth ult, The."
Canto XXII: "So this is Glastonbury. A green
    hill far away."
Canto XXIII: "December continues mild. The
    rose garden."
Canto XXIV: "December the Twenty-third: I
    visit the Ancient East."
Canto XXV: "And today is Christmas Eve.
    Once more to work."
Canto XXVI: "Morning bright as summer.
    The job on hand, A."
Carol: "To end all carols, darling."
Carrick Revisited.
Carrickfergus.
Casualty, The.
Cats.
Charon.
Château Jackson.
Chess.
Children's Games.
Christina.
Christmas Shopping.
Circe.
Circus.
Closing Album, The.
Clowns.
Cock o' the North *sels.*
Cock o' the North.
Coda.
Conscript, The.
Constant.
Contact, A.
Conversation.
Convoy.
Corncrakes.
Corner Seat.

Country Week-End.
Cradle Song for Eleanor.
Cradle Song for Miriam.
Creditor, The.
Cromlech, The.
Crossword Puzzles.
Cuckoo.
Cushendun.
Cyclist, The.
Dandelions.
Dark Age Glosses.
Darts.
Day of Renewal.
Day of Returning.
"Death of a cat, The."
Death of an Actress.
Death of an Old Lady.
Death-Wish, The.
Débâcle.
Déjà Vu.
Didymus.
Dogs in the Park.
Donegal Triptych.
Dowser, The.
Dreams in Middle Age.
'Drunk again! Where do you think you are?'
Drunkard, The.
Dublin.
Ear, The.
East.
Easter Returns.
Eclogue between the Motherless.
Eclogue by a Five-Barred Gate.
Eclogue for Christmas, An.
Eclogue from Iceland.
Elegy for Minor Poets.
Elephant Trunk.
Elephants.
Empty Shoes.
Entered in the Minutes.
Entirely.
Epitaph for Liberal Poets.
Evening in Connecticut.
Evening Indoors.
Explorations.
Figure of Eight.
Finale.
Flight of the Heart.
Flower Show.
Flowers in the Interval.
Fresh from the knife and coming to.
Galway.
Gardener, The.
Genesis.
Glacier, The.
Glass Falling.
Godfather.
Gone-Tomorrow, The.
Good Dream.
Goodbye to London.
Grey Ones, The.
Greyness Is All.
Gulf between us and the brutes, The.
Habits, The.
Half Truth from Cape Town.
Hand of Snapshots, A.
Hands and Eyes.
Happy Families.
Heated Minutes, The.
Hebrides, The.
Here-and-Never, The.
Hiatus.
Hidden Ice.
Hold-up.
Homage to Clichés.
Homage to Wren.
Horses.
House on a Cliff.
Icebergs.
Iceland.
Idle Talk.
Il Piccolo Rifiuto.
In Lieu.
Indian Village.
Individualist Speaks, The.
Indoor Sports.
Intimations of Mortality.

Introduction, The.
Invocation: "Dolphin plunge, fountain play."
Island, The.
Jehu.
Jericho.
Jigsaws *sels.*
Jigsaws.
Jingles of the Morning, The.
June Thunder.
Jungle Clearance, Ceylon.
Kingdom, The *sels.*
Kingdom, The.
Lake in the Park, The.
Last before America.
Leaving Barra.
Left-Behind, The.
Les Neiges d'Antan.
Les Sylphides.
Letter from India.
Letter to Graham and Anna.
Libertine, The.
Littoral.
London Rain.
Lugubrious, Salubrious Seaside, The.
Mahabalipuram.
Mahavveray.
Mayfly.
Meeting Point.
Memoranda to Horace.
Messiah, The.
Mixer, The.
Morning Sun.
Munich Agreement, The.
Museums.
Mutations.
National Gallery, The.
Nature Morte.
Nature Notes.
Neutrality.
New Jerusalem.
News-Reel, The.
Night Club.
No More Sea.
Nocturne: "Dark blood of night-time, The."
North.
North Sea, The.
Nostalgia.
Notes for a Biography.
Novelettes.
Now That the Shapes of Mist.
Nuts in May.
October in Bloomsbury.
Ode: "To-night is so coarse with chocolate."
Off the Peg.
Old Masters Abroad.
Old Story, The.
On the Four Masters.
On the Grettir Saga.
On the Njal Saga.
On the Venerable Bede.
Once-in-Passing, The.
Oracle, The.
Order to View.
Other Wing, The.
Our Sister Water.
Out of the Picture.
Pale Panther, The.
Park, The.
Passage Steamer.
Perdita.
Perseus.
Perspectives.
Pet Shop.
Pindar is Dead.
Place of a Skull.
Plain Speaking.
Plant and Phantom.
Plurality.
Postscript to Iceland.
Poussin.
Prayer before Birth.
Prayer in Mid-Passage.
Preacher, The.
Precursors.
Prognosis.
Prospect.
Provence.

Ravenna.
Réchauffé.
Reflections.
Refugees.
Relics.
Rest House, The.
Restaurant Car.
Return, The.
Return to Lahore.
Revenant, The.
Riddle, The.
Riding in Cars.
Rites of War.
River in Spate.
Round the Corner.
Sailing Orders.
Sand in the Air.
Satirist, The.
Schizophrene.
Sea, The.
Selva Oscura.
Shove Halfpenny.
Sleeping Winds.
Sligo and Mayo.
Slow Movement.
Slow Starter, The.
Slum Song.
Snow.
Snow Man, The.
Soap Suds.
Solitary Travel.
Solstice.
South.
Sports Page.
Spring Cleaning.
Spring Sunshine.
Spring Voices.
Springboard, The.
Star-Gazer.
Strand, The.
Street Scene.
Streets of Laredo, The.
Stygian Banks, The.
Stylite.
Suicide, The.
Suite for Recorders.
Sunday in the Park.
Sunday Morning.
Sunlight on the Garden, The.
Swing-Song.
Taken for Granted.
Tam Cari Capitis.
Taxis, The.
Thalassa.
This Is the Life.
This Way Out.
Thyestes.
Time for a Smoke.
To a Communist.
To-day was a beautiful day, the sky was a
    brilliant.
To Hedli.
To Mary.
To Posterity.
To the Public.
Toast, A.
Train to Dublin.
Trains in the Distance.
Trapezists.
Tree of Guilt, The.
Tree Party.
Trilogy for X.
Trolls, The.
Troll's Courtship.
Truisms, The.
Turf-Stacks.
Twelfth Night.
"Two Poems in Defeat."
Under the Mountain.
Upon This Beach.
Valediction: "Their verdure dare not
    show..their verdure dare not show."
Variation on Heraclitus.
Vingt-et-un.
Visit to Rouen.
Visitations.
Vistas.

Wall, The.
War Heroes.
Week to Christmas, A.
Wessex Guidebook.
West.
Western Landscape.
What ghosts of cuckoo-spit and dew.
What is truth? says Pilate.
When she had her stroke the china dogs.
When We Were Children.
Whit Monday.
Window, The.
Windowscape.
Wiper, The.
Wolves.
Woods.
Yours Next.
Translations, Coauthored Poems, etc.:
Aequam Memento.
Carpe Diem.
Corona Virginum.
Four Medieval Latin Poems.
Jam Lucis Orto Sidere.
Legend of the Dead Soldier, The.
Lilacs and the Roses, The.
Meum Est Propositum.
My Mary.
Richard Coeur-de-Lion.
Solvitur Acris Hiems.
Three Odes of Horace.
Unoccupied Zone, The.
Ut Quid Iubes, Pusiole.

McNeill, Louise
After the Blast.
American Boating Song.
Arrow Grasses by Greenbrier River.
Aubade to Fear (Heavy with Child).
Autumn Drives (Early 1800s), The.
Backward Flight.
Ballad of Joe Bittner.
Ballad of Miss Sally.
Ballad of New River.
Ballad of the Rest Home.
Best House They Was Ever In (Retired Coal
    Operator).
Blizzard.
Burying Field.
Cassandra.
Cave, The.
Chestnut Orchard.
Clearing, The.
Coal Fern.
Company (Coal Miner), The.
Cornelius Verner.
Corner Tree.
Depression Wind (Winter 1930).
Deserted Lumber Yard.
Donna MacElmain.
Dream, The.
Epitaph in the Imperative Mode.
Faldang.
Fiddler.
First Flight.
First Train (1895).
Flame, The.
Fox and Geese.
Gabriel MacElmain, Pioneer.
Garden Moment.
Granny Saunders.
Granny's Story.
Grave Creek Inscribed Stone, The.
Great Depression, The.
Hard Road, The.
Hill Daughter.
Hill Song.
Horsemen, The.
Hounds, The.
How to Unbewitch a Backtracking Hound.
Involved (The Spider).
Jane Renick MacElmain (1).
Jane Renick MacElmain (2).
Jed Kane.
Katchie Verner's Harvest.
Life-Force.
Light.
Log Drive.
Lost in Orbit.

Lullaby:*"Herda, herda, herda, sing my sisters"*.
Lydia Verner.
Martha MacElmain.
Mayapple Hill.
Memoria.
Monongah (December 6, 1907, Marion County, West Virginia, on the Monongahela River).
Moonshiner.
Mountain Corn Song.
New Corbies, The.
Nora O'Kane.
Of Fitness to Survive.
Oil Field.
Over the Mountain.
Overheard on a Bus (Miner's Wife).
Overheard on a Bus (Woman with a Cleft Palate).
Passage of Time, The.
Pasture Line Fence.
Poet.
Potherbs (Of the Edible Wild Plants My Granny Taught Me).
Reforestation.
River, The.
Roads, The.
Runaway Team (Written a Few Days After John Glenn's Space Flight), The.
Saturday Night (1890-1910).
Saturday Night (1930s).
Second Sight (My Son's First Springtime).
Snow Angels.
Sol Brady.
Son, The.
Spark, The.
Stoic (Circa 1907).
Stories at Evening (A Suburban Mother Tells Stories to Her Son).
Susan O'Kane.
Threnody for Old Orchards.
Tillie Sage (1).
Tillie Sage (2).
Tillie Sage (3).
Timber Boom.
Time Is Our House.
To the Boys in Freshman History (Thermopylae, 480 B.C.).
Traveler and Old Sorrel.
Turnpike, The.
Verb, The.
Warning.
West Virginia.
When the Scientists Told Me of the Expanding Universe.
Wife.
Winter Day (Coal Country).
Wire Brier.
Translations, Coauthored Poems, etc.:
Pioneer Lullaby.

Mahon, Derek (b. 1941)
Achill.
After Midnight.
After Pasternak.
After the Titanic.
Afterlives.
Andean Flute, The.
Another Sunday Morning.
Antarctica.
Aran.
As It Should Be.
Attic, The.
Autobiographies.
Beyond Howth Head.
Beyond the Pale.
Bicycle, The.
Blackbird, The.
Brecht in Svendborg.
Brighton Beach.
Canadian Pacific.
Chinese Restaurant in Portrush, The.
Consolations of Philosophy.
Courtyards in Delft.
Craigvara House.
Dawn at Saint Patrick's.
Dawn Chorus, The.
Day Trip to Donegal.

De Quincey in Later Life.
Death and the Sun.
Deaths.
Dejection.
Derry Morning.
Disused Shed in Co. Wexford, A.
Dream Days.
Dying Art, A.
Ecclesiastes.
Everything Is Going to Be All Right.
Exit Molloy.
Father-in-Law.
Ford Manor.
Forger, The.
Four Walks in the Country Near Saint-Brieuc.
Garage in Co. Cork, A.
Gipsies.
Girls on the Bridge.
Glengormley.
Globe in North Carolina, The.
Going Home.
Grandfather.
Heraclitus on Rivers.
Homage to Malcolm Lowry.
Home Front, The.
Homecoming.
Hunt by Night, The.
Image from Beckett, An.
In Carrowdore Churchyard.
Joycentenary Ode.
Katie at the Pool.
Kensington Notebook, A.
Kinsale.
Knut Hamsun in Old Age.
Last of the Fire Kings, The.
Last Resort, The.
Leaves.
Light Music.
Lighthouse in Maine, A.
Lives.
Lost Girls, The.
Man and Bird.
Midsummer.
Morning.
Morning Radio.
Mt. Gabriel.
Mute Phenomena, The.
Night Drive.
North Wind: Portrush.
Nostalgias.
October in Hyde Park.
Old Lady, An.
Old Roscoff.
Old Snaps, The.
One of These Nights.
Ovid in Tomis.
Penshurst Place.
Portrait of the Artist, A.
Postcard from Berlin, A.
Preface to a Love Poem.
Rathlin.
Refusal to Mourn, A.
Rock Music.
St. Eustace.
Sea in Winter, The.
Snow Party, The.
Soles.
Songs of Praise.
Squince.
Stone Age Figure Far Below, A.
Studio, The.
Table Talk.
Terminal Bar, The.
Thinking of Inis Oírr in Cambridge, Mass.
Tithonus.
Tolerable Wisdom, A.
Tractatus.
Two Songs.
Unborn Child, An.
Woods, The.
Translations, Coauthored Poems, etc.:
1.2: How to Live.
Amores *sels.*
Hearing the thunder of the intransitive weirs.
Ignorance.
Odes *sels.*

Ovid in Love.
Three Poems by Phillipe Jaccottet.
Voice, The.
Words in the Air.
Mare, Walter De la *see* De la Mare, Walter
Markson, David
Accepted.
A.D. 2029.
Agree.
Anne-on-Avon.
As in the Aftermath.
At Malcolm Lowry's Grave.
At the Lion's Head.
Birches.
Borrowed Line.
But Yet Again, We Fought.
Contradiction.
Cummings.
Daily Reviewer-Haupt.
Dante Gabriel.
Death of the Virgin, The.
Dialogue in Milan.
Dylan.
Footnotes to "Anne-on-Avon."
Funeral.
Hartnett in Worcester.
History and Theory of Art.
Hygiene.
I Ate My Love Alive.
I Met My Love.
I Saw Old Dylan.
Imitative Fragment.
Johanna.
Julia Now.
Lament: "My love is gone."
Loss.
Lowry.
Memo to His Lady's Therapist.
Monody.
Nachtmusik.
Occupation.
Of Writings Unfinished.
On Being Denied for Being Already Took.
On the Death, after Lying Wounded in the Thigh for Twenty-Six Days, of the Author of "Astrophel and Stella."
Once, in Our Quarreling.
Preference of Metre.
Prosody.
Question of Anatomy.
Quietude.
Recitation before Bed.
Relevance.
Sans.
See Susan Read.
Sexist Stanza.
Sister's Son.
Skull.
Strange Night.
Tardy Poet: 1978.
This Vision Comes.
To a Lady, a Part of Her.
To a Mexican Poet Who Has Forsaken Drink.
Traveler's Tale.
Tricentennial: 1980.
Unfinished.
Vow, The.
We Love, But Cannot Live.
Women's House of Detention.
Writer's Lament.
Youthful Poet's Unspoke Response to a Woman Talking Too Loudly in His Favorite Bookstore, The.
Marlowe, Christopher (1564–93)
Amorous Neptune.
Bridal Song: "O come, soft rest of cares, come Night."
Epithalamion Teratos.
Hero and Leander.
Hero Feels the Shaft of Love.
Leander's Return.
Love at First Sight.
Passionate Shepherd to His Love, The.
Repentance.
Wedding of Alcmane and Mya, The.

Translations, Coauthored Poems, etc.:
1.1: Quemadmodum a Cupidine pro bellis amoris scribere coactus sit.
1.2: Quod primo amore correptus, in triumphium duci se a Cupidine patiatur.
1.3: Ad amicam.
1.4: Amicam, qua arte, quibusve nutibus in caena, presente viro uti debeat, admonet.
1.5: Corinnae concubitus.
1.6: Ad Janitorem, ut fores sibi aperiat.
1.7: Ad pacandam amicam, quam verberaverat.
1.8: Execratur lenam, quae puellam suam meretricia arte instituebat.
1.9: Ad Atticum, amantem non oportere desidiosum esse, sicuti nec militem.
1.10: Ad puellam, ne pro amore praemia poscat.
1.11: Napen alloquitur, ut paratas tabellas ad Corinnam perferat.
1.12: Tabellas quas miserat execratur, quod amica noctem negabat.
1.13: Elegy: Ad Auroram, ne properet.
1.14: Puellam consolatur cui prae nimia cura comae deciderant.
1.15: Ad invidos, quod fama poetarum sit perennis.
2.1: Quod pro gigantomachia amores scribere sit coactus.
2.2: Ad Bagoum, ut custodiam puellae sibi commissae laxiorem habeat.
2.3: Ad Eunuchum servantem dominam.
2.4: Quod amet mulieres, cuiuscunque formae sint.
2.5: Ad amicam corruptam.
2.6: In mortem psittaci.
2.7: Amicae se purgat quod ancillam non amet.
2.8: Ad Cypassim ancillam Corinnae.
2.9: Ad Cupidinem.
2.10: Ad Graecinum quod eodem tempore duas amet.
2.11: Ad amicam navigantem.
2.12: Exultat, quod amica potitus sit.
2.13: Ad Isidem, ut parientem Corinnam iuvet.
2.14: In amicam, quod abortivum ipsa fecerit.
2.15: Ad annulum, quem dono amicae dedit.
2.16: Ad amicam, ut ad rura sua veniat.
2.17: Quod Corinnae soli sit serviturus.
2.18: Ad Macrum, quod de amoribus scribat.
2.19: Ad rivalem, cui uxor curae non erat.
3.1: Deliberatio poetae, utrum elegos pergat scribere an potius tragedias.
3.2: Ad amicam cursum equorum spectantem.
3.3: De amica, quae periuraverat.
3.4: Ad virum servantem coniugem.
3.5: Ad amnem, dum iter faceret ad amicam.
3.6: Quod ab amica receptus cum ea coire non potuit, conqueritur.
3.7: Quod ab amica non recipiatur, dolet.
3.8: Tibulli mortem deflet.
3.9: Ad Cererem, conquerens quod eius sacris cum amica concumbere non permittatur.
3.10: Ad amicam, a cuius amore discedere non potest.
3.11: Dolet amicam suam ita suis carminibus innotuisse ut rivales multos sibi pararit.
3.12: De Iunonis festo.
3.13: Ad amicam, si peccatura est, ut occulte peccet.
3.14: Ad Venerem, quod elegis finem imponat.
Another of the Same Nature, Made Since.
Bait[e], The.
Elegies *sels.*
Nimphs [or Nymph's] Reply to the Sheepheard [or Shepherd], The.
Pharsalia *sels.*
Wars worse than civil on Thessalian plains.

Marvell, Andrew (1621–78)
Ad Regem Carolum Parodia [A Parody: To King Charles].
After Floods on the Wharfe.
Ametas and Thestylis Making Hay-Ropes.
Bermudas.

Bludius et Corona [Blood and the Crown].
Carrying Their Coracles.
Character of Holland, The.
Clorinda and Damon.
Coronet, The.
Damon the Mower.
Daphnis and Chloe.
Definition of Love, The.
Dialogue between the Resolved Soul and Created Pleasure, A.
Dialogue between the Soul and [the] Body, A.
Dialogue between Thyrsis and Dorinda, A.
Dignissimo Suo Amico Doctori Witty.
Dutch in the Medway, The.
Elegy upon the Death of My Lord Francis Villiers, An.
Epigramma in Duos Montes Amosclivium et Bilboreum: Farfacio [Epigram on Two Mountains, Almscliff and Bilbrough: To Fairfax].
Epitaph upon —, An.
Eyes and Tears.
Fair Singer, The.
First Anniversary of the Government under His Highness the Lord Protector, 1655, The.
First Song.
Flecknoe, an English Priest at Rome.
Gallery, The.
Garden of Appleton House, The ("When in the east the morning ray").
Garden, The.
Hewel, or Woodpecker, The.
Horatian Ode upon Cromwell's Return from Ireland, An.
Hortus.
Illustrissimo Viro Domino Lanceloto Josepho de Maniban Grammatomanti [To That Renowned Man Lord Lancelot Joseph de Maniban Graphologist].
In Eandem Reginae Sueciae Transmissam [To Christina, Queen of Sweden].
In Effigiem Oliveri Cromwell [On a Portrait of Oliver Cromwell].
In Legationem Domini Oliveri St John ad Provincias Foederatas [On the Embassy of Lord Oliver St John to the United Provinces].
Inscribenda Luparae [To Be Written on the Louvre].
King Charles on [or upon] the Scaffold.
Kingfisher, The.
Last Instructions to a Painter, The.
Letter to Doctor Ingelo, A.
Loyal Scot, The.
Match, The.
Mourning.
Mower against Gardens, The.
Mower to the Glow-Worms [or Glowworms or Glo-Worms], The.
Mower's Song, The.
Music's Empire.
Nymph and Her Fawn, The.
Nymph Complaining for the Death of Her Faun [or Fawn], The.
see also Ros.
On Mr Milton's "Paradise Lost."
On the Victory Obtained by Blake over the Spaniards, in the Bay of Santa [or Sancta] Cruz, in the Island of Tenerife, 1657.
Picture of Little T. C. in a Prospect of Flowers, The.
Pros Karolon ton Basilea [To King Charles].
Ros.
Second Song.
That Providence which had so long the care.
To His Coy Mistress.
To His Noble Friend, Mr Richard Lovelace, upon His Poems.
To His Worthy Friend Doctor Witty upon His Translation of the "Popular Errors."
To My Lord Fairfax.
Tom May's Death.
Two Songs at the Marriage of the Lord Fauconberg and the Lady Mary Cromwell.
Unfortunate Lover, The.

Upon an Eunuch: A Poet.
Upon Appleton House [To My Lord Fairfax].
Upon the Death of the Lord Hastings.
Upon the Hill and Grove at Bilbrough.
Young Love.
Translations, Coauthored Poems, etc.:
In the French Translation of Lucan by Monsieur De Brebeuf Are These Verses: Lib 3.
Pharsalia *sels.*
Second Chorus from Seneca's Tragedy "Thyestes", The.
Thyestes *sels.*

Matthews, William (b. 1942)
Accompanist, The.
And So.
Another Beer.
Bad.
Black Box.
Blue Notes.
Blues for John Coltrane, Dead at 41.
Blues, The.
Bud Powell, Paris, 1959.
Burglary.
Bystanders.
Cat, The.
Change of Address.
Civilization and Its Discontents.
Cloud, The.
Dawn.
Dog Life.
Driving Alongside the Housatonic River Alone on a Rainy April Night.
Eternally Undismayed Are the Poolshooters.
Every Tub.
Everywhere.
Eyes.
Familial.
Fellow Oddballs.
Flood.
Flood Light.
Flood Peak.
Flood Plain.
Foul Shots: A Clinic.
Funeral Homes.
Good.
Good Company.
Happy Childhood, A.
Herd of Buffalo Crossing the Missouri on Ice.
Homer's Seeing-Eye Dog.
Hope.
Housecooling.
Housework.
How Careful Fire Can Be.
Hummer, The.
Icehouse, Pointe au Baril, Ontario, The.
In Memory of the Utah Stars.
In Memory of W. H. Auden.
Interpretation of Dreams, The.
It Don't Mean a Thing If It Ain't Got That Swing.
Left Hand Canyon.
Little Blue Nude.
Living among the Dead.
Long.
Loyal.
Lust.
Lust Acts.
March Heat.
Masterful.
Men in Dark Suits.
Minuscule Things.
Mood Indigo.
Moonlight in Vermont.
Moving.
Moving Again.
Nabokov's Blues.
Nabokov's Death.
Narcissus Blues.
Needle's Eye, the Lens, The.
New.
No True Rhyme in English for "Silver."
On a Diet.
On Cape Cod a Child Is Stolen.
On the Porch at the Frost Place, Franconia, NH.

107th & Amsterdam.
Onions.
Past, The.
Photo of the Author with a Favorite Pig.
Pissing off the Back of the Boat into the
    Nivernais Canal.
Portrait, The.
Premature Ejaculation.
Psychopathology of Everyday Life, The.
Puberty.
Record Flood.
Recovery Room.
Red Silk Blouse, A.
Right.
Scenic View.
School.
School Days.
School Figures.
Schoolboys with Dog, Winter.
Search Party, The.
Sleep.
Snake, The.
Snow.
Spiritual Life.
Spring Snow.
Straight Life.
Sympathetic.
Taken at the Flood.
Tardy.
Theme of the Three Caskets, The.
39,000 Feet.
This Spud's for You.
Twins.
Vasectomy.
Visionary Picnic, The.
Waking at Dusk from a Nap.
Waste Carpet, The.
Waters, The.
Wehlener Sonnenuhr Auslese 1959.
What You Need.
Whiplash.
Why I Didn't Notice It.
Why We Are Truly a Nation.
Writer-in-Residence.
Wrong.
Translations, Coauthored Poems, etc.:
Although you fill amethyst cups.
Art and Cal have made a trade.
Babahak.
Because in December when the gifts fly—.
Epigrams *sels.*
Here he is whom you read and clamor for.
Human Hymn.
I Long For a Horse.
"It's nothing," whatever.
Long year I squeezed out a tiny book, The.
Mother.
Old friend, suppose luck grants to us.
Papylus had a dong so long.
Recollections.
Slave that Cinna's named his cook, The.
Someone we both know, Rufus, looked me.
Surrounded by eunuchs and limp as a tissue.
Ted's studio burnt down, with all his poems.
"Tell me the truth, Mark," you insist.
Ten times a year you're ill, Malingerus.
That plush hair Fabulla wears?
Untitled Poem.
Why is it modern poets are ignored.
You announce that you are beautiful.
You Dance Up There.
You lie and I concur. You "give."
You sold a slave just yesterday.
You wonder, Lupus, who's the best
    schoolmaster.
You're hot to trot? Well then I'm not.

Meinke, Peter
ABC of Aerobics, The.
Advice to My Son.
Anniversary Deer, The.
Arms and the Man.
Atomic Pantoum.
Aunt Gertrud.
Aunt Mary.
Azaleas.
Because.
Blue Morning Glories.

Byron vs. DiMaggio.
Cabaret Voltaire.
Café du Pont.
Café Vue des Alpes.
Chicken Unlimited.
Church Cemetery in St. Mary's, A.
Cloud, Florida, 1985, The.
Dead Tree, The.
Dear Reader.
Death of the Pilot Whales, The.
Easter in Neuchâtel.
Elegy for a Diver.
Everything We Do.
Exodus with Children.
Father.
50 on 50.
Fixed Stars.
Flatbush.
Fourth of July.
Gift of the Magi, The.
Growing Deaf.
Heart's Location, The.
Helen.
Hermann Ludwig Ferdinand Von Helmholtz.
Hero Worship at Key West on the 4th of
    July.
Hôtel de la Truite.
Hôtel Lion d'Or.
House, The.
In Gentler Times.
Indigo Buntings.
Liquid Paper.
Love Poem 1990.
Magic Kingdom, The.
Mendel's Laws.
Minuet in G.
Monkey's Paw, The.
Myrtle the Turtle.
Myth.
Night Watch on the Chesapeake.
Ode to Good Men Fallen Before Hero Come.
Perch, The.
Ping-Pong.
Playing Shuffleboard, Drunk, in Key West,
    Fla.
Plovers.
Poet to His Tongue, The.
Poet, Trying to Surprise God, The.
Progress.
Rage.
Robert Frost in Warsaw.
Running with the Hyenas.
Shell, The.
Slow Child, The.
Soldiers with Green Leggings.
Sonnet on the Death of the Man Who
    Invented Plastic Roses.
Stille Nacht, Heilege Nacht.
Supermarket.
Surfaces.
Talk of the Paintings.
Teaching Poetry at a Country School in
    Florida.
Third Child: June Eleven, Nineteen Sixty
    Two.
This is a poem to my son Peter.
To a Daughter with Artistic Talent.
Uncle Jim.
Uncle Joe.
Vision.
Wishing He Had a Theory in Key West.
World within World.
Writing the Great American Poem in Key
    West.
You stand in isolation like the first bloom.

Melville, Herman (1819–91)
Æolian Harp, The.
After the Pleasure Party.
Age of the Antonines, The.
America.
American Aloe on Exhibition, The.
Apathy and Enthusiasm.
Apparition, The.
Arch, The.
Archipelago, The.
Armies of the Wilderness, The.

Art.
At the Cannon's Mouth.
Ball's Bluff.
Battle of Stone River, Tennessee.
Bench of Boors, The.
Berg, The.
Billy Budd, Foretopman *sels.*
Billy in the Darbies.
Buddha.
Camoëns.
Canticle, A.
Clarel: A Poem and Pilgrimage in the Holy
    Land *sels.*
Clover.
College Colonel, The.
Coming Storm, The.
Commemoration of a Naval Victory.
Conflict of Convictions, The.
Dupont's Round Fight.
Empty Stirrups.
Enthusiast, The.
Enviable Isles, The.
Epilogue: "If Luther's day expand to
    Darwin's year."
Far Off-Shore.
Field Asters.
Formerly a Slave.
Fortitude of the North, The.
Fragments of a Lost Gnostic Poem of the
    Twelfth [*or* 12th] Century.
Garden of Metrodorus, The.
Greek Architecture.
Greek Masonry.
Haglets, The.
Hearts-Of-Gold.
Herba Santa.
House-Top, The.
Immolated.
In a Bye-Canal.
In a Church of Padua.
In a Garret.
In the Desert.
In the Turret.
Inscription: "To them who crossed the flood."
Inscription, The: "While yet Rolfe's foot in
    stirrup stood."
Jack Roy.
John Marr *sels.*
John Marr.
Little Good Fellows, The.
Lone Founts.
Maldive Shark, The.
Malvern Hill.
March to the Sea, The.
Marchioness of Brinvilliers, The.
Margrave's Birthnight, The.
Martyr, The.
Milan Cathedral.
Misgivings.
Monody.
Montaigne and His Kitten.
Mortmain Reappears.
Muster, The.
Night-March, The.
Of Wickedness the Word.
Off Cape Colona.
On Sherman's Men.
On the Grave.
On the Home Guards.
On the Photograph of Corps Commander.
On the Slain Collegians.
Parthenon, The.
Pebbles.
Pisa's Leaning Tower.
Pontoosuce.
Portent, The.
Prelusive.
Ravaged Villa, The.
Reasonable Constitution, A.
Rebel Color-Bearers at Shiloh.
Rosary Beads.
Rusty Man, The.
Sheridan at Cedar Creek.
Shiloh [A Requiem].
Since as in night's deck-watch ye show.
Sketch, A.
Stonewall Jackson.

Temeraire, The.
Timoleon.
Tom Deadlight.
Trophies of Peace.
Tuft of Kelp, The.
Ungar and Rolfe.
Utilitarian View of the Monitor's Fight, A.
Venice.
Via Crucis.
Vine and Clarel.

Meredith, George (1828–1909)
Adieu, adieu, my Friar, he cried.
Age of petty tit-for-tat, An.
Ah for that time when open daylight pours.
Ah! little Angel, child of bliss!
Aimée.
Alsace-Lorraine.
Alternation.
Ambition.
And tho' my friar's mandate is severe.
Aneurin's Harp.
Angel, be ye ne'er in doubt, An.
Angela Burdett-Coutts.
Angelic Love.
Antigone.
Appeasement of Demeter, The.
Appreciation.
Arabic Poems.
Archduchess Anne.
As from the fall of candlelight.
As I turn'd into the market-place.
As often in a bun.
Ask, is Love divine.
Ass of Balaam, The.
At the Close.
At the first ball his wicket fell, and sins.
At the Funeral.
Atkins.
Atlas.
Au voleur, au voleur, au voleur!—.
Autumn Even-Song.
Ballad of Fair Ladies in Revolt, A.
Ballad of Past Meridian, A.
Ballad of the Lady Eglantine, The.
Beetle soars, the beetle spins, The.
Beggar's Soliloquy, The.
Believe me, I have studied men.
Bellerophon.
Beyond the meadow still where sweeps.
Black Richard.
Blame me not that I refuse.
Blest is the sword that leaps from sheath.
Blue Is the Sky.
Breath of the Briar.
Britain.
Brotherhood.
Bumble Bee—the Bumble Bee, The.
Burden of Strength, The.
But see what living glory floods the west.
By Morning Twilight.
By the Passeyr.
By the Rosanna.
C B M.
Cageing of Ares, The.
Call, The.
Camelus Saltat.
Camelus Saltat: Continued.
Candid Friend who strikes because he loves, The.
Capitalist, The.
Carol of Jack Frost, A.
Cassandra.
Centenary of Garibaldi, The.
Certain People, A.
Chambers of my heart are many, dear, The.
Change in Recurrence.
Child's Prayer, A.
Chillianwallah.
Chivalry.
Cleopatra.
Congress of Nations, The.
Cool you proceed at speed.
Could we know how kin we are.
Creation and the Prophet.
Creed.
Crisis, The.
Crown of Love, The.

Dalila.
Daphne.
Dark on the ridge of the cold salt wave.
Day is going, now 'tis noon, The.
Day of the Daughter of Hades, The.
Dear Heaven! for this sweet pledge of life.
Dear, my friend & honour'd madam! of hard facts I'm not a hoarder.
Dearest Dimpling, we believe.
Death of Winter, The.
Desert vulture / jealousy, The.
Desired as Summer rain.
Despots of Manchester, Oligarchs!
Dirge: "He has hid his face, and he's gone!"
Dirge in Woods.
Discipline of Wisdom, The.
Doe: A Fragment, The.
Dost thou behold some woeful soul.
Earth and a Wedded Woman.
Earth and Man.
Earth's Preference.
Earth's Secret.
Empedocles.
Emperor Frederick of Our Time, The.
Empty Purse: A Sermon to our Later Prodigal Son, The.
England before the Storm.
Epitaph on the Tombstone of James Christopher Wilson.
Events in a Rustic Mirror.
Fair Bedfellow, The.
Faith on Trial, A.
Falling of Sally, The.
Fall'n Is Lucifer.
Familiar Things.
Fireside.
Fireside Reverie.
First-Born, The.
Flower of the Ruins, The.
For any save a lover.
Force and His Master.
Foresight and Patience.
Forest History.
Fragments for "The Harvest Home" and "The Doe."
France.
Fresh Spring has come with flower and leaf to warn.
Friar uxorious!
Friend, when the thundercloud is low.
From labours through the night, outworn.
From lamplight and an aged leaf.
Fullness of love sleeps in us like a sea.
Fusion.
Garden Idyl, A.
Garden of Epicurus, The.
Gentleness of Death, The.
Glastonbury Thorn, The.
Glee.
Gordon, Jim, / Life and Limb.
Gordon of Khartoum.
Grace and Love.
Grandfather Bridgeman.
Hail, Common Sense! most rare of all!
Hard Weather.
Hatton's "God of War."
Hawarden.
He where the great sun looks his last.
Head of Bran the Blest, The.
Hear now the mission of good wine.
Hectate.
Her trousers are red; she wears a coatee.
Hernani.
Hilda's Morning and Evening Dose of Rhyme.
Holidays.
Hueless Love, The.
Hungarian Air.
Hymn to Colour.
I Chafe at Darkness.
I have a hope that's like a star.
I humm'd an air of sweet Mozart.
I look'd for my poet—he came not!
I looked from the book of the story of men.
I saw young Spring leap over the hills.
I say, that but for black Foakes'-day.
I seize in a central knot.

I wish'd the world a blindness.
I would I were with Jean.
Iconia.
If thou art sorrowful, hide thy face!
Il y a Cent Ans.
In all our daily war of words.
In Claremont woods we wandered once.
In the clear dark lake a lady dived.
In the Dry.
In the Sap.
In the time of early love.
In the Woods.
Infancy and Age.
Inspiration of the Great West Wind, The.
Internal Harmony.
Invitation to the Country.
Ireland.
Irene ducks and runs amuck, The.
Islet the Dachs.
It is the young fresh rainy leaf.
Italy.
It's many a penny you'll pay to go.
J. C. M.
Jack & Harry.
John, John of Ottenhaw!
John Lackland.
Jolly Young Carpenter, The.
Josepha.
Joy is Fleet.
Juggling Jerry.
July.
Jump-to-Glory Jane.
Karl Onyx.
King Harald's Trance.
Kiss, and a clasp, and an eye to eye, A.
Labourer, The.
Lady C. M., The.
Lark Ascending, The.
Last Contention, The.
Last Wandering of Poor Willie, The.
Later Alexandrian, A.
Lesson of Grief, The.
Lied von Castelli.
Like a blind child is the loving heart.
Line of eve o'er the moorland, A.
Lines to a Friend Visiting America.
Linnet-Hawker, The.
Little Foot-Page, The.
Lives there a man with such base mettle.
London by Lamplight.
Long was the conflict, but now 'tis done.
Longest Day, The.
Lord of old has dealt in blood, The.
Lords debate, the Commons brawl, The.
Love.
Love in the Valley.
Love is winged for two.
Love they alone the joyful heart.
Loyal Soldier, The.
Lucifer in Starlight.
M. M.
Madrigal: "Since Tuck is faithless found, no more."
Main Regret, The.
Manfred.
Margaret's Bridal-Eve.
Marian: ("Clouds fly fast across the moon, The").
Marian: ("She can be as wise as we").
Martin's Puzzle.
May Song.
Meditation under Stars.
Meeting.
Meeting, The.
Melampus.
Men and Man.
Mentor and Pupils.
Milton.
Miracle, The.
Miss Millicent Maxse was fond of her Ma.
Modern Love.
Monmouth.
Mortesto.
Mother to Babe.
Motley.
My jolly friar, / Now lift thy cowl.
My Lady has Diana's brows.

My Theme.
My Theme: Continued.
Napoléon.
Nature and Life.
Nature and Man.
New Era the Army of the Future the Egg of
    an Army, The.
New Year's Eve.
Night of Frost in May.
Night-Walk, The.
Night walks the earth with silver feet.
No boats oar slow, no barges pass.
Now dawns all waxen to your seal of life.
Nuptials of Attila, The.
O have you seen my Tuck? my bonny bonny
    Tuck!
O Mary Barrie, Mary Barrie.
O shrive me Friar, my ghostly Friar!
O 'tis my delight / In the dead of the night.
October 21, 1905.
Ode to H.I.M. Napoleon 3d.
Ode to the Spirit of Earth in Autumn.
Of Robin Redbreast's babes I told.
Old Chartist, The.
Olive Branch, The.
On Combe Bottom: Surrey.
On Como.
On Hearing the News from Venice.
On the Danger of War.
Once the fair Romance of story.
Open horizons round.
Or the single path— / Which the cool moon
    sheds.
Orchard and the Heath, The.
Orson of the Muse, An.
Outer and Inner.
Outside the Crowd.
Over the Hills.
Parody of Alfred Austin.
Pastoral 1: "How sweet on sunny
    afternoons."
Pastoral 2: "Yon upland slope which hides
    the sun."
Pastoral 3: "Now standing on this hedgeside
    path."
Pastoral 4: "Lo, as a tree, whose wintry
    twigs."
Pastoral 5: "Now from the meadow floods
    the wild duck clamours."
Pastoral 6: "How barren would this valley
    be."
Pastoral 7: "Summer glows warm on the
    meadows, and speedwell, and gold-cups,
    and daisies."
Pastorals.
Pasture Alp is webbed with shade, The.
Patriot Engineer, The.
Penetration and Trust.
Periander.
Phaéthôn.
Phantasy.
Philosopher! 'tis said you wail.
Phoebus with Admetus.
Pictures of the Rhine.
"Poems", says the title.
Poetry of Chaucer, The.
Poetry of Coleridge, The.
Poetry of Keats, The.
Poetry of Milton, The.
Poetry of Shakespeare, The.
Poetry of Shelley, The.
Poetry of Southey, The.
Poetry of Spenser, The.
Poetry of Wordsworth, The.
Point of Taste, The.
Preaching from a Spanish Ballad, A.
Prestige.
Progress.
Progression.
Promise in Disturbance, The.
Quake, quake, let us turn Quaker all!
Queen Zuleima.
Question Whither, The.
Rape of Aurora, The.
Reason.
Red Coats & the Blue, The.
Remember what a night of storm.

Reply of the County of Surrey to the Poet's
    Pathetic Address in Dispraise of Jean.
Requiem: "Where faces are hueless, where
    eyelids are dewless."
Revolution, The.
Rhine-Land.
Richard Lionheart.
Riddle for Men, The.
Roar through the Tall Twin Elm-Trees, A.
Rosalind.
Sage Enamoured and the Honest Lady, The.
St. Thérèse.
Schubert's "Farewell."
See the star yonder.
Seed-Time.
Sense and Spirit.
Shall I again have Lilac week?
She had a secret—bonny Bess!
She marries the knight she loves.
She rides in the park on a prancing bay.
She scarce has a word for Papa.
Shemselnihar.
Shipwreck of Idomeneus, The.
Sing aloud that she is mine.
Sleeping City, The.
Society.
Solon.
Song: Autumn.
Song: "Buy, buy, buy."
Song: "Come to me in any shape!"
Song: "Daisy now is out upon the green,
    The."
Song: "Fair and false! No dawn will greet."
Song: "Flower unfolds its dawning cup, The."
Song: "Forever."
Song: "Full of thy glory am I."
Song: "God bless the little Island!"
Song: "I cannot lose thee for a day."
Song: "I would be the bounding deer."
Song: "I would I were the drop of rain."
Song: "Love within the lover's breast."
Song: "Might I lie where leans her lute."
Song: "Moon is alone in the sky, The."
Song: "My chosen bride shall bless the
    plough."
Song: "My darling's love shall close me up."
Song: "No, no, the falling blossom is no
    sign."
Song: "O the wind, the wind, the wind doth
    blow."
Song: "O they canna' do without it."
Song: "Over the ferry, and over the ferry."
Song: "Pass we to another land."
Song: "Quick bird sings and pierces me,
    The."
Song: "Should thy love die; / O bury it not
    under ice-blue eyes!"
Song: Spring.
Song: The Wren.
Song: "Thou steppest from thy splendour."
Song: "Thou to me art such a spring."
Song: "Thou tremblest O my love! thy hand
    in mine."
Song: "Twelve arrows, and a bow, and
    spear."
Song: "Two wedded lovers watched the
    rising moon."
Song: "Under boughs of breathing May."
Song: "When on my faithful charger."
Song: "Who says, she is in danger."
Song: "Woo me now & you'll win me."
Song in the Songless.
Song of Courtesy, The.
Song of Drab, The.
Song of Ruark to Bhanavar the Beautiful.
Song of the New Zealander among the Ruins
    of Old London.
Song of Theodolinda, The.
Sonnet: "Hateful are those false themes of
    speculation."
Sonnet to J.M.
Sorrows and Joys.
Soul, The.
South-West Wind in the Woodland.
South-Wester, The.
Spirit of Shakespeare: Continued, The.
Spirit of Shakespeare, The.

Squireless Kate.
Star Sirius, The.
State of Age, The.
Stave of Roving Tim, A.
Story of Sir Arnulph, The.
Sunrise.
Swallow came from over the sea, The.
Swathed round in mist and crown'd with
    cloud.
Sweet Justice of Norbiton, neighbour of
    Jones.
Sweet o' the Year, The.
Tardy Spring.
Teaching of the Blows of Fortune, The.
Teaching of the Nude, The.
Test of Manhood, The.
There fell a sudden rain.
There is for me no sweeter holiday.
There stood in her street a poor exile of
    Queen Je'n.
There was a fair footman of Torrington
    Square.
There was a young poet of Chelsea.
Think not, should your husband swear.
This love of nature, that allures to take.
Thou pirate nested over Alde!
Three Eagles and the Sleepy Lion, The.
Three Maidens, The.
Three Singers to Young Blood, The.
Thrush in February, The.
Time.
Time and Sentiment.
'Tis good to keep hinderward eyes.
'Tis I have seen the coming man.
'Tis midnight in the skies, my dear.
To a Friend Lost.
To a Nightingale.
To a Skylark.
To Alex. Smith, the "Glasgow Poet," on His
    Sonnet to "Fame."
To A.M.
To Cardinal Manning.
To Carlyle.
To Children.
To Colonel Charles.
To J.M.
To Lord Palmerston.
To-morrow I am going.
To P.A. Labouchère Esq.
To Plimmer, Verandah and Cello.
To R.H.H. with Daphne.
To Robin Redbreast.
To the Comic Spirit.
To the Merry Men of France.
Too cold for joy, too cold for woe.
Trafalgar Day.
Triad of British Evils, A.
Tuck, Demitroïa, / Ariadne, and Froyja.
Tuck, my treasure! Tuck, my pleasure!
Tuck, sweet charmer, tell me why.
Tuck, thou graceless sinner!—.
Tuck! Tuck! Once you would flatter me.
'Twas in a glimmering starlight.
'Twas yesterday such a black-dye-day.
Twilight Music.
Two Blackbirds, The.
Two Masks, The.
Union in Disseverance.
Unknown Fair Faces.
Violets.
Vital Choice, The.
Vittoria Concluding the Opera of "Camilla."
Vittoria's *Italia* Song.
Voyage of the "Ophir," The.
Wand of gold from the reaper's moon, A.
Wandering Willie.
War.
Warning, The.
Was it wise to count the ranks of teeth.
Wassail for the New Year, A.
Waves are pressing up with force, The.
We need some rallying point round which.
We sat beneath the humming pines.
We see the farther in the far.
We stood in the garden alone.
We violets white and blue.
Were men of such importance as they deem.

What makes it hard to understand.
When I Would Image.
When my little son leaps in my sight.
When stormy day is cold & gray.
When Will was at home in his palace of zinc.
While Janet eyes the Lanthorn's Magic.
While Nature mocks her truth with mimic shows.
Whimper of Sympathy.
Wild Rose and the Snowdrop, The.
Wild Rose, The.
Wilding little stubble flower, A.
Will o' the Wisp.
Will Whistle.
Willie's Dirge on Little Marian.
Wind & sea are as playmates.
Wind on the Lyre.
Windy Haymaking.
Winter Heavens.
Wisdom of Eld, The.
With the Huntress.
With the Persuader.
Woodland Peace.
Woodman and Echo.
Woods of Westermain, The.
Word from the Cannon's Mouth, A.
World is full of different fates, The.
World is young, the world is well, The.
World's Advance, The.
Ye noble Lords who bravely fight.
Years Had Worn Their Season's Belt, The.
Year's Sheddings, The.
Yes, we'll pic-nic in the woods.
Yet what is this? the spring returns.
You ask me what is Genius? 'tis that.
Young Princess, The.
Young Reynard.
Young Usurper, The.
Youth in Age.
Youth in Memory.
Youthful Quest, The.
Translations, Coauthored Poems, etc.:
Achilles over the Trench.
Agamemnon in the Fight.
Assembly of the Achaians.
Beauty Rohtraut.
Bibber besotted, with scowl of a cur, having heart of a deer, thou!
Boy's Death, The.
Clash in Arms of the Achaians and Trojans.
Confession.
Evening, after a Picture.
Field-Marshal Radetzky.
Good Comrade, The.
Hans Euler.
Helen on the Skaian Gates.
Horses of Achilles, The.
Hungarian Horse-Herd, The.
Hypnos on Ida.
Iliad, The *sels.*
Invective of Achilles, The.
Landlady's Daughter, The.
Love of the Woods.
Mares of the Camargue, The.
Marshalling of the Achaians.
Mirèio *sels.*
Moonlight Night.
My Heart.
Night Watch of the Trojans before Troy.
Nourishment before Battle.
Odysseus Encircled.
Paris and Diomedes.
Postillion, The.
Recognition, The.
Shield of Achilles, The.
Song: "Joyful / And woful."
Sweetheart of the Csikos, The.
Three Gipsies, The.
To an Old Gipsy.
To the High-Flyers.
Vengeance of Apollo, The.

Merrill, James (1926–95)
About the Phoenix.
After Greece.
After the ball.
After the Fire.

Amsterdam.
Angel.
Annie Hill's Grave.
Another August.
Banks of a Stream Where Creatures Bathe.
Black Mesa, The.
Black Swan, The.
Blue Eye, The.
Blue Grotto, The.
Book of Ephraim, The *sels.*
Broken Bowl, The.
Broken Home, The.
Bronze.
Caesarion.
Carpet Not Bought, A.
Casual Wear.
Channel 13.
Charioteer of Delphi, The.
Charles on Fire.
Childlessness.
Chimes for Yahya.
Clearing the Title.
Country of a Thousand Years of Peace, The.
Current, The.
Dandelion Sermon, The.
David's Night in Veliès.
Days of 1941 and '44.
Days of 1971.
Days of 1964.
Days of 1935.
Dedication: "Hans, there are moments when the whole mind."
Domino.
Doodler, The.
Dream (Escape from the Sculpture Museum) and Waking.
Dream of Old Vienna, A.
Dreams About Clothes.
18 West 11th Street.
Event Without Particulars.
Five Old Favorites.
Flèche d'Or.
For Proust.
Friend of the Fourth Decade, The.
From a Notebook.
From the Cupola.
Grass.
Hotel de l'Univers et Portugal.
Hourglass.
House Fly, The.
House, The.
In Nine Sleep Valley.
In the Hall of Mirrors.
Island in the Works.
Kimono, The.
Komboloi.
Kostas Tympakianákis.
Last Mornings in California.
Last Words.
Little Fanfare for Felix Magowan.
Log.
Lorelei.
Lost in Translation.
Mad Scene, The.
Maisie.
Manos Karastefanís.
Marsyas.
Matinees.
McKane's Falls.
Midnight Snack, The.
Mirror.
Mornings in a New House.
Narrow Escape, A.
Nightgown.
Nike.
Octopus, The.
Olive Grove.
Orfeo.
Ouzo for Robin.
Page from the Koran.
Parrot Fish, The.
Peacock, The.
Peter.
Pier: Under Pisces, The.
Popular Demand.
Prism.
Radiometer.

Remora.
Renewal, A.
River Poem.
Roger Clay's Proposal.
Salome.
Santo.
Santorini: Stopping the Leak.
Scenes of Childhood.
School Play, The.
16. ix. 65.
Smile, The.
Strato in Plaster.
Summer People, The.
Sundown and Starlight.
Swimming by Night.
Syrinx.
Tenancy, A.
Think Tank.
Thousand and Second Night, The.
Three Chores.
Time.
To a Butterfly.
To My Greek.
Topics.
Transfigured Bird.
Trees Listening to Bach.
Under Libra: Weights and Measures.
Up and Down.
Urban Convalescence, An.
Variations: The Air Is Sweetest That a Thistle Guards.
Verse for Urania.
Victor Dog, The.
Violent Pastoral.
Vision of the Garden, A.
Voices from the Other World.
Will, The.
Willow.
Willowware Cup.
Words for Maria.
World and the Child, The.
Yánnina.

Merton, Thomas (1915–68)
Advent.
Advice to a Young Prophet.
After the Night Office—Gethsemani Abbey.
All of the branches / None of the roots.
All the Way Down.
Anatomy of Melancholy, The.
And a Few More Cargo Songs.
And So Goodbye to Cities.
And the Children of Birmingham.
Annunciation, The.
Antipoem 1.
April.
April 4th 1968.
Argument: Of the Passion of Christ, An.
Ariadne.
Ariadne at the Labyrinth.
Ash Wednesday.
At This Precise Moment of History.
Atlas and the Fatman.
Aubade: Bermuda.
Aubade—Harlem.
Aubade: Lake Erie.
Aubade—the Annunciation.
Aubade—the City.
Baroque Gravure, A.
Be My Defender.
Bees love grass, The.
Ben's Last Fight.
Berceuse: to end the sorrow of mortals.
Betrayal, The.
Biography, The.
Birdcage Walk.
Blessed Virgin Mary Compared to a Window, The.
Bombarded City, The.
Bureaucrats: Diggers.
Burial Place of Ibn Abbad, The.
Cables to the Ace.
Cairo 1326.
Calicut.
Calypso's Island.
Cana.
Candlemas Procession, The.
Canticle for the Blessed Virgin.

Captives—a Psalm, The.
Cargo Catechism.
Cargo Songs.
Carol, A: "When Jesus got my broken back for Christmas, Juniors."
Carol: "Flocks feed by darkness with a noise of whispers."
Ce Xochitl: The Sign of Flowers.
Ceremony for Edward Dahlberg.
Chant to Be Used in Processions around a Site with Furnaces.
Chee$e.
Chilam Balam.
Christina.
Christmas as to People.
Christmas Card, A.
Christopher Columbus.
City after Noon, The.
City of God, The.
City's Spring, The.
Clairvaux.
Clairvaux Prison.
Clever Strategem: Or, How to Handle Mystics, A.
Comedy Card for a Serious Case.
Communion, The.
Conversations.
Crusoe.
Darjeeling.
Dark Encounter, The.
Dark Morning, The.
Dawn. The Hour of Lauds.
Day Six O'Hare Telephane.
Death.
Delhi.
Desolation.
Dialog with Mister Clapcott.
Dirge: "Some one who hears the bugle neigh will know."
Dirge for a Town in France.
Dirge for the City of Miami.
Dirge for the Proud World.
Dirge for the World Joyce Died In.
Dramas of the Evening.
Dream at Arles on the Night of the Mistral, A.
Dreaming Trader, The.
Dry Places.
Duns Scotus.
Dzules.
Early Blizzard.
Early Legend, The.
Early Mass.
Early Morning. The Hour of Prime.
Earthquake.
East.
East with Ibn Battuta.
East with Malinowski.
Elegy for a Trappist.
Elegy for Ernest Hemingway, An.
Elegy for Five Old Ladies, An.
Elegy for James Thurber.
Elegy for the Monastery Barn.
Elias—Variations on a Theme.
Epitaph for a Public Servant.
Evening.
Evening of the Visitation, The.
Evening Prayer.
Evening: Zero Weather.
Exploits of a Machine Age.
Fable for a War.
Fall of Night, The.
Fall '66.
Fall, The.
Famous engines support type B network.
Figures for an Apocalypse *sels.*
Figures for an Apocalypse.
First Lesson about Man.
Five breaths pray in me: sun moon.
Five Virgins, The.
Flight into Egypt, The.
For My Brother: Reported Missing In Action, 1943.
For the Spanish Poet Miguel Hernandez.
Found Macaronic Antipoem.
Freedom as Experience.
From the Legend of St. Clement.

From the Second Chapter of a Verse History of the World.
Fugitive.
Geography of Lograire, The.
Ghost Dance.
Ghost Dance: Prologue.
Gloss on the Sin of Ixion.
God Said "They Did Not Hear.."
Grace's House.
Great Men of Former Times, The.
Greek Women, The.
Guns of Fort Knox, The.
Hagia Sophia.
Hare's Message.
Harmonies of Excess, The.
Heavenly City, The.
High Morning. The Hour of Tierce.
Holy Child's Song, The.
Holy Communion: the City.
Holy Sacrament of the Altar, The.
Hopeless and Felons.
House of Caiphas, The.
How Long We Wait.
How to Enter a Big City.
Hrishikesa, destroyer of Titans, ogres and canailles.
Hymn for the Feast of Duns Scotus.
Hymn of Not Much Praise for New York City.
Hymns of Lograire.
I Have Called You.
Ibn Abbad Described by a Friend (Ibn Qunfud).
Image of True Lovers' Death, The.
In Memory of the Spanish Poet Federico Garcia Lorca.
In Silence.
In the Rain and the Sun.
In the Ruins of New York.
Invocation to St. Lucy, An.
Iphigenia: Politics.
Isfahan.
It would be wrong to let one man.
Je Crois En L'Amour.
John the Volcano.
Kandy Express.
Kane Relief Expedition.
King Solomon: my master and the imbeciles.
La Comparsa en Oriente.
La Salette.
Ladies of Tlatilco, The.
Lament for Javier Heraud.
Landfall, The.
Landscape.
Landscape: Beast.
Landscape, Prophet and Wild-dog.
Landscape: Wheatfields.
Le Secret.
Legacy of Herakleitos, The.
Legend of the Tower, The.
Lent.
Lent in a Year of War.
Les Cinq Vierges.
Letter to a Sufi Who Has Abandoned Sufism to Study Law.
Letter to America, A.
Letter to My Friends, A.
Letter to One Who Has Abandoned The Way.
Letter to Pablo Antonio Cuadra Concerning Giants, A.
Letters to Che: Canto Bilingue.
Like Ilium.
Lion, The.
Listen, Saints.
Litany: "All holy souls / pray for us fellows."
Litany: "It yawns at me the cavernous gulf."
Litany: "Sing miserere / For the men who must die."
Long Enough.
Lord Is Good, The.
Love Winter When the Plant Says Nothing.
Lubnan.
Macarius and the Pony.
Macarius the Younger.
Man in the Wind, The.

Man the Master.
Marks and numbers / Cut in skin.
Martin's Predicament or Atlas Watches Every Evening.
Mecca.
Merlin and the Deer.
Message to Be Inscribed on Mark Van Doren's Hamilton Medal.
Messenger from the Horizon, A.
Messenger, The.
Messias.
Miami You Are About to Be Surprised.
Moment of Truth, The.
Moon smiles like a queen, The.
Moslems' Angel of Death, The.
Mothers you have met before still need you.
Mysterious Song in the Spring of the Year, A.
Natural History.
Never Call a Babysitter in a Thunderstorm.
New Ribbon.
News from the School at Chartres.
Newscast.
Night-Flowering Cactus.
Night of Destiny, The.
Night Train, The.
Nocturne: "Night has a sea which quenches the machine."
Nombril Walketh on the Loam.
North.
Note in Honor of Machiavelli, A.
Notes for a New Liturgy.
Now the official nerve is analyzed.
Nusayris, The.
O cross, more splendid than all the stars.
O Sweet Irrational Worship.
Ode to the Present Century.
Ohio River—Louisville, The.
Ointment, The.
Old.
Old monk is turned loose / And can travel!, The.
On a Day in August.
On the Anniversary of My Baptism.
1. Now you are all here you might as well know this is America we do what we like.
Oracle, The.
Origen.
Original Child Bomb.
Original Sin.
Originators, The.
Paper Cranes.
Peril, The.
Philosophers, The.
Picture of a Black Child with a White Doll.
Picture of Lee Ying, A.
Pilgrims' Song.
Place Names.
Planet over Eastern Parkway, The.
Plessy vs Ferguson: Theme and Variations.
Poem: "Here is the man of the islands."
Poem in the Rain and the Sun.
Poem: "Light plays like a radio in the iron tree."
Poem: 1939.
Poem: "Watching, among the rifled branches, for the sun, our hero."
Poet, to His Book, The.
Practical Program for Monks, A.
Prayer and Sermon of Ibn Abbad.
Prayer of Thanksgiving Written for Victor Hammer, A ("O Thou Father of splendor, Giver of light").
Prayer of Thanksgiving Written for Victor Hammer, A ("O Tu Pater splendoris Dator luminis").
Prayer to Saint Anatole.
Prelude: For the Feast of St. Agnes, A.
Pride of the Dead, The.
Prologo.
Prologue: The Endless Inscription.
Prologue: Why I Have a Wet Footprint on Top of My Mind.
Prophet.
Prospects of Nostradamus, The.
Proverbs.

Psalm, A: "When psalms surprise me with their music."
Psalm 132: A Modern Monastic Revision.
Public Affairs.
Queens Tunnel.
Quickening of St. John the Baptist, The.
Rahab's House.
Ranter and Their Pleads, The.
Reader, The.
Reading Translated Poets, Feb. 1.
Readings from Ibn Abbad.
Reduced to This.
Regret, The.
Responsory, A.
Responsory, 1948, A.
Rievaulx: St. Ailred.
Rilke's Epitaph.
Rites for the Extrusion of a Leper.
Round and a Hope for Smithgirls, A.
Sacred Heart 2.
St. Agnes: A Responsory.
St. Alberic.
Saint Jason.
St. John Baptist.
St. John's Night.
St. Maedoc.
St. Malachy.
St. Paul.
St. Thomas Aquinas.
Secret, The.
Secular Signs.
Selection of Concrete Poems, A.
Semiotic Poem from Racine's "Iphigenie."
Seneca.
Senescente Mundo.
Seven Archaic Images.
Sewende (Seven Day).
Silver bird is E backward in cool pond water, The.
Sincerity.
Snare, The.
Solemn Music.
Solitary Life.
Some Bloody Mutiny.
Song, A: "When it was day, we heard the panes of windows."
Song: "Bottom of the sea has come, The."
Song: "Come where the grieving rivers of the night."
Song: Contemplation.
Song: If You Seek.
Song: In the Shows of the Round Ox.
Song: Sensation Time at the Home, A.
Song: "When rain, (sings light) rain has devoured my house."
Song for Nobody.
Song for Our Lady of Cobre.
Song for the Blessed Sacrament.
Song for the Death of Averroës.
Song of the Traveller, The.
Songs.
Songs of Experience; India, One.
South.
Sowing of Meanings, The.
Special continuations: the Gethsemani racetrack.
Sponge Full of Vinegar, The.
Sports without Blood—a Letter to Dylan Thomas (1948).
Spring: Monastery Farm.
Spring Storm.
Storm at Night, The.
Stranger.
Strife between the Poet and Ambition, The.
Submerged Dragon.
Sundown.
Sunset. The Hour of Compline. Salve Regina.
Syria.
Then from Tomorrow.
Theory of Prayer.
There Has to Be a Jail for Ladies.
There is a little ceremony to be performed.
There Is a Way.
These Years a Winter.
Things and people goodbye / It is not that I prefer.
Thonga Lament.

Three Postcards from the Monastery.
Tibud Maclay.
To a Novice ("Avoid three kinds of Master").
To a Novice ("Be a son of this instant").
To a Novice ("Fool is one, The").
To a Severe Nun.
To Alfonso Cortes.
To Belong to Allah.
To Daughters: To Study History.
To Sons: Not to Be Numb.
To the Immaculate Virgin, on a Winter Night.
Tonight There Is a Showing of Champion Lights.
Tower of Babel.
Tower of Babel—A Morality, The.
Transformation: For the Sacred Heart, The.
Trappist Abbey: Matins, The.
Trappist Cemetery—Gethsemani, The.
Trappists, Working.
Tropics.
Tune for Festive Dances in the Nineteen Sixties, A.
Twenty Three Point Prospectus for Small College in the Badlands.
Two British Airmen.
Two Desert Fathers.
Two Moralities.
Two States of Prayer.
Victory, The.
Vine, The.
Vital Imperatives for Chester.
Welcome.
West.
Western Fellow Students Salute with Calypso Anthems the Movie Career of Robert Lax.
What are the marks of the enemy? / He has no wit.
What is beyond reproof / Is done in this building.
What to Think When It Rains Blood.
What Troubles I Have Seen in Birdlegged Spring.
When class was in the garden at Greylands.
When in the Soul of the Serene Disciple.
Whether There Is Enjoyment in Bitterness.
Whitsun Canticle, A.
Why Some Look up to Planets and Heroes.
Widow of Naim, The.
Winter Afternoon.
Winter's Night, The.
Wisdom.
With the World in My Blood Stream.
Word—a Responsory, The.
Translations, Coauthored Poems, etc.:
A Solis Ortus Cardine.
Action and Non-Action.
Active Life.
Advising the Prince.
Aegeus in Prison.
Air.
Allegiance.
Anger.
Apologies.
At the Gates of Aerea.
Autumn.
Autumn Floods.
Birth of the Sun, The.
Black Stone on Top of a White Stone.
Breath of Nature, The.
Butterfly.
Celebrating Giacometti.
Chagall.
Cloud, The.
Cocoa Tree.
Come Dance in Baronies.
Confucius and the Madman.
Convergence of the Many.
Cracking the Safe.
Cup with a Jaguar for the Drinking of Health.
Cutting up an Ox.
Despairing Man Draws a Serpent, The.
Diatribe Against the Old Gods *sels.*
Dirty Souls.
Dog Barks Far Out, A.
Drake in the Southern Sea.

Duke Hwan and the Wheelwright.
Empty Boat, The.
Estais Muertos.
Eurydice.
Every Evening the L & N.
Eye Is a Dog Howling in the Distance, The.
Faces of Girls Looking at Themselves in the River.
Faction du Muet.
Fighters.
Fighting Cock, The.
Five Enemies, The.
Flight of Lin Hui, The.
Flower of the Fruit, The.
From empty windows / Voice of dead eyes.
Gethsemani, KY *sels.*
Glass Orchard.
Gloria in Excelsis, The.
Glove, The.
Good Fortune.
Great and Small.
Great Knowledge.
Great Prayer.
Hat Salesman and a Capable Ruler, A.
I do not know who is out in the snow.
I Move that We Adjourn the Meeting.
I turned out the light to see the snow.
Idol of Sarapis, The.
Imperfect Lover, The.
Importance of Being Toothless, The.
In My End Is My Beginning.
Inner Law, The.
Jaguar Myth, The.
Joy of Fishes, The.
Jubilemus omnes una Deo nostro qui creavit omnia.
Keng Sang Chu.
Keng's Disciple.
Kingly Man, The.
Lake, The.
Lament of a Maiden for the Warrior's Death.
Lao Tzu's Wake.
Like empty beer cans, like cigarette butts.
Like the flights of ducks.
Logos Our Teacher, The.
Long freight train / Wakes me in my cell, The.
Lost Pearl, The.
Man from Ecuador beneath the Eiffel Tower, A.
Man Is Born in Tao.
Man of Tao, The.
Man with One Foot and the Marsh Pheasant, The.
Manifesto *sels.*
Meditation before an Ancient Poem.
Memories of the Ancient World.
Metamorphosis.
Mirror's Mission, The.
Mosaic: St. Praxed's.
Mummies.
Nahoa Urn, for a Woman.
Need to Win, The.
New Song, The.
Nights belong to / What hurts.
Notes of a Parachute Jumper.
Organ.
Other night I saw.. / Who did I see?, The.
Owl and Phoenix.
Ox Mountain Parable, The.
Pain Is an Eagle Clinging to Your Name.
Paradise of Squares.
Peace, the Wasp.
Perfect Joy.
Pillars.
Poetry Ends with Me.
Priests of the Old Gods, The.
Prisoner, The.
Prose in Advent Time.
Radicals.
Recipe.
Restoration of the Pictures, The.
Roman Nocturnes *sels.*
Secret of the Burning Stars, The.
Septentrion.
Shots were heard last night / Out by the burial ground.

Soda Fountains.
Soldiers of Peace.
Song of Purification.
Sound of passing cars, (if a car comes), The.
Space Song.
Splendor Paternae Gloriae.
Spring has come with its smell of Nicaragua.
Starlight and Non-Being.
Suddenly in the night the sirens.
Sundown.
Symphony for a Sea Bird.
Take, O take the key of Rome.
Tao.
That auto horn sounds familiar.
Three Epigrams *sels.*
Three Friends.
Three Sisters, The.
Tomb Cover of Imam Riza.
Tower of the Spirit, The.
True Man, The.
Truth, The.
Turtle, The.
Twelve Poems from *The Keeper of the Flocks.*
Two Kings and No-Form.
Two Palm Trees, The.
Urn with a Political Profile.
Useless, The.
Useless Tree, The.
Ut Queant.
We wake up with guns going off.
Weathercock on the Cathedral of Quito, The.
What the Deceased Had to Say about Himself.
When a Hideous Man.
When Knowledge Went North.
When the first signs go on.
When the Shoe Fits.
When You Point Your Finger.
Where Is Tao?
Wholeness.
Woodcarver, The.
World Is a Round Earthenware Plate, The.
Written Next to a Blue Flower.
You did not come to Rome to dream.
Zeus Is Dead.
Zinc roofs in the moonlight, The.

**Millay, Edna St. Vincent ("Nancy Boyd")
(1892–1950)**
Above These Cares.
Admetus, from my marrow's core I do.
Afternoon on a Hill.
Agnostic, The.
Alms.
Amorphous is the mind; its quality.
Ancient Gesture, An.
And if I die, because that part of me.
And is indeed truth beauty?—at the cost.
And must I then, indeed, Pain, live with you.
And you as well must die, belovèd dust.
Anguish, The.
Animal Ball, The.
Apostrophe to Man.
Apple-trees bud, but I do not, The.
Armenonville.
As men have loved their lovers in times past.
As sharp as in my childhood, still.
As to some lovely temple, tenantless.
Ashes of Life.
Assault.
At least, my dear.
Aubade: "Cool and beautiful as the blossom of the wild carrot."
Autumn Chant.
Autumn Daybreak.
Baccalaureate Hymn.
Ballad of Chaldon Down, The.
Ballad of the Harp-Weaver, The.
Be sure my coming was a sharp offense.
Bean-Stalk, The.
Being Young and Green.
Believe, if ever the bridges of this town.
Betrothal, The.
Black hair you'd say she had, or rather.
Blight.
Blue-Flag in the Bog, The.
Bluebeard.

Bobolink, The.
Buck in the Snow, The.
Burial.
By goodness and by evil so surrounded, how can the heart.
Cairn, The.
Cameo, The.
Cap D'Antibes.
Cave Canem.
Cherish you then the hope I shall forget.
Childhood Is the Kingdom Where Nobody Dies.
Chorus: "Give away her gowns."
Christmas Canticle.
City Trees.
Clearly my ruined garden as it stood.
Come home, victorious wounded!—let the dead.
Concert, The.
Conscientious Objector.
Count them unclean, these tears that turn no mill.
Counting-out Rhyme.
Courage that my mother had, The.
Curse, The.
Czecho-Slovakia.
Daphne.
Dawn.
Death of Autumn, The.
Deep in the muck of unregarded doom.
Departure.
Desolation Dreamed Of.
Dirge: "Boys and girls that held her dear."
Dirge Without Music.
Doubt No More that Oberon.
Dragonfly, The.
Dream of Saba.
Dream, The.
Ebb.
Eel-Grass.
Elaine.
Elegy: "Let them bury your big eyes."
Elegy before Death.
English Sparrows.
Enormous moon, that rise behind these hills.
Epitaph: "Grieve not for happy Claudius, he is dead."
Epitaph: "Heap not on this mound."
Epitaph for the Race of Man *sels.*
Epitaph for the Race of Man.
Establishment is shocked. Stir no adventure.
Euclid alone has looked on Beauty bare.
Even in the moment of our earliest kiss.
Evening on Lesbos.
Exiled.
Fatal Interview.
Fawn, The.
Feast.
Felicity of Grief!—even Death being kind.
Few come this way; not that the darkness.
First Fig.
Fitting, The.
Fledgling, The.
Fontaine, Je Ne Boirai Pas De Ton Eau!
For Pao-Chin, a Boatman on the Yellow Sea.
For Warmth Alone, for Shelter Only.
From a Train Window.
From a Very Little Sphinx.
Gardener in Haying-Time, The.
God's World.
Gone in good sooth you are: not even in dream.
Goose-Girl, The.
Grief that is grief and properly so hight.
Grow not too high, grow not too far from home.
Grown-up.
Hangman's Oak.
Hardy Garden, The.
Hawkweed, The.
He heard the coughing tiger in the night.
Hearing your words, and not a word among them.
Heart, have no pity on this house of bone.
Heart once broken is a heart no more, The.
Hedge of Hemlocks, The.
Here in a Rocky Cup.

Here is a wound that never will heal, I know.
His stalk the dark delphinium.
How did I bear it—how could I possibly as a child.
How healthily their feet upon the floor.
How innocent of me and my dark pain.
How innocent we lie among.
How Naked, How Without a Wall.
Humoresque.
Huntsman, What Quarry?
Hyacinth.
I, being born a woman and distressed.
I do but ask that you be always fair.
I dreamed I moved among the Elysian fields.
I, in disgust with the living, having read.
I know I am but summer to your heart.
I know my mind and I have made my choice.
I know the face of Falsehood and her tongue.
I must not die of pity; I must live.
I pray you if you love me, bear my joy.
I said in the beginning, did I not?
I said, seeing how the winter gale increased.
I see so clearly now my similar years.
I shall forget you presently, my dear.
I shall go back again to the bleak shore.
I think I should have loved you presently.
I will put Chaos into fourteen lines.
I woke in the night and heard the wind, and it blowing half a gale.
If I die solvent—die, that is to say.
If I should learn, in some quite casual way.
If, in the Foggy Aleutians.
If in the years to come you should recall.
If it should rain—(the sneezy moon).
If Still Your Orchards Bear.
If to be left were to be left alone.
Impression: Fog Off the Coast of Dorset.
In the Grave No Flower.
Indifference.
Inert Perfection.
Inland.
Intense and terrible, I think, must be the loneliness.
Intention to Escape from Him.
Interim.
Into the golden vessel of great song.
Invocation to the Muses.
It is the fashion now to wave aside.
Jesus to His Disciples.
Journal.
Journey.
Justice Denied in Massachusetts.
Keen.
Kin to Sorrow.
Lament: "Listen, children: / Your father is dead."
Leaf and the Tree, The.
Let you not say of me when I am old.
Lethe.
Life, were thy pains as are the pains of hell.
Light comes back with Columbine,; she brings, The.
Lines for a Grave-Stone.
Lines Written in Recapitulation.
Little Ghost, The.
Little Hill, The.
Look how the bittersweet with lazy muscle moves aside.
Lord Archer, Death, whom sent you in your stead?
Love is not all: it is not meat nor drink.
Love is not blind. I see with single eye.
Love me no more, now let the god depart.
Love, though for this you riddle me with darts.
Loving you less than life, a little less.
Low-Tide.
Macdougal Street.
Mariposa.
Memorial to D. C. *sels.*
Memorial to D. C.
Memory of Cape Cod.
Memory of Cassis.
Memory of England.
Men Working.
Menses.

Merry Maid, The.
Midnight Oil.
Mindful of you the sodden earth in spring.
Mist in the Valley.
Modern Declaration.
Moon, that against the lintel of the west.
Moriturus.
Mortal Flesh, Is Not Your Place in the Ground?
Most wicked words!-forbear to speak them out.
My earnestness, which might at first offend.
My Heart, Being Hungry.
My most distinguished guest and learnèd friend.
My Spirit, Sore from Marching.
My words that once were virtuous and expressed.
My worship from this hour the Sparrow-Drawn.
Nay, learnèd doctor, these fine leeches fresh.
Never May the Fruit Be Plucked.
New England Spring, 1942.
Night is my sister, and how deep in love.
No Earthly Enterprise.
No further from me than my hand.
No lack of counsel from the shrewd and wise.
No rose that in a garden ever grew.
Northern April.
Not for a Nation.
Not in a silver casket cool with pearls.
Not in this chamber only at my birth.
Not only love plus awful grief.
Not So Far as the Forest.
Not that it matters, not that my heart's cry.
Not, to me, less lavish—though my dreams have been splendid.
Not with libations, but with shouts and laughter.
Now by the path I climbed, I journey back.
Now by this moon, before this moon shall wane.
Now let the mouth of wailing for a time.
Now sits the autumn cricket in the grass.
Now that the west is washed of clouds and clear.
Nuit Blanche.
O ailing Love, compose your struggling wing!
Oak-Leaves, The.
October—An Etching.
Ode to Silence.
Of all that ever in extreme disease.
Of what importance, O my lovely girls, my dancers, O my lovely boys.
Oh, my belovèd, have you thought of this.
Oh, oh, you will be sorry for that word!
Oh, sleep forever in the Latmian cave.
Oh, think not I am faithful to a vow!
Olympian gods, mark now my bedside lamp.
On First Having Heard the Skylark.
On Hearing a Symphony of Beethoven.
On the Wide Heath.
On Thought in Harness.
Once more into my arid days like dew.
Only until this cigarette is ended.
Parsi Woman, The.
Passer Mortuus Est.
Pastoral: "If it were only still!"
Pear Tree, The.
Penitent, The.
Peril upon the paths of this desire.
Philosopher, The.
Pigeons, The.
Pity me not because the light of day.
Plaid Dress, The.
Plum Gatherer, The.
Poem and Prayer for an Invading Army.
Poet and His Book, The.
Pond, The.
Portrait.
Portrait by a Neighbour.
Prayer to Persphone.
Pretty Love, I Must Outlive You.
Princess Recalls Her One Adventure, The.
Pueblo Pot.

Rabbit, The.
Ragged Island.
Read history: so learn your place in Time.
Read history: thus learn how small a space.
Recuerdo.
Renascence.
Rendezvous.
Return from Town, The.
Return, The.
Road to Avrillé, The.
Road to the Past, The.
Rosemary.
Sappho Crosses the Dark River into Hades.
Say that We Saw Spain Die.
Say what you will, and scratch my heart to find.
Scrub.
Sea at sunset can reflect, The.
Second Fig.
See how these masses mill and swarm.
Shall I be prisoner till my pulses stop.
She Is Overheard Singing.
Short Story.
Shroud, The.
Siege.
Since I cannot persuade you from this mood.
Since of no creature living the last breath.
Singing-Woman from the Wood's Edge, The.
Sky-coloured bird, blue wings with no more spots of spotless white.
Small Hands, Relinquish All.
Snow Storm, The.
Solid Sprite Who Stands Alone, The.
Some Things Are Dark.
Sometimes, oh, often, indeed, in the midst of ugly adversity, beautiful.
Sometimes when I am wearied suddenly.
Song: "Beautiful Dove, come back to us in April."
Song for Young Lovers in a City.
Song: "Gone, gone again is Summer the lovely."
Song of a Second April.
Sonnet: "Time, that renews the tissues of this frame."
Sonnet to Gath.
Sonnets from an Ungrafted Tree.
Sorrow.
Sorrowful dreams remembered after waking.
Souvenir.
Spring.
Spring and the Fall, The.
Spring in the Garden.
Spring Song.
Steepletop.
Still will I harvest beauty where it grows.
Strange thing that I, by nature nothing prone.
Strawberry Shrub, The.
Suicide, The.
Summer, be seen no more within this wood.
Sweet love, sweet thorn, when lightly to my heart.
Tavern.
Thanksgiving Dinner.
That Love at length should find me out and bring.
Theme and Variations.
There at Dusk I Found You.
There is a well into whose bottomless eye.
Think not, nor for a moment let your mind.
This / Is mine, and I can hold it.
This beast that rends me in the sight of all.
This Dusky Faith.
This should be simple; if one's power were great.
Those hours when happy hours were my estate.
Thou art not lovelier than lilacs,—no.
Thou famished grave, I will not fill thee yet.
Three Songs from "The Lamp and the Bell."
Three Songs of Shattering.
Through the Green Forest.
Thursday.
Time does not bring relief; you all have lied.
Time, that is pleased to lengthen out the day.
To a Calvinist in Bali.
To a Friend Estranged from Me.

To a Musician.
To a Poet that Died Young.
To a Snake.
To a Young Girl.
To a Young Poet.
To Elinor Wylie.
To hold secure the province of Pure Art.
To Inez Milholland.
To Jesus on His Birthday.
To Kathleen.
To One Who Might Have Borne a Message.
To S. M.
To S. V. B.—June 15, 1940.
To the Maid of Orleans.
To the Not Impossible Him.
To the Wife of a Sick Friend.
To Those Without Pity.
To whom the house of Montagu.
Tranquility at length, when autumn comes.
Travel.
Tree Ceremonies.
Tristan.
Truce for a Moment.
Truck-Garden Market-Day.
True Encounter, The.
Two Voices.
Underground System.
Unexplorer, The.
Upon this age, that never speaks its mind.
Valentine.
Visit to the Asylum, A.
We have gone too far; we do not know how to stop: impetus.
We talk of taxes, and I call you friend.
Weeds.
Well, I have lost you; and I lost you fairly.
West Country Song.
What chores these churls do put upon the great.
What lips my lips have kissed, and where, and why.
What rider spurs him from the darkening east.
What Savage Blossom.
What's this of death, from you who never will die?
When Caesar Fell.
When did I ever deny, though this was fleeting.
When I too long have looked upon your face.
When It Is Over.
When the tree-sparrows with no sound through the pearl-pale air.
When the Year Grows Old.
When we are old and these rejoicing veins.
When we that wore the myrtle wear the dust.
When you are dead, and your disturbing eyes.
When you, that at this moment are to me.
Where can the heart be hidden in the ground.
Whereas at morning in a jeweled crown.
Who hurt you so.
Wild-cat, gnat and I.
Wild Swans.
Wine from These Grapes.
Winter Night.
Witch-Wife.
Women have loved before as I love now.
Wood Road, The.
Wraith.
Yet in an hour to come, disdainful dust.
You loved me not at all, but let it go.
You say: "Since life is cruel enough at best."
Your face is like a chamber where a king.

Miller, Chuck
Albina.
Behind a large truck.
Black November.
Dark men are speaking to dark men.
Dawn.
Day Born Without a Mouth.
Dead Dog (For Goo).
Desperate, The.
Dislocado.
Distance Between Us.
Down the Lanes and Paths (For Stack).
Dusk.

Dusk in the Woods.
End of the Negotiable Beggar Bond Banquet, The.
Ensamhet.
Flood.
For Barbara.
For César Vallejo and his Profound Oxides of Sadness.
For Dr. Dewey.
For Han Shan on His Cold Mountain.
For Juan Rulfo.
For Judy.
For Mickey.
For Mike and Kim.
For Mrs. Jones.
For My Friend John Lying on the Bed with Morning Heaves.
For Phil.
For Richard Hopper (Dies 1978).
For Schnu.
For Those Who Pray for the Souls of Broken Dolls.
Free Clinic.
From Oslo.
Gentle as the Lamb of God Made into Mad Cutlets.
Gray light awakening.
Harvesters.
Hasta la Victoria Siempre.
Hookah.
How this morning.
If you can't make a joke.
In Celebration of Surviving.
In the Parking Lot of the Supermarket.
In the typewriter shop.
Invincible Summer.
Kattegat.
Late September.
Lighted Windows (For Judy).
Luftpost (For Levy).
Meditations on an Old Shoe.
Men and Women (the Boltzmann Distribution).
Mixed Signals.
Moment of Sleep (For Schnu), A.
Near Old Fort Pike on the Des Moines River.
Nicaraguan Journal.
No and I don't know where.
Northern Fields (For Carol).
November Dusk.
On Getting My Poems Back from the Typist.
On some night a train is going past the library.
Panhandle (For Annette).
Poets, The.
Putting Up Snow Fence.
Riding the bus in the evening again.
Rising Up.
River of long standing, bridge abut-ment.
Room in a Penitentiary.
Saw 'er at a temple on the outskirts of Hangzhou.
Semantic Drift.
Shocks Brakes (For Kurt and Yansky).
So in evening there is still light.
So Long It's Been Good to Know You.
Some days / the sunlight has a clarity.
Sometimes I want to take them in.
Spade a Spade (Grocery for the Poor), A.
Start Up the Music Again.
Stumble into the great red sunset.
Stumbling and weeping.
Summer Evening.
Sun Now or Never (For Barbara), The.
Swimming in the last of September.
They came furtively.
To be against to resist everything.
When you live in your car.
Wind, The.
Winter / form across the road tumult of a schoolyard.
Winter Dawn.
Wondered why the building was so small.
You feel the hollowness of being excluded.

Milton, John (1608–74)
Adam Fallen ("Descended, Adam to the bower where Eve").

Adam Speaks.
Adam Unfallen.
All Is Best.
Another on the Same.
Arcades.
As Lords.
Ascent of Species.
At a Solemn Music[k].
At a Vacation Exercise [in the Col[l]e[d]ge [, Part Latin, Part English]].
Atonement, The.
Bacchus.
Banquet, The.
Before the starry threshold of *Jove[']s* court.
Blindness of Samson, The.
Book I.
Book II.
Book III.
Book IV.
Book V.
Book VI.
Book VII.
Book VIII.
Book IX.
Book X.
Book XI.
Book XII.
Canzone: "Scoffing, amorous maidens and young men."
Chastity.
Chastity ("I Mean That Too, But Yet a Hidden Strength").
Comus's Praise of Nature.
Council of Satan, The.
Creation.
Damon's Epitaph.
Delilah.
Desire of Wine.
Echo.
Elegiac Verses.
Elegy 1: To Charles Diodati.
Elegy 2: On the Death of the Beadle of Cambridge University.
Elegy 3: On the Death of the Bishop of Winchester.
Elegy 4: To Thomas Young.
Elegy 5: On the Coming of Spring.
Elegy 6: To Charles Deodati.
Elegy 7: "Not yet did I know your laws, enticing Amathusia."
Epitaph on the Marchioness of Winchester, An.
Eve Penitent.
Expulsion from Eden, The.
Expulsion from Paradise.
Fable of the Peasant and the Overlord, The.
Fall, The.
Flood, The.
Heaven.
Hell ("At once with him they rose").
Heroic Vengeance.
Hobsons Epitaph.
Hymn on the Morning of Christ's Nativity [or On the Morning of Christ's Nativity].
I with foolish mind and heedless zeal formerly.
Il Penseroso.
Immortal Hate.
L'Allegro.
Last Came, and Last Did Go.
Leave Taking.
Leviathan.
Lycidas.
Magi, The.
Manso.
Mask, A.
Mirth and Poetry.
Morning Hymn of Adam.
Mulciber.
Nature Does Not Suffer Decay.
New Worlds.
Nothing For Tears.
Now Came Still Evening On.
Occupations of Hell.
On Shakespear[e].
On the Death of a Fair Infant Dying of a Cough.

On the Death of the Bishop of Ely.
On the Death of the Vice-Chancellor, a Physician.
On the Engraver of His Likeness.
On the Fifth of November.
On the Forcers of Conscience.
On the Gunpowder Plot.
On the Inventor of Gunpowder.
On the Morning of Christs Nativity.
On the Platonic Idea as Aristotle Understood It.
On the Same ["James derided the Purgatorial fire of the soul"].
On the Same ["Thus did you strive to vouchsafe James to Heaven"].
On the Same ["Whom impious Rome had just marked out for her curses"].
On the University Carrier Who Sick'n'd [or Sickened] in the Time of His Vacancy [, Being Forbid to go to London, by Reason of the Plague].
On Time.
Panorama, The.
Paradise ("Another side, umbrageous Grots and Caves").
Paradise ("His fair large front and eye sublime declared").
Paradise ("In narrow room nature's whole wealth, yea more").
Paradise Lost.
Paradise Regained [or Regain'd].
Paraphrase on Psalm 114, A.
Parthians, The.
Passion, The.
Philosopher on His Way to His Death Suddenly Sent This Message to a Certain King Who Had Unawares Condemned Him, Unrecognized and Innocent, When He Was Seized by Chance Among Criminals, A.
Place of the Damned, The.
Plan of Salvation, The.
Poetry and the Melancholy Man.
Psalm 114.
Psalm 136.
Raphael's Descent.
Resources.
Rome ("He brought our saviour to the western side").
Rome ("The City which thou seest no other deem").
Sabrina.
Sabrina Fair.
Sabrina's Song.
Samson Agonistes.
Samson's Complaint.
Satan and His Host.
Satan and the Fallen Angels.
Satan Beholds Adam and Eve in Eden.
Satan Defiant.
Satan ("He ceased; and Satan stayed not to reply").
Satan ("His pride / Had cast him out from Heaven, with all his host").
Satan Journeys to the Garden of Eden.
Satan's Guile ("Whom thus answer'd th' Arch Fiend now undisguis'd").
Satan's Journey.
Satan's Legions and the Beech Leaves of the Casentino.
Satan's Soliloquy.
Slothful Sleep.
Song: on [or of] May Morning.
Sonnet 1: "O Nightingale, that on yon bloomy spray."
Sonnet 2: "Charming lady, she whose beautiful name honors."
Sonnet 3: "As on a rugged mountain at the darkening of evening."
Sonnet 4: "Diodati, and I will say it to you with wonder."
Sonnet 5: "In truth your fair eyes, my lady."
Sonnet 6: "Young, gentle, and candid lover that I am."
Sonnet 7: "How soon hath Time the suttle theef of youth."

Sonnet 8: "Captain or Colonel, or Knight in Arms."
Sonnet 9: "Ladie, that in the prime of earliest youth."
Sonnet 10: "Daughter to that good Earle, once President."
Sonnet 11: "I did but prompt the age to quit their [*or* thir] clogs."
Sonnet 12: "Book was writt of late call'd Tetrachordon, A."
Sonnet 13: "Harry, whose tunefull and well-measur'd song."
Sonnet 14: "When Faith and Love which parted from thee never."
Sonnet 15: "Fairfax, whose name in armes through Europe rings."
Sonnet 16: "Cromwell, our cheif of men, who through a cloud."
Sonnet 17: "Vane, young in yeares, but in sage counsell old."
Sonnet 18: "Avenge O Lord thy slaughter'd Saints, whose bones."
Sonnet 19: "When I consider how my light is spent."
Sonnet 20: "Lawrence of vertuous Father vertuous Son."
Sonnet 21: "Cyriack, whose Grandsire on the Royal Bench."
Sonnet 22: "Cyriack, this three years day these eyes, though clear."
Sonnet 23: "Mee thought I saw my late espoused saint."
Standing on Earth.
Star That Bids the Shepherd Fold, The.
Table Richly Spread, A.
Temperance and Virginity.
Temptation of Eve, The.
Tempter Disarmed, The.
Their Banishmnet.
Their Wedded Love.
Then when I Am Thy Captive, Talk of Chains.
Thus Eve to Adam.
To John Rouse.
To Leonora Singing in Rome.
To My Father.
To Salzilli, a Roman Poet, Being Ill.
To the Same ["Another Leonora captured the poet Torquato"].
To the Same ["Why, credulous Naples, do you vaunt your clear-voiced Siren"].
Transcendence of God, The.
True and False Glory.
Uncloistered Virtue.
Upon the Circumcision.
Verse from Defensio Secunda.
Verse from Pro Populo Anglicano Defensio.
Ways of God to Men, The.
What Though the Field Be Lost?
What Words Have Passed.
Woman.
Translations, Coauthored Poems, etc.:
Among the holy Mountains high.
Answer me when I call / God of my righteousness.
Be not thou silent now at length.
Blest is the man who hath not walk'd astray.
Fifth Ode of Horace, The.
God in the great assembly stands.
par. by Milton.
How lovely are thy dwellings fair!
Jehovah to my words give ear.
Lord God that dost me save and keep.
Lord how many are my foes.
Lord in thine anger do not reprehend me.
Lord my God to thee I flie / Save me and secure me under.
O Jehovah our Lord, how wondrous great.
Odes *sels.*
Psalms *sels.*
Thou Shepherd that dost Israel keep.
Thy gracious ear, O Lord, encline.
Thy Land to favour graciously.
To God our strength sing loud, and clear.
Why do the Gentiles tumult, and the Nations.

Montgomery, Mary Sidney Wroth, Countess of
see Wroth, Mary Sidney, Countess of Montgomery

Moore, Marianne Craig (1887–1972)
Animals Sick of the Plague, The.
Apparition of Splendor.
Arctic Ox (or Goat), The.
Armor's Undermining Modesty.
Arthur Mitchell.
Avec Ardeur.
Baseball and Writing.
Bear and the Garden-Lover, The.
Bird-witted.
Blessed Is the Man.
Blue Bug.
Bowls.
Buffalo, The.
By Disposition of Angels.
Camellia Sabina.
Camperdown Elm, The.
Carnegie Hall: Rescued.
Carriage from Sweden, A.
Charity Overcoming Envy.
Combat Cultural.
Critics and Connoisseurs.
Dream.
Efforts of Affection.
Egyptian Pulled Glass Bottle in the Shape of a Fish, An.
Elephants.
England.
Enough.
Expedient, An—Leonardo da Vinci's—and a Query.
Fables of La Fontaine *sels.*
Face, A.
Fish, The.
For February 14th.
Four Quartz Crystal Clocks.
Fox and the Grapes, The.
Frigate Pelican, The.
Granite and Steel.
Grave, A.
He "Digesteth Harde Yron."
He Wrote the History Book.
Hero, The.
His Shield.
Hometown Piece for Messrs. Alston and Reese.
I May, I Might, I Must.
Icosasphere, The.
In Distrust of Merits.
In Lieu of the Lyre.
In the Days of Prismatic Color.
In the Public Garden.
In This Age of Hard Trying, Nonchalance Is Good and.
Injudicious Gardening.
Jellyfish, A.
Jerboa, The.
Keeping Their World Large.
Labors of Hercules, The.
Leonardo Da Vinci's.
Light is Speech.
Like a Bulwark.
Lion In Love, The.
Logic and The Magic Flute.
Love in America.
Magician's Retreat, The.
Marriage.
Melchior Vulpius.
Mercifully.
Mind, Intractable Thing, The.
Mind Is an Enchanting Thing, The.
Monkey Puzzle, The.
Monkeys, The.
Mouse Metamorphosed Into a Maid, The.
Nevertheless.
New York.
Nine Nectarines.
No Better Than a "Withered Daffodil."
No Swan So Fine.
Nothing Will Cure the Sick Lion But To Eat an Ape.
Novices.
O to Be a Dragon.
Octopus, An.

Old Amusement Park.
Pangolin, The.
Paper Nautilus, The.
Part of a Novel, Part of a Poem, Part of a Play *sels.*
Past Is the Present, The.
Pedantic Literalist.
People's Surroundings.
Peter.
Picking and Choosing.
Plumet Basilisk, The.
Poetry.
Prevalent At One Time.
Propriety.
Reminiscent of a Wave At the Curl.
Rescue With Yul Brynner.
Rigorists.
Rosemary.
Saint Nicholas.
Saint Valentine.
Sea Unicorns and Land Unicorns.
Silence.
Smooth Gnarled Crape Myrtle.
Snakes, Mongooses, Snake-Charmers, and the Like.
Sojourn in the Whale.
Spenser's Ireland.
Staff of Aesculapius, The.
Steeple-Jack, The.
Student, The.
Style.
Sun.
Sycamore, The.
Tell Me, Tell Me.
Then the Ermine.
Those Various Scalpels.
Tippoo's Tiger.
To a Chameleon.
To a Giraffe.
To a Prize Bird.
To a Snail.
To a Steam Roller.
To Military Progress.
To Statecraft Embalmed.
To the Peacock of France.
To Victor Hugo of My Crow Pluto.
Tom Fool at Jamaica.
Too Much.
Values in Use.
Virginia Britannia.
Voracities and Verities Sometimes Are Interacting.
W. S. Landor.
Web One Weaves of Italy, The.
What Are Years?
When I Buy Pictures.
Wood Weasel, The.

Morgan, Frederick (b. 1922)
Abenaki Poem.
Adamson.
Adventure, The.
Aegir.
After.
Alexander.
Anaktoria.
Anger at my heart one April morning.
As It Was.
Aubade: "Who has hold of Juliet's nipples."
Autobiographies.
Balder.
Being, I.
Being, II.
Bianca.
Blue Hill Poems.
Body, The.
Bones.
Canadaigua.
Captain Blaze.
Castle Rock.
Centaurs.
Choice, The.
Christmas Tree, The.
Closed House, The.
Death Mother.
Demonstration, The.
Diagrams, The.
Dialogue.

Door, The.
Eight Triolets.
Encounter.
End, The.
Enigmas.
Etude.
Exile.
Exiles, The.
Exotica.
February 11, 1977.
Freya.
Frigg.
From a Diary.
From a Forgotten Book.
From the Kuan-Tzu.
From the Terrace.
Gawain.
Ghost, The.
Gorge, The.
Grandfather Poem.
Greenwich 1930's, I.
Greenwich 1930's, II.
Heimdall.
Hideyoshi.
His Last Case.
History.
I remember the sea when I was six.
In a five-minute stillness in September.
In Mexico.
In Silence.
Interiorly.
Irvington.
Jormungand.
Katahdin.
Letter, The.
Leviathan.
Loki.
Loki's Song.
Lucky black man in my dream.
Maitreya.
Mary.
Master, The.
May 1, 1974.
Meditations for Autumn.
Memories.
Mermaid, The.
Metamorphosis.
Mirror.
Mr. Boyd.
Moments.
Murder, The.
Music.
Night Skater, The.
1904.
1928.
1949.
Njord.
Nocturne: "Dear Wanderer, on your
    unimagined journey."
Now that at last I must forego.
Odin.
Odin's Song.
Omen.
Oppositions, The.
Orpheus to Eurydice.
Past, The.
Pirate Poem.
Poem of the Gold Coin.
Poem of the Self.
Poems of the Two Worlds.
Port Caradoc.
President Poem.
Promise, The.
Ran.
Reflection, The.
Reprieve, The.
Rescue, The.
River, The.
Samson.
Saying.
Scotch Mary.
Shame.
Skulls, The.
Sometimes I hear my father's voice,
    sometimes my son's, in mine.
Song: "Devastation / of being, The."
Step, The.

Summit, The.
Thaw.
Then.
Thor.
Three Children Looking Over the Edge of the
    World.
Touch, The.
Trader, The.
Tree, The.
Turn, The.
Turtle, The.
Two.
Two Poems to a Dead Woman.
Tyr.
Vantage, The.
Way, The.
We took a room at the Westbury.
Whale Poem.
When it rained and rained.
Winter Poem.
World of Purple Light, The.
Wrong Side, The.
Translations, Coauthored Poems, etc.:
Carmina *sels.*
Catullus: *Carmen xi.*
Catullus: *Carmen v.*
Catullus: *Carmen xli.*
Catullus: *Carmen ci.*

Morrison, Jim (1943–71)
Afternoon of Summer, An.
Ah, The Rule.
Always a Playground Instructor.
America As Bullring Arena.
American Prayer, An.
& the Cool Fluttering.
Augment of Re-Birth.
Bibulous Compound Of.
Blues, The.
Can We Resolve the Past.
Car Cemetery.
Celebration of the Lizard.
Cock-pit.
Crossroads, The.
Curses & Invocations.
Dancing & Thrashing.
Dark American Sunset, The.
Desert, The.
Do You Have.
Don't Start That.
Electric Storm.
End of the Dream, The.
End of the Rainbow, The.
End, The.
Ensenada.
Enter the Slip.
Fear is a Porch.
Feast Green Beast.
Flesh of Her.
Flowering, The.
Form Is an Angel, The.
Guided Tour, The.
He Follows a Woman.
Heaven or Hell.
Hitchhiker, The.
Hole in the Clouds, A.
Hope Is Just.
Horse Latitudes.
Hurricane and Eclipse.
I Bring These.
I Fucked the Dregs.
I Walked Thru.
I Want to Tell You.
If It's No Problem.
If Only I.
In That Year.
In This Dim Cave.
It Has Been Said.
L.A. Woman.
Lament for the Death of My Cock.
L'America.
Leave the Informed Sense.
Lessons on Becoming.
Maids Are Bickering.
Money.
Moonlight Drive.
Moving, A.
Mystery of the Dream.

Now Listen to This.
Original Temptation, The.
Paris Journal.
Pencilled Heaven.
Planes Are Groaning Mothers.
Please Like Me.
Promises.
Scour the Mind.
Sex For You.
Sidewalkers Moved, The.
Soft Parade, The.
Soul Kitchen.
Stand There Listening.
Star Fish Gluttony.
Start Again.
Still Wet From.
Sudden Attack.
Tales of the American Night.
Tender Island Night.
Thank You, O Lord.
There's Blood in the Streets.
There's Someone At the Door.
This Is My Forest.
Time Works Like Acid.
Times Change, Damaged.
To Be Alone.
Translations of the Divine.
Untrampled Footsteps.
Very Brave.
Wake, A.
We Awoke, Talking.
Wedding-Dress, The.
Welcome to the American Night.
When the Music's Over.
Wild Whore Laughs, The.
Woman in the Window.
Woman's Voice.
You Must Confront.
You Think I Don't Know.

Muldoon, Paul (b. 1951)
Aisling.
Anseo.
Armageddon, Armageddon.
Bearded Woman, by Ribera, The.
Ben.
Big House, The.
Blemish.
Boundary Commission, The.
Bran.
Carson.
Cass and Me.
Cherish the Ladies.
Chester.
Chinook.
Christo's.
Coney, The.
Cuba.
Cure for Warts, The.
Dancers at the Moy.
Duffy's Circus.
Elizabeth.
Field Hospital, The.
Fox, The.
Frog, The.
Gathering Mushrooms.
Glanders.
Good Friday, 1971. Driving Westward.
Gypsy.
Hedgehog.
Holy Thursday.
Identities.
Immram.
Immrama.
Louis.
Lunch with Pancho Villa.
Ma.
Making the Move.
Meeting the British.
Mink.
Mixed Marriage, The.
More a Man Has the More a Man Wants,
    The.
Mules.
My Grandfather's Wake.
Ned Skinner.
Ontario.
Our Lady of Ardboe.

Profumo.
Promises, Promises.
Quoof.
Right Arm, The.
Salvador.
7, Middagh Street.
Sightseers, The.
Soap-Pig, The.
Sushi.
Thrush.
Trance.
Truce.
Waking Father, The.
Weepies, The.
Why Brownlee Left.
Wind and Tree.
Wishbone, The.
Wystan.
Yggdrasill.

N

Nash, Ogden (1902–71)
A Bas Ben Adhem.
Abominable Snowman, The.
Absence Makes the Heart Grow Heart
    Trouble.
Absentees, The.
Advice outside a Church.
After the Christening.
All, All Are Gone, the Old Familiar
    Quotations.
Allow Me, Madam, But It Won't Help.
All's Brillig in Tin Pan Alley.
Always Marry an April Girl.
And How Keen Was the Vision of Sir
    Launfal?
And Three Hundred and Sixty-Six in Leap
    Year.
Anniversary, The.
Ant, The.
Any Milleniums Today, Lady?
Anybody Else Hate Nickynames?
Anybody for Money? or, Just Bring Your
    Own Basket.
April Yule, Daddy!
Are You a Snodgrass?
Arthur.
Aside to Husbands.
Ask Daddy, He Won't Know.
Asp, The.
Assorted Chocolates.
Astigmatic Naturalist, The.
Away from It All.
Bankers Are Just Like Anybody Else, Except
    Richer.
Banquet, The.
Barmaids Are Diviner Than Mermaids.
Bat, The.
Beginner's Guide to the Ocean, A.
Big Tent Under the Roof, The.
Biological Reflection.
Birdies, Don't Make Me Laugh.
Birds, The.
Birth Comes to the Archbishop.
Birthday on the Beach.
Boop-Boop-Adieup, Little Group!
Boy's Will is the Wind's Will?, A.
Brief Guide to New York, A.
Brief Guide to Rhyming, or, How Be the
    Little Busy Doth?, A.
Bugs.
Bulletin Has Just Come In, A.
Buses Headed for Scranton, The.
Caesar Knifed Again, or, Culture Biz Gets
    Hep, Boffs Profs.
Calendar-Watchers, or, What's So Wonderful
    about Being a Patriarch, The.
Calf, The.
Calling Spring VII-MMMC.
Camel, The.
Can I Get You a Glass of Water? or, Please
    Close the Glottis after You.
Canary, The.
Cantaloupe, The.
Captain John Smith.

Caraway Seed, The.
Caribou, The.
Carol for Children, A.
Cat Naps Are Too Good for Cats.
Caterpillar, The.
Caution to Everybody, A.
Celery.
Centipede, The.
Chacun à Son Berlitz.
Change Here for Wichita Falls, or, Has
    Anybody Seen My Wanderlust?
Cherub, The.
Child Is Father to the Man, But with More
    Authority, The.
Children's Party.
Child's Guide to Parents, A.
Chipmunk, The.
Chloe and the Roué.
City, The.
Clean Conscience Never Relaxes, A.
Clean Platter, The.
Club Car, The.
Cobra, The.
Coffee with the Meal.
Columbus.
Come On In, the Senility Is Fine.
Common Cold, The.
Complaint to Four Angels.
Compliments of a Friend.
Confession to Be Traced on a Birthday Cake.
Confound You, December Twenty-sixth, I
    Apologize.
Consider the Lapel, Sir.
Correction: *Eve* Delved and *Adam* Span.
Cousin Euphemia Knows Best, or, Physician,
    Heal Somebody Else.
Cow, The.
Creeps and Crawls.
Crossing the Border.
Cuckoo, The.
Curl Up and Diet.
Daddy's Home, See You Tomorrow.
Dance Unmacabre.
Do, Do, Do What You Done, Done, Done
    Before, Before, Before.
Do You Plan to Speak Bantu? or
    Abbreviation is the Thief of Sanity.
Dr. Fell and Points West.
Doctor Fell? I Thought So.
Dog's Best Friend Is His Illiteracy, A.
Don't Be Cross, Amanda.
Don't Cry, Darling, It's Blood All Right.
Don't Even Tell Your Wife, Particularly.
Don't Grin, or You'll Have to Bear It.
Don't Guess, Let Me Tell You.
Don't Look for the Silver Lining, Just Wait
    for It.
Don't Look Now.
Don't Wait, Hit Me Now!
Down the Mousehole, and What Science
    Missed There.
Dragons Are Too Seldom.
Drink with Something in It, A.
Drop of a Hat, The.
Drusilla.
Duck, The.
Edouard.
Eel, The.
Eheu! Fugaces, or, What a Difference a Lot
    of Days Make.
Eight O'Clock Peril, The.
Election Day Is a Holiday.
Electra Becomes Morbid.
Emancipation of Mr. Poplin, or, Skoal to the
    Skimmerless.
Enthusiast Is a Devotee Is a Rooter, or, Mr.
    Hemingway, Meet Mr. Stengel, An.
Epilogue to Mother's Day, Which Is To Be
    Published on Any Day But Mother's Day.
Epstein, Spare That Yule Log!
Eternal Vernal, or, In All My Dreams My
    Fair Face Beams, The.
Evening Out, The.
Every Day Is Monday.
Everybody Eats Too Much Anyhow.
Everybody Makes Poets.
Everybody Tells Me Everything.

Everybody Wants to Get into the Baedeker.
Everybody's Mind to Me a Kingdom Is, or,
    A Great Big Wonderful World It's.
Everything's Haggis in Hoboken, or, Scots
    Wha Hae Hae.
Exit, Pursued by a Bear.
Experience to Let.
Fables Bullfinch Forgot.
Fahrenheit *Gesundheit.*
Family Court.
Father, Dear Father, Go Jump in the Lake,
    or, You're Costlier than You Think.
Fee Fi Ho Hum, No Wonder Baby Sucks
    Her Thumb.
First Chime.
First Families Move Over!
First Limick.
First Payment Deferred.
Fish, The.
Fly, The.
For a Good Dog.
Fourth Limick.
Fragonard.
Frailty, Thy Name Is a Misnomer.
Friendly Touch, The.
From a Manhattan Tomb.
Funebrial Reflection.
Further Reflection on Parsley.
Gander, The.
Genealogical Reflection.
Germ, The.
Glossina Morsitans, or, the Tsetse.
Golly, How Truth Will Out.
Good-By, Old Year, You Oaf or Why Don't
    They Pay the Bonus.
Good Night, Sweet Mind.
Good Parent's Garden of Vision, A.
Good Riddance, but Now What?
Goody for Our Side and Your Side Too.
Grackle, The.
Grasshoppers Are Very Intelligent.
Grin and Bear Left.
Guppy, The.
Ha! Original Sin!
Hamster, The.
Hand Me Down My Old School Sliding
    Pads, or, There's a Hint of Strawberry
    Leaves in the Air.
Happy Ending of Mr. Train, The.
Has Anybody Seen My Noumenon?
Have a Seat behind the Potted Palm, Sir.
Have You Tried Staying Awake? or, They'll
    Find a Way to Stop That, Too.
He Digs, He Dug, He Has Dug.
Hearts and Flowers or What I Know about
    Bolivar Black.
Hearts of Gold.
Here Usually Comes the Bride.
Here We Go Quietly Nuts in May.
Hi-Ho the Ambulance-O.
Hippopotamus, The.
Ho, Varlet! My Two Cents' Worth of Penny
    Postcard!
How Do You Say Ha-Ha in French.
How Long Has This Been Going On? Oh,
    Quite Long.
How Now, Sirrah? Oh, Anyhow.
How to Be Married without a Spouse, or,
    Mr. Kipling, What Have You Done with
    Mr. Hauksbee?
How to Harry a Husband, or, Is That
    Accessory Really Necessary?
Hunter, The.
Hush, Here They Come.
I Always Say There's No Place Like New
    York in the Summer, or, That Cottage
    Small by a Waterfall Was Snapped Up
    Last February.
I Am Full of Previous Experience.
I Burn Money.
I Can Hardly Wait for the Sandman.
I Can't Have a Martini, Dear, but You Take
    One, or, Are You Going to Sit There
    Guzzling All Night?
I Didn't Say a Word, or, Who Called That
    Piccolo Player a Father?
I Do, I Will, I Have.

Second Limick.
Second Month It's Not Itemized, The.
Sedative Reflection.
Seeing Eye to Eye Is Believing.
Self-Effacement of Electra Thorne, The.
September Is Summer, Too.
September Morn.
Seven Spiritual Ages of Mrs. Marmaduke Moore, The.
Shad, The.
Shark, The.
Shinking Song.
Sic Semper Mr. Sherman's Temper, or Kindly Place Your Order in English.
Skink, The.
Slow Down, Mr. Ganderdonk, You're Late.
Smelt, The.
Snark Was a Boojum Was a Prawn, The.
Sniffle, The.
So Does Everybody Else, Only Not So Much.
So I resigned from the Chu Chin Chowder and Marching Club.
So Penseroso.
So That's Who I Remind Me Of.
Soliloquy in Circles.
Solitude of Mr. Powers, The.
Some of My Best Friends Are Children.
Song Before Breakfast.
Song for a Temperature of a Hundred and One.
Song for Ditherers.
Song for Pier Something or Other.
Song of the Open Road.
Song to Be Sung by the Father of Infant Female Children.
Splash!
Spring Comes to Murray Hill.
Spring Song.
Squab, The.
Squid, The.
Squirrel, The.
Stitch Too Late Is My Fate, A.
Strange Case of Mr. Ballantine's Valentine, The.
Strange Case of Mr. Fortague's Disappointment, The.
Strange Case of Mr. Niobob's Transmogrification, The.
Strange Case of Mr. O'Banion's Come-Uppance, The.
Strange Case of Mr. Palliser's Palate, The.
Strange Case of Mr. Pauncefoot's Broad Mind, The.
Strange Case of Mr. Wood's Frustration, or, A Team that Won't Be Beaten Better Stay off the Field, The.
Strange Case of Mr. Donnybrooks's Boredom, The.
Strange Case of the Ambitious Caddy, The.
Strange Case of the Blackmailing Dove, The.
Strange Case of the Cautious Motorist, The.
Strange Case of the Dead Divorcee, The.
Strange Case of the Entomologist's Heart, The.
Strange Case of the Girl o' Mr. Sponsoon's Dreams, The.
Strange Case of the Irksome Prude, The.
Strange Case of the Lovelorn Letter Writer, The.
Strange Case of the Lucrative Compromise, The.
Strange Case of the Pleasing Taxi-Driver, The.
Strange Case of the Renegade Lyric Writer, The.
Summer Serenade.
Summergreen for President.
Suppose He Threw It in Your Face.
Suppose I Darken Your Door.
Swan, The.
Sweetbread, The.
Table Talk.
Tableau at Twilight.
Taboo to Boot.
Tale of Custard the Dragon, The.

Tarkington, Thou Should'st Be Living in This Hour.
Tell It to the Eskimos or Tell it to the Esquimaux.
Termite, The.
Terrible People, The.
That Reminds Me.
That's Funny, Wasn't It? No, It Won't Be.
Theatrical Reflection.
There Are More Ways to Roast a Pig than Burning the House Down or You Can Always Stick Your Head in a Volcano.
There Were Giants in Those Days or Maybe There Weren't.
There'll Always Be a War between the Sexes, or, A Woman Can Be Sometimes Pleased, but Never Satisfied.
There's Always an Ubblebub.
There's Nothing Like Instinct, Fortunately.
They Won't Believe, on New Year's Eve, that New Year's Day Will Come What May.
Third Limick.
Thirteenth Labor of Hercules, The.
This Is My Own, My Native Tongue.
This Was Told Me in Confidence.
Thoughts Thought after a Bridge Party.
Thoughts Thought on an Avenue.
Thoughts Thought While Waiting for a Pronouncement from a Doctor, an Editor, a Big Executive, the Department of Internal Revenue or Any Other Momentous Pronouncer.
Thunder over the Nursery.
Time Marches On.
Tin Wedding Whistle.
To a Lady Passing Time Better Left Unpassed.
To Ee Is Human.
Tomorrow, Partly Cloudy.
Tortoise, The.
Toucan, The.
Traveler's Rest.
Trouble with Women Is Men, The.
Try It Suns. and Hols.; It's Closed Then.
Tune for an Ill-Tempered Clavichord.
Turkey, The.
Turns in a Worm's Lane.
Turtle, The.
Tweedledee and Tweedledoom.
Two and One Are a Problem.
Two Dogs Have I.
Two Goes into Two Once, If You Can Get It There.
Two Songs for a Boss Named Mr. Longwell.
Unanswered by Request.
Under the Floor.
Unselfish Husband, The.
Unwinged Ones, The.
Up from the Egg; the Confessions of a Nuthatch Avoider.
Up from the Wheelbarrow.
Very Funny, Very Funny.
Very Unclubbable Man, The.
Visit From Dr. Fell, A.
Visit, The.
Voluble Wheel Chair, The.
Wapiti, The.
Warning to Wives, A.
Wasp, The.
Watched Example Never Boils, A.
Watchman, What of the First First Lady?
We Don't Need to Leave Yet, Do We? Or, Yes We Do.
We Would Refer You to Our Service Department, If We Had One.
Wednesday Matinee.
Wendigo, The.
What Almost Every Woman Knows Sooner or Later.
What I Know About Life.
What Is Bibbidi-Bobbidi-Boo in Sanskrit?
What, No Oysters?
What, No Sheep?
What the Well-Read Patient Is Talking About, or, Look, Ma, What I Got!

What to Do until the Doctor Goes or It's Tomorrow Than You Think.
What's in a Name? Here's What's in a Name, or, I Wonder What Became of John and Mary.
What's in a Name? Some Letter I Always Forget.
What's the Matter, Haven't You Got Any Sense of Humor?
What's the Use.
When the Devil Was Sick Could He Prove It?
When You Say That, Smile! or All Right Then, Don't Smile.
Where There's a Will, There's Velleity.
Who Called That Robin a Piccolo Player?
Who Did Which? or Who Indeed?
Who Taught Caddies to Count? or A Burnt Golfer Fears the Child.
Who Understands Who Anyhow?
Why the Postman Has to Ring Twice, or, Yellow Envelope, Where Have You Gone?
Wild Jackass, The.
Will Consider Situation.
Will You Have Your Tedium Rare or Medium?
Woman Pulls the Wires.
Wombat, The.
Word about Winter, A.
Word on Wind, A.
Yes and No.
Yorkshire Pudding.
You and Me and P.B. Shelley.
You Bet Travel Is Broadening.
You Can Be a Republican, I'm a Genocrat.
You Have More Freedom in a House.
Your Lead, Partner, I Hope We've Read the Same Book.
Translations, Coauthored Poems, etc.:
Do Sphinxes Think?
Old Is for Books.

Nathan, Leonard (b. 1924)
And Finally.
Around the Fire.
As We Walked.
At the Well.
Audit.
Before Even This.
Bladder Song.
Body Count.
Breathing Exercises.
Carrying On.
Certain Prospects and Spectacular Diversions.
Chosen, The.
Closure.
Concluding Remarks.
Confession.
Conversation Piece.
Coup.
Creed.
Day the Perfect Speakers Left, The.
Diver, The.
Election, The.
Ellora.
Evolution.
Explanation.
Family Circle.
Feeding the Ducks.
Fourth Dimension, The.
Gap.
Great.
Haakon Jarl.
Hay Fever.
Hello Again.
Hieroglyph.
Highway, The.
Holding Pattern.
Hole.
Honorable Mention.
I write you out of fear.
Icon.
If you start in loneliness.
It Looks As If It Were Just Sleeping.
It's a brand new morning.
Jane Seagrim's Party.
Jubilee.
Just Looking, Thank You.

Keeping the Faith.
Kind.
Law and Order.
Learning Experience.
Letter.
Letter to the Patrol Twenty Years After.
Like Us, Maybe.
Likeness, The.
Lion Farm, The.
Loophole, The.
Master of the Winter Landscape, The.
Meadow Foam.
Mocking Bird Song.
Morning Song.
Musical Offering, A.
Near Things.
News from the Low Country.
Niño Leading an Old Man to Market.
Nurse.
On the sink of the Golden Motel washroom.
One for Beauty.
Opportunity.
Outside the Wall.
Parade.
Penance, The.
Pocket Song.
Poet's House Preserved as a Museum, The.
Powerful Little Stove, A.
Progress Report.
Pumpernickel.
Reading of History, A.
Revival Meeting for Wheelchairs and
  Stretchers.
Scroll, The.
Season's Greetings.
Servant of Stars, The.
Sick Leave.
Snake Charming.
So?
Solemn Music.
Sorry.
Soundings, The.
Spirit.
Surprise.
Table Talk.
Tendril.
That the Unexamined Life Is Not Worth
  Living.
There's too much to consecrate.
Third Wish, The.
Thirty Rings.
Through the thin hill fog.
To Be Read to Yourself in a Public Place,
  July 4, 1976 sels.
To Somewhere.
To Transcend the Cat.
Toast.
Twin Snakes.
Understanding, The.
Waiting Room Only.
Washing Socks.
Waving Good-Bye.
Widowhood.
Winter Morning of the Village.
Wisdom of the Talmud.
Word, The.
Yours Truly.

Nemerov, Howard (b. 1920)
Above.
Absent-Minded Professor.
According to His Seasons.
Advice from the Holy Tomb.
After Commencement.
Aftermath.
Again.
Ahasuerus.
Amnesty.
Analogue.
..And Is Silent.
Angel and Stone.
Anniversary.
Antigone.
April.
Armistice.
Ars Poetica.
Art Song.
At a Country Hotel.

At the Airport.
August, 1945.
Autumnal.
Backward Look, The.
Bacterial War, The.
Baron Baedeker Blew His Nose and, Sighing,
  Departed, The.
Beautiful Lawn Sprinkler, The.
Beekeeper Speaks.., The.
Beginner's Guide.
Behavior.
Being of Three Minds.
Between the Window and the Screen.
Beyond the Pleasure Principle.
Blue Suburban.
Blue Swallows, The.
Bluebeard's Wife.
Book of Kells, The.
Boom!
Boy with Book of Knowledge.
Brainstorm.
Breaking of Rainbows, The.
Brief Journey West, The.
Brueghel: The Triumph of Time.
Burning the Leaves.
Cabinet of Seeds Displayed, A.
Cain.
Canossa.
Capitals.
Carol: "Now is the world withdrawn all."
Casting.
Celestial Globe.
Central Park.
Cherry Tree, The.
Christmas Morning.
Chromium-Plated Hat. Inlaid with Scenes
  from Siegfried, A.
Clock With No Hands, A.
Cloud Seeding.
Common Saw, A.
Common Wisdom, The.
Companions, The.
Consent, The.
Conversing with Paradise.
Cosmic Comics.
Creation Myth on a Moebius Band.
Creation of Anguish.
Critic.
Crocodile at the Ancient Tombs.
Crossing, The.
Cuckoo King, The.
Cybernetics.
Daily Globe, The.
Dancer's Reply, The.
Dandelions.
Day on the Big Branch, A.
De Anima.
Dead River.
Death and the Maiden.
Death of God, The.
Debate with the Rabbi.
Decorated Skull in a University Museum.
Deep Woods.
Departure of the Ships.
Dependencies, The.
Deposition, The.
Dial Tone, The.
Dialectical Songs.
Dialogue.
Distances They Keep, The.
Distraction.
Don Juan to the Statue.
Doomsday Books, The.
Dragonfly, The.
Drama.
Drawing Lessons.
Dream, A.
Dream of Flying Comes of Age, The.
Druidic Rimes.
Du rêve, de la mathématique, et de la mort.
Earthquake in the West, The.
Ecstasies of Dialectic, The.
Einstein & Freud & Jack.
Elegy for a Nature Poet.
Elegy of Last Resort.
End of Summer School, The.
Endegeeste.

Ending, An.
Endor.
Enthusiasm for Hats.
Epigrams: "Wasp, climbing the window
  pane."
Epitaph: "Crazy, girls, crazy. Don is gone."
Epitaph: "Of the Great World he knew not
  much."
Epitaph on a Philosopher the Reports of
  Whose Death Have Been Grossly
  Minimized.
Equations of a Villanelle.
Europe.
Eve.
Exasperations of a Novelist.
Extract from Memoirs.
Fable of the War, A.
Fables of the Moscow Subway.
Fall Again, The.
Fall Song.
False Solomon's Seal.
Fiction.
Figures of Thought.
Firelight in Sunlight.
First Day, The.
First Leaf, The.
First Point of Aries, The.
First Snow.
Flame of a Candle, The.
Flower Arrangements.
Fontenelle.
For Robert Frost, in the Autumn, in Vermont.
For the Squadron.
For W———, Who Commanded Well.
Fortune Teller, The.
Four Ages, The.
Four Sonnets.
Fourth of July, The.
Fragment from Correspondence.
From a Record of Disappointment.
From the Desk of the Laureate: For
  Immediate Release.
From the Last Dream of a Dying Woman
  Aged Eighty.
Frozen City, The.
Fugue.
Full Professor, A.
Ginkgoes in Fall.
Glass Dialectic.
Gnomes.
God of This World, The.
Going Away.
Goldfish.
Goose Fish, The.
Grace to Be Said at the Supermarket.
Grace to Be Said before Committee
  Meetings.
Grand Central, with Soldiers, in Early
  Morning.
Great Society, Mark X, The.
Growing a Ghost.
Guide to the Ruins.
Gulls, The.
Gyroscope.
Harvest Home, A.
He.
Hero Comes Home in His Hamper, and Is
  Exhibited at the World's Fair, The.
Hero with Girl and Gorgon.
Hide & Seek.
History of a Literary Movement.
History of Hair from World War II to the
  Present.
Holding the Mirror Up to Nature.
Home for the Holidays.
Hope.
Human Condition, The.
Human Things.
Hunt Goes By, The.
I Only Am Escaped Alone to Tell Thee.
Icehouse in Summer, The.
Idea.
In the Black Museum.
In the Commercial Gardens.
In the Glass of Fashion.
Instructions for Use of This Toy.
Interiors.

Interview, An.
Invocation: "Wasp, climbing the window pane."
Iron Characters, The.
Issue of Life, An.
Journey of the Snowmen.
Junction, on a Warm Afternoon, The.
Keeping Informed in D.C.
Kicks.
Knowledge.
Landscape with Figures.
Late Butterflies.
Late Late Show.
Late Summer.
Lean and Hungry Look, A.
Learning by Doing.
Learning the Trees.
Life, A.
Life Cycle of Common Man.
Lightning Storm on Fuji.
Limits.
Lines & Circularities.
Lion & Honeycomb.
Lives of Gulls and Children, The.
Lobsters.
Loon's Cry, The.
Lore.
Lot Later.
Lot's Wife.
Love.
Lucifer.
Lucilius.
Madrigal: "She is the darkness where I wander."
Maestria.
Maia.
Maiden with Orb and Planets.
Make Big Money at Home! Write Poems in Spare Time!
Make Love Not War.
Mapmaker on His Art, The.
Market-Place, The.
Mars.
Master at a Mediterranean Port, The.
May Day Dancing, The.
Measure of Poetry, The.
Memory of My Friend, A.
Memory of the War, A.
Metamorphoses.
Metaphysical Automobile, The.
Metropolitan Sunday.
Midsummer's Day.
Minim.
Mirror, The.
Mrs. Mandrill.
Modern Poet, A.
Moment.
Money.
Moonshine.
Morality, A.
Morning Sun.
Moses.
Most Expensive Picture in the World, The.
Mousemeal.
Mud Turtle, The.
Murder of William Remington, The.
Mystery Story.
Myth & Ritual.
Mythological Beast.
Nature Morte.
Near the Old People's Home.
Nebuchadnezzar, Solus.
Negro Cemetery Next to a White One, A.
New Weapons in the Old War.
Nicodemus.
Night before Christmas, The.
Nightmare.
Nothing Will Yield.
Novelists.
Observation of October.
Of Experience.
Old Colonial Imperialist, An.
Old Country, The.
Old Days, The.
Old Photograph, An.
Old Picture, An.
Old Soldiers' Home, The.

Old Story, An.
Old Warplane, An.
On a Text: Jonah IV, xi.
On Being a Member of the Jury for a Poetry Prize.
On Being Asked for a Peace Poem.
On Certain Wits.
On Getting Out Of Vietnam.
On Reading "The Love and Death of Cornet Christopher Rilke."
On the Platform.
On the Threshold of His Greatness, the Poet Comes Down With a Sore Throat.
One Forever Alien.
One Moment in Eternity.
One Way.
Origin.
Orphic Scenario.
Ozymandias II.
Painter Dreaming in the Scholar's House, The.
Painting a Mountain Stream.
Paraphrase from Notebooks.
Peace in Our Time.
Philosophy.
Phoenix, The.
Photograph of a Girl, The.
Picture, A.
Place of Value, The.
Plane.
Playing Skittles.
Playing the Inventions.
Pockets.
Poem of Margery Kempe, A.
Poet as Eagle Scout, The.
Poet at Forty, The.
Political Reflexion [or Reflection].
Polonius Passing Through a Stage.
Pond, The.
Portrait of Three Conspirators.
Poverty Programs, The.
Power to the People.
Praising the Poets of That Country.
Predecessor of Perseus, A.
Presidential Address to a Party of Exiles.
Priest's Curse on Dancing, The.
Primer of the Daily Round, A.
Prism.
Private Eye, The.
Projection.
Puzzle, The.
Quaerendo Invenietis.
Quarry, The.
Questions.
Race, The.
Realities.
Redeployment.
Reflexion of a Novelist.
Reflexions on the Seizure of the Suez, and on a Proposal to Line the Banks of That Canal with Billboard Advertisements.
Refusal of a Kindness Offered.
Relation of Art and Life, A.
Remorse for Time, The.
Rent in the Screen, The.
Returning to Europe.
Riddle the Sphinx Forgot, A.
Rope's End, The.
Route Two.
Runes.
Sacrificed Author, A.
Salt Garden, The.
Sanctuary, The.
Sandpipers.
Santa Claus.
Sarabande.
Sarajevo.
Scales of the Eyes, The.
Second-Best Bed, The.
Seeing Things.
September Shooting.
September, the First Day of School.
Sestina I: "Thickness of paint or flesh cannot deface."
Sestina II: "No waste is trackless: all terrain the lost."
Seven Macabre Songs.

Shells.
Sightseers.
Singular Metamorphosis, A.
Situation Does Not Change, The.
Sleeping Beauty.
Small Moment.
Small Moon.
Snow Globe, The.
Snowflakes.
Soldier Who Lived Through the War, The.
Solipsism & Solecism.
Somewhere.
Song of Degrees, A.
Song: "Provide your friend with almanacs."
Sonnet at Easter.
Sonnet: "Form of Christ cut from dark wood, the pale, A."
Sonnet: "It seems to be the trouble, everyone."
Speculation.
Spell before Winter, A.
Spiral Shell, A.
Spy, The.
Stare of the Man from the Provinces, The.
Statues in the Public Gardens, The.
Steps for a Dancer.
Still Life I.
Still Life II.
Still Life III.
Storm Windows.
Strange Metamorphosis of Poets.
Student Dies in 100 Yard Dash.
Style.
Suburban Prophecy.
Succession.
Summer's Elegy.
Sunday.
Sunday at the End of Summer.
Sunderland.
Sunglasses, The.
Sweeper of Ways, The.
Tale.
Tapestry, The.
There.
These Words Also.
Thirtieth Anniversary Report of the Class of '41.
This, That, & the Other.
Thought.
Thought of Trees, The.
Threshold.
To a Friend.
To a Scholar in the Stacks.
To Clio, Muse of History.
To D———, Dead by Her Own Hand.
To David, about His Education.
To H. M.
To Lu Chi.
To My Least Favorite Reviewer.
To the Babylonians.
To the Bleeding Hearts Association of American Novelists.
To the Governor & Legislature of Massachusetts.
To the Mannequins.
To the Memory of John Wheelwright.
To the Poets.
To the Rulers.
Town Dump, The.
Translation.
Trees.
Trial and Death, a Double Feature.
Triumph of Education, The.
Truth.
Truth of the Matter, The.
TV.
Two Girls.
Two Pair.
Two Poems.
Two Sides to an Outside: Meditation from Empson.
Two Views of a Philosopher.
Under the Bell Jar.
Unscientific Postscript.
Vacuum, The.
Vermeer.
View from an Attic Window, The.

View from Pisgah, The.
View, The.
Virgin and Martyr.
Waiting Rooms.
Walking Down Westgate in the Fall.
Warning: Children at Play.
Watching Football on TV.
Way of Life, A.
Weather of the World, The.
Western Approaches, The.
What Kind of a Guy Was He?
Wheel King, The.
Who Did Not Die in Vain.
Winter Exercise.
Winter Lightning, The.
Wolves in the Zoo.
World as Brueghel Imagined It, The.
Writing.
Young Woman.
Zalmoxis.
Zander on God.
Translations, Coauthored Poems, etc.:
Banquaet, The.
Childhood.
Convito *sels.*

Neruda, Pablo (Neftalí Ricardo Reyes Basualto) (1904–73)
All Seated.
Ambassador, The.
And why is the sun such a poor friend.
Another.
Another One.
Are the salt and the sugar at work.
At whom is the rice grinning.
Bell-Ringer, The.
Bell Tower of Authenay, The.
Bird.
Bomb (II).
Can't you think death lives.
Century Dying, A.
Cherries.
Child of the Moon.
Cold.
Coming Back.
Conditions.
Danger, The.
Dead Dog.
Different Ship, A.
Do you hear yellow detonations.
Don't you also feel danger.
Dying.
Earth.
Egoist.
Final.
First Winter.
From the breach to the iron explosion.
Gift, The.
Heavy Surf, A.
Herbalist's Rose, The.
Homecomings.
How long would a rhinoceros last.
I Come Back from a Journey.
I entered the cave of the amethysts.
I want the jailed / light to awaken: I want.
I Went.
If all rivers are sweet.
If I'm dead and don't know it.
Initial.
Inside.
Is all peace a dove's peace?
Is 4 always 4 for everybody?
Is it true that amber contains.
Is there anything crazier in this life.
Island (VII), The.
Island (VIII), The.
Island (XII), The.
Island (XVII), The.
Island (XX), The.
Let's Wait.
Little Devils.
Men (II), The.
Men (IV), The.
Men (IX), The.
Men (XVIII), The.
Men (XIX), The.
Midday Construction.
Negative Hands.

XIX, The.
Oliverio Girondo.
One Comes Back.
Pardon Me.
Pedro Is When.
Physics.
Possessions.
Quartz opens its eyes in the snow.
Question Book *sels.*
Runaway Sun.
Same Story.
Search.
Separate Rose, The *sels.*
Sick Man in the Sun.
Sitting Down.
Skystones *sels.*
Some Creature.
Spelling book, can you love me.
Star.
Stone, toppled by water and mountain, The.
Successions.
Tell me, is the rose really naked.
That solemn Senator / who claimed I had castles.
This Broken Bell.
This Is Simple.
To Puente Curvo on the Maldonado Spit in Uruguay.
To whom does the raggedy condor.
Today How Many Hours.
Today Isn't Everything.
2 8 3 2 5 6 7 4 5 4 9.
Untenable Situation, An.
Wars, The.
What are you hiding under your hump?
What can it mean to endure.
What forced labor / for Hitler in Hell?
What will the Poles think of my hat.
When all turned to altitude.
When does the butterfly read.
Where is the child that I was.
Who can persuade the sea.
Whom can I ask / what I meant to achieve in this world?
Winter.
Won't our life be a tunnel.

Notley, Alice (b. 1945)
Alice Ordered Me to be Made.
At Night the States.
Backyard.
Bus Stop.
But He Says I Misunderstood.
Dear Dark Continent.
Descent of Alette, The *sels.*
Desert for All of Music to Take Place.
Flowers of the Foothills & Mountain Valleys.
From *The Descent of Alette*, Book 3.
Goddess Who Created This Passing World, The.
Homer's *Art.*
How Spring Comes.
It Would.
Jack Would Speak through the Imperfect Medium of Alice.
January.
Love.
Margaret & Dusty.
Mother Mask.
Perfect Point.
Poem: "St. Marks Place caught at night in hot summer."
Poem: "You hear that heroic big land music?"
Poem:"Who do I want to tell it."
Prophet, The.
Red Zinnias.
September's Book.
Sonnet:"Late Gracie Allen was a very lucid comedienne, The."
Sweetheart.
30th Birthday.
True Account of Talking to Judy Holiday, October 13, A.
Untitled.
Waltzing Matilda.
When I Was Alive.
White Phosphorus.

World's Bliss.
Your Dailiness.

O

O'Hara, Frank (1926–66)
Adieu to Norman, Bon Jour to Joan and Jean-Paul.
Alma.
Animals.
Ann Arbor Variations.
Answer to Voznesensky and Evtushenko.
Anxiety.
Argonauts, The.
Ashes on a Saturday Afternoon.
Aus Einem April.
Autobiographia Literaria.
Ave Maria.
Avenue A.
Biotherm [for Bill Berkson].
Blocks.
Captain Bada.
Chez Jane.
Colloque Sentimental.
Commercial Variations.
Cornkind.
Critic, The.
Day and Night in 1952.
Day Lady Died, The.
Easter.
Essay on Style.
F. (Missive & Walk) I. #53.
Fantasy.
First Dances.
For Grace, after a Party.
For James Dean.
For the Chinese New Year & for Bill Berkson.
Getting Up Ahead of Someone (Sun).
Hatred.
Having a Coke with You.
Heroic Sculpture.
Hôtel Transylvanie.
Hunter, The.
Image of Leda, An.
Image of the Buddha Preaching.
In Favor of One's Time.
In Memory of My Feelings.
Interior (With Jane).
Invincibility.
Jane Awake.
Joe's Jacket.
John Button Birthday.
July Is Over and There's Very Little Trace.
Kitville.
Les Étiquettes Jaunes.
Les Luths.
Lover, The.
Mary Desti's Ass.
Mayakovsky.
Meditations in an Emergency.
Memorial Day 1950.
Mexican Guitar, A.
Mozart Chemisier.
Muse Considered As a Demon Lover, The.
Music.
My Heart.
My Heat.
Naphtha.
1951.
Now That I Am in Madrid and Can Think.
Ode: "Idea of justice may be precious, An."
Ode on Causality.
Ode on Necrophilia.
Ode: Salute to the French Negro Poets.
Ode (To Joseph Lesueur) on the Arrow That Flieth by Day.
Ode to Michael Goldberg ('s Birth and Other Births).
Ode to Tanaquil Leclercq.
On Looking at *La Grande Jatte,* the Czar Wept Anew.
On Rachmaninoff's Birthday.
On Rachmaninoff's Birthday ("Blue windows, blue rooftops").
On Seeing Larry Rivers' *Washington*

Crossing the Delaware at the Museum of Modern Art.
Pastoral Dialogue, A.
Personal Poem.
Petit Poème en Prose.
Pleasant Thought from Whitehead, A.
Poem: "And tomorrow morning at 8 o'clock in Springfield, Massachusetts."
Poem: "At night Chinamen jump."
Poem: "Eager note on my door said "Call me", The."
Poem: "Hate is only one of many responses."
Poem: "I don't know as I get what D.H. Lawrence is driving at."
Poem: "I ran through the snow like a young Czarevitch!"
Poem: "I watched an armory combing its bronze bricks."
Poem in Envy of Cavalcanti, A.
Poem In January.
Poem: "Instant coffee with slightly sour cream."
Poem: "Ivy is trembling in the hammock, The."
Poem: "Khrushchev is coming on the right day!"
Poem: "Let's take a walk, you."
Poem: "Light clarity avocado salad in the morning."
Poem: "Now it is the 27th."
Poem: "Now the violets are all gone, the rhinoceroses, the cymbals."
Poem: "O sole mio, hot diggety, nix 'I wather think I can' ."
Poem Read at Joan Mitchell's.
Poem: "So many echoes in my head."
Poem: "That's not a cross look it's a sign of life."
Poem: "There I could never be a boy."
Poem: "To be idiomatic in a vacumm."
Poem: "Twin spheres full of fur and noise."
Poem V (F) W.
Poem: "When I am feeling depressed and anxious sullen."
Poetry.
Post the Lake Poets Ballad.
Postcard from John Ashbery, A.
Radio.
Rant, A.
Rhapsody.
Romanze, or the Music Students.
Saint.
St. Paul and All That.
Savoy.
Second Avenue.
Sleeping on the Wing.
Song: "Is it dirty."
Sonnet for Jane Freilicher, A.
Spirit Ink, The.
Spleen.
Step Away from Them, A.
Steps.
Summer Breezes.
Tarquin.
Terrestrial Cuckoo, A.
Three-Penny Opera, The.
To a Poet.
To Gottfried Benn.
To Hell with It.
To Jane; and in Imitation of Coleridge.
To the Film Industry in Crisis.
To the Harbormaster.
Today.
True Account of Talking to the Sun at Fire Island, A.
"Unfinished," The.
Variations on Pasternak's "Mein Liebchen, Was Willst Du Noch Mehr?"
Walking to Work.
What Appears to Be Yours.
Why I Am Not a Painter.
You Are Gorgeous and I'm Coming.
Young Poet, A.

Oliver, Mary (b. 1935)
Acid.
Alex.
Alligator Poem.

Anne.
Answers.
At Blackwater Pond.
August.
Aunt Elsie's Night Music.
Aunt Leaf.
Bailing the Boat.
Being Country Bred.
Beyond the Snow Belt.
Bitterness, A.
Black Snake, The.
Black Walnut Tree, The.
Blossom.
Bone Poem.
Buck Moon—From the Field Guide to Insects.
Buddha's Last Instruction, The.
Certain Sharpness in the Morning Air, A.
Clam Man.
Creeks.
Crossing the Swamp.
Crows.
Dogfish.
Dream of Trees, A.
Dreams.
Egret, The.
Egrets.
Encounter.
Entering the Kingdom.
Esquimos Have No Word for "War," The.
Family, The.
Farm Country.
Field near Linden, Alabama.
First Snow.
Fish, The.
Five A.M. in the Pinewoods.
Gannets.
Ghosts.
Going to Walden.
Goldenrod.
Goldfinches.
Happiness.
Hattie Bloom.
Hawk.
Her Grave.
Hermit Crab, The.
House, The.
Hummingbird Pauses at the Trumpet Vine.
Humpbacks.
Hunter's Moon—Eating the Bear.
Ice.
In Blackwater Woods.
Indonesia.
Journey, The.
Kookaburras, The.
Lamps, The.
Landscape.
Last Days.
Learning About the Indians.
Letter from Home, A.
Lightning.
Lilies.
Lilies Break Open Over the Dark Water, The.
Little Owl Who Lives in the Orchard.
Lonely, White Fields.
Magellan.
Marengo.
Maybe.
Meeting, A.
Moccasin Flowers.
Morning.
Morning in a New Land.
Morning Poem.
Moths, The.
Murderer's House, The.
Mushrooms.
Mussels.
Nature.
Night Flight.
Night Traveler, The.
1945—1985: Poem for the Anniversary.
No Voyage.
October.
On Winter's Margin.
One or Two Things.
Peonies.

Picking Blueberries, Austerlitz, New York, 1957.
Ponds, The.
Poppies.
Rabbit, The.
Rage.
Rain.
Rain in Ohio.
Return, The.
Rice.
River Styx, Ohio, The.
Robert Schumann.
Roses.
Roses, Late Summer.
Sea, The.
Singapore.
Skunk Cabbage.
Sleeping in the Forest.
Snowshoe Hare, The.
Some Herons.
Some Questions You Might Ask.
Spring.
Spring Azures.
Spring in the Classroom.
Stanley Kunitz.
Starfish.
Strawberry Moon.
Summer Day, The.
Sun, The.
Sunflowers, The.
Sunrise.
Swan, The.
Swans on the River Ayr.
Swimming Lesson, The.
Tecumseh.
This Morning Again It Was in the Dusty Pines.
Three Poems for James Wright.
Truro Bear, The.
Turtle, The.
Two Kinds of Deliverance.
University Hospital, Boston.
Visitor, A.
Vultures.
Water Snake.
Waterfall, The.
Whelks.
When Death Comes.
White Flowers.
White Night.
White Owl Flies Into and Out of the Field.
Wild Geese.
Winter.
Winter in the Country.
Wolf Moon.

Olson, Charles (1910–70)
A B Cs.
A B Cs (2).
A B Cs (3—for Rimbaud).
À Constance, This Day.
Absolutely Vernal.
Abstract #1, Yucatan.
Abt the dead he sd.
Across Space and Time.
Adamo Me.
Added to / making a Republic.
Advantage, The.
Afica.
Afternoon.
Alba, The.
All Havens Astern.
All Pink from the Bath She Slept.
All things stand out against the sky.
All You Can Do.
Allegory of Wealth, The.
Americans, The ("Cosmologist says, The").
Americans, The ("What the cosmologist meant by what constitutes").
And now let all the ships come in.
Anecdotes of the Late War.
Anniversary.
Anubis will stare.
Applause.
April Today Main Street.
As I went in and out I heard pieces.
As if Hallam Movius had placed a grid over it, and plumb-.

Motion, The.
Move Over.
Muse / is the "fate" of the poem, The.
My apple branch dressed.
My belly / sounds like an owl.
My Love Is Also / Like.
My poor dumb body.
Name-Day Night.
Nerves Are Staves, and When the Tears Come There Is Voice, The.
New England March.
New Poem.
Newly Discovered "Homeric" Hymn, A.
Night, The.
Not a rat-hole, a cat-hole: the knife of time; on the ledge, overlooking.
Not to permit himself to be.
Obit.
Objects, The.
Ode on Nativity, An.
Of Lady, of Beauty, of Stream.
Of Mathilde.
Of the United States.
On All Sides.
On the equator east of my son I Orion bequeath to him my riches.
On the Shore.
One Night Ma / Lay with Pa.
One Word as the Complete Poem.
Only the Red Fox, Only the Crow.
O'Ryan.
O'Ryan 11-15.
Other Than.
Out of the light of Heaven   the flower.
Pacific Lament.
Part of the Series on the Paths, A.
Pavement, The.
Pente cōst   under the body of the gull flying directly over.
Peograms.
Perfume!, The.
Perfume / of flowers! A haw, The.
Perfume / of flowers! A quince, The.
Personality and dourness of winter, The.
Picture, The.
Pitcher, how / exactly is.
Plantation a Beginning, A.
Po-sy, a Po-sy, A.
Poemless Rhymes for the Times.
Post Virginal, The.
Praises, The.
Proensa.
Promise, A.
Proper Soul / in the Proper Body, The.
Purgatory Blind.
Put him this way.
Quail.
Quatrain: "Do not, at this high time, desert."
R².
Real, The.
Red Fish-of-Bones, The.
Red Mallows.
Return, The.
Right in My Eye.
Ring of, The.
Rosy, It Was.
Round & A Canon, A.
Rufus Woodpecker visited the President.
Said Adam.
Sans Name.
Scream to the Editor, A.
2nd Musical Form, for Dave Young, A.
Seven Songs, The.
17th century men / who founded this land.
Shang Dynasty Oracle Bone 2 Say.
Sea / is an archeology, The.
She.
She-Bear, The.
She-Bear (II), The.
She, Thus.
She Who Hits at Will.
Shenandoah.
Shut in   kept off.
Siena.
Signs.
Sin is inferiority. The mother's cooperation in the birth of her daughter.

Sing, Mister, Sing.
Sit by the Window and Refuse.
Six Inch Chapter—in Verse, A.
Small Birds, to Agree with the Leaves, Come in the Fall.
Snow, The.
Snow White was always waiting for The Prince.
So the Norse / were neurotic.
Some Good News.
Some partial cloudiness will flow locally, mostly.
Song, The: "More than the sennet of the solstice pipe."
Soul, The.
Spring Song for Cagli, A.
Stevens Song.
Stone and Flower Series.
Story, A.
Story of an Olson, and Bad Thing, The.
Sut Lovingood.
Swimming through the air, in schools upon the highways.
Tanto e Amara.
Telesphere, The.
Tenement twilightish landscape.
There Are Sounds.
There Is No River Which Is Called Lethe.
There they were.
There Was a Youth Whose Name Was Thomas Granger.
These Days.
Thing Was Moving, The.
This.
This Man's Weakness Is Straw.
This Year.
Thoughts of the Time.
Thy Gleeman Who Flattered Thee.
To a Poet Who Read in Gloucester Before the Cape Ann Historical Literary and Scientific Society.
To Empty the Mind.
To Gerhardt, There, among Europe's Things of Which He Has Written Us in His "Brief an Creely und Olson."
To the Algae.
To the She-Bear: The 1st Song.
To Try to Get Down One Citizen as Against Another.
Tomorrow.
Toss, for John Cage, A.
Town, The.
Translation, A.
Treatment, The.
Trinacria.
Troilus.
True Numbers.
Turn now and rise.
Twist, The.
Two Poems.
2 Propositions and 3 Proof.
Undazzled, keen, / love sits.
Under every green tree, sex.
Unfinished (raw) hero—un-, The.
Variations Done for Gerald Van de Wiele.
War on the Mind in a Time of Love.
Well.
West.
West Gloucester.
West 4 and 5.
West 6.
What Had to Go.
What's Wrong with Pindar.
When do poppies bloom   I ask myself, stopping again.
When One Age Goes with It Suddenly Its Errors Evaporate.
White Horse.
Who.
Who slays the Spanish sun.
Whole World, The.
Wholly absorbed / into my own conduits to.
Will: termite mothers.
Will: the rat.
Will To, The.
Willie Francis and the Electric Chair.
Winds / which blew my daughter, The.

Winter After, The.
Winter Solstice.
With what I got out.
Without the Season of Structure, Modes Lie Like Gods Thrown Down, Helpless Before the Newness Upsets Genesis When the Young Men Pour In.
Woman's Nipples Is the Rose of the World, A.
Writ, The.
X to the Nth.
Year Is a Great Circle or the Year Is a Great Mistake, The.
Yellow of the Mask, The.
You, Hart Crane.
You know, verse.
Your Eyes.

Oppen, George (b. 1908)
Alpine.
And Their Winter and Night in Disguise.
Animula.
Anniversary Poem.
Antique.
Armies of the Plain.
Bahamas.
Ballad: "Astrolabes and lexicons."
Bicycles and the Apex, The.
Birthplace: New Rochelle.
Blood from the Stone.
Book of Job and a Draft of a Poem to Praise the Paths of the Living, The.
Boy's Room.
Building of the Skyscraper, The.
But So As by Fire.
California.
Carpenter's Boat.
Chartres.
City of Keansburg, The.
Coastal Strip.
Confession.
Crowded Countries of the Bomb, The.
Daedalus: The Dirge.
Debt.
Drawing.
Eclogue: "Men talking / Near the room's center. They have said, The."
Eros.
Exodus.
Five Poems about Poetry.
Flight.
Forms of Love, The.
Founder, The.
From a Photograph.
From a Phrase of Simone Weil's and Some Words of Hegel's.
From Disaster.
From Virgil.
Gesture, The.
Giovanni's Rape of the Sabine Women at Wildenstein's.
Guest Room.
Hills, The.
Historic Pun.
Image of the Engine.
Impossible Poem, The.
Inlet.
Kind of Garden: A Poem for my Sister, A.
Knowledge not of sorrow, you were, The.
Language of New York, A.
Latitude, Longitude.
Leviathan.
Lighthouses, The.
Little Hole, The.
Little Pin: Fragment, The.
Mayan Ground, The.
Men of Sheepshead, The.
Monument.
Morality Play: Preface, A.
Myself I Sing.
Myth of the Blaze.
Narrative, A.
Niece.
Night Scene.
O Western Wind.
Occurrences, The.
Of Being Numerous.
Of Hours.

Of This All Things..
Ozymandias.
Parousia.
Part of the Forest.
Party on Shipboard.
Pedestrian.
Penobscot.
People, the People, The.
Philai Te Kou Philai.
Population.
Power, the Enchanted World.
Primitive.
Pro Nobis.
Product.
Psalm: "In the small beauty of the forest."
Quotations.
Rationality.
Red Hook: December.
Resort.
Return.
Route.
Sara in Her Father's Arms.
Seated Man.
Semite.
Solution.
Some San Francisco Poems.
Song, the Winds of Downhill.
Source, The.
Speech at Soli, The.
Squall.
Still Life.
Stranger's Child.
Street.
Sunnyside Child.
Survival: Infantry.
Taste, The.
Technologies.
That Land.
Theological Definition, A.
Three wide / Funnels raked aft, and the
  masts slanted, The.
Time of the Missile.
To C. T.
To Memory.
To the Poets: To Make Much of Life.
Tourist Eye.
Translucent Mechanics, The.
Travelogue.
Tugs of Hull, The.
Two Romance Poems.
Undertaking in New Jersey, The.
Vulcan.
West.
White. From the / Under arm of T.
Who Shall Doubt.
Workman.
World, World—.
Zulu Girl, The.

Owen, Wilfred (1893–1918)
All Sounds Have Been As Music.
Antaeus: A Fragment.
Anthem for Doomed Youth.
Apologia Pro Poemate Meo.
Arms and the Boy.
Asleep.
At a Calvary near the Ancre.
Beauty.
Bold Horatius.
Bugles Sang.
Calls, The.
Chances, The.
Conscious.
Dead-Beat, The.
Disabled.
Dulce Et Decorum Est.
Elegy in April and September.
End, The.
Exposure.
Fates, The.
Fragment: "As bronze may be much
  beautified."
Fragment: "Cramped in that funnelled hole,
  they watched the dawn."
Fragment: "I saw his round mouth's crimson
  deepen as it fell."
Fragment: "Not one corner of a foreign
  field."

From My Diary, July 1914.
Futility.
Greater Love.
Happiness.
Has Your Soul Sipped?
Hospital Barge at Cérisy.
Imbecile, The.
Insensibility.
Inspection.
Kind Ghosts, The.
Last Laugh, The.
Le Christianisme.
Letter, The.
Long Ages Past.
Maundy Thursday.
Mental Cases.
Miners.
Music.
My Shy Hand.
Next War, The.
1914.
O World of Many Worlds.
On My Songs.
One Remains, The.
Parable of the Old Man and the Young, The.
Promisers, The.
Purple.
Roads Also, The.
Send-Off, The.
Sentry, The.
Shadwell Stair.
Show, The.
S.I.W.
Six o'clock in Princes Street.
Sleeping Beauty, The.
Smile, Smile, Smile.
Soldier's Dream.
Song of Songs.
Sonnet Autumnal.
Sonnet: "Be slowly lifted up, thou long black
  arm."
Sonnet, to a Child.
Spells and Incantation (a Fragment).
Spring Offensive.
Storm.
Strange Meeting.
Terre, A.
This is the Track.
To ———: "Three rompers run together,
  hand in hand."
To a Comrade in Flanders.
To Eros.
To My Friend.
To the Bitter Sweet-heart: a Dream.
Training.
Unreturning, The.
Winter Song.

P

Pack, Robert (b. 1929)
After All.
After Returning from Camden Harbor.
Archeology.
Autumn Warmth.
Bear on the Unicycle, The.
Beating Time.
Big Bang.
Black Hole, The.
Bounty.
Camp Wakonda, 1940.
Cave of Lascaux, The.
Champ.
Clayfeld Among the Quarks.
Clayfeld Prunes His Apple Trees.
Clayfeld Renews His Vow to Evelyn.
Clayfeld's Anniversary Song.
Clayfeld's Campaign.
Clayfeld's Daughter Reveals Her Plans.
Clayfeld's Duck.
Clayfeld's Glove.
Clayfeld's Infancy.
Clayfeld's Metamorphosis.
Clayfeld's Microscope.
Clayfeld's Operatic Debut.
Clayfeld's Son Selects His Specialty.

Clayfeld's Twin.
Closer.
Coincidence.
Cord of Wood, A.
Cracked Apple Tree, The.
Dead King, The.
Departing Words to a Son.
Display.
Drowning.
Dwarf and Doctor Freud, The.
Early and Late.
Ecstasy of the Rat, The.
Einstein's Pegasus.
Empathy.
Fathering the Map.
First Word at Last, The.
Forgetting to Forget.
Ghost Story.
Grandeur.
Hole in the Sky, A.
Human Pile, The.
Hunting.
Inheritance.
Invisible Hand, The.
It Comes to This.
It Would Have Been Enough.
Kiss, The.
Landscape Goat.
Last Drowning, The.
Let There Be Colored Light.
Letter to My Widow.
Leviathan.
Long and the Short of What's Good and
  What's Bad, The.
Look, there it is—I'm sure that is the oak.
Looking at a Mountain Range While
  Listening to a Mozart Piano Concerto.
Messages.
Modest Boast at Meridian, A.
Mountain Ash Without Cedar Waxwings.
Neanderthal Poem, "Ah," Number One.
Neutrinos.
Number.
Ode to a Lovesick Moose.
Ode to October Mist.
Orchid.
Out of Nothing.
Outlasting You.
Pantoum Approaching the Speed of Light.
Place.
Prayer for Prayer.
Proton Decay.
Quasars.
Red Shift, The.
Remains.
Reversing.
Robot.
Robot Romance.
Rondo of the Familiar.
Secrets.
Snowy Owl, The.
South Bronx, 1939.
Stellar Thanksgiving.
Stepping Out.
Still Passing.
Stolen Clothes.
Thrasher in the Willow by the Lake, The.
Trillium.
Trying to Reconcile.
Trying to Separate.
Twin, The.
Unburying the Birch.
Villanelle for Pamela.
Waking to My Name.
Walnut.
Watchers.
Waterfall.
Wild Turkeys in Paradise.
Wolf Pack, The.
Translations, Coauthored Poems, etc.:
Cherry Robbers.

Paley, Grace (b. 1922)
Age.
Ant! / lugging half an ounce, An.
Arboreal Mystery, An.
At the Battery.
Autumn.

Bee! / drowning in, A.
Bob Visits Friends.
Boys from Saint Bernard's, The.
Bridges.
Choir Singing, The.
Connections: Vermont   Vietnam (I).
Connections: Vermont   Vietnam (II).
Dance in Jinoteca, The.
Definition.
Drowning (I).
Drowning (II).
False strawberry is.
Families.
Family.
Fear.
Five Day Week, The.
For Danny.
For George (I).
For George (II).
For Mike and Jeannie: Resisters Fifteen
     Years Later.
For My Friend Who Planted a Tree for His
     Daughter Jane.
Fund Appeal.
Having Arrived by Bike at Battery Park.
Housing.
I cannot keep my mind on Jerusalem.
I don't think / the rain will end.
I Gave Away That Kid.
If you have acquired a taste for happiness.
Illegal Aliens.
In Aix.
In deepest summer / the milkweed flower.
In France.
In Hanoi   1969.
In San Salvador (I).
In San Salvador (II).
In the Bus.
Learning From Barbara Deming.
Leaves   Apples.
Letter.
Life.
Love.
Middle Age Poem.
Mulberry Street ends in good works.
My Father at 85.
My Father at 89.
My Mother: 33 Years Later.
Nature of This City, The.
No love / no love cried the last fling.
Note to Grandparents.
Now time himself   the master streamer.
Oh the dreamer said.
Old Age Porch.
Old Dog's Song, The.
On certain days I am not in love.
On Mother's Day.
On the Bank Street Pier.
On the Fourth Floor.
On the Ramblas / A Tree   A Girl.
On the Subway Station.
One Day.
People in My Family.
Poem About Storytelling, A.
Poets! / Madness is a gift.
Psalm: "Their shoes are stuccoed with
     sawdust and blood."
Quarrel.
Question.
Responsibility.
Sad Children's Song, The.
St. Johnswort!
Some days I am lonesome   I want to talk to
     my mother.
Song Stanzas of Private Luck.
South Window.
Standing in high grass at home imagining
     farm.
Stanzas: Old Age and the Conventions of
     Retirement Have Driven My Friends from
     the Work They Love.
Stranger calling a dog whistled, A.
Street Corner Dialogue.
That Country.
Then the flowers became very wild.
Then Vera stopped at the flower called
     fireweed.

34th Street Song.
Traveler.
20th Street   Spring.
Two Villages.
Veins that stand on the back of my
     sunburned hand, The.
Warning, A.
We quarreled / Alone I.
What has happened?
What is this whiteness on the fields?
What would happen / if there were a terrific
     shortage of goldenrod.
When the wild strawberry leaves turn.
Winter Afternoon.
Woman invented fire and called it, A.
Women let the tide go out, The.
Women's Prison: El Salvador / The Ballad of
     Visiting Day, The.

Patchen, Kenneth (1911–72)

After an Old Song.
Age of Pericles, The.
Ah, God, dear Brother, the mild and
     frowning rose.
All Is Safe.
All That Night Lights Were Seen Moving in
     Every Direction.
All the Bright Foam of Talk.
All the Day.
All the Flowery.
All the Roses of the World.
Always Another Viewpoint.
Among Ourselves and with All Nations.
And a Man Went Out Alone.
And He Had Wilder Moments.
And her look touching the air between us
     like a hand alive to the.
And I, Too, Am Something of a Stranger
     Here, My Friend.
And in Another Place Uses the Same Phrase.
And What with the Blunders.
And When Freedom Is Achieved.
Animal I wanted, The.
Anna Karenina and the Love-sick River.
Appian Way, The.
Ark: Angelus: Anvil.
As Frothing Wounds of Roses.
As in the green sky.
As She Was Thus Alone in the Clear
     Moonlight.
As we are so wonderfully done with each
     other.
At Grandmother's Wake.
At the Entrance to the Other World.
At the New Year.
Attila.
Authority of Krajova, The.
Autobiographical Note.
Autumn Is the Crows' Time.
Avarice and Ambition Only Were the First
     Builders of Towns and Founders of
     Empire.
Backcountry Blues.
Battle of Unameit, The.
Be music, night, / That her sleep may go.
Beautiful You Are.
Behold, One of Several Little Christs.
Being as hideous that the air weeps blood.
Beyond the Dark Cedars.
Billion Freedoms, The.
Biography of Southern Rain.
Bird-Queen, The.
Black Panther and the Little Boy, The.
Blind Maidens of Our Homelessness, The.
Blind'd be the last of men.
Blood of the Sun.
Body Beside the Ties, The.
Boxers Hit Harder When Women Are
     Around.
Breathe on the living.
Builders, The.
But of Life?
But the Images of His Former Dreams Still
     Haunted Him.
Can the Harp Shoot Through Its Propellers?
Career for a Child of Five.
Carts of the wee blind lass, The.
Catfish River Lullaby.

Character of Love Seen as a Search for the
     Lost, The.
Childhood of the Hero.
Christ! Christ! Christ! that the world.
Class of 1934.
Cleveland, Oh?
Climate of War, The.
Cloth of the Tempest, The.
Colony of the Sun, The.
Constant Bridegrooms, The.
Continual Ministry of Thy Anger, The.
Continuation of the Landscape.
Country Excursion.
Court of First Appeal.
Creation.
Crossing on Staten Island Ferry.
Crowded Net, The.
Cruelkind Swans, The.
Cruelties of the Sportive Power.
Curly Blue Buppo, The.
Daft Little Shoe Clerk Decided It Would Be
     Fun to Go Up and See What Things Are
     Like above the Sky, The.
Day of Rabblement.
Dazzling Burden, The.
Death Will Amuse Them.
Deathsong for a Maiden.
Deer and the Snake, The.
Delighted with Bluepink.
Demonstration.
Destruction of Carthage, The.
Devotion, A.
Do me that love.
Do the Dead Know What Time It Is?
Don't Wash Your Hair in the Streetcar, Nora
     Dear.
Dostoyevsky.
Down in Ol' Dontcaradama.
Down in the Lone Valley.
Each Is Alone, Each Is Everything.
Early in the Morning.
Easy Decision, An.
Easy Rider.
Ecstasy of the Pure.
Egypt.
Eight Early Poems.
Elegy for the Silent Voices and the Joiners of
     Everything.
Empire of Persia, The.
Encounter at Nightfall.
Eve of St. Agony, or the Middle Class Was
     Sitting on Its Fat.
Event at Konna, The.
Everlasting Contenders, The.
Evidence? What Evidence..?
Examination into Life and Death, An.
Executions in Moscow, The.
Expectant Shelters, The.
Fall of the Evening Star.
Family Portrait.
Farewell to the Bluewoman.
Fellow Soul, Sound Hunting to Thy
     Immeasurable Heart.
Fields of Earth.
Fifth Dimension.
Figure Motioned with Its Mangled Hand
     Toward the Wall Behind It, The.
Firing, The.
First came the Lion-Rider, across the green
     fields of the morning.
First Crusades, The!
Flowers to the House.
Fog.
Fog Over the Sea and the Sun Going Down.
Folly of Clowns.
For losing her love all would I profane.
For Miriam.
For the Mother of My Mother's Mother.
For whose adornment the mouths.
Forms of Knowledge, The.
Fox, The.
Fragment from "A Schoolboy's Odyssey."
From my high love I look at that poor world
     there.
Gautama in the Deer Park at Benares.
"Gentle and Giving" and Other Sayings.
Geography of Music.

Give you a lantern.
Grand Palace of Versailles, The.
Great Birds, The.
Great Sadnesses, The.
Great-Sledmakers, The.
Green Fires, The.
Hangman's Great Hands, The.
Harrowed by These Apprehensions He
    Resolved to Commit Himself to the Mercy
    of the Storm.
Have You Killed Your Man for Today?
Having Been Near.
He Is an.
He Is Guarded by Crowds and Shackled with
    Formalities.
He Thought of Mad Ellen's Ravings and of
    the Wretched Skeleton on the Rock.
He Was Alone (As in Reality) Upon His
    Humble Bed.
Heaven and Earth.
Heine, Too, Lived in Germany.
Her Talents..Of.
Here might have been the thinking of
    mountains.
History in a Minor Key.
History Is a Throne and a Gate.
Hold thy tongue, death!
House, and a Dead Man In It.
Hovenweep.
How God Was Made.
How Jimsey O'Roon and Peter Stack, Coal
    Miners, Came to Be Put in the Ferbettville
    (Pa.) Jail Early One Saturday Night.
How Old the World Is!
How silent are the things of heaven.
Hunted City, The.
Hunter, The.
Hymn to a Trench Gun.
I always return to this place.
I Can't Understand! I Can't Understand!
I Care What Happens.
I Don't Want To Startle You But They Are
    Going To Kill Most of Us.
I Feel Drunk All the Time.
I Got the Fat Poet into a Corner.
I have lighted the candles, Mary.
I Have No Place to Take Thee.
I Never Had Any Other Desire So Strong.
I Sent a Mental to My Love.
I Suddenly Became Conscious That This
    Thing Was Looking at Me Intently.
I suggest that this day be made holy.
I'd want her eyes to fill with wonder.
If a Poem Can Be Headed into Its Proper
    Current.
If We Are to Know Where We Live.
In a Crumbling.
In horror the God-thrown lie.
In Judgment of the Leaf.
In Memory of Kathleen.
In Order to.
In shadings of an obscure punishment.
In the Courtyard of Secret Life.
In the footsteps of the walking air.
In Your Body All Bodies Lie.
Instructions for Angels.
Intimate Guest, The.
Into another mission / Circling my exposed
    continent.
Investigation of Certain Interesting Questions.
Irate Songster, The.
Irkalla's White Caves.
It Depends on Whose Science.
It Is Big Inside a Man.
It Is for Us the Living.
It Takes Few Kinds.
It Was a Bomby Evening.
It Was Being.
It's a Smallworld.
It's Because Your Heart Is Pure, Honey.
It's My Town!
Joe Hill Listens to the Praying.
Just outside Tombstone.
Kibali-Ituri.
Knowledge of Old Towns, The.
Known Soldier, The.
Ladder, The.

Lament for the Makers of Songs.
Lao Tsze.
Last Full Measure of Devotion, The.
Lasting Seasons, The.
Leaflet (One).
Leaflet (Two).
Legend for a Little Child.
Lenada.
Let Me In!
Let Us Have Madness Openly.
Letter on Liberty, A.
Letter on the Use of Machine Guns at
    Weddings, A.
Letter to a Policemen in Kansas City, A.
Letter to the Inventors of a Tradition, A.
Letter to the Liberals, A.
Letter to the Old Men.
Letter to the Young Men, A.
Letter to Those Who Are About to Die.
Like a Mourningless Child.
Limpidity of Silences.
Lions of fire, The.
Little Black Train, The.
Little Cannibal's Bedtimesong.
Lives of the Swan.
Lonesome Boy Blues.
Lost Poem, A.
Lowellville Cemetery: Twilight.
Loyalty Is the Life You Are.
Lunch Wagon on Highway 57.
Lute in the Attic, The.
Magic Car, The.
Magical Mouse, The.
Man Is to Man a Beast.
Man Lives Here, A.
Man with the Golden Adam's Apple, The.
Manifold Fusions, The.
Matchstick-Viewed-without-Regard-to-Its-
    Outer-Surface, A.
May I Ask You a Question, Mr. Youngstown
    Sheet & Tube?
Meaning of Life, The.
Meben.
Mechanical Heart, The.
Meditation of My Lady of Sorrows.
Message from the Assistant Chief of the Fly
    People, A.
Midnight Special.
Mirru.
Mohammed.
Moon came out full, you could see the white
    breathing of the.
Moon "Continued."
Morning, My Prince—the Eye That Walks.
Mule of water, The.
Murder of Two Men by a Young Kid
    Wearing Lemon-colored Gloves, The.
My Coat Is Dirty.
My Generation Reading the Newspapers.
My Pretty Animals.
Naked Land, The.
Nervousness of Memory, The.
New Being, The.
Nice Day for a Lynching.
Night Has Been as Beautiful as Virginia.
1935.
Niobe.
No one ever works alone.
Nocturne for the Heirs of Light.
Not If He Has Any Sense, He Won't Be
    Back.
Not Many Kingdoms Left.
Note for a Diary.
November in Ohio.
Now I Went Down to the Ringside and Little
    Henry Armstrong Was There.
Now If You.
O All Down within the Pretty Meadow.
O Everliving Queen!
O fiery river / Flow out over the land.
O Fill Your Sack with Tiger Cubs.
O Howling Cells.
O kind watchers came.
O my darling troubles heaven.
O my love / The pretty towns.
O now the drenched land wakes.
O She Is as Lovely-Often as Every Day.

O sleeping falls the maiden snow.
O terrible is the highest thing.
O the sledbirds rides over the willow.
O What a Revolution!
O when I take my love out walking.
Of the same beauty were stars made.
Often Was It.
Ohio River Blues.
Old Lean Over the Tombstones, The.
Old Man.
Old Pair of Shoes, An.
Oldest Conversation, The.
On My Side.
On the South-West Coast of Erehwemos
    Stands a Romantic Little Village.
Opening the Window.
Orange Bears, The.
Origin of Baseball, The.
Other Side: The Green Home, The.
Outlaw of the Lowest Planet, The.
Overworld, The.
Palms for a Catholic Child.
Pastoral: "Dove walks with sticky feet, The."
Pathway, The.
Paxdominisit Sem Pervobiscum Etcumspiri
    Tutuo.
Peace in this green field.
Permanent Migrations, The.
Peter's Diary in Goodentown.
Pick Up the Evening Paper.
Plate of Steaming Fish, A.
Pleasures of This Gentle Day.
Plow Horses.
Poem: "Feeling chilled in that cold country."
Poem in the Form of a Letter: to Lauro de
    Bosis.
Poem Written after Reading Certain Poets
    Sired by the English School and Bitched
    by the C.P.
Poems which are written by the soul.
Polly—An Almost-True Story.
Poor Child with the Hooked Hands, The.
Poor Gorrel.
Portrait of the Artist as an Interior Decorator.
Portrait on an American Theme.
Prayer Not To Go to Paradise with the
    Asses.
Preparation for the Highest Being.
Pretty glow on the water.
Progress to a View of Life.
Put the rest away, O put the rest away!
Quantity of Mercy, The.
Queer Client and the Forest-Inn, The.
Question Is, Who Is Afraid of What, The?
Radiance in a Dark Wood, The.
Reason for Skylarks, The.
Red Wine and Yellow Hair.
Religion Is That I Love You.
Rest, heart of the tired world.
Rising a Little.
Rites of Darkness, The.
Roses of Life, The.
Saturday Night in the Parthenon.
Sea Has Caves and Urns, The.
Second People, The.
Shadows and Spring Flowers.
Shapes.
Shapes and Intensities of This Man, This
    Confucius, The.
She Had Concealed Him in a Deep Dark
    Cave.
She is the prettiest of creatures.
Should Be Sufficient.
Slums, The.
Small but Brilliant Fire Blazed in the Grate,
    A.
Snow is deep on the ground, The.
So Be It.
So It Ends.
So Near—And Yet.
Soldier and the Star, The.
Soon It Will.
Sovereign of the wilderness!
Spirit of Noplace, The.
Stars go to sleep so peacefully, The.
State of the Nation, The.

Stayed No Longer in the Place Than to Hire a Guide for the Next Stage.
Strange, Moving Lights of People Handle Holinesses Unknown, The.
Strange thing I said to Sam is the way they die, The.
Stranger, The.
Street Corner College.
Sturdy Legs, That.
Sure There Is Food.
Temple, A.
That We Here Highly Resolve.
Theory of Nato-geography as Advanced by the Tiaphidian Man, With a Comment on the Character of His Penal System, A.
There are no losses.
There Are Two.
There is nothing false in thee.
There Is One Who Watches.
There is the hand that has nothing attached to it, no arm no chest.
There's a Train Leaving Soon.
These are my great ones.
These Have Gone with Silent Hands, Seeking.
These Unreturning Destinies.
Thinking Rock.
This Early Day.
This Man Was Your Brother.
This Summer Day.
This summer earth.
Those Upon Whom God Has Labored.
Though I Had Much More To Say.
Thus Far So Nobly Advanced.
Time to Believe!, A.
To Be Charmed.
To Be Holy, Be Wholly Your Own.
To Say If You Love Someone.
To the Jewish People.
To the Tune of an Ancient Song.
To Whom It May Concern.
Tomorrow.
Tribes of Rakala, The.
Trueblue Gentleman, A.
Turner.
23rd Street Runs into Heaven.
Two for History.
Two Ghosts Together.
Unanswering Correspondences, The.
Under a Tree.
Under the green ledge.
Unfulfilling Brightnesses, The.
Unnatural History of Peru, The.
Unreturning Hosts, The.
Valley-sleeper, the Children, the Snakes, and the Giant, The.
Vanishing Institution, A.
Village Tudda, The.
Vines with Their.
Virtue.
Waiting Can Be Pretty Lousy.
Waking into Sleep.
Wanderers of the Pale Wood.
Watcher, The.
Watching Neighbors' Children.
Way men live is a lie, The.
We Are Not Worthy, Lord.
We go out together into the staring town.
We Hold These Truths to Be Self-Evident.
We Leave You Pleasure.
We Must Be Slow.
We Mutually Pledge to Each Other.
Weekend Bathers.
What Happened in the Camps.
What I'd like to know is.
What Is the Beautiful?
What Splendid Birthdays.
What the Grecian Earns.
What There Is.
When in the Course of Human Events.
When the stones burst into flame.
When We Were Here Together.
Where Every Prospect.
Where my stag-antlered love moves.
Where Two O'clock Came From.
White lions are roaring on the water.
Who Walks There?

Who'll that be.
Wide, wide in the rose's side.
Winter at the Inn.
Winter Poem.
Wolf of winter, The.
World Whose Sun Retreats Before the Brave, A.
World Will Little Note, The.
Worn on the.
Wouldn't You Be after a Jaunt of 964,000,000,000,000 Million Miles?
Written after Reading an Item in the Paper about a Young Lady Who Went Mad upon Forsaking Her Lover. He Is Here Assumed to Speak.
Yellow Stones—Sea of Majestic Doves.
Yesterday They Tried.
You May All Go Home Now.
You Must Have Some Idea Where They've Gone.

Piercy, Marge (b. 1936)
Ache's End.
All Clear.
Apologies.
At the Core.
Athena in the Front Lines.
Attack of the Squash People.
Barbie Doll.
Beauty I Would Suffer For.
Behold: A Relationship.
Best Defense is Offensive, The.
Breaking Camp.
Bridging.
Bronchitis on the 14th Floor.
Bumpity Road to Mutual Devotion, The.
Burying Blues for Janis.
Butt of Winter, The.
Cast Off, The.
Cats Like Angels.
Cats of Greece, The.
Cod Summer.
Community.
Concerning the Mathematician.
Consumer, The.
Councils.
Crabs.
Crescent Moon Like a Canoe.
Crippling, The.
Crows.
Curse of the Earth Magician on a Metal Land.
Cyclist, The.
Daily Life of the Worker Bee, The.
Death of the Small Commune, The.
Development, The.
Difference of Ages.
Digging In.
Doing It Differently.
Doors in the Wind and the Water.
Eight of Swords, The.
Emperor, The.
Erasure.
Excursions, Incursions.
Few Ashes for Sunday Morning, A.
For Jeriann's Hands.
For Shoshana Rihn—Pat Swinton.
For Strong Women.
For the Young Who Want To.
Friend, The.
Gasman Invites the Skyscrapers to Dance.
Gift of Light, A.
Girl in White.
Going In.
Gracious Goodness.
Greater Grand Rapids Lover, The.
Half Past Home.
Hallow Eve with Spaces for Ghosts.
Hand Games.
Hello Up There.
High Frequency.
Homely War, The.
Homesick.
I Am A Light You Could Read By.
I Awoke with the Room Cold.
I Will Not Be Your Sickness.
Icon.
If They Come in the Night.

In the Men's Room(s).
In the Wet.
Inside Chance, The.
Intruding.
It Breaks.
Juan's Twilight Dance.
Judgment, The.
Just Anger, A.
Kneeling at the Pipes.
Knight of Swords, The.
Landed Fish.
Lansing Bad Penny Come Again Blues, The.
Laocoön is the Name of the Figure.
Laying Down the Tower.
Learning Experience.
Let Us Gather at the River.
Letter to be Disguised as a Gas Bill.
Little Scandal, A.
Living in the Open.
Long Death, The.
Longest Night, The.
Looking at Quilts.
Love of Lettuce, The.
Magician, The.
Market Economy, The.
Married Walk in a Hot Place, A.
Martha as the Angel Gabriel.
Meditation in My Favorite Position.
Meetings Like Hungry Beaks.
Morning Athletes.
Morning Half-Life Blues, The.
Neighbor, The.
Never-Never.
Night Flight.
Night Letter.
Nine of Cups, The.
Noon of the Sunbather.
Nuisance, The.
On Castle Hill.
Peaceable Kingdom, The.
Perpetual Migration, The.
Phyllis Wounded.
Poet Dreams of a Nice Warm Motel, The.
Postcard from the Garden.
Proposal for Recycling Wastes, A.
Provocation of the Dream, The.
Queen of Pentacles, The.
Rainy 4th.
Rape Poem.
Right Thinking Man.
Right to Life.
Road Behind the Last Dune, The.
Root Canal, The.
Rough Times.
S. Dead.
Sabbath of Mutual Respect, The.
Sand Roads *sels*.
Secretary Chant, The.
Seedlings in the Mail.
September Afternoon at Four O'Clock.
Seven of Pentacles, The.
Shadow Play For Guilt, A.
Shadows of the Burning.
Sign.
Simple-Song.
Skimpy Day at the Solstice.
Skyscrapers of the Financial District Dance with Gasman, The.
Smalley Bar.
Snow in May.
Snow, Snow.
Sojourners.
Some Collisions Bring Luck.
Somehow.
Song of the Fucked Duck.
Spring Offensive of the Snail, The.
Sun, The.
Three of Cups, The.
Thrifty Lover, The.
To Be of Use.
To the Pay Toilet.
Tower Struck by Lightning Reversed; the Overturning of the Tower, The.
Track of the Master Builder, The.
Trajectory of the Traveling Susan.
Twelve-Spoked Wheel Flashing, The.
Unclench Yourself.

Under the Grind.
Unlearning to Not Speak.
Valley Where I Don't Belong, A.
Visiting a Dead Man on a Summer Day.
Walking into Love.
We Become New.
What Feeling Is This?
What the Owl Sees.
What You Waited For.
What's That Smell in the Kitchen?
Why the Soup Tastes Like the *Daily News*.
Wind is the Wall of the Year.
Window of the Woman Burning, The.
Woman in the Ordinary, The.
Women's Laughter.
Words Are Said, the Love Is Made, The.
Work of Artifice, A.
You Ask Why Sometimes I Say Stop.

Plath, Sylvia (1932–63)
Above the Oxbow.
Admonitions.
Aerialist.
Aftermath.
Alicante Lullaby.
All the Dead Dears.
Amnesiac.
Among the Narcissi.
Appearance, An.
Applicant, The.
Apprehensions.
April Aubade.
April 18.
Aquatic Nocturne.
Ariel.
Arrival of the Bee Box, The.
Babysitters, The.
Balloons.
Barren Woman.
Battle-Scene.
Bee Meeting, The.
Beekeeper's Daughter, The.
Beggars, The.
Berck-Plage.
Birthday Present, A.
Bitter Strawberries.
Black Pine Tree in an Orange Light.
Black Rook in Rainy Weather.
Blackberrying.
Blue Moles.
Bluebeard.
Brasilia.
Bucolics.
Bull of Bendylaw, The.
Burning the Letters.
Burnt-Out Spa, The.
By Candlelight.
Candles.
Channel Crossing.
Child.
Childless Woman.
Child's Park Stones.
Cinderella.
Circus in Three Rings.
Colossus, The.
Companionable Ills, The.
Contusion.
Conversation among the Ruins.
Courage of Shutting-Up, The.
Couriers, The.
Crossing the Water.
Crystal Gazer.
Cut.
Daddy.
Danse Macabre.
Dark Wood, Dark Water.
Dead, The.
Death & Co.
Death of Myth-making, The.
Denouement.
Departure.
Detective, The.
Dialogue between Ghost and Priest.
Dialogue *En Route*.
Dirge for a Joker.
Dispossessed, The.
Disquieting Muses, The.
Doom of Exiles.

Doomsday.
Dream, The.
Dream with Clam-Diggers.
Eavesdropper.
Edge.
Electra on Azalea Path.
Ella Mason and Her Eleven Cats.
Elm.
Epitaph for Fire and Flower.
Epitaph in Three Parts.
Event.
Everlasting Monday, The.
Eye-Mote, The.
Fable of the Rhododendron Stealers.
Face Lift.
Family Reunion.
Faun.
Fearful, The.
Female Author.
Fever 103°.
Fiesta Melons.
Finisterre.
Firesong.
For a Fatherless Son.
Frog Autumn.
Full Fathom Five.
Getting There.
Ghost's Leavetaking, The.
Gigolo.
Glutton, The.
Go Get the Goodly Squab.
Goatsucker.
Gold Mouths Cry.
Goring, The.
Great Carbuncle, The.
Green Rock, Winthrop Bay.
Gulliver.
Hanging Man, The.
Hardcastle Crags.
Heavy Women.
Hermit at Outermost House, The.
I Am Vertical.
I Want, I Want.
In Midas' Country.
In Plaster.
Incommunicado.
Insolent Storm Strikes at the Skull.
Insomniac.
Jailer, The.
Jilted.
Kindness.
Lady and the Earthenware Head, The.
Lady Lazarus.
Lament: "Sting of bees took away my father, The."
Landowners.
Last Words.
Leaving Early.
Lesbos.
Lesson in Vengeance, A.
Letter in November.
Letter to a Purist.
Life, A.
Little Fugue.
Lorelei.
Love Is a Parallax.
Love Letter.
Lyonnesse.
Magi.
Magnolia Shoals.
Man in Black.
Manor Garden, The.
Mary's Song.
Maudlin.
Mayflower.
Medallion.
Medusa.
Memoirs of a Spinach-Picker.
Metamorphoses of the Moon.
Metaphors.
Midsummer Mobile.
Mirror.
Miss Drake Proceeds to Supper.
Monologue at 3 A.M.
Moon and the Yew Tree, The.
Moonrise.
Moonsong at Morning.

Morning in the Hospital Solarium.
Morning Song.
Munich Mannequins, The.
Mushrooms.
Mussel Hunter at Rock Harbor.
Mystic.
Natural History.
Net-Menders, The.
Never Try to Trick Me with a Kiss.
New Year on Dartmoor.
Nick and the Candlestick.
Night Dances, The.
Night Shift.
Notes to a Neophyte.
November Graveyard.
Ode for Ted.
Old Ladies' Home.
On Deck.
On Looking into the Eyes of a Demon Lover.
On the Decline of Oracles.
On the Difficulty of Conjuring Up a Dryad.
On the Plethora of Dryads.
Other, The.
Other Two, The.
Ouija.
Owl.
Paralytic.
Parliament Hill Fields.
Perseus.
Pheasant.
Poem for a Birthday.
Poems, Potatoes.
Point Shirley.
Polly's Tree.
Poppies in July.
Poppies in October.
Princess and the Goblins, The.
Private Ground.
Prologue to Spring.
Prospect.
Purdah.
Pursuit.
Queen's Complaint, The.
Rabbit Catcher, The.
Ravaged Face, The.
Recantation.
Resolve.
Rhyme.
Rival, The.
Sculptor.
Secret, A.
Sheep in Fog.
Shrike, The.
Sleep in the Mojave Desert.
Sleepers, The.
Snakecharmer.
Snowman on the Moor, The.
Soliloquy of the Solipsist.
Song for a Revolutionary Love.
Song for a Summer's Day.
Sonnet: To Eva.
Sonnet to Satan.
Sonnet: To Time.
Sorcerer Bids Farewell to Seem, A.
Southern Sunrise.
Sow.
Spider.
Spinster.
Stars over the Dordogne.
Stillborn.
Stings.
Stopped Dead.
Street Song.
Strumpet Song.
Suicide off Egg Rock.
Surgeon at 2 A.M., The.
Swarm, The.
Tale of a Tub.
Temper of Time.
Terminal.
Thalidomide.
Thin People, The.
Three Women.
Times Are Tidy, The.
Tinker Jack and the Tidy Wives.
To a Jilted Lover.

To Eva Descending the Stair.
Totem.
Touch-and-Go.
Tour, The.
Trial of Man, The.
Trio of Love Songs.
Tulips.
Two Campers in Cloud Country.
Two Lovers and a Beachcomber by the Real Sea.
Two Sisters of Persephone.
Two Views of a Cadaver Room.
Two Views of Withens.
Vanity Fair.
Virgin in a Tree.
Waking in Winter.
Watercolor of Grantchester Meadows.
Whiteness I Remember.
Whitsun.
Widow.
Winter Landscape, with Rooks.
Winter Ship, A.
Winter Trees.
Wintering.
Winter's Tale, A.
Words.
Words for a Nursery.
Words Heard, by Accident, over the Phone.
Wreath for a Bridal.
Wuthering Heights.
Yaddo: The Grand Manor.
Yadwigha, on a Red Couch, among Lilies.
Years.
You're.
Zoo Keeper's Wife.

Poe, Edgar Allan (1809–49)
Al Aaraaf.
Annabel Lee.
Bells, The.
Bridal Ballad.
City in the Sea, The.
Coliseum, The.
Conqueror Worm, The.
Dream, A.
Dream-Land [or Dreamland].
Dream within a Dream, A.
Dreams.
Eldorado.
Enigma, An.
Eulalie—A Song.
Evening Star.
Fairyland [or Fairy-Land].
For Annie.
Happiest Day, the Happiest Hour, The.
Haunted Palace, The.
Hymn: "At morn—at noon—at twilight dim."
Israfel.
Lake: To———, The.
Lenore.
Raven, The.
Romance.
Scenes from Politian.
Sleeper, The.
Song: "Neath blue-bell or streamer."
Song: "Young flowers were whispering in melody."
Sonnet—Silence.
Sonnet—To Science.
Spirits of the Dead.
Stanzas: "How often we forget all time, when lone."
Tamerlane.
To———: "Bowers whereat, in dreams, I see, The."
To———: "I heed not that my earthly lot."
To———: "I saw thee on thy bridal day."
To———: "Not long ago, the writer of these lines."
To F———.
To F—S S. O—D.
To Helen ("Helen, thy beauty is to me").
To Helen ("I saw thee once—once only—years ago").
To M. L. S———.
To My Mother.
To One in Paradise.
To the River—.

Ulalume [or Ulalume—a Ballad].
Valentine, A.
Valley of Unrest, The.
Translations, Coauthored Poems, etc.:
Sonnet to Zante.

Pope, Alexander (1688–1744)
Alley, The.
Another [Epigram].
Answer to the Following Question of Mrs. Howe.
Apologia pro Vita Sua.
Argus.
Art of Poetry, The.
Artemisia.
Atticus ("How did they fume, and stamp, and roar, and chafe").
Atticus ("Peace to all such! but were there one whose fires").
Autumn, the Third Pastoral, or Hylas and Ægon.
Balance of Europe, The.
Bookful Blockhead, The.
Bufo.
Carnations and Butterflies.
Certain Type of Scientist Speaks, A.
Challenge: A Court Ballad, The.
Character of Marlborough, A.
Chorus of Athenians.
Chorus of Youths and Virgins.
Coxcomb Bird, The.
Descend, Ye Nine.
Dialogue, A.
Duke of Buckingham, The.
Dunciad, The.
Elegy to the Memory of an Unfortunate Lady.
Eloisa.
Eloisa to Abelard.
Epigram: "My Lord complains, that Pope, stark mad with gardens."
Epigram on the Toasts of the Kit-Cat Club, Anno 1716.
Epigram: "Peter complains, that God has given."
Epigram: "When other Ladies to the Groves go down."
Epigram from the French: "Sir, I admit your general [or gen'ral] Rule."
Epigram in a Maid of Honour's Prayer-Book.
Epigrams Occasion'd by an Invitation to Court.
Epigrams Occasioned by Cibber's Verses in Praise of Nash.
Epilogue to Mr. Rowe's *Jane Shore*.
Epilogue to the Satires, in Two Dialogues.
Epistle I, to Sir Richard Temple, Lord Cobham.
Epistle II, to a Lady: Of the Characters of Women.
Epistle III, to Allen Lord Bathurst.
Epistle IV, to Richard Boyle, Earl of Burlington.
Epistle V, to Mr. Addison.
Epistle to Dr. Arbuthnot.
Epistle to James Craggs, Esq., Secretary of State.
Epistle to Miss [or Miss Teresa] Blount, on Her Leaving the Town after the Coronation.
Epistle to Miss Blount, with the Works of Voiture.
Epistle to Mr. Jervas, with Dryden's Translation of Fresnoy's *Art of Painting*.
Epistle to Robert Earl of Oxford and Earl Mortimer.
Epitaph: "Well then, poor G——— lies under ground!"
Epitaph for One Who Would Not Be Buried in Westminster Abbey ("Heroes, and Kings! your distance keep").
Epitaph for One Who Would Not Be Buried in Westminster Abbey ("Under this Marble, or under this Sill").
Epitaph Intended for Mr. Rowe, in Westminster Abbey.
Epitaph Intended for Sir Isaac Newton, in Westminster Abbey.

Epitaph (of By-Words).
Epitaph on Charles Earl of Dorset. *see also* Epitaph on the Count of Mirandula.
Epitaph on Dr. Francis Atterbury, Bishop of Rochester, Who Died in Exile at Paris, 1732; a Dialogue.
Epitaph on Edmund Duke of Buckingham, Who Died in the Nineteenth Year of His Age, 1735.
Epitaph on General Henry Withers, in Westminster-Abbey, 1729.
Epitaph on James Craggs, Esq., in Westminster Abbey.
Epitaph on John Knight, Who Died Oct. 2, 1733.
Epitaph on Mr. Elijah Fenton, at Easthamstead in Berks, 1730.
Epitaph on Mrs. Corbet, Who Died of a Cancer in Her Breast.
Epitaph on Sir Godfrey Kneller, in Westminster-Abbey, 1723.
Epitaph on Sir William Trumbal.
Epitaph on the Count of Mirandula.
Epitaph on the Hon. Simon Harcourt.
Epitaph on the Monument of the Honourable Robert Digby, and of his Sister Mary, erected by their Father the Lord Digby, in the Church of Sherborne in Dorsetshire, 1727.
Essay on Criticism, An.
Essay on Man, An.
Faith.
Farewell to London in the Year 1715, A.
First Epistle of the First Book of Horace Imitated, The.
First Epistle of the Second Book of Horace Imitated, The.
First Ode of the Fourth Book of Horace Imitated, The.
First Satire of the Second Book of Horace [Imitated], The.
For Sir W. Trumbull.
Fragment of *Brutus*, an Epic.
Garden, The.
Ghosts of Beauty, The.
Happy Life of a Country Parson, The.
Hunt, The.
Ideals of Satire, The.
Impromptu to Lady Winchelsea.
Lamentation of Glumdalclitch for the Loss of Grildrig, The.
Life's Poor Play.
Lines on a Drawing of a Monument to Swift's Grandfather.
Macer: A Character.
Messiah [a Sacred Eclogue, in Imitation of Virgil's Pollio].
Occasioned by Some Verses of His Grace the Duke of Buckingham.
Ode: The Dying Christian to His Soul.
Ode for Music on St. Cecilia's Day.
Ode on Solitude.
Of a Lady Singing to Her Lute.
Of Her Picture.
Of Her Sickness.
Of Her Sighing.
Of Her Walking in a Garden after a Shower.
Of the Lady Who Could Not Sleep in a Stormy Night.
On a Certain Lady at Court.
On a Fan of the Author's Design, in Which Was Painted the Story of CEPHALUS and PROCRIS, with the Motto, AURA VENI.
On a Lady Who P-ssed [or P———st] at the Tragedy of Cato.
On His Grotto at Twickenham.
On Lady Mary Wortley Montagu's Portrait.
On Mr. Gay, in Westminster Abbey, 1732.
On Receiving from the Right Hon. the Lady Frances Shirley a Standish and Two Pens.
On Silence.
On the Countess of Burlington Cutting Paper.
Paraphrase on Thomas à Kempis, A.
Part of the Ninth Ode of Horace Imitated.
Pastorals.
Phryne.

Plain Fools.
Playing Cards, The.
Pleasure of Hope, The.
Presentation Verses to Nathaniel Pigott.
Presenting a *Lark*.
Progress.
Prologue Design'd for Mr. Durfy's Last Play.
Prologue to a Play for Mr. Dennis's Benefit, in 1733, when He Was Old, Blind, and in Great Distress, a Little before His Death, A.
Prologue to Mr. Addison's *Tragedy of Cato*.
Prologue to the *Three Hours after Marriage*.
Question of Libel, A.
Rape of the Lock[, an Heroi-Comical Poem], The.
Reign of Chaos, The.
Rise, Crowned with Light Imperial Salem Rise.
River, The.
Sandys's Ghost, or a Proper New Ballad on the New Ovid's Metamorphosis as it Was Intended to Be.
Sappho to Phaon.
Satire II of Dr. John Donne, Versified.
Satire IV of Dr. John Donne, Versified.
Second Epistle of the Second Book of Horace Imitated, The.
Second Satire of the First Book of Horace Imitated, The.
Second Satire of the Second Book of Horace Imitated, The.
Servile Herd, The.
Seventh Epistle of the First Book of Horace Imitated, The.
Six Maidens, The.
Sixth Epistle of the First Book of Horace Imitated, The.
Sixth Satire of the Second Book of Horace Imitated, The.
Soul's Calm Sunshine, The.
Spring, the First Pastoral, or Damon.
Summer, The Second Pastoral, or Alexis.
Sylvan Delights.
Temple of Fame, The.
Three Gentle Shepherds, The.
To a Lady.
To a Lady with the Temple of Fame.
To Belinda on the Rape of the Lock.
To Dr. Jonathan Swift.
To Eustace Budgell, Esq., on His Translation of the Characters of Theophrastus.
To Mr. Gay, Congratulating Pope on Finishing His House and Gardens.
To Mr. John Moore, Author of the Celebrated Worm-Powder.
To Mr. Thomas Southern, on His Birth-Day, 1742.
To Mrs. M. B. on Her Birth-Day.
To Quinbus Flestrin the Man-Mountain, a Lilliputian Ode.
To Sir Godfrey Kneller, on His Painting for Me the Statues of Apollo, Venus and Hercules.
To the Earl of Burlington Asking Who Writ the Libels against Him.
Translator, The.
Triumph of Dullness, The.
Two Chorus's to the Tragedy of Brutus.
Two or Three, or a Receipt to Make a Cuckold.
Umbra.
Universal Prayer [Deo Opt. Max.], The.
Verbatim from Boileau.
Verses Left by Mr. Pope, on His Lying in the Same Bed which Wilmot, the Celebrated Earl of Rochester, Slept in, at Adderbury, then Belonging to the Duke of Argyle, July 9th, 1739.
Verses Occasioned by an &c. at the End of Mr. D'Urfy's Name in the Title to One of His Plays.
Verses to Be Placed under the Picture of England's Arch-Poet: Containing a Compleat Catalogue of His Works.
Verses to be Prefix'd before Bernard Lintot's New Miscellany.

Version of the First Psalm, for the Use of a Young Lady, A.
Vestal, The.
Weeping.
Wild Garden, The.
Windsor-Forest [*or* Windsor Forest].
Winter, the Fourth Pastoral, or Daphne.
Women ben full of ragerie.
Young Traveller Is Presented to the Goddess Dulness, A.
Translations, Coauthored Poems, etc.:
Canterbury Tales, The *sels.*
Consolation of Philosophy, The ("De Consolacione Philosophie") *sels.*
Episode of Sarpedon, The.
Fable of Dryope, The.
Fraternal Rage, the guilty Thebes alarms.
Gardens of Alcinous, The.
He who beneath thy shelt'ring wing resides.
Iliad, The *sels.*
January and May, or the Merchant's Tale.
Mary Gulliver to Capt. Lemuel Gulliver.
Metamorphoses *sels.*
O thou, whose all-creating hands sustain.
Odyssey, The *sels.*
On the Statue of *Cleopatra*, Made into a Fountain by *Leo* the Tenth.
Psalms *sels.*
Stanzas: "At length, my soul! thy fruitless hopes give o'er."
Sun descending, see the *Phœacian* train, The.
Thebais *sels.*
Translation of a Hymn of St. Francis Xavier.
Vertumnus and Pomona.
Wife of Bath, The.

Pound, Ezra (1885–1972)
Addendum for C ("Evil is Usury, *neschek*, The.")
Addendum for C ("Now sun rises in Ram sign.")
Age Demanded, The.
Alba ("As cool as the pale wet leaves").
Alba ("When the nightingale to his mate").
All at Sea.
Amitites.
Apparuit.
April.
Arides.
As he was standing below the altars.
Autumn leaves blow from my hand.
Ballad of the Goodly Fere.
Beautiful Toilet, The.
Blandula, Tenella, Vagula.
Brennbaum.
Canto 1: "And then went down to the ship."
Canto 2: "Hang it all, Robert Browning."
Canto 3: "I sat on the Dogana's steps."
Canto 4: "Palace in smoky light."
Canto 5: "Great bulk, huge mass, thesaurus."
Canto 6: "What you have done, Odysseus."
Canto 7: "Eleanor (she spoiled in a British climate)."
Canto 8: "These fragments you have shelved (shored)."
Canto 9: "One year floods rose."
Canto 10: "And the poor devils dying of cold, outside Sorano."
Canto 11: "Egradment li antichi cavaler romanj."
Canto 12: "And we sit here / under the wall."
Canto 13: "Kung walked / by the dynastic temple."
Canto 14: "Io venni luogo d'ogni luce muto."
Canto 14: "Slough of unamiable liars, The."
Canto 15: "Saccharescent, lying in glucose, The."
Canto 16: "And before hell mouth; dry plain."
Canto 17: "So that the vines burst from my fingers."
Canto 18: "And of Kublai: / 'I have told you of that emperor's city in detail'."
Canto 19: "Sabotage? Yes, he took it up to Manhattan."
Canto 20: "And from the floating bodies, the incense."

Canto 20: "Sound slender, quasi tinnula."
Canto 21: " 'Keep the peace, Borso!' Where are we?"
Canto 22: "An' that man sweat blood."
Canto 23: " 'Et omniformis,' Psellos, 'omnis' ."
Canto 24: "Thus the book of the mandates."
Canto 25: "Because of the stink of the dungeons: 1344."
Canto 25: "Book of the council major."
Canto 26: "And / I came here in my young youth."
Canto 27: "Formando di disio nuova persona."
Canto 28: "And God the Father Eternal (Boja d'un Dio!)."
Canto 29: "Pearl, great sphere, and hollow."
Canto 30: "Compleynt, compleynt I hearde upon a day."
Canto 31: "Tempus loquendi, tempus tacendi."
Canto 32: " 'Revolution,' said Mr. Adams, The."
Canto 33: "Is that despotism."
Canto 34: "Oils, beasts, grasses, petrifactions, birds, incrustations."
Canto 35: "So this is (may we take it) Mitteleuropa."
Canto 36: "Lady asks me, A / I speak in season."
Canto 37: " 'Thou shalt not covet,' said Martin Van Buren, 'jail 'em for debt' ."
Canto 38: "An' that year Metevsky went over to America del Sud."
Canto 39: "Desolate is the room where the cat sat."
Canto 40: "Esprit de corps in permanent bodies."
Canto 41: " 'Ma questo,' / said the Boss, 'è divertente' ."
Canto 42: "We ought, I think, to say in civil terms: You be damned."
Canto 43: "To the serenissimo Dno (pronounced Domino)."
Canto 44: "And thou shalt not, Firenze 1766, and thou shalt not."
Canto 45: "With Usura."
Canto 46: "And if you will say that this tale teaches.."
Canto 47: "Who even dead, yet hath his mind entire!"
Canto 48: "And if the money be rented?"
Canto 49: "For the seven lakes, and by no man these verses."
Canto 50: " 'Revolution' said Mr Adams 'took place in the' ."
Canto 51: "Shines / in the mind of heaven God [*or* heaven God]."
Canto 52: "And I have told you of how things were under Duke Leopold in Siena."
Canto 53: "Yeou taught men to break branches."
Canto 54: "So that Tien-tan chose bulls, a thousand."
Canto 55: "Orbem bellis, urbem gabellis."
Canto 56: "Billets, biglietti, as coin was too heavy for transport."
Cant 57: "And when KIEN OUEN was throned."
Canto 58: "Sinbu put order in Sun land, Nippon, in the beginning of all things."
Canto 59: "De libro CHI-KING sic censeo."
Canto 60: "So the Jesuits brought in astronomy."
Canto 61: "YONG TCHING / his fourth son, to honour his forebears."
Canto 62: "Acquit of evil intention."
Canto 63: "Towards sending of Ellsworth."
Canto 64: "To John's bro, the sheriff, we lay a kind word in passing."
Canto 65: "Jurors refuse to take oath."
Canto 66: "Could not let us bring their sugar to Europe."
Canto 67: "Whereof memory of man runneth not to the contrary."
Canto 68: "Philosophers say, The: one, the few, the many."

Canto 69: "In which case a minister here from Congress wd / be useful."
Canto 70: "My situation almost the only one in the world."
Canto 71: "German ambassador once told me he cdn't bear St Paul, A."
Canto 72: "Purché si cominci a ricordare la guerra di merda."
Canto 73: "E poi dormii."
Canto 74: "Enormous tragedy of the dream in the peasant's bent shoulders, The."
Canto 75: "Out of Phlegethon!"
Canto 76: "And the sun high over horizon hidden in cloud bank."
Canto 77: "And this day Abner lifted a shovel."
Canto 78: "By the square elm of Ida."
Canto 79: "Moon, cloud, tower, a patch of the battistero all of a whiteness."
Canto 80: "Ain' committed no federal crime."
Canto 81: "Zeus lies in Ceres' bosom."
Canto 82: "When with his hunting dog I see a cloud."
Canto 83: "Hudor / HUDOR et Pax."
Canto 84: "8th October: / Si tuit li dolh elh plor."
Canto 85: "LING / Our dynasty came in because of a great sensibility."
Canto 86: "WITH solicitude / that mirrored turbationem."
Canto 87: "Between the usurer and any man who / wants to do a good job."
Canto 88: "It was Saturday the 1st day of April, toward noon."
Canto 89: "To know the histories / to know good from evil."
Canto 90: "From the colour the nature."
Canto 91: "Ab lo dolchor qu'al cor mi vai."
Canto 92: "And from this Mount were blown / seed."
Canto 93: "A man's paradise is his good nature."
Canto 94: " 'Brederode' / (to Rush, Ap 4. 1790)."
Canto 95: "LOVE, gone as lightning."
Canto 96: "Kredemon .. / kredemon .. / and the wave concealed her."
Canto 97: "Melik & Edward struck coins-with-a-sword."
Canto 98: "Boat of Ra-Set moves with the sun, The."
Canto 99: "Till the blue grass turn yellow."
Canto 100: "Has packed the Supreme Court."
Canto 101: "Finding scarcely anyone save Monsieur de Rémusat."
Canto 102: "This I had from Kalupso."
Canto 103: "1850: gt objection to any honesty in the White House."
Canto 104: "Na Khi talk made out of wind noise."
Canto 105: "Feb. 1956 / Is this a divagation."
Canto 106: "And was her daughter like that."
Canto 107: "Azalea is grown while we sleep, The."
Canto 108: "COMMINUIT / there is frost on the rock's face."
Canto 109: "Pro Veritate.. / curtiliagia teneant."
Canto 110: "Thy quiet house / The crozier's curve runs in the wall."
Canto 111, Notes for: "I, one thing, as relation to one thing."
Canto 112, From: "Owl, and wagtail / and huo-hu, the fire-fox."
Canto 113: "Thru the 12 Houses of Heaven."
Canto 114: "Pas même Fréron / hais personne / pas même Fréron."
Canto 115, From: "Scientists are in terror, The."
Canto 116: "Came Neptunus / his mind leaping / like dolphins."
Canto 117 et seq., Notes for: "For the blue flash and the moments / benedetta."
Cantos sels.
Cantos.
Cino.

Coda.
Coitus.
Coming of War, The; Actaeon.
Contemporania sels.
Dance Figure.
Difference of Opinion with Lygdamus.
Doria.
Encounter, The.
Envoi (1919).
Epitaphs: "Fu I loved the high cloud and the hill."
Erat Hora.
Fragment (1966): "That her acts / Olga's acts / of beauty."
From CXV: "Scientists are in terror, The."
From CXII: "Owl, and wagtail / and huo-hu, the fire-fox."
Garden, The.
Garret, The.
Homage to Sextus Propertius.
House of Splendour, The.
Hugh Selwyn Mauberley. (Life and Contacts).
Imerro.
In a Station of the Metro.
Ité.
Lake Isle, The.
Langue d'Oc sels.
L'ara sul rostro / 20 years of the dream.
Les Millwin.
Lustra sels.
Mauberly (1920).
Meditatio.
Moon has a swollen cheek, The.
Mr. Nixon.
Na Audiart.
Nancy where art thou?
Near Perigord.
Notes for CXI: "I, one thing, as relation to one thing."
Object, An.
Of Jacopo del Sellaio.
Pact, A.
Pagani's, November 8.
Planh for the Young English King.
Portrait d'une Femme.
Rest, The.
Return, The.
Salutation.
Salvationists.
Seafarer, The.
Sestina: Altaforte.
Siena Mi Fe'; Disfecemi Maremma.
Song of the Bowmen of Shu.
Song of the Degrees, A.
Spring, The.
Tame Cat.
Tea Shop, The.
Tenzone.
Tomb of Akr Caar, The.
Tree, The.
Villanelle: The Psychological Hour.
Villonaud for This Yule.
Virginal, A.
White Stag, The.
Yet / Ere the season died a-cold.
Yeux Glauques.
Translations, Coauthored Poems, etc.:
Exile's Letter.
Jewel Stairs' Grievance, The.
Lament of the Frontier Guard.
PHOEBUS, Phoebus, ere thou slay.
Poem by the Bridge at Ten-shin.
River Song, The.
Taking Leave of a Friend.
Women of Trachis sels.

Prince, Frank Templeton (b. 1912)
Afterword on Rupert Brooke.
Apollo and the Sibyl.
At Beaulieu.
Autumn Journey.
Babiaantje, The.
Book, The.
Byron-Shelley Conversation, A.
Campanella.
Cefalù.
Chaka.
Chapel-at-Ease.

Coeur de Lion.
Creation Myth.
Diamond, The.
Dice, The.
Drypoints of the Hasidim.
Ecumenical Exchange, 1989.
Epistle to a Patron, An.
False Bay.
Family Mottoes.
Finis Coronat Opus.
For Fugitives.
For the Deserted.
For Thieves and Beggars.
Gregory Nazianzen.
Handfast Point.
He Bathes in the Morning.
He Compares Old Customs with Those of His Kingdom.
His Dog and Pilgrim.
How Festivals Were Celebrated.
In a Province.
In the Wood.
Inn, The.
Intention, The.
Keeper's Wood.
King watches at Night, The.
Last Attachment, A.
Last Poem.
Les Congés du Lépreux.
Letter.
Memoirs in Oxford.
Moonflower, The.
Mortimer.
Moult sont Prud'hommes les Templiers.
Not a Paris Review Interview.
Old Age of Michelangelo, The.
On a Cold Night.
On a Report That in Some Rest Homes Residents Who Are Depressed Will be Charged at a Higher Rate.
People Rest after Conquests, The.
Question, The.
Renouncing an Epigram.
Sea View.
Soldiers Bathing.
Stolen Heart, The.
Strafford.
Strambotti.
Tears of a Muse in America, The.
To a Friend on His Marriage.
To a Granddaughter on One of Her Suggestions for a Christmas Present.
To a Man on His Horse.
To My Sister.
Token, The.
Two Beggars: A Reminiscence.
Vivat.
Walks in Rome.
Watching Song.
Wind in the Tree, The.
Words from Edmund Burke.
Youth and Age.
Yüan Chên Variations.

Psalms, The Book of (Bible O.T.)
Psalm 1: "Blessed is the man that walketh.."
Psalm 2: "Why do the heathen rage."
Psalm 3: "Lord, how are the increased.."
Psalm 4: "Hear me when I call, O God of my righteousness."
Psalm 5: "Give ear to my words, O Lord, consider my meditation."
Psalm 6: "O Lord, rebuke me not in thine anger."
Psalm 7: "O Lord my God, in thee do I put my trust."
Psalm 8: "O Lord our Lord, how excellent.."
Psalm 9: "I will praise thee, O Lord.."
Psalm 10: "Why standest thou afar off, O Lord?"
Psalm 11: "In the name of the Lord.."
Psalm 12: "Help, Lord; for the godly man ceaseth."
Psalm 13: "How long wilt thou forget me, O Lord?"
Psalm 14: "Fool hath said in his heart, The.."
Psalm 15: "Lord, who shall abide in thy tabernacle?"

Psalm 16: "Preserve me, O God: for in thee do I put my trust."
Psalm 17: "Hear the right, O Lord.."
Psalm 18: "I will love thee, O Lord, my strength."
Psalm 19: "Heavens declare the glory of God, The."
Psalm 20: "Lord hear thee in the day of trouble, The."
Psalm 21: "King shall rejoice in thy strength, O Lord, The."
Psalm 22: "My God, my God, why hast thou forsaken me?"
Psalm 23: "Lord is my shepherd, I shall not want, The."
Psalm 24: "Earth is the Lord's and the fulness thereof, The."
Psalm 25: "Unto thee, O Lord, do I lift up my soul."
Psalm 26: "Judge me, O Lord; for I have walked in mine integrity."
Psalm 27: "Lord is my light and my salvation, The.."
Psalm 28: "Unto thee will I cry, O Lord my rock."
Psalm 29: "Give unto the Lord, O ye mighty."
Psalm 30: "I will extol thee, O Lord; for thou hast lifted me up."
Psalm 31: "In thee, O Lord, do I put my trust. . . ."
Psalm 32: "Blessed is he whose transgression is forgiven, whose sin is covered."
Psalm 33: "Rejoice in the Lord, O ye righteous.."
Psalm 34: "I will bless the Lord at all times."
Psalm 35: "Plead my cause, O Lord, with them that strive with me."
Psalm 36: "Transgression of the wicked.."
Psalm 37: "Fret not thyself because of evildoers."
Psalm 38: "O Lord, rebuke me not in thy wrath."
Psalm 39: "I said, I will take heed to my ways."
Psalm 40: "I waited patiently for the Lord."
Psalm 41: "Blessed is he that considereth the poor."
Psalm 42: "As the hart panteth after the water brooks."
Psalm 43: "Judge me, O God.."
Psalm 44: "We have heard with our ears, O God."
Psalm 45: "My heart is inditing a good matter."
Psalm 46: "God is our refuge and strength.."
Psalm 47: "O clap your hands, all ye people."
Psalm 48: "Great is the Lord.."
Psalm 49: "Hear this, all ye people.."
Psalm 50: "Mighty God, even the Lord, hath spoken, The."
Psalm 51: "Have mercy upon me, O God.."
Psalm 52: "Why boastest thou thyself in mischief.."
Psalm 53: "Fool hath said in his heart, The. . . ."
Psalm 54: "Save me, O God, by thy name. . . ."
Psalm 55: "Give ear to my prayer, O God."
Psalm 56: "Be merciful unto me. . . ."
Psalm 57: "Be merciful unto me, O God. . . ."
Psalm 58: "Do ye indeed speak righteousness, O congregation?"
Psalm 59: "Deliver me from mine enemies, O my God."
Psalm 60: "O God, thou hast cast us off. . . ."
Psalm 61: "Hear my cry, O God.."
Psalm 62: "Truly my soul waiteth upon God."
Psalm 63: "O God, thou art my God.."
Psalm 64: "Hear my voice, O God, in my prayer."

Psalm 65: "Praise waiteth for thee, O God, in Sion."
Psalm 66: "Make a joyful unto God, all ye lands."
Psalm 67: "God be merciful unto us, and bless us."
Psalm 68: "Let God arise, let his enemies be scattered."
Psalm 69: "Save me, O God.."
Psalm 70: "Make haste, O God, to deliver me."
Psalm 71: "In thee, O Lord, do I put my trust.."
Psalm 72: "Give the king thy judgments, O God."
Psalm 73: "Truly God is good to Israel, even to such as are of a clean heart."
Psalm 74: "O God, why hast thou cast us off for ever?"
Psalm 75: "Unto thee, O God, do we give thanks."
Psalm 76: "In Judah is God known.."
Psalm 77: "I cried unto God with my voice.."
Psalm 78: "Give ear, O my people, to my law."
Psalm 79: "O God, the heathen are come.."
Psalm 80: "Give ear, O Shepherd of Israel.."
Psalm 81: "Sing aloud unto God our strength."
Psalm 82: "God standeth in the congregation of the mighty."
Psalm 83: "Keep not thou silence, O God."
Psalm 84: "How amiable are thy tabernacles, O Lord of hosts!"
Psalm 85: "Lord, thou hast been favourable unto thy land."
Psalm 86: "Bow down thine ear, O Lord, hear me."
Psalm 87: "His foundation is in the holy mountains."
Psalm 88: "O God of my salvation."
Psalm 89: "I will sing of the mercies of the Lord for ever."
Psalm 90: "Lord, thou hast been our dwelling place in all generations."
Psalm 91: "He that dwelleth in the secret place.."
Psalm 92: "It is a good thing to give thanks unto the Lord."
Psalm 93: "Lord reigneth, The.."
Psalm 94: "O Lord God, to whom vengeance belongeth."
Psalm 95: "O come, let us sing unto the Lord."
Psalm 96: "O sing unto the Lord a new song."
Psalm 97: "Lord reigneth, let the earth rejoice, The."
Psalm 98: "O sing unto the Lord a new song.."
Psalm 100: "Make a joyful noise unto the Lord, all ye lands."
Psalm 101: "I will sing of mercy and judgment."
Psalm 102: "Hear my prayer, O Lord, and let my cry.." ["*Domine exaudi orationem meam*"].
Psalm 103: "Bless the Lord, O my soul.."
Psalm 104: "Bless the Lord, O my soul.."
Psalm 105: "O give thanks unto the Lord.."
Psalm 106: "Praise ye the Lord. O give thanks.."
Psalm 107: "O give thanks unto the Lord, for he is good: for.."
Psalm 108: "O God, my heart is fixed."
Psalm 109: "Hold not thy peace, O God of my praise."
Psalm 110: "Lord said unto my Lord, The."
Psalm 111: "Praise ye the Lord. I will praise.."
Psalm 112: "Praise ye the Lord. Blessed.."
Psalm 113: "Praise ye the Lord. Praise, O ye servants.."
Psalm 114: "When Israel went out of Egypt."
Psalm 115: "Not unto us, O Lord, not unto us."
Psalm 116: "I love the Lord.."

Psalm 117: "O praise ye the Lord, all ye nations."
Psalm 118: "O give thanks unto the Lord; for he is good: because.."
Psalm 119: "Blessed are the undefiled in the way."
Psalm 120: "In my distress I cried unto the Lord.."
Psalm 121: "I will lift up mine eyes unto the hills."
Psalm 122: "I was glad when they said unto me.."
Psalm 123: "Unto thee lift I up mine eyes.."
Psalm 124: "If it had not been the Lord who was on our side.."
Psalm 125: "They that trust in the Lord shall be as mount Zion.."
Psalm 126: "When the Lord turned again the captivity of Zion.."
Psalm 127: "Except the Lord build the house."
Psalm 128: "Blessed is every one that feareth the Lord."
Psalm 129: "Many a time have they afflicted me from my youth.."
Psalm 130: "Out of the depths have I cried unto thee, O Lord."
Psalm 131: "Lord, my heart is not haughty, nor mine eyes lofty."
Psalm 132: "Lord, remember David, and all his afflictions."
Psalm 133: "Behold, how good and how pleasant it is."
Psalm 134: "Behold, bless ye the Lord, all ye servants of the Lord."
Psalm 135: "Praise ye the Lord. Praise ye the name of the Lord; praise him, O ye servants of the Lord."
Psalm 136: "O give thanks unto the Lord.."
Psalm 137: "By the rivers of Babylon.."
Psalm 138: "I will praise thee with my whole heart."
Psalm 139: "O Lord, thou hast searched me, and known me."
Psalm 140: "Deliver me, O Lord, from the evil man."
Psalm 141: "Lord, I cry unto thee.."
Psalm 142: "I cried unto the Lord with my voice."
Psalm 143: "Hear my prayer, O Lord, give ear.."
Psalm 144: "Blessed be the Lord my strength."
Psalm 145: "I will extol thee, my God, O king."
Psalm 146: "Praise ye the Lord. Praise the Lord.."
Psalm 147: "Praise ye the Lord: for it is good.."
Psalm 148: "Praise ye the Lord. Praise ye the Lord from the heavens."
Psalm 149: "Praise ye the Lord. Sing unto the Lord a new song."
Psalm 150: "Praise ye the Lord. Praise God in his sanctuary."
Psalms.
Sparrow, The.

R

Raine, Kathleen Jessie (b. 1908)
Acacia Tree.
After Fifty-five Years.
Afternoon sunlight plays.
Ah, many, many are the dead.
All that is: / The unbroken surface of the sea.
All things new / But I: no shadow.
Amo Ergo Sum.
Ancient Speech, The.
And that was all his life.
Angelus.
April's new apple buds on an old lichened tree.
Bad Dream, A.
Banked winter cloud.

Behind the lids of sleep.
Bheinn Naomh.
Binah.
Blue butterflies' eyed wings.
Bright cloud, / Bringer of rain to far fields.
By the River Eden.
Campanula.
Canna's Basalt Crags.
Chartres Annunciation, The.
Childhood.
Childhood Memory.
Cloud.
Columbines.
Crossing the sound I summoned you in
    thought.
Daisies of Florence.
Dead, The.
Dear ones in the house of the dead.
Descent Into Hades.
Dream.
Dream-flowers.
Dream of Roses, A.
Dreams.
Eider afloat in the bay.
Eileann Chanaidh.
Elementals, The.
Eternal Child, The.
Eudaimon.
Exile.
Falling Leaves.
Fateless Ones, The.
Flower, memory—.
For the Visitors' Book.
Forest is multitude.
From vague regions of sleep I come again.
Frost-rime edges blades of grass.
Golden Flowers.
Golden Leaf, The.
Halt, The.
Harvest of learning I have reaped.
Heirloom.
Her Room.
Hieros Gamos.
High Summer.
Highland Graveyard.
Hollow Hill, The.
Holy Isles, The.
House of Music, A.
House, The.
Hyacinth, The.
I breathe the air you have breathed.
I could have told much by the way.
I felt, under my old breasts, this April day.
I went out in the naked light.
If I choose remorse.
If, into this evening as the grass receives the
    dew.
If you have ceased.
Images.
In the Beck.
Instrument, The.
Into what pattern, into what music have the
    spheres whirled us.
Iona.
Island Cross, The.
It is in us they burn.
I've read all the books but one.
Journey, The.
Kore.
Lachesis.
Last night I seemed in your embrace.
Leaf, The.
Letter to Pierre Emmanuel.
Lifelong ago such days.
Lindisfarne.
Loch, The.
London air dims.
Long ago I thought you young, bright
    daimon.
Man.
Marriage of Psyche, The.
Medea.
Message.
Message from Home.
Mirage, The.
Moment, The.
Monessie Gorge.

Moon golden towards the full.
My day's plan to write.
My Father's Birthday.
My feet in the ever-moving sea.
My Mother's Birthday.
My sight with the clouds'.
Nameless Islets.
Natura Naturans.
Night in Martindale.
Night Sky.
Night Thought.
Nocturne: "Night comes, an angel stands."
Old Paintings on Italian Walls.
On a Shell-strewn Beach.
On an Ancient Isle.
On its way I see.
On Leaving Ullswater.
Once I heard your voice.
Oracles.
Oval Portrait: Jessie Wilkie, The.
Oval the golden moon.
Painting by Winifred Nicholson, A.
Path, The.
Peace of Mind.
Petal of white rose.
Poet Answers the Accuser, The.
Poet is of those, The.
Polluted tide, / Desecrated earth destroyed.
Quenching the Red.
Rainbow, beautiful and clear light, A.
Return, The.
Returning from Church.
Ring, The.
Rock.
Rose.
Scala Coeli.
Self.
Seventh Day.
Shadow.
Shells.
Silver Stag, The.
Six calices yellow gold.
Soliloquy Upon Love.
Spell Against Sorrow.
Spell of Sleep.
Spell to Bring Lost Creatures Home.
Sphere, The.
Star, The.
Star of Bethlehem.
Statues.
Still skies, still seas.
Stone on High Crag.
Summit, The.
Sun.
Testimony.
There Shall Be No More Sea.
These watery diamond spheres.
This house / No smaller than the world.
Three Poems of Incarnation.
Three Poems on Illusion.
To the Sun.
Today: / This leafy apple-tree, gray.
Today as I / Looked up at the sky's great
    face.
Traveller, The.
Triad.
Turner's Seas.
Two Invocations of Death.
Under these hills too high and bare.
Unloved, The.
Vegetation.
Water.
Whales.
What does this day bestow?
What have I to regret.
What message from imagined Paradise.
When I woke up to the snow.
Who listens, when in the concert-hall.
Wilderness, The.
Wind.
Winds.
Winter Paradise.
Winter Solstice.
With a Wave of Her Old Hand.
Word Made Flesh.
World: / Image on water, waves.
World, The.

Young or old / What was I but a story told.
Your gift of life was idleness.

Ralegh, Sir Walter (1552?–1618)
Advice, The.
Ah wretched they that worship vanities.
Anaphora, or the Figure of Report.
Ancients called me Chaos: my great yeares.
Another of the Same.
Arcadians the earth inhabited, The.
Arte of English Poesie, The.
Authours Epitaph, Made by Himself, The.
Because that stealing immortalitie.
Calybes plough not their barren soile, The.
Commendatory Verses to Edmund Spenser's
    Fairy Queen sels.
Conjectural First Draft of the Petition to
    Queen Anne.
Cretians ever lyars were, they care not what
    they say, The.
Description of Love, A.
Diseases, famine, enemies, in us no change
    have wrought.
11th: and Last Booke of the Ocean to
    Scinthia, The.
End of the Boo[c]k[e]s, of the Ocean's Love
    to Cynthia [or Scinthia], and the
    Beginning[e] of the 12 [or 22] Boo[c]k,
    Entreating of Sorrow, The.
Epitaph on the Earl of Leicester [or
    Leceister].
Epitaph upon the Right Hono[u]rable Sir
    Philip Sidney Knight, Lord Governor of
    Flushing, An.
Epizeuxis, the Underlay, or Coocko-spel.
Even they that have no murdrous will.
Excuse, The.
Farewell to False Love, A.
Farewell to the Court.
Fayne Would I But I Dare Not.
First of all is God, and the same last is he,
    The.
From the Diary of John Manningham of the
    Middle Temple.
From the Earth, and from thy bloud, O
    heaven, they came.
From wisedome Fortune differs farre.
Giants did advance their wicked hand, The.
Have speciall care, that valiant povertie.
Heaven and Earth one forme did beare.
I have no wine of Gaza, nor Falerna wine.
I sacrifice to God the Beefe, which you
    adore.
If a Phoenincian born I am, what then?
If Croesus over Halys goe.
If Synthia Be a Queene, a Princes, and
    Supreame.
In the Grace of Wit, of Tongue and Face.
Lie, The.
Like to a Hermit[e] Poor[e].
My Body in the Walls Captived.
Nimphs [or Nymph's] Reply to the
    Sheepheard [or Shepherd], The.
Nine furlongs strecht lies Tityus, who for his
    wicked deedes.
No Pleasure, Without Some Payne.
Ocean's Love to Cynthia, The sels.
On the Card[e]s, and Dice.
On the Life of Man.
One fire than other burnes more forcibly.
Passionate Man[']s Pilgrimage, The.
Ploche, or the Doubler.
Poem of Sir Walter Rawleighs, A.
Poem Put into My Lady Laiton's Pocket by
    Sr W. Rawleigh, A.
Poesie to Prove Affection is Not Love, A.
Praisd Be Dianas Faire and Harmles Light.
Saturne to be the fatter is not knowne.
Shall I, Like an Hermit, Dwell.
Sir W. Ralegh, on the Snuff of a Candle the
    Night Before He Died.
Sir Walter Ralegh to the Queen.
Sir Walter Ralegh's [or S.W. Raghlies]
    Petition to the Queene 1618.
Sir Walter Ra[u]le[i]gh to His Son[ne].
Things thus agreed: Titan made Saturne
    sweare.

To the Translator of Lucan [*or* Lucan's Pharsalia, 1614].
Vision upon This Concei[p]t of the Faerie [*or* Faery] Queen[e], A.
Walter Rawley [*or* Ralegh *or* Rawely] of the Middle Temple, in Commendation of the Steel[e] Glass[e].
Yet though thou fetch thy pedegree so farre.
Translations, Coauthored Poems, etc.:
Aeneid [*or* Eneados, Aeneis], The *sels.*
Against Eutropius *sels.*
Amazons with Crescent-formed shield, The.
Amores *sels.*
As You Came from the Holy Land [of Walsingham].
Brasen tower [*or* Tower] with doors [*or* dores] close barred [*or* bar'd], The.
Bura and Helice on Achaian ground.
But Fortune governed all their works[,] till when.
3.16: "By gifts the Macedon clave Gates a-sunder."
Carmina *sels.*
De Rerum Natura (On the Nature of Things) *sels.*
East winde with Aurora hath abiding, The.
Egyptians [*or* Aegyptians] think[e] it sin[ne] to root[e] up, or to bite.
Epitaph on the Earl of Salisbury.
From thence our kinde hard-hearted is, enduring paine and care.
Gainst Fate no counsell can prevaile.
Heaven, the earth, and all the liquid mayne, The.
Here Tantalus in water seek[e]s for water, and doth miss[e].
Heroides *sels.*
Hesperia the Gr[a]ecians call the place.
Hortatory Address to the Greeks *sels.*
I am that Dido which thou here do'st see.
If all this world had no original[l].
In the main[e] sea the i[s]le of Cre[e]te doth lie.
Joyfull Spring did ever last, The.
4.9: "Many by valour have deserved renown."
Metamorphoses *sels.*
Mindes of men are ever so affected, The.
Moist[e]ned Osyer [*or* osier] of the hoarie Willow, The.
More holy than the rest, and understanding more.
No man was better, nor more just than hee.
3.24: "Nor Southerne heat nor Northerne snow."
O wastfull Riot, never well content.
Odes *sels.*
Odyssey *sels.*
Over the Medes and light Sabaeans reigns [*or* raignes].
Pharsalia *sels.*
Phoenicians first (if Fame may credit have).
Plants and trees made poore and old, The.
Prometheus Bound *sels.*
Queene anone commands the waightie bowle, The.
Satires *sels.*
3.2: "Seldome the villaine, though much hast he make."
Shall I, Like an Hermit, Dwell.
Some old Auruncans, I remember well.
Songe Made by Sir Walter Rawley, A.
Strong Ilion thou shalt see with walls and towers high.
4.2: "Such as like heavenly wights doe come."
Sunne may set and rise, The.
Then marking this my sacred speech, but truly lend.
There is a Land which Greekes Hesperia name.
2.13: "Thirsting Tantalus doth catch at stream[e]s that from him flee, The."
To his Singular Friend, William Lithgow.
Tristium *sels.*
Vertue the Best Monument.

3.4: "Who rules the duller earth, the wind-swolne streames."
World discernes it selfe, while I the world behold, The.

"Ramal, Walter" *see* De la Mare, Walter
Ransom, John Crowe (1888–1974)
Agitato Ma Non Troppo ("I have a grief").
Agitato Ma Non Troppo ("This is what the man said").
Antique Harvesters.
April Treason.
Armageddon.
Bad News.
Bells for John Whiteside's Daughter.
Birthday of an Aging Seer.
Blackberry Winter ("If there be a power of sweetness, let it lie").
Blue Girls.
Captain Carpenter.
Conrad Sits in Twilight.
Crocodile.
Dead Boy.
Dog.
Eclogue: "JANE SNEED BEGAN IT: My poor John, alas."
Emily Hardcastle, Spinster.
Epithalamion of a Peach.
Equilibrists, The.
Fait Accompli.
First Travels of Max.
Good Ships.
Her Eyes.
Here Lies a Lady.
Hilda.
In Bed Not Dead.
Injured Sire.
Jack's Letter.
Janet Waking.
Judith of Bethulia.
Kingdom Come.
Lady Lost.
L'ETAT C'est Moi.
Man without Sense of Direction.
Master's in the Garden Again.
Miriam Tazewell.
Misanthrope.
Moments of Minnie.
Morning.
Necrological.
Nocturne: "Where now has our young Adam."
Of Margaret ("Frost, and a leaf has quit the tulip tree").
Of Margaret ("With the fall of the first leaf that winds rend").
Old Man Playing with Children.
Old Mansion.
On the Road to Wockensutter.
Our Two Worthies.
Overtures.
Painted Head.
Parting at Dawn.
Parting, without a Sequel.
Persistent Explorer.
Philomela.
Piazza Piece.
Pink and Pale.
Prelude to an Evening.
Primer for Statesmen.
Prometheus in Straits.
Puncture.
Rain.
Romance of a Youngest Daughter.
Rose, The.
Semi-Centennial.
Sixteen Poems in Eight Pairings.
Somewhere Is Such a Kingdom.
Spectral Lovers.
Spiel of [the] Three Mountebanks.
Survey of Literature.
Tall Girl, The.
Thinking, Drinking.
To the Scholars of Harvard.
Tom, Tom, the Piper's Son.
Two Gentlemen in Bonds.
Two Gentlemen Scholars.
Two in August.

Vanity of the Bright Boys, The.
Vaunting Oak.
Vision by Sweetwater.
What Ducks Require.
Winter Remembered.

"Reed, Lou" (Louis Firbank) (b. 1944)
Afterhours.
All Tomorrow's Parties.
Andy's Chest.
Average Guy.
Bed, The.
Beginning of a Great Adventure.
Betrayed.
Black Angel's Death Song.
Blue Mask, The.
Bottoming Out.
Busload of Faith.
Calm before the Storm, The.
Candy Says.
Caroline Says II.
Chelsea Girls.
Xmas in February.
City Lights.
Day John Kennedy Died, The.
Dime Store Mystery.
Dirt.
Dirty Blvd.
Doin' the Things That We Want To.
Dream, A.
Endless Cycle.
Families.
Ferryboat Bill.
Fly into the Sun.
Gift, The.
Good Evening Mr. Waldheim.
Gun, The.
Halloween Parade, The.
Hello It's Me.
Heroin.
Heroine, The.
Hold On.
Home of the Brave.
How Do You Think It Feels.
I Wanna Be Black.
I'll Be Your Mirror.
I'm Waiting for the Man.
It Wasn't Me.
Kicks.
Kids, The.
Kill Your Sons.
Lady Godiva's Operation.
Last Great American Whale.
Last Shot, The.
Legendary Hearts.
Letters to the Vatican.
Little Sister.
Make Up Mind.
Mama's Got a Lover.
Men of Good Fortune.
Murder Mystery, The.
My Friend George.
My House.
My Old Man.
New Sensations.
N.Y. Telephone Conversation.
Nobody But You.
Original Wrapper, The.
Pale Blue Eyes.
Power of Positive Drinking, The.
Rock 'N' Roll.
Romeo Had Juliette.
Sad Song.
Sick of You.
Since Half the World is H$_2$O.
Slide, The.
Small Town.
Some Kinda Love.
Standing on Ceremony.
Strawman.
Street Hassle: Street Hassle.
Street Hassle: Waltzing Matilda.
Sweet Jane.
Teach the Gifted Children.
Tell It to Your Heart.
Temporary Thing.
That's the Story of My Life.
There Is No Time.

Think It Over.
Underneath the Bottle.
Venus in Furs.
Vicious Circle.
Video Violence.
Walk on the Wild Side.
Waves of Fear.

Rexroth, Kenneth (1905–82)
Aardvark.
Aging pilgram on a, An.
"And what is love?" said Pilate.
Andrée Rexroth ("Now once more gray
    mottled buckeye branches").
Andrée Rexroth ("Years have gone. It is
    spring, The.").
Another Spring.
Art of Worldly Wisdom, The.
As I came from the.
Asking is / Dream of deign.
August 22, 1939.
Autumn in California.
Autumn of Many Years, The.
Bad Old Days, The.
Bell / Too softly and too slowly tolled, The.
Bestiary, A sels.
Between Myself and Death.
Between Two Wars.
Black / Blue Black / Blue.
Boswell: Sir, what is the chief.
Casual reverberation is not restitution, The.
Cat.
Dark within dark I cling to sleep.
Delia Rexroth.
Dialogue of Watching, A.
Discursive knowledge, knowledge by.
Double Hellas, The.
Dragon and the Unicorn, The sels.
Drowned moon plunges, The.
Dust of man's trouble rises, The.
Eve of Ch'ing Ming—Clear Bright, The.
Fish Peddler and Cobbler.
Floating.
For Eli Jacobson.
Fox.
Gathering early morning / Mushrooms, the
    music of the.
Goat.
Grammar of cause, The.
Great Nebula of Andromeda, The.
Halley's Comet.
Heart of Herakles, The.
Heaven is full of definite stars.
Herring.
Homestead Called Damascus, The sels.
Hototogisu—horobirete.
I.
I am cold in my folded blanket.
I cannot forget.
I come back to the cottage in.
I Dream of Leslie.
I hold your head tight between.
In those days / In a pool of noise.
Inversely, As the Square of Their Distances
    Apart.
It is now a decline.
Kings River Canyon.
La Vie En Rose.
Lesson in Geography, A.
Letter to William Carlos Williams, A.
Light / Light / The sliver in the firmament.
Lights in the Sky are Stars, The sels.
Lights in the Sky are Stars, The.
Lion.
Living Pearl, A.
Love Poems of Marichiko sels.
Lute Music.
Lyell's Hypothesis Again.
Making love with you.
Man.
Married Blues.
Marthe Away (She is Away).
Mary and the Seasons sels.
Mary and the Seasons.
New York a grey haze with flights of.
No leaf stirs. I am alone.
Now the Starlit Moonless Spring.

On Flower Wreath Hill sels.
On What Planet.
Over Switzerland broods the.
Pausing in my sixth decade.
Phoenix and the Tortoise, The sels.
Prolegomenon to a Theodicy, A sels.
Raccoon.
Reflecting Trees of Being and Not Being,
    The.
Requiem for the Spanish Dead.
Seven Poems for Marthe, My Wife sels.
Signature of All Things, The.
Silver Swan, The sels.
Softly and singly an owl.
Some day in six inches of.
Song at the Winepresses, A.
Sound of gongs, the songs of birds, The.
Spark in the Tinder of Knowing, The.
Spring Rain.
Stigmata of Fact, The.
Suchness.
Sword in a Cloud of Light, A.
Tea drinking, garden viewing.
They were in an unstable condition.
Thin Edge of Your Pride, The.
This is the winter of the hardest year.
This the mortared stone.
This world of ours, before we.
Thou Shalt Not Kill.
Toward An Organic Philosophy.
Uncle Sam.
Under the full moon strange birds.
Under the half moon.
Unicorn.
Vulture.
Water in a bottle, The.
Water is always the same.
We were interested in ways of being.
Webs of misery spread in the brain.
When We with Sappho.
Wolf.
Written to Music sels.
You wake me.
Young rice plants are just being.
Your tongue thrums and moves.
Zoraster long ago / Said poetry presents us.
Translations, Coauthored Poems, etc.:
    Advantages of Learning, The.

Reyes Basualto, Neftalí Ricardo *see* Neruda,
    Pablo

Rich, Adrienne (b. 1929)
Abnegation.
Absent-Minded Are Always to Blame, The.
After a Sentence in "Malte Laurids Brigge."
After Dark.
After Twenty Years.
Afterwake, The.
Afterward.
Air without Incense.
Always the Same.
Amnesia.
Annotation for an Epitaph.
Antinoüs: The Diaries.
Any Husband to Any Wife.
Apology.
Apparition.
Artificial Intelligence.
At a Bach Concert.
At a Deathbed in the Year Two Thousand.
At Hertford House.
At Majority.
At the Jewish New Year.
Atlas of the Difficult World, An.
Attention.
August.
8/8/68: i.
8/8/68: ii.
8/1/68.
8/4/68.
Aunt Jennifer's Tigers.
Autumn Equinox.
Autumn Sequence.
Bears.
Blood-Sister.
Blue Ghazals, The.
Book, The.
Boundary.

Break, The.
Breakfast in a Bowling Alley in Utica, New
    York.
Burden Baskets.
Burning of Paper instead of Children, The.
Burning Oneself In.
Burning Oneself Out.
By No Means Native.
Capital, The.
Cartographies of Silence.
Celebration in the Plaza, The.
Change of World, A.
Charleston in the Eighteen-Sixties.
Classmate, The.
Clock in the Square, A.
Colophon.
Concord River.
Continuum.
Contradictions: Tracking Poems sels.
Corpse-Plant, The.
Culture and Anarchy.
Darklight sels.
Days: Spring, The.
Dear Adrienne, / I feel signified by pain.
Dear Adrienne: / I'm calling you up tonight.
Delta.
Demon Lover, The.
Desert as Garden of Paradise, The.
Design in Living Colors.
Dialogue.
Diamond Cutters, The.
Dien Bien Phu.
Diving into the Wreck.
Double Monologue.
Dreamwood.
Eastern War Time sels.
Eastport to Block Island.
Education of a Novelist.
Epilogue for a Masque of Purcell.
Essential Resources.
Euryclea's Tale.
Explorers, The.
Face.
Face to Face.
Fact of a Doorframe, The.
Final Notations.
First Things.
Five O'Clock, Beacon Hill.
5:30 A.M.
Flesh and Blood.
Floating Poem, Unnumbered, The.
Focus.
For a Russian Poet.
For a Sister.
For Ethel Rosenberg.
For Julia in Nebraska.
For L.G.: Unseen for Twenty Years.
For Memory.
For the Conjunction of Two Planets.
For the Dead.
For the Felling of an Elm in the Harvard
    Yard.
For the Record.
Frame.
Friend I can trust is the one who will let me
    have my death, The.
From a Chapter on Literature.
From a Survivor.
From an Old House in America.
From Morning-Glory to Petersburg.
From the Prison House.
Gabriel.
Ghazal V.
Ghazals: Homage to Ghalib sels.
Ghazals: Homage to Ghalib.
Ghost of a Chance.
Granddaughter.
Grandmothers.
Halfway.
Hattie Rice Rich.
He Remembereth That We Are Dust.
Heroines.
Hohokam.
Holding Out.
Holiday.
House at the Cascades, The.
Hunger.

I Am in Danger—Sir—.
I Dream I'm the Death of Orpheus.
I Heard a Hermit Speak.
I was looking for a way out of a lifetime's
  consolations.
Ideal Landscape.
Images for Godard.
Implosions.
In my imagination I was the pivot of a fresh
  beginning.
In the Evening.
In the North.
In the Wake of Home.
In the Woods.
In Time of Carnival.
Incipience.
Innocents, The.
Insomniacs, The.
Insusceptibles, The.
Integrity.
Itinerary.
Jerusalem.
7/12/68.
7/13/68.
7/14/68: i.
7/14/68: ii.
7/16/68: i.
7/16/68: ii.
7/17/68.
7/26/68: i.
7/26/68: II.
Juvenilia.
Key, The.
Knight, The.
Knot, The.
Kursaal at Interlaken, The.
Lag, The.
Landscape of the Star.
Last Song.
Leaflets.
Letter from the Land of Sinners.
Letters: March 1969.
Life and Letters.
Like This Together.
Likeness.
Living in Sin.
Living Memory.
Location.
Loser, The.
Love in the Museum.
Lovers Are like Children.
Lucifer in the Train.
Mare's skeleton in the clearing: another sign
  of life, The.
Marriage in the 'Sixties, A.
Marriage Portion, The.
Mary Gravely Jones.
Mary Jane Colter, 1904.
Mathilde in Normandy.
Meditations for a Savage Child.
Memory says: Want to do right? Don't
  count on me.
Merely to Know.
Middle-aged, The.
Mirror in Which Two Are Seen as One, The.
Missing the Point.
Moth Hour.
Mother-in-Law.
Mother-Right.
Mourning Picture.
Moving in Winter.
My mouth hovers across your breasts.
Natural Resources.
Necessities of Life.
New Year Morning.
Newsreel.
Night.
Night in the Kitchen.
Night-Pieces: For a Child.
Night Watch.
Nightbreak.
Ninth Symphony of Beethoven Understood at
  Last as a Sexual Message, The.
Noon.
North American Time.
Not like That.
Novella.

November 1968.
Observer, The.
Of simple choice they are the villagers; their
  clothes come.
Old blanket. The crumbs of rubbed wool
  turning up, The.
On Edges.
Open-Air Museum.
Orient Wheat.
Orion.
Orion plunges like a drunken hunter.
Our Whole Life.
Particularity.
Parting: I, The.
Parting: II, The.
Passing On.
Paula Becker to Clara Westhoff.
Peace.
Peeling Onions.
Perennial Answer, The.
Phantasia for Elvira Shatayev.
Phenomenology of Anger, The.
Photograph of the Unmade Bed, The.
Picnic.
Pictures by Vuillard.
Pieces.
Pierrot Le Fou.
Planetarium.
Platform, The.
Poetry: I.
Poetry: III.
Postcard.
Power.
Prisoners, The.
Problem, unstated until now, is how, The.
Prospect, The.
Prospective Immigrants Please Note.
Purely Local.
Rafts, The.
Rain of Blood, The.
Rape.
Raven, The.
Re-forming the Crystal.
Readings of History.
Recorders in Italy.
Reliquary.
Return of the Evening Grosbeaks, The.
Revivalist in Boston, A.
Road to the great canyon always feels, The.
Roadway, The.
Roofwalker, The.
Roots.
Rural Reflections.
Rustication.
Sapling springs, the milkweed blooms, The:
  obsolete Nature.
Self-hatred.
September 21.
Shooting Script *sels*.
Shooting Script.
Side by Side.
Sisters.
6/21.
Snapshots of a Daughter-in-Law.
Snow.
Snow Queen, The.
So many minds in search of bodies.
Solfeggietto.
Song: "You're wondering if I'm lonely."
Sources.
Spirit of Place, The *sels*.
Spirit of Place, The.
Splittings.
Spring Thunder.
Springboard, The.
Stand Up.
Stelae, The.
Stepping Backward.
Storm Warnings.
Stranger, The.
Strayed Village, The.
Study of History.
Sunday Evening.
Tattered Kaddish.
Tear Gas.
They come to you with their descriptions of
  your soul.

This Beast, This Angel.
This high summer we love will pour its light.
To Frantz Fanon.
To Judith, Taking Leave.
To the Airport.
Tourist and the Town, The.
Transcendental Etude.
Transit.
Translations.
Tree, The.
Trees, The.
Trying to Talk with a Man.
Turning *sels*.
Turning the Wheel *sels*.
Turning the Wheel.
Twenty-one Love Poems.
Two Poems.
Two Songs.
Ultimate Act, The.
Uncle Speaks in the Drawing Room, The.
Unsaid Word, An.
Unsounded.
Upcountry.
Upper Broadway.
Valediction Forbidding Mourning, A.
Versailles.
Vertigo.
View of Merton College, A.
View of the Terrace, A.
Villa Adriana.
Violence.
Waking in the Dark.
Walden 1950.
Walk by the Charles, A.
Wave, The.
We are driven to odd attempts; once it would
  not have occurred to.
We were bound on the wheel of an endless
  conversation.
Well, The.
What Ghosts Can Say.
Whatever it was: the grains of the glacier
  caked in the boot-cleats.
Whatever you are that has tracked us this far.
When heat leaves the walls at last.
When This Clangor in the Brain.
When We Dead Awaken.
When your sperm enters me, it is altered.
When/Then.
White Night.
Why Else but to Forestall This Hour.
Wild Sky, The.
Will to Change, The.
Winter.
Woman Dead in Her Forties, A.
Woman Mourned by Daughters, A.
Woman waking behind grimed blinds slatted
  across a courtyard, A.
Women.
Yom Kippur 1984.
You: air-driven reft from the tuber-bitten
  soil.
You are beside me like a wall; I touch you
  with my fingers and.
You who think I find words for everything.
Your Letter.
Translations, Coauthored Poems, etc.:
Accountability.
City.
Dwingelo.
Eben Haëzer.
Fever.
Homecoming.
My Brother.
Our Family.
Poem of Women.
Sleepwalking.
Song of the Foolish Bees.
Statue.
There Are Such Springlike Nights.
White Night.

Robinson, Edwin Arlington (1869–1935)
Aaron Stark.
Afterthoughts.
Alma Mater.
Altar, The.
Amaryllis.

Another Dark Lady.
Archibald's Example.
As a World Would Have It.
Atherton's Gambit.
Aunt Imogen.
Avon's Harvest.
Ballade by the Fire.
Ballade of Broken Flutes.
Ben Jonson Entertains a Man from Stratford.
Ben Trovato.
Bewick Finzer.
Bokardo.
Bon Voyage.
Book of Annandale, The.
Boston.
Burning Book [or The Contented
  Metaphysician], The.
But for the Grace of God.
Calvary.
Calverly's.
Captain Craig.
Caput Mortuum.
Cassandra.
Charles Carville's Eyes.
Chorus of Old Men in "Ægeus", The.
Clavering.
Clerks, The.
Cliff Klingenhagen.
Clinging Vine, The.
Companion, The.
Corridor, The.
Cortège.
Credo.
Dark Hills, The.
Dark House, The.
Dead Village, The.
Dear Friends.
Demos.
Discovery.
Doctor of Billiards.
Erasmus.
Eros Turannos.
Evangelist's Wife, An.
Exit.
False Gods, The.
Field of Glory, The.
Firelight.
Flammonde.
Fleming Helphenstine.
Flying Dutchman, The.
For a Dead Lady.
For Arvia.
Fragment: "Faint white pillars that seem to
  fade."
Garden, The.
George Crabbe.
Gift of God, The.
Growth of "Lorraine," The.
Her Eyes.
Hillcrest.
Horace to Leuconoë.
House on the Hill, The.
How Annandale Went Out.
Inferential.
Isaac and Archibald.
Island, An.
Job the Rejected.
John Brown.
John Evereldown.
John Gorham.
Klondike, The.
Lancelot.
Late Summer.
Lazarus.
Leffingwell.
L'Envoi.
Leonora.
Lingard and the Stars.
Lisette and Eileen.
Llewellyn and the Tree.
London Bridge.
Long Race, The.
Lost Anchors.
Luke Havergal.
Man against the Sky, The.
Many Are Called.
Master, The.

Merlin.
Mill, The.
Miniver Cheevy.
Mr. Flood's Party.
Modernities.
Momus.
Monadnock through the Trees.
Neighbors.
New Tenants, The.
Nimmo.
Octaves.
Old King Cole.
Old King's New Jester, The.
Old Story, An.
Old Trails.
On the Night of a Friend's Wedding.
On the Way.
Partnership.
Pasa Thalassa Thalassa.
Peace on Earth.
Pilot, The.
Pity of the Leaves, The.
Poor Relation, The.
Rahel to Varnhagen.
Rat, The.
Recalled.
Rembrandt to Rembrandt.
Return of Morgan and Fingal, The.
Reuben Bright.
Revealer, The.
Richard Cory.
Sage, The.
Sainte-Nitouche.
Shadrach O'Leary.
Siege Perilous.
Song at Shannon's, A.
Sonnet: "Master and the slave go hand in
  hand, The."
Sonnet: "Oh for a poet—for a beacon
  bright."
Sonnet: "When we can all so excellently
  give."
Souvenir.
Stafford's Cabin.
Story of the Ashes and the Flame, The.
Sunken Crown, The.
Supremacy.
Tact.
Tasker Norcross.
Tavern, The.
Theophilus.
Thomas Hood.
Three Quatrains.
Three Taverns, The.
Torrent, The.
Town Down the River, The.
Tree in Pamela's Garden, The.
Twilight Song.
Two Gardens in Linndale.
Two Men.
Two Quatrains.
Two Sonnets.
Uncle Ananias.
Unforgiven, The.
Vain Gratuities.
Valley of the Shadow, The.
Verlaine.
Veteran Sirens.
Vickery's Mountain.
Villanelle of Change.
Voice of Age, The.
Wandering Jew, The.
Whip, The.
White Lights, The.
Wilderness, The.
Wise Brothers, The.
Woman and the Wife, The.
Zola.
Translations, Coauthored Poems, etc.:
Aretemias.
Doricha.
Dust of Timas, The.
Eutychides.
Happy Man, A.
Inscription by the Sea, An.
Lais to Aphrodite.
Mighty Runner, A.

Old Story, The.
Raven, The.
To-morrow.
Variations of Greek Themes.

Roethke, Theodore (1908–63)
Abyss, The.
Academic.
Adamant, The.
Against Disaster.
All Morning.
All the Earth, All the Air.
Apparition, The.
Auction, The.
Ballad of the Clairvoyant Widow.
Bat, The.
Beast, The.
Big Wind.
Boy and the Bush, The.
Bring the Day!
Carnations.
Ceiling, The.
Centaur, The.
Chair, The.
Changeling, The.
Child on Top of a Greenhouse.
Chums, The.
Coming of the Cold, The.
Cow, The.
Cuttings ("Sticks-in-a-drowse droop over
  sugary loam").
Cuttings ("This urge, wrestle, resurrection of
  dry sticks").
Cycle, The.
Dance, The.
Death Piece.
Decision, The.
Dinky.
Dolor.
Donkey, The.
Double Feature.
Dream, The.
Duet.
Dying Man, The.
Elegy: "Her face like a rain-beaten stone on
  the day she rolled off."
Elegy: "Should every creature be as I have
  been."
Elegy for Jane.
Epidermal Macabre.
Far Field, The.
Favorite, The.
Feud.
Field of Light, A.
First Meditation.
Flight, The.
Flower Dump.
Follies of Adam, The.
For an Amorous Lady.
Forcing House.
Four for Sir John Davies.
Fourth Meditation.
Frau Bauman, Frau Schmidt, and Frau
  Schwartze.
Genesis.
Gentle, The.
Geranium, The.
Gibber, The.
Give Way, Ye Gates.
Gnu, The.
Gob Music.
Goo Girl.
Happy Three, The.
Harsh Country, The.
Heard in a Violent Ward.
Her Becoming.
Her Longing.
Her Reticence.
Her Time.
Her Words.
Her Wrath.
Heron, The.
Highway: Michigan.
Hippo, The.
His Foreboding.
I Cry, Love! Love!
I Knew a Woman.
I Need, I Need.

I Waited.
Idyll: "Now as from maple to elm the
    flittermice skitter and twirl."
I'm Here.
In Evening Air.
In Praise of Prairie.
Infirmity.
Interlude.
It Was Beginning Winter.
Journey to the Interior.
Judge Not.
Kitty-Cat Bird, The.
Lady and the Bear, The.
Lamb, The.
Last Words.
Light Breather, A.
Light Comes Brighter, The.
Light Listened.
Light Poem.
Lines upon Leaving a Sanitarium.
Lizard, The.
Long Alley, The.
Long Live the Weeds.
Long Waters, The.
Longing, The.
Lost Son, The.
Love's Progress.
Lull.
Manifestation, The.
Marrow, The.
Meadow Mouse, The.
Meditation at Oyster River.
Meditation in Hydrotherapy.
Meditations of an Old Woman.
Memory.
Mid-Country Blow.
Minimal, The.
Mistake, The.
Moment, The.
Monotony Song, The.
Moss-Gathering.
Motion, The.
My Dim-Wit Cousin.
My Papa's Waltz.
Myrtle.
Myrtle's Cousin.
Night Crow.
Night Journey.
No Bird.
North American Sequence.
O Lull Me, Lull Me.
O, Thou Opening, O.
Old Florist.
On the Quay.
On the Road to Woodlawn.
Once More, the Round.
Open House.
Orchids.
Orders for the Day.
Other, The.
Otto.
Our Lady's Winter Words.
Philander.
Pickle Belt.
Pike, The.
Pipling.
Pit, The.
Plaint.
Poetaster.
Praise to the End!
Prayer: "If I must of my Senses lose."
Prayer before Study.
Premonition, The.
Prognosis.
Pure Fury, The.
Reckoning, The.
Reminder, The.
Renewal, The.
Reply, The.
Reply to a Lady Editor.
Reply to Censure.
Restored, The.
Return, The.
Right Thing, The.
River Incident.
Root Cellar.
Rose, The.

Rouse for Stevens, A.
Saginaw Song, The.
Sale.
Sensibility! O La!
Sensualists, The.
Sententious Man, The.
Sequel, The.
Serpent, The.
Shape of the Fire, The.
She.
Shimmer of Evil, The.
Shy Man, The.
Signals, The.
Silence.
Siskins, The.
Sloth, The.
Slow Season.
Slug.
Small, The.
Snake.
Song: "From whence cometh song?"
Song: "My wrath, where's the edge."
Song, The: "I met a ragged man."
Song: "This fair parcel of summer's."
Song for the Squeeze-Box.
Storm, The.
Supper with Lindsay.
Surly One, The.
Swan, The.
Thing, The.
Three Epigrams.
To My Sister.
Tranced, The.
Transplanting.
Tree, the Bird, The.
Unextinguished, The.
Unfold! Unfold!
Vernal Sentiment.
Verse with Allusions.
Visitant, The.
Voice, The.
Wagtail, The.
Waking, The.
Walk in Late Summer, A.
Weed Puller.
Whale, The.
What Can I Tell My Bones?
Where Knock Is Open Wide.
Wish for a Young Wife.
Words for the Wind.
Yak, The.
Young Girl, The.

Rolfe, Edwin (1909–54)
About Eyes.
After Tu Fu (A.D. 713-770).
After Wang Chi.
All Ghouls' Night.
And If You Don't See What You Want, Ask
    for It.
Any Slave.
Arctic Remembered, The.
Are You Now or Have You Ever Been.
Asbestos.
At the Moment of Victory.
Bal Masqué.
Ballad: "What are we having for dinner
    tonight?"
Ballad of the Noble Intentions.
Barn in Wisconsin.
Bequest.
Biography.
Blues.
Bon Voyage.
Brickyards at Beacon.
Brigadas Internacionales.
Casualty.
Catalogue.
Catalogue of I.
Cell, The.
Cheliuskin.
City of Anguish.
Communists.
Conscript's Song.
Credo.
Dawn Song.
Death by Water.

Dedication, A: "Here, then, the equivocal
    catch of a long voyage."
Definition.
Elegia.
Elegy for Our Dead.
Entry.
Epitaph: "Deep in this earth."
Essay on Dreiser (1871-1945).
Exodus 1947.
Eyes of a Blind Man.
Eyes of a Boy.
Faces No Longer White.
First Love.
Georgia Nightmare.
Glory Set, The.
Guerrillas, The.
Homage to Karl Marx.
Homecoming (August 7, 1934).
Hunter Went Killing: A Fable, A.
Idiot Joe Prays in Pershing Square and Gets
    Hauled in for Vagrancy.
In Praise Of.
In the Time of Hesitation.
June 19, 1953.
Kentucky.
Kill the Umpire!
Lanes of Death and Birth.
Letter.
Letter for One in Russia.
Letter to the Denouncers, A.
Little Ballad for Americans—1954.
Manuela.
Many an Outcast.
Marching Song of the Children of Darkness.
May Day Song.
May 22nd 1939.
Melancholy Comus, The.
More than Flesh to Fathom.
Munich.
Mystery.
Mystery II.
Night World.
Nine, The.
1949 (After Reading a News Item).
Not Hatred.
Not Men Alone.
Now the Fog.
Nuthin but Brass.
On Rico LeBrun's Crucifixion.
Paris—Christmas 1938.
Pastoral: "Lonely evening crouches, darkens
    as the hour, The."
Pastoral: "Now, on this bluest of mornings,
    we wake."
Pastoral—1954.
Pattern of Our Lives, The.
Poem: "*Consciousness*, said Don Miguel, *is a
    disease*."
Poem: "Girl lashed to the stake, The."
Poem for May First.
Poem To Delight My Friends Who Laugh at
    Science-Fiction, A.
Poisoned Air Befouled the Whole Decade,
    The.
Political Prisoner 123456789.
Portrait of a Death.
Postscript to a War.
Primer Amor.
Prophecy in Stone.
Radio Madrid—1937.
Recruit.
Room with Revolutionists.
Season of Death.
Sentry.
Ship, The.
Sixth Winter, The.
Soledad.
Somebody and Somebody Else and You.
Something Still Lives.
Song: "Keep the dream alive and growing
    always."
Song: "There is indeed now reason for
    rejoicing."
Song: "Through all the cowering world,
    crouching, shrinking."
Song for a Birth Day in Exile.
Still Must I Love You.

Sunday Evening Revery.
Survival Is of the Essence.
Testament to a Flowering Race.
These Men Are Revolution.
Three Who Died.
To My Contemporaries.
To Thine Own Self.
To Those Who Fear To Join Us.
Undersea Poem.
Unit Assignment.
Unit Meeting.
Vincent.
War Guilt.
What Does the Novice Soldier Think.
Where Buildings Congregate.
Winds of Another Sphere.
Winter's Ghost Plagues Them.
Witness at Leipzig.
Words Found on a Cave's Wall.

Rossetti, Christina Georgina (1830–94)
A Tirsi.
Acme.
Advent.
Advent Sunday.
After Communion.
After Death.
After This the Judgement.
Afterthought, An.
Afterward He Repented, and Went.
Agnellina orfanellina.
Ah Lord, Lord, if my heart were right with
   Thine.
Ah welladay and wherefore am I here?
Ahi culla vuota! ed ahi sepolcro pieno.
Alas, alas! for the self-destroyed / Vanish as
   images from a glass.
Alas my Lord, / How should I wrestle all the
   livelong night.
All beneath the sun hasteth, / All that hath
   begun wasteth.
All Flesh Is Grass.
All heaven is blazing yet / With the meridian
   sun.
All night I dream you love me well.
All Saints.
All Saints: Martyrs.
All the bells were ringing / And all the birds
   were singing.
"All Thy Works Praise Thee, O Lord": A
   Processional of Creation.
Alleluia! or Alas! my heart is crying.
Alone Lord God, in Whom our trust and
   peace.
Along the highroad the way is too long.
Alphabet, An.
Amami, t'amo / Figliolin mio.
Amen.
Amicizia: Sirocchia Son D'Amor.
Amico e Più Che Amico Mio.
Amico pesce, poiver vorrà.
Amor Dormente?
Amor Mundi.
Amor Si Sveglia?
Amore E Dispetto.
Amore E Dovere.
And is this August weather? nay not so.
And Now Why Tarriest Thou?
And There Was No More Sea.
Angeli al capo, al piede.
Angels at the foot,/ And Angels at the head.
Animuccia, vagantucccia, morbiduccia.
Annie.
Another Spring.
Answer, An.
Antipas.
Apple Gathering, An.
April.
Are They Not All Ministering Spirits?
Are Ye Not Much Better Than They?
Ariadne To Theseus.
Arrossisce la rosa: e perchè mai?
As a King, ..Unto the King.
As Cold Water to a Thirsty Soul, So Is Good
   News from a Far Country.
As dying, and behold we live!
As froth on the face of the deep, / As foam
   on the crest of the sea.

As the Apple Tree among the Trees of the
   Wood.
As the dove which found no rest / For the
   sole of her foot, flew back.
As the Doves to Their Windows.
As the Sparks Fly Upwards.
As Thy Days, So Shall Thy Strength Be.
Ascension Day.
Ascension Eve.
Ash Wednesday.
At Home.
At Last.
August.
Aura dolcissima, ma donde siete?
Autumn.
Autumn Violets.
Awake, Thou That Sleepest.
Baby cry— / Oh fie!
Baby lies so fast asleep / That we cannot
   wake her.
Babylon the Great.
Baby's cradle with no baby in it, A.
Ballad: "Soft white lamb in the daisy
   meadow."
Ballad of Boding, A.
Balm in Gilead.
Basta una notte a maturare il fungo.
Beautiful For Situation.
Beauty Is Vain.
Because He First Loved Us.
Because Thy Love hath sought me, / All
   mine is Thine and Thine is mine.
Bed of Forget-Me-Nots, A.
Before the Beginning.
Before the Paling of the Stars.
Before the Throne, and Before the Lamb.
Behold a Shaking.
Behold, I stand at the door and knock.
Behold, It Was Very Good.
Behold the Man!
"Beloved, let us love one another," says St.
   John.
Beloved, yield thy time to God, for He / Will
   make eternity thy recompense.
Better Resurrection, A.
Better So.
Birchington Churchyard.
Bird or Beast?
Bird Raptures.
Bird Song, A.
Bird's-Eye View, A.
Birthday, A.
Bitter for Sweet.
Blind from my birth, / Where flowers are
   springing.
"Blumine" Risponde.
Boats sail on the rivers, / And ships sail on
   the seas.
Books In the Running Brooks.
Bourne, The.
Boy Johnny.
Brandons Both.
Bread and Milk for Breakfast.
Bride Song.
Bride Song, A.
Brother Bruin.
Brown and furry / Caterpillar in a hurry.
Brownie, Brownie, let down your milk.
Bruised Reed Shall He Not Break, A.
Buds and Babies.
Bundle of Myrrh Is My Well-Beloved unto
   Me, A.
Burial Anthem.
Bury Hope out of sight, / No book for it and
   no bell.
But Thy Commandment Is Exceeding Broad.
By the Sea.
By the Waters of Babylon.
By the Waters of Babylon. B.C. 570.
By Way of Remembrance.
Called To Be Saints.
Can I know it?—Nay.— / Shall I know it?—
   Yea.
Candlemas Dialogue, A.
Cannot Sweeten.
Capo che chinasi, / Occhi che chiudonsi.
Cardinal Newman.

Care flieth, / Hope and fear together.
Cast down but not destroyed, chastened not
   slain.
Castle-Builder's World, A.
Cavalli marittimi / Urtansi in guerra.
Changing Chimes.
Charade.
Charades.
Charity.
Charity Never Faileth.
Charon.
Chiefest among Ten Thousand, The.
Chiesa E Signore.
Child's Talk in April.
Chill, A.
Chill blank world. Yet over the utmost sea,
   A.
Chilly Night, A.
Chinaman, The.
Christian and Jew. A Dialogue.
Christmas Carol, A: "In the bleak mid-
   winter."
Christmas Carol, A: "Thank God, thank God,
   we do believe."
Christmas Carol, for My Godchildren, A.
Christmas Carols.
Christmas Day.
Christmas Eve.
Christmastide.
Chruchyard Song of Patient Hope, A.
City Mouse and the Garden Mouse, The.
City mouse lives in a house, The.
City plum is not a plum, A.
Clever little Willie wee, / Bright eyed, blue
   eyed little fellow.
Coast-Nightmare, A.
Cobwebs.
Come cheer up, my lads, 'tis to glory we
   steer!
Come Unto Me.
Confluents.
Consider.
Consider the Lilies of the Field.
Contemptuous of his home beyond.
Convent Threshold, The.
Conversion of St. Paul.
Cor Mio.
Cor mio, cor mio / Più non ti veggo, ma mi
   rammento.
Corydon's Lament and Resolution.
Counsel, A.
Counterblast on Penny Trumpet.
Cousin Kate.
Cried Out with Tears.
Crimson curtains round my mother's bed.
Crying, my little one, footsore and weary?
Cuccurucù! Cuccurucù! / All'alba il gallo
   canta.
Currants on a bush, / And figs upon a stem.
Dancing on the hill-tops, / Singing in the
   valleys.
Darkness and light are both alike to Thee.
Daughter of Eve, A.
Day and night the Accuser makes no pause.
Day Is At Hand, The.
Days are clear, / Day after day, The.
Days of Vanity.
De Profundis.
Dead before Death.
Dead Bride, The.
Dead City, The.
Dead Hope.
Dead in the cold, a song-singing thrush.
Dear Angels and dear disembodied Saints.
Dear old woman in the lane, The.
Death.
Death Is Swallowed Up in Victory.
Death of a First-Born, A.
Death-Watches.
Death's Chill Between.
December.
Descent from the Cross, The.
Despair.
Despised and Rejected.
Diamond or a coal? / A diamond, if you
   please, A.
"Ding a ding," / The sweet bells sing.

Dirge, A: "She was as sweet as violets in the Spring."
Dirge, A: "Why were you born when the snow was falling?"
Discovery, A.
Divine and Human Pleading.
Do This, and He Doeth It.
Doeth Well..Doeth Better.
Dog lies in his kennel, The.
Dost Thou Not Care?
Dream, A.
Dream, The.
Dream Land.
Dream-Love.
Dumb Friend, A.
D'un sonno profondissimo.
Dying Man to His Betrothed, The.
E babbo e mamma ha il nostro figliolino.
Earth and Heaven.
Earth has clear call of daily bells, / A chancel-vault of gloom and star.
Earth Shall Tremble at the Look of Him, The.
Easter Carol, An.
Easter Day.
Easter Even.
Easter Monday.
Easter Morning.
Easter Tuesday.
Echo.
Echo from Willowwood, An.
Eight o'clock; / The postman's knock!
1880.
1885. St. Valentine's Day.
1884.
1886, St. Valentine's Day.
1878.
1879.
Eleanor.
Eleventh Hour, The.
Ellen Middleton.
Embertide.
Emerald is as green as grass, An.
End, An.
End Is Not Yet, The.
End of Time, The.
Endure Hardness.
Enrica, 1865.
Epiphany.
Epiphanytide.
Epitaph: "Slave yet wearing on my head a crown, A."
Eppure Allora Venivi.
Escape to the Mountain.
Eva.
Eve.
Every One That Is Perfect Shall Be as His Master.
Everything that is born must die.
Exceeding Bitter Cry, An.
Experience bows a sweet contented face.
Exultate Deo.
Eye Hath Not Seen.
Faint, Yet Pursuing.
Fair Margaret.
Fair World Tho' a Fallen, A.
Faith and Hope are wings to Love.
Faithless Shepherdess, The.
Farm Walk, A.
Fata Morgana.
Feast of the Annunciation.
Feast of the Presentation.
February.
February 14. 1883.
Ferry Me across the Water.
Finestra Mia Orientale.
First Spring Day, The.
Fisher-Wife, A.
Flint.
Floral Teaching.
Flowers Appear on the Earth, The.
Fluttered Wings.
Fly Away, Fly Away.
For a Mercy Received.
For Advent.
For All.
For Each.

For H.P.
For One Sake.
For Rosaline's Album.
For Thine Own Sake, O My God.
Forget Me Not.
Foss'io regina / Tu re saresti.
4th May Morning.
Freaks of Fashion.
Frisky Lamb, A.
From early dawn until the flush of noon.
From House to Home.
From Mestastasio.
From Sunset to Star Rise.
From the Antique.
General Assembly and Church of the Firstborn, The.
German-French Campaign, 1870–1871, The.
Ghost's Petition, The.
Go In Peace.
Goal in sihgt! Look up and sing, / Set faces full against the light, The.
Goblin Market.
God Is Our Hope and Strength.
God's Acre.
Gold of that Land is Good, The.
Golden Glories.
Golden Holly.
Golden Silences.
Gone Before.
Gone for Ever.
Gone to his rest / Bright little Bouby!
Good Friday.
Good Friday Evening.
Good Friday Morning.
Good Lord, today / I scarce find breath to say.
Good Shepherd, The.
Goodbye in fear, goodbye in sorrow.
Gran freddo è infuori, e dentro è freddo un poco.
Grant us such grace that we may work Thy Will.
Greatest of These Is Charity, The.
Green Cornfield, A.
Growing in the vale / By the uplands hilly.
Grown and Flown.
Grown Cold.
Guesses.
Had Fortune parted us / Fortune is blind.
Hail, noble face of noble friend!
Half Dead.
Half Moon Shows a Face of Plaintive Sweetness, The.
Handy Mole who plied no shovel, A.
Hark! the Alleluias of the great salvation.
Have I not striven, my God, and watched and prayed?
Have Patience.
Have You Forgotten?
He and She.
He Cannot Deny Himself.
He Shall Go No More Out.
Hear what the mournful linnets say.
Heart Knoweth Its Own Bitterness, The.
Heart's Chill Between.
Heartsease in my garden bed, / With sweetwilliam white and red.
Heaven.
Heaven overarches earth and sea.
Heaven's chimes are slow, but sure to strike at last.
Heaviness May Endure for a Night, But Joy Cometh in the Morning.
Heavy heart, if ever heart was heavy, A.
Helen Grey.
Helpmeet for Him, A.
Henry Hardiman.
Her Seed; It Shall Bruise Thy Head.
Herself a Rose Who Bore the Rose.
Hills are tipped with sunshine, while I walk / In shadows dim and cold.
His Banner over Me Was Love.
Hollow-Sounding and Mysterious.
Holy City, New Jerusalem, The.
Holy Innocents.
Hop-o'-my-thumb and little Jack Horner.
Hope Carol, A.

Hope in Grief.
Hope is like a harebell trembling from its birth.
Hope is the counterpoise of fear / While night enthralls us here.
Hopeless Case, A.
Hopping frog, hop here and be seen.
Horses of the Sea, The.
Hour and the Ghost, The.
House of cards / Is neat and small, A.
How great is little man! / Sun, moon, and stars respond to him.
How many authors are my first!
How Many Seconds in a Minute?
How One Chose.
Hurt No Living Thing.
Husband and Wife.
Hymn: "O the bitter shame and sorrow."
Hymn: "To the God Who reigns on high."
Hymn for Christmas Day, A.
I am a King, / Or an Emperor rather.
I Am Small and of No Reputation.
I caught a little ladybird / That flies far away.
I Do Set My Bow in the Cloud.
I dreamt I caught a little owl.
I dug and dug amongst the snow.
I fancy the good fairies dressed in white.
I followed Thee, my God, I followed Thee / To see the end.
I Gave a Sweet Smell.
I have a little husband / And he is gone to sea.
I Have a Message unto Thee.
I have a Poll parrot, / And Poll is my doll.
I have but one rose in the world.
I have done with hope.
I Have Fought a Good Fight.
I know a baby, such a baby,— / Round blue eyes and cheeks of pink.
I Know You Not.
I lift mine eyes to see: earth vanisheth.
I Look for the Lord.
I, Lord, Thy foolish sinner low and small.
I love you and you know it—this at least.
I planted a hand / And there came up a palm.
I said "All's over"—& I made my.
I said within myself: I am a fool.
I See That All Things Come to an End.
I seek among the living & I seek.
I sit a queen, and am no widow, and shall see no sorrow.
I sit among the green shady valleys oft.
I toiled on, but thou.
I Will Arise.
I Will Come and Heal Him.
I Will Lift Up Mine Eyes unto the Hills.
I wish I were a little bird.
Iddio C'illumini!
If.
If a mouse could fly, / Or if a crow could swim.
If a pig wore a wig, / What could we say?
If all were rain and never sun.
If hope grew on a bush, / And joy grew on a tree.
If I Could Trust Mine Own Self.
If I Had Words.
If I should ever say "my heart is in my home."
If I Were a Queen.
If love is not worth loving, then life is not worth living.
If not with hope of life, / Begin with fear of death.
If Only.
If stars dropped out of heaven, / And if flowers took their place.
If the moon came from heaven, / Talking all the way.
If the sun could tell us half / That he hears and sees.
If thou be dead, forgive and thou shalt live.
If Thou Sayest, Behold, We Knew It Not.
Il Rosseggiar Dell'Oriente Canzoniere.

Imitated From the Arpa Evangelica: Page 121.
Immalee.
"Immurata" Sister, An.
In a Certain Place.
In an Artist's Studio.
In July / No goodbye.
In Patience.
In Progress.
In resurrection is it awfuller.
In tema e in pena addio.
In the Day of His Espousals.
In the Lane.
In the meadow—what in the meadow?
In the Round Tower at Jhansi, June 8, 1857.
In the Willow Shade.
In weariness and painfulness St. Paul.
Iniquity of the Fathers upon the Children, The.
Introspective.
Is It Well with The Child?
Is the Moon Tired?
Isidora.
It Is Finished.
It is not death, O Christ, to die for Thee: / Nor is that silence of a silent land.
Italia, Io Ti Saluto!
January.
January cold desolate; / February all dripping wet.
Jerusalem of fire / And gold and pearl and gem.
Jessie Cameron.
Jesus alone:—if thus it were to me.
Johnny.
Joy is but sorrow, / While we know.
Joy of Saints, like incense turned to fire, The.
Judge Not According to the Appearance.
Judge Nothing before the Time.
July.
June.
Key-Note, The.
King of Kings and Lord of Lords.
"Kookoorookoo! kookoorookoo!" / Crows the cock before the morn.
L. E. L.
La rosa china il volto rosseggiato.
Lady Isabella.
Lady Montrevor.
Lambs of Grasmere, 1860, The.
Lassù Fia Caro Il Rivederci.
Lassuso Il Caro Fiore.
Last Answer, The.
Last *Complaint*, The.
Last Look, The.
Last Night.
Last Words of St. Telemachus, The.
Later Life: A Double Sonnet of Sonnets.
Laughing Life cries at the feast.
Laura and Lizzie Asleep.
Lay Up for Yourselves Treasures in Heaven.
Leaf from leaf Christ knows; / Himself the Lily and the Rose.
Lent.
Let Everything That Hath Breath Praise the Lord.
Let Patience Have Her Perfect Work.
Let Them Rejoice in Their Beds.
Let's Be Merry.
Lie a-bed, / Sleepy head, / Shut up eyes, bo-peep.
Life and Death.
Life Hidden.
Life Out of Death.
Life that was born today / Must make no stay.
Life's Parallels, A.
Lift up thine eyes to seek the invisible.
Light Love.
Light of Light.
Like As the Hart Desireth the Water Brooks.
Lily has a smooth stalk, / Will never hurt your hand, The.
Lily has an air, / And the snowdrop a grace, The.
L'Incognita.

Lines Given with a Penwiper.
Lines to My Grandfather.
Linnet in a gilded cage,— / A linnet on a bough, A.
Lisetta all' Amante.
Listen, and I will tell you of a face.
Listening.
Long Barren.
Long Looked For.
Look on This Picture and on This.
Looking back along life's trodden way.
Looking Forward.
Lord, by what inconceivable dim road / Thou leadest man on footsore pilgrimage!
Lord, carry me.—Nay, but I grant thee strength.
Lord, comest Thou to me?
Lord, dost Thou look on me, and will not I.
Lord, give me love that I may love Thee much.
Lord God of Hosts, most Holy and most High.
Lord, grant me grace to love Thee in my pain.
Lord, Grant Us Calm.
Lord, grant us eyes to see and ears to hear, / And souls to love and minds to understand.
Lord, grant us grace to rest upon Thy word.
Lord, hast Thou so loved us, and will not we.
Lord, I am feeble and of mean account.
Lord, I am here.—But, child, I look for thee.
Lord, It Is Good for Us to Be Here.
Lord Jesu, Thou art sweetness to my soul.
Lord Jesus, who would think that I am Thine?
Lord, make me one with Thine own faithful ones.
Lord, make me pure: / Only the pure shall see Thee as Thou art.
Lord, make us all love all: that when we meet / Even myriads of earth's myriads at Thy Bar.
Lord, Save Us, We Perish.
Lord Thomas and Fair Margaret.
Lord, Thou art fulness, I am emptiness.
Lord, we are rivers running to Thy sea.
Lord, what have I that I may offer Thee?
Lord, what have I to offer? sickening fear.
Lotus-Eaters: Ulysses to Penelope, The.
Love and Death.
Love and Hope.
Love Attacked.
Love builds a nest on earth and waits for rest.
Love Defended.
Love Ephemeral.
Love from The North.
Love hath a name of Death.
Love is all happiness, love is all beauty.
Love Is Strong as Death. ("As flames that consume").
Love Is Strong as Death. ("I have not sought Thee, I have not found Thee").
Love Lies Bleeding.
Love loveth Thee, and wisdom loveth Thee.
Love me,—I love you / Love me, my baby.
Love of Christ Which Passeth Knowledge, The.
Love, to be love, must walk Thy way / And work Thy Will.
Lowest Place, The.
Lowest Room, The.
Lugubre e vagabondo in terra e in mare.
Lullaby, oh lullaby! / Flowers are closed and lambs are sleeping.
Luscious and Sorrowful.
Maggie a Lady.
Maiden May.
Maiden-Song.
Man's life is but a working day / Whose tasks are set aright.
March.
Margaret has a milking-pail, / And she rises early.
Margery.

Mariana.
Martyr, A.
Martyr, The.
Martyrs' Song.
Marvel of Marvels.
Mary Magdalene and the Other Mary.
Massacre of Perugia, The.
Master Is Come, and Calleth for Thee, The.
Maude Clare.
Maundy Thursday.
May.
Me and my gift: kind Lord, behold.
Me you often meet / In London's crowded street.
Meeting.
Memento Mori.
Memory.
Methinks the ills of life I fain would shun.
Michael F. M. Rossetti.
Mid-Lent.
Minnie and Mattie.
Minnie bakes oaten cakes, / Minnie brews ale.
Mirage.
Mirrors of Life and Death.
Mr. and Mrs. Scott, and I.
Mix a Pancake.
Monday in Holy Week.
Monna Innominata.
Months: A Pageant, The.
Moonshine.
Mother and Child.
Mother Country.
Mother shake the cherry-tree.
Motherless baby and babyless mother.
Motherless soft lambkin / Alone upon a hill.
My baby has a father and a mother.
My baby has a mottled fist.
My Dream.
My Friend.
My Gift.
My God, wilt Thou accept, and will not we / Give aught to Thee?
My Mouse.
My old admiration before I was twenty.
My Old Friends.
Name of Jesus, The.
Ne' sogni ti veggo.
Nel verno accanto al fuoco.
New creatures; the Creator still the Same.
New Enigmas.
Next of Kin.
Night and Death.
Ninna nanna, ninna nanna!
No, Thank You, John.
Noble Sisters.
Non Son Io La Rosa Ma Vi Stetti Appresso.
None Other Lamb None Other Name.
None With Him.
Nostre Voluntà Quieti Virtù di Carità.
Not Yours But You.
November.
Novice, The.
Now They Desire.
Now They Desire a Better Country.
O Christ my God Who seest the unseen.
O Christ our All in each, our All in all!
O ciliegia infiorita.
O Death Where Is Thy Sting?
O foolish Soul! to make thy count / For languid falls and much forgiven.
O glorious sea that in each climbing wave.
O Lady Moon.
O Lord, I am ashamed to seek Thy Face / As tho' I loved Thee as Thy saints love Thee.
O Lord, I cannot plead my love of Thee.
O Lord, on Whom we gaze and dare not gaze, / Increase our faith that gazing we may see.
O Lord, when Thou didst call me, didst Thou know.
O Lucifer, Son of the Morning!
O marinaro che mi apporti tu?
O mine enemy / Rejoice not over me!
O Sailor, Come Ashore.
O thou who tell'st me that all hope is over.

O uommibatto / Agil, giocondo.
O wind, where have you been.
O wind, why do you never rest.
O ye, who are not dead and fit.
O ye who love today, / Turn away / From Patience with her silver ray.
October.
October Garden, An.
Of each sad word which is more sorrowful.
Of Him That Was Ready to Perish.
Of My Life.
Offering of the New Law, the One Oblation Once Offered, The.
Oggi.
Oh fair to see / Bloom-laden cherry tree.
Oh, Fair to See.
Oh Forza Irresistibile Dell'umile Preghiera.
Oh knell of a passing time, / Will it never cease to chime?
Oib ò, piccina / Tutto atterrita.
Old and New Year Ditties.
Old-World Thicket, An.
On Albina.
On Keats, 18 January, 1948 (Eve of St Agnes).
On the Death of a Cat.
On the grassy banks / Lambkins at their pranks.
On the note you do not send me.
On the Wing.
Once.
Once for All. (Margaret).
1 and 1 are 2— / That's for me and you.
One Certainty, The.
One Day.
One Foot on Sea, and One on Shore.
One of the Dead.
One of the Soldiers with a Spear Pierced His Side.
One Sea-Side Grave.
One Swallow Does Not Make a Summer.
One woe is past. Come what come will.
Only Believe.
Otto ore suonano: / Picchia il postino!
Our Church Palms are Budding Willow Twigs.
Our heaven must be within ourselves / Our home and heaven the work of faith.
Our life is long. Not so, wise Angels say.
Our little baby fell asleep.
Our Mothers, lovely women pitiful; / Our sisters, gracious in their life and death.
Our Widowed Queen.
Out of the Deep.
P.R.B., The.
Palm Sunday.
Paradise.
Paradise: in a Symbol.
Parting after parting, / Sore loss and gnawing pain.
Passing and Glassing.
Passing Away.
Passing away the bliss, / The anguish passing away.
Passion Flower hath sprung up tall, The.
Passiontide.
Pastime.
Patience must dwell with Love, for Love and Sorrow.
Patience of Hope.
Pause, A.
Pause of Thought, A.
Peace I Leave with You.
Peach tree on the southern wall, The.
Peacock has a score of eyes, The.
Peal of Bells, A.
Per Preferenza.
Perfect Love Casteth Out Fear.
Pesano rena e pena.
Peter Grump.
Pin has a head, but has no hair, A.
Piteous my rhyme is / What while I muse of love and pain.
Pitia a Damone.
Plague, The.
Playing at bob cherry / Tom and Nell and Hugh.

Pocket handkerchief to hem, A.
Poor Ghost, The.
Porco la zucca / Fitta in parrucca!
Portrait, A.
Portraits.
Praise of Love.
Praying Always.
Present and Future.
Prince's Progress, The.
Prodigal Son, A.
Promises like Pie-Crust.
Purification of St. Mary the Virgin, The.
Purpurea rosa / Dolce, odorosa.
Pussy has a whiskered face, / Kitty has such pretty ways.
Quanto a Lei grata io sono.
Queen of Hearts, The.
Queen Rose.
Quinquagesima.
Ransomed of the Lord, The.
Redeeming the Time.
Reflection.
Rejoice with Me.
Remember [Me].
Repining.
Rest.
Resurgam.
Resurrection Eve.
Ring Posy, A.
Ring upon her finger, / Walks the bride, A.
Ripetizione.
Rivals.
River Thames (?).
Rogationtide.
Rosalind.
Rose, The.
Rose has thorns as well as honey, A.
Rose Plant in Jericho, A.
Rose that blushes rosy red, The.
Rose with such a bonny blush, The.
Roses blushing red and white, / For delight.
Roses on a brier, / Pearls from out the bitter sea.
Rosy maiden Winifred, / With a milkpail on her head.
Roundel seems to fit a round of days, A.
Royal Princess, A.
Ruin.
Ruined Cross, The.
Rushes in a watery place, / And reeds in a hollow.
S'addorment ò la nostra figliolina.
Safe where I cannot lie yet, / Safe where I hope to lie too.
St. Andrew's Church.
St. Barnanbas.
St. Bartholomew.
St. Elizabeth of Hungary.
St. John, Apostle.
St. Mark.
St. Michael and all Angels.
St. Peter.
St. Peter once: "Lord, dost Thou wash my feet?"
St. Valentine's Day 1881.
Saints and Angels.
Salta, ranocchio, e mostrati.
Sapessi Pure!
Sappho.
Scarce tolerable life, which all life long.
Scavai la neve,—sì che scavai!
Se Cossi Fosse.
Se Fossi Andata a Hastings.
Seasons.
Seeking Rest.
Seldom "can't," / Seldom "don't."
September.
Septuagesima.
Serenade: "Come, wander forth with me!"
Seven vials hold Thy wrath: but what can hold.
Sexagesima.
Shadows Today.
Shall I Forget?
Shall not the Judge of all the earth do right?
She Came from The Uttermost Part of the Earth.

She Shall Be Brought unto the King.
Short is time, and only time is bleak.
Shut Out.
Sì che il fratello s'ha falconcello.
Si Rimanda La Tocca-Caldaja.
Sick Child's Meditation, A.
Sing me a song— / What shall I sing?
Sing-Song sels.
Sing-Song.
Sinner's own fault? So it was, The.
Sir Eustace Grey.
Sir Winter.
Sister Maude.
Sit Down in the Lowest Room.
Sketch, A.
Slain from the Foundation of the World.
Slain in their high places: fallen on rest.
Sleep at Sea.
Sleep, Sleep Happy Child; All Creation Slept and Smiled.
Sleeping at last, the trouble and tumult over.
Smile and a Sigh, A.
So Great a Cloud of Witnesses.
So I began my walk of life; no stop.
So I grew half delirious and quite sick.
Soeur Louise De La Miséricorde.
Solitary Rose, The.
Some ladies dress in muslin full and white.
Somewhere or Other.
Son, Remember.
Song: "I have loved you for long years Ellen."
Song: "I saw her; she was lovely."
Song: "It is not for her even brow."
Song: "Oh roses for the flush of youth."
Song: "Oh what comes over the sea."
Song: "She sat and sang alway."
Song: "Stream moaneth as it floweth, The."
Song: "Two doves upon the selfsame branch."
Song: "We buried her among the flowers."
Song: "When I am dead, my dearest."
Songs in a Cornfield.
Song for the Least of All Saints, A.
Song of Flight, A.
Song of the Star, The.
Sonnet: "Some say that love and joy are one: and so."
Sonnet from the Psalms.
Sonnets are full of love, and this my tome.
Sooner or later: yet at last / The Jordan must be past.
Sorrow hath a double voice, / Sharp today but sweet tomorrow.
Soul rudderless, unbraced.
Sound Sleep.
Sposa velata, / Innanellata.
Spring.
Spring Fancies sels.
Spring Fancies.
Spring is come again not as at first.
Spring Quiet.
Spunta la margherita.
Standing Afar Off for the Fear of Her Torment.
Strange voices sing among the planets which.
Stroke a flint, and there is nothing to admire.
Study. (A Soul), A.
Subject To Like Passions as We Are.
Succession of Kings, The.
Summer.
Summer Is Ended.
Summer Is Ended, The.
Summer nights are short, / Where northern days are long, The.
Summer Wish, A.
Sunday Before Advent.
Sunshine.
Surely He Hath Borne Our Griefs.
Surely there is an aching void within.
Sursum Corda.
Sweet Death.
Sweetness of rest when Thou sheddest rest.
Swift and sure the swallow.
Symbols.
Take Care Of Him.
Take No Thought for The Morrow.

Tasso and Leonora.
Tempus Fugit.
Testimony, A.
That Eden of earth's sunrise cannot vie.
That No Man Take Thy Crown.
That Where I Am, There Ye May Be Also.
That Which Hath Been Is Named Already, and It Is Known That It Is Man.
Then I Commended Mirth.
Then Shall Ye Shout.
Then They That Feared the Lord Spake Often One to Another.
Then Whose Shall Those Things Be?
There Is a Budding Morrow in Midnight.
There is but one May in the year.
There is one that has a head without an eye.
There Remaineth Therefore a Rest.
There Remaineth Therefore a Rest for the People of God ("Come blessed sleep...").
There Remaineth Therefore a Rest to the People of God ("Rest remains when all is done...").
There's Snow on the Fields.
These All Wait upon Thee.
They Desire a Better Country.
They lie at rest, our blessed dead.
They Put Their Trust in Thee, and Were Not Confounded.
They Shall Be as White as Snow.
They Toil Not, Neither Do They Spin.
This Life Is Full of Numbness.
This near-at-hand land breeds pain by measure.
Thou Art Fairer Than the Children of Men.
Thou, God, Seest Me.
Thou Knewest..Thou Oughtest Therefore.
Thou sleepest where the lilies fade.
Thread of Life, The.
Three Enemies, The.
Three little children / On the wide wide earth.
Three Moments.
Three Nuns.
Three Plum Buns.
Three Seasons.
Three Stages *sels.*
Three Stages.
Thro' burden and heat of the day.
Thy Brother's Blood Crieth.
Thy fainting spouse, yet still Thy spouse.
Thy Friend and Thy Father's Friend Forget Not.
Thy lilies drink the dew, / Thy lambs the rill, and I will drink them too.
Thy Name, O Christ, as incense streaming forth.
Thy Servant Will Go and Fight with This Philistine.
Till Tomorrow.
Time lengthening, in the lengthening seemeth long.
Time of Waiting, The.
Time passeth away with its pleasure and pain.
Time seems not short: / If so I call to mind.
To Every Seed His Own Body.
To Lalla, Reading My Verses Topsy-Turvy.
To Love and to Remember.
To Mary Rossetti.
To My Fior-Di-Lisa.
To My Friend Elizabeth.
To My Mother on Her Birthday.
To the End.
To What Purpose Is This Waste?
Toadstool comes up in a night, A.
Today For Me.
Today's Burden.
Toll, bell, toll. For hope is flying / Sighing from the earthbound soul.
Touching "Never."
Trees' Counselling, The.
Triad, A.
Trinity Sunday.
True Story, A.
Truly the Light Is Sweet.
Tu scendi dalle stelle, O Re del Cielo.
Tuesday in Holy Week.

Tune Me, O Lord, into One Harmony.
Twice.
Twilight Calm.
Twilight Night.
Twist me a crown of wind-flowers.
Two Parted.
Two Pursuits.
Two Rossettis (Brothers They), The.
Two Thoughts of Death.
Udite, si dolgono mesti fringuelli.
Under the ivy bush / One sits sighing.
Under Willows.
Undine.
Unforgotten.
Unspotted lambs to follow the one Lamb.
Until the Day Break.
Uphill [*or* Up-Hill].
Vain Shadow, A.
Valentine, 1882, A.
Valentine, 1877, A.
Valentines From C.G.R.
Vanity of Vanities.
Venus's Looking-Glass.
Versi.
Vigil of all Saints.
Vigil of St. Bartholomew.
Vigil of St. Peter.
Vigil of the Annunciation.
Vigil of the Presentation.
Was Thy Wrath against the Sea?
Watchers, The.
Water Spirit's Song, The.
Way of the World, The.
We are of those who tremble at Thy word.
We know not when, we know not where.
Weary in Well-Doing.
Wednesday in Holy Week.
Wee wee husband, / Give me some money.
Weigh all my faults and follies righteously.
What?
What Are Heavy?
What are these lovely ones, yea, what are these?
What do the stars do / Up in the sky.
What Does the Bee Do?
What does the donkey bray about?
What Good Shall My Life Do Me?
What Hath God Wrought!
What is it Jesus saith unto the soul?
What is Pink?
What Is That to Thee? Follow Thou Me.
What is the beginning? Love. What the course? Love still.
What is this above thy head, / O Man?
What Sappho Would Have Said Had Her Leap Cured Instead of Killing Her.
What to Do?
What will it be, O my soul, what will it be.
What will you give me for my pound?
What Would I Give?
What's in a Name?
Whatsoever Is Right, That Shall Ye Receive.
When a mounting skylark sings / In the sunlit summer morn.
When fishes set umbrellas up / If the rain-drops run.
When I Was in Trouble I Called upon the Lord.
When My Heart Is Vexed, I Will Complain ("O Lord, how canst Thou say...").
When My Heart Is Vexed I Will Complain ("Fields are white to harvest, look and see, The").
When the cows come home the milk is coming.
When wickedness is broken as a tree / Paradise comes to light, ah holy land!
Where Innocent Bright-Eyed Daisies Are.
Where love is, there comes sorrow / Today or else tomorrow.
Where Neither Rust Nor Moth Doth Corrupt.
Where never tempest heaveth, / Nor sorrow grieveth.
Where shall I find a white rose blowing?
Where Their Worm Dieth Not, and the Fire Is Not Quenched.
White hen sitting / On white eggs three, A.

Whither the Tribes Go Up, Even the Tribes of the Lord.
Whitsun Day.
Whitsun Eve.
Whitsun Monday.
Whitsun Tuesday.
Who cares for earthly bread tho' white?
Who Has Seen the Wind?
Who Hath Despised the Day of Small Things?
Who Have a Form of Godliness.
Who is this that cometh up not alone.
Who Shall Deliver Me?
Who shall my wandering thoughts steady & fix.
Who sits with the King in His Throne? Not a slave but a Bride.
Who would wish back the Saints upon our rough.
Whole Head Is Sick, and the Whole Heart Faint, The.
Whom the Lord Loveth He Chasteneth.
Why?
Why did baby die, / Making Father sigh.
Wife to Husband.
Will of the Lord Be Done, The.
Will These Hands Ne'er Be Clean?
Will you be there? my yearning heart has cried.
Wind has such a rainy sound, The.
Wind of January, The.
Winter: My Secret.
Winter Rain.
Wintry Sonnet, A.
Wishes: Sonnet.
Within the Veil.
Word for the Dumb, A.
World, The.
World's Harmonies, The.
Worship God.
Would that I were a turnip white.
Wouldst thou give me a heavy jewelled crown.
Wrens and robins in the hedge.
Yawn, A.
Ye Are Come unto Mount Sion.
Ye Have Forgotten the Exhortation.
Ye That Fear Him, Both Small and Great.
Yea, blessed and holy is he that hath part in the First / Resurrection!
Yea, I Have a Goodly Heritage.
Yea, if Thou wilt, Thou canst put up Thy sword.
Yea, the Sparrow Hath Found Her an House.
Year Afterwards, A.
Year's Windfalls, A.
Yes, I too could face death and never shrink.
Yet a Little While ("I dreamed and did not seek...").
Yet a Little While ("These days are long...").
You who looked on passed ages as a glass.
Young Death.
Young Men Aye Were Fickle Found Since Summer Trees Were Leafy.
Your brother has a falcon.
Zara.
Zion Said.

Rukeyser, Muriel (1913–80)
Absalom.
Adventures, Midnight.
After Melville.
After Their Quarrel.
Afterwards.
Air.
Ajanta.
Akiba.
All Souls.
All the Little Animals.
All the way through the forest, a sound of birdsong.
Alloy.
Along History.
Among Grass.
And a girl singing in the symbol air, crossing of gold, a.
Anemone.
Ann Burlak.

Another Day. A Game of Toys. Paul, Telling the Game.
Another Day (And then the cow).
Another Day (Child among his powers).
Another Day (Day Lilies, Yellow Daisies).
Another Day. For a Moment Slipping Back, Again the Unreal King.
Another Day (I will now sing).
Another Day. In a Field of Peace the Child, Playing. The Child Preparing for Daytime Sleep.
Another Day (Miss Lorence).
Another Day. Paul in the Mountains of Fantasy. Paul Tells His Adventure.
Another Day. The Children Are All Eating.
Another Day (You can't come).
Another Day (You sit there).
Are You Born? / I.
Are You Born? / II.
Arthur Peyton.
Artifact.
As he stood near the plane, they heard him say.
Asleep and Awake.
Asylum Song.
Back Tooth.
Backside of the Academy, The.
Ballad of Orange and Grape.
Ballad Theme, A.
Beast in View.
Before Danger.
Believing in Those Inexorable Laws.
Bill, The.
Birth, A.
Birth of Venus, The.
Blood is Justified, The.
Blue Flower, The.
Blue Spruce.
Book of the Dead, The.
Born in December.
Boy with His Hair Cut Short.
Boys in the Branches.
Boys of These Men Full Speed.
Breaking Open.
Breaking the nets of the world, in glimpses going.
Breathing Landscape.
Brilliant, the full-bodied, the real of the world in their powers, The.
Bringing.
Bubble of Air.
Bunk Johnson Blowing.
Burlesque.
Burning Bush.
Burnishing, Oakland.
But in these years, what is free, what is strong?
Canal.
Cannibal Bratuscha.
Cats and a Cock.
Certain Music, A.
Chapman.
Chapultepec Park / I.
Chapultepec Park / II.
Charm for Cantinflas, A.
Child and Mother.
Child Asleep, The.
Child in the Great Wood.
Child of the root, among your apples and forests.
Child wakes in the morning to enter a country, The.
Children, the Sandbar, That Summer.
Children's Orchard, The.
Christmas Eve.
Citation for Horace Gregory.
City of Monuments.
Clouds, Airs, Carried me Away.
Clues.
Conjugation of the Paramecium, The.
Cornfield, The.
Correspondences.
Course.
Crayon House.
Cries from Chiapas.
Cruise, The.
Dam, The.

Darkness Music.
Deep in the Century of Opposites.
Delta Poems.
Desdichada.
Despisals.
Destruction of Grief.
Disease, The.
Disease: After-Effects, The.
Divining Water.
Do you know Hitler? Does he like you?
Do you know what I play to be, in bed at night?
Doctors, The.
Don Baty, the Draft Resister.
Double Dialogue: Homage to Robert Frost.
Double Ode.
Down from Chicago Bryan came.
Down the stairs flying, looks at the surfaces.
Dream-Drumming.
Dreaming we were awake, we heard the rivers.
Driveway.
Drowning Young Man, The.
Drunken Girl.
During the journey there come moments of waking.
Easter Eve 1945.
Eccentric Motion.
Eel.
Effort at Speech between Two People.
Eighth Elegy. Children's Elegy.
Endless.
Evening Plaza, San Miguel.
Everything here is real and of our joy.
Exile of Music.
Eyes of Night-Time.
F.O.M.
Fable: "Yes it was the prince's kiss."
Facing Sentencing.
Father dreams that he was hid in a tree, The.
Fields where we slept.
Fifth Elegy. A Turning Wind.
Fighting for Roses.
Filament carrying morning through the waves, A.
First Elegy. Rotten Lake.
Flashing Cliff, A.
Flying Red Horse, The.
Flying to Hanoi.
Foghorn in Horror.
For a Mexican Painter.
For Fun.
For Kayle Boyle.
For Memory.
For My Son.
Forerunners.
Formosa.
Four in a Family.
Fourth Elegy. The Refugees.
From a Play: Publisher's Song.
From the Duck-Pond to the Carousel.
From the throat he can rally strength. Remembering.
Game of Ball, A.
Game of Darts at the Chesterfield Arms, A.
Gates, The.
Gauley Bridge.
George Robinson: Blues.
Gibbs.
Gift.
Gift-Poem ("December steel done...").
Gift-Poem ("Year in its cold beginning").
Girl at the Play.
Gold Leaf.
Gradus ad Parnassum.
Grand Central Station.
Green Limits.
Gullies as deep as halls held these surveyors.
Gyroscope, The.
Handclap.
Haying Before Storm.
He Had a Quality of Growth.
He is breaking the nets in his wildness for the real.
He starts awake in the city. Orion believing.
He turned cruel. Absorbed in his own cruelty.
He turns through the lucid stars of a lit city.

He would do as he had done in other states.
Hero Speech.
His Dream of Flood: And Eden.
His father is lost and away.
His gay words, words of delight.
His Head is Full of Faces.
Holy Family.
Homage to Literature.
How was he first aware he would never walk again?
How We Did It.
I have tried to show the atom as a source.
I used to press tools in the Texas oil fields.
Ice from the wings, a rattle against metal. All right, come down.
Ice-gate over the land, a shock of closure.
If you look at your succession of desires.
In a Dark House.
In a summer forest, when the profuse season.
In Hades, Orpheus.
In Her Burning.
In Our Time.
In the last hour of night, a zebra racing dawn.
In the Night the Sound Woke Us.
In the Underworld.
In yo ur time, there have been those who spoke clearly.
Into the the air far. Into the opposites.
Iris.
Iris-Eaters, The.
Islands.
It is the sixth year of the war in China.
It Is There.
Ives.
Jetty. Dover, The.
Juanita Tinsley.
Judith.
Junk-Heap at Murano.
Käthe Kollwitz.
Key, The.
King's Mountain.
Knowledge my nakedness.
Landscpe with Wave Approaching.
Lat. 10 Degrees North, Long. 45 Degrees West.
Leaving New York, I looked back fourteen times.
Leg in a Plaster Cast, A.
Letter to the Front.
Letter, Unposted.
Light falling on that filled will drives.
Lilienthal said : I heard him saying words like these.
Little Stone in the Middle of the Road, in Florida, A.
Loan, The.
Long Enough. Long Enough.
Long Past Moncada.
Looking.
Looking at Each Other.
Lost Romans, The.
Louis Sonnet, A.
Love and its Doors and Windows.
Lover as Fox.
Lynchings of Jesus, The.
M-Day's Child is Fair of Face.
Madboy's Song.
Make and be eaten, the poet says.
Man in a plane looks at the surface of land, A.
Man sits in the rocking bedroom, claws, The.
Martin Luther King, Malcolm X.
Mary Sleeth.
Mearl Blankenship.
Mediterranean.
Meeting, The.
Mendings.
Metaphor to Action.
Minotaur, The.
Miss Lorence, you are a tree with leaves on.
More Clues.
More of a Corpse than a Woman.
Mortal Girl.
Mother Garden's Round.
Motive of All of It, The.
Mountain: One from Bryant.

Movie.
Mrs. Walpurga.
Ms. Lot.
My name is Timmy Torin.
My toes feel like nothing they are so cold.
Myth.
Neruda, the Wine.
Network that emerges. At the ocean, A.
Nevertheless the Moon.
Night Feeding.
Night Flight New York.
Night-Music.
Nine Poems for the Unborn Child.
Ninth Elegy. The Antagonists.
Niobe Now.
Noguchi.
Not leaves, not lightning, not the greatness of
    rivers.
Not to Be Printed, Not to Be Said, Not to Be
    Thought.
Not Yet.
Notes for a Poem.
Now Green, Now Burning.
Now he plays with the other children.
Now that the river has changed, my dear.
Nuns in the Wind.
Of Money. And the Past.
Oh, he *is* sweet. I do love him sometimes.
On the Death of Her Mother.
One Month.
One Soldier.
Orgy.
Orpheus.
Otherworld.
Outer Banks, The.
Outpost.
Overthrow of One o'Clock at Night, The.
Painters.
Palos Verdes Cliffs.
Panacea.
Paper Anniversary.
Parades. Rattle of palm trees. The silver
    planes.
Parallel Invention.
Peace the great meaning has not been
    defined.
Phaneron.
Place at Albert Bay, The.
Place-Rituals.
Poem as Mask, The.
Poem: "Green going through the jungle of
    those years."
Poem: "I lived in the first century of world
    wars."
Poem Out of Childhood.
Poem White Page White Page Poem.
Portrait of a Man, with a Background of
    Holdings.
Pouring Milk Away.
Power.
Power never dominion. / Some other power.
Power of Suicide, The.
Power of war leads to a plan of lives, The.
Praise of the Committee.
Preamble.
Private Life of the Sphinx.
Professionals see the signs in the dice, the
    signs in the cards and clouds, The.
Question, The.
Radio silence of aircraft over the dense
    ocean.
Rang and rang, rang in a small boy's head.
Reading Time : 1 Minute 26 Seconds.
Recovering.
Red bridge fastening this city to the forest,
    A.
Resurrection of the Right Side.
Return, The.
Ringling.
Risen Image Shines, The.
Rite.
Road, The.
Rock Flow, River Mix.
Rondel: "Now that I am fifty-six."
Rune.
Running of the Grunion, The.
Ryder.

Sacred Lake.
St. Roach.
Salamander.
Sand-Quarry with Moving Figures.
Say it depends on the interpretation.
Sea has opened, the limit of his dream, The.
Sea Mercy.
Searching / Not Searching.
Second Elegy. Age of Magicians.
Secrets of American Civilization.
Seeming, The.
Segre Song.
Sestina: "Coming to Spain on the first day of
    the fighting."
Seventh Avenue.
Seventh Elegy. Dream-Singing Elegy.
Shooting Gallery.
Shortest Way Home, The.
Silence of Volcanoes.
Simple Experiment, A.
Six Canons, The.
Sixth Elegy. River Elegy.
Sixth Night: Waking, The.
Slow Death of the Dragon.
Slow Dialogue between Pain and Roosevelt.
Song for Dead Children.
Song, from "Mr. Amazeen on the River."
Song from *Puck Fair.*
Song: Love in Whose Rich Honor.
Song: Lying in Daylight.
Song of Another Tribe, A.
Song: Remembering Movies.
Song, the Brain-Coral.
Song: The Star in the Nets of Heaven.
Song: "Voice flew out of the river as
    morning flew, A."
Song: "World is full of loss; bring, wind, my
    love, The."
Sonnet:"My thoughts through yours refracted
    into speech."
Soul and Body of John Brown, The.
Sound of screaming for thirteen centuries, A.
Sounds of night in the country of the
    opposites.
Speaking Tree, The.
Speech for the Assistant, from Houdini.
Speech of the Mother, from "The Middle of
    the Air."
Speed of Darkness, The.
Speed, We Say.
Spirals and Fugues.
Statement by Willkie after Returning from
    England.
Statement: Philippa Allen.
Story, A.
Street corner to corner he will talk all day.
Structure is rising. It takes on shape, it takes
    on meaning, A.
Structure of the Plane, The.
Study in a Late Subway.
Suicide Blues.
Suite for Lord Timothy Dexter.
Summer, the Sacramento.
Sun-Artist, The.
Sun on the faces. On the knotted rocks.
Sundays, They Sleep Late.
Surrounded, The.
Target Practice.
Tarpaper shack and the red rose bush, The.
Tenth Elegy. Elegy in Joy.
Then.
Then I forget / The star in the nets of
    heaven.
Then I Saw What the Calling Was.
Theory of Flight.
There is a knotless line westward, past
    terraces.
There they slept. They left the train.
They Came to Me and Said, "There Is a
    Child."
They dug up the grave, while a banjo and
    two guitars.
They pray. Security against oldness.
They rule out of our justice and our despair.
They talk to each other, and he holds her
    hand.
Third Elegy. The Fear of Form.

This House, This Country.
This is going to be about smoke.
This is what lit the hunters of smoke and the
    paths of the forest.
This Place in the Ways.
Thousands of Days.
Three Black Women.
Three Sides of a Coin.
Time Exposures.
Time Hinder Not Me; His Arms Reach Here
    and There.
Time of finks and nobles, A.
To Enter That Rhythm Where the Self Is
    Lost.
To follow the hard sunlight on the northern
    harbor.
To keep the weakness secret. To deny it and
    break through.
Track cuts west. Slant roof, sun-catcher, The.
Traditional Tune.
Transgress, The.
Tree.
Tree of rivers flowing through our lives, A.
Tree of rivers seen and forgotten, The.
Trinity Churchyard.
Trophies.
Tunnel, The.
Two Illuminations, The.
Two Years.
Unborn Song.
Until I stand on the January platform.
Up past the burnt hills. Distance and the
    crowd.
Victims, a Play for the Home, The.
Voices.
Voices of Waking.
Waiting for Icarus.
Waking this Morning.
War Comes into my Room, The.
Wards, The.
Watchers, The.
Water-hammer, the history of ice, The.
Water Night.
Waterlily Fire.
Wedding Presents.
Welcome from War.
West Virginia.
What Do I Give You?
What Do We See?
What do you know of America? I asked a
    little Russian schoolgirl.
What do you write?
What Have You Brought Home from the
    Wars?
What I See.
What They Said.
Whatever roams the air is traveling.
Wheels and galleries of the control of tears.
When he began to witness, it was not to a
    journey.
When the true things meet us at the place we
    reach, they are all.
When the young man reaches his full height.
Where will you be tonight? Past Lisbon,
    flying.
Wherever.
Who in One Lifetime.
Willkie in the *Gulliver.*
Willkie—Stopless Falling through Air.
Willkie: Words from Russia.
Wind arrow, wind rose, the wind currents in
    air.
Woman and Emblems.
Woman as Market.
Wooden Spring.
Word of Mouth.
Work, for the Day Is Coming.
Work in the loss of mass, The.
Wreath of Women.
Writer, The.
Young Girl of the Mississippi Valley, The.
Young Men, The.

S

St. John, David (b. 1949)
    Art of Argument, the Argument of Art, The.

At Italo's.
Avenues, The.
Black Poppy (At the Temple).
Blue Waves.
Boathouse, The.
Body of Desire, The.
Chapter Forever.
Day of the Sentry, The.
Desire.
Dolls.
Doors, The.
Elegy: "Who keeps the owl's breath? Whose
    eyes desire?"
Essay on Liberation, An.
Fan Sketched with Silver Egrets, A.
Francesco and Clare.
Gin.
Guitar.
Hard & Noble Patience, A.
Hotel of Ash.
Hotel Sierra.
Hush.
I Know.
Interlude: Hephaestion's Prayer.
Iris.
Last Night with Rafaella.
Leap of Faith.
Lemons, The.
Los Angeles, 1954.
Love for the Dragon.
Lucifer in Starlight.
Man in the Yellow Gloves, The.
Meditation.
Mercenary Muse.
Meridian.
Merlin.
My Friend.
My Tea with Madame Descartes.
1984.
No Heaven.
Of Time & the Body.
Ostia.
Reef, The.
Shadow.
Shore, The.
Six/Nine/Forty-Four.
Slow Dance.
Song without Forgiveness.
Study for the World's Body.
Swan at Sheffield Park, The.
Terraces of Rain.
To Pasolini.
Una Vita Violenta (1955).
Until the Sea Is Dead.
Wavelength.
Wedding Preparations in the Country.
Who is she, coming along the street, turning
    the heads.
Winter Fires.
Winter Sun.
Woman and Leopard.

Sandburg, Carl (1878–1967)
A. E. F.
Abracadabra Boys, The.
Accomplished Facts.
Acquaintance with Death, Sir.
Adelaide Crapsey.
Again?
Air Circus.
Alice Corbin Is Gone.
Alix.
All Day Long.
Alley Rats.
Almanac.
Alone and Not Alone.
Aloof.
Altgeld.
Always the Mob.
Ambassadors of Grief.
Among the Red Guns.
And So Today.
And They Obey.
And This Will Be All?
Anecdote of Hemlock for Two Athenians.
Anna Imroth.
Answer, The.
Anywhere and Everywhere People.

Aprons of Silence.
Arithmetic.
Ashurnatsirpal III.
Aster, a farewell-summer flower, stays long
    in the last fall weeks, An.
At a Window.
At the Gates of Tombs.
Atlas, How Have You Been?
Auburn.
Auctioneer.
Autumn Movement.
Aztec.
Aztec Mask.
Baby Face.
Baby Song of the Four Winds.
Baby Toes.
Baby Vamps.
Back Yard.
Balloon Faces.
Baltic Fog Notes.
Band Concert.
Bars.
Bas-Relief.
Basket.
Bath.
Be Ready.
Beat, Old Heart.
Bee Song.
Between Two Hills.
Between Worlds.
Bilbea.
Biography.
Bird Footprint.
Bird Talk.
Bitter Summer Thoughts.
Bitter Summer Thoughts—No. 3.
Bitter Summer Thoughts—No. XXII.
Black Horizons.
Blacklisted.
Blizzard Notes.
Blossom Themes.
Blue Island Intersection.
Blue Maroons.
Blue Ridge.
Bluebird, What Do You Feed On?
'Boes.
Bones.
Books Men Die For.
Boxes and Bags.
Boy and Father.
Brainwashing.
Branches.
Brancusi.
Brass Keys.
Bricklayer Love.
Bright Conversation with Saint-Ex.
Brim.
Bringers.
Broadway.
Broken-Face Gargoyles.
Broken Hearted Soprano.
Broken Sky.
Broken Sonnet.
Broken Tabernacles.
Bronzes.
Brown Gold.
Bubbles.
Buckwheat.
Buffalo Bill.
Buffalo Dusk.
Bug Spots.
Bundles.
Butter Colors.
Buttons.
Buyers and Sellers.
Caboose Thoughts.
Cadenza.
Cahokia.
Cahoots.
Caligari.
Call the Next Witness.
Calls.
Canadians and Pottawatomies.
Carlovingian Dreams.
Cartoon.
Chamfort.
Changing Light Winds.

Chasers.
Cheap Blue.
Cheap Rent.
Chicago Boy Baby.
Chicago Poet.
Chicks.
Child.
Child Face.
Child Margaret.
Child Moon.
Child of the Romans.
Chillicothe.
Choices.
Choose.
Chords.
Chromo.
Circle of Doors.
City Number.
Clark Street Bridge.
Clean Curtains.
Clean Hands.
Clefs.
Clinton South of Polk.
Clocks.
Coin, A.
Consolation Sonata.
Cool Tombs.
Corn and Beans.
Corn Hut Talk.
Corn Prattlings.
Cornfield Ridge and Stream.
Cornucopia.
Counting.
Couple, A.
Couples.
Crabapple Blossoms.
Crabapples.
Crapshooters.
Cricket Match.
Crimson.
Crimson Changes People.
Crimson Rambler.
Cripple.
Crisscross.
Crossed Numbers.
Crossing the Ohio When Poppies Bloom in
    Ashtabula.
Crossing the Paces.
Crucible.
Cumulatives.
Cups of Coffee.
Curse of a Rich Polish Peasant on His Sister
    Who Ran Away with a Wild Man.
Dan.
Dancer.
Daybreak.
Death Snips Proud Men.
Deep Sea Wandering.
Destroyers.
Dialogue.
Different Kinds of Good-by.
Dinosaur Bones, The.
Do You Want Affidavits?
Docks.
Dogheads.
Doors.
Dragoons, I tell you the white hydrangeas
    turn rust and go soon.
Dream Girl.
Dreaming Fool.
Dreams in the Dusk.
Drowsy.
Drumnotes.
Dunes.
Dust.
Dusty Doors.
Dynamiter.
Early Copper.
Early Hours.
Early Lynching.
Early Moon.
Electric Sign Goes Dark, An.
Elephants Are Different to Different People.
Eleventh Avenue Racket.
Elm Buds.
Enemy Number One.
Epistle: "Jesus loved the sunsets on Galilee."

Even Numbers.
Evening Questions.
Evening Sea Wind.
Evening Sunsets Witness and Pass On, The.
Evening Waterfall.
Ever a Seeker.
Explanations of Love.
Face.
Falltime.
Fame If Not Fortune.
Far Rockaway Night Till Morning.
Fate.
Feather Lights.
Fellow Citizens.
Fence, A.
Field People.
Fifty-Fifty.
Fight.
Films.
Finish.
Fins.
Fire Dreams.
Fire-Logs.
Fire Pages.
Fireborn Are at Home in Fire, The.
First Sonata for Karlen Paula.
Fish Crier.
Five Cent Balloons.
Five Towns on the B. and O.
Flanders.
Flash Crimson.
Flat Lands.
Flat Waters of the West in Kansas.
Flowers Tell Months.
Flux.
Flying Fish.
Fog.
Fog Numbers.
Fog Portrait.
Follies.
Foolish About Windows.
For You.
Forgotten Wars.
Four Brothers, The.
Four Preludes on Playthings of the Wind.
Four Steichen Prints.
Fourth of July Night.
Foxgloves.
François Villon Forgotten.
Freedom is a Habit.
Frog Songs.
From the Shore.
Galoots.
Garden Wireless.
Gargoyle.
Girl in a Cage.
Glass House Canticle.
Glimmer.
God Is No Gentleman.
Gold Mud.
Goldwing Moth.
Gone.
Gong of Time, The.
Good Morning, America.
Good Night.
Government.
Graceland.
Grass.
Grassroots.
Graves.
Great Hunt, The.
Great Proud Wagon Wheels Go On, The.
Grieg Being Dead.
Guaranteed Antique.
Gypsy.
Gypsy Mother.
Half Moon In a High Wind.
Half Way.
Halsted Street Car.
Hammer, The.
Hammers Pounding.
Handfuls.
Hangman at Home, The.
Happiness.
Harmonica Humdrums.
Harrison Street Court.
Harsk, Harsk.

Harvest.
Harvest Sunset.
Has-Been, The.
Hate.
Hats.
Haunts.
Have Me.
Have you seen men handed refusals.
Hazardous Occupations.
Haze.
Haze Gold.
Head.
Heavy and Light.
Helga.
Hell on the Wabash.
Hells and Heavens.
Hemlock and Cedar.
High Moments.
His Own Face Hidden.
Hits and Runs.
Hogh Conspiratorial Persons.
Hold down the skylines now with your
    themes.
Home Fires.
Home Thoughts.
Honey and Salt.
Honky Tonk in Cleveland, Ohio.
Hoodlums.
Hoof Dusk.
Horse Fiddle.
Horses and Men in the Rain.
House.
How Much?
How Yesterday Looked.
Humdrum.
Hummingbird Woman.
Hunger and Cold.
Hungry and Laughing Men.
I Am the People, the Mob.
I Sang.
Ice Handler.
If So Hap May Be.
Iglits and His Wife.
Illinois Farmer.
Impasse.
Implications.
Impossible Iambics.
Improved Farm Land.
In a Back Alley.
In a Breath.
In paper sacks the customers carry away
    millions of tons of goods daily.
In Tall Grass.
In the days of the cockade and the brass
    pistol.
In the Shadow of the Palace.
Instructions.
Interior.
Iron.
Is There Any Easy Road to Freedom?
Is Wisdom a Lot of Language?
Isle of Patmos.
It Is Much.
Jabberers.
Jack.
Jack London and O. Henry.
Jan Kubelik.
Jan, the Son of Thomas.
Jaws.
Jazz Fantasia.
John Ericsson Day Memorial, 1918.
Joke Gold.
Joliet.
Joy.
Jug.
June.
Jungheimer's.
Junk Man, The.
Just Before April Came.
Kansas Lessons.
Keepsake Boxes.
Killers.
Kin.
Kisses, Can You Come Back Like Ghosts?
Kisses Forgotten.
Knucks.
Kreisler.

Lackawanna Twilight.
Lake Michigan Morning.
Landscape.
Landscape Including Three States of the
    Union.
Languages.
Last Answers.
Laughing Blue Steel.
Laughing Corn.
Lavender Lilies.
Lawyer.
Lawyers Know Too Much, The.
Leather Leggings.
Legends.
Lesson.
Let Love Go On.
Let the nickels and dimes explain.
Let Them Ask Your Pardon.
Letter S.
Letters to Dead Imagists.
Liars, The.
Lief the Lucky.
Light and Moonbells.
Limited.
Lines Written for Gene Kelly to Dance To.
Little Candle.
Little Girl, Be Careful What You Say.
Little Sketch.
Little Word, Little White Bird.
Loam.
Localities.
Loin Cloth.
Long Guns.
Long Shadow of Lincoln: A Litany, The.
Losers.
Losses.
Lost.
Lovable Babblers.
Love Beyond Keeping.
Love in Labrador.
Love Is a Deep and a Dark and a Lonely.
Love Letter to Hans Christian Andersen.
Lumber Yard Pools at Sunset.
Madison and 42nd.
Mag.
Mamie.
Mammy Hums.
Man and Dog on an Early Winter Morning.
Man, the Man-Hunter.
Man the Moon Shooter.
Man with the Broken Fingers, The.
Manitoba Childe Roland.
Manual System.
Manufactured Gods.
Many Handles.
Many Hats.
March of the Hungry Mountains.
Margaret.
Maroon with Silver Frost.
Mascots.
Mask.
Masses.
Maybe.
Mayor of Gary, The.
Meadow in Summer.
Medallion.
Medley.
Memoir.
Memoir of a Proud Boy.
Memoranda.
Metamorphosis.
Methusaleh Saw Many Repeaters.
Milk-White Moon, Put the Cows to Sleep.
Mill-Doors.
Million Young Workmen, 1915, A.
Mist Forms.
Mist Marches Across the Valley.
Mist, The.
Mr. Attila.
Mr. Longfellow and His Boy.
M'Liss and Louie.
Mockers Go to Kansas in Spring.
Mohammed Bek Hadjetlache.
Moist Moon People.
Moments of Dawn Riders.
Momus.
Money, Politics, Love, and Glory.

Monkey of Stars.
Monosyllabic.
Monotone.
Moon Hammock.
Moon Path.
Moon Riders.
Moon Rondeau.
Moonlight and Maggots.
Moonset.
More Country People.
Morning Glory Blue.
Muckers.
Mummy.
Murmurings in a Field Hospital.
My People.
Mysterious Biography.
Name Us a King.
Near Keokuk.
Neighbors.
Never Born.
Never Two Songs the Same.
New Farm Tractor.
New Feet.
New Hampshire Again.
New Song for Indiana Ophelias.
New Weather.
Nigger.
Night Bells.
Night Movement—New York.
Night Stuff.
Night's Nothings Again.
Nightsong.
Nocturn Cabbage.
Nocturn IV: "Claims of the sea, of the tide, move out, The."
Nocturne in a Deserted Brickyard.
Noon Hour.
North Atlantic.
Now They Bury Her Again.
Number Man.
Oak Arms.
October Paint.
Offering and Rebuff.
Old Deep Sing-Song.
Old-Fashioned Requited Love.
Old Flagman, The.
Old Hokusai Print.
Old Music for Quiet Hearts.
Old Osawatomie.
Old Timers.
Old Woman.
Omaha.
On a Flimmering Floom You Shall Ride.
On a Railroad Right of Way.
On the Breakwater.
On the Way.
One Modern Poet.
One Parting.
Onion Days.
Oomba.
Open Letter to the Poet Archibald MacLeish Who Has Forsaken His Massachusetts Farm to Make Propaganda for Freedom.
Osawatomie.
Our Hells.
Our Prayer of Thanks.
Out of the Rainbow End.
Out of White Lips.
Palladiums.
Pals.
Panels.
Paper I.
Paper II.
Pass, Friend.
Passers-by.
Paula.
Peace Between Wars.
Peace, Night, Sleep.
Peach Blossoms.
Pearl Fog.
Pearl Horizons.
Pencils.
Pennsylvania.
People of the Eaves, I Wish You Good Morning.
People Who Must.
People with Proud Chins.

People, Yes, The *sels.*
People, Yes, The.
Personalia.
Personality.
Phizzog.
Pick-Offs.
Picnic Boat.
Pigeon.
Places.
Plaster.
Plowboy.
Plunger.
Pods.
Poems Done on a Late Night Car.
Pool.
Pool of Bethesda.
Poplar and Elm.
Poppies.
Population Drifts.
Portrait.
Portrait of a Child Settling Down for an Afternoon Nap.
Portrait of a Motorcar.
Potato Blossom Songs and Jigs.
Potomac River Mist.
Potomac Town in February.
Prairie.
Prairie Waters by Night.
Prairie Woodland.
Prayer after World War.
Prayers of Steel.
Precious Moments.
Press is Peculiar, The.
Primer Lesson.
Props.
Proud and Beautiful.
Proud of Their Rags.
Proud Torsos.
Psalm of the Bloodbank.
Psalm of Those Who Go Forth before Daylight.
Public Letter to Emily Dickinson.
Purple Martins.
Put Off the Wedding Five Times and Nobody Comes to It.
Questionnaire.
Quotations.
Rain Winds Blow Doors Open.
Rakeoff and the Getaway, The.
Rat Riddles.
Ready to Kill.
Real Avenue News.
Red and White.
Red-Headed Restaurant Cashier.
Red Son, The.
Redhaw Rain.
Remembered Women.
Remorse.
Repetitions.
Riddles and Whims.
Right to Grief, The.
Ripe Corn.
River Moon.
River Moons.
River Roads.
Road and the End, The.
Rose Bawn.
Runaway Colors.
Rusty Crimson.
Salvage.
Sand Scribblings.
Sandhill People.
Sandpipers.
Santa Fe Sketches.
Sarah's Letter to Peter.
Savoir Faire.
Sayings of Henry Stephens.
Scriptsmith.
Scripture.
Scroll.
Sea Chest.
Sea Hold, The.
Sea Slant.
Sea-Wash.
Sea Wisdom.
Seven Eleven.
Seventeen Months.

Shadows Fall Blue on the Mountains.
Shag-Bark Hickory.
She Opens the Barn Door Every Morning.
Sheep.
Shenandoah.
Shenandoah Journey.
Shirt.
Shoes of Travel.
Shovel Man, The.
Silver Nails.
Silver Point.
Silver Wind.
Singing Nigger.
Sins of Kalamazoo, The.
Sixteen Months.
Sketch.
Sketch of a Poet.
Sky Pieces.
Sky Talk.
Skyscraper.
Skyscraper Loves Night, The.
Skyscrapers Stand Proud.
Slabs of the Sunburnt West.
Slants at Buffalo, New York.
Sleep Impression.
Sleep Song.
Sleepyheads.
Slippery.
Slow Program.
Small Homes.
Smoke.
Smoke and Steel.
Smoke Blue.
Smoke Rose Gold.
Smoke Shapes.
Snatch of Sliphorn Jazz.
Snow.
So to Speak.
Soiled Dove.
Solo for Saturday Night Guitar.
Soup.
South Wind Says So, The.
Southern Pacific.
Spanish.
Special Starlight.
Speech.
Sphinx, A.
Splinter.
Spray.
Spring Carries Surprises.
Spring Cries.
Spring Grass.
Spring Wind.
Star Silver.
Stars.
Stars, Songs, Faces.
Statistics.
Still Life.
Storms Begin Far Back.
Street Window.
Streets Too Old.
Striped Cats, Old Men and Proud Stockings.
Stripes.
Style.
Suburban Sicilian Sketches.
Subway.
Sumach and Birds.
Summer Grass.
Summer Shirt Sale.
Summer Stars.
Sun Dancer.
Sunset from Omaha Hotel Window.
Sunsets.
Sweeping Wendy: Study in Fugue.
Swell People.
Swirl.
Tall Man, A.
Tall Timber.
Tangibles.
Tawny.
Teamster's Farewell, A.
Telegram.
Tentative (First Model) Definitions of Poetry.
Testament.
Testimony Regarding a Ghost.
Theme in Yellow.
Themes in Contrast.

Theorem.
There Are Different Gardens.
They All Want to Play Hamlet.
They Ask Each Other Where They Came From.
They Ask: Is God, Too, Lonely.
They Buy with an Eye to Looks.
They Met Young.
They Will Say.
Thimble Islands.
Thin Strips.
This—For the Moon—Yes?
This Street Never Sleeps.
Thou Art Like a Flower.
Three Balls.
Three Fragments for Fishers of Destiny.
Three Ghosts.
Three Hills Look Different in the Moonshine.
Three Pieces on the Smoke of Autumn.
Three Shrines.
Three Slants at New York.
Three Spring Notations on Bipeds.
Three Violins.
Threes.
Throw Roses.
Throwbacks.
Timber Moon.
Timber Wings.
Timesweep.
To a Contemporary Bunkshooter.
To a Dead Man.
To Beachey, 1912.
To Certain Journeymen.
To Know Silence Perfectly.
To the Ghost of John Milton.
Trafficker.
Trinity Place.
Troths.
Turn of the Wheel.
Two.
Two Fish.
Two Humpties.
Two Items.
Two Moon Fantasies.
Two Neighbors.
Two Nocturns.
Two Strangers Breakfast.
Two Women.
Two Women and Their Fathers.
Under.
Under a Hat Rim.
Under a Telephone Pole.
Under the Capitol Dome.
Under the Harvest Moon.
Understandings in Blue.
Unintentional Paint.
Unknown War, The.
Uplands in May.
Upstairs.
Upstream.
Useless Words.
Valley Song.
Variations on a Theme.
Vaudeville Dancer.
Very Very Important.
Village in Late Summer.
Waiting.
Waiting for the Chariot.
Walking Man of Rodin, The.
Wall Shadows.
Wanting the Impossible.
Wars.
Was Ever a Dream a Drum?
Washerwoman.
Washington Monument by Night.
Way of the World, The.
We Have Gone Through Great Rooms Together.
We Must Be Polite.
Webs.
Wedding Postponed.
Weeds.
When Death Came April Twelve 1945.
Whiffletree.
Whiffs of the Ohio River at Cinncinnati.
Whirls.
White Ash.

White Hands.
White Shoulders.
Whitelight.
Who Am I?
Wilderness.
Wind Horses.
Wind on the Way, The.
Wind Sings Welcome in Early Spring, The.
Wind Song.
Windflower Leaf.
Window.
Windy City, The.
Wingtip.
Winter Gold.
Winter Milk.
Winter Weather.
Wistful.
Without Notice Beforehand.
Without the Cane and the Derby.
Woman with a Past.
Women Washing Their Hair.
Work Gangs.
Working Girls.
Worms and the Wind.
Year, The.
Yellow Evening Star.
Yes, the Dead Speak to Us.
You Shall Have Homes.
Young Bullfrogs.
Young Sea.

Sarton, May (1914–95)
Action of Therapy, The.
All Souls.
Annunciation.
Apple Tree in May.
Approach—Calcutta, The.
At Delphi.
At Lindos.
At Muzot.
Autumn Sonnets, The *sels.*
Ballad of Johnny, The.
Ballad of the Sixties.
Baroque Image.
Bears and Waterfalls.
Because What I Want Most Is Permanence.
Behind What Little Mirror.
Binding the Dragon.
Birthday on the Acropolis.
Burial.
Caged Bird, The.
Celebration for George Sarton, A.
Charleston Plantations.
Child's Japan, A.
Christmas Letter to a Psychiatrist.
Clavichord, The.
Composition.
Concentration Camps, The.
Death and the Lovers.
Der Abschied.
Divorce of Lovers, A *sels.*
Dutch Interior.
Easter Morning.
Easter, 1968.
Eine Kleine Snailmusik.
Evening Music.
Evening Walk in France.
Exchange of Gifts, An.
Fear of Angels, The.
Fig, The.
First Autumn, The.
First Snow.
Flower-Arranging Summer, A.
Franz, a Goose.
Frog, that Naked Creature, The.
Furies, The.
Garden of Childhood, The.
Gestalt at Sixty.
Giant in the Garden.
Girl with 'Cello.
Glass of Water, A.
Godhead as Lynx, The.
Greeting.
Guest, A.
Hard Death, A.
House in Winter, The.
How faint the horn sounds in the mountain passes.

Humpty Dumpty.
I shall not see the end of this unweaving.
If I could let you go as trees let go.
In Time Like Air.
Intruder, An.
Invocation: "Come out of the dark earth."
Invocation to Kali, The.
Italian Garden.
Japanese Prints.
Jonah.
Journey toward Poetry.
Kingdom of Kali, The.
Lady and the Unicorn, The.
Lady with a Falcon.
Lament for Toby, a French Poodle.
Letter from Chicago.
Letter to James Stephens, A.
Light Left On, A.
Lion and the Rose, The.
March-Mad.
Mediterranean.
Memory of Swans.
Metamorphosis.
Metaphysical Garden, The.
Monticello.
Moth in the Schoolroom.
Mud Season.
Muse as Medusa, The.
My Father's Death.
My Sisters, O My Sisters.
Myself to Me.
Myth.
Narcissus.
Nativity.
Night Watch.
Nostalgia for India.
Notes from India.
Now I Become Myself.
Nursery Rhyme.
Of Grief.
Of the Seasons.
Olive Grove, The.
On a Winter Night.
On Being Given Time.
Parrot, A.
Phoenix, The.
Portrait by Holbein.
Prayer before Work.
Prisoner at a Desk.
Proteus.
Prothalamion.
Puritan, The.
Recognition, A.
Return.
Return of Aphrodite, The.
Snow Light, The.
Song: "No, I will never forget you and your great eyes."
Song: "Now let us honor with violin and flute."
Stone Walls.
Storm of Angels, A.
Strangers.
Sun Boat.
Swans, The.
These Images Remain.
These Pure Arches.
These Were Her Nightly Journeys.
Time of Burning, The.
To the Living *sels.*
To the North.
Tortured, The.
Village Tale, A.
We Sat Smoking at a Table..
We'll to the Woods No More, the Laurels Are Cut Down.
Where Dream Begins.
Who Wakes.
Winter Carol.
Work of Happiness, The.

Schuyler, James (1923–91)
Advent.
Adverts.
After Joe Was at the Island.
Afterward.
Ajaccio Violets.
Alice Faye at Ruby Foo's.

Almanac, An.
Amy Lowell Thoughts.
Andrew Lord Poems.
April and Its Forsythia.
Arches.
At Darragh's I.
At the Beach.
August First, 1974.
August Night.
Autumn Leaves.
Await.
Awoke.
Back.
Beaded Balustrade.
Beautiful Funerals.
Belated Birthday Poem, A.
Below the Stairs.
Birds.
Bleeding Gums.
Blizzard.
Blossoming Oakwood.
Blue.
Blue Towel, A.
Bluet, The.
Boer War Bread Strike.
Buildings.
Buried at Springs.
Cardinal, A.
Cenotaph, The.
Chapel, A.
Closed Gentian Distances.
Cornflowers.
Crocus Night.
Crystal Lithium, The.
Day, The.
Daylight.
Dear Joe.
December.
Dec. 28, 1974.
Deep Winter.
Dining Out with Doug and Frank.
Dog Wants His Dinner, The.
Dorabella's Naples Watercolor.
Dreams.
Earth's Holocaust.
East Window on Elizabeth Street, An.
Edge in the Morning, The.
8/12/70.
Elizabethans Called It Dying, The.
Empathy and New Year.
En Route to Southampton.
Evening.
Evening Wind.
Evenings in Vermont.
Eyes.
Eyes at the Window.
Fabergé.
Fauré Ballade, The.
Fauré's Second Piano Quartet.
February.
February 13, 1975.
Few Days, A.
Flashes.
Footnote.
For Bob Dash.
Four Poems.
Frank! Frank!
Freely Espousing.
Frock.
"From the next."
Going.
Good Morning.
Grand Duo.
Grave, A.
Gray Day.
Gray, Intermittently Blue, Eyed Hero.
Green Door, The.
Greenwich Avenue.
Greetings from the Chateau.
Growing Dark.
Gulls.
Hats.
Haze.
Head, A.
Heather and Calendulas.
Held Breath, A.
Horse-Chestnut Trees and Roses.

Hudson Ferry.
Hymn to Life.
I Sit Down to Type.
I Think.
Ilford Rose Book.
In a Churchyard.
In Earliest Morning.
In January.
In the Round.
In Wiry Winter.
Industrial Archaeology.
Janis Joplin's Dead: Long Live Pearl.
Jelly Jelly.
Joint.
June.
June 30, 1974.
Just before Fall.
Korean Mums.
Labor Day.
Let's All Hear It for Mildred Bailey!
Letter Poem #3.
Letter Poem #2.
Letter to a Friend: Who Is Nancy Daum?
Light Blue Above.
Light from Canada.
Light Within, The.
Like Lorraine Ellison.
Lilacs.
Linen.
Looking Forward to See Jane Real Soon.
Man in Blue, A.
March Here.
Mark.
Mass. Ave., Cambridge, Mass.
Master of the Golden Glow, The.
May, 1972.
May 24th or So.
Mike.
Milk.
Moneses Uniflora.
Money Musk.
Mood Indigo.
Moon.
Morning of the Poem, The.
Morning, The.
Name Day, A.
New Yorker, A.
Night, The.
Noon Office.
November.
Now and Then.
O Sleepless Night.
October.
October 5, 1981.
On the Dresser.
Oriane.
Our Father.
Over the Hills.
Overcast, Hot.
Pastime.
Penobscot.
People Who See Bubbles Rise.
Perhaps.
Photograph, A.
Picnic Cantata, A.
Poem, A: "Tags of songs, like salvaged
    buttons."
Poem: "How about an oak leaf."
Poem: "I do not always understand what you
    say."
Poem: "I got my hair cut."
Poem: "This beauty that I see."
Poem: "Wind tears up the sun, The."
Poem: "Your enchantment / enchants me,
    stretched."
Princess Di.
Procession.
Quick, Henry, the Flit!
Rachmaninoff's Third.
Rain.
Red Brick and Brown Stone.
Reunion, A.
Roof Garden.
Rose of Marion, The.
Roxy.
Royals.
Running Footsteps.

Salute.
Saturday Night.
Scarlet Tanager.
Seeking.
Self-Pity Is a Kind of Lying, Too.
September.
Sestina: "I have reached, alas, the long
    shadow."
Shadowy Room.
Shaker.
Shimmer.
Simone Signoret.
Six Something.
Sky Eats Up the Trees, The.
Sleep.
Sleep-Gummed Eyes.
Snow, The.
Snowdrop, The.
So Good.
Sometimes.
Song: "I'm about to go shopping."
Song: "Light lies layered in the leaves, The."
Sonnet: "August, tasting of ripe grapes and
    afternoon sleep."
Sorting, Wrapping, Packing, Stuffing.
Sparks.
Spring.
Standing and Watching.
Steaming Ties.
Stone Knife, A.
Stun.
Suddenly.
Sun Cab, A.
Sunday.
Sunset.
Table of Green Fields, A.
Things to Do.
Thinness.
This Dark Apartment.
This Notebook.
This Soft October.
Three Gardens.
3/23/66.
Thursday.
To Frank O'Hara.
Today.
Tom.
Tomorrow.
Tom's Attempt to Seduce Big Brother Steve.
Tom's Dream.
Trash Book, The.
Trip.
Two.
Under the Hanger.
Unlike Joubert.
Up.
"Used Handkerchiefs 5[dc]."
Velvet Roses.
Vermont Diary, A.
View, A.
Virginia Woolf.
Voyage Autour de Mes Cartes Postales.
Walk, The.
Walter Scott.
Was It.
Watching You.
We Are Leaves.
We See Seals. Boats Go By.
We Walk.
What.
What Ails My Fern?
White.
White Boat, Blue Boat.
White City, A.
Wild Eggs.
With Frank and George at Lexington.
Witley Court.
Wonderful World.
Wystan Auden.
Yellow Flowers.
You're.

Schwartz, Delmore (1913–66)
Albert Einstein to Archibald MacLeish.
"All is forgiven when guilt is accepted."
All Night, All Night.
America, America!

Apollo Musagete, Poetry, and the Leader of the Muses.
Aria.
"At last! the present darkness! all is known!"
At This Moment of Time.
Choir and Music of Solitude and Silence, The.
Christmas Poem for Nancy.
Come, let us rejoice in James Joyce, in the greatness of this poet.
Dances and the Dancers, The.
Dream of Whitman Paraphrased, Recognized and Made More Vivid by Renoir, A.
Famous Resort in Late Autumn, The.
First Night of Fall and Falling Rain, The.
Genesis *sels.*
Greatest Thing in North America, The.
He Who Excuses Himself Also Accuses Himself.
How Can He Possess.
"Interpretation! that's the act of mind."
Journey of a Poem Compared to All the Sad Variety of Travel, The.
Kilroy's Carnival; A Poetic Prologue for TV.
King of Kings, A King among the Kings, A *sels.*
"Lo, we descend like light. Light. Light."
Love and Marilyn Monroe.
Maxims of Sisyphus, The.
Metro-Goldwyn-Mayer.
News of the Gold World of May.
Now He Knows All There Is to Know: Now He Is Acquainted With the Day and Night.
"Now we approach the darkness of to-night!"
"O Death, great captain, lift anchor!"
"O New York boy, this is Life, Life in which."
"O what a mess of judgment we have made."
Occasional Poems.
Overture.
Philology Recapitulates Ontology, Poetry Is Ontology.
Phoenix Lyrics.
Poem: "Faithful to your commands, o consciousness, o."
Poem for Jacques Maritain and Leon Trotzky.
Poem: How Marvelous Man's Kind Is.
Poem: "In the morning, when it was raining."
Poem: "Old man in the crystal morning after snow."
Poem: "Remember midsummer: the fragrance of box, of white roses."
Poem to Johann Sebastian Bach.
Poem: "Window winter."
Poem: "You, my photographer, you, most aware."
Poet, The.
Power and Glory of Language, The.
Praise Is Traditional and Appropriate.
Prologue: "Narcissus, speaking in the first person."
Rabbi to Preach.
Salute Valentine.
Sand upon the Red Sea shore, or on the beach, The.
Sequel, the Conclusion, the Endlessness, The.
Song: "Under the yellow sea."
Sonnet: "I follow thought and what the world announces."
Sonnet on Famous and Familiar Sonnets and Experiences.
Sonnet Suggested by Homer, Chaucer, Shakespeare, Edgar Allan Poe, Paul Valéry, James Joyce, et al.
Spiders.
This Is a Poem I Wrote at Night, Before the Dawn.
Two Lyrics from Kilroy's Carnival: A Masque.
What Curious Dresses All Men Wear.
When I Remember the Advent.
Words for a Trumpet Chorale Celebrating the Autumn.
Yeats Died Saturday in France.
Translations, Coauthored Poems, etc.:
Graveyard by the Sea, The *sels.*
Late Autumn in Venice.

Spring, The.
This hushed surface where the doves parade.
To a Fugitive.
To Helen.

Scott, Sir Walter (1771–1832)
Allan-Bane's Lament.
Ambuscade, The.
Autumn on Tweedside.
Bale-Fire, The.
Boat Song.
Branksome Hall.
Bridal of Trierman, The *sels.*
Brooch of Lorn, The.
Caledonia.
Coronach.
County Guy.
Dawn and Sunrise.
Death of Argentine, The.
Death of Marmion, The.
Defenceless Border, The.
Douglas and Marmion.
Edinburgh From Blackford Hill.
Edmund's Songs.
Ellen's Song.
Enchanted Goblet, The.
English Advance at Flodden, The.
Evening.
Farewell.
Fiery Cross, The.
Fitz-Eustace's Song.
Gray Brother, The.
Harold's Song.
Hellvellyn.
Hunting Song.
Hymn for the Dead.
Invocation: "Harp of the North! that mouldering long hast hung."
Ivanhoe *sels.*
Jock of Hazeldean.
Lady of the Lake, The *sels.*
Lay of the Imprisoned Huntsman.
Lay of the Last Minstrel, The *sels.*
Loch Coruisk.
Lochinvar.
Lord of the Isles, The *sels.*
Lords Strand of Northumberland, The.
Magic Castle, The.
Marmion *sels.*
Melrose by Moonlight.
Norham Castle.
On the Massacre of Glencoe, 1692.
Palmer, The.
Pibroch of Donuil Dhu.
Quentin Durward *sels.*
Rebecca's Hymn.
Ride to Stirling, The.
Rokeby *sels.*
Saint of Holy Island, The.
Song of Albert Graeme.
Spindle Song, The.
Thorsgill.
Trossachs, The.
Voyage to Arran, The.
Translations, Coauthored Poems, etc.:
Lady of the Pearls, The *sels.*
Trossachs, The.

Sexton, Anne (1928–74)
Abortion, The.
Addict, The.
Admonitions to a Special Person.
After Auschwitz.
Again and Again and Again.
All My Pretty Ones.
Ambition Bird, The.
And One for My Dame.
Angel Food Dogs, The.
Angel of Beach Houses and Picnics.
Angel of Blizzards and Blackouts.
Angel of Clean Sheets.
Angel of Fire and Genitals.
Angel of Flight and Sleigh Bells.
Angel of Hope and Calendars.
Angels of the Love Affair.
Anna Who Was Mad.
As It Was Written.
Assassin, The.
August 8th.

August 17th.
Author of the Jesus Papers Speaks, The.
Baby Picture.
Ballad of the Lonely Masturbator, The.
Barefoot.
Bat.
Bayonet.
Begat.
Bells, The.
Big Boots of Pain, The.
Big Heart, The.
Black Art, The.
Boat, The.
Break Away, The.
Break, The.
Breast, The.
Briar Rose (Sleeping Beauty).
Buying the Whore.
Child Bearers, The.
Children, The.
Christmas Eve.
Cigarettes and Whiskey and Wild, Wild Women.
Cinderella.
Civil War, The.
Clothes.
Cockroach.
Consecrating Mother, The.
Consorting with Angels.
Courage.
Cripples and Other Stories.
Crossing the Atlantic.
Curse against Elegies, A.
"Daddy" Warbucks.
Dead Heart, The.
Death Baby, The.
Death King, The.
Death of the Fathers, The.
Demon.
Despair.
Division of Parts, The.
Divorce.
Divorce, Thy Name Is Woman.
Doctor of the Heart, The.
Doctors.
Doors, Doors, Doors.
Double Image, The.
Dreaming the Breasts.
Earth Falls Down, The.
Earth, The.
Earthworm.
Eighteen Days without You.
Eighth Psalm.
Elegy in the Classroom.
Elizabeth Gone.
End, Middle, Beginning.
Errand, The.
Evil Eye, The.
Evil Seekers, The.
Exorcists, The.
Expatriates, The.
Fallen Angels, The.
Falling Dolls, The.
Farmer's Wife, The.
Faustus and I.
February 3rd.
February 4th.
February 11th.
February 17th.
February 20th.
February 21st.
Fierceness of Female, The.
Fifth Psalm.
Fire Thief, The.
Firebombers, The.
First Psalm.
Fish That Walked, The.
Flee on Your Donkey.
Flight.
Food.
For Eleanor Boylan Talking with God.
For God While Sleeping.
For John, Who Begs Me Not to Enquire Further.
For Johnny Pole on the Forgotten Beach.
For Mr. Death Who Stands with His Door Open.

For My Lover, Returning to His Wife.
For the Year of the Insane.
Fortress, The.
45 Mercy Street.
Fourth Psalm.
Frenzy.
Friends.
Frog Prince, The.
From the Garden.
Funnel.
Furies, The.
Fury of Abandonment, The.
Fury of Beautiful Bones, The.
Fury of Cocks, The.
Fury of Cooks, The.
Fury of Earth, The.
Fury of Flowers and Worms, The.
Fury of God's Good-bye, The.
Fury of Guitars and Sopranos, The.
Fury of Hating Eyes, The.
Fury of Jewels and Coal, The.
Fury of Overshoes, The.
Fury of Rain Storms, The.
Fury of Sundays, The.
Fury of Sunrises, The.
Fury of Sunsets, The.
Ghosts.
God-Monger, The.
Godfather Death.
Gods.
God's Backside.
Going Gone.
Gold Key, The.
Grandfather, Your Wound.
Gull.
Hangman, The.
Hansel and Gretel.
Her Kind.
Hex, The.
Hoarder, The.
Hog.
Hornet.
Horse.
House, The.
Housewife.
How We Danced.
Hurry Up Please It's Time.
Hutch.
I Remember.
Imitations of Drowning.
In Celebration of My Uterus.
In Excelsis.
In the Beach House.
In the Deep Museum.
Interrogation of the Man of Many Hearts,
The.
Inventory of Goodbyes, The.
Iron Hans.
Is It True?
It is a Spring Afternooon.
January 1st.
January 19th.
January 24th.
Jesus Asleep.
Jesus Awake.
Jesus Cooks.
Jesus Raises Up the Harlot.
Jesus Suckles.
Jesus Summons Forth.
Jesus, the Actor, Plays the Holy ghost.
Jesus Unborn.
Jesus Walking.
June Bug.
Just Once.
KE 6-8018.
Keeping the City.
Killing the Love.
Killing the Spring.
Kind Sir: These Woods.
Kiss, The.
Kite, The.
Knee Song.
Lament: "Someone is dead."
Landscape Winter.
Leaves That Talk.
Legend of the One-Eyed Man, The.
Lessons in Hunger.

Letter Written During a January Northeaster.
Letter Written on a Ferry While Crossing
Long Island Sound.
Letters to Dr. Y.
Little Girl, My String Bean, My Lovely
Woman.
Little Peasant, The.
Little Uncomplicated Hymn, A.
Live.
Lobster.
Locked Doors.
Lost Ingredient, The.
Lost Lie, The.
Love Letter Written in a Burning Building.
Love Plant, The.
Love Song for K. Owyne.
Love Song: "I was / the girl of the chain
letter."
Loving the Killer.
Lullaby: "It is a summer evening."
Madame Arrives in the Mail.
Maiden without Hands, The.
Making a Living.
Man and Wife.
March 4th.
March 7th.
Mary's Song.
May 30th.
Menstruation at Forty.
Money Swing, The.
Moon Song, Woman Song.
Moose.
Moss of His Skin, The.
Mother and Daughter.
Mother and Jack and the Rain.
Mothers.
Mr. Mine.
Music Swims Back to Me.
Ninth Psalm.
No So. Not So.
Noon Walk on the Asylum Lawn.
Now.
Nude Swim, The.
O Ye Tongues.
Oh.
Old.
Old Dwarf Heart.
One-Eye, Two-Eyes, Three-Eyes.
One-Legged Man, The.
Operation, The.
Other, The.
Oysters.
Pain for a Daughter.
Papa and Mama Dance, The.
Passion of the Mad Rabbit, The.
Play, The.
Poet of Ignorance, The.
Porcupine.
Portrait of an Old Woman on the College
Tavern Wall.
Praying on a 707.
Praying to Big Jack.
Protestant Easter.
Raccoon.
Rapunzel.
Rats Live on No Evil Star.
Red Dance, The.
Red-Riding Hood.
Red Roses.
Red Shoes, The.
Riding the Elevator into the Sky.
Ringing the Bells.
Risk, The.
Road Back, The.
Room of My Life, The.
Rowing.
Rowing Endeth, The.
Rumpelstiltskin.
Said the Poet to the Analyst.
Saints Come Marching In, The.
Santa.
Sea Corpse, The.
Seal.
Second Psalm.
Self in 1958.
Sermon of the Twelve Acknowledgements,
The.

Seventh Psalm.
Sheep.
Shout, The.
Sickness unto Death, The.
Silence, The.
Sixth Psalm.
Small Wire.
Snail.
Snake.
Snow.
Snow White and the Seven Dwarfs.
Some Foreign Letters.
Somewhere in Africa.
Song for a Lady.
Song for a Red Nightgown.
Speaking Bitterness.
Stand-Ins, The.
Star-Nosed Mole.
Starry Night, The.
Story for Rose on the Midnight Flight to
Boston, A.
Suicide Note.
Sun, The.
Surgeon, The.
Sweeney.
Sylvia's Death.
Taker, The.
Talking to Sheep.
Telephone.
Tenth Psalm.
That Day.
There You Were.
Those Times.
Three Green Windows.
To a Friend Whose Work Has Come to
Triumph.
To Like, to Love.
To Lose the Earth.
Torn Down from Glory Daily.
Touch, The.
Truth the Dead Know, The.
Twelve Dancing Princesses, The.
Twelve-Thousand-Day Honeymoon, The.
Two Hands.
Two Sons.
Unknown Girl in the Maternity Ward.
Us.
Uses.
Venus and the Ark.
Waiting Head, The.
Waking Alone.
Walking in Paris.
Wall, The.
Wallflower.
Wanting to Die.
Water.
Wedding Night, The.
Wedding Ring Dance, The.
Wedlock, The.
Welcome Morning.
Whale.
What the Bird with the Human Head Knew.
What's That.
When Man Enters Woman.
When the Glass of My Body Broke.
Where I Live in This Honorable House of
the Laurel Tree.
Where It Was at Back Then.
White Snake, The.
Wifebeater, The.
Witch's Life, The.
With Mercy for the Greedy.
Woman with Girdle.
Wonderful Musician, The.
Words.
Yellow.
You All Know the Story of the Other
Woman.
You, Doctor Martin.
Young.
Your Face on the Dog's Neck.
Translations, Coauthored Poems, etc.:
Buttered Greens.

Shakespeare, William (1564–1616)
As it fell upon a day.
Beauty is but a vain and doubtful good.

Crabbed age and youth cannot live together.
Did not the heavenly rhetoric of thine eye.
Fair is my love, but not so fair as fickle.
Fair was the morn when the fair queen of love.
Good night, good rest. Ah, neither be my share.
If love make me forsworn, how shall I swear to love?
If music and sweet poetry agree.
It was a lording's daughter, the fairest one of three.
Live with me, and be my love.
Lord, how mine eyes throw gazes to the east!
Lover's Complaint, A.
Lucrece's Death.
Midnight.
My flocks feed not.
On a day, alack the day!
Opportunity.
Passionate Pilgrim, The *sels.*
Passionate Pilgrim, The.
Phoenix and the Turtle, The.
Rape of Lucrece, The.
Scarce had the sun dried up the dewy morn.
Sonnet 1: "From fairest creatures we desire increase."
Sonnet 2: "When forty winters shall besiege thy brow."
Sonnet 3: "Look in thy glass, and tell the face thou viewest."
Sonnet 4: "Unthrifty loveliness, why dost thou spend."
Sonnet 5: "Those hours, that with gentle work did frame."
Sonnet 6: "Then let not winter's ragged hand deface."
Sonnet 7: "Lo! in the orient when the gracious light."
Sonnet 8: "Music[k] to hear[e], why hear'st thou music[k]."
Sonnet 9: "Is it for fear to wet a widow's eye."
Sonnet 10: "For shame! deny that thou bear'st love to any."
Sonnet 11: "As fast as thou shall wane, so fast thou growest."
Sonnet 12: "When I do count the clock that tells the time."
Sonnet 13: "Oh [or O] that you were yourself! but, love, you are."
Sonnet 14: "Not from the stars do I my judgement pluck."
Sonnet 15: "When I consider everything that grows."
Sonnet 16: "But wherefore do not you a mightier way."
Sonnet 17: "Who will believe my verse in time to come."
Sonnet 18: "Shall I compare thee to a summer's day?"
Sonnet 19: "Devouring Time, blunt thou the lion's paws."
Sonnet 20: "Woman's face with Nature's own hand painted, A."
Sonnet 21: "So is it not with me as with that Muse."
Sonnet 22: "My glass shall not persuade me I am old."
Sonnet 23: "As an unperfect actor on the stage."
Sonnet 24: "Mine eye hath play'd the painter, and hath stell'd."
Sonnet 25: "Let those who are in favour with their stars."
Sonnet 26: "Lord of my love, to whom in vassalage."
Sonnet 27: "Weary with toil, I haste me to my bed."
Sonnet 28: "How can I then return in happy plight."
Sonnet 29: "When, in disgrace with fortune and men's eyes."
Sonnet 30: "When to the sessions of sweet silent thought."
Sonnet 31: "Thy bosom is endeared with all hearts."

Sonnet 32: "If thou survive my well-contented day."
Sonnet 33: "Full many a glorious morning have I seen[e]."
Sonnet 34: "Why didst thou promise such a beauteous day."
Sonnet 35: "No more be grieved at that which thou hast done."
Sonnet 36: "Let me confess that we two must be twain."
Sonnet 37: "As a decrepit father takes delight."
Sonnet 38: "How can my muse want subject to invent."
Sonnet 39: "O, how thy worth with manners may I sing."
Sonnet 40: "Take all my loves, my Love, yea, take them all."
Sonnet 41: "Those petty [or pretty] wrongs that liberty commits."
Sonnet 42: "That thou hast her, it is not all my grief[e]."
Sonnet 43: "When most I wink, then do mine eyes best see."
Sonnet 44: "If the dull substance of my flesh were thought."
Sonnet 45: "Other two, slight air and purging fire, The."
Sonnet 46: "Mine eye and heart are at a mortal war."
Sonnet 47: "Betwixt mine eye and heart a league is took."
Sonnet 48: "How careful was I, when I took my way."
Sonnet 49: "Against that time, if ever that time come."
Sonnet 50: "How heavy do I journey on the way."
Sonnet 51: "Thus can my love excuse the slow offence."
Sonnet 52: "So am I as the rich, whose blessed key."
Sonnet 53: "What is your substance, whereof are you made."
Sonnet 54: "O [or Oh], how much more doth beauty beauteous seem."
Sonnet 55: "Not marble, nor the gilded monuments."
Sonnet 56: "Sweet love, renew thy force; be it not said."
Sonnet 57: "Being your slave, what should I do[e] but tend."
Sonnet 58: "That god forbid that made me first your slave."
Sonnet 59: "If there be nothing new, but that which is."
Sonnet 60: "Like as the waves make towards the pebbled shore."
Sonnet 61: "Is it thy will thy image should keep open."
Sonnet 62: "Sin [or Sinne] of self-love [or selfe-love] possesseth all mine eye [or eie]."
Sonnet 63: "Against my love shall be, as I am now."
Sonnet 64: "When I have seen by Time's fell hand defac'd."
Sonnet 65: "Since brass, nor stone, nor earth, nor boundless sea."
Sonnet 66: "Tired [or Tyr'd, or Tir'd] with all these, for restful death I cry."
Sonnet 67: "Ah! wherefore with infection should he live."
Sonnet 68: "Thus is his cheek the map of days outworn."
Sonnet 69: "Those parts of thee that the world's eye doth view."
Sonnet 70: "That thou art blamed shall not be thy defect."
Sonnet 71: "No longer mourn for me when I am dead."
Sonnet 72: "O! Lest the world should task you to recite."
Sonnet 73: "That time of year thou may'st [or maist] in me behold."
Sonnet 74: "But be contented: when that fell arrest."

Sonnet 75: "So are you to my thoughts as food to life."
Sonnet 76: "Why is my verse so barren of new pride."
Sonnet 77: "Thy glass will show thee how thy beauties wear."
Sonnet 78: "So oft I invoked thee for my Muse."
Sonnet 79: "Whilst I alone did call upon thy aid."
Sonnet 80: "O, how I faint when I of you do write."
Sonnet 81: "Or I shall live your epitaph to make."
Sonnet 82: "I grant thou wert not married to my Muse."
Sonnet 83: "I never saw that you did painting need."
Sonnet 84: "Who is it that says most? which can say more."
Sonnet 85: "My tongue-tied Muse in manners holds her still."
Sonnet 86: "Was it the proud full sail of his great verse."
Sonnet 87: "Farewell! Thou art too dear[e] for my possessing."
Sonnet 88: "When thou shalt be dispos'd to set me light."
Sonnet 89: "Say that thou didst forsake me for some fault."
Sonnet 90: "Then hate me when thou wilt; if ever, now."
Sonnet 91: "Some glory in their birth, some in their skill."
Sonnet 92: "But do thy worst to steal thyself away."
Sonnet 93: "So shall I live, supposing thou art true."
Sonnet 94: "They that have power to hurt[e], and will do[e] none."
Sonnet 95: "How sweet and lovely dost thou make the shame."
Sonnet 96: "Some say thy fault is youth, some wantonness."
Sonnet 97: "How like a winter hath my absence been[e]."
Sonnet 98: "From you have I been absent in the spring."
Sonnet 99: "Forward violet thus did I chide, The."
Sonnet 100: "Where art thou, Muse, that thou forget'st so long."
Sonnet 101: "O truant Muse, what shall be thy amends."
Sonnet 102: "My love is strengthen'd, though more weak in seeming."
Sonnet 103: "Alack, what poverty my Muse brings forth."
Sonnet 104: "To me, fair[e] friend, you never can be old."
Sonnet 105: "Let not my love be call'd idolatry."
Sonnet 106: "When in the chronicle of wasted time."
Sonnet 107: "Not mine own fears nor the prophetic soul."
Sonnet 108: "What's in the brain that ink may character."
Sonnet 109: "O [or Oh], never say that I was false of heart."
Sonnet 110: "Alas, 'tis true I have gone here and there."
Sonnet 111: "O, for my sake do you with Fortune chide."
Sonnet 112: "Your love and pity doth the impression fill."
Sonnet 113: "Since I left you, mine eye is in my mind."
Sonnet 114: "Or whether doth my mind, being crowned with you."
Sonnet 115: "Those lines that I before have writ do lie."
Sonnet 116: "Let me not to the marriage of true minds."
Sonnet 117: "Accuse me thus; that I have scanted all."

Sonnet 118: "Like as, to make our appetites more keen."
Sonnet 119: "What potions have I drunk of Siren tears."
Sonnet 120: "That you were once unkind befriends me now."
Sonnet 121: "'Tis better to be vile than vile esteem'd."
Sonnet 122: "Thy gift, thy tables, are within my brain."
Sonnet 123: "No, Time, thou shalt not boast that I do change."
Sonnet 124: "If my dear love were but the child of state."
Sonnet 125: "Were't aught to me I bore the canopy."
Sonnet 126: "O thou, my lovely boy, who in thy power."
Sonnet 127: "In the old age black was not counted fair."
Sonnet 128: "How oft, when thou, my music, music play'st."
Sonnet 129: "Expense of spirit in a waste of shame, The [or Th']."
Sonnet 130: "My mistress' eyes are nothing like the sun."
Sonnet 131: "Thou art as tyrannous, so as thou art."
Sonnet 132: "Thine eyes I love, and they, as pitying me."
Sonnet 133: "Beshrew that heart that makes my heart to groan."
Sonnet 134: "So, now I have confess'd that he is thine."
Sonnet 135: "Whoever hath her wish, thou hast thy Will."
Sonnet 136: "If thy soul check thee that I come so near."
Sonnet 137: "Thou blind fool, Love, what dost thou to mine eyes."
Sonnet 138: "When my love swears [or sweares] that she is made of truth."
Sonnet 139: "O, call me not to justify the wrong."
Sonnet 140: "Be wise as thou art cruel; do not press."
Sonnet 141: "In faith, I do[e] not love thee with mine eyes."
Sonnet 142: "Love is my sin and thy dear virtue hate."
Sonnet 143: "Lo! as a careful housewife runs to catch."
Sonnet 144: "Two loves I have of comfort and despair."
Sonnet 145: "Those lips that Love's own hand did make."
Sonnet 146: "Poor[e] soul[e], the centre of my sinful[l] earth."
Sonnet 147: "My love is as a fever [or feaver], longing still."
Sonnet 148: "O me, what eyes hath Love put in my head."
Sonnet 149: "Canst thou, O cruel! say I love thee not."
Sonnet 150: "O! From [or O! From] what power hast thou this powerful might."
Sonnet 151: "Love is too young to know what conscience is."
Sonnet 152: "In loving thee thou know'st I am forsworn."
Sonnet 153: "Cupid laid by his brand, and fell asleep."
Sonnet 154: "Little love-god lying once asleep, The."
Sonnets.
Sweet Cytherea, sitting by a brook.
Sweet rose, fair flower, untimely pluck'd, soon vaded.
Time's Glory.
Troy Depicted.
Two loves I have, of comfort and despair.
Venus and Adonis.
Venus, with young Adonis sitting by her.
When as thine eye hath chose the dame.
When my love swears that she is made of truth.
[Before the Rape].

Shapiro, Karl (b. 1913)
Adam and Eve.
Adult Bookstore.
Alphabet, The.
And Now, the Weather..
At Auden's Grave.
Auto Wreck.
Back, The.
Boy-Man.
Buick.
Calder, A.
California Petrarchan.
Cathedral Bells, The.
Confession, The.
Conscientious Objector, The.
Crucifix in the Filing Cabinet, The.
Cut Flower, A.
Dirty Word, The.
Dome of Sunday, The [or A].
Drug Store.
Essay on Chess.
Exile.
Figurehead, The.
First Time, The.
Fly, The.
Girls Fighting, Broadway.
Glass Poem.
Grant's Tomb Revisited.
Haircut.
Homewreck.
Hospital.
Humanities Building, The.
I Am an Atheist Who Says His Prayers.
Impact.
Intellectual, The.
Interlude, The.
Israel.
Kiss, The.
Leg, The.
Love for a Hand.
Manhole Covers.
Messias.
Mongolian Idiot.
My Grandmother.
Nebraska.
Necropolis.
New Ring, The.
Nigger.
Office Love.
Olive Tree, The.
Pigeons, The.
Poet.
Poet in Residence.
Premises.
Progress of Faust, The.
Recognition of Eve, The.
Retirement.
Room in Rome, A.
Scyros.
Shame.
Sickness of Adam, The.
Solipsism.
Spider Mums, The.
Statue of Liberty.
Synagogue, The.
Tingling Back, The.
Tornado Warning.
Travelogue for Exiles.
Tree of Guilt, The.
Twins, The.
University.
V-Letter.
Vietnam Memorial.
Waitress.
Washington Cathedral.
White Negress, The.
Translations, Coauthored Poems, etc.:
Giantess.

Shelley, Percy Bysshe (1792–1822)
Adonais; An Elegy on the Death of John Keats.
Alastor; or, The Spirit of Solitude.
Allegory, An.
Another Fragment to Music.
Another Version of the Same.
Arethusa.
At Pompeii.

Athens.
Autumn: A Dirge.
Aziola, The.
Beatrice's Last Words.
Bereavement.
Bigotry's Victim.
Birth of Pleasure, The.
Boat on the Serchio, The.
Bridal Song, A: "Golden gates of Sleep unbar, The."
Buona Notte.
see also Ode to Heaven.
Cancelled Passage.
Cancelled Passages of the Poem.
Cancelled Stanza.
Cancelled Stanza of the Mask of Anarchy.
Cenci, The.
Cenci's Curse upon His Daughter, The.
Charles the First.
Child of Twelve, A.
Cloud, The.
Daemon of the World, The; A Fragment.
Death.
Death knell is ringing, The.
Despair.
Devil's Walk, The.
Dialogue, A.
Dirge, A: "Rough wind, that moanest loud."
Dirge for the Year.
Drowned Lover, The.
Epipsychidion.
Epitaph: "These are two friends whose lives / were undivided."
Epitaphium.
Epithalamium: "Night, with all thine eyes look down!"
Evening: Ponte al Mare, Pisa.
Evening: To Harriet.
Ever as We Sailed.
Exhortation, An.
Eyes: A Fragment.
Feelings of a Republican on the Fall of Bonaparte.
Fiordispina.
Fragment: A Roman's Chamber.
Fragment: A Serpent-Face.
Fragment: A Tale Untold.
Fragment: A Wanderer.
Fragment: "Alas! this is not what I thought life was."
Fragment: Amor Aeternus.
Fragment: "And that I walk thus proudly crowned withal."
Fragment: Apostrophe to Silence.
Fragment: Beauty's Halo.
Fragment: Death in Life.
Fragment: "Follow to the deep wood's weeds."
Fragment from the Wandering Jew.
Fragment: "Gentle story of two lovers young, A."
Fragment: "Great Spirit."
Fragment: Home.
Fragment: "I faint, I perish with my love! I grow."
Fragment: "I stood upon a heaven-cleaving turret."
Fragment: "I would not be a king—enough."
Fragment: Igniculus Desiderii.
Fragment: "Is it that in some brighter sphere."
Fragment: Life Rounded with Sleep.
Fragment: Love the Universe To-day.
Fragment: Love's Tender Atmosphere.
Fragment: May the Limner.
Fragment: "Methought I was a billow in the crowd."
Fragment: Milton's Spirit.
Fragment: Music and Sweet Poetry.
Fragment: "My head is wild with weeping for a grief."
Fragment: "O thou immortal deity."
Fragment of a Ghost Story.
Fragment of a Satire on Satire.
Fragment of a Sonnet: Farewell to North Devon.
Fragment of a Sonnet: To Harriet.

Fragment: Omens.
Fragment on Keats.
Fragment, or The Triumph of Conscience.
Fragment: Pater Omnipotens.
Fragment: Rain ("Fitful alternations of the rain, The").
Fragment: Rain ("Gentleness of rain was in the wind, The").
Fragment: Rome and Nature.
Fragment: "Rude wind is singing, The."
Fragment: Satan Broken Loose.
Fragment: "Such hope, as is the sick despair of good."
Fragment: Sufficient Unto the Day.
Fragment: The Deserts of Dim Sleep.
Fragment: The False Laurel and the True.
Fragment: The Lady of the South.
Fragment: The Lake's Margin.
Fragment: The Sepulchre of Memory.
Fragment: The Vine-Shroud.
Fragment: Thoughts Come and Go in Solitude.
Fragment: " 'Tis midnight now—athwart the murky air."
Fragment: To a Friend Released from Prison.
Fragment: To Byron.
Fragment: To Italy.
Fragment: To Music, A.
Fragment: To One Singing.
Fragment: To the Mind of Man.
Fragment: To the Moon.
Fragment: To the People of England.
Fragment: "Unrisen splendour of the brightest sun."
Fragment: "Viewless and invisible Consequence, The."
Fragment: "Wake the serpent not—lest he."
Fragment: Wedded Souls.
Fragment: "What men gain fairly—that they should possess."
Fragment: "When a lover clasps his fairest."
Fragment: "When soft winds and sunny skies."
Fragment: Wine of the Fairies.
Fragment: "Ye gentle visitations of calm thought."
Fragment: "Yes! all is past—swift time has fled away."
Fragment: Zephyrus the Awakener.
see also Epipsychidion.
Fragments of an Unfinished Drama.
Fragments Supposed to Be Parts of Otho.
Fragments Written for Hellas.
From the Arabic: An Imitation.
From the Original Draft of the Poem to William Shelley.
Fugitives, The.
Ghasta; or, The Avenging Demon!!!
Ginevra.
Go Thou to Rome.
Good-Night.
Hate-Song, A.
Hellas.
Hymn of Pan.
Hymn to Intellectual Beauty.
In Horologium.
Indian Serenade, The.
Invocation: "Earth, ocean, air, belovèd brotherhood!"
Invocation to Misery.
Irishman's Song, The.
Isle, The.
Lament, A: "O world! O life! O time!"
Letter to Maria Gisborne.
Liberty.
Life of Life.
Lines: "Cold earth slept below, The."
Lines: "Far, far away, O ye."
Lines: "That time is dead for ever, child!"
Lines to a Critic.
Lines to a Reviewer.
Lines: "We meet not as we parted."
Lines: "When the lamp is shattered."
Lines Written among the Euganean Hills.
Lines Written During the Castlereagh Administration.
Lines Written in the Bay of Lerici.

Lines Written on Hearing the News of the Death of Napoleon.
Longest Journey, The.
Love.
Love, Hope, Desire and Fear.
Love's Philosophy.
Love's Rose.
Magic Car Moved On, The.
Magnetic Lady to Her Patient, The.
Marenghi.
Marianne's Dream.
Mask [or Masque] of Anarchy, The.
Melody to a Scene of Former Times.
Mighty Eagle.
Mont Blanc.
Music.
Mutability.
New National Anthem, A.
O that a chariot of cloud were mine!
Ode to Heaven.
Ode to Liberty.
Ode to Naples.
Ode to the West Wind.
Ode Written October, 1819, An.
Oedipus Tyrannus; or, Swellfoot the Tyrant.
On a Faded Violet.
On a Fête at Carlton House: Fragment.
On an Icicle That Clung to the Grass of a Grave.
On Death.
On Fanny Godwin.
On Leaving London for Wales.
On Robert Emmet's Grave.
On the Dark Height of Jura.
On the Medusa of Leonardo da Vinci in the Florentine Gallery.
Original Poetry by Victor and Cazire.
Orpheus.
Otho.
Ozymandias [of Egypt].
Passage of the Apennines.
Past, The.
Peter Bell the Third.
Pine Forest of the Cascine Near Pisa, The.
Poems from St. Irvyne, or, The Rosicrucian.
Posthumous Fragments of Margaret Nicholson.
Prince Athanase; a Fragment.
Prometheus Unbound.
Queen Mab.
Question, The.
Remembrance.
Retrospect, The: CWM Elan, 1812.
Revenge.
Revolt of Islam, The.
Rosalind and Helen; A Modern Eclogue.
Saint Edmond's Eve.
St. Irvyne's Tower.
Scene from "Tasso."
Sensitive Plant, The.
Similes for Two Political Characters of 1819.
Sister Rosa: A Ballad.
Solitary, The.
Song: "Cold, cold is the blast when December is howling."
Song: "Come [Harriet]! sweet is the hour."
Song: "Fierce roars the midnight storm."
see also Scene from "Tasso."
Song from the Wandering Jew.
Song: Hope.
Song of Proserpine.
Song: "Rarely, rarely, comest thou."
Song: To——[Harriet] ("Ah! sweet is the moonbeam..").
Song: To—— [Harriet] ("Stern, stern is the voice..").
Song: "To me this world's a dreary blank."
Song to the Men of England.
Song: Translated from the German.
Song: Translated from the Italian.
Sonnet: England in 1819.
Sonnet: "Lift not the painted veil which those who live."
Sonnet: On Launching Some Bottles Filled with Knowledge into the Bristol Channel.
Sonnet: Political Greatness.
Sonnet: To a Balloon Laden with Knowledge.

Sonnet to Byron.
Sonnet: "Ye hasten to the grave! What seek ye there."
Spectral Horseman, The.
Stanza from a Translation of the Marseillaise Hymn.
Stanza: "If I walk in Autumn's even."
Stanza, Written at Bracknell.
Stanzas—April, 1814.
Stanzas Written in Dejection, near Naples [or —December 1818, near Naples].
Summer and Winter.
Summer Evening Churchyard, A.
Sunset, The.
Tale of Society As It Is, A: From Facts, 1811.
Time.
Time Long Past.
To ———: "I fear thy kisses, gentle maiden."
To ———: "Music, when soft voices die."
To ———: "Oh! there are spirits of the air."
To ———: "One word is too often profaned."
To ———: "When passion's trance is overpast."
To ———: "Yet look on me—take not thine eyes away."
To a Skylark.
To a Star.
To Constantia.
To Constantia, Singing.
To Death.
To Edward Williams.
To Emilia Viviani.
To Harriet ("It is not blasphemy to hope that Heaven").
To Harriet ("Thy look of love has power to calm").
To Ianthe.
To Ireland.
To Jane: The Invitation.
To Jane: The Keen Stars Were Twinkling.
To Jane: The Recollection.
To Maria Gisborne in England, from Italy.
To Mary———.
To Mary.
To Mary Shelley ("My dearest Mary, wherefore hast thou gone").
To Mary Shelley ("World is dreary, The / And I'm weary").
To Mary, Who Died in This Opinion.
To Mary Wollstonecraft Godwin.
To Miss — — [Harriet Grove] from Miss —— [Elizabeth Shelley].
To-Morrow.
To Night.
To Sophia [Miss Stacey].
To the Lord Chancellor.
To the Moonbeam.
To the Nile.
To the Queen of My Heart.
To the Republicans of North America.
To William Shelley ("Billows on the beach are leaping around it, The").
To William Shelley ("My lost William, thou in whom").
To William Shelley ("Thy little footsteps on the sands").
To Wordsworth.
Tower of Famine, The.
Triumph of Life, The.
Two Spirits[: An Allegory], The.
Variation of the Song of the Moon.
Verses on a Cat.
Victoria.
Vision of the Sea, A.
Wandering Jew's Soliloquy, The.
Waning Moon, The.
War.
War Is the Statesman's Game.
Who Reigns?
Witch of Atlas, The.
With a Guitar, to Jane.
Woodman and the Nightingale, The.
World's Wanderers, The.
Zucca, The.

Translations, Coauthored Poems, etc.:
Chorus of Satyrs, Driving Their Goats.
Circumstance.
Cisma de Inglaterra *sels.*
Cyclops, The.
Divina Commedia *sels.*
Eclogues *sels.*
Faust *sels.*
First Canzone of the Convito, The.
Fragment of the Elegy on the Death of
 Adonis.
Fragment of the Elegy on the Death of Bion.
From the Greek of Moschus.
From Vergil's Fourth Georgic.
From Vergil's Tenth Eclogue.
Georgics *sels.*
Hast thou not seen, officious with delight.
Homeric Hymns *sels.*
Homer's Hymn to Castor and Pollux.
Homer's Hymn to Minerva.
Homer's Hymn to the Earth: Mother of All.
Homer's Hymn to the Moon.
Homer's Hymn to the Sun.
Homer's Hymn to Venus.
Hymn to Mercury.
In the sweet solitude of this calm place.
Kissing Helena.
La Vita Nuova *sels.*
Love Song: "One with eyes the fairest."
Magico Prodigioso *sels.*
Matilda Gathering Flowers.
Pan, Echo, and the Satyr.
Prologue in Heaven.
Sonnet: From the Italian of Guido Cavalcanti.
 Cavalcanti to Dante Alighieri.
Sonnet: [From the Italian of Dante.] Dante
 Alighieri to Guido Cavalcanti.
Spirit of Plato.
To Stella.
Ugolino.
What Mary is when she a little smiles.
Would you not like a broomstick? As for me.

Shelton, Richard (b. 1933)
After Thirty Years.
Age of Desire, The.
Age of Despair, The.
Age of Elegance, The.
Age of Miracles, The.
Age of Progress, The.
Age of Romance, The.
Age of War, The.
Alone.
And the Greatest of These.
And the Scars Will Be Covered.
Angel and the Anchorite.
April.
As I Grow Older.
At Forty.
August.
Bird in the Hand: Two Solos, A.
Boojum Tree, The.
Bottom Line, The.
Brother.
Building.
Bus to Veracruz, The.
Certain Choices.
Choose One From Among Them.
Coda.
Comfort.
Connais-Tu le Pays?
Cortege.
Courage.
Crossing, The.
Dear Life.
Death.
Death Row.
Desert.
Desert Water.
Disintegration.
Dry Season.
Dtran of Return.
Encounter.
Excerpts from the Notebook of the Poet of
 Santo Tomas.
Face.
Farmer's Testimony, The.
Five Lies About the Moon.

For Lois.
Fourteenth Anniversary, The.
Full Daytime Moon, The.
Full Harvest Moon, The.
Future, The.
Gambit, The.
Gibbous Moon, The.
Grandfathering.
Great Gulf, The.
Guilt.
Half-Moon, The.
Harry Orchard.
He who remains.
Heaven of the Poor, The.
Her.
Heroes of Our Times, The.
History.
Housecleaning.
How to Amuse a Stone.
I Have No Wings.
In the Beginning Was the Word.
Job the Father.
Kind of Glory, A.
Kingdom of the Moon, The.
Landscape With A Woman.
Language of Postcards, The.
Letter From an Inland Province.
Letter to a Dead Father.
Letter to a Lost Friend.
Letting Go.
Local Knowledge.
Machines, The.
Mexico.
Monster, The.
My Hands Are My Enemies.
My Love.
Navajo Song.
Negative Virtues, The.
New Road, The.
New Year's Eve.
Notes Towards an Autobiography.
November.
November 1st.
On Lake Pend Oreille.
One More Time.
Other World, The.
Out Here.
Outcast.
Pain.
Poet As Equestrian, The.
Point of View.
Princes of Exile, The.
Promises.
Prophet, The.
Prophets, The.
Rain the Stones the Darkness, The.
Reaching For the Gun.
Requiem for Sonora.
Reservations.
Reunion.
San Juan's Day.
Saturday Night at the Elk's Club.
Seven Ages of Man, The.
Seven Preludes to Silence.
Softly Softly.
Soldiers Returning, The.
Song of the Hogan.
Sonora.
Sonora for Sale.
Stone Garden, The.
Stones, The.
Stranger.
Strangers.
Surgery.
Survival.
Tattooed Desert, The.
Teeth of These Mountains, The.
Territorial Rights.
Three Poems For A Twenty-Fifth
 Anniversary.
To My Other Self.
To You.
Valediction: "I Who Witnessed the Nail's
 Desire."
Voice of the Moon, The.
Waning Crescent Moon, The.
War.

Whatever Became of Me.
White Hotel, The.
Why I Never Went into Politics.
Winter.
Wonders of the World.

Sidney, Sir Philip (1554–86)
All what you are still one, his own to find.
Apollo great, whose beams the greater world
 do light.
Arcadia *sels.*
As I my little flock on Ister Bank.
Astrophil and Stella.
Aurora, now thou show'st thy blushing light.
Beauty hath force to catch the human sight.
Come, *Dorus*, come, let the songs thy
 sorrows signify.
Come, *Espilus*, come now declare thy skill.
Come shepherd's weeds, become your
 master's mind.
Do not disdain, O straight upraised pine.
Dorus, tell me, where is thy wonted motion.
Eighth Song.
Eleventh Song.
Fair rocks, goodly rivers, sweet woods, when
 shall I see peace?
Feed on my sheep; my charge, my comfort,
 feed.
Fifth Song.
Fortune, Nature, Love, long have contended
 about me.
Fourth Song.
Get hence foul[e] grief[e], the canker of the
 mind[e].
Hark, plaintful ghosts! Infernal furies, hark.
Hateful cure with hate to heal, A.
How Is My Sun.
I joy in grief, and do detest all joys.
If mine eyes can speak to do hearty errand.
In Vain, Mine Eyes.
Lady of May, The *sels.*
Lady, reserved by the heav'ns to do pastors'
 company honour.
Leave me, O Love which reachest but to
 dust.
Leave off my sheep: it is no time to feed.
Let mother Earth now deck herself in
 flowers.
Let not old age disgrace my high desire.
Like as the dove which seeled-up doth fly.
Like diverse flowers, whose diverse beauties
 serve.
Lock up, fair lids, the treasure of my heart.
Love which is imprinted in my soul, The.
Loved I am, and yet complain[e] of Love.
Merchant man, whom many seas have taught,
 The.
My lute, within thyself thy tunes enclose.
My Muse what ails this ardour.
My sheep are thoughts, which I both guide
 and serve.
My words, in hope to blaze my steadfast
 mind.
Ninth Song.
Now thanked be the great god *Pan*.
Now was our heav'nly vault deprived of the
 light.
O night, the ease of care, the pledge of
 pleasure.
O stealing time, the subject of delay.
O sweet woods, the delight of solitariness!
O words, which fall like summer dew on me!
Oft have I mused, but now at length I find.
Over these brooks trusting to ease mine eyes.
Phoebus farewell, a sweeter saint I serve.
Reason, tell me thy mind, if here be reason.
Scourge of life, and death's extreme disgrace,
 The.
Second Song.
Seventh Song.
Silvanus long in love, and long in vain.
Since Nature's works be good, and death
 doth serve.
Since, shunning pain, I ease can never find.
Since so mine eyes are subject to your sight.
Since wailing is a bud of causeful sorrow.
Sixth Song.

Sonnet 1: "Loving in truth, and fain[e] in verse my love to show."

Sonnet 2: "Not at [the] first sight, nor with a dribbed shot."

Sonnet 3: "Let dainty wits cry on the sisters nine."

Sonnet 4: "Virtue, alas, now let me take some rest."

Sonnet 5: "It is most true that eyes are formed to serve."

Sonnet 6: "Some lovers speak, when they their Muses entertain."

Sonnet 7: "When Nature made her chief work, Stella's eyes."

Sonnet 8: "Love, born in Greece, of late fled from his native place."

Sonnet 9: "Queen Virtue's court, which some call Stella's face."

Sonnet 10: "Reason, in faith thou art well served, that still."

Sonnet 11: "In truth, O Love, with what a boyish kind."

Sonnet 12: "Cupid, because thou shin'st in Stella's eyes."

Sonnet 13: "Phoebus was judge between Jove, Mars, and Love."

Sonnet 14: "Alas, have I not pain enough, my friend."

Sonnet 15: "You that do search for every purling spring."

Sonnet 16: "In nature apt to like when I did see."

Sonnet 17: "His mother dear Cupid offended late."

Sonnet 18: "With what sharp checks I in myself am shent."

Sonnet 19: "On Cupid's bow how are my heart-strings bent."

Sonnet 20: "Fly, fly, my friends, I have my death-wound, fly."

Sonnet 21: "Your words my friend (right healthful caustics) blame."

Sonnet 22: "In highest way of heav'n the sun did ride."

Sonnet 23: "Curious wits,, seeing dull pensiveness, The."

Sonnet 24: "Rich fools there be, whose base and filthy heart."

Sonnet 25: "Wisest scholar of the wight most wise, The."

Sonnet 26: "Though dusty wits dare scorn astrology."

Sonnet 27: "Because I oft, in dark abstracted guise."

Sonnet 28: "You that with allegory's curious frame."

Sonnet 29: "Like some weak lords, neighboured by mighty kings."

Sonnet 30: "Whether the Turkish new moon minded be."

Sonnet 31: "With how sad steps, O Moon, thou climb'st the skies."

Sonnet 32: "Morpheus, the lively son of deadly sleep."

Sonnet 33: "I might, unhappy word, O me, I might."

Sonnet 34: "Come, let me write. 'And to what end?' To ease."

Sonnet 35: "What may words say, or what may words not say."

Sonnet 36: "Stella, whence doth this new assault arise."

Sonnet 37: "My mouth doth water, and my breast doth swell."

Sonnet 38: "This night, while sleep begins with heavy wings."

Sonnet 39: "Come sleep, O sleep, the certain knot of peace."

Sonnet 40: "As good to write as for to lie and groan."

Sonnet 41: "Having this day my horse, my hand, my lance."

Sonnet 42: "O eyes, which do the spheres of beauty move."

Sonnet 43: "Fair eyes, sweet lips, dear heart, that foolish I."

Sonnet 44: "My words I know do well set forth my mind."

Sonnet 45: "Stella oft sees the very face of woe."

Sonnet 46: "I cursed thee oft, I pity now thy case."

Sonnet 47: "What, have I thus betrayed my liberty?"

Sonnet 48: "Soul's joy, bend not those morning stars from me."

Sonnet 49: "I on my horse, and Love on me doth try."

Sonnet 50: "Stella, the fullness of my thoughts of thee."

Sonnet 51: "Pardon mine ears; both I and they do pray."

Sonnet 52: "Strife is grown between Virtue and Love, A."

Sonnet 53: "In martial sports I had my cunning tried."

Sonnet 54: "Because I breathe not love to every one."

Sonnet 55: "Muses, I oft invoked your holy aid."

Sonnet 56: "Fie, school of Patience, fie; your lesson is."

Sonnet 57: "Woe, having made with many fights his own."

Sonnet 58: "Doubt there hath been, when with his golden chain."

Sonnet 59: "Dear, why make you more of a dog than me?"

Sonnet 60: "When my good angel guides me to the place."

Sonnet 61: "Oft with true sighs, oft with uncalled tears."

Sonnet 62: "Late tired with woe, e'en ready for to pine."

Sonnet 63: "O grammar rules, O now your virtues show."

Sonnet 64: "No more, my dear, no more these counsels try."

Sonnet 65: "Love, by sure proof I may call thee unkind."

Sonnet 66: "And do I see some cause a hope to feed."

Sonnet 67: "Hope, art thou true, or dost thou flatter me?"

Sonnet 68: "Stella, the only planet of my light."

Sonnet 69: "O joy, too high for my low style to show."

Sonnet 70: "My Muse may well grudge at my heav'nly joy."

Sonnet 71: "Who will in fairest book of Nature know."

Sonnet 72: "Desire, though thou my old companion art."

Sonnet 73: "Love still a boy, and oft a wanton is."

Sonnet 74: "I never drank of Aganippe well."

Sonnet 75: "Of all the kings that ever here did reign."

Sonnet 76: "She comes, and straight therewith her shining twins do move."

Sonnet 77: "Those looks, whose beams be joy, whose motion is delight."

Sonnet 78: "O how the pleasant airs of true love be."

Sonnet 79: "Sweet kiss, thy sweets I fain would sweetly indite."

Sonnet 80: "Sweet swelling lip, well mayst thou swell in pride."

Sonnet 81: "O kiss, which dost those ruddy gems impart."

Sonnet 82: "Nymph of the garden where all beauties be."

Sonnet 83: "Good brother Philip, I have borne you long."

Sonnet 84: "Highway, since you my chief Parnassus be."

Sonnet 85: "I see the house; my heart thyself contain."

Sonnet 86: "Alas, whence came this change of looks? If I."

Sonnet 87: "When I was forced from Stella ever dear."

Sonnet 88: "Out, traitor absence: dar'st thou counsel me."

Sonnet 89: "Now that of absence the most irksome night."

Sonnet 90: "Stella, think not that I by verse seek fame."

Sonnet 91: "Stella, while now by honour's cruel might."

Sonnet 92: "Be your words made (good sir) of Indian ware."

Sonnet 93: "O fate, O fault, O curse, child of my bliss."

Sonnet 94: "Grief, find the words, for thou hast made my moan."

Sonnet 95: "Yet sighs, dear sighs, indeed true friends you are."

Sonnet 96: "Thought, with good cause thou lik'st so well the night."

Sonnet 97: "Dian, that fain would cheer her friend the Night."

Sonnet 98: "Ah bed, the field where joy's peace some do see."

Sonnet 99: "When far-spent night persuades each mortal eye."

Sonnet 100: "O tears, no tears, but rain from beauty's skies."

Sonnet 101: "Stella is sick, and in that sick-bed lies."

Sonnet 102: "Where be those roses gone, which sweetened so our eyes?"

Sonnet 103: "O happy Thames, that didst my Stella bear."

Sonnet 104: "Envious wits, what hath been mine offence."

Sonnet 105: "Unhappy sight, and hath she vanished by."

Sonnet 106: "O absent presence, Stella is not here."

Sonnet 107: "Stella, since thou so right a Princess art."

Sonnet 108: "When sorrow (using mine own fire's might)."

Sweet glove, the witness of my secret bliss.

Tenth Song.

Third Song.

Thou blind man's mark, thou fool's self-chosen snare.

Thou Pain, the only guest of loathed constraint.

Thy elder care shall from thy careful face.

To one whose state is raised over all.

Transformed in show, but more transformed in mind.

Unto the caitiff wretch whom long affliction holdeth.

Virtue, beauty, and speech, did strike, wound, charm.

What length of verse can serve brave *Mopsa*'s good to show?

What tongue can her perfections tell.

When Love, puffed up with rage of high disdain.

When two suns do appear.

Why dost thou haste away.

With two strange fires of equal heat possessed [*or* possest].

Ye [*or* you] goat-herd gods, [that love the grassy mountains].

Ye living powers enclosed in stately shrine.

You better sure shall live, not evermore.

You goodly pines, which still with brave ascent.

Translations, Coauthored Poems, etc.:

Lord, help, it is high time for me to call.

Lord, the Lord my shepherd is, The.

Psalm 22: "My God, my God, why hast thou forsaken me?"

Psalms *sels.*

Speak Thou for me against wrong-speaking foes.

To Thee, Lord, my cry I send.

Silverstein, Shel [*or* Shelley] (b. 1932)

Acrobats, The.

Afraid of the Dark.

Alice.

Bagpipe Who Didn't Say No, The.

Band-Aids.

Bang-Klang.
Battle, The.
Benjamin Bunnn.
Bloath, The.
Boa Constrictor.
Captain Hook.
Chester.
Colors.
Crocodile's Toothache, The.
Dancing Pants.
Dirtiest Man in the World, The.
Double-Tail Dog.
Drats.
Dreadful.
Early Bird.
Edge of the World, The.
Eighteen Flavors.
Enter This Deserted House.
Farmer and the Queen, The.
Fish?
Flag.
Flying Festoon, The.
For Sale.
Forgotten Language.
Fourth, The.
Fred?
Garden, The.
Generals, The.
Googies Are Coming, The.
Hat.
Hector the Collector.
Helping.
Homemade Boat.
Hug o' War.
Hungry Mungry.
I Must Remember.
I Won't Hatch.
Ickle Me, Pickle Me, Tickle Me Too.
If I Had A Brontosaurus.
If the World Was Crazy.
I'm Making a List.
Instructions.
Invention.
Invisible Boy.
Invitation.
It's Dark In Here.
Jimmy Jet and His TV Set.
Joey.
Jumping Rope.
Just Me, Just Me.
Land of Happy, The.
Lazy Jane.
Lester.
Listen To The Mustn'ts.
Little Blue Engine, The.
Long-Haired Boy, The.
Longest Nose.
Loser, The.
Love.
Ma and God.
Magic.
Magical Eraser.
Me and My Giant.
Me-Stew.
Melinda Mae.
Merry.
Minnow Minnie.
My Beard.
My Hobby.
My Rules.
No Difference.
Oh Have You Heard.
One Inch Tall.
One Who Stayed, The.
Ourchestra.
Pancake?
Paul Bunyan.
Peanut-Butter Sandwich.
Pirate Captain Jim.
Planet of Mars, The.
Poem on the Neck of a Running GIraffe, A.
Point of View.
Poor Angus.
Rain.
Razor-Tailed Wren, The.
Recipe For A Hippopotamus Sandwich.
Ridiculous Rose.

Rudy Flesh.
Santa and the Reindeer.
Sarah Cynthia Sylvia Stout Would Not Take
    the Garbage Out.
Search, The.
Shadow Wash.
Sick.
Silver Fish, The.
Skinny.
Sky Seasoning.
Sleeping Sardines.
Smart.
Snowman.
Spaghetti.
Standing.
Stone Telling.
Thumbs.
Tight Hat.
Toucan, The.
Traffic Light.
Tree House.
True Story.
Two Boxes.
Unicorn, The.
Upstairs.
Us.
Warning.
What a Day.
What's In the Sack?
Where the Sidewalk Ends.
Who.
Wild Boar.
With His Mouth Full of Food.
Won't You?
Worst, The.
Yipiyuk, The.

Simic, Charles (b. 1938)
Animal Acts.
Austerities.
Autumn Air.
Ax.
Baby Pictures of Famous Dictators.
Ballad of the Wheel, The.
Ballad: "What's that approaching like dust
    like poverty."
Bedtime Story.
Begotten of the Spleen.
Bestiary for the Fingers of My Right Hand.
Breasts.
Brooms.
Butcher Shop.
Charles Simic.
Charon's Cosmology.
Chicken Without a Head, The.
Childhood of Parmenides, The.
Chorus for One Voice.
Classic Ballroom Dances.
Cold Blue Tinge.
Concerning My Neighbors, the Hittites.
Crows.
Day Marked with a Small White Stone, A.
December Trees.
Description.
Dismantling the Silence.
Drawing the Triangle.
Drawn to Perspective.
East European Cooking.
Elegy: "Note / as it gets darker."
Elementary Cosmogony.
Empire of Dreams.
Eraser.
Errata.
Especially forlorn human specimen, An.
Euclid Avenue.
Evening.
Evening with the Master, An.
Explorers.
Eyes Fastened with Pins.
Fall Day, A.
Fear.
February.
Figuring.
Forest Birds.
Fork.
Furniture Mover.
Gallows Etiquette.
Game, The.

Gravity.
Great Horned Owl, The.
Great Infirmities.
Grocery.
Happy End.
Harsh Climate.
Help Wanted.
History.
History Book.
Hurricane Season.
In Midsummer Quiet.
Inheritance.
Inner Man, The.
Interlude.
Invention of Nothing.
Knife.
Landscape with Crutches, A.
Lesson, The.
Little Tear Gland That Says, The.
Madonnas Touched Up with a Goatee.
Man, The.
Marching.
Midpoint.
My Shoes.
My Weariness of Epic Proportions.
Navigator.
Northern Exposure.
Note.
Note Slipped Under a Door.
Nursery Rhyme.
Old Couple.
Old Mountain Road.
Partial Explanation, The.
Pastoral: "I came to a meadow."
Peaceful Kingdom.
Peaceful Trees.
Piety.
Pillow, The.
Place, The.
Poem: "Every morning I forget how it is."
Poem: "My father writes all day, all night."
Poem without a Title.
Point, The.
Position without a Magnitude.
Primer.
Prisoner, The.
Prodigy.
Psalm: "Old ones to the side."
Quiet Talk with Oneself, A.
Rosalia sels.
Rosalia.
Rough Outline.
Rural Delivery.
School for Dark Thoughts.
Shaving at Night.
Shirt.
Solitude.
Solving the Riddle.
Soup, The.
Spoon.
Spoons with Realistic Dead Flies on Them.
Stone.
Stream, The.
Strictly Bucolic.
Suitcase Strapped with a Rope, A.
Summer Morning.
Summons, The.
Terms, The.
Thus.
Tomb of Stéphane Mallarmé, The.
Toy Factory.
Travelling.
Travelling Slaughterhouse.
Trees at Night.
Two Riddles.
Variant, The.
Wall, A.
Watch Repair.
Watermelons.
Way It Is, The.
What the White Had to Say.
Whispers in the Next Room.
White.
Window Washer.
Winter Night.
Writings of the Mystics, The.

Smart, Christopher (1722–71)
Accession of King George III, The.
Against Despair.
All Saints.
Annunciation of the Blessed Virgin.
Apollo and Daphne.
Ascension of Our Lord Jesus Christ, The.
Ash Wednesday. First Day of Lent.
At Dressing in the Morning.
At Undressing in the Evening.
Author Apologizes to a Lady, for His Being
   a Little Man, The.
Beauteous, Yea Beauteous More than These.
Beauty.
Care and Generosity.
Charity.
Christmas Day.
Circumcision.
Conclusion of the Matter, The.
Conversion of St. Paul.
Country Squire and the Mandrake, The.
Crucifixion of Our Blessed Lord.
Easter Day.
Elegance.
Epiphany.
Epistle to Dr. Nares.
Epistle to John Sherratt, Esq., An.
Epitaph on Henry Fielding, Esq.
Faith.
Fifth of November, The.
For Saturday.
For Sunday.
Fortitude.
Fragment A.
Fragment B.
Fragment C.
Fragment D.
Generosity.
God Hath Sent Me to Sea for Pearls.
Good-Nature to Animals.
Gratitude.
Hail Energeia! hail, my native tongue.
Holy Innocents, The.
Honesty.
Honour.
Hope.
Hymn to the Supreme Being.
Hymns and Spiritual Songs for the Fasts and
   Festivals of the Church of England.
Hymns for the Amusement of Children.
Immortality.
Inscriptions on an Aeolian Harp.
Jubilate Agno.
Justice.
King Charles the Martyr.
King's Restoration, The.
Learning.
Let Elizur Rejoice with the Partridge.
Lines with a Pocket Book.
Long-Suffering of God.
Loveliness.
Melancholy.
Mercy.
Mineral Rejoicings.
Mirth.
Moderation.
Munificence and Modesty.
Mutual Subjection.
Nativity of Our Lord and Saviour Jesus
   Christ, The.
Nativity of St. John the Baptist, The.
New Year.
Ode to Admiral Sir George Pocock.
Ode to General Draper.
Ode to Lady Harriot.
On a Bed of Guernsey Lilies.
On an Eagle Confined in a College-Court.
On Gratitude.
On Taking a Batchelor's Degree.
On the Eternity of the Supreme Being.
On the Goodness of the Supreme Being.
On the Immensity of the Supreme Being.
On the Omniscience of the Supreme Being.
On the Power of the Supreme Being.
Patience.
Peace.
Plenteous Redemption.

Praise.
Pray Remember the Poor.
Prayer.
Presentation of Christ in the Temple, The.
Prudence.
Reason and Imagination.
St. Andrew.
St. Barnabas.
St. Bartholomew.
St. James.
St. John the Evangelist.
St. Luke.
St. Mark.
St. Matthew.
St. Matthias.
St. Michael and All Angels.
St. Peter.
St. Philip and St. James.
St. Simon and St. Jude.
St. Stephen.
St. Thomas.
Silence.
Song to David, A.
Story of a Cock and a Bull, A.
Sweets of Evening, The.
Taste.
Temperance.
To Ethelinda.
To Mrs. Dacosta.
To My Worthy Friend, Mr. T.B. One of the
   People Called Quakers.
To the Rev. Mr. Powell.
Trinity Sunday.
Truth.
Watching.
Whitsunday.
Translations, Coauthored Poems, etc.:
  1.1: To Maecenas.
  1.4: "Tibullus, whom I love and praise."
  1.4: To Sextius, a Person of Consular
    Dignity.
  1.20: "You seem to cast, my vent'rous
    book."
  2.6: "This was the summit of my views."
  2.15: Upon the Luxury of the Age He Lived
    in.
  2.16: To Grosphus.
  2.18: "Gold or iv'ry's not intended."
  3.12: To Neobule.
  3.16: To Maecenas.
  4.3: To Melpomene.
  4.11: To Phyllis.
  Arouse—and let thy foes disperse.
  Attend to the music divine.
  Carmina *sels.*
  Disertissime Romuli Nepotum.
  Earth is God's, with all she bears, The.
  Epistles *sels.*
  Hallelujah! kneel and sing / Praises to the
    heav'nly king.
  Hosanna! God be prais'd.
  Hosanna! praise the Lord, and bless.
  If the work be not direct.
  Lord and Master, to thine altar.
  Miser and the Mouse, The.
  O Frame the strains anew.
  O Lord, thy land has favour found.
  O Praise the Lord, and bless his name.
  Odes *sels.*
  Pensive we sat the silent hours.
  Psalms *sels.*
  Queen of the mountains far and near.
  Rejoice in God, ye saints above.
  Satires *sels.*
  Secular Ode, The.
  Thee will I love, O Lord, my tow'r.
  To Antonius Julus, the Son of Mark Antony,
    tof the Triumvirate.
  To His Servant.
  To L. Manlius Torquatus.
  To Posthumus.

Smith, Charlotte (1749–1806)
Apostrophe to an Old Tree.
April.
Beachy Head.
Blest is yon shepherd, on the turf reclined.
By the Same.

By the Same. Just before His Death.
By the Same. To Solitude.
By the Same. To the North Star.
Captive Escaped in the Wilds of America.
   Addressed to the Hon. Mrs. O'Neill, The.
Close of Summer, The.
Composed During a Walk on the Downs, in
   November 1787.
Dead Beggar, an Elegy Addressed to a Lady,
   The.
Descriptive Ode, Supposed to Have Been
   Written under the Ruins of Rufus's Castle,
   A.
Dictatorial Owl, The.
Disillusion with the French Revolution.
Early Butterfly, The.
Elegy: "Dark gathering clouds involve the
   threatening skies."
Emigrants, The.
Epilogue [A] to *What Is She?*
Epilogue [B] to *What Is She?*
Epilogue [C] to *What Is She?*
Evening.
Evening Walk by the Sea-Side, An.
Fairest flowers are gone! for tempests fell,
   The.
Far on the sands, the low, retiring tide.
Farewel, ye lawns!—by fond remembrance
   blest.
Female Exile. Written at Brighthelmstone in
   November 1792, The.
Flora.
Forest Boy, The.
Glow-Worm, The.
Gossamer, The.
He may be envied, who with tranquil breast.
Heath, The.
Hedge-Hog Seen in a Frequented Path, The.
Hope. A Rondeau.
Horologe of the Fields, The.
Hymn to Love and Life.
Inscription on a Stone, in the Church-Yard at
   Boreham.
Invitation to the Bee.
Jay in Masquerade, The.
Laplander, The.
Lark's Nest, The.
Lines Composed in Passing through a Forest
   in Germany.
Lydia.
Montalbert *sels.*
Moth, The.
Nepenthe.
Ode to Death.
Ode to Despair.
Ode to the Missel Thrush.
Ode to the Olive Tree.
On Being Cautioned against Walking on an
   Headland Overlooking the Sea, because It
   Was Frequented by a Lunatic.
On Leaving a Part of Sussex.
On Passing Over a Dreary Tract of Country,
   and Near the Ruins of a Deserted Chapel,
   During a Tempest.
On the Aphorism "L'Amitié est l'Amour sans
   Ailes."
On the Departure of the Nightingale.
Origin of Flattery, The.
Partial Muse, has from my earliest hours,
   The.
Peasant of the Alps, The.
Pilgrim, The.
Prologue to *What is She?* A Comedy, in Five
   Acts.
Prologue to William Godwin, *Antonio: or,
   The Soldier's Return.*
Reflections on Some Drawings of Plants.
Return of the Nightingale. Written in May
   1791, The.
Saint Monica.
Sea View, The.
Sent to the Honorable Mistress O'Neill, with
   Painted Flowers.
Should the lone Wanderer, fainting on his
   way.
Sighing I see yon little troop at play.

Sleeping Woodman. Written in April 1790,
The.
Snowdrops.
Song: "Does Pity give, tho' Fate denies."
Sonnet to the Forest Ytene.
Stanzas: "Ah! think'st thou, Laura, then, that
wealth."
Studies by the Sea.
Supposed To Be Written by Werter.
Supposed to Have Been Written in a Church-
yard, over the Grave of a Young Woman
of Nineteen.
Supposed To Have Been Written in America.
Supposed to Have Been Written in the
Hebrides.
Swallow, The.
Thirty-Eight (Addressed to Mrs. H----Y).
To a Butterfly in a Window.
To a Friend.
To a Geranium Which Flowered during the
Winter.
To a Green-Chafer, on a White Rose.
To a Nightingale.
To a Querulous Acquaintance.
To a Young Man Entering the World.
To an Amiable Girl.
To Dependence.
To Dr. Parry of Bath, with Some Botanic
Drawings Which Had Been Made Some
Years.
To Fancy.
To Fortitude.
To Friendship.
To Hope.
To Melancholy. Written on the Banks of the
Arun, October 1785.
To Miss C—on Being Desired To Attempt
Writing a Comedy.
To Mr. Hayley, on Receiving Some Elegant
Lines from Him.
To Mrs. ****.
To Mrs. G.
To My Lyre.
To Night.
To Oblivion.
To Sleep.
To Spring.
To the Countess of A—. Written on the
Anniversary of Her Marriage.
To the Earl of Egremont.
To the Fire-Fly of Jamaica, Seen in a
Collection.
To the Goddess of Botany.
To the Insect of the Gossamer.
To the Invisible Moon.
To the Moon.
To the Morning Star. Written Near the Sea.
To the Mulberry-Tree.
To the Muse.
To the Naiad of the Arun.
To the River Arun.
To the Shade of Burns.
To the Snow-Drop.
To the South Downs.
To the Sun.
To the Winds.
To Tranquillity.
To Vesper.
Truant Dove from Pilpay, The.
Unhappy exile, whom his fates confine, The.
Verses Intended to Have Been Prefixed to the
Novel of Emmeline, but Then Suppressed.
Verses, on the death of [Henrietta O'Neill],
written in September, 1794.
Verses Supposed to Have Been Written in
the New Forest, in Early Spring.
Violets.
Walk by the Water, A.
Walk in the Shrubbery, A.
What is She? sels.
Wheat-Ear, The.
When welcome slumber sets my spirit free.
Where the wild woods and pathless forests
frown.
Wild Flowers.
Winter Night, The.

Written at Bignor Park in Sussex, in August,
1799.
Written at Bristol in the Summer of 1794.
Written at Exmouth, Midsummer, 1795.
Written at Penshurst, in Autumn 1788.
Written at the Same Place, on Seeing a
Seaman Return Who Had Been Imprisoned
at Rochfort.
Written at Weymouth in Winter.
Written for the Benefit of a Distressed
Player, Detained at Brighthelmstone for
Debt, November 1792.
Written in a Tempestuous Night, on the
Coast of Sussex.
Written in Farm Wood, South Downs, in
May 1784.
Written in October.
Written in the Church-yard at Middleton in
Sussex.
Written near a Port on a Dark Evening.
Written on Passing by Moon-Light through a
Village, While the Ground Was Covered
with Snow.
Written on the Sea Shore.—October, 1784.
Written September 1791, During a
Remarkable Thunder Storm, in which the
Moon Was Perfectly Clear, While the
Tempest Gathered in Various Directions
Near the Earth.
Translations, Coauthored Poems, etc.:
From Petrarch ("Oh! place me where the
burning noon").
Loose to the wind her golden tresses
stream'd.
Love and Folly.
Oh! place me where the burning noon.
On thy grey bark, in witness of my flame.
Song from the French.
Song: "Fruit of Aurora's tears, fair Rose."
Sonnets to Laura *sels.*
Where the green leaves exclude the summer
beam.
Ye vales and woods! fair scenes of happier
hours.

Smith, Patti (b. 1946)
After/Words.
Amazing Tale of Skunkdog, The.
Amelia Earhart.
Anna of the Harbor.
Babelfield.
Babelogue.
Balance.
Ballad of a Bad Boy.
Ballad of Hagan Waker, The.
Ballad of Isabelle Eberhardt.
Burning Roses.
Combe.
Conversation with the Kid.
Corps de Plane.
Death by Water.
December.
Doctor Love.
Dog Dream.
Dream of Rimbaud.
Easter.
Fire of Unknown Origin, A.
Fleet of Deer, A.
Florence.
Georgia O'Keeffe.
Gibralto.
Grant.
Ha! Ha! Houdini!
Health Lantern.
High on Rebellion.
Hymn: "We hadn't eaten in two days. we
were entirely intoxicated."
Italy.
Jeanne D'Arc.
Jet Flakes.
Judith Revisited.
K.O.D.A.K.
Land.
Munich.
Neo Boy.
Notebook.
Notice.
Notice 2.

Oath.
Penicillin.
Picasso Laughing.
Piss Factory.
Prayer.
Ps/alm 23 Revisited.
Rape.
Rimbaud Dead.
Robert Bresson.
Salvation of Rock, The.
Schinden.
Scream of the Butterfly.
Seventh Heaven.
Sheep Lady from Algiers, The.
16 February.
Sohl.
Suite.
Thermos.
Thread.
Translators.
True Music.
Wave.
Wing.
Witt.
Work Song.
Y.

Smith, Stevie (1902–71)
Abominable Lake, The.
Actress, The.
Adelaide Abner.
Admire Cranmer!
Advice to Young Children.
After-Thought, The.
Agnostic, An.
Ah, Will the Saviour..?
Airy Christ, The.
Alfred the Great.
All Things Pass.
Alone in the Woods.
Ambassador, The.
Analysand.
And the Clouds Return after the Rain.
Angel Boley.
Angel Face.
Angel of Grace.
Anger's Freeing Power.
Animula, Vagula, Blandula.
Appetite.
Après la Politique, la Haine des Bourbons.
Arabella.
Archie and Tina.
Ass, The.
At School.
Aubade: "My dove, my doe."
Autumn.
Avondale.
Avondall.
Away, Melancholy.
Bag-Snatching in Dublin.
Bandol (Var).
Barlow.
Be Off!
Behind the Knight.
Bereaved Swan, The.
Bereavement.
Best Beast of the Fat-Stock Show at Earls
Court, The.
Beware the Man.
Bishops of the Church of England, The.
Black March.
Blood Flows Back, The.
Blue from Heaven, The.
Boat, The.
Bog-Face.
Bottle of Aspirins, The.
Breughel.
Brickenden, Hertfordshire.
British Song, A.
Broken Friendship, The.
Broken Heart, The.
But Murderous.
Bye Baby Bother.
Can It Be?
Castle, The.
Cat Asks Mouse Out.
Ceci est digne de gens sans dieu.
Celtic Fringe, The.

Celts, The.
Ceux Qui Luttent.
Childe Rolandine.
Children of the Cross, The.
Choosers, The.
Christmas.
Cock-a-Doo.
Cock and the Hen, The.
Coeur Simple.
Come.
Come, Death (1).
Come, Death (2).
Come On, Come Back.
Commuted Sentence, The.
Company.
Conventionalist, The.
Conviction (i).
Conviction (ii).
Conviction (iii).
Conviction (iv).
Cool and Plain.
Cool as a Cucumber.
Correspondence between Mr. Harrison in
  Newcastle and Mr. Sholto Peach Harrison
  in Hull.
Cousin, The.
Croft.
Crown of Bays, The.
Crown of Gold, The.
Darling Daughters.
Days of Yore, The.
Dear Child of God.
Dear Female Heart.
Dear Karl.
Dear Muse.
Death-Bed of a Financier.
Death Bereaves Our Common Mother Nature
  Grieves for My Dead Brother.
Death Came to Me.
Death in the Rose Garden.
Death of Mr. Mounsel.
Death of the Dog Belvoir.
Death Sentence, The.
Deathly Child, The.
Death's Ostracism.
Dedicated Dancing Bull and the Water Maid,
  The.
Deeply Morbid.
Deserter, The.
Devil-My-Wife, The.
Dido's Farewell to Aeneas.
Die Lorelei.
Dirge: "From a friend's friend I taste
  friendship."
Distractions and the Human Crowd.
Do Not!
Do Take Muriel Out.
Doctor, The.
Does No Love Last?
Donkey, The.
Dream.
Dream of Comparison, A.
Dream of Nourishment, A.
Drugs Made Pauline Vague.
Duty Was His Lodestar.
Easy.
Edmonton, Thy Cemetery..
Egocentric.
Emily Writes Such a Good Letter.
Eng.
Engine Drain, The.
English, The.
English Visitor, The.
Es War Einmal.
Eulenspiegelei.
Evangelie, or, The Figure of Literary
  Corruption, Seeking Glory Not Truth.
Every Lovely Limb's a Desolation.
Everything Is Swimming.
Exeat.
Face, The.
Fafnir and the Knights.
Failed Spirit, The.
Fairy Bell, The.
Fairy Story.
Fallen, Fallen.
Farewell: "Farewell dear friends."

Father for a Fool, A.
Feminine Charm.
Film Star, The.
Fish, Fish.
Flow, Flow, Flow.
Fool, The.
Forgive Me, Forgive Me.
Forgot!
Forlorn Sea, The.
Francesca in Winter.
Freddy.
Friend, The.
Friends of the River Trent.
Friskers, or, Gods and Men.
Frog Prince, The.
From My Notes for a Series of Lectures on
  Murder.
From the Coptic.
From the County Lunatic Asylum.
From the French (1).
From the French (2).
From the Greek.
From the Italian.
Frozen Lake, The.
Fugitive's Ride, The.
Fuite d'Enfance.
Full Well I Know.
Galloping Cat, The.
Ghost of Ware, The.
Girls!
Gnädiges Fräulein.
God and Man.
God and the Devil.
God Speaks.
God the Drinker.
God the Eater.
Goodnight.
Governess, The.
Grange, The.
Grave by a Holm-Oak.
Great Unaffected Vampires and the Moon.
Happiness.
Harold's Leap.
Hast Du Dich Verirrt?
Hat, The.
Heavenly City, The.
Heber.
Hendecasyllables.
Her-zie.
Hippy-Mo.
Homage to John Cowper Powys.
Hostage, The.
Hound of Ulster, The.
House of Mercy, A.
House of Over-Dew, The.
How Cruel Is the Story of Eve.
How Do You See?
How Far Can You Press a Poet?
How Slowly Time Lengthens.
Human Affection.
Humane Materialist at the Burning of a
  Heretic, A.
Hymn to the Seal.
I Am.
I Am a Girl Who Loves to Shoot.
I Could Let Tom Go—But What about the
  Children.
I Do Not Speak.
I Had a Dream.
I HATE THIS GIRL.
I Like to Play with Him.
I Love.
I Remember.
I Rode with My Darling.
I Was So Full.
I Wish.
If I Lie Down.
I'll Have Your Heart.
In Canaan's Happy Land.
In My Dreams.
In Protocreation.
In the Night.
In the Park.
Infant.
Infelice.
Intimation of Immortality.
Is It Happy?

Is It Wise?
It Filled My Heart with Love.
Jew Is Angry with His Friend Who Does Not
  Believe in Circumcision, A.
Jumbo.
Jungle Husband, The.
King Hamlet's Ghost.
King in Funeral Procession, A.
La Gretchen de Nos Jours (I).
La Gretchen de Nos Jours (II).
La Speakerine de Putney.
Lads of the Village, The.
Lady of the Well-Spring, The.
Lady "Rogue" Singleton.
Lament of a Slug-a-Bed's Wife.
Last Turn of the Screw, The.
Le Désert de l'Amour.
Le Majeur Ydow.
Le Revenant.
Le Singe qui swing.
Leader, The.
Light of Life, The.
Lightly Bound.
Listener, The.
Little Boy Lost.
Little Boy Sick.
Little Child of Brightest Face.
Little Daughters of America, The.
Loin de l'Être.
Longing for Death because of Feebleness.
Look!
Look, Look.
Lord Barrenstock.
Lord Mope.
Lord Say-and-Seal.
Lot's Wife.
Louise.
Love Me!
Magic Morning, The.
Magna Est Veritas.
Magnificent Words.
Major Macroo.
Man I Am, A.
Man Is a Spirit.
Man Saul, The.
Maximilian Esterhazy.
Mr. Over.
Mrs. Arbuthnot.
Mrs. Blow and her Animals.
Mrs Simpkins.
Mistress Osmosis.
Monsieur Pussy-Cat, Blackmailer.
Mother.
Mother, among the Dustbins.
Mother's Hearse, A.
Murder.
Murderer, The.
Mutchmore and Not-So.
My Cat Major.
My Cats.
My Hat.
My Heart Goes Out.
My Heart Was Full.
My Muse.
My Soul.
Nature and Free Animals.
N'est-ce pas assez de ne me point haïr?
Never Again.
New Age, The.
Night Thoughts.
Night-Time in the Cemetery.
Nipping Pussy's Feet in Fun.
No Categories!
No More People.
No Respect.
Noble and Ethereal.
Nodding.
Nor We of Her to Him.
Northumberland House.
Not Waving but Drowning.
Nourish Me on an Egg.
November.
Now Pine-Needles.
Numbers.
O Happy Dogs of England.
O Pug!
Oblivion.

Occasional Yarrow, The.
Oh Christianity, Christianity.
Oh Grateful Colours, Bright Looks!
Oh, If Only.
Oh Stubborn Race of Cadmus' Seed.
Oh What Is the Thing He Done?
Old Ghosts.
Old Sweet Dove of Wiveton, The.
On the Death of a German Philosopher.
On Walking Slowly after an Accident.
One of Many.
Orphan Reformed, The.
Our Bog is Dood.
Our Office Cat.
Out of Time.
Pad, Pad.
Papa Love Baby.
Parents.
Parklands, The.
Parrot.
Passing Cloud, The.
Past, The.
Pearl.
Persephone.
Persian, The.
Phèdre.
Photograph, The.
Piggy to Joey.
Pleasures of Friendship, The.
Poet!
Poet Hin, The.
Poets Are Silent, The.
Poor Soul, Poor Girl!
Portrait (I).
Portrait (II).
Pretty.
Private Means Is Dead.
Progression.
Proud Death with Swelling Port.
Quand on n'a pas ce que l'on aime, il faut
    aimer ce que l'on a—.
Queen and the Young Princess, The.
Reason, The.
Recluse, The.
Recognition Not Enough.
Rehearsal, The.
Religious Man, A.
Rencontres Funestes.
Repentance of Lady T, The.
Reversionary.
Ride, The.
River Deben, The.
River God, The.
River Humber, The.
Road Up.
Roman Road, The.
Rothebât.
Sad Heart, The.
Sad Mother, The.
Saffron.
Saint Anthony and the Rose of Life.
Sallow Bird, The.
Satin-Clad.
Scorpion.
Sea-Widow, The.
Seymour and Chantelle or Un Peu de Vice.
She Said..
Shooting Incident, The.
Si Peu Séduisante.
Siesta.
Silence and Tears.
Singing Cat, The.
Sliding Mountain, The.
Small Lady, The.
Smile, The.
So Can Anger.
So to Fatness Come.
Soldier Dear to Us, A.
Some Are Born.
Songe d'Athalie.
Songster, The.
Sorrowful Girl, The.
Souvenir de Monsieur Poop.
Spanish School.
Starling, The.
Story I Have Told, The.
Stroke, The.

Study to Deserve Death.
Suburb.
Suburban Classes, The.
Suicide's Epitaph.
Sunt Leones.
Tableau de l'Inconstance des Mauvais Anges.
Tender Only to One.
Tenuous and Precarious.
Thank You.
This Englishwoman.
This Is Disgraceful and Abominable.
Thought Is Superior.
Thoughts about the Christian Doctrine of
    Eternal Hell.
Thoughts about the Person from Porlock.
To a Dead Vole.
To a Lady in a Train.
To an American Publisher.
To Carry the Child.
To Dean Inge Lecturing on Origen.
To School!
To the Dog Belvoir.
To the Tune of the Coventry Carol.
Toll of the Roads, The.
Torquemada.
Touch and Go.
True Tyrant or the Spirit of Duty Rebuked,
    The.
Under Wrong Trees.. or Freeing the Colonial
    Peoples.
Unpopular, Lonely and Loving.
Unser Vater.
Up and Down.
Upon a Grave.
V.
Valuable.
Venus When Young Choosing Death.
Villains.
Violent Hand, The.
Virtuoso, The.
Voice from the Tomb (1).
Voice from the Tomb (2).
Voice from the Tomb (3).
Voice from the Tomb (4).
Voice from the Tomb (5).
Voices about the Princess Anemone.
Voices against England in the Night.
Votaries of Both Sexes Cry First to Venus.
Wanderer, The.
Warden, The.
Was He Married?
Was It Not Curious?
Watchful.
Weak Monk, The.
Wedding Photograph, The.
What Is She Writing? Perhaps It Will Be
    Good.
What Is the Time? or St. Hugh of Lincoln.
When the Sparrow Flies.
When the Wind.
When Walking.
Where Are You Going?
White Thought, The.
Who Is This Who Howls and Mutters?
Who Killed Lawless Lean?
Who Shot Eugenie?
Why Are the Clergy..?
Why Do I.
Why Do You Rage?
Widowhood or The Home-Coming of Lady
    Ross.
Wild Dog, The.
Will Ever?
Will Man Ever Face Fact and Not Feel Flat?
Word, The.
Wretched Woman.
Yes, I Know.
Zoo, The.
Translations, Coauthored Poems, etc.:
Carmina *sels.*
Dear Little Sirmio.
Written at the Close of Spring.

Snodgrass, William DeWitt ("S. S. Gardons")
(b. 1926)
Adolf Hitler ("Better stuffed in a bag;
    drowned").

Adolf Hitler ("More than fifty millions.
    More").
After Experience Taught Me..
April Inventory.
Assuming Fine Feathers, W. D. Takes Flight.
At the Park Dance.
Auction.
Boy Made of Meat, The; A Poem for
    Children.
Call for Clues.
Campus on the Hill, The.
Cardinal, A.
Charges Against Cock Robin, The.
Cherry Saplings.
Child of My Winter Born.
Coming Down from the Acropolis.
Coroner's Inquest.
Darkling Alphabet, A.
D.D. Byrde Callyng Jennie Wrenn.
Diplomacy: The Father.
Disguised as Cock Robin, W. D. Escapes.
Disguised as Humpty-Dumpty, W. D.
    Practices Tumbling.
Disposal.
Dr. Joseph Goebbels, Minister for
    Propaganda.
Dostoievsky Warns W. D. about Wearing
    Raskolnikov's Hat.
Dr. Joseph Goebbels ("Say goodbye to the
    help, the ranks").
Dr. Joseph Goebbels ("Stand back, make
    way, you mindless scum").
Elm Tree, An.
Eva B Hitler, geb. Braun.
Eva Braun.
Examination, The.
First Leaf, The.
Flash Flood.
Flat One, A.
Fourth of July.
Friend, A.
Führer Bunker, The *sels.*
Führer Bunker, The.
Heart's Needle.
HEINRICH•HIMMLER,
    FORMER•REICHSFUEHRER•SS—
    1•MAY•1945•.
HEINRICH•HIMMLER,
    FORMER•REICHSFUEHRER•SS—
    29•APRIL•1945•.
HEINRICH•HIMMLER,
    •REICHSFUEHRER•SS—8•APRIL•1945•.
Hermann Göring, Former Reichsmarschall.
Home Town.
House the Poet Built, The.
Inquest.
Last Time, The.
Leaving the Motel.
Lobsters in the Window.
Locked House, A.
Looking.
Lovers Go Fly a Kite, The.
Lullaby: The Comforting of Cock Robin.
Lying Awake.
Magda Goebbels ("How could you dare stay
    constant to").
Magda Goebbels ("This is the needle that we
    give").
Manet: "The Execution of the Emperor
    Maximilian."
Marsh, The.
Matisse: "The Red Studio."
Mementos, 1.
Monet: "Les Nymphéas."
Mother, The.
Mouse, The.
Mutability.
Old Apple Trees.
Old Jewelry.
Operation, The.
Orpheus.
Owls.
Papageno.
Partial Eclipse.
Phoebe's Nest, A.
Poet Ridiculed by Hysterical Academics, The.
Reconstructions.

Regraduating the Lute.
Reichsmarschall Hermann Göring ("And why, Herr Reichsmarschall, is Italy").
Reichsmarschall Hermann Göring ("Dear friends, the moment's come to ask").
Riddle:"So small it is, there must be at least two."
Seashell, A.
Seasoning Barn.
Seeing You Have..
September.
September in the Park.
Setting Out.
Silver Poplars.
Song: "Observe the cautious toadstools."
Song: "Sweet beast, I have gone prowling."
Survivors, The.
Ten Days Leave.
These Trees Stand.
Through the Nursery Window.
To a Child.
Valediction, A.
Van Gogh: "The Starry Night."
Viewing the Body.
Vuillard: "The Mother and Sister of the Artist."
W. D. Attempts to Save Cock Robin.
W. D. Attempts to Swallow the Symbol · · · · · · · · · · · · · · · · · · .
W. D. Creates a Device for Escaping.
W. D. Disguised as Cock Robin and Hidden Deep in Crimson.
W. D., Don't Fear That Animal.
W. D. Is Concerned About the Character Assassination of Cock Robin.
W. D. Lifts Ten Times the Weight of His Own Body.
W. D. Meets Mr. Evil while Removing the Record of Bartok and Replacing It with a Recent Recording by the Everly Brothers in Order to Create a Mood Conducive to Searching for Cock Robin.
W. D. Sits in Kafka's Chair and Is Interrogated Concerning the Assumed Death of Cock Robin.
W. D. Tries to Warn Cock Robin.
What We Said.

Snyder, Gary (b. 1930)
Above Pate Valley.
Across Lamarck Col.
After Work.
Aged Tamba Temple Plum Tree Song.
Alabaster.
All through the Rains.
Amitabha's Vow.
Anasazi.
Ancient forests of China logged, The.
April.
Arktos.
Arts Council Meets in Eureka, The.
As for Poets.
At Tower Peak.
At White River Roadhouse in the Yukon.
August.
August on Sourdough, a Visit from Dick Brewer.
Autumn Morning in Shokoku-ji, An.
Axe Handles.
Bath, The.
Bed in the Sky, The.
Beneath My Hand and Eye the Distant Hills, Your Body.
Berry Feast, A.
Berry Territory.
Blue Sky, The.
Bomb Test.
Bubbs Creek Haircut.
Building.
Burning Island.
Burning the Small Dead.
But ye shall destroy their altars.
By Frazier Creek Falls.
Call of the Wild, The.
Canyon Wren, The.
Cartagena.
Changing Diapers.
Circumambulating Arunachala.

Cold Mountain is a house.
Control Burn.
Cool around the Fire, The.
Could She See the Whole Real World with Her Ghost Breast Eyes Shut under a Blouse Lid?
Crash.
Dead by the Side of the Road, The.
December.
December at Yase.
Dillingham, Alaska, the Willow Tree Bar.
Dogs, Sheep, Cows, Goats.
Dullness in February: Japan.
Each dawn is clear.
Egg, The.
Elk Trails.
Engine Room, S.S. Sappa Creek, The.
Envoy to Six Years.
Ethnobotany.
Everybody Lying on Their Stomachs, Head toward the Candle, Reading, Sleeping, Drawing.
Face in the crook of her neck.
Fear Not.
Feathered Robe, The.
February.
Felix Baran / Hugo Gerlot.
Fence Posts.
Fire in the Hole.
Firing, The.
First Shaman Song.
Flung from demonic wombs.
For a Stone Girl at Sanchi.
For All.
For Example.
For John Chappell.
For Lew Welch in a Snowfall.
For Nothing.
For the Boy Who Was Dodger Point Lookout Fifteen Years Ago.
For the Children.
For the West.
For/From Lew.
Four Poems for Robin.
Foxtail Pine.
Front Lines.
Gen.
Getting in the Wood.
Go Round.
Goofing Again.
Green limb hangs in the crotch, A.
Groves are down, The.
Hay for the Horses.
He Shot Arrows, but Not at Birds Perching.
High Quality Information.
Hop, Skip, and Jump.
How Poetry Comes to Me.
How rare to be born a human being!
I can't stand these bird-songs.
I have lived at Cold Mountain.
I settled at Cold Mountain long ago.
I Went into the Maverick Bar.
In a tangle of cliffs I chose a place.
In my first thirty years of life.
In the House of the Rising Sun.
In the mountains it's cold.
It.
It Pleases.
I've lived at Cold Mountain—how many autumns.
January.
John Muir on Mt. Ritter.
July.
June.
Kai, Today.
Kisiabaton.
Kušiwoqqóbt
Kyoto Born in Spring Song.
Kyoto: March.
L M F B R.
Late October Camping in the Sawtooths.
Late Snow & Lumber Strike of the Summer of Fifty-four, The.
Lines on a Carp.
Little Songs for Gaia.
Lodgepole / cone/seed waits for fire.
Lodgepole Pine: the wonderful reproductive.

Long Hair.
Longitude 170° West, Latitude 35° North.
Look Back.
Love.
Magpie's Song.
Maitreya the Future Buddha.
Makings.
Manichaeans, The.
Manzanita.
March.
Marin-An.
Maudgalyâyana Saw Hell.
May.
Meeting the Mountains.
Men ask the way to Cold Mountain.
Message from Outside.
Mid-August at Sourdough Mountain Lookout.
Migration of Birds.
Milton by Firelight.
Morning star is not a star, The.
Mother Earth: Her Whales.
Mother of the Buddhas, Queen of Heaven, Mother of the Sun; Marici, Goddess of the Dawn.
My home was at Cold Mountain from the start.
Myths and Texts *sels.*
Nanao Knows.
Nansen.
Night.
Night Herons.
No Matter, Never Mind.
No Shoes No Shirt No Service.
Nooksack Valley.
North Beach Alba.
North Coast, The.
Not Leaving the House.
November.
Now I'll also tell what food.
O Mother Gaia.
October.
Off the Trail.
Oil.
Old Dutch Woman, The.
Old Rotting Tree Trunk Down.
Old Woman Nature.
On Climbing the Sierra Matterhorn Again after Thirty-One Years.
On Our Way to Khajuraho.
On Vulture Peak.
Once at Cold Mountain, troubles cease.
Once Only.
"One Should Not Talk to a Skilled Hunter about What Is Forbidden by the Buddha."
One Year.
Painting the North San Juan School.
Path to Han-shan's place is laughable, The.
Persimmons, The.
Pine River.
Pine Tree Tops.
Pines, under pines.
Piute Creek.
Poem Left in Sourdough Mountain Lookout.
Point Reyes.
Prayer for the Great Family.
Public Bath, The.
Rainbow Body.
Ray Wells, a big Nisqually, and I.
Real Work, The.
Regarding Wave.
Removing the Plate of the Pump on the Hydraulic System of the Backhoe.
Revolution in the Revolution in the Revolution.
Right in the Trail.
Ripples on the Surface.
Riprap.
River in the Valley.
Roots.
Running Water Music.
Running Water Music II.
Sappa Creek, The.
Saying Farewell at the Monastery After Hearing the Old Master Lecture on "Return to the Source."
Sealion, salmon, offshore.
Seaman's Ditty.

Second Shaman Song.
September.
7.IV.64.
7:VII.
Shark Meat.
Sinecure for P. Whalen, A.
Siwashing It Out Once in Siuslaw Forest.
Six Years.
Sixth-Month Song in the Foothills.
Some critic tried to put me down.
Song of the Slip.
Song of the Tangle.
Song of the Taste.
Sours of the Hills.
Soy Sauce.
Spel Against Demons.
Spikes of new smell driven up nostrils.
Spring, The.
Spring Night in Shokoku-ji, A.
Spring water in the green creek is clear.
Stone-flake and salmon.
Straight-Creek—Great Burn.
Straits of Malacca 24 Oct 1957.
Surrounded by Wild Turkeys.
Sweat, The.
Talking Late with the Governor about the Budget.
Target Practice.
Text, The.
There's a naked bug at Cold Mountain.
Thin Ice.
This Poem Is for Bear.
This Poem Is for Birds.
This Poem Is for Deer.
This Tokyo.
Thoughts on Looking at a Samuel Palmer Etching at the Tate.
Three Deer One Coyote Running in the Snow.
Three Poems for Joanne.
Through the Smoke Hole.
Tiny Energies.
To Fire.
Tōji.
Tomorrow's Song.
Toward Climax.
Trade, The.
Travelling to the Capital.
True Night.
Truth Like the Belly of a Woman Turning, The.
Twelve Hours Out of New York After Twenty-Five Days at Sea.
Two Fawns That Didn't See the Light This Spring.
Two Immortals.
Uluru Wild Fig Song.
Under the Skin of It.
Vapor Trails.
Volcano in Kyushu, A.
Walk, A.
Wash me on home, mama.
Water.
Wave.
Way West, Underground, The.
We Make Our Vows Together with All Beings.
What Happened Here Before.
What Have I Learned.
What You Should Know to Be a Poet.
When men see Han-Shan.
Why Log Truck Drivers Rise Earlier than Students of Zen.
Wild Edge, The.
Without.
Word Basket Woman.
Work to Do Toward Town.
Working on the '58 Willys Pickup.
Yase: September.
Years, The.
Translations, Coauthored Poems, etc.:
Clambering up the Cold Mountain path.
Sorrentino, Gilbert (b. 1929)
Abstraction, The.
Across the water sits a shore.
Address to the National Council on the Arts.
Ambassador, The.

Anatomy.
Annie from Miami.
Ars Longa.
As with a Simple Gesture of the Fingers.
At twenty love disintegrates.
Ave atque Vale.
Bar Games.
Bare Tree, The.
Barely Aware of the Insistent Loud Roars.
Beautiful Soup.
Big Brown Eyes.
Billy McCoy.
Blackburn's Dream.
Blue Turning Grey.
Boilermakers.
Bright Nightgown.
Broadway! Broadway!
But the light is imagined.
Calling Dr. Dunninger.
Canta Naranja.
Canzone: "On the tropical coast of Java."
Captain Marvell.
Cards.
Cautious Circumspection Does Not Win the West.
Celebration of Sorts, A.
Charles and Arthur.
Charm, The.
Chez Macadam.
Classic Case, A.
Closet, The.
Coast of Texas.
Come all ye Sons of Art.
Come from the whirling zodiac.
Crisis, The.
Crool Time.
Crown, The.
Cruel Experiments Continue!
Cynical.
De Pré Est Vénéneux Mais Joli en Automne.
Deluxe Assorted.
Detail, A.
Deux Morceaux en Forme de Banane.
Diaghilev Did Not Say "Étonnez-Moi."
Disappearance of Oilcloth, The.
Dominoes.
Door that opens on, A.
Drifting South.
Edges, The.
Elegiacs of Sulpicia.
Evening News, The.
Everybody would soon change.
Everything Is a Still-Life.
Evils of the City.
Faces of Doom and Sterility.
Fiction, The.
Fights, The.
Fixture, A.
Fragments of an Old Song 1.
Fragments of an Old Song 2.
From the Journal of Immutable Truths.
George C. Tilyou Smiles.
Gimlet.
Girl at Sixteen with Lightning.
Give Them Blood.
Good Night!
Handbook of Versification.
He walks on the street, in.
Hit Album, A.
Homage to Arnaut.
How I loved that melody.
Huge Man in Tight Pants.
Iceman, Again, The.
Impromptu Solo on a Balcony.
In a fantastic light.
In Memoriam P.B.
In the blue, singa.
In Which There is Nothing Up the Sleeve.
Insane Waiters, The.
Interesting Glass, The.
It is one man alone, what.
Jaime Valerosa y Borracho Consults His Journal.
Je Connai Gens de Toutes Sortes.
King of the dark tower is a lug, The.
L the simple shape.
Land of Cotton.

Language Barrier, The.
Le Bateau d'Amour Descried on the Briny.
Lecture on Time and Space, The.
Lemonade Panel, The.
Let's Call This.
Long Gone Blues.
Long Goodbye, The.
Lost in the Stars.
Man and Wife.
Man in Old Blue Suit at the Plaza.
Man in the Moon, The.
Marjorie.
Marvellous.
Mathematics, The.
Maytime.
Meeting, The.
Memory, The.
Midnight Special.
Miss and Hit.
Mr. America last seen crossing the road.
Morning Roundup, The.
Mosquitoes in New Jersey.
Mother, this is a ball of color.
Mysteries Sacred and Profane.
New York Times: A Poem for the Ross Feld, The.
Nightpiece.
1939 World's Fair.
Nothing grimmer than dawn at noon.
Now the night is here. Blood.
Old Tale.
Oleo Strut.
Open Boat, The.
Open Your Mouth and Say.
Oranges Returned, The.
Où Sont Ils, Où, Vierge Souvrain?
Out of Their Butchered Hearts.
Pail.
Particular density: in the center, rises, A.
Pastorale: "Rushing darkness of the summer evening, The."
Pentagram.
People in Hell are clothed.
Perceive.
Poem: "Clear objects / one grows to love. The clarity, The."
Poem for My Wife, A.
Poem: "Living friends live / in the past so they bore us."
Poem to Read in August, A.
Poet Tires of Those Who Disparage His City, The.
Prince Rupert's Drop.
Razzmatazz.
Red sun is going down somewhere, A.
Remember the story of Columbus and the orange?
Research, Again.
Rose Room.
Sappho in Paris.
See America First.
Senorita's Bouquet, A.
September in Kittery.
Shapes of Winter.
She was all in Black. A statement.
She whom no one ever found.
Silences.
Silk Ascot for the Terrorist, A.
Simplicity.
Sinking, Swimming.
16 Lines.
Solitary Man Discovered in a Field of Daisies.
Some hawk-nosed man.
Some Sap Sings a Poor Pantoum.
Something plus something else is not one thing.
Sonnet with X's.
Spouse, The.
Stinking city full of stinking, A.
Strambotto.
Stupid painter paints. He, The.
There is no instance that was not love.
They Die Over and Over. In the Movies.
3 Quatrains.
Tilt.
Totem, The.

Toward the End of Winter.
Transcript, The.
Trouble in Paradise.
Twelve Études for Voice and Kazoo.
Ultima Despedida del Principe Poniatowski
  de Su Familia.
Vapid Transit.
Variations 2.
Variations 3.
Verlaine's Innocents.
Veterans of Foreign Wars.
Vision of the City from a Window.
Waltz of the Empty Roadhouse.
What intense colloquy with the self.
What is past is here, as we.
What is to be understood.
Where are the rose-colored cities.
White Lemons.
Who Goes There?
Whole World Coal, The.
Woman Irritable because of Her Menses.
You Are My Heart's Bouquet.
Zoo, The.
Zukofsky.

Southwell, Robert (1561?–1595)
Ad sanctam catherinam, virginem et
  martyrem.
Assumption of Our Lady, The.
At Home in Heaven.
Author to the Reader, The ("Deare eye, that
  daynest to let fall a looke").
Author to the Reader, The ("Deare eye that
  doost peruse my Muses stile").
Burning Babe, The.
Child[e] My Choice [or Choyse], A.
Christe's Retorne out of Egipt.
Christe's Sleeping Frendes.
Christ's Bloody Sweate.
Christ[e]'s Childhood[e].
Circumcision, The.
Conception of our Ladie, The.
Content and Ri[t]ch[e].
David's Peccavi.
Death of our Ladie, The.
Decease, Release.
Dyer's Phancy Turned to a Sinner's
  Complainte.
Elegia VIII.
Elegia IX.
Epiphanye, The.
Fear.
Filii prodigi porcos pascentis ad patrem
  epistola.
Flight into Egipt, The.
Fortune's Falsehoode.
Fragment of a Series of Elegies.
From Fortune's Reach.
I Dye Alive.
I Dye Without Desert.
In festum pentecostes, anno domini 1580, 21
  maii.
In renovationem votorum, festis natalis
  domini.
Jesus. Marye.
Josephe's Amazement.
Laments for a Noble Lady.
Lewd Love Is Loss[e].
Life is But Losse.
Life's Death, Love's Life.
Look[e] Home.
Loss[e] in Delay[e].
Love's Gardyne Greife.
Love's Servile Lot[t].
Man to the Wound in Christ's Side.
Man's Civil[l] War[re].
Mary Magdalen's Blushe.
Mary Magdalen's Complaint at Christ's
  Death.
Nativity of Christ[e], The.
New Heaven, New War[re].
New Prince, New Pomp[e].
Of the Blessed Sacrament of the Altar [or
  Aulter].
Our Ladie's Nativitye.
Our Ladye's Spousalls.
Our Lady's [or Ladie's] Salutation.
Poema de assumptione b.v.m.

Presentation, The.
Prodigall Chyld's Soule Wracke, The.
Saint Peter's Afflicted Mynde.
Saint Peter's Complaint.
Saint Peter's Remorse.
Saint Thomas of Aquines Hymne Read on
  Corpus Christy Daye.
Scorne Not the Leaste.
Seek[e] Flowers of Heaven.
Sleep.
Stanzas from Saint Peter's Complaint.
Synne's Heavy Loade.
Times [or Tymes] Go[e] By Turn[e]s.
To the Christian Reader of "Short Rules of
  Good Life."
Upon the Image of Death.
Vale of Tear[e]s, A.
Virgin Mary to Christ on the Crosse, The.
Visitation, The.
What Joy to Live.

Spender, Stephen (1909–95)
Absence.
Acts Passed Beyond.
Adam.
Air Raid across the Bay at Plymouth.
Airman.
Art Student.
Auden at Milwaukee.
Auden's Funeral.
Awaking.
Barn, The.
Beethoven's Death Mask.
Boy, Cat, Canary.
Chalk Blue.
Conscript, The.
Cornet Cornelius Rilke.
Coward, The.
Cyril Connolly.
Double Shame, The.
Dream, The.
Driving through Snow.
Drowned under Grass.
Dusk.
Elegy for Margaret.
Elementary School Classroom in a Slum, An.
Empty House.
Epilogue to a Human Drama.
Exiles, The.
Express, The.
Footnote, A.
From My Diary.
Furies, The.
Generous Days, The.
Girl Who Has Drowned Herself Speaks, A.
Grandparents.
Hamburg, 1929.
Helmut.
Ice.
In Attica.
In 1929.
In Railway Halls.
Landscape near an Aerodrome, The.
Late Stravinsky Listening to Late Beethoven.
Little Coat, The.
Lost Days.
Louis MacNeice.
Man-Made World, A.
Marston.
Mosquito in Florence.
My Brother Luis.
My Parents.
Never Being.
Nocturne: "Their six-weeks-old daughter."
Not to You.
One.
One More New Botched Beginning.
Perhaps.
Photograph, The.
Polar Exploration.
Port Bou.
Prisoners, The.
Public Son of a Public Man, The.
Pylons, The.
Question of Identity, A.
Rejoice in the Abyss.
Remembering Cincinnatti, 1953.
Room above the Square, The.

Seascape.
Shadow of War.
Sign *Faehre nach Wilm*, The.
Sleepless.
Solipsist.
Song: "Stranger, you who hide my love."
Spiritual Explorations.
Stopwatch and an Ordnance Map, A.
Subject, Object, Sentence.
The Truly Great.
Thoughts During an Air Raid.
To Manuel Altolaguirre.
To My Daughter.
Tom's a-Cold.
Trigorin.
Two Armies.
Uncreating Chaos (Double Portrait in a
  Mirror), The.
Unemployed.
Us.
Van der Lubbe.
War God, The.
Word.
Translations, Coauthored Poems, etc.:
Antigone *sels.*
Autumn Day.
Face of the Dam: Vivian Jones.
Happy are those who have never tasted evil.
Oedipus at Colonus *sels.*
Oedipus Rex.
Oedipus the King [*or* Oedipus Rex] *sels.*
Stranger, this is shining Colonos.

Spenser, Edmund ("Colin Clout") (1552?–1599)
Address to Venus.
LXIII. "After long storms and tempests sad
  assay."
Amoretti.
Another of the Same.
Aprill.
Artegall and Radigund.
Arthur's Fight with Orgoglio and Duessa.
Astrophel.
August.
Autumn.
Balme.
Behold, O Man.
Bower of Bliss, The.
Britomart at Isis' Church.
Britomart in the House of Busirane.
By Her That Is Most Assured to Her Self.
Cave of Despair, The.
Colin Clouts Come Home Againe.
"Coming [or Comming] to kiss [or kisse] her
  lips [or lyps], (such grace I found)."
Commendatory Sonnets.
Cymochles and Phaedria.
Dame Nature.
Dance of the Graces, The.
Daphnaïda.
Despair.
Dido My Dear, Alas, Is Dead.
Ditty, A: In Praise of Eliza, Queen of the
  Shepherds.
LXV. "Doubt which ye misdeeme, fayre
  love, is vaine, The."
Dragon, The.
Elegie, or Friends Passion, for His Astrophill,
  An.
Elisa ("Ye dainty nymphs, that in this blessed
  brook").
Envy.
Epitaph upon the Right Honourable Sir
  Phillip Sidney, Knight: Lord Governor of
  Flushing, An.
Epithalamion: "Ye learned sisters, which have
  oftentimes."
Faerie Queene, The.
LXXVI. "Fair bosom! fraught with virtue's
  richest treasure."
LXXXI. "Fair [or Fayre] is my love, when
  her fair [or fayre] golden heares."
XXVII. "Fair proud, now tell me, why
  should fair be proud."
LVI. "Fair ye be sure, but cruel and unkind."
February.
Fight of the Red Cross Knight and the
  Heathen Sansjoy, The.

Fowre Hymnes.
LXX. "Fresh Spring, the herald of love's mighty king."
Garden of Adonis, The.
Garden of Proserpina, The.
LXI. "Glorious image of the Maker's beauty, The."
Guyon's Voyage to the Bower of Bliss.
Happy Isle.
I. "Happy ye leaves whenas those lily [or lilly] hands."
Hill of the Graces, The.
House of Ate, The.
House of Busyrane, The.
House of Richesse, The.
Hymne in Honour of Beautie, An.
Hymne in Honour of Love, An.
Hymne of Heavenly Beautie, An.
Hymne of Heavenly Love, An.
LXXI. "I joy to see how, in your drawen work."
XIII. "In That proud port, which her so goodly graceth."
It Fell upon a Holy [or Holly] Eve.
January Eclogue.
LXXXII. "Joy of my life, full oft for loving you."
Kinds of Trees to Plant.
Legend of Britomartis, or of Chastitie, The.
Legend of the Knight of the Red Crosse, or of Holinesse, The.
LXXXIII. "Let not one sparke of filthy lustfull fyre."
Like a huntsman.
XXXIV. "Like as a ship, that through the ocean wide."
LXXXIX. "Like as the culver on the bared bough."
XL. "Mark when she smiles with amiable cheer."
Mask of Cupid, The.
Mask of Mutability, The.
May.
LXXIX. "Men call you fair [or fayre], and you do[e] credit it."
Mermaids, The.
XIX. "Merry cuckoo, messenger of spring, The."
VIII. "More than most fair [or fayre], full of the living fire [or fyre]."
LXXIV. "Most happy letters framed by skilfull trade."
Mourning Muse of Thestylis, The.
Muiopotmos: or The Fate of the Butterflie.
Mutability.
Mutability Claims to Rule the World.
My Love Is Like to Ice.
Nature's Reply to Mutability.
Nought is on earth more sacred or divine.
November.
Nymphs and Graces Dancing, The.
Oak and the Brere, The.
October.
LIV. "Of this world's theatre in which we stay."
LXXII. "Oft when my spirit doth spread her bolder wings."
XVI. "One day as I unwarily did gaze."
Panther, knowing that his spotted hide, The.
Pastorall Aeglogue upon the Death of Sir Phillip Sidney, Knight, etc, A.
Prince Arthur.
Prosopopoia: or Mother Hubberds Tale.
Prothalamion.
Rivers Come to the Hall of Proteus for the Marriage of the Thames and the Medway, The.
Rivers of Ireland, The.
V. "Rudely thou wrongst my dear heart's desire."
Ruines of Time, The.
Scudamor in the Temple of Venus.
Sea Monsters.
Sea Nymphs, The.
Shepheardes [or Shepeards or Shepherd's] Calender, The.
Since I Have Lacked the Comfort.

LV. "So oft as I her beauty do behold."
III. "Soverayne beauty which I doo admire, The."
Summer.
XXVI. "Sweet is the rose, but grows upon a brere."
Teares of the Muses, The.
Temple of Venus, The.
XXII. "This holy season, fit to fast and pray."
To the Right Worshipfull, My Singular Good Frend, Master Gabriell Harvey, Doctor of the Lawes.
XLVII. "Trust not the treason of those smiling looks."
X. "Unrighteous Lord of love, what law is this."
Virgils Gnat.
Vision of the Graces, The.
Visions of the World's Vanity [or Vanitie].
LXXVII. "Was it a dream, or did I see it plain?"
LXII. "Weary year his race now having run, The."
XXXVII. "What guile [or guyle] is this, that those her golden tresses."
What If Some Little Paine the Passage Have.
XLIV. "When those renowned noble peers of Greece."
Who Is the Same, Which at My Window Peepes?
Winter.
XV. "Ye tradeful merchants that, with weary toil."

Translations, Coauthored Poems, etc.:
Ruines of Rome.
Visions of Bellay, The.
Visions of Petrarch, The.

Stafford, William (1914–93)
Adults Only.
Allegiances.
Any Time.
Archival Print, An.
Ask Me.
At Our House.
At the Bomb Testing Site.
At the Un-National Monument along the Canadian Border.
Aunt Mabel.
Bi-Focal.
By a River in the Osage Country.
Catechism, A.
Ceremony.
Clash.
Concealment: Ishi, the Last Wild Indian, The.
Consolations.
Dedication, A: "We stood by the library. It was an August night."
Earth Dweller.
Fall Journey.
Family Turn, A.
Farm on the Great Plains, The.
Father's Voice.
Fifteen.
First Grade.
For a Lost Child.
For My Young Friends Who Are Afraid.
Found in a Storm.
From the Move to California.
How It Is.
How These Words Happened.
How to Regain Your Soul.
If I Could Be Like Wallace Stevens.
In Camp.
In Fur.
In the Deep Channel.
In the Night Desert.
In the Oregon Country.
In the White Sky.
Indian Caves in the Dry Country.
Light by the Barn, The.
Listening.
Living on the Plains.
Long Distance.
Looking across the River.
Meditation.
Memorial: Son Bret, A.

Mr. or Mrs. Nobody.
Mother's Day.
My Father: October 1942.
My Hands.
My Mother Was a Soldier.
Near.
1940.
Objector.
One Home.
108 East 19th.
Oregon Message, An.
Our Kind.
Parentage.
Passing Remark.
Peace Walk.
People of the South Wind.
Prairie Town.
Purifying the Language of the Tribe.
Remembering.
Remembering Brother Bob.
Report to Crazy Horse.
Rescued Year, The.
Research Team in the Mountains, The.
Returned to Say.
Ritual to Read to Each Other, A.
Run before Dawn.
Saint Matthew and All.
Salvaged Parts.
Sayings from the Northern Ice.
Serving with Gideon.
Sioux Haiku.
So Long.
Some Shadows.
Song in the Manner of Flannery O'Connor, A.
Star in the Hills, The.
Stories to Live in the World With.
Story That Could Be True, A.
Thanksgiving for My Father, A.
Things I Learned Last Week.
Thinking for Berky.
Time Capsule.
Traveling through the Dark.
Troubleshooting.
Turn Over Your Hand.
Ultimate Problems.
Vacation Trip.
Vocation.
Waiting in Line.
Watching the Jet Planes Dive.
Weather Report.
Well Rising, The.
Wind World.
With Kit, Age Seven, at the Beach.

Starkey, Richard *see* Beatles, The
"Starr, Ringo" *see* Beatles, The
Stein, Gertrude (1874–1946)
Birthday Book, A.
Brim Beauvais.
Comedy like That, A.
Dates.
Emp Lace.
Go in Green.
Hotel François Ier.
Lifting Belly.
Little Novel, A.
Mark Twain Centenary.
Marry Nettie.
Men.
More Grammar for a Sentence.
New.
One or Two. I've Finished.
Painted Lace.
Patriarchal Poetry.
Practice of Oratory.
Prudence Caution and Foresight: A Story of Avignon.
Sonatina Followed by Another, A.
Stanzas in Meditation.
Study Nature.
Subject-Cases: The Background of a Detective Story.
Tillie.
What Does She See When She Shuts Her Eyes.
With a Wife.
Yet Dish.

Stevens, Wallace (1879–1955)

Academic Discourse at Havana.
Add This to Rhetoric.
Adult Epigram.
American Sublime, The.
Analysis of a Theme.
Anatomy of Monotony.
Anecdote of Canna.
Anecdote of Men by the Thousand.
Anecdote of the Jar.
Anecdote of the Prince of Peacocks.
Angel Surrounded by Paysans.
Anglais Mort à Florence.
Another Weeping Woman.
Anything Is Beautiful If You Say It Is.
Apostrophe to Vincentine, The.
Arcades of Philadelphia the Past.
Arrival at the Waldorf.
Asides on the Oboe.
Attempt to Discover Life.
Auroras of Autumn, The.
Autumn Refrain.
Bagatelles the Madrigals, The.
Banal Sojourn.
Bantams in Pine-Woods.
Bed of Old John Zeller, The.
Beginning, The.
Bird with the Coppery, Keen Claws, The.
Blue Buildings in the Summer Air, The.
Botanist on Alp (No. 1).
Botanist on Alp (No. 2).
Bouquet, The.
Bouquet of Belle Scavoir.
Bouquet of Roses in Sunlight.
Brave Man, The.
Burghers of Petty Death.
Candle a Saint, The.
Celle Qui Fût Héaulmiette.
Certain Phenomena of Sound.
Chaos in Motion and Not in Motion.
Chocorua to Its Neighbor.
Colloquy with a Polish Aunt.
Comedian as the Letter C, The.
Common Life, The.
Completely New Set of Objects, A.
Connoisseur of Chaos.
Continual Conversation with a Silent Man.
Contrary Theses (I).
Contrary Theses (II).
Cortege for Rosenbloom.
Country Words.
Countryman, The.
Creations of Sound, The.
Credences of Summer.
Crude Foyer.
Cuban Doctor, The.
Cuisine Bourgeoise.
Curtains in the House of the Metaphysician, The.
Cy Est Pourtraicte, Madame Ste Ursule, et Les Unze Mille Vierges.
Dance of the Macabre Mice.
Death of a Soldier, The.
Debris of Life and Mind.
Delightful Evening.
Depression before Spring.
Description without Place.
Dezembrum.
Dish of Peaches in Russia, A.
Disillusionment of Ten O'Clock.
Doctor of Geneva, The.
Domination of Black ("At night, by the fire").
Dove in the Belly, The.
Dry Loaf.
Dutch Graves in Bucks County.
Dwarf, The.
Earthy Anecdote.
Emperor of Ice-Cream, The.
Esthétique du Mal.
Evening without Angels.
Examination of the Hero in a Time of War.
Explanation.
Extracts from Addresses to the Academy of Fine Ideas.
Extraordinary References.
Fabliau of Florida.

Fading of the Sun, A.
Farewell to Florida.
Final Soliloquy of the Interior Paramour.
Fish-Scale Sunrise, A.
Floral Decorations for Bananas.
Flyer's Fall.
Forces, the Will & the Weather.
Frogs Eat Butterflies. Snakes Eat Frogs. Hogs Eat Snakes. Men Eat Hogs.
From the Misery of Don Joost.
From the Packet of Anacharsis.
Gallant Château.
Ghosts as Cocoons.
Gigantomachia.
Girl in a Nightgown.
Glass of Water, The.
God is Good. It Is a Beautiful Night.
Golden Woman in a Silver Mirror, A.
Good Man Has No Shape, The.
Gray Stones and Gray Pigeons.
Great Statue of the General Du Puy, The.
Green Plant, The.
Gubbinal.
Hand as a Being, The.
Hermitage at the Center, The.
Hibiscus on the Sleeping Shores.
High-Toned Old Christian Woman, A.
Holiday in Reality.
Homunculus et la Belle Étoile.
House Was Quiet and the World Was Calm, The.
How to Live. What to Do.
Human Arrangement.
Hymn from a Watermelon Pavilion.
Idea of Order at Key West, The.
Idiom of the Hero.
Imago.
In a Bad Time.
In the Carolinas.
In the Clear Season of Grapes.
In the Element of Antagonisms.
Indian River.
Infanta Marina.
Invective against Swans.
Irish Cliffs of Moher, The.
It Must Be Abstract.
It Must Change.
It Must Give Pleasure.
Jack-Rabbit, The.
Jasmine's Beautiful Thoughts Underneath the Willow.
Jouga.
Jumbo.
Lack of Repose, The.
Landscape with Boat.
Large Red Man Reading.
Last Looks at the Lilacs.
Late Hymn from the Myrrh-Mountain.
Latest Freed Man, The.
Le Monocle de Mon Oncle.
Lebensweisheitspielerei.
Les Plus Belles Pages.
Less and Less Human, O Savage Spirit.
Life Is Motion.
Like Decorations in a Nigger Cemetery.
Lions in Sweden.
Load of Sugar-Cane, The.
Loneliness in Jersey City.
Long and Sluggish Lines.
Looking across the Fields and Watching the Birds Fly.
Lot of People Bathing in a Stream, A.
Lunar Paraphrase.
Madame La Fleurie.
Man and Bottle.
Man Carrying Thing.
Man on the Dump, The.
Man Whose Pharynx Was Bad, The.
Man with the Blue Guitar, The.
Martial Cadenza.
Meditation Celestial & Terrestrial.
Men Made Out of Words.
Men That Are Falling, The.
Metamorphosis.
Metaphor as Degeneration.
Metaphors of a Magnifico.
Mrs. Alfred Uruguay.

Montrachet-le-Jardin.
Motive for Metaphor, The.
Mountains Covered with Cats.
Mozart, 1935.
Mud Master.
Negation.
New England Verses.
News and the Weather, The.
No Possum, No Sop, No Taters.
Nomad Exquisite.
Not Ideas about the Thing but the Thing Itself.
Note on Moonlight.
Notes toward a Supreme Fiction.
Novel, The.
Nuances of a Theme by Williams.
Nudity at the Capital.
Nudity in the Colonies.
O Florida, Venereal Soil.
Oak Leaves Are Hands.
Of Bright & Blue Birds & the Gala Sun.
Of Hartford in a Purple Light.
Of Heaven Considered as a Tomb.
Of Modern Poetry.
Of the Surface of Things.
Old Lutheran Bells at Home, The.
Old Man Asleep, An.
On an Old Horn.
On the Adequacy of Landscape.
On the Manner of Addressing Clouds.
On the Road Home.
One of the Inhabitants of the West.
Ordinary Evening in New Haven, An.
Ordinary Women, The.
Our Stars Come from Ireland.
Owl in the Sarcophagus, The.
Page from a Tale.
Paisant Chronicle.
Palace of the Babies.
Paltry Nude Starts on a Spring Voyage, The.
Parochial Theme.
Pastor Caballero, The.
Pastoral Nun, A.
Pediment of Appearance, The.
Peter Quince at the Clavier.
Phosphor Reading by His Own Light.
Pieces.
Place of the Solitaires, The.
Plain Sense of Things, The.
Planet on the Table, The.
Pleasures of Merely Circulating, The.
Plot against the Giant, The.
Ploughing on Sunday.
Poem That Took the Place of a Mountain, The.
Poem with Rhythms.
Poem Written at Morning.
Poems of Our Climate, The.
Poesie Abrutie.
Poetry Is a Destructive Force.
Postcard from the Volcano, A.
Prejudice against the Past, The.
Prelude to Objects.
President Ordains the Bee to Be, The.
Primitive like an Orb, A.
Prologues to What Is Possible.
Public Square, The.
Puella Parvula.
Pure Good of Theory, The.
Questions Are Remarks.
Quiet Normal Life, A.
Rabbit as King of the Ghosts, A.
Re-statement of Romance.
Reader, The.
Red Fern, The.
Repetitions of a Young Captain.
Reply to Papini.
Revolutionists Stop for Orangeade, The.
River of Rivers in Connecticut, The.
Rock, The.
Sad Strains of a Gay Waltz.
Sailing after Lunch.
St. Armorer's Church from the Outside.
Saint John and the Back-Ache.
Sea Surface Full of Clouds.
Search for Sound Free from Motion.
Sense of the Sleight-of-Hand Man, The.

Six Significant Landscapes.
Sketch of the Ultimate Politician.
Snow and Stars.
Snow Man, The.
So-and-So Reclining on Her Couch.
Some Friends from Pascagoula.
Somnambulisma.
Sonatina to Hans Christian.
Song of Fixed Accord.
Stars at Tallapoosa.
Statue against a Clear Sky.
Study of Images I.
Study of Images II.
Study of Two Pears.
Sun This March, The.
Sunday Morning.
Surprises of the Superhuman, The.
Tattoo.
Tea.
Tea at the Palaz of Hoon.
Theory.
Things of August.
Thinking of a Relation between the Images
    of Metaphors.
Thirteen Ways of Looking at a Blackbird.
This Solitude of Cataracts.
Thought Revolved, A.
Thunder by the Musician.
To an Old Philosopher in Rome.
To the One of Fictive Music.
To the Roaring Wind.
Two at Norfolk.
Two Figures in Dense Violet Night.
Two Illustrations That the World Is What
    You Make of It.
Two Tales of Liadoff.
Two Things of Opposite Natures Seem to
    Depend.
Two Versions of the Same Poem.
Ultimate Poem Is Abstract, The.
United Dames of America.
Vacancy in the Park.
Valley Candle.
Variations on a Summer Day.
Virgin Carrying a Lantern, The.
Waving Adieu, Adieu, Adieu.
Weak Mind in the Mountains, A.
Weeping Burgher, The.
Well Dressed Man with a Beard, The.
What We See Is What We Think.
Whistle Aloud, Too Weedy Wren.
Wild Ducks, People and Distances.
Wind Shifts, The.
Winter Bells.
Woman in Sunshine, The.
Woman Looking at a Vase of Flowers.
Woman Sings a Song for a Soldier Come
    Home, A.
Word with José Rodríguez-Feo.
World as Meditation, The.
World without Peculiarity.
Worms at Heaven's Gate, The.
Yellow Afternoon.

Stevenson, Robert Louis (1850–94)
About the sheltered garden ground.
Ad Martialem.
Ad Nepotem.
Ad Olum.
Ad Piscatorem.
Ad Quintilianum.
Ad Se Ipsum.
After Reading "Antony and Cleopatra."
Air of Diabelli's.
All influences were in vain.
All night through, raves or broods.
All things on earth and sea.
And thorns, but did the sculptor spare.
Angler rose, he took his rod, The.
Apologetic Postscript of a Year Later.
Armies in the Fire.
As in their flight the birds of song.
As one who having wandered all night long.
At morning on the garden seat.
At the Seaside [or Sea-Side].
Auntie's Skirts.
Autumn Fires.
Away with funeral music—set.

Aye mon, it's true; I'm no' that weel.
Bed in Summer.
Before this little gift was come.
Behold, as goblins dark of mien.
Blast—1875, The.
Block City.
Bour-Tree Den, The.
Bright is the ring of words.
Camp, A.
Canoe Speaks, The.
Celestial Surgeon, The.
Christmas at Sea.
Cock's clear voice into the clearer air, The.
Come, here is adieu to the city.
Come, my beloved, hear from me.
Come, my little children, here are songs for
    you.
Counterblast—1886, The.
Counterblast Ironical, The.
Country of the Camisards, The.
Cow, The.
Cruel Mistress, The.
Daughter of Herodias, The.
Daughter, Teuila, Native Name for Adorner,
    The.
De Erotio Puella.
De Hortis Julii Martialis.
De M. Antonio.
Death.
Death, to the dead for evermore.
Dedication: "My first gift and my last, to
    you."
Dedicatory Poem.
Ditty: "Cock shall crow, The."
Duddingstone.
Dumb Soldier, The.
Early in the morning I hear on your piano.
Eh, man Henley, you're a Don!
Embro Hie Kirk.
End of Travel, An.
English Breeze, An.
Envoy: "Go, little book, and wish to all."
Epistle to Albert Dew-Smith.
Epistle to Charles Baxter.
Epitaphium Erotii.
Escape at Bedtime.
Et Tu In Arcadia Vixisti.
Evensong.
Fair Isle at Sea—thy lovely name.
Fairy Bread.
Family, The.
Far-Farers, The.
Far over seas an island is.
Farewell: "Farewell, and when forth."
Farewell to the Farm.
Fear not, dear friend, but freely live your
    days.
Feast of Famine: Marquesan Manners, The.
Fixed is the doom; and to the last of years.
Flower god, god of the spring, beautiful,
    bountiful.
Flowers, The.
For Richmond's Garden Wall.
Foreign Children.
Foreign Lands.
From a Railway Carriage.
From Wishing-Land.
Gardener, The.
Gather ye roses while ye may.
Go, little book—the ancient phrase.
God gave to me a child in part.
Good and Bad Children.
Good Boy, A.
Good old ale, mild or pale.
Good Play, A.
Had I the power that have the will.
Hail! Childish slaves of social rules.
Hail, guest, and enter freely! All you see.
Happy Thought.
Hayloft, The.
He hears with gladdened heart the thunder.
Heather Ale: A Galloway Legend.
Henry James.
Her name is as a word of old romance.
Here he comes, big with statistics.
Here Lies Erotion.

Here you rest among the valleys, maiden
    known to but a few.
Historical Associations.
Home from the daisied meadows, where you
    linger yet.
Home no more home to me, whither must I
    wander?
Hopes.
House Beautiful, The.
House of Tembinoka, The.
I am a hunchback, yellow faced.
I am like one that for long days had sate.
I am like one that has sat alone.
I do not fear to own me kin.
I dreamed of forest alleys fair.
I have a friend; I have a story.
I have trod the upward and the downward
    slope.
I know not how, but as I count.
I know not how it is with you.
I look across the ocean.
I love to be warm by the red fireside.
I, now, O friend, whom noiselessly the
    snows.
I saw red evening through the rain.
I sit up here at midnight.
I who all the winter through.
I whom Apollo sometime visited.
I will make you brooches and toys for your
    delight.
If I could arise and travel away.
If I had wings, my lady, like a dove.
If This Were Faith.
Ille Terrarum.
In autumn when the woods are red.
In Charidemum.
In Lupum.
In Maximum.
In Memoriam, E.H.
In Memoriam F. A. S.
In the green and gallant Spring.
In the highlands, in the country places.
In the States.
Indefensible impulse of my blood, The.
Infinite shining heavens, The.
It blows a snowing gale in the winter of the
    year.
It is not yours, O mother, to complain.
It is the season now to go.
It's an overcome sooth for age an' youth.
It's forth across the roaring foam, and on
    towards the west.
Katharine.
Keepsake Mill.
Know you the river near to Grez.
Lamplighter, The.
Land of Counterpane, The.
Land of Nod, The.
Land of Story-Books, The.
Last night we had a thunderstorm in style.
Last Sight, The.
Late in the nicht in bed I lay.
Late, O miller.
Let Beauty awake in the morn from beautiful
    dreams.
Let Love go, if go she will.
Light as my heart was long ago.
Light as the linnet on my way I start.
Light-Keeper, The.
Link your arm in mine, my lad.
Little Land, The.
Lo! in thine honest eyes I read.
Lo, now, my guest, if aught amiss were said.
Long time I lay in little ease.
Look of Death is both severe and mild, The.
Looking Forward.
Looking-Glass River.
Lost Occasion, The.
Loud and low in the chimney.
Love is the very heart of spring.
Love—what is love? A great and aching
    heart.
Love's Vicissitudes.
Lowden Sabbath Morn, A.
Maker to Posterity, The.
Man sails the deep a while.
Marching Song.

Mater Triumphans.
Men are Heaven's piers; they evermore.
Men marvel at the works of man.
Mile an' a Bittock, A.
Mill-House, The.
Mine eyes were swift to know thee, and my heart.
Mirror Speaks, The.
Moon is sinking—the tempestuous weather, The.
Moon, The.
Morning drum-call on my eager ear, The.
Mother and Daughter.
Music at the Villa Marina.
My Bed Is a Boat.
My body which my dungeon is.
My brain swims empty and light.
My Conscience!
My heart, when first the blackbird sings.
My house, I say. But hark to the sunny doves.
My Kingdom.
My love was warm; for that I crossed.
My Shadow.
My Ship and I.
My Treasures.
My Wife.
My wife and I, in one romantic cot.
Nay, but I fancy somehow, year by year.
Ne Sit Ancillae Tibi Amor Pudori.
Nest Eggs.
New House, The.
Night and Day.
North-West Passage.
Not roses to the rose, I trow.
Not yet, my soul, these friendly fields desert.
Now bare to the beholder's eye.
Now when the number of my years.
O dull cold northern sky.
O Henley, in my hours of ease.
O Lady fair and sweet.
O now, although the year be done.
Of Schooners, Islands, and Maroons.
Old Chimæras, old receipts, The.
Old world moans and topes, The.
On His Pitiable Transformation.
On Some Ghostly Companions at a Spa.
On the gorgeous hills of morning.
Our Lady of the Snows.
Over the land is April.
Picture-Books in Winter.
Piper, The.
Pirate Story.
Plain as the glistering planets shine.
Pleasant river gushes, The.
Poem for a Class Re-Union.
Portrait, A.
Prayer: "I ask good things that I detest."
Prelude: "By sunny market-place and street."
Rain.
Rain is over and done, The.
Relic taken, what avails the shrine?, The.
Requiem: "Under the wide and starry sky."
Rivers and winds among the twisted hills.
Rondels.
St. Martin's Summer.
Say not of me that weakly I declined.
Scotsman's Return from Abroad, The.
Sick Child, The.
Since thou hast given me this good hope, O God.
Since years ago for evermore.
Sing clearlier, Muse, or evermore be still.
Sing me a song of a lad that is gone.
Singing.
Sit doon by me, my canty freend.
Skerryvore.
Skerryvore: the Parallel.
Small is the trust when love is green.
So live, so love, so use that fragile hour.
Song at Dawn.
Song: "Light foot and tight foot."
Song of Rahéro: A Legend of Tahiti, The.
Song of the Road, A.
Sonnets.
Soon our friends perish.
Spaewife, The.

Spring Carol.
Spring Song.
Still I love to rhyme, and still more, rhyming, to wander.
Storm.
Stormy evening closes now in vain, The.
Stormy Nights.
Stout marches lead to certain ends.
Strange are the ways of men.
Summer Night.
Summer Sun.
Summer sun shone round me, The.
Sun's Travels, The.
Susquehanna and the Delaware, The.
Swallows travel to and fro.
Swing, The.
System.
Take not my hand as mine alone.
Tales of Arabia.
Tempest tossed and sore afflicted, sin defiled and care oppressed.
Their Laureate to an Academy Class Dinner Club.
There where the land of love.
This gloomy northern day.
Thou strainest through the mountain fern.
Though deep indifference should drowse.
Thought, A.
Ticonderoga: A Legend of the West Highlands.
Time to Rise.
To ———: "I knew thee strong and quiet like the hills."
To A Gardener.
To a Youth.
To Alison Cunningham.
To all that love the far and blue.
To an Island Princess.
To Andrew Lang.
To Any Reader.
To Auntie.
To Charles Baxter.
To Dr. Hake.
To Doctor John Brown.
To F.J.S.
To friends at home, the lone, the admired, the lost.
To H.C. Bunner.
To Henry James.
To H.F. Brown.
To Kalakaua.
To K. de M.
To Madame Garschine.
To Marcus.
To Master Andrew Lang.
To Mesdames Zassetsky and Garschine.
To Minnie.
To Minnie (With a Hand-Glass).
To Miss Cornish.
To Miss Rawlinson.
To Mrs. MacMarland.
To Mrs. Will H. Low.
To Mother Maryanne.
To My Father.
To My Mother.
To My Name-Child.
To My Old Familiars.
To My Wife.
To N.V. de G.S.
To Ottilie.
To Priapus.
To Princess Kaiulani.
To Rosabelle.
To S. R. Crockett.
To S.C.
To Sydney.
To the Commissioners of Northern Lights.
To the Muse.
To the Stormy Petrel.
To W.E. Henley.
To what shall I compare her.
To Will H. Low.
To Willie and Henrietta.
To you, let snow and roses.
Travel.
Travels with a Donkey *sels*.
Tropic Rain.

Tropics vanish, and meseems that I, The.
Unforgotten I, The ("In dreams, unhappy, I behold you stand").
Unforgotten II, The ("She rested by the Broken Brook").
Unseen Playmate, The.
Vagabond, The.
Vanquished Knight, The.
Verses Written in 1872.
Visit from the Sea, A.
Voluntary.
We Have Loved of Yore.
We uncommiserate pass into the night.
Well-Head, The.
What man may learn, what man may do.
When aince Aprile has fairly come.
When the sun comes after rain.
Where Go the Boats?
Who would think, herein to look.
Whole day thro', in contempt and pity, The.
Whole Duty of Children.
Wind blew shrill and smart, The.
Wind is without there and howls in the trees, The.
Wind, The.
Windy Nights.
Winter.
Winter Time [*or* Winter-Time].
Woodman, The.
Yes, I remember, and still remember wailing.
You looked so tempting in the pew.
Young Night Thought.
Youth and Love I ("Once only by the garden gate").
Youth and Love II ("To the heart of youth the world is a highwayside").
Translations, Coauthored Poems, etc.:
De Cœnatione Micae.

Stuart, Dabney (b. 1937)

Audition.
Ballad of the Scarecrow, The.
Ballad of the Three Birds.
Barker, The.
Begging on North Main.
Birds, The.
Boston: From the Embankment.
Breakwater.
Cabbage in History, The.
Cambridge: From the Cowley Fathers Monastery.
Canned Goods.
Casting.
Charles River, The.
Coming To.
Commencement.
Common Ground.
Confirmation.
Deer.
Discovering My Daughter.
Don't Look Back.
Dressing.
Elect, The.
Elegies for Walker Dabney Stuart, Jr.
Exeutive Discovers Poetry, The.
Fence.
Finding One of the Ghosts.
Fireworks.
Flatfish.
Funeral, The.
Gesture, A.
Girl at Play.
Girl of My Dreams Is Dying.
Girl of My Dreams, The.
Goshen Pass: Winter.
Gospel Singer.
Harpist's Dream, The.
Hermaphrodite, The.
Hidden Meanings.
High Wire.
His Granddaughter Arrives.
Hospital of Lies, The.
Hunter, Prey.
I Can't Live Without You.
Interlude at the Grand Hotel, An.
Keeping Clear.
Killdeer.
Last Words.

Leaf Eater, The.
Leavetaking.
Light Years.
Lines.
Long Goodbye, The.
Love Poems.
Love Song.
Love's Body.
Lyric Meditation on Sour Locker Rooms, A.
Major Work.
Midget, The.
My Children Going.
My Hostess at the Renovated Inn.
Mystic.
Narcissus Dreaming.
Next Step, The.
No Yellow Jackets on the Mountain.
Nomads.
Once More for My Lady.
Opposite Field, The.
People Asleep.
Percussion.
Prayer, A.
Presence.
Real World, The.
Rescue.
Return, The.
River, The.
Sexual Disappointments.
Sharp Words in the Men's Room.
Sleepwalker.
Snorkeling in the Caribbean.
Song for Champagne Saturday.
Soup Jar, The.
Speakers from the Vietnam War.
Spell.
Spring Song.
Sticks and Stones.
Student, The.
Sunburst.
Taking Sides.
Taking the Wheel.
Tending.
That'll Be the Day.
This Is No Dream, This Is My Life.
Ties.
Timeshare.
Turntables.
Birthday.
Umpire.
Urban Hunting Scenes.
Warehouse Chute, The.
Water's Fine, I'm Fine, The.
We Never Close.
Widow, The.
Writing Machine, The.

Suckling, Sir John (1609–42)
Against Absence.
Against Fruition ("Fie upon hearts that burn with mutual fire!").
Against Fruition ("Stay here, fond youth, and ask no more, be wise").
Aglaura.
Answer to Some Verses Made in His Praise, An.
Ballad[e] [upon a Wedding], A.
Barber, A.
Brennoralt.
Bride, The.
Candle, A.
Cantilena Politica-Jocunda Facta Post Principis Discessum In Hispaniam.
Careless Lover, The.
Deformed Mistress, The.
Desdain ("A quoy servent tant d'artifices").
Desdain ("To what end serve the promises").
Detraction Execrated.
Ei Men Een Mathein.
Epilogue: "And how, and how, in faith—a pretty plot."
Epilogue for the Court.
Epilogue: "Our play is done; and yours doth now begin."
Epilogue: "Plays are like feasts; and every act should be."
Expostulation, The.
Farewell to Love.

Fifth Act of Aglaura As Presented to the Court, The.
Goblins, The.
Guiltless Inconstant, The.
His Dream.
If when Don Cupid's dart.
Invocation, The: "Ye juster Powers of Love and Fate."
Love and Debt Alike Troublesome.
Love, Reason, Hate, did once bespeak.
Love Turned to Hatred.
Lover's Clock, The.
Love's Burning-Glass.
Love's Representation.
Love's World.
Loving and Beloved.
Lutea Allison.
Metamorphosis, The.
Miracle, The.
My dearest rival, lest [or least] our love.
Non Est Mortale Quod Opto.
On New-Year's Day 1640, to the King.
Pedlar of Small-Wares, A.
Perjury Excused.
Poem with the Answer, A.
Proffered Love Rejected.
Prologue: "'Fore love, a mighty session; and (I fear)."
Prologue: "I've thought upon't; and cannot tell which way."
Prologue of the Author's to a Masque at Witten, A.
Prologue to the Court ("Those common passions, hopes, and fears, that still").
Prologue to the Court ("'Tis strange, perchance you'll think, that she, that died").
Prologue: "Wit in a prologue poets justly may."
Sad One, The.
Session[s] of the Poets, A.
Siege, The.
Sir, / Whether these lines do find you out.
Sir John Suckling's Answer.
Sir Toby Matthews.
Soldier, A.
Song: "Crafty boy that had full oft assay'd, The."
Song: "Honest lover whosoever."
Song: "I prithee send me back my heart."
Song: "I prithee spare me, gentle boy."
Song: "If you refuse me once and think again."
Song: "No, no, fair heretic[k], it needs must be."
Song to a Lute, A.
Song: "Unjust decrees, that do at once exact."
Sonnet: "Dost see how unregarded now."
Sonnet: "Of thee (kind boy) I ask no red and white."
Supplement of an Imperfect Copy of Verses of Mr. William Shakespeare's, By the Author, A.
There never yet was woman made.
To a Lady That Forbade to Love before Company.
To B.C.
To His Much Honoured the Lord Lepington upon His Translation of Malvezzi, His "Romulus" and "Tarquin."
To His Rival.
To Mr. Davenant for Absence.
To My Friend Will. Davenant, on His Other Poems.
To My Friend Will. Davenant, upon His Poem of "Madagascar."
To My Lady E.C. at Her Going Out of England.
To the King.
Upon A.M.
Upon L.M. Weeping.
Upon My Lady Carlisle's Walking in Hampton Court Garden.
Upon My Lord Brohall's Wedding.
Upon Sir John Lawrence's Bringing Water

over the Hills [to My L. Middlesex His House at Witten].
Upon T.C. Having the Pox.
Upon the Black Spots Worn, by My Lady D.E.
Upon the First Sight of My Lady Seymour.
Upon Two Sisters.
Verses: "I confirm'd a woman can."
Translations, Coauthored Poems, etc.:
Song: "When, dearest, I but think on [or of] thee."

Sutter, Barton (b. 1949)
Beaverhouse Downriver, The.
Cedarhome.
Celebration of Rust, A.
Cold, The.
Daybreak.
Deathwatch.
Declaration of Dependence.
Driftrose.
First Hard Frost, The.
Fishing at Forty.
Geneva.
George.
Good Night, A.
Halloween on Hennepin.
Hoarfrost and Fog.
Homing.
Husbandry.
I Love Your Crazy Bones.
Icehouse.
Little Litany for Moving Day, A.
Lost in *Antarctica.*
Love Poem.
Man Selling Pencils Outside the B. Dalton Bookstore, The.
Mrs.
My Father at His Height.
Night Out.
Night Shift: the Composing Room.
Nordeast.
November Seven, Nineteen Eighty-Four.
Old Mrs. Court and Her Quilt.
Pine Creek Parish Hall.
Real Estate.
Shoe Shop.
Sky.
Small White Flower that Contains the Sun, The.
Snowman, The.
Stalking the Wild Mushroom.
Stallion, The.
Static.
Swedish Lesson.
Taconite Harbor.
Talking To Grandpa Eastman.
Third Use of the Penis, The.
Tools.
Trying to Dream Up an Answer.
Visitor, The.
Warmth.
What the Country Man Knows By Heart.
Why Birch Trees Are White.
Wife.
Witch Tree.
Work, The.

Swift, Jonathan (1667–1745)
Addenda Quaedam.
Advice to a Parson.
Advice to the Grub Street Verse-Writers.
Anglo-Latin Verses.
Another Reply by the Dean.
Answer, An.
Answer to Delany's Riddle, The.
Answer to Dr. Delany, The.
Answer to Dr. Delany's Fable of the Pheasant and the Lark, An.
Answer to "Paulus," The.
Answer to the Ballyspellin Ballad, An.
Answer to Vanessa's Rebus, The.
Apollo.
Apollo Outwitted.
Apollo to the Dean.
Apollo's Edict.
Apology to the Lady Carteret, An.
Apples.
Asparagus.

Atlas.
Author upon Himself, The.
Author's Manner of Living, The.
Aye and No.
Aye and No: A Fable.
Ballad on the Game of Traffic, A.
Ballad to the Tune of the Cutpurse [or "The Cut-Purse"], A.
Bank Thrown Down, The.
Beasts' Confession to the Priest, The.
Beau's Reply to the Five Ladies' Answer, The.
Beautiful Young Nymph Going to Bed, A.
Bec's Birthday.
Behold! a proof of Irish sense!
Billet to the Company of Players.
Blessings of a Country Life, The.
Cadenus and Vanessa.
Can you match with me.
Cantata, A.
Cassinus and Peter.
Character of Sir Robert Walpole, The.
Character, Panegyric, and Description of the Legion Club, A.
Clad All in Brown.
Clever Tom Clinch Going to Be Hanged.
Copy of Verses upon Two Celebrated Modern Poets, A.
Corinna.
Dan Jackson's Reply.
Daphne.
Dean and the Duke, The.
Dean of St. Patrick's to Thomas Sheridan, The.
Dean Smedley Gone to Seek His Fortune.
Dean Swift's Answer to the Reverend Dr. Sheridan.
Dean to Himself on St. Cecilia's Day, The.
Dean to Thomas Sheridan, The.
Dean's Answer to "Upon Stealing a Crown," The.
Dean's Reasons for Not Building at Drapier's Hill, The.
Death and Daphne.
Description of a City Shower, A.
Description of a Salamander, The.
Description of an Irish Feast, The.
Description of Mother Ludwell's Cave, A.
Description of the Morning, A.
Desire and Possession.
Dialogue between an Eminent Lawyer and Dr. Swift, Dean of St. Patrick's.
Dialogue between Captain Tom and Sir Henry Dutton Colt, A.
Dick, a Maggot.
Dick's Variety.
Dingley and Brent.
Directions for a Birthday Song.
Discovery, The.
Dr. Swift to Mr. Pope.
Dr. Swift's Answer to Dr. Sheridan.
Dog and the Thief, The.
Dorinda dreams of dress abed.
Drapier's Hill.
Dunkirk to be Let *sels.*
Elegy on Dicky and Dolly, An.
Elegy on the Much Lamented Death of Mr. Demar, the Famous Rich Usurer, An.
Elegy On the Supposed Death of Mr. Partridge, the Almanac Maker.
Elephant, The.
Epigram, An: "Friend Rundle fell with grievous bump."
Epigram, An: "In your indignation what mercy appears."
Epigram: "Lord Pam in the church (could [or cou'd] you think it) kneeled [or kneel'd] down."
Epigram on Fasting.
Epigram on Scolding, An.
Epigram on the Hermitage at Richmond.
Epigram on Wood's Brass Money, An.
Epilogue to a Play for the Benefit of the Weavers in Ireland, An.
Epistle upon an Epistle, An.
Excellent New Ballad, An.
Excellent New Song, An.

Excellent New Song on a Seditious Pamphlet, An.
Excellent New Song upon His Grace Our Good Lord Archbishop of Dublin, An.
Fable of Midas, The.
Fable of the Bitches, The.
Fable of the Widow and Her Cat, A.
Faggot, The.
Famous Prediction of Merlin, A *sels.*
First Ode of the Second Book of Horace Paraphrased and Addressed to Richard Steele, Esq., The.
First of April, The.
From Dr. Swift to Dr. Sheridan.
From The Life and Character of Dean Swift.
Furniture of a Woman's Mind, The.
George Nim-Dan-Dean, Esq. to Mr. Sheridan.
George Nim-Dan-Dean's Invitation to Mr. Thomas Sheridan.
Grand Question Debated, The.
Gulf of All Human Possessions, The.
Hardship Put upon Ladies, The.
Helter Skelter.
Herrings.
His Grace's Answer to Jonathan.
History of Vanbrug's House, The.
Holyhead. September 25, 1727.
Horace, Book I, Ode XIV.
Horace, Epistle VII, Book I: Imitated and Addressed to the Earl of Oxford.
Horace, Lib. 2, Sat. 6.
I Walk before No Man (Composed While Asleep).
In pity to the emptying town.
In Sickness.
Ireland.
Journal of a Modern Lady, The.
Judas.
Lady Acheson Weary of the Dean.
Lady's Dressing Room, The.
Left-Handed Letter to Dr. Sheridan, A.
Letter from Dean Swift to Dean Smedley, A.
Letter to the Reverend Dr. Sheridan, A.
Libel on the Reverend Dr. Delany and His Excellency John, Lord Carteret.
Life and Genuine Character of Dr Swift, The.
Lines from Cadenus to Vanessa.
Lines to Pope.
Louisa to Strephon.
Love Song in the Modern Taste, A.
Mad Mullinix and Timothy.
Mary the Cook-Maid's Letter to Dr. Sheridan.
Mr. Jason Hassard, a Woolen Draper in Dublin.
Mrs. Harris's Petition.
My Lady's Lamentation and Complaint against the Dean.
New Year's Gift for Bec, A.
Occasioned by Sir William Temple's Late Illness and Recovery.
Ode to Dr. William Sancroft.
Ode to the Athenian Society.
Ode to the Honourable Sir William Temple.
Ode to the King.
Old Lewis thus the terms of peace to burnish.
On a Printer's Being Sent to Newgate.
On a Very Old Glass.
On Burning a Dull Poem.
On Censure.
On Cutting Down the Old Thorn at Market Hill.
On Dan Jackson's Picture.
On Dr. Rundle.
On Dreams.
On His Own Deafness.
On Lord Carteret's Arms.
On Mr. Pulteney Being Put Out of the Council.
On Mrs. Biddy Floyd.
On Noisy Tom.
On Paddy's Character of "The Intelligencer."
On Poetry: a Rhapsody.
On Psyche.
On Reading Dr. Young's Satires.

On Seeing Verses Written upon Windows in Inns.
On Stella's Birthday, 1718/1719.
On Stephen Duck, the Thresher, and Favourite Poet.
On the Archbishop of Cashel and Bettesworth.
On the Burning of Whitehall in 1698.
On the Collar of Mrs. Dingley's Lap-Dog.
On the Day of Judgement.
On the Five Ladies at Sot's Hole, with the Doctor at Their Head.
On the Irish Bishops.
On the Irish Club.
On the Little House by the Churchyard of Castleknock.
On the Words "Brother Protestants and Fellow Christians."
On Wisdom's Defeat in a Learned Debate.
On Wood the Ironmonger.
Onions.
Oranges.
Oysters.
Panegyric on the Dean, A.
Panegyric on the Reverend Dean Swift, A.
Paper book is sent by Boyle, A.
Parson's Case, The.
Part of a Summer, The.
Part of the Ninth Ode of the Fourth Book of Horace.
Pastoral Dialogue, A.
Pastoral Dialogue between Richmond Lodge and Marble Hill, A.
Peace and Dunkirk.
Pethox the Great.
Phyllis [or Phillis or Progress of Love, The].
Place of the Damned [or Damn'd], The.
Plagues of a Country Life.
Poetical Epistle to Dr. Sheridan, A.
Portrait from the Life, A.
Power of Time, The.
Probatur Aliter.
Problem, The.
Progress of Beauty, The.
Progress of Marriage, The.
Progress of Poetry, The.
Prometheus.
Quibbling Elegy on the Worshipful Judge Boat, A.
Quiet Life and a Good Name, A.
Receipt to Restore Stella's Youth, A.
Revolution at Market Hill, The.
Riddles.
Riddling Letter, A ("Sir, / Pray discruciate what follows: / The dullest beast, and gentleman's liquor").
Robin and Harry.
Run upon the Bankers, The.
Satire on an Inconstant Lover, A.
Satirical Elegy on the Death of a Late Famous General, A.
Scriblerian Verses.
Serious Poem upon William Wood, A.
Seven and Ten addyd to nyne.
Sheridan, a Goose.
Sheridan's Submission.
Simile, A.
Stella at Woodpark.
Stella's Birthday (1725).
Stella's Birthday (1723).
Stella's Birthday; Written in the Year 1720–21.
Stella's Birthday ([March 13,] 1727).
Storm, The.
Story of Baucis & Philemon, The.
Strephon and Chloe.
Swift to Sheridan.
Three Epigrams.
Tim and the Fables.
To a Friend Who Had Been Much Abused in Many Inveterate Libels.
To a Lady.
To Betty the Grisette.
To Charles Ford, Esq. on His Birthday.
To Dean Swift.
To Dr. Delany, on the Libels Writ against Him.

To Dr. Helsham.
To Dr. Sheridan.
To His Grace the Archbishop of Dublin.
To Janus.
To Lord Harley, since Earl of Oxford, on His
    Marriage.
To Mr. Congreve.
To Mr. Delany.
To Mr. Gay.
To Mr. Harley's Surgeon.
To Mr. Sheridan, upon His Verse, Written in
    Circles.
To Mrs. Houghton of Bormount.
To Quilca.
To Stella.
To Stella on Her Birthday, Written AD
    1721–2.
To Stella, Visiting Me in My Sickness.
To Stella, Who Collected and Transcribed
    His Poems.
To the Earl of Oxford, Late Lord Treasurer.
To the Earl of Peterborough.
To Thomas Sheridan.
Toland's Invitation to Dismal to Dine with
    the Calves' Head Club.
Tom Mullinex and Dick.
Town Eclogue, A.
Traulus.
Twelve Articles.
Upon Four Dismal Stories in the Doctor's
    Letter.
Upon the Horrid Plot Discovered by
    Harlequin the Bishop of Rochester's
    French Dog.
Upon the South Sea Project.
Vanbrug's House.
Verses from Quilca.
Verses Left in a Window of Dublin Castle.
Verses Made for the Women Who Cry
    Apples, etc.
Verses Occasioned by the Sudden Drying Up
    of St. Patrick's Well near Trinity College,
    Dublin.
Verses on I Know Not What.
Verses on the Death of Dr. Swift, D.S.P.D.
Verses on the Revival of the Order of the
    Bath.
Verses on the Upright Judge.
Verses Said to Be Written on the Union.
Verses Spoken Extempore by Dean Swift on
    His Curate's Complaint of Hard Duty.
Verses Wrote in a Lady's Ivory Table-Book.
Virtues of Sid Hamet the Magician's Rod,
    The.
When Mrs. Welch's chimney smokes.
Whitshed's Motto on His Coach.
Windsor Prophecy, The.
Wood, an Insect.
Yahoo's Overthrow, The.
Translations, Coauthored Poems, etc.:
Bounce to Fop.
Carmina *sels.*
Description of an Irish Feast, The.
Lesbia.

Swinburne, Algernon Charles (1837–1909)
After Death.
Anactoria.
At Eleusis.
Atalanta in Calydon *sels.*
August.
Ballad of Burdens, A.
Ballad of Death, A.
Ballad of Life, A.
Before Parting.
Before the Beginning of Years.
Christmas Carol, A.
Hendecasyllabics.
Hounds of Spring, The.
In the Orchard.
Interlude, An.
Itylus.
Laus Veneris.
Leave-taking, A.
Leper, The.
Les Noyades.
Lyke-Wake Song, A.
Masque of Queen Bersabe, The.

May Janet.
Not as with Sundering of the Earth.
O That I Now.
Old Saying, An.
Phaedra.
Rondel:"Kissing her hair."
Sapphics.
Sundew, The.
Triumph of Time, The.
We Have Seen Thee, O Love.
Who Hath Given Man Speech?
Translations, Coauthored Poems, etc.:
Complaint of the Fair Armoress [*or*
    Armouress], The.
Epitaph in Form of a Ballad, The.

T

Tate, Allen (1899–1979)
Aeneas at New York.
Aeneas at Washington.
Anabasis, The.
Ancestors, The.
Art.
Battle of Murfreesboro.
Bizarre.
Bored to Choresis.
Brief Message.
Buried Lake, The.
Calidus Juventa?
Causerie.
Cold Pastoral.
Credo in Intellectum Videntem.
Cross, The.
Cul-de-Sac.
Day.
Death of Little Boys.
Debt.
Ditty: "Moon will run all consciences to
    cover, The."
Divagation.
Dusk.
Eager Youths to a Dead Girl.
Eagle, The.
Eclogue of the Liberal and the Poet.
Edges.
Elegy for Eugenesis.
Elegy: "No more the white refulgent streets."
Emblems.
Epilogue to Œnia.
Euthanasia.
Eye, The.
Fair Cuirass Shattered.
Farewell Rehearsed.
Flapper, The.
For a Dead Citizen.
Fragment of a Meditation.
Historical Epitaphs.
Hitch Your Wagon to a Star.
Homily.
Horatian Epode to the Duchess of Malfi.
Idiot.
Idyl: "In a valley late bees with whining
    gold."
In Wintertime.
Inside and Outside.
Intellectual Detachment.
Ivory Tower, The.
John Milton.
Jubilo.
Last Days of Alice.
Light.
Lityerses.
Long Fingers.
Lycambes Talks to John.
Madness.
Madrigale: "Seed in your heart, warm dust
    transmuted."
Maimed Man, The.
Mary McDonald.
Meaning of Death, The.
Meaning of Life, The.
Mediterranean, The.
Message from Abroad.
Mr. Pope.
More Sonnets at Christmas.

Mother and Son.
Non Omnis Moriar.
Nuptials.
Oath, The.
Ode to Fear.
Ode to Our Young Pro-consuls of the Air.
Ode to the Confederate Dead.
On the Father of Liberty.
On the Founder of the Industrial System in
    the United States.
On the Great Conciliator: Now Honored in
    the Old Dominion.
On the Martyr of Harpers Ferry.
Paradigm, The.
Parthenia.
Pastoral: "Enquiring fields, courtesies, The."
Pauper, A.
Perimeters.
Procession.
Progress of Œnia, The.
Quality of Mercy.
Records.
Red Stains.
Reflections in an Old House.
Resurgam.
Retroduction to American History.
Robber Bridegroom, The.
Seasons of the Soul.
Shadow and Shade.
Sinbad.
Sonnet: "Could I be sure that I shall see the
    day."
Sonnet to Beauty.
Sonnets at Christmas.
Sonnets of the Blood.
Stranger.
Subway, The.
Suicide.
Swimmers, The.
Tercets of the Triad.
These Deathy Leaves.
To a Prodigal Old Maid.
To a Romantic.
To a Romantic Novelist.
To the Lacedemonians.
To the Romantic Traditionists.
Traveller, The.
Trout Map, The.
True Believer.
Twelve, The.
Two Conceits.
Unnatural Love.
Vigil.
Vision Beatific.
William Blake.
Winter Mask.
Wolves, The.
Translations, Coauthored Poems, etc.:
Adaption of a Theme from Catullus.
Carmina *sels.*
Carrion, A.
Correspondences.
Farewell to Anactoria.
Pervigilium Veneris.
Sulpicia to Cerinthus.

Tennyson, Alfred Tennyson, 1st Baron (1809–
92)
And buds and blossoms like the rest.
As through [*or* thro'] the Land [at Eve We
    Went].
As When a Man.
Ask Me No More [the Moon May Draw the
    Sea].
At Farringford.
Audley Court.
Baby New to Earth and Sky, The.
Balin and Balan.
Break, Break, Break.
Character, A.
Charge of the Light Brigade, The.
Come Down, O Maid, [from Yonder
    Mountain Height].
Coming of Arthur, The.
"Courage!" he said, and pointed toward the
    land.
Crossing the Bar.
Daisy, The.

Dead Prophet, The.
Dedication: "These to His Memory—since he held them dear."
Dream of Fair Women, A.
Dying Swan, The.
Eagle, The.
Edwin Morris.
Enid's Song.
Enoch Arden.
Epic, The [Morte d'Arthur].
Far-Far-Away.
Farewell, A: "Flow down, cold rivulet, to the sea."
Fatima.
Flower in the Crannied Wall.
For I Dipped [or Dipt] into the Future.
Frater Ave Atque Vale.
Gareth and Lynette.
Geraint and Enid.
Golden Year, The.
Guinevere.
Hendecasyllabics.
Holy Grail, The.
How Pure at Heart and Sound in Head.
I Envy Not in Any Moods.
I Held It Truth (with Him Who Sings).
Idylls of the King.
If Sleep and Death Be Truly One.
In Love, If Love Be Love.
In Memoriam A. H. H.
In the Garden at Swainston.
In the Valley of Cauteretz.
June Bracken and Heather.
Kraken, The.
Lady of Shalott, The.
Lancelot and Elaine.
Last Tournament, The.
Lincolnshire Shores ("A still salt pool locked in with bars of sand").
Locksley Hall.
Locksley Hall Sixty Years After.
Mariana.
Mariana in the South.
Marriage of Geraint, The.
Maud [A Monodrama].
Merlin and Vivien.
Merlin's Riddling.
Morte d'Arthur.
Move Eastward, Happy Earth, and Leave.
My Day.
Northern Farmer: New Style.
November in the Isle of Wight.
Now Sleeps the Crimson Petal, Now the White.
Ode on the Death of the Duke of Wellington.
Œnone.
Oh Yet We Trust.
On a Mourner.
Palace of Art, The.
Parnassus.
Passing of Arthur, The.
Pelleas and Ettarre.
Percivale's Quest.
Prayer: "More things are wrought by prayer."
Prayer: "Pray for my soul. More things are wrought by prayer."
Prefatory Poem to My Brother's Sonnets.
Princess, The.
Prologue: "Sir Walter Vivian all a summer's day."
Roses on the Terrace, The.
St. Simeon Stylites.
Sir Galahad [or The Purple Heart].
Sir Launcelot and Queen Guinevere.
Sir Walter Vivian's House.
Sleeping House, The.
Song at the Ruin'd Inn.
Song of Love and Death, The.
Song: "Spirit haunts the last year's hours, A."
Strong Son of God (Immortal Love).
Supposed Confessions of a Second-rate Sensitive Mind.
Sweet and Low [Sweet and Low].
Tears, Idle Tears.
There Is Sweet Music Here.
Tithonus.
To —. With the Following Poem.

To Alfred Tennyson, My Grandson.
To E.L., on His Travels in Greece.
To J. S. [James Spedding].
To Mary Boyle.
To-night the Winds Begin.
To the Marquis of Dufferin and Ava.
To the Queen.
To the Rev. F. D. Maurice.
To Ulysses.
To Virgil [or Vergil].
Tristram's Song.
Two Voices, The.
Ulysses.
Vision of Sin, The.
Vivien's Song.
What Hope Is Here for Modern Rhyme.
When on My Bed the Moonlight Falls.
Will.
Translations, Coauthored Poems, etc.:
Battle of Brunanburh.

Thomas, Dylan (1914–53)
After the Funeral.
All All and All the Dry Worlds Lever.
Altarwise by Owl-Light.
Among Those Killed in the Dawn Raid Was a Man Aged a Hundred.
And Death Shall Have No Dominion.
Author's Prologue.
Ballad of the Long-legged Bait.
Because the Pleasure-Bird Whistles.
Before I Knocked.
Ceremony after a Fire Raid.
Conversation of Prayer, The.
Deaths and Entrances.
Do Not Go Gentle into That Good Night.
Do You Not Father Me.
Ears in the Turrets Hear.
Elegy: "Too proud to die; broken and blind he died."
Especially When the October Wind.
Fern Hill.
Find Meat on Bones.
Force That through the Green Fuse Drives the Flower, The.
Foster the Light.
From Love's First Fever to Her Plague.
Grief Ago, A.
Grief Thief of Time.
Hand That Signed the Paper, The.
Here in This Spring.
Hold Hard, These Ancient Minutes in the Cuckoo's Month.
Holy Spring.
How Shall My Animal.
How Soon the Servant Sun.
Hunchback in the Park, The.
I Dreamed My Genesis.
I Fellowed Sleep.
I Have Longed to Move Away.
I, in My Intricate Image.
I Make This in a Warring Absence.
I See the Boys of Summer.
If I Were Tickled by the Rub of Love.
If My Head Hurt a Hair's Foot.
In Country Sleep.
In My Craft or Sullen Art.
In the Beginning.
In the White Giant's Thigh.
Incarnate Devil.
Into Her Lying Down Head.
It Is the Sinner's Dust-Tongued Bell.
Lament: "When I was a windy boy and a bit."
Lie Still, Sleep Becalmed.
Light Breaks Where No Sun Shines.
Love in the Asylum.
My Hero Bares His Nerves.
My World Is Pyramid.
Not from This Anger.
Now.
O Make Me a Mask.
On a Wedding Anniversary.
On No Work of Words.
On the Marriage of a Virgin.
Once below a Time.
Once It Was the Colour of Saying.
Our Eunuch Dreams.

Out of the Sighs.
Over Sir John's Hill.
Poem in October.
Poem on His Birthday.
Process in the Weather of the Heart, A.
Refusal to Mourn the Death, by Fire, of a Child in London, A.
Saint About to Fall, A.
Seed-at-Zero, The.
Shall Gods Be Said to Thump The Clouds.
Should Lanterns Shine.
Spire Cranes, The.
Then Was My Neophyte.
There Was a Saviour.
This Bread I Break.
This Side of the Truth.
To-day, This Insect.
To Others than You.
Tombstone Told When She Died, The.
Twenty-four Years.
Unluckily for a Death.
Vision and Prayer.
Was There a Time.
We Lying by Seasand.
When All My Five and Country Senses See.
When I woke.
When, Like a Running Grave.
When Once the Twilight Locks No Longer.
Where Once the Waters of Your Face.
Why East Wind Chills.
Winter's Tale, A.
Translations, Coauthored Poems, etc.:
Complaint on the Miseries of Life, A.
Upon Happiness.

Thomson, James ("B. V." or "Bysshe Vanolis") (1834–82)
Translations, Coauthored Poems, etc.:
Address to the Shade of Thomson.
Alfred: A Masque sels.
Ancient and Modern Italy Compared.
Autumn.
Britain.
Britannia.
Castle of Indolence, The.
Come, Gentle God.
Contentment.
Elegy on Parting, An.
Elegy upon James Therburn, An.
Epilogue to Agamemnon.
Epilogue to Tancred and Sigismunda.
Epitaph on Miss Stanley.
Fragment of a Poem on the Works and Wonders of Almighty Power.
"From Those Eternal Regions."
Greece.
Happy Britannica.
Happy Man, The.
Hymn on Solitude.
Hymn on the Seasons, A.
Hymn to God's Power.
Incomparable Soporific Doctor, The.
Liberty.
Lines on Marlefield.
Lisy's Parting with Her Cat.
Lover's Fate, The.
Morning in the Country, The.
Nuptial song, A.
Ode on Æolus's Harp, An.
Ode on the Death of [Mr.] Thomson.
On a Country Life.
On Beauty [orBeauety].
On May.
On Mrs. Mendez' Birthday.
On the Death of his Mother.
On the Death of Mr. Aikman.
On the Hoop.
On the Report that a Wooden Bridge.
Paraphrase on the Latter Part of the Sixth Chapter of St. Matthew's, A.
Pastoral Between Thirsis and Corydon, upon the Death of Damon, A.
Pastoral Betwixt David, Thirsis, and the Angel Gabriel, upon the Birth of our Saviour, A.
Pastoral Entertainment, A.
Poem to the Memory of Mr. Congreve, A.

Poem to the Memory of the Righ Honourable
the Lord Talbot, A.
Poetical Epistle to Sir William Bennet, Bart.
of Grubbat.
Prologue to Mallet's Mustapha.
Prologue to Tancred and Sigismunda.
Prospect, The.
Psalm CIV Paraphrased.
Rome.
Rule, Britannia!
Seasons, The.
Sent to George Lyttleton, Esq., Soon After
the Death of His Wife.
Song: "When blooming spring."
Spring.
Spring Flowers.
Summer.
Sweet Tyrant Love.
"Sweet Valley, Say."
To Alfred.
To Amanda ("Come, dear Amanda, quit the
town").
To Amanda ("Unless with my Amanda
blest").
To Fortune.
To Her I Love.
To His Royal Highness the Prince of Wales.
To Mr. Thomson.
To Mr. Thomson, on his Blooming Winter.
To Myra.
To Peace.
To Seraphina.
To the God of Fond Desire.
To the Memory of Sir Isaac Newton.
To the Nightingale.
To the Reverend Patrick Murdoch.
To the Same.
Verses Addressed to Amanda.
Verses on Receiving a Flower from his
Mistress.
Verses to Amanda. In Imitation of Tibullus.
Wild Shakespeare.
Winter.
Winter Night, A.

Tomlinson, Charles (b. 1927)
Abiquiu.
Above Carrara.
Above Manhattan.
Adam.
Aesthetic.
After a Death.
After the Storm.
Against Extremity.
Against Portraits.
Albuquerque.
All Afternoon.
Anecdote.
Antecedents.
Apparition, The.
Appearance.
Aqueduct.
Arch, The.
Archer, The.
Ariadne and the Minotaur.
Arizona Desert.
Arizona Highway.
Arrival, The.
Arroyo Hondo.
Arroyo Seco.
Ars Poetica.
Art of Poetry, The.
Assassin.
At a Glance.
At Barstow.
At Dawn.
At Delft.
At Holwell Farm.
At Saint Mary's Church.
At Sant' Antimo.
At Stoke.
At the Edge.
At the Hill Fort.
At the Trade Center.
At Trotsky's House.
At Wells: Polyphony.
Atlantic, The.
Autumn.

Autumn Piece.
Awakening, The.
Barometer, The.
Barque Nornen.
Bead, The.
Beautiful Aeroplane, The.
Beech, The.
Beethoven Attends the C Minor Seminar.
Before the Dance.
Bells: a Period Piece, The.
Below Tintern.
Biography of the Author: A Cento, A.
Black Brook.
Black Nude.
Bone.
Bootblack, The.
Bridges.
Brilliant Silence.
Byzantium.
Canal.
Carscape.
Casarola.
Castle, The.
Cavern, The.
Ceci n'est pas une Pipe.
Cézanne at Aix.
Chaconne for Unaccompanied Violin.
Chances of Rhyme, The.
Charlotte Corday.
Château de Muzot.
Chestnut Avenue: at Alton House, The.
Chief Standing Water.
Churchyard Wall, The.
Civilities of Lamplight.
Class.
Cloud Change.
Clouds.
Cochiti.
Comedy.
Compact: at Volterra, The.
Composition.
Confluence.
Consolations for Double Bass.
Conspiracy, The.
Constitution Day.
Couplet.
Cradock Newton: From an Epitaph.
Crane, The.
Cronkhite Beach.
Crossing Brooklyn Ferry.
Crow.
Curtain Call.
Da Capo.
Daisies, The.
Dates: Penkhull New Road.
De Sole.
Death in the Desert, A.
Death in Venice.
Death of Elizabeth Grieve, The.
Death of the Infanta, The.
Death of Will, The.
Departure.
Descartes and the Stove.
Desert Autumn.
Dialectic.
Dialogue.
Discrepancies.
Distinctions.
Door, The.
Double Rainbow, The.
Dream, A.
Dream, The.
Drive.
During Rain.
Eden.
Eight Observations on the Nature of Eternity.
Elegy for Henry Street.
Elemental.
Embassy.
Encounter.
End, The.
Epilogue, The: "It was a dream delivered the
epilogue."
Epitaph: Enamoured by / Brevity in method.
Etruria Vale.
Event.
Face and Image.

Farewell to Van Gogh.
Faring, The.
Farmer's Wife: at Fostons Ash, The.
Fiascherino.
Fire in a Dark Landscape.
Fireflies.
Flame.
Flight, The.
Flood, The.
Flute Music.
Focus.
For Danton.
For Miriam.
Four Kantian Lyrics.
Fox Gallery, The.
Fox, The.
Foxes' Moon.
From the Motorway.
Frondes Agrestes.
Frost.
Fruit, for sculpture.
Gap, The.
Garland for Thomas Eakins, A.
Gate, The.
Geneva Restored.
Giovanni Diodati.
Given Grace, A.
Glacier, The.
Gladstone Street.
Glass Grain.
Gli Scafari.
Good Friday.
Gorge, The.
Gossamers, The.
Green Quinces.
Greeting, The.
Gull.
Hand at Callow Hill Farm, The.
Harvest Festival: at Ozleworth.
Hawks.
Hay.
Head Hewn with an Axe.
Hedgerows.
Hero Sandwiches.
Hesitation, The.
High Summer.
Hill, The.
Hill Walk.
History.
History of a Malady.
Hokusai on the Trent.
How Far.
How It Happened.
How Still the Hawk.
Hyphens.
Ice Cream at Blauenberg.
Icos.
Idrigill.
Idyll: "Door: / PER L'UNIVERSO / is what
it says, A."
Images of Perfection.
Impalpabilities, The.
In a Brooklyn Park.
In April.
In Arden.
In Connecticut.
In December.
In Defence of Metaphysics.
In Longfellow's Library.
In March.
In Memoriam Thomas Hardy.
In Michoacán.
In October.
In the Balance.
In the Estuary.
In the Fullness of Time.
In the Intensity of Final Light.
In the Studio.
In the Ward.
In Verdi Square.
In Winter Woods.
Insistence of Things, The.
Instance, The.
Instead of an Essay.
Insufficiency of Earth, An.
Into Distance.
Jam Trap, The.

Jemez.
John Maydew or The Allotment.
Journey, The.
Juliet's Garden.
La Promenade de Protée.
Lacoste.
Lacunae.
Lament for Doormen.
Landing, The.
Las Trampas U. S. A.
Last Days of the Miser.
Last Judgement.
Last of Night, The.
Le Musée Imaginaire.
Le Rendez-Vous des Paysages.
Legend.
Lesson, The.
Letter from Costa Brava.
Letters from Amherst.
Liebestod.
Lighthouse, The.
Lines.
Lines Written in the Euganean Hills.
Little Night Music, A.
Littleton Whale, The.
Logic.
Los Pobrecitos.
Macduff.
Machiavelli in Exile.
Mackinnon's Boat.
Maillol.
Maine Winter.
Maintenant.
Marat Dead.
Marine.
Marl Pits, The.
Matachines, The.
Mausoleum, The.
Meditation on John Constable, A.
Mediterranean, The.
Meeting, The.
Mélisande.
Melody.
Metamorphosis, The.
Mictlantecuhtli.
Midlands.
Milieux.
Mirror in the Roadway, The.
Misprint.
Mr. Brodsky.
Mistlines.
Moment, The.
Montage.
More Foreign Cities.
Morwenna's Cliff.
Movements.
Mushrooms.
Music's Trinity.
Nature Poem.
Near and the Far, The.
Near Ceibwr.
Near Corinium.
Near Hartland.
Near York.
Night at the Opera, A.
Night Fishers.
Night-Piece: The Near and the Far.
Night Ride.
Night-Train, The.
Night Transfigured.
Nine Variations in a Chinese Winter Setting.
Nocturnal.
Northern Spring.
Nothing: a Divagation.
Oaxaca Bus, The.
Object in a Setting.
Observation of Facts.
October.
Ode to Arnold Schoenberg.
Of Beginning Light.
Of Lady Grange.
Of the Winter Ball Game.
Old Man at Valdez.
Old Man's Beard.
On a Landscape by Li Ch'eng.
On a May Night.
On a Mexican Straw Christ.

On a Pig's Head.
On a Theme of Pasternak.
On Eleventh Street.
On Madison.
On the Hall at Stowey.
On the Mountain.
On the Principle of Blowclocks.
On the Tlacolula Bus.
On Water.
One Day of Autumn.
One World.
Oppositions.
Or Traveller's Joy.
Order of Saying, The.
Over Brooklyn Bridge.
Over Elizabeth Bridge: a Circumvention.
Oxen: Ploughing at Fiesole.
Palm of the Hand.
Paring the Apple.
Parsnips.
Perfection, The.
Picture of J. T. in a Prospect of Stone, The.
Poem for My Father.
Poem: It falls onto my page like rain.
Poem: "Muscles which move the eyeballs."
Poem: "Space / window / that looks into
    itself."
Poem: "Upended, it crouches on broken
    limbs."
Poem: "Wakening with the window over
    fields."
Ponte Veneziano.
Poolville, N.Y.
Portobello Carnival 1973.
Portrait in Stone.
Portrait of Mrs. Spaxton.
Portrait of the Artist I.
Portrait of the Artist II.
Potion, The.
Praeludium.
Prelude, A.
Process, A.
Programme Note.
Prometheus.
Promise, The.
Prose Poem.
Providence.
Quarai.
Quarry, The.
Question, The.
Race, The.
Recompense, The.
Reeds.
Reflections.
Remembering Williams.
Request, The.
Return to Hinton.
Rhenish Winter.
Rhymes.
Rich, The.
Ritornello.
Roe Deer, The.
Rose-hips.
Rower.
Rubh An' Dunain.
Ruin, The.
Rumour.
San Fruttuoso.
Santa Maria delle Nevi.
Saving the Appearances.
Scar, The.
Sconset.
Scream, The.
Sea Change.
Sea is Open to the Light, The.
Sea Poem.
Self-Portrait: David, A.
Sense of Distance, A.
Severnside.
Shaft, The.
Shell, The.
Ship's Waiters.
Shout, The.
Sight and Flight.
Skullshapes.
Sky Writing.
Small Action Poem.

Snow Fences, The.
Snow Sequence.
Snow Signs.
Something: a Direction.
Sound of Time, The.
Spring Symphony, The.
Square, The.
Steel.
Stone Speech.
Stone Walls: at Chew Magna.
Suggestions for the Improvement of a Sunset.
Swimming Chenango Lake.
Tarquinia.
Teotihuacán.
Terminal Tramps.
Their Voices Rang.
Theory of Regress.
Thief's Journal, The.
Three Wagnerian Lyrics.
Through Binoculars.
Through Closed Eyes.
Thunder in Tuscany.
Tiger Skull.
To Be Engraved on the Skull of a
    Cormorant.
To Ivor Gurney.
To See the Heron.
Tout Entouré de Mon Regard.
Tramontana at Lerici.
Translating the Birds.
Tree.
Tree, The.
Two Poems on titles proposed by Octavio
    and Marie José Paz.
Two Views of Two Ghost Towns.
Under the Bridge.
Under the Moon's Reign.
Up at La Serra.
Urlicht.
Ute Mountain.
Valle de Oaxaca.
Van Gogh.
Variant on a Scrap of Conversation.
Variation on Paz.
Venice.
View, The.
Walking to Bells.
Way In, The.
Way of a World, The.
Weathercocks, The.
Weatherman.
Weeper in Jalisco.
Well, The.
What It Was Like.
What Virginia Said.
Whip, The.
White Van, The.
Wind.
Windshield, The.
Winter.
Winter Encounters.
Winter-Piece.
Witnesses, The.
Word in Edgeways, A.
Words for the Madrigalist.
Wrestlers on the Vase, The.
Writing on Sand.
Translations, Coauthored Poems, etc.:
Landscape.
Unstill Universe.
Veneris Venefica Agrestis.

Turco, Lewis (b. 1934)
Attic Poem.
Attic, The.
Awaken, Bells Falling.
Barn, The.
Blood Deeper than Night.
Bordello.
Burning the News.
Cancer.
Cat, The.
Church, The.
College, The.
Colony, The.
Conceit.
Corral.
Courthouse, The.

Covered Bridge, The.
Daughter Moves Out, A.
Death.
Dedication, A: "If it is true that."
Depot, The.
Desert of Melancholy, The.
Door, The.
Dream, The.
Dybbuk.
Envoi: The Wind Carol.
Epistles: "I am writing you."
Failed Fathers.
Farewell to Melancholy.
Ferry, The.
Fetch.
Forest Beyond the Glass, The.
Fort, The.
Girl You Thought You Loved, The.
Grendel.
Habitation, The.
Hank Fedder.
Home Thoughts.
Homestead, The.
Homunculus.
House, The.
Hunting Moon.
Ice House, The.
Jason Potter.
Jasper Olson.
Jonathan Hawkins.
Juggernaut.
Kitchen, The.
Lafe Grat.
Leviathan.
Lorrie.
Louie the Barber.
Lovers.
Maple Works, The.
Mary Moody Emerson, R.I.P.
Meetinghouse, The.
Menu of Melancholy, The.
Mill, The.
Millpond.
Minotaur.
Moon of Melancholy, The.
My Country Wife.
Nasnas.
Observation Tower, The.
Odradek.
Old Acquaintance, An.
Old Professor and the Sphinx, The.
Ordinary Evening in Cleveland, An.
Pharmacy, The.
Photograph, The.
Pilot, The.
Pocoangelini 1 ("Pocoangelini sat").
Pocoangelini 5 ("Pocoangelini said").
Pocoangelini 7 ("Sir. Your Head. It is stuck into the sand").
Pocoangelini 8 ("First thing in the morning, The").
Pocoangelini 12 ("She is caught in her frail house").
Pocoangelini 26 ("In the empty stadium he stood").
Pocoangelini 38 ("You have many wrinkles").
Poem: "It is time to write a poem."
Recurring Dream, The.
Reflections at Forty-Nine.
Rick De Travaille.
Roc.
Ropewalk, The.
Sasquatch.
School Drawing.
Schooner, The.
Scythe, The.
Silo, The.
Simon Judson.
Stable, The.
Stockyard, The.
Stone and Shadow.
Street Meeting.
Tavern, The.
That Particular Air.
Tick.
Tobacco Shed, The.
Tollhouse, The.

Townsfolk, The.
Trading Post, The.
Trestle, The.
Vigilance.
Visitor.
Weed Garden, The.
Werewind.
Will Somers.
Winter in Muscovy.
Xoanon.
Zombie.

U

Updike, John (b. 1932)

À l'École Berlitz.
Academy.
Accumulation.
Aerie.
Agatha Christie and Beatrix Potter.
Air Show.
Airport.
All the While.
Amish, The.
Amoeba.
Angels, The.
Another Dog's Death.
Antigua.
Apologies to Harvard.
At the End of the Rainbow.
At the Piano.
Authors' Residences.
Average Egyptian Faces Death, The.
Azores.
Back Bay.
Back from Vacation.
Bath after Sailing.
Beautiful Bowel Movement, The.
Bendix.
Bicycle Chain, A.
Bindweed.
Bitter Life, A.
Blessing, The.
Blked.
Boil.
Brazil.
Burning Trash.
Business Acquaintances.
B.W.I.
Calder's Hands.
Calendar.
Caligula's Dream.
Camera.
Capacity.
Cars in Caracas, The.
Celery.
Charleston.
Chloë's Poem.
Clan, The.
Classical Optical.
Cloud Shadows.
Code, The.
Commencement, Pingree School.
Comp. Religion.
Conclusion: "Easy Humanism plagues the land, An."
Condo Moon.
Conversation.
Cosmic Gall.
Courtesy Call.
Crab Crack.
Cunts.
Dance of the Solids, The.
Daughter.
Dea ex Machina.
Décor.
Deities and Beasts.
Déjà, Indeed.
Descent of Mr. Aldez, The.
Die Neuen Heiligen.
Dilemma in the Delta.
Dog's Death.
Dream and Reality.
Dream Objects.
Due Respect.
Duet, with Muffled Brake Drums.

During Menstruation.
Dutch Cleanser.
Dying Phobiac Takes His Fears with Him, The.
Each Summer's Swallows.
Earthworm.
East Hampton—Boston by Air.
Elderly Sex.
Elm.
Enemies of a House.
Energy: A Villanelle.
English Train Compartment.
Erotic Epigrams.
Eurydice.
Even Egrets Err.
Ex-Basketball Player.
Exposé.
Exposure.
Fall.
Farewell to the Shopping District of Antibes.
Fargo.
February 22.
Fellatio.
Fever.
Fireworks.
Fleckings, The.
Flirt.
Flurry.
Fly.
Food.
Fritillary, The.
From Above.
Frost.
Furniture, The.
Generic College.
Glasses.
Golfers.
Goodbye, Göteborg.
Gradations of Black.
Granite.
Great Scarf of Birds, The.
Grief of Cafeterias, The.
Handkerchiefs of Khaibar Khan, The.
Heading for Nandi.
High-Hearts, The.
Hoeing.
Home Movies.
Hot Water.
House Growing, The.
How to Be Uncle Sam.
Humanities Course.
I Missed His Book, but I Read His Name.
Imaginable Conference, An.
In Extremis.
In Memoriam.
In Memoriam Felis Felis.
In Praise of $(C_{10}H_9O_5)x$.
In the Tub.
Indianapolis.
Insomnia the Gem of the Ocean.
Introduction: "Of nothing but me, me."
Iowa.
Island Sun.
Jolly Greene Giant, The.
July.
Kenneths.
Kiev.
Klimt and Schiele Confront the Cunt.
L.A.
Lament, for Cocoa.
Lamplight.
Landing in the Rain at La Guardia.
Late January.
Leaving Church Early.
Leningrad.
Les Saints Nouveaux.
Light Switches.
Literary Dublin.
Little Poems.
Living with a Wife.
Long Shadow.
Maples in a Spruce Forest.
March: A Birthday Poem.
Marching through a Novel.
Marriage Counsel.
Meditation on a News Item.
Melancholy of Storm Windows, The.

Melting.
Menagerie at Versailles in 1775, The.
Miami.
Midpoint.
Milady Reflects.
Millipede, The.
Mime.
Minority Report.
Miss Moore at Assembly.
Mr. High-Mind.
Mites.
Mobile of Birds.
Moderate, The.
Modest Mound of Bones, A.
Modigliani's Death Mask.
Moons of Jupiter, The.
Moscow.
Mosquito.
Mountain Impasse.
Mouse Sex.
Movie House.
Munich.
My Children at the Dump.
Naked Ape, The.
Natural Question.
Nature.
Neotony.
Newlyweds, The.
News from the Underworld.
Night Flight, over Ocean.
No More Access to Her Underpants.
Note to the Previous Tenants.
November.
Nuda Natens.
Oddly Lovely Day Alone, An.
Ode, An: "I'm going to write a novel, hey."
Ode to Entropy.
Ode to Growth.
Ode to Healing.
Ode to Rot.
Ohio.
Old-Fashioned Lightning Rod.
Omega.
On an Island.
On the Inclusion of Miniature Dinosaurs in
    Breakfast Cereal Boxes.
On the Recently Minted Hundred-Cent Piece.
On the Way to Delphi.
One-Year-Old, The.
Open Letter to Voyager II, An.
Origin of Laughter, The.
Orthodontia.
Oxford, Thirty Years After.
Pain.
Painted Wives.
Pale Bliss.
Party Knee.
Pear like a Potato, A.
Penumbrae.
Perfection Wasted.
Phenomena.
Philological.
Pillow.
Planting a Mailbox.
Planting Trees.
Play of Memory, The.
Player Piano.
Plow Cemetery.
Poem for a Far Land.
Poisoned in Nassau.
Pompeii.
Pooem.
Pop Smash, Out of Echo Chamber.
Popular Revivals 1956.
Postcards from Soviet Cities.
Publius Vergilius Maro, the Madison Avenue
    Hick.
Query.
Rack of Paperbacks, A.
Raining in Magens Bay.
Rats.
Recital.
Reel.
Relatives.
Report of Health.
Returning Native.
Revelation.

Richmond.
Rio de Janeiro.
Rockettes, The.
Roman Portrait Busts.
Room 28.
Sails on All Saints' Day.
Sand Dollar.
São Paulo.
Scenic.
Sea Knell.
Seagulls.
Seal in Nature.
Seattle Uplift.
Self-Service.
Sensualist, The.
Seven New Ways of Looking at the Moon.
Seven Odes to Seven Natural Processes.
Seven Stanzas at Easter.
Shaving Mirror.
Shillington.
Shipbored.
Short Days, The.
Shuttle, The.
Sin City, D.C.
Skyey Developments.
Sleeping with You.
Sleepless in Scarsdale.
Small-City People.
Snapshots.
Snowdrops 1987.
Solitaire.
Solitary Pond, The.
Some Frenchmen.
Sometime Sportsman Greets the Spring, The.
Somewhere.
Song of Paternal Care, A.
Song of the Open Fireplace.
Sonic Boom.
Sonnet to Man-Made Grandeur.
South of the Alps.
Spanish Sonnets.
Spring Song.
Squirrels Mating.
Story of My Life, The.
Stunt Flier, The.
Styles of Bloom.
Suburban Madrigal.
Summer: West Side.
Sunday.
Sunday in Boston.
Sunday Rain.
Sunflower.
Sunglasses.
Sunshine on Sandstone.
Superman.
Switzerland.
Tao in the Yankee Stadium Bleachers.
Taste.
Tax-Free Encounter.
Tbilisi.
Telephone Poles.
Thin Air.
Thoughts While Driving Home.
3 A.M.
Time's Fool.
To a Box Turtle.
To a Dead Flame.
To a Waterbed.
To an Usherette.
To Crystallization.
To Ed Sissman.
To Evaporation.
To Fragmentation.
Tome-Thoughts, from the *Times*.
Toothache Man.
Topsfield Fair.
Tossing and Turning.
Touch of Spring.
Trees Eat Sunshine.
Tropical Beetles.
Tsokadze O Altitudo.
Tulsa.
Tune, in American Type.
Two Hoppers.
Two Sonnets Whose Titles Came to Me
    Simultaneously.
Typical Optical.

Under the Sunlamp.
Upon Learning That a Bird Exists Called the
    Turnstone.
Upon Learning That a Town Exists in
    Virginia Called Upperville.
Upon Looking into Sylvia Plath's *Letters
    Home.*
Upon Shaving Off One's Beard.
Upon the Last Day of His Forty-Ninth Year.
V. B. Nimble, V. B. Quick.
Vermont.
Vibration.
Vision, A.
Visions of Mackenzie King, The.
Vow.
Wash.
Washington.
Washington: Tourist View.
White Dwarf.
Why the Telephone Wires Dip and the Poles
    Are Cracked and Crooked.
Widener Library, Reading Room.
Wind.
Winter Ocean.
Within a Quad.
Wooden Darning Egg, A.
Working Outdoors in Winter.
Yerevan.
You Who Swim.
Young Matrons Dancing.
Youth's Progress.
ZIP Code Ode.
Zoo Bats.
Zulus Live in Land without a Square.

V

"V., B." *see* Thomson, James
Van Duyn, Mona (b. 1921)
    Advice to a God.
    After midnight, and my sister Lizzie.
    Along the Road.
    Annual and Perennial Problem, An.
    At Père Lachaise.
    Ballad of Blossom, The.
    Bedtime Stories.
    Billings and Cooings from "The Berkeley
        Barb."
    Birthday Card for a Psychiatrist.
    Caring for Surfaces.
    Case of The, The.
    Causes.
    Challenger, The.
    Christmas Card, After the Assassinations, A.
    Cinderella's Story.
    Cities of the Plain, The.
    Colorado.
    Creation, The.
    Day in Late October, A.
    Death By Aesthetics.
    Dwarf in the Woods.
    Earth Tremors Felt in Missouri.
    Economics.
    Elementary Attitudes.
    End of May.
    Eros to Howard Nemerov.
    Essay on Criticism, An.
    Evening Stroll in the Suburbs.
    Fall.
    Fear of Flying, The.
    First Flight.
    Folks built that barn, your great grandfather,
        and them, The.
    Footnotes to "The Autobiography of Bertrand
        Russell."
    From Yellow Lake: An Interval.
    Gardener to His God, The.
    Garland for Christopher Smart, A.
    Gentle Snorer, The.
    Good Man, The.
    Good Resolution, The.
    Goodbye, A.
    Goya's "Two Old People Eating Soup."
    Gray's Apocrypha.
    Growing Up Askew.
    Hermit of Hudson Pond, The.

Homework.
In the Cold Kingdom.
In the Hospital for Tests.
In the Missouri Ozarks.
In the Old Country, then, two ladies and two boys.
Insight.
Into Mexico.
Ja, we had it hard.
Just full of springs the world was in Illinois.
Kind of Music, A.
Learners, The.
Leda.
Leda Reconsidered.
Letters from a Father.
Lives of the Poets.
Madrid, May, 1977.
Madrid, 1974.
Marriage, with Beasts.
Midas and Wife.
Miser, The.
Moose in the Morning, Northern Maine.
Nap.
New Land.
Notes from a Suburban Heart.
Oh well, they had such a big garden.
Old widow lady, and went out to do her chore, An.
Open Letter from a Constant Reader.
Open Letter, Personal.
Outlandish Agon.
Paratrooper.
Peony Stalks.
Photographs.
Pietà, Rhenish, 14th C., the Cloisters, The.
Placet Experiri.
Postcards from Cape Split.
Pot-au-feu.
Quebec Suite.
Quiet Afternoon at Home, A.
Reading of Rex Stout, A.
Recovery.
Relationships.
Relative and an Absolute, A.
Remedies, Maladies, Reasons.
Ringling Brothers, Barnum and Bailey.
Saleswomen in Bakery Shops.
Sentimental Delusion, A.
Serious Case, A.
Sestina for Warm Seasons.
Since You Asked Me.
Small Excursion, A.
Speak, Memory!
Spell of Conjunctivitis, A.
Stream, The.
Such things there are, we don't know.
Talker, The.
That was in 1875, and we come through.
That was in 1875, then we moved here.
That was my grandfather, nearly went to prison.
3 A. M. in a War Year.
Three Valentines to the Wide World.
Time of Bees, A.
To My Godson, on His Christening.
To Poets' Worksheets in the Air-Conditioned Vault of a Library.
To Record One Must Be Unwary.
Toward a Definition of Marriage.
Twins, The.
Two Poems for Sub-Zero Times.
Two Poems, with Birds.
View, A.
Vision Test, The.
Voyeur, The.
Walking the Dog: A Diatribe.
We alwus had to herd cattle.
Well, that old big fat man.
Well, that was Saturday, day before Easter.
West Branch Ponds, Kokadjo, Maine.
What I Want to Say.
What the Motorcycle Said.
Winter's Tale, by a Wife, A.
Wish to Be Believed, The.
With Warm Regards to Miss Moore and Mr. Ransom.
Woman Waiting.

"Vanolis, Bysshe" *see* Thomson, James

W

Wakoski, Diane (b. 1937)
Apology, An.
Apparitions Are Not Singular Occurrences.
Belly Dancer.
Birds of Paradise Being Very Plain Birds, The.
Blessing Ode for a Man with Fishbones Around His Neck.
Blue Monday.
Braised Leeks & Framboise.
Breakfast.
Buddha Inherits 6 Cars on His Birthday, The.
Cannon Beach.
Civilization.
Cobra Lilies in the Supermarket.
Coins and Coffins under My Bed.
Dancing on the Grave of a Son of a Bitch.
Dark Clack of Morays, The.
David.
Donna.
Dream, The.
Driving Gloves.
Duchess Potatoes, The.
Eat your Rose Hips, C'est La Vie.
Elizabeth and the Golden Oranges.
Emerald Ice.
Exorcism.
Fanny's Cold Blue Eyes.
Father of My Country, The.
Few Silver Scales, The.
Fifteen Poems for a Lunar Eclipse None of Us Saw *sels.*
Fifteen Poems for a Lunar Eclipse None of Us Saw.
Fifth Universe.
Filling the Boxes of Joseph Cornell.
First Universe.
Follow That Stagecoach.
For Michael, Armoured with Roses.
Fourth Universe.
From A Go to B, If You Can Find It.
George Washington Slept Here.
George Washington: The Whole Man.
George Washington Writes Home About Harvesting His Hemp.
George Washington's Camp Cups.
Girls, The.
Helms Bakery Man, The.
Hermit, The.
How Do You Tell a Story?
I Have Had to Learn to Live with My Face.
Ice Eagle, The.
In the Secret Room, East of the Sun, West of the Moon.
Incident of Cherries and Peaches.
Inside Out.
Joyce Carol Oates Plays the Saturn Piano.
Justice Is Reason Enough.
Lady Who Sang, The.
Life Is Like a Game of Cards, Or Another One of Those Metaphysical Statements from a Distant Reader.
Light.
Love Letter Postmarked Van Beethoven.
Love Passes Beyond the Incredible Hawk of Innocence.
Magellanic Clouds, The.
Making a Sacher Torte.
Mechanic, The.
Moon Explodes in Autumn as a Milkweed Pod, The.
My Aunt Ella Meets the Buddha on His Birthday.
My Knees Go Before the Firing Squad at Dawn.
My Trouble.
Night Rides of My Neighbor, Lorca, That Prevent Sleep, The.
Not the Blood a Dreamer Kissed from My Mouth.
Ode to a Lebanese Crock of Olives.
On Barbara's Shore.

On the Subject of Roses.
Ordinary Poem.
Overnight Projects with Woods.
Overweight Poem.
Patriotic Poem.
Photos, The.
Pink Dress, The.
Placing a $2 Bet for a Man Who Will Never Go to the Horse Races Any More.
Poem for a Little Boy on the Buddha's Birthday.
Poet at Carpenter's Bench.
Poetry, the Unpredictable.
Precisely, Not Violets.
Precision.
Preface.
Pumpkin Pie, Or Reassurances Are Always Fake Though We Love Them, Only Physics Counts.
Reaching Out with the Hands of the Sun.
Recognizing That My Wrists Always Have Salmon Leaping for Spring in Them.
Red Runner.
Reminded of One of Those Girls I Never Was.
Removed from Natural Habitat.
Rescue Poem.
Ring, The.
Ring of Irony, The.
Ringless.
Roses Were Talking, The.
Screw, a Technical Love Poem.
Searching for the Canto Fermo.
Second Universe.
Sestina from the Home Gardener.
Silver.
Skier, The.
Slicing Oranges for Jeremiah.
Smudging.
Some Brilliant Sky.
Some Constantly Besieged Castle.
Sometimes Even My Knees Smile.
Sour Milk.
Standing at the Door.
Steely Silence.
Story of Richard Maxfield, The.
Sun.
Sun with Hands for Rays.
Tango-ing.
Telling You True, About My Fantasy Life.
Thanking My Mother for Piano Lessons.
There's Plenty of Anguish at the Railroad.
Third Universe.
Those Mythical Silver Pears.
Three of Swords.
To an Autocrat.
To the Thin and Elegant Woman Who Resides Inside of Alix Nelson.
Un Morceau en Forme de Poire.
Uncle Sam in the White House.
Universes, The.
Virtuoso Literature for Two and Four Hands.
Walking Past Paul Blackburn's Apt. on 7th St.
Warning to the Man in Receiving at Sears, A.
Water.
Western Music.
What Happened.
When You Throw Amber into the Well of the Moon.
Why My Mother Likes Liberace.
Wind Secrets.
Winter Ode.
Winter Poem for Tony Weinburger Written on the Occasion of Feeling Very Happy, A.
With Words.
Write.

Walcott, Derek (b. 1930)
Adam's Song.
Air.
Another Life.
As John to Patmos.
At the Queen's Park Hotel, with its white, high-ceilinged rooms.
Banyan Tree, Old Year's Night, The.

Beachhead.
Before that thundercloud breaks from its hawsers.
Bleecker Street, Summer.
Blues.
Brise Marine.
Camps hold [*or* held] their distance— [of] brown chestnuts and grey smoke, The.
Castaway, The.
Certain things here are quietly American.
Che.
Chicago's avenues, as white as Poland.
City's Death by Fire, A.
Codicil.
Cold Spring Harbor.
Companion in Rome, whom Rome makes as old as Rome.
Coral.
Crusoe's Island.
Crusoe's Journal.
Dark August.
Early Pompeian.
Easter.
Egypt, Tobago.
Elegy: "Our hammock swung between Americas."
Endings.
Europa.
Exile.
Far Cry from Africa, A.
Fist, The.
Flock, The.
Forest of Europe.
Fortunate Traveller, The.
From This Far.
Glory Trumpeter, The.
Goats and Monkeys.
God Rest Ye Merry, Gentlemen.
Gold dung and urinous straw from the horse garages.
Grey English road hissed emptily under the tires, The.
Gulf, The.
Guyana.
Harbour, The.
Homage to Edward Thomas.
Homecoming: Anse La Raye.
Hotel Normandie Pool, The.
Hurucan.
I can sense it coming from far, too, Maman, the tide.
I heard them marching the leaf-wet roads of my head.
I once gave my daughters, separately, two conch shells.
In a Green Night.
In the other 'eighties, a hundred midsummers gone.
Islands.
Jean Rhys.
Koenig of the River.
Lampfall.
Landfall, Grenada.
Laventille.
Lesson for This Sunday, A.
Letter from Brooklyn, A.
Liberator, The.
Long, white, summer cloud, like a cleared linen table, A.
Love after Love.
Love in the Valley.
Man Who Loved Islands, The.
Map of Europe, A.
Map of the New World.
Mass Man.
Midsummer *sels.*
Midsummer sea, the hot pitch road, this grass, these shacks that made me, The.
Midsummer stretches beside me with its cat's yawn.
Midsummer, Tobago.
Missing the Sea.
Morning Moon, The.
Mud. Clods. The sucking heel of the rain-flinger.
My double, tired of morning, closes the door.
Names.

Nearing Forty.
Negatives.
New World.
Nights in the Gardens of Port of Spain.
North and South.
Oak inns creak in their joints as light declines, The.
Oddjob, a Bull Terrier.
Old New England.
Orient and Immortal Wheat.
Origins.
Our houses are one step from the gutter. Plastic curtains.
Parang.
Piano Practice.
Pocomania.
Polish Rider, The.
Prelude: "I, with legs crossed along the daylight, watch."
Preparing for Exile.
Return to D'Ennery; Rain.
Ruins of a Great House.
Sabbaths, W.I.
Saddhu of Couva, The.
Sainte Lucie.
Schooner Flight, The.
Sea Canes.
Sea-Chantey, A.
Sea Grapes.
Sea is History, The.
Season of Phantasmal Peace, The.
Since all of your work was really an effort to appease.
Something primal in our spine makes the child swing.
Spoiler's Return, The.
Star.
Star-Apple Kingdom, The.
Sun has fired my face to terra-cotta, The.
Sunday Lemons.
Swamp, The.
Tales of the Islands.
Tarpon.
There was one Syrian, with his bicycle, in our town.
Those grooves in that forehead of sand-coloured flesh.
To Return to the Trees.
Tropic Zone.
Two Poems on the Passing of an Empire.
Upstate.
Verandah.
Village Life, A.
Volcano.
Wales.
Walk, The.
Watteau.
Wind-scraped headland, a sludgy, dishwater sea, A.
Winding Up.
With the frenzy of an old snake shedding its skin.
With the stampeding hiss and scurry of green lemmings.

Waldman, Anne (b. 1945)

After "Les Fleurs."
Ancient Song Rising.
& do what I know best.
Baby & the Gypsy.
Baby Breakdown.
Baby's Pantoum.
Ballade: "My heart's felt no wounds big or small."
Battery.
Blue That Reminds Me of the Boat When She Left, The.
Cabin.
College Under Water.
Colors.
Complaynt.
Coup de Grace.
Crack in the World.
Cure, The.
De Carlo Lots, The.
Dialogue Between the Self & the Soul.
Diaries.
Distance Traveled.

Divorce Work.
8/9.
Eyes in All Heads to Be Looked out Of.
Face the Orient.
Fast Speaking Woman.
For J.A. As Dusk Deepens Canyon.
George Sand.
Giant Night.
Going In.
He catches my eye, my fancy.
Helping the Dreamer.
Hopes & Fears.
How the Sestina (Yawn) Works.
I Digress.
Incantation.
Iovis Omnia Plena *sels.*
It Sounds It.
Leonardo.
Lie, The.
Light & Shadow.
Lindsay Speaks.
Makeup on Empty Space.
Matriarchy.
Mature love you say but my wounds come out through inner temple.
Mirror Meditation.
Mother & Child.
Mother Country.
Mother's Curse.
Musical Garden.
My Kind of Man.
Napping in the Shadow of Day.
Number Song.
Out There.
Paris Day.
Paul Eluard.
Philosophia Perennis.
Phonecall from Frank O'Hara, A.
Pictures From Tofukuji.
Poeme en Forme de la Bouche.
Revolution.
Romance.
Scallop Song.
Sidney's Complaynt.
Sisters.
Slowly.
Snow.
Some of the Things I See for You.
Song: Time Drawes Neere.
Sonnet: O Husband!
Stick, The.
Sun the Blond Out.
3 Epiphanies.
Throw Matches at the Sun!
Triolet: "Perfectly clear liquid like water, A."
True Story of Being at the Pool.
Two Hearts.
White Eyes.
Translations, Coauthored Poems, etc.:
Artemis.

Walker, Alice (b. 1944)

Abduction of Saints, The.
African Images, Glimpses from a Tiger's Back.
After the Shrink.
Armah: October 12, 1990.
At First.
Attentiveness.
Awakening, The.
Ballad of the Brown Girl.
Baptism.
Be Nobody's Darling.
Beast.
Beyond What.
Black Mail.
Black Prince, The.
Burial.
Chic Freedom's Reflection.
Clutter-up People.
Compulsory Chapel.
Confession.
Dedication.
Democratic Order, The: Such Things in Twenty Years I Understood.
Diamonds on Liz's Bosom, The.
Did This Happen to Your Mother? Did Your Sister Throw Up a Lot?

Each One, Pull One.
Eagle Rock.
Early Losses: a Requiem.
Ending.
Enemy, The.
Even as I Hold You.
Every Morning.
Excuse.
Exercises on Themes from Life.
Expect Nothing.
Facing the Way.
Family Of.
Few Sirens, A.
First, They Said.
For My Sister Molly Who in the Fifties.
Forbidden Things.
Forgive Me If My Praises.
Forgiveness.
Gift.
Girl Who Died #1, The.
Girl Who Died #2, The.
Good Night, Willie Lee, I'll See You in the
　Morning.
Gray.
Having Eaten Two Pillows.
He Said:.
He Said Come.
How Poems Are Made: A Discredited View.
Hymn: "I well remember / A time when."
I Said to Poetry.
If There Was Any Justice.
If "Those People" Like You.
I'm Really Very Fond.
In Answer to Your Silly Question.
In These Dissenting Times.
In Uganda an Early King.
Instant of Our Parting, The.
J, My Good Friend (Another Foolish
　Innocent).
Janie Crawford.
January 10, 1973.
Johann.
Judge Every One with Perfect Calm.
Karamojongs.
Killers.
Kiss, The.
Last Time, The.
Light Baggage.
Listen.
Lonely Particular.
Lost My Voice? Of Course.
Love Is Not Concerned.
Malcolm.
Medicine.
Mississippi Winter I.
Mississippi Winter II.
Mississippi Winter III.
Mississippi Winter IV.
Moody.
More Love to His Life.
Mornings / of an impossible love.
My Daughter Is Coming!
My Heart Has Reopened to You.
My Husband Says.
Mysteries.
Natural Star.
Nature of This Flower Is to Bloom, The.
Ndebele.
Never Offer Your Heart to Someone Who
　Eats Hearts.
New Face.
1971.
No Fixed Place.
No One Can Watch the Wasichu.
Nothing Is Right.
Now That the Book Is Finished.
Old Warrior Terror, The.
On Being Asked to Leave a Place of Honor
　for One of Comfort, Preferably in the
　Northern Suburbs.
On Sight.
On Stripping Bark from Myself.
Once.
Once, Again.
Overnights.
Pagan.
Perfection.

Poem at Thirty-nine.
QPP, The.
Rage.
Reassurance.
Remember?
Representing the Universe.
Revolutionary Petunias.
Right to Life, The: What Can the White Man
　Say to the Black Woman?
S M.
She Said:.
Smell of Lebanon, The.
So We've Come at Last to Freud.
Some Things I Like about My Triple Bloods.
Song: "World is full of colored / people,
　The."
Songless.
South: The Name of Home.
Storm.
Streaking (A Phenomenon Following the
　Sixties).
Talking to My Grandmother Who Died Poor.
Telling.
There are no tigers.
There were palm trees.
These Days.
These Mornings of Rain.
They Who Feel Death.
Thief.
Thing Itself, The.
Threatened.
To Die before One Wakes Must Be Glad.
To the Man in the Yellow Terry.
Torture.
View from Rosehill Cemetery: Vicksburg.
Walker.
Warning.
We Alone.
We Have a Beautiful Mother.
We Have a Map of the World.
Well.
What Ovid Taught Me.
What the Finger Writes.
When Golda Meir Was in Africa.
While Love Is Unfashionable.
Who?
Will.
Winnie Mandela We Love You.
Without Commercials.
Woman Is Not a Potted Plant, A.
Women.
"Women of Color" Have Rarely Had the
　Opportunity to Write about Their Love
　Affairs.
Your Soul Shines.

Warren, Robert Penn (1905–89)
　After Night Flight Son Reaches Bedside of
　　Already Unconscious Father, Whose Right
　　Hand Lifts in a Spasmodic Gesture, as
　　Though Trying to Make Contact: 1955.
　Afterwards.
　And All That Came Thereafter.
　And Don't Forget Your Corset Cover, Either.
　Answer to Prayer.
　Answer Yes or No.
　Apology for Domitian.
　Arrogant Law.
　At the Hour of the Breaking of the Rocks.
　Audubon.
　Ballad: Between the Boxcars.
　Ballad of a Sweet Dream of Peace.
　Ballad of Billie Potts, The.
　Ballad of Mister Dutcher and the Last
　　Lynching in Gupton.
　Be Something Else.
　Bear and the Last Person to Remember, The.
　Bear Track Plantation: Shortly after Shiloh.
　Bearded Oaks.
　Birth of Love.
　Blow, West Wind.
　Boy's Will, Joyful Labor without Pay, and
　　Harvest Home (1918).
　Brightness of Distance.
　Brotherhood in Pain.
　Butterflies over the Map.
　Chain Saw at Dawn in Vermont in Time of
　　Drouth.

Child Next Door, The.
Clearly about You.
Colder Fire.
Composition in Gold and Red-Gold.
Confederate Veteran Tries to Explain the
　Event, A.
Country Burying (1919).
Court-Martial.
Crime.
Dark Night of the Soul.
Dark Woods.
Dawn.
Dead Language: Circa 1885, A.
Debate: Question, Quarry, Dream.
Deciduous Spring.
Does the Wild Rose?
Dogwood, The.
Dragon Country: To Jacob Boehme.
Dream He Never Knew the End of, The.
Driver, Driver.
Eidolon.
Elijah on Mount Carmel.
Enclave, The.
End of Season.
Evening Hawk.
Event, The.
Fall Comes in Back-Country Vermont.
Faring, The.
Flaubert in Egypt.
Flower, The.
Fog.
Folly on Royal Street before the Raw Face of
　God.
Foreign Shore, Old Woman, Slaughter of
　Octopus.
Forever O'Clock.
Founding Fathers, Nineteenth-Century Style,
　Southeast U.S.A.
Fox-Fire: 1956.
Friends of the Family, or Bowling a Sticky
　Cricket.
Garden, The.
Go it, Granny—Go it, Hog!
Gold Glade.
Gull's Cry.
Hands Are Paid.
Harvard '61: Battle Fatigue.
Hazel Leaf, The.
He Was Formidable.
Her Hat.
His Smile.
History.
History among the Rocks.
Holly and Hickory.
Homage to Theodore Dreiser.
Human Fabric, The.
I Am Dreaming of a White Christmas: The
　Natural History of a Vision.
I Can't Even Remember the Name.
I Guess You Ought to Know Who You Are.
In Moonlight, Somewhere, They Are Singing.
In the Turpitude of Time: N.D.
Infant Boy at Midcentury.
Insomnia.
Interim, The.
Interjection #8: Or, Sometimes, Night.
Interjection #5: Solipsism and Theology.
Interjection #4: Bad Year, Bad War: A New
　Year's Card, 1969.
Interjection #1: The Need For Re-evaluation.
Interjection #7: Remarks of Soul to Body.
Interjection #6: What You Sometimes Feel on
　Your Face at Night.
Interjection #3: I Know a Place Where All Is
　Real.
Interjection #2: Caveat.
Into Broad Daylight.
Intuition.
Ivy, The.
Jet Must Be Hunting for Something, The.
Keep That Morphine Moving, Cap.
Keepsakes.
Kentucky Mountain Farm.
Late Subterfuge.
Leaf, The.
Letter about Money, Love, or Other Comfort,
　If Any.

Letter from a Coward to a Hero.
Little Boy and Lost Shoe.
Loss, of Perhaps Love, in Our World of
  Contingency.
Love and Knowledge.
Love: Two Vignettes.
Love's Parable.
Lullaby: A Motion Like Sleep.
Lullaby: Moonlight Lingers.
Lullaby: Smile in Sleep.
Mad Druggest, The.
Mad Young Aristocrat on Beach.
Man in Moonlight.
Man in the Street.
Mango on the Mango Tree, The.
Masts at Dawn.
Mediterranean Beach, Day after Storm.
Mexico Is a Foreign Country: Four Studies in
  Naturalism.
Midnight Outcry.
Modification of Landscape.
Monologue at Midnight.
Moonlight Observed from Ruined Fortress.
Moral Assessment.
Morning.
Mortmain.
Multiplication Table.
Myth on Mediterranean Beach: Aphrodite as
  Logos.
Natural History.
Natural History I.
Nature of a Mirror, The.
Night is Personal.
Night: The Motel down the Road from the
  Pen.
Not to Be Trusted.
Old Nigger on One-Mule Cart Encountered
  Late at Night When Driving Home from
  Party in the Back Country.
One Drunk Allegory.
One Voter out of Sixteen.
Only Trouble, The.
Original Sin; a Short Story.
Paradox.
Patriotic Tour and Postulate of Joy.
Paul Valéry Stood on the Cliff and
  Confronted the Furious Energies of Nature.
Penological Study: Southern Exposure.
Picnic Remembered.
Picture of Little Rory in a Municipal Park,
  The.
Place and Time.
Place Where Nothing Is, A.
Place Where the Boy Pointed, The.
Pondy Woods.
Problem in Spatial Composition, A.
Psychological Profile.
Pursuit.
Ransom.
Rattlesnake Country.
Reading Late at Night, Thermometer Falling.
Rebuke of the Rocks.
Red Mullet, The.
Return, The.
Return: An Elegy, The.
Revelation.
Riddle in the Garden.
Rumor Unverified Stop Can You Confirm
  Stop.
Saul at Gilboa.
School Lesson Based on Word of Tragic
  Death of Entire Gillum Family.
Scream, The.
Season Opens on Wild Boar in Chianti.
Shoes In Rain Jungle.
Sign Whereby He Knew, The.
Sirocco.
Skiers.
Small Soldiers with Drum in Large
  Landscape.
Small White House.
Snake, The.
Something Is Going to Happen.
Sound of That Wind, The.
Spider, The.
Stargazing.

Summer Storm (Circa 1916), and God's
  Grace.
Sunset Walk in Thaw-Time in Vermont.
Switzerland.
Tale of Time.
Tell Me a Story.
Terror.
There's a Grandfather's Clock in the Hall.
Tiberius on Capri.
Time as Hypnosis.
To a Face in a Crowd.
To a Friend Parting.
To a Little Girl, One Year Old, in a Ruined
  Fortress.
Tomorrow Morning.
Tonight the Woods Are Darkened.
Treasure Hunt.
True Nature of Time, The.
Trying to Tell You Something.
Two Poems about Suddenly and a Rose.
Two Studies in Idealism: Short Survey of
  American and Human History.
Vision: Circa 1880, A.
Vision under the October Mountain: A Love
  Poem.
Vital Statistics.
Walk by Moonlight in Small Town.
Wart, The.
Was Not the Lost Dauphin.
Way to Love God, A.
Ways of Day.
We Are Only Ourselves.
Well House, The.
Wet Hair: If Now His Mother Should Come.
What Day Is.
What Happened.
What Was the Promise That Smiled from the
  Maples at Evening?
What Were You Thinking Dear Mother?
When the Century Dragged.
Where Purples Now the Fig.
Where the Slow Fig's Purple Sloth.
Where They Come to Wait for the Body: A
  Ghost Story.
Wind.
Work.
World Comes Galloping: A True Story, The.
World Is a Parable, The.
You Never Knew Her Either, Though You
  Thought You Did.

Whitman, Walt (1819–92)
Aboard at a Ship's Helm.
Abraham Lincoln, Born Feb. 12, 1809.
Adieu to a Soldier.
After an Interval.
After the Argument.
After the Dazzle of Day.
After the Sea-Ship.
After the Supper and Talk.
Ages and Ages Returning at Intervals.
Ah Poverties, Wincings, and Sulky Retreats.
All Is Truth.
Ambition.
America.
Among the Multitude.
Apostroph.
Apparitions.
Are You the New Person Drawn toward Me?
Army Corps on the March, An.
Artilleryman's Vision, The.
As Adam Early in the Morning.
As at Thy Portals Also Death.
As Consequent, Etc.
As I Ebb'd with the Ocean of Life.
As I Lay with My Head in Your Lap
  Camerado.
As I Ponder'd [or Pondered] in Silence.
As I Sit Writing Here.
As I Walk These Broad Majestic Days.
As I Watch'd the Ploughman Ploughing.
As If a Phantom Caress'd Me.
As in a Swoon.
As the Greek's Signal Flame.
As the Time Draws Nigh.
As They Draw to a Close.
As Toilsome I Wander'd Virginia's Woods.
Ashes of Soldiers.

Ashes of Soldiers: Epigraph.
Assurances.
Base of All Metaphysics, The.
Bathed in War's Perfume.
Beat! Beat! Drums!
Beautiful Women.
Beauty of the Ship, The.
Beginners.
Beginning My Studies.
Behold This Swarthy Face.
Bivouac on a Mountain Side.
Blood-Money.
Boston Ballad, A [or A Boston Ballad 1854].
Bravest Soldiers, The.
Bravo, Paris Exposition!
Broad-Ax, The.
Broadway.
Broadway Pageant, A.
By Blue Ontario's Shore.
By Broad Potomac's Shore.
By That Long Scan of Waves.
By the Bivouac's Fitful Flame.
Calming Thought of All, The.
Camps of Green.
Carol Closing Sixty-Nine.
Cavalry Crossing a Ford.
Centenarian's Story, The.
Chanting the Square Deific.
Child's Amaze, A.
Christmas Greeting, A.
City Dead-House, The.
City of Orgies.
City of Ships.
Clear Midnight, A.
Columbian's Song, The.
Come, said my soul.
Come Up from the Fields Father.
Commonplace, The.
Continuities.
Crossing Brooklyn Ferry.
Dalliance of the Eagles, The.
Darest Thou Now O Soul.
Dead Emperor, The.
Dead Tenor, The.
Death and Burial of McDonald Clarke, a
  Parody, The.
Death of General Grant.
Death of the Nature-Lover, The.
Death's Valley.
Debris.
Delicate Cluster.
Dirge for Two Veterans.
Dismantled Ship, The.
Drayman, The.
Dying Veteran, The.
Earth, My Likeness.
Eidolons.
Eighteen Sixty-One.
Election Day, November, 1884.
End of All, The.
Ended Day, An.
Ethiopia Saluting the Colors.
Europe, the 72d and 73d Year of These
  States.
Evening Lull, An.
Excelsior.
Faces.
Facing West from California's Shores.
Fame's Vanity.
Fancies at Navesink.
Farm Picture, A.
Fast-Anchor'd Eternal O Love!
Few Drops Known, The.
First Dandelion, The.
First O Songs for a Prelude.
Font of Type, A.
For Him I Sing.
For Queen Victoria's Birthday.
For Us Two, Reader Dear.
For You O Democracy.
France, The 18th Year of These States.
From Far Dakota's Cañons (June 25, 1876).
From Montauk Point.
From My Last Years.
From Paumanok Starting I Fly Like a Bird.
From Pent-up Aching Rivers.
Full of Life Now.

Germs.
Gigantic Beauty of a Stallion, A.
Give Me the Splendid Silent Sun.
Gliding o'er All.
Glimpse, A.
Gods.
Going Somewhere.
Good-Bye, My Fancy! ("Good-bye, my Fancy! / Farewell dear mate, dear love!").
Good-Bye My Fancy ("Good-bye my fancy— (I had a word to say,)").
Grand is the Seen.
Great Are the Myths.
Had I the Choice.
Halcyon Days.
Hand-Mirror, A.
Has Any One Supposed It Lucky to Be Born?
Hast Never Come to Thee an Hour.
Here the Frailest Leaves of Me.
Hours Continuing Long.
House of Friends, The.
How Solemn as One by One.
Hush'd be the Camps To-day.
I Am He That Aches with Love.
I Am He That Walks with the Tender and Growing Night.
I Am of Old and Young.
I Dream'd in a Dream.
I Hear America Singing.
I Hear It Was Charged against Me.
I Heard You Solemn-Sweet Pipes of the Organ.
I Saw in Louisiana a Live-Oak Growing.
I Saw Old General at Bay.
I sing the body electric.
I Sit and Look Out.
I Thought That Knowledge Alone Would Suffice.
I Was Looking a Long While.
In Cabin'd Ships at Sea.
In Former Songs.
In Paths Untrodden.
In the New Garden.
Inca's Daughter, The.
Infinity.
Interpolation Sounds.
Italian Music in Dakota.
Joy, Shipmate, Joy!
Kiss to the Bride, A.
Kosmos.
L of G.
L. of G.'s Purport.
Last Droplets.
Last Invocation, The.
Laws for Creations.
Leaf for Hand in Hand, A.
Leaflets.
Lessons.
Life.
Life and Death.
Lingering Last Drops.
Lo, Victress on the Peaks.
Locations and Times.
Long, Long Hence.
Long, Too Long America.
Look Down Fair Moon.
Love That Is Hereafter, The.
Mannahatta: ("I was asking for something specific and perfect for my city").
Mannahatta: ("My city's fit and noble name resumed").
March in the Ranks Hard-Prest, and the Road Unknown, A.
Me Imperturbe.
Mediums.
Memories.
Memories of President Lincoln.
Miracles.
Mirages.
Mississippi at Midnight, The.
Mother and Babe.
Muse in the New World, The.
My Canary Bird.
My Departure.
My Legacy.
My Picture-Gallery.

My 71st Year.
Myself and Mine.
Mystic Trumpeter, The.
Native Moments.
Nay, Tell Me Not To-day the Publish'd Shame.
New Year's Day, 1848.
Night on the Prairies.
No Labor-Saving Machine.
Noiseless Patient Spider.
Not Heat Flames Up and Consumes.
Not Heaving from My Ribb'd Breast Only.
Not Meagre, Latent Boughs Alone.
Not My Enemies Ever Invade Me.
Not the Pilot.
Not Youth Pertains to Me.
Now Finalè to the Shore.
Now Lift Me Close.
Now Precedent Songs, Farewell.
O Captain! My Captain!
O Hymen! O Hymenee!
O Living Always, Always Dying.
O Magnet-South.
O Me! O Life!
O Star of France (1870–71).
O Sun of Real Peace.
O Tan-Faced Prairie-Boy.
O You Whom I Often and Silently Come.
Ode: "O, God of Columbia! O, Shield of the Free!"
Of Him I Love Day and Night.
Of Many a Smutch'd Deed Reminiscent.
Of That Blithe Throat of Thine.
Of the Terrible Doubt of Appearances.
Offerings.
Old Age's Lambent Peaks.
Old Age's Ship & Crafty Death's.
Old Chants.
Old Ireland.
Old Man's Thought of School, An.
Old Salt Kossabone.
Old War-Dreams.
On Journeys through the States.
On, on the Same, Ye Jocund Twain!
On the Beach at Night.
On the Beach at Night Alone.
On the Same Picture.
Once I Pass'd through a Populous City.
One Hour to Madness and Joy.
One Song, America, Before I Go.
One Thought Ever at the Fore.
One's-Self I Sing.
Or, from That Sea of Time.
Orange Buds by Mail from Florida.
Osceola.
Others May Praise What They Like.
Our Future Lot.
Our Old Feuillage.
Out from Behind This Mask.
Out of May's Shows Selected.
Out of the Cradle Endlessly Rocking.
Out of the Rolling Ocean the Crowd.
Outlines for a Tomb.
Over the Carnage Rose Prophetic a Voice.
Ox-Tamer, The.
Pallid Wreath, The.
Passage to India.
Patrolling Barnegat.
Paumanok.
Paumanok Picture, A.
Pensive and Faltering.
Pensive on Her Dead Gazing.
Perfections.
Persian Lesson, A.
Pioneers! O Pioneers!
Place Where a Great City Stands, The.
Play-Ground, The.
Poem of Remembrances for a Girl or a Boy of These States.
Poet, The.
Poets to Come.
Portals.
Prairie-Grass Dividing, The.
Prairie States, The.
Prairie Sunset, A.
Prayer of Columbus.
Promise to California, A.

Proud Music of the Storm.
Punishment of Pride, The.
Queries to My Seventieth Year.
Quicksand Years.
Race of Veterans.
Reconciliation.
Recorders Ages Hence.
Red Jacket (from Aloft).
Respondez!
Resurgemus.
Return of the Heroes, The.
Reversals.
Riddle Song, A.
Rise O Days from Your Fathomless Deeps.
Roaming in Thought.
Roots and Leaves Themselves Alone.
Rounded Catalogue Divine Complete, The.
Runaway Slave, The.
Runner, The.
Sail Out for Good, Eidólon Yacht!
Salut au Monde!
Savantism.
Says.
Scented Herbage of My Breast.
Shakspeare-Bacon's Cipher.
Ship Ahoy!
Ship Starting, The.
Shut Not Your Doors.
Sight in Camp [or] Sight in Camp in the Daybreak Gray and Dim, A.
Singer in the Prison, The.
Sleepers, The.
Small the Theme of My Chant.
So Far, and So Far, and On toward the End.
So Long!
Sobbing of the Bells, The.
Solid, Ironical, Rolling Orb.
Sometimes with One I Love.
Song at Sunset.
Song for All Seas, All Ships.
Song for Certain Congressmen.
Song for Occupations, A.
Song of Joys, A.
Song of Myself.
Song of Prudence.
Song of the Answerer.
Song of the Banner at Daybreak.
Song of the Broad-Axe [or Broad-Ax].
Song of the Exposition.
Song of the Open Road.
Song of the Redwood-Tree.
Song of the Rolling Earth, A.
Song of the Universal.
Soon Shall the Winter's Foil Be Here.
Sounds of the Winter.
Souvenirs of Democracy.
Spain, 1873–74.
Spanish Lady, The.
Sparkles from the Wheel.
Spirit That Form'd This Scene.
Spirit Whose Work Is Done.
Spontaneous Me.
Starting from Paumanok.
States!
Still Though the One I Sing.
Stronger Lessons.
Supplement Hours.
Swiftly Arose.
Tears.
Tests.
Thanks in Old Age.
That Music Always Round Me.
That Shadow My Likeness.
Then Shall Perceive.
There Was a Child Went Forth.
These Carols.
These I Singing in Spring.
Thick-Sprinkled Bunting.
Think of the Soul.
This Compost.
This Day, O Soul.
This Dust Was Once the Man.
This Moment Yearning and Thoughtful.
Thou Mother with Thy Equal Brood.
Thou Orb Aloft Full-Dazzling.
Thou Reader.
Thought: ("As I sit with others at a great

feast, suddenly while the music is playing").
Thought of Columbus, A.
Thought ("Of Equality..").
Thought ("Of Justice—as if Justice could be any thing but the same ample law, expounded by natural judges and saviors").
Thought ("Of obedience, faith, adhesiveness").
Thought: ("Of persons arrived at high positions, ceremonies, wealth, scholarships, and the like").
Thoughts ("Of ownership—as if one fit to own things could not at pleasure enter upon all, and incorporate them into himself or herself").
Thoughts: ("Of public opinion").
Thoughts ("Of these years I sing").
Thoughts—I: Visages.
Thoughts—6: "Of What I Write."
Time to Come.
To a Certain Cantatrice.
To a Certain Civilian.
To a Common Prostitute.
To a Foil'd European Revolutionaire.
To a Historian.
To a Locomotive in Winter.
To a President.
To a Pupil.
To a Stranger.
To a Western Boy.
To Be at All.
To-day and Thee.
To Foreign Lands.
To Get the Final Lilt of Songs.
To Him That Was Crucified.
To Old Age.
To One Shortly to Die.
To Rich Givers.
To Soar in Freedom and in Fullness of Power.
To the East and to the West.
To the Garden the World.
To the Leaven'd Soil They Trod.
To the Man-of-War Bird.
To the Pending Year.
To the Reader at Parting.
To the States.
To the States, To Identify the 16th, 17th, or 18th Presidentiad.
To the Sun-set Breeze.
To Thee Old Cause.
To Think of Time.
To Those Who've Fail'd.
To You ("Let us twain walk aside from the rest").
To You ("Stranger, if you passing meet me and desire to speak to me, why should you not speak to me?").
To You ("Whoever you are, I fear you are walking the walks of dreams").
Torch, The.
Transpositions.
Trickle Drops.
True Conquerors.
Turn O Libertad.
Twenty Years.
Twilight.
Twilight Song, A.
Two Rivulets.
Unexpress'd, The.
Unfolded Out of the Folds.
United States to Old World Critics, The.
Unnamed Lands.
Unseen Buds.
Untold Want, The.
Vigil Strange I Kept on the Field One Night.
Virginia—the West.
Visor'd.
Vocalism.
Voice from Death, A.
Voice of the Rain, The.
Wallabout Martyrs, The.
Walt Whitman.
Wandering at Morn.
Warble for Lilac-Time.
Washington's Monument, February, 1885.

We All Shall Rest at Last.
We Two Boys Together Clinging.
We Two, How Long We Were Fool'd.
Weave In, My Hardy Life.
What Am I After All.
What Best I See in Thee.
What Place Is Besieged?
What Ship Puzzled at Sea.
What Think You I Take My Pen in Hand?
When I Heard at the Close of the Day.
When I Heard the Learn'd Astronomer.
When I Peruse the Conquer'd Fame.
When I Read the Book.
When Lilacs Last in the Dooryard Bloom'd.
When the Full-Grown Poet Came.
While behind All, Firm and Erect.
While Not the Past Forgetting.
Whispers of Heavenly Death.
Who Is Now Reading This?
Who Learns My Lesson Complete.
Whoever You Are Holding Me Now in Hand.
With All Thy Gifts.
With Antecedents.
With Husky-Haughty Lips, O Sea!
Woman Waits for Me, A.
World below the Brine, The.
World Take Good Notice.
Would You Hear of an Old-Time [*or* Old-Fashioned] Sea fight?
Wound-Dresser, The.
Wounded Person, The.
Year of Meteors(1859–60).
Year That Trembled and Reel'd beneath Me.
Years of the Modern.
Yet, Yet Ye Downcast Hours.
Yonnondio.
You Felons on Trial in Courts.
You Lingering Sparse Leaves of Me.
Young Grimes.
Youth, Day, Old Age and Night.

Whittier, John Greenleaf (1807–92)
Abraham Davenport.
Abram Morrison.
Adjustment.
After Election.
Album Verses.
All's Well.
Among the Hills.
Amy Wentworth.
Andrew Rykman's Prayer.
Angel of Patience, The.
Angels of Buena Vista, The.
Anniversary Poem.
Answer, The.
April.
Arisen at Last.
Artist of the Beautiful, An.
Astræa.
Astræa at the Capitol.
At Eventide.
At Last.
At Port Royal.
At School-Close.
At Washington.
Autograph, An.
Autumn Thoughts.
Banished from Massachusetts.
Barbara Frietchie.
Barclay of Ury.
Barefoot Boy, The.
Bartholdi Statue, The.
Battle Autumn of 1862, The.
Bay of Seven Islands, The.
Bayard Taylor.
Benedicite.
Benevolence.
Between the Gates.
Birchbrook Mill.
Birthday Wreath, The.
Bolivar.
Book, The.
Book Our Mothers Read, The.
Branded Hand, The.
Brewing of Soma, The.
Bridal of Pennacook, The.
Brother of Mercy, The.

Brown Dwarf of Rügen, The.
Brown of Ossawatomie.
Bryant on His Birthday.
Burial of Barber.
Burning Drift-Wood.
Burns.
By Their Works.
Cable Hymn, The.
Calef in Boston.
Call of the Christian, The.
Captain's Well, The.
Cassandra Southwick.
Centennial Hymn.
Chalkley Hall.
Changeling, The.
Channing.
Chapel of the Hermits, The.
Chicago.
Child-Songs.
Christian Slave, The.
Christian Tourists, The.
Christmas Carmen, A.
Christmas of 1888, The.
Cities of the Plain, The.
Clear Vision, The.
Clerical Oppressors.
Cobbler Keezar's Vision.
Common Question, The.
Conductor Bradley.
Conquest of Finland, The.
Corn-Song, The.
Countess, The.
Crisis, The.
Cross, The.
Crucifixion, The.
Cry of a Lost Soul, The.
Curse of the Charter-Breakers, The.
Cypress-Tree of Ceylon, The.
Daniel Neall.
Daniel Wheeler.
Day, A.
Day's Journey, A.
Dead Feast of the Kol-Folk, The.
Dead Ship of Harpswell, The.
Dedication: "I would the gift I offer here."
Deity, The.
Democracy.
Demon of the Study, The.
Derne.
Disarmament.
Disenthralled, The.
Divine Compassion.
Dole of Jarl Thorkell, The.
Double-Headed Snake of Newbury, The.
Dream of Pio Nono, The.
Dream of Summer, A.
Drovers, The.
Drunkard to His Bottle, The.
Earthquake, The.
Easter Flower Gift, An.
Ego.
Ein Feste Burg Ist Unser Gott.
Elliott.
Emancipation Group, The.
Eternal Goodness, The.
Eva.
Eve of Election, The.
Evening in Burmah.
Exile's Departure, The.
Exiles, The.
Expostulation.
Extract from "A New England Legend."
Ezekiel.
Fair Quakeress, The.
Familist's Hymn, The.
Farewell, A: "What shall I say, dear friends, to whom I owe."
Farewell, The: "Gone, gone,—sold and gone."
Female Martyr, The.
First-Day Thoughts.
First Flowers, The.
Fishermen, The.
Fitz-Greene Halleck.
Flowers in Winter.
Follen.
For an Autumn Festival.

For Righteousness' Sake.
Forgiveness.
Fountain, The.
Fragment, A: "Dreadful burden of our sins we feel, The."
Fratricide, The.
Freed Islands, The.
Freedom in Brazil.
Frémont Campaign Song, A.
Friend's Burial, The.
From Perugia.
Frost Spirit, The.
Fruit-Gift, The.
Funeral Tree of the Sokokis.
Gallows, The.
Garden.
Garibaldi.
Garrison.
Garrison of Cape Ann, The.
George L. Stearns.
Gift of Tritemius, The.
Giving and Taking.
Godspeed.
Golden Wedding of Longwood, The.
Gone.
Grave by the Lake, The.
Greeting.
Greeting, A.
Hampton Beach.
Harvest Hymn.
Haschish, The.
Haverhill.
Hazel Blossoms.
Healer, The.
Help.
Henchman, The.
Hermit of the Thebaid, The.
Hero, The.
Hill-Top, The.
Hive at Gettysburg, The.
Holy Land, The.
Home-Coming of the Bride, The.
Homestead, The.
How Mary Grew.
How the Robin Came.
How the Women Went from Dover.
Howard at Atlanta.
Human Sacrifice, The.
Hunters of Men, The.
Huskers, The.
Hymn for the Celebration of Emancipation at Newburyport.
Hymn for the House of Worship at Georgetown.
Hymn for the Opening of Plymouth Church.
Hymn for the Opening of Thomas Starr King's House of Worship.
Hymn: "O Holy Father! just and true."
Hymn: "O Thou, whose presence went before."
Hymn of the Children.
Hymn of the Dunkers.
Hymn Sung at Christmas by the Scholars of St. Helena's Island, S.C.
Hymns from the French of Lamartine.
Hymns of the Brahmo Somaj.
"I Was a Stranger and Ye Took Me in."
Ichabod[!].
In Memory.
In Peace.
In Quest.
In Remembrance of Joseph Sturge.
In School-Days.
In the Evil Days.
In the "Old South."
Inscription: "Eagle, stooping from yon snow-blown peaks, The."
Inscriptions.
Invocation: "Through Thy clear spaces, Lord, of old."
Isabel.
Isabella of Austria.
Italy.
James Russell Lowell.
John Underhill.
Jubilee Singers, The.
Judith at the Tent of Holofernes.

June on the Merrimac.
Kallundborg Church.
Kansas Emigrants, The.
Kathleen.
Kenoza Lake.
Khan's Devil, The.
King Solomon and the Ants.
King Volmer and Elsie.
King's Missive, The.
Kinsman.
Knight of St. John, The.
Kossuth.
Lakeside, The.
Lament, A: "Circle is broken, one seat is forsaken, The."
Landmarks, The.
Last Eve of Summer, The.
Last Walk in Autumn, The.
Laurels, The.
Laus Deo!
Lay of Old Time, A.
Le Marais du Cygne.
Legacy, A.
Legend of St. Mark, The.
Legend of the Lake, A.
Leggett's Monument.
Letter, A.
Letter from a Missionary of the Methodist Episcopal Church South, in Kansas, to a Distiguished Politician.
Letter to Lucy Larcom.
Lexington.
Library, The.
Light That Is Felt, The.
Lines from a Letter to a Young Clerical Friend.
Lines on a Fly-Leaf.
Lines on Leaving Appledore.
Lines on the Death of S. Oliver Torrey.
Lines on the Portrait of a Celebrated Publisher.
Lines Written in an Album.
Lost Occasion, The.
Lost Statesman, The.
Lucy Hooper.
Lumbermen, The.
Lydia H. Sigourney.
Mabel Martin.
Maids of Attitash, The.
Mantle of St. John de Matha, The.
Marguerite.
Mary Garvin.
Massachusetts.
Massachusetts to Virginia.
Maud Muller.
Mayflowers, The.
Meeting, The.
Memorial, A.
Memories.
Memory, A.
Memory of Burns, The.
Men of Old, The.
Merrimac, The.
Metacom.
Milton.
Minister's Daughter, The.
Miriam.
Missionary, The.
Mrs. Choate's House-Warming.
Mithridates at Chios.
Mogg Megone.
Moloch in State Street.
Moral Warfare, The.
Mother.
Mount Agiochook.
Mountain Pictures.
Mulford.
My Birthday.
My Dream.
My Namesake.
My Playmate.
My Psalm.
My Soul and I.
My Thanks.
My Triumph.
Mystery, A.
Mystic's Christmas, The.

Name, A.
Naples.
New Exodus, The.
New Hampshire.
New Wife and the Old, The.
New Year, The.
Norembega.
Norsemen, The.
Norumbega Hall.
O. W. Holmes on His Eightieth Birthday.
Ocean.
Official Piety.
Old Burying-Ground, The.
On a Fly-Leaf of Longfellow's Poems.
On a Prayer-Book.
On Receiving an Eagle's Quill from Lake Superior.
On the Big Horn.
One of the Signers.
Oriental Maxims.
Our Autocrat.
Our Country.
Our Master.
Our River.
Our State.
Outdoor Reception, An.
Over-Heart, The.
Overruled.
Pæan.
Pageant, The.
Palatine, The.
Palestine.
Palm-Tree, The.
Panorama, The.
Pass of the Sierra, The.
Past and Coming Year, The.
Pastoral Letter, The.
Peace Autumn, The.
Peace Convention at Brussels, The.
Peace of Europe, The.
Pennsylvania Hall.
Pennsylvania Pilgrim, The.
Pentucket.
Pictures.
Pine-Tree, The.
Pipes at Lucknow, The.
Poet and the Children, The.
Poor Voter on Election Day, The.
Prayer of Agassiz, The.
Prayer-Seeker, The.
Preacher, The.
Prelude: "Along the roadside, like the flowers of gold."
Pressed Gentian, The.
Prisoner for Debt, The.
Prisoners of Naples, The.
Problem, The.
Proclamation, The.
Proem: "I love the old melodious lays."
Prophecy of Samuel Sewall, The.
Prophetess.
Pumpkin, The.
Quaker Alumni, The.
Quaker of the Olden Time, The.
Quakers Are Out, The.
Questions of Life.
R. S. S., at Deer Island on the Merrimac.
Rabbi Ishmael.
Randolph of Roanoke.
Ranger, The.
Rantoul.
Raphael.
Red Riding-Hood.
Red River Voyageur, The.
Reformer, The.
Relic, The.
Remembrance.
Rendition, The.
Requirement.
Requital.
Response.
Reunion, The.
Revelation.
Revisited.
Reward, The.
Ritner.

River Path, The.
Robin, The.
"Rock" in El Ghor, The.
Rock-Tomb of Bradore, The.
Sabbath Scene, A.
Saddest Words, The.
Saint Gregory's Guest.
St. John.
St. Martin's Summer.
Samuel E. Sewall.
Samuel J. Tilden.
Sea Dream, A.
Seed-Time and Harvest.
Seeking of the Waterfall, The.
Sentence of John L. Brown, The.
Shadow and the Light, The.
Ship-Builders, The.
Shoemakers, The.
Sicilian Vespers, The.
Singer, The.
Sister.
Sisters, The.
Sisters: A Picture by Barry, The.
Skipper Ireson's Ride.
Slave-Ships, The.
Slaves of Martinique, The.
Snow-Bound [or Snow-Bound; a Winter
    Idyl].
Song, A: "Beneath thy skies, November!"
Song for the Time, A.
Song of Harvest, A.
Song of Slaves in the Desert.
Song of the Negro Boatmen.
Song of the Vermonters, 1779, The.
Spirit of the North, The.
Spiritual Manifestation, A.
Stanzas: "Bind up thy tresses, thou beautiful
    one."
Stanzas for the Times.
Star of Bethlehem, The.
Storm on Lake Asquam.
Story of Ida, The.
Summer by the Lakeside.
Summer Pilgrimage, A.
Summons, A.
Summons, The.
Sumner.
Sunset on the Bearcamp.
Swan Song of Parson Avery, The.
Sweet Fern.
Sycamores, The.
Tauler.
Telling the Bees.
Tent on the Beach, The.
Texas.
Thiers.
Thomas Starr King.
Three Bells, The.
Thy Will Be Done.
To ———: "Fair Nature's priestesses! to
    whom."
To ———: "Maiden! with the fair brown
    tresses."
To a Cape Ann Schooner.
To a Friend.
To a Poetical Trio in the City of Gotham.
To a Southern Statesman.
To Avis Keene.
To Charles Sumner.
To Delaware.
To E. C. S.
To Englishmen.
To Faneuil Hall.
To Fredrika Bremer.
To G. G.
To George B. Cheever.
To J. P.
To James T. Fields.
To John C. Frémont.
To Lucy Larcom.
To Lydia Maria Child.
To Massachusetts.
To My Friend on the Death of His Sister.
To My Old Schoolmaster.
To My Sister.
To Oliver Wendell Holmes.
To Pennsylvania.

To Pius IX.
To Ronge.
To Samuel E. Sewall and Harriet W. Sewall.
To the Memory of Charles B. Storrs.
To the Memory of Thomas Shipley.
To the Reformers of England.
To the Thirty-Ninth Congress.
To William H. Seward.
To William Lloyd Garrison.
Toussaint L'Ouverture.
Trailing Arbutus, The.
Trinitas.
Truce of Piscataqua, The.
Trust.
Two Angels, The.
Two Elizabeths, The.
Two Loves, The.
Two Rabbins, The.
Utterance.
Vale of the Merrimac, The.
Valuation.
Vanishers, The.
Vaudois Teacher, The.
Vesta.
Vision of Echard, The.
Voices, The.
Vow of Washington, The.
Voyage of the Jettie.
Waiting, The.
Watchers, The.
Welcome to Lowell, A.
Well of Loch Maree, The.
What of the Day?
What State Street Said to South Carolina, and
    What South Carolina Said to State Street.
What the Birds Said.
What the Traveller Said at Sunset.
What the Voice Said.
Wife of Manoah to Her Husband, The.
William Forster.
William Francis Bartlett.
Wilson.
Wind of March, The.
Winter Night.
Winter Roses.
Wish of To-day, The.
Wishing Bridge, The.
Witch of Wenham, The.
Within the Gate.
Woman, A.
Wood Giant, The.
Word for the Hour, A.
Word, The.
Wordsworth.
World Transformed, The.
World's Convention, The.
Worship.
Worship of Nature, The.
Wreck of Rivermouth, The.
Yankee Girl, The.
Yorktown.

Wilbur, Richard (b. 1921)
Advice from the Muse.
Advice to a Prophet.
After the Last Bulletins.
Agent, The.
Alatus.
All That Is.
All These Birds.
Altitudes.
&.
Another Voice.
Apology.
April 5, 1974.
Aspen and the Stream, The.
Attention Makes Infinity.
Avowal, The.
Ballade for the Duke of Orléans.
Baroque Wall-Fountain in the Villa Sciarra,
    A.
Beacon, The.
Beasts.
Beautiful Changes, The.
Bell Speech.
Beowulf.
Black Birch in Winter, A.
Black November Turkey, A.

Boy at the Window.
C Minor.
Caserta Garden.
Castles and Distances.
Catch, The.
Ceremony.
Children of Darkness.
Christmas Hymn, A.
Chronic Condition, A.
Cicadas.
Clearness.
Complaint.
Conjuration.
Cottage Street, 1953.
Courtyard Thaw, A.
Death of a Toad, The.
Digging for China.
Driftwood.
Dubious Night, A.
Dutch Courtyard, A.
Eight Riddles from Symphosius.
Epistemology.
Event, An.
Exeunt.
Eye, The.
Fable, A.
Fall in Corrales.
Fern-Beds in Hampshire County.
Finished Man, A.
Fire-Truck, A.
First Snow in Alsace.
Five Women Bathing in Moonlight.
Flippancies.
Flumen Tenebrarum.
Folk Tune.
For Dudley.
For Ellen.
For K. R. on Her Sixtieth Birthday.
For the New Railway Station in Rome.
For the Student Strikers.
For W. H. Auden.
Fourth of July, The.
From the Lookout Rock.
Games One.
Games Two.
Gemini.
Giacometti.
Giaour and the Pacha, The.
Gifts, The.
Glance from the Bridge, A.
Gnomons.
Good Servant, The.
Grace.
Grasse: The Olive Trees.
Grasshopper, A.
Hamlen Brook.
He Was.
Hole in the Floor, A.
Icarium Mare.
In a Bird Sanctuary.
In a Churchyard.
In Limbo.
In the Elegy Season.
In the Field.
In the Smoking-Car.
John Chapman.
John Chrysostom.
Juggler.
June Light.
Junk.
La Rose des Vents.
Lamarck Elaborated.
Lament: "Nashe's old queens who bartered
    young and fair."
Late Aubade, A.
Leaving.
L'Etoile.
Lightness.
Lilacs, The.
Looking into History.
Love Calls Us to the Things of This
    World.
Loves of the Puppets.
Lying.
March.
Marché aux Oiseaux.
Marginalia.

Matthew VIII, 28 ff.
Mechanist, The.
Melongène.
Merlin Enthralled.
Mill, The.
Miltonic Sonnet for Mr. Johnson on His
    Refusal of Peter Hurd's Official Portrait,
    A.
Mind.
Mind-Reader, The.
Mined Country.
Museum Piece.
My Father Paints the Summer.
Next Door.
O.
Objects.
October Maples, Portland.
Ode to Pleasure.
On Freedom's Ground.
On Having Mis-identified a Wild Flower.
On the Eyes of an SS Officer.
On the Marginal Way.
Orchard Trees, January.
Pangloss's Song: A Comic-Opera Lyric.
Parable.
Pardon, The.
Part of a Letter.
Peace of Cities, The.
Pelican, The.
Peter.
Piazza di Spagna, Early Morning.
Piccola Commedia.
Pity.
Place Pigalle.
Plain Song for Comadre, A.
Playboy.
Poplar, Sycamore.
Potato.
Praise in Summer.
Prisoner of Zenda, The.
Problem from Milton, A.
Proof, The.
Puritans, The.
Regatta, The.
Riddle, A.
Ride, The.
Rillons, Rillettes.
Rule, The.
Running.
Seed Leaves.
Shad-Time.
Shallot, A.
Shame.
She.
Simile for Her Smile, A.
Simplification, A.
Sirens, The.
Sketch, A.
Sleepless at Crown Point.
Some Riddles from Symphosius.
Someone Talking to Himself.
Song, A: "As at the bottom of a seething
    well."
Sonnet.
Speech for the Repeal of the McCarran Act.
Star System, The.
Statues.
Still, Citizen Sparrow.
Stop.
Storm in April, A.
Summer Morning, A.
Sun and Air.
Sunlight Is Imagination.
Superiorities.
Teresa.
Terrace, The.
Then.
Thyme Flowering among Rocks.
To an American Poet Just Dead.
To His Skeleton.
To Ishtar.
To the Etruscan Poets.
Transit.
Trolling for Blues.
Two Quatrains for First Frost.
Two Riddles from Aldhelm.
Two Songs in a Stanza of Beddoes'.

Two Voices in a Meadow.
Tywater.
Undead, The.
Under a Tree.
Under Cygnus.
Up, Jack.
Violet and Jasper.
Voice from under the Table, A.
Walgh-Vogel, The.
Walking to Sleep.
Water Walker.
Waters, The.
Wedding Toast, A.
Wellfleet: The House.
What's Good for the Soul is Good for Sales.
Winter Spring.
Wood, A.
"World without Objects Is a Sensible
    Emptiness, A."
Worlds.
Writer, The.
Wyeth's Mild Cans.
Year's End.
Translations, Coauthored Poems, etc.:
Agrigentum Road, The.
Antéros.
Antiworlds.
Arrow in the Wall, An.
Ballade in Old French.
Ballade of Forgiveness.
Ballade of the Ladies of Time Past.
Ballade to End With, A.
Compass.
Dead Still.
Death, from a Distance.
Everness.
Ewigkeit.
Foggy Street.
Funeral of Bóbo, The.
Grasshopper and the Ant, The.
Happy the Man.
Harbor, The.
Helen.
Horses, The.
L'Invitation au Voyage.
Lot's Wife.
Mirabeau Bridge.
Phone Booth.
Prayer to Go to Paradise with the Donkeys, A.
Rondeau: "Year has cast its cloak away,
    The."
Six Years Later.
Song.
Tartuffe.
To Madame du Châtelet.
Two Poems.

Williams, Charles Kenneth (b. 1936)
Acids.
Admiral Fan, The.
After That.
Allies: According to Herodotus.
Alzheimer's: The Husband.
Alzheimer's: The Wife.
Another Dollar.
Ashes Ashes We All Fall Down.
Baby, I don't want.
Bad Mouth.
Becoming Somebody Else.
Before This.
Beginning of April, The.
Being Alone.
Beyond.
Bishop Tutu's Visit to the White House:
    1984.
Blades.
Blame.
Body, The.
Bread.
Bringing It Home.
Call, The.
Cautionary, The.
Cave, The.
Cellophane.
Child Psychology.
Clay out of Silence.
Color of Time, The.
Combat.

Conscience.
Covenant, The.
Cracks.
Crawl.
Creams.
Crime.
Crime, The.
Critic, The.
Dawn.
Day for Anne Frank, A.
Did I write this.
Dimensions.
Dirty Talker: D Line, Boston, The.
Dog, The.
Dominion: Depression.
Don't.
Downwards.
Dream, The.
Drought.
Easter.
Elms.
End of Drought.
Ethics.
Even If I Could.
Experience.
Failure.
Faint Praise.
Fast Food.
Fat.
Fifteen.
Fire.
First Desires.
Flat.
Fleas, too, / have fled, The.
Flight.
Floor.
For Children When They Grow Up.
For Gail, When I Was Five.
Friends.
From My Window.
From Now On.
Game, The.
Gap, The.
Gas Station, The.
Gift, The.
Giving It Up.
Good Mother: Out.
Greed.
Guatemala: 1964.
Hail goes / dancing, The.
Halves.
Hard Part, The.
Harm.
Helen.
Herakles.
Hercules, Deianira, Nessus.
History.
Hog Heaven.
Holiday: / every / yard or, A.
Hood.
Hooks.
Hounding Mercy.
How Humble We Were before This.
I Am the Bitter Name.
I know / nothing anymore.
I sit in my room.
I'd forgotten and / how could I ever.
Image, The.
In the Heart of the Beast.
In the middle / of a bite of.
In the next life.
In There.
Inches.
Innings.
Instinct.
Insult, The.
Interrogation II.
It Is Teeming.
It Is This Way with Men.
It's over now. I watch.
Jetsam.
Junior High School Concert: Salle Rossini.
Just Right.
Keep It.
Kin.
Kingdom of Stinking Wishes, The.
Knot, The.

Last, The.
Last Deaths, The.
Le Petit Salvié.
Like Little Birds.
Listen carefully. / I'm meditating.
Little Shirt, The.
Long Bells, The.
Long Naked Walk of the Dead, The.
Loss.
Love: Beginnnings.
Love: Wrath.
Love: Youth.
Madder.
Man Who Owns Sleep, The.
Matter, The.
Medusa.
Men.
Mirror, The.
Modern, The.
Mornings: Catherine.
Most excruciating / thing, The.
My Book, My Book.
My Fly.
My Mother's Lips.
Near the Haunted Castle.
Neglect.
New Car.
Next to the Last Poem about God, The.
Nickname of Hell, The.
Nostalgia.
Nut, The.
Of What Is Past.
On Learning of a Friend's Illness.
On the Other Hand.
On the Roof.
One of the Muses.
Or.
Orchid, The.
Other Side, The.
Park, The.
Past, The.
Patience Is When You Stop Waiting.
Peace.
Penance.
Philadelphia: 1978.
Poem for the Governments, A.
Politics.
Poor Hope.
Portions of Manslayer.
Prodigy, The.
Question, The.
Rabbit Fights for His Life the Leopard Eats
    Lunch, The.
Race of the Flood, The.
Racists.
Rampage, The.
Reading: Early Sorrow.
Reading: Winter.
Refuge, Serpent-Riders.
Regulars, The.
Repression.
Resentment.
Ribbons.
Room.
Rungs.
Saint Sex.
Sanctity, The.
Saturday.
Scar.
Secrets.
Shade, The.
Shadows.
Shame.
Shells.
Signs.
Silence, The.
Sky, Water.
Sleeping Over.
Snow: I.
Snow: II.
So / mucked up with.
Solid, The.
Soliliquies.
Soon.
Sorrow, The.
Souls.
Spider Psyche.

Spirit the Triumph, The.
Spit.
Spring: another / joke. / This run-down.
Still Life.
Sting, The.
Storm, The.
Suicide: Anne.
Tails.
Tar.
Ten Below.
That night, / winter, / rain.
That the world / is going.
Then the Brother of the Wind.
They Warned Him Then They Threw Him
    Away.
They wash you / when.
Thinking Thought.
Thirst.
This Day.
This Is a Sin.
This is what, / at last, it is.
Three Seasons and a Gorilla.
Time: 1978.
Time: 1976.
To Listen.
To Market.
Toil.
Trappers.
Trash.
Travelers.
Twice More.
Undead, The.
Vehicle: Absence.
Vehicle: Conscience.
Vehicle: Violence.
Villanelle of the Suicide's Mother.
Waking Jed.
War.
What a sound his.
What Did the Man Do with the Clouds?
What Is and Is Not.
What Must I Do To Be Lost?
What we are / given.
When / you were small, I.
When.
Winter, / damn, / again.
With Ignorance.
Work.
World's Greatest Tricycle-Rider, The.
You're two, that's great.
Yours.

Williams, Miller (b. 1930)
Aesthetic Distance.
After a Brubeck Concert.
After the Revolution for Jesus a Secular Man
    Prepares His Final Remarks.
After You Die You Don't Give a Piddling
    Damn.
Aging Actress Sees Herself a Starlet on the
    Late Show, The.
Allende at the End.
And Then.
And When in Scenes of Glory.
Animals.
Associate Professor Delivers an Exhortation
    to His Failing Students, The.
August Evening Outside of Nashville, An.
Before.
Being Here.
Believing in Symbols.
Book, The.
Caterpillar, The.
Divorce.
Documenting It.
Entropy.
Euglena.
Evening: A Studio in Rome.
Everything Is Fine Here How Are You.
Firebreathers at the Café Deux Magots, The.
Fly Me to the Moon.
For Lucinda, Robert, and Karyn.
For Lucy, on Her Birthday.
For Reuben, at Twelve Months.
For Victor Jara.
Form and Theory of Poetry.
Friend, The.
Getting Experience.

Getting the Message.
Ghost of His Wife Comes to Tell Him How
    It Is.
Ghosts.
Gift of Prophecy Lost, The.
Glass Darkly, A.
He Glimpses a Nobler Vision.
He Speaks to His Arguing Friends and to
    Himself.
House in the Vacant Lot, The.
How Does a Madsong Know That's What It
    Is?
How the Elephant Got His Hump.
How to Stop Smoking.
Husband.
I Go Out of the House for the First Time.
In a Gradually Moving Car Somewhere in
    Calcutta.
In Another Town.
In Extremis in Hardy, Arkansas.
In Nashville, Standing in the Wooden Circle
    Sawed Out from the Old Ryman Stage, the
    Picker has a vision.
In Your Own Words Without Lying Tell
    Something of Your Background With
    Particular Attention to Anything Relating
    to the Position For Which You Are
    Applying. Press Down.
Jonathan Aging.
Journalist Buys a Pig Farm, The.
La Ultima Carta: A Young Wife Writes to
    Her Husband in the Mountains.
Late Show.
Let Me Tell You.
Little Poem, A.
Living on the Surface.
Logos.
Lost in Ladispoli.
Love and How It Becomes Important in Our
    Day to Day Lives.
Love in the Cathedral.
Love Poem.
Main Street.
Man Who Stays Up Late, The.
Mecanic on Duty at All Times.
Memphis, 2 P.M.
Missing Persons.
Muse, The.
My Wife Reads the Paper at Breakfast on the
    Birthday of the Scottish Poet.
Newspaper Picture of Spectators at a Hotel
    Fire, A.
Normandy Beach.
Notes from the Agent on Earth: How to be
    Human.
On a Photograph of My Mother at Seventeen.
On a Trailways Bus a Man Who Holds His
    Head Strangely Speaks to the Seat Behind
    Him.
On Hearing About the Death of Mitzi
    Mayfair.
On the Death of a Middle-Aged Man.
On the Symbolic Consideration of Hands and
    the Significance of Death.
On the Way Home From Nowhere, New
    Year's Eve.
One Day a Woman.
One of the Crowd on the Shore Tells How It
    Was.
One of Those Rare Occurrences on a City
    Bus.
Ones that Are Thrown Out, The.
Original Sin.
Paying Some Attention to His Birthday the
    Associate Professor Goes About His
    Business Considering What He Sees and a
    Kind of Praise.
People.
Picker.
Pity and Fear.
Plain.
Poem for Emily, A.
Promotion, The.
Reading the Newsapaper on Microfilm.
Rebecca at Play.
Rituals.
Rock.

Rubaiyat for Sue Ella Tucker.
Ruby Tells All.
Running into Things.
Sale.
Schumann Adds Trombones to His Second
  Symphony After Mendelssohn Conducts
  the First Performance.
Senator Explains a Vote, The.
Sir.
Sitting Alone at Sunrise: Problems in the
  Space-Time Continuum.
Some Lines Finished Just Before Dawn at the
  Bedside of a Dying Student / It has
  Snowed all Night.
Staying.
Story, The.
Style.
Summer Afternoon an Old Man Gives Some
  Thought to the Central Questions, A.
Survivor, The.
Tearing Down the Hotel.
Thinking about Bill, Dead of AIDS.
Thinking Friday Night with a Gothic Storm
  Going About Final Causes and Logos and
  Mitzi Mayfair.
Toast to Floyd Collins, A.
Today is Wednesday.
Trying.
Trying to Remember.
Vanishing Point, The.
Vision and Prayer.
Voice of America.
Waiting for the Paper to be Delivered.
We.
Well-Ordered Life, The.
Why God Permits Evil: For Answers to This
  Question of Interest to Many Write Bible
  Answers Dept. E-7.
Widow, The.
Wiedersehen.
Woman on the Porch, The.
Words.
WW I.

Williams, William Carlos (1883–1963)
A, B & C of It, The.
A La Lune.
Act, The.
Ad Infinitum.
Adam.
Address.
Address, An.
Advent of Today.
Africa.
After Song, An.
Aftermath, The.
Aginst the Sky.
Agonized Spires, The.
Aigeltinger.
Alighting from my horse to drink with you.
All That is Perfect in Woman.
All the Fancy Things.
And Thus with All Praise.
And Who Do You Think "They" Are?
Another Old Woman.
Another Year.
Apology.
Apparition, The.
Appeal.
Approach of Winter.
Approach to a City.
Approaching Hour, The.
Après le Bain.
April.
April is the Saddest Month.
Arrival.
Art, The.
Artist, The.
Asphodel, That Greeny Flower.
At Dawn.
At Kenneth Burke's Place.
At Night.
At the Ball Game.
At the Bar.
At the Brink of the Winter.
At the Faucet of June.
Atlantic City Convention, The.
Attic Which Is Desire, The.

Autumn.
Aux Imagistes.
Avenue of Poplars, The.
Ballad of Faith.
Ballad: "To a man and his wife."
Ballet.
Banner Bearer, The.
Bare Tree, The.
Bastard Peace, A.
Berket and the Stars.
Better than flowers.
Between Walls.
Bird.
Bird Song.
Birds and Flowers.
Bird's Companion, The.
Birds, The.
Birdsong, The.
Birth of Venus, The.
Birth, The.
Bitter World of Spring, The.
Black Winds, The.
Blizzard.
Blueflags.
Botticellian Trees, The.
Breakfast.
Brief Lief.
Brilliance, The.
Brilliant Sad Sun.
Bull, The.
Burning the Christmas Greens.
Butterandeggs.
Calypsos.
Canthara.
Catastrophic Birth.
Catholic Bells, The.
Cats' Month, The.
Ce-Lia The Immortal Beauty.
Celebration, A.
Centenarian, The.
Cézanne.
Chanson.
Cherry Blossoms at Evening.
Chicory and Daisies.
Child and Vegetables.
Childe Harold to the Round Tower Came.
Children, The.
Chinese Nightingale.
Chinese Toy, A.
Choral: The Pink Church.
Christmas 1950.
Chrysanthemum, The.
Classic Picture.
Classic Scene.
Clock of the Years, The.
Clouds, The.
Cod Head, The.
Cold Front, A.
Cold Night, The.
Come On!
Comfort.
Complaint.
Complete Destruction.
Complexity, The.
Composition.
Con Brio.
Confidence, A.
Conquest.
Construction.
Contemporania.
Controversy, The.
Conventional Ballad.
Convivio.
Corn Harvest, The.
Coronal, A.
Counter, The.
Crimson Cyclamen, The.
Crude Lament.
Crystal Maze, A.
Cuchulain.
Cure, The.
Daisy.
Dance, The.
Danse Russe.
Dark Day, The.
Dawn.
Daybreak.

Dead Baby, The.
Death.
Death by Radio.
Death of Franco of Cologne, The: His
  Prophecy of Beethoven.
Death of See, The.
Death the Barber.
December.
Deceptrices, The.
Dedication for a Plot of Ground.
Deep Religious Faith.
Defective Record, The.
Defense.
Defiance to Cupid.
Delicacies, The.
Della Primavera Transportata al Morale.
Descent.
Descent of Winter, The.
Descent, The.
Desert Music, The.
Design for November.
Desolate Field, The.
Detail.
Details for Paterson.
Dish of Fruit, The.
Disputants, The.
Divertimiento.
Drink.
Drugstore Library.
Drunk and the Sailor, The.
Drunkard, The.
Early Martyr, An.
East Coocoo.
Education a Failure.
El Hombre.
Election Day.
Elegy for D.H. Lawrence, An.
End of the Parade, The.
End of the Rope, The.
Entity, The.
Epigramme: "Hast ever seen a man."
Episode 17.
Epitaph; "Old willow with hollow branches,
  An."
Eternity.
Eternity, An.
Eve.
Every Day.
Exercise.
Exercise, An.
Exercise No. 2.
Exultation, An.
Eyeglasses, The.
Farmer, The.
Fertile.
15 Years Later.
Fight, The.
Figueras Castle.
Fine Work with Pitch and Copper.
Fire Spirit.
First Praise.
Fish.
Flattery.
Flight to the City.
Flower, The.
Flowers Alone, The.
Flowers by the Sea.
Flowing River, A.
Folded Skyscraper, A *sels.*
Fond Farewell, A.
Fool's Song, The.
Foot-Note, A.
For a Low Voice.
For Eleanor and Bill Monahan.
For G.B.S., Old.
For Viola: De Gustibus.
Foreign.
Formal Design, A.
4th of July.
Fragment: "As for him who."
Fragment: "My God, Bill, what have you
  done?"
Franklin Square.
From a Book.
From a Play.
From a Window.
From "The Birth of Venus," Song.

Fruit, The.
Full Moon.
Gayest of Bright Flowers, The.
Genesis.
Genius, The.
Gentle Man, The.
Gentle Negress, The.
Gentle Rejoinder, The.
Gift, The.
Girl, The.
Goat, The.
Good Night.
Goodnight, A.
Gossips, The.
Gothic Candor.
Graceful Bastion, The.
Graph.
Graph for Action.
Great Figure, The.
Great Mullen.
Green Eyes.
Greeting for Old Age.
Grotesque.
Gulls.
Halfworld, The.
Hard Core of Beauty, The.
Hard Listener, The.
Hard Times.
Haymaking.
He Has Beaten about the Bush Long Enough.
Healall.
Heel & Toe to the End.
Hemmed-in Males.
Hermaphroditic Telephones, The.
Hero.
Hey Red!
Hic Jacet.
High Bridge above the Tagus River at
    Toledo, The.
His Daughter.
History.
History of Love, A.
Homage.
Horned Purple.
Horse Show, The.
Horse, The.
Host, The.
Hounded Lovers, The.
House, The.
How Bad It Is to Say.
How Has the Way Been Found?
Hula-Hula.
Hunter, The.
Hunters in the Snow, The.
Hurricane, The.
Hymn to Love Ended.
I bought a new.
I Will Sing a Joyous Song.
"I Would Not Change For Thine."
Idyl: "They say to me, 'There is'."
Idyl: "Wine of the grey sky."
Illegitimate Things.
Immortal.
Impromptu: The Suckers.
In Chains.
In Harbor.
In San Marco, Venezia.
In Sisterly Fashion.
In the 'Sconset Bus.
Incognito.
Informative Object, An.
Injury, The.
Intelligent Sheepman and the New Cars, The.
Interests of 1926.
Invitation.
Invocation and Conclusion.
Io Baccho!
It Is a Living Coral.
It Is a Small Plant.
Italian Garden, The.
Item.
Ivy Crown, The.
January.
Jersey Lyric.
Jingle.
June 9.
Jungle, The.

K. McB.
Keller Gegen Dom.
King!, The.
La Belle Dame de Tous les Jours.
La Flor.
Labrador.
Lady speaks, The.
Lament: "What face, in the water."
Landscape with the Fall of Icarus.
Last Turn, The.
Last Words of My English Grandmother,
    The.
Last Words of My Grandmother.
Late for Summer Weather.
Late Singer, The.
Le Médecin Malgré Lui.
Lear.
Lesson, The.
Libertad! Igualdad! Fraternidad!
Light Becomes Darkness.
Light Hearted William.
Light Shall Not Enter.
Lily, The.
Lines: "Leaves are greygreen."
Lines on Receiving *The Dial's* Award: 1927.
Lion, The.
Locust Tree in Flower, The.
Lonely Street, The.
Look, there goes the young lady across the
    street.
Love.
Love Charm, The.
Love Poem, A:"Basic hatred / Sometimes has
    a flower."
Love Song: "Daisies are broken."
Love Song: First Version, 1915, A.
Love Song: "I lie here thinking of you."
Love Song: "You have come between me
    and the terrifying presence."
Love Song;"Sweep the house clean."
Lovely Ad.
Loving Dexterity, The.
Lustspiel.
Mama.
Man and Nature.
Man in a Room.
Man to a Woman, A.
Maneuver [*or* Manoeuvre], The.
March.
March Is a Light.
Marianne Moore.
Marriage.
Marriage of Souls, The.
Marriage Ritual, A.
Martin and Katherine.
May 1st Tomorrow.
M.B.
Memory of April.
Men, The.
Mental Hospital Garden, The.
Metric Figure.
Mezzo Forte.
Middle.
Midwinter.
Min Schleppner.
Mind Hesitant, The.
Mind's Games, The.
Mirrors, The.
Misericordia.
Mistrust of the Beloved.
Mists over the River.
Modest Achievement, The.
Monstrous Marriage, The.
Moon, The.
Moon and Stars.
Moral, The.
Morning.
Motor-Barge, The.
Mounted as an Amazon.
Mujer.
My Luv.
Naked.
Nantucket.
Navajo.
Negro Woman, A.
New Cathedral Overlooking the Park, The.
New Clouds, The.

New England.
New Mexico.
Night.
Night Rider, The.
Nightingales, The.
No Good Too.
Non-Entity, The.
Note, A.
Note to Music: Brahms 1st Piano Concerto.
Nun's Song.
Observer, The.
Offering.
Ogre, The.
Ol' Bunk's Band.
Old-Fashioned German Christmas Card, An.
Old House, The.
Old Men, The.
Old Worshipper, The.
On a Proposed Trip South.
On First Opening the Lyric Year.
On Gay Wallpaper.
On St. Valentine's Day.
Orchard, The.
Orchestra, The.
Ordeal, The.
Our (American) Ragcademicians.
Overture to a Dance of Locomotives.
Painting, The.
Parable of the Blind, The.
Passaic, N.J.
Passer Domesticus.
Pastoral 1; "Old man who goes about, The."
Pastoral 2: "If I talk to things."
Pastoral; "If I say I have heard voices."
Pastoral: "Little sparrows, The."
Pastoral; "When I was younger."
Paterson *sels.*
Paterson.
Paterson, Book V: The River of Heaven.
Paterson: The Falls.
Paul.
Pause, The.
Peace.
Peace on Earth.
Perfection.
Period Piece: 1834.
Perpetuum Mobile: The City.
Petunia, The.
Philomena Andronico.
Phoenix and the Tortoise, The.
Picture of a Nude in a Machine Shop.
Picture Showing.
Pictures from Brueghel *sels.*
Pictures from Brueghel.
Pigheaded Poet.
Pink Locust, The.
Place (Any Place) to Transcend All Places,
    A.
Play.
Plea for Mercy, A.
Poem: "As the cat."
Poem: "Daniel Boone, the father of
    Kentucky."
Poem for Norman Macleod, A.
Poem: "Looking up, of a sudden."
Poem: "On getting a card."
Poem: "Plastic surgeon who has, The."
Poem: "Rose fades, The."
Poem, The: "It's all in / the sound. A song."
Poet and His Poems, The.
Polar Bear, The.
Poor, The.
Porous.
Portent.
Portrait in Greys, A.
Portrait of a Lady.
Portrait of a Woman at Her Bath.
Portrait of a Woman in Bed.
Portrait of a Young Man with a Bad Heart.
Portrait of the Author.
Portrait of the Times, A.
Postlude.
Pot of Flowers, The.
Predicter of Famine, The.
Prelude, A; "I know only the bare rocks of
    today."
Prelude to Winter.

Primrose.
Problem, The.
Proletarian Portrait.
Promenade.
Province, The.
Quality of Heaven, The.
Queen-Anne's-Lace.
Question and Answer.
Quietness.
R R Bums, The.
Rain.
Raindrops on a Briar.
Raleigh Was Right.
Raper from Passenack, The.
Rapid Transit.
Rare Gist, The.
Rat, The.
Readie Pome.
Red Lily, The.
Red Wheelbarrow, The.
Red-Wing Blackbird, The.
Rendezvous.
Resemblance, The.
Return to Work, The.
Revelation, The.
Reverie and Invocation.
Rewaking, The.
Rhymed Address: The Lobster.
Rigamarole.
Right of Way, The.
Riposte.
Ritualists, The.
River Rhyme.
River Rhyme II.
Rock-Old Dogma, The.
Rocking Woman, The.
Rogation Sunday.
Romance Moderne.
Rose, The.
Rosebush in an Unlikely Garden, A.
Rumba! Rumba!
Russia.
Sadness of the Sea, The.
Sale, The.
Sappho, Be Comforted.
Savage Beast, The.
Sea, The.
Sea-Elephant, The.
Sea-Trout and Butterfish.
Seafarer.
Self, The.
Self-Portrait.
Self-Portrait 1.
Self-Portrait 2.
Semblables, The.
Seraph.
Shadow, The.
Shadows.
She Who Turns Her Head.
Shoot It Jimmy!
Short Poem.
Sicilian Emigrant's Song.
Sick African.
Silence.
Simplex Sigilum Veri: A Catalogue.
Sketch for a Portrait of Henry Ford.
Sleeping Brute, The.
Slow Movement.
Sluggishly.
Smell.
Smiling Dane, A.
Snow Begins, The.
Solstice.
Some Simple Measures in the American
    Idiom and the Variable Foot.
Sometimes It Turns Dry and the Leaves Fall
    before They Are Beautiful.
Song: "Beauty is a shell."
Song: "Black-winged gull, The."
Song: "I'd rather read an account."
Song: "If I / could count the silence."
Song: "Pluck the florets from."
Song: "Russia! Russia! you might say."
Song: "You are forever April."
Sonnet in Search of an Author.
Sort of a Song, A.
Soughing Wind, The.

Sound of Waves, The.
Source, The.
Sparrow, The.
Sparrows among Dry Leaves.
Spirit of '76.
Spouts.
Spring.
Spring and All.
Spring is Here Again, Sir.
Spring Song.
Spring Storm.
Spring Strains.
St. Francis Einstein of the Daffodils.
St. Valentine.
Still Life.
Still Lifes.
Stillness.
Stone Crock, The.
Storm, The.
Stormy.
Stroller.
Struggle of Wings.
Stylist, The.
Sub Terra.
Summer Song.
Sun, The.
Sun Bathers, The.
Sunday.
Sunflowers.
Suzanne.
Suzy.
Swaggering Gait, The.
Sympathetic Portrait of a Child.
Tailpiece.
Tapiola.
10/14.
Term, The.
Testament of Perpetual Change, The.
These.
These Purists.
Thing, The.
Thinker, The.
Thinking Back Toward Christmas: A
    Statement for the Virgin.
This Florida: 1924.
This Is Just to Say.
This Is Pioneer Weather.
Thistle.
Thoughtful Lover, The.
3 A.M. The Girl with the Honey Colored
    Hair.
Three Graces, The.
Three Nahuatl Poems.
Three Sonnets.
3 Stances.
Threnody: "Christian coin, The."
Thursday.
Time the Hangman.
Title, The.
To.
To a Chinese Woman.
To a Dead Journalist.
To a Dog Injured in the Street.
To a Friend.
To a Friend Concerning Several Ladies.
To a Lovely Old Bitch.
To a Man Dying on His Feet.
To a Mexican Pig-Bank.
To a Poor Old Woman.
To a Solitary Disciple.
To a Sparrow.
To a Woman Seen Once.
To a Wood Thrush.
To a Woodpecker.
To All Gentleness.
To an Elder Poet.
To an Old Jaundiced Woman.
To Be Closely Written on a Small Piece of
    Paper Which Folded into a Tight Lozenge
    Will Fit Any Girl's Locket.
To Be Hungry Is to Be Great.
To Be Recited to Flossie on Her Birthday.
To Close.
To Daphne and Virginia.
To Elsie.
To Flossie.
To Ford Madox Ford in Heaven.

To Greet a Letter-Carrier.
To Have Done Nothing.
To Mark Anthony in Heaven.
To My Friend Ezra Pound.
To the Dean.
To the Ghost of Marjorie Kinnan Rawlings.
To the Outer World.
To the Shade of Po Chü-I.
To Waken an Old Lady.
To Wish Myself Courage.
Tolstoy.
Tract.
Tragic Detail.
Trala Trala Trala La-le-la.
Transitional.
Translation.
Translations from the Spanish.
Tree.
Tree and Sky.
Trees.
Trees, The.
Tribute to Neruda the Poet Collector of
    Seashells.
Tribute to the Painters.
Tulip Bed, The.
Turkey in the Straw.
Turtle, The.
Twelve Line Poem.
Two Aspects of April.
Two Deliberate Exercises.
Two Pendants: For the Ears.
Unfrocked Priest, The.
Unison, A.
United Front, The.
United States, The.
Unknown, The.
Uses of Poetry, The.
Usurers of Heaven, The.
Venus Over the Desert.
View.
View by Color Photography on a Commercial
    Calendar.
View of a Lake.
Virtue.
Virtuous Agent, The.
Visit, The.
Vision of Labor, A: 1931.
Waiting.
Wanderer, The.
Wanderer, The: A Rococo Study.
War, the Destroyer.
Weasel Snout.
Well Disciplined Bargeman, The.
When Fresh, It Was Sweet.
When I saw.
When Structure Fails Rhyme Attempts to
    Come to the Rescue.
Wide Awake, Full of Love.
Widow's Lament in Springtime, The.
Wild Orchard.
Wildflower, The.
Willow Poem.
Wind Increases, The.
Wind of the Village.
Winds, The.
Winter.
Winter Quiet.
Winter Sunset.
Winter Trees.
Woman in Front of a Bank, A.
Woman Walking.
Woodpecker, The.
Woodthrush, The.
Words Lying Idle, The.
Words, the Words, the Words, The.
World Contracted to a Recognizable Image,
    The.
World Narrowed to a Point, The.
Writer's Prologue to a Play in Verse.
Wrong Door, The.
Yachts, The.
Yellow Chimney, The.
Yellow Flower, The.
Yellow Season, The.
Yellow Tree Peony, The.
You Have Pissed Your Life.
Young Cat and the Chrysanthemums, The.

Young Housewife, The.
Young Laundryman, The.
Young Love.
Young Sycamore.
Young Woman at a Window.
Your lovely hands.
Youth and Beauty.
Translations, Coauthored Poems, etc.:
After the Party.
Agony Among the Crowd, The.
Bella Donna Iu.
Birds have flown away from the mountains, The.
Chant of the Frontiersman.
Curfew.
Drinking Together.
From the Inside.
From the Outside.
Hymn Among the Ruins.
In Dream's Wake.
In spring you sleep and never know when the morn comes.
In the Wineshop of Chinling.
Infinite Horses, The.
Jean Sans Terre at the Final Port.
Jean Sans Terre Circles the Earth Seven Times.
Jean Sans Terre Discovers the West Pole.
Jean Sans Terre Leads the Caravan.
Jean Sans Terre Reviews the Fathers.
Knight, The.
Lament of a Graying Woman.
Late Spring.
Letter, A.
Long Banister Lane.
Maid, The.
March, The.
Naked.
Narcissus in the Desert.
Newlywed's Cuisine, The.
Ode to Laziness.
Old Man and the Child, The.
Phoenix Undying, *sel.*
Piano Solo.
Prelude in Boricua.
Profile of a Lady.
Returning after I left my home in childhood.
Sappho.
Silently I ascend the western pavilion.
Solo.
Spotting the moonlight at my bedside.
Spring in the Snow-Drenched Garden.
Spring Song.
Steering my little boat towards a misty islet.
Summer Song.
Three Generations.
To Friend-Tree of Counted Days.
To Li Po.
To Meng Hao-Jan.
To Regain the Day Again.
To Wang Wei.
Uncertain of the Crime.
Visit.
Visitor, The.
Wanderings of the Tribe, The.
Widower's Monologue.
Wolf, A.
Wrested from Mirrors.
Youth on Horseback, The.

Wordsworth, William (1770–1850)
Abuse of Monastic Power.
Acquittal of the Bishops.
Address from the Spirit of Cockermouth Castle.
Address to Kilchurn Castle, upon Loch Awe.
Address to My Infant Daughter, Dora on Being Reminded That She Was a Month Old That Day, September 16.
Address to Silence.
Address to the Ocean.
Address to the Scholars of the Village School of—1798.
Admonition.
Advance—come forth from the Tyrolean ground.
Aërial Rock—Whose Solitary Brow.
Affliction of Margaret—, The.

Afflictions of England.
After Landing—The Valley of Dover, Nover, 1820.
After Leaving Italy.
After Leaving Italy, Continued.
After-Thought ("Oh Life! without thy chequered scene").
After Visiting the Field of Waterloo.
Airey-Force Valley.
Aix-la-Chapelle.
Alas! what boots the long laborious quest.
Alcaeus to Sappho.
Alfred.
Alice Fell; or, Poverty.
Along the mazes of this song I go.
American Tradition.
Among all lovely things my Love had been.
Among the Ruins of a Convent in the Apennines.
Anacreon.
And is it among rude untutored Dales.
Andrew Jones.
Anecdote for Fathers.
Animal Tranquility and Decay.
Anticipation. October, 1803.
Apology.
Apology ("Nor scorn the aid which Fancy oft doth lead").
Apology ("Not utterly unworthy to endure").
Archbishop Chichely to Henry V.
Argument for Suicide.
Armenian Lady's Love, The.
Artegal and Elidure.
As when, upon the smooth pacific deep.
Aspects of Christianity in America— Concluded—American Episcopacy.
Aspects of Christianity in America— Continued.
Aspects of Christianity in America—the Pilgrim Fathers.
At Albano.
At Applethwaite, near Keswick.
At Bala-Sala, Isle of Man.
At Bologna, in Remembrance of the Late Insurrections, 1837.
At Bologna, in Remembrance of the Late Insurrections, 1837, Continued: "As leaves are to the tree wheron they grow."
At Bologna, in Remembrance of the Late Insurrections, 1837, Continued: "Hard task! exclaim the undisciplined, to lean."
At Dover.
At Florence.
At Florence.—from Michelangelo.
At Furness Abbey ("Here, where, of havoc tired and rash undoing").
At Furness Abbey ("Well have yon Railway Labourers to THIS ground").
At Rome ("Is this, ye Gods, the Capitolian Hill?").
At Rome.—Regrets.—In Allusion to Niebuhr and Other Modern Historians.
At Rome.—Regrets.—In Allusion to Niebuhr and Other Modern Historians, Continued.
At Rome ("They—who have seen the noble Roman's scorn").
At Sea off the Isle of Man.
At the Convent of Camaldoli.
At the Convent of Camaldoli, Continued.
At the Eremite or Upper Convent of Camaldoli.
At the Grave of Burns (1803, Seven Years After His Death).
At the Isle of Wight. 1793.
At Vallombrosa.
Author's Voyage down the Rhine (Thirty Years Ago).
Avaunt all specious pliancy of mind.
Avon, The.
Away, away, it is the air.
Ballad, A: "And will you leave me thus alone."
Baptism.
Beauty and Moonlight.
Before the Picture of the Baptist, by Raphael, in the Gallery at Florence.
Beggars.

"Beloved Vale!" I said, "when I shall con."
Between Namur and Liege.
Birth of Love, The.
Black Stones of Iona, The.
Blest Statesman He, Whose Mind's Unselfish Will.
Blind Highland Boy, The; A Tale Told by the Fire-side, After Returning to the Vale of Grasmere.
Books.
Borderers, The. A Tragedy.
Bothwell Castle.
Brave Schill! by death delivered, take thy flight.
Brook! whose society the Poet seeks.
Brothers, The.
Brownie, The.
Brownie's Cell, The.
Brugès ("Bruges I saw attired with golden light").
Brugès ("Spirit of Antiquity—enshrined, The").
By a Blest Husband Guided, Mary Came.
By a Retired Mariner (A Friend of the Author).
By Moscow Self-Devoted to a Blaze.
By the Sea-Shore, Isle of Man.
By the Sea-Side.
By the Side of Rydal Mere.
Calais, August, 1802.
Calais, August 15, 1802.
Call not the royal Swede unfortunate.
Calm Is the Fragrant Air, and Loth to Lose.
Cambridge and the Alps.
Cantata, from Metastasio.
Canute.
Captivity.—Mary Queen of Scots.
Casual Incitement.
Catechizing.
Cathedrals, etc.
Cave of Staffa ("Thanks for the lessons of this Spot—fit school").
Cave of Staffa ("We saw, but surely, in the motley crowd").
Cave of Staffa ("Ye shadowy Beings, that have rights and claims").
Cenotaph.
Cento Made By Wordsworth, A.
Change Me, Some God, Into That Breathing Rose!
Character, A.
Character of the Happy Warrior.
Characteristics of a Child Three Years Old.
Charles the Second.
Childless Father, The.
Church of San Salvador Seen from the Lake of Lugano.
Church to Be Erected.
Churchyard among the Mountains, The.
Churchyard among the Mountains (Continued), The.
Cistertian Monastery.
Clerical Integrity.
Coleridge's Mind a Life Unto Itself.
Column Intended by Buonaparte for a Triumphal Edifice in Milan, Now Lying by the Way-Side in the Simplon Pass, The.
Come ye that are disturbed, this steady voice.
Commination Service, The.
Companion to the Foregoing [Love Lies Bleeding].
Complaint, A.
Complaint of a Forsaken Indian Woman, The.
Composed after a Journey across the Hamilton Hills, Yorkshire.
Composed after Reading a Newspaper of the Day.
Composed among the Ruins of a Castle in North Wales.
Composed at Cora Linn in Sight of Wallace's Tower.
Composed at Rydal on May Morning, 1838.
Composed at the Same Time and on the Same Occasion.
Composed by the Sea-Shore.
Composed by the Sea-Side, near Calais, August, 1802.

Composed by the Side of Grasmere Lake.
Composed During a Storm.
Composed in One of the Catholic Cantons.
Composed in One of the Valleys of Westmoreland, on Easter Sunday.
Composed in Roslin Chapel, During a Storm.
Composed in the Glen of Loch Etive.
Composed in the Valley near Dover, on the Day of Landing.
Composed Near Calais on the Road Leading to Ardres, August 7, 1802.
Composed on a May Morning.
Composed on the Banks of a Rocky Stream.
Composed on the Eve of the Marriage of a Friend in the Vale of Grasmere, 1812.
Composed upon an Evening of Extraordinary Splendour and Beauty.
Composed upon Westminster Bridge, September 3, 1802.
Composed When a Probability Existed of Our Being Obliged to Quit Rydal Mount as a Residence.
Composed While the Author Was Engaged in Writing a Tract, Occasioned by the Convention of Cintra.
Conclusion: "But here no cannon thunders to the gale."
Conclusion: "In one of these excursions, travelling then."
Conclusion: "In one of those excursions (may they ne'er)."
Conclusion: "Why Sleeps the future, as a snake enrolled."
Conclusion: "Yes, though He well may tremble at the sound."
Confirmation.
Confirmation Continued.
Congratulation.
Conjectures.
Consummate Happiness.
Continued [Church to Be Erected].
Continued [Dissolution of the Monasteries].
Continued [Inside of King's College Chapel, Cambridge].
Continued [Other Benefits].
Continued [Seclusion].
Contrast; the Parrot and the Wren, The.
Conversion.
Convict, The.
Corruptions of the Higher Clergy.
Could I the priest's consent have gained.
Council of Clermont, The.
Countess' Pillar.
Cranmer.
Crescent-Moon, the Star of Love, The.
Crusaders.
Crusades.
Cuckoo and the Nightingale, The.
Cuckoo at Laverna May 25, 1837 The.
Cuckoo-Clock, The.
Cumberland Water Authority.
Danish Boy; A Fragment, The.
Danish Conquests.
Decay of Piety.
Dedicated Spirit, A.
Dedication (Sent with These Poems, in Ms., To —).
Departure from the Vale of Grasmere. August, 1803.
Descriptive Sketches Taken During a Pedestrian Tour among the Alps.
Despondency.
Despondency Corrected.
Desponding Father! Mark This Altered Bough.
Desultory Stanzas, upon Receiving the Preceding Sheets from the Press.
Devotional Incitements.
Dion.
Dirge Sung by a Minstrel.
Discourse of the Wanderer and an Evening Visit to the Lake.
Dissensions.
Dissolution of the Monasteries.
Distractions.
Distressful gift! this Book receives.
Dog—An Idyllium, The.

Druidical Excommunication.
Dunlolly Eagle, The.
Eagle and the Dove, The.
Eagles.
Earl of Breadalbane's Ruined Mansion, and Family Burial-Place, near Killin, The.
Ecclesiastical Sonnets.
Echo, upon the Gemmi.
Eclipse of the Sun, 1820, The.
Edward Signing the Warrant for the Execution of Joan of Kent.
Edward VI.
Effusion in the Pleasure-Ground on the Banks of the Bran, Near Dunkeld.
Effusion in the Presence of the Painted Tower of Tell, at Altorf.
Egyptian Maid; or, The Romance of the Water Lilly, The.
1811 ("Power of Armies is a visible thing, The").
1811 ("Here pause: the poet claims at least this praise").
1801.
1810.
1830.
Ejaculation.
Elegiac Musings in the Grounds of Coleorton Hall, the Seat of the Late Sir G.H. Beaumont, BART.
Elegiac Stanzas.
Elegiac Stanzas (Addressed to Sir G.H.B. upon the Death of His Sister-in-Law).
Elegiac Stanzas Composed in the Churchyard of Grasmere.
Elegiac Stanzas Suggested by a Picture of Peele Castle, in a Storm [Painted by Sir George Beaumont].
Elegiac Verses in Memory of My Brother, John Wordsworth.
Elegy Written in the Same Place upon the Same Occasion.
Elizabeth.
Ellen Irwin; or, The Braes of Kirtle.
Emigrant French Clergy.
Emigrant Mother, The.
Eminent Reformers.
Emperors and Kings, How Oft Have Temples Rung.
Engelberg, the Hill of Angels.
England! the time is come when thou shouldst wean.
English Reformers in Exile.
Epigram on an Event in Col. Evans's Redoubted Performances in Spain.
Epistle to Sir George Howland Beaumont, BART.
Epitaph: "Six months to six years added he remained."
Epitaph in Grasmere Church.
Epitaph in the Chapel Yard of Langdale, Westmoreland.
Ere with Cold Beads of Midnight Dew.
Eternal Lord! Eased from a Cumbrous Load.
Even as a dragon's eye that feels the stress.
Evening Walk Addressed to a Young Lady, An.
Excursion, The.
Expostulation and Reply.
Extempore Effusion upon the Death of James Hogg.
Extract from the Conclusion of a Poem, Composed in Anticipation of Leaving School.
Fact, and an Imagination or, Canute and Alfred, on the Sea-Shore, A.
Faery Chasm, The.
Fair below Helvellyn, The.
Fair Prime of Life! Were It Enough to Gild.
Fairest, brightest, hues of ether fade, The.
Fall of the Aar—Handec, The.
Fancy and Tradition.
Farewell, A: "Farewell, thou little Nook of mountain-ground."
Farewell Lines.
Farmer of Tilsbury Vale, The.
Feel for the Wrongs of Universal Ken.
Feelings of a French Royalist, on the

Disinterment of the Remains of the Duke D'Enghien.
Feelings of a Noble Biscayan at One of Those Funerals 1810.
Feelings of the Tyrolese.
Fidelity.
Filial Piety.
Fish-Women.—On Landing at Calais.
Fishing.
Flower Garden at Coleorton Hall, Leicestershire, A.
Flowers.
Flowers on the Top of the Pillars at the Entrance of the Cave.
Fly, some kind Harbinger, to Grasmere-dale!
For a Seat in the Groves of Coleorton.
For the Spot Where the Hermitage Stood on St Herbert's Island, Derwent-Water.
Force of Prayer, The; or, The Founding of Bolton Priory; A Tradition.
Foregoing Subject Resumed, The.
Foresight.
Forms of Prayer at Sea.
Forsaken, The.
Fort Fuentes.
Forth from a Jutting Ridge, Around Whose Base.
Fountain, The.
Four Fiery Steed Impatient of the Rein.
Fragment: "For let the impediment be what it may."
Fragment: "In vain did Time and Nature.."
Fragment: "Witness Thou."
Fragment: "Yet once again."
Fragment: A Somersetshire Tragedy.
Fragment from Dove Cottage Manuscript 44 (I).
Fragment of a "Gothic" Tale.
Fragment of an Intended Poem on Milton, Written in the Copy of *Paradise Lost* Which Belonged to Wordsworth at Cambridge.
Fragment: Redundance.
Fragment: The Baker's Cart.
Fragments: Drafts, Mostly or All for a Poem on a Heroic Theme.
Fragments from Dove Cottage Manuscript 44 (II).
Fragments from the Alfoxden Notebook (I).
Fragments from the Alfoxden Note-Book (II).
Fragments from the Alfoxden Note-Book (III).
Fragments from the "Christabel" Note-book.
France (Concluded).
French and the Spanish Guerrillas, The.
French Army in Russia 1812–1813, The.
French Revolution as It Appeared to Enthusiasts at Its Commencement. Reprinted from "The Friend."
From the Alban Hills, Looking towards Rome.
From the Dark Chambers of Dejection Freed.
Funeral Service.
General View of the Troubles of the Reformation.
Gentle Spenser.
Germans on the Heights of Hochheim, The.
Glad Sight Wherever New with Old.
Glad Tidings.
Gleaner (Suggested By a Picture), The.
Glen-Almain; Or, the Narrow Glen.
Go Back to Antique Ages, If Thine Eyes.
Gold and Silver Fishes in a Vase.
Goody Blake and Harry Gill.
Gordale.
Grace Darling.
Gravestone upon the Floor in the Cloisters of Worcester Cathedral, A.
Great men have been among us; hands that penned.
Green Linnet, The.
Greenock.
Grief, thou hast lost an ever ready friend.
Guilt and Sorrow; or Incidents upon Salisbury Plain.
Gunpowder Plot.
Gypsies.

Hail, Twilight, sovereign of one peaceful hour!
Hail, Zaragoza! If with unwet eye.
Hark! 'Tis the Thrush, Undaunted, Undeprest.
Hart-Leap Well.
Hart's-Horn Tree, near Penrith.
Haunted Tree; To———, The.
Help for the Memory of the Grand Independent; A New Song, A.
Her Eyes Are Wild.
Her Only Pilot the Soft Breeze, the Boat.
Highland Broach, The.
Highland Hut.
Hint from the Mountains for Certain Political Pretenders.
Hints for the Fancy.
His Descendents.
Hofer.
Home at Grasmere.
Horn of Egremont Castle, The.
Horse, The.
Hour-bell sounds, and I must go, The.
How Beautiful the Queen of Night, on High.
How Rich That Forehead's Calm Expanse!
How sweet it is, when mother Fancy rocks.
Humanity.
Hymn for the Boatmen, as They Approach the Rapids under the Castle of Heidelberg.
I find it written of SIMONIDES.
I Heard (Alas! 'Twas Only in a Dream).
I Know an Aged Man Constrained to Dwell.
I love upon a stormy night.
I Wandered Lonely as a Cloud.
I Watch, and Long Have Watched [with Calm Regret].
Idiot Boy, The.
Idle Shepherd-Boys, The; or, Dungeon-Ghyll Force. A Pastoral.
If This Great World of Joy and Pain.
If thou indeed derive thy light from Heaven.
Illustrated Books and Newspapers.
Illustration; the Jung-Frau and the Fall of the Rhine near Schaffhausen.
Imagination.
Imagination and Taste, How Impaired and Restored.
Imagination, How Impaired and Restored.
Imaginative Regrets.
Imitation of Juvenal — Satire VIII.
In a Carriage, upon the Banks of the Rhine.
In Allusion to Various Recent Histories and Notices of the French Revolution.
In Allusion to Various Recent Histories and Notices of the French Revolution, Concluded.
In Allusion to Various Recent Histories and Notices of the French Revolution, Continued.
In due observance of an ancient rite.
In Lombardy.
In My Mind's Eye a Temple, Like a Cloud.
In Part from Moschus's Lament for Bion.
In Patterdale.
In Sight of the Town of Cockermouth.
In the Cathedral at Cologne.
In the Channel, between the Coast of Cumberland and the Isle of Man.
In the First Page of an Album by One Whose Handwriting Is Wretchedly Bad.
In the Firth of Clyde, Ailsa Crag.
In the Sound of Mull.
In the Woods of Rydal.
In These Fair Vales Hath Many a Tree.
Incident at Bruges.
Incident Characteristic of a Favourite Dog.
Incipient Madness.
Indignation of a High-Minded Spaniard 1810.
Infant M— M—, The.
Influence Abused.
Influence of Natural Objects [in Calling Forth and Strengthening the Imagination in Boyhood and Early Youth].
Inscribed upon a Rock.
Inscription for a Monument in Crossthwaite Curch, in the Vale of Keswick.
Inscription for a Seat by a Roadside, Half Way up a Steep Hill, Facing the South.

Inscription for a Seat by the Pathway Side Ascending to Windy Brow.
Inscription in a Garden of Stone.
Inscription in the Grounds of Coleorton, the Seat of Sir George Beaumont, BART., Leicestershire
Inscription on a Rock at Rydal Mount.
Inscriptions Supposed to Be Found in and near a Hermit's Cell; 1818.
Inside of King's College Chapel, Cambridge.
Intent on Gathering Wool from Hedge and Brake.
Interdict, An.
Intimations of Sublimity.
Introduction: "I, who accompanied with faithful pace."
Introduction—Childhood and School-Time.
Invocation to the Earth; February, 1816.
Iona ("How sad a welcome! To each voyager").
Iona ("On to Iona!—What can she afford").
Is there a power that can sustain and cheer.
Isle of Man ("Did pangs of grief for lenient time too keen").
Isle of Man ("Youth too certain of his power to wade, A").
It is a beauteous Evening, calm and free.
It is no spirit who from heaven hath flown.
It is not to be thought of that the Flood.
It was an April morning: fresh and clear.
Italian Itinerant, and the Swiss Goatherd, The.
Jewish Family (in a Small Valley Opposite St Goar, upon the Rhine), A.
Journey Renewed.
June, 1820.
Just Vengeance Claims Thy Soul for Rights Invaded?
King of Sweden, The.
Kitten and [the] Falling Leaves, The.
Kitten at Play, The.
Labourer's Noon-Day Hymn, The.
Lady Whom You here Behold, The.
Lament of Mary Queen of Scots on the Eve of a New Year.
Laodamia.
Last of the Flock, The.
Last Supper, by Leonardo da Vinci, in the Refectory of the Convent of Maria della Grazia—Milan, The.
Latimer and Ridley.
Latitudinarianism.
Laud.
Leaves That Rustled on THis Oak-Crowned Hill, The.
Let More Ambitious Poets Take the Heart.
Liberty.
Lines Composed a Few Miles above Tintern Abbey on Revisiting the Banks of the Wye during a Tour, July 13, 1798.
Lines Inscribed in a Copy of His Poems Sent to the Queen for the Royal Library at Windsor.
Lines: "Loud is the Vale! the Voice is up."
Lines: "Nay, Traveller! rest. This lonely Yew-tree stands."
Lines on the Expected Invasion 1803.
Lines Suggested By a Portrait from the Pencil of F. Stone.
Lines Written as a School Exercise at Hawkshead, Anno Aetatis 14.
Lines Written in Early Spring.
Lines Written in the Album of the Countess of Lonsdale.
Lines Written on a Blank Leaf in a Copy of the Author's Poem "The Excursion", upon Hearing of the Death of the Late Vicar of Kendal.
Lines Written While Sailing in a Boat at Evening.
LITTLE Onward Lend Thy Guiding Hand, A.
Liturgy, The.
Lo! Where She Stands Fixed in a Saint-like Trance.
London, 1802.
London, from Hampstead Heath.

Longest Day; Addressed to My Daughter, The.
Look now on that Adventurer who hath paid.
Louisa; After Accompanying Her on a Mountain Excursion.
Love Lies Bleeding.
Lowther.
Lucy.
Lucy Gray; or, Solitude.
Lyre! Though Such Power Do in Thy Magic Live.
Malham Cove.
Mark the concentrated hazels that enclose.
Marriage Ceremony, The.
Martial courage of a day is vain, The.
Mary Queen of Scots.
Massy Ways Carried across These Heights, The.
Maternal Grief.
Matron of Jedborough and Her Husband, The.
Matthew.
Memorial near the Outlet of the Lake of Thun.
Memorials of a Tour in Italy, 1837.
Memorials of a Tour of the Continent; 1820.
Memory.
Men of the Western World! In Fate's Dark Book.
Me thought I saw the footsteps of a throne.
Michael [A Pastoral Poem].
Missions and Travels.
Modern Athens, The.
Monastery of Old Bangor.
Monastic Voluptuousness.
Monks and Schoolmen.
Monument Commonly Called Long Meg and Her Daughters, near the River Eden, The.
Monument of Mrs Howard.
More May not Be by Human Art Exprest.
Morning Exercise, A.
Most Alluring Clouds That Mount the Sky, The.
Most Sweet It Is with Unuplifted Eyes.
Motto Intended for Poems on the Naming of Places.
Musings near Aquapendente April, 1837.
Mutability.
My heart leaps up when I behold.
Narrow girdle of rough stones and crags, A.
Near Rome, in Sight of St Peter's.
Near the Lake of Thrasymene.
Near the Same Lake [Thrasymene].
Near the Spring of the Hermitage.
New Church-Yard.
New Churches.
Newton.
Night-Piece, A.
Night Thought, A.
No spade for leagues had won a rood of earth.
No whimsy of the purse is here.
Noble, The.
Norman Boy, The.
Norman Conquest, The.
Not in the Lucid Intervals of Life.
Not Love, not War, nor the Tumultuous Swell.
November, 1806.
November, 1813.
November, 1836.
November 1.
Nunnery.
Nuns fret not at their convent's narrow room.
Nun's Well, Brigham.
Nutting.
O Nightingale! thou surely art.
Oak and the Broom, The; A Pastoral.
Oak of Guernica! Tree of holier power.
Obligations of Civil to Religious Liberty.
Occasioned by the Battle of Waterloo February, 1816.
Occasioned by the Battle of Waterloo (the Last Six Lines Intended for an Inscription) February, 1816.

October, 1803 ("One might believe that natural miseries").
October, 1803 ("These times strike monied worldlings with dismay").
October, 1803 ("When, looking on the present face of things").
Ode Composed on May Morning.
Ode: 1815.
Ode: 1814.
Ode: Intimations of Immortality [from Recollections of Early Childhood].
Ode on the Installation of His Royal Highness Prince Albert as Chancellor of the University of Cambridge, July, 1847.
Ode: The Morning of the Day Appointed for a General Thanksgiving. January 18, 1816.
Ode to Apollo.
Ode to Duty.
Ode to Lycoris.
Ode to Lycoris; May, 1817.
Ode: "Who rises on the banks of Seine."
O'er the wide earth, on mountain and on plain.
Oh What a Wreck! How Changed in Mien and Speech!
Old Abbeys.
Old Cumberland Beggar, The.
On a Celebrated Event in Ancient History.
On a High Part of the Coast in Cumberland.
On a Portrait of the Duke of Wellington upon the Field of Waterloo, by Haydon.
On Approaching the Staub-Bach, Lauterbrunnen.
On Being Stranded near the Harbour of Boulogne.
On Entering Douglas Bay, Isle of Man.
On Hearing the "Ranz des Vaches" on the Top of the Pass of St Gothard.
On Revisiting Dunlolly Castle.
On Seeing a Needlecase in the Form of a Harp; the Work of E.M.S.
On Seeing Some Tourists of the Lakes Pass by Reading; a Practice Very Common.
On the Banks of a Rocky Stream.
On the Death of an Unfortunate Lady.
On the Death of His Majesty (George the Third).
On the Departure of Sir Walter Scott from Abbotsford, for Naples.
On the Detraction Which Followed the Publication of a Certain Poem.
On the Extinction of the Venetian Republic.
On the Final Submission of the Tyrolese.
On the Firth of Clyde.
On the Power of Sound.
On the Projected Kendal and Windermere Railway.
On the Same Occasion.
On the Same Occasion [on Seeing the Foundation Preparing for the Erection of Rydal Chapel].
On the Sight of a Manse in the South of Scotland.
On Windermere; Bowness Bay and Belle Isle.
Once I Could Hail (Howe'er Serene the Sky).
Open Prospect.
Orchard Pathway, The.
Other Benefits.
Other Influences.
Our Lady of the Snow.
Oxford, May Thirtieth, Eighteen Twenty ("Shame on this faithless heart! that could allow").
Oxford, May 30, 1820 ("Ye sacred Nurseries of blooming Youth!").
Papal Abuses.
Papal Dominion.
Parsonage in Oxfordshire, A.
Parsonage, The.
Pass of Kirkstone, The.
Passage from John Wilson's *The Angler's Tent*.
Passage from Mary Barker's *Lines Addressed to a Noble Lord* (His Lordship Will Know Why).
Pastor, The.

Pastoral Character.
Patriotic Sympathies.
Paulinus.
Pelayo.
Pelion and Ossa flourish side by side.
Persecution.
Persecution of the Scottish Covenanters.
Personal Talk.
Persuasion.
Pet Lamb, The; A Pastoral.
Peter Bell; a Tale.
Pibroch's note, discountenanced or mute.
Picture of Daniel in the Lions' Den, at Hamilton Palace.
Pilgrim's Dream; or, The Star and the Glow-Worm, The.
Pillar of Trajan, The.
Pine of Monte Mario at Rome, The.
Placard for a Poll Bearing an Old Shirt.
Place of Burial in the South of Scotland, A.
Places of Worship.
Plain of Donnerdale, The.
Plea for Authors, May, 1838, A.
Plea for the Historian.
Poems Composed or Suggested During a Tour, in the Summer of 1833.
Poet and the Caged Turtledove, The.
Poet!—He Hath Put His Heart to School, A.
Poet to His Grandchild; Sequel to "A Plea for Authors."
Poet's Dream, The.
Poet's Epitaph, A.
Point at Issue, The.
Poor Robin.
Power of Music.
Prelude; Growth of a Poet's Mind [1805 vers.], The.
Prelude; Growth of a Poet's Mind [1850 vers.], The.
Prelude, Prefixed to the Volume Entitled "Poems Chiefly of Early and Late Years."
Presentiments.
Primitive Saxon Clergy.
Primrose of the Rock, The.
Prithee, Gentle Lady, List.
Processions Suggested on a Sabbath Morning in the Vale of Chamouny.
Prophecy, A.
Prophecy February, 1807, A.
Protest against the Ballot.
Proud Were Ye, Mountains, When, in Times of Old.
Rains at length have ceased, the winds are stilled, The.
Recluse; Home at Grasmere, The *sels*.
Recollection of the Portrait of King Henry Eighth, Trinity Lodge, Cambridge.
Recovery.
Redbreast Chasing the Butterfly, The.
Redbreast, The [Suggested in a Westmoreland Cottage].
Reflections.
Regrets.
Remembrance of Collins, Composed upon the Thames near Richmond.
Repentance; A Pastoral Ballad.
Reproof.
Residence at Cambridge.
Residence in France and French Revolution.
Residence in France ("As oftentimes a river, it might seem").
Residence in France ("Even as a river,—partly (it might seem)").
Residence in London.
Resolution and Independence.
Rest and Be Thankful!
Resting-Place, The.
Retirement.
Retrospect Love of Nature Leading to Love of Mankind.
Return.
Reverie of Poor Susan, The.
Revival of Popery.
Richard I.
River Duddon [A Series of Sonnets], The.
River Eden, Cumberland, The.
Road extended o'er a heath, The.

Rob Roy's Grave.
Roman Antiquities.
Roman Antiquities Discovered at Bishopstone, Herefordshire.
Rural Architecture.
Rural Ceremony.
Rural Illusions.
Russian Fugitive, The.
Ruth [or, The Influences of Nature].
Sacheverel.
Sacrament.
Said Secrecy to Cowardice and Fraud.
Sailor's Mother, The.
St Paul's.
St Catherine of Ledbury.
Saints.
Salisbury Plain and Stonehenge.
Same, The [Eminent Reformers].
Same, The [Inside of King's College Chapel, Cambridge].
Same Subject, The [Stepping-Stones].
Same Subject, The [Dissolution of the Monasteries].
Same Subject (Continued) [Imagination and Taste, How Impaired and Restored].
Same Subject (Continued) [Imagination].
Saxon Conquest.
Saxon Monasteries, and Lights and Shades of the Religion.
Say, what is Honour?—'Tis the finest sense."
Scene in Venice.
Scene on the Lake of Brientz.
School-Time.
Scorn Not the Sonnet [Critic, You Have Frowned].
Seathwaite Chapel.
Seclusion.
September, 1815.
September, 1819 ("Departing summer hath assumed").
September, 1819 ("Sylvan slopes with corn-clad fields, The").
September, 1802. Near Dover.
September 1, 1802.
Septimi Gades.
Sequel to *Beggars* Composed Many Years After.
Seven Sisters, or, the Solitude of Binnorie, The.
She was a phantom of delight.
Sheep-Washing.
Shepherd, looking eastward softly said, The.
Shepherd, The.
Siege of Vienna Raised by John Sobieski February, 1816.
Simon Lee [the Old Huntsman].
Simplon Pass, The.
Skating.
Sky-Prospect—From the Plain of France.
Small Celandine, The.
So Fair, So Sweet, Withal So Sensitive.
Soft As a Cloud Is Yon Blue Ridge.
Solitary Reaper, The.
Solitary, The.
Somnambulist, The.
Song at the Feast of Brougham Castle upon the Restoration of Lord Clifford, the Shepherd, to the Estates and Honours of His Ancestors.
Song for the Spinning Wheel (Founded upon a Belief Prevalent among the Pastoral Vales of Westmoreland).
Song for the Wandering Jew.
Sonnet Composed at—Castle.
Sonnet in the Pass of Killicranky.
Sonnet on Milton.
Sonnet on Seeing Miss Helen Maria Williams Weep at a Tale of Distress.
Sonnet to a Picture by Lucca Giordano in the Mureo Borbonico at Naples.
Sonnet (To an Octogenarian).
Sonnet Translated from the Italian of Milton.
Sonnet: "Why should we weep or mourn, Angelic boy."
Sonnet Written by Mr — Immediately after the Death of His Wife.
Sonnets upon the Punishment of Death.

Source of the Danube, The.
Spanish Guerillas 1811.
Sparrow's Nest, The.
Sponsors.
Squib on Colonel Evans, A.
Stanzas Composed in the Simplon Pass.
Stanzas Suggested in a Steamboat off Saint Bees' Head, on the Coast of Cumberland.
Stanzas Written in My Pocket-Copy of Thomson's "Castle of Indolence."
Star-Gazers.
Stars Are Mansions Built by Nature's Hand, The.
Steamboats, Viaducts and Railways.
Stepping-Stones, The.
Stepping Westward.
Stray Pleasures.
Struggle of the Britons against the Barbarians.
Suggested at Tyndrum in a Storm.
Suggested by a Picture of the Bird of Paradise.
Suggested by a View from an Eminence in Inglewood Forest.
Suggested by Mr W. Westall's Views of the Caves, etc., in Yorkshire.
Suggested by the Foregoing [Monument of Mrs Howard].
Suggested by the View of Lancaster Castle (on the Road from the South).
Summer Vacation.
Sun has long been set, The.
Surprised by Joy [Impatient as the Wind].
Sweet was the walk along the narrow lane.
Tables Turned, The.
Temptations from Roman Refinements.
Thanksgiving after Childbirth.
There is a bondage worse, far worse, to bear.
There is a little unpretending Rill.
There Is a Pleasure in Poetic Pains.
There is an Eminence,—of these our hills.
There Was a Boy.
There was a spot.
This Lawn, a Carpet All Alive.
Thorn, The.
Those words were uttered as in pensive mood.
Though narrow be that old Man's cares, and near.
Though Pulpits and the Desk May Fail.
Though the Bold Wings of Poesy Affect.
Thought[s] of a Briton on the Subjugation of Switzerland.
Thoughts on the Seasons.
Thoughts Suggested the Day Following, on the Banks of Nith, near the Poet's Residence.
Three Cottage Girls, The.
Three Graves, The.
Through Cumbrian wilds, in many a mountain cove.
Tinker, The.
'Tis He Whose Yester-Evening's High Disdain.
'Tis said that some have died for love.
To ———: " 'Wait, prithee, wait!' this answer Lesbia threw."
To ———: "Happy the feeling from the bosom thrown."
To ———: "If these brief Records, by the Muses' art."
To ———: "Let other bards of angels sing."
To ———: "Look at the fate of summer flowers."
To ———: "O dearer far than light and life are dear."
To —, in Her Seventieth Year.
To — Upon the Birth of Her First-Born Child, March, 1833.
To—, on Her First Ascent to the Summit of Helvellyn.
To a Butterfly *sels*.
To a Butterfly.
To a Child [Written in Her Album].
To a Friend.
To a Lady.

To a Painter ("All praise the Likeness by thy skill portrayed").
To a Painter ("Though I beheld at first with blank surprise").
To a Sexton.
To a Sky-Lark.
To a Skylark ("Ethereal minstrel! pilgrim of the sky").
To a Snow-Drop.
To a Young Lady Who Had Been Reproached for Taking Long Walks in the Country.
To B.R. Haydon.
To B.R. Haydon, On Seeing His Picture of Napoleon Buonaparte on the Island of St Helena.
To Coleridge in Sicily.
To Cordelia M———.
To Enterprise.
To H. C.[, Six Years Old].
To Henry Crabbe Robinson.
To I.F.
To Joanna.
To Lady Beaumont.
To Lucca Giordano.
To M. H.
To May.
To Melpomene.
To My Sister.
To Rotha Q—.
To S.H.
To Sleep ("Flock of sheep that leisurely pass by, A").
To Sleep ("Fond words have oft been spoken to thee, sleep!").
To Sleep ("O gentle Sleep! do they belong to thee").
To the Author's Portrait.
To the Clouds.
To the Cuckoo.
To the Daisy ("Bright Flower! whose home is everywhere").
To the Daisy ("In youth from rock to rock I went").
To the Daisy ("Sweet Flower! belike one day to have").
To the Earl of Lonsdale.
To the Evening Star over Grasmere Water.
To the Highland Girl of Inversneyde.
To the Lady E.B. and the Hon. Miss P.
To the Lady Fleming on Seeing the Foundation Preparing for the Erection of Rydal Chapel, Westmoreland.
To the Lady Mary Lowther.
To the Memory of Raisley Calvert.
To the Men of Kent (October, 1803).
To the Moon (Composed by the Seaside,—on the Coast of Cumberland).
To the Moon (Rydal).
To the Pennsylvanians.
To the Planet Venus.
To the Planet Venus, an Evening Star.
To the Poet, John Dyer.
To the Rev. Christopher Wordsworth, D.D., Master of Harrow School.
To the Rev. Dr Wordsworth (with the Sonnets to the River Duddon, and Other Poems in This Collection, 1820).
To the River Derwent.
To the River Greta, near Keswick.
To the Same Flower [The Daisy].
To the Same Flower [The Small Celandine].
To the Small Celandine.
To the Sons of Burns, after Visiting the Grave of Their Father.
To the Spade of a Friend (An Agriculturist).
To the Torrent at the Devil's Bridge, North Wales, 1824.
To the Utilitarians.
To Thomas Clarkson, on the Final Passing of the Bill for the Abolition of the Slave Trade. March, 1807.
To Toussaint L'Ouverture.
Town of Schwytz, The.
Tradition.
Tradition of Oker Hill in Darley Dale, Derbyshire, A.

Translation of a Celebrated Greek Song.
Translation of the Bible.
Transubstantiation.
Travelling.
Trepidation of the Druids.
Triad, The.
Tributary Stream.
Tribute to the Memory of the Same Dog.
Troilus and Cresida.
Trosachs, The.
Troubles of Charles the First.
Tuft of Primroses, The.
Two April Mornings, The.
Two Epigrams on Byron's *Cain*.
Two Thieves, The; or, the Last Stage of Avarice.
Tynwald Hill.
Types and Symbols of Eternity.
Uncertainty.
Unremitting Voice of Nightly Streams, The.
Upon a Portrait.
Upon Perusing the "Epistle [To Sir George Howland Beaumont"] Thirty Years after Its Composition.
Upon seeing a Coloured Drawing of the Bird of Paradise in an Album.
Upon the Late General Fast. March, 1832.
Upon the Same Event.
Upon the Sight of a Beautiful Picture.
Upon the Sight of the Portrait of a Female Friend.
Vale of Esthwaite, The.
Valedictory Sonnet.
Vaudois, The.
Vaudracour and Julia.
Vernal Ode.
View from the Top of Black Comb.
Virgin, The.
Visitation of the Sick.
Volant Tribe of Bards on Earth Are Found, A.
Waggoner, The.
Waldenses.
Walton's Book of Lives.
Wanderer, The.
Wanderer Recalls the Past, The.
Wansfell! This Household Has a Favoured Lot.
Warning, The.
Wars of York and Lancaster.
Water Fowl.
Waterfall and the Eglantine, The.
We Are Seven.
We Poets in Our Youth.
Weak is the will of man, his judgement blind
Western clouds a deepening gloom display, The.
Westmoreland Girl, The.
What Heavenly Smiles! O Lady Mine.
What if our numbers barely could defy.
What is it that tells my soul the Sun is setting?
When Haughty Expectations Prostrate Lie.
When I have borne in memory what has tamed.
When Philoctetes in the Lemnian Isle.
When Severn's Sweeping Flood Had Overthrown.
When slow from pensive twilight's latest gleams.
When, to the attractions of the busy world.
Where lies the land to which your Ship must go?
Where Lies the Truth? Has Man in Wisdom's Creed.
While Anna's Peers and Early Playmates Tread.
While Beams of Orient Light Shoot Wide and High.
Whirl-blast from behind the hill, A.
White Doe of Rylstone, The; or, The Fate of the Nortons.
Who but Is Pleased to Watch the Moon on High.
Who fancied what a pretty sight.
Why Art Thou Silent [Is Thy Love a Plant].
Why, Minstrel, These Untuneful Murmurings.

Wicliffe.
Widow on Windmere Side, The.
Wild Duck's Nest, The.
William the Third.
Winter's Evening, A.
Wishing-Gate Destroyed, The.
Wishing-Gate, The.
With a Small Present.
With how sad steps, O Moon, thou climb'st the sky.
With Ships the sea was sprinkled far and nigh.
Wordsworth Reading Chaucer.
Wordsworth Skates on Esthwaite Water.
World is too much with us; late and soon, The.
Wren's Nest, A.
Written after the Death of Charles Lamb.
Written in a Blank Leaf of MacPherson's *Ossian*.
Written in a Grotto.
Written in Germany on One of the Coldest Days of the Century.
Written in London, September, 1802.
Written in March [While Resting on the Bridge at the Foot of Brother's Water].
Written in Mrs Field's Album opposite a Pen-and-Ink Sketch in the Manner of a Rembrandt Etching Done by Edmund Field.
Written in the Strangers' Book at "The Station," Opposite Bowness.
Written in Very Early Youth.
Written upon a Blank Leaf in "The Compleat Angler."
Written with a Pencil upon a Stone in the Wall of the House (an Out-House), on the Island at Grasmere.
Written with a Slate Pencil on a Stone, on the Side of the Mountain of Black Comb.
Written with a Slate Pencil upon a Stone, the Largest of a Heap Lying near a Deserted Quarry, upon One of the Islands at Rydal.
Yarrow Revisited.
Yarrow Unvisited [1803].
Yarrow Visited [September, 1814].
Yes, it was the mountain Echo.
Yes! Thou Art Fair, Yet Be Not Moved.
Yew-Trees.
Young England—What Is Then Become of Old.
Young Wordsworth's London, The.
Translations, Coauthored Poems, etc.:
3.13: Translation of Horace's Ode III, xiii.
Aeneid [*or Eneados, Aeneis*], The *sels*.
All breathed in silence, and intensely gazed.
And sweet it is to see in summer time.
Arms, and the Man I sing, the first who bore.
Barberry-Tree, The.
Camoëns, he the accomplished and the good.
Canterbury Tales, The *sels.*
Carmina *sels.*
Come, gentle sleep, death's image though thou art.
Cottager to Her Infant, (By My Sister), The.
Death of a Starling, The.
Destined to war from very infancy.
Georgics *sels.*
Grateful is Sleep, my life in stone bound fast.
Lesbia.
Maniple's Tale—A Modernization, The.
No mortal object did these eyes behold.
Not without heavy grief of heart did He.
Now when the Gods had crushed the Asian State.
O flower of all that springs from gentle blood.
O Lelius, beauteous flower of gentleness.
O Thou who movest onward with a mind.
Odes *sels.*
Orlando Furioso *sels.*
Orlando who great length of time had been.
Orpheus and Eurydice.
Pause, courteous Spirit!—Baldi supplicates.
Perhaps some needful service of the State.

Prioress' Tale—A Modernization, The.
Rid of a vexing and a heavy load.
Septimius and Acme.
She who to lift her heavy eyes had tried.
Sonnet: "If grief dismiss me not to them that rest."
There never breathed a man who, when his life.
This scarcely uttered they advance, and straight.
To the grove, the meadow, the well.
To the Supreme Being.
Torquato Tasso rests within this tomb.
Translation of Virgil's Georgic IV. 511–15.
True it is that Ambrosio Salinero.
Voice from the Side of Etna, The; or, the Mad Monk.
Weep not, belovèd Friends! nor let the air.
Well-nigh the voyage now is overpast.
Yes! hope may with my strong desire keep pace.

Wright, Charles (b. 1935)
Arkansas Traveller.
Ars Poetica.
Bar Giamaica, 1959-60.
Bicoastal Journal.
California Dreaming.
California Spring.
Called Back.
Childhood's Body.
China Journal.
Chinese Journal.
Composition in Grey and Pink.
Cryopexy.
Dead Color.
December Journal.
Dog Day Vespers.
Dog Yoga.
Driving through Tennessee.
Driving to Passalacqua, 1960.
Gate City Breakdown.
George Trakl Journal.
Hawaii Dantesca.
Holy Thursday.
Homage to Cesare Pavese.
Homage to Claude Lorrain.
Homage to Paul Cézanne.
Italian Days.
Journal of English Days, A.
Journal of One Significant Landscape, A.
Journal of Southern Rivers, A.
Journal of the Year of the Ox, A.
Journal of Three Questions, A.
Journal of True Confessions, A.
Laguna Blues.
Laguna Dantesca.
Landscape with Seated Figure and Olive Trees.
Language Journal.
Last Journal.
Light Journal.
Local Journal.
Lonesome Pine Special.
Looking at Pictures.
Lost Bodies.
Lost Souls.
Mantova.
March Journal.
May Journal.
Monastery at VrLOWSCARONac, The.
Mount Caribou at Night.
New Year's Eve, 1979.
Night Journal.
Night Journal II.
October.
Other Side of the River, The.
Portrait of the Artist with Hart Crane.
Portrait of the Artist with Li Po.
Primitive Journal.
Primitive Journal II.
Roma I.
Roma II.
Saturday Morning Journal.
Self-Portrait ("In Murray, Kentucky, I lay once").
Self-Portrait ("Pictures in the air have few visitors, The").

Self-Portrait ("Charles on the Trevisan, night bridge").
Self-Portrait ("Marostica, Val di Ser. Bassano del Grappa").
Self-Portrait ("Someday they'll find me out, and my lavish hands").
Silent Journal.
Southern Cross, The.
Spring Abstract.
T'ang Notebook.
Three Poems for the New Year *sels.*
Three Poems for the New Year [1].
Three Poems for the New Year [2].
Three Poems for the New Year [3].
Three Poems of Departure.
To Giacomo Leopardi in the Sky.
Two Stories.
Vesper Journal.
Virginia Reel.
Yard Journal.

Wright, James (1927–80)
Accusation, The.
Alarm, The.
All the Beautiful are Blameless.
American Twilights, 1957.
American Wedding.
Angel, The.
Arrangements with Earth for Three Dead Friends.
Arriving in the Country Again.
As I Step over a Puddle at the End of Winter, I Think of an Ancient Chinese Governor.
Assignation, The.
At the Executed Murderer's Grave.
At the Slackening of the Tide.
At Thomas Hardy's Birthplace, 1953.
Autumn Begins in Martins Ferry, Ohio.
Autumnal.
Before a Cashier's Window in a Department Store.
Beginning.
Blessing, A.
Blue Teal's Mother.
Breath of Air, A.
Brush Fire.
But Only Mine.
By a Lake in Minnesota.
Centenary Note: Inscribed to Little Crow, Leader of the Sioux Rebellion in Minnesota, 1862, A.
Christmas Greeting, A.
Cold Divinities, The.
Come Forth.
Complaint.
Confession to J. Edgar Hoover.
Depressed by a Book of Bad Poetry, I Walk toward an Unused Pasture and Invite the Insects to Join Me.
Devotions.
Dog in a Cornfield.
Dream of Burial, A.
Echo for the Promise of Georg Trakl's Life.
Eclogue at Nash's Grove.
Eisenhower's Visit to Franco, 1959.
Elegy for the Poet Morgan Blum, An.
Elegy in a Firelit Room.
Eleutheria.
Erinna to Sappho.
Evening.
Father.
Fear Is What Quickens Me.
Fishermen, The.
Fit against the Country, A.
For the Marsh's Birthday.
From a Bus Window in Central Ohio, Just before a Thunder Shower.
Frontier, The.
Gambling in Stateline, Nevada.
Gemela.
Gesture by a Lady with an Assumed Name, A.
Ghost, The.
Girl in a Window, A.
Goodbye to the Poetry of Calcium.
Having Lost My Sons, I Confront the Wreckage of the Moon: Christmas, 1960.

Horse, The.
How My Fever Left.
Humming a Tune for an Old Lady in West
   Virginia.
I Am a Sioux Brave, He Said in
   Minneapolis.
I Try to Waken and Greet the World Once
   Again.
I Was Afraid of Dying.
Idea of the Good, The.
In a Viennese Cemetery.
In Fear of Harvests.
In Memory of a Spanish Poet.
In Memory of Leopardi.
In Memory of the Horse David, Who Ate
   One of my Poems.
In Ohio.
In Response to a Rumor that the Oldest
   Whorehouse in Wheeling, West Virginia,
   Has Been Condemned.
In Shame and Humiliation.
In Terror of Hospital Bills.
In the Cold House.
In the Face of Hatred.
Inscription for the Tank.
Jewel, The.
Katy Did.
Lament for My Brother on a Hayrake.
Larry.
Late November in a Field.
Learning from MacDiarmid.
Life, The.
Lifting Illegal Nets by Flashlight.
Lights in the Hallway, The.
Listening to the Mourners.
Little Girl on Her Way to School, A.
Living by the Red River.
Lying in a Hammock at William Duffy's
   Farm in Pine Island, Minnesota.
Mad Fight Song for William S. Carpenter,
   1966, A.
Many of Our Waters: Variaitons on a Poem
   by a Black Child.
March.
Mary Bly.
Mesage Hidden in an Empty Wine Bottle that
   I Threw into a Gully of Maple Trees One
   Night at an Indecent Hour, A.
Message from the Mountain Pool Where the
   Deer Come Down, A.
Milkweed.
Miners.
Minneapolis Poem, The.
Moon.
Moral Poem Freely Accepted from Sappho,
   A.
Morality of Poetry, The.
Morning Hymn to a Dark Girl.
Mutterings over the Crib of a Deaf Child.
My Grandmother's Ghost.
Northern Pike.
Note Left in Jimmy Leonard's Shack, A.
Offense, The.
Offering for Mr. Bluehart, An.
Old Age Compensation.
Old Man Drunk.
On Minding One's Own Business.
On the Skeleton of a Hound.
On the Way to the Planetarium.
Outside Fargo, North Dakota.
Paul.
Poem about Breasts, A.
Poem about George Doty in the Death
   House, A.
Poem by Garnie Braxton, A.
Poem for Kathleen Ferrier.
Poem Written under an Archway in a
   Discontinued Railroad Station, Fargo,
   North Dakota, A.
Poems to a Brown Cricket.
Poor Washed Up by Chicago Winter, The.
Prayer in My Sickness, A.
Prayer to Escape from the Market Place, A.
Prayer to the Lord Ramakrishna, A.
Presentation of Two Birds to My Son, A.
Quail, The.
Quest, The.

Rain.
Red Jacket's Grave.
Refusal, The.
Revelation, The.
RIP.
River Down Home, The.
Saint Judas.
Sappho.
Seasonless, The.
Secret Gratitude, A.
Shadow and the Real, The.
She Hid in the Trees from the Nurses.
Sitting in a Small Screenhouse on a Summer
   Morning.
Small Blue Heron, The.
Small Frogs Killed on the Highway.
Snowstorms in the Midwest.
So She Said.
Song for the Middle of the Night, A.
Sparrows in a Hillside Drift.
Speak.
Spring Images.
Stages on a Journey Westward.
Summer Memory in the Crowded City, A.
Sun Tan at Dusk.
Three Sentences for a Dead Swan.
Three Stanzas From Goethe.
Three Steps to the Graveyard.
To a Dead Drunk.
To a Defeated Savior.
To a Friendly Dun.
To a Fugitive.
To a Hostess Saying Goodnight.
To a Troubled Friend.
To Flood Stage Again.
To Harvey, Who Traced the Circulation.
To the August Fallen.
To the Evening Star: Central Minnesota.
To the Muse.
To the Ohio.
To the Poets in New York.
Today I Was So Happy, So I Made this
   Poem.
Trouble.
Trying to Pray.
Twilights.
Two Hangovers.
Two Horses Playing in the Orchard.
Two Poems about President Harding.
Two Postures beside a Fire.
Two Spring Charms.
Undermining of the Defense Economy, The.
Way to Make a Living, A.
What the Earth Asked Me.
Willy Lyons.
Winter Day in Ohio, A.
Witches Waken the Natural World in Spring.
Written in a Copy of Swift's Poems, for
   Wayne Burns.
Youth.
Translations, Coauthored Poems, etc.:
Anacreon's Grave.
Big People, The.
De Profundis.
Divine Falling of Leaves, A.
Down to the Dregs.
Dreaming.
Eternal Dice, The.
Girl Walking into a Shadow, A.
Heights of Macchu Picchu, III, The.
I am Freed.
I Want to Sleep.
Life.
Love Song to a Morning.
Moguer.
Nature Alive.
Not in Marble Palaces.
On the City Ramparts of Cádiz.
Our Daily Bread.
Pretty Redhead, The.
Rats, The.
Rose of the Sea.
Rosebushes.
Sleep.
Some Beasts.
Ten Short Poems.
Trumpets.

White Rose.
Winter Night, A.

Wroth [*or* Wroath], Mary Sidney, Countess of
   Montgomery (1587?–1651?)
Crowne of Sonetts Dedicated to Love, A.
Dialogue: Sheapherd, and Sheapherdess.
Lindamira's Complaint.
Love's Victorie.
Pamphilia to Amphilanthus.
Song 1: "Spring now come att last, The."
Song 1: "Sweet lett mee injoye thy sight."
Song 2: "All night I weep[e], all day I cry,
   Ay me[e]."
Song 2: "Sweet Silvia in a shadie wood."
Song 3: "Come merry spring delight us."
Song 3: "Stay, my thoughts, do nott aspire."
Song 4: "Lovers learne to speake butt
   truthe."
Song 4: "Sweetest love returne againe."
Song 5: "Time only cause of my unrest."
Song 6: "You happy blessed eyes."
Song 7: "Sorrow, I yeeld, and grieve that I
   did miss."
Song: "Beeing past the paines of love."
Song: "Birds doe sing, day doth apeere,
   The."
Song: "Deerest if I by my deserving."
Song: "Fairest, and still truest eyes."
Song: "Gon is my joy while heere I
   mourne."
Song: "I, that ame of all most crost."
Song: "Love a child is ever criing [*or*
   crying]."
Song: "Love as well can make abiding."
Song: "Love what art thou? A vaine
   thought."
Song: "O[h] me[e] the time is [*or* has] come
   to part."
Song: "Say Venus how long have I lov'd,
   and serv'd you heere?"
Song: "Springing time of my first loving,
   The."
Song: "Who can blame mee if I love?"
Sonnet 1: "Deare eyes farewell, my Sunne
   once, now my end."
Sonnet 1: "In night yett may wee see some
   kind of light."
Sonnet 1: "In this strang labourinth how shall
   I turne?"
Sonnet 1: "My hart is lost, what can I now
   expect."
Sonnet 1: "When night's [*or* nights] black
   mantle could most darknes prove."
Sonnet 2: "Deare eyes how well (indeed) you
   doe adorne."
Sonnet 2: "Is to leave all, and take the thread
   of love."
Sonnet 2: "Late in the Forest I did Cupid
   see."
Sonnet 2: "Love like a jugler, comes to play
   his prise."
Sonnet 2: "O deadly rancour to a constant
   heart."
Sonnet 3: "His flames ar joyes, his bands
   true lovers might."
Sonnet 3: "Juno still jealouse of her husband
   Jove."
Sonnet 3: "Most blessed Night, the happy
   time for love."
Sonnet 3: "Surgeon I would aske, but 'tis too
   late."
Sonnet 3: "Yett is ther hope: Then Love butt
   play thy part."
Sonnet 4: "And bee in his brave court a
   gloriouse light."
Sonnet 4: "Cruell suspition, O! bee now att
   rest."
Sonnet 4: "Forbeare darke night, my joyes
   now budd againe."
Sonnet 4: "When I beeheld the Image of my
   deere."
Sonnet 5: "And burne, yett burning you will
   love the smart."
Sonnet 5: "Can pleasing sight, misfortune
   ever bring?"
Sonnet 5: "How many nights have I with
   paine indur'd."

Sonnet 5: "Leave me vain Hope, too long thou hast posses[s]t."

Sonnet 5: "Like to huge clowds of smoke which well may hide."

Sonnet 6: "Ô strive nott still to heape disdaine on mee."

Sonnet 6: "Hee may owr profitt, and out Tuter prove."

Sonnet 6: "My pain[e], still smothered [or smother'd] in my grievèd bre[a]st."

Sonnet 6: "O! that noe day would ever more appeere."

Sonnet 6: "Though you forsake me, yet alas permit."

Sonnet 7: "End fond jealousie alas I know, An."

Sonnet 7: "How blest bee they then, who his favors prove."

Sonnet 7: "Love leave to urge, thou know'st thou hast the hand."

Sonnet 7: "No time, noe roome, noe thought, or writing can."

Sonnet 7: "Some doe, perhaps, both wrong my love, and care."

Sonnet 8: "Hee that shunns love doth love him self the less."

Sonnet 8: "How gloewoorme like the sunn doth now apeere."

Sonnet 8: "Led by the powre of griefe, to waylings brought."

Sonnet 8: "Poore Love in chaines, and fetters like a thiefe."

Sonnet 9: "Be[e] you all pleased [or pleas'd]? your pleasures grieve not[t] me[e]."

Sonnet 9: "But wher they may returne with honors grace."

Sonnet 9: "My muse now hapy, lay thy self to rest."

Sonnet 9: "'Pray doe nott use thes words I must bee gone."

Sonnet 10: "Bee from court of Love, and reason torne."

Sonnet 10: "Folly would needs make mee a lover bee."

Sonnet 10: "Weary traveller who tired sought, The."

Sonnet 11: "Unprofitably pleasing, and unsound."

Sonnet 11: "You endless torments that my rest opress."

Sonnet 12: "Bee given to him who triumphs in his right."

Sonnet 12: "Cloy'd with the torments of a tedious night."

Sonnet 13: "Deare fammish nott what you your self gave food."

Sonnet 13: "Free from all fogs butt shining faire, and cleere."

Sonnet 14: "Am I thus conquered? [or conquer'd]? have I lost the powers."

Sonnet 14: "Except my hart which you beestow'd before."

Sonnet 15: "Truly poore Night thou wellcome art to mee."

Sonnet 16: "Sleepe fy possess mee nott, nor doe nott fright."

Sonnet 17: "Sweet shades why doe you seeke to give delight."

Sonnet 18: "Which should I better like of, day, or night."

Sonnet 19: "Come darkest night, be[e]coming sorrow best."

Sonnet 20: "Sunn which glads, the earth att his bright sight, The."

Sonnet 21: "When last I saw thee, I did not[t] thee see."

Sonnet 22: "Like to the Indians, scorched with the sun[ne]."

Sonnet 23: "When every one to pleasing pastime hies."

Sonnet 24: "Once did I heere an aged father say."

Sonnet 25: "Poore eyes bee blind, the light behold noe more."

Sonnet 26: "Deare cherish this, and with it[t] my soules will."

Sonnet 27: "Fie [or Fy] tedious Hope, why do[e] you still rebel[l]?"

Sonnet 28: "Griefe, killing griefe: have nott my torments binn."

Sonnet 29: "Fly hence O! joy noe longer heere abide."

Sonnet 30: "You blessed shades, which give mee silent rest."

Sonnet 31: "After long trouble in a taedious way."

Sonnet 32: "How fast thou fliest, O Time, on loves swift wings."

Sonnet 33: "How many eyes poore Love hast thou to guard."

Sonnet 34: "Take heed mine eyes, how you your lookes doe cast."

Sonnet 35: "False [or Faulce] hope which feeds but[t] to destroy, and spill."

Sonnet 36: "How well poore hart thou wittnes canst I love."

Sonnet 37: "Night, welcome art thou to my mind destrest."

Sonnet 38: "What pleasure can a bannish'd creature have."

Sonnet 39: "Iff I were giv'n to mirthe 't'wowld be more cross."

Sonnet 40: "Itt is nott love which you poore fooles do deeme."

Sonnet 41: "You blessed starrs which doe heavns glory show."

Sonnet 42: "If ever love had force in huma[i]ne brest?"

Sonnet 43: "O dearest eyes the lights, and guids of love."

Sonnet 44: "How fast thou hast'st (O spring) with sweetest speed."

Sonnet 45: "Good now bee still, and doe nott mee torment."

Sonnet 46: "Love, thou hast all, for now thou hast mee made."

Sonnet 47: "O stay mine eyes, shed nott thes fruitles tears."

Sonnet 48: "How like a fire doth love increase in me[e]."

Sonnet: "Can the lov'd Image of thy deerest face."

Sonnet: "Eyes, can you tell mee wher my hart remaines?"

Sonnet: "Fly traiter joye whose end brings butt dispaire."

Sonnet: "Lett griefe as farr bee from your deerest brest."

Sonnet: "O Memory [or Memorie], could I but loose thee now."

Sonnet: "Oft did I wounder why the sweets of Love."

Sonnet: "Unquiet griefe search farder, in my hart."

see also Pamphilia to Amphilanthus.

Wyatt, Sir Thomas (1503?–1542)

Absence, alas, / Causeth me pass.

Accused though I be without desert.

After great storms the calm returns.

Against the rock I climb, both high and hard.

Ah, my heart, ah, what aileth thee.

Ah, Robin, / Jolly Robin.

Alas, dear heart! what hap [or hope] had I.

Alas, Fortune, what aileth thee.

Alas, madam[e], for stealing [or stelying] of a kiss [or kysse].

Alas! my dear, the word thou spakest.

Alas, poor man, what hap have I.

Alas, the grief and deadly wo[e]ful smart[!].

All heavy minds.

All in thy sight my life doth whole depend.

All ye that know of care and heaviness.

Alone musing, / Remembering.

And if an eye may save or slay.

And wilt [or wylt] thou le[a]ve me thus?

Answer, The.

Answer that ye made to me, my dear, The [or Th'].

Argument, Th'.

As power and wit will me assist.

At last withdraw your cruelty.

At mo[o]st mischief.

Avising the bright beams of these fair eyes.

Ballad of Will, The.

Because I have thee still kept from lies and blame.

Behold, love, thy power how she despiseth!

Being as none is, I do complain.

Blame not my lute, for he must sound [or sssnd or Sownde].

But sithens you it assay to kill.

By bolstered words I am borne in hand.

Caesar, when that the traitor of Egypt.

Comfort at hand! Pluck up thy heart.

Comfort thyself, my wo[e]ful heart.

Complaining, alas, without redress.

Deem as ye list. Upon good cause.

Defamed guiltiness by silence unkempt.

Desire, alas, my master and my foe.

Desire to sorrow doth me constrain.

Dido am I, the founder first of Carthage.

Disdain me not without desert.

Disdain not, madam, on him to look.

Divers[e] [or Dyvers] doth[e] use, as I have heard and kno[w].

Do way, do way, ye little wily prat!

Double, diverse, sullen, and strange.

Driven by desire, I did this deed.

Driven by desire to set affection.

Driving to desire, adread also to dare.

Duress of pains and grievous smart.

Each man me telleth I change most my device [or devise].

Enemy [or en'my] of life, decayer of all kind, The [or Th'].

Epitaph of Sir Thomas Gravener, [Knight], An.

Face that should content me wonders [or wondrous] well, A.

Farewell, all my welfare.

Farewell, love, and all thy law[e]s forever.

Farewell, the reign of cruelty!

Flaming sighs that boil within my breast, The.

For shamefast harm of great and hateful need.

For to love her for her looks lovely.

For want of [or I] will in woe I plain.

Forget not yet the tried intent.

Fortune doth frown.

Fortune, what aileth thee.

From these high [or hie] hill[e]s as when a spring doth fall.

From thought to thought, from hill to hill love doth me lead.

Fruit of all the service that I serve, The.

Full well it may be seen.

Furious in his raging ire, The.

Give place all ye that doth rejoice.

Go, burning sighs, unto the frozen heart.

Greeting to you both in hearty wise.

Grudge on who list, this is my lot.

Had I wist that now I wot.

Hap happeth oft unlooked for.

Hate whom ye list for I care not.

He is not de[a]d that sometime [or somtyme] hath a fall.

Heart and service to you proffered, The.

Heart oppressed [or oppress'd] with desperate thought.

Heaven and earth, and all that hear me plain.

Help[e] me to seek [or seke] for I lost it there.

Horrible of hue, hideous to behold.

How should I / Be so pleasant.

I abide and abide and better abide.

I am as I am and so will I be.

I am ready and ever will be.

I have been a lover.

I have sought long with steadfastness.

I know not where my heavy sighs to hide.

I lead a life unpleasant, nothing glad.

I love, loved, and so doth she.

I might by no means surmise.

I must go walk[e] the woods so wild.

I see my plaint with open ears.

I see that chance hath chosen me.

I see the change from that that was.

If amorous faith in heart unfeigned.

If chance assigned [or assign'd].

If ever man might him avaunt.
If fancy [or fansy] would favour.
If I might have at mine own will.
If in the world there be more woe.
If it be so that I forsake thee.
If thou wilt mighty be, flee from the rage.
If waker care, if sudden [or sodayne] pale
  colo[u]r.
If with complaint the pain might be
  expressed.
In aeternum I was once determed.
In court to serve, decked with fresh array.
In doubtful breast whilst motherly Pity.
In faith I not [well] what to say.
In mourning wise since daily I increase.
In wilful riches I have found poverty.
Iopas's Song.
Is it possible.
It burneth yet, alas, my heart's desire.
It may be good, like it who list.
It was my choice, it was no chance.
Joy so short alas, the pain so near, The.
Knot which first my heart did strain, The.
Lady gave me a gift she had not, A.
Lament my loss[e], my labo[u]r, and my pain
  [or payne].
Like as the bird in the cage enclosed.
Like as the swan towards her death.
Like as the wind with raging blast.
Live thou gladly if so thou may.
Lively sparks that issue from those eyes, The.
Lo, how I seek and sue to have.
Lo, what it is to love!
Longer to muse.
Longer to trow ye.
Loss is small to lose such one, The.
Love and Fortune and my mind, rememb'rer.
Love hath again.
Love whom ye list and spare not.
Lucks, my fair falcon, and your fellows all.
Madam, I you require.
Madam, withouten many words.
Marvel [or Marvaill] no more although [or
  all tho].
Me list no more to sing.
Might I as well within my song belay.
Mine [or Myne] own[e] John Poyntz, since
  [or sins] ye delight to know.
Mistrustful minds be moved.
Most wretched heart, most miserable.
Mourning my heart doth sore oppress.
My heart I gave thee not to do it pain.
My hope, alas, hath me abused.
My love is like unto th'eternal fire.
My love took scorn my service to retain.
My lute, awake! Perform [the] last.
My mother's maids [or maydes] when they
  did sew [or sowe] and spin [or spynne].
My pen, take pain a little space.
My sweet, alas, forget me not.
Nature that gave the bee so feat a grace.
Now all of change.
Now must I learn to feign.
Now must I le[a]rn[e] to live [or lyve] at
  rest.
O, cruel heart, where is thy faith?
O goodly hand.
O miserable sorrow withouten cure!
O, what undeserved cruelty.
Of Carthage he, that worthy warrior.
Of purpose Love chose first for to be blind.
Once [or Ons], as methought, Fortune me
  kissed [or kist or kyst].
Once in your grace I know I was.
Pain of all pain, the most grievous pain.
Pass forth, my wonted cries.
Patience, for I have wrong.
Patience for my device.
Patience of all my smart.
Patience though I have not.
Penitential Psalms *sels.*
Perdy [or Perdie or Perdye], I said[e] it [or
  yt] not.
Pillar [or Piller] perished [or pearisht] is
  whe[a]rto I le[a]nt, The.
Plain ye, mine eyes. Accompany my heart.
Process of time worketh such wonder.

Prologue: "Love, to give law unto his subject
  hearts."
Prove whether I do change, my dear.
Quondam was I in my lady's grace.
Resound my voice [or voyse], ye woods [or
  wodes] that hear [or here] me plain.
Restful place, reviver of my smart, The.
Right true it is and said full yore ago.
Satires *sels.*
Shall she never out of my mind.
She sat and sewed that hath done me the
  wrong.
She that should most, perceiveth least.
Sighs are my food, drink are my tears.
Since love is such that, as ye wot.
Since Love will needs that I shall love.
Since so ye please to hear me plain.
Since that my language without eloquence.
Since ye delight to know.
Since you will needs that I shall sing.
Sith I myself displease thee.
Sith it is so that I am thus refused.
So unwarely was never no man caught.
Sometime I fled the fire that me brent.
Sometime I sigh, sometime I sing.
Speak thou and speed, where will or power
  ought [or aught] help'th.
Spending hand that alway poureth [or
  powreth] out [or owte], A.
Spite hath no power to make me sad.
Spite of their spite which they in vain.
Stand whoso list upon the slipper top.
Such hap as I am happed in.
Such is the course that nature's kind hath
  wrought.
Such vain thought as wonted to mislead me.
Suffering in sorrow, in hope to attain.
Sufficed not, madame, that you did tear.
Tagus farewell, that westward with thy
  streams.
Take heed betime, lest ye be spied.
Tangled [or Tanglid] I was [or was I] in [or
  yn] Love's snare.
That time that mirth did steer my ship.
There was never file half so well filed.
There was never nothing more me pained [or
  payned].
They fle[e] from me that sometime [or
  sometyme] did me se[e]k[e].
Thou hast no faith of him that hath none.
Thou sleepest fast and I with woeful heart.
Though I cannot your cruelty constrain.
Though I myself be bridled of my mind.
Though of the sort there be that feign.
Though some do grudge to see me joy.
Though this the [or thy] port and I thy
  servant true.
Throughout the world, if it were sought.
Thy promise was to love me best.
To cause accord or to ag[g]re[e].
To make an end of all this strife.
To my mishap, alas, I find.
To rail or jest, ye know I use it not.
To seek each where where man doth live.
To wet your eye withouten tear.
To whom should I sue to ease my pain?
To wish and want and not obtain.
Unstable dream[e] [or dreme], according [or
  accordyng] to the place.
Venomous thorns that are so sharp and keen.
Venus, in sport, to please therewith her dear.
Vulcan begat me. Minerva me taught.
Wandering gadling in the summer tide, The.
Was I never yet of your love grieved.
What death is worse than this?
What means [or meaneth or menethe] this
  when I lie [or lye] alone.
What needeth these threnning words and
  wasted wind?
What no, Perdy [or Perdie or perdie][!] ye
  may be sure[!].
What rage is this? What furo[u]r of what
  kind [or kynd]?
What should I say.
What thing is that that I both have and lack.
What vaileth [or 'vaileth] truth [or trouth]?
  or by it to take pain [or payn]?

What word is that that changeth not.
What would ye more of me, your slave,
  require.
When first mine eyes did view and mark.
When that I call unto my mind.
Where shall I have at mine own will.
Who hath he[a]rd of such[e] cruelty before.
Who list his wealth and ease retain.
Who would have ever thought.
Whoso list to hunt, I know where is an hind.
Will ye see what wonders love hath wrought?
With serving still.
Within my breast I never thought it gain.
Ye know my heart, my lady dear.
Ye old mule, that thin[c]k your self so fair
  [or fayre].
You that in love find[e] luck[e] and
  [h]abunda[u]nce.
Your looks so often cast.
Translations, Coauthored Poems, etc.:
  Although thou see th'outrageous climb aloft.
  Ever mine [or myn] hap[pe] is slack and
    slo[w] in coming [or commyng].
  F[f]rom depth of[f] sin[n] and from a deep
    despair [or diepe dispaire].
  Hear my prayer, O Lord, hear my request.
  How oft have I, my dear [or dere] and
    cruel[l] foe.
  I find no peace and all my war[r] is done.
  Like to these unme[a]surable montains [or
    mountayns].
  Long[e] love that in my thought do[e]th [or
    I] harbour [or harber or harbar], The.
  Lord hear [or here] my prayer [or prayre]
    and let my cry[e] pass[e].
  Mine old dear enemy [or en'my] , my
    froward master.
  My galley [or galy] charged with
    forgetfulness.
  O happy are they that have forgiveness got.
  O Lord, as I thee have both prayed and pray.
  O Lord, since in my mouth thy mighty name.
  Psalms *sels.*
  Rue on me, Lord, for thy goodness and
    grace.
  So feeble is the thread that doth the burden
    stay.
  Some fowls there be that have so perfect
    sight.
  Sonnets to Laura *sels.*

Y

Yau, John (b. 1950)
  After Moving.
  After removing the anodized plate, the two
    electricians discover an.
  All This Changing Trouble Luck and
    Suddenness.
  Avenue of Americans.
  Bare Sheets I.
  Bare Sheets II.
  Bare Sheets III.
  Beneath sky's broken tiles, ancient barns are
    embedded in plaster.
  Blessed flagellants set forth, mounted on
    tatters of flaming horses, The.
  Box mountain of hardened tears is hoisted up
    the scaffold, two, A.
  Broken Off by the Music.
  Cameo of a Chinese Woman on Mulberry
    Street.
  Carp and Goldfish *sels.*
  Cascade.
  Casual solitude that is beyond casualness, A.
  Cenotaph of Snow.
  Certainty of being part of the atmosphere,
    The.
  Charred hansom is discovered on Bubbling
    Well Road. In the shade.
  Charred Voice of Max Ernst, The.
  Choral Amphisbaena.
  Clay Nursing Home, The.
  Confessions.
  Corpse and Mirror I *sels.*
  Corpse and Mirror II *sels.*

Corpse and Mirror III *sels.*
Counting the times as if they added up.
Dear . . .
Different Cereal, A.
Different Prince, A.
Discovery of Honey, The.
Dragon's Blood I.
Dragon's Blood II.
Dragon's Blood III.
Dragon's Blood IV.
Dream Life of a Coffin Factory in Lynn, Massachussetts, The.
Dream Report.
"E Pluribus Unum."
Electric Drills.
Engines of Gloom and Affection.
Eskimo Tales.
Eskimo Villanelle.
Flying Inland.
Genghis Chan: Private Eye I.
Genghis Chan: Private Eye II.
Genghis Chan: Private Eye III.
Genghis Chan: Private Eye IV.
Genghis Chan: Private Eye V.
Genghis Chan: Private Eye VI.
Genghis Chan: Private Eye VII.
Halfway to China.
I do not imagine anyone I know, including myself, would like to.
I learn to count without pointing at my fingers. This is Pinocchio.
If you asked.
January 18, 1979.
La Brea.
Late Night Movies I.
Late Night Movies II.
Late Night Movies III.
Late Night Movies IV.
Manhattan Miniature.
Marco Polo.
Medusa.
Missing Pages.
Modern Love.
Nantucket.
No One Ever Tried To Kiss Anna May Wong.
Noise of Life, The.
Paradise.
Picture Book.
Pieces of a piece. The face in the window larger.
Pleasures of Exile, The.
Postcards are fragments of an encyclopedia; and typical of one an- / nouncing.
Postcards from Nebraska.
Predella *sels.*
Preoella: "Blue woolen..."
Radiant Silhouette I.
Radiant Silhouette II.
Radiant Silhouette III.
Radiant Silhouette IV.
Radiant Silhouette V.
Reading of an Ever-Changing Tale, The.
Realizing that any certainty is an old one.
Recoil.
Red Fountain.
Return of the Hunters, The.
Return of Ulysses I.
Return of Ulysses II.
Rising cost of heart attacks. Different, The.
Robert Herrick.
Roof shaped like a strawberry. Hurriedly torn.
Room with open windows facing a street, A.
Rubbing her sable with long thoughtful.
Rumors.
Sam Spade Haiku.
Scenes from the Life of Boullee *sels.*
Scotch tape scars on the wall. Scared, The.
Seance Music.
Serenade: "Windows reflect the fuscous clouds."
Shanghai Shenanigans.
She descends the stairway of the last ditch beyond the horizon. I.
Sheets dangling from the line, The.
Shimmering Pediment.

Sleepness Night of Eugene Delacroix, The.
So much of the proscenium burned.
Some fish we peel back, leaving only the bones. Others devour us.
Sometimes.
Spin, Spell, Spill.
Stuffing yourself into a blizzard.
Stumbling blocks are realigned, The.
Suite of Imitations Written After Reading Translations of Poems by Li He And Li Shang-yin, A.
Telephone Call, The.
Ten Songs.
Texas Sprawl.
Their Shadows.
To the young boy standing in front of the large glass tanks, each.
Toy Trucks and Fried Rice.
Two Kinds of Song.
Two Meditations on Guanajuato *sels.*
Variations on Corpse and Mirror.
Variations on Corpse and Mirror (Second Set).
We Are All Vultures.
When a comet passes over the town, whoever sees it knows a corpse.
When one of our citizens dies, his corpse is placed in his chariot.
When one of our citizens dies, his head is cut off and placed inside.
When the movie ends and the lights come on, the audience is puzzled.
When the movie ends, the lights come on. The audience is puzzled.
When you break a mirror, you must count up the pieces to see if.
Why Did What Was When.
Without noticing the fire descending into the.
You Must Remember.
Zebra-striped pillow. The restlessness.

Yeats, William Butler (1865–1939)
Acre of Grass, An.
Adam's Curse.
After Long Silence.
Against Unworthy Praise.
All Souls' Night.
All Things Can Tempt Me.
Alternative Song for the Severed Head in "The King of the Great Clock Tower."
Among School Children.
Anashuya and Vijaya.
Ancestral Houses.
Another Song of a Fool.
Apparitions, The.
Appointment, An.
Are You Content.
Arrow, The.
At Algeciras—a Meditation upon Death.
At Galway Races.
At The Abbey Theatre.
Baile and Aillinn.
Ballad of Father Gilligan, The.
Ballad of Father O'Hart, The.
Ballad of Moll Magee, The.
Ballad of the Foxhunter, The.
Balloon of the Mind, The.
Beautiful Lofty Things.
Before the World Was Made.
Beggar to Beggar Cried.
Black Tower, The.
Blessed, The.
Blood and the Moon.
Broken Dreams.
Bronze Head, A.
Brown Penny.
Byzantium.
Cap and Bells, The.
Cat and the Moon, The.
Chambermaid's First Song, The.
Chambermaid's Second Song, The.
Choice, The.
Chosen.
Church and State.
Circus Animals' Desertion, The.
Cloak, the Boat, and the Shoes, The.
Coat, A.
Cold Heaven, The.

Collarbone [*or* Collar-Bone] of a Hare, The.
Colonel Martin.
Come Gather Round Me Parnellites.
Come Let Us Mock at the Great.
Coming of Wisdom with Time, The.
Conjunctions.
Consolation.
Coole Park and Ballylee, 1931.
Coole Park, 1929.
Countess Cathleen in Paradise, The.
Cradle Song, A: "Angels are stooping, The."
Crazed Girl, A.
Crazed Moon, The.
Crazy Jane and Jack the Journeyman.
Crazy Jane and the Bishop.
Crazy Jane Grown Old Looks at the Dancers.
Crazy Jane on God.
Crazy Jane on the Day of Judgment.
Crazy Jane Reproved.
Crazy Jane Talks with the Bishop.
Cuchulain Comforted.
Cuchulain's Fight with the Sea.
Curse of Cromwell, The.
Dancer at Cruachan and Cro-Patrick, The.
Dawn, The.
Death.
Death of the Hare, The.
Dedication to a Book of Stories Selected from the Irish Novelists.
Deep-sworn Vow, A.
Delphic Oracle upon Plotinus, The.
Demon and Beast.
Dialogue of Self and Soul, A.
Dolls, The.
Double Vision of Michael Robartes, The.
Down by the Salley Gardens.
Dream of Death, A.
Drinking Song, A.
Drunken Man's Praise of Sobriety, A.
Easter, 1916.
Ego Dominus Tuus.
Empty Cup, The.
Ephemera.
Everlasting Voices, The.
Faery Song, A.
Fallen Majesty.
Falling of the Leaves, The.
Fascination of What's Difficult, The.
Father and Child.
Fergus and the Druid.
Fiddler of Dooney, The.
First Confession, A.
First Love.
Fish, The.
Fisherman, The.
Folly of Being Comforted, The.
Fool by the Roadside, The.
For Anne Gregory.
Four Ages of Man, The.
Fragments; "Locke sank into a swoon."
Friends.
Friend's Illness, A.
Friends of his Youth, The.
From "Oedipus at Colonus."
From the "Antigone."
Ghost of Roger Casement, The.
Gift of Harun Al-Rashid, The.
Girl's Song.
Gratitude to the Unknown Instructors.
Great Day, The.
Grey Rock, The.
Gyres, The.
Happy Townland, The.
Harp of Aengus, The.
Hawk, The.
He and She.
He Bids His Beloved Be at Peace.
He Gives His Beloved Certain Rhymes.
He Hears the Cry of the Sedge.
He Mourns for the Change That Has Come upon Him and His Beloved, and Longs for the End of the World.
He Remembers Forgotten Beauty.
He Reproves the Curlew.
He Tells a Valley Full of Lovers.
He Tells of the Perfect Beauty.

He Thinks of His Past Greatness When a
    Part of the Constellations of Heaven.
He Thinks of Those Who Have Spoken Evil
    of His Beloved.
He Wishes for the Cloths of Heaven.
He Wishes His Beloved Were Dead.
Heart of the Woman, The.
Her Anxiety.
Her Dream.
Her Praise.
Her Triumph.
Her Vision in the Wood.
High Talk.
His Bargain.
His Confidence.
His Dream.
His Memories.
His Phoenix.
His Wildness.
Host of the Air, The.
Hosting of the Sidhe, The.
Hound Voice.
Hour before Dawn, The.
Human Dignity.
I Am of Ireland.
I See Phantoms of Hatred and of the Heart's
    Fullness and of the Coming Emptiness.
I walked among the seven woods of Coole.
Image from a Past Life, An.
Imitated from the Japanese.
In Memory of Alfred Pollexfen.
In Memory of Eva Gore-Booth and Con
    Markievicz.
In Memory of Major Robert Gregory.
In Tara's Halls.
In the Seven Woods.
Indian to His Love, The.
Indian upon God, The [or An].
Into the Twilight.
Irish Airman Foresees His Death, An.
John Kinsella's Lament for Mrs. Mary
    Moore.
King and No King.
Lady's First Song, The.
Lady's Second Song, The.
Lady's Third Song, The.
Lake Isle of Innisfree, The.
Lamentation of the Old Pensioner, The.
Lapis Lazuli.
Last Confession, A.
Leaders of the Crowd, The.
Leda and the Swan.
Lines Written in Dejection.
Living Beauty, The.
Long-legged Fly.
Lover Asks Forgiveness because of His Many
    Moods.
Lover Mourns for the Loss of Love, The.
Lover Pleads with His Friend for Old
    Friends, The.
Lover Speaks to the Hearers of His Songs in
    Coming Days, The.
Lover Tells of the Rose in His Heart, The.
Lover's Song, The.
Love's Loneliness.
Lullaby: "Beloved, may your sleep be
    sound."
Mad as the Mist and Snow.
Madness of King Goll, The.
Magi, The.
Maid Quiet.
Man and the Echo.
Man Who Dreamed of Faeryland, The.
Man Young and Old, A.
Mask, The.
Meditation in Time of War, A.
Meditation of the Old Fisherman, The.
Meditations in Time of Civil War *sels*.
Meditations in Time of Civil War.
Meeting.
Memory.
Memory of Youth, A.
Men Improve with the Years.
Mermaid, The.
Meru.
Michael Robartes and the Dancer.
Model for the Laureate, A.

Mohini Chatterjee.
Moods, The.
Mother of God, The.
Mountain Tomb, The.
Municipal Gallery Revisited, The.
My Descendants.
My House.
My Table.
Nativity, A.
Needle's Eye, A.
Never Give All the Heart.
New Faces, The.
News for the Delphic Oracle.
Nineteen Hundred and Nineteen.
Nineteenth Century and After, The.
No Second Troy.
O Do Not Love Too Long.
Oil and Blood.
Old Age of Queen Maeve, The.
Old Man Stirs the Fire to a Blaze, An.
Old Memory.
Old Men Admiring Themselves in the Water,
    The.
Old Stone Cross, The.
Old Tom Again.
On a Picture of a Black Centaur by Edmund
    Dulac.
On a Political Prisoner.
On Being Asked for a War Poem.
On Those That Hated "The Playboy of the
    Western World," 1907.
On Woman.
O'Rahilly, The.
Owen Aherne and His Dancers.
Pardon, old fathers, if you still remain.
Parnell.
Parnell's Funeral.
Parting.
Paudeen.
Peace.
Peacock, The.
People, The.
Phases of the Moon, The.
Pilgrim, The.
Pity of Love, The.
Players Ask for a Blessing on the Psalteries
    and on Themselves, The.
Poet Pleads with the Elemental Powers, The.
Poet to His Beloved, A.
Politics.
Prayer for My Daughter, A.
Prayer for My Son, A.
Prayer for Old Age, A.
Prayer on Going into My House.
Presences.
Quarrel in Old Age.
Ragged Wood, The.
Realists, The.
Reconciliation.
Red Hanrahan's Song about Ireland.
Remorse for Intemperate Speech.
Results of Thought, The.
Resurrection, The *sels*.
Ribh at the Tomb of Baile and Aillinn.
Ribh Considers Christian Love Insufficient.
Ribh Denounces Patrick.
Ribh in Ecstasy.
Road at My Door, The.
Roger Casement.
Rose of Battle, The.
Rose of Peace, The.
Rose of the World, The.
Rose Tree, The.
Running to Paradise.
Sad Shepherd, The.
Sailing to Byzantium.
Saint and the Hunchback, The.
Scholars, The.
Second Coming, The.
Secret Rose, The.
Secrets of the Old, The.
September 1913.
Seven Sages, The.
Shadowy Waters, The.
Shepherd and Goatherd.
Sixteen Dead Men.
Solomon and the Witch.

Solomon to Sheba.
Song, A; "I thought no more was needed."
Song from "The Player Queen,"A.
Song of the Happy Shepherd, The.
Song of the Old Mother, The.
Song of Wandering Aengus, The.
Sorrow of Love, The ("Brawling of a
    sparrow in the eaves, The").
Spilt Milk.
Spirit Medium, The.
Spur, The.
Stare's Nest by My Window, The.
Statistics.
Statues, The.
Stick of Incense, A.
Stolen Child, The.
Stream and Sun at Glendalough.
Summer and Spring.
Sweet Dancer.
Swift's Epitaph.
Symbols.
That the Night Come.
There.
These Are the Clouds.
Those Dancing Days Are Gone.
Those Images.
Thought from Propertius, A.
Three Beggars, The.
Three Bushes, The.
Three Hermits, The.
Three Marching Songs.
Three Monuments, The.
Three Movements.
Three Songs to the One Burden.
Three Things.
To a Child Dancing in the Wind.
To a Friend Whose Work Has Come to
    Nothing.
To a Poet, Who Would Have Me Praise
    Certain Bad Poets, Imitators of His and
    Mine.
To a Shade.
To a Squirrel at Kyle-na-no.
To a Wealthy Man Who Promised a Second
    Subscription to the Dublin Municipal
    Gallery if It Were Proved the People
    Wanted Pictures.
To a Young Beauty.
To a Young Girl.
To an Isle in the Water.
To Be Carved on a Stone at Thoor Ballylee.
To Dorothy Wellesley.
To His Heart, Bidding It Have No Fear.
To Ireland in the Coming Times.
To Some I Have Talked with by the Fire.
To the Rose upon the Rood of Time.
Tom at Cruachan.
Tom O'Roughley.
Tom the Lunatic.
Towards Break of Day.
Tower, The.
Travail of Passion, The.
Two Kings, The.
Two Songs from a Play.
Two Songs of a Fool.
Two Songs Rewritten for the Tune's Sake.
Two Trees, The.
Two Years Later.
Unappeasable Host, The.
Under Ben Bulben.
Under Saturn.
Under the Moon.
Under the Round Tower.
Upon a Dying Lady.
Upon a House Shaken by the Land Agitation.
Vacillation.
Valley of the Black Pig, The.
Veronica's Napkin.
Vision, A *sels*.
Wanderings of Oisin, The.
What Magic Drum?
What Then?
What Was Lost.
Wheel, The.
When Helen Lived.
When You Are Old.
Whence Had They Come?

While I, from that reed-throated whisperer.
White Birds, The.
Who Goes with Fergus?
Wild Old Wicked Man, The.
Wild Swans at Coole, The.
Wisdom.
Witch, The.
Withering of the Boughs, The.
Woman Homer Sung, A.
Words.
Young Man's Song.
Youth and Age.
Translations, Coauthored Poems, etc.:
Colonus' Praise.
Oedipus at Colonus *sels.*

Young, Al (b. 1939)
Absent from the United States.
Afraid.
After Visiting Arl at the Hospital.
Afternoon After, The.
Again / Who am I?
Alba.
Always it's either.
American Glamour.
American Time.
Any Inner City Blues.
April Blue.
Arabia.
Are You the Lover or Loved?
Ars Poetica.
Art of Benny Carter, The.
Aunt.
Available Light.
Backtracking.
Bear Gulch Road.
Beauty of Milwaukee Cold with Rain, The.
Belgrade Moon.
Berkeley Pome.
Big Ocean-Waving, Woman-Pulling Moon.
Big Sur.
Billie.
Birthday Poem.
Bitter Spring Again, The.
Black Queen for More Than a Day.
Blues Don't Change, The.
Blues in December.
Boogie With O.O. Gabugah.
Brand New Morning Love Song, A.
Breathing in morning.
By Heart.
California Peninsula: El Camino Real.
Carolina Moon.
Chemistry.
Citizen CB.
City Home Detroit.
Coastal Moon.
Continuing.
Curative Powers of Silence, The.
Dance for Aging Hipsters, A.
Dance for Li Po, A.
Dance for Ma Rainey, A.
Dance for Militant Dilettantes, A.
Dance of the Infidels.
Dancer, The.
Dancing.
Dancing All Alone.
Dancing Day to Day.
Dancing in the Laundromat [or] Dust: an
    Ordinary Song.
Dancing in the Street.
Dancing Naked.
Dancing Pierrot.
Dancing Together.
Day Kennedy Died.
Dear Arl.
Dear Old Stockholm.
Dear Ravi Shankar.
Demerol.
Detroit 1958.
Dexter Gordon at Keystone Korner.
Dock Song Crazy.
Drawing.
Dream Take: 22.
Dreamjot: 1962.
Dreams of Paradise.
Dude in Denver.
East Boston.

Election Night Pome.
Elegy: "Good morning!"
Erosong.
Eternity.
Everywhere.
Falling Asleep in a Darkening Room.
Flirt.
Flu.
Foggy Morning.
For Arl in Her Sixth Month.
For Janet Kafka, Dead at 30.
For Joanne in Poland.
For Kenneth & Miriam Patchen.
For Poets.
Fort Collins, Colorado.
Friday the 12th.
From Bowling Green.
Fun City Samba.
Geography of the Near Past.
Get that feeling sometimes.
Going Back Home.
Green Is a Feeling, Not a Color.
Grizzly Peak.
Groupie.
H$_2$O.
Hallucinogenic Halleluuuu.
Hangover.
Hawk Revisited, The.
Head of a Woman.
Here in Violet Light.
Herrick Hospital, Fifth Floor.
Ho.
Hoboken Broken Down: A Hasty
    Recollection.
Hot House.
Houston in October.
How Stars Start.
How the Rainbow Works.
I Arrive in Madrid.
I violinize peace.
Ian.
Identities.
Imitation Dance, The.
Improvisation.
In a Twinkling, the Green.
In Marin Again.
In the Tender Woodland.
Indiana Gig, The.
Intimacy.
Invitation.
It Is God that Moves in Your Heart.
It's India.
Jackie McLean: Alto Saxophone.
James Cotton Band at Keystone, The.
January.
Jazz as Was.
John Coltrane Dance, The.
Jolt.
Joy/Spring.
Jungle Strut.
Kicking.
Kiss.
Koto Music/Singing.
Leadbelly Song, The.
Leaving Home for Home.
Leaving Rochester.
Leaving Syracuse.
Lemons, Lemons.
Lesson.
Lester Leaps In.
Life at the Back of the Plane.
Lightning, Divine Lightning.
Little More Traveling Music, A.
Little Poem About Jazz, A.
Loneliness.
Lonesome in the Country.
Look Good, Smell Good, Feel.
Lovesong of O. O. Gabugah.
Madness.
Madrid 1963: Some Changes.
Making Love After Hours.
Malagueña Salerosa.
Malcolm's Messasge.
Manhattan March, The 1970s.
Maya.
Mexico City Lover.
Michael At Sixteen Months.

Mid-Life Crises: A Critical Review.
Midnight Special Revisited, The.
Moon, How Do I Measure Up?
Moon of No Return.
Moon Over Matter.
Moon, the Whole Moon, and Nothing but the
    Moon, The.
Moon Up Close in Winter by the Telescope,
    The.
Moon Watching by Lake Chapala.
Moonlessness.
More Clues to the Blues.
Morning Poem for Michael, A.
Moss.
Mountains of California: Part 1, The.
Mountains of California: Part 2, The.
Move Continuing, The.
Moving, Merging, Fading, Standing Still.
My Spanish Heart.
Myself When I Am Real.
Myth Science of Our Time, The.
New Autumn, New York.
New Mode of Production, The.
New Moon Over Grove Street.
New Mystic, The.
New Orleans Intermission.
Night Before Michael Was Born, The.
No More Doors Tonight.
No Strings Attached.
No Trespassing.
Not Her, She Aint No Gypsy.
Now's the Time.
O!
Ocean Springs Missippy.
October Variations, The.
October Window.
Odds, The.
Old Fashioned Cincinnati Blues, The.
Old Light.
Old O.O. Blues, The.
Old Woman.
One West Coast.
Only Race There Is, The.
Orchard at Night in Rain Light, The.
Pachuta, Mississippi / a Memoir.
Palm Drive Palo Alto.
Paris.
People of Letters.
Physics of Loneliness, The.
Pidgin Moon.
Poem for Dorothy Dandridge, A.
Poem for Dylan Thomas, A.
Poem for Lena Horne, A.
Poem for Omar Khayyam (1050?-1123?
    A.D.).
Poem for Players, A.
Poem for Willard Motley, A.
Poem Found Emptying Out My Pockets.
Poem with Orange.
Poetry.
Politics As History.
Ponce de León: A Morning Walk.
Prelude.
Prestidigitator 1, The.
Prestidigitator 2, The.
Problem of Identity, The.
Process.
Providence, Rhode Island.
Reading Nijinsky's Diary.
Real Time.
Realism.
Rediscovered Diary Entry.
Reggie's Version.
Robbie's Dance, The.
Roland Navarro (1939-1961).
Romance.
Romance Without Finance.
Rundown at Ned's Bar B.Q., The.
Sad Hour of Your Peace, The.
Sarajevo Moon.
Sarajevo Moonlight.
Saudades: The Portuguese Blues.
Sea Level.
See, See, Moon.
Selectric II.
Self-Portrait: Holding On.
Sentience.

Seventh April.
Sing a Song of Singapore.
Singular Yen, A.
Sleepy Day at Half Moon Bay.
So is there life on you, moon?
Some Recent Fiction.
Some Spice for Jack Spicer.
Sometimes With the Waves.
Son.
Song skips around, The.
Song Turning Back Into Itself 1.
Song Turning Back into Itself, The *sels.*
Squirrels.
Still Lives.
Studio up over in Your Ear.
Suicide.
Summer.
Sunday Illumination.
Sunday Sonnet for My Mother's Mother, A.
Sweet Sixteen Lines.
Teaching.
Thelonious: An Intro.
There Is a Sadness.
Tiny Self-Portrait.
Topsy: Part 2.
Total Incandescence.
Tribute.
Tune.
Tutti Colori Quality of Light, The.
Two A.M.
2 takes from *Love in Los Angeles.*
Visiting Day.
W. H. Auden & Mantan Moreland.
Waking Up in Santa Cruz at Sea.
Watsonville after the Quake.
What Have You Got of Your Own.
What Is the Blues?
What You Seize Is What You Git.
Whatever Becomes of the Living.
Where the Danube and Sava Rivers Meet.
Why a Hush Should Not Be Rushed.
Winter Leaves.
Yes, the Secret Mind Whispers.
You Don't Know What Love Is.
Your Basic Black Poet.

Z

Zimmer, Paul (b. 1934)
Ancient Wars, The.
Barney Hung Over.
Cecil Sliding Away from the Memory of
    Wanda.
Cecil, Zimmer, and the Man-Made Lake.
Christian Fearing the Sky.
Confession, Curse and Prayer.
Curse of the Frogs, The.
Day Zimmer Lost Religion, The.
Death Demonstrates His Presence to Zimmer.
Death of the Hired Zimmer.
Dogs of Zimmer, The.
Driving North from Savannah on My
    Birthday.
Duke Ellington Dream, The.
Eisenhower Years, The.
Entering the Storm, Unable to Swim,
    Zimmer, Rollo, and Cecil Are Saved.
Enzyme Poem for Suzanne, An.
Father Animus and Zimmer.
Final Affection, A.
Games in the Field, The.
Great House, The.
Gus in the Streets.
Gus Sees Wanda Drinking.
History of Bears, The.
I Go Out in the Long Nights.
Irene Gogle.
Julian Barely Misses Zimmer's Brains.
Leaves of Zimmer.
Lester Tells of the End of the Summer.
Lester Tells of Wanda and the Big Snow.
Once as a Child I Had Bad Dreams.
One for the Ladies at the Troy Laundry Who
    Cooled Themselves for Zimmer.
Rollo's Miracle.
Sonnet: Zimmer Imagines Himself Being
    Poet-in-Residence.

Sweet Night Bleeds From Zimmer, The.
Thurman Dreaming in Right Field.
Thurman's Slumping Blues.
Wanda and the Fish.
Wanda and Zimmer.
Wanda Being Beautiful.
What Zimmer Would Be.
When Angels Came to Zimmer.
Work.
Worrying About You All the Time.
Zimmer and the Ghost.
Zimmer at the Diggings.
Zimmer Directs Himself Home from the
    Diggings.
Zimmer Drunk and Alone, Dreaming of Old
    Football Games.
Zimmer Envying Elephants.
Zimmer Fearing Anemia.
Zimmer Finds Imbellis in the Ancient
    Graves.
Zimmer Guilty of the Burnt Girl.
Zimmer Imagines Heaven.
Zimmer in Grade School.
Zimmer Loathing the Gentry.
Zimmer Remembering Wanda.
Zimmer the Drugstore Cowboy.
Zimmer Warns Himself with Vivid Images
    Against Old Age.
Zimmer with Lester Under the Moon.
Zimmer's Head Thudding against the
    Blackboard.
Zimmer's Last Gig.
Zimmer's Love Poem After A Hard Dream.
Zimmershire Lad, A.
Zumer Is Icumen In.

Zimmerman, Robert *see* "Dylan, Bob"

Zukofsky, Louis (1904–78)
African Violet.
After Charles Sedley.
After Reading.
Ah spring, when with a thaw of blue.
Air.
Alba (1952).
All of December Toward New Year's.
All Wise.
Aloe.
Alpine Rosy Bells.
And so till we have died.
And Without.
Anew, sun, to fire summer.
Another Ashtray.
Arizona.
Artemisia.
As to How Much.
Ashtray.
Aster.
Atque in Perpetuum   A.W.
Aubade, 1925.
Azalea.
Barely and *widely.*
Bayberry.
Bearded Iris.
Belly Locks Shnooks Oakie.
Bird that cries like a baby, The.
Butter-and-Eggs.
Can a mote of sunlight defeat its purpose.
Catullus viii.
Celia's Birthday Poem.
Charlock per Winkle.
Che Di Lor Suona Su Nella Tua Vita.
Chicory.
Chloride of Lime and Charcoal.
Chokecherry.
Chrysanthemum.
Cinquefoil.
Claims.
Clover.
Cockle.
Coleus.
Crocus.
Dahlia.
Daisy.
Dandelion.
Daruma.
Deutzia.
Dogwood.
Drive, fast kisses.

During the Passaic Strike of 1926.
Dutch White Iris.
1892-1941.
Even if love convey.
Ferry.
Finally a Valentine.
Flushing Meadows.
For Selma Gubin's Umbrellas.
For you I have emptied the meaning.
For Zadkine.
Forsythia.
Four-o'clock.
4 Other Countries.
"Further than."
Gamut.
George Washington.
Glad they were there.
Grape-Hyacinth.
Grassflower.
Grecian Windflower.
Green leaf that will outlast the winter.
Green plant grows, The.
Guests, The.
Guillaume de Machault (1300-1377) Ballade:
    Plourès, dames.
Gulls over a rotting hull.
Happiest February.
Has the sum.
Head Lines.
Heart us invisbly thyme time.
Heart's Ease.
Heights, The.
Her face the Book of—Love Delights in—
    Praises.
—"Her Soil's Birth."
Hill.
Homage.
Home for Aged Bomb Throwers—U.S.S.R.
Honesty.
Honeysuckle.
H.T.
Hyacinth.
I Sent Thee Late.
I walk in the old street.
Imitation.
Immature Pebbles.
"Immediate Aim, The."
Impatiens.
In the midst of things.
Incident, An.
I's (Pronounced *Eyes*).
It's a Gay Li-ife.
It's hard to see but think of a sea.
Jade.
Jaunt.
Judge and the Bird, The.
Junction, A.
Last cigarette / a companion, A.
Lavender Cotton.
Laws Can Say, The.
Lese-Wiat, from Caul Gate.
Letter of Poor Birds, The.
Light.
Lilac.
Lilies.
Lily-of-the-Valley.
Lily-of-the-Valley Fortunei.
Lines of this new song are nothing, The.
Liveforever.
Madison, Wis., Remembering the Bloom of
    Monticello (1931).
Madrigal for 3 Voices, A.
"Mantis."
"Mantis," An Interpretation.
March First.
Marigold.
Marriage Song for Florence and Harry, A.
Memory of V. I. Ulianov.
Men in the kitchens, The.
Michtam.
Motet.
Mountain Laurel.
My nephew / And my new.
Narcissus.
1959 Valentine.
No One Inn.
Non Ti Fidar.

Nor did the prophet.
Not it was no dream of coming death.
N.Y.
Old.
Old Poet Moves to a New Aprtment 14
   Times, The.
On Valentine's Day to Friends.
One friend.
One lutenist played *look*; your through was
   drink.
"One oak fool box";—the pun.
Or a Valentine.
Oxalis.
Pachysandra.
Pamphylian.
Perch Less.
Peri Poietikes.
Petunia.
Phlox.
Poem Beginning "The."
Poppy Anemone.
Pretty.
Privet.
Prop. LXI.
Pussy Willow.
Que J'ay Dit Devant.
Queen Anne's Lace.
Rains, the rains, The.
Raspberry.
Reading and Talking.
Record, The.
Romatic Portrait.
Rose-of-Sharon.
Roses.
Run on, you still dead to the sound of a
   name.
(Ryokan's scroll).
Send regards to Ida the bitch.
Sequence 1944-6.
Shang Cup.
Slipperwort.
Snow-Wreath.
Snowdrop.
Snowflake.
So sounds grass, and if it is sun or no sun.
So That Even a Lover.
Some time has gone.
Song for the Year's End, A.
Song Theme.
Song—3/4 time.
Songs of Degrees.
Spearmint.
Spider or Ribbon Plant.
Spirea.
Spook's Sabbath, Five Bowings.
Sprengeri.
Starglow.
Strange / To reach that age.
Stratford-on-Avon.
Stubbing the cloud-fields—the searchlight,
   high.
Tam Cari Capitis.
Telephus Sedum.
The.
This Fall, 1933.
This is after all vacation. All that.
This year / that Valentine is / late.
Thyme.
To Friends, for Good Health.
To My Baby Paul.
To My Valentines.
Train-Signal.
Translation, The.
Tulip.
29 Poems.
29 Songs.
Two Dedications: D.R.
Two Dedications: Tibor Serly.
Valentine, A.
Venus's Looking-glass.
Vines.
Violet.
W.
Ways, The.
Weeds.
What are these songs.
When the crickets.

White Begonia.
Wild Geranium.
Wild Honeysuckle.
William Carlos Williams Alive!
Windflower.
Wire.
Wish, A.
With a Capital P.
With a Valentine (the 12 February).
With a Valentine (the 14 February).
World autumn, The.
"X."
Xenophanes.
Yarrow.
Yaupon.
You three:—my wife.
You who were made for this music.
Zebrina etc.
Zinnia.
Translations, Coauthored Poems, etc.:
Acme, Septimius, sighs so amorous.
Alfenus, remember *kind intimacies*? false?
   They elated us.
Ameana pulling, a foot touted high.
Annals of Volusius, cock at his offal.
At hest, hendecasyllabics, what is this.
Aufilena—*bonnie, simple,* laud and they're
   amicable.
Aufilena, virile content him weave her her
   solo.
Aurelius, father, assure that the o numb.
Bononian, sis Rufa, Rufus' lum fell at.
'c-hommodating he'd bait, seeking
   accomodating willed.
Caelius Aufilenus' mate, Quintius Aufilena's
   am.
Caelius, Lesbia new star, Lesbia a light.
Canapés, my Fabullus, at home any.
Carmina *sels.*
Cold how mean, fortune consuming you
   oppresses your care, your.
Commend to you my cares for the love I
   love.
Conniving Thallus, mulley, you, cony cully,
   cop below.
Consul (ere) Pompei O preened a duo, Cinna,
   so lay bound.
Credit me poor to say of my life *maledictory
   weed die.*
Cute boy arm in elbow prize con man, kid,
   what do we see.
Day, see no day—choke, qualm, quick
   qualm—benevolence, merit are.
Decay bars one time, 'solely to know, see
   Catullus.'
Diana, sum us in faith a.
Egnatius, candid as his horse-bit white
   dentures.
Facile as can be the boat you see, my guests,
   says.
Firmum is all too known fails so Meantool a
   Dives.
Flavius—that delicate lass—to Catullus.
Furius, Aurelius: comities—Catullus.
Furius, "Little Villa" has no nod for Auster.
Furius, with no key to service, no key.
Gallus ha' but brothers: bro one's lady slip's
   make so young she's.
Gellius how he'd rare at pot true uncle
   objurgate soul array.
Gellius is thin why yes: kiddin'? quite a
   bonny mater.
He'll hie me, par *is* he? the God divide her.
How cast down is the mind that took to my
   Lesbia, culprit.
Human all key mog knee this pecks it loom
   in a moon the.
I'm a bow, my dual kiss, Ipsithilla.
In the, same in (when qualm?) thick wee
   poetry, putrid Victi.
Lament, o graces of Venus, and Cupids.
Lesbia may dicker simper maul or nag talk at
   whom, come.
Lesbia (my price scent t'her hero) mauls and
   deplores me, '*dig it*'.
Lesbius has pooled her: kidney? whom
   Lesbia my—lit.

Marrucinus Asinius, that sinister.
Master of eloquence and Rome's potent line.
May we live, my Lesbia, love while we may.
Meantool amuck with her. Muck with her
   mean tool ah? Geared I.
Meantool inhabits in style three times ten
   hewed acres, forty.
Meantool reconnoiters Pipléa scanning Their
   mountain.
Mellowed *those*, I call *those* eyes, Juventius.
Minister wet to lee, pour the Falernian.
Miss her, Catullus? don't be so inept to rail.
Mool 'tis homos,' Naso 'n' queer take 'im
   mool 'tis ho most *he.*
Mulled hosts their countries yet mulled there
   by a core of wake tossed.
My last—Cornificius—your Catullus'.
Newly say dickered my love air my own
   would marry me all.
Nil, not my aim to study you, Caesar, to
   be—well, a placater.
No idea, Gelli, spurred me to mirror you
   faithful.
No it would not mean a damn (quick whim
   referred to pure.
No lift odd mere horror, harrowed (why
   boy?) that no woman will.
No love by test, my love, 'll air then, time,
   say the care of all my time.
None but a lioness moaned this, Libya's
   mountains.
Not many enchant you (put to it) popular is
   he, Juventi.
Not that I look to my eyes more than your
   love.
Now seed their Magus (of Gelli's mother
   wrestling confounded.
O Colonia, whose wishes build a long bridge
   to dance on.
O dear cool you couldn't be virile—you
   couldn't a parent he.
O farm, dear nest, or say Sabine, ah say
   Tibur's.
O quick floss silk of the Juventii, form.
O ram ridicule home, Cato, the jokes some.
O th'hate I move love. Quarry it fact I am,
   for that's so re queries.
Offer 'em up to me—bullneck crook of the
   baths.
Otho's scooped nut its pusillanimity.
Out—so this means you render them, ten
   sestertia, Silo.
Pelion could one time prong its top worthy
   keel in pines.
Peninsular arm, Sirmio, insular arm, well.
Piping, beaus, I'll go *whoosh* and I'll rumble
   you.
Piso's own comates, his, corps an inane as.
Poet I'm too near your and my sod daily.
Porky and Socration, two-eye sins as try.
"Pull! crew" 's convenient to reprobate kin
   hides.
Queries, you ask how many times must I
   kiss.
Quick death, Catullus! what more horrors
   may hurry!
Quid, fact it is Gelli? quick'ning mother, at
   (queer) sis, all three.
Quiddity, Gelli, quarry, rosy as these too lips
   belie.
Quinti, see if't be wish of cool eyes day bear
   your Catullus.
Quintia's *foremost* to multitudes; my eye can
   deed her *long, e—*.
Risible nice go when from mud a crony.
Rufey my how frustrate unquickened and
   craved the tie I'm equal.
Rum asks—see, fortune won't molest you.
Salt hacks, tavern boys, what skews, can't
   you burn alleys.
Salvé, next, minimal, poor little nosey.
Secret I take it a commitment hushed to feed
   amic—.
Securer a bo? no sacred armpits lair hops as
   that he-goat's.
See, Comini, popular arbitrer turned on
   uncanny senescence.

See could we quit coveting hope taunting where hope hid and.

See quick calm moot as gratifying the tombed—sepulchres.

Seek or record then the benefactor—pree or voluptuous.

Sigh paid to be studious when I moved went on to (queer) once.

Sparrow, my girl's pleasure, delight of my girl.

Spurred altering wake toss Attis his craft racing till marled in the.

Suffenus is, stay Varus,—whom you've proven—is the.

Surreptitious you at bay doom loot is, my little Juventi.

Varus old crony had me visit his love.

Veranius of all my beloved friends.

Vesper out there, you vain knees can sure get up: Vesper, Olympus.

Warm gale, a dose of spring—revert to the pores.

What demented malice, my silly Ravidus.

Who lives o on Helicon hill.

Whom do I give my neat little volume.

Whose hoax to put up with, outstare, protest patience.

Yesterday, Licinius, what a day it was.

Yet see (may as I do) a confect of my cure—a dolor.

You could then, my heart, wit, eye, mean in proposing love our aim.

Zmyrna, my own Cinna, nine harvests passed making his hymn.

SUBJECT INDEX

Poems under each subject heading are listed alphabetically by author. Subjects range from specific (for example, persons) to general (for example, Faith*).*
Some subject headings show cross-references to related subjects. Some subjects, such as Love*, are so broad that they appear here only to refer the user to related subjects.*

A

Aaron (Bible)
Herbert. Aaron.
Abandonment
Atwood. Beauharnois.
Auden. Dying House, The.
Blake. Never seek [*or* pain] to tell thy love.
Boyle. Painter Speaks—the Woman Answers, The.
Bunting. Search under every veil.
Campion. My Love Hath Vowd.
Carew. Lady, Rescued from Death by a Knight, Who in the Instant Leaves Her, Complains Thus, A.
To His Mistress Retiring in Affection.
To Master W. Montague.
Carroll, Jim. It is afternoon   a sailor is crying above the waterfall.
"Carroll, Lewis." Coronach.
Miss Jones.
Carruth. Abandoned Ranch, Big Bend.
Catullus. Carmen 30: "Alfenus from Cremona / forsakes the friendship of friends."
Clark. Afternoons.
"Like Musical Instruments."
Withdrawal.
De la Mare. Abandoned Church, An.
Dickey, William. Dog Under False Pretences.
Donne. To Mr I. L. ("Blessed [*or* Blesst] are your north parts, for all this long time").
Dove. Adolescence—III.
"Dylan." Abandoned Love.
Fox. Letter to Peter Wilkins.
Galvin. Stone Arabia Farm.
Gardner. Feminine Ending or, Abandoned, She Died.
Garrigue. For Such a Bird He Had No Convenient Cage.
Griffiths. Fathers.
Unmetalled Road.
Hacker. Celles.
Hayden. Incense of the Lucky Virgin.
Sub Specie Aeternitatis.
Hemingway. Black-Ass Poem After Talking to Pamela Churchill.
Hill. My little son, when you could command marvels.
Hughes, Langston. Mama and Daughter.
Midwinter Blues.
Hugo. Death of the Kapowsin Tavern.
Degrees of Gray in Philipsburg.
Ghosts at Garnet.
Graves at Mukilteo.
House on 15th S.W., The.
Houses Lie, Believe the Lying Sea.
Kapowsin.
Montana Ranch Abandoned.
Ode to the Trio Fruit Company of Missoula.
River Now, The.
Silver Star.
1614 Boren.
Wheel of Fortune.
Why I Think of Dumar Sadly.
Knight. Keeping of a Promise, The.
Kooser. Abandoned Farmhouse.
Kunitz. Your turn, Grass of confusion.
Longfellow. Tale of Acadie, A.

Lorde. And Don't Think I Won't Be Waiting.
Story Books on a Kitchen Table.
McAuley. Go on, stir up your tiresome wavelets.
You've mastered the bleak art of Changes.
MacNeice. On the Njal Saga.
Valediction: "Their verdure dare not show...their verdure dare not show."
McNeill. Jane Renick MacElmain (1).
Markson. Lament: "My love is gone."
Meinke. Arms and the Man.
Merton. Letter to One Who Has Abandoned The Way.
Morrison. Car Cemetery.
Untrampled Footsteps.
Nash. Exit, Pursued by a Bear.
Maybe You Can't Take It with You, but Look What Happens When You Leave It Behind.
Neruda. This Broken Bell.
Pack. Drowning.
Hole in the Sky, A.
Piercy. It Breaks.
Prince. For the Deserted.
Psalms. Psalm 22: "My God, my God, why hast thou forsaken me?"
Ransom. Lady Lost.
Rich. In the Wake of Home.
Rolfe. Ship, The.
Rossetti. Margery.
Sexton. Fury of Abandonment, The.
Sidney. Psalm 22: "My God, my God, why hast thou forsaken me?"
Smith, Charlotte. Saint Monica.
Sorrentino. Closet, The.
Coast of Texas.
Land of Cotton.
Long Goodbye, The.
Marjorie.
Mr. America last seen crossing the road.
Spender. Song: "Stranger, you who hide my love."
Tomlinson. Idrigill.
Three Wagnerian Lyrics.
Two Views of Two Ghost Towns.
Turco. Colony, The.
Williams, Charles Kenneth. Neglect.
Williams, Miller. Rubaiyat for Sue Ella Tucker.
Yeats. John Kinsella's Lament for Mrs. Mary Moore.
Zukofsky. Alfenus, remember *kind intimacies*? false? They elated us.

Abbey Theatre, Dublin
Yeats. At The Abbey Theatre.
Abbeys. *see* Monasteries.
Abel. *see* Cain and Abel.
Abelard and Heloise
Pope. Eloisa to Abelard.
Wilbur. Ballade of the Ladies of Time Past.
Aberdeen, Scotland
Hardy. Aberdeen.
Whittier. Barclay of Ury.
Abishag
Glück. Abishag.
Abolitionists
Cullen. Negro Mother's Lullaby, A.
Dove. David Walker (1785–1830).

Dunbar. Douglass.
Hayden. Runagate Runagate.
Rukeyser. Soul and Body of John Brown, The.
Whittier. Brown of Ossawatomie.
Burial of Barber.
Cross, The.
Daniel Neall.
Daniel Wheeler.
Emancipation Group, The.
Follen.
For Righteousness' Sake.
George L. Stearns.
How Mary Grew.
James Russell Lowell.
Leggett's Monument.
Lines from a Letter to a Young Clerical Friend.
Massachusetts.
New Year, The.
Panorama, The.
Randolph of Roanoke.
Song, A: "Beneath thy skies, November!"
Song for the Time, A.
Sumner.
To Charles Sumner.
To George B. Cheever.
To Lydia Maria Child.
To the Memory of Charles B. Storrs.
To the Memory of Thomas Shipley.
To William Lloyd Garrison.
William Forster.
World's Convention, The.
Wordsworth. To Thomas Clarkson, on the Final Passing of the Bill for the Abolition of the Slave Trade. March, 1807.
Aborigines
Ginsberg. Ayers Rock / Uluru Song.
Snyder. Uluru Wild Fig Song.
Abortion
Atwood. Christmas Carols.
Brooks. Mother, The.
Glück. Egg, The.
Hardy. Reluctant Confession.
Jonson. To Fine Lady Would-Be.
Piercy. Provocation of the Dream, The.
Right to Life.
Sabbath of Mutual Respect, The.
Sexton. Abortion, The.
Snodgrass. Mother, The.
Walker. Ballad of the Brown Girl.
Williams, William Carlos. Cold Front, A.
Abraham
Cohen. You Have Sweetened Your Word.
Dickinson. Abraham to kill him.
Gardner. Abraham and Isaac.
Milton. Paraphrase on Psalm 114, A.
Nemerov. Nicodemus.
Owen. Parable of the Old Man and the Young, The.
Smart. Circumcision.
Faith.
Absalom
Auden. Pride.
Absence
Angelou. After.
Arnold. Summer Night, A.
Auden. Bawbee.

Rookery, The.
Seen when nights are silent.
Stop all the clocks, cut off the telephone.
Beckett. Vieil aller / vieux arrêts.
Berg. Remembering and Forgetting.
Two Fragments.
Visit, The.
Berry. Praise.
Turning always in my mind toward you.
Berryman. Great citadels whereon the gold sun falls.
I expect you from the North. The path winds in.
I lift—lift you five States away your glass.
Most strange, my change, this nervous interim—.
Mutinous in the half-light, & malignant, grind.
Boyle. After New York—May Seventeenth.
Brontë. From our evening fireside now.
Browning, Robert. Never the Time and the Place.
Campion. Harden now thy tyred hart, with more than flinty rage.
Carew. Mr. Carew to His Friend.
Separation of Lovers.
To Her in Absence; a Ship.
Upon Some Alterations in My Mistress, after My Departure into France.
Carroll, Jim. Leaving N.Y.C.
"Carroll, Lewis." Valentine, A.
Catullus. Carmen 8: "Break off / fallen Catullus."
Carmen 66: "Who scans the bright machinery of the skies."
Cohen. For Anne.
There Are No Traitors.
You're Not Supposed to Be Here.
Coleridge. Day-Dream, The ("If thou wert here, these tears were tears of light").
Hour When We Shall Meet Again, The.
Something Childish, but Very Natural.
Stanger Minstrel, A.
Cooper. For My Mother in Her First Illness, from a Window Overlooking Notre Dame.
Crane. Exile.
Old Song.
Creeley. Away.
Berlin: First Night & Early Morning.
Knokke.
Little Time—and Place.
Passage, The.
Place.
Sight, A.
Sign Board, The.
Smoke.
Song: "Those rivers run from that land."
Turn, The.
De la Mare. Alone.
Spectre, The.
Voice, The.
Dickinson. Absence disembodies—so does Death.
Is not an absent friend as mysterious.
It was not Death, for I stood up.
They say that absence conquers.
To the faithful Absence is condensed presence.
Dobyns. Absence.
Separate Time, A.
Donne. To Mr I. L. ("Blessed [or Blesst] are your north parts, for all this long time").
To Mr. T. W. ("At once, from hence, my lines and I depart").
Dunbar. Absence.
Waiting.
"Dylan." Corrina, Corrina.
Ford. It Seems You Never Were.
Gallagher. Kidnap[p]er.
Ginsberg. Dakar Doldrums.
Love Letter.
Gunn. Annihilation of Nothing, The.
Colour Machine, The.
During an Absence.
Hacker. "That was in another country," but the wench.
Haines. We were away for a long time.
Hardy. Voice, The.
Herrick. Presence and Absence.

Hughes, Langston. So Long.
Knott. Goodbye.
Prophet in a Landscape of Immemorial Time.
Summoning, The.
Lawrence. Quite Forsaken.
Return.
Lewis. Home Thoughts from Abroad.
Song (On Seeing Dead Bodies Floating Off the Cape).
Liddy. For Jimin in Manchuria II.
Lovelace. Elinda's [or Ellinda's] Glove.
Lowell. Home after Three Months Away.
Lowry. With Sweetest Love from All the Little Animals As from 2 Old Friends.
"MacDiarmid." Empty Vessel.
Markson. Writer's Lament.
Melville. Empty Stirrups.
Merton. Starlight and Non-Being.
Nathan. Surprise.
Nemerov. Small Moon.
Neruda. Dying.
Pack. Unburying the Birch.
Patchen. This room has mystery like trance.
Piercy. All Clear.
Breaking Camp.
You are an opening in me.
Pope. Autumn, the Third Pastoral, or Hylas and Ægon.
Raine. All that is: / The unbroken surface of the sea.
Angelus.
Wilderness, The.
Ransom. Jack's Letter.
Winter Remembered.
Rich. 7/13/68.
7/12/68.
Splittings.
Rossetti. Fisher-Wife, A.
St. John. Hush.
Shakespeare. Sonnet 113: "Since I left you, mine eye is in my mind."
Sidney. Sonnet 106: "O absent presence, Stella is not here."
Sonnet 60: "When my good angel guides me to the place."
Sonnet 89: "Now that of absence the most irksome night."
Simic. Rosalia and her mother moved away.
Smith, Stevie. When the Sparrow Flies.
Spender. Absence.
Spenser. LXXXIX. "Like as the culver on the bared bough."
Stevens. Gallant Château.
Stuart. Song for Champagne Saturday.
Suckling. Against Absence.
To Mr. Davenant for Absence.
Tennyson. Daisy, The.
Thomas. I Make This in a Warring Absence.
Turco. Visitor.
Wilbur. "World without Objects Is a Sensible Emptiness, A."
Williams, Charles Kenneth. Hard Part, The.
Williams, Miller. Missing Persons.
Wordsworth. Why Art Thou Silent [Is Thy Love a Plant].
Wyatt. Absence, alas, / Causeth me pass.
Yau. Late Night Movies IV.
Suite of Imitations Written After Reading Translations of Poems by Li He And Li Shang-yin, A.
Young. Absent from the United States.
Moonlessness.
Moving, Merging, Fading, Standing Still.
Odds, The.
Zukofsky. Guests, The.
Human all key mog knee this pecks it loom in a moon dew.
Miss her, Catullus? don't be so inept to rail.

See also **Loneliness; Separation.**

Abundance
Berry. Arrival, The.
Song (1).
Bukowski. Sexpot.
Emerson. Nature ("Day by day for her darlings to her much she added more").
Jeffers. Trap, The.

Acacia
Raine. Acacia Tree.
Wilbur. Part of a Letter.

Academia
Berryman. College of cocktails, a few gentlemen.
Farewell to Miles.
Professor's Song, A.
Burns. Dean of Faculty—a New Ballad, The.
"Carroll, Lewis." Bachanalian Ode, A.
Deserted Parks, The.
Examination Statute.
Majesty of Justice, The.
Carruth. Sonnet: "Most brainy woman, the sexuality of your thought."
To dig at Luxor, to peer.
Cummings. Yonder deadfromtheneckup graduate of a.
Davie. Liverpool Epistle, A.
Hall. Brief Lives.
Hopkins. By Mrs. Hopley.
Jarrell. Esthetic Theories: Art as Expression.
Time and the Thing-in-Itself in a Textbook.
Koch. At the Poem Society a black-haired man stands up to say.
Larkin. Posterity.
Lovelace. To the Genius of Mr. John Hall.
"MacDiarmid." It is possible that a change may come.
Nemerov. Decorated Skull in a University Museum.
Full Professor, A.
Relation of Art and Life, A.
Olson. I'm With You.
Ransom. Prometheus in Straits.
Rich. Autumn Equinox.
Roethke. Academic.
Rossetti. P.R.B., The.
Rukeyser. Gibbs.
Updike. Academy.
Generic College.
Humanities Course.
Story of My Life, The.
Williams, William Carlos. He Has Beaten about the Bush Long Enough.
Our (American) Ragcademicians.

Acadia and Acadians
Longfellow. Evangeline, a Tale of Acadie.
Part the First.

Accent
Davie. At Knaresborough.
Lawrence. Oxford Voice, The.
Meinke. Myrtle the Turtle.
Nash. Chacun à Son Berlitz.
Everybody's Mind to Me a Kingdom Is, or, A Great Big Wonderful World It's.
This Is My Own, My Native Tongue.
Stevens. Search for Sound Free from Motion.

Acceptance
Angelou. John J.
Berg. In the Evening.
Berry. He Is in the Habit of the World.
September 2, 1969.
Burns. Orananaoig, or, the Song of Death.
Song: "Contented wi' little, and cantie wi' mair."
Though fickle fortune has deceiv'd me.
Written in Friar's Carse Hermitage on the Banks of Nith—June—1788.
Ye Jacobites By Name.
Ceravolo. Don't Break It.
Cooper. If the weather breaks.
Creeley. "Bolinas and Me.."
Days and Days.
For Martin.
Cummings. Gee i like to think of dead it means nearer because deeper firmer.
It may not always be so; and i say.
Let it go—the.
Dickinson. It ceased to hurt me, though so slow.
Dunn. Essay on the Personal.
Some Things I Wanted to Say to You.
Woman with Five Hearts, The.
Eberhart. Life and Death.
Emerson. Come!—the palace of heaven rests

on aëry pillars.
Terminus ("It is time to be old").
Ferlinghetti. Elegy to Dispel Gloom, An.
Ford. Impossibility of Dying in Your Arms Does Not Sadden Me, The.
Gardner. Letter from Slough Pond.
Panic Vine, The.
Glück. My Cousin in April.
Hardy. Looking Back.
New Dawn's Business, The.
Herrick. To Vulcan.
Hewitt. Disaster on the Box.
Expectancy.
Her situation seemed a piteous thing.
Lake Bled, Slovenia.
Raindrop.
Hugo. Good View from Flagstaff, A.
Joseph. Dog Body and Cat Mind.
Kipling. Ex-Clerk.
Refined Man, The.
Knott. Poem: "Beach holds and sifts us through her dreaming fingers, The."
Kunitz. I was happy you were born.
Mens Creatrix.
You cried. You cried.
Levine. On My Own.
Lewis. Gates of my palace are opened wide, The.
Renewal.
Liddy. Holden.
Lindsay. One Brief Hour of Grown-up Glory on the Gulf of Mexico.
MacLeish. It is time we should accept.
Back-Again, The.
Selva Oscura.
To Mary.
Meredith. All other joys of life he strove to warm.
Faith on Trial, A.
Outer and Inner.
Philosopher! 'tis said you wail.
Merton. Metamorphosis.
Morrison. Curses & Invocations.
Please Like Me.
Olson. Kingfishers, The.
Pack. Clayfeld Renews His Vow to Evelyn.
Paley. Women let the tide go out, The.
Piercy. I Will Not Be Your Sickness.
Rich. Letter from the Land of Sinners.
Loser, The.
Rossetti. Advent.
Cried Out with Tears.
Death's Chill Between.
Had Fortune parted us / Fortune is blind.
Heart's Chill Between.
Lord, what have I to offer? sickening fear.
My God, wilt Thou accept, and will not we / Give aught to Thee?
Of Him That Was Ready to Perish.
When I Was in Trouble I Called upon the Lord.
Rukeyser. Desdichada.
Shelley. To ———: "One word is too often profaned."
Warren. We Are Only Ourselves.
Whitman. Me Imperturbe.
To a Common Prostitute.
Whittier. Woman, A.
Williams, Miller. He Speaks to His Arguing Friends and to Himself.
Summer Afternoon an Old Man Gives Some Thought to the Central Questions, A.
Wroth. After long trouble in a taedious way.
Zukofsky. Catullus viii.

Accidents
Atwood. This is a mistake, / these arms and legs.
Those south of us are lavish.
Berryman. Damn You, Jim D., You Woke Me Up.
Bishop. Trouvée.
Bukowski. Jack-Knife.
Carruth. House out to sea.
Wreck of the Circus Train, The.
Creeley. Place, The.
Davie. After an Accident.

Dickey, James. Falling.
Sustainment.
Everson. Reaper.
Frost. Door in the Dark, The.
Objection to Being Stepped On, The.
Out, Out —.
Gardner. Bronchitis at the Chelsea—or Salud Raul.
Gildner. Letter From My Good Hand, A.
Hardy. I Worked No Wile to Meet You.
Herrick. Bracelet of Pearle: To Silvia, The.
Broken Christall, The.
Casualties.
Hewitt. Dustcart, The.
Great Event, A.
Mosaic.
Prelude to Consternation.
Townland of Peace.
21st September 1912.
Hoffman. That Morning.
Witnesses.
Joseph. There are more accidents in the home than on the roads.
Kipling. Destroyers in Collision.
Dove of Dacca, The.
Knight. Poem of Attrition, A.
Lawrence. Collier's Wife, The.
Lieberman. Stubby Carrot.
MacNeice. After the Crash.
Matthews. Black Box.
Meredith. Gordon, Jim, / Life and Limb.
Hungarian Horse-Herd, The.
Merrill. Broken Bowl, The.
Merton. Cup with a Jaguar for the Drinking of Health.
Nash. Lather as You Go.
Oppen. Cars on the highway filled with speech.
Pack. Clayfeld Prunes His Apple Trees.
Clayfeld's Twin.
Paley. For Mike and Jeannie: Resisters Fifteen Years Later.
Piercy. S. Dead.
Plath. Cut.
Roethke. Elegy for Jane.
Rolfe. Poem To Delight My Friends Who Laugh at Science-Fiction, A.
Sexton. Break, The.
Silverstein. Band-Aids.
Bang-Klang.
Snyder. Crash.
Stuart. Soup Jar, The.
Van Duyn. Reading of Rex Stout, A.
Warren. Ballad: Between the Boxcars.
Williams, Charles Kenneth. Child Psychology.
Williams, Miller. Running into Things.
Williams, William Carlos. Detail.
Young. Roland Navarro (1939-1961).
See also **Airplane Crashes; Automobile Accidents; Disasters; Nuclear Accidents; Railroad Wrecks; Shipwrecks.**

Accordions
Hall. Wedding Party.
Accounting and Accountants
Frost. Hardship of Accounting, The.
Achilles
Auden. Shield of Achilles, The.
Campion. Breake now my heart and dye! Oh no, she may relent.
Catullus. Carmen 64: "In old days / driving through soft waters."
Cullen. Sonnet: "I have not loved you in the noblest way'".
Doolittle. Chorus of the Women of Chalkis.
Duncan. Achilles' Song.
"Dylan." Temporary Like Achilles.
Glück. Triumph of Achilles, The.
Graves. Penthesileia.
Meredith. Achilles over the Trench.
Bibber besotted, with scowl of a cur, having heart of a deer, thou!
Horses of Achilles, The.
Invective of Achilles, The.
Nourishment before Battle.
Shield of Achilles, The.
Zukofsky. Pelion could one time prong its top worthy keel in pines.

Acorns
Dickey, James. Seeking the Chosen.
Hall. Acorns.
Acquiescence
Atwood. Not you I fear but that other.
Carruth. Smallish Son, The.
Cowper. Acquiescence of Pure Love, The.
Entire Surrender, The.
Figurative Description of the Procedure of Divine Love, A.
Nativity, The.
On the same.
Season.
Self-Diffidence.
Gardner. Sonnet for My Acquaintances.
Herrick. Event of Things Not in Our Power.
No Luck in Love.
To Fortune.
Kunitz. Knot, The.
MacLeish. What Any Lover Learns.
Piercy. When did I first become aware—.
Wroth. After long trouble in a taedious way.
Sonnet 7: "Love leave to urge, thou know'st thou hast the hand."
Sonnet 48: "How like a fire doth love increase in me[e]."
Acrobatics and Acrobats
Fox. Acrobat, The.
Graves. Acrobats.
Gunn. Before the Carnival.
Rukeyser. Ringling.
Silverstein. Acrobats, The.
Smith, Stevie. Look, Look.
See also **Circus; Gymnastics and Gymnasts; Tightropes and Tightrope Walkers; Trapezes and Trapeze Artists.**
Acrostic (form)
"Carroll, Lewis." Acrostic: A boat, beneath a sunny sky.
Acrostic: Around my lonely hearth, to-night.
Acrostic: Dreams, that elude the Waker's frenzied grasp—.
Acrostic: Is all our Life, then, but a dream.
Acrostic: Little maidens, when you look.
Acrostic: Maiden, though thy heart may quail.
Double Acrostic: I sing a place wherein agree.
Double Acrostic: Two little girls near London dwell.
Examination Statute.
Nursery Darling, A.
Puck Lost and Found.
To My Child-Friend.
Two Acrostics: Round the wondrous globe / Maidens, if a maid you meet.
Stuart. Discovering My Daughter.
Actaeon
Pound. Canto 4: "Palace in smoky light."
Acting and Actors
Ashbery. Popular Songs.
Berryman. Meeting.
Burns. On Seeing Miss Fontenelle in a Favourite Character.
Prologue: "When by a generous Public's kind acclaim."
Campion. In Ligonem.
"Carroll, Lewis." Prologue: "Ladies and Gentlemen seems stiff and cold."
Prologue to "La Guida Di Bragia."
Clark. Theatre.
Coleridge. Mrs. Siddons.
Crabbe. Arrival of the Players, The.
Eberhart. Man's Greed and Envy Are So Great.
Ford. We each play our roles.
Gardner. Not At All What One Is Used To.
Garrigue. Movie Actors Scribbling Letters Very Fast in Crucial Scenes.
Studies for an Actress.
Ginsberg. Blue Angel, The.
Gunn. Looks.
Hardy. Noble Lady's Tale, The.
To an Actress.
Tragedian to Tragedienne.
Herrick. Upon Comely a Good Speaker but an Ill Singer.
Hewitt. Dedication.
First Pantomime.

Lines on the Opening of the Belgrade Theatre.
Prelude to an Ode for Barnum.
Jonson. To Edward Alleyn.
Joseph. Puppet Show, The.
Kipling. Actors.
Koertge. Sidekicks.
Lieberman. Psychodrama: Tokyo Mime Film.
Lindsay. Epitaphs for Two Players.
Knight in Disguise, The.
Mae Marsh, Motion Picture Actress.
Tramp's Refusal, The.
Lowry. This business of evil / Like brokers the weevil.
McAuley. Actor: Decline and Death, The.
MacNeice. CantoV: "Hence these arrears, this filing cabinet crammed."
Melville. Coming Storm, The.
Merrill. School Play, The.
Nash. Boop-Boop-Adieup, Little Group!
Queen Is in the Parlor, The.
Self-Effacement of Electra Thorne, The.
Notley. True Account of Talking to Judy Holiday, October 13, A.
O'Hara. Mexican Guitar, A.
To the Film Industry in Crisis.
Sandburg. They All Want to Play Hamlet.
Schuyler. Two.
Schwartz. Love and Marilyn Monroe.
Sexton. Play, The.
Smith, Charlotte. Written for the Benefit of a Distressed Player, Detained at Brighthelmstone for Debt, November 1792.
Smith, Patti. K.O.D.A.K.
Smith, Stevie. Actress, The.
Sorrentino. Rose Room.
Stevens. Of Modern Poetry.
Repetitions of a Young Captain.
Wilbur. Prisoner of Zenda, The.
Williams, Miller. Aging Actress Sees Herself a Starlet on the Late Show, The.
Williams, William Carlos. 15 Years Later.
Yau. Late Night Movies I.
Yeats. Players Ask for a Blessing on the Psalteries and on Themselves, The.
Young. Poem for Dorothy Dandridge, A.

See also **Show Business.**

Adam and Eve
Angelou. Couple, The.
Blake. Ghost of Abel, The.
Browning, Elizabeth Barrett. Drama of Exile, A.
Poet's Vow, The.
Byron. Impromptu.
Carruth. Museum Piece.
Clough. Adam and Eve.
Cohen. Photograph, The.
This Marriage.
Crane. Garden Abstract.
Cullen. One Day We Played a Game.
Davie. Eden.
De la Mare. Dream, A.
Exile, The.
Dickey, James. Eagle's Mile, The.
Poisoned Man, The.
Dobyns. Gardener, The.
"Dylan." Man Gave Names to All the Animals.
Eberhart. Ineffable, The.
Throwing the Apple.
Emerson. But never yet the man was found.
Dæmonic and the Celestial Love, The.
Eve roved in Paradise, I've heard.
Fletcher. And God, looking out upon earth, said, "Lo, it is time / To create mankind."
August, 1940.
Cain and Abel in the meantime had grown.
In the still evening of the sixth long day.
Then the archangels all together abandoned the black menacing sky.
Graves. History of the Fall.
Apple Island.
Hesketh. Scapegoat.
Hewitt. Name and Number.
Hill. Assisi Fragments, The.
Hughes, Ted. Apple Tragedy.
Childish Prank, A.
Theology.

Koertge. Excerpts from God's Secret Diary.
Lawrence. Birth Night.
Renaissance.
Lindsay. Eden in Winter.
Genesis.
To Eve, Man's Dream of Wifehood as Described by Milton.
Lowry. And yet his suffering got involved with all this.
MacLeish. What Adam Said.
Milton. Adam Unfallen.
Banquet, The.
Now Morn her rosie steps in th' eastern clime.
Paradise ("His fair large front and eye sublime declared").
Satan Beholds Adam and Eve in Eden.
Thus talking hand in hand alone they pass'd.
Uncloistered Virtue.
Olson. Anubis will stare.
Patchen. Man with the Golden Adam's Apple, The.
Plath. Dialogue *En Route*.
Roethke. Follies of Adam, The.
Rossetti. Bird or Beast?
That Eden of earth's sunrise cannot vie.
Sexton. Rats Live on No Evil Star.
Shapiro. Adam and Eve.
Stevenson. Men are Heaven's piers; they evermore.
Stuart. Hermaphrodite, The.
Tomlinson. Adam.
In Arden.
Walcott. Adam's Song.
New World.
Williams, William Carlos. Adam.
Eve.
Yeats. Adam's Curse.

See also **Eve.**

Adams, Henry
Auden. Henry Adams / Was mortally afraid of Madams.

Addison, Joseph
Pope. Atticus ("Peace to all such! but were there one whose fires").

Admiration
Angelou. Just for a Time.
Auden. Gipsy Girl, The.
Richard Jefferies.
Berg. Lowell: Self-Portrait.
New Year's.
Ollie, Answer Me.
William Carlos Williams Reading His Poems.
Bishop. To a Tree.
Boyle. For Marianne Moore's Birthday.
Bukowski. Eulogy to a Hell of a Dame—.
Mother and Son.
Bunting. O, it is godlike to sit selfpossessed.
Yes, it's slow, docked of amours.
Burns. Address, to the Shade of Thomson, on Crowning His Bust, at *Ednam, Roxburghshire*, with Bays.
Answer, The [To the Guidwife of Wauchope-House].
Epistle to Mr Tytler of Woodhouselee, Author of a Defence of Mary Queen of Scots.
Extempore Epistle to Mr. McAdam of Craigengillian, (Wrote in Nanse Tinnock's, Mauchline) in Answer to an Obliging Letter He Sent in the Commencement of My Poetic Career.
Extempore—on Some Commemorations of Thomson.
I Love My Jean.
O had the malt thy strength of mind.
To Renton of Lamerton.
Verses Intended to Be Written below a Noble Earl's Picture.
While new-ca'd kye rowte at the stake.
Byron. She Walks in Beauty.
Translation from Catullus ("Equal to Jove that youth must be").
Campion. Another Dialogue, To Be Sung at the Same Time.
O Joyes exceeding!
To the Right Noble and Vertuous Theophilus Howard, Lorde of Walden, Sonne and Heire to the Right Honorable the Earle of Suffolke.

To the Right Vertuous, and Honorable, the Lord and Lady Hayes.
To the Worthy Author.
Welcome to this flowrie place.
Carew. Comparison, The.
Complement, The.
Divine Love, A.
Eyes of a Blind Man.
Good Counsel to a Young Maid ("When you the sun-burnt pilgrim see").
Lips and Eyes.
Mistake, The.
New Years Gift. To the Queen, A.
On a Damask[e] Rose, Sticking upon a Lady's Breast.
To A. L.; Persuasions [or Perswasions] to Love.
To My Worthy Friend Master George Sands [or Sandys], on His Translation of the Psalms.
Catullus. Carmen 18: "I dedicate, I consecrate this grove to thee."
Carmen 51: "Godlike the man who."
Carmen 86: "We have heard of Quintia's beauty. To me she is tall, slender."
Carmen 95: "Nine harvests & nine winters since its inception."
Clare. Love and Solitude.
Cohen. Peace.
Petitions.
Coleridge. To Matilda Betham from a Stranger.
Creeley. Birds, The.
Dear Dorothy.
Flower, The.
For a Friend.
Wind, The.
Cullen. To John Keats, Poet, at Springtime.
Cummings. Because you take life in your stride(instead.
Spirit colossal / (& daunted by always).
Dickey, William. Narcissus Unbound.
Dickinson. Adulation is inexpensive.
I always ran Home to Awe when a child.
Dunn. About the Elk and the Coyotes That Killed Her Calf.
Loves.
Walking the Marshland.
"Dylan." Covenant Woman.
Sara.
She Belongs to Me.
Tough Mama.
Everson. But masked of the self.
So him in dream.
Ferlinghetti. Pound at Spoleto.
Fisher. Paraphrases.
Fletcher. As I wandered over the city through the night.
Gallagher. Horse in the Drugstore, The.
Garrigue. Primer of Plato.
Graves. Your Private Way.
Griffiths. Hairdresser, Age 55, Dalston.
Gunn. Bone.
Selves.
Thomas Bewick.
Hacker. Elektra on Third Avenue.
Hemingway. I Like Americans.
I Like Candians.
Herrick. On Tomasin Parsons.
School or Perl of Putney, the Mistress of All Singular Manners, Mistresse Portman, The.
To the Most Accomplist Gentleman, Master Edward Norgate, Clark of the Signet to His Majesty.
Upon the Nipples of Julia's Breast.
Weeping Cherry, The.
Hesketh. Bleasdale: The Wooden Circle.
Hewitt. After Reading *Sonnets* by Rev. Charles Turner (1864) and *The New Day*, Sonnets by Dr T. Gordon Hake (1890).
College Fence, The.
Dedication.
Holy Place, A.
J.B. Shelton (1876–1958), The Coventry Antiquarian.
Lagan in October, The.
Last Call, The.

Lonely Heart, The.
Mary Hagan, Islandmagee, 1919.
My Sister.
Paper Banners.
Reference, The.
Roman Fort, The.
Sunset.
To Be Used in an Address Delivered at the Unveiling of a Plaque Commemorating "George A. Birmingham."
To the Memory of James Connolly.
Variations on a Theme.
Winter Park.
W.R. Rodgers.
Hughes, Ted. I see the oak's bride in the oak's grasp.
Song: "O lady, when the tipped cup of the moon blessed you."
Keats. Addressed to Haydon.
Extracts from an Opera.
To Charles Cowden Clarke.
Kinnell. Hen Flower, The.
Last River, The.
Knight. For Mary Ellen McAnally.
You Are.
Knott. (Poem): "Like a room."
Koch. Burning Mystery of Anna in 1951, The.
In Love with You.
On Beauty.
Summery Weather.
To Marina.
Koertge. In the Underground Station.
Kunitz. Particular Lullaby.
Unwithered Garland, The.
Liddy. Debt, The.
Eugene Connolly.
Letter to Sainte-Beuve.
Miles II.
Lindsay. Being the Dedication of a Morning.
Life Transcendent.
My Lady in Her White Silk Shawl.
My Lady Is Compared to a Young Tree.
Roosevelt.
To a Golden-Haired Girl in a Louisiana Town.
To Gloriana.
To Lady Jane.
Town of American Visions, The.
We Meet at the Judgement and I Fear It Not.
Lorde. Dear Toni Instead of a Letter of Congratulation.
Hard Love Rock.
Mentor.
Poem for a Poet.
To a Girl Who Knew What Side Her Bread Was Buttered On.
Lovelace. Quintia is handsome, fair, tall, straight, all these.
Lowell. Alfred Corning Clark.
Lowry. And Who Is It That With Snow-Freaked Antlers Vicariously Musheth.
Welcome Home Oh Our Beloved Hartebeeste.
With Devotion Entire from All Your Little Animals We Thought Fit to Revive the Following Ditty.
MacNeice. But to turn in on the world, you are all the places.
Solstice.
Under the Mountain.
With you, pray not without you, trapped on the edge of the world.
Mahon. Aran.
Markson. Cummings.
To a Lady, a Part of Her.
Unfinished.
Matthews. Cloud, The.
Twins.
Melville. College Colonel, The.
Jack Roy.
Marchioness of Brinvilliers, The.
On the Photograph of Corps Commander.
Sheridan at Cedar Creek.
Meredith. To a Friend Lost.
When I Would Image.
Merton. Allegiance.
Nahoa Urn, for a Woman.
When You Point Your Finger.
Morrison. Money.

Neruda. Are the salt and the sugar at work.
Do you hear yellow detonations.
Tell me, is the rose really naked.
Olson. For Sappho, Back.
Owen. Long Ages Past.
Pack. Looking at a Mountain Range While Listening to a Mozart Piano Concerto.
Ode to a Lovesick Moose.
Prince. Being *incontentabile* / Like Foscolo, in making verse.
Raine. Old Paintings on Italian Walls.
Ralegh. If Synthia Be a Queene, a Princes, and Supreame.
Rolfe. Eyes of a Blind Man.
Eyes of a Boy.
Night World.
Rossetti. My old admiration before I was twenty.
Roundel seems to fit a round of days, A.
Two Rossettis (Brothers They), The.
St. John. Who is she, coming along the street, turning the heads.
Sarton. Recognition, A.
Schuyler. Belated Birthday Poem, A.
Sestina: "I have reached, alas, the long shadow."
Sidney. Eighth Song.
Sonnet 29: "Like some weak lords, neighboured by mighty kings."
Sonnet 37: "My mouth doth water, and my breast doth swell."
Sonnet 52: "Strife is grown between Virtue and Love, A."
Sonnet 77: "Those looks, whose beams be joy, whose motion is delight."
Sonnet 91: "Stella, while now by honour's cruel might."
Sonnet 100: "O tears, no tears, but rain from beauty's skies."
Sonnet 103: "O happy Thames, that didst my Stella bear."
Third Song.
Transformed in show, but more transformed in mind.
Smart. Ode to Lady Harriot.
Smith, Charlotte. Epilogue [C] to *What Is She?*
Verses, on the death of [Henrietta O'Neill], written in September, 1794.
Smith, Patti. Dog Dream.
Ha! Ha! Houdini!
Sorrentino. Annie from Miami.
Stafford. Parentage.
Passing Remark.
Stevenson. As one who having wandered all night long.
I know not how it is with you.
Katharine.
Plain as the glistering planets shine.
To Andrew Lang.
To H.F. Brown.
To K. de M.
To Princess Kaiulani.
To W.E. Henley.
Stuart. Fence.
Love Poems.
My Hostess at the Renovated Inn.
Timeshare.
Swift. Ode to Dr. William Sancroft.
Ode to the Athenian Society.
Ode to the Honourable Sir William Temple.
Warren. Birth of Love.
Wilbur. Piazza di Spagna, Early Morning.
Praise in Summer.
Williams, Charles Kenneth. Just Right.
New Car.
Silence, The.
Young. Bear Gulch Road.
Brand New Morning Love Song, A.
Dear Arl.
Election Night Pome.
Groupie.
Moon, the Whole Moon, and Nothing but the Moon, The.
Mountains of California: Part 1, The.
Poem for Lena Horne, A.
Whatever Become of the Living.

Zukofsky. Celia's Birthday Poem.
Chloride of Lime and Charcoal.
Do not leave me.
He'll hie me, par *is* he? the God divide her.
Her face the Book of—Love Delights in—Praises.
Like the oceans, or the leaves of fine Southern.
Quintia's *foremost* to multitudes; my eye can deed her *long, e—*.
Stubbing the cloud-fields—the searchlight, high.
Zmyrna, my own Cinna, nine harvests passed making his hymn.

Adolescence
Auden. Adolescence.
Beatles. Cry Baby Cry.
Berryman. Freshman Blues.
Ciardi. Encounter.
Cohen. Memories.
Davie. Nosegay, The.
Dickey, James. Sheep Child, The.
Dove. Adolescence—II.
"Dylan." My Back Pages.
Times They Are A-Changin', The.
Glück. From the Suburbs.
Graves. Dream of Frances Speedwell, A.
Growing Pains.
Griffiths. Cemaes Songs.
Gunn. Adolescence.
London returned to after twelve years, A.
Slow Waker.
Jeffers. October Week-End.
Jong. At the Museum of Natural History.
Kunitz. Game, The.
Lewis. Lines on a Young Girl.
Lowell. Ivana.
Lowry. Poem Influenced By John Davenport and Cervantes.
Matthews. Mood Indigo.
Meinke. Helen.
Merrill. Matinees.
Muldoon. Profumo.
Nash. Tarkington, Thou Should'st Be Living in This Hour.
Olson. Gloss, A.
Pack. Clayfeld's Microscope.
Roethke. Pickle Belt.
Rukeyser. Question, The.
Sandburg. Father sees a son nearing manhood, A.
Sexton. Little Girl, My String Bean, My Lovely Woman.
Love Song: "I was / the girl of the chain letter."
Young.
Shapiro. Drug Store.
Smith, Stevie. Conventionalist, The.
What Is She Writing? Perhaps It Will Be Good.
Stafford. Fifteen.
Updike. Orthodontia.
Williams, Charles Kenneth. Child Psychology.
Fifteen.
Hood.
Williams, Miller. In Your Own Words Without Lying Tell Something of Your Background With Particular Attention to Anything Relating to the Position For Which You Are Applying. Press Down.
Williams, William Carlos. Horned Purple.
Suzy.

Adonis
Auden. Easter Monday.
Browning, Elizabeth Barrett. Lament for Adonis.
Doolittle. Adonis.
Lovelace. Princesse Löysa drawing.
Lowry. Port has a sweeter name than Saigon, The.
Shakespeare. Venus and Adonis.
Shelley. Fragment of the Elegy on the Death of Adonis.
Wroth. Sonnet 9: "But wher they may returne with honors grace."

Adoption and the Adopted
Brontë. A.E. And R.C.

Adultery and Adulterers

Gunn. Blank, A.
Hughes, Langston. Madam and the Charity Child.
Rossetti. Motherless baby and babyless mother.

Adultery and Adulterers
Angelou. They Went Home.
Berg. Bandage.
Berry. Marriage.
Berryman. I owe you, do I not, a roofer: though.
Outlaws claw mostly to a riddled end.
Burns. Epitaph on a Wag in Mauchline.
Byron. Parisina.
Campion. Epigramme: "Smith, by sute divorst, the knowne adultres."
In Crispinum.
Carew. Secrecy [or Secresie] Protested.
To His Mistress Retiring in Affection.
Catullus. Carmen 57: "Caesar Mamurraque! / A peerless pair of brazen buggers."
Carmen 67: "Sweet entrance to a husband's pleasure."
Carmen 71: "If every anyone / was deservedly plagued by a goat under his armpits."
Carmen 74: "Gellius, / hearing his uncle anathematise the mere mention."
Carmen 78: "Gallus's brothers possess / one, the most attractive of wives."
Carmen 113: "In The Year of Pompey's First Consulate, Cinna."
Clough. Clergyman's Second Tale, The.
Creeley. Anger.
Dickey, James. Adultery.
Donne. Tale of a Citizen and His Wife, A.
Gunn. Adultery.
Hacker. One master, aged, as I am, thirty-two.
Hall. Adultery At Forty.
Edward's Anecdote.
Hardy. In the Restaurant.
On Martock Moor.
War-Wife of Catknoll, The.
Heaney. Punishment.
Herrick. Upon Letcher: Epigram.
Upon Scobble [Epigram].
Hewitt. Palmist, The.
Hughes, Langston. Sister.
Jonson. On Old Colt.
On Sir Voluptuous Beast.
On the Same Beast.
Koertge. Zenith and After, The.
Lawrence. Two Wives.
Liddy. Many Mansions.
Lovelace. Her jealous Husband an Adultresse gave.
Lowell. Death of Anne Boleyn.
MacLeish. Or play the strong boy, spit in the world's face, shout.
MacNeice. Provence.
Marlowe. 3.4: Ad virum servantem coniugem.
Meredith. It chanced his lips did meet her forehead cool.
Preaching from a Spanish Ballad, A.
Pack. Trillium.
Plath. Other, The.
Poe. Scenes from Politian.
Sandburg. Couples.
Sexton. For My Lover, Returning to His Wife.
Little Peasant, The.
Shakespeare. Sonnet 92: "In loving thee thou know'st I am forsworn."
Walcott. Adam's Song.
Waldman. Divorce Work.
Williams, William Carlos. Great Mullen.
Zukofsky. Consul (ere) Pompei O preened a duo, Cinna, so lay bound.
Gallus ha' but brothers: bro one's lady slip's make so young she's.
Gellius how he'd rare at pot true uncle objurgate soul array.
O dear cool you couldn't be virile—you couldn't a parent he.
"Pull! crew" 's convenient to reprobate kin hides.
Securer a bo? no sacred armpits lair hops as that he-goat's.

Advent
Auden. For the Time Being; a Christmas Oratorio.
Herrick. Christs Twofold Coming.
Merton. Advent.
Rossetti. Advent.
Advent Sunday.
Sooner or later: yet at last / The Jordan must be past.
Sunday Before Advent.
Schuyler. Advent.

Adventure and Adventurers
Auden. History of Science, The.
Berrigan. Lines for Lauren Owen.
Berryman. Captain's Song, The.
Bukowski. On Being 20.
Eberhart. American Hakluyt.
Height of Man, The.
Sea Storm.
Stealth and Subtleties of Growth.
Fisher. Knight.
Hewitt. Little Ships.
Jong. In the Glass-Bottomed Boat.
Merrill. Narrow Escape, A.
Thousand and Second Night, The.
Merton. Ben's Last Fight.
Crusoe.
Nathan. Family Circle.
"Reed." New Sensations.
Rossetti. Lotus-Eaters: Ulysses to Penelope, The.
Sandburg. Moments of Dawn Riders.
Red Son, The.
Silverstein. Alice.
Stafford. Run before Dawn.
Stevenson. Historical Associations.
Keepsake Mill.
Mile an' a Bittock, A.
To N.V. de G.S.
What glory for a boy of ten.
Wright, James. Pretty Redhead, The.

Advertising
Bunting. As to my heart, that may as well be forgotten.
Burns. Versicles on Sign-Posts.
Cohen. Don't Go Home with Your Hard-on.
Cummings. Poem, or Beauty Hurts Mr. Vinal.
Dickinson. I'm Nobody! Who are you?
"Dylan." I Shall Be Free.
Ginsberg. Junk Mail.
Hardy. Circular, A.
Kipling. Advertisement, The.
Lindsay. There were open boxes of fine cigars.
Merton. Now leaning over the salt nerve of our wave length we have decided to send you the frozen exports of a compromised musician.
Proverbs.
Nash. Roll On, Thou Deep and Dark Blue Copy Writer—Roll!
Song of the Open Road.
Strange Case of the Lucrative Compromise, The.
What, No Sheep?
Sandburg. From what graveyards and sepulchers have they come.
Schuyler. Adverts.
Updike. Publius Vergilius Maro, the Madison Avenue Hick.
Williams, William Carlos. Lovely Ad.
See also **Billboards.**

Advice
Atwood. After all you are quite.
Beatles. You're Going to Lose That Girl.
Berry. Manifesto: the Mad Farmer Liberation Front.
Blake. Song 3rd By an Old Shepherd.
Bogan. Young Mage, The.
Browning, Elizabeth Barrett. Wisdom Unapplied.
Bukowski. Counsel.
Friendly Advice to a Lot of Young Men.
How to Be a Great Writer.
Now, If You Were Teaching Creative Writing, He Asked, What Would You Tell Them?
Burns. Country Lassie.

Epistle to a Young Friend.
Prologue: "No song nor dance I bring from yon great city."
Written in Friar's Carse Hermitage on the Banks of Nith—June—1788.
Carew. Conquest by Flight.
"Carroll, Lewis." Rules and Regulations.
Catullus. Carmen 23: "Friend Furius, / who has no slaves & no money'."
Chaucer. Nun's Priest's Tale, The.
Proverbs: "What shul these clothes thus manyfold."
Truth.
Coleridge. On Revisiting the Sea-Shore, after Long Absence.
Creeley. Way, The.
Dickey, William. Being Asked To Define Bourgeois Individuality.
Life Moving More Rapidly Than Hands Can Manage.
Donne. To E. of D. with Six Holy Sonnets.
Dunn. Some Things I Wanted to Say to You.
To a Friend in Love with the Wrong Man Again.
"Dylan." Advice for Geraldine on Her Miscellaneous Birthday.
I Am a Lonesome Hobo.
It Ain't Me, Babe.
She's Your Lover Now.
Sweetheart Like You.
To Ramona.
Emerson. Discontented Poet: A Masque, The.
Do that which you can do.
Drink, hear my counsel, my son, that the world fret thee not.
I said to the East wind.
Kind & holy were the words.
Novice, hear me what I say.
Suum Cuique ("Wilt thou seal up the avenues of ill?").
To Rhea.
Way of love is unlimited, The.
Graves. Advice from a Mother.
Hardy. Young Man's Exhortation, A.
Hemingway. Advice to a Son.
Lines to a Girl 5 Days After Her 21st Birthday.
Travel Poem.
Herbert. Perirrhanterium.
Herrick. Advice the Best Actor.
Caution in Councell.
Consultation.
Counsell.
Good Precepts, or Counsell.
Paranæticall, or Advisive Verse, to His Friend, M. John Wicks.
To his Booke ("Take mine advise, and go not neere").
Hewitt. Great Event, A.
My Own and Not My Own.
Housman. Carpenter's Son, The.
Sage to the Young Man, The.
When I was one-and-twenty.
Hughes, Langston. Mother to Son.
Prayer: "I ask you this."
Warning.
Warning: Augmented.
Jarrell. Hanged man on the gallows, The.
Jong. For My Sister, against Narrowness.
Jonson. Martial. Epigram XLVII, Book X.
Kipling. If.
One Viceroy Resigns.
Koch. Art of Love, The.
Art of Poetry, The.
On Beauty.
Some General Instructions.
Kunitz. Goodies are shaken / from the papatree.
Lewis. Sacco Writes to His Son.
Lorde. For Each of You.
For My Singing Sister.
Lovelace. Advice to My Best Brother, Colonel Francis Lovelace.
MacLeish. Seafarer.
McNeill. Grave Creek Inscribed Stone, The.
Meinke. Advice to My Son.

Millay. If in the years to come you should
  recall.
Morrison. Crossroads, The.
  Lessons on Becoming.
Notley. Prophet, The.
Olson. Rufus Woodpecker visited the
  President.
Piercy. Seven of Pentacles, The.
Prince. To a Granddaughter on One of Her
  Suggestions for a Christmas Present.
Ralegh. Sir Walter Ra[u]le[i]gh to His
  Son[ne].
"Reed." Vicious Circle.
Rich. I Heard a Hermit Speak.
Robinson. Old King's New Jester, The.
  Voice of Age, The.
Rolfe. Blues.
Rossetti. Versi.
Sandburg. Father sees a son nearing manhood,
  A.
He was a king or a shah, an ahkoond or rajah.
  Snatch of Sliphorn Jazz.
Three Fragments for Fishers of Destiny.
Sexton. Sermon of the Twelve
  Acknowledgements, The.
Sidney. Fair rocks, goodly rivers, sweet
  woods, when shall I see peace?
  Sonnet 85: "I see the house; my heart thyself
  contain."
Silverstein. Instructions.
Smart. Praise.
Snodgrass. Diplomacy: The Father.
Williams, Miller. For Reuben, at Twelve
  Months.
Young. O!
Zukofsky. Furius, with no key to service, no
  key.

Aegean Sea
Hewitt. Cape Sunion.

Aeneas
Campion. Ballad, A: "Dido was the Carthage
  Queene."
Merton. Like Ilium.
Spenser. Then all astoined with this mighty
  ghoast.
Tate. Aeneas at New York.
  Aeneas at Washington.

Aeneid, The (Virgil)
Liddy. Vir.
Lovelace. Asse Eating the Ænieds, The.

Aengus
Yeats. Harp of Aengus, The.
  Song of Wandering Aengus, The.

Aesop
Catullus. Carmen 22: "I must, Varus, tell
  you."
Crane. Black Tambourine.
Zukofsky. Suffenus is, stay Varus,—whom
  you've proven—is the.

Affection
Auden. Four sat on in the bare room, The.
Beatles. And I Love Her.
  Ask Me Why.
  Can't Buy Me Love.
  Every Little Thing.
  For You Blue.
  Her Majesty.
  I Want to Hold Your Hand.
  I'm Happy Just to Dance with You.
  I've Just Seen a Face.
  Julia.
  Old Brown Shoe.
  She's a Woman.
  Something.
  Wild Honey Pie.
  You Like Me Too Much.
Berry. Beginning and end.
  Freedom of Loving, The.
Bly. Good Silence, The.
  In the Month of May.
  Indigo Bunting, The.
Bradstreet. Another ("Phoebus, make haste").
  Letter to Her Husband, Absent upon Public[k]
  Employment, A.
  To Her Father, with Some Verses.
Browning, Elizabeth Barrett. L. E. L.'s Last
  Question.

My Kate.
  Parting Lovers.
  Proof and Disproof.
  Question and Answer.
  Sonnet: "And therefore if to love can be
  desert."
  Sonnet: "And wilt thou have me fashion into
  speech."
  Sonnet: "Because thou hast the power and
  own'st the grace."
  Sonnet: "Beloved, thou hast brought me many
  flowers."
  Sonnet: "But only three in all God's universe."
  Sonnet: "Can it be right to give what I can
  give."
  Sonnet: "Face of all the world is changed, I
  think, The."
  Sonnet: "I lift my heavy heart up solemnly."
  Sonnet: "I never gave a lock hair away."
  Sonnet: "I thank all who have loved me in
  their hearts."
  Sonnet: "I thought once how Theocritus had
  sung."
  Sonnet: "If I leave all for thee, wilt thou
  exchange."
  Sonnet: "Indeed this very love which is my
  boast."
  Sonnet: "Is it indeed so? If I lay here dead."
  Sonnet: "My own Beloved, who hast lifted
  me."
  Sonnet: "Oh, yes! they love through all this
  world of ours."
  Sonnet: "Pardon, oh, pardon, that my soul
  should make."
  Sonnet: "Say over again, and yet once over
  again."
  Sonnet: "Soul's Rialto hath its merchandise,
  The."
  Sonnet: "When we first met and loved, I did
  not build."
  Sonnet: "With the same heart, I said, I'l
  answer thee."
  Sonnet: "Yes, call me by my pet-name! let me
  hear."
  Void in Law.
Burns. Extempore Epistle to Mr. McAdam of
  Craigengillian, (Wrote in Nanse Tinnock's,
  Mauchline) in Answer to an Obliging Letter
  He Sent in the Commencement of My Poetic
  Career.
It is na, Jean, thy bonie face.
  My Eppie.
  My Wife's a Winsome Wee Thing.
  O May Thy Morn.
  Reply to Robert Riddell.
  Scotish Song.
  She Says She Lo'es Me Best of A'.
  Song: " 'Twas na her bonie blue e'e was my
  ruin."
  Song: "O this is no my ain lassie."
  Song: "O wat ye wha's in yon town."
  To Chloris.
  To Mr. McMurdo, with a Pound of Lundiefoot
  Snuff.
  Young Jockey was the blythest lad.
Byron. So We'll Go No More a Roving.
  Stanzas: "Could Love for ever."
  Stanzas to Jessy.
  To Thyrza.
Campion. My Sweetest Lesbia [Let Us Live
  and Love].
Carew. Fly That Flew into My Mistress'[s]
  Eye, A.
  In Praise of His Mistress.
  To my Friend G.N. from Wrest.
  To My Rival.
  Tooth-Ache Cured by a Kiss, The.
Catullus. Carmen 5: "Lesbia / live with me."
  Carmen 45: "Phyllis Corydon clutched to
  him."
Chaucer. Romance [or Romaunt] of the Rose,
  The.
Clark. Ace of Destiny.
  Got to be there, so that she'll know.
  My Hypertrophic Devotion.
Coleridge. Her Thoughts.
  Imitated from the Welch.

Lines on a Portrait of a Lady.
  To the Rev. George Coleridge.
Crabbe. On Receiving from a Lady a Present
  of a Ring.
Creeley. Act of Love, The.
  Air: "Cat Bird Singing."
  Boy, the.
  Fall.
  For Walter Chappell.
  Love Comes Quietly.
  Night.
  Oh Mabel.
  Song, A: "I had wanted a quiet testament."
  To Bobbie.
Cullen. To One Not There.
Cummings. But if a living dance upon dead
  minds.
  Clown's smirk in the skull of a baboon, A.
  Great advantage of being alive, The.
  Hate blows a bubble of despair into.
  If everything happens that can't be done.
  If i love You.
  If(touched by love's own secret)we,like
  homing.
  In spite of everything.
  Love is more thicker than forget.
  Love is the every only god.
  Love's function is to fabricate unknownness.
  Now all the fingers of this tree(darling)have.
  O by the by / has anybody seen.
  Somewhere I have never travelled,gladly
  beyond.
  Yes is a pleasant country.
Dickinson. Affection is like bread.
  Affection wants you to know it is here.
  Genius is the ignition of affection.
  Is not the distinction of Affection.
  It stills, incites, infatuates.
  Ravenousness of fondness, The.
  Were the Velocity of Affection.
Dunbar. Negro Love Song, A.
Dunn. All That We Have.
"Dylan." Absolutely Sweet Marie.
  All I Really Want to Do.
  Buckets of Rain.
  Coming from the Heart (The Road Is Long).
  Emotionally Yours.
  Farewell: "Oh it's fare thee well my darlin'
  true."
  From a Buick 6.
  I'll Keep It with Mine.
  It Takes a Lot to Laugh, It Takes a Train to
  Cry.
  Leopard-Skin Pill-Box Hat.
  Love Minus Zero/No Limit.
  Mama, You Been on My Mind.
  Man in Me, The.
  Never Say Goodbye.
  New Pony.
  Nobody 'Cept You.
  One of Us Must Know (Sooner or Later).
  Pledging My Time.
  Sara.
  Something's Burning, Baby.
  Tight Connection to My Heart (Has Anybody
  Seen My Love).
  To Be Alone with You.
  Tonight I'll Be Staying Here with You.
  Wedding Song.
  When the Night Comes Falling from the Sky.
  Winterlude.
  You Angel You.
  You're Gonna Make Me Lonesome When You
  Go.
Emerson. Kind & holy were the words.
Gallagher. Hug, The.
Gardner. Accomplices, The.
  Baldur Was Beautiful Too.
  Cock-a-Hoop.
  Convalescence in Summer 1949.
  Cowardice.
  Disenchanted, The.
  Eros in May at MacDowell.
  Feminine Ending or, Abandoned, She Died.
  Fixing the Clock.
  Folkways.
  Fright among the Runes.

Grocery Bouquet, The.
In the Museum.
Incantate the Cockatrice.
Jean Sans Terre Wraps Himself in a Red Coat.
Letter from Slough Pond.
Lines to a Seagreen Lover.
Man of Faith, The.
Mathematics of Encounter.
Prospero's Isle.
Salt.
Searchlight, The.
Tango for Zither.
Two Sapphics.
Your Fearful Symmetries.
Zei Gesund.
Garrigue.   For Anybody's Martyr's Song.
Glück.   Hawk's Shadow.
Graves.   Circus Ring.
Colophon.
Compact.
Depth of Love.
Five.
Gorge, The.
Her Brief Withdrawal.
Iago.
In Perspective.
Love Charms.
Necklace, The.
None the Wiser.
On Giving.
Pity.
Poet's Curse, The.
Pride of Progeny.
Quinque.
Records.
Reiteration, The.
Risk, The.
Seven Years.
Sincèrement.
Song: Cherries or Lilies.
Song: Dew-Drop and Diamond.
Song: Victims of Calumny.
Strangeness.
Strangling in Merrion Square, The.
Three Locked Hoops.
Three Words Only.
Timeless Meeting.
To Be in Love.
Touch My Shut Lips.
When Love Is Not.
Griffiths.   Still Too Quick to Hold.
Gunn.   High Fidelity.
Hall.   Gold.
Hemingway.   To Crazy Christian.
Herrick.   3.9: Dialogue between Horace and
   Lydia, A ("Donec gratus eram").
Another ("Where love begins, there dead thy
   first desire").
Eclipse, The.
His Mistris to Him at His Farwell.
How His Soule Came Ensnared.
Martha, Martha.
No Action Hard to Affection.
On Julias Lips.
On Love ("That love 'twixt men do's ever
   longest last").
Parliament of Roses to Julia, The.
To Anthea ("Anthea I am going hence").
To Electra ("Let not thy Tomb-stone").
To Julia ("I am zeellesse, prethee pray").
To Mistresse Dorothy Parsons.
To My Dearest Sister M. Mercie Herrick.
To Sapho ("Thou saist thou lov'st me Sapho; I
   say no").
Upon Love ("Love is a circle").
Upon Lucia Dabled in the Deaw.
Hewitt.   My Parents' Courtship.
Of a Professor.
R.P.M.
Hopkins.   Love me as I love thee. O double
   sweet!
Keats.   To ———: "Had I a man's fair form,
   then might my sighs."
To Emma.
To Georgiana Augusta Wylie.
To Some Ladies.
Upon My Life, Sir Nevis, I Am Piqued.

Kinnell.   Two Seasons.
Koertge.   Getting the License.
Lewis.   And now we seek once more the
   burning breeze.
And still the heart breaks, wakeful all the
   night?
Atropos to Ophelia.
Beloved Beware.
Corfe Castle.
Dancer, The.
Desperate, The.
Destruction.
Encirclement.
Fever.
Goodbye.
I send you a Christmas present, sweet.
Lament: "Oh Absalom, beloved, what can I
   say?"
Merchants Wife, The.
Mid-Winter.
Miniature on a Book of Hours.
On a Bereaved Girl.
On Leave: Marriage.
Post-Script: for Gweno.
Separation, A.
Shadows.
She Comes To Him in the Night.
She Remains.
She Wakes Early, While He Still Sleeps.
Song: "I lay in sheets of softest linen."
Song: "Oh journeyman, Oh journeyman."
Sonnet (Aboard a Troopship) to Gweno.
*They Part at Daybreak, Returning Their
   Inevitable Ways.*
Valediction.
Victory.
*Vigil: He Lies Awake in the Barracks Room,
   Fearful She Will Not Come, The.*
*Vigil: She Tarries, Far-Off, in a Strange
   Anguish, The.*
Water Music.
Wood Song.
Liddy.   Enchanter of Yellow Gold to the Old
   Friend, The.
In a Blue Smoke.
Sergeant Valentine Function, at Hollyfort.
Third Letter to Jimin in Manchuria.
Lorde.   Dozens, The.
Poem for a Poet.
Progress Report.
Lowell.   Dunbarton.
Grandparents.
Lowry.   Margeries and the malcolms did, The.
Port has a sweeter name than Saigon, The.
Welcome Home Oh Gladsome Springhorned
   Beloved and Famed Harteebeeste.
"MacDiarmid."   His attitude towards woman is
   the basic point.
MacLeish.   Old Gray Couple (2), The.
Markson.   Contradiction.
Merton.   Flight of Lin Hui, The.
Morgan.   Catullus: *Carmen v.*
Morrison.   Please Like Me.
Nash.   Love Me but Leave My Dog Alone.
Reflection on Caution.
Nemerov.   New Weapons in the Old War.
Neruda.   Dead Dog.
O'Hara.   Kitville.
Poem: "So many echoes in my head."
To Jane; and in Imitation of Coleridge.
Olson.   À Constance, This Day.
Heart is a clock, The.
She.
Owen.   Song of Songs.
Pack.   Kiss, The.
Prince.   Chapel-at-Ease.
Strambotti.
Raine.   Hieros Gamos.
Soliloquy Upon Love.
Ralegh.   Arte of English Poesie, The.
As You Came from the Holy Land [of
   Walsingham].
Excuse, The.
Poesie to Prove Affection is Not Love, A.
Rossetti.   Death's Chill Between.
Dog lies in his kennel, The.
Heart's Chill Between.

My Mouse.
Piteous my rhyme is / What while I muse of
   love and pain.
So I grew half delirious and quite sick.
Sonnets are full of love, and this my tome.
To My Friend Elizabeth.
Rukeyser.   Among Grass.
Orpheus.
Song, the Brain-Coral.
Sarton.   Letter to James Stephens, A.
Schuyler.   Letter Poem #2.
Letter Poem #3.
Oriane.
Watching You.
You're.
Shapiro.   Twins, The.
Sidney.   All what you are still one, his own to
   find.
Like diverse flowers, whose diverse beauties
   serve.
Sonnet 25: "Wisest scholar of the wight most
   wise, The."
Sonnet 87: "When I was forced from Stella
   ever dear."
Silverstein.   Hug o' War.
Sorrentino.   Big Brown Eyes.
Diaghilev Did Not Say "Étonnez-Moi."
Marjorie.
You Are My Heart's Bouquet.
Spender.   One.
Stein.   Sonatina Followed by Another, A.
Stevenson.   All things on earth and sea.
To you, let snow and roses.
Stuart.   Finding One of the Ghosts.
Girl of My Dreams, The.
That'll Be the Day.
Suckling.   Desdain ("To what end serve the
   promises").
Sutter.   Warmth.
Thomson.   To Myra.
Verses on Receiving a Flower from his
   Mistress.
Van Duyn.   Garland for Christopher Smart, A.
Notes from a Suburban Heart.
Warren.   Answer to Prayer.
Whitman.   Base of All Metaphysics, The.
Sometimes with One I Love.
Wilbur.   June Light.
Williams, Charles Kenneth.   Being Alone.
Dog, The.
Snow: II.
Williams, Miller.   Fly Me to the Moon.
Ghost of His Wife Comes to Tell Him How It
   Is.
Love in the Cathedral.
Notes from the Agent on Earth: How to be
   Human.
Paying Some Attention to His Birthday the
   Associate Professor Goes About His Business
   Considering What He Sees and a Kind of
   Praise.
Poem for Emily, A.
Sir.
Wordsworth.   Lesbia.
Septimius and Acme.
Wroth.   Sonnet 3: "His flames ar joyes, his
   bands true lovers might."
Young.   Only Race There Is, The.
Zukofsky.   Acme, Septimius, sighs so amorous.
Barely and *widely.*
Cactus rose-mauve and gray, twin overturned.
Celia's Birthday Poem.
Finally a Valentine.
Madison, Wis., Remembering the Bloom of
   Monticello (1931).
May we live, my Lesbia, love while we may.
On Valentine's Day to Friends.
Passing tall.
Record, The.
Tam Cari Capitis.
With a Valentine (the 12 February).
With a Valentine (the 14 February).

Affliction

Beatles.   I Me Mine.
Berg.   Wanting to Be Heavier.
Cowper.   ˙ To a Friend in Distress.

Vicissitudes Experienced in the Christian Life, The.
Gardner. Convalescence in Summer 1949.
Herrick. Affliction.
Comforts in Crosses.
Good Men Afflicted Most.
Pain[e] Ends in Pleasure.
Persecutions Profitable.
Kipling. Natural Theology.
Lewis. Black dog barking at the moon.
Country Gentleman, The.
Polish girls singing, in the wind's soughing.
White brain crossing, The.
Milton. Lord God that dost me save and keep.
Psalms. Psalm 88: "O God of my salvation."
Psalm 120: "In my distress I cried unto the Lord.."
Psalm 132: "Lord, remember David, and all his afflictions."
Psalm 140: "Deliver me, O Lord, from the evil man."
Psalm 142: "I cried unto the Lord with my voice."
Psalm 143: "Hear my prayer, O Lord, give ear.."
Wyatt. Hear my prayer, O Lord, hear my request.

Afghanistan
Kipling. Ballad of the King's Jest, The.
Ballad of the King's Mercy, The.

Africa
Angelou. Africa.
For Us, Who Dare Not Dare.
Browning, Robert. Home-Thoughts, from the Sea.
Through the Metidja to Abd-el-Kadr.
Carroll, Jim. Words from Babylon.
Carruth. Algeria.
Cullen. Brown Boy to Brown Girl.
Heritage.
Dunbar. Ode to Ethiopia.
Eberhart. Lions Copulating.
Eliot. To the Indians Who Died in Africa.
Hardy. Drummer Hodge.
Hewitt. Art and Technology.
Hughes, Langston. Africa.
Afro-American Fragment.
Danse Africaine.
Negro.
Kipling. This Uninhabited Island.
Koch. Geography.
Lawrence. Tropic.
Lindsay. Congo, The.
Meredith. Gordon of Khartoum.
Moore. Jerboa, The.
Nemerov. Two Poems.
Walcott. Far Cry from Africa, A.
Walker. African Images, Glimpses from a Tiger's Back.
Karamojongs.
There are no tigers.
There were palm trees.
Williams, William Carlos. Gentle Negress, The.

African-American Power
Angelou. No No No No.
Pusher, The.
Knight. Dark Prophecy: I Sing of Shine.
Lorde. NOW.

African Americans
Angelou. Ain't That Bad.
Amoebaean for Daddy.
Black Ode.
Calling of Names, The.
Family Affairs.
On Working White Liberals.
Passing Time.
Sepia Fashion Show.
Song for the Old Ones.
Still I Rise.
Thank You, Lord.
Through the Inner City to the Suburbs.
To a Husband.
To a Suitor.
Weekend Glory.
Bishop. Cootchie.
Songs for a Colored Singer.

Blake. Little Black Boy, The.
Brooks. Ballad of Rudolph Reed, The.
I Love Those Little Booths at Benvenuti's.
We Real Cool.
Browning, Elizabeth Barrett. Runaway Slave at Pilgrim's Point, The.
Carruth. Mountain, The.
Sam and Poll Go Back to the City.
Crane. Black Tambourine.
Cullen. Black Christ, The.
Black Majesty.
Colored Blues Singer.
From the Dark Tower.
Heritage.
Litany of the Dark People, The.
Pagan Prayer.
Shroud of Color, The.
Song of Praise, A.
Yet Do I Marvel.
Cummings. Theys sO alive.
Dunbar. Black Samson of Brandywine.
Colored Band, The.
Colored Soldiers, The.
Unsung Heroes, The.
We Wear the Mask.
When Dey 'Listed Colored Soldiers.
"Dylan." Baby black's / been had.
Hurricane.
Emerson. I am not black in my mind.
Ford. Plaint.
Hemingway. Road to Avallon, The.
To Will Davies.
Hughes, Langston. Brothers.
Consider Me.
Cross.
Dream Variation[s].
Flatted Fifths.
Freedom Train.
Freedom's Plow.
Graduation.
High to Low.
I, Too.
Low to High.
Me and the Mule.
Merry-Go-Round.
Migrant.
Negro.
Negro Mother, The.
Negro Speaks of Rivers, The.
Neighbor.
Nightmare Boogie.
One-Way Ticket.
Porter.
Prayer Meeting.
Ruby Brown.
Seashore through Dark Glasses (Atlantic City).
Shame on You.
South, The.
Stars.
Sun Song.
Theme for English B.
Trumpet Player.
Uncle Tom.
What? So Soon!
Jarrell. Lady Bates.
Jonson. Sound, sound aloud / The welcome of the orient flood.
Kinnell. Avenue Bearing the Initial of Christ into the New World, The.
Knight. Another Poem for Me (after Recovering from an O.D.).
Black Poet Leaps to His Death, A.
Bones of My Father, The.
Con/tin/u/way/shun Blues.
Fable: "Once upon a today and yesterday and nevermore there were 7 men."
For Black Poets Who Think of Suicide.
Haiku: "Two hours I've walked."
Memo #32.
My Life, the Quality of Which.
On Seeing the Black Male as #1 Sex Object in America.
Once on a Night in the Delta: A Report From Hell.
Various Protestations From Various People.
Warden Said to Me the Other Day, The.

Lindsay. Booker Washington Trilogy, The.
Congo, The.
Lorde. Coal.
Generation II.
Lowell. For the Union Dead.
Mad Negro Soldier Confined at Munich, A.
Melville. Formerly a Slave.
Merton. Plessy vs Ferguson: Theme and Variations.
Nemerov. Negro Cemetery Next to a White One, A.
Rukeyser. George Robinson: Blues.
Three Black Women.
Sandburg. Nigger.
Singing Nigger.
Shapiro. Nigger.
Walker. It is true--/ I've always loved.
Whitman. Ethiopia Saluting the Colors.
Williams, William Carlos. Sick African.
Time the Hangman.
Wordsworth. September 1, 1802.
Wright, James. Confession to J. Edgar Hoover.
Young. Birthday Poem.
Boogie With O.O. Gabugah.
Dance for Militant Dilettantes, A.
Identities.
Old O.O. Blues, The.
Some Recent Fiction.
What You Seize Is What You Git.
Your Basic Black Poet.

Afterlife
Berrigan. Wrong Train.
Berry. But do not let your ignorance.
Brontë. Lines: "I die; but when the grave shall press."
Wide cathedral aisles are lone, The.
Cowper. Acquiescence of Pure Love, The.
Child of God Longing To See Him Beloved, A.
On the Death of the Bishop of Ely.
Translation of Epitaph to Northcot.
Crane. Circumstance, The.
Cullen. Poet, The.
Cummings. If there are any heavens my mother will(all by herself)have.
Eberhart. Ides of March, The.
Emerson. Spirits of the wise, sit on the clouds, The.
Fenton. Kingfisher's Boxing Gloves, The.
Hartley. Alice Miriam.
Herrick. His Charge to Julia at His Death.
Plaudite, or End of Life, The.
Hewitt. Dungannon Cattle Market.
Hill. Not as we are but as we must appear.
Housman. They shall have breath that never were.
Hughes, Ted. Risen, The.
Jeffers. Inscription for a Gravestone.
Kunitz. Time swings her burning hands.
Lawrence. Like the Green Candles of Malintzi.
My Way Is Not Thy Way.
Song of the Dead.
Levine. Breath.
MacNeice. This Is the Life.
Mahon. Leaves.
Marvell. Dialogue between Thyrsis and Dorinda.
Tom May's Death.
Merrill. Voices from the Other World.
Milton. On the Death of the Bishop of Ely.
Neruda. When all turned to altitude.
Oliver. Roses, Late Summer.
Patchen. At the Entrance to the Other World.
Rolfe. Something Still Lives.
Rukeyser. My name is Timmy Torin.
Sandburg. To a Dead Man.
Stevenson. Death.
Nor judge me light, tho' light at times I seem.
Whitman. Unnamed Lands.
Williams, Charles Kenneth. Giving It Up.
Williams, Miller. After You Die You Don't Give a Piddling Damn.
Wright, James. Willy Lyons.
Yau. When one of our citizens dies, his corpse is placed in his chariot.

When one of our citizens dies, his head is cut off and placed inside.

Afternoon
"Carroll, Lewis." Dedication: "All in the golden afternoon."
Carruth. Backyard in California, A.
Davie. Tuscan Morning.
De la Mare. In the Garden.
Fisher. Mounted on all four walls, the neat.
Galvin. Pollen.
Hartley. Invitation.
Lowry. Afternoon Nocturne.
Millay. Afternoon on a Hill.
Nemerov. Harvest Home, A.
O'Hara. Tarquin.
Olson. Afternoon.
Tomlinson. All Afternoon.
Carscape.
Eight Observations on the Nature of Eternity.
Hokusai on the Trent.
Wright, James. Down to the Dregs.
Young. Afternoon After, The.

Afton River, Scotland
Burns. Afton Water.

Agamemnon
Jeffers. Tower beyond Tragedy, The.
Meredith. Agamemnon in the Fight.
Marshalling of the Achaians.
Merton. Greek Women, The.
Ralegh. 4.9: "Many by valour have deserved renown."

Agassiz, Louis
Whittier. Prayer of Agassiz, The.

Aggression
Bukowski. Transformation and Disfiguration.
Carruth. Sonnet: Sin.
Cohen. My Honour.
Lawrence. Attila.
Lindsay. Lion, The.
Nash. Tweedledee and Tweedledoom.
Notley. Bus Stop.
Thomas. If My Head Hurt a Hair's Foot.
Young. Are You the Lover or Loved?
Dance for Militant Dilettantes, A.

Aging
Ammons. Late Look.
Angelou. On Reaching Forty.
Arnold. Growing Old.
Ashbery. Tone Poem, A.
Atwood. After all you are quite.
Aging Female Poet on Laundry Day.
Aging Female Poet Sits on the Balcony.
Girl and Horse, 1928.
Keep.
Auden. At Twenty we find our friends for ourselves, but it takes Heaven.
Babies in their mothers' arms.
Cave of Nakedness, The.
Doggerel by a Senior Citizen.
His ageing nature is the same.
No window in his suburb lights that bedroom where.
None of us are as young.
Old People's Home.
Price, The.
Prologue at Sixty.
Waste.
With what conviction the young man spoke.
Beatles. When I'm Sixty Four.
Beckett. Saint-Lô.
Berg. To Charlie.
William Carlos Williams Reading His Poems.
Berry. Ripening.
Berryman. At Chinese Checkers.
Clots of age, grovel and palsy, crave, The.
Damned.
Marble nor monuments where of then we spoke.
Point of Age, A.
Betjeman. Fruit.
Senex.
Bishop. Mountain, The.
Bly. Defeated.
Night Frogs.
Visiting the Farallones.
Watcher, The.
Boyle. Poem about Black Power, A.

Bradstreet. Of the Four Ages of Man.
Brontë. O evening, why is thy light so sad?
Why do I hate that lone green dell?
Brooks. Old Mary.
Browning, Robert. By the Fire-Side.
Prologue: "Poet's age is sad: for why?, The."
Rabbi Ben Ezra.
Youth and Art.
Bukowski. American Express, Athens, Greece.
Clean Old Man.
Doom and Siesta Time.
For Al—.
One of the Hottest.
Poem for My 43rd Birthday.
This Then—.
Bunting. Slinking by the jug-and-bottle.
You can't grip years, Postume.
Burns. Broom Besoms ["Young and souple was I, when I lap the dyke"].
Deuks Dang o'er My Daddie, The.
John Anderson, My Jo.
Lazy Mist, The.
Sketch. New Year's Day. To Mrs. Dunlop.
Byron. Fill the Goblet.
L'Amitié Est L'Amour Sans Ailes.
So We'll Go No More a Roving.
Stanzas for Music ("There's not a joy the world can give like that it takes away").
To Edward Noel Long, Esq.
To the Countess of Blessington.
To Time.
Campion. First Love.
My Dearest Mistress.
Carew. Disdain Returned.
"Carroll, Lewis." Air is bright with hues of light, The.
Father William.
Game of Fives, A.
Carruth. Capper Kaplinski at the North Side Cue Club.
Essay on Love.
Excursus of Reassurance in Begonia Time, An.
For thon demgeorne dreorigne oft.
He thinks how, often when his semen spews.
His body, caught there in the mirror, lean.
Insomniac Sleeps Well for Once and, The.
Last year of youth, The.
Living Alone.
Marge.
New Hartford.
No Supervening Thought of Grace.
Opusthirteen.
Rummage.
Sex.
Shall he then finally "put away childish things."
Silence.
Song: Luxury.
Song: The Old, Old Man.
Sonnet: "Fear of falling is why the old men walk."
Sonnet: "I want to do a complaint now. Which is to say."
Sonnet: "To rebel. So I have saved my life, not once."
Sonnet: "You rose from our embrace and the small light spread."
Tanck's Epilogue.
Tanck's Song About His Birthday.
Tanck's Song About His Unicameral Mind.
Tanck's Song About the Younger Generation.
Tanck's Song About Youth and Age.
That I Had Had Courage When Young.
Twilight Comes.
Valentine.
Ciardi. Washing Your Feet.
Clough. Dance on, dance on, we see, we see.
Here am I yet, another twelvemonth spent.
July's Farewell.
Cohen. Angelica.
I Left a Woman.
I Left a Woman Waiting.
Is This What You Wanted.
Marita.
My Honour.

This Is for You.
Tower of Song, The.
Coleridge. Improvisatore, The.
Cowper. Inscription for a Stone.
Lines for a Memorial of Ashley Cowper.
Moralizer Corrected, The.
See'st thou yon mountains laden with deep snow.
Song: "No more shall hapless Celia's ears."
To Mary.
To William Hayley, Esq.: In Reply to His Solicitation to Write with Him in a Literary Work.
Crabbe. Phoebe Dawson.
Creeley. Chanson.
For Irving.
For the Graduation.
Testament, A.
Cummings. Harder perhaps than a newengland bed.
My uncle / Daniel fought in the civil.
Nobody wears a yellow.
Noone" autumnal this great lady's gaze.
oDE: "O / the sweet & aged people."
Somebody knew Lincoln somebody Xerxes.
Time,be kind;herself and i.
Tw / oo / ld / o / nce upo / n.
Whatever's merely wilful, / and not miraculous.
When hair falls off and eyes blur And.
When time delicately is sponging sum after.
Davie. And Our Eternal Home.
Artifex in Extremis.
Autumn Imagined.
Heigh-ho on a Winter Afternoon.
Liverpool Epistle, A.
Penelope.
Recollections of George Oppen in a Letter to an English Friend.
Selina, Countess of Huntingdon.
So Make Them Melt as the Dishoused Snail.
They, to Me.
Though Dry, Not Dry.
Trip to Huntsville, The.
De la Mare. Brother and Sister.
Karma.
News.
On the Esplanade.
Time Passes.
Dickey, William. At Your Old House.
Dickinson. Little Snow was here and there, A.
My Wars are laid away in Books.
We outgrow love like other things.
We turn not older with years.
Dobyns. Body's Weight, The.
Fatal Kisses.
What You Have Come To Expect.
Doolittle. "I love you," / spoken in rhapsodic metre.
Dunbar. At Sunset Time.
Lost Dream, A.
Vengeance is Sweet.
Dunn. Carpenter's Song, The.
Eberhart. Edgar Lee Masters.
Experience Evoked.
God and Man.
Half-bent Man.
Hardy Perennial.
Haystack, The.
Lovely were the fruit trees in the evening.
Eliot. Cooking Egg, A.
Emerson. Brother, no decrepitude.
Climacteric.
I know the appointed hour.
Only three things lengthen life.
Salve Senescentem.
Terminus ("For thought & not praise").
Terminus ("It is time to be old").
Thanks to those who go & come.
This effervescing gentleman who despises a secret.
Valedictory Poem.
Wo is me woe's me when I think.
Woods.
Fisher. There's a time, finally.
Fox. And the lovers meet again.
Frost. In the Home Stretch.

Span of Life, The.
To Earthward.
What Fifty Said.
Gallagher. Borrowed Ones, The.
My Mother Remembers That She Was Beautiful.
Some with Wings, Some with Manes.
Galvin. Sengekontacket.
Gardner. Children Are Game.
Nor Good Red Herring.
On Looking in the Looking Glass.
This Room Is Full of Clocks.
Ginsberg. Aether.
Don't Grow Old ("Old Poet").
Don't Grow Old ("Twenty-eight years").
Growing Old Again.
Old Village before I Die, The.
Some Love.
Glück. End of the World, The.
For My Mother.
Portrait of the Queen in Tears.
To Autumn.
Graves. Change.
Dazzle of Darkness.
Imminent Seventies, The.
Suicide in The Copse, The.
Griffiths. Climber.
Gunn. For a Birthday.
Hall. Dancers.
Days, The.
Friend Revisited, A.
Grown-Ups, The.
Hole, The.
In the Kitchen of the Old House.
Mr. Wakeville on Interstate 90.
My Son, My Executioner.
Old Timer's Day.
Hardy. Ageing House, The.
At Madame Tussaud's in Victorian Years.
At the Dinner-Table.
Circus-Rider to Ringmaster.
Colonel's Soliloquy, The.
Ghost of the Past, The.
God's Education.
Her Apotheosis.
In a Eweleaze near Weatherbury.
In the Night She Came.
Lament of the Looking-Glass, The.
Revisitation, The.
Seeing the Moon Rise.
She, to Him.
Ten Years Since.
Under High-Stoy Hill.
Voice of Things, The.
When you shall see me in the toils of Time.
Woman Who Went East, The.
Hartnett. Old Catechism, The.
Sibelius in Silence.
Hayden. Lear Is Gay.
Hemingway. Age Demanded, The.
Along with Youth.
Herbert. Answer, The.
Mortification.
Herrick. Changes to Corinna, The.
Courage Cool'd.
His Age, Dedicated to His Peculiar Friend, Master John Wickes, under the Name of Posthumus.
On Himselfe ("Young I was, but [or who] now am old").
To a Bed of Tulips.
To a Gentlewoman Objecting to Him His Grey Hairs.
To His Friend, on the Untunable Times.
To His Mistresses.
Upon Silvia, a Mistresse.
Upon Wrinkles.
Hesketh. All Hallows.
Call of the North.
Comparison with a Sunflower.
From the Day Room.
House In the Tree.
Second Childhood.
Sundowner.
Violet at Ninety.
Walled In.

Wordsworth's Old Age.
Yew Tree Guest House.
Hewitt. Age and Youth.
Autumnal.
Bifocal in Gaza.
College Fence, The.
Modelled Head, The.
My Own and Not My Own.
Neglected Lane, The.
Of course, the gruffest prompting comes from age.
On the Canal.
Retreaded Rhymes.
R.K.
Sonnet in Autumn.
Souterrain, The.
Variations on a Theme.
Young Womanhood.
Hoffman. Himself.
Jogger.
Ode to Joy.
Holmes. Statements in a Personal Winter.
Housman. Loveliest of trees, the cherry now.
Say, lad, have you things to do?
When first my way to fair I took.
When summer's end is nighing.
Hughes, Langston. Little Green Tree.
Young Gal's Blues.
Hugo. Again, Kapowsin.
Art of Poetry, The.
Flying, Reflying, Farming.
From Altitude, the Diamonds.
Hot Springs.
In Your Young Dream.
Letter to Blessing from Missoula.
Letter to Libbey from St. Regis.
Letter to Mayo from Missoula.
Letter to Wright from Gooseprairie.
Other Grave, The.
Park at Villammare, The.
Places and Ways to Live.
Storm in Acquafredda.
Jarrell. Aging.
All or None.
Bad Music, The.
Face, The.
Faded.
Island, The.
Next Day.
Old Song, An.
Player Piano, The.
Jeffers. Age in Prospect.
Birthday.
For Una.
I have been warned. It is more than thirty years since I wrote.
Johnson. Succeeding years thy early frame destroy.
Jong. Aging.
Poem for Molly's Fortieth Birthday.
Reading, A.
Jonson. My Picture Left in Scotland.
To the World [A Farewell for a Gentlewoman, Virtuous and Noble].
Joseph. Butcher's.
Genus: Homo.
Homo Sapiens.
Patient old cripple, A.
Warning.
Watching a child watching a witch.
Keats. In Drear-nighted December.
Kinnell. Still Time, The.
Kipling. His Apologies.
What of the hunting, hunter bold?
Knight. Poem For a Certain Lady on Her 33rd Birthday, The.
Koch. Magic of Numbers, The.
Koertge. He ("Was looking for work at forty-seven and the owner of a").
Larkin. Age.
Breadfruit.
Dockery and Son.
I Have Started to Say.
Long Last.
Long Sight in Age.
Love Songs in Age.
Nothing to Be Said.

Old Fools, The.
On Being Twenty-Six.
Reference Back.
Triple Time.
View, The.
Winter Palace, The.
Lawrence. Beware, O My Dear Young Men.
Monologue of a Mother.
So There!
Young Are Not Mean in Material Things, The.
Levertov. Man, A.
Levine. Breath.
For Fran.
Late Moon.
Look.
My Son and I.
New Day, A.
Red Dust.
Salts and Oils.
28.
Lewis. Encirclement.
Prelude and Fugue.
Longfellow. For age is opportunity no less.
Morituri Salutamus.
Nature.
Lorde. As I Grew Up Again.
Generation II.
Lowry. Beside Oneself.
"Portly & middleaged" can never.
McGrath. Changeling, The.
Dream Range, The.
Orphan, The.
Progress of the Soul, The.
Uses of the Lost Poets.
MacLeish. Bed, The.
Conway Burying Ground.
Definitions of Old Age.
Dozing on the Lawn.
Hebrides.
Old Gray Couple (2), The.
Old Man's Journey.
Old Men in the Leaf Smoke, The.
Ship's Log.
They Come No More, Those Words, Those Finches.
With Age Wisdom.
McNeill. Second Sight (My Son's First Springtime).
Markson. But Yet Again, We Fought.
Johanna.
Meinke. Vision.
Meredith. Atlas.
But see what living glory floods the west.
Fresh Spring has come with flower and leaf to warn.
I have a hope that's like a star.
Motley.
Time.
Time and Sentiment.
Wisdom of Eld, The.
Youth in Age.
Youth in Memory.
Merrill. After the Fire.
Black Mesa, The.
Hourglass.
Kimono, The.
Lorelei.
Mirror.
Prism.
Tenancy, A.
Time.
Verse for Urania.
Will, The.
Millay. Grown-up.
Oh, my belovèd, have you thought of this.
What lips my lips have kissed, and where, and why.
Miller. In the typewriter shop.
Milton. Sonnet 7: "How soon hath Time the suttle theef of youth."
Morrison. In That Year.
Time Works Like Acid.
Nash. Birthday on the Beach.
Calendar-Watchers, or, What's So Wonderful about Being a Patriarch, The.
Crossing the Border.
Eheu! Fugaces, or, What a Difference a Lot of

Days Make.
For a Good Dog.
Good Parent's Garden of Vision, A.
Lines on Facing Forty.
Lines to Be Scribbled on Somebody Else's
    Thirtieth Milestone.
Old Is for Books.
Preface to the Past.
Nathan. Table Talk.
Nemerov. Boy with Book of Knowledge.
First Leaf, The.
Landscape with Figures.
Old Soldiers' Home, The.
Poet at Forty, The.
Thirtieth Anniversary Report of the Class of
    '41.
Young Woman.
Neruda. Ambassador, The.
O'Hara. Hatred.
Oppen. And if at 80.
Birthplace: New Rochelle.
Fifty years / Sidereal time.
Guest Room.
Occurring "neither for self."
Tell the beads of the chromosomes like a
    rosary.
Thirties. And / A spectre, The.
You are the last.
Owen. Sonnet, to a Child.
Paley. Age.
Choir Singing, The.
Old Dog's Song, The.
One Day.
Sad Children's Song, The.
Piercy. Sign.
Plath. Mirror.
Old Ladies' Home.
Tinker Jack and the Tidy Wives.
Poe. Happiest Day, the Happiest Hour, The.
Pope. Prologue Design'd for Mr. Durfy's Last
    Play.
Prologue to a Play for Mr. Dennis's Benefit,
    in 1733, when He Was Old, Blind, and in
    Great Distress, a Little before His Death, A.
To Mrs. M. B. on Her Birth-Day.
Pound. Beautiful Toilet, The.
Tea Shop, The.
Prince. Old Age of Michelangelo, The.
On a Report That in Some Rest Homes
    Residents Who Are Depressed Will be
    Charged at a Higher Rate.
Raine. What can I tell you, future ones.
Winter Paradise.
Young or old / What was I but a story told.
Ransom. Blue Girls.
Conrad Sits in Twilight.
Master's in the Garden Again.
Rich. Autumn Equinox.
Dear Adrienne: / I'm calling you up tonight.
Halfway.
Life and Letters.
Necessities of Life.
Since we're not young, weeks have to do
    time.
Transcendental Etude.
Upper Broadway.
When This Clangor in the Brain.
Robinson. Amaryllis.
Isaac and Archibald.
Veteran Sirens.
Roethke. Feud.
Other, The.
Our Lady's Winter Words.
Sententious Man, The.
Rolfe. Biography.
Dedication, A.
Rossetti. Dumb Friend, A.
Lowest Room, The.
Youth gone, and beauty gone if ever there.
Rukeyser. In Her Burning.
Letter, Unposted.
Sandburg. Ever a Seeker.
Glimmer.
Junk Man, The.
Let Them Ask Your Pardon.
Streets Too Old.

Trafficker.
Working Girls.
Schuyler. Few Days, A.
Tomorrow.
Shakespeare. Sonnet 2: "When forty winters
    shall besiege thy brow."
Sonnet 5: "Those hours, that with gentle work
    did frame."
Sonnet 22: "My glass shall not persuade me I
    am old."
Sonnet 60: "Like as the waves make towards
    the pebbled shore."
Sonnet 63: "Against my love shall be, as I am
    now."
Sonnet 67: "Ah! wherefore with infection
    should he live."
Sonnet 73: "That time of year thou may'st [or
    maist] in me behold."
Sonnet 104: "To me, fair[e] friend, you never
    can be old."
When my love swears that she is made of
    truth.
Shapiro. Retirement.
Shelton. As I Grow Older.
At Forty.
Smith, Charlotte. Fairest flowers are gone! for
    tempests fell, The.
Prologue to What is She? A Comedy, in Five
    Acts.
Song: "Fruit of Aurora's tears, fair Rose."
Thirty-Eight (Addressed to Mrs. H----Y).
Where the green leaves exclude the summer
    beam.
Smith, Stevie. Pad, Pad.
Progression.
Snyder. Sweat, The.
Sorrentino. Bare Tree, The.
Blue Turning Grey.
Everybody would soon change.
Silk Ascot for the Terrorist, A.
Some hawk-nosed man.
Toward the End of Winter.
Spender. From My Diary.
Stafford. Waiting in Line.
Stevenson. Air of Diabelli's.
He hears with gladdened heart the thunder.
I know not how, but as I count.
Light as my heart was long ago.
Now bare to the beholder's eye.
Now when the number of my years.
Old lady (so they say) but I, The.
On His Pitiable Transformation.
Though deep indifference should drowse.
To F.J.S.
To Minnie.
To My Old Familiars.
To Will H. Low.
To Willie and Henrietta.
We Have Loved of Yore.
What man may learn, what man may do.
Stuart. Casting.
His Granddaughter Arrives.
Birthday.
Sutter. First Hard Frost, The.
Fishing at Forty.
Swift. On Stella's Birthday, 1718/1719.
Receipt to Restore Stella's Youth, A.
Stella's Birthday (1725).
Stella's Birthday; Written in the Year 1720–
    21.
Tate. Last Days of Alice.
Meaning of Life, The.
To a Prodigal Old Maid.
Tennyson. June Bracken and Heather.
Thomas. I See the Boys of Summer.
Lament: "When I was a windy boy and a bit."
Process in the Weather of the Heart, A.
When Once the Twilight Locks No Longer.
Tomlinson. On the Hall at Stowey.
Turco. Habitation, The.
Homunculus.
Photograph, The.
Reflections at Forty-Nine.
Street Meeting.
Updike. Dutch Cleanser.
Golfers.
Melancholy of Storm Windows, The.

Shillington.
To a Dead Flame.
Upon the Last Day of His Forty-Ninth Year.
Van Duyn. Challenger, The.
Colorado.
Sestina for Warm Seasons.
Stream, The.
Wakoski. Sour Milk.
Walcott. Codicil.
I once gave my daughters, separately, two
    conch shells.
Nearing Forty.
Parang.
Waldman. Mirror Meditation.
Walker. Mississippi Winter III.
Whitman. Apparitions.
My 71st Year.
Queries to My Seventieth Year.
Whittier. At Eventide.
Greeting.
My Birthday.
O. W. Holmes on His Eightieth Birthday.
Reunion, The.
Sea Dream, A.
To My Old Schoolmaster.
To Oliver Wendell Holmes.
Voyage of the Jettie.
Wilbur. Black Birch in Winter, A.
For K. R. on Her Sixtieth Birthday.
Next Door.
Williams, Charles Kenneth. Alzheimer's: The
    Wife.
Fifteen.
Tails.
World's Greatest Tricycle-Rider, The.
Williams, Miller. And Then.
Jonathan Aging.
On a Photograph of My Mother at Seventeen.
Ruby Tells All.
Summer Afternoon an Old Man Gives Some
    Thought to the Central Questions, A.
Vanishing Point, The.
Williams, William Carlos. Another Old
    Woman.
Death of Franco of Cologne, The: His
    Prophecy of Beethoven.
Descent, The.
For G.B.S., Old.
Lament of a Graying Woman.
Old Worshipper, The.
Poem: "Looking up, of a sudden."
Rocking Woman, The.
Three Graces, The.
To a Man Dying on His Feet.
To Wish Myself Courage.
Wide Awake, Full of Love.
Wordsworth. September, 1819 ("Departing
    summer hath assumed").
Sequel to Beggars Composed Many Years
    After.
To ———: "Look at the fate of summer
    flowers."
Wright, Charles. Hawaii Dantesca.
Journal of Southern Rivers, A.
Wright, James. Fishermen, The.
In the Cold House.
Many of Our Waters: Variaitons on a Poem
    by a Black Child.
Many of Our Waters: Variations on a Poem
    by a Black Child.
Mesage Hidden in an Empty Wine Bottle that
    I Threw into a Gully of Maple Trees One
    Night at an Indecent Hour, A.
Old Age Compensation.
Old Man Drunk.
Three Steps to the Graveyard.
Youth.
Wyatt. There was never file half so well filed.
Ye old mule, that thin[c]k your self so fair [or
    fayre].
Yeats. Broken Dreams.
Coming of Wisdom with Time, The.
Crazy Jane Grown Old Looks at the Dancers.
Crazy Jane Talks with the Bishop.
Fallen Majesty.
Folly of Being Comforted, The.
Her Vision in the Wood.

Lines Written in Dejection.
Living Beauty, The.
Man Young and Old, A.
Memory of Youth, A.
Men Improve with the Years.
New Faces, The.
Song, A; "I thought no more was needed."
Sweet Dancer.
Wild Swans at Coole, The.
Young Man's Song.
Youth and Age.
Young. Morning Poem for Michael, A.
Move Continuing, The.
Real Time.
Zukofsky. Strange / To reach that age.
Valentine, A.
See also **Middle Age; Old Age.**
Agnosticism and Agnostics
Hardy. Impercipient, The.
Meredith. Thou pirate nested over Alde!
Millay. Agnostic, The.
Smith, Stevie. Agnostic, An.
See also **Doubt.**
Agoraphobia
Nash. On Waking to the Third Rainy Morning
of a Long Week End.
Agriculture. *see* **Farming and Farmers.**
Agustini, Delmira
Olson. Grinning monster out side the system.
AIDS (acquired immune deficiency syndrome)
Carroll, Jim. In Time, AIDS.
Carruth. Your dream: / The letters HIV
appear.
Gunn. Courtesies of the Interregnum.
J Car, The.
Lament: "Your dying was a difficult
enterprise."
Man With Night Sweats, The.
Memory Unsettled.
Missing, The.
Reassurance, The.
Sacred Heart.
Still Life.
Terminal.
To the Dead Owner of a Gym.
Words for Some Ash.
Hacker. Nights of 1964-1966: The Old
Reliable.
Liddy. Richard, Oremus.
Williams, Miller. Thinking about Bill, Dead of
AIDS.
Air
Bishop. Colder the Air, The.
Carroll, Jim. Poem: "This country invades
me."
Carruth. Aer.
Creeley. For Allen.
De la Mare. Spirit of air, The.
Dickey, James. Immortals.
Night Bird.
Dickinson. Air has no Residence, no
Neighbor.
'Tis whiter than an Indian Pipe.
Eberhart. Imagining How It Would Be to Be
Dead.
Now Is The Air Made of Chiming Balls.
Emerson. Score of airy miles will smooth, A.
Ford. Wind is the breath of it.
Hesketh. Shaping Spirit, The.
Hewitt. April Awake.
On Colinward: The Scattering.
This Antrim Air in Summer.
Hopkins. Blessed Virgin Compared to the Air
We Breathe, The.
Larkin. To a Very Slow Air.
Lawrence. Four, The.
Notley. When I Was Alive.
Oppen. Approached the window as if to see.
Raine. Lifelong ago such days.
Rukeyser. Air.
Sarton. Composition.
Schuyler. Deep Winter.
In Wiry Winter.
Light Blue Above.
Simic. Autumn Air.
Stuart. Light Years.
Love's Body.

Wilbur. Attention Makes Infinity.
Sun and Air.
Wright, James. Breath of Air, A.
Air Plants
Crane. Air Plant, The.
Emerson. See yonder leafless trees against the
sky.
Air Travel
Dunn. On Hearing the Airlines Will Use a
Psychological Profile to Catch Potential
Skyjackers.
Eberhart. United 555.
Ginsberg. Over Laramie.
Wings Lifted over the Black Pit.
Larkin. Naturally the Foundation Will Bear
Your Expenses.
Nash. Unwinged Ones, The.
Sexton. Flight.
Story for Rose on the Midnight Flight to
Boston, A.
Tomlinson. Landing, The.
Updike. Airport.
East Hampton—Boston by Air.
From Above.
Landing in the Rain at La Guardia.
Night Flight, over Ocean.
Shuttle, The.
Van Duyn. Elementary Attitudes.
Fear of Flying, The.
First Flight.
See also **Airports.**
Air Warfare
Dickey, James. Firebombing, The.
Doolittle. Erige Cor Tuum ad Me in Caelum.
R.A.F.
Eberhart. Dam Neck, Virginia.
Fury of Aerial Bombardment, The.
Everson. Raid, The.
Hall. Airstrip in Essex, 1960, An.
Hill. To the Nieuport Scout.
Hugo. Mission to Linz.
Jarrell. Dead Wingman, The.
Death of the Ball Turret Gunner, The.
Eighth Air Force.
Field Hospital, A.
Front, A.
Gunner.
Losses.
Perfectly Free Association, A.
Pilot from the Carrier, A.
Pilots, Man Your Planes.
Range in the Desert, The.
Second Air Force.
Siegfried.
Jeffers. Air-Raid Rehearsals.
Fantasy.
Great Sunset, The.
Two Christmas-Cards.
Kipling. R.A.F. (Aged Eighteen).
Lawrence. Bombardment.
Zeppelin Nights.
MacNeice. Brother Fire.
In the misty night humming to themselves like
morons.
Merton. Long Enough.
Nemerov. Old Warplane, An.
Rolfe. City of Anguish.
Rukeyser. Radio silence of aircraft over the
dense ocean.
Structure of the Plane, The.
Spender. Air Raid across the Bay at Plymouth.
Thoughts During an Air Raid.
Tate. Ode to Our Young Pro-consuls of the
Air.
Thomas. Ceremony after a Fire Raid.
Refusal to Mourn the Death, by Fire, of a
Child in London, A.
Williams, Miller. We.
Yeats. Irish Airman Foresees His Death, An.
Airline Stewardesses
Dickey, James. Falling.
Ferlinghetti. Ascending over Ohio.
Airplane Crashes
Dickey, James. Liberator Explodes, The.
Patience: In the Mill.
Ginsberg. Crash.
Hall. Man in the Dead Machine, The.

Hesketh. More than Grass.
Hugo. Where We Crashed.
Jarrell. Front, A.
Pilot from the Carrier, A.
Lowry. Chilliwack.
McAuley. Death of Fathers.
Updike. On an Island.
Airplanes
Ammons. Sitting Down, Looking Up.
Clark. Autorotation without Gravity.
Motion, 1953.
Dickey, James. Liberator Explodes, The.
Two Poems of Flight Sleep.
Dunn. Bringing It Down.
Frost. Wrights' Biplane, The.
Gunn. Small Plane in Kansas.
Hall. Grave The Well, The.
Old Pilot, The.
Persistence of 1937.
Hesketh. More than Grass.
Hewitt. By Air to Birmingham on a Mid-June
Evening.
21st September 1912.
Wheel, The.
Hill. To the Nieuport Scout.
Hugo. Flying, Reflying, Farming.
Jeffers. Machine, The.
Jong. Flight to Catalina.
Kinnell. Flying Home.
Kipling. Hymn of the Triumphant Airman.
Lowry. Prelude to Another Drink.
Sun, Aeroplane, Lovers.
Yvonne stood there silently / the roar of the
plane still in her ears.
McAuley. For the Humanism Class at
Fairchild Airforce Base, in Place of a Session
on the Book of Job.
Matthews. 39,000 Feet.
Oppen. Flight.
Pack. Black Hole, The.
Piercy. Night Flight.
Rolfe. About Eyes.
Rukeyser. Structure of the Plane, The.
Sandburg. Air Circus.
Bas-Relief.
Smith, Patti. Corps de Plane.
Tomlinson. Beautiful Aeroplane, The.
Sky Writing.
Updike. Air Show.
Young. American Glamour.
Life at the Back of the Plane.
Zukofsky. Jaunt.
See also **Aviation and Aviators.**
Airports
Edmunds. Landing in Cairo.
Meinke. Church Cemetery in St. Mary's, A.
Merton. Day Six O'Hare Telephane.
Nemerov. At the Airport.
Paley. Illegal Aliens.
See also **Air Travel.**
Ajanta, India
Rukeyser. Ajanta.
Akhmatova, Anna
Berg. Memory.
With Akhmatova at the Black Gates.
Gallagher. Stepping Outside.
Southwell. Filii prodigi porcos pascentis ad
patrem epistola.
Alabama (state)
Hughes, Langston. Croon.
Daybreak in Alabama.
Sorrentino. Fragments of an Old Song 2.
Some Sap Sings a Poor Pantoum.
Williams, Miller. Plain.
Alaska
Haines. Invaders, The.
To Vera Thompson.
Train Stops at Healy Fork, The.
Hewitt. Romantic, The.
Kipling. Lukannon.
Albatrosses
Coleridge. Rime of the Ancient Mariner, The.
Edmunds. Albatross.
Hartley. Bird, in Soliloquizing Voices a
Woman's Wish, The.
Alcestis
Robinson. As a World Would Have It.

Alchemy and Alchemists
Bogan. Alchemist, The.
Browning, Robert. Paracelsus.
Chaucer. Canon's Yeoman's Tale, The.
Donne. Love's Alchemy [or Alchemie].
Emerson. Chemist of love, The.
Hopkins. Alchemist in the City, The.
Jonson. To Alchemists.
Olson. Bagatto.
Double, double, root and branch.
Plath. Recantation.
Simic. Poem without a Title.

Alcoholism and Alcoholics
Bukowski. Beer.
Spider, The.
Bunting. I'm the worse for drink again, it's.
Light of my eyes, there *is* something to be said.
Carruth. Aw, Dylan, have you left us? Have you gone?
Diagnosis is / Anxiety psychoneurosis, The.
Incorrigible Dirigible, The.
Marge.
Glück. Seconds.
Heaney. Casualty.
Herrick. To M. Kellam.
Upon Blinks.
Upon Guesse.
Upon Punchin.
Upon Tap.
Hesketh. Meths Men, The.
Hughes, Langston. Drunkard.
Wine-O.
Hugo. Hilltop, The.
Letter to Logan from Milltown.
Kooser. For a Friend.
Liddy. Cantico Per Lo Tuo Amore V.
Lowell. Drinker, The.
Lowry. Alcoholic.
Alternative.
At the Bar.
Boatmen swing their lanterns on the Caribbean, The.
Don't, Have One for the Road.
I have known a city of dreadful night.
Most nauseous of all drinks, what is your spell?
No Time to Stop and Think.
Old Blake was warm, he got down to the hub.
Poem: "When drunk he crawled home on his knees."
Prelude to Another Drink.
Prelude To Mammon.
When I was young I broke all drinking records.
Markson. Dylan.
Notley. Jack Would Speak through the Imperfect Medium of Alice.
Pound. Epitaphs: "Fu I loved the high cloud and the hill."
Roethke. My Papa's Waltz.
Schuyler. Over the Hills.
Updike. To Ed Sissman.
Van Duyn. Fall.
Recovery.
Williams, William Carlos. Aigeltinger.
Io Baccho!
Young. Old Woman.
See also **Drunkards.**

Alder Trees
Carruth. Coarse leaf, alder leaf.
Once More.
Hewitt. Alder Stick, The.
Levertov. Victors, The.

Ale
Burns. Lady Onlie.
O gude ale comes and gude ale goes.
Campion. Epigramme: "Tosts as snakes or as the mortall Henbane."
Stevenson. Good old ale, mild or pale.

Alexander the Great, King of Macedon
De la Mare. Alexander.
Dryden. Alexander's Feast; or, The Power of Music [or Musique].
Gunn. From an Asian Tent.
Lowell. Alexander.
Death of Alexander.

Morgan. Alexander.
Rukeyser. Speaking Tree, The.
Wilbur. Worlds.

Alfonso X, King of Castile and León
Emerson. Alphonso of Castile.

Alice in Wonderland
Ferlinghetti. I am waiting for my case to come up.
Graves. Alice.
Silverstein. Alice.
Wilbur. Fourth of July, The.

Alienation
Angelou. Chicken-Licken.
Detached, The.
Faces.
Arnold. Buried Life, The.
Ashbery. Errors.
Wet Casements.
Auden. Motherhood.
Song: "Merriest cuckoo / Which haunted us in May, The."
To throw away the key and walk away.
Beatles. Fool on the Hill, The.
Berg. Dust.
One.
Wife Talks to Herself, A.
Berryman. Traveller, The.
Bly. Snowbanks North of the House.
Winter Poem.
Brontë. Deep, deep down in the silent grave.
It is not pride, it is not shame.
Lonely at her window sitting.
Weaned from life and torn away.
Woods, you need not frown on me.
Brooks. Bronzeville Man with a Belt in the Back.
Garbageman: the Man with the Orderly Mind.
Cohen. Death of a Lady's Man.
First We Take Manhattan.
Creeley. Form of Women, A.
Moon, The.
Dickey, William. Here There Are Three of Us Driving South in This Expensive Car.
Dobyns. Refusing the Necessary.
Eliot. Burnt Norton.
Gerontion.
Journey of the Magi.
Love Song of J. Alfred Prufrock, The.
Portrait of a Lady.
Emerson. Blight.
Intellect.
Ferlinghetti. Director of Alienation.
Ford. Is he a blood relation of yourd.
Fox. Blue Dress, The.
Frost. In Neglect.
Gallagher. Boat Ride.
Gardner. Disenchanted, The.
Southwest of True North.
To Thoreau on Rereading Walden.
Hacker. She twists scraps of her hair in unshelled snails.
Sisterhood.
Hall. Exile.
Umbrella, The.
Hayden. Soledad.
Heaney. Guttural Muse, The.
Herrick. Once Seen, and No More.
Hewitt. Alien Harvest.
Hopkins. To Seem the Stranger.
Housman. There pass the careless people.
Jong. My Daughter Says.
Joseph. Modern Witches 2: Sentinels.
Larkin. Importance of Elsewhere, The.
Lewis. Polish girls singing, in the wind's soughing.
Lorde. Dozens, The.
Lowry. Of the Francia.
Meredith. London by Lamplight.
Merton. Cables to the Ace.
I have sought for myself.
Nash. Very Unclubbable Man, The.
Nathan. As We Walked.
Nemerov. You too will cool, though from your distance light.
Neruda. Century Dying, A.
Men (XVIII), The.

Men (XIX), The.
Where is the child that I was.
Oppen. Anniversary Poem.
Chorus (androgynous): "Find me."
Enclave / Filled with their own, An.
I cannot even now / Altogether disengage myself.
Moving over the hills, crossing the irrigation.
Now in the helicopters the casual will.
Resort.
Return.
Roots of words, The.
Thirties. And / A spectre, The.
Unable to begin / At the beginning, the fortunate.
Whether, as the intensity of seeing increases, one's distance.
Raine. Unloved, The.
Ransom. Tom, Tom, the Piper's Son.
Rich. After Dark.
Stranger, The.
Robinson. Mr. Flood's Party.
Rukeyser. Effort at Speech between Two People.
Sandburg. Useless Words.
Shapiro. My Grandmother.
Retirement.
Solipsism.
Travelogue for Exiles.
Washington Cathedral.
Smith, Patti. Doctor Love.
Grant.
Tomlinson. Aqueduct.
Mr. Brodsky.
Winter.
Williams, Charles Kenneth. Park, The.
Shame.
Solid, The.
Williams, Miller. Aesthetic Distance.
Divorce.
I Go Out of the House for the First Time.
Well-Ordered Life, The.
Williams, William Carlos. Pigheaded Poet.
Wordsworth. World is too much with us; late and soon, The.
Wyatt. Fortune, what aileth thee.
I must go walk[e] the woods so wild.
Young. Ian.
Zukofsky. "Further than."

Aliens
Mahon. Mt. Gabriel.
Nash. Period II.
Silverstein. Planet of Mars, The.
Williams, Miller. He Glimpses a Nobler Vision.

All Souls' Day
Hardy. I Rose Up as My Custom Is.
Lawrence. All Souls' Day.
Rukeyser. All Souls.

All Souls' Night
Glück. All Hallows.

Allen, Ethan
Carruth. It's French, of course—our name. And I must think.

Alligators
Dickey, William. Alligators and Paris and North America.
Nash. Purist, The.
Oliver. Alligator Poem.
See also **Crocodiles.**

Alliteration
Berrigan. Epithalamion: "Pussy put her paw into the pail of paint."

Almanacs
Bishop. Sestina: "September rain falls on the house."

Almond Trees and Almonds
Herrick. Upon His Kinswoman Mistresse Bridget Herrick.
Upon Sibilla.
Hewitt. Agrigento, Sicily.
Lawrence. Bare Almond-Trees.
Flowers.
Letter from Town: The Almond-Tree.
Meredith. Her arms two branches of the almond-tree that sway at morn in the.

Alphabet
Beckett. Home Olga.
Burns. Tale, A.
Coleridge. Indifference of the Heavens, The.
Graves. H.
Hesketh. Paint Box.
Marvell. In the French Translation of Lucan by Monsieur De Brebeuf Are These Verses: Lib 3.
Rossetti. Alphabet, An.
Shapiro. Alphabet, The.
Silverstein. Love.
Snodgrass. Darkling Alphabet, A.

Alphabet Poems
"Carroll, Lewis." Examination Statute.
Nemerov. Primer of the Daily Round, A.
Snodgrass. Darkling Alphabet, A.

Alpheus
Levertov. Well, The.
Shelley. Arethusa.

Alps
Bunting. On the Fly-Leaf of Pound's Cantos.
Coleridge. Hymn before Sunrise, in the Vale of Chamouni.
Dickinson. Our lives are Swiss.
Hardy. Schreckhorn, The.
Meinke. Café du Pont.
  Café Vue des Alpes.
  Easter in Neuchâtel.
Meredith. By the Rosanna.
Wordsworth. Advance—come forth from the Tyrolean ground.
  Descriptive Sketches Taken During a Pedestrian Tour among the Alps.

Alsace, France
Wilbur. First Snow in Alsace.

Altars
Ginsberg. Voice of Rock, The.
Herbert. Altar, The.
Robinson. Altar, The.
Tomlinson. In Michoacán.

Altgeld, John Peter
Lindsay. Bryan, Bryan, Bryan, Bryan.
  Eagle That Is Forgotten, The.
Sandburg. Altgeld.

Altolaguirre, Manuel
Spender. To Manuel Altolaguirre.

Alumni
Eberhart. I Went to See Irving Babbitt.
Merton. Western Fellow Students Salute with Calypso Anthems the Movie Career of Robert Lax.
Nemerov. Thirtieth Anniversary Report of the Class of '41.
Whittier. Reunion, The.

Amaryllis (mythology)
Campion. I Care Not for These Ladies.

Amazons
Burns. Should he escape the slaughter of thine Eyes.
Ralegh. Amazons with Crescent-formed shield, The.

Ambition
Atwood. Eating Fire.
Bly. Watering the Horse.
Browning, Elizabeth Barrett. Night and the Merry Man.
Bukowski. Talking to My Mailbox..
Bunting. On highest summits dawn comes soonest.
Burns. On J-hn M-rne, Laird of L-gg-n.
Campion. Ad Rob. Caraeum Equitem Auratum Nobilissimum.
  In Cambrum.
Carruth. Rummage.
Ciardi. Crate of Sterling Loving Cups, A.
Cohen. Price of This Book, The.
  When I Left the King.
  Wrong Man, The.
Davie. Vying.
De la Mare. Miracle, The.
Dunn. My Brother's Work.
Emerson. On prince or bride no diamond stone.
Gardner. Reveille for a Rockinghorse Poet.

Herrick. Ambition: ("In man, ambition is the common'st thing").
  Ambition ("In wayes to greatnesse, think on this").
Hewitt. Great Headmaster, A.
  Minister.
  Poet's Trade, The.
Hugo. Bay of Sad Loss.
Jeffers. Margrave.
  Such Counsels You Gave to Me.
  What's the best life for a man?
Joseph. This nut withering on the shelf.
Koertge. Royce Newport Money.
Kunitz. Goodies are shaken / from the papa-tree.
Liddy. Swinburne on the Playing Fields.
Lieberman. Song of the Thrush.
Longfellow. Mezzo Cammin.
Lowry. I do not wish to live.
Meredith. Ambition.
  Internal Harmony.
Merton. Strife between the Poet and Ambition, The.
Nash. Strange Case of the Irksome Prude, The.
  There'll Always Be a War between the Sexes, or, A Woman Can Be Sometimes Pleased, but Never Satisfied.
Paley. When she was young she wanted.
Pope. Macer: A Character.
Prince. Mine old dear enemy.
  Strafford.
  Words from Edmund Burke.
Ransom. Tom, Tom, the Piper's Son.
  Vanity of the Bright Boys, The.
Rukeyser. Citation for Horace Gregory.
  Hero Speech.
  Metaphor to Action.
  What do you know of America? I asked a little Russian schoolgirl.
Schwartz. How Can He Possess.
Sexton. Ambition Bird, The.
Sidney. Sonnet 27: "Because I oft, in dark abstracted guise."
Smith, Patti. Ha! Ha! Houdini!
  Piss Factory.
Spender. Public Son of a Public Man, The.
Warren. He Was Formidable.
Williams, Charles Kenneth. Refuge, Serpent-Riders.
Williams, Miller. Notes from the Agent on Earth: How to be Human.
Wordsworth. To Enterprise.
Wyatt. Against the rock I climb, both high and hard.
  Speak thou and speed, where will or power ought [or aught] help'th.

Ambulances
Larkin. Ambulances.
Nash. Hi-Ho the Ambulance-O.

America
Angelou. America.
Ashbery. Pyrography.
Atwood. Two-Headed Poems.
Berrigan. Lady.
Berry. We Who Prayed and Wept.
Berryman. Have a Genuine American Horror-&-Mist on the Rocks.
  Lightning, The.
Blake. Prophecy, A.
Boyle. For an American.
  To America.
  United States, The.
Carruth. Song: The Famous Vision of America.
Coleridge. On the Prospect of Establishing a Pantisocracy in America.
Cummings. He does not have to feel because he thinks.
  I sing of Olaf glad and big.
  Next to of course god america i.
  O pr / gress verily thou art m.
  O to be in finland.
  Remarked Robinson Jefferson.
  Woman / of bronze / unhappy, A.
Davie. Agave in the West.
  Depravity: Two Sermons.

  Letter to Curtis Bradford, A.
  Pastor Errante.
  Third Epistle.
Dickinson. Sweet Land of Liberty.
Donne. Cales and Guiana.
"Dylan." Bob Dylan's 115th Dream.
  Clean-Cut Kid.
  Highway 61 Revisited.
  Hurricane.
  Last Thoughts on Woody Guthrie.
  Motorpsycho Nightmare.
  My Life in a Stolen Moment.
  Slow Train.
  Tangled Up in Blue.
  Union Sundown.
Eberhart. Inchiquin Lake, Penobscot Bay.
  Yonder.
Emerson. Poem, Spoken Before the ΦBK Society, August, 1834.
Ferlinghetti. Autobiography.
  I am waiting for my case to come up.
  Poet's eye obscenely seeing, The.
  Sailing thru the straits of Demos.
Fletcher. America.
Ford. Special Effects.
Frost. America Is Hard to See.
Ginsberg. After Dead Souls.
  America.
  Bayonne Turnpike to Tuscarora.
  Beginning of a Long Poem of These States.
  Beginning of a Poem of These States.
  Crazy Spiritual, A.
  Crossing Nation.
  Ecologue.
  Footnote to Howl.
  Have You Seen This Movie?
  Hiway Poesy: L.A.–Albuquerque–Texas–Witchita.
  In the Baggage Room at Greyhound.
  Independence Day.
  Iron Horse.
  Over Kansas.
  Poem on America, A.
  Reflections in Sleepy Eye.
  Stotras to Kali Destroyer of Illusions.
  Television Was a Baby Crawling toward That Deathchamber.
  These States: Into L.A.
  Who Will Take Over the Universe?
  Wichita Vortex Sutra.
  Wings Lifted over the Black Pit.
Hall. Grave The Well, The.
Hayden. American Journal.
Hewitt. My Brooklyn Uncle.
Hill. Locust Songs.
  Martyrdom of Saint Sebastian.
Hughes, Langston. Freedom's Plow.
Hugo. Belt.
Jarrell. Jamestown.
  To the New World.
Jeffers. July Fourth by the Ocean.
  Shine, Empire.
  Shine, Republic.
  Teheran.
Jong. House-Hunting in the Bicentennial Year.
Lawrence. Evening Land, The.
Levine. One for the Rose.
  Silent in America.
  Sources.
Lindsay. Bryan, Bryan, Bryan, Bryan.
  Gospel of Beauty, A.
Lorde. Vietnam Addenda.
McGrath. Topography of History, The.
  Two Songs from "The Hunted Revolutionaries."
MacLeish. America Was Promises.
  At the Lincoln Memorial.
  Background with Revolutionaries.
  Ballad of the Corn-Cob and the Lie, The.
  Bernál Díaz' Preface to his Book.
  Conversation in a Belfry.
  Invocation to the Social Muse.
  Oil Painting of the Artist as the Artist.
  Sixth Book, The.
Matthews. Every Tub.
  39,000 Feet.
Meinke. Supermarket.

Melville. America.
Ungar and Rolfe.
Meredith. Lines to a Friend Visiting America.
Merton. Christopher Columbus.
Ghost Dance: Prologue.
Letter to America, A.
1. Now you are all here you might as well know this is America we do what we like.
Moore. Love in America.
Morgan. Promise, The.
Morrison. Welcome to the American Night.
Nash. Look What You Did, Christopher!
Nathan. If you start in loneliness.
There's too much to consecrate.
Nemerov. Boy with Book of Knowledge.
One Forever Alien.
O'Hara. Hatred.
Mozart Chemisier.
Olson. Abt the dead he sd.
Across Space and Time.
Ballad for Americans.
Being Altogether Literal, & Specific, and Seeking at the Same Time to be Successfully Explicit.
"Enthusiasm", An.
Got Me Home, the Light Snow Gives the Air, Falling.
Gulf of Maine, The.
Having descried the nation.
I have been an ability—a machine—up to.
Nerves Are Staves, and When the Tears Come There Is Voice, The.
17th century men / who founded this land.
Oppen. In this nation.
Patchen. Joe Hill Listens to the Praying.
Lenada.
Letter to Those Who Are About to Die.
O fiery river / Flow out over the land.
When in the Course of Human Events.
Piercy. Peaceable Kingdom, The.
Visiting a Dead Man on a Summer Day.
Rich. Open-Air Museum.
Sources.
Rolfe. Winds of Another Sphere.
Rukeyser. Blood is Justified, The.
Book of the Dead, The.
Juanita Tinsley.
Movie.
Road, The.
This House, This Country.
West Virginia.
What do you know of America? I asked a little Russian schoolgirl.
Sandburg. And So Today.
Ever a Seeker.
Good Morning, America.
Out of White Lips.
Smoke and Steel.
So you want to divide all the money there is.
Threes.
Schuyler. Industrial Archaeology.
Schwartz. Kilroy's Carnival; A Poetic Prologue for TV.
Sexton. Firebombers, The.
Shout, The.
Sixth Psalm.
Shapiro. And Now, the Weather..
I Am an Atheist Who Says His Prayers.
Manhole Covers.
Statue of Liberty.
Snyder. Dullness in February: Japan.
For the West.
I Went into the Maverick Bar.
Two Immortals.
What Happened Here Before.
Sorrentino. See America First.
Stevenson. I look across the ocean.
Ticonderoga: A Legend of the West Highlands.
Updike. Fargo.
Walcott. Elegy: "Our hammock swung between Americas."
Upstate.
Waldman. Mother Country.
Whitman. Ages and Ages Returning at Intervals.
America.

And thou, America, / For the scheme's culmination.
Apostroph.
As Consequent, Etc.
Bravo, Paris Exposition!
By Blue Ontario's Shore.
Carol Closing Sixty-Nine.
Columbian's Song, The.
Election Day, November, 1884.
For You O Democracy.
Full of Life Now.
House of Friends, The.
O Magnet-South.
Ode: "O, God of Columbia! O, Shield of the Free!"
On Journeys through the States.
One Song, America, Before I Go.
Or, from That Sea of Time.
Orange Buds by Mail from Florida.
Our Old Feuillage.
Poem of Remembrances for a Girl or a Boy of These States.
Prairie-Grass Dividing, The.
Prairie States, The.
Respondez!
Return of the Heroes, The.
Small the Theme of My Chant.
Song of the Banner at Daybreak.
Starting from Paumanok.
States!
Thou Mother with Thy Equal Brood.
Thou Orb Aloft Full-Dazzling.
Thoughts ("Of these years I sing").
To-day and Thee.
To Foreign Lands.
To the East and to the West.
To the Leaven'd Soil They Trod.
Twilight Song, A.
United States to Old World Critics, The.
Washington's Monument, February, 1885.
When Lilacs Last in the Dooryard Bloom'd.
With All Thy Gifts.
With Antecedents.
Years of the Modern.
Yonnondio.
Whittier. On Receiving an Eagle's Quill from Lake Superior.
Our Country.
Wilbur. On Freedom's Ground.
Williams, Charles Kenneth. Admiral Fan, The.
In the Heart of the Beast.
Williams, William Carlos. Song: "Russia! Russia! you might say."
To Elsie.
Wright, Charles. Lonesome Pine Special.
Wright, James. American Twilights, 1957.
Eclogue at Nash's Grove.
Frontier, The.
In Memory of a Spanish Poet.
Stages on a Journey Westward.
Young. American Time.
Zimmer. Eisenhower Years, The.
Leaves of Zimmer.
Zukofsky. Jaunt.
See also **United States.**

American Indians. see **Native Americans.**

American Revolution
Burns. Fragment, A: "When *Guilford* good our Pilot stood."
Cowper. Modern Patriot, The.
Dunbar. Black Samson of Brandywine.
Emerson. Hymn[:] Sung at the Completion of the Concord Monument, April 19, 1836.
Song: "Shout for those whose course is done."
Kipling. American Rebellion, The.
Longfellow. Landlord's Tale: Paul Revere's Ride, The.
MacNeice. Jehu.
Olson. King's Mountain.
To Empty the Mind.
Whitman. Centenarian's Story, The.
Wallabout Martyrs, The.
Whittier. Lexington.
Yorktown.
Wilbur. On Freedom's Ground.

Americans
Auden. On the Circuit.

Boyle. American Citizen.
For an American.
Crane. America's Plutonic Ecstasies.
Pillar and the Post, The.
Davie. To an American Classicist.
Eberhart. Statue of Liberty.
Emerson. Ancient drop of feudal blood, An.
At Sea, September 1833.
Ferlinghetti. Baseball Canto.
Buddha in the Woodpile, A.
Home Home Home.
Two Scavengers in a Truck, Two Beautiful People in a Mercedes.
Hughes, Langston. Madam's Calling Cards.
Hugo. What Thou Lovest Well Remains American.
Jeffers. Ave Caesar.
July Fourth by the Ocean.
Kipling. American, An.
Choice, The.
Koch. You Were Wearing.
Lawrence. O! Americans.
Nash. Ms. Found under a Serviette in a Lovely Home.
Scram, Lion!
Nathan. It's a brand new morning.
Olson. Americans, The ("Cosmologist says, The").
Americans, The ("What the cosmologist meant by what constitutes").
I, Mencius, Pupil of the Master.
17th century men / who founded this land.
"Reed." Last Great American Whale.
Shapiro. Boy-Man.
Shelley. To the Republicans of North America.
Smith, Patti. Combe.
Notebook.
Sorrentino. Mr. America last seen crossing the road.
Walcott. Certain things here are quietly American.
Warren. Founding Fathers, Nineteenth-Century Style, Southeast U.S.A.
Whitman. For You O Democracy.
I Hear America Singing.
Mediums.
Nay, Tell Me Not To-day the Publish'd Shame.
Our Old Feuillage.
Prairie-Grass Dividing, The.
Race of Veterans.
Starting from Paumanok.
Williams, William Carlos. Impromptu: The Suckers.
Poem: "Daniel Boone, the father of Kentucky."
Question and Answer.

Amherst, Massachusetts
Wilbur. Altitudes.

Amish, The
Updike. Amish, The.

Amnesia
Plath. Amnesiac.

Amputees
Cohen. Morning Song.
Herrick. Upon the Losse of His Finger.
Jarrell. Terms.
Lewis. "Your leg must go. Okay?" the surgeon said.
"MacDiarmid." In the Children's Hospital.
Owen. Disabled.
Shapiro. Leg, The.

Amsterdam, Netherlands
Davie. At the Café Parnasse.
Ferlinghetti. Two Amsterdams.
Garrigue. Amsterdam Letter.
Merrill. Amsterdam.
Schuyler. Sometimes.

Amusement Parks
Gildner. Blue Like the Heavens.
Lieberman. Inside the Gyroscope.
Meinke. Magic Kingdom, The.
Moore. Old Amusement Park.

Anacreon
Wright, James. Anacreon's Grave.

Analysis
Berg. Kiss, The.
  Page 256.
Creeley. Pedigree, The.
Hesketh. Analyst.
  Brain Child.
MacNeice. Cromlech, The.
Pack. Landscape Goat.
Piercy. Learning to manage the process.
Zukofsky. "Mantis," An Interpretation.

Anarchism and Anarchists
Bukowski. This.
Carruth. Republicans? We've got a few. In
  fact.
Cullen. For an Anarchist.
Frost. Case for Jefferson, A.
Hewitt. Lilibulero.
Merrill. 18 West 11th Street.
Rolfe. To My Contemporaries.
Shelley. Mask [or Masque] of Anarchy, The.

Ancestry and Ancestors
Angelou. Family Affairs.
Atwood. Book of Ancestors.
Berryman. Ancestor.
Brooks. Sundays of Satin-Legs Smith, The.
Carroll, Jim. Poem: "I snatch a grape from her
  breast."
Clark. Ancestors.
Cowper. On Pedigree.
Creeley. And.
Cullen. Heritage.
Eberhart. Statue of Liberty.
Emerson. Forerunners.
  Thank the gods thy governors.
  Thou shalt make thy house.
  Why honor the new men.
Fenton. Chosun.
Galvin. Donegal.
  My Grandmother Steals Her Last Trout.
Graves. Ancestors.
  Flowering Aloe, The.
  Front Door Soliloquy.
  Song: The Queen of Time.
Hardy. Pedigree, The.
  She, I, and They.
  Sine Prole.
Herrick. Upon Clunn.
Hewitt. Search, The.
Jeffers. Patronymic.
Kipling. British-Roman Song, A.
  Heritage, The.
Knight. Bones of My Father, The.
  Idea of Ancestry, The.
"MacDiarmid." Direadh III.
Meinke. Flatbush.
Miller. For Barbara.
Olson. Chain of memory is resurrection   I am
  a vain man, The.
  So the Norse / were neurotic.
  To Gerhardt, There, among Europe's Things of
  Which He Has Written Us in His "Brief an
  Creely und Olson."
  Winds / which blew my daughter, The.
Pack. Archeology.
Patchen. We Leave You Pleasure.
Raine. Highland Graveyard.
Ralegh. Yet though thou fetch thy pedigree so
  farre.
Rich. Poem of Women.
Rukeyser. Bubble of Air.
  For My Son.
Sandburg. Turn of the Wheel.
  We'll see what we'll see.
Shapiro. Messias.
  Nigger.
Shelton. Prophets, The.
Smart. For man is between the pinchers while
  his soul is shaping and purifying.
Stevens. Extraordinary References.
Stevenson. Say not of me that weakly I
  declined.
  To Princess Kaiulani.
Sutter. Swedish Lesson.
Tate. Ancestors, The.
  Emblems.
Updike. Toothache Man.

Walcott. Grey English road hissed emptily
  under the tires, The.
Walker. In These Dissenting Times.
Wilbur. Nights rolled upon the river's face.
Williams, Miller. After a Brubeck Concert.
Wordsworth. Song at the Feast of Brougham
  Castle upon the Restoration of Lord Clifford,
  the Shepherd, to the Estates and Honours of
  His Ancestors.
Wright, Charles. Arkansas Traveller.
Yeats. Dedication to a Book of Stories
  Selected from the Irish Novelists.
  Three Marching Songs.

Anchors
Herrick. End of His Work, The.
  His Hope or Sheet-Anchor.
Kipling. Anchor Song.

Andersen, Hans Christian
Sandburg. Love Letter to Hans Christian
  Andersen.
Stevens. Sonatina to Hans Christian.

Andrea del Sarto. *see* **Sarto, Andrea del.**

Andromache
Browning, Elizabeth Barrett. Hector and
  Andromache.
Ford. Andromache, I think of you! / When the
  war goes on forever.

Andromeda
Fox. Finding the Andromeda Nebula.
Hill. Slime; the residues of refined tears.
Hopkins. Andromeda.

Anemones
Ford. In the tentacles.
Lawrence. Purple Anemones.
Liddy. Pools where it offers to our curiosity,
  The.
MacLeish. Hearts' and Flowers'.
Oppen. Words cannot be wholly transparent.
  And that is the.

Anesthesia
Matthews. Recovery Room.

Angels
Ammons. Lofty.
Blake. Memorable Fancy, A ("Angel came to
  me and said").
  Memorable Fancy, A ("Once I saw a Devil in
  a flame of fire").
Boyle. Angels for Djuna Barnes.
Browning, Elizabeth Barrett. Heaven and
  Earth.
  Seraphim, The.
Browning, Robert. Guardian-Angel, The.
Burns. To a Painter.
"Carroll, Lewis." Beatrice.
Clark. Angel's Choice.
  Millennial Icon.
De la Mare. Tom's Angel.
Dickinson. Again—his voice is at the door.
  Angel begins in the morning, The.
  Angels, in the early morning.
  Cloud withdrew from the Sky, A.
  Forever honored be the Tree.
  God permits industrious Angels.
  Little East of Jordan, A.
  Many an angel, with its needle.
  What did They do since I saw Them?
Dobyns. Noise the Hairless Make, The.
Donne. Air[e] and Angels.
  Angels, The.
  At the round earth's imagined corners, blow.
  Bracelet, The.
Doolittle. This is no rune nor riddle.
Dunbar. Jack Frost at Bedtime.
Dunn. Bad Angels, The.
  Between Angels.
  Guardian Angel, The.
"Dylan." Precious Angel.
  Three Angels.
Eberhart. Angels, The.
  Incomparable Light, The.
  Portrait of Rilke.
  Vision.
Emerson. Around the man who seeks a noble
  end.
  Bended to fops who bent to him.
  Discontented Poet: A Masque, The.

Dull uncertain brain, A.
  Excelsior.
  He whom God had thus preferred.
  Shall the Muse sing for thousands & not sing.
Fox. Angel of Death, The.
Graves. Birth of Angels.
  True Joy.
Herrick. Angells.
  Upon Teares.
Hewitt. Mary's Lullaby.
  Tumbling Spore, The.
Hill. Copper clouds / are not of this light,
  The.
  Requite this angel whose.
Hughes, Langston. Angels Wings.
Jarrell. Archangel's' Song, The.
Kipling. Azrael's Count.
  Legend of Mirth, The.
  Supports, The.
Lawrence. Hymn to Nothingness.
  Lucifer.
  Old Archangels.
  Walk Warily.
Levertov. Vision, A.
Levine. Angel Butcher.
  Waking an Angel.
Lindsay. Our Guardian Angels and Their
  Children.
Lovelace. Amyntor's Grove.
Lowry. Glaucous Winged Gull, The.
McGrath. Two Songs from "The Hunted
  Revolutionaries."
MacNeice. When the stranger came out of the
  night.
Meredith. Story of Sir Arnulph, The.
Merrill. Angel.
  Dedication: "Hans, there are moments when
  the whole mind."
Merton. Angels again / Farmers of the mind.
  Moslems' Angel of Death, The.
  Restoration of the Pictures, The.
  Song of Purification.
Nash. Cherub, The.
O'Hara. In Favor of One's Time.
  Muse Considered As a Demon Lover, The.
Olson. Hear my prayer my father.
  I met my Angel last night on Cinvat Bridge.
Patchen. Instructions for Angels.
Poe. Israfel.
Raine. Chartres Annunciation, The.
  Nocturn: "Night comes, an angel stands."
Rich. Gabriel.
  This Beast, This Angel.
Rossetti. Advent.
  Angels at the foot,/ And Angels at the head.
  Are They Not All Ministering Spirits?
  Baby lies so fast asleep / That we cannot
  wake her.
  Dear Angels and dear disembodied Saints.
  Divine and Human Pleading.
  From House to Home.
  Holy Innocents.
  If stars dropped out of heaven, / And if
  flowers took their place.
  Our life is long. Not so, wise Angels say.
  This near-at-hand land breeds pain by
  measure.
  Three little children / On the wide wide earth.
  Watchers, The.
  Ye Have Forgotten the Exhortation.
Sandburg. Isle of Patmos.
Sarton. Annunciation.
  Fear of Angels, The.
  Nativity.
  Song: "No, I will never forget you and your
  great eyes."
  Storm of Angels, A.
Schuyler. Head, A.
Sexton. Angel of Clean Sheets.
  Angel of Fire and Genitals.
  Angel of Flight and Sleigh Bells.
  Consorting with Angels.
  Fallen Angels, The.
  Locked Doors.
Shakespeare. Sonnet 144: "Two loves I have
  of comfort and despair."
  Two loves I have, of comfort and despair.

Shapiro. Exile.
Sickness of Adam, The.
Shelley. Prologue in Heaven.
Smart. St. Michael and All Angels.
Smith, Patti. Witt.
Smith, Stevie. Angel Face.
Angel of Grace.
Crown of Bays, The.
Fallen, Fallen.
From the Coptic.
Galloping Cat, The.
I Rode with My Darling.
No Categories!
No More People.
Tableau de l'Inconstance des Mauvais Anges.
Violent Hand, The.
Southwell. New Heaven, New War[re].
Spenser. And is there care in heauen [or heaven]? and is there loue [or love].
Stevens. Angel Surrounded by Paysans.
Whitman. Play-Ground, The.
Whittier. Two Angels, The.
Williams, Charles Kenneth. Saint Sex.
Williams, William Carlos. Incognito.
Wordsworth. Engelberg, the Hill of Angels.
Scene on the Lake of Brientz.
Wright, James. Alarm, The.
Angel, The.
De Profundis.
Larry.
Secret Gratitude, A.
Zimmer. When Angels Came to Zimmer.
Zukofsky. Lilac.

Anger
Berry. Anger against Beasts.
Berryman. Cloud and Flame.
I say I laid siege—you enchanted me.
You, Chris, contrite I never thought to see.
Blake. Christian Forbearance.
Poison Tree, A.
Was I angry with Hayley who used me so ill.
Boyle. To a Proud Old Woman Watching the Tearing Down of the Hurricane Shed.
Browning, Robert. Halbert and Hob.
Bukowski. Love Is a Piece of Paper Torn to Bits.
Report Upon the Consumption of Myself, A.
Byron. And Dost Thou Ask the Reason of My Sadness?
Campion. See Where She Flies.
Carruth. Sonnet: "Women in anger, it seems, become theatrical."
Catullus. Carmen 16: "Pedicabo et irrumabo."
Carmen 21: "Impresario of neediness."
Clark. De Ira Dei.
Cohen. Commentary—Death to This Book.
Commentary—The News You Really Hate.
Death to This Book.
News You Really Hate, The.
This Marriage.
Creeley. Anger.
Crisis, The.
Dream, The.
Friends, The.
Goodbye.
Hands, The.
Out of Sight.
Temper, The.
Davie. Being Angry with God.
Depravity: Two Sermons.
De la Mare. Be angry now no more!
How Blind!
Making a fire.
Dobyns. Anger.
Spleen.
Spring Rain.
Doolittle. Ariadne.
Chance Meeting.
"Dylan." Playboys and Playgirls.
This Wheel's on Fire.
Eberhart. Hatred of the Old River.
Throwing the Apple.
Ford. There's No Place to Sleep in This Bed, Tanguy.
Gardner. Your Fearful Symmetries.
Glück. Labor Day.
Graves. No Letter.

Griffiths. Glyndŵr Subdued.
Mines in Sepia Tint, The.
Gunn. At an Intersection.
Glamorous and difficult friend.
Pig Pig she cries.
Hacker. Fifteen to Eighteen.
Iva's Pantoum.
1976.
Hall. "Between the Clock and the Bed."
Edward's Anecdote.
Herrick. Anger.
Gods Anger.
Gods Anger without Affection.
To His Angrie God.
To the Rose; a Song.
Upon Irene.
Hewitt. Drypoint.
I Still Had a Friend.
My Own and Not My Own.
Sonnet: "I have no time to worship. I must live."
Hugo. Eileen.
Letter to Hanson from Miami.
Joseph. If you can't join them beat them.
Modern Witches 1: Crouching.
Modern Witches 2: Sentinels.
Keats. Lines Written on 29 May / The Anniversary of the Restoration of Charles the 2nd.
Kipling. Et Dona Ferentes.
Knight. Apology for Apostasy?
Kunitz. Portrait, The.
Lawrence. What Ails Thee?
Working Man, The.
Levine. Fist.
Fox, The.
Horse, The.
Letters for the Dead.
Longfellow. Meanwhile the stalwart Miles Standish was marching steadily northward.
Lovelace. Hand of sacred Cato bad to tear, The.
Meinke. Rage.
Meredith. Agamemnon in the Fight.
Black Richard.
Invective of Achilles, The.
It ended, and the morrow brought the task.
Misery is greater, as I live!, The.
No state is enviable. To the luck alone.
Merton. Anger.
Milton. Lord God that dost me save and keep.
Nash. Don't Be Cross, Amanda.
There'll Always Be a War between the Sexes, or, A Woman Can Be Sometimes Pleased, but Never Satisfied.
O'Hara. Rant, A.
Oliver. Acid.
Rage.
Oppen. Down-town / Swarms. Surely the oldest city.
Pack. After Returning from Camden Harbor.
Paley. Muncipal center / the morning of anger, The.
Patchen. Hangman's Great Hands, The.
Irate Songster, The.
Piercy. Just Anger, A.
Neighbor, The.
Plath. Courage of Shutting-Up, The.
Purdah.
Psalms. Psalm 88: "O God of my salvation."
Psalm 89: "I will sing of the mercies of the Lord for ever."
Ransom. Agitato Ma Non Troppo ("This is what the man said").
"Reed." Bottoming Out.
Rich. Nightbreak.
Phenomenology of Anger, The.
Roethke. Song: "My wrath, where's the edge."
Rossetti. Seven vials hold Thy wrath: but what can hold.
Rukeyser. Gift-Poem ("Year in its cold beginning").
St. John. Lemons, The.
Sandburg. Choose.
Sarton. Stone Walls.
Sexton. Again and Again and Again.
Assassin, The.

Bayonet.
Telephone.
Shakespeare. Sonnet 142: "Love is my sin and thy dear virtue hate."
Sidney. Sonnet 74: "Love still a boy, and oft a wanton is."
Smith, Patti. Gibralto.
Smith, Stevie. Anger's Freeing Power.
Dear Child of God.
So Can Anger.
Spender. Prisoners, The.
Sutter. November Seven, Nineteen Eighty-Four.
Thomas. Not from This Anger.
Wakoski. Exorcism.
Filling the Boxes of Joseph Cornell.
Love Letter Postmarked Van Beethoven.
Williams, Charles Kenneth. Blame.
Reading: Early Sorrow.
Williams, William Carlos. Fond Farewell, A.
Wordsworth. Indignation of a High-Minded Spaniard 1810.
Wright, James. Revelation, The.
Zukofsky. Aurelius, father, assure that the o numb.
Piping, beaus, I'll go whoosh and I'll rumble you.

See also **Quarrels.**

Animals
Atwood. Animals in That Country, The.
Cyclops.
Dreams of the Animals.
Auden. Address to the Beasts.
Our Hunting Fathers.
Berry. To the Unseeable Animal.
Berryman. Animal Trainer, The.
Bishop. Armadillo, The.
Word with You, A.
Bogan. Variation on a Sentence.
Boyle. Comeallye for Robert Carlton Brown, A.
Browning, Elizabeth Barrett. Island, An.
Browning, Robert. White Witchcraft.
Bukowski. Seahorse.
Byron. Wild Gazelle, The.
"Carroll, Lewis." Little Man That Had a Little Gun, The.
Carruth. Essay.
Harlequin / is said to assimilate himself to a condition.
Creeley. Animal, The.
Herd, The.
Cullen. Thoughts in a Zoo.
Cummings. O the sun comes up-up-up in the opening.
Davie. Dissent. A Fable.
Dickey, James. Deer among Cattle.
For the Last Wolverine.
Heaven of Animals, The.
Hedge Life.
Dickey, William. Love among the Manichees.
Dickinson. Little Dog that wags his tail, A.
Most important population, The.
Pretty boarders are leaving the trees, The.
Dobyns. Name-Burning.
Donne. Why are we[e] by all creatures waited on?
Doolittle. Scribe.
Dunbar. Critters' Dance, De.
Duncan. Back to the figure.
Dunn. Turning Fifty.
Workers.
"Dylan." Man Gave Names to All the Animals.
Eberhart. Illusion of Eternity, The.
Mystical Beast in the Shadows, The.
Vastness and Indifference of the World, The.
Emerson. On the chamber, on the stairs.
Fenton. Wild Ones[, The].
Ford. Baby's in Jail; the Animal Day Plays Alone.
Gallagher. Cows, a Vision.
Gardner. At the Zoo.
Masked Shrew, The.
This Room Is Full of Clocks.
Garrigue. False Country of the Zoo.
Song in Sligo.

Graves. Allie.
Griffiths. Guardianship.
Hacker. Exiles.
Haines. Book of the Jungle.
Hall. Child's Garden, A.
New Animals.
Hartnett. I Heard Him Whistle.
Heaney. Sweeney Astray.
Hemingway. Translations from the Esquimaux:
There Are Seasons.
Hesketh. Animals' Last Words.
Cats.
Giraffes.
Mallard, The.
Truant.
Hewitt. Beastie, The.
Dry Summer, Islandmagee, 1921.
Name and Number.
Pet Shop, The.
Stoat, The.
Those Swans Remember; A Poem.
Hoffman. Moving among the Creatures.
Hughes, Ted. Bull Moses, The.
Crow Hill.
Jeffers. Animals.
Jong. Assuming Our Dominance.
How to Name Your Familiar.
Kinnell. Another Night in the Ruins.
Kipling. Eddi's Service.
Man goes to Man! Cry the challenge though
the Jungle!
Night we felt the earth would move, The.
Parade-Song of the Camp Animals.
What of the hunting, hunter bold?
When ye say to Tabaqui, "My Brother!" when
ye call the Hyena to meat.
Kooser. How to Foretell a Change in the
Weather.
Larkin. Little Lives of Earth and Form, The.
Lawrence. Glory.
Him with His Tail in His Mouth.
Morality.
St Matthew.
Self-Pity.
Levertov. Come into Animal Presence.
Else a great Prince in prison lies.
Levine. Animals Are Passing from Our Lives.
To get west you go east.
Lovelace. Her Muffe.
Lowry. And Who Is It That With Snow-
Freaked Antlers Vicariously Museth.
As from All the Little Animals.
But we little animaux have gone.
Conclusion—Poem, A.
Duckturne.
Little Ditty for This Day to the Beloved
Harteebeeste, A.
Morning bird is singing, the.
My Beloved Harteebeeste.
Mysterious Hint, A.
Platinum sun rising. / Platinum frost on porch.
Spark Poetry.
Welcome Home Oh Gladsome Springhorned
Beloved and Famed Harteebeeste.
Welcome Home Oh Most Loved and Famed
Harteebeeste.
With Sweetest Love from All the Little
Animals As from 2 Old Friends.
With Sweetest Love from All the Little
Animals to Their Beloved Harteebeeste.
Xochitepec.
McAuley. Short Journeys Before Daybreak.
MacNeice. Gulf between us and the brutes,
The.
Pet Shop.
McNeill. Cave, The.
Merrill. Channel 13.
Millay. Animal Ball, The.
Miller. For Schnu.
Moore. Animals Sick of the Plague, The.
Jerboa, The.
Monkeys, The.
Pangolin, The.
Morrison. Celebration of the Lizard.
Feast Green Beast.
Hole in the Clouds, A.
Stand There Listening.

Nash. Bulletin Has Just Come In, A.
Caribou, The.
Exit, Pursued by a Bear.
I Happen To Know.
Mr. Burgess, Meet Mr. Barmecide.
Nemerov. Tale.
Neruda. To whom does the raggedy condor.
What are you hiding under your hump?
O'Hara. Heroic Sculpture.
Olson. Lower Field—Enniscorthy.
Obit.
Only the Red Fox, Only the Crow.
Oppen. They await / War, and the news.
Pack. Beating Time.
Ode to a Lovesick Moose.
Patchen. Animal I wanted, The.
Animals of the morning wood watching in
silence as, The.
But the Beast of the Wood came as a smiling
man.
My Pretty Animals.
Then did the wind move sunful fingers
through her hair.
Plath. Go Get the Goodly Squab.
Wuthering Heights.
Zoo Keeper's Wife.
Ransom. Spiel of [the] Three Mountebanks.
Rossetti. 1885. St. Valentine's Day.
Hurt No Living Thing.
If a mouse could fly, / Or if a crow could
swim.
Mirrors of Life and Death.
Peacock has a score of eyes, The.
What does the donkey bray about?
When the cows come home the milk is
coming.
Rukeyser. Afterwards.
Sandburg. Sky Talk.
Sarton. Godhead as Lynx, The.
Schuyler. Dog Wants His Dinner, The.
Sexton. White Snake, The.
Shelton. There is a bird.
Sidney. As I my little flock on Ister Bank.
Silverstein. Farmer and the Queen, The.
Instructions.
Unicorn, The.
Simic. Animal Acts.
Smart. Good-Nature to Animals.
Smith, Stevie. Best Beast of the Fat-Stock
Show at Earls Court, The.
Can It Be?
I Am a Girl Who Loves to Shoot.
It Filled My Heart with Love.
Listener, The.
Mrs. Blow and her Animals.
Nature and Free Animals.
Photograph, The.
Shooting Incident, The.
Snyder. Berry Territory.
Dogs, Sheep, Cows, Goats.
Maitreya the Future Buddha.
Thoughts on Looking at a Samuel Palmer
Etching at the Tate.
Three Deer One Coyote Running in the Snow.
Stevens. Jouga.
Poetry Is a Destructive Force.
Stevenson. Portrait, A.
Stuart. Killdeer.
Swift. Beasts' Confession to the Priest, The.
Thomas. How Shall My Animal.
Updike. Deities and Beasts.
High-Hearts, The.
Menagerie at Versailles in 1775, The.
Philological.
Popular Revivals 1956.
Topsfield Fair.
Van Duyn. Good Man, The.
Goodbye, A.
Kind of Music, A.
Marriage, with Beasts.
Whitman. I think I could turn and live awhile
with animals.
Ox-Tamer, The.
Whittier. Red Riding-Hood.
Wilbur. Beasts.
Walgh-Vogel, The.

Williams, Charles Kenneth. Ribbons.
Sky, Water.
Wright, James. Brush Fire.
In Shame and Humiliation.
Some Beasts.
To the Evening Star: Central Minnesota.
Zukofsky. Arizona.
See also **Death of Animals.**
Animism
De la Mare. Spirit of air, The.
Strange Spirit, The.
Wanderers, The.
Ford. I love my animal heart.
Gardner. Sloth, The.
Southwest of True North.
That "Craning of the Neck."
Lewis. Tiger of Camden Town, The.
Rich. Trees, The.
Wright, Charles. Journal of One Significant
Landscape, A.
Anne, Queen of England
Clark. "Himself let him unknown contain."
Anniversaries
Berry. Anniversary, An.
Burns. Seventh of November, The.
Dickey, William. Anniversary, The.
Donne. Anniversary [*or* Anniversarie], The.
Hardy. Looking at a Picture on an
Anniversary.
Hopkins. Silver Jubilee, The.
Lovelace. Anniversary on the Hymeneals of
My Noble Kinsman, Thomas Stanley,
Esquire, An.
McGrath. Anniversaries.
Meinke. Anniversary Deer, The.
Nash. Anniversary, The.
Nemerov. Anniversary.
Pack. Clayfeld's Anniversary Song.
Robinson. Woman and the Wife, The.
Smith, Charlotte. To the Countess of A—.
Written on the Anniversary of Her Marriage.
Thomas. On a Wedding Anniversary.
Annunciation of the Virgin
Donne. Annunciation.
Upon the Annunciation and Passion Falling
upon One Day. 1608.
Gunn. Jesus and His Mother.
Merton. Annunciation, The.
Aubade—the Annunciation.
Messenger, The.
Rossetti. Feast of the Annunciation.
Vigil of the Annunciation.
Smart. Annunciation of the Blessed Virgin.
Antaeus
Heaney. Hercules and Antaeus.
Owen. Antaeus: A Fragment.
Antarctica
Sutter. Lost in *Antarctica.*
Anteaters
Moore. Pangolin, The.
Antelopes
Hesketh. Panther and the Antelope, The.
Wright, James. Spring Images.
See also **Elands.**
Anthropology and Anthropologists
Hewitt. On the Choice of a Title.
Merton. Cargo Songs.
East with Malinowski.
Williams, Miller. Tearing Down the Hotel.
Anticipation
Auden. Christmas Eve.
Winter Afternoon.
Beatles. I Don't Want to Spoil the Party.
Berryman. All we were going strong last night
this time.
Cold rewards trail in, when the man is blind,
The.
Darling I wait O in my upstairs box.
Dew is drying fast, a last drop glistens, The.
Four oval shadows, paired, ringed each by
sun.
I expect you from the North. The path winds
in.
If long enough I sit here, she, she'll pass.
Night and the City.
Today is it? Is it today? I shudder.

Browning, Elizabeth Barrett. Sonnet: "Beloved, my beloved, when I think."
Browning, Robert. In Three Days.
Burns. Carl an the King Come.
Extempore Reply to an Invitation.
Song, Composed in August.
Campion. Come away, arm'd with loves delights.
Clark. On Marine Silence Street.
Cohen. Waiting for the Miracle.
Coleridge. Ballad of the Dark Ladié, The.
Blossoming of the Solitary Date-Tree, The.
Crane. Persuasion, A.
Dickinson. Consummation is the hurry of fools.
Dobyns. Body's Hope, The.
Dunbar. Expectation.
Waiting.
"Dylan." Seven Days.
Emerson. Borrowing from the French.
Ferlinghetti. Along the Appian Way / children are playing.
Heap of Broken Images, A.
I am waiting for my case to come up.
Garrigue. Incantatory Poem.
Graves. Expect Nothing.
No Letter.
Not to Sleep.
Griffiths. Island with Army, Pines and Wind.
Hardy. On the Way.
Riddle, The.
Timing Her.
Hewitt. At Shottery, Anne Hathaway's Cottage.
Bogside, Derry, 1971.
Hugo. Bay of Resolve.
Good Day for Seeing Your Limitations, A.
Hawk in Uig.
History of the Sketch, A.
Maratea Porto: The Dear Postmistress There.
Or Another Place.
Point No Point.
Skykomish River Running.
Jong. In My Cauldron under the Full Moon.
Kinnell. Wait.
Koch. Bricks, The.
Kooser. Late February.
Larkin. Next, Please.
Lawrence. Craving for Spring.
Endless Anxiety.
No News.
Suspense.
Turned Down.
Lorde. Father, the Year Has Fallen.
Memorial III—from a Phone Booth on Broadway.
Rooming Houses are Old Women.
McGrath. Fatigue of Objects, The.
McNeill. Blizzard.
Meredith. Along the garden terrace, under which.
Appreciation.
But Joan, where is Bessy?—She.
Lords debate, the Commons brawl, The.
Marian: "Clouds fly fast across the moon, The."
Shall I again have Lilac week?
Tuck, my treasure! Tuck, my pleasure!
Wand of gold from the reaper's moon, A.
Nathan. Poet's House Preserved as a Museum, The.
O'Hara. Lover, The.
St. Paul and All That.
What Appears to Be Yours.
Oppen. There can be a brick.
Rexroth. La Vie En Rose.
Roethke. Song: "My wrath, where's the edge."
Schuyler. Await.
Schwartz. At This Moment of Time.
Shakespeare. Sonnet 118: "Like as, to make our appetites more keen."
Sidney. Tenth Song.
Silverstein. Traffic Light.
Sorrentino. Red sun is going down somewhere, A.
Tennyson. Move Eastward, Happy Earth, and Leave.

Williams, Charles Kenneth. Past, The.
Young. Night before Michael Was Born, The.
Zukofsky. Valentine, A.

Antigone
Davie. Creon's Muse.
Meredith. Antigone.
Nathan. Letter.
Nemerov. Antigone.
Smith, Stevie. Oh Stubborn Race of Cadmus' Seed.
Spender. Happy are those who have never tasted evil.

Antiques
Bukowski. 56 Year Old Poem, A.
Burns. Ken ye ought o' Captain Grose?
On the Late Captain Grose's Peregrinations thro' Scotland, Collecting the Antiquities of That King.
Dickinson. We outgrow love like other things.
Graves. Hung Wu Vase, The.
Hugo. Antiques in Ellettsville.
Schuyler. "Used Handkerchiefs 5[dc]."
Zukofsky. Shang Cup.

Anti-Semitism
Boyle. Poem about the Jews, A.
Pack. South Bronx, 1939.

Antony (Marc Antony)
Dickinson. I never knew a broken Heart.
Lawrence. Universe Flows, The.
Stevenson. After Reading "Antony and Cleopatra."
Williams, William Carlos. To Mark Anthony in Heaven.

Antrim. *see* **County Antrim, Northern Ireland.**

Ants
Bly. Ant Mansion, The.
Ants.
Bukowski. Ants, The.
Carruth. One ant turns backward.
Emerson. Forbore the ant hill, shunned to tread.
Frost. Departmental.
Hoffman. Ants.
Knott. Ant Dodger.
Lovelace. Ant, The.
Whilst in an Amber-shade the Ant doth feast.
Nash. Ant, The.
Nemerov. Between the Window and the Screen.
Paley. Ant! / lugging half an ounce, An.
Then Vera stopped at the flower called fireweed.
Simic. Solitude.
Wilbur. Grasshopper and the Ant, The.
Wright, Charles. Journal of Three Questions, A.

Anxiety
Ammons. For Doyle Fosso.
Auden. Only a smell had feelings to make known.
Berg. Two Little Songs.
Berrigan. Clarity! clarity! a semblance of motion, omniscience. / There is no such thing as a breakdown.
Berryman. How Do You Do, Dr Berryman, Sir?
Bukowski. Big Bastard with a Sword.
Burns. Song: "Blythe hae I been on yon hill."
Campion. Ad Melleam.
Dolus.
If she forsake me, I must die.
Pin'd I am, and like to die.
What harts content can he finde.
Carruth. Arthritic gray snowlight hobbles down the valley westward.
Expectantly and fearfully I sing.
Living Alone.
One called Next steps up, The.
Tanck's Song About Fear of Falling.
To dig at Luxor, to peer.
Catullus. Carmen 38: "Angst, / ennui & angst."
Clark. Up in Here.
Cohen. Asthmatic, The.
Commentary—The Asthmatic.
Everybody Knows.

Future, The.
I Had It for a Moment.
Invisible Trouble, The.
Creeley. Going to Bed.
Kid.
Names.
NYC—.
Rites, The.
Something.
Waiting.
Window, The.
Dickinson. Crisis is a Hair.
Dunn. Midnight.
Night Truths.
Worrier, The.
"Dylan." Tell Me, Momma.
Trouble.
Walkin' Down the Line.
Eberhart. Anxiety I Felt in Guanajuato, The.
Fisher. Here comes the modulation.
Garrigue. Civilization Constantly Worrying about Itself as It Goes on Doing What It Is Worrying About That It Is Doing, A.
Forest.
Lead in the Water.
My Frantic Heart.
Smoke Shop Owner's Daughter, The.
Hall. Fathers and Sons.
Shudder [, The].
Hardy. Homecoming, The.
Suspense.
Hayden. Ice Storm.
Herbert. Conscience.
Herrick. Sorrows Succeed.
Hewitt. Dissertation II.
Second Front: Double Summertime, July 1943.
Hoffman. Dread, A.
Holmes. Instructions for the World Librarian.
Hopkins. She Schools the Flighty Pupils of Her Eyes.
Hugo. In Your Blue Dream.
In Your Racing Dream.
Joseph. High Devil, Deep Pit.
Man as Image (MASSIF; CHEMISTRY).
Mirror, Mirror.
Round: "Body of a child lay in the pool, The."
Kunitz. No Word.
Plot Against Hitler, The.
What wakes me now.
Lawrence. Endless Anxiety.
Levertov. Looking-glass.
Lorde. Memorial III—from a Phone Booth on Broadway.
Lowry. Death of an Oaxaqueñian.
McGrath. Enemy, The.
Heroes of Childhood, The.
In Dream Time.
Legendary Progress.
Letter for Marian, A.
Parable.
Poem: "Light flares from the tombstones.."
Restless Night, The.
MacNeice. Prognosis.
Marlowe. 1.2: Quod primo amore correptus, in triumphium duci se a Cupidine patiatur.
Meredith. Call, The.
Il y a Cent Ans.
In all our daily war of words.
Waves are pressing up with force, The.
Merrill. Komboloi.
Merton. First Lesson about Man.
Owl and Phoenix.
Morgan. Abenaki Poem.
Morrison. Soft Parade, The.
Nash. "My Child Is Phlegmatic.."—Anxious Parent.
Strange Case of Mr. Fortague's Disappointment, The.
Under the Floor.
We Don't Need to Leave Yet, Do We? Or, Yes We Do.
When the Devil Was Sick Could He Prove It?
O'Hara. Anxiety.
Oppen. Department of Plants and Structures— obsolete, the old name.

Guest Room.
They await / War, and the news.
Piercy. Under the Grind.
Rich. Picnic.
Sunday Evening.
Roethke. Silence.
Sarton. Gestalt at Sixty.
Shakespeare. Sonnet 58: "That god forbid that made me first your slave."
Smith, Charlotte. Female Exile. Written at Brighthelmstone in November 1792, The.
To a Friend.
Sorrentino. Faces of Doom and Sterility.
Stevenson. Ad Se Ipsum.
Long time I lay in little ease.
Warren. Driver, Driver.
Treasure Hunt.
Williams, Charles Kenneth. Fire.
Wright, Charles. Laguna Blues.
Zukofsky. And so till we have died.
Aubade, 1925.
My last—Cornificius—your Catullus'.
You three:—my wife.

Apartments
Carroll, Jim. One Flight Up.
Cooper. Rent.
Gunn. Apartment Cats.
Hall. Old Houses.
Hughes, Langston. Madam and the Rent Man.
Hugo. 1614 Boren.
Jarrell. Hope.
Koch. In the Morning.
Levertov. From the Roof.
Lorde. Moving Out Or the End of Cooperative Living.
Merrill. Tenancy, A.
Oppen. Rectangular, rearing / Black windows into daylight: the sound.
Solitary are obsessed, The.
Strange that the youngest people I know.
Paley. On the Fourth Floor.
Rich. Living in Sin.
Tomlinson. Lament for Doormen.
Updike. Note to the Previous Tenants.
Williams, Charles Kenneth. Flight.

Apathy
Atwood. Notes towards a Poem That Can Never Be Written.
Auden. Musée des Beaux Arts.
Bukowski. Winter.
Bunting. As appleblossom to crocus.
Clark. Milky Turqoise Cloud.
Clough. Here have I been these one and twenty years.
Cummings. Lis / -ten / you know what i mean when.
Most(people / simply / can't).
Of all the blessings which to man.
Eliot. Love Song of J. Alfred Prufrock, The.
Emerson. He walked the streets of great New York.
Glück. Returning a Lost Child.
Griffiths. Shamanism, Dalston.
Hewitt. Bradford Millionaire.
Knife, The.
Ulster Landowner's Song, An.
Hughes, Ted. View of a Pig.
Kipling. Russia to the Pacifists.
Lewis. Suicide, The.
Lindsay. Leaden-eyed, The.
McAuley. Lecture.
MacNeice. Easter Returns.
Merton. Lightly, lightly, so lightly.
Piercy. Knight of Swords, The.
"Reed." Heroin.
Men of Good Fortune.
Rolfe. Not Hatred.
Sixth Winter, The.
Shapiro. Hospital.
Sorrentino. Bright Nightgown.
Iceman, Again, The.
Out of Their Butchered Hearts.
Stafford. Ritual to Read to Each Other, A.
Stevenson. Celestial Surgeon, The.
Williams, Charles Kenneth. Ethics.
Ten Below.

Apes
Cohen. When I Left the King.
Donne. It quickened [or quickned] next a toyful[l] ape, and so.
Larkin. Ape Experiment Room.
Smith, Stevie. Le Singe qui swing.

Aphrodite
Browning, Robert. Oh Love, Love, thou that from the eyes diffusest.
Doolittle. Men you strike.
Simaetha.
Glück. Aphrodite.
Hoffman. Aphrodite.
Lawrence. Man of Tyre, The.
Meredith. Vital Choice, The.
With the Persuader.
Olson. Ring of, The.
Robinson. Lais to Aphrodite.
Warren. Myth on Mediterranean Beach: Aphrodite as Logos.
See also **Venus (goddess).**

Apocalypse
"Dylan." Talkin' World War III Blues.
Ford. I Wonder.
Graves. Interruption.
Haines. Choosing a Stone.
Dürer's Vision.
Hill. Day clacks and birds, The.
Lawrence. Dies Illa.
Stoic.
Merton. Figures for an Apocalypse.
Landscape: Beast.
Olson. End of the World / is the Turn-About, The.
Rukeyser. Third Elegy. The Fear of Form.
Williams, Miller. He Glimpses a Nobler Vision.
See also **End of the World; Judgment Day.**

Apollinaire, Guillaume
Berrigan. It is night. You are asleep. And beautiful tears.
Ferlinghetti. Reading Apollinaire by the Rogue River.
Ginsberg. At Apollinaire's Grave.
Sorrentino. Coast of Texas.

Apollo
Beatles. Sun King.
Browning, Robert. Apollo and the Fates.
Burns. To Mr. John Taylor.
Campion. To his sweet Lute *Apollo* sung the motions of the Spheares.
Carruth. Little Old Funky Homeric Blues for Herm, A.
Cowper. Ode to Apollo.
Doolittle. Evadne.
Emerson. Comrade or the book is good, The.
Graves. Apollo of the Physiologists.
Herrick. Canticle to Apollo, A.
To Apollo ("Thou mighty lord and master of the Lyre").
To Apollo ("Phoebus! When that I a Verse").
Hesketh. Sun Up.
Keats. Apollo to the Graces.
Ode to Apollo ("God of the golden bow").
Ode to Apollo ("In thy western halls of gold").
Kunitz. Flight of Apollo, The.
Liddy. Kerouac's Ronsard Dance.
Lovelace. Princesse Löysa drawing.
Meredith. Evening, after a Picture.
Phoebus with Admetus.
Rape of Aurora, The.
Vengeance of Apollo, The.
Millay. Daphne.
Robinson. Many Are Called.
Sexton. Where I Live in This Honorable House of the Laurel Tree.
Sidney. *Apollo* great, whose beams the greater world do light.
Phoebus farewell, a sweeter saint I serve.
Smart. Apollo and Daphne.
Swift. Apollo.
Apollo Outwitted.
Apollo to the Dean.
Apollo's Edict.
First of April, The.
Williams, William Carlos. After Song, An.

Apoplexy. *see* **Strokes.**

Apostles
Auden. Twelve, The.
Browning, Robert. Death in the Desert, A.
Davie. Pentecost.
Dickinson. Of Paul and Silas it is said.
Donne. Apostles, The.
Herrick. Salutation.
Pound. Ballad of the Goodly Fere.
Robinson. Three Taverns, The.
Rossetti. Ascension Day.
Smart. Let Peter rejoice with the Moon Fish who keeps up the life in the waters by night.
St. James.
St. Mark.
St. Matthew.
St. Philip and St. James.
Tate. Twelve, The.
Wilbur. Peter.

Apple Blossoms
Sandburg. Crabapple Blossoms.
June.

Apple Trees and Apples
Bogan. Crossed Apple, The.
"Carroll, Lewis." Dreaming of apples on a wall.
Crane. Sunday Morning Apples.
Creeley. Juggler's Thought.
Surgeons.
Cummings. It's over a(see just).
Dunbar. Old Apple-Tree, The.
Unlucky Apple, The.
"Dylan." Apple Suckling Tree.
Don't Ya Tell Henry.
Eberhart. Apple Buds.
Emerson. Always day & night.
Frost. After Apple-picking.
Gold Hesperidee, The.
Unharvested.
Wood-Pile, The.
Galvin. Apple Trees, The.
Wild Apple Trees.
Hall. Apples.
Hesketh. Scapegoat.
Hewitt. Mad Applegrower, The.
Hughes, Ted. Apple Dumps.
Joseph. First Spring Dawn.
Keats. O Blush Not So! O Blush Not So!
Kinnell. Apple Tree, The.
Larkin. As Bad as a Mile.
Lawrence. Medlars and Sorb-Apples.
Mystic.
Old Orchard, The.
Lindsay. Fairy from the Apple-Seed, The.
In Praise of Johnny Appleseed.
Meredith. Breath of the Briar.
Nathan. Opportunity.
Olson. My apple branch dressed.
Oppen. Still Life.
Pack. Clayfeld Prunes His Apple Trees.
Kiss, The.
Wild Turkeys in Paradise.
Paley. For My Friend Who Planted a Tree for His Daughter Jane.
Leaves Apples.
Patchen. Carts of the wee blind lass, The.
Rossetti. Apple Gathering, An.
Rukeyser. Tree.
Simic. History.
Interlude.
Snodgrass. Old Apple Trees.
Swift. Apples.
Tomlinson. Paring the Apple.
Wilbur. John Chapman.
Williams, Charles Kenneth. I'd forgotten and / how could I ever.
Williams, William Carlos. Perfection.
Wild Orchard.
Wright, James. Two Horses Playing in the Orchard.

Apprentices
Chaucer. Cook's Tale, The.
Hartnett. Poet as Mastercraftsman, The.
Jonson. To My Old Faithful Servant: And (by His Continued Virtue) My Loving Friend: The Author of this Work, M[r] Rich[ard] Brome.

Merton. To a Novice ("Avoid three kinds of Master").
Muldoon. Sushi.

Approval
Bukowski. Twins.
Cohen. Commentary—Hurry to Your Dinner.
Dickinson. I thought your approbation Fame.
Hewitt. Ballad, The.
  Collector's Choice.
  Island Folk Tale, An.
  Neglected Lane, The.
Merton. King Solomon: my master and the imbeciles.
Piercy. I Will Not Be Your Sickness.
Sorrentino. Lemonade Panel, The.
Young. Moon, How Do I Measure Up?

Apricot Trees and Apricots
Sorrentino. Memory, The.

April
Auden. Alston Moor.
  April.
  April in a Town.
Browning, Robert. Home-Thoughts, from Abroad.
Carruth. Where the snow bank leans.
Cummings. "but why should" / the / greatest.
  If(among / silent skies).
  When faces called flowers float out of the ground.
De la Mare. April.
  Cherry Trees, The.
Eberhart. This Fevers Me.
Emerson. April.
  Gentle Spring has charmed the earth.
  More sweet than my refrain.
Glück. My Cousin in April.
Hewitt. April.
Jeffers. Gale in April.
Levine. Sleepless Night, A.
  Told.
Merton. April.
Millay. Northern April.
  Road to Avrillé, The.
  Song of a Second April.
  Spring.
Nash. Always Marry an April Girl.
Nemerov. April.
Oliver. Blossom.
Rossetti. If it's weary work to live.
Sandburg. Branches.
  Just Before April Came.
  Plowboy.
  Three Spring Notations on Bipeds.
Shelley. Fragment: May the Limner.
Snodgrass. April Inventory.
Stevenson. Over the land is April.
Tomlinson. In April.
Whittier. April.
Wilbur. Gnomons.
  Storm in April, A.
Williams, William Carlos. Della Primavera Transportata al Morale.
  Two Aspects of April.

April Fool's Day
MacNeice. April Fool.
Swift. First of April, The.

Aquinas, St. Thomas. *see* **Thomas Aquinas, Saint.**

Arab-Israeli Wars
Ginsberg. Jaweh and Allah Battle.
Hoffman. 1956.

Arabia
De la Mare. Arabia.
Lindsay. Doll's "Arabian Nights," A.
Stevenson. Tales of Arabia.
Young. Arabia.

Arabs
Browning, Robert. Through the Metidja to Abd-el-Kadr.
Emerson. Arabian Ballad.
Gallagher. Rijl.

Arachne
Ford. Being nor whim nor.
Hayden. Richard Hunt's "Arachne."

Aran Islands, Ireland
Mahon. Aran.

Arbus, Diane
Nemerov. To D———, Dead by Her Own Hand.

Arbutus
Dickinson. Pink—small—and punctual.
Whitman. For Queen Victoria's Birthday.
Whittier. Mayflowers, The.
  Trailing Arbutus, The.

Arcadia
Auden. Vespers.
"Carroll, Lewis." Three Little Maids.
Dunbar. Ballade: "By Mystic's banks I held my dream."
  Farewell to Arcady.
Ralegh. Arcadians the earth inhabited, The.
Stevenson. To H.C. Bunner.

Archaeology and Archaeologists
Auden. Archaeology.
Betjeman. Archaeological Picnic, The.
Eberhart. Dry Rot, The.
Gardner. Only Relic, The.
Hardy. Clasped Skeleton, The.
Pack. Archeology.
Rich. In my imagination I was the pivot of a fresh beginning.
  Of simple choice they are the villagers; their clothes come.
Rukeyser. Artifact.
Schuyler. Industrial Archaeology.
Updike. Toothache Man.
Williams, William Carlos. Smiling Dane, A.
Yau. Late Night Movies I.

Archery
Frost. Version.
Graves. Blind Arrow, A.
Merton. Need to Win, The.
Tomlinson. Archer, The.
Wilbur. Arrow in the Wall, An.

Architecture and Architects
Atwood. City Planners, The.
Auden. Prologue: The Birth of Architecture.
Carruth. Meadow House.
Duncan. Architecture, The.
Emerson. Problem, The.
Fenton. South Parks Road.
Fletcher. Elegy on an Empty Skyscraper.
  Evening Clouds, The.
  Tower, The.
Garrigue. Grand Canyon, The.
Hardy. Abbey Mason, The.
  Heiress and Architect.
Hopkins. Boughs being pruned, birds preenèd, show more fair.
Jonson. Expostulation with Inigo Jones, An.
  To Inigo, Marquess Would Be, a Corollary.
Kipling. My New-Cut Ashlar.
Mahon. Mt. Gabriel.
Melville. Greek Architecture.
  Greek Masonry.
Piercy. Track of the Master Builder, The.
Rich. Mary Jane Colter, 1904.
Sandburg. Scaffolding holds the arch in place, The.
Tomlinson. Albuquerque.
  Dates: Penkhull New Road.
Yau. Rumors.
Zukofsky. Imitation.

Arctic
Carruth. Afterword: What the Poet Had Written.
Davie. After the Calamitous Convoy (July 1942).
  Behind the North Wind.
Gunn. From the Highest Camp.
Hall. Wolf Knife.
Spender. Polar Exploration.
Whitman. Of That Blithe Throat of Thine.
Whittier. Spirit of the North, The.

Arethusa
Shelley. Arethusa.

Argentina
Lowell. Buenos Aires.
Rolfe. Song for a Birth Day in Exile.

Arguments. *see* **Quarrels.**

Ariadne
Browning, Elizabeth Barrett. Bacchus and Ariadne.
  How Bacchus Comforts Ariadne.
Dobyns. Theseus Within the Labyrinth.
Lovelace. Princesse Löysa drawing.
Merton. Ariadne.
  Ariadne at the Labyrinth.
Simic. In Midsummer Quiet.
Tomlinson. Ariadne and the Minotaur.

Aristocracy
Berry. Aristocracy, The.
Betjeman. County.
Burns. Address of Beelzebub.
  Extempore Verses on Dining with Lord Daer.
  Verses Intended to Be Written below a Noble Earl's Picture.
Dickey, William. Dog Under False Pretences.
Graves. Cloak, The.
Hill. Funeral Music.
Lawrence. Aristocracy of the Sun.
  Magnificent Democracy.
  Rise in the World, A.
Meredith. Miss Millicent Maxse was fond of her Ma.
Rich. Uncle Speaks in the Drawing Room, The.
Wilbur. Complaint.
Williams, William Carlos. Impromptu: The Suckers.

Aristotle
Auden. Megalopsych, The.
Cowper. On the Platonic Idea as Aristotle Understood It.
Eberhart. Commitment, A.
  Great Principles Are Thrown Down by Time.
  Kaire.
Meinke. Fixed Stars.
Milton. On the Platonic Idea as Aristotle Understood It.

Arithmetic
Hewitt. Arithmetic.
Sandburg. Arithmetic.

Arizona (state)
Carruth. Rimrock, Where It Is.
Clark. Gift of Tongue.
Cohen. I Can't Forget.
Fletcher. Cliff-dwelling.
  Fuel Vendor, The.
  Mexican Quarter.
  Rain in the Desert.
  Well in the Desert, The.
  Windmills, The.
Hacker. Country & Western II.
Tomlinson. Arizona Desert.
Zukofsky. Arizona.
  In Arizona / (how many years in the mountains).

Ark, The
Cohen. Etiquette.
Graves. Ark, The.
Silverstein. Unicorn, The.
Thomas. Author's Prologue.
Warren. Gold Glade.
See also **Noah.**

Arkansas (state)
Angelou. My Arkansas.
Davie. Siloam.
Williams, Miller. Getting Experience.
Wright, Charles. Arkansas Traveller.

Arlington National Cemetery, Virginia
Haines. Arlington.

Armada. *see* **Spanish Armada.**

Armenia and Armenians
Davie. Mandelstam's Hope for the Best.
Hemingway. They All Made Peace—What Is Peace?
Updike. Yerevan.

Armies
Everson. Eastward the armies.
Jeffers. Ghosts in England.
Lewis. Now only beggars still go singing.
  This stunted pine whose knotted roots.
Melville. Armies of the Wilderness, The.
  Night-March, The.
Patchen. Knowledge of Old Towns, The.
Prince. How Festivals Were Celebrated.
Stevenson. Our Lady of the Snows.

Armistice
Frost. November.
Graves. Armistice Day, 1918.
Hardy. And There Was a Great Calm.
Peace Peal, The.
Kipling. London Stone.
Longfellow. Message of Peace, A.
Nemerov. Armistice.
See also **Peace.**

Armstrong, Louis
Schuyler. Beautiful Funerals.

Army Life
Housman. Grenadier.
New Mistress, The.
Jarrell. Absent with Official Leave.
Good-bye, Wendover; Good-bye, Mountain
Home.
Lines, The.
Mail Call.
Second Air Force.
Soldier [T. P.].
Transient Barracks.
Kipling. Back to the Army Again.
Boots.
Cholera Camp.
Danny Deever.
'Eathen, The.
Gentlemen-Rankers.
Gunga Din.
Jacket, The.
Loot.
Mandalay.
Men That Fought at Minden, The.
Oonts.
Parade-Song of the Camp Animals.
Private Ortheris's Song.
Roman Centurion's Song, The.
Route Marchin'.
Shut-Eye Sentry, The.
Snarleyow.
Troopin'.
Young British Soldier, The.
Lawrence. Drill in the Heat.
Young Soldier with Bloody Spurs, The.
Lewis. All Day It Has Rained.
Infantry.
On Embarkation.
Lowry. Deserter.
McNeill. Saturday Night (1930s).
Morgan. Letter, The.
Nathan. Letter to the Patrol Twenty Years
After.
Rolfe. Sentry.
Stevenson. Country of the Camisards, The.
Prelude: "By sunny market-place and street."
Whitman. Adieu to a Soldier.
Bivouac on a Mountain Side.
By the Bivouac's Fitful Flame.
Camps of Green.
Cavalry Crossing a Ford.
Wright, Charles. Italian Days.
See also **Soldiers.**

Arnold, Matthew
Ferlinghetti. Sea Is Calm Tonight, The.

Arranged Marriage. *see* **Marriage, Arranged.**

Arrows
De la Mare. Hunter, The.
Dickinson. I've got an arrow here.
Dobyns. Six Poems on Moving.
Emerson. I have an arrow that can find its
mark.
Ye have Grace.
Psalms. Psalm 64: "Hear my voice, O God, in
my prayer."
Wakoski. Elizabeth and the Golden Oranges.
Wilbur. Arrow in the Wall, An.

Art and Artists
Ammons. Orchard.
Atwood. Later in Belleville: Career.
Auden. Composer, The.
Dethroned.
Geography of the House, The.
Portrait.
Thomas Epilogizes.
Berrigan. In Joe Brainard's collage its white
arrow.

Berryman. Ecce Homo.
Bishop. Monument, The.
Blake. All Pictures thats Panted with sense &
with Thought.
Blakes apology for His Catalogue.
I asked [*or* askd] my Dear Friend, Orator
Prigg.
Now Art has lost its mental Charms.
O dear Mother outline of knowledge most
sage.
On the Great Encouragement Given By
English Nobility & Gentry to Correggio
Rubens Rembrandt Reynolds Gainsborough
Catalani Ducrowe & Dilbury Doodle.
On the Venetian Painter.
Pretty Epigram for [Those] the Entertainment
of Those Who [Pay] Have Paid Great Sums
in the Venetian & Flemish Ooze, A.
Rafael Sublime Majestic Graceful Wise.
To Venetian Artists.
Venetian; all thy Colouring is no more.
When I see a Rubens Rembrandt [or]
Correggio.
You say their Pictures well Painted be.
Bogan. To an Artist, to Take Heart.
Boyle. Artist Speaks..the Woman Answers,
The.
Print from a Lucite Block.
This Is Not a Letter.
Brooks. Spaulding and Francois.
Browning, Elizabeth Barrett. Hiram Powers'
"Greek Slave."
Browning, Robert. At the "Mermaid."
Beatrice Signorini.
Cleon.
Deaf and Dumb.
Fra Lippo Lippi.
How It Strikes a Contemporary.
Lady and the Painter, The.
One Word More.
Youth and Art.
Bukowski. Bring Down the Beams.
Experience.
On Going Back to the Street after Viewing an
Art Show.
Bunting. Gertie Gitana's hymn to waltzing.
Burns. To a Painter.
Byron. Condolatory Address.
Carruth. Buddhist Painter Prepares to Paint,
The.
Lana.
Museum Piece.
Post-Impressionist Susurration for the First of
November, 1983, A.
This Decoration.
Wheel of Being II, The.
Catullus. Carmen 36: "Volusian sheets / shit-
shotten Annals."
Carmen 65: "Although entangled in prolonged
grief."
Carmen 68: "Borne down by bitter
misfortune."
Carmen 105: "O'Toole / attempting an entry
of the *mons Parnassus.*"
Ciardi. Annals.
Conversation with Leonardo, A.
On Passion As a Literary Tradition.
Clark. Baby Book Fate Dream.
Cohen. Commentary—How to Speak Poetry.
How to Speak Poetry.
Coleridge. Apologia pro Vita Sua.
To a Critic.
To Matilda Betham from a Stranger.
To Mr. Pye.
To the Young Artist.
With Fielding's *Amelia.*
Cooper. In a Room with Picassos.
Cowper. Denner's Old Woman.
Tears of a Painter, The.
Creeley. Figures, The.
Cummings. Conversation with my friend is
particularly.
If i have made,my lady,intricate.
If you like my poems let them.
Mr youse needn't be so spry.
My naked lady framed.
Picasso / you give us Things.

Pity his how illimitable plight.
Some ask praise of their fellows.
S.T.
This mind made war.
To start,to hesitate;to stop.
Davie. Cherry Ripe.
Dublin Georgian.
Dublin Georgian (2).
Feeders, The.
Hill Field, The.
Limited Achievement.
Nonconformist, The.
Portrait of the Artist as a Farmyard Fowl.
Resolutions.
To a Brother in the Mystery.
Tuscan Brutus, The.
With the Grain.
Dickinson. Artists wrestled here!
I work to drive the awe away.
Nature is a Haunted House.
Dobyns. Velocity of Cows, The.
Donne. To Mr. B. B.
Doolittle. Red Roses for Bronze.
Dunbar. Nature and Art.
Duncan. Architecture, The.
Nel Mezzo del Cammin di Nostra Vita.
"Dylan." Bringing It All Back Home.
I end up then.
So at last at least.
Yes, I am a thief of thoughts.
Eberhart. Art, the holy care of life.
Cancer Cells, The.
Commitment, A.
Fortune's Mist.
Looking Head On.
On the Fragility of Mind.
Emerson. Art.
Artist.
By art, by music, overthrilled.
Enough is done highminded friend go sleep.
Loss and Gain.
My Garden.
Try the might the Muse affords.
Ferlinghetti. London / crossfigured / creeping
with trams.
Plan du Centre de Paris à Vol D'Oiseau.
Triumph of the Postmodern.
Fisher. Artists, Providers, Places to Go.
In the Black Country.
Lesson in Composition, The.
Fletcher. Fragments of Eternity.
Oiran and Her Kamuso, An.
Portrait, The.
Ford. I do put art before.
Fox. Peaches.
Garrigue. Improvisation upon the Theme of
the Lady and the Unicorn, An.
Ginsberg. Cézanne's Ports.
Ignu.
This Is about Death.
Gray. Ode for Music.
Gunn. Confessions of the Life Artist.
Expression.
Selves.
Hall. This Poem.
Hardy. Figure in the Scene, The.
Hartnett. Sibelius in Silence.
Heaney. Artist, An.
Herrick. Art above Nature, to Julia.
Painting Sometimes Permitted.
Upon Man.
Hewitt. After Reading *Sonnets* by Rev.
Charles Turner (1864) and *The New Day,*
Sonnets by Dr T. Gordon Hake (1890).
Art Room in a City School.
Art's Duped Riddle.
August 1939.
Drypoint.
From a Museum Man's Album.
I Learn About Art.
Lagan in October, The.
Portrait, The.
Roll Call.
Roseblade's Visitants and Mine.
Sonnet: "I have no time to worship. I must
live."
Sunset.

Artemis
                    SUBJECT INDEX
                    1410

To Any Dweller in Lewis Street.
Valediction Lines to My WEA Students.
Variations on a Theme.
Watercolour, The.
William Conor RHA, 1881–1968.
William J. McClughin.
With a Little Book of Pottery.
Hill. Pre-Raphaelite Notebook, A.
Holmes. Work on in the faith.
Hugo. Back of Gino's Place.
1614 Boren.
Jarrell. Head of Wisdom, The.
In Galleries.
Old and the New Masters, The.
Jeffers. Artist, An.
To a Young Artist.
Vices.
Jong. Artist as an Old Man, The.
Empty.
Jonson. Soft, subtle fire, thou soul of art.
Joseph. Cutting Off One's Ears for Someone
Else Is Wrong.
Keats. On Seeing the Elgin Marbles.
Kipling. Conundrum of the Workshops, The.
Evarra and His Gods.
Jubal and Tubal Cain.
Story of Ung, The.
When Earth's Last Picture Is Painted.
Knott. Poem (How I Lost My Pen-Name).
Sculpture, The.
Koch. Artist, The.
Our Hearts.
Kunitz. Artist, The.
At the Porch of the Caryatids.
Liddy. Art Is Not for Grown-ups.
Price, The.
Lindsay. Mae Marsh, Motion Picture Actress.
Lowell. Beethoven.
Lost Tune, The.
Lowry. Stoker Tom's Ukulele.
McAuley. Artist, Reclining, The.
"MacDiarmid." And thus a poetry which fully
understands.
So, like him, we cry *"l'honneur des hommes:
Saint Langage."*
MacLeish. Corporate Entity.
Markson. Death of the Virgin, The.
Dialogue in Milan.
History and Theory of Art.
Marlowe. 3.14: Ad Venerem, quod elegis
finem imponat.
Meinke. To a Daughter with Artistic Talent.
Melville. Art.
Merrill. Dreams About Clothes.
Merton. Mosaic: St. Praxed's.
Originators, The.
Paradise of Squares.
Millay. And if I die, because that part of me.
To hold secure the province of Pure Art.
Moore. When I Buy Pictures.
Muldoon. Christo's.
Nash. Everybody Makes Poets.
Nemerov. To Clio, Muse of History.
O'Hara. Memorial Day 1950.
Why I Am Not a Painter.
Oliver. Dream of Trees, A.
Olson. Bottled up for days, mostly.
"Enthusiasm", An.
For Cy Twombly Faced with His First
Chicago & N.Y. Shows.
Knowing All Ways, Including the
Transposition of Continents.
So the Norse / were neurotic.
Oppen. Constant singing / Of the radios, and
the art, The.
Drawing.
Giovanni's *Rape of the Sabine Women* at
Wildenstein's.
Or, in that light, New arts!
Pack. Trying to Separate.
Patchen. Continual Ministry of Thy Anger,
The.
Portrait of the Artist as an Interior Decorator.
Pope. Epitaph on Sir Godfrey Kneller, in
Westminster-Abbey, 1723.
To Sir Godfrey Kneller, on His Painting for

Me the Statues of Apollo, Venus and
Hercules.
Pound. Of Jacopo del Sellaio.
Prince. My last morning and so, here.
Sun floats in sublime, The.
Ransom. Painted Head.
Rich. At a Bach Concert.
Aunt Jennifer's Tigers.
Burning Oneself Out.
Diamond Cutters, The.
Ghazals: Homage to Ghalib.
Pierrot Le Fou.
Rural Reflections.
They come to you with their descriptions of
your soul.
Robinson. Caput Mortuum.
Rolfe. Bequest.
On Rico LeBrun's Crucifixion.
Rossetti. In an Artist's Studio.
Rukeyser. Käthe Kollwitz.
Painters.
Sun-Artist, The.
Schuyler. After Joe Was at the Island.
Back.
Dear Joe.
Fauré Ballade, The.
Morning of the Poem, The.
Red Brick and Brown Stone.
Trash Book, The.
Shakespeare. It was a lording's daughter, the
fairest one of three.
Sonnet 68: "Thus is his cheek the map of days
outworn."
Shapiro. Poet.
Poet in Residence.
Room in Rome, A.
White Negress, The.
Smith, Patti. Babelogue.
Balance.
Easter.
Florence.
Neo Boy.
Picasso Laughing.
Robert Bresson.
Salvation of Rock, The.
Scream of the Butterfly.
Y.
Smith, Stevie. Choosers, The.
Full Well I Know.
New Age, The.
Snodgrass. Matisse: "The Red Studio."
Snyder. Thoughts on Looking at a Samuel
Palmer Etching at the Tate.
Sorrentino. Come all ye Sons of Art.
16 Lines.
Spender. Art Student.
Grandparents.
Mosquito in Florence.
Stevens. Add This to Rhetoric.
Anecdote of the Jar.
From the Packet of Anacharsis.
Man with the Blue Guitar, The.
Prelude to Objects.
So-and-So Reclining on Her Couch.
Stevenson. To Sydney.
To the Muse.
Tate. Art.
Intellectual Detachment.
Tennyson. Palace of Art, The.
Tomlinson. Chances of Rhyme, The.
Distinctions.
Updike. Angels, The.
Calder's Hands.
Fleckings, The.
Gradations of Black.
Les Saints Nouveaux.
Modigliani's Death Mask.
Two Hoppers.
Van Duyn. Homework.
Learners, The.
Wakoski. Roses Were Talking, The.
Walcott. In the other 'eighties, a hundred
midsummers gone.
Map of Europe, A.
Waldman. Lie, The.
Walker. Songless.
Whitman. Eidolons.

Whittier. Artist of the Beautiful, An.
Flowers in Winter.
On a Prayer-Book.
Wilbur. Museum Piece.
Ode to Pleasure.
Williams, Charles Kenneth. Refuge, Serpent-
Riders.
Williams, Miller. Style.
Williams, William Carlos. All the Fancy
Things.
Art, The.
Painting, The.
Title, The.
Two Deliberate Exercises.
Wordsworth. At the Convent of Camaldoli.
Foregoing Subject Resumed, The.
Gleaner (Suggested By a Picture), The.
How Rich That Forehead's Calm Expanse!
Lyre! Though Such Power Do in Thy Magic
Live.
On Seeing a Needlecase in the Form of a
Harp; the Work of E.M.S.
Poet!—He Hath Put His Heart to School, A.
To Lucca Giordano.
Upon the Sight of a Beautiful Picture.
Vale of Esthwaite, The.
Written in Mrs Field's Album opposite a Pen-
and-Ink Sketch in the Manner of a
Rembrandt Etching Done by Edmund Field.
Yau. Bare Sheets III.
January 18, 1979.
Sleepness Night of Eugene Delacroix, The.
Yeats. Curse of Cromwell, The.
Lapis Lazuli.
Nativity, A.
Zukofsky. *Annals* of Volusius, cock at his
offal.
Ask of the sun.
Cold how mean, fortune consuming you
oppresses your care, your.
Even if love convey.
Meantool reconnoiters Pipléa scanning Their
mountain.
Shang Cup.
Spook's Sabbath, Five Bowings.
Two Dedications: D.R.
Yet see (may as I do) a confect of my cure—
a dolor.
You three:—my wife.

See also **Artists' Colonies.**

Artemis
Browning, Robert. Artemis Prologizes.
Doolittle. Chorus of Troizenian Women.
Daemon initiate, spirit.
No more, O my spirit.
Meredith. Vital Choice, The.
Waldman. Artemis.

Arthritis
Hugo. Hot Springs.

Arthurian Legend
Auden. Arthur's Quoit, Dyffryn.
Campion. Epigram, An: "Merlin, the great
King Arthur being slaine."
Hewitt. Pendragon.
Hill. Merlin.
Robinson. Lancelot.
Merlin.
Scott. Magic Castle, The.
Smith, Stevie. Blue from Heaven, The.
Tennyson. Lady of Shalott, The.
Morte d'Arthur.
Pelleas and Ettarre.
Prayer: "Pray for my soul. More things are
wrought by prayer."
Wordsworth. Egyptian Maid; or, The Romance
of the Water Lilly, The.

Artifacts
Burns. On the Late Captain Grose's
Peregrinations thro' Scotland, Collecting the
Antiquities of That King.
Galvin. With Anne at the Peabody.
Hughes, Ted. Relic.
Rich. Open-Air Museum.

Artists' Colonies
Liddy. Death of Artists, The.
Robinson. Hillcrest.

Ascension Day
Auden. Ascension Day, 1964.
Beckett. Ascension.
Donne. Ascension [or Ascention].
Herrick. Clouds.
Rossetti. Ascension Day.
Ascension Eve.
Smart. Ascension of Our Lord Jesus Christ,
The.

Ash Trees
Auden. Dark Fiddler, The.
Hopkins. Ashboughs.
Kipling. Tree Song, A.
Meinke. Dead Tree, The.

Ashbery, John
Koch. Circus, The.
Fate.
O'Hara. Postcard from John Ashbery, A.
"Unfinished," The.
Schuyler. Dining Out with Doug and Frank.
Fauré Ballade, The.
Waldman. For J.A. As Dusk Deepens Canyon.

Ashes
Bukowski. Ashes.
Clark. After the Fire—The Woman.
Hall. Coal Fire, The.
Hesketh. Sundowner.
Levine. Ashes.
Sandburg. Pool.
White Ash.
Simic. Primer.

Asia
Berg. Endings.
1945.
Eberhart. Rape of the Cataract, The.
Ginsberg. Angkor Wat.
Jarrell. Wide Prospect, The.
Lowell. Father's Bedroom.
Merrill. Willoware Cup.
Nash. So I resigned from the Chu Chin
Chowder and Marching Club.

Asian-Americans
Carruth. Eternity Blues.
Cohen. When This American Woman.
Hugo. Letter to Matthews from Barton Street
Flats.
Yau. Cameo of a Chinese Woman on
Mulberry Street.
No One Ever Tried To Kiss Anna May Wong.
Toy Trucks and Fried Rice.
See also **Chinese, The; Japanese, The.**

Aspen Trees
Carruth. Leaves, The.
Hopkins. Binsey Poplars (Felled 1879).
Wilbur. Aspen and the Stream, The.
See also **Poplar Trees.**

Asphodels
Williams, William Carlos. Of asphodel, that
greeny flower.

Aspirations
Beatles. Drive My Car.
I'll Get You.
Paperback Writer.
Berrigan. In my paintings for they are present.
Carroll, Jim. Fear and Trembling.
Dove. Magic.
Duncan. Nel Mezzo del Cammin di Nostra
Vita.
Hughes, Langston. Deferred.
Negro Mother, The.
To Be Somebody.
Lewis. Prelude and Fugue.
Lindsay. On the Road to Nowhere.
Lorde. Seventh Sign, The.
"MacDiarmid." Dytiscus.
Meredith. Open horizons round.
Nash. Eheu! Fugaces, or, What a Difference a
Lot of Days Make.
Rolfe. Brickyards at Beacon.
Song: "Keep the dream alive and growing
always."
Undersea Poem.
Stevenson. I, now, O friend, whom noiselessly
the snows.
Take not my hand as mine alone.
Sutter. Good Night, A.

My Father at His Height.
Night Shift: the Composing Room.

Assassinations and Assassins
Berryman. Formal Elegy.
Carruth. I was watching the telly not serious
you know just looking.
Dobyns. Body of Romulus, The.
Ferlinghetti. Assassination Raga.
Elegy to Dispel Gloom, An.
Gunn. Claus von Stauffenberg.
Julian the Apostate.
Hall. "Marat's Death."
Kipling. Ave Imperatrix!
Knight. It Was a Funky Deal.
Kunitz. His innocence was to trust.
Plot Against Hitler, The.
Lorde. Equinox.
MacLeish. State Funeral: March 31, 1969.
Melville. Martyr, The.
Merton. April 4th 1968.
Oppen. Armies of the Plain.
Rolfe. Epitaph: "Deep in this earth."
Rukeyser. Martin Luther King, Malcolm X.
Tomlinson. Assassin.
At Trotsky's House.
Charlotte Corday.
Marat Dead.
Wakoski. Second Universe.
Whitman. Spanish Lady, The.
Williams, Miller. Allende at the End.
Young. Day Kennedy Died.

Asses. *see* **Donkeys.**

Assisi, Italy
St. John. Francesco and Clare.

Assistance
Beatles. Help!
Cowper. Human Frailty.
Lindsay. Flower of Mending, The.
Piercy. Gracious Goodness.
Rolfe. To Thine Own Self.
Silverstein. Helping.
Stuart. High Wire.
Williams, Charles Kenneth. When.

Assurance
Bukowski. Out of the Blue.
Clough. But whether in the uncoloured light
of truth.
Creeley. Window, The.
Dickey, William. Confidence.
Rossetti. Until the Day Break.
Tomlinson. Request, The.

Assyrians
Bishop. Wading at Wellfleet.
Byron. Destruction of Sennacherib, The.
Walcott. There was one Syrian, with his
bicycle, in our town.

Astrology and Astrologers
Cowper. On the Astrologers.
Crashaw. Love's Horoscope.
Dickey, James. Zodiac, The.
Dickey, William. Sagittarius, Scorpio Rising.
Dickinson. Nature assigns the Sun.
Emerson. Horoscope.
Ford. Your Horoscope.
Graves. Non Cogunt Astra.
Kipling. Astrologer's Song, An.
Unto whose use the pregnant suns are poised.
Lowry. Consolation.
Stars have simple paradigms, The.
Virgo.
Rich. For the Conjunction of Two Planets.
Schuyler. Picnic Cantata, A.
Sexton. Madame Arrives in the Mail.
Sidney. Sonnet 26: "Though dusty wits dare
scorn astrology."
Sorrentino. Impromptu Solo on a Balcony.
Wilbur. Flumen Tenebrarum.

Astronauts
Hayden. Astronauts.
Williams, William Carlos. Heel & Toe to the
End.

Astronomy and Astronomers
Auden. Song: "Relation seemed ordained for
us."
Carroll, Jim. Evening News.
For John Donne.
Prologue: "Starting with little in mind."

Clough. Uranus.
Coleridge. Translation of a Greek Ode on
Astronomy.
Dickinson. Nature assigns the Sun.
Edmunds. Egypt.
Emerson. Song of Seyd [or Seid] Nimetollah
of Kuhistan.
Star seer Copernicus / Only could earn a
curse.
Ferlinghetti. Olbers' Paradox.
Fox. Finding the Andromeda Nebula.
Letters from the Astronomers.
Megrez.
Hewitt. Nebula.
Jeffers. Great Explosion, The.
Lawrence. Astronomical Changes.
Pack. Stellar Thanksgiving.
Rich. For the Conjunction of Two Planets.
Planetarium.
Rukeyser. Sacred Lake.
Whitman. When I Heard the Learn'd
Astronomer.

Atalanta
Olson. Atalanta.

Atheism
Cullen. For an Atheist.
Dunn. At the Smithville Methodist Church.
Hardy. Impercipient, The.
Lawrence. There Are No Gods.
Lowell. For George Santayana.
MacNeice. Although we say we disbelieve.
And the Lord was not in the whirlwind.
Didymus.
Nemerov. Memory of My Friend, A.
Schuyler. I Sit Down to Type.
Sexton. Play, The.
Swift. Lines to Pope.
Wright, Charles. Composition in Grey and
Pink.

Athena
Cowper. On Pallas Bathing.
Doolittle. Helios and Athene.
Muse, / tell me of this man of wit.
Piercy. Athena in the Front Lines.
See also **Minerva.**

Athens, Greece
Browning, Robert. Pheidippides.
Byron. Maid of Athens, Ere We Part.
Cohen. You Went to Work.
Hugo. Gull Hardly Explained, The.
MacNeice. Gorged on red, green, purple,
tomatoes, peppers, aubergine.
Meredith. Solon.
Milton. Look once more ere we leave this
specular Mount.
Muldoon. Dancers at the Moy.
Nemerov. On Getting Out Of Vietnam.
Patchen. Age of Pericles, The.
Sandburg. Anecdote of Hemlock for Two
Athenians.
Swift. Ode to the Athenian Society.
Wordsworth. Modern Athens, The.
Translation of a Celebrated Greek Song.

Athletics and Athletes
Davie. After the Match.
Dickey, James. Olympian, The.
Gunn. Courtesies of the Interregnum.
Hemingway. Punt, The.
Safety Man, The.
Hewitt. Uncle Sam and Aunt Edie.
Housman. To an Athlete Dying Young.
Matthews. Foul Shots: A Clinic.
In Memory of the Utah Stars.
Masterful.
Olson. I Mean, No.
Piercy. Morning Athletes.
Updike. Ex-Basketball Player.
Whitman. Runner, The.

Atlanta, Georgia
Whittier. Howard at Atlanta.

Atlantic Ocean
Cowper. Castaway, The.
Eberhart. Child, The.
Glück. Lady in the Single, The.
Kipling. Deep-Sea Cables, The.
When the cabin port-holes are dark and green.

Atlantis
Longfellow. Seaweed.
Sandburg. North Atlantic.
Sexton. Crossing the Atlantic.
Tomlinson. Atlantic, The.

Atlantis
Crane. Atlantis.
Lindsay. Song in July, A.

Atomic Bomb
Cooper. Atom bellies like a cauliflower, The.
Eberhart. On Shooting Particles beyond the
  World.
Frost. U. S. 1946 King's X.
Haines. Dürer's Vision.
Merton. La Salette.
  Original Child Bomb.
Rolfe. Idiot Joe Prays in Pershing Square and
  Gets Hauled in for Vagrancy.
Stafford. At the Bomb Testing Site.
Williams, Charles Kenneth. Dream, The.
See also **Hiroshima, Japan; Nuclear War.**

Atoms
Emerson. Atom displaces all atoms beside,
  The.
  Atom from atom yawns as far.
  Principle of all things; entrails made.
Nemerov. White water now in the snowflake's
  prison.
Raine. Scala Coeli.
Rukeyser. I have tried to show the atom as a
  source.

Atonement
Arnold. Sick King in Bokhara, The.
Byron. Lines Addressed to a Young Lady.
Herrick. Abels Bloud.
  Recompence, The.
Hill. As with torches we go, at wild
  Christmas.
Jeffers. Fire.
Smart. Hymn to the Supreme Being.

Attics
Auden. Up There.
Davie. Intervals in a Busy Life.
Sandburg. Upstairs.
Turco. Attic Poem.
  Attic, The.
  Odradek.

Attucks, Crispus
Hayden. Crispus Attucks.

Auctions
Hardy. Bags of Meat.
Hughes, Ted. Formal Auctioneer, The.
Koertge. My Father ("Once owned a blind
  horse, a big gray who").
Levine. Buying and Selling.
Roethke. Auction, The.
Sandburg. Auctioneer.
Silverstein. For Sale.
Snodgrass. Auction.

Auden, Wystan Hugh
Berryman. Shirley & Auden.
Davie. Cheshire.
Eberhart. To Auden on His Fiftieth.
  Trying to Hold It All Together.
Hoffman. Letter to W.H. Auden, A.
Muldoon. Louis.
  Wystan.
Schuyler. Wystan Auden.
Shapiro. At Auden's Grave.
Spender. Auden at Milwaukee.
  Auden's Funeral.
Wilbur. For W. H. Auden.
Young. W. H. Auden & Mantan Moreland.

Audubon, John James
Eberhart. Key West.

August
Atwood. Late August.
Bly. August Rain.
Clare. August.
Dunbar. In August.
Eberhart. Loon Call, A.
Fisher. Leaden August with the life gone out
  of it.
Hardy. August Midnight, An.
  Wet August, A.
Hartley. Very Languor, The.
Lawrence. August Holidays.

Merton. On a Day in August.
Millay. If Still Your Orchards Bear.
Nemerov. Ending, An.
Oliver. August.
Plath. In Midas' Country.
Rich. August.
Rossetti. And is this August weather? nay not
  so.
Schuyler. Sonnet: "August, tasting of ripe
  grapes and afternoon sleep."
Schwartz. Purple black cloud at sunset: it is
  late August.
Snyder. Mid-August at Sourdough Mountain
  Lookout.
Swinburne. August.
Walcott. Dark August.
Williams, Miller. August Evening Outside of
  Nashville, An.

Augustine, Saint
Cohen. You Have Sweetened Your Word.
"Dylan." I Dreamed I Saw St. Augstine.
Herrick. Confession.
Nemerov. Frozen City, The.
Whittier. Shadow and the Light, The.

Aunt Jemima
Hayden. Aunt Jemima of the Ocean Waves.

Aunts
Ciardi. Aunt Mary.
Cooper. In the House of the Dying.
Davie. Abbeyforde.
De la Mare. Mrs. Grundy.
Dunbar. Appreciation.
Eliot. Aunt Helen.
Ferlinghetti. Photo of Emily, The.
Galvin. Weave a Circle Round Me Thrice.
Ginsberg. To Aunt Rose.
Hewitt. Aunt Cis and Uncle Tom.
Kooser. Carrie.
Lawrence. Change of Government.
McAuley. Labor and Tribulation.
Meinke. Aunt Gertrud.
  Aunt Mary.
Plath. Tour, The.
Rich. Aunt Jennifer's Tigers.
Robinson. Aunt Imogen.
Roethke. Elegy: "Her face like a rain-beaten
  stone on the day she rolled off."
Sexton. Some Foreign Letters.
  Walking in Paris.
Stafford. Family Turn, A.
Stevenson. Auntie's Skirts.
  To Auntie.
Wakoski. My Aunt Ella Meets the Buddha on
  His Birthday.
Young. Aunt.

Auschwitz, Poland
Hill. Statesman have known visions. And, not
  alone.
McGrath. Remembering the Children of
  Auschwitz.
Rukeyser. Breaking Open.

Australia
Ginsberg. Ayers Rock / Uluru Song.
Kipling. Lichtenberg.
  Ode: "So long as memory, valour, and faith
  endure."
  This is the mouth-filling song of the race that
  was run by a Boomer.
  Young Queen, The.

Authorship and Authors
Bradstreet. Author to Her Book, The.
Browning, Elizabeth Barrett. Vision of Poets,
  A.
Catullus. Carmen 14: "If, my irrepressible
  Calvus, I didn't."
  Carmen 35: "Fetch, papyrus / our soft-
  measured poet."
Chaucer. Chaucer's Retraction.
Hardy. At a Rehearsal of One of J.M.B.'s
  Plays.
Herrick. Argument of His Book, The.
  On His Booke ("Bound (almost) now of my
  book I see, The").
  Poetry Perpetuates the Poet.
  To His Booke ("Goe thou forth my booke,
  though late").
  To His Book[e] ("If hap it must, that I must

see thee lye").
  To His Learned Friend M. Jo. Harmar,
  Phisitian to Colledge of Westminster.
  To Sir George Parrie, Doctor of the Civill
  Law.
Johnson. Young Author, The.
Jonson. To His Much and Worthily Esteemed
  Friend the Author.
  To the Worthy Author on *The Husband.*
Lovelace. Epilogue, The: "Stubborne Author
  of the trifle, Crime, The."
Nash. So That's Who I Remind Me Of.
Piercy. For the Young Who Want To.
Pope. Prologue to the *Three Hours after
  Marriage.*
Pound. Lake Isle, The.
Rich. Frame.
Robinson. Book of Annandale, The.
  George Crabbe.
  Verlaine.
Updike. Agatha Christie and Beatrix Potter.
Authors' Residences.
  Clan, The.
  Die Neuen Heiligen.
  I Missed His Book, but I Read His Name.
  Jolly Greene Giant, The.
  Tome-Thoughts, from the *Times.*
Wordsworth. Plea for Authors, May, 1838, A.
  Poet to His Grandchild; Sequel to "A Plea for
  Authors."
Zukofsky. Not that I look to my eyes more
  than your love.
  Poet I'm too near your and my sod daily.

Autism
Meinke. Slow Child, The.

Automation
Hesketh. Brief Encounter.
Moore. Four Quartz Crystal Clocks.

Automobile Accidents
Carruth. As the broken front differential pops
  and jumps.
  Late. The back road "slicker than owl shit."
  Snow.
  Poem moves. / After the fierce intention, The.
Dobyns. Santaigo: In Praise of Community.
Glück. Racer's Widow, The.
Haines. Driving through Oregon (Dec. 1973).
Kipling. Arterial.
  Ballad of the Cars, The.
  Idiot Boy, The.
  Lady Geraldine's Hardship.
  Landau, The.
  When the Journey Was Intended to the City.
Matthews. Bystanders.
  Whiplash.
Muldoon. Good Friday, 1971. Driving
  Westward.
Nash. Strange Case of the Cautious Motorist,
  The.
Roethke. Highway: Michigan.
Schuyler. Stun.
Shapiro. Auto Wreck.
Smith, Patti. Ballad of a Bad Boy.
Stafford. My Father: October 1942.
Warren. Old Nigger on One-Mule Cart
  Encountered Late at Night When Driving
  Home from Party in the Back Country.
Williams, Charles Kenneth. Travelers.
Williams, William Carlos. Man and Nature.
  Romance Moderne.

Automobile Racing
Glück. Racer's Widow, The.

Automobiles
Auden. Trippers.
Beatles. Drive My Car.
Betjeman. Meditation on the A30.
Bly. Driving toward the Lac Qui Parle River.
Bukowski. Dogs.
  Stolen.
  20 minutes later.
Carruth. Eternity Blues.
  Sociology of Toyotas and Jade
  Chrysanthemums, The.
  Song: Luxury.
Ciardi. Craft.
Cummings. She being Brand.
Dickey, James. Cherrylog Road.

Dickey, William. Things Kept.
Dobyns. Cuidadores de Autos.
Frost. Were I in Trouble.
Ginsberg. Wrote This Last Night.
Gunn. All Do Not All Things Well.
Haines. End of the Street, The.
Hewitt. Erice, Western Sicily.
  Suburb.
Kipling. Advertisement, The.
  Braggart, The.
  Child's Garden, A.
  Consolations of Memory, The.
  Contradictions.
  Dying Chauffer, The.
  Fastness.
  Inventor, The.
  Justice's Tale, The.
  Marrèd Drives of Windsor, The.
  Moral, The.
  Progress of the Spark, The.
  Sepulchral.
  To a Lady, Peruading Her to a Car.
  To Motorists.
Kunitz. On Twelfth Street in Manhattan.
Lindsay. In Which Many Autos Pass
  Westward.
Lowry. Three Little Dog-Gone Mice.
Matthews. Moving.
Miller. Shocks Brakes (For Kurt and Yansky).
  When you live in your car.
Nash. Poor Mr. Strawbridge.
  Strange Case of Mr. Niobob's
  Transmogrification, The.
  Strange Case of the Cautious Motorist, The.
Nemerov. Fugue.
Oppen. Cars run in a void of utensils, The.
  Part of the Forest.
Patchen. Magic Car, The.
Sandburg. Portrait of a Motorcar.
Shapiro. Buick.
Tomlinson. Arch, The.
Updike. Cars in Caracas, The.
  Duet, with Muffled Brake Drums.
  Neumático punturado—we stopped.
  Self-Service.
  Short Days, The.
  Thin Air.
Wakoski. Buddha Inherits 6 Cars on His
  Birthday, The.
Williams, Charles Kenneth. New Car.
Williams, William Carlos. Ballad of Faith.
  Intelligent Sheepman and the New Cars, The.
Zukofsky. Cars once steel and green, now old.
  Pretty.

See also **Driving and Drivers.**

Autumn
Angelou. Late October.
Auden. Autumn.
Berg. Last Meeting.
Berry. October 10.
  Snake, The.
Blake. To Autumn.
Bly. Fire of Despair Has Been Our Savior,
  The.
  In Rainy September.
  Uneasiness in Fall.
Bogan. Simple Autumnal.
Brontë. Fall, leaves, fall; die, flowers, away.
  O come with me, thus ran the song.
  Old church tower and garden wall, The.
Browning, Robert. By the Fire-Side.
Burns. Song, Composed in August.
"Carroll, Lewis." Humpty Dumpty's
  Recitation.
Carruth. Coarse leaf, alder leaf.
  Emergency Haying.
  Excellence requires / leaf-rakers to sweep one
  spot.
  Fall, The.
  November: Indian Summer.
  Once More.
  Sonnet: "Like the magnificent stationary
  animal it is."
  Sonnet: "This is our perfect silver maple's
  day."
  Tanck's Song About November.
  This Song.

Ceravolo. Autumn Break.
  In My Crib.
  Song of Autumn, A.
Clark. Difference, A.
  October.
Crane. October-November.
  Pastorale.
  Sunday Morning Apples.
Creeley. Knokke.
Cummings. Allbutnotquitemost.
  Always before your voice my soul.
  Autumn is:that between there and here.
  !blac / k / agains / t.
  Cruelly,love / walk the autumn long.
  Dim / i / nu / tiv / e this park is e.
  It's over a(see just).
  O purple finch / please tell me why.
  Timeless / ly this / (merely and whose).
  To stand(alone)in some.
  Wind has blown the rain away and blown, A.
Dickey, James. Autumn.
Dickinson. As Summer into Autumn slips.
  Autumn is among us.
  Autumn—overlooked my Knitting.
  I remember the leaves were falling.
  It consoles the happy Sorrow of Autumn.
  Morns are meeker than they were, The.
  Name—of it—is "Autumn", The.
  Red Leaves take the Green Leaves place, The.
  Summer has been wide and deep, The.
Dobyns. Music One Looks Back On, The.
Dunbar. Merry Autumn.
  Signs of the Times.
Eberhart. Autumnal.
  Book of Nature, The.
  Hornets by the Sill.
  In the Garden.
  Loon Call, A.
  Man of Summer, The.
  Spider, The.
  Vermont Idyll.
Ferlinghetti. New York—Albany.
Fletcher. From the Chinese.
Ford. Prevalence of the.
  Soleil d'automne. Do.
Frost. Clear and Colder.
  My November Guest.
  Quest of the Purple-Fringed, The.
Galvin. Light from Fundy.
Gardner. Autumn: Early Morning.
  Fall in Massachusetts.
  Grocery Bouquet, The.
  Tango for Zither.
Garrigue. Address to the Migrations.
  Flux of Autumn, The.
  One for the Roses.
Glück. All Hallows.
  Thanksgiving.
Graves. September Landscape.
Gunn. Autumn Chapter in a Novel.
Hacker. Late August.
Haines. Listening in October.
  Poem: "Immense sadness / of approaching
  winter, the."
Hall. Kicking the Leaves.
  Stone Walls.
Hardy. Autumn in King's Hintock Park.
  Autumn Rain-Scene, An.
  Best She Could, The.
  Days to Recollect.
  Last Chrysanthemum, The.
  Last Week in October.
  Later Autumn, The.
  News for Her Mother.
  Night in November, A.
  Shortening Days at the Homestead.
  Upper Birch-Leaves, The.
Hartley. Chromatism in Red.
Hartnett. Oatwoman, The.
Hesketh. And Fall.
  Autumn at Whitewell.
  St. Luke's Summer.
  Sundowner.
  Widowhood.
Hewitt. Already autumn silently / has come to
  sky and field and tree.
  Autumn Gale.

Autumn Valley.
Frost.
  Here at the Tide's Turn.
  Leaf.
  Lyric: "Chestnut and beech / sycamore and
  willow."
  November Park.
  Shortened Day, The.
  Sonnet in Autumn.
  Sonnets in October.
  Swan's Nest.
Hopkins. Hurrahing in Harvest.
  Now I am minded to take a pipe in hand.
  Spring and Fall.
Housman. Tell Me Not Here [It Needs Not
  Saying].
Hughes, Ted. October Dawn.
Jeffers. Autumn Evening.
Keats. To Autumn.
Kipling. Two Months.
Knott. Widower's Winter.
Kunitz. Approach of Autumn.
  End of Summer.
Larkin. Afternoons.
  Autumn.
  Autumn Has Caught Us in Our Summer Wear.
  Mother, Summer, I.
  Past Days of Gales.
Lawrence. At the Window.
  Autumn at Taos.
  Autumn Sunshine.
  Dolour of Autumn.
  Guelder Roses.
  Song-Day in Autumn.
Levertov. Air of November.
  Coming Fall, The.
Levine. Zaydee.
Lewis. Autumn, 1939.
Lindsay. Sweetheart Autumn.
Longfellow. Aftermath.
Lowry. October Sunset.
McGrath. Another Season.
  Autumn Song.
  Beyond the Red River.
  Black Train, The.
  In Early Autumn.
MacLeish. Autumn.
  Immortal Autumn.
  Old Men in the Leaf Smoke, The.
  Survivor.
  Tourist Death.
  Winter Is Another Country.
MacNeice. Canto XVII: "This was the night
  that specially we went down."
Meredith. Autumn Even-Song.
  Ode to the Spirit of Earth in Autumn.
  Seed-Time.
  Song: Autumn.
Merton. Autumn.
Millay. Autumn Chant.
  Autumn Daybreak.
  Death of Autumn, The.
  God's World.
  Now sits the autumn cricket in the grass.
  Now that the west is washed of clouds and
  clear.
  Song: "Gone, gone again is Summer the
  lovely."
  Spring and the Fall, The.
Miller. November Dusk.
Nathan. To Transcend the Cat.
Nemerov. Again.
  Autumnal.
  Burning the Leaves.
  Consent, The.
  Elegy of Last Resort.
  First Leaf, The.
  For Robert Frost, in the Autumn, in Vermont.
  Late Butterflies.
  Walking Down Westgate in the Fall.
Owen. Sonnet Autumnal.
Paley. Autumn.
  Leaves Apples.
Patchen. Autumn Is the Crows' Time.
Piercy. Some Collisions Bring Luck.
Plath. Gold Mouths Cry.
  Letter in November.

Pope. Autumn, the Third Pastoral, or Hylas and Ægon.
Rich. This high summer we love will pour its light.
Roethke. Slow Season.
Rossetti. Autumn.
Bitter for Sweet.
Can I know it?—Nay.— / Shall I know it?— Yea.
Death-Watches.
October Garden, An.
Rukeyser. Salamander.
Sandburg. Auburn.
Autumn Movement.
Buckwheat.
Corn Prattlings.
Cornucopia.
Falltime.
First Sonata for Karlen Paula.
Lake Michigan Morning.
On a Railroad Right of Way.
Poplar and Elm.
Sleep Impression.
Tawny.
Theme in Yellow.
Three Pieces on the Smoke of Autumn.
Timber Moon.
Under the Harvest Moon.
Sarton. First Autumn, The.
If I could let you go as trees let go.
Schuyler. Autumn Leaves.
Held Breath, A.
Master of the Golden Glow, The.
People Who See Bubbles Rise.
Schwartz. First Night of Fall and Falling Rain, The.
Purple black cloud at sunset: it is late August.
Scott. Autumn on Tweedside.
Shakespeare. Sonnet 73: "That time of year thou may'st [or maist] in me behold."
Shapiro. Exile.
Shelley. Autumn: A Dirge.
Ode to the West Wind.
Shelton. On Lake Pend Oreille.
Some years the birds.
Simic. Fall Day, A.
Smith, Charlotte. To Melancholy. Written on the Banks of the Arun, October 1785.
Written in October.
Snodgrass. September in the Park.
Sorrentino. De Pré Est Vénéneux Mais Joli en Automne.
Spender. Autumn Day.
Stevens. Autumn Refrain.
Like Decorations in a Nigger Cemetery.
Lunar Paraphrase.
Stevenson. Autumn Fires.
In autumn when the woods are red.
Swinburne. Hendecasyllabics.
Thomas. Poem in October.
Tomlinson. At Holwell Farm.
Autumn.
Autumn Piece.
Gossamers, The.
One Day of Autumn.
White Van, The.
Updike. Great Scarf of Birds, The.
November.
Van Duyn. Day in Late October, A.
Warren. Composition in Gold and Red-Gold.
Whittier. Autumn Thoughts.
Battle Autumn of 1862, The.
Day, A.
Fruit-Gift, The.
Last Eve of Summer, The.
Last Walk in Autumn, The.
St. Martin's Summer.
Song of Harvest, A.
Wilbur. Alatus.
Fall in Corrales.
October Maples, Portland.
Williams, Charles Kenneth. Listen carefully. / I'm meditating.
Williams, William Carlos. Autumn.
Pause, The.
Prelude to Winter.
Sometimes It Turns Dry and the Leaves Fall

before They Are Beautiful.
10/14.
Yellow Season, The.
Wordsworth. Let More Ambitious Poets Take the Heart.
Longest Day; Addressed to My Daughter, The.
September, 1815.
September, 1819 ("Departing summer hath assumed").
September, 1819 ("Sylvan slopes with corn-clad fields, The").
Wright, James. Autumn Begins in Martins Ferry, Ohio.
Autumnal.
Lament for My Brother on a Hayrake.
Rats, The.
Yeats. Falling of the Leaves, The.
Young. New Autumn, New York.
October Variations, The.
Zukofsky. Ears beringed with fuzz.
World autumn, The.

Avalanches
Frost. On Taking from the Top to Broaden the Base.
Griffiths. Fluidity, Charmouth.
Hewitt. On Hearing a Traveller's Tale of the Alps.
Smith, Charlotte. Peasant of the Alps, The.

Aviation and Aviators
Cooper. Meteors.
Hall. Airstrip in Essex, 1960, An.
Old Pilot, The.
Hoffman. First Flight.
Jarrell. Dead Wingman, The.
Death of the Ball Turret Gunner, The.
Learners, The.
Losses.
Siegfried.
Levine. Poem of Flight, The.
Nemerov. Dream of Flying Comes of Age, The.
Sandburg. To Beachey, 1912.
Snyder. Vapor Trails.
Spender. Landscape near an Aerodrome, The.
Updike. Sonic Boom.
See also **Air Travel; Air Warfare; Airports.**

Avignon, France
Glück. Letter from Provence.
Stein. Prudence Caution and Foresight: A Story of Avignon.

Axes
Frost. Axe-Helve, The.
Simic. Ax.
Snyder. Axe Handles.

Ayr, Scotland
Burns. Afton Water.
Braes o' Ballochmyle, The.
Brigs of Ayr, a Poem. Inscribed to J. B*********, Esq; Ayr, The.
Song, A: "Thou lingering Star with lessening ray."
Song: "Gloomy night is gath'ring fast, The."

Azaleas
Meinke. Azaleas.
Zukofsky. Azalea.

Aztecs
Berrigan. Poem in the Modern Manner.
Ferlinghetti. Baja Beatitudes.
Lowell. Lizard rusty as a leaf rubbed rough.
Sandburg. Aztec Mask.
Dusty Doors.
Stafford. Ultimate Problems.
Tomlinson. In Michoacán.
Mictlantecuhtli.
Williams, William Carlos. Three Nahuatl Poems.

B

Babel, Tower of
Merton. Tower of Babel.
Tower of Babel—A Morality, The.
Sandburg. From the four corners of the earth.
Babies
Auden. Babies in their mothers' arms.
Mundus et Infans.

Blake. Cradle Song, A: "Sleep, sleep, beauty bright."
Infant Joy.
Infant Sorrow.
Browning, Elizabeth Barrett. Sleeping and Watching.
Burns. Bonie Dundee.
Rowin 't in Her Apron, The.
Carroll, Jim. Poem: "This country invades me."
"Carroll, Lewis." Maggie's Visit to Oxford.
Two Poems to Rachel Daniel.
Ciardi. For Myra out of the Album.
Clark. Air.
Nimble Rays of Day Bring Oxygen to Her Blood.
Coleridge. Frost at Midnight.
Sonnet to a Friend Who Asked[,] How I Felt When the Nurse First Presented My Infant to Me.
To an Infant.
Cooper. For a Boy Born in Wartime.
Cummings. Youful / larger / of smallish).
Davie. Christening, A.
Dickey, James. Magus, The.
Dickey, William. For Every Last Batch When the Next One Comes Along.
Dobyns. Faces.
Greedy Child, The.
Dunbar. Little Brown Baby.
Poet and the Baby, The.
Puttin' the Baby Away.
Turning of the Babies in the Bed, The.
Two Little Boots.
Fenton. Come and eat your Pablum.
Glück. Egg, The.
My Cousin in April.
Graves. To Lucia at Birth.
Griffiths. Courage.
Gunn. Baby Song.
Hacker. Country & Western II.
Hardy. New Toy, The.
Herrick. Upon a Child.
Johnson. Parodies of Bishop Percy's *Hermit of Warkworth.*
Kinnell. Under the Maud Moon.
Koch. Girl and Baby Florist Sidewalk Pram Nineteen Seventy Something.
Larkin. Born Yesterday.
Lawrence. Baby Asleep after Pain, A.
Baby-Movements.
Baby Running Barefoot.
Baby Songs Ten Months Old.
War-Baby.
Lorde. Now That I Am Forever with Child.
MacLeish. Adam's Jealousy: Eve's Answer.
Adam's Riddle.
Babe's Riddle, The.
Eve's Rebuke to Her Child.
MacNeice. Aubade for Infants.
Mahon. Unborn Child, An.
Merrill. Little Fanfare for Felix Magowan.
Merton. Never Call a Babysitter in a Thunderstorm.
Nash. After the Christening.
Come On In, the Senility Is Fine.
It Must Be the Milk.
Our Child Doesn't Know Anything.
Pediatric Reflection.
Reflection on Babies.
Song to Be Sung by the Father of Infant Female Children.
Thunder over the Nursery.
Oppen. Sara in Her Father's Arms.
Plath. By Candlelight.
Candles.
Death & Co.
Event.
For a Fatherless Son.
Gulliver.
I Want, I Want.
Magi.
Morning Song.
New Year on Dartmoor.
Night Dances, The.
You're.

Raine. November rain with thin fingers tapping.
Rolfe. Song: "Keep the dream alive and growing always."
Rossetti. Angels at the foot,/ And Angels at the head.
Baby cry— / Oh fie!
Baby lies so fast asleep / That we cannot wake her.
Baby's cradle with no baby in it, A.
Ballad: "Soft white lamb in the daisy meadow."
Christmas Day.
Crimson curtains round my mother's bed.
Crying, my little one, footsore and weary?
Dog lies in his kennel, The.
Holy Innocents.
Husband and Wife.
I know a baby, such a baby,— / Round blue eyes and cheeks of pink.
Lie a-bed, / Sleepy head, / Shut up eyes, bo-peep.
Light Love.
Love me,—I love you / Love me, my baby.
Lullaby, oh lullaby! / Flowers are closed and lambs are sleeping.
Motherless baby and babyless mother.
My baby has a father and a mother.
My baby has a mottled fist.
Our little baby fell asleep.
Why did baby die, / Making Father sigh.
Your brother has a falcon.
Rukeyser. Do you know what I play to be, in bed at night?
Night Feeding.
Sandburg. Baby Vamps.
Chicago Boy Baby.
Portrait of a Child Settling Down for an Afternoon Nap.
Sixteen Months.
Slippery.
Sexton. Death Baby, The.
Falling Dolls, The.
Hangman, The.
Unknown Girl in the Maternity Ward.
Silverstein. Dreadful.
Smith, Charlotte. To Tranquillity.
Smith, Stevie. But Murderous.
Bye Baby Bother.
Dream of Nourishment, A.
Infant.
Sad Mother, The.
She Said..
Valuable.
Snyder. Changing Diapers.
Kyoto Born in Spring Song.
Stevenson. Mater Triumphans.
To My Name-Child.
Turco. Pocoangelini 8 ("First thing in the morning, The").
Updike. Stunt Flier, The.
Waldman. Baby & the Gypsy.
Baby's Pantoum.
Napping in the Shadow of Day.
Scallop Song.
Williams, Charles Kenneth. Creams.
Kingdom of Stinking Wishes, The.
Rampage, The.
You're two, that's great.
Williams, Miller. Ones that Are Thrown Out, The.
Poem for Emily, A.
Williams, William Carlos. Struggle of Wings.
Wordsworth. Cottager to Her Infant, (By My Sister), The.
Emigrant Mother, The.
Her Eyes Are Wild.
Infant M— M—, The.
Wright, James. Gemela.
Mary Bly.
Song for the Middle of the Night, A.
Yeats. Dolls, The.
Song from "The Player Queen,"A.
Young. Michael At Sixteen Months.

See also **Infant Death.**

Babylon
Auden. Cinders.

Bishop. Burglar of Babylon, The.
Carroll, Jim. Words from Babylon.
De la Mare. Bitter Waters.
Lindsay. Babylon, Babylon, Babylon the Great.
Darling Daughter of Babylon.
Merton. Captives—a Psalm, The.
Nemerov. To the Babylonians.
Rossetti. Babylon the Great.
By the Waters of Babylon.
By the Waters of Babylon. B.C. 570.
Sandburg. Ashurnatsirpal III.
Bilbea.

Baby-Sitting and Baby-Sitters
Merton. Never Call a Babysitter in a Thunderstorm.
Plath. Babysitters, The.

Bacchus
Browning, Elizabeth Barrett. Bacchus and Ariadne.
Catullus. Carmen 27: "Falernian, / old Falernian!"
Doolittle. Choros Translations.
Herrick. Bacchanalian Verse, A.
Hymn[e] to Bacchus, A ("Bacchus, let...").
Hymne to Bacchus, A ("I sing...").
To Bacchus, a Canticle.
Jonson. Dedication of the King's New Cellar.
To Bacchus, The.
Milton. Bacchus.
Ransom. Nocturne: "Where now has our young Adam."
Zukofsky. Cocktails / and signs of.
Minister wet to lee, pour the Falernian.

Bach, Johann Sebastian
Auden. Bach and the Lady.
J.S. Bach.
Bly. Six Winter Privacy Poems.
Hartley. B. is for Bach—.
Markson. Strange Night.
Merrill. Trees Listening to Bach.
Moore. Dream.
Nathan. Musical Offering, A.
Sandburg. Number Man.
Williams, William Carlos. Divertimiento.
Zukofsky. Wish, A.

Bachelors
"Carroll, Lewis." Game of Fives, A.
Eberhart. New England Bachelor, A.
Herrick. Single Life Most Secure.
To His Tomb-Maker.
Upon the Loss[e] of His Mistresses.
Nash. Tune for an Ill-Tempered Clavichord.
Sorrentino. Research, Again.

Backs
Lorde. Monkeyman.
Shapiro. Back, The.

Bacon, Sir Francis
Campion. Ad ampliss. totius Angliae Cancellarium, Fr. Ba.
De la Mare. Polonius.
Herbert. To the Right Hon. the Lord Chancellor (Bacon).
Jonson. Lord Bacon's Birthday.
Updike. He omits, Goya, not even the good news.
Whitman. Shakspeare-Bacon's Cipher.

Bacteria
Nemerov. Bacterial War, The.

Badgers
"Carroll, Lewis." Three Badgers, The.
Clare. Badger ("When midnight comes a host of dogs and men").
Heaney. Badgers, The.
Hewitt. Watchers, The.
Hughes, Ted. Coming Down through Somerset.
Tomlinson. Scream, The.

Baggage
Dickey, James. Baggage King, The.
Ginsberg. In the Baggage Room at Greyhound.

Bagpipes
"MacDiarmid." Bagpipe Music.
MacNeice. Bagpipe Music.
Silverstein. Bagpipe Who Didn't Say No, The.

Tomlinson. Mr. Brodsky.
Whittier. Pipes at Lucknow, The.

Bahamas
Eberhart. Scouring, The.
MacLeish. Bahamas.
Oppen. Bahamas.

Balaam
Meredith. Ass of Balaam, The.

Baldness
Donne. Licentious Person, A.
Herrick. On Jone.
Spenser. High on a hill a goodly cedar grewe.

Baldwin, James
Boyle. For James Baldwin.

Ballet
Crane. To Portapovitch.
Dickinson. I cannot dance upon my Toes.
Graves. Casse-Noisette.
Two Disciplines.
Hardy. Ballet, The.
St. John. Of Time & the Body.
Wilbur. L'Etoile.

Balloons
Bishop. Armadillo, The.
Dickinson. You've seen Balloons set—Haven't You?
Plath. Balloons.
Sandburg. Balloon Faces.
Five Cent Balloons.

Ballrooms
Hemingway. Big Dance on the Hill, The.

Balls
Berryman. Ball Poem, The.
Clark. Superballs.
Oppen. White. From the / Under arm of T.
Wilbur. Juggler.

Ballylee, Ireland
Yeats. Coole Park and Ballylee, 1931.
To Be Carved on a Stone at Thoor Ballylee.

Baltimore, Maryland
Cullen. Incident.
Sarton. Night Watch.

Bananas
Kipling. Song of Bananas, A.
Lieberman. Banana Dwarf, The.
Banana Madonna, The.
Sandburg. Unintentional Paint.
Stevens. Floral Decorations for Bananas.

Bands
Dunbar. Colored Band, The.
Hewitt. Bandstand.
Lowry. Lament in the Pacific Northwest.
"Reed." Sweet Jane.

Bangkok, Thailand
Eberhart. Rape of the Cataract, The.

Banjos
Dunbar. Banjo Song, A.
Voice of the Banjo, The.
Kipling. Song of the Banjo, The.

Banking and Bankers
Bukowski. Sweater.
Graves. Bank Account.
Lowry. Song: "Pity the blind and the halt but yet pity."
Merton. But did you ever know the whole world was once held prisoner in a bank?
Nash. Anybody for Money? or, Just Bring Your Own Basket.
Bankers Are Just Like Anybody Else, Except Richer.
Ma, What's a Banker? or, Hush, My Child.
Olson. Friend, The.
"Reed." Sweet Jane.
Swift. Bank Thrown Down, The.
Run upon the Bankers, The.
Williams, William Carlos. Simplex Sigilum Veri: A Catalogue.
To a Mexican Pig-Bank.
Woman in Front of a Bank, A.

See also **Financiers.**

Baptism
Ciardi. Evil Eye, The.
Coleridge. My Baptismal Birthday [*or* Birth-Day].

Crashaw. Acts 8; On the Baptized Æthiopian.
On the Water of Our Lord's Baptism[e].
Hardy. Christening, The.
  Royal Sponsors.
Herbert. Love ("Thou art too hard for me in
  Love").
Herrick. Baptisme.
  To Julia ("Holy waters hither bring").
Hesketh. Jolly Good Fellow, A.
Lovelace. Elegie. Princesse Katherine, An.
Merton. On the Anniversary of My Baptism.
Walcott. City's Death by Fire, A.
Walker. Baptism.
Williams, Charles Kenneth. Acids.
Williams, Miller. And When in Scenes of
  Glory.
Wordsworth. To Rotha Q—.
See also **Christenings.**

Bar Mitzvah
Schwartz. Rabbi to Preach.

Barbecues. see Picnics and Barbecues.

Barbers
Carroll, Jim. My needs were few and pure.
Carruth. Sonnet: "Why extremely do we
  observe more of."
Hugo. Cattails.
Kooser. Self-Portrait at Thirty-Nine.
Levine. To a Child Trapped in a Barber Shop.
Nash. I'll Get One Tomorrow.
Suckling. Barber, A.
Turco. Louie the Barber.
Updike. Aerie.

Barcelona, Spain
Hewitt. Camaradas Y Compañeros.
Levine. Francisco, I'll Bring You Red
  Carnations.
  Hear Me.
Paley. On the Ramblas / A Tree A Girl.

Bards
Blake. Introduction: "Hear the voice of the
  Bard!"
Burns. Epistle to J. L*****k, an Old Scotch
  Bard.
  Lament for James, Earl of Glencairn.
Byron. Ballad: "Of all the twice ten thousand
  bards."
  Lines Written in the Travellers' Book at
  Orchomenus.
  Soliloquy of a Bard in the Country.
Emerson. And though he dearly prized the
  bards of fame.
  Bard or dunce is blest, but hard.
  Divine Inviters! I accept.
  Genial spark the poet felt, The.
  James Russell Lowell.
  On that night the poet went.
  Song of Taliesin.
Everson. Bard.
Graves. Bards, The.
Gray. Bard, The [A Pindaric Ode].
  Long Story, A.
  Progress of Poesy, The.
Hewitt. Fame.
  Ossian's Grave, Lubitavish, County Antrim.
  True Smith of Tieveragh, The.
Keats. How Many Bards Gild the Lapses of
  Time!
  Sonnet: "Where didst thou find, young Bard,
  thy sounding lyre?"
Kipling. In the Neolithic Age.
  Last Rhyme of True Thomas, The.
Meredith. Aneurin's Harp.
Whitman. As I Ponder'd [*or* Pondered] in
  Silence.
  By Blue Ontario's Shore.
Wordsworth. Idle Shepherd-Boys, The; or,
  Dungeon-Ghyll Force. A Pastoral.

Barges
Levertov. Music, A.
Williams, William Carlos. Motor-Barge, The.
  Well Disciplined Bargeman, The.

Barley
Burns. John Barleycorn [a Ballad].
Hesketh. Second Childhood.

Barns
Bly. Opening the Door of a Barn I Thought
  Was Empty on New Year's Eve.

Frost. Old Barn at the Bottom of the Fogs,
  The.
Garrigue. Doggerel of a Diehard Who Sleeps
  in a Nest of Newspapers.
Gildner. Old Farm in Northern Michigan.
Hall. Great Day in the Cows' House.
Kooser. Tom Ball's Barn.
Merton. Elegy for the Monastery Barn.
Nemerov. Human Things.
Rolfe. Barn in Wisconsin.
Sandburg. For sixty years the pine lumber
  barn.
Snodgrass. Seasoning Barn.
Spender. Barn, The.
Turco. Barn, The.
Wright, James. Summer Memory in the
  Crowded City, A.

Baroque
Bogan. Baroque Comment.
Fenton. Lollipops of the Pomeranian Baroque.

Barrel Organs. see Hurdy-Gurdies.

Bars and Bartenders
Betjeman. Public House Drunk.
Bukowski. Don't Touch the Girls.
  My Friend.
  Training for Kid Aztec.
  Yellow Cab.
Cohen. Closing Time.
Creeley. Billfold.
Cummings. Dick Mid's large bluish face
  without eyebrows.
  I was sitting in mcsoreley's.   outside it was
  New York and beauti- / fully snowing.
  In Healey's Palace I was sitting.
  Infinite jukethrob smoke & swallow to dis.
  Oil tel duh woil doi sez.
  She sits dropping on a caret of clenched arms.
  Them which despair.
  Waddling / madam star, The.
Dickey, William. Confidence.
Dobyns. Kentucky Derby Day, Belfast, Maine.
Fox. To Do More Than Hair.
Gallagher. Instructions to the Double.
Gunn. Fever.
Hacker. Gino hummed an epthialamium.
Hall. Repeated Shapes, The.
Hewitt. Bombed Public House, The.
  Burnt Post, The.
  In a Lurgan Pub.
  Word, The.
Hoffman. High Society.
Hughes, Langston. Bar.
Hugo. Cantina Iannini.
  Hilltop, The.
  Letter to Reed from Lolo.
  Letter to Welch from Browning.
  Milltown Union Bar, The.
  Only Bar in Dixon, The.
Lawrence. Ships in Bottles.
Levine. Midget, The.
  Poem Circling Hamtramck, Michigan, All
  Night in Search of You, The.
Liddy. All the journeys / To be made for
  instance, over the seas.
  Evening at Axel's.
  Every Evening in Axel's.
  Taking One's Students to Avondale.
  To the Liberal Magistrates.
Lowry. Cantinas, The.
  Closed Pub, The.
  Drunkards, The.
  November, 1937.
  Three Little Dog-Gone Mice.
McAuley. Signs.
Mahon. Terminal Bar, The.
Markson. At the Lion's Head.
Meinke. Writing the Great American Poem in
  Key West.
Nash. How Do You Say Ha-Ha in French.
Nathan. Servant of Stars, The.
Patchen. State of the Nation, The.
"Reed." Power of Positive Drinking, The.
Sandburg. Jungheimer's.
Snyder. I Went into the Maverick Bar.
Sorrentino. Bar Games.
Sutter. Nordeast.
Turco. Lorrie.

Updike. Décor.
Whitman. Glimpse, A.
Wilbur. Violet and Jasper.
Williams, Charles Kenneth. Medusa.
Williams, Miller. Glass Darkly, A.
Williams, William Carlos. At the Bar.
  Hemmed-in Males.
Wright, James. Old Man Drunk.
Young. Topsy: Part 2.

Baseball
Clark. Baseball and Classicism.
  Clemente (1934-1972).
Creeley. Ball Game, The.
"Dylan." Catfish.
Eberhart. Ball Game.
Ferlinghetti. Baseball Canto.
Galvin. Knot Hole Gang, The.
Gardner. Are Poets Ball Players?
Gildner. Around the Horn.
  4th Base.
Hall. Baseball Players, The.
  Old Home Week.
  Old Timer's Day.
Hemingway. Opening Game, The.
Hugo. Ballpark at Moiese, The.
  From Altitude, the Diamonds.
  Letter to Mantsch from Havre.
Knott. Mitts and Gloves.
Koertge. Night Games.
Lieberman. My Father Dreams of Baseball.
Markson. Hartnett in Worcester.
Matthews. Hummer, The.
  Masterful.
Moore. Baseball and Writing.
  Hometown Piece for Messrs. Alston and
  Reese.
Nash. Hand Me Down My Old School Sliding
  Pads, or, There's a Hint of Strawberry
  Leaves in the Air.
Olson. Pitcher, how / exactly is.
Pack. Clayfeld's Glove.
Patchen. Origin of Baseball, The.
Rolfe. Kill the Umpire!
  Nine, The.
Sandburg. Hits and Runs.
Stuart. Opposite Field, The.
  Umpire.
Turco. Pocoangelini 26 ("In the empty
  stadium he stood").
Updike. Tao in the Yankee Stadium Bleachers.
Williams, William Carlos. At the Ball Game.
Zimmer. Thurman Dreaming in Right Field.
  Thurman's Slumping Blues.

Basketball
Hemingway. Safety Man, The.
Hugo. In Your Young Dream.
Matthews. Foul Shots: A Clinic.
  In Memory of the Utah Stars.
Updike. Ex-Basketball Player.

Baths and Bathing
Auden. Encomium Balnei.
Berryman. Young Woman's Song.
Clark. Nimble Rays of Day Bring Oxygen to
  Her Blood.
Cohen. Good Fight, The.
Cowper. On a Bath.
  On Pallas Bathing.
Crane. Bathers, The.
Davie. After the Match.
Gunn. Bath House, The.
Hacker. I'll dabble in specifics in my bath.
Hardy. Aquae Sulis.
Jonson. On the New Hot-House.
Kipling. Naaman's Song.
Lawrence. Bathing Resort.
  Forte Dei Marmi.
  Gloire de Dijon.
  Gods! The Gods!, The.
  Sea-Bathers.
Nash. And Three Hundred and Sixty-Six in
  Leap Year.
  Samson Agonistes.
  Splash!
Olson. All Pink from the Bath She Slept.
  Carrying water to the Youth in Honor of
  Sappho Jane Harrison & Miss Duncan if She
  Had.

Patchen. Weekend Bathers.
Plath. Battle-Scene.
Tale of a Tub.
Roethke. Meditation in Hydrotherapy.
Rukeyser. From a Play: Publisher's Song.
Sandburg. Slippery.
Schuyler. March Here.
Silverstein. Instructions.
Skinny.
Snyder. Bath, The.
Public Bath, The.
Wilbur. Five Women Bathing in Moonlight.
Williams, William Carlos. I bought a new.
Portrait of a Woman at Her Bath.
Zukofsky. "Further than."

Bats
"Carroll, Lewis." Mad Hatter's Song, The.
Cummings. I'd think "wonder / if" if.
Dickinson. Bat is dun, with wrinkled Wings,
The.
Ford. Jeweled Bat, The.
Serenade to Leonor.
Galvin. Bats, The.
Jarrell. Bats.
Kooser. Man with the Hearing Aid, The.
Lawrence. Bat.
Man and Bat.
Lowry. Note, A.
MacNeice. Million simmering kettles: in the
Destroyer's shrine, A.
Nash. Bat, The.
Roethke. Bat, The.
Sexton. Bat.
Silverstein. Enter This Deserted House.
Updike. Zoo Bats.
Wilbur. Mind.

Battlefields
Boyle. Battlefield, The.
Brontë. There swept adown that dreary glen.
Burns. Battle of Sherra-Moor, The.
Bonie Laddie, Highland Laddie.
Killiecrankie.
Cummings. Earth like a tipsy.
Davie. Battlefield, A.
Emerson. Hymn[:] Sung at the Completion of
the Concord Monument, April 19, 1836.
I am not black in my mind.
In Memoriam.
Fenton. Wind.
Graves. Dawn Bombardment.
Gunn. Beach Head, The.
Haines. Dusk of the Revolutionaries.
Hall. "O Flodden Field."
Hardy. In Time of Wars and Tumults.
San Sebastian.
Valenciennes.
Hewitt. Crossing, The.
Hill. Distant Fury of Battle, The.
Mobile, immaculate and austere.
Prowess, vanity, mutual regard.
Keats. King Stephen. A Fragment of a
Tragedy.
Lewis. Raid, The.
Melville. Inscription: "To them who crossed
the flood."
Shiloh [A Requiem].
Prince. Cefalù.
Sandburg. Grass.
New Feet.
Stevenson. Ticonderoga: A Legend of the
West Highlands.
Vanquished Knight, The.
Tennyson. Morte d'Arthur.
Warren. History among the Rocks.
Whittier. Watchers, The.
Williams, William Carlos. March, The.
Wordsworth. After Visiting the Field of
Waterloo.

Baucis and Philemon
Gunn. Philemon and Baucis.
Swift. Story of Baucis & Philemon, The.

Baudelaire, Charles
Bunting. Baudelaire in Cythera.
Dobyns. Cézanne's Love of Poetry.
Fletcher. Lid, The.
Ford. Ballad for Baudelaire.
Gunn. Readings in French.

Liddy. Letter to Sainte-Beuve.
Sorrentino. Give Them Blood.
Poem: "Clear objects / one grows to love. The
clarity, The."

Bavaria
Carruth. To Know in Reverie the Only
Phenomenology of the Absolute.
Updike. Munich.

Bay Trees. *see* **Laurels.**

Beaches
Arnold. Dover Beach.
Betjeman. Beside the Seaside.
East Anglian Bathe.
Green shutters, shut your shutters! Windyridge.
Greenaway.
Bishop. End of March, The.
Bukowski. On a Night You Don't Sleep.
Carroll, Jim. Blue Poles.
Cold Faces.
"Carroll, Lewis." Lady of the Ladle, The.
Size and Tears.
Three Voices, The.
Ceravolo. Wind Is Blowing West, The.
Creeley. Obscene Poem, An.
Cummings. Because i love you)last night.
How many moments must(amazing each).
I remark that this beach has been used
too. much Too. originally.
Maggie and milly and molly and may.
Dickey, James. Circuit.
Immortals.
Two Women.
Eberhart. Ceremony By the Sea, A.
Emerson. Lobster-car, boat, or fishbasket.
Gardner. At a Summer Hotel.
Summers Ago.
Glück. Lady in the Single, The.
Silverpoint.
Graves. Beach, The.
Griffiths. Geriatrics.
Taking Shelter.
Gunn. Beach Head, The.
Three.
Hardy. At the Aquatic Sports.
Heaney. Sandstone Keepsake.
Strand at Lough Beg, The.
Hesketh. On Iona.
Hewitt. Brown's Bay, Islandmagee, Spring
1917.
Seaside Town, A.
Sonnet: "By the sea's edge, on gravel and on
sand."
Housman. Smooth between sea and land.
Hugo. Changes in Policy at Taholah.
Jeffers. Beach, The.
Knott. Poem (the Starfish One).
Kunitz. Prophecy on Lethe.
Lawrence. Restlessness.
Levine. We sat by the shore.
Liddy. Shore.
Sister Beach, Sister Garden.
McAuley. Glory.
MacNeice. Lugubrious, Salubrious Seaside,
The.
Provence.
Strand, The.
Upon This Beach.
Millay. Low-Tide.
Nash. Don't Look Now.
Pretty Halcyon Days.
Seaside Serenade.
Nemerov. Salt Garden, The.
Olson. Lordly and Isolate Satyrs, The.
Pack. Red Shift, The.
Patchen. Fifth Dimension.
Plath. Point Shirley.
Two Lovers and a Beachcomber by the Real
Sea.
Raine. On a Shell-strewn Beach.
Rich. Parting: I, The.
Rukeyser. Children, the Sandbar, That
Summer.
Sandburg. Sandhill People.
Schuyler. Edge in the Morning, The.
We See Seals. Boats Go By.
You're.
Sexton. Kite, The.

Sea Corpse, The.
There You Were.
Shelley. Fragment: The Lake's Margin.
Silverstein. Generals, The.
Snyder. North Coast, The.
Point Reyes.
Running Water Music.
Spenser. One day I wrote her name upon the
strand.
Stafford. With Kit, Age Seven, at the Beach.
Stevens. Fabliau of Florida.
Tomlinson. Stone Speech.
Writing on Sand.
Updike. Antigua.
Raining in Magens Bay.
Rio de Janeiro.
Sunglasses.
Wakoski. Cannon Beach.
Walcott. Beachhead.
Before that thundercloud breaks from its
hawsers.
Something primal in our spine makes the child
swing.
Warren. Mad Young Aristocrat on Beach.
Myth on Mediterranean Beach: Aphrodite as
Logos.
Paradox.
Whitman. On the Beach at Night.
On the Beach at Night Alone.
Whittier. Tent on the Beach, The.
Wilbur. On the Marginal Way.
Waters, The.
Wright, James. At the Slackening of the Tide.
Young. Sad Hour of Your Peace, The.
Zukofsky. Sand: For the cigarette finished,
The.
See also **Seacoasts; Shores.**

Beads
Dunbar. She Told Her Beads.
Merrill. Komboloi.
Tomlinson. Bead, The.

Beans
Browning, Robert. Bean-Feast, The.
Clare. Bean Field, The.
Herrick. Littlenesse No Cause of Leanesse.
Jarrell. Gleaning.
Sandburg. Corn and Beans.
Silverstein. Sleeping Sardines.

Beards
Creeley. Boy, the.
Updike. Upon Shaving Off One's Beard.

Bears
Atwood. Dream 3: Night Bear Which
Frightened Cattle.
Bly. Schoolcraft's Diary Written on the
Missouri: 1830.
Carruth. Bears at Raspberry Time.
Cummings. Like a little bear twilight.
Dunbar. Cabin Tale, A.
Dunn. Good Life, A.
Eberhart. Winter Kill.
Everson. Bride of the Bear.
Frost. Bear, The.
Gardner. Part of the Darkness.
Graves. To Be Called A Bear.
Haines. Bear loped before me, A.
Old, root-crowded cemetery, An.
Hall. Self-Portrait as a Bear.
Kinnell. Bear, The.
Lastness.
Kipling. Truce of the Bear, The.
Moore. Bear and the Garden-Lover, The.
Oliver. Happiness.
Spring.
Truro Bear, The.
Rich. Bears.
Roethke. Lady and the Bear, The.
Rossetti. Brother Bruin.
Sarton. Bears and Waterfalls.
Snyder. Right in the Trail.
This Poem Is for Bear.
Way West, Underground, The.
Wright, James. March.
Zimmer. History of Bears, The.

Beatings
Angelou. Kind of Love, Some Say, A.
"Carroll, Lewis." Duchess's Lullaby, The.

Dobyns. How Could You Ever Be Fine.
"Reed." Caroline Says II.

Beatniks
Berrigan. Pandora's Box, An Ode.
Ginsberg. Bop Lyrics.
  Dream Record: June 8, 1955.
  Footnote to Howl.
  Fragment 1956.
  Fragment: The Names II.
  Howl.
  Many Loves.
Smith, Patti. Ps/alm 23 Revisited.

Beatrice Portinari
Graves. Beatrice and Dante.

Beaumont, Francis
Jonson. To Francis Beaumont.
Wordsworth. At Applethwaite, near Keswick.
  For a Seat in the Groves of Coleorton.

Beauty
Angelou. Black Ode.
Arnold. Growing Old.
Auden. Appletreewick.
  Blind Lead the Blind, The.
  Dawn.
  Dichtung und Wahrheit.
  Dragon-fly, The.
  Everest.
  Helen.
  March.
  Moment, A.
  My Lady of the Wood.
  Prayer.
  Sonnet: "This world is full of lovely things."
  Vision.
  Walk, The.
  Woods in Rain.
Beatles. I Saw Her Standing There.
Beckett. Scarcely Disfigured.
Berry. River Bridged and Forgot, The.
Berryman. Astronomies and slangs to find
  you, dear.
  Canto Amor.
  If not white shorts—then in a princess gown.
  Meeting.
  Sigh as it ends. I keep an eye on your.
Bogan. Question in a Field.
Brontë. I've been wandering in the
  greenwoods.
Browning, Elizabeth Barrett. Best Thing in the
  World, The.
  Daughters of Pandarus, The.
  Hiram Powers' "Greek Slave."
  May's Love.
  So the storms bore the daughters of Pandarus
  out into thrall.
  Song of the Rose.
  Sonnet: "Yet, love, mere love, is beautiful
  indeed."
  Where's Agnes?
Browning, Robert. Guardian-Angel, The.
  Magical Nature.
  Pretty Woman, A.
  Song: "Nay but you, who do not love her."
  Women and Roses.
Bukowski. Girls at the Green Hotel, The.
  Huge Ear Rings.
Burns. Answer to the Foregoing—Extempore
  [Clarinda].
  Beware o' Bonie Ann.
  Bonnie Peg.
  Bonnie [or Bonny] Wee Thing, The.
  Delia.
  Fragment: "Her flowing locks, the raven's
  wing."
  Fragment, Which Was Meant for the
  Beginning of an Elegy on the Late Miss
  Burnet of Monboddo, A.
  Hey for a Lass wi' a Tocher.
  Humble Petition of Bruar Water to the Noble
  Duke of Athole, The.
  I do confess thou art sae fair.
  Jessie—A New Scots Song.
  Lovely Davies.
  Lovely Polly Stewart.
  Lover's Morning Salute to His Mistress, The.
  My Lady's Gown There's Gairs upon't.
  My Peggy's Face.

O Mally's Meek, Mally's Sweet.
O once I loved [or lov'd] a bonnie lass.
O saw ye bonny Lesley.
She Says She Lo'es Me Best of A'.
Song: "Adown winding Nith I did wander."
Song, Altered from an Old English One.
Song: "Anna, thy charms my bosom fire."
Song.—Composed at Auchtertyre on Miss
  Euphemia Murray of Lentrose.
Song: "In Mauchline there dwells six proper
  young Belles."
Song: "O wat ye wha's in yon town."
Song: "On Cessnock banks a lassie dwells."
Song. On Miss P——— K———, A.
Theniel Menzies' Bony Mary.
To Maria.
To Miss C*********, a Very Young Lady.
To Miss Ferrier.
Where braving angry Winter's storms.
Yon wild, mossy mountains sae lofty and
  wide.
Byron. Girl of Cadiz, The.
  Oh! Snatch'd Away in Beauty's Bloom.
  On the Eyes of Miss A——— H———.
  She Walks in Beauty.
  Sonnet, to Genevra.
  Sonnet, to the Same.
  Stanzas for Music ("There be none of
  Beauty's daughters").
  To M———.
  To Mary on Receiving Her Picture.
Campion. Ad Cambricum.
  Are you what your faire lookes expresse?
  Art Thou That She.
  Beautie Without Love Deformitie.
  Do Not, Oh, Do Not Prize.
  Epigram: "None then should through thy
  beawty, Lawra, pine."
  Her rosie cheekes, her ever smiling eyes.
  I must complain, yet doe enjoy my Love.
  In Melleam.
  Just beguiler, / Kindest love, yet only chastest.
  Rose-cheeked Laura[, Come].
  Rose-cheekt Lawra, come.
  So sweet is thy discourse to me.
  There Is a Garden in Her Face.
  There Is None, O None but You.
  Thou Joy'st, Fond Boy.
  Though You Are Young [or Yoong].
  Vain Men, Whose Follies.
  When Laura smiles her sight revives both
  night and day.
  Where She Her Sacred Bower Adorns.
  Why presumes thy pride on that, that must so
  private be.
Carew. Carver. To His Mistress, The.
  Comparison, The.
  Complement, The.
  Disdain Returned.
  Divine Mistress, A.
  Fancy, A.
  First of Jealousy. Dialogue, The.
  Hue and Cry, The.
  Incommunicability of Love.
  Ingrateful[l] Beauty Threatened.
  Lover, in the Disguise of an Amazon, Is
  Dearly Beloved of His Mistress, A.
  My Mistress Commanding Me to Return Her
  Letters.
  Obsequies to the Lady Anne Hay.
  On Mistress N.
  On Sight of a Gentlewoman's Face in the
  Water.
  On the Marriage of T. K. and C. C.: The
  Morning Stormy.
  Pastoral[l] Dialogue, A.
  Song, [A]: "Ask[e] me no more where Jove
  bestows."
  Song: Beautiful Mistress, A.
  Song: Murdering Beauty.
  Tinder, The.
  To A. L.; Persuasions [or Perswasions] to
  Love.
  To a Lady, That Desired I Would Love Her.
  To A.D., Unreasonable, Distrustful of Her
  Own Beauty.
  To my Friend G.N. from Wrest.

To One Who, When I Praised My Mistress'
  Beauty, Said I Was Blind.
  To the Painter.
"Carroll, Lewis." Beatrice.
  Double Acrostic: I sing a place wherein agree.
  Turtle Soup.
Carruth. Birth of Venus, The.
  Sonnet: "Last night, I don't know if from
  habit or intent."
Catullus. Carmen 9: "Veraniolus, / first of
  friends."
  Carmen 86: "We have heard of Quintia's
  beauty. To me she is tall, slender."
Chaucer. Book of the Duchesse, The.
  Merciles[s] Beaute [or Beautée or Beauty].
  To Rosamounde.
  Womanly Noblesse.
Ciardi. Bees and Morning Glories.
  Catalpa, The.
Clark. Birds.
  Blue Dress.
  Sedge.
Cohen. Beneath My Hands.
  Dance Me to the End of Love.
  Petitions.
  Portrait of a Girl.
Coleridge. Complaint of Ninathóma, The.
  Genevieve.
  Song, ex improviso.
Cowper. Song, A: "Sparkling eye, the
  mantling cheek."
  Song: "No more shall hapless Celia's ears."
  Sonnet 2: "Charming lady, she whose beautiful
  name honors."
Crane. Bathers, The.
Crashaw. Upon the Faire Ethiopian Sent to a
  Gentlewoman.
  [With Some Poems Sent to a Gentlewoman. I].
Creeley. Birthday, A.
  Chance, The.
  Was.
  Water Music.
  Women, The.
Cullen. Advice to a Beauty.
  Bright Bindings.
  Life's Rendezvous.
  Medusa.
  Song of Praise, A.
  To John Keats, Poet, at Springtime.
Cummings. 4.7: "Farewell,runaway
  snows! For the meadow is green,and the
  tree stands."
  Christ but they're few.
  Cleopatra built / like a smooth arrow or.
  Every one of the red roses opened.
  Except in your / honour.
  Helen.
  Here's s / omething round(& so).
  I love you / for your little,startled,thoughtless
  ways.
  I shall imagine life.
  "I think you like."
  If i love You.
  Is there a flower(whom).
  Let's,from some loud unworld's most rightful
  wrong.
  Life is more true than reason will deceive.
  Mr youse needn't be so spry.
  Moon-lit snow is falling like strange candy
  into the big eyes of the, The.
  Morsel miraculous and meaningless.
  My love / thy hair is one kingdom.
  My naked lady framed.
  Nothing whichful about / thick big this.
  O purple finch / please tell me why.
  Open green house / (dear).
  Perhaps it is to feel strike.
  Poem, or Beauty Hurts Mr. Vinal.
  Pretty a day, A.
  Puella Mea.
  River of Mist, The.
  These from my mother's greatgrandmother's
  rosebush white.
  This young question mark man.
  Thy face is a still white house of holy things.
  Time,be kind;herself and i.
  To start,to hesitate;to stop.

Until and i heard.
Whatever's merely wilful, / and not miraculous.
When my love comes to see me it's.
Where's Madge then / Madge and her men?
White guardians of the universe of sleep.
Who are you,little i.
Why / do the / fingers.
Without the mercy of / your eyes your.
You are like the snow only.
You said Is / there anything which.
Davie. Derbyshire Turf.
De la Mare. Age.
Epitaph, An: "Here lies a most beatiful lady."
Looking Glass, The.
Ophelia.
Phantom, The.
Shadow.
Sleeper, The.
Three Cherry Trees, The.
Treachery.
Unchanging, The.
Vain Finding.
Veil, The.
When the rose is faded.
Dickinson. Acts of Light which beautified, The.
All we secure of Beauty.
Awkward as the homely are.
Beauty be not caused—It Is.
Beauty crowds me till I die.
Beauty is often timidity.
Charm invests a face, A.
Definition of Beauty is, The.
Estranged from Beauty, none can be.
How vast is the chastisement of Beauty.
I died for Beauty—but was scarce.
In a World too full of Beauty for Peace.
"Infinite Beauty"—of which you speak, The.
Neither in Heaven nor Earth.
Parents of Beauty, The.
So gay a Flower.
Dobyns.
Donne. Letter to the Lady Carey, and Mistress Essex Rich, from Amiens, A.
Doolittle. Ancient Wisdom Speaks.
I Said.
Song: "You are as gold."
Dunbar. Alice.
Love's Pictures.
Song, A: "On a summer's day as I sat by a stream."
Duncan. Poetry, a Natural Thing.
Salvages: An Evening Place.
Torso, The.
Dunn. Beautiful Women.
Loves.
Snowmass Cycle, The.
Walking the Marshland.
"Dylan." Eternal Circle.
Hazel.
Eberhart. Opulence.
Prometheus.
Transformation.
Whenever I See Beauty I See Death.
White Pines, Felled 1984.
Emerson. And do I waste my time.
Beauty.
Chladni strewed on glass the sand.
Dear Ellen, many a golden year.
Dearest, where thy shadow falls.
Each and All.
For joy & beauty planted it.
From Omar Chiam.
Harp, The.
I call her beautiful;—she says.
Illusions like the tints of pearl.
In the deep heart of man a poet dwells.
O what are heroes prophets men.
Ode to Beauty.
Power of a beautiful face lifts me to heaven, The.
Rhodora, The [On Being Asked Whence Is the Flower].
She had wealth of mornings in her year.
Tell me maiden dost thou use.
To Eva.

When in eternity the light.
Would you know what joy is hid.
Ferlinghetti. Carrara, Looking Seaward.
I have not lain with beauty all my life.
Light, The.
Fisher. Death music sounds for a boy by a stream.
Wells of shadow by the stream.
Fletcher. Elegy on a Nordic White Protestant.
Ford. And oh what a beautiful child you are.
Hair of her head could be a bed, The.
Gallagher. Present.
Garrigue. Primer of Plato.
Glück. Letter from our Man in Blossomtime.
Mirror, The.
Graves. Blessed Sun.
Dangerous Gift, The.
Down, Wanton, Down!
Green Woods of Unrest, The.
Her Beauty.
Love in Barrenness.
Necklace, The.
September Landscape.
Tousled Pillow.
Gunn. Glamorous and difficult friend.
Hardy. Aberdeen.
Background and the Figure, The.
Beauty, The.
Beauty's Soliloquy during Her Honeymoon, A.
Best She Could, The.
Concerning Agnes.
Eunice.
Faithful Wilson.
To an Imposter of Rosalind.
To Outer Nature.
Hartley. Immortal Face.
Whoever dies—dies for the love.
Hartnett. Some white academy of grace.
Hemingway. Inexpressible, The.
Herrick. Another Upon Her.
Apron of Flowers, The.
Art above Nature, to Julia.
Beauty.
Candor of Julias Teeth, The.
Cloud, The.
Definition of Beauty, The.
Delight in Disorder.
Descripcion; of a Woman, The.
Eclipse, The.
Elegy: "Since louely sweete, much like unto a Dewe."
Epitaph upon a Virgin, An.
Mrs. Eliz. Wheeler, Under the Name of the Lost Shepardesse.
Neglect.
On Tomasin Parsons.
Request to the Graces, An.
Rosarie, The.
To a Mayd.
To Anthea Lying in Bed.
To Electra.
To Mistresse Mary Willand.
To Perenna ("When I thy parts runne o're, I can't espie").
To the Handsome Mistresse Grace Potter.
To the Most Comely and Proper M. Elizabeth Finch.
Upon a Comely, and Curious Maide.
Upon a Painted Gentlewoman.
Upon Her Blush.
Upon Her Feet.
Upon His Julia.
Upon Julia's Clothes.
Upon Julia's Haire, Bundled up in a Golden Net.
Upon Silvia, a Mistresse.
Upon the Nipples of Julia's Breast.
Upon the Roses in Julias Bosome.
Upon Wrinkles.
Weeping Cherry, The.
Hesketh. Bolton-Le-Moors, 1960.
Hewitt. Art's Duped Riddle.
Nettles of Offence.
Sonnet: "Since brooding men put beauty in a rime."
Hoffman. At Provincetown.
He was the first who had returned.

Hopkins. Although she be more white.
As it fell upon a day.
Boughs being pruned, birds preenèd, show more fair.
Confirmed beauty will not bear a stress.
Daphne.
Floris in Italy.
Pied Beauty.
To What Serves Mortal Beauty?
Hughes, Langston. My People.
When Sue Wears Red.
Hughes, Ted. Fallgrief's Girlfriends.
Hugo. Brown Stone.
Jarrell. Head of Wisdom, The.
Jeffers. At the Fall of an Age.
Beauty of Things, The.
Birds and Fishes.
Divinely Superfluous Beauty.
Give Your Heart to the Hawks.
Hope is Not for the Wise.
Invasion.
Irish Headland, An.
It was good of my father, whom I hated at times.
Life from the Lifeless.
New Year's Eve.
Ocean's Tribute, The.
Rearmament.
Red Mountain.
Such Counsels You Gave to Me.
Their Beauty Has More Meaning.
Johnson. To Lady Firebrace.
Jonson. Elegy, An: "By those bright eyes, at whose immortal fires."
Elegy [or Elegie], An: "Let me be what I am, as Virgil cold."
Elegy [or Elegie] on the Lady Jane Pawlet [or Paulet], [Marchioness of Winton], An.
Fair friend, 'tis true, your beauties move.
It Was a Beauty That I Saw.
Ode, An: "Helen, did Homer never see."
Ode Enthusiastic.
On Lucy Countess[e] of Bedford.
Sound, sound aloud / The welcome of the orient flood.
Still turn, and imitate the heaven.
To Mary, Lady Wroth ("Madam, had all antiquity been lost").
When Love at first did move.
Joseph. INTERIOR: The Man Turns the Sheet for the Musician (Dutch).
STUDY: A Lady in her Bedroom (Bonnard).
Keats. Thing of Beauty, A.
To ———: "Time's sea hath been five years at its slow ebb."
To Georgiana Augusta Wylie.
To the Ladies Who Saw Me Crowned.
Kinnell. Falls, The.
Saint Francis and the Sow.
Knott. Poem: "Beach holds and sifts us through her dreaming fingers, The."
Poem: "With the toys of your nape."
Sonnet: "Way the world is not, The."
Koch. On Beauty.
Kunitz. For Proserpine.
Particular Lullaby.
Larkin. Latest Face.
Like the Train's Beat.
Lawrence. Bodiless God.
Early Spring.
Fronleichnam.
One Woman to All Women.
Pomegranate.
Roses on the Breakfast Table.
Shows.
So Let Me Live.
Levertov. Love Song.
March, A.
Lewis. Belief.
Bequest.
Defeat.
Song: "O have you seen the thorn that grows."
Victory.
Liddy. He'd be alive today if he wasn't pretty.
Lady/Lord in Doorway.
May Day Song.
Translate into Latin for my Epitaph.

Lindsay. Alone in the Wind, on the Prairie.
My Lady in Her White Silk Shawl.
My Lady Is Compared to a Young Tree.
To Gloriana.
To Lady Jane.
Lovelace. Ode: "You are deceiv'd; I sooner may dull fair."
Quintia is handsome, fair, tall, straight, all these.
Lowry. Asperin tree outside told me to say, The.
I set this down as humble prayer.
Little Ditty for This Day to the Beloved Harteebeeste, A.
Love of a Seagull.
Song for My Wife.
That's What I Mean.
Very dark and clear with an onshore wind.
Welcome Home Oh Gladsome Springhorned Beloved and Famed Harteebeeste.
"MacDiarmid." Milk-Wort and Bog Cotton.
MacLeish. Adam in the Evening.
Beauty is that Medusa's head.
But she was both,—she was both loved and love.
Excavation of Troy.
First I will tell you something of these two.
Landscape as a Nude.
No doubt he'd once had eyes to see.
Not Marble nor the Gilded Monuments.
Things he had loved because he knew them lost.
Two Poems from the War.
Under an elm tree where the river reaches.
Years of the Dog.
MacNeice. Circe.
Corona Virginum.
Old Story, The.
Markson. But Yet Again, We Fought.
Matthews. Straight Life.
Meinke. Sonnet on the Death of the Man Who Invented Plastic Roses.
Meredith. Angel, be ye ne'er in doubt, An.
Ballad of the Lady Eglantine, The.
Grace and Love.
Hectate.
Her arms two branches of the almond-tree that sway at morn in the.
Her cheeks are as a crystal goblet held to the sun.
Now the youth was not ware of the beams.
One fairest of the ripe unwedded left.
She issues radiant from her dressing-room.
She rides in the park on a prancing bay.
To A.M.
When I Would Image.
Years Had Worn Their Season's Belt, The.
Merrill. Peacock, The.
Merton. Philosophers, The.
Millay. And is indeed truth beauty?—at the cost.
And you as well must die, belovèd dust.
Euclid alone has looked on Beauty bare.
How did I bear it—how could I possibly as a child.
Love is not blind. I see with single eye.
Portrait.
Still will I harvest beauty where it grows.
To Kathleen.
What's this of death, from you who never will die?
When I too long have looked upon your face.
Milton. Sonnet 2: "Charming lady, she whose beautiful name honors."
Nash. Aside to Husbands.
Biological Reflection.
Nathan. One for Beauty.
Nemerov. Dandelions.
Young Woman.
Neruda. Can't you think death lives.
O'Hara. Having a Coke with You.
Poem: "O sole mio, hot diggety, nix 'I wather think I can'."
Olson. Beauty / is to lay hold of Love.
Epigon.
For a Lady of Whom I Speak.
For Sappho, Back.

Imbued / with the light.
Kingfishers, The.
La Chute.
Lordly and Isolate Satyrs, The.
Out of the light of Heaven the flower.
Red Mallows.
Thing Was Moving, The.
When do poppies bloom I ask myself, stopping again.
Your Eyes.
Oppen. Only that it should be beautiful.
Owen. Beauty.
Imbecile, The.
Purple.
Paley. No love / no love cried the last fling.
Patchen. Beautiful You Are.
Demonstration.
Hold thy tongue, death!
Hovenweep.
O my love / The pretty towns.
O She Is as Lovely-Often as Every Day.
Of the same beauty were stars made.
She is the prettiest of creatures.
What Is the Beautiful?
Piercy. Barbie Doll.
Beauty I Would Suffer For.
Poe. Al Aaraaf.
Eulalie—A Song.
Israfel.
Lake: To————, The.
Sleeper, The.
Stanzas: "How often we forget all time, when lone."
To————: "Not long ago, the writer of these lines."
To Helen ("Helen, thy beauty is to me").
To Helen ("I saw thee once—once only—years ago").
To the River————.
Valley of Unrest, The.
Pope. Of Her Picture.
Of Her Walking in a Garden after a Shower.
Presenting a Lark.
Pound. Dance Figure.
Prince. Token, The.
Youth and Age.
Raine. Amo Ergo Sum.
Cloud.
Turner's Seas.
Ralegh. As You Came from the Holy Land [of Walsingham].
In the Grace of Wit, of Tongue and Face.
Poem of Sir Walter Rawleighs, A.
Ransom. Hilda.
Judith of Bethulia.
Rexroth. Autumn in California.
Rolfe. Manuela.
Rossetti. Annie.
Beauty Is Vain.
Behold, It Was Very Good.
Books In the Running Brooks.
Buds and Babies.
Cousin Kate.
De Profundis.
Earth and Heaven.
Easter Morning.
Eleanor.
Exultate Deo.
Floral Teaching.
Fluttered Wings.
For Advent.
From early dawn until the flush of noon.
Growing in the vale / By the uplands hilly.
Helen Grey.
His Banner over Me Was Love.
Holy City, New Jerusalme, The.
If stars dropped out of heaven, / And if flowers took their place.
Immalee.
Lady Isabella.
Last Look, The.
Lily has a smooth stalk, / Will never hurt your hand, The.
Lily has an air, / And the snowdrop a grace, The.
Listen, and I will tell you of a face.
Lord, make me one with Thine own faithful

ones.
Love is all happiness, love is all beauty.
Luscious and Sorrowful.
On Albina.
Once.
Peter Grump.
Praise of Love.
Queen Rose.
Rose, The.
Rose with such a bonny blush, The.
Seasons.
Serenade ("Come, wander forth with me! the orange flowers").
Song: "I saw her; she was lovely."
Song: "It is not for her even brow."
Summer.
There Is a Budding Morrow in Midnight.
To What Purpose Is This Waste?
Valentines from C.G.R.
Versi.
What Is Pink?
What is this above thy head, / O Man?
Who Hath Despised the Day of Small Things?
Within the Veil.
World's Harmonies, The.
Rukeyser. Woman and Emblems.
St. John. Hard & Noble Patience, A.
Who is she, coming along the street, turning the heads.
Sandburg. Autumn Movement.
Baby Face.
Flash Crimson.
Foxgloves.
Monotone.
Murmurings in a Field Hospital.
My People.
Personalia.
Proud and Beautiful.
Sumach and Birds.
They Buy with an Eye to Looks.
Two.
Sarton. Memory of Swans.
Portrait by Holbein.
Swans, The.
Schuyler. Poem: "This beauty that I see."
Schwartz. Dream of Whitman Paraphrased, Recognized and Made More Vivid by Renoir, A.
When I Remember the Advent.
Scott. Dawn and Sunrise.
Harold's Song.
Invocation: "Harp of the North! that mouldering long hast hung."
Thorsgill.
Sexton. Snow White and the Seven Dwarfs.
Shakespeare. Beauty is but a vain and doubtful good.
Phoenix and the Turtle, The.
Sonnet 4: "Unthrifty loveliness, why dost thou spend."
Sonnet 5: "Those hours, that with gentle work did frame."
Sonnet 10: "For shame! deny that thou bear'st love to any."
Sonnet 14: "Not from the stars do I my judgement pluck."
Sonnet 18: "Shall I compare thee to a summer's day?"
Sonnet 20: "Woman's face with Nature's own hand painted, A."
Sonnet 24: "Mine eye hath play'd the painter, and hath stell'd."
Sonnet 53: "What is your substance, whereof are you made."
Sonnet 54: "O [or Oh], how much more doth beauty beauteous seem."
Sonnet 65: "Since brass, nor stone, nor earth, nor boundless sea."
Sonnet 95: "How sweet and lovely dost thou make the shame."
Sonnet 101: "O truant Muse, what shall be thy amends."
Sonnet 103: "Alack, what poverty my Muse brings forth."
Sonnet 104: "To me, fair[e] friend, you never can be old."
Sonnet 106: "When in the chronicle of wasted

time."
Sonnet 127: "In the old age black was not counted fair."
Sonnet 130: "My mistress' eyes are nothing like the sun."
Sonnet 132: "Thine eyes I love, and they, as pitying me."
Shapiro.   Cut Flower, A.
Shelley.   Fragment: Beauty's Halo.
Hymn to Intellectual Beauty.
To Sophia [Miss Stacey].
Sidney.   Doubt you to whom my Muse these notes intendeth [or entendeth].
Seventh Song.
Sixth Song.
Sonnet 11: "In truth, O Love, with what a boyish kind."
Sonnet 5: "It is most true that eyes are formed to serve."
Sonnet 9: "Queen Virtue's court, which some call Stella's face."
What tongue can her perfections tell.
Smart.   Beauty.
Loveliness.
Ode to Lady Harriot.
Smith, Charlotte.   Song: "Fruit of Aurora's tears, fair Rose."
To the Fire-Fly of Jamaica, Seen in a Collection.
Smith, Stevie.   Lady of the Well-Spring, The.
Rehearsal, The.
Sorrowful Girl, The.
Sorrentino.   Shapes of Winter.
Spender.   From My Diary.
Spenser.   At last, so faire a ladie did I spie.
Being one day at my window all alone.
XV. "Ye tradeful merchants that, with weary toil."
High on a hill a goodly cedar grewe.
Hymne in Honour of Beautie, An.
Panther, knowing that his spotted hide, The.
Stevens.   Anything Is Beautiful If You Say It Is.
Peter Quince at the Clavier.
Stevenson.   Her name is as a word of old romance.
Here you rest among the valleys, maiden known to but a few.
In Memoriam, E.H.
Katharine.
Let Beauty awake in the morn from beautiful dreams.
Mother and Daughter.
To Henry James.
To Madame Garschine.
Stuart.   My Hostess at the Renovated Inn.
Suckling.   Non Est Mortale Quod Opto.
Song: "When, dearest, I but think on [or of] thee."
Sonnet: "Dost see how unregarded now."
Sonnet: "Of thee (kind boy) I ask no red and white."
To B.C.
Upon the First Sight of My Lady Seymour.
Upon Two Sisters.
Swift.   Lady's Dressing Room, The.
On Stella's Birthday, 1718/1719.
Progress of Beauty, The.
Swinburne.   Ballad of Death, A.
Ballad of Life, A.
Complaint of the Fair Armoress [or Armouress], The.
Sapphics.
Tate.   Sonnet to Beauty.
Tennyson.   To —. With the Following Poem.
Thomson.   Morning in the Country, The.
Updike.   Eurydice.
Penumbrae.
South of the Alps.
Sunshine on Sandstone.
Youth's Progress.
Van Duyn.   Midas and Wife.
Wakoski.   Ode to a Lebanese Crock of Olives.
Reaching Out with the Hands of the Sun.
Walcott.   As John to Patmos.
Warren.   Child Next Door, The.
Interjection #8: Or, Sometimes, Night.

Whitman.   Beautiful Women.
Had I the Choice.
Love That Is Hereafter, The.
My Canary Bird.
Song of the Answerer.
Song of the Rolling Earth, A.
Then Shall Perceive.
Whittier.   Artist of the Beautiful, An.
Clear Vision, The.
Fair Quakeress, The.
Hazel Blossoms.
Pictures.
Sea Dream, A.
Stanzas: "Bind up thy tresses, thou beautiful one."
Sunset on the Bearcamp.
To ——: "Maiden! with the fair brown tresses."
Wilbur.   Beautiful Changes, The.
Caserta Garden.
Piazza di Spagna, Early Morning.
Potato.
Still, Citizen Sparrow.
Thyme Flowering among Rocks.
Transit.
Williams, Charles Kenneth.   Hooks.
Love: Wrath.
Williams, Miller.   Book, The.
Williams, William Carlos.   At Dawn.
Ce-Lia The Immortal Beauty.
Green Eyes.
Hard Core of Beauty, The.
Homage.
La Belle Dame de Tous les Jours.
Red Lily, The.
Song: "Beauty is a shell."
Wordsworth.   Anacreon.
Between Namur and Liege.
Bruges ("Bruges I saw attired with golden light").
Composed upon an Evening of Extraordinary Splendour and Beauty.
Composed upon Westminster Bridge, September 3, 1802.
Contrast; the Parrot and the Wren, The.
Dedication (Sent with These Poems, in Ms., To —).
Glad Sight Wherever New with Old.
Gleaner (Suggested By a Picture), The.
Gold and Silver Fishes in a Vase.
How Rich That Forehead's Calm Expanse!
I Heard (Alas! 'Twas Only in a Dream).
Jewish Family (in a Small Valley Opposite St Goar, upon the Rhine), A.
Lady Whom You here Behold, The.
Lyre! Though Such Power Do in Thy Magic Live.
November 1.
Prithee, Gentle Lady, List.
So Fair, So Sweet, Withal So Sensitive.
Suggested by a Picture of the Bird of Paradise.
To ——: "Let other bards of angels sing."
To —, in Her Seventieth Year.
To—, on Her First Ascent to the Summit of Helvellyn.
To a Skylark ("Ethereal minstrel! pilgrim of the sky").
To the Highland Girl of Inversneyde.
Vernal Ode.
While Beams of Orient Light Shoot Wide and High.
Wild Duck's Nest, The.
Written in the Strangers' Book at "The Station," Opposite Bowness.
Yes! Thou Art Fair, Yet Be Not Moved.
Wright, Charles.   Night Journal.
Spring Abstract.
Wright, James.   All the Beautiful are Blameless.
Eleutheria.
Pretty Redhead, The.
Shadow and the Real, The.
To a Hostess Saying Goodnight.
Wroth.   Sonnet 2: "Deare eyes how well (indeed) you doe adorne."
Sonnet 12: "Bee given to him who triumphs in

his right."
Sonnet 41: "You blessed starrs which doe heavns glory show."
Wyatt.   Nature that gave the bee so feat a grace.
Yeats.   Arrow, The.
Beautiful Lofty Things.
Broken Dreams.
Crazed Girl, A.
Dream of Death, A.
He Remembers Forgotten Beauty.
He Tells of the Perfect Beauty.
His Phoenix.
Living Beauty, The.
Memory.
Michael Robartes and the Dancer.
No Second Troy.
Secret Rose, The.
Symbols.
Thought from Propertius, A.
To a Young Beauty.
Zimmer.   Wanda Being Beautiful.
Zukofsky.   H.T.
In Arizona / (how many years in the mountains).
Not much more than being.
Quintia's *foremost* to multitudes; my eye can deed her *long, e—*.
Veranius of all my beloved friends.
World autumn, The.

Beauty and the Beast
Duncan.   Four Songs the Night Nurse Sang.

Beavers
Schuyler.   Awoke.
Sutter.   Beaverhouse Downriver, The.

Bedrooms
Auden.   Cave of Nakedness, The.
Carroll, Jim.   My Debt.
Lowell.   Father's Bedroom.
Mahon.   Studio, The.
"Reed."   Bed, The.
Sexton.   February 4th.
Now.
Smith, Stevie.   Goodnight.

Beds
Bukowski.   Beds, Toilets, You and Me—.
Burns.   Bonie Lass Made the Bed to Me, The.
Cummings.   Bed is not very big, The.
Dunn.   Emptiness.
Eberhart.   Day-Bed, The.
Graves.   Window Pane, The.
Gunn.   Bed, The.
Herrick.   Her Bed.
Hesketh.   Widowhood.
Johnson.   Translation of Benserade's Verses À Son Lit.
Koch.   In Bed.
Larkin.   Talking in Bed.
Lovelace.   Ode to Lucasta: The Rose.
Lowry.   Oh welcome Home /To thy cot by the foam.
Piercy.   Beds that are mirrors.
Rossetti.   Crimson curtains round my mother's bed.
Sexton.   Angel of Clean Sheets.
Song for a Red Nightgown.
Sidney.   Sonnet 98: "Ah bed, the field where joy's peace some doe see."
Simic.   Inheritance.
Stevenson.   Come, my little children, here are songs for you.
Land of Counterpane, The.
Late in the nicht in bed I lay.
My Bed Is a Boat.
North-West Passage.
Walker.   Overnights.
Yau.   Zebra-striped pillow. The restlessness.
Zukofsky.   Madison, Wis., Remembering the Bloom of Monticello (1931).

Beech Trees and Beechnuts
Carruth.   Coming of winter / is a beech sapling.
Dove.   Copper Beech, The.
Fletcher.   Midwinter Sunset.
Frost.   Beech.
Boundless Moment, A.
Heaney.   In the Beech.

Spender. Barn, The.
Tomlinson. Beech, The.
Near Hartland.

Beef
Griffiths. Llangefni Market.
Nash. Calf, The.

Beer
Bukowski. Beer.
Burns. O had the malt thy strength of mind.
Carruth. Marvin McCabe.
Dunbar. Lager Beer.
Eberhart. Clerihew for Alan Gaylord, A.
Herrick. Coblers Catch, The.
Tinkers Song, The.
Upon Prig ("Prig now drinks Water, who before drank Beere").
Upon Spunge.
Housman. Terence, This Is Stupid Stuff.
Lovelace. Being Treated to Ellinda.
Lowry. Danish Sailor's Song.
Noble City Full of Pigeons or Everyone a Hypocrite Including Me.
McGrath. Mediterranean.
Trinc: Praises II.
McNeill. Moonshiner.
Matthews. Another Beer.
Meredith. O have you seen my Tuck? my bonny bonny Tuck!
Schuyler. Trash Book, The.
Stevenson. Good old ale, mild or pale.
Sit doon by me, my canty freend.
Williams, Miller. Glass Darkly, A.

Bees and Beekeeping
Ammons. Cousins.
Hype.
Oblivion's Room.
Transfer.
Bogan. Animal, Vegetable and Mineral.
Bukowski. Pansies.
Carew. Upon a Mole in Celia's Bosom.
"Carroll, Lewis." What is most like a bee in May?
Ciardi. Bees and Morning Glories.
Cohen. Politics of This Book, The.
Cowper. Bee and the Pine-Apple, The.
Innocent Thief, The.
Pine-Apple and the Bee, The.
Davie. Hornet.
De la Mare. Quiet Enemy, The.
Dickinson. Bee his burnished Carriage, A.
Bee! I'm expecting you!
Bees are Black, with Gilt Surcingles.
Come slowly—Eden!
Could I but ride indefinite.
Did the Harebell loose her girdle.
His Feet are shod with Gauze.
His oriental heresies.
Like Trains of Cars on Tracks of Plush.
Of Silken Speech and Specious Shoe.
Single clover Plank, A.
We—Bee and I—live by the quaffing.
What tenements of clover.
Duncan. After Reading H.D.'s *Hermetic Definitions.*
Dunn. Workers.
Eberhart. In the Garden.
Sunday in October.
Emerson. Humble-Bee, The.
Sparrow is rich in her nest, THe.
Frost. White-Tailed Hornet, The.
Hartley. Nature.
Herrick. Captived Bee; or, The Little Filcher, The.
Dream, The.
Present: or, The Bag of the Bee, The.
Kinnell. Fly, The.
Kipling. Bee-Boy's Song, The.
Lawrence. Coming Awake.
Lorde. Bees, The.
Lovelace. Black Patch on Lucasta's Face, A.
Both lurks and shines hid in an Amber-tear.
Meredith. Bumble Bee—the Bumble Bee, The.
Fullness of love sleeps in us like a sea.
Merton. Bees love grass, The.
Nemerov. And Is Silent.
Beekeeper Speaks.., The.
Oppen. Latitude, Longitude.

Paley. Bee! / drowning in, A.
Piercy. Daily Life of the Worker Bee, The.
Plath. Arrival of the Bee Box, The.
Beekeeper's Daughter, The.
Stings.
Swarm, The.
Wintering.
Rich. Song of the Foolish Bees.
Rossetti. When the cows come home the milk is coming.
Sandburg. Bee Song.
In Tall Grass.
Sexton. Hornet.
Smith, Charlotte. Invitation to the Bee.
Van Duyn. Time of Bees, A.
Wright, Charles. Journal of Three Questions, A.

Beethoven, Ludwig van
Berryman. Beethoven Triumphant.
Bukowski. Bee's 5th.
Note Upon the Love Letters of Beethoven.
Sardines in Striped Dresses.
Eberhart. Kinaesthesia.
Ginsberg. Eroica.
Jarrell. Head of Wisdom, The.
Lowell. Beethoven.
MacLeish. Pablo Casals.
Millay. On Hearing a Symphony of Beethoven.
Rich. Ninth Symphony of Beethoven Understood at Last as a Sexual Message, The.
Spender. Beethoven's Death Mask.
Late Stravinsky Listening to Late Beethoven.
Tomlinson. Beethoven Attends the C Minor Seminar.
Wakoski. Sometimes Even My Knees Smile.
Zukofsky. This is after all vacation. All that.

Beetles
Cohen. Beetle, The.
Commentary—The Beetle.
Dove. Roses.
Gardner. Cockchafer.
Hewitt. Providence 2.
Olson. I had had / a beetle.
Pack. Clayfeld's Anniversary Song.
Sorrentino. Zoo, The.
Updike. Tropical Beetles.

Beets
Nash. Parsnip, The.

Begging and Beggars
Berry. Guest, The.
Music, A.
Bishop. Pink Dog.
Browning, Robert. Twins, The.
Burns. Jolly Gauger, The.
Ciardi. October 18: Boston.
Cooper. He came all this way.
Cummings. But mr can you maybe listen there's.
Right here the other night something.
De la Mare. Owl, The.
Dickinson. Beggar Lad—dies early, The.
It came his turn to beg.
Most she touched me by her muteness.
There comes an hour when begging stops.
When a Lover is a Beggar.
Donne. Lame Beggar, A.
To Mr. T. W. ("Pregnant again with th' old twins hope, and fear").
"Dylan." Please, Mrs. Henry.
Emerson. There are beggars in Iran and Araby.
Gunn. Improvisation.
St. Martin and the Beggar.
Sparrow.
Hayden. Kid.
Herrick. Beggar to Mab, the Fairy [*or* Fairie] Queen, The.
Beggars.
Begger, The.
Biting of Beggars.
His Petition.
No Bashfulnesse in Begging.
Upon Guesse.
Upon Her Almes.
Hewitt. Father Explains, A.

Knife, The.
Scissors For a One-Armed Tailor.
Housman. He looked at me with eyes I thought.
Hugo. Beggar in Sapri.
Joseph. Subscription.
Lawrence. From a College Window.
Lieberman. Skateboard Throne: an Ode to Citizen Amputees, The.
Lindsay. Honor Among Scamps.
Prologue to "Rhymes to be Traded for Bread."
Lovelace. Faire Begger, The.
McGrath. Emblems of Exile.
Meredith. Beggar's Soliloquy, The.
Bellerophon.
Nathan. Ellora.
Oliver. Acid.
Pack. Stolen Clothes.
Plath. Beggars, The.
Prince. For Thieves and Beggars.
Rukeyser. Adventures, Midnight.
Suckling. Song: "I prithee send me back my heart."
Wordsworth. Beggars.
Old Cumberland Beggar, The.
Wright, James. Dreaming.
Wroth. Sonnet 2: "Late in the Forest I did Cupid see."
Yeats. Beggar to Beggar Cried.
Hour before Dawn, The.
Three Beggars, The.
Under the Round Tower.
See also **Homeless, The; Vagabonds.**

Belfast, Northern Ireland
Davie. Belfast on a Sunday Afternoon.
Hewitt. Methodists.
MacNeice. Belfast.
Mahon. Afterlives.
Brighton Beach.
Muldoon. Aisling.

Belgium
Auden. Brussels in Winter.
Cummings. Belgium.
Davie. Hyphens.
Hardy. Appeal to America on Behalf of the Belgian Destitute, An.
Cry of the Homeless.
On the Belgian Expatriation.
Wordsworth. After Visiting the Field of Waterloo.
Between Namur and Liege.
Bruges ("Bruges I saw attired with golden light").
Bruges ("Spirit of Antiquity—enshrined, The").
Incident at Bruges.

Belief
Auden. Belief.
Berry. Below.
Carruth. I don't say you can't find him in New Hampshire.
La colline du mystère. Solitary here. The stone.
Clough. O happy they whose hearts receive.
Creeley. Mirror, The.
Dickinson. Incredible never surprises us, The.
Neither fearing Extinction.
Spirit lasts, but in what mode, The.
We cannot believe for each other.
Duncan. Song of the Borderguard, The.
Dunn. Naturally.
"Dylan." In the Garden.
Need a Woman.
Eberhart. Height of Man, The.
Emerson. I have found a nobler love.
Everson. Narrows of Birth, The.
Fisher. There's a belief to fix. It feels strong.
Ford. Comedy of Belief.
Fox. Letter to Peter Wilkins.
Frost. They Were Welcome to Their Belief.
We vainly wrestle with the blind belief.
Hardy. Graveyard of Dead Creeds, The.
Hartley. Vesper Hymn for Tuesday and June, after the Visit of Henry Wells.
Herrick. To Silvia ("No more my Silvia, do I mean to pray").
Hesketh. Credo.
Hewitt. MacDonnell's Question.

Revenant.
Rome Sunday[,] June 1960.
Hill.   Bidden Guest, The.
Holmes.   Doctor Trustus: Man of Good Will.
Kipling.   Yet at the last, ere our spearmen had found him.
Lawrence.   Belief.
Levine.   Belief.
I Could Believe.
Lowry.   Cap and gown instead of a sweatrag, A.
Rich man, poor man, beggarman, thief.
Where Did That One Go to, 'Erbert.
MacLeish.   America Was Promises.
Melville.   Margrave's Birthnight, The.
Merton.   Je Crois En L'Amour.
Nash.   Seeing Eye to Eye Is Believing.
Neruda.   Dead Dog.
Olson.   I hang on by.
Quatrain: "Do not, at this high time, desert."
Patchen.   Court of First Appeal.
Time to Believe!, A.
Rexroth.   Sword in a Cloud of Light, A.
Rolfe.   Credo.
Rossetti.   Have I not striven, my God, and watched and prayed?
Lord, carry me.—Nay, but I grant thee strength.
Rukeyser.   Lilienthal said : I heard him saying words like these.
This Place in the Ways.
Willkie—Stopless Falling through Air.
Sandburg.   Manufactured Gods.
Who shall speak for the people?
Smith, Stevie.   God the Eater.
Sorrentino.   Maytime.
Stevens.   Well Dressed Man with a Beard, The.
Whittier.   Cypress-Tree of Ceylon, The.
Williams, Miller.   Believing in Symbols.
How Does a Madsong Know That's What It Is?

See also **Faith.**

Bells
Auden.   Autumn Evening.
"Carroll, Lewis."   Acrostic: "Maiden, though thy heart may quail."
Bruno's Song.
Clough.   See! the faint green tinge from the western sky has.
Cohen.   Anthem: "Birds they sang, The."
Crane.   Broken Tower, The.
Cummings.   B / eLl / s? / bE.
De la Mare.   Bells, The.
Dickinson.   How still the Bells in Steeples stand.
When Bells stop ringing—Church—begins.
Emerson.   I love thy music, mellow bell.
Fletcher.   Sea-Sounding Bells.
Hardy.   Chimes, The.
Christmas in the Elgin Room.
Drawing Details in an Old Church.
Peace Peal, The.
Herrick.   Bellman, The.
Hewitt.   Bell, The.
Housman.   Bredon Hill.
When the bells justle in the tower.
Hugo.   No Bells to Believe.
Kipling.   Bell Buoy, The.
Bells and Queen Victoria, The.
Clerks and the Bells, The.
Lawrence.   Bells.
Passing-Bell, A.
Lindsay.   He Climbs the Hill Where the Tree Grows.
He Gives What He Won to the Indian Girl.
He Receives the Bells.
He Starts on the Return Journey.
In Memory of My Friend, Joyce Kilmer, Poet and Soldier.
Lowry.   Duckturne.
Fiesta.
MacLeish.   Signal, The.
Merrill.   Chimes for Yahya.
Neruda.   This Broken Bell.
Olson.   Mind's Notice, The.
Poe.   Bells, The.

Rossetti.   All the bells were ringing / And all the birds were singing.
"Ding a ding," / The sweet bells sing.
Peal of Bells, A.
Toll, bell, toll. For hope is flying / Sighing from the earthbound soul.
Sandburg.   Light and Moonbells.
Night Bells.
When Death Came April Twelve 1945.
Schwartz.   Christmas Poem for Nancy.
Sexton.   Ringing the Bells.
Smith, Stevie.   Fairy Bell, The.
Tomlinson.   Bells: a Period Piece, The.
Walking to Bells.
Turco.   Pocoangelini 5 ("Pocoangelini said").
Whittier.   Red River Voyageur, The.
Skipper Ireson's Ride.
Wilbur.   Bell Speech.
Dubious Night, A.
Williams, William Carlos.   Catholic Bells, The.

Belshazzar
Byron.   Vision of Belshazzar, The.
Stevens.   Country Words.

Ben Bulben, Ireland
Yeats.   Under Ben Bulben.

Beowulf
Turco.   Grendel.
Wilbur.   Beowulf.

Berkeley, George
Davie.   Fountain, The.

Berlin, Germany
Bunting.   Herr Lignitz knows Old Berlin. It is near the Post Office.
Carruth.   August 14, 1961.
Cohen.   First We Take Manhattan.
Mahon.   Postcard from Berlin, A.
Snodgrass.   Dr. Joseph Goebbels, Minister for Propaganda.

Bermuda
Cooper.   Bermuda.
Marvell.   Bermudas.
Merton.   Aubade: Bermuda.

Berrigan, Daniel
Rich.   Burning of Paper instead of Children, The.

Berryman, John
Bishop.   Thank-You Note.
Ciardi.   Trying to Feel Something.
Holmes.   Berryman's Dead.

Bertrand de Born
Pound.   Near Perigord.
Sestina: Altaforte.

Bestiality
Cummings.   In hammamet did camping queers et al).
Dickey, James.   Sheep Child, The.
Dobyns.   Bowlers Anonymous.

Bethlehem
Browning, Elizabeth Barrett.   Virgin Mary to the Child Jesus, The.
Raine.   Star of Bethlehem.
Sandburg.   Star Silver.

Betrayal
Angelou.   Communication I.
Beatles.   Sexy Sadie.
What Goes On?
Berg.   Nothingness.
Bly.   In Mourning for Betrayal.
Brontë.   But the hearts that once adored me.
His land may burst the galling chain.
I'm standing in the forest now.
To A.G.A.
Written in the Gaaldine Prison Caves to A.G.A.
Browning, Elizabeth Barrett.   Romance of the Ganges, A.
Bunting.   Duke Valentine had been in Lombardy with the King.
Burns.   As I was a wand'ring ae midsummer e'enin.
Awa Whigs Awa.
Can You Leave Me Thus, My Katy.
Hughie Graham.
Laddies by the banks o' Nith, The.
Lord Gregory.
Robin Shure in Hairst.

Saw Ye My Phely (Quasi Dicat, Phillis).
Song: "Had I a cave on some wild, distant shore."
Thou hast left me ever, Jamie.
Byron.   Endorsement to the Deed of Separation, in the April of 1816.
Carruth.   Event Itself, The.
Catullus.   Carmen 21: "Impresario of neediness."
Carmen 36: "Volusian sheets / shit-shotten Annals."
Cohen.   Disguises.
Field Commander Cohen.
Paper-Thin Hotel.
Singer Must Die, A.
Traitor, The.
Warning.
Coleridge.   Eros aei lalethros hetairos.
Pitt.
To One Who Published in Print.
Creeley.   Anger.
Places.
Cullen.   Judas Iscariot.
Cummings.   It started when Bill's chip let on to.
Davie.   Black Hoyden.
Dickinson.   That she forgot me was the least.
Dobyns.   Under the Green Ceiling.
"Dylan."   Union Sundown.
Emerson.   Traitors tho' plumed & steel equipped.
Webster.
Gardner.   Man of Faith, The.
Graves.   Above the Edge of Doom.
Golden Anchor.
Horizon.
Impossible, The.
Lamia in Love.
Lost Jewel, A.
Not at Home.
Pardon, The.
Wreath, The.
Hardy.   At Shag's Heath.
Mongrel, The.
Rose-Ann.
Herrick.   Cock-Crow.
Gods Price, and Mans Price.
His Words to Christ, Going to the Cross.
Hesketh.   Scapegoat.
Hewitt.   1957–1972.
Hopkins.   Did Helen steal my love from me?
Hughes, Langston.   Could Be.
Joseph.   Version of the Phoenix Story, A.
Kipling.   Declaration of London, The.
Disciple, The.
Memories.
Song at Cock-Crow, A.
Ulster.
Kunitz.   Next to Last Things.
Lawrence.   Traitors.
Two Wives.
Liddy.   Lesbos.
Lowry.   And yet I am of England too; odi et amo.
Another Immorality.
Hangover—Reading Rilke, Schnitzler or Someone, A.
McAuley.   Nun of St. Michan's, The.
MacLeish.   Woman on the Stair, The.
Marlowe.   2.6: In mortem psittaci.
3.11: Dolet amicam suam ita suis carminibnus innotuisse ut rivales multos sibi pararit.
Meredith.   It chanced his lips did meet her forehead cool.
It ended, and the morrow brought the task.
Love ere he bleeds, an eagle in high skies.
Misery is greater, as I live!, The.
Once the fair Romance of story.
Out in the yellow meadows, where the bee.
She issues radiant from her dressing-room.
She yields: my Lady in her noblest mood.
What may the woman labour to confess?
Yet it was plain she struggled, and that salt.
Merton.   Betrayal, The.
House of Caiphas, The.
Letter to One Who Has Abandoned The Way.
Millay.   My Spirit, Sore from Marching.

Raine. And that was all his life.
Ralegh. Farewell to False Love, A.
Ransom. Winter Remembered.
"Reed." Betrayed.
Rolfe. Letter to the Denouncers, A.
Rossetti. Dying Man to His Betrothed, The.
  Easter Even.
  Two Parted.
Rukeyser. Handclap.
  Sixth Elegy. River Elegy.
Sexton. Legend of the One-Eyed Man, The.
Shakespeare. Lover's Complaint, A.
  Sonnet 41: "Those petty [or pretty] wrongs
    that liberty commits."
Shelley. Love's Rose.
Sorrentino. Waltz of the Empty Roadhouse.
Stevens. Good Man Has No Shape, The.
Swift. Judas.
Wakoski. Recognizing That My Wrists
    Always Have Salmon Leaping for Spring in
    Them.
Whitman. Blood-Money.
Whittier. Ichabod[!].
Williams, Charles Kenneth. Soliliquies.
Wyatt. And if an eye may save or slay.
  Behold, love, thy power how she despiseth!
  But sithens you it assay to kill.
  Defamed guiltiness by silence unkempt.
  How should I / Be so pleasant.
  Longer to trow ye.
  O, cruel heart, where is thy faith?
  Once in your grace I know I was.
  Who would have ever thought.
Zimmer. Worrying About You All the Time.
Zukofsky. *Annals* of Volusius, cock at his
    offal.
  Aurelius, father, assure that the o numb.

Betrothal
Browning, Elizabeth Barrett. Crowned and
    Wedded.
  Rhyme of the Duchess May.
  Romance of the Ganges, A.
Coleridge. Keepsake, The.
Stein. Marry Nettie.

Bible
Auden. Memento Creatoris Tui.
Berryman. Search, The.
Bishop. Over 2000 Illustrations and a
    Complete Concordance.
Blake. Memorable Fancy, A ("Once I saw a
    Devil in a flame of fire").
Cohen. Altar, The.
  Commentary—The Altar.
Cowper. Sonnet to Mrs. Unwin.
Dickinson. Bible is an antique Volume, The.
Donne. Apostles, The.
  Doctors, The.
  Upon the Translation of the Psalms by Sir
    Philip Sidney, and the Countess of Pembroke
    His Sister.
Dryden. Scriptures, The.
Emerson. But never yet the man was found.
  We sauntered amidst miracles.
Fletcher. On My Father's Hundredth Birthday.
Graves. After the Flood.
Hall. Maundy Thursday's Candles.
Hardy. After Reading Psalms XXXIX, XL,
    etc.
  Respectable Burgher, The.
Heaney. Other Side, The.
Herbert. Holy Scriptures (1), The.
  Holy Scriptures (2), The.
  Thanksgiving, The.
Herrick. His Wish to God.
  Lip Labour.
  Montes Scripturarum, the Mounts of the
    Scriptures.
Hewitt. Evangelist.
  Free Mason.
  Going to Church.
  Grim Dean, who sleeps within his pulpit's
    shade.
  In the Lenin Library, Dushanbe.
  Our Sunday School Teacher.
  When my wife's sister's husband came to die.
Knight. Genesis 11.
Knott. My Mother's List of Names.

Liddy. To the Memory of Bernard Berenson.
Lowry. Search, The.
Mahon. Ecclesiastes.
Merrill. Salome.
Nemerov. Book of Kells, The.
Olson. In the Hills South of Capernaum, Port.
Raine. My day's plan to write.
Sandburg. Methusaleh Saw Many Repeaters.
  Scripture.
Sarton. Jonah.
Shelton. In the Beginning Was the Word.
Simic. Begotten of the Spleen.
  Concerning My Neighbors, the Hittites.
Smart. Jubilate Agno.
  Song to David, A.
  Taste.
Smith, Stevie. Magnificent Words.
Walcott. Long, white, summer cloud, like a
    cleared linen table, A.
Wilbur. Lot's Wife.
  Matthew VIII, 28 ff.
  Peter.
  Simplification, A.
Williams, Miller. Why God Permits Evil: For
    Answers to This Question of Interest to
    Many Write Bible Answers Dept. E-7.

Bicycles and Bicycling
Berryman. It was the sky all day I grew to
    and saw.
MacNeice. Cyclist, The.
Mahon. Bicycle, The.
Piercy. Cyclist, The.
Williams, Charles Kenneth. World's Greatest
    Tricycle-Rider, The.

Bigamy and Bigamists
Hardy. Wife and Another, A.

Billboards
Larkin. Sunny Prestatyn.
Lindsay. Buzzing autos, like black bees.
Nash. Song of the Open Road.

Billiards
Betjeman. Clash went the Billiard Balls.
Cummings. Newly / cued / motif smites truly
    to beautifully.
  Surely / Cued / motif smites truly to
    Beautifully, The.
Lieberman. Queen of the Billiards.
Robinson. Doctor of Billiards.

"Billy the Kid" (William H. Bonney)
"Dylan." Billy.

Biography
Auden. Change of Air, A.
Cooper. Long View from the Suburbs.
Creeley. I.
Dickinson. Biography first convinces us.
  Like a Memoir of the Sun.
Larkin. Posterity.
Sandburg. Biography.
Snodgrass. Manet: "The Execution of the
    Emperor Maximilian."
Whitman. When I Read the Book.
Williams, William Carlos. Visit, The.

Birch Trees
Carruth. Five / jays / discuss / goodandevil.
  Meadow House.
  Trees, The.
  Under the hill a winter twilight.
Frost. Birches.
  Pea Brush.
  Young Birch, A.
Hardy. Upper Birch-Leaves, The.
Lewis. Poet, The.
Meinke. Robert Frost in Warsaw.
Schuyler. 8/12/70.
Sutter. Why Birch Trees Are White.
Wilbur. Black Birch in Winter, A.
Williams, William Carlos. Portrait of the
    Author.

Birds
Ammons. After Yesterday.
  Glass Speciality.
  Mirrorment.
  Squall Ball.
Auden. At last, down in the lane.
  Bird-Language.
  Decoys, The.
  Sower, The.

Berg. It Is.
Berry. Architecture, An.
  Bird Killer, The.
  For the Future.
  Hidden Singer, The.
  Outside the window.
  Still sleeping, he heard.
  There is a sort of vertical.
  Wild, The.
Bishop. Five Flights Up.
  Love is feathered like a bird.
  Rain Towards Morning.
  Some Dreams They Forgot.
Blake. Birds, The.
Bly. Loon's Cry, The.
Bogan. Statue and Birds.
Boyle. Dialogue of Birds for Howard
    Nemerov, A.
  Dreams Dreamed.
  Only Bird That Sang, The.
  Two Twilights for William Carlos Williams.
Brontë. Redbreast, Early in the morning.
Brooks. Light and diplomatic bird, A.
Browning, Elizabeth Barrett. Deserted Garden,
    The.
  Island, An.
  Man and Nature.
Browning, Robert. In the Doorway.
Bukowski. Singing Is Fire.
Burns. Hunting Song.
  On Scaring Some Waterfowl in Loch Turit, a
    Wild Scene among the Hills of Oughtertyre.
  Phillis the Fair.
Carroll, Jim. Wing and Claw.
"Carroll, Lewis." Lang Coortin', The.
Carruth. Birds of Vietnam, The.
  Imagine bird bones.
  In filthy Puerto Rico lives a bird with no.
  Small things / hardest to believe.
  Wild Swans at Norfolk, The.
  Wind in the pines, a dark, damp, Novemb'ring
    wind.
Catullus. Carmen 2: "Lesbia's sparrow! /
    Lesbia's plaything!"
Chaucer. Dream, The.
Ciardi. Bird in Whatever Name, The.
  Birds, Like Thoughts.
  No White Bird Sings.
  Size of Song, The.
Clark. Birds.
Cohen. Anthem: "Birds they sang, The."
  I Like the Way You Opposed Me.
Coleridge. Answer to a Child's Question.
  Song: "Sunny shaft did I behold, A."
Cooper. Morning on the St. John's.
Cowper. Faithful Friend, The.
  On Mrs. Montagu's Feather-Hangings.
  Pairing Time Anticipated.
  Tale, A: "In Scotland's realm, where trees are
    few."
Creeley. Bird, The.
  Birds, The.
  Chanson.
  3 in 1.
Cummings. At just 5 a / m i hear eng.
  Birds(/ here,inven / ting air).
  Birds meet above the new Moon.
  For any ruffian of the sky.
  Hills chime with thrush.
  May my heart always be open to little.
  Nine birds(rising / through a gold
    moment)climb.
  Now(more near ourselves than we).
  SNOW / cru / is / ingw Hi.
  Swi(/ across!gold's / rouNdly.
  Until and i heard.
  Without the mercy of / your eyes your.
Davie. Screech-Owl.
De la Mare. Dawn.
  Estranged.
  Martins: September.
  Riddlers, The.
  Rooks In October.
  Speech.
  Thomas Hardy.
  Titmouse.
  Who?

Dickey, James. Owl King, The.
Reincarnation (II).
Three, The.
Dickinson. Before you thought of Spring.
Bird came down the Walk, A.
Bird her punctual music brings, The.
Bird must sing to earn the Crumb, The.
Birds are very bold this Morning, The.
Birds begun at Four o'clock, The.
Birds reported from the South, The.
For every Bird a Nest.
High from the earth I heard a bird.
His Bill an Auger is.
His Bill is clasped—his Eye forsook.
I have a Bird in spring.
I have seen one Bird and part of another.
Lady feeds Her little Bird, The.
Mama never forgets her birds.
Most triumphant Bird I ever knew or met,
The.
No ladder needs the bird but skies.
Of Being is a Bird.
Ones that disappeared are back, The.
Out of sight? What of that?
Saddest noise, the sweetest noise, The.
She sights a Bird—she chuckles.
Upon his Saddle sprung a Bird.
Dobyns. Song for Making the Birds Come.
Doolittle. Birds in Snow.
Dunbar. Crumb, a Crumb, and a Little Seed,
A.
Oh little fledgling out of the nest.
Preparation.
Sympathy.
Two Songs.
Dunn. As It Moves.
Nova Scotia.
Walking the Marshland.
Eberhart. By the Stream.
Evening Bird Song.
Go to the Shine That's on a Tree.
I Walked Out to the Graveyard to See the
Dead.
Incidence of Flight.
Learning from Nature.
Now Is the Air Made of Chiming Balls.
Old Tom.
Opulence.
Thrush Song at Dawn.
Truncated Bird, The.
Ultimate Song.
Young Hunter, The.
Emerson. As I walked in the woods.
From "Bird Conversations."
If bright the sun, he tarries.
May.
Miracle, The.
Everson. Canticle to the Waterbirds, A.
Fenton. Sweden. Lapp. Pouch made from a
blackthroated diver.
Ferlinghetti. General Song of Humanity, The.
He with the Beating Wings.
L'Occupation Obsédée.
Fisher. Dawn birds at noon.
Fletcher. Sailboats.
Ford. Chakora bird / Like a partridge. It is
said, The.
Do birds need to fly so much.
Fox. Beasts Have Entered, The.
Hands.
Offering.
Ornithology.
Frost. Exposed Nest, The.
Looking for a Sunset Bird in Winter.
Minor Bird, A.
Never Again Would Birds' Song Be the Same.
On a Bird Singing in its Sleep.
Oven Bird, The.
Gallagher. Bird-Window-Flying.
Candle, Lamp & Firefly.
Some Painful Butterflies Pass Through.
Unsteady Yellow.
Galvin. Chickadee.
Grackles, The.
Willow, Wishbone, Warblers.
Gardner. Roundelay: "Blood-red bird with one

green eye, A."
Southwest of True North.
Garrigue. Address to the Migrations.
Ginsberg. Very Dove, A.
Graves. Ambience.
P'eng That Was a K'un, The.
Gray. Couplet about Birds.
Gunn. On the Move.
Haines. House of the Injured, The.
Victims.
Hall. "Internal and External Forms."
Hardy. Bird-Catcher's Boy, The.
Bird-Scene at a Rural Dwelling, A.
Blinded Bird, The.
Boy's Dream, The.
Puzzled Game-Birds, The.
Selfsame Song, The.
Yellow-Hammer, The.
Hartley. Flight, The.
If We Could.
Sestets.
Hartnett. I Have Exhausted the Delighted
Range.
Heaney. Drifting Off.
First Flight, The.
Oracle.
Hemingway. Bird of Night.
Herrick. To His Maid Prew.
Hesketh. How to Do It.
St. Luke's Summer.
Survival.
Hewitt. Country Walk in March, A.
Erice, Western Sicily.
First Snow in the Glens.
For R.
July.
Late Spring.
Lettered Snow, The.
March Day.
Note on Intellectuals.
Sap in the Sticks Again.
Sparrowhawk.
Hoffman. In the Pitch of Night.
Hopkins. As kingfishers catch fire, dragonflies
draw flame.
Windhover, The.
Hughes, Ted. Crow and the Birds.
Curlews Lift.
Heptonstall Cemetery.
Swift Comes the Swift, The.
Swifts.
Hugo. Beachthieves.
Colors of a Bird, The.
Cripples, The.
Duwamish No. 2.
Orcas in the Eyes.
Resulting from Magnetic Interference.
Triangle for Green Men.
Jarrell. Country Life, A.
Loss.
Mockingbird, The.
Jeffers. Birds.
Birds and Fishes.
Winged Rock.
Joseph. Muse.
Patient old cripple, A.
Version of the Phoenix Story, A.
Kinnell. Gray Heron, The.
Last Songs.
Kipling. Darzee's Chaunt.
Knott. Widower's Winter.
Kooser. New Year's Day.
Lawrence. Blue Jay, The.
Living, A.
Many Mansions.
Sigh No More.
Levertov. Claritas.
Stems.
Levine. Red Dust.
Liddy. Cormorants / By the pollock holes
diving.
Hesperian evenings certainly.
Voyage to Cytherea, A.
Lieberman. Corners.
Longfellow. Poet's Tale: The Birds of
Killingworth, The.

Lorde. Ballad from Childhood.
Trip on the Staten Island Ferry, A.
Lovelace. Falcon, The.
Lowry. And now the seagulls feed on the
front porch.
Au clair de la lune.
Billetin.
Bird in the Tree, The.
Contemplation of Dead Reckoning.
Fiesta.
Fragments from the Duck Anthology to Greet
Our Beloved Harteebeeste in the Morning
Watch.
Happiest of Hartebeeste Days and Devoted
Love Eterne.
Lyrical Morning Poem.
Marathon of gulls / a chiming of chickadees,
A.
Morning bird is bathing, The.
Morning rain is raining / A morning pain is
paining, The.
Morning Song for the Harteebeeste.
New Guinea Gardener Bird, The.
Oh love / Oh Shame, we are late.
Reveille.
Singing. / The morning bird. / (Humphum!).
Sweet Good Night Poem to Our Beloved
Hartebeeste from All the Little Animals.
With Sweetest Morning Love to Their Beloved
Harteebeeste.
McAuley. Making Repairs.
"MacDiarmid." Caledonian Antisyzygy, The.
Ex Vermibus.
Glen of Silence, The.
On a Raised Beach.
McGrath. Face of the Precipice is Black with
Lovers, The.
Inheritance, The.
MacLeish. Critics on the Lawn.
Voyage en Provence.
MacNeice. Canto XV: "Been here before?
Whether he has or no."
Corncrakes.
On the Venerable Bede.
McNeill. Backward Flight.
Markson. At Malcolm Lowry's Grave.
Marlowe. 2.6: In mortem psittaci.
Meinke. Indigo Buntings.
Plovers.
Meredith. July.
Night of Frost in May.
Pastoral 5: "Now from the meadow floods the
wild duck clamours."
Song: "Quick bird sings and pierces me, The."
Song: "Under boughs of breathing May."
Song: The Wren.
South-Wester, The.
Two Blackbirds, The.
We saw the swallows gathering in the sky.
Merton. Autumn.
Silver bird is E backward in cool pond water,
The.
Symphony for a Sea Bird.
Millay. Black hair you'd say she had, or
rather.
Bobolink, The.
Pigeons, The.
Sky-coloured bird, blue wings with no more
spots of spotless white.
Milton. Meanwhile the tepid caves and fens
and shores.
Moore. Bird-witted.
Smooth Gnarled Crape Myrtle.
To a Prize Bird.
To the Peacock of France.
Morgan. Poem of the Self.
Muldoon. Elizabeth.
Nash. Birdies, Don't Make Me Laugh.
Birds, The.
Grackle, The.
Toucan, The.
Up from the Egg; the Confessions of a
Nuthatch Avoider.
Nathan. Holding Pattern.
Mocking Bird Song.
Nemerov. Distances They Keep, The.

Neruda. Bird.
Do you hear yellow detonations.
Oliver. Rabbit, The.
Olson. Grinning monster out side the system.
Round & a Canon, A.
Small Birds, to Agree with the Leaves, Come in the Fall.
Variations Done for Gerald Van de Wiele.
Oppen. From a Phrase of Simone Weil's and Some Words of Hegel's.
Undertaking in New Jersey, The.
Workman.
Pack. Thrasher in the Willow by the Lake, The.
Paley. For George (II).
Patchen. Bird-Queen, The.
Great Birds, The.
O the sledbirds rides over the willow.
Poor Gorrel.
Piercy. Crippling, The.
Plath. Goatsucker.
Poe. Romance.
Prince. He Bathes in the Morning.
Raine. Lapwing's wavering flight, The.
London air dims.
My day's plan to write.
Ransom. Lady Lost.
Somewhere Is Such a Kingdom.
Rich. Return of the Evening Grosbeaks, The.
Roethke. All Morning.
Kitty-Cat Bird, The.
Reply, The.
Siskins, The.
Tree, the Bird, The.
Young Girl, The.
Rolfe. Hunter Went Killing: A Fable, A.
Rossetti. All the bells were ringing / And all the birds were singing.
Another Spring.
Bird Song, A.
Child's Talk in April.
1885. St. Valentine's Day.
Freaks of Fashion.
Gone for Ever.
Green Cornfield, A.
If the sun could tell us half / That he hears and sees.
Mirrors of Life and Death.
Paradise: in a Symbol.
Rushes in a watery place, / And reeds in a hollow.
Summer nights are short, / Where northern days are long, The.
When a mounting skylark sings / In the sunlit summer morn.
White hen sitting / On white eggs three, A.
Sandburg. Among the shapes and shadow-shapes.
Bird Footprint.
Bird Talk.
Cheap Rent.
Little Word, Little White Bird.
Margaret.
Outstraw green turns gold turns ashen and, The.
River Roads.
Sandhill People.
Santa Fe Sketches.
Spring Cries.
Three Spring Notations on Bipeds.
Wingtip.
Sarton. Caged Bird, The.
Franz, a Goose.
Parrot, A.
Phoenix, The.
Swans, The.
Schuyler. In Wiry Winter.
Schwartz. Poem: "In the morning, when it was raining."
Sexton. Torn Down from Glory Daily.
What the Bird with the Human Head Knew.
Shelley. Fragment: Omens.
Silverstein. Early Bird.
Toucan, The.
Smith, Charlotte. Dictatorial Owl, The.
Evening Walk by the Sea-Side, An.
Jay in Masquerade, The.

Supposed To Have Been Written in America.
Wheat-Ear, The.
Ye vales and woods! fair scenes of happier hours.
Smith, Stevie. Avondall.
British Song, A.
Hippy-Mo.
Sallow Bird, The.
Snodgrass. Charges Against Cock Robin, The.
D.D. Byrde Callyng Jennie Wrenn.
Elm Tree, An.
Examination, The.
Papageno.
Phoebe's Nest, A.
W. D. Attempts to Save Cock Robin.
Snyder. This Poem Is for Birds.
Sorrentino. Who Goes There?
Spender. Boy, Cat, Canary.
Spenser. Then heavenly branches did I see arise.
Upon an hill a bright flame I did see.
Stafford. Troubleshooting.
Stevens. On an Old Horn.
Somnambulisma.
Stevenson. As in their flight the birds of song.
Nest Eggs.
Time to Rise.
To Ottilie.
Stuart. Ballad of the Scarecrow, The.
Ballad of the Three Birds.
Love's Body.
Thomas. Over Sir John's Hill.
Spire Cranes, The.
Tomlinson. Encounter.
In the Estuary.
Translating the Birds.
Updike. Each Summer's Swallows.
Great Scarf of Birds, The.
Mobile of Birds.
Upon Learning That a Bird Exists Called the Turnstone.
Van Duyn. Letters from a Father.
Wakoski. Elizabeth and the Golden Oranges.
Few Silver Scales, The.
Removed from Natural Habitat.
Walcott. Flock, The.
Season of Phantasmal Peace, The.
Warren. Love and Knowledge.
Patriotic Tour and Postulate of Joy.
Whitman. Of That Blithe Throat of Thine.
To the Man-of-War Bird.
Wilbur. All These Birds.
Event, An.
From the Lookout Rock.
Games Two.
In a Bird Sanctuary.
Marché aux Oiseaux.
Sketch, A.
Still, Citizen Sparrow.
Williams, Charles Kenneth. That the world / is going.
Williams, William Carlos. Bird.
Bird's Companion, The.
Birdsong, The.
Breakfast.
Passer Domesticus.
Struggle of Wings.
To Waken an Old Lady.
Unknown, The.
Wanderer: A Rococo Study, The.
Wordsworth. Contrast; the Parrot and the Wren, The.
In the Woods of Rydal.
Incipient Madness.
June, 1820.
Morning Exercise, A.
Redbreast, The [Suggested in a Westmoreland Cottage].
Reverie of Poor Susan, The.
Sailor's Mother, The.
Suggested by a Picture of the Bird of Paradise.
Upon seeing a Coloured Drawing of the Bird of Paradise in an Album.
Water Fowl.
Wren's Nest, A.
Wright, James. Little Girl on Her Way to

School, A.
Presentation of Two Birds to My Son, A.
RIP.
Summer Memory in the Crowded City, A.
Yeats. White Birds, The.
Zukofsky. For Zadkine.
Gulls over a rotting hull.
Perch Less.
Sparrow, my girl's pleasure, delight of my girl.
See also **Waterfowl; Listings for specific Birds.**

Birds' Nests
Cummings. I / never / guessed any / thing(even a).
Heaney. Nesting-Ground.
Wilbur. Lightness.
Williams, Charles Kenneth. That the world / is going.
Wordsworth. Wren's Nest, A.

Birds of Paradise
Graves. Bird of Paradise.
Lovelace. Lucasta's Fan[ne], with a Looking-Glass[e] in It.
Wakoski. Birds of Paradise Being Very Plain Birds, The.
Wordsworth. Suggested by a Picture of the Bird of Paradise.

Bird-watching
Berry. Outside the window.
There is a sort of vertical.
Eberhart. Snowy Owl.
Galvin. Whirl Is King.
Kinnell. Gray Heron, The.
Mahon. Man and Bird.
Nash. Up from the Egg; the Confessions of a Nuthatch Avoider.
Schuyler. In Wiry Winter.
Van Duyn. Letters from a Father.

Birmingham, Alabama
Merton. And the Children of Birmingham.
Picture of a Black Child with a White Doll.

Birmingham, England
Lowry. Letter from Oaxaca to North Africa 1936.
MacNeice. Birmingham.

Birth
Arnold. In Utrumque Paratus.
Auden. Crocus stars the border, The.
Beckett. Chaque jour envie.
Sanies I.
Berry. Birth (Near Port William), The.
Her First Calf.
Bishop. All the heaven and earth.
Bly. December 23, 1926.
Bradstreet. Before the Birth of One of Her Children.
Byron. On the Birth of John William Rizzo Hoppner.
Carroll, Jim. I am trying to abide by the clues.
Carruth. His dream: / He is dressed in a white sheet, riding.
Cooper. For a Boy Born in Wartime.
Cowper. On Hermocratia.
Crashaw. Upon the birth of the Princesse Elizabeth.
Cummings. And i imagine.
Little horse is newlY, The.
Pity his how illimitable plight.
De la Mare. Birthnight: To F., The.
Of a Son.
Dickey, James. Daughter.
For a Time and Place.
Dobyns. Birth Report.
Dove. Variation on Guilt.
Dunn. For Fathers of Girls.
Waiting with Two Members of a Motorcycle Gang for My Child to Be Born.
Eberhart. Return of Odysseus, The.
Emerson. What from this barren being do we reap.
Everson. Out of the Ash.
Ferlinghetti. True Confessional.
Fisher. Poem to Be Watched, A.
Ford. Baby on the way!
Glück. Garden, The.

Graves. Name.
Song of Blodeuwedd, The.
Woman of Greece.
Gunn. Being Born.
Hacker. Christmas Crown, A.
Haines. I keep a fire and tell a story.
Hardy. Life and Death at Sunrise.
To an Unborn Pauper Child.
Unborn, The.
Herrick. Epitaph upon a Sober Matron, An.
Upon a Lady That Dyed in Child-Bed, and
Left a Daughter behind Her.
Upon Batt.
Hesketh. Boy Drowning.
First Day, The.
I Give Death to a Son.
Hewitt. Doctor Muses, The.
Doctor's Bag, The.
Hughes, Langston. S-sss-ss-sh!
Hughes, Ted. Birth of Rainbow.
February 17th.
Jeffers. Birthday (Autobiography).
Jong. Birth of the Water Baby, The.
Demeter at Dusk.
Nursing You.
Jonson. Epigram on the Prince's Birth. 1630,
An.
Epigram to the Queen, Then Lying In. 1630,
An.
Kipling. Nursing Sister, The.
Knight. On the Birth of a Black / Baby / Boy.
Stretching of the Belly, The.
Knott. Closet, The.
Larkin. This Was Your Place of Birth, This
Daytime Palace.
Lawrence. God Is Born.
Levine. Let Me Be.
Lieberman. 82 X 48.
Lindsay. Star of My Heart.
Lorde. And What About the Children.
Now That I Am Forever with Child.
Lovelace. Elegie. Princesse Katherine, An.
Lowry. El Leon Sends His Greetings.
For Nordahl Grieg Ship's Fireman.
From This Acceptance, Sir, We Might
Proceed.
Marina—.
"MacDiarmid." Lo! A Child Is Born.
MacLeish. Carrion Spring, The.
Morrison. It Has Been Said.
Muldoon. Mules.
Oliver. Meeting, A.
Olson. Epigon.
Ferrini—I.
La Chute III.
Ode on Nativity, An.
Ring of, The.
Sin is inferiority. The mother's cooperation in
the birth of her daughter.
Translation, A.
Oppen. Eclogue: "Men talking / Near the
room's center. They have said, The."
There can be a brick.
Pack. Clayfeld Prunes His Apple Trees.
Patchen. After an Old Song.
Piercy. Provocation of the Dream, The.
Raine. At the day's end I found.
Ransom. Of Margaret ("Frost, and a leaf has
quit the tulip tree").
Of Margaret ("With the fall of the first leaf
that winds rend").
Rich. There Are Such Springlike Nights.
Rolfe. Song for a Birth Day in Exile.
Rossetti. Before the Paling of the Stars.
Blind from my birth, / Where flowers are
springing.
Christmas Eve.
Death.
Everything that is born must die.
Hymn for Christmas Day, A.
Purification of St. Mary the Virgin, The.
To Mary Rossetti.
Rukeyser. Are You Born? / I.
Are You Born? / II.
Ballad Theme, A.
Birth, A.

Unborn Song.
Woman and Emblems.
Sandburg. Between Worlds.
Chicks.
Ever a Seeker.
Fog Numbers.
Harsk, Harsk.
I was born in the morning of the world.
Jan Kubelik.
Marshall Field the First was spick and span
while alive.
Sacred legion of the justborn, The.
Special Starlight.
Striped Cats, Old Men and Proud Stockings.
Shapiro. Recognition of Eve, The.
Shelley. Fragment: Life Rounded with Sleep.
Snodgrass. Through the Nursery Window.
Spender. Grandparents.
Stevens. Ghosts as Cocoons.
Stevenson. Nest Eggs.
To Miss Cornish.
Stuart. Killdeer.
Thomas. In the Beginning.
Vision and Prayer.
Thomson. To His Royal Highness the Prince
of Wales.
Updike. Amoeba.
Van Duyn. Paratrooper.
To My Godson, on His Christening.
Waldman. Number Song.
Warren. Brotherhood in Pain.
Vital Statistics.
Williams, Charles Kenneth. They wash you /
when.
Williams, Miller. For Lucy, on Her Birthday.
People.
Williams, William Carlos. Birth, The.
Catastrophic Birth.
Wordsworth. To — Upon the Birth of Her
First-Born Child, March, 1833.
Yeats. Consolation.
Stick of Incense, A.

Birth Control
Jonson. To Fine Lady Would-Be.
Matthews. Vasectomy.
Pack. Trying to Reconcile.
See also **Abortion.**

Birth Defects
Muldoon. Blemish.
Williams, Miller. Ones that Are Thrown Out,
The.

Birthdays
Angelou. On Reaching Forty.
Auden. Many Happy Returns.
Beatles. Birthday.
Berrigan. 44th Birthday Evening, at Harris's.
Something Amazing Just Happened.
Boyle. Poem for Arthur, A.
Bukowski. Poem for My 43rd Birthday.
Burns. Impomptu, on Mrs. W. Riddell's
Birthday, 4th Novr. 1793.
To Terraughty, on His Birth-Day.
Byron. On This Day I Complete My Thirty-
sixth Year.
Through Life's Dull Road, So Dim and Dirty.
Carroll, Jim. For Sue's Birthday.
I hope that George enjoys the gifts.
Poem on My Son's Birthday.
Ron Padgett is holding two birthday gifts.
Carruth. Tanck's Song About His Birthday.
Ciardi. Birthday.
Cowper. To Miss Creuzé.
Cummings. Your birthday comes to tell me
this.
De la Mare. Lucy.
Dickinson. Birthday of but a single pang.
One Year ago—jots what?
Eberhart. To Auden on His Fiftieth.
Ginsberg. To P.O.
Gunn. Lines for My 55th Birthday.
Hacker. Iva's Birthday Poem.
Hall. On Reaching the Age of Two Hundred.
Hemingway. Lines to a Girl 5 Days After Her
21st Birthday.
Hesketh. Party, The.
Hopkins. Complaint, A.
Jeffers. Birthday.

Johnson. Short Song of Congratulation [*or* To
a Young Heir], A.
To Mrs Thrale [on Her Thirty-fifth Birthday].
Jonson. Ode, or Song, by All the Muses, An.
Ode. To Sir William Sydney, on His Birthday.
Knight. Birthday Poem.
Larkin. Dear CHARLES, My Muse, Asleep or
Dead.
Lawrence. Birthday.
Lorde. Birthday Memorial to Seventh Street,
A.
Lowry. Happy birthday to you.
MacNeice. Turn again, Whittington. Riding
the surf.
Markson. Tardy Poet: 1978.
Meinke. 50 on 50.
Merrill. Ouzo for Robin.
Merton. We wake up with guns going off.
Nash. Birthday on the Beach.
Lady Thinks She Is Thirty, A.
Lines to Be Scribbled on Somebody Else's
Thirtieth Milestone.
Not George Washington's, Not Abraham
Lincoln's, but Mine.
Party, The.
O'Hara. John Button Birthday.
Poem: "Now it is the 27th."
Patchen. What Splendid Birthdays.
Plath. Birthday Present, A.
Pope. To Mr. Thomas Southern, on His Birth-
Day, 1742.
To Mrs. M. B. on Her Birth-Day.
Rossetti. Birthday, A.
To My Mother on Her Birthday.
Rukeyser. Rondel: "Now that I am fifty-six."
Voices of Waking.
Schuyler. November.
Smith, Patti. 16 February.
Sorrentino. Do you know that sad journey is
lifted from your darling's heart?
My hated birthday looms. In the rude and
wretched country.
Toward the End of Winter.
Stein. Birthday Book, A.
Stevenson. From Wishing-Land.
To Miss Cornish.
Stuart. Birthday.
Swift. Bec's Birthday.
On Stella's Birthday, 1718/1719.
Stella's Birthday (1725).
Stella's Birthday (1723).
Stella's Birthday; Written in the Year 1720–
21.
Stella's Birthday ([March 13,] 1727).
To Stella on Her Birthday, Written AD 1721–
2.
Thomas. Poem in October.
Poem on His Birthday.
Van Duyn. Birthday Card for a Psychiatrist.
Sestina for Warm Seasons.
Whitman. For Queen Victoria's Birthday.
Whittier. My Birthday.
To Oliver Wendell Holmes.
Wilbur. For K. R. on Her Sixtieth Birthday.
Williams, Charles Kenneth. Saturday.
Williams, William Carlos. Trala Trala Trala
La-le-la.
Turkey in the Straw.
Zimmer. Driving North from Savannah on My
Birthday.
Zukofsky. In the midst of things.

Birthmarks
Wright, James. Accusation, The.

Birthplaces
Berry. I sit in the shade of the trees of the
land I was born in.
Coleridge. Tell's Birth-Place.
Frost. Birthplace, The.
Hardy. Domicilium.
Hewitt. Glittering Sod, The.
Hughes, Langston. New Yorkers.
Levine. I Was Born in Lucerne.
Williams, Charles Kenneth. Most excruciating
/ thing, The.

Bismarck, Otto von
Hill. There is an ancient landscape of green
branches.

Bison. *see* **Buffaloes.**

Bitterness
Atwood. Beauharnois.
Auden. His care-free swagger was a fine invention.
Stark bewölkt.
We Too Had Known Golden Hours.
Beatles. Not a Second Time.
You Won't See Me.
Berryman. I owe you, do I not, a roofer: though.
Ménage à trois, like Tristan's,—difficult.
"Ring us up when you want to see us."— "Sure."
Bukowski. Blackbirds Are Rough Today, The.
Day I Kicked Away a Bankroll, The.
Empire of Coins, An.
I Am with the Roots of Flowers.
I Wait in the White Rain.
Man with the Hot Nose, The.
Mercy, Wherever You Are, Come Running in to Me and Grab Me in Your Good Arms—.
Minor Impulse to Complain, A.
O, We are the Outcasts.
One Hundred and Ninety-Nine Pounds of Clay Leaning Forward.
Practice.
Regard Me.
Bunting. You, with my enemy, strolling down my street.
Carew. In the Person of a Lady To Her Inconstant Servant.
Lover, in the Disguise of an Amazon, Is Dearly Beloved of His Mistress, A.
To Celia, upon Love's Ubiquity.
To Her Again, She Burning in a Fever.
To My Inconstant Mistress [or Mistris].
Carruth. Of course make love not.
Clark. I'm on an Island.
Davie. Artifex in Extremis.
De la Mare. They Told Me.
Donne. Julia.
Doolittle. Eros.
Red Roses for Bronze.
Dove. Definition in the Face of Unnamed Fury.
Dunbar. Then and Now.
"Dylan." All Over You.
Down in the Flood.
Quit Your Low Down Ways.
Shot of Love.
Eberhart. Hill Dream of Youth, Thirty Years Later.
Eliot. Lines for an Old Man.
Ford. There's No Place to Sleep in This Bed, Tanguy.
Graves. Laureate, The.
Hacker. "That was in another country," but the wench.
Haines. Deserted Cabin.
Hardy. He Abjures Love.
Old Excursions.
Torn Letter, The.
Hartnett. Small Farm, A.
Hemingway. Portrait of a Lady.
Herrick. Another on Love ("Love's of it self, too sweet").
To M. Laurence Swetnaham.
Hewitt. Breastplate.
Holmes. Decline of the West.
Statements in a Personal Winter.
Hughes, Ted. Her Husband.
Hugo. Leaving the Dream.
Maratea Porto: The Bitter Man.
Jong. Blood & Honey.
Joseph. If you can't join them beat them.
Modern witches 1: crouching.
Modern witches 2: sentinels.
Keats. All Gentle Folks Who Owe a Grudge.
Kinnell. Meditation Among the Tombs.
Kooser. Old Photograph, An.
Widow, A.
Kunitz. Thief, The.
Lawrence. Grudge of the Old, The.
Monologue of a Mother.
Lewis. They have clipped the wings of my doves, my messengers.

Lorde. American Cancer Society Or There Is More Than One Way to Skin a Coon.
And Don't Think I Won't Be Waiting.
Cables To Rage Or I've Been Talking On This Street Corner..
Conversations in Crisis.
New York City.
Spring People.
Who Said It Was Simple.
MacNeice. Il Piccolo Rifiuto.
Markson. Daily Reviewer-Haupt.
Memo to His Lady's Therapist.
On Being Denied for Being Already Took.
Marlowe. 1.12: Tabellas quas miserat execratur, quod amica noctem negabat.
Meredith. Distraction is the panacea, Sir!
Merton. Whether There Is Enjoyment in Bitterness.
Miller. End of the Negotiable Beggar Bond Banquet, The.
Morgan. We took a room at the Westbury.
Morrison. I Fucked the Dregs.
L'America.
Oliver. Bitterness, A.
Certain Sharpness in the Morning Air, A.
Patchen. Letter to the Old Men.
Piercy. Crippling, The.
Letter to be Disguised as a Gas Bill.
Poe. To ———: "I heed not that my earthly lot."
Raine. Columbines.
Rolfe. Definition.
Rossetti. So I began my walk of life; no stop.
Spring is come again not as at first.
Shelton. November 1st.
Smith, Stevie. I'll Have Your Heart.
In the Night.
Lightly Bound.
Mother.
Night Thoughts.
Smile, The.
Snodgrass. Diplomacy: The Father.
Sorrentino. Address to the National Council on the Arts.
Fixture, A.
Poet Tires of Those Who Disparage His City, The.
Silk Ascot for the Terrorist, A.
Some hawk-nosed man.
Something plus something else is not one thing.
Stinking city full of stinking, A.
That you allow yourself this vast neglect of me.
Who Goes There?
Stevenson. O now, although the year be done.
Rain is over and done, The.
Tennyson. My Day.
Turco. Jonathan Hawkins.
Williams, Charles Kenneth. Flat.
Herakles.
Kin.
Philadelphia: 1978.
Yeats. Her Vision in the Wood.

Black (color)
Coleridge. Ne Plus Ultra.
Creeley. Lady in Black.
Donne. Oh my black[e] soul[e]! now thou art summoned.
Graves. Black.
Knott. Goodbye.
Levertov. Wings, The.
Lowry. Lament—June 1944.
Sandburg. Sweeping Wendy: Study in Fugue.
Sidney. Sonnet 7: "When Nature made her chief work, Stella's eyes."
Sorrentino. Who Goes There?
Walcott. Goats and Monkeys.

Black Power. *see* **African-American Power.**

Blackberries
Heaney. Blackberry-Picking.
Kinnell. Blackberry Eating.
Oliver. August.
Plath. Blackberrying.

Blackbirds
Ammons. Bay Bank.
Beatles. Blackbird.

Emerson. Blackbird's song the blackbird's song, The.
Everson. Dusk, The.
Winter Ploughing.
Hardy. I Watched a Blackbird.
Hesketh. At Four A.M.
Dead Blackbird.
Hewitt. Black and White.
Knight. Vigo County.
Liddy. June 16, 1992.
Mahon. Blackbird, The.
Raine. Frost-rime edges blades of grass.
Stevens. Thirteen Ways of Looking at a Blackbird.
Williams, Charles Kenneth. Greed.
Williams, William Carlos. Birds, The.
Red-Wing Blackbird, The.

Blackouts
Dickey, James. Ice Skin, The.

Blacks. *see* **African Americans.**

Blacksmiths
Burns. To Mr. John Taylor.
Everson. Cutting the Firebreak.
Graves. Red Shower, The.
Hopkins. Felix Randal.
Lindsay. North Star Whispers to the Blacksmith's Son, The.
Longfellow. Village Blacksmith, The.

Blake, William
Auden. Contra Blake.
Self-educated WILLIAM BLAKE.
Dunn. Eggs.
Emptiness.
Fisher. Elohim Creating Adam, The.
Ginsberg. Psalm IV.
Hewitt. Rhyme for Blake, A.
Lawrence. Dark Satanic Mills.
Levine. My Poets.
Liddy. Proverbs of Corca Bascinn.
Lowry. Old Blake was warm, he got down to the hub.
Schoolboy's Complaint, The.
Nemerov. Frozen City, The.
Oliver. Spring Azures.
Roethke. Supper with Lindsay.
Rukeyser. Homage to Literature.
Tate. William Blake.

Blasphemy
Herrick. Upon Brock.
Lowry. Oh gentle Jesus of the hymnal once.
MacNeice. Blasphemies, The.
Wilbur. Simplification, A.

Blessings
Berry. Woods.
Burns. At Roslin Inn.
On John McMurdo.
Phillis the Fair.
To a Young Lady, *Miss Jessy L———, Dumfries; with Books which the Bard Presented Her.*
To Miss C*********, a Very Young Lady.
To Terraughty, on His Birth-Day.
Campion. Ad Graios.
To the Right Vertuous, and Honorable, the Lord and Lady Hayes.
Catullus. Carmen 100: "Undone or done up with love."
De la Mare. Prayer, A.
Dickinson. One Blessing had I than the rest.
"Dylan." Forever Young.
Everson. High Embrace, The.
Frost. Answer, An.
Griffiths. At the Consecration.
Herrick. Crutches.
Gods Blessing.
Gods Bounty ("God, as He's potent, so He's likewise known").
Gods Bounty ("Gods Bounty, that ebbs lesse and lesse").
Good-Night, or Blessing, The.
Graces for Children.
Loading and Unloading.
None Truly Happy Here.
Poores Portion, The.
Riches and Poverty.
To Biancha, to Blesse Him.
To Dianeme; a Ceremonie in Glocester.

To God ("God gives not onely corne").
Wassaile, The.
Welcome What Comes.
Hewitt. Blessing.
Booleys, The.
Colour.
Evening in Spring.
Hymn: "Noon in an English county."
Jarrell. Blind Sheep, The.
Jonson. Ben Jonson's Grace before King James.
Kipling. Outsong in the Jungle.
Kunitz. Blessing of Women, A.
Lorde. Relevant Is Different Points on the Circle.
Lowry. Never in a comedian's life have I laughed till then!
With Sweet Devotion and True from All the Little Animals.
McAuley. Blessing.
MacNeice. Ode: "To-night is so coarse with chocolate."
Merton. Secular Signs.
Psalms. Psalm 67: "God be merciful unto us, and bless us."
Psalm 128: "Blessed is every one that feareth the Lord."
Rolfe. 1949 (After Reading a News Item).
Song for a Birth Day in Exile.
Rossetti. Gold of that Land is Good, The.
Hail, noble face of noble friend!
Heavy heart, if ever heart was heavy, A.
Love builds a house on earth and waits for rest.
Perfect Love Casteth Out Fear.
Rukeyser. Voices of Waking.
St. John. Shadow.
Stevenson. New House, The.
Wakoski. Blessing Ode for a Man with Fishbones Around His Neck.
Whittier. Benedicite.
Yeats. Blessed, The.
Players Ask for a Blessing on the Psalteries and on Themselves, The.
Prayer on Going into My House.
Zukofsky. Caelius Aufilenus' mate, Quintius Aufilena's am.

Blindness
Berry. Music, A.
To Know the Dark.
Blake. How to Know Love from Deceit.
Browning, Elizabeth Barrett. Hugh Stuart Boyd [His Blindness].
Browning, Robert. Blind man to the maiden said, The.
Campion. In Morachum.
Carew. Eyes of a Blind Man.
To One Who, When I Praised My Mistress' Beauty, Said I Was Blind.
"Carroll, Lewis." Matilda Jane.
Cooper. Blind Girl.
Door, The.
Crashaw. Mark 10; The Blind Cured by the Word of Our Saviour.
Samson to His De[ora]lilah.
De la Mare. Euphrasy.
Dickey, James. Reading *Genesis* to a Blind Child.
Dickinson. Before I got my eye put out.
Who saw no Sunrise cannot say.
Dobyns. Santaigo: In Praise of Community.
Duncan. Master of Rime told me, You must learn to lose heart, The.
Eberhart. Going.
Oedipus.
Ferlinghetti. Just as I used to say.
That fellow on the boattrain who insisted.
Frost. Haec Fabula Docet.
Gallagher. Reading Aloud.
Graves. Those Blind from Birth.
Haines. To a Man Going Blind.
Hardy. At a Country Fair.
Blinded Bird, The.
Herrick. Being Once Blind, His Request to Biancha.
Upon His Eye-Sight Failing Him.
Upon Reape.
Jarrell. Blind Man's Song, The.

Blind Sheep, The.
Sphinx's Riddle to Oedipus, The.
Jeffers. I saw a regiment of soldiers shuffling and stumbling.
Kipling. Put forth to watch, unschooled, alone.
Kooser. Blind Always Come as Such a Surprise, The.
Boarding House.
Levertov. Solitude, A.
Lieberman. Unblinding, The.
Lowry. Song: "Pity the blind and the halt but yet pity."
McGrath. Parable.
Meinke. Café Vue des Alpes.
Milton. Blindness of Samson, The.
Hail holy Light, ofspring [*or* offspring] of Heav'n [*or* Heaven] first-born.
Sonnet 22: "Cyriack, this three years day these eyes, though clear."
Paley. Fund Appeal.
Rolfe. Eyes of a Blind Man.
Rossetti. Blind from my birth, / Where flowers are springing.
Sketch, A.
Stuart. Begging on North Main.
Sutter. Man Selling Pencils Outside the B. Dalton Bookstore, The.
Williams, Miller. Some Lines Finished Just Before Dawn at the Bedside of a Dying Student / It has Snowed All Night.
Williams, William Carlos. Parable of the Blind, The.
Wright, James. You know / if a blind boy.

Blizzards
Carruth. Blizzard trampling past has left.
Frost. Willful Homing.
Hacker. Third Snowfall.
McNeill. Blizzard.
Merton. Early Blizzard.
Oliver. Beyond the Snow Belt.
Schuyler. Blizzard.
Spender. Remembering Cincinnatti, 1953.
Williams, William Carlos. Blizzard.
See also **Storms.**

Blocks (toys)
Stevenson. Block City.

Blood
Carew. Celia Bleeding, to the Surgeon.
Carroll, Jim. Saint Theresa.
Coleridge. Loss.
Dickey, James. Poisoned Man, The.
Scratch, The.
Dickey, William. Performances.
Duncan. My Mother Would Be a Falconress.
Stage Directions.
Edmunds. Appalachia.
Emerson. Ancient drop of feudal blood, An.
Everson. Blood of the Poet, The.
Burning Book, The.
Passion Week.
Ford. ABC's.
Frost. Flood, The.
Gunn. Book of the Dead, The.
Cannibal.
Faustus Triumphant.
Hesketh. Letter to Vincent.
Truth Game.
Hugo. Ballpark at Moiese, The.
Jeffers. So Many Blood-Lakes.
That Noble Flower.
Joseph. Lure.
Lawrence. Cold Blood.
Red.
Shedding of Blood.
Lewis. Defeat.
Lorde. Need: A Chorale for Black Woman Voices.
Separation.
Lowry. I don't want to criticize war.
"MacDiarmid." One of the Principal Causes of War.
Meinke. Shell, The.
Merton. What to Think When It Rains Blood.
Neruda. Danger, The.
Rich. Rain of Blood, The.
Rossetti. Babylon the Great.
Cannot Sweeten.

I Have Fought a Good Fight.
Whitsun Eve.
Sandburg. Crimson Changes People.
Fight.
Psalm of the Bloodbank.
Smoke and Steel.
Sorrentino. Abstraction, The.
Gimlet.
Oleo Strut.
Shapes of Winter.
Southwell. Christ's Bloody Sweate.
Stafford. Ceremony.
Stuart. Harpist's Dream, The.
Tate. Red Stains.
Sonnets of the Blood.
Turco. Blood Deeper than Night.
Warren. You Never Knew Her Either, Though You Thought You Did.
Whitman. Trickle Drops.
Wright, James. Living by the Red River.
To Harvey, Who Traced the Circulation.

Blue (color)
Bogan. Variation on a Sentence.
Dunn. Man Who Never Loses His Balance, The.
Emerson. Heavy blue chain, The.
Fox. Blue Dress, The.
Frost. Fragmentary Blue.
Hartley. Crucifixion of Noel, The.
Hugo. Blue Stone.
Keats. Blue! 'Tis the Life of Heaven, the Domain.
Lawrence. Blueness.
Lowry. About Ice.
Merrill. Blue Eye, The.
Patchen. Curly Blue Buppo, The.
Sandburg. Bluebird, What Do You Feed On?
Cheap Blue.
Morning Glory Blue.
Understandings in Blue.
Schuyler. Footnote.
Snyder. Blue Sky, The.
Sorrentino. Man in Old Blue Suit at the Plaza.
Wakoski. Blue Monday.
Young. Pidgin Moon.

Blue Jays
Ciardi. One Jay at a Time.
Cummings. Crazy jay blue) / demon laughshriek.
Dickinson. Jay his Castanet has struck, The.
Sorrentino. Man and Wife.
Wright, James. I Try to Waken and Greet the World Once Again.

Bluebells
Brontë. To the Bluebell.
Tomlinson. Metamorphosis, The.

Bluebirds
Dickinson. After all Birds have been investigated and laid aside.
Eberhart. Now Is The Air Made of Chiming Balls.
Frost. Last Word of a Bluebird, The.
Sandburg. Bluebird, What Do You Feed On?

Bluefish
Wilbur. Trolling for Blues.

Blues (mood)
Angelou. Good Woman Feeling Bad, A.
My Life Has Turned to Blue.
Carruth. Cowshed Blues, The.
Dunbar. Blue.
"Dylan." Black Crow Blues.
Bob Dylan's Blues.
Corrina, Corrina.
Living the Blues.
Meet Me in the Morning.
Poor Boy Blues.
Stuck Inside of Mobile with the Memphis Blues Again.
Walkin' Down the Line.
Hughes, Langston. Bound No'th Blues.
Hard Daddy.
Misery.
Miss Blues'es Child.
Monroe's Blues.
Knight. Con/tin/u/way/shun Blues.
Memo #43.
Lowry. Cold Roast Hamlet Blues,

Blubberhouses Blues, Ugley Blues.
Nagging at myself something awful.
Matthews. Blue Notes.
Rolfe. Brickyards at Beacon.
Schuyler. Roxy.
Young. Any Inner City Blues.
Blues Don't Change, The.
James Cotton Band at Keytstone, The.
More Clues to the Blues.
See, See, Moon.
What Is the Blues?
See also **Melancholy.**

Blues (music)
Carruth. Billie Holiday.
Called him "Big Joe" yes and Joe Turner it
was his name.
Expatiation on the Combining of Weathers at
Thirty-Seventh and Indiana Where the
Southern More or Less Crosses the Dog, An.
High above themselves. Above everything,
flux, ooze.
In the mind's house of heaven the great night
never.
Named she was a Smith, born Smith, but how
related.
Your dream: / His name was Hermes, and he
was all to all.
Cullen. Colored Blues Singer.
Cummings. One slipslouch twi / tterstamp.
Dove. Shakespeare Say.
Hayden. Homage to the Empress of the Blues.
Hughes, Langston. Misery.
Monroe's Blues.
Note on Commercial Theatre.
Weary Blues, The.
Lowry. Got a date with a bottle of / gin.
Matthews. Blues, The.
Morrison. Very Brave.
Rolfe. Blues.
Schuyler. Beautiful Funerals.
Roxy.
Young. Blues Don't Change, The.
Old Fashioned Cincinnati Blues, The.
Old O.O. Blues, The.

Boarding Houses
Atwood. Roominghouse, Winter.
Kipling. Ballad of Fisher's Boardinghouse,
The.
Larkin. Mr. Bleaney.

Boasting
Angelou. Little Girl Speakings.
Cummings. Buncha hardboil guys frum duh
A.C. fulla.
Dunbar. Career, A.
Hardy. Epitaph for George Moore.
Herrick. Great Boast, Small Rost.
Upon Mease.
Upon One Who Said She Was Alwayes
Young.
Upon Pievish.
Upon Spunge.
Hewitt. Sonnet: "I thought tonight of all the
lovers gone."
Kipling. Braggart, The.
Markson. See Susan Read.
Nash. Oh, Stop Being Thankful All over the
Place.
People.
Psalms. Psalm 52: "Why boastest thou thyself
in mischief."
Sandburg. Primer Lesson.
Stevenson. Apologetic Postscript of a Year
Later.

Boats and Boating
Atwood. Boat, A.
Beckett.
Berry. Plan, The.
Bishop. Arrival at Santos.
Browning, Elizabeth Barrett. Romance of the
Ganges, A.
Catullus. Carmen 4: "My bean-pod boat you
see here."
Clark. Time.
Coleridge. Water Ballad.
Cooper. Now it's our turn. Three a.m.
Dickey, James. Drifting.
Facing Africa.

Dunbar. On the River.
Passage, The.
Duncan. There are memories everywhere then.
Rememberd, we go out, as in.
Eberhart. Angels, The.
Ship Burning and a Comet All in One Day, A.
Slow Boat Ride.
Waiting To Lean to the Master's Command.
Ford. Pleasure boat, pleasure boat where has it
gone?
Frost. Flower Boat, The.
Gallagher. Boat Ride.
Woman-Enough.
Words Written Near a Candle.
Galvin. October Dory Race.
Garrigue. Song in Sligo.
Hall. Long River, The.
Hesketh. Credo.
Integration.
Hewitt. Lost *Argo*, Islandmagee, Summer
1919.
My First Reported Words.
Hopkins. As it fell upon a day.
Jeffers. Boats in a Fog.
Kipling. Lowestoft Boat, The.
Koch. Poem: "Thing / To do / Is organize /
The Sea, The."
Lawrence. In a Boat.
Lindsay. Empty Boats, The.
Path in the Sky, The.
Lowry. Hypocrite! Oxford Grouper! Yahoo!
Oh Storms / Oh The Seal!
MacLeish. Boatmen of Santorin, The.
McNeill. American Boating Song.
Mahon. Hearing the thunder of the intransitive
weirs
Meredith. Song: "Over the ferry, and over the
ferry."
There is for me no sweeter holiday.
Merrill. Blue Grotto, The.
Parrot Fish, The.
Miller. Kattegat.
Oliver. Bailing the Boat.
Olson. Boat, The.
Measure.
Oppen. Product.
Tugs of Hull, The.
Plath. Crossing the Water.
Rich. We are driven to odd attempts; once it
would not have occurred to.
Rossetti. Boats sail on the rivers, / And ships
sail on the seas.
Charon.
O glorious sea that in each climbing wave.
River Thames (?).
Sandburg. Docks.
Lost.
Picnic Boat.
Sarton. Sun Boat.
Schuyler. Edge in the Morning, The.
Sexton. Boat, The.
Shelley. Startled by his own thoughts, he
looked around.
Sidney. Sonnet 103: "O happy Thames, that
didst my Stella bear."
Silverstein. Homemade Boat.
Smith, Stevie. Magic Morning, The.
Sorrentino. Le Bateau d'Amour Descried on
the Briny.
Stevens. Load of Sugar-Cane, The.
Sailing after Lunch.
Stevenson. Where Go the Boats?
Tomlinson. Venice.
Turco. Schooner, The.
Whittier. Voyage of the Jettie.
Wilbur. Regatta, The.
Wordsworth. Hymn for the Boatmen, as They
Approach the Rapids under the Castle of
Heidelberg.
Zukofsky. Facile as can be the boat you see,
my guests, says.
Ways, The.

See also **Ferry Boats; Freighters; Ships and
Shipbuilding; Yachts.**

Bobolinks
Dickinson. Bobolink is gone, The.

No Bobolink—reverse His Singing.
Way to know the Bobolink, The.

Bobwhites
Merton. O Sweet Irrational Worship.

Bodies
Ammons. Ah.
Atwood. Deaths of the Other Children, The.
Fortification, A.
We are hard on each other.
Your flawed body, sickle.
Auden. Mind to body spoke the whole night
through, The.
Prime.
Beckett. D'abord / à plat sur du dur.
Out of Sight in the Direction of My Body.
Berryman. Fall and rise of her midriff bells. I
watch.
Freshman Blues.
Huddle of Need, A.
Blake. Voice of the Devil, The.
Bly. Horse of Desire, The.
Origin of the Praise of God, The.
We Love This Body.
Bogan. Cartography.
Bradstreet. Of the Four Humors in Man's
Constitution.
Brooks. Still Do I Keep My Look, My
Identity.
Carruth. Assignment.
Sonnet: "You in a tallness slenderly, as a
lone."
Clark. Energy of the Pre-World as a Bungee
Cable Jumper.
Cohen. When Even The.
Coleridge. Body Imaging Soul.
Life in Death.
Veil of Spirit, The.
Written after a Walk before Supper.
Cooper. Conversation by the Body's Light.
Waiting.
Creeley. Alba.
Circle.
Enough.
Eye, The.
Flesh.
For a Screaming Lady.
Let something else be / the question—.
Looking Out.
Places.
Plan Is the Body, The.
Trees.
Wall, A.
Cummings. But   turning   a   corner   ,i.
In making Marjorie god hurried.
Liz.
Look / my fingers,which.
Perhaps it was Myself sits down in this
chair. There were two chairs,in fact.
Sometimes i am alive because with.
You said Is / there anything which.
Dickey, William. Narcissus Unbound.
Dickinson. Body grows without, The.
Dobyns. Belly, The.
Body's Journey, The.
Body's Strength, The.
Body's Weight, The.
Community, The.
Sweat.
Donne. Ecstasy, The.
Holy Ghost, The.
Love's Progress.
Resurrection, Imperfect.
Doolittle. Contest, The.
Duncan. I Am a Most Fleshly Man.
Dunn. Desire.
Long Term.
Primer for Swimming at Black Point, A.
Eberhart. Ball Game.
Face, Ocean.
Giantess, The.
Nothing But Change.
Refrains.
Wedding, The.
Emerson. Crowning hour when bodies vie
with souls, The.
Eternal Watcher, who doth wake, The.

If thy body pine.
Poets are colorpots.
Fisher. Garden, The.
Ford. Sorer the joints, The.
Untouched ones, the, The.
Fox. In the factory where dolls are made.
Miss Pimberton Of.
My Father's Oldest Sister.
Your Nipples.
Gallagher. Each Bird Walking.
Graves. Cock in Pullet's Feathers.
Thieves, The.
Trudge, Body!
Gunn. Stealer, The.
Hacker. Mother II.
Presentation Piece.
Herrick. Body, The.
Great Spirits Supervive.
Life Is the Body's [or Bodies] Light.
Hesketh. He Saved Others.
Skeleton Bride.
Hughes, Ted. Face was necessary—I found
face.
If mouth could open its cliff.
Joseph. To achieve knowledge, salting away
Faust's stock—.
Knott. Ritual.
Lawrence. Bodiless God.
Body of God, The.
Eloi, Eloi, Lama Sabachthani?
She Said as Well to Me.
Levertov. Gone Away.
Our Bodies.
McAuley. Astronomy.
"MacDiarmid." All life's million conflicting
interests and relationships.
McGrath. Behold the Woman.
Rediscovery.
MacLeish. What the Lion Said to the Child.
What the Serpent Said to Adam.
Markson. Question of Anatomy.
To a Lady, a Part of Her.
Unfinished.
Marvell. Dialogue between the Soul and [the]
Body, A.
Merton. Metamorphosis.
Miller. Gentle as the Lamb of God Made into
Mad Cutlets.
Morgan. Body, The.
Omen.
Two bodies in the river.
Morrison. Guided Tour, The.
Nash. Don't Look Now.
O'Hara. Poem: "When I am feeling depressed
and anxious sullen."
Olson. Cross-Legged, the Spider and the Web.
Elements of clothes, an arm and hand the head
of a cock.
Gate Is Prouti, The.
It is a nation of nothing but poetry.
Lalage!
Moebius Strip, The.
My poor dumb body.
Woman's Nipples Is the Rose of the World,
A.
Piercy. Cats Like Angels.
Friend, The.
"Reed." Candy Says.
Rich. Splittings.
Roethke. Epidermal Macabre.
Orders for the Day.
Rossetti. Soul rudderless, unbraced.
Rukeyser. Endless.
Handclap.
St. John. Study for the World's Body.
Sandburg. Cadenza.
No matter how thick or how thin you slice it
it's still baloney.
Walking Man of Rodin, The.
Sexton. August 17th.
In Celebration of My Uterus.
Mr. Mine.
Mother and Daughter.
Sidney. What tongue can her perfections tell.
Silverstein. Band-Aids.
Smart. Author Apologizes to a Lady, for His
Being a Little Man, The.

Smith, Stevie. Man Is a Spirit.
This Englishwoman.
Snyder. Alabaster.
Bath, The.
Egg, The.
Sorrentino. Oleo Strut.
Stevenson. My body which my dungeon is.
Stuart. Love's Body.
Sutter. I Love Your Crazy Bones.
Third Use of the Penis, The.
Updike. In Extremis.
Ode to Healing.
Van Duyn. Gray's Apocrypha.
Wakoski. To the Thin and Elegant Woman
Who Resides Inside of Alix Nelson.
Waldman. Crack in the World.
Mirror Meditation.
Whitman. Come, said my soul.
I am the poet of the Body and I am the poet
of the Soul.
I sing the body electric.
Wilbur. Shallot, A.
Williams, Charles Kenneth. Fat.
For Gail, When I Was Five.
I know / nothing anymore.
To Market.
Williams, Miller. I Go Out of the House for
the First Time.
Sale.
Williams, William Carlos. United States, The.
Wright, Charles. Lost Bodies.
Wright, James. Dog in a Cornfield.
Girl in a Window, A.
Jewel, The.
Offense, The.
Yeats. Lady's Second Song, The.
Lady's Third Song, The.
Michael Robartes and the Dancer.
Oil and Blood.
Young. Flu.
Green Is a Feeling, Not a Color.
Tiny Self-Portrait.
Zimmer. Zimmer Remembering Wanda.
Zukofsky. Junction, A.
Prop. LXI.
So That Even a Lover.
Who endure days like this.
See also **Nudity and Nudists.**
Boer War
Hardy. At the War Office, London.
Christmas Ghost-Story, A.
Colonel's Soliloquy, The.
Departure.
Drummer Hodge.
Embarcation.
Going of the Battery, The.
Song of the Soldiers' Wives and Sweethearts.
Souls of the Slain, The.
Wife in London, A.
Kipling. Absent-Minded Beggar, The.
Bridge-Guard in the Karroo.
Chant-Pagan.
Columns.
Dirge of Dead Sisters.
General Joubert.
Islanders, The.
Lesson, The.
Lichtenberg.
M. I.
Old Issue, The.
Parting of the Columns, The.
Piet.
Return, The.
Rimmon.
Settler, The.
Stellenbosch.
Two Kopjes.
Meredith. At the Close.
Schuyler. Boer War Bread Strike.
Boethius, Anicius Manlius Severinus
Hill. At Pavia, a visitation of some sorrow.
Boethius'.
Bogart, Humphrey
Berg. To My Friends.
Stuart. This Is No Dream, This Is My Life.
Bogs
Heaney. Bog Queen.

Bogland.
Tollund Man, The.
Hugo. Sneosdal.
Smith, Stevie. Our Bog is Dood.
Boleyn, Anne
Lowell. Death of Anne Boleyn.
Wyatt. Whoso list to hunt, I know where is an
hind.
Bolsheviks
Kunitz. Bolsheviks.
Lawrence. Bourgeois and Bolshevist.
Choice of Evils.
Cowardice and Impudence.
Half-Blind, The.
Hard-Boiled Conservatives.
Property and No-Property.
Property Question, The.
Bombs and Bombing
Carroll, Jim. Dresden to Chesapeake Bay.
Carruth. Any fire will do - you who are
sleeping.
People burned, came apart, suffocated, melted.
Your dream: / Its peculiar name is Hydrogen
Bomb.
Ginsberg. Hūṃ Bom!
Hewitt. Bombed Public House, The.
Street Names.
Hughes, Ted. Woman Unconscious, A.
Jarrell. Angels at Hamburg, The.
Siegfried.
Truth, The.
Jeffers. Great Explosion, The.
Kipling. Bombed in London.
Knott. Depressionism.
MacNeice. Swing-Song.
Merrill. 18 West 11th Street.
Popular Demand.
Merton. Bombarded City, The.
Sports without Blood—a Letter to Dylan
Thomas (1948).
Morgan. His Last Case.
Morrison. Hurricane and Eclipse.
We Awoke, Talking.
Rolfe. After Tu Fu (A.D. 713-770).
Casualty.
City of Anguish.
Death by Water.
Paris—Christmas 1938.
Radio Madrid—1937.
Sexton. Firebombers, The.
Smith, Stevie. No More People.
Spender. Epilogue to a Human Drama.
Rejoice in the Abyss.
Stafford. At the Bomb Testing Site.
Wilbur. Mined Country.
See also **Air Warfare.**
Bones
De la Mare. Thus Her Tale.
Dickey, James. Rib, The.
Garrigue. Song: "O beautiful, my relic bone."
Graves. Broken Neck.
Hall. Columns of the Parthenon, The.
Heaney. Bone Dreams.
Herrick. Proof to No Purpose.
Hesketh. Skeleton Bride.
Hughes, Ted. Relic.
Hugo. Sandbanks, The.
Kinnell. Poem of Night.
Koertge. What She Wanted.
Morgan. Bones.
Nathan. Wisdom of the Talmud.
Oliver. Bone Poem.
Olson. Marry the Marrow.
Roethke. I Cry, Love! Love!
Sandburg. Dinosaur Bones, The.
Sexton. Fury of Beautiful Bones, The.
Stevens. Postcard from the Volcano, A.
Updike. Dream and Reality.
Modest Mound of Bones, A.
See also **Skeletons.**
Bonney, William H.. *see* **"Billy the Kid"**
(William H. Bonney).
Bonsai
Piercy. Work of Artifice, A.
Books
Bradstreet. Author to Her Book, The.

Browning, Elizabeth Barrett. Hugh Stuart Boyd [Legacies].
Little Friend, The.
Browning, Robert. Sibrandus Schafnaburgensis.
Burns. Book-Worms, The.
O leave novels, ye Mauchline belles.
To a Young Lady, *Miss Jessy L———, Dumfries; with Books which the Bard Presented Her.*
To Miss L———.
Byron. You Ask for a "Volume of Nonsense."
Campion. Ad Librum.
To the Reader.
Writer to his Booke, The.
"Carroll, Lewis." Acrostic: "Are you deaf, Father William?"
Lesson in Latin, A.
Three Little Maids.
To Three Puzzled Little Girls, from the Author.
Catullus. Carmen 1: "To whom should I present this."
Carmen 22: "I must, Varus, tell you."
Cohen. Commentary—She Has Given Me the Bullet.
Cowper. Ode to Rouse.
On Madan's Answer to Newton.
Davie. Grace in the Fore Street.
Dickinson. Book is only the Heart's Portrait, A.
He ate and drank the precious Words.
Hour for books, those enthralling friends, An.
It is still as distinct as Paradise.
It stills, incites, infatuates.
Precious—moldering pleasure—'tis, A.
There is no Frigate like a Book.
Unto my Books—so good to turn.
Donne. Valediction, A: Of the Book.
Dove. One Volume Missing.
Dunbar. On a Clean Book.
Sonnet; "Emblem of blasted hope and lost desire."
Eberhart. Request.
Ruby Daggett.
Emerson. Ancient lady who dwelt in Rome, An.
Inspired we must forget our books.
What all the books of ages paint, I have.
Written in a Volume of Goethe.
Fisher. Correspondence.
Graves. Colophon.
Gunn. To a Dead Graduate Student.
Hall. Illustration.
Three Movements, The.
Herrick. Lines Have Their Linings, and Bookes Their Buckram.
On His Booke ("Bound (almost) now of my book I see, The").
To God ("If any thing delight me for to print").
To His Book[e] ("Have I not blest thee? Then go forth; nor fear").
To His Booke ("Be bold my Booke, nor be abasht, or feare").
To His Booke ("Goe thou forth my booke, though late").
To His Booke ("Like to a Bride, come forth my Book, at last").
To His Booke ("Thou art a plant sprung up to wither never").
To His Booke ("While thou didst keep thy candor undefil'd").
To His Book[e] ("If hap it must, that I must see thee lye").
To His Closet-Gods.
To Momus.
To My Ill Reader.
To Sir George Parrie, Doctor of the Civill Law.
To the High and Noble Prince, George, Duke, Marquesse, and Earle of Buckingham.
To the Lady Mary Villars, Governesse to the Princesse Henretta.
To the Most Illustrious and Most Hopefull Prince, Charles, Prince of Wales.
To the Most Learned, Wise, and Arch-

Antiquary, M. John Selden.
To the Right Honourable, Philip, Earle of Pembroke, and Montgomerie.
Hewitt. Oh, ban the books and save the children's lives.
Reading.
Jarrell. Author to the Reader, The.
Carnegie Library, Juvenile Division, The.
Children Selecting Books in a Library.
Forest Murmurs.
Reader, The.
Jong. Books.
Jonson. Author ad Librum.
On the Honoured Poems of His Honoured Friend, Sir John Beaumont, Baronet.
To Mrs Alice Sutcliffe, on Her Divine *Meditations.*
To My Bookseller.
To the Reader ("This figure, that thou here seest put").
To the Same [Sir Henry Goodyere].
Vision of Ben Jonson, on the Muses of His Friend M. Drayton, The.
Keats. Keen, Fitful Gusts Are Whispering Here and There.
Larkin. New Eyes Each Year.
Study of Reading Habits, A.
Lawrence. My Naughty Book.
To Pino.
Liddy. Tray-Carrier of Laurels, Liam Miller.
Lowell. Father's Bedroom.
McGrath. Use of Books, The.
Markson. Daily Reviewer-Haupt.
I Saw Old Dylan.
Quietude.
See Susan Read.
Meredith. I looked from the book of the story of men.
"Poems", says the title.
Merton. Duke Hwan and the Wheelwright.
Poet, to His Book, The.
Milton. Sonnet 12: "Book was writt of late call'd Tetrachordon, A."
To John Rouse.
Muldoon. Making the Move.
Nash. Lecturer in Bookstore.
Nathan. And Finally.
Nemerov. Du rêve, de la mathématique, et de la mort.
Oppen. Light / Of the closed pages, tightly closed, packed against each other, The.
Paley. Traveler.
Raine. I've read all the books but one.
Rich. Burning of Paper instead of Children, The.
Sandburg. Books Men Die For.
He was a king or a shah, an ahkoond or rajah.
Medley.
This—For the Moon—Yes?
Who was that antique Chinese crook who put over his revolution and.
Schuyler. This Notebook.
Sexton. February 20th.
Simic. History Book.
Writings of the Mystics, The.
Smart. 1.20: "You seem to cast, my vent'rous book."
Lines with a Pocket Book.
Stevens. House Was Quiet and the World Was Calm, The.
Poem That Took the Place of a Mountain, The.
Stevenson. Envoy: "Go, little book, and wish to all."
Go, little book—the ancient phrase.
Land of Story-Books, The.
Maker to Posterity, The.
Picture-Books in Winter.
So shall this book wax like unto a well.
To Any Reader.
To H.F. Brown.
To Master Andrew Lang.
Who would think, herein to look.
Tomlinson. Chief Standing Water.
Updike. Ode, An: "I'm going to write a novel, hey."

Rack of Paperbacks, A.
Tome-Thoughts, from the *Times.*
Van Duyn. Day in Late October, A.
Wakoski. Precisely, Not Violets.
Walcott. Volcano.
Whitman. As the Time Draws Nigh.
By Broad Potomac's Shore.
In Cabin'd Ships at Sea.
L of G.
L. of G.'s Purport.
Shut Not Your Doors.
Whoever You Are Holding Me Now in Hand.
Williams, Charles Kenneth. Critic, The.
My Book, My Book.
Williams, Miller. Book, The.
Williams, William Carlos. Coronal, A.
Wordsworth. Desultory Stanzas, upon Receiving the Preceding Sheets from the Press.
Distressful gift! this Book receives.
Expostulation and Reply.
On the Detraction Which Followed the Publication of a Certain Poem.
Prelude, Prefixed to the Volume Entitled "Poems Chiefly of Early and Late Years."
Tables Turned, The.
To the Rev. Christopher Wordsworth, D.D., Master of Harrow School.
Written upon a Blank Leaf in "The Compleat Angler."
Yeats. Realists, The.
Ribh at the Tomb of Baile and Aillinn.
Zukofsky. Song—3/4 time.
Suffenus is, stay Varus,—whom you've proven—is the.
Whom do I give my neat little volume.

Bookworms
Burns. Book-Worms, The.
Hartley. Rapture.

Booth, Edwin
Lindsay. Edwin Booth.
Melville. Coming Storm, The.

Booth, William
Lindsay. General William Booth Enters into Heaven.

Boots
Carruth. Where two boots labored yesterday across the.
Dunbar. Two Little Boots.
Hardy. New Boots, The.
Lowry. Poor Butterfly that stamped.
MacNeice. Forth from a sack of fishing-reels and deck-quoits.

Borden, Lizzie
Gallagher. Instructions to the Double.
Koertge. Coign of Vantage.

Boredom
Ammons. Stills.
Atwood. Letter from Persephone.
Berryman. How shall I do, to pass the weary time.
Bukowski. Not Quite So Soon.
Training for Kid Aztec.
Carruth. I came to this place one November day.
I know there is a country where we go.
Catullus. Carmen 44: "It depends who's talking if you're a 'Sabine'."
Cummings. Ballad of the Scholar's Lament.
Davie. Blank of the Wall, The.
Limited Achievement.
Dobyns. Syracuse Nights.
Dunn. Round Trip.
Fletcher. Empty Days, The.
Hesketh. Yew Tree Guest House.
Hewitt. Great Headmaster, A.
Lawrence. Boredom, Ennui, Depression.
Last Lesson of the Afternoon.
To a Certain Friend.
Nash. Our Child Doesn't Know Anything.
Spring Comes to Murray Hill.
Strange Case of Mr. Donnybrooks's Boredom, The.
Nathan. Chosen, The.
Oppen. Approached the window as if to see.
Words cannot be wholly transparent. And that is the.

Rexroth. Advantages of Learning, The.
Sandburg. Humdrum.
Silverstein. Land of Happy, The.
  My Hobby.
Stevenson. Rain is over and done, The.
  Since years ago for evermore.
Thomson. Elegy upon James Therburn, An.
Williams, Charles Kenneth. End of Drought.
Zukofsky. O farm, dear nest, or say Sabine,
  ah say Tibur's.

Bores
Betjeman. Reproof Deserved; or After the
  Lecture.
Nash. So Does Everybody Else, Only Not So
  Much.
  There Were Giants in Those Days or Maybe
  There Weren't.
  Will You Have Your Tedium Rare or
  Medium?
Shelton. Pain.

Borgia, Lucretia
Smith, Stevie. Yes, I Know.

Bosch, Hieronymus
Hugo. Prado: Bosch: S. Antonio, The.

Boston, Massachusetts
Ciardi. Bedlam Revisited.
  Benefits of an Education, The.
  Cal Coolidge and the Co.
  Feasts.
  Five-Year Step, A.
  Highest Place in Town, The.
  Knothole in Spent Time, A.
  River, The.
  Romancing with Our Beasts.
  Shaft, The.
Cummings. My humorous ghost precisely will.
  When i am in boston,i do not speak.
Edmunds. November.
Emerson. Boston.
  Last Farewell, The.
  O Boston city lecture-hearing.
  Trimountain.
Hall. Woolworth's.
Lowell. At the Indian Killer's Grave.
  For the Union Dead.
  Mary Winslow.
  Public Garden, The.
  Where the Rainbow Ends.
McGrath. Driving toward Boston I Run across
  One of Robert Bly's Old Poems.
MacLeish. Night Watch in the City of Boston.
Moore. In the Public Garden.
Plath. Winter's Tale, A.
Robinson. Boston.
Sexton. Just Once.
Updike. Back Bay.
  Sunday in Boston.
Walcott. Gold dung and urinous straw from
  the horse garages.
Whitman. Boston Ballad, A [or A Boston
  Ballad 1854].
Whittier. Calef in Boston.
  In the "Old South."
  King's Missive, The.
  Landmarks, The.
  Moloch in State Street.
  To Faneuil Hall.
  Young. East Boston.

Boston Tea Party
Emerson. Boston.

Boswell, James
Jong. To James Boswell in London.

Bosworth Field, Battle of (1485)
Lowell. Bosworth Field.

Bottles
Griffiths. Old Hope.
Kinnell. Milk Bottle, The.
Kooser. Beer Bottle.
Lawrence. Ships in Bottles.
Stevens. Anecdote of the Jar.

Bourgeoisie
Angelou. Sepia Fashion Show.
Auden. Unknown Citizen, The.
Brooks. Man of the Middle Class, A.
Bukowski. Day I Kicked Away a Bankroll,
  The.

Carruth. I am a fanatic lover of liberty,
  considering it.
  World as Will and Representation, The.
Cummings. Cambridge ladies who live in
  furnished souls, The.
  I say no world.
Dickey, William. Being Asked To Define
  Bourgeois Individuality.
Griffiths. Crossing Lady-Stanley, Here, 1868.
  Education.
  Out of a Descended Generation.
  Shrinking Horizon.
Hardy. Lady in the Furs, The.
Hemingway. Big Dance on the Hill, The.
Larkin. Toads.
Lawrence. Bourgeois and Bolshevist.
  Choice of Evils.
  Climbing Up.
  Cowardice and Impudence.
  Half-Blind, The.
  How Beastly the Bourgeois Is.
  Ignoble Procession, The.
  Middle Classes, The.
  Prestige.
  Property and No-Property.
  Property Question, The.
  Red-Herring.
  Worm Either Way.
Lowry. Is there no song that I can sing.
  What Sigbjørn Said.
Nash. What the Well-Read Patient Is Talking
  About, or, Look, Ma, What I Got!
Nemerov. Life Cycle of Common Man.
Rolfe. Sixth Winter, The.

Bowery, The, New York City
Lowry. Epitaph: "Dear Scipio Sprague / sans
  plague sans blague."

Bowlers. see Bowling and Bowlers.

Bowles, William Lisle
Byron. William Lisle Bowles.
Coleridge. To the Rev. [or Reverend] W. L.
  Bowles.

Bowling and Bowlers
Dobyns. Bowlers Anonymous.
Liddy. In the Bowling Alley.

Boxing and Boxers
Bukowski. Art, An.
  Empire of Coins, An.
  Loser, The.
"Dylan." Hurricane.
  Who Killed Davey Moore?
Hartley. Light-Heavy at Prayer.
Hayden. Free Fantasia: Tiger Flowers.
Hughes, Langston. Joe Louis.
Kipling. NOVEMBER (Boxing).
Nathan. Twin Snakes.
Patchen. Now I Went Down to the Ringside
  and Little Henry Armstrong Was There.
Sandburg. Boxes and Bags.
Williams, Charles Kenneth. Vehicle: Violence.

Boy Scouts
Kipling. Boy Scouts' Patrol Song, A.

Boys
Auden. Photograph of a Boy in Costume, The.
Betjeman. False Security.
Bishop. Casabianca.
Boyle. Career.
Burns. My Bonie Laddie's Young but He's
  Growin Yet.
Carew. Dart, The.
"Carroll, Lewis." Duchess's Lullaby, The.
  Love among the Roses.
Ciardi. Boy.
Dickey, James. Little More, The.
Dunbar. Boy's Summer Song, A.
Ford. Pre-puberty boys.
Gunn. Allegory of the Wolf Boy, The.
  Blackie, the Electric Rembrandt.
Hall. Young Watch Us, The.
Hardy. Boy's Dream, The.
  Boys Then and Now.
Hartley. Local Boys and Girls Small Town
  Stuff.
Hewitt. Sheep Fair.
Hughes, Langston. Tag.
Kinnell. First Song.

Lawrence. Discipline.
  Little-Boy Brilliant.
Longfellow. My Lost Youth.
Lorde. Bees, The.
Lovelace. With a fair boy a Cryer we behold.
Lowry. Oh the Pyrrus boys are we.
Morgan. Poem of the Gold Coin.
Olson. Anniversary.
  Spring Song for Cagli, A.
Patchen. Street Corner College.
Schuyler. Head, A.
Silverstein. Hungry Mungry.
  Pirate Captain Jim.
Snodgrass. Boy Made of Meat, The; A Poem
  for Children.
Wakoski. Poem for a Little Boy on the
  Buddha's Birthday.
Warren. He Was Formidable.
Whitman. We Two Boys Together Clinging.
Whittier. Oh for boyhood's painless play.
Williams, William Carlos. Hard Times.
  Horned Purple.
Wordsworth. Rural Architecture.
See also **Childhood and Children; Youth.**

Bradstreet, Anne
Berryman. Winters close, springs open, no
  child stirs, The.
Bradstreet. Anagram, An.
  Another ("Artes bred neat *An*").
  Another to Mrs. Anne Bradstreet, Author of
  this Poem.
  Funeral Elegy Upon that Pattern and Patron of
  Virtue, A.
  I cannot wonder at Apollo now.
  In Praise of the Author, Mistress Anne
  Bradstreet, Virtue's True and Lively Pattern.
  To My Dear Sister, the Author of these
  Poems.
  Upon Mrs. Anne Bradstreet, Her Poems, Etc.
  Upon the Author.
  Upon the Author. By a Known Friend.

Brahma
Emerson. Brahma.
  Proteus.

Brahms, Johannes
Stevens. Anglais Mort à Florence.

Brains
Auden. Ode to the Diencephalon.
Campion. In Nervam.
"Carroll, Lewis." Photography Extraordinary.
Carruth. Tanck's Song About Brains.
Dickinson. Where the Treasure is.
Gunn. Listening to Jefferson Airplane.
Hesketh. What Is a Person?
Hoffman. Brainwaves.
Kunitz. Organic Bloom.
Nemerov. Cybernetics.
Pack. Empathy.
"Reed." Lady Godiva's Operation.
Rolfe. Bon Voyage.
Sandburg. Brainwashing.
Snodgrass. Examination, The.
Stuart. We Never Close.
Turco. Tick.
Williams, William Carlos. Play.

Brancusi, Constantin
Shapiro. White Negress, The.
Smith, Patti. Salvation of Rock, The.

Brandy
MacNeice. Brandy Glass, The.

Brazil
Bishop. Four Sambas.
Davie. Helena Morley.
Kipling. I've never sailed the Amazon.
Lewis. Port of Call: Brazil.
Updike. Brazil.
  Rio de Janeiro.
  São Paulo.
Whittier. Freedom in Brazil.

Bread
Atwood. All Bread.
Auden. Daily Bread.
Burns. Bannocks o' Bear-Meal.
Crashaw. On the Miracle of Multiplied [or
  Multiplyed] Loaves.
Dunbar. Dinah Kneading Dough.

Breakfast
Hall. Valley of Morning.
Hartnett. Bread.
Herrick. Larr's Portion, and the Poets Part.
  Upon Pennie.
McGrath. Bread of this World; Praises III,
  The.
Schuyler. Boer War Bread Strike.
Simic. Austerities.

Breakfast
Dobyns. Oatmeal Deluxe.
Eberhart. Angels, The.
Graves. Breakfast Table.
Lawrence. Roses on the Breakfast Table.
Lowry. Eye-Opener.
  For Our Sweetharteebeeste on Hartebeeste
  Day.
  With Sweetest Morning Love to Their Beloved
  Harteebeeste.
MacLeish. Hotel Breakfast.
Nash. Eight O'Clock Peril, The.
Rich. Breakfast in a Bowling Alley in Utica,
  New York.
Rossetti. Bread and Milk for Breakfast.
Sandburg. Two Strangers Breakfast.
Silverstein. Early Bird.
Sorrentino. White Lemons.
Wakoski. Breakfast.
Williams, William Carlos. Promenade.
Yau. Different Cereal, A.

Breasts
Berg. Lament: "My mother wants to be
  burned, she told me."
Carew. On a Damask[e] Rose, Sticking upon a
  Lady's Breast.
  Upon a Mole in Celia's Bosom.
Carroll, Jim. Poem: "I snatch a grape from her
  breast."
Cohen. I Perceived the Outline of Your
  Breasts.
Crashaw. Luke 11; Blessed Be the Paps
  Which Thou Hast Sucked.
Cummings. Gert.
  Life boosts herself rapidly at me.
  Wing Wong,uninterred at twice.
Gallagher. Breasts.
Herrick. Fresh Cheese and Cream.
  How Roses Came Red.
  To Roses in Julia's Bosome.
  Upon Julia's Breasts.
  Upon the Nipples of Julia's Breast.
Lawrence. Song of a Man Who Is Loved.
McGrath. Rediscovery.
Markson. To a Lady, a Part of Her.
Oppen. Zulu Girl, The.
Sexton. Breast, The.
  Dreaming the Breasts.
  Mr. Mine.
Simic. Breasts.
Smart. To Ethelinda.
Smith, Stevie. Dream of Nourishment, A.
  This Englishwoman.
Spenser. LXXVI. "Fair bosom! fraught with
  virtue's richest treasure."
Stuart. Girl of My Dreams Is Dying.
Williams, William Carlos. Still Life.
Wright, James. Poem about Breasts, A.

Breath
Berry. Cold Pane, The.
Byron. Song: "Breeze of the night in gentler
  sighs."
Clark. Nimble Rays of Day Bring Oxygen to
  Her Blood.
Creeley. "Do You Think."
  Le Fou.
Dickey, James. Basics.
  Breath.
Dickinson. I breathed enough to take the
  Trick.
Duncan. For a Muse Meant.
Gardner. And Thou No Breath at All?
Herrick. On Julia's Breath.
  To Julia ("Julia, when thy Herrick dies").
  Upon a Free Maid, with a Foule Breath.
  Upon a Sowre-Breath Lady.
  Upon Jone and Jane.
  Upon Linnit.
  Upon Lungs.

Hewitt. Hedgehog.
  My dear spouse died—a tumour on the brain.
Levine. Breath.
Nathan. Breathing Exercises.
Sidney. Sonnet 95: "Yet sighs, dear sighs,
  indeed true friends you are."
Stuart. High Wire.

Brecht, Bertolt
Mahon. Brecht in Svendborg.

Breughel, Pieter. see Brueghel, Pieter.

Bricks and Bricklayers
Carruth. Listen, in night's last tender hour.
Koch. Bricks, The.
Sandburg. Bricklayer Love.

Brides
Browning, Elizabeth Barrett. Lay of the
  Brown Rosary, The.
  Rhyme of the Duchess May.
Byron. Sonnet on the Nuptials of the Marquis
  Antonio Cavalli with the Countess Clelia
  Rasponi of Ravenna.
Campion. Breath you now, while Io Hymen.
  Song: "Now hath Flora rob'd [or robbed] her
  bowers."
Carew. Hymneal Song, on the Nuptials of the
  Lady Ann Wentworth and the Lord Lovelace.
  Married Woman, A.
  To Mistress Katherine Neville, on Her Green
  Sickness.
Carruth. "Shock? Is that what you're asking?
  My dear, I was a."
Coleridge. To Mary Pridham.
De la Mare. Episodes.
Donne. Eclogue 1613. December 26.
Doolittle. Hymen.
Eberhart. Wedding, The.
Emerson. Stately bride is the shining world,
  A.
  World is a bride superbly dressed, The.
Herrick. Delaying Bride, The.
  Tithe [or Tythe]: To the Bride, The.
  Upon a Maid That Died [or Dyed] the Day
  She Was Married [or Marryed].
Hill. Dead Bride, The.
Lovelace. Anniversary on the Hymeneals of
  My Noble Kinsman, Thomas Stanley,
  Esquire, An.
  Sonnet. To Generall Goring.
Meredith. Flat as to an eagle's eye.
  Margaret's Bridal-Eve.
Morrison. Wedding-Dress, The.
Olson. Bride, The.
Patchen. O out of that feast in the blond wood
  of the morning.
Poe. Bridal Ballad.
  To ———: "I saw thee on thy bridal day."
Ransom. Epithalamion of a Peach.
Robinson. Dust of Timas, The.
Rossetti. Advent Sunday.
  Boy Johnny.
  Bride Song, A.
  Ring upon her finger, / Walks the bride, A.
  Who sits with the King in His Throne? Not a
  slave but a Bride.
Simic. Rough Outline.
Smith, Stevie. I Remember.
Whitman. Kiss to the Bride, A.
Whittier. Home-Coming of the Bride, The.

See also **Weddings.**

Bridges, Robert
Hopkins. To R. B.

Bridges
Berg. From the Bridge.
Burns. Brigs of Ayr, a Poem. Inscribed to J.
  B********, Esq; Ayr, The.
Carruth. Why was the passenger pigeon
  exterminated?
Catullus. Carmen 17: "Cologna Veneta - /
  where the good folk."
Crane. Bridge of Estador, The.
  To Brooklyn Bridge.
De la Mare. Bridge, The.
Dickey, James. At Darien Bridge.
  Meadow Bridge.
Fisher. In long shapes over the channel's.
Hardy. On Sturminster Foot-Bridge.

Hartley. Whole Creation Groans to Be
  Delivered, The.
Hewitt. Long Bridge, The.
Hugo. District in the City, A.
Kipling. Akbar's Bridge.
Levine. 7 Years from Somewhere.
Nash. Poor Mr. Strawbridge.
Neruda. To Puente Curvo on the Maldonado
  Spit in Uruguay.
Paley. Bridges.
Piercy. Bridging.
Rossetti. Boats sail on the rivers, / And ships
  sail on the seas.
Rukeyser. Network that emerges. At the
  ocean, A.
  Red bridge fastening this city to the forest, A.
Sandburg. Clark Street Bridge.
Tomlinson. Aqueduct.
  Bridges.
  Over Elizabeth Bridge: a Circumvention.
  Ponte Veneziano.
Turco. Covered Bridge, The.
Wilbur. Glance from the Bridge, A.
  Simile for Her Smile, A.
Williams, Miller. In Another Town.
Williams, William Carlos. Spirit of '76.
Zukofsky. O Colonia, whose wishes build a
  long bridge to dance on.

Bristol, England
Betjeman. Bristol.
Graves. Invitation to Bristol.

British Columbia, Canada
Lowry. Beneath the Malebolge lies Hastings
  street.

British Empire
Blake. Song of Liberty, A.
Davie. Demi-Exile. Howth.
Emerson. Song: "Shout for those whose
  course is done."
Graves. Single Fare.
Hardy. Coronation, The.
Hewitt. Test, The.
Hill. Short History of British India (I), A.
  Short History of British India (II), A.
  Short History of British India (III), A.
Kipling. Arithmetic on the Frontier.
  Army Headquarters.
  Ballad of Boh Da Thone, The.
  Ballad of East and West, The.
  "Birds of Prey" March.
  Boots.
  Burial, The.
  China-going P. & O.'s.
  Cholera Camp.
  Christmas in India.
  Dedication from "Barrack-Room Ballads."
  Delilah.
  England's Answer.
  Flowers, The.
  Ford o' Kabul River.
  Grave of the Hundred Dead, The.
  Gunga Din.
  Houses, The.
  Irish Guards, The.
  Jobson's Amen.
  Kitchener's School.
  Legend of the Foreign Office, A.
  Lesson, The.
  Lichtenberg.
  Lost Legion, The.
  Man Who Could Write, The.
  Mandalay.
  Masque of Plenty, The.
  Moon of Other Days, The.
  Native-Born, The.
  New Knighthood, The.
  One Viceroy Resigns.
  Oonts.
  Our Lady of the Snows.
  Overland Mail, The.
  Pagett, M. P.
  Parade-Song of the Camp Animals.
  Pharaoh and the Sergeant.
  Plea of the Simla Dancers, The.
  Post That Fitted, The.
  Private Ortheris's Song.
  Pro-Consuls, The.

Public Waste.
Recessional.
Rhodes Memorial, Table Mountain.
Route Marchin'.
Screw-Guns.
Settler, The.
Song for the Women, The.
Song of the Banjo, The.
Song of the Cities, The.
Song of the Sons, The.
Study of an Elevation, in Indian Ink.
Tale of Two Cities, A.
Things and the Man.
To the City of Bombay.
To Thomas Atkins.
What the People Said.
Widow at Windsor, The.
Widow's Party, The.
Young Queen, The.
Muldoon. Meeting the British.
Smart. Accession of King George III, The.
King's Restoration, The.
Ode to Admiral Sir George Pocock.
Ode to General Draper.
St. Simon and St. Jude.
Story of a Cock and a Bull, A.
Thomson. Britannia.
Walcott. In the small coffin of his house, the
pensioner.

British Museum, London
Auden. I'm afraid there's many a spectacled
sod.
Hardy. In the British Museum.
MacNeice. British Museum Reading Room,
The.
Wordsworth. Ode on the Installation of His
Royal Highness Prince Albert as Chancellor
of the University of Cambridge, July, 1847.

Brittany, France
Browning, Robert. Hervé Riel.

Broadway, New York City
Lowry. Morning coat is walking, A.
Rich. Upper Broadway.
Robinson. White Lights, The.
Sandburg. Broadway.
Electric Sign Goes Dark, An.
Whitman. Broadway.
Broadway Pageant, A.

Brodsky, Joseph
Walcott. Forest of Europe.

Brontë, Charlotte
Arnold. Turn we next to the dead.
Dickinson. All overgrown by cunning moss.

Brontë, Emily
Carruth. Your dream: / His name was
Heathcliff, and he was clearly.
Hughes, Ted. Emily Brontë.

Bronx, The, New York City
Levine. Walk with Tom Jefferson, A.
Updike. Tao in the Yankee Stadium Bleachers.

Brooke, Rupert
Lowry. Those who die young will look
forever young.
Prince. Afterword on Rupert Brooke.

Brooklyn, New York City
Berrigan. Personal Poem #9.
Crane. With a Photograph to Zell, Now Bound
for Spain.
Davie. For Doreen. A Voice from the Garden.
"Dylan." Joey.
Gallagher. Conversation with a Fireman from
Brooklyn.
Meinke. Aunt Mary.
Cloud, Florida, 1985, The.
Flatbush.
Muldoon. Carson.
Oppen. Heart pounds / To be among them, the
buildings, The.
Red Hook: December.
Tomlinson. Crossing Brooklyn Ferry.
In a Brooklyn Park.
Whitman. Centenarian's Story, The.
Crossing Brooklyn Ferry.

Brooklyn Bridge
Berrigan. Lord, it is time. Summer was very
great.

Crane. To Brooklyn Bridge.
Moore. Granite and Steel.
Oppen. Great stone / Above the river, The.
Tomlinson. Over Brooklyn Bridge.

Brooks and Streams
Ammons. Close Relations.
Deaf Zone.
Auden. Streams.
Berryman. Sullen brook hardly would satisfy,
A.
Burns. Birks of Aberfeldy, The [Composed on
the Spot].
Down the Burn Davie.
Humble Petition of Bruar Water to the Noble
Duke of Athole, The.
Carruth. Brook has holes in its cover, The.
Brook, The.
Day the brook went out, The.
Frozen / brook sprawls, The.
Of Brook and Stone.
Water, The.
Clough. Sweet streamlet bason! at thy side.
Coleridge. Imitated from Ossian.
Lines to a Beautiful Spring in a Village.
Water Ballad.
Wish, A.
De la Mare. Who?
Dickinson. Have you got a Brook in your
little heart.
Dunbar. Wadin' in de Crick.
Emerson. Old Age.
Frost. Brook in the City, A.
Going for Water.
Hyla Brook.
West-running Brook.
Garrigue. Brook, The.
Hall. Cold Water.
Hopkins. Inversnaid.
Winter with the Gulf Stream.
Levertov. Resolve, The.
Merrill. Banks of a Stream Where Creatures
Bathe.
Olson. Afica.
Day Song.
Smith, Stevie. Brickenden, Hertfordshire.
Occasional Yarrow, The.
Snyder. Water.
Stevens. Lot of People Bathing in a Stream,
A.
Tennyson. Farewell, A: "Flow down, cold
rivulet, to the sea."
Tomlinson. Black Brook.
Confluence.
Wilbur. Hamlen Brook.
Wordsworth. Brook! whose society the Poet
seeks.
Fragment from Dove Cottage Manuscript 44
(I).
It was an April morning: fresh and clear.
On the Banks of a Rocky Stream.
There is a little unpretending Rill.

See also **Rivers.**

Brooms
Carruth. Women like new brooms.
Davie. Sorting the Personae.
Jong. Her Broom, or the Ride of the Witch.
Lawrence. New Brooms.
Levine. Saturday Sweeping.
Simic. Brooms.
Wordsworth. Oak and the Broom, The; A
Pastoral.

Brotherhood
Berry. Gathering, The.
Horses.
In the thought of you I imagine myself free of
the weapons and the official hates that I have
borne on my back like a hump.
Little farm, motherland, made.
Peace. May he waken.
Blake. Divine Image, The ("To Mercy, Pity,
Peace, and Love").
Little Black Boy, The.
Burns. On Fergusson.
Song—For A' That and A' That.
Sons of Old Killie, The.
Carew. Second Rapture, The.

Ceravolo. Wild Provoke of the Endurance
Sky.
Emerson. Rex.
Frost. Tuft of Flowers, The.
Gardner. Jean Sans Terre Wraps Himself in a
Red Coat.
Ginsberg. Who Be Kind To.
Hardy. Wind Blew Words, The.
Hewitt. Song for May Day.
To Robert Telford Hewitt.
To the People of Dresden.
Hoffman. When my wiser brother.
Kipling. Ballad of East and West, The.
Banquet Night.
Mother-Lodge, The.
Pilgrim's Way, A.
Prayer, The: "My brother kneels, so saith
Kabir."
Two Races.
MacLeish. Speech to Those Who Say
Comrade.
Melville. Vine and Clarel.
Meredith. Creed.
Moore. In Distrust of Merits.
Oppen. Wars that are just? A simpler
question: In the event.
Psalms. Psalm 133: "Behold, how good and
how pleasant it is."
Ransom. Armageddon.
Rolfe. After Wang Chi.
Definition.
First Love.
Poem for May First.
These Men Are Revolution.
To Those Who Fear To Join Us.
Sandburg. Long Shadow of Lincoln: A Litany,
The.
Shelley. Over the utmost hill at length I sped.
Shelton. Saturday Night at the Elk's Club.
Whitman. Full of Life Now.
I Dream'd in a Dream.
I Hear It Was Charged against Me.
One Thought Ever at the Fore.
Salut au Monde!
Starting from Paumanok.
To Him That Was Crucified.
To the East and to the West.
Williams, William Carlos. Convivio.
Wordsworth. Feel for the Wrongs of Universal
Ken.

Brothers
Angelou. Kin.
Berryman. Letter to His Brother.
Travelling South.
Bly. Dream of a Brother, A.
Browning, Elizabeth Barrett. Court Lady, A.
Campion. To the Most High and Mighty
Prince Charles.
"Carroll, Lewis." John gave his brother James
a box.
Lyceum, The.
Two Brothers, The.
Catullus. Carmen 101: "Journeying over many
seas and through many countries."
Creeley. World, The.
De la Mare. Brother and Sister.
Dickey, James. In the Tree House at Night.
String, The.
Vessels.
Dickinson. Vivid in our immortal Group.
Dove. Song. Summer.
Dunbar. Ione.
Dunn. My Brother's Work.
Emerson. In Memoriam.
Ford. Seis Hermanos.
Fox. Five Stanzas for My Two Brothers.
Frost. To E.T.
Gunn. Cannibal.
Invitation, An.
Herrick. To His Brother in Law Master John
Wingfield.
To His Dying Brother, Master William
Herrick.
Hewitt. Brothers, The.
Hopkins. Brothers.
Jonson. Speech Presented unto King James at
a Tilting in the Behalf of the Two Noble

Brown

Brothers S[ir] Robert and S[ir] Henry Rich, Now Earls of Warwick and Holland, A.

Keats. To My Brother George.
  To My Brothers.

Lawrence. Dust in the East.

Levine. You Can Have It.

Lovelace. Advice to My Best Brother, Colonel Francis Lovelace.
  To His Deare Brother Colonel F.L.

Lowell. Her Dead Brother.

MacLeish. Family Group.

Melville. Timoleon.

Merton. For My Brother: Reported Missing In Action, 1943.

Morgan. Catullus: *Carmen ci.*

Pack. Clayfeld's Twin.
  Twin, The.

Patchen. Moon came out full, you could see the white breathing of the.

Prince. Two Beggars: A Reminiscence.

Ransom. Two Gentlemen in Bonds.

Robinson. Two Gardens in Linndale.

Rossetti. Portraits.

Sexton. For Johnny Pole on the Forgotten Beach.
  Fourth Psalm.
  Papa and Mama Dance, The.

Shelton. Brother.

Silverstein. Two Boxes.
  What a Day.

Smith, Stevie. Death Bereaves Our Common Mother Nature Grieves for My Dead Brother.

Spender. My Brother Luis.

Stafford. Remembering Brother Bob.

Stuart. Opposite Field, The.

Tate. Adaption of a Theme from Catullus.
  Sonnets of the Blood.

Tennyson. Prefatory Poem to My Brother's Sonnets.

Van Duyn. Twins, The.

Wakoski. David.
  Some Brilliant Sky.

Williams, William Carlos. Portrait of the Author.

Wordsworth. Brothers, The.
  Elegiac Verses in Memory of My Brother, John Wordsworth.
  Tradition of Oker Hill in Darley Dale, Derbyshire, A.
  When, to the attractions of the busy world.

Wright, James. Lament for My Brother on a Hayrake.

Zukofsky. Mulled hosts their countries yet mulled there by a core of wake tossed.

Brown, Jerry (Edmund Gerald Brown, Jr.)

Snyder. He Shot Arrows, but Not at Birds Perching.
  Talking Late with the Governor about the Budget.

Brown, John

Cullen. Negro Mother's Lullaby, A.

Hayden. John Brown.

Hughes, Langston. October 16[: The Raid].

Lindsay. John Brown.

Melville. Portent, The.

Robinson. John Brown.

Rukeyser. Soul and Body of John Brown, The.

Sandburg. And you take hold of a handle.
  Osawatomie.

Tate. On the Martyr of Harpers Ferry.

Whittier. Brown of Ossawatomie.

Brown (color)

Dunn. Clarities, The.

Hugo. Brown Stone.

Browning, Elizabeth Barrett

Browning, Robert. Flight of the Duchess, The.
  Lost Mistress, The.

Dickinson. Her—"last Poems."

McGrath. Near Pah-Gotzin-Kay.

Nash. Old Is for Books.

Browning, Robert

Browning, Robert. Inscription for a Sketch.

Meredith. On Hearing the News from Venice.

Nash. Old Is for Books.

Sandburg. Manitoba Childe Roland.

Bruce, Robert

Burns. Robert Bruce's March to Bannockburn.

Brueghel, Pieter

Auden. Musée des Beaux Arts.

De la Mare. Breughel's Winter.

Hugo. Brueghel in the Doria.

Nemerov. Brueghel: The Triumph of Time.
  Hope.
  World as Brueghel Imagined It, The.

Plath. Two Views of a Cadaver Room.

Williams, William Carlos. Dance, The ("In Brueghel's great picture").
  Dance, The ("When the snow falls").
  Parable of the Blind, The.
  Pictures from Brueghel.

Zukofsky. Ask of the sun.

Brussels, Belgium

Auden. Brussels in Winter.

Whittier. Peace Convention at Brussels, The.

Brutus (Marcus Junius Brutus)

Pope. Two Chorus's to the Tragedy of Brutus.

Bryan, William Jennings

Carruth. But once winds lightened, freshening fair from the West.

Lindsay. Bryan, Bryan, Bryan, Bryan.

Bryant, William Cullen

Rukeyser. Mountain: One from Bryant.

Whittier. Bryant on His Birthday.

Bubbles

Herrick. Bubble; a Song, The.

Markson. Hygiene.

Sandburg. Bubbles.

Schuyler. People Who See Bubbles Rise.

Buckingham, George Villiers, 2d Duke of

Dryden. In the first rank of these did Zimri stand.

Budapest, Hungary

Tomlinson. Over Elizabeth Bridge: a Circumvention.

Buddha and Buddhism

Auden. To a Small Buddha.

Carruth. Buddhist Painter Prepares to Paint, The.

Cooper. Jittoku, Buddhist Mystic—15th Century.

Eberhart. Way Out, A.

Ferlinghetti. Buddha in the Woodpile, A.

Fletcher. Buddha and Christ.

Ginsberg. For Creely's Ear.
  Guru Om.
  Reflections at Lake Louise.
  Sakyamuni Coming Out from the Mountain.
  What Would You Do If You Lost It.

Jeffers. Meditation on Saviors.
  Theory of Truth.

Kipling. Buddha at Kamakura.

Lieberman. Daibutsu.
  God's Measurements.

Lindsay. Poems Speaking of Buddha, Prince Siddartha.

Melville. Buddha.

Meredith. 'Tis good to keep hinderward eyes.

Merton. Five breaths pray in me: sun moon.

Morrison. Afternoon of Summer, An.
  End of the Dream, The.

Oliver. Buddha's Last Instruction, The.

Snyder. Amitabha's Vow.
  Circumambulating Arunachala.
  How rare to be born a human being!
  Maudgalyâyana Saw Hell.
  Regarding Wave.

Wakoski. Buddha Inherits 6 Cars on His Birthday, The.
  My Aunt Ella Meets the Buddha on His Birthday.

Waldman. Pictures From Tofukuji.

See also **Zen Buddhism.**

"Buffalo Bill" (William Frederick Cody)

Cummings. Buffalo Bill's / defunct / who used to.

Sandburg. Buffalo Bill.

Buffaloes

Atwood. Buffalo in Compound: Alberta.

Haines. Head on the Table, The.

Kipling. Dark children of the mere and marsh.

Lindsay. Ghost of the Buffaloes, The.

Matthews. Herd of Buffalo Crossing the Missouri on Ice.

Moore. Buffalo, The.

Oliver. Ghosts.

Pack. Cave of Lascaux, The.

Sandburg. Buffalo Dusk.

Bugles and Buglers

Nash. Edouard.

Owen. Bugles Sang.

Buildings and Builders

Ammons. Cracking a Few Hundred Million Years.

Berry. For the Rebuilding of a House.

Bishop. Along Galeana Street.

Browning, Robert. Apparent Failure.

Cooper. Builder of Houses, The.

Cowper. Epigrams on His Garden Shed.
  Inscription for an Hermitage.

Creeley. Invitation, The.

Dove. Corduroy Road.

Duncan. Nel Mezzo del Cammin di Nostra Vita.

Emerson. One night he dreamed of a palace fair.

Graves. Fallen Tower of Siloam, The.

Gunn. Diagrams.

Hacker. Forage Sestina.

Hall. Traffic.

Hartnett. Visit to Castletown House, A.

Jonson. To Penshurst.

Keats. Fragment of the "Castle Builder."
  My New-Cut Ashlar.
  Palace, The.
  Romulus and Remus.
  Truthful Song, The.

Kipling. Hymn of Breaking Strain.

Koertge. Urban Renewal.

Levine. Making It New.

Lewis. Pharaoh has seen me in the hovels of Israel.

Lieberman. Tilemaker's Hill Fresco, The.

Lorde. Workers Rose on May Day or Postcript to Karl Marx, The.

Lowry. New Guinea Gardener Bird, The.

MacLeish. Burying Ground by the Ties.
  Fifteenth Book, The.

Marvell. Inscribenda Luparae [To Be Written on the Louvre].
  Upon Appleton House [To My Lord Fairfax].

Neruda. Midday Construction.

Oppen. Lights that blaze and promise, The.

Piercy. Gasman Invites the Skyscrapers to Dance.

Ralegh. Strong Ilion thou shalt see with walls and towers high.

Sandburg. Shovel Man, The.

Schuyler. Buildings.
  East Window on Elizabeth Street, An.
  Green Door, The.
  Greenwich Avenue.
  Witley Court.

Sidney. Sonnet 9: "Queen Virtue's court, which some call Stella's face."

Snyder. Building.

Sorrentino. Chez Macadam.

Stevens. Public Square, The.
  Sketch of the Ultimate Politician.

Tomlinson. Above Manhattan.
  Crane, The.

Turco. Observation Tower, The.

Updike. Sonnet to Man-Made Grandeur.

Whittier. Norumbega Hall.

Wilbur. For the New Railway Station in Rome.

Williams, Charles Kenneth. Sanctity, The.

Williams, Miller. Tearing Down the Hotel.

Williams, William Carlos. Defective Record, The.
  Vision of Labor, A: 1931.

Wordsworth. Written with a Pencil upon a Stone in the Wall of the House (an Out-House), on the Island at Grasmere.

Zukofsky. Imitation.

Bull Run, Battles of (1861, 1862)

Melville. Fortitude of the North, The.

Bullets

Cohen. She Has Given Me the Bullet.

Hartley. Eagle of the Inner Eye.
"Reed." Nobody But You.

Bullfights and Bullfighters
Atwood. Bull Song.
Bukowski. Brave Bull.
Dobyns. Querencia.
Eberhart. Lorca.
  Matador.
Hayden. La Corrida.
Hemingway. Poem Is By Maera, The.
Liddy. La Muerte de Joselito.
Olson. This.
Plath. Goring, The.
Tomlinson. Theory of Regress.

Bullfinches
Cowper. On Mrs. Throckmorton's Bulfinch.
Hardy. Bullfinches, The.

Bulls
Atwood. Bull Song.
Cowper. On a Mischievous Bull.
Eberhart. Matador.
Edmunds. Black Bull, The.
Ford. Butterfly and the Bull, The.
Glück. Brooding Likeness.
Griffiths. Llangefni Market.
  Villa-Famès, August 1986.
Hesketh. Bull Alone.
Hewitt. Dry Summer, Islandmagee, 1921.
Hughes, Ted. Bull Moses, The.
Lawrence. St Luke.
Olson. He / in the dark stall, no day now for
  him, to paw.
Smart. Story of a Cock and a Bull, A.
Smith, Stevie. Dedicated Dancing Bull and the
  Water Maid, The.
Spenser. In summers day, when Phœbus fairly
  shone.
Williams, William Carlos. Bull, The.

Bullying and Bullies
Angelou. Thirteens (Black), The.
  Thirteens (White), The.
Bukowski. Bee, The.
  Big Max.
Dobyns. Bleeder.
Griffiths. Shamanism, Dalston.
Hesketh. Different.
Lindsay. Dangerous Little Boy Fairies, The.
Nash. Introduction, The.
Pack. South Bronx, 1939.
"Reed." My Old Man.
Spender. My Parents.
Williams, Charles Kenneth. Hood.
  Love: Wrath.

Bunyan, John
Kipling. Holy War, The.

"Bunyan, Paul"
Silverstein. Paul Bunyan.

Bureaucracy and Bureaucrats
Auden. Unknown Citizen, The.
Davie. Pilate.
Fisher. 3rd November 1976.
Frost. Departmental.
Hewitt. Administration.
Kipling. Army Headquarters.
  China-going P. & O.'s.
  General Summary, A.
  Last Department, The.
  Man Who Could Write, The.
  Masque of Plenty, The.
  Pagett, M. P.
  Plea of the Simla Dancers, The.
  Public Waste.
  Rupaiyat of Omar Kal'vin, The.
  Study of an Elevation, in Indian Ink.
Piercy. Emperor, The.
Smith, Stevie. Choosers, The.

Burglars
Koertge. Moving Day.
Matthews. Burglary.
  Little Blue Nude.

Burial
Beckett. Malacoda.
Berry. So treat me, even dead.
Berryman. Poet's Final Instructions, The.
Carruth. French Hill.
  My Father's Face.

Ciardi. Box Comes Home, A.
  Sea Burial.
Cowper. Another.
  By Callimachus.
  Inscription for a Stone.
De la Mare. Never More, Sailor.
Dickey, James. Sled Burial, Dream Ceremony.
  Sleepers.
Dobyns. How It Was at the End.
Eberhart. Dead Skunk.
  Gesture, The.
  Sea Burial from the Cruiser *Reve*.
Galvin. Carrowkeel.
Hardy. Her Late Husband.
  I Found Her Out There.
Herrick. Bed-Man, or Grave-Maker, The.
  Buriall.
  Rosemarie Branch, The.
  To Anthea: ("Now is the time, when all the
    lights wax dim").
  To the Passenger.
  Upon Himselfe Being Buried.
  Upon Prue [*or* Prew], His Maid.
Hesketh. Walking Back.
Hewitt. Lifting, The.
  Rite.
Hill. Down in the river-garden a grey-gold.
  Strange church smelled a bit 'high,' of
    censers, The.
Jeffers. Delusion of Saints.
  I have told you in another poem, whether
    you've read it or not.
  In the Hill at Newgrange.
  Shane O'Neill's Cairn.
Kipling. Ballade of Burial, A.
Knight. Last Words By "Slick."
Knott. Ritual.
Lawrence. Let the Dead Bury Their Dead.
Lowry. Old Woman who Buried Cats, The.
"MacDiarmid." I mind when ny first wife
  died.
MacLeish. Burial, The.
  Conway Burying Ground.
  Why—what men were they that beneath the
    moon.
MacNeice. Canto XX: "To Wales once more,
  though not on holiday now."
Millay. Burial.
Morgan. There was no bulldozer handy, so.
Nash. Tweedledee and Tweedledoom.
Prince. At Beaulieu.
Robinson. Leonora.
Rossetti. Ye Have Forgotten the Exhortation.
Stevenson. Here Lies Erotion.
  My wife and I, in one romantic cot.
  Now when the number of my years.
  To Priapus.
Warren. Country Burying (1919).
Whitman. Of Him I Love Day and Night.
Wright, James. Alarm, The.
  Dream of Burial, A.
Yau. When one of our citizens dies, his head
  is cut off and placed inside.
See also **Cemeteries; Funerals; Graves;
  Mausoleums; Tombs.**

Burke, Edmund
Coleridge. Burke.
Wilbur. Marché aux Oiseaux.

Burlesque. see Striptease.

Burma
Kipling. Ballad of Boh Da Thone, The.
  Grave of the Hundred Dead, The.
  Mandalay.
Lewis. Burma Casualty.
Whittier. Evening in Burmah.

Burns, Robert
Burns. There was a lad was born in Kyle.
Crane. Song for Happy Feast Days, A.
Keats. On Visiting the Tomb of Burns.
  This Mortal Body of a Thousand Days.
Nash. Everything's Haggis in Hoboken, or,
  Scots Wha Hae Hae.
Smith, Charlotte. To the Shade of Burns.
Stevenson. Thou strainest through the
  mountain fern.
Whittier. Burns.
  Memory of Burns, The.

Williams, William Carlos. Address.
Wordsworth. At the Grave of Burns (1803,
  Seven Years After His Death).
  Thoughts Suggested the Day Following, on the
    Banks of Nith, near the Poet's Residence.
  To the Sons of Burns, after Visiting the Grave
    of Their Father.

Burr, Aaron
Robinson. On the Way.
Schuyler. Eyes at the Window.

Burr, Theodosia
Schuyler. Eyes at the Window.

Burros. see Donkeys.

Bus Terminals
Ginsberg. In the Baggage Room at
  Greyhound.
Lowry. Dollarton Bus Stop, The.
  Singing smell of tar, of the highway, A.

Buses
Atwood. Bus to Alliston, Ontario, The.
Bishop. Moose, The.
Creeley. Peace.
Dobyns. Santiago: la Avenida Pedro de
  Valdivia.
Gunn. Smoking Pot on the Bus.
Hewitt. On a Country Bus Forty Years Ago.
Levine. Ordinary Morning, An.
Liddy. Orpheus as a Christian Scientist.
Lieberman. Creole Mephistopheles, The.
  Tartine's Banishment.
Lowry. Canadian Turned Back at the Border,
  The.
  Dollarton Bus Stop, The.
McGrath. Love in a Bus.
Matthews. Every Tub.
Miller. Riding the bus in the evening again.
Nash. Buses Headed for Scranton, The.
Notley. Bus Stop.
Oppen. I saw from the bus.
Paley. In the Bus.
Tomlinson. Oaxaca Bus, The.
Williams, William Carlos. In the 'Sconset
  Bus.

Business and Businessmen
Betjeman. Business Girls.
  Executive.
Bukowski. Dow Jones: Down.
Carruth. Your dream: / Its name apparently is
  Honeywell.
Clark. "In the Bond Scandals.."
Crabbe. Wager, The.
Cummings. Exit a kind of unkindness exit.
De la Mare. Isaac Meek.
Dickinson. I asked no other thing.
Eberhart. Emerson's Concord.
  Old Fashioned American Business Man, An.
Ginsberg. Who Runs America?
Hewitt. Erice, Western Sicily.
Hughes, Langston. Madam's Past History.
MacLeish. Corporate Entity.
Merton. Corporate posture: variables of fat.
  Gloss on the Sin of Ixion.
  Hat Salesman and a Capable Ruler, A.
Nash. Snark Was a Boojum Was a Prawn,
  The.
Olson. Business, The.
  Dramatis Personae.
Oppen. City of the corporations, A.
Rukeyser. Dam, The.
  Time of finks and nobles, A.
Stuart. Executive Discovers Poetry, The.
  Warehouse Chute, The.
Updike. Business Acquaintances.
  Imaginable Conference, An.
  Tax-Free Encounter.
Williams, Miller. Promotion, The.
See also **Accounting and Accountants;
  Advertising; Banking and Bankers;
  Capitalism; Financiers; Commerce.**

Butchering and Butchers
Atwood. Song of the Hen's Head.
Dobyns. White Pig.
Hardy. Bags of Meat.
Joseph. Butcher's.
Levine. Angel Butcher.
  Animals Are Passing from Our Lives.

McGrath. Another Season.
Merton. Cutting up an Ox.
Nash. Calf, The.
Paley. Psalm: "Their shoes are stuccoed with sawdust and blood."
Robinson. Reuben Bright.
Simic. Butcher Shop.
Tomlinson. On a Pig's Head.
Updike. Modest Mound of Bones, A.
Williams, Charles Kenneth. Racists.

Butter
Hardy. Pat of Butter, The.

Buttercups
Hesketh. Buttercup Children, The.
Second Childhood.

Butterflies
Browning, Robert. Amphibian.
Carruth. Chase in Spring, The.
Rhopaloceral.
Clark. Slow Life.
Crane. Moth That Made God Blind, The.
Dickinson. Butterfly in honored Dust, The.
Butterfly obtains, The.
Butterfly upon the Sky, The.
Butterfly's Assumption Gown, The.
Butterfly's Numidian Gown, The.
Cocoon above! Cocoon below!
Defrauded I a Butterfly.
From Cocoon forth a Butterfly.
Fuzzy fellow, without feet, A.
His oriental heresies.
My Cocoon tightens—Colors tease.
Some such Butterfly be seen.
Two Butterflies went out at Noon.
What tenements of clover.
Duncan. Roots and Branches.
Dunn. Instead of You.
Eberhart. Undercliff Evening.
Emerson. Have ye seen the caterpillar.
Ford. Butterfly and the Bull, The.
Frost. Blue-Butterfly Day.
My Butterfly.
Tuft of Flowers, The.
Gildner. Last Monarch of the Season, The.
Graves. Flying Crooked.
Hayden. Butterfly Piece.
Joseph. Butterfly is dainty flippant fragile, The.
Kipling. Butterflies.
There was never a queen like Balkis.
Lawrence. Butterfly.
Liddy. Churros.
Clare, the Butterflies.
For Jimin in Manchuria II.
Lindsay. King of Yellow Butterflies, The.
Song for Elizabeth, A.
Soul of a Butterfly, The.
Lowry. !Bulletin!
Poor Butterfly that stamped.
Merrill. To a Butterfly.
Merton. Butterfly.
Nathan. Gap.
Nemerov. Crossing, The.
Late Butterflies.
Minim.
Oliver. One or Two Things.
Raine. Blue butterflies' eyed wings.
Smith, Charlotte. Early Butterfly, The.
To a Butterfly in a Window.
Spender. Chalk Blue.
Van Duyn. Speak, Memory!
Walcott. Lesson for This Sunday, A.
Warren. Butterflies over the Map.
Williams, Charles Kenneth. Friends.
In the next life.
Williams, William Carlos. Graceful Bastion, The.
Informative Object, An.
Wright, James. Spring Images.
Zukofsky. Daruma.

Buzzards
Auden. Buzzards.
Stevens. Jack-Rabbit, The.
Tomlinson. High Summer.
Translating the Birds.
Warren. Pondy Woods.

See also **Vultures.**
Byron, George Gordon Noel Byron, 6th Baron
Arnold. Memorial Verses.
When Byron's eyes were shut in death.
Auden. You lived and moved among the best society.
Byron. On This Day I Complete My Thirty-sixth Year.
"Carroll, Lewis." Melancholetta.
Gunn. Lerici.
Hugo. Lake Byron, Maybe Gordon Lord.
Keats. To Lord Byron.
Koch. Art of Poetry, The.
Meinke. Byron vs. DiMaggio.
Meredith. Manfred.
Nash. Chloe and the Roué.
Prince. Byron-Shelley Conversation, A.
Shelley. Fragment: To Byron.
Sonnet to Byron.
Wordsworth. Passage from Mary Barker's *Lines Addressed to a Noble Lord* (His Lordship Will Know Why).
Two Epigrams on Byron's *Cain.*
Byzantium
Gunn. Punch Rubicundus.
Yeats. Byzantium.
Sailing to Byzantium.

C

Cabbages
Lawrence. Rose Is Not a Cabbage, A.
Oliver. Skunk Cabbage.
Sandburg. Nocturn Cabbage.
Cactus
Hartley. Flatterers, The.
Lowry. Sunrise.
Zukofsky. Arizona.
Cactus rose-mauve and gray, twin overturned.
Cadavers. see Corpses.
Cadiz, Spain, Battle of (1596)
Donne. Cales and Guiana.
Sir John Wingfield.
Cads
Herrick. Upon Dundrige.
Upon Rumpe.
Upon Urles.
Kipling. Delilah.
Caesar, Julius
Bukowski. Anthony.
Catullus. Carmen 93: "Utter indifference to your welfare, Caesar."
Crashaw. Mark 12; (Give to Cæsar———) (And to God———).
Jonson. To Clement Edmonds, on His *Caesar's Commentaries* Observed, and Translated.
Lindsay. Trial of the Dead Cleopatra in Her Beautiful and Wonderful Tomb, The.
Millay. When Caesar Fell.
Zukofsky. Nil, not my aim to study you, Caesar, to be—well, a placater.
Cafés
Cohen. Café, The.
Commentary—The Café.
Cummings. 5 / derbies-with-men-in-them smoke Helmar.
Davie. At the Café Parnasse.
Hewitt. Montelepre.
Meinke. Café du Pont.
Sorrentino. Annie from Miami.
Sappho in Paris.
Updike. Grief of Cafeterias, The.
Wright, Charles. Bar Giamaica, 1959-60.
Cain and Abel
Blake. Ghost of Abel, The.
Byron. Oh! thou dead/ And everlasting witness! whose unsinking.
Clough. Adam and Eve.
Coleridge. Wanderings of Cain, The.
Dobyns. Long Story.
Fletcher. Cain and Abel in the meantime had grown.
Then the archangels all together abandoned the

black menacing sky.
There was a pool that rippled in the silence of the north.
They buried Abel at sunset in the red wet earth.
Herrick. Abels Bloud.
Another ("Bloud of Abel was a thing, The").
Kipling. Cain and Abel.
Merton. Will a narrow lane / Save Cain?
Nemerov. Cain.
Cakes
Beatles. Savoy Truffle.
Bishop. Going to the Bakery.
Cummings. This little bride & groom are.
Joseph. Feast, The.
St. John. Wedding Preparations in the Country.
Calais, France
"Carroll, Lewis." Acrostic: Love-lighted eyes, that will not start.
Calcutta, India
Ginsberg. Heat.
Kinnell. To a Child in Calcutta.
Williams, Miller. In a Gradually Moving Car Somewhere in Calcutta.
Calder, Alexander
Shapiro. Calder, A.
Updike. Calder's Hands.
Caliban
Browning, Robert. Caliban upon Setebos; or, Natural Theology in the Island.
California (state)
Angelou. California Prodigal.
Carruth. Backyard in California, A.
Tanck's Song About Dying Young.
Davie. Across the Bay.
In California.
Gunn. Flying Above California.
Geysers, The.
Lights among Redwood.
Hugo. Mendocino, Like You Said.
Jarrell. In Montecito.
Jeffers. Carmel.
Carmel Point.
Clouds of Evening.
Loving Shepherdess, The.
Morro Bay.
Return.
Thurso's Landing.
Women at Point Sur, The.
Koertge. Life on the Edge of the Continent.
Lindsay. Golden Whales of California.
Oppen. And Their Winter and Night in Disguise.
California.
Plath. Sleep in the Mojave Desert.
Rukeyser. Burnishing, Oakland.
St. John. Hotel Sierra.
Until the Sea Is Dead.
Shapiro. California Petrarchan.
Snyder. Burning the Small Dead.
Hay for the Horses.
Marin-An.
Wakoski. Smudging.
Whitman. Promise to California, A.
Song of the Redwood-Tree.
Whittier. Pass of the Sierra, The.
Wright, Charles. California Dreaming.
Young. California Peninsula: El Camino Real.
One West Coast.
Caligula
Updike. Caligula's Dream.
Calligraphy
Zukofsky. (Ryokan's scroll).
Calliope (muse)
Lindsay. Kallyope Yell, The.
Calm
Atwood. Boat, A.
Beckett. Bon bon il est un pays.
Sitôt sorti de l'ermitage.
Berry. Envoy: "Love, all day there has been at the edge of my mind."
Grace.
Browning, Elizabeth Barrett. Sonnet: "Accuse me not, beseech thee, that I wear."
Bukowski. Not Quite So Soon.

Carroll, Jim. I rest with the dogs across the feathers of birds.
Clare. Evening.
Cohen. Commentary—Hurry to Your Dinner.
Cowper. R.S.S. Written in a Fit of Illness.
Cummings. Love is a guess / that deepens.
N / OthI / n / g can / s / urPas / s.
Donne. Calm[e], The.
Eberhart. Sea Storm.
Fisher. If I declare *Peace.*
Fletcher. Hour of Peace, The.
Graves. Poisoned Day.
Hardy. Epigraph to "The Woodlanders."
Hayden. Islands, The.
Herrick. To Music, to Becalm a Sweet-sick Youth.
Hewitt. I Told My Heart to Rest.
In the Luxembourg Gardens.
Hoffman. Stillness, A.
Hughes, Langston. Sea Calm.
Hughes, Ted. Horses, The.
Jeffers. Now Returned Home.
Kunitz. Death In Moonlight.
MacNeice. Evening Indoors.
Oppen. Likely as not a ruined head gasket.
"Reed." Calm before the Storm, The.
Rossetti. Grant us such grace that we may work Thy Will.
In Progress.
There Remaineth Therefore a Rest for the People of God.
What Sappho Would Have Said Had Her Leap Cured Instead of Killing Her.
Shelley. Fragment: "Ye gentle visitations of calm thought."
Southwell. From Fortune's Reach.
Stafford. Near.
Stevenson. I am like one that has sat alone.
Voluntary.
Stuart. Flatfish.
Warren. Lullaby: A Motion Like Sleep.
Masts at Dawn.
Wordsworth. Composed by the Side of Grasmere Lake.
Rains at length have ceased, the winds are stilled, The.
Stars Are Mansions Built by Nature's Hand, The.

Calvary
Dickinson. That I did always love.
See also **Crucifixion, The.**

Calves
Berry. Her First Calf.
In the predicament of other lives.
Ford. Baby on the way!
Hall. Great Day in the Cows' House.
Hardy. Calf, The.
Hughes, Ted. Birth of Rainbow.
March Calf, A.
Nash. Calf, The.
Sweetbread, The.
Tomlinson. Macduff.

Calvinism
Betjeman. Calvinistic Evensong.
Eighteenth-Century Calvinistic Hymn, An.
Clough. Latest Decalogue, The.
Hall. Impossible Marriage, The.
Kipling. McAndrew's Hymn.
Lowell. Mr. Edwards and the Spider.
Millay. To a Calvinist in Bali.

Calypso (mythology)
MacLeish. Calypso's Island.
Merton. Calypso's Island.

Camaraderie
Fletcher. Morning is clean and blue and the wind blows up the clouds, The.
Jonson. Epistle Answering to One That Asked to Be Sealed of the Tribe of Ben, An.
McGrath. Blues for Jimmy.
Restless Night, The.
Triumphal March.
See also **Friendship.**

Cambodia and Cambodians
Clark. Sleepwalker's Fate.
Fenton. Cambodia.
Dead Soldiers.

Cambridge, England
Coleridge. Absence.
Wilbur. Violet and Jasper.
Wordsworth. Inside of King's College Chapel, Cambridge.

Cambridge, Massachusetts
Cummings. Awful darkness of the town, The.
Eberhart. How It Is.
Schuyler. Four Poems.
See also **Harvard University.**

Cambridge University
Berryman. London.
Message.
Other Cambridge, The.
Transit.
Cowper. Elegy 1: To Charles Diodati.
Sparrows Self-Domesticated.
Davie. On Bertrand Russell's "Portraits from Memory."
Kipling. Scholars, The.
Milton. Elegy 1: To Charles Diodati.
Wordsworth. Inside of King's College Chapel, Cambridge.

Camden, William
Campion. Ad Guil. Camdenum.
Jonson. To William Camden.

Camellias
Moore. Camellia Sabina.
Schuyler. Chapel, A.

Camelot
Robinson. Lancelot.
Merlin.
Tennyson. Lady of Shalott, The.
Morte d'Arthur.

Camels
Ford. Oh, a patch of green.
Hewitt. Twisted Heart, The.
Kipling. Camel's hump is an ugly lump, The.
Oonts.
Nash. Camel, The.

Cameras
Ciardi. On a Photo of Sgt. Ciardi a Year Later.
Thanks to a Botanist, A.
Gunn. Song of a Camera.
See also **Photography and Photographers.**

Campaigns, Political
Lindsay. Bryan, Bryan, Bryan, Bryan.
Rukeyser. Professionals see the signs in the dice, the signs in the cards and clouds, The.
They pray. Security against oldness.
See also **Voting and Voters.**

Campanula
Raine. Campanula.

Campbell, Roy
"MacDiarmid." Left-wing poetry represents a rise in the price of bread.

Camping
Dickey, James. Place of the Skull, The.
Sleeping Out at Easter.
Emerson. Adirondacs, The.
Everson. Bride of the Bear.
Jeffers. Oh, Lovely Rock.
Plath. Two Campers in Cloud Country.
Rexroth. Fish Peddler and Cobbler.
Floating.
Snyder. August on Sourdough, a Visit from Dick Brewer.
Bubbs Creek Haircut.
Cool around the Fire, The.
For the Boy Who Was Dodger Point Lookout Fifteen Years Ago.
Late October Camping in the Sawtooths.
Stuart. River, The.
Wright, Charles. Other Side of the River, The.
Young. No More Doors Tonight.

Campuses. *see* **Colleges and Universities.**

Canaan
Milton. Paraphrase on Psalm 114, A.
Smith, Stevie. In Canaan's Happy Land.

Canada
Atwood. At the Tourist Centre in Boston.
Thoughts from Underground.
Two-Headed Poems.

Cohen. Cherry Orchards.
Creeley. Canada.
Davie. Bougainville.
Jesuits in North America, The.
Letter to Curtis Bradford, A.
Dunn. Walking the Marshland.
Kipling. Our Lady of the Snows.
Prairie, The.
Two Canadian Memorials.
Lowry. Old Blake was warm, he got down to the hub.
Walk in Canada.
Whittier. St. John.

Canals
Hewitt. Word, The.
Hugo. Crinan Canal.
Lowry. Peter Gaunt and the Canals.
Melville. In a Bye-Canal.
Tomlinson. Canal.

Canaries
Nash. Canary, The.
Whitman. My Canary Bird.
Wilbur. Pity.

Cancer (disease)
Auden. Miss Gee.
Cohen. I Wanted to Be a Doctor.
Dickey, James. Cancer Match, The.
For the Death of Vince Lombardi.
Dickey, William. Elegy Before the Time.
Eberhart. Cancer Cells, The.
Lovely were the fruit trees in the evening.
Hewitt. My dear spouse died—a tumour on the brain.
Hugo. Green Stone.
Jarrell. Christmas Roses, The.
Lorde. American Cancer Society Or There Is More Than One Way to Skin a Coon.
Lowell. Death from Cancer.
Rich. Woman Dead in Her Forties, A.
Sexton. Operation, The.
Spender. Elegy for Margaret.
Stuart. Girl of My Dreams Is Dying.
Turco. Cancer.

Candlemas
Herrick. Ceremonies for Candlemasse Day, The.
Ceremonies for Candlemas[se] Eve.
Ceremony upon Candlemas Eve.
To Perenna ("I a Dirge will pen for thee").
Upon Candlemasse Day.
Merton. Candlemas Procession, The.

Candles
Carruth. Have you ever seen.
Creeley. Of Years.
Warning, The.
De la Mare. Reverie.
Rose in Candlelight, A.
Dunbar. At Candle-Lightin' Time.
Dunn. One Side of the Story.
Herrick. Tapers.
To Mistresse Mary Willand.
Lawrence. All Souls.
Liddy. Death of Lovers, The.
"MacDiarmid." Servant Girl's Bed.
MacNeice. Candle in his white grave-clothes, always turning his cowled head, The.
Finale.
I have no clock, yet I can hear.
Millay. Second Fig.
Nemerov. Flame of a Candle, The.
Piercy. I Am A Light You Could Read By.
Plath. By Candlelight.
Candles.
Stevens. Valley Candle.
Suckling. Candle, A.
Wilbur. For K. R. on Her Sixtieth Birthday.

Candy
Carruth. Sonnet: "Cindy, the secret's out. Yes, you're addict-."
Ferlinghetti. Pennycandystore beyond the El, The.
Hugo. La Push.

Candy Stores
Ferlinghetti. Pennycandystore beyond the El, The.

Cannibalism and Cannibals
Dobyns. Pablo Neruda.

Eberhart. Came lassitude and despair of the mind.
 Explorer on Main Street, The.
Joseph. Man as Cannibal (PLAIN; BIOLOGY).
MacNeice. Thyestes.
Patchen. Little Cannibal's Bedtimesong.
Rukeyser. Cannibal Bratuscha.
Silverstein. Dreadful.
Stevenson. Feast of Famine: Marquesan Manners, The.

Canning
Van Duyn. Homework.

Canoes and Canoeing
O'Hara. Terrestrial Cuckoo, A.
Oppen. Travelogue.
Rexroth. Floating.
Snyder. Canyon Wren, The.
Stevenson. Canoe Speaks, The.
 On the great streams the ships may go.

Canonical Hours
Davie. Horae Canonicae.

Canova, Antonio
Byron. In This Beloved Marble View.

Cape Breton Island, Nova Scotia
Bishop. Cape Breton.

Cape Cod, Massachusetts
Galvin. Old Map of Barnstable County.
Knight. Television Speaks.
Matthews. On Cape Cod a Child Is Stolen.
Millay. Memory of Cape Cod.
Schuyler. Rose of Marion, The.

Capital Punishment
"Dylan." Ballad of Donald White.
Jeffers. Margrave.
"MacDiarmid." Facing the Chair.
Olson. Willie Francis and the Electric Chair.
Plath. Trial of Man, The.
Warren. Where They Come to Wait for the Body: A Ghost Story.
Whittier. Gallows, The.
 Human Sacrifice, The.
Wordsworth. Sonnets upon the Punishment of Death.

See also **Executions and Executioners.**

Capitalism
Carruth. Your dream: / Its name apparently is Honeywell.
Cummings. Memorabilia.
"Dylan." I Pity the Poor Immigrant.
 Maggie's Farm.
 Money Blues.
 Union Sundown.
Emerson. New England Capitalist.
 Since the devil hopping on.
Hewitt. Cape Sunion.
Knight. Memo #9.
Larkin. Homage to a Government.
Lawrence. Always This Paying.
 But I Say unto You: Love One Another.
 Cry of the Masses.
 For All That.
 Latent Desire, The.
 Love as an Escape.
 Money.
 Money-Madness.
 Why—?
 Young Are Not Greedy, The.
"MacDiarmid." My Songs Are Kandym in the Waste Land.
McGrath. Vision of Three Angels Viewing the Progress of Socialism.
MacLeish. Empire Builders.
Meredith. Capitalist, The.
 Song: "Buy, buy, buy."
Merrill. Clearing the Title.
Merton. Proverbs.
 Songs of Experience; India, One.
Olson. Being Altogether Literal, & Specific, and Seeking at the Same Time to be Successfully Explicit.
Sandburg. So you want to divide all the money there is.
Shapiro. Drug Store.
 Humanities Building, The.
Snyder. Trade, The.

Williams, William Carlos. Libertad! Igualdad! Fraternidad!
Zukofsky. Arizona.
 Two Dedications: D.R.

See also **Banking and Bankers; Business and Businessmen; Financiers.**

Captivity
Cowper. On a Goldfinch Starved to Death in His Cage.
De la Mare. Bitter Waters.
 Captive, The.
Dickinson. Prison gets to be a friend, A.
Dunbar. Sympathy.
Garrigue. Iowa City Zoo.
Graves. Moon's Tear, The.
Hewitt. Prisoners on the Roof, The.
Kipling. Captive, The.
 Half-Ballad of Waterval.
Lawrence. There Is No Way Out.
 Wild Things in Captivity.
Lewis. Fishes inhabit the deep rock crannies, the worm the dry.
 Swallows are nesting in the hovels of Israel, The.
 They have clipped the wings of my doves, my messengers.
Lovelace. Lady A. L., My Asylum [in a Great Extremity], The.
Lowry. With Sweetest Love and Welcome from All the Little Animals.
MacLeish. Captivity of the Fly.
Meredith. Two Blackbirds, The.
Morrison. Enter the Slip.
Rich. For a Sister.
Rukeyser. Woman and Emblems.
Sidney. Like as the dove which seeled-up doth fly.
Smart. On an Eagle Confined in a College-Court.
Williams, Charles Kenneth. Souls.
Wordsworth. Gold and Silver Fishes in a Vase.
Wroth. Sonnet 14: "Am I thus conquered? [or conquer'd]? have I lost the powers."

Caravaggio, Michelangelo Merisi da
Gunn. In Santa Maria del Popolo.
Markson. Death of the Virgin, The.
Prince. Sun floats in sublime, The.

Card Games
Dickey, William. Face-Paintings of the Caduveo Indians.
Dobyns. Card Game, The.
Dove. Sailor in Africa, The.
Duncan. Poem in Stretching, A.
"Dylan." Jack o' diamonds / jack o' diamonds.
Frost. In Divés' Dive.
Graves. Song: Sword and Rose.
Larkin. Card-Players, The.
MacNeice. Vingt-et-un.
Nash. Your Lead, Partner, I Hope We've Read the Same Book.
Rossetti. House of cards / Is neat and small, A.
 Queen of Hearts, The.
Sexton. Angel of Beach Houses and Picnics.
Sorrentino. Cards.
 Woman Irritable because of Her Menses.
Updike. Solitaire.
Wakoski. Life Is Like a Game of Cards, Or Another One of Those Metaphysical Statements from a Distant Reader.

Cardiff, Wales
Wordsworth. When Severn's Sweeping Flood Had Overthrown.

Cardinals (ornithology)
Carruth. Meditation in the Presence of "Ostrich Walk."
 Song: The Old, Old Man.
Schuyler. Cardinal, A.

Cargoes
Lewis. Consider this silent disciplined assembly.
Merton. Cargo Catechism.
 Cargo Songs.
 Dialog with Mister Clapcott.

John the Volcano.
 Sewende (Seven Day).

See also **Freighters.**

Caribbean Islands. *see* **West Indies.**

Caribbean Sea
Crane. To the Empress Josephine's Statue.
Merton. Poem: "Here is the man of the islands."
Millay. Dream of Saba.
Walcott. Sea-Chantey, A.

See also **West Indies.**

Caring
Berg. Tashkent Blossoms, 1944.
Carroll, Jim. For Sue's Birthday.
Cooper. Rent.
De la Mare. Mrs. Grundy.
Everson. Bride of the Bear.
Gardner. Mea Culpa.
Gildner. All Hallows' Eve in Kansas.
Glück. Portrait.
Graves. Crucibles of Love.
 Should I Care.
 Song: How Can I Care?
 Virgin Mirror.
Hewitt. Aesthete's Renunciation.
 Aristocratic Area.
 For Deirdre.
 Gentle Bush, The.
 King Concerned, The.
 Mister Faintheart Middleclass.
Kooser. Boarding House.
MacNeice. Flight of the Heart.
Notley. Sonnet:"Late Gracie Allen was a very lucid comedienne, The."
Pack. Clayfeld's Duck.
 Out of Nothing.
Piercy. Hand Games.
 In the Wet.
 We are all hustling and dealing.
Rossetti. Because He First Loved Us.
 Lord, carry me.—Nay, but I grant thee strength.
Stafford. Remembering Brother Bob.
Stevenson. For Richmond's Garden Wall.
 To Madame Garschine.
Wright, James. Arrangements with Earth for Three Dead Friends.
 Mutterings over the Crib of a Deaf Child.

Carlyle, Thomas
Graves. Something to Say.
Meredith. To Carlyle.

Carmel, California
Hugo. Mission in Carmel.
Jeffers. Carmel.
 Carmel Point.
 Tor House.

Carnivals
Bishop. Pink Dog.
Boyle. Carnival 1927.
"Dylan." Dusty Old Fairgrounds.
Ginsberg. Big Beat.
Gunn. Before the Carnival.
Hugo. One by Twachtman at the Frye.
Merrill. Think Tank.
Nash. Lecturer in Bookstore.
Rich. In Time of Carnival.
Tomlinson. Portobello Carnival 1973.

Carousels. *see* **Merry-Go-Rounds.**

Carp
Wright, James. Lifting Illegal Nets by Flashlight.

Carpe Diem
Angelou. Come, And Be My Baby.
Auden. Now from far eastern wolds, the bay.
 Two Triolets.
Beatles. Love You To.
Berrigan. I Heard Brew Moore Say, One Day.
Browning, Robert. Youth and Art.
Bunting. Snow's on the fellside, look! How deep.
Burns. Here's, a bottle and an honest friend.
 Hey Ca' thro'.
 Sketch. New Year's Day. To Mrs. Dunlop.
 Song: "My father was a farmer upon the Carrick border O."

Byron. To Caroline ("When I hear you express an affection so warm").
Campion. My Dearest Mistress.
Carew. To A. L.; Persuasions [or Perswasions] to Love.
Clough. Mari Magno II.
Cowper. Written in a Quarrel.
Cullen. I Have a Rendezvous with Life.
Cummings. For him alone life's worse than worst.
Granted the all / saving our young kiss only.
My father moved through dooms of love.
One's not half two. It's two are halves of one.
Ponder,darling,these busted statues.
Song: "But we've the may / (for you are in love)."
What freedom's not some under's mere above.
What if a much of a which of a wind.
Dobyns. Uprising.
"Dylan." Desire (Liner Notes).
Emerson. Fame.
Fine presentiments controlled him.
Go build forth, and feast on being's banquet.
Heri, Cras, Hodie.
How drearily in College hall.
I said to the East wind.
In thy holiday of life.
Frost. Carpe Diem.
Gardner. Cadenza.
Canzonetta.
Fixing the Clock.
Garrigue. Note to La Fontaine, A.
Hardy. Best She Could, The.
Queen Caroline to Her Guests.
Herrick. Anacreontike.
Best To Be Merry.
Corinna's Going a-Maying.
End Decreed, An.
Paranæticall, or Advisive Verse, to His Friend, M. John Wicks.
To Electra ("'Tis Ev'ning, my Sweet").
To Enjoy the Time.
To Live Freely.
To Sappho.
To Silvia to Wed.
To [the] Virgins, to Make Much of Time.
To Youth.
Jong. To X. (With Ephemeral Kisses).
Jonson. O know to end, as to begin.
Song. To Celia: ("Come my Celia, let us prove").
Keats. Fancy.
Ode on a Grecian Urn.
Lewis. Lines on a Tudor Mansion.
Lindsay. Tiger on Parade, The.
Lovelace. To Amarantha, That She Would Dishevel[l] Her Hair[e].
MacLeish. Speech to a Crowd.
MacNeice. Carpe Diem.
Marlowe. Nimphs [or Nymph's] Reply to the Sheepheard [or Shepherd], The.
Marvell. To His Coy Mistress.
Young Love.
Meinke. Advice to My Son.
Melville. Rosary Beads.
Millay. I shall forget you presently, my dear.
Oliver. Peonies.
Ralegh. Nimphs [or Nymph's] Reply to the Sheepheard [or Shepherd], The.
Ransom. Blue Girls.
Morning.
Old Man Playing with Children.
Rich. Floating Poem, Unnumbered, The.
Robinson. Horace to Leuconoë.
Rossetti. Maiden May.
Sandburg. If So Hap May Be.
Moments of Dawn Riders.
Two Neighbors.
Sidney. Fourth Song.
Southwell. Loss[e] in Delay[e].
Spenser. Whiles someone did chant this lovely lay, The.
Stevenson. Away with funeral music—set.
Gather ye roses while ye may.
Tennyson. Now Sleeps the Crimson Petal, Now the White.

Williams, Miller. In Nashville, Standing in the Wooden Circle Sawed Out from the Old Ryman Stage, the Picker has a vision.
Thinking Friday Night with a Gothic Storm Going About Final Causes and Logos and Mitzi Mayfair.
Williams, William Carlos. Song: "Pluck the florets from."
Young. Sunday Illumination.

Carpentry and Carpenters
Davie. With the Grain.
Dickinson. Myself was formed—a Carpenter.
Oppen. Carpenter's Boat.
Workman.
Wilbur. Hole in the Floor, A.

Carpets. see Rugs and Carpets.

Carriages
Burns. To the Honble Mr. R. M———, of P-nm-re, on His High Phaeton.
De la Mare. Last Coachload, The.
Moore. Carriage from Sweden, A.
Tomlinson. Poem: "Wakening with the window over fields."

Cars. see Automobiles.

Carving and Carvers
Atwood. Some Objects of Wood and Stone.
Davie. On Generous Lines.
McAuley. Ritual.
Merton. Woodcarver, The.
Sidney. Do not disdain, O straight upraised pine.
You goodly pines, which still with brave ascent.

Cary, Sir Lucius
Jonson. To the Immortal[l] Memory [or Memorie] and Friendship of That Noble Pair[e], Sir Lucius Cary and Sir H. [or Henry] Morison.

Casement, Roger David
Yeats. Ghost of Roger Casement, The.
Roger Casement.

Cassandra
Bogan. Cassandra.
Jeffers. Cassandra.
Tower beyond Tragedy, The.
Keats. Translated from Ronsard.
Meredith. Cassandra.
Paley. Responsibility.
Robinson. Cassandra.

Castile. see Spain.

Castlereagh, Robert Stewart, 2d Viscount
Byron. Epigrams: "Oh, Castlereagh! thou art a patriot now."
Shelley. Similes for Two Political Characters of 1819.

Castles
Brontë. Written in Aspin Castle.
Burns. Castle Gordon—*Intended to Be Sung to Morag.*
Lines on Stirling.
Cummings. My love is building a building.
Dunn. Happiness.
Graves. Castle, The.
Gunn. Down panic, down. The castle is still here.
Jack Straw sits.
My coldness wakes me.
Hacker. Celles.
Hopkins. Escorial, The.
Hugo. Duntulm Castle.
Ferniehirst Castle.
Levertov. Psalm Concerning the Castle.
Lewis. Pharaoh has seen me in the hovels of Israel.
McAuley. Baldungan Castle.
Poe. Haunted Palace, The.
Scott. Magic Castle, The.
Smith, Stevie. Castle, The.
Tomlinson. Castle, The.
Château de Muzot.
Legend.
Wilbur. Castles and Distances.
Wordsworth. Address to Kilchurn Castle, upon Loch Awe.
Bothwell Castle.
Composed among the Ruins of a Castle in

North Wales.
Elegiac Stanzas Suggested by a Picture of Peele Castle, in a Storm [Painted by Sir George Beaumont].
Fragment of a "Gothic" Tale.
Horn of Egremont Castle, The.
Vale of Esthwaite, The.
Yeats. Blood and the Moon.

Castration
Carruth. As doctor Peter said.
Jeffers. Oysters.

Castro, Fidel
Carruth. He reads: / "That is one of the great tragedies."
Cohen. Field Commander Cohen.
Updike. Meditation on a News Item.

Catalpa Trees
Ciardi. Catalpa, The.

Catbirds
Creeley. Air: "Cat Bird Singing."

Catechism
Emerson. We sauntered amidst miracles.
Stafford. Catechism, A.

Caterpillars
Bly. Caterpillar, A.
Dickinson. Fuzzy fellow, without feet, A.
How soft a Caterpillar steps.
Emerson. Have ye seen the caterpillar.
Nash. Caterpillar, The.
Rossetti. Brown and furry / Caterpillar in a hurry.
Brown and furry.
Silverstein. Standing.
Williams, Miller. Caterpillar, The.

Cathedrals
Davie. Under St Paul's.
Edmunds. Nocturne.
Hardy. Abbey Mason, The.
Cathedral Façade at Midnight, A.
Melville. Milan Cathedral.
Merton. Weathercock on the Cathedral of Quito, The.
Oppen. Chartres.
Rukeyser. Evening Plaza, San Miguel.
Shapiro. Cathedral Bells, The.
Williams, William Carlos. New Cathedral Overlooking the Park, The.
Wordsworth. In the Cathedral at Cologne.

Cather, Willa
Rich. For Julia in Nebraska.

Catherine of Siena, Saint
Dove. Catherine of Siena.

Catholicism and Catholics
Auden. Macao.
Beckett. Zone.
Betjeman. Anglo-Catholic Congresses.
Browning, Robert. Holy-Cross Day.
Cohen. Montreal.
Coleridge. Sancti Dominici Pallium.
Cummings. Candles and / Here Comes a glass box.
Donne. Show me dear[e] Christ, thy spouse, so bright and clear.
Doolittle. This is no rune nor riddle.
Eberhart. Irish Catholic.
Edmunds. Doña Sebastiana.
El Santuario de Chimayó.
Eliot. Hippopotamus, The.
Gildner. Harold Fogel Could Be Anywhere.
They Have Turned the Church Where I Ate God.
Graves. Cuirassiers of the Frontier, The.
Herbert. To the Lady Elizabeth Queen of Bohemia.
Hewitt. After the Fire.
Green Shoot, The.
Irish Dimension, The.
May Alter.
Kinnell. Avenue Bearing the Initial of Christ into the New World, The.
Lawrence. Church, The.
Liddy. Miles.
To the Liberal Magistrates.
Lowell. Beyond the Alps.
For George Santayana.
Thanksgiving's Over.

Melville. Vine and Clarel.
Patchen. Palms for a Catholic Child.
Prince. My last morning and so, here.
Robinson. Erasmus.
Schuyler. I Sit Down to Type.
  Mark.
Tomlinson. On a Mexican Straw Christ.
Whittier. Pastoral Letter, The.
Williams, Miller. In Your Own Words
  Without Lying Tell Something of Your
  Background With Particular Attention to
  Anything Relating to the Position For Which
  You Are Applying. Press Down.
Williams, William Carlos. Catholic Bells, The.
  Light Becomes Darkness.
Wordsworth. Composed in One of the
  Catholic Cantons.
  Near Rome, in Sight of St Peter's.

Cats
Auden. Cat, The.
  Single creature leads a partial life, The.
Bishop. Lullaby for the Cat.
Boyle. Winter Fable, A.
Bukowski. History of a Tough Motherfucker,
  The.
  I Was Born to Hustle Roses Down the
  Avenues of the Dead.
  Little Tigers Everywhere.
  One for the Old Boy.
  Terminology.
Bunting. Pious Cat, The.
"Carroll, Lewis." Mouse's Tale, The: "We
  lived beneath the mat."
  Three sisters at breakfast were feeding the cat.
Catullus. Carmen 59: "Menenius' wife, / a
  red-headed cat from Bologna."
Cowper. Colubriad, The.
  Familiarity Dangerous.
  Retired Cat, The.
Crane. Chaplinesque.
Creeley. Love ("Thing comes / of itself,
  The").
Cullen. Cat, The.
  Cats.
Cummings. Float / ing / ly) / i / (in Khoury's
  warm).
  (Im)c-a-t(mo).
  Why did you go.
De la Mare. Comfort.
  Maerchen.
Dickey, William. Lady of Shalott, Her Mirror
  Broken, The.
Dickinson. She sights a Bird—she chuckles.
Dobyns. Getting Up.
  Way It Goes or the Proper Use of Leisure
  Time, The.
Dunn. After Losses.
  Cleanliness.
Eberhart. Concord Cats.
  Key West.
  Old Tom.
  Vastness and Indifference of the World, The.
Eliot. Lines to a Persian Cat.
Emerson. Comfort with a purring cat.
Ferlinghetti. Cat, The.
Fisher. Cat's glinting face as it stared, The.
  Woman across the lane, The.
Ford. Christine is the girl I adore.
  There's a howling stray.
Garrigue. Epitaph for My Cat.
  Rain Song.
Graves. Frightened Men.
Gray. Ode on the Death of a Favourite [or
  Favorite] Cat, Drowned in a Tub [or Bowl]
  of Gold Fishes.
Griffiths. Small Substantial Shadow.
Gunn. Apartment Cats.
  Cat and the Wind, The.
Hall. Alligator Bride, The.
Hardy. Last Words to a Dumb Friend.
  Roman Gravemounds, The.
Hartley. V—Is for Victory as You Can Plainly
  See.
Hemingway. Earnest Liberal's Lament, The.
  To Crazy Christian.
Herrick. Upon Pusse and her Prentice.
Hesketh. Cats.

Hughes, Ted. Esther's Tomcat.
Jarrell. Happy Cat, The.
  Lonely Man, The.
Joseph. Fifty-thousand cats cross our garden—
  .
Keats. To Mrs. Reynolds's Cat.
Kinnell. Supper after the Last, The.
Kipling. Pussy can sit by the fire and sing.
Kooser. Sleeping Cat.
Levertov. Cat as Cat, The.
Levine. Theory of Prosody, A.
Lindsay. Dirge for a Righteous Kitten, A.
  Mysterious Cat, The.
Lowry. Old Woman who Buried Cats, The.
MacLeish. Cat in the Wood, The.
MacNeice. Cats.
Matthews. Cat, The.
Merrill. Maisie.
Moore. Peter.
Nash. Cat Naps Are Too Good for Cats.
  Kitten, The.
Oliver. Morning.
Olson. Not a rat-hole, a cat-hole: the knife of
  time; on the ledge, overlooking.
Piercy. Cats of Greece, The.
  I Awoke with the Room Cold.
Plath. Ella Mason and Her Eleven Cats.
Rossetti. On the Death of a Cat.
  Pussy has a whiskered face, / Kitty has such
  pretty ways.
Sandburg. Three Slants at New York.
Shelley. Verses on a Cat.
Silverstein. Drats.
Smart. For I will consider my Cat Jeoffry.
Smith, Stevie. Cat Asks Mouse Out.
  Celtic Fringe, The.
  Conviction (iii).
  Friskers, or, Gods and Men.
  Galloping Cat, The.
  Monsieur Pussy-Cat, Blackmailer.
  My Cat Major.
  My Cats.
  Nipping Pussy's Feet in Fun.
  Nodding.
  Our Office Cat.
  Singing Cat, The.
Stevens. Rabbit as King of the Ghosts, A.
Stuart. Canned Goods.
Swift. Fable of the Widow and Her Cat, A.
Thomson. Lisy's Parting with Her Cat.
Turco. Cat, The.
Updike. Daughter.
Van Duyn. At Père Lachaise.
Williams, William Carlos. Cats' Month, The.
  Complete Destruction.
  Mujer.
  Poem: "As the cat."
  Young Cat and the Chrysanthemums, The.
Yeats. Cat and the Moon, The.
  Two Songs of a Fool.
Zukofsky. Bononian, sis Rufa, Rufus' lum fell
  at.
See also **Kittens.**

Cattle
Glück. Thanksgiving.
Hardy. Bags of Meat.
Herrick. Bucolick betwixt Two: Lacon and
  Thyrsis, A.
Hughes, Ted. Birth of Rainbow.
  March Calf, A.
Jeffers. Wind-Struck Music, The.
Kipling. Alnaschar and the Oxen.
  Lament of the Border Cattle Thief, The.
  Mulholland's Contract.
Muldoon. Cherish the Ladies.
See also **Bulls; Cowboys; Cows; Meat.**

Catullus
Campion. De Catullo et Martiale.
  In Cambrum.
Davie. Catullus on Friendship.
MacLeish. You Also, Gaius Valerius Catullus.
Tennyson. Frater Ave Atque Vale.
Zukofsky. Catullus viii.
  In the midst of things.

Caution
Browning, Elizabeth Barrett. Wisdom
  Unapplied.

Bukowski. Counsel.
Clark. Bathed.
Creeley. First Time, The.
  For Benny and Sabina.
Cullen. Advice to a Beauty.
  To a Brown Girl.
Eberhart. Scouring, The.
Emerson. Pericles.
Everson. Spotfire.
Garrigue. Note to La Fontaine, A.
Hacker. Adult Entertainment.
Herrick. Safety on the Shore.
  Safety To Look to Ones Selfe.
Hewitt. Ocean, 1940.
  Search, The.
Joseph. Overbold, The.
Kipling. Carmen Circulare.
  Four Points, The.
Kunitz. So Intricately Is This World Resolved.
Lewis. To a Comrade in Arms.
Lowry. Homoeopathic Blues in J.
Matthews. How Careful Fire Can Be.
Meredith. England before the Storm.
  'Tis good to keep hinderward eyes.
Nash. Strange Case of the Cautious Motorist,
  The.
Piercy. Girl in White.
Rolfe. Little Ballad for Americans—1954.
Silverstein. Captain Hook.
  Warning.
Smart. Watching.
Sorrentino. Ars Longa.
Stuart. Ballad of the Scarecrow, The.
Wroth. Sonnet 34: "Take heed mine eyes, how
  you your lookes doe cast."
Yeats. Never Give All the Heart.

Cavalcanti, Guido
O'Hara. Poem in Envy of Cavalcanti, A.
Shelley. Sonnet: [From the Italian of Dante.]
  Dante Alighieri to Guido Cavalcanti.

Cavaliers
Browning, Robert. Cavalier Tunes.
Herrick. His Cavalier.

Cavalry
Brooks. Riders to the Blood-Red Wrath.
Housman. Lancer.
  Soldier from the wars returning.
Tennyson. Charge of the Light Brigade, The.
Whitman. Cavalry Crossing a Ford.

Cavemen
Fletcher. Epilogue: "By the glare of the
  guttering torch."
Kipling. Story of Ung, The.
Mahon. Hunt by Night, The.
Rukeyser. Painters.
See also **Man, Primitive.**

Caves
Carroll, Jim. Caves, The.
"Carroll, Lewis." Ye Fattale Cheyse.
Coleridge. Catullian Hendecasyllables.
  Complaint of Ninathóma, The.
Gunn. Merlin in the Cave: He Speculates
  without a Book.
Hall. Child, The.
Jeffers. Hands.
McNeill. Cave, The.
Notley. Poem: "Who do I want to tell it."
Olson. On All Sides.
Pack. Cave of Lascaux, The.
Patchen. Irkalla's White Caves.
Pope. On His Grotto at Twickenham.
Rukeyser. Ajanta.
Stafford. Indian Caves in the Dry Country.
  Long rope of gray smoke was, A.
Tomlinson. Cavern, The.
Williams, William Carlos. Avenue of Poplars,
  The.
Wordsworth. Cave of Staffa ("We saw, but
  surely, in the motley crowd").
  Cave of Staffa ("Ye shadowy Beings, that
  have rights and claims").
  Suggested by Mr W. Westall's Views of the
  Caves, etc., in Yorkshire.
  To the Lady Mary Lowther.

Caviar
Williams, William Carlos. For Viola: De
  Gustibus.

Cecilia, Saint
Auden. Anthem for St. Cecilia's Day.
Crane. Sonnet: "Ere elfish Night shall sift another day."
Davie. Nashville Mornings.
Dryden. Alexander's Feast; or, The Power of Music [or Musique].
Song for St Cecilia's Day [1687], A.
Pope. Ode for Music on St. Cecilia's Day.

Celandine
Wordsworth. Small Celandine, The.
To the Same Flower [The Small Celandine].
To the Small Celandine.

Celery
Nash. Celery.
Updike. Celery.

Celibacy
Bukowski. Almost Made Up Poem, An.
Everson. Sea: / And in its flaw the sprung silence.
Graves. Starred Coverlet, The.
Lowell. Like Henry VIII, Mohammed got religion.
Nash. Tune for an Ill-Tempered Clavichord.
See also **Bachelors; Virginity and Virgins.**

Cellars
Auden. Down There.
Gunn. Bringing to Light.
Down in the cellars, nothing is visible.
Roethke. Root Cellar.

Cellos
McAuley. Dying Swan, The.

Celts
Hugo. Standing Stones of Callanish, The.
"MacDiarmid." Celtic genius—Cornwall, Scotland, Ireland, Wales—, The.
Wreck of the *Swan*, The.
Smith, Stevie. Celts, The.

Cemeteries
Auden. Island Cemetery, An.
Beckett. Ne manquez pas à Tanger.
Berry. He Looks out the Window at the Town.
Meadow, The.
Bishop. Cemetery of Childhood.
Bunting. Now that sea's over that island.
Carruth. Ain't that something? Why, I knowed old Tom.
Cooper. Graveyard, The.
Creeley. I.
Cummings. Allbutnotquitemost.
One / t / hi / s / snowflake.
Dickinson. Chilly Peace infests the Grass, A.
This quiet Dust was Gentlemen and Ladies.
Where every bird is bold to go.
Dobyns. Cemetery Nights.
Cemetery Nights II.
Cemetery Nights IV.
Cemetery Nights V.
Eberhart. Soul Longs to Return Whence It Came, The.
Fenton. Bus is waiting at the southern gate, The.
But when so many had died, so many and at such speed.
Fisher. Looking for life, I lost my mind.
Griffiths. Llantysilio, Overgrown.
Haines. At Slim's River.
Hardy. Friends Beyond.
Levelled Churchyard, The.
Merrymaking in Question, A.
Paying calls.
Sexton at Longpuddle, The.
Supplanter, The.
Voices from Things Growing in a Churchyard.
While Drawing in a Churchyard.
Hill. Distant Fury of Battle, The.
Housman. God's Acre.
Hughley Steeple.
Hugo. Antisocial Easter.
Digging Is an Art.
Graves at Coupeville.
Graves at Mukilteo.
St. John's Chapel.
Two Graves in a Day.
Keats. On Visiting the Tomb of Burns.

Kipling. King's Pilgrimage, The.
Knight. Crown Hill Cemetary, Indianapolis.
Kooser. In a Country Cemetery in Iowa.
There Is Always a Little Wind.
Lawrence. Giorno dei Morti.
Levine. Cemetery at Academy, California, The.
Longfellow. Jewish Cemetery at Newport, The.
Lowell. Dunbarton.
Quaker Graveyard in Nantucket, The.
McGrath. Poem: "Light flares from the tombstones.."
McNeill. Burying Field.
Meinke. Church Cemetery in St. Mary's, A.
Merton. Trappist Cemetery—Gethsemani, The.
Nathan. Meadow Foam.
Nemerov. Negro Cemetery Next to a White One, A.
Piercy. Visiting a Dead Man on a Summer Day.
Rossetti. Birchington Churchyard.
Rukeyser. Trinity Churchyard.
Sandburg. Cool Tombs.
Trinity Place.
Schuyler. In a Churchyard.
Schwartz. This hushed surface where the doves parade.
Smith, Charlotte. Written in the Church-yard at Middleton in Sussex.
Smith, Stevie. Edmonton, Thy Cemetery..
English Visitor, The.
Great Unaffected Vampires and the Moon.
Night-Time in the Cemetery.
Out of Time.
Stevens. Two at Norfolk.
Stevenson. Ditty: "Cock shall crow, The."
Stuart. Funeral, The.
Tate. Ode to the Confederate Dead.
Tomlinson. After a Death.
Ice Cream at Blauenberg.
Updike. Plow Cemetery.
Van Duyn. At Père Lachaise.
Whitman. Camps of Green.
Ode: "O, God of Columbia! O, Shield of the Free!"
Whittier. Hive at Gettysburg, The.
Old Burying-Ground, The.
Wilbur. In a Churchyard.
Williams, William Carlos. Children, The.
For a Low Voice.
On First Opening the Lyric Year.
Wordsworth. Elegiac Stanzas Composed in the Churchyard of Grasmere.
Place of Burial in the South of Scotland, A.
Wright, James. Three Steps to the Graveyard.
Way to Make a Living, A.
Yeats. Under bare Ben Bulben's head.
See also **Burial; Graves; Mausoleums; Tombs.**

Censorship
Bishop. Word with You, A.
Boyle. Poem for Vida Hadjebi Tabrizi, A.
Byron. Canto the Eleventh.
Donne. Raderus.
Edmunds. White Nights, 1938.
Fox. Mother Was a Good.
Hewitt. Grim Dean, who sleeps within his pulpit's shade.
Oh, ban the books and save the children's lives.
Lawrence. Auto-Da-Fé.
Broadcasting to the G.B.P.
Censors.
Censors.
13 Pictures.
Lowry. Those Coke to Newcastle Blues.
Nash. Invocation: "Senator Smoot (Republican, Ut.)."
Legal Reflection.
Swift. On Censure.

Centaurs
Gunn. Light is in the pupil.
Kipling. Centaurs, The.
Morgan. Centaurs.
Williams, Charles Kenneth. Hercules, Deianira, Nessus.

Yeats. On a Picture of a Black Centaur by Edmund Dulac.

Centipedes
Dove. Centipede.
Nash. Centipede, The.

Central America. *see* **Latin America and Latin Americans.**

Central Park, New York City
Cohen. I Knelt Beside a Stream.
Ferlinghetti. Sherman's March Reglitterized.
Hughes, Langston. Dive.
Lowell. Central Park.
Nemerov. Central Park.
Rukeyser. From the Duck-Pond to the Carousel.
Schuyler. Dining Out with Doug and Frank.
Tomlinson. In Verdi Square.

Ceremonial Songs (genre). *see* **Wedding Songs.**

Ceres. *see* **Demeter.**

Cereus, Night-blooming
Hayden. Night-Blooming Cereus, The.
Merton. Night-Flowering Cactus.

Certainty
Berg. 1922.
Creeley. Down Home.
For a Friend.
For Somebody's Marriage.
Je Vois dans le Hasard Tous les Biens Que J'espere.
Kate's.
Persons.
Cullen. Brown Boy to Brown Girl.
Hartley. How like the sea / to be.
M.T.—a Relative in Certain Aspects of Metaphysical Divination.
Hesketh. My Faithful Lover.
Hewitt. Poetry, Then..
Jeffers. Nova.
Liddy. Holden, a Thought From Abroad.
Inscribed on the Flyleaf of Richard Shay's Copy of Rimbaud's *Illuminations*.
MacNeice. Greyness Is All.
Yau. Realizing that any certainty is an old one.

Ceylon. *see* **Sri Lanka.**

Cézanne, Paul
Dobyns. Cézanne and the Love of Color.
Cézanne and Zola.
Cézanne's Ambition.
Cézanne's Doubts.
Cézanne's Love of Poetry.
Cézanne's Outrageousness.
Dunn. Amidst the Faltering.
Tomlinson. Cézanne at Aix.
Williams, William Carlos. Cézanne.
Delicacies, The.

Chagall, Marc
Ferlinghetti. Don't let that horse.
Hewitt. Remembering a Conversation: Itzik Manger at the PEN Conference, Edinburgh, 1950.
Merton. Chagall.

Chainmail
Dickey, James. Lakes of Värmland.

Chairs
Hewitt. Child, the Chair, the Leaf, The.
Kipling. My Father's Chair.
Neruda. All Seated.
Sitting Down.
Roethke. Chair, The.
Stevens. Human Arrangement.
Whittier. Legend of the Lake, A.

Chameleons
Kinnell. Gray Heron, The.
Moore. To a Chameleon.

Champions
Dickey, James. Olympian, The.

Chance
Beckett. À l'instant de s'entendre dire.
Blake. If you play a Game of Chance know before you begin.
Carew. Dart, The.
Clark. Moira's Messages.
Now She Dwells Here.
Creeley. Business, The.
Conspiracy, The.

Epigraph: "Lot's wife, / married to chance."
Happy love, this.
Place, The.
Song: "Those rivers run from that land."
Dobyns. Santiago: la Avenida Pedro de
Valdivia.
Dunn. What.
White Collar.
Fox. Roads in That Town Have No Name,
The.
Graves. Pandora.
Griffiths. Hymns and Backward Glances.
Returning I live with a huge space.
Hardy. Philosophical Fantasy, A.
Herrick. Casualties.
Large Bounds Doe but Bury Us.
Hewitt. In a Lurgan Pub.
Jeffers. Stone Axe, The.
Jonson. Eye of looking back were well, An.
Kinnell. Little Sleep's-Head Sprouting Hair in
the Moonlight.
Knott. At the Crossroads.
Levine. Theory of Prosody, A.
Lindsay. Tiger on Parade, The.
Morrison. Heaven or Hell.
Nash. Don't Look for the Silver Lining, Just
Wait for It.
Nemerov. Sonnet: "It seems to be the trouble,
everyone."
Prince. Dice, The.
Rolfe. Mystery II.
Rukeyser. Willkie—Stopless Falling through
Air.
Sandburg. If So Hap May Be.
Sarton. Strangers.
Shapiro. Pigeons, The.
Shelley. Circumstance.
Simic. Elementary Cosmogony.
Tomb of Stéphane Mallarmé, The.
Williams, Miller. Believing in Symbols.
Wyatt. He is not de[a]d that sometime [or
somtyme] hath a fall.
Young. Now's the Time.

See also **Fate; Fortune.**

Change
Angelou. Changes.
In Retrospect.
To a Man.
Atwood. Eventual Proteus.
She Considers Evading Him.
Wereman, The.
Auden. As I Walked Out One Evening.
Certainly praise: let song mount again and
again.
Change of Air, A.
Dark Years, The.
Forty Years On.
In a Train.
Last of the Old Year, The.
On Receiving a Christmas Card.
Prologue at Sixty.
Shock, A.
So an age ended, and its last deliverer died.
Tarn, The.
Thomas Prologizes.
Beatles. I'll Follow the Sun.
I'm Looking Through You.
In My Life.
Night Before, The.
Revolution.
Something.
Berry. Awake at Night.
Dance, The.
Goods.
How fine / to have a long-legged house.
In the heron's eye.
Let the great song come.
Meeting, A.
Old Elm Tree by the River, The.
Recognition.
Rising, the river.
Traveling at Home.
Berryman. It will seem strange, no more this
range on range.
Our love conducted as in tropic rain.
Betjeman. Delectable Duchy.
Meditation on a Constable Picture.

Browning, Elizabeth Barrett. Change Upon
Change.
Island, An.
Browning, Robert. Prologue: "Poet's age is
sad: for why?, The."
Bukowski. On Being 20.
Reunion.
Sardines in Striped Dresses.
Take It.
Bunting. Two hundred and seven paces.
Burns. Extempore.
Song: "Let not Woman e'er complain."
Carew. Persuasions to Enjoy.
Upon Some Alterations in My Mistress, after
My Departure into France.
"Carroll, Lewis." Warden's Charm, The.
Carruth. Coming of winter / is a beech
sapling.
Clark. Change.
Moira.
October.
Clough. If it is thou whose casual hand
withdraws.
July's Farewell.
Coleridge. Constancy to an Ideal Object.
Duty Surviving Self-Love.
Pang More Sharp Than All, The.
To a Friend, in Answer to a Melancholy
Letter.
Cooper. If the weather breaks.
Cowper. On the Shortness of Life.
To a Friend in Distress.
Yardley Oak.
Crane. Van Winkle.
Creeley. Change.
Diction.
For Love.
Littleton, N.H.
Rain (2) ("Thoughtful of you, I was /
anticipating change in").
Surgeons.
Cummings. As freedom is a breakfastfood.
As is the sea marvelous.
If seventy were young / and death uncommon.
Metamorphosis.
My mind is.
Think of it:not so long ago.
You are like the snow only.
You are not going to,dear. You are not going
to and.
De la Mare. Looking Glass, The.
Dickinson. At Half past Three, a single Bird.
Changelessness / is Nature's change.
He touched me, so I live to know.
Presentiment—is that long Shadow—on the
Lawn.
Sic transit gloria mundi.
Donne. Change.
Oh, to vex me, contraries [or conraryes] meet
in one.
Dove. Jiving.
Ö.
Straw Hat.
Sunday Greens.
Wingfoot Lake.
Dunbar. Change Has Come, The.
"Dylan." Ballad of a Thin Man.
Changing of the Guards.
Farewell Angelina.
Gonna Change My Way of Thinking.
It's All Over Now, Baby Blue.
Long Ago, Far Away.
Never Gonna Be the Same Again.
Off the Top of My Head.
Paths of Victory.
Playboys and Playgirls.
Restless Farewell.
Tangled Up in Blue.
Times They Are A-Changin', The.
When the Ship Comes In.
Eberhart. Haystack, The.
Incarcerating sunlight, world damnation.
Inchiquin Lake, Penobscot Bay.
Nothing But Change.
Redemption.
Stopping a Kaleidoscope.
Tobacconist of Eighth Street, The.

Eliot. East Coker.
Emerson. Amulet, The.
Holidays.
Once the priest / Lived in an age.
Proteus.
To Ellen, at the South.
Everson. October Tragedy.
Scout, The.
Fisher. Also.
Magritte Imitated Himself.
Something has to happen here.
Ford. Bala Krishna's voice.
Bedraggled rose, The.
Chinaberries / Change from green to yellow.
In, The.
Heartfelt installations. / Beginnings are
benevolent.
Fox. Islanders.
On the Other Side of Uji Bridge.
Frost. Nothing Gold Can Stay.
Ginsberg. Brooklyn College Brain.
Change: *Kyoto-Tokyo Express*, The.
Complaint of the Skeleton to Time.
Understand That This Is a Dream.
Glück. Cottonmouth Country.
Here Are My Black Clothes.
Graves. Change.
Finding of Love, The.
Freehold.
Good Night to the Old Gods.
If No Cuckoo Sings.
Griffiths. Optimism.
Unwritten Chapters.
Gunn. Rites of Passage.
That was fifteen years ago.
Words.
Hacker. Letter from Goose Creek: April.
Orpheus and animus, / drawing back to
journeys now.
Rooms in Bloomsbury.
Haines. Guevara.
Mothball Fleet: Benicia, California.
Rolling Back.
Hall. Exile.
"King and Queen."
Love Is Like Sounds.
September Ode.
Tree and the Cloud, The.
Wedding Party.
Hardy. According to the Mighty Working.
Ancient to Ancients, An.
Chimes, The.
Going and Staying.
His Visitor.
In a Former Resort after Many Years.
Jubilee of a Magazine, The.
Man Who Forgot, The.
Night of Questionings, A.
Places.
Second Visit, The.
Starlings on the Roof.
Temporary the All, The.
There Seemed a Strangeness.
Voice of Things, The.
Where They Lived.
Hartley. Androscoggin.
Fence Between.
Metaphysic.
Yes, I Know—Yes.
Hayden. Theme and Variation.
Herrick. Change Common to All.
Change Gives Content.
Fair[e] Days; or, Dawn[e]s Deceitful[l].
Hope Well and Have Well: or, Faire after
Foule Weather.
Impossibilities to His Friend.
Speake in Season.
Upon Judith.
Upon Shift.
Upon Skrew.
Upon Trap.
Hesketh. Changing Colour.
So Little It Can Take.
Violet at Ninety.
Widowhood.
Hewitt. Agitator.
Autumnal.

Young. California Peninsula: El Camino Real.
  Imitation Dance, The.
  Leadbelly Song, The.
  Madrid 1963: Some Changes.
  Odds, The.
  Tune.
See also **Transience.**

Changelings
Burns. Tam Lin.
Ransom. Tom, Tom, the Piper's Son.
  Vanity of the Bright Boys, The.
Roethke. Changeling, The.
Smith, Stevie. Eulenspiegelei.

Channing, William Henry
Emerson. Ode, Inscribed to W. H. Channing.
Whittier. Channing.

Chanteys. *see* **Sea Chanteys.**

Chaos
Bukowski. Simplicity of Everything in Viet
  Nam, The.
Burns. Ode to the Departed Regency-Bill—
  1789.
Carruth. Final Version, The.
Duncan. Years As Catches, The.
"Dylan." Groom's Still Waiting at the Altar,
  The.
  Hard Rain's A-Gonna Fall, A.
  Off the Top of My Head.
Eberhart. Extremity.
  My mind was heavy and my luck was dark.
  O Wild Chaos!
Emerson. Who saw the hid beginnings.
Everson. Spotfire.
Fisher. Rules and Ranges for Ian Tyson.
Frost. Pertinax.
Ginsberg. Angkor Wat.
  Friday the Thirteenth.
  I Beg You Come Back & Be Cheerful.
  Magic Psalm.
  Reply, The.
Graves. Ecstasy of Chaos.
Hardy. What's There to Tell?
Hughes, Ted. All the dreary Sunday morning.
Hugo. Keen to Leaky Flowers.
Joseph. Muse.
Kunitz. Reflection by a Mailbox.
Lawrence. Think—!
Liddy. Night / We went running to the
  garden.
MacNeice. Aftermath.
Merton. Out of the rain and the darkness and
  the depths, the bottomless holes in the green
  sea.
Millay. I will put Chaos into fourteen lines.
Morrison. Original Temptation, The.
Ralegh. Ancients called me Chaos: my great
  yeares.
Rolfe. City of Anguish.
Rukeyser. Nuns in the Wind.
Sandburg. People, yes, The.
Sarton. Action of Therapy, The.
Stevens. Connoisseur of Chaos.
  Idiom of the Hero.
Updike. Ode to Entropy.
Williams, Charles Kenneth. Crime, The.
Williams, William Carlos. Descent.
Wroth. Sonnet 4: "And bee in his brave court
  a gloriouse light."
Yeats. Second Coming, The.

Chaplin, Charlie
Crane. Chaplinesque.
"Reed." City Lights.
Sandburg. Without the Cane and the Derby.
Tomlinson. Lacunae.

Chapman, George (1559?-1634)
Jonson. To My Worthy and Honoured Friend,
  Mr George Chapman, on His Translation of
  Hesiod's *Works and Days.*
Keats. On First Looking into Chapman's
  Homer.

Chapman, John ("Johnny Appleseed")
Lindsay. In Praise of Johnny Appleseed.
  Johnny Appleseed Speaks of the Appleblossom
  Amaranth That Will Come to This City.
  Johnny Appleseed's Ship Comes In.
  Johnny Appleseed's Wife from the Palace of

Eve.
  Johnny Appleseed's Wife of the Mind.
Wilbur. John Chapman.

Charity
Berry. Guest, The.
  Outside the window.
Bishop. Brazilian Tragedy.
  Miracle for Breakfast, A.
Browning, Robert. Twins, The.
Chaucer. Man of Law's Tale, The.
  Second Nun's Prologue, The.
Cohen. Morocco.
  Take this Longing.
Coleridge. Faith, Hope, and Charity.
Cowper. Charity.
Crashaw. C[h]aritas Nimia; or, The Dear[e]
  Bargain.
Dickinson. If I can stop one Heart from
  breaking.
Emerson. Motto to "Considerations by the
  Way."
Fletcher. Levite and the Samaritan, The.
Graves. Certain Mercies.
Herbert. To My Successor.
Herrick. Almes.
  Biting of Beggars.
  Cheerfulnesse in Charitie: or, The Sweet
  Sacrifice.
  His Almes.
  Upon Grudgings.
  Upon Her Almes.
  Upon Sibilla.
  Upon Urles.
Hewitt. For Certain Subscribers to the Miners'
  Fund.
  Little Bourgeois is Upset, The.
Hopkins. To him who ever thought with love
  of me.
Hugo. Medicine Bow.
Jarrell. Money.
Kipling. Song for the Women, The.
Lawrence. Embankment at Night, before the
  War: Charity.
Lindsay. Net to Snare the Moonlight, A.
  Prologue to "Rhymes to be Traded for Bread."
Lovelace. Faire Begger, The.
MacNeice. When the stranger came out of the
  night.
Meredith. Burden of Strength, The.
  Main Regret, The.
Moore. Charity Overcoming Envy.
Paley. Fund Appeal.
Rossetti. Behold, I stand at the door and
  knock.
  Charity.
  Charity Never Faileth.
  Despised and Rejected.
Smart. Charity.
  Pray Remember the Poor.
Smith, Charlotte. Written for the Benefit of a
  Distressed Player, Detained at
  Brighthelmstone for Debt, November 1792.
Stevenson. I am a hunchback, yellow faced.
Whitman. To Rich Givers.
Whittier. Captain's Well, The.
  Giving and Taking.
  Hymn of the Children.
  "I Was a Stranger and Ye Took Me in."
  In the Evil Days.
  Red Riding-Hood.
  Saint Gregory's Guest.
  Trust.
  Valuation.
  Voices, The.
Wordsworth. Narrow girdle of rough stones
  and crags, A.
  To the Lady Fleming on Seeing the
  Foundation Preparing for the Erection of
  Rydal Chapel, Westmoreland.
See also **Philanthropy and Philanthropists.**

Charlemagne
Wordsworth. Aix-la-Chapelle.

Charles I, King of England
Herrick. Bad Season Makes the Poet Sad,
  The.
  To the King.
  To the King and Queene, upon Their Unhappy

Distances.
  To the King ("If when these Lyricks (Cesar)
  You shall heare").
  To the King, upon His Com[m]ing with His
  Army into the West.
  To the King, upon His Taking of Leicester.
  To the King, upon His Welcome to Hampton-
  Court.
Jonson. Epigram on the Prince's Birth. 1630,
  An.
  Epigram. To K[ing] Charles for a[n] Hundred
  Pounds He Sent Me in My Sickness. 1629,
  An.
  Epigram. To our Great and Good K[ing]
  Charles on his Anniversary Day. 1629, An.
  Epigram. To the Household. 1630, An.
  Humble Petition of Poor Ben to the Best of
  Monarchs, Masters, Men, King Charles, The.
  New years [*or* yeares], expect new gifts: sister,
  your harp[e].
  New Year's Gift Sung to King Charles. 1635,
  A.
  On the King's Birthday.
  Song of Welcome to King Charles, A.
  To K[ing] Charles and Q[ueen] Mary, for the
  Loss of Their First-Born. An Epigram
  Consolatory. 1629.
  To My L[ord] the King, on the Christening
  His Second Son James.
  To the King. On His Birthday. An Epigram
  Anniversary. Novem[ber] 19, 1632.
Lovelace. To My Worthy Friend Mr. Peter
  Lely [*or* Lilly].
Marvell. What field of all the civil wars.
Shelley. Charles the First.
Smart. King Charles the Martyr.

Charles II, King of England
Dryden. Absalom and Achitophel, Pt. I.
  In pious times ere [*or* e'r] priest-craft did
  begin.
Herrick. Pastorall Upon the Birth of Prince
  Charles, A.
  To His Muse.
  To Prince Charles upon his coming to Exeter.
  To the Most Illustrious and Most Hopefull
  Prince, Charles, Prince of Wales.
Keats. Lines Written on 29 May / The
  Anniversary of the Restoration of Charles the
  2nd.
Lovelace. Mock Song, A.
Marvell. Ad Regem Carolum Parodia [A
  Parody: To King Charles].
  Last Instructions to a Painter, The.
  Pros Karolon ton Basilea [To King Charles].
Smart. King's Restoration, The.

Charles, Prince of Wales
Schuyler. Overcast, Hot.

Charles River, Massachusetts
Ciardi. River, The.
Rich. Walk by the Charles, A.
Schuyler. Frank! Frank!

Charleston, South Carolina
Rich. Charleston in the Eighteen-Sixties.
Updike. Charleston.

Charm
Burns. Blue-Eyed Lassie, The.
Coleridge. Snow-Drop, The.
Dunn. Dinner, The.
Herrick. Another ("If ye fear to be
  affrighted").
  Charme, or an Allay for Love, A.
  Charmes.
Lowry. Hartebeeste Both Grave and Gay, The.
Ransom. Vision by Sweetwater.
Rossetti. Helpmeet For Him, A.
Tomlinson. Request, The.
Yeats. Memory.

Charms (genre)
Campion. Bring away this Sacred Tree.
  Goe, happy man, like th' Evening Starre.
  Thrice Toss[e] These Oaken Ashes in the Air
  [*or* Ayre].
Garrigue. Incantatory Poem.
Herrick. Another Charme for Stables.
  Another to Bring in the Witch.
  Another("Let the superstitious wife").
Kipling. Charm, A.

Rukeyser. Charm for Cantinflas, A.

Charon
Auden. Lost.
Cowper. On Niobe.
Eberhart. Enigma, The.
Herrick. Charon and Phylomel, a Dialogue Sung.
New Charon, The.
MacNeice. Charon.
Millay. Sappho Crosses the Dark River into Hades.
Simic. Charon's Cosmology.

Chartres, France
Eberhart. Retrospective Forelook.
Hill. Eia ergo. For this is Sion's twin city.
Kipling. Chartres Windows.
MacLeish. Chartres.
Merton. News from the School at Chartres.
Oppen. Chartres.

Chastity
Atwood. Women's Issue, A.
Bogan. Ad Castitatem.
Campion. Ad Cambricum.
Ad Leam.
With spotles mindes now mount we to the tree.
Crashaw. To [Mrs. M. R.] Councel Concerning Her Choise.
Donne. Virgins, The.
Doolittle. She Rebukes Hippolyta.
Ford. Modesty, chastity.
Herrick. Another ("Love he that will; it best likes me").
His Recantation.
Like Loves His Like.
No Spouse but a Sister.
To His Tomb-Maker.
To Love.
To the Little Spinners.
Upon Himselfe ("I co'd never love indeed").
Upon Love ("In a Dreame, Love bad me go").
Jong. Becoming a Nun.
Lawrence. Chastity.
Virgin Youth.
Lovelace. To Lucasta. Ode Lyrick.
Marlowe. 2.3: Ad Eunuchum servantem dominam.
Meredith. Vital Choice, The.
With the Huntress.
Ralegh. Shall I, Like an Hermit, Dwell.
Shall I, Like an Hermit, Dwell.
Sidney. Ye living powers enclosed in stately shrine.
Smart. Circumcision.
Stevenson. Ne Sit Ancillae Tibi Amor Pudori.
Suckling. Lutea Allison.
Wroth. Sonnet 2: "Is to leave all, and take the thread of love."
Yeats. Three Bushes, The.

Chatterton, Thomas
Coleridge. Monody on the Death of Chatterton.
Keats. To Chatterton.
Lowry. Port has a sweeter name than Saigon, The.
"Portly & middleaged" can never.
Those who die young will look forever young.

Chaucer, Geoffrey
Campion. Elegeia I (1595).
Cummings. Chaucer.
Keats. Written on a Blank Space at the End of Chaucer's Tale of "The Floure and the Lefe."
Meredith. Poetry of Chaucer, The.
Spenser. Whilom, as antique stories tellen us.
Wordsworth. Edward VI.
Wordsworth Reading Chaucer.

Cheerfulness
Browning, Elizabeth Barrett. Cheerfulness Taught by Reason.
Cummings. Jack's white horse(up).
Graves. Song: Come, Enjoy Your Sunday!
Herrick. Cheerfulnesse in Charitie: or, The Sweet Sacrifice.
Kipling. English Way, The.
Lowry. Good Luck.
Rossetti. Gone to his rest / Bright little

Bouby!
Rosy maiden Winifred, / With a milkpail on her head.
Wordsworth. From the Dark Chambers of Dejection Freed.

Cheese
Hall. O Cheese.
Herrick. Fresh Cheese and Cream.
Merton. Chee$e.
Patchen. Rising a Little.

Chekhov, Anton
Berg. Gooseberries.
Kiss, The.
Prayer: "Nobody understands so let the Rabbi."
Dunn. Observer, The.
Garrigue. Why the Heart Has Dreams Is Why the Mind Goes Mad.
Heaney. Chekhov on Sakhalin.
Mahon. Old Snaps, The.

Chemical Warfare
Auden. James Honeyman.
Cummings. Lis / -ten / you know what i mean when.
Kipling. Gethsemane.
Morrison. I Fucked the Dregs.
Owen. Dulce Et Decorum Est.

Chemistry and Chemists
Graves. Research and Development: Classified.
Young. Chemistry.

Cherry Trees and Cherries
Berry. Fall.
De la Mare. Cherry Trees, The.
Gunn. Cherry Tree, The.
Herrick. Cherrie-Ripe.
Cherry-Pit.
To Cherry-Blossomes.
Upon Mistresse Susanna Southwell, Her Cheeks.
Housman. Loveliest of trees, the cherry now.
Joseph. Cherry.
Lawrence. Cherry Robbers.
Song: "Up in the high."
Lowry. Wild Cherry, The.
Nemerov. Cherry Tree, The.
Neruda. Cherries.
Pack. Cherry Robbers.
Rossetti. Let's Be Merry.
Mother shake the cherry-tree.
Oh fair to see / Bloom-laden cherry tree.
Playing at bob cherry / Tom and Nell and Hugh.
Sidney. Sonnet 82: "Nymph of the garden where all beauties be."
Snodgrass. Cherry Saplings.
Williams, William Carlos. Bare Tree, The.
Cherry Blossoms at Evening.
Orchard, The.

Chesapeake Bay
Dunbar. Night on the Chesapeake.
To the Eastern Shore.
Galvin. Pitch Pines.
Meinke. Night Watch on the Chesapeake.
Sandburg. Sea Hold, The.

Chess
Ferlinghetti. Deep Chess.
Lovelace. To Dr. F. B. on His Book of Chess[e].
MacNeice. Chess.
Robinson. Atherton's Gambit.
Shapiro. Essay on Chess.
Simic. Prodigy.

Chesterton, Gilbert Keith
Hardy. Epitaph for G. K. Chesterton.

Chestnut Trees and Chestnuts
Frost. Evil Tendencies Cancel.
McNeill. Chestnut Orchard.
Tomlinson. Chestnut Avenue: at Alton House, The.

Chicago, Illinois
Berrigan. Chicago Morning.
Carruth. Michigan Water: a Few Riffs before Dawn.
Once on a night in spring.
Snow, The.

Ginsberg. Open Window on Chicago, An.
Written on Hotel Napkin: Chicago Futures.
Hughes, Langston. Migrant.
Levine. New Day, A.
McGrath. Migration of Cities, The.
Rexroth. Bad Old Days, The.
Rukeyser. Third Elegy. The Fear of Form.
Sandburg. Chicago Boy Baby.
Chicago seems all fox and swine.
Clinton South of Polk.
Mamie.
Real Avenue News.
Windy City, The.
Walcott. Chicago's avenues, as white as Poland.
Whittier. Chicago.
Wright, James. Poor Washed Up by Chicago Winter, The.

Chickadees
Emerson. In Walden wood the chickadee.
Titmouse, The.
See also **Titmice.**

Chickens
Burns. To Alexander Findlater.
"Carroll, Lewis." Lays of Sorrow, No. 1.
Carruth. Classical.
Missing the Bo in the Henhouse.
Dickey, William. Chickens in San Francisco.
Dobyns. Spiritual Chickens.
Emerson. No song so tuneful, quoth the fox.
Frost. Blue Ribbon at Amesbury, A.
Hall. Henyard Round, The.
Herrick. Upon Cock.
Kinnell. Supper after the Last, The.
Lawrence. Flat-Foot's Song.
Lowry. For Nordahl Grieg Ship's Fireman.
Meinke. Chicken Unlimited.
Rossetti. White hen sitting / On white eggs three, A.
Sandburg. Chicks.
Sexton. Fury of Cocks, The.
Silverstein. I Won't Hatch.
Simic. Chicken Without a Head, The.
Smith, Stevie. Cock and the Hen, The.
Wright, James. Presentation of Two Birds to My Son, A.

Child Abuse
Angelou. To Beat the Child Was Bad Enough.
Bly. Snow Geese.
"Carroll, Lewis." Duchess's Lullaby, The.
Davie. Grazia Deledda, Young.
Hayden. Whipping, The.
Joseph. Untitled.
Lawrence. Discord in Childhood.
Meinke. This is a poem to my son Peter.
"Reed." Endless Cycle.
Sexton. Friends.
Wifebeater, The.
Shelton. Reaching For the Gun.
Smith, Stevie. Lord Barrenstock.
Papa Love Baby.

Child Labor
Blake. Chimney Sweeper, The ("A little black thing among the snow").
Chimney Sweeper, The ("When my mother died I was very young").
Galvin. Photo of Miners, A.
Sandburg. They Will Say.

Childhood and Children
Angelou. Elegy: "I lay down in my grave."
John J.
Kin.
Little Girl Speakings.
Atwood. Children like the block, The.
Children on the lawn / joined hand to hand, The.
However, / in all their games.
Auden. Babies in their mothers' arms.
Bawbee.
His peasant parents killed themselves with toil.
In the Nursery.
No window in his suburb lights that bedroom where.
Price, The.
Schoolchildren.
To a Child in Tears.
Berg. Bandage.

Brothers.
Don't Forget.
Dust.
Following It.
Nothingness.
Tashkent Blossoms, 1944.
Times.
Berry. Old Man Is Older in History than in
  Time, The.
Our Children, Coming of Age.
To Tanya at Christmas.
Berryman. At Chinese Checkers.
Ball Poem, The.
Hello.
Betjeman. Child Ill, A.
False Security.
Group Life: Letchworth.
Indoor Games near Newbury.
Lines Written to Martyn Skinner Before His
  Departure from Oxfordshire in Search of
  Quiet—1961.
Narcissus.
Norfolk.
North Coast Recollections.
NW5 and N6.
Original Sin on the Sussex Coast.
Bishop. All the heaven and earth.
Cemetery of Childhood.
In the Waiting Room.
Infancy.
Squatter's Children.
Blake. Holy Thursday (" 'Twas on a Holy
  Thursday, their innocent faces clean").
Holy Thursday ("Is this a holy thing to see").
Infant Joy.
Infant Sorrow.
Nurse's Song ("When the voices of children
  are heard on the green / And laughing is
  heard on the hill").
Nurse's Song ("When the voices of children
  are heard on the green / And whisperings [or
  whisprings] are in the dale").
Bogan. Kept.
Boyle. Dedicated to Terre des Hommes.
Poem in One Sentence, A.
What Parents Do Not Yet Know.
Bradstreet. In Reference to Her Children, 23
  June, 1659 [or 1656].
Brontë. A.E. And R.C.
I saw thee, child, one summer's day.
I.M. to I.G.
Mild the mist upon the hill.
Song to A.A.
Upon her soothing breast.
Brooks. Mother, The.
Notes from the Childhood and the Girlhood.
Browning, Elizabeth Barrett. Child Asleep, A.
Cry of the Children, The.
Deserted Garden, The.
Fourfold Aspect, The.
Hector in the Garden.
Isobel's Child.
Life.
Lost Bower, The.
Pet-Name, The.
Romance of the Ganges, A.
Song against Singing, A.
Sonnet: "Yes, call me by my pet-name! let me
  hear."
Tale of Villafranca, A.
To Bettine.
Void in Law.
Browning, Robert. Epigram on School Days.
Bukowski. Bee, The.
Seahorse.
Upon First Reading the Immortal Literature of
  the World—.
Bunting. Search under every veil.
Burns. O That I Had Ne'er Been Married.
On the Birth of a Posthumous Child, Born in
  Peculiar Circumstances of Family Distress.
To Miss C********, a Very Young Lady.
Byron. And I have loved thee, Ocean! and my
  joy.
Childish Recollections.
On a Distant View of the Village and School
  of Harrow on the Hill.

Carroll, Jim. You hear the call.
"Carroll, Lewis." Acrostic: A boat, beneath a
  sunny sky.
Acrostic: Around my lonely hearth, to-night.
Acrostic: Dreams, that elude the Waker's
  frenzied grasp—.
Acrostic: Little maidens, when you look.
Canto IV: Hys Nouryture.
Christmas Greetings.
Dedication: "All in the golden afternoon."
Dedication: "Child of the pure unclouded
  brow."
Duchess's Lullaby, The.
Echoes.
Lays of Mystery, Imagination, and Humour,
  No. 1: The Palace of Humbug.
Love among the Roses.
Lyceum, The.
Nursery Darling, A.
Puck Lost and Found.
Song of Love, A.
Those Horrid Hurdy-Gurdies!
Three Children.
Two Thieves.
Carruth. Child, The.
Child's Being, The.
Sigh, you seven seas.
Sonnet: "If you see a child that shivers when
  it hears."
Sonnet: "The Bo was three when we slugged
  through Arizona."
Sound of Snow, The.
Wise child is born, The.
World as Will and Representation, The.
Ceravolo. Cool Breeze.
Indian Suffering.
Lighthouse.
Sea Level.
Ciardi. One Morning.
Clark. Superballs.
Clough. I watched them from the window, thy
  children at their play.
Incident, An.
Thou bidd'st me mark how swells with rage.
Cohen. Another Family.
Front Lawn.
Reason I Write, The.
Stay.
You Who Question Souls.
Coleridge. Anthem for the Children of Christ's
  Hospital.
Encinctured with a twine of leaves.
On the Christening of a Friend's Child.
Youth and Age.
Cooper. Builder of Houses, The.
Leaving Water Hyacinths.
My Young Mother.
Cowper. Hymn for the Sunday School at
  Olney.
On the Picture of a Sleeping Child.
Prayer for Children.
Crane. Idiot, The.
Creeley. Cantos, The.
Charm, The.
Fragment, A: "On the street I am met with
  constant hostility."
Hey.
Method of Actuality, The.
People.
Sitting Here.
Cullen. Incident.
Saturday's Child.
Cummings. Being / twelve / who hast merely.
Here pasture ends— / this girl and boy.
Hist   whist / little ghostthings.
I walked the boulevard.
I'd think "wonder / if" if.
In Just- / spring   when the world is mud-.
Little man / (in a hurry).
Little tree / little silent Christmas tree.
One nonsufficiently inunderstood.
Sitting in a tree-.
So little he is.
Sonnet entitled how to run the world).
These children singing in stone a.
Who are you,little i.
Davie. Baptist Childhood, A.

Derbyshire.
Housekeeping.
Northamptonshire.
Prolific Spell, The.
Shropshire.
Stratford on Avon.
Wide France.
De la Mare. Children of Stare, The.
Dry August Burned.
Incantation.
Irrevocable, The.
Keys of Morning, The.
Massacre, The.
Myself.
O Childish Mind!
Pollie.
Reserved.
Reverie.
Slum Child, The.
Sunday, A.
Sunken Garden, The.
To My Mother.
Unheard Melodies.
Universe, The.
Winter Dusk.
Young Girl, A.
Dickey, James. Form.
Rafters, The.
Voyage of the Needle, The.
Dickey, William. Dolls Play at Hansel and
  Gretel, The.
For Every Last Batch When the Next One
  Comes Along.
Memoranda.
Dickinson. Bliss is the plaything of the child.
Child's faith is new, The.
From all the Jails the Boys and Girls.
God permits industrious Angels.
It troubled me as once I was.
Let Us play Yesterday.
Little Dog that wags his tail, A.
New feet within my garden go.
One Sister have I in our house.
Ravenousness of fondness, The.
They won't frown always—some sweet Day.
Trudging to Eden, looking backward.
With Leopards for Playmates, the beautiful
  Child.
Dobyns. Bleeder.
Gun, The.
Pastel Dresses.
Silence.
Streetlight.
Ten Feet of Rope.
What You Have Come To Expect.
Doolittle. At Eleusis.
Dedication: "When everything was over."
Dream.
Grown Up.
No.
Dunbar. Boy's Summer Song, A.
Charity.
Liza May.
Lullaby: "Bedtime's come fu' little boys."
Scamp.
Wadin' in de Crick.
When a Feller's Itchin' to be Spanked.
Duncan. Old women came from their caves to
  close the too many doors, The.
Dunn. As It Moves.
Photograph Album, The.
Regardless.
Worrier, The.
Eberhart. Book of Nature, The.
Child, The.
If I Could Only Live at the Pitch That Is near
  Madness.
Incomparable Light, The.
Lost Children, The.
Old Tree by the Penobscot.
Orchard.
Recollection of Childhood.
Three Kids.
Eliot. Animula.
Cultivation of Christmas Trees, The.
Emerson. Awed I behold once more.
Dirge: "Knows he who tills this lonely field."

Motto to "The Poet."
Teach your child to earn his meal.
Fenton. Adult: That's a tattooed man.
Nest of Vampires.
Ferlinghetti. Along the Appian Way / children are playing.
In woods where many rivers run.
Pennycandystore beyond the El, The.
Fisher. Rudiments.
Fletcher. Old Nursery.
Ford. And oh what a beautiful child you are.
Little boys, faces smeared.
Realization / Of fantasy, yes. This, A.
Standing on the garden.
Fox. Child Called *Morte*, A.
Rescue.
Roads in That Town Have No Name, The.
Frost. Birches.
Home Burial.
Maple.
Gallagher. Amplitude.
Disappearances in the Guarded Sector.
View from an Empty Chair.
Galvin. Knot Hole Gang, The.
Weave a Circle Round Me Thrice.
Gardner. Card Island or Cod Island?
Children Are Game.
Summer Remembered.
Summers Ago.
That Princeling.
West of Childhood.
Garrigue. Bleecker Street.
Smoke Shop Owner's Daughter, The.
Gildner. Edward.
Farm, The.
Harold Fogel Could Be Anywhere.
Is My Heart Really Big As My Fist?
Wean Poem.
Ginsberg. Gregory Corso's Story.
Two Boys Went Into a Dream Diner.
Glück. Apple Trees, The.
Beginning, The.
Descending Figure.
Drowned Children, The.
End of the World, The.
Firstborn.
Gift, The.
Grandmother in the Garden.
Illuminations.
Portrait.
Returning a Lost Child.
School Children, The.
Scraps.
Tree House, The.
Graves. Alice.
Child with Veteran.
Dreaming Children.
Hero, The.
Sweet-Shop Round The Corner, The.
Warning to Children.
Wm. Brazier.
Gray. Ode on a Distant Prospect of Eton College.
Griffiths. Children in a Walled Garden.
Expectations.
Fathers.
Few Bars Over Again, A.
Guesthouse, The.
Optimism.
Spanish Providence, A.
Still Too Quick to Hold.
Gunn. Blank, A.
Courage, a Tale.
Hide and Seek.
Three.
Hacker. Geographer.
Iva's Pantoum.
Little Robber Girl Considers the Wide World, The.
1976.
Sword.
Third Snowfall.
Haines. These images and their hidden voices.
Hall. Child, The.
Exile.
Illustration.

Sleeping Giant, The.
Toy Bone, The.
Hardy. Childhood among the Ferns.
Children and Sir Nameless, The.
Her Death and After.
In a Waiting-Room.
Hartley. "Lewiston Is a Pleasant Place."
Hartnett. Poem for Lara, 10.
Hayden. Rabbi, The.
Those Winter Sundays.
Whipping, The.
Year of the Child, The.
Heaney. Bye-Child.
England's Difficulty.
Follower.
Railway Children, The.
Terminus.
Herbert. Holy Baptism (2).
Herrick. Upon Gubbs.
Upon Jolly and Jilly.
Upon Ralph.
Hesketh. Call of the North.
Journey.
Second Childhood.
Hewitt. Aunt Cis and Uncle Tom.
Balloons and Wooden Guns.
Carol Singers.
Carson at Six Road Ends.
Child, the Chair, the Leaf, The.
Encounter Nineteen Twenty.
First Pantomime.
Folk for Tea.
Free Foot, The.
House Demolished, A.
I Go to School.
I Remember.
Incident, An.
Interval.
Irish Dimension, The.
Lead Soldiers and Regimental Uniforms.
Lost *Argo*, Islandmagee, Summer 1919.
Miss Murdoch.
No Cresta Run.
October's Child.
On Dunmore's Waste.
Periodicity.
Pet Shop, The.
Portstewart, 1914.
River Streets, The.
Seaside Town, A.
Strangers and Neighbors.
Teetotal Master.
Victorian Steps Out, A.
Hill. Cowan Bridge; At the Site of 'Lowood School.'
Princes of Mercia were badger and raven, The.
Stone Man, The.
Hoffman. Battle of Hastings, The.
In the Beginning.
Hopkins. By Mrs. Hopley.
Handsome Heart, The.
Spring and Fall.
Hughes, Langston. Children's Rhymes.
Genius Child.
Kid in the Park.
To Be Somebody.
Hughes, Ted. Deaf School.
Hugo. Guns at Fort Flagler.
Iowa Déjà Vu.
Saying Goodbye to Mrs. Noraine.
Schoolgirl at Seola.
Time to Remember Sangster.
White Center.
Jarrell. Carnegie Library, Juvenile Division, The.
Childhood.
Children Selecting Books in a Library.
Cinderella.
Elementary Scene, The.
Gleaning.
Head of Wisdom, The.
Hope.
Lady Bates.
Lost Children, The.
Lost World, The.
Moving.
Quilt-Pattern, A.

Sick Child, A.
Thinking of the Lost World.
Truth, The.
Jeffers. Solstice.
Johnson. In Rivum a Mola Stoana Lichfeldiæ Diffluentem.
Joseph. Animal Story, An.
Jack and the Beanstalk.
Round: "Body of a child lay in the pool, The."
Keats. 'Tis the Witching Time [*or* Hour] of Night.
Kinnell. First Song.
Freedom, New Hampshire.
Little Sleep's-Head Sprouting Hair in the Moonlight.
To a Child in Calcutta.
Kipling. Butterflies.
I keep six honest serving-men.
So we settled it all when the storm was done.
Knight. Indianapolis War Memorial.
On the Projects Playground.
Knott. Closet, The.
Two Vietnam Poems: (1966).
Koch. Aus Einer Kindheit.
You Were Wearing.
Kooser. North of Alliance.
Kunitz. At breakfast mother sipped her buttermilk.
Testing-Tree, The.
Your first dog was a Pekinese.
Larkin. I Remember, I Remember.
Lawrence. After School.
Child and the Soldier, The.
I Heard Her Say.
Piano.
Piano, The.
Punisher, The.
Snowy Day in School, A.
Young Fathers.
Levine. Belle Isle, 1949.
Children's Crusade, The.
Hold Me.
How many lives were torn apart.
Lost and Found.
Milkweed.
On My Own.
Pili's Wall.
To a Child Trapped in a Barber Shop.
Lewis. *Merchants Wife, The.*
Liddy. For all who trod / Golden North American streets.
Pools where it offers to our curiosity, The.
To the Memory of Sylvia Plath: A Personal Note.
Lieberman. Girard, Girard.
House Skin, The.
Lindsay. Doll Upon the Topmost Bough, The.
How Dulcenia del Toboso Is Like the Left Wing of a Bird.
Like the woods of old Kentucky.
Master of the Dance, The.
Longfellow. Children's Hour, The.
My Lost Youth.
Lorde. And What About the Children.
As I Grew Up Again.
Ballad from Childhood.
Blackstudies.
Bloodbirth.
Conclusion.
Equinox.
Release Time.
Relevant Is Different Points on the Circle.
Rites of Passage.
Sacrifice.
Seventh Sign, The.
Signs.
Song for a Thin Sister.
To My Daughter the Junkie on a Train.
What My Child Learns of the Sea.
Lowell. Child's Song.
Harriet.
My Last Afternoon with Uncle Devereux Winslow.
Returning.
Lowry. Autopsy on this childhood then reveals, An.

Child may find no words for its sorrow, A.
Glaucous Winged Gull, The.
Margeries and the malcolms did, The.
Midnight denies poursuivant of the dawn.
Poem Influenced By John Davenport and
    Cervantes.
McAuley. Owen at Play.
"MacDiarmid." First Love.
Of John Davidson.
McGrath. Heroes of Childhood, The.
Remembering the Children of Auschwitz.
Uses of the Lost Poets.
MacLeish. Ancestral.
Eleven.
Eve Quiets Her Children.
Hebrides.
Revolution of the Children.
MacNeice. Canto XVII: "This was the night
    that specially we went down."
Canto XXII: "So this is Glastonbury. A green
    hill far away."
Carrick Revisited.
Children's Games.
Oranges (sweet) and lemons (bitter) childhood,
    An.
Soap Suds.
Taken for Granted.
To keep themselves young—Is that why
    people have children?
McNeill. Chestnut Orchard.
First Flight.
Fox and Geese.
Mayapple Hill.
Over the Mountain.
Wire Brier.
Marvell. Picture of Little T. C. in a Prospect
    of Flowers, The.
Matthews. Blues, The.
Happy Childhood, A.
Housework.
Recollections.
School Days.
Schoolboys with Dog, Winter.
Search Party, The.
Meinke. Growing Deaf.
Minuet in G.
Myrtle the Turtle.
Ping-Pong.
Running with the Hyenas.
Shell, The.
Slow Child, The.
Third Child: June Eleven, Nineteen Sixty Two.
To a Daughter with Artistic Talent.
When Eve was cloned from Adam's rib, and
    stood.
Meredith. Ah! little Angel, child of bliss!
Child's Prayer, A.
Fair Bedfellow, The.
First-Born, The.
Holidays.
Infancy and Age.
Mother to Babe.
Motley.
Orchard and the Heath, The.
Philosopher! 'tis said you wail.
World is young, the world is well, The.
Merrill. Broken Home, The.
Chimes for Yahya.
Days of 1941 and '44.
Days of 1935.
Dream of Old Vienna, A.
Salome.
Scenes of Childhood.
School Play, The.
Up and Down.
Verse for Urania.
Vision of the Garden, A.
World and the Child, The.
Merton. Birdcage Walk.
Landscape.
Winter's Night, The.
Millay. As sharp as in my childhood, still.
Cairn, The.
Childhood Is the Kingdom Where Nobody
    Dies.
Morgan. 1928.
Past, The.

Scotch Mary.
Then.
Three Children Looking Over the Edge of the
    World.
When it rained and rained.
Morrison. Hole in the Clouds, A.
If Only I.
In That Year.
Wake, A.
You Think I Don't Know.
Muldoon. Cass and Me.
Right Arm, The.
Nash. Absentees, The.
Birdies, Don't Make Me Laugh.
Child Is Father to the Man, But with More
    Authority, The.
Children's Party.
Come On In, the Senility Is Fine.
Crossing the Border.
Don't Cry, Darling, It's Blood All Right.
Father, Dear Father, Go Jump in the Lake, or,
    You're Costlier than You Think.
Fee Fi Ho Hum, No Wonder Baby Sucks Her
    Thumb.
Guppy, The.
I Want a Drink of Water, but Not from the
    Thermos.
I'll Take the High Road Commission.
Little Feet.
One Third of a Calendar.
Piano Tuner, Untune Me That Tune.
Preface to the Past.
Queen Is in the Parlor, The.
Some of My Best Friends Are Children.
Nathan. I write you out of fear.
Nemerov. Central Park.
Childhood.
Home for the Holidays.
Icehouse in Summer, The.
Lives of Gulls and Children, The.
Mars.
Puzzle, The.
Remorse for Time, The.
Sleeping Beauty.
Snow Globe, The.
Triumph of Education, The.
Warning: Children at Play.
Neruda. Where is the child that I was.
Notley. January.
O'Hara. Autobiographia Literaria.
Cornkind.
Ode on Causality.
Ode to Michael Goldberg ('s Birth and Other
    Births).
Poem: "There I could never be a boy."
Olson. Fable for Slumber.
Ferrini—I.
One Night Ma / Lay with Pa.
Oppen. Birthplace: New Rochelle.
From a Photograph.
Pedestrian.
Street.
Sunnyside Child.
West.
Owen. Happiness.
To ———: "Three rompers run together, hand
    in hand."
Pack. Camp Wakonda, 1940.
Clayfeld's Infancy.
Invisible Hand, The.
Stolen Clothes.
Paley. Boys from Saint Bernard's, The.
For Danny.
In the Bus.
My Mother: 33 Years Later.
Note to Grandparents.
Sad Children's Song, The.
Patchen. Black Panther and the Little Boy,
    The.
Career for a Child of Five.
Childhood of the Hero.
Event at Konna, The.
Mirru.
Reason for Skylarks, The.
Watching Neighbors' Children.
Plath. Brasilia.

Child.
Childless Woman.
Pope. Behold the child, by Nature's kindly
    law.
Prince. Intention, The.
Raine. Beside the river Eden.
Childhood.
Childhood Memory.
Eternal Child, The.
I used to watch you, sleeping.
Message.
My Father's Birthday.
Spell to Bring Lost Creatures Home.
Three Poems of Incarnation.
"Reed." Beginning of a Great Adventure.
Teach the Gifted Children.
Rich. Afterwake, The.
Bears.
Classmate, The.
In the Wake of Home.
Innocents, The.
Night-Pieces: For a Child.
Not like That.
Robinson. For Arvia.
Roethke. Child on Top of a Greenhouse.
My Papa's Waltz.
Where Knock Is Open Wide.
Rolfe. Pattern of Our Lives, The.
Song: "There is indeed now reason for
    rejoicing."
Rossetti. Charade.
Child's Talk in April.
Clever little Willie wee, / Bright eyed, blue
    eyed little fellow.
Frisky Lamb, A.
Isidora.
Mother and Child.
Three little children / On the wide wide earth.
Rukeyser. Another Day. A Game of Toys.
Paul, Telling the Game.
Another Day (And then the cow).
Another Day (Child among his powers).
Another Day (Day Lilies, Yellow Daisies).
Another Day (I will now sing).
Another Day (Miss Lorence).
Another Day. The Children Are All Eating.
Another Day (You can't come).
Another Day (You sit there).
Are You Born? / II.
Boy with His Hair Cut Short.
Child and Mother.
Child Asleep, The.
Child wakes in the morning to enter a country,
    The.
Children, the Sandbar, That Summer.
Crayon House.
Destruction of Grief.
Do you know Hitler? Does he like you?
Eighth Elegy. Children's Elegy.
Father dreams that he was hid in a tree, The.
Fourth Elegy. The Refugees.
From the Duck-Pond to the Carousel.
Gift.
He turned cruel. Absorbed in his own cruelty.
His father is lost and away.
In the last hour of night, a zebra racing dawn.
My toes feel like nothing they are so cold.
Not Yet.
Now he plays with the other children.
Poem Out of Childhood.
Sea has opened, the limit of his dream, The.
That is what they say, who were broken off
    from love.
Victims, a Play for the Home, The.
When he began to witness, it was not to a
    journey.
Sandburg. Baby Face.
Buffalo Bill.
Child.
Child Face.
Child Margaret.
Child Moon.
Chillicothe.
Clinton South of Polk.
Five Cent Balloons.
Helga.
House.

Margaret.
Mildred Klinghofer whirled through youth in bloom.
Neither wife nor child had Mr. Eastman and the manner of his death.
Never Born.
People with Proud Chins.
Seventeen Months.
Spring Wind.
Three Spring Notations on Bipeds.
Why did the children.
Winter Milk.
Sarton. Ballad of Johnny, The.
Garden of Childhood, The.
Giant in the Garden.
Schwartz. Spring, The.
Sexton. Angel of Blizzards and Blackouts.
Baby Picture.
Children, The.
Death Baby, The.
Double Image, The.
Fortress, The.
Fury of Overshoes, The.
January 1st.
Little Uncomplicated Hymn, A.
Praying to Big Jack.
Red Roses.
Shout, The.
Those Times.
Shakespeare. Sonnet 6: "Then let not winter's ragged hand deface."
Sonnet 11: "As fast as thou shall wane, so fast thou growest."
Sonnet 13: "Oh [or O] that you were yourself! but, love, you are."
Sonnet 17: "Who will believe my verse in time to come."
Shapiro. Solipsism.
Shelley. To William Shelley ("Billows on the beach are leaping around it, The").
Silverstein. Googies Are Coming, The.
Hat.
If I Had A Brontosaurus.
Listen To The Mustn'ts.
One Inch Tall.
Ourchestra.
Rudy Flesh.
Sick.
Smart.
True Story.
Where the Sidewalk Ends.
Simic. Austerities.
Childhood of Parmenides, The.
Figuring.
Game, The.
Primer.
Prodigy.
Smith, Charlotte. Glow-Worm, The.
Sighing I see yon little troop at play.
Smith, Stevie. Advice to Young Children.
Archie and Tina.
Bog-Face.
Children of the Cross, The.
Cousin, The.
Deathly Child, The.
Governess, The.
Last Turn of the Screw, The.
Little Child of Brightest Face.
Louise.
Maximilian Esterhazy.
Mother's Hearse, A.
My Heart Was Full.
Northumberland House.
One of Many.
Our Bog is Dood.
Parklands, The.
Queen and the Young Princess, The.
Soldier Dear to Us, A.
To Carry the Child.
Unser Vater.
Snodgrass. Boy Made of Meat, The; A Poem for Children.
Mouse, The.
Reconstructions.
To a Child.
Sorrentino. Classic Case, A.
Midnight Special.

Spender. Elementary School Classroom in a Slum, An.
Empty House.
Footnote, A.
My Parents.
To My Daughter.
Stafford. Adults Only.
First Grade.
Living on the Plains.
Mother's Day.
Remembering Brother Bob.
Stevens. Celle Qui Fût Héaulmiette.
Questions Are Remarks.
Stevenson. Ad Nepotem.
Auntie's Skirts.
Bed in Summer.
Before this little gift was come.
Come, my little children, here are songs for you.
Cow, The.
De Erotio Puella.
Early in the morning I hear on your piano.
Escape at Bedtime.
Et Tu In Arcadia Vixisti.
Fairy Bread.
Farewell to the Farm.
Foreign Children.
Foreign Lands.
God gave to me a child in part.
Good and Bad Children.
Good Boy, A.
Good Play, A.
Hayloft, The.
Here Lies Erotion.
Home from the daisied meadows, where you linger yet.
In Charidemum.
Keepsake Mill.
Lamplighter, The.
Land of Counterpane, The.
Land of Nod, The.
Land of Story-Books, The.
Looking Forward.
Looking-Glass River.
Marching Song.
My Bed Is a Boat.
My Kingdom.
My Shadow.
My Ship and I.
My Treasures.
North-West Passage.
Picture-Books in Winter.
Pirate Story.
Sick Child, The.
Singing.
Stormy Nights.
Sun's Travels, The.
Swing, The.
System.
Thought, A.
Time to Rise.
To Alison Cunningham.
To Any Reader.
To Minnie.
To My Mother.
To My Name-Child.
To Rosabelle.
To Willie and Henrietta.
Unseen Playmate, The.
What glory for a boy of ten.
Where Go the Boats?
Whole Duty of Children.
Winter Time [or Winter-Time].
Young Night Thought.
Stuart. Rescue.
Soup Jar, The.
Tending.
Warehouse Chute, The.
Sutter. Beaverhouse Downriver, The.
Swift. Corinna.
Tate. Eye, The.
Tennyson. Baby New to Earth and Sky, The.
Thomas. Fern Hill.
This Side of the Truth.
Tomlinson. Picture of J. T. in a Prospect of Stone, The.

Turco. School Drawing.
Werewolf.
Updike. Conversation.
July.
One-Year-Old, The.
Van Duyn. Bedtime Stories.
Three Valentines to the Wide World.
Wakoski. Coins and Coffins under My Bed.
Walcott. At the Queen's Park Hotel, with its white, high-ceilinged rooms.
Camps hold [or held] their distance— [of] brown chestnuts and grey smoke, The.
Cold Spring Harbor.
Lesson for This Sunday, A.
With the frenzy of an old snake shedding its skin.
Waldman. De Carlo Lots, The.
Lindsay Speaks.
Mother & Child.
Warren. Little Boy and Lost Shoe.
Picture of Little Rory in a Municipal Park, The.
Whitman. After the Argument.
Play-Ground, The.
There Was a Child Went Forth.
Whittier. Autograph, An.
Barefoot Boy, The.
Child-Songs.
Hymn of the Children.
In School-Days.
Light That Is Felt, The.
Lines Written in an Album.
My Namesake.
My Playmate.
Name, A.
Oh for boyhood's painless play.
Poet and the Children, The.
Wilbur. Boy at the Window.
Digging for China.
Pardon, The.
Statues.
Williams, Charles Kenneth. Before This.
Blades.
Body, The.
Color of Time, The.
For Gail, When I Was Five.
Gift, The.
Good Mother: Out.
I Am the Bitter Name.
I'd forgotten and / how could I ever.
My Mother's Lips.
Of What Is Past.
Park, The.
Reading: Early Sorrow.
Scar.
Sorrow, The.
Still Life.
Tails.
Ten Below.
Waking Jed.
When / you were small, I.
Williams, Miller. For Lucinda, Robert, and Karyn.
Getting Experience.
Rebecca at Play.
Vanishing Point, The.
Williams, William Carlos. Child and Vegetables.
Death of Franco of Cologne, The: His Prophecy of Beethoven.
Hic Jacet.
Portent.
Sympathetic Portrait of a Child.
To.
Waiting.
Wordsworth. Anecdote for Fathers.
"Beloved Vale!" I said, "when I shall con."
Characteristics of a Child Three Years Old.
Infant M— M—, thou.
Intent on Gathering Wool from Hedge and Brake.
LITTLE Onward Lend Thy Guiding Hand, A.
My heart leaps up when I behold.
Ode: Intimations of Immortality [from Recollections of Early Childhood].
Ruth [or, The Influences of Nature].
To a Child [Written in Her Album].

To H. C.[, Six Years Old].
We Are Seven.
While Anna's Peers and Early Playmates Tread.
Wright, James. Big People, The.
Evening.
Little Girl on Her Way to School, A.
Mutterings over the Crib of a Deaf Child.
Note Left in Jimmy Leonard's Shack, A.
Poem by Garnie Braxton, A.
Sappho.
Song for the Middle of the Night, A.
Trumpets.
Twilights.
Yau. Shimmering Pediment.
To the young boy standing in front of the large glass tanks, each.
Yeats. Among School Children.
Cradle Song, A: "Angels are stooping, The."
Prayer for My Daughter, A.
To a Child Dancing in the Wind.
Zimmer. Father Animus and Zimmer.
Irene Gogle.
One for the Ladies at the Troy Laundry Who Cooled Themselves for Zimmer.
What Zimmer Would Be.
Zimmer Guilty of the Burnt Girl.
Zimmer's Head Thudding against the Blackboard.
Zukofsky. March First.
See also **Adolescence; Boys; Death in Childhood; Girls; Youth.**

Chile
Coleridge. Nightingale, The.
Dobyns. Cuidadores de Autos.
General Matthei Drives Home through Santiago.
Williams, Miller. Allende at the End.

Chillon Castle, Switzerland
Byron. Sonnet on Chillon.

Chimney Sweepers
Blake. Chimney Sweeper, The ("A little black thing among the snow").
Chimney Sweeper, The ("When my mother died I was very young").
Graves. Wm. Brazier.

Chimneys
Cummings. Death's Chimney.
Frost. Kitchen Chimney, The.
Graves. Under the Pot.
Williams, William Carlos. Yellow Chimney, The.

China
Auden. Macao.
Berg. For the Ghost of Li Po.
Bunting. Vestiges.
Cohen. Democracy.
Eberhart. Ode to the Chinese Paper Snake.
Pull of Memory, The.
Ultimate Song.
Fox. On the Other Side of Uji Bridge.
Hall. Photographs of China.
Hoffman. Twentieth Century, The.
Lindsay. Chinese Nightingale, The.
Incense.
Shantung[, or The Empire of China is Crumbling Down].
Lowry. I've Said Goodbye to Shanghai.
Marching down the road to China.
Merton. Picture of Lee Ying, A.
Miller. Saw 'er at a temple on the outskirts of Hangzhou.
Nathan. Letter.
O'Hara. Poem: "At night Chinamen jump."
Rolfe. After Wang Chi.
Rukeyser. It is the sixth year of the war in China.
Tomlinson. Nine Variations in a Chinese Winter Setting.
Wilbur. Digging for China.
Williams, William Carlos. Spring in the Snow-Drenched Garden.
Summer Song.
Wright, Charles. China Journal.
Yau. Halfway to China.
Marco Polo.
Shanghai Shenanigans.

Chinaware
Merrill. Willowware Cup.
Moore. No Swan So Fine.

Chinese, The
Carruth. "My mother did it. She had to, she said. She took."
Of Distress Being Humiliated by the Classical Chinese Poets.
Clark. Sounding Chinese at Inspiration Point.
Cohen. Event, The.
Eberhart. Bells of a Chinese Temple, The.
Gallagher. Rijl.
Some Painful Butterflies Pass Through.
Hewitt. Sunset.
Jeffers. On an Anthology of Chinese Poems.
Nemerov. To Lu Chi.
O'Hara. For the Chinese New Year & for Bill Berkson.
Rossetti. Chinaman, The.
Sandburg. Bronzes.
Yau. Their Shadows.
Zukofsky. Imitation.

Chipmunks
Cummings. & sun & / sil / e / nce.
Eberhart. Vastness and Indifference of the World, The.
Jarrell. Chipmunk's Day, The.
Nash. Chipmunk, The.
Pack. Cherry Robbers.

Chivalry
Chaucer. Squire's Tale, The.
De la Mare. Keep Innocency.
Graves. Absent Crusader.
Hardy. Then and Now.
Keats. Calidore. A Fragment.
Specimen of an Induction to a Poem.
To [Mary Frogley].
Melville. Rusty Man, The.
Meredith. Archduchess Anne.
Ballad of the Lady Eglantine, The.
Lives there a man with such base mettle.
Nash. How Now, Sirrah? Oh, Anyhow.
Silverstein. Tight Hat.

Chocolates
Creeley. Song: "Were I myself more blithe."
Nash. Assorted Chocolates.

Choices
Bukowski. 35 Seconds.
Byron. God Maddens Him Whom 'T Is His Will to Lose.
Campion. Could my poore hart whole worlds of toungs employ.
What meanes this folly, now to brave it so.
Carew. Married Woman, A.
Carroll, Jim. Child Growing Up with the Sun, A.
Judging the Pageant.
Carruth. Lost.
Sonnet: "To have been Diogenes. Why not? Or de Sade."
Clough. Shall I decide it by a random shot?
Dickey, William. Coyote's Song.
Donne. To Mr. B. B.
Frost. Lovely Shall Be Choosers, The.
Graves. Dans un Seul Lit.
Down, Wanton, Down!
Sharp Ridge, The.
Whole Love.
Hardy. Private Man on Public Men, A.
Herrick. Choose for the Best.
Will the Cause of Woe, The.
Hewitt. Poem: "My name is Revolution—let me speak."
Terrible Choice, The.
Volunteer, The.
Hoffman. Keys.
Hugo. Snoqualmie.
Jarrell. Conversation with the Devil, A.
Jong. In My Cauldron under the Full Moon.
Jonson. Epode: "Not to know vice at all, and keep[e] true state."
It follows now you are to prove.
Kunitz. Beyond Reason.
Larkin. After-Dinner Remarks.
Dockery and Son.
How Distant.
Places, Loved Ones.

Lawrence. Free Will.
Impulse.
Lowry. I tried to think of something good.
Is there no song that I can sing.
Markson. We Love, But Cannot Live.
Merton. Rock shot chasms / Promise unplanned flight.
Nash. Strange Case of the Lucrative Compromise, The.
Olson. In Cold Hell, in Thicket.
Pack. Trying to Reconcile.
Paley. Life.
Piercy. Right to Life.
Ransom. Romance of a Youngest Daughter.
"Reed." Black Angel's Death Song.
Rich. Roofwalker, The.
Rossetti. All heaven is blazing yet / With the meridian sun.
Ballad of Boding, A.
Brandons Both.
If a mouse could fly, / Or if a crow could swim.
Sandburg. Choices.
Choose.
Stafford. Passing Remark.
Stuart. Taking Sides.
Wilbur. Sirens, The.
Williams, Charles Kenneth. Halves.
What we are / given.
Wright, Charles. Lost Souls.
Wroth. Sonnet 1: "In this strang labourinth how shall I turne?"
Wyatt. Like as the bird in the cage enclosed.
Yeats. Choice, The.

Choking
Creeley. End, The.
Koch. Summer in the trees! "It is time to strangle several bad poets."
Pack. Dwarf and Doctor Freud, The.

Cholera
Dove. Cholera.
Kipling. Cholera Camp.

Chopin, Frédéric François
Davie. In Chopin's Garden.

Christenings
Coleridge. On the Christening of a Friend's Child.
Hardy. To C.F.H.
Hewitt. Outside the Creeds.
Van Duyn. To My Godson, on His Christening.
See also **Baptism.**

Christianity and Christians
Angelou. Lord, in My Heart.
Beatles. Let It Be.
Bishop. Brazil, January 1, 1502.
Blake. Vision of Christ that thou dost see, The.
Bly. Empty Place, An.
Boyle. Angels for Djuna Barnes.
Bradstreet. Occasional Meditations: "By night, when others soundly slept."
Brooks. Spaulding and Francois.
Browning, Elizabeth Barrett. Earth and Her Praisers.
View Across the Roman Campagna.
Work and Contemplation.
Browning, Robert. Death in the Desert, A.
Easter-Day.
Gold Hair.
Holy-Cross Day.
Campion. Come Let Us Sound With Melodie.
To the World.
Clough. Sa Majestá Très Chrétienne.
Cohen. Be with Me.
Deep Happiness, A.
Embrace, The.
Fragment from a Journal.
Great Feast in Quebec, A.
Coleridge. Religious Musings.
Cowper. Hymn for the Sunday School at Olney.
Progress of Error, The.
Reflection on the Foregoing Ode.
Song of Mercy and Judgment, A.
Truth.

Crashaw. Howres for the Hours of Matines, The.
Cullen. Mood.
Sonnet: "I know now how a man whose blood is hot."
Davie. Christian Hero, A.
Helena Morley.
Dickinson. I'm ceded—I've stopped being Theirs.
Is it a joyous expanse of Year.
Donne. And whilst [or whil'st] this universal choir [or universall Quire].
Confessors, The.
From tempting Satan to tempt us.
Show me dear[e] Christ, thy spouse, so bright and clear.
Dunbar. Light, The.
Religion.
Dunn. At the Smithville Methodist Church.
"Dylan." I Believe in You.
Precious Angel.
Property of Jesus.
Eberhart. Once More, O Ye.
United 555.
Emerson. We sauntered amidst miracles.
Everson. In All These Acts.
Ferlinghetti. Sometime during eternity / some guys show up.
Fox. Galileo Galilei (1564–1642).
Galvin. Holy Well, A.
Gardner. Ballade: "Lady of Heaven, Queen of nature."
Graves. Awakening, The.
Griffiths. At the Consecration.
Hymns and Backward Glances.
Hartnett. He'll to the Moors.
Mountains, Fall on Us.
No Avail.
Heaney. Westering.
Herbert. British Church, The.
Church Militant, The.
Church-Rents and Schisms.
Cross[e], The.
Priesthood, The.
Herrick. Christian Militant.
Crosses.
Good Christians.
On Himselfe ("Here down my wearyed limbs Ile lay").
Hewitt. Conversations in Hungary, August 1969.
Simple-Minded Christian, The.
Hill. Fidelities.
Hopkins. On the Portrait of Two Beautiful Young People.
Housman. New Year's Eve.
Hugo. Letter to Hill from St. Ignatius.
Joseph. CENTERPIECE: St. Sebastian (Italian).
Kinnell. Avenue Bearing the Initial of Christ into the New World, The.
In the Twentieth Century of my trespass on earth.
Knott. Brighton Rock by Graham Greene.
Racist Poem.
Lawrence. Cross, The.
Jesus' Farewell.
Retort to Jesus.
Song of Don Ramon, The.
Liddy. Holden.
Kerouac's Ronsard Dance.
Lady/Lord in Doorway.
Proverbs of Corca Bascinn.
Roses of Parnell & Mellowes, The.
Lindsay. See how the generations pass.
MacNeice. Belfast.
Meredith. Garden of Epicurus, The.
Song of Theodolinda, The.
Merton. Letter to Pablo Antonio Cuadra Concerning Giants, A.
New Song, The.
Two Desert Fathers.
Milton. Sonnet 19: "When I consider how my light is spent."
Muldoon. Our Lady of Ardboe.
Nemerov. Frozen City, The.
Sonnet: "Form of Christ cut from dark wood, the pale, A."

Olson. Easter.
Obit.
Owen. Maundy Thursday.
Paley. Choir Singing, The.
Plath. Medusa.
Prince. Book, The.
Ecumenical Exchange, 1989.
Raine. Harvest of learning I have reaped.
Robinson. Three Taverns, The.
Rossetti. Christian and Jew. A Dialogue.
I Know You Not.
Testimony, A.
Scott. Gray Brother, The.
Shapiro. Synagogue, The.
Smart. Epistle to John Sherratt, Esq., An.
Hymns and Spiritual Songs for the Fasts and Festivals of the Church of England.
Hymns for the Amusement of Children.
Jubilate Agno.
Song to David, A.
Smith, Stevie. House of Over-Dew, The.
How Do You See?
Noble and Ethereal.
Oh Christianity, Christianity.
Sunt Leones.
Thoughts about the Christian Doctrine of Eternal Hell.
Why Do You Rage?
Stevens. High-Toned Old Christian Woman, A.
Sunday Morning.
Stevenson. Lowden Sabbath Morn, A.
Scotsman's Return from Abroad, The.
Swift. Lines to Pope.
On the Words "Brother Protestants and Fellow Christians."
Thomas. Altarwise by Owl-Light.
Before I Knocked.
Vision and Prayer.
Updike. Each day's tour, I gather sandy castles.
Van Duyn. Old widow lady, and went out to do her chore, An.
Pietà, Rhenish, 14th C., the Cloisters, The.
Relative and an Absolute, A.
Whitman. To Him That Was Crucified.
Whittier. Brown Dwarf of Rŭgen, The.
By Their Works.
Call of the Christian, The.
Christian Tourists, The.
Holy Land, The.
How Mary Grew.
Nauhaught, the Deacon.
Red River Voyageur, The.
Wilbur. Christmas Hymn, A.
Rule, The.
Williams, Miller. Vision and Prayer.
Wordsworth. Composed in Roslin Chapel, During a Storm.
Decay of Piety.
Eagle and the Dove, The.
Inscription for a Monument in Crossthwaite Curch, in the Vale of Keswick.
On the Same Occasion [on Seeing the Foundation Preparing for the Erection of Rydal Chapel].
Wright, Charles. Lost Bodies.
Yeats. Ribh Considers Christian Love Insufficient.
Veronica's Napkin.
Zimmer. Father Animus and Zimmer.

Christmas
Auden. Blessed Event.
Berrigan. For You.
Seurat and Juan Gris combine this season.
Berry. To Tanya at Christmas.
Betjeman. Beaumaris, December 21, 1963.
Christmas.
Boyle. Christmas Carol for Emanuel Carnevali, A.
Browning, Elizabeth Barrett. Christmas Gifts.
Virgin Mary to the Child Jesus, The.
"Carroll, Lewis." Christmas Greetings.
Carruth. Essay on Death.
Song: The Young Man with the Guitar, Testing.
Coleridge. Christmas Carol, A: "Shepherds

went their hasty way, The."
Homeless.
Crashaw. To the Queen's Majesty.
Creeley. Christmas: May 10, 1970.
Xmas.
Cullen. Christus Natus Est.
Cummings. And i imagine.
Little tree / little silent Christmas tree.
Davie. Hawkshead and Dachau in a Christmas Glass.
De la Mare. Before Dawn.
Donne. Nativity [or Nativitie].
Doolittle. Christmas 1944.
Dunbar. Back-Log Song, A.
Chrismus Is A-Comin'.
Christmas.
Christmas Carol: "Ring out, ye bells!"
Christmas Folksong, A.
Christmas in the Heart.
Little Christmas Basket, A.
Speakin' o' Christmas.
Eberhart. Christmas Tree.
Eliot. Cultivation of Christmas Trees, The.
Frost. To a Young Wretch.
Gildner. Xmas.
Ginsberg. These States: Into L.A.
Graves. Carol of Patience.
Christmas Robin, The.
Griffiths. Christmas Night.
Hymns and Backward Glances.
Hacker. Christmas Crown, A.
Hall. Carol, A.
Family, The.
Waiting on the Corners.
Hardy. Burning the Holly.
Christmastide.
House of Hospitalities, The.
Nightmare, and the Next Thing, A.
Oxen, The.
Reminder, The.
Yuletide in a Younger World.
Hemingway. Poem to Mary (Second Poem).
Herbert. Christmas.
Herrick. Ceremonies for Christmas[se].
Christs Birth.
Ode on the Birth of Our Saviour, An.
Saint Distaffs Day, or the Morrow after Twelfth Day.
Upon Candlemasse Day.
Upon Tuck.
Hesketh. No Reply at Christmas.
Single Footprints.
Hewitt. Christmas Rhymers, Ballynure, 1941, The.
Filled Stocking, The.
Rhyme for Christmas Morning, A.
Hopkins. Moonless darkness stands between.
Hugo. Christmas with Shepherds in Brefaro.
December 24 and George McBride Is Dead.
Letter to Annick from Boulder.
Jarrell. Christmas Roses, The.
Night before the Night before Christmas, The.
Jeffers. Two Christmas-Cards.
Jonson. Hum drum, sauce for a cony.
Hymn[e] on the Nativity [or Nativitie] of My Saviour, A.
Nor do you think that their legs is all.
Kinnell. To Christ Our Lord.
Kipling. Christmas in India.
Eddi's Service.
Lindsay. Doll Upon the Topmost Bough, The.
Lowell. Christmas.
Lowry. Deserter.
McGrath. Bread of this World; Praises III, The.
MacNeice. Canto VII: "Cloud of witnesses. To whom? To what?, A."
Canto XXIII: "December continues mild. The rose garden."
Canto XXIV: "December the Twenty-third: I visit the Ancient East."
Canto XXV: "And today is Christmas Eve. Once more to work."
Canto XXVI: "Morning bright as summer. The job on hand, A."
Meinke. Stille Nacht, Heilege Nacht.
Melville. Margrave's Birthnight, The.

Liddy. Many Mansions.
Lieberman. Daibutsu.
  Organist's Black Carnation, The.
Lindsay. In the Immaculate Conception
  Church.
MacLeish. St. Philip's Church in Antigua.
Mahon. Songs of Praise.
Meinke. Church Cemetery in St. Mary's, A.
Melville. In a Church of Padua.
Merton. Notes for a New Liturgy.
Neruda. Bell Tower of Authenay, The.
Owen. Le Christianisme.
Paley. Choir Singing, The.
Raine. Returning from Church.
Rossetti. St. Andrew's Church.
Schuyler. Mark.
Simic. Gravity.
  Winter Night.
Stevens. Blue Buildings in the Summer Air,
  The.
  Gray Stones and Gray Pigeons.
  St. Armorer's Church from the Outside.
  Winter Bells.
Stevenson. You looked so tempting in the
  pew.
Sutter. Pine Creek Parish Hall.
Swift. Verses on the Upright Judge.
Tate. Sonnets at Christmas.
Thomas. It Is the Sinner's Dust-Tongued Bell.
Tomlinson. Arroyo Seco.
  At Saint Mary's Church.
  Idyll: "Door: / PER L'UNIVERSO / is what it
    says, A."
  In Michoacán.
  Las Trampas U. S. A.
  Santa Maria delle Nevi.
  Turco. Church, The.
Whitman. March in the Ranks Hard-Prest, and
  the Road Unknown, A.
Whittier. Book, The.
  Hymn for the House of Worship at
    Georgetown.
  Hymn for the Opening of Plymouth Church.
  Hymn for the Opening of Thomas Starr King's
    House of Worship.
  In the "Old South."
  Kallundborg Church.
  Landmarks, The.
Wilbur. Dubious Night, A.
  Plain Song for Comadre, A.
Williams, William Carlos. Problem, The.
Wordsworth. Church of San Salvador Seen
  from the Lake of Lugano.
  Composed in Roslin Chapel, During a Storm.
  For a Seat in the Groves of Coleorton.
  Inscription for a Monument in Crossthwaite
    Curch, in the Vale of Keswick.
  Inside of King's College Chapel, Cambridge.
  On the Same Occasion [on Seeing the
    Foundation Preparing for the Erection of
    Rydal Chapel].
  When Severn's Sweeping Flood Had
    Overthrown.
Yau. Cenotaph of Snow.

Churchill, Winston Leonard Spencer
Hill. Innocent soul / ghosting for its lost.

Churchyards
Auden. In a Country Churchyard.
Mahon. In Carrowdore Churchyard.
Rossetti. Birchington Churchyard.
Tomlinson. Churchyard Wall, The.

Cibber, Colley
Johnson. Epigram on Colley Cibber.
Pope. Cibber! write all thy Verses upon
  Glasses.

Cicadas
Eberhart. Largess, The.
Hartley. Cicada.
Kooser. August.
McGrath. Poem: "Long wound of the
  summer—, The."
Van Duyn. Walking the Dog: A Diatribe.
Wilbur. Cicadas.

Cigarettes
Cohen. I Knelt Beside a Stream.
Cummings. This cigarette is extremely long.
Kunitz. Hand-Rolled Cigarettes.

Lorde. American Cancer Society Or There Is
  More Than One Way to Skin a Coon.
Lowry. Men With Coats Thrashing.
Nash. There Are More Ways to Roast a Pig
  than Burning the House Down or You Can
  Always Stick Your Head in a Volcano.
  Thoughts Thought after a Bridge Party.
Zukofsky. Incident, An.
  Last cigarette / a companion, A.
  Sand: For the cigarette finished, The.
See also **Smoking and Smokers.**

Cigars
Kipling. Betrothed, The.
Sandburg. Crimson.
  Noon Hour.

Cinderella
Jarrell. Cinderella.
Plath. Cinderella.
Sexton. Cinderella.
Van Duyn. Cinderella's Story.

Circe
Atwood. Circe / Mud Poems.
Auden. Circe.
Doolittle. Circe.
Gunn. Moly.
MacNeice. Canto XI: "Golden guineas filter
  through the mist, The."
  Circe.

Circumcision
Crashaw. Our Lord in His Circumcision to
  His Father.
Herrick. Another New-Yeeres Gift, or Song
  for the Circumcision.
  New-Yeeres Gift, or Circumcisions Song, Sung
  to the King in the Presence at White Hall,
  The.
  To His Savior [or Saviour]. The New Years
  [or yeers] Gift.
  Upon Zelot.
Milton. Upon the Circumcision.
Smart. Circumcision.
Smith, Stevie. Jew Is Angry with His Friend
  Who Does Not Believe in Circumcision, A.
Southwell. Circumsision, The.

Circus
Auden. Circus, The.
Beatles. Being for the Benefit of Mr. Kite.
Berryman. Animal Trainer, The.
Bishop. Cirque d'Hiver.
Dove. Hill of Beans, A.
Edmunds. Treblinka.
Emerson. Like vaulters in the circus round.
Gardner. Three Rings or Five rings.
Koch. Circus, The.
Kooser. Geek, The.
Lawrence. On the Drum.
  Two Performing Elephants.
  When I Went to the Circus.
Lindsay. Born of mobs, born of steam.
  Every soul / Resident / In the earth's one
  circus tent!
  I am the Gutter Dream.
MacNeice. Circus.
Muldoon. Duffy's Circus.
Nash. Big Tent Under the Roof, The.
Olson. Her Dream, Half Remembered.
Plath. Circus in Three Rings.
  Denouement.
Rukeyser. Destruction of Grief.
  Ringling.
Sandburg. Air Circus.
  Hazardous Occupations.
  We live only once.
Sexton. Bells, The.
Silverstein. Acrobats, The.
Smith, Stevie. This Is Disgraceful and
  Abominable.
Van Duyn. Ringling Brothers, Barnum and
  Bailey.
Williams, William Carlos. Phoenix and the
  Tortoise, The.

Cities
Angelou. Through the Inner City to the
  Suburbs.
Arnold. In Utrumque Paratus.
Ashbery. Unctuous Platitudes.

Atwood. City Planners, The.
Auden. In villages from which their
  childhoods came.
  Paysage Moralisé.
  Plane Tree, The.
Beckett. Scene.
Berrigan. Lord, it is time. Summer was very
  great.
Berry. Going into the city, coming.
  Mad Farmer in the City, The.
Betjeman. City.
  City, The.
Bishop. From the Country to the City.
  Night City.
Browning, Elizabeth Barrett. My Doves.
  Soul's Travelling, The.
Browning, Robert. Up at a Villa—Down in
  the City.
Bukowski. Night on a Visa Card.
Bunting. Two hundred and seven paces.
Carroll, Jim. Love Rockets.
  Moss under your fingernails it feeds, The.
  One Flight Up.
  What matter for thick armchairs and fine
  shelves for books?
Carruth. Gray dawn seeping through stone.
  It was our city too. Chrome and glass.
  Snow, The.
  Sonnet: "Dearest, I never knew such loving.
  There."
  Sonnet: "From our very high window at the
  Sheraton."
  Thaw.
Clough. As, at a railway junction, men.
  To the Great Metropolis.
Cohen. I Wonder How Many People in This
  City.
Coleridge. Hope and Time.
  Silent City, A.
Crane. Euclid Avenue.
  Porphyro in Akron.
Creeley. City, The.
  Night in NYC.
Cummings. As usual i did not find him in
  cafes,the more dissolute atmosphere.
  At the head of this street a gasping organ is
  waving moth-eaten.
  Because / an obstreperous grin minutely floats.
  Blue woman with sticking out breasts hanging,
  A.
  Even if all desires things moments be.
  —GON splashes-sink.
  He as o, A / ld as who stag.
  Helves surling out of eakspeasies
  per(reel)hapsingly.
  I walked the boulevard.
  My sonnet is A light goes on in.
  (One!) / the wisti-twisti barber.
  One winter afternoon / (at the magical hour).
  Only as what(out of a flophouse)floats.
  Paris,thou art non.
  Phonograph's voice like a keen spider
  skipping, The.
  Spring(side / walks are)is.
  Taxis toot whirl people moving perhaps laugh
  into the slowly.
  Twentyseven bums give a prostitute the once.
  What a proud dreamhorse
  pulling(smoothloomingly)through.
  When / from a sidewalk.
Davie. Agave in the West.
  Scythian Charioteers, The.
  Zion.
Donne. To Sir Henry Wotton ("Sir, more than
  kisses, letters mingle souls").
Doolittle. Cities.
  It is no madness to say.
  Other Sea-Cities.
  Tribute, The.
Dove. Spy.
  Straw Hat.
  Under the Viaduct, 1932.
Duncan. Everything Speaks to Me.
  Household, The.
Dunn. Round Trip.
"Dylan." Sign on the Window.
  To Ramona.

Eberhart. To Harriet Monroe.
Eliot. *Boston Evening Transcript*, The.
　His soul stretched tight across the skies.
　Morning at the Window.
　Morning comes to consciousness, The.
　Preludes (I–IV).
　Rhapsody on a Windy Night.
　Winter evening settles down, The.
　You tossed a blanket from the bed.
Fisher. After Working.
　By the Pond.
　City.
　For Realism.
　Lullaby and Exhortation for the Unwilling
　　Hero.
　107 Poems.
　Sun Hacks, The.
Fletcher. City Lights.
　Elegy on London.
　Flickering of incessant rain.
　Houses of the city no longer hum and play,
　　The.
　Lake Shore at Night.
Garrigue. Bleecker Street.
Ginsberg. Describe: The Rain on
　　Dasaswamedh Ghat.
　My Sad Self.
　Two Sonnets.
Gunn. Bringing to Light.
　In Praise of Cities.
　Map of the City, A.
　Night Taxi.
　Tenderloin.
Hacker. Two Cities.
Hall. Poem With One Fact.
　Transcontinent.
Hardy. From Her in the Country.
　Nightmare, and the Next Thing, A.
Hartley. Midnight—the City.
　Outcast City on the Kennebec, The.
　This Little City.
Herrick. Peace not Permanent.
　To His Muse ("Whither, mad maiden, wilt
　　thou roame?").
　Upon Hinmself ("Come, leave this loathed
　　Country-life, and then").
Hewitt. City Morning.
　Hymn: "Noon in an English county."
　Sunset over Glenaan.
Hopkins. Alchemist in the City, The.
Housman. In my own shire, if I was sad.
Hughes, Langston. Summer Evening (Calumet
　　Avenue).
Hugo. What the Brand New Freeway Won't
　　Go By.
Jarrell. City, City!
Jeffers. What are Cities For?
Joseph. Instant on the Viaduct, An.
　Married People Going to Work.
　On the Embankment.
　Timetable for a Town.
Kipling. Song of Seven Cities, The.
　Song of the Cities, The.
　To the City of Bombay.
　Your patience, Sirs. The Devil took me up.
Larkin. Arrival.
　Bridge for the Living.
Lawrence. City-Life.
　In the Cities.
　North Country, The.
Levertov. City Psalm.
　Whisper, The.
　Window, A.
　World Outside, The.
Levine. These Streets.
Lewis. *Civil Servant, The.*
Lindsay. Springfield Magical.
Lowry. Beneath the Malebolge lies Hastings
　　street.
　Fisherman's Return.
　Of the Francia.
　There is no poetry when you live there.
McGrath. Dawn Song.
　Migration of Cities, The.
　Return to Marsh Street.
　Underground, The.
MacNeice. Birmingham.

Morning Sun.
Street Scene.
Meinke. ABC of Aerobics, The.
　Anniversary Deer, The.
Meredith. Linnet-Hawker, The.
　Sleeping City, The.
　Tardy Spring.
Merton. And So Goodbye to Cities.
　Aubade—the City.
　City's Spring, The.
　Holy Communion: the City.
　How to Enter a Big City.
Miller. Hookah.
Nash. City, The.
Nemerov. From a Record of Disappointment.
　Frozen City, The.
　Sestina II: "No waste is trackless: all terrain
　　the lost."
　Situation Does Not Change, The.
　Stare of the Man from the Provinces, The.
O'Hara. Poem "Now the violets are all gone,
　　the rhinoceroses, the cymbals."
　Song: "Is it dirty."
Olson. Part of the Series on the Paths, A.
　To Try to Get Down One Citizen as Against
　　Another.
Oppen. *Amor fati* / The love of fate.
　Enclave / Filled with their own, An.
　I cannot even now / Altogether disengage
　　myself.
　Impossible Poem, The.
　Moving over the hills, crossing the irrigation.
　Now in the helicopters the casual will.
　Obsessed, bewildered / By the shipwreck.
　Or define / Man beyond rescue.
　Or, in that light, New arts!
　Pedestrian.
　So spoke of the existence of things.
　Source, The.
　Strange that the youngest people I know.
　Streets, in a poor district.
　Sunnyside Child.
　Tourist Eye.
　Unable to begin / At the beginning, the
　　fortunate.
　We are pressed, pressed on each other.
Paley. Fear.
Patchen. All That Night Lights Were Seen
　　Moving in Every Direction.
　He Was Alone (As in Reality) Upon His
　　Humble Bed.
　That blue hole, Heaven, carry its tide over the
　　wounded within.
　23rd Street Runs into Heaven.
Piercy. Learning Experience.
Poe. City in the Sea, The.
"Reed." City Lights.
Rossetti. Dead City, The.
　Mr. and Mrs. Scott, and I.
　True Story, A.
Rukeyser. Eel.
　Sixth Elegy. River Elegy.
　Wooden Spring.
Sandburg. Blue Island Intersection.
　Cahoots.
　City Number.
　Fellow Citizens.
　Flat Lands.
　Good Morning, America.
　Hats.
　Osawatomie.
　Passers-by.
　People Who Must.
　Santa Fe Sketches.
　Skyscraper.
　Slants at Buffalo, New York.
　Smoke Blue.
　Streets Too Old.
　They Will Say.
　Windy City, The.
Schuyler. Morning, The.
Schwartz. America, America!
Sexton. Keeping the City.
Snyder. Cartagena.
　7:VII.
Spender. Hamburg, 1929.

Spenser. Long having deeply gron'd these
　　visions sad.
Stevenson. My brain swims empty and light.
　O Lady fair and sweet.
Swift. Description of a City Shower, A.
Tomlinson. Geneva Restored.
　More Foreign Cities.
Updike. São Paulo.
　Small-City People.
Wakoski. Walking Past Paul Blackburn's Apt.
　　on 7th St.
Walcott. City's Death by Fire, A.
　Midsummer stretches beside me with its cat's
　　yawn.
Warren. Her Hat.
Whitman. Sparkles from the Wheel.
Wilbur. For the New Railway Station in
　　Rome.
　Peace of Cities, The.
　Shame.
Williams, Charles Kenneth. Snow: I.
Williams, William Carlos. Approach to a City.
　Bastard Peace, A.
　Bitter World of Spring, The.
　Construction.
　Flower, The.
　Grotesque.
　Metric Figure.
　Perpetuum Mobile: The City.
　Predicter of Famine, The.
Wordsworth. Aix-la-Chapelle.
　Composed upon Westminster Bridge,
　　September 3, 1802.
Wright, James. On the City Ramparts of
　　Cádiz.
　River Down Home, The.
Yau. Counting the times as if they added up.
　Pieces of a piece. The face in the window
　　larger.
　Predella.
　Room with open windows facing a street, A.
　Without noticing the fire descending into the.
Zimmer. Gus in the Streets.
Zukofsky. Cocktails / and signs of.
See also **Towns; Villages.**
Citizenship
　Atwood. Is this what we wanted.
　Hewitt. Memorandum for the Moderates.
Civil Defense
　Williams, Miller. We.
Civil Rights Movement. *see* **Protest, Social.**
Civil War, Spain
　Jarrell. For the Madrid Road.
　Levine. Francisco, I'll Bring You Red
　　Carnations.
　Hear Me.
　MacNeice. And I remember Spain.
　Merton. In Memory of the Spanish Poet
　　Federico Garcia Lorca.
　Rukeyser. Mediterranean.
　Sestina: "Coming to Spain on the first day of
　　the fighting."
　Spender. Port Bou.
　To Manuel Altolaguirre.
　Two Armies.
　Williams, William Carlos. Figueras Castle.
See also **Spain.**
Civil War, United States
　Berryman. Ancestor.
　Bishop. From Trollope's Journal.
　Dickey, James. Hunting Civil War Relics at
　　Nimblewill Creek.
　Dunbar. Colored Soldiers, The.
　News, The.
　Robert Gould Shaw.
　Unsung Heroes, The.
　When Dey 'Listed Colored Soldiers.
　Emerson. Boston Hymn.
　Voluntaries.
　Fletcher. Elegy in a Civil War Cemetery.
　Passing of the South, The.
　Frost. Black Cottage, The.
　Gildner. Dear and most Loved wife it is with
　　pleasure.
　Dear and Mutch Loved One with pleasure I
　　take.

Dear Cecelia we hav hat some warm times.
Dear Cecelia well its shel and shel and.
Dear loved one did I mention General Grants.
Dear loved one well the last 2 days I spent.
Dear wife and bosom friend I hat seen hart.
Dear wife and friend I dozed but now will try.
Dear wife and friend I hav not mutch to write.
Dear wife I feal prety rested now.
Dear woman I again take pen in hand.
Dear woman I am sor a littel bit.
Dear woman I am well and hope you ar.
Dear woman I was glat to hear from you.
I went with General Logans men and we.
Letters from Vicksburg.
Mrs. Blood. Dear Madam. Yours of Sept. 13.
Some boys ar playing cards but I dont feal.
We left the River seven days ago.
Hayden. Dream, The.
Hill. Shiloh Church, 1862: Twenty–Three Thousand.
Jarrell. Description of Some Confederate Soldiers, A.
Kunitz. His innocence was to trust.
Lowell. For the Union Dead.
Melville. Apparition, The.
Armies of the Wilderness, The.
At the Cannon's Mouth.
Ball's Bluff.
Battle of Stone River, Tennessee.
Canticle, A.
College Colonel, The.
Fortitude of the North, The.
House-Top, The.
Malvern Hill.
March to the Sea, The.
On Sherman's Men.
On the Grave.
On the Home Guards.
On the Slain Collegians.
Portent, The.
Rebel Color-Bearers at Shiloh.
Sheridan at Cedar Creek.
Shiloh [A Requiem].
Stonewall Jackson.
Utilitarian View of the Monitor's Fight, A.
Olson. Anecdotes of the Late War.
As if Hallam Movius had placed a grid over it, and plumb-.
Civil War, The.
Connection, The.
Rich. Charleston in the Eighteen-Sixties.
Rukeyser. City of Monuments.
Sandburg. Hammers Pounding.
Shenandoah.
Tate. Ode to the Confederate Dead.
Updike. Richmond.
Warren. Bear Track Plantation: Shortly after Shiloh.
History among the Rocks.
Whitman. Adieu to a Soldier.
Army Corps on the March, An.
Artilleryman's Vision, The.
As I Lay with My Head in Your Lap Camerado.
As Toilsome I Wander'd Virginia's Woods.
Ashes of Soldiers: Epigraph.
Bathed in War's Perfume.
Beat! Beat! Drums!
Bivouac on a Mountain Side.
By the Bivouac's Fitful Flame.
Cavalry Crossing a Ford.
City of Ships.
Come Up from the Fields Father.
Death of General Grant.
Delicate Cluster.
Dirge for Two Veterans.
Eighteen Sixty-One.
Ethiopia Saluting the Colors.
First O Songs for a Prelude.
From Paumanok Starting I Fly Like a Bird.
Give Me the Splendid Silent Sun.
How Solemn as One by One.
I Saw Old General at Bay.
Lo, Victress on the Peaks.
March in the Ranks Hard-Prest, and the Road Unknown, A.
O Sun of Real Peace.

Over the Carnage Rose Prophetic a Voice.
Race of Veterans.
Reconciliation.
Sight in Camp [or] Sight in Camp in the Daybreak Gray and Dim, A.
Song of the Banner at Daybreak.
Spirit Whose Work Is Done.
To a Certain Civilian.
Turn O Libertad.
Twilight Song, A.
Vigil Strange I Kept on the Field One Night.
Virginia—the West.
While Not the Past Forgetting.
World Take Good Notice.
Wound-Dresser, The.
Year That Trembled and Reel'd beneath Me.
Whittier. Anniversary Poem.
At Port Royal.
Barbara Frietchie.
Battle Autumn of 1862, The.
Ein Feste Burg Ist Unser Gott.
Hymn for the Celebration of Emancipation at Newburyport.
Hymn Sung at Christmas by the Scholars of St. Helena's Island, S.C.
Laus Deo!
Lost Occasion, The.
Peace Autumn, The.
Thy Will Be Done.
To Englishmen.
To John C. Frémont.
To Samuel E. Sewall and Harriet W. Sewall.
Watchers, The.
What the Birds Said.
Word for the Hour, A.

Civil Wars, England
Browning, Robert. Cavalier Tunes.
Herrick. Bad Season Makes the Poet Sad, The.
Obedience.
Upon the Troublesome Times.
Kipling. Edgehill Fight.
Marvell. Elegy upon the Death of My Lord Francis Villiers, An.
Milton. On the Forcers of Conscience.
Sonnet 8: "Captain or Colonel, or Knight in Arms."
Sonnet 15: "Fairfax, whose name in armes through Europe rings."
Sonnet 16: "Cromwell, our cheif of men, who through a cloud."

Civilization
Auden. Road's Your Place, The.
Ciardi. Measurements.
Cowper. Thracian, The.
Davie. Among Artisans' Houses.
"Dylan." Tombstone Blues.
Eliot. Choruses from "The Rock."
Waste Land, The.
Emerson. Adirondacs, The.
Enough is done highminded friend go sleep.
Water.
World-Soul, The.
Ferlinghetti. Vast Confusion, A.
Ford. There's No Place to Sleep in This Bed, Tanguy.
Fox. In the Land of Shinar.
Ovid.
Hall. New Hampshire.
Hartley. And, if the Popocatapetl.
Hesketh. From Walden.
Hill. After Cumae.
Decembrist blood! We are taxed.
Elegiac Stanzas: On a Visit to Dove Cottage.
Lowlands of Holland, The.
Of Commerce and Society: Variations on a Theme.
Holmes. Obituary for Jan Masaryk.
Jeffers. Decaying Lambskins.
Hellenistics.
New Mexican Mountain.
Sign-Post.
Still the Mind Smiles.
That light blood-loving weasel, a tongue of yellow.
What is Worthless?
Kipling. Benfactors, The.

City of Brass, The.
For All We Have and Are [1914].
White Man's Burden, The.
Koch. Our Hearts.
Kunitz. Gladiators, The.
Revolving Meditation.
Lawrence. Man, A.
Lindsay. Gospel of Beauty, A.
MacLeish. Fifteenth Book, The.
Sheep in the Ruins, The.
Mahon. Beyond Howth Head.
Image from Beckett, An.
Matthews. Civilization and Its Discontents.
Merton. Martin's Predicament or Atlas Watches Every Evening.
Natur / aabho / rrret / vacuu / uuuum.
Morrison. Flowering, The.
Now Listen to This.
Nash. Tell It to the Eskimos or Tell it to the Esquimaux.
We Would Refer You to Our Service Department, If We Had One.
Nathan. Loophole, The.
Neruda. Danger, The.
Olson. Plantation a Beginning, A.
Patchen. Man Is to Man a Beast.
Rich. Meditations for a Savage Child.
Rukeyser. Lost Romans, The.
Outpost.
Sandburg. At the Gates of Tombs.
Chillicothe.
Good Morning, America.
Shelton. Sonora for Sale.
Stevens. Anecdote of the Jar.
Frogs Eat Butterflies. Snakes Eat Frogs. Hogs Eat Snakes. Men Eat Hogs.
Tomlinson. Theory of Regress.
Wakoski. Civilization.
Wright, James. Horse, The.
Yeats. Long-legged Fly.

Clams and Clamming
Eberhart. Clam Diggers and Diggers of Sea Worms, The.
Hartley. At Half Past Anything.
Hoffman. Clams, The.
Oliver. Clam Man.
See also **Oysters; Shells.**

Clans
Burns. Campbells Are Comin, The.
Scott. Brooch of Lorn, The.
Wordsworth. Brownie, The.
See also **Culloden, Battle of (1746).**

Class. *see* **Social Class.**

Classicism
Clough. Resignation—to Faustus.
Coleridge. Garden of Boccaccio, The.
Tombless Epitaph, A.
Cummings. Ballad of the Scholar's Lament.
When i am in boston,i do not speak.
Davie. Sculptures in Hungary.
Scythian Charioteers, The.
Thyestes.
To an American Classicist.
Doolittle. I Said.
Nossis.
Emerson. I rake no coffined clay, nor publish wide.
Hardy. Liddell and Scott.
Jarrell. English Garden in Austria, An.
Jonson. Fit of Rhyme [or Rime] against Rhyme [or Rime], A.
Merrill. To My Greek.
Olson. At midnight, after hours of love, I ate.
Rolfe. Not Men Alone.
Sandburg. Child of the Romans.
I am zero, naught, one ciper.
In the days of the cockade and the brass pistol.
Southern Pacific.
Stevenson. Et Tu In Arcadia Vixisti.
Walcott. Sea Grapes.
Williams, William Carlos. After Song, An.
Yeats. Bronze Head, A.

Cleanliness
Carroll, Jim. Little Ode on St. Anne's Day.
Love Rockets.

Dunn. Cleanliness.
Emerson. We wish like the glass.
Herrick. Meane, The ("Tis much among the filthy to be clean").
Upon Brock.
Lovelace. Lucasta at the Bath.
Nash. Child Is Father to the Man, But with More Authority, The.
O'Hara. Song: "Is it dirty."
Silverstein. Dirtiest Man in the World, The.
Smith, Patti. Munich.
Stuart. Tending.
Wilbur. Plain Song for Comadre, A.

Clemens, Samuel Langhorne. see "Twain, Mark" (Samuel Langhorne Clemens).

Cleopatra
Berryman. Song from "Cleopatra."
Cummings. Cleopatra built / like a smooth arrow or.
Eberhart. Dry Rot, The.
Edmunds. Fire, The.
Landing in Cairo.
Hughes, Ted. Cleopatra to the Asp.
Kunitz. Cleopatra.
Lawrence. Universe Flows, The.
Lindsay. Trial of the Dead Cleopatra in Her Beautiful and Wonderful Tomb, The.
Lowell. Nunc Est Bibendum, Cleopatra's Death.
Meredith. Cleopatra.
Nash. Asp, The.
Pope. On the Statue of *Cleopatra*, Made into a Fountain by *Leo* the Tenth.
Stevenson. After Reading "Antony and Cleopatra."
Updike. Dilemma in the Delta.

Clergy
Berryman. Song of the Demented Priest, The.
Browning, Robert. Bishop Blougram's Apology.
Bishop Orders His Tomb at Saint Praxed's Church, The.
Soliloquy of the Spanish Cloister.
Burns. Calf, The.
Elegy on Peg Nicholson.
Holy Tulzie, The.
Kirk of Scotland's Garland—a New Song, The.
Lines *Written on a Window, at the King's Arms Tavern, Dumfries.*
On a Celebrated Ruling Elder.
To the Rev. John McMath, Inclosing a Copy of *Holy Willie's Prayer*, Which He Had Requested.
Byron. Bowles and Campbell.
New Vicar of Bray, The.
Chaucer. Canon's Yeoman's Tale, The.
Good man ther[e] was of religioun [or religion], A.
Cowper. Elegy 2: On the Death of the Beadle of Cambridge University.
Yearly Distress, The.
Crabbe. Election, The.
Vicar, The.
Crashaw. Luke 10; And a Certaine Priest Comming that Way Looked on Him and Passed by.
Upon Bishop Andrewes's [or Andrewes His] Picture before His Sermons.
Donne. To Mr. Tilman after He Had Taken Orders.
Dryden. Priestcraft and Private Judgement.
Emerson. Blame me not thou hoarse preacher.
Hymn Sung at the Second Church, Boston, at the Ordination of Rev. Chandler Robbins.
Once the priest / Lived in an age.
Fenton. Staffordshire Murderer, A.
Hardy. In Church.
Heaney. Cleric, The.
Herbert. Aaron.
Priesthood, The.
Windows, The.
Herrick. To Jos: Lo: Bishop of Exeter.
Upon Glass: Epigram.
Upon Trap.
Hill. Fantasia on 'Horbury'; John Bacchus Dykes, 1859.

Hopkins. Habit of Perfection, The.
Hughes, Langston. Madam and the Minister.
Sunday Morning Prophecy.
Jonson. Epigram, An: "That you have seen the pride, beheld the sport."
On Lip the Teacher.
Kipling. Curé, The.
Eddi's Service.
Our Lady of the Sackcloth.
Lawrence. At the Bank in Spain.
Death of the Baron, The.
Liddy. Cliffs with sea breaking at their.
Lowry. Those Coke to Newcastle Blues.
MacLeish. Acknowledgement.
Marvell. Flecknoe, an English Priest at Rome.
Milton. Elegy 2: On the Death of the Beadle of Cambridge University.
Prince. Moult sont Prud'hommes les Templiers.
Ralegh. Epitaph on the Earl of Salisbury.
Robinson. Sainte-Nitouche.
Smith, Charlotte. Slow in the Wintry Morn, the struggling light.
Stevens. Blue Buildings in the Summer Air, The.
Gray Stones and Gray Pigeons.
Swift. Ode to Dr. William Sancroft.
On the Irish Bishops.
Tennyson. To the Rev. F. D. Maurice.
Thomson. To the Reverend Patrick Murdoch.
Turco. Simon Judson.
Whittier. Clerical Oppressors.
Gallows, The.
Inscriptions.
Letter from a Missionary of the Methodist Episcopal Church South, in Kansas, to a Distiguished Politician.
Lines from a Letter to a Young Clerical Friend.
Minister's Daughter, The.
Official Piety.
Pastoral Letter, The.
Sabbath Scene, A.
Yeats. Ballad of Father Gilligan, The.

See also **Rabbis.**

Clerks
Dobyns. Window, The.
Robinson. Clerks, The.
Roethke. Dolor.

See also **Office Workers.**

Cleveland, Ohio
Ginsberg. Cleveland, the Flats.
Koch. Artist, The.
Patchen. Cleveland, Oh?
Sandburg. Honky Tonk in Cleveland, Ohio.
Simic. Euclid Avenue.
Turco. Ordinary Evening in Cleveland, An.

Clichés
Clough. That out of sight is out of mind.
Merton. Anatomy of Melancholy, The.
Found Macaronic Antipoem.
Nash. Oh, Stop Being Thankful All over the Place.
Sandburg. Put Off the Wedding Five Times and Nobody Comes to It.

Cliff Dwellers
Williams, William Carlos. Testament of Perpetual Change, The.

Cliffs
Betjeman. Cornish Cliffs.
Winter Seascape.
Doolittle. Cliff Temple, The.
Hardy. To a Sea-Cliff.
Liddy. At castle shadowed mouth of the / Doonbeg.
At castle shadowed mouth of the.
Lowry. Pilgrim passes through the town by night, A.
McAuley. Creed.
Plath. Finisterre.
Raine. Canna's Basalt Crags.
Tomlinson. Morwenna's Cliff.
Near Ceibwr.
Warren. Paul Valéry Stood on the Cliff and Confronted the Furious Energies of Nature.
Wordsworth. Gordale.

Clocks
Atwood. Beauharnois.
Bishop. Paris, 7 A.M.
Browning, Elizabeth Barrett. Hugh Stuart Boyd [Legacies].
Bunting. Song of the Ackworth Clock, The.
Campion. De horologio portabili.
"Carroll, Lewis." Miss Jones.
Coleridge. For a Market-Clock.
Cowper. Motto on the King's Clock.
Cummings. There are so many tictoc.
Dickinson. Clock stopped, A.
Emerson. To the Clock.
Graves. Counting the Beats.
Gunn. Clock, The.
Hall. "Between the Clock and the Bed."
Hardy. Clock-Winder, The.
Copying Architecture in an Old Minster.
Hemingway. Three traveling clocks.
Hesketh. Mill Clock, The.
MacLeish. Why the Face of a Clock is not Truly a Circle.
MacNeice. Slow Starter, The.
Moore. Four Quartz Crystal Clocks.
Nemerov. Clock With No Hands, A.
Rich. Clock in the Square, A.
Sandburg. Clocks.
Solo for Saturday Night Guitar.
Tomlinson. At Delft.
Warren. Forever O'Clock.
There's a Grandfather's Clock in the Hall.
Wilbur. Bell Speech.
Wordsworth. Cuckoo-Clock, The.

See also **Watches.**

Clothing
Burns. Wee Willie Gray.
Carruth. November Jeans Song.
Cowper. Methinnks I see thee decently array'd.
Dunbar. Bohemian, The.
"Dylan." Clothes Line.
Ferlinghetti. Underwear.
Fisher. Crumpled clothes come slowly off.
Ford. Ram wears a cowboy.
Fox. Help Me with the Buttons.
Gallagher. Black Silk.
Coats, The.
I Save Your Coat, But You Lose It Later.
Galvin. Old Clothes, The.
Gildner. Last Articles.
Hacker. Part of a True Story.
Hall. Pictures of Philippa.
Hardy. Gentleman's Second-Hand Suit, A.
Old Gown, The.
Pink Frock, The.
Herrick. Art above Nature, to Julia.
Cloathes, Are Conspirators.
Cloaths for Continuance.
Clothes Do But Cheat and Cozen [or Cousen] Us.
Delight in Disorder.
Julia's Petticoat.
Leprosie in Cloathes.
Lilly in a Christal, The.
Raggs.
Upon Cuts.
Upon Electra.
Upon Julia's Ribband.
Upon Julia's Unlacing Her Self.
Upon Lupes.
Upon Shift.
Upon Skrew.
Hughes, Langston. When Sue Wears Red.
Jonson. Still to be neat, still to be dressed [or Drest].
Koertge. He ("Has a new double-knit suit with slightly flared").
Kunitz. Old Clothes Man, The.
Larkin. Large Cool Store, The.
Lawrence. Moral Clothing.
Levine. Suit, The.
Lovelace. To a Lady with Child that Asked [or Ask'd] an Old Shirt.
Markson. Julia Now.
Merrill. Dreams About Clothes.
Sundown and Starlight.
Nash. Man With Two New Suits, The.

Requiem: "There was a young belle of old Natchez."
Nathan. Pocket Song.
Nemerov. Old Story, An.
Pockets.
Olson. Elements of clothes, an arm and hand the head of a cock.
Patchen. My Coat Is Dirty.
"Reed." All Tomorrow's Parties.
Rossetti. Bread and Milk for Breakfast.
St. John. Woman and Leopard.
Sandburg. Films.
Summer Shirt Sale.
Schuyler. Frock.
Velvet Roses.
Schwartz. What Curious Dresses All Men Wear.
Sexton. Clothes.
Song for a Red Nightgown.
Silverstein. Benjamin Bunnn.
Simic. Piety.
Smith, Stevie. Si Peu Séduisante.
Snyder. No Shoes No Shirt No Service.
Sorrentino. Huge Man in Tight Pants.
Spender. Little Coat, The.
Stevens. Explanation.
Stevenson. Auntie's Skirts.
Updike. Courtesy Call.
Wakoski. Pink Dress, The.
Wilbur. Catch, The.
Love Calls Us to the Things of This World.
Williams, Charles Kenneth. Vehicle: Absence.
See also **Jewelry.**

Clouds
Brontë. Still as she looked the iron clouds.
Browning, Elizabeth Barrett. House of Clouds, The.
Man and Nature.
Clark. "sun shoots high..", The.
Coleridge. Fancy in Nubibus.
Crane. To the Cloud Juggler.
Dickey, James. Wall and Cloud.
Dickinson. Curious Cloud surprised the Sky, A.
Dobyns. Clouds.
Fletcher. Evening Clouds, The.
Midsummer Dawn at Sea.
Midwinter Sunset.
Over the roof-tops race the shadows of clouds.
Ford. Clouds covered it, The.
Frost. Lost in Heaven.
Hall. Tree and the Cloud, The.
Hardy. Sheep-Boy, The.
Herrick. Her Bed.
Hewitt. Thresher, The.
Hugo. Clouds of Uig, The.
Joseph. Cloud.
Even Over the Flat Land.
Levertov. Clouds.
Levine. Clouds.
Roofs.
Liddy. Blue Mountain.
Meinke. Cloud, Florida, 1985, The.
Meredith. On Como.
South-Wester, The.
Merton. Cloud, The.
Nash. Cherub, The.
Olson. Clouds, The.
Raine. Bright cloud, / Bringer of rain to far fields.
Cloud.
Lifelong ago such days.
My sight with the clouds'.
Rossetti. Boats sail on the rivers, / And ships sail on the seas.
Sandburg. Broken Sky.
Evening Sea Wind.
Sky Talk.
Schuyler. Gray Day.
Shelley. Cloud, The.
Sorrentino. Maytime.
Stevens. Sea Surface Full of Clouds.
Swift. Answer, An.
Tomlinson. Clouds.
Into Distance.
Updike. Cloud Shadows.
Descent of Mr. Aldez, The.

Wakoski. Magellanic Clouds, The.
Walcott. Long, white, summer cloud, like a cleared linen table, A.
Williams, William Carlos. Clouds, The.
Idyl: "Wine of the grey sky."
Wordsworth. Most Alluring Clouds That Mount the Sky, The.
Sky-Prospect—From the Plain of France.
To the Clouds.
Yau. Box mountain of hardened tears is hoisted up the scaffold, two, A.
Genghis Chan: Private Eye VI.
Suite of Imitations Written After Reading Translations of Poems by Li He And Li Shang-yin, A.
Yeats. These Are the Clouds.

Clough, Arthur Hugh
Arnold. Thyrsis.

"Clout, Colin." *see* **Spenser, Edmund ("Colin Clout").**

Clover
Berry. February 2, 1968.
Dickinson. His oriental heresies.
Eberhart. Cover Me Over.
Melville. Clover.
Zukofsky. Clover.

Clowns
Clare. Clown, The.
Creeley. Out of Sight.
Cummings. One winter afternoon / (at the magical hour).
Fletcher. Clown's Song.
Fox. Clown, The.
Hall. Clown, The.
Hartley. Three Friends: Outline for a Picture.
Hesketh. Clown.
MacNeice. Clowns.
Patchen. Folly of Clowns.
See also **Circus.**

Clumsiness
Dunbar. My Best Girl.
Olson. Day Song, the Day After.
Siena.

Coal Mining and Coal Miners
Lawrence. Collier's Wife, The.
McNeill. Best House They Was Ever In (Retired Coal Operator).
Company (Coal Miner), The.
Monongah (December 6, 1907, Marion County, West Virginia, on the Monongahela River).
Overheard on a Bus (Miner's Wife).
Stoic (Circa 1907).
Winter Day (Coal Country).
Owen. Miners.
Rossetti. Diamond or a coal? / A diamond, if you please, A.
Sorrentino. Fights, The.
Whole World Coal, The.

Cobblers. *see* **Shoes and Shoemakers.**

Coca Cola
O'Hara. Having a Coke with You.
Olson. Being Altogether Literal, & Specific, and Seeking at the Same Time to be Successfully Explicit.

Cocaine
Gunn. Smoking Pot on the Bus.
Sandburg. Snow.

Cockfighting
Cowper. Cock-Fighters Garland.
Tale, Founded on a Fact, A.
Merton. Fighting Cock, The.
See also **Roosters.**

Cockroaches
Bukowski. Cockroach.
Kooser. In the Kitchen, at Midnight.
Piercy. Kneeling at the Pipes.
Rukeyser. St. Roach.
Sexton. Cockroach.
Williams, Charles Kenneth. What a sound his.

Cocks. *see* **Roosters.**

Cocoa
Merton. Cocoa Tree.
Silverstein. Minnow Minnie.

Cody, William Frederick. *see* **"Buffalo Bill" (William Frederick Cody).**

Coercion
Auden. Don't you dream of a world, a society, with no coercion?
Kunitz. Approach to Thebes, The.
Sotto Voce.
Lindsay. Harps in Heaven.
Williams, Charles Kenneth. Interrogation II.

Coffee
Bukowski. Luck.
Nash. Coffee with the Meal.
Smith, Patti. Thermos.

Coffins
Byron. On a Royal Visit to the Vaults.
Windsor Poetics.
Cohen. Wheels, Fireclouds.
Dickinson. Coffin—is a small Domain, A.
Hardy. Not Only I.
Six Boards, The.
Three Tall Men, The.
Robinson. Leonora.
Rolfe. Something Still Lives.

Coins
Donne. Bracelet, The.
Duncan. Salvages: An Evening Place.
Emerson. Since you set no worth on the heart.
Understanding's copper coin, The.
Hill. Coins handsome as Nero's; of good substance and.
Hughes, Langston. Fact.
Tomorrow.
Meredith. Cleopatra.
Nemerov. Money.
Sandburg. Coin, A.
In a Back Alley.
Sorrentino. Bar Games.
Updike. On the Recently Minted Hundred-Cent Piece.

Cold
Ammons. Grisly Grit.
Atwood. Midwinter, Presolstice.
You Are Happy.
Berry. Cold, The.
Snake, The.
Bishop. Colder the Air, The.
Burns. Cauld Frosty Morning.
Cauld Is the E'enin Blast.
Lines Written in the Kirk of Lamington.
Carew. To Her Again, She Burning in a Fever.
To My Mistress [or Mistris], I Burning in Love.
Carruth. After the thaw after.
In cold / the snow.
Twenty-two degrees below zero.
Wet fire / it turns out.
When some amazonian indians for whom.
Cooper. High deck. Blue skies overhead.
White distance, A.
Creeley. As Now It Would Be Snow.
Blue.
Davie. Samuel Beckett's Dublin.
Dickey, James. Form.
Ice Skin, The.
Dickinson. 'Twas warm—at first—like Us.
Dunbar. Misty Day, A.
Eberhart. Commas in Wintertime.
Lost Children, The.
Emerson. Winds are cold, the days are dark, The.
Fox. Alkaid.
Ice.
Frost. There Are Roughly Zones.
Gildner. Day Before Thanksgiving, a Call Comes to Me Concerning Insulation, The.
Gunn. My coldness wakes me.
Haines. Fairbanks Under the Solstice.
Into the Glacier.
Snowy Night.
Winter News.
Hall. Table, The.
Waiting on the Corners.
Herrick. Health.
Upon Himselfe ("I lately fri'd, but now behold").
Hesketh. After Verlaine.

Invitation.
Letter to Vincent.
Hewitt.   Braes O' Layde, The.
Footing Turf.
Hughes, Ted.   November.
Hugo.   Drums in Scotland.
Duwamish.
Sandbanks, The.
Kipling.   Open Door, The.
Lawrence.   Coldness in Love.
Lowry.   Morning sneat is snewing, The.
Morning stove is wheezing, The.
Old Blake was warm, he got down to the hub.
Poor Butterfly that stamped.
Two frozen claws / In two frozen minutes.
With Dearest Morning Love and Kisses.
MacNeice.   Another Cold May.
Mahon.   Tolerable Wisdom, A.
Matthews.   Pissing off the Back of the Boat
into the Nivernais Canal.
Meredith.   Carol of Jack Frost, A.
Night of Frost in May.
Or the single path— / Which the cool moon
sheds.
Tardy Spring.
Merrill.   David's Night in Veliès.
Nightgown.
Millay.   When the Year Grows Old.
Morgan.   Past, The.
Rose dawn, in smoke, over the East River, A.
Nash.   Samson Agonistes.
Nemerov.   Of fire and of lust proceeds the
world.
Winter Lightning, The.
Neruda.   Cold.
O'Hara.   Poem In January.
Roethke.   Coming of the Cold, The.
Rolfe.   Arctic Remembered, The.
Rossetti.   Chill, A.
Crying, my little one, footsore and weary?
There's Snow on the Fields.
Rukeyser.   Speech for the Assistant, from
Houdini.
Sandburg.   Hunger and Cold.
Sarton.   To the North.
Sexton.   God's Backside.
Silverstein.   Poor Angus.
Simic.   Winter Night.
Spenser.   My Love Is Like to Ice.
Stafford.   Weather Report.
Tomlinson.   In the Balance.
Object in a Setting.
Tramontana at Lerici.
Warren.   Trying to Tell You Something.
Wilbur.   Wyeth's Mild Cans.
Williams, Charles Kenneth.   Snow: II.
Williams, William Carlos.   Cold Night, The.
Wright, James.   In the Cold House.

Colds (illness)
Ammons.   Cold Rheum.
Nash.   Fahrenheit *Gesundheit*.
Sniffle, The.
Sutter.   Cold, The.
Williams, Charles Kenneth.   Shade, The.

Coleridge, Samuel Taylor
Eberhart.   Bones of Coleridge, The.
Frost.   Most of It, The.
Gunn.   Keats at Highgate.
Lowell.   Coleridge.
Coleridge and Richard II.
Meredith.   Poetry of Coleridge, The.
Nash.   I Can Hardly Wait for the Sandman.
Schwartz.   Philology Recapitulates Ontology,
Poetry Is Ontology.
Shelley.   He was a might poet—and.
You will see Coleridge, he who sits obscure.
Smith, Stevie.   Thoughts about the Person from
Porlock.
Wordsworth.   Coleridge's Mind a Life Unto
Itself.

Colette (Sidonie Gabrielle Colette)
Garrigue.   Cortège for Colette.
Jong.   Dear Colette.

Colleges and Universities
Berryman.   Crisis.
In & Out.

Nowhere.
Two Organs.
Burns.   Dean of Faculty—a New Ballad, The.
"Carroll, Lewis."   Bachanalian Ode, A.
"Dylan."   Alternatives to College.
Emerson.   Valedictory Poem.
Frost.   Lucretius versus the Lake Poets.
Gunn.   His Rooms in College.
Heaney.   Cloistered.
Herrick.   To His Kinsman, Master Thomas
Herrick, Who Desired to Be in His Book.
Jarrell.   Randall Jarrell, Office Hours 10-11.
Soldier Walks under the Trees of the
University, The.
Jong.   Exam Dream, The.
Kipling.   Clerks and the Bells, The.
Koch.   Oh to be seventeen years old.
Koertge.   Loving Ugly.
Orientation Week.
Lawrence.   From a College Window.
In Nottingham.
Nottingham's New University.
Lowry.   Cap and gown instead of a sweatrag,
A.
MacNeice.   Canto XII: "Now to dissolve in
port. I take the train."
Canto XIII: "Leaving the colleges then and
their half-remembered."
Markson.   Accepted.
Johanna.
Merton.   Twenty Three Point Prospectus for
Small College in the Badlands.
Moore.   Student, The.
Nash.   Caesar Knifed Again, or, Culture Biz
Gets Hep, Boffs Profs.
One Man's Meed Is Another Man's
Overemphasis.
Olson.   It is a nation of nothing but poetry.
Plath.   Resolve.
Prince.   Fretted discoloured towers and domes.
Sun shines on the gliding river, The.
Shapiro.   Humanities Building, The.
University.
Smart.   On an Eagle Confined in a College-
Court.
Spender.   One More New Botched Beginning.
Turco.   College, The.
Updike.   Generic College.
Waldman.   College Under Water.
Whittier.   Norumbega Hall.
Spiritual Manifestation, A.
Wilbur.   Finished Man, A.
Wordsworth.   Oxford, May 30, 1820 ("Ye
sacred Nurseries of blooming Youth!").
See also **Students.**

Collins, Michael
Liddy.   Note.

Cologne, Germany
Coleridge.   Cologne.
On My Joyful Departure from the Same City.
Wordsworth.   In the Cathedral at Cologne.

Colonialism
Bradstreet.   Dialogue between Old England and
New, A.
Cowper.   Charity.
Creeley.   America.
Dunbar.   Conquerors, The.
Fletcher.   England Again.
Hewitt.   Colonial Consequence.
Motives.
Hill.   Locust Songs.
Kipling.   Song of the White Men, A.
South Africa.
White Man's Burden, The.
Merton.   Dzules.
Tibud Maclay.
Morgan.   Adventure, The.
Trader, The.
Nathan.   If you start in loneliness.
Olson.   Got Me Home, the Light Snow Gives
the Air, Falling.
Gulf of Maine, The.
Rich.   Location.
Self-hatred.
Rukeyser.   Suite for Lord Timothy Dexter.
Updike.   B.W.I.
Walcott.   North and South.

See also **British Empire; Imperialism.**

Colorado (state)
Boyle.   American Citizen.
Dunn.   Belly Dancer at the Hotel Jerome.
Fletcher.   On Mesa Verde.
Morgan.   Castle Rock.
Waldman.   Incantation.
Whitman.   Spirit That Form'd This Scene.

Colorado River
Sandburg.   Many Hats.

Colors
Bishop.   Pleasure Seas.
Bukowski.   It's Nothing to Laugh About.
Clark.   Eos.
"First cold winter twilights.."
Rojo.
Creeley.   Greendoon's Song.
Cullen.   Colors.
Cummings.   Come a little further—why be
afraid.
De la Mare.   Window, The.
Dickinson.   Who is the East?
Eberhart.   Vermont Idyll.
Fisher.   Trace, The.
Gunn.   Colour Machine, The.
Hall.   No Color Man.
Pictures of Philippa.
Hardy.   Colour, The.
Hesketh.   Changing Colour.
Emily Dickinson.
Paint Box.
Hewitt.   Colour.
Difficult Man, A.
Eye for Color, An.
Grey and White.
Swan.
Turban, The.
Knott.   Brighton Rock by Graham Greene.
Lowry.   Ex-Poet, The.
Port Moody.
Matthews.   Red Silk Blouse, A.
Morrison.   Desert, The.
Olson.   Color is image.
Oppen.   White. From the / Under arm of T.
Pound.   Song of the Degrees, A.
Rossetti.   Freaks of Fashion.
What is Pink?
Sandburg.   Brown Gold.
Butter Colors.
Haze Gold.
Lake Michigan Morning.
Maroon with Silver Frost.
My People.
Never Two Songs the Same.
October Paint.
Runaway Colors.
Small Homes.
Themes in Contrast.
Two Fish.
What did Hiamovi, the red man, Chief of.
Wind Sings Welcome in Early Spring, The.
Winter Gold.
Schuyler.   Standing and Watching.
Silverstein.   Colors.
Garden, The.
Smith, Stevie.   Oh Grateful Colours, Bright
Looks!
Sorrentino.   Across the water sits a shore.
Cautious Circumspection Does Not Win the
West.
Crown, The.
Deux Morceaux en Forme de Banane.
Drifting South.
Homage to Arnaut.
Lost in the Stars.
She was all in Black. A statement.
Some Sap Sings a Poor Pantoum.
Waltz of the Empty Roadhouse.
Stevens.   Domination of Black ("At night, by
the fire").
Sutter.   Why Birch Trees Are White.
Tomlinson.   Distinctions.
Suggestions for the Improvement of a Sunset.
Waldman.   Colors.
Williams, William Carlos.   Portrait in Greys,
A.
Wright, Charles.   Cryopexy.

Zukofsky. Blue light is the night harbor-slip. For Selma Gubin's Umbrellas.

Colosseum, Rome
Poe. Coliseum, The.

Coltrane, John
Carruth. Sonnet: "Must genius always struggle, always exaggerate."
Matthews. Blues for John Coltrane, Dead at 41.
Young. John Coltrane Dance, The.

Colts
Coleridge. On the broad mountain-top.
Frost. Runaway, The.
Lindsay. Broncho That Would Not Be Broken, The.
See also **Horses.**

Columbia University
Merton. Western Fellow Students Salute with Calypso Anthems the Movie Career of Robert Lax.

Columbus, Christopher
Clough. How in all wonder Columbus got over.
Crane. Ave Maria.
Dunbar. Columbian Ode.
Emerson. Poem, Spoken Before the ΦBK Society, August, 1834.
Valedictory Poem.
Hughes, Ted. Fourth of July.
McGrath. Columbus.
Merton. Christopher Columbus.
Nash. Columbus.
Look What You Did, Christopher!
Sandburg. Destroyers.
Mysterious Biography.
Silverstein. Edge of the World, The.
Simic. Navigator.
Sorrentino. Remember the story of Columbus and the orange?
Whitman. Passage to India.
Thought of Columbus, A.

Comas
Kooser. Failed Suicide, The.
Meredith. King Harald's Trance.

Combs
Clark. Ah—There.

Comedians
"Dylan." Lenny Bruce.
Hewitt. Prelude to an Ode for Barnum.
Lindsay. Knight in Disguise, The.
Meredith. As often in a bun.
Plath. Dirge for a Joker.
St. John. Chapter Forever.
Sorrentino. Marvellous.
Variations 3.

Comets
Eberhart. Ship Burning and a Comet All in One Day, A.
Fox. In the Planetarium.
Hardy. Comet at Yell'ham, The.
Hopkins. —I am like a slip of comet.
Johnson. Translation of a Distich on the Duke of Modena.
Lindsay. Comet of Prophecy, The.
Tomlinson. Recompense, The.
Yau. When a comet passes over the town, whoever sees it knows a corpse.

Comfort
Beatles. She's a Woman.
Beckett. Mots survivants.
Berry. Envoy: "Love, all day there has been at the edge of my mind."
He Is in the Habit of the World.
He stood on the ground.
How many times have I come to you out of my head.
In Rain.
New House, The.
Thought of Something Else, The.
Warm day in December, A.
Wild Geese, The.
You lean at ease in your warm house at night after supper.
Young Man, Thinking of the Old, The.
Browning, Elizabeth Barrett. Comfort.
Thought for a Lonely Death-Bed, A.

Burns. Song: "I murder hate by field or flood."
Carruth. Dawn. Hoar on the grass.
Clark. Afternoons.
Every Day.
Nimble Rays of Day Bring Oxygen to Her Blood.
Cohen. In the Eyes of Men.
Our Lady of Solitude.
Window, The.
Creeley. Comfort.
Phone.
Cullen. To France.
Emerson. Comfort with a purring cat.
Maiden Speech of the Æolian Harp.
Nature saith / I am not infinite.
Sunshine was he.
Fisher. Provision.
Hall. Edward's Anecdote.
Hardy. At the Railway Station, Upway.
Problem, The.
To a Lady Playing and Singing in the Morning.
Herrick. Comfort In Calamity.
Comfort to a Youth That Had Lost His Love.
His Comfort.
His Letanie, To the Holy Spirit.
On Fortune.
Hesketh. After Ecclesiastes.
Meths Men, The.
Partridge.
Hewitt. E.H.
Ellendene.
House Demolished, A.
One I Loved, The.
Orientations.
Paid Quarterly.
Shortened Day, The.
Holmes. Women in A.M.
Housman. In my own shire, if I was sad.
Jong. Gazing Out, Gazing In.
Joseph. To Keep Each Other Warm.
Keats. Why Did I Laugh Tonight?
Lewis. Fragment, A: "Where aloneness fiercely."
In Hospital: Poona (2).
Monologue.
River Temple: Wai, The.
Lindsay. O prodigal son, O recreant daughter.
Lowry. Child may find no words for its sorrow, A.
Melville. Herba Santa.
Morrison. I Bring These.
Very Brave.
Nash. Eheu! Fugaces, or, What a Difference a Lot of Days Make.
Have You Tried Staying Awake? or, They'll Find a Way to Stop That, Too.
Oppen. You are the last.
Raine. Binah.
Rossetti. Balm in Gilead.
Charity Never Faileth.
Fair World Tho' a Fallen, A.
Methinks the ills of life I fain would shun.
Standing Afar Off for the Fear of Her Torment.
There's Snow on the Fields.
Thou Knewest...Thou Oughtest Therefore.
What Is That to Thee? Follow Thou Me.
Zion Said.
Sandburg. At a Window.
Haunts.
Smith, Charlotte. To the Goddess of Botany.
Sorrentino. Poem: "Clear objects / one grows to love. The clarity, The."
Stevenson. New House, The.
Walker. Facing the Way.

Comic Strips
Ashbery. Farm Implements and Rutabagas in a Landscape.
Sandburg. Cartoon.
Sorrentino. Zoo, The.

Commandments. *see* **Ten Commandments.**

Commencement Day
Emerson. Valedictory Poem.
Nemerov. After Commencement.
Smart. On Taking a Batchelor's Degree.

Commerce
Emerson. Poets are colorpots.
Herrick. Society.
Hesketh. Clown Flowers.
Jarrell. Soldier, The.
Kipling. Big Steamers.
Merchantmen, The.
Peace of Dives, The.
Such As in Ships.
Meredith. Olive Branch, The.
Merton. Dreaming Trader, The.
Nemerov. Guide to the Ruins.
Olson. Being Altogether Literal, & Specific, and Seeking at the Same Time to be Successfully Explicit.
Zukofsky. Song for the Year's End, A.
Two Dedications: D.R.
See also **Business and Businessmen.**

Communes
Piercy. Death of the Small Commune, The.

Communication
Angelou. Communication I.
Communication II.
Atwood. Against Still Life.
Their Attitudes Differ.
We hear nothing these days.
Auden. At the Maison Lyons.
To E.T.
Beatles. Hey Bulldog.
Julia.
Michelle.
Norwegian Wood.
She Came in Through the Bathroom Window.
She Said She Said.
Things We Said Today.
What You're Doing.
When I Get Home.
Within You Without You.
Word, The.
You Never Give Me Your Money.
Beckett. Tailpiece.
Bly. Hawk, The.
Bukowski. Out of the Blue.
Carroll, Jim. Loft, The.
Carruth. Hey, Basho, you there!
Marvin McCabe.
Names.
Renaissance.
Sonnet: "Key-reist, I am fed and sick unto death with this."
Sonnet: "Well, she told me I had an aura. 'What?' I said."
They Accuse Me of Not Talking.
Ceravolo. Contrast.
Ciardi. Encounter.
Requisitioning.
Sorrow of Obedience, The.
Week That Was, The.
Clark. Moira's Messages.
"Point is Fixed.., A."
Radio.
Cohen. I Had It for a Moment.
Creeley. Act of Love, The.
Answer, The.
Conspiracy, The.
Rain ("Things one sees through").
Than I.
Cummings. If you and i awakening.
Lady,i will touch you with my mind.
May i feel said he.
O / sure)but / nobody unders(no).
Dickinson. Speech is one symptom of Affection.
Doolittle. You'll go on, talking away.
Duncan. Human Communion. Traces, The.
Upon Taking Hold.
Dunn. Something.
"Dylan." Joan Baez in Concert, Part 2.
Let's Keep It Between Us.
Sign Language.
We Better Talk This Over.
Eliot. Conversation Galante.
Ferlinghetti. At the *Gare Bruxelles-Midi.*
Come lie with me and be my love.
Fisher. Poet's Message, The.
Ford. I felt my forefinger.
That first and last word.

Frost. Missive Missile, A.
Gallagher. Refusing Silence.
Gardner. Disenchanted, The.
Southwest of True North.
That "Craning of the Neck."
To Thoreau on Rereading Walden.
Two Sapphics.
Glück. Seated Figure.
Graves. Starred Coverlet, The.
What Did You Say?
Hacker. And I shout at Iva, whine at you.
Easily.
Culled from the brambled ceiling of my wide.
Hardy. Last Signal, The.
Herrick. His Answer to a Friend.
Upon Love, by Way of Question and Answer.
Hesketh. Evergreen.
Paint Box.
Words.
Hewitt. Man from the Mountains, The.
Hill. Scarcely speaking: it becomes as a.
Hoffman. Signatures.
Joseph. Chorale.
Figure in a Landscape.
Little dots.
Lost Continent, The.
Not able to resist the spring.
Kipling. Code of Morals, A.
Dove of Dacca, The.
Fabulists, The.
Puzzler, The.
Knott. Juggler to His Audience, The.
Kunitz. Silence.
Lewis. Prologue: The Grinder.
Liddy. Last Light in Clare's Mind.
McGrath. Letter for Marian, A.
MacNeice. Babel.
Business Men.
Idle Talk.
To Posterity.
Mahon. Preface to a Love Poem.
Markson. Nachtmusik.
Matthews. Straight Life.
Merton. Conversations.
Nahoa Urn, for a Woman.
Morrison. Moving, A.
Nathan. Sorry.
Olson. There Are Sounds.
Oppen. And if at 80.
Possible / To use.
Roots of words, The.
Unable to begin / At the beginning, the
fortunate.
Pack. Display.
Paley. In France.
Poem About Storytelling, A.
What has happened?
Piercy. Councils.
Hand Games.
Simple-Song.
Ransom. Two in August.
Rich. Cartographies of Silence.
Ghazal V.
Implosions.
Nightbreak.
Our Whole Life.
That conversation we were always on the
edge.
Valediction Forbidding Mourning, A.
We were bound on the wheel of an endless
conversation.
Robinson. Tact.
Rukeyser. Effort at Speech between Two
People.
Sonnet:"My thoughts through yours refracted
into speech."
War Comes into my Room, The.
Watchers, The.
Schwartz. "Interpretation! that's the act of
mind."
Power and Glory of Language, The.
Silverstein. Forgotten Language.
Smith, Patti. True Music.
Wave.
Stafford. Ritual to Read to Each Other, A.
Stevens. Continual Conversation with a Silent
Man.

Tomlinson. How Far.
Something: a Direction.
Updike. A l'École Berlitz.
Bicycle Chain, A.
Lamplight.
Van Duyn. Quiet Afternoon at Home, A.
Toward a Definition of Marriage.
Wish to Be Believed, The.
Warren. Trying to Tell You Something.
Wilbur. Phone Booth.
Williams, Charles Kenneth. To Listen.
Williams, Miller. Love in the Cathedral.
People.
Trying.
Williams, William Carlos. Love Song: "You
have come between me and the terrifying
presence."
Young. After Visiting Arl at the Hospital.
By Heart.
Lightning, Divine Lightning.
Moving, Merging, Fading, Standing Still.
Zukofsky. Rains, the rains, The.

Communion. *see* **Eucharist.**
Communism
Berryman. Communist.
Bukowski. 22,000 Dollars in 3 Months.
Cummings. Kumrads die because they're told).
Red Front, The.
Red-rag and pink-flag.
Thanksgiving (1956).
Dove. Eastern European Eclogues.
"Dylan." Russian has three an' a half red
eyes, A.
Talkin' John Birch Paranoid Blues.
Ginsberg. Kral Majales.
Lowry. Communist, The.
Where Did That One Go to, 'Erbert.
"MacDiarmid." Seamless Garment, The.
MacNeice. To a Communist.
Merton. Radicals.
Rich. For Ethel Rosenberg.
Rolfe. Room with Revolutionists.
Unit Assignment.
Unit Meeting.
Tomlinson. Assassin.
Prometheus.
Up at La Serra.
Williams, William Carlos. Choral: The Pink
Church.
Foot-Note, A.
Jingle.
Rogation Sunday.
Commuting and Commuters
Clark. Aubade: "Truck gears grinding up
Marin."
Ferlinghetti. Home Home Home.
Fisher. Commuter.
Hewitt. City Morning.
Sutter. Halloween on Hennepin.
See also **Suburbs and Suburban Life.**
Companionship and Companions
Ammons. That Day.
Angelou. Alone.
Conceit, A.
Ashbery. Love Poem, A.
Atwood. After the agony in the guest /
bedroom, you lying by the.
Circle Game, The.
Eventual Proteus.
Hesitations Outside the Door.
Is / Not.
Lying here, everything in me.
Their Attitudes Differ.
They Are Hostile Nations.
They were all inaccurate.
This is a mistake, / these arms and legs.
What is it, it does not.
You are the sun / in reverse, all energy.
You take my hand and.
Auden. Glad.
Lullaby: "Lay your sleeping head, my love."
Two Climbs.
When he is well.
Beatles. Here, There and Everywhere.
Two of Us.
When I'm Sixty Four.
You Like Me Too Much.

Beckett. Mots survivants.
Berrigan. Coda: Song.
She.
Berry. And then, one by one, he moved me.
Except.
Finally, he brought me to a hill.
To Tanya at Christmas.
Bukowski. Another Bed.
Blue Cheese and Chili Peppers.
Lady Poet, The.
Miracle is the Shortest Time, The.
Night on a Visa Card.
Bunting. As to my heart, that may as well be
forgotten.
Women swarm in Tauentsienstrasse.
Burns. Dainty Davie.
O May Thy Morn.
O [or Oh] Wert Thou in the Cauld Blast.
Carroll, Jim. August.
Blue Poles.
Distances, The.
Green Bus, The.
Narrows, The.
Poem: "Yesterday you past / into your lips..
your hips."
3 hours into the afternoon of March 9th.
Carruth. Tanck's Song About Silence.
Catullus. Carmen 13: "I shall expect / you in
to dine."
Carmen 43: "O elegant whore!"
Carmen 50: "Other day we spent, The."
Carmen 75: "Reason blinded by sin, Lesbia."
Ceravolo. I Like to Collapse.
Clare. Song: "Say What Is Love—To Live In
Vain."
Clark. Got to be there, so that she'll know.
I draw a head. You ask.
Village Minstrel, The.
Coleridge. Day-Dream, A ("My eyes make
pictures, when they are shut").
To Two Sisters.
Cooper. Door, The.
Earthquake, The.
Faithful, The.
Feathers.
Graveyard, The.
Racetrack, The.
Rent.
Creeley. For Love.
Of Years.
Rose, The.
Cullen. Ghosts.
Cummings. Love's function is to fabricate
unknownness.
Davie. Treviso, the Pescheria.
De la Mare. Comfort.
Disguise, The.
Flower, The.
Good Company.
Remonstrance, The.
Dickinson. He was my host—he was my
guest.
I hope you may not go.
I learned—at least—what Home could be.
I was with you in all the loneliness.
Lifetime is for two.
When thou goest through the Waters.
Dunbar. To Her.
Dunn. Romance, A.
"Dylan." Buckets of Rain.
Don't Fall Apart on Me Tonight.
Emotionally Yours.
Fourth Time Around.
I and I.
If Not for You.
If You Gotta Go, Go Now.
In the Summertime.
Is Your Love in Vain?
It Ain't Me, Babe.
It Takes a Lot to Laugh, It Takes a Train to
Cry.
Just Like a Woman.
Mama, You Been on My Mind.
Most Likely You Go Your Way (and I'll Go
Mine).
Need a Woman.
Obviously Five Believers.

Odds and Ends.
One More Weekend.
Positively 4th Street.
She's Your Lover Now.
Tight Connection to My Heart (Has Anybody Seen My Love).
To Be Alone with You.
Tonight I'll Be Staying Here with You.
Tough Mama.
True Love Tends to Forget.
Wedding Song.
Where Are You Tonight? (Journey through Dark Heat).
You're Gonna Make Me Lonesome When You Go.
Everson. Bride of the Bear.
Stone Face Falls.
Fisher. Experimenting.
Of the Empirical Self and for Me.
Steam Crane, The.
Wrestler, The.
Frost. Pasture, The.
Galvin. In Egg Time.
Garrigue. Invitation to a Hay.
Moralizing Overheard in a Forest.
Waking, I Always Waked You Awake.
Graves. Narrow Sea, The.
Song: Once More.
Terraced Valley, The.
Gunn. Crosswords.
Thoughts on Unpacking.
Touch.
Hacker. Companion, The.
Dear Jool, I Miss You in Saint-Saturnin.
Little Robber Girl Gets On in the Wide World, The.
Hartley. Encompassed.
Hayden. Dogwood Trees, The.
Herrick. Not To Love.
To Phyllis to Love and Live with Him.
To the Maids to Walke Abroad.
Wounded Heart, The.
Hesketh. Walking Away.
Hoffman. His Steps.
Night Fishing.
Hugo. Letter to Libbey from St. Regis.
Night with Cindy at Heitman's, A.
Old Scene.
Jong. For My Husband.
Gazing Out, Gazing In.
Kinnell. Flying Home.
Kooser. Boarding House.
Five P.M.
Kunitz. After the Last Dynasty.
Last Question, The.
Lovers Relentlessly.
Night-Piece.
Route Six.
Sotto Voce.
Strange Calendar.
Lawrence. Compari.
Levertov. Bedtime.
From the Roof.
Losing Track.
Luxury.
Sequence, A.
Levine. To a Fish Head Found on the Beach Near Málaga.
Lindsay. For All Who Ever Sent Lace Valentines.
Genesis.
Johnny Appleseed's Wife from the Palace of Eve.
Slender maiden found me sleeping, The.
Spice-Tree, The.
We Meet at the Judgement and I Fear It Not.
Lorde. Memorial I.
To the Girl Who Lives In a Tree.
Lovelace. By thy fault is my mind brought to that pass.
Fabullus I will treat you handsomely.
Lowell. Man and Woman.
Lowry. How did all this begin, and why am I here.
In Praise of an Understudy.
McGrath. Celebration.
Perpetual Motion.

MacLeish. Old Gray Couple (1), The.
MacNeice. All Over Again.
Canto XI: "Golden guineas filter through the mist, The."
Coda.
In still grey dawn a delicate tendril.
McNeill. Wife.
Mahon. Two Songs.
Meinke. Myth.
Meredith. Appreciation.
Dost thou behold some woeful soul.
Good Comrade, The.
He felt the wild beast in him betweenwhiles.
Hueless Love, The.
In Claremont woods we wandered once.
Jack & Harry.
Love is winged for two.
Marian: "Clouds fly fast across the moon, The."
Pastoral 6: "How barren would this valley be."
Song: "I cannot lose thee for a day."
Time and Sentiment.
Merrill. Bronze.
Merton. Convergence of the Many.
Miller. For Barbara ("Crawling out").
For Barbara ("Wandering in").
For Schnu.
Morgan. As the sun dims we begin to think.
Sleeping, we boarded a boat.
Trader, The.
Nash. You Can Be a Republican, I'm a Genocrat.
Nathan. And Finally.
Hello Again.
Near Things.
Progress Report.
Nemerov. Blue Suburban.
Day on the Big Branch, A.
Realities.
Neruda. Successions.
Olson. Telesphere, The.
Oppen. I cannot even now / Altogether disengage myself.
To C. T.
Troubled that you are not, as they say.
Owen. Apologia Pro Poemate Meo.
Pack. After Returning from Camden Harbor.
Clayfeld's Metamorphosis.
Paley. South Window.
Piercy. It Breaks.
Prince. Handfast Point.
Watching Song.
"Reed." Pale Blue Eyes.
Rich. Across a city from you, I'm with you.
After Twenty Years.
Autumn Equinox.
Blood-Sister.
Can it be growing colder when I begin.
Five O'Clock, Beacon Hill.
Flesh and Blood.
Holding Out.
I wake up in your bed. I know I have been dreaming.
If I lay on that beach with you.
In the Evening.
It was your vision of the pilot.
July seventeenth nineteen sixty eight.
7/13/68.
Marriage in the 'Sixties, A.
No one's fated or doomed to love anyone.
Old blanket. The crumbs of rubbed wool turning up, The.
Paula Becker to Clara Westhoff.
Photograph of the Unmade Bed, The.
Pieces.
Pierrot Le Fou.
Prisoners, The.
Rain on the West Side Highway.
Roots.
Side by Side.
Stepping Backward.
To Judith, Taking Leave.
When We Dead Awaken.
When/Then.
Woman Dead in Her Forties, A.
You are beside me like a wall; I touch you with my fingers and.

Your dog, tranquil and innocent, dozes through.
Your silence today is a pond where drowned things live.
Robinson. Captain Craig.
Companion, The.
Firelight.
Tasker Norcross.
Vain Gratuities.
Rolfe. Pattern of Our Lives, The.
Rossetti. Portraits.
Rukeyser. Back Tooth.
They talk to each other, and he holds her hand.
Shelley. From the Arabic: An Imitation.
Letter to Maria Gisborne.
Silverstein. Two Boxes.
Us.
Stevenson. As Daniel, bird-alone, in that far land.
My Wife.
Swift. Stella's Birthday (1725).
To Stella.
To Stella, Visiting Me in My Sickness.
Twelve Articles.
Tate. Perimeters.
Red Stains.
Walcott. Lampfall.
Village Life, A.
Waldman. My Kind of Man.
Walker. Forgive Me If My Praises.
Gift.
Warren. In Moonlight, Somewhere, They Are Singing.
Wilbur. Gifts, The.
Williams, Charles Kenneth. Covenant, The.
Friends.
Hard Part, The.
In There.
One of the Muses.
Ribbons.
Sting, The.
To Market.
Toil.
Williams, Miller. Plain.
Williams, William Carlos. My Luv.
Sub Terra.
Wright, Charles. Self-Portait ("In Murray, Kentucky, I lay once").
Wyatt. If it be so that I forsake thee.
Young. Making Love After Hours.
Mexico City Lover.
No Trespassing.
Zukofsky. Canapés, my Fabullus, at home any.
How cast down is the mind that took to my Lesbia, culprit.
One friend.
Reading and Talking.
Salvé, next, minimal, poor little nosey.
Yesterday, Licinius, what a day it was.

See also **Friendship.**

Compassion
Angelou. I Almost Remember.
Auden. Some say that handsome raider still at large.
Berg. Brothers.
Dreaming with a Friend.
In Death I Know Well Enough All Things End in Emptiness.
Bukowski. One for Old Snaggle-Tooth.
Byron. Sonnet to the Prince Regent.
Tear, The.
Carroll, Jim. Compassion.
Ceravolo. Note from St. Francis.
Coleridge. Inward Light.
Crane. Chaplinesque.
Crashaw. Luke 10; And a Certaine Priest Comming that Way Looked on Him and Passed by.
Creeley. Ballad, A: "We have a song for the death in her body."
Phone.
Token, A.
World, The.
Cullen. Magnets.
Davie. Bent, The.
Sext.

Dickinson. I wish I might say one liquid word.
Tenderness has not a Date.
Donne. Ralphius.
What if this present were the world's last night?
"Dylan." Baby, Stop Crying.
Love Minus Zero/No Limit.
Only a Hobo.
Sweetheart Like You.
Eberhart. Question Mark.
Rumors of liberation. We could not believe it.
Galvin. Fear of the Waldorf Cafeteria.
For a Little Girl of Pompeii.
Hemingway. Poem to Mary (Second Poem).
Hesketh. Christmas Blackmail.
Hewitt. Little Bourgeois is Upset, The.
Holmes. Suzy Q, The.
Jeffers. Crumbs or the Loaf.
Knott. Consolations of Sociobiology, The.
Two Vietnam Poems: (1966).
Lawrence. Tender Reverence.
Levertov. Skew Lines.
Levine. Coming Home, *Detroit*, 1968.
Lewis. Compassion.
Liddy. Litany of Satan, The.
Meredith. Across his path the spouseless Lady cast.
Nathan. Nurse.
Olson. West Gloucester.
Oppen. Technologies.
Ransom. Puncture.
Rich. Knight, The.
Your dog, tranquil and innocent, dozes through.
Rossetti. Lines Given with a Penwiper.
Sidney. Sonnet 46: "I cursed thee oft, I pity now thy case."
Smith, Stevie. Full Well I Know.
Whittier. Healer, The.
Minister's Daughter, The.
Wilbur. Gifts, The.
Williams, Charles Kenneth. Color of Time, The.
Day for Anne Frank, A.
Neglect.
Williams, William Carlos. Seraph.
Wordsworth. Fragment: The Baker's Cart.
Sonnet on Seeing Miss Helen Maria Williams Weep at a Tale of Distress.
Wright, James. Saint Judas.
Zimmer. Irene Gogle.
Zukofsky. Reading and Talking.
Song for the Year's End, A.

Competition
Berry. Who has invented our enmity? Who has prescribed us.
Bukowski. Ants, The.
Cowper. Strada's Nightingale.
Doolittle. Toward the Piraeus.
Ferlinghetti. Deep Chess.
Graves. Woman Poet and Man Poet.
Hesketh. Christmas Blackmail.
Housman. This time of year a twelvemonth past.
Hugo. O-Mok-See at Nine Mile.
Lieberman. Eros at the World Kite Pageant.
Queen of the Billiards.
Merrill. Marsyas.
Nash. Malice Domestic.
O'Hara. Hôtel Transylvanie.
Pack. Camp Wakonda, 1940.
Ransom. Two Gentlemen in Bonds.
Rolfe. Nine, The.
Rukeyser. Trophies.
Sidney. Come, *Dorus*, come, let the songs thy sorrows signify.
Sonnet 13: "Phoebus was judge between Jove, Mars, and Love."
Sonnet 59: "Dear, why make you more of a dog than me?"
Swift. Tom Mullinex and Dick.
Williams, Charles Kenneth. Love: Youth.
Young. Roland Navarro (1939-1961).

See also **Rivalry.**

Complacency
Auden. Contra Blake.

Browning, Elizabeth Barrett. Loved Once.
Cohen. Cherry Orchards.
Creeley. End of the Day, The.
Same.
Warning, The.
Cummings. Of all the blessings which to man.
Dickinson. Complacency! My Father!
Dunn. Good Life, A.
Nova Scotia.
Hewitt. Coasters, The.
Meredith. Familiar Things.
Merton. What do you teach me / Mama my cow?
Shapiro. Buick.
Smith, Stevie. Eng.
Leader, The.
Sorrentino. King of the dark tower is a lug, The.
Something plus something else is not one thing.
Williams, Charles Kenneth. Experience.
What we are / given.

Computers
Carroll, Jim. Fragment, A: "When I see a rabbit."
Merton. Write a prayer to a computer?
Pack. Ode to October Mist.
Robot.
Rich. Artificial Intelligence.

Comraderie
Ammons. Resolve.
Herrick. Jack and Jill.
Hewitt. Hired Lad's Farewell, The.
Peter Peri (1899-1967).
Roll Call.
Valediction Lines to My WEA Students.
Kipling. Banquet Night.
Changelings, The.
Rolfe. Eyes of a Boy.
Many an Outcast.
Primer Amor.
Sorrentino. Veterans of Foreign Wars.
Williams, Charles Kenneth. Sanctity, The.

Concentration
Atwood. Children on the lawn / joined hand to hand, The.
Merton. Butterfly.
Ibn Abbad Described by a Friend (Ibn Qunfud).
Woodcarver, The.

Concentration Camps
Berg. Desnos Reading the Palms of Men on Their Way to the Gas Chambers.
Ciardi. Gift, The.
Cohen. All There Is to Know about Adolph Eichmann.
Failure of a Secular Life, The.
Heirloom.
Invisible Trouble, The.
It Uses Us!
Hayden. Belsen, Day of Liberation.
Jarrell. Camp in the Prussian Forest, A.
In the Camp There Was One Alive.
Protocols.
Kunitz. Extermination Camp, The.
Merton. Chant to Be Used in Processions around a Site with Furnaces.
Sarton. Concentration Camps, The.
Williams, Charles Kenneth. Day for Anne Frank, A.

See also **Auschwitz, Poland; Holocaust.**

Conception
Berrigan. Poem upon the page is as massive as, The.
Berry. I dream of you walking at night along the streams.
Dickinson. Solemn thing—it was—I said, A.
Dunn. For Fathers of Girls.
Fox. In the Planetarium.
Heaney. Act of Union.
Herrick. Observation.
Tithe [*or* Tythe]: To the Bride, The.
Upon a Lady Faire, but Fruitlesse.
Jeffers. Dead Men's Child, The.
"MacDiarmid." Harry Semen.
Rukeyser. Running of the Grunion, The.
Williams, Miller. Voice of America.

Concerts
Coleridge. Lines Composed in a Concert-Room.
Dunbar. Concert, The.
Duncan. Concert, The.
Gunn. Monterey.
Outdoor Concert, The.
Sandburg. Band Concert.
Williams, Charles Kenneth. Junior High School Concert: Salle Rossini.
Prodigy, The.
Williams, Miller. Schumann Adds Trombones to His Second Symphony After Mendelssohn Conducts the First Performance.

Concord, Massachusetts
Emerson. At Plymouth in the friendly crowd.
Hymn[:] Sung at the Completion of the Concord Monument, April 19, 1836.
Musketaquid.
Rich. Concord River.
Walden 1950.

Concrete Poetry. *see* **Shaped Poetry.**

Confederacy
Tate. Ode to the Confederate Dead.
See also **Civil War, United States.**

Confessions
Berg. On This Side of the River.
Berry. Purification, A.
Browning, Elizabeth Barrett. Confessions.
Browning, Robert. Confessional, The.
Forgiveness, A.
Carruth. Event, The.
Chaucer. Parson's Tale, The.
Cohen. I Tried to Leave You.
Sisters of Mercy.
What I'm Doing Here.
Creeley. Europeans, The.
Hill, The.
Song: "I wouldn't / embarrass you."
Donne. To the Countess of Bedford ("Though I be dead, and buried, yet I have").
Dunn. On Hearing the Airlines Will Use a Psychological Profile to Catch Potential Skyjackers.
What They Wanted.
Gunn. Confessions of the Life Artist.
Hall. Carlotta's Confession.
Hemingway. Ultimately.
Herbert. Trinity Sunday.
Herrick. Confession.
His Confession.
To God ("I'le come, I'le creep").
Hewitt. Evangelist.
Hughes, Langston. Third Degree.
Lowell. Between the Porch and the Altar.
Melville. In a Church of Padua.
Meredith. O shrive me Friar, my ghostly Friar!
Tuck, Demitroïa, / Ariadne, and Froyja.
What may the woman labour to confess?
Muldoon. Cuba.
Schwartz. He Who Excuses Himself Also Accuses Himself.
Sexton. Talking to Sheep.
Shapiro. Confession, The.
Smith, Stevie. Hostage, The.
Man I Am, A.
Swift. Beasts' Confession to the Priest, The.
Walker. Confession.
Wilbur. Mind-Reader, The.
Williams, William Carlos. Keller Gegen Dom.
Wright, James. Confession to J. Edgar Hoover.
Yau. Confessions.
Zimmer. Confession, Curse and Prayer.

Confidence
Browning, Elizabeth Barrett. Apprehension, An.
Clark. "In the Bond Scandals.."
Davie. Expecting Silence.
Fenton. Tauler.
Fisher. Tapicer.
Herrick. First Marrs or Makes, The.
Larkin. He Hears That His Beloved Has Become Engaged.
Nash. There's Nothing Like Instinct, Fortunately.
Piercy. Unlearning to Not Speak.

Sandburg. Fireborn Are at Home in Fire, The.
Striped Cats, Old Men and Proud Stockings.
Stevenson. What glory for a boy of ten.
Williams, William Carlos. Swaggering Gait, The.
Yeats. His Confidence.

Conflict
Atwood. They Are Hostile Nations.
This is not something that can be renounced.
Yes at first you / go down smooth as.
Auden. Summer quickens grass, The.
Berg. Both.
In the Evening.
On This Side of the River.
Shoeshine.
What I Wanted to Say.
Boyle. This Is Not a Letter.
Bunting. That filly couldn't carry a rider nor.
Carew. To Master W. Montague.
To My Friend, Will. Davenant.
To One That Desired to Know My Mistress [or Mistris].
Carroll, Jim. Poem: "People down / The hallway who, The."
Catullus. Carmen 85: "I hate and I love. And if you ask me how."
Cohen. I Like the Way You Opposed Me.
There Is a War.
This Is War.
Creeley. Eros.
Fancy.
Friends, The.
Question, The.
Sopa.
Whip, The.
Wife, The.
Davie. Gripping Serial.
Dunn. Amidst the Faltering.
At the Smithville Methodist Church.
In the House.
Eberhart. Laocoön.
Fisher. Wrong Time, The.
Graves. Pearl, The.
To Lucia at Birth.
Hewitt. Breach, The.
Cultra Manor: The Ulster Folk Museum.
Nineteen Sixteen, or the Terrible Beauty.
Scottish Interlude.
Those Swans Remember; A Poem.
Ulsterman in England Remembers, An.
Wheel, The.
Hoffman. Battle of Hastings, The.
Larkin. If My Darling.
Lawrence. Woe.
Liddy. Maud Gonne Rode Out on a White Horse to Coolgreany.
Lorde. Love, Maybe.
Lovelace. I hate and love, wouldst thou the reason know?
Lowry. Bright as the Pleiades Upon the Soul.
Marlowe. 1.9: Ad Atticum, amantem non oportere desidiosum esse, sicuti nec militem.
2.2: Ad Bagoum, ut custodiam puellae sibi commissae laxiorem habeat.
2.13: Ad Isidem, ut parientem Corinnam iuvet.
2.14: In amicam, quod abortivum ipsa fecerit.
2.18: Ad Macrum, quod de amoribus scribat.
3.1: Deliberatio poetae, utrum elegos pergat scribere an potius tragedias.
3.7: Quod ab amica non recipiatur, dolet.
Melville. After the Pleasure Party.
America.
Armies of the Wilderness, The.
Meredith. Sonnet to J.M.
Merton. Advising the Prince.
All things change. / The sun is new everyday.
Homer was wrong in saying: "Would that conflict might perish from among gods and men."
Morrison. Blues, The.
Nash. What's the Matter, Haven't You Got Any Sense of Humor?
Nathan. Reading of History, A.
Nemerov. Deposition, The.
On Getting Out of Vietnam.
Rukeyser. Ninth Elegy. The Antagonists.
Sarton. Jonah.

Snodgrass. Call for Clues.
Southwell. Man's Civil[l] War[re].
Swift. Description of an Irish Feast, The.
Walcott. I heard them marching the leaf-wet roads of my head.
North and South.
Wyatt. To make an end of all this strife.
Will ye see what wonders love hath wrought?
Yeats. Meeting.
Young. Belgrade Moon.
Zukofsky. O th'hate I move love. Quarry it fact I am, for that's so re queries.

Conformity
Auden. Unknown Citizen, The.
Bly. Executive's Death, The.
Carruth. He used to think his escape was in lucidity.
One ant turns backward.
Sonnet: "To have been Diogenes. Why not? Or de Sade."
Spring 1967.
Clark. "Because They Are Desiring.."
Cohen. Aquarian Age.
I Am Punished.
Style.
There Is a War.
Cummings. Everybody happy? / WE-WE-WE. IN) all those who got.
Most(people / simply / can't).
My specialty is living said.
Of Ever-Ever Land i speak.
Peopleshaped toomany-ness far too, A.
There are possibly 2 1/2 or impossibly 3.
Dickinson. Much madness is divinest sense.
"Dylan." Advice for Geraldine on Her Miscellaneous Birthday.
I Am a Lonesome Hobo.
It's Alright, Ma (I'm Only Bleeding).
Johnny (little johnny) / with his father's hammer.
Lenny Bruce.
Maggie's Farm.
Subterranean Homesick Blues.
To Ramona.
Emerson. Easy to match what others do.
Herrick. Conformitie.
Conformity Is Comely.
Jeffers. Intellectuals.
Joseph. High life.
Just a snack for lunch.
Warning.
Kunitz. Harsh Judgment, The.
Lieberman. Corners.
Lindsay. Congo, The.
McGrath. Ode for the American Dead in Asia.
MacNeice. Habits, The.
Hidden Ice.
Melville. Enthusiast, The.
Neruda. Men (XVIII), The.
Olson. Conqueror.
Piercy. At the big round table in the university.
Sarton. Frog, that Naked Creature, The.
Prisoner at a Desk.
Shapiro. University.
Snodgrass. Charges Against Cock Robin, The.
Poet Ridiculed by Hysterical Academics, The.
Sorrentino. King of the dark tower is a lug, The.
Stevens. Disillusionment of Ten O'Clock.
Thomas. I Fellowed Sleep.
Williams, Charles Kenneth. Flat.

Confusion
Auden. Consequences.
Beckett. Saint-Lô.
Berg. Fragment, 1959.
Memory.
Burns. O Dear Minny What Shall I Do?
Carew. Lover, upon an Accident Necessitating His Departure, Consults with Reason, A. Methodus Amandi.
To His Mistress Retiring in Affection.
To Mistress Katherine Neville, on Her Green Sickness.
Clark. Tones of voice are petty, The.
Cowper. See Where the Thames, the Purest Stream.

Creeley. Chasing the Bird.
Fancy.
Mind's Heart.
Plan, The.
Please.
Snow, The.
That day / in an oak tree—.
Thinking.
Dickey, William. History of the Moon, The.
"Dylan." Mixed Up Confusion.
Ferlinghetti. Overpopulation.
Vast Confusion, A.
Fox. Alioth.
Alkor/Mizar.
Frost. Cabin in the Clearing, A.
Gallagher. 3 A.M. Kitchen: My Father Talking.
Graves. Sincèrement.
Sweet-Shop Round The Corner, The.
Hardy. I Was the Midmost.
Herrick. Confusion of Face.
Hesketh. Christmas Blackmail.
Hewitt. Fool's Cap, The.
I Told My Heart to Rest.
Monastary, Tourliani, Mykonos.
Revenant.
Twisted Heart, The.
Jarrell. Story, A.
Jeffers. Triad.
Knight. Various Protestations From Various People.
Lawrence. Embankment at Night, before the War: Charity.
Lorde. Bloodbirth.
New Year's Day.
October.
Pirouette.
Lowry. Outward Bound.
Markson. Contradiction.
Prosody.
Matthews. Waking at Dusk from a Nap.
Merton. Mothers you have met before still need you.
1. Now you are all here you might as well know this is America we do what we like.
Nash. Calling Spring VII-MMMC.
Do Sphinxes Think?
Song for Ditherers.
Strange Case of Mr. Pauncefoot's Broad Mind, The.
Thirteenth Labor of Hercules, The.
Unanswered by Request.
What's in a Name? Some Letter I Always Forget.
Who Did Which? or Who Indeed?
Nathan. Explanation.
Plath. Appearance, An.
Rolfe. In Praise Of.
Still Must I Love You.
Sandburg. Under the Capitol Dome.
Silverstein. Ma and God.
Smith, Patti. Penicillin.
Sorrentino. Charm, The.
Fiction, The.
Mathematics, The.
Silences.
Stevenson. Rivers and winds among the twisted hills.
Stuart. Confirmation.
Williams, Charles Kenneth. Dirty Talker: D Line, Boston, The.
History.
I sit in my room.
Shadows.

Congo River
Angelou. For Us, Who Dare Not Dare.

Congreve, William
Dryden. To My Dear Friend Mr Congreve [on His Comedy Called "The Double-Dealer"].

Connecticut (state)
Carruth. Sound of Snow, The.
Eberhart. Project, The.
River Water Music.
Scouring, The.
Hall. Days, The.
Sleeping Giant, The.
Wreckage, The.

Hugo. Overlooking Yale.
Stevens. River of Rivers in Connecticut, The.
Tomlinson. In Connecticut.

Connecticut River
Stevens. River of Rivers in Connecticut, The.

Conquistadors
Crane. Imperator Victus.
Frost. Vindictives, The.
MacLeish. Conquistador.
McNeill. Cornelius Verner.

Conrad, Joseph
Berg. Talking.
Carruth. Eternity Blues.
Cullen. For Joseph Conrad.
Walcott. Volcano.

Conscience
Bly. Getting Up Late.
Byron. Answer to ——'s Professions of
Affection.
Clark. Daring to Be the Same.
De la Mare. Memory.
Dickinson. Who is it seeks my Pillow Nights.
Dunbar. Conscience and Remorse.
Dunn. With No Experience in Such Matters.
"Dylan." Shot of Love.
Fenton. Vacant Possession, A.
Gardner. Of Conscience.
Graves. With Her Lips Only.
Hardy. He Follows Himself.
Heaney. From the Republic of Conscience.
Herrick. Sabbaths.
To His Conscience.
To Oenone ("What conscience, say, is it in
thee").
Hewitt. Wedding Present, The.
Hopkins. Candle Indoors, The.
Jeffers. New Year's Dawn, 1947.
Knott. Beddybye.
Kunitz. Firesticks.
Lawrence. Conscience.
Young Want to Be Just, The.
Lowell. Symptoms.
Lowry. Ladder, The.
Not all of us were heroes said my brother wit.
Perhaps for Eridanus.
Soul's Pentonville, The.
Merton. Soda Fountains.
Nash. Clean Conscience Never Relaxes, A.
Inter-Office Memorandum.
My Conscience.
Reflection of the Fallibility of Nemesis.
Piercy. Knight of Swords, The.
Rich. Over the hills in Shutesbury, Leverett.
Sandburg. Clean Hands.
Cups of Coffee.
Shakespeare. Sonnet 151: "Love is too young
to know what conscience is."
Simic. Inner Man, The.
Stevens. High-Toned Old Christian Woman,
A.
Stevenson. My Conscience!
Wilbur. Mind-Reader, The.
Peter.
Williams, Charles Kenneth. Conscience.
How Humble We Were before This.

Conscientious Objectors
Bunting. Keep Troth.
Lawrence. Rondeau of a Conscientious
Objector.
Lowell. Memories of West Street and Lepke.
Shapiro. Conscientious Objector, The.
See also **Pacifism and Pacifists.**

Consciousness
Atwood. Out.
Beatles. Strawberry Fields Forever.
While My Guitar Gently Weeps.
Berg. Homage to the Afterlife.
Memory.
Self-Portrait at Six.
Sister Ann.
Berry. Observance.
Thought of Something Else, The.
Carruth. And there in the sky is the known
face half-hidden.
Child's Being, The.
Final Version, The.

Nine, he thinks, and every one a failure.
Spirit / let there be even in the last hour.
Then from beyond, from nowhere, from the
wilderness.
Water, The.
Why is the face in the water a woman?
Because.
Coleridge. Lovely was the death.
Creeley. Divisions.
Lion and the Dog, The.
Little Time—and Place.
Measure, The.
Numbers.
On Acid.
Poem for D. H. Lawrence.
Cummings. Take for example this.
De la Mare. Riddle, A.
Snowdrop, The.
Dickinson. Consciousness is the only home.
My Cocoon tightens—Colors tease.
Of Consciousness, her awful Mate.
Too little way the House must lie.
We learned the Whole of Love.
Dunn. Insomnia.
Everson. Sixty Five.
Ford. In struggling to get.
Ginsberg. Do We Understand Each Other?
Eastern Ballad, An.
Eye Altering Alters All, The.
Manifesto.
Mind Breaths.
Refrain.
Haines. Inside the shell of our skulls.
Hardy. Aerolite, The.
I Travel as a Phantom Now.
New Year's Eve.
Jeffers. Consciousness.
Lawrence. Climbing Down.
Nemesis.
Nullus.
Terra Incognita.
Liddy. Coolgreany.
From This Distance: The Last Poem of the
Clare Bards in Praise of the MacDonnells of
Kilkee.
MacNeice. Good Dream.
Oliver. Spring.
Oppen. Who Shall Doubt.
Rolfe. Poem: "*Consciousness*, said Don
Miguel, *is a disease.*"
Rukeyser. Sea has opened, the limit of his
dream, The.
Tree of rivers seen and forgotten, The.
Sandburg. Fireborn Are at Home in Fire, The.
Simic. Inner Man, The.
Sorrentino. Handbook of Versification.
Stafford. Ritual to Read to Each Other, A.
Tomlinson. Bootblack, The.
Movements.
Tout Entouré de Mon Regard.
Van Duyn. Kind of Music, A.
Three Valentines to the Wide World.
Two Poems, with Birds.
Warren. Return, The.
Williams, Charles Kenneth. Waking Jed.
Zukofsky. "Mantis," An Interpretation.
Or a Valentine.
You three:—my wife.

Conscription, Military
Cummings. Why must itself up every of a
park.
MacNeice. Conscript, The.

Conservation. *see* **Ecology and Ecologists.**

Consolation
Atwood. People come from all over to consult
me, bringing their limbs.
What is it, it does not.
Berg. Dreaming with a Friend.
1911.
Prayer: "Nobody understands so let the
Rabbi."
Boyle. Painter Speaks—the Woman Answers,
The.
Browning, Elizabeth Barrett. Consolation.
Cowper. Epistle to a Protestant Lady in
France, An.
Dove. Five Elephants.

Emerson. Patch of meadow & upland, A.
Griffiths. For the Irish Sea.
Kunitz. Postcript.
Lowry. Consolation.
Mahon. Consolations of Philosophy.
Rich. Fact of a Doorframe, The.
Rossetti. Death of a First-Born, A.
Sidney. Sonnet 106: "O absent presence, Stella
is not here."
Sonnet 57: "Woe, having made with many
fights his own."
Van Duyn. Open Letter from a Constant
Reader.
Williams, Charles Kenneth. Call, The.
Wyatt. Comfort at hand! Pluck up thy heart.
Young. Elegy: "Good morning!"
For Joanne in Poland.
Grizzly Peak.

Conspiracy
Byron. Marino Faliero, Doge of Venice.
Ginsberg. Hadda Be Playing on the Jukebox.
Gunn. Court Revolt, The.
Kipling. Cleared.
Nemerov. Portrait of Three Conspirators.
Tomlinson. Conspiracy, The.

Constable, John
Betjeman. Meditation on a Constable Picture.
Tomlinson. Meditation on John Constable, A.

Constancy. *see* **Fidelity.**

Constantinople, Turkey
Lowry. Byzantium: Or Where the Great Life
Begins.
Stevenson. Strange are the ways of men.

Constellations
Bradstreet. Element Fire Boasts of the
Constellations, The.
Catullus. Carmen 66: "Who scans the bright
machinery of the skies."
Cummings. What time is it i wonder never
mind.
Eliot. Sweeney among the Nightingales.
Emerson. For Lyra yet shall be the pole.
Frost. On Looking Up by Chance at the
Constellations.
Lovelace. On the Best, Last, and Only
Remaining Comedy of Mr. Fletcher.
Mahon. Globe in North Carolina, The.
Merton. Lion, The.
Solemn Music.
Muldoon. Armageddon, Armageddon.
Rich. Orion.
Orion plunges like a drunken hunter.
Planetarium.
Wilbur. In the Field.
Under Cygnus.
Wyatt. Iopas's Song.
Zukofsky. Human all key mog knee this pecks
it loom in a moon the.
See also **Sky; Stars.**

Constitution (ship)
Sandburg. In the days of the cockade and the
brass pistol.

Construction Workers. *see* **Buildings and
Builders.**

Consumerism
Beatles. Paperback Writer.
Piggies.
Cummings. Jehovah buried,Satan dead.
Poem, or Beauty Hurts Mr. Vinal.
Emerson. Since the devil hopping on.
Hewitt. Rotterdam.
Jeffers. Trap, The.
Lieberman. Moonlighters.
Meredith. Song: "Buy, buy, buy."
Merton. Proverbs.
Nash. I Remember Yule.
Nemerov. Life Cycle of Common Man.
Olson. War on the Mind in a Time of Love.
Sandburg. Name Us a King.

Contempt
Bukowski. Man with the Hot Nose, The.
Thank God for Alleys.
Burns. Extempore [on the *Loyal Natives'*
Verses].
Cohen. I Decided.

Creeley. Ballad, A: "We have a song for the death in her body."
Cullen. Song of Sour Grapes, A.
Dobyns. Spite.
Emerson. I've found the dainty malice out.
Hemingway. Defense of Luxembourg.
Oily Weather.
Hugo. Goodbye, Iowa.
Joseph. Beyond Descartes.
Keats. All Gentle Folks Who Owe a Grudge.
Lowry. From This Acceptance, Sir, We Might Proceed.
You think you are a man shaking the hands of that dog.
McGrath. Proletarian in Abstract Light.
Rolfe. Kill the Umpire!
Rossetti. Contemptuous of his home beyond.
Some ladies dress in muslin full and white.
Sarton. Of Grief.
Sidney. Virtue, beauty, and speech, did strike, wound, charm.
Sorrentino. Blue Turning Grey.
Stuart. Hidden Meanings.
Warren. Psychological Profile.

Contentment
Auden. Mill (Hempstead), The.
Rain.
Beatles. I Feel Fine.
If I Needed Someone.
I'm Happy Just to Dance with You.
Octopus's Garden.
Bly. In the Month of May.
Love Poem in Twos and Threes.
Man and a Woman Sit Near Each Other.
Browning, Elizabeth Barrett. Past and Future.
Bukowski. Hello, Willie Shoemaker.
One for the Shoeshine Man.
Plate Glass Window, A.
Poem for My 43rd Birthday.
We Will Taste the Islands and the Sea.
Bunting. Yan tan tethera pethera pimp.
Burns. Bess[y] and Her Spinning-Wheel.
Birks of Aberfeldy, The [Composed on the Spot].
Country Lassie.
Fragment: "Altho' my bed were in yon muir."
Galla Water.
Lea-Rig, The.
Louis, What Reck I by Thee.
My Collier Laddie.
Ronalds of the Bennals, The.
Song: "Behind yon hills where Lugar flows."
Song: "Contented wi' little, and cantie wi' mair."
Song: "No Churchman am I for to rail and to write."
Song: "Yestreen I had a pint o' wine."
Sonnet—On Hearing a Thrush Sing on a Morning Walk in January.
Written in Friar's Carse Hermitage on the Banks of Nith—June—1788.
Campion. Ad Lucium.
Canto Quinto.
Epigramme: "Wiseman wary lives, yet most secure, A."
In eosdem.
O what unhop't for sweet supply!
Though far from joy, my sorrowes are as far.
Carroll, Jim. Fragment: Little N.Y. Ode.
Carruth. I was watching the telly not serious you know just looking.
Renaissance.
Twilight Comes.
Clare. Sonnet: "I love to see the summer beaming forth."
Cowper. Contentment.
How blest the youth whom Fate ordains.
To Lady Austen.
Creeley. Innocence, The.
Rain, The.
Song: "How simply / for another."
Thank You.
Two Ways of Looking in a Mirror.
Cullen. To France.
Davie. Cold Spring in Essex.
Heigh-ho on a Winter Afternoon.
Dickey, William. Joy.

Dickinson. I'm sorry for the Dead—Today.
Their Height in Heaven comforts not.
Dunbar. Content.
Foolin' wid de Seasons.
Limitations.
Dunn. I Come Home Wanting to Touch Everyone.
Something Like Happiness.
"Dylan." Guess I'm Doin' Fine.
Watching the River Flow.
Emerson. Day's Ration, The.
I have no hoarded treasure.
Everson. August.
Ferlinghetti. At midnight on the next balcony.
Fletcher. Calm, The.
Court Lady Standing under Cherry Tree.
On the Verandah.
Ford. These days of small but.
When you close your eyes.
Garrigue. Song for "Buvez les Vins du Postillion"—Advt.
Graves. Everywhere Is Here.
Nothing Now Astonishes.
Strangeness.
What Will Be, Is.
Hacker. April Interval.
Haines. To Turn Back.
Hemingway. At night I lay with you.
Herbert. Family [or Familie], The.
Jesu.
Herrick. Content, Not Cates.
His Content in the Country.
His Grange.
His Grange, or Private Wealth.
His Wish ("Fat be my Hinde").
Lots to Be Liked.
Repletion.
Short and Long Both Likes.
To His Deere God.
Welcome What Comes.
Hewitt. Dissertation I.
First Corncrake.
For Roberta in the Garden.
Isaac McKeown.
Labour Victory, A.
Last Summer, For Roberta (1975), The.
Leaving for Holiday.
My Own and Not My Own.
Old Men Sitting.
With a Little Book of Pottery.
Housman. Here are the skies, the planets seven.
Hughes, Ted. Mountains.
Wadsworth Moor.
Hugo. Fairfield.
Getty.
Second Chances.
Johnson. Chearful sage, when solemn dictatees fail.
Joseph. Gentleman that my black hen lays eggs for, The.
Inland Sea, The.
Sun Has Burst the Sky, The.
Unlooked-For Season, The.
Keats. For There's Bishop's Teign.
Kipling. These are the four that are never content, that have never been filled since the Dews began.
Lawrence. Beautiful Old Age.
Lonely, Lonesome, Loney—O!
Song of a Man Who Is Loved.
Levine. Suit, The.
Words.
Longfellow. Day Is Done, The.
McAuley. Coming & Going.
McGrath. Celebration for June 24.
Poem: "Down the small and crooked road."
Progress of the Soul, The.
MacNeice. Canto XXVI: "Morning bright as summer. The job on hand, A."
Now That the Shapes of Mist.
Marvell. Garden, The.
Meredith. Beyond the meadow still where sweeps.
Could we know how kin we are.
Desert vulture / jealousy, The.
Desired as Summer rain.

Fullness of love sleeps in us like a sea.
Love they alone the joyful heart.
Pastoral 1: "How sweet on sunny afternoons."
Song: "I cannot lose thee for a day."
There is for me no sweeter holiday.
To the High-Flyers.
Woodland Peace.
World is full of different fates, The.
Nathan. Icon.
Near Things.
O'Hara. Saint.
Paley. Middle Age Poem.
Piercy. If They Come in the Night.
Poe. Eulalie—A Song.
Prince. To a Friend on His Marriage.
Rexroth. Advantages of Learning, The.
Robinson. Burning Book [or the Contented Metaphysician], The.
Firelight.
Rossetti. And There Was No More Sea.
Do This, and He Doeth It.
Sandburg. Anywhere and Everywhere People.
Honey and Salt.
Sarton. Work of Happiness, The.
Schuyler. Blue towel, A.
Letter Poem #3.
Sexton. Fury of Sundays, The.
I Remember.
Shakespeare. Sonnet 29: "When, in disgrace with fortune and men's eyes."
Silverstein. Sky Seasoning.
Smart. 2.6: "This was the summit of my views."
Smith, Charlotte. To Spring.
To the Moon.
To Tranquillity.
Written September 1791, During a Remarkable Thunder Storm, in which the Moon Was Perfectly Clear, While the Tempest Gathered in Various Directions Near the Earth.
Smith, Stevie. Ass, The.
Deeply Morbid.
My Heart Was Full.
Stafford. Earth Dweller.
Stevenson. Winter.
Thomas. Once below a Time.
Thomson. Contentment.
Updike. Upon Learning That a Town Exists in Virginia Called Upperville.
Van Duyn. Winter has stiffened the ground, the birds are gone.
Warren. Mediterranean Beach, Day after Storm.
Whitman. Glimpse, A.
Wilbur. Ballade for the Duke of Orléans.
Williams, William Carlos. Idyl: "They say to me, 'There is'."
Wordsworth. And sweet it is to see in summer time.
Danish Boy; A Fragment, The.
Farmer of Tilsbury Vale, The.
Ode to Apollo.
Stray Pleasures.
Yeats. Are You Content.
Lake Isle of Innisfree, The.
Peacock, The.
Young. Ars Poetica.
Dance for Li Po, A.
Look Good, Smell Good, Feel.
Romance.
Sunday Illumination.
Zukofsky. Pretty.

See also **Happiness.**

Continuity
Atwood. Circle Game, The.
Auden. Progress.
Stone Walls.
Bunting. Weeping oaks grieve, chestnuts raise.
Carroll, Jim. On Tour.
Carruth. Over and over.
Song: "Summer burns on the edges of day."
Cohen. Cross Didn't Fall on Me, A.
Creeley. Again.
For the Graduation.
Night in NYC.
Sentence, The.
Testament, A.

Duncan.　Beginning of Writing, The.
Eberhart.　Big Rock.
Parker River, The.
Eliot.　Dry Salvages, The.
Little Gidding.
Emerson.　Brother, no decrepitude.
Fisher.　Continuity.
If I Didn't.
Periodicity: the crack.
Ford.　St.-John Perse.
Tender blows the leaf, tender drops the eye.
This same sea, there.
Garrigue.　Clovers, The.
Giralda, The.
Haines.　Alive in the World.
Hardy.　Heredity.
In a Museum.
In the British Museum.
Life Laughs Onward.
Hill.　Cycle.
Hoffman.　In That High House.
Hughes, Ted.　Sometimes it comes, a gloomy flap of lightning.
Hugo.　Announcement.
Gray Stone.
In Your Good Dream.
Sound Track Conditional.
Jeffers.　Hope is Not for the Wise.
Point Pinos and Point Lobos.
Torch-Bearers' Race, The.
Joseph.　Against the Personality Cult.
Certain Weathers.
Even Over the Flat Land.
Kipling.　Truthful Song, The.
Kunitz.　Layers, The.
Levine.　Milkweed.
Lindsay.　Preface to "Bob Taylor's Birthday."
McAuley.　Allegro Moderato.
McGrath.　Drowned Man: Death Between Two Rivers, The.
Mediterranean.
Political Song for the Year's End.
MacNeice.　Broken bollard, rusted hawser.
Pindar is Dead.
Why, now it has happened.
McNeill.　Arrow Grasses by Greenbrier River.
Matthews.　Hope.
Merton.　In My End Is My Beginning.
Nemerov.　Dependencies, The.
Rope's End, The.
Neruda.　Initial.
Oliver.　Bone Poem.
In Blackwater Woods.
Olson.　Hour of evening—supper hour, for my neighbors—quietness, The.
Other Than.
Toss, for John Cage, A.
Oppen.　Endlessly, endlessly, / The definition of mortality.
In these explanations it is presumed.
Pack.　Waking to My Name.
Piercy.　Martha as the Angel Gabriel.
On Castle Hill.
Raine.　In the Beck.
Shells.
Water.
Snodgrass.　Leaving the Motel.
Snyder.　Makings.
Warren.　Arrogant Law.
Scream, The.
Whittier.　Sunset on the Bearcamp.
Young.　Black Queen for More Than a Day.
Green Is a Feeling, Not a Color.
How Stars Start.
Zukofsky.　Cactus rose-mauve and gray, twin overturned.
Memory of V. I. Ulianov.

Contrariness
Beatles.　Hello Goodbye.
We Can Work It Out.
Berry.　Contrariness of the Mad Farmer, The.
"Carroll, Lewis."　Elections to the Hebdomadal Council, The.
Donne.　Cross, The.
Griffiths.　Contractions.
Herrick.　Contention.

Hesketh.　Cats.
Child's Guide to Philosophy, A.
Melville.　Parthenon, The.
Contrition
Creeley.　Letter, The.
Convalescence
Coleridge.　To a Young Lady [Miss Lavinia Poole] on Her Recovery from a Fever.
Dickinson.　I shall watch your passage from Crutch to Cane.
My first well Day—since many ill.
Emerson.　Give All to Love.
Glück.　To Florida.
Lowry.　How overjoyed I am to get your letter.
Plath.　Among the Narcissi.
Schuyler.　Afterward.
Conventionality
Beckett.　À peine à bien mené.
Ainsi a-t-on beau.
Ford.　Break up conventional.
Garden of Disorder, The.
Hardy.　Christening, The.
Recalcitrants, The.
Lowry.　Rocksie Ann was a Roxy and she live on Histon, Eng.
Ransom.　Nocturne: "Where now has our young Adam."
Snodgrass.　Poet Ridiculed by Hysterical Academics, The.
Warren.　And Don't Forget Your Corset Cover, Either.
Convents
Hugo.　Montesano Unvisited.
Wordsworth.　Incident at Bruges.
Stanzas Suggested in a Steamboat off Saint Bees' Head, on the Coast of Cumberland.
See also **Nuns.**
Conversation
Atwood.　Conversation, A.
Berg.　Behind Us.
Milk.
On This Side of the River.
Berry.　Conversation, The.
For a night and a day.
In Memory: Stuart Egnal.
Berryman.　On the wheat-sacks sullen with the ceaseless damp.
Poem for Bhain, A.
Tea.
You sailed in sky-high, with your speech askew.
Bishop.　Conversation.
Wit, The.
Boyle.　Artist Speaks...the Woman Answers, The.
Bukowski.　Got to the track early to study my figures and here's this.
I park, get out, lock the car, it's a perfect day, warm and.
She Came Out of the Bathroom With Her Flaming Red Hair and Said—.
She Said.
Campion.　Awake, thou spring of speaking grace, mute rest becomes not thee.
Carew.　Methodus Amandi.
"Carroll, Lewis."　Three Voices, The.
Carruth.　Sam and Poll Go Back to the City.
Septic Tank.
Catullus.　Carmen 10: "Alfenus Varus / buttonholes me."
Ciardi.　October 18: Boston.
Clark.　Her voice is heard, and then the child's.
Cohen.　Café, The.
Commentary—The Café.
Cowper.　Conversation.
Crane.　Praise for an Urn.
Creeley.　Interview, The.
Rites, The.
Cummings.　Logeorge / lo / wellifitisn't eddy how's the boy.
Now two old ladies sit peacefully knitting.
Oil tel duh woil doi sez.
Davie.　Berkshire.
Owl Minerva, The.
De la Mare.　In the Garden.
Dickinson.　Writing is brief and fleeting.

Dobyns.　Explaining the Nature of Evidence.
Dunbar.　Drizzle.
Eberhart.　At The Canoe Club.
Frost.　Meeting and Passing.
Gallagher.　When You Speak to Me.
Gardner.　Conversation at Midnight with Oscar Williams.
Gunn.　Conversation of Old Men, The.
Conversation, The.
Jamesian.
Keats at Highgate.
Hacker.　Villanelle: Late Summer.
Hall.　Speeches.
Hartley.　Word and Its Meaning, A.
Hesketh.　Naked Ostrich.
Hewitt.　Hour with E.M.F. at Ninety, An.
In the Rosses.
Kinnell.　Meditation Among the Tombs.
Lawrence.　Drawing-Room.
Talk.
Longfellow.　Fire of Drift-Wood, The.
Lorde.　Conversations in Crisis.
Fantasy and Conversation.
Meinke.　Talk of the Paintings.
Meredith.　At dinner, she is hostess, I am host.
Madam would speak with me. So, now it comes.
My lady unto Madam makes her bow.
Merrill.　Charles on Fire.
Narrow Escape, A.
Merton.　Conversations.
Nash.　Is This Seat Taken? Yes, or, My Neck Is Sticking In.
Let's Not Play Lotto, Let's Just Talk.
Mr. Barcalow's Breakdown.
Olson.　As I went in and out I heard pieces.
Oppen.　Eclogue: "Men talking / Near the room's center. They have said, The."
Paley.　On the Bank Street Pier.
Patchen.　There's a Train Leaving Soon.
"Reed."　N.Y. Telephone Conversation.
Rich.　Dialogue.
We were bound on the wheel of an endless conversation.
Roethke.　Supper with Lindsay.
Rolfe.　Winter's Ghost Plagues Them.
Sidney.　Sonnet 30: "Whether the Turkish new moon minded be."
Sonnet 51: "Pardon mine ears; both I and they do pray."
Sorrentino.　Evils of the City.
Stein.　Sonatina Followed by Another, A.
Stevens.　On the Road Home.
Stuart.　Flatfish.
Tomlinson.　Rhenish Winter.
Word in Edgeways, A.
Turco.　Old Acquaintance, An.
Updike.　Thoughts While Driving Home.
Van Duyn.　Footnotes to "The Autobiography of Bertrand Russell."
Talker, The.
Wakoski.　Steely Silence.
Williams, Charles Kenneth.　Politics.
Williams, Miller.　On a Trailways Bus a Man Who Holds His Head Strangely Speaks to the Seat Behind Him.
Yau.　Genghis Chan: Private Eye V.
Yeats.　To Some I Have Talked with by the Fire.
Young.　Dancer, The.
Zukofsky.　Reading and Talking.
Varus old crony had me visit his love.
Conversion
Berryman.　After a Stoic, a Peripatetic, a Pythagorean.
Emerson.　William Rufus and the Jew.
Hewitt.　Evangelist.
Year of Grace and My Great-Grandfather.
Merton.　St. Paul.
Ransom.　Persistent Explorer.
Smart.　Conversion of St. Paul.
St. Andrew.
Whittier.　Call of the Christian, The.
Conviction
Berg.　Daughters, The.
"Carroll, Lewis."　Canto VI: Dyscomfyture.

Creeley. As Now It Would Be Snow.
Way, The.
Dunn. Wanting to Get Closer.
Lowry. What was that story of an older
  dream.
Rolfe. Unit Assignment.

Convoys
Kipling. Convoy Escort.
MacNeice. Convoy.

Cook, Captain James
Atwood. Reincarnation of Captain Cook, The.
Davie. Fifth Epistle.
  I Have Said, Ye Are Gods.

Cooking and Cooks
Berry. Grandmother, The.
Bishop. Lines Written in the Fannie Farmer
  Cookbook.
Catullus. Carmen 94: "Stuffing, O'Toole
  naturally stuffs with his tool."
Cowper. Salad, The.
Dunbar. Capture, The.
  Curiosity.
Fisher. Cook.
  Today / let us think.
Fox. Like a Woman in the Kitchen.
  My Father's Oldest Sister.
Gardner. Widow's Yard, The.
Graves. Under the Pot.
Gunn. Meat.
Herrick. Upon Dol.
  Upon Hog.
Kipling. Master-Cook, The.
Levine. Grandmother in Heaven.
Lowry. Cook in the Galley, The.
  That she could cook.
McGrath. Bread of this World; Praises III,
  The.
Muldoon. Sushi.
Nash. Malice Domestic.
  Second Limick.
  Strange Case of Mr. Palliser's Palate, The.
Piercy. What's That Smell in the Kitchen?
Rossetti. Minnie bakes oaten cakes, / Minnie
  brews ale.
  Mix a Pancake.
Schuyler. Joint.
Sexton. Fury of Cooks, The.
  Jesus Cooks.
Silverstein. Me-Stew.
Stuart. Cabbage in History, The.
Van Duyn. Reading of Rex Stout, A.
  Saleswomen in Bakery Shops.
Wakoski. Making a Sacher Torte.
  Pumpkin Pie, Or Reassurances Are Always
  Fake Though We Love Them, Only Physics
  Counts.
  Un Morceau en Forme de Poire.
Williams, Charles Kenneth. So / mucked up
  with.
Williams, William Carlos. Newlywed's
  Cuisine, The.
Zukofsky. Meantool amuck with her. Muck
  with her mean tool ah? Geared I.

Coole, Ireland
Yeats. Coole Park and Ballylee, 1931.
  Coole Park, 1929.
  I walked among the seven woods of Coole.
  In the Seven Woods.
  Wild Swans at Coole, The.

Copernicus, Nicholas
Emerson. Star seer Copernicus / Only could
  earn a curse.
Fox. Nicholas Copernicus (1473–1543).
Wilbur. Fourth of July, The.

Coral
Emerson. Coral worm beneath the sea, The.
Lieberman. Coral Reef, The.
Walcott. Coral.

Corinth, Greece
Byron. Siege of Corinth, The.
Doolittle. Antipater of Sidon.
Hewitt. Old Corinth.

Cormorants
Liddy. Cormorants / By the pollock holes
  diving.
  Hesperian evenings certainly.

Tomlinson. To Be Engraved on the Skull of a
  Cormorant.

Corn
Bly. Snowfall in the Afternoon.
Byron. Oh! might I kiss those eyes of fire.
Catullus. Carmen 48: "Iuventius, / were I
  allowed."
Davie. By the Road to Upper Midhope.
Dunbar. Corn-Stalk Fiddle, The.
Lawrence. Fireflies in the Corn.
Lindsay. Cornfields, The.
  Life Transcendent.
Lovelace. To Juventius.
Melville. Trophies of Peace.
Rukeyser. Cornfield, The.
Sandburg. Bitter Summer Thoughts—No. 3.
  Corn and Beans.
  Corn Prattlings.
  Cornfield Ridge and Stream.
  Cricket Match.
  Early Copper.
  Harvest.
  Laughing Corn.
  Ripe Corn.
  Wind in the corn leaves among the naked
  stalks, The.
Whittier. Huskers, The.
Zukofsky. Mellowed *those*, I call *those* eyes,
  Juventius.

Corncrakes
Hewitt. Arithmetic.
  Company.
  Corncrake.
  First Corncrake.
  July.

Cornwall, England
Betjeman. Delectable Duchy.
  Trebetherick.
  Tregardock.
Davie. Cornwall.
  Short Run to Camborne.
"MacDiarmid." I sing of Cornwall.

Corpses
Atwood. Corpse Song.
Bly. Counting Small-boned Bodies.
Bukowski. On Seeing an Old Civil War
  Painting with My Love.
Dickinson. Do People moulder equally.
Eberhart. When Golden Flies Upon My
  Carcass Come.
Fletcher. Blessing of the Worms, The.
Ford. Seeking out corpses.
Garrigue. Gravepiece.
Gunn. Lazarus Not Raised.
Heaney. Graubelle Man, The.
Hesketh. Very Small Casualty, A.
Housman. Some can gaze and not be sick.
Jarrell. To Be Dead.
  Washing the Corpse.
Lowry. Thoughts While Drowning: But Try to
  Eliminate the Argument.
"MacDiarmid." Dead Liebknecht, The.
Plath. Two Views of a Cadaver Room.
Rolfe. Mystery.
  Something Still Lives.
Rossetti. In a Certain Place.
Snodgrass. Old Apple Trees.
  Viewing the Body.
Swinburne. After Death.
Tate. Carrion, A.
Turco. Pilot, The.
Yau. Variations on Corpse and Mirror.
  Variations on Corpse and Mirror (Second Set).
  When a comet passes over the town, whoever
  sees it knows a corpse.
  When one of our citizens dies, his corpse is
  placed in his chariot.
  When the movie ends and the lights come on,
  the audience is puzzled.
See also **Necrophilia.**

Corruption
Auden. Last Bus, Saturday Night.
  We Too Had Known Golden Hours.
Berry. River Bridged and Forgot, The.
Blake. I wander thro each dirty street.
  London ("I wander through each chartered

street").
To see a World in a Grain of Sand.
Bly. Executive's Death, The.
Browning, Elizabeth Barrett. View Across the
  Roman Campagna.
Byron. Answer to ——'s Professions of
  Affection.
Catullus. Carmen 52: "Drop dead, Catullus, lie
  right down & die."
  Carmen 77: "Whom I have trusted to no end
  (Rufus)."
Chaucer. Canon's Yeoman's Tale, The.
  Former Age, The.
  Friar's Tale, The.
  Pardoner's Prologue, The.
  Summoner's Tale, The.
Coleridge. To an Unfortunate Woman Whom
  the Author Had Known in the Days of Her
  Innocence.
"Dylan." Jokerman.
  Tombstone Blues.
Ford. Convalescence, The.
Gardner. Part of the Darkness.
Graves. Accomplice, The.
  Man of Evil.
  Questions in a Wood.
  Wigs and Beards.
Griffiths. Children in a Walled Garden.
Herrick. Bad Princes Pill Their People.
Jeffers. Be Angry at the Sun.
  Delusion of Saints.
  Going to Horse Flats.
  Ink-Sack.
  Ordinary Newscaster, An.
  Sinverguenza.
  Skunks.
  Stars Go Over the Lonely Ocean, The.
Kipling. Bees and the Flies, The.
  Legend of the Foreign Office, A.
  What Happened.
Kunitz. Revolving Meditation.
  Tutored Child, The.
Lawrence. Nottingham's New University.
  Riches.
Lewis. Belief.
  Yet we are safely at this port of call.
Lindsay. What the Moon Saw.
Lowry. Words on a Grave.
McAuley. From the burly give-and-take.
MacLeish. Black Day, The.
  Conversation in a Belfry.
  Good Man in a Bad Time, A.
  Tricked by Eternity the Heart.
MacNeice. Canto XI: "Golden guineas filter
  through the mist, The."
Marlowe. 3.13: Ad amicam, si peccatura est,
  ut occulte peccet.
Nathan. Before Even This.
  Confession.
Nemerov. Poverty Programs, The.
Olson. What Had to Go.
Plath. Firesong.
Ralegh. Epitaph on the Earl of Salisbury.
Roethke. Prognosis.
Rolfe. Poisoned Air Befouled the Whole
  Decade, The.
Rossetti. Babylon the Great.
  Thy Friend and Thy Father's Friend Forget
  Not.
Sandburg. Hogh Conspiratorial Persons.
  Soiled Dove.
Shakespeare. Sonnet 35: "No more be grieved
  at that which thou hast done."
  Two loves I have, of comfort and despair.
Shapiro. Washington Cathedral.
Shelley. Fragment: "Gentle story of two lovers
  young, A."
  Lines Written During the Castlereagh
  Administration.
Smith, Stevie. Evangelie, or, The Figure of
  Literary Corruption, Seeking Glory Not
  Truth.
Sutter. Celebration of Rust, A.
Swift. On the Burning of Whitehall in 1698.
  On the Five Ladies at Sot's Hole, with the
  Doctor at Their Head.
Williams, Miller. Love and How It Becomes

Cortés

Important in Our Day to Day Lives.
Senator Explains a Vote, The.
Zukofsky. Quick death, Catullus! what more horrors may hurry!
Rufey my how frustrate unquickened and craved the tie I'm equal.

Cortés, Hernán

MacLeish. Eleventh Book, The.
First Book, The.
Seventh Book, The.
Sixth Book, The.

Cosmetics

Campion. Epigramme: "Cease, fond wretch, to love, so oft deluded."
Cowper. On a Battered Beauty.
On a Similar Character.
Donne. Phryne.
Herrick. Neglect.
Upon Judith.
Upon Sibilla.
Jonson. Still to be neat, still to be dressed [or Drest].

Cosmology

Beatles. I'm Only Sleeping.
Cummings. Kind) / YM&WC / (of sort of).
Fox. Almagest, Last Letter to Zakarias.
Morrison. Star Fish Gluttony.

Cosmos

Browning, Robert. Reverie.
Clark. "Point is Fixed..., A."
Merton. All things are fire.
Space Song.
Olson. Celestial Evening, October 1967.
Sandburg. Scriptsmith.
Shelley. Daemon of the World, The; A Fragment.

See also **Creation.**

Cotton

Angelou. Miss Scarlet, Mr. Rhett and other Latter-Day Saints.
Hesketh. Master Cotton Spinner.
Levine. Ashes.
Liddy. Cottage by the Bridge.

Counterfeiting and Counterfeiters

Lawrence. Aloof in Gaiety.

Counting

Dickinson. 'Tis One by One—the Father counts.
Eberhart. Soldier Rejects His Times Addressing His Contemporaries, A.
Lowry. Abacus, The.
Olson. Kin.
Rossetti. 1 and 1 are 2— / That's for me and you.
Schuyler. Six Something.

Country Dialects

Stafford. Song in the Manner of Flannery O'Connor, A.

Country Life

Auden. Houses rolled into the sun, The.
Thanksgiving for a Habitat.
Berry. At a Country Funeral.
Dream, The.
Berryman. Long Home, The.
Betjeman. On Leaving Wantage 1972.
Bishop. From the Country to the City.
Bogan. Old Countryside.
Browning, Elizabeth Barrett. Soul's Travelling, The.
Bukowski. Countryside.
Burns. As I Went Out Ae May Morning.
Ballad, A: "There was a lass and she was fair."
Bess[y] and Her Spinning-Wheel.
Bob o' Dumblane, The.
Brose and Butter.
Cotter's Saturday Night [Inscribed to Robert Aiken [or R. A****], Esq.], The.
Country Lassie.
Epistle to Hugh Parker.
Grim Grizzle.
To the Weaver's Gin Ye Go.
Waukrife Minnie, A.
Carruth. *Better, goddamn it. Why, whenever I see folks.*
It's awful, Amos.

Or independence, call it what you blame well like.
Our own hearts too like, seems's-zo, whenever.
Clare. August.
Mole-Catcher, The.
Clough. "There is no God," the wicked saith.
Coleridge. Reflections on Having Left a Place of Retirement.
Cowper. Salad, The.
Task, The.
Crabbe. Election, The.
Rural Life.
Truth in Poetry.
Creeley. City, The.
Farm, The.
Davie. Bedfordshire.
County Durham.
Gemona-del-Friuli, 1961–1976.
Gloucestershire.
Grazia Deledda, Young.
Idyll: "As a horn of the high moon veers in clear skies over Main Street."
Iowa.
Looking Out from Ferrara.
Sounds of a Devon Village.
Through Bifocals.
West Virginia's Auburn.
Donne. To Sir Henry Wotton ("Sir, more than kisses, letters mingle souls").
Dryden. To My Honoured [or Honour'd] Kinsman, John Driden [of Chesterton in the County of Huntingdon, Esquire].
Dunbar. At Loafing-Holt.
Diplomacy.
Land o' Used to Be, The.
Dunn. Round Trip.
"Dylan." Clothes Line.
Country Pie.
New Morning.
Time Passes Slowly.
Tiny Montgomery.
Everson. Residual Years, The.
Frost. Case for Jefferson, A.
Directive.
Need of Being Versed in Country Things, The.
Roadside Stand, A.
Galvin. Defending the Provinces.
Old Woodsroads.
Rural Mailboxes.
Stealing the Christmas Greens.
Warmth.
Garrigue. After Reading "The Country of the Pointed Firs."
Gildner. Johann Gaertner (1793–1887).
Graves. On Dwelling.
Hall. Merle Bascom's .22.
Names of Horses.
Ox Cart Man.
Twelve Seasons.
Hardy. Bird-Scene at a Rural Dwelling, A.
In Time of "The Breaking of Nations."
Hartley. Back Road Country.
Why talk of cities.
Hemingway. Country Poem with Little Country.
Inexpressible, The.
Herrick. Bucolick betwixt Two: Lacon and Thyrsis, A.
Country Life: To His Brother, M. Tho. Herrick.
Country Life, to the Honored Mr. Endymion Porter[, Groome of the Bed-Chamber to His Maj.], The.
Eclogue, or Pastorall between Endimion Porter and Lycidas Herrick, An.
His Content in the Country.
His Grange.
Larr's Portion, and the Poets Part.
Saint Distaffs Day, or the Morrow after Twelfth Day.
To His Muse ("Whither, mad maiden, wilt thou roame?").
To Phyllis to Love and Live with Him.
Upon Himnself ("Come, leave this loathed Country-life, and then").
Hewitt. Country Talk.

Drift of Petals, The.
Encounter With R.J. Welch, The Antiquary.
Glenaan.
Homestead.
Hymn: "Noon in an English county."
O Country People.
Sunset over Glenaan.
This Is No Land of Constable and Clare.
This Then My Country.
Way to School, The.
Hugo. In Stafford Country.
Jarrell. Country Life, A.
Jonson. Praises of a Country Life, The.
Keats. For There's Bishop's Teign.
Over the Hill and Over the Dale.
To One Who Has Been Long in City Pent.
Where Be You [or Ye] Going, You [or Ye] Devon Maid?
Lawrence. Letter from Town: The Almond-Tree.
Love on the Farm.
Whether or Not.
Levine. These Streets.
Lewis. *Civil Servant, The.*
Corfe Castle.
Country Gentleman, The.
Liddy. Country Life.
Vir IX.
Longfellow. Fire of Drift-Wood, The.
Lowry. There is no poetry when you live there.
McGrath. Ah... to the Villages!
MacNeice. Coffee leaps in a crystal knob.
Forth from a sack of fishing-reels and deck-quoits.
McNeill. Faldang.
Saturday Night (1890-1910).
Mahon. Woods, The.
Marvell. Garden, The.
Melville. Immolated.
Meredith. Beyond the meadow still where sweeps.
Grandfather Bridgeman.
Here Jack and Tom are paired with Moll and Meg.
Invitation to the Country.
Or the single path— / Which the cool moon sheds.
Poor things! we know not what they suffer.
To the High-Flyers.
Millay. Return, The.
Nash. Nine Miles to the Railroad.
Nathan. News from the Low Country.
Nemerov. At a Country Hotel.
Oliver. Being Country Bred.
Farm Country.
Winter in the Country.
Olson. Main Street / is deserted, the hills.
Patchen. Backcountry Blues.
We Must Be Slow.
Plath. Song for a Summer's Day.
Pope. Happy Life of a Country Parson, The.
Rich. Rural Reflections.
Rolfe. Barn in Wisconsin.
Rossetti. Farm Walk, A.
Sandburg. Flanders.
More Country People.
Potato Blossom Songs and Jigs.
Sarton. Apple Tree in May.
Charleston Plantations.
Puritan, The.
Schuyler. Evenings in Vermont.
Korean Mums.
Vermont Diary, A.
Walk, The.
Simic. Ballad: "What's that approaching like dust like poverty."
Old Mountain Road.
Rural Delivery.
Smart. To My Worthy Friend, Mr. T.B. One of the People Called Quakers.
Smith, Charlotte. He may be envied, who with tranquil breast.
Peasant of the Alps, The.
Smith, Stevie. I Love.
Sorrentino. Fragments of an Old Song 2.

Pastorale: "Rushing darkness of the summer evening, The."
Stevenson. De Hortis Julii Martialis.
Not undelightful, friend, our rustic ease.
Stuart. Killdeer.
Sutter. Geneva.
George.
He would never say any of this.
Husbandry.
Mrs.
Visitor, The.
What the Country Man Knows By Heart.
When loons laugh he does not.
Why he lives there he can't say.
Swift. To Quilca.
Verses from Quilca.
Thomas. In Country Sleep.
Thomson. On a Country Life.
Tomlinson. Portrait of Mrs. Spaxton.
Turco. Homestead, The.
My Country Wife.
Silo, The.
Townsfolk, The.
Van Duyn. Postcards from Cape Split.
Walcott. Upstate.
Whitman. Farm Picture, A.
Williams, Charles Kenneth. It Is Teeming.
Sleeping Over.
Williams, Miller. Love and How It Becomes Important in Our Day to Day Lives.
Main Street.
Williams, William Carlos. Aftermath, The.
Raleigh Was Right.
Wordsworth. 1830.
Wright, Charles. December Journal.
Three Poems of Departure.
Two Stories.
Wright, James. Arriving in the Country Again.
Summer Memory in the Crowded City, A.
Yeats. Lake Isle of Innisfree, The.
Young. Lonesome in the Country.
Pachuta, Mississippi/a Memoir.
Zukofsky. Che Di Lor Suona Su Nella Tua Vita.

County Antrim, Northern Ireland
Hewitt. This Antrim Air in Summer.
MacNeice. Carrickfergus.
Mahon. North Wind: Portrush.
Rathlin.

County Cork, Ireland
Mahon. Garage in Co. Cork, A.
Kinsale.
Penshurst Place.

County Donegal, Ireland
Muldoon. Good Friday, 1971. Driving Westward.

County Galway, Ireland
MacNeice. Galway.

County Mayo, Ireland
MacNeice. Sligo and Mayo.

County Meath, Ireland
Muldoon. My Grandfather's Wake.

County Sligo, Ireland
MacNeice. Sligo and Mayo.
Yeats. Lake Isle of Innisfree, The.

Courage
Atwood. Notes towards a Poem That Can Never Be Written.
Berryman. Dangerous Year, The.
Germanicus leapt upon the wild lion in Smyrna.
To a Woman.
Brontë. No coward soul is mine.
Brooks. Strong Men, Riding Horses.
Browning, Robert. Arcades Ambo.
Burns. McPherson's Farewell.
O Kenmure's on and awa, Willie.
Byron. On the Star of "The Legion of Honour."
"Carroll, Lewis." Ye Fattale Cheyse.
Clough. Say not the struggle nought [or naught] availeth.
Cowper. On Miltiades.
Creeley. Dishonest Mailmen, The.
Cummings. You which could grin three smiles into a dead.

Davie. Schubert from water, from birdsong's gamut Mozart.
Vancouver.
De la Mare. Courage.
Dickinson. Bless God, he went as soldiers.
I took my Power in my Hand.
If your Nerve, deny you.
Dunbar. To Dr. James Newton Matthews, Mason, Ill.
Dunn. Essay on Sanity.
"Dylan." Lenny Bruce.
Eliot. Defense of the Islands.
Emerson. In an Age of Fops and Toys.
Look danger in the eye it vanishes.
Titmouse, The.
Frost. Courage to Be New, The.
Glück. From the Japanese.
Graves. Until We Both.
Griffiths. Courage.
Herrick. More Mighty, the More Merciful, The.
More Modest, More Manly.
On Love ("Love is a kind of warre").
To His Muse, Another to the Same.
To the Lord Hopton, on His Fight in Cornwall.
Hewitt. On the Choice of a Title.
River Streets, The.
Uncle Dick and Aunt Bertha.
Hoffman. Poem, The: "Arriving at last."
Unchosen, The.
Housman. Loitering with a vacant eye.
Sage to the Young Man, The.
Hugo. Kilmuir Cemetery: The Knight in Blue-Green Relief.
Joseph. Another Old Tale.
Butterfly is dainty flippant fragile, The.
Lawrence. Courage.
Lewis. Defeated: for Wales, The.
Parable.
Lovelace. It is not, y' are deceav'd, it is not blisse.
Lowell. Marcus Cato 95–42 B.C.
Sir Thomas More.
Lowry. Arise, arrogant arsemongers / Come! clashing clowns.
Courage is not standing on the crosstrees.
Give me a poem / To wring the hearts of men.
Pilgrim passes through the town by night, A.
Rocksie Ann was a Roxy and she live on Histon, Eng.
Song for My Wife.
McGrath. Poem: "Down the small and crooked road."
MacLeish. Pablo Casals.
Melville. At the Cannon's Mouth.
Rebel Color-Bearers at Shiloh.
Meredith. Crown of Love, The.
Song of Drab, The.
Squireless Kate.
To Cardinal Manning.
To J.M.
Merton. Fighters.
Millay. Courage that my mother had, The.
Morrison. You Must Confront.
Nash. How Now, Sirrah? Oh, Anyhow.
It's Snug to Be Smug.
Notley. 30th Birthday.
Oppen. Kind of Garden: A Poem for my Sister, A.
Owen. Spring Offensive.
Paley. Learning From Barbara Deming.
Standing in high grass at home imagining farm.
Psalms. Psalm 27: "Lord is my light and my salvation, The."
Ralegh. Sir W. Ralegh, on the Snuff of a Candle the Night Before He Died.
Rich. Trying to Talk with a Man.
Roethke. Reply to Censure.
Rossetti. For a Mercy Received.
I Have Fought a Good Fight.
Lady Montrevor.
Yes, I too could face death and never shrink.
Rukeyser. To keep the weakness secret. To deny it and break through.

Schwartz. Choir and Music of Solitude and Silence, The.
Scott. Death of Marmion, The.
Douglas and Marmion.
Sexton. Courage.
Shelton. Courage.
Smith, Stevie. Can It Be?
Harold's Leap.
Stafford. For My Young Friends Who Are Afraid.
Tennyson. Charge of the Light Brigade, The.
Whitman. Bravest Soldiers, The.
Whittier. Barbara Frietchie.
Conductor Bradley.
Three Bells, The.
Wordsworth. Martial courage of a day is vain, The.
Occasioned by the Battle of Waterloo (the Last Six Lines Intended for an Inscription) February, 1816.
Ode: The Morning of the Day Appointed for a General Thanksgiving. January 18, 1816.
Westmoreland Girl, The.
Wright, James. Mad Fight Song for William S. Carpenter, 1966, A.

Courtesy
Auden. Private faces in public places.
Hall. Grave the Well, The.
Hewitt. Folk for Tea.
In the Lenin Library, Dushanbe.
Wake, The.
Lowry. Devil is a gentleman, The.
Meredith. Song of Courtesy, The.
Robinson. Flammonde.
Silverstein. I'm Making a List.
Tight Hat.
Sorrentino. Diaghilev Did Not Say "Étonnez-Moi."
Tilt.
Stuart. Gesture, A.
Whittier. To ———: "Fair Nature's priestesses! to whom."
Williams, Miller. Entropy.

Courtiers
Browning, Elizabeth Barrett. Romaunt of Margret, The.
Browning, Robert. In a Balcony.
De la Mare. Heresy.
Donne. Satire 4: "Well, I may now receive, and die: my sin."
To Sir Henry Wotton ("Here's no more news, than virtue, I may as well").
To Sir Henry Wotton ("Sir, more than kisses, letters mingle souls").
To the Countess of Bedford ("Madam, / You have refined me, and to worthiest things").
Graves. Son Altesse.
Hardy. Royal Sponsors.
Herrick. Dialogue Betwixt Himselfe and Mistresse Eliza: Wheeler, Under the Name of Amarillis, A.
Eclogue, or Pastorall between Endimion Porter and Lycidas Herrick, An.
Jonson. Epigram, An: "That you have seen the pride, beheld the sport."
On Court-Parrot.
On Court-Worm[e].
To Courtling.
Keats. Cap and Bells; or, The Jealousies, The.
Ransom. Vaunting Oak.
Rossetti. I am a King, / Or an Emperor rather.

Courtship
Angelou. To a Suitor.
Where We Belong, A Duet.
Ashbery. Long Novel, A.
More Pleasant Adventures.
Auden. As I Walked Out One Evening.
Ballad: "He offered her his paucity."
Chloe to Daphnis in Hyde Park.
Say Yes!
Beatles. Love Me Do.
Ob-La-Di Ob-La-Da.
Beckett. Song: "Age is when to a man."
Berryman. I wished, all the mild days of middle March.
Betjeman. Subaltern's Love-Song, A.
Blake. Some look. to see the sweet Outlines.

Brooks. Independent Man, The.
Lovely Love, A.
Browning, Elizabeth Barrett. Amy's Cruelty.
Lady Geraldine's Courtship.
Man's Requirements, A.
Question and Answer.
Sonnet: "First time he kissed me, he but only kissed."
Sonnet: "First time that the sun rose on thine oath, The."
Sonnet: "My letters! All dead paper, mute and white."
Sonnet: "Pardon, oh, pardon, that my soul should make."
Year's Spinning, A.
Browning, Robert. In a Balcony.
Light Woman, A.
Serenade at the Villa, A.
Burns. Allan Water.
Ballad, A: "There was a lass and she was fair."
Ca' the Ewes [or Yowes] [to the Knowes].
Ca' the Yowes [to the Knowes].
Comin[g] thro' [or through] the Rye.
Dainty Davie.
Down the Burn Davie.
Duncan Davison.
Duncan Gray.
Halloween.
I Love My Love in Secret.
I'll Mak You Be Fain to Follow Me.
John Come Kiss Me Now.
Lassie wi' the Lintwhite Locks.
Lea-Rig, The.
Leezie Lindsay.
Mary Morison.
O Lay Thy Loof in Mine Lass.
O Steer Her Up and Haud Her Gaun.
On Willie Chalmers.
Scotish Ballad.
She Says She Lo'es Me Best of A'.
Song: "Behind yon hills where Lugar flows."
Song, Composed in August.
Song: "It was upon a Lammas night."
Song: "O Philly, happy be that day."
Song: "O whistle, and I'll come to ye, my lad."
There Grows a Bonie Brier-Bush.
Tibbie Dunbar.
Tibbie Fowler.
Waukrife Minnie, A.
Byron. Reply to Some Verses of J.M.B. Pigot, Esq., on the Cruelty of His Mistress.
Stanzas to a Lady, with the Poems of Camoëns.
To a Vain Lady.
To Romance.
Campion. Ad Caspiam.
As on a day Sabina fell asleepe.
Aye me, that love should natures workes accuse!
Be Wise, and Fly Not.
Canto Secundo.
Come, you pretty false-eyed wanton [or false-ey'd wanton].
Dance, The.
Dear If I with Guile.
Dolus.
Elegye, An: "Constant to none, but ever false to me."
Follow, follow[e] / Though with mischiefe.
Hide not, sweetest Love, a sight so pleasing.
If any hath the heart to kill.
If I urge my kinde desires.
If thou longst so much to learne (sweet boy) what 'tis to love.
In Laurentiam.
In Melleam.
Kinde in unkindnesse, when will you relent.
Lords Welcome, sung before the Kings Good-night, The.
Love Me or Not.
Maydes are simple, some men say.
Never love unlesse you can.
Now Winter Nights Enlarge.
Shall I Come, Sweet Love.
So many loves have I neglected.

So Quicke, So Hot, So Mad is Thy Fond Sute.
Song, The: "Wooe her, and win her, he that can."
Sweete, come againe.
Tarry sweete love.
Think'st thou to seduce me then with words that have no meaning?
Though your strangenesse frets my hart.
What meanes this folly, now to brave it so.
Whether away my sweetest deerest?
Carew. Boldness[e] in Love.
Good Counsel to a Young Maid ("When you the sun-burnt pilgrim see").
Love's Courtship.
Methodus Amandi.
Pastoral[l] Dialogue, A.
Third Song, The.
To A. L.; Persuasions [or Perswasions] to Love.
To a Lady, That Desired I Would Love Her.
To His Mistress [or Mistris] Confined.
"Carroll, Lewis." King-Fisher [or King-Fisher's] Song, The.
Lang Coortin', The.
Carruth. Near Addison now.
Chaucer. Anelida and Arcite.
Complaint unto His Lady, A.
Complaynt d'Amours.
Franklin's Tale, The.
Knight's Tale, The.
Parlement of Foules, The.
Romance [or Romaunt] of the Rose, The.
Squire's Tale, The.
To Rosamounde.
Troilus and Criseyde [or Criseide].
Womanly Noblesse.
Coleridge. Kiss, The.
Night-Scene, The.
To an Unfortunate Woman at the Theatre.
To the Evening Star.
Crabbe. Frank Courtship, The.
Crashaw. Out of the Italian; a Song.
[With Some Poems Sent to a Gentlewoman. I].
[With Some Poems Sent to a Gentlewoman. II].
Cummings. As freedom is a breakfastfood.
Except in your / honour.
If i love You.
Let it go—the.
Who knows if the moon's.
Yes is a pleasant country.
Davie. Dule of a Dewsbury Matron.
Donne. Expostulation, The.
Letter Written by Sir H. G. and J. D. alternis vicibus, A.
Nature's lay idiot [or Ideot], I taught thee to love.
Prohibition, The.
To the Countess of Huntingdon ("That unripe side of earth, that heavy clime").
Dove. Courtship.
Courtship, Diligence.
Dryden. Song: "Fair, sweet and young, receive a prize."
Dunbar. Circumstances Alter Cases.
Confidence, A.
Coquette Conquered, A.
Discovered.
How Shall I Woo Thee.
Howdy, Honey, Howdy!
Li'l' Gal.
My Best Girl.
On the Road.
Sling Along.
Spring Wooing, A.
Suitor, The.
Wooing, The.
Eberhart. When Doris Danced.
Ford. Christine is the girl I adore.
Gardner. Lines to a Seagreen Lover.
Summer Evening.
Garrigue. Again, Again.
Cracked Looking Glass.
Grenoble Café.
Suite.
To Speak of My Influences.
Glück. Swans.

Graves. Arrow Shots.
Bites and Kisses.
Bower-Bird.
Coronet of Moonlight.
Five.
For Ever.
Green-Sailed Vessel, The.
Hazel Grove, The.
Hills of May, The.
Hoopoe Tells Us How, The.
Inkidoo and the Queen of Babel.
Love and Night.
Love Gifts.
Perfectionists.
Possibly.
Promised Ballad, The.
Quinque.
She to Him.
Song: The Promise.
Song: To Become Each Other.
Uncut Diamond, The.
Unnamed Spell, The.
Hacker. Thursday, the eighth of August, four o'clock.
Hardy. Catching Ballet of the Wedding Clothes, The.
Flirt's Tragedy, The.
Gallant's Song.
I Was Not He.
I Worked No Wile to Meet You.
Letter's Triumph, The.
Why Be at Pains?
Hartnett. He'll to the Moors.
Herrick. Conjuration, to Electra, A.
Corinna's Going a-Maying.
Hymne to the Graces, A.
Leven.
On Love("Love is a kind of warre").
To Electra. Love Looks for Love.
To His Valentine, on S. Valentines Day.
To Mistresse Amie Potter.
To Rosemary and Baies.
To Silvia ("Pardon my trespasse").
To the Lark.
Up Tail[e]s All.
Upon a Cherrystone Sent to the Tip of the Lady Jemmonia Walgraves Eare.
Upon a Delaying Lady.
Zeal Required in Love.
Hewitt. In a Suburban Avenue.
My Parents' Courtship.
Hopkins. Castara Victrix.
Continuation of R. Garnett's Nix.
Daphne.
Lover's Stars, The.
Tomorrow meet you? O not tomorrow.
Housman. Along the field as we came by.
Delight it is in youth and May.
Oh see how thick the goldcup flowers.
Sloe was lost in flower, The.
This time of year a twelvemonth past.
Hughes, Langston. Up-Beat.
Jong. After the Earthquake.
Jonson. Song. To Celia ("Drink to me only with thine eyes").
To the Same [Sir Luckless Woo-All].
Keats. Stanzas: "You say you love; but with a voice."
To ———: "Had I a man's fair form, then might my sighs."
To Fanny.
To [Mary Frogley].
Where Be You [or Ye] Going, You [or Ye] Devon Maid?
Kipling. MAY (Fishing).
Koch. For there are numerous questions remaining which one must consider.
Koertge. Getting the License.
Lawrence. Cherry Robbers.
Drained Cup, The.
Hands of the Betrothed, The.
I Wish I Knew a Woman.
Liaison.
Sunday Afternoon in Italy.
Turned Down.
Lewis. Jason and Medea.
Merchants Wife, The.

Lieberman. Courtship of the Jersey Lineman.
Loves of the Peacocks.
Lindsay. Blacksmith's Serenade, The.
For All Who Ever Sent Lace Valentines.
Lovelace. To Chloe, Courting Her for His
Friend.
Markson. I Met My Love.
Marlowe. Nimphs [orNymph's] Reply to the
Sheepheard[orShepherd], The.
Passionate Shepherd to His Love, The.
Meredith. Am I failing? For no longer can I
cast.
Crown of Love, The.
I think she sleeps: it must be sleep, when low.
Iconia.
Lord Dusiote sprang from priest and squire.
Lords of the Court they sighed heart-sick, The.
Love in the Valley.
My Heart.
O shrive me Friar, my ghostly Friar!
Open hither, open hence.
Sing aloud that she is mine.
Song: Spring.
Song: "Under boughs of breathing May."
Song: "Woo me now & you'll win me."
Vital Choice, The.
What soul would bargain for a cure that
brings.
Merrill. From the Cupola.
Miller. Sun Now or Never (For Barbara), The.
Nash. Advice outside a Church.
Chloe and the Roué.
Daddy's Home, See You Tomorrow.
Emancipation of Mr. Poplin, or, Skoal to the
Skimmerless.
Sedative Reflection.
Strange Case of Mr. Ballantine's Valentine,
The.
Strange Case of the Girl o' Mr. Sponsoon's
Dreams, The.
Strange Case of the Lovelorn Letter Writer,
The.
That Reminds Me.
To a Lady Passing Time Better Left Unpassed.
O'Hara. Lover, The.
Olson. Day Song, the Day After.
Soul, The.
Pack. Robot Romance.
Patchen. Figure Motioned with Its Mangled
Hand Toward the Wall Behind It, The.
Fragment from "A Schoolboy's Odyssey."
Great Birds, The.
Not If He Has Any Sense, He Won't Be
Back.
O when I take my love out walking.
On the South-West Coast of Erehwemos
Stands a Romantic Little Village.
Polly—An Almost-True Story.
We go out together into the staring town.
Who'll that be.
Pope. Spring, the First Pastoral, or Damon.
Prince. I think of waking / In the country inn.
To begin with he was undoubtedly in love.
We cannot disinter the girls of nineteen-eight.
Ralegh. Arte of English Poesie, The.
Description of Love, A.
11th: and Last Booke of the Ocean to
Scinthia, The.
Excuse, The.
Fayne Would I But I Dare Not.
In the Grace of Wit, of Tongue and Face.
Nimphs [or Nymph's] Reply to the
Sheepheard [or Shepherd], The.
Sir Walter Ralegh to the Queen.
Ransom. Thinking, Drinking.
Roethke. For an Amorous Lady.
Rossetti. Amor Mundi.
Cousin Kate.
Jessie Cameron.
Maiden-Song.
No, Thank You, John.
Noble Sisters.
Prince's Progress, The.
Triad, A.
Schwartz. Spiders.
Scott. Song of Albert Graeme.
Sexton. White Snake, The.

Shakespeare. Live with me, and be my love.
Scarce had the sun dried up the dewy morn.
Sweet Cytherea, sitting by a brook.
Venus, with young Adonis sitting by her.
When as thine eye hath chose the dame.
Shelley. Longest Journey, The.
Sidney. Come, Dorus, come, let the songs thy
sorrows signify.
Come, Espilus, come now declare thy skill.
Eighth Song.
Eleventh Song.
Fourth Song.
If mine eyes can speak to do hearty errand.
Lady, reserved by the heav'ns to do pastors'
company honour.
Silvanus long in love, and long in vain.
Since so mine eyes are subject to your sight.
Sonnet 6: "Some lovers speak, when they their
Muses entertain."
Sonnet 61: "Oft with true sighs, oft with
uncalled tears."
Sonnet 64: "No more, my dear, no more these
counsels try."
Sonnet 66: "And do I see some cause a hope
to feed."
Sonnet 67: "Hope, art thou true, or dost thou
flatter me?"
Sonnet 69: "O joy, too high for my low style
to show."
Sonnet 107: "Stella, since thou so right a
Princess art."
Smith, Charlotte. Love and Folly.
On the Aphorism "L'Amitié est l'Amour sans
Ailes."
Stanzas: "Ah! think'st thou, Laura, then, that
wealth."
Smith, Stevie. Barlow.
I Like to Play with Him.
Le Désert de l'Amour.
Magic Morning, The.
Snodgrass. D.D. Byrde Callyng Jennie Wrenn.
Sorrentino. Charm, The.
Verlaine's Innocents.
Spender. Acts Passed Beyond.
Stevens. Last Looks at the Lilacs.
Stevenson. I will make you brooches and toys
for your delight.
To Miss Rawlinson.
Unforgotten II, The ("She rested by the
Broken Brook").
Stuart. Girl of My Dreams, The.
Suckling. Detraction Execrated.
Love, Reason, Hate, did once bespeak.
Love's World.
Loving and Beloved.
Siege, The.
Song: "Honest lover whosoever."
Song: "No, no, fair heretic[k], it needs must
be."
Sonnet: "Of thee (kind boy) I ask no red and
white."
Why so pale and wan, fond lover?
Swinburne. Ballad of Burdens, A.
May Janet.
Old Saying, An.
Thomson. Sweet Tyrant Love.
To Amanda ("Unless with my Amanda blest").
To Her I Love.
To Seraphina.
To the Same.
Verses on Receiving a Flower from his
Mistress.
Verses to Amanda. In Imitation of Tibullus.
Turco. Zombie.
Wakoski. From A Go to B, If You Can Find
It.
Williams, Miller. On the Death of a Middle-
Aged Man.
Williams, William Carlos. First Praise.
Portrait of a Young Man with a Bad Heart.
Wordsworth. Ellen Irwin; or, The Braes of
Kirtle.
Wyatt. For to love her for her looks lovely.
I have sought long with steadfastness.
If waker care, if sudden [or sodayne] pale
colo[u]r.
Madam, withouten many words.

Since Love will needs that I shall love.
What needeth these threnning words and
wasted wind?
When first mine eyes did view and mark.
Yau. Modern Love.
Yeats. Cap and Bells, The.
Her Triumph.
Cousins
Eliot. Cousin Nancy.
Roethke. My Dim-Wit Cousin.
Rossetti. Maggie a Lady.
Coventry, England
Hewitt. Prologue for an Evening at the
Whitefriars.
Larkin. I Remember, I Remember.
Cowardice and Cowards
Browning, Robert. Martin Relph.
Burns. Johnie Cope.
Laddies by the banks o' Nith, The.
On Capt. W——— R-dd-ck of C-rb—ton.
Campion. Epigramme: "His late losse the
Wiveless Higs in order."
"Carroll, Lewis." Canto I: The Trystyng.
Edmunds. El Niño.
Eliot. Gerontion.
Emerson. This world is tedious.
Herrick. Fear[e] Gets Force.
No Despight to the Dead.
Hewitt. Belfastman Abroad Argues with
Himself.
Housman. Day of Battle, The.
My dreams are of a field afar.
Jonson. On Mongrel Esquire.
To Brain-Hardy.
Kipling. Braggart, The.
Coward, The.
Heriot's Ford.
Knight. Cop-Out Session.
Lawrence. Cowardice and Impudence.
Cowards.
Laughter.
Willy Wet-Leg.
Levine. Heaven.
Lovelace. It is not, y' are deceav'd, it is not
blisse.
Meredith. Bibber besotted, with scowl of a
cur, having heart of a deer, thou!
Oliver. Kookaburras, The.
Prince. Moult sont Prud'hommes les
Templiers.
Roethke. Prognosis.
Rolfe. Munich.
Smith, Stevie. No Respect.
Cowboys
Atwood. Backdrop Addresses Cowboy.
Boyle. Career.
Cohen. Ballad of the Absent Mare.
"Dylan." John Wesley Harding.
Ford. Dicty Glide in Central Park Menagerie.
Ram wears a cowboy.
Hall. Lone Ranger, The.
Koertge. He ("Got drunk once with another
cowpuncher").
Silverstein. True Story.
Tomlinson. At Barstow.
Warren. Rattlesnake Country.
Williams, Miller. Pity and Fear.
Cowper, William
Blake. William Cowper Esqre.
Browning, Elizabeth Barrett. Cowper's Grave.
Davie. Homage to William Cowper.
Huntingdonshire.
Cows
Berry. Her First Calf.
Bly. Opening the Door of a Barn I Thought
Was Empty on New Year's Eve.
Burns. Calf, The.
Grim Grizzle.
Carruth. Cows at Night, The.
Cowshed Blues, The.
Godhulivela.
Johnny Spain's White Heifer.
Sanskrit root word, The.
Sonnet: "Poor little book, The Sleeping Beauty
died."
Which ain't much barn at that, maybe twenty
head.

Creeley. Don't Sign Anything.
Dickey, James. Trees and Cattle.
Dobyns. Conviviality of Cows, The.
Eberhart. Barn, The.
Frost. Cow in Apple Time, The.
Gallagher. Cows, a Vision.
Hall. Great Day in the Cows' House.
Herrick. Supreme Fortune Falls Soonest.
Lieberman. Swimming Pool Pastoral.
Lowry. Three Little Dog-Gone Mice.
Nash. Cow, The.
Roethke. Cow, The.
Rossetti. Brownie, Brownie, let down your
  milk.
  When the cows come home the milk is
  coming.
Rukeyser. Another Day (And then the cow).
Sandburg. Milk-White Moon, Put the Cows to
  Sleep.
Stevenson. Cow, The.
Tomlinson. Macduff.
Van Duyn. Ballad of Blossom, The.
  Just full of springs the world was in Illinois.

Coyotes
Dunn. About the Elk and the Coyotes That
  Killed Her Calf.
Tomlinson. Anecdote.

Crab Apple Trees and Crab Apples
Sandburg. Crabapples.

Crabbe, George
Davie. Trevenen.
Robinson. George Crabbe.

Crabs and Crabbing
Atwood. Landcrab I.
  Landcrab II.
Bishop. Strayed Crab.
Graves. With the Gift of a Lion's Claw.
Hughes, Ted. Ghost Crabs.
Lowry. Kraken, Eagles, in British Columbia.
Plath. Mussel Hunter at Rock Harbor.
Updike. Crab Crack.
See also Hermit Crabs.

Craftsmanship
Cowper. Flatting Mill, The.
Hewitt. Instead of an Elegy.
  Irish Glass.
  Palimpsest.
  Tinker's Answer, The.
Kipling. My New-Cut Ashlar.
Kunitz. Trompe L'oeil.
Lieberman. Moonlighters.
  Tilemaker's Hill Fresco, The.
Morgan. Abenaki Poem.
Sorrentino. Stupid painter paints. He, The.

Crane, Hart
Creeley. Hart Crane.
Hartley. Un Recuerdo—Hermano—Hart Crane
  R.I.P.
Lowell. Words for Hart Crane.
Markson. Relevance.
Muldoon. Louis.
Olson. Birth's Obituary.
  You, Hart Crane.
Sorrentino. Deluxe Assorted.
Wright, Charles. Portrait of the Artist with
  Hart Crane.

Cranes (ornithology)
Bukowski. About Cranes.
Carruth. Too Tenuous.
Ceravolo. Migratory Noon.
Dunn. Nova Scotia.
Haines. Cranes.
Hugo. Lone Cheer from the Stands for a
  Bitter Crane.
Lowry. Crane over seas and forests seeks her
  home, The.
Olson. Landscape, Without Color.

Cranmer, Thomas
Davie. Widower.
Smith, Stevie. Admire Cranmer!

Crazy Horse (Oglala Sioux Chief)
MacLeish. Wildwest.
Smith, Patti. Salvation of Rock, The.
Stafford. Report to Crazy Horse.
  Sioux Haiku.

Creation
Ashbery. Other Cindy, The.
Auden. Anthem: "Let us praise our Maker,
  with true passion extol Him."
Sonnet I: "There was desolate silence on the
  world."
Blake. Tiger [or Tyger][!], The.
Bogan. Homunculus.
Browning, Elizabeth Barrett. Measure, The.
Browning, Robert. Johannes Agricola in
  Meditation.
Bunting. Darling of Gods and Men, beneath
  the gliding stars.
Carruth. And in the town, in neon-blaring
  twilight.
As movement seen, so is the sound, the
  singing.
He goes out with his chainsaw into the cold
  bright.
Point is (maybe) that the woman's face was
  made, The.
Princess, the poem is born and you have
  woken.
Ceravolo. Data.
Ciardi. On Wet Iota.
Cooper. Where is the simple myth we used to
  have?
Crashaw. Matthew 27; And He Answered
  Them Nothing.
Cummings. As if as / if a mys.
Here's to opening and upward,to leaf and to
  sap.
Love is the every only god.
Pity his how illimitable plight.
Swim so now million many worlds in each.
Take for example this.
This is the vase, Here.
We love each other very dearly.
When god decided to invent.
De la Mare. Glance, The.
Riddle, A.
Scribe, The.
Snowdrop, The.
Dickey, James. Reading Genesis to a Blind
  Child.
Dickinson. It's easy to invent a Life.
Just as He spoke it from his Hands.
Dobyns. Gardener, The.
Nihilist, The.
Oatmeal Deluxe.
Eberhart. Goal of Intellectual Man, The.
Maze.
Spring Mountain Climb.
Wisdom of Insecurity, The.
Emerson. From the stores of eldest Matter.
Hold of the Maker, not the made.
Rhodora, The [On Being Asked Whence Is the
  Flower].
Stand up, that we may sacrifice the soul.
Upon a rock yet uncreate.
Everson. South Coast, The.
Fisher. Elohim Creating Adam, The.
Fletcher. And God, looking out upon earth,
  said, "Lo, it is time / To create mankind."
In the still evening of the sixth long day.
Out of the waves they clomb, plant, insect,
  fish, and bird.
Prelude: "Before the beginning of things."
Six long days was the unseen God in labour
  with the earth.
Frost. Sitting by a Bush in Broad Sunlight.
Galvin. Assembling a Street.
Glück. Lamentations.
Graves. Five.
Hell.
Quinque.
Herbert. Man.
Pulley, The.
Herrick. Eye, The.
Hesketh. Edward Thomas.
Imagination.
Unicorn.
Hewitt. I Learn About Art.
Man Fish and Bird.
Sonnet: "Among the many selves that throng
  my flesh."
Hill. Genesis.

Hoffman. After God.
Housman. 'Tis five years since, "An end,"
  said I.
Hughes, Ted. Bride and Groom Lie Hidden
  for Three Days.
Crow's First Lesson.
Widdop.
Jarrell. Birth of Venus, The.
In the Ward: The Sacred Wood.
Man in Majesty.
Unicorn, The.
Jeffers. De Rerum Virtute.
There is this infinite energy, the power of God
  forever working.
Kipling. Dedication, A: "And they were
  stronger hands than mine."
Hymn of Breaking Strain.
If I have taken the common clay.
Kunitz. Cold-eyed, in Naples once.
Trompe L'oeil.
Lawrence. End, The Beginning, The.
God Is Born.
Him with His Tail in His Mouth.
Let There Be Light!
Michael Angelo.
Work of Creation, The.
Levine. Children's Crusade, The.
Pili's Wall.
Rain Downriver.
Liddy. At a Czech Tomb in Tuam.
Lindsay. Sunshine.
McAuley. Astronomy.
"MacDiarmid." My Love Is to the Light of
  Lights.
MacLeish. Creator.
Vicissitudes of the Creator.
MacNeice. Canto IX: "Master closed the door.
  The unmodern words, The."
McNeill. After the Blast.
Melville. Venice.
Meredith. You ask me what is Genius? 'tis
  that.
Merton. Perfect Joy.
Prose in Advent Time.
Secret of the Burning Stars, The.
Millay. This should be simple; if one's power
  were great.
Milton. And God created the great whales,
  and each.
Earth was form'd, but in the womb as yet,
  The.
For man to tell how human life began.
Forthwith the sounds and seas, each creek and
  bay.
Heaven opened wide / Her ever during gates,
  harmonious sound.
Meanwhile the tepid caves and fens and
  shores.
Morning Hymn of Adam.
Thus God the Heav'n created, thus the Earth.
Nathan. Confession.
Nemerov. Creation Myth on a Moebius Band.
First Day, The.
Neruda. From the breach to the iron
  explosion.
Gift, The.
Midday Construction.
Sitting Down.
Notley. Goddess Who Created This Passing
  World, The.
Olson. Added to / making a Republic.
Blow is Creation, / & the Twist   the
  Nasturtium, The.
Celestial Evening, October 1967.
Having descried the nation.
Hour of evening—supper hour, for my
  neighbors—quietness, The.
Lamp, The.
Liturgical / eighth day, The.
Pack. After All.
First Word at Last, The.
Robot.
Patchen. How God Was Made.
Theory of Nato-geography as Advanced by the
  Tiaphidian Man, With a Comment on the
  Character of His Penal System, A.
Piercy. Athena in the Front Lines.

Prince. Creation Myth.
Psalms. Psalm 104: "Bless the Lord, O my soul.."
Ralegh. From the Earth, and from thy bloud, O heaven, they came.
Heaven and Earth one forme did beare.
Rossetti. "All Thy Works Praise Thee, O Lord": A Processional of Creation.
Rukeyser. All the way through the forest, a sound of birdsong.
Child of the root, among your apples and forests.
During the journey there come moments of waking.
Gyroscope, The.
He Had a Quality of Growth.
Power of war leads to a plan of lives, The.
Sixth Night: Waking, The.
Structure is rising. It takes on shape, it takes on meaning, A.
Sandburg. Earth is a forgotten cinder, The.
Glass House Canticle.
I have been woven among meshes of long ropes.
Special Starlight.
There is only one horse on the earth.
Shapiro. Recognition of Eve, The.
Sickness of Adam, The.
Simic. Austerities.
Smith, Patti. Y.
Smith, Stevie. God and the Devil.
God Speaks.
Nature and Free Animals.
Passing Cloud, The.
Snyder. No Matter, Never Mind.
Sorrentino. Man in the Moon, The.
Southwell. Vale of Tear[e]s, A.
Spender. Adam.
Stevens. Completely New Set of Objects, A.
Negation.
Stevenson. And thorns, but did the sculptor spare.
Men marvel at the works of man.
Of Schooners, Islands, and Maroons.
Thomas. In the Beginning.
Upon Happiness.
Tomlinson. Maillol.
Portrait in Stone.
Small Action Poem.
Waldman. Scallop Song.
Warren. Where the Slow Fig's Purple Sloth.
Whitman. Laws for Creations.
Love That Is Hereafter, The.
Whittier. Clear Vision, The.
Invocation: "Through Thy clear spaces, Lord, of old."
Last Walk in Autumn, The.
Revelation.
Summer by the Lakeside.
Wilbur. Games Two.
On the Marginal Way.
Praise in Summer.
Two Voices in a Meadow.
Williams, Charles Kenneth. Nut, The.
Williams, Miller. He Speaks to His Arguing Friends and to Himself.
Wright, Charles. Night Journal.
Yeats. Rose of the World, The.
See also **Cosmology.**

Creativity
Bly. Meditation on Philosophy, A.
Boyle. Poem for a Painter Who Drinks Wine.
Creeley. Figures, The.
Moment.
Pryaer, A.
Cummings. Move / deeply,rain / (dream hugely)wish.
No man,if men are gods;but if gods must.
To start,to hesitate;to stop.
Dobyns. Velocity of Cows, The.
Duncan. Illustrative Lines.
Ferlinghetti. Adieu À Charlot.
Populist Manifesto.
Gardner. Are Poets Ball Players?
Ginsberg. Aether.
Contest of Bards.
Mescaline.

Hall. This Poem.
Hardy. Plaint to Man, A.
Jarrell. Cow wandering in the bare field, The.
Forest Murmurs.
Man in Majesty.
Jonson. Epistle to Elizabeth, Countess of Rutland.
Ode to James, Earl of Desmond, An.
To a Weak Gamester in Poetry.
Lawrence. Absolute Reverence.
Things Men Have Made.
Whatever Man Makes.
Levertov. To the Muse.
Liddy. I know nothing but this scene.
Marvell. Upon an Eunuch: A Poet.
Merton. Three Sisters, The.
Oppen. Little Hole, The.
Piercy. For Jeriann's Hands.
Rich. Diamond Cutters, The.
Schuyler. For Bob Dash.
Sidney. Sonnet 50: "Stella, the fullness of my thoughts of thee."
Snodgrass. Matisse: "The Red Studio."
Stevens. Man with the Blue Guitar, The.
Walcott. Since all of your work was really an effort to appease.
Walker. Beast.
Wright, Charles. Journal of True Confessions, A.
Young. Breathing in morning.

Creatures
Blake. Memorable Fancy, A ("I was in a printing house in Hell & I saw the method in").
Bunting. You idiot! What makes you think decay will.
De la Mare. Ariel.
Fog.
Forests.
Idleness.
Eberhart. Mystical Beast in the Shadows, The.
Fox. Letter to Peter Wilkins.
Herrick. Like Loves His Like.
Kinnell. Milk Bottle, The.
Lindsay. Yet Gentle Will the Griffin Be.
Neruda. Some Creature.
Raine. Spell to Bring Lost Creatures Home.
Rossetti. So I grew half delirious and quite sick.
Sandburg. There is only one horse on the earth.
Silverstein. Bloath, The.
Worst, The.
Yipiyuk, The.
Stuart. Next Step, The.
Turco. Odradek.
Xoanon.
Yeats. High Talk.
See also **Animals.**

Cremation
Eberhart. New Entrepreneurial Plan.
Hesketh. Brief Encounter.
Dilemma.
Hewitt. On Colinward: The Scattering.
Jeffers. It nearly cancels my fear of death, my dearest said.
Williams, William Carlos. Complete Destruction.

Cressida. *see* **Troilus and Cressida.**

Crete
Doolittle. Phaedra.
Ralegh. Cretians ever lyars were, they care not what they say, The.
In the main[e] sea the i[s]le of Cre[e]te doth lie.
Robinson. Chorus of Old Men in "Ægeus", The.

Crew and Crew Racing
Kipling. APRIL (*Rowing*).

Cricket (game)
Betjeman. Cricket Master.
"Carroll, Lewis." Deserted Parks, The.
Hewitt. Away Match: June 1924.
Dry Summer, Islandmagee, 1921.
Kipling. JUNE (*Cricket*).
Meredith. At the first ball his wicket fell, and sins.

Merton. Sports without Blood—a Letter to Dylan Thomas (1948).

Crickets
Bishop. Behind Stowe.
Browning, Robert. What a pretty tale you told me.
Carroll, Jim. For Ezra Pound.
Cohen. Roshi.
Song to Make Me Still.
Summer Haiku.
Cowper. Cricket, The.
Cummings. Cri / C / k / et / in.
Dunn. Petty Thing, A.
Round Trip.
Frost. One Guess.
Galvin. Last Open-Air Concert, The.
Hewitt. My Father.
Keats. On the Grasshopper and [the] Cricket.
Lindsay. Crickets on a Strike.
Lovelace. Ant, The.
Pack. Cord of Wood, A.
Sandburg. Buckwheat.
Cricket Match.
Splinter.
Silverstein. Enter This Deserted House.
Wright, James. Poems to a Brown Cricket.
Zukofsky. Crickets' / thickets / light, / delight.
When the crickets.

Crime and Criminals
Atwood. Marrying the Hangman.
Beatles. Maggie Mae.
Bishop. Burglar of Babylon, The.
Bukowski. Cold Plums.
Burns. Geordie [An Old Ballad].
Chaucer. Former Age, The.
Crabbe. Condemned Felon, The.
Smugglers and Poachers.
Cummings. Dick Mid's large bluish face without eyebrows.
It started when Bill's chip let on to.
Dickinson. I know some lonely Houses off the Road.
It comforts the Criminal little to know.
Dobyns. Beauty.
Dunn. White Collar.
"Dylan." Ballad of Donald White.
Billy.
Hurricane.
I Am a Lonesome Hobo.
Joey.
Lily, Rosemary, and the Jack of Hearts.
Fenton. GIRL ATTACKED.
Fletcher. Requiem for a Twentieth-Century Outlaw.
Ford. To Christopher Marlowe.
Ginsberg. Mugging.
Tonite I walked out of my red apartment door on East tenth street's dusk.
Hall. Cops and Robbers.
Hardy. In the Servants' Quarters.
Herrick. Rules for Our Reach.
Upon Boreman. Epig.
Upon Letcher: Epigram.
Hugo. Kilmuir Cemetery: Stone with Two Skulls and No Name.
Reading at the Old Federal Courts Building, St. Paul.
Jonson. My masters and friends, and good people draw near.
On a Robbery.
Kipling. Outlaws, The.
Koertge. Burglar, The.
I Wanted My Name on the Side of a Building
I Wanted to Be as Feared as the Word Biopsy.
Kunitz. System, The.
Lowry. Soul's Pentonville, The.
Marlowe. 2.2: Ad Bagoum, ut custodiam puellae sibi commissae laxiorem habeat.
Marvell. Bludius et Corona [Blood and the Crown].
Merton. Cracking the Safe.
Milton. On the Gunpowder Plot.
Morrison. Hitchhiker, The.
Muldoon. Immram.
More a Man Has the More a Man Wants, The.
Olson. Gonfalon Raised Tonight, The.

"Reed." Kicks.
Sandburg. Alley Rats.
Cahoots.
People, yes, the people, The.
Rakeoff and the Getaway, The.
Schwartz. To a Fugitive.
Smith, Patti. Rape.
Whitman. You Felons on Trial in Courts.
Whittier. Curse of the Charter-Breakers, The.
Slave-Ships, The.
Williams, Charles Kenneth. Crime.
Crime, The.
Williams, Miller. *In Extremis* in Hardy, Arkansas.
Williams, William Carlos. Uncertain of the Crime.
Wordsworth. Borderers, The. A Tragedy.
Peter Bell; a Tale.
Wright, James. To a Fugitive.

See also **Prisons and Prisoners.**

Crimean War
"Carroll, Lewis." Path of Roses, The.
Kipling. Last of the Light Brigade, The.
Meredith. Loyal Soldier, The.
Red Coats & the Blue, The.
Tennyson. Charge of the Light Brigade, The.

Cripples
Angelou. Willie.
Gunn. Dolly.
Hewitt. Child, the Chair, the Leaf, The.
Joseph. Inverts.
Kipling. Dead Statesman, A.
Lieberman. Stubby Carrot.
Oppen. Vulcan.
Owen. Disabled.
Sandburg. Cripple.
Sexton. One-Eye, Two-Eyes, Three-Eyes.
One-Legged Man, The.
Smith, Stevie. Bereavement.

See also **Handicaps and the Handicapped.**

Criticism and Critics
Ammons. Theory Center.
Berryman. Crisis.
Olympus.
Browning, Elizabeth Barrett. Summing Up in Italy.
Browning, Robert. Dialogue between Father and Daughter.
Bukowski. Dear Pa and Ma.
She Said.
Burns. On Critics.
Robert Burns' Answer [to Epistle from a Taylor].
To Captain Riddell.
Byron. Answer to Some Elegant Verses.
Behold! in various throngs the scribbling crew.
Canto the Eleventh.
Dear Doctor, I Have Read Your Play.
Parenthetical Address.
To a Knot of Ungenerous Critics.
To Lord Thurlow.
To the Author of a Sonnet Beginning " 'Sad Is My Verse,' You Say, 'And Yet No Tear' ."
Campion. Ad Nashum.
Coleridge. Lines to a Comic Author, on an Abusive Review.
To a Critic.
Cowper. Lines Written in the Monthly Review.
On a Review Condemning Thelyphthora.
Cullen. To Certain Critics.
Cummings. American critic ad 1935.
Davie. July, 1964.
Rejoinder to a Critic.
Dickinson. Your relentless Music.
Dunbar. To a Captious Critic.
Eberhart. Critic With His Pained Eye, The.
Fisher. Critics Can Bleed.
Hartnett. Man Who Wrote Yeats, the Man Who Wrote Mozart, The.
Hemingway. Valentine.
Herrick. Hymne to Sir Clipseby Crew, A.
To Critic[k]s.
To His Muse ("Whither, mad maiden, wilt thou roame?").
To the Detracter.

Upon Nis.
Upon the Same.
Hewitt. Because I Paced My Thought.
B.O.W.
Raindrop.
Hopkins. Proved Etherege prudish, selfish, hypocrite, heartless.
Hugo. Wheel of Fortune.
Jonson. Epigram to My Bookseller.
Epistle to a Friend, An ("Censure not sharply then, but me advise").
Ode to Himself.
On Cheveril.
On the Magnetic Lady.
To Censorious Courtling.
To Courtling.
To Fool, or Knave.
To Mr Jonson upon these Verses.
To My Mere English Censurer.
To Playwright.
To the Learnèd Critic.
To the Same [Alphonso Ferrabosco].
To the Worthy Author Mr John Fletcher.
Keats. House of Mourning Written by Mr Scott, The.
Koch. Pleasures of Peace, The.
Kunitz. Choice of Weapons, A.
Lawrence. Editorial Office.
Mr Squire.
My Little Critics.
Thomas Earp.
Lowry. I don't want to criticize war.
McAuley. Aor Against the Bad Reviewer.
Late Afternoon, Running: Close Reasoning, Listening Closely.
Prelude in Darkness.
Press Conference: King James Version.
Sunset.
"MacDiarmid." To distinctly English writers in England.
McGrath. For a Critic Who Tries to Write Poems.
MacLeish. Brooks Atkinson.
MacNeice. Prayer in Mid-Passage.
Markson. Daily Reviewer-Haupt.
Death of the Virgin, The.
Dialogue in Milan.
Prosody.
Marvell. To His Noble Friend, Mr Richard Lovelace, upon His Poems.
Meinke. Playing Shuffleboard, Drunk, in Key West, Fla.
Meredith. Camelus Saltat.
Camelus Saltat: Continued.
Point of Taste, The.
Nash. If He Scholars, Let Him Go.
Nemerov. Critic.
On Certain Wits.
Refusal of a Kindness Offered.
Sacrificed Author, A.
To My Least Favorite Reviewer.
O'Hara. Answer to Voznesensky and Evtushenko.
Critic, The.
Olson. Having descried the nation.
Issues from the Hand of God.
Piercy. Letter to be Disguised as a Gas Bill.
Pope. Essay on Criticism, An.
Prologue to the *Three Hours after Marriage.*
Where'er you find the cooling western breeze.
Rich. They come to you with their descriptions of your soul.
Rolfe. And If You Don't See What You Want, Ask for It.
May Day Song.
Shakespeare. Sonnet 112: "Your love and pity doth the impression fill."
Sonnet 140: "Be wise as thou art cruel; do not press."
Shelley. Lines to a Critic.
Lines to a Reviewer.
Smart. 1.4: "Tibullus, whom I love and praise."
Smith, Charlotte. Epiologue [B] to *What Is She?*
Epilogue [C] to *What Is She?*
Snyder. Some critic tried to put me down.

Swift. Hobbes clearly proves that every creature.
Tennyson. Hendecasyllabics.
Updike. Moderate, The.
Vision, A.
Whittier. To Charles Sumner.
Williams, Charles Kenneth. Critic, The.
Wordsworth. On the Detraction Which Followed the Publication of a Certain Poem.
Scorn Not the Sonnet [Critic, You Have Frowned].
Yeats. On Those That Hated "The Playboy of the Western World" 1907.
To a Poet, Who Would Have Me Praise Certain Bad Poets, Imitators of His and Mine.

Crockett, Samuel Rutherford
Stevenson. To S. R. Crockett.

Crocodiles
"Carroll, Lewis." How doth the little crocodile.
Ford. Large bead on the.
Tonguless crocodile / Meets eyeless tiger darted.
Nash. Purist, The.
Rossetti. My Dream.
Spenser. Beside the fruitfull shore of muddie Nile.

See also **Alligators.**

Crocuses
Berry. Planting Crocuses.
Hesketh. Invitation.
Schuyler. Spring.

Cromwell, Oliver
Emerson. Fate ("Deep in the man sits fast his fate").
Lovelace. Mock Song, A.
Marvell. First Anniversary of the Government under His Highness the Lord Protector, 1655, The.
Horatian Ode upon Cromwell's Return from Ireland, An.
I saw him dead, a leaden slumber lyes [*or* lies].
In Effigiem Oliveri Cromwell [On a Portrait of Oliver Cromwell].
That Providence which had so long the care.
Milton. Sonnet 16: "Cromwell, our cheif of men, who through a cloud."
Yeats. Curse of Cromwell, The.

Croquet
MacNeice. Soap Suds.

Cross, The
Cowper. Joy of the Cross, The.
Crane. Mermen, The.
Donne. Cross, The.
"Dylan." Sign on the Cross.
Hardy. Wood Fire, The.
Herrick. Christs Words on the Crosse, My God, My God.
Crosses.
Hesketh. Cross.
Lawrence. Cross, The.
Lewis. Lovers who among the grasses.
Lowry. And, when you go—much as a meteor.
And yet his suffering got involved with all this.
What the Irish Soldier Said.
Melville. Inscription, The: "While yet Rolfe's foot in stirrup stood."
Merton. O cross, more splendid than all the stars.
Raine. Island Cross, The.
"Reed." Dime Store Mystery.
Rossetti. Behold the Man!
Lord, what have I to offer? sickening fear.
Ruined Cross, The.
Watchers, The.
What is it Jesus saith unto the soul?
Sandburg. Loin Cloth.
Sexton. With Mercy for the Greedy.
Shapiro. Crucifix in the Filing Cabinet, The.
Smith, Stevie. Children of the Cross, The.
Stevens. Botanist on Alp (No. 2).
Tate. Cross, The.

Whittier. Mantle of St. John de Matha, The.
See also **Crucifixion, The.**

Crowds
Auden. Sext.
"Carroll, Lewis." Lays of Sorrow, No. 2.
Carruth. What does this wind say, plunging upon the land.
Cummings. People who, The.
Emerson. And he like me is not too proud.
Look danger in the eye it vanishes.
Hartley. To Partridge Merrithew.
Herrick. Crowd and Company, The.
Way in a Crowd.
Hewitt. On a Country Bus Forty Years Ago.
Hoffman. Center of Attention, The.
Hughes, Langston. Subway Rush Hour.
Kunitz. He steps out from the crowd.
Lawrence. Submergence.
Sandburg. Always the Mob.
I Am the People, the Mob.
In the chain store or the independent it is the people meeting the people.
Tomlinson. What Virginia Said.
Williams, Miller. Newspaper Picture of Spectators at a Hotel Fire, A.
Williams, William Carlos. At the Ball Game.

Crowns
Browning, Elizabeth Barrett. Crowned and Wedded.
Herrick. To his deare Valentine, Mistresse Margaret Falconbrige.
Hill. On the morning of the crowning we chorused our.
Marvell. Coronet, The.
Robinson. Sunken Crown, The.
Rossetti. Twist me a crown of wind-flowers.
Smith, Stevie. Crown of Gold, The.

Crows
Ammons. Clarifications.
Crow Ride.
Atwood. Crow Song.
Chaucer. Manciple's Tale, The.
Clark. Crows.
Creeley. Crow, The.
Dickey, James. Veer-Voices: Two Sisters under Crows.
Dickinson. Spring, and not a Blue Bird.
Dobyns. Six Poems on Moving.
Ferlinghetti. Triste Corbiére.
Ford. On a high branch two.
Lindsay. Being a Seven-Year-Old Boy's Elaborate Memory of the Day of His Birth.
Two Old Crows.
MacLeish. Black Humor.
McNeill. New Corbies, The.
Nash. Chacun à Son Berlitz.
Oliver. Crows.
Patchen. Autumn Is the Crows' Time.
Piercy. Crows.
Roethke. Night Crow.
Simic. Crows.
Tomlinson. Crow.
In March.
Maine Winter.
Updike. Why the Telephone Wires Dip and the Poles Are Cracked and Crooked.

Crucifixion, The
Auden. Shield of Achilles, The.
Berryman. Disciple, The.
Blake. Nail his neck to the cross nail it with a nail.
Browning, Elizabeth Barrett. Seraphim, The.
Carruth. Crucifixion.
Emergency Haying.
Crashaw. In Cicatrices Domini Jesu.
On Our Crucified Lord Naked, and Bloody.
On the Bleeding Wounds of Our Crucified Lord.
On the Still Surviving Markes of Our Saviours Wounds.
To Pontius Washing His Blood-Stained Hands.
To Pontius Washing His Hands.
Upon Our Saviour's Tomb[e] Wherein Never Man Was Laid.
Upon the Thornes Taken Downe from Our Lords Head Bloody.
Cullen. Simon the Cyrenian Speaks.

Dickinson. I should have been too glad, I see.
Must be a Woe.
One Crucifixion is recorded—only.
"Remember me" implored the Thief!
To put this World down, like a Bundle.
Donne. Crucifying.
Good Friday [*or* Goodfriday], 1613. Riding Westward.
Son, The.
Edmunds. El Santuario de Chimayó.
Hill Village, A.
Fletcher. Crucifixion, The.
Hall. Maundy Thursday's Candles.
Hardy. Wood Fire, The.
Herbert. Home.
Sacrifice, The.
Herrick. Gods Price, and Mans Price.
His Anthem, to Christ on the Crosse.
His Saviour['']s Words, Going to the Cross[e].
His Words to Christ, Going to the Cross.
Observation ("Virgin-Mother stood at distance [there], The").
Summe, and the Satisfaction, The.
This cross-tree here.
Hill. Canticle for Good Friday.
Hopkins. Pilate.
Hughes, Ted. Contender, The.
God, A.
Jeffers. Dear Judas.
What is Worthless?
Lewis. Crucifixion, The.
Lieberman. Mural of Wakeful Sleep, The.
Lowry. Imprisoned in a Liverpool of self.
Melville. Via Crucis.
Meredith. Song of Theodolinda, The.
Merton. Biography, The.
Sponge Full of Vinegar, The.
Prince. Soldiers Bathing.
Robinson. Calvary.
Rossetti. Behold the Man!
Bundle of Myrrh Is My Well-Beloved unto Me, A.
Good Friday.
Good Friday Evening.
Good Friday Morning.
It Is Finished.
Mary Magdalene and the Other Mary.
One of the Soldiers with a Spear Pierced His Side.
Rukeyser. Gates, The.
Sandburg. Early Lynching.
Silver Nails.
Sexton. In the Deep Museum.
Shapiro. New Ring, The.
Southwell. Christ's Bloody Sweate.
Man to the Wound in Christ's Side.
Virgin Mary to Christ on the Crosse, The.
Van Duyn. Pietà, Rhenish, 14th C., the Cloisters, The.
Whittier. Crucifixion, The.
Yeats. Two Songs from a Play.
See also **Cross, The; Calvary.**

Cruelty
Beatles. Run for Your Life.
Berryman. *Luftmenschen* dream, the men who live on air.
Burns. Man's Inhumanity to Man.
Campion. Her fayre inflaming eyes.
Carew. Cruel Mistress, A.
Elegy on the La: Pen: Sent to My Mistress Out of France, An.
Looking-Glass, A.
To His Mistress.
To My Mistress [*or* Mistris], I Burning in Love.
"Carroll, Lewis." Alice's Recitation.
Carruth. Sonnet: "While you stood talking at the counter, cutting."
Ciardi. Faces.
Creeley. Dream, The.
Hill, The.
Operation, The.
Dickey, William. Memoranda.
Dickinson. She dealt her pretty words like Blades.
Doolittle. Ariadne.
We have seen how the most amiable.

Hacker. Why We Are Going Back to Paradise Island.
Hall. September Ode.
Hardy. Face at the Casement, The.
God's Education.
Son's Portrait, The.
Herrick. Biting of Beggars.
Cruelties.
Cruelty.
Cruelty Base in Commanders.
To Dianeme ("I co'd but see thee").
Upon Grubs.
Upon Grudgings.
Hugo. For a Northern Woman.
Maratea Porto: The Bitter Man.
Why Sapri Will Never Be Italian.
Jarrell. Snow-Leopard, The.
Jeffers. Orca.
Joseph. Man as Cannibal (PLAIN; BIOLOGY).
Untitled.
Lawrence. Cherry Robbers.
Lovelace. A La Bourbon.
Courante Monsieur.
Ode To My Lady H.
Lowell. Attila, Hitler.
Meredith. Society.
Millay. To Those Without Pity.
O'Hara. Invincibility.
Olson. Allegory of Wealth, The.
Piercy. Always you were dancing before the altar of guilt.
Rich. Burning Oneself In.
Photograph of the Unmade Bed, The.
Rossetti. A Tirsi.
Amore E Dovere.
Ariadne To Theseus.
Behold, I stand at the door and knock.
Shelley. Bigotry's Victim.
Shelton. Monster, The.
Smith, Charlotte. Blest is yon shepherd, on the turf reclined.
Smith, Stevie. Adelaide Abner.
How Cruel Is the Story of Eve.
Stevenson. Cruel Mistress, The.
I have a friend; I have a story.
Williams, Charles Kenneth. Conscience.
Dirty Talker: D Line, Boston, The.
Love: Wrath.
Wordsworth. When Philoctetes in the Lemnian Isle.
Wyatt. Alas! my dear, the word thou spakest.
Alone musing, / Remembering.
At last withdraw your cruelty.
Disdain not, madam, on him to look.
Heart oppressed [*or* oppress'd] with desperate thought.
If with complaint the pain might be expressed.
Longer to muse.
Love hath again.
Since ye delight to know.
Thou sleepest fast and I with woeful heart.
Though I cannot your cruelty constrain.
Who hath he[a]rd of such[e] cruelty before.

Cruelty to Animals
Bukowski. Brave Bull.
I Cannot Stand Tears.
Love Is a Piece of Paper Torn to Bits.
Object Lesson.
Burns. Elegy on Peg Nicholson.
On Seeing a Wounded Hare Limp by Me, Which a Fellow Had Just Shot At.
Clare. Badger ("When midnight comes a host of dogs and men").
Dunbar. Forest Greeting, The.
Hardy. Blinded Bird, The.
Compassion.
Jeffers. Memoir.
Kinnell. Bear, The.
Porcupine, The.
Kipling. Beasts Are Very Wise, The.
Kunitz. Scourge, The.
Nemerov. Kicks.
Rossetti. Brother Bruin.
Sarton. Village Tale, A.
Silverstein. Point of View.
Smart. Good-Nature to Animals.

Smith, Stevie. Es War Einmal.
This Is Disgraceful and Abominable.
Walcott. Lesson for This Sunday, A.
Williams, Charles Kenneth. Ten Below.

Crusades
Ferlinghetti. Spirit of the Crusades.
Graves. Absent Crusader.
Hugo. Picnic in the Saracen Ruin, The.
Lowell. Joinville and Louis IX.
Patchen. First Crusades, The!

Crystals
Emerson. Put in, drive home the sightless wedges.
Lawrence. Why Does She Weep?
"MacDiarmid." Crystals like Blood.
Updike. To Crystallization.

Cuba
Patchen. Leaflet (One).

Cuchulain (Irish legendary hero)
Smith, Stevie. Hound of Ulster, The.
Williams, William Carlos. Cuchulain.
Yeats. Cuchulain Comforted.
Cuchulain's Fight with the Sea.

Cuckoldry and Cuckolds
Burns. Dost blush, my dear Billy, asham'd of thyself.
O An Ye Were Dead Gudeman.
We'll Hide the Couper behint the Door.
Campion. Epigramme: "At all thou frankly throwst, while, Frank, thy wife."
Epigramme: "Barnzy stiffly vowes that hees no Cuckold."
Epigramme: "Thou telst me, Barnzy, Dawson hath a wife."
Chaucer. Merchant's Tale, The.
Shipman's Tale, The.
Cohen. Cuckold's Song, The.
Jonson. To Hornet.
"MacDiarmid." Focherty.
Pope. Two or Three, or a Receipt to Make a Cuckold.
See also **Adultery and Adulterers.**

Cuckoos
Auden. Short Ode to the Cuckoo.
Doolittle. Cuckoo Song.
Hopkins. Repeat That, Repeat.
When cuckoo calls and I may hear.
Kipling. Cuckoo Song.
MacNeice. Cuckoo.
Nash. Cuckoo, The.
Nemerov. Cuckoo King, The.
Wordsworth. Cuckoo and the Nightingale, The.
Cuckoo at Laverna May 25, 1837 The.
Cuckoo-Clock, The.
To the Cuckoo.
To the Cuckoo.

Cucumbers
Cowper. How to Grow Cucumbers.

Culloden, Battle of (1746)
Burns. Lovely Lass o' Inverness, The.

Culture
Atwood. Charivari.
Those south of us are lavish.
Burns. Scots Prologue, For Mrs. Sutherland's Benefit Night, Spoken at the Theatre Dumfries.
Ciardi. Bicentennial.
Davie. Meeting of Cultures, A.
Emerson. Culture.
Fenton. Lollipops of the Pomeranian Baroque.
Sweden. Lapp. Pouch made from a blackthroated diver.
This Octopus Exploits Women.
Ginsberg. Studying the Signs.
Hewitt. Dedication of "The Rhyming Weavers."
Hour with E.M.F. at Ninety, An.
Once Alien Here.
Levine. Sources.
Liddy. In the Bowling Alley.
Lindsay. For All Who Ever Sent Lace Valentines.
Merton. Letter to Pablo Antonio Cuadra Concerning Giants, A.
Sewende (Seven Day).

Nash. Caesar Knifed Again, or, Culture Biz Gets Hep, Boffs Profs.
Exit, Pursued by a Bear.
Oliver. Esquimos Have No Word for "War," The.
Olson. Kingfishers, The.
Oppen. Bicycles and the Apex, The.
Sandburg. Always the storm of propaganda blows.
Shapiro. Drug Store.
Tomlinson. Le Musée Imaginaire.
Waldman. Face the Orient.
Williams, William Carlos. All the Fancy Things.
Young. American Time.

Cumberland, England
Davie. Cumberland.
Wordsworth. Stanzas Suggested in a Steamboat off Saint Bees' Head, on the Coast of Cumberland.

Cunningham, Merce
Olson. Merce of Egypt.

Cupid
Bishop. Love with his gilded bow and crystal arrows.
Blake. To Chloes breast young Cupid slily stole.
Why was Cupid a Boy.
Browning, Elizabeth Barrett. Marriage of Psyche and Cupid.
Psyche Gazing on Cupid.
Byron. From Anacreon ("'Twas now the hour when Night had driven").
Campion. Ad Amorem.
Mistris [or Mistress] Since You So Much Desire.
O Love, where are thy Shafts, thy Quiver, and thy Bow?
Umbra.
When the God of Merrie Love.
Carew. Love's Courtship.
Willing Prisoner to His Mistress, The.
Chaucer. Romance [or Romaunt] of the Rose, The.
Coleridge. Kisses.
Cowper. By Moschus.
Elegy 7: "Not yet did I know your laws, enticing Amathusia."
Crashaw. Out of the Greeke Cupid's Cryer.
Out of the Italian.
De la Mare. Encounter, The.
Last Arrow, The.
Tired Cupid, The.
Emerson. Cupido.
Initial, Dæmonic, and Celestial Love.
Glück. Reproach, The.
Herrick. Bag of the Bee, The.
Cheat of Cupid; or, The Ungentle Guest, The.
How Lillies Came White.
How Roses Came Red.
Hymne to Cupid, An.
Hymne to Love, An.
Hymne to Venus, and Cupid, A.
Showre of Blossomes, The.
To Cupid.
To Oenone ("Thou saist Love's dart").
Upon Cupid ("As lately I a Garland bound").
Upon Cupid ("Love, like a Beggar, came to me").
Upon Cupid ("Love, like a Gypsie, lately come").
Upon Cupid ("Old wives have often told, how they").
Upon Love ("Christall Violl Cupid brought, A").
Upon Love ("Love brought me to a silent Grove").
Wounded Cupid, The.
Lovelace. Amyntor's Grove.
Cupid Far Gone.
Sir Thomas Wortley's Sonnet Answered.
Marlowe. 2.9: Ad Cupidinem.
Milton. Elegy 7: "Not yet did I know your laws, enticing Amathusia."
Shakespeare. Sonnet 153: "Cupid laid by his brand, and fell asleep."
Sidney. Sonnet 8: "Love, born in Greece, of

late fled from his native place."
Sonnet 12: "Cupid, because thou shin'st in Stella's eyes."
Sonnet 13: "Phoebus was judge between Jove, Mars, and Love."
Sonnet 17: "His mother dear Cupid offended late."
Sonnet 20: "Fly, fly, my friends, I have my death-wound, fly."
Sonnet 43: "Fair eyes, sweet lips, dear heart, that foolish I."
Sonnet 65: "Love, by sure proof I may call thee unkind."
Suckling. Metamorphosis, The.
To B.C.
Wroth. Love's Victorie.
O pardon, Cupid I confess my fault.
Song 2: "Sweet Silvia in a shadie wood."
Sonnet: "Oft did I wounder why the sweets of Love."
Sonnet 1: "My hart is lost, what can I now expect."
Sonnet 2: "Late in the Forest I did Cupid see."
Sonnet 3: "His flames ar joyes, his bands true lovers might."
Sonnet 5: "And burne, yett burning you will love the smart."
Sonnet 6: "O! that noe day would ever more appeere."
Sonnet 8: "Poore Love in chaines, and fetters like a thiefe."
Sonnet 33: "How many eyes poore Love hast thou to guard."
Venus unto the Gods a sure did move.

Cupidity
Herrick. Any Way for Wealth.

Cups
"Carroll, Lewis." Lyceum, The.
Dickey, William. Fred and the Holy Grail.
Doolittle. When I Am a Cup.
Fox. Story of Toile, The.
Herrick. Sincerity.
Lawrence. Cups.
Schuyler. Shimmer.
Scott. Enchanted Goblet, The.
Zukofsky. Shang Cup.

Curie, Marie
Rich. Power.

Curiosity
Berg. Bread.
Shoeshine.
Carruth. West Bolton is due north of Bolton, East.
Crane. Shall I Subsume..
Creeley. Time.
Dickinson. Unknown is the largest need, The.
Duncan. Helmet of Goliath, The.
Hacker. More circumspect good friend, if by "deceive."
Nights of 1962: The River Merchant's Wife.
Hewitt. Beastie, The.
Dissertation II.
Encounter With R.J. Welch, The Antiquary.
Fairy-Man at Layde, The.
Great Event, A.
Portrait, The.
Kinnell. For Robert Frost.
Kipling. I keep six honest serving-men.
Knott. My Mother's List of Names.
Lawrence. Tease.
Lorde. Ballad from Childhood.
Nash. Do Sphinxes Think?
I Spy, or, The Depravity of Privacy.
Never Mind the Overcoat, Button Up That Lip.
Schuyler. East Window on Elizabeth Street, An.
Sidney. Sonnet 92: "Be your words made (good sir) of Indian ware."
Silverstein. Stone Telling.
What's In the Sack?
Smith, Charlotte. Truant Dove from Pilpay, The.
Snodgrass. Orpheus.
Sorrentino. Barely Aware of the Insistent Loud Roars.

Stuart. Girl at Play.
Warren. Does the Wild Rose?
Williams, Charles Kenneth. For Gail, When I Was Five.
Knot, The.

Curses
Burns. Epitaph on Mr. Burton.
Carruth. Tanck's Song About the Jinx.
Coleridge. Devonshire Road, A.
Rime of the Ancient Mariner, The.
Three Graves, The.
Donne. Curse, The.
"Dylan." Seven Curses.
Emerson. Burn your literary verses.
If curses be the wage of love.
Graves. Return.
Hardy. No Bell-Ringing.
Herrick. Another [To His Booke].
Curse. A Song, The.
To the Sour[e] Reader.
Joseph. Modern witches 1: crouching.
Koertge. My Father ("Said, 'What the devil!' when he dropped").
Lindsay. Curse for Kings, A.
Lowry. No prayer for the people.
Nash. Lines To Be Mumbled At Ovington's.
Oh, Shucks, Ma'am, I Mean Excuse Me.
Nemerov. Priest's Curse on Dancing, The.
Rukeyser. Transgress, The.
Sandburg. Curse of a Rich Polish Peasant on His Sister Who Ran Away with a Wild Man.
Whiffletree.
Shelley. Cenci's Curse upon His Daughter, The.
Smith, Stevie. Cool as a Cucumber.
Waldman. Mother's Curse.
Wordsworth. Three Graves, The.
Wright, James. Song for the Middle of the Night, A.
Yeats. Crazy Jane and the Bishop.

Custer, George Armstrong
MacLeish. Wildwest.
Whitman. From Far Dakota's Cañons (June 25, 1876).

Custom
Betjeman. Beaumaris, December 21, 1963.
Carruth. Great Death, The.
He thinks of classical women.
Gardner. Prospero's Isle.
Herrick. Lawes ("Who violates the Customes, hurts the Health").
MacNeice. Off the Peg.
Prince. He Compares Old Customs with Those of His Kingdom.

Cyclamen
Lawrence. Sicilian Cyclamens.

Cyclops
Browning, Elizabeth Barrett. Cyclops, The.

Cynicism and Cynics
Bukowski. Freedom: The Unmolested Eagle of Myself.
Kind of Lecture on a Dull Day When There Isn't Even a Fly Around to Kill, A.
Report Upon the Consumption of Myself, A.
60 Yard Pass.
Soul.
Swans Walk My Brain in April It Rains, The.
With Vengeance Like a Tiger Crawls.
Bunting. Isn't it poetical, a chap's mind in the dumps?
Catullus. Carmen 25: "From Thallus the pederast."
Carmen 49: "Silver-tongued among the sons of Rome."
Creeley. Citizen.
Stomping with Catullus.
Cummings. Crazy jay blue) / demon laughshriek.
Dickinson. Hereafter, I will pick no Rose.
Dunbar. Vengeance is Sweet.
Dunn. Desire.
His Music.
Kindness.
Eberhart. Old Fashioned American Business Man, An.
Frost. Demiurge's Laugh, The.
Gunn. To His Cynical Mistress.

Hardy. Christmas: 1924.
Cynic's Epitaph.
He Never Expected Much.
Kunitz. Bottom of the Glass, The.
To the Reader.
Lawrence. Little-Boy Brilliant.
Liddy. Evening at Axel's.
Lovelace. Cynicks narrow houshold stuffe of Crutch, The.
To Marcus T. Cicero.
Meinke. Magic Kingdom, The.
Melville. Apparition, The.
Nash. Strange Case of Mr. O'Banion's Come-Uppance, The.
Piercy. Poet Dreams of a Nice Warm Motel, The.
Rolfe. Little Ballad for Americans—1954.
Smart. Disertissime Romuli Nepotum.
Smith, Stevie. Infant.
Sorrentino. Cynical.
Stafford. Meditation.
Wilbur. Matthew VIII, 28 ff.
Williams, Charles Kenneth. Hog Heaven.
You're two, that's great.
Zukofsky. Conniving Thallus, mulley, you, cony cully, cop below.
Immature Pebbles.
Master of eloquence and Rome's potent line.

Cypress Trees
Carruth. Look, a cypress tree.
Davie. Cypress Avenue, The.
Herrick. To the Yew and Cypress to Grace His Funeral.
Jeffers. Granite and Cypress.
Lawrence. Cypresses.
Meinke. Soldiers with Green Leggings.
Snyder. Kisiabaton.
Tomlinson. At Sant' Antimo.

Cyprus
Rossetti. St. Barnanbas.

Czechoslovakia
Auden. Forty Years On.
Millay. Czecho-Slovakia.

D

Da Vinci, Leonardo. *see* **Leonardo da Vinci.**

Dachau, Germany
Davie. Hawkshead and Dachau in a Christmas Glass.

Dachshunds
Meredith. Islet the Dachs.

Daedalus
Oppen. Daedalus: The Dirge.

Daffodils
Beckett. Thither.
Herrick. Divination by a Daffadill [or Daffodil].
To Daffodils [or Daffadills].
Hesketh. Winter Daffodils.
Hopkins. —And on their brittle green quils.
Johnson. On a Daffodil, the First Flower the Author Had Seen That Year.
MacLeish. Companions.
Rossetti. Growing in the vale / By the uplands hilly.
Schuyler. In a Churchyard.
Wordsworth. I Wandered Lonely as a Cloud.

Daggers
"Reed." Kicks.

Dahlias
Fletcher. Dahlias, The.
Zukofsky. Dahlia.

Daisies
Bunting. Three Michaelmas daisies.
Burns. To a Mountain Daisy [On Turning One Down, with the Plough, in April—1786].
Cohen. Photograph, The.
Coleridge. Fragment: "O'er the raised earth the gales of evening sigh."
Hartley. There Is Spit upon the Daisy Stem.
Herrick. To Daisies, Not to Shut So Soon[e].
Hesketh. Joke, The.
Lowry. Blepharipappus Glandulosus or White Tidy-Tips.

Rossetti. Where Innocent Bright-Eyed Daisies Are.
Who Hath Despised the Day of Small Things?
Sexton. Break Away, The.
Fury of Flowers and Worms, The.
Sorrentino. Solitary Man Discovered in a Field of Daisies.
Tennyson. Daisy, The.
Tomlinson. Daisies, The.
Wilbur. Mechanist, The.
Williams, William Carlos. Chicory and Daisies.
Wordsworth. To a Child [Written in Her Album].
To the Daisy ("Bright Flower! whose home is everywhere").
To the Daisy ("In youth from rock to rock I went").
To the Daisy ("Sweet Flower! belike one day to have").
To the Same Flower [The Daisy].
Zukofsky. Close your eyes.
Daisy.

Dali, Salvador
Muldoon. Salvador.

Damnation and the Damned
Burns. Epitaph on D—— C——.
Epitaph on Holy Willie.
Graves. Descent into Hell.
Red Shower, The.
Song: Lift-Boy.
Hughes, Langston. Fire.
Merton. Ranter and Their Pleads, The.
Rossetti. I Know You Not.
Toll, bell, toll. For hope is flying / Sighing from the earthbound soul.
Shelley. To the Lord Chancellor.
Swift. Place of the Damned [or Damn'd], The.
Walcott. Orient and Immortal Wheat.
Whittier. Cry of a Lost Soul, The.

Dams
Auden. Damming Stream.
Hall. Town of Hill, The.
Hewitt. On the Grand Dublin Canal: Musing on the "Two Nations" Theory.
Kipling. Giffen's Debt.
Lowry. Peter Gaunt and the Canals.
Rukeyser. Dam, The.
Statement: Philippa Allen.
Spender. Face of the Dam: Vivian Jones.

Danae
Bogan. Stanza: "No longer burn the hands that seized."
Duncan. Mirror, The.
Joseph. Danaë.
Zenith.
Ralegh. Brasen tower [or Tower] with doors [or dores] close barred [or bar'd], The.
Yeats. Unappeasable Host, The.

Dancing and Dancers
Beatles. I Saw Her Standing There.
I'm Happy Just to Dance with You.
Your Mother Should Know.
Berry. Dance, A.
Dance, The.
Having danced until nearly.
Our Children, Coming of Age.
Song (3).
Wheel, The.
Berryman. King David Dances.
Bly. Praise for All Dancers.
Boyle. American Citizen.
Square Dance for a Square, A.
Browning, Elizabeth Barrett. Dance, The.
Bukowski. Don't Touch the Girls.
Bunting. All the cants they peddle.
Coryphée gravefooted precise, dance to the gracious music.
Burns. On the Duchess of Gordon's Reel Dancing.
Reel o' Stumpie, The.
Byron. Muse of the many-twinkling feet! whose charms.
Campion. Dance, dance, and visit now the shadowes of our joy.
Dance, The.
Stars Dance, The.

Carroll, Jim. Nightclubbing.
"Carroll, Lewis." Mock Turtle's Song, The.
Mock Turtle's Song, The: "Beneath the waters
  of the sea."
There was an ancient City, stricken down.
Carruth. Woman, The.
Cohen. Dance Me to the End of Love.
Memories.
Crane. To Portapovitch.
Creeley. Dancing.
Fragments: "Decorous, and forbearing further
  correction."
Los Guitaristas.
Quick-Step.
Cullen. She of the Dancing Feet Sings.
Cummings. FloatfloaflofIf / lloloa.
Jimmie's got a goil.
Ladies and gentlemen this little girl.
Six / are in a room's dark around).
Ta / ppin / g / toe / hip.
Davie. Dancing Measures.
Dickinson. I cannot dance upon my Toes.
Dobyns. Window, The.
Dunbar. Angelina.
Critters' Dance, De.
Dance, The.
Frolic, A.
Valse, The.
Virginia Reel, A.
Dunn. Belly Dancer at the Hotel Jerome.
Dancing with God.
Danse Manhattanique.
Eberhart. When Doris Danced.
Ferlinghetti. Retired Ballerinas, Central Park
  West.
Gallagher. Four Dancers at an Irish Wedding.
Gardner. Jig for Harmonica.
Tango for Zither.
Waltz for Accordion.
Glück. Tango.
Graves. How It Started.
Gunn. Lofty in the Palais de Danse.
1975.
Hall. Dancers.
Hardy. At a Pause in a Country Dance.
Ballet, The.
Dance at the Phoenix, The.
Dawn after the Dance, The.
Fiddler, The.
In the Marquee.
Night of the Dance, The.
Reminiscences of a Dancing Man.
Hartley. Festival of the Corn, The.
Hartnett. Some white academy of grace.
Hemingway. Lines to a Young Lady on Her
  Having Very Nearly Won a Vögel.
Herrick. Song to the Maskers, A.
Hesketh. Changing Colour.
Jolly Good Fellow, A.
Hewitt. In a Lurgan Pub.
Housman. Fancy's Knell.
Hughes, Langston. College Formal:
  Renaissance Casino.
Dancer.
Dream Boogie.
Dream Variation[s].
Sunday by the Combination.
Hugo. Dancer at Kozani's.
Jarrell. Girl Dreams That She Is Giselle, The.
Jeffers. New Mexican Mountain.
Kipling. Plea of the Simla Dancers, The.
Knott. Rigor Vitus.
(Sergey) (Yesenin) Speaking (Isadora)
  (Duncan).
Koch. Our Hearts.
Larkin. Dancer, The.
Lawrence. Fronleichnam.
Swing Song of a Girl and a Soldier.
Tarantella.
Lewis. Dancer, The.
Liddy. Poem for My Sister Nora, at the
  Reading.
Thursdays Are Sacred.
Lindsay. Dancing for a Prize.
How a Little Girl Danced.
Lovelace. Courante Monsieur.
Gratiana Dancing [or Dauncing] and [or &]

Singing.
Loose Saraband, A: ("Nay, prethee [or prithee]
  dear, draw nigher").
To Lucasta ("I laugh and sing, but cannot
  tell").
Lowry. Good Luck.
I don't want to criticize war.
With Midsummer Devotion from All the Little
  Animals to Their Beloved Harteebeeste.
MacNeice. Les Sylphides.
McNeill. Faldang.
Fiddler.
Mahon. Andean Flute, The.
Matthews. You Dance Up There.
Meredith. I would I were with Jean.
Millay. Of what importance, O my lovely
  girls, my dancers, O my lovely boys.
Moore. Arthur Mitchell.
Nemerov. Dancer's Reply, The.
May Day Dancing, The.
Priest's Curse on Dancing, The.
Steps for a Dancer.
O'Hara. Alma.
First Dances.
Olson. Merce of Egypt.
Moebius Strip, The.
Sing, Mister, Sing.
Paley. Dance in Jinoteca, The.
Piercy. Three of Cups, The.
Pound. Dance Figure.
Prince. How Festivals Were Celebrated.
Roethke. Dance, The.
Once More, the Round.
Rossetti. Brother Bruin.
Rukeyser. Rock Flow, River Mix.
Three Black Women.
St. John. Slow Dance.
Sandburg. Cadenza.
Couples.
Dancer.
Lines Written for Gene Kelly to Dance To.
Mask.
Vaudeville Dancer.
Schuyler. Alice Faye at Ruby Foo's.
Schwartz. Dances and the Dancers, The.
Sexton. How We Danced.
Red Dance, The.
Twelve Dancing Princesses, The.
Wedding Ring Dance, The.
Silverstein. Dancing Pants.
Smith, Stevie. Dedicated Dancing Bull and the
  Water Maid, The.
Sorrentino. Rose Room.
Stevens. Dance of the Macabre Mice.
Stuart. That'll Be the Day.
Tomlinson. Before the Dance.
Cochiti.
Updike. Rockettes, The.
Young Matrons Dancing.
Wakoski. Belly Dancer.
Dancing on the Grave of a Son of a Bitch.
Tango-ing.
Wilbur. Grace.
Williams, William Carlos. Artist, The.
Canthara.
Dance, The ("In Brueghel's great picture").
Dance, The ("When the snow falls").
Danse Russe.
Heel & Toe to the End.
Hula-Hula.
Philomena Andronico.
Rumba! Rumba!
When Fresh, It Was Sweet.
Yeats. Double Vision of Michael Robartes,
  The.
Fiddler of Dooney, The.
Sweet Dancer.
When Loie Fuller's Chinese dancers enwound.

See also **Ballet; Ghosts; Waltzes and Waltzing.**

Dandelions
Dickinson. Dandelion's pallid tube, The.
Its little Ether Hood.
We should not mind so small a flower.
Lindsay. Dandelion, The.
MacNeice. Dandelions.
Nemerov. Dandelions.
Whitman. First Dandelion, The.

Zukofsky. Dandelion.

Daniel
Emerson. Γνωθι Σεαυτον.
Glück. Gretel in Darkness.
Lindsay. Daniel.

Dante Alighieri
Berryman. Dante's Tomb.
Byron. Prophecy of Dante, The.
Carruth. Excursus of Reassurance in Begonia
  Time, An.
There was this girl 18, 19 and slight.
Chaucer. House of Fame, The.
Creeley. Guido, i' vorrei che tu e Lapo ed io.
Cummings. Great Dante stands in Florence,
  looking down.
Davie. Mandelstam, on Dante.
Dobyns. This Life.
Duncan. Before the Judgment.
Household, The.
Emerson. Dante's Vita Nuova.
Solution.
Graves. Beatrice and Dante.
Keats. Dream, after Reading Dante's Episode
  of Paolo and Francesca, A.
Kunitz. Dante.
Lowell. Dante 3. Buonconte.
Lowry. Search, The.
McGrath. Migration of Cities, The.
Roethke. Her Wrath.
Sandburg. Our Hells.
Tomlinson. Idyll: "Door: / PER L'UNIVERSO
  / is what it says, A."
Wordsworth. At Florence.
Wright, Charles. Southern Cross, The.

Danube
Meredith. Square along the couch, and stark.
Wordsworth. Source of the Danube, The.
Young. Where the Danube and Sava Rivers
  Meet.

Daphne
Doolittle. If You Will Let Me Sing.
Glück. Mythic Fragment.
Undertaking, The.
Haines. Of yourself and your beginnings.
Joseph. Women at Streatham Hill.
Lovelace. Princesse Löysa drawing.
Meredith. Daphne.
Millay. Daphne.
Pound. Tree, The.
Smart. Apollo and Daphne.
Swift. Death and Daphne.
Zukofsky. For Zadkine.

Daredevils
Cowper. Card, A.
Sandburg. Hazardous Occupations.

Darkness
Atwood. Interlunar.
Projected Slide of an Unknown Soldier.
Solstice Poem.
Beckett. Noire soeur.
Berg. At the Door.
Behind Us.
Heartache.
1914.
Berry. At night make me one with the
  darkness.
Bird Killer, The.
Breaking.
Creation Myth.
Current, The.
Farmer and the Sea, The.
Fear of Darkness, The.
He Has Lived through Another Night.
In the heron's eye.
..it is not too soon to provide by every.
Returning.
Seventeen Years.
Sometimes our life reminds me.
Song in a Year of Catastrophe.
To Know the Dark.
Brontë. Night is darkening round me, The.
Byron. Darkness.
Carew. Song: Beautiful Mistress, A.
Carroll, Jim. Marked by a more distant sky, I
  hold.
Carruth. Fourth Version, The.
Metaphysical.

Mountain Cabin, The.
Shadow sprang out, The.
Clark. Dark Continent.
Out of Darkness I Came.
Retro.
Cowper. Scenes Favourable to Meditation.
Creeley. Anger.
For Leslie.
Hero, The.
I Know a Man.
Persons.
Rhythm, The.
Shame, The.
Somewhere.
You.
Cummings. I was considering how.
When citied day with the sonorous homes.
De la Mare. Disguise, The.
Juliet's Nurse.
Unforeseen.
Dickey, James. Rafters, The.
Spring-Shock.
Dickinson. We grow accustomed to the Dark.
Dunbar. Love is the light of the world, my dear.
Slow through the Dark.
Duncan. Albigenses, The.
Bring It Up from the Dark.
Huon of Bordeaux.
Dunn. Loveliness.
Eberhart. Bath Room, The.
Light, Time, Dark.
Parker River, The.
Poet, The.
Emerson. And as the light divided the dark.
Good Charles the springs adorer.
Winds are cold, the days are dark, The.
Everson. Dusk, The.
Fisher. Dark on Dark.
No dark in the body.
Rules and Ranges for Ian Tyson.
Fox. Alioth.
Night and Day.
Ukiyo-E.
Gallagher. Reading Aloud.
Gardner. That Princeling.
Garrigue. Forest.
Graves. Children of Darkness.
Jealous Man, A.
Griffiths. Shrinking Horizon.
Gunn. Annihilation of Nothing, The.
Down in the cellars, nothing is visible.
Feel of Hands, The.
Vigil of Corpus Christi, The.
Hartley. It is as if at times.
Hemingway. Night comes with soft and drowsy plumes.
Herrick. In the Dark None Dainty.
Hesketh. At Four A.M.
Changing Colour.
I Cannot Look into the Sun.
Prayer for Sun.
Vision.
Hewitt. For R.
Glens of Atrim, The.
Man Fish and Bird.
Monastary, Tourliani, Mykonos.
Hill. Masque of Blackness, The.
Of Coming-into-Being and Passing-Away.
Hopkins. In the staring darkness.
Jarrell. Afterwards.
90 North.
Joseph. Moon.
On the Embankment.
Kinnell. Meditation Among the Tombs.
Middle of the Way.
Knott. Funny Poem.
Kooser. Late Lights in Minnesota.
Kunitz. One summer, like a stone.
Lawrence. After Dark.
At Midnight.
Blueness.
Glory of Darkness.
Grief.
Hark in the Dusk!
In the Dark.

Reach Over.
Young Wife, A.
Levine. Late Moon.
Lewis. Port of Call: Brazil.
Stars seem gilded nipples.
Welsh Night, A.
Liddy. Spring tide swept 'em to the hills.
Talking to Clare as.
Vir V.
Lowry. Dark Path.
Darkness has its compensations, both.
McGrath. In Sickness Like Sleep.
Remembering the Children of Auschwitz.
MacLeish. Night after night I lie like this listening.
MacNeice. Canto XVI: "Young man cannot answer. Is this life?, The."
Merton. Dark Encounter, The.
Responsory, A.
Milton. Samson's Complaint.
Morrison. Bibulous Compound Of.
Dark American Sunset, The.
Nemerov. Advice from the Holy Tomb.
Madrigal: "She is the darkness where I wander."
Of fire and of lust proceeds the world.
Oliver. Lamps, The.
Olson. Sans Name.
Oppen. But at night the park.
Patchen. Rites of Darkness, The.
Raine. Quenching the Red.
Who stands at my door in the storm and rain.
Robinson. Valley of the Shadow, The.
Roethke. Shimmer of Evil, The.
Rolfe. Faces No Longer White.
Pastoral: "Lonely evening crouches, darkens as the hour, The."
Rossetti. O Lucifer, Son of the Morning!
Shadows Today.
Strange voices sing among the planets which.
Sarton. Girl with 'Cello.
Sidney. How Is My Sun.
Silverstein. Afraid of the Dark.
It's Dark In Here.
Joey.
Simic. Forest Birds.
Stafford. Traveling through the Dark.
Stevens. Sun This March, The.
Stevenson. Late, O miller.
Stuart. Love Song.
Tomlinson. Civilities of Lamplight.
Fire in a Dark Landscape.
Fireflies.
Turco. Epistles: "I am writing you."
Warren. Dark Woods.
Monologue at Midnight.
Wilbur. Beacon, The.
Williams, Miller. Being Here.
On the Way Home From Nowhere, New Year's Eve.
Wright, James. Beginning.
Big People, The.
Lights in the Hallway, The.
On Minding One's Own Business.
Revelation, The.
Wroth. Sonnet 19: "Come darkest night, be[e]coming sorrow best."
Sonnet 22: "Like to the Indians, scorched with the sun[ne]."
Sonnet 43: "O dearest eyes the lights, and guids of love."
Zukofsky. Aubade, 1925.
Can a mote of sunlight defeat its purpose.

Darling, Grace Horsley
Wordsworth. Grace Darling.
Darwin, Charles
Dickinson. Why the Thief ingredient accompanies all Sweetness.
Pack. Grandeur.
See also **Evolution.**
Dating
Angelou. Country Lover.
Beatles. Lovely Rita.
Brooks. Independent Man, The.
Bukowski. Parts of an Opera, Parts of a Guitar, Part of Nowhere.
Dove. Planning the Perfect Evening.

Dunbar. Negro Love Song, A.
Gunn. Lofty in the Palais de Danse.
Koch. For there are numerous questions remaining which one must consider.
Of course you must stop her. Say anything: "Hello!" "Good-bye!"
Which cannot be begun, however, until you meet somebody.
Kunitz. Downtown at the Front St. Bi-jo (spelt Bijou).
Lowry. Got a date with a bottle of / gin.
Updike. To an Usherette.
Yau. Discovery of Honey, The.
Daughters
Atwood. Red Shirt, A.
Berrigan. In the 51st State.
Berryman. Holy, & holy. The damned are said to say.
Browning, Elizabeth Barrett. Romaunt of Margret, The.
Bukowski. Sitting in a Sandwich Joint.
Burns. Written under the Picture of the Celebrated Miss Burns.
Byron. Jephtha's Daughter.
Translation from Vittorelli.
Campion. Ad Cambricum.
"Carroll, Lewis." Lyceum, The.
Carruth. Essay on Death.
Coleridge. Old Man of the Alps, The.
Three Graves, The.
Cooper. For My Mother in Her First Illness, from a Window Overlooking Notre Dame.
Creeley. Fire, The.
Sitting Here.
De la Mare. Glance, The.
On the Esplanade.
Owl, The.
Dickey, James. Root-light, or the Lawyer's Daughter.
Dobyns. Faces.
Shaving.
Doolittle. Zeus-Provider.
Dove. Variation on Guilt.
Dunn. Midnight.
Substitute, The.
Walking the Marshland.
"Dylan." Tears of Rage.
Eberhart. Vastness and Indifference of the World, The.
Eliot. Marina.
Emerson. What from this barren being do we reap.
Fletcher. Father's Thought of His Daughter, The.
Fox. Peregrine Falcon.
Gallagher. Borrowed Ones, The.
Gardner. At a Summer Hotel.
Daughter.
Gildner. To My Daughter.
Glück. Morning.
Graves. Frosty Night, A.
Hacker. Iva's Birthday Poem.
Mother.
No better lost than any other woman.
Prayer for my Daughter.
Robber Woman, The.
Towards Autumn.
Hardy. Lorna the Second.
Statue of Liberty, The.
Sunday Morning Tragedy, A.
Herrick. Mr. Hericke his Daughter's Dowrye.
To the Lady Mary Villars, Governesse to the Princesse Henretta.
Hewitt. Cushkib Fair.
For Jean.
Hughes, Langston. Mama and Daughter.
Jarrell. Lost Children, The.
Jong. Dear Marys, Dear Mother, Dear Daughter.
My Daughter Says.
Jonson. On My First Daughter.
Kipling. Merrow Down.
Knight. Circling the Daughter.
Koertge. Coming Out.
For My Daughter.
Orientation Week.
Lawrence. Daughter of the Great Man, The.

Longfellow. Theologian's Tale: Torquemada, The.
Wreck of the *Hesperus*, The.
Lorde. Dear Toni Instead of a Letter of Congratulation..
Lovelace. Paris's Second Judgement.
Lowell. Home after Three Months Away.
MacLeish. White-Haired Girl.
Markson. Johanna.
Matthews. Babahak.
Meinke. Soldiers with Green Leggings.
To a Daughter with Artistic Talent.
Meredith. Doe: A Fragment, The.
Nor had saffron and sapphire and red.
She scarce has a word for Papa.
Nash. Boy's Will is the Wind's Will?, A.
Good Parent's Garden of Vision, A.
In Which the Poet Is Ashamed but Pleased.
Olson. Winds / which blew my daughter, The.
Oppen. Exodus.
My daughter, my daughter, what can I say.
Pack. Clayfeld's Daughter Reveals Her Plans.
Closer.
Plath. I see her in my sleep, my red, terrible girl.
Ransom. Bells for John Whiteside's Daughter.
Rexroth. Living Pearl, A.
Rich. Woman Mourned by Daughters, A.
Rossetti. There Is a Budding Morrow in Midnight.
Versi.
Sexton. Little Girl, My String Bean, My Lovely Woman.
Mother and Daughter.
Pain for a Daughter.
Smith, Stevie. Bereavement.
Darling Daughters.
Feminine Charm.
Human Affection.
Spender. To My Daughter.
Stevens. Sonatina to Hans Christian.
Stevenson. Mother and Daughter.
Stuart. Discovering My Daughter.
Fireworks.
Water's Fine, I'm Fine, The.
Turco. Daughter Moves Out, A.
Updike. Commencement, Pingree School.
Daughter.
Song of Paternal Care, A.
Walcott. Early Pompeian.
Walker. Forgiveness.
My Daughter Is Coming!
Poem at Thirty-nine.
Warren. Colder Fire.
Whittier. Farewell, The: "Gone, gone,—sold and gone."
Wilbur. Song.
Writer, The.
Williams, Charles Kenneth. Fifteen.
Gift, The.
Nickname of Hell, The.
Williams, Miller. Poem for Emily, A.
Williams, William Carlos. Ogre, The.
Youth and Beauty.
Wordsworth. Address to My Infant Daughter, Dora on Being Reminded That She Was a Month Old That Day, September 16.
Three Graves, The.
Yeats. Father and Child.
Prayer for My Daughter, A.

David (Bible)
Berryman. King David Dances.
Bradstreet. David's Lamentation for Saul and Jonathan.
Browning, Robert. Saul.
Byron. Harp the Monarch Minstrel Swept, The.
Cohen. Hallelujah.
Transmission, The.
Davie. Creature David, The.
David Dancing.
De la Mare. Goliath.
Dryden. Malcontents, The.
Glück. Abishag.
Parable, A.
Jarrell. Bronze David of Donatello, The.

Lindsay. In Which Roosevelt Is Compared to Saul.
Lowry. Lines on the Poet Being Informed That His Epic About the Philistines Etc. Needed Cutting.
Psalms. Psalm 18: "I will love thee, O Lord, my strength."
Psalm 132: "Lord, remember David, and all his afflictions."
Rossetti. Thy Servant Will Go and Fight with This Philistine.
Smart. Song to David, A.
Thee will I love, O Lord, my tow'r.
Swinburne. Masque of Queen Bersabe, The.
Thomson. Pastoral Betwixt David, Thirsis, and the Angel Gabriel, upon the Birth of our Saviour, A.
Zukofsky. Nor did the prophet.

Davies, Sir John
Campion. Ad Io. Davisium.
Roethke. Four for Sir John Davies.

Dawn
Angelou. Brief Innocence.
Auden. Dawn.
Dawn.
February Dawn, A.
Beckett. Alba.
Bly. Dawn in Threshing Time.
Browning, Elizabeth Barrett. Sabbath Morning at Sea, A.
Burns. Song, Altered from an Old English One.
Carruth. Arthritic gray snowlight hobbles down the valley westward.
Dawn. Hoar on the grass.
Michigan Water: a Few Riffs before Dawn.
Not night now. Dawn. Six o'clock, a November morning.
Pale dawnlight spooks the mist.
Stepping Backward.
Cooper. Morning on the St. John's.
Crashaw. Beginning of Heliodorus, The.
Cummings. Dawn / and now.begins / feeling.
Lady of Silence.
De la Mare. Before Dawn.
Break of Morning.
Dawn.
Forests.
Glimpse, The.
Stranger, The.
Dickinson. Not knowing when the Dawn will come.
Dunbar. Dawn.
"Dylan." Night passes fast for me now, The.
Eberhart. Four Lakes' Days.
Hoot Owls.
Line of Verse of Yeats, A.
Parker River, The.
Thrush Song at Dawn.
Emerson. Coin the daydawn into lines.
Ferlinghetti. Upon Reflection.
Fletcher. Midsummer Dawn at Sea.
Gardner. Autumn: Early Morning.
Ginsberg. Fourth Floor, Dawn, Up All Night Writing Letters.
Glück. Aubade: "Today above the gull's call."
Graves. Return of the Goddess [Artemis].
Griffiths. Ciudadela, 1991.
Hardy. Dawn after the Dance, The.
Herrick. To Anthea Lying in Bed.
To Julia, in Her Dawn, or Day-breake.
Hesketh. Brain Child.
Hewitt. Little House, The.
Skypiece.
Splendid Dawn, The.
Hoffman. Aubade: "Weaned from moon."
Hopkins. Dawn that the pebbly low-down East.
In more precision now of light and dark.
Housman. Fairies break their dances, The.
Reveille.
Hughes, Langston. Black Maria.
Hugo. Last Words from Maratea.
Jeffers. Dawn.
Johnson. Aurora Est Musis Amica.
Keats. Imitation of Spenser.

Kipling. Hymn of the Triumphant Airman.
Last Ode, The.
Larkin. Quite Forsaken.
Winter Dawn.
Lawrence. Making Light of It.
New Day, A.
Words.
Lewis. Dawn on the East Coast.
Lindsay. In the Beginning.
Lowry. Jokes on the Poop.
Lapis dawn is gleaming, A.
Mad Poem: Wind Blowing Through the Shack.
Sunrise.
McAuley. Behind a brightening cloud.
McGrath. Dawn Song.
MacLeish. Midsummer Dawn.
Melville. Clover.
Meredith. By Morning Twilight.
Full loud & fresh crows Chaunticlere!
Now the youth footed swift to the dawn.
Pastoral 2: "Yon upland slope which hides the sun."
Sunrise.
Millay. Autumn Daybreak.
Dawn.
Miller. Dawn.
Start Up the Music Again.
Winter Dawn.
Owen. Fragment: "Cramped in that funnelled hole, they watched the dawn."
Prince. He Bathes in the Morning.
Rolfe. Dawn Song.
Rossetti. "Kookoorookoo! kookoorookoo!" / Crows the cock before the morn.
Rukeyser. Chapultepec Park / I.
During the journey there come moments of waking.
Sandburg. Alone and Not Alone.
Daybreak.
First Sonata for Karlen Paula.
Nightsong.
Sarah's Letter to Peter.
She Opens the Barn Door Every Morning.
Since death is there in the light of the sun, in the song of the.
Themes in Contrast.
Schwartz. Poem: "Remember midsummer: the fragrance of box, of white roses."
This Is a Poem I Wrote at Night, Before the Dawn.
Sidney. *Aurora*, now thou show'st thy blushing light.
Sonnet 99: "When far-spent night persuades each mortal eye."
Smith, Charlotte. To the Morning Star.
Written Near the Sea.
To the Sun.
Smith, Stevie. Aubade: "My dove, my doe."
Snyder. Each dawn is clear.
Stevens. Brave Man, The.
Stevenson. Song at Dawn.
Stuart. Percussion.
Sutter. Daybreak.
Thomas. Light Breaks Where No Sun Shines.
Tomlinson. At Dawn.
Cloud Change.
Last of Night, The.
Of Beginning Light.
Warren. Dawn.
Williams, Charles Kenneth. Dawn.
Williams, William Carlos. Chinese Nightingale.
Dawn.
Daybreak.
Wordsworth. Ode Composed on May Morning.
While Beams of Orient Light Shoot Wide and High.
Wright, James. Dawn brings with it, The.
Little Girl on Her Way to School, A.
Yeats. Dawn, The.
Zukofsky. Alba (1952).

See also **Morning; Sunrise.**

Day
Angelou. Plagued Journey, A.

Auden. On the frontier at dawn getting down.
  Skyreholme Mill.
Berrigan. Peace.
Berryman. Meditation.
Browning, Elizabeth Barrett. Island, An.
Campion. Tell me, gentle howre of night.
Carroll, Jim. Burning of Bustin's Island, The.
"Carroll, Lewis." Air is bright with hues of
  light, The.
Clark. Magic Arrival No. 7.
Creeley. Every Day.
  For Benny and Sabina.
  Hi There!
Cummings. Hours rise up putting off stars and
  it is, The.
  Out of midsummer's blazing most not night.
  Put off your faces,Death:for day is over.
De la Mare. Disguise, The.
Dickinson. Day came slow—till Five o'clock,
  The.
  Some say goodnight—at night.
Dobyns. Morning Song.
Doolittle. Mid-day.
Dunbar. Day.
  Drowsy Day, A.
  Warm Day in Winter, A.
Dunn. Halves.
  Here and There.
Eberhart. Autumnal.
  Bells of a Chinese Temple, The.
  By the Stream.
  Clam Diggers and Diggers of Sea Worms,
    The.
  Commitment, A.
  Four Exposures.
  Four Lakes' Days.
  Off Spectacle Island.
  Soldier Rejects His Times Addressing His
    Contemporaries, A.
Emerson. Always day & night.
  Days.
  Days pass over me, The.
  If bright the sun, he tarries.
  My days roll by me like a train of dreams.
  What flowing central forces, say.
Ford. Day has twenty-four hours, The.
Graves. Children of Darkness.
Hartley. Hollander's Animal Faith.
  To H.C.
Hesketh. Buttercup Children, The.
  Days.
  Love's Advocate.
  Winter Daffodils.
Hewitt. Winter Day.
Hopkins. Windy Day in Summer, A.
Keats. To My Brother George.
Kinnell. Middle of the Way.
Kipling. Hymn of the Triumphant Airman.
  Morning Song in the Jungle.
Larkin. Days.
  Lift through the Breaking Day.
  Long Lion Days.
Lawrence. Fall of Day, The.
Lowry. Heat Wave.
  Hostage.
  How overjoyed I am to get your letter.
  Mad Poem: Wind Blowing Through the Shack.
  Those were the days / And never again.
  With Midsummer Devotion from All the Little
    Animals to Their Beloved Harteebeeste.
MacNeice. Canto VI: "Everydayness is good;
  particular-dayness."
McNeill. Winter Day (Coal Country).
Merton. Song, A: "When it was day, we heard
  the panes of windows."
Miller. For Judy.
  Some days / the sunlight has a clarity.
Morgan. Fresh June morning, A.
Nash. Midsummer's Daymare.
Neruda. First Winter.
  Inside.
Olson. Dragon-Fly, The.
  Going from Battle to Battle.
  Seven Songs, The.
Rossetti. Awake, Thou That Sleepest.
  Day Is At Hand, The.
  Days are clear, / Day after day, The.

Easter Even.
Is the Moon Tired?
"Kookoorookoo! kookoorookoo!" / Crows the
  cock before the morn.
Let Them Rejoice in Their Beds.
Oh knell of a passing time, / Will it never
  cease to chime?
Praying Always.
Smile and a Sigh, A.
Summer nights are short, / Where northern
  days are long, The.
Sandburg. Clark Street Bridge.
  Daybreak.
  Harmonica Humdrums.
  Skyscraper.
Schuyler. White Boat, Blue Boat.
Shapiro. Shame.
Smith, Stevie. Aubade: "My dove, my doe."
Stevens. Brave Man, The.
  Prejudice against the Past, The.
Stevenson. Bed in Summer.
  Moon, The.
  Night and Day.
  Song at Dawn.
Whittier. Day's Journey, A.
Wilbur. Death of a Toad, The.
  Sun and Air.
  Sunlight Is Imagination.
Williams, William Carlos. Advent of Today.
  Full Moon.
Wordsworth. Composed on a May Morning.
Zukofsky. Que J'ay Dit Devant.

Daydreams

Ashbery. Instruction Manual, The.
  Mixed Feelings.
Berry. Thought of Something Else, The.
Bishop. End of March, The.
Bukowski. Eaten by Butterflies.
  Interviewed by a Guggenheim Recipient.
  Parts of an Opera, Parts of a Guitar, Part of
    Nowhere.
  Thermometer.
Clough. Come pleasant thoughts; sweet
  thoughts, at will.
Coleridge. Day-Dream, A ("My eyes make
  pictures, when they are shut").
  Day-Dream, The ("If thou wert here, these
    tears were tears of light").
Dunbar. By the Stream.
Gildner. Porch, The.
Hall. Days, The.
  In the Kitchen of the Old House.
Kipling. Alnaschar and the Oxen.
"MacDiarmid." Gin but the oor 'ud chop and
  set me free.
  Harry Semen.
  Here in the hauf licht hoo I've grown!
Nash. Spring Comes to Murray Hill.
Nathan. Table Talk.
Rexroth. Between Two Wars.
  Thin Edge of Your Pride, The.
Sarton. Nostalgia for India.
  We Sat Smoking at a Table..
Stevenson. Mill-House, The.
Young. Afternoon After, The.
  Loneliness.

See also **Dreams and Dreaming.**

De Hooch, Pieter. *see* **Hooch, Pieter de.**

Deafness

"Carroll, Lewis." Acrostic: "Are you deaf,
  Father William?"
  Matilda Jane.
Davie. Reflections on Deafness.
Hughes, Ted. Deaf School.
Kooser. Boarding House.
  Man with the Hearing Aid, The.
Lowell. Marcus Cato 234–149 B.C.
Meinke. Growing Deaf.
Swift. On His Own Deafness.
Wright, James. Mutterings over the Crib of a
  Deaf Child.

Dean, James

O'Hara. For James Dean.

Death and the Dead

Ammons. Merchandise.
  Songlet.
Angelou. Elegy: "I lay down in my grave."

Gamut, The.
Lesson, The.
Mourning Grace.
Arnold. How changed is here each spot man
  makes or fills!
  Memorial Verses.
  Requiescat.
  Thyrsis.
  Turn we next to the dead.
  What though the music of thy rustic flute.
Ashbery. Flowering Death.
  Saying It to Keep It from Happening.
Atwood. Another Elegy.
  Deaths of the Other Children, The.
  Dufferin, Simcoe, Grey.
  Machine. Gun. Nest.
  Settlers, The.
  This Is a Photograph of Me.
Auden. After the Burial.
  Amor Vincit Omnia.
  As the poets have mournfully sung.
  Carter's Funeral, The.
  Clocks cannot tell our time of day.
  Colonel to be shot at dawn, The.
  Death's Echo.
  Elegy: "Wagtail splutters in the stream, A."
  Elegy: "Why was it that you gave us no
    warning."
  Friday's Child.
  Humpty Dumpty.
  In a Country Churchyard.
  In Memoriam L. K.-A. 1950–1952.
  Maria Hat Geholfen.
  Miner's Wife, The.
  No, not from this life, not from this life is
    any.
  Nones.
  November at Weybourne.
  O What Is That Sound [Which So Thrills the
    Ear].
  Often the man, alone shut, shall consider.
  Old People's Home.
  On a Greek Tomb Relief.
  Recitative by Death.
  Rookhope (Weardale, Summer 1922).
  Since the Autumn day.
  Sonnet: "April is here but when will Easter
    come?"
  Stop all the clocks, cut off the telephone.
Beatles. I Am the Walrus.
Beckett. Alba.
  I would like my love to die.
  Je voudrais que mon amour meure.
  Jusque dans la caverne ciel et sol.
  La nuit venue où l'âme allait.
  Mort de A.D.
  Morte parmi.
  Plus loin un autre commémore.
  Sleep till death.
  Song: "Age is when to a man."
  Trouble with tragedy is the fuss it makes, The.
Berg. At the Door.
  Dreaming with a Friend.
  Holes, The.
  Homage to the Afterlife.
  In Death I Know Well Enough All Things
    End in Emptiness.
  Lament: "My mother wants to be burned, she
    told me."
  Remembering and Forgetting.
  Uncle Will, the Gardener.
  What I Wanted to Say.
Berrigan. Dear Margie, hello. It is 5:15 a.m.
  How strange to be gone in a minute / Bearden
    is dead Gallup is dead Margie is dead.
  I Heard Brew Moore Say, One Day.
  Last Poem.
  People Who Died.
Berry. Any man's death could end the story.
  As the vision of labor grows.
  At last, completed in his rest.
  Beneath this stone a Berry is planted.
  Beware of the machinery of longevity. When a
    man's life is over.
  Boone.
  But do not let your ignorance.
  Canticle.

Clear Days, The.
Cold Pane, The.
Dark with power.
Dear relatives and friends, when my last breath.
Discipline, A.
Elegy: "All day our eyes could find no resting place."
Farmer among the Tombs, The.
Fern, The.
Finally, he brought me to a hill.
For the Hog Killing.
Freedom of Loving, The.
Grandmother, The.
He Is in the Habit of the World.
He Takes His Time.
I have come to the end.
I saw one standing aside, alone.
In Memory: Stuart Egnal.
In the predicament of other lives.
Man Walking and Singing, A.
Marriage, an Elegy, A.
Meadow, The.
Meeting, A.
Morning's News, The.
My life's wave is at its crest.
My mind was overborne with questions.
Necessity of Faith, The.
Old Man Is Older in History than in Time, The.
Poem for J.
Poem: "Willing to die, / you give up."
Praise, A.
Requiem: "We will see no more."
Ripening.
Slip, The.
So treat me, even dead.
Sparrow.
Sycamore, The.
Though He Can't Know Death, He Must Study Dying.
Three Elegiac Poems.
To be at home on its native ground.
We came then to his time of pain.
We stood on a height.
What I am learning to give you is my death.
Wheel, The.
When I think of death I see.
Wish to Be Generous, The.
World's one song is passing, The.
Berryman. Dante's Tomb.
Epilogue: "He died in December. He must descend."
Grandfather, sleepless in a room upstairs.
Handshake, the Entrance, The.
Message.
Poet's Final Instructions, The.
Possessed, The.
Sanctuary.
Scots Poem.
Whether There Is Sorrow in the Demons.
You come blonde visiting through the black air.
Betjeman. Aldershot Crematorium.
Before the Anæsthetic; or, A Real Fright.
Child Ill, A.
City.
Commander, The.
Cottage Hospital, The.
Death in Leamington.
Dorset.
Five O'Clock Shadow.
For Nineteenth-Century Burials.
Fruit.
Good-bye.
Hon. Sec., The.
House of Rest.
I.M. Walter Ramsden, Ob. March 26, 1947, Pembroke College, Oxford.
In Memory of George Whitby, Architect.
In Willesden Churchyard.
Inevitable.
Last Laugh, The.
Loneliness.
Monody on the Death of a Platonist Bank Clerk.
Mortality.

Old Friends.
On a Portrait of a Deaf Man.
Variation on a Theme by T. W. Rolleston.
Bishop. Cootchie.
First Death in Nova Scotia.
Man-Moth, The.
Table, The.
Thy senses are too different to please me.
Whom are you carrying.
Blake. And his legs carried it like a long fork.
Another [Epitaph]: "Here lies John Trot, the Friend of all mankind."
Another [Epitaph]: "I was buried near this Dike."
Epitaph, An: "Come knock your heads against this stone."
Sick Rose, The.
Bly. Ant Mansion, The.
Christmas Eve Service at Midnight at St. Michael's.
Hawk, The.
In Mourning for Betrayal.
Bogan. Exhortation.
From Heine.
My Voice Not Being Proud.
Sonnet: "Dark, underground, is furnished with the bone."
Boyle. Branded for Slaughter.
Christmas Carol for Emanuel Carnevali, A.
Complaint for Mary and Marcel, A.
Dedicated to Robert McAlmon.
Evening Grass, The.
Funeral in Hungary.
Letter to Archibald Craig, A.
Letter to Francis Picabia, A.
O This Is Not Spring.
On the Death of My Student, the Poet Serafin.
Only Bird That Sang, The.
Poem for Samuel Beckett, A.
Poem for the Students of Greece, A.
World Tour.
Bradstreet. Before the Birth of One of Her Children.
Epitaph on my Dear and Ever Honored Mother Mrs. Dorothy Dudley.
In Memory of My Dear Grandchild Anne Bradstreet.
Of the Four Ages of Man.
To the Memory of My Dear and Ever Honored Father Thomas Dudley Esq. Who Deceased July 31, 1653, and of His Age 77.
To the Memory of My Dear Daughter in Law, Mrs. Mercy Bradstreet.
Upon a Fit of Sickness, Anno 1632.
Brontë. A.S. to G.S.
At such a time, in such a spot.
Battle had passed from the height, The.
Come, walk with me.
Death.
Death Of A.G.A., The.
Deep, deep down in the silent grave.
Enough of Thought, Philosopher.
E.W. to A.G.A.
Far, far away is mirth withdrawn.
From a D— W— in the N. C.
H.A. and A.S.
Heaven's glory shone where he was laid.
Here, with my knee upon thy stone.
How Clear She Shines!
I gazed within thine earnest eyes.
I saw thee, child, one summer's day.
I see around me tombstones grey.
I.M. to I.G.
It is too late to call thee now.
Lines by Claudia.
Long Neglect Has Worn Away.
Methinks this heart should rest awhile.
Night of storms has passed, The.
Night was dark, yet winter breathed, The.
No coward soul is mine.
None but one beheld him dying.
Not many years but long enough to see.
O come again; what chains withhold.
O mother, I am not regretting.
O wander not so far away!
R. Alcona to J. Brenzaida.
Remembrance.

Rosina.
Shed no tears o'er that tomb.
Sleep brings no joy to me.
Song: "King Julius left the south country."
Song: "Linnet in the rocky dells, The."
Song: "O between distress and pleasure."
Stanzas: "I'll not weep that thou art going to leave me."
Stanzas to———.
Start not! upon the minister wall.
There shines the moon, at noon of night.
There swept adown that dreary glen.
Thousand sounds of happiness, A.
'Tis moonlight, summer moonlight.
To A.S., 1830.
Warning and Reply.
Why ask to know the date—the clime?
Wind was rough which tore, The.
Yes, holy be thy resting place.
Brooks. In Honor of David Anderson Brooks, My Father.
Last Quatrain of the Ballad of Emmett Till, The.
Mentors.
Of De Witt Williams on His Way to Lincoln Cemetery.
Rites for Cousin Vit, The.
Southeast Corner.
White Troops Had Their Orders but the Negroes Looked Like Men.
Browning, Elizabeth Barrett. Bacchus and Ariadne.
Dead Rose, A.
Died..
Felicia Hemans.
Fourfold Aspect, The.
Hugh Stuart Boyd [His Death, 1848].
L. E. L.'s Last Question.
Lament for Adonis.
Life and Love.
Mother and Poet.
Sleep, The.
Sonnet: "Unlike are we, unlike, O princely heart!"
Sounds.
Thought for a Lonely Death-Bed, A.
Browning, Robert. After.
Arcades Ambo.
Dance of Death, The.
Doctor———.
Evelyn Hope.
Gold Hair.
Lines on Swinburne.
Lines to the Memory of James Dow.
Lost Leader, The.
May and Death.
Prospice.
Bukowski. Bedpans.
Beds, Toilets, You and Me—.
Conversation in a Cheap Room.
Conversation on Morality, Eternity and Copulation, A.
Death Wants More Death.
Doom and Siesta Time.
Eat.
Eulogy to a Hell of a Dame—.
Everything.
Farewell Thing While Breathing, A.
Freedom: The Unmolested Eagle of Myself.
Gift, The.
Goodbye.
I Wait in the White Rain.
I Write This Upon the Last Drink's Hammer.
Japanese Note.
Kind of Lecture on a Dull Day When There Isn't Even a Fly Around to Kill, A.
Meek Have Inherited, The.
Naked at 92 Degrees.
Nothing Subtle.
Old Man, Dead in a Room.
On Seeing an Old Civil War Painting with My Love.
One for the Old Boy.
Our Curious Position.
Poem for Liz.
Practice.
Practice.

Result.
Rose, Rose.
Sky Sign.
Sleep.
Suggestion for an Arrangement.
There Once Was a Woman Who Put Her
Head into an Oven.
Truce.
Up Your Yellow River.
What They Want.
When I Think of Myself Dead.
Worst and the Best, The.
You Smoke a Cigarette.
Bunting. Amru'l Qais and Labīd and Akhtal
and blind A'sha and Qais.
Farewell ye sequent graces.
Faridun watched the road.
He whom we anatomized.
I'm the worse for drink again, it's.
Let his days be few and let.
Man's life so little worth.
Many well-known people have been packed
away in cemeteries.
Night is hard by. I am vexed and bothered by
sleep.
Poor soul! Softy, whisperer.
Song for Rustam, A.
Stuck in the mud they are saying: "We were
sad."
These tracings from a world that's dead.
Under the olive trees.
You can't grip years, Postume.
Burns. Address, to the Shade of Thomson, on
Crowning His Bust, at *Ednam, Roxburgh-*
shire, with Bays.
Another [Epigram on Said Occasion].
Bard's Epitaph, A.
Death and Doctor Hornbook [A True Story].
Elegy on Captain Matthew Henderson [*or*
Capt. M——— H———] [*A Gentleman*
Who Held the Patent for His Honours
Immediately from Almighty God!].
Elegy on Mister William Cruikshank A. M.
Elegy on the Death of Robert Ruisseaux.
Epigram on Said Occasion.
Epitaph Extempore, on a Person Nicknamed
the Marquis, Who Desired Burns to Write
One on Him.
Epitaph for H——— L———, Esq., of L———
—.
Epitaph for J. H. Writer in Ayr.
Epitaph for William Nicol.
Epitaph. Here Lies Robert Fergusson, Poet.
Epitaph: "Lo worms enjoy the seat of bliss."
Epitaph on D——— C———.
Epitaph on Holy Willie.
Epitaph on J-hn B-shby.
Epitaph on John Dove [Innkeeper, Mauchline].
Epitaph on Mr. Burton.
Epitaph on My Own Friend, and My Father's
Friend, Wm Muir in Tarbolton Miln.
Epitaph on R. Muir.
Extempore—on Some Commemorations of
Thomson.
For G. H. Esq.
For R. A. Esq.
For the Author's Father.
Fragment, Which Was Meant for the
Beginning of an Elegy on the Late Miss
Burnet of Monboddo, A.
Highland Mary.
Ill-fated Genius! Heaven-taught Fergusson.
Lament for James, Earl of Glencairn.
Lines Addressed to Mr. John Ranken.
Lines: "He who of R--k-n sang, lies stiff and
dead."
Lines Sent to Sir John Whiteford, of
Whiteford, Bart. with the Foregoing Poem.
Man Was Made to Mourn, a Dirge.
McPherson's Farewell.
Merry Hae I Been Teethin a Heckle.
Monody on Maria.
On a Celebrated Ruling Elder.
On a Noisy Polemic.
On a Schoolmaster in Cleish Parish, Fifeshire.
On an Innkeeper in Tarbolton.
On Captn. L———lles.

On Fergusson.
On Gabriel Richardson.
On Jas. Grieve, Laird of Boghead, Tarbolton.
On J-hn M-r-ne, Laird of L-gg-n.
On Reading, in a Newspaper, the Death of
J——— McL———, Esq. Brother to a
Young Lady, a Particular Friend of the
Author's.
On Robert Riddel.
On Tam the Chapman.
On the Death of Sir J. Hunter Blair.
On the Death of the Late Lord President
Dundas.
On W. R———, Esq.
On Wee Johnie.
On William Graham [*or* W——— Gr-h-m],
Esq., of Mossknowe [*or* M-sskn-w].
Orananaoig, or, the Song of Death.
Prayer, in the Prospect of Death, A.
Say, sages, what's the charm on earth.
Sketch for an Elegy.
Song, A: "Thou lingering Star with lessening
ray."
Sonnet on the Death of Robert Riddel, Esq. *of*
Glen Riddel, April 1794.
Stanzas on the Same Occasion [in the Prospect
of Death].
Tam Samson's Elegy.
Where Helen Lies.
Byron. Adieu, The.
And Thou Art Dead, as Young and Fair.
Answer to a Beautiful Poem, Entitled "The
Common Lot."
Aristomenes.
Bright Be the Place of Thy Soul!
Churchill's Grave.
Destruction of Sennacherib, The.
Duel, The.
Elegiac Stanzas on the Death of Sir Peter
Parker, Bart.
Epigram on an Old Lady Who Had Some
Curious Notions Respecting the Soul.
Epitaph for Joseph Blacket.
Epitaph on John Adams, of Southwell.
Euthanasia.
Fragment, A: "Could I remount the river of
my years."
If Sometimes in the Haunts of Men.
If That High World.
Inscription on the Monument of a
Newfoundland Dog.
Lines Written beneath an Elm in the
Churchyard of Harrow.
Love and Death.
Monody on the Death of the Right Hon. R. B.
Sheridan.
Ode from the French.
Ode to a Lady Whose Lover Was Killed by a
Ball, Which at the Same Time Shivered a
Portrait next His Heart.
Oh factious viper! whose envenom'd tooth.
Oh! Snatch'd Away in Beauty's Bloom.
On the Death of a Young Lady.
One Struggle More, and I Am Free.
Stanzas: "I heard thy fate without a tear."
Thoughts for a Speech of Lucifer, in the
Tragedy of "Cain."
To Caroline ("Oh when shall the grave hide
for ever my sorrow?").
To Thyrza.
Translation from Vittorelli.
Youth, Nature, and Relenting Jove.
Campion. De obitu Phil. Sydnaei equitis aurati
generosissimi.
Elegie upon the Untimely Death of Prince
Henry, An.
In Morachum.
In obitum Gual. Devoreux fratris clariss.
Comitus Essexiae.
In Obitum Hen. Mag. Brit. Principis.
Lamentation, A.
Leave prolonging thy distresse.
To the Most High and Mighty Prince Charles.
To the Most Illustrious and Mighty Fredericke
the Fift, Count Palatine of the Rhein.
To the Most Princely and Vertuous the Lady

Elizabeth.
To The Most Sacred King James.
Umbra.
When Thou Must Home.
Carew. Another [Epitaph on Lady Mary
Villiers] ("This little vault, this narrow
room").
Another [On the Duke of Buckingham].
Can we not force from widowed poetry.
Elegy on the La: Pen: Sent to My Mistress
Out of France, An.
For a Picture Where a Queen Laments over
the Tomb of a Slain Knight.
Grief Engrossed.
Maria Wentworth.
On the Duke of Buckingham.
To the Countess of Anglesey.
Upon the Sickness of E.S.
Carroll, Jim. Calm Under Fire.
Chelsea May.
Compassion.
Dead Salamander's Song.
For Elizabeth.
Found it once more in the ocean's rush.
I am trying to abide by the clues.
Into a swamp this heart is flying.
Light rising into her features where.
Loft, The.
Love Story.
M. Verdoux, The Wife Killer.
Maybe I'm Amazed.
Some detectives in worn suits slide at my
door.
Traffic.
Window in Cherry Valley, A.
Winter's Age.
"Carroll, Lewis." Acrostic: Dreams, that elude
the Waker's frenzied grasp—.
Acrostic: Is all our Life, then, but a dream.
As It Fell upon a Day.
Dreamland.
Empress of Art, for thee I twine.
Sailor's Wife, The.
Stolen Waters.
Three Sunsets.
Valley of the Shadow of Death, The.
Willow-Tree, The.
Carruth. Algeria.
Anent Socrates, or Somebody.
Another hard, hard morning with a hard snow.
Bearer, The.
Cold hunger tripped her but her years.
Crucifixion.
Death, he thinks. In fact he thought it
every day.
Essay on Death.
Essay on Marriage.
Études de Plusiers Paysages de l'Âme.
Fat Lady, The.
Fragment: "Who can know more deeply than I
your loneliness there?"
French Hill.
Ho-Hum Again.
Homecoming.
In deep winter the sea roams.
Mother.
No Supervening Thought of Grace.
None.
Not Transhistorical Death, or at Least Not
Quite.
Persimmon wind, lost names raining. Thwart.
Questions.
Ravine, The.
Sigh, you seven seas.
Song: So Often, So Long I Have Thought.
Song: So Why Does This Dead Carnation.
Sonnet: "Thy sting sufficeth, Death. If
Heidegger first."
Tanck's Song About Dying Young.
There was this girl 18, 19 and slight.
'Tis a fine deceit.
Catullus. Carmen 52: "Drop dead, Catullus, lie
right down & die."
Carmen 68: "Borne down by bitter
misfortune."
Carmen 96: "If, Calvus, effects of grief."
Carmen 101: "Journeying over many seas and

through many countries."
Sunne may set and rise, The.
Ceravolo. Autumn-Time, Wind and the Planet
  Pluto.
Contrast.
Chaucer. This olde man gan looke in his
  visage.
Ciardi. Alec.
Apartment with a View, A.
Aunt Mary.
Epilogue: The Burial of the Last Elder.
Epithalamium at St. Michael's Cemetary.
Graph, The.
Highest Place in Town, The.
Invasion of Sleep Walkers, The.
It Took Four Flowerboats to Convoy My
  Father's Black.
Minus One.
One Dull Thing You Did Was to Die,
  Fletcher, The.
Sea Burial.
Thousandth Poem for Dylan Thomas, The.
Two Saints.
Was a Man.
What *Was* Her Name.
Clark. Diary of Desert War.
In the Dark Mountains, Brilliant.
Nodding.
Clough. Epi-Strauss-ium.
That children in their loveliness should die.
Cohen. Commentary—Final Examination.
Commentary—She Has Given Me the Bullet.
Final Examination.
If It Be Your Will.
Roshi Again.
She Has Given Me the Bullet.
Song for My Assassin.
This Wretch.
Who by Fire?
Your Death.
Coleridge. Death Wish, A.
Elegy Imitated from One of Akenside's Blank-
  Verse Inscriptions.
Epitaph: "Stop, Christian passer-by!—Stop,
  child of God."
Epitaphium Testamentarium.
Israel's Lament.
Koskiusko.
Life in Death.
Lines on a Friend.
Monody on the Death of Chatterton.
Ne Plus Ultra.
Old Man of the Alps, The.
On an Insignificant.
On Receiving an Account That His Only
  Sister's Death Was Inevitable.
On Seeing a Youth Affectionately Welcomed
  by a Sister.
Separation from Asra.
W. H. *Eheu!*
Cooper. All is closed in.
Breslau, November-December 1917.
Faithful, The.
In the House of the Dying.
Nightmare of the Suburbs, A.
Roman Dream.
Yesterday a letter / spoke of our parting.
Cowper. Epitaph on a Hare.
Epitaph on Dr. Johnson.
Epitaphium Alterum.
Inscription for the Tomb of Hamilton.
Ode on the Death of a Lady.
On a Good Man.
On Invalids.
On the Death of Damon.
On the Death of Russell.
On the Death of the Vice-Chancellor, a
  Physician.
On the Shortness of Life.
Crabbe. Ancient Mansion, The.
Ellen.
Crane. Broken Tower, The.
Circumstance, The.
Her Eyes Had..
Paraphrase.
Possessions.
Praise for an Urn.

Crashaw. Another on [Mr. Herrys].
Death's Lecture.
Elegie on the Death of Doctor Porter, An.
Elegy upon the Death of Mr. Stanninow
  Fellow of Queenes Colledge.
Epitaph upon a Young Married Couple, An.
John 15; Upon Our Lords Last Comfortable
  Discourse with His Disciples.
Matthew 28; Come See the Place where the
  Lord Lay.
[Mr. Herrys,] His Epitaph.
Recommendation, The.
Upon the Death of a Freind.
Upon the Death of a Gentleman.
Upon the Death of Mister Herrys.
Upon the Death of the Most Desired Mister
  Herrys.
Creeley. After Lorca.
And.
Days and Days.
Death of Venus, The.
Dying.
Festival, The.
For My Mother: Genevieve Jules Creeley.
Heroes.
Message, The.
Moment.
Rhythm, The.
Swinging Down Central.
That day / in an oak tree—.
World, The.
Cullen. Brown Girl Dead, A.
Death to the Poor.
Epilogue: "Lily, being white not red, The."
Foolish Heart, The.
For an Anarchist.
For an Evolutionist and His Opponent.
In Spite of Death.
Only the Polished Skeleton.
Poet, The.
Proud Heart, The.
Requiescam.
Sonnet Dialogue.
Threnody for a Brown Girl.
Two Thoughts of Death.
Wise, The.
Cummings. 2.14: "Ah, Postumus, fleet-footed
  are the years!"
After Seeing French Funeral.
Am was. are leaves few this. is these a or.
Annie died the other day.
Buffalo Bill's / defunct / who used to.
But the other / day i was passing a certain.
Come nothing to my comparable soul.
Connotation of infinity, A.
Death is more than.
Death(having lost)put on his universe.
Death's Chimney.
Dedicated to Dear Nana Clarke.
Don't get me wrong oblivion.
Dying is fine)but Death.
First president to be loved by his, The.
Gee i like to think of dead it means nearer
  because deeper firmer.
Glory is fallen out of, The.
Great, A / man / is / gone.
Handsome and clever and he went cruising.
Hate blows a bubble of despair into.
Here is little Effie's Head.
Hips lOOsest OOping shoulders blonde&
  pastoral hair,strong.
How dark and single,where he ends,the earth.
I am going to utter a tree,Noboby.
I like / to think that on.
If i should sleep with a lady called death.
It is funny,you will be dead some day.
It)It will it.
It's just like a coffin's.
Let us suspect,chérie,this not very big.
Lively and loathesome moe's respectably dead.
Memory believes / fragrance of a
  town(whose).
My love is building a building.
Nobody loses all the time.
Nor woman / (just as it be).
Now that fierce few.
Now two old ladies sit peacefully knitting.

Of all things under our.
Only as what(out of a flophouse)floats.
Put off your faces,Death:for day is over.
Quick i the death of thing.
Rain or hail / sam done.
S.F.D.
Since feeling is first.
Softly from its still lair in Plympton Street.
Somebody knew Lincoln somebody Xerxes.
Suppose / Life is an old man carrying flowers
  on his head.
That which we who're alive in spite of
  mirrors.
The(/ Wistfully / dead seem generous)don't.
This is a rubbish of human rind.
This is the garden:clours come and go.
Whatever's merely wilful, / and not
  miraculous.
When god lets my body be.
When life is quite through with.
When thou art dead,dead,and far from the
  splendid sin.
When unto nights of autumn do complain.
Who before dying demands not rebirth.
Who's most afraid of death?thou.
You no / tice / nobod / y wants.
Young / man sitting, The.
Davie. After an Accident.
Anglican Lady, An.
Ars Poetica.
Artifex in Extremis.
Death in the West, A.
Death of a Painter.
Death of a Voice.
Departed, The.
G. M. B.
Harrow, The.
Intervals in a Busy Life.
Measured Tread, A.
Mother.
Nineteen-Seventeen.
Penelope.
Rutland.
Three Beyond.
Widowers.
De la Mare. Age.
Anatomy.
Assignation, The.
Autumn.
Away.
Betrayal.
Bottle, The.
Bridge, The.
Bright Life.
Cage, The.
Death-Dream, The.
Defeat.
Epitaph, An: "Here lies a most beatiful lady."
Even In The Grave.
Faithless.
Familiar, The.
Fare Well.
Flotsam.
Goliath.
Good Company.
Here Sleeps.
Hospital.
How Sleep the Brave.
Imogen.
Isaac Meek.
Juliet's Nurse.
Keep Innocency.
Keys of Morning, The.
Life.
Marionettes, The.
Mistress Fell.
Motley.
Music Unheard.
Peace.
Reconciliation.
Remembrance.
Revenant, The.
Sallie's Musical Box.
Satire, The.
Shadow.
Shadow.
Snowflake, The.

Sorcery.
Taciturn, The.
Thorn, The.
To E. T.: 1917.
Truce.
Virtue.
Waiting.
What?
Where?
Where Is Thy Victory?
Dickey, James. Attempted Departure.
Breath.
Deborah as Scion.
Eagle's Mile, The.
Farmers.
For Robert Bhain Campbell.
Gila Bend.
Hospital Window, The.
Island, The.
Poem: "For having left the birds that left me."
Poem: "O death, so dear to me."
Sled Burial, Dream Ceremony.
Sleepers.
String, The.
To Be Done in Winter.
Tomb Stone.
Vessels.
Via appia.
Dickey, William. Elegy Before the Time.
G.F. Died 1954, Aged 27.
His Death from Cancer.
In The Dreaming.
Part Song, With Concert of Recorders.
Dickinson. Absence disembodies—so does Death.
Admirations—and Contempts—of time, The.
Advance is Life's condition.
Afraid! Of whom am I afraid?
After a brief unconsciousness.
After a hundred years.
After the great intrusion of Death.
Ah! dainty—dainty Death!
All but Death can be Adjusted.
As by the dead we love to sit.
As from the earth the light Balloon.
Back from the cordial Grave I drag thee.
Because I could not stop for Death.
Believing that we are to have no Face.
Bereavement in their death to feel.
Brain—is wider than the Sky, The.
Brain, within its Groove, The.
Bustle in a House, The.
By a departing light.
Color, Caste, Denomination.
Could I visit the Beds.
Dear friend, can you walk.
Death blow is a Life blow to Some, A.
Death cannot plunder half so fast.
Death goes far around.
Death has only to touch a trifle.
Death is a Dialogue between.
Death is like the insect.
Death is perhaps an intimate friend.
Death is potential to that Man.
Death is the supple Suitor.
Death leaves Us homesick, who behind.
Death obtains the Rose.
Death sets a Thing significant.
Death warrants are supposed to be.
Did she suffer—except to leave you?
Distance that the dead have gone, The.
Do People moulder equally.
Doom is the House without the Door.
Doomed—regard the Sunrise, The.
Dreams are the subtle Dower.
Dust is the only Secret.
Dust like the Mosquito, The.
Dying! Dying in the night!
Dying is a wild Night.
Dying need but little, Dear, The.
Dying! To be afraid of thee.
Each Second is the last.
Endow the Living—with the Tears.
Except to Heaven, she is nought.
Face I carry with me—last, The.
Fear—like Dying, dilates trust.
Finite life, little sister, A.

First We knew of Him was Death, The.
Footlights cannot improve the grave.
For Death—or rather.
Frost of Death was on the Pane, The.
Great Hope fell, A.
Grief of wonder at her fate.
Had I presumed to hope.
He fought like those Who've nought to lose.
Heart asks Pleasure—first, The.
Her dying feels to me.
Her final Summer was it.
His Life was so shy and his tastes so unknown.
Home itself is far from home.
How fortunate the Grave.
How many times these low feet staggered.
How sweet that he rose in the morning.
How sweet the "Life that now is."
How to repair my shattered ranks.
I died for Beauty—but was scarce.
I felt a Funeral, in my Brain.
I haven't told my garden yet.
I heard a fly buzz—when I died.
I keep my pledge.
I know of people in the Grave.
I like a look of Agony.
I meant to find Her when I came.
I never hear that one is dead.
I never lost as much but twice.
I notice where Death has been introduced.
I see thee clearer for the Grave.
I should not dare to leave my friend.
If any sink, assure that this, now standing.
If anybody's friend be dead.
If He were living—dare I ask.
If I may have it, when it's dead.
If I should cease to bring a Rose.
If I should die.
If I shouldn't be alive.
If this is "fading."
In falling Timbers buried.
It came at last but prompter Death.
It don't sound so terrible—quite—as it did.
It perished with beautiful reluctance.
It was not Death, for I stood up.
It's coming—the postponeless Creature.
I've seen a Dying Eye.
Last Night that She lived, The.
Let down the Bars, Oh Death.
Life is death we're lengthy at.
Long—long Sleep—a famous—Sleep, A.
Manner of its Death, The.
Me prove it now—Whoever doubt.
Meeting is well worth parting.
Midsummer, was it, when They died.
Mighty dying of my Father, The.
More Life—went out—when He went.
More than the Grave is closed to me.
Mother's dying almost stunned my spirit.
My life closed twice before its close.
My Triumph lasted till the Drums.
Not all of life to live, is it.
Nothing in her Life became her.
Of Death I try to think like this.
Oh give it Motion—deck it sweet.
On this long storm the Rainbow rose.
One dignity delays for all.
Only Balmless Wound, The.
Overtakelessness of those, The.
Pain has but one Acquaintance.
Praise it—'tis dead.
Promise This, When You be Dying.
Right to perish might be thought, The.
Robbed by Death—but that was easy.
Safe in their Alabaster Chambers.
Said Death to Passion.
Shade upon the mind there passes, A.
She bore it till the simple veins.
She died at play,/ Gambolled away.
She died—this was the way she died.
She lay as if at play.
Sickness of this World it most occasions, A.
So give me back to Death.
So proud she was to die.
Some Wretched creature, savior take.
Somehow myself survived the Night.
Soul must go by Death alone, The.

Soul should always stand ajar, The.
Soul, take thy risk.
Stem of a departed Flower, The.
Still own thee—still thou art.
Summer has two Beginnings.
Sun kept setting—setting—still, The.
Suspense—is Hostiler than Death.
Sweet Acclamation of Death divulges it, The.
Sweet hours have perished here.
Sweet is it as Life.
Sweet—safe—Houses.
Sweet, to have had them lost.
Test of Love—is Death, The.
That after Horror—that 'twas us.
That Bareheaded life under the grass.
That odd old man is dead a year.
That short—potential stir.
That the Divine has been human.
That this should feel the need of Death.
That we are permanent.
There is a finished feeling.
There is a word/ Which bears a sword.
There's a certain Slant of light.
There's been a Death, in the Opposite House.
There's something quieter than sleep.
They put Us far apart.
This Consciousness that is aware.
This docile one inter.
This heart that broke so long.
This Me—that walks and works—must die.
Those not live yet.
Those that die seem near me.
Those who have been in the Grave the longest.
Three times—we parted—Breath—and I.
Throe upon the features, A.
Tie the Strings to my Life, My Lord.
'Tis easier to pity those when dead.
'Tis so appalling—it exhilarates.
'Tis Sunrise—Little Maid—Hast Thou.
To die before it feared to die.
To die—takes just a little while.
To forget you would be impossible.
To him to whom Events and Omens.
To know just how He suffered—would be dear.
Toad, can die of Light, A.
Too scanty 'twas to die for you.
Train went through a burial gate, A.
Tried always and Condemned by thee.
'Twas comfort in her Dying Room.
'Twas fighting for his Life he was.
'Twas just this time, last year, I died.
'Twas warm—at first—like Us.
Two swimmers wrestled on the spar.
Two Travellers perishing in Snow.
Under the Light, yet under.
Unit, like Death, for Whom?
Upon Concluded Lives.
Vision of Immortal Life has been fulfilled, The.
Visitor in Marl, A.
Vivid in our immortal Group.
Wait till the Majesty of Death.
We all have moments with the dust.
We can but follow to the Sun.
We don't cry—Tim and I.
We go by detachments to the strange Home.
We must be less than Death.
We never know we go when we are going.
We wear our sober Dresses when we die.
What care the Dead, for Chanticleer.
What if I say I shall not wait!
What Inn is this.
Whatever it is—she has tried it.
When One has given up One's life.
While it is alive.
Who knows where our hearts go.
Whole of it came not at once, The.
With closer clutch for that which remains.
With sorrow that the Joy is past.
World—feels Dusty, The.
You'll find—it when you try to die.
Your little mental gallantries.
You're right—"the way is narrow."
Dobyns. Beauty.
Cemetery Nights.

Cemetery Nights II.
Cemetery Nights IV.
Cemetery Nights V.
Counterparts.
Delicate, Plummeting Bodies, The.
Footstep.
Fragments.
Grandfather Poem, The.
Hidden Within the Sleeves of Those Dark
    Robes.
Tomatoes.
Donne. As due by many titles I resign[e].
Blossom [or Blossome], The.
Computation, The.
Contemplation of Our State in Our Deathbed.
Death[,] be not proud, though some have
    called thee.
Dissolution, The.
Elegy on Mistress Boulstred.
Elegy on the L. C.
Elegy on the Lady Markham.
Elegy upon the Death of Mistress Boulstred,
    An.
Elegy upon the Untimely Death of the
    Incomparable Prince Henry.
Epitaph on Himself.
Funeral Elegy, A.
Funeral[l], The.
Hero and Leander.
Hymn[e] to God My God, In My Sickness[e].
Hymn to the Saints, and to Marquis
    Hamilton[, An].
Obsequies to the Lord Harrington, Brother to
    the Lady Lucy, Countess of Bedford.
Oh my black[e] soul[e]! now thou art
    summoned.
Paradox, The.
Pyramus and Thisbe.
Second Anniversary [or Anniversarie], The.
Since she whom I loved [or lov'd] hath paid
    [or payd] her last debt.
Through thy submitting all, to blow[e]s.
To the Lady Bedford.
Doolittle. Body and Soul.
Charioteer.
Choros Sequence.
Dead Priestess Speaks, A.
Envy.
Epigram: "Golden one is gone from the
    banquets, The."
Epitaph: "So I may say."
For Bryher and Perdita.
Loss.
Never let it be said.
Priest.
Prisoners.
She is dead.
Time breaks the barrier.
Dove. Company.
Event, The.
Oriental Ballerina, The.
Thomas at the Wheel.
Tou Wan Speaks to Her Husband Liu Sheng.
Zeppelin Factory, The.
Dryden. Epilogue to *Tyrannic[k] Love.*
To the Memory of Mr Oldham.
Dunbar. Alexander Crummel—Dead.
Behind the Arras.
Border Ballad, A.
"Chronic Kicker," The.
Communion.
Compensation.
Dead.
Death.
Death of the First Born, The.
Death Song[, A].
Dirge: "Place this bunch of mignonette."
Frederick Douglass.
Goin' Home.
In the Tents of Akbar.
Love-Song: "If Death should claim me for her
    own to-day."
Masters, The.
My dear love died last night.
News, The.
On the Death of W. C.
Paradox, The.

Premonition.
Puttin' the Baby Away.
Remembered.
Right to Die, The.
To a Dead Friend.
To Alice Dunbar.
To the Memory of Mary Young.
Two Little Boots.
W'en I Gits Home.
When All Is Done.
Duncan. After a Long Illness.
Huon of Bordeaux.
In Blood's Domaine.
Reaper, The.
Dunn. Legacy.
Letter About Myself to You.
Return, The.
"Dylan." Ballad for a Friend.
Ballad of Hollis Brown.
Dead Man, Dead Man.
I Wanna Be Your Lover.
Knockin' on Heavin's Door.
Last Thoughts on Woody Guthrie.
Lenny Bruce.
Let Me Die in My Footsteps.
Man on the Street.
Only a Hobo.
Rambling, Gambling Willie.
Whatcha Gonna Do.
Who Killed Davey Moore?
Eberhart. And the first, the father, with
    indomitable will.
Apple Buds.
At Night.
Cage, The.
Cemetery, The.
Ceremony By the Sea, A.
Death in the Mines.
Edgar Lee Masters.
Emily Dickinson.
Examination of Psyche: Thoughts of Home.
Flux.
Forgotten Rock, The.
Gesture, The.
Grave Piece.
Hardy Perennial.
I Walked over the Grave of Henry James.
I Will Not Dare to Ask One Question.
Ides of March, The.
Images of death arise.
Imagining How It Would Be to Be Dead.
John Finley.
John Ledyard.
Largess, The.
Life and Death.
Loss.
Man Who Was Blown Down by the Wind, A.
Meditation, A.
New Entrepreneurial Plan.
Nexus.
Nostalgia for Edith Sitwell.
Old Tom.
On Seeing an Egyptian Mummy in Berlin,
    1932.
Once More, O Ye.
Passage, The.
Perception as a Guided Missile.
Poet, The.
Rumination.
Scouring, The.
Sestina: "I die, no matter what I do I die."
Sometimes the Longing for Death.
Suite in Prison.
Swallows Return, The.
There Is an Evil in the Air.
To Kenya Tribesmen, the Turkana.
Track.
Truncated Bird, The.
Trying to Hold It All Together.
Two Loves.
Ur Burial.
Virgin, The.
Ways and Means.
When Golden Flies Upon My Carcass Come.
Whenever I See Beauty I See Death.
Young Greek, Killed In The Wars, A.
Young Hunter, The.

Edmunds. Back Home.
December Frost.
Doña Sebastiana.
Jonathan Lazarus Wright, 1702–1729.
Lunes.
Morada La Muerte, The.
One Look at the Creation.
Eliot. Aunt Helen.
Dans le Restauramt.
Hollow Men, The.
Lines to a Yorkshire Terrier.
Marina.
Wind Sprang Up at Four o'Clock, The.
Emerson. All the great & good.
Arabian Ballad.
Dirge: "Knows he who tills this lonely field."
Dust unto dust! and shall no more be said.
Epitaph: "Bethink, poor heart, what bitter kind
    of jest."
From Omar Chiam.
From the Persian of Hafiz.
Good-bye.
Hearst thou, sweet spirit, thou hast heard
    before.
I am alone. Sad is my solitude.
I am: what I am.
I love thy music, mellow bell.
I shall go from my sickbed to heaven.
In Memoriam.
Leave me, Fear! thy throbs are base.
Lines on the Death of Miss M. B. Farnham.
My days roll by me like a train of dreams.
Nun's Aspiration.
On the Death of Mr. John Haskins.
On two days it steads not to run from thy
    grave.
Original—"Apropos."
Shall the Muse sing for thousands & not sing.
She never comes to me.
So long as there's a trace.
Spirits of the wise, sit on the clouds, The.
Sweet, sweet, is sleep,—Ah! sweeter, to be
    stone.
Teach me I am forgotten by the dead.
Teach me your mood, O patient stars!
Terminus ("It is time to be old").
Thousand dangers of ruin has the street of
    love.
To J. W.
Visit, The.
What avails it me.
Why fear to die.
Why should I live.
Everson. Danse Macabre.
In the Breach.
Poet Is Dead, The.
Reaper.
Fenton. Cambodia.
Dead Soldiers.
God, A Poem.
Letter to John Fuller.
Prison Island.
Ferlinghetti. Elegy on the Death of Kenneth
    Patchen, An.
Man Who Rode Away, The.
Old Italians Dying, The.
Queens Cemetery, Setting Sun.
Fisher. As He Came near Death.
Occasional Poem 7.1.72.
Wonders of Obligation.
Fletcher. Bedroom.
Blessing of the Worms, The.
Blue Symphony.
Elegy in a Civil War Cemetery.
Fuel Vendor, The.
Groundswell, The.
Last Frontier, The.
Old South, The.
Poppies of the Red Year.
Requiem for a Twentieth-Century Outlaw.
Reunion.
Scythe, The.
Ford. ABC's.
Andromache, I think of you! / When the war
    goes on forever.
Ballad for Baudelaire.
Candy Darling.

Curse for the War Machine, A.
Death in all its forms.
Death's-head moth, A.
Do birds need to fly so much.
Even when the heart of the world is found.
I Wonder.
Max Ernst.
Fox.   Angel of Death, The.
   At Nightfall.
   Child Called *Morte*, A.
   Dead Women.
   Juggler, The.
   Servants of the Emperor, The.
   White and the River.
Frost.   Away!
   Death of the Hired Man, The.
   Home Burial.
   In a Disused Graveyard.
   Out, Out —.
   Place for a Third.
   Times Table, The.
   To E.T.
   Wind and the Rain, The.
Gallagher.   Accomplishment.
   Candle, Lamp & Firefly.
   Coats, The.
   Dim House, Bright Face.
   Small Garden Near a Field.
   Sugar.
   Survival of a Heart.
   Tableau Vivant.
   Their Heads Bent Toward Each Other Like
     Flowers.
   With Stars.
Galvin.   Carrowkeel.
   Field of Inheritance, The.
   Tautog.
   Widow at "Whaleroad's End," The.
Gardner.   And Thou No Breath at All?
   Ballade: "You who outlive us, you, our mortal
     brothers."
   Bronchitis at the Chelsea—or Salud Raul.
   Cock-a-Hoop.
   Feminine Ending or, Abandoned, She Died.
   In Memory of Lemuel Ayers, Scene Designer,
     Dead of Cancer in His Fortieth Year.
   Knowing.
   Nursery Rhyme No. 1.
   Of Flesh and Bone.
   Spendthrift.
   Telephone, The.
   Triolet: "Bad die old, The."
   When a Warlock Dies.
   Whole World's in a Terrible Chassis, The.
   Zei Gesund.
Garrigue.   Gravepiece.
Gildner.   Edward.
   Prayer for My Father.
   Szostak.
Ginsberg.   At Apollinaire's Grave.
   Atypical Affair, An.
   Death News.
   Death on All Fronts.
   Don't Grow Old.
   Dream Record: June 8, 1955.
   Epigram on a Painting of Golgotha.
   Father Death Blues.
   Fragment: The Names II.
   Hymmnn.
   Hymn: "No hyacinthine imagination can
     express this clock of meat bleakly pining."
   In Memoriam: William Cannastra, 1922–1950.
   Memory Gardens.
   Names, The.
   On Neal's Ashes.
   On Neruda's Death.
   On Reading William Blake's "The Sick Rose."
   Reply, The.
   Sad Dust Glories.
   Television Was a Baby Crawling toward That
     Deathchamber.
   Western Ballad, A.
   What's Dead?
Glück.   Adult Grief.
   Apple Trees, The.
   Chicago Train, The.
   Descending Figure.

Dream of Mourning, The.
Drowned Children, The.
Fire, The.
Firstborn.
Garden, The.
Hyacinth.
Japonica.
La Force.
Late Snow.
Metamorphosis.
Phenomenal Survivals of Death in Nantucket.
Racer's Widow, The.
Swimmer, The.
Graves.   Dead Hand.
   Down.
   Dreaming Children.
   Iago.
   It Was All Very Tidy.
   Leaving the Rest Unsaid.
   Narrow Sea, The.
   Presence, The.
   Pure Death.
   Reiteration, The.
   Sharp Ridge, The.
   Song: Cherries or Lilies.
   Song: To Become Each Other.
   Suicide in The Copse, The.
   Sweet-Shop Round The Corner, The.
   Theme of Death, The.
   Title of Poet, The.
   To Be Poets.
   To Bring the Dead to Life.
   Toast to Death, A.
   True Evil.
   Twice Of The Same Fever.
   Twin of Sleep, The.
   Undead, The.
   Villagers and Death, The.
   Virus, The.
Gray.   Concluding Lines of Epitaph on Mrs
     Mason.
   Descent of Odin, The.
   Elegy Written in a Country Churchyard.
   Epitaph on Mrs Jane Clarke.
   Epitaph on Sir William Williams.
   Ode on the Death of a Favourite [*or* Favorite]
     Cat, Drowned in a Tub [*or* Bowl] of Gold
     Fishes.
   Sonnet [on the Death of Mr. Richard West].
Griffiths.   Elegy for John Tripp.
   From Waterloo Bridge, Ensuing Dark.
   Geriatrics.
   Shooting of Levellers, Burford, 1649.
Gunn.   Beautician, The.
   Book of the Dead, The.
   Corporal, The.
   Death's Door.
   Elegy: "I can almost see it."
   From an Asian Tent.
   Garden of the Gods, The.
   In Time of Plague.
   Inherited Estate, The.
   J Car, The.
   Lament: "Your dying was a difficult
     enterprise."
   Lerici.
   Monterey.
   My Sad Captains.
   Old Woman, The.
   Reassurance, The.
   Sacred Heart.
   Sketch of the Great Dejection, A.
   To a Dead Graduate Student.
   To Isherwood Dying.
   To the Dead Owner of a Gym.
   Unsettled Motorcyclist's Vision of His Death,
     The.
   Victim, The.
   Words for Some Ash.
Hacker.   Autumn 1980.
   Ballad of Ladies Lost and Found.
   Elegy: "Crying from exile, I."
   Elevens.
   For Elektra.
   Geographer.
   Mother.
   Nights of 1964-1966: The Old Reliable.

Presentation Piece.
Sword.
Haines.   Arlington.
   Calendar, The.
   Fairbanks Under the Solstice.
   Flight, The.
   Listening in October.
   On Banner Dome.
   People fell back, a field of wheat, The.
   Pitcher of Milk, The.
   Poem About Birch Trees.
   To Vera Thompson.
Hall.   Beau of the Dead.
   Body Politic, The.
   Carlotta's Confession.
   Child's Garden, A.
   Christmas Eve in Whitneyville, 1955.
   Coffee Cup, The.
   Eleanor's Letters.
   Elegy for Wesley Wells.
   Exile.
   Flies.
   Hole, The.
   Hut of the man alone, The.
   Idea of Flying, The.
   In the Kitchen of the Old House.
   Man in the Dead Machine, The.
   Mr. and Mrs. Billings.
   My Friend Felix.
   My Son, My Executioner.
   No Deposit.
   Praise for Death.
   Raisin, The.
   Red Branch, The.
   Religious Articles.
   Shudder [, The].
   Sleeping.
   Small Fig Tree, A.
   Snow, The.
   Traffic.
   White Apples.
Hardy.   After the Death of a Friend.
   After the Last Breath.
   Afterwards.
   A.H., 1855–1912.
   Amabel.
   Announcement, The.
   At Castle Boterel.
   At Mayfair Lodgings.
   At the Mill.
   Beeny Cliff.
   Casual Acquaintance, The.
   Channel Firing.
   Choirmaster's Burial, The.
   Concerning Agnes.
   Conversation at Dawn, A.
   Dead Quire, The.
   Death-Day Recalled, A.
   Death of Regret, The.
   Drummer Hodge.
   Duel, The.
   During Wind and Rain.
   Epitaph: "I never cared for Life: Life cared for
     me."
   Evening Shadows.
   Every Artemisia.
   Fading Rose, The.
   Felled Elm and She, The.
   Fragment: "At last I entered a long dark
     gallery."
   Friends Beyond.
   Going, The.
   Harvest-Supper, The.
   Her Death and After.
   Her Secret.
   I Found Her Out There.
   I Met a Man.
   In the Evening.
   Inquiry, An.
   Intra Sepulchrum.
   Julie-Jane.
   King's Soliloquy, A.
   Lament: "How she would have loved."
   Last Journey, A.
   Last Performance, The.
   Life and Death at Sunrise.
   Lodging-House Fuchsias, The.

Looking Across.
Nettles, The.
New Dawn's Business, The.
Night of Questionings, A.
Not Only I.
Nothing Matters Much.
Old Likeness, An.
On One Who Lived and Died Where He Was Born.
One Ralph Blossom Soliloquizes.
Paradox.
Rash Bride, The.
Regret Not Me.
Seen by the Waits.
Sexton at Longpuddle, The.
Slow Nature, The.
Squire Hooper.
Subalterns, The.
Sun's Last Look on the Country Girl, The.
Thoughts of Phena.
To-Be-Forgotten, The.
To Louisa in the Lane.
Upbraiding, An.
Voice, The.
When Dead.
Where the Picnic Was.
While Drawing in a Churchyard.
Whipper-In, The.
Who's in the Next Room?
Why She Moved House.
Wife in London, A.
Woman's Fancy, A.
Your Last Drive.
Hartley. Afterlude.
Going Man, A.
Modigliani's Death Mask.
Three Loving Men.
Hartnett. Death of an Irishwoman.
Last Vision of Eoghan Rua Ó Súilleabháin, The.
Oatwoman, The.
Prayer at Death.
Sickroom.
That Actor Kiss.
Hayden. Approximations.
Broken Dark, The.
Burly Fading One, The.
Day of the Dead (Tehuantepec).
Mourning Poem for the Queen of Sunday.
Heaney. Badgers, The.
Casualty.
Funeral Rites.
Graubelle Man, The.
In Memoriam Francis Ledwidge.
King of the Ditchbacks, The.
Mid-Term Break.
Sweeney's Last Poem.
Triptych.
Wishing Tree, The.
Hemingway. Killed Piave—July 8—1918.
Poem: "Only man I ever loved, The."
Poem to Mary (Second Poem).
Sequal.
To a Tragic Poetess.
To Chink Whose Trade Is Soldiering.
Herbert. Death.
Dialogue-Anthem, A.
Doomsday.
Life.
Virtue [or Vertue].
Herrick. After Autumne, Winter.
Age Unfit for Love.
Bed-Man, or Grave-Maker, The.
Comfort to a Youth That Had Lost His Love.
Death Ends All Woe.
Dirge of Jephthah's Daughter, The.
Elegy: "Since louely sweete, much like unto a Dewe."
Gods Keyes.
Good Death, A.
His Answer to a Friend.
His Last Request to Julia.
His Meditation upon Death.
His Winding-Sheet.
No Despight to the Dead.
Ode to Master Endymion Porter, upon His Brother's Death, An.

On Himselfe ("I will no longer kiss").
On Himselfe: ("If that my Fate has now fulfill'd my yeere").
On Himselfe ("I'll write no more of Love; but now repent").
On Himselfe ("Weep for the dead, for they have lost this light").
Parkinsons Shade to the House of Mr. Pallauicine Taking His Death Ill.
Posting to Printing.
Teares, and Laughter.
To Anthea: ("If, deare Anthea, my hard fate it be").
To Biancha.
To Death.
To Electra ("Let not thy Tomb-stone").
To God, on His Sickness[e].
To His Kinswoman, Mistresse Susanna Herrick.
To His Lovely Mistresses.
To His Paternall Countrey.
To Julia ("Julia, when thy Herrick dies").
To Julia ("Saints-bell calls; and Julia, I must read, The").
To Perilla.
To the Nightingale, and Robin-Red-Brest.
To the Passenger.
To the Reverend Shade of His Religious Father.
Transfiguration, The.
Upon a Maide ("Hence a blessed soule is fled").
Upon a Wife That Dyed Mad with Jealousie.
Upon an Old Man a Residenciarie.
Upon Hanch a Schoolmaster.
Upon Prue [or Prew], His Maid.
Upon the Losse of His Finger.
Widow's Tears [or Widdowes Teares]: or, Dirge of Dorcas, The.
Hesketh. Brief Encounter.
Cap, The.
Comparison with a Sunflower.
Dead Blackbird.
Death of a Gardener.
Dilemma.
He Saved Others..
I Give Death to a Son.
Journey.
July 2nd, 1916.
Leave Train, The.
More than Grass.
Naked Ostrich.
Party, The.
Prayer for Sun.
Reclaimed.
Skeleton Bride.
Walking Away.
Walking Back.
Wordsworth's Old Age.
Hewitt. Aquarium.
Case of Mistaken Identity, A.
Corridor.
Doctor Muses, The.
Drypoint.
Dungannon Cattle Market.
Eager Journey.
Epitaph for a Gardener.
Fairy-Man at Layde, The.
Father's Death, A.
First Funeral.
First Ride.
Gathering Praties.
Ghosts.
Grandfather Robinson Dies in 1898.
Grief ("I thought when the grave was sodded").
Grief ("When men lie down for ever / and names their tombstones take").
Hesitant Memorial.
I Lie Alone.
Immortality.
In Recollection of Drumcliffe, September 1948.
Last Call, The.
Late Spring, 1912.
Lifting, The.
Memorial Service.

My Father's Death in Hospital.
My Father's Ghost.
My Grandfather Dies, 1923.
My Uncle Johnny.
My Uncle Willy.
Neither an Elegy Nor a Manifesto.
October Sonnets.
Of a Professor.
On Choosing Some Verses for My Sister's Cremation.
Ophelia.
Peter Peri (1899-1967).
Poem: "My name is Revolution—let me speak."
Providence 3.
Providence 2.
Rebel, The.
Rite.
Romantic, The.
Salute to Matthew Arnold.
Sarcophagus.
Scar, The.
Sonnet: "I think of Glasgow, where reluctantly."
To the Memory of James Connolly.
21st September 1912.
Uncle Dick and Aunt Bertha.
Unnecessary Dread, The.
Wake, The.
With E.M.F. on 28th December 1965.
W.R. Rodgers.
Hill. Anguish bloated by the replete scream.
Domaine Public.
Down in the orchard.
Funeral Music.
Guardians, The.
In Memory of Jane Fraser [or Frazer].
Merlin.
Not as we are but as we must appear.
Statesman have known visions. And, not alone.
Two Formal Elegies.
White Ship, The.
Hoffman. Asleep.
I Dreamt My Love A-Dying Lay.
Ode to Joy.
That Morning.
Holmes. Death Drag (The Elegist).
For Walker Evans.
Out of a Fever: For Robert Lowell (Sept. 13, 1977).
Petition Concerning the Death-Wish.
Too-Late Words to My Father.
Hopkins. Felix Randal.
Glimmer'd along the square-cut steep.
Her prime of life—cut down too soon.
No worst, there is none. Pitched past pitch of grief.
O Death, Death, He is come.
Spring and Death.
Why should their foolish bands, their hopeless hearses.
Housman. A. J. J.
Along the field as we came by.
Ask me no more, for fear I should reply.
Bredon Hill.
Farms of home lie lost in even, The.
For My Funeral.
Half-moon westers low, my love, The.
Here dead lie we because we did not choose.
Hughley Steeple.
I shall not die for you.
Illic Jacet.
Is my team ploughing.
Isle of Portland, The.
Like mine, the veins of these that slumber.
Night is freezing fast, The.
Now to her lap the incestuous earth.
Oh on my breast in days hereafter.
On your midnight pallet lying.
Rain, it streams on stone and hillock, The.
Say, lad, have you things to do?
Shot? so quick, so clean an ending?
Some can gaze and not be sick.
Stone, steel, dominions pass.
This time of year a twelvemonth past.
To an Athlete Dying Young.

Wake not for the world-heard thunder.
When I came last to Ludlow.
When I watch the living meet.
When smoke stood up from Ludlow.
When the eye of day is shut.
With rue my heart is laden.
Yon flakes that fret the eastern sky.
Hughes, Langston. Drum.
Fantasy in Purple.
Stony Lonesome.
Sylvester's Dying Bed.
Wake.
Widow Woman.
Young Gal's Blues.
Hughes, Ted. Bayonet Charge.
Bowled Over.
Dead man in his cave beginning to sweat, The.
Dead, she became space-earth.
Examination at the Womb-Door.
Executioner, The.
Heptonstall.
I know well / You are not infallible.
Life Is Trying to Be Life.
New Moon in January.
Prospero and Sycorax.
Ravens.
Remembrance Day.
Risen, The.
So the leaves trembled.
Soliloquy: "Whenever I am got under my gravestone."
Suddenly his poor body.
Waving goodbye, from your banked hospital bed.
Woman Unconscious, A.
Hugo. Ayr.
Cattails.
Death in the Aquarium.
December 24 and George McBride Is Dead.
Digging Is an Art.
Elegy: "I expected him to look dead in the casket."
Farmer, Dying.
Good Day for Seeing Your Limitations, A.
Graves in Queens.
Graves in Uig.
Here, but Unable to Answer.
Kilmuir Cemetery: Stone with Two Skulls and No Name.
Last Words to James Wright.
Mill at Romesdal.
Montgomery Hollow.
Other Grave, The.
Piping to You on Skye from Lewis.
Right Madness on Skye, The.
To Die in Milltown.
Tony.
Two Graves in a Day.
Uig Registrar.
With Ripley at the Grave of Albert Parenteau.
Jarrell. Afterwards.
Automaton, The.
Black Swan, The.
Boyg, Peer Gynt, the One Only One, The.
Che Farò Senza Euridice.
Dead, The.
Death of the Ball Turret Gunner, The.
Difficult Resolution, The.
Dream of Waking, The.
Essay on the Human Will, An.
Hanged man on the gallows, The.
Iceberg, The.
In the Camp There Was One Alive.
In the Ward: The Sacred Wood.
Islands, The.
January 1938.
Knight, Death, and the Devil, The.
La Belle au Bois Dormant.
Laboratory, The.
Losses.
Mother, Said the Child.
One Who Was Different, The.
Place of Death, The.
Poem for Someone Killed in Spain, A.
Prince, The.
Say Good-bye to Big Daddy.

Scherzo.
Seele im Raum.
Sleeping Beauty: Variation of the Prince, The.
To Be Dead.
Truth, The.
Utopian Journey, A.
Washing the Corpse.
Well-to-Do Invalid, A.
What was longed for and, once, certain.
When I Was Home Last Christmas.
Women on a Bus.
Jeffers. Battle.
Bed by the Window, The.
Birth and Death.
Cawdor.
Come Little Birds.
Deer Lay Down Their Bones, The.
Drunken Charlie.
Eagle and hawk with their great claws and hooked heads.
Ghosts in England.
Give Your Wish Light.
Greater Grandeur.
Hungerfield.
I am seventy-four years old and suddenly all my strength.
I have told you in another poem, whether you've read it or not.
In the Hill at Newgrange.
Inhumanist, The.
Iona: the Graves of the Kings.
It nearly cancels my fear of death, my dearest said.
Loving Shepherdess, The.
Low Sky, The.
Medea.
Monument.
No Resurrection.
Ode to Hengist and Horsa.
Old age hath clawed me with his scaly clutch.
Original Sin.
Ossian's Grave.
Purse-Seine, The.
Seventieth Birthday.
Shears, The.
Shooting Season.
Sirens, The.
To Death.
Vulture.
Where I?
Johnson. On the Death of Dr [or Mr] Robert Levet [a Practiser in Physic].
Translation of the Latin Epitaph on Sir Thomas Hanmer, Written by Doctor Freind, A.
Verses on the Death of His Mother.
Jonson. By this time had they reached the Stygian pool.
Charles Cavendish to His Posterity.
Elegy [or Elegie] on the Lady Jane Pawlet [or Paulet], [Marchioness of Winton], An.
Epitaph, An: "What beauty would have lovely styled."
Epitaph on Elizabeth, L. H.
Epitaph, on Henry L[ord] La-ware. To the Passer-By, An.
Epitaph on Master Philip Gray, An.
Epitaph on Master Vincent Corbet[t], An.
Eptiaph on Katherine, Lady Ogle.
Ode. To Himself, An.
Of Death.
Of Life and Death.
On Margaret Ratcliffe.
On Sir John Roe ("In place of scutcheons, that should deck thy hearse").
Stay, view this stone: and, if thou beest not such.
To the Memory of That Most Honoured Lady Jane, Eldest Daughter to Cuthbert, Lord Ogle: and Countess of Shrewsbury.
To the World [A Farewell for a Gentlewoman, Virtuous and Noble].
Joseph. Eurydice to Orpheus.
LANDSCAPE: *Jungle Days* (Dutch).
Lazarus.
Old Man Going.
Recovered from the Sea.

Keats. Ah! Ken Ye What I Met the Day.
As from the Darkening Gloom a Silver Dove.
Can Death Be Sleep, When Life Is But a Dream.
Song: "I had a dove and the sweet dove died."
To Chatterton.
Written in Disgust of Vulgar Superstition.
Kinnell. Freedom, New Hampshire.
Goodbye.
Kipling. Answer, The.
Appeal, The.
Azrael's Count.
Ballad of the Cars, The.
Ballade of Burial, A.
Burial, The.
Chil's Song.
Dead King, The [Edward VII; 1910].
Dedication from "Barrack-Room Ballads."
Doctors.
Dying Chauffer, The.
En-dor.
Explanation, The.
Follow Me 'Ome.
Gift of the Sea, The.
Harp Song of the Dane Women.
Heriot's Ford.
Jane's Marriage.
Last Department, The.
Last Suttee, The.
L'Envoi; Departmental Ditties.
Mary Gloster, The.
My Boy Jack.
Nativity, A.
Neighbours.
Old Mother Laidinwool.
Possibilities.
Queen's Men, The.
Ripple Song, A.
Snarleyow.
Song of the Dead, The.
Song to Mithras, A.
There were three friends that buried the fourth.
Things and the Man.
Tomlinson.
Undertaker's Horse, The.
Widower, The.
Yet at the last, ere our spearmen had found him.
Knight. Last Words By "Slick."
Knott. At the Crossroads.
Closet, The.
Death.
Funny Poem.
Shorts / Excerpts ("I write these lines to cripple the dead").
Shorts / Excerpts ("Searching it goes").
Two Vietnam Poems: (1966).
Koch. Circus, The.
Koertge. Day Alvero Pineda Was Killed, The.
Kooser. After My Grandmother's Funeral.
After the Funeral: Cleaning Out the Medicine Cabinet.
Death at the Office, A.
For a Friend.
Goldfish Floats to the Top of His Life, The.
My Grandfather Dying.
Notes on the Death of Nels Paulssen, Farmer, at the Ripe Old Age of 93.
Uncle Adler.
Widow Lester, The.
Kunitz. Approach of Autumn.
Blessing of Women, A.
Clouds took me by the hand.
Customs Collector's Report, The.
Dragonfly, The.
Etcher of the secret wrinkles.
Gladiators, The.
Last Words.
O sister of the shadow.
Probing the deepest selves.
Sacred to the Memory.
Single Vision.
Sotto Voce.
Unquiet Ones, The.
Way Down, The.
When the magician died, I wept.
Larkin. Ambulances.

April Sunday Brings the Snow, An.
At the Chiming of Light upon Sleep.
Aubade: "I work all day, and get half-drunk at night."
Compline.
Dublinesque.
Hospital Visits.
I Have Started to Say.
Local Snivels through the Field, The.
Mower, The.
Next, Please.
Sympathy in White Major.
Unfinished Poem.
Lawrence. All Souls.
At Last.
Beware the Unhappy Dead!
Birthday.
Bride, The.
Call into Death.
Cherry Robbers.
Dead People.
Death.
Death of Our Era, The.
Death of the Baron, The.
Difficult Death.
Drama, A.
Dust in the East.
Endless Anxiety.
Erinnyes.
Everlasting Flowers.
Fatality.
Full Life.
Giorno dei Morti.
Gladness of Death.
Grief.
Houseless Dead, The.
Huitzilopochtli Gives the Black Blade of Death.
Huitzilopochtli's Watch.
Hymn to Priapus.
Initiation Degrees.
Let the Dead Bury Their Dead.
Like the Green Candles of Malintzi.
Litany of Grey Nurses.
Man Who Died, A.
My Way Is Not Thy Way.
Neither Moth Nor Rust.
New Heaven and Earth.
New Word, The.
New Year's Night.
No News.
Obsequial Ode.
On That Day.
Pear-Blossom.
People Who Care.
Rabbit Snared in the Night.
Resurrection.
Revolutionary, The.
Shadow of Death, The.
Shadows.
Ship of Death, The.
Sleep.
So Let Me Live.
Song of Death.
Song of the Dead.
Spirits Summoned West.
Sympathy.
To Lettice, My Sister.
Troth with the Dead.
Two Wives.
Violets.
Violets for the Dead.
We Have Gone Too Far.
Welcome Death.
What Quetzalcoatl Saw in Mexico.
When Most Men Die.
When the Ripe Fruit Falls.
Levertov. Another Spring.
Clouds.
Didactic Poem.
Note to Olga (1966), A.
Olga Poems.
Three Meditations.
Levine. Angel Butcher.
Baby Villon.
Belief.
Cemetery at Academy, California, The.

Children's Crusade, The.
Face, The.
Francisco, I'll Bring You Red Carnations.
Having Been Asked "What is a Man?" I Answer.
Hear Me.
Horse, The.
How Much Can It Hurt?
I Could Believe.
Jewish Graveyards, Italy.
Late Answer, A.
Let Me Be.
Letters for the Dead.
L'Homme et La Bête.
Lost and Found.
Miracle, The.
1933.
No One Remembers.
On a Drawing by Flavio.
On the Birth of Good & Evil During the Long Winter of '28.
On the Murder of Lieutenant José Del Castillo by the Falangist Bravo Martinez, July 12, 1936.
Red Dust.
To a Fish Head Found on the Beach Near Málaga.
To Cipriano, in the Wind.
To My God in His Sickness.
To P.L., 1916–1937.
Uncle.
Voice, The.
Waking an Angel.
Lewis. Autumn, 1939.
Compassion.
Dancer, The.
Defeat.
East, The.
Easter at Christmas.
Finale.
Greetings.
Lady in Black.
Lying in the hospital he often thought.
Mending, with books and papers and a fan.
Midnight in India.
Now only beggars still go singing.
Observation Post: Forward Area.
Odi et Amo.
Olwen and Taliesin.
On a Bereaved Girl.
Parable.
Peace.
Sacco Writes to His Son.
She Remains.
Socrates on the frozen lake.
Song: "I lay in sheets of softest linen."
Song: "Oh journeyman, Oh journeyman."
Song (On Seeing Dead Bodies Floating Off the Cape).
Sweet Mother Chruch, beleaguered on the hill.
Swimmer, The.
Unknown Soldier, The.
Vigil: She Tarries, Far-Off, in a Strange Anguish, The.
Village Funeral: Maharashtra.
Westminster Abbey.
White brain crossing, The.
White frost; intricate bare branches.
Liddy. Bright Crown of Freedom, The.
Clare, the Butterflies.
Death of the Poor.
Eugene Connolly.
Hesperian evenings certainly.
La Muerte de Joselito.
Poison, The.
Richard, Oremus.
Sound of a Moment at Scariff, The.
We saw the star of knowledge.
Wild curlew whistle I offer my death to.
Lindsay. Drunkard's Funeral, The.
Hearth Eternal, The.
Hope of the Resurrection, The.
I Want to Go Wandering.
O prodigal son, O recreant daughter.
Prairie Battlements, The.
Prayer to All the Dead Among Mine Own People, A.

What the Sexton Said.
Written in a Year When Many of My People Died.
Longfellow. Cross of Snow, The.
Hawthorne.
Lorde. Day They Eulogized Mahalia, The.
Equinox.
Father Son and Holy Ghost.
Martha.
Memorial I.
Memorial II.
Suffer the Children.
Lovelace. A La Bourbon.
Amyntor's Grove.
Answer, The.
Black Patch on Lucasta's Face, A.
Both lurks and shines hid in an Amber-tear.
Ode To My Lady H.
On the Death of Mrs. Elizabeth Filmer.
Sir Thomas Wortley's Sonnet Answered.
To His Deare Brother Colonel F.L.
Treasure found one entring at death's gate, A.
Whilst in an Amber-shade the Ant doth feast.
Lowell. Alfred Corning Clark.
Dante 3. Buonconte.
Death and the Bridge.
Death of Alexander.
For Robert Kennedy Nineteen Twenty-Five to Sixty-Eight.
For Sale.
Her Dead Brother.
History.
Ice.
Mary Winslow.
Mills of the Kavanaughs, The.
Mr. Edwards and the Spider.
Mother Marie Therese.
Nunc Est Bibendum, Cleopatra's Death.
Quaker Graveyard in Nantucket, The.
Sailing Home from Rapallo.
Two Walls.
Where the Rainbow Ends.
Lowry. And partly they deserve dishonest death.
Comfort.
Communal Message.
Correcting Manuscript.
Deserter.
Dream of the Departing Soldier.
Elsinore was the battlements of Oaxaca.
For Under the Volcano.
Give me the money, / Give me the money.
Glory of the Sea, The.
Homoeopathic Blues in J.
I wrote: In the dark cavern of our birth.
Illegal Heart, The.
In Memoriam; Ingvald Bjorndal and His Comrade.
In Praise of an Understudy.
Jokes in the Galley.
Lines on the Poet Being Informed That His Epic About the Philistines Etc. Needed Cutting.
Lusty Advice of a Fortune-Teller.
Marina—.
Names of Mexican rivers I forgot, The.
Note, A.
Note For a Poem.
Pacific is a feeble symbol of death.
Poem: "When drunk he crawled home on his knees."
Song about Madrid, Useful Any Time.
Songs for Second Childhood.
They will be ashamed after they are dead.
Thirty Five Mescals in Cuautla.
Those who die young will look forever young.
Thou was not born for death, immortal Duck.
To Herr Toller, Who Hanged Himself.
Volcano is dark and suddenly thunder, The.
Words on a Grave.
McAuley. "Alle Herrlichkeit Des Menschen."
Confession, The.
De Mortuis.
Death of Fathers.
Labor and Tribulation.
Mourners.
Vigil.

"MacDiarmid." At My Father's Grave.
Dead Liebknecht, The.
I mind when my first wife died.
Island Funeral.
John Maclean (1879-1923).
Of John Davidson.
On a Raised Beach.
Skald's Death.
Stony Limits.
Watergaw, The.
Wreck of the *Swan*, The.
McGrath. Blues for Jimmy.
Blues for Warren.
Death for the Dark Stranger.
Drowned Man: Death Between Two Rivers, The.
Epitaph: "Again, traveller, you have come a long way led by that star."
Go Ask the Dead.
Memorial.
Passages.
People Are So Busy: Or: That's Life!
Poem: "Down the small and crooked road."
MacLeish. Boatmen of Santorin, The.
Burial, The.
Conway Burying Ground.
Cummings.
Dozing on the Lawn.
1892—19—.
Eleventh Book, The.
Epistle to Be Left in the Earth.
Eternity, An.
For the Anniversary of my Mother's Death.
Fourteenth Book, The.
Great Contemporary Discoveries.
Hemingway.
Immortal Helix.
Interrogate the Stones.
Man!
Mark Van Doren and the Brook.
Mother Goose's Garland.
My Naked Aunt.
Nat Bacon's Bones.
Old Gray Couple (1), The.
Old Gray Couple (2), The.
Prologue: "And the way goes on in the worn earth."
What the Wind Said to the Water: What the Water Replied.
William Adams Delano.
Words to be Spoken.
MacNeice. Aequam Memento.
After the Crash.
All is well, said the voice from the tiny pulpit.
Bar-Room Matins.
Beni Hasan.
Burnt Bridge, The.
Candle in his white grave-clothes, always turning his cowled head, The.
Canto II: "'On the other hand,' said Gavin—or could have said."
Canto XVIII: "Lament for the Makers. Monday comes; at noon."
Casualty, The.
Charon.
Death of an Actress.
Death-Wish, The.
Eclogue between the Motherless.
Empty Shoes.
Epitaph for Liberal Poets.
Gardener, The.
On the Grettir Saga.
On the Njal Saga.
Pindar is Dead.
Place of a Skull.
Revenant, The.
Rites of War.
Sunlight on the Garden, The.
Than which not any. Time.
This Is the Life.
Wall, The.
War Heroes.
When she had her stroke the china dogs.
McNeill. Aubade to Fear (Heavy with Child).
Ballad of Joe Bittner.
Ballad of the Rest Home.
Burying Field.

Jane Renick MacElmain (2).
Lydia Verner.
Monongah (December 6, 1907, Marion County, West Virginia, on the Monongahela River).
Second Sight (My Son's First Springtime).
Snow Angels.
Susan O'Kane.
Tillie Sage (3).
Mahon. Deaths.
Exit Molloy.
Image from Beckett, An.
In Carrowdore Churchyard.
Markson. Agree.
At Malcolm Lowry's Grave.
Dylan.
Funeral.
On the Death, after Lying Wounded in the Thigh for Twenty-Six Days, of the Author of "Astrophel and Stella."
Skull.
Marlowe. 1.15: Ad invidos, quod fama poetarum sit perennis.
2.6: In mortem psittaci.
Marvell. Damon the Mower.
Dialogue between Thyrsis and Dorinda, A.
Elegy upon the Death of My Lord Francis Villiers, An.
Epitaph upon —, An.
That Providence which had so long the care.
Tom May's Death.
Upon the Death of the Lord Hastings.
Matthews. Blues for John Coltrane, Dead at 41.
Bystanders.
Driving Alongside the Housatonic River Alone on a Rainy April Night.
Funeral Homes.
Hope.
Living among the Dead.
Long.
Mother.
Nabokov's Death.
On Cape Cod a Child Is Stolen.
School.
Theme of the Three Caskets, The.
Meinke. Because.
Dead Tree, The.
Monkey's Paw, The.
Melville. Ball's Bluff.
Haglets, The.
Monody.
On the Grave.
On the Home Guards.
On the Slain Collegians.
Meredith. Angela Burdett-Coutts.
Ballad of Past Meridian, A.
C B M.
Cassandra.
Dirge: "He has hid his face, and he's gone!"
Dirge in Woods.
Emperor Frederick of Our Time, The.
Epitaph on the Tombstone of James Christopher Wilson.
Force and His Master.
Gentleness of Death, The.
Good Comrade, The.
Gordon of Khartoum.
Hawarden.
Hear now the mission of good wine.
Horses of Achilles, The.
Hueless Love, The.
J. C. M.
Lady C. M., The.
Landlady's Daughter, The.
Love.
Love they alone the joyful heart.
M. M.
Margaret's Bridal-Eve.
On Hearing the News from Venice.
Requiem: "Where faces are hueless, where eyelids are dewless."
Soft night–wind went laden to death, The.
State of Age, The.
Then said she, quick as the cries.
To a Friend Lost.

Vittoria Concluding the Opera of "Camilla."
Year's Sheddings, The.
Merrill. Annie Hill's Grave.
Broken Home, The.
Country of a Thousand Years of Peace, The.
Flèche d'Or.
Friend of the Fourth Decade, The.
Hotel de l'Univers et Portugal.
Salome.
Smile, The.
Yánnina.
Merton. Black Stone on Top of a White Stone.
Death.
Dirge: "Some one who hears the bugle neigh will know."
Elegy for Ernest Hemingway, An.
Elegy for Five Old Ladies, An.
Elegy for James Thurber.
Estais Muertos.
Faces of Girls Looking at Themselves in the River.
Ghost Dance.
Great Men of Former Times, The.
Guns of Fort Knox, The.
Hare's Message.
Lament for Javier Heraud.
Lament of a Maiden for the Warrior's Death.
Lao Tzu's Wake.
Litany: "Sing miserere / For the men who must die."
Moslems' Angel of Death, The.
Mysterious Song in the Spring of the Year, A.
Picture of a Black Child with a White Doll.
Poem: 1939.
Pride of the Dead, The.
Prisoner, The.
Prologo.
Responsory, 1948, A.
Rilke's Epitaph.
Songs.
Sponge Full of Vinegar, The.
There await men when they die.
Three Friends.
Two British Airmen.
What the Deceased Had to Say about Himself.
Millay. And you as well must die, belovèd dust.
Buck in the Snow, The.
Childhood Is the Kingdom Where Nobody Dies.
Conscientious Objector.
Elegy before Death.
Epitaph: "Grieve not for happy Claudius, he is dead."
If I die solvent—die, that is to say.
Keen.
Lines for a Grave-Stone.
Moriturus.
Passer Mortuus Est.
Shroud, The.
To S. V. B.—June 15, 1940.
Valentine.
Wine from These Grapes.
Miller. Dead Dog (For Goo).
For Juan Rulfo.
For Mike and Kim.
Milton. Another on the Same.
Damon's Epitaph.
Epitaph on the Marchioness of Winchester, An.
Hobsons Epitaph.
Lycidas.
Meanwhile [*or* Mean while] the Adversary of God and Man.
On the Death of the Vice-Chancellor, a Physician.
On the Same ["Thus did you strive to vouchsafe James to Heaven"].
On the University Carrier Who Sick'n'd [*or* Sickened] in the Time of His Vacancy [, Being Forbid to go to London, by Reason of the Plague].
On Time.
Pensive here I sat.
Sonnet 14: "When Faith and Love which parted from thee never."

Sonnet 23: "Mee thought I saw my late
  espoused saint."
Then both ourselves and seed at once to free.
Moore.   Grave, A.
What Are Years?
Morgan.   Body, The.
Captain Blaze.
Catullus: *Carmen ci.*
Death is the least of things to be feared.
Lady, the strange malignancy.
Omen.
Skulls, The.
Step, The.
Summit, The.
Vantage, The.
Whitish dawn had just appeared, The.
Who will laugh / in coldest glee.
Morrison.   & the Cool Fluttering.
Car Cemetery.
End, The.
He Follows a Woman.
Hurricane and Eclipse.
If It's No Problem.
If Only I.
Mystery of the Dream.
There's Blood in the Streets.
When the Music's Over.
Muldoon.   Big House, The.
Fox, The.
Soap-Pig, The.
Nash.   Crossing the Border.
Old Men.
People.
Tweedledee and Tweedledoom.
Nathan.   Closure.
It Looks As If It Were Just Sleeping.
Kind.
Wisdom of the Talmud.
Nemerov.   According to His Seasons.
Anniversary.
August, 1945.
Baron Baedeker Blew His Nose and, Sighing,
  Departed, The.
Between the Window and the Screen.
Elegy for a Nature Poet.
Epitaph: "Crazy, girls, crazy. Don is gone."
For W——— Who Commanded Well.
From the Last Dream of a Dying Woman
  Aged Eighty.
Grace to Be Said at the Supermarket.
In the Glass of Fashion.
My death with a nail in his foot.
Officer wore a thin smile, The.
On Reading "The Love and Death of Cornet
  Christopher Rilke."
One Moment in Eternity.
Photograph of a Girl, The.
Place of Value, The.
Sestina I: "Thickness of paint or flesh cannot
  deface."
Situation Does Not Change, The.
Small Moment.
Speculation.
Student Dies in 100 Yard Dash.
To a Friend.
To go low, to be as nothing, to die.
To the Memory of John Wheelwright.
Under the Bell Jar.
Virgin and Martyr.
Who Did Not Die in Vain.
You too will cool, though from your distance
  light.
Neruda.   Bell-Ringer, The.
Can't you think death lives.
Coming Back.
Different Ship, A.
Final.
Herbalist's Rose, The.
Initial.
Midday Construction.
Oliverio Girondo.
Search.
Sick Man in the Sun.
Today How Many Hours.
Untenable Situation, An.
What can it mean to endure.

Where is the child that I was.
Won't our life be a tunnel.
Notley.   Poem: "St. Marks Place caught at
  night in hot summer."
Poem: "You hear that heroic big land music?"
Poem: "Who do I want to tell it."
Sonnet: "Late Gracie Allen was a very lucid
  comedienne, The."
World's Bliss.
Your Dailiness.
O'Hara.   Alma.
Ashes on a Saturday Afternoon.
Day Lady Died, The.
Hatred.
Hôtel Transylvanie.
Poem: "And tomorrow morning at 8 o'clock in
  Springfield, Massachusetts."
Poem: "Eager note on my door said "Call
  me", The."
"Unfinished," The.
Oliver.   Black Snake, The.
Ghosts.
Marengo.
Rain.
Visitor, A.
When Death Comes.
White Flowers.
White Owl Flies Into and Out of the Field.
Olson.   Abt the dead he sd.
Anubis will stare.
As snow lies on the hill love's blackness lies.
As the Dead Prey upon Us.
At Yorktown.
Birth's Obituary.
Burial Ground.
Cole's Island.
Conqueror.
Death of Europe, The.
Diaries of Death.
He / in the dark stall, no day now for him, to
  paw.
Just Inside the Vigil of Christmas.
La Chute.
La Chute II.
La Préface.
Marry the Marrow.
Maximus, from Dogtown-1.
Newly Discovered "Homeric" Hymn, A.
Part of the Series on the Paths, A.
Sans Name.
Story of an Olson, and Bad Thing, The.
Tanto e Amara.
There Was a Youth Whose Name Was
  Thomas Granger.
Thing Was Moving, The.
Town, The.
Variations Done for Gerald Van de Wiele.
Oppen.   Now we do most of the killing.
Pro Nobis.
They await / War, and the news.
Which act is / Violence.
You are the last.
Owen.   Asleep.
End, The.
Futility.
Last Laugh, The.
Miners.
Next War, The.
Strange Meeting.
Unreturning, The.
Pack.   Clayfield's Son Selects His Specialty.
Fathering the Map.
Last Drowning, The.
Letter to My Widow.
Long and the Short of What's Good and
  What's Bad, The.
Prayer for Prayer.
Secrets.
Paley.   Drowning (I).
For George (II).
For Mike and Jeannie: Resisters Fifteen Years
  Later.
Old Age Porch.
Some days I am lonesome   I want to talk to
  my mother.
Patchen.   Ah, God, dear Brother, the mild and
  frowning rose.

All That Night Lights Were Seen Moving in
  Every Direction.
All the Bright Foam of Talk.
And a Man Went Out Alone.
At Grandmother's Wake.
Battle of Unameit, The.
Body Beside the Ties, The.
Breathe on the living.
Creation.
Crossing on Staten Island Ferry.
Death Will Amuse Them.
Deathsong for a Maiden.
Destruction of Carthage, The.
Devotion, A.
Do the Dead Know What Time It Is?
Early in the Morning.
Encounter at Nightfall.
Everlasting Contenders, The.
Examination into Life and Death, An.
Executions in Moscow, The.
Fox, The.
From my high love I look at that poor world
  there.
Have You Killed Your Man for Today?
Hold thy tongue, death!
House, and a Dead Man In It.
I Feel Drunk All the Time.
I Have No Place to Take Thee.
I saw three hundred fat cattle putting their
  forlornly comic faces.
In a Crumbling.
In Memory of Kathleen.
In shadings of an obscure punishment.
In the Courtyard of Secret Life.
Irkalla's White Caves.
It Is for Us the Living.
Lament for the Makers of Songs.
Last Full Measure of Devotion, The.
Lasting Seasons, The.
Lowellville Cemetery: Twilight.
Matchstick-Viewed-without-Regard-to-Its-
  Outer-Surface, A.
Now If You.
O All Down within the Pretty Meadow.
O Everliving Queen!
O Howling Cells.
O terrible is the highest thing.
Old Man.
Oldest Conversation, The.
Pathway, The.
Permanent Migrations, The.
Portrait on an American Theme.
Prayer Not To Go to Paradise with the Asses.
Radiance in a Dark Wood, The.
Religion Is That I Love You.
So It Ends.
There Is One Who Watches.
These are my great ones.
These Have Gone with Silent Hands, Seeking.
These Unreturning Destinies.
This Early Day.
Those Upon Whom God Has Labored.
To the Tune of an Ancient Song.
Tomorrow.
Unreturning Hosts, The.
We Hold These Truths to Be Self-Evident.
We Leave You Pleasure.
White lions are roaring on the water.
You May All Go Home Now.
Piercy.   Barbie Doll.
Hallow Eve with Spaces for Ghosts.
Knight of Swords, The.
Landed Fish.
Long Death, The.
Married Walk in a Hot Place, A.
On Castle Hill.
Proposal for Recycling Wastes, A.
S. Dead.
What You Waited For.
Plath.   All the Dead Dears.
April 18.
Bee Meeting, The.
Berck-Plage.
Birthday Present, A.
Daddy.
Dead, The.
Death & Co.

Detective, The.
Dirge for a Joker.
Edge.
Electra on Azalea Path.
Epitaph in Three Parts.
Getting There.
Lament: "Sting of bees took away my father, The."
Last Words.
Point Shirley.
Stings.
Totem.
Poe. Annabel Lee.
City in the Sea, The.
Conqueror Worm, The.
For Annie.
Lenore.
Raven, The.
Sleeper, The.
Spirits of the Dead.
To My Mother.
To One in Paradise—a Ballad].
Ulalume [or Ulalume—a Ballad].
Pope. Epitaph for One Who Would Not Be Buried in Westminster Abbey ("Heroes, and Kings! your distance keep").
Epitaph for One Who Would Not Be Buried in Westminster Abbey ("Under this Marble, or under this Sill").
Epitaph Intended for Mr. Rowe, in Westminster Abbey.
Epitaph (of By-Words).
Epitaph on Charles Earl of Dorset.
Epitaph on Dr. Francis Atterbury, Bishop of Rochester, Who Died in Exile at Paris, 1732; a Dialogue.
Epitaph on Edmund Duke of Buckingham, Who Died in the Nineteenth Year of His Age, 1735.
Epitaph on General Henry Withers, in Westminster-Abbey, 1729.
Epitaph on James Craggs, Esq., in Westminster Abbey.
Epitaph on John Knight, Who Died Oct. 2, 1733.
Epitaph on Mr. Elijah Fenton, at Easthamstead in Berks, 1730.
Epitaph on Mrs. Corbet, Who Died of a Cancer in Her Breast.
Epitaph on Sir Godfrey Kneller, in Westminster-Abbey, 1723.
Epitaph on Sir William Trumbal.
Epitaph on the Hon. Simon Harcourt.
Epitaph on the Monument of the Honourable Robert Digby, and of his Sister Mary, erected by their Father the Lord Digby, in the Church of Sherborne in Dorsetshire, 1727.
Epitaph: "Well then, poor G—— lies under ground!"
Ode: The Dying Christian to His Soul.
On Mr. Gay, in Westminster Abbey, 1732.
Winter, the Fourth Pastoral, or Daphne.
Pound. Planh for the Young English King.
Prince. And yet the Sibyl parches, caught and clutched within a fist of dust!
For Thieves and Beggars.
Last Attachment, A.
Last Poem.
On a Cold Night.
To believe is above all to be in love.
Two and a half years later the interpreter.
Raine. After Fifty-five Years.
Ah, many, many are the dead.
All that is: / The unbroken surface of the sea.
And that was all his life.
Crossing the sound I summoned you in thought.
Dead, The.
Dear ones in the house of the dead.
Descent Into Hades.
Dream.
Eider afloat in the bay.
From vague regions of sleep I come again.
Highland Graveyard.
If, into this evening as the grass receives the dew.
If you have ceased.

Instrument, The.
It crossed my mind.
Journey, The.
Kore.
Last night I seemed in your embrace.
November rain with thin fingers tapping.
One night in a dream.
Outside, sun, frost, wind, rain.
Rock is written with the sign, The.
These watery diamond spheres.
Two Invocations of Death.
Whiteness of moonlight builds a house that is not there.
With a Wave of Her Old Hand.
Ralegh. Epitaph upon the Right Hono[u]rable Sir Philip Sidney Knight, Lord Governor of Flushing, An.
Passionate Man['] s Pilgrimage, The.
Sir W. Ralegh, on the Snuff of a Candle the Night Before He Died.
Songe Made by Sir Walter Rawley, A.
Sunne may set and rise, The.
Vertue the Best Monument.
Ransom. Here Lies a Lady.
Piazza Piece.
Rain.
"Reed." Heroin.
Street Hassle: Street Hassle.
Rexroth. Andrée Rexroth ("Now once more gray mottled buckeye branches").
Andrée Rexroth ("Years have gone...").
Between Myself and Death.
Delia Rexroth.
For Eli Jacobson.
Requiem for the Spanish Dead.
Rich. At a Deathbed in the Year Two Thousand.
Corpse-Plant, The.
Final Notations.
For the Dead.
From a Survivor.
I Dream I'm the Death of Orpheus.
Moth Hour.
Mourning Picture.
Our Family.
Paula Becker to Clara Westhoff.
Phantasia for Elvira Shatayev.
Sleepwalking.
Stelae, The.
Tattered Kaddish.
To Frantz Fanon.
Why Else but to Forestall This Hour.
Woman Dead in Her Forties, A.
Woman Mourned by Daughters, A.
Robinson. Amaryllis.
Aretemias.
Chorus of Old Men in "Ægeus", The.
Cortège.
Exit.
For a Dead Lady.
Fragment: "Faint white pillars that seem to fade."
Happy Man, A.
Inferential.
Lisette and Eileen.
Luke Havergal.
Old Story, An.
Raven, The.
Recalled.
We shriek to live, but no man ever lives.
Where does a dead man go?—The dead man dies.
Whip, The.
Roethke. Death Piece.
Dying Man, The.
Elegy for Jane.
Elegy: "Her face like a rain-beaten stone on the day she rolled off."
Flight, The.
Frau Bauman, Frau Schmidt, and Frau Schwartze.
Journey to the Interior.
No Bird.
Plaint.
Sale.
Tranced, The.
Unfold! Unfold!

Rolfe. Asbestos.
Elegy for Our Dead.
Essay on Dreiser (1871-1945).
May 22nd 1939.
Paris—Christmas 1938.
Portrait of a Death.
Season of Death.
Somebody and Somebody Else and You.
Something Still Lives.
Survival Is of the Essence.
Rossetti. After Death.
Afterward He Repented, and Went.
All Flesh Is Grass.
All heaven is blazing yet / With the meridian sun.
All Saints.
Alleluia! or Alas! my heart is crying.
Amen.
Answer, An.
Are They Not All Ministering Spirits?
As dying, and behold we live!
As Thy Days, So Shall Thy Strength Be.
At Home.
Autumn.
Awake, Thou That Sleepest.
Ballad: "Soft white lamb in the daisy meadow."
Before the Beginning.
Behold a Shaking.
Beloved, yeild thy time to God, for He / Will make eternity thy recompense.
Better So.
Bird's-Eye View, A.
Bourne, The.
Burial Anthem.
Bury Hope out of sight, / No book for it and no bell.
But Thy Commandment Is Exceeding Broad.
Can I know it?—Nay.— / Shall I know it?— Yea.
Cardinal Newman.
Charon.
Chill blank world. Yet over the utmost sea, A.
Chilly Night, A.
Chruchyard Song of Patient Hope, A.
Convent Threshold, The.
Counsel, A.
Day and night the Accuser makes no pause.
Days of Vanity.
Dead before Death.
Dead Bride, The.
Dead City, The.
Death.
Death Is Swallowed Up in Victory.
Death-Watches.
Death's Chill Between.
Despair.
Dirge, A: "She was as sweet as violet..."
Dirge, A: "Why were you born when the snow was falling?"
Doeth Well. Doeth Better.
Dream Land.
Dying Man to His Betrothed, The.
Easter Monday.
Easter Tuesday.
Eleventh Hour, The.
Ellen Middleton.
End, An.
End Is Not Yet, The.
Eve.
Everything that is born must die.
Faint, Yet Pursuing.
Fair World Tho' a Fallen, A.
Floral Teaching.
Flowers Appear on the Earth, The.
For Advent.
For All.
For Each.
For Rosaline's Album.
From the Antique.
General Assembly and Church of the Firstborn, The.
Goal in sihgt! Look up and sing, / Set faces full against the light, The.
Golden Silences.
Gone Before.
Gone to his rest / Bright little Bouby!

Guesses.
Half Dead.
He Shall Go No More Out.
Heaven's chimes are slow, but sure to strike at last.
Heaviness May Endure for a Night, But Joy Cometh in the Morning.
Henry Hardiman.
Husband and Wife.
I Have a Message unto Thee.
I have but one rose in the world.
I lift mine eyes to see: earth vanisheth.
I love you and you know it—this at least.
I See That All Things Come to an End.
If not with hope of life, / Begin with fear of death.
If thou be dead, forgive and thou shalt live.
"Immurata" Sister, An.
In a Certain Place.
In resurrection is it awfuller.
Iniquity of the Fathers upon the Children, The.
Isidora.
It is not death, O Christ, to die for Thee: / Nor is that silence of a silent land.
Judge Nothing before the Time.
Lady Isabella.
Last Answer, The.
Last *Complaint*, The.
Last Look, The.
Last Words of St. Telemachus, The.
Laughing Life cries at the feast.
Lent.
Let Them Rejoice in Their Beds.
Life and Death.
Life Hidden.
Life Out of Death.
Long Looked For.
Looking back along life's trodden way.
Looking Forward.
Lord, make me one with Thine own faithful ones.
Lord, make us all love all: that when we meet / Even myriads of earth's myriads at Thy Bar.
Lord Thomas and Fair Margaret.
Love and Death.
Love hath a name of Death.
Love Is Strong as Death ("As flames that consume...").
Love Is Strong as Death ("I have sought Thee...").
Martyr, A.
May.
Mirrors of Life and Death.
Mother Country.
My Friend.
My Old Friends.
Next of Kin.
Night and Death.
None With Him.
Now They Desire.
O Death Where Is Thy Sting?
O Lucifer, Son of the Morning!
Of My Life.
On the Death of a Cat.
One Day.
One of the Dead.
One Sea-Side Grave.
One woe is past. Come what come will.
Only Believe.
Our Church Palms are Budding Willow Twigs.
Our heaven must be within ourselves / Our home and heaven the work of faith.
Our Mothers, lovely women pitiful; / Our sisters, gracious in their life and death.
Parting after parting, / Sore loss and gnawing pain.
Passing and Glassing.
Pause, A.
Peal of Bells, A.
Peter Grump.
Pitia a Damone.
Plague, The.
Poor Ghost, The.
Portrait, A.
Prince's Progress, The.
Remember [Me].

Repining.
Rest.
Resurrection Eve.
Rosalind.
Ruined Cross, The.
Safe where I cannot lie yet, / Safe where I hope to lie too.
Sappho.
Scarce tolerable life, which all life long.
Septuagesima.
Shall I Forget?
Sir Eustace Grey.
Slain in their high places: fallen on rest.
Sleep at Sea.
Sleeping at last, the trouble and tumult over.
Son, Remember.
Song: "Oh roses for the flush of youth."
Song: "Stream moaneth as it floweth, The."
Song: "We buried her among the flowers."
Song: "When I am dead, my dearest."
Songs in a Cornfield.
Summer Is Ended, The.
Sweet Death.
Take Care Of Him.
Then They That Feared the Lord Spake Often One to Another.
Then Whose Shall Those Things Be?
There Remaineth Therefore a Rest.
There Remaineth Therefore a Rest for the People of God ("Come blessed sleep...").
There Remaineth Therefore a Rest for the People of God ("Rest remains when all is done...").
They lie at rest, our blessed dead.
Thou sleepest where the lilies fade.
Three Moments.
Three Nuns.
Thy Servant Will Go and Fight with This Philistine.
Toll, bell, toll. For hope is flying / Sighing from the earthbound soul.
Triad, A.
Two Thoughts of Death.
Under Willows.
Uphill [*or* Up-Hill].
Watchers, The.
We are of those who tremble at Thy word.
Wednesday in Holy Week.
What Good Shall My Life Do Me?
What to Do?
Whatsoever Is Right, That Shall Ye Receive.
When My Heart Is Vexed I Will Complain ("Fields are white to harvest, look and see, The").
When wickedness is broken as a tree / Paradise comes to light, ah holy land!
Where never tempest heaveth, / Nor sorrow grieveth.
Where Their Worm Dieth Not, and the Fire Is Not Quenched.
Whither the Tribes Go Up, Even the Tribes of the Lord.
Who cares for earthly bread tho' white?
Who shall my wandering thoughts steady & fix.
Who would wish back the Saints upon our rough.
Why?
Ye Have Forgotten the Exhortation.
Year Afterwards, A.
You who looked on passed ages as a glass.
Young Death.
Young Men Aye Were Fickle Found Since Summer Trees Were Leafy.
Zara.
Rukeyser. Arthur Peyton.
Book of the Dead, The.
Course.
Delta Poems.
Doctors, The.
Dreaming we were awake, we heard the rivers.
Driveway.
For Memory.
Gibbs.
In the Night the Sound Woke Us.
Iris.
Madboy's Song.

Mary Sleeth.
Mearl Blankenship.
Mother Garden's Round.
On the Death of Her Mother.
Outer Banks, The.
Power.
Power of Suicide, The.
Sea Mercy.
Shooting Gallery.
Slow Death of the Dragon.
Sun on the faces. On the knotted rocks.
Then.
What They Said.
St. John. Elegy: "Who keeps the owl's breath? Whose eyes desire?"
Hard & Noble Patience, A.
Sandburg. Acquaintance with Death, Sir.
And So Today.
Anecdote of Hemlock for Two Athenians.
Anna Imroth.
Black Horizons.
Bones.
Books Men Die For.
Brancusi.
Chamfort.
Cool Tombs.
Death Snips Proud Men.
Drumnotes.
Dunes.
Dusty Doors.
Electric Sign Goes Dark, An.
Fence, A.
Finish.
Fog Numbers.
Four Brothers, The.
Grass.
Graves.
Grieg Being Dead.
Guaranteed Antique.
Have Me.
Haze.
Hunger and only hunger changes worlds?
Illinois Farmer.
In a Breath.
In the folded and quiet yesterdays.
Instructions.
Iron.
Jaws.
Junk Man, The.
Killers ("I am put high...").
Killers ("I am singing...").
Kindest and gentlest here are the, The.
Lavender Lilies.
Liars, The.
Losers.
Losses.
Man, the Man-Hunter.
Man with the Broken Fingers, The.
Marshall Field the First was spick and span while alive.
Memoir of a Proud Boy.
Mildred Klinghofer whirled through youth in bloom.
Million Young Workmen, 1915, A.
Mist Forms.
Mummy.
Murmurings in a Field Hospital.
Never Born.
Now They Bury Her Again.
Old Osawatomie.
On Lang Syne Plantation they had a prayer.
Pals.
People, yes, The.
People, yes, the people, The.
Places.
Ready to Kill.
Repetitions.
Response of wild birds, The.
Right to Grief, The.
Sandhill People.
Since death is there in the light of the sun, in the song of the.
Slabs of the Sunburnt West.
Smoke.
Swirl.
Testament.
Themes in Contrast.

Throw Roses.
To a Dead Man.
To Certain Journeymen.
Troths.
Under the Harvest Moon.
Waiting for the Chariot.
When Death Came April Twelve 1945.
Woman with a Past.
Yes, the Dead Speak to Us.
Sarton. All Souls.
Burial.
Celebration for George Sarton, A.
Death and the Lovers.
How faint the horn sounds in the mountain passes.
Letter from Chicago.
Moth in the Schoolroom.
My Father's Death.
Of Grief.
Schuyler. "From the next .."
Grave, A.
Heather and Calendulas.
Mike.
Schwartz. "All is forgiven when guilt is accepted."
Now He Knows All There Is to Know: Now He Is Acquainted With the Day and Night.
Sequel, the Conclusion, the Endlessness, The.
Yeats Died Saturday in France.
Scott. Coronach.
Death of Argentine, The.
Fitz-Eustace's Song.
Lay of the Imprisoned Huntsman.
Palmer, The.
Song of Albert Graeme.
Sexton. All My Pretty Ones.
Assassin, The.
Clothes.
Curse against Elegies, A.
Death King, The.
Elizabeth Gone.
For Johnny Pole on the Forgotten Beach.
For Mr. Death Who Stands with His Door Open.
Godfather Death.
Hex, The.
Hurry Up Please It's Time.
KE 6-8018.
Lament: "Someone is dead."
Leaves That Talk.
Letters to Dr. Y.
Live.
Making a Living.
May 30th.
Oh.
Sea Corpse, The.
Somewhere in Africa.
Starry Night, The.
Sweeney.
Taker, The.
Tenth Psalm.
Truth the Dead Know, The.
Waiting Head, The.
Wanting to Die.
Shakespeare. Sonnet 32: "If thou survive my well-contented day."
Sonnet 71: "No longer mourn for me when I am dead."
Sonnet 72: "O! Lest the world should task you to recite."
Sonnet 73: "That time of year thou may'st [or maist] in me behold."
Sonnet 74: "But be contented: when that fell arrest."
Sonnet 81: "Or I shall live your epitaph to make."
Sonnet 107: "Not mine own fears nor the prophetic soul."
Sonnet 110: "Alas, 'tis true I have gone here and there."
Sonnet 146: "Poor[e] soul[e], the centre of my sinful[l] earth."
Sweet rose, fair flower, untimely pluck'd, soon vaded.
Shapiro. Auto Wreck.
Cut Flower, A.
Hospital.

Interlude, The.
My Grandmother.
Necropolis.
Scyros.
Vietnam Memorial.
Shelley. Daemon of the World, The; A Fragment.
Death.
Death knell is ringing, The.
Dialogue, A.
Fragment: Death in Life.
Fragment: Life Rounded with Sleep.
Fragment: Omens.
Mask [or Masque] of Anarchy, The.
On a Faded Violet.
On Death.
Song for "Tasso."
Sonnet: "Ye hasten to the grave! What seek ye there."
Summer Evening Churchyard, A.
To Death.
To Night.
Shelton. Cortege.
Death.
Rain the Stones the Darkness, The.
Reunion.
Softly Softly.
Sidney. Oft have I mused, but now at length I find.
Since Nature's works be good, and death doth serve.
Since wailing is a bud of causeful sorrow.
Silverstein. Boa Constrictor.
Fred?
Paul Bunyan.
Simic. Charon's Cosmology.
Eyes Fastened with Pins.
Marching.
Navigator.
Smart. At Undressing in the Evening.
Epitaph on Henry Fielding, Esq.
To Posthumus.
Smith, Charlotte. April.
By the Same.
By the Same. Just before His Death.
Dead Beggar, an Elegy Addressed to a Lady, The.
Inscription on a Stone, in the Church-Yard at Boreham.
Ode to Death.
Supposed to Have Been Written in a Church-yard, over the Grave of a Young Woman of Nineteen.
To the Shade of Burns.
To Tranquillity.
To Vesper.
Verses, on the death of [Henrietta O'Neill], written in September, 1794.
Winter Night, The.
Smith, Patti. Ballad of a Bad Boy.
Ballad of Isabelle Eberhardt.
Combe.
Death by Water.
Jeanne D'Arc.
Picasso Laughing.
Rimbaud Dead.
Robert Bresson.
Smith, Stevie. Ambassador, The.
Angel Boley.
Après la Politique, la Haine des Bourbons.
Arabella.
Ass, The.
Bereavement.
Black March.
Boat, The.
Come, Death (1).
Come, Death (2).
Company.
Crown of Bays, The.
Death-Bed of a Financier.
Death Bereaves Our Common Mother Nature Grieves for My Dead Brother.
Death Came to Me.
Death of Mr. Mounsel.
Death of the Dog Belvoir.
Death Sentence, The.
Death's Ostracism.

Die Lorelei.
Do Take Muriel Out.
Edmonton, Thy Cemetery..
Exeat.
Farewell: "Farewell dear friends."
Flow, Flow, Flow.
From the Coptic.
Fuite d'Enfance.
God the Drinker.
Grave by a Holm-Oak.
Harold's Leap.
How Far Can You Press a Poet?
If I Lie Down.
Le Revenant.
Longing for Death because of Feebleness.
Mrs. Arbuthnot.
Mr. Over.
Mrs Simpkins.
Murder.
My Heart Goes Out.
Night-Time in the Cemetery.
Not Waving but Drowning.
Parklands, The.
Poet!
Poor Soul, Poor Girl!
Private Means Is Dead.
Progression.
Proud Death with Swelling Port.
Quand on n'a pas ce que l'on aime, il faut aimer ce que l'on a—.
Reversionary.
River Deben, The.
Siesta.
Silence and Tears.
Study to Deserve Death.
Tender Only to One.
To a Lady in a Train.
To the Dog Belvoir.
Toll of the Roads, The.
Upon a Grave.
Venus When Young Choosing Death.
Voice from the Tomb (1).
Who Killed Lawless Lean?
Who Shot Eugenie?
Why Do I.
Zoo, The.
Snodgrass. Adolf Hitler ("More than fifty millions. More").
Disposal.
Eva B Hitler, geb. Braun.
Flat One, A.
Monet: "Les Nymphéas."
Old Jewelry.
Song: "Observe the cautious toadstools."
Survivors, The.
To a Child.
Viewing the Body.
Snyder. For John Chappell.
For Lew Welch in a Snowfall.
For/From Lew.
I have lived at Cold Mountain.
Word Basket Woman.
Sorrentino. Anatomy.
Blackburn's Dream.
But the light is imagined.
In Memoriam P.B.
Nothing grimmer than dawn at noon.
Now the night is here. Blood.
Poem: "Living friends live / in the past so they bore us."
She whom no one ever found.
Ultima Despedida del Principe Poniatowski de Su Familia.
Zoo, The.
Southwell. I Dye Alive.
I Dye Without Desert.
Laments for a Noble Lady.
Life is But Losse.
Life's Death, Love's Life.
Upon the Image of Death.
What Joy to Live.
Spender. Beethoven's Death Mask.
Boy, Cat, Canary.
Coward, The.
Cyril Connolly.
Elegy for Margaret.
Furies, The.

Girl Who Has Drowned Herself Speaks, A.
In Attica.
My Brother Luis.
Never Being.
Perhaps.
Spiritual Explorations.
Stopwatch and an Ordnance Map, A.
Trigorin.
Spenser.   At last, so faire a ladie did I spie.
Pastorall Aeglogue upon the Death of Sir
   Phillip Sidney, Knight, etc, A.
What If Some Little Paine the Passage Have.
Stafford.   Aunt Mabel.
Dedication, A: "We stood by the library. It
   was an August night."
Fall Journey.
My Father: October 1942.
Once a man killed another, to rob him.
108 East 19th.
Weather Report.
Stevens.   Burghers of Petty Death.
Death of a Soldier, The.
Flyer's Fall.
Of Heaven Considered as a Tomb.
Owl in the Sarcophagus, The.
Postcard from the Volcano, A.
Sunday Morning.
Two at Norfolk.
Worms at Heaven's Gate, The.
Stevenson.   Ad Martialem.
After Reading "Antony and Cleopatra."
Angler rose, he took his rod, The.
As starts the absent dreamer, when a train.
Before this little gift was come.
Behold, as goblins dark of mien.
Celestial Surgeon, The.
Counterblast—1886, The.
Daughter of Herodias, The.
De M. Antonio.
Death.
Death, to the dead for evermore.
Ditty: "Cock shall crow, The."
End of Travel, An.
Fear not, dear friend, but freely live your
   days.
Feast of Famine: Marquesan Manners, The.
For Richmond's Garden Wall.
He hears with gladdened heart the thunder.
Here Lies Erotion.
Here you rest among the valleys, maiden
   known to but a few.
I am like one that for long days had sate.
I do not fear to own me kin.
I have trod the upward and the downward
   slope.
I, now, O friend, whom noiselessly the snows.
I whom Apollo sometime visited.
If I had wings, my lady, like a dove.
In Memoriam F. A. S.
It is not yours, O mother, to complain.
It's an owercome sooth for age an' youth.
Light as my heart was long ago.
Look of Death is both severe and mild, The.
Loud and low in the chimney.
Love—what is love? A great and aching heart.
Man sails the deep a while.
My wife and I, in one romantic cot.
Not roses to the rose, I trow.
Not yet, my soul, these friendly fields desert.
Now when the number of my years.
Our Lady of the Snows.
Poem for a Class Re-Union.
Requiem: "Under the wide and starry sky."
Rivers and winds among the twisted hills.
Since thou hast given me this good hope, O
   God.
So live, so love, so use that fragile hour.
Soon our friends perish.
Strange are the ways of men.
There where the land of love.
Ticonderoga: A Legend of the West
   Highlands.
To ———: "I knew thee strong and quiet like
   the hills."
To Charles Baxter.
To H.F. Brown.
To K. de M.

To Mrs. Will H. Low.
To Priapus.
To W.E. Henley.
To Will H. Low.
To you, let snow and roses.
Tropics vanish, and meseems that I, The.
Unforgotten I, The ("In dreams, unhappy, I
   behold you stand").
Vanquished Knight, The.
Verses Written in 1872.
We uncommiserate pass into the night.
When the sun comes after rain.
Wind blew shrill and smart, The.
Stuart.   Birds, The.
Elegies for Walker Dabney Stuart, Jr.
Funeral, The.
Girl of My Dreams Is Dying.
I Can't Live Without You.
Major Work.
Spell.
Taking the Wheel.
Widow, The.
Sutter.   Can you believe it?
Deathwatch.
First Hard Frost, The.
Friends find the family.
Geneva.
I didn't used to care much.
Mrs.
Sky.
Talking To Grandpa Eastman.
This woman is nobody's woman.
Warming up in their truck.
Swift.   Death and Daphne.
Elegy on Dicky and Dolly, An.
Elegy on the Much Lamented Death of Mr.
   Demar, the Famous Rich Usurer, An.
Elegy On the Supposed Death of Mr.
   Partridge, the Almanac Maker.
Paper book is sent by Boyle, A.
Quibbling Elegy on the Worshipful Judge
   Boat, A.
Swinburne.   After Death.
Ballad of Death, A.
Les Noyades.
Lyke-Wake Song, A.
Triumph of Time, The.
Tate.   Adaption of a Theme from Catullus.
Anabasis, The.
Calidus Juventa?
Carrion, A.
Cross, The.
Eager Youths to a Dead Girl.
Elegy for Eugenesis.
Emblems.
For a Dead Citizen.
Intellectual Detachment.
Light.
Non Omnis Moriar.
Nuptials.
Oath, The.
Our elder brother whom we had not seen.
Procession.
Reflections in an Old House.
Stranger.
Then, brother, you would never think me vain.
This message hastens lest we both go down.
Vigil.
Tennyson.   Crossing the Bar.
Dead Prophet, The.
Far-Far-Away.
In the Garden at Swainston.
In the Valley of Cauteretz.
Lady of Shalott, The.
Mariana in the South.
Morte d'Arthur.
Old yew, which graspest at the stones.
Prefatory Poem to My Brother's Sonnets.
St. Simeon Stylites.
Sweet after showers, ambrosial air.
Tithonus.
To J. S. [James Spedding].
Thomas.   After the Funeral.
Among Those Killed in the Dawn Raid Was a
   Man Aged a Hundred.
And Death Shall Have No Dominion.
Conversation of Prayer, The.

Death is all metaphors, shape in one history.
Deaths and Entrances.
Do Not Go Gentle into That Good Night.
Elegy: "Too proud to die; broken and blind he
   died."
Force That through the Green Fuse Drives the
   Flower, The.
Hand That Signed the Paper, The.
Lament: "When I was a windy boy and a bit."
Now.
Poem on His Birthday.
Then Was My Neophyte.
To-day, This Insect.
Tombstone Told When She Died, The.
Unluckily for a Death.
When, Like a Running Grave.
Thomson.   On the Death of his Mother.
On the Death of Mr. Aikman.
Poem to the Memory of Mr. Congreve, A.
To the Memory of Sir Isaac Newton.
Tomlinson.   Cradock Newton: From an
   Epitaph.
Curtain Call.
De Sole.
Death in the Desert, A.
Death of Elizabeth Grieve, The.
For Miriam.
In Memoriam Thomas Hardy.
Mausoleum, The.
Remembering Williams.
Tree, The.
Turco.   Death.
Dream, The.
Dybbuk.
Forest Beyond the Glass, The.
Pilot, The.
Scythe, The.
Updike.   Bath after Sailing.
Fall.
Millipede, The.
Perfection Wasted.
To Ed Sissman.
Van Duyn.   Creation, The.
Reading of Rex Stout, A.
Stream, The.
Wakoski.   Apparitions Are Not Singular
   Occurrences.
David.
Story of Richard Maxfield, The.
Walcott.   Landfall, Grenada.
Letter from Brooklyn, A.
Sea Canes.
Verandah.
Village Life, A.
Walker.   Burial.
Girl Who Died #1, The.
Girl Who Died #2, The.
Good Night, Willie Lee, I'll See You in the
   Morning.
To Die before One Wakes Must Be Glad.
Warren.   After Night Flight Son Reaches
   Bedside of Already Unconscious Father,
   Whose Right Hand Lifts in a Spasmodic
   Gesture, as Though Trying to Make Contact:
   1955.
Answer Yes or No.
Bear Track Plantation: Shortly after Shiloh.
Butterflies over the Map.
Chain Saw at Dawn in Vermont in Time of
   Drouth.
Confederate Veteran Tries to Explain the
   Event, A.
Country Burying (1919).
Death I have entered is a death, The.
Dream He Never Knew the End of, The.
Event, The.
Fall Comes in Back-Country Vermont.
Harvard '61: Battle Fatigue.
I Am Dreaming of a White Christmas: The
   Natural History of a Vision.
Insomnia.
Interim, The.
Mad Druggest, The.
Old Nigger on One-Mule Cart Encountered
   Late at Night When Driving Home from
   Party in the Back Country.
Reading Late at Night, Thermometer Falling.

School Lesson Based on Word of Tragic
  Death of Entire Gillum Family.
South shoulder of the pass, The.
There once, on that goat island, I.
There's a Grandfather's Clock in the Hall.
Way to Love God, A.
What Happened.
Whitman.　As at Thy Portals Also Death.
As I Watch'd the Ploughman Ploughing.
As If a Phantom Caress'd Me.
As They Draw to a Close.
Ashes of Soldiers.
Assurances.
City Dead-House, The.
Come Up from the Fields Father.
Dead Tenor, The.
Death and Burial of McDonald Clarke, a
  Parody, The.
Death of the Nature-Lover, The.
Death's Valley.
Dying Veteran, The.
End of All, The.
Gliding o'er All.
Great Are the Myths.
Hush'd be the Camps To-day.
In Former Songs.
Joy, Shipmate, Joy!
Last Invocation, The.
My Departure.
Now Finalè to the Shore.
O Captain! My Captain!
O Living Always, Always Dying.
Of Him I Love Day and Night.
Old Age's Ship & Crafty Death's.
Old Salt Kossabone.
On the Same Picture.
Or, from That Sea of Time.
Osceola.
Outlines for a Tomb.
Pallid Wreath, The.
Pensive and Faltering.
Portals.
Sleepers, The.
Sobbing of the Bells, The.
This Compost.
This Dust Was Once the Man.
Thought: ("As I sit with others at a great
  feast, suddenly while the music is playing").
Time to Come.
To One Shortly to Die.
To Think of Time.
Two Rivulets.
We All Shall Rest at Last.
When Lilacs Last in the Dooryard Bloom'd.
Whispers of Heavenly Death.
Yet, Yet Ye Downcast Hours.
Whittier.　Andrew Rykman's Prayer.
At Last.
Autumn Thoughts.
Between the Gates.
Bolivar.
Dead Feast of the Kol-Folk, The.
Dead Ship of Harpswell, The.
Eva.
Female Martyr, The.
Friend's Burial, The.
Gone.
In Memory.
In Peace.
In Remembrance of Joseph Sturge.
Isabella of Austria.
Kinsman.
Lament, A: "Circle is broken, one seat is
  forsaken, The."
Lines on the Death of S. Oliver Torrey.
Lucy Hooper.
Marguerite.
Memorial, A.
Missionary, The.
Mulford.
Naples.
New Wife and the Old, The.
Old Burying-Ground, The.
Palatine, The.
Poet and the Children, The.
R. S. S., at Deer Island on the Merrimac.
Rantoul.

Samuel J. Tilden.
Sisters, The: A Picture by Barry
Telling the Bees.
Thomas Starr King.
To the Memory of Charles B. Storrs.
To the Memory of Thomas Shipley.
William Forster.
Wilbur.　Another Voice.
Ballade in Old French.
Ballade to End With, A.
Bell Speech.
Beowulf.
Castles and Distances.
Death, from a Distance.
For Dudley.
For W. H. Auden.
Funeral of Bobò, The.
In a Churchyard.
Lightness.
Lilacs, The.
Merlin Enthralled.
Mill, The.
Pardon, The.
Pity.
Prayer to Go to Paradise with the Donkeys, A.
Puritans, The.
To an American Poet Just Dead.
To His Skeleton.
Tywater.
Up, Jack.
Voice from under the Table, A.
Year's End.
Williams, Charles Kenneth.　Becoming
  Somebody Else.
Clay out of Silence.
Covenant, The.
Dream, The.
Even If I Could.
Faint Praise.
Friends.
From Now On.
Giving It Up.
Hail goes / dancing, The.
Helen.
Inches.
Le Petit Salvié.
Little Shirt, The.
Long Naked Walk of the Dead, The.
They wash you / when.
This Day.
To Listen.
Villanelle of the Suicide's Mother.
Williams, Miller.　And Then.
For Victor Jara.
Ghosts.
In Nashville, Standing in the Wooden Circle
  Sawed Out from the Old Ryman Stage, the
  Picker has a vision.
Notes from the Agent on Earth: How to be
  Human.
On Hearing About the Death of Mitzi Mayfair.
On the Death of a Middle-Aged Man.
On the Symbolic Consideration of Hands and
  the Significance of Death.
People.
Rituals.
Some Lines Finished Just Before Dawn at the
  Bedside of a Dying Student / It has Snowed
  All Night.
Story, The.
Survivor, The.
Widow, The.
Williams, William Carlos.　Complete
  Destruction.
Death.
Death of Franco of Cologne, The: His
  Prophecy of Beethoven.
Death the Barber.
End of the Rope, The.
Eternity, An.
Last Words of My English Grandmother, The.
Last Words of My Grandmother.
Note, A.
Observer, The.
Picture Showing.
Rapid Transit.
Smiling Dane, A.

Spring Song.
Stone Crock, The.
To a Dead Journalist.
To a Dog Injured in the Street.
To the Ghost of Marjorie Kinnan Rawlings.
Tragic Detail.
Two Pendants: For the Ears.
Widow's Lament in Springtime, The.
Wordsworth.　Address to the Scholars of the
  Village School of—1798.
Argument for Suicide.
Ballad, A: "And will you leave me thus
  alone."
By a Blest Husband Guided, Mary Came.
Cenotaph.
Could I the priest's consent have gained.
Destined to war from very infancy.
Dirge Sung by a Minstrel.
Elegiac Stanzas.
Elegiac Stanzas (Addressed to Sir G.H.B. upon
  the Death of His Sister-in-Law).
Elegiac Verses in Memory of My Brother,
  John Wordsworth.
Elegy Written in the Same Place upon the
  Same Occasion.
Ellen Irwin; or, The Braes of Kirtle.
Epitaph in Grasmere Church.
Epitaph in the Chapel Yard of Langdale,
  Westmoreland.
Forth from a Jutting Ridge, Around Whose
  Base.
Glen-Almain; Or, the Narrow Glen.
Hour-bell sounds, and I must go, The.
Laodamia.
Lines Written on a Blank Leaf in a Copy of
  the Author's Poem "The Excursion", upon
  Hearing of the Death of the Late Vicar of
  Kendal.
Matthew.
Methought I saw the footsteps of a throne.
Not without heavy grief of heart did He.
November, 1836.
O flower of all that springs from gentle blood.
O Lelius, beauteous flower of gentleness.
O Thou who movest onward with a mind.
On the Death of an Unfortunate Lady.
On the Death of His Majesty (George the
  Third).
Pause, courteous Spirit!—Baldi supplicates.
Perhaps some needful service of the State.
Seven Sisters, or, the Solitude of Binnorie,
  The.
She dwelt among the untrodden ways.
She was a phantom of delight.
Slumber did my spirit seal, A.
Sonnet Written by Mr — Immediately after
  the Death of His Wife.
Sonnets upon the Punishment of Death.
There never breathed a man who, when his
  life.
Thoughts Suggested the Day Following, on the
  Banks of Nith, near the Poet's Residence.
To ——: "O dearer far than light and life
  are dear."
To a Sexton.
To the Memory of Raisley Calvert.
Torquato Tasso rests within this tomb.
True it is that Ambrosio Salinero.
Two April Mornings, The.
Upon Perusing the "Epistle [To Sir George
  Howland Beaumont"] Thirty Years after Its
  Composition.
Upon the Sight of the Portrait of a Female
  Friend.
Weep not, belovèd Friends! nor let the air.
Well-nigh the voyage now is overpast.
Wright, Charles.　Arkansas Traveller.
Called Back.
Hawaii Dantesca.
Homage to Cesare Pavese.
Homage to Paul Cézanne.
Lost Bodies.
Portrait of the Artist with Li Po.
Southern Cross, The.
To Giacomo Leopardi in the Sky.
Wright, James.　Alarm, The.
All the Beautiful are Blameless.

Angel, The.
Arrangements with Earth for Three Dead
   Friends.
Assignation, The.
At the Executed Murderer's Grave.
At the Slackening of the Tide.
At Thomas Hardy's Birthplace, 1953.
Before a Cashier's Window in a Department
   Store.
But Only Mine.
Centenary Note: Inscribed to Little Crow,
   Leader of the Sioux Rebellion in Minnesota,
   1862, A.
Christmas Greeting, A.
De Profundis.
Devotions.
Dream of Burial, A.
Echo for the Promise of Georg Trakl's Life.
Eclogue at Nash's Grove.
Elegy for the Poet Morgan Blum, An.
Erinna to Sappho.
Eternal Dice, The.
Frontier, The.
Gesture by a Lady with an Assumed Name, A.
Girl Walking into a Shadow, A.
Heights of Macchu Picchu, III, The.
Humming a Tune for an Old Lady in West
   Virginia.
I Am a Sioux Brave, He Said in Minneapolis.
I Was Afraid of Dying.
Idea of the Good, The.
In a Viennese Cemetery.
Inscription for the Tank.
Katy Did.
Lament for My Brother on a Hayrake.
Life, The.
Many of Our Waters: Variations on a Poem
   by a Black Child.
Mesage Hidden in an Empty Wine Bottle that
   I Threw into a Gully of Maple Trees One
   Night at an Indecent Hour, A.
Miners.
Minneapolis Poem, The.
Moguer.
Northern Pike.
Note Left in Jimmy Leonard's Shack, A.
Offense, The.
Offering for Mr. Bluehart, An.
Old Age Compensation.
Old Man Drunk.
On the Skeleton of a Hound.
Our Daily Bread.
Paul.
Poem about George Doty in the Death House,
   A.
Refusal, The.
Saint Judas.
Small Blue Heron, The.
Speak.
Three Sentences for a Dead Swan.
To a Dead Drunk.
To a Defeated Savior.
To a Friendly Dun.
To Harvey, Who Traced the Circulation.
To the Muse.
Today I Was So Happy, So I Made this
   Poem.
Two Poems about President Harding.
Way to Make a Living, A.
White Rose.
Willy Lyons.
Winter Day in Ohio, A.
Wroth.   Sonnet 30: "You blessed shades,
   which give mee silent rest."
Wyatt.   Enemy [or en'my] of life, decayer of
   all kind, The [or Th'].
   In mourning wise since daily I increase.
   Plain ye, mine eyes. Accompany my heart.
   Stand whoso list upon the slipper top.
   To make an end of all this strife.
Yau.   When a comet passes over the town,
   whoever sees it knows a corpse.
   When one of our citizens dies, his corpse is
   placed in his chariot.
   When one of our citizens dies, his head is cut
   off and placed inside.
Yeats.   Baile and Aillinn.

Ballad of Father O'Hart, The.
Ballad of the Foxhunter, The.
Circus Animals' Desertion, The.
Countess Cathleen in Paradise, The.
Crazy Jane and the Bishop.
Death.
Double Vision of Michael Robartes, The.
Dream of Death, A.
Fool by the Roadside, The.
He Thinks of His Past Greatness When a Part
   of the Constellations of Heaven.
He Wishes His Beloved Were Dead.
His Dream.
In Memory of Alfred Pollexfen.
In Tara's Halls.
Irish Airman Foresees His Death, An.
Last Confession, A.
Man and the Echo.
Man Who Dreamed of Faeryland, The.
Mountain Tomb, The.
Sailing to Byzantium.
Shepherd and Goatherd.
That the Night Come.
Three Bushes, The.
Three Things.
To a Shade.
Tom O'Roughley.
Two Songs from a Play.
Upon a Dying Lady.
Vacillation.
Young.   Why a Hush Should Not Be Rushed.
Zimmer.   Christiaan Fearing the Sky.
   Curse of the Frogs, The.
   Death Demonstrates His Presence to Zimmer.
   Zimmer and the Ghost.
   Zimmer Finds Imbellis in the Ancient Graves.
Zukofsky.   Air.
   Cold how mean, fortune consuming you
   oppresses your care, your.
   During the Passaic Strike of 1926.
   H.T.
   Mulled hosts their countries yet mulled there
   by a core of wake tossed.
   Quick death, Catullus! what more horrors may
   hurry!
   Sand: For the cigarette finished, The.
   See quick calm moot as gratifying the
   tombed—sepulchres.
   Song Theme.

Death in Childhood
Angelou.   Child Dead in Old Seas.
   To Beat the Child Was Bad Enough.
Atwood.   Death of a Young Son by Drowning.
Betjeman.   Child Ill, A.
Bishop.   First Death in Nova Scotia.
Bradstreet.   In Memory of My Dear Grandchild
   Anne Bradstreet.
   In Memory of My Dear Grandchild Elizabeth
   Bradstreet Who Deceased August, 1665,
   Being a Year and a Half Old.
   On My Dear Grandchild Simon Bradstreet,
   [Who Died on 16TH November, 1669, Being
   But A Month And One Day Old].
Brontë.   Farewell To Alexandria, A.
   To the Bluebell.
Browning, Elizabeth Barrett.   Child's Grave at
   Florence, A.
   Isobel's Child.
   Little Mattie.
   They look up with their pale and sunken faces.
Burns.   To the Memory of the Unfortunate
   Miss Burns 1791.
Carew.   Another [Epitaph on the Lady Mary
   Villiers] ("Purest soul that e'er was sent,
   The").
   Epitaph on the Lady Mary Villiers.
Clare.   Dying Child, The.
Coleridge.   Epitaph on an Infant.
   On an Infant Which Died before Baptism.
Cowper.   On an Infant.
Dickinson.   How the Waters closed above Him.
   Is his sweet wife too faint to remember.
   Not all die early, dying young.
   Some, too fragile for winter winds.
   Taken from men—this morning.
   Vision of Immortal Life has been fulfilled,
   The.

Who "meddled" with the costly Hearts.
Dobyns.   Night Swimmer.
   Song of the Drowned Boy.
Donne.   Niobe.
Dunbar.   Death of the First Born, The.
Eberhart.   Lost Children, The.
Emerson.   In Senahar, my first born sleeps.
   Threnody: "South-wind brings, The."
   What from this barren being do we reap.
Fox.   Five Stanzas for My Two Brothers.
   Horses, The.
Frost.   Out, Out —.
Galvin.   For a Little Girl of Pompeii.
Garrigue.   Beheld in Naples.
Gray.   Epitaph on a Child.
Hall.   Baseball Players, The.
   Child's Garden, A.
Hardy.   Dead Bastard, The.
Hartley.   Present to the Sun, A.
   Two Drowned at the Gateway.
Heaney.   Limbo.
   Mid-Term Break.
Herrick.   Epitaph upon a Child, An.
   To the Lady Crew, Upon the Death of her
   Child.
   Upon a Child. An Epitaph.
   Upon a Child That Died [or Dyed].
Hewitt.   Breach, The.
   Faded Leaf: A Chapter of Family History,
   The.
   Return (1885), The.
Hugo.   Small Oil Left in the House We Rented
   in Boulder, The.
   Somersby.
Jarrell.   Come to the Stone.
   Lady Bates.
   Lost Children, The.
   Protocols.
   Requiem for the Death of a Boy.
Jonson.   Epitaph on S.P. [Salomon or Salathiel
   Pavy], a Child of Q[ueen] El[izabeth's]
   Chapel.
   On My First Daughter.
   On My First Son [or Sonne].
   Why I Write Not of Love.
Kipling.   Gift of the Sea, The.
   Return of the Children, The.
Levine.   Goodbye.
Lindsay.   In Memory of a Child.
Lorde.   Rites of Passage.
Lovelace.   Elegie. Princesse Katherine, An.
Meredith.   Willie's Dirge on Little Marian.
Milton.   On the Death of a Fair Infant Dying
   of a Cough.
Morgan.   February 11, 1977.
Pope.   Epigram: "Peter complains, that God
   has given."
Ransom.   Bells for John Whiteside's Daughter.
   Dead Boy.
Rexroth.   Delia Rexroth.
Rossetti.   Baby lies so fast asleep / That we
   cannot wake her.
   Baby's cradle with no baby in it, A.
   Death.
   Death of a First-Born, A.
   Is It Well with The Child?
   Michael F. M. Rossetti.
   Sleep, Sleep Happy Child; All Creation Slept
   and Smiled.
   Why did baby die, / Making Father sigh.
Rukeyser.   Song for Dead Children.
Schuyler.   Head, A.
Smith, Patti.   Fire of Unknown Origin, A.
Snodgrass.   Mouse, The.
Stafford.   Consolations.
   For a Lost Child.
   Memorial: Son Bret, A.
Stevenson.   De Erotio Puella.
   Epitaphium Erotii.
Tate.   Death of Little Boys.
Thomas.   Refusal to Mourn the Death, by Fire,
   of a Child in London, A.
Thomson.   Epitaph on Miss Stanley.
Whittier.   Legend of the Lake, A.
   Vesta.
Williams, Charles Kenneth.   Vehicle: Absence.

Wordsworth. By a Blest Husband Guided, Mary Came.
Childless Father, The.
Epitaph: "Six months to six years added he remained."
In due observance of an ancient rite.
Lucy Gray; or, Solitude.
Maternal Grief.
Sonnet: "Why should we weep or mourn, Angelic boy."
Surprised by Joy [Impatient as the Wind].
Three years she grew in sun and shower.
We Are Seven.

Death in War. *see* **War Dead.**

Death of Animals
Atwood. Song of the Hen's Head.
Auden. Cat, The.
Owl, The.
Berry. Snake, The.
Bly. Dead Seal [near McClure's Beach], The.
Dried Sturgeon, The.
Hollow Tree, A.
Browning, Elizabeth Barrett. Sea-Mew, The.
Bukowski. Coupons.
Dogs.
One for the Old Boy.
Singing Is Fire.
Winter.
Burns. Auld Man's Mare's Dead, The.
Death and Dying Words of Poor Mailie, the Author's Only Pet Yowe, an Unco Mournfu' Tale, The.
Elegy on Peg Nicholson.
On the Death of Echo, a Lap-Dog.
Poor Mailie's Elegy.
What Will I Do Gin My Hoggie Die.
Byron. Translation from Catullus ("Ye Cupids, droop each little head").
"Carroll, Lewis." Lays of Sorrow, No. 1.
Carruth. Bears at Raspberry Time.
Cave Painting.
Classical.
Essay.
Sonnet: "Poor little book, *The Sleeping Beauty* died."
Why was the passenger pigeon exterminated?
Catullus. Carmen 3: "Who loves beauty / vel her statues."
Cummings. Me Up at Does.
Dickey, James. Heaven of Animals, The.
Dickinson. His Bill is clasped—his Eye forsook.
Eberhart. Dead Skunk.
For a Lamb.
Everson. Hare: An Earlier Episode, The.
Rattlesnake August.
Spikehorn.
Steelhead.
Ferlinghetti. Rough Song of Animals Dying.
Ford. Jeweled Bat, The.
Poem for Paul Eluard.
Fox. Raccoon, A.
Frost. Draft Horse, The.
Gardner. Widow's Yard, The.
Garrigue. Epitaph for My Cat.
Mouse, The.
Gildner. Rustling a Hog.
Gray. Ode on the Death of a Favourite [or Favorite] Cat, Drowned in a Tub [or Bowl] of Gold Fishes.
Griffiths. Rivers Are Running Beneath Us.
Villa-Famès, August 1986.
Haines. East from Glacier Park.
Ghost Hunter, The.
Goshawk, The.
Moosehead, The.
Victims.
Hardy. Last Words to a Dumb Friend.
Robin, The.
Hartley. As the Buck Lay Dead.
Plover.
This Portrait of a Seadove—Dead.
Hayden. Gulls.
Killing the Calves.
Plague of Starlings, A.
Hemingway. To Crazy Christian.

Herrick. Upon His Spaniel[l] Tracie [or Tracy].
Hesketh. Animals' Last Words.
Dead Blackbird.
Gone Away.
How to Do It.
Mallard, The.
Owl.
Panther and the Antelope, The.
Survival.
Survivors.
Very Small Casualty, A.
Hewitt. Dungannon Cattle Market.
Gap, The.
Sheep Skull, The.
Hoffman. Last Lynx.
Rats.
Hughes, Ted. Coming Down through Somerset.
Manacled with blood.
View of a Pig.
When we sat his mother on her tail, he mouthed her teat.
Hugo. Again, Kapowsin.
Jarrell. Laboratory, The.
Jeffers. House Dog's Grave, The.
Hurt Hawks.
Joseph. In Memory of God.
Kinnell. Hen Flower, The.
Kipling. Power of the Dog, The.
Kooser. Fort Robinson.
Geek, The.
Kunitz. Robin Redbreast.
Levertov. Day Begins, A.
Lieberman. Island Trashfires.
Lindsay. Dirge for a Righteous Kitten, A.
Eagle That Is Forgotten, The.
Tiger on Parade, The.
Longfellow. Poet's Tale: The Birds of Killingworth, The.
Lovelace. Fly Caught in a Cobweb, A.
Toad and Spyder, The.
Lowry. Crane over seas and forests seeks her home, The.
Note, A.
Old Woman who Buried Cats, The.
Salmon Drowns Eagle.
Warning from False Cape Horn.
McAuley. For the Humanism Class at Fairchild Airforce Base, in Place of a Session on the Book of Job.
Path, The.
McGrath. Used Up.
Marvell. Nymph Complaining for the Death of Her Faun [or Fawn], The.
Matthews. Loyal.
Meredith. Islet the Dachs.
No boats oar slow, no barges pass.
Young Reynard.
Muldoon. Ned Skinner.
Nash. For a Good Dog.
Nathan. Learning Experience.
Neruda. Dead Dog.
Oliver. Encounter.
Ghosts.
Her Grave.
Olson. Round & a Canon, A.
Raine. Silver Stag, The.
Whales.
Ransom. Janet Waking.
Rich. Mare's skeleton in the clearing: another sign of life, The.
Rossetti. Dead in the cold, a song-singing thrush.
On the Death of a Cat.
Sandburg. Half Way.
Sarton. Lament for Toby, a French Poodle.
Shapiro. Impact.
Smith, Charlotte. Hedge-Hog Seen in a Frequented Path, The.
To a Butterfly in a Window.
Snodgrass. Auction.
Coroner's Inquest.
Mouse, The.
Snyder. Dead by the Side of the Road, The.
Spenser. Being one day at my window all alone.

Stafford. Meditation.
Traveling through the Dark.
Tate. Carrion, A.
Updike. Another Dog's Death.
Dog's Death.
Mouse Sex.
Warren. Love and Knowledge.
Season Opens on Wild Boar in Chianti.
Was Not the Lost Dauphin.
Wilbur. Death of a Toad, The.
Pardon, The.
Williams, Charles Kenneth. Shells.
Williams, Miller. Animals.
Wordsworth. Death of a Starling, The.
Dog—An Idyllium, The.
Last of the Flock, The.
Wright, James. Brush Fire.
Small Frogs Killed on the Highway.
Sparrows in a Hillside Drift.
Zukofsky. Lament, o graces of Venus, and Cupids.

Debauchery
Beckett. Dortmunder.
Bunting. O everlastingly self-deluded!
Byron. Damaetas.
Emerson. Ghaselle.
Graves. Blue-Fly, The.
Johnson. Short Song of Congratulation [or To a Young Heir], A.
Jonson. On Gut.
Keats. Give Me Women, Wine, and Snuff.
Marlowe. 2.10: Ad Graecinum quod eodem tempore duas amet.
Sutter. Night Out.
Whitman. Hand-Mirror, A.
Wyatt. In court to serve, decked with fresh array.

Debt
Carroll, Jim. My Debt.
"Carroll, Lewis." Peter and Paul.
Catullus. Carmen 26: "Your cottage, Furius, sheltered."
Carmen 103: "Either give me my hundred pounds back, Silo."
Dickinson. Where we owe so much it defies Money.
Donne. Ralphius.
Emerson. And hungry Debt beseiged my door.
Nature will not lose.
Suum Cuique ("Wilt thou seal up the avenues of ill?").
Frost. Closed for Good.
Ingenuities of Debt, The.
Graves. Bank Account.
Herrick. Bell-Man, The.
Long Lookt for Comes at Last.
Summe, and the Satisfaction, The.
To God ("With golden Censers..").
Upon Bunce: Epigram.
Upon Paske a Draper.
Hughes, Langston. Little Lyric (of Great Importance).
Jonson. Epistle to a Friend ("They are not, sir, worst owers, that do pay").
Epistle to Mr Arthur Squib.
Kipling. Rowers, The.
Lovelace. Sylo pray pay me my ten Sesterces.
Lowry. Men With Coats Thrashing.
When I was young I broke all drinking records.
Meredith. Sweet Justice of Norbiton, neighbour of Jones.
Nash. First Payment Deferred.
Friendly Touch, The.
Second Month It's Not Itemized, The.
Plath. Dispossessed, The.
Shelton. Bottom Line, The.
Suckling. Love and Debt Alike Troublesome.
Tate. Debt.
Whittier. Prisoner for Debt, The.
Williams, William Carlos. Detail.
Wright, James. Before a Cashier's Window in a Department Store.
Zukofsky. Furius, "Little Villa" has no nod for Auster.
Out—so this means you render them, ten sestertia, Silo.

Deception

Angelou. How I Can Lie to You.
Beatles. I'm Looking Through You.
Berg. Mother Political.
Berryman. Here too you came and sat a time once, drinking.
Blake. How to Know Love from Deceit.
Browning, Elizabeth Barrett. Queen Annelida and False Arcite.
Bukowski. Ass But No Class.
Killer, A.
Madness.
Bunting. Shall I sulk because my love has a double heart?
Thundercloud fills meadows with heavenly beauty, The.
You've come! O how flustered and anxious I've been.
Burns. Fragment: "Why, why tell thy lover."
Stay, my Charmer, can you leave me.
Byron. Chain I Gave, The.
From the French.
Parisina.
Thou Art Not False, But Thou Art Fickle.
To a Lady.
To Anne.
Written in "Letters to an Italian Nun and an English Gentleman: by J.J. Rousseau: Founded on Facts."
Campion. Are you what your faire lookes expresse?
Elegye, An: "Constant to none, but ever false to me."
Faine would I my love disclose.
How eas'ly wert thou chained.
I must complain, yet doe enjoy my Love.
If I urge my kinde desires.
If Love loves truth, then women doe not love.
Shall then a traiterous kis or a smile.
Carew. Deposition from Love, A.
Looking-Glass, A.
Carroll, Jim. Poem: "Some trust the wolf."
Saint Theresa.
"Carroll, Lewis." How doth the little crocodile.
Peter and Paul.
Prologue: "Ladies and Gentlemen seems stiff and cold."
Catullus. Carmen 6: "Your most recent acquisition, Flavius."
Carmen 29: "What man could stomach the sight."
Carmen 36: "Volusian sheets / shit-shotten Annals."
Carmen 42: "From the quarters of the compass."
Chaucer. Epilogue to the Merchant's Tale.
Merchant's Tale, The.
Miller's Prologue, The.
Reeve's Tale, The.
Cohen. Music Crept by Us, The.
Stranger Song, The.
When Even The.
Coleridge. Lines in the Manner of Spenser.
To an Unfortunate Woman at the Theatre.
Westphalian Song.
Cowper. Anti-Thelyphthora.
Apology, An.
Creeley. But You.
"Do You Think.."
Echo Of.
If You.
Place, A.
Song: "What I took in my hand."
Davie. Frontenac.
De la Mare. Stratagem, The.
Donne. And through that bitter agony [or agonie].
On His Mistress [or Mistris].
Dunbar. Ballad: "I know my love is true."
Parted.
Dunn. Biography in the First Person.
On Hearing the Airlines Will Use a Psychological Profile to Catch Potential Skyjackers.
What They Wanted.
"Dylan." Denise.

Man of Peace.
Seeing the Real You at Last.
Emerson. Maia.
O sun! take off thy hood of clouds.
Panoply of Paradise is mine.
Fenton. Voice disguiser with membrane of a spider's egg-case, A.
Frost. Revelation.
Graves. Beauty in Trouble.
Blind Arrow, A.
Cock in Pullet's Feathers.
Friday Night.
Full Moon.
Hung Wu Vase, The.
In Disguise.
Inkidoo and the Queen of Babel.
Leda.
Recognition.
Sick Love.
Theseus and Ariadne.
Gunn. To His Cynical Mistress.
Haines. Tunnel, The.
Hardy. He Did Not Know Me.
Mock Wife, The.
Outside the Casement.
Woman's Trust, A.
Herrick. Anacreontike.
Fair[e] Days; or, Dawn[e]s Deceitful[l].
Upon Shark.
Hewitt. Belfastman Abroad Argues with Himself.
Prime Minister.
To a Modern Irish Poet.
Hopkins. Cockle's Antibilious Pills.
Hughes, Ted. Childish Prank, A.
Speech Out of Shadow.
Jonson. On Captain Hazard the Cheater.
On Playwright ("Playwright, by chance, hearing some toys I had writ").
To Fine Grand.
To Prowl the Plagiary.
Kipling. Post That Fitted, The.
Truce of the Bear, The.
Knott. Poem: "Beach holds and sifts us through her dreaming fingers, The."
Shorts / Excerpts ("Other strangers than our own may remember").
Kunitz. Again! Again!
Confidential Instructions.
Dark and the Fair, The.
Fitting of the Mask, The.
What wakes me now.
Lawrence. Aloof in Gaiety.
She Looks Back.
Lindsay. Master of the Dance, The.
Lovelace. Ode: "You are deceiv'd; I sooner may dull fair."
Lowry. Plagiarist, The.
Tortures of hell are stern, their fires burn fiercely, The.
McAuley. From the burly give-and-take.
What the Recent Survey Has Revealed.
MacNeice. That roses are red is home—and homesickness.
McNeill. Mayapple Hill.
Marlowe. 3.3: De amica, quae periuraverat.
3.13: Ad amicam, si peccatura est, ut occulte peccet.
Matthews. Little Blue Nude.
Meredith. What soul would bargain for a cure that brings.
Merton. Sincerity.
Nash. Hush, Here They Come.
Neruda. Little Devils.
Olson. Cinos.
Loves of Anat, I, The.
Patchen. Let Me In!
Yesterday They Tried.
Piercy. Girl in White.
Juan's Twilight Dance.
Man can lie to himself, A.
You speak of the collective.
Psalms. Psalm 10: "Why standest thou afar off, O Lord?"
Psalm 12: "Help, Lord; for the godly man ceaseth."

Ransom. April Treason.
In Bed Not Dead.
Rich. Knight, The.
Rolfe. Pastoral—1954.
Rossetti. Cannot Sweeten.
Fair Margaret.
Faithless Shepherdess, The.
Last Night.
Look on This Picture and on This.
Margery.
Sister Maude.
Undine.
Zara.
Rukeyser. Deep in the Century of Opposites.
Down from Chicago Bryan came.
Schuyler. Princess Di.
Sexton. Errand, The.
Red-Riding Hood.
Shakespeare. Fair is my love, but not so fair as fickle.
Sonnet 92: "But do thy worst to steal thyself away."
Sonnet 93: "So shall I live, supposing thou art true."
Sonnet 95: "How sweet and lovely dost thou make the shame."
Sonnet 137: "Thou blind fool, Love, what dost thou to mine eyes."
Sonnet 148: "O me, what eyes hath Love put in my head."
When my love swears that she is made of truth.
Sidney. Lord, help, it is high time for me to call.
Silverstein. Dreadful.
Hat.
Razor-Tailed Wren, The.
Sick.
Snodgrass. Assuming Fine Feathers, W. D. Takes Flight.
W. D. Disguised as Cock Robin and Hidden Deep in Crimson.
Sorrentino. King of the dark tower is a lug, The.
Maytime.
Spender. Song: "Stranger, you who hide my love."
Stafford. Archival Print, An.
Stevenson. Heather Ale: A Galloway Legend.
Stuart. Nomads.
Swift. Upon the South Sea Project.
Warren. Interjection #1: The Need For Re-evaluation.
Mango on the Mango Tree, The.
Not to Be Trusted.
Picnic Remembered.
Williams, William Carlos. Great Mullen.
Wroth. Song: "Love a child is ever criing [or crying]."
Sonnet 2: "Love like a jugler, comes to play his prise."
Sonnet 5: "Can pleasing sight, misfortune ever bring?"
Sonnet 7: "End fond jealousie alas I know, An."
Sonnet 35: "False [or Faulce] hope which feeds but[t] to destroy, and spill."
Wyatt. Caesar, when that the traitor of Egypt.
Do way, do way, ye little wily prat!
Mistrustful minds be moved.
To wet your eye withouten tear.
What vaileth [or 'vaileth] truth [or trouth]? or by it to take pain [or payn]?
Ye old mule, that thin[c]k your self so fair [or fayre].
Yeats. Three Bushes, The.
Zukofsky. *Annals* of Volusius, cock at his offal.
At hest, hendecasyllabics, what is this.
Flavius—that delicate lass—to Catullus.
Whose hoax to put up with, outstare, protest patience.

Decisions

Ammons. *De* / on one, The.
Angelou. Last Decision, The.
Atwood. I made no choice / I decided nothing.

Berryman. Point of Age, A.
Byron. Journal in Cephalonia.
Creeley. Two Times ("It takes so long to look down").
Cummings. Well)here's looking at ourselves.
"Dylan." If You Gotta Go, Go Now.
Frost. Road Not Taken, The.
Graves. Next Time, The.
Griffiths. Decision.
Herrick. Will Makes the Work, or Consent Makes the Cure, The.
Hesketh. Master Cotton Spinner.
Koch. Departure from Hydra, The.
Lawrence. Bad Beginning, A.
To Let Go Or to Hold on—?
Merton. I Move that We Adjourn the Meeting.
Morgan. Decisions of afternoon: as.
Pack. Clayfeld's Son Selects His Specialty.
Dead King, The.
Patchen. Easy Decision, An.
"Reed." Make Up Mind.
Think It Over.
Roethke. Decision, The.
Sandburg. Chillicothe.
Silverstein. Pancake?
Stafford. At a little pond in the woods.
Wilbur. Sirens, The.
Williams, Charles Kenneth. Halves.
See also **Free Will.**

Decorum
Fox. Blanc de Blanc.
Glück. My Neighbor in the Mirror.
Kinnell. To William Carlos Williams.

Deer
Boyle. Print from a Lucite Block.
Carruth. I Know, I Remember, But How Can I Help You.
In the snowy woods of morning.
Late. The back road "slicker than owl shit."
Snow.
Once More.
Song of the gray, The.
Spaniel flies with his ears, The.
Ciardi. At First Flower of the Easy Day.
Coleridge. Timorous Hind, The.
Dickey, James. Deer among Cattle.
Everson. Canticle to the Christ in the Holy Eucharist, A.
Ferlinghetti. Wild Life Cameo, Early Morn.
Frost. Two Look at Two.
Galvin. Winter Runner, The.
Garrigue. Iowa City Zoo.
Glück. Messengers.
Haines. Ghost Hunter, The.
Hardy. Fallow Deer at the Lonely House, The.
Hartley. As the Buck Lay Dead.
Hesketh. First Day, The.
Hughes, Ted. Roe-Deer.
Jeffers. Deer Lay Down Their Bones, The.
Fawn's Foster-Mother.
Kunitz. Death In Moonlight.
Lawrence. Doe at Evening, A.
Lieberman. Nara Park: Twilight Deer Feeding.
Lovelace. La Bella Bona Roba.
Lowry. Warning from False Cape Horn.
Marvell. Nymph Complaining for the Death of Her Faun [or Fawn], The.
Meinke. Anniversary Deer, The.
Meredith. Doe: A Fragment, The.
Poor things! we know not what they suffer.
Merton. Merlin and the Deer.
Millay. Buck in the Snow, The.
Fawn, The.
Oliver. Five A.M. in the Pinewoods.
Picking Blueberries, Austerlitz, New York, 1957.
Oppen. Psalm: "In the small beauty of the forest."
Patchen. Deer and the Snake, The.
Raine. Silver Stag, The.
Snyder. Long Hair.
Soy Sauce.
This Poem Is for Deer.
Two Fawns That Didn't See the Light This Spring.
Stafford. Traveling through the Dark.
Stuart. Deer.

Tomlinson. At Dawn.
Roe Deer, The.
Wright, James. Moral Poem Freely Accepted from Sappho, A.
Wyatt. Whoso list to hunt, I know where is an hind.
See also **Hunting and Hunters.**
Defeat
Beatles. I'm a Loser.
Cohen. Captain, The.
Dickinson. I took my Power in my Hand.
My Portion is Defeat—today.
Emerson. Archangel Hope / Looks to the azure cope, The.
Herrick. Some Comfort in Calamity.
To Virgins.
Hewitt. Defeat.
East Antrim Winter.
Limitations.
Nineteen Sixteen, or the Terrible Beauty.
November Wood.
Salute to Matthew Arnold.
Hugo. Degrees of Gray in Philipsburg.
Jarrell. Winter's Tale, The.
Jeffers. We Are Those People.
Kunitz. Cleopatra.
Dragonfly, The.
Lewis. *She Remains.*
Lindsay. Broncho That Would Not Be Broken, The.
Election night at midnight.
MacNeice. Richard Coeur-de-Lion.
Meredith. Ah, what a dawn of splendour, when her sowers.
At the first ball his wicket fell, and sins.
Behind the Northern curtain-folds he passed.
Behold, the Gods are with her, and are known.
Bellerophon.
Desire and terror then had each of each.
Eastward of Paris morn is high.
Henceforth of her the Gods are known.
In Nature is no rearward step allowed.
Lo, where hurricane flocks of the North-wind rattle their thunder.
Look not for spreading boughs.
Mark where a credible ghost pulls bridle to view that bare.
Monmouth.
O she that made the brave appeal.
On her lost arm love bade her look.
She shall rise worthier of her prototype.
She snatched at heaven's flame of old.
Soon felt she in her shivered frame.
They are with her now, and in her ears, and known.
We look for her that sunlike stood.
Piercy. Eight of Swords, The.
Ransom. Prelude to an Evening.
Prelude to an Evening.
Robinson. Mighty Runner, A.
Rolfe. Vincent.
Sandburg. Ashurnatsirpal III.
Sidney. Sonnet 36: "Stella, whence doth this new assault arise."
Stevenson. O dull cold northern sky.
Wright, James. Speak.
Deformities
Ford. Roots.
Shapiro. Mongolian Idiot.
Warren. Child Next Door, The.
Degas, Edgar
Hesketh. Poem is a Painting, A.
Wilbur. L'Etoile.
Museum Piece.
De Hooch, Pieter
Sarton. Dutch Interior.
Tomlinson. Paring the Apple.
Wilbur. Objects.
De la Mare, Walter
Eliot. To Walter de la Mare.
Dehumanization
Angelou. Junkie Monkey Reel.
Ashbery. This Configuration.
Emerson. New England Capitalist.
Griffiths. Guardianship.
Kooser. They Had Torn Off My Face at the Office.

Lindsay. Celestial Circus, The.
Owen. Anthem for Doomed Youth.
Plath. Applicant, The.
Williams, Charles Kenneth. Crime, The.
See also **Bureaucracy and Bureaucrats.**
Déjà Vu
Beckett. Ne manquez pas à Stuttgart.
MacNeice. Déjà Vu.
Ransom. Vision by Sweetwater.
Dejection
Auden. Stark bewölkt.
"Carroll, Lewis." Rules and Regulations.
Cohen. Invisible Tonight.
Coleridge. Dejection; an Ode.
Letter to Sara Hutchinson.
Gunn. Sketch of the Great Dejection, A.
Lowry. Need it be so niggardly of meaning too?
Mahon. Dejection.
Exit Molloy.
Shelley. Stanzas Written in Dejection, near Naples [or —December 1818, near Naples].
Snodgrass. W. D. Is Concerned About the Character Assassination of Cock Robin.
See also **Melancholy.**
Del Sarto, Andrew. see Sarto, Andrea del.
Delaware (state)
Hugo. Imagining Delaware.
Kinnell. Memory of Wilmington.
Silverstein. Benjamin Bunnn.
Whittier. To Delaware.
Delft, Holland
Mahon. Courtyards in Delft.
Tomlinson. At Delft.
Delight
Browning, Elizabeth Barrett. Deserted Garden, The.
Burns. Delia.
Carruth. In the snowy woods of morning.
Creeley. Hélas.
Dickinson. Delight—becomes pictorial.
Delight has no Competitor.
Delight is as the flight.
Oh Sumptuous moment.
Rather arid delight.
Eliot. Dedication to My Wife, A.
Hartley. Canticle for October.
8 Words.
Hollander's Animal Faith.
To C———.
Hesketh. Gymnasts, The.
House In the Tree.
On Iona.
Second Childhood.
What Is God?
Jong. Raspberries in My Driveway, The.
Merton. Harmonies of Excess, The.
When You Point Your Finger.
Oliver. Summer Day, The.
Patchen. Ark: Angelus: Anvil.
Rossetti. These All Wait upon Thee.
Shelley. Song: "Rarely, rarely, comest thou."
Stevens. Poems of Our Climate, The.
Stevenson. To Rosabelle.
Warren. Into Broad Daylight.
Love: Two Vignettes.
Not to Be Trusted.
Young. Morning Poem for Michael, A.
Deliverance
Ciardi. Gift, The.
Clough. Bethesda: A Sequel.
Donne. And through that bitter agony [or agonie].
Deliver us for thy descent.
From being anxious, or secure.
From needing danger, to be[e] good.
From tempting Satan to tempt us.
In churches, when the infirmity [or the'infirmitie].
Through thy submitting all, to blow[e]s.
When senses, which thy so[u]ldiers are.
Hewitt. Grief ("When men lie down for ever / and names their tombstones take").
Jarrell. Jews at Haifa.
Jeffers. Home.
Women at Point Sur, The.

Lawrence. Elysium.
Merton. Prisoner, The.
Nemerov. Morality, A.
Oliver. Two Kinds of Deliverance.
Pope. He who beneath thy shelt'ring wing resides.
Psalms. Psalm 54: "Save me, O God, by thy name. . . ."
Psalm 59: "Deliver me from mine enemies, O my God."
Psalm 69: "Save me, O God.."
Psalm 70: "Make haste, O God, to deliver me."
Psalm 71: "In thee, O Lord, do I put my trust."
Psalm 91: "He that dwelleth in the secret place.."
Psalm 116: "I love the Lord.."
Psalm 118: "O give thanks unto the Lord; for he is good: because.."
Psalm 126: "When the Lord turned again the captivity of Zion.."
Psalm 140: "Deliver me, O Lord, from the evil man."
Psalm 144: "Blessed be the Lord my strength."
Rossetti. Whom the Lord Loveth He Chasteneth.
Sandburg. Waiting for the Chariot.
Waldman. Coup de Grace.
Warren. Letter about Money, Love, or Other Comfort, If Any.
Wordsworth. Composed During a Storm.
Siege of Vienna Raised by John Sobieski February, 1816.

Delphi, Oracle of
Doolittle. Delphi.
Hall. At Delphi.
Merrill. Charioteer of Delphi, The.
Merton. Lord whose is the oracle at Delphi neither utters nor hides his meaning, The.
Robinson. Chorus of Old Men in "Ægeus", The.
Sidney. Thy elder care shall from thy careful face.
Yeats. News for the Delphic Oracle.

Demeter
Browning, Elizabeth Barrett. Psyche Propitiating Ceres.
Doolittle. Demeter.
Meredith. Appeasement of Demeter, The.
Then said she, quick as the cries.

Democracy
Bukowski. Troops, The.
Cohen. Democracy.
Cummings. Thanksgiving (1956).
Emerson. Ancient drop of feudal blood, An.
Ferlinghetti. Sailing thru the straits of Demos.
Hall. Impossible Marriage, The.
Hughes, Langston. Democracy.
Kipling. Declaration of London, The.
Lawrence. Democracy Is Serivce.
Future Relationships.
Robot-Democracy.
True Democracy.
Piercy. Councils.
Robinson. Demos.
Sandburg. Four Brothers, The.
LINCOLN? / He was a mystery in smoke and flags.
When was it long ago the murmurings began.
Whitman. City of Ships.
Commonplace, The.
Election Day, November, 1884.
For You O Democracy.
Song of the Banner at Daybreak.
States!
Whittier. Democracy.
Wilbur. On Freedom's Ground.

See also **Campaigns, Political; Voting and Voters.**

Demons
Auden. Merax & Mullin.
Berryman. Whether There Is Sorrow in the Demons.
Bishop. Patience of an Angel.

Burns. De'il's [*or* Deil's] Awa wi' th' [*or* the] Exciseman, The.
Eberhart. Salem.
Emerson. Asmodaean feat be mine, The.
Dæmonic and the Celestial Love, The.
Ford. Neurotic demon, / Trying to convince himself.
Graves. Beware, Madam!
Deliverance.
Gratitude for a Nightmare.
Haunted House, The.
That Was the Night.
This Holy Month.
Hill. Asmodeus.
Do words make up the majesty.
Lawrence. Be a Demon!
Levertov. Novices, The.
Lorde. Blackstudies.
Lowry. Devil is a gentleman, The.
Devil was a Gentleman, The.
McGrath. Two Songs from "The Hunted Revolutionaries."
Milton. Next came one / Who mourn'd in earnest, when the Captive Ark.
Olson. Stevens Song.
Rich. This Beast, This Angel.
Sexton. Demon.
Sorrentino. Faces of Doom and Sterility.
Whittier. Demon of the Study, The.
Williams, Miller. One of the Crowd on the Shore Tells How It Was.
Wright, James. Poem about George Doty in the Death House, A.
Yeats. Demon and Beast.

See also **Monsters.**

Denial
Angelou. Remembering.
We Saw Beyond Our Seeming.
Auden. Say Yes!
Browning, Elizabeth Barrett. Denial, A.
"Carroll, Lewis." My Fairy.
Carruth. And he stood at his window and shook his fist at a cloud.
Event, The.
Opusthirteen.
Phone.
Creeley. Loop, A.
Song: "I wouldn't / embarrass you."
Dickinson. Denial—is the only fact.
Renunciation—is a piercing Virtue.
"Dylan." It Ain't Me, Babe.
Eberhart. Life and Death.
Graves. Cool Web, The.
Is Now the Time?
Nobody.
She Is No Liar.
Hardy. In the Servants' Quarters.
Hemingway. To Chink Whose Trade Is Soldiering.
Herrick. Anthea's Retractation.
Maids Nay's Are Nothing.
Nor Buying or Selling.
Hewitt. My Great-Grandfather's Refusal.
Knott. Depressionism.
Fear of Domesticity.
Levertov. Lamentation, A.
Liddy. Notes towards a Video of Avondale House.
Lowry. My hate is as a wind that buffets me.
MacNeice. Canto XX: "To Wales once more, though not on holiday now."
Mixer, The.
Morrison. There's Someone At the Door.
Ransom. Good Ships.
Nocturne: "Where now has our young Adam."
Parting at Dawn.
Rossetti. If I should ever say "my heart is in my home."
Mariana.
Williams, Charles Kenneth. Good Mother: Out.
Zukofsky. Happier, happier, now.

Denmark
Hewitt. Braes O' Layde, The.
Meredith. Hatton's "God of War."

Dentistry and Dentists
Liddy. City of Dreadful Knight, The.

Silverstein. Crocodile's Toothache, The.

Dentures
Herrick. Upon Glasco. Epig.

Deportation
Griffiths. Refugees.

Depression (economic). *see* **Great Depression.**

Depression (psychological)
Beatles. I'm Down.
Yer Blues.
Berryman. Lightning, The.
Some sketch sweat' out, unwilling swift & crude.
Brontë. And first an hour of mournful musing.
I'll come when thou art saddest.
O God of heaven! the dream of horror.
That dreary lake, that midnight sky.
Wind, sink to rest in the heather.
Bukowski. Beer.
For Al—.
Something.
Weather Report.
Campion. No grave for woe, yet earth my watrie teares devoures.
Carroll, Jim. I have walked these streets so often I could.
Love Poem: "I see myself, sad now, as in a mirror."
Cohen. Invisible Trouble, The.
Only Poem, The.
Dunn. Urgencies.
Fisher. Leaden August with the life gone out of it.
Trouble coming, on a Saturday or a Monday.
Fletcher. November Days.
Hayden. Ice Storm.
Hesketh. It Was Not I.
Hughes, Langston. Neighbor.
Hugo. Letter to Bell from Missoula.
Letter to Sister Madeline from Iowa City.
Why Sapri Will Never Be Italian.
Jong. Depression in Early Spring.
Keats. To J. H. Reynolds, Esq.
Knott. Depressionism.
Lawrence. Boredom, Ennui, Depression.
Lowry. Foul, or Twenty-Five.
Thoughts While Drowning: But Try to Eliminate the Argument.
McAuley. Noon Apocrypha.
Meredith. Long was the conflict, but now 'tis done.
Nash. So Penseroso.
Pack. Villanelle for Pamela.
Patchen. Crowded Net, The.
Ohio River Blues.
Prince. On a Report That in Some Rest Homes Residents Who Are Depressed Will be Charged at a Higher Rate.
Rossetti. When My Heart Is Vexed I Will Complain ("Fields are white to harvest, look and see, The").
Sexton. Fury of Rain Storms, The.
Smith, Charlotte. To Night.
Smith, Patti. Fleet of Deer, A.
Smith, Stevie. My Muse.
Sorrentino. It is one man alone, what.
Stevens. Anglais Mort à Florence.
Stevenson. After Reading "Antony and Cleopatra."
Tempest tossed and sore afflicted, sin defiled and care oppressed.
Waldman. Out There.
Wright, Charles. Dog Yoga.

See also **Melancholy; Mental Illness.**

Dereliction
Lovelace. Forsaken Lady to Her False Servant, A.
Wordsworth. Decay of Piety.

Descartes, René
Beckett. Whoroscope.
Dunn. Something Like Happiness.
Eberhart. Retrospective Forelook.
Joseph. Descartes—You There?
Nemerov. Endegeeste.
Tomlinson. Descartes and the Stove.

Deserts
Bishop. Travelling in the Family.

Carroll, Jim. Desert Casino, The.
For Robert Smithson.
Carruth. Abandoned Ranch, Big Bend.
Coming Down to the Desert at Lordsburg, N.M.
Rimrock, Where It Is.
Ciardi. Driving across the American Desert and Thinking of the Sahara.
Clark. Desert Wars.
Diary of Desert War.
Creeley. Night Sky, A.
De la Mare. Image, The.
Dickey, James. Gila Bend.
Dove. Sahara Bus Trip, The.
"Dylan." Amazon chick / with an amazin' pancho villa face, An.
Fletcher. Cliff-dwelling.
Fuel Vendor, The.
On Mesa Verde.
Rain in the Desert.
Well in the Desert, The.
Windmills, The.
Garrigue. Pays Perdu.
Hewitt. Tiphead.
Hughes, Langston. Desert.
Hughes, Ted. Bar-Room TV.
Jarrell. Range in the Desert, The.
Joseph. Meteorology, A.
Kipling. Pelicans in the Wilderness (A Grave near Halfa).
Song in the Desert, A.
Kunitz. Old Cracked Tune, An.
Lindsay. I Went Down into the Desert.
Lowry. Death of an Oaxaqueñian.
Kraken, Eagles, in British Columbia.
Matthews. Moving Again.
Melville. In the Desert.
Meredith. Song: "Thou to me art such a spring."
Merton. Dry Places.
Plath. Sleep in the Mojave Desert.
Raine. Moment, The.
Rich. Turning the Wheel.
Rossetti. I dug and dug amongst the snow.
Sandburg. People know what the land knows, The.
Shelley. Ozymandias [of Egypt].
Shelton. Boojum Tree, The.
Desert.
Landscape With A Woman.
New Road, The.
Teeth of These Mountains, The.
Whatever Became of Me.
When a man loves the desert.
Tomlinson. Arizona Desert.
Death in the Desert, A.
Near and the Far, The.
Walker. On Sight.
Whittier. Song of Slaves in the Desert.
Williams, William Carlos. New Mexico.
Zukofsky. In Arizona / (how many years in the mountains).

Desire

Ammons. Gardening.
Angelou. Black Ode.
Here's to Adhering.
On Diverse Deviations.
Prescience.
Zorro Man, A.
Ashbery. Blessing in Disguise, A.
Lament upon the Waters, The.
Atwood. Against Still Life.
I look up, you are standing.
Now it is winter. / By winter I mean: white, silent.
Spring again, can I stand it.
There Is Only One of Everything.
Variation on the Word *Sleep.*
Woman Who Could Not Live With Her Faulty Heart, The.
Your flawed body, sickle.
Auden. Aware.
Beatles. All I've Got to Do.
Dig a Pony.
Eight Days a Week.
For You Blue.
I Wanna Be Your Man.

I Will.
I'll Get You.
It's Only Love.
Little Child.
Long Long Long.
Love Me Do.
Old Brown Shoe.
Beckett. Cascando.
Être là sans mâchoires sans dents.
Sanies I.
Berg. From the Bridge.
Gooseberries.
Berry. Deepest sleep holds us, The.
Design of a House, The.
I saw one standing aside, alone.
Marriage.
Turning always in my mind toward you.
We don't bother nobody.
Berryman. Desire Is a World by Night.
Desires of Men and Women.
Down & Back.
In a poem made by Cummings, long since, his.
Languid the songs I wish I willed . . . I try.
Song of the Young Hawaiian, The.
Still it pleads and rankles: "Why do you love *me?*"
Tyranny of your car—so far resembles.
Why can't, Chris, why shouldn't *they* fall in love?
Blake. Abstinence sows sand all over.
Beneath the white thorn lovely May.
What is it men in women do require?
Bly. At Midocean.
Cry Going Out over Pastures, The.
Bogan. Dream, The.
Brooks. Ballad of Chocolate Mabbie, The.
Browning, Elizabeth Barrett. Man's Requirements, A.
Sonnet: "Can it be right to give what I can give."
Sonnet: "Let the world's sharpness, like a clasping knife."
Browning, Robert. In a Gondola.
Pretty Woman, A.
Song: "Nay but you, who do not love her."
Burns. Allan Water.
Bonie Lass Made the Bed to Me, The.
Bonnie [or Bonny] Wee Thing, The.
Cardin o't, The.
Cauld Frosty Morning.
Delia.
Duncan Davison.
Dusty Miller.
Gallant Weaver, The.
Green Sleeves [and Tartan Ties].
I'll Ay[e] Ca' in by Yon Town.
It is na, Jean, thy bonie face.
Jamie Come Try Me.
Let Me in This Ae Night.
Mary Morison.
O Lay Thy Loof in Mine Lass.
O Saw Ye My Maggie.
O Were My Love Yon Lilac[k] Fair.
Passion's Cry.
Revision for Clarinda.
Scotish Song.
Song: "As I cam down by yon castle wa' ."
Song: "Blythe hae I been on yon hill."
Song: "O Philly, happy be that day."
Song: "O wat ye what that lo'es me."
Song: "Yestreen I had a pint o' wine."
Talk not to me of savages.
Tam Glen.
There's News Lasses News.
Thine am I, my Chloris fair.
Tibbie Dunbar.
To Chloris.
To Miss Isabella Macleod.
To the Weaver's Gin Ye Go.
Wilt thou be my Dearie.
Young Jockey was the blythest lad.
Byron. Lucietta. A Fragment.
To a Beautiful Quaker.
To M.S.G. ("Whene'er I view those lips of thine").

Translation from Catullus ("Equal to Jove that youth must be").
Campion. Ad Melleam.
And would you faine the reason know.
And Would You See My Mistress' Face?
Art Thou That She.
Be thou then my beauty named.
Be Wise, and Fly Not.
Beauty, Since You So Much Desire.
Dear If I with Guile.
Epigram: "None then should through thy beawty, Lawra, pine."
Fain Would I Wed.
Faine would I my love disclose.
Fire, fire, fire, fire!
First Love.
Follow, follow[e] / Though with mischiefe.
Hide not, sweetest Love, a sight so pleasing.
How eas'ly wert thou chained.
In eosdem.
In Lycium et Clytham.
In Pandarum.
Kinde in unkindnesse, when will you relent.
Leave prolonging thy distresse.
Love Me or Not.
My Life's Delight.
My Sweetest Lesbia [Let Us Live and Love].
O deare, that I with thee might live.
O Love, where are thy Shafts, thy Quiver, and thy Bow?
Oft have I sigh'd for him that heares me not.
Respect my faith, regard my service past.
Shal I come, if I swim? wide are the waves, you see.
So Quicke, So Hot, So Mad is Thy Fond Sute.
Sweete, come againe.
Tarry sweete love.
There Is None, O None but You.
Unlesse there were consent twixt hell and heaven.
Vaile, love, mine eyes, O hide from me.
What meanes this folly, now to brave it so.
Where She Her Sacred Bower Adorns.
Whether away my sweetest deerest?
Young and Simple though I Am.
Your Fair[e] Look[e]s Inflame [My Desire].
Carew. Guiltless Inconstant, The.
Love's Courtship.
Mediocrity in Love Rejected.
New Years Gift. To the Queen, A.
Separation of Lovers.
To My Worthy Friend Master George Sands [or Sandys], on His Translation of the Psalms.
To One That Desired to Know My Mistress [or Mistris].
Carroll, Jim. Our Desires.
Poem: "We are very much a part of the boredom."
Wing and Claw.
Carruth. Afternoon of a Faun.
Almanach du Printemps Vivarois.
August.
Concerning Necessity.
Ekstase, Alptraum, Schlaf in einem Nest von Flammen.
Fourth.
Green Mountain Idyl.
His Dream.
If It Were Not for You.
Incident of May.
Purana, Meaning Once Upon a Time.
Sonnet: "You in a tallness slenderly, as a lone."
Three Songs.
Catullus. Carmen 2: "Lesbia's sparrow! / Lesbia's plaything!"
Carmen 5: "Lesbia / live with me."
Carmen 7: "Curious to learn / how may kiss- / es of your lips."
Carmen 32: "Call me to you / at siesta."
Carmen 35: "Fetch, papyrus / our soft-measured poet."
Carmen 45: "Phyllis Corydon clutched to him."
Carmen 51: "Godlike the man who."

Carmen 66: "Who scans the bright machinery of the skies."
Clark. Ace of Destiny.
"Because They Are Desiring.."
I Was Born to Speak Your Name.
Somnambulism.
Clough. Come pleasant thoughts; sweet thoughts, at will.
Whence are ye, vague desires.
Cohen. Ain't No Cure for Love.
Beneath My Hands.
Dark at Four O'Clock.
End of My Life in Art.
Escape, The.
Fingerprints.
Fly, The.
I Am Dying.
I Long to Hold Some Lady.
I Perceived the Outline of Your Breasts.
I Try to Keep in Touch.
I'm Your Man.
Light as the Breeze.
Memories.
My Room.
1967.
One of Us Cannot Be Wrong.
Paper-Thin Hotel.
Promise.
So Long, Marianne.
Stay.
Take this Longing.
Traitor, The.
Ugly in My Own Eyes.
Way Back, The.
When Even The.
You Do Not Have to Love Me.
You Know Who I Am.
You Live like a God.
Coleridge. Desire.
Cowper. Delia, th' unkindest girl on earth.
Of Himself.
Sonnet 2: "Charming lady, she whose beautiful name honors."
Symptoms of Love, The.
Crane. Legend.
Possessions.
Thou Canst Read Nothing..
Creeley. Ballad of the Despairing Husband.
"Bolinas and Me.."
Comfort.
Flesh.
For W.C.W. ("Rhyme is after, The").
Kid, The.
Menu, The.
Night.
Now Then.
Old Song.
Smell of gum wrappers as of Saturday afternoon at movies.
Snow, The.
Song: "What do you / want, love. To be."
To Bobbie.
Two Times ("Image / docteur").
Cummings. After your poppied hair inaugurates.
Ballade: "White night roared with a huge north-wind, The."
Because i love you)last night.
Before the fragile gradual throne of night.
Except in your / honour.
First of All My Dreams, The.
Goodby Betty,don't remember me.
How / tinily / of / squir(two be).
I have looked upon thee—and I have loved thee.
I have loved,let us see if that's all.
I spoke to thee.
If learned darkness from our searched world.
In front of your house i.
In the rain- / darkness, the sunset.
It is at moments after i have dreamed.
Item.
I've come to ask you if there isn't a.
Lady will you come with me into.
Lean candles hunger in.
Love is a guess / that deepens.
Mind is its own beautiful prisoner, The.

My eyes are fond of the east side.
My humorous ghost precisely will.
My lady is an ivory garden.
My sweet old etcetera.
Notice the convulsed orange inch of moon.
O Thou to whom the musical white spring.
On the Madam's best april the.
Open your heart: / i'll give you a treasure.
Puella Mea.
Silently if,out of not knowable.
Skies may be blue;yes.
So isn't small one littlest why.
Somewhere I have never travelled,gladly beyond.
Speaking of love(of).
Spring has been exquisite and the, The.
Sweet spring is your.
Thee will i praise between those rivers whose.
Thing most new complete fragile intense, A.
This cigarette is extremely long.
Thy fingers make early flowers of.
Unto thee i / burn incense.
We love each other very dearly.
When my love comes to see me it's.
When my sensational moments are no more.
When of your eyes one smile entirely brings down.
Which is the very.
Willing pitifully to bewitch.
Davie. Blank of the Wall, The.
Master & Man.
Winter Landscape Near Ely, A.
De la Mare. Homesick.
Invocation: "Burning fire shakes in the night, The."
Out Of Bounds.
Dickey, William. Læestrygonians, The.
Dickinson. Heart wants what it wants, The.
I cannot live with You.
When we have ceased to care.
Dobyns. Belly, The.
Tenderly.
Donne. Lovers' Infiniteness[e].
Love's Diet.
Doolittle. Cassandra.
Helmsman, The.
She Contrasts with Herself Hippolyta.
Simaetha.
Dove. Happenstance.
His Shirt.
Secret Garden, The.
Sunday Greens.
Dunbar. Change, The.
If I Could But Forget.
In a English Garden.
Night, Dim Night.
Retort.
Duncan. This potion is love's portion. This herb.
Torso, The.
Dunn. Desire.
Landscape at the End of the Century.
Tenderness.
Truck Stop: Minnesota.
"Dylan." Abandoned Love.
Dirge: "I hate myself for lovin' you and the weakness that it showed."
Hazel.
I Wanna Be Your Lover.
I Want You.
I'd Have You Any Time.
Isis.
Lay, Lady, Lay.
Love You Too Much.
Meet Me in the Morning.
Oh, Sister.
One More Cup of Coffee (Valley Below).
One More Weekend.
Peggy Day.
Sara.
Something There Is About You.
Spanish Harlem Incident.
Temporary like Achilles.
You Angel You.
Eberhart. Art, the holy care of life.
Lord, stabilise me. My legs.
On Seeing an Egyptian Mummy in Berlin,

1932.
On the Fragility of Mind.
Passage, The.
Request.
Request for Offering.
Supreme Authority of the Imagination, The.
Transfer, The.
Edmunds. Weathering.
Eliot. Dedication to My Wife, A.
Emerson. Ode to Beauty.
See how the roses burn!
To Rhea.
Everson. Challenge, The.
Ferlinghetti. Astonished Heart, The.
Love Nut, The.
Short Story on a Painting of Gustav Klimt.
Fisher. Timelessness of Desire.
Fletcher. Aster Flower, The.
Blue Symphony.
Father's Thought of His Daughter, The.
Love and Suspicion.
Memory: The Walk on the Beach.
Night Song.
Vision.
Ford. Happy? The very eye of the world.
Fox. Ukiyo-E.
Frost. Discovery of the Madeiras, The.
Gallagher. Photograph of a Lighthouse Through Fog.
Galvin. Dog Love.
Garrigue. Again, Again.
Bleecker Street.
Demon Came to Me, A.
From Venice Was That Afternoon.
Grenoble Café.
Last Letter to the Scholar.
Mask and Knife, The.
Moralizing Overheard in a Forest.
To Speak of My Influences.
Ginsberg. Done, Finished with the Biggest Cock.
Fie My Fum.
Green Automobile, The.
Kaddish.
Night Gleam.
Rain-Wet Asphalt Heat, Garbage Curbed Cans Overflowing.
Shrouded Stranger, The.
Why Is God Love, Jack?
Glück. Aubade: "Today above the gull's call."
Early December in Croton-on-Hudson.
Elms.
Embrace, The.
Encounter, The.
Mirror, The.
Northwood Path.
Portrait of the Queen in Tears.
Graves. Ample Garden, The.
Arrears of Moonlight.
Beds of Grainne and Diarmuid, The.
Between Trains.
Black Goddess, The.
Cure, The.
Endless Pavement.
Fire Walker.
Fragment: "Are you shaken, are you stirred."
Hoopoe Tells Us How, The.
Judgement of Paris.
La Mejicana.
Lamia in Love.
Last Poem, A.
Leap, The.
Lure of Murder.
Name Day.
Patience.
Possessed.
Snap-Comb Wilderness, The.
Snapped Thread, The.
Song: The Far Side of Your Moon.
Stolen Jewel.
Symptoms of Love.
To Myrto About Herself.
To the Teumessian Vixen.
Troughs of Sea.
True Joy.
Under the Olives.
Unnamed Spell, The.

Watch, The.
Wild Cyclamen.
Young Cordwainer, The.
Hacker. Another poet, woman and alive.
One master, aged, as I am, thirty-two.
Haines. Way We Live, The.
Hall. Exile.
"Kiss, The."
Love Is Like Sounds.
Passage to Worship.
"Reclining Figure."
Wells.
Hardy. Chosen, The.
From Victor Hugo.
In the Street.
Love Watches a Window.
Lover to Mistress.
Maiden's Pledge, A.
Seven Times, The.
To Meet, or Otherwise.
Hartley. Lay warm gentle hand upon me.
Metaphysic.
Hartnett. He'll to the Moors.
Sad Singing in Darkness.
Hemingway. Oily Weather.
Herrick. Against Love.
Another ("Love he that will; it best likes
me").
Begger, The.
Change Gives Content.
Charme, or an Allay for Love, A.
Frozen Zone; or, Julia Disdainful, The.
His Misery in a Mistresse.
Hymne to Love, An.
Julia's Petticoat.
Love Kill'd by Lack.
Night-Piece, to Julia, The.
Of Love: ("I do not love, nor can it be").
Of Love ("Ile get me hence").
Of Love ("Instruct me now, what love will
do").
On Himselfe ("Love-sick I am, and must
endure").
On Love.
Pastorall Sung to the King: Montano, Silvio,
and Mirtillo, Shepards, A.
Things of Choice, Long a Comming.
To All Young Men That Love.
To Anthea ("Come Anthea, know thou this").
To Anthea: ("Lets call for Hymen if agreed
thou art").
To Bacchus, a Canticle.
To Cupid.
To Dewes. A Song.
To Electra.
To Electra ("'Tis Ev'ning, my Sweet").
To Perenna: ("How long, *Perenna*, wilt thou
see").
To Springs and Fountains.
To the Little Spinners.
Upon Cupid ("As lately I a Garland bound").
Upon Irene.
Upon Julia['s] Washing Herself in the River.
Upon Love, by Way of Question and Answer.
Upon Love ("Christall Violl Cupid brought,
A").
Upon Love ("I held Love's head while it did
ake").
Upon Love: ("I plaid with Love, as with the
fire").
Upon Love ("In a Dreame, Love bad me go").
Upon Love: ("Love, I have broke").
Upon Love: ("Love scorch'd my finger, but
did spare").
Upon Love: ("Love's a thing, (as I do
heare)").
Want.
What Kind of Mistress[e] He Would Have.
Hewitt. Aesthete's Renunciation.
Little Ships.
My Future Wife.
New Jerusalem.
On Reading Wallace Stevens' *Collected Poems*
after Many Years.
On the Choice of a Title.
This Narrative.
Hill. And you my spent heart's treasure.

Coplas.
He wounds with ecstasy. All.
Love, oh my love, it will come.
Pentecost Castle, The.
Stupefying images of grief-in-dream.
Holmes. Mouth.
Hughes, Langston. Desire.
Hugo. Bay of Recovery.
December 24, Alone.
Letter to Kathy from Wisdom.
Letter to Welch from Browning.
Upper Voight's, to All the Cutthroat There.
Jarrell. Over the florid capitals.
Jeffers. Cawdor.
Divinely Superfluous Beauty.
Maid's Thought, The.
Thurso's Landing.
Johnson. Song, A: "Not the soft sighs of
vernal gales."
Jong. Beast, Book, Body.
Demon Lover, The.
Pane Caldo.
Paper Cuts.
Jonson. Elegy, An: "By those bright eyes, at
whose immortal fires."
Song, A: "Come, let us here enjoy the shade."
Joseph. Danaë.
High Devil, Deep Pit.
Old Man Going.
Keats. Extracts from an Opera.
Fill for Me a Brimming Bowl.
Hither, Hither, Love.
Lines: "Unfelt, unheard, unseen."
Of Late Two Dainties Were before Me Placed.
Stanzas: "You say you love; but with a
voice."
To Emma.
Woman! When I Behold Thee Flippant, Vain.
Kipling. Oldest Song, The.
Knight. On Seeing the Black Male as #1 Sex
Object in America.
Larkin. Wants.
Lawrence. After Many Days.
And Jude the Obscure and His Beloved.
Appeal, The.
Bad Beginning, A.
Basta!
Come Spring, Come Sorrow.
December Night.
Deeper Than Love.
Desire.
Desire Goes Down into the Sea.
Desire Is Dead.
Dog-Tired.
Elixir.
Failure, A.
Forecast.
Frost Flowers.
Grasshopper Is a Burden.
Hands of the Betrothed, The.
In Trouble and Shame.
Latent Desire, The.
Lotus and Frost.
Love Message.
Man Reaches a Point.
Manifesto.
Mess of Love, The.
Narcissus.
On the Balcony.
Other Women Have Reared in Me.
Paradise Re-entered.
Primal Passions, The.
Red.
Restlessness.
Rose of All the World.
She Was a Good Little Wife.
Sighs.
Snap-Dragon.
Spiritual Woman, A.
Sunday Afternoon in Italy.
Temples.
To Toss the Troubled Night Long.
Virgin Youth.
Wedding Morn.
What Does She Want?
Witch I, The.

Witch II, The.
Women Want Fighters for Their Lovers.
Levertov. Unknown, The.
Levine. Poem Circling Hamtramck, Michigan,
All Night in Search of You, The.
Liddy. Death of Artists, The.
Delphine and Hippolyta.
Donn, / though you are cousin.
Evening at Axel's.
Tips of the fronds become swollen, The.
Translate into Latin for my Epitaph.
Waters by this music.
We saw the star of knowledge.
Lorde. Conversations in Crisis.
Lovelace. Dialogue. Lucasta, Alexis.
Guiltlesse Lady Imprisoned; after Penanced, A.
Love Made in the First Age[: To Chloris].
To a Lady That Desired Me I Would Bear My
Part with Her in a Song.
Lowry. Pacific is a feeble symbol of death.
To account for this, but it cannot be.
Virgo.
McGrath. Celebration for June 24.
Sometimes.
War Resisters' Song.
MacLeish. And he had used love's dream of
love before.
First I will tell you something of these two.
Here, O wanderer, here is the hill and the
harbor.
O hide your eyes.
This was not love but love's true negative.
Thunderhead.
Whom do you love, she said, when you look
out.
MacNeice. Troll's Courtship.
Markson. Question of Anatomy.
To a Lady, a Part of Her.
Marlowe. 2.19: Ad rivalem, cui uxor curae
non erat.
3.2: Ad amicam cursum equorum spectantem.
Marvell. Ametas and Thestylis Making Hay-
Ropes.
Match, The.
Mower's Song, The.
Melville. After the Pleasure Party.
In a Bye-Canal.
Meredith. Adieu, adieu, my Friar, he cried.
Am I failing? For no longer can I cast.
As the egg of an ostrich at the bottom [of] a
bubbling spring.
Ask, is Love divine.
Breath of the Briar.
Full faith I have she holds that rarest gift.
Give to imagination some pure light.
He felt the wild beast in him betweenwhiles.
Her cheeks are as a crystal goblet held to the
sun.
How many a thing which we cast to the
ground.
I bade my Lady think what she might mean.
I met at morn a girl of the tribes, bearing a
milk-bowl.
I must be flattered. The imperious.
Love is winged for two.
O Mary Barrie, Mary Barrie.
See the star yonder.
This golden head has wit in it. I live.
Was it wise to count the ranks of teeth.
We three are on the cedar-shadowed lawn.
Merrill. Kimono, The.
Lorelei.
Octopus, The.
Variations: The Air Is Sweetest That a Thistle
Guards.
Merton. Five Enemies, The.
It is hard to fight / against one's heart's
desire.
Last evening a city man.
Miami You Are About to Be Surprised.
Two Palm Trees, The.
Millay. Fatal Interview.
Philosopher, The.
To a Musician.
Milton. Sonnet 2: "Charming lady, she whose
beautiful name honors."
Morgan. Catullus: *Carmen v.*

Morrison. Soul Kitchen.
Nash. Chloe and the Roué.
Emancipation of Mr. Poplin, or, Skoal to the Skimmerless.
Song for Pier Something or Other.
Strange Case of the Girl o' Mr. Sponsoon's Dreams, The.
Strange Case of the Lovelorn Letter Writer, The.
To a Lady Passing Time Better Left Unpassed.
Nathan. Third Wish, The.
Nemerov. Sestina I: "Thickness of paint or flesh cannot deface."
O'Hara. Poem: "I don't know as I get what D.H. Lawrence is driving at."
Poem: "O sole mio, hot diggety, nix 'I wather think I can' ."
St. Paul and All That.
Variations on Pasternak's "Mein Liebchen, Was Willst Du Noch Mehr?"
Oliver. Blossom.
Hattie Bloom.
Olson. À Constance, This Day.
Maximus Letter # Whatever.
Of Mathilde.
Troilus.
War on the Mind in a Time of Love.
White Horse.
Oppen. Forms of Love, The.
Owen. Fates, The.
Long Ages Past.
Music.
Song of Songs.
To the Bitter Sweet-heart: a Dream.
Patchen. I Never Had Any Other Desire So Strong.
I'd want her eyes to fill with wonder.
Piercy. Nuisance, The.
Poe. Dream within a Dream, A.
To ———: "Not long ago, the writer of these lines."
To F——.
To F—S S. O—D.
To Helen ("I saw thee once—once only—years ago").
Pope. Presenting a *Lark.*
Pound. Na Audiart.
Prince. Byron-Shelley Conversation, A.
Ralegh. Poesie to Prove Affection is Not Love, A.
Rich. Re-forming the Crystal.
Sex, as they harshly call it.
Robinson. John Evereldown.
Roethke. Favorite, The.
Four for Sir John Davies.
Her Longing.
I Knew a Woman.
Long Waters, The.
Longing, The.
Love's Progress.
Marrow, The.
Memory.
Other, The.
Pure Fury, The.
Renewal, The.
Rose, The.
Sententious Man, The.
Sequel, The.
She.
Swan, The.
Verse with Allusions.
Voice, The.
Rolfe. Manuela.
Rossetti. Come back to me, who wait and watch for you.
Hope Carol, A.
"I, if I perish, perish"—Esther spake.
Like As the Hart Desireth the Water Brooks.
Margery.
Ransomed of the Lord, The.
Roses on a brier, / Pearls from out the bitter sea.
Soeur Louise De La Miséricorde.
Subject To Like Passions as We Are.
Till Tomorrow.
Trust me, I have not earned your dear rebuke.
What Would I Give?

Rukeyser. Cries from Chiapas.
Eyes of Night-Time.
If you look at your succession of desires.
Looking at Each Other.
Meeting, The.
Song of Another Tribe, A.
Two Illuminations, The.
What I See.
St. John. Desire.
Sandburg. Adelaide Crapsey.
At a Window.
Aztec.
Bricklayer Love.
Broken Hearted Soprano.
Calls.
Circle of Doors.
Dream Girl.
Evening Questions.
Evening Waterfall.
Gone.
Great Hunt, The.
Have Me.
Horse Fiddle.
Jan Kubelik.
Joy.
Love Beyond Keeping.
Manitoba Childe Roland.
M'Liss and Louie.
Moon Rondeau.
Offering and Rebuff.
Old-Fashioned Requited Love.
On the Breakwater.
One Parting.
Paula.
Poems Done on a Late Night Car.
Red-Headed Resstaurant Cashier.
Red Son, The.
Sarah's Letter to Peter.
Shirt.
Spanish.
They Met Young.
Thou Art Like a Flower.
Two Moon Fantasies.
Variations on a Theme.
White Ash.
Sarton. Death and the Lovers.
Prothalamion.
Schuyler. Sleep.
Table of Green Fields, A.
Tom.
Schwartz. Overture.
Sexton. Ambition Bird, The.
Farmer's Wife, The.
Jesus Asleep.
To Like, to Love.
Where I Live in This Honorable House of the Laurel Tree.
Shakespeare. Sonnet 46: "Mine eye and heart are at a mortal war."
Sonnet 51: "Thus can my love excuse the slow offence."
Sonnet 52: "So am I as the rich, whose blessed key."
Sonnet 56: "Sweet love, renew thy force; be it not said."
Sonnet 114: "Or whether doth my mind, being crowned with you."
Sonnet 147: "My love is as a fever [or feaver], longing still."
Sonnet 150: "O! From what power..." what power hast thou this powerful might."
Sonnet 154: "Little love-god lying once asleep, The."
Shapiro. Back, The.
Glass Poem.
Haircut.
Shelley. Love, Hope, Desire and Fear.
To the Queen of My Heart.
Shelton. Her.
My Love.
Sidney. Phoebus farewell, a sweeter saint I serve.
Second Song.
Sonnet 14: "Alas, have I not pain enough, my friend."
Sonnet 46: "I cursed thee oft, I pity now thy case."

Sonnet 56: "Fie, school of Patience, fie; your lesson is."
Sonnet 60: "When my good angel guides me to the place."
Sonnet 66: "And do I see some cause a hope to feed."
Sonnet 72: "Desire, though thou my old companion art."
Thou blind man's mark, thou fool's self-chosen snare.
Smith, Patti. Ballad of Isabelle Eberhardt.
Dream of Rimbaud.
Smith, Stevie. Appetite.
Fool, The.
I Could Let Tom Go—But What about the Children.
La Gretchen de Nos Jours (II).
Longing for Death because of Feebleness.
Love Me!
Shooting Incident, The.
Tender Only to One.
Snyder. Beneath My Hand and Eye the Distant Hills, Your Body.
Four Poems for Robin.
Manichaeans, The.
Three Poems for Joanne.
Sorrentino. Light, my light, let me never be again.
Spenser. My Love Is Like to Ice.
Stein. Lifting Belly.
Stevens. Bouquet of Belle Scavoir.
Dezembrum.
Men That Are Falling, The.
Stevenson. Ad Olum.
Hopes.
Mater Triumphans.
Old world moans and topes, The.
Plain as the glistering planets shine.
To Minnie (With a Hand-Glass).
To what shall I compare her.
Unforgotten II, The ("She rested by the Broken Brook").
We Have Loved of Yore.
Stuart. Begging on North Main.
Once More for My Lady.
Suckling. Against Absence.
Guiltless Inconstant, The.
Love's Burning-Glass.
Miracle, The.
Song: "Crafty boy that had full oft assay'd, The."
Song: "Unjust decrees, that do at once exact."
Sonnet: "Dost see how unregarded now."
Swift. Desire and Possession.
Swinburne. Sapphics.
Tate. Sulpicia to Cerinthus.
Thomas. If I Were Tickled by the Rub of Love.
Into Her Lying Down Head.
Thomson. Come, Gentle God.
Lover's Fate, The.
To Fortune.
To the God of Fond Desire.
Tomlinson. Death of Will, The.
Updike. No More Access to Her Underpants.
Van Duyn. Billings and Cooings from "The Berkeley Barb."
Wakoski. Screw, a Technical Love Poem.
Waldman. Ballade: "My heart's felt no wounds big or small."
Musical Garden.
My Kind of Man.
Sidney's Complaynt.
Warren. Birth of Love.
Sound of That Wind, The.
Whitman. As Adam Early in the Morning.
Fast-Anchor'd Eternal O Love!
From Pent-up Aching Rivers.
I Heard You Solemn-Sweet Pipes of the Organ.
Not Heat Flames Up and Consumes.
O You Whom I Often and Silently Come.
Out of the Rolling Ocean the Crowd.
To the Garden the World.
When I Heard at the Close of the Day.
Whittier. Henchman, The.
Wilbur. Apology.

Complaint.
L'Etoile.
Piccola Commedia.
Playboy.
She.
To Madame du Châtelet.
Voice from under the Table, A.
Williams, Charles Kenneth. Game, The.
Love: Beginnnings.
Love: Youth.
On the Other Hand.
Orchid, The.
Sting, The.
With Ignorance.
Williams, Miller. How to Stop Smoking.
Williams, William Carlos. Appeal.
Attic Which Is Desire, The.
Chanson.
Design for November.
Sappho.
Song: "You are forever April."
Spring Song.
Venus Over the Desert.
Wordsworth. Lesbia.
Septimius and Acme.
To ———: " 'Wait, prithee, wait!' this answer
   Lesbia threw."
Yes! hope may with my strong desire keep
   pace.
Wright, Charles. Laguna Dantesca.
Wright, James. Accusation, The.
Angel, The.
Assignation, The.
Before a Cashier's Window in a Department
   Store.
Erinna to Sappho.
Girl in a Window, A.
Girl Walking into a Shadow, A.
I am Freed.
In a Viennese Cemetery.
Lights in the Hallway, The.
Offense, The.
On the Way to the Planetarium.
Poem about Breasts, A.
Sappho.
Shadow and the Real, The.
This morning / My beloved rose, before I did.
Wroth. Song 6: "You happy blessed eyes."
Song: "Love a child is ever criing [or
   crying]."
Song: "Say Venus how long have I lov'd, and
   serv'd you heere?"
Sonnet 1: "My hart is lost, what can I now
   expect."
Sonnet 2: "Love like a jugler, comes to play
   his prise."
Sonnet 4: "When I beeheld the Image of my
   deere."
Sonnet 5: "And burne, yett burning you will
   love the smart."
Sonnet 7: "How blest bee they then, who his
   favors prove."
Sonnet 8: "Hee that shunns love doth love him
   self the less."
Sonnet 11: "Unprofitably pleasing, and
   unsound."
Sonnet 17: "Sweet shades why doe you seeke
   to give delight."
Sonnet 34: "Take heed mine eyes, how you
   your lookes doe cast."
Sonnet 35: "False [or Faulce] hope which
   feeds but[t] to destroy, and spill."
Wyatt. Desire, alas, my master and my foe.
Desire to sorrow doth me constrain.
Driven by desire, I did this deed.
For want of [or I] will in woe I plain.
From these high [or hie] hill[e]s as when a
   spring doth fall.
Furious gun in his raging ire, The.
Grudge on who list, this is my lot.
If amorous faith in heart unfeigned.
If fancy [or fansy] would favour.
If thou wilt mighty be, flee from the rage.
It burneth yet, alas, my heart's desire.
Lively sparks that issue from those eyes, The.
So feeble is the thread that doth the burden
   stay.

So unwarely was never no man caught.
Sometime I fled the fire that me brent.
Such vain thought as wonted to mislead me.
Though I myself be bridled of my mind.
Yau. Recoil.
Yeats. Arrow, The.
First Confession, A.
Love's Loneliness.
What Magic Drum?
What Then?
Young. Black Queen for More Than a Day.
Zukofsky. Acme, Septimius, sighs so amorous.
He'll hie me, par is he? the God divide her.
Home for Aged Bomb Throwers—U.S.S.R.
Human all key mog knee this pecks it loom in
   a moon the.
I'm a bow, my dual kiss, Ipsithilla.
May we live, my Lesbia, love while we may.
1959 Valentine.
One lutenist played look; your through was
   drink.
Poet I'm too near your and my sod daily.
Prop. LXI.
Queries, you ask how many times must I kiss.
Sparrow, my girl's pleasure, delight of my
   girl.
The.

See also **Erotic Love; Lust.**

Desks
Mahon. Table Talk.

Desolation
Auden. Landscape.
Motherhood.
Truly our fathers had the gout.
Berg. Dreaming with a Friend.
Thread.
Berry. Desolation.
Brontë. Coldly, bleakly, drearily.
It was night, and on the mountains.
Old Hall of Elbë, ruined, lonely now.
R. Alcona to J. Brenzaida.
Remembrance.
Browning, Elizabeth Barrett. Sonnet: "Thou
   hast thy calling to some palace floor."
Campion. Raving warre, begot / In the thirstye
   sands.
Carruth. Cappadocian Song.
Gunmetal snow icecolored sky.
Catullus. Carmen 37: "Nine posts, five doors,
   up the Clivus."
Clark. Easter Sunday.
Cohen. Diamonds in the Mine.
Creeley. Enough.
Marriage, A.
Night Sky, A.
Cullen. Black Magdalens.
De la Mare. Bitter Waters.
Defeat.
Doolittle. Tribute, The.
Duncan. Back to the figure.
Dunn. Atlantic City.
Observer, The.
Snow Leopard, The.
Ford. Feet of his days have been mangled,
   The.
Gallagher. Bonfire.
Ginsberg. In Back of the Real.
Vulture Peak: Gridhakuta Hill.
Haines. Driving through Oregon (Dec. 1973).
Hesketh. Northern Stone.
Hill. Tristia: 1891–1938.
Hughes, Ted. That Moment.
Hugo. Letter to Scanlon from Whitehall.
South Italy, Remote and Stone.
Jeffers. Place for No Story, The.
Knight. Feeling Fucked Up.
Liddy. Mistress on her white horse at, The.
Lowry. As the poor end of each dead day
   drew near.
De Lesseps, he said, was not the only one.
Delirium in Vera Cruz.
Drunkards, The.
Ghosts in New Houses.
MacNeice. Order to View.
Windowscape.
McNeill. Deserted Lumber Yard.
Merton. Desolation.

Millay. Desolation Dreamed Of.
Feast.
Miller. Black November.
So in evening there is still light.
Morgan. End, The.
Exile.
Oliver. River Styx, Ohio, The.
Prince. For the Deserted.
Ransom. Emily Hardcastle, Spinster.
Rossetti. Castle-Builder's World, A.
I Look for the Lord.
Rukeyser. Certain Music, A.
Shelley. Tower of Famine, The.
Simic. Fall Day, A.
Smith, Charlotte. Descriptive Ode, Supposed
   to Have Been Written under the Ruins of
   Rufus's Castle, A.
Unhappy exile, whom his fates confine, The.
Smith, Stevie. Every Lovely Limb's a
   Desolation.
Sorrentino. Coast of Texas.
Thomas. Hand That Signed the Paper, The.
Williams, Charles Kenneth. Neglect.
Zimmer. Cecil Sliding Away from the
   Memory of Wanda.
Eisenhower Years, The.
Zukofsky. Dying away as of trees, A.
Salt hacks, tavern boys, what skews, can't you
   burn alleys.

Despair
Arnold. Self-Dependence.
Auden. Happy Tree, The.
He Revisits the Spot.
Beckett. Cascando.
Scarcely Disfigured.
Berg. For the Ghost of Li Po.
Sticks.
To the Being We Are.
Berry. Desolation.
Berryman. As usual I'm up before the sun.
Demand me again what Kafka's riddles mean.
Despair.
Form, The.
If long enough I sit here, she, she'll pass.
It will seem strange, no more this range on
   range.
No.
Once when they found me, some refrain "*Quoi
   faire?*."
Song of the Bridegroom, The.
Wasp skims nearby up the bright warm air, A.
What was Ashore, then? Cargoed with Forget.
Where the lane from the highway swerves the
   first drops fell.
Betjeman. Tregardock.
Blake. Sick Rose, The.
Song: "My silks and line array."
Bly. Fire of Despair Has Been Our Savior,
   The.
Snowbanks North of the House.
When the Dumb Speak.
Boyle. And Winter.
Dedicated to *Terre des Hommes*.
Brontë. Castle Wood.
Darkness was overtraced on every face.
F. de Samara to A. G. A.
I know not how it falls on me.
I would have touched the heavenly key.
In dungeons dark I cannot sing.
It will not shine again.
Sleep brings no joy to me.
Sympathy.
What use is it to slumber here.
Wind, I hear it sighing, The.
Written on Returning to the P. of I. on the
   10th of January, 1827.
Browning, Elizabeth Barrett. Loved Once.
Mask, The.
Nature's Remorses.
Proof and Disproof.
Bukowski. Blackbirds Are Rough Today, The.
One Hundred and Ninety-Nine Pounds of Clay
   Leaning Forward.
Rat Rises, A.
When the Berry Bush Dies I'll Swim Down
   the Green River with My Hair on Fire.
Wrong Number.

Bunting. Last night without sight of you my brain was ablaze.
Now we've no hope of going back.
Burns. Despondency, an Ode.
Fragment: "Now health forsakes that angel face."
Raving winds around her blowing.
Thou hast left me ever, Jamie.
To Ruin.
Byron. And Wilt Thou Weep When I Am Low?
Epistle to a Friend.
Herod's Lament for Mariamne.
Julian [A Fragment].
La Revanche.
Lament of Tasso, The.
Lines Written beneath a Picture.
Remembrance.
Reply to Some Verses of J.M.B. Pigot, Esq., on the Cruelty of His Mistress.
Stanzas: "Chill and mirk is the nightly blast."
Campion. Breake now my heart and dye! Oh no, she may relent.
O never to be moved.
Spyres Curten, The.
"Carroll, Lewis." Third Voice, The.
Carruth. Arthritic gray snowlight hobbles down the valley westward.
Because in the heart / of darkness I could not see.
Eternal City.
Now tell me if we don't need a revolution!
Black.
Of the rights of each to zero. No, I mean the only.
Some don't get much, Amos.
Sonnet: "Why complain, brothers, to you, my writing."
Spring 1967.
Clark. Crisis on the Savannah.
Easter Sunday.
Clough. My wind is turned to bitter north.
Cohen. Everybody Knows.
Future, The.
I Draw Aside the Curtain.
Invisible Tonight.
My Honour.
Coleridge. Despair.
Visionary Hope, The.
Work without Hope.
Cowper. Castaway, The.
Lines Written During a Period of Insanity.
Crashaw. On Hope.
Creeley. Ballad of the Despairing Husband.
Dream, The.
For Love.
Woman, The.
Cullen. At a Parting.
Therefore, Adieu.
De la Mare. Euphrasy.
Futility.
Macbeth.
Mirage.
Dickinson. Despair's advantage is achieved.
Doubt if it be Us, A.
I cannot live with You.
It might be lonelier.
It was not Death, for I stood up.
I've dropped my Brain—My Soul is numb.
No Man can compass a Despair.
One joy of so much anguish.
Safe Despair it is that raves.
Somewhat, to hope for.
This Chasm, Sweet, upon my life.
Dobyns. Ways of Keys, The.
Doolittle. Cassandra.
Envy.
Fragment 40: "Keep love and he wings."
Let me be / a splinter in your side.
Sea-Choros.
Dove. Aurora Borealis.
Dunbar. Blue.
Despair.
One Life.
River of Ruin, The.
Ships That Pass in the Night.
There are brilliant heights of sorrow.

Worn Out.
Wraith, The.
Duncan. Bring It Up from the Dark.
"Dylan." Every Grain of Sand.
No Time to Think.
Poor Boy Blues.
Standing on the Highway.
Eberhart. Despair.
I turned where the sun came up and he held my hand.
Incarcerating sunlight, world damnation.
Lost, The.
Necessity.
Sestina: "I die, no matter what I do I die."
Suicide Note.
Ferlinghetti. In Golden Gate Park that day.
Rough Song of Animals Dying.
Fletcher. Elegy on Tintern Abbey.
Last Frontier, The.
Sharaku Dreams.
Frost. Not All There.
Gallagher. Ballad of Ballymote, The.
Garrigue. Homage to Ghosts.
My Frantic Heart.
Gildner. Girl in the Red Convertible, The.
Ginsberg. Yes and It's Hopeless.
Glück. Memo from the Cave.
World Breaking Apart.
Graves. Raft, The.
Hacker. 1976.
Hall. Praise for Death.
Hardy. Coming Up Oxford Street: Evening.
Darkling Thrush, The.
Her Love-Birds.
Meeting with Despair, A.
Murmurs in the Gloom.
Hartnett. Mountains, Fall on Us.
Naked Surgeon, The.
Poet Down, The.
Hemingway. God is away for the summer.
Herbert. Affliction (4).
Assurance.
Collar, The.
Decay.
Denial[l].
Glimpse, The.
Home.
Longing.
Herrick. Fear[e] Gets Force.
No Danger to Men Desperate.
Hesketh. Bull Alone.
It Was Not I.
Hewitt. Boy Seen in a Bus Journey.
Fairy Thresher, The.
Habit of Mercy, The.
Heart of Joy, The.
I Turned My Touch to Campion.
Leaf.
Lyric: "Let but a thrush begin."
Poem: "Consider Wordsworth in his withered age."
Postscript, 1984.
Hill. Scarcely speaking: it becomes as a.
Hoffman. Thought I Was Dying.
Holmes. Bad Turn, A.
Cold Window.
Hopkins. Alchemist in the City, The.
Carrion Comfort.
Fragment of Anything You Like, A.
I wake and feel the fell of dark, not day.
Leaden Echo and the Golden Echo, The.
My prayers must meet a brazen heaven.
No worst, there is none. Pitched past pitch of grief.
Pilate.
Stephen and Barberie.
Trees by their yield.
Voice from the World, A.
Why if it be so, for the dismal morn.
Housman. I promise nothing: friends will part.
Spring Morning.
Twice a week the winter thorough.
World goes none the lamer, The.
Hugo. Approaching the Castle.
Beggar in Sapri.
Birthday.
Brief History.

Keokuk.
Letter to Levertov from Butte.
Montgomery Hollow.
My Buddy.
Jarrell. Forsaken Girl, The.
Jeffers. Air-Raid Rehearsals.
Johnson. Winter's Walk, The.
Joseph. Beyond Descartes.
Man in a Bar.
Round: "Body of a child lay in the pool, The."
Wet Sunday.
Keats. Day Is Gone and All Its Sweets Are Gone, The.
To Hope.
Knight. Report to the Mother.
Kunitz. Night Letter.
Larkin. Life with a Hole in It, The.
There Is No Language of Destruction.
Lawrence. And Oh—That the Man I Am Might Cease to Be.
Ballad of Another Ophelia.
Erotic.
Forsaken and Forlorn.
Impulse.
Labour Battalion.
Loggerheads.
Misery.
Next Morning.
Stoic.
Under the Oak.
What Do I Care?
What Is a Man to Do?
Lewis. At dusk in my garden the flowers are waiting.
Atropos to Ophelia.
Karanje Village.
Mountain over Aberdare, The.
Southend at Dusk.
Suicide, The.
Yet we are safely at this port of call.
Liddy. Icarus.
Litany of Satan, The.
Lorde. Generation.
Lowry. Correcting Manuscript.
Death of an Oaxaqueñian.
I tried to think of something good.
Like the black iron steps.
Poem to be Placed at the Conclusion of a Long Obscure Passionate and Eloquent Book of Poems.
Search, The.
There is no poetry when you live there.
McAuley. Dust-Devils.
Mnemosyne: The Empty Room.
McGrath. Citizen Dreaming, The.
Don't Think You Know My Name!
End of the Line, The.
Everything in Order.
Nuclear Winter.
McNeill. Great Depression, The.
Mahon. Girls on the Bridge.
Meredith. Blame me not that I refuse.
I am to follow her. There is much grace.
I Chafe at Darkness.
Love they alone the joyful heart.
Song: "Forever."
Too cold for joy, too cold for woe.
Merrill. Time.
Merton. Despairing Man Draws a Serpent, The.
Litany: "It yawns at me the cavernous gulf."
Millay. No Earthly Enterprise.
Miller. Day Born Without a Mouth.
Desperate, The.
November Dusk.
Nemerov. Redeployment.
Notley. Poem: "You hear that heroic big land music?"
O'Hara. Meditations in an Emergency.
Olson. As snow lies on the hill love's blackness lies.
Cry pain, & the dogs of yrself devour.
February 10, One Year Too Late.
Jas Jargon.
Return, The.

She, Thus.
Tanto e Amara.
Oppen. But at night the park.
Cars on the highway filled with speech.
Crowded Countries of the Bomb, The.
Fifty years / Sidereal time.
Lights / Shine, the fire, The.
People, the People, The.
Power ruptures at a thousand holes.
Survival: Infantry.
There was no other guarantee.
They carry nativeness / To a conclusion.
Patchen. Blind Maidens of Our Homelessness,
The.
Christ! Christ! Christ! that the world.
Eve of St. Agony, or the Middle Class Was
Sitting on Its Fat.
Lost Poem, A.
Morning, My Prince—the Eye That Walks.
O Fill Your Sack with Tiger Cubs.
Stars go to sleep so peacefully, The.
Piercy. Eight of Swords, The.
Plath. Event.
Moon and the Yew Tree, The.
Purdah.
Ravaged Face, The.
Sonnet: To Eva.
Street Song.
Winter Landscape, with Rooks.
Raine. Medea.
Ralegh. My Body in the Walls Captived.
Rexroth. Requiem for the Spanish Dead.
Rich. Antinoüs: The Diaries.
Roethke. Against Disaster.
Feud.
Surly One, The.
Rolfe. Letter for One in Russia.
Season of Death.
Words Found on a Cave's Wall.
Rossetti. Better Resurrection, A.
Dead Hope.
Fair Margaret.
If Only.
L. E. L.
Old-World Thicket, An.
What Would I Give?
When My Heart Is Vexed, I Will Complain.
Rukeyser. Down from Chicago Bryan came.
St. John. No Heaven.
Sarton. Christmas Letter to a Psychiatrist.
How faint the horn sounds in the mountain
passes.
My Father's Death.
Prisoner at a Desk.
Where Dream Begins.
Schwartz. Sequel, the Conclusion, the
Endlessness, The.
Sexton. Angel of Hope and Calendars.
Big Boots of Pain, The.
Despair.
Eighteen Days without You.
End, Middle, Beginning.
February 17th.
Flight.
45 Mercy Street.
Her Kind.
Sickness unto Death, The.
Shelley. Circumstance.
Fragment: "Such hope, as is the sick despair
of good."
Invocation to Misery.
Lament, A: "O world! O life! O time!"
Lines Written among the Euganean Hills.
see also Scene from "Tasso."
Sonnet: England in 1819.
Stanza, Written at Bracknell.
Stanzas Written in Dejection, near Naples [or
—December 1818, near Naples].
Shelton. Great Gulf, The.
Sidney. I joy in grief, and do detest all joys.
Sonnet 108: "When sorrow (using mine own
fire's might)."
Sonnet 19: "On Cupid's bow how are my
heart-strings bent."
Silverstein. Long-Haired Boy, The.
What a Day.
Simic. Cold Blue Tinge.

Smart. Against Despair.
Smith, Charlotte. April.
By the Same. To the North Star.
Composed During a Walk on the Downs, in
November 1787.
Far on the sands, the low, retiring tide.
Laplander, The.
Nepenthe.
Ode to Death.
Ode to Despair.
On Leaving a Part of Sussex.
On Passing Over a Dreary Tract of Country,
and Near the Ruins of a Deserted Chapel,
During a Tempest.
Return of the Nightingale. Written in May
1791, The.
Should the lone Wanderer, fainting on his
way.
Sleeping Woodman. Written in April 1790,
The.
To Fancy.
To Mrs. ****.
To Oblivion.
To Spring.
To the Morning Star. Written Near the Sea.
To the Muse.
To the Sun.
To the Winds.
Unhappy exile, whom his fates confine, The.
Where the wild woods and pathless forests
frown.
Winter Night, The.
Written at Bignor Park in Sussex, in August,
1799.
Written at Exmouth, Midsummer, 1795.
Written in a Tempestuous Night, on the Coast
of Sussex.
Written on Passing by Moon-Light through a
Village, While the Ground Was Covered with
Snow.
Smith, Patti. Gibralto.
Smith, Stevie. Appetite.
Bereaved Swan, The.
Blood Flows Back, The.
Bog-Face.
Do Take Muriel Out.
Does No Love Last?
Forgot!
Friend, The.
I Am.
I Rode with My Darling.
Poor Soul, Poor Girl!
Rothebât.
Sad Heart, The.
Sea-Widow, The.
Sorrentino. Cerinthus, don't you have some
soft thought for your girl.
He walks on the street, in.
Nightpiece.
Nothing grimmer than dawn at noon.
Now the night is here. Blood.
Ultima Despedida del Principe Poniatowski de
Su Familia.
Spender. Oedipus Rex.
Trigorin.
Spenser. Cave of Despair, The.
Despair.
Hard by a rivers side a virgin faire.
When I behold this tickle trustles state.
Stevenson. Cruel Mistress, The.
Love—what is love? A great and aching heart.
Man sails the deep a while.
O dull cold northern sky.
Swift. Phyllis [or Phillis or Progress of Love,
The].
Tennyson. Mariana.
Œnone.
Supposed Confessions of a Second-rate
Sensitive Mind.
Two Voices, The.
Thomas. Saint About to Fall, A.
Where Once the Waters of Your Face.
Updike. By the light of insomnia, truths.
Walcott. Laventille.
Williams, Charles Kenneth. Bread.
Dimensions.

Loss.
Portions of Manslayer.
Williams, William Carlos. Drunkard, The.
Portrait of the Author.
Wordsworth. Away, away, it is the air.
Ballad, A: "And will you leave me thus
alone."
Complaint of a Forsaken Indian Woman, The.
Composed Near Calais on the Road Leading
to Ardres, August 7, 1802.
In Part from Moschus's Lament for Bion.
Lament of Mary Queen of Scots on the Eve of
a New Year.
Reverie of Poor Susan, The.
Sonnet Written by Mr — Immediately after
the Death of His Wife.
'Tis said that some have died for love.
Written in London, September, 1802.
Wright, Charles. Primitive Journal.
Wroth. Song 1: "Spring now come att last,
The."
Song 2: "All night I weep[e], all day I cry,
Ay me[e]."
Song 7: "Sorrow, I yeeld, and grieve that I did
miss."
Sonnet 6: "My pain[e], still smothered [or
smother'd] in my grievèd bre[a]st."
Sonnet 8: "Led by the powre of griefe, to
waylings brought."
Sonnet 9: "Be[e] you all pleased [or pleas'd]
your pleasures grieve not[t] me[e]."
Sonnet 9: "'Pray doe nott use thes words I
must bee gone."
Sonnet 11: "You endless torments that my rest
opress."
Sonnet 12: "Cloy'd with the torments of a
tedious night."
Sonnet 18: "Which should I better like of,
day, or night."
Sonnet 25: "Poore eyes bee blind, the light
behold noe more."
Sonnet 30: "You blessed shades, which give
mee silent rest."
Sonnet 42: "If ever love had force in
huma[i]ne brest?"
Sonnet: "Fly traiter joye whose end brings butt
dispaire."
Wyatt. After great storms the calm returns.
Alas, poor man, what hap have I.
All heavy minds.
All in thy sight my life doth whole depend.
Because I have thee still kept from lies and
blame.
Comfort thyself, my wo[e]ful heart.
Enemy [or en'my] of life, decayer of all kind,
The [or Th'].
For shamefast harm of great and hateful need.
Fruit of all the service that I serve, The.
Heart oppressed [or oppress'd] with desperate
thought.
I lead a life unpleasant, nothing glad.
I see that chance hath chosen me.
Joy so short alas, the pain so near, The.
Like as the swan towards her death.
Love and Fortune and my mind, remem'rer.
Most wretched heart, most miserable.
My hope, alas, hath me abused.
O, what undeserved cruelty.
Pillar [or Piller] perished [or pearisht] is
whe[a]rto I le[a]nt, The.
Plain ye, mine eyes. Accompany my heart.
Restful place, reviver of my smart, The.
She sat and sewed that hath done me the
wrong.
Since you will needs that I shall sing.
Suffering in sorrow, in hope to attain.
There was never nothing more me pained [or
payned].
To wish and want and not obtain.
What death is worse than this?
Yeats. He Mourns for the Change That Has
Come upon Him and His Beloved, and Longs
for the End of the World.
Reconciliation.
Two Songs Rewritten for the Tune's Sake.
Young. Herrick Hospital, Fifth Floor.
January.

Zimmer. Gus Sees Wanda Drinking.
Zimmer Remembering Wanda.
Destiny
Atwood. It's the story that counts.
  There must be more for you to do.
Auden. Like a Vocation.
  Standing among the ruins, the horror-struck
    conqueror exclaimed.
Beatles. Martha My Dear.
Beckett. Je suis ce cours de sable qui glisse.
  My way is in the sand flowing.
Browning, Elizabeth Barrett. Sonnet: "Unlike
  are we, unlike, O princely heart!"
Bukowski. Blackbirds Are Rough Today, The.
Carruth. Destinies, destinations: In Morrisville.
  Lost.
  Stronger than destiny is pain.
Clark. Fate.
  I Was Born to Speak Your Name.
  Moira.
  Moirai, The.
  Spiritual.
  Withdrawal.
Cohen. Avalanche.
  Song for My Assassin.
  Who by Fire?
Cowper. Boadicea: An Ode.
Creeley. Curse.
  Oh No.
  Prejudice, The.
  Window, The.
Cullen. Judas Iscariot.
Eberhart. American Hakluyt.
  Necessity.
  Oedipus.
  Recognition.
Emerson. All that thy virgin soul can ask be
  thine.
  Epitaph: "Bethink, poor heart, what bitter kind
    of jest."
  I must not borrow light.
  Reach me wine No counsel weakens the
    conclusion of the lot.
  Ruler after word & thought.
  Turtle in swamp.
Fisher. Staffordshire Red.
Glück. Liberation.
Graves. Bweteen Hyssop and Axe.
Hardy. Destined Pair, The.
  Man Was Drawing Near to Me, A.
  Mismet.
  Turnip-Hoer, The.
Hartley. Blandly she lies.
Hesketh. Leave Train, The.
Hugo. Three Stops to Ten Sleep.
Kunitz. King of the River.
Lawrence. Destiny.
Levine. Salts and Oils.
Lovelace. To His Deare Brother Colonel F.L.
Lowry. Minstrel in Labrador, A.
  That's What I Mean.
  Ye pow'rs who make mankind oyour care.
"MacDiarmid." Poetry that never for a
  moment forgets, A.
MacNeice. Birthright.
Mahon. Girls on the Bridge.
Meredith. Karl Onyx.
Merton. Glove, The.
Moore. Those Various Scalpels.
Morrison. Form Is an Angel, The.
  Heaven or Hell.
Nemerov. Sunderland.
Patchen. These Unreturning Destinies.
Prince. Dice, The.
  Plato says that in Heaven there is.
Rukeyser. Game of Ball, A.
Sandburg. Scriptsmith.
  Sky Pieces.
  Three Fragments for Fishers of Destiny.
  Webs.
Sarton. At Delphi.
Sorrentino. What is to be understood.
Stevenson. To Andrew Lang.
Stuart. Love Song.
Warren. From landscape the color of lions.
  Leaf, The.

Wilbur. Death, from a Distance.
  Under Cygnus.
Williams, Charles Kenneth. Even If I Could.
Williams, Miller. Believing in Symbols.
  Getting the Message.
See also **Fate.**
Destruction
Atwood. Beauharnois, Glengarry.
  It Is Dangerous to Read Newspapers.
  Newsreel: Man and Firing Squad.
  Well, we felt / we were almost getting
    somewhere.
Auden. No trenchant parting this.
  Old Mine, The.
  Sawmill, The.
Berry. Against the War in Vietnam.
  Bloodroot is white, The.
  Dark with power.
  In This World.
  Sometimes he thinks the earth.
  Supplanting, The.
  Want of Peace, The.
  Who has invented our enmity? Who has
    prescribed us.
  Window grows fragile, The.
Berryman. Long Home, The.
Bukowski. Change of Habit, A.
  Destroying Beauty.
  Dogs.
  I've Seen Too Many Glazed-Eyed Bums
    Sitting under a Bridge Drinking Cheap Wine.
Bunting. Chorus of Furies.
Byron. On the Day of the Destruction of
  Jerusalem by Titus.
Carroll, Jim. After St. John of the Cross.
  I stored daylight in secret attics.
  Traffic.
Carruth. Great Death, The.
Catullus. Carmen 36: "Volusian sheets / shit-
  shotten Annals."
Ciardi. Divorced, Husband Demolishes Home.
Clark. After the Fire—The Woman.
  Commanders, The.
  Milky Turqoise Cloud.
Crane. Eternity.
Creeley. Answer, The.
  "Oh My Love.."
  Some Afternoon.
Dickey, William. Afternoon Evening and
  Night in the Courtyard of the Museum of
  Modern Art.
Dobyns. Somewhere It Still Moves.
Duncan. Passage over Water.
Dunn. Bringing It Down.
Eberhart. Came lassitude and despair of the
  mind.
  Dream, A.
  Fantasy of a Small Idea.
  Groundhog Revisiting, The.
  Incarcerating sunlight, world damnation.
  Laocoön.
  Necessity.
  Protagonists.
  Swinging Bridge, The.
  Testimony.
  Truncated Bird, The.
  United 555.
  White Pines, Felled 1984.
  Words.
  World War.
Emerson. Water.
Everson. Attila.
Fenton. Wind.
Frost. Bursting Rapture.
  Fire and Ice.
Gallagher. Death of the Horses by Fire.
  Unsteady Yellow.
Graves. Mist.
  Twins.
Gray. Impromptu.
Griffiths. From Waterloo Bridge, Ensuing
  Dark.
  Guesthouse, The.
Gunn. Lofty in the Palais de Danse.
Haines. In Nature.
Hall. Corner, The.

Hesketh. From Walden.
  Joke, The.
Hewitt. House Demolished, A.
  September Lull.
Hughes, Ted. Executioner, The.
  Littleblood.
  Lovepet, The.
  Once I said lightly.
  Stone, The.
  That Moment.
  When Men Got to the Summit.
Hugo. End of Krim's Pad, The.
Jarrell. Traveler, The.
Jeffers. Beautiful Captive, The.
  Decaying Lambskins.
  End of the World.
  Little Scraping, A.
  Love and the Hate, The.
  Rain, hail and brutal sun, the plow in the
    roots.
  Summer Holiday.
  What of It?
Jonson. Execration upon Vulcan, An.
Joseph. Think of the minute amount a mouse
  eats.
Kinnell. Another Night in the Ruins.
  Ruins under the Stars.
Kipling. Song of Seven Cities, The.
Kooser. Grandfather.
  Shooting a Farmhouse.
Kunitz. Ambergris.
  Approach to Thebes, The.
  Dark and the Fair, The.
  Last Picnic, The.
  Thing That Eats the Heart, The.
  You have closed your eyes.
Lawrence. At Last.
  Breath of Life, The.
  Dies Illa.
Lewis. Destruction.
  Raiders' Dawn.
  Sweet Mother Chruch, beleaguered on the hill.
  Three endless weeks of sniping all the way.
Liddy. Voyage to Cytherea, A.
  We saw the star of knowledge.
Lieberman. Santana.
  Wreckage of the Pagoda Moons.
Lindsay. Soul of a Spider, The.
Lowry. Lament in the Pacific Northwest.
  S.O.S Sinking fast by both bow and stern.
"MacDiarmid." Glen of Silence, The.
McGrath. Citizen Dreaming, The.
MacLeish. Night Watch in the City of Boston.
  Population Explosion.
MacNeice. Canto XXV: "And today is
  Christmas Eve. Once more to work."
  Débâcle.
  Jungle Clearance Ceylon.
Markson. Women's House of Detention.
Melville. Pisa's Leaning Tower.
  Ravaged Villa, The.
Meredith. Under the thin hoop of gold.
Merrill. Nike.
  Urban Convalescence, An.
Merton. Letter to Pablo Antonio Cuadra
  Concerning Giants, The.
  Ox Mountain Parable, The.
Morrison. Original Temptation, The.
  Wild Whore Laughs, The.
Olson. La Torre.
  Mathematical Secret, and the Apron, The.
  Scream to the Editor, A.
  Town, The.
Oppen. It is the air of atrocity.
  Survival: Infantry.
Owen. To Eros.
Patchen. Destruction of Carthage, The.
Piercy. Emperor, The.
  Kneeling at the Pipes.
  Long Death, The.
Poe. Sonnet—To Science.
Raine. It is in us they burn.
  Polluted tide, / Desecrated earth destroyed.
Rich. For the Record.
Rolfe. Prophecy in Stone.
Rossetti. Alas, alas! for the self-destroyed /
  Vanish as images from a glass.

God Is Our Hope and Strength.
Hear what the mournful linnets say.
Rukeyser. For Fun.
Sand-Quarry with Moving Figures.
Sandburg. At the Gates of Tombs.
Shapiro. Tornado Warning.
Shelley. Lines Written During the Castlereagh Administration.
Tower of Famine, The.
Silverstein. Hungry Mungry.
Smith, Patti. Robert Bresson.
Snodgrass. Cherry Saplings.
Mother, The.
Silver Poplars.
What We Said.
Spender. Nocturne: "Their six-weeks-old daughter."
Perhaps.
Spenser. I saw raynde up on yvorie pillours tall.
Long having deeply gron'd these visions sad.
Stevens. Public Square, The.
Swift. On the Burning of Whitehall in 1698.
Warren. Natural History I.
What Day Is.
Williams, Charles Kenneth. Don't.
Downwards.
Williams, William Carlos. Jean Sans Terre Reviews the Fathers.
Wordsworth. Nunnery.
Rural Architecture.
Sonnet Composed at—Castle.
Steamboats, Viaducts and Railways.
Wyatt. Like as the wind with raging blast.
Will ye see what wonders love hath wrought?
Young. Old Woman.
Watsonville after the Quake.
Zukofsky. *Annals* of Volusius, cock at his offal.

Detectives
Hughes, Langston. Café: 3 A.M.
Nash. Don't Guess, Let Me Tell You.
Plath. Detective, The.
Yau. Genghis Chan: Private Eye I.
Genghis Chan: Private Eye II.
Genghis Chan: Private Eye III.
Genghis Chan: Private Eye IV.
Late Night Movies II.
Sam Spade Haiku.

Determination
Angelou. Still I Rise.
Atwood. Planters, The.
Cohen. I Tried to Leave You.
"Dylan." Open the Door, Homer.
Eberhart. Bath Room, The.
Old Question.
Hardy. In the Seventies.
Hewitt. Spring Restored, The.
Hughes, Ted. Crueller than owl or eagle.
Kunitz. Knot, The.
Lindsay. Mouse That Gnawed the Oak-Tree Down, The.
Lowry. Poem Inspired By Auden and Clare's Snail.
Oliver. Journey, The.
Piercy. For the Young Who Want To.
Rich. Power.
Rolfe. Kentucky.
Sarton. Humpty Dumpty.
Schwartz. Sonnet Suggested by Homer, Chaucer, Shakespeare, Edgar Allan Poe, Paul Valéry, James Joyce, et al.
Sidney. Sonnet 64: "No more, my dear, no more these counsels try."
Silverstein. Little Blue Engine, The.
Melinda Mae.
Stevenson. Ad Se Ipsum.
Stuart. Midget, The.
Once More for My Lady.
Williams, William Carlos. Dedication for a Plot of Ground.
To an Old Jaundiced Woman.
Wyatt. Lo, how I seek and sue to have.
Though some do grudge to see me joy.
What no, Perdy [*or* Perdie *or* perdie][!] ye may be sure[!].

Detroit, Michigan
Levine. Belle Isle, 1949.
Coming Home, *Detroit*, 1968.
Detroit Grease Shop Poem.
Ordinary Morning, An.
Saturday Sweeping.
Snow.
You Can Have It.
O'Hara. Alma.
Young. City Home Detroit.

Developing Countries
Van Duyn. Economics.

Devil. *see* **Satan.**

Devonshire, England
Davie. Devonshire.
Livingshayes.
Sounds of a Devon Village.
Herrick. Discontents in Devon.
To His Household Gods.

Dew
Bishop. What's that shining in the leaves.
Creeley. My Love.
Ford. Dew falls but the, The.
Graves. Song: Dew-Drop and Diamond.
Herrick. To Dewes. A Song.
To Primroses Filled with Morning Dew.
Upon Julia's Haire Fill'd with Dew.
Marvell. On a Drop of Dew.
Ros.

Diabetes
Hacker. Fifteen to Eighteen.
Fourteen.

Diana (mythology)
Catullus. Carmen 34: "Moving in her radiant care."
Cullen. To Endymion.
Gallagher. Instructions to the Double.
Jonson. Queen and huntress, chaste and fair.
Meredith. My Lady has Diana's brows.
Ralegh. Praisd Be Dianas Faire and Harmles Light.
Sidney. Now was our heav'nly vault deprived of the light.
Smart. Queen of the mountains far and near.
Zukofsky. Diana, sum us in faith a.
See also **Artemis.**

Diaries
Bishop. From Trollope's Journal.
Koch. Artist, The.
Larkin. Forget What Did.
Lorde. Martha.
Patchen. Note for a Diary.
Prince. Vivat.
"Reed." Dream, A.
Swift. Verses Wrote in a Lady's Ivory Table-Book.
Walcott. Islands.
Waldman. Diaries.

Dickens, Charles
Browning, Robert. Reflections on Reading a Life of Dickens.

Dickinson, Emily
Berryman. Your Birthday in Wisconsin You Are 140.
Crane. To Emily Dickinson.
Eberhart. Wedding on Cape Rosier, A.
MacLeish. In and Come In.
Nash. Chipmunk, The.
Rich. I Am in Danger—Sir—.
Strangers are an endangered species.
Sandburg. Letters to Dead Imagists.
Public Letter to Emily Dickinson.
Tomlinson. Letters from Amherst.
Wilbur. Altitudes.

Dictionaries
Carruth. RAVAGE, v.t. To lay waste; to subject.
Hardy. Liddell and Scott.
Johnson. Gnothi Seauton (Post Lexicon Anglicanum Auctum et Emendatum).
McGrath. Need for Dictionaries II, The.

Dido
Campion. Ballad, A: "Dido was the Carthage Queene."
Ralegh. I am that Dido which thou here do'st see.

Smith, Stevie. Dido's Farewell to Aeneas.
Wyatt. Dido am I, the founder first of Carthage.

Dieting
Herrick. Diet.
Matthews. On a Diet.
Nash. I Can't Have a Martini, Dear, but You Take One, or, Are You Going to Sit THere Guzzling All Night?
Snodgrass. W. D. Lifts Ten Times the Weight of His Own Body.

Digby, Lady Venetia
Jonson. Epigram to My Muse, the Lady Digby, on Her Husband, Sir Kenelm Digby, An.
Eupheme.

Digging and Diggers
Atwood. Digging.
Bunting. Under sand clay. Dig, wait.
Ciardi. In the Hole.
Gildner. Digging for Indians.
Hall. Digging.
Hewitt. Gathering Praties.
Souterrain, The.
Koertge. To Impress the Girl Next Door.
Sandburg. Muckers.
Stuart. Spell.
Wilbur. Digging for China.
Zimmer. Zimmer at the Diggings.

Dikes
Kipling. Dykes, The.

Dillinger, John
Bukowski. John Dillinger Marches On.

DiMaggio, Joe
Meinke. Byron vs. DiMaggio.

Diners
Atwood. They Eat Out.
Ceravolo. Route.
Eberhart. Hand, The.
Gunn. Cafeteria in Boston.
St. John. Avenues, The.
Simic. Partial Explanation, The.
Williams, Charles Kenneth. Regulars, The.

Dinosaurs
Sandburg. Dinosaur Bones, The.
Silverstein. If I Had A Brontosaurus.
Updike. On the Inclusion of Miniature Dinosaurs in Breakfast Cereal Boxes.

Diocletian
Donne. Confessors, The.

Diogenes
Melville. Apparition, The.
Schwartz. Albert Einstein to Archibald MacLeish.

Dionysus
Carruth. Gods.
Clark. Change.
Crane. Lachrymae Christi.
Doolittle. Choros Translations.
Graves. Ambrosia of Dionysus and Semele, The.
Levertov. Prayer, The.

Diplomacy and Diplomats
Davie. From the New World.
Donne. To Sir Henry Wotton, at His Going Ambassador to Venice.
Emerson. Tact.
Hewitt. Going up to Dublin.
Jonson. To the Right Hon[oura]ble Hierome, L[ord] Weston. An Ode Gratulatory for His Return from His Embassy. 1632.
Marvell. In Legationem Domini Oliveri St John ad Provincias Foederatas [On the Embassy of Lord Oliver St John to the United Provinces].
Letter to Doctor Ingelo, A.
Meredith. While Nature mocks her truth with mimic shows.
Paley. In Hanoi 1969.
Smith, Stevie. Ambassador, The.

Dirigibles
Carruth. Incorrigible Dirigible, The.

Disabilities
Dickinson. Anatomical dishabille.
Fisher. Pete Brown's Old Eggs Still Hatch.

Glück. Cripple in the Subway, The.
Late Snow.
Koertge. Coming Out.
Kunitz. Silence.
Lindsay. Lame Boy and the Fairy, The.
Owen. Disabled.
Imbecile, The.
Rich. Transit.
Rukeyser. Slow Dialogue between Pain and Roosevelt.

Disappointment
Auden. We Too Had Known Golden Hours.
Beatles. For No One.
I Don't Want to Spoil the Party.
Betjeman. Costa Blanca, The.
Bukowski. Trapped.
Burns. Here's a Health to Ane I Lo'e Dear.
I dream'd I lay where flowers were springing.
Carruth. Ideas hit life like / planks hitting water. Some skim.
Incident of May.
Catullus. Carmen 28: "In Piso's suite / are empty pockets."
Carmen 77: "Whom I have trusted to no end (Rufus)."
Carmen 91: "In this hopeless & wasting love of mine."
Clark. Ace of Destiny.
Cohen. Commentary—Death to This Book.
Death to This Book.
Price of This Book, The.
Cooper. After Fever.
Cowper. Hope, like the short-liv'd ray that gleams awhile.
Love Abused.
Creeley. Echo.
Love ("Not enough. The question: what is").
Thinking.
Dickinson. It would never be Common—more—I said.
This is the place they hoped before.
Whoever disenchants.
Dove. Lightnin' Blues.
Dunn. All That We Have.
Mon Semblable.
Photograph in the Hallway, The.
Response to a Letter from France.
"Dylan." Went to See the Gypsy.
Eberhart. Address to you.
Eliot. Cooking Egg, A.
Ginsberg. Long Live the Spiderweb.
Graves. Timeless Meeting.
Griffiths. News of a Marriage.
Hardy. Broken Appointment, A.
Expectation and Experience.
Homecoming, The.
I Said and Sang Her Excellence.
John and Jane.
No Buyers [or No Buyers: A Street Scene].
O I Won't Lead a Homely Life.
Herrick. Invitation, The.
Hewitt. At Shottery, Anne Hathaway's Cottage.
Failed Image.
Mainland, The.
No Cresta Run.
21st September 1912.
Housman. Yonder see the morning blink.
Hugo. Fairfield.
Hawk in Uig.
Maratea Porto: The Dear Postmistress There.
Jeffers. Local Legend.
Self-Criticism in February.
Joseph. Feast, The.
There are more accidents in the home than on the roads.
Levine. Blasting from Heaven.
Liddy. To the Memory of Bernard Berenson.
Lorde. My Fifth Trip to Washington Ended in Northeast Delaware.
Sewerplant Grows In Harlem Or I'm a Stranger Here Myself..
Lowry. Communist, The.
Welcome Home, Oh Our Sweetest Harteebeeste Beloved.
MacLeish. Against Illuminations.
White-Haired Girl.

Meredith. I look'd for my poet—he came not!
Madrigal: "Since Tuck is faithless found, no more."
Once the fair Romance of story.
Reply of the County of Surrey to the Poet's Pathetic Address in Dispraise of Jean.
'Twas yesterday such a black-dye-day.
Was it wise to count the ranks of teeth.
Waves are pressing up with force, The.
We stood in the garden alone.
While Nature mocks her truth with mimic shows.
Nash. Have a Seat behind the Potted Palm, Sir.
Strange Case of Mr. Fortague's Disappointment, The.
Strange Case of Mr. Wood's Frustration, or, A Team that Won't Be Beaten Better Stay off the Field, The.
Try It Suns. and Hols.; It's Closed Then.
Nathan. Letter.
Servant of Stars, The.
Table Talk.
Through the thin hill fog.
Nemerov. Your beauty once the profit of your scorn.
Oppen. People, the People, The.
What ends / Is that.
Ralegh. Farewell to False Love, A.
"Reed." Families.
Sad Song.
Rich. Prospect, The.
Rossetti. Of each sad word which is more sorrowful.
Schuyler. August Night.
Schwartz. Maxims of Sisyphus, The.
"O New York boy, this is Life, Life in which."
"O what a mess of judgment we have made."
Poem: "Faithful to your commands, o consciousness, o."
Shelley. Fragment: "Alas! this is not what I thought life was."
Silverstein. Eighteen Flavors.
Invention.
Snowman.
Smith, Charlotte. Elegy: "Dark gathering clouds involve the threatening skies."
To Mrs. G.
Sorrentino. Research, Again.
They Die Over and Over. In the Movies.
Where are the rose-colored cities.
Stuart. Sexual Disappointments.
Sutter. November Seven, Nineteen Eighty-Four.
Wordsworth. Star-Gazers.
Yarrow Visited [September, 1814].
Wroth. Sonnet 27: "Fie [or Fy] tedious Hope, why do[e] you still rebel[l]?"
Wyatt. Answer that ye made to me, my dear, The [or Th'].
Give place all ye that doth rejoice.
If ever man might him avaunt.
In wilful riches I have found poverty.
Sith it is so that I am thus refused.
Thou hast no faith of him that hath none.
Zukofsky. No idea, Gelli, spurred me to mirror you faithful.
Piso's own comates, his, corps an inane as.
Rufey my how frustrate unquickened and craved the tie I'm equal.

Disarmament. *see* **Militarism; Pacifism and Pacifists.**

Disasters
Beckett. Imagine si ceci.
Berryman. Tampa Stomp.
Carroll, Jim. Fragment, A: "When I see a rabbit."
Dickinson. It was a quiet seeming Day.
"Dylan." Talking Bear Mountain Picnic Massacre Blues.
Eberhart. Three Kids.
Graves. Fallen Tower of Siloam, The.
Herrick. Comfort In Calamity.
Hewitt. Disaster on the Box.
Lyric: "Let this last lyric of a passing day."
To the People of Dresden.

Hoffman. Halflives.
Jeffers. Night Without Sleep.
Kipling. Dove of Dacca, The.
Giffen's Debt.
Larkin. Explosion, The.
Meredith. Phaéthôn.
Plath. Doomsday.
"Reed." Fly into the Sun.
Rolfe. Poem To Delight My Friends Who Laugh at Science-Fiction, A.
Survival Is of the Essence.
Three Who Died.
Rossetti. Repining.
Snodgrass. Flash Flood.
Warren. Brightness of Distance.
Summer Storm (Circa 1916), and God's Grace.
Whitman. Voice from Death, A.
Whittier. Chicago.
Williams, Miller. Survivor, The.

Discipline
Berry. Discipline, A.
Ciardi. Boy.
Cohen. Queen Victoria and Me.
Graves. Two Disciplines.
Herbert. Discipline.
Kipling. That Day.
Lawrence. Discipline.
Schoolmaster [A], The.
Matthews. Foul Shots: A Clinic.
Meredith. To Children.
Merton. When in the Soul of the Serene Disciple.
Rossetti. Seldom "can't," / Seldom "don't."
Stevenson. Good and Bad Children.
In Charidemum.
Williams, Charles Kenneth. Good Mother: Out.

Discontent
Atwood. Summer again; / in the mirrors of this room.
They were all inaccurate.
Beatles. I Should Have Known Better.
Berg. Both.
Day, A.
Betjeman. Meditation on the A30.
Browning, Elizabeth Barrett. Adequacy.
Discontent.
Exaggeration.
Bukowski. I Have Lived in England.
I Write This Upon the Last Drink's Hammer.
Literary Life, The.
Look:, The.
9 Rings.
With Vengeance Like a Tiger Crawls.
Burns. O Ay My Wife She Dang Me.
O That I Had Ne'er Been Married.
Byron. I Would I Were a Careless Child.
Carroll, Jim. Poem: "Tea is boiling, The."
Carruth. Ho-Hum Again.
Catullus. Carmen 23: "Friend Furius, / "who has no slaves & no money.""
Clare. "Poets are born"—and so are whores—the trade is.
Clark. Human Life.
Cohen. Change, The.
Commentary—The Change.
Cooper. High deck. Blue skies overhead. White distance, A.
Cowper. By Philemon.
Creeley. Chicago.
For an Anniversary.
For the New Year.
Gift, The.
Irish.
Roads.
Sick.
Something for Easter.
There Is.
Tunnel, The.
Yellow.
Dobyns. How To Like It.
It's Like This.
Emerson. Discontented Poet: A Masque, The.
O Hafiz! speak not of thy need.
Fletcher. Discontent.
Ford. And the Path of Least.
Ginsberg. Paterson.

Graves. Lovers in Winter.
Gunn. Autumn Chapter in a Novel.
Hardy. Rift, The.
Hartley. This Living in Small Place.
Hemingway. Black-Ass Poem After Talking to Pamela Churchill.
Flat Roofs.
Herrick. Adversity ("Love is maintain'd by wealth; when all is spent").
Discontents in Devon.
Not To Love.
Hewitt. Clink of Rhyme, The.
Domestic Help.
Joseph. This nut withering on the shelf.
Kipling. Four Angels, The.
Koertge. Sunday.
Kooser. Goldfish Floats to the Top of His Life, The.
Widow Lester, The.
Kunitz. Night Letter.
Larkin. Sinking Like Sediment through the Day.
Who Called Love Conquering.
Lawrence. Beware the Unhappy Dead!
Courage.
Elderly Discontented Women.
Lindsay. Song of the Garden-Toad, The.
Springfield Magical.
Voice of the Man Impatient with Visions and Utopias, The.
Lowry. And lights a cigarette, noting, far off.
Morning rain is rained, The.
McGrath. Ah.. to the Villages!
MacNeice. Corner Seat.
Nature Morte.
Splinters under the nails, weals on the buttocks.
To Hedli.
Wolves.
McNeill. Jane Renick MacElmain (1).
Markson. Tardy Poet: 1978.
Youthful Poet's Unspoke Response to a Woman Talking Too Loudly in His Favorite Bookstore, The.
Matthews. Left Hand Canyon.
March Heat.
Melville. Mortmain Reappears.
Meredith. Promise in Disturbance, The.
Millay. Rendezvous.
Neruda. What can it mean to endure.
Notley. But He Says I Misunderstood.
O'Hara. Ode (To Joseph Lesueur) on the Arrow That Flieth by Day.
Pack. Trying to Reconcile.
Plath. Lesbos.
Spinster.
Pope. Mary Gulliver to Capt. Lemuel Gulliver.
Rolfe. And If You Don't See What You Want, Ask for It.
Brickyards at Beacon.
Winds of Another Sphere.
Shakespeare. Sweet rose, fair flower, untimely pluck'd, soon vaded.
Silverstein. Santa and the Reindeer.
Smith, Stevie. Actress, The.
Easy.
Repentance of Lady T, The.
Warden, The.
Snodgrass. Seeing You Have..
Stevenson. Since years ago for evermore.
To My Old Familiars.
Stuart. Commencement.
Thomas. I Have Longed to Move Away.
Tomlinson. Way In, The.
Updike. Academy.
Warren. World Is a Parable, The.
Williams, Charles Kenneth. Fat.
I sit in my room.
Rampage, The.
What Did the Man Do with the Clouds?
Williams, William Carlos. Raleigh Was Right.
Wordsworth. Fragment: A Somersetshire Tragedy.
Song for the Wandering Jew.
Yeats. He Hears the Cry of the Sedge.
Zukofsky. Even if love convey.
Furius, with no key to service, no key.

Discothèques
Ginsberg. Chances "R."

Discovery
Beatles. Got to Get You into My Life.
I Should Have Known Better.
Bly. Finding the Father.
Browning, Robert. Reverie.
Bukowski. Greek, The.
One Night Stand.
Carew. Ingrateful[l] Beauty Threatened.
Cooper. She is like that man.
Creeley. They.
Cummings. Here's s / omething round(& so).
Davie. Bolyai, the Geometer.
Homage to John L. Stephens.
Eberhart. Nostalgia for Edith Sitwell.
Everson. Screed of the Flesh, The.
Ferlinghetti. Plough of Time, The.
Fisher. Near Garmsley Camp.
Ford. Fortune's Wheel. In the.
Fox. Caroline Herschel (1750–1848).
Galileo Galilei (1564–1642).
Nicholas Copernicus (1473–1543).
Gardner. Searchlight, The.
Gunn. Discovery of the Pacific, The.
To Natty Bumppo.
Haines. Guevara.
Hall. Poem, The: "It discovers by night."
Three Movements, The.
Hesketh. Return.
Hewitt. Dissertation I.
No Second Troy.
Tryst.
Hoffman. Folk Tale.
Hughes, Ted. Fourth of July.
Keats. There was a naughty boy.
Kipling. Explorer, The.
Kooser. At the Bus Stop Next to the Funeral Home.
Levertov. Garden Wall, The.
Secret, The.
Lorde. Ballad from Childhood.
MacLeish. Bernál Díaz' Preface to his Book.
Voyage West.
MacNeice. All Over Again.
Truisms, The.
Vistas.
With you, pray not without you, trapped on the edge of the world.
Morgan. Summit, The.
Three Children Looking Over the Edge of the World.
Owen. Music.
Piercy. Erasure.
Raine. Winds.
Rich. In my imagination I was the pivot of a fresh beginning.
Robinson. Discovery.
Rolfe. Undersea Poem.
Rukeyser. West Virginia.
Sandburg. Child Moon.
Leather Leggings.
Schuyler. Bluet, The.
Shapiro. Leg, The.
Sorrentino. Solitary Man Discovered in a Field of Daisies.
Stafford. Watching the Jet Planes Dive.
Warren. History.
Whitman. Thought of Columbus, A.
Yau. Charred hansom is discovered on Bubbling Well Road. In the shade.
Young. No Strings Attached.

Disdain
Bunting. You idiot! What makes you think decay will.
Campion. Fire that must flame is with apt fuell fed.
Catullus. Carmen 17: "Cologna Veneta - / where the good folk."
Carmen 24: "Best sprig of the clan."
Carmen 29: "What man could stomach the sight."
Carmen 69: "Do not wonder when the wench declines."
Carmen 88: "What, Gellius, of the man."
Carmen 97: "As God is my witness where is the difference between."

Carmen 103: "Either give me my hundred pounds back, Silo."
Cohen. Letter.
Creeley. Gift, The.
Memory, The.
Davie. Revulsion.
Donne. To the Countess of Bedford ("Honour is so sublime perfection").
Glück. My Neighbor in the Mirror.
Hemingway. They All Made Peace—What Is Peace?
Hewitt. Aesthete's Renunciation.
At the Newsagent's.
Domimie's Log, A.
Glens, The.
Green Shoot, The.
Lines for a Dead Alderman.
My Grandmother Robinson.
Salute to Matthew Arnold.
Turf-Carrier [or Turf Carrier] on Aranmore.
Joseph. Exile in Devon, An.
Koertge. Man like a Curtain, A.
Liddy. Dinner Menu a Burnt Offering, A.
Orpheus as a Christian Scientist.
Lorde. Suffer the Children.
Lovelace. Sylo pray pay me my ten Sesterces.
To Rufus.
Lowry. Loathing is as beautiful as the scourge.
McGrath. Proletarian in Abstract Light.
Plath. Daddy.
Pope. Epigram: "My Lord complains, that Pope, stark mad with gardens."
Ransom. Misanthrope.
Sidney. Sonnet 104: "Envious wits, what hath been mine offence."
Wilbur. Simplification, A.
Williams, Charles Kenneth. Kin.
Williams, William Carlos. Unfrocked Priest, The.
Wyatt. Behold, love, thy power how she despiseth!
Zukofsky. No it would not mean a damn (quick whim referred to pure.
No lift odd mere horror, harrowed (why boy?) that no woman will.
O Colonia, whose wishes build a long bridge to dance on.
O quick floss silk of the Juventii, form.
Out—so this means you render them, ten sestertia, Silo.
Quid, fact it is Gelli? quick'ning mother, at (queer) sis, all three.
Whose hoax to put up with, outstare, protest patience.

Disease
Beckett. Ooftish.
Carruth. Marge.
New Hartford.
Sonnet: "I want to do a complaint now. Which is to say."
Sonnet: "Why extremely do we observe more of."
Catullus. Carmen 71: "If every anyone / was deservedly plagued by a goat under his armpits."
Cohen. Asthmatic, The.
Commentary—The Asthmatic.
I Wanted to Be a Doctor.
Cummings. Come,gaze with me upon this dome.
Davie. Alzheimer's Disease.
Hypochondriac Logic.
Recollections of George Oppen in a Letter to an English Friend.
Dobyns. Bleeder.
Duncan. In Blood's Domaine.
"Dylan." Legionnaire's Disease.
Eberhart. My mind was heavy and my luck was dark.
Virgin, The.
Emerson. For fifteen winter days.
Written in Sickness.
Glück. Fortress, The.
Hayden. As My Blood Was Drawn.
Herrick. Leprosie in Houses.
Physitians.

Prognostick, A.
Upon Urles.
Hesketh. He Saved Others..
Ward F4.
Kunitz. Children at play in a field.
Lowry. Prelude To Mammon.
Morgan. It takes me aback at times.
Mr. Boyd.
Muldoon. Aisling.
Nash. Bulletin Has Just Come In, A.
Piercy. Crabs.
Ransom. Here Lies a Lady.
Rossetti. Henry Hardiman.
Rukeyser. Bill, The.
Cornfield, The.
Disease: After-Effects, The.
Disease, The.
Sandburg. Cripple.
Schuyler. What Ails My Fern?
Wilbur. Pangloss's Song: A Comic-Opera
Lyric.
Williams, Charles Kenneth. Alzheimer's: The
Husband.
Alzheimer's: The Wife.
Williams, Miller. Thinking about Bill, Dead of
AIDS.
Zukofsky. Securer a bo? no sacred armpits lair
hops as that he-goat's.

Disgrace
Cohen. In the Eyes of Men.
Creeley. Penitent, The.
De la Mare. In Disgrace.
Hewitt. No Second Troy.
Prague, or Novotny, If You Remember Him.
Merton. Faction du Muet.
Prince. White sunlight and the dripping oars!
"Reed." Kids, The.
Rich. Book, The.
Rolfe. Political Prisoner 123456789.
Sidney. Sonnet 21: "Your words my friend
(right healthful caustics) blame."
Snodgrass. Reichsmarschall Hermann Göring
("And why, Herr Reichsmarschall, is Italy").

Dishonesty
Bly. Letter to Her.
Cohen. Everybody Knows.
Dove. Compendium.
"Dylan." Odds and Ends.
Gardner. Abraham and Isaac.
Hardy. To a Sea-Cliff.
Herrick. Upon Eeles.
Hewitt. Belfastman Abroad Argues with
Himself.
Jonson. On Bawds and Usurers.
On Cheveril the Lawyer.
Nemerov. Sonnet: "It seems to be the trouble,
everyone."
Pack. Camp Wakonda, 1940.
Piercy. People ask questions.
Rolfe. Pastoral—1954.
Wordsworth. To the Pennsylvanians.

Dishonor
Brontë. A.A.A.
Hewitt. Jenny Geddes.
Jonson. On Mongrel Esquire.
To Captain Hungry.
Kipling. Hadramauti.
Last of the Light Brigade, The.
Melville. Stonewall Jackson.
Morrison. I Bring These.

Disillusion
Angelou. Accident.
Auden. He Revisits the Spot.
Beatles. For No One.
Bly. Aban Kavost and Ivar Oakeson.
Woman Bewildered, The.
Browning, Robert. Patriot, The [An Old
Story].
Saint Martin's Summer.
Carew. Ingrateful[l] Beauty Threatened.
Catullus. Carmen 72: "There was a time,
Lesbia, when."
Carmen 115: "O'Toole is the proud master
of."
Ceravolo. Caught in the Swamp.
Cohen. Poems Don't Love Us Any More,
The.

Coleridge. On a Discovery Made Too Late.
Creeley. Changes, The.
Hunger.
Roads.
Same.
There.
Cullen. Bright Bindings.
La Belle, La Douce, La Grande.
Dickinson. Loss of something ever felt I, A.
Split the Lark—and you'll find the Music.
Dobyns. Great Doubters of History, The.
"Dylan." Abandoned Love.
Clean-Cut Kid.
Hard Times in New York Town.
Idiot Wind.
In times behind, I too.
John Brown.
Just Like Tom Thumb's Blues.
Like a Rolling Stone.
Love Is Just a Four-Letter Word.
My Back Pages.
Nothing Was Delivered.
Seeing the Real You at Last.
Talking New York.
Tight Connection to My Heart (Has Anybody
Seen My Love).
Ferlinghetti. Poet's eye obscenely seeing, The.
See / it was like this when.
We squat upon the beach of love.
Gallagher. In Maceio.
Ginsberg. My Alba.
Hewitt. Encounter Nineteen Twenty.
New Jerusalem 1.
Holmes. Doctor Trustus: Man of Good Will.
Unwanted 1943 Chappaqua Flashback.
Hugo. Graves.
Joseph. Animal Story, An.
Koch. Thanksgiving.
Levertov. Remembering.
Lewis. Now only beggars still go singing.
This stunted pine whose knotted roots.
Lovelace. That me alone you lov'd, you once
did say.
MacNeice. Refugees.
Mahon. I wake in a dark flat.
Meredith. Aimée.
Am I failing? For no longer can I cast.
But where began the change; and what's my
crime?
It is the young fresh rainy leaf.
Not solely that the Future she destroys.
What are we first? First, animals; and next.
Merton. Whether There Is Enjoyment in
Bitterness.
Morgan. Promise, The.
Nathan. Servant of Stars, The.
Nemerov. Your beauty once the profit of your
scorn.
Oliver. House, The.
Olson. Knowing All Ways, Including the
Transposition of Continents.
Owen. Dulce Et Decorum Est.
Sleeping Beauty, The.
Sonnet Autumnal.
Sonnet, to a Child.
To ———: "Three rompers run together, hand
in hand."
Patchen. Among Ourselves and with All
Nations.
I Care What Happens.
Lament for the Makers of Songs.
Let Us Have Madness Openly.
1935.
So Be It.
Watcher, The.
World Will Little Note, The.
Piercy. Curse of the Earth Magician on a
Metal Land.
Raine. Star, The.
"Reed." My Old Man.
Sad Song.
Rich. Afterward.
Snow Queen, The.
Robinson. Another Dark Lady.
Old Story, The.
Rossetti. Whole Head Is Sick, and the Whole
Heart Faint, The.

Schuyler. Labor Day.
Poem: "How about an oak leaf."
Shelley. Alastor; or, The Spirit of Solitude.
Prince Athanase; a Fragment.
Sidney. Fifth Song.
Virtue, beauty, and speech, did strike, wound,
charm.
Smith, Charlotte. Fairest flowers are gone! for
tempests fell, The.
Hope. A Rondeau.
Swift. Cassinus and Peter.
Tomlinson. Jam Trap, The.
Warren. Be Something Else.
Wilbur. Someone Talking to Himself.
Williams, Charles Kenneth. In the Heart of the
Beast.
Most excruciating / thing, The.
Then the Brother of the Wind.
Williams, William Carlos. Jean Sans Terre
Discovers the West Pole.
Wyatt. Mine [or Myne] own[e] John Poyntz,
since [or sins] ye delight to know.
Yeats. Old Stone Cross, The.
Young. Providence, Rhode Island.
Zukofsky. Decay bars one time, 'solely to
know, see Catullus.'
Meantool inhabits in style three times ten
hewed acres, forty.

Disorder
Atwood. Solstice Poem.
Berry. February 2, 1968.
Carruth. Terra.
Dickinson. I have felt like a troubled Top.
Eberhart. Passage, The.
Ferlinghetti. Rebels, The.
San Jose Symphony Reception.
Fisher. At No Distance.
Half reconciled, half healed: but.
Ford. Candy Darling.
Garden of Disorder, The.
Griffiths. Misrule, Towyn, 1990.
Small Substantial Shadow.
Gunn. Wheel of Fortune, The.
Herrick. Delight in Disorder.
His Change.
Lowry. Welcome Home Oh Our Most
Beloved Harteebeeste.
Meredith. Age of petty tit-for-tat, An.
Triad of British Evils, A.
Merrill. Broken Bowl, The.
Nash. Mules, The.
Stevens. Connoisseur of Chaos.
Young. Son.

Disraeli, Benjamin
Browning, Robert. On Benjamin Disraeli.

Distrust
Beatles. You Can't Do That.
Berg. 1914.
Byron. On Sam Rogers.
Carew. Guiltless Inconstant, The.
To His Jealous Mistress.
Catullus. Carmen 25: "From Thallus the
pederast."
Carmen 30: "Alfenus from Cremona / forsakes
the friendship of friends."
Carmen 36: "Volusian sheets / shit-shotten
Annals."
Creeley. Of Years.
Place, A.
Stomping with Catullus.
Dunn. Man Who Closed Shop, The.
Graves. Love Letter, The.
Herrick. Distrust ("To safeguard man from
wrongs, there nothing must").
Distrust ("What ever men for Loyalty
pretend").
Suspicion Makes Secure.
Hughes, Langston. Madam and Her Might-
Have-Been.
Ransom. Her Eyes.
Rich. Like This Together.
Rolfe. Hunter Went Killing: A Fable, A.
Little Ballad for Americans—1954.
Sorrentino. Spouse, The.
Trouble in Paradise.
Stuart. Urban Hunting Scenes.
Suckling. Guiltless Inconstant, The.

Williams, Charles Kenneth. Mirror, The.
Question, The.
Zukofsky. Alfenus, remember *kind intimacies?*
false? They elated us.
Annals of Volusius, cock at his offal.
Conniving Thallus, mulley, you, cony cully,
cop below.

Diversity
Dunbar. Accountability.
Emerson. Once the priest / Lived in an age.
Hardy. So Various.
Hewitt. Frontier, The.
Glens, The.
In Recollection of Drumcliffe, September
1948.
O Country People.
Hughes, Langston. Mystery.
Kipling. Two Races.
We and They.
MacLeish. Colloquy for the States.
Oppen. In this nation.
Ralegh. I sacrifice to God the Beefe, which
you adore.
Rossetti. To My Fior-Di-Lisa.
Sidney. Like diverse flowers, whose diverse
beauties serve.

Dives (Bible)
Crashaw. Luke 16; Dives *Asking a Drop.*
Kipling. Peace of Dives, The.

Diving and Divers
Atwood. Younger Sister, Going Swimming.
Dunn. Insomnia.
Gunn. Plunge, The.
Hayden. Diver, The.
Housman. Oh fair enough are sky and plain.
Knight. Poem of Attrition, A.
Lewis. *He Gives Her Botticelli's Birth of
Venus as a Wedding Gift.*
Lieberman. Diving Ballet, The.
Spearing, The.
Lowry. Kraken, Eagles, in British Columbia.
Meinke. Elegy for a Diver.
Meredith. In the clear dark lake a lady dived.
Nathan. Diver, The.
Rich. Diving into the Wreck.
Springboard, The.
Tomlinson. San Fruttuoso.

Divining and Diviners
Herrick. Divination by a Daffadill [*or
Daffodil*].
Rukeyser. Divining Water.
Swift. Virtues of Sid Hamet the Magician's
Rod, The.

Divorce
Bly. Woman Bewildered, The.
Bukowski. Drill, The.
Imagination and Reality.
Sundays Kill More Men Than Bombs.
Byron. To Eliza.
Cooper. Holding Out.
Dobyns. Kentucky Derby Day, Belfast, Maine.
Dunbar. Chappie, A.
Ferlinghetti. People Getting Divorced.
Fox. She Used to Water the Plants.
Graves. In the Vestry.
Jong. Divorce.
Kunitz. River Road.
Lieberman. Woman's Tongue.
McAuley. After Yeats, After Ronsard,
*Pace*Hopkins.
Meredith. Thus piteously Love closed what he
begat.
Merrill. Broken Home, The.
Nash. Strange Case of the Dead Divorcee,
The.
Piercy. Laocoön is the Name of the Figure.
Sandburg. Fifty-Fifty.
Sarton. I shall not see the end of this
unweaving.
Sexton. Break Away, The.
Divorce.
February 21st.
Sutter. Driftrose.
Static.
Wife.
Turco. Jason Potter.
Updike. My Children at the Dump.

Waldman. Divorce Work.
Williams, Miller. Divorce.
Williams, William Carlos. Genesis.

Doctors. *see* **Physicians.**

Dodo Birds
Wilbur. Walgh-Vogel, The.

Dogs
Auden. Single creature leads a partial life,
The.
Talking to Dogs.
Bishop. Five Flights Up.
Pink Dog.
Boyle. Hunt.
Lost Dogs of Phnom Penh, The.
Browning, Elizabeth Barrett. Flush or Faunus.
To Flush, My Dog.
Browning, Robert. Tray.
Bukowski. Dog.
Dogs, The.
Monday Beach, Cold Day.
Bunting. Passport Officer, The.
Burns. On a Dog of Lord Eglinton's.
On the Death of Echo, a Lap-Dog.
Twa Dogs, The.
'Twas in that place o' Scotland's isle.
Byron. Inscription on the Monument of a
Newfoundland Dog.
Carroll, Jim. Dog Crunch.
"Carroll, Lewis." Lang Coortin', The.
Mouse's Tale, The: "We lived beneath the
mat."
Carruth. Reversions, always.
Underground the Darkness Is the Light.
Ciardi. Between.
Knowing Bitches.
Suburban.
Cowper. Beau's Reply.
Dog and the Water-Lily, The.
Epitaph on Fop.
On a Spaniel Called Beau Killing a Young
Bird.
Crane. Great Western Plains, The.
Creeley. For Allen.
Lion and the Dog, The.
Messengers, The.
Walking the Dog.
Dickey, James. Madness.
Dickey, William. Dog Under False Pretences.
Dunn. Something Like Happiness.
Eberhart. Key West.
Eliot. Lines to a Yorkshire Terrier.
Emerson. I have an arrow that can find its
mark.
Ferlinghetti. Dog.
Ford. Black dog in a, A.
Fox. Dog Days.
Frost. Canis Major.
On Our Sympathy with the Under Dog.
One More Brevity.
Span of Life, The.
Gallagher. Story of a Citizen, The.
Galvin. Dog Love.
Gildner. Geisha.
Gunn. Her Pet.
Vigil of Corpus Christi, The.
Yoko.
Hall. Kill, The.
Hardy. Ah, Are You Digging on My Grave?
Dead "Wessex" the Dog to the Household.
Mongrel, The.
Popular Personage at Home, A.
Why She Moved House.
Hartley. Bulldog on the Roof—Avenue C.
Pot-Luck among the Casuals.
Hesketh. Gone Away.
Hoffman. In the Days of Rin-Tin-Tin.
Hughes, Langston. Warning: Augmented.
Jeffers. House Dog's Grave, The.
Johnson. Translation of Du Bellay's *Epigram
on a Dog.*
Jong. Best Friends.
If God is a Dog.
Jubilate Canis.
Joseph. Going to Sylvie's.
Kinnell. Supper after the Last, The.
Kipling. Dinah in Heaven.
For our white and our excellent nights—for

the nights of swift running.
Four-Feet.
His Apologies.
Power of the Dog, The.
Pussy can sit by the fire and sing.
Supplication of the Black Aberdeen.
This is the mouth-filling song of the race that
was run by a Boomer.
Knight. Crown Hill Cemetary, Indianapolis.
Kooser. First Snow.
Kunitz. Rover.
Lawrence. As Thyself!
Bibbles.
Lords of Life Are the Masters of Death, The.
Song of the Grey Dog, The.
Levertov. Shlup, shlup, the dog.
Levine. Dog Poem.
"MacDiarmid." And a poetry in which as in a
film.
MacNeice. Dogs in the Park.
McNeill. How to Unbewitch a Backtracking
Hound.
Matthews. Dog Life.
Homer's Seeing-Eye Dog.
Loyal.
Meredith. As I turn'd into the market-place.
Over the Hills.
To Children.
Merrill. Victor Dog, The.
Merton. Dog barks far out, A.
Miller. Dead Dog (For Goo).
Morrison. Ensenada.
Muldoon. Bran.
Nash. Dog's Best Friend Is His Illiteracy, A.
For a Good Dog.
Love Me but Leave My Dog Alone.
Please Pass the Biscuit.
Two Dogs Have I.
Neruda. Dead Dog.
Oliver. Her Grave.
Olson. She Who Hits at Will.
Paley. Old Dog's Song, The.
Stranger calling a dog whistled, A.
Patchen. He Is an.
Pope. Argus.
Prince. His Dog and Pilgrim.
Rossetti. Hop-o'-my-thumb and little Jack
Horner.
Pussy has a whiskered face, / Kitty has such
pretty ways.
Sandburg. Dan.
Dogheads.
Sarton. Lament for Toby, a French Poodle.
Village Tale, A.
Schuyler. Oriane.
Sexton. Your Face on the Dog's Neck.
Sidney. Sonnet 59: "Dear, why make you
more of a dog than me?"
Silverstein. Double-Tail Dog.
Simic. Variant, The.
Smith, Patti. Amazing Tale of Skunkdog, The.
Smith, Stevie. Après la Politique, la Haine des
Bourbons.
Death of the Dog Belvoir.
Goodnight.
Hound of Ulster, The.
Jumbo.
O Happy Dogs of England.
O Pug!
To the Dog Belvoir.
Wild Dog, The.
Swift. Bounce to Fop.
On the Collar of Mrs. Dingley's Lap-Dog.
Updike. Dog's Death.
Van Duyn. Ballad of Blossom, The.
Footnotes to "The Autobiography of Bertrand
Russell."
Goodbye, A.
We alwus had to herd cattle.
Who says the world is mud? For the fifth day.
Wilbur. Pardon, The.
Williams, Charles Kenneth. Dog, The.
Williams, William Carlos. April is the Saddest
Month.
Banner Bearer, The.
Complexity, The.
In the 'Sconset Bus.

Savage Beast, The.
  To a Dog Injured in the Street.
Wordsworth. Dog—An Idyllium, The.
  Fidelity.
  Incident Characteristic of a Favourite Dog.
  Tribute to the Memory of the Same Dog.
Wright, James. Dog in a Cornfield.
  On the Skeleton of a Hound.
Zimmer. Dogs of Zimmer, The.
Zukofsky. "Immediate Aim, The."
See also **Puppies; Listings for specific Dogs.**

Dollhouses
Liddy. His Refugees.

Dolls
Atwood. Five Poems for Dolls.
"Carroll, Lewis." Matilda Jane.
Cummings. Dominic has / a doll wired.
Fox. In the factory where dolls are made.
Gunn. Dolly.
Levertov. Partial Resemblance.
MacNeice. Christina.
Miller. For Those Who Pray for the Souls of
  Broken Dolls.
Rossetti. All the bells were ringing / And all
  the birds were singing.
  I have a Poll parrot, / And Poll is my doll.
St. John. Dolls.
  Hush.
Sexton. Falling Dolls, The.
Yau. I learn to count without pointing at my
  fingers. This is Pinocchio.
Yeats. Dolls, The.

Dolphins
Bishop. Riverman, The.
Fletcher. Steamers.
Gunn. Aquarium, The.
Lawrence. They Say the Sea Is Loveless.
Lowell. Dolphin.
Nash. Porpoise, The.

Dominican Republic
Dove. Parsley.

Don Juan
Byron. Don Juan.
Lawrence. Don Juan.
Nemerov. Don Juan to the Statue.

Don Quixote
Melville. Rusty Man, The.
Wilbur. Parable.

Donegal. *see* **County Donegal, Ireland.**

Donkeys
"Carroll, Lewis." Lays of Sorrow, No. 2.
Coleridge. To a Young Ass.
Hall. At Delphi.
Hewitt. Turf-Carrier [*or* Turf Carrier] on
  Aranmore.
Kipling. Legends of Evil, The.
Meredith. Ass of Balaam, The.
Nash. Wild Jackass, The.
Roethke. Donkey, The.
Smith, Stevie. Donkey, The.
Wilbur. Prayer to Go to Paradise with the
  Donkeys, A.

Donne, John
Carew. Can we not force from widowed
  poetry.
Coleridge. On Donne's Poetry.
Hartley. John Donne in His Shroud.
Jonson. To John Donne ("Donne, the delight
  of Phoebus, and each Muse").
  To John Donne ("Who shall doubt, Donne,
  where I a poet be").
Lowry. Donne He's Regular.
Rukeyser. Homage to Literature.

Dons
Eberhart. To Auden on His Fiftieth.
See also **Teaching and Teachers.**

Doors
Auden. Out of it steps our future, through this
  door.
"Carroll, Lewis." As It Fell upon a Day.
Carruth. It was our city too. Chrome and
  glass.
Cooper. Door, The.
Creeley. Box, The.
  Chicago.

Door, The ("It is hard").
Door, The ("Thump, Thump.").
  Return.
Cummings. There are 6 doors.
Dunn. Room and the World, The.
Eberhart. Perception as a Guided Missile.
Emerson. Tell men what they knew before.
  Unbar the door, since thou the Opener art.
Frost. Lockless Door, The.
Graves. Door, The.
Haines. Down the turning stairway.
Hardy. She Opened the Door.
Herrick. No Lock against Lechery.
Kipling. Open Door, The.
Lawrence. Doors.
Piercy. Doors in the Wind and the Water.
Sandburg. Circle of Doors.
  Doors.
Tomlinson. Door, The.
  Small Action Poem.
Turco. Door, The.
Whitman. Portals.

Dorset, England
Davie. Dorset.
Hardy. Domicilium.
  Once at Swanage.
  Overlooking the River Stour.
  Roman Road, The.

Dostoyevsky, Feodor
Ginsberg. Fyodor.
Lawrence. Reading in the Evening.
Patchen. Dostoyevsky.

Doubt
Ammons. Lost and Found.
Arnold. Dover Beach.
Auden. Tale, A.
Beatles. Don't Pass Me By.
Berg. Day, A.
  Through Glass.
Berryman. Nones.
  Rackman and victim twist: sounds all these
  weeks.
  Vespers.
Brooks. Love Note I: Surely.
Browning, Elizabeth Barrett. Sonnet: "And
  wilt thou have me fashion into speech."
  Sonnet: "Beloved, my beloved, when I think."
Bukowski. Fuck.
Burns. Primrose, The.
Clark. Greeks, The.
  Love (after La Rochefoucauld).
Cowper. Vicissitudes Experienced in the
  Christian Life, The.
Creeley. Happy Man, The.
  Mechanic, The.
  They (2).
  Token, A.
Dickinson. Split the Lark—and you'll find the
  Music.
  Sweet Skepticism of the Heart.
  Those—dying then.
Dunn. Guardian Angel, The.
  Hard Work 1956.
"Dylan." Is Your Love in Vain?
  Standing on the Highway.
Emerson. We sauntered amidst miracles.
Ford. Comedy of Belief.
Gallagher. Into the Known.
  On Your Own.
  Time Lapse with Tulips.
Hacker. Last Time, The.
Herrick. Seek[e] and Find[e].
Hesketh. What Is God?
Hewitt. B.O.W.
  Carol Singers.
  Fool's Cap, The.
  For Busha.
  Substance and Shadow.
  To such a gap as this our love has come.
  Who Was C.B. Fry?
Kipling. As the Bell Clinks.
Knott. Lesson.
Lawrence. Can't Be Borne.
Lewis. *Vigil: He Lies Awake in the Barracks
  Room, Fearful She Will Not Come, The.*
Lowell. Tenth Muse.

Lowry. Fear ringed by doubt is my eternal
  moon.
MacNeice. Oh but my doubt is a sea harsher
  than this that I see.
Merrill. Carpet Not Bought, A.
Nathan. Feeding the Ducks.
O'Hara. Ode: "Idea of justice may be
  precious, An."
  To the Harbormaster.
Oppen. West.
Ransom. Somewhere Is Such a Kingdom.
Rexroth. August 22, 1939.
Rossetti. After Communion.
  Until the Day Break.
Sandburg. Impossible Iambics.
  Maybe.
Schuyler. Daylight.
Silverstein. Magical Eraser.
Smart. Honesty.
  St. Thomas.
Smith, Stevie. Why Do You Rage?
Sorrentino. Mathematics, The.
  Spouse, The.
Stevens. Blue Buildings in the Summer Air,
  The.
  Landscape with Boat.
Stuart. Mystic.
Tennyson. Supposed Confessions of a Second-
  rate Sensitive Mind.
Wilbur. Agent, The.
  Dubious Night, A.
Williams, Charles Kenneth. Mirror, The.
  Politics.
  Question, The.
Williams, Miller. He Speaks to His Arguing
  Friends and to Himself.
Zukofsky. Do not leave me.
  Tam Cari Capitis.
See also **Agnosticism and Agnostics.**

Douglass, Frederick
Dunbar. Douglass.
  Frederick Douglass.
Hayden. Frederick Douglass.

Dover, England
Arnold. Dover Beach.
Auden. Dover.
Dickey, James. Dover: Believing in Kings.
Ferlinghetti. Sea Is Calm Tonight, The.
Rukeyser. Jetty. Dover, The.
Wordsworth. At Dover.

Doves
Browning, Elizabeth Barrett. My Doves.
Campion. What Harvest Half So Sweet Is.
Cohen. Anthem: "Birds they sang, The."
  Dove, The.
Davie. Woodpigeons at Raheny.
De la Mare. Dove, The.
Dickinson. Once more, my now bewildered
  Dove.
Dunbar. Dove, The.
Eberhart. Child, The.
Gallagher. Zero.
Hughes, Ted. Bang—a burning, A.
  Dove Came, The.
Keats. Song: "I had a dove and the sweet
  dove died."
Kipling. Dove of Dacca, The.
Lowry. Communal Message.
  Still speeding to your heart.
MacLeish. Wood Dove at Sandy Spring, The.
Millay. Song: "Beautiful Dove, come back to
  us in April."
Nash. Strange Case of the Blackmailing Dove,
  The.
Paley. In Aix.
Rossetti. As the dove which found no rest /
  For the sole of her foot, flew back.
  As the Doves to Their Windows.
  Look on This Picture and on This.
  Thy fainting spouse, yet still Thy spouse.
Sidney. Like as the dove which seeled-up doth
  fly.
Smith, Stevie. Old Sweet Dove of Wiveton,
  The.
Southwell. Presentation, The.
Stevens. Dove in the Belly, The.
  Song of Fixed Accord.

Stevenson. If I had wings, my lady, like a dove.
Wordsworth. Near Anio's stream, I spied a gentle Dove.
Poet and the Caged Turtledove, The.
To ———: " 'Wait, prithee, wait!' this answer Lesbia threw."
Young. Sentience.
Zukofsky. Wire.
See also **Turtle Doves.**

Down's Syndrome. *see* **Mental Retardation.**

Dowries
Burns. My Tocher's the Jewel.
Herrick. Mr. Hericke his Daughter's Dowrye.

Dragonflies
Auden. Dragon-fly, The.
Bogan. Dragonfly, The.
Kunitz. Dragonfly, The.
Millay. Dragonfly, The.
Nemerov. Dragonfly, The.
Olson. Dragon-Fly, The.

Dragons
Auden. Evolution of the Dragon, The.
"Carroll, Lewis." Jabberwocky.
Ford. Prevalence of the.
Hall. Some Oddities.
Meredith. Forest History.
You must love the light so well.
Merton. Landscape: Beast.
Submerged Dragon.
Moore. O to Be a Dragon.
Plumet Basilisk, The.
Nash. Dragons Are Too Seldom.
Tale of Custard the Dragon, The.
Patchen. Where Two O'clock Came From.
Rukeyser. Slow Death of the Dragon.
Sarton. Binding the Dragon.
Smith, Stevie. Fafnir and the Knights.
Spenser. Hideous dragon, dreadfull to behold, A.
Warren. Dragon Country: To Jacob Boehme.
Yau. Dragon's Blood III.

Drake, Sir Francis
Campion. De Fran. Draco.
Incipit Thomas Campianus Medicinae Doctor.
In Peragrantissimi, Itinerosissimi,
Montiscandentissimique Peditis, Thomae
Coryati, viginti-hebdomadarium *Diarium, sex*
pedibus gradiens, partim vero claudicans,
Encomiasticon.
Davie. Devonshire.
Kipling. Frankie's Trade.
With Drake in the Tropics.
Merton. Drake in the Southern Sea.

Drawing
Bukowski. Bring Down the Beams.
Clark. I draw a head. You ask.
Clough. Upon the water in the boat.
Cowper. To Romney.
Graves. Wild Cyclamen.
Haines. Eye in the Rock, The.
Hall. Illustration.
Hardy. Why Did I Sketch.
Hugo. History of the Sketch, A.
Levine. On a Drawing by Flavio.
Merrill. Doodler, The.
Vision of the Garden, A.
Milton. On the Engraver of His Likeness.
Nemerov. Drawing Lessons.
Pack. Cave of Lascaux, The.
Rukeyser. Crayon House.
Simic. Drawing the Triangle.
Smith, Charlotte. Reflections on Some Drawings of Plants.
To Dr. Parry of Bath, with Some Botanic Drawings Which Had Been Made Some Years.
Turco. School Drawing.
Waldman. Pictures From Tofukuji.
Young. Drawing.

Drayton, Michael
Jonson. Vision of Ben Jonson, on the Muses of His Friend M. Drayton, The.

Dreams and Dreaming
Angelou. To a Freedom Fighter.
Ashbery. Hop o' My Thumb.
Landscape (After Baudelaire).

Atwood. Dream 1: the Bush Garden.
Dream 3: Night Bear Which Frightened Cattle.
Dreams of the Animals.
Flying Inside Your Own Body.
Nightshade on the Way to School.
Surely in your language.
Variation on the Word *Sleep.*
Auden. Dream, A.
Humpty Dumpty.
Lesson, The.
Misunderstanding, A.
Beckett. Rêve / sans fin.
Serena II.
Berg. Answer, The.
Fragment, 1959.
In the Evening.
One.
Roses.
Berrigan. Banging around in a cigarette she isn't "in love."
Crystal.
My dream a drink with Lonnie Johnson we discuss the code.
Berry. Dream, The.
In the early morning dark.
Meeting, A.
This comes after silence. Was it something I said.
Berryman. Desire Is a World by Night.
I dreamt he drove me back to the asylum.
Search, The.
Bishop. Sleeping Standing Up.
Summer's Dream, A.
Blake. Dream, A.
Land of Dreams, The.
Bly. Cornpicker Poem.
Dream of a Brother, A.
Dream of Retarded Children, A.
Dream of What Is Missing, A.
Dream on the Night of First Snow, A.
Four Ways of Knowledge.
Orchard Keeper, The.
Bogan. Come, Sleep.
Dream, The.
Meeting, The.
Boyle. Dreams Dreamed.
Brontë. Day Dream, A.
High waving heather, 'neath stormy blasts bending.
How Clear She Shines!
Night of storms has passed, The.
Brooks. Kitchenette Building.
Browning, Elizabeth Barrett. Isobel's Child.
Memory and Hope.
Romaunt of Margret, The.
Sonnet: "I lived with visions for my company."
Browning, Robert. Bad Dreams I.
Bad Dreams II.
Bad Dreams III.
Bad Dreams IV.
Statue and the Bust, The.
Women and Roses.
Bukowski. Nice Try.
On the Continent.
Burns. I dream'd I lay where flowers were springing.
Byron. Away, Away, Ye Notes of Woe!
Darkness.
Dream, The.
To ———: "But once I dared to lift my eyes."
To M.S.G. ("When I dream that you love me, you'll surely forgive").
Carroll, Jim. Dresden to Chesapeake Bay.
Fear of Dreaming.
Next Door.
Wing and Claw.
"Carroll, Lewis." Acrostic: A boat, beneath a sunny sky.
Acrostic: Dreams, that elude the Waker's frenzied grasp—.
Acrostic: Love-lighted eyes, that will not start.
Dreaming of apples on a wall.
Dreamland.
Lays of Mystery, Imagination, and Humour,

No. 1: The Palace of Humbug.
Love among the Roses.
Carruth. Always this special / secret feeling, the failure.
Dornröschen, princess.
Fifth Version, The.
Sleeping Beauty, The.
'Tis a fine deceit.
Chaucer. Book of the Duchesse, The.
House of Fame, The.
Clark. Baby Book Fate Dream.
"Before Dawn.."
Mist Sleeve Flight.
Sleepwalker.
Clough. I dreamed a dream: I dreamt that I espied.
Cohen. Beside My Son.
Dream, The.
Morning Song.
When I Left the King.
Coleridge. Kubla Khan; or, A Vision in a Dream.
Lines in the Manner of Spenser.
Something Childish, but Very Natural.
Two Founts, The.
Wish for Dreamful Sleep, A.
Cooper. All These Dreams.
And here is that part of my dream I would like to forget.
El Sueño de la Razón.
Cowper. Morning Dream, The.
Crabbe. World of Dreams, The.
Crane. Echoes.
Creeley. Death of Venus, The.
Dream, The ("A lake").
Dream, The ("Such perfection").
Dreams.
For No Clear Reason.
Saints, The.
Sleep.
That day / in an oak tree—.
Three Ladies, The.
Woman, The.
Cullen. For a Poet.
Hunger.
Cummings. And what were · roses. Perfume?for i do.
An(fragrance)Of / (Begins) / millions.
Be unto love as rain is unto colour;create.
Blue the triangular why.
Dive for dreams / or a slogan may topple you.
Doll's boy's asleep / under a stile.
Fair ladies tall lovers / riding are through the.
Fea / therr / ain / :dreamin.
First of All My Dreams, The.
Here pasture ends— / this girl and boy.
If a cheerfulest Elephantangelchild should sit.
If being mortised with a dream.
If the Lovestar grows most big.
I'll tell you a dream i had once i was away up in the sky Blue,everything.
It is at moments after i have dreamed.
Leastlessly / out / of this.
Listen / beloved / i dreamed.
Long ago,between a dream and a dream.
My darling since / you and.
My eyes are fond of the east side.
My sweet old etcetera.
Now i lay(with everywhere around).
Out of the mountain of his soul comes.
Perfectly a year,we watched Together les enfants jumping and.
Perished have safe small.
Poets yeggs and thirsties.
Precisely as unbig a why as i'm.
Sonnet entitled how to run the world).
Sonnet: "I dreamed I was among the conquerors."
Supposing i dreamed this).
Thethe / the pink / Tartskids with.
Tw / oo / ld / o / nce upo / n.
2 little whos / (he and she).
What a proud dreamhorse pulling(smoothloomingly)through.
When you are silent,shining host by guest.
White guardians of the universe of sleep.

Why why / How many winds make wonderful.
  You are tired, / (I think).
Davie. David Dancing.
  Dream Forest.
  Hermes and Mr Shaw.
De la Mare. Anatomy.
  Assignation, The.
  Dark Château, The.
  Death-Dream, The.
  Dream, A.
  Dreamer, The ("O Thou who").
  Dreamer, The ("Woods were still").
  Dreams ("Be gentle").
  Dreams ("Ev'n one").
  Epitaph, An: "Last, Stone, a little yet."
  Flotsam.
  Glimpse, The.
  Massacre, The.
  Miss Loo.
  Nocturne: "'Tis not my voice now speaks; but
    as a bird."
  Remembrance.
  Reverie.
  Shade, The.
  Stranger, The.
  Three Strangers, The.
  Unfinished Dream, The.
  Universe, The.
  Unregarding.
  Voices.
  Where Is Thy Victory?
Dickey, James. Birthday Dream, The.
Dickey, William. Avalanche.
Dickinson. Dreams—are well—but Waking's
  better.
  I dream about father every night.
  I have a King, who does not speak.
  In Winter in my Room.
  Night's capacity varies.
  We dream—it is good we are dreaming.
  Within that little Hive.
Donne. Dream[e], The.
Doolittle. At Baia.
  Dream.
Dove. Oriental Ballerina, The.
  This Life.
  Upon Meeting Don L. Lee, in a Dream.
Dunbar. Dream Song I.
  Dream Song II.
  Dreamer, The.
  Dreamin' Town.
  Dreams.
  Ere Sleep Comes Down to Soothe the Weary
    Eyes.
  He Had His Dream.
  If.
  Lost Dream, A.
  Over the Hills.
  Pool, The.
  Why Fades a Dream?
Duncan. Dreamers, The.
  Festivals, The.
  Often I Am Permitted to Return to a Meadow.
  Sentinels, The.
Dunn. In a Dream of Horses.
"Dylan." Bob Dylan's 115th Dream.
  I Dreamed I Saw St. Augstine.
  Talkin' World War III Blues.
Eberhart. Book of Nature, The.
  Caravan of Silence.
  Dream, A.
  Dream Journey of the Head and Heart.
  Dream, The.
  In after Time.
  Love Poem, A: "I am the lightness that I
    know."
  Only in the Dream.
  Passage, The.
  Verbalist of Summer, The.
  When Doris Danced.
Eliot. Wind Sprang Up at Four o'Clock, The.
Emerson. Ah! not to me these dreams belong.
  Memory.
  Terminus ("For thought & not praise").
Everson. Black Hills, The.
  Danse Macabre.

Narrows of Birth, The.
Sixty Five.
Ferlinghetti. Late Impressionist Dream.
  Painter's Dream, The.
  Sueño Real.
Fisher. Don't Ask.
  Masterpieces in my sleep. A suppressed.
  Report on August.
Fletcher. Court Lady Standing under Cherry
  Tree.
  Life.
  Spattering of the rain upon pale terraces, The.
Ford. Dreaming of walking.
  In a dream you had.
  Real dreams. More real than.
  Sandman, I'd tear you limb from limb.
  This dream of burnt ivory.
  What am I dreaming of?
Fox. Dog Days.
  Megrez.
  Phekda.
Gallagher. As If It Happened.
  Candle, Lamp & Firefly.
  Disappearances in the Guarded Sector.
  Meeting, The.
  Tableau Vivant.
Galvin. Old Trip by Dream Train, The.
Gardner. Nightmare.
  Telephone, The.
Garrigue. Enemy of Those Who Are Enemies
  of Sleep.
Gildner. Shy Roofer, The.
Ginsberg. Dream, A.
  Drowse Murmurs.
  Meaningless Institution, A.
  Understand That This Is a Dream.
  Vision 1948.
Glück. Dream of Mourning, The.
  12. 6. 71.
Graves. Arrears of Moonlight.
  Dawn Bombardment.
  Dream of Frances Speedwell, A.
  Dream Recalled on Waking.
  Friday Night.
  Garden, The.
  Hag-Ridden.
  In Procession.
  In Trance At A Distance.
  Promised Ballad, The.
  Secret Land, The.
  Song: Dream Warning.
  Song: Once More.
  Theseus and Ariadne.
  Through Nightmare.
  To Sleep.
  What Did I Dream?
  Window Sill, The.
Griffiths. Continuity.
Gunn. Barren Leaves.
  Bath House, The.
  Down panic, down. The castle is still here.
  Dream sponsors: / Charles Manson, tongue.
  I spin like a solitary star, I swoon.
  Small Town in Kansas.
  Waking Dream, A.
  Wheel of Fortune, The.
  Without a Counterpart.
Haines. Red Trees in the Wind.
  Skagway.
  South Wind.
Hall. Milkers Broken Up.
  New Animals.
  Six Naps in One Day.
  Town of Hill, The.
  White Apples.
  Woolworth's.
Hardy. Bereft, She Thinks She Dreams.
  Dream-Follower, The.
  Dream Is—Which? The.
  Dream or No, A.
  In the Marquee.
  In the Small Hours.
  Last Journey, A.
  Self-Unseeing, The.
  Shadow on the Stone, The.
Hayden. Bone-Flower Elegy.
Herrick. Dreame, The.

Dream[e]s.
  His Dream[e].
  Upon Love ("In a Dreame, Love bad me go").
  Vine, The.
  Vision, The ("Methought I saw").
  Vision, The ("Sitting alone").
  Vision to Electra, The.
Hesketh. Horses, The.
  July 2nd, 1916.
  Master Cotton Spinner.
  Waiting.
Hewitt. From the Chinese of Wang Li Shi.
  Interval.
  My Father's Ghost.
  Reference, The.
  Roseblade's Visitants and Mine.
Hill. What other men do with other women.
Hoffman. Dreamer, The.
  Possession.
Hughes, Langston. Beale Street.
  Dream.
  Dream Variation[s].
  Havana Dreams.
  Morning After.
  Water-Front Streets.
Hugo. Anacortes-Sydney Run, The.
  In Your Bad Dream.
  In Your Big Dream.
  In Your Dream after Falling in Love.
  In Your Dream on the Eve of Success.
  In Your Fugitive Dream.
  In Your Good Dream.
  In Your Hot Dream.
  In Your Racing Dream.
  In Your War Dream.
  In Your Wild Dream.
  In Your Young Dream.
  Poem for Zen Hofman.
  With Kathy in Wisdom.
Jarrell. Afterwards.
  Dead Wingman, The.
  Dream of Waking, The.
  Dream, The.
  Dreams.
  Girl Dreams That She Is Giselle, The.
  Girl in a Library, A.
  House in the Wood, The.
  Lost Love, The.
  Night before the Night before Christmas, The.
Jong. Without Parachutes.
Jonson. Dream[e], The.
  Give end unto thy pastimes, Love.
Joseph. Inland Sea, The.
  Reported Missing.
  Waking.
Keats. Dream, A.
  Dream, after Reading Dante's Episode of
    Paolo and Francesca, A.
  Nebuchadnezzar's Dream.
  To J. H. Reynolds, Esq.
Kipling. Divided Destinies.
  Fairies' Siege, The.
Larkin. Morning Has Spread Again.
  Traumerai.
  Why Did I Dream of You Last Night?
Lawrence. Ah life, God, Law, whatever name
  you have.
  Dissolute.
  Dream-Confused.
  Dreams Old and Nascent.
  Dreams Old and Nascent: Nascent.
  Dreams Old and Nascent: Old.
  Martyr à la Mode.
  Thief in the Night.
  To Toss the Troubled Night Long.
Levertov. Runes, The.
Levine. Ask the Roses.
Lewis. Fever.
  His mind is an inarticulated question.
  She Comes To Him in the Night.
  Vigil: She Tarries, Far-Off, in a Strange
    Anguish, The.
Lieberman. Increasing Night.
Lindsay. Alone in the Wind, on the Prairie.
  Last Song of Lucifer, The.
Lorde. Barren.
  Dreams Bite.

Rites of Passage.
Song: "Wild trees have bought me."
Sowing.
St. Louis Out of Time.
Lovelace. Triumphs of Philamore and Amoret, The.
Lowell. Couple, The.
Harriet's Dream.
Lowry. Alas, there is no still path in my soul.
Days Like Smitten Cymbals of Brass, The.
El Leon Sends His Greetings.
Joseph Cconrad.
Peter Gaunt and the Canals.
Villaknell.
Young Man From Oaxaca, The.
McAuley. I dream a flag snaps in a cold wind.
McGrath. Dream Range, The.
In Dream Time.
In the Sleep of Reason.
MacLeish. Lines for a Prologue.
Night Dream, The.
Two Women Talking.
MacNeice. Bad Dream.
Dreams in Middle Age.
Good Dream.
McNeill. Dream, The.
Mahon. Dawn Chorus, The.
Markson. Borrowed Line.
Matthews. Interpretation of Dreams, The.
Waking at Dusk from a Nap.
Meredith. Phantasy.
Merrill. Dream (Escape from the Sculpture Museum) and Waking.
Dreams About Clothes.
Mad Scene, The.
Olive Grove.
Merton. Dream at Arles on the Night of the Mistral, A.
Great Prayer.
Restoration of the Pictures, The.
Secret, The.
You did not come to Rome to dream.
Millay. Dream of Saba.
Dream, The.
Miller. Ensamhet.
Milton. Sonnet 23: "Mee thought I saw my late espoused saint."
Morgan. Demonstration, The.
From the Terrace.
Lucky black man in my dream.
One sweltering Sunday afternoon in August.
Voice spoke in the night, A.
Morrison. Still Wet From.
Nash. Cat Naps Are Too Good for Cats.
I Can Hardly Wait for the Sandman.
I Saw Euterpe Kissing Santa Claus.
It Figures.
My Dream.
Nathan. Conversation Piece.
Morning Song.
Scroll, The.
Nemerov. Dream, A.
Frozen City, The.
Mythological Beast.
Poet as Eagle Scout, The.
Rent in the Screen, The.
Returning to Europe.
Sleeping Beauty.
Winter Exercise.
O'Hara. Fantasy.
Sleeping on the Wing.
Oliver. Dreams.
Rage.
Olson. As though there were no flowing.
Conversation Galante.
Her Dream, Half Remembered.
Translation, A.
Oppen. Alpine.
Owen. Soldier's Dream.
Strange Meeting.
To the Bitter Sweet-heart: a Dream.
Paley. Oh the dreamer said.
One Day.
Patchen. Irkalla's White Caves.
Plath. Dream, The.
Dream with Clam-Diggers.

Ghost's Leavetaking, The.
Sleepers, The.
Terminal.
Waking in Winter.
Poe. Dream, A.
Dream-Land [or Dreamland].
Dream within a Dream, A.
Dreams.
Fairyland [or Fairy-Land].
Oh! that my young life were a lasting dream!
To ———: "Bowers whereat, in dreams, I see, The."
Prince. Autumn Journey.
Raine. Behind the lids of sleep.
Dream.
Dream-flowers.
Dream of Roses, A.
Dreams.
Elementals, The.
Hieros Gamos.
Last night I seemed in your embrace.
Still skies, still seas.
Ransom. Prelude to an Evening.
"Reed." Day John Kennedy Died, The.
Dream, A.
Rexroth. Between Myself and Death.
Fish Peddler and Cobbler.
Rich. I wake up in your bed. I know I have been dreaming.
Incipience.
Jerusalem.
Lag, The.
Night Watch.
Robinson. Altar, The.
Miniver Cheevy.
Roethke. Dream, The.
Memory.
Rolfe. Song: "Keep the dream alive and growing always."
Undersea Poem.
Rossetti. All night I dream you love me well.
Ballad of Boding, A.
Coast-Nightmare, A.
Echo.
Fata Morgana.
For One Sake.
Hopeless Case, A.
I dream of you to wake: would that I might.
I dreamt I caught a little owl.
Mirage.
My Dream.
On the Wing.
Reflection.
Sound Sleep.
Tasso and Leonora.
Two Parted.
What?
Yet A Little While.
Rukeyser. Cannibal Bratuscha.
Child in the Great Wood.
Clues.
Dream-Drumming.
His Dream of Flood: And Eden.
In a Dark House.
Much later, I lie in a white seaport night.
Nevertheless the Moon.
Phaneron.
Recovering.
Seventh Elegy. Dream-Singing Elegy.
Three Black Women.
Water Night.
Whatever roams the air is traveling.
Sandburg. Among the Red Guns.
Between Two Hills.
Bringers.
Buffalo Bill.
Carlovingian Dreams.
Chicago seems all fox and swine.
Consolation Sonata.
Dream Girl.
Dreaming Fool.
Dreams in the Dusk.
Dusty Doors.
Fire-Logs.
Gone.
Mamie.
Mildred Klinghofer whirled through youth in

bloom.
Monkey of Stars.
Moonlight and Maggots.
Murmurings in a Field Hospital.
Pick-Offs.
Portrait of a Motorcar.
Prayers of Steel.
Rain Winds Blow Doors Open.
Sixteen Months.
Smoke and Steel.
Tangibles.
Waiting.
Was Ever a Dream a Drum?
Sarton. Nursery Rhyme.
These Were Her Nightly Journeys.
Where Dream Begins.
Schuyler. Dreams.
Sleep.
Tom's Dream.
Velvet Roses.
Schwartz. Poem: "Remember midsummer: the fragrance of box, of white roses."
To a Fugitive.
Sexton. Author of the Jesus Papers Speaks, The.
45 Mercy Street.
Old.
Stand-Ins, The.
Three Green Windows.
Where It Was at Back Then.
Shakespeare. Sonnet 27: "Weary with toil, I haste me to my bed."
Sonnet 42: "When most I wink, then do mine eyes best see."
Shapiro. Love for a Hand.
Shelley. Marianne's Dream.
Sidney. Now was our heav'nly vault deprived of the light.
Sonnet 32: "Morpheus, the lively son of deadly sleep."
Sonnet 38: "This night, while sleep begins with heavy wings."
Simic. Empire of Dreams.
Smith, Charlotte. To Sleep.
When welcome slumber sets my spirit free.
Where the wild woods and pathless forests frown.
Smith, Patti. Grant.
Munich.
Smith, Stevie. Avondall.
Be Off!
Death's Ostracism.
Dream.
Dream of Nourishment, A.
I Had a Dream.
In My Dreams.
My Hat.
Songe d'Athalie.
Voice from the Tomb (2).
Snyder. For a Stone Girl at Sanchi.
Sorrentino. Blackburn's Dream.
Canta Naranja.
Everybody would soon change.
Spender. Dream, The.
Dusk.
Spenser. At length, even at the time when Morpheus.
Stafford. Vocation.
Stevens. Cuban Doctor, The.
Disillusionment of Ten O'Clock.
Sketch of the Ultimate Politician.
Stevenson. Escape at Bedtime.
I dreamed of forest alleys fair.
Land of Nod, The.
North-West Passage.
To what shall I compare her.
Young Night Thought.
Stuart. Casting.
Dressing.
Exeutive Discovers Poetry, The.
Sleepwalker.
Suckling. His Dream.
Sutter. Trying to Dream Up an Answer.
Swift. On Dreams.
Thomas. I Fellowed Sleep.
Our Eunuch Dreams.
When Once the Twilight Locks No Longer.

Tomlinson. Dream, A.
Dream, The.
Epilogue, The: "It was a dream delivered the epilogue."
Scream, The.
Variation on Paz.
Turco. Dream, The.
Recurring Dream, The.
Updike. Caligula's Dream.
Dream and Reality.
Dream Objects.
Visions of Mackenzie King, The.
Van Duyn. Nap.
Wakoski. Dream, The.
Waldman. Helping the Dreamer.
Matriarchly.
Warren. I Am Dreaming of a White Christmas: The Natural History of a Vision.
Lullaby: Smile in Sleep.
Whitman. Old War-Dreams.
Ship Ahoy!
Whittier. Dream of Pio Nono, The.
My Dream.
Mystery, A.
Pageant, The.
Sabbath Scene, A.
Wilbur. Antiworlds.
Folk Tune.
In Limbo.
In the Smoking-Car.
Merlin Enthralled.
Walking to Sleep.
Williams, Charles Kenneth. Covenant, The.
Crime, The.
Gap, The.
History.
Knot, The.
Last, The.
Long Bells, The.
Room.
Shadows.
Shells.
To Listen.
Williams, Miller. Man Who Stays Up Late, The.
Williams, William Carlos. In Dream's Wake.
Libertad! Igualdad! Fraternidad!
Revelation, The.
Thursday.
Two Pendants: For the Ears.
Wordsworth. Expostulation and Reply.
Fragments from the Alfoxden Note-Book (II).
I Heard (Alas! 'Twas Only in a Dream).
Pilgrim's Dream; or, The Star and the Glow-Worm, The.
Wright, Charles. Mantova.
Wright, James. American Twilights, 1957.
But Only Mine.
Dream of Burial, A.
Dreaming.
I slouch in bed.
Moral Poem Freely Accepted from Sappho, A.
Poem about Breasts, A.
To a Defeated Savior.
To a Fugitive.
Wyatt. They fle[e] from me that sometime [or sometyme] did me se[e]k[e].
Yau. Dragon's Blood I.
Dream Report.
Suite of Imitations Written After Reading Translations of Poems by Li He And Li Shang-yin, A.
Two Kinds of Song.
Yeats. Dream of Death, A.
He Wishes for the Cloths of Heaven.
Her Dream.
His Dream.
Host of the Air, The.
Lover Tells of the Rose in His Heart, The.
Poet to His Beloved, A.
Presences.
Towards Break of Day.
Under the Moon.
Under the Round Tower.
White Birds, The.
Withering of the Boughs, The.
Young. Curative Powers of Silence, The.

Dream Take: 22.
Dreamjot: 1962.
Falling Asleep in a Darkening Room.
It Is God that Moves in Your Heart.
Joy/Spring.
2 takes from *Love in Los Angeles*.
Zimmer. Great House, The.
Sonnet: Zimmer Imagines Himself Being Poet-in-Residence.
Thurman Dreaming in Right Field.
Zimmer's Love Poem After A Hard Dream.
Zukofsky. Not it was no dream of coming death.

Dress. *see* **Clothing.**

Driftwood
Hesketh. Waiting.
Notley. True Account of Talking to Judy Holiday, October 13, A.
Wilbur. Driftwood.

Drinking Water
Bishop. Under the Window: Ouro Prêto.
Silverstein. Lazy Jane.

Drinks and Drinking
Atwood. After the agony in the guest / bedroom, you lying by the.
Beckett. Bois seul.
Berryman. Audacities and fetes of the drunken weeks!
I lift—lift you five States away your glass.
Sigh as it ends . I keep an eye on your.
Bishop. Table, The.
Browning, Elizabeth Barrett. Wine of Cyprus.
Bukowski. ..American Express, Athens, Greece.
I Am Visited by an Editor and a Poet.
I Am with the Roots of Flowers.
Nice Place, A.
Practice.
Soirée.
Somebody Always Breaking My Dainty Solitude.
Suicide.
Thank God for Alleys.
3:30 A.M. Conversation.
Bunting. Light of my eyes, there *is* something to be said.
Burns. Epistle to J. R******, Enclosing Some Poems.
Epitaph on John Dove [Innkeeper, Mauchline].
Friend Commissar, since we're met and are happy.
Grace after Dinner.
Gudeen to You Kimmer.
Here's, a bottle and an honest friend.
Hey Tuti Tatey.
Inscription on a Goblet.
Lady Onlie.
My bottle is a holy pool.
My Love She's But a Lassie Yet.
On Gabriel Richardson.
Scotch Drink.
Song: "No Churchman am I for to rail and to write."
Tam o' Shanter [A Tale].
Then Guidwife Count the Lawin.
Theniel Menzies' Bony Mary.
There was twa wives, and twa witty wives.
To Clarinda.
To Mr. John Kennedy.
To Mr. S. McKenzie.
To William Stewart.
Weary Pund o' Tow, The.
Whistle. A Ballad, The.
Willie Brew'd [or Brewed] a Peck o' Maut.
Byron. Fill the Goblet.
Hock and Soda Water.
Lines Inscribed upon a Cup Formed from a Skull.
Campion. Epigramme: "Tosts as snakes or as the mortall Henbane."
"Carroll, Lewis." Stolen Waters.
Carruth. Notes from Robin Hill Cottage.
Ciardi. Two Saints.
Coleridge. Drinking versus Thinking.
Ode in the Manner of Anacreon, An.
Crane. Wine Menagerie, The.
Davie. Dancing Measures.

Dickey, William. G.F. Died 1954, Aged 27.
Dickinson. I would distil a cup.
We—Bee and I—live by the quaffing.
Dunbar. At the Tavern.
Preference, A.
Stirrup Cup, The.
Eberhart. Ship Burning and a Comet All in One Day, A.
Emerson. Drink till the turbans are all unbound.
Spare thou neither time nor blood for thy friend.
Who dedicates himself to the glass.
Ford. And music is still a mystery!
Frost. In a Glass of Cider.
Garrigue. Song for "Buvez les Vins du Postillion"—Advt.
Graves. Ouzo Unclouded.
Gunn. Another All-Night Party.
Donahue's Sister.
Sparrow.
Hall. Cider 5[dc] A Glass.
Hardy. Great Things.
Hartnett. Poet as Black Sheep, The.
Poet Down, The.
Heaney. Sloe Gin.
Hemingway. I'm off'n wild wimmen.
Little drops of grain alcohol.
Some day when you are picked up.
Herbert. Drink not the third glass, which thou canst not tame.
Herrick. Anacrontik Verse.
Bacchanalian Verse, A.
Coblers Catch, The.
Frolic[k], A.
Hymn[e] to Bacchus, A.
Hymne, to the Lares, A.
To Live Merrily, and To Trust to Good Verses.
Upon Spunge.
Wassaile, The.
Welcome to Sack, The.
Hesketh. Meths Men, The.
Hewitt. No Second Troy.
Hoffman. Old Reprobate.
Housman. Terence, This Is Stupid Stuff.
Hughes, Langston. Flatted Fifths.
Neighbor.
Hughes, Ted. Apple Tragedy.
Hugo. Cantina Iannini.
Dixon.
Hilltop, The.
Letter to Sister Madeline from Iowa City.
Only Bar in Dixon, The.
Keats. Hence Burgundy, Claret, and Port.
Kipling. Jacket, The.
When the Journey Was Intended to the City.
Larkin. Livings.
Lawrence. Cups.
Drunk.
Song to the Tune of *La Cucaracha*.
Liddy. All the journeys / To be made for instance, over the seas.
Bright Crown of Freedom, The.
Lady Fitzwilliam.
To the Memory of Sylvia Plath: A Personal Note.
Vir II.
Lovelace. Sonnet. To Generall Goring.
Vintage to the Dungeon, The.
Lowry. Alternative.
Cantinas, The.
Closed Pub, The.
Eye-Opener.
Fisherman's Return.
Got a date with a bottle of / gin.
Jokes Aloft.
My hate is as a wind that buffets me.
Names of Mexican rivers I forgot, The.
No prayer for the people.
No Time to Stop and Think.
Old Blake was warm, he got down to the hub.
Pijijiapan.
Prayer, A.
Prelude to Another Drink.
Prelude To Mammon.
Promises made drunk should be kept drunk.

Sunrise.
We Sit Unhackled Drunk and Mad to Edit.
What Sigbj[do]orn Said.
McAuley. Mnemosyne: The Empty Room.
"MacDiarmid." Old Wife in High Spirits.
MacLeish. Well, he was drunk. That much
  was clear.
MacNeice. Alcohol.
Brandy Glass, The.
Toast, A.
Yours Next.
Mahon. Terminal Bar, The.
Markson. At the Lion's Head.
Lowry.
To a Mexican Poet Who Has Forsaken Drink.
Meinke. Hero Worship at Key West on the
  4th of July.
Uncle Joe.
Writing the Great American Poem in Key
  West.
Meredith. Her trousers are red; she wears a
  coatee.
Yes, we'll pic-nic in the woods.
Merrill. Ouzo for Robin.
Morrison. Bibulous Compound Of.
Very Brave.
Nash. Club Car, The.
Drink with Something in It, A.
It Must Be the Milk.
Nevertheless.
Reflections on Ice-breaking.
Sic Semper Mr. Sherman's Temper, or Kindly
  Place Your Order in English.
Nemerov. Day on the Big Branch, A.
Fourth of July, The.
Moonshine.
Notley. Bus Stop.
O'Hara. Anxiety.
Joe's Jacket.
Mozart Chemisier.
Patchen. Great-Sledmakers, The.
"Reed." Last Shot, The.
Power of Positive Drinking, The.
Underneath the Bottle.
Robinson. Miniver Cheevy.
Mr. Flood's Party.
Roethke. Gob Music.
Song for the Squeeze-Box.
St. John. Gin.
Silverstein. Minnow Minnie.
Sorrentino. Jaime Valerosa y Borracho
  Consults His Journal.
Stevenson. At morning on the garden seat.
Aye mon, it's true; I'm no' that weel.
Blast—1875, The.
Counterblast—1886, The.
Good old ale, mild or pale.
Heather Ale: A Galloway Legend.
Sit doon by me, my canty freend.
To Charles Baxter.
Wind blew shrill and smart, The.
Stuart. Song for Champagne Saturday.
Suckling. Come, let the State stay.
Hall, a hall, A.
Some drink! what, boy, some drink!
That box, fair mistress, which thou gavest to
  me.
Swift. Poetical Epistle to Dr. Sheridan, A.
Van Duyn. Fall.
Warren. One Drunk Allegory.
Wilbur. Voice from under the Table, A.
Williams, Charles Kenneth. Friends.
Williams, Miller. Friend, The.
Glass Darkly, A.
Toast to Floyd Collins, A.
Williams, William Carlos. Drink.
Lines on Receiving *The Dial's* Award: 1927.
World Narrowed to a Point, The.
Yeats. Drinking Song, A.
Zimmer. Curse of the Frogs, The.

See also **Alcoholism and Alcoholics; Drunkards.**

Driving and Drivers
Berg. Driving Out Again at Night.
In It.
Iowa.
Betjeman. Meditation on the A30.

Bly. Driving toward the Lac Qui Parle River.
Three Kinds of Pleasures.
Creeley. "Follow the Drinking Gourd.."
I Know a Man.
Mobile Homes.
Cummings. She being Brand.
Dobyns. General Matthei Drives Home
  through Santiago.
Dove. Nigger Song: An Odyssey.
Dunn. Coming Home, Garden State Parkway.
Smiles.
Toward the Verrazano.
Woman on Edgehill Road, The.
Ginsberg. Bayonne Turnpike to Tuscarora.
Hall. My Friend Felix.
Heaney. Night Drive.
Peninsula, The.
Hewitt. Distances, The.
Double-Ended Tram, The.
Kipling. Beginner, The.
Carmen Circulare.
Four Points, The.
Fox-Hunting.
Justice's Tale, The.
To a Lady, Peruading Her to a Car.
When the Journey Was Intended to the City.
Kooser. Drive in the Country, A.
Liddy. Cantico Per Lo Tuo Amore V.
Lieberman. Bulwark.
MacNeice. Wiper, The.
Meinke. Cloud, Florida, 1985, The.
Miller. For Mike and Kim.
Muldoon. Good Friday, 1971. Driving
  Westward.
Olson. De Los Cantares.
Rich. Over the hills in Shutesbury, Leverett.
Sexton. Road Back, The.
Spender. Driving through Snow.
Stuart. Goshen Pass: Winter.
Tomlinson. Arch, The.
Arroyo Hondo.
Carscape.
Drive.
Night Ride.
Van Duyn. Vision Test, The.
Wakoski. Driving Gloves.
Williams, William Carlos. Right of Way, The.
Young. Palm Drive Palo Alto.
Zukofsky. Jaunt.

See also **Automobiles.**

Drought
Everson. Rattlesnake August.
Frost. Broken Drought, The.
Hewitt. For a Moment of Darkness over the
  Nations.
Lewis. Indian Day.
Mahratta Ghats, The.
Observation Post: Forward Area.
McAuley. Dust-Devils.
MacLeish. Bearing the long lance, their
  banners before them.
Williams, Charles Kenneth. Drought.
Williams, William Carlos. Words Lying Idle,
  The.

Drowning
Atwood. Death of a Young Son by Drowning.
This Is a Photograph of Me.
Carroll, Jim. Window in Cherry Valley, A.
Cowper. Castaway, The.
Dickinson. Drowning is not so pitiful.
Dobyns. Song of the Drowned Boy.
Donne. Hero and Leander.
Doolittle. Loss.
Fox. If He Had Not Had Two Hands Tattooed
  on His Chest.
Lemons, Limes.
Glück. Drowned Children, The.
Graves. Miller's Man, The.
Gunn. Behind the Mirror.
Lerici.
Hartley. Fishermen's Last Supper.
Two Drowned at the Gateway.
Heaney. Limbo.
Herrick. Deluge, The.
Faire Shewes Deceive.
Leanders Obsequies.
Hesketh. Boy Drowning.

Hill. White Ship, The.
Hopkins. Wreck of the Deutschland, The.
Hugo. Lady in Kicking Horse Reservoir, The.
Jeffers. Beach, The.
Liddy. Afterword.
Lowell. Margaret Fuller Drowned.
Mother Marie Therese.
Lowry. Alas, there is no still path in my soul.
Injured Choriant or Paeonic.
Salmon Drowns Eagle.
S.O.S Sinking fast by both bow and stern.
Thought While Drowning (Acapulco).
MacNeice. Death of an Old Lady.
Olson. Pacific Lament.
Pack. Drowning.
Secrets.
Paley. Drowning (I).
Drowning (II).
Plath. Epitaph in Three Parts.
Ralegh. Bura and Helice on Achaian ground.
Robinson. Inscription by the Sea, An.
Rolfe. Death by Water.
Rossetti. Love and Death.
Rukeyser. Drowning Young Man, The.
Exile of Music.
Schuyler. Grave, A.
Sexton. Imitations of Drowning.
Silverstein. Skinny.
Smith, Charlotte. To Vesper.
Smith, Stevie. Boat, The.
Not Waving but Drowning.
Thomson. On the Report that a Wooden
  Bridge.
Updike. Pop Smash, Out of Echo Chamber.
Wilbur. Marginalia.
Wright, James. All the Beautiful are
  Blameless.
In Response to a Rumor that the Oldest
  Whorehouse in Wheeling, West Virginia, Has
  Been Condemned.
Note Left in Jimmy Leonard's Shack, A.
River Down Home, The.
To a Defeated Savior.
To the Muse.

Drowsiness
Clark. Nodding.
Dunbar. Drowsy Day, A.
Rossetti. Lotus-Eaters: Ulysses to Penelope,
  The.
Thomson. Incomparable Soporific Doctor, The.
Young. American Glamour.

Drug Addiction
Angelou. Junkie Monkey Reel.
Letter to an Aspiring Junkie.
Beatles. Everybody's Got Something to Hide
  Except Me and My Monkey.
Bukowski. Girls.
Junkies.
Carroll, Jim. Paregoric Babies.
Withdrawal Letter.
Gunn. Street Song.
Jarrell. Say Good-bye to Big Daddy.
Knight. Another Poem for Me (after
  Recovering from an O.D.).
Idea of Ancestry, The.
Welcome Back, Mr. Knight: Love of My Life.
Lorde. To My Daughter the Junkie on a Train.
Mahon. De Quincey in Later Life.
"Reed." Waves of Fear.
Schuyler. Mike.
Sexton. Addict, The.
Shelton. Certain Choices.
Smith, Stevie. Drugs Made Pauline Vague.
Young. Ho.

Drugs
Angelou. Pusher, The.
Beatles. Day in the Life, A.
Doctor Robert.
Everybody's Got Something to Hide Except
  Me and My Monkey.
Fixing a Hole.
Happiness Is a Warm Gun.
Helter Skelter.
I Am the Walrus.
Berrigan. Dear Margie, hello. It is 5:15 a.m.
Berryman. Drugs Alcohol Little Sister.
Bukowski. Big John of Echo Park.

Girls.
Old Gang, The.
Overhead Mirrors.
Carroll, Jim. Back Home.
Blue Pill, The.
For Elizabeth.
Maybe I'm Amazed.
New Year 1970.
Cohen. Café, The.
Commentary—The Café.
Stranger Song, The.
Creeley. Jack's Blues.
Xmas Poem: Bolinas.
"Dylan." Mr. Tambourine Man.
Subterranean Homesick Blues.
Fenton. Psychopharmacological drugs.
Ginsberg. Aether.
Auto Poesy: On the Lam from Bloomington.
Laughing Gas.
Mescaline.
Methedrine Vision in Hollywood, A.
News Bulletin.
Pertussin.
Griffiths. Shamanism, Dalston.
Gunn. Another All-Night Party.
In Time of Plague.
Painkillers.
Victim, The.
Liddy. Vir V.
Lorde. For My Singing Sister.
MacNeice. Messiah, The.
Muldoon. Gathering Mushrooms.
Nemerov. Frozen City, The.
"Reed." Chelsea Girls.
Heroin.
How Do You Think It Feels.
I'm Waiting for the Man.
Kill Your Sons.
Slide, The.
Walk on the Wild Side.
St. John. Meridian.
Thomson. Incomparable Soporific Doctor, The.
Waldman. How the Sestina (Yawn) Works.
Whittier. Brewing of Soma, The.
Young. Demerol.
Hallucinogenic Halleluuuu.
Lovesong of O. O. Gabugah.
Moss.

Druids
Carew. First Song, The.
Galvin. Carrowkeel.
Graves. Druid Love.
Hewitt. Saint Patrick.
Hugo. Druid Stones at Kensaleyre.
Wordsworth. Trepidation of the Druids.
Yeats. Fergus and the Druid.

Drums
Bogan. Drum, The.
Graves. Death by Drums.
Hardy. Drummer Hodge.
Hughes, Langston. Danse Africaine.
Knight. Ilu, the Talking Drum.
MacLeish. Music and Drum.
Merton. When night falls / beat one drum / in honor of night.
Olson. Drum World, The.
For My Friend.
La Chute.
Rukeyser. Dream-Drumming.
Sandburg. Was Ever a Dream a Drum?
Stevenson. Prelude: "By sunny market-place and street."
Whole day thro', in contempt and pity, The.
Whitman. Beat! Beat! Drums!

Drunkards
Betjeman. Public House Drunk.
Bukowski. As Crazy As I Ever Was.
Dear Friend.
Farewell, Foolish Objects.
4:30 A.M.
I have a saying, "You will find the lowest of the breed at there."
Night They Took Whitey, The.
Not All That Bad.
On and Off the Road.
Overhead Mirrors.
Shit Time.

Some Picnic.
Star, The.
Training for Kid Aztec.
Twins.
Bunting. O everlastingly self-deluded!
Burns. Gudeen to You Kimmer.
Johnie Blunt.
O ken ye what Meg o' the mill has gotten.
Song: "No Churchman am I for to rail and to write."
Then Guidwife Count the Lawin.
Byron. Epitaph on John Adams, of Southwell.
Ciardi. Joshua on Eighth Avenue.
Cummings. Glazed mind layed in a, A).
Gr, a / eyhaire / d(m).
He as o, A / ld as who stag.
In Healey's Palace I was sitting.
Softly from its still lair in Plympton Street.
The / nimble / heat / had.
Davie. Nones.
De la Mare. Drugged.
Dickinson. Ditch is dear to the Drunken man, The.
Drunkard cannot meet a Cork, A.
Dunbar. Delinquent, The.
Lager Beer.
Emerson. Ghaselle.
I will be drunk and down with wine.
Secretly to love & to drink, what is it? tis a dissolute day's work.
To whom a glass full of red wine.
Fenton. Skip, The.
Gardner. Jig for Harmonica.
Graves. Point of No Return.
Gunn. Outside the Diner.
Herrick. Upon Blisse.
Upon Buggins.
Upon Huncks: Epigram.
Upon One-Ey'd Broomsted.
Upon Parrat.
Vision, The.
Housman. Could man be drunk for ever.
Hugo. Late Summer, Drummond.
Neighbor.
Phoning from Sweathouse Creek.
To Die in Milltown.
Villager.
Jeffers. Drunken Charlie.
Jonson. On Captain Hazard the Cheater.
Kipling. Cells.
Giffen's Debt.
Private Ortheris's Song.
Shut-Eye Sentry, The.
Kunitz. There was a big blond uncle-bear.
Levine. Sweet Will.
Liddy. Orpheus as a Christian Scientist.
Lindsay. Drunkard's Funeral, The.
Drunkards in the Street, The.
Lovelace. Cup of Drunkard, A.
Lowry. Cantinas, The.
Danish Sailor's Song.
Don't, Have One for the Road.
Drunkards, The.
I met a man who had got drunk with Christ.
Playing drunk / Drunk and bored.
Poem: "When drunk he crawled home on his knees."
Prayer, A.
Promises made drunk should be kept drunk.
R. Usher.
When I was young I broke all drinking records.
Young Fellow Named Crane, A.
Young Man From Oaxaca, The.
MacNeice. Drunkard, The.
Meinke. Elegy for a Diver.
Miller. For My Friend John Lying on the Bed with Morning Heaves.
Milton. As Lords.
Oliver. Alex.
Oppen. Night Scene.
"Reed." Underneath the Bottle.
Robinson. Miniver Cheevy.
Mr. Flood's Party.
Roethke. Surly One, The.
Sandburg. Jack London and O. Henry.
Schuyler. Ajaccio Violets.

Sexton. Cigarettes and Whiskey and Wild, Wild Women.
Shelton. After Thirty Years.
Stevenson. Cruel Mistress, The.
In Charidemum.
Sutter. Night Out.
Tomlinson. Terminal Tramps.
Van Duyn. Fall.
Warren. Folly on Royal Street before the Raw Face of God.
Wilbur. Voice from under the Table, A.
Williams, Charles Kenneth. Toil.
Williams, William Carlos. Drinking Together.
Drunkard, The.
Late Spring.
Wright, James. Christmas Greeting, A.
I Am a Sioux Brave, He Said in Minneapolis.
I slouch in bed.
Inscription for the Tank.
Larry.
Note Left in Jimmy Leonard's Shack, A.
To a Dead Drunk.
Yeats. Drunken Man's Praise of Sobriety, A.
Hour before Dawn, The.
Zimmer. Barney Hung Over.
Death of the Hired Zimmer.
Gus Sees Wanda Drinking.
Lester Tells of the End of the Summer.
Zimmer Drunk and Alone, Dreaming of Old Football Games.

See also **Alcoholism and Alcoholics.**

Dryads
Doolittle. Acon.

Dryden, John
Byron. Verses Found in a Summer-House at Hales-Owen.
Lowry. Schoolboy's Complaint, The.
Pope. Epitaph Intended for Mr. Rowe, in Westminster Abbey.

Du Bois, William Edward Burghardt
Walker. "Women of Color" Have Rarely Had the Opportunity to Write about Their Love Affairs.

Dublin, Ireland
Davie. North Dublin.
Samuel Beckett's Dublin.
Heaney. Viking Dublin: Trial Pieces.
Hewitt. Bangor, Spring 1916.
Going up to Dublin.
His Majesty's Inspectors.
Nineteen Sixteen, or the Terrible Beauty.
Paper Banners.
Larkin. Dublinesque.
Liddy. June 16, 1992.
Patrick Kavanagh's Dublin.
Vir V.
MacNeice. Dublin.
Mahon. Dawn at Saint Patrick's.
Updike. Literary Dublin.

Duchamp, Marcel
Fisher. Duchamp and Man Ray.
Ford. Flag of Ecstasy.

Ducks
Campion. De Fran. Draco.
"Carroll, Lewis." Little Man That Had a Little Gun, The.
Carruth. Ducks, waking at sea.
Ceravolo. Grass.
Coleridge. Parliamentary Oscillators.
Dunbar. Capture, The.
Eliot. Lines to a Duck in a Park.
Galvin. Seals in the Inner Harbor.
Hughes, Ted. Wild Duck, The.
Joseph. Here Lies Treasure: Here Be Monsters.
Lowry. Duck Train—Vocal Arctic Fox-Trot.
El Leon Sends His Greetings.
Goldeneye and Goldfish.
I am very small.
Morning Address of Love to the Beloved Harteebeeste.
3 Happy Little Ducks.
Welcome Home Oh Our Beloved Harteebeeste.
Welcome Home Oh Sweetest Harteebeeste with Quadruple Devotion from All the Little Animals.

Wild-duck swam in the gold-fish pond, The.
With a Great Goodmorning Kiss and Luck and Love to Our Beloved Harteeste from All the Little Animals.
With Devotion Entire from All Your Little Animals We Thought Fit to Revive the Following Ditty.
Nash. Duck, The.
Nathan. Feeding the Ducks.
Pack. Clayfeld's Duck.
Patchen. Trueblue Gentleman, A.
Ransom. What Ducks Require.
Rossetti. When the cows come home the milk is coming.
Stevens. Sonatina to Hans Christian.
Wild Ducks, People and Distances.
Wordsworth. Wild Duck's Nest, The.

Dudevant, Baronne. *see* **"Sand, George"** (Amandine Aurore Lucie Dupin, Baronne Dudevant).

Duels
Browning, Robert. After.
Before.
Count Gismond.
Byron. Duel, The.
Hardy. Duel, The.
Lovelace. Toad and Spyder, The.

Dullness
Ashbery. Old heavens, you used to tweak above us.
Bukowski. Good Loser, The.
Unkind Poem, An.
Burns. Dulness, with redoubted sway.
Symon Gray.
Hall. No Color Man.
Lawrence. No! Mr Lawrence!
Worm Turns, The.
Piercy. Trying to enter each other.
Pound. Les Millwin.

Dumbness
"Carroll, Lewis." Matilda Jane.
Crashaw. Mark 7; The Dumbe Healed, and the People Enjoyned Silence.
Hill. Song Contest.

Dumps
Nemerov. Town Dump, The.
Rich. Open-Air Museum.
Stevens. Man on the Dump, The.
Tomlinson. From the Motorway.
Updike. My Children at the Dump.

Dunbar, Paul Laurence
Cullen. For Paul Laurence Dunbar.
Hayden. Paul Laurence Dunbar.

Duncan, Robert
Zukofsky. Her face the Book of—Love Delights in—Praises.

Dunes
Frost. Sand Dunes.
Piercy. Road Behind the Last Dune, The.
St. John. Until the Sea Is Dead.
Sandburg. Dunes.

Dunkirk, France
Lewis. After Dunkirk.
Swift. Peace and Dunkirk.

Duns Scotus
Hopkins. Duns Scotus's Oxford.
Merton. Duns Scotus.
Hymn for the Feast of Duns Scotus.

Dürer, Albrecht
Haines. Dürer's Vision.
Middle Ages, The.
Jarrell. Knight, Death, and the Devil, The.
Moore. Steeple-Jack, The.

Dusk. *see* **Twilight.**

Dust
Burns. Dusty Miller.
Eberhart. Imagining How It Would Be to Be Dead.
Frost. Peck of Gold, A.
Gunn. Elegy on the Dust.
Words for Some Ash.
Hesketh. Meths Men, The.
Kooser. Carrie.
Notley. Margaret & Dusty.
Oppen. Approached the window as if to see.

Rich. He Remembereth That We Are Dust.
Rukeyser. George Robinson: Blues.
Sandburg. Dust.
Mummy.
Warren. Forever O'Clock.

Dutch, The
Robinson. Rembrandt to Rembrandt.
Stevens. Dutch Graves in Bucks County.

Dutch Wars
Kipling. Dutch in the Medway, The.
Marvell. Character of Holland, The.
Last Instructions to a Painter, The.
Loyal Scot, The.

Duty
Brontë. M. Douglas to E.R. Gleneden.
Clough. Do duty feeling nought and truth believe.
Duty—that's to say, complying.
Cowper. Hope.
Love of God the End of Life, The.
De la Mare. How Sleep the Brave.
Donne. From needing danger, to be[e] good.
Eberhart. Burden.
Images of death arise.
Emerson. Duty.
Voluntaries.
Frost. Stopping by Woods on a Snowy Evening.
Graves. Her Brief Withdrawal.
Lion-Gentle.
Pride of Love.
Herrick. Duty to Tyrants.
Hewitt. Nicolai, Courier in Belgrade.
Scattering, The.
Volunteer, The.
Jeffers. Historical Choice.
Thurso's Landing.
Kipling. Eddi's Service.
Glory of the Garden, The.
King's Job, The.
King's Task, The.
Pro-Consuls, The.
Reformers, The.
Song in Storm, A.
McNeill. Son, The.
Melville. In the Turret.
Merton. Mysterious Song in the Spring of the Year, A.
Nash. Kind of an Ode to Duty.
Prince. Words from Edmund Burke.
Ralegh. Sir Walter Ralegh to the Queen.
Ransom. Bad News.
Roethke. Last Words.
Rolfe. Not Hatred.
Sentry.
What Does the Novice Soldier Think.
Words Found on a Cave's Wall.
Rossetti. Praise of Love.
Sandburg. And They Obey.
Without the daily chores of the people.
Shakespeare. Sonnet 26: "Lord of my love, to whom in vassalage."
Smith, Stevie. Duty Was His Lodestar.
I Could Let Tom Go—But What about the Children.
Queen and the Young Princess, The.
True Tyrant or the Spirit of Duty Rebuked, The.
Stevenson. Say not of me that weakly I declined.
Tennyson. Charge of the Light Brigade, The.
Whittier. Abraham Davenport.
Anniversary Poem.
Samuel E. Sewall.
Wordsworth. Fragment: "For let the impediment be what it may."
Occasioned by the Battle of Waterloo (the Last Six Lines Intended for an Inscription) February, 1816.
Ode to Duty.

Dwarfs
Coleridge. Two Founts, The.
Fox. Dwarfs, The.
Patchen. I Suddenly Became Conscious That This Thing Was Looking at Me Intently.
Sexton. Rumpelstiltskin.

Smart. Author Apologizes to a Lady, for His Being a Little Man, The.

E

Eagles
Browning, Robert. Eagle, The.
Carruth. Aer.
Coleridge. Eagle and the Tortoise, The.
Cummings. Eagle, The.
Dickey, James. Eagles.
Eagle's Mile, The.
Edmunds. Cabin Site Christmas Island, N.S.
Frost. Auspex.
Hoffman. Eagles.
Hughes, Langston. Fact.
Hughes, Ted. Eagle.
Jeffers. Beaks of Eagles, The.
Fire on the Hills.
Kunitz. Eagle.
Lawrence. American Eagle, The.
Eagle in New Mexico ("On a low").
Eagle in New Mexico ("Towards the sun").
St John.
Towards the sun, towards the south-west.
Lindsay. Eagle That Is Forgotten, The.
Lowry. Kraken, Eagles, in British Columbia.
Salmon Drowns Eagle.
Merrill. Violent Pastoral.
Nash. Strange Case of Mr. O'Banion's Come-Uppance, The.
Rossetti. "Beloved, let us love one another," says St. John.
Shelley. Mighty Eagle.
Smart. On an Eagle Confined in a College-Court.
Spenser. Kingly bird, that beares Joves thunder-clap, The.
Stevens. Some Friends from Pascagoula.
Tate. Eagle, The.
Tennyson. Eagle, The.
Tomlinson. Cochiti.
Wakoski. Ice Eagle, The.
Whitman. Dalliance of the Eagles, The.
Whittier. On Receiving an Eagle's Quill from Lake Superior.
Wordsworth. Dunlolly Eagle, The.
Eagles.

Ears
Boyle. Lesson in Anatomy, A.
Donne. That learning, thine ambassador.
That living law, the magistrate.
That our ears' sickness we [*or* eares sicknesse wee] may cure.
Emerson. Dost thou not hear me Ellen.
Fisher. Half hearing, half in a veil, to lope.
Lovelace. To a Lady That Desired Me I Would Bear My Part with Her in a Song.

Earth
Atwood. You Begin.
Auden. Bucolics.
Earth's Praises.
Et in Arcadia Ego.
Ode to Gaea.
Sonnet I: "There was desolate silence on the world."
Sonnet: "This world is full of lovely things."
Beckett. Serena II.
Berry. Awake at Night.
Below.
Broken Ground, The.
Current, The.
Earth and Fire.
Enriching the Earth.
Let my marriage be brought to the ground.
Mad Farmer's Love Song, The.
Marriage, an Elegy, A.
Now that April with sweet rain.
On the Hill Late at Night.
Satisfactions of the Mad Farmer, The.
Silence, The.
Sowing the seed, / my hand is one with the earth.
Stones, The.
Sycamore gathers / out of the sky, white, The.
To be sane in a mad time.

Want of Peace, The.
World's one song is passing, The.
Bishop. Elegy for Maria Alves.
Boyle. World Tour.
Browning, Elizabeth Barrett. Earth and Her Praisers.
Heaven and Earth.
Man and Nature.
Sonnet: "When our two souls stand up erect and strong."
Browning, Robert. Reverie.
Bukowski. Sun Wields Mercy, The.
Byron. When Coldness Wraps This Suffering Clay.
Wild Gazelle, The.
Carroll, Jim. Mercury Clouds.
Carruth. Introspectional.
Terra.
Clark. You (V) (after Holderlin).
Coleridge. Delinquent Travellers, The.
Faith, Hope, and Charity.
Hymn to the Earth.
Ode on the Departing Year.
Crane. Interior.
Shall I Subsume..
To Earth.
Creeley. Envoi: "Particulars they want."
For a Friend.
For the Graduation.
Here.
June 6, 1970.
Kiki.
Province, The.
Sunset.
Cummings. All worlds have halfsight,seeing either with.
As if as / if a mys.
Bigness of cannon, The.
I say no world.
Maker of many mouths.
O sweet spontaneous.
Old mr ly / fresh from a fu.
Silent unday by silently not night.
Davie. Metals.
De la Mare. Bright Life.
Futility.
Gloria Mundi.
Music.
Sleep.
Snow.
Dickey, James. For a Time and Place.
Immortals.
Moon Flock.
Dickinson. If roses had not faded.
Oh Matchless Earth—We underrate.
What indeed is Earth but a Nest.
Donne. First Anniversary [or Anniversarie], The.
Through thy submitting all, to blow[e]s.
To Mr. Tilman after He Had Taken Orders.
To the Praise of the Dead, and the Anatomy.
Duncan. Ballad of the Enamord Image, The.
Dunn. Local Time.
Room and the World, The.
Eberhart. Cover Me Over.
Fantasy of a Small Idea.
Forms of the Human.
Go to the Shine That's on a Tree.
Grove, The.
Hard Structure of the World, The.
Ideal and the Real, The.
Maze.
Memory.
Pasture, The.
Soul Longs to Return Whence It Came, The.
Spring Mountain Climb.
Stopping a Kaleidoscope.
Summery Windermere, sweet lake!
Emerson. Atom from atom yawns as far.
Builder of heaven, The.
Desire no bread, forsake the guest hall of the earth.
Drink wine, and the heaven.
Had I the world for my enemy.
Hamatreya.
In this sour world, o summerwind.
None spares another yet it pleases me.

Now tells the flower.
Patch of meadow & upland, A.
Patient Pan / Drunken with nectar, The.
Softens the air so cold & rude.
Stand up, that we may sacrifice the soul.
Stately bride is the shining world, A.
That each should in his house abide.
This world is tedious.
World is a bride superbly dressed, The.
Everson. Winter Ploughing.
Fisher. Open— / and away.
Wonders of Obligation.
Fletcher. Black Rock, The.
Six long days was the unseen God in labour with the earth.
Ford. Face of the Earth, The.
Wind is the breath of it.
World's a mirror. Break it and you die!, The.
Frost. No Holy Wars for Them.
Gardner. Conversation at Midnight with Oscar Williams.
Gunn. Aqueduct.
First Man, The.
Haines. Hermitage, The.
Tundra, The.
Hartley. To the Nameless One.
Tree that bears—, A.
Heaney. Bog Queen.
Hemingway. I think that I have never trod.
Herrick. Another ("Thou bidst me come; I cannot come; for why").
To His Paternall Countrey.
White Island: or Place of the Blest, The.
Hesketh. Imagination.
Hewitt. Because I Paced My Thought.
Booleys, The.
Colney Hatch.
For R.S. Thomas.
Garron Top.
Palimpsest.
September Lull.
Those Swans Remember; A Poem.
Vigil.
Hill. Emblem, The.
Genesis.
I was invested in mother-earth, the crypt of roots.
In Piam Memoriam.
Hoffman. Reflections.
Hopkins. God's Grandeur.
Ribblesdale.
Housman. Here are the skies, the planets seven.
Hughes, Ted. Like those flailing flames.
Jarrell. Archangel's' Song, The.
Blind Sheep, The.
Jeffers. Beautiful Captive, The.
Broken Balance, The.
Eye, The.
Flight of Swans.
Hope is Not for the Wise.
Irish Headland, An.
It flows out of mystery into mystery: there is no beginning—.
Life from the Lifeless.
Metamorphosis.
Subjected Earth.
Unformed volcanic earth, a female thing, The.
Kinnell. Westport.
Kipling. Sestina of the Tramp-Royal.
Koch. Geography.
Lawrence. Four, The.
Mediterranean in January.
There Are Too Many People.
Transformations.
Travel Is Over.
Levertov. Earth Psalm.
O Taste and See.
Levine. Clouds.
How Much Earth.
On a Drawing by Flavio.
Rain Downriver.
Snow.
They Feed They Lion.
To My God in His Sickness.
To P.L., 1916–1937.
Walk with Tom Jefferson, A.

Liddy. Republic 1939, The.
Lindsay. Comet of Prophecy, The.
Sew the Flags Together.
Lorde. Dreams Bite.
Sowing.
Lovelace. Female Glory.
Paradox, A.
Paris's Second Judgement.
To my Dear Friend Mr. E.R.
To My Noble Kinsman T.S. Esq.
Lowry. Communist, The.
Lament—June 1944.
Lying awake beside a sleeping girl.
Need it be so niggardly of meaning too?
McAuley. Beyond the crowding spires of pine, the hill.
"MacDiarmid." Bonnie Broukit Bairn, The.
But shairly, shairly, there maun be.
I was better with the sounds of the sea.
Little White Rose, The.
O Ease My Spirit.
MacLeish. Hands.
Seafarer.
Speech to a Crowd.
Sunset Piece, The.
MacNeice. Canto X: "Daily news. And today? There is not so much to note."
McNeill. Son, The.
Mahon. Tractatus.
Matthews. Wehlener Sonnenuhr Auslese 1959.
Meinke. World within World.
Merrill. Childlessness.
Merton. Space Song.
Millay. God's World.
Morgan. From the Kuan-Tzu.
Morrison. Desert, The.
Nash. Any Milleniums Today, Lady?
Nemerov. Celestial Globe.
Earth orbits on the sun and has no sign.
Knowledge.
Loon's Cry, The.
O'Hara. Invincibility.
Oliver. Night Flight.
Olson. Binnacle, The.
Canto One Hundred and One.
Drum World, The.
Flower grows, The.
King of the Wood / King of the Dead.
Maximus, from Dogtown-1.
May 31, 1961.
Sing, Mister, Sing.
Whole World, The.
Pack. Watchers.
Patchen. Early in the Morning.
Eve of St. Agony, or the Middle Class Was Sitting on Its Fat.
Great Birds, The.
How Old the World Is!
In Your Body All Bodies Lie.
Instructions for Angels.
Lao Tsze.
Lenada.
Letter to the Old Men.
Message from the Assistant Chief of the Fly People, A.
My Coat Is Dirty.
My Generation Reading the Newspapers.
O kind watchers came.
O my love / The pretty towns.
Other Side: The Green Home, The.
Overworld, The.
Pick Up the Evening Paper.
Preparation for the Highest Being.
Red Wine and Yellow Hair.
Rest, heart of the tired world.
Snow is deep on the ground, The.
Sure There Is Food.
Valley-sleeper, the Children, the Snakes, and the Giant, The.
What the Grecian Earns.
What There Is.
World Whose Sun Retreats Before the Brave, A.
World Will Little Note, The.
Raine. Into what pattern, into what music have the spheres whirled us.
Sun, great giver of all that is.

This little house / No smaller than the world.
Word Made Flesh.
World: / Image on water, waves.
World, The.
Ralegh. World discernes it selfe, while I the world behold, The.
Rexroth. Lute Music.
Lyell's Hypothesis Again.
Rich. Atlas of the Difficult World, An.
Rossetti. Advent.
De Profundis.
Earth and Heaven.
Earth has clear call of daily bells, / A chancel-vault of gloom and star.
Heaven overarches earth and sea.
Heaven's chimes are slow, but sure to strike at last.
His Banner over Me Was Love.
Horses of the Sea, The.
I Look for the Lord.
If stars dropped out of heaven, / And if flowers took their place.
Look on This Picture and on This.
Present and Future.
Roses on a brier, / Pearls from out the bitter sea.
Sexagesima.
Strange voices sing among the planets which.
This near-at-hand land breeds pain by measure.
Thou sleepest where the lilies fade.
To What Purpose Is This Waste?
Vain Shadow, A.
What is this above thy head, / O Man?
When a mounting skylark sings / In the sunlit summer morn.
Who cares for earthly bread tho' white?
Rukeyser. He Had a Quality of Growth.
Sandburg. Atlas, How Have You Been?
Be Ready.
Breathing of the earth, The.
Early Copper.
Earth is a forgotten cinder, The.
Leather Leggings.
Loam.
People, yes, The.
There is only one horse on the earth.
These wheels within wheels.
Sarton. At Muzot.
Composition.
Invocation: "Come out of the dark earth."
Prothalamion.
Puritan, The.
Stone Walls.
Schuyler. Earth's Holocaust.
Sexton. As It Was Written.
Earth, The.
First Psalm.
Shelley. Prologue in Heaven.
Silverstein. Edge of the World, The.
Simic. Poem: "Every morning I forget how it is."
Smart. On the Immensity of the Supreme Being.
Smith, Stevie. In Protocreation.
Snodgrass. Song: "Observe the cautious toadstools."
Snyder. For Nothing.
Little Songs for Gaia.
O Mother Gaia.
Wash me on home, mama.
Sorrentino. Come from the whirling zodiac.
Detail, A.
Southwell. Vale of Tear[e]s, A.
Spender. Drowned under Grass.
Stevens. Anatomy of Monotony.
Gubbinal.
Planet on the Table, The.
Ultimate Poem Is Abstract, The.
Yellow Afternoon.
Stuart. Cabbage in History, The.
Confirmation.
Suckling. Love's World.
Thomas. This Bread I Break.
Tomlinson. Dialogue.
Turco. Pocoangelini 7 ("Sir. Your Head. It is stuck into the sand").

Updike. Vibration.
Walker. We Have a Beautiful Mother.
Whitman. Earth, My Likeness.
I am the poet of the Body and I am the poet of the Soul.
Love That Is Hereafter, The.
Song of the Rolling Earth, A.
Wilbur. Antiworlds.
Attention Makes Infinity.
Caserta Garden.
On Having Mis-identified a Wild Flower.
Worlds.
Williams, Charles Kenneth. Clay out of Silence.
Don't.
Williams, William Carlos. At Kenneth Burke's Place.
Jean Sans Terre Circles the Earth Seven Times.
Wright, James. Alarm, The.
Arrangements with Earth for Three Dead Friends.
At Thomas Hardy's Birthplace, 1953.
Eternal Dice, The.
Fit against the Country, A.
Ghost, The.
Goodbye to the Poetry of Calcium.
Horse, The.
Poem for Kathleen Ferrier.
Rosebushes.
What the Earth Asked Me.
Yau. She descends the stairway of the last ditch beyond the horizon. I.
Yeats. Before the World Was Made.
Zukofsky. Gamut.
Memory of V. I. Ulianov.
World autumn, The.

Earthquakes
Boyle. After the Earth Quaked.
Cooper. Earthquake, The.
Davie. Gemona-del-Friuli, 1961–1976.
"Dylan." Black Diamond Bay.
Lindsay. Voice of the Earthquake, The.
Merton. Atlas and the Fatman.
Earthquake.
Schuyler. Shadowy Room.
Spenser. On high hills top I saw a stately frame.
Van Duyn. Earth Tremors Felt in Missouri.
Whittier. Earthquake, The.
Young. Watsonville after the Quake.

"Eastaway, Edward." see Thomas, Edward ("Edward Eastaway").

Easter
Auden. Easter Monday.
Berryman. Heaven.
Browning, Robert. Easter-Day.
"Carroll, Lewis." Acrostic: "Are you deaf, Father William?"
Carruth. Æolian.
Ciardi. Lamb, The.
Two Egrets.
Clough. Easter Day II.
Easter Day. Naples, 1849.
Crashaw. Easter Day.
Dunbar. Easter Ode, An.
Glück. Easter Season.
Hardy. Drizzling Easter Morning, A.
Herbert. Easter.
Easter Wings.
Hewitt. Easter Flock.
Easter Tuesday.
Hopkins. Easter.
Easter Communion.
That Nature Is a Heraclitean Fire and of the Comfort of the Resurrection.
Housman. Easter Hymn.
MacNeice. Easter Returns.
Meinke. Easter in Neuchâtel.
Nemerov. Sonnet at Easter.
Olson. Easter.
Rossetti. Easter Carol, An.
Easter Day.
Easter Even.
Easter Monday.
Easter Morning.
Our Church Palms are Budding Willow Twigs.

Rukeyser. Easter Eve 1945.
Sarton. Easter Morning.
Sexton. Passion of the Mad Rabbit, The.
Protestant Easter.
Smith, Stevie. Conviction (ii).
Spenser. Most glorious lord of life that on this day.
Updike. Seven Stanzas at Easter.
Van Duyn. Well, that was Saturday, day before Easter.
Walcott. Easter.
Whittier. Easter Flower Gift, An.
Williams, Charles Kenneth. Easter.
Wordsworth. Composed in One of the Valleys of Westmoreland, on Easter Sunday.

Easter Island
Neruda. Island (VIII), The.
Island (VII), The.
Island (XVII), The.
Island (XII), The.
Island (XX), The.
Men (IX), The.
Men (XIX), The.

Easter Rebellion (1916)
Yeats. Easter, 1916.
Rose Tree, The.
Sixteen Dead Men.
Three Songs to the One Burden.

Eating
Atwood. Carrying Food Home in Winter.
Eating Snake.
Auden. To-night at Seven-thirty.
Berry. If a man finds it necessary to eat garbage, he should resist the.
Prayer after Eating.
There is a sort of vertical.
Bishop. Table, The.
Bukowski. Eat.
"Carroll, Lewis." Canto I: The Trystyng.
First Voice, The.
Walrus and the Carpenter, The.
Catullus. Carmen 13: "I shall expect / you in to dine."
Cowper. To the Halibut.
Creeley. Apple Uppfle.
Dickey, James. Bread.
Dickinson. Deprived of other Banquet.
Dobyns. Spiritual Chickens.
Donne. Liar, The.
To Mr. T. W. ("Pregnant again with th' old twins hope, and fear").
Dunbar. Possum.
Emerson. God only knew how Saadi dined.
Ford. Owlet pulls / Pieces of meat from between the, The.
Fox. Like a Woman in the Kitchen.
My Father's Oldest Sister.
Griffiths. Llangefni Market.
Gunn. J Car, The.
Waitress.
Hall. Moon, The.
Self-Portrait as a Bear.
Hemingway. Ship Translated Being La Paquebot, The.
Herrick. Content, Not Cates.
Custard, The.
Hymne, to the Lares, A.
Littlenesse No Cause of Leanesse.
Meat without Mirth.
Panegyric to Sir Lewis Pemberton, A.
To Sir Clipseby Crew ("Give me wine, and give me meate").
Upon Grubs.
Upon Gryll.
Upon Jack and Jill: Epigram.
Upon Lungs.
Upon Magot a Frequenter of Ordinaries.
Upon Mease.
Upon Showbread [or Shewbread]: Epigram.
Upon Skinns.
Upon Skurffe.
Upon Tooly.
Hewitt. In the Lenin Library, Dushanbe.
Jong. Catch, The.
Jonson. Inviting a Friend to Supper.
Kinnell. Supper after the Last, The.
Knight. Eat Helen B Happy (a Found Poem).

Lawrence. Bowls.
Lovelace. Fabullus I will treat you
    handsomely.
Meredith. Tuck, thou graceless sinner!—.
Nash. Bugs.
    Celery.
    Everybody Eats Too Much Anyhow.
    Isn't That a Dainty Dish? No!
    Pizza, The.
    Squab, The.
O'Hara. Essay on Style.
Silverstein. Boa Constrictor.
    Fish?
    I Must Remember.
    Melinda Mae.
    Pancake?
    Recipe For A Hippopotamus Sandwich.
    Ridiculous Rose.
    Silver Fish, The.
    Sky Seasoning.
    Sleeping Sardines.
Simic. East European Cooking.
    Spoon.
Stevenson. At morning on the garden seat.
    Aye mon, it's true; I'm no' that weel.
    Thought, A.
Stuart. Ballad of the Three Birds.
Updike. Trees Eat Sunshine.
Williams, Charles Kenneth. For Gail, When I
    Was Five.
    Greed.
    Modern, The.
Zukofsky. Canapés, my Fabullus, at home any.

See also **Food; Gluttony and Gluttons.**

Eating Disorders
Nash. Curl Up and Diet.
Silverstein. Hungry Mungry.

Echo (mythology)
Campion. Elegia I (1619).
Schwartz. Prologue: "Narcissus, speaking in
    the first person."

See also **Narcissus (mythology).**

Echoes
Ashbery. Late Echo.
Bishop. Chemin de Fer.
Clough. See! the faint green tinge from the
    western sky has.
Creeley. Characteristically.
    Echo.
    Some Echoes.
    Variations.
De la Mare. Echo.
Fletcher. From the Japanese, III.
Hardy. Echo-Elf Answers, The.
Sidney. Fair rocks, goodly rivers, sweet
    woods, when shall I see peace?
Tomlinson. Walking to Bells.
Wordsworth. Yes, it was the mountain Echo.

Eclipses
Graves. Near Eclipse, The.
Hardy. At a Lunar Eclipse.
Lovelace. On the Best, Last, and Only
    Remaining Comedy of Mr. Fletcher.
Schuyler. Moon.
Snodgrass. Partial Eclipse.
Wordsworth. Eclipse of the Sun, 1820, The.

Ecology and Ecologists
Carruth. Cave Painting.
    Names.
    Now tell me if we don't need a revolution!
    Black.
    Oldest Killed Lake in North America, The.
    Slums par excellence that were your farms!
    And all.
    Sonnet: "I think continually of the
    differences."
    Too Tenuous.
    Ugly, evil, dying. The old soft lines.
    Why was the passenger pigeon exterminated?
Cowper. Poplar Field, The.
Frost. To a Young Wretch.
Garrigue. Lead in the Water.
Hopkins. Binsey Poplars (Felled 1879).
Hugo. Duwamish Head.
    Plans for Altering the River.
Joseph. In Memory of God.

Kunitz. War against the Trees, The.
"MacDiarmid." My Songs Are Kandym in the
    Waste Land.
McNeill. Clearing, The.
    Oil Field.
Piercy. Why the Soup Tastes Like the *Daily
    News.*
Roethke. Moss-Gathering.
Snyder. Call of the Wild, The.
    Dillingham, Alaska, the Willow Tree Bar.
    For All.
    Front Lines.
    Mother Earth: Her Whales.
    Tomorrow's Song.
    Toward Climax.
Waldman. White Eyes.

See also **Pollution.**

Economics and Economists
Griffiths. Fruits of Virtue.
Kunitz. Economist's Song, The.
Prince. Sun shines on the gliding river, The.
Smart. Care and Generosity.
Van Duyn. Economics.
Wright, James. Undermining of the Defense
    Economy, The.

Ecstasy
Berryman. Mysteries, The.
Carruth. "Ecstasy is the / disaster of pleasure":
    this.
    Ecstasy, The.
Cummings. Her careful distinct sex whose
    sharp lips comb.
    (Let us tremble)a personal radiance sits.
Dickinson. I hope that you are well.
    Take all away from me, but leave me Ecstasy.
    Transport one cannot contain, A.
Doolittle. Psyche.
Dove. Catherine of Alexandria.
Duncan. Years As Catches, The.
Eberhart. On Seeing an Egyptian Mummy in
    Berlin, 1932.
Ferlinghetti. Euphoria.
    Making Love in Poetry.
Graves. Ecstasy of Chaos.
Hall. Fête.
Hardy. On Stinsford Hill at Midnight.
Hewitt. Sonnet: "There in the lonely quarry
    where at dawn."
Hopkins. Late I fell in the ecstasy.
Jarrell. Man in Majesty.
Joseph. Zenith.
Meredith. Song: "Joyful / And woful."
Merton. Air.
Millay. As sharp as in my childhood, still.
Schuyler. Photograph, A.
Whitman. One Hour to Madness and Joy.
Yeats. Ribh in Ecstasy.

Eden
Auden. Dethroned.
    Vespers.
Browning, Elizabeth Barrett. Drama of Exile,
    A.
Cohen. Not Going Back.
Cummings. Devil crept in eden wood.
Davie. Eden.
De la Mare. Exile, The.
Dickey, James. Poisoned Man, The.
Dickinson. Did the Harebell loose her girdle.
    Eden is that old-fashioned House.
    Expulsion from Eden grows indistinct.
    Not seeing, still we know.
Dobyns. Gardener, The.
Dunbar. Unlucky Apple, The.
"Dylan." Gates of Eden.
Eberhart. Adam Cast Forth.
    Throwing the Apple.
Emerson. Eve roved in Paradise, I've heard.
Fox. Letters from the Island.
    There was, perhaps, a time.
Graves. History of the Fall.
Hesketh. Reclaimed.
Hopkins. Spring.
Housman. When Adam walked in Eden
    young.
Hughes, Ted. Theology.
Joseph. First Spring Dawn.
Larkin. At the Chiming of Light upon Sleep.

Lawrence. Eve.
    Paradise Re-entered.
Lindsay. Eden in Winter.
MacLeish. Eve's Exile.
MacNeice. Apple Blossom.
Milton. Adam Fallen ("Descended, Adam to
    the bower where Eve").
    Paradise ("Another side, umbrageous Grots
    and Caves").
    So spake our Mother Eve, and Adam heard.
    Tempter Disarmed, The.
Raine. On its way I see.
    Under these hills too high and bare.
Rossetti. Sexagesima.
    That Eden of earth's sunrise cannot vie.
Shapiro. Exile.
    Sickness of Adam, The.
Spender. Adam.
Thomas. Incarnate Devil.
Tomlinson. Adam.
    Eden.
    In Arden.
    To Ivor Gurney.
Walcott. New World.
Whittier. Lay of Old Time, A.
Wilbur. Problem from Milton, A.

See also **Adam and Eve; Paradise.**

Edinburgh, Scotland
Burns. Address to Edinburgh.

Edison, Thomas Alva
Jeffers. Edison.
Koertge. Excerpts from God's Secret Diary.

Editors
Byron. Strahan, Tonson, Lintot of the Times.
"Carroll, Lewis." Double Acrostic: I sing a
    place wherein agree.
Lawrence. Great Newspaper Editor to His
    Subordinate, The.
Roethke. Reply to a Lady Editor.

Education
Boyle. Crow, The.
Coleridge. Love, Hope, and Patience in
    Education.
Cowper. Tirocinium; or, A Review of Schools.
Cummings. As Joe Gould says in.
    Bud(spiggy nuvduh fienus).
Dickinson. Through the Dark Sod—as
    Education.
Eberhart. Killer, The.
Emerson. Easy to match what others do.
    He must have / Droll fancies sometimes cross
    his quiet thoughts.
Gardner. Little Rock Arkansas 1957.
Ginsberg. Sather Gate Illumination.
Gray. Alliance of Education and Government,
    The.
Hardy. Young Man's Epigram on Existence,
    A.
Hesketh. Academic.
    Truant.
Hoffman. Peaceable Kingdom, The.
Keats. In After-Time, a Sage of Mickle Lore.
Koertge. He: "Was taken out of school after."
Lowry. Der Tag.
Meredith. Discipline of Wisdom, The.
    Empty Purse: A Sermon to our Later Prodigal
    Son, The.
Millay. Intention to Escape from Him.
Milton. Sonnet 21: "Cyriack, whose Grandsire
    on the Royal Bench."
Nemerov. Sweeper of Ways, The.
    To David, about His Education.
    Triumph of Education, The.
Oliver. Answers.
"Reed." Teach the Gifted Children.
Rexroth. Advantages of Learning, The.
Smart. Learning.
Snodgrass. Campus on the Hill, The.
Spender. Elementary School Classroom in a
    Slum, An.
Stevenson. Here he comes, big with statistics.
Updike. À l'École Berlitz.
Whitman. To a Pupil.
Wordsworth. Lines Written as a School
    Exercise at Hawkshead, Anno Aetatis 14.

See also **Colleges and Universities; Scholarship and Scholars; Students; Teaching and Teachers.**

Edward III, King of England
Blake. King Edward the Third.

Edward IV, King of England
Blake. Prologue, Intended for a Dramatic Piece of King Edward the Fourth.
Sidney. Sonnet 75: "Of all the kings that ever here did reign."

Edward VII, King of England
Kipling. Dead King, The [Edward VII; 1910].

Edwards, Jonathan
Lowell. After the Surprising Conversions.
Jonathan Edwards in Western Massachusetts.
Mr. Edwards and the Spider.
Warren. Worst Sinner, Jonathan Edwards' God, The.

Eels
Gunn. Seabed, The.
Lowry. Eels.
Nash. Eel, The.
Wakoski. Dark Clack of Morays, The.

Eggs
"Carroll, Lewis." Lays of Sorrow, No. 1.
Ciardi. Tommy's Pond.
Dunn. Eggs.
Herrick. Her Legs.
Upon Tooly.
Hewitt. Hen and the Cock: A Glens Folk Rhyme, The.
Hoffman. Egg.
Hughes, Langston. Bar.
Joseph. Gentleman that my black hen lays eggs for, The.
Lowry. Eels.
Just a Merry Little Ditty of Welcome for the Most Beloved Harteebeeste on Easter Sunday.
MacLeish. Vicissitudes of the Creator.
Merrill. Transfigured Bird.
Rossetti. Hear what the mournful linnets say.
White hen sitting / On white eggs three, A.
Sandburg. Chicks.
Smoke Shapes.
Two Humpties.
When we say fresh eggs we mean fresh.
Schuyler. Wild Eggs.
Silverstein. I Won't Hatch.
Smith, Stevie. Nourish Me on an Egg.

Egotism and Egotists
Boyle. Crow, The.
Bukowski. 56 Year Old Poem, A.
Macho Man.
Campion. Epigramme: "What though Harry braggs, let him be noble."
Carew. Ingrateful[l] Beauty Threatened.
Catullus. Carmen 15: "*My love & I* are yours to command."
Carmen 47: "Lucius Calpurnius Piso Caesoninus."
Clare. Braggart.
Clark. "In the Bond Scandals.."
Creeley. Immoral Proposition, The.
Davie. In the Stopping Train.
Eberhart. If I Could Only Live at the Pitch That Is near Madness.
My Brains Are Slipping in the Fields of Eros.
Scouring, The.
Usurper.
Ginsberg. Ego Confession.
Griffiths. Crossing Lady-Stanley, Here, 1868.
Knott. Shorts / Excerpts ("I write these lines to cripple the dead").
Lawrence. Be It So.
Ego-Bound.
Ego-Bound Women.
Egoists, The.
Escape.
Gulf, The.
Jealousy.
Self-Conscious People.
Self-Sacrifice.
Strife.
Lindsay. What the Scarecrow Said.
Lowry. And now the seagulls feed on the front porch.
McAuley. Catnap, with Nightmare.

MacNeice. Budgie.
To the Public.
Nash. Self-Effacement of Electra Thorne, The.
Nemerov. Hero Comes Home in His Hamper, and Is Exhibited at the World's Fair, The.
Olson. Fable for Slumber.
Pack. Camp Wakonda, 1940.
Rukeyser. Chapman.
Sandburg. From what graveyards and sepulchers have they come.
Smith, Stevie. Dear Karl.
Egocentric.
Spender. Subject, Object, Sentence.
Trigorin.
Stuart. Elect, The.
Van Duyn. Talker, The.
Warren. Interjection #5: Solipsism and Theology.
Mad Young Aristocrat on Beach.
Williams, Charles Kenneth. Alzheimer's: The Husband.
Zukofsky. Commend to you my cares for the love I love.
Porky and Socration, two-eye sins as try.
See also **Individualism and Individualists.**

Egrets
Carruth. Parting up/down from / one on the shore, two egrets—.
Ciardi. Two Egrets.
Oliver. Egret, The.
Egrets.
St. John. Fan Sketched with Silver Egrets, A.
Updike. Even Egrets Err.

Egypt
Browning, Robert. First-Born of Egypt, The.
Carruth. Fact of the Matter, The.
Clark. Egypt, Everything.
Pharoahs Sacrifice Themselves before Her, The.
Clough. When Israel Came Out of Egypt.
Crane. By Nilus Once I Knew.
Cummings. Cleopatra built / like a smooth arrow or.
Doolittle. Egypt.
Eberhart. Dry Rot, The.
Sphinx.
Ultimate Song.
Edmunds. Landing in Cairo.
Hartley. King Amenemhat III.
Hewitt. Sarcophagus.
Hopkins. Soliloquy of One of the Spies Left in the Wilderness, A.
Jong. Egyptology.
Kipling. Grave Near Cairo, A.
Naaman's Song.
Pharaoh and the Sergeant.
Lindsay. Trial of the Dead Cleopatra in Her Beautiful and Wonderful Tomb, The.
McAuley. My earliest memory? why, the lassitude!
MacNeice. Réchauffé.
Meredith. Foresight and Patience.
Merton. Cairo 1326.
Idol of Sarapis, The.
Patchen. Egypt.
Pope. On the Statue of *Cleopatra*, Made into a Fountain by *Leo* the Tenth.
Ralegh. Egyptians [*or Aegyptians*] think[e] it sin[ne] to root[e] up, or to bite.
Shelley. Ozymandias [of Egypt].
Updike. Average Egyptian Faces Death, The.
Dilemma in the Delta.
Walcott. Egypt, Tobago.
Warren. All is nothing, nothing all.
Flaubert in Egypt.
Whittier. New Exodus, The.
Zukofsky. So sounds grass, and if it is sun or no sun.

Eichmann, Adolf
Carruth. Adolf Eichmann.
Cohen. All There Is to Know about Adolph Eichmann.
Levertov. During the Eichmann Trial.
Merton. Epitaph for a Public Servant.

Einstein, Albert
Coleridge. Xmas Gift.
Fox. Albert Einstein (1879–1955).

Ginsberg. Xmas Gift.
MacLeish. Einstein.
Pack. Einstein's Pegasus.
Williams, William Carlos. St. Francis Einstein of the Daffodils.

Eisenhower, Dwight David
Dickey, James. Two Poems of the Military.
Lowell. Inauguration Day: January 1953.
Wright, James. Eisenhower's Visit to Franco, 1959.

El Dorado
Poe. Eldorado.

El Greco. *see* **Greco, El.**

El Salvador
Paley. In San Salvador (I).
In San Salvador (II).
Women's Prison: El Salvador / The Ballad of Visiting Day, The.

Elands
Jarrell. Seele im Raum.

Electric Appliances
Nash. What, No Sheep?

Electricity
Dickey, James. Power and Light.
Haines. Men Against the Sky.
Kipling. Song of the Dynamo.
Lawrence. Storm in the Black Forest.
Lieberman. Courtship of the Jersey Lineman.
Lindsay. Rhyme About an Electrical Advertising Sign, A.
Yau. After removing the anodized plate, the two electricians discover an.

Elephants
Cummings. Silently little blue elephant shyly(he was terri), The.
Kipling. I will remember what I was. I am sick of rope and chain.
'Less you want your toes trod off you'd better get back at once.
Municipal.
Torn boughs trailing o'er the tusks aslant, The.
Lawrence. Elephant.
Elephant Is Slow to Mate, The.
Elephants in the Circus.
Elephants Plodding.
On the Drum.
Two Performing Elephants.
MacNeice. Elephant Trunk.
Elephants.
Moore. Elephants.
Sandburg. Elephants Are Different to Different People.
Spenser. Soone after this I saw an elephant.
Swift. Elephant, The.
Zimmer. Zimmer Envying Elephants.

Elevators
Hughes, Langston. Elevator Boy.
Nemerov. Fiction.
Sexton. Riding the Elevator into the Sky.

Elgin Marbles
Hardy. Christmas in the Elgin Room.
Keats. On Seeing the Elgin Marbles.

Elijah (Bible)
Dickinson. Elijah's Wagon knew no thill.
Warren. Elijah on Mount Carmel.

"Eliot, George" (Mary Ann [*or Marian*] Evans Lewes Cross)
Dickinson. She is the Lane to the Indes.

Eliot, Thomas Stearns
Auden. To T. S. Eliot on His Sixtieth Birthday.
Cummings. Out of the pants which cover me.
Eliot. Lines for Cuscuscaraway and Mirza Murad Ali Beg.
Ferlinghetti. Sea and Ourselves at Cape Ann, The.
Lowry. Thing to know is how to write a verse, The.
Rukeyser. Citation for Horace Gregory.

Elizabeth I, Queen of England
Bishop. Britannia Rules the Waves.
Bradstreet. In Honour of That High and Mighty Princess Queen Elizabeth of Happy Memory.
Burns. Lament of Mary Queen of Scots on the Approach of Spring.

Campion. Ad Thamesin.
English *Sapphick*, The.
Greatest in thy wars.
Shadowes before the shining sunne do vanish.
Dickinson. Elizabeth told Essex.
Kipling. Looking Glass, The.
Pageant of Elizabeth, A.
Together.
Spenser. Colin Clouts Come Home Againe.
Tomlinson. At Saint Mary's Church.

Elk
Ceravolo. Ho Ho Ho Caribou.
Dunn. About the Elk and the Coyotes That Killed Her Calf.
Haines. Field of the Caribou, The.
Nash. Wapiti, The.

Elliot, Ebenezer
Whittier. Elliott.

Elm Trees
Berry. Old Elm Tree by the River, The.
Byron. Lines Written beneath an Elm in the Churchyard of Harrow.
Carruth. Like a frozen lake the sky in the bitterest.
October. Twilight / flutters like cloth of silver.
Hardy. Felled Elm and She, The.
Levertov. Living While It May.
MacLeish. Long Hot Summer.
Two Trees, The.
Melville. Malvern Hill.
Moore. Camperdown Elm, The.
Plath. Elm.
Sandburg. Elm Buds.
Poplar and Elm.
Snodgrass. Elm Tree, An.
Tomlinson. Tree.
Updike. Elm.
Williams, Charles Kenneth. Elms.
Zukofsky. Memory of V. I. Ulianov.

Elopement
"Carroll, Lewis." Miss Jones.
Hardy. In Sherborne Abbey.
Hill. Who Are These Coming to the Sacrifice?
Hopkins. Elopement, The.
Lewis. *Marriage Bed, The.*
Longfellow. Skeleton in Armor [*or* Armour], The.
Sandburg. Curse of a Rich Polish Peasant on His Sister Who Ran Away with a Wild Man.
Scott. Jock of Hazeldean.
Lochinvar.

Elves
Bishop. Behind Stowe.
Burns. Tam Lin.
De la Mare. Unfinished Dream, The.
Dunbar. Discovery, The.
Levertov. Elves, The.
See also **Fairies.**

Ely, England
Cowper. On the Death of the Bishop of Ely.
Eberhart. Slow Boat Ride.
Milton. On the Death of the Bishop of Ely.

Emancipation (1863-1865)
Dunbar. Deserted Plantation, The.
Emancipation.
To the South.
Whittier. Astræa at the Capitol.
At Port Royal.
Hymn for the Celebration of Emancipation at Newburyport.
Jubilee Singers, The.
Laus Deo!
Proclamation, The.

Embryos
"MacDiarmid." All life's million conflicting interests and relationships.
Poetry that never for a moment forgets, A.
Rukeyser. For a Mexican Painter.

Emerson, Ralph Waldo
Dickinson. Emerson's intimacy with his "Bee."
Eberhart. Emerson's Concord.
Turco. Mary Moody Emerson, R.I.P.

Emigration
Boyle. New Emigration, The.
On Taking up Residence in Virginia.

Bunting. Complaint of the Morpethshire Farmer, The.
Gin the Goodwife Stint.
Burns. Address of Beelzebub.
Lines Written on a Bank-Note.
On a Scotch Bard Gone to the West Indies.
Dickinson. Away from Home are some and I.
To an Emigrant, Country is idle.
Fenton. Children in Exile.
Hall. Sister on the Tracks, A.
Hewitt. Mainland, The.
My Aunt Sarah and Uncle Joe.
My Brooklyn Uncle.
Jarrell. To the New World.
Smith, Charlotte. Disillusion with the French Revolution.

Emmet, Robert
Shelley. On Robert Emmet's Grave.

Empedocles
Emerson. Brave Empedocles defying fools, The.
Meredith. Empedocles.

Empire State Building, New York City
Oppen. It is *that* light.
Schuyler. Six Something.

Emptiness
Ammons. Hollows.
Angelou. After.
Atwood. I am sitting on the / edge of the impartial.
Paper Bag, A.
Berg. Holes, The.
Berry. Wild, The.
Blake. Opposition Is True Friendship.
Bukowski. Girls From Nowhere.
Carruth. Emptiness—you know.
Words in a Certain Appropriate Mode.
Ceravolo. Warmth.
Clark. "Like Musical Instruments.."
What the picture tells me is itself.
Cohen. Drawer's Condition on November 28, 1961, The.
You Have No Form.
Cooper. Waiting.
Yesterday a letter / spoke of our parting.
Cowper. My pens are all spilt, and my ink-glass is dry.
Creeley. Dishonest Mailmen, The.
Envoi: "Particulars they want."
Flesh.
Hole, The.
Ice Cream.
Joy.
Language, The.
On Vacation.
Rain (2) ("Thoughtful of you, I was / anticipating change in").
Sign Board, The.
Cullen. After a Visit.
Hunger.
Cummings. Emptied.hills.listen.
De la Mare. Empty House, The.
Dunn. After Losses.
Emptiness.
"Dylan." I Dreamed I Saw St. Augstine.
Sad-Eyed Lady of the Lowlands.
Eberhart. Waiting To Lean to the Master's Command.
Eliot. Burbank with a Baedeker: Beistein with a Cigar.
Conversation Galante.
Dans le Restauramt.
Gerontion.
Hollow Men, The.
Waste Land, The.
Everson. Sixty Five.
Fletcher. Empty Days, The.
Ford. Theatre of winter, The.
Gallagher. Coming Home.
Ginsberg. Land O'Lakes, Wisc.
Glück. Solstice.
Graves. Florist Rose, The.
Not at Home.
Recognition.
Thief.
Griffiths. Contact.
In the Railway Hotel at Cordoba.

Hacker. Last Time, The.
Haines. Denali Road.
That mid-fall morning, driving north.
Hardy. Exeunt Omnes.
Hartley. Pistols for Pleasure—Guitars for Defense.
Herbert. Dotage.
Hesketh. Cross.
Hughes, Ted. You are a wild look—out of an egg.
Hugo. In Stafford Country.
Joseph. Dead of Night.
Kinnell. Another Night in the Ruins.
Kipling. Derelict, The.
Knott. Obsolescent and His Deity (Polyptych), An.
Lawrence. Tarantella.
Winter Dawn.
Liddy. Dream of a Strange One.
Mistress on her white horse at, The.
To the Memory of Bernard Berenson.
Lindsay. Leaden-eyed, The.
McGrath. Encounter.
MacLeish. Carrion Spring, The.
Mahon. Achill.
Markson. *Sans.*
Matthews. Fellow Oddballs.
Meredith. Song: "Fair and false! No dawn will greet."
Merton. Action and Non-Action.
Desolation.
Empty Boat, The.
Perfect act is empty. Who can see it?, The.
Useless Tree, The.
Where Is Tao?
Morrison. L.A. Woman.
To Be Alone.
When the Music's Over.
Woman in the Window.
Nathan. Carrying On.
Servant of Stars, The.
Neruda. Sick Man in the Sun.
Oppen. Population.
Pack. Archeology.
Out of Nothing.
Patchen. I always return to this place.
Piercy. Gasman Invites the Skyscrapers to Dance.
Morning Half-Life Blues, The.
Raine. Her Room.
Unloved, The.
Whiteness of moonlight builds a house that is not there.
Rich. Blue Ghazals, The.
Demon Lover, The.
Rolfe. Letter for One in Russia.
Sunday Evening Revery.
Rossetti. Castle-Builder's World, A.
Shapiro. Nebraska.
Simic. Eraser.
Sorrentino. It is one man alone, what.
Meeting, The.
Woman Irritable because of Her Menses.
Waldman. Makeup on Empty Space.
Warren. Only Trouble, The.
What Happened.
Williams, Charles Kenneth. Admiral Fan, The.
For Children When They Grow Up.
Hounding Mercy.
Madder.
Rabbit Fights for His Life the Leopard Eats Lunch, The.
Spring: another / joke. / This run-down.
Undead, The.
Williams, William Carlos. These.
Wright, Charles. Dog Yoga.
Wright, James. I Want to Sleep.
Not in Marble Palaces.
Zukofsky. Dying away as of trees, A.
Happier, happier, now.
Lines of this new song are nothing, The.

Enchantment
Brontë. Night is darkening round me, The.
Browning, Robert. Isle's Enchantress, The.
Burns. Answer to the Foregoing—Extempore [Clarinda].

Campion. Goe, happy man, like th' Evening Starre.
Carew. In Praise of His Mistress.
Tinder, The.
To One Who, When I Praised My Mistress' Beauty, Said I Was Blind.
Coleridge. Silver Thimble, The.
Crane. Your eyes, those pools with soft rushes.
Cummings. Emperor / sleeps in a palace of porphyry, The.
To stand(alone)in some.
Ferlinghetti. Café Notre Dame.
Graves. Or To Perish Before Day.
Hardy. As 'Twere To-night.
First Sight of Her and After.
In a Whispering Gallery.
Paphian Ball, The.
Shiver, The.
Herrick. To Music: A Song.
Hewitt. By Air to Birmingham on a Mid-June Evening.
Clogh-Oir: September 1971.
Et Tu In Arcadia Vixisti.
Glen of Light, The.
Holy Place, A.
Mass.
Seaside Town, A.
Swan.
Joseph. Language Teaching: Naming.
Road from Glastonbury, The.
Lawrence. Witch I, The.
Lindsay. Master of the Dance, The.
Meredith. Enter these enchanted woods.
Here the snake across your path.
Pope. Of Her Picture.
Raine. Your gift of life was idleness.
Shelley. Fragments of an Unfinished Drama.
Stevenson. Mother and Daughter.
Young. Billie.
Erosong.

End of the World
Angelou. On a Bright Day, Next Week.
Beckett. Imagine si ceci.
Browning, Robert. Childe Roland to the Dark Tower Came.
Bukowski. End, The.
On the Failure of a Poet.
10 Lions and the End of the World.
Worst and the Best, The.
Cummings. If in beginning twilight of winter will stand.
Now does our world descend.
What if a much of a which of a wind.
When god decided to invent.
While a once world slips from.
De la Mare. Sign, A.
Dobyns. Day the World Ends, The.
Donne. At the round earth's imagined corners, blow.
"Dylan." Man of Peace.
Talkin' World War III Blues.
Eberhart. Ides of March, The.
Ferlinghetti. Reading Apollinaire by the Rogue River.
Frost. Once by the Pacific.
Glück. End of the World, The.
Haines. Dürer's Vision.
Holmes. Premonitory July.
Jarrell. Dialogue between Soul and Body, A.
Jeffers. End of the World.
I Shall Laugh Purely.
McGrath. End of the World, The.
MacLeish. End of the World, The.
McNeill. Cassandra.
Mahon. Morning Radio.
Meredith. Creation and the Prophet.
Merton. Martin's Predicament or Atlas Watches Every Evening.
Senescente Mundo.
Olson. Hotel Steinplatz, Berlin, December 25 (1966).
Pack. Proton Decay.
Raine. It is in us they burn.
Rukeyser. Noguchi.
Shapiro. Scyros.
Smart. On the Eternity of the Supreme Being.

Snyder. L M F B R.
Van Duyn. Relative and an Absolute, A.
Wilbur. Advice to a Prophet.
Williams, Charles Kenneth. Clay out of Silence.
Downwards.
That the world / is going.
Wright, Charles. October.

See also **Apocalypse; Judgment Day.**
Endangered Species
Atwood. Elegy for the Giant Tortoises.
Oliver. Ghosts.
Endurance
Beckett. Pas à pas.
Berryman. "I *couldn't leave* you" you confessed next day.
Sanctuary.
Bishop. Night City.
Burns. O, for Ane-and-Twenty Tam.
Byron. Love and Death.
To a Lady.
To the Earl of Clare.
Carroll, Jim. In This Room Particularly.
"Carroll, Lewis." There was an ancient City, stricken down.
Carruth. After the thaw after.
Coleridge. Forbearance.
Cowper. Nature Unimpaired by Time.
Ode on the Death of a Lady.
Cullen. Harsh World That Lashest Me.
Davie. Break, The.
Trip to Huntsville, The.
Wombwell on Strike.
De la Mare. Courage.
Doolittle. Ancient Wisdom Speaks.
"I love you," / spoken in rhapsodic metre.
Dunn. Beyond Hammonton.
Edmunds. Black Bull, The.
Stone.
Emerson. Character.
Ferlinghetti. Thoughts to a Concerto of Telemann.
Fletcher. Black Rock, The.
Gunn. Rastignac at 45.
Hardy. Coming of the End, The.
Hewitt. For Busha.
If I had given you that love and care.
R.K.
Sonnet: "Our love is full of memorable things."
Stone.
Jeffers. All the Little Hoof-Prints.
Granite and Cypress.
It is a pity the shock-waves.
Old Stone-Mason, The.
Kipling. Old Men, The.
after Horace, Book 5, Ode 22.
Kunitz. Welcome the Wrath.
Larkin. I See a Girl Dragged by the Wrists.
Lawrence. Race and Battle.
Lovelace. Valiant Love.
Lowry. Foul, or Twenty-Five.
Stars have simple paradigms, The.
MacLeish. Actfive.
Chartres.
Snowflake Which Is Now and Hence Forever, The.
Merrill. After Greece.
Merton. Autumn Floods.
Milton. Nature Does Not Suffer Decay.
O'Hara. Poem: "Light clarity avocado salad in the morning."
Olson. He treads on edges of being where the drop.
I hang on by.
Piercy. Ache's End.
Plath. Firesong.
Psalms. Psalm 129: "Many a time have they afflicted me from my youth.."
Ralegh. From thence our kinde hard-hearted is, enduring paine and care.
Shelley. But Greece and her foundations are.
Simic. Terms, The.
Smart. St. Matthias.
Smith, Stevie. Study to Deserve Death.
Snodgrass. September in the Park.

Spenser. What time the Romaine Empire bore the raine.
Stafford. Consolations.
Warren. Keep That Morphine Moving, Cap.
To a Face in a Crowd.
Whittier. Within the Gate.
Wroth. Sonnet 45: "Good now bee still, and doe nott mee torment."
Yeats. Travail of Passion, The.
Young. Breathing in morning.
Thelonious: An Intro.
Zukofsky. Cactus rose-mauve and gray, twin overturned.
Passing tall.
Who endure days like this.

See also **Fortitude.**
Endymion
Cullen. To Endymion.
Emerson. Manners.
Keats. Endymion: Poetic Romance.
Millay. Oh, sleep forever in the Latmian cave.
Enemies
Byron. Imitation of Tibullus.
Carew. Truce in Love Intreated.
Catullus. Carmen 52: "Drop dead, Catullus, lie right down & die."
Carmen 116: "Conscientiously bringing my mind to bear on this problem."
De la Mare. Hare, A.
Emerson. Bended to fops who bent to him.
For two rewards, & nought beside.
Had I the world for my enemy.
Has thine enemy slandered thy house.
Skeptic, The.
To the Shah, from Hafiz.
Hardy. Enemy's Portrait, The.
Man He Killed, The.
Hemingway. Defense of Luxembourg.
Herrick. Discord Not Disadvantageous.
Pitie to the Prostrate.
Hewitt. Drypoint.
Peace Pact.
Kipling. France.
Piet.
Lawrence. My Enemy.
Lovelace. Fly Caught in a Cobweb, A.
Merton. What are the marks of the enemy? / He has no wit.
Milton. Be not thou silent now at length.
What Though the Field Be Lost?
Psalms. Psalm 41: "Blessed is he that considereth the poor."
Psalm 54: "Save me, O God, by thy name. . . ."
Psalm 68: "Let God arise, let his enemies be scattered."
Psalm 83: "Keep not thou silence, O God."
Psalm 129: "Many a time have they afflicted me from my youth."
Robinson. New Tenants, The.
Rolfe. Entry.
Nine, The.
Sentry.
To Those Who Fear To Join Us.
Smart. Arouse—and let thy foes disperse.
Whitman. Reconciliation.
Wyatt. Right true it is and said full yore ago.
Zukofsky. Quick death, Catullus! what more horrors may hurry!
Sigh paid to be studious when I moved went on to (queer) once.
Energy
Blake. Voice of the Devil, The.
Carruth. Being, The.
Ceravolo. Dangers of the Journey to the Happy Land.
Cowper. Inscription for a Stone.
Moralizer Corrected, The.
Creeley. Massachusetts.
Gunn. My Sad Captains.
Joseph. Man as Matter (ISLAND; PHYSICS).
Lawrence. We Are Transmitters.
Liddy. Donn na Duimche.
In the Bowling Alley.
Lowry. Save that the optimistic ones are worse.
Rossetti. I Will Arise.

Rukeyser. I have tried to show the atom as a source.
Not leaves, not lightning, not the greatness of rivers.
Tree of rivers flowing through our lives, A.
Sorrentino. Razzmatazz.
Updike. Energy: A Villanelle.
Waldman. Battery.
Revolution.
Slowly.
Wilbur. Star System, The.
Young. Jolt.

Engineers
Hewitt. Volunteer, The.
Kipling. Hymn of Breaking Strain.
McAndrew's Hymn.
Nurses, The.
Sappers.
Study of an Elevation, in Indian Ink.
Moore. Icosasphere, The.
Tomlinson. On the Principle of Blowlocks.
Williams, William Carlos. Aigeltinger.

England
Auden. On This Island.
Beatles. Mean Mr. Mustard.
Berryman. Shirley & Auden.
Betjeman. Christmas.
Dear Old Village, The.
Great Central Railway, Sheffield Victoria to Banbury.
In Westminster Abbey.
Matlock Bath.
Old Liberals, The.
Town Clerk's Views, The.
Blake. And Did Those Feet in Ancient Time.
Fields from Islington to Marybone, The.
When Klopstock England defied.
Bradstreet. Dialogue between Old England and New, A.
Old England.
Browning, Elizabeth Barrett. Sweetness of England, The.
Browning, Robert. Home-Thoughts, from Abroad.
Home-Thoughts, from the Sea.
Nationality in Drinks.
Bunting. Keep Troth.
Burns. Dumfires Volunteers, The.
Scots Ballad.
Such a Parcel of Rogues in a Nation.
Byron. Canto the Eleventh.
Irish Avatar, The.
Italy.
Oh factious viper! whose envenom'd tooth.
Campion. Ad Guil. Camdenum.
Ad Invictissimum Serenissimumque Iacobvm *Magnae Britanniae Regem.*
Elegeia I (1595).
Epigram, An: "Merlin, the great King Arthur being slaine."
Epigramma: "Haeredem (ut spes est) pariet nova nupta Scot Anglum."
Shewes and nightly revels, signes of joy and peace.
To the Most Puisant and Gratious James King of Great Britaine.
Carruth. Once and Again.
Coleridge. O My Mother Isle! ("Not yet enslaved, not wholly vile").
To the Honourable Mr. Erskine.
Cowper. Address to the Mob, An.
Boadicea: An Ode.
Effeminate Englishmen.
Expostulation.
Lily and the Rose, The.
On the Promotion of Thurlow.
Table Talk.
To Sir Joshua Reynolds.
Crashaw. To the Queen, Upon her Numerous Progeny, a Panegyricke.
Davie. Bedfordshire.
Cambridgeshire.
County Durham.
Derbyshire.
Dissent. A Fable.
Dudwood.
England.

English Revenant, An.
Fourth Epistle.
Gloucestershire.
Hampshire.
Herefordshire.
Hertfordshire.
Low Lands.
Out of East Anglia.
Rain on South-East England.
Rutland.
Sixth Epistle.
Some Shires Revisited.
Stratford on Avon.
Third Epistle.
Trevenen.
Westmorland.
Wild Boar Clough.
Winter's Talents.
De la Mare. England.
How Sleep the Brave.
Dickinson. Robin's my Criterion for Tune, The.
Dunn. Substitute, The.
Eberhart. Ultimate Song.
Fletcher. England Again.
Gunn. Between the pastel boutiques.
Hall. Village in East Anglia, A.
Hardy. Call to National Service, A.
Herbert. British Church, The.
Hill. Funeral Music.
Herefordshire Carol, The.
Laurel Axe, The.
Loss and Gain.
Mercian Hymns.
Hopkins. To Seem the Stranger.
What Shall I Do for the Land that Bred Me.
Housman. Clunton and Clunbury.
1887.
New Mistress, The.
On Wenlock Edge the wood's in trouble.
Jeffers. Ghosts in England.
Subjected Earth.
Two Christmas-Cards.
Jonson. Epigram to the Queen, Then Lying In. 1630, An.
New Year's Gift Sung to King Charles. 1635, A.
On the Union.
To My L[ord] the King, on the Christening His Second Son James.
To the King. On His Birthday. An Epigram Anniversary. Novem[ber] 19, 1632.
To the Right Hon[oura]ble Hierome, L[ord] Weston. An Ode Gratulatory for His Return from His Embassy. 1632.
Keats. Happy Is England! I Could Be Content.
Lines Written on 29 May / The Anniversary of the Restoration of Charles the 2nd.
On Peace.
Kipling. Absent-Minded Beggar, The.
American Rebellion, The.
Anvil, The.
Bells and Queen Victoria, The.
Big Steamers.
Broken Men, The.
Brown Bess.
Chant-Pagan.
Charm, A.
Coastwise Lights, The.
Dane-Geld.
Dawn Wind, The.
Deep-Sea Cables, The.
Dutch in the Medway, The.
Edgehill Fight.
England's Answer.
English Flag, The.
Et Dona Ferentes.
Fastness.
Flowers, The.
France.
French Wars, The.
Glory of the Garden, The.
In Springtime.
Islanders, The.
James I.
King Henry VII. And the Shipwrights.
King's Job, The.

King's Task, The.
Land, The.
Last of the Light Brigade, The.
Memories.
My Father's Chair.
Norman and Saxon.
Open Door, The.
Pirates in England, The.
Puck's Song.
Reeds of Runnymede, The.
Return, The.
River's Tale, The.
Roman Centurion's Song, The.
Secret of the Machines, The.
Sir Richard's Song.
Together.
Tree Song, A.
Ulster.
Vineyard, The.
With Drake in the Tropics.
Larkin. Having Grown Up in Shade of Church and State.
Naturally the Foundation Will Bear Your Expenses.
MCMXIV.
Lawrence. As for Me, I'm a Patriot.
Clydesider.
England in 1929.
English Are So Nice!, The.
Flapper Vote.
Innocent England.
My Native Land.
Rose and Cabbage.
Rose Is Not a Cabbage, A.
Rose of England, The.
Spirits Summoned West.
Lovelace. Mock Song, A.
Lowry. And yet I am of England too; odi et amo.
April 1937 In the Oaxaca Train.
In the Oaxaca Train.
MacNeice. Bad Lord Byron went to the firing, helmet and dogs and all.
Canto XXI "Thirtieth inst., too soon the thirtieth ult, The."
I ought to be glad.
October in Bloomsbury.
Marvell. First Anniversary of the Government under His Highness the Lord Protector, 1655, The.
Last Instructions to a Painter, The.
On the Victory Obtained by Blake over the Spaniards, in the Bay of Santa [or Sancta] Cruz, in the Island of Tenerife, 1657.
That Providence which had so long the care.
Upon Appleton House [To My Lord Fairfax].
Meredith. Aneurin's Harp.
Atkins.
Britain.
Call, The.
Congress of Nations, The.
England before the Storm.
Head of Bran the Blest, The.
Ireland.
John Lackland.
Labourer, The.
Lines to a Friend Visiting America.
Loyal Soldier, The.
New Era the Army of the Future the Egg of an Army, The.
Old Chartist, The.
Outside the Crowd.
Patriot Engineer, The.
Poetry of Chaucer, The.
Poetry of Shakespeare, The.
Red Coats & the Blue, The.
Song: "God bless the little Island!"
Song of the New Zealander among the Ruins of Old London.
Song: "Twelve arrows, and a bow, and spear."
Song: "Who says, she is in danger."
Three Eagles and the Sleepy Lion, The.
To Colonel Charles.
To Lord Palmerston.
To the Merry Men of France.
Voyage of the "Ophir," The.
Warning, The.

Wassail for the New Year, A.
Ye noble Lords who bravely fight.
Merton. When class was in the garden at Greylands.
Millay. Memory of England.
Oppen. Tugs of Hull, The.
Pope. Epitaph on Dr. Francis Atterbury, Bishop of Rochester, Who Died in Exile at Paris, 1732; a Dialogue.
Fragment of *Brutus*, an Epic.
Windsor-Forest [*or* Windsor Forest].
Ralegh. Sir Walter Ralegh's [*or* S.W. Raghlies] Petition to the Queene 1618.
Rossetti. Succession of Kings, The.
Rukeyser. Otherworld.
Scott. English Advance at Flodden, The.
Shelley. Fragment: To the People of England.
New National Anthem, A.
Song to the Men of England.
Sonnet: England in 1819.
Smith, Charlotte. Beachy Head.
Prologue to William Godwin, *Antonio: or, The Soldier's Return.*
Slow in the Wintry Morn, the struggling light.
Smith, Stevie. I Love.
O Happy Dogs of England.
Suburban Classes, The.
Voices against England in the Night.
Spenser. Ruines of Time, The.
Suckling. Cantilena Politica-Jocunda Facta Post Principis Discessum In Hispaniam.
Tennyson. To the Marquis of Dufferin and Ava.
Thomson. Britain.
Happy Britannica.
Prospect, The.
Rule, Britannia!
"Sweet Valley, Say."
Tomlinson. Bridges.
Dates: Penkhull New Road.
Midlands.
Return to Hinton.
To Ivor Gurney.
Updike. English Train Compartment.
Walcott. Exile.
Grey English road hissed emptily under the tires, The.
Mud. Clods. The sucking heel of the rain-flinger.
With the stampeding hiss and scurry of green lemmings.
Whittier. Freed Islands, The.
Hymn: "O Holy Father! just and true."
To the Reformers of England.
Williams, William Carlos. Exultation, An.
Wordsworth. After Landing—The Valley of Dover, Nover, 1820.
Artegal and Elidure.
Composed by the Sea-Side, near Calais, August, 1802.
Composed in the Valley near Dover, on the Day of Landing.
England! the time is come when thou shouldst wean.
It is not to be thought of that the Flood.
Lines on the Expected Invasion 1803.
Lines Written as a School Exercise at Hawkshead, Anno Aetatis 14.
London, 1802.
Ode: The Morning of the Day Appointed for a General Thanksgiving. January 18, 1816.
Sonnet in the Pass of Killicranky.
View from the Top of Black Comb.
When I have borne in memory what has tamed.
Young England—What Is Then Become of Old.
Wright, Charles. Journal of English Days, A.
Yeats. Ghost of Roger Casement, The.
On a Political Prisoner.
Zukofsky. Stratford-on-Avon.
See also **Civil Wars, England.**

England, Church of. *see* **Church of England.**

English, The
Blake. Thames.
Byron. Girl of Cadiz, The.
World Is a Bundle of Hay, The.

Campion. Bravely deckt, come forth, bright day.
Debetur alto iure Principium Iovi.
To the Most Disconsolate Great Brittaine.
"Carroll, Lewis." Acrostic: Maidens! if you love the tale.
To M. A. B.
Coleridge. Fears in Solitude.
Cummings. Flotsam and jetsam / are gentlemen poeds.
It was a goodly co.
Q:dwo / we know of anything which can.
Dryden. In pious times ere [*or* e'r] priest-craft did begin.
Dunbar. Letter, A.
Hartnett. Inchicore Haiku.
Hemingway. Robert Graves.
Hewitt. Prologue for an Evening at the Whitefriars.
Kipling. Absent-Minded Beggar, The.
Anvil, The.
Beginnings, The.
Belts.
Birthright, The.
English Way, The.
Et Dona Ferentes.
Flowers, The.
Fuzzy-Wuzzy.
General Joubert.
Gentlemen-Rankers.
Islanders, The.
Jacket, The.
Jobson's Amen.
Kitchener's School.
Ladies, The.
Loot.
Lost Legion, The.
Native-Born, The.
Norman and Saxon.
Puzzler, The.
Song of the Dead, The.
Song of the English, A.
To Thomas Atkins.
Waster, The.
Young British Soldier, The.
Koch. Departure from Hydra, The.
Lawrence. British Boy, The.
British Sincerity.
Brittania's Baby.
Broadcasting to the G.B.P.
Emasculation.
English Are So Nice!, The.
Gentleman, The.
How Beastly the Bourgeois Is.
I Know a Noble Englishman.
Little-Boy Brilliant.
Lucky Little Britisher.
Man in the Street, The.
Middle-Class Children.
My Native Land.
Rose and Cabbage.
We Can't Be Too Careful.
Liddy. City Life.
"MacDiarmid." To distinctly English writers in England.
MacNeice. Solitary Travel.
Nash. Ms. Found under a Serviette in a Lovely Home.
Oafishness Sells Good, Like an Advertisement Should.
Scram, Lion!
Schuyler. Witley Court.
Shelley. Song to the Men of England.
Smart. Ode to General Draper.
Whitsunday.
Smith, Stevie. Eng.
English, The.
Oh, If Only.
This Englishwoman.
Tomlinson. Class.
Whittier. To Englishmen.
Wordsworth. Decay of Piety.
Incident at Bruges.
Protest against the Ballot.

English Channel
Kipling. French Wars, The.
Wet Litany, The.

Smith, Charlotte. Beachy Head.

Engraving and Engravers
Boyle. Seascape for an Engraver.
Donne. Valediction, A: Of My Name in the Window.
Hartley. Sea Engraving—Style of 1880.
Tomlinson. To Be Engraved on the Skull of a Cormorant.

Envy
Ammons. Upshot, The.
Berg. Daughters, The.
Sad Invective.
Bukowski. Millionaire, The.
Byron. To D———.
Campion. Ad Lucium.
My Sweetest Lesbia [Let Us Live and Love].
"Carroll, Lewis." Canto IV: Hys Nouryture.
Catullus. Carmen 5: "Lesbia / live with me."
Carmen 12: "While everyone else is laughing & drinking."
Carmen 81: "Surely, Iuventius, one of this throng in Rome."
Carmen 83: "Lesbia is extraordinarily vindictive."
Cowper. On Envy.
Crashaw. On Nanus Mounted on an Ant.
Creeley. Europeans, The.
Dickinson. I envy seas—whereon He rides.
Dobyns. Envy.
Dunn. American Film, An.
Eberhart. Man's Greed and Envy Are So Great.
Edmunds. In Memoriam: Robert Fitzgerald.
Emerson. Free thyself from wo.
I have found a nobler love.
Fenton. Skip, The.
Gallagher. Same Kiss After Many Years, The.
Hardy. Singing Lovers.
Herrick. Not to Covet Much Where Little is the Charge.
Jonson. On the Right Honourable and Virtuous Lord Weston, L[ord] High Treasurer of England, upon the Day He Was Made Earl of Portland, 17. Febr. 1632. To the Envious.
Joseph. Exile in Devon, An.
Kipling. Divided Destinies.
My Rival.
Lovelace. To Chloe, Courting Her for His Friend.
Meredith. Brotherhood.
How many a thing which we cast to the ground.
I must be flattered. The imperious.
Morgan. Catullus: *Carmen v.*
Morrison. Can We Resolve the Past.
Nash. Possessions Are Nine Points of Conversation.
Psalms. Psalm 73: "Truly God is good to Israel, even to such as are of a clean heart."
Rolfe. Munich.
Shakespeare. Sonnet 70: "That thou art blamed shall not be thy defect."
Sidney. Sonnet 59: "Dear, why make you more of a dog than me?"
Smith, Stevie. Barlow.
Night Thoughts.
Spenser. Envy.
Tomlinson. Green Quinces.
Wilbur. All These Birds.
Wordsworth. Lesbia.
Zukofsky. Lesbia (my price scent t'her hero) mauls and deplores me, '*dig it*'.
Marrucinus Asinius, that sinister.
May we live, my Lesbia, love while we may.
Not many enchant you (put to it) popular is he, Juventi.
See also **Jealousy.**

Epic Poetry
Browning, Elizabeth Barrett. Critics say that epics have died out, The.
Byron. From Anacreon ("I wish to tune my quivering lyre").
Koch. Art of Poetry, The.
Pope. To Belinda on the Rape of the Lock.
Simic. My Weariness of Epic Proportions.
Tennyson. Morte d'Arthur.

Epictetus
Arnold. To a Friend.

Epigrams
Byron. Martial, Lib. I. Epig. I.
Campion. Ad Castricum.
De Epigrammate.
De Fran. Draco.
In Bretonem.
In Nervam.
Cowper. Epigram is but a feeble thing, An.
Herrick. Upon Pusse and her Prentice.
Jonson. To All, to Whom I Write.
To My Book.
To My Mere English Censurer.
To the Ghost of Martial.
Mahon. As It Should Be.
Dying Art, A.

Epiphany. *see* **Twelfth Night.**

Epitaphs
Bradstreet. Epitaph on my Dear and Ever
  Honored Mother Mrs. Dorothy Dudley.
Byron. Here's a Happy New Year! But with
  Reason.
Substitute for an Epitaph.
Crashaw. Epitaph. Upon Doctor Brooke, An.
Epitaph upon Mr. Ashton, a Conformable
  Citizen, An.
[Mr. Herrys,] His Epitaph.
Davie. No Epitaph.
De la Mare. Epitaph, An: "Last, Stone, a little
  yet."
Hardy. Gentleman's Epitaph on Himself and a
  Lady, Who Were Buried Together, A.
Herrick. Epitaph on the Tomb of Sir Edward
  Giles and His Wife in the South Aisle of
  Dean Prior Church.
To His Tomb-Maker.
Hewitt. Cold Warrior: Anzac Day, 1946.
With E.M.F. on 28th December 1965.
Jeffers. George Sterling's Death.
Lovelace. On the Death of Mrs. Elizabeth
  Filmer.
Lowry. Epitaph on Our Gardener, Dead Near
  Liverpool.
Words on a Grave.
Merton. Rilke's Epitaph.
Tomb Cover of Imam Riza.
Ralegh. Authours Epitaph, Made by Himself,
  The.
Epitaph on the Earl of Leicester [*or* Leceister].
Songe Made by Sir Walter Rawley, A.
Rich. Annotation for an Epitaph.
Tomlinson. Cradock Newton: From an
  Epitaph.
Epitaph: Enamoured by / Brevity in method.
Whitman. As Toilsome I Wander'd Virginia's
  Woods.
Williams, William Carlos. Address, An.
Wordsworth. Could I the priest's consent have
  gained.
Epitaph in Grasmere Church.
Epitaph in the Chapel Yard of Langdale,
  Westmoreland.
Gravestone upon the Floor in the Cloisters of
  Worcester Cathedral, A.

Equality
Auden. Recitative by Death.
Bradstreet. Mercury showed Apollo Bartas'
  book.
Burns. Extempore Verses on Dining with Lord
  Daer.
Song—For A' That and A' That.
To the Beautiful Miss Eliza J———n, on Her
  Principles of Liberty and Equality.
"Carroll, Lewis." Alice's Recitation.
Ceravolo. Autumn Break.
Chaucer. Franklin's Tale, The.
Tale of Melibee, The.
Wife of Bath's Tale, The.
Creeley. Eye, The.
Night.
Davie. I Have Said, Ye Are Gods.
Dickey, James. Basics.
Dickinson. Color, Caste, Denomination.
Emerson. Boston.
Gardner. Little Rock Arkansas 1957.
Herrick. Conformity Is Comely.

Hewitt. Equality.
Hughes, Ted. Fallgrief's Girlfriends.
Kipling. Equality of Sacrifice.
Merton. All of the branches / None of the
  roots.
Dogs bark at everyone they do not know.
Plessy vs Ferguson: Theme and Variations.
Rossetti. There Remaineth Therefore a Rest.
Sandburg. Graceland.
Psalm of the Bloodbank.
Whitman. Song for Occupations, A.
Thought ("Of Equality.").
Thoughts—I: Visages.
Whittier. Our Country.
Poor Voter on Election Day, The.
Wordsworth. What if our numbers barely
  could defy.
Yeats. Paudeen.
See also **Social Class.**

Erne (river), Ireland
Muldoon. Yggdrasill.

Ernst, Max
Ford. Max Ernst.
Yau. Charred Voice of Max Ernst, The.

Eros. *see* **Cupid.**

Erosion
Berry. Dance, A.
Hewitt. Stone.
"MacDiarmid." My Songs Are Kandym in the
  Waste Land.
Morrison. Time Works Like Acid.
Sandburg. Handfuls.
Sutter. Celebration of Rust, A.
Tomlinson. Compact: at Volterra, The.
Poem: "Upended, it crouches on broken
  limbs."
Sea Poem.
Wilbur. On the Marginal Way.

Erotic Love
Ammons. Market Adviser.
Tryst.
Angelou. Remembrance.
Shaker, Why Don't You Sing?
Zorro Man, A.
Ashbery. My Erotic Double.
Atwood. I look up, you are standing.
Auden. Alston Moor.
Amor Vincit Omnia.
Autumn Evening.
Chloe to Daphnis in Hyde Park.
Coming of Love, The.
Earth's Praises.
Ebes Anthos Apollumenon.
Encounter.
Extract.
Four sat on in the bare room, The.
From the very first coming down.
In Due Season.
Letter, The.
Lovers' Lane.
My Lady of the Wood.
Song: "Crocus stars the border, The."
Sunken Lane, The.
Suppose they met, the inevitable procedure.
There is so much that I can share with you.
Thomas Epilogizes.
Uncle Henry.
Vision.
Whenever I see for the first time.
Yes and No.
Beatles. Day Tripper.
Don't Let Me Down.
For You Blue.
Hold Me Tight.
I Wanna Be Your Man.
Love You To.
Please Please Me.
Beckett. Lady Love.
Out of Sight in the Direction of My Body.
Scarcely Disfigured.
Universe-Solitude.
Berg. Summer Twilight.
Sunday Afternoon.
You.
Berry. And when we speak together.
Dance passes beyond us, The.
Dance, The.

Earth and Fire.
Fear of Love, The.
Song: "I tell my love in rhyme."
To Tanya at Christmas.
Berryman. Ah when you drift hover before
  you kiss.
Great citadels whereon the gold sun falls.
Betjeman. Agricultural Caress.
Hearts Together.
Invasion Exercise on the Poultry Farm.
Lake District.
Licorice Fields at Pontefract, The.
Myfanwy at Oxford.
Narcissus.
North Coast Recollections.
Potpourri from a Surrey Garden.
Russell Flint, A.
Bishop. Late Air.
Love is feathered like a bird.
Now a conundrum Love propounds.
Three Valentines.
Bly. At Midocean.
At the Time of Peony Blossoming.
Ferns.
Horse of Desire, The.
Listening to the Köln Concert.
Bogan. Frightened Man, The.
Rhyme.
Browning, Elizabeth Barrett. Psyche Gazing
  on Cupid.
Sonnet: "And yet, because thou overcomest
  so."
Sonnet: "Go from me. Yet I feel that I shall
  stand."
Sonnet: "How do I love thee? Let me count
  the ways."
Sonnet: "I think of thee! My thoughts do
  twine and bud."
Sonnet: "If thou must love me, let it be for
  nought."
Sonnet: "Indeed this very love which is my
  boast."
Sonnet: "Is it indeed so? If I lay here dead."
Sonnet: "My own Beloved, who hast lifted
  me."
Sonnet: "Thou comest! all is said without a
  word."
Sonnet: "What can I give thee back, O
  liberal."
Sonnet: "When our two souls stand up erect
  and strong."
Sonnet: "When we first met and loved, I did
  not build."
Sonnet: "Yet, love, mere love, is beautiful
  indeed."
Browning, Robert. Last Ride Together, The.
Burns. Bonie Lass Made the Bed to Me, The.
Had I the Wyte She Bade Me.
Muirland Meg.
O May Thy Morn.
O Saw Ye My Maggie.
Ode to Spring.
Patriarch, The.
Song: "It was upon a Lammas night."
Song: "My girl she's airy, she's buxom and
  gay."
Trogger, The.
Byron. To a Lady Who Presented to the
  Author a Lock of Hair Braided with His
  Own, and Appointed a Night in December to
  Meet Him in the Garden.
Translation from Catullus ("Equal to Jove that
  youth must be").
Campion. Ad Amorem.
Follow, follow[e] / Though with mischiefe.
I Care Not for These Ladies.
It Fell on a Summer's [*or* Sommers] Day [*or*
  Daie].
My Dearest Mistress.
Secret Love or Two I Must Confess[e], A.
Carew. Rapture, A.
Catullus. Carmen 51: "Godlike the man who."
Carmen 55: "Where / if it's not too much to
  ask."
Carmen 58: "Lesbia, our Lesbia, the same old
  Lesbia."
Carmen 61: "Hill (breeder) of Helicon."

Ceravolo. Fly.
 Red Sun.
Ciardi. Two Hours.
Clough. Ah, what is love, our love, she said.
 Do duty feeling nought and truth believe.
 Homo Sum, Nihil Humani—.
 Natura Naturans.
 O Theos Meta Sou.
 Oh, ask not what is love, she said.
 Thought may well be ever ranging.
 To be, be thine.
Cohen. All Right, Edith.
Coleridge. First Advent of Love.
 Love and Friendship Opposite.
 Ode in the Manner of Anacreon, An.
 Rose, The.
 To an Unfortunate Woman Whom the Author
  Had Known in the Days of Her Innocence.
Cooper. Letters.
 Obligations.
 Pencil Sketch of Self & Other.
 Song: "Here I am yours, and here, and here."
Crashaw. Out of the Italain.
 Out of the Italian; a Song.
Creeley. Places.
 Question, The.
 Sight, A.
 Two Times ("Image / docteur").
 Woman, The.
Cullen. At a Parting.
 Bright Bindings.
 Brown Boy to Brown Girl.
 If You Should Go.
 Love Tree, The.
 Love's Way.
 One Day We Played a Game.
 Pity the Deep in Love.
 Song of Praise.
 Song of Praise, A.
 Sonnet: "I have not loved you in the noblest
  way."
 Street Called Crooked, The.
 To a Brown Girl.
 Variations on a Theme.
 Wind Bloweth Where It Listeth, The.
Cummings. After your poppied hair
  inaugurates.
 Amiable putrescence carpenters, An.
 And this day it was Spring..us.
 As / we lie side by side.
 Because i love you)last night.
 Bed is not very big, The.
 Before the fragile gradual throne of night.
 Dirty colours of her kiss have just, The.
 Five Americans.
 Her / flesh / Came / at.
 Her careful distinct sex whose sharp lips
  comb.
 I like my body when it is with your.
 I will be / M o ving in the Street of her.
 If i believe / in death be sure.
 I'll tell you a dream i had once i was away up
  in the sky Blue,everything.
 Light cursed falling in a singular block.
 Luminous tendril of celestial wish.
 May i feel said he.
 Moon is hiding in, The.
 My deathly body's deadly lady.
 My lady is an ivory garden.
 My love / thy hair is one kingdom.
 My strength becoming wistful in a glib.
 My sweet old etcetera.
 O It's Nice To Get Up In,the slipshod mucous
  kiss.
 Reason let others give and realness bring.
 Sapphics.
 Sh estiffl / ystrut sal.
 She,straddling my lap.
 Sunlight was over.
 Thee will i praise between those rivers whose.
 There is a / moon sole.
 Upon the room's / silence,i will sew.
 Voices to voices, lip to lip.
 What is thy mouth to me?
 When i have thought of you somewhat too.
 When the spent day begins to frail.

 When you went away it was morning.
 You asked me to come:it was raining a little.
Dickey, James. Cherrylog Road.
 On the Hill below the Lighthouse.
Dickey, William. Making Love.
Dickinson. Rose did caper on her cheek, The.
 We went to sleep as if it were a country.
Dobyns. Roughhousing.
Donne. Confined Love.
 Dissolution, The.
 Farewell to Love.
 Flea, The.
 Good Morrow, The.
 Love's Alchemy [or Alchemie].
 Love's Deity [or Deitie].
 Love's Growth.
 Love's Progress.
 Love's Usury.
 Love's War.
 Nature's lay idiot [or Ideot], I taught thee to
  love.
 Sun[ne] Rising, The.
 To His Mistress Going to Bed.
 To Mr. C.B.
 To the Countess of Huntingdon ("That unripe
  side of earth, that heavy clime").
Doolittle. Epigrams.
 O Spirit, / spark by spark.
Dove. For Kazuko.
Dunn. One Side of the Story.
"Dylan." I'll Be Your Baby Tonight.
 Lay, Lady, Lay.
 On a Night Like This.
 Peggy Day.
Eberhart. My Brains Are Slipping in the
  Fields of Eros.
Edmunds. Farewell: "Farewell, my love,
  goodbye."
 Lancaster Street.
 One Look at the Creation.
 Thirteen Years.
 Willows Coming into Leaf.
Emerson. And since round lines are drawn.
 Casella.
 Eros.
 Give All to Love.
 Love and Thought.
 Ode to Beauty.
Ferlinghetti. Come lie with me and be my
  love.
 Tunisian Nostalgia.
Ford. I do put art before.
 What hard work it takes.
Fox. Letter to Peter Wilkins.
 Offering.
 There was, perhaps, a time.
Galvin. Summer School.
Gardner. Compleat Anglers, The.
 Gimboling.
 Mathematics of Encounter.
 Summer Evening.
Ginsberg. I Lay Love on My Knee.
 Love Poem on Theme by Whitman.
 Love Replied.
 Love Returned.
 Many Loves.
 Song: "Weight of the world, The."
Glück. Aubade: "Today above the gull's call."
 Encounter, The.
 Garden, The.
 Happiness.
 Lady in the Single, The.
 Mirror, The.
 Northwood Path.
 Reproach, The.
 Summer.
Graves. Age Gap.
 Bites and Kisses.
 Crystal, The.
 Dancing Flame.
 Discarded Love Poem, The.
 Dream of Hell, A.
 Druid Love.
 Earlier Lovers.
 Elsewhere.
 Envoi: "There is no now for us but always."
 Jus Primae Noctis.

 Loving True, Flying Blind.
 Moon's Tear, The.
 Mountain Lovers.
 Ours is No Wedlock.
 Poet's Curse, The.
 Prohibition, The.
 Song: Seven Fresh Years.
 Song: The Queen of Time.
 Testament.
 To Come of Age.
 Two Crucial Generations.
Gunn. Bed, The.
 For a Birthday.
 Hug, The.
 Lines for My 55th Birthday.
 Monster, The.
Hacker. Aube Provençale.
 Between us on our wide bed we cuddle an
  incubus.
 Elektra on Third Avenue.
 For K.J., Leaving and Coming Back.
 I will never be only a Lesbian.
 I'll tell you what I don't want: an affair.
 My child wants dolls, a tutu, that girls' world
  made.
 Orpheus and animus, / drawing back to
  journeys now.
 Pantoum.
 Presentation Piece.
 Separate Lives.
 Sestina: "For a week now our bodies have
  whispered."
 Villanelle: "Every day our bodies seperate."
 Villanelle: Late Summer.
 When I read poems to the art students.
 When that jackbooted choreography.
 When you told me that he was in jail.
 You made algebra: his tastes in food.
Herrick. Bride-Cake, The.
 Her Legs.
 Lawne, The.
 Love Dislikes Nothing.
 Love Perfumes All Parts.
 No Loathsomnesse in Love.
 To Anthea: ("Lets call for Hymen if agreed
  thou art").
 To Anthea, Who May Command Him
  Anything.
 To Dianeme ("Show me thy feet; show me thy
  legs, thy thighs").
 To Electra ("I'll [or Ile] come to thee in all
  those shapes").
 To Julia, in Her Dawn, or Day-breake.
 Upon Julia's Breasts.
 Upon Loach.
 Vine, The.
 Vision to Electra, The.
Hesketh. Love without Frontiers.
 Love's Advocate.
 My Faithful Lover.
 Protean Lover.
 Reclaimed.
 Traitor.
 Vine, The.
Hewitt. Nettles of Offence.
Hill. From the Latin.
 Troublesome Reign, The.
 Veni Redemptor, but not in our time.
Holmes. Les Italiennes.
 Suzy Q, The.
 Watching Morning In.
 Weekend Away.
Housman. When I was one-and-twenty.
Jeffers. For Una.
 Hungerfield.
 Resurrection.
Jong. Long Tunnel of Wanting You, The.
 Sailing Home.
 We Learned.
Jonson. Fragmentum Petron. Arbitr. The Same
  Translated.
Keats. Over the Hill and Over the Dale.
Knott. Poem: "Beach holds and sifts us
  through her dreaming fingers, The."
 Sculpture, The.
Koch. Art of Love, The.
 Days and Nights.

In Bed.
Sleeping with Women.
Koertge. Life on the Edge of the Continent.
Sex Object.
Lawrence. All of Roses.
New Year's Eve.
Paradise Re-entered.
Young Wife, A.
Levertov. Eros at Temple Stream.
Face to Face.
Hymn to Eros.
Lewis. *Marriage Bed, The.*
She Comes To Him in the Night.
Under each starry leafless tree.
Liddy. Along a leafy lonely river God-shy-
eyed fisher boys.
Death of Lovers, The.
Deaths and Electrocutions.
Delphine and Hippolyta.
Tell us, streaming lady.
Lorde. Bridge Through My Window.
Echo.
Love Poem.
On a Night of the Full Moon.
Progress Report.
Lovelace. Love Made in the First Age[: To
Chloris].
Lowry. And, when you go—much as a
meteor.
And who is it through the forest after the.
Arctic fox / With snow white hocks, The.
As to report, / Within his court.
Asperin tree outside told me to say, The.
Au clair de la lune.
Ballad: "Twas in the springtime of the year."
Burnt pier: the last passenger: the farewells,
The.
Communal Message.
Conclusion—Poem, A.
For Our Sweetharteebeeste on Hartebeeste
Day.
Harteebeeste Is Here Again, The.
Hindu Babe / I love you.
I am very small.
Illegal Heart, The.
I've Said Goodbye to Shanghai.
Just some love and kisses.
Little Ditty for This Day to the Beloved
Harteebeeste, A.
Love and wisdom have no home.
Morning bird sits mutely, The.
Morning rain is sleeting, The.
Morning rain is weeping, The.
Morning sleet is sleeting, The.
Morning stove is wheezing, The.
My Beloved Harteebeeste.
My love now lies upon his rump.
New Guinea Gardener Bird, The.
Oh and / Who is it unforlorn.
Oh love / Oh Shame, we are late.
Oh the Harteebeeste is*dear*to us.
Oh welcome Home /To thy cot by the foam.
Rich man, poor man, beggarman, thief.
Simple Seabird's Tribute to Her Harteebeeste,
A.
Slough of Despond: Or the House of Hope,
The.
Spark Poetry.
Still speeding to your heart.
Sun, Aeroplane, Lovers.
Sun was almost shining, The.
There's something burning, you said, when we
were hammering.
Though we are but *sea* birds.
To account for this, but it cannot be.
Two frozen claws / In two frozen minutes.
Volcano is dark and suddenly thunder, The.
Welcome Home Oh Gladsome Springhorned
Beloved and Famed Harteebeeste.
Welcome Home oh Harteebeeste beloved who
doth with thy.
Welcome Home oh Harteebeeste mio.
Welcome Home—Oh Most Beloved
Harteebeeste.
Welcome Home Oh Our Beloved Harteebeeste.
Welcome Home, Oh Sweetest Harteebeeste.
Who made this suicide pact of love?

With Dearest Love Enfolded and Enclosed
from *All* the Litle Animals.
With Midsummer Devotion from All the Little
Animals to Their Beloved Harteebeeste.
With Sweet Devotion and True from All the
Little Animals.
With Sweetest Devotion from *All* the Little
Animals to Their Most Beloved Harteebeeste.
With Sweetest Love and Sunday Anthems or
Sweetest Goodnight from All the Little
Animals.
"MacDiarmid." Water of Life.
MacLeish. What Must.
Woman on the Stair, The.
MacNeice. Libertine, The.
Shelley and jazz and lieder and love and
hymn-tunes.
Marvell. To His Coy Mistress.
Meinke. Everything We Do.
In Gentler Times.
Love Poem 1990.
Merrill. From the Cupola.
Millay. She Is Overheard Singing.
Morgan. In Mexico.
May 1, 1974.
Morrison. I Walked Thru.
Sex For You.
Untrampled Footsteps.
Neruda. Physics.
Olson. Boats' lights in the dawn going so
swiftly, the, The.
It's Not / the Erotic.
Patchen. All That Night Lights Were Seen
Moving in Every Direction.
And her look touching the air between us like
a hand alive to the.
And What with the Blunders.
As Frothing Wounds of Roses.
As She Was Thus Alone in the Clear
Moonlight.
As we are so wonderfully done with each
other.
Be music, night, / That her sleep may go.
Beautiful You Are.
Builders, The.
Character of Love Seen as a Search for the
Lost, The.
Colony of the Sun, The.
Do me that love.
Early in the Morning.
Fall of the Evening Star.
Farewell to the Bluewoman.
First came the Lion-Rider, across the green
fields of the morning.
For here indeed was the unassailable kingdom
of the heart itself.
For losing her love all would I profane.
For Miriam.
Give you a lantern.
Harrowed by These Apprehensions He
Resolved to Commit Himself to the Mercy of
the Storm.
Having Been Near.
He Thought of Mad Ellen's Ravings and of
the Wretched Skeleton on the Rock.
Heaven and Earth.
Her Talents...Of.
I know the hair, tissue, skin.
I Sent a Mental to My Love.
In Judgment of the Leaf.
In Memory of Kathleen.
It is a lonely walk into the mind's retreat.
It's Because Your Heart Is Pure, Honey.
Lute in the Attic, The.
Meditation of My Lady of Sorrows.
Not Many Kingdoms Left.
O my darling troubles heaven.
O my love / The pretty towns.
O sleeping falls the maiden snow.
Pretty glow on the water.
Put the rest away, O put the rest away!
Religion Is That I Love You.
She Had Concealed Him in a Deep Dark
Cave.
She is the prettiest of creatures.
Stayed No Longer in the Place Than to Hire a
Guide for the Next Stage.

Then at last the Lovers began to speak
together.
There's a Train Leaving Soon.
Thinking Rock.
To Say If You Love Someone.
Waiting Can Be Pretty Lousy.
When We Were Here Together.
Where my stag-antlered love moves.
Written after Reading an Item in the Paper
about a Young Lady Who Went Mad upon
Forsaking Her Lover. He Is Here Assumed to
Speak.
Yellow Stones—Sea of Majestic Doves.
Your name includes the shadow flight of
birds.
Piercy. You Ask Why Sometimes I Say Stop.
Pope. Summer, The Second Pastoral, or
Alexis.
Ransom. Equilibrists, The.
"Reed." Some Kinda Love.
Street Hassle: Waltzing Matilda.
Rexroth. Between Myself and Death.
Rich. Floating Poem, Unnumbered, The.
I come home from you through the early light
of spring.
I wake up in your bed. I know I have been
dreaming.
My mouth hovers across your breasts.
Night Watch.
Rossetti. A Tirsi.
All night I dream you love me well.
Amore E Dispetto.
Amore E Dovere.
Annie.
Ariadne To Theseus.
At Last.
Bed of Forget-Me-Nots, A.
Brandons Both.
Cor Mio.
Corydon's Lament and Resolution.
Despair.
Dream, A.
Dream, The.
Echo from Willowwood, An.
Fair Margaret.
Faithless Shepherdess, The.
From Mestastasio.
Grown Cold.
Have You Forgotten?
If I Were a Queen.
Il Rosseggiar Dell'Oriente Canzoniere.
In the Lane.
Isidora.
Lisetta all' Amante.
Listening.
Long Looked For.
Look on This Picture and on This.
Lord Thomas and Fair Margaret.
Love and Death.
Love Attacked.
Love Defended.
"Love me, for I love you"—and answer me.
Mariana.
Moonshine.
Novice, The.
O thou who tell'st me that all hope is over.
One Foot on Sea, and One on Shore.
Pitia a Damone.
Rosalind.
Song: "I have loved you for long years Ellen."
Song: "I saw her; she was lovely."
Song: "It is not for her even brow."
Till Tomorrow.
To My Fior-Di-Lisa.
To the End.
Touching "Never."
Two Parted.
Undine.
Versi.
Year Afterwards, A.
Young Men Aye Were Fickle Found Since
Summer Trees Were Leafy.
Zara. ("I dreamed")
Zara. ("Now the pain")
Zara. ("Pale sad face")
Zion Said.
Rukeyser. Anemone.

Drunken Girl.
Nevertheless the Moon.
Parallel Invention.
Song: Lying in Daylight.
Song: Remembering Movies.
Three Sides of a Coin.
Tunnel, The.
What I See.
St. John. Body of Desire, The.
Fan Sketched with Silver Egrets, A.
My Friend.
Sandburg. Explanations of Love.
Let Love Go On.
Love Is a Deep and a Dark and a Lonely.
Moon Rondeau.
Offering and Rebuff.
Schuyler. Await.
Blue towel, A.
Daylight.
Perhaps.
Photograph, A.
Sleep.
Steaming Ties.
Up.
Was It.
Watching You.
We Are Leaves.
Schwartz. Aria.
Sexton. Song for a Lady.
That Day.
Us.
Shapiro. Girls Fighting, Broadway.
Sidney. Second Song.
Simic. Breasts.
Elegy: "Note / as it gets darker."
Hurricane Season.
Smith, Patti. Gibralto.
Hymn: "We hadn't eaten in two days. we
were entirely intoxicated."
Penicillin.
Schinden.
Thermos.
Thread.
Snyder. After Work.
Sorrentino. Charm, The.
Stein. Lifting Belly.
Stevenson. As in the hostel by the bridge, I
sate.
Come, my beloved, hear from me.
Duddingstone.
Feast of Famine: Marquesan Manners, The.
From Wishing-Land.
I am like one that for long days had sate.
I dreamed of forest alleys fair.
I have a friend; I have a story.
I love to be warm by the red fireside.
I who all the winter through.
If I had wings, my lady, like a dove.
In the green and gallant Spring.
Know you the river near to Grez.
Let Love go, if go she will.
Lo! in thine honest eyes I read.
Love is the very heart of spring.
Love—what is love? A great and aching heart.
Men are Heaven's piers; they evermore.
Mine eyes were swift to know thee, and my
heart.
Music at the Villa Marina.
My love was warm; for that I crossed.
My wife and I, in one romantic cot.
Nay, but I fancy somehow, year by year.
O now, although the year be done.
Piper, The.
Rain is over and done, The.
Relic taken, what avails the shrine?, The.
Small is the trust when love is green.
Spring Song.
Swallows travel to and fro.
Though deep indifference should drowse.
To what shall I compare her.
You looked so tempting in the pew.
Suckling. Against Fruition ("Fie upon hearts
that burn with mutual fire!").
Careless Lover, The.
Desdain ("To what end serve the promises").
Expostulation, The.
Farewell to Love.

Love Turned to Hatred.
Lover's Clock, The.
Love's Representation.
Miracle, The.
My dearest rival, lest [or least] our love.
Perjury Excused.
Siege, The.
Song: "If you refuse me once and think
again."
Song: "No, no, fair heretic[k], it needs must
be."
To a Lady That Forbade to Love before
Company.
Upon A.M.
Upon My Lady Carlisle's Walking in Hampton
Court Garden.
Verses: "I confirm'd a woman can."
Swinburne. In the Orchard.
Interlude, An.
Laus Veneris.
Updike. Blessing, The.
Chloë's Poem.
Erotic Epigrams.
Nuda Natens.
Sleeping with You.
You Who Swim.
Van Duyn. Footnotes to "The Autobiography
of Bertrand Russell."
Leda.
Leda Reconsidered.
Sentimental Delusion, A.
3 A. M. in a War Year.
Wakoski. Follow That Stagecoach.
Inside Out.
Love Passes Beyond the Incredible Hawk of
Innocence.
Mechanic, The.
Pink Dress, The.
Preface.
Rescue Poem.
Sometimes Even My Knees Smile.
To an Autocrat.
Walker. I'm Really Very Fond.
Smell of Lebanon, The.
Whitman. As Adam Early in the Morning.
From Pent-up Aching Rivers.
Spontaneous Me.
When I Heard at the Close of the Day.
Whoever You Are Holding Me Now in Hand.
Wilbur. Apology.
Dead Still.
Late Aubade, A.
Loves of the Puppets.
Pangloss's Song: A Comic-Opera Lyric.
Someone Talking to Himself.
Williams, Charles Kenneth. Game, The.
Orchid, The.
Williams, Miller. August Evening Outside of
Nashville, An.
Before.
How to Stop Smoking.
Williams, William Carlos. Curfew.
Queen-Anne's-Lace.
St. Valentine.
Wright, James. Eleutheria.
Gesture by a Lady with an Assumed Name, A.
Lights in the Hallway, The.
On the Way to the Planetarium.
Sappho.
So She Said.
To the bridge of love.
Wyatt. Ah, my heart, ah, what aileth thee.
I have been a lover.
My love is like unto th'eternal fire.
With serving still.
Yau. Different Prince, A.
Noise of Life, The.
Yeats. Last Confession, A.
Ribh in Ecstasy.
Young. In Marin Again.
Zukofsky. Caelius, Lesbia new star, Lesbia a
light.
Catullus viii.
Drive, fast kisses.
He'll hie me, par *is* he? the God divide her.
Rum asks—see, fortune won't molest you.
Who lives *o* on Helicon hill.

See also **Sex.**

Error
Beatles. She Loves You.
Beckett. De pied ferme.
Catullus. Carmen 81: "Surely, Iuventius, one
of this throng in Rome."
Cowper. Four Ages, The.
Progress of Error, The.
Creeley. Eye, The.
Sight, A.
Water.
Donne. Doctors, The.
Herrick. Truth and Error.
Lowry. No road in existence strikes such
terror.
Report on Conditions.
Matthews. Wrong.
Ransom. Parting, without a Sequel.
Robinson. While we are drilled in error, we
are lost.
Rolfe. Political Prisoner 123456789.
Simic. Errata.
Zukofsky. Not many enchant you (put to it)
popular is he, Juventi.

Escalators
Dunn. As It Moves.

Escapes
Auden. Half Way.
Beatles. She's Leaving Home.
Browning, Robert. Flight of the Duchess, The.
Bukowski. Hangover and Sick Leave.
Carroll, Jim. Leaving N.Y.C.
Clark. Lyric, The: "Suffering / lament, sorrow
and wild."
Cooper. All These Dreams.
Roman Dream.
Cummings. Notice the convulsed orange inch
of moon.
You are tired, / (I think).
Dickey, James. Attempted Departure.
Dickey, William. Rainbow Grocery, The.
Dickinson. Escape is such a thankful Word.
I never hear the word "escape."
Dobyns. Favorite Iraqi Soldier.
Doolittle. Calliope.
Lift my head, help me up.
Dove. Pamela.
Three Days of Forest, a River, Free.
"Dylan." Billy.
Can You Please Crawl Out Your Window?
Drifter's Escape.
Mr. Tambourine Man.
Motorpsycho Nightmare.
Romance in Durango.
Eberhart. Grave Piece.
Edmunds. One for the Road.
Emerson. Builder of heaven, The.
Fisher. Running Changes, The.
Frost. Escapist—Never.
How Hard It Is to Keep from Being King
When It's in You and in the Situation.
Garrigue. Attempting to Persuade You to Go
for a Walk in the Public Gardens.
Griffiths. Shooting of Levellers, Burford,
1649.
Gunn. I spin like a solitary star, I swoon.
Hardy. Wish for Unconsciousness, A.
Hesketh. Meths Men, The.
Tunnel, The.
Widowhood.
Hewitt. Troubles, 1922, The.
Hughes, Ted. At the bottom of the Arctic sea,
they say.
Kipling. Ballad of Minepit Shaw, The.
Wilful-Missing.
Knott. Shorts / Excerpts ("Suddenly I
understood").
Koch. Brassiere Factory, The.
Kunitz. Artist, The.
Postcript.
Lawrence. Love as an Escape.
Levine. And the Trains Go On.
Walk with Tom Jefferson, A.
Lovelace. Calling Lucasta from Her
Retirement.
Lowry. Peter Gaunt, as Gynt then, climbs a

dune.
Some years ago he started to escape.
McGrath. Get Out of Town.
MacNeice. Cradle Song for Eleanor.
Flight of the Heart.
Spring Sunshine.
Woods.
Merton. Look in the night, look, look in the night.
Morrison. Celebration of the Lizard.
Crossroads, The.
Ensenada.
Moonlight Drive.
Sex For You.
Olson. All Havens Astern.
Ransom. Morning.
Rich. Mother-Right.
Prospect, The.
Rolfe. City of Anguish.
Rukeyser. Target Practice.
Schwartz. To a Fugitive.
Shelley. Fugitives, The.
Silverstein. Flying Festoon, The.
Ickle Me, Pickle Me, Tickle Me Too.
Where the Sidewalk Ends.
Simic. Suitcase Strapped with a Rope, A.
Smith, Patti. Doctor Love.
Smith, Stevie. Come On, Come Back.
Fugitive's Ride, The.
I Wish.
Who Shot Eugenie?
Snodgrass. Disguised as Cock Robin, W. D.
Escapes.
W. D. Creates a Device for Escaping.
Stevenson. Far over seas an island is.
O Lady fair and sweet.
Stuart. Leavetaking.
Tate. Light.
Warren. Interjection #3: I Know a Place
Where All Is Real.
Skiers.
Williams, Charles Kenneth. History.
Wright, James. In the Face of Hatred.
Prayer to Escape from the Market Place, A.
Small Blue Heron, The.
Snowstorms in the Midwest.
To a Fugitive.
Wyatt. Double, diverse, sullen, and strange.
Farewell, the reign of cruelty!
If I might have at mine own will.
Longer to muse.
Now all of change.
Now must I le[a]rn[e] to live [or lyve] at rest.
Sith I myself displease thee.
Tangled [or Tanglid] I was [or was I] in [or
yn] Love's snare.
To make an end of all this strife.

Eschatology. *see* **End of the World.**

Eskimos
Dobyns. After the War With the Eskimos.
Dunn. Loneliness.
"Dylan." Quinn the Eskimo.
Haines. Among the quiet people of the frost.
Kipling. Angutivaun Taina.
People of the Eastern Ice, they are melting
like the snow, The.
Koch. Geography.
Oliver. Esquimos Have No Word for "War,"
The.
Yau. Eskimo Tales.
Eskimo Villanelle.

Essex, England
Betjeman. Essex.
Davie. Essex.
Levertov. Map of the Western Part of the
County of Essex in England, A.

Esther, Book of (Bible)
Lindsay. Rhyme for All Zionists, A.

Estrangement
Atwood. I can't tell you my name.
Berg. Nothingness.
On the Steps.
Berryman. For you am I collared to quit my
dear.
Her & It.
I say *I laid siege—you enchanted me.*
Impossible to speak to her, and worse.

Is it possible, poor kids, you must not come
out?
Ménage à trois, like Tristan's,—difficult.
Our lives before hopelessly our mistake!—.
Our Sunday morning when dawn-priests were
applying.
Sunderings and luxations, *luxe,* and grief.
Bly. In Rainy September.
Browning, Robert. In a Year.
Rephan.
Worst of It, The.
Byron. Lines on Hearing That Lady Byron
Was Ill.
Remind Me Not, Remind Me Not.
So We'll Go No More a Roving.
To George, Earl Delawarr.
To Lesbia.
To the Same.
Catullus. Carmen 72: "Cancel, Catullus, the
expectancies of friendship."
Creeley. Place.
Dickey, James. Turning Away.
Dobyns. Community, The.
Letter Beginning with the First Line of Your
Letter.
Party, The.
Place between Us, The.
Separations.
Doolittle. In the Rain.
Let me be / a splinter in your side.
Dunbar. Parted.
Song, A: "Thou art the soul of a summer's
day."
Dunn. Coming Home, Garden State Parkway.
Romance, A.
"Dylan." I Don't Believe You (She Acts Like
We Never Have Met).
Idiot Wind.
Seeing the Real You at Last.
Silent Weekend.
Tears of Rage.
Walk Out in the Rain.
When the Night Comes Falling from the Sky.
You're a Big Girl Now.
Fisher. Epitaph: Lorine Niedecker.
Gallagher. Photograph of a Lighthouse
Through Fog.
Graves. Iago.
Moon's Last Quarter, The.
Semi-Detached.
This Holy Month.
Unposted Letter.
Wall, The.
Wand, The.
Winged Heart, The.
Woman Poet and Man Poet.
Hardy. Side by Side.
What Did It mean?
Hewitt. Neighbor's Funeral, A.
Hill. Distance is on edge.
Hoffman. Chosen, The.
Thought I Was Dying.
Trip, A.
When my wiser brother.
Hopkins. Beginning of the End, The.
Lover's Stars, The.
Voice from the World, A.
Jeffers. Birth-Dues.
Lowell. Man and Wife.
To Speak of Woe That Is in Marriage.
MacNeice. Bluebells.
Selva Oscura.
Merrill. Renewal, A.
Merton. I have sought for myself.
Miller. Distance Between Us.
Olson. Distances, The.
Plath. Conversation among the Ruins.
Ransom. Parting at Dawn.
Two in August.
Rich. After Dark.
Like This Together.
Mother-in-Law.
Rain on the West Side Highway.
St. John. Blue Waves.
Song without Forgiveness.
Winter Fires.

Sexton. Fury of Beautiful Bones, The.
Love Letter Written in a Burning Building.
Shakespeare. Sonnet 89: "Say that thou didst
forsake me for some fault."
Sonnet 120: "That you were once unkind
befriends me now."
Sonnet 148: "Lo! as a careful housewife runs
to catch."
Smith, Stevie. Adelaide Abner.
Broken Friendship, The.
La Gretchen de Nos Jours (I).
Rothebât.
Sea-Widow, The.
Stuart. People Asleep.
Updike. No More Access to Her Underpants.
Wilbur. Arrow in the Wall, An.
Williams, Charles Kenneth. Crawl.
Trash.
Twice More.
Williams, William Carlos. Postlude.
Wyatt. I must go walk[e] the woods so wild.
Yeats. Ephemera.
Memory of Youth, A.
O Do Not Love Too Long.
Young. Dance of the Infidels.
Dancing in the Street.
East Boston.
Zukofsky. Day, see no day—choke, qualm,
quick qualm—benevolence, merit are.

Eternity
Auden. Dream, A.
Sonnet II: "It matters not that we shall cease
to be."
Berryman. *Are we?* You murmur "not." What
of the night.
Betjeman. NW5 and N6.
Blake. Each Man is in His Spectres power.
Eternity ("He who binds [*or* bends] to himself
a joy").
Bogan. I Saw Eternity.
Brontë. I'm happiest when most away.
Lines: "I die; but when the grave shall press."
Was it with the fields of green.
Browning, Elizabeth Barrett. Sonnet: "I
thought once how Theocritus had sung."
Sonnet: "If thou must love me, let it be for
nought."
Browning, Robert. Love.
Rephan.
Bukowski. Our Curious Position.
Byron. If That High World.
When Coldness Wraps This Suffering Clay.
Carruth. Oaks and dark pines, remote, the
northern forest.
Point is (maybe) that the woman's face was
made, The.
Cowper. Living Water.
Simple Trust.
Cummings. Connotation of infinity, A.
I was considering how.
If i believe / in death be sure.
Noone and a star stand,am to am.
(One fine day) / let's take the train.
Out of the mountain of his soul comes.
Stand with your lover on the ending earth.
True lovers in each happening of their hearts.
Davie. I come in out of Space, and with a
rake.
Those plaguy; needling games of ours, where
stooks.
De la Mare. Moment, The.
Snowing.
Dickinson. Always begins.
As if the Sea should part.
Because I could not stop for Death.
Blunder is an estimate, The.
Eternity may imitate.
How firm Eternity must look.
I cannot tell how Eternity seems.
Is it a joyous expanse of Year.
It was a quiet way.
Only News I know, The.
Our journey had advanced.
Show me Eternity, and I will show you
Memory.
There is no first, or last, in Forever.

Time feels so vast that were it not.
Writing is brief and fleeting.
Dunbar. Forever.
Eberhart. Emily Dickinson.
Illusion of Eternity, The.
Once More, O Ye.
Emerson. Dear Ellen, many a golden year.
Eternal Watcher, who doth wake, The.
Roomy Eternity / Casts her schemes rarely.
Spiritual Laws.
Ferlinghetti. Cro-Magnons.
River Still To Be Found, A.
Fletcher. And at these words there rose
against the ark.
Garrigue. Circle, The.
Graves. Always.
Envoi: "There is no now for us but always."
Fast Bound Together.
For Ever.
Half-Finished Letter, The.
Hazel Grove, The.
Impossible Day, The.
New Eternity, The.
Song: Yesterday Only.
Tomorrow's Envy of Today.
Hall. Shudder [, The].
Hartnett. I have been stone, dust of space, sea
and sphere.
Herrick. Eternity [or Eternitie].
Love What It Is.
No Time in Eternity.
Penitence.
Sabbaths.
Sin and Strife.
To His Honoured Kinsman, Sir Richard Stone.
Wages.
White Island: or Place of the Blest, The.
Hewitt. Chinese Fluteplayer.
Delos.
Dungannon Cattle Market.
Hill. Not as we are but as we must appear.
Housman. Bring, in this timeless grave to
throw.
If truth in hearts that perish.
Immortal Part, The.
Hughes, Ted. Pibroch.
Jarrell. Venetian Blind, The.
Jeffers. It flows out of mystery into mystery:
there is no beginning—.
Jong. People Who Live.
Kunitz. Change.
Lawrence. Fatality.
Non-Existence.
Sickness.
Lindsay. In Memory of a Child.
Lowry. Ship is Turning Homeward, The.
We Sit Unhackled Drunk and Mad to Edit.
McAuley. Photographer's Model, The.
MacLeish. Eternity, An.
Eve's First Prophecy.
Pole Star.
Mahon. Tithonus.
Melville. Montaigne and His Kitten.
Morgan. Touch, The.
Nemerov. Somewhere.
Olson. Day Song.
Drum World, The.
For My Friend.
Later Note on Letter #15, A.
Raine. Banked winter cloud.
Hyacinth, The.
If you have ceased.
Not that light is holy, but that the holy is the
light—.
Rock.
Rich. 7/16/68: i.
Robinson. Sage, The.
Rossetti. As the Doves to Their Windows.
Bed of Forget-Me-Nots, A.
Beloved, yeild thy time to God, for He / Will
make eternity thy recompense.
Birchington Churchyard.
Earth Shall Tremble at the Look of Him, The.
End of Time, The.
For Each.
From the Antique.
Goodbye in fear, goodbye in sorrow.

Let Patience Have Her Perfect Work.
Life's Parallels, A.
New creatures; the Creator still the Same.
Parting after parting, / Sore loss and gnawing
pain.
Patience of Hope.
Short is time, and only time is bleak.
There Remaineth Therefore a Rest to the
People of God.
Time lengthening, in the lengthening seemeth
long.
Time passeth away with its pleasure and pain.
Time seems not short: / If so I call to mind.
Trinity Sunday.
Unforgotten.
Sandburg. Sea-Wash.
Schuyler. Daylight.
Shakespeare. Sonnet 6: "Then let not winter's
ragged hand deface."
Sonnet 109: "O [or Oh], never say that I was
false of heart."
Smart. On the Eternity of the Supreme Being.
Smith, Stevie. Intimation of Immortality.
Thomas. All All and All the Dry Worlds
Lever.
Tomlinson. Eight Observations on the Nature
of Eternity.
Wordsworth. Lines Written While Sailing in a
Boat at Evening.
Wright, Charles. Composition in Grey and
Pink.
To Giacomo Leopardi in the Sky.
Yeats. Ephemera.
Needle's Eye, A.
Tom at Cruachan.
Whence Had They Come?
Young. H₂O.
See also **Immortality.**

Ethiopia
Crashaw. Acts 8; On the Baptized Æthiopian.
Dunbar. Ode to Ethiopia.

Etiquette
Beckett. À peine à bien mené.
Betjeman. How to Get On in Society.
Bishop. Manners.
Browning, Robert. Respectability.
Byron. To Marion.
"Carroll, Lewis." Canto II: Hys Fyve Rules.
Cohen. Etiquette.
Herrick. Good Manners at Meat.
Panegyric to Sir Lewis Pemberton, A.
To a Gentlewoman on Just Dealing.
Upon Showbread [or Shewbread]: Epigram.
Merton. Apologies.
"Reed." Standing on Ceremony.
Sandburg. We Must Be Polite.
Silverstein. Rudy Flesh.
With His Mouth Full of Food.
Simic. Gallows Etiquette.
Smart. Elegance.
Mutual Subjection.
Sorrentino. Tilt.
Stevenson. Good Boy, A.
Hail! Childish slaves of social rules.
Whole Duty of Children.

Eton College
Gray. Ode on a Distant Prospect of Eton
College.

Etruscan Civilization
Lawrence. Cypresses.
Tomlinson. Tarquinia.
Wilbur. To the Etruscan Poets.

Eucharist
Berryman. Our Sunday morning when dawn-
priests were applying.
Hartley. This Piece of Eucharist.
Herbert. Agony [or Agonie], The.
Banquet, The.
H[oly] Communion, The.
Holy Communion, The.
Love.
Superliminare.
Herrick. Eucharist, The.
Hill. At dawn the Mass.
Hopkins. Bugler's First Communion, The.
Liddy. Churros.

Merton. Communion, The.
Holy Sacrament of the Altar, The.
Southwell. Of the Blessed Sacrament of the
Altar [or Aulter].
Saint Thomas of Aquines Hymne Read on
Corpus Christy Daye.
Thomas. This Bread I Break.
See also **Last Supper.**

Euclid
"Carroll, Lewis." To My Pupil.
Emerson. Loose the knots of the heart; never
think on thy fate.
Lovelace. Snail [or Snayl], The.
Millay. Euclid alone has looked on Beauty
bare.

Europa
Walcott. Europa.

Europe
Beckett. Zone.
Blake. Europe; A Prophecy.
Boyle. Confession to Eugene Jolas, A.
Browning, Elizabeth Barrett. North and the
South, The.
Cummings. Hanged / if n / y in a real hot
spell.
Dove. Eastern European Eclogues.
Eberhart. Yonder.
Emerson. At Sea, September 1833.
Ginsberg. Europe! Europe!
Hemingway. Some day when you are picked
up.
Hewitt. Brown's Bay, Islandmagee, Spring
1917.
Glendun.
Second Front: Double Summertime, July 1943.
Hill. Lowlands of Holland, The.
Martyrdom of Saint Sebastian.
Of Commerce and Society: Variations on a
Theme.
Jeffers. Bowl of Blood, The.
Lowell. Beyond the Alps.
MacLeish. Cinema of a Man.
Memory Green.
Oil Painting of the Artist as the Artist.
Meredith. Mother who gave birth to Jeanne,
The.
Poured streams of Europe's veins the flood.
To Lord Palmerston.
Wassail for the New Year, A.
Merton. Night Train, The.
Nash. My Trip Daorba.
Nemerov. Europe.
Returning to Europe.
Olson. To Gerhardt, There, among Europe's
Things of Which He Has Written Us in His
"Brief an Creely und Olson."
Plath. Stopped Dead.
Pope. Balance of Europe, The.
Rossetti. Massacre of Perugia, The.
Simic. East European Cooking.
Sorrentino. Old Tale.
Tomlinson. Mediterranean, The.
Waldman. Going In.
Whitman. Europe, the 72d and 73d Year of
These States.
Wordsworth. Desultory Stanzas, upon
Receiving the Preceding Sheets from the
Press.
Memorials of a Tour of the Continent; 1820.

Eurydice
Atwood. Eurydice.
Browning, Robert. Eurydice to Orpheus.
Dobyns. Orpheus.
Doolittle. Eurydice.
Graves. Eurydice.
Hill. Orpheus and Eurydice.
Jarrell. Che Farò Senza Euridice.
Joseph. Eurydice to Orpheus.
Lovelace. Orpheus to Beasts.
Lowry. You cannot, must not, Orpheus, look
back, my soul.
Merton. Eurydice.

Euthanasia
Jeffers. Hurt Hawks.
Tate. Euthanasia.
Williams, Charles Kenneth. When.

Evangelism and Evangelists
Cummings. Skinny voice / of the leatherfaced, The.
This evangelist / buttons with his big gollywog voice.
Davie. Evangelist, The.
Hayden. Witch Doctor.
Hewitt. Evangelist.
Rich. Revivalist in Boston, A.
Robinson. Evangelist's Wife, An.
Rossetti. St. Bartholomew.
Vigil of St. Bartholomew.
Sandburg. To a Contemporary Bunkshooter.

Eve
Berryman. Gislebertus' Eve.
Carruth. I Tell You For Several Years of My Madness I Heard the Voice of Lilith Singing in the Trees of Chicago.
Cooper. Eve.
Eberhart. Throwing the Apple.
Frost. Never Again Would Birds' Song Be the Same.
Graves. History of the Fall.
Hughes, Ted. Theology.
Lawrence. Eve.
MacLeish. Serpent's Cradle Song, The.
What Eve Said.
Meinke. When Eve was cloned from Adam's rib, and stood.
Milton. As when of old some orator renowed.
Eve Penitent.
In bower and field he sought, where any tuft.
Temptation of Eve, The.
Rossetti. Afterthought, An.
Eve.
Smith, Patti. Seventh Heaven.
Smith, Stevie. Dream of Comparison, A.
How Cruel Is the Story of Eve.
Wilbur. She.
Yeats. Adam's Curse.

Evening
Auden. Autumn Evening.
Berry. Evening comes / when we finish work and go, An.
Bishop. Going to the Bakery.
Blake. To the Evening Star.
Bly. Surprised by Evening.
Bukowski. I Kneel.
Imbecile Night.
Burns. Lea-Rig, The.
Carruth. Tabula Rasa.
Clare. Evening.
Evening.
Winter Evening.
Coleridge. Pensive at eve on the hard world I mus'd [or mused].
Cowper. Just when our drawing-rooms begin to blaze.
Cummings. At the ferocious phenomenon of 5 o'clock i find myself gently decompos.
Fragrant sag of fruit distinctly grouped, A.
Sometime,perhaps in Paris we will.
Windows go orange in the slowly.
De la Mare. Evening.
Evening.
Myself.
Spark, The.
Tailor, The.
Thomas Hardy.
Dickinson. As willing lid o'er weary eye.
Crickets sang, The.
It's evening and the orchestra of winds.
Lightly stepped a yellow star.
Doolittle. Evening.
Dove. Reading Hölderlin on the Patio with the Aid of a Dictionary.
Eberhart. Evening Bird Song.
Memory.
Eliot. His soul stretched tight across the skies.
Winter evening settles down, The.
Fisher. In the evening the smoke blows far away.
Fletcher. Grey Symphony.
Invocation to Evening.
On the Banks of the Sumida.
Ford. First owl of the evening.

Frost. Stopping by Woods on a Snowy Evening.
Haines. Green smoke and white ash.
Lake in the Sky, The.
Hartley. Go Lightly.
Robin Hood Cove—Georgetown, Maine.
Summer Evening.
West cheek to rose.
Hemingway. Night comes with soft and drowsy plumes.
Stevenson.
Hesketh. And Fall.
Hoffman. At Evening.
Evening.
Hughes, Langston. Wonder.
Hughes, Ted. Full Moon and Little Frieda.
Jarrell. Evening.
Jeffers. Autumn Evening.
Johnson. Evening Ode, An.
Kinnell. Another Night in the Ruins.
Larkin. Coming.
Going.
Longfellow. Fire of Drift-Wood, The.
Lovelace. Another ("As I beheld a winters evening air").
Lowry. Boatmen swing their lanterns on the Caribbean, The.
Duckturne.
Nocturne: "This evening Venus signs alone."
Meinke. Talk of the Paintings.
Merton. Evening.
Song, A: "When it was day, we heard the panes of windows."
Morgan. As the sun dims we begin to think.
Morrison. Electric Storm.
Roethke. In Evening Air.
Rolfe. Pastoral: "Lonely evening crouches, darkens as the hour, The."
Sandburg. Evening Questions.
Evening Sea Wind.
Evening Waterfall.
How Yesterday Looked.
Moon Path.
Sarton. Evening Music.
Light Left On, A.
Schuyler. Poem: "How about an oak leaf."
Scott. Evening.
Shelley. Evening: To Harriet.
Simic. Evening.
Smart. Sweets of Evening, The.
Smith, Charlotte. Evening.
Snyder. Work to Do Toward Town.
Stevens. Delightful Evening.
Evening without Angels.
Stevenson. Evensong.
Night and Day.
Williams, William Carlos. Steering my little boat towards a misty islet.
Wordsworth. Composed upon an Evening of Extraordinary Splendour and Beauty.
Crescent-Moon, the Star of Love, The.
Wright, James. Brush Fire.
De Profundis.
See also **Twilight.**

Evening Star
Blake. To the Evening Star.
Bogan. Evening-Star.
Campion. Goe, happy man, like th' Evening Starre.
Carruth. Anima.
Tabula Rasa.
Coleridge. To the Evening Star.
Cummings. Thou / firsting a hugeness of twi / -light.
Jeffers. Evening Ebb.
Millay. Now that the west is washed of clouds and clear.
Smith, Charlotte. To Vesper.
Stevens. Homunculus et la Belle Étoile.
Martial Cadenza.
See also **Venus (planet).**

Evers, Medgar
"Dylan." Only a Pawn in Their Game.

Evictions
Griffiths. Giving Them What For.
Waldman. Cabin.
Wordsworth. Composed When a Probability

Existed of Our Being Obliged to Quit Rydal Mount as a Residence.

Evil
Auden. Danse Macabre.
Berryman. Amos.
Nothing there? nothing up the sky alive.
Opus Dei.
Blake. Marriage of Heaven and Hell, The.
Bogan. At a Party.
Bukowski. In a Neighborhood of Murder.
Byron. Sketch, A.
Thoughts for a Speech of Lucifer, in the Tragedy of "Cain."
To Dives (William Beckford). A Fragment.
Carruth. Sonnet: Sin.
Chaucer. Pardoner's Tale, The.
Cohen. You Who Question Souls.
Coleridge. Christabel.
Cowper. Cock-Fighters Garland.
Davie. Eight Years After.
Ironist, The.
Donne. In churches, when the infirmity [or the'infirmitie].
Duncan. Albigenses, The.
Fire, The.
Eberhart. Evil.
Fantasy of a Small Idea.
Formative Mastership.
Ineffable, The.
Laocoön.
Meditation Two.
Emerson. I will not live out of me.
O Boston city lecture-hearing.
There is no evil but can speak.
Fletcher. Hard Sayings.
New Beatitudes, The.
Frost. Bearer of Evil Tidings, The.
Quandary.
Gardner. Triolet: "Bad die old, The."
Garrigue. Only the Irresistible Abides.
Graves. Man of Evil.
Succubus, The.
True Evil.
Gray. Tophet.
Hayden. As My Blood Was Drawn.
Theory of Evil.
Herrick. Evill.
His Confession.
Neutrality Loathsome.
Spell, The.
Hesketh. Lyric Evening.
Hewitt. Man Fish and Bird.
On Hearing a Traveller's Tale of the Alps.
Rhyme for Blake, A.
Hoffman. Crop-Dusting.
Housman. Delight it is in youth and May.
Epitaph, An: "Stay, if you list, O passer by the way."
Jarrell. Blind Sheep, The.
Jeffers. Orca.
Kunitz. Between the Acts.
Next to Last Things.
To the Reader.
Lawrence. Dark Satanic Mills.
Departure.
Doors.
Evil Is Homeless.
Evil World-Soul, The.
First Song of Huitzilopochtli.
Immorality.
Men Are Not Bad.
Murder.
Murderous Weapons.
Our Moral Age.
Root of Our Evil, The.
Second Song of Huitzilopochtli.
Song of the Grey Dog, The.
Strife.
Third Song of Huitzilopochtli.
What Then Is Evil?
Lindsay. Above the Battle's Front.
Simon Legree—A Negro Sermon.
Lowry. Alas, there is no still path in my soul.
Conversations With Goethe.
Curse, A.
I sing the joy of poverty, not such.
This business of evil / Like brokers the

weevil.
  Those Coke to Newcastle Blues.
McAuley. Aor Against the Warmonger.
"MacDiarmid." Think not that I forget a
  single pang.
McGrath. Death for the Dark Stranger.
MacLeish. Black Humor.
MacNeice. Canto XIX: "All out!" the voices
  cry in the Park, "All out!"
Matthews. Bad.
Meredith. Black Richard.
  We see the farther in the far.
Nemerov. August, 1945.
Olson. Evil.
Oppen. Serpent, Ouroboros / Whose tail is in
  his mouth: he is the root.
Patchen. Where Every Prospect.
Plath. Lesson in Vengeance, A.
Psalms. Psalm 14: "Fool hath said in his
  heart, The.."
Psalm 50: "Mighty God, even the Lord, hath
  spoken, The."
Psalm 53: "Fool hath said in his heart,
  The. . . ."
Rossetti. True Story, A.
  Who shall my wandering thoughts steady &
  fix.
Sandburg. Mazuma, the jack, the shekels, the
  kale, The.
Sarton. Intruder, An.
Sexton. After Auschwitz.
  Dead Heart, The.
  Evil Eye, The.
  Evil Seekers, The.
  Is It True?
Smith, Stevie. Angel Boley.
  To the Tune of the Coventry Carol.
Snodgrass. Mother, The.
Spender. Happy are those who have never
  tasted evil.
Walcott. Camps hold [or held] their
  distance— [of] brown chestnuts and grey
  smoke, The.
  God Rest Ye Merry, Gentlemen.
Whitman. I Sit and Look Out.
  Roaming in Thought.
Williams, Charles Kenneth. Bishop Tutu's
  Visit to the White House: 1984.
  How Humble We Were before This.
Williams, Miller. Why God Permits Evil: For
  Answers to This Question of Interest to
  Many Write Bible Answers Dept. E-7.
Williams, William Carlos. Mirrors, The.
Wyatt. Nature that gave the bee so feat a
  grace.

Evolution
Auden. Progress?
  We've covered enough ground since that
  awkward day.
Cooper. Wronke, Spring 1917.
Cullen. For an Evolutionist and His Opponent.
Emerson. Motto to "Nature" ("Subtle chain of
  countless rings, A").
  Three Dimensions, The.
Frost. Accidentally on Purpose.
Ginsberg. Falling Asleep in America.
Graves. Hearth, The.
Gunn. First Man, The.
Hewitt. Consequences.
Lawrence. Self-Protection.
Morrison. Flowering, The.
Nathan. Evolution.
Nemerov. Tale.
Pack. Grandeur.
Paley. Veins that stand on the back of my
  sunburned hand, The.
Sandburg. Among the shapes and shadow-
  shapes.
  Man the Moon Shooter.
  Since death is there in the light of the sun, in
  the song of the.
  These wheels within wheels.
  Tylor believed it important; he put it down; he
  asks us to read it, to look.
  Wilderness.
Smith, Stevie. Religious Man, A.
Updike. Naked Ape, The.

Wilbur. Lamarck Elaborated.
See also Darwin, Charles; Extinction; Genetics
  and Geneticists.

Excavations
Hill. Solomon's Mines.
MacNeice. Dowser, The.
  Legend of the Dead Soldier, The.
Tomlinson. Near Corinium.

Excrement
Auden. Geography of the House, The.
Ciardi. Suburban.
Updike. Beautiful Bowel Movement, The.

Executions and Executioners
Atwood. Newsreel: Man and Firing Squad.
Auden. Colonel to be shot at dawn, The.
Browning, Robert. Martin Relph.
  Muckle-Mouth Meg.
Bukowski. Big Bastard with a Sword.
Burns. Hughie Graham.
Catullus. Carmen 108: "If, by general consent,
  it should be decided."
Clark. "Himself let him unknown contain."
Cullen. Not Sacco and Vanzetti.
Dickinson. Upon the gallows hung a wretch.
Fisher. Barnardine's Reply.
Gardner. Ballade: "You who outlive us, you,
  our mortal brothers."
Gunn. No Speech from the Scaffold.
Hall. Sums.
Hardy. Stranger's Song, The.
Heaney. Strange Fruit.
Housman. Carpenter's Son, The.
  Eight O'Clock.
  On moonlit heath and lonesome bank.
Hughes, Ted. Executioner, The.
Kipling. Ballad of the King's Mercy, The.
  Danny Deever.
Lowell. Death of Anne Boleyn.
  Saint-Just 1767–93.
  Sir Thomas More.
MacLeish. Galán.
Marvell. King Charles on [or upon] the
  Scaffold.
Melville. Billy in the Darbies.
Meredith. Josepha.
Milton. Philosopher on His Way to His Death
  Suddenly Sent This Message to a Certain
  King Who Had Unawares Condemned Him,
  Unrecognized and Innocent, When He Was
  Seized by Chance Among Criminals, A.
Patchen. Executions in Moscow, The.
  Joe Hill Listens to the Praying.
Prince. Strafford.
Sandburg. Hangman at Home, The.
Simic. Toy Factory.
Smith, Stevie. Death Sentence, The.
  Humane Materialist at the Burning of a
  Heretic, A.
  One of Many.
Snodgrass. Manet: "The Execution of the
  Emperor Maximilian."
Swift. Clever Tom Clinch Going to Be
  Hanged.
Swinburne. Epitaph in Form of a Ballad, The.
Wyatt. In mourning wise since daily I
  increase.
Zukofsky. See, Comini, popular arbitrer turned
  on uncanny senescence.
See also Capital Punishment; Hanging.

Exercise
Gunn. Exercise, The.
Hardy. Pedestrian, The.
Koertge. Urban Renewal.
Lowry. Fisherman's Return.
Meinke. ABC of Aerobics, The.
Meredith. Beetle soars, the beetle spins, The.
Walker. Every Morning.

Exhilaration
Ammons. Blue Skies.
Beatles. It's All Too Much.
Browning, Robert. Prologue: "O the old wall
  here! How I could pass."
Dickinson. Exhilaration is the Breeze.
  Exhiliration—is within.
  How small the furniture of bliss!
  Impossibility, like Wine.

No Rose, yet felt myself a'bloom.
  'Tis Anguish grander than Delight.
  Transport's mighty price is.
  Why the full heart is speechless.
  Withdrawal of the Fuel of Rapture, The.
Dobyns. Syracuse Nights.
Eberhart. Hardening into Print.
  Ichetucknee.
Hemingway. Opening Game, The.
Hewitt. Great Event, A.
Levertov. City Psalm.
  Letter to William Kinter of Muhlenberg, A.
  Sparks.
Lorde. NOW.
Nash. No Doctors Today, Thank You.
Nemerov. First Point of Aries, The.
  Frozen City, The.
Rich. Night in the Kitchen.
Shelley. O that a chariot of cloud were mine!
Stuart. His Granddaughter Arrives.
Young. Get that feeling sometimes.
  I violinize peace.

Exile
Auden. Deemed this an outpost, I.
  Exiles, The.
Betjeman. Sir John Piers.
Brontë. Lines by Claudia.
  Loud without the wind roaring.
  Visionary, The.
Browning, Elizabeth Barrett. Exile's Return,
  The.
Burns. Birth-Day Ode. December 31st 1787,
  A.
  Frae the friends and Land I love.
  My Harry was a gallant gay.
Byron. Prophecy of Dante, The.
Campion. As by the streames of Babilon.
Carruth. Ovid, Old Buddy, I Would Discourse
  with You a While.
  Your dream: / His name was Hannibal, i.e., by
  Baal's.
Cohen. For E. J. P.
Cowper. Soul That Loves God Finds Him
  Every Where, The.
  To Babylon's proud waters brought.
Crane. Purgatorio.
Crashaw. On the proud banks of great
  Euphrates' flood.
Davie. Letter to Curtis Bradford, A.
De la Mare. Exile.
  Exile, The.
Doolittle. No more, O my spirit.
Emerson. Exile, The.
  I am an exile from my home; heavily.
Gunn. First Meeting with a Possible Mother-
  in-Law.
  Right Possessor, The.
Hacker. Exiles.
Hall. Exile.
Herbert. see also To the Lady Elizabeth
  Queen of Bohemia.
Hewitt. Boat-Builder's Caulking Irons, The.
  Exile.
  1957–1972.
Hoffman. Last Arrival, The.
  When my wiser brother.
Hugo. Clearances, The.
Joseph. Man in a Bar.
Kipling. Broken Men, The.
  St. Helena Lullaby, A.
Liddy. After Hal'amová.
  For all who trod / Golden North American
  streets.
  Republic 1939, The.
Lieberman. Tartine's Banishment.
Lovelace. Another ("The centaur, siren I
  forgo").
Lowry. Exile is the luckiest of men, The.
McAuley. Actor: Decline and Death, The.
  Prologue: "Not for me, the crusader cross."
MacLeish. Eve's Exile.
MacNeice. Eclogue from Iceland.
  Ut Quid Iubes, Pusiole.
Mahon. Ovid in Tomis.
Meredith. Song: "Forever."
Merton. Pillars.
Millay. Exiled.

Morgan. Exiles, The.
Morrison. Start Again.
Nathan. Pumpernickel.
Nemerov. Presidential Address to a Party of
  Exiles.
  To the Babylonians.
Oppen. Of Hours.
Plath. Doom of Exiles.
Pope. Epitaph on Dr. Francis Atterbury,
  Bishop of Rochester, Who Died in Exile at
  Paris, 1732; a Dialogue.
Prince. Drypoints of the Hasidim.
  His old fame is dumb.
Psalms. Psalm 137: "By the rivers of
  Babylon.."
Ralegh. Farewell to the Court.
Rich. Book, The.
  By No Means Native.
Robinson. Aaron Stark.
  Island, An.
Rukeyser. Another Day. Paul in the Mountains
  of Fantasy. Paul Tells His Adventure.
  Fourth Elegy. The Refugees.
  Judith.
  Mediterranean.
  Song: "World is full of loss; bring, wind, my
  love, The."
Shapiro. Exile.
  Synagogue, The.
  Travelogue for Exiles.
Smart. Pensive we sat the silent hours.
Smith, Charlotte. Female Exile. Written at
  Brighthelmstone in November 1792, The.
  Lines Composed in Passing through a Forest
  in Germany.
Southwell. Christe's Retorne out of Egipt.
Spender. Exiles, The.
Tomlinson. Of Lady Grange.
Walcott. Banyan Tree, Old Year's Night, The.
  Exile.
  Hotel Normandie Pool, The.
  Midsummer sea, the hot pitch road, this grass,
  these shacks that made me, The.
  North and South.
  Our houses are one step from the gutter.
  Plastic curtains.
  Preparing for Exile.
  Return to D'Ennery; Rain.
Walker. Be Nobody's Darling.
Whittier. Exile's Departure, The.
Wyatt. I must go walk[e] the woods so wild.
Yau. Pleasures of Exile, The.

Existentialism and Existentialists
Beckett. Flux cause.
Dickey, William. Therefore.
Roethke. Duet.
Rossetti. Ah welladay and wherefore am I
  here?
Sandburg. Cumulatives.
  Man in the street is fed, The.
  People is a myth, an abstraction, The.
  Somebody has to make the tubs and pails.
Spender. Solipsist.
Tomlinson. Juliet's Garden.
Williams, Charles Kenneth. Gas Station, The.
Wright, James. As I Step over a Puddle at the
  End of Winter, I Think of an Ancient
  Chinese Governor.

Exodus
Dunbar. Ante-Bellum Sermon, An.
Meinke. Exodus with Children.
Nemerov. Moses.
Oppen. Exodus.
Psalms. Psalm 78: "Give ear, O my people, to
  my law."
  Psalm 105: "O give thanks unto the Lord.."
  Psalm 106: "Praise ye the Lord. O give
  thanks.."
  Psalm 114: "When Israel went out of Egypt."
Tomlinson. Flight, The.

Experience
Angelou. Wonder.
Atwood. Yes at first you / go down smooth
  as.
Auden. Inn Song.
Beatles. Baby You're a Rich Man.

Dear Prudence.
  Two of Us.
Berrigan. Ann Arbor Song.
  Around the Fire.
  Last Poem.
  Wrong Train.
Brontë. Why do I hate that lone green dell?
Browning, Elizabeth Barrett. Fourfold Aspect,
  The.
  Perplexed Music.
Bukowski. Friendly Advice to a Lot of Young
  Men.
  I've been going to the track for years.
Carroll, Jim. I drank cough syrup in alcoves.
Ceravolo. May.
  Passivation.
  Route.
Chaucer. Wife of Bath's Prologue, The.
Clough. Currente Calamo.
Coleridge. Christabel.
Cooper. Knowledge That Comes through
  Experience, The.
Cowper. Upon a Venerable Rival.
Creeley. Lover, The.
  That day / in an oak tree—.
  Wisdom.
Cummings. All ignorance toboggans into
  know.
  But if a living dance upon dead minds.
  Conceive a man,should he have anything.
  Here's to opening and upward,to leaf and to
  sap.
  If everything happens that can't be done.
  May my heart always be open to little.
  Of Ever-Ever Land i speak.
  One's not half two. It's two are halves of
  one.
  Since feeling is first.
  Sonnet entitled how to run the world).
  This mind made war.
  Voices to voices, lip to lip.
  What a proud dreamhorse
  pulling(smoothloomingly)through.
Davie. Advise me, draftsman of the drifting
  sands.
  Schubert from water, from birdsong's gamut
  Mozart.
Dickinson. Experience is the Angled Road.
  Far from Love the Heavenly Father.
  I stepped from Plank to Plank.
Dunn. Tenderness.
"Dylan." Desolation Row.
  Jim Jim / where is our party?
  My Life in a Stolen Moment.
  Shelter from the Storm.
  Stuck Inside of Mobile with the Memphis
  Blues Again.
  Town I was born in holds no memories, The.
Eberhart. Experience Evoked.
  Rumination.
Emerson. Experience.
Fenton. Pitt-Rivers Museum, Oxford, The.
Ferlinghetti. Autobiography.
Ford. He Cut His Finger on Eternity.
  Let us make of day a delirium.
Gardner. Cadenza.
  Canzonetta.
  Collage of Echoes.
  Minotaur, The.
  Panic Vine, The.
  That Was Then.
  Whole World's in a Terrible Chassis, The.
Ginsberg. Howl.
Graves. Those Who Came Short.
Hacker. Hang-Glider's Daughter, The.
Hardy. Two Houses, The.
Hartley. Gulls at Gloucester.
  Sea Engraving—Style of 1880.
Hemingway. Poem, 1928.
  Travel Poem.
Hesketh. Love without Frontiers.
Hewitt. Domestic Help.
  Feathers on Turf.
Hill. God's Little Mountain.
Holmes. Vignette.
Jeffers. To a Young Artist.
Kipling. Bonfires, The.

Craftsman, The.
  Men That Fought at Minden, The.
  Nurses, The.
  Sestina of the Tramp-Royal.
Tomlinson.
  When 'Omer Smote 'Is Bloomin' Lyre.
Knott. Poem (How I Lost My Pen-Name).
Lawrence. Courage.
  Wealth.
  When the Ripe Fruit Falls.
Levine. One for the Rose.
  Salts and Oils.
  28.
Lewis. After Dunkirk.
  I within me holding.
  Prologue: The Grinder.
  Sacco Writes to His Son.
  Wood Song.
Liddy. Letter to Eamonn Wall, A.
MacLeish. L'An Trentiesme de Mon Eage.
Merton. All the Way Down.
  Marks and numbers / Cut in skin.
Nash. Experience to Let.
Nemerov. Of Experience.
Neruda. Bell-Ringer, The.
Oppen. Little Hole, The.
Owen. All Sounds Have Been As Music.
  Sonnet Autumnal.
Piercy. Married Walk in a Hot Place, A.
  Perpetual Migration, The.
Pope. Epistle I, to Sir Richard Temple, Lord
  Cobham.
Raine. Child in a little boat.
  High Summer.
  I breathe the air you have breathed.
Ransom. Blue Girls.
"Reed." Some Kinda Love.
Robinson. Isaac and Archibald.
  Twilight Song.
Rossetti. Experience bows a sweet contented
  face.
  If the moon came from heaven, / Talking all
  the way.
Sandburg. Almanac.
  Anywhere and Everywhere People.
  Australian mounted infantryman now teaches,
  The.
  Explanations of Love.
  Localities.
  Love Is a Deep and a Dark and a Lonely.
  Methusaleh Saw Many Repeaters.
  Sketch of a Poet.
  We Have Gone Through Great Rooms
  Together.
  We live only once.
  Worms and the Wind.
Schwartz. If nature is life, nature is death.
Silverstein. Alice.
  Stone Telling.
Smith, Patti. Jet Flakes.
  Prayer.
  Wing.
Stafford. Looking across the River.
Stevens. Poem Written at Morning.
Stevenson. I have a hoard of treasure in my
  breast.
  What man may learn, what man may do.
Stuart. Casting.
Van Duyn. Insight.
  New Land.
  Paratrooper.
  To My Godson, on His Christening.
Waldman. Dialogue Between the Self & the
  Soul.
Warren. I am the past time, am old, but.
Whitman. Beautiful Women.
  Myself and Mine.
  Song of Joys, A.
  Stronger Lessons.
Williams, Charles Kenneth. This is what, / at
  last, it is.
  Undead, The.
Williams, Miller. After the Revolution for
  Jesus a Secular Man Prepares His Final
  Remarks.
  Associate Professor Delivers an Exhortation to
  His Failing Students, The.

Fly Me to the Moon.
For Reuben, at Twelve Months.
How Does a Madsong Know That's What It Is?
In Nashville, Standing in the Wooden Circle Sawed Out from the Old Ryman Stage, the Picker has a vision.
Ruby Tells All.
Thinking Friday Night with a Gothic Storm Going About Final Causes and Logos and Mitzi Mayfair.
Williams, William Carlos. Old Man and the Child, The.
Wright, James. Pretty Redhead, The.
Young. For Poets.
Leadbelly Song, The.
Poem for Omar Khayyam (1050?-1123? A.D.).
Poetry.
Prestidigitator 1, The.
W. H. Auden & Mantan Moreland.

Exploring and Explorers
Atwood. Explorers, The.
Further Arrivals.
Reincarnation of Captain Cook, The.
Berry. July, 1773.
Bukowski. Best Way to Get Famous Is to Run Away, The.
Carruth. Afterword: What the Poet Had Written.
Your dream: / His name was Hendryk Hudson. And oh, the glory!
Clough. As one who shoots an arrow overhead.
How in all wonder Columbus got over.
Davie. Homage to John L. Stephens.
Killala.
Lasalle.
Second Epistle.
Donne. Cales and Guiana.
Calm[e], The.
Storm[e], The.
To Mr. R. W. ("If, as mine is, thy life a slumber be").
Eberhart. Cage, The.
Ford. Fortune's Wheel. In the.
Hardy. Rover Come Home, The.
Hoffman. Exploration.
Folk Tale.
Hugo. Troubadour Removed, A.
Kipling. Explorer, The.
I am the Most Wise Baviaan, saying in most wise tones.
Lost Legion, The.
Merchantmen, The.
Song of Travel, A.
Voortrekker, The.
With Drake in the Tropics.
Levertov. Into the Interior.
Levine. Across the world / in the high mountains of the West.
New Day, A.
7 Years from Somewhere.
McGrath. Poem—Unfinished Poem.
MacLeish. Voyage West.
Marvell. Bermudas.
Merton. Christopher Columbus.
Drake in the Southern Sea.
Kane Relief Expedition.
Place Names.
Milton. New Worlds.
Nash. Look What You Did, Christopher!
Oliver. Magellan.
Rich. Explorers, The.
Unsounded.
Rolfe. Cheliuskin.
Faces No Longer White.
Sandburg. Lief the Lucky.
Shapiro. Waitress.
Silverstein. Edge of the World, The.
Simic. Explorers.
Stuart. Snorkeling in the Caribbean.
Walcott. Liberator, The.
Warren. History.
Whitman. Of That Blithe Throat of Thine.
Passage to India.
Thought of Columbus, A.
Whittier. Seeking of the Waterfall, The.

Explosions
Carroll, Jim. Evening News.
Clark. Millennial Icon.
Emerson. Put in, drive home the sightless wedges.
Kooser. Letter From Aunt Belle, A.
Larkin. Explosion, The.
Lowry. Never seek to tell thy stove.
Pack. Big Bang.
Wyatt. Furious gun in his raging ire, The.

Exterminating and Exterminators
Browning, Robert. Pied Piper of Hamelin, The.
Bukowski. Terminology.
Gardner. Cockchafer.
Last Trump, The.
Lorde. Vietnam Addenda.
Silverstein. Drats.

Extinction
Dickey, James. For the Last Wolverine.
Garrigue. Pays Perdu.
Jeffers. Extinct Vertebrate, An.
Passenger Pigeons.
Nash. Caution to Everybody, A.
Next!
Neruda. Island (VII), The.
Oliver. Ghosts.
Pack. Mountain Ash Without Cedar Waxwings.
Remains.
Piercy. Homesick.
Rich. Hohokam.
Sandburg. Buffalo Dusk.
Updike. Popular Revivals 1956.
Wilbur. Walgh-Vogel, The.

Extrasensory Perception
Graves. Foreboding, The.
Wilbur. Mind-Reader, The.
Young. Process.

Extreme Unction
Walcott. My double, tired of morning, closes the door.
Wilbur. Rule, The.

Eyeglasses
Herrick. Upon Center a Spectacle-Maker with a Flat Nose.
Hewitt. Spectacle of Truth, The.
Nash. And How Keen Was the Vision of Sir Launfal?
Updike. Glasses.
Typical Optical.
Williams, William Carlos. Eyeglasses, The.

Eyes
Berg. Last Meeting.
1922.
This Cold.
Berryman. Of all that weeks-long day, though call it back.
Bishop. Britannia Rules the Waves.
They all kept looking at each other's eyes.
Three Sonnets for the Eyes.
Thy senses are too different to please me.
Tidal Basin.
Burns. Blue-Eyed Lassie, The.
Song: "O this is no my ain lassie."
Byron. On the Eyes of Miss A—— H—— —.
"Carroll, Lewis." Acrostic: Love-lighted eyes, that will not start.
After Three Days.
Beatrice.
When the King found that his money was nearly all.
Catullus. Carmen 82: "My eyes in your pledge, Quintius."
Clark. Fate Spinners in Time-Editing Studio, Eternity Blvd., 2 A.M.
Cohen. Your Eyes.
Cooper. Blind Girl.
Crane. Modern Craft.
Your eyes, those pools with soft rushes.
Creeley. Alice.
As real as thinking.
Disappointment, The.
Eye, The.
For Leslie.
Friend, The.

Hello.
Some Echoes.
Cummings. Life hurl my.
Open green those / (dear).
So isn't small one littlest why.
The(oo)is / lOOk / (aliv / e)e / yes.
De la Mare. Clear Eyes.
Euphrasy.
Eyes.
Happy Encounter, The.
Treachery.
Twilight.
Vain Finding.
Window, The.
Dickey, James. Daughter.
Dobyns. Eyelids.
Donne. Message, The.
Witchcraft by a Picture.
Doolittle. If Your Eyes Had Been Blue.
"Dylan." Dark Eyes.
Eberhart. Mystical Beast in the Shadows, The.
Eliot. Eyes That Last I Saw in Tears.
Emerson. Dost thou not hear me Ellen.
Far seen the river glides below.
Illusions like the tints of pearl.
Pair of crystal eyes will lead me, A.
Plunge in yon angry waves.
Since you set no worth on the heart.
They strew in the path of kings and czars.
What are all the flowers.
When Jane was absent Edgar's eye.
Fisher. Only target / is the eyeball, The.
Ford. Only one destiny.
Fox. In the taxidermist's shop.
Gallagher. Accomplishment.
Ritual of Memories, The.
Gunn. Kiss at Bayreuth, The.
Looks.
To Natty Bumppo.
Hartley. For the Shut Eye.
Herrick. Bashfulnesse.
Eye, The.
Eyes, The.
Upon Franck.
Upon Her Eyes.
Upon His Julia.
Hewitt. Bifocal in Gaza.
Hopkins. She Schools the Flighty Pupils of Her Eyes.
Jonson. Oh Do Not Wanton with Those Eyes.
Knight. I And Your Eyes.
Knott. Goodbye.
(Poem): "Like a room."
Shorts / Excerpts ("Night, in whose death did your ennui take refuge?").
Liddy. Notes towards a Video of Avondale House.
Lovelace. Lucasta Weeping.
To Quintius.
Lowell. Eye and Tooth.
Lowry. Little Ditty for This Day to the Beloved Harteebeeste, A.
McAuley. Exile on His Failing Vision, The.
"MacDiarmid." Milk-Wort and Bog Cotton.
MacNeice. Grey Ones, The.
Marvell. Eyes and Tears.
Matthews. Eyes.
Merton. Eye Is a Dog Howling in the Distance, The.
Millay. Tavern.
Muldoon. Blemish.
Olson. Babe, The.
Dura.
Your Eyes.
Owen. Fates, The.
Pack. Thrasher in the Willow by the Lake, The.
Patchen. I always return to this place.
I Suddenly Became Conscious That This Thing Was Looking at Me Intently.
Plath. Eye-Mote, The.
On Looking into the Eyes of a Demon Lover.
Raine. Seventh Day.
Ransom. Her Eyes.
Rolfe. About Eyes.
Rukeyser. Eyes of Night-Time.
Sandburg. Brim.

Pick-Offs.
Shag-Bark Hickory.
Spanish.
Sweeping Wendy: Study in Fugue.
Under a Hat Rim.
Valley Song.
Schuyler. Eyes.
Sexton. Fury of Hating Eyes, The.
Shakespeare. Sonnet 24: "Mine eye hath play'd the painter, and hath stell'd."
Sonnet 137: "Thou blind fool, Love, what dost thou to mine eyes."
Shelley. Eyes: A Fragment.
Sidney. Sonnet 105: "Unhappy sight, and hath she vanished thy."
Sonnet 42: "O eyes, which do the spheres of beauty move."
Sonnet 48: "Soul's joy, bend not those morning stars from me."
Sonnet 7: "When Nature made her chief work, Stella's eyes."
Sorrentino. Ultima Despedida del Principe Poniatowski de Su Familia.
Stevens. Tattoo.
Stevenson. Plain as the glistering planets shine.
Unforgotten II, The ("She rested by the Broken Brook").
Stuart. Long Goodbye, The.
Suckling. Bright star o' th' lower orb, twinkling inviter.
Thomson. To Myra.
Tomlinson. Poem: "Muscles which move the eyeballs."
Through Closed Eyes.
Updike. Typical Optical.
Wakoski. Fanny's Cold Blue Eyes.
Wilbur. On the Eyes of an SS Officer.
Williams, William Carlos. Weasel Snout.
Wroth. Sonnet: "Eyes, can you tell mee wher my hart remaines?"
Zukofsky. Quinti, see if't wish of cool eyes day bear your Catullus.
World autumn, The.

Ezra
Berryman. Prayer of the Middle-Aged Man, The.

F

Faces
Atwood. Head against White.
My face, my other faces.
Auden. First Meeting.
Private faces in public places.
Beatles. I've Just Seen a Face.
Berg. Alone.
Burns. Fragment: "Her flowing locks, the raven's wing."
Campion. There Is a Garden in Her Face.
Carew. Lips and Eyes.
"Carroll, Lewis." Faces in the Fire.
Carruth. Wind sighing, crying, singing in the pines. Who knows.
Creeley. Just Friends.
Sign Board, The.
Soup.
To Bobbie.
Cummings. Babylon slim / -ness of / evenslicing.
De la Mare. Anatomy.
Cage, The.
Veil, The.
Widow, The.
Dickey, James. Faces Seen Once.
Dickinson. Face devoid of love or grace, A.
Lovely Face to sit by, A.
Dobyns. Fatal Kisses.
Eberhart. Face, Ocean.
Fisher. Corner.
Ford. He has a luminous.
Fox. My Father's Face.
Gallagher. Even Now You Are Leaving. Not There.
Gunn. Rastignac at 45.
Hall. Raisin, The.

Herrick. Upon a Scarre in a Virgins Face.
Upon Crab.
Upon His Julia.
Upon Mistresse Susanna Southwell, Her Cheeks.
Upon Spalt.
Hewitt. Mirror.
Hopkins. In her cheeks that dwell.
Think of an opening page illuminèd.
Hughes, Langston. Chord.
125th Street.
Kinnell. Fly, The.
Poem of Night.
Knott. (Face) (Autumn) (En Face).
Kooser. Self-Portrait at Thirty-Nine.
Kunitz. Fitting of the Mask, The.
Lawrence. Human Face, The.
Portraits.
Levertov. Looking-glass.
Lewis. Unknown Soldier, The.
Lovelace. Another ("As I beheld a winters evening air").
Black Patch on Lucasta's Face, A.
Lowry. Song for a Marimba.
Matthews. My friend said Auden died.
Miller. Moment of Sleep (For Schnu), A.
Moore. Face, A.
Nemerov. Sestina I: "Thickness of paint or flesh cannot deface."
Olson. True Numbers.
Rich. Face.
Rossetti. Descent from the Cross, The.
I know a baby, such a baby,— / Round blue eyes and cheeks of pink.
Sandburg. Aztec Mask.
Child Face.
Face.
Halsted Street Car.
Mask.
Momus.
Monotone.
Passers-by.
Phizzog.
Under a Hat Rim.
Shelley. Fragment: A Serpent-Face.
Shelton. Face.
Sidney. Sonnet 9: "Queen Virtue's court, which some call Stella's face."
Smith, Stevie. Face, The.
Repentance of Lady T, The.
Sorrentino. Particular density: in the center, rises, A.
Trouble in Paradise.
Stuart. Charles River, The.
Long Goodbye, The.
Tomlinson. Face and Image.
Updike. Shaving Mirror.
Wakoski. I Have Had to Learn to Live with My Face.
Whitman. Faces.
Williams, Charles Kenneth. In There.
Waking Jed.
With Ignorance.
Wright, James. Accusation, The.
Wroth. Sonnet: "Can the lov'd Image of thy deerest face."
Sonnet: "Oft did I wounder why the sweets of Love."
Wyatt. Face that should content me wonders [or wondrous] well, A.

Factories
Bishop. Varick Street.
Bukowski. Sparks.
Dickey, William. Life Moving More Rapidly Than Hands Can Manage.
Fox. In the factory where dolls are made.
Hall. Traffic.
Heaney. Milk Factory, The.
Hewitt. Cultra Manor: The Ulster Folk Museum.
Kipling. Song of the Lathes, The.
Koch. Brassiere Factory, The.
Lawrence. Factory Cities, The.
Lindsay. Factory Windows Are Always Broken.
Longfellow. Ropewalk, The.
Lowry. Magic World, The.

Miller. Wondered why the building was so small.
Oppen. Debt.
Sandburg. Anna Imroth.
Mill-Doors.
Smith, Patti. Piss Factory.
Tomlinson. Dates: Penkhull New Road.
Etruria Vale.
Williams, Charles Kenneth. To Market.
Williams, William Carlos. Classic Scene.

Faerie Queene, The
Koch. Art of Poetry, The.
Ralegh. Another of the Same.
Vision upon This Concei[p]t of the Faerie [or Faery] Queen[e], A.
Wordsworth. White Doe of Rylstone, The; or, The Fate of the Nortons.

Failure
Auden. Candles Gutter Low, The.
Berryman. Nones.
Bly. August Rain.
Browning, Elizabeth Barrett. Romance of the Ganges, A.
Romaunt of Margret, The.
Bukowski. Word on the Quick and Modern Poem-Makers, A.
Cowper. Distressed Travellers, The.
Creeley. For Lewis, to Say It.
For the New Year.
Pay.
Something for Easter.
Cummings. Nobody loses all the time.
Dickinson. Success is counted sweetest.
Dunbar. For the Man Who Fails.
Dunn. Instead of You.
Emerson. Cloud upon cloud / Clouds after rain.
Ginsberg. How Come He Got Canned at the Ribbon Factory.
I feel as if I am at a dead.
Last Night in Calcutta.
Ode to Failure.
Walking Home at Night.
Glück. Legend.
Hacker. Satisfied loves eat big breakfasts. I.
Hardy. He Did Not Know Me.
Her Confession.
Hemingway. Poetry.
Herrick. Paines without Profit.
Plots Not Still Prosperous.
Hewitt. Late Spring, 1912.
Little Death, The.
Pavane for a Dead Professor.
Peter Peri (1899-1967).
Ruins Answer, The.
Uncle Sam and Aunt Edie.
Hughes, Langston. Dancer.
Hughes, Ted. Crow's First Lesson.
Hugo. Why I Think of Dumar Sadly.
Jonson. Ode: "If men, and times were now."
Ode to Himself.
Ode. To Himself, An.
Kipling. That Day.
Koertge. Burglar, The.
Kooser. Abandoned Farmhouse.
Larkin. Success Story.
To Failure.
Lewis. Had I ever a young field.
Separation, A.
Liddy. Death of Artists, The.
Litany of Satan, The.
Lowry. Autopsy on this childhood then reveals, An.
Foul, or Twenty-Five.
Poem Inspired By Auden and Clare's Snail.
Scribner's Sons.
MacLeish. Hands.
Pack. Clayfeld's Campaign.
Piercy. Death of the Small Commune, The.
Prince. His old fame is dumb.
Words from Edmund Burke.
Robinson. Bewick Finzer.
Clavering.
Old Trails.
Shadrach O'Leary.
Wise Brothers, The.
Rolfe. Postscript to a War.

Rossetti. Septuagesima.
Swift and sure the swallow.
Symbols.
Rukeyser. Paper Anniversary.
Schwartz. "O what a mess of judgment we have made."
Silverstein. Little Blue Engine, The.
Stevenson. Ad Se Ipsum.
Lost Occasion, The.
Turco. Failed Fathers.
Old Professor and the Sphinx, The.
Whitman. To Those Who've Fail'd.
Wilbur. In the Smoking-Car.
Williams, Charles Kenneth. Failure.
Yeats. To a Friend Whose Work Has Come to Nothing.
Zimmer. Zimmer in Grade School.

Fairies
Auden. Belief.
Campion. Tell me, gentle howre of night.
"Carroll, Lewis." Bruno's Song.
My Fairy.
Puck Lost and Found.
Chaucer. Sir Thopas.
Coleridge. Songs of the Pixies.
De la Mare. Fairy in Winter, The.
Dunbar. Discovery, The.
Graves. Lollocks.
Hardy. On a Midsummer Eve.
Herrick. Beggar to Mab, the Fairy [or Fairie] Queen, The.
Fairies, The.
Fairy Temple; or, Oberon's Chapel, The.
Oberon's Feast.
Oberon's Palace.
Temple, The.
Housman. Fairies break their dances, The.
Keats. Cap and Bells; or, The Jealousies, The.
Faery Bird's Song.
Faery Song.
La Belle Dame Sans Merci.
Song of Four Faeries.
When They Were Come unto the Faery's Court.
Kipling. And you may lead a thousand men.
Ballad of Minepit Shaw, The.
Lindsay. Cold Sunbeams.
Dancing for a Prize.
Dangerous Little Boy Fairies, The.
Fairy from the Apple-Seed, The.
Lame Boy and the Fairy, The.
What the Gray-Winged Fairy Said.
Poe. Fairyland [or Fairy-Land].
Rossetti. I fancy the good fairies dressed in white.
Shelley. Fragment: Wine of the Fairies.
Smith, Stevie. Cool as a Cucumber.
Stevenson. Fairy Bread.
Little Land, The.
Wright, James. Evening.
Yeats. Faery Song, A.
Stolen Child, The.
See also Elves; Goblins.

Fairs
Auden. Fairground.
Berryman. World's Fair.
Burns. Rattlin, Roarin Willie.
Gunn. At the Barriers.
Fair in the Woods, The.
Hardy. At a Country Fair.
At Casterbridge Fair.
Ballad-Singer, The.
Expectation and Experience.
Former Beauties.
Last Look round St. Martin's Fair.
Sheep Fair, A.
Larkin. Show Saturday.
Sandburg. Honky Tonk in Cleveland, Ohio.
Stafford. Adults Only.
Updike. Topsfield Fair.
Whitman. Bravo, Paris Exposition!
Williams, William Carlos. Dance, The.
Young. People of Letters.

Fairy Tales
Ashbery. Märchenbilder.
Auden. In the Nursery.
"Carroll, Lewis." Dedication: "Child of the

pure unclouded brow."
To M. A. B.
Dickey, William. Dolls Play at Hansel and Gretel, The.
Glück. Gretel in Darkness.
Graves. To Juan at the Winter Solstice.
Jarrell. Forest Murmurs.
House in the Wood, The.
Märchen, The.
Joseph. Still Reading Fairy Stories.
Nash. Fee Fi Ho Hum, No Wonder Baby Sucks Her Thumb.
Olson. Snow White was always waiting for The Prince.
Plath. Battle-Scene.
Prince. Autumn Journey.
Rukeyser. Fable: "Yes it was the prince's kiss."
Sandburg. Love Letter to Hans Christian Andersen.
Silverstein. Captain Hook.
Smith, Stevie. Fairy Story.
Frog Prince, The.
Spenser. Prosopopoia: or Mother Hubberds Tale.
Stuart. Hidden Meanings.
Van Duyn. Cinderella's Story.
Williams, Charles Kenneth. Near the Haunted Castle.

Fairyland
Auden. Tale, A.
Graves. Land of Whipperginny, The.

Faith
Angelou. Just Like Job.
Arnold. Dover Beach.
Berry. Homecoming, A.
Necessity of Faith, The.
Berryman. Facts & Issues, The.
Faith like the warrior ant swarming, enslaving.
Pacifist's Song, The.
Under new management, Your Majesty.
Blake. Divine Image, The ("To Mercy, Pity, Peace, and Love").
Hes a Blockhead who wants a proof of what he Cant Percieve.
Lamb, The.
Mock On, Mock On, Voltaire, Rousseau.
Night.
You dont believe I wont attempt to make ye.
Bly. Conversation with a Holy Woman Not Seen for Many Years.
Brontë. No coward soul is mine.
Visionary, The.
Brooks. Firstly Inclined to Take What It Is Told.
People protest in sprawling lightless ways.
Browning, Elizabeth Barrett. Drama of Exile, A.
Romance of the Ganges, A.
Browning, Robert. Bad Dreams I.
Byron. Stanzas to Augusta.
Were My Bosom As False As Thou Deem'st It to Be.
Campion. Epigramme: "Wiseman wary lives, yet most secure, A."
Out of My Soul's Depth.
Carruth. Names.
Once and Again.
Chaucer. Second Nun's Tale, The.
Clough. In controversial foul impureness.
O happy they whose hearts receive.
"There is no God," the wicked saith.
Cohen. Veil, A.
Coleridge. Faith, Hope, and Charity.
Mythology in an Age of Reason.
Cowper. Aspirations of the Soul after God.
Divine Love Endures No Rival.
Glory to God Alone.
Hope.
Love Faithful in the Absence of the Beloved.
Love of God the End of Life, The.
Necessity of Self-Abasement.
Olney Hymns.
Perfect Sacrifice, The.
Secrets of Divine Love Are To Be Kept, The.
Self-Diffidence.
Truth and Divine Love Rejected by the World.

Crane. Recitative.
Crashaw. Adoro Te. The Hymn of Saint Thomas in Adoration of the Blessed Sacrament.
Mark 4; Why Are Yee Afraid, O Yee of Little Faith?
Creeley. Circle.
Mechanic, The.
Poem, A: "If the water forms."
Cullen. Counter Mood.
Lines to My Father.
Sonnet: "These are no wind-blown rumors, soft say-sos."
Cummings. Here is little Effie's Head.
I thank You God for most this amazing.
Jehovah buried,Satan dead.
No time ago / or else a life.
That melancholy / fellow'll play / his handorgan.
Davie. Articulacy. Hints from the Koran.
De la Mare. Catechism, The.
Dickinson. Child's faith is new, The.
Dust like the Mosquito, The.
"Faith" is a fine invention.
Faith—is the Pierless Bridge.
"Faithful to the end" Amended.
He strained my faith.
How brittle are the Piers.
I know that He exists.
I never lost as much but twice.
I never saw a Moor.
My Faith is larger than the Hills.
Nearest Dream recedes—unrealized, The.
On a Columnar Self.
Read—Sweet—how others—strove.
This is a Blossom of the Brain.
Those—dying then.
To lose one's faith—surpass.
To mend each tattered Faith.
To pile like Thunder to its close.
What I see not, I better see.
Donne. Angels, The.
Elegy upon the Untimely Death of the Incomparable Prince Henry.
Patriarchs, The.
To Mr. Roland Woodward ("Like one who in [or who'in] her third widowhood [or widdowhood] doth profess[e]").
Dryden. Thus man by his own strength to Heaven would soar.
Dunbar. After Many Days.
After While.
By Rugged Ways.
Faith.
Mare Rubrum.
Resignation.
Slow through the Dark.
Dunn. At the Smithville Methodist Church.
Guardian Angel, The.
"Dylan." Ain't No Man Righteous, No Not One.
Are You Ready?
Covenant Woman.
Gonna Change My Way of Thinking.
I and I.
I Believe in You.
I Dreamed I Saw St. Augstine.
In the Garden.
In the Summertime.
Nobody 'Cept You.
Precious Angel.
Pressing On.
Property of Jesus.
Saved.
Saving Grace.
Solid Rock.
Trouble in Mind.
What Can I Do for You?
When You Gonna Wake Up?
Eberhart. On the Fragility of Mind.
Emerson. Character.
Honor bright o muse.
Problem, The.
Sacrifice.
Unbar the door, since thou the Opener art.
Worship.
Everson. Annul in Me My Manhood.

Burning Book, The.
Encounter, The.
Frost Lay White on California, A.
I Am Long Weaned.
You, God.
Fenton. God, A Poem.
Fisher. There's a belief to fix. It feels strong.
Frost. Innate Helium.
Gardner. Abraham and Isaac.
Ballade: "Lady of Heaven, Queen of nature."
Ballade: "You who outlive us, you, our mortal brothers."
Man of Faith, The.
Timeo.
Word From the Piazza del Limbo, A.
Garrigue. Giralda, The.
In Memory.
Glück. Jeanne d'Arc.
Graves. Ample Garden, The.
Dancing Flame.
Poet's Curse, The.
Possessed.
Woman and Tree.
Hardy. Between Us Now.
Impercipient, The.
Hartley. Nameless Speaks, The.
Water from the Rock.
Hartnett. Naked Surgeon, The.
There Will Be a Talking.
Herbert. Afflction (5).
Affliction (1).
Affliction (2).
Artillery [or Artillerie].
Assurance.
Banquet, The.
Bitter-Sweet.
Charms and Knots.
Church-Floor[e], The.
Collar, The.
Complaining.
Content.
Discharge, The.
Discipline.
Divinity.
Elixir [or Elixer], The.
Employment (1).
see also To the Lady Elizabeth Queen of Bohemia.
Faith.
Flower, The.
Forerunners, The.
Glance, The.
Grace.
Holy Baptism (2).
Justice (1).
Knell, The.
Love (1).
Love ("Thou art too hard for me in Love").
Love Unknown.
Method, The.
Nature.
Peace.
Pearl. Matthew 13:45, The.
Perseverance.
Pilgrimage, The.
Praise (1).
Quidditie [or Quiddity], The.
Repentance.
Search, The.
Sepulchre.
Sin (1).
Sonnet: "My God, where is that ancient heat towards Thee."
Sonnet: "Sure Lord, there is enough in thee to dry."
Submission.
Superliminare.
Temper (1), The.
Temper (2), The.
Thanksgiving, The.
Trinity Sunday.
Twenty-third Psalm, The.
Windows, The.
Herrick. Faith.
Faith Four-square.
His Creed.
His Words to Christ, Going to the Cross.

Lamp, The.
Parasceve, or Preparation, The.
To God ("Lord, I am like to mistletoe").
To God ("Make, make me Thine").
Upon Spenke.
Upon Woman and Mary.
Hesketh. My Faithful Lover.
Hewitt. Carol Singers.
Nebula.
Rite, Lubitavish, Glenaan.
Salute to Matthew Arnold.
Torcello.
When the Bell Rings in the Steeple.
Hill. Risen Christ! Once more, The.
Hoffman. Companion, The.
Hopkins. Carrion Comfort.
God's Grandeur.
He hath abolished the old drouth.
Nondum.
O Deus, Ego Amo Te.
Trees by their yield.
Housman. If it chance your eye offend you.
Jeffers. Credo.
No Resurrection.
Quia Absurdum.
Thebaid.
Joseph. Road from Glastonbury, The.
Keats. O Thou Whose Face Hath Felt the Winter's Wind.
Kinnell. Wait.
Kipling. Obedient, The.
Old Song, An.
Recessional.
Song of the English, A.
To the True Romance.
Lawrence. Talk of Faith.
Levine. 28.
Lewis. Boy who climbed the creaking stairs, The.
Lovers who among the grasses.
Liddy. Patrick Kavanagh's Dublin.
Lindsay. Come let us pray to the Lord of the sky.
Heart of God.
Hope of the Resurrection, The.
In the Immaculate Conception Church.
Johnny Appleseed Speaks of the Appleblossom Amaranth That Will Come to This City.
Shield of Faith, The.
Sun Says His Prayers, The.
Where Is the Real Non-Resistant?
Lowry. And yet I am of England too; odi et amo.
Communist, The.
Consider what you have lost by lack of faith.
Shakespeare's house is safe and sound.
McAuley. Nun of St. Michan's, The.
Prelude in Darkness.
Press Conference: King James Version.
Sunset.
McGrath. Against the False Magicians.
MacLeish. Actfive.
Eve's Second Prophecy.
MacNeice. Carol: "To end all carols, darling."
Creditor, The.
Nothing more simple. Among the tarnished.
Tall story over a dark sanctum, A.
Ut Quid Iubes, Pusiole.
Melville. Arch, The.
Conflict of Convictions, The.
Epilogue: "If Luther's day expand to Darwin's year."
Meredith. Ass of Balaam, The.
Boy's Death, The.
"Dream is the thought in the ghost, The."
Faith on Trial, A.
Lord of old has dealt in blood, The.
Sense and Spirit.
Song of Theodolinda, The.
Test of Manhood, The.
To J.M.
Merton. Death.
Splendor Paternae Gloriae.
Millay. Oh, think not I am faithful to a vow!
This Dusky Faith.
Milton. Answer me when I call / God of my

righteousness.
On Time.
Morgan. May 1, 1974.
Nathan. Creed.
Keeping the Faith.
Nemerov. Sonnet: "Form of Christ cut from dark wood, the pale, A."
O'Hara. Poem: "When I am feeling depressed and anxious sullen."
Olson. Babe, The.
In one age or other, if not in this.
Quatrain: "Do not, at this high time, desert."
Willie Francis and the Electric Chair.
Owen. Has Your Soul Sipped?
Last Laugh, The.
Pack. Prayer for Prayer.
Paley. Standing in high grass at home imagining farm.
Piercy. Seedlings in the Mail.
Pope. Faith.
Psalms. Psalm 4: "Hear me when I call, O God of my righteousness."
Psalm 115: "Not unto us, O Lord, not unto us."
Ransom. Eclogue: "JANE SNEED BEGAN IT: My poor John, alas."
"Reed." Busload of Faith.
Robinson. Credo.
Just as I wonder at the twofold screen.
Siege Perilous.
When one that you and I had all but sworn.
Rossetti. All beneath the sun hasteth, / All that hath begun wasteth.
Behold, I stand at the door and knock.
Charades.
Charity.
Come Unto Me.
Divine and Human Pleading.
Fair Margaret.
Faith and Hope are wings to Love.
For a Mercy Received.
Greatest of These Is Charity, The.
Hope is like a harebell trembling from its birth.
I followed Thee, my God, I followed Thee / To see the end.
I Know You Not.
I lift mine eyes to see: earth vanisheth.
In weariness and painfulness St. Paul.
Leaf from leaf Christ knows; / Himself the Lily and the Rose.
Lord God of Hosts, most Holy and most High.
Lord, It Is Good for Us to Be Here.
Lord Jesu, Thou art sweetness to my soul.
Lord Jesus, who would think that I am Thine?
Lowest Room, The.
Moonshine.
O Lord, on Whom we gaze and dare not gaze, / Increase our faith that gazing we may see.
O Lord, when Thou didst call me, didst Thou know.
Offering of the New Law, the One Oblation Once Offered, The.
Our heaven must be within ourselves / Our home and heaven the work of faith.
Ransomed of the Lord, The.
Ruined Cross, The.
Somewhere or Other.
Song for the Least of All Saints, A.
Take No Thought for The Morrow.
Vigil of St. Peter.
Ye Are Come unto Mount Sion.
St. John. Leap of Faith.
Schuyler. I Sit Down to Type.
Sexton. Small Wire.
Shakespeare. Sonnet 92: "But do thy worst to steal thyself away."
Smart. Conclusion of the Matter, The.
Faith.
Fortitude.
Strong is the horse upon his speed.
Smith, Charlotte. To Mrs. ****.
Smith, Stevie. Dream of Comparison, A.
God the Eater.
Snodgrass. Magda Goebbels ("How could you dare stay constant to").
Sorrentino. Celebration of Sorts, A.

Spenser. Since I Have Lacked the Comfort.
When I behold this tickle trustles state.
Stevens. Blue Buildings in the Summer Air,
The.
Stevenson. Embro Hie Kirk.
Evensong.
If This Were Faith.
To Marcus.
Wind is without there and howls in the trees,
The.
Stuart. Mystic.
Sutter. As a boy my father preached to trees.
Can you believe it?
My Father at His Height.
Pine Creek Parish Hall.
Visitor, The.
Tennyson. On a Mourner.
Supposed Confessions of a Second-rate
Sensitive Mind.
That which we dare invoke to bless.
Two Voices, The.
You say, but with no touch of scorn.
Thomas. Where Once the Waters of Your
Face.
Walcott. City's Death by Fire, A.
Whittier. Adjustment.
Answer, The.
Eternal Goodness, The.
Hermit of the Thebaid, The.
In Quest.
Mantle of St. John de Matha, The.
My Dream.
Questions of Life.
Requirement.
"Rock" in El Ghor, The.
Sisters, The: A Picture by Barry, The.
Tauler.
Trust.
Watchers, The.
Well of Loch Maree, The.
Williams, Charles Kenneth. Gap, The.
They Warned Him Then They Threw Him
Away.
Williams, Miller. After the Revolution for
Jesus a Secular Man Prepares His Final
Remarks.
After You Die You Don't Give a Piddling
Damn.
And When in Scenes of Glory.
He Speaks to His Arguing Friends and to
Himself.
In Your Own Words Without Lying Tell
Something of Your Background With
Particular Attention to Anything Relating to
the Position For Which You Are Applying.
Press Down.
Notes from the Agent on Earth: How to be
Human.
Picker.
Some Lines Finished Just Before Dawn at the
Bedside of a Dying Student / It has Snowed
All Night.
Vision and Prayer.
Wordsworth. At the Convent of Camaldoli.
Forsaken, The.
In due observance of an ancient rite.
O Thou who movest onward with a mind.
Wright, Charles. Journal of English Days, A.
Journal of Southern Rivers, A.
Journal of True Confessions, A.
Lost Bodies.
Wroth. Song: "Love as well can make
abiding."
Song: "O[h] me[e] the time is [or has] come
to part."
Wyatt. After great storms the calm returns.
Argument, Th'.
Give place all ye that doth rejoice.
Live thou gladly if so thou may.
Thou hast no faith of him that hath none.
What should I say.
Ye know my heart, my lady dear.
Yeats. Tom the Lunatic.
Zukofsky. Tam Cari Capitis.

Faith Healers
Larkin. Faith Healing.

Falcons
Bukowski. Sky Sign.
Duncan. My Mother Would Be a Falconress.
Emerson. While roses bloomed along the
plain.
Fox. Peregrine Falcon.
Graves. Falcon Woman, The.
Hopkins. Windhover, The.
Hughes, Ted. And the Falcon Came.
Jeffers. New Year's Eve.
Lovelace. Lady with a Falcon on Her Fist, A.
Sarton. Lady with a Falcon.

Fall. *see* **Autumn.**

Falling
Berry. When I rise up.
"Carroll, Lewis." As It Fell upon a Day.
Carruth. Little Death, The.
Creeley. Entre Nous.
Look.
Place, The.
Dunn. Meditation on Two Themes.
Emerson. I read on the porch of a palace
bold.
Hewitt. Descent, The.
Omens and Auguries.
Kinnell. Falls, The.
Kipling. By the Hoof of the Wild Goat.
Lowry. No prayer for the people.
Merton. Notes of a Parachute Jumper.
Raine. Falling Leaves.
Snodgrass. Disguised as Humpty-Dumpty, W.
D. Practices Tumbling.
Tomlinson. Elemental.
Williams, Charles Kenneth. Vehicle:
Conscience.

Fame
Ashbery. He.
Auden. Iceland Revisited.
Beatles. Drive My Car.
Honey Pie.
Bradstreet. To My Dear Sister, the Author of
these Poems.
Browning, Robert. Popularity.
Bukowski. Best Way to Get Famous Is to Run
Away, The.
Byron. Lines: "Dear Becher, you tell me to
mix with mankind."
Stanzas Written on the Road between Florence
and Pisa.
Thy Days Are Done.
What is the end of fame? 'Tis but to fill.
Campion. Ad Carolum Fitz Geofridum.
Ad Tho. Munsonium, equitem Auratum et
Baronetum.
In Cambrum.
Neither buskin now, nor bayes.
Some from the starry throne his fame derives.
To. Campiani Epigramma de Instituto
Authoris.
Cohen. Chelsea Hotel.
Coleridge. Epitaph: "Stop, Christian passer-
by!—Stop, child of God."
Cowper. Another Version.
Answer to Stanzas Addressed to Lady
Hesketh.
On the Biographia Britannica.
To Dr. Austin.
To Sir John Fenn.
Translation of Verses to Lloyd.
Crane. Thou Canst Read Nothing..
Cummings. Hokku.
?
Sonnet: "I dreamed I was among the
conquerors."
Davie. Surrey.
Dickinson. Above Oblivion's Tide there is a
Pier.
Be Mine the Doom.
Beggar at the Door for Fame, The.
Fame is a bee.
Fame is a fickle food.
Fame is the one that does not stay.
Fame is the tint that Scholars leave.
Fame of Myself, to justify.
Fame's Boys and Girls, who never die.
First We knew of Him was Death, The.

I'm Nobody! Who are you?
Publication—is the Auction.
"Dylan." I Shall Be Free.
Oh where were these magazines.
Emerson. Fame.
His instant thought the Poet spoke.
Fisher. Paraphrases.
Frost. Provide, Provide.
Ginsberg. After Whitman & Reznikoff.
Graves. Singleness in Love.
Troublesome Fame.
Hacker. Elegy: "Crying from exile, I."
Hardy. Abbey Mason, The.
To an Actress.
Hartnett. Old Catechism, The.
Herrick. Fame.
Fame Makes Us Forward.
Glorie.
Glory.
To His Book[e]: ("Have I not blest thee? Then
go forth; nor fear").
To the Most Accomplisht Gentleman Master
Michael Oulsworth.
To the Right Honourable Edward Earle of
Dorset.
Upon Himself: ("Thou shalt not All die").
Wit Punisht, Prospers Most.
Hewitt. Portraits on the Walls.
Hughes, Langston. Joe Louis.
Hughes, Ted. Famous Poet.
Jeffers. Giant's Ring, The.
Let Them Alone.
Jonson. To Alphonso Ferrabosco, on His
Book.
To My Truly-Beloved Friend, Mr Browne: on
His Pastorals.
To the Same [Alphonso Ferrabosco].
Who, Virtue, can thy power forget.
Keats. Addressed to Haydon.
On Fame ("Fame, like a wayward girl, will
still be coy").
On Fame ("How fever'd is the man who
cannot look").
This Mortal Body of a Thousand Days.
To Kosciusko.
Lowry. Donne He's Regular.
Success is like some horrible disaster.
Tibute to the Renowned Harteebeeste, A.
Melville. On Sherman's Men.
Meredith. Chivalry.
To Alex. Smith, the "Glasgow Poet," on His
Sonnet to "Fame."
Merton. Elegy for Ernest Hemingway, An.
Turtle, The.
Milton. True and False Glory.
Morgan. His Last Case.
Nash. Parable for Sports Writers, Society
Columnists, Bond Salesmen, and Poets or Go
Get a Reputation, A.
Nathan. So?
Nemerov. Modern Poet, A.
Neruda. Another One.
Owen. To My Friend.
Pope. To a Lady with the Temple of Fame.
Pound. White Stag, The.
Prince. His old fame is dumb.
Ralegh. 4.9: "Many by valour have deserved
renown."
Rich. Focus.
Robinson. Old Trails.
Three Quatrains.
Sandburg. Fame If Not Fortune.
Soup.
Vaudeville Dancer.
Schwartz. "Lo, we descend like light. Light.
Light."
Shakespeare. Sonnet 125: "Were't aught to me
I bore the canopy."
Shelley. Ozymandias [of Egypt].
Shelton. Harry Orchard.
Sidney. Sonnet 90: "Stella, think not that I by
verse seek fame."
Smith, Stevie. Crown of Bays, The.
Film Star, The.
Spender. Question of Identity, A.
Stevenson. Strange are the ways of men.
Updike. At the End of the Rainbow.

Little Poems.
Newlyweds, The.
Pop Smash, Out of Echo Chamber.
Whitman. Fame's Vanity.
Wilbur. Ballade of the Ladies of Time Past.
Williams, Miller. My Wife Reads the Paper at Breakfast on the Birthday of the Scottish Poet.
Yeats. While I, from that reed-throated whisperer.

See also **Greatness.**

Family
Auden. Household, A.
Through the Looking-Glass.
Beatles. Ob-La-Di Ob-La-Da.
Berry. My Great-Grandfather's Slaves.
There is no government so worthy as your son who fishes with you in silence beside the forest pool.
Bishop. My name is Severino.
Poem: "About the size of an old-style dollar bill."
Table, The.
Travelling in the Family.
Browning, Robert. Family, The.
Bukowski. Not To Worry.
Some Picnic.
Carruth. Abandoned Ranch, Big Bend.
Family Reunion.
Sonnet: "Like the magnificent stationary animal it is."
Catullus. Carmen 23: "Friend Furius, / "who has no slaves & no money.""
Ciardi. Bedlam Revisited.
Clark. One.
Cooper. In the House of the Dying.
Creeley. Family, The.
"For Some Weeks.."
Heaven.
I.
Dickey, James. Deborah as Scion.
Dunn. That Saturday Without a Car.
Under the Black Oaks.
"Dylan." Down Along the Cove.
Eberhart. Orchard.
Spite Fence.
Edmunds. Back Home.
Ferlinghetti. Home Home Home.
I Genitori Perduti.
Ford. Whole family weeping.
Fox. White and the River.
Gallagher. Ballad of Ballymote, The.
Cougar Meat.
Woodcutting on Lost Mountain.
Glück. From the Japanese.
From the Suburbs.
Returning a Lost Child.
Scraps.
Still Life.
Thanksgiving.
Graves. Brother.
Great-Grandmother, The.
Pride of Progeny.
Gunn. Hide and Seek.
Slow Waker.
Three.
Hacker. And I shout at Iva, whine at you.
Easily.
Callers, The.
Elevens.
For Elektra.
Inheritances.
Hall. Family, The.
Tomorrow.
Hardy. After the Burial.
Hartley. Family Album in Red Plush.
Heaney. Funeral Rites.
Hemingway. Blood is thicker than water.
Hesketh. Single Footprints.
Hewitt. Aunt Cis and Uncle Tom.
Breach, The.
Covenanter's Grave, The.
Cushkib Fair.
Faded Leaf: A Chapter of Family History, The.
Fairy Thresher, The.

First Ride.
From a Museum Man's Album.
Incident, An.
Lonely Heart, The.
Lonsdale Street.
My Aunt Sarah and Uncle Joe.
My Grandmother's Garter.
Orchard Country.
Portstewart, 1914.
Return (1885), The.
Ruins Answer, The.
Scattering, The.
Scottish Interlude.
Sunset over Glenaan.
Teetotal Master.
Vida, Mykonos.
Wheel, The.
Hopkins. Epithalamion: "Hark, hearer, hear what I do; lend a thought now, make believe."
Jeffers. At the Birth of an Age.
Such Counsels You Gave to Me.
Knight. My Uncle is My Honor and a Guest in My House.
Kooser. Christmas Eve.
Kunitz. Father and Son.
Quinnapoxet.
Levine. I Was Born in Lucerne.
Letters for the Dead.
Memory of rain falling slowly, The.
Sources.
Lewis. Prelude and Fugue.
Lieberman. Family Tree, The.
Lindsay. Perfect Marriage, The.
Lowry. Personal.
McAuley. Behind a brightening cloud.
Mother, sisters, brother.
Questions for my Grandfather.
MacLeish. Family Group.
MacNeice. Back-Again, The.
Happy Families.
When she had her stroke the china dogs.
McNeill. Nora O'Kane.
Overheard on a Bus (Woman with a Cleft Palate).
Snow Angels.
Stories at Evening (A Suburban Mother Tells Stories to Her Son).
Matthews. Moving Again.
Meinke. Hôtel de la Truite.
House, The.
Ping-Pong.
Running with the Hyenas.
Meredith. We saw the swallows gathering in the sky.
Merrill. Dream of Old Vienna, A.
Nemerov. Midsummer's Day.
Notley. Dear Dark Continent.
Oliver. Family, The.
Pack. Inheritance.
Leviathan.
Look, there it is—I'm sure that is the oak.
Remains.
Rondo of the Familiar.
Trillium.
Waking to My Name.
Paley. Family.
Patchen. Family Portrait.
Kibali-Ituri.
Ransom. First Travels of Max.
"Reed." Families.
Rich. Our Family.
Rolfe. Testament to a Flowering Race.
Rossetti. Gone Before.
Valentine, 1877, A.
Rukeyser. Absalom.
Another Day. The Children Are All Eating.
Double Ode.
Four in a Family.
Green Limits.
Word of Mouth.
Sandburg. Home Fires.
Sarton. Child's Japan, A.
Schuyler. Over the Hills.
Sexton. All My Pretty Ones.
Papa and Mama Dance, The.

Smith, Stevie. Is It Happy?
Tenuous and Precarious.
Sorrentino. Fragments of an Old Song 1.
Spender. Elegy for Margaret.
Stafford. Catechism, A.
Family Turn, A.
One Home.
Stevenson. Family, The.
Fixed is the doom; and to the last of years.
These rings, O my beloved pair.
To Auntie.
Stuart. Commencement.
Don't Look Back.
Lines.
Taking Sides.
Sutter. Just learning to talk, I watched.
Tate. Farewell Rehearsed.
Not power nor the casual [*or* storied] hand of God.
Updike. Due Respect.
Wakoski. Slicing Oranges for Jeremiah.
There's Plenty of Anguish at the Railroad.
Walcott. I once gave my daughters, separately, two conch shells.
Something primal in our spine makes the child swing.
Waldman. De Carlo Lots, The.
Walker. Dedication.
Warren. Ballad of Billie Potts, The.
Flower, The.
Williams, William Carlos. Three Generations.
Wordsworth. Fragment: "For let the impediment be what it may."
Jewish Family (in a Small Valley Opposite St Goar, upon the Rhine), A.
Wright, Charles. Self-Portait ("Pictures in the air have few visitors, The").
Virginia Reel.
Wright, James. Cold Divinities, The.
Old Man Drunk.
Willy Lyons.
Zukofsky. Furius, with no key to service, no key.
H.T.
Men in the kitchens, The.
My nephew / And my new.

Family Life
Atwood. And you play the safe game / the orphan game.
In this house (in a dying orchard).
Beatles. Lady Madonna.
Berg. And the Scream.
In Blue Light.
Berry. And I am here in Kentucky in the place I have made myself.
You lean at ease in your warm house at night after supper.
Betjeman. Beside the Seaside.
Green shutters, shut your shutters! Windyridge.
Group Life: Letchworth.
Winthrop Mackworth Redivivus.
Bishop. Family Portrait.
Brooks. Vacant Lot, The.
Byron. Blues, The.
Creeley. Boy, the.
Gift of Great Value, A.
Davie. Abbeyforde.
Liverpool Epistle, A.
Dove. Taking in Wash.
Dunbar. At Candle-Lightin' Time.
'Long To'ds Night.
Dunn. I Come Home Wanting to Touch Everyone.
Legacy.
Loves.
Regardless.
Fox. Letters from the Island.
Gardner. That Was Then.
Gildner. After World War II.
Around the Kitchen Table.
House on Buder Street, The.
Nails.
Hartnett. Poet as Black Sheep, The.
Small Farm, A.
Hayden. Those Winter Sundays.
Herrick. Upon Grubs.
Hewitt. Hill-Farm, The.

Jeffers. Cawdor.
Tamar.
Knight. Idea of Ancestry, The.
Kunitz. Three Floors.
Your turn, Grass of confusion.
Lawrence. Red-Herring.
Lewis. Prelude and Fugue.
Lowell. My Last Afternoon with Uncle
Devereux Winslow.
McAuley. Exile, *En Famille*, The.
Meinke. Chicken Unlimited.
Meredith. Orchard and the Heath, The.
Millay. Lament: "Listen, children: / Your
father is dead."
Muldoon. Mixed Marriage, The.
Nash. Family Court.
O'Hara. Ave Maria.
Olson. All Pink from the Bath She Slept.
Incunabula, 1958.
Paley. 20th Street Spring.
Prince. Family Mottoes.
Psalms. Psalm 128: "Blessed is every one that
feareth the Lord."
"Reed." Standing on Ceremony.
Rich. In the Wake of Home.
Woman Mourned by Daughters, A.
Roethke. Happy Three, The.
Rossetti. What Does the Bee Do?
Rukeyser. Victims, a Play for the Home, The.
Sandburg. Boy and Father.
Population Drifts.
Sexton. Boat, The.
Funnel.
Mother and Jack and the Rain.
Smith, Stevie. Emily Writes Such a Good
Letter.
House of Over-Dew, The.
Mutchmore and Not-So.
Sliding Mountain, The.
Snodgrass. Fourth of July.
Friend, A.
Stafford. Family Turn, A.
Rescued Year, The.
Stein. Prudence Caution and Foresight: A
Story of Avignon.
Stuart. Canned Goods.
Updike. Home Movies.
House Growing, The.
Leaving Church Early.
Living with a Wife.
Relatives.
Van Duyn. Bedtime Stories.
Folks built that barn, your great grandfather,
and them, The.
Growing Up Askew.
Relationships.
Waldman. De Carlo Lots, The.
Wilbur. Tartuffe.
Williams, Charles Kenneth. Sanctity, The.
Time: 1978.
Time: 1976.
Wordsworth. Even as a dragon's eye that feels
the stress.
Young. Elegy: "Good morning!"

Famine
Lewis. Observation Post: Forward Area.
Stevenson. Feast of Famine: Marquesan
Manners, The.
Walker. Few Sirens, A.
Wyatt. In doubtful breast whilst motherly Pity.

Fancy
Burns. Mary Morison.
Cowper. Anti-Thelyphthora.
Smith, Charlotte. To Fancy.
Sorrentino. She was all in Black. A statement.
See also **Imagination.**

Fans
Bukowski. My Groupie.
What to Do with Contributor's Copies?
Lovelace. Lucasta's Fan[ne], with a Looking-
Glass[e] in It.
Nash. Enthusiast Is a Devotee Is a Rooter, or,
Mr. Hemingway, Meet Mr. Stengel, An.
St. John. Fan Sketched with Silver Egrets, A.
Stuart. Ties.

Fantasies
Berrigan. Something Amazing Just Happened.

Browning, Elizabeth Barrett. Romance of the
Swan's Nest, The.
Bukowski. Notations from a Muddled
Indolence.
Seahorse.
"Carroll, Lewis." Dedication: "All in the
golden afternoon."
My Fancy.
Clark. I Was Born to Speak Your Name.
Last Poem (after Robert Desnos), The.
Coleridge. Frost at Midnight.
Lines Written at the King's Arms, Ross,
Formerly the House of the "Man of Ross."
Written at Shurton Bars, near Bridgewater,
September 1795, in Answer to a Letter from
Bristol.
Creeley. Flesh.
Cummings. Boy and the Man, The.
Doll's boy's asleep / under a stile.
My sweet old etcetera.
Paper Palace, The.
Than(by yon sunset's wintry glow).
Will i ever forget that precarious moment?
De la Mare. Fog.
Which?
Dove. Adolescence—III.
Eberhart. Commas in Wintertime.
Lament of a New England Mother, The.
Eliot. Cooking Egg, A.
Ferlinghetti. Imaginary Happening, London,
An.
Wild Dreams of a New Beginning.
Fletcher. Isle Iranim.
Life.
Tower, The.
Griffiths. Unwritten Chapters.
Hacker. I'll dabble in specifics in my bath.
Hardy. Dream of the City Shopwoman.
Dream or No, A.
Imaginings.
Let Me Believe.
Herrick. To the Maids to Walke Abroad.
Hesketh. Horses, The.
Tunnel, The.
Hughes, Langston. Flatted Fifths.
Jarrell. Seele im Raum.
Levine. Roofs.
Lowry. Just a Merry Little Ditty of Welcome
for the Most Beloved Harteebeeste on Easter
Sunday.
MacLeish. Two Women Talking.
Morrison. Hope Is Just.
Moonlight Drive.
Tales of the American Night.
Wedding-Dress, The.
Woman in the Window.
Neruda. Is it true that amber contains.
Pound. Dance Figure.
Rexroth. I Dream of Leslie.
Rolfe. Cell, The.
Rossetti. Echo.
In an Artist's Studio.
Rukeyser. Along History.
Make and be eaten, the poet says.
Sarton. Bears and Waterfalls.
Metaphysical Garden, The.
Nursery Rhyme.
Song: "No, I will never forget you and your
great eyes."
These Were Her Nightly Journeys.
Silverstein. Flying Festoon, The.
Ickle Me, Pickle Me, Tickle Me Too.
If the World Was Crazy.
Invitation.
True Story.
Spenser. Muiopotmos: or The Fate of the
Butterflie.
Stuart. Girl of My Dreams, The.
Narcissus Dreaming.
Wakoski. Preface.
Telling You True, About My Fantasy Life.
Walker. She Said:.
Wilbur. Antiworlds.
Attention Makes Infinity.
Baroque Wall-Fountain in the Villa Sciarra, A.
Williams, Charles Kenneth. Don't.

Williams, Miller. Man Who Stays Up Late,
The.
Williams, William Carlos. Good Night.
Wyatt. Answer, The.
Yeats. He Tells of the Perfect Beauty.
Young. Brand New Morning Love Song, A.

Farewell
Atwood. Goodbye, mother / of my mother,
old bone.
Beckett. Da Tagte Es.
Berryman. And Plough-month peters out . its
thermal power.
Farewell to Miles.
Purgatory.
Bogan. Fifteenth Farewell.
Bukowski. Saying Goodbye to Love.
Byron. Adieu, The.
Farewell Petition to J.C.H., Esq.
Farewell to the Muse.
From the French.
Napoleon's Farewell.
To Florence.
To Romance.
Catullus. Carmen 101: "Journeying over many
seas and through many countries."
Coleridge. Sonnet on Quitting Christ's
Hospital.
Crane. With a Photograph to Zell, Now Bound
for Spain.
Davie. Fare Thee Well.
Donne. Expiration, The.
Fever, A.
Dunbar. My Love Irene.
"Dylan." Boots of Spanish Leather.
Don't Think Twice, It's All Right.
Farewell Angelina.
Farewell: "Oh it's fare thee well my darlin'
true."
Never Say Goodbye.
One of Us Must Know (Sooner or Later).
Walk Out in the Rain.
Fletcher. On the Beach.
Glück. Last Letter.
Herrick. His Tears to Thamesis [*or* Thamasis].
To Dianeme ("Dear, though to part it be a
hell").
To His Booke ("Goe thou forth my booke,
though late").
To His Peculiar Friend Master Thomas
Shapcott, Lawyer.
Hesketh. After Ecclesiastes.
Love's Advocate.
Hewitt. Uncle Dick and Aunt Bertha.
Housman. Now hollow fires burn out to black.
Kunitz. Tristia.
Lawrence. Seven Seals.
Virgin Mother, The.
Levine. I reenter a day in a late summer.
Lowry. Freighter 1940.
McAuley. Andante Cantabile.
MacLeish. Cat in the Wood, The.
What Must.
Merton. Things and people goodbye / It is not
that I prefer.
Morgan. Catullus: *Carmen ci.*
Pope. Farewell to London in the Year 1715,
A.
Ralegh. Farewell to False Love, A.
Farewell to the Court.
Poem Put into My Lady Laiton's Pocket by Sr
W. Rawleigh, A.
Rolfe. Recruit.
Rossetti. On the note you do not send me.
Till Tomorrow.
Sandburg. Different Kinds of Good-by.
Epistle: "Jesus loved the sunsets on Galilee."
One Parting.
Spray.
Smith, Stevie. Farewell: "Farewell dear
friends."
Sorrentino. Ave atque Vale.
Some hawk-nosed man.
Stevens. Farewell to Florida.
Waving Adieu, Adieu, Adieu.
Stevenson. Farewell to the Farm.
Suckling. Farewell to Love.
Song: "I prithee send me back my heart."

Tate. Adaption of a Theme from Catullus.
Wordsworth. Farewell, A: "Farewell, thou little Nook of mountain-ground."
Wright, James. To a Hostess Saying Goodnight.
Wyatt. Farewell, love, and all thy law[e]s forever.
Zukofsky. Mulled hosts their countries yet mulled there by a core of wake tossed.

Fargo, North Dakota
Wright, James. Outside Fargo, North Dakota.

Farming and Farmers
Angelou. Southeast Arkanasia.
Atwood. Planters, The.
Auden. Punchard.
   Skyreholme Mill.
Berg. Iowa.
Berry. And that is our story.
   And then, one by one, he moved me.
   As the vision of labor grows.
   Beginning, A.
   Beginning and end.
   Beneath this stone a Berry is planted.
   Boy must learn the man, The.
   Contrariness of the Mad Farmer, The.
   Current, The.
   Don't worry and fret about the crops. After you have done all you can for them, let them stand in the weather on their own.
   Ended, a story is history.
   Enriching the Earth.
   Evening comes / when we finish work and go, An.
   Farm travels in snow, The.
   Farmer among the Tombs, The.
   Farmer and the Sea, The.
   Farmer, Speaking of Monuments, The.
   February. A cloudy day.
   February 2, 1968.
   Going into the city, coming.
   Having danced until nearly.
   Horses.
   I saw one standing aside, alone.
   I worked by will then, he.
   In the predicament of other lives.
   In This World.
   Lineage, A.
   Little farm, motherland, made.
   Mad Farmer in the City, The.
   Mad Farmer Revolution, The.
   Man Born to Farming, The.
   Man who does not ask too much, A.
   My life's wave is at its crest.
   Planting Trees.
   Rain.
   River Bridged and Forgot, The.
   Satisfactions of the Mad Farmer, The.
   Seeds, The.
   September 2, 1969.
   Since then I have arrived here.
   Song in a Year of Catastrophe.
   Sowing.
   Sowing the seed, / my hand is one with the earth.
   Standing Ground, A.
   Streets, guns, machines.
   What we leave behind to sleep.
   Wish to Be Generous, The.
Betjeman. Harvest Hymn.
Bishop. Prodigal, The.
   Sonnet of Intimacy.
Bly. Snowfall in the Afternoon.
Bunting. Complaint of the Morpethshire Farmer, The.
   Gin the Goodwife Stint.
   Soil sandy and the plow light, neither, The.
Burns. Cotter's Saturday Night [Inscribed to Robert Aiken [or R. A****], Esq.], The.
Campion. *Jacke* and *Jone*, they thinke no ill.
Carruth. And so with paragraphics.
   Another hard, hard morning with a hard snow.
   As you or I, but at least he fights hard to get.
   Baler, The.
   Concerning Necessity.
   Emergency Haying.
   Green Mountain Idyl.
   Lady.

Marshall Washer.
   Slows. A bent figure in the dark, thickly clothed.
   Slums par excellence that were your farms! And all.
   Some don't get much, Amos.
   Store, more'n likely, in one of those tenements.
   Those Indians who came and didn't stay.
   When them old hooters had plenty eating material.
   Which ain't much barn at that, maybe twenty head.
Clare. January: A Winters Day.
Cowper. Another ["Take to thy bosom, gentle earth, a swain"].
   Yearly Distress, The.
Creeley. Counterpoint, A.
Cummings. Nobody loses all the time.
   Wee people / dwelling / between serene.
Davie. Back of Affluence.
   By the Road to Upper Midhope.
Dickey, James. Farmers.
Dickinson. Products of my Farm are these, The.
Dunbar. Disappointed.
"Dylan." Motorpsycho Nightmare.
Eberhart. Recollection of Childhood.
   Sunday in October.
   Van Black, an Old Farmer in His Dell.
Emerson. Husband has the nearest acres, The.
   King. If farmers make my land secure.
   Musketaquid.
Fenton. Fruit-Grower in War-time (and Some of His Enemies), The.
Fletcher. Thunderstorm in the Ozarks.
Frost. Code, The.
   Death of the Hired Man, The.
   Impulse, The.
   Mowing.
   Pasture, The.
   Putting in the Seed.
   Range-finding.
   Strong Are Saying Nothing, The.
Gildner. Memory, A.
   Old Farm in Northern Michigan.
   Wheat.
Griffiths. Courting Prosperity.
   Expectations.
   Llangefni Market.
Hall. Elegy for Wesley Wells.
   Farm, The.
   Henyard Round, The.
   New Animals.
   Ox Cart Man.
Hartnett. Retreat of Ita Cagney, The.
   Small Farm, A.
Heaney. Follower.
   Harvest Bow, The.
   Wife's Tale, The.
Herrick. His Grange, or Private Wealth.
Hewitt. Alien Harvest.
   Blue Lias Inn, The.
   Ceilidhe, The.
   Cushkib Fair.
   East Antrim Winter.
   Farmer's Second Son, The.
   Gap, The.
   Glenaan.
   Glens of Atrim, The.
   J.B. Shelton (1876–1958), The Coventry Antiquarian.
   Lint Pulling, The.
   Mid-April.
   On a Country Bus Forty Years Ago.
   Ploughman, The.
   Real Estate.
   Resource.
   Seedsman, The.
   Sunset over Glenaan.
   This Then My Country.
   Thresher, The.
   Threshing, The.
   Triad ("Three sounds of peace and rich increase").
   Tricycle, The.
Hill. Emblem, The.
   Good Husbandry.

Hughes, Ted. February 17th.
Hugo. Brief History.
   Centuries near Spinnazola.
   Farmer, Dying.
   Politely like Snakes in the Oats.
   Remote Farm on the Dubrovnik-Sarajevo Run.
   South Italy, Remote and Stone.
Jarrell. Field and Forest.
Kooser. Abandoned Farmhouse.
Lawrence. Love on the Farm.
Lewis. *Country Gentleman, The.*
   Had I ever a young field.
   Peasant Song.
Lieberman. Woman's Tongue.
Lindsay. Cornfields, The.
   Proud Farmer, The.
Longfellow. Tale of Acadie, A.
MacLeish. Eleven.
Meinke. Rage.
Meredith. Noise of the hollow ground, A.
   Now the valley in ruin of fields.
   Pastoral 2: "Yon upland slope which hides the sun."
   Phoebus with Admetus.
   Then said she, quick as the cries.
Muldoon. Why Brownlee Left.
Nemerov. Harvest Home, A.
Oliver. Farm Country.
Olson. Dry Ode, The.
Pack. Inheritance.
Paley. Dance in Jinoteca, The.
Patchen. Autumn Is the Crows' Time.
Plath. Dispossessed, The.
   Memoirs of a Spinach-Picker.
Rich. Roots.
Rossetti. Margaret has a milking-pail, / And she rises early.
Sandburg. Harvest Sunset.
   Illinois Farmer.
   Improved Farm Land.
   Laughing Corn.
   More Country People.
   Omaha.
   Onion Days.
   Plowboy.
   Prairie.
   Redhaw Rain.
   She Opens the Barn Door Every Morning.
   Smoke Blue.
   Village in Late Summer.
   Weeds.
Sarton. Prothalamion.
Schuyler. Under the Hanger.
Sexton. Farmer's Wife, The.
Shelton. Farmer's Testimony, The.
Silverstein. Farmer and the Queen, The.
Smith, Charlotte. Lark's Nest, The.
Snyder. Hay for the Horses.
Stevens. From the Packet of Anacharsis.
Stevenson. Farewell to the Farm.
   In Lupum.
Sutter. Geneva.
   George.
   Husbandry.
   Mrs.
   Real Estate.
Tennyson. Northern Farmer: New Style.
Tomlinson. At Holwell Farm.
   Farmer's Wife: at Fostons Ash, The.
   How It Happened.
   In December.
   Oxen: Ploughing at Fiesole.
Turco. Barn, The.
   Homestead, The.
   Silo, The.
Updike. Hoeing.
   Pear like a Potato, A.
Van Duyn. Folks built that barn, your great grandfather, and them, The.
   Nap.
   Old widow lady, and went out to do her chore, An.
   Well, that old big fat man.
Warren. Boy's Will, Joyful Labor without Pay, and Harvest Home (1918).
Whitman. Farm Picture, A.
Whittier. Seed-Time and Harvest.

Wilbur. Sonnet.
Williams, Charles Kenneth. Loss.
Williams, William Carlos. Farmer, The.
Wordsworth. Farmer of Tilsbury Vale, The.
　Solitary Reaper, The.
Wright, James. From a Bus Window in
　Central Ohio, Just before a Thunder Shower.
　Milkweed.
　Rats, The.

Farmworkers
Boyle. Comeallye for Robert Carlton Brown,
　A.
Carruth. Marvin McCabe.
　Pa McCabe.
Clare. January: A Winters Day.
Hardy. We Field-Women.
Hugo. Bad Vision at the Skagit.
Lawrence. Beloved.
　Land-Worker.
Oliver. Indonesia.
Warren. Boy's Will, Joyful Labor without
　Pay, and Harvest Home (1918).
See also **Migrant Workers.**

Fascism and Fascists
Bukowski. 22,000 Dollars in 3 Months.
Cullen. Apostrophe to the Land.
Cummings. Red-rag and pink-flag.
Griffiths. Guardianship.
Hemingway. D'Annunzio.
Hill. Christmas Trees.
Lowry. Where Did That One Go to, 'Erbert.

Fashion
Beatles. Polythene Pam.
Cohen. Paris Models.
Jonson. On English Monsieur.
Lieberman. Tartine, for All Her Bulk.
Merton. BROnze fasHIONs / RONZEfa
　shIONS BR.
Nash. Allow Me, Madam, But It Won't Help.
　Don't Look Now.
　Man With Two New Suits, The.
　Thoughts Thought on an Avenue.
　What's the Use.
Nemerov. History of a Literary Movement.
Rossetti. Freaks of Fashion.
　If a pig wore a wig, / What could we say?
　Some ladies dress in muslin full and white.
Sandburg. Proud and Beautiful.
　Style.
Stevens. Explanation.
Thomson. On the Hoop.
See also **Clothing.**

Fate
Auden. Episode, An.
　Two friends who met here and embraced are
　　gone.
　Walk After Dark, A.
Beatles. I've Just Seen a Face.
Berrigan. Red Shift.
Berryman. October's both, back in the Sooner
　State.
Bogan. Didactic Piece.
Brontë. Now trust a heart that trusts in you.
　Will the day be bright or cloudy?
Browning, Elizabeth Barrett. Sonnet: "Heavy
　heart, Beloved, have I borne, A."
　Sonnet: "Let the world's sharpness, like a
　clasping knife."
　Sonnet: "My future will not copy fair my
　past."
Browning, Robert. Saint Martin's Summer.
Bukowski. Got to the track early to study my
　figures and here's this.
　Love.
Burns. Tam Glen.
　To a Mountain Daisy [On Turning One Down,
　with the Plough, in April—1786].
Byron. To the Same.
Campion. Elegie upon the Untimely Death of
　Prince *Henry*, An.
　In Obitum Hen. Mag. Brit. Principis.
　Song: "Shadowes darking our intents, The."
　Vanish, vanish hence, confusion.
Carew. For a Picture Where a Queen Laments
　over the Tomb of a Slain Knight.
　Hue and Cry, The.

To Celia, upon Love's Ubiquity.
To His Mistress.
Ceravolo. Ocean.
Chaucer. Fortune.
Ciardi. Minus One.
Clark. Antiquarian.
　Baby Book Fate Dream.
　Coral.
　Domestic Life of Ghosts, The.
　Fate.
　"Himself let him unknown contain."
　Out of Darkness I Came.
　Personal Angel Glimpsed.
　Spiritual.
Cohen. Avalanche.
　Song for My Assassin.
　Who by Fire?
Coleridge. To a Friend, in Answer to a
　Melancholy Letter.
Cowper. Fragment: "He came to him in the
　extasy of pray'r."
　How blest the youth whom Fate ordains.
　Mortals around your destin'd heads.
Creeley. Kore.
　Song: "What I took in my hand."
Cullen. Ultimatum.
De la Mare. Captive, The.
　Even In The Grave.
　Iago.
　Round, The.
Dickinson. Belshazzar had a Letter.
　Ended, ere it begun.
　It dropped so low—in my Regard.
　It is very wrong that you were ill.
　To earn it by disdaining it.
　Uncertain lease—develops lustre.
Donne. Elegy upon the Untimely Death of the
　Incomparable Prince Henry.
Dunbar. Crisis, The.
Duncan. Poem Beginning with a Line by
　Pindar, A.
"Dylan." Black Diamond Bay.
　If Dogs Run Free.
　Simple Twist of Fate.
Eberhart. Flux.
　Later or Sooner.
Lorca.
　Lost, The.
　Recognition.
Emerson. Alas! till now I had not known.
　All that thy virgin soul can ask be thine.
　Archangel Hope / Looks to the azure cope,
　　The.
　Day's Ration, The.
　Divine Inviters! I accept.
　Fate ("Deep in the man sits fast his fate").
　Fate ("Her planted eye to-day controls").
　Guy.
　Is Jove immortal / So is Cerberus at his
　　portal.
　Loose the knots of the heart; never think on
　　thy fate.
　Love / Asks nought his brother cannot give.
　Motto to "Fate."
　Nemesis.
　No fate, save by the victim's fault, is low.
　On two days it steads not to run from thy
　　grave.
　Perhaps thy lot in life is higher.
　Puff of air or dry or damp, A.
　See & hear the fraud, the malice of the
　　change of fortune.
　'Tis write on Paradise's gate.
Frost. Design.
　Draft Horse, The.
Galvin. After Midnight.
Garrigue. Why the Heart Has Dreams Is Why
　the Mind Goes Mad.
Ginsberg. Wrote This Last Night.
Graves. Bank Account.
　Meeting, The.
　Second-Fated, The.
Hardy. Hap.
　Last Love-Word.
Hayden. For King, for Robert Kennedy.
Herrick. Change Common to All.
　Doomes-Day.

End Decreed, An.
Good Luck Not Lasting.
Lots to Be Liked.
Man's Dying-Place Uncertain.
On Fortune.
Parcæ, The; or, Three Dainty Destinies: The
　Armilet.
Suffer Thou that Canst not Shift.
Three Fatal[l] Sisters.
To the Fever, Not To Trouble Julia.
Hesketh. Animals' Last Words.
Hewitt. Glendun.
　Providence 3.
　Songs I Sing, The.
Hoffman. It cannot come because desired.
　Way It Is, The.
Housman. Along the field as we came by.
　As I gird on for fighting.
　Ask me no more, for fear I should reply.
　I promise nothing: friends will part.
　I to my proofs.
　Now dreary dawns the eastern light.
　Young is the blood that yonder.
Hughes, Langston. Bad Luck Card.
Jarrell. Widow's Song, The.
Keats. Endymion: Poetic Romance.
Kipling. Answer, The.
　By the Hoof of the Wild Goat.
　Gertrude's Prayer.
Lewis. Socrates on the frozen lake.
Lovelace. Advice to My Best Brother, Colonel
　Francis Lovelace.
　To Ellinda. Upon His Late Recovery.
　To His Deare Brother Colonel F.L.
Lowry. Chilliwack.
　Dead men tell cryptic tales and this is one.
　Lusty Advice of a Fortune-Teller.
　Sonnet: "This ruin now, where moonlight
　　walks alone."
　There is a sort of conspiracy about the great.
McGrath. Political Song for the Year's End.
Marvell. Definition of Love, The.
Matthews. Whiplash.
Melville. Apathy and Enthusiasm.
　Camoëns.
　Haglets, The.
　Immolated.
Meredith. Behold, the Gods are with her, and
　are known.
　Karl Onyx.
　What makes it hard to understand.
　Will Whistle.
　World is full of different fates, The.
Merton. World Is a Round Earthenware Plate,
　The.
Morrison. Heaven or Hell.
Nash. Necessary Dirge, A.
Neruda. Sitting Down.
Olson. Some Good News.
Oppen. *Amor fati* / The love of fate.
Owen. Fates, The.
　O World of Many Worlds.
　This is the Track.
Patchen. And He Had Wilder Moments.
Poe. To ———: "I heed not that my earthly
　lot."
Pound. Arides.
Prince. Thyme, tufa, sage, anemone.
Raine. Fateless Ones, The.
　Lachesis.
Ralegh. Gainst Fate no counsell can prevaile.
"Reed." Black Angel's Death Song.
Robinson. Eros Turannos.
Roethke. Waking, The.
Rolfe. Mystery II.
Rukeyser. Beast in View.
Sandburg. Chamfort.
　Fate.
　Fight.
　Mamie.
　On the Way.
　Wind in the corn leaves among the naked
　　stalks, The.
Shapiro. Auto Wreck.
Shelley. Fragment: "And that I walk thus
　proudly crowned withal."
Simic. Tomb of Stéphane Mallarmé, The.

Smith, Stevie. From the Greek.
Spender. Stranger, this is shining Colonos.
Stevens. Flyer's Fall.
Stevenson. Strange are the ways of men.
Ticonderoga: A Legend of the West
  Highlands.
What man may learn, what man may do.
Youth and Love I ("Once only by the garden
  gate").
Tate. These generations that have sealed your
  heart.
Tomlinson. Impalpabilities, The.
Wilbur. Good Servant, The.
Marginalia.
Wright, James. Life.
Wroth. Sonnet 31: "After long trouble in a
  taedious way."
Wyatt. For shamefast harm of great and
  hateful need.

See also **Fortune; Chance; Destiny.**

Fathers
Angelou. Amoebaean for Daddy.
Ashbery. Boy, A.
Atwood. Bedside.
Beckett. Ainsi a-t-on beau.
Berg. Answer, The.
At the Door.
Driving Out Again at Night.
Last Elegy.
Red Weed.
Remembering and Forgetting.
To the Same Place.
Visiting the Stone.
Voice, The.
Why Are We Here?
Wife Talks to Herself, A.
Berry. Elegy: "All day our eyes could find no
  resting place."
Gathering, The.
Berryman. Scholars at the Orchid Pavilion.
Betjeman. Child Ill, A.
Hertfordshire.
Bishop. Infancy.
Table, The.
Travelling in the Family.
Bly. Finding the Father.
More of the fathers are dying each day.
My Father's Wedding.
Boyle. Confession to Eugene Jolas, A.
Bradstreet. To Her Father, with Some Verses.
To Her Most Honored Father Thomas Dudley,
  Esquire, These Humbly Presented.
To the Memory of My Dear and Ever
  Honored Father Thomas Dudley Esq. Who
  Deceased July 31, 1653, and of His Age 77.
Browning, Elizabeth Barrett. Romance of the
  Ganges, A.
Romaunt of Margret, The.
Bukowski. I Was Born to Hustle Roses Down
  the Avenues of the Dead.
My Old Man.
Burns. For the Author's Father.
Byron. To My Son.
Translation from Vittorelli.
What Matter the Pangs of a Husband and
  Father.
Carroll, Jim. Poem on My Son's Birthday.
When he was young in Harlem my father.
Carruth. Fathers die, but sons.
Little Fire in the Woods, The.
My Father's Face.
Of Brook and Stone.
Catullus. Carmen 33: "Vibennius & son,
  renowned."
Ciardi. Elegy: "My father was born with a
  spade in his hand and traded it."
Epithalamium at St. Michael's Cemetary.
It Took Four Flowerboats to Convoy My
  Father's Black.
Tree Trimming.
Cohen. Another Family.
Beside My Son.
Commentary—Beside My Son.
Don't Go Home with Your Hard-on.
Night Comes On, The.
Nothing I Can Lose.
Coleridge. Exchange, The.

Sonnet Composed on a Journey Homeward;
  the Author Having Received Intelligence of
  the Birth of a Son, 20 September 1796.
Sonnet on Receiving a Letter Informing Me of
  the Birth of a Son.
To the Rev. George Coleridge.
Cowper. To His Father.
Creeley. Fragment, A: "On the street I am met
  with constant hostility."
Province, The.
Variation, A.
Cullen. Lines to My Father.
Cummings. My father moved through dooms
  of love.
Davie. Barnsley, 1966.
Father, the Cavalier.
My Father's Honour.
Obiter Dicta.
Staffordshire.
Dickey, James. Bee, The.
Daughter.
Fathers and Sons.
Hospital Window, The.
Dickinson. Home itself is far from home.
I dream about father every night.
Dobyns. Faces.
Dove. Anti-Father.
Father out Walking on the Lawn, A.
Grape Sherbet.
My Father's Telescope.
Taking in Wash.
Dunn. Briefcases.
Midnight.
Photograph Album, The.
Waiting with Two Members of a Motorcycle
  Gang for My Child to Be Born.
Worrier, The.
Eberhart. At Night.
Orchard.
Fletcher. Bedroom.
Father's Thought of His Daughter, The.
On My Father's Hundredth Birthday.
Towards the North Star.
Fox. Horses, The.
My Father's Face.
Gallagher. Black Money.
Boat Ride.
Even Now You Are Leaving.
3 A.M. Kitchen: My Father Talking.
Galvin. Sengekontacket.
Gardner. Telephone, The.
Gildner. Heart Attack.
Memory, A.
My Father after Work.
Prayer for My Father.
To My Daughter.
Ginsberg. Don't Grow Old.
Don't Grow Old.
Glück. Departure.
Metamorphosis.
Mythic Fragment.
Griffiths. Chips.
Fathers.
Unmetalled Road.
Gunn. From an Asian Tent.
Hacker. For Elektra.
Hall. Day I Was Older, The.
Fathers and Sons.
Match.
Merle Bascom's .22.
White Apples.
Hardy. After the Burial.
Forbidden Banns, The.
Her Father.
On the Doorstep.
To My Father's Violin.
Whipper-In, The.
Hartley. Man the Father, The.
Hartnett. That Actor Kiss.
Hayden. Those Winter Sundays.
Heaney. Digging.
Follower.
Hemingway. Across the Board.
Advice to a Son.
Herrick. To the Reverend Shade of His
  Religious Father.
Upon Dundrige.

Hewitt. Corridor.
Domimie's Log, A.
Epitaph for a Conscript, 1940.
Father Explains, A.
Father's Death, A.
Gap, The.
Going to Church.
House at Ballyholme, The.
I saw my father die. For two long years.
I Still Had a Friend.
Jacob and the Angel.
Lonely Heart, The.
Long Bridge, The.
My Father.
My Father's Death in Hospital.
My Father's Ghost.
My Father's Voice.
My Own and Not My Own.
Psychometrist's Remarkable Forecast, The.
Rite.
Street Names.
Those Morning Walks.
Wedding Present, The.
Year of Grace and My Great-Grandfather.
Holmes. Too-Late Words to My Father.
Hopkins. By Mrs. Hopley.
Hugo. Here, but Unable to Answer.
Jonson. Epigram on William, Lord Burl[eigh],
  Lo[rd] High Treasurer of England, An.
On My First Son [*or* Sonne].
Koertge. Coming Out.
He ("Bought a three-bedroom house in 1948").
He ("Drove a school bus for the extra
  money").
He ("Gave me 50 dollars for Christmas one
  year").
He ("Gave me his car").
He ("Got drunk once with another
  cowpuncher").
He ("Had a bay stallion once that the Triple
  Bar C").
He ("Has a new double-knit suit with slightly
  flared").
He ("Has never written me a letter himself").
He ("Told me that I shouldn't have books like
  that").
He ("Used to climb trees that were").
He ("Used to do most everything himself").
He ("Walked in the basement all winter. For
  exercise").
He ("Was looking for work at forty-seven and
  the owner of a").
He ("Was never called Wild Bill").
He: "Was taken out of school after."
My Father ("Lies on the same couch that he
  used to").
My Father ("Once owned a blind horse, a big
  gray who").
My Father ("Said, 'What the devil!' when he
  dropped").
Royce Newport Money.
Kooser. Christmas Eve.
Kunitz. Catch, The.
Portrait, The.
Your turn, Grass of confusion.
Lawrence. Question.
Young Fathers.
Levine. Across the world / in the high
  mountains of the West.
Face, The.
My Son and I.
1933.
Starlight.
Liddy. Miles II.
Lieberman. 82 X 48.
Inside the Gyroscope.
Love, the Barber.
My Father Dreams of Baseball.
Lorde. Father Son and Holy Ghost.
Love Poem.
Lowell. Commander Lowell.
Father.
Father in a Dream.
Father's Bedroom.
Home after Three Months Away.
Middle Age.
Terminal Days at Beverly Farms.

McAuley. Exile, *En Famille*, The.
Penance.
"MacDiarmid." At My Father's Grave.
McGrath. Afternoon of a McGrath.
Offering.
Poem: "My little son comes running with open arms!"
MacNeice. Strand, The.
Truisms, The.
Woods.
Markson. Accepted.
Funeral.
Matthews. Happy Childhood, A.
Meinke. Advice to My Son.
Father.
Soldiers with Green Leggings.
This is a poem to my son Peter.
Meredith. Doe: A Fragment, The.
Periander.
Merrill. Midnight Snack, The.
Scenes of Childhood.
Merton. When a Hideous Man.
Milton. To My Father.
Moore. Silence.
Morgan. Murder, The.
Sometimes I hear my father's voice, sometimes my son's, in mine.
Muldoon. Cherish the Ladies.
Coney, The.
Immram.
Immrama.
Waking Father, The.
Wishbone, The.
Nash. Ask Daddy, He Won't Know.
Daddy's Home, See You Tomorrow.
Good Parent's Garden of Vision, A.
In Which the Poet Is Ashamed but Pleased.
My Daddy.
My Trip Daorba.
Please Leave Father Alone.
Soliloquy in Circles.
Olson. Fathers, The.
Grandfather-Father Poem, The.
I have been an ability—a machine—up to.
I saw, from under Him, the beginning.
Sit by the Window and Refuse.
Oppen. Occurrences, The.
Pack. After All.
Clayfeld's Daughter Reveals Her Plans.
Clayfeld's Glove.
Clayfeld's Son Selects His Specialty.
Departing Words to a Son.
Inheritance.
Kiss, The.
Last Drowning, The.
Paley. Autumn.
My Father at 85.
My Father at 89.
On Mother's Day.
On the Subway Station.
One Day.
Patchen. Autobiographical Note.
Worn on the.
Plath. Colossus, The.
Daddy.
Electra on Azalea Path.
Lament: "Sting of bees took away my father, The."
Little Fugue.
On the Decline of Oracles.
Raine. My Father's Birthday.
"Reed." My Old Man.
Rexroth. Andree Rexroth ("Now once more gray mottled buckeye branches").
Rich. After Dark.
Roethke. My Papa's Waltz.
Premonition, The.
Reminder, The.
Rossetti. Prodigal Son, A.
Rukeyser. Ms. Lot.
St. John. Six/Nine/Forty-Four.
Sandburg. Boy and Father.
Two Women and Their Fathers.
Sarton. Celebration for George Sarton, A.
My Father's Death.
Sexton. All My Pretty Ones.
And One for My Dame.

Begat.
"Daddy" Warbucks.
Divorce, Thy Name Is Woman.
How We Danced.
Moss of His Skin, The.
Santa.
Shelton. Letter to a Dead Father.
Letting Go.
Rain the Stones the Darkness, The.
Silverstein. Smart.
Simic. Inheritance.
Poem: "My father writes all day, all night."
Smith, Patti. Grant.
Smith, Stevie. Correspondence between Mr. Harrison in Newcastle and Mr. Sholto Peach Harrison in Hull.
Father for a Fool, A.
Fuite d'Enfance.
Unser Vater.
Snodgrass. Diplomacy: The Father.
Sorrentino. Perceive.
Spender. Public Son of a Public Man, The.
Stafford. Father's Voice.
Listening.
My Father: October 1942.
Parentage.
Rescued Year, The.
Thanksgiving for My Father, A.
Stevens. Contrary Theses (II).
Irish Cliffs of Moher, The.
Stevenson. Ad Nepotem.
God gave to me a child in part.
Last Sight, The.
Stuart. Girl at Play.
Soup Jar, The.
Warehouse Chute, The.
Sutter. My Father at His Height.
Thomas. Do Not Go Gentle into That Good Night.
Do You Not Father Me.
My World Is Pyramid.
Turco. Corral.
Failed Fathers.
Minotaur.
Recurring Dream, The.
Updike. How to Be Uncle Sam.
Van Duyn. Letters from a Father.
Wakoski. Father of My Country, The.
Placing a $2 Bet for a Man Who Will Never Go to the Horse Races Any More.
Walcott. Letter from Brooklyn, A.
Walker. Forgive Me If My Praises.
Poem at Thirty-nine.
Warren. After Night Flight Son Reaches Bedside of Already Unconscious Father, Whose Right Hand Lifts in a Spasmodic Gesture, as Though Trying to Make Contact: 1955.
Lullaby: A Motion Like Sleep.
Lullaby: Moonlight Lingers.
Reading Late at Night, Thermometer Falling.
Ways of Day.
Whitman. Dirge for Two Veterans.
Williams, Charles Kenneth. Child Psychology.
Easter.
Fifteen.
Instinct.
Sorrow, The.
Williams, William Carlos. Invitation.
To a Friend.
Wordsworth. Anecdote for Fathers.
Childless Father, The.
Fragment: "For let the impediment be what it may."
Wright, James. Evening.
Father.
Having Lost My Sons, I Confront the Wreckage of the Moon: Christmas, 1960.
Revelation, The.
Two Postures beside a Fire.
Youth.
Yeats. Father and Child.
Zukofsky. Head Lines.
Offer 'em up to me—bullneck crook of the baths.

Fathers-in-Law
Mahon. Father-in-Law.

Fatigue. *see* **Weariness.**

Faults
Beckett. Ce qu'a de pis.
Hartley. This Millimeter.
Herrick. In the Dark None Dainty.
No Fault in Women.
To the Generous Reader.
Rossetti. Sinner's own fault? So it was, The.
Shakespeare. Sonnet 96: "Some say thy fault is youth, some wantonness."
Sorrentino. Everything Is a Still-Life.
Je Connai Gens de Toutes Sortes.
What intense colloquy with the self.
Wakoski. My Trouble.
Williams, Charles Kenneth. Blame.

Fauns
Eberhart. Reading Room, The New York Public Library.

Faust
Ashbery. Faust.
Crane. For the Marriage of Faustus and Helen.
Gunn. Faustus Triumphant.
Hill. Doctor Faustus.
Jarrell. Conversation with the Devil, A.
Sexton. Faustus and I.
Shapiro. Progress of Faust, The.

Fawkes, Guy
Crashaw. On the Gunpowder-Treason.
Upon the Gunpowder Treason ("Grow plumpe, leane Death").
Upon the Gunpowder Treason ("Reach me a quill").
Jonson. To William, Lord Mounteagle.
Milton. On the Gunpowder Plot.

Fear
Angelou. Life Doesn't Frighten Me.
Atwood. Highest Altitude.
Auden. Evolution of the Dragon, The.
Leap Before You Look.
Never Stronger.
Some say that handsome raider still at large.
To a Field-mouse.
Beckett. En face.
Berg. To Charlie.
Berry. Creation Myth.
Fear of Love, The.
This comes after silence. Was it something I said.
Berryman. Conversation.
Defensio in Extremis.
Despair.
Letter to His Brother.
Song of the Bridegroom, The.
Bogan. Frightened Man, The.
Browning, Elizabeth Barrett. Sonnet: "I lift my heavy heart up solemnly."
Sonnet: "When we first met and loved, I did not build."
Browning, Robert. Cardinal and the Dog, The.
Bukowski. Guru.
Burns. Cares o' love are sweeter far, The.
On the Seas and Far Away.
Prayer, in the Prospect of Death, A.
Song—(On Chloris Being Ill).
Stanzas on the Same Occasion [in the Prospect of Death].
Carew. First of Jealousy. Dialogue, The.
Carroll, Jim. Fear and Trembling.
Fear of Dreaming.
I watched a street gang heading.
Sleeplessness.
"Carroll, Lewis." Nursery Darling, A.
Valley of the Shadow of Death, The.
Clark. Dark Continent.
Coleridge. Lines Suggested by the Last Words of Berengarius.
Cooper. Approaching my life I am terrified.
Crane. Fear.
Crashaw. Out of Martiall.
Creeley. Dimensions.
For Fear.
Form of Women, A.
Hart Crane.
Hero, The.
I Am Held by My Fear of Death.
Knokke.
Sleep.

That day / in an oak tree—.
Tiger, The.
Window, The.
Cummings. Breathe with me this fear.
Even a pencil has fear to.
Right here the other night something.
This fear is no longer dear. You are not
  going to America and.
Who's most afraid of death?thou.
Davie. Butterfly-girl of the Mussulman, all.
On Not Deserving.
Winter Landscapes.
De la Mare. Fear.
I Sit Alone.
Reflections.
Tom's Angel.
Dickinson. Danger is not at first.
Did you ever stand in a Cavern's Mouth.
Fear—like Dying, dilates trust.
I lived on Dread.
Peril as a Possession.
There lurked a dread that you had gone.
While we were fearing it, it came.
Dobyns. Fear.
Doolittle. I Said.
Dove. Centipede.
Motherhood.
Nightmare.
Dunbar. Boogah Man, The.
Lullaby: "Kiver up yo' haid, my little lady."
Dunn. Letter Home.
Ordinary Days.
Primer for Swimming at Black Point, A.
Sudden Light and the Trees, The.
"Dylan." Señor (Tales of Yankee Power).
Whatcha Gonna Do.
Eberhart. Child, The.
New England Bachelor, A.
Scarf of June, The.
What Gives.
Emerson. Bluebeard. Let the gentle wife
  prepare.
Leave me, Fear! thy throbs are base.
Teach me your mood, O patient stars!
When Jane was absent Edgar's eye.
Why fear to die.
Ferlinghetti. Elegy on the Death of Kenneth
  Patchen, An.
Ford. Like a wild bird he.
Fox. Nicholas Copernicus (1473–1543).
Frost. Assurance.
Fear of Man, The.
Fear, The.
Storm Fear.
Gardner. Cowardice.
Man of Faith, The.
Minotaur, The.
Music Room, The.
Of Flesh and Bone.
Panic Vine, The.
That Princeling.
Timeo.
Garrigue. Only the Irresistible Abides.
Gildner. Heart Attack.
Kneeling in the Snow.
Ginsberg. Please Open the Window and Let
  Me In.
You Might Get in Trouble.
Glück. Garden, The.
Gretel in Darkness.
12. 6. 71.
Graves. Dreaming Children.
Frightened Men.
Straw, The.
Sun-Face and Moon-Face.
That Was the Night.
Tolling Bell.
Gunn. Man With Night Sweats, The.
Memory Unsettled.
Secret Sharer, The.
Stealer, The.
Without a Counterpart.
Hacker. After the Revolution.
Gerda in the Aerie.
His Wife at Bellevue.
Hardy. January Night, A.

Plena Timoris.
To an Unborn Pauper Child.
Hartley. What Is Sacrament.
Hartnett. Sickroom.
Hayden. Soledad.
Heaney. Sweeney in Connacht.
Wedding Day.
Herrick. Another ("If ye fear to be
  affrighted").
Empires.
Feare.
First Marrs or Makes, The.
Gods Mirth, Mans Mourning.
No Bashfulnesse in Begging.
No Danger to Men Desperate.
Reverence.
Ship-Wrack.
To His Muse, Another to the Same.
Upon Grubs.
Hesketh. Dead Blackbird.
Fox, The.
Hewitt. Anglo-Irish Accord, The.
Bogside, Derry, 1971.
Descent, The.
Encounter Nineteen Twenty.
Failed Image.
Glens, The.
Hand over Hand.
Hedgehog.
I Lie Alone.
I saw my father die. For two long years.
Minor Poet's Dilemma, 1940.
My Grandmother Robinson.
Street Names.
Unnecessary Dread, The.
Well-Intentioned Consul, The.
Witch, The.
Hoffman. Unchosen, The.
Holmes. Petition Concerning the Death-Wish.
Hughes, Langston. Situation.
Jarrell. Bird of Night, The.
Fear.
Prince, The.
Jeffers. Nerves.
Jonson. Of Death.
To Fine Lady Would-Be.
Joseph. Overbold, The.
Story.
Keats. When I Have Fears That I May Cease
  to Be.
Kinnell. Still Time, The.
Kipling. Favour, The.
Song of the Little Hunter, The.
That Day.
This I saw when the rites were done.
Knott. Fear of Domesticity.
Kooser. Presidential Poem, A.
Kunitz. Game, The.
There was a big blond uncle-bear.
Lawrence. At the Front.
Doe at Evening, A.
Don't Look at Me.
Humiliation.
Kissing and Horrid Strife.
Late at Night.
People Who Care.
Sickness.
Snake.
Song of a Man Who Has Come Through.
Walk Warily.
Why Does She Weep?
Levertov. Clouds.
Who Is at My Window.
Levine. Memory of rain falling slowly, The.
Lewis. Across seven thousand miles of sea
  and time.
And still the heart breaks, wakeful all the
  night?
Bivouac.
Black dog barking at the moon.
Departure, The.
Monologue.
Water Music.
"Your leg must go. Okay?" the surgeon said.
Liddy. After Hal'amová.
Lorde. Blackstudies.
Generation II.

Lowry. Communal Message.
Dollarton Bus Stop, The.
Faking was three times married to Faking.
Fear ringed by doubt is my eternal moon.
Here him play / That sinister melody.
How did all this begin, and why am I here.
Mr. Lowry's Good Friday under a Real
  Cactus.
No wonder it feared peace, the knees
  of years.
November, 1937.
Virgo.
"MacDiarmid." Two Memories.
McGrath. Legendary Progress.
Revisionist Poem: Machado.
MacLeish. Second Book, The.
What the Old Women Say.
MacNeice. Close the vein! It is Easter Eve.
Crouched upon sea-chiselled gravel, staring out
  and up at the sea.
Heated Minutes, The.
Intimations of Mortality.
Les Neiges d'Antan.
McNeill. Aubade to Fear (Heavy with Child).
Mahon. After Midnight.
Matthews. Burglary.
Meinke. Third Child: June Eleven, Nineteen
  Sixty Two.
You stand in isolation like the first bloom.
Meredith. Here the snake across your path.
Merrill. Days of 1941 and '44.
Midnight Snack, The.
Merton. Lament for Javier Heraud.
World Is a Round Earthenware Plate, The.
Millay. Intense and terrible, I think, must be
  the loneliness.
Morgan. From the Terrace.
Morrison. You Must Confront.
Oliver. Lightning.
Olson. As though there were no flowing.
Story of an Olson, and Bad Thing, The.
Tanto e Amara.
Translation, A.
Owen. Next War, The.
On My Songs.
Storm.
Pack. Black Hole, The.
Early and Late.
Patchen. Dazzling Burden, The.
Poor Gorrel.
Question Is, Who Is Afraid of What, The?
Radiance in a Dark Wood, The.
Rising a Little.
Piercy. Rape Poem.
Plath. Pursuit.
Pope. Shut, shut the door, good *John*!
fatigu'd, I said.
Prince. On a Cold Night.
Stolen Heart, The.
Psalms. Psalm 27: "Lord is my light and my
  salvation, The.."
Ralegh. Sir W. Ralegh, on the Snuff of a
  Candle the Night Before He Died.
Ransom. Parting at Dawn.
Two Gentlemen Scholars.
"Reed." Waves of Fear.
Robinson. Avon's Harvest.
Roethke. Against Disaster.
Lull.
Plaint.
Rolfe. Casualty.
Georgia Nightmare.
Marching Song of the Children of Darkness.
Portrait of a Death.
Song: "Through all the cowering world,
  crouching, shrinking."
To Those Who Fear To Join Us.
Rossetti. All beneath the sun hasteth, / All
  that hath begun wasteth.
Care flieth, / Hope and fear together.
Dead City, The.
Earth Shall Tremble at the Look of Him, The.
Everything that is born must die.
Fisher-Wife, A.
Goodbye in fear, goodbye in sorrow.
Hope is the counterpoise of fear / While night
  enthralls us here.

I Am Small and of No Reputation.
Last Answer, The.
Lord, I am here.—But, child, I look for thee.
On the note you do not send me.
Perfect Love Casteth Out Fear.
Will These Hands Ne'er Be Clean?
Ye Are Come unto Mount Sion.
Rukeyser. Another Day (Child among his powers).
Before Danger.
His gay words, words of delight.
Motive of All of It, The.
Sandburg. Chamfort.
In the days of the cockade and the brass pistol.
Schwartz. At This Moment of Time.
Sexton. Imitations of Drowning.
Shakespeare. Sonnet 23: "As an unperfect actor on the stage."
Sonnet 48: "How careful was I, when I took my way."
Shelley. Fragment: Sufficient Unto the Day.
Love, Hope, Desire and Fear.
To ——: "I fear thy kisses, gentle maiden."
Shelton. Negative Virtues, The.
Sidney. Since Nature's works be good, and death doth serve.
Silverstein. Afraid of the Dark.
I Won't Hatch.
Worst, The.
Simic. Fear.
Old Couple.
Smith, Charlotte. Captive Escaped in the Wilds of America. Addressed to the Hon. Mrs. O'Neill, The.
Smith, Stevie. Blood Flows Back, The.
Voices about the Princess Anemone.
Word, The.
Sorrentino. Faces of Doom and Sterility.
Stevenson. I sit up here at midnight.
In autumn when the woods are red.
Late in the nicht in bed I lay.
Sick Child, The.
This gloomy northern day.
Stuart. High Wire.
Tate. Ode to Fear.
Turco. Weed Garden, The.
Updike. Conversation.
Dying Phobiac Takes His Fears with Him, The.
Yes, self-obsession fills our daily clothes.
Walcott. God Rest Ye Merry, Gentlemen.
Waldman. Hopes & Fears.
Walker. Old Warrior Terror, The.
Threatened.
Warren. Midnight Outcry.
Stargazing.
Whittier. Song of Slaves in the Desert.
Wilbur. Peace of Cities, The.
Williams, Charles Kenneth. Bishop Tutu's Visit to the White House: 1984.
Body, The.
Dream, The.
Patience Is When You Stop Waiting.
Shells.
Thirst.
Vehicle: Conscience.
Vehicle: Violence.
Williams, Miller. Being Here.
Book, The.
On the Way Home From Nowhere, New Year's Eve.
Williams, William Carlos. Cure, The.
Light Shall Not Enter.
Misericordia.
Wordsworth. Western clouds a deepening gloom display, The.
Wright, James. Christmas Greeting, A.
Fear Is What Quickens Me.
I Was Afraid of Dying.
In Terror of Hospital Bills.
Lights in the Hallway, The.
White Rose.
Wroth. Sonnet 3: "Most blessed Night, the happy time for love."
Wyatt. Driving to desire, adread also to dare.
It may be good, like it who list.

Yeats. Presences.
To His Heart, Bidding It Have No Fear.
Who Goes with Fergus?
Young. Afraid.
Zimmer. Zimmer Fearing Anemia.
Zukofsky. Crickets' / thickets / light, / delight.
Snows' night's winds on the window rattling.
Tall and singularly dark you pass among the breakers—.

Feasts and Feasting
Browning, Robert. Founder of the Feast, The.
Gerousios Oinos.
Campion. Dialogue Sung the First Night, A.
Carew. Upon a Mole in Celia's Bosom.
"Carroll, Lewis." Red Queen's Lullaby, The.
De la Mare. Fool's Song, The.
Dunbar. Back-Log Song, A.
Glück. Thanksgiving.
Hall. Eating the Pig.
Herrick. Ceremonies for Christmas[se].
Good Manners at Meat.
Invitation, The.
Kunitz. Supper Before Last, The.
MacNeice. This Is the Life.
Marlowe. 3.12: De Iunonis festo.
Meredith. Fusion.
Tuck! Tuck! Once you would flatter me.
Nash. Private Dining Room, The.
Smart. 4.11: To Phyllis.
Swift. Description of an Irish Feast, The.
Description of an Irish Feast, The.
Turco. Winter in Muscovy.

February
Auden. February Dawn, A.
Berry. February. A cloudy day.
Carruth. On Lincoln's birthday the forest.
When conditions of frost and.
Dickinson. How luscious is the dripping.
White as an Indian Pipe.
Hoffman. February.
Levine. Saturday Sweeping.
Sandburg. Potomac Town in February.
Schuyler. February.
Thinness.
Simic. February.

Feebleness
Herrick. Crutches.
Olson. This Man's Weakness Is Straw.
Rossetti. Thy fainting spouse, yet still Thy spouse.

Feet
Burns. O Mally's Meek, Mally's Sweet.
Herrick. To Dianeme ("Show me thy feet; show me thy legs, thy thighs").
Upon Her Feet.
Upon Pimpe.
Upon Smeaton.
Sexton. Barefoot.
Silverstein. Dancing Pants.
Snodgrass. W. D. Creates a Device for Escaping.
Warren. Shoes In Rain Jungle.
See also **Toes.**

Fellowship. see **Brotherhood.**

Feminism and Feminists
Bradstreet. Mercury showed Apollo Bartas' book.
Bukowski. Beginning, A.
Some of My Readers.
Chaucer. Wife of Bath's Prologue, The.
Wife of Bath's Tale, The.
Gallagher. Conversation with a Fireman from Brooklyn.
Hacker. Ballad of Ladies Lost and Found.
Graffiti from the Gare Saint-Manqué.
Hugo. To Women.
Jong. Seventeen Warnings in Search of a Feminist Poem.
Lawrence. It's No Good!
Levertov. Hypocrite Women.
Meredith. Ballad of Fair Ladies in Revolt, A.
Millay. To Inez Milholland.
Nash. Don't Grin, or You'll Have to Bear It.
Oliver. Strawberry Moon.
Rich. Natural Resources.
Ninth Symphony of Beethoven Understood at

Last as a Sexual Message, The.
Snapshots of a Daughter-in-Law.
Translations.
Rukeyser. Myth.
Waldman. Ancient Song Rising.
Fences
Dickey, James. Fence Wire.
Eberhart. Spite Fence.
Hugo. Graves at Elkhorn.
Kooser. Snow Fence.
Larkin. Wires.
McNeill. Pasture Line Fence.
Miller. Putting Up Snow Fence.
Sandburg. Fence, A.
Snyder. Fence Posts.
Stuart. Fence.
See also **Walls.**
Fencing and Fencers
Jonson. Epigram. To William, Earl of Newcastle, An.
Fenians
Hewitt. Homestead.
Ulster Landowner's Song, An.
Meredith. Her trousers are red; she wears a coatee.
Ferns
Berry. Fern, The.
Eberhart. Velvet Rocks.
Hughes, Ted. Fern.
"MacDiarmid." Bracken Hills in Autumn.
McNeill. Coal Fern.
Hill Song.
Schuyler. What Ails My Fern?
Stevens. Red Fern, The.
Whittier. Sweet Fern.
Wilbur. Fern-Beds in Hampshire County.
Ferry Boats
Kinnell. Last River, The.
Memory of Wilmington.
Lorde. Trip on the Staten Island Ferry, A.
Millay. Recuerdo.
Rossetti. Charon.
Ferry Me across the Water.
Sexton. Letter Written on a Ferry While Crossing Long Island Sound.
Tomlinson. Crossing Brooklyn Ferry.
Turco. Ferry, The.
Whitman. Crossing Brooklyn Ferry.
Festivals
"Dylan." Million Dollar Bash.
Hartley. Festival of the Corn, The.
Herrick. Quintell, The.
Hoffman. Mi-Carême.
Hugo. Carnival Inside, The.
Lewis. Holi.
Marlowe. 3.9: Ad Cererem, conquerens quod eius sacris cum amica concumbere non permittatur.
Meredith. Here Jack and Tom are paired with Moll and Meg.
Merton. Ce Xochitl: The Sign of FLowers.
La Comparsa en Oriente.
Prince. How Festivals Were Celebrated.
Schwartz. News of the Gold World of May.
Tomlinson. Harvest Festival: at Ozleworth.
Matachines, The.
Portobello Carnival 1973.
Feuds
Hill. Florentines.
Kipling. Jubal and Tubal Cain.
Wordsworth. Brownie, The.
Fever
Browning, Robert. Fever.
Burns. Scroggam.
Cooper. After Fever.
Dickinson. These Fevered Days—to take them to the Forest.
Edmunds. Fever.
Emerson. Things oft miscalling, as the hen-.
Gunn. Fever.
Plath. Fever 103°.
Rukeyser. Girl at the Play.
St. John. Interlude: Hephaestion's Prayer.
Smith, Patti. 16 February.
Wright, James. How My Fever Left.
Fiddles and Fiddlers
Burns. Green Sleeves [and Tartan Ties].

McPherson's Farewell.
Rattlin, Roarin Willie.
Dunbar. Itching Heels.
My Sweet Brown Gal.
Temptation.
Hardy. At the Aquatic Sports.
At the Railway Station, Upway.
Country Wedding, The.
Hewitt. Instead of an Elegy.
Kinnell. First Song.
McNeill. Fiddler.
Sandburg. Hell on the Wabash.
Yeats. Fiddler of Dooney, The.

See also **Violins.**

Fidelity
Ammons. Milepost.
Beatles. Any Time at All.
Don't Let Me Down.
Eight Days a Week.
Every Little Thing.
From Me to You.
Here, There and Everywhere.
I Will.
Oh! Darling.
Something.
Tell Me What You See.
Thank You Girl.
Things We Said Today.
Wait.
When I Get Home.
When I'm Sixty Four.
Brontë. Visionary, The.
Browning, Elizabeth Barrett. Man's
Requirements, A.
Sonnet: "I never gave a lock hair away."
Burns. Bonie Bell.
Godly Girzie.
Jessie—A New Scots Song.
Jockey Fou and Jenny Fain.
Louis, What Reck I by Thee.
My Collier Laddie.
O Lay Thy Loof in Mine Lass.
Open the Door to Me, Oh!
When wild War's deadly blast was blawn.
Campion. Now let her change and spare not.
Shall I then hope when faith is fled?
Thou Joy'st, Fond Boy.
Why presumes thy pride on that, that must so
private be.
Catullus. Carmen 104: "Do you really believe
I could blacken my life."
Carmen 109: "Joy of my life! you tell me
this."
Carmen 111: "In constancy content with one
man, there."
Chaucer. Complaint unto Pity, The.
Womanly Noblesse.
Cowper. Doves, The.
Sonnet 6: "Young, gentle, and candid lover
that I am."
Tale, A: "In Scotland's realm, where trees are
few."
To Delia.
Cullen. Street Called Crooked, The.
Cummings. My youthful lady will have other
lovers.
Nothing false and possible is love.
This man's heart / is true to his.
True lovers in each happening of their hearts.
Dickinson. Fidelity never flickers.
Guest am I to have.
He found my Being—set it up.
Donne. Indifferent, The.
Lovers' Infiniteness[e].
Valediction, A: Of My Name in the Window.
"Dylan." Emotionally Yours.
I Want You.
Love Minus Zero/No Limit.
Silent Weekend.
Tell Me That It Isn't True.
Gardner. Baldur Was Beautiful Too.
Graves. Arrow on the Vane.
Broken Compact.
Jus Primae Noctis.
Poet's Curse, The.
Song: Basket of Blossom.
Song: Yesterday Only.

That Other World.
Unposted Letter.
Hardy. Catching Ballet of the Wedding
Clothes, The.
Faithful Swallow, The.
Faithful Wilson.
Harvest-Supper, The.
Postponement.
Herrick. Bondman, The.
Bracelet; to Julia, The.
His Protestation to Perilla.
Love Me Little, Love Me Long.
Parting Verse, Or Charge to His Supposed
Wife When He Travelled, The.
To Anthea, Who May Command Him
Anything.
To Julia ("Permit me, Julia, now to goe
away").
Jong. For My Husband.
Middle Aged Lovers, I.
Jonson. Epistle. To Katharine, Lady Aubigny.
Kipling. My Lady's Law.
Old Song, An.
Kunitz. Promise Me.
Lawrence. Fidelity.
Lewis. I send you a Christmas present, sweet.
Jason and Medea.
Post-Script: for Gweno.
Song: "I lay in sheets of softest linen."
Sonnet (Aboard a Troopship) to Gweno.
Marlowe. 2.3: Ad Eunuchum servantem
dominam.
Meredith. But where began the change; and
what's my crime?
Kiss, and a clasp, and an eye to eye, A.
Preaching from a Spanish Ballad, A.
So spake she her first utterance on the rack.
Soft night–wind went laden to death, The.
Song: "Love within the lover's breast."
Song: "No, no, the falling blossom is no
sign."
Song: "Two wedded lovers watched the rising
moon."
Swallow came from over the sea, The.
Their sense is with their senses all mixed in.
Think not, should your husband swear.
You like not that French novel? Tell me why.
Merton. Allegiance.
Millay. Not even my pride will suffer much.
To the Not Impossible Him.
Milton. Sonnet 6: "Young, gentle, and candid
lover that I am."
Ralegh. Ploche, or the Doubler.
Robinson. Luke Havergal.
Rossetti. Forget Me Not.
Heart's Chill Between.
Lisetta all' Amante.
Meeting.
That No Man Take Thy Crown.
Shakespeare. Sonnet 31: "Thy bosom is
endeared with all hearts."
Sonnet 116: "Let me not to the marriage of
true minds."
Sidney. Sonnet 88: "Out, traitor absence:
dar'st thou counsel me."
Sonnet 91: "Stella, while now by honour's
cruel might."
Smith, Charlotte. From Petrarch ("Oh! place
me where the burning noon").
Oh! place me where the burning noon.
On thy grey bark, in witness of my flame.
Supposed to Have Been Written in a Church-
yard, over the Grave of a Young Woman of
Nineteen.
Van Duyn. Open Letter, Personal.
Voyeur, The.
Whittier. King Volmer and Elsie.
Williams, Miller. Husband.
Pity and Fear.
Wyatt. Deem as ye list. Upon good cause.
Forget not yet the tried intent.
Hate whom ye list for I care not.
Mourning my heart doth sore oppress.
Pain of all pain, the most grievous pain.
Quondam was I in my lady's grace.
Sometime I sigh, sometime I sing.
Spite of their spite which they in vain.

What would ye more of me, your slave,
require.
Ye know my heart, my lady dear.
Zukofsky. Aufilena, virile content him weave
her her solo.
Credit me poor to say of my life *maledictory
weed die.*
You could then, my heart, wit, eye, mean in
proposing love our aim.

Fields and Pastures
Berry. Stay Home.
Browning, Robert. Two in the Campagna.
Carruth. *Better, goddamn it. Why, whenever I
see folks.*
Cowper. Poplar Field, The.
Crane. Alert Pillow..., The.
Creeley. Juggler's Thought.
Davie. Hill Field, The.
De la Mare. English Downs.
To K. M.
Dickey, James. Farmers.
Emerson. Know he who tills this lonely field.
Seyd planted where the deluge ploughed.
Everson. Muscat Pruning.
Frost. Pasture, The.
Waiting.
Gunn. Aqueduct.
For Signs.
Haines. Pickers.
Hall. Great Day in the Cows' House.
High Pasture, The.
Swan.
Hardy. Spot, A.
Heaney. Field Work.
Hewitt. Real Estate.
Riders, The.
Hopkins. Dewy fields in the morning under
the sun.
Hugo. Open Country.
Jarrell. Field and Forest.
Kooser. In the Corners of Fields.
Spring Plowing.
Lovelace. Ant, The.
Marvell. Mower's Song, The.
Olson. Dry Ode, The.
Enniscorthy Suite.
For a Man Gone to Stuttgart Who Left an
Automobile Behind Him.
Plath. In Midas' Country.
Roethke. All the Earth, All the Air.
Far Field, The.
Rossetti. Green Cornfield, A.
Rukeyser. After Their Quarrel.
Sandburg. Bitter Summer Thoughts.
Brown Gold.
Corn Hut Talk.
Cornucopia.
Field People.
Memoranda.
You Shall Have Homes.
Sarton. Baroque Image.
Sorrentino. De Pré Est Vénéneux Mais Joli en
Automne.
Wilbur. Exeunt.
Grasshopper, A.
Williams, William Carlos. Desolate Field, The.
Healall.
Winter Quiet.
Wordsworth. Repentance; A Pastoral Ballad.
Wright, James. I Was Afraid of Dying.
Late November in a Field.
To the Evening Star: Central Minnesota.
See also **Meadows.**

Fiesole, Italy
Hardy. In the Old Theatre, Fiesole.

Fig Trees and Figs
Graves. Song: Fig Tree in Leaf.
Hall. Small Fig Tree, A.
Lawrence. Bare Fig-trees.
Figs.
Sarton. Fig, The.
Warren. Where Purples Now the Fig.
Where the Slow Fig's Purple Sloth.
Williams, William Carlos. Passaic, N.J.

Fights
Bishop. Argument.
Browning, Robert. Woman's Last Word, A.

Bukowski. My Friend.
9 Rings.
Strange Moment, A.
Thank God for Alleys.
35 Seconds.
225 Pounds.
Who in the Hell is Tom Jones?
Burns. Gude Wallace.
"Carroll, Lewis." Tèma con Variazioni.
Cowper. Cause Won, The.
Crashaw. Upon the Same.
Creeley. Broken Back Blues.
Cummings. Adhuc sub Judice Lis.
I / (meet)t(touch).
Spoke joe to jack.
De la Mare. Goliath.
Dunbar. Rivals, The.
Trouble in de Kitchen.
Warrior's Prayer, The.
Eberhart. Airman Considers His Power, An.
Emerson. To the Shah, from Hafiz.
Graves. Hero, The.
Hardy. Fight on Durnover Moor, The.
Hemingway. Defense of Luxembourg.
Herrick. Satan.
Housman. As I gird on for fighting.
Joseph. Dawn Walkers.
Kipling. Belts.
Quest, The.
Rhyme of the Three Sealers, The.
Kunitz. Gladiators, The.
Lawrence. Battle of Life.
Repulsed.
What Would You Fight For?
Lindsay. John L. Sullivan, the Strong Boy of Boston.
Lowry. Harteebeeste with flying hoof, The.
Two streams came from a different source, The.
McAuley. In the Red Corner.
Merton. Ben's Last Fight.
Pack. Wolf Pack, The.
Piercy. Night Letter.
Ransom. Captain Carpenter.
Rich. Blue Ghazals, The.
Implosions.
On Edges.
Rolfe. Marching Song of the Children of Darkness.
Rossetti. I Have Fought a Good Fight.
Rukeyser. They called us to a change of heart.
Sandburg. Blue Maroons.
Silverstein. Battle, The.
Smith, Stevie. Mistress Osmosis.
Van Duyn. Outlandish Agon.
Wilbur. Giaour and the Pacha, The.
Williams, Charles Kenneth. Blades.
I Am the Bitter Name.
Peace.
Toil.
Williams, Miller. Memphis, 2 P.M.
Williams, William Carlos. Controversy, The.
Fight, The.
Wright, James. Larry.
Zimmer. Ancient Wars, The.
Barney Hung Over.
Sweet Night Bleeds From Zimmer, The.
Zimmer Finds Imbellis in the Ancient Graves.
Filipinos. see **Philippines.**
Financiers
Meredith. Capitalist, The.
See also **Banking and Bankers.**
Finches
Berry. Finches, The.
Carruth. Snow buntings whirling / on a snowy field.
Keats. Sometimes goldfinches one by one will drop.
Lewis. Now as a lover would.
Wordsworth. Green Linnet, The.
Fingers
Cohen. Fingerprints.
Dobyns. Hidden Within the Sleeves of Those Dark Robes.
Hall. Match.
Herrick. Upon the Losse of His Finger.
Meinke. Double helix and the triple star, The.

Simic. Bestiary for the Fingers of My Right Hand.
Sorrentino. As with a Simple Gesture of the Fingers.
Stuart. Harpist's Dream, The.
Finland
Fox. Alkaid.
Lowry. Passing Impatience With a Noble Country, A.
Whittier. Conquest of Finland, The.
Finns
Lowry. Passing Impatience With a Noble Country, A.
Fir Trees
Hesketh. Imprint.
Fire and Fires
Atwood. Two Fires, The.
Auden. Before.
By the Fire.
To-night when a full storm surrounds the house.
Berry. Autumn Burning, An.
Don't own so much clutter that you will be relieved to see your.
Supplanting, The.
We pile the brush high.
Bishop. Casabianca.
Night City.
Bogan. Feuer-Nacht.
Bradstreet. Here Follow[es] Some Verses upon the Burning of Our House [July 10th, 1966. Copied Out of a Loose Paper].
Carew. To Her Again, She Burning in a Fever.
To My Mistress [or Mistris], I Burning in Love.
Carruth. Fat Lady, The.
Ignis.
In Memoriam.
Mansion burned. Maids, The.
My Hut.
People burned, came apart, suffocated, melted.
Wet fire / it turns out.
Clark. After the Fire—The Woman.
Cohen. Joan of Arc.
One Night I Burned.
Coleridge. Nose, The.
Cowper. On the Burning of Lord Mansfield's Library.
On the Same.
Creeley. Fire.
Night Sky, A.
Saturday Afternoon.
De la Mare. Invocation: "Burning fire shakes in the night, The."
Making a fire.
Moth, The.
Vigil.
Dickey, James. Attempted Departure.
Purgation ["Beyond the eye, grasses go over the long fields"].
Walking the Fire Line.
Dickinson. Ashes denote that Fire was.
Dare you see a Soul at the White Heat?
Largest Fire ever known, The.
You cannot put a Fire out.
Dobyns. General and the Tango Singer, The.
Donne. I am a little world made cunningly.
Dunbar. Back-Log Song, A.
Noddin' by de Fire.
Duncan. Fire, The.
Tribal Memories.
Eberhart. Art, the holy care of life.
Enigma, The.
Extremity.
Prometheus.
Ship Burning and a Comet All in One Day, A.
Wild Swans of Inverane, The.
Edmunds. Fire, The.
Emerson. It takes a philosopher or fool.
Sun is the sole inconsumable fire, The.
That wandering fire to me appears.
Everson. Bride of the Bear.
Spotfire.
Fisher. Burning Graves at Netherton, The.
Ford. Wind is the breath of it.

Frost. Bonfire, The.
Fire and Ice.
Gallagher. Crêpes Flambeau.
Death of the Horses by Fire.
Gardner. Fall in Massachusetts.
Jean Sans Terre Wraps Himself in a Red Coat.
Gildner. Wean Poem.
Graves. Dazzle of Darkness.
Fire Walker.
Hearth, The.
Song: A Phoenix Flame.
Under the Pot.
Gunn. Door opens, The.
Faustus Triumphant.
Hall. Coal Fire, The.
Swan.
Hardy. Wood Fire, The.
Herrick. Another to the Maids.
Hell Fire ("Fire of Hell this strange condition hath, The").
Scar[e]-Fire, The.
Upon Love: ("I plaid with Love, as with the fire").
Hesketh. Brief Encounter.
Invitation.
Shaping Spirit, The.
Hewitt. After the Fire.
Eleventh Night, The.
Hoffman. Barn Burnt in Ohio, A.
Hughes, Langston. Fire.
Hughes, Ted. Notes for a Little Play.
Jeffers. Fire.
Fire on the Hills.
Jonson. Execration upon Vulcan, An.
Kinnell. Under the Maud Moon.
Kipling. Fires, The.
Kooser. Grandfather.
Lawrence. December Night.
Fire.
Four, The.
Levine. Ashes.
Coming Home, Detroit, 1968.
Miracle, The.
Liddy. Cantico Per Lo Tuo Amore III.
Personal Odyssey.
Lieberman. Kofukuji Arsonists, The.
Lindsay. Here's to the Spirit of Fire.
Lorde. Day They Eulogized Mahalia, The.
Summer Oracle.
Lovelace. Fly about a Glass[e] of Burnt Claret, A.
Lowry. And now I brood on what I think I know.
Dark Path.
Lament—June 1944.
Number 8 Fireman.
Shakespeare's house is safe and sound.
There's something burning, you said, when we were hammering.
Virgo.
McAuley. House Burning Down.
McGrath. Coal Fire in Winter, A.
MacNeice. Brother Fire.
McNeill. Spark, The.
Matthews. How Careful Fire Can Be.
Meredith. Agamemnon in the Fight.
Clash in Arms of the Achaians and Trojans.
Fireside.
Merrill. After the Fire.
Charles on Fire.
Log.
Mornings in a New House.
Merton. All things are fire.
Elegy for the Monastery Barn.
Out of the rain and the darkness and the depths, the bottomless holes in the green sea.
Morrison. & the Cool Fluttering.
Nash. There Are More Ways to Roast a Pig than Burning the House Down or You Can Always Stick Your Head in a Volcano.
Nemerov. Firelight in Sunlight.
Flame of a Candle, The.
Olson. Here i am, naked.
Li Po.
What Had to Go.
Paley. Woman invented fire and called it, A.
Patchen. Green Fires, The.

Piercy. Few Ashes for Sunday Morning, A.
I Am A Light You Could Read By.
Noon of the Sunbather.
Shadows of the Burning.
Plath. Aftermath.
Burning the Letters.
Firesong.
Raine. It is in us they burn.
Six calices yellow gold.
Ransom. Puncture.
Rich. Burning Oneself Out.
Rolfe. Poem: "Girl lashed to the stake, The."
Rossetti. Emerald is as green as grass, An.
Love Is Strong as Death.
Stroke a flint, and there is nothing to admire.
Subject To Like Passions as We Are.
Rukeyser. Burning Bush.
For Fun.
Waterlily Fire.
St. John. Winter Fires.
Sandburg. Anna Imroth.
Earth is a forgotten cinder, The.
Fire Pages.
Impossible Iambics.
Kin.
Sea only knows the bottom of the ship, The.
Schuyler. Moneses Uniflora.
Scott. Bale-Fire, The.
Sexton. Angel of Fire and Genitals.
Fire Thief, The.
Shapiro. Exile.
Simic. February.
Smith, Patti. Fire of Unknown Origin, A.
Smith, Stevie. Humane Materialist at the
Burning of a Heretic, A.
Persian, The.
Snyder. Burning the Small Dead.
Cool around the Fire, The.
Sorrentino. Land of Cotton.
Spenser. My Love Is Like to Ice.
Stafford. Salvaged Parts.
Stevenson. Armies in the Fire.
Autumn Fires.
Swift. On the Burning of Whitehall in 1698.
Tate. Fire I praise was once perduring flame,
The.
Near to me as perfection in the blood.
Tomlinson. At Holwell Farm.
Fire in a Dark Landscape.
Flame.
Night-Piece: The Near and the Far.
Turco. Burning the News.
Updike. Burning Trash.
Song of the Open Fireplace.
Working Outdoors in Winter.
Van Duyn. Along the Road.
Elementary Attitudes.
Walcott. City's Death by Fire, A.
Whitman. By the Bivouac's Fitful Flame.
Whittier. Burning Drift-Wood.
Chicago.
Legend of the Lake, A.
Wilbur. Riddle, A.
Williams, Charles Kenneth. Bringing It Home.
Fire.
Hail goes / dancing, The.
It's over now. I watch.
Williams, Miller. Newspaper Picture of
Spectators at a Hotel Fire, A.
Williams, William Carlos. Crude Lament.
Zukofsky. Incident, An.
Fire Engines
Wilbur. Fire-Truck, A.
Williams, William Carlos. Great Figure, The.
Firearms. see Guns.
Firecats
Stevens. Earthy Anecdote.
Fire-eaters
Williams, Miller. Firebreathers at the Café
Deux Magots, The.
Firefighters
Gallagher. Conversation with a Fireman from
Brooklyn.
Lowry. Hostage.
Number 8 Fireman.
Schuyler. Witley Court.
Williams, Charles Kenneth. Fire.

Wright, James. Red Jacket's Grave.
Fireflies
Clark. Fireflies.
Dickinson. Winged spark doth soar about, A.
Fox. Ukiyo-E.
Frost. Fireflies in the Garden.
Lawrence. Fireflies in the Corn.
Marvell. Mower to the Glow-Worms [or
Glowworms or Glo-Worms], The.
Meinke. Fourth of July.
Smith, Charlotte. Glow-Worm, The.
Tomlinson. Fireflies.
On a May Night.
See also **Glowworms.**
Fireworks
Lowry. Though we are all a little bit
disappointed this year there won't be any
fireworks.
Meinke. Fourth of July.
Hero Worship at Key West on the 4th of July.
Nemerov. Fourth of July, The.
Rich. Celebration in the Plaza, The.
Sandburg. Fourth of July Night.
Stuart. Fireworks.
Updike. Fireworks.
**First Church of The Millennium. see Shakers
(First Church of The Millennium).**
First World War. see World War I.
Fish
Bishop. Fish, The.
Bly. Dried Sturgeon, The.
Bukowski. Goldfish.
"Carroll, Lewis." How doth the little
crocodile.
Humpty Dumpty's Recitation.
Mock Turtle's Song, The: "Beneath the waters
of the sea."
Three sisters at breakfast were feeding the cat.
Two Brothers, The.
White Queen's Riddle, The.
Carruth. When Howitzers Began.
Ciardi. Lung Fish, The.
Cowper. On the High Price of Fish.
To the Halibut.
Dickey, James. Eagle's Mile, The.
Movement of Fish, The.
Dickey, William. Post-Therapy Room.
Eberhart. Ospreys in Cry.
Everson. Steelhead.
Ferlinghetti. Hilarious God.
Graves. P'eng That Was a K'un, The.
Haines. All spine and knotted fin-rays.
Hartley. Fishmonger.
Hewitt. Aquarium.
Providence 3.
Hoffman. Dogfish.
Hughes, Ted. Pike.
Hugo. At the Stilli's Mouth.
Bass.
Cape Alava.
Death in the Aquarium.
Dwelling.
Introduction to the Hoh.
Lone Lake, Whidbey.
Name the Mystery Fin and Win a Doll.
Sweet Piece from Fontal.
Underwater Autumn.
Jeffers. Birds and Fishes.
Joseph. Catch.
Keats. Minnows.
Kunitz. King of the River.
Lawrence. Fish.
Little Fish.
Levine. To a Fish Head Found on the Beach
Near Málaga.
Liddy. Afterword.
Country Life.
May Day Song.
Lieberman. Skin Song.
Lowell. Fishnet.
Lowry. Mackerel shouldn't take, A.
Singing. / The morning bird. / (Humphum!).
"MacDiarmid." Dytiscus.
McGrath. Beyond Seattle.
MacLeish. Vicissitudes of the Creator.
Melville. Maldive Shark, The.
Merton. Joy of Fishes, The.

Nash. Barmaids Are Diviner Than Mermaids.
Guppy, The.
Shad, The.
Smelt, The.
Nemerov. Goose Fish, The.
Oliver. Fish, The.
Olson. Abstract #1, Yucatan.
Red Fish-of-Bones, The.
Patchen. Plate of Steaming Fish, A.
Raine. In the Beck.
Rossetti. When fishes set umbrellas up / If the
rain-drops run.
Sandburg. Among the shapes and shadow-
shapes.
Fish Crier.
Flying Fish.
Two Fish.
Sexton. Fish That Walked, The.
Silverstein. Fish?
Minnow Minnie.
Silver Fish, The.
Smith, Charlotte. Walk by the Water, A.
Smith, Stevie. Fish, Fish.
Friends of the River Trent.
Look!
Snyder. Lines on a Carp.
Sealion, salmon, offshore.
Spenser. Looking far foorth into the ocean
wide.
Stuart. Flatfish.
Real World, The.
Warren. Red Mullet, The.
Whitman. Paumanok Picture, A.
Wilbur. Shad-Time.
Williams, William Carlos. Cod Head, The.
Fish.
Sea-Trout and Butterfish.
Wordsworth. Gold and Silver Fishes in a
Vase.
Wright, James. Northern Pike.
Yau. Some fish we peel back, leaving only
the bones. Others devour us.
To the young boy standing in front of the
large glass tanks, each.
Yeats. Fish, The.
Three Movements.
See also **Listings for specific Fish.**
Fishing and Fishermen
Atwood. Fishing for Eel Totems.
Berry. Don't pray for the rain to stop.
I have thought of you stepping out of your
doorway at dawn, your son in your tracks.
Now that April with sweet rain.
Plan, The.
Bishop. At the Fishhouses.
Fish, The.
Bunting. Mesh cast for mackerel.
Byron. And angling too, that solitary vice.
"Carroll, Lewis." Two Brothers, The.
Ciardi. Benefits of an Education, The.
Crane. Bacardi Spreads the Eagle's Wing.
De la Mare. Old Angler, The.
Donne. Bait[e], The.
Dunbar. Fishing.
Lazy Day, A.
Till the Wind Gets Right.
Eberhart. Angels, The.
Deep Fishing.
Ferlinghetti. Baja Beatitudes.
Fox. Ice Fishing.
Gallagher. Boat Ride.
Gardner. Compleat Anglers, The.
Haines. Sometimes in our sleep.
To My Father.
Hall. Cold Water.
Hartley. Fishermen's Last Supper.
This Little City.
Hayden. Smelt Fishing.
Heaney. Hazel Stick for Catherine Ann, A.
Hesketh. Cap, The.
Fisherman Poet.
Hewitt. Aquarium.
Silver Was the Barbèd Hook.
Hoffman. Night Fishing.
Hughes, Langston. Catch.
Hughes, Ted. Earth-Numb.
Stealing Trout on a May Morning.

Hugo. Bass.
Between the Bridges.
Changes at Meridian.
Cleggan.
Confederate Graves in Little Rock.
Cornwall, Touring.
Duwamish Head.
In Your Blue Dream.
La Push.
Langaig.
Letter to Bly from La Push.
Letter to Wagoner from Port Townsend.
Pishkun Reservoir.
Plunking the Skagit.
Shark Island.
Tahola.
West Marginal Way.
Jeffers. Drunken Charlie.
Purse-Seine, The.
Salmon Fishing.
Kipling. MAY (*Fishing*).
Kunitz. Catch, The.
Hand-Rolled Cigarettes.
Quinnapoxet.
Liddy. Along a leafy lonely river God-shy-
eyed fisher boys.
Lieberman. Lobsters in the Brain Coral.
Saltcod Red.
Lowell. Drunken Fisherman, The.
Lowry. After Labour Day.
"MacDiarmid." Ah, sweetheart, what a pool!
Broad, deep, strong, silent, and sedate!
As I have often told.
With the Herring Fishers.
MacLeish. Poet.
Mahon. Soles.
Marlowe. Bait[e], The.
Meinke. Perch, The.
Meredith. My Heart.
Merrill. Parrot Fish, The.
Pier: Under Pisces, The.
16. ix. 65.
Morgan. Mr. Boyd.
Muldoon. Waking Father, The.
Nash. Fish, The.
Nemerov. Casting.
Olson. By Cure of—Sulfa.
is an archeology: eight fathom down, on
Dogger Bank, the bones, The.
Oppen. Ballad: "Astrolabes and lexicons."
Plath. Net-Menders, The.
Roethke. Pike, The.
Rossetti. Fisher-Wife, A.
Smith, Stevie. Fish, Fish.
Snyder. Shark Meat.
Stafford. In the Deep Channel.
Stevens. Thinking of a Relation between the
Images of Metaphors.
Stevenson. Ad Piscatorem.
I sit up here at midnight.
Stuart. People Asleep.
Real World, The.
Sutter. Fishing at Forty.
Icehouse.
Tate. Trout Map, The.
Tomlinson. Mackinnon's Boat.
Night Fishers.
Updike. Crab Crack.
Walcott. Tarpon.
Whitman. Paumanok Picture, A.
Torch, The.
Whittier. Fishermen, The.
Skipper Ireson's Ride.
Wilbur. Trolling for Blues.
Williams, Miller. Trying to Remember.
Williams, William Carlos. Birds have flown
away from the mountains, The.
Gentle Rejoinder, The.
Paul.
Ritualists, The.
Wordsworth. Written upon a Blank Leaf in
"The Compleat Angler."
Wright, James. Fishermen, The.
Lifting Illegal Nets by Flashlight.
Yeats. Fish, The.
Fisherman, The.
Zimmer. Cecil, Zimmer, and the Man-Made

Lake.
Entering the Storm, Unable to Swim, Zimmer,
Rollo, and Cecil Are Saved.
See also **Clams and Clamming; Crabs and
Crabbing; Listings for specific Fish.**
Fitzgerald, Edward
Browning, Robert. To Edward FitzGerald.
Fitzgerald, F. Scott
Davie. Garden Party, The.
Flags
Eberhart. Flag, The.
Emerson. In the kingdom of Poesy Hafiz
waves like a banner.
Kipling. English Flag, The.
Kunitz. Eagle.
Whitman. Ethiopia Saluting the Colors.
Whittier. Pine-Tree, The.
Flags, United States
Cummings. Our Flag.
Emerson. To the mizen, the main, & the fore.
Frost. Not of School Age.
Silverstein. Flag.
Whitman. Bathed in War's Perfume.
Delicate Cluster.
Thick-Sprinkled Bunting.
World Take Good Notice.
Whittier. Barbara Frietchie.
Centennial Hymn.
Mantle of St. John de Matha, The.
Flamingos
Lieberman. Flamingos of the Soda Lakes.
MacLeish. Boy in the Roman Zoo.
Flanders, Belgium
Hill. Canaan.
Owen. To a Comrade in Flanders.
Flapjacks. *see* **Pancakes.**
Flattery
Bukowski. Note to the Boys in the Back
Room, A.
Burns. Brigs of Ayr, a Poem. Inscribed to J.
B*********, Esq; Ayr, The.
To Maria.
Byron. Answer to the Foregoing, Addressed to
Miss———.
Written in "Letters to an Italian Nun and an
English Gentleman: by J.J. Rousseau:
Founded on Facts."
Campion. Kind in every kinde.
Clough. Because a Lady chose to say.
Cowper. 1.9: "Saunt'ring along the street one
day."
In a Letter to the Same [C. P.].
On Flatterers.
Donne. Oh, let me not serve so, as those men
serve.
To the Countess of Huntingdon ("Madam, /
Man to God's image, Eve, to man's was
made").
Emerson. Early after the night long revel.
In this sour world, o summerwind.
Herrick. Another Upon Her.
Flatterie.
To His Brother in Law Master John
Wingfield.
To His Honoured Friend, M. John Weare,
Councellour.
To His Honoured Friend, Sir John Mynts.
To His Honoured Kinsman, Sir Richard Stone.
To His Kinsman, Sir Tho. Soame.
To His Kinswoman, Mrs. Penelope Wheeler.
To His Worthy Kinsmen, Mr. Stephen Soame.
To Oenone ("Sweet Oenone, doe but say").
To the Honoured, Master Endimion Porter.
To the Right Honourable Edward Earle of
Dorset.
Johnson. To Lyce, an Elderly Lady.
Jonson. To Robert, Earl of Salisbury ("What
need hast thou of me, or of my muse").
Koch. Of course you must stop her. Say
anything: "Hello!" "Good-bye!"
Ransom. Primer for Statesmen.
Shakespeare. Sonnet 69: "Those parts of thee
that the world's eye doth view."
Sonnet 85: "My tongue-tied Muse in manners
holds her still."
Sonnet 138: "When my love swears [*or*
sweares] that she is made of truth."

Sidney. Sonnet 35: "What may words say, or
what may words not say."
Smith, Charlotte. Origin of Flattery, The.
Smith, Stevie. Rehearsal, The.
Wordsworth. Written in the Strangers' Book at
"The Station," Opposite Bowness.
Fleas
Coleridge. On Donne's First Poem.
Donne. Flea, The.
Sandburg. Englishman in the old days, An.
Silverstein. Santa and the Reindeer.
Williams, Charles Kenneth. Fleas, too, / have
fled, The.
Fletcher, John
Herrick. Upon Master Fletchers Incomparable
Playes.
Jonson. To the Worthy Author M[r] John
Fletcher.
Lovelace. To Fletcher Reviv'd.
Flies
Beckett. La Mouche.
Blake. Fly, The.
Little Fly.
Bukowski. Not All That Bad.
Carew. Fly That Flew into My Mistress'[s]
Eye, A.
Cohen. Fly, The.
To a Fellow Student.
Cummings. Off a pane)the.
Ohld song / you Know.
Dickinson. Butterfly in honored Dust, The.
I heard a fly buzz—when I died.
Dunn. Resurrection, The.
Eberhart. When Golden Flies Upon My
Carcass Come.
Graves. Blue-Fly, The.
Hall. Flies.
Hartley. Asses' Out-House, The.
Herrick. Amber Bead, The.
Upon a Flie.
Hoffman. Ephemeridae.
Hughes, Ted. Cranefly in September, A.
Joseph. Trying to Understand Violence.
Kinnell. Fly, The.
Lovelace. Fly about a Glass[e] of Burnt
Claret, A.
Lowell. Harriet.
MacLeish. Captivity of the Fly.
La Foce.
MacNeice. Mayfly.
Merrill. House Fly, The.
Nash. Fly, The.
Nemerov. Between the Window and the
Screen.
Truth.
Olson. Big Fat Fly, A.
Tomlinson. Jam Trap, The.
Updike. Fly.
Williams, Charles Kenneth. My Fly.
Wordsworth. Written in Germany on One of
the Coldest Days of the Century.
Flight
Berry. Past the strait of kept faith.
Star, The.
There is a sort of vertical.
When I rise up.
Bishop. Invitation to Miss Marianne Moore.
Ciardi. Birds, Like Thoughts.
Clark. Birds.
De la Mare. Glimpse, The.
Dickey, James. Eagles.
Eagle's Mile, The.
Night Bird.
Eberhart. Gulled.
I turned where the sun came up and he held
my hand.
Incidence of Flight.
Tree Swallows.
Frost. Kitty Hawk.
Gunn. Flying Above California.
Small Plane in Kansas.
Hall. Idea of Flying, The.
Old Pilot, The.
Hesketh. Owl.
Hewitt. By Air to Birmingham on a Mid-June
Evening.
September Lull.

Hopkins. All as that moth call'd Underwing, alighted.
Ecquis Binas.
Hughes, Ted. Heptonstall Cemetery.
My idleness curdles.
Swift Comes the Swift, The.
Swifts.
You stop to rest, far up, you teeter.
Hugo. Lone Cheer from the Stands for a Bitter Crane.
Memoirs.
Jong. Flight to Catalina.
Kipling. Flight, The.
Levine. Poem of Flight, The.
Lovelace. Falcon, The.
McAuley. Making Repairs.
McNeill. First Flight.
Matthews. I Long For a Horse.
39,000 Feet.
Nash. Bat, The.
Caution to Everybody, A.
It's Snug to Be Smug.
Oliver. Night Flight.
Piercy. Night Flight.
Rossetti. Fly Away, Fly Away.
Paradise: in a Symbol.
Rukeyser. Flying Red Horse, The.
Night Flight : New York.
Preamble.
Theory of Flight.
Schuyler. In Wiry Winter.
Silverstein. Flying Festoon, The.
Ickle Me, Pickle Me, Tickle Me Too.
Long-Haired Boy, The.
Simic. Autumn Air.
Smith, Stevie. I Wish.
Look, Look.
No More People.
Snodgrass. Assuming Fine Feathers, W. D. Takes Flight.
Sorrentino. Captain Marvell.
Spender. Airman.
Tomlinson. Encounter.
Sight and Flight.
Warren. Evening Hawk.
Wilbur. All These Birds.
Williams, Miller. One Day a Woman.
Wright, James. Presentation of Two Birds to My Son, A.

Flirtation
Beatles. Day Tripper.
Norwegian Wood.
Browning, Elizabeth Barrett. Lady's "Yes," The.
Bunting. Carmencita's tawny paps.
Ginger, who are you going with?
Dove. Flirtation.
Gunn. Bally *Power Play*.
Fever.
Hardy. Watering-Place Lady Inventoried, A.
Herrick. Lips Tongueless[e].
Sho[o]e Tying, The.
Silken Snake, The.
To His Mistress Objecting to Him Neither Toying or Talking.
Hewitt. For Any Women Who Pass This House.
Hopkins. Castara Victrix.
Lawrence. Passing Visit to Helen.
She Was a Good Little Wife.
Lindsay. For All Who Ever Sent Lace Valentines.
Meredith. Jolly Young Carpenter, The.
Smith, Patti. Ballad of Hagan Waker, The.
Smith, Stevie. Rencontres Funestes.
Stevenson. Mine eyes were swift to know thee, and my heart.
Ne Sit Ancillae Tibi Amor Pudori.
To Miss Rawlinson.
To Rosabelle.
When aince Aprile has fairly come.
You looked so tempting in the pew.
Updike. Flirt.
Young. Flirt.

Flodden Field, Battle of (1513)
Scott. English Advance at Flodden, The.

Flood, The
Cohen. Gypsy Wife, The.
Fletcher. Night lay upon the ocean like a sword.
Now it was noonday, fortieth of the flood.
Milton. Flood, The.

Floods
Atwood. After the Flood, We.
Auden. Damming Stream.
Berry. Don't pray for the rain to stop.
Wet Time, A.
Bishop. Flood, The.
Bly. Schoolcraft's Diary Written on the Missouri: 1830.
Carruth. And the water/ the rising water.
Dunbar. Right's Security.
"Dylan." Down in the Flood.
Ferlinghetti. Wild Dreams of a New Beginning.
Fletcher. Flood Symphony, The.
Frost. Flood, The.
Galvin. Connecticut River in Flood, The.
Griffiths. Misrule, Towyn, 1990.
Gunn. Flooded Meadows.
Hayden. Burly Fading One, The.
Hewitt. East Antrim Winter.
Old Mill-Race, The.
Joseph. February Floods, 1953.
Non-communicant.
River Rising in India.
Kipling. Floods, The.
Song of Seven Cities, The.
Knight. Poem to Galway Kinnell, A.
"MacDiarmid." Cheville.
MacNeice. River in Spate.
Matthews. Everywhere.
Flood Light.
Flood Peak.
Record Flood.
Merton. Autumn Floods.
Miller. Flood.
Rukeyser. His Dream of Flood: And Eden.
Tarpaper shack and the red rose bush, The.
They dug up the grave, while a banjo and two guitars.
Snodgrass. Flash Flood.
Tomlinson. Epilogue, The: "It was a dream delivered the epilogue."
Flood, The.
Whitman. Voice from Death, A.
Wordsworth. When Severn's Sweeping Flood Had Overthrown.
Wright, James. To Flood Stage Again.
Zimmer. Cecil, Zimmer, and the Man-Made Lake.

Florence, Italy
Browning, Elizabeth Barrett. King Victor Emanuel Entering Florence, April, 1860.
Browning, Robert. Old Pictures in Florence.
Davie. Mr Sharp in Florence.
Hill. Florentines.
Holmes. Decline of the West.
Lawrence. À La Maniere De D. H. Lawrence.
Bat.
Lowell. Florence.
McGrath. Migration of Cities, The.
Raine. Daisies of Florence.
Schuyler. This Notebook.
Tomlinson. Machiavelli in Exile.
Wordsworth. At Florence.

Florida
Berryman. Tampa Stomp.
Bishop. Florida.
Carruth. Études de Plusiers Paysages de l'Âme.
Cohen. Poems Don't Love Us Any More, The.
Dunbar. Florida Night, A.
To the Miami.
Eberhart. Angels, The.
Opposition.
Emerson. For fifteen winter days.
Glück. To Florida.
Hugo. Letter to Hanson from Miami.
Jong. Keys, The.
Koertge. Mr. Big.
Meinke. Cloud, Florida, 1985, The.

Merton. Dirge for the City of Miami.
Sorrentino. Some Sap Sings a Poor Pantoum.
Stevens. Fabliau of Florida.
Farewell to Florida.
Indian River.
Nomad Exquisite.
O Florida, Venereal Soil.
Updike. Miami.
Williams, William Carlos. This Florida: 1924.
Yau. Halfway to China.

Florists
Koch. Girl and Baby Florist Sidewalk Pram Nineteen Seventy Something.
Roethke. Old Florist.

Flowers
Ammons. Mirrorment.
Auden. Flowers and Stationmaster.
Berg. Both.
Bishop. Elegy for Maria Alves.
Blake. Garden of Love, The.
Wild Thyme, The.
Bly. At the Time of Peony Blossoming.
Bogan. Animal, Vegetable and Mineral.
Browning, Elizabeth Barrett. Deserted Garden, The.
Flower in a Letter, A.
Island, An.
Man and Nature.
Sonnet: "Beloved, thou hast brought me many flowers."
Browning, Robert. Flower's Name, The.
Magical Nature.
Bukowski. Pansies.
Rose, Rose.
Burns. Banks of the Devon, The.
O Were My Love Yon Lilac[k] Fair.
Posie, The.
Campion. And Would You See My Mistress' Face?
Dance now and sing the joy and love we owe.
Song: "Now hath Flora rob'd [or robbed] her bowers."
Carew. Protestation [A Sonnet], The.
Carroll, Jim. Desert Casino, The.
So months of cool flowers close in these arms.
Carruth. Almanach du Printemps Vivarois.
Bouquet in Dog Time.
Carnations.
Chicory.
Excursus of Reassurance in Begonia Time, An.
Language of Flowers, Etc., The.
Of Distress Being Humiliated by the Classical Chinese Poets.
Song: So Why Does This Dead Carnation.
Sonnet: "To see a woman long oppressed by fear."
Survival as Tao, Beginning at 5:00 A.M.
This Decoration.
This Song.
Ceravolo. Struggling.
Coleridge. Keepsake, The.
On Observing a Blossom on the First of February 1796.
Reproof and Reply, The.
Snow-Drop, The.
Cooper. Morning on the St. John's.
Crane. Moment Fugue.
Creeley. Flower, The.
Late Comer, The.
Rhyme, The.
Snow, The.
Cummings. But the other / day i was passing a certain.
I like / to think that on.
In time of daffodils(who know.
Lily has a rose.
One winter afternoon / (at the magical hour).
Riverly is a flower.
Rosetree,rosetree / —you're a song to see:whose.
Should this fool die.
Tumbling-hair / picker of buttercups.
Davie. Chrysanthemums.
Demi-Exile. Howth.
De la Mare. April Moon.
Bottle, The.
Daisy, The.

Hawthorn Hath a Deathly Smell, The.
Imogen.
Lucy.
Miracle, The.
Noon and Night Flower.
Ophelia.
Pot Of Musk, A.
When the rose is faded.
Dickinson. As Children bid the Guest "Good Night."
Between My Country—and the Others.
Bloom—is Result—to meet a Flower.
Blossom perhaps is an introduction, A.
Bulbs are in the sod, The.
Career of flowers differs from ours, The.
Clover's simple Flame, The.
Come slowly—Eden!
Daisy follows soft the Sun, The.
Did the Harebell loose her girdle.
Ferocious as a Bee without a wing.
Flower keeps it's appointment.
Flower must not blame the Bee, The.
Flower will not trouble her, it has so small a Foot, A.
Flowers—Well—if anybody.
How many Flowers fail in Wood.
I tend my flowers for thee.
Immortality of Flowers, The.
Intrusiveness of flowers.
It would not know if it were spurned.
"Lethe" in my flower.
Lovely flowers embarrass me, The.
Nature's faithful Blossoms.
Perhaps you'd like to buy a flower.
South Winds jostle them.
Stem of a departed Flower, The.
There is a flower that Bees prefer.
They ask but our Delight.
We are snatching our jewels from the frost.
When they come back—if Blossoms do.
Whose are the little beds, I asked.
Doolittle. At Baia.
Daemon initiate, spirit.
Evening.
Garden.
Sea Rose.
Dove. Then Came Flowers.
Dunbar. Seedling, The.
Dunn. Landscape, The.
Loveliness.
Eberhart. Ceremony By the Sea, A.
Forms of the Human.
Gesture, The.
Indian Pipe.
Perception as a Guided Missile.
Emerson. Botanist.
By breath of beds of roses drawn.
Dark Flower of Cheshire garden.
Days pass over me, The.
From Omar Chiam.
Go if thou wilt ambrosial Flower.
Good Charles the springs adorer.
He must have / Droll fancies sometimes cross his quiet thoughts.
Know he who tills this lonely field.
May.
Rhodora, The [On Being Asked Whence Is the Flower].
She walked in flowers around my field.
What are all the flowers.
Fletcher. Aster Flower, The.
Dogwood.
Ford. Roots.
Some flowers come up.
Some flowers wickedly.
Fox. Nightshade.
She Used to Water the Plants.
Frost. Flower-Gathering.
Leaves Compared with Flowers.
Locked Out.
Lodged.
Passing Glimpse, A.
Rose Pogonias.
Subverted Flower, The.
Tuft of Flowers, The.
Wind and Window Flower.

Gallagher. In Maceio.
Rhododendrons.
Garrigue. Doggerel of a Diehard Who Sleeps in a Nest of Newspapers.
For an Orchard Tree.
Ginsberg. In Back of the Real.
Glück. Flowering Plum.
Japonica.
Graves. Song: Three Rings for Her.
Troll's Nosegay, The.
Gunn. Messenger, The.
Moly.
Hall. Self-Portrait as a Bear.
Hardy. Flower's Tragedy, The.
To Flowers from Italy in Winter.
Hartley. Mystical Forest, The.
Herbert. Flower, The.
Life.
Herrick. Dialogue Betwixt Himselfe and Mistresse Eliza: Wheeler, Under the Name of Amarillis, A.
How Primroses Came Green.
How the Wall-Flower Came First, and Why So Called.
Meditation for His Mistress[e], A.
Mrs. Eliz. Wheeler, Under the Name of the Lost Shepardesse.
On Gelli-Flowers Begotten.
Showre of Blossomes, The.
To Anthea: ("Sick is Anthea, sickly is the spring").
To Blossoms.
To Carnations.
To Daffodils [or Daffadills].
To Flowers.
To Violets.
Upon Electra's Teares.
Upon One Lillie, Who Marryed with a Maid Call'd Rose.
Why Flowers Change Color.
Hesketh. Buttercup Children, The.
Very Small Casualty, A.
Hewitt. Last Summer, For Roberta (1975), The.
Neighbor's Funeral, A.
We too have gone down little roads in spring.
Hill. Sobieski's Shield.
Hopkins. Basket broad of woven white rods, A.
Ends of the crisp buds she chips, The.
They came / Next to meadows abundant, pierced with flowers.
Housman. I hoed and trenched and weeded.
When green buds hang in the elm like dust.
Hugo. Bouquets from Corley.
Saying Goodbye to Mrs. Noraine.
Joseph. Cherry.
For a New Year.
Homo Sapiens.
Meteorology, A.
Keats. Sweet Peas.
Kipling. Flowers, The.
Kunitz. As Flowers Are.
Lawrence. Assuming the Burden.
Bavarian Gentians.
Flowers and Men.
Kiss, A.
Purple Anemones.
Revolutionary, The.
Levertov. Annuals.
Levine. New Season.
Liddy. Attention: First Lady of the Festival.
My Neighbours Two Brothers.
Lindsay. Fairy Bridal Hymn, The.
How the Wings Were Made.
Lovelace. Lucasta, Taking the Waters at Tunbridge.
Ode to Lucasta: The Rose.
Lowry. Dodder, The.
Isle of Man Wildflowers.
Mysterious Hint, A.
Poor Butterfly that stamped.
MacNeice. Flower Show.
Marvell. Picture of Little T. C. in a Prospect of Flowers, The.
Melville. American Aloe on Exhibition, The.

Meredith. Ballad of the Lady Eglantine, The.
Flower of the Ruins, The.
Glastonbury Thorn, The.
I saw young Spring leap over the hills.
Seed-Time.
Song: "Daisy now is out upon the green, The."
Song: "Flower unfolds its dawning cup, The."
Song: "No, no, the falling blossom is no sign."
Wild Rose and the Snowdrop, The.
Yet what is this? the spring returns.
Merrill. In Nine Sleep Valley.
Merton. Flower of the Fruit, The.
Poor flowers in geometric beds.
Nash. Max Schling, Max Schling, Lend Me Your Green Thumb.
Solitude of Mr. Powers, The.
Nathan. Honorable Mention.
Nemerov. Flower Arrangements.
Notley. Flowers of the Foothills & Mountain Valleys.
Red Zinnias.
Oliver. Moccasin Flowers.
Olson. Dogwood Comes Out Yellow, The.
Flower grows, The.
For a Man Gone to Stuttgart Who Left an Automobile Behind Him.
Hymn to Proserpine.
Perfume / of flowers! A haw, The.
Perfume / of Flowers!, The.
Perfume!, The.
Po-sy, a Po-sy, A.
She Who Hits at Will.
Oppen. Technologies.
Paley. False strawberry is.
St. Johnswort!
She did good. She stood up like a.
Patchen. All the Flowery.
Day of Rabblement.
Delighted with Bluepink.
Flowers to the House.
Shadows and Spring Flowers.
Piercy. Daily Life of the Worker Bee, The.
Plath. Among the Narcissi.
Fable of the Rhododendron Stealers.
I Am Vertical.
Leaving Early.
Pope. Garden, The.
Prince. Babiaantje, The.
Raine. Columbines.
Daisies of Florence.
Dream-flowers.
Flower, memory—.
Forest is multitude.
Golden Flowers.
Kore.
Painting by Winifred Nicholson, A.
Ransom. Here Lies a Lady.
Roethke. Carnations.
Geranium, The.
Shape of the Fire, The.
Rolfe. Testament to a Flowering Race.
Rossetti. Another Spring.
As Cold Water to a Thirsty Soul, So Is Good News from a Far Country.
Balm in Gilead.
Blind from my birth, / Where flowers are springing.
Buds and Babies.
Can I know it?—Nay.— / Shall I know it?— Yea.
Consider the Lilies of the Field ("Flowers Preach to us...").
Consider the Lilies of the Field ("Solomon most glorious...").
Dirge, A. "She was as sweet as violets..."
Flowers Appear on the Earth, The.
God's Acre.
Golden Glories.
Gone for Ever.
Heartsease in my garden bed, / With sweetwilliam white and red.
Heavy heart, if ever heart was heavy, A.
Hope is like a harebell trembling from its birth.
I dug and dug amongst the snow.

I Gave a Sweet Smell.
I Have a Message unto Thee.
If hope grew on a bush, / And joy grew on a tree.
If stars dropped out of heaven, / And if flowers took their place.
In the meadow—what in the meadow?
Lily has a smooth stalk, / Will never hurt your hand, The.
Lily has an air, / And the snowdrop a grace, The.
Love hath a name of Death.
Mirrors of Life and Death.
October Garden, An.
Passing and Glassing.
Passion Flower hath sprung up tall, The.
Queen Rose.
Ring upon her finger, / Walks the bride, A.
Rivals.
Rose has thorns as well as honey, A.
Rose that blushes rosy red, The.
Roses blushing red and white, / For delight.
Sweet Death.
These All Wait upon Thee.
To My Fior-Di-Lisa.
To the End.
Twist me a crown of wind-flowers.
Who Hath Despised the Day of Small Things?
Why did baby die, / Making Father sigh.
Within the Veil.
Rukeyser. Blue Flower, The.
Sandburg. Aster, a farewell-summer flower, stays long in the last fall weeks, An.
Bitter Summer Thoughts—No. XXII.
Bright Conversation with Saint-Ex.
Butter Colors.
Flowers Tell Months.
Follies.
Handfuls.
Harvest.
High Moments.
New Song for Indiana Ophelias.
Nightsong.
Out of the Rainbow End.
Spring Carries Surprises.
There Are Different Gardens.
Thou Art Like a Flower.
Two.
Year, The.
Sarton. Flower-Arranging Summer, A.
Schuyler. Bluet, The.
Cornflowers.
Footnote.
In the Round.
Korean Mums.
Like Lorraine Ellison.
Roof Garden.
Three Gardens.
Yellow Flowers.
Schwartz. Poem: "Remember midsummer: the fragrance of box, of white roses."
Sexton. Love Plant, The.
Shakespeare. Sonnet 99: "Forward violet thus did I chide, The."
Shapiro. Cut Flower, A.
Spider Mums, The.
Shelley. On a Faded Violet.
Silverstein. Enter This Deserted House.
Forgotten Language.
Smart. For the doubling of flowers is the improvement of the gard'ner's talent.
Smith, Charlotte. Horologe of the Fields, The.
Invitation to the Bee.
Reflections on Some Drawings of Plants.
Sent to the Honorable Mistress O'Neill, with Painted Flowers.
Snowdrops.
Song: "Fruit of Aurora's tears, fair Rose."
To Dr. Parry of Bath, with Some Botanic Drawings Which Had Been Made Some Years.
Walk in the Shrubbery, A.
Smith, Patti. Sohl.
Smith, Stevie. Written at the Close of Spring.
Sorrentino. But the light is imagined.
De Pré Est Vénéneux Mais Joli en Automne.
Drifting South.

Homage to Arnaut.
Marvellous.
Poem to Read in August, A.
Senorita's Bouquet, A.
Stinking city full of stinking, A.
Spenser. Behold, O Man.
Stevens. Attempt to Discover Life.
Cy Est Pourtraicte, Madame Ste Ursule, et Les Unze Mille Vierges.
Woman Looking at a Vase of Flowers.
Stevenson. Flowers, The.
To A Gardener.
To Miss Rawlinson.
Sutter. First Hard Frost, The.
Small White Flower that Contains the Sun, The.
Swinburne. Sundew, The.
Tennyson. Flower in the Crannied Wall.
Thomson. Spring Flowers.
Updike. Fleckings, The.
Natural Question.
Query.
Styles of Bloom.
Van Duyn. Annual and Perennial Problem, An.
Peony Stalks.
Wakoski. Donna.
Warren. Flower, The.
Whitman. Orange Buds by Mail from Florida.
These I Singing in Spring.
Unseen Buds.
Whittier. First Flowers, The.
Flowers in Winter.
Hazel Blossoms.
Star of Bethlehem, The.
Trailing Arbutus, The.
Wilbur. In a Churchyard.
In the Field.
On Having Mis-identified a Wild Flower.
Williams, William Carlos. Ad Infinitum.
Aux Imagistes.
Blueflags.
Chicory and Daisies.
Daisy.
Flower, The.
Flowers Alone, The.
Flowers by the Sea.
Gayest of Bright Flowers, The.
Ivy Crown, The.
La Flor.
Locust Tree in Flower, The.
Loving Dexterity, The.
Modest Achievement, The.
Petunia, The.
Pink Locust, The.
Pot of Flowers, The.
Self-Portrait 2.
Song: "Russia! Russia! you might say."
Yellow Flower, The.
Wordsworth. Flower Garden at Coleorton Hall, Leicestershire, A.
Flowers on the Top of the Pillars at the Entrance of the Cave.
Foresight.
Love Lies Bleeding.
Poor Robin.
Primrose of the Rock, The.
So Fair, So Sweet, Withal So Sensitive.
To a Lady.
To a Snow-Drop.
Young. For Kenneth & Miriam Patchen.
Realism.
Zukofsky. African Violet.
Aloe.
Alpine Rosy Bells.
Artemisia.
Aster.
Azalea.
Bayberry.
Bearded Iris.
Butter-and-Eggs.
Charlock per Winkle.
Chicory.
Chokecherry.
Chrysanthemum.
Cinquefoil.
Clover.

Cockle.
Coleus.
Crocus.
Dahlia.
Daisy.
Dandelion.
Deutzia.
Dogwood.
Dutch White Iris.
Ears beringed with fuzz.
Forsythia.
Four-o'clock.
Grape-Hyacinth.
Grassflower.
Grecian Windflower.
Heart us invisbly thyme time.
Heart's Ease.
Honesty.
Honeysuckle.
Hyacinth.
Impatiens.
Jade.
Lavender Cotton.
Lilac.
Lilies.
Lily-of-the-Valley.
Lily-of-the-Valley Fortunei.
Liveforever.
Marigold.
Mountain Laurel.
Narcissus.
Oxalis.
Pachysandra.
Petunia.
Phlox.
Poppy Anemone.
Privet.
Pussy Willow.
Queen Anne's Lace.
Raspberry.
Rose-of-Sharon.
Roses.
Slipperwort.
Snow-Wreath.
Snowdrop.
Snowflake.
Spearmint.
Spider or Ribbon Plant.
Spirea.
Sprengeri.
Starglow.
Telephus Sedum.
Thyme.
Tulip.
Venus's Looking-glass.
Vines.
Violet.
Weeds.
White Begonia.
Wild Geranium.
Wild Honeysuckle.
Windflower.
"X."
Yarrow.
Yaupon.
Zebrina etc.
Zinnia.

Flutes
Browning, Elizabeth Barrett. Musical Instrument, A.
Browning, Robert. Flute-Music, with an Accompaniment.
Dobyns. Marsyas, Midas and the Barber.
Doolittle. Flute Song.
Eberhart. Kinaesthesia.
Emerson. Flute, The.
Hewitt. Chinese Fluteplayer.
Lindsay. Flute of the Lonely, The.
Sexton. To Lose the Earth.
Tomlinson. Flute Music.

Flying Dutchman (ship)
Robinson. Flying Dutchman, The.

Flying Saucers
Hayden. Unidentified Flying Object.

Foals
Cummings. Life / shuts &)opens the world.

See also **Horses.**

Fog
Auden. Thank You, Fog.
Carruth. Look, a cypress tree.
Cummings. Un / der fog / 's / touch.
De la Mare. Fog.
Dickey, James. Fog Envelops the Animals.
Dickinson. Sun and Fog contested, The.
Dunn. Dinner, The.
Eberhart. Flux.
Galvin. Fog Township.
  Sea Fogs at the Chequammitt Inn.
  This Fog.
Gunn. Night Piece, The.
Hayden. Traveling through Fog.
Jarrell. Front, A.
Jeffers. Boats in a Fog.
Joseph. Diary.
Levertov. Ground-Mist, The.
Lowry. As from All the Little Animals.
Matthews. On Cape Cod a Child Is Stolen.
Meinke. Café Vue des Alpes.
Millay. Impression: Fog Off the Coast of
  Dorset.
Olson. Measure.
  Mind's Notice, The.
Oppen. Forms of Love, The.
Patchen. Fog.
  Fog Over the Sea and the Sun Going Down.
Plath. Prospect.
Rolfe. Now the Fog.
Rukeyser. Foghorn in Horror.
Sandburg. Baltic Fog Notes.
  Far Rockaway Night Till Morning.
  Feather Lights.
  Fog.
  Fog Numbers.
  Fog Portrait.
  In the Shadow of the Palace.
  Lost.
  New Weather.
  Pearl Fog.
  Sea Slant.
Schuyler. Gray, Intermittently Blue, Eyed
  Hero.
Sutter. Hoarfrost and Fog.
Tomlinson. In December.
Warren. Fog.
Wilbur. Foggy Street.
Wordsworth. As when, upon the smooth
  pacific deep.
Zukofsky. Ferry.

Folly
Burns. Greybeard, old wisdom, may boast of
  his treasures, The.
  Wisdom and Science—honor'd Powers!
Campion. Canto Quarto.
"Carroll, Lewis." My First is singular at best.
Catullus. Carmen 74: "Gellius, / hearing his
  uncle anathematise the mere mention."
  Carmen 83: "Lesbia is extraordinarily
  vindictive."
Jeffers. What Odd Expedients.
Kipling. Blue Roses.
  City of Brass, The.
Lowry. Prelude To Mammon.
Sandburg. They have yarns / Of a skyscraper
  so tall they had to put hinges.
Smith, Charlotte. Love and Folly.
Suckling. Love, Reason, Hate, did once
  bespeak.
Wroth. Sonnet 10: "Folly would needs make
  mee a lover bee."
Zukofsky. Gellius how he'd rare at pot true
  uncle objurgate soul array.
  Lesbia (my price scent t'her hero) mauls and
  deplores me, *'dig it'*.

Food
Angelou. Health-Food Diner, The.
Atwood. Carrying Food Home in Winter.
Auden. To-night at Seven-thirty.
Browning, Robert. Prologue: "Pray, Reader,
  have you eaten ortolans."
Bukowski. Windy Night.
Burns. At Brownhill Inn.
  Grace after Dinner.
  To a Haggis.

Cowper. Lines after the Manner of Homer.
Dickinson. Am told that fasting gives to food.
  God gave a Loaf to every Bird.
Doolittle. There is no sign-post to say.
Dunbar. Curiosity.
  When de Co'n Pone's Hot.
Eberhart. Tree Swallows.
  Winter Kill.
Gardner. Nursery Rhyme No. 2.
Gunn. Cafeteria in Boston.
Haines. It is nearly thirty years.
Herrick. Custard, The.
  Graces for Children.
  Manna.
  To God ("God! to my little meale and oyle").
  To His Book[e] ("Make haste away, and let
  one be").
  Upon Jack and Jill: Epigram.
  Upon Ralph.
Hesketh. Survival.
Jonson. Hymn: "Room, room, make room for
  the bouncing belly."
  Inviting a Friend to Supper.
Kipling. Big Steamers.
  Master-Cook, The.
  Such As in Ships.
Lawrence. Bread upon the Waters.
  Food of the North.
  Living, A.
Levine. Salts and Oils.
Lovelace. Being treated to Ellinda.
Lowry. And now the seagulls feed on the
  front porch.
  Goldeneye and Goldfish.
  Hunger.
  Wild-duck swam in the gold-fish pond, The.
McNeill. Katchie Verner's Harvest.
Matthews. On a Diet.
Nash. Absentees, The.
  Are You a Snodgrass?
  Banquet, The.
  Caraway Seed, The.
  Clean Platter, The.
  Further Reflection on Parsley.
  I Can't Have a Martini, Dear, but You Take
  One, or, Are You Going to Sit THere
  Guzzling All Night?
  Isn't That a Dainty Dish? No!
  Lines to Be Embroidered on a Bib, or, The
  Child Is Father of the Man, but Not for
  Quite a While.
  My Dear, How Ever Did You Think Up This
  Delicious Salad?
  Parsley for Vice-President!
  Parsnip, The.
  Private Dining Room, The.
  Table Talk.
  What, No Oysters?
Nemerov. Grace to Be Said at the
  Supermarket.
  Lobsters.
Piercy. Attack of the Squash People.
  Beauty I Would Suffer For.
  Consumer, The.
Ransom. Survey of Literature.
Rolfe. Ballad: "What are we having for dinner
  tonight?"
Rossetti. Three Plum Buns.
  Wee wee husband, / Give me some money.
Schuyler. Joint.
Sexton. Food.
Silverstein. I Must Remember.
  Point of View.
Smith, Stevie. Nourish Me on an Egg.
Snodgrass. Boy Made of Meat, The; A Poem
  for Children.
Snyder. Now I'll also tell what food.
  Song of the Taste.
Stuart. Cabbage in History, The.
  Canned Goods.
Sutter. Stalking the Wild Mushroom.
Swift. Epigram on Fasting.
Turco. Menu of Melancholy, The.
Updike. Food.
  On the Inclusion of Miniature Dinosaurs in
  Breakfast Cereal Boxes.

Van Duyn. Reading of Rex Stout, A.
  Saleswomen in Bakery Shops.
Wakoski. Braised Leeks & Framboise.
  Overweight Poem.
Wilbur. Rillons, Rillettes.
Williams, William Carlos. Host, The.
Young. Night before Michael Was Born, The.
See also **Cooking and Cooks; Eating; Gluttony
  and Gluttons.**

Food Poisoning
Young. Rundown at Ned's Bar B.Q, The.

Fools
Blake. Cromek Speaks.
  Great Men & Fools do often me Inspire.
  He has observed the golden rule.
  Lacedemonian Instruction.
  Madman I have been calld Fool they call thee.
  Sussex Men are Noted Fools, The.
  These are the Idiots chiefest arts.
Burns. C———d faithful likeness, friend
  Painter, would'st seize?
  Dost blush, my dear Billy, asham'd of thyself.
  He clench'd his pamphlets in his fist.
  Holy Fair, The.
  Monody on Maria.
  On Capt. W——— R-dd-ck of C-rb—ton.
  On Commissary Goldie's Brains.
  On J-hn M-r-ne, Laird of L-gg-n.
  On W. R———, Esq.
  On William Graham [*or* W——— Gr-h-m],
  Esq., of Mossknowe [*or* M-sskn-w].
  Postscript [To W. S*****n, Ochiltree].
  Pray who are these *Natives* the Rabble so
  ven'rate.
  To the Honble Mr. R. M———, of P-nm-re,
  on His High Phaeton.
Byron. Verses Found in a Summer-House at
  Hales-Owen.
Clare. Lout, The: "For Sunday's play he never
  makes excuse."
Cowper. 1.9: "Saunt'ring along the street one
  day."
  Card, A.
  Lines with Two Cockscombs.
Creeley. Counterpoint, A.
  Epigraph: "Lot's wife, / married to chance."
Cummings. May my heart always be open to
  little.
  Out of the lie of no.
De la Mare. Iago.
Eberhart. Man Who Was Blown Down by the
  Wind, A.
Emerson. Bard or dunce is blest, but hard.
  It takes a philosopher or fool.
Herrick. Foolishnesse.
Hewitt. Epitaph for a Conscript, 1940.
  Ireland.
  Passion.
Hopkins. On a Dunce Who Had Not a Word
  to Say for Himself.
Jonson. On Don Surly.
  On the Famous Voyage.
  On the Magnetic Lady.
  To a Friend, an Epigram of Him.
  To Courtling.
  To Fool, or Knave.
  To Groom Idiot.
  To Inigo, Marquess Would Be, a Corollary.
  To Mime.
Kipling. Now it is not good for the Christian's
  health to hustle the Aryan brown.
Lindsay. On the Road to Nowhere.
Lovelace. Fool much bit by fleas put out the
  light, A.
  When Portia her dear I Lord's sad fate did
  hear.
Lowry. Villaknell.
  You think you are a man shaking the hands of
  that dog.
"MacDiarmid." Fool, The.
MacLeish. Ship of Fools.
Melville. Montaigne and His Kitten.
Meredith. Camelus Saltat: Continued.
Merton. Antipoem 1.
  I have sought for myself.
  To a Novice ("Fool is one, The").

Olson. Fool, The.
Green Man, The.
Patchen. Spirit of Noplace, The.
Pope. Another [Epigram].
Epigram from the French: "Sir, I admit your
general [or gen'ral] Rule."
Prologue to the *Three Hours after Marriage*.
Verses to Be Placed under the Picture of
England's Arch-Poet: Containing a Compleat
Catalogue of His Works.
Sandburg. Dreaming Fool.
Silverstein. Silver Fish, The.
Smith, Stevie. Father for a Fool, A.
Sorrentino. Open Your Mouth and Say.
Williams, William Carlos. Hero.
Naked.
Yeats. Another Song of a Fool.
Symbols.
See also **Jesters.**

Football
Bukowski. Gentleman and the Bastard, The.
Dickey, James. Bee, The.
For the Death of Vince Lombardi.
In the Pocket.
Eberhart. Harvard Stadium.
Gildner. First Practice.
Meeting My Best Friend from the Eighth
Grade.
Hemingway. Dedicated to F. W.
Punt, The.
Tackle, The.
Hewitt. Summer Park.
Hughes, Ted. Football at Slack.
Jarrell. Nursery Rhyme, A.
Say Good-bye to Big Daddy.
Nash. One Man's Meed Is Another Man's
Overemphasis.
Nemerov. Watching Football on TV.
Stuart. Ties.
Tomlinson. Of the Winter Ball Game.
Wright, James. Autumn Begins in Martins
Ferry, Ohio.
See also **Soccer.**

Forbidden Fruit
Carew. Secrecy [or Secresie] Protested.
Cowper. Bee and the Pine-Apple, The.
Pine-Apple and the Bee, The.
Creeley. Now Then.
Hewitt. Tryst.
Jong. Demon Lover, The.
Marlowe. 2.19: Ad rivalem, cui uxor curae
non erat.
Milton. As when of old some orator renowed.
Shapiro. Tree of Guilt, The.

Ford, Ford Madox
Cummings. Possibly thrice we glimpsed.
Lowell. Ford Madox Ford ("Lobbed ball
plops, then dribbles up the cup, The").
Williams, William Carlos. To Ford Madox
Ford in Heaven.

Forest Fires
Atwood. Two Fires, The.
Dickey, James. Walking the Fire Line.
Levine. Late Answer, A.
Snyder. Control Burn.
Stone-flake and salmon.
Text, The.
Wright, James. Brush Fire.

Foresters
Emerson. Forester.
Hoffman. Dijon.
Sidney. Come, *Espilus*, come now declare thy
skill.
Whittier. Ranger, The.

Forests
Atwood. Paths and Thingscape.
Auden. Reflections in a Forest.
Berry. Beware of the machinery of longevity.
When a man's life is over.
Country where he lives, The.
I have thought of you stepping out of your
doorway at dawn, your son in your tracks.
Sometimes our life reminds me.
Bishop. Chemin de Fer.
Bly. Solitude Late at Night in the Woods.
Browning, Robert. Forest Thought, A.

Burns. On a Bank of Flowers.
Carruth. Beginning with the palest and softest
lavender.
First Version, The.
On Lincoln's birthday the forest.
Clark. Door to the Forest, The.
Cummings. This / forest pool / A so.
Davie. Sylvae.
Tunstall Forest.
De la Mare. Dwelling-Place, The.
Mourn'st Thou Now?
Sorcery.
Dickey, James. By Canoe through the Fir
Forest.
Sleeping Out at Easter.
Doolittle. Pursuit.
Dunbar. Forest Greeting, The.
Eliot. Usk.
Emerson. I sat upon the ground.
Waldeinsamkeit.
Fox. Exposing Fox and Artifice.
Frost. Dream Pang, A.
In winter in the woods alone.
Into My Own.
Stopping by Woods on a Snowy Evening.
Garrigue. Forest.
Motifs from the Dark Wood.
Graves. Gift of Sight.
Haines. Book of the Jungle.
Hardy. In a Wood.
Yell'ham-Wood's Story.
Hartley. Mystical Forest, The.
Jarrell. Forest Murmurs.
House in the Wood, The.
Kipling. Way through the Woods, The.
Levertov. Novices, The.
Lewis. Oh in a slim spaced forest.
Lindsay. What the Forester Said.
Lowry. Welcome Home oh Harteebeeste mio.
With Sweet Devotion and True from All the
Little Animals.
With Sweet Sweet Love from All Your
Amused Little Animals.
McGrath. Remembering the Children of
Auschwitz.
MacNeice. Woods.
Meredith. South-West Wind in the Woodland.
Millay. Through the Green Forest.
Nemerov. Deep Woods.
Oliver. Rain.
Sleeping in the Forest.
Olson. Part of the Series on the Paths, A.
Paley. For My Friend Who Planted a Tree for
His Daughter Jane.
Prince. In the Wood.
Ransom. First Travels of Max.
Rolfe. Georgia Nightmare.
Rukeyser. All the way through the forest, a
sound of birdsong.
Child in the Great Wood.
Gullies as deep as halls held these surveyors.
Sexton. Expatriates, The.
Simic. Ballad: "What's that approaching like
dust like poverty."
December Trees.
Forest Birds.
Smith, Charlotte. Sonnet to the Forest Ytene.
Snyder. Green limb hangs in the crotch, A.
Sorrentino. Man and Wife.
Sutter. Small White Flower that Contains the
Sun, The.
Tomlinson. In Arden.
Turco. Fort, The.
Walcott. Air.
Warren. Chain Saw at Dawn in Vermont in
Time of Drouth.
Monologue at Midnight.
Whittier. Ranger, The.
Wood Giant, The.
Wilbur. Riddle, A.
Williams, Charles Kenneth. Insult, The.
Wordsworth. Suggested by a View from an
Eminence in Inglewood Forest.
Wright, James. Fit against the Country, A.
On the Skeleton of a Hound.
Quail, The.

See also **Woods.**

Forgery and Forgers
Mahon. Forger, The.
Nemerov. To Clio, Muse of History.

Forges
Heaney. Casualty.

Forgetfulness
Beckett. Live and clean forget from day to
day.
Clark. Night Patrol.
Cowper. Epistle to Hill.
Crane. Forgetfulness.
You Are That Frail..
Creeley. Anywhere.
For the New Year.
It Is at Times.
Names.
Song: "What do you / want, love. To be."
De la Mare. Clear Eyes.
Dreamer, The.
Dickey, William. Face-Paintings of the
Caduveo Indians.
Dickinson. If recollecting were forgetting.
Knows how to forget!
Sweet—You forgot—but I remembered.
To be forgot by thee.
Whether they have forgotten.
Dobyns. Pastel Dresses.
Putting It All Away.
Slipping Away.
"Dylan." True Love Tends to Forget.
Eberhart. Formative Mastership.
Fisher. Some Loss.
Garrigue. Song for "Buvez les Vins du
Postillon"—Advt.
Hardy. Death of Regret, The.
Tess's Lament.
Lawrence. Forget.
Lowry. Midnight denies poursuivant of the
dawn.
Names of Mexican rivers I forgot, The.
McGrath. Memorial.
MacLeish. 1892—19—.
Meredith. Dear, my friend & honour'd
madam! of hard facts I'm not a hoarder.
Distraction is the panacea, Sir!
Merton. Take thought, man, tonight.
When the Shoe Fits.
Nash. Mr. Betts's Mind a Kingdom Is.
Olson. Gulf of Maine, The.
Pack. Forgetting to Forget.
Rossetti. Exceeding Bitter Cry, An.
Forget Me Not.
He and She.
Long Looked For.
Zara.
Rukeyser. He starts awake in the city. Orion
believing.
Tree of rivers seen and forgotten, The.
Wind arrow, wind rose, the wind currents in
air.
Sandburg. Forgotten Wars.
François Villon Forgotten.
Jan, the Son of Thomas.
Silverstein. Homemade Boat.
Smith, Charlotte. Nepenthe.
Verses Supposed to Have Been Written in the
New Forest, in Early Spring.
Sorrentino. Long Gone Blues.
Swinburne. Interlude, An.
Williams, Charles Kenneth. Alzheimer's: The
Wife.
Williams, Miller. Documenting It.
Wright, Charles. In steeps and sighs.
Zukofsky. Incident, An.

Forgiveness
Auden. Pardon.
Beatles. Tell Me Why.
Berry. Anger against Beasts.
Do Not Be Ashamed.
Berryman. Penny, pity, for the runaway ass!,
A.
Browning, Elizabeth Barrett. That Day.
Browning, Robert. Adam, Lilith, and Eve.
Byron. On Revisiting Harrow.
To Anne.
Campion. Wise men patience never want.

Carruth. Reflexive.
Sonnet: "To the aged, trembling, illiterate woman yesterday."
Ciardi. Fast As You Can Count to Ten.
Clough. Well, well,—Heaven bless you all from day to day!
Cohen. Bird on the Wire.
Famous Blue Raincoat.
Coleridge. Epitaph: "Stop, Christian passer-by!—Stop, child of God."
Cooper. Pencil Sketch of Self & Other.
Creeley. Flowers.
So Big.
De la Mare. Be angry now no more!
Clear Eyes.
Forgiveness.
How Blind!
Dickey, William. In The Dreaming.
Dickinson. Of God we ask one favor.
"Remember me" implored the Thief!
'Tis true—They shut me in the Cold.
Donne. Hymn to God the Father, A.
If poisonous [or poysonous] mineral[l]s, and if that tree.
Dunbar. How Lucy Backslid.
Duncan. Adoration of the Virgin, The.
Dunn. After the Argument.
Long Term.
Everson. Black Hills, The.
Frost. Forgive, O Lord, my little jokes on Thee.
Gardner. Ballade: "You who outlive us, you, our mortal brothers."
Ginsberg. Love Forgiven.
Graves. Gold and Malachite.
Hedges Freaked With Snow.
In Her Only Way.
Return.
Song: Reconciliation.
Three Words Only.
Hardy. Burghers, The.
Husband's View, The.
Peace-Offering, The.
Tolerance.
Wife and Another, A.
Herbert. Justice (2).
Love.
Herrick. His Prayer for Absolution.
Hewitt. Bloody Brae, The.
Mother and Son.
Prague, or Novotny, If You Remember Him.
Take the intention then and let me live.
Hopkins. Complaint, A.
Kipling. Supplication of the Black Aberdeen.
Kunitz. I wake to a glittering world.
Liddy. Holden.
Lindsay. Soul of a Butterfly, The.
Lowry. Exile's Return.
I bet you don't know who I am.
McAuley. Labor and Tribulation.
Meinke. Father.
Meredith. Hans Euler.
Love ere he bleeds, an eagle in high skies.
Merton. Ode to the Present Century.
Milton. To whom the Tempter impudent replied.
Morrison. End of the Dream, The.
O'Hara. Poem: "Light clarity avocado salad in the morning."
Oppen. They await / War, and the news.
Psalms. Psalm 25: "Unto thee, O Lord, do I lift up my soul."
Psalm 32: "Blessed is he whose transgression is forgiven, whose sin is covered."
Psalm 130: "Out of the depths have I cried unto thee, O Lord."
Raine. Dear ones in the house of the dead.
Robinson. Partnership.
Unforgiven, The.
Rolfe. War Guilt.
Rossetti. Afterward He Repented, and Went.
Alas my Lord, / How should I wrestle all the livelong night.
Ash Wednesday.
Good Lord, today / I scarce find breath to say.
Hymn: "O the bitter shame and sorrow."
If thou be dead, forgive and thou shalt live.

Look on This Picture and on This.
O Lord, when Thou didst call me, didst Thou know.
Weigh all my faults and follies righteously.
Young Men Aye Were Fickle Found Since Summer Trees Were Leafy.
St. John. Song without Forgiveness.
Schwartz. Sand upon the Red Sea shore, or on the beach, The.
Smart. Hymn to the Supreme Being.
Justice.
Lord and Master, to thine altar.
Smith, Stevie. Forgive Me, Forgive Me.
When Walking.
Sorrentino. Midnight Special.
Stevenson. Lo, now, my guest, if aught amiss were said.
Our Lady of the Snows.
Tennyson. As through [or thro'] the Land [at Eve We Went].
Warren. Interjection #4: Bad Year, Bad War: A New Year's Card, 1969.
Revelation.
Whittier. Forgiveness.
Requital.
Two Angels, The.
Two Rabbins, The.
Wilbur. Ballade of Forgiveness.
Williams, Charles Kenneth. Penance.
Williams, William Carlos. This Is Just to Say.
Wordsworth. Rid of a vexing and a heavy load.
Wright, James. Message from the Mountain Pool Where the Deer Come Down, A.
Wyatt. F[f]rom depth of[f] sin[n] and from a deep despair [or diepe dispaire].
O happy are they that have forgiveness got.
Yeats. He Wishes His Beloved Were Dead.
Lover Asks Forgiveness because of His Many Moods.

Forks
Lovelace. Being treated to Ellinda.
Simic. Fork.

Fortitude
Ammons. Fortitude.
Emerson. I batter the wheel of heaven.
Hartley. Listening to the Music.
Kipling. If.
Winners, The.
Moore. Nevertheless.
Smart. Fortitude.
Smith, Charlotte. Ode to the Missel Thrush.
To Fortitude.
See also **Endurance.**

Fortune
Auden. Bank Holiday.
Beckett. À l'instant de s'entendre dire.
Browning, Elizabeth Barrett. But Fortune governed all their works[,] till when.
Burns. Ill-fated Genius! Heaven-taught Fergusson.
Byron. Love and Gold.
Campion. In obitum Gual. Devoreux fratris clariss. Comitus Essexiae.
Carruth. Tanck's Song About the Transportation Business.
Chaucer. Fortune.
Coleridge. To a Friend, in Answer to a Melancholy Letter.
Cowper. Verses Written at Bath on Finding the Heel of a Shoe.
Crashaw. Epithalamium: "Come virgin Tapers of pure waxe."
Cummings. That melancholy / fellow'll play / his handorgan.
De la Mare. Dust to Dust.
Eberhart. Fortune's Mist.
Emerson. Divine Inviters! I accept.
Fortune and Hope! I've made my port.
Guy.
If thy darling favor thee.
Van Buren.
Woods.
Ford. Beautiful new / Character may enter the, A.
Gray. Now the golden morn aloft.
Gunn. Wheel of Fortune, The.

Hardy. Hap.
He Fears His Good Fortune.
Herrick. Adversity ("Adversity hurts none, but onely such").
All Things Run Well for the Righteous.
Change Common to All.
Discord Not Disadvantageous.
Felicitie Knowes No Fence.
Fortune.
Fortune Favours.
Good Luck Not Lasting.
No Paines, No Gaines.
Potentates.
Reverence to Riches.
Speake in Season.
Suffer Thou that Canst not Shift.
Supreme Fortune Falls Soonest.
To Fortune.
To His Sister in Law, M. Susanna Herrick.
Hewitt. Host.
Housman. Lads in their hundreds to Ludlow come in for the fair, The.
Kipling. Wishing-Caps, The.
Koch. Locks.
Lowry. There is a tide in the affairs of men.
MacNeice. After long trouble in a taedious way.
Meredith. My Theme.
Merton. Good Fortune.
Septentrion.
Song: In the Shows of the Round Ox.
Psalms. Psalm 16: "Preserve me, O God: for in thee do I put my trust."
Ralegh. But Fortune governed all their works[,] till when.
Epizeuxis, the Underlay, or Coocko-spel.
From wisedome Fortune differs farre.
Rukeyser. Slow Death of the Dragon.
Sandburg. Fame If Not Fortune.
Joke Gold.
Shakespeare. As it fell upon a day.
Sidney. Fortune, Nature, Love, long have contended about me.
Spenser. At last, so faire a ladie did I spie.
Wroth. Sonnet 1: "In night yett may wee see some kind of light."
Wyatt. Alas, Fortune, what aileth thee.
Fortune doth frown.
In faith I not [well] what to say.
Marvel [or Marvaill] no more although [or all tho].
Once [or Ons], as methought, Fortune me kissed [or kist or kyst].
See also **Fate; Luck; Chance.**

Fortunetelling and Fortunetellers
Auden. Model, The.
Campion. Song: "Shadowes darkning our intents, The."
Carruth. Fat Lady, The.
Sonnet: "Well, she told me I had an aura. 'What?' I said."
Cohen. I See You on a Greek Mattress.
So Long, Marianne.
Emerson. Hear what the glass will tell thee.
Gildner. Meeting the Reincarnation Analyst.
Graves. Man Does, Woman Is.
Hardy. Echo-Elf Answers, The.
Herrick. Upon Cupid ("Love, like a Gypsie, lately come").
Hewitt. Palmist, The.
Hoffman. Fortune, A.
Hughes, Langston. Ballad of the Fortune Teller.
Ballad of the Gypsy.
Madam and the Fortune Teller.
Jeffers. Reference to a Passage in Plutarch's Life of Sulla.
Lawrence. There Was a Gay Bird Named Christine.
Lindsay. I Know All This When Gipsy Fiddles Cry.
Marvell. Illustrissimo Viro Domino Lancelot Josepho de Maniban Grammatomanti [To That Renowned Man Lord Lancelot Joseph de Maniban Graphologist].
Merrill. Last Mornings in California.
Nemerov. Fortune Teller, The.

Plath. Crystal Gazer.
Sandburg. Gypsy Mother.
Stevenson. Spaewife, The.

Fossils
Dove. Fish in the Stone, The.
Ferlinghetti. Cro-Magnons.
Haines. All spine and knotted fin-rays.
Nash. Next!
Williams, William Carlos. Smiling Dane, A.

Fountains
Bogan. Roman Fountain.
Coleridge. Inscription for a Fountain on a
  Heath.
  Ovidian Elegiac Metre, The.
Cowper. Living Water.
Davie. Fountain of Arethusa, The.
  Fountain of Cyanë, The.
  Fountain, The.
Dunbar. Fount of Tears, The.
Eberhart. Garden God, The.
Fisher. Memorial Fountain, The.
Garrigue. For the Fountains and Fountaineers
  of Villa d'Este.
Herrick. To Springs and Fountains.
  To the Water Nymphs, Drinking at the
  Fountain.
Levertov. Fountain, The.
Olson. Gate Is Prouti, The.
  I Weep, Fountain of Jazer.
  Story, A.
Pope. On the Statue of *Cleopatra*, Made into
  a Fountain by *Leo* the Tenth.
Rukeyser. Beast in View.
Whittier. Fountain, The.
Wilbur. Ballade for the Duke of Orléans.
  Baroque Wall-Fountain in the Villa Sciarra, A.
Williams, William Carlos. Spouts.
Wordsworth. Fountain, The.
Yau. Red Fountain.

Fourth of July
Berry. Independence Day.
Lowell. Fourth of July in Maine.
Meinke. Fourth of July.
  Hero Worship at Key West on the 4th of July.
Nemerov. Fourth of July, The.
Piercy. Rainy 4th.
Sandburg. Fourth of July Night.
Schuyler. At the Beach.
  Quick, Henry, the Flit!
Silverstein. Fourth, The.
Snodgrass. Fourth of July.
Wilbur. Fourth of July, The.
Williams, William Carlos. 4th of July.
Young. Summer.

Fox, Charles James
Wordsworth. Lines: "Loud is the Vale! the
  Voice is up."

Foxes
Atwood. Song of the Fox.
Burns. Fragment—on Glenriddel's Fox
  Breaking His Chain, A.
"Carroll, Lewis." Ye Fattale Cheyse.
Dickey, James. Dog Sleeping on My Feet, A.
  Listening to Foxhounds.
Eberhart. Wild Life and Tamed Life.
Edmunds. My Love Has Been.
Emerson. No song so tuneful, quoth the fox.
Graves. To the Teumessian Vixen.
Hesketh. Fox, The.
  Gone Away.
Hughes, Ted. Thought-Fox, The.
Kipling. Fox-Hunting.
Levine. Fox, The.
Lowry. Arctic fox / With snow white hocks,
  The.
  As to report, / Within his court.
McNeill. Timber Boom.
Meredith. Young Reynard.
Moore. Fox and the Grapes, The.
Muldoon. Fox, The.
Patchen. Fox, The.
Rexroth. Fox.
Rich. Abnegation.
Sandburg. Early Moon.
Tomlinson. Fox Gallery, The.
  Fox, The.
  Foxes' Moon.

Wright, James. Blue Teal's Mother.

Foxgloves
Gunn. Crystal.
Sandburg. Foxgloves.

France
Beckett. Dieppe ("Again the last ebb").
  Dieppe ("Encore le dernier reflux").
Byron. Napoleon's Farewell.
Carroll, Jim. El Hombre del Ombre.
Carruth. In France, through archways, the
  archaic stonework.
Cowper. In Seditionem Horrendum.
Crane. I Rob My Breast.
Cullen. La Belle, La Douce, La Grande.
  To France ("I have a dream...").
  To France ("Though I am not the first...").
Cummings. Little ladies more / than dead
  exactly dance.
Davie. Brantôme.
  Killala.
  Right Wing Sympathies.
  Wide France.
Dunn. Response to a Letter from France.
Eberhart. Mediterranean Song.
Ferlinghetti. *Firenze*, a Lifetime Later.
  Late Impressionist Dream.
  L'Occupation Obsédée.
  Morlaix: Into the Future with Neil Young.
Garrigue. Beaucaire.
Hacker. Graffiti from the Gare Saint-Manqué.
Heaney. Night Drive.
Hemingway. Lines to Be Read at the Casting
  of Scott FitzGerald's Balls into the Sea from
  Eden Roc (Antibes, Alpes Maritimes).
Hill. Mystery of the Charity of Charles Péguy,
  The.
Jeffers. Dead to Clemenceau: November 1929,
  The.
Johnson. French Distichs.
Kipling. Curé, The.
  France.
  French Wars, The.
  King's Pilgrimage, The.
  Song of French Roads, A.
  Song of Seventy Horses.
Liddy. Vir.
  Vir III.
  Vir IV.
Meredith. Ah, what a dawn of splendour,
  when her sowers.
  Behold, the Gods are with her, and are known.
  Eastward of Paris morn is high.
  He, did he love her? France was his weapon,
  shrewd.
  In Nature is no rearward step allowed.
  Let but the rational prevail.
  Look not for spreading boughs.
  Mark where a credible ghost pulls bridle to
  view that bare.
  Mother who gave birth to Jeanne, The.
  New Era the Army of the Future the Egg of
  an Army, The.
  Not yet had History's Ætna smoked the skies.
  Now her face white waves in the
  tempest's sharp flame-blink.
  O she that made the brave appeal.
  On her lost arm love bade her look.
  She hailed him Saint.
  She shall rise worthier of her prototype.
  She snatched at heaven's flame of old.
  Three Eagles and the Sleepy Lion, The.
  To P.A. Labouchère Esq.
  To the Merry Men of France.
  We look for her that sunlike stood.
Millay. To the Maid of Orleans.
Moore. Light is Speech.
  To the Peacock of France.
Paley. In Aix.
Raine. Letter to Pierre Emmanuel.
Rexroth. La Vie En Rose.
Sarton. Evening Walk in France.
Smith, Stevie. Bandol (Var).
Suckling. Cantilena Politica-Jocunda Facta
  Post Principis Discessum In Hispaniam.
Swinburne. Les Noyades.
Tomlinson. Lacoste.
Updike. Farewell to the Shopping District of

Antibes.
  Some Frenchmen.
Whitman. France, The 18th Year of These
  States.
  O Star of France (1870–71).
Whittier. Bartholdi Statue, The.
  Thiers.
Wordsworth. Calais, August 15, 1802.
  Great men have been among us; hands that
  penned.
  October, 1803 ("One might believe that natural
  miseries").
  September, 1802. Near Dover.
Zukofsky. 4 Other Countries.

Francesca, Piers delta. *see* **Piero della
  Francesca.**

Francis of Assisi, Saint
Kinnell. Saint Francis and the Sow.
Lindsay. Voice of St. Francis of Assisi, The.
St. John. Francesco and Clare.
Williams, William Carlos. Mental Hospital
  Garden, The.
Young. Berkeley Pome.

Franco, Francisco
Wright, James. Eisenhower's Visit to Franco,
  1959.

Franco-Prussian War
Meredith. Let but the rational prevail.
Rossetti. German-French Campaign, 1870–
  1871, The.
Whitman. O Star of France (1870–71).
Whittier. Thiers.

Frank, Anne
Williams, Charles Kenneth. Day for Anne
  Frank, A.

Frankenstein
Atwood. Speeches for Dr Frankenstein.
Cohen. Believe Me, Edith.
Hewitt. Fables for Stormont.

Franklin, Aretha
Cohen. Different Drum, A.

Franklin, Benjamin
Sandburg. Open Letter to the Poet Archibald
  MacLeish Who Has Forsaken His
  Massachusetts Farm to Make Propaganda for
  Freedom.

Fraternity. *see* **Brotherhood.**

Fratricide
Kipling. Romulus and Remus.
Melville. Battle of Stone River, Tennessee.
Whittier. Fratricide, The.

Free Will
Atwood. Torture.
Cullen. Ultimatum.
Frost. Road Not Taken, The.
Herrick. Another ("Art thou not destin'd?
  then, with hast, go on").
  Another ("Sin is an act so free, that if we
  shall").
  Predestination.
Jarrell. Conversation with the Devil, A.
Jonson. Epode: "Not to know vice at all, and
  keep[e] true state."
Lowry. Dead men tell cryptic tales and this is
  one.
Neruda. Island (XII), The.
Ralegh. Mindes of men are ever so affected,
  The.
Schwartz. "At last! the present darkness! all is
  known!"
Whittier. Overruled.
Wroth. Sonnet 48: "How like a fire doth love
  increase in me[e]."

Freedom
Angelou. Caged Bird.
  To a Freedom Fighter.
Atwood. Lying here, everything in me.
  This is not something that can be renounced.
Auden. Chilled by the Present, its gloom and
  its noise.
  Free One, A.
  They wondered why the fruit had been
  forbidden.
Beckett. Second Nature.
  Sitôt sorti de l'ermitage.

Berry. He goes free of the earth.
Independence Day.
It is not too soon to provide by every.
Law That Marries All Things, The.
Mad Farmer's Love Song, The.
Berryman. Captain's Song, The.
Christian to Try: "I am so coxed in it."
Heaven.
Bishop. Sonnet: "Caught—the bubble."
Blake. Song of Liberty, A.
Browning, Elizabeth Barrett. Calls on the Heart.
Hiram Powers' "Greek Slave."
King Victor Emanuel Entering Florence, April, 1860.
Runaway Slave at Pilgrim's Point, The.
Sword of Castruccio Castracani, The.
Browning, Robert. Why I Am a Liberal.
Bukowski. Friendly Advice to a Lot of Young Men.
Hello, Willie Shoemaker.
Poem to a Most Affectionate Lady.
Burns. Address of Beelzebub.
Caledonia.
Castle Gordon—*Intended to Be Sung to Morag.*
De'il's [or Deil's] Awa wi' th' [or the] Exciseman, The.
Fragment, A: "When *Guilford* good our Pilot stood."
Fragment—on Glenriddel's Fox Breaking His Chain, A.
Grant me, indulgent Heaven, that I may live.
I Hae a Wife o' My Ain.
Ode [for General Washington's Birthday].
On Johnson's Opinion of Hampden.
Perish their names, however great or brave.
Poetical Inscription, for an Altar to Independence at Kerrouchtry, the Seat of Mr. Heron, Written in Summer 1795.
Robert Bruce's March to Bannockburn.
Song—For A' That and A' That.
To the Beautiful Miss Eliza J———n, on Her Principles of Liberty and Equality.
Tree of Liberty, The.
Byron. Canto the Eleventh.
Sonnet on Chillon.
Translation of the Famoue Greek War Song *Deute Paides Tov Ellenon.*
When a Man Hath No More Freedom to Fight for at Home.
Campion. Could my poore hart whole worlds of toungs employ.
Carew. Willing Prisoner to His Mistress, The.
Carruth. Against the wall he / gropes like ivy, you pray, I.
As Rousseau was another, singing.
Book, The.
Came in upon him once how he might find.
I am a fanatic lover of liberty, considering it.
Of the rights of each to zero. No, I mean the only.
Then rapture is self in itself entranced. And love?
Cohen. Bird on the Wire.
Coleridge. Foster-Mother's Tale, The.
La Fayette.
To Earl Stanhope.
To the Honourable Mr. Erskine.
Cooper. Breslau, Spring 1918.
Cowper. Gratitude and Love to God.
Morning Dream, The.
Crane. To Brooklyn Bridge.
Creeley. Ballad of the Despairing Husband.
Places.
Cullen. Karenge Ya Marenge.
Wind Bloweth Where It Listeth, The.
Cummings. Am was. are leaves few this. is these a or.
As freedom is a breakfastfood.
Be of love(a little).
F is for foetus(a).
I say no world.
If(touched by love's own secret)we,like homing.
Let's,from some loud unworld's most rightful wrong.

O to be in finland.
There are possibly 2 1/2 or impossibly 3.
Unlove's the heavenless hell and homeless home.
What freedom's not some under's mere above.
Why must itself up every of a park.
De la Mare. Little Salamander, The.
Dickinson. Could I but ride indefinite.
No Prisoner be.
No Rack can torture me.
Power to fly is sweet, The.
Sweet Land of Liberty.
They shut me up in Prose.
Donne. Batter my heart, three-personed [or three person'd] God; for you.
Doolittle. Helmsman, The.
I could say, / red.
In the Rain.
Dove. Geometry.
Pamela.
Three Days of Forest, a River, Free.
Transport or Slaves From Maryland to Mississippi, The.
Dunbar. Ante-Bellum Sermon, An.
Awakening, The.
Emancipation.
Duncan. Old women came from their caves to close the too many doors, The.
Dunn. Hard Work 1956.
"Dylan." As I Went Out One Morning.
Chimes of Freedom.
Eberhart. Critic With His Pained Eye, The.
Humanist, The.
Life as Visionary Spirit.
Secret Heart, The.
To the Mad Poets.
Wedding, The.
Eliot. Burnt Norton.
Emerson. Ancient drop of feudal blood, An.
Boston.
Etienne de la Boéce.
Few are free / All might be.
Freedom.
Ode Sung in the Town Hall.
Pilgrims, The.
Rhyme of the poet, The.
See how Romance adheres.
Skeptic, The.
Trimountain.
Everson. And then that humming.
Ferlinghetti. Dog.
Fisher. Freedoms / out of contrivance.
Without Location.
Ford. Prison Life.
Fox. Ukiyo-E.
Ginsberg. To the Punks of Dawlish.
Glück. Legend.
Undertaking, The.
Graves. Freehold.
Gooseflesh Abbey.
Song: Come, Enjoy Your Sunday!
Gunn. Aquarium, The.
Hall. Friend Revisited, A.
Hardy. At the Railway Station, Upway.
Orphaned Old Maid, The.
Hartley. Little Known Bird of the Inner Eye.
Hayden. Frederick Douglass.
Runagate Runagate.
Hemingway. There was Ike and Tony and Jaque and me.
Herrick. His Answer to a Question.
Liberty.
More Potent, Lesse Peccant.
To All Young Men That Love.
To Love.
Upon Love ("Love, I have broke").
Hesketh. Comparison with a Sunflower.
Defeathered.
Hewitt. Fontanel.
Free Foot, The.
Mobile Mollusc, A.
My Father's Death in Hospital.
Oh, ban the books and save the children's lives.
Tribunes, The.
Valediction Lines to My WEA Students.
YCVS and the Ulster Division, The.

Hill. Beautiful lady, / in reverence.
Hughes, Langston. Democracy.
Dream Variation[s].
Freedom Train.
Freedom's Plow.
Refugee in America.
Hughes, Ted. Bull Moses, The.
Gnat-Psalm.
Jaguar, The.
Jarrell. Emancipators, The.
Lines, The.
Port of Embarkation.
Woman at the Washington Zoo, The.
Jeffers. Coast-Road, The.
Shine, Republic.
Jong. In the Glass-Bottomed Boat.
Sunjuice.
Joseph. Warning.
Keats. Song: "I had a dove and the sweet dove died."
Kipling. Benfactors, The.
Ex-Clerk.
Greek National Anthem, The.
I will remember what I was. I am sick of rope and chain.
Song of Travel, A.
Knight. Various Protestations From Various People.
We Free Singers Be.
Lawrence. Free Will.
Let Us Talk, Let Us Laugh.
Liberty's Old Old Story.
Neptune's Little Affair with Freedom.
Levine. Ashes.
Children's Crusade, The.
Liddy. Maud Gonne Rode Out on a White Horse to Coolgreany.
Wine of Lovers.
Lindsay. Old Horse in the City, The.
Over the Appalachian Barricade.
Longfellow. Slave Singing at Midnight, The.
Lovelace. To Althea, from Prison.
To Lucasta, from Prison.
Triumphs of Philamore and Amoret, The.
Vintage to the Dungeon, The.
What doubt'st thou hand? sad Cato 'tis to kill.
Lowry. Conversations With Goethe.
Glaucous Winged Gull, The.
We Sit Unhackled Drunk and Mad to Edit.
Where Did That One Go to, 'Erbert.
MacLeish. Boy in the Roman Zoo.
Brave New World.
Good Man in a Bad Time, A.
Liberty.
MacNeice. Canto VII: "Cloud of witnesses. To whom? To what?, A."
Matthews. Untitled Poem.
Meinke. Supermarket.
Meredith. This, no more, doth Callistes recall.
Merton. All of the branches / None of the roots.
And the Children of Birmingham.
Elias—Variations on a Theme.
Freedom as Experience.
Millay. Not for a Nation.
Morgan. Loki's Song.
Morrison. End, The.
Translations of the Divine.
Nathan. Sick Leave.
Olson. Fool, The.
Pack. Clayfeld's Duck.
Patchen. And When Freedom Is Achieved.
Billion Freedoms, The.
Letter on Liberty, A.
Piercy. Noon of the Sunbather.
Sabbath of Mutual Respect, The.
Sojourners.
Raine. Eudaimon.
Wind.
Ransom. Dog.
Rolfe. At the Moment of Victory.
Homecoming (August 7, 1934).
Rossetti. Linnet in a gilded cage,— / A linnet on a bough, A.
Promises like Pie-Crust.
Song of the Star, The.
Rukeyser. Ann Burlak.

Game of Darts at the Chesterfield Arms, A.
In Our Time.
Juanita Tinsley.
Long Enough. Long Enough.
Secrets of American Civilization.
When the young man reaches his full height.
St. John. Essay on Liberation, An.
Sandburg. Cahokia.
Freedom is a Habit.
Is There Any Easy Road to Freedom?
Limited.
Nickels click off fares in the slot machines of the subway, the elevated, The.
Noon Hour.
Open Letter to the Poet Archibald MacLeish Who Has Forsaken His Massachusetts Farm to Make Propaganda for Freedom.
People learn, unlearn, learn, The.
Shoes of Travel.
Who were those editors picking the most.
Sarton. Caged Bird, The.
On Being Given Time.
Phoenix, The.
Prisoner at a Desk.
Schwartz. To a Fugitive.
Shelley. Cancelled Stanza.
Liberty.
Ode to Liberty.
Smith, Patti. High on Rebellion.
Smith, Stevie. Anger's Freeing Power.
Snodgrass. Assuming Fine Feathers, W. D. Takes Flight.
Valediction, A.
Snyder. High Quality Information.
Off the Trail.
Once at Cold Mountain, troubles cease.
Sorrentino. Gimlet.
Stevens. Latest Freed Man, The.
Stevenson. Ad Martialem.
Ad Olum.
In Maximum.
Voluntary.
Stuart. This Is No Dream, This Is My Life.
Thomson. Prospect, The.
Walcott. Elegy: "Our hammock swung between Americas."
Warren. Night: The Motel down the Road from the Pen.
Whitman. Broadway Pageant, A.
Columbian's Song, The.
Commonplace, The.
Election Day, November, 1884.
France, The 18th Year of These States.
House of Friends, The.
Inca's Daughter, The.
Lo, Victress on the Peaks.
Old Age's Ship & Crafty Death's.
Old Salt Kossabone.
Poem of Remembrances for a Girl or a Boy of These States.
Song of the Banner at Daybreak.
Spain, 1873–74.
Thoughts ("Of these years I sing").
To Soar in Freedom and in Fullness of Power.
To the States.
Turn O Libertad.
Washington's Monument, February, 1885.
We Two, How Long We Were Fool'd.
Years of the Modern.
Whittier. After Election.
Arisen at Last.
Astræa at the Capitol.
At Port Royal.
Bartholdi Statue, The.
Brown Dwarf of Rŭgen, The.
Democracy.
Derne.
Eve of Election, The.
Exiles, The.
Expostulation.
Freed Islands, The.
Freedom in Brazil.
Garibaldi.
Greeting, A.
Hymn: "O Holy Father! just and true."
Hymn: "O Thou, whose presence went before."

Hymn Sung at Christmas by the Scholars of St. Helena's Island, S.C.
In the "Old South."
Jubilee Singers, The.
Kansas Emigrants, The.
King's Missive, The.
Kossuth.
Laus Deo!
Legend of St. Mark, The.
Letter, A.
Lexington.
Lines from a Letter to a Young Clerical Friend.
Lost Occasion, The.
Lost Statesman, The.
Massachusetts.
Mayflowers, The.
Moloch in State Street.
Moral Warfare, The.
New Hampshire.
New Year, The.
One of the Signers.
Pæan.
Pass of the Sierra, The.
Pennsylvania Hall.
Pennsylvania Pilgrim, The.
Pine-Tree, The.
Proclamation, The.
Proem: "I love the old melodious lays."
Rantoul.
Relic, The.
Rendition, The.
Ritner.
Song of the Vermonters, 1779, The.
Stanzas for the Times.
Summons, A.
Summons, The.
Sumner.
Thiers.
Thomas Starr King.
To Delaware.
To Faneuil Hall.
To Pennsylvania.
To the Memory of Charles B. Storrs.
To William H. Seward.
Toussaint L'Ouverture.
Vow of Washington, The.
What of the Day?
World's Convention, The.
Wilbur. Harbor, The.
On Freedom's Ground.
Regatta, The.
Still, Citizen Sparrow.
Williams, William Carlos. In Chains.
Wordsworth. Composed at Cora Linn in Sight of Wallace's Tower.
Eagle and the Dove, The.
Italian Itinerant, and the Swiss Goatherd, The.
Just Vengeance Claims Thy Soul for Rights Invaded?
Liberty.
Ode to Lycoris.
On a Celebrated Event in Ancient History.
Thought[s] of a Briton on the Subjugation of Switzerland.
To a Skylark ("Ethereal minstrel! pilgrim of the sky").
Town of Schwytz, The.
Upon the Same Event.
Wright, James. I am Freed.
To a Fugitive.
Wroth. Song: "Beeing past the paines of love."
Sonnet 14: "Am I thus conquered? [or conquer'd]? have I lost the powers."
Wyatt. Ah, my heart, ah, what aileth thee.
If chance assigned [or assign'd].
Now must I le[a]rn[e] to live [or lyve] at rest.
Tangled [or Tanglid] I was [or was I] in [or yn] Love's snare.
Young. Now's the Time.
October Window.

Freemasonry
Burns. Farewell. To the Brethren of St. James' Lodge, Tarbolton, The.
Sons of Old Killie, The.

Kipling. Banquet Night.
Mother-Lodge, The.
Freighters
Lowry. From Helsinki to Liverpool with Lumber.
Zukofsky. Buoy—no, how.
See also **Cargoes.**
Frémont, John Charles
Whittier. Frémont Campaign Song, A.
Song, A: "Beneath thy skies, November!"
Song for the Time, A.
To John C. Frémont.
French, The
Eberhart. Retrospective Forelook.
Gunn. Readings in French.
Hartley. From a Paris Window—High.
Hoffman. Letter to William Frohock.
Koertge. Pronouncing My Name.
Nash. Chacun à Son Berlitz.
How Do You Say Ha-Ha in French.
If He Scholars, Let Him Go.
Strange Case of Mr. Palliser's Palate, The.
Try It Suns. and Hols.; It's Closed Then.
What Is Bibbidi-Bobbidi-Boo in Sanskrit?
O'Hara. Ode: Salute to the French Negro Poets.
St. John. My Tea with Madame Descartes.
Schuyler. Fauré Ballade, The.
Simone Signoret.
Sorrentino. Crown, The.
She whom no one ever found.
Tomlinson. Milieux.
French Revolution
Blake. Fayette beside King Lewis stood.
French Revolution, The.
Let the Brothels of Paris be opened.
Louis XVI.
When France got free Europe 'twixt Fools & Knaves.
Coleridge. Destruction of the Bastile.
Domestic Peace.
Fears in Solitude.
France; an Ode.
Ode on the Departing Year.
Priestley.
Recantation.
To a Young Lady.
To the Honourable Mr. Erskine.
Jarrell. 1789–1939.
Smith, Charlotte. Disillusion with the French Revolution.
Long wintry months are past; the Moon that now.
Slow in the Wintry Morn, the struggling light.
Tomlinson. Charlotte Corday.
For Danton.
Marat Dead.
Wordsworth. French Revolution as It Appeared to Enthusiasts at Its Commencement. Reprinted from "The Friend."
Freud, Sigmund
Auden. In Memory of Sigmund Freud.
Berg. At a Friend's Birthday Party in the Garden at Night.
Cohen. Is This What You Wanted.
Doolittle. Dedication: "When everything was over."
Master, The.
Hacker. For Elektra.
MacLeish. Dr. Sigmund Freud Discovers the Sea Shell.
Paley. One Day.
Stevens. Mountains Covered with Cats.
Walker. So We've Come at Last to Freud.
Friars
Chaucer. Friar's Prologue, The.
Summoner's Prologue, The.
Summoner's Tale, The.
Meredith. Adieu, adieu, my Friar, he cried.
Ransom. Necrological.
Friends, Society of
Longfellow. Proclamation, The.
Whittier. Abram Morrison.
Anniversary Poem.
Banished from Massachusetts.

Barclay of Ury.
Cassandra Southwick.
Chalkley Hall.
Cross, The.
Daniel Wheeler.
Exiles, The.
Fair Quakeress, The.
First-Day Thoughts.
How the Women Went from Dover.
King's Missive, The.
Meeting, The.
Pennsylvania Pilgrim, The.
Quaker Alumni, The.
Quaker of the Olden Time, The.
Quakers Are Out, The.
Revelation.
Two Elizabeths, The.

Friendship
Ashbery. Friends.
Auden. At Twenty we find our friends for
   ourselves, but it takes Heaven.
Envoi: "Take up your load and go, lad."
For Friends Only.
Friendship.
I'm beginning to lose patience.
None of us are as young.
On Receiving a Christmas Card.
Robin, The.
So I must go my way.
Song: "I have a little book."
Thank You, Fog.
Two friends who met here and embraced are
   gone.
We Sat.
Beatles. Any Time at All.
With a Little Help from My Friends.
Berg. Brothers.
Berrigan. New Personal Poem.
So Going Around Cities.
Berry. Beginning and end.
For a night and a day.
In Memory: Stuart Egnal.
Kentucky River Junction.
Meeting, A.
Plan, The.
To Gary Snyder.
We stood on a height.
Berryman. I've met your friend at last, your
   violent friend.
Ménage à trois, like Tristan's,—difficult.
To Bhain Campbell.
Winter-Piece to a Friend Away, A.
Betjeman. Old Friends.
Bishop. Letter to N. Y.
Manuelzinho.
Shampoo, The.
Blake. If Men will act like a maid smiling
   over a Churn.
[*Look Flaxman & Stothard do*] old
   acquaintance well.
Mr Stothard to Mr Cromek.
On H[ayle]ys Friendship.
To forgive Enemies H[ayley] does pretend.
To Hayley [*or* To H[ayley]].
To John Flaxman, 12 September 1800.
Was I angry with Hayley who used me so ill.
Bly. After Drinking All Night with a Friend,
   We Go Out in a Boat at Dawn to See Who
   Can Write the Best Poem.
Boyle. Letter to Archibald Craig, A.
Ode to a Maintenance Man and His Family.
Brontë. But the hearts that once adored me.
Love and Friendship.
Not many years but long enough to see.
O hinder me by no delay.
Browning, Elizabeth Barrett. Hugh Stuart
   Boyd [His Blindness].
Little Friend, The.
Sea-side walk, A.
Sleep, The.
Sonnet: "I thank all who have loved me in
   their hearts."
To Bettine.
To Mary Russell Mitford.
Browning, Robert. Clive.
Fears and Scruples.

Light Woman, A.
Waring.
Bukowski. Letter from the North.
Reunion.
What to Do with Contributor's Copies?
Burns. Epistle to Captn Willm Logan at Park.
Here's, a bottle and an honest friend.
Interpolation.
Reply to Robert Riddell.
Second Epistle to Davie.
Third Epistle to J. Lapraik.
To Chloris.
To Chloris.
To J. S****.
To Mr. John Kennedy.
To Mrs. C———.
To Renton of Lamerton.
To Terraughty, on His Birth-Day.
While new-ca'd kye rowte at the stake.
Byron. L'Amitié Est L'Amour Sans Ailes.
Lines Written on a Blank Leaf of the
   "Pleasures of Memory."
On Revisiting Harrow.
Pignus Amoris.
To a Youthful Friend.
To Edward Noel Long, Esq.
To George, Earl Delawarr.
To the Earl of Clare.
Campion. Were My Heart as Some Men's
   Are.
Carew. To My Worthy Friend, Master
   Davenant Upon His Excellent Play, *The Just
   Italian.*
"Carroll, Lewis." Double Acrostic: I sing a
   place wherein agree.
Madrigal: "He shouts amain, he shouts again."
To My Child-Friend.
Valentine, A.
Carruth. Pa McCabe.
Catullus. Carmen 1: "To whom should I
   present this."
Carmen 9: "Veraniolus, / first of friends."
Carmen 12: "While everyone else is laughing
   & drinking."
Carmen 30: "Alfenus from Cremona / forsakes
   the friendship of friends."
Carmen 38: "Angst, / ennui & angst."
Carmen 68: "Borne down by bitter
   misfortune."
Carmen 72: "Cancel, Catullus, the expectancies
   of friendship."
Carmen 91: "In this hopeless & wasting love
   of mine."
Chaucer. Romance [*or* Romaunt] of the Rose,
   The.
Clough. Mari Magno I.
Sectantem levia nervi deficiunt.
Coleridge. Duty Surviving Self-Love.
Hexameters.
Love and Friendship Opposite.
Scars Remaining, The.
To a Gentleman.
To a Young Friend.
To W. Wordsworth.
Cowper. 1.5: "'Twas a long journey lay before
   us."
Catharina.
Catharina, the Second Part.
Contemporaries all surpassed, see one.
Epistle to Hill.
Epistle to Lady Austen.
Faithful Friend, The.
Friendship.
On Flatterers.
On the Death of Damon.
On the Death of Russell.
This ev'ning, Delia, you and I.
To Hayley.
To Unwin.
Valediction, The: "Farewell, false hearts!
   whose best affections fail."
Winter Nosegay, The.
Crabbe. On Receiving from a Lady a Present
   of a Ring.
Crane. Postscript, A.
Crashaw. Upon Two Greene Apricockes Sent

to Cowley by Sir Crashaw.
With a Picture Sent to a Friend.
Creeley. Damon & Pythias.
For a Friend.
For Anybody.
For Friendship.
For Joel.
For Rainer Gerhardt.
For Tom.
For Walter Chappell.
Friend, The.
Friends, The.
Hart Crane.
Poem, A: "If the water forms."
Saturday Afternoon.
Trees.
Cullen. Dear Friends and Gentle Hearts.
Little Sonnet to Little Friends.
Tableau.
Cummings. 2.14: "Ah, Postumus, fleet-footed
   are the years!"
"But / he" i / staring / into winter twi.
W.H.W., Jr.
Davie. Catullus on Friendship.
Recollections of George Oppen in a Letter to
   an English Friend.
Rutland.
Shropshire.
De la Mare. Faithless.
Dickinson. Are Friends Delight or Pain?
Believing that we are to have no Face.
By Chivalries as tiny.
Friend is a / solemnity, A.
Friends are nations in themselves.
Gift of neither Heaven nor Earth, The.
I am speechlessly grateful for a friend.
I cannot depict a friend to my mind.
I have the friend who loves me.
I think it sad to have a friend.
If anybody's friend be dead.
Is not an absent friend as mysterious.
Must I lose the Friend that saved my Life.
My friend must be a Bird.
Shady friend—for Torrid days, A.
Small weight is obnoxious, A.
Sweet and soft as summer, Darlings.
That you return to us alive.
To which as to a Reservoir.
Trudging to Eden, looking backward.
Who loves you most.
You asked me if I wrote now?
Donne. To Mr I. L. ("Blessed [*or* Blesst] are
   your north parts, for all this long time").
To Mr I. L. ("Of that short roll of friends writ
   in my heart").
To Mr. R. W. ("If, as mine is, thy life a
   slumber be").
To Mr. T. W. ("All hail, sweet poet, more full
   of more strong fire").
To Mr. T. W. ("Haste thee harsh verse as fast
   as thy lame measure").
To Mr. C.B.
To the Lady Bedford.
Dunbar. After the Quarrel.
Comrade.
Silence.
To a Dead Friend.
To Dr. James Newton Matthews, Mason, Ill.
Dunn. Letter About Myself to You.
"Dylan." All I Really Want to Do.
Ballad for a Friend.
Bob Dylan's Dream.
I'll Remember You.
Joan Baez in Concert, Part 2.
Let's Keep It Between Us.
Night passes fast for me now, The.
Restless Farewell.
Eberhart. Wild Swans of Inverane, The.
Emerson. Always day & night.
Drink, hear my counsel, my son, that the
   world fret thee not.
For Genius made his cabin wide.
For two rewards, & nought beside.
Friend is he, who, hunted as a foe, A.
Friends to me are frozen wine.
Friendship ("Ruddy drop of manly blood, A").
Friendship ("Thou foolish Hafiz! Say, do

churls").
From Frodmer's Drama "The Friends."
Had I the world for my enemy.
Hard is it to persuade the public mind of its
  plain duty & true interest.
I live among ideal men.
I must not borrow light.
It is certain that who his mind.
Knowst thou the luck the friends face to see.
Maiden Speech of the Æolian Harp.
Motto to "Considerations by the Way."
No physician has a balsam for my wo.
O friend blame not Hafiz.
Rubies.
Spare thou neither time nor blood for thy
  friend.
Whilst I disdain the populace.
Who loves his friend with his heart of hearts.
Fisher. Debt for Tomorrow, A.
Frost. In the Long Night.
Telephone, The.
Time to Talk, A.
Gallagher. Hug, The.
Gardner. In Memory of Lemuel Ayers, Scene
  Designer, Dead of Cancer in His Fortieth
  Year.
Man of Faith, The.
Sonnet for My Acquaintances.
Word From the Piazza del Limbo, A.
Gildner. Meeting My Best Friend from the
  Eighth Grade.
Glück. Triumph of Achilles, The.
Graves. At First Sight.
At the Well.
Song: Just Friends.
Gray. Epitaph on Sir William Williams.
Gunn. Between the pastel boutiques.
But I came back, after the last bus.
Glamorous and difficult friend.
J Car, The.
Reassurance, The.
Terminal.
To a Friend in Time of Trouble.
Hacker. Against Silence.
Another poet, woman and alive.
Chaplet for Judith Landry, A.
Country & Western II.
Dear Jool, I Miss You in Saint-Saturnin.
Elevens.
Gerda in the Aerie.
Late August Letter.
Letter from Goose Creek: April.
Little Robber Girl Gets On in the Wide
  World, The.
Nights of 1964-1966: The Old Reliable.
Nights of 1962: The River Merchant's Wife.
This is a high and sprawling wooden flat.
Towards Autumn.
Hall. Body Politic, The.
Cider 5[dc] A Glass.
Friend Revisited, A.
Milkers Broken Up.
My Friend Felix.
Hartnett. Person as Dreamer: We Talk about
  the Future, The.
Hayden. Letter.
Hemingway. Modern Version of Polonius'
  Advice, A.
Herbert. Church-Porch, The.
Unkindness.
Herrick. Deluge, The.
His Age, Dedicated to His Peculiar Friend,
  Master John Wickes, under the Name of
  Posthumus.
Hymne to Sir Clipseby Crew, A.
To his Friend, Master J. Jincks.
To His Friend to Avoid Contention of Words.
To His Honoured and Most Ingenious Friend,
  Mr. Charles Cotton.
To M. Leonard Willan His Peculiar Friend.
True Friendship.
True Safety.
Hewitt. After the Fire.
Country Walk in May, A.
For Busha.
Irish Dimension, The.
Man from the Mountains, The.

River Streets, The.
Storm, The.
Townland of Peace.
W.R. Rodgers.
Holmes. For Walker Evans.
Housman. Hughley Steeple.
Shake hands, we shall never be friends, all's
  over.
West, The.
When I came last to Ludlow.
When I would muse in boyhood.
Hughes, Ted. Six Young Men.
Jeffers. George Sterling.
No Resurrection.
Johnson. Ode on Friendship, An.
Jonson. Epigram. To a Friend and Son.
Epistle to a Friend, An ("Sir, I am thankful,
  first, to heaven, for you").
Epistle to Master Arth[ur] Squib, An.
Epistle to Master John Selden, An.
Poem Sent Me by Sir William Burlase, A.
To the Immortal[l] Memory [or Memorie] and
  Friendship of That Noble Pair[e], Sir Lucius
  Cary and Sir H. [or Henry] Morison.
To the Same [Benjamin Rudyerd] ("If I would
  wish, for truth, and not for show").
Turn him, and see his threads; look if he be.
Keats. To a Friend Who Sent Me Some
  Roses.
To Charles Cowden Clarke.
To George Felton Mathew.
Kipling. Follow Me 'Ome.
France.
Friends, The.
Pussy can sit by the fire and sing.
There were three friends that buried the fourth.
Thousandth Man, The.
Koch. Circus, The.
Departure from Hydra, The.
Fate.
Secret, The.
Lawrence. Emotional Friend, The.
Henriette.
Lies About Love.
Refused Friendship.
To a Certain Friend.
Levine. Making It New.
Liddy. La Muerte de Joselito.
Little Song for Ivy Day, 1991.
Sister Beach, Sister Garden.
Lorde. Dear Toni Instead of a Letter of
  Congratulation..
Sister, Morning Is a Time for Miracles.
Lovelace. Grasse-Hopper, The.
Lowell. Randall Jarrell 1. October 1965.
Randall Jarrell 2.
Randall Jarrell 3.
Lowry. Doggerel.
I bet you don't know who I am.
S.O.S Sinking fast by both bow and stern.
With Great Love Oh Beloved Harteebeeste
  from El Leon.
"MacDiarmid." To a Friend and Fellow Poet.
MacNeice. Canto XIII: "Leaving the colleges
  then and their half-remembered."
Casualty, The.
Markson. Agree.
To a Mexican Poet Who Has Forsaken Drink.
Matthews. Little Blue Nude.
Meredith. Candid Friend who strikes because
  he loves, The.
I look'd for my poet—he came not!
It's many a penny you'll pay to go.
Madrigal: "Since Tuck is faithless found, no
  more."
To-morrow I am going.
Tuck, sweet charmer, tell me why.
Tuck! Tuck! Once you would flatter me.
Merrill. Black Mesa, The.
Clearing the Title.
Days of 1971.
Friend of the Fourth Decade, The.
Manos Karastefanís.
16. ix. 65.
Strato in Plaster.
Words for Maria.
Merton. Flight of Lin Hui, The.

Message to Be Inscribed on Mark Van
  Doren's Hamilton Medal.
Three Friends.
Miller. Dead Dog (For Goo).
So Long It's Been Good to Know You.
Milton. Damon's Epitaph.
Morgan. Encounter.
Letter, The.
Morrison. Lessons on Becoming.
Muldoon. Soap-Pig, The.
Nash. Compliments of a Friend.
Crossing the Border.
Hush, Here They Come.
I Know You'll Like Them.
I'll Write Their Number Down When We Get
  Home.
Suppose I Darken Your Door.
Nemerov. Blue Suburban.
Day on the Big Branch, A.
Memory of My Friend, A.
Song: "Provide your friend with almanacs."
To a Friend.
Neruda. Oliverio Girondo.
Notley. Margaret & Dusty.
O'Hara. Aus Einem April.
Biotherm [for Bill Berkson].
John Button Birthday.
Poem Read at Joan Mitchell's.
Olson. Death of Europe, The.
Pack. Unburying the Birch.
Paley. For George (I).
Piercy. Bumpity Road to Mutual Devotion,
  The.
Friend, The.
Morning Athletes.
My friend, on the deck we sit.
My old friend, how we sustain.
Night Letter.
We are all hustling and dealing.
Pope. On Mr. Gay, in Westminster Abbey,
  1732.
Presentation Verses to Nathaniel Pigott.
Pound. Amitites.
Ralegh. To his Singular Friend, William
  Lithgow.
"Reed." Vicious Circle.
Robinson. I grant you friendship is a royal
  thing.
Long Race, The.
Old Story, An.
Old Story, The.
Sainte-Nitouche.
Roethke. Chums, The.
Rolfe. Room with Revolutionists.
Rossetti. Along the highroad the way is too
  long.
Care flieth, / Hope and fear together.
Dumb Friend, A.
Hail, noble face of noble friend!
I seek among the living & I seek.
Me you often meet / In London's crowded
  street.
Peal of Bells, A.
Promises like Pie-Crust.
River Thames (?).
To My Friend Elizabeth.
Zara.
Rukeyser. Born in December.
Cats and a Cock.
Course.
St. John. My Friend.
Wavelength.
Schuyler. Dear Joe.
June 30, 1974.
Poem: "I do not always understand what you
  say."
Sexton. Big Heart, The.
Shakespeare. Sonnet 30: "When to the
  sessions of sweet silent thought."
Sonnet 42: "That thou hast her, it is not all
  my grief[e]."
Sonnet 133: "Beshrew that heart that makes
  my heart to groan."
Sonnet 134: "So, now I have confess'd that he
  is thine."
Shelley. Sonnet: [From the Italian of Dante.]
Dante Alighieri to Guido Cavalcanti.

Shelton. After Thirty Years.
Certain Choices.
Silverstein. Helping.
Hug o' War.
Me and My Giant.
Razor-Tailed Wren, The.
Tree House.
Smart. To Posthumus.
Smith, Charlotte. Captive Escaped in the
Wilds of America. Addressed to the Hon.
Mrs. O'Neill, The.
On the Aphorism "L'Amitié est l'Amour sans
Ailes."
To Friendship.
Walk in the Shrubbery, A.
Smith, Stevie. Broken Friendship, The.
Dirge: "From a friend's friend I taste
friendship."
Freddy.
Nor We of Her to Him.
Pleasures of Friendship, The.
Voice from the Tomb (4).
Snodgrass. Friend, A.
Sorrentino. Mathematics, The.
Spender. Auden's Funeral.
Stevenson. Fear not, dear friend, but freely
live your days.
Here Lies Erotion.
It's an overcome sooth for age an' youth.
Mile an' a Bittock, A.
My Shadow.
To Charles Baxter.
To friends at home, the lone, the admired, the
lost.
To Marcus.
Verses Written in 1872.
Sutter. Third Use of the Penis, The.
Swift. Dean and the Duke, The.
Part of a Summer, The.
To Stella, Visiting Me in My Sickness.
Twelve Articles.
Tennyson. In the Garden at Swainston.
Thomas. To Others than You.
Thomson. Lover's Fate, The.
Van Duyn. Open Letter, Personal.
Walcott. Sea Canes.
Village Life, A.
Walker. These Days.
Warren. To a Friend Parting.
Whitman. As Toilsome I Wander'd Virginia's
Woods.
I Dream'd in a Dream.
I Saw in Louisiana a Live-Oak Growing.
In Paths Untrodden.
Not Heat Flames Up and Consumes.
Recorders Ages Hence.
Whittier. Benedicite.
Ego.
Greeting.
Laurels, The.
Legacy, A.
My Namesake.
My Thanks.
Remembrance.
Response.
To ———: "Fair Nature's priestesses! to
whom."
To Avis Keene.
To Fredrika Bremer.
Williams, Charles Kenneth. Signs.
Williams, Miller. Friend, The.
Thinking about Bill, Dead of AIDS.
Williams, William Carlos. Old Worshipper,
The.
Wordsworth. In the First Page of an Album
by One Whose Handwriting Is Wretchedly
Bad.
To a Child [Written in Her Album].
To I.F.
To the Lady E.B. and the Hon. Miss P.
Travelling.
Wright, Charles. To Giacomo Leopardi in the
Sky.
Yeats. Friends.
Lover Pleads with His Friend for Old Friends,
The.

Young. Again / Who am I?
Roland Navarro (1939-1961).
Zukofsky. Alfenus, remember *kind intimacies*?
false? They elated us.
Cold how mean, fortune consuming you
oppresses your care, your.
Day, see no day—choke, qualm, quick
qualm—benevolence, merit are.
Marrucinus Asinius, that sinister.
My last—Cornificius—your Catullus'.
No idea, Gelli, spurred me to mirror you
faithful.
On Valentine's Day to Friends.
To Friends, for Good Health.
Veranius of all my beloved friends.
Whom do I give my neat little volume.

Frietchie, Barbara
Whittier. Barbara Frietchie.

Frog Prince, The
Smith, Stevie. Frog Prince, The.

Frogs
Bly. Night Frogs.
Bukowski. It's Nothing to Laugh About.
Dickinson. His Mansion in the Pool.
Long sigh of the Frog, The.
Eberhart. On Returning to a Lake in Spring.
Fenton. Frog hunts on land by vision. He
escapes, A.
Graves. Frog and the Golden Ball, The.
Heaney. Death of a Naturalist.
Kinnell. First Song.
Vapor Trail Reflected in the Frog Pond.
Lowry. No wonder it feared peace, the knees
of years.
MacLeish. Peepers in Our Meadow, The.
Muldoon. Frog, The.
Rossetti. Contemptuous of his home beyond.
Hopping frog, hop here and be seen.
Sandburg. Frog Songs.
Spring Cries.
Young Bullfrogs.
Sarton. Frog, that Naked Creature, The.
Sexton. Elegy in the Classroom.
Frog Prince, The.
Smith, Stevie. Frog Prince, The.
Tomlinson. Poolville, N.Y.
Wright, James. Small Frogs Killed on the
Highway.

Frontiers
Everson. Scout, The.
Hugo. Fort Benton.
MacLeish. Definition of the Frontiers.
Geography of this Time.
Nathan. If you start in loneliness.
Turco. Trading Post, The.

Frontiersmen
Garrigue. Land We Did Not Know, The.
McNeill. Turnpike, The.
Williams, William Carlos. Chant of the
Frontiersman.
Poem: "Daniel Boone, the father of
Kentucky."

Frost
Beckett. Vive morte ma seule saison.
Carruth. On Lincoln's birthday the forest.
Thaw, The.
When conditions of frost and.
Dickinson. Apparently with no surprise.
Frost was never seen, The.
Doolittle. Blue-geese, white-geese, you may
say.
Frost. Peril of Hope.
Herrick. Farewell Frost; or, Welcome the
Spring.
Hewitt. Frost.
Spring of the Year.
Joseph. Diary.
Lovelace. Grasse-Hopper, The.
Lowry. Fragment: "Dead tree that, frozen,
utters at the top, The."
Walk in Canada.
With Dearest Morning Love and Kisses.
Meredith. Carol of Jack Frost, A.
Raine. Frost-rime edges blades of grass.
Sandburg. Maroon with Silver Frost.
Thomson. What art thou, frost? and whence
are thy keen stores.

Tomlinson. Frost.
Instance, The.
Winter-Piece.
Updike. Frost.
Whittier. Frost Spirit, The.
Wilbur. Two Quatrains for First Frost.

Frost, Robert
Berryman. Lines to Mr Frost.
Brooks. Of Robert Frost.
Carruth. I live where Frost lived.
West Bolton is due north of Bolton, East.
Eberhart. Worldly Failure.
Hewitt. Clink of Rhyme, The.
Kinnell. For Robert Frost.
Lowell. Robert Frost.
MacLeish. In and Come In.
Markson. Birches.
Matthews. On the Porch at the Frost Place,
Franconia, NH.
Meinke. Robert Frost in Warsaw.
Nemerov. For Robert Frost, in the Autumn, in
Vermont.
Rukeyser. Double Dialogue: *Homage to
Robert Frost.*
Schwartz. Now He Knows All There Is to
Know: Now He Is Acquainted With the Day
and Night.

Fruit Trees and Fruit
Bishop. Elegy for Maria Alves.
Cowper. On Thurlow.
Davie. Cherry Ripe.
Dickinson. We are snatching our jewels from
the frost.
Eberhart. Lovely were the fruit trees in the
evening.
Emerson. Color, taste, and smell, smaragdus,
sugar, and musk.
Fenton. Fruit-Grower in War-time (and Some
of His Enemies), The.
Ford. Chinaberries / Change from green to
yellow. In, The.
This year's jackfruit hang.
Garrigue. Catch What You Can.
Hacker. Late August.
Hesketh. St. Luke's Summer.
Hoffman. That the Pear Delights Me Now.
Hugo. Ode to the Trio Fruit Company of
Missoula.
Jong. Fruits & Vegetables.
Raspberries in My Driveway, The.
Lawrence. Grapes.
Lovelace. Being treated to Ellinda.
Lowry. Christ I am tired of fruit im poetry.
McGrath. Praises.
McNeill. Mayapple Hill.
Merton. Flower of the Fruit, The.
Millay. Never May the Fruit Be Plucked.
Moore. Nevertheless.
Nine Nectarines.
Nash. Cantaloupe, The.
Piercy. September Afternoon at Four O'Clock.
Roethke. Pickle Belt.
Rossetti. Currants on a bush, / And figs upon
a stem.
Goblin Market.
Lily has a smooth stalk, / Will never hurt your
hand, The.
Oh fair to see / Bloom-laden cherry tree.
Peach tree on the southern wall, The.
Rushes in a watery place, / And reeds in a
hollow.
Sarton. Olive Grove, The.
Schuyler. Jelly Jelly.
Whittier. Fruit-Gift, The.
Williams, William Carlos. Brief Lief.
This Is Just to Say.
Zukofsky. Pretty.
Raspberry.

Fry, Elizabeth
Whittier. Two Elizabeths, The.

Fuchsia
Hardy. Lodging-House Fuchsias, The.

Fulfillment
Ammons. Holding On.
Angelou. Unmeasured Tempo.
Atwood. There must be more for you to do.
Beatles. All You Need Is Love.

And I Love Her.
Ask Me Why.
End, The.
Bly. Love Poem in Twos and Threes.
   Man and a Woman Sit Near Each Other.
Browning, Elizabeth Barrett. Lay of the Early
   Rose, A.
Browning, Robert. At the "Mermaid."
Bukowski. Another Bed.
Carruth. Summer, The.
Clough. In controversial foul impureness.
   O stream, descending to the sea.
Cohen. Owning Everything.
"Dylan." Need a Woman.
Eberhart. Transfer, The.
Graves. Vow, The.
Keats. Character of Charles Brown.
Levertov. Part, The.
Levine. Words.
Meredith. Line of eve o'er the moorland, A.
Merton. Man Is Born in Tao.
Nathan. Chosen, The.
Oliver. Stanley Kunitz.
Olson. Maximus, at the Harbor.
   Maximus Letter # Whatever.
Piercy. Shadows of the Burning.
"Reed." Doin' the Things That We Want To.
Robinson. Three Quatrains.
Rossetti. Buds and Babies.
Tomlinson. Their Voices Rang.
Young. Erosong.
   What Is the Blues?
Zimmer. Enzyme Poem for Suzanne, An.

Fuller, Margaret
Hacker. Ballad of Ladies Lost and Found.

Fulton, Robert
Sandburg. Trinity Place.

Fun
Beatles. Yellow Submarine.
Cowper. Impromptu ["So I have seen the
   maids in vain"].
"Dylan." Goin' to Acapulco.
Eberhart. Clerihew for Alan Gaylord, A.
Gardner. Prospero's Isle.
Gunn. Falstaff.
Herrick. Anacreontike.
   Frolic[k], A.
Merton. Old.
Silverstein. My Hobby.
   Oh Have You Heard.
See also **Play; Pleasure; Libraries and**
   Librarians.

Funerals
Auden. Carter's Funeral, The.
   Stop all the clocks, cut off the telephone.
Berry. At a Country Funeral.
Boyle. Funeral in Hungary.
Carruth. None.
   Sonnet: "If I die today, which statistically
   speaking."
Ciardi. It Took Four Flowerboats to Convoy
   My Father's Black.
Cullen. Brown Girl Dead, A.
Cummings. After Seeing French Funeral.
   Old mr ly / fresh from a fu.
Dickinson. Element of Elegy, The.
   I felt a Funeral, in my Brain.
Dobyns. Counterparts.
   How It Was at the End.
Donne. Funeral[l], The.
Dove. Tou Wan Speaks to Her Husband Liu
   Sheng.
Eberhart. Irish Catholic.
   New England Protestant.
Edmunds. Highlands 1966, The.
Emerson. Bird was gone the ghastly trees,
   The.
Fenton. Better for the widow, that she should
   not live in fear of surprise, The.
   Bus is waiting at the southern gate, The.
Fisher. Aside to a Children's Tale.
Fletcher. Grandfather's Grave.
Ford. St.-John Perse.
Fox. At Nightfall.
Gardner. Whole World's in a Terrible Chassis,
   The.
   Zei Gesund.

Garrigue. Beheld in Naples.
Gildner. Szostak.
Hardy. Choirmaster's Burial, The.
   Farmer Dunman's Funeral.
   Hatband, The.
   Leaving, A.
   Retty's Phases.
   She at His Funeral.
Heaney. Funeral Rites.
Herrick. Bucolick betwixt Two: Lacon and
   Thyrsis, A.
   Funeral[l] Rites of the Rose, The.
   His Embalming to Julia.
   To Flowers.
   To the Yew and Cypress to Grace His
   Funeral.
   Upon a Maid That Died [*or* Dyed] the Day
   She Was Married [*or* Marryed].
Hewitt. First Funeral.
   Lifting, The.
   Neighbor's Funeral, A.
   Rite.
Hill. For whom do we scrape our tribute of
   pain.
   Processionals in the exemplary cave.
Housman. Bredon Hill.
Hughes, Langston. As Befits a Man.
   Ballad of the Man Who's Gone.
   Dead in There.
   Night Funeral in Harlem.
Lawrence. Violets.
   Violets for the Dead.
Levine. Goodbye.
Lewis. Village Funeral: Maharashtra.
   Westminster Abbey.
Lindsay. Drunkard's Funeral, The.
Longfellow. Hawthorne.
Lovelace. Elegie. On the Death of Mrs.
   Cassandra Cotton, an.
Lowell. Death of the Sheriff, The.
Lowry. Give me the money, / Give me the
   money.
   Hangover—Reading Rilke, Schnitzler or
   Someone, A.
"MacDiarmid." Island Funeral.
McNeill. Jane Renick MacElmain (2).
Markson. Funeral.
   Nachtmusik.
Matthews. Funeral Homes.
Meredith. Soft night–wind went laden to
   death, The.
Merrill. Annie Hill's Grave.
Millay. Without Music.
Nash. Maybe You Can't Take It with You,
   but Look What Happens When You Leave It
   Behind.
Nathan. It Looks As If It Were Just Sleeping.
Nemerov. One Moment in Eternity.
Olson. Absolutely Vernal.
Plath. Bee Meeting, The.
Poe. Lenore.
Ransom. Bells for John Whiteside's Daughter.
   Emily Hardcastle, Spinster.
Robinson. Cortège.
   Whip, The.
Roethke. On the Road to Woodlawn.
Rossetti. "Ding a ding," / The sweet bells
   sing.
Sandburg. And So Today.
   Pals.
   Repetitions.
   Waiting for the Chariot.
Schuyler. Beautiful Funerals.
   Chapel, A.
Smith, Stevie. King in Funeral Procession, A.
   Silence and Tears.
Snodgrass. Old Apple Trees.
   Viewing the Body.
Stuart. Funeral, The.
Sutter. Friends find the family.
   This woman is nobody's woman.
   Warming up in their truck.
Tate. Stranger.
Thomas. After the Funeral.
Walker. Burial.
Whitman. Interpolation Sounds.
Whittier. Funeral Tree of the Sokokis.

Williams, Miller. On the Death of a Middle-
   Aged Man.
   On the Symbolic Consideration of Hands and
   the Significance of Death.
   Widow, The.
Williams, William Carlos. Tract.
Wright, James. Refusal, The.
Yeats. Mountain Tomb, The.

Furnaces
Kooser. Furnace.

Furniture
Cowper. Gratitude.
   Sofa, The.
Eberhart. Day-Bed, The.
Gunn. Pierce Street.
Hardy. Little Old Table, The.
Hartley. Furnished Rooms.
Lawrence. Furniture.
Nash. Have You Tried Staying Awake? or,
   They'll Find a Way to Stop That, Too.
Rich. Dreamwood.
Simic. Furniture Mover.
Updike. Furniture, The.
Wright, James. Nature Alive.

Fuseli, Henry
Blake. To Hunt.
   William Cowper Esqre.
Browning, Robert. Mary Wollstonecraft and
   Fuseli.

Future
Atwood. Here are the holy birds.
Auden. Out of it steps our future, through this
   door.
   We Sat.
Berry. For the Future.
   How fine / to have a long-legged house.
   To Tanya at Christmas.
   To What Listens.
   What we leave behind to sleep.
Berryman. Search, The.
Betjeman. Planster's Vision, The.
Bly. Two Sounds When We Sit by the Ocean.
Browning, Elizabeth Barrett. Sonnet: "My
   future will not copy fair my past."
Clark. Moirai, The.
Clough. Mari Magno I.
   Nay draw not yet the cork, my friend.
Coleridge. Superstition.
Cooper. Blue Anchor, The.
Creeley. Eye, The.
   Going to Bed.
   Massachusetts.
Cummings. But being not amazing:without
   love.
   If(touched by love's own secret)we,like
   homing.
   In time's a noble mercy of proportion.
Davie. Prolific Spell, The.
   Some Future Moon.
De la Mare. Humanity.
Dickinson. Future—never spoke, The.
   If the future is mighty as the past.
   Oh Future! thou secreted peace.
Dobyns. General and the Tango Singer, The.
   Inappropriate Gestures.
Dunbar. Beyond the Years.
   To Kelly Miller, Jr.
Dunn. Almost Everyone.
   Worrier, The.
"Dylan." Whatcha Gonna Do.
   When the Ship Comes In.
Eberhart. May Evening.
Emerson. Future, The.
   Heri, Cras, Hodie.
   Shun passion, fold the hands of thrift.
   There is in all the sons of men.
   Valedictory Poem.
Frost. Something for Hope.
Graves. Non Cogunt Astra.
   Olive-Yard, The.
   Tomorrow's Envy of Today.
Griffiths. Contractions.
   Hymns and Backward Glances.
   Returning I live with a huge space.
   Shrinking Horizon.
Hardy. At a Fashionable Dinner.
   He Wonders about Himself.

If You Had Known.
1967.
Strange House, The.
Hartnett. There Will Be a Talking.
Heaney. Triptych.
Hesketh. Gymnasts, The.
Hewitt. Boy Seen in a Bus Journey.
Parallels Never Meet.
Ulsterman in England Remembers, An.
Hoffman. Stop the Deathwish! Stop It! Stop!
Housman. Lads in their hundreds to Ludlow
come in for the fair, The.
Jarrell. On the Railway Platform.
Up in the sky the star is waiting.
Winter's Tale, The.
Jeffers. Granite and Cypress.
Watch the Lights Fade.
Kipling. Ballad of the *Clampherdown*, The.
Before a Midnight Breaks in Storm.
Storm Cone, The.
Larkin. Arundel Tomb, An.
Lawrence. Future States.
Future War.
Return of Returns.
Signs of the Times.
Wandering Cosmos, The.
Wellsian Futures.
Liddy. For all who trod / Golden North
American streets.
Lindsay. Amaranth, The.
Johnny Appleseed Speaks of Great Cities in
the Future.
On the Road to Nowhere.
MacLeish. Eve Explains Everything to the
Thrush Who Repeats Everything.
Poetical Remains.
MacNeice. Gone-Tomorrow, The.
Prospect.
Mahon. Squince.
Markson. A.D. 2029.
Melville. Of Wickedness the Word.
Merton. Prospects of Nostradamus, The.
Public Affairs.
Morrison. Thank You, O Lord.
Nathan. Hieroglyph.
Neruda. Let's Wait.
O'Hara. Poem: "Instant coffee with slightly
sour cream."
Patchen. Soon It Will.
Piercy. Seedlings in the Mail.
"Reed." There Is No Time.
Rich. Prospective Immigrants Please Note.
Robinson. Ballade by the Fire.
To-morrow.
Rossetti. Cobwebs.
Dost Thou Not Care?
I sit a queen, and am no widow, and shall see
no sorrow.
Passing away the bliss, / The anguish passing
away.
Where love is, there comes sorrow / Today or
else tomorrow.
Where shall I find a white rose blowing?
Rukeyser. King's Mountain.
Victims, a Play for the Home, The.
Sandburg. Answer, The.
Between Worlds.
Broken-Face Gargoyles.
Haze.
Kindest and gentlest here are the, The.
One memorial stone reads.
Wars.
You can drum on immense drums.
Shelley. Lines: "Far, far away, O ye."
To-Morrow.
Shelton. Future, The.
Spender. Pylons, The.
Uncreating Chaos (Double Portrait in a
Mirror), The.
Stafford. In the White Sky.
Stevenson. Wind is without there and howls in
the trees, The.
Walcott. Prelude: "I, with legs crossed along
the daylight, watch."
Whitman. Apostroph.
As in a Swoon.
Full of Life Now.

Going Somewhere.
In the New Garden.
Long, Long Hence.
New Year's Day, 1848.
One Song, America, Before I Go.
Our Future Lot.
Poets to Come.
Recorders Ages Hence.
So Far, and So Far, and On toward the End.
Thou Mother with Thy Equal Brood.
Thoughts ("Of these years I sing").
To a Historian.
To the Pending Year.
Turn O Libertad.
Years of the Modern.
Wilbur. Nights rolled upon the river's face.
Williams, Charles Kenneth. In the next life.
Williams, Miller. After a Brubeck Concert.
For Reuben, at Twelve Months.
Wordsworth. Composed at the Same Time and
on the Same Occasion.
Presentiments.
Wright, Charles. Mount Caribou at Night.
Yau. Genghis Chan: Private Eye VII.
Yeats. Happy Townland, The.
Zukofsky. Happiest February.
I Sent Thee Late.
My nephew / And my new.

G

Gabriel
Browning, Elizabeth Barrett. Drama of Exile,
A.
Hopkins. Angelus Ad Virginem.
Rich. Gabriel.
Rossetti. Feast of the Annunciation.
Smart. St. Michael and All Angels.
Thomson. Pastoral Betwixt David, Thirsis, and
the Angel Gabriel, upon the Birth of our
Saviour, A.
Galatea
"Carroll, Lewis." Air is bright with hues of
light, The.
Galilee, Israel
Sandburg. Epistle: "Jesus loved the sunsets on
Galilee."
Galileo
Fox. Galileo Galilei (1564–1642).
Hugo. Galileo's Chair.
Jarrell. Emancipators, The.
Smith, Stevie. Thought Is Superior.
Gallantry
Dickinson. Your little mental gallantries.
Fenton. In September greasebands are put on
standard apple,.
Koertge. Getting the License.
Galley Slaves
Kipling. Song of the Galley-Slaves.
Muldoon. My Grandfather's Wake.
Gallows
Simic. Gallows Etiquette.
See also **Hanging.**
Galuppi, Baldassaro
Browning, Robert. Toccata of Galuppi's, A.
Galway. *see* **County Galway, Ireland.**
Gambling and Gamblers
Auden. Casino.
Bukowski. Day the Epileptic Spoke, The.
Driving in for a wash and.
Fat Mexican woman in front of me in line, A.
I am sitting in the stands with a.
I don't know where they come from.
I have a saying, "You will find the lowest of
the breed at the."
I lost a dollar at the track today and I know
that's.
I was out there again today. There are some
creatures out there.
Some fat son-of-a-bitch with.
Two old guys behind me were talking, The.
Valentine Gift, A.
Carroll, Jim. Desert Casino, The.
Coleridge. To Fortune.

Cowper. Tale, Founded on a Fact, A.
Dickey, William. Gambling at Reno.
Dickinson. We lose—because we win.
Dunn. Legacy.
"Dylan." Lily, Rosemary, and the Jack of
Hearts.
Rambling, Gambling Willie.
Fenton. Obsolete Oxfordshire game of "A-
All," The.
Gardner. Writing Poetry.
Graves. Man Does, Woman Is.
Hemingway. Sport of Kings, The.
Herrick. Upon Raspe.
Hughes, Langston. Madam and the Number
Writer.
Numbers.
Situation.
Jonson. Epistle to Mr Arthur Squib.
Kipling. Maxim.
Koertge. Day Alvero Pineda Was Killed, The.
Jockey, A.
Liddy. My Neighbours Two Brothers.
Lindsay. Gamblers, The.
What the Ghost of the Gambler Said.
Muldoon. Immram.
Nash. How Long Has This Been Going On?
Oh, Quite Long.
Olson. Friday, Good Friday, which.
With what I got out.
Sandburg. Cahoots.
Crapshooters.
Tomlinson. Biography of the Author: A Cento,
A.
Wakoski. Placing a $2 Bet for a Man Who
Will Never Go to the Horse Races Any
More.
Wright, James. Gambling in Stateline, Nevada.
Games
Atwood. And you play the safe game / the
orphan game.
Game after Supper.
However, / in all their games.
Berryman. At Chinese Checkers.
Blake. Blind-Man's Buff.
Bukowski. It's the Way You Play the Game.
Burns. Johnie Blunt.
Whistle. A Ballad, The.
Cummings. May i feel said he.
Dobyns. Santiago: Five Men in the Street:
Number One.
Dunn. Competition.
Eberhart. Ball Game.
Time Passes.
Vastness and Indifference of the World, The.
Fenton. Obsolete Oxfordshire game of "A-
All," The.
Gardner. Writing Poetry.
Gunn. Bally *Power Play*.
Elegy: "I can almost see it."
Hide and Seek.
Inside-Outside Game, The.
Seesaw.
Heaney. England's Difficulty.
Herrick. Beucolick, or Discourse of Neatherds,
A.
Cherry-Pit.
Draw Gloves.
Love's Play at Push-Pin.
Stool-Ball.
To the Maids to Walke Abroad.
Upon Raspe.
Hewitt. Balloons and Wooden Guns.
Dry Summer, Islandmagee, 1921.
Dustcart, The.
On Dunmore's Waste.
Hugo. Guns at Fort Flagler.
Kipling. Verses on Games.
MacNeice. Children's Games.
Indoor Sports.
Sports Page.
McNeill. Fox and Geese.
Wire Brier.
Meinke. Playing Shuffleboard, Drunk, in Key
West, Fla.
Merton. Song: In the Shows of the Round Ox.
Nash. Queen Is in the Parlor, The.

Your Lead, Partner, I Hope We've Read the Same Book.
Nemerov. Playing Skittles.
Sonnet: "It seems to be the trouble, everyone."
Patchen. Mirru.
Rossetti. Hop-o'-my-thumb and little Jack Horner.
Rukeyser. Another Day. A Game of Toys.
Paul, Telling the Game.
Game of Darts at the Chesterfield Arms, A.
Simic. Game, The.
Stevenson. Good Play, A.
Marching Song.
My Kingdom.
My Ship and I.
Pirate Story.
To Willie and Henrietta.
Unseen Playmate, The.
Swift. Ballad on the Game of Traffic, A.
Wilbur. Statues.
Williams, Charles Kenneth. Baby, I don't want.
Game, The.
Yau. Why Did What Was When.
Zimmer. Games in the Field, The.

See also **Card Games; Sports.**

Gandhi, Mohandas Karamchand
Boyle. Poem about Black Power, A.
Cullen. Karenge Ya Marenge.
"MacDiarmid." Why.

Ganges River, India
Oppen. Tugs of Hull, The.

Gangs and Gangsters
Carroll, Jim. I watched a street gang heading.
Creeley. Gangster.
Cummings. Come from his gal's.
"Dylan." Joey.
Fenton. Wild Ones[, The].
Gunn. Black Jackets.
Muldoon. Immram.
Sightseers, The.
Weepies, The.

Gannets
Oliver. Gannets.

Ganymede
Olson. Borne down by the inability to lift the heaviness.

Garages
McGrath. Excursion: Or: O Columbus!, The.
Mahon. Garage in Co. Cork, A.

Garbage and Garbage Men
Berry. If a man finds it necessary to eat garbage, he should resist the.
Wild, The.
Dobyns. Santiago: Five Men in the Street: Number Two.
Ferlinghetti. Two Scavengers in a Truck, Two Beautiful People in a Mercedes.
Nemerov. Town Dump, The.
Rich. Open-Air Museum.
Silverstein. Sarah Cynthia Sylvia Stout Would Not Take the Garbage Out.
Tomlinson. From the Motorway.
Updike. Accumulation.
Burning Trash.
Ode to Rot.
Wilbur. After the Last Bulletins.
Junk.
Williams, Charles Kenneth. Men.
Trash.
Zukofsky. Wire.

García Lorca, Federico
Cohen. Take This Waltz (*After Lorca*).
Merton. In Memory of the Spanish Poet Federico Garcia Lorca.
Muldoon. Louis.

Garda, Lake, Italy
Tennyson. Frater Ave Atque Vale.

Gardens and Gardening
Ammons. Spring Clearing.
Atwood. Dream 1: the Bush Garden.
Auden. Their Lonely Betters.
Berry. Planting Crocuses.
Bishop. Manuelzinho.
Bly. Glimpse of the Waterer.

Browning, Elizabeth Barrett. Deserted Garden, The.
Burns. Gardener wi' His Paddle—or, The Gardener's March, The.
Campion. And Would You See My Mistress' Face?
Carruth. "I've Never Seen Such a Real Hard Time Before": Three-Part Invention.
Song of the Two Crows.
Ciardi. On the Patio.
Suburban.
Cowper. Epigrams on His Garden Shed.
I was a stricken deer, that left the herd.
Crane. Fernery, The.
Postscript.
Creeley. Door, The.
Cummings. This is the garden:clours come and go.
Davie. For Doreen. A Voice from the Garden.
Gardens No Emblems.
Hermes and Mr Shaw.
Pietà.
De la Mare. In the Garden.
Myself.
Old Ben.
Quiet Enemy, The.
Sunken Garden, The.
Dickey, William. Lady of Shalott, Her Mirror Broken, The.
Dickinson. Little garden within, The.
My Garden—like the Beach.
Doolittle. Garden.
Sheltered Garden, The.
Dunbar. In a English Garden.
Emerson. Dark Flower of Cheshire garden.
Gardener.
Go into the garden.
I to my garden went.
In my garden three ways meet.
Fisher. I work in my garden.
Religious garden.
Fletcher. In the Garden of Dreams.
Fox. Mother Is.
Frost. Atmosphere.
Girl's Garden, A.
Late Walk, A.
Winter Eden, A.
Galvin. War in the Garden.
Garrigue. Cortège for Colette.
Strike of the Night, The.
Glück. Garden, The.
Graves. Ample Garden, The.
Garden, The.
Gardener.
Hidden Garden, The.
Gunn. Garden of the Gods, The.
Interruption.
Kent.
Last Days at Teddington.
Looking Glass.
Hall. Child's Garden, A.
Digging.
Hartnett. Green Room.
Herbert. Paradise.
Hesketh. Death of a Gardener.
Invitation.
Limbo.
Tom Rich.
Walled In.
Hewitt. At Shottery, Anne Hathaway's Cottage.
Epitaph for a Gardener.
For Roberta in the Garden.
In the Luxembourg Gardens.
Suburban Spring in Warwickshire.
Jarrell. In a Hospital Garden.
Jeffers. Carmel.
Kipling. Glory of the Garden, The.
Knott. Depressionism.
Lawrence. Guelder Roses.
Prophet in the Rose Garden, The.
Snap-Dragon.
Trees in the Garden.
Levertov. Figure of Time, A.
Lewis. Public Gardens, The.
Liddy. Attention: First Lady of the Festival.
Sister Beach, Sister Garden.

Lindsay. On the Garden Wall.
Song of the Garden-Toad, The.
Lowell. Public Garden, The.
Lowry. Epitaph on Our Gardener, Dead Near Liverpool.
McAuley. I planned a little fountain.
McGrath. Residencies.
MacNeice. Gardener, The.
Marvell. Garden, The.
Hortus.
Mower against Gardens, The.
Meinke. Love Poem 1990.
Melville. Garden of Metrodorus, The.
Meredith. Grace and Love.
Merrill. Words for Maria.
Millay. Gardener in Haying-Time, The.
Hardy Garden, The.
Spring in the Garden.
Steepletop.
Nash. Correction: *Eve* Delved and *Adam* Span.
He Digs, He Dug, He Has Dug.
Nemerov. In the Commercial Gardens.
Salt Garden, The.
Pack. Autumn Warmth.
Piercy. Digging In.
Love of Lettuce, The.
Queen of Pentacles, The.
Seven of Pentacles, The.
Plath. Manor Garden, The.
Pope. Garden, The.
Raine. April's new apple buds on an old lichened tree.
High Summer.
Ransom. Master's in the Garden Again.
Miriam Tazewell.
Rich. Design in Living Colors.
For Memory.
Robinson. Tree in Pamela's Garden, The.
Two Gardens in Linndale.
Roethke. Flower Dump.
Frau Bauman, Frau Schmidt, and Frau Schwartze.
Otto.
Transplanting.
Weed Puller.
Rossetti. Beloved, yeild thy time to God, for He / Will make eternity thy recompense.
God's Acre.
Heartsease in my garden bed, / With sweetwilliam white and red.
In the meadow—what in the meadow?
October Garden, An.
On Keats, 18 January, 1948 (Eve of St Agnes).
Shut Out.
Rukeyser. Fighting for Roses.
In Hades, Orpheus.
Mother Garden's Round.
Sandburg. Garden Wireless.
Poppies.
Sarton. Garden of Childhood, The.
Metaphysical Garden, The.
Schuyler. August First, 1974.
Belated Birthday Poem, A.
Blossoming Oakwood.
For Bob Dash.
Horse-Chestnut Trees and Roses.
In the Round.
Roof Garden.
Three Gardens.
We Walk.
What Ails My Fern?
Sexton. Angel of Blizzards and Blackouts.
Snyder. Roots.
Southwell. Love's Gardyne Greife.
Stein. What Does She See When She Shuts Her Eyes.
Stevens. Cy Est Pourtraicte, Madame Ste Ursule, et Les Unze Mille Vierges.
Stevenson. About my fields, in the broad sun.
Autumn Fires.
De Hortis Julii Martialis.
Gardener, The.
To A Gardener.
Tomlinson. Juliet's Garden.
Near and the Far, The.
Under the Bridge.

Turco. Weed Garden, The.
Updike. Planting a Mailbox.
Van Duyn. Elementary Attitudes.
 Gardener to His God, The.
 Garland for Christopher Smart, A.
 Notes from a Suburban Heart.
 Oh well, they had such a big garden.
Wakoski. Sestina from the Home Gardener.
Warren. Garden, The.
Whittier. Chalkley Hall.
 Garden.
 Song of Harvest, A.
Wilbur. Caserta Garden.
 He Was.
Williams, William Carlos. At the Brink of the
 Winter.
 Every Day.
 Italian Garden, The.
 Quality of Heaven, The.
Wordsworth. Inscription in the Grounds of
 Coleorton, the Seat of Sir George Beaumont,
 BART., Leicestershire.
 Inscription in a Garden of the Same.
 Written at the Request of Sir George
 Beaumont, BART., and in His Name, for an
 Urn, Placed by Him at the Termination of a
 Newly-Planted Avenue, in the Same Grounds.

Garfield, James Abram
Whitman. Sobbing of the Bells, The.

Gargoyles
Sandburg. Broken-Face Gargoyles.
 Gargoyle.

Garibaldi, Giuseppe
Browning, Elizabeth Barrett. Garibaldi.
 King's Gift, The.
Meredith. Centenary of Garibaldi, The.
Whittier. Garibaldi.

Garrick, David
Johnson. Prologue Spoken by Mr[.] Garrick at
 the Opening of the Theatre in Drury Lane,
 1747.

Garrison, William Lloyd
Whittier. Garrison.
 To William Lloyd Garrison.

Gasoline Stations
Bishop. Filling Station.
Stafford. From the Move to California.
Williams, Miller. Mecanic on Duty at All
 Times.

Gates
Dunbar. Old Front Gate, The.
Graves. Hidden Garden, The.
Kunitz. Open the Gates.
Pack. Cord of Wood, A.
Patchen. It Was Being.
Tomlinson. Gap, The.
 Gate, The.

Gauguin, Paul
Dunn. My Brother's Work.
Hill. Terribilis Est Locus Iste; *Gaugin and the
 Pont-Aven School.*

Gawaine, Sir
Meredith. Song of Courtesy, The.
Robinson. Lancelot.
 Merlin.

Gazelles
Lawrence. Gazelle Calf, The.
 Tales.

Geese
Berry. To Gary Snyder.
 Wild Geese, The.
Bly. Snow Geese.
Bukowski. I Cannot Stand Tears.
Carroll, Jim. Withdrawal Letter.
Carruth. All Things.
 No Matter What, After All, and That Beautiful
 Word So.
Dobyns. Geese.
Fisher. Park, The.
Fletcher. Jade Elegy, The.
Glück. Messengers.
Herrick. Upon Gander.
Hughes, Ted. Goose.
Kipling. Flight, The.
Mahon. Canadian Pacific.
Nash. Gander, The.

Olson. Landscape, Without Color.
Piercy. Postcard from the Garden.
Plath. Rhyme.
Sandburg. Seven Eleven.
Tomlinson. Prelude, A.
 Weatherman.
Warren. Tell Me a Story.

Gems
Byron. Cornelian, The.
Carew. Epitaph on the Lady S.: Wife of Sir
 W.S.
Dickinson. Diamond on the Hand, A.
 I held a Jewel in my fingers.
 I'll clutch—and clutch.
 'Tis little—I could care for Pearls.
Emerson. I wear no badge; no tinsel star.
 Rubies.
Herrick. Amber Bead, The.
 Rock of Rubies: and The Quarrie of Pearls,
 The.
 To Julia: ("How rich and pleasing thou, my
 Julia, art").
 To the Right Honourable Mildmay, Earl of
 Westmorland.
Kipling. Birthright, The.
Rossetti. Diamond or a coal? / A diamond, if
 you please, A.
 Emerald is as green as grass, An.
Schuyler. Fabergé.
Silverstein. Garden, The.
Smart. Fragment D.

Generals
Burns. Address to General Dumourier.
Cummings. Neither awake / (there's your
 general).
Dobyns. General Matthei Drives Home
 through Santiago.
Hemingway. Roosevelt.
Hughes, Ted. Mascot, The.
 Wit's End.
Kipling. Bobs.
 General Joubert.
 Lord Roberts.
 Stellenbosch.
Lovelace. Sonnet. To Generall Goring.
Marvell. Upon Appleton House [To My Lord
 Fairfax].
 Upon the Hill and Grove at Bilbrough.
Patchen. Attila.
Pope. Epitaph on General Henry Withers, in
 Westminster-Abbey, 1729.
Smart. Ode to General Draper.
Williams, William Carlos. Visitor, The.

Generosity
Browning, Elizabeth Barrett. Sonnet: "What
 can I give thee back, O liberal."
Campion. Come follow me, my wandring
 mates.
Carruth. Pa McCabe.
Creeley. Testament, A.
Dickinson. Seraphic shame generosity causes,
 The.
Dunn. Emptiness.
 From the Manifesto of the Selfish.
Gallagher. In Maceio.
Hacker. She Bitches About Boys.
Hewitt. Homestead.
Hughes, Langston. Preference.
Jonson. Epigram. To K[ing] Charles for a[n]
 Hundred Pounds He Sent Me in My
 Sickness. 1629. An.
MacLeish. Rape of the Swan, The.
Merton. Convergence of the Many.
Rossetti. Will you be there? my yearning heart
 has cried.
Smart. Care and Generosity.
 Generosity.
 Munificence and Modesty.
 St. Barnabas.
Spender. Generous Days, The.
Wroth. Sonnet: "Lett griefe as farr bee from
 your deerest brest."

Genetics and Geneticists
Creeley. Name, The.
Hewitt. Unnecessary Dread, The.
Knott. Consolations of Sociobiology, The.

Meinke. Double helix and the triple star, The.
 Monk can do his work on bended knees, A.
Pack. Messages.
Rolfe. Testament to a Flowering Race.
See also **Evolution.**

Genius
Blake. All Religions Are One.
Carruth. Sonnet: "If you see a child that
 shivers when it hears."
Coleridge. Character of Wallenstein, The.
 To Richard Brinsley Sheridan, Esq.
Crabbe. Edward Shore.
Crane. Masters, The.
Davie. At the Cradle of Genius.
 Brilliance.
Dickinson. Genius is the ignition of affection.
Emerson. Atom displaces all atoms beside,
 The.
Graves. Casse-Noisette.
Herrick. To the Genius of His House.
Hughes, Langston. Genius Child.
Jarrell. Boyg, Peer Gynt, the One Only One,
 The.
Meredith. To P.A. Labouchère Esq.
 You ask me what is Genius? 'tis that.
Robinson. Ben Jonson Entertains a Man from
 Stratford.
Smith, Charlotte. Written at Bristol in the
 Summer of 1794.
Thomson. To Alfred.
 To the Memory of Sir Isaac Newton.
Williams, William Carlos. Poem: "Plastic
 surgeon who has, The."

Gentians
Dickinson. Gentian has a parched Corolla,
 The.
 God made a little Gentian.
Lawrence. Bavarian Gentians.
Whittier. Pressed Gentian, The.

Geography and Geographers
Donne. Hymn[e] to God My God, In My
 Sickness[e].
Hacker. Art of a Novel, The.
Hugo. Graves in Queens.
Koch. Geography.
Rexroth. Lesson in Geography, A.
Sandburg. Turn of the Wheel.
Whitman. Broadway Pageant, A.
 Passage to India.

Geology and Geologists
Carruth. Essay on Stone.
Ciardi. Goodnight.
Hewitt. For Any Irishman.
Rexroth. Lyell's Hypothesis Again.
Snyder. What Happened Here Before.
Tomlinson. Gli Scafari.

Geometry
Cummings. Newly / cued / motif smites truly
 to beautifully.
 Surely / Cued / motif smites truly to
 Beautifully, The.
Davie. Bolyai, the Geometer.
Dickinson. Best Witchcraft is Geometry.
Dove. Geometry.
Hartley. Geometric Death.
Stevens. Common Life, The.
Tomlinson. Head Hewn with an Axe.
Zukofsky. "Further than."
See also **Euclid.**

George I, King of England
Burns. German Lairdie, The.

George III, King of England
Byron. George the Third.
 Saint Peter sat by the celestial gate.
Cowper. Annus Memorabilis, 1789.
 On His Majesty's Sea Bathing.
 On the Queens's Visit to London.
Koch. You Were Wearing.
Smart. Accession of King George III, The.
Wordsworth. November, 1813.
 On the Death of His Majesty (George the
 Third).

George V, King of England
Betjeman. Death of King George V.
Kipling. King and the Sea, The.
 King's Pilgrimage, The.

Georgia (state)
Angelou. Georgia Song, A.
Dickey, James. In the Marble Quarry.
Hughes, Langston. Georgia Dusk.
Sun Song.
Kunitz. Mounds rise up on every side, The.
Melville. March to the Sea, The.

Geraniums
Carruth. August First.
Joseph. Geranium.
Lawrence. Red Geranium and Godly
Mignonette.
Olson. I was stretched out on the earth   so
that a wild geranium.
Oppen. Drawing.
Roethke. Geranium, The.
Smith, Charlotte. To a Geranium Which
Flowered during the Winter.
Wordsworth. Poor Robin.
Zukofsky. Millennium of sun—.

German (language)
Dickey, William. Die Älte Frau, Die Älte
Marschallin.
Jarrell. Deutsch durch Freud.
Koertge. Pronouncing My Name.
Meinke. Stille Nacht, Heilege Nacht.

Germans, The
Carroll, Jim. Crossed Wires.
Clark. Sedge.
Dove. At the German Writers Conference in
Munich.
Ferlinghetti. Expressionist History of German
Expressionism.
Hemingway. Schwarzwald.
Jarrell. Germans Are Lunatics, The.
Jeffers. Fourth Act.
Kipling. Justice.
Outlaws, The.
Liddy. His Refugees.
Robinson. Rahel to Varnhagen.
Rukeyser. As he stood near the plane, they
heard him say.
Williams, William Carlos. Rare Gist, The.
Wordsworth. Germans on the Heights of
Hochheim, The.

Germany
Beckett. Ne manquez pas à Stuttgart.
Bogan. Kapuzinerberg (Salzburg).
Bukowski. Some of My Readers.
Bunting. Women swarm in Tauentsienstrasse.
Carruth. People burned, came apart,
suffocated, melted.
Spring Notes from Robin Hill.
Cowper. Elegy 4: To Thomas Young.
Dunn. When the Revolution Came.
Fenton. It is not what they built. It is what
they knocked down.
Ginsberg. Ruhr-Gebiet.
Tübingen–Hamburg Schlafwagen.
Hardy. England to Germany in 1914.
Hill. De Jure Belli ac Pacis.
Jarrell. Angels at Hamburg, The.
Kipling. Justice.
Outlaws, The.
Rowers, The.
Lowell. Exile's Return, The.
Meredith. Emperor Frederick of Our Time,
The.
Let but the rational prevail.
Pictures of the Rhine.
Rhine-Land.
Merton. Fable for a War.
Milton. Elegy 4: To Thomas Young.
O'Hara. Image of the Buddha Preaching.
Rukeyser. Another Day (Day Lilies, Yellow
Daisies).
Sandburg. In the Shadow of the Palace.
Snodgrass. Reichsmarschall Hermann Göring
("And why, Herr Reichsmarschall, is Italy").
Spender. Helmut.
Van der Lubbe.
Whitman. Dead Emperor, The.
Williams, Miller. Normandy Beach.
Wordsworth. Alas! what boots the long
laborious quest.
Prophecy February, 1807, A.

Germs
Nash. Germ, The.
Williams, Miller. Euglena.
See also **Bacteria.**

Gethsemane
Dickinson. Gethsemene and Cana.
Hewitt. New Jerusalem 1.
Southwell. Christe's Sleeping Frendes.

Gettysburg, Battle of (1863)
Whittier. Hive at Gettysburg, The.

Ghettos
Griffiths. Llantysilio, Overgrown.
Lorde. New York City.
Piercy. Community.
Williams, Charles Kenneth. Bread.

Ghosts
Auden. April.
Family Ghosts.
No, not from this life, not from this life is
any.
Berryman. Who for those ages ever without
some blood.
You come blonde visiting through the black
air.
Brooks. Mentors.
Carroll, Jim. Heroes.
"Carroll, Lewis." Acrostic: Around my lonely
hearth, to-night.
Acrostic: Dreams, that elude the Waker's
frenzied grasp—.
Phantasmagoria.
Clark. Domestic Life of Ghosts, The.
Coleridge. Phantom or Fact?
Crabbe. Lady Barbara; or, The Ghost.
Crane. To Conquer Variety.
Creeley. Passage, The.
Cullen. Ghosts.
Two Who Crossed a Line (She Crosses).
Cummings. Round face near the top of the
stairs, A.
Davie. Apparition, An.
Departed, The.
House, The.
My Father's Honour.
De la Mare. Betrayal.
Familiar, The.
Ghost, The.
Ghost, The.
Hospital.
Imogen.
Listeners, The.
News.
Revenant, The.
Shadow.
Solitude.
Spectre, The.
Thus Her Tale.
Tryst, The.
Twilight.
Which Way?
Who's that?
Dickey, James. Craters.
Dickey, William. In The Dreaming.
Dickinson. Distance that the dead have gone,
The.
I lift the lid to my box of Phantoms.
My family of Apparitions.
Only Ghost I ever saw, The.
Donne. Apparition, The.
Dryden. Epilogue to *Tyrannic[k] Love.*
Dunbar. Wraith, The.
Fletcher. Back Stairs, The.
Fox. Visitor, The.
Graves. Ancestors.
Coronation Murder, The.
Country Mansion, A.
No More Ghosts.
Or To Perish Before Day.
Outlaws.
Restless Ghost, A.
Welsh Incident.
Hall. Mount Kearsarge.
Hardy. At Shag's Heath.
At the Piano.
Bird-Catcher's Boy, The.
Dead Man Walking, The.
Family Portraits.

Garden Seat, The.
Glimpse, The.
Haunter, The.
Head above the Fog, The.
Her Haunting-Ground.
I Have Lived with Shades.
Monument-Maker, The.
My Spirit Will Not Haunt the Mound.
Noble Lady's Tale, The.
Phantom Horsewoman, The.
Re-Enactment, The.
Second Night, The.
Souls of the Slain, The.
Spectres That Grieve.
Spellbound Palace, A.
Vagg Hollow.
Wistful Lady, The.
Woman Driving, A.
Woman I Met, The.
Heaney. King of the Ditchbacks, The.
Herrick. Upon an Old Man a Residenciarie.
Hesketh. All Hallows.
Hewitt. Apparition.
Blue Lias Inn, The.
Cold Warrior: Anzac Day, 1946.
Ghosts.
Jacob and the Angel.
Hill. Innocent soul / ghosting for its lost.
Housman. In midnights of November.
When I watch the living meet.
Hugo. Way a Ghost Behaves, The.
Way a Ghost Dissolves, The.
Jarrell. Ghost, a Real Ghost, A.
Jeffers. As the eye fails through age or
disease.
Ghost.
Mara.
Joseph. Walk in the woods at the hour when
the fuddled sun.
Kipling. Doors were wide, the story saith,
The.
Looking Glass, The.
Old Mother Laidinwool.
Possibilities.
Kunitz. Master and Mistress.
Lawrence. Erinnyes.
Houseless Dead, The.
Nostalgia.
Spirits Summoned West.
We Have Gone Too Far.
Liddy. Dorcas.
Sound of a Moment at Scariff, The.
Lindsay. Ghosts in Love.
Lowell. Ghost, The.
Lowry. Ghosts in New Houses.
Lines Written on Reading Dostoievski.
Never in a comedian's life have I laughed till
then!
Roar of the Sea and the Darkness, The.
Western Ocean, The.
When I am in the purgatory of the unread.
McGrath. All the Dead Soldiers.
MacLeish. Where wilt thou lead me? Speak.
MacNeice. Never so lithe in the green dingle.
McNeill. Ballad of Joe Bittner.
Millay. Little Ghost, The.
Wraith.
Morgan. Ghost, The.
Nocturne: "Dear Wanderer, on your
unimagined journey."
People dressed in the styles.
Reprieve, The.
Oliver. Aunt Elsie's Night Music.
Olson. As the Dead Prey upon Us.
At Yorktown.
Owen. Kind Ghosts, The.
Shadwell Stair.
Pack. Cracked Apple Tree, The.
Ghost Story.
Plath. Danse Macabre.
Dialogue between Ghost and Priest.
Poe. Conqueror Worm, The.
Haunted Palace, The.
Pope. Most souls, 'tis true, but peep out once
an age.
Raine. One night in a dream.
Ransom. Spectral Lovers.

"Reed." My House.
Rich. What Ghosts Can Say.
Robinson. Lingard and the Stars.
Rossetti. Chilly Night, A.
  Coast-Nightmare, A.
  Ghost's Petition, The.
  Hour and the Ghost, The.
  Poor Ghost, The.
Sandburg. Kisses, Can You Come Back Like
  Ghosts?
  Testimony Regarding a Ghost.
  Three Ghosts.
Sexton. Ghosts.
Shelley. Fragment of a Ghost Story.
Shelton. On stormy nights.
  Reunion.
Simic. Navigator.
Smith, Charlotte. Lydia.
  On Leaving a Part of Sussex.
Smith, Stevie. Ghost of Ware, The.
  King Hamlet's Ghost.
  Longing for Death because of Feebleness.
  Old Ghosts.
  Parklands, The.
  Wanderer, The.
Spender. Us.
Stevens. Two Tales of Liadoff.
Stevenson. On Some Ghostly Companions at a
  Spa.
Thomas. Do You Not Father Me.
Tomlinson. Apparition, The.
Turco. Fetch.
  Weed Garden, The.
  Werewind.
Van Duyn. In the Old Country, then, two
  ladies and two boys.
  Just full of springs the world was in Illinois.
Walcott. Verandah.
Whittier. Garrison of Cape Ann, The.
  New Wife and the Old, The.
  Prayer-Seeker, The.
  Sisters, The.
Williams, Charles Kenneth. Giving It Up.
Williams, Miller. Ghost of His Wife Comes to
  Tell Him How It Is.
  Ghosts.
  Story, The.
Wordsworth. I find it written of SIMONIDES.
  Lucy Gray; or, Solitude.
Wright, James. Assignation, The.
  Erinna to Sappho.
  Ghost, The.
  My Grandmother's Ghost.
  Youth.
Yeats. All Souls' Night.
  Apparitions, The.
  Crazy Jane and Jack the Journeyman.
  To a Shade.
Zimmer. Zimmer and the Ghost.
Giacometti, Alberto
Berg. Three Voices.
Merton. Celebrating Giacometti.
Wilbur. Giacometti.
Giants
Bly. Near the Giant's House.
Hall. Sleeping Giant, The.
Jeffers. Giant's Ring, The.
Millay. Bean-Stalk, The.
Patchen. Reason for Skylarks, The.
Plath. Queen's Complaint, The.
Pope. Lamentation of Glumdalclitch for the
  Loss of Grildrig, The.
  To Quinbus Flestrin the Man-Mountain, a
  Lilliputian Ode.
Ralegh. Giants did advance their wicked hand,
  The.
Silverstein. Me and My Giant.
  Paul Bunyan.
Wilbur. Giaour and the Pacha, The.
Gibbon, Edward
Hardy. Lausanne: In Gibbon's Old Garden:
  11–12 p.m.
Gibbs, Josiah Willard
Rukeyser. Gibbs.
Gibraltar
Dickinson. I have seen one Bird and part of
  another.

Gifts and Giving
Beatles. I Feel Fine.
Berrigan. Something Amazing Just Happened.
Berry. Gift of Gravity, The.
Betjeman. Christmas.
Browning, Elizabeth Barrett. Hugh Stuart
  Boyd [Legacies].
  King's Gift, The.
  Sonnet: "Beloved, thou hast brought me many
  flowers."
Browning, Robert. Lines for a Gift.
Burns. Cardin o't, The.
  O had the malt thy strength of mind.
  Posie, The.
  To a Young Lady, *Miss Jessy L——,
  Dumfries; with Books which the Bard
  Presented Her.*
  To Miss L——.
  To Mr. McMurdo, with a Pound of Lundiefoot
  Snuff.
Byron. Chain I Gave, The.
"Carroll, Lewis." Maggie B——.
Carruth. I Could Take.
  Impossible Indispensability of the Ars Poetica,
  The.
  Leaf from Mr. Dyer's Woods, A.
Clark. Greeks, The.
Cohen. Gift.
Coleridge. Silver Thimble, The.
Cooper. Long View from the Suburbs.
Cowper. Lines with Two Cockscombs.
  Thanks for a Gift of Pheasants.
  To Anne Bodham.
  To John Johnson.
  To Mrs. King.
  To Mrs. Newton.
  To Mrs. Throckmorton.
Creeley. Gift, The.
  Kiki.
Dickinson. We are snatching our jewels from
  the frost.
  Your Gifts are from the Sky.
Doolittle. Acon.
  At Croton.
  Fragment Forty one: "Am I blind alas."
  Gift, The.
Dunbar. She Gave Me a Rose.
Eberhart. Mistaken Identity.
  To Evan.
Emerson. He whom God had thus preferred.
  Motto to "Gifts."
  Oft have I said, I say it once more.
Ford. In my hair he's put.
Glück. Swans.
Graves. Love Gifts.
  Name Day.
  On Giving.
  Song: Basket of Blossom.
  Song: Beyond Giving.
  Song: Come, Enjoy Your Sunday!
Hall. Merle Bascom's .22.
Herrick. Almes.
  Carkanet, The.
  Christs Part.
  Gods Hands.
  His Dream[e].
  Jimmall Ring, or True-Love-Knot, The.
  Larr's Portion, and the Poets Part.
  New-Year's [*or* New-Yeares] Gift Sent to Sir
  Simeon Steward, A.
  New-Yeeres Gift, The.
  Pomander Bracelet, The.
  Primrose, The.
  Ring Presented to Julia, A.
  Short Hymne to Larr, A.
  Ternarie of Littles, upon a Pipkin of Jellie [*or*
  Jelly] Sent to a Lady, A.
  To His Saviour, a Child; a Present, by a
  Child.
Hewitt. Carol Singers from the Church, The.
  Wedding Present, The.
Hopkins. Morning, Midday, and Evening
  Sacrifice.
Johnson. To Miss —: On Her Giving the
  Author a Gold and Silk Net-work Purse.
Jonson. To Mr John Burges.
Keats. To a Friend Who Sent Me Some

Roses.
  To a Young Lady Who Sent Me a Laurel
  Crown.
Koertge. He ("Drove a school bus for the
  extra money").
  He ("Gave me 50 dollars for Christmas one
  year").
Lawrence. New Year's Night.
  Sick.
Lewis. I send you a Christmas present, sweet.
Liddy. His Refugees.
  Vir VIII.
Lindsay. Doll Upon the Topmost Bough, The.
  He Gives What He Won to the Indian Girl.
Lovelace. Dedication to Anne Lovelace, The.
Lowry. I am speeding through the northern
  lights.
MacLeish. Revenant, The.
Meredith. To R.H.H. with Daphne.
Merton. Macarius the Younger.
  Ointment, The.
Nash. I Remember Yule.
  I'll Eat My Split-Level Turkey in the
  Breezeway.
  I'm a Pleasure to Shop for.
Oliver. Night Traveler, The.
Olson. Friend, The.
  On the equator east of my son I Orion
  bequeath to him my riches.
Pope. On Receiving from the Right Hon. the
  Lady Frances Shirley a Standish and Two
  Pens.
Prince. Token, The.
Raine. Heirloom.
Roethke. Her Reticence.
Rolfe. Glory Set, The.
Rossetti. Epiphany.
  Lord, what have I that I may offer Thee?
  Me and my gift: kind Lord, behold.
  O Sailor, Come Ashore.
  Ransomed of the Lord, The.
Rukeyser. Gift.
Sandburg. Englishman in the old days, An.
Schuyler. Stone Knife, A.
  This Notebook.
Shelley. To ——: "One word is too often
  profaned."
  To Emilia Viviani.
Silverstein. Santa and the Reindeer.
Smith, Stevie. Dear Karl.
Sorrentino. Oranges Returned, The.
Stafford. Mother's Day.
Stevenson. Dedication: "My first gift and my
  last, to you."
  Envoy: "Go, little book, and wish to all."
  Go, little book—the ancient phrase.
  These rings, O my beloved pair.
  To Kalakaua.
  To Minnie (With a Hand-Glass).
Swift. Paper book is sent by Boyle, A.
Tomlinson. Picture of J. T. in a Prospect of
  Stone, The.
Walker. Gift.
Whittier. To Avis Keene.
Wilbur. Gifts, The.
Wordsworth. To ——: "Happy the feeling
  from the bosom thrown."
  With a Small Present.
Wyatt. Lady gave me a gift she had not, A.
  To seek each where where man doth live.
Yeats. Gift of Harun Al-Rashid, The.
  He Gives His Beloved Certain Rhymes.
  Never Give All the Heart.
  To a Wealthy Man Who Promised a Second
  Subscription to the Dublin Municipal Gallery
  if It Were Proved the People Wanted
  Pictures.
Young. Reggie's Version.
Ginkgo Trees
Nemerov. Ginkgoes in Fall.
Sorrentino. Big Brown Eyes.
Ginsberg, Allen
Berrigan. Pandora's Box, An Ode.
  Red Shift.
Carruth. Thaw.
Creeley. Please.
Williams, William Carlos. Cézanne.

Herrick. Excesse.
Upon Chub.
Upon Magot a Frequenter of Ordinaries.
Upon Spokes.
Jonson. Hymn: "Room, room, make room for
the bouncing belly."
On Gut.
Nash. Nevertheless.
Pizza, The.
Quick, Hammacher, My Stomacher!
Piercy. Consumer, The.
Plath. Glutton, The.
Roethke. Goo Girl.
Myrtle's Cousin.
Verse with Allusions.
Shakespeare. Sonnet 75: "So are you to my
thoughts as food to life."
Yeats. Chambermaid's First Song, The.

Gnats
Eberhart. Equivalence of Gnats and Mice.
Gnat on My Paper.
Gnats.
Graves. One Hard Look.
Hughes, Ted. Gnat-Psalm.

Gnus
Roethke. Gnu, The.

Goats
Creeley. Disappointment, The.
Edmunds. Going Out to Look at the Year's
First Blossoms.
Ford. Small black goat with, A.
Gallagher. Woman Who Raised Goats, The.
Haines. West of Logan Pass, where.
Hughes, Ted. Meeting.
Kipling. By the Hoof of the Wild Goat.
They killed a Child to please the Gods.
Lawrence. He-Goat.
She-Goat.
Lovelace. Swain, Hind, Knight; I fed, till'd,
did command, A.
Plath. Goatsucker.
Simic. Old Mountain Road.
Williams, William Carlos. Goat, The.

Goblins
"Carroll, Lewis." Canto IV: Hys Nouryture.
Herrick. Ceremony upon Candlemas Eve.
Plath. Princess and the Goblins, The.
Silverstein. Lester.
Magic.

See also **Elves; Fairies; Ghosts.**

God
Atwood. Resurrection.
Auden. Cinders.
Friday's Child.
I'm afraid there's many a spectacled sod.
Pride.
Sonnet I: "There was desolate silence on the
world."
Beckett. Serena I.
Berg. In the Evening.
Music.
1945.
To the Being We Are.
Berryman. Amos.
Apparition, The.
Back.
Certainty Before Lunch.
Compline.
Eleven Addresses to the Lord.
Facts & Issues, The.
Form, The.
Interstitial Office.
Lauds.
Matins.
Nones.
Nothing there? nothing up the sky alive.
Opus Dei.
Overseas Prayer.
Pacifist's Song, The.
Prayer After All, A.
Prayer of the Middle-Aged Man, The.
Prime.
Sext.
Somber Prayer.
Terce.
Unknowable? Perhaps Not Altogether.

Usual Prayer, A.
Vespers.
Betjeman. In Westminster Abbey.
Bishop. Rainbow.
Blake. Divine Image, The ("To Mercy, Pity,
Peace, and Love").
I rose up at the dawn of day.
Memorable Fancy, A ("I was in a printing
house in Hell & I saw the method in").
There Is No Natural Religion.
Tiger [*or* Tyger][!], The.
To Nobodaddy.
To see a World in a Grain of Sand.
Bradstreet. Here Follow[es] Some Verses upon
the Burning of Our House [July 10th, 1966.
Copied Out of a Loose Paper].
My soul, rejoice thou in thy God.
My thankful heart with glorying tongue.
What God is like to him I serve?
Brontë. No coward soul is mine.
Brooks. God Works in a Mysterious Way.
Preacher: Ruminates Behind the Sermon, The.
Browning, Elizabeth Barrett. Child's Thought
of God, A.
Confessions.
Heaven and Earth.
Hugh Stuart Boyd [His Death, 1848].
Human Life's Mystery.
Island, An.
Isobel's Child.
Measure, The.
Only a Curl.
Seraphim, The.
Since Without Thee We Do No Good.
Sleep, The.
Sonnet: "But only three in all God's universe."
Soul's Travelling, The.
Browning, Robert. Boy and the Angel, The.
Epilogue: "On the first of the Feast of Feasts."
Johannes Agricola in Meditation.
Rephan.
Reverie.
Burns. First Psalm, The.
First Six Verses of the Ninetieth Psalm, The.
Grace after Meat.
Grace before Dinner, Extempore, A.
Lying at a Reverend Friend's House One
Night, the Author Left the Following *Verses*
in the Room Where He Slept.
Prayer, under the Pressure of Violent Anguish,
A.
Stanzas on the Same Occasion [in the Prospect
of Death].
Byron. God Maddens Him Whom 'T Is His
Will to Lose.
Heaven and Earth.
Prayer of Nature, The.
Campion. Author of light, revive my dying
spright.
Bravely deckt, come forth, bright day.
Come Let Us Sound With Melodie.
Heart's Music.
Lift up to heav'n, sad wretch, thy heavy
spright.
Seek the Lord.
Sing a song of joy.
To Music Bent Is My Retired Mind.
Triumph now with Joy and mirth.
Carew. Second Song, The.
Carruth. Ontological Episode of the Asylum.
Sonnet: "Was Yahweh chosen by the chosen
people?"
Ceravolo. Data.
Fill and Illumined.
Sea Level.
Chaucer. All human kind on earth.
Ciardi. In Place of a Curse.
Memo: Preliminary Draft of a Prayer to God
the Father.
On Wet Iota.
Clark. De Ira Dei.
Clough. Hymnos Aymnos.
Irritability unnatural.
It fortifies my soul to know.
Light words they were, and lightly, falsely
said.
Look you, my simple friend, 'tis one of those.

Though to the vilest things beneath the moon.
What we, when face to face we see.
When Israel Came Out of Egypt.
Cohen. All My Life.
Holy Is Your Name.
I Draw Aside the Curtain.
I Lost My Way.
If It Be Your Will.
It Is All Around Me.
It Is to You I Turn.
Magic Is Alive.
My Teacher.
Not Knowing Where to Go.
We Cry Out.
When I Have Not Rage.
You Who Pour Mercy into Hell.
Coleridge. Lovely was the death.
Philosophical Trinity, The.
To Nature.
Cooper. Now I have thought the very thoughts
of God!
Where is the simple myth we used to have?
Cowper. God Hides His People.
Olney Hymns.
Season.
Repose in God.
Soul That Loves God Finds Him Every
Where, The.
Crashaw. John 16; Verily I Say unto You,
Yee Shall Weep and Lament.
Mark 12; (Give to Cæsar———) (And to
God———).
Matthew 27; And He Answered Them
Nothing.
Matthew 8; I Am Not Worthy that Thou
Should'st Come Under my Roofe.
Creeley. Awakening, The.
From Pico & the Women: A Life.
Song: "God give you pardon from gratitue."
Cullen. Death to the Poor.
Dictum.
Epitaph: "She leans across a golden table."
For a Mouthy Woman.
For an Atheist.
Shroud of Color, The.
Sonnet: "These are no wind-blown rumors,
soft say-sos."
To the Three for Whom the Book.
Yet Do I Marvel.
Cummings. By little accurate saints thickly
which tread.
God.
God,Thine the hand that doth extend.
I am a little church(no great cathedral).
I thank You God for most this amazing.
Jehovah buried,Satan dead.
Maybe god / is a child.
On souls robbed of their birth-right's better
part.
Round a so moon could dream(i sus).
These from my mother's greatgrandmother's
rosebush white.
Vision.
When any mortal(even the most odd).
When god decided to invent.
World is very big, and we, The.
Davie. Articulacy. Hints from the Koran.
Being Angry with God.
Brilliance.
Cannibals.
Church Militant.
Curtains!
God of Details, The.
I Have Said, Ye Are Gods.
If I Take the Wings of the Morning.
Inditing a Good Matter.
Just You Wait!
Levity.
Mandelstam's Hope for the Best.
Meteorologist, September.
Nosegay, The.
Ordinary God.
Sing unto the Lord a New Song.
Standings.
Their Rectitude Their Beauty.
Thirty-Ninth Psalm, Adapted, The.
Thou Art Near at Hand, O Lord.

Though Dry, Not Dry.
To get past harping on the laws of Nature.
De la Mare. Hour-Glass, The.
Last Chapter, The.
Sunrise.
Universe, The.
Dickey, James. Daughter.
Dickey, William. Ezekiel's Rabbit.
Dickinson. All Circumstances are the Frame.
Expanse cannot be lost.
God is a distant—stately Lover.
God is indeed a jealous God.
God made no act without a cause.
God seems much more friendly.
"Heavenly Father"—take to thee.
How ruthless are the gentle.
I got so I could take his name.
I had some things that I called mine.
I never felt at Home—Below.
It was too late for Man.
Love of God may be taught, The.
My Maker—let me be.
Nature and God—I neither knew.
Of God we ask one favor.
Only God—detect the Sorrow.
Only News I know, The.
Spring is the Period.
Sun and Moon must make their haste, The.
Truth—is as old as God.
"We thank thee Oh Father" for these strange
Minds.
Who is it seeks my Pillow Nights.
Dobyns. Gardener, The.
Nihilist, The.
Donne. As due by many titles I resign[e].
Father, The.
Hear[e] us, O hear[e] us Lord; to thee.
Hymn [or Hymne] to Christ, at the Author's
Last Going into Germany, A.
Hymn[e] to God My God, In My Sickness[e].
That our ears' sickness we [or eares sicknesse
wee] may cure.
Doolittle. Magician [Master].
Orestes Theme.
Priest.
Two Poems for Christmas, 1937.
Dunbar. Compensation.
Equipment.
God Reigns.
Hymn, A: "Lead gently, Lord, and slow."
Hymn: "When storms arise."
Night.
Not They Who Soar!
Plantation Melody, A.
Possession.
Resignation.
Spiritual, A.
To the Memory of Mary Young.
Too Busy.
Duncan. This Place Rumord to Have Been
Sodom.
Dunn. Dancing with God.
Moralists.
"Dylan." Ain't No Man Righteous, No Not
One.
Every Grain of Sand.
Father of Night.
Gonna Change My Way of Thinking.
Pressing On.
Saved.
Solid Rock.
Trouble in Mind.
What Can I Do for You?
Whatcha Gonna Do.
When He Returns.
When You Gonna Wake Up?
With God on Our Side.
Eberhart. Book of Nature, The.
Fury of Aerial Bombardment, The.
God and Man.
Harvard Stadium.
John Finley.
Meditation, A.
On a Squirrel Crossing the Road in Autumn,
in New England.
Parker River, The.
Redemption.

Sometimes the Longing for Death.
Throwing the Apple.
Edmunds. Passion Week Monday after Palm
Sunday.
Eliot. Blessed sister, holy mother, spirit of the
fountain.
Choruses from "The Rock."
Emerson. And the best gift of God.
Be of good cheer, brave spirit; steadfastly.
Bohemian Hymn, The.
But God will keep his promise yet.
Come!—the palace of heaven rests on aëry
pillars.
Dæmonic and the Celestial Love, The.
Dear brother, would you know the life.
Dull uncertain brain, A.
From "Bird Conversations."
Γνωθι Σεαυτον.
Hard is it to persuade the public mind of its
plain duty & true interest.
He walked the streets of great New York.
He whom God had thus preferred.
I will not hesitate to speak the word.
I will not live out of me.
Is Jove immortal / So is Cerberus at his
portal.
Leave me, Fear! thy throbs are base.
Lines on the Death of Miss M. B. Farnham.
Love / Asks nought his brother cannot give.
No fate, save by the victim's fault, is low.
No. 13 Hymn Written in Concord Sept. 1814.
On the Death of Mr. John Haskins.
Phoenix, The.
Rules to men made evident, The.
Sun is the sole inconsumable fire, The.
There is in all the sons of men.
Threnody: "South-wind brings, The."
When success exalts thy lot.
Everson. Burning Book, The.
Canticle for the Feast of the Most Precious
Blood, 1954, A.
Canticle of the Rose, The.
Canticle to the Waterbirds, A.
Encounter, The.
Frost Lay White on California, A.
God Germed in Raw Granite.
Out of the Ash.
Screed of the Flesh, The.
Song the Body Dreamed in the Spirit's Mad
Behest, The.
South Coast, The.
You, God.
Fenton. God, A Poem.
Tauler.
Fletcher. And God, looking out upon earth,
said, "Lo, it is time / To create mankind."
As Adam, clutching earth, lay stunned within
the darkness.
Fourfold is made the divine nature of man.
In the still evening of the sixth long day.
Now it was the ninth morning and the unseen
God.
Out of the waves they clomb, plant, insect,
fish, and bird.
Prelude: "Before the beginning of things."
Six long days was the unseen God in labour
with the earth.
Fox. If He Had Not Had Two Hands Tattooed
on His Chest.
Johannes Kepler (1571–1630).
Frost. Concept Self-Conceived, A.
Fear of God, The.
Forgive, O Lord, my little jokes on Thee.
Masque of Reason, A.
Not All There.
Gardner. Ballade: "Lady of Heaven, Queen of
nature."
Timeo.
Ginsberg. Holy Ghost on the Nod over the
Body of Bliss.
Jaweh and Allah Battle.
Psalm II: "Ah, still Lord, ah sweet Divinity."
Glück. Baskets.
Gift, The.
Lamentations.
Graves. Knobs and Levers.

Griffiths. At the Consecration.
Chiming at Trwyn Du, The.
Hall. Fathers and Sons.
Small Fig Tree, A.
Hardy. Agnosto Theo [To an Unknown God].
Bedridden Peasant, The.
Fragment: "At last I entered a long dark
gallery."
God-Forgotten.
God's Education.
God's Funeral.
New Year's Eve.
Philosophical Fantasy, A.
Hartnett. Old Catechism, The.
Sad Singing in Darkness.
Whom I ask for no gift.
Hemingway. God is away for the summer.
I think that I have never trod.
Neothomist Poem.
Herbert. Antiphon (2): "Praised be the God of
love."
Artillery [or Artillerie].
Bitter-Sweet.
Call, The.
Church-Floor[e], The.
Church-Lock and Key.
Clasping of Hands.
Collar, The.
Decay.
Dedication, The: "Lord, my first fruits present
themselves to thee."
Discipline.
Easter Wings.
Elixir [or Elixer], The.
Employment (1).
Evensong.
Evensong [or Even-Song].
Family [or Familie], The.
Forerunners, The.
Frailty.
Grace.
Home.
Hope.
Invitation, The.
Judgement.
Justice (1).
Knell, The.
L'Envoy.
Man.
Method, The.
Misery [or Miserie].
Obedience.
Odour, The. (2 Corinthians 2).
Offering, An.
Paradise.
Pearl. Matthew 13:45, The.
Perseverance.
Posy [or Posie], The.
Praise (3).
Praise (2).
Prayer (2).
Providence.
Pulley, The.
Search, The.
Sepulchre.
Sion.
Thanksgiving, The.
To All Angels and Saints.
Twenty-third Psalm, The.
Unkindness.
Vanity [or Vanitie] (1).
Whitsunday.
World, The.
Herrick. Affliction.
Angells.
Another ("God is *Jehovah* cal'd; which name
of His").
Another of God.
Another ("That there's a God").
Another, to God ("Lord, do not beat me").
Another, to God ("Though thou beest").
Calling, and Correcting.
Charroll Presented to Dr. Williams Bp. of
Lincolne as a Newyears Guift, A.
Clouds.
Confusion of Face.
Correction.

Free Welcome.
God, and Lord.
God, and the King.
God ("God (as the learned Damascen write)").
God ("God, in the *holy Tongue*, they call").
God ("God is more here, then in another place").
God Has a Twofold Part.
God Heares Us.
God ("In God there's nothing, but 'tis known to be").
God is One.
God Not To Be Comprehended.
God Sparing in Scourging.
God to Be First Served.
Gods Anger.
Gods Anger without Affection.
Gods Blessing.
Gods Descent.
Gods Dwelling.
Gods Grace.
Gods Hands.
Gods Keyes.
Gods Mercy.
Gods Mirth, Mans Mourning.
Gods Power.
Gods Presence ("God is all-present to what e'er we do").
Gods Presence ("God's evident, and may be said to be").
Gods Presence ("God's present ev'ry where; but most of all").
Gods Time Must End Our Trouble.
Hardning of Hearts.
His Dream[e].
His Ejaculation to God.
His Petition.
His Power.
His Recantation.
JEHOVAH.
Judgment-Day, The.
Knowledge.
Manna.
Neutrality Loathsome.
No Coming to God without Christ.
No Escaping the Scourging.
North and South.
Ode, or Psalme, to God, An.
Of all the good things whatsoe're we do.
Paine and Pleasure.
Pardon.
Position in the Hebrew Divinity, A.
Prayers Must Have Poise.
Prescience.
Reverence.
Riches and Poverty.
Right Hand, The.
Silence.
Staffe and Rod, The.
Teares: ("God from our eyes all teares..").
This, and the Next World.
To Find[e] God.
To God ("Come to me God; but do not come").
To God ("God gives not onely corne").
To God ("God is all-sufferance here").
To God ("God's undivided, One in Persons Three").
To God ("If any thing delight me for to print").
To God ("I'le come, I'le creep").
To God ("Lord, I am like to mistletoe").
To God ("Make, make me Thine").
To God ("Thou hast promis'd, Lord, to be").
To God ("With golden Censers..").
To God ("Work is done, The").
To His Angrie God.
To His Ever-Loving God.
To His Saviour.
To Marygolds.
Upon God ("God is all fore-part; for, we never see").
Upon God ("God when He takes my goods and chattels hence").
Upon Time.
Virgin Mary, The ("Virgin Marie was [as I have read], The").

What God Is.
Whips.
Youth, and Age.
Hesketh. Imagination.
More than Grass.
Reclaimed.
Sun Up.
Unicorn.
What Is God?
Hewitt. Priest Goes through the Motions of the Play, The.
Providence 3.
Providence 2.
Retreaded Rhymes.
Hill. Good Husbandry.
Hoffman. After God.
Hopkins. As kingfishers catch fire, dragonflies draw flame.
At the Wedding March.
Barnfloor and Winepress.
God's Grandeur.
Half-way House, The.
He hath abolished the old drouth.
In the Valley of the Elwy.
Justus Quidem Tu Es, Domine.
Let me be to Thee as the circling bird.
Nondum.
O Death, Death, He is come.
O Deus, Ego Amo Te.
On Saturday sailed from Bremen.
Pied Beauty.
Spring and Fall.
Summa.
Thee, God, I come from, to thee go.
Where art thou friend, whom I shall never see.
Housman. Laws of God, the laws of man, The.
'Tis five years since, "An end," said I.
Hughes, Langston. Personal.
Jarrell. Archangel's' Song, The.
Let's love each other for what we are.
Jeffers. As the eye fails through age or disease.
Birds and Fishes.
Birth-Dues.
Consciousness.
Excesses of God, The.
Fog.
Going to Horse Flats.
Inhumanist, The.
Intellectuals.
Noon.
Not Our Good Luck.
Patronymic.
Pearl Harbor.
Pleasures.
Point Pinos and Point Lobos.
Silent Shepherds, The.
Soul's Desert, The.
Teheran.
There is no God but God; he is all that exists.
There is this infinite energy, the power of God forever working.
Triad.
Johnson. On Losing the Power of Speech.
Prayer: "Summe Deus, cui caeca patent penetralia cordis."
Jong. For Molly, Concerning God.
If God is a Dog.
On the Avenue.
Jonson. From *The Touchstone of Truth.*
Hymn[e] to God the Father, A.
Reverse on the Back Side, The.
Sinner's Sacrifice, The.
To Heaven.
To K[ing] Charles and Q[ueen] Mary, for the Loss of Their First-Born. An Epigram Consolatory. 1629.
Keats. God of the Meridian.
Kipling. Answer, The.
Carol, A: "Our Lord Who did the Ox command."
Evarra and His Gods.
Late Came the God.
My New-Cut Ashlar.
Natural Theology.
Necessitarian, The.

Non Nobis Domine!
Obedient, The.
Prayer of Miriam Cohen, The.
Rabbi's Song, The.
Rahere.
Rebel, The.
Recessional.
Song of the English, A.
Supports, The.
Threshold, The.
Two-Sided Man, The.
Yet at the last, ere our spearmen had found him.
Koertge. Excerpts from God's Secret Diary.
Mr. Big.
Kunitz. Very Tree.
Lawrence. Abysmal Immortality.
Ah, with His Blessing Bright on Thy Mouth and Thy Brow.
At Midnight.
Bells.
Body of God, The.
Eloi, Eloi, Lama Sabachthani?
God.
God Is Born.
Hands of God, The.
Hymn to Nothingness.
Irreverent Thoughts.
Living Quetzalcoatl, The.
Lord of the Morning Star.
Lord's Prayer.
Man of Tyre, The.
Martyr à la Mode.
Mills of God, The.
Moth and Rust.
Neither Moth Nor Rust.
Only Man.
Pax.
Rainbow.
Religion.
Sight of God, The.
Silence.
Son of the Morning Star.
Song of Don Ramon, The.
Spanish Privilege.
Vengeance Is Mine.
When Wilt Thou Teach the People?
Why Does She Weep?
Work of Creation, The.
Levine. On a Drawing by Flavio.
To My God in His Sickness.
Liddy. Homage to Conor Cruise O'Brien.
On a Protestant Mystic.
Lindsay. Heart of God.
Lorde. When the Saints Come Marching In.
Lovelace. Paradox, A.
Lowell. Death and the Bridge.
Mr. Edwards and the Spider.
Watchmaker God.
Words.
Lowry. And Samson said if yo' shave ma hair.
And yet his suffering got involved with all this.
Ballad: "Twas in the springtime of the year."
Conversations With Goethe.
Dead men tell cryptic tales and this is one.
Death of an Oaxaqueñian.
I think that I shall never see.
Mr. Lowry's Good Friday under a Real Cactus.
New Guinea Gardener Bird, The.
Number 8 Fireman.
Pacific is a feeble symbol of death.
Poets are Godlike in that they.
Prayer: "I pray that I may form a prayer, oh Lord."
Prayer ("Oh thou who art not above").
Prelude to Another Drink.
What the Gardener Said to Mrs. Trail.
Who made this suicide pact of love?
McAuley. Late Afternoon, Running: Close Reasoning, Listening Closely.
"MacDiarmid." Cheville.
Dying Earth, The.
Focherty.

Fool, The.
Think not that I forget a single pang.
MacLeish. Creator.
Infinite Reason, The.
Learned Men, The.
Ship in the Tomb.
MacNeice. Although we say we disbelieve.
And the Lord was not in the whirlwind.
Blasphemies, The.
Creditor, The.
Hands and Eyes.
Jam Lucis Orto Sidere.
Mahon. Ecclesiastes.
Mute Phenomena, The.
Soles.
Marvell. Bermudas.
Meinke. Plovers.
Poet to His Tongue, The.
Poet, Trying to Surprise God, The.
Melville. Conflict of Convictions, The.
In the Desert.
Meredith. As from the fall of candlelight.
Succourful daughters of men are the rosed and
starred.
Test of Manhood, The.
Merton. After the Night Office—Gethsemani
Abbey.
Candlemas Procession, The.
Desolation.
Elias—Variations on a Theme.
Freedom as Experience.
God is day and night, winter and summer,
conflict and peace.
God Said "They Did Not Hear.."
Hagia Sophia.
Heavenly City, The.
I Have Called You.
Landscape: Wheatfields.
Logos Our Teacher, The.
Lord Is Good, The.
Natural History.
New Song, The.
On a Day in August.
Prose in Advent Time.
Psalm, A: "When psalms surprise me with
their music."
Reader, The.
Round and a Hope for Smithgirls, A.
Sincerity.
Sowing of Meanings, The.
Stranger.
To a Novice ("Be a son of this instant").
To a Novice ("Fool is one, The").
To Belong to Allah.
Way of man has no wisdom, but the way of
God has, The.
Wisest man is an ape compared to God.
Word—a Responsory, The.
Millay. Blue-Flag in the Bog, The.
Milton. Psalm 136.
Sonnet 19: "When I consider how my light is
spent."
Transcendence of God, The.
Morgan. Being, I.
Being, II.
Jormungand.
Leviathan.
Njord.
Morrison. & the Cool Fluttering.
Blues, The.
Flowering, The.
Leave the Informed Sense.
Soft Parade, The.
Translations of the Divine.
Nash. Fly, The.
Oh, Stop Being Thankful All over the Place.
Nemerov. Death of God, The.
God of This World, The.
View from Pisgah, The.
Zander on God.
Neruda. Gift, The.
When all turned to altitude.
Olson. Bottled up for days, mostly.
Go / Make a Bridge.
I saw, from under Him, the beginning.
This Year.
To a Poet Who Read in Gloucester Before the

Cape Ann Historical Literary and Scientific
Society.
Winter Solstice.
Oppen. To Memory.
Pack. After All.
Paley. Standing in high grass at home
imagining farm.
Patchen. All the Roses of the World.
At the Entrance to the Other World.
Behold, One of Several Little Christs.
Billion Freedoms, The.
Breathe on the living.
Builders, The.
Christ! Christ! Christ! that the world.
Deer and the Snake, The.
Easy Rider.
Expectant Shelters, The.
How God Was Made.
How silent are the things of heaven.
In horror the God-thrown lie.
Instructions for Angels.
Lions of fire, The.
Man Lives Here, A.
Meben.
Mohammed.
Overworld, The.
Palms for a Catholic Child.
Paxdominisit Sem Pervobiscum Etcumspiri
Tutuo.
Permanent Migrations, The.
Poems which are written by the soul.
Progress to a View of Life.
Rites of Darkness, The.
Snow is deep on the ground, The.
Temple, A.
There is nothing false in thee.
There Is One Who Watches.
Unfulfilling Brightnesses, The.
We Are Not Worthy, Lord.
Plath. Faun.
Pope. All are but parts of one stupendous
whole.
Messiah [a Sacred Eclogue, in Imitation of
Virgil's Pollio].
Paraphrase on Thomas à Kempis, A.
Translation of a Hymn of St. Francis Xavier.
What if the foot, ordain'd the dust to tread.
Prince. Question, The.
Psalms. Psalms.
Raine. It is in us they burn.
Lindisfarne.
Six calices yellow gold.
Young or old / What was I but a story told.
Ralegh. First of all is God, and the same last
is he, The.
Then marking this my sacred speech, but truly
lend.
Rexroth. Suchness.
Rich. Ghazal V.
Robinson. Just as I wonder at the twofold
screen.
Octaves.
Sonnet: "When we can all so excellently
give."
Roethke. Abyss, The.
Decision, The.
Elegy: "Should every creature be as I have
been."
Marrow, The.
Rossetti. Advent.
After Communion.
Afterthought, An.
Afterward He Repented, and Went.
Ah Lord, Lord, if my heart were right with
Thine.
Alas my Lord, / How should I wrestle all the
livelong night.
All Saints.
"All Thy Works Praise Thee, O Lord": A
Processional of Creation.
Alone Lord God, in Whom our trust and
peace.
And Now Why Tarriest Thou?
And There Was No More Sea.
Annie.
Answer, An.
Antipas.

Are They Not All Ministering Spirits?
Are Ye Not Much Better Than They?
As a King, ..Unto the King.
As froth on the face of the deep, / As foam
on the crest of the sea.
As the dove which found no rest / For the
sole of her foot, flew back.
As the Sparks Fly Upwards.
As Thy Days, So Shall Thy Strength Be.
Beautiful For Situation.
Before the Beginning.
Before the mountains were brought forth,
before.
Behold a Shaking.
Behold, It Was Very Good.
Books In the Running Brooks.
By Way of Remembrance.
Called To Be Saints.
Chiefest among Ten Thousand, The.
Chill blank world. Yet over the utmost sea, A.
Christmas Carol, A: "Thank God, thank God,
we do believe."
Consider.
Cried Out with Tears.
Darkness and light are both alike to Thee.
Day Is At Hand, The.
Dead Bride, The.
Death Is Swallowed Up in Victory.
Divine and Human Pleading.
Do This, and He Doeth It.
Dost Thou Not Care?
Dying Man to His Betrothed, The.
Earth Shall Tremble at the Look of Him, The.
Easter Even.
Easter Even.
Easter Morning.
Ellen Middleton.
Escape to the Mountain.
Eva.
Experience bows a sweet contented face.
Eye Hath Not Seen.
Feast of the Presentation.
For a Mercy Received.
For Advent.
For Thine Own Sake, O My God.
From House to Home.
Go In Peace.
Gold of that Land is Good, The.
Grant us such grace that we may work Thy
Will.
Had Fortune parted us / Fortune is blind.
Have I not striven, my God, and watched and
prayed?
He Cannot Deny Himself.
Heart Knoweth Its Own Bitterness, The.
Heaven.
Her Seed; It Shall Bruise Thy Head.
Holy City, New Jerusalme, The.
Holy Innocents.
Hymn: "O the bitter shame and sorrow."
Hymn: "To the God Who reigns on high."
I Do Set My Bow in the Cloud.
I followed Thee, my God, I followed Thee /
To see the end.
I Have Fought a Good Fight.
I Look for the Lord.
I, Lord, Thy foolish sinner low and small.
I Will Arise.
I Will Come and Heal Him.
I Will Lift Up Mine Eyes unto the Hills.
If I Could Trust Mine Own Self.
If not with hope of life, / Begin with fear of
death.
If Thou Sayest, Behold, We Knew It Not.
Imitated From the Arpa Evangelica: Page 121.
In Patience.
Is It Well with The Child?
It is not death, O Christ, to die for Thee: /
Nor is that silence of a silent land.
Joy of Saints, like incense turned to fire, The.
Let Everything That Hath Breath Praise the
Lord.
Let Patience Have Her Perfect Work.
Life Out of Death.
Life that was born today / Must make no stay.
Like As the Hart Desireth the Water Brooks.
Long Barren.

Lord, by what inconceivable dim road / Thou leadest man on footsore pilgrimage!
Lord, comest Thou to me?
Lord, give me love that I may love Thee much.
Lord, grant me grace to love Thee in my pain.
Lord, grant us eyes to see and ears to hear, / And souls to love and minds to understand.
Lord, grant us grace to rest upon Thy word.
Lord, hast Thou so loved us, and will not we.
Lord, I am feeble and of mean account.
Lord, I am here.—But, child, I look for thee.
Lord, make me one with Thine own faithful ones.
Lord, make me pure: / Only the pure shall see Thee as Thou art.
Lord, make us all love all: that when we meet / Even myriads of earth's myriads at Thy Bar.
Lord, Thou art fulness, I am emptiness.
Lord, we are rivers running to Thy sea.
Lord, what have I to offer? sickening fear.
Love builds a nest on earth and waits for rest.
"Love Is Strong As Death."
Love loveth Thee, and wisdom loveth Thee.
Love, to be love, must walk Thy way / And work Thy Will.
Lowest Place, The.
Martyr, A.
Martyr, The.
Martyrs' Song.
Master Is Come, and Calleth for Thee, The.
Maundy Thursday.
Me and my gift: kind Lord, behold.
Mid-Lent.
My God, wilt Thou accept, and will not we / Give aught to Thee?
O Death Where Is Thy Sting?
O Lord, I am ashamed to seek Thy Face / As tho' I loved Thee as Thy saints love Thee.
O Lord, I cannot plead my love of Thee.
O Lord, on Whom we gaze and dare not gaze, / Increase our faith that gazing we may see.
O Lord, when Thou didst call me, didst Thou know.
Offering of the New Law, the One Oblation Once Offered, The.
Our Widowed Queen.
Out of the Deep.
Palm Sunday.
Passiontide.
Patience of Hope.
Peace I Leave with You.
Perfect Love Casteth Out Fear.
Quinquagesima.
Rogationtide.
Rose Plant in Jericho, A.
St. Elizabeth of Hungary.
St. Mark.
St. Michael and all Angels.
St. Peter.
Seven vials hold Thy wrath: but what can hold.
Shadows Today.
Shall not the Judge of all the earth do right?
Sinner's own fault? So it was, The.
Sit Down in the Lowest Room.
Slain in their high places: fallen on rest.
Song for the Least of All Saints, A.
Song: "We buried her among the flowers."
Sursum Corda.
Sweetness of rest when Thou sheddest rest.
Take No Thought for The Morrow.
That Which Hath Been Is Named Already, and It Is Known That It Is Man.
Then They That Feared the Lord Spake Often One to Another.
There Remaineth Therefore a Rest.
There Remaineth Therefore a Rest to the People of God.
They lie at rest, our blessed dead.
They Shall Be as White as Snow.
They Toil Not, Neither Do They Spin.
Three Nuns.
Thy fainting spouse, yet still Thy spouse.
Thy lilies drink the dew, / Thy lambs the rill, and I will drink them too.

Thy Servant Will Go and Fight with This Philistine.
Time of Waiting, The.
To Every Seed His Own Body.
To the End.
To What Purpose Is This Waste?
Trust me, I have not earned your dear rebuke.
Tune Me, O Lord, into One Harmony.
Twice.
Two Pursuits.
Until the Day Break.
Vanity of Vanities.
Vigil of St. Bartholomew.
Vigil of the Presentation.
Was Thy Wrath against the Sea?
Watchers, The.
We are of those who tremble at Thy word.
Weary in Well-Doing.
What do the stars do / Up in the sky.
What Good Shall My Life Do Me?
What Hath God Wrought!
Whatsoever Is Right, That Shall Ye Receive.
When I Was in Trouble I Called upon the Lord.
When My Heart Is Vexed, I Will Complain.
Where Neither Rust Nor Moth Doth Corrupt.
Whitsun Day.
Whitsun Eve.
Who Have a Form of Godliness.
Who sits with the King in His Throne? Not a slave but a Bride.
Who would wish back the Saints upon our rough.
Why?
Will of the Lord Be Done, The.
Worship God.
Wouldst thou give me a heavy jewelled crown.
Ye Have Forgotten the Exhortation.
Yea, the Sparrow Hath Found Her an House.
Young Death.
Zion Said.
Rukeyser.   Akiba.
Little Stone in the Middle of the Road, in Florida, A.
Mortal Girl.
Nuns in the Wind.
Place at Albert Bay, The.
Silence of Volcanoes.
Sandburg.   Ambassadors of Grief.
Brancusi.
Brass Keys.
Fire Dreams.
Four Brothers, The.
Glass House Canticle.
God Is No Gentleman.
Good Morning, America.
I have been woven among meshes of long ropes.
Manufactured Gods.
Many Hats.
Night's Nothings Again.
Our Prayer of Thanks.
Public Letter to Emily Dickinson.
Slabs of the Sunburnt West.
There is only one horse on the earth.
They Ask: Is God, Too, Lonely.
Wanting the Impossible.
Sarton.   Invocation to Kali, The.
Schuyler.   Six Something.
Schwartz.   "All is forgiven when guilt is accepted."
Choir and Music of Solitude and Silence, The.
"Now we approach the darkness of to-night!"
"O Death, great captain, lift anchor!"
Sexton.   Author of the Jesus Papers Speaks, The.
Earth, The.
Faustus and I.
Fifth Psalm.
First Psalm.
For Eleanor Boylan Talking with God.
Fury of God's Good-bye, The.
Fury of Sunrises, The.
God's Backside.
Is It True?
Keeping the City.

May 30th.
No So. Not So.
Praying to Big Jack.
Rowing Endeth, The.
Sickness unto Death, The.
Small Wire.
Wall, The.
Welcome Morning.
What the Bird with the Human Head Knew.
Shelley.   Prologue in Heaven.
Silverstein.   Ma and God.
Unicorn, The.
Smart.   Gratitude.
Hymn to the Supreme Being.
Jubilate Agno.
Long-Suffering of God.
On the Eternity of the Supreme Being.
On the Goodness of the Supreme Being.
On the Immensity of the Supreme Being.
On the Omniscience of the Supreme Being.
On the Power of the Supreme Being.
Smith, Charlotte.   Evening Walk by the Sea-Side, An.
Studies by the Sea.
Smith, Patti.   Grant.
Smith, Stevie.   Breughel.
Conviction (i).
Dear Child of God.
Distractions and the Human Crowd.
Egocentric.
Fuite d'Enfance.
God and the Devil.
God Speaks.
God the Eater.
How Do You See?
I Was So Full.
Man Saul, The.
Mother, among the Dustbins.
Nature and Free Animals.
Never Again.
No Categories!
Oh Christianity, Christianity.
Passing Cloud, The.
Reason, The.
To Dean Inge Lecturing on Origen.
Sorrentino.   Celebration of Sorts, A.
Southwell.   At Home in Heaven.
Spenser.   I saw raysde up on yvorie pillours tall.
It was the time, when rest, soft sliding downe.
Stafford.   Ultimate Problems.
Stevens.   Cy Est Pourtraicte, Madame Ste Ursule, et Les Unze Mille Vierges.
Les Plus Belles Pages.
Stevenson.   All influences were in vain.
Angler rose, he took his rod, The.
As one who having wandered all night long.
Blast—1875, The.
Counterblast Ironical, The.
Embro Hie Kirk.
English Breeze, An.
Hail, guest, and enter freely! All you see.
House Beautiful, The.
I am a hunchback, yellow faced.
If I could arise and travel away.
If This Were Faith.
It's forth across the roaring foam, and on towards the west.
Last night we had a thunderstorm in style.
Late in the nicht in bed I lay.
Men marvel at the works of man.
Nor judge me light, tho' light at times I seem.
Prayer: "I ask good things that I detest."
Scotsman's Return from Abroad, The.
Since thou hast given me this good hope, O God.
Stout marches lead to certain ends.
Strange are the ways of men.
Susquehanna and the Delaware, The.
Tempest tossed and sore afflicted, sin defiled and care oppressed.
This gloomy northern day.
Well-Head, The.
Stuart.   Confirmation.
Swinburne.   Leper, The.
Tennyson.   Flower in the Crannied Wall.
Supposed Confessions of a Second-rate

Sensitive Mind.
Wish, that of the living whole, The.
Thomas. Upon Happiness.
Thomson. Fragment of a Poem on the Works and Wonders of Almighty Power.
Hymn on the Seasons, A.
Hymn to God's Power.
Psalm CIV Paraphrased.
Updike. Trees Eat Sunshine.
Wind.
Warren. Fox-Fire: 1956.
Interjection #6: What You Sometimes Feel on Your Face at Night.
Way to Love God, A.
Whitman. Chanting the Square Deific.
Persian Lesson, A.
While behind All, Firm and Erect.
Whittier. All's Well.
Andrew Rykman's Prayer.
Benevolence.
Book, The.
Clear Vision, The.
Deity, The.
Divine Compassion.
Eternal Goodness, The.
Familist's Hymn, The.
Female Martyr, The.
Fragment, A: "Dreadful burden of our sins we feel, The."
Grave by the Lake, The.
Hermit of the Thebaid, The.
Hymn for the House of Worship at Georgetown.
Hymn for the Opening of Plymouth Church.
Hymn for the Opening of Thomas Starr King's House of Worship.
Hymns from the French of Lamartine.
Hymns of the Brahmo Somaj.
Invocation: "Through Thy clear spaces, Lord, of old."
Lakeside, The.
Last Walk in Autumn, The.
Lines on Leaving Appledore.
Mary Garvin.
Miriam.
My Dream.
My Psalm.
My Soul and I.
On a Prayer-Book.
Our River.
Over-Heart, The.
Palestine.
Palm-Tree, The.
Quaker Alumni, The.
Questions of Life.
Rabbi Ishmael.
Requirement.
Revelation.
River Path, The.
"Rock" in El Ghor, The.
Saint Gregory's Guest.
Song of Harvest, A.
Summer by the Lakeside.
Tauler.
Thy Will Be Done.
Vaudois Teacher, The.
What the Traveller Said at Sunset.
What the Voice Said.
Wife of Manoah to Her Husband, The.
Wish of To-day, The.
Word, The.
Wilbur. Dubious Night, A.
Everness.
Prayer to Go to Paradise with the Donkeys, A.
Proof, The.
Williams, Charles Kenneth. Becoming Somebody Else.
Dominion: Depression.
Even If I Could.
For Children When They Grow Up.
For Gail, When I Was Five.
Innings.
Like Little Birds.
Little Shirt, The.
Loss.
Next to the Last Poem about God, The.
Poor Hope.

Race of the Flood, The.
Spit.
They Warned Him Then They Threw Him Away.
Williams, Miller. Entropy.
Why God Permits Evil: For Answers to This Question of Interest to Many Write Bible Answers Dept. E-7.
Wordsworth. Cuckoo at Laverna May 25, 1837 The.
Fact, and an Imagination or, Canute and Alfred, on the Sea-Shore, A.
Flowers on the Top of the Pillars at the Entrance of the Cave.
In My Mind's Eye a Temple, Like a Cloud.
Matron of Jedborough and Her Husband, The.
On a High Part of the Coast in Cumberland.
Suggested at Tyndrum in a Storm.
Though Pulpits and the Desk May Fail.
Thoughts Suggested the Day Following, on the Banks of Nith, near the Poet's Residence.
To the Supreme Being.
Wright, James. Eternal Dice, The.
Speak.
Wyatt. After great storms the calm returns.
Argument, Th'.
Yeats. At Algeciras—a Meditation upon Death.
Black Tower, The.
Crazy Jane on God.
Dancer at Cruachan and Cro-Patrick, The.
Indian upon God, The [or An].
Paudeen.
Ribh Denounces Patrick.
Rose of the World, The.
Unappeasable Host, The.
Veronica's Napkin.
Young. By Heart.
Kicking.
Myself When I Am Real.
Zukofsky. For you I have emptied the meaning.

Gods and Goddesses
Berrigan. Poem in the Modern Manner.
Berry. Hidden Singer, The.
Observance.
Walking on the River Ice.
Berryman. Long Home, The.
Blake. If it is True What the Prophets write.
Browning, Elizabeth Barrett. Dead Pan, The.
Browning, Robert. Artemis Prologizes.
Carew. Coelum Britannicum.
Cruel Mistress, A.
To the King, at His Entrance into Saxham: By Master John Crofts.
Carruth. Your dream: / Her name was Hestia, sister of God.
Chaucer. House of Fame, The.
Clark. Daring to Be the Same.
Egypt, Everything.
Withdrawal.
Coleridge. Visit of the Gods, The.
Cummings. 4.6: "O, blessed of the gods."
Epithalamion: "Thou aged unreluctant earth who dost."
No man,if men are gods;but if gods must.
Davie. Idyll: "As a horn of the high moon veers in clear skies over Main Street."
Zodiac, The.
De la Mare. Exile.
Mourn'st Thou Now?
Music.
Quarry, The.
Dickey, William. Coyote's Song.
Doolittle. Are we unfathomable night.
Ariadne.
At Croton.
At Eleusis.
Dodona.
Evadne.
God, The.
Helios.
Helios and Athene.
Hermonax.
Muse, / tell me of this man of wit.
Myrtle Bough.
Phaedra.

Psyche.
Pygmalion.
Sea Gods.
Sitalkas.
Thetis.
Tribute, The.
We have seen how the most amiable.
Eberhart. Difficulty of Ideas, The.
Gods of Washington, D.C., The.
Skier and the Mountain, The.
Eliot. Dry Salvages, The.
Emerson. Around the man who seeks a noble end.
Culture.
For every god.
From high to higher forces.
Gods walk in the breath of the woods, The.
I have supped with the gods tonight.
If curses be the wage of love.
Think not the gods receive thy prayer.
Ford. Activity without / Attachment. One link with the.
Glück. Embrace, The.
Graves. Between Moon and Moon.
Friday Night.
In Her Praise.
Knobs and Levers.
Pandora.
Problems of Gender.
Return of the Goddess [Artemis].
Rhea.
Tousled Pillow.
Weather of Olympus, The.
White Goddess, The.
Gunn. Garden of the Gods, The.
Goddess, The.
Odysseus on Hermes.
Hemingway. Mitrailliatrice.
Herrick. Devotion Makes the Deity.
Evensong.
Griefes.
Hymne to Juno, An.
Hymne, to the Lares, A.
Littlenesse No Cause of Leanesse.
Meane in Our Meanes, A.
Short Hymne to Venus, A.
To His Closet-Gods.
To His Household Gods.
To the Genius of His House.
Hill. Doctor Faustus.
Jong. To the Goddess.
To the Horned God.
Jonson. Queen and huntress, chaste and fair.
To His Lady, Then Mrs Cary.
Kipling. Giffen's Debt.
Gods of the Copybook Headings, The.
Poseidon's Law.
Sack of the Gods, The.
Sacrifice of Er-Heb, The.
Shiv and the Grasshopper.
Song of the Men's Side.
Song of the Red War-Boat.
Song to Mithras, A.
Kunitz. Among the Gods.
Lawrence. All Sorts of Gods.
Be It So.
Cabbage-Roses.
Cold Blood.
False Democracy and Real.
For a Moment.
Give Us Gods.
Glimpses.
Gods.
Gods, The.
Gods! The Gods!, The.
Goethe and Pose.
Huitzilopochtli Gives the Black Blade of Death.
Huitzilopochtli's Watch.
Like the Green Candles of Malintzi.
Lords of Life Are the Masters of Death, The.
Man Is More Than *Homo Sapiens*.
Man of Tyre, The.
Maximus.
Men Like Gods.
Men Like Gods.
Name the Gods!

Old Men.
Return of Returns.
Service.
Song of the Grey Dog, The.
Spiral Flame.
There Are No Gods.
Third Song of Huitzilopochtli.
Two Ways of Living and Dying.
What Are the Gods?
Worship.
Levertov. Eros.
Postcards: A Triptych, The.
Lindsay. Queen of Bubbles, The.
Lorde. Oya.
Lovelace. As once I bad good morning to the day.
Ask'd in the Country, what I did, I said.
If you are Phœbus Sister Delia, pray.
Princesse Löysa drawing.
Sanazar's Hexaflick.
MacLeish. Renovated Temple, The.
MacNeice. But even so, he said, daily I hanker, daily.
Canto XXIV: "December the Twenty-third: I visit the Ancient East."
Too large in feature for a world of cuties.
Mahon. Tithonus.
Marlowe. 3.9: Ad Cererem, conquerens quod eius sacris cum amica concumbere non permittatur.
Melville. Trophies of Peace.
Meredith. Hypnos on Ida.
Teaching of the Nude, The.
Merrill. After Greece.
Nike.
Merton. Atlas and the Fatman.
Autumn Floods.
Chilam Balam.
Lord whose is the oracle at Delphi neither utters nor hides his meaning, The.
Songs of Experience; India, One.
Milton. Next came one / Who mourn'd in earnest, when the Captive Ark.
Morgan. Freya.
Frigg.
Loki.
Ran.
Nemerov. Companions, The.
Distraction.
Olson. Advantage, The.
Applause.
Distances, The.
I Am So Small You Can Hardly See Me.
In Cold Hell, in Thicket.
In Wiro language.
Lordly and Isolate Satyrs, The.
She-Bear, The.
Some partial cloudiness will flow locally, mostly.
There Is No River Which Is Called Lethe.
Unfinished (raw) hero—un-, The.
Patchen. Outlaw of the Lowest Planet, The.
Plath. Full Fathom Five.
Lorelei.
Ouija.
Ralegh. 3.4: "Who rules the duller earth, the wind-swolne streames."
Brasen tower [or Tower] with doors [or dores] close barred [or bar'd], The.
Egyptians [or Aegyptians] think[e] it sin[ne] to root[e] up, or to bite.
From the Earth, and from thy bloud, O heaven, they came.
Mindes of men are ever so affected, The.
Praisd Be Dianas Faire and Harmles Light.
Saturne to be the fatter is not knowne.
Things thus agreed: Titan made Saturne sweare.
Robinson. False Gods, The.
Rukeyser. Game of Ball, A.
Sandburg. Cheap Rent.
Hammer, The.
Sarton. Myth.
Proteus.
Return of Aphrodite, The.
Sexton. Gods.
Shelton. Sonora for Sale.

Sidney. Sonnet 13: "Phoebus was judge between Jove, Mars, and Love."
Sonnet 17: "His mother dear Cupid offended late."
Smith, Patti. Ballad of Isabelle Eberhardt.
Smith, Stevie. God the Drinker.
River God, The.
Venus When Young Choosing Death.
Spender. In Attica.
Spenser. Upon an hill a bright flame I did see.
Stevens. Less and Less Human, O Savage Spirit.
Thomas. Shall Gods Be Said to Thump The Clouds.
Tomlinson. Mictlantecuhtli.
Updike. Deities and Beasts.
Milady Reflects.
Wilbur. To Ishtar.
Yeats. Conjunctions.
Grey Rock, The.

God's Protection
Angelou. Just Like Job.
Browning, Elizabeth Barrett. Soul's Travelling, The.
Burns. On the Birth of a Posthumous Child, Born in Peculiar Circumstances of Family Distress.
Clough. That there are powers above us I admit.
Cummings. 4.6: "O, blessed of the gods."
Ballade of Soul.
De la Mare. Imagination's Pride, The.
"Dylan." Every Grain of Sand.
Emerson. Novice, hear me what I say.
Nun's Aspiration.
Worship.
Everson. Frost Lay White on California, A.
Herbert. Afflction (5).
Affliction (4).
Evensong [or Even-Song].
Invitation, The.
L'Envoy.
Providence.
Herrick. Goodnesse of His God, The.
Rod, The.
Way, The.
Holmes. Petition Concerning the Death-Wish.
Kipling. Ave Imperatrix!
Covenant, The.
Hymn before Action.
Mulholland's Contract.
Song of the Fifth River.
What the People Said.
Koertge. Excerpts from God's Secret Diary.
Kunitz. Benediction.
Lindsay. Invocation for "The Map of the Universe."
Johnny Appleseed's Ship Comes In.
Lowry. Dead men tell cryptic tales and this is one.
McAuley. Press Conference: King James Version.
MacNeice. Prayer before Birth.
Merton. Be My Defender.
Rossetti. Consider.
I Will Arise.
Lord, I am here.—But, child, I look for thee.
Smart. Gratitude.
On the Goodness of the Supreme Being.
Stevenson. Our Lady of the Snows.
Whittier. Ein Feste Burg Ist Unser Gott.
Familist's Hymn, The.
Wordsworth. Effusion in the Presence of the Painted Tower of Tell, at Altorf.
Hymn for the Boatmen, as They Approach the Rapids under the Castle of Heidelberg.
Jewish Family (in a Small Valley Opposite St Goar, upon the Rhine), A.

Godwin, William
Coleridge. To William Godwin.
Shelley. Mighty Eagle.

Goebbels, Joseph
Snodgrass. Dr. Joseph Goebbels ("Say goodbye to the help, the ranks").
Dr. Joseph Goebbels ("Stand back, make way, you mindless scum").

Magda Goebbels ("This is the needle that we give").

Goethe, Johann Wolfgang von
Arnold. Memorial Verses.
Auden. To Goethe: a Complaint.
Browning, Elizabeth Barrett. To Bettine.
Browning, Robert. Burlesque for Palgrave on the Pronunciation of "Metamorphosis."
Emerson. Solution.
Written in a Volume of Goethe.
Koertge. Pronouncing My Name.
Lawrence. Goethe and Pose.
Stevenson. To Charles Baxter.
Wright, James. Three Stanzas From Goethe.

Gogh, Vincent van. see Van Gogh, Vincent.

Gold
Crane. Key West.
De la Mare. Gold.
Dickinson. I never told the buried gold.
Donne. Bracelet, The.
Doolittle. Song: "You are as gold."
Dunbar. Real Question, The.
Emerson. Chemist of love, The.
High heart, O Hafiz! though not thine.
Understanding's copper coin, The.
Frost. Vindictives, The.
Gunn. Value of Gold, The.
Hall. Gold.
Herrick. Gold and Frankincense.
Hewitt. Golden Boy, The.
Hugo. Gold Man on the Beckler, The.
Gold Stone.
Jonson. Those that in blood such violent pleasure have.
Kipling. Runes on Weland's Sword, The.
Song of the Fifth River.
Lindsay. Voice of the Earthquake, The.
Lorde. Family Resemblance, A.
Lowry. Poem On Gold.
MacLeish. Rainbow at Evening.
Rossetti. Golden Glories.
Johnny.
Sandburg. Crucible.
Gold Mud.
Joke Gold.
Silverstein. Garden, The.
Search, The.

Gold Mining and Gold Miners
Merrill. McKane's Falls.
Robinson. Klondike, The.
Williams, William Carlos. Epigramme: "Hast ever seen a man."

Golden Age
Frost. Lost Follower, The.
Whittier. My Triumph.

Golden Mean
Cowper. On Envy.
Donne. From being anxious, or secure.
When senses, which thy so[u]ldiers are.
Eberhart. Somewhere Else.
Sidney. You better sure shall live, not evermore.

Golden Rule, The
Angelou. Lord, in My Heart.
"Dylan." Do Right to Me Baby (Do Unto Others).
Herrick. Like Pattern, Like People.

Goldenrod
Lowry. Dodder, The.
Poem On Gold.
Oliver. Goldenrod.
Paley. What would happen / if there were a terrific shortage of goldenrod.

Goldfinches
Ammons. For Louise and Tom Gossett.
Cowper. Faithful Friend, The.
On a Goldfinch Starved to Death in His Cage.
Hardy. Caged Goldfinch, The.
Lowry. Poem On Gold.
Oliver. Goldfinches.
Wilbur. Sketch, A.

Goldfish
Lowry. Goldeneye and Goldfish.
Wild-duck swam in the gold-fish pond, The.
Nemerov. Goldfish.

Golf
Berg. Last Elegy.
Betjeman. Seaside Golf.
Hewitt. My Father.
Kipling. OCTOBER (*Golf*).
Liddy. Woodenbridge Golf Club.
Lieberman. Black Lotus of the Links.
Lowell. Ford Madox Ford ("Lobbed ball plops, then dribbles to the cup, The").
Lowry. In Praise of an Understudy.
Though I Have More.
Nash. Slow Down, Mr. Ganderdonk, You're Late.
Strange Case of the Ambitious Caddy, The.
Who Taught Caddies to Count? or A Burnt Golfer Fears the Child.
Updike. Golfers.

Goliath
De la Mare. Goliath.
Duncan. Helmet of Goliath, The.
Lowry. Lines on the Poet Being Informed That His Epic About the Philistines Etc. Needed Cutting.

Good
Berry. Necessity of Faith, The.
Blake. Marriage of Heaven and Hell, The.
Browning, Elizabeth Barrett. Futurity.
Bukowski. Strange Moment, A.
Burns. At Whigham's Inn, Sanquar.
First Psalm, The.
Written in Friar's Carse Hermitage on the Banks of Nith—June—1788.
Clough. To think that men of former days.
Dunbar. God Reigns.
Eberhart. Fantasy of a Small Idea.
Ineffable, The.
Meditation Two.
Emerson. Around the man who seeks a noble end.
Good is what goes on the road of Nature.
I will not live out of me.
We would do nought but good.
Frost. Quandary.
Gardner. Triolet: "Bad die old, The."
Hardy. Unkept Good Fridays.
Heaney. Disappearing Island, The.
Herrick. Almes.
His Confession.
Sin ("Sin no Existence; Nature none it hath").
Hewitt. Man Fish and Bird.
On Hearing a Traveller's Tale of the Alps.
Hopkins. How all is one way wrought!
Kipling. Curé, The.
Kunitz. Between the Acts.
Lindsay. Above the Battle's Front.
Lowry. Epitaph on Our Gardener, Dead Near Liverpool.
Hartebeeste Both Grave and Gay, The.
Morning Song for the Hartebeeste.
Morning tanker gleameth, The.
My two hands broke in two: and they broke me!
Those Coke to Newcastle Blues.
Piercy. My old friend, how we sustain.
Pope. Version of the First Psalm, for the Use of a Young Lady, A.
Rossetti. At Last.
Watchers, The.
Who shall my wandering thoughts steady & fix.
Spenser. One day, whiles that my daylie cares did sleepe.
Stevens. Good Man Has No Shape, The.
Whitman. Roaming in Thought.
Young Grimes.
Whittier. Answer, The.
Eternal Goodness, The.
Lines Written in an Album.
Requirement.
Wordsworth. O'er the wide earth, on mountain and on plain.
Wright, James. Trying to Pray.

Good Friday
Donne. Good Friday [*or* Goodfriday], 1613.
Riding Westward.
Hardy. Unkept Good Fridays.
Herbert. Good Friday.

Herrick. Good Friday: Rex Tragicus, or, Christ Going to His Cross[e].
Hill. Canticle for Good Friday.
Hugo. St. Ignatius Where the Salish Wail.
Olson. Friday, Good Friday, which.
Rossetti. Bundle of Myrrh Is My Well-Beloved unto Me, A.
Good Friday.
Good Friday.
Good Friday Evening.
Good Friday Morning.

Good Samaritan
Cummings. Man who had fallen among thieves, A.
Dickey, William. Coyote's Song.
Rossetti. Half Dead.

Goodman, Benny
Carruth. "Sure," Said Benny Goodman.

Gore-Booth, Eva
Yeats. In Memory of Eva Gore-Booth and Con Markievicz.

Gorillas
Carruth. My Chicago, city of all.

Gorse
Browning, Elizabeth Barrett. Lessons from the Gorse.

Gospel Music
Dove. Gospel.
Stuart. Gospel Singer.

Gossip and Gossips
Auden. Love Feast, The.
Bukowski. Fleg.
I Have Shit Stains in My Underwear Too.
Clare. Scandal.
Davie. Against Confidences.
De la Mare. Juliet's Nurse.
Donne. Mercurius Gallo-Belgicus.
Dunbar. Circumstances Alter Cases.
Protest.
"Dylan." Tell Me That It Isn't True.
Emerson. Hush!
Quoth Saadi, when I stood before.
Hardy. Victorian Rehearsal, A.
Herrick. On Himselfe ("One Eare tingles; some there be").
Suspition upon His Over-much Familiarity with a Gentlewoman, The.
Hewitt. I Still Had a Friend.
Hopkins. Miss Story's character! too much you ask.
Hughes, Langston. Joe Louis.
Koertge. Primary Considerations.
Nash. Don't Even Tell Your Wife, Particularly.
I Have It on Good Authority.
Never Mind the Overcoat, Button Up That Lip.
This Was Told Me in Confidence.
O'Hara. Personal Poem.
Piercy. I am sitting on a kitchen chair.
"Reed." N.Y. Telephone Conversation.
Shakespeare. Sonnet 121: "'Tis better to be vile than vile esteem'd."
Sidney. Sonnet 92: "Be your words made (good sir) of Indian ware."
Snodgrass. Charges Against Cock Robin, The.
Williams, Charles Kenneth. Regulars, The.
Wordsworth. Personal Talk.
See also **Rumor; Reputation.**

Government
Berry. Against the War in Vietnam.
Sometimes he thinks the earth.
There is no government so worthy as your son who fishes with you in silence beside the forest pool.
Bishop. Four Sambas.
Bly. Johnson's Cabinet Watched by Ants.
Burns. Act Sederunt of the Session—A Scots Ballad.
Carruth. Sonnet: "All revolutions in modern times have led."
Those Indians who came and didn't stay.
Cowper. Table Talk.
Duncan. Everything Speaks to Me.
Emerson. Ode, Inscribed to W. H. Channing.
Politics.

Ginsberg. Capitol Air.
Gray. Alliance of Education and Government, The.
Griffiths. Giving Them What For.
Herrick. Another on the Same.
Gentlenesse.
Ill Government.
Obedience.
Obedience in Subjects.
Power in the People, The.
Present Government Grievous.
Rules for Our Reach.
Hewitt. Agenda.
Resource.
Hill. Respublica.
Kipling. Death-Bed, A.
MacDonough's Song.
Lawrence. Change of Government.
Flapper Vote.
Liddy. Sergeant Valentine Function, at Hollyfort.
Lindsay. Preface to "Bob Taylor's Birthday."
Lorde. Revolution Is One Form of Social Change.
MacLeish. Twelfth Book, The.
Marvell. First Anniversary of the Government under His Highness the Lord Protector, 1655, The.
Last Instructions to a Painter, The.
Music's Empire.
Merton. Cracking the Safe.
Note in Honor of Machiavelli, A.
Nemerov. Poverty Programs, The.
Rukeyser. Disease: After-Effects, The.
Sandburg. And They Obey.
Death Snips Proud Men.
Government.
Liars, The.
Mr. Longfellow and His Boy.
Nickels click off fares in the slot machines of the subway, the elevated, The.
People learn, unlearn, learn, The.
People, yes, The.
Snow.
Trinity Place.
Was he preaching or writing poetry or talking through his hat? He was.
Turco. Courthouse, The.
Williams, Charles Kenneth. Another Dollar.
Bishop Tutu's Visit to the White House: 1984.
Poem for the Governments, A.
Yeats. Appointment, An.
Church and State.
Old Stone Cross, The.

Goya y Lucientes, Francisco José de
Duncan. Poem Beginning with a Line by Pindar, A.
Ferlinghetti. Goya & the Sleep of Reason.
In Goya's greatest scenes we seem to see.
Updike. He omits, Goya, not even the good news.
Van Duyn. Goya's "Two Old People Eating Soup."

Grace
Beckett. À elle l'acte calme.
Nuit qui fais tant.
Berrigan. Dear Ron: Keats was a baiter of bears etc.
Berry. Gift of Gravity, The.
Grace.
Browning, Elizabeth Barrett. Work.
Campion. Author of light, revive my dying spright.
Loe, when backe mine eye.
View Mee, Lord.
Chaucer. ABC, An.
Cowper. Song of Mercy and Judgment, A.
Triumph of Heavenly Love Desired, The.
Creeley. Birds, The.
Fire, The.
Le Fou.
Cullen. Atlantic City Waiter.
Dickinson. Anatomical dishabille.
Day that I was crowned, The.
Grace—Myself—might not obtain, The.
Her Grace is all she has.
How spacious must be the Heart.

I cross till I am weary.
Love a Life can show Below, The.
Oh what a Grace is this.
Sweetest Heresy received, The.
Donne. Thou hast made me, and shall thy work[e] decay?
"Dylan." Saving Grace.
Eberhart. Incidence of Flight.
Words.
Emerson. Grace.
Ye have Grace.
Fox. Figure Eights.
Glück. Gift, The.
Herbert. Conscience.
Grace.
Love.
Temper (2), The.
Herrick. Affliction.
God ("God is more here, then in another place").
Gods Dwelling.
Gods Grace.
Hardning of Hearts.
Humility.
To God ("If I have plaid the Truant").
To the Handsome Mistresse Grace Potter.
Upon Gryll.
Hewitt. Boy Seen in a Bus Journey.
Rome Sunday[,] June 1960.
Hill. Ascend through declension.
Hopkins. Handsome Heart, The.
To What Serves Mortal Beauty?
Jonson. To Susan, Countess of Montgomery.
Levertov. Grace-Note, The.
McAuley. Dying Swan, The.
MacLeish. Crossing.
Meinke. Hermann Ludwig Ferdinand Von Helmholtz.
Merton. Grace's House.
Image of True Lovers' Death, The.
Snare, The.
Nemerov. Behavior.
Dancer's Reply, The.
Steps for a Dancer.
Patchen. For whose adornment the mouths.
Raine. Returning from Church.
Ralegh. Passionate Man['s] Pilgrimage, The.
Robinson. But for the Grace of God.
Rossetti. Changing Chimes.
Do This, and He Doeth It.
Feast of the Presentation.
Grant us such grace that we may work Thy Will.
Helen Grey.
Lady Isabella.
Listening.
Lord, grant me grace to love Thee in my pain.
Lord, grant us grace to rest upon Thy word.
Lord, I am feeble and of mean account.
Lord, Thou art fulness, I am emptiness.
Night and Death.
O Lord, I am ashamed to seek Thy Face / As tho' I loved Thee as Thy saints love Thee.
St. Mark.
Seven vials hold Thy wrath: but what can hold.
Sit Down in the Lowest Room.
Valentines From C.G.R.
We know not when, we know not where.
What is it Jesus saith unto the soul?
Rukeyser. Ninth Elegy. The Antagonists.
Shakespeare. Did not the heavenly rhetoric of thine eye.
Sonnet 53: "What is your substance, whereof are you made."
Southwell. Author to the Reader, The ("Deare eye that doost peruse my Muses stile").
Stevenson. Thought, A.
To Miss Cornish.
Stuart. Gesture, A.
Wilbur. Grace.
Lament: "Nashe's old queens who bartered young and fair."
Wordsworth. Composed During a Storm.
Yeats. Countess Cathleen in Paradise, The.
Zukofsky. Cactus rose-mauve and gray, twin overturned.

Grackles
Ammons. Modality.
Nash. Grackle, The.
Stevens. Snow and Stars.

Graffiti
Ginsberg. Graffiti 12th Cubicle Men's Room Syracuse Airport.
Larkin. Sunny Prestatyn.
Meinke. Helen.
Oppen. Power, which hides what it can.
Rukeyser. Backside of the Academy, The.

Grammar
Creeley. Not Again.
Sentence, The.
Cummings. First president to be loved by his, The.
Love's the i guess most only verb that lives.
Graves. O.
Koch. Permanently.
Nash. Oafishness Sells Good, Like an Advertisement Should.
Sidney. Sonnet 63: "O grammar rules, O now your virtues show."
Silverstein. Chester.
Spender. Subject, Object, Sentence.

Grand Canyon
Garrigue. Grand Canyon, The.
Rich. Road to the great canyon always feels, The.
Turning the Wheel.
Sandburg. Many Hats.

Grandchildren
Berry. Conversation, The.
Matthews. Recollections.
Tennyson. To Alfred Tennyson, My Grandson.
Williams, William Carlos. Paul.
Wordsworth. Poet to His Grandchild; Sequel to "A Plea for Authors."
Sonnet: "Why should we weep or mourn, Angelic boy."

Granddaughters
Jeffers. Granddaughter.
Rossetti. Lines to My Grandfather.
Williams, William Carlos. Suzy.
3 Stances.

Grandfathers
Berrigan. Cranston Near the City Line.
Berry. Conversation, The.
Berryman. Grandfather, sleepless in a room upstairs.
Bishop. Manners.
Bukowski. Gold Pocket Watch, A.
Coleridge. To the Rev. George Coleridge.
Dobyns. Grandfather Poem, The.
Dove. Roast Possum.
Sunday Night at Grandfather's.
Fletcher. Grandfather's Grave.
Fox. Grandfather.
Glück. Legend.
Graves. Age Gap.
Hacker. Sword.
Hall. Child's Garden, A.
Flies.
Maple Syrup.
Table, The.
Hewitt. Carnations.
Eager Journey.
Ghosts.
Grandfather Robinson Dies in 1898.
I Lie Alone.
My Grandfather Dies, 1923.
Orchard Country.
Seedsman, The.
Townland of Peace.
Jong. Horse from Hell, The.
Kooser. My Grandfather Dying.
Levine. Goodbye.
Nitrate.
Zaydee.
Lowell. Dunbarton.
McAuley. Questions for my Grandfather.
Mahon. Grandfather.
Morgan. Grandfather Poem.
Muldoon. My Grandfather's Wake.
Olson. Grandfather-Father Poem, The.
Rossetti. Lines to My Grandfather.

Sexton. Funnel.
Grandfather, Your Wound.
Shelton. Grandfathering.
Kind of Glory, A.
Stuart. Breakwater.
Hospital of Lies, The.

Grandmothers
Atwood. Five Poems for Grandmothers.
Berry. Grandmother, The.
Bishop. Sestina: "September rain falls on the house."
Carruth. Mother, The.
Crane. My Grandmother's Love Letters.
Cullen. For My Grandmother.
Davie. Housekeeping.
Dunbar. Opportunity.
Duncan. Old women came from their caves to close the too many doors, The.
Fox. Grandmother.
Gallagher. Coats, The.
Glück. Grandmother in the Garden.
Graves. Great-Grandmother, The.
Hall. Flies.
Hartnett. For My Grandmother, Bridget Halpin.
Hewitt. Faded Leaf: A Chapter of Family History, The.
Filled Stocking, The.
House at Ballyholme, The.
My Father's Mother.
My Grandmother Robinson.
My Grandmother's Mother.
Suburban Spring in Warwickshire.
Victorian Steps Out, A.
Hughes, Langston. Dime.
Koertge. My Grandmother.
Levine. Grandmother in Heaven.
Oliver. Answers.
Patchen. At Grandmother's Wake.
Piercy. Snow in May.
Plath. Point Shirley.
Rich. Grandmothers.
St. John. Iris.
Schuyler. Quick, Henry, the Flit!
So Good.
Shapiro. My Grandmother.
Snyder. Old Dutch Woman, The.
Stevenson. Dedicatory Poem.
Stuart. Gesture, A.
Walker. Medicine.
Williams, Charles Kenneth. What Did the Man Do with the Clouds?
Williams, William Carlos. Last Words of My English Grandmother, The.
Last Words of My Grandmother.
Wright, James. My Grandmother's Ghost.
Young. Sunday Sonnet for My Mother's Mother, A.

Grandparents
"Carroll, Lewis." Poeta Fit, Non Nascitur.
Lowell. Grandparents.
Matthews. Recollections.
Nash. Come On In, the Senility Is Fine.
Olson. To Gerhardt, There, among Europe's Things of Which He Has Written Us in His "Brief an Creely und Olson."
Paley. Note to Grandparents.
Spender. Grandparents.
Sutter. Talking To Grandpa Eastman.
Yau. Their Shadows.

Grant, Ulysses Simpson
Gildner. Dear loved one did I mention General Grants.
Sandburg. Bronzes.
Hammers Pounding.
Shapiro. Grant's Tomb Revisited.
Whitman. Death of General Grant.
What Best I See in Thee.
Wilbur. Fourth of July, The.

Grapes
Dickinson. Grapes were big and fresh, The.
Emerson. On a raisin stone.
Frost. Wild Grapes.
Hartley. Violet Grape—and Shadowy Myrtle Leaf.
Hughes, Ted. Wino.
Lawrence. Grapes.

Moore. Fox and the Grapes, The.
Rexroth. Song at the Winepresses, A.

Grass
Berry. On the Hill Late at Night.
Bly. Grass from Two Years.
Dickinson. Grass so little has to do, The.
Eberhart. Cover Me Over.
Emerson. For Lyra yet shall be the pole.
Gunn. Grasses.
Haines. To Turn Back.
Hall. Granite and Grass.
Hemingway. I think that I have never trod.
Larkin. Cut Grass.
Lawrence. Leaves of Grass, Flowers of Grass.
Lovelace. Grasse-Hopper, The.
Merrill. Grass.
Merton. Bees love grass, The.
Rossetti. Thou Knewest...Thou Oughtest
　Therefore.
Sandburg. Grass.
　Grassroots.
　In Tall Grass.
　Man and Dog on an Early Winter Morning.
　Never Two Songs the Same.
　Spring Grass.
　Summer Grass.
　Who was that early sodbuster in Kansas? He
　　leaned at the gatepost and.
Simic. Variant, The.
Spender. Drowned under Grass.
Williams, William Carlos. Province, The.
Wordsworth. This Lawn, a Carpet All Alive.
Wright, James. Two Spring Charms.
Zukofsky. And so till we have died.

Grasshoppers
Clare. Grasshoppers.
Cowper. On the Grasshopper.
Cummings. R-P-O-P-H-E-S-S-A-G-R.
Garrigue. Maimed Grasshopper Speaks Up,
　The.
Keats. On the Grasshopper and [the] Cricket.
Kipling. Shiv and the Grasshopper.
Lindsay. Explanation of the Grasshopper, An.
Lovelace. Grasse-Hopper, The.
Tomlinson. Desert Autumn.
Wilbur. Grasshopper, A.
　Grasshopper and the Ant, The.

Gratitude
Berryman. Prayer for the Self, A.
Boyle. Poem of Gratitude, A.
Browning, Elizabeth Barrett. Sonnet: "I thank
　all who have loved me in their hearts."
　Sonnet: "What can I give thee back, O
　liberal."
Burns. To Mr. Graham of Fintry, On Being
　Appointed to My Excise Division.
Byron. Stanzas to Augusta.
Campion. To My Honourable Friend, Sr.
　Thomas Mounson, *Knight and Baronet.*
To My Worthy Friend, Mr. John Mounson,
　Sonne and Heyre to Sir Thomas Mounson,
　Knight and Baronet.
To the Right Honourable, Both in Birth and
　Vertue, Francis, Earle of Cumberland.
Carruth. Dedication in These Days.
　When I Wrote a Little.
Catullus. Carmen 44: "It depends who's
　talking if you're a 'Sabine'."
　Carmen 100: "Undone or done up with love."
Cowper. Gratitude.
　Gratitude and Love to God.
　To Manso.
Creeley. Song: "God give you pardon from
　gratitue."
　Thank You.
Dickinson. Gratitude—is not the mention.
　Gratitude is the timid wealth.
Dunbar. To an Ingrate.
Dunn. Routine Things Around the House, The.
"Dylan." Covenant Woman.
　In the Summertime.
　Man in Me, The.
　Nobody 'Cept You.
　Saving Grace.
　Solid Rock.
　Wedding Song.

What Can I Do for You?
　You Angel You.
Emerson. Kind & holy were the words.
Everson. Canticle to the Waterbirds, A.
Frost. Closed for Good.
　On Being Chosen Poet of Vermont.
Glück. Gratitude.
Hacker. Chaplet for Judith Landry, A.
Herrick. Primitiæ to Parents, The.
To his Faithfull Friend, Master John Crofts,
　Cup-bearer to the King.
To Sir Clipsebie Crew ("Since to th'Country
　first I came").
To the Most Virtuous Mistress Pot, Who
　Many Times Entertained Him.
Upon Flood, Or a Thankfull Man.
Hewitt. Dedication.
　Drift of Petals, The.
　E.H.
　Ex-Serviceman, The.
　First Honey.
　For Jean.
　Nourish Your Heart.
Hopkins. In the staring darkness.
Jonson. To Esmé, Lord Aubigny.
Koch. Thank You.
Lawrence. Wild Common, The.
Lowry. Pines write a Chinese poem upon the
　white-gold sun.
　With Sweet Devotion and True from All the
　Little Animals.
　Ye pow'rs who make mankind your care.
Meredith. No knightly sword to serve, nor
　harp of bard.
　Now the valley in ruin of fields.
　Question Whither, The.
To Plimmer, Verandah and Cello.
Milton. Manso.
Notley. Sweetheart.
Poe. To M. L. S——.
Rossetti. Christmas Carol, A: "Thank God,
　thank God, we do believe."
Smart. Epistle to John Sherratt, Esq., An.
Smith, Charlotte. To Dr. Parry of Bath, with
　Some Botanic Drawings Which Had Been
　Made Some Years.
Snyder. Prayer for the Great Family.
Stevenson. To Alison Cunningham.
Young. It's India.
　Two A.M.
Zukofsky. Caelius Aufilenus' mate, Quintius
　Aufilena's am.
　O farm, dear nest, or say Sabine, ah say
　Tibur's.

See also **Thankfulness.**

Graves
Auden. Arthur's Quoit, Dyffryn.
Beckett. Plus loin un autre commémore.
Berry. Any man's death could end the story.
Betjeman. Lord Cozens Hardy.
Browning, Robert. Bad Dreams IV.
　Bishop Orders His Tomb at Saint Praxed's
　Church, The.
　Childe Roland to the Dark Tower Came.
　Fame.
Bukowski. Beautiful Young Girl Walking Past
　the Graveyard—, The.
Byron. Churchill's Grave.
Ciardi. Epithalamium at St. Michael's
　Cemetary.
Coleridge. Knight's Tomb, The.
Crashaw. Upon the Sepulchre of our Lord.
Creeley. For Leslie.
Davie. No Epitaph.
De la Mare. Beneath a motionless yew.
　England.
　Even In The Grave.
　Hawthorn Hath a Deathly Smell, The.
Dickey, James. Escape, The.
Dickinson. Ample make this Bed.
　Coffin—is a small Domain, A.
　Color of the Grave is Green, The.
　It was a Grave, yet bore no Stone.
　Not any higher stands the Grave.
　We do not play on Graves.
　Who could be motherless.
Donne. Relic, The.

Eberhart. Bones of Coleridge, The.
　Cemetery, The.
　Ceremony By the Sea, A.
　Concord Cats.
　Dead Skunk.
　Gesture, The.
　Grave Piece.
　I Walked Out to the Graveyard to See the
　　Dead.
　I Walked over the Grave of Henry James.
　Ides of March, The.
　Suite in Prison.
　Ur Burial.
Edmunds. Hill Village, A.
　Taos.
Emerson. In Memoriam.
　Why fear to die.
Frost. In a Disused Graveyard.
Garrigue. Gravepiece.
Hall. Maple Syrup.
　Sister on the Tracks, A.
Hardy. Ah, Are You Digging on My Grave?
　Before My Friend Arrived.
　By the Barrows.
　Evening Shadows.
　In the Evening.
　Marble Tablet, The.
　Nettles, The.
　Poet, A.
　Rain on a Grave.
　Roman Gravemounds, The.
　Sexton at Longpuddle, The.
Herrick. Dirge upon the Death of the Right
　Valiant Lord, Bernard Stuart, A.
　Tapers.
To Anthea: ("Now is the time, when all the
　lights wax dim").
To Biancha.
To Laurels.
To Perenna, A Mistresse ("Deare Perenna,
　prethee come").
To Perenna ("I a Dirge will pen for thee").
To the Yew and Cypress to Grace His
　Funeral.
Upon an Old Man a Residenciarie.
Upon His Departure Hence.
Hesketh. Days.
Hewitt. Covenanter's Grave, The.
　Ossian's Grave, Lubitavish, County Antrim.
Housman. Hughley Steeple.
　Rain, it streams on stone and hillock, The.
　Sigh that heaves the grasses, The.
　With rue my heart is laden.
Hugo. Confederate Graves in Little Rock.
　G. I. Graves in Tuscany.
　Graves at Elkhorn.
　Graves in Queens.
　Indian Graves at Jocko.
　Kilmuir Cemetery: Stone with Two Skulls and
　　No Name.
　Kilmuir Cemetery: The Knight in Blue-Green
　　Relief.
　Somersby.
Jarrell. Come to the Stone.
Jeffers. I have told you in another poem,
　whether you've read it or not.
　Iona: the Graves of the Kings.
　Shakespeare's Grave.
　Subjected Earth.
Knott. Widower's Winter.
Larkin. To Write One Song, I Said.
Lawrence. All Souls.
　Birthday.
　Giorno dei Morti.
Levine. Jewish Graveyards, Italy.
Lindsay. What the Sexton Said.
Lorde. Father Son and Holy Ghost.
Lowell. At the Indian Killer's Grave.
　Sailing Home from Rapallo.
Lowry. Hostage.
　Rain Fell Heavily, The.
MacNeice. Beni Hasan.
　Introduction, The.
Merton. Burial Place of Ibn Abbad, The.
Millay. In the Grave No Flower.
　Lines for a Grave-Stone.
Moore. Grave, A.

Plath. November Graveyard.
Pope. Epitaph Intended for Mr. Rowe, in Westminster Abbey.
Raine. Outside, sun, frost, wind, rain.
Rainbow, beautiful and clear light, A.
Robinson. Cortège.
Leonora.
Rolfe. Epitaph: "Deep in this earth."
Rossetti. Baby's cradle with no baby in it, A.
Flowers Appear on the Earth, The.
For Rosaline's Album.
Gone to his rest / Bright little Bouby!
One Sea-Side Grave.
Song: "When I am dead, my dearest."
There Remaineth Therefore a Rest.
Two Thoughts of Death.
What to Do?
Year Afterwards, A.
Sandburg. Cool Tombs.
Graves.
Smith, Charlotte. By the Same.
Smith, Stevie. Dream.
English Visitor, The.
Grave by a Holm-Oak.
Upon a Grave.
Stevenson. Epitaphium Erotii.
Requiem: "Under the wide and starry sky."
Stuart. Spell.
Sutter. Warming up in their truck.
Thomas. Tombstone Told When She Died, The.
Tomlinson. Arroyo Seco.
Death in the Desert, A.
Epitaph: Enamoured by / Brevity in method.
Wakoski. Dancing on the Grave of a Son of a Bitch.
Whitman. As Toilsome I Wander'd Virginia's Woods.
Dirge for Two Veterans.
Whittier. Grave by the Lake, The.
Naples.
Rock-Tomb of Bradore, The.
Wordsworth. Gravestone upon the Floor in the Cloisters of Worcester Cathedral, A.
Wright, James. Anacreon's Grave.
Eclogue at Nash's Grove.
In a Viennese Cemetery.
Red Jacket's Grave.
Refusal, The.
Way to Make a Living, A.
Zukofsky. For Zadkine.
I Sent Thee Late.
See also **Burial; Cemeteries; Mausoleums; Tombs.**

Graves, Morris
Hartley. Word Arrangements for Pictures by Morris Graves.

Graves, Robert
Graves. Face in the Mirror, The.
My Name and I.
Hoffman. Her Obedient Servant.

Gravevards. see Cemeteries.

Gravity
Berry. Gift of Gravity, The.
Eberhart. Quanta.
Triptych.
Simic. Gravity.
Wilbur. Juggler.
Lightness.
Williams, Miller. One Day a Woman.

Gray, Thomas
Gray. Sketch of His Own Character.
Smith, Charlotte. To the South Downs.
Wilbur. In a Churchyard.

Great Britain. see **England; Northern Ireland; Scotland; Wales.**

Great Depression
Auden. Economics.
Ciardi. Cal Coolidge and the Co.
Dove. Hill of Beans, A.
Hall. 1934.
Hughes, Langston. Madam's Past History.
Relief.
McNeill. Depression Wind (Winter 1930).
Great Depression, The.
Sutter. My dad's old man was a carpenter.

Williams, William Carlos. Portrait of the Times, A.

Great Lakes
Merton. Aubade: Lake Erie.
Sandburg. Lost.

Great Wall, China
Williams, William Carlos. World Contracted to a Recognizable Image, The.

Greatness
Byron. Thou glorious mirror, where the Almighty's form.
Cummings. All ignorance toboggans into know.
Dickinson. Go thy great way!
You said that I "was Great"—one Day.
Eberhart. John Ledyard.
Emerson. For pearls, plunge in the sea.
Γνωθι Σεαυτον.
Shah Sandschar, whose lowest slave.
Jeffers. Great Men.
Ocean.
Teheran.
Lowry. There is a sort of conspiracy about the great.
Melville. On the Photograph of Corps Commander.
Milton. O Jehovah our Lord, how wondrous great.
Nemerov. Chromium-Plated Hat. Inlaid with Scenes from Siegfried, A.
Piercy. Woman in the Ordinary, The.
Psalms. Psalm 8: "O Lord our Lord, how excellent.."
Psalm 93: "Lord reigneth, The.."
Psalm 98: "O sing unto the Lord a new song.."
Psalm 111: "Praise ye the Lord. I will praise.."
Psalm 113: "Praise ye the Lord. Praise, O ye servants.."
Ralegh. No man was better, nor more just than hee.
Spender. The Truly Great.
Spenser. When these sad sights were overpast and gone.
Suckling. Non Est Mortale Quod Opto.
Whitman. Ambition.
By Blue Ontario's Shore.
Wordsworth. Great men have been among us; hands that penned.
See also **Fame.**

Greco, El
Rolfe. Exodus 1947.

Greece
Betjeman. Greek Orthodox.
Boyle. Poem for February First 1975, A.
Poem for the Students of Greece, A.
Browning, Robert. Cleon.
Greece.
Byron. Isles of Greece, the isles of Greece!, The.
On This Day I Complete My Thirty-sixth Year.
Translation of the Famous Greek War Song Deute Paides Tov Ellenon.
Written after Swimming from Sestos to Abydos.
Cohen. Café, The.
Commentary—The Café.
Days of Kindness.
Fragment from a Journal.
Cummings. One April dusk the.
Doolittle. In Our Town.
Islands, The.
Lais.
Nossis.
Dove. Ants of Argos, The.
Nestor's Bathtub.
Pithos.
Eberhart. Cousin Florence.
Love among The Ruins.
Young Greek, Killed In The Wars, A.
Emerson. Elizabeth Hoar.
Poem on Eloquence by R. W. Emerson.
Ferlinghetti. Sailing thru the straits of Demos.
Graves. Ouzo Unclouded.
Gray. Agrippina.

Hall. At Delphi.
Mycenae.
Hemingway. Modern Version of Polonius' Advice, A.
Hewitt. Delos.
Monastary, Tourliani, Mykonos.
Mycenae and Epidaurus.
Mykonos.
Lawrence. Argonauts, The.
MacNeice. Close the vein! It is Easter Eve.
Tall story over a dark sanctum, A.
Which still is much. Here in this mountain village.
McNeill. To the Boys in Freshman History (Thermopylae, 480 B.C.).
Meredith. Foresight and Patience.
Merrill. After Greece.
Charioteer of Delphi, The.
Kostas Tympakianákis.
Piercy. Cats of Greece, The.
Prince. Gregory Nazianzen.
Rolfe. Glory Set, The.
Rukeyser. Canal.
His Head is Full of Faces.
Sandburg. Isle of Patmos.
Near Keokuk.
Sarton. At Lindos.
Birthday on the Acropolis.
Mediterranean.
Myth.
Narcissus.
Shelley. But Greece and her foundations are.
World's great age begins anew, The.
Snodgrass. Coming Down from the Acropolis.
Stevens. From the Packet of Anacharsis.
Thomson. Greece.
Updike. Classical Optical.
Whittier. Hero, The.
Wordsworth. On a Celebrated Event in Ancient History.
Upon the Same Event.

Greed
Berry. Don't own so much clutter that you will be relieved to see your.
We Who Prayed and Wept.
Berryman. Desires of Men and Women.
Browning, Elizabeth Barrett. King's Gift, The.
Browning, Robert. Gold Hair.
Ponte dell' Angelo, Venice.
Burns. Ken Ye What Meg o' the Mill Has Gotten.
Ode, Sacred to the Memory of Mrs. ——— of ———.
Song: "O poortith cauld, and restless love."
Song: "Tibby I hae seen the day."
Such a Parcel of Rogues in a Nation.
There's a youth in this city, it were a great pity.
Tibbie Fowler.
Byron. Love and Gold.
Chaucer. Pardoner's Prologue, The.
Pardoner's Tale, The.
Proverbs: "What shul these clothes thus manyfold."
Cohen. Future Night, A.
My Greed.
Take this Longing.
Cowper. Another ["Art thou some individual of a kind"].
Another ["Miser, traversing his house, A"].
Cottager and His Landlord, The.
From Menander.
On a Miser.
Crane. Pillar and the Post, The.
You Are That Frail..
Cummings. Greedy the people, The.
My(his from daughter's mother's zero mind).
You no / tice / nobod / y wants.
Dobyns. Covetousness.
Greedy Child, The.
Dunbar. For the Man Who Fails.
"Dylan." I'd Hate to Be You on That Dreadful Day.
Talking Bear Mountain Picnic Massacre Blues.
Union Sundown.
Who Killed Davey Moore?

Eberhart. Man's Greed and Envy Are So
  Great.
Emerson. Hamatreya.
  Wealth.
  World is a bride superbly dressed, The.
Ferlinghetti. Director of Alienation.
Frost. Vindictives, The.
Gardner. Nursery Rhyme No. 1.
Graves. Accomplice, The.
  Beggar Maid and King Cophetua, The.
  Lack.
Hardy. Vampirine Fair, The.
Herbert. Size, The.
Herrick. Again.
  Any Way for Wealth.
  Covetous Still Captives, The.
  Upon Greedy.
  Upon Much-More.
  Upon Rush.
Hewitt. Cape Sunion.
Jarrell. Money.
  Nollekens.
  Wide Prospect, The.
Jonson. On Bank the Usurer.
  On Chuff, Banks the Usurer's Kinsman.
  Those that in blood such violent pleasure
  have.
Joseph. In Memory of God.
  Think of the minute amount a mouse eats.
Kipling. Rupaiyat of Omar Kal'vin, The.
Lawrence. Modern Prayer.
  What Is a Man to Do?
  Young Are Not Greedy, The.
McNeill. Lydia Verner.
Meredith. Fusion.
  Josepha.
  Quake, quake, let us turn Quaker all!
  Triad of British Evils, A.
Merton. Keng Sang Chu.
Milton. Fable of the Peasant and the Overlord,
  The.
Morrison. Feast Green Beast.
Nash. Anybody for Money? or, Just Bring
  Your Own Basket.
Olson. *Scream* to the Editor, A.
  War on the Mind in a Time of Love.
Pope. Epistle IV, to Richard Boyle, Earl of
  Burlington.
  Epistle III, to Allen Lord Bathurst.
  On His Grotto at Twickenham.
Robinson. Aaron Stark.
  To curse the chilled insistence of the dawn.
Sandburg. So you want to divide all the
  money there is.
  Unemployed / Without a stake in the country,
  The.
Sexton. March 4th.
  With Mercy for the Greedy.
Shapiro. Waitress.
Silverstein. Fish?
  Just Me, Just Me.
  Lester.
Smart. 2.18: "Gold or iv'ry's not intended."
  Miser and the Mouse, The.
Smith, Stevie. Crown of Gold, The.
  Death-Bed of a Financier.
  Villains.
Tennyson. Northern Farmer: New Style.
Van Duyn. Miser, The.
Whittier. Haschish, The.
  Valuation.
Williams, William Carlos. Con Brio.
  Question and Answer.
Wordsworth. Andrew Jones.
  At Furness Abbey ("Well have yon Railway
  Labourers to THIS ground").
  October, 1803 ("These times strike monied
  worldlings with dismay").
  Proud Were Ye, Mountains, When, in Times
  of Old.
  Repentance; A Pastoral Ballad.
  Star-Gazers.
  To the Pennsylvanians.
  Two Thieves, The; or, the Last Stage of
  Avarice.
  Written in London, September, 1802.

Yeats. Three Beggars, The.
  Witch, The.
Zukofsky. Arizona.
Green (color)
Berry. Green and White.
Carruth. Four greens / the poplar trunk.
  Leaves, The.
Creeley. Christmas: May 10, 1970.
Dickey, James. Poem: "For having left the
  birds that left me."
Eberhart. Spring was never his fort. Suspect at
  first.
Graves. Variables of Green.
Lawrence. Green.
Schuyler. I Think.
Sorrentino. Variations 2.
Stein. Go in Green.
Stevens. Candle a Saint, The.
  Phosphor Reading by His Own Light.
Tomlinson. Focus.
  Green Quinces.
Young. Green Is a Feeling, Not a Color.
Zukofsky. —"Her Soil's Birth."
  Que J'ay Dit Devant.
Greene, Graham
Knott. Brighton Rock by Graham Greene.
Liddy. Homage to Conor Cruise O'Brien.
Greenhouses
Cowper. Winter Nosegay, The.
Hardy. Frozen Greenhouse, The.
Roethke. Big Wind.
  Child on Top of a Greenhouse.
  Forcing House.
Rossetti. How many authors are my first!
Stevens. Poesie Abrutie.
Greenwich Village, New York City
Carruth. Re-Acquaintance.
Markson. Women's House of Detention.
Paley. Boys from Saint Bernard's, The.
"Reed." Halloween Parade, The.
Gregory, Lady Augusta
Yeats. Municipal Gallery Revisited, The.
Gregory, Robert
Yeats. In Memory of Major Robert Gregory.
Grenada
Walcott. Landfall, Grenada.
Greyhounds
Kipling. FEBRUARY (*Coursing*).
Grief
Berg. Heartache.
  In Washington Square.
  To the Same Place.
  Why Are We Here?
Berry. Grief.
  Poem for J.
  To be at home on its native ground.
Berryman. "Broken heart.." but *can* a heart
  break, now?, A.
  Epilogue: "He died in December. He must
  descend."
  For you an idyl, was it not, so far.
  Impossible to speak to her, and worse.
  Parting as Descent.
  Surviving Love.
  Three, almost, now into the ass's years.
Blake. On Another's Sorrow.
Brontë. Castle Wood.
  Day Dream, A.
  E.W. to A.G.A.
  Stanzas: "Often rebuked, yet always back
  returning."
Browning, Elizabeth Barrett. Bereavement.
  Claim, The.
  Exaggeration.
  Felicia Hemans.
  Grief.
  Sea-Mew, The.
  Sonnet: "If I leave all for thee, wilt thou
  exchange."
Bukowski. You Smoke a Cigarette.
Bunting. Song for Rustam, A.
Burns. Elegy on Captain Matthew Henderson
  [*or* Capt. M——— H———] [A *Gentleman*
  Who Held the Patent for His Honours
  Immediately from Almighty God!].
  Fair Jenny.

Fragment, Which Was Meant for the
  Beginning of an Elegy on the Late Miss
  Burnet of Monboddo, A.
  Lament for James, Earl of Glencairn.
  On Reading, in a Newspaper, the Death of
  J——— McL———, Esq. Brother to a
  Young Lady, a Particular Friend of the
  Author's.
  Raving winds around her blowing.
  Song: "Had I a cave on some wild, distant
  shore."
  Song.—In the Character of a Ruined Farmer.
Byron. And Wilt Thou Weep When I Am
  Low?
  Away, Away, Ye Notes of Woe!
  Ode to a Lady Whose Lover Was Killed by a
  Ball, Which at the Same Time Shivered a
  Portrait next His Heart.
  Oh! Snatch'd Away in Beauty's Bloom.
  Stanzas for Music.
  Stanzas: "I heard thy fate without a tear."
  To Florence.
  Translation from Catullus ("Ye Cupids, droop
  each little head").
Campion. Could my heart more tongues
  imploy.
  Elegie upon the Untimely Death of Prince
  Henry, An.
  If any hath the heart to kill.
  Illustrissimo, Potentissimoque Principi,
  Frederico Quinto, Rheni Comiti Palatino,
  Duci Bavariae, &c.
  Since she, ev'n shee, for whom I liv'd.
  To the Most Disconsolate Great Brittaine.
  To The Most Sacred King James.
Carew. Grief Engrossed.
  To the Countess of Anglesey.
  Upon the King's Sickness.
"Carroll, Lewis." Melancholetta.
Carruth. Niobe, your tears.
Catullus. Carmen 3: "Who loves beauty / vel
  her statues."
  Carmen 65: "Although entangled in prolonged
  grief."
  Carmen 96: "If, Calvus, effects of grief."
  Carmen 101: "Journeying over many seas and
  through many countries."
Cohen. My Lady Can Sleep.
  To a Fellow Student.
Coleridge. Monody on the Death of
  Chatterton.
  On Receiving an Account That His Only
  Sister's Death Was Inevitable.
Cooper. Holding Out.
Creeley. For Leslie.
  Greendoon's Song.
Cummings. 1.24: "Who chides the tears that
  weep so dear a head?"
Davie. Break, The.
De la Mare. Argument, The.
  Captive, The.
  Clear Eyes.
  Courage.
  Disguise, The.
  For All the Grief.
  Music.
  Oh, Why?
  Reflections.
  Riddlers, The.
  Widow, The.
Dickinson. After great pain, a formal feeling
  comes.
  Bereavement in their death to feel.
  Bustle in a House, The.
  Butterfly upon the Sky, The.
  Grief is a Mouse.
  Grief of wonder at her fate.
  I can wade Grief.
  I measure every Grief I meet.
  If all the griefs I am to have.
  Perhaps the dear, grieved Heart.
  So glad we are—a Stranger'd deem.
  Summers of bloom—and months of frost.
  'Tis good—the looking back on Grief.
Dobyns. Grief.
Donne. Elegy on the L. C.
  If faithful soul[e]s be alike glorified [*or*

glorifi'd].
O might those sigh[e]s and tear[e]s return[e] again[e].
Triple Fool, The.
Valediction, A: Forbidding Mourning.
Dunbar. Change Has Come, The.
In the Tents of Akbar.
Love and Grief.
Love's Chastening.
Phyllis.
Sea speaks to me of you, The.
Yesterday and Tomorrow.
Dunn. Sweetness.
"Dylan." Tears of Rage.
Eberhart. Loss.
New England Protestant.
Trying to Hold It All Together.
Emerson. I grieve that better souls than mine.
There resides in the grieving.
Fletcher. From the Japanese, IV.
Gallagher. Rhododendrons.
Garrigue. Grief Was to Go Out, Away.
Glück. Last Letter.
Triumph of Achilles, The.
Graves. Brief Reunion.
Gentleman, The.
Hooded Flame.
Prison Walls.
Reproach.
Gray. Amatory Lines.
Death of Hoel, The.
Epitaph on Mrs Jane Clarke.
Song: "Thyrsis, when we parted, swore."
Sonnet [on the Death of Mr. Richard West].
Gunn. Blank, A.
Monster, The.
Hall. Our Walk in Yorkshire.
Sister by the Pond, A.
Hardy. Bereft.
Confession to a Friend in Trouble, A.
He Prefers Her Earthly.
Hartley. It was to learn that grief is a major.
Hartnett. Prayer at Death.
Herbert. Affliction (3).
Confession.
Grief.
Herrick. Anacreontike.
Bucolick betwixt Two: Lacon and Thyrsis, A.
Crosses.
Ease.
Faire after Foule.
Felicity, Quick of Flight.
Griefe ("Consider sorroowes, how they are aright").
Griefe ("Sorrowes divided amongst many, lesse").
Griefes.
Happinesse.
His Comfort.
His Weaknesse in Woes.
Observation ("Virgin-Mother stood at distance [there], The").
To His Kinswoman, Mistresse Susanna Herrick.
To Primroses Filled with Morning Dew.
Upon the Bishop of Lincolne's Imprisonment.
Will Makes the Work, or Consent Makes the Cure, The.
Hesketh. All Hallows.
Hewitt. For Jean.
Grief ("I thought when the grave was sodded").
Grief ("When men lie down for ever / and names their tombstones take").
Ocean, 1940.
Hill. As he is wounded.
Coplas.
Hopkins. Nightingale, The.
No worst, there is none. Pitched past pitch of grief.
Spring and Fall.
Housman. Bredon Hill.
Land of Biscay, The.
Hughes, Langston. Widow Woman.
Hugo. Remember Graham.
Jonson. On My First Son [or Sonne].

Slow, slow, fresh fount, keep time with my salt tears.
Joseph. Man as Image (MASSIF; CHEMISTRY).
Kipling. Children, The.
Kingdom, The.
London Stone.
Night we felt the earth would move, The.
Only Son, An.
Son, A.
Knott. Widower's Winter.
Larkin. Deep Analysis.
If Grief Could Burn Out.
Portrait.
Thaw.
Lawrence. Another Ophelia.
Bereavement.
Brooding Grief.
Change of Life.
Dust in the East.
Going Back.
Grief.
Hymn to Priapus.
Sorrow.
Levertov. Lamentation, A.
Lewis. Renewal.
Songs of Sleep.
Liddy. For Jimin in Manchuria II.
Longfellow. Cross of Snow, The.
Lorde. Memorial I.
Suffer the Children.
Lovelace. Guiltlesse Lady Imprisoned; after Penanced, A.
In Allusion to the French Song.
Lucasta Paying Her Obsequies.
To His Deare Brother Colonel F.L.
Vintage to the Dungeon, The.
When Portia her dear I Lord's sad fate did hear.
Lowry. Jokes Aloft.
Mr. Lowry's Good Friday under a Real Cactus.
Old Woman who Buried Cats, The.
Sadness is so much a part of me.
Thoughts While Drowning: But Try to Eliminate the Argument.
McAuley. "Alle Herrlichkeit Des Menschen."
Secret.
"MacDiarmid." At My Father's Grave.
MacLeish. He leans against the window-sill.
Marvell. Mourning.
Melville. Martyr, The.
Monody.
Meredith. Chillianwallah.
Dost thou behold some woeful soul.
Ever invoking fire from heaven, the fire.
Flower of the Ruins, The.
Horses of Achilles, The.
If thou art sorrowful, hide thy face!
Lesson of Grief, The.
Two Blackbirds, The.
Merrill. Willow.
Millay. As to some lovely temple, tenantless.
Felicity of Grief!—even Death being kind.
Grief that is grief and properly so hight.
Interim.
Lament: "Listen, children: / Your father is dead."
Once more into my arid days like dew.
Song of a Second April.
Three Songs of Shattering.
Time does not bring relief; you all have lied.
To One Who Might Have Borne a Message.
When the tree-sparrows with no sound through the pearl-pale air.
Wood Road, The.
Milton. Sonnet 23: "Mee thought I saw my late espoused saint."
Morgan. Catullus: Carmen ci.
Nemerov. Ahasuerus.
Anniversary.
Oliver. Murderer's House, The.
Three Poems for James Wright.
Olson. All You Can Do.
Owen. Happiness.
Hospital Barge at Cérisy.

Patchen. O now the drenched land wakes.
Unanswering Correspondences, The.
Plath. Departure.
Poe. Annabel Lee.
For Annie.
Pope. Weeping.
Raine. Spell Against Sorrow.
Ralegh. Farewell to the Court.
Rexroth. Andrée Rexroth.
Robinson. Reuben Bright.
Roethke. Apparition, The.
Sequel, The.
Rossetti. All Flesh Is Grass.
Alleluia! or Alas! my heart is crying.
Better So.
By the Waters of Babylon.
Cried Out with Tears.
Death of a First-Born, A.
Death's Chill Between.
Despair.
Gone Before.
Heart Knoweth Its Own Bitterness, The.
Heart's Chill Between.
Hope in Grief.
If I Had Words.
Life Out of Death.
Love Defended.
Margery.
Novice, The.
On the Death of a Cat.
One of the Dead.
Passing away the bliss, / The anguish passing away.
Seeking Rest.
Song: "Stream moaneth as it floweth, The."
Song: "When I am dead, my dearest."
Sonnet from the Psalms.
Summer Is Ended, The.
Surely He Hath Borne Our Griefs.
Three Moments.
Undine.
Vanity of Vanities.
Yet a Little While.
Rukeyser. Christmas Eve.
Flattered by grief, the changeable spirit.
Sandburg. Right to Grief, The.
Sarton. Of Grief.
Scott. Coronach.
Shakespeare. Sonnet 28: "How can I then return in happy plight."
Sonnet 40: "Take all my loves, my Love, yea, take them all."
Sonnet 50: "How heavy do I journey on the way."
Sonnet 90: "Then hate me when thou wilt; if ever, now."
Shelley. Dirge, A: "Rough wind, that moanest loud."
Fragment: "My head is wild with weeping for a grief."
Lament, A: "O world! O life! O time!"
Sunset, The.
Sidney. Hark, plaintful ghosts! Infernal furies, hark.
How Is My Sun.
I joy in grief, and do detest all joys.
Leave off my sheep: it is no time to feed.
Sonnet 93: "O fate, O fault, O curse, child of my bliss."
Sonnet 94: "Grief, find the words, for thou hast made my brain."
Smith, Charlotte. Lydia.
Ode to Despair.
Reflections on Some Drawings of Plants.
Snowdrops.
Verses Intended to Have Been Prefixed to the Novel of Emmeline, but Then Suppressed.
Smith, Stevie. And the Clouds Return after the Rain.
Ceux Qui Luttent.
English Visitor, The.
Happiness.
No Respect.
So to Fatness Come.
Spanish School.
Story I Have Told, The.
Stevens. Another Weeping Woman.

Stevenson. Before this little gift was come.
Suckling. Upon the Black Spots Worn, by My Lady D.E.
Sutter. This woman is nobody's woman.
Swift. Occasioned by Sir William Temple's Late Illness and Recovery.
Tate. Adaption of a Theme from Catullus.
Tennyson. Break, Break, Break.
Calm is the morn without a sound.
Dark house, by which once more I stand.
I Held It Truth (with Him Who Sings).
Sweet after showers, ambrosial air.
Tears, Idle Tears.
Thomas. Grief Ago, A.
Grief Thief of Time.
Out of the Sighs.
Thomson. On the Death of his Mother.
Turco. Cancer.
Walker. At First.
Warren. Leaf, The.
Whitman. Come Up from the Fields Father.
Whittier. Funeral Tree of the Sokokis.
Telling the Bees.
To My Friend on the Death of His Sister.
Vesta.
Williams, William Carlos. Widow's Lament in Springtime, The.
Wordsworth. Death of a Starling, The.
Force of Prayer, The; or, The Founding of Bolton Priory; A Tradition.
Maternal Grief.
O flower of all that springs from gentle blood.
O Lelius, beauteous flower of gentleness.
Sonnet: "If grief dismiss me not to them that rest."
Wright, James. Complaint.
Down to the Dregs.
Listening to the Mourners.
Song: "Love as well can make abiding."
Wroth. Song 1: "Spring now come att last, The."
Song 7: "Sorrow, I yeeld, and grieve that I did miss."
Sonnet 4: "Cruell suspition, O! bee now att rest."
Sonnet 4: "Forbeare darke night, my joyes now budd againe."
Sonnet 8: "How gloewoorme like the sunn doth now apeere."
Sonnet 8: "Led by the powre of griefe, to waylings brought."
Sonnet 28: "Griefe, killing griefe: have nott my torments binn."
Sonnet 36: "How well poore hart thou wittnes canst I love."
Wyatt. Alas, the grief and deadly wo[e]ful smart[!].
All heavy minds.
And wilt [or wylt] thou le[a]ve me thus?
At mo[o]st mischief.
Blame not my lute, for he must sound [or sssnd or Sownde].
Complaining, alas, without redress.
Duress of pains and grievous smart.
Flaming sighs that boil within my breast, The.
If in the world there be more woe.
Sighs are my food, drink are my tears.
Young. Day Kennedy Died.
Dreams of Paradise.
Zukofsky. Lament, o graces of Venus, and Cupids.
Mulled hosts their countries yet mulled there by a core of wake tossed.
See quick calm moot as gratifying the tombed—sepulchres.
Yet see (may as I do) a confect of my cure— a dolor.
See also **Sorrow; Mourning and Mourners.**

Grocers
Simic. Grocery.
Williams, Charles Kenneth. Bread.
Racists.

Groundhogs
Eberhart. Groundhog Revisiting, The.
Groundhog, The.
Frost. Drumlin Woodchuck, A.
Plath. Incommunicado.

Growth
Ashbery. Boy, A.
Grapevine, The.
Spring Day.
Young Son, The.
Berry. Broken Ground, The.
Familiar, The.
Farmer among the Tombs, The.
Seeds, The.
Sycamore, The.
Boyle. What Parents Do Not Yet Know.
Brooks. Big Bessie Throws Her Son into the Street.
Browning, Elizabeth Barrett. Isobel's Child.
Carroll, Jim. Growing Up.
Clough. Shall I decide it by a random shot?
Cowper. On a Plant of Virgin's Bower.
Cummings. Am was. are leaves few this. is these a or.
But also dying / (as well as).
If everything happens that can't be done.
Might these be thrushes climbing through almost(do they).
Dickinson. Could you tell me how to grow.
Growth of Man—like Growth of Nature.
Her Sweet turn to leave the Homestead.
I could not prove the Years had feet.
Solemn thing within the Soul, A.
Doolittle. I could say, / red.
Dunbar. Old Front Gate, The.
Song: "My heart to thy heart."
Eberhart. Cage, The.
Forms of the Human.
In after Time.
Mind and Nature.
Rumination.
Stealth and Subtleties of Growth.
Truncated Bird, The.
What Gives.
Emerson. Cloud upon cloud / The world is seeming.
Coral worm beneath the sea, The.
Go out into Nature and plant trees.
Holidays.
Principle of all things; entrails made.
To Ellen, at the South.
To every creature / Adam gave its name.
What never was no, & still will be.
Who saw the hid beginnings.
Galvin. Mayflies.
Gunn. Aqueduct.
Value of Gold, The.
Haines. For Anne, at a Little Distance.
Sun on Your Shoulder, The.
Tree, The.
Hall. Exile.
Hardy. Second Attempt, A.
Herrick. To God ("Lord, I am like to mistletoe").
Hewitt. House Demolished, A.
Interval.
Periodicity.
Hoffman. Folk Tale.
Housman. Loitering with a vacant eye.
Jong. Autumn Perspective.
Kipling. 'Eathen, The.
Kooser. North of Alliance.
Levine. Pili's Wall.
Winter Words.
Lorde. Dear Toni Instead of a Letter of Congratulation.
Lowell. Growth (Harriet).
"MacDiarmid." All life's million conflicting interests and relationships.
To a Friend and Fellow Poet.
MacNeice. And what when the glass breaks when the Note sounds?
How, yes how! To achieve in a world of flux and bonfires.
McNeill. Garden Moment.
Nemerov. Mars.
Notley. January.
O'Hara. Poem: "There I could never be a boy."
Olson. Imbued / with the light.
Out of the light of Heaven the flower.
Plantation a Beginning, A.

Piercy. Perpetual Migration, The.
Raine. Rose.
Rolfe. Pastoral: "Now, on this bluest of mornings, we wake."
Rukeyser. He is breaking the nets in his wildness for the real.
Hero Speech.
Work in the loss of mass, The.
Sandburg. Crabapple Blossoms.
Follies.
Laughing Corn.
Loam.
Out of the Rainbow End.
Shelton. Outcast.
Southwell. Times [or Tymes] Go[e] By Turn[e]s.
Stevenson. As in their flight the birds of song.
Looking Forward.
My Shadow.
Nay, but I fancy somehow, year by year.
Nest Eggs.
To My Name-Child.
Stuart. Midget, The.
Birthday.
Tomlinson. How Far.
Witnesses, The.
Updike. Ode to Growth.
Planting Trees.
Whitman. Return of the Heroes, The.
Wilbur. Fern-Beds in Hampshire County.
Seed Leaves.
Wood, A.
Williams, Charles Kenneth. When / you were small, I.
Wordsworth. Companion to the Foregoing [Love Lies Bleeding].
My heart leaps up when I behold.
Wright, Charles. Self-Portait ("Pictures in the air have few visitors, The").
Young. Dancing Naked.
Winter Leaves.
Zukofsky. Mountain Laurel.

Guadalajara, Mexico
Ashbery. Instruction Manual, The.

Guatemala
Koertge. In South America on Business He Does Something He Is Ashamed of yet on the Way Home Dreams of It Again and Again.
Stevens. Arrival at the Waldorf.
Williams, Charles Kenneth. Guatemala: 1964.

Guerrillas
Heaney. Requiem for the Croppies.
Kipling. Arithmetic on the Frontier.
Ballad of Boh Da Thone, The.
Grave of the Hundred Dead, The.
Stevens. Revolutionists Stop for Orangeade, The.
Wordsworth. French and the Spanish Guerrillas, The.
Spanish Guerilas 1811.

Guest, Edgar A.
Nash. Lines to a World-famous Poet Who Failed to Complete a World-famous Poem; or, Come Clean, Mr. Guest!

Guests
Auden. For Friends Only.
Berry. Guest, The.
Berryman. Mysteries, The.
Bishop. House Guest.
Campion. Ad Ge. Chapmannum.
De la Mare. Feckless Dinner Party, The.
Hall. Wedding Party.
Hewitt. Folk for Tea.
Hospitality: For E.K.
Jonson. Inviting a Friend to Supper.
Nash. I Know Exactly Who Dropped the Overalls in Mrs. Murphy's Chowder.
Polterguest, My Polterguest.
There's Always an Ubblebub.
Patchen. Intimate Guest, The.
Silverstein. Spaghetti.
Stevenson. Hail, guest, and enter freely! All you see.
Lo, now, my guest, if aught amiss were said.

See also **Hospitality; Visiting and Visitors.**
Guilt
Angelou. My Guilt.
Atwood. Last year I abstained / this year I devour.
Berg. In Blue Light.
Visit, The.
Berry. Throwing away the Mail.
Burns. Penitential Thought, in the Hour of Remorse—Intended for a Tragedy, A.
Remorse.
Byron. Prayer of Nature, The.
Stanzas for Music.
Campion. What harts content can he finde.
Carroll, Jim. Dresden to Chesapeake Bay.
It is afternoon a sailor is crying above the waterfall.
Carruth. For thon demgeorne dreorigne oft.
Chaucer. Physician's Tale, The.
Ciardi. Two Saints.
Clough. In Stratis Viarum II.
Like a child.
Crashaw. To Pontius Washing His Hands.
Creeley. Teachings, The.
Cummings. Ballade: "Does something lie who'd rather stand."
Guilt is the cause of more disauders.
It started when Bill's chip let on to.
Davie. Machineries of Shame.
Dunbar. Debt, The.
Dunn. Cleanliness.
"Dylan." Only a Pawn in Their Game.
Who Killed Davey Moore?
Emerson. For that a man is a mark.
No fate, save by the victim's fault, is low.
Everson. Black Hills, The.
Hare: An Earlier Episode, The.
Fenton. Vacant Possession, A.
Gallagher. Small Garden Near a Field.
Gardner. Mea Culpa.
Of Conscience.
Of Mercy.
Who Spilled the Salt?
Ginsberg. Blame the Thought, Cling to the Bummer.
"Drive All Blames into One."
Graves. Blanket Charge.
Semi-Detached.
Trial of Innocence.
Gunn. High Fidelity.
Haines. Inside the shell of our skulls.
Hall. By the Exeter River.
September Ode.
Hardy. Blow, The.
Brother, The.
Caricature, The.
Rake-hell Muses.
Vampirine Fair, The.
Herbert. Conscience.
Herrick. Blame.
Upon Paske a Draper.
Hesketh. Betterwear Man, The.
Hewitt. My Teachers.
Simple-Minded Christian, The.
Jarrell. Bamberg.
Eighth Air Force.
Today is almost over.
Jeffers. Blood-Guilt, The.
Kunitz. Guilty Man, The.
Lewis. Slug, The.
Soubrettes, The.
Lieberman. Skateboard Throne: an Ode to Citizen Amputees, The.
Lowry. Deserter.
Thoughts While Drowning: But Try to Eliminate the Argument.
MacLeish. Carrion Crow, The.
Morrison. End of the Rainbow, The.
There's Blood in the Streets.
Nash. Down the Mousehole, and What Science Missed There.
Inter-Office Memorandum.
Period I.
Strange Case of the Blackmailing Dove, The.
Nathan. Season's Greetings.
Neruda. Child of the Moon.

Danger, The.
Wars, The.
Prince. He Bathes in the Morning.
Letter.
Rich. Education of a Novelist.
If I lay on that beach with you.
Poem of Women.
Rape.
Upcountry.
Rolfe. Season of Death.
War Guilt.
Rossetti. Escape to the Mountain.
Surely there is an aching void within.
Weigh all my faults and follies righteously.
Rukeyser. Cannibal Bratuscha.
Song of Another Tribe, A.
Sandburg. Smoke.
Sarton. Tortured, The.
Who Wakes.
Schwartz. He Who Excuses Himself Also Accuses Himself.
Sexton. Earth Falls Down, The.
Hex, The.
Shapiro. Tree of Guilt, The.
Shelton. Guilt.
Smith, Stevie. Oh What Is the Thing He Done?
Snodgrass. Inquest.
Sorrentino. Gimlet.
Midnight Special.
Southwell. Mary Magdalen's Blushe.
Spender. Double Shame, The.
Sutter. Talking To Grandpa Eastman.
Warren. Crime.
Pursuit.
Red Mullet, The.
Revelation.
Whitman. Of Many a Smutch'd Deed Reminiscent.
Wilbur. Peter.
Pity.
Williams, Charles Kenneth. Another Dollar.
Blame.
Combat.
Image, The.
That night, / winter, / rain.
Williams, Miller. For Victor Jara.
Wright, Charles. California Spring.
Guitars
Beatles. While My Guitar Gently Weeps.
Brontë. Lady to Her Guitar, The.
Dickey, James. Rain Guitar, The.
Larkin. Two Guitar Pieces.
Lieberman. Tartine, Strumming Her Opera.
Lowry. Stoker Tom's Ukulele.
St. John. Guitar.
Stevens. Jouga.
Man with the Blue Guitar, The.
Gulls
Browning, Elizabeth Barrett. Sea-Mew, The.
Ciardi. Gulls Land and Cease to Be.
Coleridge. Looking Seaward.
Swallows interweaving there mid the paired, The.
Dunn. Update.
Eberhart. Gulled.
Fletcher. Gulls, The.
Hartley. Confidence.
We have broken bread.
Hayden. Gulls.
Hewitt. Grey and White.
Hoffman. At Provincetown.
Hugo. Gull Hardly Explained, The.
Jeffers. Storm blowing up, rain and dark weather and the roaring wind, The.
Joseph. False Postulate.
Lowry. Love of a Seagull.
McGrath. Poem: "Through the fog / The gulls."
MacLeish. Before March.
Nash. Sea-Gull, The.
Nemerov. Gulls, The.
Lives of Gulls and Children, The.
Olson. Pente cōst under the body of the gull flying directly over.
Oppen. On that water / Grey with morning.
Sexton. Gull.

Smith, Stevie. Numbers.
Stevenson. Visit from the Sea, A.
Tomlinson. Faring, The.
Gull.
Updike. Seagulls.
Warren. Gull's Cry.
Wilbur. Harbor, The.
Two Songs in a Stanza of Beddoes'.
Williams, William Carlos. Gulls.
Song: "Black-winged gull, The."
Wright, James. Morality of Poetry, The.
Poem by Garnie Braxton, A.
Zukofsky. Gulls over a rotting hull.
Gum Trees
Frost. Gum-Gatherer, The.
Gunpowder Plot. *see* **Fawkes, Guy.**
Guns
Beatles. Happiness Is a Warm Gun.
Rocky Raccoon.
"Carroll, Lewis." Facts.
Puck Lost and Found.
Cooper. Nightmare of the Suburbs, A.
Cowper. On the Inventor of Guns.
Creeley. Two Times ("It takes so long to look down").
Cummings. Bigness of cannon, The.
Dobyns. Gun, The.
Dunn. Sudden Light and the Trees, The.
Graves. Shot, The.
Hall. Merle Bascom's .22.
Hardy. Channel Firing.
Hewitt. Case of Mistaken Identity, A.
Iron Circle, The.
Nineteen Sixteen, or the Terrible Beauty.
Second Front: Double Summertime, July 1943.
Two Spectres Haunt Me.
Ulsterman in England Remembers, An.
Kipling. Jacket, The.
Screw-Guns.
Snarleyow.
Knight. Boone County.
Knott. Beddybye.
Kunitz. Careless Love.
Lawrence. Murderous Weapons.
MacLeish. Hemingway.
Merton. Guns of Fort Knox, The.
Milton. On the Inventor of Gunpowder.
Nemerov. September Shooting.
Owen. Arms and the Boy.
Sonnet: "Be slowly lifted up, thou long black arm."
"Reed." Gun, The.
Rolfe. Casualty.
City of Anguish.
St. John. Lemons, The.
Sandburg. A. E. F.
Iron.
Long Guns.
Whitman. Artilleryman's Vision, The.
Williams, Charles Kenneth. Crime.
Wright, James. Echo for the Promise of Georg Trakl's Life.
Gustavus II (Gustavus Adolphus), King of Sweden
Carew. In Answer of an Elegiacal[l] Letter, Upon the Death of the King of Sweden [from Aurelian Townsend, Inviting Me to Write on That Subject].
Wordsworth. Call not the royal Swede unfortunate.
Guy Fawkes Day. *see* **Fawkes, Guy.**
Guyana
Walcott. Guyana.
Gwyn, Nell
Williams, William Carlos. King!, The.
Gymnastics and Gymnasts
Hesketh. Gymnasts, The.
See also **Acrobatics and Acrobats.**
Gypsies
Auden. Gipsy Girl, The.
Campion. Song: "Shadowes darking our intents, The."
Clare. Gipsies: "Gipsies seek wide sheltering woods again, The."
Gipsies: "Snow falls deep; the forest lies alone, The."

Cohen. Gypsy Wife, The.
"Dylan." Spanish Harlem Incident.
Went to See the Gypsy.
Emerson. Romany Girl, The.
Graves. Batxóca.
Hewitt. Tinker's Answer, The.
Jonson. From the famous Peak of Derby.
Joseph. Subscription.
Keats. Old Meg She Was a Gipsy.
Kipling. Gipsy Trail, The.
Gipsy Vans.
Lawrence. Gipsy.
Lindsay. I Know All This When Gipsy
Fiddles Cry.
Tramp's Refusal, The.
Mahon. Gipsies.
Matthews. Babahak.
Meredith. Sweetheart of the Csikos, The.
Three Gipsies, The.
To an Old Gipsy.
Sandburg. Fame If Not Fortune.
Gypsy.
Gypsy Mother.
Wordsworth. Gypsies.

H

Habits
Atwood. You take my hand and.
Beckett. Vieil aller / vieux arrêts.
Clark. Clemente (1934-1972).
Creeley. Mountains in the Desert, The.
One Day.
Operation, The.
Gallagher. Sugar.
Graves. Love Charms.
Herrick. Upon Ralph ("Ralph pares his
nayles").
Upon Tubbs.
Lowry. Men With Coats Thrashing.
Markson. At the Lion's Head.
Marlowe. 1.10: Ad puellam, ne pro amore
praemia poscat.
Nathan. Closure.
Surprise.
Rolfe. Now the Fog.
Sorrentino. Je Connai Gens de Toutes Sortes.
Young. Kicking.
Zukofsky. Immature Pebbles.

Hades
Browning, Elizabeth Barrett. Psyche and
Cerberus.
Psyche and Proserpine.
Carruth. None.
Cowper. By Heraclides.
De la Mare. Shade, The.
Herrick. Orpheus and Pluto.
Meredith. Then again in disorderly woods.
Merton. Souls smell in hades.
Raine. Descent Into Hades.
These watery diamond spheres.
Robinson. Aretemias.
Rukeyser. In the Underworld.

Hafiz
Emerson. 'ΑΔΑΚΡΥΝ ΝΕΜΟΝΤΑΙ ΑΙΩΝΑ.
Friendship ("Thou foolish Hafiz! Say, do
churls").
Hafiz.

Haggard, Sir Henry Rider
Auden. Sir Rider Haggard / Was completely
staggered.

Haggis
Burns. To a Haggis.

Haiku (form)
Hewitt. Gloss, on the Difficulties of
Translation.
Wilbur. Sleepless at Crown Point.
Yau. Sam Spade Haiku.

Hail
Heaney. Hailstones.
Hopkins. Strike, churl; hurl, cheerless wind,
then; heltering hail.
Lowry. Morning rain is sleeting, The.
Williams, Charles Kenneth. Hail goes /
dancing, The.

Zukofsky. Rains, the rains, The.

Hair
Bishop. Shampoo, The.
Bly. Conversation, A.
Browning, Elizabeth Barrett. Sonnet: "Soul's
Rialto hath its merchandise, The."
Bukowski. Red Up and Down.
Texan.
Burns. Bonie Mary.
Fragment: "Her flowing locks, the raven's
wing."
"Carroll, Lewis." Lang Coortin', The.
Only a Woman's Hair.
Clark. Ah—There.
Cowper. Delia, th' unkindest girl on earth.
On an Old Woman.
To a Lady ["Star that beams on Anna's breast,
The"].
Cummings. Hair your a brook.
Dickey, William. Pruned Roses, The.
Dunn. Turning Fifty.
Emerson. And rival Coxcombs with enamored
stare.
Plunge in yon angry waves.
Samson stark at Dagon's knee.
Fox. To Do More Than Hair.
Gallagher. Ever After.
Graves. Snap-Comb Wilderness, The.
Gunn. Skateboard.
Hardy. Tresses, The.
Herrick. On Jone.
Upon Blanch.
Upon His Gray Haires.
Upon Julia's Haire, Bundled up in a Golden
Net.
Upon Julia's Haire Fill'd with Dew.
Housman. Oh who is that young sinner with
the handcuffs on his wrists?
Jong. On Sending You a Lock of My Hair.
Knott. Shorts / Excerpts ("Hope...goosestep").
Lawrence. So There!
Levertov. Psalm Praising the Hair of Man's
Body, A.
Lieberman. Love, the Barber.
Lindsay. In Praise of Gloriana's Remarkable
Golden Hair.
On Suddenly Receiving a Curl Long Refused.
To Lady Jane.
Lovelace. To Amarantha, That She Would
Dishevel[l] Her Hair[e].
Lowry. And Samson said if yo' shave ma
hair.
Pigs—For T.H.
Marlowe. 1.14: Puellam consolatur cui prae
nimia cura comae deciderant.
Nash. Electra Becomes Morbid.
I'll Get One Tomorrow.
My Dream.
Nathan. Tendril.
Nemerov. History of Hair from World War II
to the Present.
Piercy. Hello Up There.
Sign.
Rich. Parting: II, The.
Rossetti. Johnny.
Rukeyser. Boy with His Hair Cut Short.
Sandburg. Red-Headed Resstaurant Cashier.
Women Washing Their Hair.
Schuyler. Suddenly.
Silverstein. Colors.
Long-Haired Boy, The.
My Beard.
Upstairs.
Snodgrass. Phoebe's Nest, A.
Spenser. XXXVII. "What guile [or guyle] is
this, that those her golden tresses."
Stuart. My Hostess at the Renovated Inn.
Swinburne. Rondel: "Kissing her hair."
Updike. Klimt and Schiele Confront the Cunt.
Williams, William Carlos. Spring.
Yeats. For Anne Gregory.

Hairdressers
Griffiths. Hairdresser, Age 55, Dalston.

Haiti
Cullen. Black Majesty.
Lieberman. Creole Mephistopheles, The.
Prayer against the Curse Bomb.

Whittier. Toussaint L'Ouverture.

Halloween
Atwood. Paper Bag, A.
Burns. Halloween.
Carruth. Metaphysical.
Cummings. Hist whist / little ghostthings.
Glück. All Hallows.
Lowry. I am speeding through the northern
lights.
Mysterious Hint, A.
Piercy. Hallow Eve with Spaces for Ghosts.
"Reed." Halloween Parade, The.
Sandburg. Theme in Yellow.

Hamlet
Auden. Thomas Prologizes.
Bukowski. Weather Report.
Carruth. Your dream is Hamlet again.
De la Mare. Hamlet.
Eberhart. Broken Pen, The.
Hamlet Father, The.
Fox. April Fool.
Lewis. Atropos to Ophelia.
Lindsay. Epitaphs for Two Players.
Hamlet.
Nash. Strange Case of the Lovelorn Letter
Writer, The.
Nemerov. Orphic Scenario.
Sandburg. They All Want to Play Hamlet.
Smith, Stevie. Easy.
Tomlinson. Lacunae.

Hammers and Hammering
Creeley. For Fear.
Silverstein. Bang-Klang.
Wilbur. Folk Tune.

Hammocks
Davie. Amazonian.

Hamsters
Nash. Hamster, The.

Handball
Dunn. Day and Night Handball.

Handicaps and the Handicapped
Herrick. Upon Truggin.
Hugo. Freaks at Spurgin Road Field, The.
Merton. Man with One Foot and the Marsh
Pheasant, The.
Owen. Disabled.
Patchen. Poor Child with the Hooked Hands,
The.
Thomas. Hunchback in the Park, The.
Williams, Charles Kenneth. Hooks.
Wordsworth. Idiot Boy, The.
See also **Amputees; Birth Defects; Blindness;
Cripples; Deafness; Mental Retardation.**

Hands
Atwood. You Begin.
Auden. Hands.
Beatles. I Want to Hold Your Hand.
Berg. People Trying to Love.
Berry. Current, The.
Put your hands into the mire.
Bogan. Heard by a Girl.
Clark. Garland of Red, A.
Crane. Episode of Hands.
Creeley. Box, The.
Dimensions.
Figures, The.
For Friendship.
In an Act of Pity.
Medallion.
People, The.
Tally, A.
You.
Davie. Hot Hands.
Duncan. Upon Taking Hold.
Eberhart. Hand and the Shadow, The.
Hand, The.
Ferlinghetti. At the *Gare Bruxelles-Midi*.
Fox. Hands.
Rescue.
Gallagher. Meeting, The.
Some with Wings, Some with Manes.
Gildner. Letter From My Good Hand, A.
Gunn. Feel of Hands, The.
Herrick. Hand and Tongue, The.
Right Hand, The.
Housman. As through the wild green hills of
Wyre.

Jeffers. Hand.
   Hands.
Keats. This Living Hand, Now Warm and
   Capable.
Kinnell. Poem of Night.
Knott. (Face) (Autumn) (En Face).
Kooser. Old Soldiers' Home.
Levine. Fist.
Lorde. Pirouette.
Lovelace. Her Muffe.
Lowry. My two hands broke in two: and they
   broke me!
   Two frozen claws / In two frozen minutes.
McGrath. Praises IV.
MacNeice. Nothing more simple. Among the
   tarnished.
Paley. Veins that stand on the back of my
   sunburned hand, The.
Patchen. There is the hand that has nothing
   attached to it, no arm no chest.
Piercy. Friend, The.
St. John. Man in the Yellow Gloves, The.
Sandburg. Sayings, sentences, what of them?
   White Hands.
Sexton. Maiden without Hands, The.
   Touch, The.
   Two Hands.
   When the Glass of My Body Broke.
Shapiro. Love for a Hand.
Shelton. My Hands Are My Enemies.
Smith, Stevie. Ceci est digne de gens sans
   dieu.
Stafford. My Hands.
   Turn Over Your Hand.
Stevens. Hand as a Being, The.
Sutter. Motto above my table says, The.
Thomas. Hand That Signed the Paper, The.
Tomlinson. Palm of the Hand.
Updike. Calder's Hands.
Wilbur. Good Servant, The.
Williams, Charles Kenneth. Hooks.
   Other Side, The.
Williams, William Carlos. Your lovely hands.
Wright, James. Red Jacket's Grave.
Yeats. Balloon of the Mind, The.
Zukofsky. Glad they were there.

Handwriting
Nemerov. Writing.

Hanging
Angelou. We Saw Beyond Our Seeming.
Atwood. Marrying the Hangman.
Bishop. Hanging of the Mouse, The.
Burns. Geordie [An Old Ballad].
   McPherson's Farewell.
Campion. Epigramme: "Smith, by sute divorst,
   the knowne adultres."
Eberhart. Snowy Owl.
Gardner. Ballade: "You who outlive us, you,
   our mortal brothers."
Hemingway. To Will Davies.
Herrick. Upon Letcher: Epigram.
Housman. Carpenter's Son, The.
   Culprit, The.
   Eight O'Clock.
   On moonlit heath and lonesome bank.
Kipling. Danny Deever.
Levine. L'Homme et La Bête.
Lowry. To Herr Toller, Who Hanged Himself.
MacLeish. Galán.
Melville. Portent, The.
Millay. Hangman's Oak.
Plath. Hanging Man, The.
Sandburg. Hangman at Home, The.
Smith, Stevie. Hostage, The.
Swift. Clever Tom Clinch Going to Be
   Hanged.
Warren. Ballad of Mister Dutcher and the Last
   Lynching in Gupton.
See also **Executions and Executioners;**
   Lynching.

Hangovers
Burns. To William Stewart.
Lowry. Hangover—Reading Rilke, Schnitzler
   or Someone, A.
   Morning bird sits mutely, The.
   With Great Love Oh Beloved Harteebeeste
   from El Leon.

Wright, James. Two Hangovers.
Young. Hangover.

Hansel and Gretel
Glück. Gretel in Darkness.
Jarrell. Quilt-Pattern, A.
Koertge. Gretel.
McGrath. Remembering the Children of
   Auschwitz.
Sexton. Hansel and Gretel.

Happiness
Ammons. Salute.
Atwood. You Are Happy.
Auden. After the Storm.
   Detective Story.
   Early Morning Bathing.
   Frost.
   Glad.
   Memento Creatoris Tui.
   Two Triolets.
Beatles. Good Day Sunshine.
Boyle. Glad Day for Laurence Vail, A.
Brontë. How still, how happy! These [or
   Those] are words.
Browning, Robert. At the "Mermaid."
Bukowski. Skaters, The.
Burns. First Psalm, The.
   My Eppie.
   O gude ale comes and gude ale goes.
   Song: "My father was a farmer upon the
   Carrick border O."
   Young Jockey was the blythest lad.
Byron. Well! Thou Art Happy.
Carew. To My Cousin (C.R.) Marrying My
   Lady (A.).
Catullus. Carmen 9: "Veraniolus, / first of
   friends."
Clare. Old Man, The.
Coleridge. Angel Visitant, An.
   Happy Husband, The.
   Homeless.
   To Asra.
Cowper. Poet's New-Year's Gift, The.
   To Health.
Creeley. Air: "The Love of a Woman."
   For Betsy and Tom.
   For Joel.
   Indians.
   Je Vois dans le Hasard Tous les Biens Que
   J'espere.
   Lady Bird.
   Soup.
Cullen. One Day We Played a Game.
   Spring Reminiscence.
Cummings. I am so glad and very.
   Out of more find than seeks.
   You shall above all things be glad and young.
De la Mare. I Sit Alone.
   Self to self.
Dickinson. Accept my timid happiness.
   By Chivalries as tiny.
   Enough is so vast a sweetness.
   Good times are always mutual.
   "Happiness" without a cause, The.
   I fear you have much happiness.
   I had a daily Bliss.
   She's happy, with a new Content.
   Such is the Force of Happiness.
Dove. Pearls.
Dunbar. Love Letter, A.
Duncan. O Outrider! / when you come to the
   threshold of the stars.
Dunn. Observer, The.
"Dylan." Al's wife claimed I can't be happy.
   Down Along the Cove.
   New Morning.
Eberhart. Adam Cast Forth.
Emerson. O sun! take off thy hood of clouds.
Ferlinghetti. Heaven / was only half as far
   that night.
Ford. If someone asked you to be happy.
Frost. Happiness Makes Up in Height for
   What It Lacks in Length.
Gildner. Wean Poem.
Ginsberg. Scribble.
Glück. Happiness.
   Letter from our Man in Blossomtime.

Graves. As When the Mystic.
   Everywhere Is Here.
Griffiths. Chips.
Hacker. Late August Letter.
Hardy. Occultation, The.
Hayden. Islands, The.
Herrick. Anacreontike.
   Felicitie Knowes No Fence.
   Felicity, Quick of Flight.
   Few Fortunate.
   Four[e] Things Make Us Happy Here.
   Happinesse.
   None Truly Happy Here.
Hesketh. Party, The.
   Violet at Ninety.
Hewitt. For Roberta in the Garden.
   Happy Man, The.
   We too have gone down little roads in spring.
   Winter Day.
Hoffman. It cannot come because desired.
Hughes, Ted. Bull Moses, The.
Jarrell. Happy Cat, The.
Knight. Eat Helen B Happy (a Found Poem).
Kunitz. First Love.
Lawrence. Wedlock.
Levertov. Joy.
Levine. Starlight.
Lindsay. Sunshine.
Lowry. But we little animaux have gone.
   Doggerel.
   Good Luck.
   Happiness.
   Happy birthday to you.
   Hartebeeste Both Grave and Gay, The.
   Harteebeeste Is Here Again, The.
   Lusty Advice of a Fortune-Teller.
   Moon in Scandinavia, The.
   3 Happy Little Ducks.
   "MacDiarmid." To Hell wi' Happiness!
MacNeice. Take this old man with the
   soldierly straight back.
   With you, pray not without you, trapped on
   the edge of the world.
Marlowe. Another of the Same Nature, Made
   Since.
Meredith. Here Jack and Tom are paired with
   Moll and Meg.
J. C. M.
   Joy is Fleet.
Merton. All of the branches / None of the
   roots.
   Joy of Fishes, The.
Morgan. Summit, The.
Nathan. Certain Prospects and Spectacular
   Diversions.
Neruda. Possessions.
Oliver. Goldfinches.
   Happiness.
   Hummingbird Pauses at the Trumpet Vine.
   Morning Poem.
   Poppies.
   Sunrise.
Oppen. Theological Definition, A.
Owen. Happiness.
Paley. If you have acquired a taste for
   happiness.
Patchen. What There Is.
Piercy. Apologies.
Poe. Dreams.
Pope. Ode on Solitude.
   Version of the First Psalm, for the Use of a
   Young Lady, A.
Pound. Salutation.
Raine. Leaf, The.
   Oval Portrait: Jessie Wilkie, The.
Rich. In the Woods.
Robinson. Cliff Klingenhagen.
   Happy Man, A.
Roethke. Waking, The.
Rossetti. Dancing on the hill-tops, / Singing in
   the valleys.
   I toiled on, but thou.
   In resurrection is it awfuller.
   Love is all happiness, love is all beauty.
   Trees' Counselling, The.
   Will you be there? my yearning heart has

cried.
Young Death.
Rukeyser. Chapultepec Park / I.
Sandburg. Fellow Citizens.
Happiness.
Shag-Bark Hickory.
Snatch of Sliphorn Jazz.
Two Neighbors.
Shelley. Past, The.
Song: "Rarely, rarely, comest thou."
Sidney. Sonnet 70: "My Muse may well grudge at my heav'nly joy."
Silverstein. Land of Happy, The.
Simic. Happy End.
Smith, Charlotte. He may be envied, who with tranquil breast.
To the Countess of A—. Written on the Anniversary of Her Marriage.
Smith, Stevie. And the Clouds Return after the Rain.
Conviction (iv).
Happiness.
Is It Happy?
Mother.
V.
Written at the Close of Spring.
Sorrentino. Prince Rupert's Drop.
Stevens. Crude Foyer.
Of Bright & Blue Birds & the Gala Sun.
Stevenson. Happy Thought.
Unseen Playmate, The.
Sutter. Nordeast.
Thomas. Upon Happiness.
Thomson. Happy Man, The.
Updike. Pale Bliss.
Wakoski. Winter Poem for Tony Weinburger Written on the Occassion of Feeling Very Happy, A.
Walcott. Something primal in our spine makes the child swing.
Walker. Mississippi Winter II.
Warren. Mediterranean Beach, Day after Storm.
Whitman. Halcyon Days.
Song of Joys, A.
When I Heard at the Close of the Day.
Wilbur. Happy the Man.
Wedding Toast, A.
What's Good for the Soul is Good for Sales.
Williams, William Carlos. Better than flowers.
Wordsworth. Fragments from Dove Cottage Manuscript 44 (II).
Wright, James. Blessing, A.
Moon.
Northern Pike.
Today I Was So Happy, So I Made this Poem.
Way to Make a Living, A.
White Rose.
Yau. Stumbling blocks are realigned, The.
Young. In Marin Again.
Madness.
O!
Zimmer. Julian Barely Misses Zimmer's Brains.
Zukofsky. Happier, happier, now.
Happiest February.
Marriage Song for Florence and Harry, A.
Veranius of all my beloved friends.

See also **Contentment.**

Harbors and Ports
Carroll, Jim. Poem: "My footsteps in the shallow."
Cooper. Leaving Water Hyacinths.
Crane. Harbor Dawn, The.
Dickinson. To multiply the Harbors.
Galvin. Seals in the Inner Harbor.
Hardy. Harbour Bridge, The.
Marble-Streeted Town, The.
Hugo. Letter to Peterson from the Pike Place Market.
Port Townsend.
Jarrell. Metamorphoses, The.
Lewis. Port of Call: Brazil.
Southend at Dusk.
Lowry. On Reading R.L.S.
Olson. Intended Angle of Vision Is from My Kitchen, The.

Oppen. Heart pounds / To be among them, the buildings, The.
Men of Sheepshead, The.
Monument.
Time of the Missile.
Plath. Green Rock, Winthrop Bay.
Rukeyser. Formosa.
Wind arrow, wind rose, the wind currents in air.
Sandburg. Destroyers.
Docks.
Smith, Patti. Anna of the Harbor.
Tomlinson. Arrival, The.
Sconset.
Walcott. Harbour, The.
Wilbur. Harbour, The.
Zukofsky. Heights, The.

Harding, John Wesley
"Dylan." John Wesley Harding.

Harding, Warren Gamaliel
Ashbery. Qualm.
Cummings. First president to be loved by his, The.
O'Hara. Poem: "That's not a cross look it's a sign of life."
Wright, James. Two Poems about President Harding.

Hardy, Thomas
Betjeman. Heart of Thomas Hardy, The.
De la Mare. Thomas Hardy.
Fletcher. Black Rock, The.
Lawrence. And Jude the Obscure and His Beloved.
Tomlinson. In Memoriam Thomas Hardy.
Walcott. Love in the Valley.
Wright, James. At Thomas Hardy's Birthplace, 1953.

Hares
Burns. On Seeing a Wounded Hare Limp by Me, Which a Fellow Had Just Shot At.
Cowper. Epitaph on a Hare.
Epitaphium Alterum.
De la Mare. Hare, A.
Everson. Hare: An Earlier Episode, The.
Hesketh. Imprint.
Hewitt. At Shottery, Anne Hathaway's Cottage.
"MacDiarmid." Ross-shire Hills, The.
Merton. Hare's Message.
Smart. To the Rev. Mr. Powell.
Walcott. Grey English road hissed emptily under the tires, The.
Yeats. Two Songs of a Fool.

See also **Rabbits.**

Harlem, New York City
Angelou. Harlem Hopscotch.
"Dylan." Spanish Harlem Incident.
Edmunds. December 27, 1988.
Nocturne.
Hughes, Langston. College Formal: Renaissance Casino.
Comment on Curb.
Dive.
Good Morning.
Harlem.
Island.
Juke Box Love Song.
Likewise.
Neighbor.
Night Funeral in Harlem.
Not a Movie.
Passing.
Projection.
Knight. Harlem.
Merton. Aubade—Harlem.
Rukeyser. Ballad of Orange and Grape.
Schuyler. Mood Indigo.
Updike. Eurydice.

Harper's Ferry, West Virginia
Sandburg. Landscape Including Three States of the Union.

Harps and Harpists
Brontë. Harp of wild and dream-like strain.
Coleridge. Ad Lyram.
Eolian Harp, The.
Snow-Drop, The.

Dunbar. Master-Player, The.
To a Lady Playing the Harp.
Eberhart. Play, The.
Emerson. He loved to watch & wake.
Thy trivial harp will never please.
Haines. Stone Harp, The.
Liddy. June 16, 1992.
Lindsay. Harps in Heaven.
Melville. Æolian Harp, The.
Millay. Ballad of the Harp-Weaver, The.
Smart. Inscriptions on an Aeolian Harp.
Stuart. Harpist's Dream, The.
Wordsworth. On Seeing a Needlecase in the Form of a Harp; the Work of E.M.S.

Hartley, Marsden
Hartley. Soliloquy in Dogtown, Cape Ann.

Harvard University
Cummings. Little joe gould has lost his teeth and doesn't know where.
Eberhart. I Went to See Irving Babbitt.
Sanders Theater.
Moore. In Lieu of the Lyre.
Nash. Mind of Professor Primrose, The.
Updike. Apologies to Harvard.
Widener Library, Reading Room.
Within a Quad.

Harvest
Atwood. November.
Bly. Dawn in Threshing Time.
Carruth. Emergency Haying.
In late winter cold nights.
De la Mare. Scarecrow, The.
Dryden. Song by Comus and Three Peasants, A.
Glück. All Hallows.
Haines. Harvest.
Hartley. Five Women.
Herrick. Hock-Cart, or Harvest Home, The.
Upon Nodes.
Hewitt. Alien Harvest.
Failed Image.
Threshing, The.
Hopkins. Hurrahing in Harvest.
Lawrence. Youth Mowing, A.
Longfellow. Aftermath.
MacLeish. Sowing of the Dead Corn, The.
McNeill. Clearing, The.
Katchie Verner's Harvest.
Mountain Corn Song.
Marlowe. 3.9: Ad Cererem, conquerens quod eius sacris cum amica concumbere non permittatur.
Melville. Trophies of Peace.
Meredith. Desired as Summer rain.
Song: "My chosen bride shall bless the plough."
Miller. Harvesters.
Nash. Not Even for Brunch.
Nemerov. Fat time of the year is also time, The.
Harvest Home, A.
Rossetti. For All.
For Each.
Rogationtide.
Seasons.
When My Heart Is Vexed I Will Complain ("Fields are white to harvest, look and see, The").
Yea, I Have a Goodly Heritage.
Sandburg. Corn Hut Talk.
Harvest.
You Shall Have Homes.
Stevenson. In Lupum.
Swinburne. August.
Tomlinson. Harvest Festival: at Ozleworth.
Turco. Scythe, The.
Whittier. Huskers, The.
Wordsworth. Solitary Reaper, The.
Wright, James. In Fear of Harvests.

Harvey, Gabriel (1545?–1630)
Spenser. To the Right Worshipfull, My Singular Good Frend, Master Gabriell Harvey, Doctor of the Lawes.

Hashish
Ford. Unwashed, unbedded. / He has fine bones and a.

Smith, Patti. Hymn: "We hadn't eaten in two days. we were entirely intoxicated."
Whittier. Haschish, The.

Hasidism
Prince. Drypoints of the Hasidim.

Hate
Angelou. Artful Pose.
Faces.
Atwood. Holding my arms down.
Auden. There Will Be No Peace.
Berry. In the thought of you I imagine myself free of the weapons and the official hates that I have borne on my back like a hump.
Morning's News, The.
Who has invented our enmity? Who has prescribed us.
Window grows fragile, The.
Browning, Robert. Halbert and Hob.
Soliloquy of the Spanish Cloister.
Bukowski. Genius of the Crowd, The.
Carew. First of Jealousy. Dialogue, The.
Catullus. Carmen 108: "If, by general consent, it should be decided."
Ciardi. My Tribe.
Cohen. Commentary—The News You Really Hate.
News You Really Hate, The.
What I'm Doing Here.
Crashaw. But Now They Have Seen, and Hated.
Creeley. Crow, The.
Cullen. Apostrophe to the Land.
Black Christ, The.
Dickinson. I had no time to Hate.
Doolittle. Epigrams.
She is dead.
To love, one must slay.
Dunbar. To an Ingrate.
Duncan. Up Rising.
"Dylan." I used t' hate enzo.
Only a Pawn in Their Game.
Eberhart. Assassin, The.
Hatred of the Old River.
Edmunds. Black Bull, The.
Everson. Eastward the armies.
Frost. Beyond Words.
Hemingway. Captives.
Hewitt. Iron Circle, The.
Lines for a Dead Alderman.
Little House, The.
Parallels Never Meet.
Street Names.
Well-Intentioned Consul, The.
Hill. Dead Bride, The.
Hopkins. Love me as I love thee. O double sweet!
Housman. In my own shire, if I was sad.
Hughes, Langston. Georgia Dusk.
Jeffers. Bird with the Dark Plumes, The.
Jonson. Little Shrub Growing By, A.
Kipling. Beginnings, The.
Jubal and Tubal Cain.
Poison of Asps.
Lawrence. Both Sides of the Medal.
Can't Be Borne.
Dead People.
Eloi, Eloi, Lama Sabachthani?
History.
Love.
Repulsed.
Lowry. Loathing is as beautiful as the scourge.
My hate is as a wind that buffets me.
Passing Impatience With a Noble Country, A.
Schoolboy's Complaint, The.
Visiting the Wreck: An Able Seaman Explains.
Wild Cherry, The.
McAuley. Aor Against the Bad Reviewer.
Aor Against the Philistine Who Destroyed Lovely Dublin Vistas With His Ugly Erections, Then Absconded to London.
MacNeice. Belfast.
Millay. Blight.
Milton. What Though the Field Be Lost?
Nash. One Night in Oz.
O'Hara. Poem: "Hate is only one of many

responses."
Spleen.
Olson. Fable for Slumber.
Hate.
Leader, The.
Poemless Rhymes for the Times.
Patchen. Don't Wash Your Hair in the Streetcar, Nora Dear.
Piercy. Letter to be Disguised as a Gas Bill.
Rape Poem.
"Reed." Original Wrapper, The.
Robinson. Avon's Harvest.
Roethke. Lull.
Rolfe. Not Hatred.
Sandburg. Accordingly, they commenced by an insidious.
From the people the countries get their names.
Hate.
Man, the Man-Hunter.
Sexton. Children, The.
Fury of Hating Eyes, The.
Shakespeare. Sonnet 10: "For shame! deny that thou bear'st love to any."
Sonnet 145: "Those lips that Love's own hand did make."
Sonnet 149: "Canst thou, O cruel! say I love thee not."
Shelley. Hate-Song, A.
Lines to a Critic.
Sidney. Love which is imprinted in my soul, The.
Smith, Stevie. I HATE THIS GIRL.
Stevenson. I have a friend; I have a story.
Suckling. Love, Reason, Hate, did once bespeak.
Love Turned to Hatred.
Walker. First, They Said.
January 10, 1973.
Warren. Child Next Door, The.
Williams, Charles Kenneth. Beyond.
In the Heart of the Beast.
Poor Hope.
Williams, William Carlos. Love Poem, A:"Basic hatred / Sometimes has a flower."
Mistrust of the Beloved.
Wright, James. In the Face of Hatred.
Wyatt. Such is the course that nature's kind hath wrought.
Zukofsky. "Immediate Aim, The."
Old.
See, Comini, popular arbitrer turned on uncanny senescence.

Hats
Bishop. Exchanging Hats.
Manuelzinho.
Burns. Cock up Your Beaver.
"Carroll, Lewis." First Voice, The.
Dove. Headdress.
"Dylan." Leopard-Skin Pill-Box Hat.
Emerson. Comfort with a purring cat.
Hall. Second Stanza, A.
Hardy. In the Days of Crinoline.
Herrick. Upon Shift.
Kooser. Grandfather Cap, The.
Nash. Drop of a Hat, The.
Nemerov. Enthusiasm for Hats.
Sandburg. Hats.
Quotations.
Sky Pieces.
Schuyler. Hats.
Silverstein. Upstairs.
Smith, Stevie. Hat, The.
Magna Est Veritas.
My Hat.
Snodgrass. Dostoievsky Warns W. D. about Wearing Raskolnikov's Hat.
Stevens. Pastor Caballero, The.

Haunted Houses
"Carroll, Lewis." Canto I: The Trystyng.
Canto IV: Hys Nouryture.
Canto V: Byckerment.
Davie. House, The.
De la Mare. Feckless Dinner Party, The.
Who's that?
Frost. Ghost House.
Graves. Country Mansion, A.
Haunted House, The.

Hill. Asmodeus.
Neruda. Untenable Situation, An.
Silverstein. Enter This Deserted House.

Havana, Cuba
Crane. Eternity.
Ginsberg. Havana 1953.
Stevens. Academic Discourse at Havana.

Hawaii
Berryman. Song of the Young Hawaiian, The.
Dickey, William. Heroine, The.
Updike. Heading for Nandi.

Hawks
Atwood. Marsh, Hawk.
Eberhart. Forgotten Rock, The.
Gunn. Tamer and Hawk.
Hopkins. Windhover, The.
Hughes, Ted. Hawk Roosting.
Hugo. Hawk in Uig.
Jeffers. Hurt Hawks.
Old half blinded hawk—but how can he hunt with only one eye?—, The.
Rock and Hawk.
Jonson. To Sir Henry Goodyere.
McAuley. Gesture, A.
MacLeish. Poem for the Time of Change.
Oliver. Hawk.
Oppen. Workman.
Thomas. Over Sir John's Hill.
Tomlinson. Hawks.
How Still the Hawk.
Warren. Evening Hawk.
Problem in Spatial Composition, A.
Yeats. Hawk, The.
Young. Sentience.

Hawthorn (botany)
Heaney. Haw Lantern, The.
Hesketh. Mary.
Jarrell. Trees in Spring, The.
Raine. Frost-rime edges blades of grass.
Swift. On Cutting Down the Old Thorn at Market Hill.
Tomlinson. Providence.

Hawthorne, Nathaniel
Creeley. Nathaniel Hawthorne.
Longfellow. Hawthorne.
Lowell. Hawthorne.
Melville. Monody.
Walcott. Love in the Valley.

Hay and Haymaking
Dickinson. I'm sorry for the Dead—Today.
Gunn. At the Back of the North Wind.
Hall. Table, The.
Hewitt. Fame.
Footing Turf.
Hay.
Haymaking in the Low Meadow.
MacLeish. Where the Hayfields Were.
Meredith. Windy Haymaking.
Stevenson. Hayloft, The.
Tomlinson. Hay.
Wright, James. Lament for My Brother on a Hayrake.

Haydon, Benjamin Robert
Browning, Elizabeth Barrett. On a Portrait of Wordsworth by B. R. Haydon.
Keats. Addressed to Haydon.
To B.R. Haydon, with a Sonnet Written on Seeing the Elgin Marbles.
Wordsworth. To B.R. Haydon.
To B.R. Haydon, On Seeing His Picture of Napoleon Buonaparte on the Island of St Helena.

Haymaking. see **Hay and Haymaking.**

Haze. see **Fog.**

Hazlitt, William
Coleridge. W. H. *Eheu!*

Heads
Bukowski. Big Bastard with a Sword.
Sword, The.
12:18 A.M.
Eberhart. Dream Journey of the Head and Heart.
Haines. Head on the Table, The.
Herrick. Head-Ake, The.
Sandburg. Head.
Schuyler. Head, A.

Silverstein. Chester.
Young. Head of a Woman.

Health Clubs
Gunn. To the Dead Owner of a Gym.

Heaney, Seamus
Davie. Summer Lightning.

Hearts
Angelou. Greyday.
Atwood. Heart Test with an Echo Chamber.
This is the secret: these hearts.
Woman Makes Peace with Her Faulty Heart,
The.
Woman Who Could Not Live With Her Faulty
Heart, The.
Beckett. How hollow heart and full.
Berryman. "Broken heart.." but *can* a heart
break, now?, A.
Bishop. Weed, The.
Browning, Elizabeth Barrett. Calls on the
Heart.
False Step, A.
My Heart and I.
Byron. On a Cornelian Heart Which Was
Broken.
Carew. Celia Bleeding, to the Surgeon.
Mistake, The.
"Carroll, Lewis." Christmas Greetings.
Miss Jones.
Stolen Waters.
Carruth. Apology for Using the Word "Heart"
in Too Many Poems, An.
Clark. Superballs.
Clough. I have seen higher holier things than
these.
In Stratis Viarum IV.
Coleridge. Loss.
Crane. Hive, The.
Creeley. Echo.
Mind's Heart.
Trap, The.
Wanting You.
Cullen. Foolish Heart, The.
Proud Heart, The.
Cummings. Dedication: "White rose my soul,
The."
I carry your heart with me(i carry it in).
Lady you have written me a letter.
Must being shall.
These people socalled were not given hearts.
Three wealthy sisters swore they'd never part.
Davie. Heart Beats.
De la Mare. Be angry now no more!
Fleeting, The.
Night.
Dickey, James. Angina.
Dickinson. Heart has narrow Banks, The.
Poor little Heart!
Donne. Blossom [*or* Blossome], The.
Dream, The.
Legacy [*or* Legacie], The.
Message, The.
Doolittle. To love, one must slay.
Dunn. That Saturday Without a Car.
"Dylan." Heart of Mine.
Eberhart. Anima.
Dream Journey of the Head and Heart.
Going.
Secret Heart, The.
Ways and Means.
Emerson. Dost thou not hear me Ellen.
Fair fall thy soft heart!
I know this perilous love-lane.
I will not live out of me.
If he go apart.
Loose the knots of the heart; never think on
thy fate.
Perhaps thy lot in life is higher.
Roomy Eternity / Casts her schemes rarely.
Since you set no worth on the heart.
This effervescing gentleman who despises a
secret.
Though her eye seek other forms.
Frost. Devotion.
Glück. Portrait.
Gunn. Sacred Heart.
Herrick. Christs Part.
Frozen Heart, The.

Heart, The.
His Weaknesse in Woes.
Of Love. A Sonnet.
To Oenone ("What conscience, say, is it in
thee").
Upon Lupes.
Wounded Heart, The.
Hesketh. Christmas Blackmail.
Traitor.
Hewitt. Ballad, The.
Bell, The.
Dichotomy.
Grief ("I thought when the grave was
sodded").
I've Known Her Turn from Bitter Phrase.
Nourish Your Heart.
Twisted Heart, The.
Hill. If the night is dark.
Koch. Simplicity of the Unknown Past, The.
Larkin. If Hands Could Free You, Heart.
Lawrence. Heart of Man, The.
Metal for Resistance.
Liddy. Talking to Clare as.
Lovelace. Answer, The.
Loose Saraband, A: (Ah me! the little Tyrant
Theefe!).
To Lucasta ("Like to the sentinel [*or* Sent'nel]
stars, I watch all night").
Lowell. Colloquy in Black Rock.
Lowry. Born ailing on a hemisphere apart.
But we little animaux have gone.
Fisherman's Return.
Give me a poem / To wring the hearts of
men.
Harteebeeste Is Here Again, The.
Prayer: "Oh thou who art not above."
Queer Poem.
Simple Seabird's Tribute to Her Harteebeeste,
A.
Song for a Marimba.
Still speeding to your heart.
Villanelle, an Interviewo on Morale.
Welcome Home oh Harteebeeste beloved who
doth with thy.
Welcome Home oh Harteebeeste mio.
Welcome Home, Oh Sweetest Harteebeeste.
With Sweetest Love and Sunday Anthems or
Sweetest Goodnight from All the Little
Animals.
Meinke. Heart's Location, The.
Merton. Sacred Heart 2.
Transformation: For the Sacred Heart, The.
Millay. Heart, do not bruise the breast.
Olson. Heart is a clock, The.
Patchen. Mechanical Heart, The.
Prince. At Beaulieu.
"Reed." Tell It to Your Heart.
Rexroth. Spark in the Tinder of Knowing,
The.
Rossetti. As a King, ...Unto the King.
Because Thy Love hath sought me, / All mine
is Thine and Thine is mine.
From early dawn until the flush of noon.
Hope Carol, A.
If I should ever say "my heart is in my
home."
Like as the Hart Desireth the Water Brooks.
Lord, comest Thou to me?
Sunday Before Advent.
When I Was in Trouble I Called upon the
Lord.
Sandburg. Beat, Old Heart.
Sexton. Dead Heart, The.
Doctor of the Heart, The.
Old Dwarf Heart.
Shakespeare. Sonnet 151: "In faith, I do[e] not
love thee with mine eyes."
Shelley. From the Arabic: An Imitation.
Lines: "When the lamp is shattered."
Sidney. Sonnet 12: "Cupid, because thou
shin'st in Stella's eyes."
Smith, Stevie. La Gretchen de Nos Jours (II).
Voice from the Tomb (3).
Sorrentino. Anatomy.
Oleo Strut.
Thomas. When All My Five and Country
Senses See.

Walcott. Fist, The.
Waldman. Matriarchly.
Throw Matches at the Sun!
Two Hearts.
Walker. Never Offer Your Heart to Someone
Who Eats Hearts.
Warren. Debate: Question, Quarry, Dream.
Williams, Charles Kenneth. Shells.
Williams, William Carlos. Portrait of a Young
Man with a Bad Heart.
Wright, James. At Thomas Hardy's Birthplace,
1953.
Jewel, The.
Wroth. Love's Victorie.
Song: "Deerest if I by my deserving."
Sonnet 13: "Free from all fogs butt shining
faire, and cleere."
Sonnet: "Eyes, can you tell mee wher my hart
remaines?"
Yeats. Her Vision in the Wood.
Owen Aherne and His Dancers.
Song, A; "I thought no more was needed."
Zukofsky. Ashtray.
Finally a Valentine.
On Valentine's Day to Friends.
Sequence 1944-6.

Heat
Bukowski. Thermometer.
Carruth. When some amazonian indians for
whom.
Clark. Diary of Desert War.
Gift of Tongue.
Coleridge. Perspiration: A Travelling Eclogue.
Davie. Barnsley Cricket Club.
Hardness of Light, The.
Dickey, James. Basics.
Gila Bend.
Dunbar. Summer Pastoral, A.
Eberhart. Great Praises.
Man of Autumn, The.
Nexus.
Galvin. Warmth.
Graves. Cool Web, The.
Hall. Table, The.
Hemingway. Flat Roofs.
God is away for the summer.
Herrick. Frozen Heart, The.
Health.
Hesketh. Heat-Wave.
Hughes, Ted. Sunstroke.
Kipling. Pagett, M. P.
Koch. Boiling Water, The.
Lawrence. Drill in the Heat.
Lowry. Heat Wave.
With a Great Goodmorning Kiss and Luck and
Love to Our Beloved Harteeste from All the
Little Animals.
Markson. This Vision Comes.
Matthews. Eternally Undismayed Are the
Poolshooters.
March Heat.
Merton. Tropics.
Morrison. Tender Island Night.
Nash. September Is Summer, Too.
O'Hara. My Heat.
Pack. Autumn Warmth.
Rich. Burning Oneself In.
Rolfe. Winter's Ghost Plagues Them.
Sorrentino. Drifting South.
Spenser. My Love Is Like to Ice.
Tomlinson. Las Trampas U. S. A.
Walcott. Midsummer, Tobago.
Sun has fired my face to terra-cotta, The.
Warren. Place and Time.
Rattlesnake Country.
Small White House.
Young. Hot House.

Heather
Hewitt. Mist.
Whittier. Burns.

Heaven
Angelou. Arrival.
Atwood. Resurrection.
Auden. Sonnet: "This world is full of lovely
things."
Two Triolets.
Bishop. Seascape.

Blake. Marriage of Heaven and Hell, The.
Bradstreet. As weary pilgrim, now at rest.
Brontë. Heaven's glory shone where he was laid.
Lines: "Far away is the land of rest."
Brooks. Hunchback Girl: She Thinks of Heaven.
Browning, Elizabeth Barrett. Heaven and Earth.
Isobel's Child.
Soul's Travelling, The.
Browning, Robert. Reverie.
Byron. Heaven and Earth.
Saint Peter sat by the celestial gate.
Campion. Most sweet and pleasing are thy wayes, O God.
Carew. Second Song, The.
Clough. O Heaven, and thou most loving family.
Coleridge. Faith, Hope, and Charity.
Kubla Khan; or, A Vision in a Dream.
Cowper. Epitaph on Mrs. Higgins.
Crane. And Bees of Paradise.
Crashaw. I Am the Doore.
It Is Better To Go into Heaven with One Eye.
Upon the Infant Martyrs.
Creeley. Drums, The.
Saints, The.
Cullen. For a Lady I Know.
She of the Dancing Feet Sings.
Cummings. If there are any heavens my mother will(all by herself)have.
Davie. Jacob's Ladder.
Three Beyond.
De la Mare. Night.
Sunrise.
Tryst, The.
Where Is Thy Victory?
Dickey, James. Heaven of Animals, The.
Dickey, William. Self Prepares for an Unwilling Journey, The.
Dickinson. "Arcturus" is his other name.
Cloud withdrew from the Sky, A.
Fact that Earth is Heaven, The.
Forever at His side to walk.
Going to Heaven!
"Heaven" has different Signs—to me.
Heaven is but a little way.
Heaven is so far of the Mind.
"Heaven"—is what I cannot reach!
Heaven will not be as good as Earth.
How far is it to Heaven?
I am glad you are in the open Air.
I never saw a Moor.
I reason, Earth is short.
I think just how my shape will rise.
I went to Heaven.
If roses had not faded.
Immortal is an ample word.
Immured in Heaven!
Is Heaven a Physician?
I've known a Heaven, like a Tent.
Lest this be Heaven indeed.
Like Flowers, that heard the news of Dews.
Meeting is well worth parting.
Of Tolling Bell I ask the cause?
Pit—but Heaven over it, A.
She's happy, with a new Content.
Should you but fail at—Sea.
So much of Heaven has gone from Earth.
Take Your Heaven further on.
Thank God there is a world.
There is a Zone whose even Years.
'Tis so much joy! 'Tis so much joy!
To come from Heaven is casual.
To make even Heaven more heavenly.
We pray—to Heaven.
We shun it ere it comes.
What is—"Paradise."
Where bells no more affright the morn.
Which is best? Heaven.
Who has not found the Heaven—below.
Why—do they shut Me out of Heaven?
You're right—"the way is narrow."
Donne. Hymn to the Saints, and to Marquis Hamilton[, An].

Our Companie in the Next World.
To Mr. Tilman after He Had Taken Orders.
Dunbar. Path, The.
Theology.
W'en I Gits Home.
Eberhart. Birth and Death.
Blessed Are the Angels in Heaven.
Ideal and the Real, The.
Sestina: "I die, no matter what I do I die."
Emerson. Come!—the palace of heaven rests on aëry pillars.
Drink wine, and the heaven.
For Lucifer, that old athlete.
Ghaselle.
Go if thou wilt ambrosial Flower.
Hearst thou, sweet spirit, thou hast heard before.
Inscription on a Well in Memory of the Martyrs of the War.
Ninefold table of Heaven, The.
Now tells the flower.
O what is Heaven but the fellowship.
Phoenix, The.
Power of a beautiful face lifts me to heaven, The.
Shall the Muse sing for thousands & not sing.
Soul, The.
Spiritual Laws.
To the Shah, from Enweri ("From thy worth and weight the stars gravitate").
Frost. Trial by Existence, The.
Graves. Green Castle, The.
Heaven.
True Joy.
Hacker. Partial Analysis.
Hartnett. Wounded Otter, The.
Herbert. Heaven.
Obedience.
Star[re], The.
Herrick. Another ("Thou bidst me come; I cannot come; for why").
Comfort to a Youth That Had Lost His Love.
God Heares Us.
Heaven ("Heav'n is most fair").
Heaven ("Heaven is not given").
His Creed.
Honours Are Hindrances.
Humility.
No Time in Eternity.
Ode, or Psalme, to God, An.
On Heaven.
Tapers.
Teares: ("Our present Teares here (not our present laughter)").
This, and the Next World.
To Heaven.
To His Ever-Loving God.
White Island: or Place of the Blest, The.
Hopkins. Ashboughs.
Earth and heaven, so little known, The.
Handsome Heart, The.
Heaven-Haven.
—Hill / Heaven and every field, are still.
Il Mystico.
My prayers must meet a brazen heaven.
Not kind! to freeze me with forecast.
O Death, Death, He is come.
Hughes, Langston. Heaven.
Jonson. To Heaven.
Keats. As from the Darkening Gloom a Silver Dove.
Ode: "Bards of passion and of mirth."
Kipling. Dinah in Heaven.
Lawrence. Ah, with His Blessing Bright on Thy Mouth and Thy Brow.
Fallen Leaves.
Hymn to Nothingness.
Someone Will Enter between the Gates.
Levine. Grandmother in Heaven.
Heaven.
Miracle, The.
Liddy. Scott Rautmann, Saturday Night.
Lindsay. Celestial Circus, The.
General William Booth Enters into Heaven.
Harps in Heaven.
How Johnny Appleseed Walked Alone in the Jungles of Heaven.

In Memory of a Child.
In Praise of Gloriana's Remarkable Golden Hair.
Last Song of Lucifer, The.
Lovelace. Dialogue. Lute and Voice, A.
Elegie. Princesse Katherine, An.
Falcon, The.
Parent and Prince of Heav'n O lead I pray.
To my Dear Friend Mr. E.R.
To My Noble Kinsman T.S. Esq.
Lowry. Fragment: "Dead tree that, frozen, utters at the top, The."
No prayer for the people.
Matthews. Familial.
Merton. Heavenly City, The.
How Long We Wait.
Psalm 132: A Modern Monastic Revision.
Millay. Blue-Flag in the Bog, The.
Milton. Heaven.
Love thou saist.
On the Same ["Thus did you strive to vouchsafe James to Heaven"].
Paradise Lost.
Morrison. He Follows a Woman.
Nathan. Certain Prospects and Spectacular Diversions.
Nemerov. Backward Look, The.
Morality, A.
Oliver. Roses, Late Summer.
Olson. Out of the light of Heaven the flower.
Patchen. How silent are the things of heaven.
Outlaw of the Lowest Planet, The.
What the Grecian Earns.
Plath. Sheep in Fog.
Pope. Epigram: "Peter complains, that God has given."
Epitaph on the Monument of the Honourable Robert Digby, and of his Sister Mary, erected by their Father the Lord Digby, in the Church of Sherborne in Dorsetshire, 1727.
Prince. Plato says that in Heaven there is.
Psalms. Psalm 19: "Heavens declare the glory of God, The."
Ralegh. 4.2: "Such as like heavenly wights doe come."
Passionate Man[']s Pilgrimage, The.
Robinson. Supremacy.
Rossetti. Afterthought, An.
Ah Lord, Lord, if my heart were right with Thine.
All heaven is blazing yet / With the meridian sun.
All Saints.
All Saints.
And Now Why Tarriest Thou?
Annie.
Antipas.
As Cold Water to a Thirsty Soul, So Is Good News from a Far Country.
As the Doves to Their Windows.
As the Sparks Fly Upwards.
As Thy Days, So Shall Thy Strength Be.
Awake, Thou That Sleepest.
Beautiful For Situation.
Before the Throne, and Before the Lamb.
Behold a Shaking.
Behold, It Was Very Good.
Burial Anthem.
But Thy Commandment Is Exceeding Broad.
By Way of Remembrance.
Called To Be Saints.
Cast down but not destroyed, chastened not slain.
Chiefest among Ten Thousand, The.
Christian and Jew. A Dialogue.
Convent Threshold, The.
Counsel, A.
Darkness and light are both alike to Thee.
Day Is At Hand, The.
De Profundis.
Death.
Death Is Swallowed Up in Victory.
Dirge, A.
Discovery, A.
Doeth Well..Doeth Better.
Earth and Heaven.

Earth has clear call of daily bells, / A chancel-vault of gloom and star.
Earth Shall Tremble at the Look of Him, The. 1878.
Eleventh Hour, The.
Ellen Middleton.
Eva.
Eye Hath Not Seen.
Faint, Yet Pursuing.
Flowers Appear on the Earth, The.
From House to Home.
General Assembly and Church of the Firstborn, The.
Goal in sihgt! Look up and sing, / Set faces full against the light, The.
Gold of that Land is Good, The.
Gone Before.
Had Fortune parted us / Fortune is blind.
Hark! the Alleluias of the great salvation.
He Shall Go No More Out.
Heaven.
Heaven overarches earth and sea.
Heaven's chimes are slow, but sure to strike at last.
Heaviness May Endure for a Night, But Joy Cometh in the Morning.
Heavy heart, if ever heart was heavy, A.
Her Seed; It Shall Bruise Thy Head.
His Banner over Me Was Love.
Holy City, New Jerusalem, The.
Holy Innocents.
How great is little man! / Sun, moon, and stars respond to him.
I Am Small and of No Reputation.
I Do Set My Bow in the Cloud.
I have done with hope.
I Look for the Lord.
I Will Lift Up Mine Eyes unto the Hills. ("I am pale with sick desire").
I Will Lift Up Mine Eyes unto the Hills. ("When sick of life and all the world-").
If stars dropped out of heaven, / And if flowers took their place.
Jerusalem of fire / And gold and pearl and gem.
Jesus alone:—if thus it were to me.
Joy of Saints, like incense turned to fire, The.
Lady Isabella.
Last Words of St. Telemachus, The.
Lay Up for Yourselves Treasures in Heaven.
Life Hidden.
Life that was born today / Must make no stay.
Lift up thine eyes to seek the invisible.
Look on This Picture and on This.
Lord, by what inconceivable dim road / Thou leadest man on footsore pilgrimage!
Lord God of Hosts, most Holy and most High.
Lord, grant us eyes to see and ears to hear, / And souls to love and minds to understand.
Lord Jesus, who would think that I am Thine?
Lord, make me one with Thine own faithful ones.
Lord Thomas and Fair Margaret.
Lord, we are rivers running to Thy sea.
Love and Hope.
Man's life is but a working day / Whose tasks are set aright.
Martyr, The.
Marvel of Marvels.
Michael F. M. Rossetti.
Moonshine.
Mother and Child.
Mother Country.
Now They Desire.
O mine enemy / Rejoice not over me!
Only Believe.
Our heaven must be within ourselves / Our home and heaven the work of faith.
Paradise.
Paradise: in a Symbol.
Passion Flower hath sprung up tall, The.
Pause, A.
Resurrection Eve.
Rivals.
Rose Plant in Jericho, A.
St. Andrew's Church.

Saints and Angels.
Shadows Today.
She Shall Be Brought unto the King.
Slain in their high places: fallen on rest.
Sleep, Sleep Happy Child; All Creation Slept and Smiled.
So Great a Cloud of Witnesses.
Son, Remember.
Song of the Star, The.
Song: "We buried her among the flowers."
Strange voices sing among the planets which.
Sunday Before Advent.
Sweetness of rest when Thou sheddest rest.
That Where I Am, There Ye May Be Also.
They lie at rest, our blessed dead.
This near-at-hand land breeds pain by measure.
Thou Knewest..Thou Oughtest Therefore.
Thou sleepest where the lilies fade.
Thy Name, O Christ, as incense streaming forth.
Till Tomorrow.
Time of Waiting, The.
To Every Seed His Own Body.
To the End.
To What Purpose Is This Waste?
Truly the Light Is Sweet.
Two Thoughts of Death.
Uphill [or Up-Hill].
Watchers, The.
We know not when, we know not where.
What are these lovely ones, yea, what are these?
What Good Shall My Life Do Me?
What Hath God Wrought!
What will it be, O my soul, what will it be.
When a mounting skylark sings / In the sunlit summer morn.
Where Neither Rust Nor Moth Doth Corrupt.
Where never tempest heaveth, / Nor sorrow grieveth.
Where shall I find a white rose blowing?
Whither the Tribes Go Up, Even the Tribes of the Lord.
Who cares for earthly bread tho' white?
Who is this that cometh up not alone.
Who sits with the King in His Throne? Not a slave but a Bride.
Who would wish back the Saints upon our rough.
Why?
Yawn, A.
Ye Are Come unto Mount Sion.
Ye Have Forgotten the Exhortation.
Ye That Fear Him, Both Small and Great.
Yet a Little While. ("Heaven is not far, tho' luv the shy").
Yet a Little While. ("I dreamed and did not seek: today I seek").
St. John. No Heaven.
Sandburg. Hells and Heavens.
Sarton. Annunciation.
Sexton. Frenzy.
Shelley. see also Ode to Heaven.
Daemon of the World, The; A Fragment.
Ode to Heaven.
Shelton. Heaven of the Poor, The.
Silverstein. Paul Bunyan.
Smith, Stevie. Heavenly City, The.
Noble and Ethereal.
Snodgrass. Monet: "Les Nymphéas."
Southwell. At Home in Heaven.
Seek[e] Flowers of Heaven.
Spenser. Bower of Bliss, The.
Stevens. Botanist on Alp (No. 2).
Of Heaven Considered as a Tomb.
Waving Adieu, Adieu, Adieu.
Stevenson. It's forth across the roaring foam, and on towards the west.
Tempest tossed and sore afflicted, sin defiled and care oppressed.
To all that love the far and blue.
Walcott. Orient and Immortal Wheat.
Return to D'Ennery; Rain.
Whittier. Between the Gates.
Mystery, A.

Norembega.
To My Friend on the Death of His Sister.
Wilbur. Icarium Mare.
Prayer to Go to Paradise with the Donkeys, A.
Wordsworth. If thou indeed derive thy light from Heaven.
Though narrow be that old Man's cares, and near.
Yeats. Cold Heaven, The.
He Thinks of His Past Greatness When a Part of the Constellations of Heaven.
He Wishes for the Cloths of Heaven.
Rose of Peace, The.
Young. Not Her, She Aint No Gypsy.
Palm Drive Palo Alto.
Zimmer. Zimmer Imagines Heaven.
Zukofsky. Pamphylian.
See also **Paradise.**

Hebe
Graves. To Ogmian Hercules.
Hebrew
Smart. Fragment C.
Whitsunday.
Hebrides
Hugo. Letter to Garber from Skye.
Jeffers. Now Returned Home.
Lowry. Eels.
MacLeish. Hebrides.
Thrush in the Gaelic Islands, The.
MacNeice. Hebrides, The.
Mahon. Sea in Winter, The.
Smith, Charlotte. Supposed to Have Been Written in the Hebrides.
Hector
Browning, Elizabeth Barrett. Hector and Andromache.
Hector in the Garden.
Carruth. Existence Before Essence.
Was she innocent? Too beautiful for that.
Hedgehogs
Clare. Hedgehog, The.
Cummings. Porky & porkie.
Hewitt. Hedgehog.
Hedgehog: For R., The.
Larkin. Mower, The.
Muldoon. Hedgehog.
Smith, Charlotte. Hedge-Hog Seen in a Frequented Path, The.
Tomlinson. Scream, The.
Hedonism
Blake. Proverbs of Hell.
Cummings. Since feeling is first.
Herrick. Pleasures Pernicious.
Housman. Think no more, lad; laugh, be jolly.
Lindsay. Johnny Appleseed's Wife from the Palace of Eve.
Melville. After the Pleasure Party.
Olson. Laughing Ones, The.
Heine, Heinrich
Bogan. From Heine.
Carruth. Essay on Stone.
Helen of Troy
Browning, Robert. Helen's Tower.
Carruth. Light in the Locust Tree.
Was she innocent? Too beautiful for that.
Your dream: / His name was Homer. He was blind.
Crane. For the Marriage of Faustus and Helen.
Cummings. Helen.
De la Mare. Mirage.
Doolittle. And Pergamos, / City of the Phrygians.
Crowd of the Greek force, The.
Helen.
Paris came to Ida.
Duncan. This potion is love's portion. This herb.
Gunn. Helen's Rape.
Hewitt. Ashes in the Wind.
Jeffers. Ah, Faustus,/ Now hast thou but one bare hour [or hower] to live.
At the Fall of an Age.
Tower beyond Tragedy, The.
Was This the Face.
Jonson. Ode, An: "Helen, did Homer never see."

Lovelace. Clitophon and Lucippe.
Lowry. Canny Castor, Punching Pollux.
MacLeish. But she was both,—she was both loved and love.
Well, he was drunk. That much was clear.
Meredith. Helen on the Skaian Gates.
Poe. To Helen: ("Helen, thy beauty is to me").
Schwartz. To Helen.
Smith, Stevie. I Had a Dream.
Van Duyn. Winter has stiffened the ground, the birds are gone.
Walcott. Map of the New World.
Wilbur. Helen.
Voice from under the Table, A.
Yeats. When Helen Lived.

Hell
Auden. Christ in Hades.
Hell.
Beckett. Jusque dans la caverne ciel et sol.
Noire soeur.
Bishop. Hell is Graduated.
Blake. Marriage of Heaven and Hell, The.
Browning, Robert. Doctor——.
Bukowski. How Do They Get Your Number?
Sad-Eyed Mules of Men.
Burns. Kellyburnbraes.
Carroll, Jim. Compassion.
Coleridge. Alla Sua Amica.
Crashaw. But Men loved Darkness[e] Rather Than [or Then] Light.
De la Mare. Making a fire.
Outskirts, The.
Dickey, William. Self Prepares for an Unwilling Journey, The.
Dickinson. Pit—but Heaven over it, A.
To attempt to speak of what has been.
You're right—"the way is narrow."
Dunbar. Theology.
Eberhart. Blessed Are the Angels in Heaven.
Enigma, The.
Sestina: "I die, no matter what I do I die."
Emerson. Ghaselle.
Everson. Vision of Felicity, The.
Glück. Day Without Night.
Graves. Descent into Hell.
Encounter, The.
Hell.
Instructions to the Orphic Adept.
Sharp Ridge, The.
Gray. Descent of Odin, The.
Hacker. Partial Analysis.
Herrick. Barley-Break; or, Last in Hell.
Hell Fire ("Fire of Hell this strange condition hath, The").
Hell Fire ("One onely fire has Hell; but yet it shall").
Hell ("Hell is no other, but a soundlesse pit").
Hell ("Hell is the place where whipping-cheer abounds").
Sin and Strife.
Hewitt. Those Morning Walks.
Housman. Hell Gate.
Mill-stream, now that noises cease, The.
Jeffers. Where are you damn'd?
Wilson in Hell.
Keats. Dream, after Reading Dante's Episode of Paolo and Francesca, A.
Kipling. We meet in an evil land.
Lawrence. Someone Will Enter between the Gates.
Lieberman. Creole Mephistopheles, The.
Lindsay. Last Song of Lucifer, The.
Simon Legree—A Negro Sermon.
Lovelace. Dialogue. Lute and Voice, A.
Lowry. Doggerel.
I met a man who suffered more than I.
No prayer for the people.
No words assess, no pencil knows.
Tortures of hell are stern, their fires burn fiercely, The.
McGrath. Passages.
Meredith. Nor had saffron and sapphire and red.
Now the meadows with crocus besprent.
Now the youth footed swift to the dawn.
Merton. All the Way Down.

Millay. Some Things Are Dark.
Milton. Anon out of the earth a fabric huge.
Dungeon horrible, on all sides round, A.
Hell ("At once with him they rose").
Occupations of Hell.
Paradise Lost.
Place of the Damned, The.
Olson. Flower grows, The.
I Believe in You.
In Cold Hell, in Thicket.
Loves of Anat, I, The.
Owen. Strange Meeting.
Robinson. Eutychides.
Supremacy.
Rossetti. Sunday Before Advent.
Where Their Worm Dieth Not, and the Fire Is Not Quenched.
Sandburg. Hells and Heavens.
Our Hells.
Shelley. Hell is a city much like London.
Smith, Stevie. Ambassador, The.
Thoughts about the Christian Doctrine of Eternal Hell.
Snodgrass. Orpheus.
Sorrentino. People in Hell are clothed.
Tate. Cross, The.
Tomlinson. Last Judgement.
Walcott. Orient and Immortal Wheat.
Wright, James. Ghost, The.
Yeats. Rose of Peace, The.

Hell's Angels
Gunn. Black Jackets.

Heloise. *see* **Abelard and Heloise.**

Help
Atwood. I see you fugitive, stumbling across the prarie.
Beatles. Help!
With a Little Help from My Friends.
Berry. Creation Myth.
Browning, Elizabeth Barrett. Sea-Mew, The.
Carew. Lady, Rescued from Death by a Knight, Who in the Instant Leaves Her, Complains Thus, A.
Clark. I'm on an Island.
Dickinson. These Strangers, in a foreign World.
To offer brave assistance.
"Dylan." Ballad of Frankie Lee and Judas Priest, The.
Fourth Time Around.
Minstrel Boy.
Graves. Grotesques.
Hartley. O lift me—majestic Sire.
Hesketh. Defeathered.
Lindsay. Flower of Mending, The.
Lorde. To My Daughter the Junkie on a Train.
Lowry. Conversations With Goethe.
S.O.S Sinking fast by both bow and stern.
Merton. Litany: "All holy souls / pray for us fellows."
Song of Purification.
Milton. Lord how many are my foes.
Nash. Everybody Wants to Get into the Baedeker.
Olson. All You Can Do.
Psalms. Psalm 3: "Lord, how are the increased.."
Psalm 35: "Plead my cause, O Lord, with them that strive with me."
Psalm 38: "O Lord, rebuke me not in thy wrath."
Psalm 40: "I waited patiently for the Lord."
Psalm 43: "Judge me, O God.."
Psalm 44: "We have heard with our ears, O God."
Psalm 46: "God is our refuge and strength.."
Psalm 60: "O God, thou hast cast us off. . . ."
Psalm 70: "Make haste, O God, to deliver me."
Psalm 108: "O God, my heart is fixed."
Psalm 121: "I will lift up mine eyes unto the hills."
Psalm 124: "If it had not been the Lord who was on our side.."
Psalm 146: "Praise ye the Lord. Praise the Lord.."

Rossetti. Out of the Deep.
Sidney. Speak Thou for me against wrong-speaking foes.
Silverstein. Helping.
Wyatt. O Lord, as I thee have both prayed and pray.

Hemingway, Ernest
Eberhart. Key West.
Koch. On Beauty.
MacLeish. Hemingway.
Merton. Elegy for Ernest Hemingway, An.
Nash. Roll On, Thou Deep and Dark Blue Copy Writer—Roll!
Updike. Meditation on a News Item.

Hemlocks
Ammons. Celestial Dealings.
Dickinson. I think the Hemlock likes to stand.
Millay. Hedge of Hemlocks, The.

Henry VIII, King of England
Wordsworth. Recollection of the Portrait of King Henry Eighth, Trinity Lodge, Cambridge.

"Henry, O." (William Sydney Porter)
Lindsay. Knight in Disguise, The.

Hens
Atwood. Song of the Hen's Head.
Bishop. Trouvée.
"Carroll, Lewis." Lays of Sorrow, No. 1.
Davie. Portrait of the Artist as a Farmyard Fowl.
Emerson. Things oft miscalling, as the hen-.
Joseph. Gentleman that my black hen lays eggs for, The.
Kinnell. Hen Flower, The.
Schuyler. Wild Eggs.
Updike. Wooden Darning Egg, A.
Wilbur. Black November Turkey, A.
See also **Chickens.**

Heraclitus
Atwood. After Heraclitus.
Carruth. Your dream: / His name is Heraclitus, and he is huge.
Hopkins. That Nature Is a Heraclitean Fire and of the Comfort of the Resurrection.
MacNeice. Variation on Heraclitus.
Mahon. Heraclitus on Rivers.
Merton. Legacy of Herakleitos, The.

Herbs
Carruth. Spring Notes from Robin Hill.
Emerson. Blight.
Where the fungus broad & red.
Fox. Nightshade.
Gunn. Fennel.
Jong. Bitter Herb.
Deadly Nightshade.
Henbane.
Mandrake.
Monkshood.
Thorn Apple.
Kipling. Our Fathers of Old.
Smart. Fragment D.
Updike. Sensualist, The.

Hercules
Emerson. Turtle in swamp.
Graves. Hercules at Nemea.
To Ogmian Hercules.
Heaney. Hercules and Antaeus.
Nash. Thirteenth Labor of Hercules, The.
Nemerov. It is forbidden to go further.
Owen. Antaeus: A Fragment.
Williams, Charles Kenneth. Hercules, Deianira, Nessus.

Herding
Hewitt. Saint Patrick.
Whittier. Drovers, The.
See also **Shepherds and Shepherdesses.**

Heresy and Heretics
Coleridge. Foster-Mother's Tale, The.
Cowper. Lines Written in the Monthly Review.
Hewitt. Consequences.
Meredith. John Lackland.
Merton. Nusayris, The.
Syria.
Prince. Campanella.

Hermaphrodites
Carruth. Your dream: / His name was unheard of, very strange.
Gardner. Three Rings or Five rings.
Stuart. Hermaphrodite, The.

Hermit Crabs
Oliver. Hermit Crab, The.

Hermits
Bishop. Chemin de Fer.
Carruth. He was a soldier, he was a madman, he was a hermit.
Coleridge. This Hermit good lives in that wood.
Emerson. Hermione.
Galvin. Last Man in the Quabbin, The.
Gunn. Last Man, The.
Haines. Hermitage, The.
Hall. Oysters and Hermits.
Hartley. It is as if at times.
Hoffman. Hermit of Cape Rosier, The.
Hugo. Ballad of the Upper Bumping.
Oliver. Strawberry Moon.
Plath. Hermit at Outermost House, The.
Robinson. Stafford's Cabin.
Van Duyn. Hermit of Hudson Pond, The.
Wakoski. Hermit, The.
Walcott. Winding Up.
Williams, William Carlos. Stylist, The.
Wordsworth. Brownie, The.
Brownie's Cell, The.
Yeats. Three Hermits, The.

Hero and Leander
Byron. Written after Swimming from Sestos to Abydos.
Campion. Shal I come, if I swim? wide are the waves, you see.
Donne. Hero and Leander.
Keats. On a Leander Gem which Miss Reynolds, My Kind Friend, Gave Me.

Heroes and Heroines
Atwood. My beautiful wooden leader.
There must be more for you to do.
Auden. O What Is That Sound [Which So Thrills the Ear].
Brooks. Negro Hero.
Browning, Elizabeth Barrett. Critics say that epics have died out, The.
Fourfold Aspect, The.
Sword of Castruccio Castracani, The.
Browning, Robert. Hervé Riel.
Burns. Duan First.
Byron. Elegiac Stanzas on the Death of Sir Peter Parker, Bart.
Monody on the Death of the Right Hon. R. B. Sheridan.
On the Star of "The Legion of Honour."
Thy Days Are Done.
Translation from Horace.
Translation of the Epitaph on Virgil and Tibullus.
Carew. First Song, The.
"Carroll, Lewis." Dreamland.
Creeley. Heroes.
Cummings. My father moved through dooms of love.
Davie. Corrib: An Emblem.
Pacer in the Fresco. John the Baptist, The.
De la Mare. Absalom.
Peace.
Dickinson. Gleam of an heroic Act, The.
To have been the missing Hero.
We never know how high we are.
"Dylan." Quinn the Eskimo.
Woody Guthrie was my last idol.
Eberhart. Protagonists.
Emerson. Forerunners.
From high to higher forces.
Heroism.
Ford. Death in all its forms.
Frost. Trial by Existence, The.
Gardner. Folkways.
Glück. Parable, A.
Graves. Miller's Man, The.
To Ogmian Hercules.
Gray. Conan.
Gunn. Byrnies, The.
Hall. Persistence of 1937.

Hardy. By the Barrows.
Herrick. Ultimus Heroum: or, To the Most Learned, and to the Right Honourable, Henry, Marquesse of Dorchester.
Hewitt. College Fence, The.
Hugo. Kilmuir Cemetery: The Knight in Blue-Green Relief.
Jeffers. Broadstone, The.
Epic Stars, The.
Jonson. To William, Lord Mounteagle.
Keats. To Kosciusko.
Kipling. Giffen's Debt.
Grave Near Cairo, A.
Koertge. Sidekicks.
Lawrence. For the Heroes Are Dipped in Scarlet.
Levine. Francisco, I'll Bring You Red Carnations.
Liddy. Since the splendour of MacDonnell of the cliffs.
Vir III.
Lindsay. Galahad, Knight Who Perished.
Litany of the Heroes.
Longfellow. Skeleton in Armor [or Armour], The.
Lovelace. Being treated to Ellinda.
Hand by which no King but Serjeant dies, The.
Lowell. For the Union Dead.
Lowry. And partly they deserve dishonest death.
Days Like Smitten Cymbals of Brass, The.
Peter Gaunt and the Canals.
There is a sort of conspiracy about the great.
McGrath. Heroes of Childhood, The.
Marvell. Loyal Scot, The.
To My Lord Fairfax.
Meinke. Ode to Good Men Fallen Before Hero Come.
Melville. Commemorative of a Naval Victory.
Meredith. Flood that swept her to be slave, The.
October 21, 1905.
On him the long enchained, released.
Merton. Wounded football hero / Is nominated to share / In the human condition, The.
Moore. Hero, The.
Nemerov. Hero Comes Home in His Hamper, and Is Exhibited at the World's Fair, The.
Who Did Not Die in Vain.
Olson. Unfinished (raw) hero—un-, The.
Patchen. Childhood of the Hero.
Plath. Times Are Tidy, The.
Ralegh. 4.9: "Many by valour have deserved renown."
Some old Aurancans, I remember well.
"Reed." Heroine, The.
Rukeyser. Hero Speech.
Trophies.
Shelton. Heroes of Our Times, The.
Smart. Ode to Admiral Sir George Pocock.
Ode to General Draper.
Smith, Patti. Amazing Tale of Skunkdog, The.
Spender. Seascape.
The Truly Great.
Stevens. Examination of the Hero in a Time of War.
Paisant Chronicle.
Thunder by the Musician.
Stevenson. Lost Occasion, The.
Whole day thro', in contempt and pity, The.
Tomlinson. Hero Sandwiches.
Whitman. Return of the Heroes, The.
Wallabout Martyrs, The.
Whittier. Derne.
Hero, The.
Wilbur. Beowulf.
Williams, Charles Kenneth. Herakles.
Williams, William Carlos. Childe Harold to the Round Tower Came.
Hero.
Wordsworth. Memorial near the Outlet of the Lake of Thun.

Heroin. *see* **Drug Addiction.**

Herons
Berry. Heron, The.
Cooper. Leaving Water Hyacinths.

Galvin. Great Blue.
Gardner. That "Craning of the Neck."
Hartley. Two grey herons flying.
Hesketh. Cap, The.
Hoffman. Stillness, A.
Jeffers. People and a Heron.
Oliver. Some Herons.
Roethke. Heron, The.
Tomlinson. To See the Heron.
Walcott. Heron flies across the morning marsh and brakes, A.
Wright, James. Old Age Compensation.
Small Blue Heron, The.

Herrick, Robert
Herrick. On Himselfe ("Aske me, why I do not sing").
On Himselfe: ("Born[e] I was to meet with Age").
On Himselfe ("I fear no Earthly Powers").
On Himselfe ("I will no longer kiss").
On Himselfe ("Ile sing no more, nor will I longer write").
On Himselfe ("I'll write no more of Love; but now repent").
On Himselfe ("Let me not live, if I not love").
On Himselfe ("Live by thy Muse thou shalt; when others die").
On Himselfe ("Some parts may perish; dye thou canst not all").
On Himselfe ("Weep for the dead, for they have lost this light").
On Himselfe ("Work is done: young men, and maidens set, The").
Upon Himself: ("I dislikt but even now").
Upon Himself ("Mop-eyed I am, as some have said").
Upon Himself: ("Th'art hence removing, (like a Shepherds Tents)").
Upon Himself: ("Thou shalt not All die").
Upon Himselfe ("I am Sive-like, and can hold").
Upon Himselfe ("I co'd never love indeed").
Upon Hinmself ("Come, leave this loathed Country-life, and then").
Hewitt. Hollyhocks against the Wall, The.
Yau. Robert Herrick.

Herring
"Carroll, Lewis." Three Badgers, The.
"MacDiarmid." With the Herring Fishers.
Swift. Herrings.

Hiawatha
"Carroll, Lewis." Hiawatha's Photographing.

Hiccups
MacNeice. Messiah, The.

Highlands of Scotland. *see* **Scottish Highlands.**

Highways. *see* **Roads.**

Hiking and Hikers
Betjeman. Hike on the Downs, A.
Dobyns. Gottéron Landscape.
Pack. Invisible Hand, The.
Tomlinson. Hill, The.
Young. Bear Gulch Road.
Sunday Illumination.

Hills and Mountains
Berry. Song (2).
Bogan. Last Hill in a Vista.
Brontë. What is that smoke that ever still.
Browning, Elizabeth Barrett. Olives and Mountains.
Burns. Written with a Pencil over the Chimney-Piece, in the Parlour of the Inn at Kenmore, Taymouth.
Ciardi. Highest Place in Town, The.
Coleridge. Stanger Minstrel, A.
To a Young Friend.
Cummings. At dusk / just when.
Perished have safe small.
Sunset.
De la Mare. Crazed.
Mountains, The.
Dickinson. Mountain sat upon the Plain, The.
Mountains grow—unnoticed, The.
Eberhart. Summery Windermere, sweet lake!
Emerson. Fable: "Mountain and the squirrel, The."
Frost. Mountain, The.

Hall. Sleeping Giant, The.
Southwest of Buffalo.
Hardy. Rome: On the Palatine.
Schreckhorn, The.
Under High-Stoy Hill.
Hewitt. Descent, The.
Hopkins. —Hill / Heaven and every field, are
still.
Hugo. Triangle for Green Men.
Kipling. Ballade of Burial, A.
Floods, The.
Sea and the Hills, The.
Larkin. Hills in Their Recumbent Postures,
The.
Lawrence. At the Cearne.
Hills, The.
"MacDiarmid." Ross-shire Hills, The.
MacLeish. Pony Rock.
Robinson. Dark Hills, The.
Rukeyser. Alloy.
Sandburg. Cornfield Ridge and Stream.
Three Hills Look Different in the Moonshine.
Uplands in May.
Schuyler. Awoke.
Silverstein. Little Blue Engine, The.
Snyder. Mid-August at Sourdough Mountain
Lookout.
Sours of the Hills.
Spender. Pylons, The.
Stuart. Killdeer.
Tomlinson. Hill, The.
Meeting, The.
Ute Mountain.
Whittier. Hill-Top, The.
Williams, William Carlos. Stroller.
Wordsworth. Engelberg, the Hill of Angels.
Trosachs, The.
Wansfell! This Household Has a Favoured
Lot.
See also **Mountain Climbing.**

Hinduism and Hindus
Ford. I'd like to linger.
Illness, The.
I'm attached, and he's.
Ginsberg. On Illness.
Kipling. Hindu Sepoy in France.
Lewis. Village Funeral: Maharashtra.
Lowry. Hindu Babe / I love you.
MacNeice. Mahabalipuram.
Merton. Hrishikesa, destroyer of Titans, ogres
and canailles.
Yeats. Indian upon God, The [*or* An].

Hippies
Angelou. Take Time Out.
Dickey, James. False Youth: Autumn: Clothes
of the Age.
Ferlinghetti. John Lennon in the Porto Santo
Stefano.
Koertge. Quiz, The.

Hippopotamuses
Eliot. Hippopotamus, The.
Nash. Hippopotamus, The.
Roethke. Hippo, The.
Silverstein. Recipe For A Hippopotamus
Sandwich.

Hiroshima, Japan
Carruth. Your dream: / At first its name is
Heliopolis.
Levine. Horse, The.
Merton. Original Child Bomb.

History and Historians
Angelou. Family Affairs.
Ashbery. Tapestry.
Atwood. Comic Books vs. History.
1837 War in Retrospect.
Marrying the Hangman.
You can't live here without breathing.
Auden. Certainly praise: let song mount again
and again.
Fall of Rome, The.
Homage to Clio.
Makers of History.
Beckett. Ainsi a-t-on beau.
Berg. Page 256.
Berry. All the lives this place.
Design of a House, The.
Dream, The.

Ended, a story is history.
He Looks out the Window at the Town.
How fine / to have a long-legged house.
Look in / and see him looking out.
Meditation in the Spring Rain.
Old Man Is Older in History than in Time,
The.
Since then I have arrived here.
Sowing.
Streets, guns, machines.
Where.
Berryman. Boston Common.
Bukowski. It's Not Who Lived Here.
Burns. Caledonia.
Epistle to Mr Tytler of Woodhouselee, Author
of a Defence of Mary Queen of Scots.
Campion. Ad Guil. Camdenum.
Carew. To My Friend, Will. Davenant.
Carruth. I hurt. Hungrier flowers try my rank
ground.
Sociology of Toyotas and Jade
Chrysanthemums, The.
Sparrows.
Spirit / whatever you are wherever.
Spring Notes from Robin Hill.
Therefore to us, time's / final lesson: be
content.
Tsar, who knew you? Who.
Your dream: / His name was Hero, and his
other name.
Clark. Moirai, The.
1968.
Clough. To think that men of former days.
Cohen. On Hearing a Name Long Unspoken.
Streetcars.
You Live like a God.
Cowper. Ode on *Sir Charles Grandison.*
Cummings. All nearness pauses,while a star
can grow.
Puella Mea.
Remarked Robinson Jefferson.
Thou in whose swordgreat story shine the
deeds.
Davie. Behind the North Wind.
Creature David, The.
First Epistle.
Second Epistle.
Seur, near Blois.
Sixth Epistle.
Third Epistle.
Vancouver.
Vindication of Jovan Babic, The.
Dobyns. Body of Romulus, The.
Where We Are.
Dunn. Privilege.
When the Revolution Came.
"Dylan." Long Ago, Far Away.
Eliot. Defense of the Islands.
Little Gidding.
Lune de Miel.
Emerson. History & prophecy are alike.
I must not borrow light.
Solution.
Thanks to those who go & come.
Ferlinghetti. Cro-Magnons.
History of the World: a TV Docu-Drama.
Fletcher. Journey Day.
On Mesa Verde.
Song of Natchez Under the Hill, The.
Ford. Simple is madness, like a kick in the
pants.
Frost. Never Naught Song, A.
Peaceful Shepherd, The.
Planners, The.
Gallagher. Small Garden Near a Field.
Garrigue. Beaucaire.
Ginsberg. Café in Warsaw.
Eroica.
Seabattle of Salamis Took Place off Perama.
Stotras to Kali Destroyer of Illusions.
Glück. Saturnalia.
Graves. End of Play.
Gray. Ode for Music.
Griffiths. Craig-y-Don.
Gunn. Claus von Stauffenberg.
Hall. Letter to an English Poet.
Hardy. Aged Newspaper Soliloquizes, The.

Clasped Skeleton, The.
One We Knew.
Rome: Building a New Street in the Ancient
Quarter.
Rome: On the Palatine.
Zermatt: To the Matterhorn.
Hartnett. Bereft of Its Great Poets.
Herbert. Church Militant, The.
Hesketh. Violet at Ninety.
Hewitt. Anglo-Irish Accord, The.
Clogh-Oir: September 1971.
Conacre.
Conversations in Hungary, August 1969.
Cultra Manor: The Ulster Folk Museum.
Demagogue.
Dilemma, The.
Glittering Sod, The.
House on the Hill, The.
In That Fair and Pleasant Land.
In This Year of Grace.
Little People, A.
MacDonnell's Question.
Mosaic.
Municipal Gallery Revisited, October 1954.
Orchard Country.
Paraphrase of Verses by Mayakovsky.
Prologue for an Evening at the Whitefriars.
Sonnet: "By the sea's edge, on gravel and on
sand."
This Is No Land of Constable and Clare.
Timber.
Twelfth of July, The.
Ulsterman, An.
Hill. Crack of a starting pistol. Jean Jaurès.
History as Poetry.
Martyrdom of Saint Sebastian.
Of Rumor, of Clamor.
There is an ancient landscape of green
branches.
Hoffman. At the Roman Wall, 1956.
Historian, A.
Tree.
Holmes. Instructions for the World Librarian.
Hugo. Carloway Broch.
Castel Sant'Angelo.
Centuries near Spinnazola.
Chysauster.
Ferniehirst Castle.
First South and Cambridge.
Glen Uig.
Map of Skye, A.
Ness.
On Hearing a New Escalation.
St. Clement's: Harris.
Schoolgirl at Seola.
Uig Registrar.
Jarrell. Dead, The.
Memoirs of Glückel of Hameln, The.
Jeffers. I Shall Laugh Purely.
Moon and Five Planets.
Ode to Hengist and Horsa.
Real and Half Real.
Jonson. Mind of the Frontispiece to a Book,
The.
To My Chosen Friend the Learnèd Translator
of Lucan, Thomas May, Esquire.
To Sir Henry [*or* Henrie] Savile [upon His
Translation of Tacitus].
Keats. Lines Written in the Highlands after a
Visit to Burns's Country.
Kipling. Flies, The.
France.
General Summary, A.
King's Task, The.
Land, The.
Philadelphia.
Pirates in England, The.
River's Tale, The.
Knight. And Tell Me Poet, Can Love Exist in
Slavery?
Kunitz. Hand-Rolled Cigarettes.
Larkin. Arundel Tomb, An.
Plymouth.
Lawrence. Death of Our Era, The.
Under the Oak.
Levertov. Shalom.
Levine. Gift for a Believer.

New Season.
Sources.
Liddy. Coolgreany.
To the Liberal Magistrates.
Lindsay. After Reading the Sad Story of the
    Fall of Babylon.
Litany of the Heroes.
"MacDiarmid." Major Road Ahead.
McGrath. Anniversaries.
In Praise of Necessity.
Political Song for the Year's End.
Theory, A.
MacNeice. If shepherd to nymph were the
    whole story.
In a little room, a little plot, a little lifetime.
Pride in your history is pride.
Markson. History and Theory of Art.
Marvell. Upon Appleton House [To My Lord
    Fairfax].
Meinke. Flatbush.
Meredith. I looked from the book of the story
    of men.
Il y a Cent Ans.
Karl Onyx.
Outside the Crowd.
Remember what a night of storm.
Merton. At the Gates of Aerea.
At This Precise Moment of History.
King Solomon: my master and the imbeciles.
Slowly slowly / Comes Christ through the
    garden.
Tower of Babel.
Nathan. Reading of History, A.
Nemerov. From a Record of Disappointment.
To Clio, Muse of History.
Truth of the Matter, The.
O'Hara. In Memory of My Feelings.
Olson. April Today Main Street.
At Yorktown.
Ballad for Americans.
Bigmans II.
Buffalo Ode.
Collected Poems of, The.
Got Me Home, the Light Snow Gives the Air,
    Falling.
Gulf of Maine, The.
He, Who, in His Abandnoned Infancy, Spoke
    of Jesus, Caesar, Those Who Beg, and Hell.
John Burke.
Kingfishers, The.
Later Note on Letter #15, A.
Main Street / is deserted, the hills.
Mathematical Secret, and the Apron, The.
Maximus, in Gloucester Sunday, LXV.
Maximus, to Gloucester.
Plantation a Beginning, A.
Praises, The.
Some Good News.
Stevens Song.
To Gerhardt, There, among Europe's Things of
    Which He Has Written Us in His "Brief an
    Creely und Olson."
Oppen. Alpine.
Founder, The.
Mayan Ground, The.
Solitary are obsessed, The.
There are things / We live among "and to see
    them."
Which act is / Violence.
Patchen. History in a Minor Key.
History Is a Throne and a Gate.
Two for History.
Piercy. For Shoshana Rihn—Pat Swinton.
Pope. Fragment of *Brutus*, an Epic.
Windsor-Forest [*or* Windsor Forest].
Raine. Oracles.
Rock is written with the sign, The.
Ralegh. Arcadians the earth inhabited, The.
If all this world had no original[l].
Rich. Culture and Anarchy.
Education of a Novelist.
I was looking for a way out of a lifetime's
    consolations.
In my imagination I was the pivot of a fresh
    beginning.
Living Memory.
Mathilde in Normandy.

No one's fated or doomed to love anyone.
Readings of History.
Study of History.
Turning the Wheel.
Whatever it was: the grains of the glacier
    caked in the boot-cleats.
Whatever you are that has tracked us this far.
Rolfe. Poem for May First.
Rukeyser. Book of the Dead, The.
Correspondences.
Sea Mercy.
Theory of Flight.
St. John. Woman and Leopard.
Sandburg. Accomplished Facts.
Bilbea.
Bronzes.
Coin, A.
Deep roots moving in lush soil to send a
    silver-gray beech tree.
From what graveyards and sepulchers have
    they come.
Good Morning, America.
He was a king or a shah, an ahkoond or rajah.
I Am the People, the Mob.
Many Hats.
Nigger.
Old Timers.
One memorial stone reads.
Poobahs rise and hold their poobah sway, The.
Santa Fe Sketches.
Savoir Faire.
Singing Nigger.
Statistics.
They Buy with an Eye to Looks.
Wars.
Was he preaching or writing poetry or talking
    through his hat? He was.
We'll see what we'll see.
Who was that antique Chinese crook who put
    over his revolution and.
Windy City, The.
Schuyler. Eyes at the Window.
Fauré Ballade, The.
Sidney. Sonnet 30: "Whether the Turkish new
    moon minded be."
Simic. History Book.
Smith, Charlotte. Beachy Head.
Smith, Stevie. How Cruel Is the Story of Eve.
Ride, The.
Snyder. Building.
What Happened Here Before.
Spender. Exiles, The.
Footnote, A.
Stuart. No Yellow Jackets on the Mountain.
Speakers from the Vietnam War.
Tate. Historical Epitaphs.
Tomlinson. Compact: at Volterra, The.
History.
On the Tlacolula Bus.
Turco. Fort, The.
Updike. Comp. Religion.
Klimt and Schiele Confront the Cunt.
Literary Dublin.
Sonnet to Man-Made Grandeur.
Walcott. Sea is History, The.
Warren. Founding Fathers, Nineteenth-Century
    Style, Southeast U.S.A.
Shoes In Rain Jungle.
Whitman. Death of General Grant.
Few Drops Known, The.
On the Same Picture.
To a Historian.
To-day and Thee.
With Antecedents.
Whittier. Landmarks, The.
Sycamores, The.
Yorktown.
Wilbur. Ballade of the Ladies of Time Past.
Compass.
Looking into History.
Speech for the Repeal of the McCarran Act.
Waters, The.
Williams, Charles Kenneth. This Is a Sin.
Williams, Miller. Sir.
Tearing Down the Hotel.
Wordsworth. Aix-la-Chapelle.
Apology.

Artegal and Elidure.
At Rome.—Regrets.—In Allusion to Niebuhr
    and Other Modern Historians.
At Rome.—Regrets.—In Allusion to Niebuhr
    and Other Modern Historians, Continued.
Ecclesiastical Sonnets.
From the Alban Hills, Looking towards Rome.
Go Back to Antique Ages, If Thine Eyes.
In Allusion to Various Recent Histories and
    Notices of the French Revolution.
In Allusion to Various Recent Histories and
    Notices of the French Revolution, Concluded.
In Allusion to Various Recent Histories and
    Notices of the French Revolution, Continued.
In the Sound of Mull.
Massay Ways Carried across These Heights,
    The.
Near the Lake of Thrasymene.
Near the Same Lake [Thrasymene].
On the Same Occasion [on Seeing the
    Foundation Preparing for the Erection of
    Rydal Chapel].
Pillar of Trajan, The.
Plea for the Historian.
Roman Antiquities.
Roman Antiquities Discovered at Bishopstone,
    Hereforshire.
To the Rev. Christopher Wordsworth, D.D.,
    Master of Harrow School.
Wright, Charles. Journal of the Year of the
    Ox, A.
Yeats. Lapis Lazuli.
Young. Politics As History.
Zukofsky. Poem Beginning "The."

Hitchhiking and Hitchhikers
Ciardi. Faces.
"Dylan." Standing on the Highway.
Gunn. Hitching into Frisco.
Kinnell. Memory of Wilmington.
Knight. Talking in the Woods with Karl
    Amorelli.
Muldoon. Good Friday, 1971. Driving
    Westward.

Hitler, Adolf
Berg. Not That.
Carruth. Adolf Eichmann.
Your dream: / His name was Hitler and he
    lived over.
Cohen. Hitler.
Opium and Hitler.
Dunn. Introduction to the 20th Century.
Gunn. Claus von Stauffenberg.
Jeffers. Bowl of Blood, The.
Day is a Poem, The.
Liddy. Enchanter of Yellow Gold to the Old
    Friend, The.
Lowell. Attila, Hitler.
Neruda. What forced labor / for Hitler in
    Hell?
Rukeyser. Another Day. A Game of Toys.
Paul, Telling the Game.
Another Day (You can't come).
Traditional Tune.
Snodgrass. Adolf Hitler ("Better stuffed in a
    bag; drowned").
Adolf Hitler ("More than fifty millions.
    More").
Eva B Hitler, geb. Braun.
Updike. Munich.

Hoboes. see Vagabonds.

Hogarth, William
Johnson. Epitaph on William Hogarth, An.

Hogg, James
Wordsworth. Extempore Effusion upon the
    Death of James Hogg.

Hogue, La, Battle of (1692)
Cummings. No time ago / or else a life.

Hokusai, Katsushika
Sandburg. His Own Face Hidden.

Hölderlin, Friedrich
Carruth. Your dream: / His name was
    Hölderlin. Ah, name, name!

"Holiday, Billie" (Eleanora Fagan McKay)
Carruth. Billie Holiday.
Hughes, Langston. Song for Billie Holiday.
O'Hara. Day Lady Died, The.

Holidays
Auden.   Easter Monday.
"Carroll, Lewis."   Acrostic: Little maidens,
    when you look.
Dickinson.   Lest any doubt that we are glad
    that they were born Today.
Gunn.   At the Barriers.
Hardy.   Yuletide in a Younger World.
Herrick.   Ceremonies for Candlemas[se] Eve.
Hewitt.   Leaving for Holiday.
Lawrence.   August Holidays.
MacNeice.   Postcript to Iceland.
Merton.   Old.
Nemerov.   Home for the Holidays.
O'Hara.   Ashes on a Saturday Afternoon.
Silverstein.   I Must Remember.
Spender.   Sign *Faehre nach Wilm*, The.
Williams, Charles Kenneth.   Holiday: / every /
    yard or, A.
See also **Listings for specific Holidays.**
Holland. *see* **Netherlands.**
Holly
Heaney.   Holly.
Rossetti.   Golden Holly.
Rose has thorns as well as honey, A.
Hollywood, California
Cohen.   End of My Life in Art.
Jarrell.   Lost World, The.
Thinking of the Lost World.
Sandburg.   Landscape.
Holmes, Oliver Wendell
Whittier.   O. W. Holmes on His Eightieth
    Birthday.
Our Autocrat.
To Oliver Wendell Holmes.
Holocaust
Berg.   Desnos Reading the Palms of Men on
    Their Way to the Gas Chambers.
Berry.   Discipline, A.
Berryman.   Lover & child, a little sing.
Bukowski.   When the Berry Bush Dies I'll
    Swim Down the Green River with My Hair
    on Fire.
Carruth.   Adolf Eichmann.
Event Itself, The.
"They tossed my baby like a cat in the air."
Cohen.   All There Is to Know about Adolph
    Eichmann.
Failure of a Secular Life, The.
Davie.   Hawkshead and Dachau in a Christmas
    Glass.
Edmunds.   Treblinka.
Glück.   Parable, A.
Hayden.   From the Corpse Woodpiles, from the
    Ashes.
Hewitt.   Strangers and Neighbors.
Hill.   I Had Hope When Violence Was Ceas't.
September Song.
Two Formal Elegies.
Jarrell.   Camp in the Prussian Forest, A.
In the Camp There Was One Alive.
Protocols.
Jong.   Bed of the World, The.
By Train from Berlin.
Heidelberg Landlady, The.
Levertov.   During the Eichmann Trial.
Lindsay.   Scissors-Grinder, The.
McGrath.   Remembering the Children of
    Auschwitz.
Merton.   Epitaph for a Public Servant.
Oliver.   1945—1985: Poem for the
    Anniversary.
Olson.   La Préface.
Oppen.   It is the air of atrocity.
Plath.   Mary's Song.
Schuyler.   Let's All Hear It for Mildred
    Bailey!
Sexton.   After Auschwitz.
Uses.
Williams, Charles Kenneth.   Spit.
Zukofsky.   Song for the Year's End, A.
Holy Baptism. *see* **Baptism.**
Holy Communion. *see* **Eucharist.**
Holy Family
Merton.   Holy Child's Song, The.
Rukeyser.   Holy Family.

Whitman.   Swiftly Arose.
Holy Ghost
Davie.   Comforter, The.
Eberhart.   Track.
Herbert.   Whitsunday.
Lawrence.   God and the Holy Ghost.
Rossetti.   Whitsun Day.
Smith, Stevie.   How Do You See?
Holy Innocents
Rossetti.   Holy Innocents.
Unspotted lambs to follow the one Lamb.
Holy Roman Empire
Lowell.   Charles Vby Titian.
Holy Spirit
Berry.   To the Holy Spirit.
Cohen.   Dove, The.
Coleridge.   O Spirit blest! / Whether th' eternal
    Throne around.
Davie.   Cannibals.
Donne.   Holy Ghost, The.
Show me dear[e] Christ, thy spouse, so bright
    and clear.
Herrick.   Gods Dwelling.
His Letanie, To the Holy Spirit.
Holy Thursday
Blake.   Holy Thursday (" 'Twas on a Holy
    Thursday, their innocent faces clean").
Holy Thursday ("Is this a holy thing to see").
Rossetti.   Maundy Thursday.
Home
Ammons.   Calling.
Berry.   Beneath this stone a Berry is planted.
In place with you, as I come and go.
Returning.
Stay Home.
Burns.   Banks of Nith, The.
My Heart's in the Highlands.
Song: "Their groves o' sweet myrtle let
    Foreign Lands reckon."
Wren's Nest, The.
Byron.   Wild Gazelle, The.
"Carroll, Lewis."   Acrostic: Maidens! if you
    love the tale.
Nursery Darling, A.
Carruth.   This nation was asylum when we
    came.
Your dream: / Her name was Hestia, sister of
    God.
Catullus.   Carmen 46: "Now spring bursts."
Ciardi.   Talking Myself to Sleep at One More
    Hilton.
Clough.   Come home, come home! and where
    an home hath he.
Coleridge.   Happy Home, The.
Cooper.   Little Vesper, A.
Cowper.   Soul That Loves God Finds Him
    Every Where, The.
Creeley.   Away.
For the Graduation: Bolinas, 1972.
Mobile Homes.
Please.
Cummings.   Home means that / when the
    certainly.
Davie.   Blank of the Wall, The.
Conditioned Air, A.
De la Mare.   Comfort.
Tryst, The.
Dickey, James.   Coming Back to America.
Dickinson.   Fairest Home I ever knew, The.
Home is the riddle of the wise.
Home itself is far from home.
I learned—at least—what Home could be.
Where Thou art—that—is Home.
You spoke of "Hope" surpassing "Home."
Donne.   Jealousy.
To Sir Henry Wotton ("Sir, more than kisses,
    letters mingle souls").
Dunbar.   Hope.
Possum Trot.
Dunn.   Letter Home.
"Dylan."   On the Road Again.
Town I was born in holds no memories, The.
Eberhart.   Examination of Psyche: Thoughts of
    Home.
Edmunds.   Back Home.
Eliot.   To the Indians Who Died in Africa.
Emerson.   For his constant dwelling place has

Hafiz.
I never went out of my country.
Poet is at home, A.
That each should in his house abide.
They strew in the path of kings and czars.
Thou shalt make thy house.
Una.
Fisher.   At the end of the familiar.
Frost.   Death of the Hired Man, The.
Thatch, The.
Gallagher.   Coming Home.
View from an Empty Chair.
Galvin.   Old Trip by Dream Train, The.
Garrigue.   Why the Heart Has Dreams Is Why
    the Mind Goes Mad.
Glück.   Adult Grief.
Gunn.   Thoughts on Unpacking.
Hacker.   Two Cities.
Haines.   Incurable Home, The.
Hardy.   Concerning His Old Home.
Hartley.   Recognition of Region.
Herrick.   Thanksgiving to God for His House,
    A.
Hesketh.   I Am Not Resigned.
Walking Back.
Hewitt.   Belfastman, The.
Cushkib Fair.
Disaster on the Box.
Homestead.
House at Ballyholme, The.
House Demolished, A.
Lonsdale Street.
Man from Malabar, The.
Mycenae and Epidaurus.
1957–1972.
96 Clifton Park Avenue and the Robinsons.
Our Avenue.
Substance and Shadow.
Townland of Peace.
Holmes.   Dire Coasts.
Old Saybrook House, The.
Housman.   Recruit, The.
Hughes, Langston.   Croon.
Kid in the Park.
Hugo.   Houses.
How to Use a Storm.
Last Day There.
Listen, Ripley.
Living Alone.
Only Bar in Dixon, The.
Jeffers.   Salvage.
Joseph.   Exorcism.
Kipling.   Coastwise Lights, The.
Flowers, The.
Lichtenberg.
Native-Born, The.
Recall, The.
Roman Centurion's Song, The.
Song of the Wise Children.
Sussex.
Virginity, The.
Larkin.   Story.
Lawrence.   End of Another Home Holiday.
Levine.   How many lives were torn apart.
7 Years from Somewhere.
We sat by the shore.
Lewis.   Destruction.
Fishes inhabit the deep rock crannies, the
    worm the dry.
Home Thoughts from Abroad.
Island, The.
Lovelace.   Another ("The centaur, siren I
    forgo").
Lowry.   Crane over seas and forests seeks her
    home, The.
In Memoriam; Ingvald Bjorndal and His
    Comrade.
Love and wisdom have no home.
New Guinea Gardener Bird, The.
With Midsummer Devotion from All the Little
    Animals to Their Beloved Harteebeeste.
MacLeish.   New England Weather.
Sketch for a Portrait of Mme. G——M——
—.
Where a Poet's From.
MacNeice.   Canto IX: "Master closed the door.
    The unmodern words, The."

Mahon. Ford Manor.
Meinke. Liquid Paper.
  Monkey's Paw, The.
Merrill. Another August.
Millay. On the Wide Heath.
Nemerov. Home for the Holidays.
  Succession.
Piercy. Concerning the Mathematician.
  Homesick.
  Spring Offensive of the Snail, The.
Raine. House, The.
  Iona.
  Message from Home.
  Nameless Islets.
  Spell to Bring Lost Creatures Home.
Rich. Strayed Village, The.
  Tourist and the Town, The.
  Wild Sky, The.
Robinson. House on the Hill, The.
Roethke. Return, The.
Rossetti. Discovery, A.
  End Is Not Yet, The.
  Hear what the mournful linnets say.
  How One Chose.
  Ruin.
Rukeyser. Book of the Dead, The.
  Home thoughts from home; we read you every
  day.
  Man in a plane looks at the surface of land,
  A.
  Song, from "Mr. Amazeen on the River."
  This House, This Country.
Sandburg. Crimson Rambler.
  Knucks.
Sarton. Der Abschied.
Sexton. January 19th.
Shelley. Fragment: Home.
Simic. Euclid Avenue.
Snodgrass. Mutability.
Snyder. Cold Mountain is a house.
  Not Leaving the House.
Stafford. At Our House.
  One Home.
Stevenson. Ille Terrarum.
  My body which my dungeon is.
  New House, The.
  Not undelightful, friend, our rustic ease.
  Scotsman's Return from Abroad, The.
  When the sun comes after rain.
Sutter. Homing.
Turco. Home Thoughts.
Updike. House Growing, The.
Walcott. Exile.
  Return to D'Ennery; Rain.
Walker. On Being Asked to Leave a Place of
  Honor for One of Comfort, Preferably in the
  Northern Suburbs.
Whitman. O Magnet-South.
Whittier. Homestead, The.
Wordsworth. Admonition.
  Composed by the Sea-Shore.
  Composed When a Probability Existed of Our
  Being Obliged to Quit Rydal Mount as a
  Residence.
  Farewell, A: "Farewell, thou little Nook of
  mountain-ground."
  On Being Stranded near the Harbour of
  Boulogne.
Wright, James. Father.
Wroth. Sonnet 10: "Weary traveller who tired
  sought, The."
Yau. Stuffing yourself into a blizzard.
Yeats. Under Saturn.
Young. Dancing Day to Day.
  Going Back Home.
  Indiana Gig, The.
Zukofsky. Warm gale, a dose of spring—
  revert to the pores.

Homecoming
Ammons. I Went Back.
Angelou. Mothering Blackness, The.
Arnold. Resignation.
Atwood. Bus to Alliston, Ontario, The.
Auden. Out of sight assuredly, not out of
  mind.
Beckett. Sanies I.
Berry. Homecoming, A.

Berryman. Home Ballad, The.
Blake. Dream, A.
Boyle. Confession to Eugene Jolas, A.
Burns. When wild War's deadly blast was
  blawn.
Carew. Upon Master W. Montague, His
  Return from Travel.
Carruth. Arctic owl moved across the
  snowsmooth, The.
  Third Version, The.
Cummings. Your homecoming will be my
  homecoming.
Davie. Rodez.
Dickey, James. Coming Back to America.
Dove. Son, The.
Dunbar. Bein' Back Home.
  Goin' Back.
Emerson. Saadi loved the new & old.
  What lovelier forms things wear.
Graves. Home-Coming, The.
Hardy. Geographical Knowledge.
  His Visitor.
  Rover Come Home, The.
  Welcome Home.
Hartley. Return of the Native.
Heaney. Trial Runs.
Hugo. Ashville.
Jarrell. Transient Barracks.
Jeffers. Northern Heather.
  Return.
Kinnell. Flying Home.
Kipling. Return, The.
  Troopin'.
Knight. Poem for Myself (or Blues for a
  Mississippi Black Boy), A.
  Welcome Back, Mr. Knight: Love of My Life.
Lewis. And still the heart breaks, wakeful all
  the night?
  Before he sails a man may go on leave.
  Odyssey, The.
  She Wakes Early, While He Still Sleeps.
Lowry. Oh welcome Home /To thy cot by the
  foam.
  Ship is Turning Homeward, The.
  Welcome Home Oh Harteebeeste.
  Welcome Home, Oh Sweetest Harteebeeste.
  Welcome Home Our Own.
MacLeish. Journey Home.
Mahon. Homecoming.
  I am going home by sea.
Meredith. Moonlight Night.
  Periander.
  Recognition, The.
  Richard Lionheart.
Merrill. Island in the Works.
Merton. Poem in the Rain and the Sun.
Morrison. Augment of Re-Birth.
Neruda. Homecomings.
Olson. How Things Change.
Owen. Send-Off, The.
Pope. Mary Gulliver to Capt. Lemuel Gulliver.
Raine. On an Ancient Isle.
Ransom. Prelude to an Evening.
  Prelude to an Evening.
"Reed." Families.
Rolfe. Homecoming (August 7, 1934).
Rossetti. Minnie bakes oaten cakes, / Minnie
  brews ale.
Rukeyser. Fifth Elegy. A Turning Wind.
  Shortest Way Home, The.
  Welcome from War.
Sarton. Return.
  To the North.
Schuyler. Elizabethans Called It Dying, The.
  Up.
Shelton. Dtran of Return.
Smith, Charlotte. Written at the Same Place,
  on Seeing a Seaman Return Who Had Been
  Imprisoned at Rochfort.
Walcott. Homecoming: Anse La Raye.
Whitman. Twenty Years.
Williams, William Carlos. Returning after I
  left my home in childhood.
Wordsworth. After Landing—The Valley of
  Dover, Nover, 1820.
  Composed at Rydal on May Morning, 1838.

Composed in the Valley near Dover, on the
  Day of Landing.
Zimmer. Zimmer Directs Himself Home from
  the Diggings.

Homeless, The
Ashbery. Street Musicians.
Berg. In Washington Square.
Berryman. Boston Common.
Bukowski. Private First Class.
Clare. Tramp, The.
Dickey, James. Bums, on Waking.
Dobyns. Frenchie.
  Invisibles, The.
"Dylan." Man on the Street.
  Only a Hobo.
Edmunds. December 27, 1988.
Emerson. There are beggars in Iran and
  Araby.
Griffiths. Giving Them What For.
Gunn. Improvisation.
  Old Meg.
  Outside the Diner.
Hartley. She Sauntered Most Elegantly Down.
Hewitt. Mister Faintheart Middleclass.
Hughes, Langston. Vagabonds.
Hughes, Ted. November.
Lawrence. Embankment at Night, before the
  War: Outcasts.
Merrill. House, The.
Rolfe. Season of Death.
  Sixth Winter, The.
  Winter's Ghost Plagues Them.
Sandburg. Old Woman.
Stevenson. Ille Terrarum.
Thomas. Hunchback in the Park, The.
Warren. Dark Night of the Soul.
Williams, Charles Kenneth. Harm.
  Park, The.
  Philadelphia: 1978.
  Thirst.
  Toil.
Williams, William Carlos. To a Poor Old
  Woman.

Homer
Atwood. Circe / Mud Poems.
Browning, Robert. Development.
Carruth. Light in the Locust Tree.
  Was she innocent? Too beautiful for that.
  Your dream: / His name was Homer. He was
  blind.
Cowper. Answer to Stanzas Addressed to
  Lady Hesketh.
  Inscription for a Bust of Homer.
  It is a maxim of much weight.
  On a Mistake in His Translation of Homer.
  To John Johnson.
Eberhart. Garden God, The.
Emerson. Solution.
Hewitt. To Piraeus.
Jeffers. Epic Stars, The.
Keats. On First Looking into Chapman's
  Homer.
  To Homer.
Kipling. When 'Omer Smote 'Is Bloomin'
  Lyre.
Matthews. Homer's Seeing-Eye Dog.
Notley. Homer's *Art*.
Oliver. Return, The.
Tennyson. "Courage!" he said, and pointed
  toward the land.
Yeats. Woman Homer Sung, A.

Homesickness
Browning, Robert. Home-Thoughts, from
  Abroad.
Byron. Lachin y Gair.
Clough. Ye flags of Piccadilly, / Where I
  posted up and down.
Coleridge. Home-Sick.
  Lines Written in the Album at Elbingerode, in
  the Har[t]z Forest.
De la Mare. Homesick.
Dunbar. Home Longings.
  Letter, A.
  To the Eastern Shore.
Glück. Legend.
Hemingway. First Poem to Mary in London.
Jarrell. Island, The.

Kinnell. Flying Home.
Kipling. Broken Men, The.
  Fires, The.
  Moon of Other Days, The.
Lewis. In Hospital: Poona (1).
Lowry. Outward Bound.
McAuley. Draft Balance Sheet.
MacLeish. American Letter.
MacNeice. But even so, he said, daily I
  hanker, daily.
  Nostalgia.
Ransom. Crocodile.
Spender. Cornet Cornelius Rilke.
Waldman. Paris Day.
Wordsworth. Why, Minstrel, These Untuneful
  Murmurings.
Wright, James. Outside Fargo, North Dakota.

Homesteaders
Whittier. Kansas Emigrants, The.

Homophobia
Hughes, Langston. Café: 3 A.M.
Lorde. Poem for Women in Rage, A.
"Reed." Slide, The.

Homosexuality and Homosexuals
Beatles. Polythene Pam.
Berryman. Shirley & Auden.
Betjeman. Narcissus.
Blake. Why was Cupid a Boy.
Boyle. In Defense of Homosexuality.
Catullus. Carmen 16: "Pedicabo et irrumabo."
  Carmen 33: "Vibennius & son, renowned."
  Carmen 56: "Matter for mirth, Cato, & a
    smile, A."
  Carmen 80: "How is it, Gellius."
  Carmen 106: "When an auctioneer's seen with
    a good-looking boy."
  Carmen 112: "Naso! an elevated personage."
  Hymeneal.
Creeley. All That Is Lovely in Men.
Cummings. In hammamet did camping queers
  et al).
Dickey, William. Alligators and Paris and
  North America.
  Rainbow Grocery, The.
Ginsberg. Archetype Poem, The.
  Chances "R."
  Come All Ye Brave Boys.
  I Have Increased Power.
  Many Loves.
  Maybe Love.
  Tethnakin D'oligo Pideuis Fainom Alaia.
  This Form of Life Needs Sex.
Gunn. At the Barriers.
  Blank, A.
  Bone.
  But I came back, after the last bus.
  Differences, The.
  London returned to after twelve years, A.
  Menace, The.
  Miracle, The.
  Punch Rubicundus.
  San Francisco Streets.
  Sweet Things.
  Venetian Blind.
Hacker. Graffiti from the Gare Saint-Manqué.
  I will never be only a Lesbian.
  Partial Analysis.
Hughes, Langston. Café: 3 A.M.
Jonson. On Sir Voluptuous Beast.
Knight. For Freckle-Faced Gerald.
Koch. Aus Einer Kindheit.
Lawrence. Ego-Bound Women.
  I Know a Noble Englishman.
  Modern Problems.
Liddy. Art Is Not for Grown-ups.
  Cantico.
  Correspondences.
  Delphine and Hippolyta.
  Lesbos.
  Reply of the Friend, The.
  Sound of a Moment at Scariff, The.
  Wine of Lovers.
Lowell. Words for Hart Crane.
Olson. Issues from the Hand of God.
Plath. Lesbos.
Prince. Old Age of Michelangelo, The.

"Reed." Halloween Parade, The.
  Slide, The.
Rexroth. When We with Sappho.
Schuyler. Morning of the Poem, The.
  Tom.
  Tom's Attempt to Seduce Big Brother Steve.
Sexton. Rapunzel.
Shapiro. Girls Fighting, Broadway.
Smith, Stevie. Lord Barrenstock.
Stein. Men.
Van Duyn. Cities of the Plain, The.
Whitman. In Paths Untrodden.
  Not Heat Flames Up and Consumes.
  Recorders Ages Hence.
  When I Heard at the Close of the Day.
  Whoever You Are Holding Me Now in Hand.
Wright, James. Sappho.
Zukofsky. Cute boy arm in elbow prize con
  man, kid, what do we see.
  Mool 'tis homos,' Naso 'n' queer take 'im
    mool 'tis ho most he.
  O ram ridicule home, Cato, the jokes some.
  Offer 'em up to me—bullneck crook of the
    baths.
  Piping, beaus, I'll go whoosh and I'll rumble
    you.
  Quiddity, Gelli, quarry, rosy as these too lips
    belie.

Honduras
Lorde. To the Girl Who Lives In a Tree.

Honesty
Atwood. We are hard on each other.
Burns. Epitaph on J-hn B-shby.
Campion. Dear If I with Guile.
Epigramme: "Phoebe all the rights Elisa
  claymeth."
  Faire If You Expect Admiring.
  Heart's Music.
  Maydes are simple, some men say.
  Some can flatter, some can faine.
  Were My Heart as Some Men's Are.
Cowper. Conversation.
  Friendship.
Creeley. Again.
  For Somebody's Marriage.
  Somebody Died.
Davie. Against Confidences.
Dunbar. My Sort o' Man.
Dunn. Return, The.
Emerson. Hard is it to persuade the public
  mind of its plain duty & true interest.
  Papas Blondine / Grew tall & wise.
  Romany Girl, The.
Graves. Song: To Become Each Other.
Hall. Friend Revisited, A.
Hewitt. Difficult Man, A.
  Faded Leaf: A Chapter of Family History,
    The.
  Hospitality: For E.K.
Hughes, Ted. Soliloquy: "Whenever I am got
  under my gravestone."
Meredith. Their sense is with their senses all
  mixed in.
Rukeyser. Poem as Mask, The.
Sandburg. Great Sphinx and the Pyramids say,
  The.
  Hogh Conspiratorial Persons.
  Implications.
  Tall Timber.
Shelley. Fragment: "What men gain fairly—
  that they should possess."
Smart. Truth.
Sorrentino. Let's Call This.
  3 Quatrains.
Stafford. Fifteen.
Van Duyn. What I Want to Say.
Whittier. Nauhaught, the Deacon.
Wyatt. Throughout the world, if it were
  sought.
Zukofsky. You three:—my wife.

Honey
Dickinson. Within that little Hive.
Doolittle. Fragment 113: "Not honey, / not the
  plunder of the bee."
  Socratic.
Eberhart. Sunday in October.
Graves. Song: To a Rose.

Rossetti. Golden Glories.
  When the cows come home the milk is
    coming.
Sandburg. In Tall Grass.

Honey Eaters
Oliver. Happiness.

Honeymoons
Eliot. Lune de Miel.
Glück. Bridal Piece.
Hardy. Four Footprints.
Herrick. Epithalamy to Sir Thomas Southwell
  and His Lady, An.
Prince. Inn, The.
Rukeyser. Wedding Presents.
Updike. Newlyweds, The.

Honeysuckle
Ford. Typhoid and smallpox.
Rossetti. O wind, where have you been.
Zukofsky. Honeysuckle.
  Wild Honeysuckle.

Hong Kong
Merton. Picture of Lee Ying, A.

Honor
Berryman. Scholars at the Orchid Pavilion.
Boyle. People's Cry, The.
Brontë. M. Douglas to E.R. Gleneden.
Browning, Robert. After.
  At the "Mermaid."
  Count Gismond.
Byron. On Leaving Newstead Abbey.
Campion. Ad Leam.
  Ballad, A: "Dido was the Carthage Queene."
  O griefe, O spight, to see poore Vertue
    scorn'd.
  Shall then a traiterous kis or a smile.
Carew. Feminine Honour.
  To My Much Honoured Friend, Henry, Lord
    Carey of Leppington, Upon His Translation
    of Malvezzi.
Chaucer. Lak of Stedfastnesse.
Clark. You (V) (after Holderlin).
Cowper. To Dr. Darwin.
De la Mare. Here Sleeps.
Dickinson. All men for Honor hardest work.
  Judgment is justest.
  Sown in dishonor!
  There is nothing sweeter than Honor, but
    Love.
Donne. To the Countess of Bedford ("Honour
  is so sublime perfection").
Emerson. Quoth Saadi, when I stood before.
  Rex.
  Why honor the new men.
Graves. Charm for Sound Sleeping, A.
  Song: Sword and Rose.
Hemingway. To Good Guys Dead.
Herrick. God to Be First Served.
  Studies to Be Supported.
  To His Learned Friend M. Jo. Harmar,
    Phisitian to Colledge of Westminster.
Hewitt. On Choosing Some Verses for My
  Sister's Cremation.
Hughes, Langston. Shame on You.
Jeffers. Tower beyond Tragedy, The.
Jonson. Ode. To Sir William Sydney, on His
  Birthday.
  Song. To Celia ("Drink to me only with thine
    eyes").
  To Sir Edward Herbert.
  To Sir Henry Cary.
  To Sir Henry Nevil.
  To Thomas, Earl of Suffolk.
Kipling. Dedication from "Barrack-Room
  Ballads."
  Hindu Sepoy in France.
  Pro-Consuls, The.
  Two Canadian Memorials.
Levine. Jewish Graveyards, Italy.
  My Poets.
  On the Murder of Lieutenant José Del Castillo
    by the Falangist Bravo Martinez, July 12,
    1936.
  To Cipriano, in the Wind.
Lindsay. Hearth Eternal, The.
  Honor Among Scamps.
Lovelace. Mock Charon, A.
  To Lucasta, [on] Going to the War[re]s.

Lowry.   No wonder it feared peace, the knees
  of years.
Melville.   College Colonel, The.
  On the Home Guards.
Meredith.   Preaching from a Spanish Ballad, A.
Olson.   Dramatis Personae.
Owen.   S.I.W.
  To a Comrade in Flanders.
Roethke.   Reply to Censure.
Rolfe.   Elegy for Our Dead.
Sandburg.   Bronzes.
  John Ericsson Day Memorial, 1918.
  Letters to Dead Imagists.
Shakespeare.   Sonnet 25: "Let those who are in
  favour with their stars."
Sidney.   Sonnet 35: "What may words say, or
  what may words not say."
Smart.   Honour.
Smith, Charlotte.   Apostrophe to an Old Tree.
Stevenson.   In Memoriam, E.H.
  Vanquished Knight, The.
Stuart.   Return, The.
Suckling.   Loving and Beloved.
Whitman.   To a Certain Cantatrice.
Wilbur.   Up, Jack.
Williams, Miller.   My Wife Reads the Paper at
  Breakfast on the Birthday of the Scottish
  Poet.
Wordsworth.   Pause, courteous Spirit!—Baldi
  supplicates.
  Say, what is Honour?—"Tis the finest sense."
Wright, James.   Centenary Note: Inscribed to
  Little Crow, Leader of the Sioux Rebellion in
  Minnesota, 1862, A.
  In Memory of a Spanish Poet.
Wyatt.   Dido am I, the founder first of
  Carthage.
Young.   Dancing Naked.

Hooch, Pieter de
Mahon.   Courtyards in Delft.

Hood, Thomas
Robinson.   Thomas Hood.

Hooker, Joseph
Davie.   Anglican Lady, An.

Hoopoes
Graves.   Hoopoe Tells Us How, The.

Hope
Angelou.   No No No No.
  Plagued Journey, A.
Arnold.   Self-Dependence.
Atwood.   In this house (in a dying orchard.
Auden.   Christ in Hades.
Beatles.   Sun King.
  This Boy.
Beckett.   Ce qu'ont les yeux.
  Hope is a knave befools us evermore.
Berry.   Since then I have arrived here.
  Young Man, Thinking of the Old, The.
Berryman.   For you my all, was it not, so far.
  Man who made her let me climb the derrick,
  The.
  Most strange, my change, this nervous
  interim—.
  Musculatures and skulls. Later some throng.
Bly.   Poem in Three Parts.
Brontë.   And first an hour of mournful musing.
  Anticipation.
  Hope.
  Ierne's eyes were glazed and dim.
  What use is it to slumber here.
Browning, Elizabeth Barrett.   Memory and
  Hope.
Browning, Robert.   Prologue: "O the old wall
  here! How I could pass."
Bukowski.   Crunch, The.
  One for the Shoeshine Man.
Bunting.   Now we've no hope of going back.
Burns.   Nithsdale's Welcome Hame.
  Song: "Anna, thy charms my bosom fire."
Byron.   Stanzas for Music.
Carroll, Jim.   Cosmopolitan Sense, The.
Carruth.   Return to Love.
  Sonnet: "It's said by the thoughtful masters
  that to know death."
Ceravolo.   Wild Provoke of the Endurance
  Sky.
Clare.   Ballad: "Summer morning is risen."

Clark.   Crisis on the Savannah.
Clough.   To see the rich autumnal tints depart.
Coleridge.   Faith, Hope, and Charity.
  Fragment: "O'er the raised earth the gales of
  evening sigh."
  Hope and Tranquillity.
  Indifference of the Heavens, The.
  Lewti.
  Lines Suggested by the Last Words of
  Berengarius.
  Love, Hope, and Patience in Education.
  Love's Apparition and Evanishment.
  To Fortune.
  To the Autumnal Moon.
  Visionary Hope, The.
  Work without Hope.
Cowper.   Hope.
  Hope, like the short-liv'd ray that gleams
  awhile.
Crane.   Ave Maria.
Crashaw.   On Hope.
Creeley.   Business, The.
  Carnival, The.
  For a Screaming Lady.
  Fragment, A: "On the street I am met with
  constant hostility."
  Mechanic, The.
  "Oh My Love.."
  Wall, A.
  Walls.
Cullen.   Brown Boy to Brown Girl.
  From the Dark Tower.
Cummings.   Air, / be / comes / or.
  Chilly,murky night, A.
  !Hope / faith! / !life / love!
  So many selves(so many fiends and gods).
  Though your sorrows not.
  Thy face is a still white house of holy things.
  Unnoticed woman from whose kind large
  flesh.
De la Mare.   Cage, The.
  Catechism, The.
  Euphrasy.
  Rachel.
  Virtue.
Dickinson.   Could Hope inspect her Basis.
  Faithful "I am sorry", A.
  Hope is a strange invention.
  Hope is a subtle Glutton.
  "Hope" is the thing with feathers.
  I dwell in Possibility.
  I hope you may sometime be.
  Is this the Hope that opens and shuts.
  Promise is firmer than a Hope, A.
  Way Hope builds his House, The.
  You spoke of "Hope" surpassing "Home."
Dobyns.   Body's Hope, The.
Donne.   To Mr. T. W. ("Pregnant again with
  th' old twins hope, and fear").
Doolittle.   So if you love me.
Dove.   Fiammetta Breaks Her Peace.
  First Kiss.
Dunbar.   Disappointed.
Dunn.   Almost Everyone.
  Homage to the Divers.
  Waiting with Two Members of a Motorcycle
  Gang for Two Children to Be Born.
"Dylan."   Ain't Gonna Grieve.
  Baby, I'm in the Mood for You.
  I Shall Be Released.
  Paths of Victory.
  Seven Days.
  Shelter from the Storm.
Eberhart.   Angels, The.
  Austere Poem.
  Breathless, The.
  Lost, The.
  Man Who Was Blown Down by the Wind, A.
  Poet, The.
Emerson.   And Ellen, when the greybeard
  years.
  Fortune and Hope! I've made my port.
  Maiden Speech of the Æolian Harp.
Galvin.   Field of Inheritance, The.
  Willow, Wishbone, Warblers.
Ginsberg.   In Back of the Real.
  Sunflower Sutra.

Graves.   Desert Fringe.
  Home-Coming, The.
  Love without Hope.
  Lovers in Winter.
  Poor Others.
Griffiths.   Chips.
  Contractions.
  Old Hope.
Hall.   Sun, The.
Hardy.   Darkling Thrush, The.
  Song of Hope.
  To an Unborn Pauper Child.
Herbert.   Hope.
  Pilgrimage, The.
  Size, The.
Herrick.   Faith.
  His Hope or Sheet-Anchor.
  Hope Heartens.
  Hope Well and Have Well: or, Faire after
  Foule Weather.
  Impossibilities to His Friend.
  Sufferance.
  To God, on His Sickness[e].
  To Sapho ("Sapho, I will chuse to go").
Hesketh.   Evergreen.
  No Reply at Christmas.
  Winter Daffodils.
Hewitt.   Already autumn silently / has come to
  sky and field and tree.
  Christmas Eve.
  Curfew Tower, The.
  Exile.
  For Busha.
  For One Who Did Not March.
  Happy Boy, A.
  He Suggests a Solution.
  Interim.
  King Concerned, The.
  Limitations.
  Lyric: "Let but a thrush begin."
  Lyric: "Let this last lyric of a passing day."
  Northern Spring.
  Poet's Trade, The.
  Pro Tanto Quid Retribuamas.
  Rank-and-Filer, The.
  Ruins Answer, The.
  To the People of Dresden.
  Two Spectres Haunt Me.
  Watercolour, The.
Holmes.   Fayetteville Dawn (2).
  Night Music.
  Watching Morning In.
  Weekend Away.
  Work on in the faith.
Hopkins.   Leaden Echo and the Golden Echo,
  The.
Housman.   How clear, how lovely bright.
Hughes, Langston.   Hope.
Hugo.   Good View from Flagstaff, A.
Jarrell.   Hope.
  Jews at Haifa.
  Lament of the Children of Israel in Rome.
  Utopian Journey, A.
Jeffers.   Hope is Not for the Wise.
  Local Legend.
Johnson.   Winter's Walk, The.
Jong.   Middle Aged Lovers, II.
Joseph.   Man as Real (CITY; HUMAN).
  Road from Glastonbury, The.
Keats.   To Hope.
Knight.   Green Grass and Yellow Balloons.
Knott.   Lesson.
Kooser.   Leaky Faucet, The.
Larkin.   Slight Relax of Air Where Cold Was,
  A.
Levine.   Planting.
Lewis.   Greetings.
Liddy.   In a Blue Smoke.
  Little Song for Ivy Day, 1991.
  My Neighbours Two Brothers.
  Narcissus and the Young Men.
  Orpheus as a Christian Scientist.
Lindsay.   Amaranth, The.
  Invocation for "The Map of the Universe."
  Speak Now for Peace.
  Town of American Visions, The.
Lowry.   April 1937 In the Oaxaca Train.

Chilliwack.
Faking was three times married to Faking.
In the Oaxaca Train.
Lusty Advice of a Fortune-Teller.
Poem to be Placed at the Conclusion of a Long Obscure Passionate and Eloquent Book of Poems.
Sadness is so much a part of me.
Scribner's Sons.
Some years ago he started to escape.
MacLeish. Pole Star.
Two Poems from the War.
MacNeice. Home beyond this life? Or through it? If through, how?
Prospect.
This year, last year, one time, ever.
McNeill. Epitaph in the Imperative Mode.
Mahon. Everything Is Going to Be All Right.
I wake in a dark flat.
Markson. Loss.
Meinke. In Gentler Times.
Melville. Immolated.
Meredith. Friend, when the thundercloud is low.
Hilda's Morning and Evening Dose of Rhyme.
In all our daily war of words.
In the time of early love.
Linnet-Hawker, The.
Nature and Man.
New Year's Eve.
Persistent through the brazen chorus round.
Promise in Disturbance, The.
Song: "Pass we to another land."
Sonnet: "Hateful are those false themes of speculation."
Soul, The.
Vittoria's *Italia* Song.
Merton. Round and a Hope for Smithgirls, A.
Nash. Has Anybody Seen My Noumenon?
Song Before Breakfast.
Nemerov. Hope.
Oliver. Aunt Elsie's Night Music.
Olson. And now let all the ships come in.
Distances, The.
Oppen. Also he has set the world.
From Disaster.
That Land.
Pack. Clayfeld's Metamorphosis.
Piercy. Magician, The.
Sun, The.
Poe. Dreams.
Pope. Pleasure of Hope, The.
Prince. To a Friend on His Marriage.
Psalms. Psalm 42: "As the hart panteth after the water brooks."
Psalm 43: "Judge me, O God.."
Raine. Polluted tide, / Desecrated earth destroyed.
Robinson. Old Trails.
Rolfe. Guerrillas, The.
Rossetti. All beneath the sun hasteth, / All that hath begun wasteth.
All heaven is blazing yet / With the meridian sun.
Alone Lord God, in Whom our trust and peace.
As froth on the face of the deep, / As foam on the crest of the sea.
Bury Hope out of sight, / No book for it and no bell.
But Thy Commandment Is Exceeding Broad.
Care flieth, / Hope and fear together.
Charity.
Come Unto Me.
Dead Hope.
Doeth Well...Doeth Better.
End of Time, The.
Everything that is born must die.
Experience bows a sweet contented face.
Faith and Hope are wings to Love.
Greatest of These Is Charity, The.
Hope Carol, A.
Hope in Grief.
Hope is like a harebell trembling from its birth.
Hope is the counterpoise of fear / While night enthralls us here.

I have done with hope.
I said "All's over"—& I made my.
If hope grew on a bush, / And joy grew on a tree.
If Only.
Last Answer, The.
Love and Hope.
Now They Desire a Better Country.
O Christ my God Who seest the unseen.
Of each sad word which is more sorrowful.
On the note you do not send me.
Our heaven must be within ourselves / Our home and heaven the work of faith.
Redeeming the Time.
Serenade.
Song for the Least of All Saints, A.
Song: "Oh what comes over the sea."
Song: "She sat and sang alway."
Sorrow hath a double voice, / Sharp today but sweet tomorrow.
Sunshine.
Three Seasons.
Three Stages.
Toll, bell, toll. For hope is flying / Sighing from the earthbound soul.
We are of those who tremble at Thy word.
Where Their Worm Dieth Not, and the Fire Is Not Quenched.
Worship God.
Ye Are Come unto Mount Sion.
Yet A Little While.
Rukeyser. Chapultepec Park / II.
Dreaming we were awake, we heard the rivers.
Juanita Tinsley.
Noguchi.
Who in One Lifetime.
Sandburg. Dream Girl.
Hope is a tattered flag and a dream out of time.
It Is Much.
Passers-by.
Scaffolding holds the arch in place, The.
Sea only knows the bottom of the ship, The.
Tangibles.
There have been thousands of Andy Adams.
Sarton. Greeting.
March-Mad.
Schwartz. Poem: "Faithful to your commands, o consciousness, o."
Poem for Jacques Maritain and Leon Trotzky.
Poem: How Marvelous Man's Kind Is.
Sexton. Snow.
Shelley. Circumstance.
Lines: "Far, far away, O ye."
Lines Written among the Euganean Hills.
Love, Hope, Desire and Fear.
Sidney. Get hence foul[e] grief[e], the canker of the mind[e].
Merchant man, whom many seas have taught, The.
Sonnet 66: "And do I see some cause a hope to feed."
Sonnet 67: "Hope, art thou true, or dost thou flatter me?"
Sonnet 68: "Stella, the only planet of my light."
Smart. Against Despair.
Hope.
Smith, Charlotte. By the Same. To the North Star.
Hope. A Rondeau.
Hymn to Love and Life.
Ode to the Missel Thrush.
To Hope.
Smith, Stevie. Friend, The.
La Gretchen de Nos Jours (II).
Reason, The.
Spenser. One day, whiles that my daylie cares did sleepe.
Stevens. Thought Revolved, A.
Stevenson. Et Tu In Arcadia Vixisti.
Farewell: "Farewell, and when forth."
Hopes.
I have trod the upward and the downward slope.
I look across the ocean.
Light as the linnet on my way I start.

Man sails the deep a while.
St. Martin's Summer.
To Marcus.
Tomlinson. Ars Poetica.
Updike. Pooem.
Waldman. Hopes & Fears.
Warren. Brightness of Distance.
When the Century Dragged.
Whittier. Star of Bethlehem, The.
Trust.
Williams, Charles Kenneth. Dimensions.
In the Heart of the Beast.
Next to the Last Poem about God, The.
Poor Hope.
Williams, William Carlos. Min Schleppner.
To the Outer World.
Wordsworth. Composed Near Calais on the Road Leading to Ardres, August 7, 1802.
Evening Walk Addressed to a Young Lady, An.
Near Anio's stream, I spied a gentle Dove.
October, 1803 ("These times strike monied worldlings with dismay").
sequel to To — Upon the Birth of Her First-Born Child, March, 1833.
Wishing-Gate, The.
Wright, Charles. Hawaii Dantesca.
Wright, James. Arrangements with Earth for Three Dead Friends.
Wroth. Song 3: ("Come merry spring delight us").
Song 3: ("Stay, my thoughts, do nott aspire").
Song: "I, that ame of all most crost."
Sonnet 27: "Fie [*or* Fy] tedious Hope, why do[e] you still rebel[l]?"
Wyatt. I abide and abide and better abide.
Young. Dreams of Paradise.
For Kenneth & Miriam Patchen.
Poem Found Emptying Out My Pockets.
Problem of Identity, The.
Seventh April.
Zukofsky. Ah spring, when with a thaw of blue.
Glad they were there.
Green leaf that will outlast the winter.
Happiest February.
—"Her Soil's Birth."
Homage.
Honesty.
Valentine, A.
See also **Optimism.**

Hopi, The
Rich. Mary Jane Colter, 1904.
Tomlinson. Arizona Desert.
Death in the Desert, A.

Hopkins, Gerard Manley
Eberhart. Killer, The.

Horace
Auden. Horatians, The.
"Carroll, Lewis." Lesson in Latin, A.
Cowper. Reflection on the Foregoing Ode.
To Mrs. Throckmorton.
Davie. Wombwell on Strike.
MacNeice. Memoranda to Horace.
Robinson. Horace to Leuconoë.
Smart. 1.1: To Maecenas.
4.3: To Melpomene.
On Taking a Batchelor's Degree.

Horse Chestnut Trees and Horse Chestnuts
Gunn. Hampstead; the Horse Chestnut Trees.
Schuyler. Horse-Chestnut Trees and Roses.

Horse Racing
Bukowski. Bad Action.
Bravo.
Horsemeat.
Longshot.
Space Creatures.
Valentine Gift, A.
Dobyns. Kentucky Derby Day, Belfast, Maine.
Hacker. Late August Letter.
Hemingway. Across the Board.
Sport of Kings, The.
Kipling. AUGUST (*Coaching*).
MARCH (*Racing*).
Mare's Nest, The.
Koertge. Day Alvero Pineda Was Killed, The.

Jockey, A.
Last-Minute Change of Plans.
Larkin. At Grass.
Lowry. Draft Board.
Moore. Tom Fool at Jamaica.
Olson. There they were.
Sandburg. Alix.
Remorse.
Wakoski. Placing a $2 Bet for a Man Who Will Never Go to the Horse Races Any More.
Yeats. At Galway Races.

Horse Shows
Sidney. Sonnet 41: "Having this day my horse, my hand, my lance."

Horseback Riding
Browning, Robert. How They Brought the Good News from Ghent to Aix.
Cummings. This(that / grey)white / (man)horse.
Dickey, James. Sustainment.
Dobyns. Triangular Field, The.
Gardner. Reveille for a Rockinghorse Poet.
When in Rome..
Hardy. Circus-Rider to Ringmaster.
Jonson. Epigram. To William, Earl of Newcastle, An.
Kipling. Then we brought the lances down—then the trumpets blew.
Lowry. Sunrise.
McNeill. Gabriel MacElmain, Pioneer.
Scott. Ride to Stirling, The.
Shelton. Poet As Equestrian, The.
Sidney. Sonnet 41: "Having this day my horse, my hand, my lance."
Sonnet 49: "I on my horse, and Love on me doth try."
Wilbur. Ride, The.

Horses
Auden. Landscape.
Ploughing.
Berg. 1922.
Berry. Horses.
Sorrel Filly, The.
Berryman. Whether There Is Sorrow in the Demons.
Bly. Watering the Horse.
Browning, Robert. How They Brought the Good News from Ghent to Aix.
Bunting. That filly couldn't carry a rider nor.
Burns. Auld Farmer's New-Year-Morning Salutation to His Auld Mare, Maggie, on Giving Her the Accustomed Ripp of Corn to Hansel in the New-Year, The.
Auld Man's Mare's Dead, The.
Elegy on Peg Nicholson.
Epistle to Hugh Parker.
Tam o' Shanter [A Tale].
To Mr. John Taylor.
Carroll, Jim. Silver Mirrors.
"Carroll, Lewis." Ye Capete Knyghte.
Carruth. Sonnet: " 'Whut do you spose thet thing is,' Oi said. 'Whut?' ."
Cohen. Ballad of the Absent Mare.
Change, The.
Commentary—The Change.
Cooper. Racetrack, The.
Cowper. Cantab, The.
Creeley. Don't Sign Anything.
Folk Song, A: "Hitch up honey for the / market race all."
Gift of Great Value, A.
Rescue, The.
Cummings. What a proud dreamhorse pulling(smoothloomingly)through.
Davie. Equestrian Sestina.
De la Mare. Assignation, The.
To K. M.
Dickey, James. Dusk of Horses, The.
Horses and Prisoners.
Dickinson. I like to see it lap the Miles.
Dunbar. Dat Ol' Mare o' Mine.
Dunn. In a Dream of Horses.
Emerson. Like vaulters in the circus round.
Fletcher. Saturday Night: Horses Going to Pasture.

Fox. Horses, The.
Letters from the Island.
Frost. Draft Horse, The.
Runaway, The.
Gallagher. From Dread in the Eyes of Horses.
His Shining Helmet; Its Horsehair Crest.
Horse in the Drugstore, The.
If Poetry Were Not a Morality.
Glück. Horse.
Graves. Last Fistful, The.
Haines. South Wind.
Hall. Names of Horses.
On a Horse Carved in Wood.
Hardy. Horses Aboard.
Hartley. Beyond the Broken House.
Hemingway. Country Poem with Little Country.
Herrick. Upon Spur.
Hesketh. Horses, The.
Rivals, The.
Hewitt. Crossing, The.
Great Event, A.
King's Horses, The.
Leaving for Holiday.
Lettered Snow, The.
Mile-Long Street, The.
Ploughman, The.
Riders, The.
Stallion.
Way to School, The.
Hoffman. Great Horse Strode without a Rider, The.
Inviolable.
Hughes, Ted. Horses, The.
Hugo. O-Mok-See at Nine Mile.
Scene.
Time to Remember Sangster.
Topographical Map.
Jeffers. Roan Stallion.
Jonson. Epigram. To William, Earl of Newcastle, An.
Kipling. Contradictions.
Mare's Nest, The.
Snarleyow.
Undertaker's Horse, The.
With Scindia to Delhi.
Koertge. He ("Had a bay stallion once that the Triple Bar C").
My Father ("Once owned a blind horse, a big gray who").
Larkin. At Grass.
Lawrence. White Horse, The.
Levertov. Ce bruit da la mer.
Levine. Horse, The.
Liddy. Maud Gonne Rode Out on a White Horse to Coolgreany.
You are going to fall in love.
Lieberman. House Skin, The.
Lindsay. Broncho That Would Not Be Broken, The.
Old Horse in the City, The.
Lowry. Draft Board.
McGrath. Dreams of Wild Horses, The.
Used Up.
MacNeice. Horses.
River in Spate.
McNeill. Horsemen, The.
Traveler and Old Sorrel.
Matthews. I Long For a Horse.
Meredith. Horses of Achilles, The.
Hungarian Horse-Herd, The.
Mares of the Camargue, The.
Postillion, The.
Sweetheart of the Csikos, The.
Merrill. Charioteer of Delphi, The.
Moore. Tom Fool at Jamaica.
Morrison. Horse Latitudes.
Muldoon. Dancers at the Moy.
Oliver. Bailing the Boat.
Spring.
Patchen. It Takes Few Kinds.
Plow Horses.
Plath. Whiteness I Remember.
Prince. To a Man on His Horse.
Rossetti. Horses of the Sea, The.
Horses of the sea, The.
Rukeyser. Flying Red Horse, The.

Schwartz. Dances and the Dancers, The.
This Is a Poem I Wrote at Night, Before the Dawn.
Sexton. Horse.
Pain for a Daughter.
Simic. Little Tear Gland That Says, The.
Smith, Stevie. Fugitive's Ride, The.
Snyder. All through the Rains.
Sutter. Stallion, The.
Tomlinson. Poem: "Wakening with the window over fields."
Saving the Appearances.
Whitman. Gigantic Beauty of a Stallion, A.
Wilbur. Horses, The.
Ride, The.
Williams, Charles Kenneth. On Learning of a Friend's Illness.
Work.
Williams, William Carlos. Horse, The.
Infinite Horses, The.
When Structure Fails Rhyme Attempts to Come to the Rescue.
Wordsworth. Four Fiery Steed Impatient of the Rein.
Horse, The.
Wright, James. Blessing, A.
Horse, The.
Poems to a Brown Cricket.
Sitting in a Small Screenhouse on a Summer Morning.
Two Horses Playing in the Orchard.
Yau. Blessed flagellants set forth, mounted on tatters of flaming horses, The.
See also Colts; Foals; Horse Racing; Horse Shows; Horseback Riding.

Horseshoes
Burns. To Mr. John Taylor.

Hospitality
Atwood. We think of you as one.
Burns. At Whigham's Inn, Sanquar.
Verse Composed and Repeated by *Burns,* to the Master of the House, on Taking Leave at a Place in the Highlands, Where He Had Been Hospitably Entertained, A.
Verses Written on a Window of the Inn at Carron.
Campion. Ad Ge. Chapmannum.
Come follow me, my wandring mates.
De la Mare. Hospital.
Dickinson. Soul that hath a Guest, The.
Hardy. At an Inn.
Squire Hooper.
Herrick. Happinesse to Hospitalitie, or a Hearty Wish to Good House-Keeping.
To His Peculiar Friend M. Jo: Wicks.
To the Most Virtuous Mistress Pot, Who Many Times Entertained Him.
Upon Showbread [*or* Shewbread]: Epigram.
Hewitt. In the Rosses.
My Father's Mother.
Hugo. Places and Ways to Live.
Jonson. Inviting a Friend to Supper.
Kipling. Ballad of East and West, The.
Hadramauti.
Lowry. Hospitality.
Mahon. Tolerable Wisdom, A.
Merton. Isfahan.
Nash. Just Keep Quiet and Nobody Will Notice.
Polterguest, My Polterguest.
Suppose I Darken Your Door.
Visit From Dr. Fell, A.
Piercy. Poet Dreams of a Nice Warm Motel, The.
Robinson. Cliff Klingenhagen.
Tomlinson. Quarai.
Updike. Neotony.
Whittier. "I Was a Stranger and Ye Took Me in."
Williams, Charles Kenneth. Guatemala: 1964.
See also Guests.

Hospitals
Berg. Ollie, Answer Me.
Berryman. Hell Poem, The.
I Know.
Purgatory.

Bukowski. Bedpans.
Mexican Girls, The.
Carruth. Diagnosis is / Anxiety psychoneurosis, The.
Sonnet: "At the hospital where I had the echocardiagram."
Cohen. Teachers.
Creeley. Heaven.
Cullen. Lines for a Hospital.
Dickey, James. Poem: "For having left the birds that left me."
Dobyns. In the Hospital.
Fisher. Hospital in Winter, The.
Fox. Rescue.
Transvestite, The.
Graves. Surgical Ward: Men.
Griffiths. Courage.
Gunn. Still Life.
Hacker. His Wife at Bellevue.
Hall. Tubes.
Hayden. Broken Dark, The.
Hesketh. Tunnel, The.
Ward F4.
What Is a Person?
Hewitt. Geriatric Ward, The.
Jarrell. Christmas Roses, The.
Field Hospital, A.
In a Hospital Garden.
Utopian Journey, A.
X-Ray Waiting Room in the Hospital, The.
Kipling. Nursing Sister, The.
Knight. At a VA Hospital in the Middle of the United States of America: An Act in a Play.
Larkin. Building, The.
Hospital Visits.
Levine. Having Been Asked "What is a Man?" I Answer.
Lewis. Greetings.
In Hospital: Poona (1).
In Hospital: Poona (2).
"MacDiarmid." In the Children's Hospital.
Matthews. Recovery Room.
Merton. I seek you in the hospital where you work.
Miller. Free Clinic.
Muldoon. Field Hospital, The.
Oliver. University Hospital, Boston.
Owen. Conscious.
Hospital Barge at Cérisy.
Mental Cases.
Pack. Dwarf and Doctor Freud, The.
Plath. Face Lift.
Morning in the Hospital Solarium.
Poem for a Birthday.
Surgeon at 2 A.M., The.
Tulips.
Rukeyser. In Hades, Orpheus.
Sarton. Night Watch.
Schuyler. Arches.
Linen.
Pastime.
Sleep.
Sexton. August 17th.
Break, The.
Lullaby: "It is a summer evening."
Operation, The.
Unknown Girl in the Maternity Ward.
You, Doctor Martin.
Snodgrass. Flat One, A.
Operation, The.
Stuart. Hospital of Lies, The.
Tomlinson. In the Ward.
Updike. Aerie.
Van Duyn. In the Hospital for Tests.
Recovery.
Williams, William Carlos. Between Walls.
From a Window.
Wright, James. She Hid in the Trees from the Nurses.
Yau. Telephone Call, The.
Young. Herrick Hospital, Fifth Floor.

Hotels
Carroll, Jim. On Tour.
Cohen. Another Room.
Commentary—Another Room.
Fisher. Foyer, The.

Gardner. At a Summer Hotel.
Gunn. Corridor, The.
1975.
Larkin. Friday Night in the Royal Station.
Meinke. Hôtel de la Truite.
Hôtel Lion d'Or.
Merrill. Hotel de l'Univers et Portugal.
Nash. Change Here for Wichita Falls, or, Has Anybody Seen My Wanderlust?
Have a Seat behind the Potted Palm, Sir.
Mrs. Purvis Dreads Room Service.
Traveler's Rest.
Rossetti. Uphill [or Up-Hill].
St. John. Hotel Sierra.
Shelton. White Hotel, The.
Stein. Hotel François Ier.
Stuart. Interlude at the Grand Hotel, An.
Walcott. At the Queen's Park Hotel, with its white, high-ceilinged rooms.

See also **Motels.**
Houdini, Harry
Smith, Patti. Ha! Ha! Houdini!
Hourglasses
De la Mare. Hour-Glass, The.
Hesketh. Days.
Jonson. Hour-Glass [or Houre-Glasse], The.
Merrill. Hourglass.
House Painting
Schuyler. White.
Housekeeping
Bukowski. Fragile!
Davie. Sorting the Personae.
Dove. Dusting.
Pomade.
Frost. Housekeeper, The.
Jong. Woman Enough.
Koertge. Night Games.
Lowry. Deal was here, / Oh love alas, The.
Morning bird sits mutely, The.
Welcome Home Oh Our Most Beloved Harteebeeste.
Merrill. Three Chores.
Nash. You Have More Freedom in a House.
Schuyler. Below the Stairs.
Song: "I'm about to go shopping."
Things to Do.
White.
See also **Housewives.**
Houses
Atwood. Small Cabin, The.
Auden. Dying House, The.
Thanksgiving for a Habitat.
Berry. Design of a House, The.
Don't own so much clutter that you will be relieved to see your.
For the Rebuilding of a House.
How fine / to have a long-legged house.
New House, The.
New Roof, The.
Berryman. Long Home, The.
Bishop. End of March, The.
Jerónimo's House.
Browning, Robert. House.
Carew. To Saxham.
"Carroll, Lewis." As It Fell upon a Day.
Carruth. Crow's Mark.
Mansion burned. Maids, The.
Meadow House.
My Hut.
New Hartford.
Catullus. Carmen 26: "Your cottage, Furius, sheltered."
Ciardi. Divorced, Husband Demolishes Home.
Cohen. One Night I Burned.
Coleridge. Eolian Harp, The.
Cooper. Builder of Houses, The.
Souvenirs.
Creeley. House, The.
Picture, A.
Some Place.
Davie. Among Artisans' Houses.
Priory of St Saviour, Glendalough, The.
De la Mare. Alone.
Empty House, The.
Old Summerhouse, The.
Sleeper, The.

Dickey, James. Courtship, The.
Two Poems of Going Home.
Dickinson. I know some lonely Houses off the Road.
Props assist the House, The.
Dove. House on Bishop Street, The.
Dunbar. Old Homestead, The.
Dunn. Fairy Tale.
Eberhart. Key West.
Emerson. I read on the porch of a palace bold.
These trees like tho'ts that to visions congeal.
What avails it me.
Fletcher. Journey Day.
Towards the North Star.
Ford. Crows in the fog, dogs.
Frost. Black Cottage, The.
Cocoon, The.
Directive.
Four-room shack aspiring high.
In the Home Stretch.
Steeple on the House, A.
Gallagher. Death of the Horses by Fire.
Garrigue. Beaucaire.
Country Villa.
Gildner. Ice Shanties.
Ginsberg. Strange New Cottage in Berkeley, A.
Griffiths. Craig-y-Don.
Gunn. Last Days at Teddington.
Nature of an Action, The.
Pierce Street.
Rain stops. I look round: a square of floor, The.
Waking in a Newly Built House.
Haines. Many times bound outward.
Tree that Became a House, The.
Hall. Alligator Bride, The.
Dump, The.
Flies.
In the Kitchen of the Old House.
Old Houses.
Hardy. Architectural Masks.
Domicilium.
House with a History, A.
To a Well-Named Dwelling.
Two Houses, The.
Hartley. Berry House, The.
These Six or Several Houses.
Hartnett. Visit to Castletown House, A.
Heaney. Summer Home.
Herbert. World, The.
Herrick. Observation ("Jewes, when they built Houses [I have read], The").
Thanksgiving to God for His House, A.
Hesketh. Return.
Hopkins. In the Valley of the Elwy.
Hugo. Beaverbank.
Doing the House.
Greystone Cottage.
Houses Lie, Believe the Lying Sea.
2433, First Home, Last House in Missoula.
Where the House Was.
Jeffers. To the House.
To the Rock that Will Be a Cornerstone of the House.
Joseph. Go Back to Square One.
Walk in the woods at the hour when the fuddled sun.
Koertge. He ("Bought a three-bedroom house in 1948").
Kooser. Houses at the Edge of Town.
Shooting a Farmhouse.
Kunitz. In a Strange House.
Three Floors.
Larkin. Home Is So Sad.
Lawrence. Parliament Hill in the Evening.
Lindsay. Flying House, and the May Queen Eternal, The.
Lorde. Rooming Houses are Old Women.
Lowell. For Sale.
Lowry. Ghosts in New Houses.
Lament in the Pacific Northwest.
Lament—June 1944.
Shakespeare's house is safe and sound.
MacLeish. Population Explosion.
MacNeice. Château Jackson.

House on a Cliff.
Order to View.
Selva Oscura.
McNeill. Flame, The.
Matthews. Housecooling.
Housework.
Meinke. House, The.
Meredith. Autumn Even-Song.
Merrill. House, The.
Miller. For Mickey.
Morgan. Closed House, The.
Nash. Little Feet.
Maybe You Can't Take It with You, but Look What Happens When You Leave It Behind.
No Wonder Our Fathers Died.
You Have More Freedom in a House.
Neruda. Midday Construction.
Olson. *Scream* to the Editor, A.
Oppen. Birthplace: New Rochelle.
Paley. Housing.
Sad Children's Song, The.
Patchen. If We Are to Know Where We Live.
May I Ask You a Question, Mr. Youngstown Sheet & Tube?
Plath. Landowners.
Point Shirley.
Tour, The.
Raine. For the Visitors' Book.
Ransom. Old Mansion.
What Ducks Require.
Rich. House at the Cascades, The.
Robinson. Fragment: "Faint white pillars that seem to fade."
House on the Hill, The.
Roethke. Sale.
Rukeyser. Crayon House.
Sandburg. Even Numbers.
Sexton. Buttered Greens.
February 11th.
Smith, Stevie. Grange, The.
House of Over-Dew, The.
Snodgrass. House the Poet Built, The.
Snyder. Cold Mountain is a house.
Spender. Empty House.
Stevens. Gallant Château.
Stevenson. House Beautiful, The.
My house, I say. But hark to the sunny doves.
New House, The.
Swift. On the Little House by the Churchyard of Castleknock.
To Quilca.
Tomlinson. Fox Gallery, The.
On the Hall at Stowey.
Ruin, The.
What It Was Like.
Turco. House, The.
Updike. Hot Water.
Walcott. Ruins of a Great House.
Warren. Small White House.
Wilbur. Altitudes.
Wellfleet: The House.
Williams, William Carlos. Defective Record, The.
House, The.
Old House, The.
Wordsworth. Highland Hut.
No whimsy of the purse is here.
Yau. Rising cost of heart attacks. Different, The.
Roof shaped like a strawberry. Hurriedly torn.
Zimmer. Great House, The.
Zukofsky. Furius, "Little Villa" has no nod for Auster.

See also **Home.**

Housewives
Emerson. Bluebeard. Let the gentle wife prepare.
Graves. Any Honest Housewife.
Heaney. Old Smoothing Iron.
Jarrell. Next Day.
Nash. I Know Exactly Who Dropped the Overalls in Mrs. Murphy's Chowder.
Sexton. Housewife.
Risk, The.
Smith, Stevie. Wretched Woman.
Van Duyn. Caring for Surfaces.

Williams, William Carlos. Young Housewife, The.
See also **Housekeeping.**
Housman, Alfred Edward
Auden. A. E. Housman.
Hudson, Henry
Carruth. Your dream: / His name was Hendryk Hudson. And oh, the glory!
Hudson Bay, Canada
Frost. Empty Threat, An.
Hudson River, New York
Carroll, Jim. At eighteen years of age.
Edmunds. December 27, 1988.
Levertov. From the Roof.
Lowell. Mouth of the Hudson, The.
Oppen. Time of the Missile.
Schuyler. Dining Out with Doug and Frank.
Hudson Ferry.
Hughes, Langston
Brooks. Langston Hughes.
Knight. For Langston Hughes.
Hughes, Ted
Plath. Ode for Ted.
Hugo, Victor
Meredith. Fall'n Is Lucifer.
Huguenots
Whittier. St. John.
Human Folly
Atwood. How To Tell One Country from Another.
Beatles. I Me Mine.
Beckett. Ce qu'a de pis.
Fous qui disiez.
How hollow heart and full.
Second Nature.
Boyle. Short Poem in Color, A.
Square Dance for a Square, A.
Bradstreet. Contemplations.
Bukowski. Playing It Out.
Chaucer. Monk's Tale, The.
Clark. Parish: A Satire, The.
Clough. Because a Lady chose to say.
Coleridge. Lines to Thomas Poole.
Ode to Tranquillity.
Cowper. Bee and the Pine-Apple, The.
God Neither Known Nor Loved by the World.
Human Frailty.
Pine-Apple and the Bee, The.
Cummings. Humanity i love you.
Dickinson. How Human Nature dotes.
"Dylan." Ain't No Man Righteous, No Not One.
Gotta Serve Somebody.
Idiot Wind.
Jokerman.
License to Kill.
Precious Angel.
Property of Jesus.
Trouble in Mind.
Watching the River Flow.
Watered-Down Love.
Eberhart. Big Rock.
Ferlinghetti. Endless Life.
History of the World: a TV Docu-Drama.
Morlaix. Into the Future with Neil Young.
Triumph of the Postmodern.
Uses of Poetry.
World is a beautiful place, The.
Galvin. Fear of *Gray's Anatomy.*
Graves. Fools.
Oath, The.
Shot, The.
Song: The Sundial's Lament.
Hartley. October Afternoon.
Herbert. Dotage.
Herrick. Delay.
Out of Time, Out of Tune.
Hewitt. Alder Stick, The.
Dilemma, The.
Folk Custom.
Return, The.
Stone.
Holmes. Storm in the Ozarks.
Jeffers. Advice to Pilgrims.
As the eye fails through age or disease.
Beautiful Captive, The.

Dawn.
De Rerum Virtute.
Eagle Valor, Chicken Mind.
Faith.
Orca.
Original Sin.
Roan Stallion.
Salvage.
Soul's Desert, The.
Unformed volcanic earth, a female thing, The.
World's Wonders, The.
Lowry. Lament in the Pacific Northwest.
We likened one man to a ship adrift.
Meredith. Were men of such importance as they deem.
Nash. Grasshoppers Are Very Intelligent.
Little Miss Muffet Sat on a Prophet—and Quite Right, Too!
Neruda. This Is Simple.
Owen. Arms and the Boy.
Sonnet: "Be slowly lifted up, thou long black arm."
Pope. Whate'er the passion--knowledge, fame, or pelf.
Rich. He Remembereth That We Are Dust.
Scott. Spindle Song, The.
Shapiro. Fly, The.
Stafford. Mr. or Mrs. Nobody.
Van Duyn. Causes.
Serious Case, A.
To Poets' Worksheets in the Air-Conditioned Vault of a Library.
Warren. Man in the Street.
Natural History I.
Williams, Charles Kenneth. That the world / is going.
Then the Brother of the Wind.
Wright, Charles. Language Journal.
Last Journal.
Looking at Pictures.
May Journal.
New Year's Eve, 1979.
Vesper Journal.
Wroth. Sonnet 33: "How many eyes poore Love hast thou to guard."

Human Race. see **Mankind.**
Humility
Auden. Rainy Afternoon, A.
Berry. Want of Peace, The.
We Who Prayed and Wept.
Blake. Clod and [*or* &] the Pebble, The.
Browning, Elizabeth Barrett. Confessions.
Reed, A.
Carew. On the Marriage of T. K. and C. C.: The Morning Stormy.
Ceravolo. Spring.
Chaucer. Franklin's Prologue, The.
Coleridge. Forbearance.
Humility the Mother of Charity.
Cowper. God Hides His People.
Nativity, The.
Cullen. Any Human to Another.
Davie. Creon's Muse.
Terce.
De la Mare. Imagination's Pride, The.
Dickinson. Tiniest ones are the mightiest, The.
Dunbar. Love's Humility.
"Dylan." Are You Ready?
Gotta Serve Somebody.
If You See Her, Say Hello.
Lay Down Your Weary Tune.
Emerson. And he like me is not too proud.
Experience.
I care not whither I may go.
Nature 1 ("Winters know / Easily to shed the snow").
Everson. In the Ripeness of the Weed.
Frost. Demiurge's Laugh, The.
Ginsberg. Man's Glory.
Herbert. Church-Lock and Key.
Discharge, The.
Humility.
Misery [*or* Miserie].
Posy [*or* Posie], The.
Praise (1).
Sighs and Groans [*or* Grones].

To the Right Hon. the Lord Chancellor (Bacon).
Herrick. Humility.
Meane Things Overcome Mighty.
To Worthy Friend, M. Tho. Falconbirge.
Hewitt. Dissertation I.
William Conor RHA, 1881–1968.
Hughes, Ted. Horrible Religious Error, A.
Hugo. Port Townsend, 1974.
Johnson. Ant, The.
Kipling. His spots are the joy of the Leopard: his horns are the Buffalo's pride.
If.
Non Nobis Domine!
Recessional.
Lawrence. Fireflies in the Corn.
Humility.
Humility Mongers.
Tender Reverence.
Lindsay. In the Immaculate Conception Church.
Johnny Appleseed's Hymn to the Sun.
We Meet at the Judgement and I Fear It Not.
Lowry. I set this down as humble prayer.
MacNeice. Sea, The.
Meredith. Believe me, I have studied men.
While Janet eyes the Lanthorn's Magic.
Merton. Ode to the Present Century.
Nash. Confession to Be Traced on a Birthday Cake.
Olson. Concerning Exaggeration, or How, Properly, to Heap Up.
Psalms. Psalm 123: "Unto thee lift I up mine eyes.."
Psalm 131: "Lord, my heart is not haughty, nor mine eyes lofty."
Ransom. Crocodile.
Rolfe. Political Prisoner 123456789.
Rossetti. I Will Come and Heal Him.
Lowest Place, The.
Sit Down in the Lowest Room.
Ye Are Come unto Mount Sion.
Sandburg. Why should any man try to find the distance to the moon by guessing.
Spenser. When these sad sights were overpast and gone.
Warren. I had once poured oil on his head.
Wilbur. Finished Man, A.
Williams, Charles Kenneth. Easter.
Men.
Wordsworth. Fact, and an Imagination or, Canute and Alfred, on the Sea-Shore, A.
Narrow girdle of rough stones and crags, A.
When Haughty Expectations Prostrate Lie.
Wright, Charles. Chinese Journal.
Night Journal.

Hummingbirds
Berry. Sitting among the bluebells.
Ciardi. 11:02 A.M. The Bird Disappeared.
Dickinson. Route of Evanescence, A.
Within my Garden, rides a Bird.
Eberhart. Vision.
Fletcher. Oiran and Her Kamuso, An.
Lawrence. Humming-Bird.
Levertov. Revivals.
Turn of the Head, A.
Oliver. Hummingbird Pauses at the Trumpet Vine.

Hunchbacks
Byron. Deformed Transformed, The.
Glück. Cell, The.
McGrath. Emblems of Exile.
Thomas. Hunchback in the Park, The.
Yeats. Saint and the Hunchback, The.

Hundred Years War
Cummings. Thou in whose swordgreat story shine the deeds.

Hungary
Boyle. Funeral in Hungary.
Cummings. Thanksgiving (1956).
Whittier. Kossuth.

Hunger
Angelou. Starvation.
Atwood. More and More.
Auden. Healthy Spot, A.
Beckett. Vulture, The.
Berg. Leaves.

Berry. Deepest sleep holds us, The.
Sparrow.
Creeley. Down Home.
Hunger.
Words.
Dickinson. Great Hungers feed themselves.
I had been hungry, all the Years.
It would have starved a Gnat.
Dobyns. Belly, The.
Ferlinghetti. Astonished Heart, The.
Ford. Glass violin is broken, The.
Haines. Hunger.
Hall. Wolf Knife.
Hartley. Pot-Luck among the Casuals.
Herrick. Hunger.
Hewitt. Beastie, The.
Fair Game.
Flight.
Limitations.
No Comment!
Note on Intellectuals.
Holmes. Mouth.
Kunitz. Supper Before Last, The.
Lawrence. Munitions.
Levine. They Feed They Lion.
Lowry. Hunger.
Piercy. What the Owl Sees.
Ralegh. O wastfull Riot, never well content.
Rossetti. Prodigal Son, A.
Sandburg. Big fish eat the little fish, The.
Galoots.
Horse Fiddle.
Hunger and Cold.
Hunger and only hunger changes worlds?
Schuyler. Dog Wants His Dinner, The.
Sexton. Food.
Shout, The.
Silverstein. Eighteen Flavors.
Poor Angus.
Sleeping Sardines.
Simic. Autumn Air.
Smith, Stevie. Dream of Nourishment, A.
Walker. Few Sirens, A.
Wilbur. Potato.
Williams, Charles Kenneth. With Ignorance.
Wright, James. Before a Cashier's Window in a Department Store.
To a Friendly Dun.

Hunt, Leigh
Keats. On Receiving a Laurel Crown from Leigh Hunt.
To Leigh Hunt, Esq.
Written on the Day That Mr. Leigh Hunt Left Prison.

Hunting and Hunters
Atwood. Dream 2: Brian the Still-Hunter.
Song of the Fox.
Auden. Decoys, The.
Hunting Season.
September.
Berry. For the Hog Killing.
Long Hunter, The.
Berryman. Not to Live.
Betjeman. Hunter Trials.
Boyle. Hunt.
Burns. Hunting Song.
On Seeing a Wounded Hare Limp by Me, Which a Fellow Had Just Shot At.
"Carroll, Lewis." Hunting of the Snark, The.
Little Man That Had a Little Gun, The.
Clare. Badger ("When midnight comes a host of dogs and men").
Marten.
Mole-Catcher, The.
Coleridge. Hunting Song.
Cowper. Needless Alarm, The.
On a Fowler.
Cummings. All in green went my love riding.
De la Mare. Hunter, The.
Quarry, The.
Dickey, James. Fox Blood.
Springer Mountain.
Summons, The.
Doolittle. Huntress.
Dove. Connections.
Dunbar. Forest Greeting, The.
Hunting Song.

Eberhart. Young Hunter, The.
Everson. Dark Waters.
Hare: An Earlier Episode, The.
Fletcher. Epilogue: "By the glare of the guttering torch."
Frost. Rabbit Hunter, The.
Gallagher. Cougar Meat.
Galvin. In Egg Time.
Glück. Liberation.
Gray. Caradoc.
Haines. Divided, the Man is Dreaming.
Ghost Hunter, The.
Moose Calling, A.
Thousands of years passed.
Victims.
Hall. High Pasture, The.
Hardy. Puzzled Game-Birds, The.
Hartley. As the Buck Lay Dead.
Hartnett. I Heard Him Whistle.
Hesketh. Fox, The.
Gone Away.
Owl.
Panther and the Antelope, The.
Hewitt. Fair Game.
Hoffman. At Don's Garage.
Comanches.
Last Lynx.
Safari.
Housman. Atys.
R. L. S.
Jeffers. Shooting Season.
Wind-Struck Music, The.
Jonson. To Sir Henry Goodyere.
Kinnell. Bear, The.
To Christ Our Lord.
Kipling. Angutivaun Taina.
Fox-Hunting.
Go, stalk the red dear o'er the heather.
Hunting Song of the Seeonee Pack.
JANUARY (*Hunting*).
SEPTEMBER (*Shooting*).
Song of the Little Hunter, The.
What of the hunting, hunter bold?
Koertge. He ("Used to climb trees that were").
Kunitz. Robin Redbreast.
Lawrence. Mountain Lion.
Lieberman. Spearing, The.
Tarpon.
Lorde. Woman Thing, The.
Lovelace. La Bella Bona Roba.
Love Inthron'd.
Lowry. Salmon Drowns Eagle.
McAuley. Path, The.
Mahon. Hunt by Night, The.
St. Eustace.
Marvell. Nymph Complaining for the Death of Her Faun [*or* Fawn], The.
Meinke. Plovers.
World within World.
Meredith. Gordon, Jim, / Life and Limb.
Long was the conflict, but now 'tis done.
No boats oar slow, no barges pass.
Poor things! we know not what they suffer.
Song: "I would be the bounding deer."
With the Huntress.
Young Reynard.
Millay. Huntsman, What Quarry?
October—An Etching.
Nash. Hunter, The.
Nemerov. Fat time of the year is also time, The.
Hunt Goes By, The.
O'Hara. Hunter, The.
Poem: "I ran through the snow like a young Czarevitch!"
Oliver. Hunter's Moon—Eating the Bear.
Wolf Moon.
Pack. Cave of Lascaux, The.
Hunting.
Paley. Job of hunting of shooting in hunting season of, The.
Patchen. Fox, The.
Hunter, The.
Pope. Hunt, The.
See! from the brake the whirring Pheasant springs.
When milder autumn summer's heat succeeds.

Raine. Silver Stag, The.
Rolfe. Hunter Went Killing: A Fable, A.
Rukeyser. Beast in View.
  Shooting Gallery.
Sandburg. Early Hours.
Scott. Hunting Song.
  Lay of the Imprisoned Huntsman.
Smart. Country Squire and the Mandrake, The.
Smith, Charlotte. Hedge-Hog Seen in a
  Frequented Path, The.
Smith, Stevie. Es War Einmal.
  I Am a Girl Who Loves to Shoot.
  Shooting Incident, The.
Spenser. Like a huntsman.
Stevenson. Portrait, A.
Stuart. Hunter, Prey.
Sutter. Stalking the Wild Mushroom.
Turco. Hunting Moon.
Van Duyn. Hermit of Hudson Pond, The.
Wakoski. Few Silver Scales, The.
Warren. Season Opens on Wild Boar in
  Chianti.
  Was Not the Lost Dauphin.
Wilbur. Castles and Distances.
Wordsworth. Simon Lee [the Old Huntsman].
Wright, James. Fear Is What Quickens Me.
Wyatt. Whoso list to hunt, I know where is an
  hind.
Yeats. Ballad of the Foxhunter, The.
  Hound Voice.
Young. Prelude.
Zimmer. Julian Barely Misses Zimmer's
  Brains.

Hurdy-Gurdies
Cummings. At the head of this street a
  gasping organ is waving moth-eaten.

Hurricanes
Crane. Hurricane, The.
MacLeish. Hurricane.
Millay. Dream of Saba.
See also Storms.

Husbands
Angelou. To a Husband.
Berry. Marriage.
Bradstreet. For the Restoration of My Dear
  Husband from a Burning Ague.
  In My Solitary Hours in My Dear Husband
  His Absence.
  In Thankful Acknowledgement for the Letters
  I Received from My Husband Out Of
  England.
  In Thankful[l] Remembrance for My Dear
  Husband[']s Safe Arrival[l].
  To My Dear and Loving Husband.
Byron. What Matter the Pangs of a Husband
  and Father.
Campion. In Crispinum.
Carruth. Your dream: / His name was
  Husband, his title Herr.
Coleridge. Happy Husband, The.
Donne. Jealousy.
Dove. Recovery.
Graves. Slice of Wedding Cake, A.
Hardy. Every Artemisia.
  Her Second Husband Hears Her Story.
Herrick. Good Husband, A.
  Upon Blanch: ("Blanch swears her Husband's
  lovely; when a scald").
Hughes, Langston. Madam and Her Might-
  Have-Been.
Jonson. Epigram to My Muse, the Lady
  Digby, on Her Husband, Sir Kenelm Digby,
  An.
Lawrence. Good Husbands Make Unhappy
  Wives.
  I Heard Her Say.
Lowell. To Speak of Woe That Is in
  Marriage.
Nash. How to Harry a Husband, or, Is That
  Accessory Really Necessary?
  Perfect Husband, The.
  Trouble with Women Is Men, The.
  Very Funny, Very Funny.
Pope. Mary Gulliver to Capt. Lemuel Gulliver.
Rossetti. I have a little husband / And he is
  gone to sea.
  Wee wee husband, / Give me some money.

Sexton. And One for My Dame.
  Now.
  Where It Was at Back Then.
  Your Face on the Dog's Neck.
Sorrentino. Spouse, The.
Stein. She is that kind of a wife. She can see.
Stevenson. So live, so love, so use that fragile
  hour.
Williams, Charles Kenneth. Alzheimer's: The
  Husband.

Hyacinths
Cooper. Leaving Water Hyacinths.
Doolittle. Shepherd, The.
Emerson. All day the rain.
Glück. Hyacinth.
Millay. Hyacinth.
Prince. Babiaantje, The.
Raine. Hyacinth, The.
Zukofsky. Hyacinth.

Hydrangeas
Ammons. Touching.
Sandburg. Dragoons, I tell you the white
  hydrangeas turn rust and go soon.
Williams, William Carlos. Lesson, The.

Hyenas
Kipling. Hyænas [or Hyenas], The.
  When ye say to Tabaqui, "My Brother!" when
  ye call the Hyena to meat.

Hymns
Betjeman. Olney Hymns.
Bishop. Hymn to the Virgin.
Browning, Elizabeth Barrett. Since Without
  Thee We Do No Good.
Crashaw. Apology [or Apologie] for the
  Foregoing Hymn[e], An.
  Hymn for New Year's Day.
  Hymn in the Glorious Epiphanie.
  Vexilla Regis.
Emerson. For every god.
Hardy. Barthélémon at Vauxhall.
Hugo. Chapel Further West than Most, A.
  Repairing the House, the Church, Restoring
  the Music.
Mahon. Songs of Praise.
Psalms. Psalm 33: "Rejoice in the Lord, O ye
  righteous."
Scott. Hymn for the Dead.
  Rebecca's Hymn.
Smart. Rejoice in God, ye saints above.
Thomson. Hymn on the Seasons, A.
Wilbur. Christmas Hymn, A.

Hypnosis and Hypnotists
Browning, Robert. Mesmerism.
Morrison. Promises.

Hypocrisy and Hypocrites
Beatles. Baby You're a Rich Man.
Berryman. Farewell to Miles.
Bly. Johnson's Cabinet Watched by Ants.
Browning, Elizabeth Barrett. Man's
  Requirements, A.
Browning, Robert. Bishop Blougram's
  Apology.
  Soliloquy of the Spanish Cloister.
Burns. Address to the Unco Guid, or the
  Rigidly Righteous.
  Holy Willie's Prayer.
  To the Rev. John McMath, Inclosing a Copy
  of *Holy Willie's Prayer*, Which He Had
  Requested.
Byron. New Vicar of Bray, The.
"Carroll, Lewis." Alice's Recitation.
Chaucer. Summoner's Prologue, The.
  Summoner's Tale, The.
Clough. Latest Decalogue, The.
Cowper. God Neither Known Nor Loved by
  the World.
  Love of the World Reproved, The.
Creeley. Wait for Me.
Cummings. Come, gaze with me upon this
  dome.
  Next to of course god america i.
  Opening of the chambers close.
  Season 'tis, my lovely lambs, The.
Davie. Church Militant.
Donne. When senses, which thy so[u]ldiers
  are.
Dunbar. Religion.

"Dylan." Jack o' diamonds / jack o'
  diamonds.
  Positively 4th Street.
  Slow Train.
Emerson. Hafiz thou art from Eternity.
  I've found the dainty malice out.
Graves. Sick Love.
Hemingway. Chapter Heading.
  Shock Troops.
Hewitt. Dungannon Cattle Market.
  For Certain Subscribers to the Miners' Fund.
Hughes, Langston. American Heartbreak.
Jeffers. Of all things which are living and can
  form a judgment.
Jonson. On Court-Parrot.
  On Don Surly.
  On the Town's Honest Man.
  To Sir Ra[l]ph Shelton.
Kipling. Islanders, The.
  Rhyme of the Three Captains, The.
  SEPTEMBER (*Shooting*).
  Tommy.
  Waster, The.
Knight. Memo #9.
  On Watching Politicians Perform at Martin
  Luther King's Funeral.
Lawrence. British Sincerity.
  Commandments.
  Humility Mongers.
  Keep It Up.
  Retort to Jesus.
  Retort to Whitman.
Levertov. Hypocrite Women.
Lewis. Sweet Mother Chruch, beleaguered on
  the hill.
Liddy. After Kraske.
  On a Protestant Mystic.
Lindsay. At Mass.
  Why I Voted the Socialist Ticket.
Lorde. Vietnam Addenda.
Lowry. Noble City Full of Pigeons or
  Everyone a Hypocrite Including Me.
MacLeish. Hypocrite Auteur.
Meredith. At dinner, she is hostess, I am host.
  It is no vulgar nature I have wived.
Martin's Puzzle.
Morrison. L'America.
  There's Someone At the Door.
Nash. Nevertheless.
Olson. Jas Jargon.
Piercy. Kneeling at the Pipes.
  Peaceable Kingdom, The.
Pope. Epigram in a Maid of Honour's Prayer-
  Book.
Ralegh. Epitaph on the Earl of Salisbury.
Rolfe. Definition.
  Letter to the Denouncers, A.
  On Rico LeBrun's Crucifixion.
Rukeyser. Movie.
Shapiro. Drug Store.
  Mongolian Idiot.
Smith, Charlotte. Slow in the Wintry Morn,
  the struggling light.
Sorrentino. Beautiful Soup.
  Boilermakers.
  Hit Album, A.
  Iceman, Again, The.
  Mr. America last seen crossing the road.
  Poet Tires of Those Who Disparage His City,
  The.
  Stinking city full of stinking, A.
  Stupid painter paints. He, The.
Tennyson. Character, The.
Whittier. Christian Slave, The.
  Clerical Oppressors.
  Gallows, The.
  Leggett's Monument.
  Letter from a Missionary of the Methodist
  Episcopal Church South, in Kansas, to a
  Distiguished Politician.
  Lines on the Portrait of a Celebrated
  Publisher.
  Pastoral Letter, The.
  To Englishmen.
Williams, William Carlos. Early Martyr, An.
  Graph for Action.

I

Ibsen, Henrik
Rich. Juvenilia.
Ibycus
Graves. Ibycus of Samos.
Icarus
Auden. Musée des Beaux Arts.
Dunn. Worker's Creed, A.
Liddy. Icarus.
Morrison. Tender Island Night.
Rukeyser. Waiting for Icarus.
Sexton. To a Friend Whose Work Has Come
   to Triumph.
Spender. Airman.
Wilbur. Icarium Mare.
Williams, William Carlos. Landscape with the
   Fall of Icarus.
Ice
Berrigan. Into the closed air of the slow.
Carruth. Morning ice on the window.
   Snow / ice / bitter wind.
   Thaw, The.
   When some amazonian indians for whom.
Creeley. Blue.
Dickey, James. Adam in Winter.
Dickey, William. Avalanche.
Fox. Figure Eights.
   Ice.
Frost. Fire and Ice.
Hayden. Ice Storm.
Hesketh. Letter to Vincent.
Kooser. Walking to Work.
Lowry. About Ice.
Matthews. Icehouse, Pointe au Baril, Ontario,
   The.
Nemerov. Icehouse in Summer, The.
Olson. Here i am, naked.
Rolfe. Arctic Remembered, The.
   Cheliuskin.
Rukeyser. Ice-gate over the land, a shock of
   closure.
Sandburg. Earth is a forgotten cinder, The.
   Metamorphosis.
   Wind carves sand into shapes, The.
Spenser. My Love Is Like to Ice.
Turco. Ice House, The.
Wakoski. Ice Eagle, The.
Wilbur. Glance from the Bridge, A.
   Stop.
Ice Cream
Nash. Tableau at Twilight.
Silverstein. Eighteen Flavors.
Tomlinson. Ice Cream at Blauenberg.
Van Duyn. In the Cold Kingdom.
Ice Hockey
Bly. Hockey Poem, The.
Bukowski. Hog.
Ice Skating and Ice Skaters. *see* **Skating and
Skaters.**
Icebergs
Bishop. Imaginary Iceberg, The.
Cowper. On the Ice Islands Seen Floating in
   the German Ocean.
Dickey, James. Form.
Dickinson. Icebergs italicize the Sea.
Hardy. Convergence of the Twain, The.
MacNeice. Icebergs.
Melville. Berg, The.
Merton. Kane Relief Expedition.
Rukeyser. Outpost.
Iceland
Auden. Journey to Iceland.
Dunn. Carpenter's Song, The.
Hewitt. My Uncle.
MacNeice. Eclogue from Iceland.
   Iceland.
   Letter to Graham and Anna.
Icicles
Carruth. Eye of / the hut, The.
   Small things / hardest to believe.
   Window / the icicle / the gleaming moon, The.
Wilbur. Courtyard Thaw, A.
Idaho (state)
Hugo. Cataldo Mission.
Wright, James. Frontier, The.

Idealism and Idealists
Beatles. Can't Buy Me Love.
Browning, Elizabeth Barrett. Tale of
   Villafranca, A.
Bunting. Keep Troth.
Cowper. On the Platonic Idea as Aristotle
   Understood It.
Creeley. Revelation, The.
Davie. Scythian Charioteers, The.
Dickinson. Ideals are the Fairy Oil.
   Taking up the fair Ideal.
"Dylan." Jim Jim / where is our party?
   My Back Pages.
   Romance in Durango.
   When I Paint My Masterpiece.
Eberhart. Difficulty of Ideas, The.
   Fantasy of a Small Idea.
Emerson. I live among ideal men.
   Idealism.
Graves. Perfectionists.
   What is Love?
Herrick. No Loathsomnesse in Love.
Hughes, Langston. As I Grew Older.
Lawrence. For the Heroes Are Dipped in
   Scarlet.
   Mess of Love, The.
Lindsay. Johnny Appleseed's Wife from the
   Palace of Eve.
   On the Building of Springfield.
Lowry. We Sit Unhackled Drunk and Mad to
   Edit.
MacNeice. In a little room, a little plot, a
   little lifetime.
Milton. On the Platonic Idea as Aristotle
   Understood It.
Nathan. Diver, The.
Neruda. Gift, The.
Olson. Heart is a clock, The.
Plath. Letter to a Purist.
Ransom. To the Scholars of Harvard.
Rich. Ideal Landscape.
Shelley. Prince Athanase; a Fragment.
Silverstein. My Rules.
Snodgrass. Dr. Joseph Goebbels, Minister for
   Propaganda.
Sorrentino. Mr. America last seen crossing the
   road.
Stevens. Analysis of a Theme.
   Creations of Sound, The.
Wyatt. *In aeternum* I was once determed.
Identity Crisis
Arnold. Self-Dependence.
Atwood. Double Voice, The.
   Two-Headed Poems.
Berg. Not That.
   Three Voices.
Bukowski. Last Generation, The.
"Carroll, Lewis." Third Voice, The.
Carruth. His body, caught there in the mirror,
   lean.
   Upward through the dark, this.
Ceravolo. Green Lake Is Awake, The.
   Passivation.
   Struggling.
Cohen. Fingerprints.
Creeley. Thinking.
Dunn. Substitute, The.
Eberhart. Mistaken Identity.
Hewitt. Belfastman, The.
   Colony, The.
   Name and Number.
Sonnet: "Among the many selves that throng
   my flesh."
Hughes, Ted. Wodwo.
Jarrell. Woman at the Washington Zoo, The.
Koertge. Waiting.
Lieberman. Transvestite.
Merton. Fall, The.
   With the World in My Blood Stream.
Muldoon. Identities.
Olson. In Cold Hell, in Thicket.
   Pavement, The.
Oppen. Chorus (androgynous): "Find me."
   World, World—.
"Reed." I Wanna Be Black.
Rolfe. Catalogue of I.
Sarton. Ballad of Johnny, The.

Schuyler. Poem, A: "Tags of songs, like
   salvaged buttons."
Shapiro. I Am an Athetist Who Says His
   Prayers.
Spender. Question of Identity, A.
Van Duyn. Good Resolution, The.
Waldman. Complaynt.
Young. Hoboken Broken Down: A Hasty
   Recollection.
   Problem of Identity, The.
Idleness
Ammons. Layabout.
Beatles. Mother Nature's Son.
Berryman. Young Woman's Song.
De la Mare. Idleness.
Emerson. And do I waste my time.
   Apology, The.
Herrick. Disswasions from Idlenesse.
Hesketh. Yew Tree Guest House.
Keats. Ode on Indolence.
Lindsay. Beggar Speaks, The.
McAuley. My earliest memory? why, the
   lassitude!
Sidney. Sonnet 18: "With what sharp checks I
   in myself am shent."
Silverstein. Jimmy Jet and His TV Set.
Smith, Stevie. Lament of a Slug-a-Bed's Wife.
Spender. Unemployed.
Stevenson. My brain swims empty and light.
See also **Sloth.**
Idolatry
Cohen. Altar, The.
   Commentary—The Altar.
Dickinson. Save me from the idolatry.
Frost. On Being Idolized.
Hayden. Idol.
Herrick. Devotion Makes the Deity.
Kipling. Evarra and His Gods.
Kunitz. Words of the Preacher, The.
Lawrence. Film Passion.
Lindsay. My Lady in Her White Silk Shawl.
   Slender maiden found me sleeping, The.
   To a Golden-Haired Girl in a Louisiana Town.
McAuley. Gesture, A.
   Her womanhood collected into a pale.
MacNeice. Because you intoxicate like all the
   drinks.
   Leaving Barra.
Merton. Captives—a Psalm, The.
   Idol of Sarapis, The.
   Priests of the Old Gods, The.
Psalms. Psalm 115: "Not unto us, O Lord, not
   unto us."
   Psalm 135: "Praise ye the Lord. Praise ye the
   name of the Lord; praise him, O ye servants
   of the Lord."
Ralegh. Ah wretched they that worship
   vanities.
Sandburg. Hammer, The.
   Manufactured Gods.
Shakespeare. Sonnet 105: "Let not my love be
   call'd idolatry."
Smart. O Praise the Lord, and bless his name.
Ignorance
Ammons. Course Work.
Angelou. Bump d'Bump.
Beckett. Gnome.
Berry. And I declare myself free.
   It is *ignorant* money I declare.
   We don't bother nobody.
Bunting. These tracings from a world that's
   dead.
Campion. Ad Rusticum.
Carroll, Jim. You hear the call.
Catullus. Carmen 17: "Cologna Veneta - /
   where the good folk."
Cohen. I Stopped to Listen.
Cowper. Lines Written upon a Window-
   Shutter at Weston.
   On One Ignorant and Arrogant.
Creeley. For the Graduation.
   Love Comes Quietly.
   Wisdom.
Cummings. All ignorance toboggans into
   know.
   Lis / -ten / you know what i mean when.
   Love's function is to fabricate unknownness.

lucid comedienne, The."
Untitled.
Oliver. University Hospital, Boston.
Olson. Librarian, The.
Piercy. Bronchitis on the 14th Floor.
Years ago I had a friend.
Plath. Among the Narcissi.
Pope. Of Her Sickness.
Prince. Last Attachment, A.
Ransom. Kingdom Come.
Rich. Final Notations.
Problem, unstated until now, is how, The.
When/Then.
You who think I find words for everything.
Roethke. Infirmity.
Rolfe. Song: "There is indeed now reason for
rejoicing."
Rossetti. Dear old woman in the lane, The.
Johnny.
Sick Child's Meditation, A.
Rukeyser. Absalom.
Disease, The.
George Robinson: Blues.
In Hades, Orpheus.
Mearl Blankenship.
Mendings.
Panacea.
Praise of the Committee.
Statement: Philippa Allen.
To keep the weakness secret. To deny it and
break through.
Two Years.
Wards, The.
Schuyler. Afterward.
Below the Stairs.
Name Day, A.
Shelton. He is ill.
Sidney. Sonnet 101: "Stella is sick, and in that
sick-bed lies."
Sonnet 102: "Where be those roses gone,
which sweetened so our eyes?"
Silverstein. Love.
Smart. Hymn to the Supreme Being.
Smith, Charlotte. Written at Bristol in the
Summer of 1794.
Smith, Patti. Health Lantern.
Hymn: "We hadn't eaten in two days. we
were entirely intoxicated."
Penicillin.
16 February.
Smith, Stevie. Ceci est digne de gens sans
dieu.
Deathly Child, The.
Little Boy Sick.
Loin de l'Être.
Stroke, The.
To a Lady in a Train.
Snodgrass. Flat One, A.
Sorrentino. Cerinthus, don't you have some
soft thought for your girl.
Spender. Elegy for Margaret.
Stevenson. Aye mon, it's true; I'm no' that
weel.
Land of Counterpane, The.
Old world moans and topes, The.
To W.E. Henley.
Stuart. Girl of My Dreams Is Dying.
Hospital of Lies, The.
Prayer, A.
Suckling. Upon T.C. Having the Pox.
Swift. In Sickness.
To Dr. Helsham.
To Dr. Sheridan.
To Stella.
To Stella, Visiting Me in My Sickness.
Tate. Mother and Son.
Tomlinson. History of a Malady.
Updike. Boil.
Fever.
Revelation.
Van Duyn. After midnight, and my sister
Lizzie.
Case of The, The.
In the Hospital for Tests.
Letters from a Father.
Winter's Tale, by a Wife, A.

Waldman. Triolet: "Perfectly clear liquid like
water, A."
Walker. Medicine.
Whitman. Evening Lull, An.
Wilbur. Tartuffe.
Williams, Charles Kenneth. Helen.
Le Petit Salvié.
Wordsworth. Idiot Boy, The.
Matron of Jedborough and Her Husband, The.
While Anna's Peers and Early Playmates
Tread.
Wright, James. Prayer in My Sickness, A.
Yeats. Friend's Illness, A.
Young. Flu.

Illusion
Ashbery. Forties Flick.
Illustration.
Auden. Blind Lead the Blind, The.
Beatles. Strawberry Fields Forever.
Berg. Good.
Bishop. Gentleman of Shalott, The.
Objects & Apparitions.
Blake. Memorable Fancy, A ("Angel came to
me and said").
Bukowski. Dogs of Egypt, The.
It's the Way You Play the Game.
Notations from a Muddled Indolence.
Now.
Trick to Dull Our Bleeding, A.
Carew. To T. H., a Lady Resembling My
Mistress.
Ceravolo. Note from St. Francis.
Crane. Visible the Untrue, The.
Creeley. Echo Of.
Cullen. Only the Polished Skeleton.
Davie. Those plaguy; needling games of ours,
where stooks.
De la Mare. Quiet.
Dickinson. I many times thought Peace had
come.
Donne. Dream, The.
Dunbar. We Wear the Mask.
Dunn. Belly Dancer at the Hotel Jerome.
Happiness.
Parable of the Fictionist.
Eberhart. Birth of the Spirit, The.
Gods of Washington, D.C., The.
Illusion of Eternity, The.
Vision through Timothy.
Emerson. Cloud upon cloud / The world is
seeming.
Illusions like the tints of pearl.
Maia.
Proteus.
Who dedicates himself to the glass.
Ferlinghetti. Euphoria.
Grottamare.
Morlaix: Into the Future with Neil Young.
Fisher. Rules and Ranges for Ian Tyson.
Fletcher. Oiran and Her Kamuso, An.
Ford. Indra; my house; the.
Poverty is always / Imaginary. The.
Fox. Fata Morgana.
Galvin. Fear of Gray's Anatomy.
Gardner. Cowardice.
Garrigue. Studies for an Actress.
Griffiths. Choice of Flowers, The.
Gunn. Vox Humana.
Hewitt. Fool's Cap, The.
In a Suburban Avenue.
Hoffman. Far-Off Light.
Holmes. Memoirs of an Imaginary Man, The.
Hugo. How Meadows Trick You.
Keats. And What Is Love? It Is a Doll
Dressed Up.
Knott. Poem: "Beach holds and sifts us
through her dreaming fingers, The."
Sculpture, The.
Kunitz. Illumination, The.
Illusionist, The.
Lawrence. Impulse.
Stoic.
Levertov. Gone Away.
Ground-Mist, The.
Living While It May.
Liddy. Poison, The.
Lindsay. Celestial Circus, The.

In Praise of Gloriana's Remarkable Golden
Hair.
Lovelace. Cinna seems poor in show.
Ode: "You are deceiv'd; I sooner may dull
fair."
McAuley. What the Recent Survey Has
Revealed.
MacLeish. Against Illuminations.
MacNeice. Conversation.
Drunkard, The.
Schizophrene.
Train to Dublin.
Mahon. Stone Age Figure Far Below, A.
Meredith. For any save a lover.
Merton. Delhi.
What we see of things is the things
themselves.
Morrison. Cock-pit.
Dark American Sunset, The.
L.A. Woman.
Pencilled Heaven.
Tales of the American Night.
Nemerov. Maia.
Sestina I: "Thickness of paint or flesh cannot
deface."
Owen. Kind Ghosts, The.
Pack. Ode to October Mist.
Raine. Three Poems on Illusion.
World: / Image on water, waves.
Rich. Newsreel.
Rossetti. I dreamt I caught a little owl.
Rukeyser. Palos Verdes Cliffs.
Sandburg. Kindest and gentlest here are the,
The.
Shapiro. I Am an Atheist Who Says His
Prayers.
Shelley. To ———: "Oh! there are spirits of
the air."
Silverstein. Invisible Boy.
Smith, Stevie. Conviction (iii).
Stafford. Bi-Focal.
Stevens. Add This to Rhetoric.
What We See Is What We Think.
Stuart. Nomads.
Swift. Occasioned by Sir William Temple's
Late Illness and Recovery.
Tomlinson. Mushrooms.
Wakoski. Follow That Stagecoach.
Whitman. Apparitions.
Are You the New Person Drawn toward Me?
Eidolons.
Mirages.
Of the Terrible Doubt of Appearances.
Wordsworth. Oxford, May Thirtieth, Eighteen
Twenty ("Shame on this faithless heart! that
could allow").
Wroth. Sonnet 5: "Can pleasing sight,
misfortune ever bring?"
Sonnet 40: "Itt is nott love which you poore
fooles do deeme."
Wyatt. Ye old mule, that thin[c]k your self so
fair [or fayre].
Zukofsky. Lines of this new song are nothing,
The.

Imagination
Beckett. Fin fond du néant.
Berg. Bread.
Roses.
Berry. But do not let your ignorance.
Berryman. I am interested alone in making
ready.
Bishop. ,Sleeping on the Ceiling.
Brontë. Aye, there it is! It wakes to-night.
Gleneden's Dream.
Plead for Me.
To Imagination.
Brooks. Anniad, The.
Browning, Robert. By the Fire-Side.
Bukowski. Insomnia.
"Carroll, Lewis." Mad Gardener's Song, The.
My Fancy.
My First is singular at best.
Carruth. Always this special / secret feeling,
the failure.
Existing Pool, The.
To Know in Reverie the Only Phenomenology

of the Absolute.
Une Présence Absolue.
Ceravolo. Green Lake Is Awake, The.
  Spring in This World of Poor Mutts.
Ciardi. For Instance.
Coleridge. Fancy in Nubibus.
  Reason.
  Reason for Love's Blindness.
Crane. Postscript.
Creeley. Again.
  "Do You Think.."
  Dying.
  Echo.
  Ice Cream.
  Lion and the Dog, The.
  Los Guitaristas.
  Place, A.
  Sounds.
  "There.."
  They.
  To the One in the Gray Coat.
  Up in the Air.
  Wicker Basket, A.
  Wife, The.
Cummings. Dominic has / a doll wired.
  Eagle, The.
  If a cheerfulest Elephantangelchild should sit.
  In a middle of a room.
  It really must / be Nice,never to.
  No man,if men are gods;but if gods must.
  Nothing is more exactly terrible than.
  Open your heart: / i'll give you a treasure.
  River of Mist, The.
  Sonnet entitled how to run the world).
  Thethe / the pink / Tartskids with.
  When rain whom fear.
  Whose are these(wraith a clinging with a
    wraith).
Davie. Brilliance.
  Dream Forest.
De la Mare. Dreams.
  Imagination's Pride, The.
  Memory.
  O Childish Mind!
Dickinson. I cannot dance upon my Toes.
Donne. Sappho to Philaenis.
Dove. Banneker.
  Geometry.
Dryden. Prologue to the University of Oxford,
  1674.
Dunbar. By the Stream.
Duncan. Descriptions of Imaginary Poetries.
  Imagining in Writing.
  Often I Am Permitted to Return to a Meadow.
Dunn. American Film, An.
  Danse Manhattanique.
  Instead of You.
  Landscape at the End of the Century.
  Photograph in the Hallway, The.
  Update.
Eberhart. Fables of the Moon.
  Fortune's Mist.
  Reading Room, The New York Public Library.
  Supreme Authority of the Imagination, The.
Eliot. La Figlia Che Piange.
Fisher. Artists, Providers, Places to Go.
  Counterfeit bucolic scene, A.
  Intruder, The.
  Poem: "Small / poem / the unit of feeling,
    The."
Fox. Rescue.
  Say It Has Been Snowing.
Frost. Courage to Be New, The.
  Riders.
Gardner. At the Zoo.
  Card Island or Cod Island?
Ginsberg. Imaginary Rose in a Book, An.
  Psalm I.
  Sunset S.S. Azemour.
Graves. Alice.
  Death Room, The.
  In Disguise.
  Secret Land, The.
  Troughs of Sea.
  Warning to Children.
Griffiths. Tŷ Newydd.
Gunn. Inside-Outside Game, The.

Justin.
  Pierce Street.
  Rain stops. I look round: a square of floor,
    The.
Hacker. Art of a Novel, The.
  Celles.
Hardy. After a Romantic Day.
  Meditation on a Holiday.
  Sun on the Bookcase, The.
Hartley. Going Man, A.
  Some Moments with Locatelli.
Hewitt. Comment on Verse.
  Fairy-Man at Layde, The.
  I Cannot Make a Song Tonight.
  Sanctuary.
  Substance and Shadow.
  Who Was C.B. Fry?
Hill. Imaginative Life, The.
Hoffman. Instructions to a Medium, to be
  Transmitted to the Shade of W.B. Yeats, the
  Latter Having Responded in a Séance Held
  on 13 June 1965, Its Hundredth Birthday.
  Possession.
Hugo. Imagining Delaware.
  Memoirs.
Jarrell. Carnegie Library, Juvenile Division,
  The.
  Children Selecting Books in a Library.
  Children's Arms.
  Cinderella.
  Cow wandering in the bare field, The.
  Girl in a Library, A.
  Sick Child, A.
  Unicorn, The.
Jonson. Break, Fant'sy, from thy cave of
  cloud.
Joseph. Abstract Study—Circles.
  Bound upon a Wheel.
  February Floods, 1953.
  Not a Rootless Lily.
  Translation.
  Tripping down.
Keats. Ode on a Grecian Urn.
  On Receiving a Curious Shell, and a Copy of
    Verses, from the Same Ladies.
  On "The Story of Rimini."
  To My Brother George.
Kipling. Friends, The.
Koch. In the Morning.
Kunitz. Testing-Tree, The.
Larkin. Essential Beauty.
  Observation.
Lawrence. Early Spring.
Levertov. Sequence, A.
Liddy. At a Czech Tomb in Tuam.
  Tray-Carrier of Laurels, Liam Miller.
Lindsay. When the Mississippi Flowed in
  Indiana.
Lorde. Summer Oracle.
Lowry. Hunger.
"MacDiarmid." Harry Semen.
MacLeish. And he had used love's dream of
  love before.
  She was herself, not his, not anything.
  Whom do you love, she said, when you look
    out.
MacNeice. Canto II: "'On the other hand,'
  said Gavin—or could have said."
Markson. Lowry.
Meinke. Chicken Unlimited.
  You stand in isolation like the first bloom.
Meredith. Give to imagination some pure
  light.
Merton. In the Rain and the Sun.
  Moon smiles like a queen, The.
Millay. Amorphous is the mind; its quality.
Morrison. Stand There Listening.
Muldoon. Trance.
Nemerov. Maia.
Oliver. Aunt Leaf.
  Spring Azures.
  Swan, The.
Olson. 2nd Musical Form, for Dave Young,
  A.
  What's Wrong with Pindar.
  Writ, The.
Oppen. From Virgil.

Owen. Spells and Incantation (a Fragment).
Patchen. He Was Alone (As in Reality) Upon
  His Humble Bed.
Plath. Letter to a Purist.
  November Graveyard.
  On the Difficulty of Conjuring Up a Dryad.
  On the Plethora of Dryads.
  Tale of a Tub.
Rich. Poetry: III.
Rolfe. Any Slave.
Rukeyser. Child wakes in the morning to enter
  a country, The.
  Risen Image Shines, The.
St. John. Merlin.
Sandburg. Child Margaret.
  Hummingbird Woman.
Sarton. Notes from India.
  These Images Remain.
Schuyler. Greetings from the Chateau.
Sexton. August 8th.
  February 3rd.
  Fourth Psalm.
  Gold Key, The.
Shelley. To ——: "Oh! there are spirits of
  the air."
Silverstein. If the World Was Crazy.
  Invisible Boy.
  Invitation.
  Land of Happy, The.
  One Inch Tall.
  Recipe For A Hippopotamus Sandwich.
  True Story.
  Who.
  Yipiyuk, The.
Simic. Prisoner, The.
Smart. Reason and Imagination.
Smith, Stevie. Agnostic, An.
  In Protocreation.
  My Hat.
  Our Bog is Dood.
Snodgrass. W. D., Don't Fear That Animal.
Snyder. I can't stand these bird-songs.
Sorrentino. Classic Case, A.
  Crown, The.
Stafford. Allegiances.
Stevens. Academic Discourse at Havana.
  Delightful Evening.
  Final Soliloquy of the Interior Paramour.
  Human Arrangement.
  Imago.
  Man with the Blue Guitar, The.
  Mrs. Alfred Uruguay.
  Plain Sense of Things, The.
  Puella Parvula.
  Snow Man, The.
Stevenson. Block City.
  Dumb Soldier, The.
  Far over seas an island is.
  Good Play, A.
  Historical Associations.
  Land of Counterpane, The.
  Land of Nod, The.
  Land of Story-Books, The.
  Little Land, The.
  My Bed Is a Boat.
  My Kingdom.
  Pirate Story.
  To Any Reader.
  Unseen Playmate, The.
Stuart. Exeutive Discovers Poetry, The.
  Student, The.
Suckling. Upon My Lady Carlisle's Walking
  in Hampton Court Garden.
Tomlinson. Sense of Distance, A.
Updike. Marching through a Novel.
Van Duyn. Woman Waiting.
Wakoski. Fifth Universe.
Walcott. I can sense it coming from far, too,
  Maman, the tide.
Whitman. Ambition.
  Glimpse, A.
Whittier. Tent on the Beach, The.
  To My Sister.
Wilbur. Clearness.
  In the Elegy Season.
  La Rose des Vents.

Sunlight Is Imagination.
Walking to Sleep.
Williams, Charles Kenneth. Most excruciating / thing, The.
Near the Haunted Castle.
Williams, William Carlos. Deep Religious Faith.
Wordsworth. Her Only Pilot the Soft Breeze, the Boat.
In My Mind's Eye a Temple, Like a Cloud.
Morning Exercise, A.
Pibroch's note, discountenanced or mute.
Weak is the will of Man, his judgement blind.
While Beams of Orient Light Shoot Wide and High.
Yarrow Visited [September, 1814].
Yes! Thou Art Fair, Yet Be Not Moved.
Yau. Radiant Silhouette IV.
Yeats. Those Images.
Zukofsky. Lines of this new song are nothing, The.
Some time has gone.
To my wash-stand.

See also **Fancy.**

Immigration and Immigrants
Atwood. Disembarking at Quebec.
First Neighbours.
Further Arrivals.
Immigrants, The.
Cohen. Portrait of a Girl.
Cummings. Mary green / cheerful & generous.
"Dylan." I Pity the Poor Immigrant.
Eberhart. Statue of Liberty.
Fenton. Chosun.
Ferlinghetti. Poet's eye obscenely seeing, The.
Frost. Immigrants.
Galvin. 1847.
My Grandmother Steals Her Last Trout.
Glück. Legend.
Griffiths. Giving Them What For.
Hartley. Kuzan—First Avenue.
Hugo. Tony.
Jarrell. Night before the Night before Christmas, The.
To the New World.
Joseph. Man in a Bar.
MacLeish. Burying Ground by the Ties.
MacNeice. Last before America.
Refugees.
Mahon. Canadian Pacific.
Meredith. Patriot Engineer, The.
Olson. I have been an ability—a machine—up to.
Oppen. Strange that the youngest people I know.
Paley. Autumn.
Family.
Having Arrived by Bike at Battery Park.
Illegal Aliens.
Letter.
Nature of This City, The.
Rich. Prospective Immigrants Please Note.
Shapiro. My Grandmother.
Statue of Liberty.
Sutter. Swedish Lesson.
Whittier. Pennsylvania Pilgrim, The.
Wilbur. Speech for the Repeal of the McCarran Act.
Williams, William Carlos. Sicilian Emigrant's Song.

Immortality
Angelou. Wonder.
Arnold. Shakespeare.
Atwood. Bus along St Clair: December, A.
They Eat Out.
Auden. J.S. Bach.
Yes and No.
Berg. Coat, The.
Berry. Bloodroot is white, The.
Farmer, Speaking of Monuments, The.
Bly. Poem in Three Parts.
Bogan. Homunculus.
Browning, Robert. Cleon.
Earth's Immortalities.
Bukowski. Upon First Reading the Immortal Literature of the World—.

Carruth. Contra Mortem.
Third Version, The.
Catullus. Carmen 40: "Whatever could have possessed you."
Coleridge. Human Life; on the Denial of Immortality.
Cummings. But if a living dance upon dead minds.
Fame Speaks.
Helen.
Let us suspect,chérie,this not very big.
Mortals) / climbi / ng i / nto eachness begi.
So shy shy shy(and with a).
De la Mare. Alexander.
Evening.
Not Only.
Dickey, James. Immortals.
Dickinson. Ambition cannot find him.
Because I could not stop for Death.
Extol thee—could I? Then I will.
Finite life, little sister, A.
Footlights cannot improve the grave.
Given in Marriage unto Thee.
If my Bark sink.
Immortality of Flowers, The.
Immortality she gave, The.
Is Immortality a bane.
It is an honorable Thought.
It may have been she came to show you.
It's thoughts—and just One Heart.
Letter always seemed to me, A.
My life closed twice before its close.
No heart that broke but further went.
Only News I know, The.
Reticent volcano keeps, The.
Risks of Immortality, The.
Soul's Superior instants, The.
Speculate with all our might.
Such are the inlets of the mind.
Take all away.
That Such have died enable Us.
Two—were immortal twice.
Unable are the Loved to die.
Vision of Immortal Life has been fulfilled, The.
We thirst at first—'tis Nature's Act.
Who abdicated Ambush.
Why should we hurry—why indeed?
With Pinions of Disdain.
Dobyns. Delicate, Plummeting Bodies, The.
Donne. Death[,] be not proud, though some have called thee.
Good Morrow, The.
Harbinger to the Progress, The.
Through thy submitting all, to blow[e]s.
Eberhart. Hand, The.
R. G. E.
Ways and Means.
Eliot. Whispers of Immortality.
Emerson. Brave Empedocles defying fools, The.
Eros.
Ferlinghetti. I have not lain with beauty all my life.
Ford. This is the story of fire without flames.
Fox. Susanna.
Ginsberg. Poem Rocket.
Hardy. Her Immortality.
His Immortality.
Rome: At the Pyramid of Cestius near the Graves of Shelley and Keats.
Shelley's Skylark.
Hartley. Immortal Face.
Herbert. Death.
Virtue [*or* Vertue].
Herrick. His Creed.
To His Peculiar Friend Master Thomas Shapcott, Lawyer.
Hewitt. Art Room in a City School.
Chinese Fluteplayer.
Fairy-Man at Layde, The.
Immortality.
Isaac McKeown.
Minor Poet's Dilemma, 1940.
Jeffers. Animula.
Post Mortem.

Jong. My death.
Xylophone of the Spine, The.
Jonson. To the Memory of My Beloved, the Author Mr [*or* Master] William Shakespeare[: And What He Hath Left Us].
Keats. Darkling I listen; and for many a time.
Ode: "Bards of passion and of mirth."
Lawrence. Resurrection.
Liddy. Unlike the moon.
Wild curlew whistle I offer my death to.
Lindsay. Beyond the Moon.
Lorde. Maiden, The.
Lowry. Thou was not born for death, immortal Duck.
MacLeish. Some Aspects of Immortality.
Throwing a careless pebble in the lake.
What the Wind Said to the Water: What the Water Replied.
McNeill. Lost in Orbit.
Marlowe. 1.15: Ad invidos, quod fama poetarum sit perennis.
Merton. Meditation before an Ancient Poem.
Prince. Byron-Shelley Conversation, A.
Raine. Kore.
Ralegh. Because that stealing immortalitie.
Robinson. Dark House, The.
Doricha.
Man against the Sky, The.
Rossetti. That No Man Take Thy Crown.
Rukeyser. Mortal Girl.
Shakespeare. Sonnet 55: "Not marble, nor the gilded monuments."
Sonnet 81: "Or I shall live your epitaph to make."
Sonnet 107: "Not mine own fears nor the prophetic soul."
Smart. Immortality.
Spenser. One day I wrote her name upon the strand.
Tennyson. Tithonus.
Whitman. Joy, Shipmate, Joy!
On the Beach at Night.
Whittier. Raphael.
Wordsworth. Upon a Portrait.
Wright, Charles. Laguna Dantesca.
Yeats. Sailing to Byzantium.
Zukofsky. What demented malice, my silly Ravidus.

Imperfections
Beckett. Out of Sight in the Direction of My Body.
Campion. Vaile, love, mine eyes, O hide from me.
Coleridge. Humility the Mother of Charity.
Creeley. Cantos, The.
Immoral Proposition, The.
Dickey, William. Therefore.
Eberhart. Meditation, A.
Everson. Challenge, The.
Herrick. No Loathsomnesse in Love.
To the Generous Reader.
Knott. Racist Poem.
Stevens. Poems of Our Climate, The.
Warren. Nature of a Mirror, The.

Imperialism
Auden. Standing among the ruins, the horror-struck conqueror exclaimed.
Bly. Hatred of Men with Black Hair.
Davie. Bougainville.
Frontenac.
Letter to Curtis Bradford, A.
Eberhart. Rape of the Cataract, The.
Frost. Bad Island, The—Easter.
Jeffers. Bowl of Blood, The.
Shine, Empire.
Kipling. Kitchener's School.
Recessional.
Rowers, The.
Song of the White Men, A.
White Man's Burden, The.
Lawrence. Combative Spirit, The.
Triumph.
Lindsay. Shantung[, or The Empire of China is Crumbling Down].
Lowell. Cicero, the Sacrificial Killing.
Marcus Cato 234–149 B.C.

"MacDiarmid." All dreams of "imperialism" must be exorcised.
McGrath. Columbus.
Fresco: Departure for an Imperialist War.
Meredith. Chillianwallah.
Gordon of Khartoum.
Voyage of the "Ophir," The.
Warning, The.
Merton. Letter to Pablo Antonio Cuadra Concerning Giants, A.
Tibud Maclay.
Olson. Bigmans II.
Thomas. Incarnate Devil.
Updike. B.W.I.
Waldman. Face the Orient.

Impermanence. see **Transience.**

Impotence
Bukowski. Sex and/or Love.
Carruth. Sex.
Shall he then finally "put away childish things."
Cohen. These Heroics.
Eberhart. Meditation, A.
Everson. Kingfisher Flat.
Graves. Primrose Bed, The.
Herrick. To His Mistresses.
Hewitt. Providence 1.
Marlowe. 3.6: Quod ab amica receptus cum ea coire non potuit, conqueritur.
Morrison. Lament for the Death of My Cock.
Rukeyser. Portrait of a Man, with a Background of Holdings.
Stevens. Mountains Covered with Cats.
Williams, William Carlos. Plea for Mercy, A.
Yeats. Chambermaid's Second Song, The.

Impressionism and Impressionists
Ferlinghetti. Late Impressionist Dream.
Matisse at the Modern, Magritte at the Met.
Returning to Paris with Pissarro.

Impulse
Clark. Time.
Creeley. Dancing.
Massachusetts.
Post Cards.
Koch. Departure from Hydra, The.
Zukofsky. Drive, fast kisses.

Incantations
Jong. Love Spell: against Endings.
Waldman. Incantation.

Incest
Catullus. Carmen 74: "Gellius, / hearing his uncle anathematise the mere mention."
Carmen 79: "They nickname Lesbia's brother 'pulcher' ."
Carmen 88: "What, Gellius, of the man."
Carmen 90: "Let there stem (Gellius)."
Carmen 111: "In constancy content with one man, there."
Jeffers. Such Counsels You Gave to Me.
Tamar.
Zukofsky. Aufilena, virile content him weave her her solo.
Gellius how he'd rare at pot true uncle objurgate soul array.
Lesbius has pooled her: kidney? whom Lesbia my—lit.
Now seed their Magus (of Gelli's mother wrestling confounded.
Quid, fact it is Gelli? quick'ning mother, at (queer) sis, all three.

Incomprehensibility
Berg. Cherries.
Good.
Milk.
Uncle Will, the Gardener.
Byron. Translation from Catullus ("Ye Cupids, droop each little head").
Carruth. Being as Moment, The.
Catullus. Carmen 3: "Who loves beauty / vel her statues."
Coleridge. To Mr. Pye.
Creeley. For Lewis, to Say It.
"Dylan." Ballad of a Thin Man.
Bob Dylan's 115th Dream.
Highway 61 Revisited (liner Notes).
I Shall Be Free No. 10.

On the Road Again.
Rita May.
Sitting on a Barbed-Wire Fence.
Everson. Lava Bed.
We in the Fields.
Ford. Bad Habit, The.
Griffiths. For the Irish Sea.
Hesketh. What Is God?
Hewitt. O Country People.
Joseph. Shadows Coming.
Nash. It's about Time.
Nemerov. Banquaet, The.
Neruda. Men (XIX), The.
Wordsworth. Death of a Starling, The.
Wright, Charles. December Journal.
Journal of Three Questions, A.
Saturday Morning Journal.
Zukofsky. Lament, o graces of Venus, and Cupids.

Inconstancy
Beatles. No Reply.
Beckett. Confections.
Browning, Elizabeth Barrett. Change Upon Change.
Bukowski. Sexpot.
Burns. Banks O' Doon, The.
Banks o' Doon, The: "Ye flowery banks o' bonie Doon."
Can You Leave Me Thus, My Katy.
Eppie McNab.
Scotish Ballad.
Song: "Let not Woman e'er complain."
Thou hast left me ever, Jamie.
Carruth. R.M.D.
Chaucer. Against Women Unconstant [or A Ballade against Woman Inconstant].
Cowper. Friendship.
On Female Inconstancy.
Song, A: "On the green margin of the brook."
"Dylan." Absolutely Sweet Marie.
Eberhart. Going to Maine.
Graves. Confess, Marpessa.
Hardy. Inconsistent, The.
Sun on the Letter, The.
Herbert. Giddiness.
Herrick. Upon Himself: ("I dislikt but even now").
Upon Trap.
Jonson. Another. In Defense of Their Inconstancy [or Inconstancie]. A Song.
Kipling. Ballade of Jakko Hill, A.
Pack. Still Passing.
Piercy. I lack a light touch.
Ralegh. Advice, The.
Stevenson. To Henry James.

Indecision. see **Decisions.**

Independence
Arnold. Self-Dependence.
Beatles. She's Leaving Home.
Ticket to Ride.
Brooks. Independent Man, The.
Browning, Elizabeth Barrett. Calls on the Heart.
Bunting. Ginger, who are you going with?
Please stop gushing about his pink.
Burns. I Hae a Wife o' My Ain.
Poetical Inscription, for an Altar to Independence at Kerrouchtry, the Seat of Mr. Heron, Written in Summer 1795.
To Daunton Me.
Cohen. Why Don't You Try.
Dunbar. Easy-Goin' Feller, An.
"Dylan." Like a Rolling Stone.
Trust Yourself.
Eliot. Cousin Nancy.
Emerson. But Nature whistled with all her winds.
Civil world will much forgive, The.
Gallagher. Beginning to Say No.
Hughes, Ted. Calves harshly parted from their mamas.
Jeffers. My Dear Love.
Thebaid.
Oppen. Great stone / Above the river, The.
Pack. Closer.
Prince. To a Granddaughter on One of Her Suggestions for a Christmas Present.

Rich. Mountain laurel in bloom, The.
Rolfe. Somebody and Somebody Else and You.
Smith, Charlotte. To Dependence.
Snodgrass. Valediction, A.
Stevens. Nuances of a Theme by Williams.
Waldman. Ballade: "My heart's felt no wounds big or small."
Warren. Ivy, The.
Picture of Little Rory in a Municipal Park, The.
Whittier. Hero, The.
Wilbur. On Freedom's Ground.
Wordsworth. Resolution and Independence.

India
Atwood. Sunday Drive, A.
Carruth. Godhulivela.
Purana, Meaning Once Upon a Time.
Cohen. On Seeing Kabir's Poems on Her Dressing Table.
Cullen. Karenge Ya Marenge.
Ginsberg. Describe: The Rain on Dasaswamedh Ghat.
Patna-Benares Express.
Hill. Short History of British India (I), A.
Short History of British India (III), A.
Short History of British India (II), A.
Joseph. River Rising in India.
Kipling. Army Headquarters.
Cholera Camp.
Christmas in India.
Giffen's Debt.
Grave of the Hundred Dead, The.
Gunga Din.
In Springtime.
Lament of the Border Cattle Thief, The.
Last Suttee, The.
Legend of the Foreign Office, A.
Man Who Could Write, The.
Mandalay.
Masque of Plenty, The.
Moon of Other Days, The.
Mother-Lodge, The.
Now it is not good for the Christian's health to hustle the Aryan brown.
One Viceroy Resigns.
Oonts.
Open Door, The.
Overland Mail, The.
Pagett, M. P.
Parade-Song of the Camp Animals.
Plea of the Simla Dancers, The.
Public Waste.
Route Marchin'.
Song for the Women, The.
Song of the Wise Children.
Study of an Elevation, in Indian Ink.
Tale of Two Cities, A.
To the City of Bombay.
Truce of the Bear, The.
Two Months.
What Happened.
With Scindia to Delhi.
Lewis. By the Gateway of India: Bombay.
Holi.
In Hospital: Poona (2).
Indian Day.
Journey, The.
Karanje Village.
Mahratta Ghats, The.
Midnight in India.
Night bibles India in her wilderness.
To Rilke.
Lindsay. I Know All This When Gipsy Fiddles Cry.
"MacDiarmid." Poetry like the character of Indian culture, A.
Why.
MacNeice. Letter from India.
Matthews. Scenic View.
Meredith. Chillianwallah.
Merton. Calicut.
Darjeeling.
Delhi.
Songs of Experience; India, One.
Nash. How to Be Married without a Spouse, or, Mr. Kipling, What Have You Done with

Mr. Hauksbee?
Kipling's Vermont.
Nathan. Parade.
O'Hara. Image of the Buddha Preaching.
Rukeyser. Ajanta.
Sarton. Approach—Calcutta, The.
Invocation to Kali, The.
Nostalgia for India.
Notes from India.
Snyder. On Our Way to Khajuraho.
Walcott. Exile.
Saddhu of Couva, The.
Whitman. Passage to India.
Young. It's India.

Indian Summer
Dickinson. These are the days when Birds come back—.
These Indian-Summer Days.
Lindsay. Indian Summer Day on the Prairie, An.
Sorrentino. Red sun is going down somewhere, A.
Stevenson. St. Martin's Summer.
Whittier. St. Martin's Summer.
Williams, William Carlos. Late for Summer Weather.

Indiana (state)
Levine. Helmet, The.
Sandburg. Mayor of Gary, The.
New Song for Indiana Ophelias.
Updike. Indianapolis.
Young. Indiana Gig, The.

Indians, American. *see* **Native Americans.**

Indifference
Auden. On a Greek Tomb Relief.
Beckett. Bois seul.
Bukowski. Beautiful Young Girl Walking Past the Graveyard—, The.
Byron. To Caroline ("You say you love, and yet your eye").
Catullus. Carmen 30: "Alfenus from Cremona / forsakes the friendship of friends."
Carmen 39: "Because he has bright white teeth, Eg- / natius whips out a."
Carmen 93: "Utter indifference to your welfare, Caesar."
Creeley. Crow, The.
First Time, The.
Song: "Were I myself more blithe."
Dickey, James. Nameless.
Dickey, William. More Under Saturn.
"Dylan." One More Cup of Coffee (Valley Below).
Emerson. I care not whither I may go.
Garrigue. Civilization Constantly Worrying about Itself as It Goes on Doing What It Is Worrying About That It Is Doing, A.
Glück. Return, The.
Griffiths. Glyndŵr Subdued.
Hardy. At a Bridal.
Hewitt. Hesitant Memorial.
Municipal Gallery Revisited, October 1954.
Neighbor's Funeral, A.
Joseph. Lady.
Kunitz. How Long Is the Night?
Lawrence. Loggerheads.
What Do I Care?
Levine. Coming Home, *Detroit*, 1968.
Liddy. Prayers of a Pagan.
Translate into Latin for my Epitaph.
Markson. I Met My Love.
Melville. Pebbles.
Pound. Object, An.
Rossetti. Love Attacked.
Smith, Patti. Judith Revisited.
Smith, Stevie. Voice from the Tomb (3).
Snodgrass. Disposal.
Stevenson. Love's Vicissitudes.
Williams, William Carlos. She Who Turns Her Head.
Wright, Charles. Landscape with Seated Figure and Olive Trees.
Wyatt. Love whom ye list and spare not.
Zukofsky. Alfenus, remember *kind intimacies*? false? They elated us.
Egnatius, candid as his horse-bit white dentures.

Nil, not my aim to study you, Caesar, to be— well, a placater.

Indigestion
Herrick. Upon Gut.
Lowry. Morning song of El Leon.
Stevenson. Daughter of Herodias, The.

Individualism and Individualists
Arnold. Self-Dependence.
Beatles. Fixing a Hole.
Berg. Leaves.
Boyle. Artist Speaks..the Woman Answers, The.
Bukowski. Last Generation, The.
Carroll, Jim. I Am Not Kurt Schwitters.
Narrows, The.
Clough. In Stratis Viarum I.
Coleridge. Phantom.
Creeley. Measure, The.
Cummings. There are possibly 2 1/2 or impossibly 3.
Davie. Nonconformist, The.
Dickinson. There seems a spectral power.
To be singular under plural circumstances.
Dunbar. Bohemian, The.
Path, The.
Dunn. How to Be Happy: Another Memo to Myself.
Under the Black Oaks.
"Dylan." It's Alright, Ma (I'm Only Bleeding).
Emerson. Easy to match what others do.
Elizabeth Hoar.
Etienne de la Boéce.
I will not live out of me.
Let not conceited sages laugh aloud.
Ode, Inscribed to W. H. Channing.
Simple people each with basket or tool, The.
Ferlinghetti. Adieu À Charlot.
Jack of Hearts, The.
Fisher. Epitaph: Lorine Niedecker.
Glück. Marathon.
Graves. Portrait, The.
Hewitt. Country Talk.
Our Avenue.
Jeffers. Heavy and yellow with the clay wrack from the flooded valley.
Kipling. Glories, The.
Two Races.
Lawrence. At Last.
Be a Demon!
Don'ts.
Levertov. Melody Grundy.
Liddy. Personal Odyssey.
"MacDiarmid." And a poetry in which as in a film.
MacNeice. Individualist Speaks, The.
Plurality.
Merton. New Ribbon.
Nash. Thoughts Thought on an Avenue.
O'Hara. My Heart.
Olson. "At the boundary of the mighty world" H. (T) 620 foll.
Po-sy, a Po-sy, A.
Piercy. I Will Not Be Your Sickness.
Sandburg. Always the Mob.
Personality.
Style.
Your low birth puts you beneath me.
Stevens. United Dames of America.
Walker. Light Baggage.
On Stripping Bark from Myself.
Whitman. By Blue Ontario's Shore.
Williams, William Carlos. On First Opening the Lyric Year.
Wyatt. I am as I am and so will I be.
Yeats. Coat, A.
Zukofsky. Song for the Year's End, A.

See also **Egotism and Egotists.**

Indonesia and Indonesians
Fenton. Dead Soldiers.
Oliver. Indonesia.

Indulgences
Bunting. Night is hard by. I am vexed and bothered by sleep.
Campion. Epigramme: "Buffe loves fat vians, fat ale, fat all things."

Carruth. Your dream: / Its name apparently is Honeywell.
Griffiths. Post Imperial.
Herrick. Youth, and Age.
Meredith. Certain People, A.
Patchen. I compel you to question me about my motives.
"Reed." Strawman.
Smith, Stevie. Mother's Hearse, A.
Stevenson. Good old ale, mild or pale.
Young. Hangover.
Madness.

Industrial Revolution
Bishop. Varick Street.

Industrial Workers of the World (IWW)
McGrath. Heroes of Childhood, The.

Industrialization
Auden. Allendale.
Bukowski. High-Rise of the New World, The.
Davie. Cheshire.
For an Age of Plastics. [Plymouth].
Dunbar. Ballade: "By Mystic's banks I held my dream."
Eberhart. Hard Structure of the World, The.
Emerson. New England Capitalist.
Frost. Bursting Rapture.
Hall. Foundations of American Industry, The.
Hesketh. Bolton-Le-Moors, 1960.
Hewitt. Chant for the Five-Year Plan.
Hoffman. On the Industrial Highway.
Hughes, Ted. Mayday on Holderness.
Koch. Brassiere Factory, The.
Larkin. Going, Going.
Lawrence. Cross, The.
Evening Land, The.
Factory Cities, The.
Gulf, The.
New Houses, New Clothes.
North Country, The.
Oh Wonderful Machine!
Robot Feelings.
Side-Step, O Sons of Men!
We Die Together.
What Is a Man to Do?
Why—?
Levertov. For Floss.
Levine. They Feed They Lion.
Lowry. Picture, A.
Two streams came from a different source, The.
McNeill. Oil Field.
Merton. Ohio River—Louisville, The.
Nash. First Chime.
Olson. Swimming through the air, in schools upon the highways.
Rich. Location.
Sandburg. Five Towns on the B. and O.
Prairie.
Spender. Landscape near an Aerodrome, The.
Williams, William Carlos. Sketch for a Portrait of Henry Ford.
Wright, Charles. Lonesome Pine Special.
Zukofsky. O sleep, the sky goes down behind the poplars.

Ineptitude
Burns. Dear Cimon Gray, / The other day.
To Mr. E—— on His Translation of and Commentaries on Martial.
Emerson. With the key of the secret he marches faster.
MacLeish. Ship of Fools.
Nash. He Digs, He Dug, He Has Dug.
Pope. To Eustace Budgell, Esq., on His Translation of the Characters of Theophrastus.
Translator, The.
Verses to Be Placed under the Picture of England's Arch-Poet: Containing a Compleat Catalogue of His Works.

Infant Death
Dunbar. Two Little Boots.
Hartnett. Lament for Tadhg Cronin's Children.
Jonson. On My First Daughter.
To K[ing] Charles and Q[ueen] Mary, for the Loss of Their First-Born. An Epigram Consolatory. 1629.
McNeill. Granny's Story.

Williams, William Carlos. Dead Baby, The.

See also **Death in Childhood.**

Infanticide

Browning, Elizabeth Barrett. Runaway Slave at Pilgrim's Point, The.

Carruth. "They tossed my baby like a cat in the air."

Hall. By the Exeter River.

Smith, Stevie. But Murderous.

Williams, Miller. Ones that Are Thrown Out, The.

Infants. *see* **Babies.**

Infatuation

Angelou. Senses of Insecurity.

Auden. Vision.

Brooks. Love Note II: Flags.

Browning, Robert. Beatrice Signorini.

Cristina.

Rudel to the Lady of Tripoli.

Sonnet: "Eyes, calm beside thee, (Lady couldst thou know!)."

Burns. Fragment, A: "When first I came to Stewart Kyle."

Carew. Hue and Cry, The.

Mr. Carew to His Friend.

"Carroll, Lewis." Atalanta in Camden-Town.

Three Sunsets.

Clark. Last Poem (after Robert Desnos), The.

My Hypertrophic Devotion.

Coleridge. Lewti.

Cowper. Sonnet 5: "In truth your fair eyes, my lady."

Sonnet 4: "Diodati, and I will say it to you with wonder."

Sonnet 6: "Young, gentle, and candid lover that I am."

Crane. Ah! without the moon, what white nights.

Dickinson. Her thot's tho' they are older.

I see thee better—in the Dark.

Dobyns. White Skirt, The.

Emerson. Bring wine release me.

Dante's Vita Nuova.

Pair of crystal eyes will lead me, A.

Take my heart in thy hand, O beautiful boy of Schiraz!

When Jane was absent Edgar's eye.

Graves. Circus Ring.

Dream of Frances Speedwell, A.

Growing Pains.

Invitation to Bristol.

Poor Others.

Three Times In Love.

To Be in Love.

Traditionalist, The.

Herrick. Epitaph upon a Virgin, An.

Short Hymne to Venus, A.

To Oenone ("Thou saist Love's dart").

Upon a Black Twist, Rounding the Arm of the Countess of Carlisle.

Upon Love ("Love brought me to a silent Grove").

Upon Love ("Some salve to every sore, we may apply").

Writing.

Housman. Oh, when I was in love with you.

Kipling. Fall of Jock Gillespie, The.

Koch. In Love with You.

Spring.

To Marina.

To You.

Koertge. To Impress the Girl Next Door.

Larkin. Spirit Wooed, The.

Markson. Skull.

Meredith. We three are on the cedar-shadowed lawn.

Milton. Sonnet 5: "In truth your fair eyes, my lady."

Sonnet 4: "Diodati, and I will say it to you with wonder."

Sonnet 6: "Young, gentle, and candid lover that I am."

Ralegh. Poesie to Prove Affection is Not Love, A.

Rolfe. Still Must I Love You.

Sandburg. Dancer.

Old-Fashioned Requited Love.

Shirt.

Shelley. Fragments of an Unfinished Drama.

To Constantia, Singing.

Sidney. *Dorus*, tell me, where is thy wonted motion.

Eleventh Song.

In Vain, Mine Eyes.

Since so mine eyes are subject to your sight.

Sonnet 107: "Stella, since thou so right a Princess art."

Sonnet 108: "When sorrow (using mine own fire's might)."

Sonnet 16: "In nature apt to like when I did see."

Sonnet 21: "Your words my friend (right healthful caustics) blame."

Sonnet 23: "Curious wits,, seeing dull pensiveness, The."

Sonnet 36: "Stella, whence doth this new assault arise."

Sonnet 47: "What, have I thus betrayed my liberty?"

Sonnet 49: "I on my horse, and Love on me doth try."

Sonnet 51: "Pardon mine ears; both I and they do pray."

Sonnet 53: "In martial sports I had my cunning tried."

Sonnet 54: "Because I breathe not love to every one."

Sonnet 61: "Oft with true sighs, oft with uncalled tears."

Sonnet 64: "No more, my dear, no more these counsels try."

Sonnet 67: "Hope, art thou true, or dost thou flatter me?"

Sonnet 68: "Stella, the only planet of my light."

Sonnet 69: "O joy, too high for my low style to show."

Sonnet 74: "Love still a boy, and oft a wanton is."

Sonnet 76: "She comes, and straight therewith her shining twins do move."

Sonnet 85: "I see the house; my heart thyself contain."

Sonnet 92: "Be your words made (good sir) of Indian ware."

Unto the caitiff wretch whom long affliction holdeth.

Smith, Stevie. At School.

Spenser. Nymphs and Graces Dancing, The.

Stuart. Timeshare.

Sutter. I Love Your Crazy Bones.

Williams, Charles Kenneth. Game, The.

Wyatt. Avising the bright beams of these fair eyes.

It was my choice, it was no chance.

Love hath again.

O goodly hand.

Of purpose Love chose first for to be blind.

Pain of all pain, the most grievous pain.

What would ye more of me, your slave, require.

Infidelity

Angelou. Pickin Em Up and Layin Em Down.

Poor Girl.

They Went Home.

Beatles. Another Girl.

I'll Be Back.

No Reply.

Rocky Raccoon.

Run for Your Life.

Tell Me Why.

What Goes On?

You Can't Do That.

Brooks. My Little 'Bout-Town Gal Has Gone.

Browning, Elizabeth Barrett. Bertha in the Lane.

Bianca among the Nightingales.

That Day.

Browning, Robert. Any Wife to Any Husband.

Forgiveness, A.

Worst of It, The.

Bukowski. Moaning and Groaning.

Burns. As I was a wand'ring ae midsummer

e'enin.

Eppie McNab.

My Lady's Gown There's Gairs upon't.

O An Ye Were Dead Gudeman.

Saw Ye My Phely (Quasi Dicat, Phillis).

She's fair and fause that causes my smart.

We'll Hide the Couper behint the Door.

Byron. On the Quotation "And My True Faith Can Alter Never, Though Thou Art Gone Perhaps Forever."

Remember Thee! Remember Thee!

To Woman.

When We Two Parted.

Campion. In Melleam.

Secret Love or Two I Must Confess[e], A.

Carew. Deposition from Love, A.

Guiltless Inconstant, The.

Carruth. Pray You Young Woman.

Catullus. Carmen 11: "Furius, Aurelius, friends of my youth."

Carmen 70: "Lesbia says she'ld rather marry me."

Chaucer. Anelida and Arcite.

Book of the Duchesse, The.

Cook's Tale, The.

Miller's Prologue, The.

Miller's [*or* Milleres] Tale, The.

Shipman's Tale, The.

Troilus and Criseyde [*or* Criseide].

Coleridge. Alice Du Clos.

Cowper. Love Abused.

Song, A: "On the green margin of the brook."

Cummings. It may not always be so; and i say.

Dickey, James. Adultery.

Dickey, William. Part Song, With Concert of Recorders.

Donne. Change.

Indifferent, The.

Love's Diet.

Message, The.

Nature's lay idiot [*or* Ideot], I taught thee to love.

Song: "Go, and catch a falling star."

Woman's Constancy.

Dove. Definition in the Face of Unnamed Fury.

Everson. Frost Lay White on California, A.

Fisher. Passive Partner, The.

Glück. Nurse's Song.

Graves. First Love.

Lament for Pasiphaë.

Should I Care.

Song: Though Once True Lovers.

Straw, The.

True Magic.

With Her Lips Only.

Hardy. Burghers, The.

Contretemps, The.

Dame of Athelhall, The.

Duel, The.

In the Days of Crinoline.

Military Appointment, A.

Moon Looks In, The.

Moth-Signal, The.

Newcomer's Wife, The.

Poor Man and a Lady, A.

Shiver, The.

Telegram, The.

Two Wives, The.

Wedding Morning, The.

Hayden. Burly Fading One, The.

Herrick. Chop-Cherry.

Eye, The.

To His False Mistris.

Upon Scobble [Epigram].

Housman. Along the field as we came by.

Spring Morning.

Hughes, Langston. Ultimatum.

Hughes, Ted. Kreutzer Sonata.

Jeffers. Love and the Hate, The.

Mara.

Steelhead, Wild Pig, the Fungus.

Thurso's Landing.

Jong. Parable of the Four-Poster.

Keats. Gripus.

Song: "Hush, hush! tread softly! hush, hush my dear."
Kipling. Pink Dominoes.
Koch. To Marina.
Koertge. In South America on Business He Does Something He Is Ashamed of yet on the Way Home Dreams of It Again and Again.
Last-Minute Change of Plans.
Primary Considerations.
Zenith and After, The.
Lindsay. At Mass.
Lovelace. Female Inconstancy.
Forsaken Lady to Her False Servant, A.
Scrutiny [or Scrutinie], The.
Lowell. At the Altar.
Between the Porch and the Altar.
MacNeice. Last light purples the mirrors of paddy, the tracks, The.
Prayer in Mid-Passage.
Marlowe. 2.5: Ad amicam corruptam.
2.8: Ad Cypassim ancillam Corinnae.
3.10: Ad amicam, a cuius amore discedere non potest.
Meredith. I play for Seasons; not Eternities!
She yields: my Lady in her noblest mood.
Waves are pressing up with force, The.
Millay. She Is Overheard Singing.
Thursday.
Moore. Injudicious Gardening.
Morgan. Catullus: Carmen xi.
Pope. Autumn, the Third Pastoral, or Hylas and Ægon.
Ralegh. Farewell to False Love, A.
"Reed." Gift, The.
Robinson. London Bridge.
Schuyler. This Dark Apartment.
Sexton. You All Know the Story of the Other Woman.
Shakespeare. Sonnet 138: "When my love swears [or sweares] that she is made of truth."
Sidney. Sonnet 91: "Stella, while now by honour's cruel might."
Suckling. Guiltless Inconstant, The.
Swift. Satire on an Inconstant Lover, A.
Walker. My Husband Says.
Williams, Charles Kenneth. Ethics.
Question, The.
Signs.
Williams, William Carlos. Exercise.
Wyatt. Accused though I be without desert.
Ah, Robin, / Jolly Robin.
Spite hath no power to make me sad.
Unstable dream[e] [or dreme], according [or accordyng] to the place.
Yeats. Host of the Air, The.
Zukofsky. Furius, Aurelius: comities—Catullus.
Newly say dickered my love air my own would marry me all.

See also **Adultery and Adulterers.**

Infinity
Ammons. Juice.
Blake. Memorable Fancy, A ("Prophets Isaiah and Ezekiel dined with me, and, The").
Browning, Elizabeth Barrett. Finite and Infinite.
Browning, Robert. Rephan.
Reverie.
Clough. As one who shoots an arrow overhead.
Coleridge. Traveller through Infinity, The.
Cummings. Life is more true than reason will deceive.
Structure,miraculous challenge,devout am.
Dickinson. Infinite a sudden Guest, An.
Show me Eternity, and I will show you Memory.
To the staunch Dust.
Eberhart. Seeing is Deceiving.
Emerson. Bohemian Hymn, The.
Coil of space the cones of light, The.
Roomy Eternity / Casts her schemes rarely.
Ferlinghetti. Endless Life.
Herrick. God ("God (as the learned Damascen write)").

Jong. Aura.
Nemerov. Two Sides to an Outside: Meditation from Empson.
Oppen. Like the wind in the trees and the bells.
Raine. Forest is multitude.
Rukeyser. Place-Rituals.
Sandburg. Leather Leggings.
Wilbur. All That Is.
Attention Makes Infinity.
Williams, Charles Kenneth. Even If I Could.
Young. Singular Yen, A.

Inflation
Emerson. Since the devil hopping on.
Zukofsky. This Fall, 1933.

Ingratitude
Campion. Epigramme: "Arthure brooks only those that brooke not him."
Epigramme: "Drue feasts no Puritans; the churles, he saith."
Epigramme: "Drue gives thee money, yet thou thankst not him."
Carew. In the Person of a Lady To Her Inconstant Servant.
Herbert. Unkindness.
Smith, Charlotte. To a Querulous Acquaintance.
Smith, Stevie. Will Man Ever Face Fact and Not Feel Flat?
Wordsworth. Fragment: "For let the impediment be what it may."

Inheritance
Angelou. My Guilt.
Atwood. How little I know / about you finally.
Berry. At last, completed in his rest.
Byron. Werner; or, The Inheritance.
Carruth. Mother, The.
Cowper. Grief of an Heir, The.
De la Mare. Isaac Meek.
Donne. Disinherited.
Father, part of his double interest.
Dryden. All human[e] things are subject to decay.
Gunn. Inherited Estate, The.
Hacker. Inheritances.
Sword.
Herrick. Lyric[k] for Legacies.
Upon Leech.
Hewitt. From a Museum Man's Album.
Island Folk Tale, An.
Johnson. Short Song of Congratulation [or To a Young Heir], A.
Jonson. On Chuff, Banks the Usurer's Kinsman.
Lewis. Had I ever a young field.
McNeill. Lydia Verner.
Merton. When a Hideous Man.
Ralegh. Things thus agreed: Titan made Saturne sweare.
"Reed." Endless Cycle.
Simic. Inheritance.
Tomlinson. Bells: a Period Piece, The.
History.
Jemez.
Waldman. Mature love you say but my wounds come out through inner temple.
Warren. How beautiful are the young, walking.
Whitman. My Legacy.
Wordsworth. Michael [A Pastoral Poem].

Injuries
Bly. Winter Poem.
Bunting. To abate what swells.
Crane. Episode of Hands.
Creeley. Man, The.
Dickey, James. Scarred Girl, The.
War Wound, The.
Dickinson. Anatomical dishabille.
Frost. Not to Keep.
Graves. Injuries.
Gunn. Wound, The.
Herrick. Bleeding Hand: or, The Sprig of Eglantine Given to a Maid, The.
Hewitt. Dustcart, The.
My Grandfather Dies, 1923.

Jarrell. X-Ray Waiting Room in the Hospital, The.
Kipling. DECEMBER (Skating).
Kooser. Very Old, The.
Lewis. Lying in the hospital he often thought. Three endless weeks of sniping all the way.
Lowry. Burnt pier: the last passenger: the farewells, The.
Child may find no words for its sorrow, A.
Consider what you have lost by lack of faith.
My love now lies upon his rump.
Note, A.
When I am in the purgatory of the unread.
Markson. On the Death, after Lying Wounded in the Thigh for Twenty-Six Days, of the Author of "Astrophel and Stella."
Plath. Contusion.
Psalms. Psalm 38: "O Lord, rebuke me not in thy wrath."
Ransom. Puncture.
Rossetti. Hurt No Living Thing.
Rukeyser. Another Day. For a Moment Slipping Back, Again the Unreal King.
Sandburg. Brim.
Shakespeare. Fair was the morn when the fair queen of love.
Shelley. Ode Written October, 1819, An.
Silverstein. Band-Aids.
Sorrentino. Pail.
Waltz of the Empty Roadhouse.
Williams, Charles Kenneth. Crime.
Greed.
Men.
Scar.
Williams, William Carlos. Injury, The.
Interests of 1926.
Wyatt. O Lord, as I thee have both prayed and pray.

Injustice
Beatles. Taxman.
Berryman. Interstitial Office.
Blake. Gwin, King of Norway.
Boyle. Poem for the Students of Greece, A.
Poem for the Teesto Diné of Arizona, A.
Browning, Robert. Heretic's Tragedy, The.
"Carroll, Lewis." Mouse's Tale, The.
Chaucer. Reeve's Prologue, The.
Cooper. And here is that part of my dream I would like to forget.
Cowper. Sonnet Addressed to Mr. Phillips, A.
Cullen. Scottsboro, Too, Is Worth Its Song.
Cummings. Remarked Robinson Jefferson.
Why must itself up every of a park.
"Dylan." Hurricane.
Lonesome Death of Hattie Carroll, The.
Maggie's Farm.
Oxford Town.
Percy's Song.
Playboys and Playgirls.
Seven Curses.
Hall. Small Fig Tree, A.
Herrick. Bad Wages for Good Service.
Bribes and Gifts Get All.
Upon the Bishop of Lincolne's Imprisonment.
Jonson. On a Robbery.
Kipling. Cleared.
Liddy. Bicentennial Words for the Liberal Magistrates of 1798.
Lindsay. Abraham Lincoln Walks at Midnight.
Who Knows?
Lorde. Revolution Is One Form of Social Change.
Vietnam Addenda.
MacNeice. Jericho.
Merton. But did you ever know the whole world was once held prisoner in a bank?
Millay. Justice Denied in Massachusetts.
Nash. Bankers Are Just Like Anybody Else, Except Richer.
Owen. Parable of the Old Man and the Young, The.
Patchen. Hangman's Great Hands, The.
Letter to a Policemen in Kansas City, A.
Piercy. Judgment, The.
Rich. For a Sister.
Rolfe. June 19, 1953.
Sarton. Prisoner at a Desk.

Shakespeare. Sonnet 66: "Tired [*or* Tyr'd, *or* Tir'd] with all these, for restful death I cry."
Stafford. In Camp.
Stuart. Speakers from the Vietnam War.
Whittier. Ein Feste Burg Ist Unser Gott.
Expostulation.
For Righteousness' Sake.
Human Sacrifice, The.
Hunters of Men, The.
Massachusetts to Virginia.
On a Prayer-Book.
Prisoner for Debt, The.
Sentence of John L. Brown, The.
Williams, Charles Kenneth. Rampage, The.

See also **Protest, Social.**

Innisfree, Ireland
Yeats. Lake Isle of Innisfree, The.

Innocence
Angelou. Martial Choreograph.
Ashbery. Punishing the Myth.
Auden. Robin, The.
Beatles. Rain.
Berrigan. Summer so histrionic, marvelous dirty days.
Berry. Adze, The.
Boone.
Thief, The.
Berryman. Curse, The.
Blake. Lily, The.
To see a World in a Grain of Sand.
Brontë. H.A. and A.S.
Song to A.A.
Tell me, tell me, smiling child.
Browning, Elizabeth Barrett. Child Asleep, A.
Lost Bower, The.
Browning, Robert. Pippa Passes.
Bukowski. Notations from a Muddled Indolence.
One for Old Snaggle-Tooth.
Burns. O once I loved [*or* lov'd] a bonnie lass.
Campion. Ad Amorem.
Carruth. Cows at Night, The.
For thon demgeorne dreorigne oft.
President's Speech, The.
Saving Way, The.
Clark. Air.
Cohen. Not Going Back.
Coleridge. Christabel.
To an Infant.
Cooper. Song: "Here I am yours, and here, and here."
Cowper. On the Picture of a Sleeping Child.
Creeley. Anywhere.
Joke, The.
Cullen. Dear Friends and Gentle Hearts.
Cummings. Who were so dark of heart they might not speak.
Dobyns. Gun, The.
Dunn. As It Moves.
Whiteness.
"Dylan." Bob Dylan's Dream.
Eliot. Hippopotamus, The.
Emerson. God The Lord save Massachusetts.
O sun! take off thy hood of clouds.
Fenton. Adult: That's a tattooed man.
Nest of Vampires.
Ferlinghetti. Deflowering.
With bells for hooves in sounding streets.
Fletcher. August, 1940.
Birth of Christ, The.
Ford. Baby's in Jail; the Animal Day Plays Alone.
Fox. Raccoon, A.
Gardner. Card Island or Cod Island?
Children Are Game.
When in Rome..
Word From the Piazza del Limbo, A.
Garrigue. Land We Did Not Know, The.
Gildner. Is My Heart Really Big As My Fist?
Ginsberg. Wild Orphan.
Graves. Ages of Oath, The.
Cliff Edge, The.
Trial of Innocence.
Griffiths. Fathers.
Few Bars Over Again, A.

Gunn. Innocence.
Sunlight.
Hall. Child's Garden, A.
September Ode.
Hardy. Boys Then and Now.
Child and the Sage, The.
In a Waiting-Room.
Leader of Fashion, A.
Man with a Past, The.
Sweet Hussy, The.
Hartley. Find the Face.
Herbert. Holy Baptism (2).
Herrick. To Julia ("Holy waters hither bring").
Hewitt. Age and Youth.
Easter Flock.
First Funeral.
In a Suburban Avenue.
Isaac McKeown.
Lilibulero.
Rhyme for Blake, A.
Hill. Holy Thursday.
Hoffman. Ode to Joy.
Housman. He, standing hushed, a pace or two apart.
Jarrell. And did she dwell in innocence and joy.
Joseph. First Spring Dawn.
Still Reading Fairy Stories.
Story.
Sunripe.
Knight. Circling the Daughter.
Larkin. Under a Splendid Chestnut Tree.
Lawrence. Jeune Fille, The.
Lewis. From a Play.
Lovers who among the grasses.
Sentry, The.
Soubrettes, The.
Lindsay. My Lady Is Compared to a Young Tree.
Lowry. For Nordahl Grieg Ship's Fireman.
I sing the joy of poverty, not such.
MacLeish. What the Green Tree Said.
MacNeice. Apple Blossom.
Autobiography.
To keep themselves young—Is that why people have children?
When We Were Children.
McNeill. First Flight.
Mahon. Girls on the Bridge.
Homecoming.
Meinke. Anniversary Deer, The.
Melville. On the Slain Collegians.
Meredith. In the time of early love.
It is the young fresh rainy leaf.
Like a blind milk is the loving heart.
No state is enviable. To the luck alone.
Now the youth was not ware of the beams.
One fairest of the ripe unwedded left.
Philosopher! 'tis said you wail.
What makes it hard to understand.
Merton. My gaze is clear as a sunflower.
Morrison. End of the Rainbow, The.
Wake, A.
Nash. It's Snug to Be Smug.
Passionate Pagan and the Dispassionate Public, The.
Period I.
Nemerov. Remorse for Time, The.
Snow Globe, The.
Neruda. Is all peace a dove's peace?
Oppen. In these explanations it is presumed.
Quotations.
Plath. Dream with Clam-Diggers.
Raine. Eternal Child, The.
Ransom. Bad News.
Janet Waking.
Necrological.
Vaunting Oak.
"Reed." Calm before the Storm, The.
Rich. Amnesia.
Innocents, The.
Robinson. Souvenir.
Rolfe. After Tu Fu (A.D. 713-770).
Poisoned Air Befouled the Whole Decade, The.
Song for a Birth Day in Exile.

Song: "Through all the cowering world, crouching, shrinking."
Rossetti. Once.
To Lalla, Reading My Verses Topsy-Turvy.
Word for the Dumb, A.
Rukeyser. Do you know what I play to be, in bed at night?
Sandburg. Brancusi.
Clean Curtains.
Clean Hands.
Crimson Changes People.
Sarton. Giant in the Garden.
Schwartz. He Who Excuses Himself Also Accuses Himself.
Shapiro. Mongolian Idiot.
Shame.
Shelley. Fragment: "Gentle story of two lovers young, A."
Smith, Charlotte. Glow-Worm, The.
Gossamer, The.
Sighing I see yon little troop at play.
To Fancy.
To Mrs. G.
Written in Farm Wood, South Downs, in May 1784.
Smith, Stevie. Last Turn of the Screw, The.
My Heart Was Full.
Snodgrass. Mouse, The.
Sorrentino. At twenty love disintegrates.
Girl at Sixteen with Lightning.
Où Sont Ils, Où, Vierge Souvrain?
Razzmatazz.
Silk Ascot for the Terrorist, A.
Verlaine's Innocents.
Stuart. Deer.
Sutter. Beaverhouse Downriver, The.
Thomas. Fern Hill.
Refusal to Mourn the Death, by Fire, of a Child in London, A.
Then Was My Neophyte.
Tomlinson. Mélisande.
Wakoski. Love Passes Beyond the Incredible Hawk of Innocence.
Virtuoso Literature for Two and Four Hands.
Warren. Little Boy and Lost Shoe.
Lullaby: Smile in Sleep.
Picnic Remembered.
Sirocco.
Ways of Day.
Whittier. Changeling, The.
In School-Days.
Vanishers, The.
Williams, Charles Kenneth. Acids.
Fifteen.
Gas Station, The.
Kingdom of Stinking Wishes, The.
Secrets.
Williams, Miller. Getting Experience.
Rebecca at Play.
Williams, William Carlos. Woodpecker, The.
Wordsworth. To the Highland Girl of Inversneyde.
Yeats. To a Child Dancing in the Wind.
Young. Michael At Sixteen Months.
Sweet Sixteen Lines.
Zukofsky. Ask of the sun.
It's hard to see but think of a sea.
So That Even a Lover.

Inns
Auden. Inn Song.
Betjeman. Village Inn, The.
Burns. At Brownhill Inn.
At Roslin Inn.
At Whigham's Inn, Sanquar.
Epigram: "Whoe'er he be that sojourns here."
Verses Written on a Window of the Inn at Carron.
Hardy. At an Inn.
Warren. Ballad of Billie Potts, The.

See also **Hotels; Motels.**

Inquisition, The
Browning, Robert. Delivery to the Secular Arm, The: A Scene During the Existence of the Spanish Inquisition at Antwerp, 1570.
Longfellow. Theologian's Tale: Torquemada, The.

Insanity. *see* **Madness.**

Insects

Auden. Aliens, The.
Beckett. Morte parmi.
Berryman. They Have.
De la Mare. Round, The.
Dunn. To a Friend in Love with the Wrong Man Again.
Eberhart. Largess, The.
Emerson. In Walden wood the chickadee.
 Solar insect on the wing.
Fenton. Fruit-Grower in War-time (and Some of His Enemies), The.
 In September greasebands are put on standard apple,.
Gardner. Cockchafer.
Hardy. August Midnight, An.
Hesketh. Survivors.
Hewitt. Diptera.
Joseph. Think of the minute amount a mouse eats.
Longfellow. Poet's Tale: The Birds of Killingworth, The.
Lorde. Brown Menace or Poem to the Survival of Roaches, The.
Lowry. Prelude to Another Drink.
McNeill. Of Fitness to Survive.
Meredith. Garden Idyl, A.
 O 'tis my delight / In the dead of the night.
 Sweet o' the Year, The.
Nash. Bugs.
 Creeps and Crawls.
 Glossina Morsitans, or, the Tsetse.
 Strange Case of the Entomologist's Heart, The.
Oliver. Buck Moon—From the Field Guide to Insects.
Roethke. Minimal, The.
Rossetti. These All Wait upon Thee.
Sandburg. Bug Spots.
 Purple Martins.
 Small Homes.
 Without Notice Beforehand.
Schuyler. September.
Sexton. June Bug.
Shapiro. Fly, The.
 Interlude, The.
Smith, Charlotte. Flora.
 To a Green-Chafer, on a White Rose.
 To the Fire-Fly of Jamaica, Seen in a Collection.
Spenser. In summers day, when Phœbus fairly shone.
Swift. Wood, an Insect.
Thomas. To-day, This Insect.
Updike. Fritillary, The.
Wilbur. Water Walker.
Wright, James. Depressed by a Book of Bad Poetry, I Walk toward an Unused Pasture and Invite the Insects to Join Me.
 I Was Afraid of Dying.
Zukofsky. "Mantis."

Insomnia and Insomniacs

Angelou. Insomniac.
Beatles. I Call Your Name.
 I'm So Tired.
Berg. 1909.
Berry. Awake at Night.
Berryman. As usual I'm up before the sun.
 Henry by Night.
Bukowski. Eaten by Butterflies.
 Fragile!
 Insomnia.
 On a Night You Don't Sleep.
Burns. Ay Waukin O.
Campion. Spyres Curten, The.
Carroll, Jim. Fear of Dreaming.
 Sleeplessness.
Cowper. *see also* Watching unto God in the Night-Season.
 see also Watching unto God in the Night-Season.
 Watching unto God in the Night-Season.
Creeley. Berlin: First Night & Early Morning.
Galvin. Night Ways.
Graves. Not to Sleep.
Hardy. Lying Awake.

Hayden. Broken Dark, The.
 Ice Storm.
Holmes. Midnight Oil.
Jarrell. Prayer at Morning, A.
Kipling. City of Sleep, The.
Larkin. Bottle Is Drunk Out by One, The.
Lindsay. Abraham Lincoln Walks at Midnight.
MacLeish. Night after night I lie like this listening.
MacNeice. Intimations of Mortality.
Millay. Midnight Oil.
Nash. Sedative Reflection.
Plath. Insomniac.
Pope. Of the Lady Who Could Not Sleep in a Stormy Night.
Rich. Afterwake, The.
 Insomniacs, The.
 Night.
 White Night.
Sarton. Who Wakes.
Schuyler. O Sleepless Night.
Shakespeare. Sonnet 28: "How can I then return in happy plight."
 Sonnet 61: "Is it thy will thy image should keep open."
Sidney. Sonnet 40: "As good to write as for to lie and groan."
 Sonnet 98: "Ah bed, the field where joy's peace some do see."
Spender. Sleepless.
Updike. By the light of insomnia, truths.
 Insomnia the Gem of the Ocean.
 Sleepless in Scarsdale.
 Tossing and Turning.
Wilbur. Walking to Sleep.
Williams, William Carlos. Song: "If I / could count the silence."
Zukofsky. Aubade, 1925.

Inspiration

Angelou. Impeccable Conception.
Arnold. Stanzas in Memory of the Author of "Obermann."
Berg. For the Ghost of Li Po.
Berrigan. Grace to be born and live as variously as possible.
 On the 15th day of November in the year of the motorcar.
Bly. Walking Swiftly.
Bukowski. Ah..
 On Going Back to the Street after Viewing an Art Show.
Burns. Duan Second.
 Lovely Davies.
 O were I on Parnassus hill.
 To Miss Ferrier.
 Written with a Pencil over the Chimney-Piece, in the Parlour of the Inn at Kenmore, Taymouth.
Carew. Celia Singing ("Hark, how my Celia, with the choice").
Cowper. 5.12: "You bid me write t' amuse the tedious hours."
 Elegy 6: To Charles Deodati.
Creeley. Door, The.
 Irish.
 Massachusetts.
Dunbar. Inspiration.
Dunn. Worker's Creed, A.
"Dylan." Ain't Gonna Grieve.
Emerson. Ah! not to me these dreams belong.
 Art.
 Fine presentiments controlled him.
 Honor bright o muse.
 I never knew but one.
 Inspired we must forget our books.
 O what are heroes prophets men.
 Pour the wine! pour the wine!
 S. R.
 Thy trivial harp will never please.
Fletcher. Alpine Violets.
Ginsberg. Blessed Be the Muses.
Graves. At the Gate.
 Mid-Winter Waking.
Hall. Three Movements, The.
Herrick. Departure of the Good Daemon, The.
 Draw, and Drinke.
 Not Every Day Fit for Verse.

To Sir Clipsebie Crew ("Since to th'Country first I came").
To Sir Clipseby Crew ("Give me wine, and give me meate").
To the Most Illustrious and Most Hopefull Prince, Charles, Prince of Wales.
Hesketh. Wordsworth's Old Age.
Hewitt. Art Room in a City School.
Holmes. Northfork October Return.
Johnson. Aurora Est Musis Amica.
Jonson. And Must I Sing? What Subject Shall I Choose?
Keats. How Many Bards Gild the Lapses of Time!
 On Sitting Down to Read "King Lear" Once Again.
 Poet, The.
 To B.R. Haydon, with a Sonnet Written on Seeing the Elgin Marbles.
 Welcome Joy, and Welcome Sorrow.
Koch. Artist, The.
Kunitz. Mens Creatrix.
Lowry. Jig, like Noah's donkey in the Ark, The.
Marlowe. 3.1: Deliberatio poetae, utrum elegos pergat scribere an potius tragedias.
Meredith. Later Alexandrian, A.
 Mentor and Pupils.
 On Combe Bottom: Surrey.
 Orson of the Muse, An.
 Pastoral 3: "Now standing on this hedgeside path."
 Star Sirius, The.
 To the Comic Spirit.
 You ask me what is Genius? 'tis that.
Merton. Poetry Ends with Me.
Millay. On Thought in Harness.
Milton. Elegy 6: To Charles Deodati.
Morrison. America As Bullring Arena.
Nemerov. Invocation: "Wasp, climbing the window pane."
Prince. Tears of a Muse in America, The.
Robinson. Bokardo.
 Sonnet: "Oh for a poet—for a beacon bright."
Rossetti. O ye, who are not dead and hid.
Schwartz. Song: "Under the yellow sea."
Sidney. Sonnet 15: "You that do search for every purling spring."
 Sonnet 28: "You that with allegory's curious frame."
 Sonnet 41: "Having this day my horse, my hand, my lance."
 Sonnet 74: "I never drank of Aganippe well."
 Sonnet 90: "Stella, think not that I by verse seek fame."
Smith, Charlotte. Flora.
 To My Lyre.
 To the Muse.
Stevenson. Far over seas an island is.
 Happy Thought.
 I whom Apollo sometime visited.
 Long time I lay in little ease.
 Sing clearlier, Muse, or evermore be still.
 Still I love to rhyme, and still more, rhyming, to wander.
Swift. To Mr. Congreve.
Thomson. Ode on Æolus's Harp, An.
 Poetical Epistle to Sir William Bennet, Bart. of Grubbat.
Tomlinson. Château de Muzot.
 Death of Will, The.
 Marl Pits, The.
 Praeludium.
Waldman. Phonecall from Frank O'Hara, A.
Williams, Miller. Muse, The.
Wordsworth. Not Love, not War, nor the Tumultuous Swell.
Young. By Heart.
 Dear Ravi Shankar.
 Dexter Gordon at Keystone Korner.
 Get that feeling sometimes.
 Jungle Strut.
 Poem for Dylan Thomas, A.
 Prestidigitator 2, The.
 Whatever Become of the Living.
Zukofsky. After Charles Sedley.
 Barely and *widely*.

Some time has gone.
You who were made for this music.
Instinct
Auden. Aware.
Berg. It Is.
Cowper. Beau's Reply.
Creeley. Billfold.
 Mouths Nuzz.
 Way.
 Words.
 Young Woman.
Davie. And of the sixth sense, the
 infinitesimal suffix.
Dunn. Beyond Hammonton.
Knott. Consolations of Sociobiology, The.
Lawrence. Immoral Man.
Lowry. Goldeneye and Goldfish.
Merton. Cutting up an Ox.
Oliver. Being Country Bred.
 Lilies Break Open Over the Dark Water, The.
 Turtle, The.
Roethke. Manifestation, The.
Schuyler. Running Footsteps.
Stevens. Poetry Is a Destructive Force.
Thomas. Before I Knocked.
 How Shall My Animal.
Updike. Each Summer's Swallows.
Institutionalization
Atwood. Visit to Toronto, with Companions.
Berryman. I dreamt he drove me back to the
 asylum.
Bogan. Evening in the Sanitarium.
Carruth. Asylum, The.
 December now. Winter deepens and darkens.
 Stars.
 Hall Five.
 He remembers: / There was this big house
 they called the Hatch.
 In the hot high summer I came.
 Ontological Episode of the Asylum.
 Rise up and proclaim themselves, and his skin.
 Rule of the majority is / strictly enforced in
 all matters, The.
 That I Had Had Courage When Young.
Clark. Parish: A Satire, The.
Kipling. Mother's Son, The.
Lowell. Waking in the Blue.
Morrison. Do You Have.
Plath. Face Lift.
 Miss Drake Proceeds to Supper.
Sexton. Double Image, The.
 Flee on Your Donkey.
 Music Swims Back to Me.
 Ringing the Bells.
Thomas. Love in the Asylum.
Insults
Bukowski. Poem for Liz.
Bunting. What the Chairman Told Tom.
Burns. Dost hang thy head, Billy, asham'd
 that thou knowest me?
 Extempore—On Being Shown a Beautiful
 County Seat Belonging to the Same [Maxwell
 of Cardoness].
 [On] Maxwell of Cardoness.
Catullus. Carmen 92: "Lesbia loads me night
 & day with her curses."
 Carmen 98: "Same can be said of you,
 Victius, The."
Cowper. Apology, An.
Herrick. Upon Jollies Wife.
 Upon Pearch.
Hughes, Langston. Sliver.
Meredith. Paris and Diomedes.
Oliver. Acid.
Suckling. Sir John Suckling's Answer.
Swift. Lesbia.
Williams, Charles Kenneth. Allies: According
 to Herodotus.
 Insult, The.
Yeats. Come Let Us Mock at the Great.
Zukofsky. In the, same in (when qualm?)
 thick wee poetry, putrid Victi.
 Lesbia may dicker simper maul or nag talk at
 whom, come.
Integrity
Berry. And I declare myself free.
 By the excellence of his work the workman is

a neighbor. By.
 Vision must have severity.
Brontë. All day I've toiled, but not with pain.
Byron. Thou Art Not False, But Thou Art
 Fickle.
Creeley. Like They Say.
Emerson. But if thou do thy best.
 Heartily heartily sing.
Hartley. Little Bird Alone.
Heaney. From the Canton of Expectation.
Hopkins. He mightbe slow and something
 feckless first.
Jeffers. Answer, The.
Lowell. Coleridge and Richard II.
 Marcus Cato 95–42 B.C.
Roethke. Pure Fury, The.
Rukeyser. Lilienthal said : I heard him saying
 words like these.
Shakespeare. Sonnet 125: "Were't aught to me
 I bore the canopy."
Spenser. Who so wil seeke by right deserts
 t'attaine.
Intellect and Intellectuals
Auden. Mind to body spoke the whole night
 through, the.
 To the man-in-the-street who, I'm sorry to say.
Clark. West of Eden.
Cummings. Ballad of an Intellectual.
 "Gay" is the captivating cognomen of a Young
 Woman of cambridge,mass.
 Mr youse needn't be so spry.
 My mind is.
 Since feeling is first.
 Trick of finding what you didn't lose, The.
Dickinson. Brain—is wider than the Sky, The.
 Genius is the ignition of affection.
Dobyns. Santiago: Five Men in the Street:
 Number Two.
Eberhart. Centennial For Whitman.
 Face, Ocean.
 In a Hard Intellectual Light.
 Man's Greed and Envy Are So Great.
 Poem as Trajectory, The.
 Sanders Theater.
Eliot. Cooking Egg, A.
Emerson. If he go apart.
 Intellect / Gravely broods apart on joy.
 Intellect.
 Motto to "Intellect."
Frost. At Woodward's Gardens.
Herrick. His Desire.
 Studies to Be Supported.
 Wit Punisht, Prospers Most.
Hewitt. Little Death, The.
 Mathematics.
 Note on Intellectuals.
 Poetry, Then.
 Touch of Things, The.
 William J. McClughin.
Hill. Let mind be more precious than soul; it
 will not.
Lawrence. Cerebral Emotions.
 Chastity.
 Climb Down, O Lordly Mind.
 Little-Boy Brilliant.
 Noli Me Tangere.
 Touch.
 What Matters.
Levertov. Vision, A.
"MacDiarmid." Glasgow, 1960.
Moore. Mind, Intractable Thing, The.
 Mind Is an Enchanting Thing, The.
Nash. If He Scholars, Let Him Go.
 Who Did Which? or Who Indeed?
Nemerov. Blue Swallows, The.
 Brainstorm.
Neruda. Negative Hands.
Pope. What if the foot, ordain'd the dust to
 tread.
Prince. To My Sister.
Shapiro. Essay on Chess.
 Intellectual, The.
Shelley. Hymn to Intellectual Beauty.
Simic. Harsh Climate.
Smith, Stevie. Oh, If Only.
Tomlinson. Antecedents.
Wilbur. Mind.

See also **Rationalism and Rationalists; Reason;
 Libraries and Librarians.**
Interment. *see* **Burial.**
International Brigade. *see* **Civil War, Spain.**
Interracial Love and Marriage
Cullen. Ballad of the Brown Girl, The.
Hacker. Against Silence.
St. John. Los Angeles, 1954.
Walker. Ballad of the Brown Girl.
 Johann.
Williams, Charles Kenneth. Dog, The.
Intolerance
Eberhart. Scarf of June, The.
Ginsberg. Uptown.
Hughes, Ted. Martyrdom of Bishop Farrar,
 The.
Meredith. Falling of Sally, The.
Pack. Hunting.
Warren. And Don't Forget Your Corset Cover,
 Either.
Williams, Charles Kenneth. End of Drought.
 Hog Heaven.
Introspection
Angelou. I Almost Remember.
Beatles. Strawberry Fields Forever.
 There's a Place.
 Tomorrow Never Knows.
Berg. From the Bridge.
 With Akhmatova at the Black Gates.
 Writing Class.
Berrigan. Into the closed air of the slow.
Bly. Chinese Tomb Guardians.
 Four Ways of Knowledge.
 Man Locked Inside the Oak, The.
 Meditation on Philosophy, A.
Brontë. All hushed and still within the house.
 Had there been falsehood in my breast.
 I know not how it falls on me.
 I'll come when thou art saddest.
 My Comforter.
 Self-Interrogation.
Bukowski. As I Lay Dying.
 Face While Shaving.
 Goldfish.
 Imbecile Night.
 Reprieve and Admixture.
Carruth. Asylum, The.
Creeley. Rain, The.
 Song: "You look out and you see people."
 Than I.
 Walking.
Dickinson. I often wish I was a grass.
 It is solemn to remember.
 Thousand questions rise to my lips, A.
Dunbar. Ere Sleep Comes Down to Soothe the
 Weary Eyes.
Dunn. Honesty.
 Temporarily.
Gallagher. Amplitude.
 Borrowed Ones, The.
 Simple Sonatina.
Garrigue. Bad Times Song.
 In Memory.
Gunn. Plan of Self-Subjection, A.
 Secret Sharer, The.
Herrick. His Wish.
Hewitt. Bell, The.
 Jacob and the Angel.
Liddy. Dear Anima, Show These Words.
 Personal Odyssey.
McGrath. Seekers, The.
Mahon. Dawn at Saint Patrick's.
Markson. Contradiction.
Merton. Stranger.
Milton. Il Penseroso.
Nathan. Audit.
Nemerov. From a Record of Disappointment.
 Idea.
 Loon's Cry, The.
 Paraphrase from Notebooks.
 Salt Garden, The.
 Sanctuary, The.
 This is about the stillness in moving things.
Neruda. Bell Tower of Authenay, The.
 Homecomings.
 One Comes Back.
 Possessions.

Oliver. Five A.M. in the Pinewoods.
Olson. Added to / making a Republic.
Celestial Evening, October 1967.
Maximus, to Himself.
Rexroth. Signature of All Things, The.
Rich. In the Woods.
Necessities of Life.
Storm Warnings.
Rolfe. At the Moment of Victory.
Biography.
Letter to the Denouncers, A.
St. John. Meditation.
Sarton. Action of Therapy, The.
Fear of Angels, The.
Frog, that Naked Creature, The.
Work of Happiness, The.
Shapiro. Tingling Back, The.
Silverstein. Standing.
Smith, Patti. Notebook.
Smith, Stevie. After-Thought, The.
Swift. Occasioned by Sir William Temple's
Late Illness and Recovery.
Van Duyn. Advice to a God.
From Yellow Lake: An Interval.
Two Poems, with Birds.
Walcott. Hotel Normandie Pool, The.
Return to D'Ennery; Rain.
Walk, The.
Wilbur. Aspen and the Stream, The.
Hole in the Floor, A.
Williams, Charles Kenneth. On Learning of a
Friend's Illness.
Trappers.
Wordsworth. Most Sweet It Is with Unuplifted
Eyes.
Wright, Charles. Bicoastal Journal.
T'ang Notebook.
Young. Again / Who am I?
Dancing All Alone.
Zukofsky. Not it was no dream of coming
death.
Wish, A.

Invective
Jeffers. Advice to Pilgrims.

Inventions and Inventors
Eberhart. Instruments.
Reading Room, The New York Public Library.
Fisher. Cut Worm.
Hewitt. Scissors For a One-Armed Tailor.
Jeffers. Edison.
Knott. Obsolescent and His Deity (Polyptych),
An.
McGrath. Portents.
Meinke. Sonnet on the Death of the Man Who
Invented Plastic Roses.
Nemerov. Extract from Memoirs.
Neruda. 2 8 3 2 5 6 7 4 5 4 9.
Rich. Rules break like a thermometer, The.
Rukeyser. Parallel Invention.
Sandburg. Solo for Saturday Night Guitar.
Spender. Airman.

Investment and Investors
Lowry. Peeropolis; another Petersburg!

Invocation
Beckett. Nuit qui fais tant.
De la Mare. For All the Grief.
Edmunds. Chromo.
Herrick. His Prayer to Ben[.] Jo[h]nson.
MacNeice. Invocation: "Dolphin plunge,
fountain play."
Suckling. Invocation, The: "Ye juster Powers
of Love and Fate."

Iona, Scotland
Jeffers. Iona: the Graves of the Kings.
Kipling. Threshold, The.
Wordsworth. Homeward we turn. Isle of
Columba's Cell.
Iona ("How sad a welcome! To each
voyager").
Iona ("On to Iona!—What can she afford").

Iowa (state)
Berg. Iowa.
Berrigan. Poem: "Of morning, Iowa City,
blue."
Davie. Back of Affluence.
Iowa.
Or, Solitude.

Gallagher. Boat Ride.
Sandburg. Silver Point.
Updike. Iowa.

Iphigenia
Lowry. Iphigenia in Aulis. Agamemnon
Speaks.
Merton. Iphigenia: Politics.
Semiotic Poem from Racine's "Iphigenie."

Iran and Iranians
Boyle. Poem for Vida Hadjebi Tabrizi, A.
See also **Persians.**

Ireland
Beckett. Serena I.
Betjeman. Ireland with Emily.
Small Towns of Ireland, The.
Byron. Irish Avatar, The.
Clough. O'Brien, most disconsolate of Men.
Davie. Church of Ireland.
Corrib: An Emblem.
Demi-Exile. Howth.
Killala.
Townend, 1976.
Two from Ireland.
Donne. H. W. in Hibernia Belligeranti.
Eberhart. Inchiquin Lake, Penobscot Bay.
Galvin. Inventing Ballygalvin.
Graves. Broken Girth, The.
Hartnett. Visit to Croom, 1745, A.
Heaney. Bogland.
In Memoriam Francis Ledwidge.
Requiem for the Croppies.
Singing School.
Hewitt. Anglo-Irish Accord, The.
As You Like It.
Awareness of Time.
Carson at Six Road Ends.
Colonial Consequence.
Colony, The.
Dilemma, The.
Encounter Nineteen Twenty.
Glens, The.
Glittering Sod, The.
Irish Glass.
Irishman in Coventry, An.
Little People, A.
Neither an Elegy Nor a Manifesto.
No Comment!
Overture for an Ulster Literature.
Postscript, 1984.
Return (1885), The.
Sonnet: "When I have read your hard and
lively words."
This Antrim Air in Summer.
Troubles, 1922, The.
Twelfth of July, The.
Ulster Names.
Ulster Winter (1942).
Ulsterman.
Will.
William Conor RHA, 1881–1968.
Hugo. Cleggan.
Tinker Camp, The.
Jarrell. Rhapsody on Irish Themes, A.
Jeffers. In the Hill at Newgrange.
Irish Headland, An.
Northern Heather.
Ossian's Grave.
Kipling. Ulster.
Larkin. Importance of Elsewhere, The.
Liddy. Cracks in the Pavement.
Maud Gonne Rode Out on a White Horse to
Coolgreany.
New O'Dwyer's dim lights. "You hate, The."
1949: Child Redmond to Dark Wexford Came.
Roses of Parnell & Mellowes, The.
You are going to fall in love.
McAuley. Aor Against the Philistine Who
Destroyed Lovely Dublin Vistas With His
Ugly Erections, Then Absconded to London.
On Saint Paddy's Day, the jukebox plays.
MacNeice. Belfast.
Cushendun.
Dublin.
Neutrality.
Nightmare leaves fatigue.
On the Four Masters.

Valediction: "Their verdure dare not
show...their verdure dare not show."
McNeill. Hill Daughter.
Mahon. Homecoming.
Marvell. Horatian Ode upon Cromwell's
Return from Ireland, An.
Meredith. Ireland.
Moore. Spenser's Ireland.
Muldoon. Christo's.
Duffy's Circus.
Frog, The.
Good Friday, 1971. Driving Westward.
Ma.
Sightseers, The.
Nash. It's a Grand Parade It Will Be, Modern
Design.
Shelley. To Ireland.
Stevens. Irish Cliffs of Moher, The.
Our Stars Come from Ireland.
Swift. Ireland.
On the Irish Club.
On the Words "Brother Protestants and Fellow
Christians."
Thomas. Fern Hill.
Whitman. Old Ireland.
Whittier. Exile's Departure, The.
Kathleen.
Yeats. Alternative Song for the Severed Head
in "The King of the Great Clock Tower."
Dedication to a Book of Stories Selected from
the Irish Novelists.
Easter, 1916.
Grey Rock, The.
Hosting of the Sidhe, The.
I Am of Ireland.
Into the Twilight.
Many ingenious lovely things are gone.
Municipal Gallery Revisited, The.
On a Political Prisoner.
O'Rahilly, The.
Pardon, old fathers, if you still remain.
Parnell.
Parnell's Funeral.
Prayer for My Daughter, A.
Red Hanrahan's Song about Ireland.
Rose Tree, The.
September 1913.
Three Songs to the One Burden.
To Ireland in the Coming Times.
See also **Northern Ireland; Listings for specific
Counties.**

Ireland, Northern. *see* **Northern Ireland.**

Iris (flower)
Ammons. Triplet.
Doolittle. Sea Iris.
Fletcher. Court Lady Standing under Cherry
Tree.
Lawrence. Scent of Irises.
Levine. White Iris, The.
Matthews. New.
Meredith. To A.M.
Rukeyser. Iris.
Iris-Eaters, The.
St. John. Iris.
Zukofsky. Bearded Iris.

Irish, The
Cummings. Mary green / cheerful & generous.
Davie. Belfast on a Sunday Afternoon.
Dublin Georgian.
Wearing of the Green, The.
Dunbar. John Boyle O'Reilly.
Galvin. 1847.
Hearing Irish Spoken.
My Grandmother Steals Her Last Trout.
Graves. Single Fare.
Hardy. Donaghadee.
Hartnett. Death of an Irishwoman.
Inchicore Haiku.
Pity the Man Who English Lacks.
Sibelius in Silence.
Hewitt. Aesthete's Renunciation.
Agitator.
Conversations in Hungary, August 1969.
Country Walk in May, A.
For Any Irishman.
Glittering Sod, The.
In the Rosses.

In This Year of Grace.
Ireland.
Irish Dimension, The.
Irishman in Coventry, An.
"Lass of Richmond Hill", or The Royal
  Garden Party, The.
On the Choice of a Title.
Once Alien Here.
Overture for an Ulster Literature.
Rite, Lubitavish, Glenaan.
Scar, The.
True Smith of Tieveragh, The.
Ulsterman, An.
Jarrell. Rhapsody on Irish Themes, A.
Kipling. Belts.
Irish Guards, The.
Liddy. Cracks in the Pavement.
I.M. George Fitzpatrick.
Proverbs of Corca Bascinn.
Lindsay. Potatoes' Dance, The.
McAuley. On Saint Paddy's Day, the jukebox
  plays.
MacNeice. Last before America.
Muldoon. Anseo.
Armageddon, Armageddon.
Cuba.
Louis.
More a Man Has the More a Man Wants, The.
Quoof.
Ransom. Birthday of an Aging Seer.
Sorrentino. Evils of the City.
Whittier. Abram Morrison.
Yeats. O'Rahilly, The.
Remorse for Intemperate Speech.

Irish Republican Army
Hewitt. Prisoners on the Roof, The.

Iron
Cummings. Chas sing does(who).
Hewitt. Boat-Builder's Caulking Irons, The.
Kipling. Cold Iron.
Lawrence. Things Made by Iron.
Lowry. Pigs—For T.H.
Rukeyser. Simple Experiment, A.
Sandburg. Iron.

Irony
Ammons. Quit That.
Berg. Page 256.
Bukowski. Beast, The.
86'd.
Genius of the Crowd, The.
Trick to Dull Our Bleeding, A.
Creeley. Apology, The.
Comfort.
"Do You Think."
Form of Adaptation, A.
Gift of Great Value, A.
Names, The.
The.
What's for Dinner.
Davie. Ironist, The.
Nosegay, The.
Dunn. Honesty.
Teacher Answering Young Radicals.
Gallagher. Survival of a Heart.
Graves. I'd Die for You.
Under the Olives.
Hardy. After the War.
Country Wedding, The.
In a London Flat.
Two Men, The.
You Were the Sort that Men Forget.
Hartley. Ironies out of St. George's.
Metaphysic.
Hemingway. Age Demanded, The.
Poem: "Only man I ever loved, The."
Hewitt. "Lass of Richmond Hill", or The
  Royal Garden Party, The.
Jeffers. Urchin, The.
Knott. Shorts / Excerpts ("Hope...goosestep").
Kooser. Place in Kansas, A.
Liddy. May Day Song.
Republic 1939, The.
McGrath. Three Functions of Irony.
War Resisters' Song.
Mahon. As It Should Be.
Sandburg. Lavender Lilies.
Sidney. Sonnet 63: "O grammar rules, O now

your virtues show."
What length of verse can serve brave *Mopsa*'s
  good to show?
Sorrentino. People in Hell are clothed.
Stevenson. System.
Wilbur. Parable.
Walgh-Vogel, The.
Williams, Miller. One of Those Rare
  Occurrences on a City Bus.
Young. Poem for Willard Motley, A.
Sad Hour of Your Peace, The.
Zukofsky. Ashtray.
Immature Pebbles.
It's a Gay Li-ife.
Men in the kitchens, The.
Millennium of sun—.

Isaac
Cohen. Story of Isaac.
Gardner. Abraham and Isaac.
Oppen. He who will not work shall not eat.
Owen. Parable of the Old Man and the
  Young, The.

Isaiah
Blake. Memorable Fancy, A ("Prophets Isaiah
  and Ezekiel dined with me, and, The").
Cohen. Isaiah.

Ishmael
Cohen. Israel.
Duncan. Bring It Up from the Dark.

Ishtar
Levertov. Song for Ishtar.
Wilbur. To Ishtar.

Isis
Doolittle. We have seen how the most
  amiable.
Shapiro. Interlude, The.

Islands
Atwood. You may wonder why I'm not
  describing the landscape for you.
Auden. Islands.
On This Island.
Berrigan. Stronger than alcohol, more great
  than song.
Bishop. Crusoe in England.
Browning, Elizabeth Barrett. Island, An.
Browning, Robert. Isle's Enchantress, The.
Byron. Island, The.
Cowper. Alexander Selkirk.
Davie. Emigrant, to the Receding Shore.
Dickey, William. Joy.
Eberhart. Moment of Equilibrium among the
  Islands.
Fisher. Sugar flowers.
Fox. Islanders.
Gardner. Prospero's Isle.
Hall. Stones.
Hartley. Corniche—Marseille.
How like the sea / to be.
I am an island— / My mother was a mountain
  once.
Islands in Penobscot Bay.
There Is an Island.
This Crusty Fragment.
Hewitt. Agrigento, Sicily.
Mainland, The.
Mykonos.
Hopkins. There is an island, wester'd in the
  main.
Hugo. Anacortes-Sydney Run, The.
Bannerman's Island.
Piping to You on Skye from Lewis.
Jarrell. Subway from New Britain to the
  Bronx, The.
Jong. Unrequited.
Kipling. This Uninhabited Island.
Lawrence. Greeks Are Coming!, The.
Liddy. Voyage to Cytherea, A.
Lowry. About Ice.
"MacDiarmid." Island Funeral.
MacNeice. No More Sea.
Mahon. Rathlin.
Melville. Archipelago, The.
Enviable Isles, The.
Merton. Poem: "Here is the man of the
  islands."
Millay. Ragged Island.
Oppen. Ballad: "Astrolabes and lexicons."

Poe. Sonnet to Zante.
Raine. Nameless Islets.
Rukeyser. Islands.
Lover as Fox.
Shelley. Isle, The.
Stevenson. Fair Isle at Sea—thy lovely name.
Feast of Famine: Marquesan Manners, The.
To Princess Kaiulani.
To S.C.
Walcott. As John to Patmos.
Islands.
Whittier. Brown Dwarf of Rügen, The.
Wilbur. Avowal, The.
La Rose des Vents.
Wordsworth. Brownie's Cell, The.
Yau. Missing Pages.
Yeats. Lake Isle of Innisfree, The.

Isolde. *see* **Tristram and Isolde.**

Israel
Browning, Robert. First-Born of Egypt, The.
Byron. Oh! Weep for Those.
Clough. When Israel Came Out of Egypt.
Cohen. Israel.
Politics of This Book, The.
Dove. Early Morning on the Tel Aviv-Haifa
  Freeway.
"Dylan." Neighborhood Bully.
Emerson. To transmute crime to wisdom, & to
  stem.
Ginsberg. Galilee Shore.
Housman. When Israel out of Egypt came.
Jarrell. Jews at Haifa.
Knight. Poem on the Middle East "Peace
  Process", A.
Lewis. At dusk in my garden the flowers are
  waiting.
Lindsay. Ahasuerus in his prime.
Psalms. Psalm 135: "Praise ye the Lord.
Praise ye the name of the Lord; praise him,
  O ye servants of the Lord."
Psalm 136: "O give thanks unto the Lord."
Rich. Memory says: Want to do right? Don't
  count on me.
Scott. Rebecca's Hymn.
Shapiro. Israel.
Olive Tree, The.
Smart. O Praise the Lord, and bless his name.

Italians, The
Browning, Robert. Italian in England, The.
Ciardi. Feasts.
Poems from Italy.
Ferlinghetti. Old Italians Dying, The.
Hemingway. D'Annunzio.
Grass smooth on the prairies.
Rossetti. Enrica, 1865.
Schuyler. Eyes.

Italy
Auden. Good-Bye to the Mezzogiorno.
Browning, Elizabeth Barrett. First News from
  Villafranca.
Garibaldi.
Italy and the World.
King Victor Emanuel Entering Florence, April,
  1860.
Napoleon III in Italy.
Nature's Remorses.
Olives and Mountains.
Sword of Castruccio Castracani, The.
Browning, Robert. Englishman in Italy, The.
Fra Lippo Lippi.
Love among the Ruins.
Piano di Sorrento.
Pippa Passes.
Sordello.
Up at a Villa—Down in the City.
What I love best in all the world.
Bunting. Duke Valentine had been in
  Lombardy with the King.
Byron. Italy.
Carruth. Two Romantic Pieces.
Ciardi. Poems from Italy.
Clough. Amours de Voyage.
Peschiera.
Coleridge. Garden of Boccaccio, The.
Cummings. Great Dante stands in Florence,
  looking down.
Memorabilia.

Davie. Gemona-del-Friuli, 1961–1976.
Going to Italy.
Looking Out from Ferrara.
Tuscan Morning.
Via Portello.
Dickinson. Our lives are Swiss.
Eberhart. Cousin Florence.
Love among The Ruins.
Garrigue. Country Villa.
Hemingway. Arsiero, Asiago, / Half a hundred more.
Riparto d'Assalto.
They All Made Peace—What Is Peace?
Hewitt. Erice, Western Sicily.
Hugo. April in Cerignola.
Beggar in Sapri.
Christmas with Shepherds in Brefaro.
Eighteen Days in a Tuscan World.
Galleria Umberto I.
Italian Town Abandoned.
Kennedy *Ucciso*.
Last Words from Maratea.
Letter to Ammons from Maratea.
Letter to Libbey from St. Regis.
Map of Montana in Italy, A.
Maratea Antica.
Maratea Porto: Saying Good-bye to the Vitolos.
Maratea Porto: The Bitter Man.
Montesano Unvisited.
Morning in Padova.
One Son North to Naples.
Paestum.
Pizzeria S. Biagio.
South Italy, Remote and Stone.
Spinazzola: Quella Cantina Là.
Tiberio's Cliff.
Tretitoli, Where the Bomb Group Was.
View from Cortona, A.
Viva La Resistènza.
Why Sapri Will Never Be Italian.
With Anna at Camaldoli.
Jarrell. In Galleries.
Lawrence. Cypresses.
Levine. Gift for a Believer.
I Was Born in Lucerne.
Lowry. Another Immorality.
Meredith. Centenary of Garibaldi, The.
Italy.
On Como.
Vittoria's *Italia* Song.
Merrill. Bronze.
Milton. Sonnet 18: "Avenge O Lord thy slaughter'd Saints, whose bones."
Moore. Web One Weaves of Italy, The.
Ralegh. Hesperia the Gr[a]ecians call the place.
Some old Auruncans, I remember well.
There is a Land which Greekes Hesperia name.
Rich. Recorders in Italy.
Rossetti. Italia, Io Ti Saluto!
St. John. Terraces of Rain.
Schuyler. Dorabella's Naples Watercolor.
Shelley. Fragment: To Italy.
Lines Written among the Euganean Hills.
Smith, Patti. Florence.
Italy.
Tennyson. Daisy, The.
Frater Ave Atque Vale.
Thomson. Ancient and Modern Italy Compared.
Tomlinson. Above Carrara.
Up at La Serra.
Updike. South of the Alps.
Whittier. From Perugia.
Garibaldi.
Wilbur. Agrigentum Road, The.
Wordsworth. At Bologna, in Remembrance of the Late Insurrections, 1837.
At Bologna, in Remembrance of the Late Insurrections, 1837, Continued: "As leaves are to the tree wheron they grow."
At Bologna, in Remembrance of the Late Insurrections, 1837, Continued: "Hard task! exclaim the undisciplined, to lean."
Church of San Salvador Seen from the Lake of Lugano.
Eclipse of the Sun, 1820, The.
Fort Fuentes.
Memorials of a Tour in Italy, 1837.
Stanzas Composed in the Simplon Pass.
Wright, Charles. Italian Days.
Wright, James. In Memory of Leopardi.
Young. Here in Violet Light.
So is there life on you, moon?
Tutti Colori Quality of Light, The.
Zukofsky. 4 Other Countries.

Itching
Nash. Man Bites Dog-Days.
Requiem: "There was a young belle of old Natchez."
Taboo to Boot.

Ivy
Carruth. Against the wall he / gropes like ivy, you pray, I.
Garrigue. Moralizing Overheard in a Forest.
Hardy. Ivy-Wife, The.
Hesketh. Reflections.
Rossetti. Under the ivy bush / One sits sighing.
Warren. Ivy, The.

J

Jack and the Beanstalk
Hewitt. First Pantomime.
Jarrell. Jack.

Jackdaws
Cowper. Jackdaw, The.
Tomlinson. At the Hill Fort.

Jackrabbits
Stevens. Jack-Rabbit, The.

Jackson, Andrew
Lindsay. Statue of Old Andrew Jackson, The.

Jackson, Mahalia
Lorde. Day They Eulogized Mahalia, The.

Jackson, Thomas Jonathan ("Stonewall")
Melville. Stonewall Jackson.

Jacob (Bible)
Burns. Patriarch, The.
Crane. Dust Now Is.
Davie. Jacob's Ladder.
Dickinson. Audacity of Bliss, said Jacob to the Angel.
Little East of Jordan, A.
Herrick. Beggars.
Levertov. Jacob's Ladder, The.
Milton. Paraphrase on Psalm 114, A.

Jacobites
Burns. Battle of Sherra-Moor, The.
Killiecrankie.
Song: "Small birds rejoice in the green leaves returning, The."
There'll Never Be Peace Till Jamie Comes Hame.
Up and Warn A' Willie.
Ye Jacobites By Name.

Jaguars
Hughes, Ted. Jaguar, The.
Second Glance at a Jaguar.
Merton. Jaguar Myth, The.

Jails. *see* **Prisons and Prisoners.**

Jam- and Jelly-making
Larkin. April Sunday Brings the Snow, An.

Jamaica, West Indies
Smith, Charlotte. To the Fire-Fly of Jamaica, Seen in a Collection.

James I, King of England
Burns. Lament of Mary Queen of Scots on the Approach of Spring.
Campion. Ad Invictissimum Serenissimumque Iacobvm *Magnae Britanniae Regem*.
Another Dialogue, To Be Sung at the Same Time.
De Regis reditu e Scotia.
Epigram, An: "Merlin, the great King Arthur being slaine."
Kings Good-night, The.
To the Most Puisant and Gratious James King of Great Britaine.
To The Most Sacred King James.
Truth, sprung from heaven, shall shine.
Jonson. Dedication of the King's New Cellar.
To Bacchus, The.
Panegyre, on the Happy Entrance of James, Our Sovreign, to His First High Session of Parliament in This Kingdom, the 19 of March, 1603, A.
To King James ("How, best of kings, dost thou a scepter bear[e]!").
To King James ("That we the loss might know, and thou our love").
To King James ("Who would not be thy subject, James, t'obey").
Kipling. James I.
Lovelace. If James the King of wit.
Milton. On the Gunpowder Plot.
On the Same ["James derided the Purgatorial fire of the soul"].
On the Same ["Thus did you strive to vouchsafe James to Heaven"].
On the Same ["Whom impious Rome had just marked out for her curses"].

James II, King of England
Jonson. To the Ghost of Martial.

James, Henry
Auden. At the Grave of Henry James.
Gunn. Jamesian.
Hall. Beau of the Dead.
Ransom. Old Mansion.
Schuyler. This Notebook.
Stevenson. Henry James.
Mirror Speaks, The.

Jamestown, Virginia
Jarrell. Jamestown.
Moore. Enough.

January
Eberhart. Snow Cascades.
Sandburg. Manitoba Childe Roland.
Schuyler. In January.
Snyder. January.
Williams, William Carlos. January.
Moon and Stars.
Young. January.
Zukofsky. N.Y.

Janus
Carew. To the New Year [For the Countess of Carlisle].
Eberhart. Nexus.
Swift. To Janus.

Japan
Carroll, Jim. Misery may be folded.
Fletcher. On the Banks of the Sumida.
Ginsberg. Change: *Kyoto-Tokyo Express*, The.
Jarrell. Rising Sun, The.
Siegfried.
Kipling. Buddha at Kamakura.
Lieberman. Kofukuji Arsonists, The.
Nara Park: Twilight Deer Feeding.
Wreckage of the Pagoda Moons.
Mahon. Snow Party, The.
Sandburg. Old Hokusai Print.
Sarton. Child's Japan, A.
Japanese Prints.
Snyder. Dullness in February: Japan.
Feathered Robe, The.
In the House of the Rising Sun.
Kai, Today.
Public Bath, The.
Rainbow Body.

Japanese, The
Bukowski. Japanese Wife, The.
Cohen. Roshi.
Cummings. YgUDuh / ydoan / yunnuhstan.
Davie. Chrysanthemums.
Nash. Japanese, The.
Sarton. Exchange of Gifts, An.

Jason
Dickinson. Finding is the first Act.
Lewis. Jason and Medea.
Swift. Mr. Jason Hassard, a Woolen Draper in Dublin.

Jays
Carruth. Five / jays / discuss / goodandevil.
Jays shrieking in the fir clump, a world enraged.

Dickinson. I am studying music now with the jays.
I saw the Jays this Morning.
No Brigadier throughout the Year.
Prompt—executive Bird is the Jay, A.
Lawrence. Blue Jay, The.

See also **Blue Jays.**

Jazz
Carruth. Day very solid February 12th, 1944, A.
Exact beat from—, The.
For Papa.
Freedom and Discipline.
High above themselves. Above everything, flux, ooze.
Homage to John Lyly and Frankie Newton.
How To.
It was Catlett driving, de Paris blowing strong.
Letter to Maxine Sullivan.
Little Old Funky Homeric Blues for Herm, A.
Meditation in the Presence of "Ostrich Walk."
Paragraphs.
Sonnet: "Must genius always struggle, always exaggerate."
Sonnet: "Persistent is the thought for me of that."
"Sure," Said Benny Goodman.
Tanck's Song About Earl Hines.
What a Wonder Among the Instruments Is the Walloping Tramboone!
Who Cares, Long as It's B-Flat.
Clark. Or.
Creeley. Broken Back Blues.
Cummings. God pity me whom(god distinctly has).
Hayden. Soledad.
Knight. Indiana Avenue, 1949.
Larkin. For Sidney Bechet.
Reference Back.
Levine. On the Corner.
Matthews. Accompanist, The.
Bud Powell, Paris, 1959.
O'Hara. Day Lady Died, The.
Rolfe. Nuthin but Brass.
Sandburg. Honky Tonk in Cleveland, Ohio.
Jazz Fantasia.
Vaudeville Dancer.
Sorrentino. Broadway! Broadway!
Turco. Lorrie.
Williams, William Carlos. Shoot It Jimmy!
Young. Art of Benny Carter, The.
Jackie McLean: Alto Saxophone.
Jazz as Was.
Lester Leaps In.
Little Poem About Jazz, A.
Thelonious: An Intro.
Zimmer. Duke Ellington Dream, The.
Zimmer's Last Gig.

Jealousy
Auden. Trippers.
Victor.
Beatles. If I Fell.
Rocky Raccoon.
Run for Your Life.
This Boy.
You Can't Do That.
You're Going to Lose That Girl.
Berryman. Boy twenty-one, in Donne, shied like a blow.
Itself a lightning-flash ripping the dark.
Whom undone David upto the dire van sent.
Bly. Danger of Loss, The.
Browning, Robert. In a Balcony.
My Last Duchess [Ferrara].
Byron. Translation from Catullus ("Equal to Jove that youth must be").
Campion. Ad Melleam.
Though your strangenesse frets my hart.
Turne all thy thoughts to eyes.
Carew. To His Jealous Mistress.
To One That Desired to Know My Mistress [or Mistris].
Catullus. Carmen 2: "Lesbia's sparrow! / Lesbia's plaything!"
Carmen 21: "Impresario of neediness."
Carmen 51: "Godlike the man who."

Carmen 104: "Do you really believe I could blacken my life."
Chaucer. Complaint of Mars, The.
Complaint of Venus, The.
Clark. My Hypertrophic Devotion.
Cohen. 1967.
One of Us Cannot Be Wrong.
Poem: "I heard of a man."
Coleridge. Not at Home.
Creeley. Memory, The.
Cummings. Spoke joe to jack.
Dickinson. God is indeed a jealous God.
You see we keep a jealous Heart.
Doolittle. At Ithaca.
Red Roses for Bronze.
Dunbar. Jealous.
"Dylan." I used t' hate enzo.
Lily, Rosemary, and the Jack of Hearts.
Property of Jesus.
Eberhart. Man's Greed and Envy Are So Great.
Emerson. When in eternity the light.
Fisher. Passive Partner, The.
Fletcher. Love and Suspicion.
Glück. Horse.
Graves. Cat-Goddesses.
Dialogue on the Headland.
Dream of Hell, A.
I'd Die for You.
Jealous Man, A.
Lack.
Powers Unconfessed.
Prison Walls.
Prometheus.
To Beguile and Betray.
Tower of Love, The.
Gunn. Road Map, The.
Hall. Jealous Lovers, The.
Hardy. Face at the Casement, The.
Love the Monopolist.
Rival, The.
To Carrey Clavel.
Hartnett. Old Catechism, The.
Heaney. Dream of Jealousy, A.
Herrick. How Marigolds Came Yellow.
Sonnet, A: "Ile dote noe more, nor shall mine eyes."
To Jealousie.
Upon a Wife That Dyed Mad with Jealousie.
Jeffers. Give Your Heart to the Hawks.
Mara.
Jonson. Against Jealousy [or Jealousie].
Keats. Song: "Hush, hush! tread softly! hush, hush my dear."
Kipling. Bill 'Awkins.
Koch. Down at the Docks.
Koertge. Whippersnappers.
Larkin. Dance, The.
I See a Girl Dragged by the Wrists.
Love Again.
Lawrence. Jealousy.
Tease.
Liddy. He'd be alive today if he wasn't pretty.
Miles III.
Lovelace. Cupid Far Gone.
Lowry. Days Like Smitten Cymbals of Brass, The.
Marlowe. 1.4: Amicam, qua arte, quibusve nutibus in caena, presente viro uti debeat, admonet.
2.7: Amicae se purgat quod ancillam non amet.
3.4: Ad virum servantem coniugem.
Meredith. Desert vulture / jealousy, The.
Merton. Great and Small.
Nash. Absence Makes the Heart Grow Heart Trouble.
Love Me but Leave My Dog Alone.
O'Hara. For Grace, after a Party.
Hôtel Transylvanie.
Plath. Shrike, The.
Ralegh. Excuse, The.
Ransom. Vaunting Oak.
"Reed." Gift, The.
Robinson. Evangelist's Wife, An.
Rossetti. Sister Maude.
Shakespeare. Sonnet 29: "When, in disgrace

with fortune and men's eyes."
Sonnet 41: "Those petty [or pretty] wrongs that liberty commits."
Sonnet 48: "How careful was I, when I took my way."
Sonnet 61: "Is it thy will thy image should keep open."
Sidney. Sonnet 78: "O how the pleasant airs of true love be."
With two strange fires of equal heat possessed [or possest].
Smith, Stevie. Mistress Osmosis.
Stuart. That'll Be the Day.
Wakoski. Reminded of One of Those Girls I Never Was.
Whitman. Sometimes with One I Love.
Williams, Charles Kenneth. Cautionary, The.
Image, The.
Love: Youth.
Silence, The.
Soliloquies.
Wroth. Sonnet 3: "Most blessed Night, the happy time for love."
Sonnet 4: "Cruell suspition, O! bee now att rest."
Sonnet 4: "When I beeheld the Image of my deere."
Sonnet 6: "O! that noe day would ever more appeere."
Sonnet 7: "End fond jealousie alas I know, An."
Sonnet 13: "Free from all fogs butt shining faire, and cleere."
Sonnet 14: "Except my hart which you beestow'd before."
Wyatt. Wandering gadling in the summer tide, The.
Yeats. Anashuya and Vijaya.
Zukofsky. Aurelius, father, assure that the o numb.
Catullus viii.
Credit me poor to say of my life *maledictory weed die.*
He'll hike me, par *is* he? the God divide her.
Sparrow, my girl's pleasure, delight of my girl.

See also **Envy.**

Jeffers, Robinson
Everson. Poet Is Dead, The.
Rukeyser. Citation for Horace Gregory.

Jefferson, Thomas
MacLeish. Brave New World.
Rukeyser. Secrets of American Civilization.
Sandburg. Open Letter to the Poet Archibald MacLeish Who Has Forsaken His Massachusetts Farm to Make Propaganda for Freedom.
Sarton. Monticello.
Tate. On the Father of Liberty.
Zukofsky. Madison, Wis., Remembering the Bloom of Monticello (1931).

Jellyfish
Lieberman. Flying below Sea Level.
Moore. Jellyfish, A.
Nash. Jellyfish, The.

Jeremiah (Bible)
Donne. Lamentations of Jeremy, for the Most Part According to Tremeullius.

Jericho
Merton. Rahab's House.

Jerome, Saint
Jarrell. Jerome.
Merton. Two Desert Fathers.
Moore. Leonardo Da Vinci's.

Jerusalem
Blake. And Did Those Feet in Ancient Time.
But turning toward Ololon in terrible majesty
Milton.
Jerusalem; The Emanation of the Giant Albion.
Byron. On the Day of the Destruction of Jerusalem by Titus.
Cohen. Isaiah.
Politics of This Book, The.
Cullen. At the Wailing Wall in Jerusalem.
Dickey, William. Ezekiel's Rabbit.

Duncan. Kingdom of Jerusalem, The.
Herrick. To His Brother Nicolas Herrick.
MacNeice. New Jerusalem.
Melville. Via Crucis.
Paley. I cannot keep my mind on Jerusalem.
Warning, A.
Psalms. Psalm 122: "I was glad when they said unto me."
Rich. Jerusalem.
Rossetti. All Saints.
By the Waters of Babylon.
Holy City, New Jerusalem, The.
Jerusalem of fire / And gold and pearl and gem.
Now They Desire.
Whither the Tribes Go Up, Even the Tribes of the Lord.
Rukeyser. Traditional Tune.
See also **Zion.**

Jesters
De la Mare. Falstaff.
Hesketh. Joke, The.
Kipling. Jester, The.
Lowry. Jokes Amidships.
Nash. If Fun Is Fun, Isn't That Enough?
Robinson. Old King's New Jester, The.
Yeats. Cap and Bells, The.
See also **Fools.**

Jesuits
Davie. Jesuits in North America, The.

Jesus Christ
Auden. Christ in Hades.
Pardon.
Question, The: "All of us believe."
Berryman. After a Stoic, a Peripatetic, a Pythagorean.
Disciple, The.
Blake. And Did Those Feet in Ancient Time.
Lamb, The.
Memorable Fancy, A ("Once I saw a Devil in a flame of fire").
Night.
Was Jesus Humble? or did he.
Bly. Crazy Carlson's Meadow.
Falling Asleep.
Bradstreet. Occasional Meditations: "By night, when others soundly slept."
Brooks. In Emanuel's Nightmare: Another Coming of Christ.
Browning, Elizabeth Barrett. Drama of Exile, A.
Mediator, The.
Past and Future.
Seraphim, The.
Thought for a Lonely Death-Bed, A.
Virgin Mary to the Child Jesus, The.
Browning, Robert. Death in the Desert, A.
Epistle Containing the Strange Medical Experience of Karshish, the Arab Physician, An.
"Carroll, Lewis." After Three Days.
Christmas Greetings.
Carruth. Sonnet: "O Jesus, thou who sittest up there on the right."
Sorrow Song, The.
Cohen. Embrace, The.
Suzanne [Takes You Down].
Transmission, The.
Coleridge. Epitaphium Testamentarium.
Lovely was the death.
My Baptismal Birthday [*or* Birth-Day].
Religious Musings.
Translation of a Passage in Ottfried's Metrical Paraphrase of the Gospel.
Virgin's Cradle-Hymn, The.
Cowper. I was a stricken deer, that left the herd.
Longing To Be with Christ.
Crane. After Jonah.
Lachrymae Christi.
Crashaw. Authors Motto, The.
But Now They Have Seen, and Hated.
Christs Victory.
Come we shepheards whose blest sight.
Hymn in the Assumption.
Hymn in the Glorious Epiphanie.
Hymne of the Nativity, Sung by the

Shepheards, A.
In Cicatrices Domini Jesu.
John 15; Upon Our Lords Last Comfortable Discourse with His Disciples.
Luke 11; Blessed Be the Paps Which Thou Hast Sucked.
Luke 2; Quærit Jesum Suum Maria.
Luke 7; She Began To Wash His Feet with Teares and Wipe Them with the Haires of Her Head.
Mark 10; The Blind Cured by the Word of Our Saviour.
Mark 7; The Dumbe Healed, and the People Enjoyned Silence.
Matthew 22; Neither Durst Any Man from that Day Aske Him Any More Questions.
Matthew 28; Come See the Place where the Lord Lay.
On the Bleeding Wounds of Our Crucified Lord.
On the Still Surviving Markes of Our Saviours Wounds.
On the Water of Our Lord's Baptism[e].
On the Wounds of Our Crucified Lord.
Our Lord in His Circumcision to His Father.
Out of *Grotius* his Tragedy of *Christes* Sufferinges.
Psalmus 1.
To Pontius Washing His Blood-Stained Hands.
To Pontius Washing His Hands.
To the Name above Every Name, the Name of Jesus, a Hymn.
Upon Our Saviour's Tomb[e] Wherein Never Man Was Laid.
Upon the Asse That Bore Our Saviour.
Upon the Sepulchre of our Lord.
Creeley. Women, The.
Cullen. Black Christ, The.
Christus Natus Est.
Judas Iscariot.
Cummings. After-Glow.
And i imagine.
Jehovah buried, Satan dead.
No time ago / or else a life.
There are possibly 2 1/2 or impossibly 3.
Davie. Our Lady.
De la Mare. Break of Morning.
Dickey, William. Fred and the Holy Grail.
Dickinson. At least—to pray—is left—is left.
Dying! Dying in the night!
God is a distant—stately Lover.
He gave away his Life.
I shall know why—when Time is over.
Jesus! thy Crucifix.
Just so—Jesus—raps.
Life—is what we make it.
Obtaining but our own Extent.
One crown that no one seeks.
Perhaps you think me stooping.
Proud of my broken heart, since thou didst break it.
Savior must have been, The.
Savior's only signature, The.
So well that I can live without.
To be human is more than to be divine.
To have had such Daughters is sanctity.
"Unto me?" I do not know you.
Word made Flesh is seldom, A.
Donne. And through that bitter agony [*or* agonie].
Cross, The.
Deliver us for thy descent.
Father, part of his double interest.
Oh my black[e] soul[e]! now thou art summoned.
Resurrection, Imperfect.
Son[ne] of God hear[e] us, and since thou.
Son, The.
Spit in my face ye [*or* you] Jew[e]s, and pierce my side.
Temple.
Through thy submitting all, to blow[e]s.
Upon the Annunciation and Passion Falling upon One Day. 1608.
What if this present were the world's last night?
Why are we[e] by all creatures waited on?

Wilt thou love God, as he thee? [*or* thee!] then digest.
Duncan. Adoration of the Virgin, The.
"Dylan." Ain't No Man Righteous, No Not One.
Are You Ready?
Gonna Change My Way of Thinking.
In the Garden.
Long Ago, Far Away.
Saved.
Saving Grace.
Solid Rock.
What Can I Do for You?
When He Returns.
When You Gonna Wake Up?
Eberhart. Way Out, A.
Emerson. No. 13 Hymn Written in Concord Sept. 1814.
Wine resembles the Lord Jesus.
Ferlinghetti. Sometime during eternity / some guys show up.
Fletcher. Birth of Christ, The.
Buddha and Christ.
Crucifixion, The.
Fragments of Eternity.
Last Judgment, The.
1921.
Procession, The.
Well in the Desert, The.
Gallagher. Reading Aloud.
Gardner. Ballade: "Lady of Heaven, Queen of nature."
Ginsberg. Epigram on a Painting of Golgotha.
Glück. Easter Season.
Nativity Poem.
Pietà.
Winter Morning.
Graves. Descent into Hell.
In the Wilderness.
Gunn. Jesus and His Mother.
Hacker. Christmas Crown, A.
Hall. Small Fig Tree, A.
Hardy. Evening in Galilee, An.
Panthera.
Hartley. Three Friends: Outline for a Picture.
Hartnett. I have been stone, dust of space, sea and sphere.
Heaney. Westering.
Herbert. Aaron.
Affliction (3).
Affliction (2).
Agony [*or* Agonie], The.
Bag, The.
Bunch of Grapes, The.
Business.
Church Militant, The.
Colossians 3:3.
Dawning, The.
Dialogue, The.
Dialogue-Anthem, A.
Dulness[e].
Ephesians 4:30. Grieve not the Holy Spirit, etc.
Good Friday.
Holdfast, The.
Holy Baptism (1).
Holy Communion, The.
Jesu.
Justice (2).
Lent.
Longing.
Love.
Love-Joy.
Love ("Thou art too hard for me in Love").
Mary [*or* Marie] Magdalene.
Reprisal[l], The.
Sacrifice, The.
Son[ne], The.
Sunday.
Thanksgiving, The.
Ungratefulness.
Herrick. Another, to God ("Though thou beest").
Another, to His Saviour.
Christ.
Christs Action.
Christs Incarnation.

Christs Part.
Christs Sadnesse.
Christs Suffering.
Christs Words on the Crosse, My God, My
  God.
Coheires.
Coming to Christ.
Gods Descent.
Good Friday: Rex Tragicus, or, Christ Going
  to His Cross[e].
His Coming to the Sepulcher.
His Offering, with the Rest, at the Sepulcher.
His Saviour[']s Words, Going to the Cross[e].
Martha, Martha.
New-Yeeres Gift, or Circumcision Song, Sung
  to the King in the Presence at White Hall,
  The.
No Coming to God without Christ.
To Christ.
To His Saviours Sepulcher: His Devotion.
Hesketh.   Jolly Good Fellow, A.
  Reclaimed.
  Sun Up.
Hewitt.   Christmas Eve.
  Easter Tuesday.
  Ecce Homo.
  Egyptian Night.
  Heart of Joy, The.
  Isaac McKeown.
  Last Crusade, The.
  Mary's Lullaby.
  My Great-Grandfather's Refusal.
  Rhyme for Christmas Morning, A.
  Saint Patrick.
  Terrible Choice, The.
  Year of Grace and My Great-Grandfather.
Hill.   I went out early.
  Lachrimae Amantis.
  Lachrimae Antiquae Novae.
  Lachrimae Coactae.
  Lachrimae Verae.
Holmes.   Sade on Calvary.
Hopkins.   Angelus Ad Virginem.
  As kingfishers catch fire, dragonflies draw
    flame.
  But what indeed is ask'd of me?
  Easter.
  Hope holds to Christ.
  Jesu Dulcis Memoria.
  Lantern Out of Doors, The.
  Moonless darkness stands between.
  Myself unholy, from myself unholy.
  New Readings.
  Oratio Patris Condren: O Jesu Vivens in
    Maria.
  Soldier, The.
  Spring.
  Thee, God, I come from, to thee go.
  Where art thou friend, whom I shall never see.
  Windhover, The.
Housman.   Easter Hymn.
Hughes, Langston.   Feet o' Jesus.
  Shout.
Hughes, Ted.   Your tree—your oak.
Hugo.   Holy Family.
Jeffers.   Dear Judas.
  Meditation on Saviors.
  Theory of Truth.
Jonson.   Hymn[e] on the Nativity [or Nativitie]
  of My Saviour, A.
  Reverse on the Back Side, The.
Joseph.   Lazarus.
Kipling.   Burden, The.
  Last Ode, The.
  Nativity, A.
Knott.   Racist Poem.
  Shorts / Excerpts ("Other strangers than our
    own may remember").
Kunitz.   He.
Lawrence.   Ballad of a Wilful Woman.
  Coming of Quetzalcoatl, The.
  Commandments.
  Demiurge.
  Jesus' Farewell.
  Know Thyself.
  Meeting among the Mountains.
  My Name Is Jesus.

Quetzalcoatl Looks Down on Mexico.
Retort to Jesus.
Risen Lord, The.
Son of the Morning Star.
Song of Don Ramon, The.
Lewis.   Boy who climbed the creaking stairs,
  The.
  Crucifixion, The.
Liddy.   Last Light in Clare's Mind.
Lindsay.   Daniel.
  I Heard Immanuel Singing.
  Johnny Appleseed's Hymn to the Sun.
  Star of My Heart.
  When Peter Jackson Preached in the Old
    Church.
Lowell.   Drunken Fisherman, The.
Lowry.   And yet his suffering got involved
  with all this.
  Asperin tree outside told me to say, The.
  Christ, slashed with an axe, in the humped
    church.
  I met a man who had got drunk with Christ.
  Oh gentle Jesus of the hymnal once.
  Thing to know is how to write a verse, The.
  What the Irish Soldier Said.
"MacDiarmid."   Harry Semen.
  Innumerable Christ, The.
MacLeish.   Carrion Crow, The.
  Seeing.
Markson.   Sister's Son.
Marvell.   Clorinda and Damon.
  Coronet, The.
Meinke.   Gift of the Magi, The.
Merton.   A Solis Ortus Cardine.
  Argument: Of the Passion of Christ, An.
  Betrayal, The.
  Biography, The.
  Cana.
  Carol, A: "When Jesus got my broken back
    for Christmas, Juniors."
  Early Mass.
  Flight into Egypt, The.
  Landfall, The.
  Logos Our Teacher, The.
  Ointment, The.
  Sacred Heart 2.
  Senescente Mundo.
  Slowly slowly / Comes Christ through the
    garden.
  Song for the Blessed Sacrament.
  Song of the Traveller, The.
  Sponge Full of Vinegar, The.
  Victory, The.
  Vine, The.
  Widow of Naim, The.
Millay.   Jesus to His Disciples.
Milton.   Hymn on the Morning of Christ's
  Nativity [or On the Morning of Christ's
  Nativity].
  Look once more ere we leave this specular
    Mount.
  On the Morning of Christs Nativity.
  Passion, The.
  So they in Heav'n their odes and vigils tun'd.
Morgan.   Mr. Boyd.
Morrison.   Afternoon of Summer, An.
Nemerov.   Ahasuerus.
  Carol: "Now is the world withdrawn all."
  Santa Claus.
  Sonnet: "Form of Christ cut from dark wood,
    the pale, A."
Olson.   Easter.
  Not a rat-hole, a cat-hole: the knife of time;
    on the ledge, overlooking.
  Siena.
Oppen.   That Land.
Pound.   Ballad of the Goodly Fere.
Prince.   Sun floats in sublime, The.
Raine.   Star of Bethlehem.
Ralegh.   On the Card[e]s, and Dice.
Ransom.   Armageddon.
  Our Two Worthies.
Robinson.   Calvary.
Rolfe.   Prophecy in Stone.
Rossetti.   Advent Sunday.
  After This the Judgement.
  As the Apple Tree among the Trees of the

  Wood.
Ascension Day.
Ascension Eve.
Ash Wednesday.
Because He First Loved Us.
Because Thy Love hath sought me, / All mine
  is Thine and Thine is mine.
Before the Paling of the Stars.
Before the Throne, and Before the Lamb.
Behold the Man!
Bruised Reed Shall He Not Break, A.
Candlemas Dialogue, A.
Changing Chimes.
Chiefest among Ten Thousand, The.
Christmas Carol, for My Godchildren, A.
Christmas Day.
Christmas Eve.
Come Unto Me.
Consider the Lilies of the Field.
Conversion of St. Paul.
Day and night the Accuser makes no pause.
Dear Angels and dear disembodied Saints.
Death of a First-Born, A.
Descent from the Cross, The.
Despised and Rejected.
Easter Monday.
Easter Tuesday.
Embertide.
Epiphany.
Epiphanytide.
Exceeding Bitter Cry, An.
For H.P.
God Is Our Hope and Strength.
God's Acre.
Good Friday Evening.
Good Friday Morning.
Good Shepherd, The.
Half Dead.
Heavy heart, if ever heart was heavy, A.
Her Seed; It Shall Bruise Thy Head.
Hymn for Christmas Day, A.
I Am Small and of No Reputation.
I Know You Not.
If I should ever say "my heart is in my
  home."
If Only.
It Is Finished.
Jesus alone:—if thus it were to me.
Judge Not According to the Appearance.
King of Kings and Lord of Lords.
Leaf from leaf Christ knows; / Himself the
  Lily and the Rose.
Let Them Rejoice in Their Beds.
Light of Light.
Long Barren.
Lord, carry me.—Nay, but I grant thee
  strength.
Lord, dost Thou look on me, and will not I.
Lord God of Hosts, most Holy and most High.
Lord, Grant Us Calm.
Lord Jesu, Thou art sweetness to my soul.
Lord Jesus, who would think that I am Thine?
Lord, what have I that I may offer Thee?
Love Is Strong as Death.
Love of Christ Which Passeth Knowledge,
  The.
Lowest Place, The.
Mary Magdalene and the Other Mary.
Name of Jesus, The.
New creatures; the Creator still the Same.
None Other Lamb None Other Name.
None With Him.
Not Yours But You.
O Christ my God Who seest the unseen.
O Christ our All in each, our All in all!
O mine enemy / Rejoice not over me!
Of Him That Was Ready to Perish.
Offering of the New Law, the One Oblation
  Once Offered, The.
One of the Soldiers with a Spear Pierced His
  Side.
Our Church Palms are Budding Willow Twigs.
Our life is long. Not so, wise Angels say.
Passion Flower hath sprung up tall, The.
Purification of St. Mary the Virgin, The.
Ransomed of the Lord, The.
Rejoice with Me.

Sick Child's Meditation, A.
Slain from the Foundation of the World.
St. John, Apostle.
Surely He Hath Borne Our Griefs.
Take Care Of Him.
That No Man Take Thy Crown.
That Where I Am, There Ye May Be Also.
This near-at-hand land breeds pain by measure.
Thou Art Fairer Than the Children of Men.
Thou, God, Seest Me.
Three Enemies, The.
Thy Friend and Thy Father's Friend Forget Not.
Thy Name, O Christ, as incense streaming forth.
Tuesday in Holy Week.
Vigil of all Saints.
Vigil of St. Peter.
We know not when, we know not where.
Wednesday in Holy Week.
What is it Jesus saith unto the soul?
What Is That to Thee? Follow Thou Me.
When My Heart Is Vexed I Will Complain ("Fields are white to harvest, look and see, The").
Whitsun Day.
Whitsun Eve.
Whitsun Tuesday.
Ye That Fear Him, Both Small and Great.
Yea, blessed and holy is he that hath part in the First / Resurrection!
Yea, if Thou wilt, Thou canst put up Thy sword.
Rukeyser. Holy Family.
Lynchings of Jesus, The.
Place-Rituals.
Traditional Tune.
Sandburg. Child.
Early Lynching.
Epistle: "Jesus loved the sunsets on Galilee."
Loin Cloth.
Special Starlight.
Star Silver.
To a Contemporary Bunkshooter.
Sexton. For God While Sleeping.
Is It True?
Jesus Asleep.
Jesus Awake.
Jesus Cooks.
Jesus Raises Up the Harlot.
Jesus Summons Forth.
Jesus Unborn.
Jesus Walking.
Protestant Easter.
Smart. Ascension of Our Lord Jesus Christ, The.
Crucifixion of Our Blessed Lord.
Easter Day.
Epiphany.
Generosity.
Learning.
Presentation of Christ in the Temple, The.
Smith, Patti. Oath.
Smith, Stevie. Ah, Will the Saviour.?
Airy Christ, The.
Christmas.
Conviction (i).
Conviction (ii).
Torquemada.
Was He Married?
Southwell. Burning Babe, The.
Child[e] My Choice [or Choyse], A.
Christe's Retorne out of Egipt.
Christ's Bloody Sweate.
Christ[el]'s Childhood[e].
New Heaven, New War[re].
New Prince, New Pomp[e].
Stevenson. Tempest tossed and sore afflicted, sin defiled and care oppressed.
Tennyson. Sweet after showers, ambrosial air.
Thomson. Pastoral Betwixt David, Thirsis, and the Angel Gabriel, upon the Birth of our Saviour, A.
Walcott. Easter.
Walker. Abduction of Saints, The.

J, My Good Friend (Another Foolish Innocent).
Whitman. To Him That Was Crucified.
Whittier. Chapel of the Hermits, The.
Child-Songs.
Crucifixion, The.
Dedication: "I would the gift I offer here."
Dole of Jarl Thorkell, The.
Easter Flower Gift, An.
Holy Land, The.
Meeting, The.
Our Master.
Over-Heart, The.
Palestine.
Woman, A.
Wilbur. Pelican, The.
Williams, Miller. One of the Crowd on the Shore Tells How It Was.
Vision and Prayer.
Williams, William Carlos. Gothic Candor.
Wordsworth. Fly, some kind Harbinger, to Grasmere-dale!
Inscription on a Rock at Rydal Mount.
Well-nigh the voyage now is overpast.
Yeats. Conjunctions.
Stick of Incense, A.
Two Songs from a Play.

Jewelry
Browning, Elizabeth Barrett. King's Gift, The.
Bukowski. Huge Ear Rings.
Carew. Epitaph on the Lady S.: Wife of Sir W.S.
Cowper. To a Lady ["Star that beams on Anna's breast, The"].
Donne. Bracelet, The.
Graves. Bracelet, A.
Song: Three Rings for Her.
With a Gift of Rings.
Herrick. Bracelet of Pearle: To Silvia, The.
Carkanet, The.
Eare-rings.
Pomander Bracelet, The.
Seest thou those diamonds which she wears.
To Julia: ("How rich and pleasing thou, my Julia, art").
Marvell. Bludius et Corona [Blood and the Crown].
Meredith. When I saw the jewelled girdle tied at her waist I thought of.
Sandburg. Thin Strips.
Schuyler. Fabergé.
Scott. Brooch of Lorn, The.
Snodgrass. Old Jewelry.
Wakoski. Emerald Ice.
Ring, The.

See also **Rings.**

Jews
Berg. Coat, The.
Not That.
On the Steps.
Boyle. Confession to Eugene Jolas, A.
Jews among the Nations, The.
Poem about the Jews, A.
Browning, Robert. Holy-Cross Day.
Carruth. Sonnet: "Was Yahweh chosen by the chosen people?"
Cohen. Friend, When You Speak.
This Marriage.
De la Mare. Bitter Waters.
Owl, The.
"Dylan." Neighborhood Bully.
Emerson. William Rufus and the Jew.
Gardner. That Was Then.
Glück. Parable, A.
Griffiths. Refugees.
Hacker. Days of 1944: Three Friends.
Graffiti from the Gare Saint-Manqué.
Inheritances.
Hayden. Rabbi, The.
Herbert. Jews, The.
Self-Condemnation.
Herrick. North and South.
Observation ("Jewes, when they built Houses [I have read], The").
Hewitt. Remembering a Conversation: Itzik Manger at the PEN Conference, Edinburgh, 1950.

Strangers and Neighbors.
Tiphead.
Hughes, Langston. Likewise.
Jarrell. Jews at Haifa.
Lament of the Children of Israel in Rome.
Kinnell. Avenue Bearing the Initial of Christ into the New World, The.
Kipling. Song of the Fifth River.
Levine. Jewish Graveyards, Italy.
Liddy. Vir X.
Longfellow. Jewish Cemetery at Newport, The.
Merton. Chagall.
Nemerov. Debate with the Rabbi.
Memory of My Friend, A.
To the Babylonians.
Paley. I cannot keep my mind on Jerusalem.
Letter.
Some days I am lonesome I want to talk to my mother.
Song Stanzas of Private Luck.
Street Corner Dialogue.
Warning, A.
Patchen. To the Jewish People.
Prince. Drypoints of the Hasidim.
Rich. At the Jewish New Year.
Sources.
Yom Kippur 1984.
Robinson. Wandering Jew, The.
Rossetti. Christian and Jew. A Dialogue.
Rukeyser. Akiba.
Christmas Eve.
Despisals.
To be a Jew in the twentieth century.
Writer, The.
Schwartz. Sand upon the Red Sea shore, or on the beach, The.
Sexton. Uses.
Shapiro. Alphabet, The.
Israel.
Messias.
Olive Tree, The.
Synagogue, The.
Shelley. Wandering Jew's Soliloquy, The.
Smith, Stevie. Jew Is Angry with His Friend Who Does Not Believe in Circumcision, A.
Songe d'Athalie.
Tomlinson. Byzantium.
Williams, Charles Kenneth. Spit.
Wordsworth. Jewish Family (in a Small Valley Opposite St Goar, upon the Rhine), A.
Zukofsky. Song for the Year's End, A.

Jigsaw Puzzles
Oppen. Solution.

Joan of Arc
Cohen. Joan of Arc.
Glück. Jeanne d'Arc.
Lindsay. Mark Twain and Joan of Arc.
MacNeice. Visit to Rouen.
Meredith. Brooding on her deep fall, the many strings.
In Nature is no rearward step allowed.
She hailed him Saint.
Millay. To the Maid of Orleans.

Job (Bible)
Auden. Job.
Everson. I Am Long Weaned.
Fletcher. End of Job, The.
Frost. Masque of Reason, A.
Robinson. Job the Rejected.
Shelton. Job the Father.

Jockeys
Koertge. Day Alvero Pineda Was Killed, The.
Jockey, A.

See also **Horse Racing.**

Jogging and Joggers. *see* **Running and Runners.**

John, Saint
Browning, Robert. Death in the Desert, A.
Emerson. Turtle in swamp.
Rossetti. "Beloved, let us love one another," says St. John.
St. John, Apostle.
Sandburg. Isle of Patmos.
Wilbur. John Chrysostom.
Wedding Toast, A.

John XXIII, Pope
Hewitt. Rome Sunday[,] June 1960.
"John Bull"
Byron. World Is a Bundle of Hay, The.
John the Baptist, Saint
Davie. Pacer in the Fresco. John the Baptist, The.
Merrill. Salome.
Merton. Quickening of St. John the Baptist, The.
St. John Baptist.
St. John's Night.
Ut Queant.
Rossetti. Imitated From the Arpa Evangelica: Page 121.
Smart. Nativity of St. John the Baptist, The.
Wordsworth. Before the Picture of the Baptist, by Raphael, in the Gallery at Florence.
"Johnny Appleseed." see **Chapman, John ("Johnny Appleseed").**
Johnson, Lionel
Yeats. In Memory of Major Robert Gregory.
Johnson, Lyndon Baines
Duncan. Up Rising.
Paley. My Father at 85.
Wilbur. Miltonic Sonnet for Mr. Johnson on His Refusal of Peter Hurd's Official Portrait, A.
Johnson, Samuel
Cowper. Epitaph on Dr. Johnson.
Dunbar. Then and Now.
Wilbur. Epistemology.
Jonah (Bible)
Crane. After Jonah.
Fox. Cetus, a Letter from Jonah.
Jarrell. Jonah.
Nemerov. On a Text: Jonah IV, xi.
Sexton. Making a Living.
Jonathan (Bible)
Bradstreet. David's Lamentation for Saul and Jonathan.
Jones, Ebenezer
Betjeman. Incident in the Early Life of Ebenezer Jones, Poet, 1828, An.
Jonson, Ben
Carew. To Ben Jonson.
Herrick. Another ["Thou had'st the wreath before, now take the Tree"].
Bacchanalian Verse, A.
His Prayer to Ben[.] Jo[h]nson.
Ode for Him, An.
Upon Ben Jo[h]nson.
Upon M. Ben Jo[h]nson: Epigram.
Johnson. Then Jonson came, instructed from the school.
Jonson. Humble Petition of Poor Ben to the Best of Monarchs, Masters, Men, King Charles, The.
Moore. No Better Than a "Withered Daffodil."
Suckling. First that broke silence was good old Ben, The.
Joplin, Janis
Hacker. Elegy: "Crying from exile, I."
Piercy. Burying Blues for Janis.
Schuyler. Janis Joplin's Dead: Long Live Pearl.
Mike.
Joseph, Saint
"MacDiarmid." Harry Semen.
Southwell. Josephe's Amazement.
Joseph (Bible, O.T.)
Graves. Joseph and Mary.
Herbert. Joseph's Coat.
Hewitt. Ecce Homo.
Egyptian Night.
Nemerov. September, the First Day of School.
Simic. Psalm: "Old ones to the side."
Joseph (Chief Joseph)
Hugo. Bear Paw.
Journalism and Journalists
Dobyns. Beauty.
Donne. Mercurius Gallo-Belgicus.
"Dylan." Oh where were these magazines.
Hewitt. Ulster Landowner's Song, An.
Jeffers. Be Angry at the Sun.
Ordinary Newscaster, An.

"MacDiarmid." Here in the hauf licht hoo I've grown!
Sandburg. Buttons.
Press is Peculiar, The.
Williams, Miller. Journalist Buys a Pig Farm, The.
Williams, William Carlos. To a Dead Journalist.
Zukofsky. Michtam.
See also **Magazines; Newspapers.**
Joy
Auden. Joy.
Sower, The.
Beckett. Chaque jour envie.
Berry. What I am learning to give you is my death.
When I rise up.
Berryman. Heaven.
Blake. Eternity ("He who binds [or bends] to himself a joy").
Infant Joy.
Bradstreet. As spring the winter doth succeed.
On My Son's Return Out of England.
Brontë. Fair sinks the summer evening now.
How golden bright from earth and heaven.
How long will you remain? The midnight hour.
Month after month, year after year.
That wind, I used to hear it swelling.
Through the hours of yesternight.
Browning, Elizabeth Barrett. Christmas Gifts.
Claim, The.
Dance, The.
Deserted Garden, The.
Life.
Love.
Sonnet: "Heavy heart, Beloved, have I borne, A."
Sonnet: "I lived with visions for my company."
Sonnet: "I think of thee! My thoughts do twine and bud."
Burns. Seventh of November, The.
Byron. Spell Is Broke, the Charm is Flown, The.
Translation from Anacreon.
Campion. Dance, dance, and visit now the shadowes of our joy.
If I hope, I pine; if I feare, I faint and die.
Night as well as brightest day hath her delight.
O what unhop't for sweet supply!
Time, that leads the fatall round.
While dancing rests, fit place to musicke graunting.
"Carroll, Lewis." Acrostic: Around my lonely hearth, to-night.
For The Garland of Rachel.
Carruth. Alive.
November Jeans Song.
Ceravolo. Book of Wild Flowers, The.
Happiness in the Trees.
Star Song.
White Fish in Reeds.
Clough. In Stratis Viarum II.
Coleridge. Barberry-Tree, The.
Crashaw. Upon the birth of the Princesse Elizabeth.
Creeley. For W.C.W. ("Pleasure of the wit sustains, The").
Cummings. All stars are(and not one star only)love.
Darling!because my blood can sing.
Honour corruption villainy holiness.
!Hope / faith! / !life / love!
Humble one(gifted with / illimitable joy).
If everything happens that can't be done.
If(among / silent skies).
Joyful your complete fearless and pure love.
Love our so right.
Might these be thrushes climbing through almost(the).
Open your heart: / i'll give you a treasure.
Spring!may— / everywhere's here.
Sweet spring is your.
These(whom;pretends / blue nothing).
Though your sorrows not.
Trees / were in(give).

Until and i heard.
When faces called flowers float out of the ground.
Which is the very.
Your homecoming will be my homecoming.
De la Mare. Disguise, The.
Imp Within, The.
Dickinson. Bliss is the plaything of the child.
Did life's penurious length.
Did Our Best Moment last.
Good times are always mutual.
I can wade Grief.
If all the griefs I am to have.
In many and reportless places.
Is Bliss then, such Abyss.
Joy that has no stem nor core, The.
Joy we most revere, The.
No Rose, yet felt myself a'bloom.
Oh, honey of an hour.
One Joy of so much anguish.
Rehearsal to Ourselves.
So glad we are—a Stranger'd deem.
Sweet and soft as summer, Darlings.
There are Sweets of Pathos.
Thrill came slowly like a Boon for, The.
Who never wanted—maddest Joy.
With sorrow that the Joy is past.
Dunbar. Lesson, The.
Old Cabin, The.
To J. Q.
Duncan. Years As Catches, The.
Dunn. Meditation on Two Themes.
Naturally.
Eberhart. Full of Joy Do Not Know; They Need Not, The.
I turned where the sun came up and he held my hand.
Incidence of Flight.
My Brains Are Slipping in the Fields of Eros.
Oak, The.
Ode to Silence.
Orchard, The.
Poet, The.
Request.
To Kenya Tribesmen, the Turkana.
To the Mad Poets.
Emerson. Come let us strew roses.
For joy & beauty planted it.
From the Persian of Hafiz.
Hafiz since on the world.
Intellect / Gravely broods apart on joy.
Oil & Wine, / Sparkling gems, & rich attire.
Water.
Where o where is the message which today.
Written in Naples, March, 1833.
Ferlinghetti. Voix Glauque.
Fletcher. Joy.
My stiff-spread arms / Break into sudden gesture.
Gardner. Cadenza.
Jean Sans Terre Wraps Himself in a Red Coat.
Jig for Harmonica.
Ginsberg. Today.
Glück. Nativity Poem.
Song of Invisible Boundaries.
Hardy. First or Last.
Herrick. Happinesse.
Pain[e] Ends in Pleasure.
Teares: ("Our present Teares here (not our present laughter)").
To Youth.
Upon Hanch a Schoolmaster.
Hesketh. Jolly Good Fellow, A.
Survivors.
Hewitt. Heart of Joy, The.
In Praise of Elizabeth.
Sonnet: "Our love is full of memorable things."
Hoffman. Ode to Joy.
Holmes. Sweet Charity.
Hopkins. Hurrahing in Harvest.
Hughes, Langston. Gypsy Melodies.
Joy.
Jarrell. Perfect Love Casteth Out Everything.
Jeffers. Joy.
Joseph. Sun Has Burst the Sky, The.
Keats. Fancy.

Imitation of Spenser.
Song: "Spirit here that reignest!"
Welcome Joy, and Welcome Sorrow.
Kipling. For our white and our excellent
  nights—for the nights of swift running.
To the Companions.
Kooser. Walking Beside a Creek.
Kunitz. First Love.
Larkin. Many Famous Feet Have Trod.
Lawrence. Autumn Sunshine.
Goodnight.
Kissing and Horrid Strife.
Many Mansions.
No Joy in Life.
Other Women Have Reared in Me.
She Looks Back.
Levertov. Joy.
Matins.
Lewis. *Merchants Wife, The.*
Songs of Sleep.
Lovelace. Dialogue. Lucasta, Alexis.
McGrath. Praises.
Meredith. Beyond the meadow still where
  sweeps.
Dear Heaven! for this sweet pledge of life.
First-Born, The.
In the Woods.
Love of the Woods.
Pastoral 4: "Lo, as a tree, whose wintry
  twigs."
She marries the knight she loves.
Sing aloud that she is mine.
Song in the Songless.
Song: "Joyful / And woful."
Song: "Under boughs of breathing May."
Sorrows and Joys.
Sweet o' the Year, The.
This, no more, doth Callistes recall.
To a Skylark.
To Robin Redbreast.
When my little son leaps in my sight.
Years Had Worn Their Season's Belt, The.
Merton. Perfect Joy.
Restoration of the Pictures, The.
Milton. Sonnet 16: "Cromwell, our cheif of
  men, who through a cloud."
O'Hara. Poem: "Khrushchev is coming on the
  right day!"
Oliver. Blossom.
Humpbacks.
Olson. All things stand out against the sky.
Day Song.
Only the Red Fox, Only the Crow.
Paley. Middle Age Poem.
Patchen. And then a bird that was like a great
  pale wolf flying down.
Pathway, The.
Psalms. Psalm 126: "When the Lord turned
  again the captivity of Zion.."
Raine. I could have told much by the way.
When I woke up to the snow.
Roethke. All the Earth, All the Air.
Moment, The.
Rossetti. And There Was No More Sea.
Birthday, A.
De Profundis.
Easter Carol, An.
Easter Day.
Easter Even.
From early dawn until the flush of noon.
If hope grew on a bush, / And joy grew on a
  tree.
Joy is but sorrow, / While we know.
Love and Hope.
Love Defended.
Methinks the ills of life I fain would shun.
Minnie bakes oaten cakes, / Minnie brews ale.
Praise of Love.
Present and Future.
Rose, The.
Seeking Rest.
Serenade.
Song: "We buried her among the flowers."
Sonnet: "Some say that love and joy are one:
  and so."
Then I Commended Mirth.
Unforgotten.

Valentine, 1877, A.
What will it be, O my soul, what will it be.
When My Heart Is Vexed I Will Complain
  ("Fields are white to harvest, look and see,
  The").
Will you be there? my yearning heart has
  cried.
Rukeyser. Ballad Theme, A.
Flying Red Horse, The.
Gift-Poem ("Year in its cold beginning").
Make and be eaten, the poet says.
Reading Time : 1 Minute 26 Seconds.
Tenth Elegy. Elegy in Joy.
When the true things meet us at the place we
  reach, they are all.
Sandburg. Joy.
Schwartz. Salute Valentine.
Spring, The.
Sexton. Fifth Psalm.
Seventh Psalm.
Welcome Morning.
Sidney. Sonnet 69: "O joy, too high for my
  low style to show."
Sonnet 70: "My Muse may well grudge at my
  heav'nly joy."
Smith, Stevie. Word, The.
Sorrentino. Variations 3.
Stevenson. Before this little gift was come.
De M. Antonio.
I am like one that has sat alone.
Light as my heart was long ago.
Spring Carol.
Updike. Burning Trash.
Van Duyn. Goya's "Two Old People Eating
  Soup."
Who says the world is mud? For the fifth day.
Warren. Love: Two Vignettes.
Whitman. Song of Joys, A.
Warble for Lilac-Time.
Whittier. Christmas Carmen, A.
June on the Merrimac.
Wilbur. For Ellen.
Hamlen Brook.
Williams, Charles Kenneth. Acids.
Williams, William Carlos. Martin and
  Katherine.
Wordsworth. Along the mazes of this song I
  go.
Barberry-Tree, The.
Wright, James. Blessing, A.
Wroth. Sonnet 38: "What pleasure can a
  bannish'd creature have."
Sonnet: "Fly traiter joye whose end brings butt
  dispaire."
Young. Joy/Spring.
Maya.
Zukofsky. Happiest February.
My nephew / And my new.
Perch Less.

Joyce, James
Boyle. On Taking up Residence in Virginia.
Liddy. June 16, 1992.
Notes towards an Ivy Leaf Video.
Vir XII.
Lowry. Those Coke to Newcastle Blues.
"MacDiarmid." Ah, Joyce, this is our task.
All life's million conflicting interests and
  relationships.
So, like him, we cry *"l'honneur des hommes:
  Saint Langage."*
Mahon. Joycentenary Ode.
Schwartz. Come, let us rejoice in James
  Joyce, in the greatness of this poet.
Smith, Patti. Conversation with the Kid.
Walcott. Volcano.

Judas Iscariot
Cullen. Judas Iscariot.
Judas Iscariot. (First Version).
De la Mare. Ballad of Christmas, A.
Herrick. Beginnings and Endings.
Jeffers. Dear Judas.
Lowry. Nagging at myself something awful.
Sandburg. Guaranteed Antique.
Sexton. Legend of the One-Eyed Man, The.
Swift. Judas.
Wright, James. Saint Judas.

Judges
"Carroll, Lewis." Mouse's Tale, The.
Davie. Pilate.
Dunbar. To Mary Church Terrell.
"Dylan." Lonesome Death of Hattie Carroll,
  The.
Percy's Song.
Seven Curses.
Jonson. Another to Him.
Epigram on Sir Edward Coke, when He Was
  Lord Chief Justice of England, An.
Epigram. To Thomas Lo[rd] Ellsmere, the Last
  Term He Sat Chancellor, An.
Kipling. Gallio's Song.
Gehazi.
Lady Geraldine's Hardship.
Sandburg. Killers.
What is a judge? A judge is a seated torso
  and head sworn before God.
Simic. Summons, The.
Spender. Van der Lubbe.
Swift. Verses on the Upright Judge.
Updike. Mr. High-Mind.
Whittier. Prophecy of Samuel Sewall, The.
Williams, William Carlos. To a Friend.
Zukofsky. Judge and the Bird, The.

Judgment
Beckett. Somme toute / tout compte fait.
Berry. Do Not Be Ashamed.
Boyle. For James Schevill.
Byron. Queries to Casuists.
Carew. To the Reader of Master William
  Davenant's Play [*The Wits*].
Carroll, Jim. Judging the Pageant.
M. Verdoux, The Wife Killer.
Clough. Thesis and Antithesis.
Cowper. Judgment of the Poets, The.
Lines Written During a Period of Insanity.
Davie. Three Beyond.
Witness.
Dickinson. Judgment is justest.
"Dylan." Hard Rain's A-Gonna Fall, A.
Whatcha Gonna Do.
Emerson. For that a man is a mark.
Prudence.
Everson. Answer, The.
Graves. Any Honest Housewife.
Myrrhina.
Hartley. Moralizing.
Herrick. To a Disdaynefull Fayre.
To Sir George Parrie, Doctor of the Civill
  Law.
Hewitt. This Narrative.
Hill. Psalms of Assize.
Ritornelli.
Jarrell. Variations.
Jonson. To the Worthy Author M[r] John
  Fletcher.
Kipling. Tomlinson.
Lawrence. Loggerheads.
Lewis. Shadows.
Liddy. Lesbos.
MacLeish. Eighth Book, The.
MacNeice. After anemones, after almond.
Meredith. World's Advance, The.
Merton. Dirge for the Proud World.
Great Knowledge.
Reduced to This.
Milton. God in the great assembly stands.
Lord my God to thee I flie / Save me and
  secure me under.
Piercy. Judgment, The.
Men are laughing as I approach, The.
Thrifty Lover, The.
Psalms. Psalm 7: "O Lord my God, in thee do
  I put my trust."
Psalm 9: "I will praise thee, O Lord."
Psalm 10: "Why standest thou afar off, O
  Lord?"
Psalm 26: "Judge me, O Lord; for I have
  walked in mine integrity."
Psalm 28: "Unto thee will I cry, O Lord my
  rock."
Psalm 36: "Transgression of the wicked."
Psalm 37: "Fret not thyself because of
  evildoers."
Psalm 72: "Give the king thy judgments, O

God."
Psalm 82: "God standeth in the congregation of the mighty."
Psalm 98: "O sing unto the Lord a new song."
Ransom. Armageddon.
Hilda.
Moments of Minnie.
"Reed." Vicious Circle.
Rich. 8/1/68.
Rolfe. Kill the Umpire!
Rossetti. Sooner or later: yet at last / The Jordan must be past.
Rukeyser. Facing Sentencing.
Sidney. To Thee, Lord, my cry I send.
Simic. Summons, The.
Smart. O Frame the strains anew.
Smith, Stevie. Death-Bed of a Financier.
Do Not!
Spender. Van der Lubbe.
Stevenson. Nor judge me light, tho' light at times I seem.
Walker. Judge Every One with Perfect Calm.
Whittier. By Their Works.
Wright, James. At the Executed Murderer's Grave.
Wyatt. Although thou see th'outrageous climb aloft.

Judgment Day
Byron. Vision of Judgment, The.
Clough. What we, when face to face we see.
Coleridge. For a Market-Clock.
Crashaw. Dies Irae.
Cummings. Chérie / the very,picturesque,last Day.
De la Mare. Hawthorn Hath a Deathly Smell, The.
Dickey, William. Ezekiel's Rabbit.
Dickinson. Departed—to the Judgment.
Not what We did, shall be the test.
'Twas a long Parting—but the time.
"Dylan." Are You Ready?
I'd Hate to Be You on That Dreadful Day.
Herbert. Death.
Doomsday.
Judgement.
Herrick. Comforts in Contentions.
Gods Providence.
Judgement Day, The.
Judgment-Day, The.
Upon Himselfe Being Buried.
Hill. They bespoke doomsday and they meant it by.
Hoffman. Incubus.
Jarrell. Bamberg.
Sears Roebuck.
Kipling. Last Chantey, The.
Untimely.
Kunitz. For the Word Is Flesh.
"MacDiarmid." Crowdieknowe.
Sexton. Fury of Earth, The.
Simic. Psalm: "Old ones to the side."
Swift. On the Day of Judgement.
Tomlinson. Last Judgement.
Whittier. Abraham Davenport.
Yeats. Crazy Jane on the Day of Judgment.
Second Coming, The.
See also **Apocalypse; End of the World.**

Judith (Apocrypha)
Ransom. Judith of Bethulia.

Juggling and Jugglers
Fox. Juggler, The.
Kipling. Juggler's Song, The.
Knott. Juggler to His Audience, The.
Meredith. Juggling Jerry.
Wilbur. Juggler.

Julius Caesar. *see* **Caesar, Julius.**

July
Bogan. July Dawn.
Eberhart. Coast of Maine.
Summer Landscape.
Swallows Return, The.
Tree Swallows.
Vision through Timothy.
Hartley. Reflex.
Vast rose of July.
Silverstein. Fourth, The.
Snowman.

Wilbur. My Father Paints the Summer.

Jumping
Fisher. Supposed Dancer, The.
Merton. Notes of a Parachute Jumper.
Silverstein. Jumping Rope.
Smith, Stevie. Cousin, The.
Harold's Leap.

June
Cowper. Judgment of the Poets, The.
Dickinson. I'm sorry for the Dead—Today.
Eberhart. Project, The.
Emerson. Low December vault in June be up-lifted high.
She walked in flowers around my field.
Glück. Solstice.
Gunn. June.
Kipling. Two Months.
Larkin. Cut Grass.
MacNeice. June Thunder.
Nash. Here Usually Comes the Bride.
Sandburg. Crabapple Blossoms.
Garden Wireless.
June.
Schuyler. I Think.
June.
Sexton. June Bug.
Tennyson. June Bracken and Heather.
Wilbur. June Light.

Jungles
Clark. Crisis on the Savannah.
Eberhart. Jungle, The.
Recollection of Childhood.
Kipling. Law of the Jungle, The.
Man goes to Man! Cry the challenge though the Jungle!
Morning Song in the Jungle.
Mowgli's Song against People.
Now Chil the Kite brings home the night.
Outsong in the Jungle.
Song of the Little Hunter, The.
Veil them, cover them, wall them round.
What of the hunting, hunter bold?
Lewis. Jungle, The.
Lindsay. Parvenu.
Merton. Cocoa Tree.
Nemerov. Two Poems.
Rukeyser. Poem: "Green going through the jungle of those years."
Smith, Stevie. Jungle Husband, The.
Williams, William Carlos. Jungle, The.
Wright, James. Some Beasts.

Juniper Trees
Lieberman. Family Tree, The.

Junk and Junkyards
Bukowski. Big John of Echo Park.
Carruth. Johnny Spain's White Heifer.
Dickey, James. Cherrylog Road.
Fisher. Rust. Limewash. The iron tyres.
Levine. Walk with Tom Jefferson, A.
Rukeyser. Junk-Heap at Murano.
Silverstein. Hector the Collector.
Tomlinson. Mirror in the Roadway, The.
Wilbur. Junk.

Jupiter (god)
Emerson. When wrath & terror changed Jove's regal port.
Ralegh. Arcadians the earth inhabited, The.
Wroth. Sonnet 3: "Juno still jealouse of her husband Jove."

Jupiter (planet)
Updike. Moons of Jupiter, The.

Justice
Browning, Robert. Instans Tyrannus.
Campion. Ad Tho. Munsonium, equitem Auratum et Baronetum.
Carew. Upon My Lord Chief Justice's Election of My Lady Anne Wentworth [*or* A.W.] for His Mistress.
"Carroll, Lewis." Majesty of Justice, The.
Chaucer. Tale of Melibee, The.
Coleridge. Good Great Man, The.
Pitt.
Cowper. Divine Justice Amiable.
Crashaw. Upon the Death of the Most Desired Mister Herrys.
Cummings. "Nothing" the unjust man complained.

Davie. Saw I Never the Righteous Forsaken.
So Make Them Melt as the Dishouséd Snail.
To get past harping on the laws of Nature.
Vengeance Is Mine, Saith the Lord.
De la Mare. In the Dock.
Dunbar. Justice.
To Miss Mary Britton.
"Dylan." Drifter's Escape.
Joey.
When the Ship Comes In.
Eberhart. Vastness and Indifference of the World, The.
Emerson. Astræa.
Fletcher. Levite and the Samaritan, The.
Frost. Masque of Mercy, A.
Gardner. Of Conscience.
Of Mercy.
Heaney. Stone Verdict, The.
Herbert. Justice (2).
Herrick. God Sparing in Scourging.
Good, and Bad.
Like Pattern, Like People.
Mercy and Love.
Rapine Brings Ruine.
Smart.
To God ("God is all-sufferance here").
To God ("I'le come, I'le creep").
Hewitt. Happy Boy, A.
Lines for a Dead Alderman.
Minister.
To Robert Telford Hewitt.
Hill. Cowan Bridge; At the Site of 'Lowood School.'
Sobieski's Shield.
Song Contest.
To dispense, with justice; or, to dispense.
Hughes, Langston. Freedom Train.
Freedom's Plow.
Who But the Lord?
Jeffers. Tower beyond Tragedy, The.
Jonson. On Lieutenant Shift.
Joseph. Love and Justice.
Kipling. Gallio's Song.
Gehazi.
Justice.
Lawrence. Deepest Sensuality, The.
Demon Justice.
Lies.
Vibration of Justice.
When Wilt Thou Teach the People?
Lowry. Plingen plangen auf gefangen.
Soul's Pentonville, The.
"MacDiarmid." Focherty.
Meredith. Blest is the sword that leaps from sheath.
Merton. Advising the Prince.
Atlas and the Fatman.
Those who speak with understanding must hold fast to what is common.
Milton. Jehovah to my words give ear.
Thy Land to favour graciously.
O'Hara. Ode: "Idea of justice may be precious, An."
Plath. Dialogue between Ghost and Priest.
Psalms. Psalm 5: "Give ear to my words, O Lord, consider my meditation."
Psalm 9: "I will praise thee, O Lord."
Psalm 12: "Help, Lord; for the godly man ceaseth."
Psalm 14: "Fool hath said in his heart, The."
Psalm 17: "Hear the right, O Lord."
Psalm 28: "Unto thee will I cry, O Lord my rock."
Psalm 53: "Fool hath said in his heart, The. . . ."
Psalm 62: "Truly my soul waiteth upon God."
Psalm 73: "Truly God is good to Israel."
Psalm 75: "Unto thee, O God, do we give thanks."
Psalm 76: "In Judah is God known."
Psalm 79: "O God, the heathen are come."
Psalm 85: "Lord, thou hast been favourable unto thy land."
Psalm 107: "O give thanks unto the Lord, for he is good: for."
Psalm 125: "They that trust in the Lord shall be as mount Zion."

Psalm 132: "Lord, remember David, and all his afflictions."
Psalm 140: "Deliver me, O Lord, from the evil man."
Ralegh. 3.4: "Who rules the duller earth, the wind-swolne streames."
"Reed." Dirt.
Rolfe. All Ghouls' Night.
Letter.
Witness at Leipzig.
Sandburg. And you take hold of a handle.
Implications.
In the light of the cold glimmer of what everybody knows, why should the.
"Lawyer," hiccuped a disbarred member of the bar, "is a man who", A.
What is a judge? A judge is a seated torso and head sworn before God.
When was it long ago the murmurings began.
Who was that antique Chinese crook who put over his revolution and.
Sidney. Lord, help, it is high time for me to call.
To Thee, Lord, my cry I send.
Smart. Justice.
O Lord, thy land has favour found.
Southwell. Scorne Not the Leaste.
Whitman. Thought ("Of Justice—as if Justice could be any thing but the same ample law, expounded by natural judges and saviors").
Whittier. Cities of the Plain, The.
Mithridates at Chios.
Slave-Ships, The.
To the Reformers of England.
Wilbur. Water Walker.
Williams, Miller. *In Extremis* in Hardy, Arkansas.
Williams, William Carlos. Early Martyr, An.
Impromptu: The Suckers.
Wordsworth. Feelings of a French Royalist, on the Disinterment of the Remains of the Duke D'Enghien.
Humanity.
What if our numbers barely could defy.
See also **Injustice.**

Justification
Bukowski. Darlings.
"Dylan." Restless Farewell.
Emerson. Compensation ("Why should I keep holiday").
Ferlinghetti. What could she say to the fantastic foolybear.
Hewitt. For Any Women Who Pass This House.
Lowry. And partly they deserve dishonest death.
Half of the harm that is done in this world.
Rich. Women.

Juvenile Delinquency
Brooks. We Real Cool.
"Dylan." Walls of Red Wing.

K

Kabul, Afghanistan
Kipling. Ford o' Kabul River.
Kafka, Franz (1883-1924)
Berryman. Demand me again what Kafka's riddles mean.
Knott. Keeper, The.
Kalamazoo, Michigan
Lindsay. Kalamazoo.
Sandburg. Sins of Kalamazoo, The.
Kangaroos
Kipling. This is the mouth-filling song of the race that was run by a Boomer.
Lawrence. Kangaroo.
Nash. Kangaroo, The.
Kansas (state)
Ferlinghetti. Astonished Heart, The.
Gildner. All Hallows' Eve in Kansas.
Gunn. Small Plane in Kansas.
Kooser. Place in Kansas, A.
Lindsay. Kansas.
Santa-Fé Trail (A Humoresque), The.

Sandburg. Flat Waters of the West in Kansas.
Mockers Go to Kansas in Spring.
Stafford. Ceremony.
Rescued Year, The.
Whittier. Burial of Barber.
Kansas Emigrants, The.
Le Marais du Cygne.
Letter from a Missionary of the Methodist Episcopal Church South, in Kansas, to a Distiguished Politician.
Wilbur. Piccola Commedia.

Kansas City, Kansas and Missouri
Dickey, William. Elegy Before the Time.
Katydids
Dunbar. Whip-Poor-Will and Katy-Did.
Wright, James. Katy Did.
Kavanagh, Patrick
Hartnett. Poet Down, The.
Keats, John
Auden. After Reading Keats' Ode.
Browning, Elizabeth Barrett. By Keats's soul, the man who never stepped.
Byron. Who Kill'd John Keats?
Cullen. For John Keats, Apostle of Beauty.
To John Keats, Poet, at Springtime.
Cummings. Fame Speaks.
Davie. Two Widows in Tashkent.
Gunn. Keats at Highgate.
Hardy. At a House in Hampstead.
At Lulworth Cove a Century Back.
Rome: At the Pyramid of Cestius near the Graves of Shelley and Keats.
Hugo. Lecture.
Jong. Dear Keats.
Keats. Song about Myself, A.
Lowry. More Impatience.
Port has a sweeter name than Saigon, The.
"Portly & middleaged" can never.
"MacDiarmid." Greatest poets undergo a kind of crisis in their art, The.
So, like him, we cry *"l'honneur des hommes: Saint Langage."*
Meredith. Poetry of Keats, The.
Merton. Philosophers, The.
Olson. I'm With You.
Oppen. Boy's Room.
Rossetti. On Keats, 18 January, 1948 (Eve of St Agnes).
Rukeyser. From a Play: Publisher's Song.
Homage to Literature.
Shelley. Peace, peace! he is not dead, he doth not sleep.
Stuart. I Can't Live Without You.
Keller, Helen
Cullen. For Helen Keller.
Davie. To Helen Keller.
Kennedy, John Fitzgerald
Auden. Elegy for J.F.K.
Berryman. Formal Elegy.
Bly. Kennedy's Inauguration.
Dove. 1963.
Ferlinghetti. Assassination Raga.
Frost. For John F. Kennedy; His Inauguration.
Hugo. Kennedy *Ucciso.*
Olson. Hustings, The ("Under the eyes").
Oppen. Armies of the Plain.
"Reed." Day John Kennedy Died, The.
Young. Day Kennedy Died.
Kennedy, Robert Francis
Ferlinghetti. Assassination Raga.
Hayden. For King, for Robert Kennedy.
Lowell. For Robert Kennedy Nineteen Twenty-Five to Sixty-Eight.
Kent, England
Davie. Kent.
Kentucky
Berry. And I am here in Kentucky in the place I have made myself.
Dunbar. After a Visit.
Lindsay. My Fathers Came from Kentucky.
Sandburg. Knucks.
Sarton. Night Watch.
Warren. Kentucky Mountain Farm.
Kerouac, Jack
Berrigan. Pandora's Box, An Ode.

Ferlinghetti. Canticle of Jack Kerouac, The.
Late Impressionist Dream.
Ginsberg. Malest Cornifici Tuo Catullo.
Memory Gardens.
Sunflower Sutra.
Sweet Levinsky.
Holmes. Writing the Atheneum talk, I wonder.
Liddy. After Hal'amová.
Thursdays Are Sacred.
Key West, Florida
Bishop. Norther—Key West, A.
Sunday at Key West.
Crane. Key West.
Eberhart. Key West.
Meinke. Hero Worship at Key West on the 4th of July.
Olson. Key West.
Stevens. Idea of Order at Key West, The.
Two Figures in Dense Violet Night.
Keys
De la Mare. Keys of Morning, The.
Dobyns. Ways of Keys, The.
Wakoski. Sun.
Kidnapping and Kidnappers
Dove. Abduction, The.
Koertge. Old People.
McAuley. But old Lares with the rest forgot in time.
Silverstein. Googies Are Coming, The.
Smith, Stevie. What Is the Time?; or, St. Hugh of Lincoln.
Killing and Killers
Berry. Bird Killer, The.
For the Hog Killing.
Carruth. Of course make love not.
Ciardi. Baboon and the State, The.
Cowper. On a Spaniel Called Beau Killing a Young Bird.
Eberhart. Airman Considers His Power, An.
Assassin, The.
Fisher Cat, The.
Killer, The.
Vastness and Indifference of the World, The.
Villanelle: "Christ is walking in your blood today."
Winter Kill.
Everson. Black Hills, The.
Griffiths. Shooting of Levellers, Burford, 1649.
Hall. Body Politic, The.
Kill, The.
Hayden. Killing the Calves.
Hughes, Ted. Eagle.
Esther's Tomcat.
Hawk Roosting.
Kreutzer Sonata.
Manacled with blood.
Tiger-Psalm.
Jarrell. Essay on the Human Will, An.
Jeffers. To Kill in War Is Not Murder.
Kinnell. Dead Shall Be Raised Incorruptible, The.
Kooser. Shooting a Farmhouse.
Kunitz. Bolsheviks.
Foreign Affairs.
Gladiators, The.
Lewis. Patrol, The.
McAuley. Aor Against the Warmonger.
Confession, The.
"MacDiarmid." Left-wing poetry represents a rise in the price of bread.
MacLeish. Eighth Book, The.
MacNeice. Grey Ones, The.
In the misty night humming to themselves like morons.
Than which not any could be found other.
This then is our answer under.
Matthews. Sympathetic.
Merton. Lament for Javier Heraud.
Shots were heard last night / Out by the burial ground.
Take, O take the key of Rome.
Pack. Hunting.
Patchen. Battle of Unameit, The.
Destruction of Carthage, The.
Have You Killed Your Man for Today?
Meben.

O Howling Cells.
Quantity of Mercy, The.
Under the green ledge.
Ralegh. Even they that have no murdrous will.
"Reed." Kicks.
Rolfe. Words Found on a Cave's Wall.
Sandburg. Black Horizons.
Hate.
Hoodlums.
Warren. Bear Track Plantation: Shortly after Shiloh.
Court-Martial.
Dream He Never Knew the End of, The.
Williams, Charles Kenneth. How Humble We Were before This.
Nut, The.
Williams, Miller. Missing Persons.
Voice of America.
Zimmer. Confession, Curse and Prayer.

Kimonos
Lieberman. Kimono.

Kindness
Berg. Brothers.
Rubber Rats.
Browning, Elizabeth Barrett. Island, An.
Bunting. Verse and Version.
Chaucer. Gentilesse.
Coleridge. Charity in Thought.
Genevieve.
Pang More Sharp Than All, The.
Pity.
Cowper. Reciprocal Kindness the Primary Law of Nature.
Creeley. Thank You.
Cullen. Tribute.
Davie. At Knaresborough.
Humanly Speaking.
Master & Man.
Dickinson. Had I a pleasure you had not.
To do a magnanimous thing.
Dunbar. My Sort o' Man.
Plea, A.
Dunn. Kindness.
Ginsberg. Who Be Kind To.
Glück. Gratitude.
Graves. Apples and Water.
Hartley. Somewhere, between the coming.
Hewitt. W.R. Rodgers.
Hopkins. Brothers.
Joseph. Goddess of Nature's Diatribe to her People, The.
Lawrence. All I Ask.
Lowry. This business of evil / Like brokers the weevil.
Meredith. To Children.
Millay. To Those Without Pity.
Plath. Kindness.
Rossetti. Behold, I stand at the door and knock.
Night and Death.
Rose, The.
Southwell. Scorne Not the Leaste.
Spender. Acts Passed Beyond.
Stafford. Aunt Mabel.
Stevenson. I am a hunchback, yellow faced.
To Mrs. MacMarland.
Warren. His Smile.
Whittier. Hill-Top, The.
Wright, James. Sappho.
Wroth. Song 1: "Sweet lett mee injoye thy sight."
Zukofsky. In that this happening.

King, Martin Luther, Jr
Hayden. For King, for Robert Kennedy.
Lorde. Rites of Passage.
Lowell. Two Walls.
Merton. April 4th 1968.
Rukeyser. Martin Luther King, Malcolm X.
Sarton. Easter, 1968.
Walker. Abduction of Saints, The.
Killers.

King, William, Archbishop of Dublin
Swift. Excellent New Song upon His Grace Our Good Lord Archbishop of Dublin, An.

King Lear
Auden. Encounter.

Keats. On Sitting Down to Read "King Lear" Once Again.
Nathan. Widowhood.
Williams, William Carlos. Lear.

Kingfishers
Berry. Before Dark.
Fenton. Kingfisher's Boxing Gloves, The.
Hopkins. As kingfishers catch fire, dragonflies draw flame.
Lowry. Kingfishers in British Columbia.
Oliver. Kookaburras, The.
Olson. Kingfishers, The.

Kings
Auden. He looked in all His wisdom from His throne.
Berryman. Not to Live.
Bishop. Twelfth Morning; or What You Will.
Blake. Gwin, King of Norway.
Prologue to King John.
Boyle. People's Cry, The.
Bradstreet. Four[e] Monarchies, The.
Brontë. Song: "King Julius left the south country."
Browning, Elizabeth Barrett. King Victor Emanuel Entering Florence, April, 1860.
Napoleon III in Italy.
Sword of Castruccio Castracani, The.
Browning, Robert. Solomon and Balkis.
With Daniel Bartoli.
Burns. Carl an the King Come.
Dream, A.
Byron. Harp the Monarch Minstrel Swept, The.
On a Royal Visit to the Vaults.
To Belshazzar.
Very Mournful Ballad, A.
Windsor Poetics.
Carew. New Year's Gift. To the King, A.
Upon the King's Sickness.
"Carroll, Lewis." Bruno's Song.
When the King found that his money was nearly all.
Ye Fattale Cheyse.
Clough. Sa Majestá Très Chrétienne.
Cooper. Gaza.
Cowper. Philosopher and the King, The.
Crashaw. To the Queen's Majesty.
Upon the Kings Coronation ("Sound forth, cælestiall Organs, lett heavens quire").
Upon the Kings Coronation ("Strange Metamorphosis! It was but now").
Cullen. Black Majesty.
Davie. God Saves the King.
Thyestes.
Woe unto Thee!
De la Mare. Maerchen.
Never-To-Be.
Dickinson. Belshazzar had a Letter.
I met a King this afternoon!
Emerson. A.H.
Ancient lady who dwelt in Rome, An.
Hear what the glass will tell thee.
In the kingdom of Poesy Hafiz waves like a banner.
King. If farmers make my land secure.
Our Shah's counsel is the efflux.
Shah Sandschar, whose lowest slave.
They strew in the path of kings and czars.
To the Shah, from Enweri ("Not in their houses stand the stars").
What lovelier forms things wear.
William Rufus and the Jew.
Fenton. Tauler.
Graves. Beggar Maid and King Cophetua, The.
Gunn. Court Revolt, The.
Hardy. King's Soliloquy, A.
Herrick. Bad Wages for Good Service.
Blame.
Blame the Reward of Princes.
Caution in Councell.
Clemency in Kings.
Counsell.
Cruelty.
Dangers Wait on Kings.
Difference Betwixt King and Subjects, The.
Distance Betters Dignities.

Empires.
Flatterie.
God, and the King.
Ill Government.
King and No King, A.
Kings.
Kings and Tyrants.
Love.
Obedience.
Obedience in Subjects.
Patience in Princes.
Power in the People, The.
Strength to Support Soveraignty.
To the King.
To the King, To Cure the Evill.
Twelfe Night, or King and Queene.
Upon Kings.
Warre.
Hewitt. King Concerned, The.
Monarch, The.
Hill. Requiem for the Plantagenet Kings.
Hoffman. Shaking the President's Hand.
Jeffers. Ghosts in England.
Jonson. Bow both your heads at once, and hearts.
Kipling. And since he was Master and Servant in all that we asked him.
Ballad of the King's Jest, The.
Ballad of the King's Mercy, The.
"I have a thousand men," said he.
James I.
King Henry VII. And the Shipwrights.
King's Job, The.
King's Task, The.
My Father's Chair.
Palace, The.
Reeds of Runnymede, The.
Song of Seven Cities, The.
There was never a queen like Balkis.
Lindsay. Curse for Kings, A.
Doll's "Arabian Nights," A.
He harried lions up the peaks.
King Arthur's Men Have Come Again.
Who Knows?
Lovelace. To Lucasta, from Prison.
Lowell. Death of Alexander.
MacNeice. Jehu.
Rites of War.
Meredith. Brooding on her deep fall, the many strings.
Emperor Frederick of Our Time, The.
Events in a Rustic Mirror.
Head of Bran the Blest, The.
John Lackland.
Song of Drab, The.
Olson. King of the Wood / King of the Dead.
Prince. King watches at Night, The.
Psalms. Psalm 45: "My heart is inditing a good matter."
Psalm 47: "O clap your hands, all ye people."
Ralegh. 3.16: "By gifts the Macedon clave Gates a-sunder."
Ransom. Two Gentlemen in Bonds.
Rich. In the North.
Rossetti. Maundy Thursday.
Succession of Kings, The.
What Hath God Wrought!
Sandburg. Four Brothers, The.
High Conspiratorial Persons.
Name Us a King.
Savoir Faire.
Shelley. Fragment: "I would not be a king—enough."
Fragment: Pater Omnipotens.
Sidney. Sonnet 75: "Of all the kings that ever here did reign."
Silverstein. Peanut-Butter Sandwich.
Smith, Stevie. King in Funeral Procession, A.
Sorrentino. Charles and Arthur.
Stevenson. My Kingdom.
Suckling. On New-Year's Day 1640, to the King.
Swift. Ode to the King.
Walker. In Uganda an Early King.
Warren. How beautiful are the young, walking.
Woman, who had cried out, "O thou, The."

Wilbur. Castles and Distances.
Williams, Charles Kenneth. Allies: According
to Herodotus.
Wordsworth. Edward VI.
Emperors and Kings, How Oft Have Temples
Rung.
Fact, and an Imagination or, Canute and
Alfred, on the Sea-Shore, A.
Imitation of Juvenal — Satire VIII.
King of Sweden, The.
Yau. Two Kinds of Song.
Yeats. Black Tower, The.
King and No King.
Madness of King Goll, The.
Model for the Laureate, A.
Two Kings, The.
See also **Listings for specific Kings.**

Kipling, Rudyard
Nash. How to Be Married without a Spouse,
or, Mr. Kipling, What Have You Done with
Mr. Hauksbee?
Kipling's Vermont.

Kisses
Berg. Daughters, The.
Berryman. Ah when you drift hover before
you kiss.
Audacities and fetes of the drunken weeks!
Keep your eyes open when you kiss: do:
when.
Venice, 182.
Browning, Elizabeth Barrett. Sonnet: "First
time he kissed me, he but only kissed."
Browning, Robert. Moth's kiss, first, The!
Bunting. Came to me— / Who?
Burns. And I'll kiss thee yet, yet.
Dusty Miller.
John Come Kiss Me Now.
Song: "Ae fond kiss, and then we sever."
Byron. First Kiss of Love, The.
Oh! might I kiss those eyes of fire.
Campion. Ad Caspiam.
Canto Tertio.
Come, you pretty false-eyed wanton [or false-
ey'd wanton].
In Lycium et Clytham.
In Melleam.
My Sweetest Lesbia [Let Us Live and Love].
What Harvest Half So Sweet Is.
Carew. Tooth-Ache Cured by a Kiss, The.
"Carroll, Lewis." Madrigal: "He shouts amain,
he shouts again."
Carruth. Sonnet: "In the mind of the kiss
occurs a thought so rich."
Catullus. Carmen 5: "Lesbia / live with me."
Carmen 7: "Curious to learn / how may kiss- /
es of your lips."
Carmen 48: "Iuventius, / were I allowed."
Carmen 99: "Purloining while you played in
honeyed youth."
Coleridge. Kiss, The.
Kisses.
Cummings. B / et / wee / n no / w dis.
Being(just a little).
Come a little further—why be afraid.
Dirty colours of her kiss have just, The.
I have found what you are like.
Now that,more nearest even than your fate.
O my wholly unwise and definite.
Thing most new complete fragile intense, A.
Thy fingers make early flowers of.
Up into the silence the green.
Voices to voices, lip to lip.
What over and which under.
Dobyns. Santiago: Forestal Park.
Donne. Expiration, The.
Dove. Adolescence—I.
Dunbar. Breaking the Charm.
Come and Kiss Me Sweet and Twenty.
Her Thought and His.
Phantom Kiss, The.
Dunn. Each from Different Heights.
My Brother's Work.
Emerson. Ah, could I hide me in my song.
Pair of crystal eyes will lead me, A.
Ferlinghetti. Short Story on a Painting of
Gustav Klimt.
Fox. Modern woman in search of a soul.

Gallagher. Same Kiss After Many Years, The.
Graves. Silent Visit.
Gunn. Kiss at Bayreuth, The.
Hall. "Kiss, The."
Hardy. Kiss, A.
Last Time, The.
Mock Wife, The.
Sigh, The.
That Kiss in the Dark.
Two Lips.
Hartnett. That Actor Kiss.
Herrick. Barley-Break; or, Last in Hell.
Draw Gloves.
Head-Ake, The.
His Embalming to Julia.
Hymne to Venus, and Cupid, A.
Kiss[e], A.
Kisse, The.
Kisses.
Kisses Loathesome.
Kissing and Bussing.
Kissing Usurie.
Leven.
Love Palpable.
Love Perfumes All Parts.
On Gelli-Flowers Begotten.
Teares: ("God from our eyes all teares.").
Tithe [or Tythe]: To the Bride, The.
To Dianeme ("Give me one kiss").
To Electra.
Upon a Free Maid, with a Foule Breath.
Upon a Virgin Kissing a Rose.
Upon Jack and Jill: Epigram.
Upon Lucia.
Jonson. Fragmentum Petron. Arbitr. The Same
Translated.
O, that joy so soon should waste!
To the Same [Celia].
Kunitz. Game, The.
Lawrence. After School.
Appeal, The.
Assuming the Burden.
Decision, A.
Hyde Park at Night, before the War.
Kisses in the Train.
Lightning.
Mystery.
Seven Seals.
Liddy. Dear Anima, Show These Words.
Narcissus and the Young Men.
Scott Rautmann, Saturday Night.
Vir VIII.
Vir IV.
You Came By on Bamboo Stilts, Playing
Horse.
Lindsay. By the Spring at Sunset.
Lovelace. Courante Monsieur.
To Juvencius.
Markson. Sexist Stanza.
Millay. What lips my lips have kissed, and
where, and why.
Morgan. Catullus: Carmen v.
Olson. Real, The.
Treatment, The.
Patchen. Demonstration.
Plath. Never Try to Trick Me with a Kiss.
Roethke. Shy Man, The.
Rossetti. Baby lies so fast asleep / That we
cannot wake her.
My baby has a mottled fist.
Our little baby fell asleep.
Sandburg. Counting.
Kisses, Can You Come Back Like Ghosts?
Kisses Forgotten.
Schwartz. Aria.
Sexton. Kiss, The.
Knee Song.
Shapiro. Kiss, The.
Shelley. Love's Philosophy.
Sidney. Sonnet 74: "I never drank of
Aganippe well."
Sonnet 79: "Sweet kiss, thy sweets I fain
would sweetly indite."
Sonnet 80: "Sweet swelling lip, well mayst
thou swell in pride."
Sonnet 81: "O kiss, which dost those ruddy
gems impart."

Sonnet 82: "Nymph of the garden where all
beauties be."
Smith, Stevie. I HATE THIS GIRL.
Stevenson. Small is the trust when love is
green.
To Rosabelle.
Swinburne. Rondel: "Kissing her hair."
Tennyson. As through [or thro'] the Land [at
Eve We Went].
Walker. Kiss, The.
Whitman. Behold This Swarthy Face.
Williams, Charles Kenneth. On the Other
Hand.
Wordsworth. Lesbia.
Wyatt. Alas, madam[e], for stealing [or
stelying] of a kiss [or kysse].
Yau. Paradise.
Recoil.
Young. Kiss.
Zukofsky. Drive, fast kisses.
May we live, my Lesbia, love while we may.
Mellowed *those*, I call *those* eyes, Juventius.
Queries, you ask how many times must I kiss.
Surreptitious you at bay doom loot is, my
little Juventi.
Two Dedications: Tibor Serly.

Kitchens
Crane. In a Court.
Dunbar. Trouble in de Kitchen.
Hacker. Shirland Road.
Haines. Kitchen, The.
Hartnett. Bread.
Roethke. Last Words.
Stuart. Don't Look Back.
Turco. Kitchen, The.
Wakoski. Un Morceau en Forme de Poire.

Kites (ornithology)
Kipling. Chil's Song.

Kites (toys)
Cohen. Kite Is a Victim, A.
Fisher. Kites are the best sort of gods, The.
Ford. Human kites, fantastic.
Heaney. Kite for Michael and Christopher, A.
Lieberman. Eros at the World Kite Pageant.
Sexton. Kite, The.
Snodgrass. Lovers Go Fly a Kite, The.
Stuart. Light Years.

Kittens
Eberhart. Old Tom.
Jarrell. Sign, The.
Lindsay. Dirge for a Righteous Kitten, A.
Moore. Reminiscent of a Wave At the Curl.
Nash. Kitten, The.
Smith, Stevie. Our Office Cat.
Wordsworth. Kitten and [the] Falling Leaves,
The.

Klee, Paul
Haines. Paul Klee.
Nemerov. Painter Dreaming in the Scholar's
House, The.

Klimt, Gustav
Ferlinghetti. Short Story on a Painting of
Gustav Klimt.

Knees
Sexton. Knee Song.

Knife-Grinding and Knife-Grinders
Cummings. Who sharpens every dull.
Everson. Cutting the Firebreak.
Lindsay. Scissors-Grinder, The.
Whitman. Sparkles from the Wheel.

Knighthood and Knights
Browning, Elizabeth Barrett. Romaunt of the
Page, The.
Browning, Robert. Childe Roland to the Dark
Tower Came.
Heretic's Tragedy, The.
"Carroll, Lewis." Lays of Sorrow, No. 2.
Ye Capete Knyghte.
Chaucer. Sir Thopas.
Squire's Tale, The.
Wife of Bath's Tale, The.
Coleridge. Ballad of the Dark Ladié, The.
Dunbar. Knight, The.
Emerson. Arabian Ballad.
Graves. Absent Crusader.
Son Altesse.

Herrick. To His Peculiar Friend Sir Edward Fish, Knight Baronet.
Hughes, Ted. Knight, The.
Jonson. Speech Presented unto King James at a Tilting in the Behalf of the Two Noble Brothers S[ir] Robert and S[ir] Henry Rich, Now Earls of Warwick and Holland, A.
To Sir Luckless Woo-All.
Keats. Calidore. A Fragment.
King Stephen. A Fragment of a Tragedy.
La Belle Dame Sans Merci.
Kipling. Last Rhyme of True Thomas, The.
Lollius.
Quest, The.
Lovelace. Swain, Hind, Knight; I fed, till'd, did command, A.
MacNeice. Canto XXII: "So this is Glastonbury. A green hill far away."
Meredith. Chivalry.
Song of Courtesy, The.
Song: "When on my faithful charger."
Rich. Knight, The.
Robinson. Lancelot.
Sandburg. Horses and Men in the Rain.
Scott. Branksome Hall.
Invocation: "Harp of the North! that mouldering long hast hung."
Lochinvar.
Ride to Stirling, The.
Shakespeare. It was a lording's daughter, the fairest one of three.
Smith, Charlotte. Prologue to William Godwin, Antonio: or, The Soldier's Return.
Smith, Stevie. Behind the Knight.
Blue from Heaven, The.
Fafnir and the Knights.
Frozen Lake, The.
Stevenson. Vanquished Knight, The.
Tennyson. Sir Galahad [or The Purple Heart].
Sir Launcelot and Queen Guinevere.
Whittier. Knight of St. John, The.
Wordsworth. Effusion in the Pleasure-Ground on the Banks of the Bran, Near Dunkeld.
Fragments: Drafts, Mostly or All for a Poem on a Heroic Theme.

Knights of Pythias
Kipling. New Knighthood, The.

Knitting and Knitters
Dickinson. Autumn—overlooked my Knitting.
Hartley. We are knitting now.
Hewitt. First Letters.
Pangur Ban.
Lawrence. Daughter of the Great Man, The.
Simic. Gallows Etiquette.

Knives
Dobyns. Men with Long Faces, The.
Emerson. I use the knife.
Hall. Wolf Knife.
Lorde. Poem for Women in Rage, A.
McGrath. Deprivation.
Fatigue of Objects, The.
Schuyler. Stone Knife, A.
Sexton. Bayonet.
Simic. Knife.

Knowledge
Ammons. One Thing and Another.
Pedagogy Agog.
Progress Report.
Teleology.
Atwood. Procedures for Underground.
Berg. 1914.
Berry. And that is our story.
At a Country Funeral.
Creation Myth.
Fall.
Gathering, The.
History.
Horses.
Our bond is no little economy based on the exchange.
Put your hands into the mire.
Recognition, The.
To be at home on its native ground.
To Know the Dark.
Berryman. Spinning Heart, The.
Bishop. At the Fishhouses.
Blake. All Religions Are One.

Bogan. Knowledge.
Bradstreet. Of the Four Humors in Man's Constitution.
Browning, Robert. Paracelsus.
Reverie.
Bunting. After the grimaces of capitulation.
Carruth. How Lewisburg, Pa., Escaped the Avenging Angel.
Clough. Human spirits saw I on a day, The.
Cooper. Knowledge That Comes through Experience, The.
Cowper. Conversation.
On Mrs. Montagu's Feather-Hangings.
Creeley. End, The.
Folk Song, A: "Hitch up honey for the / market race all."
For Lewis, to Say It.
Somebody Died.
Sunset.
Wisdom.
Cummings. Love's function is to fabricate unknownness.
You shall above all things be glad and young.
Davie. Life Encompassed.
Dickinson. Inferential Knowledge, The.
When overwhelmed to know.
Dobyns. Bravado.
Donne. Poor soul, in this thy flesh what dost thou know?
Doolittle. No one knows, / the heart of a child.
Duncan. Ballad of the Enamord Image, The.
Circulations of the Song.
Master of Rime told me, You must learn to lose heart, The.
"Dylan." Highway 61 Revisited (liner Notes).
John Wesley Harding (Liner Notes).
Rita May.
Eberhart. Hardening into Print.
Only in the Dream.
Testimony.
Emerson. I wear no badge; no tinsel star.
On earth's wide thoroughfares below.
Tell men what they knew before.
Who knows this or that?
Fox. At the Edge of the Suburbs.
Frost. From Plane to Plane.
Revelation.
Garrigue. Catch What You Can.
Ginsberg. Lysergic Acid.
PsalmIII: "To God: to illuminate all men. Beginning with Skid Road."
Griffiths. Belonging.
Gunn. Merlin in the Cave: He Speculates without a Book.
Hacker. Days of 1959.
Hardy. Fragment: "At last I entered a long dark gallery."
Known Had I.
Masked Face, The.
Not Known.
Hartley. This Piece of Eucharist.
Villa—I would be brief, yet say—.
Herrick. Knowledge.
To Doctor Alabaster.
Hesketh. Child's Guide to Philosophy, A.
I Am.
My Faithful Lover.
Return.
Scapegoat.
Starlings.
Truant.
Violet at Ninety.
Walking Away.
Walled In.
What Is a Person?
Hewitt. Ballad, The.
E.H.
Fool's Cap, The.
Hand over Hand.
Roseblade's Visitants and Mine.
Scissors For a One-Armed Tailor.
Those Morning Walks.
Hughes, Ted. Man Seeking Experience Enquires His Way of a Drop of Water, The.
Jeffers. Science.

Joseph. False Postulate.
Version of the Phoenix Story, A.
Keats. Read Me a Lesson, Muse, and Speak It Loud.
Kipling. Chartres Windows.
Our Fathers of Old.
Threshold, The.
Koch. Taking a Walk with You.
Larkin. Far Out.
Lawrence. All-Knowing.
Know-All.
You.
Levine. Cemetery at Academy, California, The.
On My Own.
Silent in America.
Liddy. Letter to Eamonn Wall, A.
We saw the star of knowledge.
Lowry. And now I brood on what I think I know.
Midnight denies poursuivant of the dawn.
No words assess, no pencil knows.
"MacDiarmid." Poetry the quality of which, A.
MacLeish. Autobiography.
Land's End.
Le Secret Humain.
Learned Men, The.
Meredith. From lamplight and an aged leaf.
He tells it, who knew the law.
Merton. Great Knowledge.
Learning of many things does not teach understanding, or else it would have taught Hesiod and Pythagoras, The.
Useless, The.
When Knowledge Went North.
Wisdom.
Nash. Ask Daddy, He Won't Know.
Who Did Which? or Who Indeed?
Nathan. Diver, The.
Hieroglyph.
Hole.
Opportunity.
That the Unexamined Life Is Not Worth Living.
Nemerov. Boy with Book of Knowledge.
Knowledge.
To David, about His Education.
O'Hara. Spleen.
Olson. A B Cs (2).
Oppen. Because the known and the unknown.
Clarity / In the sense of transparence.
Lighthouses, The.
Likely as not a ruined head gasket.
Not to reduce the thing to nothing.
Tell the life of the mind, the mind creates the finite.
Tho the world.
Patchen. Forms of Knowledge, The.
Should Be Sufficient.
Poe. Al Aaraaf.
Pope. Know then thyself, presume not God to scan.
Pound. Tree, The.
Psalms. Psalm 139: "O Lord, thou hast searched me, and known me."
Raine. Chartres Annunciation, The.
Dream-flowers.
Message from Home.
On a Shell-strewn Beach.
Rich. Apparition.
From Morning-Glory to Petersburg.
Merely to Know.
You are beside me like a wall; I touch you with my fingers and.
Roethke. Marrow, The.
Rossetti. Take No Thought for The Morrow.
To Lalla, Reading My Verses Topsy-Turvy.
We know not when, we know not where.
Rukeyser. Afterwards.
Knowledge my nakedness.
St. John. I Know.
Sandburg. Gang in its working clothes, The.
He was a king or a shah, an ahkoond or rajah.
I have said to the elephant and the flea, "Each of us makes his life."
I was born in the morning of the world.

Leather Leggings.
Pals.
Peace Between Wars.
People is a lighted believer and, The.
People with Proud Chins.
Sea Hold, The.
Since death is there in the light of the sun, in the song of the.
Unknown War, The.
Was he preaching or writing poetry or talking through his hat? He was.
Why repeat? I heard you the first time.
Schwartz. Albert Einstein to Archibald MacLeish.
"Now we approach the darkness of to-night!"
Praise Is Traditional and Appropriate.
Sand upon the Red Sea shore, or on the beach, The.
Shapiro. Solipsism.
Simic. Writings of the Mystics, The.
Smart. On the Omniscience of the Supreme Being.
Snyder. Magpie's Song.
My home was at Cold Mountain from the start.
Sorrentino. Detail, A.
Stevens. Somnambulisma.
Stevenson. Here he comes, big with statistics.
Tennyson. To —. With the Following Poem.
Thomas. Was There a Time.
Why East Wind Chills.
Whitman. As in a Swoon.
I Thought That Knowledge Alone Would Suffice.
Savantism.
That Music Always Round Me.
Whittier. Common Question, The.
Questions of Life.
Wilbur. In a Bird Sanctuary.
Problem from Milton, A.
Water Walker.
Williams, Charles Kenneth. I know / nothing anymore.
Next to the Last Poem about God, The.
Regulars, The.
Williams, Miller. How Does a Madsong Know That's What It Is?
One of Those Rare Occurrences on a City Bus.
Today is Wednesday.
Wordsworth. Composed on the Banks of a Rocky Stream.
Yau. So much of the proscenium burned.
Zukofsky. Ask of the sun.

Kollwitz, Käthe
Rukeyser. Käthe Kollwitz.

Koran
Davie. Articulacy. Hints from the Koran.
Merrill. Page from the Koran.
Merton. Cairo 1326.
Night of Destiny, The.

Korean War
Carruth. On a Certain Engagement South of Seoul.
Jeffers. De Rerum Virtute.
McGrath. Ode for the American Dead in Asia.

Kosciusko, Thaddeus
Coleridge. Koskiusko.
Keats. To Kosciusko.

Ku Klux Klan
Hayden. Night, Death, Mississippi.
Hughes, Langston. Ku Klux.

Kubla Khan
Coleridge. Kubla Khan; or, A Vision in a Dream.

Kyoto, Japan
Waldman. Pictures From Tofukuji.

L

La Hogue, Battle of. *see* Hogue, La, Battle of (1692).
Labor and Laborers
Ashbery. Bird's-Eye View of the Tool and Die Co.

Berry. You lean at ease in your warm house at night after supper.
Bukowski. Mexican Girls, The.
Sparks.
Winter Comes to a Lot of Places in August.
Cummings. I say no world.
Dickey, William. Life Moving More Rapidly Than Hands Can Manage.
Dickinson. Labor might fatigue.
Dobyns. Santiago: Five Men in the Street: Number Two.
Dunbar. Equipment.
Eberhart. Maine Roustabout, A.
Emerson. Use will in man new grace reveal.
Frost. Tuft of Flowers, The.
Gallagher. Black Money.
Glück. School Children, The.
Griffiths. Consequences.
Oil Terminal.
Out of a Descended Generation.
Hall. Foundations of American Industry, The.
Hemingway. Worker, The.
Herrick. End of His Work, The.
Gods Blessing.
Labour.
Recompence.
Rest.
Upon Trencherman.
Hewitt. Brothers, The.
Dedication of "The Rhyming Weavers."
End of the World, The.
For Certain Subscribers to the Miners' Fund.
"Forty-Four Hours" Strike, 1919, The.
Gathering Praties.
Lint Pulling, The.
96 Clifton Park Avenue and the Robinsons.
Palimpsest.
Song of the Shipyard Men, The.
Hopkins. God's Grandeur.
Jeffers. Bixby's Landing.
On Building with Stone.
Johnson. Ant, The.
Kipling. Wage-Slaves, The.
Koertge. He ("Was looking for work at forty-seven and the owner of a").
Streetsweeper, The.
Kooser. Late September.
Larkin. Toads.
Toads Revisited.
Lawrence. Morning Work.
Study.
Levine. Helmet, The.
Lewis. Rhondda, The.
"MacDiarmid." Seamless Garment, The.
MacLeish. Burying Ground by the Ties.
Millay. Men Working.
Nash. Grasshoppers Are Very Intelligent.
More About People.
Two Songs for a Boss Named Mr. Longwell.
Olson. O'Ryan.
Oppen. Antique.
Men of Sheepshead, The.
Piercy. To Be of Use.
Rolfe. Asbestos.
Brickyards at Beacon.
Rukeyser. Absalom.
Alloy.
Bill, The.
Burnishing, Oakland.
Disease: After-Effects, The.
Doctors, The.
George Robinson: Blues.
Mearl Blankenship.
Power.
Praise of the Committee.
Statement: Philippa Allen.
Sandburg. Child of the Romans.
Dynamiter.
Horses and Men in the Rain.
Ice Handler.
In paper sacks the customers carry away millions of tons of goods daily.
Jack.
Masses.
Mayor of Gary, The.
Mill-Doors.
Muckers.

Old Flagman, The.
Onion Days.
Psalm of Those Who Go Forth before Daylight.
Sayings, sentences, what of them?
Somebody has to make the tubs and pails.
There have been thousands of Andy Adams.
Three Ghosts.
To Certain Journeymen.
Was he preaching or writing poetry or talking through his hat? He was.
What the people learn out of lifting and hauling and waiting and losing.
Working Girls.
You do what you must—this world and then the next—one world at a.
Shelley. Song to the Men of England.
Sidney. Merchant man, whom many seas have taught, The.
Simic. Furniture Mover.
Smith, Charlotte. To Dependence.
Smith, Stevie. Alfred the Great.
Road Up.
Snyder. Hay for the Horses.
Late Snow & Lumber Strike of the Summer of Fifty-four, The.
Stevenson. Link your arm in mine, my lad.
To A Gardener.
Woodman, The.
Sutter. My dad's old man was a carpenter.
Night Shift: the Composing Room.
Snowman, The.
Swift. Description of the Morning, A.
Verses Spoken Extempore by Dean Swift on His Curate's Complaint of Hard Duty.
Tate. On the Founder of the Industrial System in the United States.
Tomlinson. Churchyard Wall, The.
Hand at Callow Hill Farm, The.
Lament for Doormen.
Steel.
Whitman. I Hear America Singing.
Whittier. Drovers, The.
Huskers, The.
Lumbermen, The.
Shoemakers, The.
Wordsworth. Labourer's Noon-Day Hymn, The.
Young. New Mode of Production, The.
See also **Work and Workers.**

Labor Day
Glück. Labor Day.
Oliver. Stanley Kunitz.
Sandburg. LINCOLN? / He was a mystery in smoke and flags.
Schuyler. Labor Day.

Labor Unions
Berryman. Thanksgiving: Detroit.
"Dylan." Union Sundown.
Hewitt. My Aunt Sarah and Uncle Joe.
Patchen. Joe Hill Listens to the Praying.
Sandburg. Ice Handler.
In paper sacks the customers carry away millions of tons of goods daily.
Teamster's Farewell, A.
See also **Strikes and Strikers.**

Labrador, Canada
Crane. North Labrador.
Sandburg. Love in Labrador.
Williams, William Carlos. Labrador.

Labyrinths
Auden. Maze, The.
Cowper. Maze, The.
Gardner. Minotaur, The.
Hewitt. Corridor.
Morrison. Guided Tour, The.
Raine. Tree of night is spangled with a thousand stars, The.
Rukeyser. Minotaur, The.

Lade, Sir John
Johnson. Short Song of Congratulation [*or* To a Young Heir], A.

Ladybirds
Eberhart. How It Is.
Rossetti. I caught a little ladybird / That flies far away.

Lafayette, Marie Joseph, Marquis de
Blake. Fayette beside King Lewis stood.
Coleridge. La Fayette.
Emerson. Poem, Spoken Before the ΦΒΚ
    Society, August, 1834.
Lake District, England
Arnold. Youth of Nature, The.
Wordsworth. Composed at Rydal on May
    Morning, 1838.
    Composed When a Probability Existed of Our
      Being Obliged to Quit Rydal Mount as a
      Residence.
    Four Fiery Steed Impatient of the Rein.
Lakes and Ponds
Ammons. Second Party.
Atwood. Younger Sister, Going Swimming.
Auden. Lakes.
Mill (Hempstead), The.
    Tarn, The.
Burns. On Scaring Some Waterfowl in Loch
    Turit, a Wild Scene among the Hills of
    Oughtertyre.
Byron. Sonnet to Lake Leman.
Carruth. Oldest Killed Lake in North America,
    The.
    Underground the Darkness Is the Light.
Ciardi. Island Galaxy, An.
Clark. Lake, The.
Creeley. Thinking.
    Way, The.
Cummings. This / forest pool / A so.
De la Mare. Visionary, The.
Dickey, James. Remnant Water.
Dunbar. Matter of Locality, A.
Eberhart. On Returning to a Lake in Spring.
Emerson. He loved to watch & wake.
    Miracle, The.
Fox. On Some Such Morning.
Frost. Spring Pools.
Garrigue. Shore.
Glück. Pond, The.
Haines. Lake in the Sky, The.
    We climbed all afternoon.
Hall. Day I Was Older, The.
    Sister by the Pond, A.
    Southwest of Buffalo.
Hewitt. Lake Bled, Slovenia.
    Little Lough, The.
Hugo. Cairn in Loch An Duin, The.
    Dog Lake with Paula.
    Kapowsin.
    Lake Byron, Maybe Gordon Lord.
    Lone Lake, Whidbey.
    Meridian.
    Sweet Piece from Fontal.
    Turtle Lake.
Joseph. Here Lies Treasure: Here Be
    Monsters.
Kunitz. Goose Pond.
MacNeice. Lake in the Park, The.
Meredith. In the clear dark lake a lady dived.
Merton. Lake, The.
Nemerov. Pond, The.
O'Hara. Mozart Chemisier.
Oliver. At Blackwater Pond.
Pack. Clayfeld's Metamorphosis.
Plath. Crossing the Water.
    Private Ground.
Poe. Lake: To———, The.
Rukeyser. Sacred Lake.
Sandburg. Dialogue.
    Flat Waters of the West in Kansas.
    Lake Michigan Morning.
    Night Stuff.
    Old Music for Quiet Hearts.
    Purple Martins.
Scott. Loch Coruisk.
Shelley. Fragment: The Lake's Margin.
Smith, Stevie. Abominable Lake, The.
    Frozen Lake, The.
Stuart. Interlude at the Grand Hotel, An.
Tomlinson. Gorge, The.
Whittier. Grave by the Lake, The.
    Kenoza Lake.
    Lakeside, The.
    Storm on Lake Asquam.
    Summer by the Lakeside.

    Voyage of the Jettie.
    Well of Loch Maree, The.
Wilbur. Marginalia.
Williams, William Carlos. View of a Lake.
Wordsworth. Passage from John Wilson's *The*
    Angler's Tent.
    Written in the Strangers' Book at "The
    Station," Opposite Bowness.
Wright, James. By a Lake in Minnesota.
    On Minding One's Own Business.
Lamb, Charles
Coleridge. This Lime-Tree Bower My Prison.
    To a Friend [Charles Lamb] Together with an
      Unfinished Poem.
    To a Friend [Charles Lamb] Who Had
      Declared His Intention of Writing No More
      Poetry.
Nash. All, All Are Gone, the Old Familiar
    Quotations.
Wordsworth. Farewell Lines.
    Written after the Death of Charles Lamb.
Lamb, Mary
Wordsworth. Farewell Lines.
Lambs
Blake. Lamb, The.
Burns. What Will I Do Gin My Hoggie Die.
Ciardi. Lamb, The.
Dunbar. Hymn: "O li'l lamb out in de col'".
Eberhart. For a Lamb.
Ford. Little lamb who made thee? / Ho but
    the egg is growing hair.
Hewitt. Rhyme for Blake, A.
Hughes, Ted. Couples Under Cover.
    February 17th.
    Ravens.
    Sheep.
Larkin. First Sight.
Lawrence. St Mark.
Merrill. Violent Pastoral.
Merton. Will a narrow lane / Save Cain?
Roethke. Lamb, The.
Rossetti. Angels at the foot,/ And Angels at
    the head.
    Frisky Lamb, A.
    Motherless soft lambkin / Alone upon a hill.
    On the grassy banks / Lambkins at their
      pranks.
    Thy lilies drink the dew, / Thy lambs the rill,
      and I will drink them too.
Smith, Stevie. Death Bereaves Our Common
    Mother Nature Grieves for My Dead Brother.
Wordsworth. Pet Lamb, The; A Pastoral.
    Westmoreland Girl, The.
Lament (form)
Burns. Galloway Tam.
    Song: "As I stood by yon roofless tower."
De la Mare. Fairy in Winter, The.
    News.
    Ophelia.
    Suicide, The.
    Sunk Lyonesse.
Eberhart. Despair.
    Ode to Silence.
Emerson. Hermione.
Herrick. To Perenna ("I a Dirge will pen for
    thee").
MacLeish. Why—what men were they that
    beneath the moon.
Markson. Writer's Lament.
Merton. Cup with a Jaguar for the Drinking of
    Health.
    Dirge for the World Joyce Died In.
    Lament of a Maiden for the Warrior's Death.
    Organ.
    Whitsun Canticle, A.
Sidney. Sonnet 33: "I might, unhappy word, O
    me, I might."
Wilbur. Lament: "Nashe's old queens who
    bartered young and fair."
Wyatt. Resound my voice [*or* voyse], ye
    woods [*or* wodes] that hear [*or* here] me
    plain.
See also **Lament in Title and First Line Index.**
Lamplighting and Lamplighters
Emerson. At Plymouth in the friendly crowd.
Kooser. Summer Night, A.
Oliver. Lamps, The.

Stevens. Tea.
Stevenson. Lamplighter, The.
Tomlinson. Civilities of Lamplight.
Lampreys. *see* **Eels.**
Lancashire, England
Carew. To Saxham.
Davie. Lancashire.
Lancelot du Lac
Robinson. Lancelot.
Williams, William Carlos. Con Brio.
Landlords and Landladies
Angelou. Contemporary Announcement.
Atwood. Landlady, The.
Berry. Companions, The.
Bukowski. Breakout.
    Buffalo Bill.
    Nice Place, A.
"Dylan." Dear Landlord.
Hughes, Langston. Ballad of the Landlord.
    Madam and the Rent Man.
Landor, Walter Savage
Moore. W. S. Landor.
Landscape
Atwood. Place: Fragments, A.
Auden. Day-dreams of a Tourist.
    I chose this lean country.
    North, The.
    Visit, A.
Beatles. Lucy in the Sky with Diamonds.
Boyle. Landscape for Wyn Henderson, A.
Browning, Elizabeth Barrett. Sea-Mew, The.
Burns. Humble Petition of Bruar Water to the
    Noble Duke of Athole, The.
Eliot. New Hampshire.
    Rannoch, by Glencoe.
    Usk.
    Virginia.
Emerson. Seemed, tho' the soft sheen all
    enchants.
Ferlinghetti. Baja Revisited.
    Carrara, Looking Seaward.
Fox. Say It Has Been Snowing.
Ginsberg. Wales Visitation.
Griffiths. Wedding Photograph.
Hardy. Death-Day Recalled, A.
    In Front of the Landscape.
Hewitt. Agrigento, Sicily.
    April.
    Below the Mournes in May.
    By Air to Birmingham on a Mid-June
      Evening.
    Cobweb.
    From the Chinese of Wang Li Shi.
    Garron Top.
    Glenarriffe and Parkmore.
    Glens of Atrim, The.
    Glens, The.
    Landscape.
    Living Landscape, The.
    March Day.
    Minor Victorian Painter, A.
    My Uncle.
    On a January Train Journey.
    On the Grand Dublin Canal: Musing on the
      "Two Nations" Theory.
    Ram's Horn, The.
    Sonnet: "When I have read your hard and
      lively words."
    This Is No Land of Constable and Clare.
    Will.
Jarrell. Country Was, The.
Jonson. To Sir Robert Wroth.
Kinnell. Supper after the Last, The.
Kipling. Run of the Downs, The.
    Three-Part Song, A.
McAuley. In six-inch scale, the Mayo
    baronies.
MacLeish. Landscape as a Nude.
Marvell. Upon Appleton House [To My Lord
    Fairfax].
    Upon the Hill and Grove at Bilbrough.
Melville. Enviable Isles, The.
    Inscription, The: "While yet Rolfe's foot in
      stirrup stood."
Patchen. Continuation of the Landscape.
Raine. Dream.
    Mirage, The.

Moon golden towards the full.
Shadow.
Rexroth. Song at the Winepresses, A.
Rossetti. Mirrors of Life and Death.
Rukeyser. Breathing Landscape.
Homage to Literature.
Notes for a Poem.
Sandburg. Back Yard.
Flat Lands.
Landscape.
Landscape.
Nocturne in a Deserted Brickyard.
Schuyler. Evening Wind.
June.
Just before Fall.
View, A.
White Boat, Blue Boat.
Stevens. In the Clear Season of Grapes.
Stuart. Goshen Pass: Winter.
Sutter. Real Estate.
Tomlinson. Appearance.
At Stoke.
Brilliant Silence.
Casarola.
Flight, The.
Hedgerows.
Hill Walk.
In Winter Woods.
Landscape.
Lines Written in the Euganean Hills.
On a Landscape by Li Ch'eng.
On the Mountain.
Snow Fences, The.
Van Duyn. View, A.
Whittier. Golden Wedding of Longwood, The.
Pictures.
Revisited.
Williams, Miller. Waiting for the Paper to be
Delivered.
Williams, William Carlos. Storm, The.
Wordsworth. Malham Cove.
On the Sight of a Manse in the South of
Scotland.
Wright, Charles. Landscape with Seated Figure
and Olive Trees.
Wright, James. In Ohio.
Quest, The.
Young. Old Light.

Landscapes
Ashbery. Haunted Landscape.
Purists Will Object.
Boyle. To America.
United States, The.
Emerson. Inspired we must forget our books.
Fox. Islanders.
Graves. Lost Acres.
Gunn. Iron Landscapes (and the Statue of
Liberty).
Hopkins. Distance / Dappled with diminish'd
trees.
Hugo. Distances.
Jong. Imaginary Landscapes.
Lowry. Contemplation of Dead Reckoning.
"MacDiarmid." And a poetry in which as in a
film.
Melville. Pontoosuce.
Olson. Tenementy twilightht landscape.
Rukeyser. Landscpe with Wave Approaching.
Sandburg. Localities.
New Hampshire Again.
Nocturn IV: "Claims of the sea, of the tide,
move out, The."
Schuyler. Beaded Balustrade.
Vermont Diary, A.
Smith, Charlotte. To the South Downs.
Tomlinson. Saving the Appearances.
Wilbur. Terrace, The.
Wordsworth. Written in Mrs Field's Album
opposite a Pen-and-Ink Sketch in the Manner
of a Rembrandt Etching Done by Edmund
Field.
Wright, Charles. Journal of the Year of the
Ox, A.

Landslides
Dickey, James. Sustainment.

Lang, Andrew
Stevenson. Not roses to the rose, I trow.

To Andrew Lang.
To Master Andrew Lang.

Language
Ammons. De / on one, The.
Ashbery. Paradoxes and Oxymorons.
Atwood. Despite us / there is only one
universe, the sun.
Fishing for Eel Totems.
Surely in your language.
We hear nothing these days.
Auden. Natural Linguistics.
Beckett. Écoute-les / s'ajouter.
Berry. Sycamore gathers / out of the sky,
white, The.
Bly. Words Rising.
Campion. Think'st thou to seduce me then
with words that have no meaning?
Carroll, Jim. El Hombre del Ombre.
Carruth. Comparative Iconography.
Fragment: "Who can know more deeply than I
your loneliness there?"
How Lewisburg, Pa., Escaped the Avenging
Angel.
Naming for Love.
No Matter What, After All, and That Beautiful
Word So.
Of Distress Being Humiliated by the Classical
Chinese Poets.
Post-Impressionist Susurration for the First of
November, 1983, A.
RAVAGE, v.t. To lay waste; to subject.
Sanskrit root word, The.
Sonnet: "Honey, darling, baby..but no
endearments."
Sonnet: "The hubbub of the Hall of
Languages, our Babel."
Sonnet: "The Word for Today is 'panoptic,'
which the goddamn."
Sonnet: "What if the psychologians, those
grand old frauds."
Steeple bush, hardhack.
Ceravolo. O gong of wept / O unviolet.
Water: How Weather Feels the Cotton Hotels.
Clark. Gift of Tongue.
Cohen. Commentary—How to Speak Poetry.
French and English.
How to Speak Poetry.
Cowper. Canzone: "Scoffing, amorous maidens
and young men."
Crane. By Nilus Once I Knew.
Creeley. Echo.
Language, The.
Message, The.
Method, A.
Pacing as with some consequent.
Pay.
To the One in the Gray Coat.
Words.
Cummings. Here is little Effie's Head.
Newly / cued / motif smites truly to
beautifully.
Oil tel duh woil doi sez.
Surely / Cued / motif smites truly to
Beautifully, The.
Davie. Hearing Russian Spoken.
Well-Found Poem.
With the Grain.
De la Mare. Incantation.
Dickinson. Could mortal lip divine.
Duncan. For a Song of the Languagers.
I ask the unyielding Sentence that shows Itself
forth in the language.
O Outrider! / when you come to the threshold
of the stars.
Poetry Disarranged.
Source.
Writing as Writing.
Dunn. Decorum.
Naturally.
"Dylan." Sign Language.
Eberhart. By the Stream.
I Went to See Irving Babbitt.
Emerson. Brave Empedocles defying fools,
The.
Muse / Can at pleasure use, The.
When thy soul / Is filled with a just image
fear not thou.

Ferlinghetti. Baja Beatitudes.
General Song of Humanity, The.
Sweet and various the woodlark.
Fisher. Walk through, minding the nettles.
Fletcher. Vowels, The.
Fox. In the Land of Shinar.
There was, perhaps, a time.
Gallagher. Poem in Translation, A.
Second Language.
Glück. Illuminations.
Graves. Cool Web, The.
Dance of Words.
In Time of Absence.
O.
Tilth.
Hacker. After the Revolution.
For Jean Migrenne.
Sestina: "For a week now our bodies have
whispered."
Hall. Je Suis une Table.
Hardy. History of an Hour, The.
Liddell and Scott.
Hartnett. Inchicore Haiku.
Pity the Man Who English Lacks.
This road is not new.
Heaney. Alphabets.
Herbert. Son[ne], The.
Hesketh. Brain Child.
Evergreen.
Hewitt. Dedication of "The Rhyming
Weavers."
My Father's Voice.
Hoffman. He was the first who had returned.
Problems of Knowledge.
Hugo. Ness.
Joseph. Figure in a Landscape.
Language Teaching: Naming.
Little dots.
Kipling. Birthright, The.
Koch. Permanently.
Liddy. Necessity of Writing in This Tongue,
The.
Slovak Tongue, The.
Lorde. Coal.
Lowry. French Pronunciation Simplified for
Julian Trevelyan.
In Cape Code with Conrad Aiken.
"MacDiarmid." All dreams of "imperialism"
must be exorcised.
Caledonian Antisyzygy, The.
I'm weary o' the shapes mere chance can
thraw.
So, like him, we cry "l'honneur des hommes:
Saint Langage."
To distinctly English writers in England.
Weapon, The.
McGrath. Flint and Steel.
Need for Dictionaries II, The.
Merrill. Lost in Translation.
To My Greek.
Merton. Decoding the looks of opposites.
Writing down their silences.
Let choirs of educated men compose.
Miller. Albina.
Milton. Canzone: "Scoffing, amorous maidens
and young men."
Hail native language, that by sinews weak.
Nash. Brief Guide to Rhyming, or, How Be
the Little Busy Doth?, A.
Enthusiast Is a Devotee Is a Rooter, or, Mr.
Hemingway, Meet Mr. Stengel, An.
Oafishness Sells Good, Like an Advertisement
Should.
Oh, Shucks, Ma'am, I Mean Excuse Me.
Scram, Lion!
This Is My Own, My Native Tongue.
To Ee Is Human.
Nathan. Understanding, The.
Word, The.
Nemerov. Capitals.
Origin.
Translation.
Neruda. Pedro Is When.
Spelling book, can you love me.
Olson. A B Cs.
A B Cs (2).
Abstract #1, Yucatan.

Applause.
For Mac Hammond.
Moon Is the Number 18, The.
Motion, The.
Promise, A.
Red Mallows.
Shenandoah.
Small Birds, to Agree with the Leaves, Come
in the Fall.
These Days.
Oppen. Building of the Skyscraper, The.
Emotions are engaged, The.
Leviathan.
Lights / Shine, the fire, The.
Possible / To use.
Song, the Winds of Downhill.
Words cannot be wholly transparent. And that
is the.
Paley. What has happened?
Plath. Incommunicado.
Magi.
Raine. Ancient Speech, The.
Sandburg. Abracadabra Boys, The.
Alley Rats.
Fifty-Fifty.
Is Wisdom a Lot of Language?
Jabberers.
Languages.
Little Girl, Be Careful What You Say.
Monosyllabic.
People is Everyman, everybody, The.
Precious Moments.
Primer Lesson.
Two Fish.
Two Nocturns.
Useless Words.
Schwartz. "Interpretation! that's the act of
mind."
Power and Glory of Language, The.
Shapiro. Dirty Word, The.
Simic. Errata.
Pastoral: "I came to a meadow."
Smart. Fragment C.
Hail Energeia! hail, my native tongue.
Whitsunday.
Smith, Patti. After/Words.
Translators.
Snyder. June.
Sorrentino. Language Barrier, The.
Spender. Word.
Stafford. Purifying the Language of the Tribe.
Stein. More Grammar for a Sentence.
New.
Patriarchal Poetry.
Practice of Oratory.
Sonatina Followed by Another, A.
Tillie.
Yet Dish.
Stevens. On the Manner of Addressing
Clouds.
Pieces.
Repetitions of a Young Captain.
Stevenson. Maker to Posterity, The.
Spring Carol.
Stuart. Coming To.
Sutter. Swedish Lesson.
Thomas. Before I Knocked.
In the Beginning.
Tomlinson. Ceci n'est pas une Pipe.
Updike. Blked.
Song of Paternal Care, A.
Van Duyn. Since You Asked Me.
To My Godson, on His Christening.
Walcott. Codicil.
Those grooves in that forehead of sand-
coloured flesh.
Waldman. Philosophia Perennis.
Some of the Things I See for You.
Warren. Brotherhood in Pain.
Dead Language: Circa 1885, A.
Williams, Miller. Words.
Williams, William Carlos. Africa.
From a Play.
Graph for Action.
Wright, Charles. Language Journal.
Vesper Journal.

Yeats. Into the Twilight.
Lady's First Song, The.
Zukofsky. I's (Pronounced *Eyes*).
Translation, The.
Wish, A.
Lanterns
Fletcher. From the Chinese.
Hewitt. Hollyhocks against the Wall, The.
Laocoön
Piercy. Laocoön is the Name of the Figure.
Lapwings
Blake. O lapwing, thou fliest around the
heath.
Larches
Carruth. Tamarack with needles lost, The.
Williams, William Carlos. To Friend-Tree of
Counted Days.
Larks
Burns. Address to the Woodlark.
Cummings. May i be gay.
Dunbar. With the Lark.
Hardy. Shelley's Skylark.
Herrick. To the Lark.
Hewitt. Arithmetic.
Hoffman. Larks, The.
Hopkins. Caged Skylark, The.
Sea and the Skylark, The.
When eyes that cast about the heights of
heaven.
Woodlark, The.
Hughes, Ted. All the dreary Sunday morning.
I suppose you just gape and let your gaspings.
Lark begins to go up, The.
Like those flailing flames.
My idleness curdles.
Lowry. !Bulletin!
Meredith. Lark Ascending, The.
Pastoral 7: "Summer glows warm on the
meadows, and speedwell, and gold-cups, and
daisies."
To a Skylark.
Millay. On First Having Heard the Skylark.
Pope. Presenting a *Lark*.
Rossetti. Bird Raptures.
Shelley. To a Skylark.
Smart. For Saturday.
Wilbur. Beowulf.
Wordsworth. To a Sky-Lark.
To a Skylark ("Ethereal minstrel! pilgrim of
the sky").
See also **Meadowlarks.**
Las Vegas, Nevada
Ginsberg. Las Vegas: Verses Improvised for
El Dorado H.S. Newspaper.
Last Judgment
Atwood. Resurrection.
Cohen. Gypsy Wife, The.
Israel.
Fletcher. Last Judgment, The.
Herbert. Self-Condemnation.
Last Rites. see Extreme Unction.
Last Supper
Rossetti. Offering of the New Law, the One
Oblation Once Offered, The.
Southwell. Of the Blessed Sacrament of the
Altar [*or* Aulter].
Walcott. Easter.
Wordsworth. Last Supper, by Leonardo da
Vinci, in the Refectory of the Convent of
Maria della Grazia—Milan, The.
Latin
Burns. Elegy on Mister William Cruikshank
A. M.
"Carroll, Lewis." Lesson in Latin, A.
Cummings. Noster was a ship of swank, The.
Graves. Jugum Improbum.
Hardy. After Reading Psalms XXXIX, XL,
etc.
Patchen. And in Another Place Uses the Same
Phrase.
Prince. Family Mottoes.
Sarton. Godhead as Lynx, The.
Zukofsky. Translation, The.
Latin America and Latin Americans
Carruth. You—Spanish-speaking.
Fletcher. Mexican Quarter.

Gallagher. Sugar.
That Kind of Thing.
Hugo. Troubadour Removed, A.
McGrath. Lament for Pablo Neruda.
Latter-Day Saints, Church of Jesus Christ of.
see **Mormons.**
Laughter
Beckett. En face.
Samedi répit.
Blake. When the Green Woods Laugh.
Bukowski. Funny.
Burns. Occasional Address, Spoken by Miss
Fontenell, on Her Bnefit-Night, Decr. 4th.
1793.—Written by Mr Burns.
"Carroll, Lewis." Beatrice.
Carruth. Have you ever seen.
Catullus. Carmen 31: "Apple of islands,
Sirmio, & bright peninsulas, set."
Carmen 53: "I laughed. Calvus. I laughed
today."
Creeley. Crisis, The.
June 6, 1970.
Laughing.
Saints, The.
Wicker Basket, A.
"You've Tried the World, Try Jesus."
De la Mare. Falstaff.
Dickey, James. Small Song.
Dunn. Amidst the Faltering.
Eliot. Hysteria.
Emerson. Stout Sparta shrined the god of
Laughter.
Fox. Clown, The.
Graves. Heaven.
Laugh, The.
Gunn. Girls Next Door, The.
Hall. Clown, The.
Hardy. Catullus: XXXI.
Herrick. Anthea's Retractation.
Laugh and Lie Downe.
Teares, and Laughter.
Upon Bice.
Hesketh. Clown.
Sally.
Hewitt. Prelude to an Ode for Barnum.
Kipling. Legend of Mirth, The.
To the Companions.
Lawrence. Laughter.
Lovelace. Lucasta Laughing.
To Lucasta ("I laugh and sing, but cannot
tell").
Lowry. Consider what you have lost by lack
of faith.
Good Luck.
Hostage.
I met the spirit of tragedy in the wood.
Never in a comedian's life have I laughed till
then!
MacLeish. Poet's Laughter.
MacNeice. Barcelona in Wartime.
Meredith. Glee.
My jolly friar, / Now lift thy cowl.
When she laughs there is a glitter as of
morning before me.
Nash. I'm Terribly Sorry for You, But I Can't
Help Laughing.
That's Funny, Wasn't It? No, It Won't Be.
Piercy. Women's Laughter.
Sandburg. Bundles.
Laughing Blue Steel.
Thin Strips.
White Shoulders.
Without the daily chores of the people.
Smith, Stevie. Dear Little Sirmio.
Persian, The.
Updike. Origin of Laughter, The.
Wyatt. Caesar, when that the traitor of Egypt.
Zukofsky. Peninsular arm, Sirmio, insular arm,
well.
Risible nice go when from mud a crony.
See also **Mirth.**
Laundry and Laundering
Ferlinghetti. Away above a harborful.
Herrick. Upon a Cheap Laundresse: Epigram.
Upon Sudds, a Laundress[e].
Housman. From the wash the laundress sends.
Jarrell. Washing.

Jong. Dirty Laundry Poem, The.
Joseph. Washing is jerked from shade into the sun, The.
Merrill. Mad Scene, The.
Sandburg. Washerwoman.
Schuyler. Closed Gentian Distances.
Steaming Ties.
Smith, Stevie. Small Lady, The.
Updike. Bendix.
Wash.
Wilbur. Love Calls Us to the Things of This World.
Williams, William Carlos. Young Laundryman, The.
Young. Dancing in the Laundromat [or] Dust: an Ordinary Song.

Laurels
Bogan. Several Voices Out of a Cloud.
Herrick. Mount of the Muses, The.
To Laurels.
To Mistress Katherine Bradshaw, the Lovely, That Crowned Him with Laurel.
Willow Garland, The.
Keats. To a Young Lady Who Sent Me a Laurel Crown.
Meredith. Daphne.
Shelley. Fragment: The False Laurel and the True.

Lavender
MacNeice. Lavender blue for love, lavender green for youth.

Law and Lawyers
Auden. Law like Love.
Beatles. Maxwell's Silver Hammer.
Berryman. "I *couldn't leave* you" you confessed next day.
Boyle. For James Schevill.
Browning, Elizabeth Barrett. Void in Law.
Browning, Robert. Ponte dell' Angelo, Venice.
"Carroll, Lewis." Lays of Mystery, Imagination, and Humour, No. 1: The Palace of Humbug.
Mouse's Tale, The.
Carruth. Lana.
Catullus. Carmen 49: "Silver-tongued among the sons of Rome."
Cohen. Singer Must Die, A.
Cowper. Report of an Adjudged Case.
Trail of Admiral Keppel, The.
Davie. Standings.
De la Mare. In the Dock.
Polonius.
Dickinson. It comforts the Criminal little to know.
Donne. Satire 2: "Sir: though (I thank God for it) I do hate."
Satire 5: "Thou shalt not laugh in this leaf, Muse, nor they."
To Mr. B. B.
Dunbar. Lawyers' Ways, The.
Frost. Self-Seeker, The.
Graves. Blanket Charge.
Gunn. Legal Reform.
Herrick. Lawes ("When Lawes full power have to sway, we see").
To His Honoured Friend, M. John Weare, Councellour.
Upon Case.
Hill. Why should I strike you with my name.
Housman. Laws of God, the laws of man, The.
Jonson. Epigram to the Coucillor That Pleaded and Carried the Cause, An.
On Cheveril.
On Cheveril the Lawyer.
Joseph. Love and Justice.
Lovelace. To Marcus T. Cicero.
Lowry. No words assess, no pencil knows.
Merton. Inner Law, The.
Letter to a Sufi Who Has Abandoned Sufism to Study Law.
Plessy vs Ferguson: Theme and Variations.
Those who speak with understanding must hold fast to what is common.
Nathan. Law and Order.
Olson. Law.
Pope. Verbatim from Boileau.

"Reed." Dirt.
Rolfe. Letter.
Rukeyser. Bill, The.
Disease: After-Effects, The.
Doctors, The.
Praise of the Committee.
Sandburg. In the light of the cold glimmer of what everybody knows, why should the.
Lawyer.
"Lawyer," hiccuped a disbarred member of the bar, "is a man who", A.
Lawyers Know Too Much, The.
Smart. Disertissime Romuli Nepotum.
Stevenson. Here he comes, big with statistics.
Swift. Helter Skelter.
Turco. Courthouse, The.
Updike. Mr. High-Mind.
Williams, Miller. *In Extremis* in Hardy, Arkansas.
Williams, William Carlos. To a Friend.
Zukofsky. Laws Can Say, The.
Master of eloquence and Rome's potent line.

Lawes, Henry
Milton. Sonnet 13: "Harry, whose tunefull and well-measur'd song."

Lawns
Ciardi. On the Orthodoxy and Creed of My Power Mower.
Creeley. For Helen.
Herrick. Lawne, The.
Hughes, Ted. Sunstroke.
Silverstein. Helping.
Razor-Tailed Wren, The.
Wordsworth. This Lawn, a Carpet All Alive.
Zukofsky. Guests, The.

Lawrence, David Herbert
Ferlinghetti. Man Who Rode Away, The.
Hewitt. In Memoriam: D.H. Lawrence.
Holmes. Dying Lawrence.
Lawrence in Taos.
Lawrence. No! Mr Lawrence!
Lowry. Those Coke to Newcastle Blues.
O'Hara. Poem: "I don't know as I get what D.H. Lawrence is driving at."
Williams, William Carlos. Elegy for D.H. Lawrence, An.

Lawrence, Edward
Milton. Sonnet 20: "Lawrence of vertuous Father vertuous Son."

Lazarus (Bible)
Browning, Robert. Epistle Containing the Strange Medical Experience of Karshish, the Arab Physician, An.
Crashaw. Upon Lazarus His Teares.
Dickey, James. Lazarus to the Assembled.
Gunn. Lazarus Not Raised.
Hill. History as Poetry.
Joseph. Lazarus.
Kunitz. When the Dead Arise.
Robinson. Lazarus.
Rossetti. Son, Remember.
Sexton. Jesus Summons Forth.
Tennyson. When Lazarus left his charnel-cave.
Wright, James. Come Forth.

Laziness
Ammons. Likely Story.
Burns. Weary Pund o' Tow, The.
Campion. Lighten, heavy hart, thy spright.
Chaucer. Cook's Tale, The.
Clough. He sate, no stiller stands a rock.
Dobyns. Sloth.
Dunbar. In the Morning.
Gardner. One Sunday in 1966.
Herrick. Ass[e], The.
Long and Lazy [or Lazie].
Hughes, Langston. Kid Sleepy.
Lawrence. Bathing Resort.
Nash. Introspective Reflection.
Let's Not Climb the Washington Monument Tonight.
Where There's a Will, There's Velleity.
Who Called That Robin a Piccolo Player?
Roethke. Poetaster.
Silverstein. Lazy Jane.
Smith, Stevie. From the French (1).
Lament of a Slug-a-Bed's Wife.
Thomson. Castle of Indolence, The.

Williams, William Carlos. Ode to Laziness.
Portrait of a Woman in Bed.
Yeats. Chambermaid's Second Song, The.

Leadership
Atwood. Our leader / is a man of water.
Auden. Sext.
Byron. Sonnet to the Prince Regent.
Cohen. Captain, The.
Cummings. To William F. Bradbury.
Dryden. All human[e] things are subject to decay.
Eberhart. Way Out, A.
Eliot. Coriolan.
Emerson. Go boldly forth, and feast on being's banquet.
Hardy. Murmurs in the Gloom.
Herrick. Examples, or Like Prince, Like People.
Like Pattern, Like People.
Society.
Hewitt. Crossing, The.
Hoffman. Blood.
Jonson. To Sir Horace Vere.
To Sir Thomas Roe.
To the Same [Sir Thomas Roe].
To True Soldiers.
To William, Earl[e] of Pembroke.
Kipling. Akbar's Bridge.
Bells and Queen Victoria, The.
Norman and Saxon.
One Viceroy Resigns.
Servant When He Reigneth, A.
Together.
Lindsay. Abraham Lincoln Walks at Midnight.
Meredith. Ambition.
Day is going, now 'tis noon, The.
Hawarden.
She shall rise worthier of her prototype.
To J.M.
To Lord Palmerston.
To weld the nation in a name of dread.
Merton. Urn with a Political Profile.
Olson. Leader, The.
Pack. Dead King, The.
Wolf Pack, The.
Rolfe. Faces No Longer White.
1949 (After Reading a News Item).
Sandburg. From what graveyards and sepulchers they come.
In the folded and quiet yesterdays.
Is There Any Easy Road to Freedom?
LINCOLN? / He was a mystery in smoke and flags.
People learn, unlearn, learn, The.
Sacred legion of the justborn, The.
Who shall speak for the people?
Snodgrass. Manet: "The Execution of the Emperor Maximilian."
Stevenson. Take not my hand as mine alone.
Warren. There once, on that goat island, I.
Whitman. Not the Pilot.
Thought ("Of obedience, faith, adhesiveness").
Wordsworth. Emperors and Kings, How Oft Have Temples Rung.

Leander. *see* **Hero and Leander.**

Lear, Edward
Auden. Edward Lear.
Tennyson. To E.L., on His Travels in Greece.

Lear, King. *see* **King Lear.**

Learning
Atwood. You Begin.
Beckett. Gnome.
Berry. And that is our story.
Boy must learn the man, The.
I worked by will then, he.
"Carroll, Lewis." Three Children.
Coleridge. Lines to Thomas Poole.
Donne. Obscure Writer, An.
Upon Mr. Thomas Coryat's Crudities.
Dunn. Eggs.
Emerson. His learning truly lifted Hafiz to Heaven.
Gardner. Zei Gesund.
Glück. Illuminations.
Graves. Plea to Boys and Girls, A.
Hartley. Horowitz.
Herrick. Precepts.

Hewitt. Farmer's Second Son, The.
I Go to School.
Who Was C.B. Fry?
Jarrell. Randall Jarrell, Office Hours 10-11.
Jonson. Epigram on Sir Edward Coke, when He Was Lord Chief Justice of England, An.
To the Same [Sir Henry Goodyere].
Kinnell. Schoolhouse, The.
Koch. Some General Instructions.
Lorde. As I Grew Up Again.
Black Mother Woman.
Lovelace. Because with bought books, Sir, your study's fraught.
To My Truely Valiant, Learned Friend, Who in His Booke Resolv'd the Art Gladiatory into the Mathematick's.
To the Genius of Mr. John Hall.
Meredith. My Theme: Continued.
Merton. Duke Hwan and the Wheelwright.
Keng's Disciple.
Learning of many things does not teach understanding, or else it would have taught Hesiod and Pythagoras, The.
My birthday was in March, when the weather was furious.
To a Novice ("Avoid three kinds of Master").
Useless, The.
Miller. If you can't make a joke.
Oliver. Learning About the Indians.
Starfish.
Olson. Of Lady, of Beauty, of Stream.
Rolfe. Testament to a Flowering Race.
Rossetti. 1 and 1 are 2— / That's for me and you.
Sandburg. Let Them Ask Your Pardon.
People learn, unlearn, learn, The.
People with Proud Chins.
We Must Be Polite.
What the people learn out of lifting and hauling and waiting and losing.
Shelley. To a Skylark.
Simic. Lesson, The.
Smart. Learning.
Snyder. For Example.
June.
Sorrentino. Razzmatazz.
Stafford. Living on the Plains.
Things I Learned Last Week.
Stevenson. Early in the morning I hear on your piano.
Tomlinson. Instead of an Essay.
Le Musée Imaginaire.
Waldman. Some of the Things I See for You.
Whitman. Lessons.
Whittier. Library, The.
Spiritual Manifestation, A.
Wilbur. Mechanist, The.
Williams, Charles Kenneth. First Desires.
Spirit the Triumph, The.
Williams, Miller. Before.
Wordsworth. Oxford, May 30, 1820 ("Ye sacred Nurseries of blooming Youth!").
Yeats. Another Song of a Fool.
Young. Teaching.

Leaves
Ammons. Poem: "In a high wind the."
Berg. Sticks.
Berry. October 10.
Bishop. Quai d'Orléans.
Carruth. Against the wall he / gropes like ivy, you pray, I.
Coarse leaf, alder leaf.
Excellence requires / leaf-rakers to sweep one spot.
I Could Take.
Leaf from Mr. Dyer's Woods, A.
Leaves, The.
Stronger than destiny is pain.
Creeley. Fall.
Cummings. !blac / k / agains / t.
D-re-A-mi-N-gl-Y / leaves / (sEe)
L(a / le / af / fa / ll / s).
Dickey, James. Vessels.
Dickinson. I remember the leaves were falling.
Dunbar. Chase, The.
Dunn. In the 20th Century.
Frost. Gathering Leaves.

In Hardwood Groves.
Leaf-Treader, A.
Leaves Compared with Flowers.
Misgiving.
Hall. Days, The.
Kicking the Leaves.
Stone Walls.
Hardy. June Leaves and Autumn.
Master and the Leaves, The.
Hartley. Geometric Death.
Hesketh. Autumn at Whitewell.
So Little It Can Take.
Hewitt. For a September Afternoon of Unexpected Brightness.
Hopkins. Silver scarce-call-silver gloss, A.
Housman. When green buds hang in the elm like dust.
Lawrence. Difference, The.
Fallen Leaves.
Leaves of Grass, Flowers of Grass.
Liddy. Poem for My Sister Nora, at the Reading.
MacLeish. Old Men in the Leaf Smoke, The.
Mahon. Leaves.
Nathan. Like Us, Maybe.
Nemerov. Burning the Leaves.
Threshold.
Neruda. What are you hiding under your hump?
O'Hara. Les Étiquettes Jaunes.
Pastoral Dialogue, A.
Paley. For George (I).
Raine. Falling Leaves.
Golden Leaf, The.
Leaf, The.
Robinson. Pity of the Leaves, The.
Sandburg. Auburn.
Bird Talk.
Cornucopia.
Little Sketch.
October Paint.
Sleep Impression.
Year, The.
Schuyler. Autumn Leaves.
8/12/70.
October.
We Are Leaves.
Sexton. Buttered Greens.
Leaves That Talk.
Stuart. Leaf Eater, The.
Tomlinson. Autumn Piece.
Elemental.
Warren. Deciduous Spring.
Leaf, The.
Wilbur. Alatus.
March.
October Maples, Portland.
Then.
Two Quatrains for First Frost.
Under a Tree.
Williams, William Carlos. Avenue of Poplars, The.
Confidence, A.
Disputants, The.
Lines: "Leaves are greygreen."
Offering.
Quietness.
Soughing Wind, The.
To Be Closely Written on a Small Piece of Paper Which Folded into a Tight Lozenge Will Fit Any Girl's Locket.
Wordsworth. Kitten and [the] Falling Leaves, The.
Whirl-blast from behind the hill, A.
Wright, James. To the August Fallen.
Zukofsky. Green leaf that will outlast the winter.
March First.
Prop. LXI.
Train-Signal.
See also **Autumn.**

Lebanon and Lebanese
Carruth. Sonnet: "To the aged, trembling, illiterate woman yesterday."
Merton. Lubnan.

Leda
Bogan. Stanza: "No longer burn the hands that seized."
Doolittle. Leda.
Graves. Leda.
Lawrence. Leda.
MacLeish. Eve's Child.
Meinke. Helen.
Merton. Zeus Is Dead.
Nash. Leda's Fortunate Gaffe.
Van Duyn. Leda.
Leda Reconsidered.
Yeats. Leda and the Swan.

Ledwidge, Francis
Heaney. In Memoriam Francis Ledwidge.

Lee, Robert Edward
Fletcher. Passing of the South, The.
Sandburg. Hammers Pounding.

Legionnaires' Disease
"Dylan." Legionnaire's Disease.

Legree, Simon
Lindsay. Simon Legree—A Negro Sermon.

Legs
Cummings. My girl's tall with hard long eyes.
Graves. Legs, The.
Herrick. Her Legs.
To Dianeme ("Show me thy feet; show me thy legs, thy thighs").
Olson. Lalage!
Sexton. Barefoot.
Silverstein. Dancing Pants.
Updike. Rockettes, The.
Williams, William Carlos. Cold Night, The.
Portrait of a Lady.

Leicester, Robert Dudley, Earl of
Ralegh. Epitaph on the Earl of Leicester [*or* Leceister].

Leisure
Berry. He Takes His Time.
Carroll, Jim. How Relaxed.
"Carroll, Lewis." Dedication: "All in the golden afternoon."
Clark. Thought is surrounded by a halo.
Dove. One Volume Missing.
Dunbar. Lazy Day, A.
Ginsberg. Bricklayer's Lunch Hour, The.
Hardy. Farmer Dunman's Funeral.
Hopkins. Penmaen Pool.
Liddy. Last Light in Clare's Mind.
Woodenbridge Golf Club.
Lowry. Glory of the Sea, The.
Merton. Let us cool your bitter sweet charm with incense and verse.
Rossetti. Pastime.
Pocket handkerchief to hem, A.
Reflection.
Song of Flight, A.
Swift and sure the swallow.
Snyder. Walk, A.
Sorrentino. Lecture on Time and Space, The.
Stevens. Ordinary Women, The.

Lemmings
Haines. Lemmings, The.

Lemons
Fox. Lemons, Limes.
Walcott. Sunday Lemons.
Young. Lemons, Lemons.

Lenin, Vladimir Ilyich
Hewitt. Moscow Moment.
"MacDiarmid." Skeleton of the Future, The.
MacLeish. Background with Revolutionaries.
Muldoon. Salvador.
Rukeyser. Motive of All of It, The.

Leningrad, Russia. *see* **Saint Petersburg** [*formerly* **Leningrad**], **Russia.**

Lennon, John
Beatles. Ballad of John and Yoko, The.
Ferlinghetti. John Lennon in the Porto Santo Stefano.

Lent
Herbert. Lent.
Herrick. Fast, or Lent, The.
To Keep a True Lent.
Upon Bungie.
Hoffman. Mi-Carême.

Merton. Lent.
Rossetti. Lent.
 Mid-Lent.
 Passiontide.
Schuyler. Blossoming Oakwood.
Smart. Ash Wednesday. First Day of Lent.

Lentils
Silverstein. Sky Seasoning.

Leonardo da Vinci
Ciardi. Conversation with Leonardo, A.
Eberhart. Cancer Cells, The.
Garrigue. For an Orchard Tree.
Moore. Expedient, An—Leonardo da
 Vinci's—and a Query.
 Leonardo Da Vinci's.
Shelley. On the Medusa of Leonardo da Vinci
 in the Florentine Gallery.
Waldman. Leonardo.
Wordsworth. Last Supper, by Leonardo da
 Vinci, in the Refectory of the Convent of
 Maria della Grazia—Milan, The.

Leopards
Dickinson. Civilization—spurns—the Leopard!
 With thee—in the Desert.
Dunn. Snow Leopard, The.
Hesketh. Snow Leopard.
Jarrell. Snow-Leopard, The.
St. John. Woman and Leopard.

Leopold III, King of the Belgians
Berryman. Moon and the Night and the Men,
 The.

Leprechauns
Millay. Singing-Woman from the Wood's
 Edge, The.

Leprosy and Lepers
Herrick. To Women, to Hide Their Teeth, if
 They Be Rotten or Rusty.
Kipling. Gehazi.
Merton. Ointment, The.
 Rites for the Extrusion of a Leper.
Prince. Les Congés du Lépreux.
Rossetti. Go In Peace.
Swinburne. Leper, The.

Lesbians. see Homosexuality and Homosexuals.

Lesbos, Greece
Liddy. Lesbos.
Millay. Evening on Lesbos.
Rexroth. When We with Sappho.

Lethargy
Duncan. Dreamers, The.
Joseph. Getting Up in Winter.
Lowry. Heat Wave.
Rolfe. Asbestos.

Letter Carriers. see Mail and Mailmen.

Letters
Atwood. Postcard.
Auden. Letter, The.
 Letter, The.
Beatles. P.S. I Love You.
Berg. Unfinished Double Sonnet.
 Wanting to Be Heavier.
Berry. To search for what belongs where it is.
Berryman. Infallible symbolist!—Tanker
 driven ashore.
 Winter-Piece to a Friend Away, A.
Bishop. Letter to N. Y.
Bogan. Packet of Letters.
Bradstreet. Letter to Her Husband, Absent
 upon Public[k] Employment, A.
 In Thankful Acknowledgement for the Letters
 I Received from My Husband Out Of
 England.
Browning, Elizabeth Barrett. Sonnet: "My
 letters! All dead paper, mute and white."
Browning, Robert. To Miss Unger.
Bukowski. Almost Made Up Poem, An.
 Artists.
 Love.
 Note to the Boys in the Back Room, A.
Carew. Elegy on the La: Pen: Sent to My
 Mistress Out of France, An.
 My Mistress Commanding Me to Return Her
 Letters.
"Carroll, Lewis." Lang Coortin', The.
 Miss Jones.

Cohen. Famous Blue Raincoat.
 Your Death.
Cooper. Letters.
 Little Vesper, A.
Cowper. On a Letter of Miss Fanshawe.
Crane. My Grandmother's Love Letters.
Creeley. Interview, The.
 Invoice, The.
 Names.
Cummings. "April" / this letter's dated.
 Ecco a letter starting "dearest we."
 Lady you have written me a letter.
 Mr. smith / is reading / his letter.
Dickinson. Going—to—Her!
 Going to Him! Happy letter!
 In Ebon Box, when years have flown.
 Interview is acres.
 Letter always seemed to me, A.
 Letter is a joy of Earth, A.
 This is but a fragment.
 Way I read a Letter's—this, The.
 What a Hazard a Letter is!
Dobyns. Letter Beginning with the First Line
 of Your Letter.
Donne. H. W. in Hibernia Belligeranti.
 Letter Written by Sir H. G. and J. D. alternis
 vicibus, A.
 To Mr. T. W. ("Pregnant again with th' old
 twins hope, and fear").
 To Mrs. M. H.
 To the Countess of Bedford ("To have written
 then, when you writ, seemed to me").
Dunbar. Love Letter, A.
Dunn. Bringing It Down.
Emerson. Letters.
 Letters ("My tongue is prone to lose the
 way").
Gallagher. Under Stars.
Graves. H.
 Half-Finished Letter, The.
 Love and Night.
 Love Letter, The.
 Song: Of Course.
 Strayed Message, The.
Gunn. Invitation, An.
Hall. Eleanor's Letters.
Hardy. Letter's Triumph, The.
 Love-Letters, The.
 Read by Moonlight.
 Sun on the Letter, The.
 Thing Unplanned, The.
 Torn Letter, The.
 Wife in London, A.
Hayden. Letter.
Hewitt. First Letters.
Hopkins. Complaint, A.
Hughes, Langston. Little Old Letter.
 Personal.
Jarrell. Burning the Letters.
Kinnell. Correspondence School Instructor
 Says Goodbye to His Poetry Students, The.
Koch. Railway Stationery, The.
 To Marina.
Kooser. Letter From Aunt Belle, A.
Kunitz. Night Letter.
Larkin. At Thirty-One, When Some Are Rich.
Lawrence. Correspondence in After Years.
 No News.
Levertov. Sparks.
Liddy. Miles III.
 Third Letter to Jimin in Manchuria.
Lorde. Martha.
 Trip on the Staten Island Ferry, A.
Lovelace. Lines Prefixed to John Davies'
 Translation of Voiture's Letters, 1657.
Lowry. How overjoyed I am to get your letter.
 I am very small.
 I bet you don't know who I am.
 Morning bird is bathing, The.
 Oh and / Who is it unforlorn.
McAuley. Questions for my Grandfather.
Marlowe. 1.11: Napen alloquitur, ut paratas
 tabellas ad Corinnam perferat.
Meinke. Dear Reader.
Meredith. Dear, my friend & honour'd
 madam! of hard facts I'm not a hoarder.
 Fair Bedfellow, The.

Grandfather Bridgeman.
 I think she sleeps: it must be sleep, when low.
 She scarce has a word for Papa.
 Thou pirate nested over Alde!
Merrill. Friend of the Fourth Decade, The.
Morgan. Letter, The.
Muldoon. Thrush.
Nash. What's in a Name? Some Letter I
 Always Forget.
Nathan. Letter.
O'Hara. Postcard from John Ashbery, A.
Oliver. Letter from Home, A.
Owen. Letter, The.
Piercy. Letter to be Disguised as a Gas Bill.
 Wrote two letters while rain.
Plath. Burning the Letters.
Pope. Verses Occasioned by an & c. at the
 End of Mr. D'Urfy's Name in the Title to
 One of His Plays.
Prince. Letter.
Ransom. Parting, without a Sequel.
Rich. On Edges.
 Postcard.
 Your Letter.
Rolfe. Glory Set, The.
 Letter for One in Russia.
Rossetti. Eight o'clock; / The postman's
 knock!
 Lines to My Grandfather.
 Otto ore suonano: / Picchia il postino!
Sandburg. Bilbea.
 One Parting.
 Sarah's Letter to Peter.
Schuyler. Ilford Rose Book.
 Stone Knife, A.
 Voyage Autour de Mes Cartes Postales.
Sexton. Letter Written During a January
 Northeaster.
 Letter Written on a Ferry While Crossing
 Long Island Sound.
 Some Foreign Letters.
Silverstein. Love.
Smart. Epistle to Dr. Nares.
Smith, Stevie. Emily Writes Such a Good
 Letter.
 Jungle Husband, The.
Sorrentino. From the Journal of Immutable
 Truths.
 Oranges Returned, The.
Stevenson. To Charles Baxter.
Stuart. Sunburst.
Tomlinson. Letter from Costa Brava.
 Letters from Amherst.
Van Duyn. Letters from a Father.
 Relative and an Absolute, A.
Wakoski. Write.
Walcott. Letter from Brooklyn, A.
Waldman. De Carlo Lots, The.
Walker. What the Finger Writes.
Whitman. Come Up from the Fields Father.
Wilbur. Part of a Letter.
Williams, Miller. La Ultima Carta: A Young
 Wife Writes to Her Husband in the
 Mountains.
Wordsworth. Upon Perusing the "Epistle [To
 Sir George Howland Beaumont"] Thirty
 Years after Its Composition.
Yau. Dear . . .
 Postcards are fragments of an encyclopedia;
 and typical of one an- / nouncing.
 Postcards from Nebraska.
See also **Mail and Mailmen.**

Lettuce
Piercy. Love of Lettuce, The.

Leukemia
Carroll, Jim. Cough Syrup.

Leven River, Scotland
Burns. Campbells Are Comin, The.

Levet, Robert
Johnson. On the Death of Dr [*or* Mr] Robert
 Levet [a Practiser in Physic].

Lexington and Concord, Battles of (1775)
Whittier. Lexington.

Li Po
Berg. For the Ghost of Li Po.
Liddy. Third Letter to Jimin in Manchuria.

MacLeish. Poet's Laughter.
Williams, William Carlos. To Li Po.
Wright, Charles. Portrait of the Artist with Li Po.
Liars. *see* **Lies and Lying.**
Liberace
Wakoski. Why My Mother Likes Liberace.
Liberalism and Liberals
Angelou. On Working White Liberals.
Betjeman. Old Liberals, The.
Browning, Robert. Lost Leader, The.
  Why I Am a Liberal.
"Dylan." You tell me about politics.
Patchen. Letter to the Liberals, A.
Tate. Eclogue of the Liberal and the Poet.
Liberty. *see* **Freedom.**
Liberty, Statue of
Cummings. Woman / of bronze / unhappy, A.
Gunn. Iron Landscapes (and the Statue of Liberty).
Lowry. Elsinore was the battlements of Oaxaca.
Whittier. Bartholdi Statue, The.
Wilbur. On Freedom's Ground.
Libraries and Librarians
Cowper. Ode to Rouse.
  On Mrs. Montagu's Feather-Hangings.
Davie. Grace in the Fore Street.
Eberhart. Reading Room, The New York Public Library.
Hartley. Daily Library Visitor.
Hewitt. Reading.
  Survival.
Jarrell. Carnegie Library, Juvenile Division, The.
  Children Selecting Books in a Library.
  Girl in a Library, A.
Jonson. Execration upon Vulcan, An.
Larkin. New Eyes Each Year.
Lewis. *Mine Host.*
Lowry. Search, The.
MacNeice. British Museum Reading Room, The.
Miller. On some night a train is going past the library.
Milton. To John Rouse.
Schwartz. Greatest Thing in North America, The.
Tomlinson. Portrait of the Artist II.
Whittier. Library, The.
Williams, Charles Kenneth. Critic, The.
Lice
Burns. To a Louse [On Seeing One on a Lady's Bonnet at Church].
Glück. Chicago Train, The.
Williams, William Carlos. Poor, The.
Lies and Lying
Angelou. How I Can Lie to You.
Atwood. We are hard on each other.
Berryman. To Bhain Campbell.
  Troubling are masks... the faces of friends, my face.
  You should be gone in winter, that Nature mourn.
Browning, Elizabeth Barrett. Garibaldi.
Browning, Robert. Confessional, The.
Bukowski. Old Gang, The.
Campion. Elegye, An: "Constant to none, but ever false to me."
  Epigramme: "All wonders Barnzy speakes, all grosely faind."
  Faine would I my love disclose.
  In Barnum.
  My Love Hath Vowd.
Catullus. Carmen 70: "Lesbia says she'ld rather marry me."
Chaucer. Summoner's Prologue, The.
Ciardi. Knothole in Spent Time, A.
Clough. Yes, I have lied, and so must walk my way.
Coleridge. Alice Du Clos.
Creeley. Bed, The.
  Mind's Heart.
  Song: "Grit / of things, The."
Cullen. To an Unknown Poet.
Cummings. This evangelist / buttons with his big gollywog voice.

Donne. Mercurius Gallo-Belgicus.
Doolittle. Lovers may come and go.
Dove. Boast, The.
Dunn. In a Dream of Horses.
"Dylan." Most Likely You Go Your Way (and I'll Go Mine).
  Positively 4th Street.
Eberhart. Critic With His Pained Eye, The.
  Hill Dream of Youth, Thirty Years Later.
Emerson. This world is tedious.
  Who royally bedded.
Glück. From the Japanese.
  Memo from the Cave.
Graves. Iron Palace.
  Prepared Statement, The.
  Word, The.
Hall. Grown-Ups, The.
Hardy. Her Dilemma.
Herrick. To Sapho ("Thou saist thou lov'st me Sapho; I say no").
  Upon Teage.
Jeffers. Faith.
  Ink-Sack.
Kipling. Dead Statesman, A.
  Pagett, M. P.
  There is pleasure in the wet, wet clay.
Lawrence. Drawing-Room.
  Emotional Lies.
  I Am in a Novel.
  Laughter.
  Lies.
  Lies About Love.
  Poison.
Lovelace. Female Inconstancy.
Lowry. Comfort.
  Elsinore was the battlements of Oaxaca.
  They will be ashamed after they are dead.
MacLeish. Ballad of the Corn-Cob and the Lie, The.
Nash. Golly, How Truth Will Out.
Oppen. I am the father of no country.
Piercy. Man can lie to himself, A.
  People ask questions.
Pope. To the Earl of Burlington Asking Who Writ the Libels against Him.
Psalms. Psalm 52: "Why boastest thou thyself in mischief.."
Ralegh. I am that Dido which thou here do'st see.
  Lie, The.
Rich. Cartographies of Silence.
  Our Whole Life.
Robinson. Lisette and Eileen.
  Uncle Ananias.
Rukeyser. One Month.
  They rule out of our justice and our despair.
Sandburg. Accordingly, they commenced by an insidious.
  Liars, The.
  Remember the chameleon. He was a well-behaved chameleon.
Schuyler. On the Dresser.
Shakespeare. Sonnet 138: "When my love swears [or sweares] that she is made of truth."
Silverstein. Hat.
  Magical Eraser.
  Oh Have You Heard.
  Sick.
  Who.
Suckling. Perjury Excused.
Wilbur. Lying.
Wordsworth. In Allusion to Various Recent Histories and Notices of the French Revolution.
  In Allusion to Various Recent Histories and Notices of the French Revolution, Concluded.
Zukofsky. Newly say dickered my love air my own would marry me all.
Life
Ammons. Coming To.
Angelou. Call Letters: Mrs. V.B.
  Lesson, The.
  Life Doesn't Frighten Me.
Ashbery. Two Scenes.
Auden. Mill, The.
  Precious Five.

Beckett. D'où / la voix qui dit.
  Hors crâne seul dedans.
  Je suis ce cours de sable qui glisse.
  My way is in the sand flowing.
  Que ferais-je sans ce monde sans visage sans questions.
  Trouble with tragedy is the fuss it makes, The.
  What would I do without this world faceless incurious.
Berrigan. In the 51st State.
  Last Poem.
  Red Shift.
  Tambourine Life.
Berry. Any man's death could end the story.
  At last, completed in his rest.
  Cold Pane, The.
  Envoy: "Love, all day there has been at the edge of my mind."
  Farmer among the Tombs, The.
  Fern, The.
  Forty Years.
  He Has Lived through Another Night.
  I give you what is unbounded, passing from dark to dark.
  May Song.
  My life's wave is at its crest.
  Our Children, Coming of Age.
  Poem of Thanks, A.
  Praise.
  Seeds, The.
  Song (4).
  Song Sparrow Singing in the Fall, A.
  Song (3).
  Sycamore, The.
  To Think of the Life of a Man.
Berryman. Sensible, coarse, and moral; in decent brown.
Bly. November Day at McClure's Beach.
  Watcher, The.
Bradstreet. Of the Four Ages of Man.
Brooks. Sadie and Maud.
  Vacant Lot, The.
Browning, Elizabeth Barrett. Felicia Hemans.
  Human Life's Mystery.
  Life.
  Love.
  Prospect, The.
  Rhapsody of Life's Progress, A.
  Sonnet: "Is it indeed so? If I lay here dead."
  Sonnet: "When our two souls stand up erect and strong."
  Sounds.
Browning, Robert. Master Hugues of Saxe-Gotha.
  Pisgah-Sights. I.
  Pisgah-Sights. II.
  Rabbi Ben Ezra.
  Reverie.
Bukowski. 86'd.
  Love Poem, A.
  One for the Shoeshine Man.
  Overhead Mirrors.
  Poem to a Most Affectionate Lady.
  Windy Night.
  Word on the Quick and Modern Poem-Makers, A.
Burns. Epistle to a Young Friend.
  Here's, a bottle and an honest friend.
  Lazy Mist, The.
  Poem on Life.
  Song: "Contented wi' little, and cantie wi' mair."
  Song: "My father was a farmer upon the Carrick border O."
  Twa Dogs, The.
Byron. Egotism. A Letter to J.T. Becher.
  If That High World.
  Spell Is Broke, the Charm is Flown, The.
  Thoughts for a Speech of Lucifer, in the Tragedy of "Cain."
Carroll, Jim. Chelsea May.
  Coda.
  Distances, The.
  Invisible Sleep.
  Poem: "Tea is boiling, The."
"Carroll, Lewis." Acrostic: Is all our Life, then, but a dream.

Acrostic: Maiden, though thy heart may quail.
Third Voice, The.
Three Sunsets.
To My Child-Friend.
Valley of the Shadow of Death, The.
Carruth. Contra Mortem.
For your love given.
He: Life is an old / casino in the park. I.
House out to sea.
Phantasmagoria, The.
Wreck of the Circus Train, The.
Ceravolo. Cross Fire.
Don't Break It.
Ciardi. Island Galaxy, An.
Lung Fish, The.
Memo: Preliminary Draft of a Prayer to God the Father.
Thoughts on Looking into a Thicket.
Clark. Coral.
Eternity.
Human Life.
1968.
Slow Life.
Clough. Enough, small Room,—though all too true.
Here have I been these one and twenty years.
O stream, descending to the sea.
To spend unsolaced years of pain.
Coleridge. Epitaph: "Stop, Christian passer-by!—Stop, child of God."
Life.
On a Cataract.
Psyche.
Suicide's Argument, The.
What Is Life?
Wish, A.
Cooper. Middle Age.
Praise.
Things.
Crashaw. Epithalamium: "Come virgin Tapers of pure waxe."
Out of Catullus.
Creeley. Flowers.
People.
Cullen. I Have a Rendezvous with Life.
Life's Rendezvous.
More Than a Fool's Song.
Protest.
Self Criticism.
Cummings. Anyone lived in a pretty how town.
As freedom is a breakfastfood.
Ci-gît l Foetus(unborn to not die).
Conceive a man,should he have anything.
Death(having lost)put on his universe.
Denied night's face / have shadowless they?
Go(perpe)go / (tu)to(al).
Great advantage of being alive, The.
Honour corruption villainy holiness.
If everything happens that can't be done.
Into the strenuous briefness.
Life is more true than reason will deceive.
May my heart always be open to little.
Might these be thrushes climbing through almost(do they).
My father moved through dooms of love.
Out of midsummer's blazing most not night.
Plant Magic dust / expect hope doubt.
Precisely as unbig a why as i'm.
Rain or hail / sam done.
Sometimes i am alive because with.
Sonnet entitled how to run the world).
Suppose / Life is an old man carrying flowers on his head.
Will out of the kindness of their hearts a few philosophers tell me.
Davie. Feeders, The.
God of Details, The.
Life Encompassed.
Prolific Spell, The.
Those plaguy; needling games of ours, where stooks.
Utterings.
Where Depths Are Surfaces.
De la Mare. Anatomy.
Argument, The.
Away.

Bright Life.
Courage.
Dreams.
Haunted.
Hunter, The.
Last Chapter, The.
Life.
Music Unheard.
Silence.
Snowflake, The.
Dickinson. Advance is Life's condition.
How sweet the "Life that now is."
I am alive—I guess.
Life is so strong a vision.
Life is the finest secret.
Life we have is very great, The.
Most of our Moments.
Not all of life to live, is it.
Sweet is it as Life.
That it will never come again.
There is not so much Life as talk of Life.
To be alive—is Power.
We all have moments with the dust.
Dobyns. Body's Journey, The.
Great Doubters of History, The.
No Map.
Toting It Up.
Wind Chimes.
Dove. Charm, The.
Fish in the Stone, The.
Ike.
This Life.
Dryden. When I Consider Life.
Dunbar. By Rugged Ways.
Common Things.
If.
Life.
Long Ago.
Passage, The.
Sum, The.
Duncan. After a Long Illness.
Dunn. Privilege.
"Dylan." All Along the Watchtower.
Ballad of Hollis Brown.
Bringing It All Back Home.
Coming from the Heart (The Road Is Long).
Desire (Liner Notes).
Desolation Row.
High treachery sails / unveils.
Highway 61 Revisited.
Jim Jim / where is our party?
Last Thoughts on Woody Guthrie.
Minstrel Boy.
Open the Door, Homer.
Song to Woody.
Trouble.
Up to Me.
You tell me about politics.
Eberhart. As If You Had Never Been.
Austere Poem.
Birth and Death.
Contend with steepness, the dark air.
Dead Skunk.
Evaluation Under a Pine Tree, Lying On Pine Needles, An.
Examination of Psyche: Thoughts of Home.
Experience Evoked.
Extremity.
Flow of Thought.
Four Exposures.
Hard Structure of the World, The.
Hardening into Print.
Hardy Perennial.
Harvard Stadium.
Hill Dream of Youth, Thirty Years Later.
Human Being is a Lonely Creature, The.
Ides of March, The.
Images of death arise.
In after Time.
John Ledyard.
Key West.
Lament of a New England Mother, The.
Later or Sooner.
Listing.
Long Swing, The.
Long Term Suffering.
Looking Head On.

Loss.
Lyric Absolute, The.
Meditation, A.
Meditation Two.
New Entrepreneurial Plan.
New Hampshire, February.
Oak, The.
Only in the Dream.
Quarrel with a Cloud.
Question Mark.
Return, The.
Rumination.
Rumors of liberation. We could not believe it.
Suite in Prison.
To Kenya Tribesmen, the Turkana.
Usurper.
Ways and Means.
What Gives.
Worldly Failure.
You Think They Are Permanent But They Pass.
Young Greek, Killed In The Wars, A.
Eliot. Dry Salvages, The.
Emerson. Ah strange strange strange.
As the drop feeds its fated flower.
Blight.
But God will keep his promise yet.
Climacteric.
Cloud upon cloud / The world is seeming.
Cup of life is not so shallow, The.
Days pass over me, The.
Day's Ration, The.
Far seen the river glides below.
Go boldly forth, and feast on being's banquet.
I am: what I am.
I use the knife.
Idealism.
In thy holiday of life.
Life.
Life is great / Men are small.
Motto to "Nominalist and Realist."
Nature.
O What have I to do.
On that night the poet went.
To J. W.
What never was no, & still will be.
Wo is me woe's me when I think.
Fenton. Skip, The.
Ferlinghetti. Autobiography.
Deep Chess.
Endless Life.
Heap of Broken Images, A.
Making Love in Poetry.
River Still To Be Found, A.
Sea Is Calm Tonight, The.
Sueño Real.
Uses of Poetry.
Voix Glauque.
We squat upon the beach of love.
World is a beautiful place, The.
Fisher. Home Pianist's Companion, The.
Toyland.
Fletcher. Invocation to Evening.
My stiff-spread arms / Break into sudden gesture.
On the Beach.
Truth of the Matter, The.
Ford. Even when the heart of the world is found.
In the maze of the.
Peaks of pleasure, peaks.
Will of the weed to startle, The.
Fox. Mother Was a Good.
Frost. On the Heart's Beginning to Cloud the Mind.
Question, A.
Road Not Taken, The.
Gallagher. Coats, The.
Gardner. At the Zoo.
Collage of Echoes.
Jean Sans Terre The Chest of Drawers.
Minotaur, The.
Panic Vine, The.
Gildner. 8/22/38–8/22/68.
In the Beginning.
Life & Death in Skokie.
Ginsberg. Four Haiku.

Gospel Noble Truths.
Old Pond.
Stool Pigeon Blues.
Graves. To Evoke Posterity.
Gunn. Confessions of the Life Artist.
Incident on a Journey.
Legal Reform.
Memoirs of the World.
Rastignac at 45.
Taylor Street.
Hacker. Nights of 1962: The River Merchant's Wife.
Haines. Alive in the World.
Stones.
What is Life?
Hall. Carlotta's Confession.
Mr. Wakeville on Interstate 90.
Raisin, The.
Hardy. Before Life and After.
Chimes Play "Life's a Bumper!"The.
Life Laughs Onward.
Masked Face, The.
Necessitarian's Epitaph, A.
On One Who Lived and Died Where He Was Born.
Placid Man's Epitaph, A.
Thoughts from Sophocles.
To Life.
What's There to Tell?
Hartley. Boston Common—Long Time Ago.
Do nothing to injure the living.
Furnished Rooms.
Like a lustrous bird threading the maze.
Heaney. From the Canton of Expectation.
Hemingway. Advice to a Son.
Herbert. Life.
Water-Course, The.
Herrick. Crosse and Pile.
Four[e] Things Make Us Happy Here.
Good Death, A.
Life Is the Body's [or Bodies] Light.
Readinesse.
To His Closet-Gods.
Upon Prickles.
Hesketh. Academic.
Dead Blackbird.
Edward Thomas.
First Day, The.
How to Do It.
I Am.
I Give Death to a Son.
Journey.
Leave Train, The.
Mill Clock, The.
Moving Staircase.
Preparing to Leave.
Shaping Spirit, The.
Survival.
Traitor.
Vine, The.
Walking Back.
What Is God?
Hewitt. Belfastman, The.
Coasters, The.
Conacre.
Defeat.
End of the World, The.
Epitaph to a Man Not Dead.
Glenarriffe and Parkmore.
Hand over Hand.
Heart of Joy, The.
Homestead.
Landscape.
Mid-April.
Nourish Your Heart.
November Wood.
October-Born.
On Colinward: The Scattering.
Periodicity.
Poem: "Consider Wordsworth in his withered age."
Pro Tanto Quid Retribuamas.
Sheep Skull, The.
Song for May Day.
Townland of Peace.
Hill. Scenes with Harlequins.
Hoffman. Folk Tale.

Keys.
Special Train, A.
Stone, A.
Housman. Be still, my soul, be still; the arms you bear are brittle.
Chestnut casts his flambeaux, and the flowers, The.
First of May, The.
From far, from eve and morning.
Immortal Part, The.
Terence, This Is Stupid Stuff.
Westward on the high-hilled plains.
Hughes, Langston. Advice.
Consider Me.
Life Is Fine.
Mother to Son.
Still Here.
Hughes, Ted. Crueller than owl or eagle.
Jarrell. Country Life, A.
Rabbit hurries to the brim of its wood, The.
Terms.
Utopian Journey, A.
Well Water.
What's the Riddle.
Jeffers. Animals.
Ante Mortem.
Praise Life.
Treasure, The.
Unformed volcanic earth, a female thing, The.
Jonson. To William Roe ("When Nature bids us leave to live, 'tis late").
Keats. Human Seasons, The.
Ode to a Nightingale.
Kinnell. Milk Bottle, The.
Kipling. Long Trail, The.
Knight. My Life, the Quality of Which.
Kooser. Advice.
Kunitz. Bottom of the Glass, The.
Crystal Cage, The.
Layers, The.
To be old and to be young.
Larkin. After-Dinner Remarks.
Afternoons.
And the Wave Sings Because It Is Moving.
Daily Things We Do, The.
Days.
Essential Beauty.
Livings.
Negative Indicative.
Nothing to Be Said.
Ultimatum.
Under a Splendid Chestnut Tree.
Lawrence. All That We Have Is Life.
Battle of Life.
Being Alive.
Breath of Life, The.
Breath of Life, The.
Corot.
Doors.
Dreams Old and Nascent.
Fatality.
Full Life.
Kissing and Horrid Strife.
Life and the Human Consciousness.
Living, A.
Non-Existence.
On the Road.
Real Democracy.
Shades.
So Let Me Live.
Wandering Cosmos, The.
We Are Transmitters.
Levertov. Living.
Levine. Ashes.
Ask the Roses.
Blasting from Heaven.
Clouds.
Conductor of Nothing, The.
Dog Poem.
Genius.
Gift for a Believer.
Hold Me.
How Much Earth.
Let Me Begin Again.
Lights I Have Seen Before.
Look.
Noon.

On the Corner.
Rain Downriver.
Salami.
Salts and Oils.
Saturday Sweeping.
Silent in America.
Suit, The.
Sweet Will.
28.
Walk with Tom Jefferson, A.
We sat by the shore.
Words.
Lewis. Bivouac.
Journey, The.
Lying in the hospital he often thought.
Mending, with books and papers and a fan.
Raid, The.
Sacco Writes to His Son.
Song: "Oh journeyman, Oh journeyman."
Westminster Abbey.
Liddy. In the Bowling Alley.
Lindsay. Being the Dedication of a Morning.
I Want to Go Wandering.
Longfellow. Psalm of Life, A.
Lovelace. A La Bourbon.
Ode To My Lady H.
Lowell. Bosworth Field.
Lowry. And now I brood on what I think I know.
Consider what you have lost by lack of faith.
Correcting Manuscript.
Dark Path.
El Leon Sends His Greetings.
I tried to think of something good.
Is there no song that I can sing.
Men With Coats Thrashing.
Minstrel in Labrador, A.
My hate is as a wind that buffets me.
Pijijiapan.
Pines write a Chinese poem upon the white-gold sun.
Poem Influenced By John Davenport and Cervantes.
Song about Madrid, Useful Any Time.
Songs for Second Childhood.
Soul, The.
When I was young I broke all drinking records.
Wild Cherry, The.
McAuley. To His Host, Who Has Asked Him To Stay Longer.
"MacDiarmid." Ah, Joyce, this is our task.
But shairly, shairly, there maun be.
Poetry full of cynghanedd, and hair-trigger relationships, A.
Poetry that never for a moment forgets, A.
Water of Life.
Wreck of the Swan, The.
MacLeish. Rue Carpenter.
Seafarer.
What Eve Said.
MacNeice. And what when the glass breaks when the Note sounds?
Birthright.
Canto VI: "Everydayness is good; particular-dayness."
Canto XVI: "Young man cannot answer. Is this life?, The."
Canto XVII: "This was the night that specially we went down."
Habits, The.
Half Truth from Cape Town.
How, yes how? In this mirrored maze—.
Milestones. My own; small things lost in a vast.
Now That the Shapes of Mist.
Prayer before Birth.
Turn again, Whittington. Riding the surf.
McNeill. Arrow Grasses by Greenbrier River.
Mahon. Sea in Winter, The.
Marlowe. 1.15: Ad invidos, quod fama poetarum sit perennis.
Matthews. Fellow Oddballs.
Good.
Theme of the Three Caskets, The.
Untitled Poem.
Whiplash.

Meinke. Heart's Location, The.
Melville. Buddha.
Meredith. Ballad of Past Meridian, A.
Force and His Master.
Gentleness of Death, The.
Hear now the mission of good wine.
Hymn to Colour.
In the Dry.
In the Woods.
Riddle for Men, The.
Sister Hours in circles linked, The.
Sonnet: "Hateful are those false themes of
speculation."
Stave of Roving Tim, A.
Succourful daughters of men are the rosed and
starred.
Merrill. Kostas Tympakianákis.
Last Words.
Peter.
Merton. Early Legend, The.
Last evening a city man.
Other night I saw... / Who did I see?, The.
Peace, the Wasp.
Three Friends.
True Man, The.
Turtle, The.
Vine, The.
What the Deceased Had to Say about Himself.
Millay. Thou famished grave, I will not fill
thee yet.
Miller. Dusk in the Woods.
For Judy.
For Mickey.
For Richard Hopper (Dies 1978).
Gray light awakening.
In the typewriter shop.
Meditations on an Old Shoe.
Panhandle (For Annette).
Poets, The.
Riding the bus in the evening again.
Shocks Brakes (For Kurt and Yansky).
Morgan. From the being born to the dying.
Greenwich 1930's, II.
Maitreya.
Rose dawn, in smoke, over the East River, A.
Song: "Devastation / of being, The."
Tree, The.
Morrison. Cock-pit.
Guided Tour, The.
Hope Is Just.
If It's No Problem.
Nash. Any Milleniums Today, Lady?
What I Know About Life.
You and Me and P.B. Shelley.
Nathan. Third Wish, The.
Nemerov. Life, A.
Life Cycle of Common Man.
Under the Bell Jar.
Neruda. Men (IX), The.
Possessions.
Runaway Sun.
Search.
Today Isn't Everything.
Won't our life be a tunnel.
Notley. January.
Your Dailiness.
O'Hara. In Favor of One's Time.
In Memory of My Feelings.
Ode (To Joseph Lesueur) on the Arrow That
Flieth by Day.
Poem: "Instant coffee with slightly sour
cream."
Steps.
Oliver. Dogfish.
Going to Walden.
In Blackwater Woods.
Magellan.
One or Two Things.
Ponds, The.
Singapore.
Summer Day, The.
When Death Comes.
Olson. A B Cs (3—for Rimbaud).
Anniversary.
Asymptotes.
Binnacle, The.
Chain of memory is resurrection I am a vain

man, The.
Conqueror.
Distances, The.
Drum World, The.
He treads on edges of being where the drop.
In one age or other, if not in this.
K, The.
Lamp, The.
Peograms.
Story of an Olson, and Bad Thing, The.
Tomorrow.
Will To, The.
Oppen. Blood from the Stone.
But So As by Fire.
From a Phrase of Simone Weil's and Some
Words of Hegel's.
Occurrences, The.
Pro Nobis.
Pack. Bounty.
Clayfeld's Anniversary Song.
Inheritance.
Outlasting You.
Robot.
Waking to My Name.
Watchers.
Patchen. And I, Too, Am Something of a
Stranger Here, My Friend.
But of Life?
Cloth of the Tempest, The.
Continual Ministry of Thy Anger, The.
Court of First Appeal.
Cruelties of the Sportive Power.
Examination into Life and Death, An.
Fellow Soul, Sound Hunting to Thy
Immeasurable Heart.
Gautama in the Deer Park at Benares.
Investigation of Certain Interesting Questions.
It Is Big Inside a Man.
It Is for Us the Living.
Meaning of Life, The.
Message from the Assistant Chief of the Fly
People, A.
Old lean over the tombstones, The.
Progress to a View of Life.
Rites of Darkness, The.
Roses of Life, The.
There are no losses.
Time to Believe!, A.
Tribes of Rakala, The.
Under the green ledge.
Piercy. Right Thinking Man.
Seven of Pentacles, The.
Plath. Appearance, An.
Channel Crossing.
Life, A.
Mystic.
Pope. Behold the child, by Nature's kindly
law.
Epistle I, to Sir Richard Temple, Lord
Cobham.
Life's Poor Play.
Raine. And that was all his life.
Ralegh. On the Life of Man.
Ransom. Here Lies a Lady. A version
Here Lies a Lady. B version
"Reed." Sweet Jane.
Rich. Atlas of the Difficult World, An.
8/8/68: i.
Burning Oneself Out.
Can it be growing colder when I begin.
Last Song.
Living Memory.
Tattered Kaddish.
Transcendental Etude.
Robinson. Ballade by the Fire.
Llewellyn and the Tree.
Man against the Sky, The.
Octaves.
We shriek to live, but no man ever lives.
Roethke. Decision, The.
Manifestation, The.
Orders for the Day.
Verse with Allusions.
Walk in Late Summer, A.
Rolfe. Biography.
Somebody and Somebody Else and You.
Rossetti. All Flesh Is Grass.

All heaven is blazing yet / With the meridian
sun.
Along the highroad the way is too long.
Annie.
Answer, An.
Autumn.
Awake, Thou That Sleepest.
Ballad of Boding, A.
Christmas Carol, for My Godchildren, A.
Cobwebs.
Days of Vanity.
Dead Bride, The.
Dear Angels and dear disembodied Saints.
Eleventh Hour, The.
End Is Not Yet, The.
February 14. 1883.
From the Antique.
Goal in sihgt! Look up and sing, / Set faces
full against the light, The.
Half Dead.
Half Moon Shows a Face of Plaintive
Sweetness, The.
Have Patience.
Heaviness May Endure for a Night, But Joy
Cometh in the Morning.
I love you and you know it—this at least.
I said within myself: I am a fool.
I See That All Things Come to an End.
If love is not worth loving, then life is not
worth living.
If not with hope of life, / Begin with fear of
death.
"Immurata" Sister, An.
In resurrection is it awfuller.
Last Complaint, The.
Laughing Life cries at the feast.
Lent.
Life and Death.
Life that was born today / Must make no stay.
Life's Parallels, A.
Long Looked For.
Looking back along life's trodden way.
Man's life is but a working day / Whose tasks
are set aright.
Methinks the ills of life I fain would shun.
Mirrors of Life and Death.
My Old Friends.
Next of Kin.
Night and Death.
None With Him.
O foolish Soul! to make thy count / For
languid falls and much forgiven.
O thou who tell'st me that all hope is over.
O ye, who are not dead and fit.
Of My Life.
Our Church Palms are Budding Willow Twigs.
Our life is long. Not so, wise Angels say.
Pastime.
Present and Future.
Redeeming the Time.
Saints and Angels.
Sappho.
Scarce tolerable life, which all life long.
So I began my walk of life; no stop.
Sonnets are full of love, and this my tome.
Summer.
Then I Commended Mirth.
Then They That Feared the Lord Spake Often
One to Another.
Three Stages.
Time of Waiting, The.
Today's Burden.
Unforgotten.
Uphill [or Up-Hill].
Vanity of Vanities.
Water Spirit's Song, The.
Wednesday in Holy Week.
What Good Shall My Life Do Me? ("Have
dead men")
What Good Shall My Life Do Me? ("No
hope")
What is the beginning? Love. What the
course? Love still.
Wrens and robins in the hedge.
Yawn, A.
Yes, I too could face death and never shrink.

Yet a Little While.
You who looked on passed ages as a glass.
Rukeyser. Six Canons, The.
St. John. Boathouse, The.
  Love for the Dragon.
  No Heaven.
Sandburg. Almanac.
  Always the Mob.
  Among the shapes and shadow-shapes.
  Anna Imroth.
  Anywhere and Everywhere People.
  Aprons of Silence.
  Band Concert.
  Bath.
  Between Two Hills.
  Between Worlds.
  Blue Island Intersection.
  Breathing of the earth, The.
  Broken-Face Gargoyles.
  Caboose Thoughts.
  Chamfort.
  Chillicothe.
  Choices.
  Clark Street Bridge.
  Clean Hands.
  Consolation Sonata.
  Cripple.
  Early Copper.
  Eleventh Avenue Racket.
  Flying Fish.
  Gone.
  Grass lives, goes to sleep, lives again, The.
  Guaranteed Antique.
  Hangman at Home, The.
  Happiness.
  Hazardous Occupations.
  Heavy and Light.
  Home Fires.
  Hoodlums.
  Humdrum.
  Iglits and His Wife.
  In a Breath.
  In the Shadow of the Palace.
  Jack.
  Joke Gold.
  Loam.
  Long Guns.
  Mag.
  Many Hats.
  Masses.
  Mayor of Gary, The.
  Methusaleh Saw Many Repeaters.
  Mill-Doors.
  Moon Riders.
  Near Keokuk.
  Night's Nothings Again.
  Old Flagman, The.
  Old Woman.
  On the Way.
  Onion Days.
  Oomba.
  Outstraw green turns gold turns ashen and,
    The.
  Passers-by.
  People of the Eaves, I Wish You Good
    Morning.
  People Who Must.
  People will live on, The.
  People, yes, the people, The.
  Personalia.
  Real Avenue News.
  Red Son, The.
  Right to Grief, The.
  Shovel Man, The.
  Silver Nails.
  Sins of Kalamazoo, The.
  Soup.
  Southern Pacific.
  Still Life.
  Teamster's Farewell, A.
  Testament.
  Themes in Contrast.
  There is only one horse on the earth.
  This Street Never Sleeps.
  Three Ghosts.
  Transient tar-paper shack, The.
  Two Items.

Two Neighbors.
Variations on a Theme.
We live only once.
What the people learn out of lifting and
  hauling and waiting and losing.
When we say fresh eggs we mean fresh.
Whiffs of the Ohio River at Cinncinnati.
Who can make a poem of the depths of
  weariness.
Why should any man try to find the distance
  to the moon by guessing.
Without Notice Beforehand.
Without the daily chores of the people.
Working Girls.
You do what you must—this world and then
  the next—one world at a.
Young Sea.
Schuyler. Few Days, A.
  Hymn to Life.
  Sky Eats Up the Trees, The.
  We must observe the amenities.
Schwartz. Sand upon the Red Sea shore, or on
  the beach, The.
Sexton. Courage.
  End, Middle, Beginning.
  Evil Eye, The.
  Just Once.
  Live.
  Lost Ingredient, The.
  Ninth Psalm.
  Room of My Life, The.
  Rowing.
  Seventh Psalm.
  Speaking Bitterness.
Shapiro. Interlude, The.
Shelley. Daemon of the World, The; A
  Fragment.
  Sonnet: "Lift not the painted veil which those
    who live."
Shelton. Coda.
  Dear Life.
  Notes Towards an Autobiography.
Simic. Ballad of the Wheel, The.
  Great Infirmities.
  Lesson, The.
  Poem: "Every morning I forget how it is."
  Terms, The.
Smith, Stevie. All Things Pass.
  Ceux Qui Luttent.
  Come, Death (1).
  Dream of Comparison, A.
  God and the Devil.
  Some Are Born.
  Up and Down.
Snodgrass. After Experience Taught Me..
  April Inventory.
  Setting Out.
Snyder. Bed in the Sky, The.
  Sinecure for P. Whalen, A.
  Tiny Energies.
Sorrentino. Cruel Experiments Continue!
  Door that opens on, A.
  Edges, The.
  Fragments of an Old Song 1.
  How I loved that melody.
  In Which There is Nothing Up the Sleeve.
  Mother, this is a ball of color.
  Sonnet with X's.
  Vision of the City from a Window.
  What intense colloquy with the self.
  What is to be understood.
Stafford. Ask Me.
  For My Young Friends Who Are Afraid.
Stevens. Contrary Theses (II).
  Men Made Out of Words.
  Parochial Theme.
  Red Fern, The.
  St. Armorer's Church from the Outside.
  Sunday Morning.
Stevenson. As starts the absent dreamer, when
  a train.
  Away with funeral music—set.
  I have a hoard of treasure in my breast.
  I, now, O friend, whom noiselessly the snows.
  Love—what is love? A great and aching heart.
  Morning drum-call on my eager ear, The.
  Rivers and winds among the twisted hills.

To all that love the far and blue.
To Will H. Low.
Stuart. Casting.
  Common Ground.
  Major Work.
  Taking the Wheel.
Suckling. Ei Men Een Mathein.
Swinburne. At Eleusis.
  Before the Beginning of Years.
Tate. Meaning of Life, The.
  Our elder brother whom we had not seen.
  Resurgam.
Thomas. All All and All the Dry Worlds
  Lever.
  Force That through the Green Fuse Drives the
    Flower, The.
  Foster the Light.
  From Love's First Fever to Her Plague.
  If I Were Tickled by the Rub of Love.
  My World Is Pyramid.
  This Bread I Break.
  Twenty-four Years.
Tomlinson. Remembering Williams.
Updike. Furniture, The.
  Hot Water.
  Light Switches.
  Ode to Rot.
  Sand Dollar.
Van Duyn. Pot-au-feu.
Wakoski. Emerald Ice.
  How Do You Tell a Story?
  In the Secret Room, East of the Sun, West of
    the Moon.
  Life Is Like a Game of Cards, Or Another
    One of Those Metaphysical Statements from
    a Distant Reader.
  Virtuoso Literature for Two and Four Hands.
Walcott. Prelude: "I, with legs crossed along
  the daylight, watch."
Warren. And All That Came Thereafter.
  Arrogant Law.
  We Are Only Ourselves.
  When the Century Dragged.
Whitman. Continuities.
  Great Are the Myths.
  Life.
  Miracles.
  My 71st Year.
  Myself and Mine.
  O Living Always, Always Dying.
  To Be at All.
  Two Rivulets.
  Weave In, My Hardy Life.
  When I Read the Book.
Whittier. At Eventide.
Wilbur. All That Is.
  C Minor.
  Driftwood.
  In a Bird Sanctuary.
  Leaving.
  Ode to Pleasure.
  Star System, The.
  Trolling for Blues.
  "World without Objects Is a Sensible
    Emptiness, A."
Williams, Charles Kenneth. Beyond.
  Bread.
  Cellophane.
  Dimensions.
  Faint Praise.
  From Now On.
  Hog Heaven.
  Innings.
  Like Little Birds.
  Or.
  Other Side, The.
  Penance.
  Race of the Flood, The.
  Shade, The.
  Sting, The.
  This is what, / at last, it is.
  Undead, The.
  What Is and Is Not.
  What Must I Do To Be Lost?
Williams, Miller. Associate Professor Delivers
  an Exhortation to His Failing Students, The.
  For Reuben, at Twelve Months.

In Nashville, Standing in the Wooden Circle
Sawed Out from the Old Ryman Stage, the
Picker has a vision.
Living on the Surface.
Notes from the Agent on Earth: How to be
Human.
People.
Rebecca at Play.
Rock.
Williams, William Carlos. Butterandeggs.
History.
Horse Show, The.
Love Song;"Sweep the house clean."
Mind's Games, The.
Pastoral 1; "Old man who goes about, The."
Pastoral: "Little sparrows, The."
Piano Solo.
Some Simple Measures in the American Idiom
and the Variable Foot.
Sunday.
Virtue.
You Have Pissed Your Life.
Wordsworth. Along the mazes of this song I
go.
Fragments from Dove Cottage Manuscript 44
(II).
If This Great World of Joy and Pain.
Longest Day; Addressed to My Daughter, The.
Sweet was the walk along the narrow lane.
Wright, Charles. Journal of the Year of the
Ox, A.
Journal of True Confessions, A.
Laguna Blues.
Lost Souls.
Wright, James. American Twilights, 1957.
Angel, The.
Blue Teal's Mother.
Dawn brings with it, The.
Down to the Dregs.
Horse, The.
In Terror of Hospital Bills.
Inscription for the Tank.
Larry.
Life.
Life, The.
Many of Our Waters: Variaitons on a Poem
by a Black Child.
Moguer.
Mutterings over the Crib of a Deaf Child.
Northern Pike.
Not in Marble Palaces.
Offense, The.
Our Daily Bread.
RIP.
River Down Home, The.
Secret Gratitude, A.
To a Defeated Savior.
To a Friendly Dun.
To Harvey, Who Traced the Circulation.
Trying to Pray.
Undermining of the Defense Economy, The.
What the Earth Asked Me.
Yau. Certainty of being part of the
atmosphere, The.
La Brea.
Late Night Movies III.
Stumbling blocks are realigned, The.
Yeats. Four Ages of Man, The.
Gyres, The.
Meru.
New Faces, The.
To Some I Have Talked with by the Fire.
What Magic Drum?
Wild Old Wicked Man, The.
Young. Afraid.
Alba.
Bitter Spring Again, The.
Blues in December.
Citizen CB.
Continuing.
Dancing.
Dancing Day to Day.
Dancing in the Street.
Detroit 1958.
Elegy: "Good morning!"
Everywhere.
From Bowling Green.

How Stars Start.
How the Rainbow Works.
Intimacy.
Invitation.
Little More Traveling Music, A.
Malcolm's Messasge.
Morning Poem for Michael, A.
Myself When I Am Real.
New Mystic, The.
Now's the Time.
Poem with Orange.
Rediscovered Diary Entry.
Some Spice for Jack Spicer.
Song Turning Back Into Itself 1.
There Is a Sadness.
Tribute.
Zukofsky. Gamut.
Spook's Sabbath, Five Bowings.

Lifeguards
Dickey, James. Lifeguard, The.
Stuart. River, The.

Light
Atwood. Eating Fire.
Auden. Sunshine.
Berg. Endings.
Good.
Berry. At night make me one with the
darkness.
Breaking.
Returning.
Star, The.
Berryman. In a poem made by Cummings,
long since, his.
Blake. To Morning.
Bogan. Evening-Star.
Brontë. Not a vapour had stained the
breezeless blue.
Still as she looked the iron clouds.
Browning, Elizabeth Barrett. Romance of the
Ganges, A.
Browning, Robert. Deaf and Dumb.
Campion. So sweet is thy discourse to me.
Carew. Song: Beautiful Mistress, A.
Carroll, Jim. Light rising into her features
where.
Painting by Flashlight.
Prell.
Carruth. Fourth Version, The.
Ignis.
Moon, The.
When conditions of frost and.
Clark. Energy of the Pre-World as a Bungee
Cable Jumper.
Personal Angel Glimpsed.
Retro.
Coleridge. Veil of Light, The.
Veil of Spirit, The.
Cooper. Morning on the St. John's.
Creeley. Christmas: May 10, 1970.
Distance.
Kitchen.
Medallion.
Revelation, The.
Some Echoes.
Tunnel, The.
Two.
World, The.
Cummings. Weazened Irrefutable unastonished.
Yes but even / 4 or(&).
Davie. Going to Italy.
Hardness of Light, The.
Sunburst.
De la Mare. Rose in Water, A.
Unforeseen.
Vigil.
Wanderers, The.
Dickey, James. Power and Light.
Spring-Shock.
Dickinson. Light exists in Spring, A.
Light is sufficient to itself.
Poets light but Lamps, The.
There's a certain Slant of light.
Donne. Nocturnal[l] upon Saint Lucy's [or S.
Lucies] Day, Being the Shortest Day, A.
Doolittle. Projector.
Projector II.

Dunbar. Light, The.
Light was on the golden sands, The.
Dunn. Clarities, The.
Naturally.
What.
Eberhart. Bath Room, The.
Goal of Intellectual Man, The.
In after Time.
Incomparable Light, The.
Light From Above.
Light, Time, Dark.
Poetry and Games.
Return, The.
Eliot. O Light Invisible, we praise Thee!
Emerson. And as the light divided the dark.
As the drop feeds its fated flower.
Coin the daydawn into lines.
On that night the poet went.
Ferlinghetti. Olbers' Paradox.
Fisher. At Once.
From an English Sensibility.
In the Wall.
Portcullis, The.
Fletcher. From the Japanese, I.
Fox. And night comes.
Blanc de Blanc.
Night and Day.
Frost. Night Light, The.
Gallagher. Bird-Window-Flying.
Gray Eyes.
Reading Aloud.
Gardner. Searchlight, The.
Whole World's in a Terrible Chassis, The.
Graves. Children of Darkness.
Lament for Pasiphaë.
Gunn. Light is in the pupil.
Lights among Redwood.
Map of the City, A.
Silver Age, The.
Sunlight.
Wrestling.
Hacker. Angry, I speak, and pass the hurt to
you.
Haines. Lamp full of shadows burned, A.
Winter Light, A.
Hardy. Youth Who Carried a Light, The.
Hartley. Light of Night.
Hesketh. At Four A.M.
Credo.
Edward Thomas.
Gymnasts, The.
It Was Not I.
Journey.
Prayer for Sun.
Sally.
Vision.
Hewitt. For a September Afternoon of
Unexpected Brightness.
Glen of Light, The.
Moon, The.
November Park.
Hughes, Langston. Wonder.
Hughes, Ted. Earth locked out the light, The.
Jonson. Howe'er the brightness may amaze.
Joseph. Man as Matter (ISLAND; PHYSICS).
Kipling. Chartres Windows.
Coastwise Lights, The.
Knight. Haiku 1: "Slender Finger of Light,
A."
Kooser. Late Lights in Minnesota.
Kunitz. When the Light Falls.
Lawrence. Street Lamps.
Levine. Belief.
Last Step, The.
Lights I Have Seen Before.
Liddy. Spring tide swept 'em to the hills.
Lowry. October Sunset.
Windows from a Machine Shop.
"MacDiarmid." Milk-Wort and Bog Cotton.
Servant Girl's Bed.
MacLeish. No Lamp Has Ever Shown Us
Where to Look.
Seeing.
MacNeice. Here too, as in my childhood,
twilight.
Star-Gazer.
McNeill. Light.

Mahon. Light Music.
Matthews. Eyes.
Melville. In the Desert.
Merton. Candlemas Procession, The.
Miller. For Judy.
  Lighted Windows (For Judy).
Milton. Hail holy Light, ofspring [*or* offspring] of Heav'n [*or* Heaven] first-born.
Nemerov. Advice from the Holy Tomb.
  Madrigal: "She is the darkness where I wander."
  Sunglasses, The.
Neruda. First Winter.
  Inside.
Oliver. Buddha's Last Instruction, The.
Oppen. But at night the park.
Pack. Einstein's Pegasus.
  Let There Be Colored Light.
Patchen. And forth from that shadow of a shadow.
Piercy. Butt of Winter, The.
Plath. Great Carbuncle, The.
Raine. Afternoon sunlight plays.
  Golden Flowers.
  Images.
  Not that light is holy, but that the holy is the light—.
  Oval the golden moon.
  Path, The.
  Sun.
Rich. Focus.
  Integrity.
Roethke. Light Listened.
Rolfe. Vincent.
Rossetti. Light of Light.
  Shadows Today.
  Truly the Light Is Sweet.
  Whither the Tribes Go Up, Even the Tribes of the Lord.
Rukeyser. Risen Image Shines, The.
  Sun-Artist, The.
Sandburg. Butter Colors.
  Evening Questions.
  Feather Lights.
  Haze Gold.
  Light and Moonbells.
  Little Candle.
  Moonlight and Maggots.
  Skyscraper Loves Night, The.
  Smoke Shapes.
  Star Silver.
  Whitelight.
  Winter Gold.
Sarton. Light Left On, A.
Schuyler. Light Within, The.
  Shimmer.
  Sun Cab, A.
  This Soft October.
Silverstein. Invention.
Smith, Stevie. Light of Life, The.
Sorrentino. But the light is imagined.
  How I loved that melody.
  In a fantastic light.
  Le Bateau d'Amour Descried on the Briny.
  Shapes of Winter.
  Silences.
Stafford. Light by the Barn, The.
Stevens. Common Life, The.
  Homunculus et la Belle Étoile.
  Note on Moonlight.
  Of Hartford in a Purple Light.
  Sun This March, The.
  Tattoo.
Stuart. Light Years.
Thomas. Light Breaks Where No Sun Shines.
Tomlinson. Bead, The.
  Brilliant Silence.
  Carscape.
  Cloud Change.
  Couplet.
  Frondes Agrestes.
  Glass Grain.
  In March.
  In the Intensity of Final Light.
  Night Ride.
  Object in a Setting.
  Of Beginning Light.

On a Theme of Pasternak.
Sea is Open to the Light, The.
Urlicht.
Turco. Epistles: "I am writing you."
Updike. Light Switches.
Waldman. Light & Shadow.
Warren. Multiplication Table.
Whittier. Light That Is Felt, The.
Wilbur. Five Women Bathing in Moonlight.
  Star System, The.
Williams, William. Gift of Prophecy Lost, The.
Williams, William Carlos. Seraph.
Wright, Charles. Cryopexy.
Wright, James. Beginning.
  Shadow and the Real, The.
  To the Evening Star: Central Minnesota.
Wroth. Song: "Birds doe sing, day doth apeere, The."
  Sonnet 4: "And bee in his brave court a gloriouse light."
  Sonnet 22: "Like to the Indians, scorched with the sun[ne]."
  Sonnet 43: "O dearest eyes the lights, and guids of love."
Yau. "E Pluribus Unum."
Yeats. He and She.
Young. Hot House.
  Lemons, Lemons.
  Moon Up Close in Winter by the Telescope, The.
  New Moon Over Grove Street.
  Sea Level.
  Tutti Colori Quality of Light, The.
Zukofsky. Light.
  Perch Less.

Lighthouses
Ceravolo. Lighthouse.
Gunn. Round and Round.
Lowry. Lighthouse invites the storm and lights it, The.
Mahon. Lighthouse in Maine, A.
Stevenson. Light-Keeper, The.
  Skerryvore.
Tomlinson. Lighthouse, The.
Wilbur. Beacon, The.

Lightning
Ammons. Time Spans.
Dickey, James. Doorstep, Lightning, Waif-Dreaming.
  Eagle's Mile, The.
  Flash, The.
Dickinson. Lightning is a yellow Fork, The.
  Lightning playeth—all the while, The.
Emerson. At last the poet spoke.
Graves. Blackening Sky.
Kinnell. Another Night in the Ruins.
Lawrence. Lightning.
  Storm in the Black Forest.
"MacDiarmid." Two Memories.
Nash. Watched Example Never Boils, A.
Oliver. Lightning.
Sandburg. Oak Arms.
Stevenson. Last night we had a thunderstorm in style.
Updike. Old-Fashioned Lightning Rod.
Young. Lightning, Divine Lightning.
Zukofsky. Crickets' / thickets / light, / delight.

Lightning Bugs. *see* **Fireflies.**

Lilacs
Carruth. Ovid, Old Buddy, I Would Discourse with You a While.
Eberhart. Transformation.
MacLeish. Critics on the Lawn.
Schuyler. Lilacs.
Stevens. Last Looks at the Lilacs.
Wilbur. Lilacs, The.
Zukofsky. Lilac.

Lilies
Atwood. Squaw Lilies: Some Notes.
Berry. Lilies, The.
Cowper. Lily and the Rose, The.
Davie. Lily at Noon, A.
Doolittle. Sea Lily.
Herrick. How Lillies Came White.
  Upon One Lillie, Who Marryed with a Maid Call'd Rose.

Hopkins. Pure gold lily, but by the pure gold lily, A.
Housman. Lent Lily, The.
Lawrence. Lilies in the Fire.
Liddy. Debt, The.
Oliver. Lilies.
  Lilies Break Open Over the Dark Water, The.
  Ponds, The.
Rossetti. Consider the Lilies of the Field.
  Lily has an air, / And the snowdrop a grace, The.
  River Thames (?).
  Rose that blushes rosy red, The.
  Thy lilies drink the dew, / Thy lambs the rill, and I will drink them too.
Sandburg. Lavender Lilies.
Sexton. From the Garden.
Smart. On a Bed of Guernsey Lilies.
Williams, William Carlos. Lily, The.
  Red Lily, The.
Zukofsky. Lilies.

Lilies of the Valley
Dunbar. Lily of the Valley, The.
Smith, Charlotte. To an Amiable Girl.

Lilith
Carruth. Why dost thou tear me? Had I done thee hurt?

Limbo
Auden. Limbo Culture.
Berrigan. After Peire Vidal, & Myself.
Coleridge. Limbo.
Poe. Al Aaraaf.
Raine. Halt, The.

Limestone
Auden. In Praise of Limestone.
Jeffers. Bixby's Landing.

Lincoln, Abraham
Dunbar. Lincoln.
Eberhart. Fortune's Mist.
Fletcher. Lincoln.
  Passing of the South, The.
Hartley. A. Lincoln—Odd, or Even.
  American Ikon—Lincoln.
Kunitz. His innocence was to trust.
  In the Great Hall of the Library.
Lindsay. Abraham Lincoln Walks at Midnight.
  Babylon, Babylon, Babylon the Great.
Lowell. Abraham Lincoln.
MacLeish. At the Lincoln Memorial.
Melville. Martyr, The.
Robinson. Master, The.
Sandburg. Cool Tombs.
  Fire-Logs.
  In a Back Alley.
  Knucks.
  LINCOLN? / He was a mystery in smoke and flags.
  Long Shadow of Lincoln: A Litany, The.
  Potomac River Mist.
  Sayings of Henry Stephens.
  Tall Man, A.
Whitman. Abraham Lincoln, Born Feb. 12, 1809.
  Hush'd be the Camps To-day.
  Memories of President Lincoln.
  O Captain! My Captain!
  This Dust Was Once the Man.
  When Lilacs Last in the Dooryard Bloom'd.
Whittier. Quakers Are Out, The.

Lincolnshire, England
Davie. Lincolnshire.

Linden Trees
MacLeish. Linden Branch, The.
  Linden Trees, The.

Lindisfarne, England
Scott. Saint of Holy Island, The.

Lindsay, Vachel
Ginsberg. To Lindsay.

Linen
Schuyler. Adverts.
  Linen.
  "Used Handkerchiefs 5[dc]."

Linnets
De la Mare. Linnet, The.
Meredith. Linnet-Hawker, The.

Rossetti. Hear what the mournful linnets say.
Linnet in a gilded cage,— / A linnet on a
bough, A.
Wordsworth. Green Linnet, The.

Lions
Bukowski. 10 Lions and the End of the
World.
Carruth. Wreck of the Circus Train, The.
Cowper. Reciprocal Kindness the Primary Law
of Nature.
Creeley. Lion and the Dog, The.
Duncan. In Waking.
Song of the Borderguard, The.
What of the structure of Rime? I said.
Eberhart. Lions Copulating.
Ford. Serenade to Leonor.
Ginsberg. Lion for Real, The.
Graves. Lion Lover.
Song: Dream Warning.
With the Gift of a Lion's Claw.
Herrick. Upon Umber: Epigram.
Hugo. Bassetti's Lions.
George Stubbs at Yale.
Lawrence. St Mark.
Lindsay. Lion, The.
Merton. Lion, The.
Moore. Lion In Love, The.
Nash. Lion, The.
Nathan. Lion Farm, The.
Patchen. Lions of fire, The.
Meben.
White lions are roaring on the water.
Sarton. Lion and the Rose, The.
Silverstein. It's Dark In Here.
Smith, Stevie. Reversionary.
Roman Road, The.
Sunt Leones.
Zoo, The.
Spenser. Mighty lyon, lord of all the wood, A.
Stevens. Lions in Sweden.

Lips
Carew. Lips and Eyes.
Cummings. Voices to voices, lip to lip.
Emerson. Ah, could I hide me in my song.
And since round lines are drawn.
Graves. Touch My Shut Lips.
Herrick. Captived Bee; or, The Little Filcher,
The.
Cherrie-Ripe.
On Julias Lips.
Rock of Rubies: and The Quarrie of Pearls,
The.
Upon His Julia.
Upon Lucie.
Weeping Cherry, The.
Liddy. You Came By on Bamboo Stilts,
Playing Horse.
Lorde. Pirouette.
Shakespeare. Sonnet 128: "How oft, when
thou, my music, music play'st."
Sidney. Sonnet 80: "Sweet swelling lip, well
mayst thou swell in pride."

Lipscomb, Eugene
Jarrell. Say Good-bye to Big Daddy.

Listening and Listeners
Berrigan. Paul Blackburn.
Berry. To What Listens.
Carruth. Aer.
Clark. Moodsville.
Creeley. Friends, The.
Here.
Mary's Fancy.
Total Parts of a World, The.
Davie. Having No Ear.
De la Mare. Dove, The.
Dunn. Listener, The.
Emerson. Dervish whined to Said, The.
Hall. "Internal and External Forms."
Hartley. To C———.
Herrick. Canticle to Apollo, A.
Upon a Hoarse Singer.
Hewitt. Listener, The.
Hughes, Langston. Lady's Boogie.
Koch. Hearing.
Lawrence. Listening.
Liddy. Death of Mathmaticians, The.
Nash. Listen.

Raine. Triad.
Who listens, when in the concert-hall.
Sorrentino. Celebration of Sorts, A.
Stuart. Writing Machine, The.
Tomlinson. Little Night Music, A.
Words for the Madrigalist.
Updike. Mountain Impasse.
Williams, Charles Kenneth. In the middle / of
a bite of.
Young. You Don't Know What Love Is.
Zukofsky. In Arizona / (how many years in
the mountains).

Literature
Auden. Dichtung und Wahrheit.
Thanksgiving, A.
Berry. Autumn Burning, An.
Berryman. Crisis.
Professor's Song, A.
Tea.
Byron. No Infant Sotheby, Whose Dauntless
Head.
Cohen. I Decided.
Cummings. Let's start a magazine.
Davie. Pentecost.
University of the South, The.
Dickey, James. Place of the Skull, The.
Donne. To Mr. R. W. ("Kindly I envy thy
song's [or songs] perfection").
"Dylan." Desolation Row.
Eberhart. Bones of Coleridge, The.
Clerihew for Alan Gaylord, A.
Nostalgia for Edith Sitwell.
Emerson. Burn your literary verses.
Fisher. News for the Ear.
Suppose—.
Gunn. Readings in French.
Hartnett. I say farewell to English verse.
Hill. Bibliographers, The.
Hoffman. Translators' Party, The.
Liddy. At castle shadowed mouth of the /
Doonbeg.
Letter to Eamonn Wall, A.
Miles.
Lowry. Gentleness of rain is in the wind, The.
Outside was the roar of the sea and the
darkness.
"MacDiarmid." Ah, Joyce, this is our task.
Archin' here and arrachin there.
Gairmscoile.
It is possible that a change may come.
So, like him, we cry "l'honneur des hommes:
Saint Langage."
To distinctly English writers in England.
Wheesht, wheesht, Joyce, and let me hear.
Moore. Picking and Choosing.
Nash. Literary Reflection.
Nemerov. History of a Literary Movement.
Ransom. Survey of Literature.
Rich. 7/14/68: i.
7/16/68: ii.
Smith, Stevie. Souvenir de Monsieur Poop.
Stevens. Poem That Took the Place of a
Mountain, The.
Suckling. To His Much Honoured the Lord
Lepington upon His Translation of Malvezzi,
His "Romulus" and "Tarquin."
Tomlinson. Antecedents.
Walcott. Love in the Valley.
Williams, William Carlos. Question and
Answer.
Wordsworth. Illustrated Books and
Newspapers.
Zukofsky. Poem Beginning "The."
See also **Authorship and Authors; Criticism
and Critics.**

Little, Malcolm. see **Malcolm X (Malcolm
Little).**

Little Bighorn, Battle of (1876)
Whitman. From Far Dakota's Cañons (June
25, 1876).

Lizards
Cohen. One.
Eberhart. Let the Tight Lizard on the Wall.
Hardy. Lizard, The.
Hughes, Ted. Earth locked out the light, The.
Kinnell. Gray Heron, The.
Lawrence. Lizard.

Lowell. Lizard rusty as a leaf rubbed rough.
MacLeish. Old Man to the Lizard, The.
Moore. Plumet Basilisk, The.
Nash. Skink, The.
Roethke. Lizard, The.
Rossetti. When fishes set umbrellas up / If the
rain-drops run.

Llamas
Nash. Lama, The.

Lobsters
"Carroll, Lewis." Alice's Recitation.
Mock Turtle's Song, The.
Mock Turtle's Song, The: "Beneath the waters
of the sea."
Lieberman. Lobsters in the Brain Coral.
Nemerov. Lobsters.
Oppen. Ballad: "Astrolabes and lexicons."
Sexton. Lobster.
Snodgrass. Lobsters in the Window.
Sorrentino. September in Kittery.
Williams, William Carlos. Rhymed Address:
The Lobster.

Loch Ness. see **Ness, Loch, Scotland.**

Locomotives
MacLeish. Grazing Locomotives.
Williams, William Carlos. East Coocoo.
See also **Trains; Railroads.**

Locusts
Berry. Seventeen Years.
"Dylan." Day of the Locusts.
Merton. Radicals.
Nash. Locust-Lovers, Attention!

Log Houses
Patchen. Vanishing Institution, A.

Lombardi, Vince
Dickey, James. For the Death of Vince
Lombardi.

London, England
Auden. Hodge Looks toward London.
Beckett. Serena I.
Berrigan. Old-Fashioned Air.
Betjeman. Hertfordshire.
Monody on the Death of Aldersgate Street
Station.
South London Sketch, 1844.
South London Sketch, 1944.
Blake. Fields from Islington to Marybone,
The.
I wander tho each dirty street.
London ("I wander through each chartered
street").
"Carroll, Lewis." Double Acrostic: Two little
girls near London dwell.
Cowper. London Suburbs.
Creeley. In London.
Davie. To Londoners.
Donne. To Mr E. G.
Fletcher. Elegy on London.
Ginsberg. Studying the Signs.
Gunn. Adolescence.
London returned to after twelve years, A.
Hardy. East-End Curate, An.
To a Tree in London.
Hemingway. First Poem to Mary in London.
Herrick. His Return to London.
Hill. Churchill's Funeral.
Housman. Eight O'Clock.
In my own shire, if I was sad.
Hugo. Walking Praed Street.
Jarrell. London.
Johnson. London: A Poem.
Joseph. Anthropomorphism Reversed.
Keats. Lines on the Mermaid Tavern.
Kipling. London Stone.
Lawrence. Piccadilly Circus at Night.
To Clarinda.
Town in 1917.
Lowry. Above all, absent yourself from that
affair.
MacNeice. Canto III: "To work—To
Beaconsfield. A suburban train."
Canto VIII: "Fair; not to say radiant. The
Twentyfifth of September."
Goodbye to London.
Homage to Wren.
Street Scene.

Streets of Laredo, The.
Whit Monday.
Mahon. Kensington Notebook, A.
Meredith. London by Lamplight.
Merton. Queens Tunnel.
Owen. Shadwell Stair.
Pope. Farewell to London in the Year 1715, A.
Raine. London air dims.
St. John. Swan at Sheffield Park, The.
Shelley. Hell is a city much like London.
On Leaving London for Wales.
You are now / In London, that great sea.
Thomas. Refusal to Mourn the Death, by Fire, of a Child in London, A.
Wordsworth. London, 1802.

Londonderry, Northern Ireland
Mahon. Derry Morning.

Lone Ranger, The
Hall. Lone Ranger, The.

Loneliness
Angelou. Greyday.
Traveler, The.
Ashbery. Ivory Tower, The.
Atwood. And you play the safe game / the orphan game.
Auden. Alone.
At Twenty we find our friends for ourselves, but it takes Heaven.
Loneliness.
Minnelied.
Pleasure Island.
Quique Amavit.
Witnesses, The.
Beatles. Eleanor Rigby.
Yer Blues.
Yesterday.
Beckett. Lueurs lisières.
Roundelay: "On all that strand."
Berg. Red Weed.
Times.
Berryman. Handshake, the Entrance, The.
He Resigns.
I've met your friend at last, your violent friend.
Sometimes the night echoes to prideless wailing.
Transit.
World's Fair.
Betjeman. Eunice.
House of Rest.
Loneliness.
Bly. Man Writes to a Part of Himself, A.
"Out of the Rolling Ocean, the Crowd . . ."
Snowbanks North of the House.
Bradstreet. In My Solitary Hours in My Dear Husband His Absence.
Brontë. And like myself lone, wholly lone.
I paused on the threshold, I turned to the sky.
If grief for grief can touch thee.
Lonely at her window sitting.
Sun Has Set, The.
Brooks. Empty Woman, The.
Preacher: Ruminates Behind the Sermon, The.
Sunset of the City, A.
Bukowski. Alone with Everybody.
Blue Cheese and Chili Peppers.
Chicago.
Christmas Eve, Alone.
Crunch, The.
Here I Am.
Love Is a Dog from Hell.
Me.
Night I Fucked My Alarm Clock, The.
Oh, Yes.
Sword, The.
Yellow Cab.
Bunting. Last night without sight of you my brain was ablaze.
Southwind, tell her what.
You've come! O how flustered and anxious I've been.
Burns. English Song.
How lang and dreary is the night.
Jockey's Ta'en the Parting Kiss.
My Nannie's Awa'.

Sae Far Awa.
Wae Is My Heart.
Byron. I Would I Were a Careless Child.
Stanzas: "Oh!—my lonely—lonely—lonely Pillow!"
Campion. My Life's Delight.
Oft have I sigh'd for him that heares me not.
Carroll, Jim. Marked by a more distant sky, I hold.
"Carroll, Lewis." Faces in the Fire.
Carruth. Loneliness[: An Outburst of Hexasyllables].
Poem moves north, The.
Catullus. Carmen 69: "Do not wonder when the wench declines."
Ceravolo. In My Crib.
Clare. Song: "I peeled bits of straw and I got switches too."
Clark. Afternoons.
Clough. Enough, small Room,—though all too true.
Cohen. Blessed Are You.
Closing Time.
Deep Happiness, A.
Diamonds in the Mine.
Guests, The.
Coleridge. Blossoming of the Solitary Date-Tree, The.
Hexameters.
Homeless.
Loss.
Crane. Legende.
Moth That Made God Blind, The.
Old Song.
Creeley. Door, The.
End, The.
Fire.
For a Friend.
For Somebody's Marriage.
Moon, The.
Not Now.
Places.
There Is.
Whip, The.
Cummings. I will cultivate within.
L(a / le / af / fa / ll / s).
Lily has a rose.
Nothing is more exactly terrible than.
Wind has blown the rain away and blown, A.
De la Mare. Alone.
Old Men, The.
Ophelia.
Dickinson. Could that sweet Darkness where they dwell.
Door just opened on a street, A.
Heart, not so heavy as mine.
I hide myself within my flower.
I thought to shun the Loneliness.
I tried to think a lonelier Thing.
I was with you in all the loneliness.
I've none to tell me to but Thee.
Loneliness One dare not sound, The.
Shade upon the mind there passes, A.
There is another Loneliness.
We don't cry—Tim and I.
Dobyns. Body's Curse, The.
Mermaid.
To Pull into Oneself as into a Locked Room.
What You Have Come To Expect.
Doolittle. Chance.
Dove. Catherine of Siena.
Dunbar. Lonesome.
Memory of Martha, The.
My Lady of Castle Grand.
Dunn. Atlantic City.
Because We Are Not Taken Seriously.
Coming Home, Garden State Parkway.
Listener, The.
Night Truths.
Smiles.
This Late in the Century.
Urgencies.
"Dylan." Black Crow Blues.
Dirge: "I hate myself for lovin' you and the weakness that it showed."
Obviously Five Believers.
Only a Hobo.

Simple Twist of Fate.
Tomorrow Is a Long Time.
You're Gonna Make Me Lonesome When You Go.
Eberhart. Human Being is a Lonely Creature, The.
Point-pushed by the wind, rain.
Edmunds. I Have Tried to Find You.
Eliot. Le Directeur.
Emerson. Alone in Rome! Why Rome is lonely too.
Good-bye.
I cannot find a place so lonely.
I grieve that better souls than mine.
Thine Eyes Still Shined.
What avails it me.
Where art thou / Thou beautiful dream.
Frost. Acquainted with the Night.
Bereft.
Desert Places.
Impulse, The.
Loneliness.
Most of It, The.
Gardner. Convalescence in Summer 1949.
Fixing the Clock.
Knowing.
Ginsberg. Asphodel, An.
Desolation, A.
Flash Back.
Nov. 23, 1963: Alone.
Glück. Return, The.
12. 6. 71.
Graves. Crane, The.
Love as Lovelessness.
Raft, The.
Griffiths. Nearness.
Hacker. Elevens.
Little Robber Girl Considers the Wide World, The.
When I read poems to the art students.
Haines. Deserted Cabin.
On the Road.
Hall. Hut of the man alone, The.
Toy Bone, The.
Hardy. Before Knowledge.
Bereft.
Lonely Days.
Nobody Comes.
Orphaned Old Maid, The.
Sailor's Mother, The.
Song to an Old Burden.
Son's Portrait, The.
Voice of the Thorn, The.
Hartley. Lonely Return to the Lonely, the divine to the Divine—Proclus, The.
Hartnett. Death of an Irishwoman.
Mo Ghrá Thú.
Mountains, Fall on Us.
Sad Singing in Darkness.
Hemingway. First Poem to Mary in London.
Hesketh. Different.
Hoffman. O Personages.
Holmes. Midnight Oil.
Year's End.
Housman. Hughley Steeple.
Rainy Pleiads wester, The.
There pass the careless people.
Weeping Pleiads wester, The.
Winds out of the west land blow, The.
Hughes, Langston. Desert.
50–50.
Hope.
Kid in the Park.
One.
Stony Lonesome.
Hugo. Letter to Hanson from Miami.
Swimmer at Lake Edward, The.
Jarrell. Eine Kleine Nachtmusik.
Game at Salzburg, A.
Ghost, a Real Ghost, A.
Island, The.
London.
Lonely Man, The.
See-er of Cities, The.
Windows.
Kinnell. Burn, The.
Kipling. Love Song of Har Dyal, The.

Knight. Poem to Galway Kinnell, A.
Kooser. Old Woman, The.
Lawrence. Drunk.
Elysium.
Loneliness.
Sighs.
Song of a Man Who Is Not Loved.
Uprooted, The.
Levertov. Gone Away.
In Abeyance.
Levine. At the Fillmore.
Memory of rain falling slowly, The.
Planting.
Poem Circling Hamtramck, Michigan, All
Night in Search of You, The.
Lewis. Bivouac.
Boy who climbed the creaking stairs, The.
Fragment, A: "Where aloneness fiercely."
Lament: "Oh Absalom, beloved, what can I
say?"
Liddy. All the journeys / To be made for
instance, over the seas.
Icarus.
New O'Dwyer's dim lights. "You hate, The."
Song about Sinn Fein for Serena.
To the Memory of Sylvia Plath: A Personal
Note.
Lorde. Keyfoods.
Lovelace. To Rufus.
Lowry. Drunkards, The.
How did all this begin, and why am I here.
Poem Inspired By Auden and Clare's Snail.
McGrath. From a Long Way Out of Pah-
Gatzin-Kay.
Little Odyssey of Jason Quint, of Science,
Doctor, The.
Orphan, The.
Parable.
MacLeish. Epitaph for John McCutcheon.
Winter Is Another Country.
MacNeice. Autobiography.
Eclogue between the Motherless.
Heated Minutes, The.
Lake in the Park, The.
Merman under the Plough, The.
Nostalgia.
Passage Steamer.
Postcript to Iceland.
Sand in the Air.
Troll's Courtship.
When clerks and navvies fondle.
Mahon. Achill.
Matthews. Blues, The.
Good Company.
Meredith. Black Richard.
Lesson of Grief, The.
Mortesto.
They that love not—are they not as blind
camels that behold no.
Millay. On the Wide Heath.
Miller. Ensamhet.
So in evening there is still light.
Stumbling and weeping.
Milton. And thus he spake, each bird and
beast behold.
Nash. Listen.
Solitude of Mr. Powers, The.
Very Unclubbable Man, The.
Nathan. Sorry.
Table Talk.
Neruda. Bird.
Notley. Sweetheart.
O'Hara. On Looking at La Grande Jatte, the
Czar Wept Anew.
Poem: "To be idiomatic in a vacuum."
Oliver. Lilies.
Oppen. Rationality.
Pack. Hole in the Sky, A.
Paley. We quarreled / Alone I.
Patchen. All the Day.
Each Is Alone, Each Is Everything.
Lonesome Boy Blues.
No one ever works alone.
Piercy. Going In.
Prince. False Bay.
Raine. Crossing the sound I summoned you in
thought.

Lachesis.
Unloved, The.
Rexroth. Inversely, As the Square of Their
Distances Apart.
Rich. Rain on the West Side Highway.
Song: "You're wondering if I'm lonely."
Robinson. Mr. Flood's Party.
Song at Shannon's, A.
Roethke. His Foreboding.
Rossetti. At Home.
Chilly Night, A.
If.
Let Patience Have Her Perfect Work.
Lowest Room, The.
Repining.
Sappho.
Song: "Stream moaneth as it floweth, The."
Who Have a Form of Godliness.
Will These Hands Ne'er Be Clean?
Zara.
Sandburg. Alone and Not Alone.
Canadians and Pottawatomies.
Love Is a Deep and a Dark and a Lonely.
M'Liss and Louie.
Stripes.
They Ask: Is God, Too, Lonely.
Schuyler. August Night.
Sexton. Angel of Beach Houses and Picnics.
January 24th.
Killing the Love.
Shelley. Remembrance.
To Mary Shelley ("World is dreary, The / And
I'm weary").
Shelton. Negative Virtues, The.
Simic. Cold Blue Tinge.
Partial Explanation, The.
Whispers in the Next Room.
Smith, Charlotte. Pilgrim, The.
To the Winds.
Smith, Stevie. Deeply Morbid.
Orphan Reformed, The.
Unpopular, Lonely and Loving.
Voice from the Tomb (4).
Widowhood or The Home-Coming of Lady
Ross.
Sorrentino. Coast of Texas.
It is one man alone, what.
Meeting, The.
Spender. Not to You.
Room above the Square, The.
Stuart. Light Years.
Tennyson. Mariana.
Tomlinson. Dream, The.
Turco. Envoi: The Wind Carol.
Homunculus.
Will Somers.
Updike. Grief of Cafeterias, The.
Van Duyn. Open Letter from a Constant
Reader.
Walker. He Said:.
Whitman. As If a Phantom Caress'd Me.
I Saw in Louisiana a Live-Oak Growing.
This Moment Yearning and Thoughtful.
When I Peruse the Conquer'd Fame.
Whittier. Autograph, An.
Missionary, The.
Williams, Charles Kenneth. Being Alone.
Fleas, too, / have fled, The.
Keep It.
Shame.
Williams, Miller. Man Who Stays Up Late,
The.
Williams, William Carlos. Ballet.
Man in a Room.
Widower's Monologue.
Wright, James. As I Step over a Puddle at the
End of Winter, I Think of an Ancient
Chinese Governor.
Assignation, The.
Big People, The.
But Only Mine.
Elegy for the Poet Morgan Blum, An.
For the Marsh's Birthday.
Having Lost My Sons, I Confront the
Wreckage of the Moon: Christmas, 1960.
I Am a Sioux Brave, He Said in Minneapolis.
Idea of the Good, The.

Inscription for the Tank.
Katy Did.
Many of Our Waters: Variations on a Poem
by a Black Child.
Moguer.
Northern Pike.
Offense, The.
Poem about Breasts, A.
Poems to a Brown Cricket.
Pretty Redhead, The.
Revelation, The.
So She Said.
Speak.
To a Dead Drunk.
To a Friendly Dun.
To Harvey, Who Traced the Circulation.
Wyatt. Lucks, my fair falcon, and your
fellows all.
What means [or meaneth or menethe] this
when I lie [or lye] alone.
Yeats. Crazy Jane and Jack the Journeyman.
Two Songs Rewritten for the Tune's Sake.
Young. Dance for Aging Hipsters, A.
Hallucinogenic Halleluuuu.
Loneliness.
Making Love After Hours.
Physics of Loneliness, The.
Rediscovered Diary Entry.
Song skips around, The.
Topsy: Part 2.
Zimmer. Christiaan Fearing the Sky.
Gus in the Streets.
Zukofsky. Dying away as of trees, A.
Homage.
No lift odd mere horror, harrowed (why boy?)
that no woman will.
Sequence 1944-6.
Who endure days like this.

Long Island, New York
Ferlinghetti. Poem for Old Walt.
Glück. Meridian.
Merton. New Ribbon.
Schuyler. Birds.
Whitman. As I Ebb'd with the Ocean of Life.
Centenarian's Story, The.
From Montauk Point.
Ode: "O, God of Columbia! O, Shield of the
Free!"
Paumanok.
Paumanok Picture, A.

Longfellow, Henry Wadsworth
Betjeman. Longfellow's Visit to Venice.
"Carroll, Lewis." Hiawatha's Photographing.
Nash. Boy's Will is the Wind's Will?, A.
Sandburg. Mr. Longfellow and His Boy.
Schuyler. Light from Canada.
Tomlinson. In Longfellow's Library.
Whittier. On a Fly-Leaf of Longfellow's
Poems.
Poet and the Children, The.

Longing
Ashbery. Business Personals.
Pursuit of Happiness, The.
Song: "Song tells us of our old way of living,
The."
37 Haiku.
Auden. Last Time, The.
North, The.
Seen when nights are silent.
Since the Autumn day.
Beatles. Baby's in Black.
Eight Days a Week.
For No One.
From Me to You.
Got to Get You into My Life.
I Call Your Name.
I Need You.
I'm So Tired.
It Won't Be Long.
Long and Winding Road, The.
Long Long Long.
Misery.
P.S. I Love You.
Yes It Is.
Berg. Cherries.
People Trying to Love.
Berrigan. Heloise.

Berryman. Fare Well.
  Mutinous in the half-light, & malignant, grind.
  On the wheat-sacks sullen with the ceaseless
    damp.
  Your shining—where?—rays my wide room
    with gold.
Bly. Cry Going Out over Pastures, The.
  Dream of What Is Missing, A.
  Finding the Father.
Bogan. Girl's Song.
Brontë. F. de Samara to A. G. A.
  Shall Earth no more inspire thee.
  Song By Julius Brenzaida To G.S.
  Wind, sink to rest in the heather.
Brooks. To Be in Love.
Browning, Elizabeth Barrett. Isobel's Child.
  May's Love.
  Romaunt of Margret, The.
  Sonnet: "Beloved, my beloved, when I think."
  Sonnet: "If I leave all for thee, wilt thou
    exchange."
Browning, Robert. In Three Days.
  Lovers' Quarrel, A.
  Never the Time and the Place.
  One Way of Love.
  Pauline [or Pauline; A Fragment of a
    Confession].
Bukowski. Dogs of Egypt, The.
Burns. Answer to the Foregoing—Extempore
    [Clarinda].
  Ay Waukin O.
  Blue-Eyed Lassie, The.
  Bonie Lad That's Far Awa, The.
  Bonnie [or Bonny] Wee Thing, The.
  Cauld Frosty Morning.
  English Song.
  For the Sake o' Somebody.
  Fragment: "Altho' my bed were in yon muir."
  Here Awa' There Awa ["Here awa', there
    awa' wandering, Willie"].
  Jockey's Ta'en the Parting Kiss.
  Mary Morison.
  Merry Hae I Been Teethin a Heckle.
  My Harry was a gallant gay.
  My Heart's in the Highlands.
  O Lay Thy Loof in Mine Lass.
  On the Seas and Far Away.
  Passion's Cry.
  Revision for Clarinda.
  Sae Far Awa.
  Song: "Behold the hour, the boat arrive."
  Song: "O, Logan, sweetly didst thou glide."
  Sweet fa's the eve on Craigieburn.
  Wilt thou be my Dearie.
  Young Highland Rover, The.
Campion. Come away, arm'd with loves
    delights.
  Harden now thy tyred hart, with more than
    flinty rage.
Carew. Divine Mistress, A.
  Lady, Rescued from Death by a Knight, Who
    in the Instant Leaves Her, Complains Thus,
    A.
  Mr. Carew to His Friend.
  To Her in Absence; a Ship.
  To My Mistress[e] in My Absence.
Carroll, Jim. Poem: "We are very much a part
    of the boredom."
"Carroll, Lewis." Lady Muriel's Song.
Carruth. And there in the sky is the known
    face half-hidden.
  He decided to live. Alone. One room.
  Quaking.
Catullus. Carmen 2: "Lesbia's sparrow! /
    Lesbia's plaything!"
  Carmen 8: "Break off / fallen Catullus."
  Carmen 55: "Where / if it's not too much to
    ask."
  Carmen 107: "If ever anyone anywhere,
    Lesbia, is looking."
Ceravolo. Cross Fire.
  Sea Level.
  Soul in Migration.
Clare. I Am.
Clark. I Was Born to Speak Your Name.
  "My heart in pieces."
Coleridge. Day-Dream, The ("If thou wert

here, these tears were tears of light").
Love.
Sigh, The.
Something Childish, but Very Natural.
Stanger Minstrel, A.
Crane. Exile.
Creeley. Away.
  Distance.
  Flesh.
  For Benny and Sabina.
  In a Boat Shed.
  Let something else be / the question—.
  Messengers, The.
  Place.
  Pryaer, A.
  Smoke.
  Song: "Those rivers run from that land."
Cullen. Lament: "Now let all lovely things
    embark."
  To the Swimmer.
Cummings. Always before your voice my
    soul.
  Ballad of Love.
  Before the fragile gradual throne of night.
  Clown's smirk in the skull of a baboon, A.
  Consider O / woman this / my body.
  Ivory performing rose, The.
  Lady / i pray to what is unimaginable.
  Longing.
  O Distinct / Lady of my unkempt adoration.
  Spring has been exquisite and the, The.
  Supposing i dreamed this).
Davie. Thou Art Near at Hand, O Lord.
De la Mare. Betrayal.
  Eyes.
  Monologue, The.
  Thorn, The.
  Vacant Day, The.
Dickey, William. Kindness, A.
Dickinson. Heart wants what it wants, The.
  I envy seas—whereon He rides.
  I many times thought Peace had come.
  It's fragrant news, to know they pine.
  Longing is like the Seed.
  What shall I do now—it whimpers so.
Donne. Fever, A.
Dove. Boccaccio: The Plague Years.
Dunbar. Longing.
Duncan. Source.
Dunn. Good Life, A.
  One Side of the Story.
"Dylan." Bob Dylan's Dream.
  Boots of Spanish Leather.
  Down the Highway.
  Golden Loom.
  Gypsy Lou.
  Heart of Mine.
  I Wanna Be Your Lover.
  I'd Have You Any Time.
  Jim Jim / where is our party?
  Need a Woman.
  Obviously Five Believers.
  Pledging My Time.
  Sign on the Window.
  Temporary Like Achilles.
  Visions of Johanna.
  Wallflower.
  Where Are You Tonight? (Journey through
    Dark Heat).
Eberhart. Sometimes the Longing for Death.
Edmunds. I Have Tried to Find You.
Emerson. Dante's Vita Nuova.
Hafiz.
  To Rhea.
Ferlinghetti. Astonished Heart, The.
  Light, The.
  Two Amsterdams.
Fletcher. Jade Elegy, The.
Gallagher. All Day the Light Is Clear.
  Coming Home.
  Under Stars.
Gardner. Convalescence in Summer 1949.
  Grocery Bouquet, The.
  Letter from Slough Pond.
  Moth Happened, The.
Garrigue. Catch What You Can.
  Incantatory Poem.

Mask and Knife, The.
Requiem: "In the sudden white silence, where
    are you?"
Stranger, The.
Ginsberg. Further Proposal, A.
  Lion for Real, The.
  NIght-Apple, The.
  Song: "Weight of the world, The."
  Stanzas: Written at Night in Radio City.
  Transcription of Organ Music.
  Western Ballad, A.
Glück. Brennende Liebe.
  Fire, The.
  Islander, The.
Graves. As All Must End.
  Crane, The.
  Shift of Scene, A.
  Song: Crown of Stars.
Griffiths. Nearness.
Gunn. Autobiography.
Hacker. Aube Provençale.
  Home, and I've.
Hardy. Conversation at Dawn, A.
  Curtains Now Are Drawn, The.
  From Her in the Country.
  Last Leaf, The.
  Musing Maiden, The.
  Something Tapped.
  Turnip-Hoer, The.
  Voice, The.
  Whitewashed Wall, The.
Hartley. Day is dark—the night, The.
Hayden. Ballad of Sue Ellen Westerfield, The.
Herbert. Glimpse, The.
Hesketh. Bull Alone.
  I Am Not Resigned.
Hewitt. Birthday Rhyme for Roberta, A.
  Epithalamion: "O who will share with me."
  Ireland.
Hill. O light of light, supreme delight.
  Pavana Dolorosa.
  Splendidly-shining darkness.
Hoffman. Vows.
Holmes. Decline of the West.
  Dire Coasts.
  Old Saybrook House, The.
Housman. Far in a western brookland.
  Oh fair enough are sky and plain.
  Spring Morning.
  'Tis time, I think, by Wenlock town.
  When the lad for longing sighs.
Hughes, Langston. Afro-American Fragment.
Hugo. Mission to Linz.
Jeffers. Maid's Thought, The.
Jong. Parable of the Four-Poster.
Joseph. Chrysanth.
  Dead of Night.
  Feast, The.
  Here Lies Treasure: Here Be Monsters.
  Inland Sea, The.
  Man as Image (MASSIF; CHEMISTRY).
  Reported Missing.
  There are more accidents in the home than on
    the roads.
  Tripping down.
  X marks the spot. A postcard from home.
Keats. Day Is Gone and All Its Sweets Are
    Gone, The.
  Endymion: Poetic Romance.
  Fill for Me a Brimming Bowl.
  I Cry Your Mercy, Pity, Love—Ay, Love!
  Isabella; or, The Pot of Basil.
  To ———: "Time's sea hath been five years
    at its slow ebb."
  To Fanny.
  What Can I Do to Drive Away.
Kipling. Brookland Road.
  Love Song of Har Dyal, The.
  Mother-Lodge, The.
  Rebirth.
  Recall, The.
  Rimini.
  Song of the Wise Children.
  To the Unknown Goddess.
  Virginity, The.
Knight. I And Your Eyes.

Knott. Consolations of Sociobiology, The.
Prophet in a Landscape of Immemorial Time.
Kunitz. I Dreamed That I Was Old.
Indian Summer at Land's End.
Last Question, The.
Lovers Relentlessly.
No Word.
Regard of Tangents.
Lawrence. Coldness in Love.
Drunk.
North Country, The.
Search for Love.
Separated.
Levertov. Unknown, The.
Lewis. Across seven thousand miles of sea and time.
And still the heart breaks, wakeful all the night?
At dusk in my garden the flowers are waiting.
Chanson Triste.
Dawn on the East Coast.
Departure, The.
Desperate, The.
Exultantly he drives his screaming pinnace.
Fever.
Fishes inhabit the deep rock crannies, the worm the dry.
Fragment, A: "Where aloneness fiercely."
His mind is an inarticulated question.
Home Thoughts from Abroad.
In Hospital: Poona (1).
Lament: "Oh Absalom, beloved, what can I say?"
Mid-Winter.
On the Welsh Mountains.
Sensual mind in the wreaths of wine, The.
Song (On Seeing Dead Bodies Floating Off the Cape).
Sonnet (Aboard a Troopship) to Gweno.
Swallows are nesting in the hovels of Israel, The.
They Part at Daybreak, Returning Their Inevitable Ways.
Tiger of Camden Town, The.
Valediction.
Vigil: He Lies Awake in the Barracks Room, Fearful She Will Not Come, The.
Water Music.
Way Back, The.
Ways.
Liddy. Dinner Menu a Burnt Offering, A.
Donn, / though you are cousin.
Third Letter to Jimin in Manchuria.
Tips of the fronds become swollen, The.
Lindsay. Alone in the Wind, on the Prairie.
Beggar's Valentine, The.
Gamblers, The.
In Praise of Songs That Die.
On Suddenly Receiving a Curl Long Refused.
Lorde. Change of Season.
Memorial II.
Sowing.
To the Girl Who Lives In a Tree.
Lovelace. In Allusion to the French Song.
Lowry. Poem Influenced By John Davenport and Cervantes.
"MacDiarmid." Wheesht, Wheesht.
McGrath. Epitaph: "Again, traveller, you have come a long way led by that star."
Poem: "In the list of one thousand false addresses."
Repeated Journey, The.
MacLeish. Broken Promise.
Mahon. Achill.
Markson. A.D. 2029.
Lament: "My love is gone."
Sans.
Writer's Lament.
Marlowe. 1.3: Ad amicam.
1.6: Ad Janitorem, ut fores sibi aperiat.
Matthews. Mood Indigo.
Melville. Since as in night's deck-watch ye show.
Meredith. Beauty Rohtraut.
Blue Is the Sky.
But Joan, where is Bessy?—She.
Grace and Love.

He found her by the ocean's moaning verge.
He passed her through the sermon's dull defile.
I wish'd the world a blindness.
I would I were with Jean.
Line of eve o'er the moorland, A.
Lords of the Court they sighed heart-sick, The.
Love in the Valley.
Marian: "Clouds fly fast across the moon, The."
Marian: "She can be as wise as we."
Message from her set his brain aflame, A.
Mortesto.
My Lady has Diana's brows.
Night-Walk, The.
Night walks the earth with silver feet.
No knightly sword to serve, nor harp of bard.
Now the valley in ruin of fields.
Persistent through the brazen chorus round.
See the star yonder.
Shall I again have Lilac week?
She rides in the park on a prancing bay.
Shemselnihar.
Song: "Come to me in any shape!"
Song: "Flower unfolds its dawning cup, The."
Song: "Full of thy glory am I."
Song: "I would be the bounding deer."
Song: "I would I were the drop of rain."
Song: "O they canna' do without it."
Song: "Thou to me art such a spring."
Their sense is with their senses all mixed in.
They say, that Pity in Love's service dwells.
This was the woman; what now of the man?
Three Maidens, The.
'Tis midnight in the skies, my dear.
We violets white and blue.
When she laughs there is a glitter as of morning before me.
With the Persuader.
Young Usurper, The.
Youthful Quest, The.
Merrill. Vision of the Garden, A.
Miller. Lighted Windows (For Judy).
How lovely are thy dwellings fair!
Morgan. Bianca.
1949.
Morrison. Please Like Me.
When the Music's Over.
Muldoon. Bran.
Neruda. Cold.
Coming Back.
Men (XVIII), The.
Runaway Sun.
Sick Man in the Sun.
Whom can I ask / what I meant to achieve in this world?
Olson. As the Dead Prey upon Us.
Maximus, at the Harbor.
When do poppies bloom I ask myself, stopping again.
Oppen. In the door, / Long legged, tall.
Party on Shipboard.
Owen. My Shy Hand.
One Remains, The.
Poe. Sonnet to Zante.
To One in Paradise.
Pope. Of the Lady Who Could Not Sleep in a Stormy Night.
Presenting a *Lark*.
Pound. Imerro.
Prince. Eight times the autumn weather.
In the Wood.
Moonflower, The.
Psalms. Psalm 42: "As the hart panteth after the water brooks."
Psalm 63: "O God, thou art my God."
Psalm 84: "How amiable are thy tabernacles, O Lord of hosts!"
Ralegh. Like to a Hermit[e] Poor[e].
Rich. Continuum.
Demon Lover, The.
For the Conjunction of Two Planets.
Key, The.
Loser, The.
Paula Becker to Clara Westhoff.
Perennial Answer, The.
Since we're not young, weeks have to do

time.
This high summer we love will pour its light.
Robinson. Luke Havergal.
Rolfe. Conscript's Song.
Elegia.
First Love.
Letter for One in Russia.
Manuela.
Primer Amor.
Still Must I Love You.
Rossetti. Amore E Dovere.
Annie.
Confluents.
De Profundis.
Dream, A.
Dream, The.
Echo from Willowwood, An.
Fair World Tho' a Fallen, A.
Hope Carol, A.
If.
Like As the Hart Desireth the Water Brooks.
Long Looked For.
Looking Forward.
Repining.
Song: "I have loved you for long years Ellen."
Twilight Night.
Two Parted.
Wishes: Sonnet.
Rukeyser. Believing in Those Inexorable Laws.
Gift.
Song: Love in Whose Rich Honor.
Song: "World is full of loss; bring, wind, my love, The."
Young Girl of the Mississippi Valley, The.
Sandburg. Ambassadors of Grief.
Aztec.
Bricklayer Love.
Calls.
Circle of Doors.
Couple, A.
Home Thoughts.
M'Liss and Louie.
Old-Fashioned Requited Love.
Remembered Women.
River Moon.
Silver Wind.
Sarton. Because What I Want Most Is Permanence.
Letter to James Stephens, A.
Schuyler. August Night.
Await.
Day, The.
Evening.
O Sleepless Night.
Saturday Night.
Steaming Ties.
Sunday.
Table of Green Fields, A.
Shakespeare. Sonnet 57: "Being your slave, what should I do[e] but tend."
Shapiro. Sickness of Adam, The.
Shelley. Fragment: Igniculus Desiderii.
To ———: "Yet look on me—take not thine eyes away."
To Mary———.
To the Queen of My Heart.
Shelton. April.
Gambit, The.
Sidney. Over these brooks trusting to ease mine eyes.
Sonnet 60: "When my good angel guides me to the place."
Sonnet 62: "Late tired with woe, e'en ready for to pine."
Sonnet 89: "Now that of absence the most irksome night."
Tenth Song.
Silverstein. Just Me, Just Me.
Won't You?
Smith, Charlotte. Loose to the wind her golden tresses stream'd.
Song: "Does Pity give, tho' Fate denies."
Stanzas: "Ah! think'st thou, Laura, then, that wealth."
Smith, Patti. Easter.
Jet Flakes.

Smith, Stevie. In the Night.
Lot's Wife.
Snyder. Four Poems for Robin.
Seaman's Ditty.
Sorrentino. Bar Games.
Coast of Texas.
Evening News, The.
Long Gone Blues.
Old Tale.
pentagram.
Research, Again.
Where are the rose-colored cities.
Spender. Not to You.
Stevens. Poem with Rhythms.
Stevenson. Fixed is the doom; and to the last
   of years.
If I had wings, my lady, like a dove.
In the green and gallant Spring.
To Minnie.
To Minnie (With a Hand-Glass).
To Miss Rawlinson.
To Mrs. Will H. Low.
To My Mother.
To what shall I compare her.
To Willie and Henrietta.
Stuart. Finding One of the Ghosts.
I Can't Live Without You.
Once More for My Lady.
Song for Champagne Saturday.
Sutter. Good Night, A.
He would never say any of this.
What the Country Man Knows By Heart.
When loons laugh he does not.
Swift. To Stella.
Tate. Edges.
To a Prodigal Old Maid.
Updike. Heading for Nandi.
Report of Health.
Van Duyn. Goodbye, A.
Walker. Will.
Warren. Fox-Fire: 1956.
Whitman. I Heard You Solemn-Sweet Pipes of
   the Organ.
O You Whom I Often and Silently Come.
Whittier. Amy Wentworth.
At Last.
Summer Pilgrimage, A.
Wilbur. Ballade for the Duke of Orléans.
Ballade to End With, A.
Complaint.
Williams, Charles Kenneth. Acids.
Being Alone.
From Now On.
Gas Station, The.
Inches.
Long Bells, The.
Of What Is Past.
They Warned Him Then They Threw Him
   Away.
Time: 1978.
What Must I Do To Be Lost?
With Ignorance.
Williams, Miller. La Ultima Carta: A Young
   Wife Writes to Her Husband in the
   Mountains.
My Wife Reads the Paper at Breakfast on the
   Birthday of the Scottish Poet.
Williams, William Carlos. Gentle Negress,
   The.
Solo.
Wordsworth. Why, Minstrel, These Untuneful
   Murmurings.
Wright, Charles. Bicoastal Journal.
Composition in Grey and Pink.
Dead are waiting for us in our rooms, The.
Journal of True Confessions, A.
May Journal.
October.
T'ang Notebook.
To Giacomo Leopardi in the Sky.
Wright, James. American Wedding.
Complaint.
For the Marsh's Birthday.
Idea of the Good, The.
Poems to a Brown Cricket.
Prayer in My Sickness, A.
She Hid in the Trees from the Nurses.

So She Said.
Sun Tan at Dusk.
To the Muse.
Wroth. Song: "Fairest, and still truest eyes."
Sonnet 3: "Yett is ther hope: Then Love butt
   play thy part."
Sonnet 17: "Sweet shades why doe you seeke
   to give delight."
Sonnet 26: "Deare cherish this, and with it[t]
   my soules will."
Sonnet 36: "How well poore hart thou wittnes
   canst I love."
Wyatt. Answer, The.
As power and wit will me assist.
Ballad of Will, The.
Comfort thyself, my wo[e]ful heart.
Desire to sorrow doth me constrain.
For want of [or I] will in woe I plain.
Go, burning sighs, unto the frozen heart.
Grudge on who list, this is my lot.
Heart oppressed [or oppress'd] with desperate
   thought.
If fancy [or fansy] would favour.
It may be good, like it who list.
Knot which first my heart did strain, The.
Madam, I you require.
Might I as well within my song belay.
My sweet, alas, forget me not.
Once [or Ons], as methought, Fortune me
   kissed [or kist or kyst].
So feeble is the thread that doth the burden
   stay.
Such hap as I am happed in.
Sufficed not, madame, that you did tear.
There was never nothing more me pained [or
   payned].
Though of the sort there be that feign.
Though this the [or thy] port and I thy servant
   true.
Was I never yet of your love grieved.
What death is worse than this?
Young. Maya.
Zimmer. I Go Out in the Long Nights.
One for the Ladies at the Troy Laundry Who
   Cooled Themselves for Zimmer.
Zimmer's Love Poem After A Hard Dream.
Zukofsky. Catullus viii.
Miss her, Catullus? don't be so inept to rail.
Rum asks—see, fortune won't molest you.
See could we quit coveting hope taunting
   where hope hid and.
Sparrow, my girl's pleasure, delight of my
   girl.

Longshoremen
Gallagher. Black Money.

Lookout Mountain, Battle of (1863)
Hayden. On Lookout Mountain.

Loons
Carruth. Loon on Forrester's Pond, The.
Eberhart. Dream, A.
Loon Call, A.

Lorelei
Clark. Sedge.
Merrill. Lorelei.
Smith, Stevie. Die Lorelei.

Los Angeles, California
Beatles. Blue Jay Way.
Clark. West of Eden.
Cohen. Commentary—It's Probably Spring.
End of My Life in Art.
   see also Commentary—It's Probably Spring.
Dickey, James. Exchanges.
Jarrell. Gleaning.
Thinking of the Lost World.
McGrath. Return to Marsh Street.
Morrison. L.A. Woman.
Rukeyser. Palos Verdes Cliffs.
Updike. L.A.
See also **Hollywood, California.**

Loss
Ammons. Permanence.
Angelou. No Loser, No Weeper.
Arnold. Forsaken Merman, The.
Ashbery. Leasing of September, The.
Atwood. At first I was given centuries.
Hesitations Outside the Door.

In the house on the cliff.
It is not the things themselves.
Precognition.
Auden. Ebes Anthos Apollumenon.
Elegy: "Why was it that you gave us no
   warning."
Letter, The.
Light strives with darkness, right with wrong.
Beatles. Baby's in Black.
Don't Bother Me.
I'm a Loser.
Berg. Between Us.
Dreaming with a Friend.
Driving Out Again at Night.
Red Weed.
To My Friends.
Berrigan. Red Shift.
Berry. Forty Years.
We came then to his time of pain.
We don't bother nobody.
Berryman. As usual I'm up before the sun.
Ball Poem, The.
Because I'd seen you not believe your lover.
Began with swirling, blind, unstilled oh still.
Cambridge friend put in,—one whom I used,
   A.
Clots of age, grovel and palsy, crave, The.
Fall and rise of her midriff bells. I watch.
Most strange, my change, this nervous
   interim—.
"Ring us up when you want to see us..."—
   "Sure."
Spendthrift Urethra—Sphincter, frugal one—.
Surviving Love.
Betjeman. Cockney Amorist, The.
Lament for Moira McCavendish, A.
Bishop. One Art.
Bly. Visiting the Farallones.
Brontë. Alcona, in its changing mood.
From our evening fireside now.
Inspiring music's thrilling sound, The.
O come again; what chains withhold.
Old Hall of Elbë, ruined, lonely now.
Was it with the fields of green.
Brooks. Appendix to the Anniad.
Browning, Elizabeth Barrett. Lost Bower, The.
Sonnet: "My letters! All dead paper, mute and
   white."
Year's Spinning, A.
Browning, Robert. Any Wife to Any Husband.
In a Year.
Lost Leader, The.
Lost Mistress, The.
Too Late.
Waring.
Youth and Art.
Bukowski. Fat Mexican woman in front of me
   in line, A.
I Made a Mistake.
Longshot.
Melancholia.
Burns. Braes o' Ballochmyle, The.
Fragment, Which Was Meant for the
   Beginning of an Elegy on the Late Miss
   Burnet of Monboddo, A.
Highland Widow's Lament, The.
Lass of Ecclefechan, The.
Lines on Stirling.
Lovely Lass o' Inverness, The.
Man Was Made to Mourn, a Dirge.
On the Death of the Late Lord President
   Dundas.
Raving winds around her blowing.
Song, A: "Thou lingering Star with lessening
   ray."
Song: "Ae fond kiss, and then we sever."
Song: "As I stood by yon roofless tower."
Song: "Farewell, thou stream that winding
   flows."
Song.—In the Character of a Ruined Farmer.
Song: "Small birds rejoice in the green leaves
   returning, The."
Sonnet on the Death of Robert Riddel, Esq. of
   Glen Riddel, April 1794.
Strathallan's Lament.
To Ruin.

To William Creech.
Winter It Is Past, The.
Byron. Fragment Written Shortly after the Marriage of Miss Chaworth.
Herod's Lament for Mariamne.
On Finding a Fan.
Remember Him Whom Passion's Power.
There Was a Time, I Need Not Name.
To a Lady.
To the Countess of Blessington.
Translation from Catullus ("Ye Cupids, droop each little head").
Campion. Ballad, A: "Dido was the Carthage Queene."
Could my heart more tongues imploy.
Epigramme: "His late losse the Wiveless Higs in order."
Let him that will be free and keep his hart from care.
Long have mine eies gaz'd with delight.
Peaceful Western Wind, The.
Carew. Deposition from Love, A.
"Carroll, Lewis." Coronach.
Faces in the Fire.
Stolen Waters.
Three Sunsets.
Carruth. *As you or I, but at least he fights hard to get.*
Bitcheries of Madison Avenue, The.
Ithiel Falls, below the Nazarene campground.
A name.
Lines Written in an Asylum.
Store, more'n likely, in one of those tenements.
Catullus. Carmen 3: "Who loves beauty / vel her statues."
Carmen 058: "Lesbia, our Lesbia, the same old Lesbia."
Carmen 65: "Although entangled in prolonged grief."
Carmen 68: "Borne down by bitter misfortune."
Carmen 76: "If evocations of past kindness shed."
Carmen 96: "If, Calvus, effects of grief."
Carmen 101: "Journeying over many seas and through many countries."
Clark. Antiquarian.
Clough. Alteram Partem.
Cohen. Ballad of the Absent Mare.
Came So Far for Beauty.
Days of Kindness.
For Anne.
I'd Like to Read.
Lovers.
Nothing I Can Lose.
Sisters of Mercy.
We Cry Out.
Coleridge. Farewell to Love.
On Seeing a Youth Affectionately Welcomed by a Sister.
Song: "Sunny shaft did I behold, A."
To a Friend [Charles Lamb] Together with an Unfinished Poem.
Crane. Ah! the divine infatuation.
Her Eyes Had.
Mermen, The.
Sad Indian, The.
Stark Major.
Voyages.
Creeley. Echoes.
In an Act of Pity.
Sanine to Leda.
To And.
Cullen. Lament: "Now let all lovely things embark."
Sonnet: "I know now how a man whose blood is hot."
Therefore, Adieu.
Threnody for a Brown Girl.
Variations on a Theme.
Wind Bloweth Where It Listeth, The.
Cummings. "Could that"i marveled"be / you?"
First Jock he / was kilt a handsome.
In heavenly realms of hellas dwelt.
Let it go—the.
My little heart is so wonderfully sorry.
Noster was a ship of swank, The.

O / the round / little man we.
Of Ever-Ever Land i speak.
Proud of his scientific attitude.
When my sensational moments are no more.
When what hugs stopping earth than silent is.
W.H.W., Jr.
Why did you go.
Workingman with hand so hairy-sturdy.
Worshipping same / they squirm and they spawn.
Davie. Revenge for Love.
Rutland.
Scythian Charioteers, The.
De la Mare. Fare Well.
Reserved.
Dickey, James. Leap, The.
To Be Done in Winter.
Dickinson. Bereaved of all, I went abroad.
Each Scar I'll keep for Him.
Except the Heaven had come so near.
Had I presumed to hope.
Her sweet Weight on my Heart a Night.
Home itself is far from home.
How much of Source escapes with thee.
How sweet that he rose in the morning.
I cannot buy it—'tis not sold.
I had a guinea golden.
I lost a World—the other day!
I trust you may have the dearest summer.
If I'm lost—now.
Loss of something ever felt I, A.
Now I knew I lost her.
Of so divine a Loss.
Only Balmless Wound, The.
Severer Service of myself.
She went as quiet as the Dew.
Stimulus of Loss, The.
Things that never can come back, are several, The.
To lose thee—sweeter than to gain.
We miss a Kinsman more.
Where I have lost, I softer tread.
Who never lost, are unprepared.
You love me—you are sure.
Donne. Bracelet, The.
Computation, The.
To Mr I. L. ("Blessed [or Blesst] are your north parts, for all this long time").
Doolittle. Calliope.
Chance Meeting.
Eros.
Fragment 40: "Keep love and he wings."
Hyacinth.
Loss.
Dove. Exeunt the Viols.
Dunbar. Golden Day, A.
Ione.
Jilted.
Wraith, The.
Yesterday and Tomorrow.
Dunn. Sister.
Vanishings, The.
"Dylan." Abandoned Love.
Absolutely Sweet Marie.
All Over You.
Ballad in Plain D.
Boots of Spanish Leather.
Girl of the North Country.
Golden Loom.
Gypsy Lou.
I Threw It All Away.
If You See Her, Say Hello.
Living the Blues.
Mama, You Been on My Mind.
Meet Me in the Morning.
One More Night.
Quit Your Low Down Ways.
Shot of Love.
Simple Twist of Fate.
Tight Connection to My Heart (Has Anybody Seen My Love).
Tomorrow Is a Long Time.
Visions of Johanna.
Where Are You Tonight? (Journey through Dark Heat).
Eberhart. Broken Wing Theory.

Haystack, The.
Loss.
Eliot. Eyes That Last I Saw in Tears.
Hollow Men, The.
Journey of the Magi.
Emerson. Dost thou not hear me Ellen.
Give All to Love.
In Memoriam.
My days roll by me like a train of dreams.
Shall the Muse sing for thousands & not sing.
Threnody: "South-wind brings, The."
Where art thou / Thou beautiful dream.
Everson. Rattlesnake August.
Fenton. Skip, The.
Wind.
Ferlinghetti. Deflowering.
Fisher. Some Loss.
Gallagher. Calm, The.
Coming Home.
Even Now You Are Leaving.
I Save Your Coat, But You Lose It Later.
Gardner. Accomplices, The.
At a Summer Hotel.
Bronchitis at the Chelsea—or Salud Raul.
Daughter.
Two Sapphics.
Garrigue. After Reading "The Country of the Pointed Firs."
Grief Was to Go Out, Away.
Requiem: "In the sudden white silence, where are you?"
Gildner. Letter From My Good Hand, A.
Ginsberg. Café in Warsaw.
Car Crash.
Elegy for Neal Cassady.
Garden State.
Over Denver Again.
Glück. Autumnal.
Dream of Mourning, The.
Egg, The.
Fire, The.
First Goodbye.
Here Are My Black Clothes.
Rosy.
Graves. As When the Mystic.
At the Gate.
Desert Fringe.
Lost Love.
Gray. Song: "Thyrsis, when we parted, swore."
Gunn. Autobiography.
Beautician, The.
Right Possessor, The.
Without a Counterpart.
Hacker. Against Silence.
Autumn 1980.
Geographer.
Sea Coming Indoors, The.
Hall. Elegy for Wesley Wells.
Red Branch, The.
Religious Articles.
Hardy. At a Seaside Town in 1869.
At Rushy-Pond.
Ballad of Love's Skeleton, The.
Boys Then and Now.
Change, The.
Evelyn G. of Christminster.
He Inadvertently Cures His Love-Pains.
I Said to Love.
Marble-Streeted Town, The.
Molly Gone.
On Martock Moor.
Re-Enactment, The.
Revulsion.
Signs and Tokens.
Song from Heine.
Song to an Old Burden.
Standing by the Mantlepiece.
That Moment.
They Would Not Come.
Under High-Stoy Hill.
Without Ceremony.
Hartley. Outcast City on the Kennebec, The.
Hartnett. No Avail.
Hayden. Road in Kentucky, A.
Hemingway. Sport of Kings, The.
Herrick. His Losse.

Losse from the Heat.
Plunder, The.
Upon a Comely, and Curious Maide.
Upon Skurffe.
Hesketh. I Cannot Look into the Sun.
No Reply at Christmas.
Hewitt. Betrayal.
Hired Lad's Farewell, The.
J.B. Shelton (1876–1958), The Coventry
  Antiquarian.
King's Horses, The.
Knife, The.
Lonsdale Street.
Lost *Argo*, Islandmagee, Summer 1919.
My dear spouse died—a tumour on the brain.
My Father's Death in Hospital.
Hill. Coplas.
Ten years without you. For so it happens.
Hopkins. Sparky air, The.
Voice from the World, A.
Housman. Give me a land of boughs in leaf.
If truth in hearts that perish.
Into my heart an air that kills.
We'll to the woods no more.
Hughes, Langston. Cora.
Homecoming.
Lament over Love.
Young Gal's Blues.
Hughes, Ted. Black Beast, The.
Hugo. Beaverbank.
Bone Hunting.
Clearances, The.
Graves.
Landscapes.
Last Words to James Wright.
Road Ends at Tahola.
Semi-Lunatics of Kilmuir, The.
Way a Ghost Behaves, The.
Where the House Was.
Jarrell. Bad Music, The.
Che Farò Senza Euridice.
I loved you, too. There was no use. I had no
  time.
Leave.
Loss.
Lost Love, The.
Moving.
Northern Snows, The.
Second Air Force.
Street Has Changed, The.
Today is almost over.
Truth, The.
Jong. Driving Me Away.
Letter to My Lover after Seven Years.
There Is Only One Story.
Jonson. Elegy, An: "Since you must go, and I
  must bid farewell."
Execration upon Vulcan, An.
To the World [A Farewell for a Gentlewoman,
  Virtuous and Noble].
Why I Write Not of Love.
Joseph. Animal Story, An.
Dawn Walkers.
Exorcism.
February Floods, 1953.
Genus: Homo.
Go Back to Square One.
High Devil, Deep Pit.
Lost Sea, The.
Lure.
Man in a Bar.
Non-communicant.
Persephone Returns.
Walk in the woods at the hour when the
  fuddled sun.
Keats. In Drear-nighted December.
Kipling. Bridegroom, The.
Children, The.
Dove of Dacca, The.
Follow Me 'Ome.
For to Admire.
Kingdom, The.
Lovers' Litany, The.
Mesopotamia.
Possibilities.
Recantation, A.
Russia to the Pacifists.

Soldier, Soldier.
Song in the Desert, A.
There were three friends that buried the fourth.
Widower, The.
With Scindia to Delhi.
Knight. Feeling Fucked Up.
No Moon Floods the Memory of that Night.
Knott. Closet, The.
Koch. To Marina.
Larkin. No Road.
So through that unripe day you bore your
  head.
Lawrence. Another Ophelia.
Bereavement.
Bread upon the Waters.
Call into Death.
Drama, A.
Elegy: "Sun immense and rosy, The."
Grey Evening.
Humiliation.
Inheritance, The.
Kiss, A.
Last Words to Miriam.
Last Words to Muriel.
Love Message.
Love Song, A: "Reject me not if I should say
  to you."
Mesopotamia.
On the Balcony.
Seekers.
Silence.
Submergence.
Witch II, The.
Levine. Buying and Selling.
Lost and Found.
Lewis. Dancer, The.
From a Play.
Greetings.
Lovers who among the grasses.
Raid, The.
She Remains.
Song: "I lay in sheets of softest linen."
Song (On Seeing Dead Bodies Floating Off
  the Cape).
Valediction.
Liddy. Eugene Connolly.
Longfellow. Cross of Snow, The.
Hawthorne.
Lorde. Sister, Morning Is a Time for Miracles.
Lovelace. Another ("I Did believe I was in
  Heav'n").
Lowry. Oh, poor Mary Ann / When she got to
  the top.
Two streams came from a different source,
  The.
McGrath. Changeling, The.
End of the Line, The.
MacLeish. Beside her in the dark the chime.
Fall!, The.
He leans against the window-sill.
Psyche with the Candle.
Things he had loved because he knew them
  lost.
MacNeice. Sand in the Air.
Markson. At Malcolm Lowry's Grave.
I Ate My Love Alive.
Johanna.
Loss.
Monody.
We Love, But Cannot Live.
Marlowe. 1.12: Tabellas quas miserat
  execratur, quod amica noctem negabat.
2.11: Ad amicam navigantem.
2.16: Ad amicam, ut ad rura sua veniat.
Marvell. Unfortunate Lover, The.
Matthews. Blues for John Coltrane, Dead at
  41.
Meredith. C B M.
Dark on the ridge of the cold salt wave.
Hilda's Morning and Evening Dose of Rhyme.
Hungarian Air.
I am to follow her. There is much grace.
I bade my Lady think what she might mean.
In our old shipwrecked days there was an
  hour.
It chanced his lips did meet her forehead cool.
Love.

Mark where the pressing wind shoots javelin-
  like.
Message from her set his brain aflame, A.
So spake she her first utterance on the rack.
Song: "Should thy love die; / O bury it not
  under ice-blue eyes!"
This was the woman; what now of the man?
'Tis Christmas weather, and a country house.
Two Blackbirds, The.
Vittoria Concluding the Opera of "Camilla."
Merton. Dirge for a Town in France.
Take thought, man, tonight.
Millay. If I should learn, in some quite casual
  way.
What lips my lips have kissed, and where, and
  why.
Milton. Mulciber.
Morgan. Catullus: *Carmen ci.*
Nathan. Morning Song.
Surprise.
Neruda. Ambassador, The.
Final.
O'Hara. Mayakovsky.
Oliver. Hattie Bloom.
In Blackwater Woods.
Olson. Maximus to Himself June 1964.
Pacific Lament.
Oppen. From Disaster.
Historic Pun.
It is a place.
Return.
Some of the young men.
Pack. Clayfeld Renews His Vow to Evelyn.
Mountain Ash Without Cedar Waxwings.
Paley. Ant! / lugging half an ounce, An.
Piercy. All Clear.
Never-Never.
Plath. Bucolics.
Denouement.
Poe. Dream, A.
Dream within a Dream, A.
Happiest Day, the Happiest Hour, The.
Sleeper, The.
To ———: "Bowers whereat, in dreams, I
  see, The."
To One in Paradise.
Valley of Unrest, The.
Pope. Lamentation of Glumdalclitch for the
  Loss of Grildrig, The.
Prince. Coeur de Lion.
For Fugitives.
Letter.
Raine. Her Room.
Ralegh. End of the Boo[c]k[e]s, of the
  Ocean's Love to Cynthia [*or* Scinthia], and
  the Beginning[e] of the 12 [*or* 22] Boo[c]k,
  Entreating of Sorrow, The.
Ransom. Dead Boy.
"Reed." Halloween Parade, The.
Hello It's Me.
Pale Blue Eyes.
Rich. Loser, The.
Of simple choice they are the villagers; their
  clothes come.
Old blanket. The crumbs of rubbed wool
  turning up, The.
Stelae, The.
Robinson. On the Night of a Friend's
  Wedding.
Roethke. Apparition, The.
Beast, The.
Visitant, The.
Rolfe. Sunday Evening Revery.
Witness at Leipzig.
Rossetti. Cousin Kate.
Despair.
Grown and Flown.
Rukeyser. His father is lost and away.
Loan, The.
Of Money. And the Past.
Waiting for Icarus.
Sandburg. And This Will Be All?
Dreams in the Dusk.
Great Hunt, The.
Schuyler. August First, 1974.
Morning of the Poem, The.
Sexton. Ballad of the Lonely Masturbator,

The.
Fury of God's Good-bye, The.
Going Gone.
Inventory of Goodbyes, The.
Lost Lie, The.
Waking Alone.
Wedding Night, The.
Shakespeare. Sonnet 42: "That thou hast her, it is not all my grief[e]."
Sonnet 49: "Against that time, if ever that time come."
Sonnet 86: "Was it the proud full sail of his great verse."
Sonnet 87: "Farewell! Thou art too dear[e] for my possessing."
Sonnet 90: "Then hate me when thou wilt; if ever, now."
Sonnet 134: "So, now I have confess'd that he is thine."
Shapiro. Haircut.
Leg, The.
Shelley. Lines: "We meet not as we parted."
On a Faded Violet.
Sunset, The.
To Mary Shelley ("My dearest Mary, wherefore hast thou gone").
To William Shelley ("My lost William, thou in whom").
Sidney. Sonnet 18: "With what sharp checks I in myself am shent."
Ye [or you] goat-herd gods, [that love the grassy mountains].
Smith, Charlotte. By the Same. Just before His Death.
Elegy: "Dark gathering clouds involve the threatening skies."
Forest Boy, The.
Lydia.
Peasant of the Alps, The.
Verses, on the death of [Henrietta O'Neill], written in September, 1794.
When welcome slumber sets my spirit free.
Where the green leaves exclude the summer beam.
Ye vales and woods! fair scenes of happier hours.
Smith, Patti. Fire of Unknown Origin, A.
Work Song.
Smith, Stevie. Arabella.
Broken Heart, The.
Gnädiges Fräulein.
House of Over-Dew, The.
Recluse, The.
Story I Have Told, The.
Sorrentino. Cerinthus, don't you have some soft thought for your girl.
Edges, The.
George C. Tilyou Smiles.
Good Night!
Poem to Read in August, A.
That you allow yourself this vast neglect of me.
Southwell. Laments for a Noble Lady.
Spender. Double Shame, The.
Spenser. Within this wood, out of a rocke did rise.
Stafford. Farm on the Great Plains, The.
Saint Matthew and All.
Stevenson. Let Love go, if go she will.
Love—what is love? A great and aching heart.
Rain is over and done, The.
Relic taken, what avails the shrine?, The.
Soon our friends perish.
Tate. Adaption of a Theme from Catullus.
Tennyson. Œnone.
Tomlinson. Death of the Infanta, The.
Elegy for Henry Street.
Tarquinia.
Updike. Lament, for Cocoa.
My Children at the Dump.
South of the Alps.
Wakoski. Few Silver Scales, The.
Lady Who Sang, The.
Ring of Irony, The.
Waldman. Cabin.
Walker. Walker.

Warren. Loss, of Perhaps Love, in Our World of Contingency.
Whitman. O Captain! My Captain!
When Lilacs Last in the Dooryard Bloom'd.
Yonnondio.
Whittier. Farewell, The: "Gone, gone,—sold and gone."
Fountain, The.
Inscription: "Eagle, stooping from yon snow-blown peaks, The."
Rendition, The.
Singer, The.
Truce of Piscataqua, The.
Williams, Charles Kenneth. Call, The.
Covenant, The.
Downwards.
Le Petit Salvié.
Loss.
Vehicle: Absence.
Williams, William Carlos. Hemmed-in Males.
Silently I ascend the western pavilion.
Wordsworth. Complaint, A.
Composed When a Probability Existed of Our Being Obliged to Quit Rydal Mount as a Residence.
Death of a Starling, The.
Elegiac Verses in Memory of My Brother, John Wordsworth.
From the Alban Hills, Looking towards Rome.
Grief, thou hast lost an ever ready friend.
Last of the Flock, The.
Peter Bell; a Tale.
She dwelt among the untrodden ways.
Sonnet in the Pass of Killicranky.
Vaudracour and Julia.
Why, Minstrel, These Untuneful Murmurings.
Wishing-Gate Destroyed, The.
Written in London, September, 1802.
Wright, James. Gambling in Stateline, Nevada.
Having Lost My Sons, I Confront the Wreckage of the Moon: Christmas, 1960.
Humming a Tune for an Old Lady in West Virginia.
In Memory of the Horse David, Who Ate One of my Poems.
Listening to the Mourners.
Quail, The.
Wroth. Love's Victorie.
Song: "I, that ame of all most crost."
Sonnet 9: "'Pray doe nott use thes words I must bee gone."
Sonnet 25: "Poore eyes bee blind, the light behold noe more."
Sonnet 29: "Fly hence O! joy noe longer heere abide."
Wyatt. Help[e] me to seek [or seke] for I lost it there.
I see the change from that that was.
Loss is small to lose such one, The.
My love took scorn my service to retain.
Where shall I have at mine own will.
Yeats. Crazy Jane Reproved.
King and No King.
Lover Mourns for the Loss of Love, The.
Never Give All the Heart.
Young. Afraid.
Zimmer. Thurman's Slumping Blues.
Zukofsky. Caelius, Lesbia new star, Lesbia a light.
Cold how mean, fortune consuming you oppresses your care, your.
Lament, o graces of Venus, and Cupids.
Marigold.
Mulled hosts their countries yet mulled there by a core of wake tossed.
See quick calm moot as gratifying the tombed—sepulchres.
Seek or record then the benefactor—pree or voluptuous.
Yet see (may as I do) a confect of my cure—a dolor.

Lot (Bible)
Housman. Half-way, for one commandment broken.
Nemerov. Lot Later.
Lot's Wife.
Rukeyser. Ms. Lot.

Wilbur. Lot's Wife.
Lotus
Hewitt. Willow Pattern.
Kunitz. Off Point Lotus.
Lawrence. Lotus and Frost.
Lindsay. Wedding of the Rose and the Lotus, The.
Louis XIV, King of France
Marvell. Inscribenda Luparae [To Be Written on the Louvre].
Louis XVI, King of France
Blake. French Revolution, The.
Smith, Charlotte. Long wintry months are past; the Moon that now.
Louisiana
Carruth. New Orleans.
L'Ouverture, Toussaint. *see* Toussaint L'Ouverture, François Dominique.
Love. *see* Affection; Companionship and Companions; Courtship; Dating; Desire; Erotic Love; Lust; Sex; Sexuality.
Lovebirds
Chaucer. Romance [*or* Romaunt] of the Rose, The.
Eberhart. Bower, The.
Hall. Young Watch Us, The.
Hardy. Her Love-Birds.
Nash. Two and One Are a Problem.
Pack. Ode to a Lovesick Moose.
Rolfe. Night World.
Wright, James. For the Marsh's Birthday.
Lovelace, Richard
Lovelace. Commendatory Poems.
Elegies, 1660.
Marvell. To His Noble Friend, Mr Richard Lovelace, upon His Poems.
Lowell, Amy
Cullen. Epitaph: "She leans across a golden table."
Cummings. Slightly before the middle of Congressman Pudd.
Schuyler. Amy Lowell Thoughts.
Lowell, James Russell
Emerson. James Russell Lowell.
Whittier. James Russell Lowell.
Welcome to Lowell, A.
Lowell, Robert
Berg. Lowell: Self-Portrait.
Bishop. North Haven.
Fox. Nail of the Index Finger, The.
Holmes. Out of a Fever: For Robert Lowell (Sept. 13, 1977).
Hugo. Graves in Uig.
Lowry, Malcolm
Lowry. Doggerel.
Epitaph: "Dear Scipio Sprague / sans plague sans blague."
Mahon. Homage to Malcolm Lowry.
Loyalty
Berryman. Troubling are masks... the faces of friends, my face.
Browning, Elizabeth Barrett. Rhyme of the Duchess May.
Sonnet: "I never gave a lock hair away."
Sonnet: "My poet, thou canst touch on all the notes."
Browning, Robert. Light Woman, A.
Burns. Bannocks o' Bear-Meal.
Here's a Health to Them That's Awa'.
Highland Laddie.
My Collier Laddie.
O, for Ane-and-Twenty Tam.
O [*or* Oh] Wert Thou in the Cauld Blast.
Sutors o' Selkirk.
Toast, A.
Catullus. Carmen 1: "To whom should I present this."
Carmen 11: "Furius, Aurelius, friends of my youth."
Chaucer. Balade of Complaint, A.
Clerk's Tale, The.
Cowper. On Loyalty.
Creeley. For Anybody.
She Went to Stay.
"Dylan." From a Buick 6.

Eberhart. Later or Sooner.
Emerson. Quoth Saadi, when I stood before.
Glück. Late Snow.
Haines. Guevara.
Hardy. I will be faithful to thee; aye, I will!
In Weatherbury Stocks.
Hewitt. Dilemma, The.
If I had given you that love and care.
Memorandum for the Moderates.
Hill. Vocations.
Housman. As through the wild green hills of Wyre.
Jeffers. At the Birth of an Age.
House Dog's Grave, The.
Kipling. Dinah in Heaven.
Gunga Din.
Ode: "So long as memory, valour, and faith endure."
Song of the Red War-Boat.
Ulster.
Kunitz. Signal from the House, The.
Lawrence. Talk of Loyalty.
Lewis. At dusk in my garden the flowers are waiting.
Lovelace. To Lucasta, from Prison.
McAuley. Here on the vast edges drear.
You've mastered the bleak art of Changes.
Markson. Vow, The.
Merton. Come Dance in Baronies.
Morgan. Catullus: Carmen xi.
Nash. Father, Dear Father, Go Jump in the Lake, or, You're Costlier than You Think.
Olson. Maximus, to Gloucester.
Prince. His Dog and Pilgrim.
Psalms. Psalm 89: "I will sing of the mercies of the Lord for ever."
Ralegh. Advice, The.
Smith, Charlotte. From Petrarch ("Oh! place me where the burning noon").
Inscription on a Stone, in the Church-Yard at Boreham.
Oh! place me where the burning noon.
Stanzas: "Ah! think'st thou, Laura, then, that wealth."
Snodgrass. Magda Goebbels ("How could you dare stay constant to").
Sorrentino. Totem, The.
Whittier. Answer, The.
Williams, Charles Kenneth. Being Alone.
Wroth. Sonnet 26: "Deare cherish this, and with it[t] my soules will."
Yeats. Black Tower, The.
Zukofsky. Barely and widely.
Furius, Aurelius: comities—Catullus.
1959 Valentine.
Tam Cari Capitis.
Whom do I give my neat little volume.

Luck
Beckett. À l'instant de s'entendre dire.
Bukowski. Luck.
Burns. O raging Fortune's withering blast.
Carruth. Tanck's Song About the Jinx.
Clark. Now She Dwells Here.
Cummings. Lucky means finding / Holes where.
Dickinson. Luck is not chance.
Dunbar. Way T'ings Come, De.
Dunn. Carpenter's Song, The.
Herrick. Coming of Good Luck, The.
Crosse and Pile.
Good Luck Not Lasting.
Large Bounds Doe but Bury Us.
No Luck in Love.
Hewitt. Knife, The.
Local Poet, A.
Housman. Now dreary dawns the eastern light.
Hughes, Langston. Bad Luck Card.
Luck.
Hugo. Green Stone.
Red Stone.
Kipling. Beat off in our last fight were we?
Wishing-Caps, The.
Lowry. Good Morning to Our Sweetest Harteebeeste!
Tibute to the Renowned Harteebeeste, A.
Nash. How Long Has This Been Going On?
Oh, Quite Long.

Outcome of Mr. Buck's Superstition, The.
Prayer at the End of a Rope.
Turns in a Worm's Lane.
You Bet Travel Is Broadening.
Nemerov. Sonnet: "It seems to be the trouble, everyone."
Rossetti. Linnet in a gilded cage,— / A linnet on a bough, A.
Queen of Hearts, The.
Sandburg. Come on, superstition, and get my goat.
Wyatt. Alas, Fortune, what aileth thee.
For shamefast harm of great and hateful need.
He is not de[a]d that sometime [or somtyme] hath a fall.
Young. Friday the 12th.
Zukofsky. Honesty.
See also **Chance; Fate; Fortune.**

Lucknow, India
Whittier. Pipes at Lucknow, The.

Luddites
Byron. Ode to the Framers of the Frame Bill, An.
Hewitt. Executives Third Tier.

Lullabies
Bishop. Lullaby. / Adult and child.
Lullaby for the Cat.
Browning, Elizabeth Barrett. Song against Singing, A.
"Carroll, Lewis." Red Queen's Lullaby, The.
Eberhart. Line of Verse of Yeats, A.
Fenton. Lullaby for a Summer Recess.
Herrick. Upon a Child.
Keats. 'Tis the Witching Time [or Hour] of Night.
McNeill. Pioneer Lullaby.
Rossetti. Holy Innocents.
Lie a-bed, / Sleepy head, / Shut up eyes, bo-peep.
Lullaby, oh lullaby! / Flowers are closed and lambs are sleeping.
Stevenson. Home from the daisied meadows, where you linger yet.
Tennyson. Sweet and Low [Sweet and Low].
Wordsworth. Cottager to Her Infant, (By My Sister), The.
See also **Cradle Song in Title and First Line Index; Lullaby in Title and First Line Index.**

Lumbering and Lumbermen
Carruth. As you or I, but at least he fights hard to get.
Dickey, James. Other, The.
Frost. In winter in the woods alone.
Hardy. Throwing a Tree.
McNeill. Deserted Lumber Yard.
Log Drive.
Saturday Night (1890-1910).
Meredith. Woodman and Echo.
Snyder. Ancient forests of China logged, The.
But ye shall destroy their altars.
Ethnobotany.
Felix Baran / Hugo Gerlot.
Getting in the Wood.
Ray Wells, a big Nisqually, and I.
Whittier. Lumbermen, The.
Wilbur. Folk Tune.
Williams, Charles Kenneth. Elms.

Lunch
Creeley. Sopa.
Hughes, Langston. Lunch in a Jim Crow Car.
Koch. Lunch.
Nash. Dance Unmacabre.
O'Hara. Step Away from Them, A.
Patchen. Lunch Wagon on Highway 57.
Stevens. Sailing after Lunch.
Tomlinson. Hero Sandwiches.
Portrait of the Artist II.

Lungs
Piercy. Bronchitis on the 14th Floor.
Rukeyser. Disease, The.

Lust
Auden. Cinders.
Love Feast, The.
Beatles. I Should Have Known Better.
Please Please Me.
Why Don't We Do It in the Road.

Berryman. Images of Elspeth.
Spot of poontang on a five-foot piece, A.
Betjeman. Late-flowering Lust.
Lenten Thoughts of a High Anglican.
Senex.
Bishop. Love with his gilded bow and crystal arrows.
Bukowski. I Kneel.
Iron Mike.
My Groupie.
99 to One.
Bunting. Dear be still! Time's start of us lengthens slowly.
Burns. Charlie He's My Darling.
Muirland Meg.
There's News Lasses News.
Trogger, The.
Carruth. Sonnet: "Dearest, I never knew such loving. There."
Sonnet: "Freedom in love? It has been questioned. Think."
Creeley. June 6, 1970.
Looking Out.
Cummings. God pity me whom(god distinctly has).
My eyes are fond of the east side.
My girl's tall with hard long eyes.
On the Madam's best april the.
Poem her belly marched through me as, The.
Sh estiffl / ystrut sal.
Twentyseven bums give a prostitute the once.
What time is it i wonder never mind.
When i have thought of you somewhat too.
When thou hast taken thy last applause,and when.
Dobyns. Desire.
Syracuse Nights.
White Thighs.
Doolittle. O for wings.
Duncan. Albigenses, The.
Mirror, The.
Eberhart. Enigma, The.
Mais L'Amour Infini Me Montera Dans L'Ame.
Everson. And it creams: from under her elbow a suffix of light, a sheen of kept being.
Annul in Me My Manhood.
But masked of the self.
Man of God. Tall man, man of oath. Mad man of ignorant causes.
So him in dream.
Gildner. My Coed Wife.
Ginsberg. Sweet Boy, Gimme Yr Ass.
Graves. Blue-Fly, The.
In Trance At A Distance.
Succubus, The.
Gunn. Modes of Pleasure.
Herrick. Julia's Petticoat.
Parting Verse, Or Charge to His Supposed Wife When He Travelled, The.
Poet Loves a Mistress, but Not to Marry, The.
To Bacchus, a Canticle.
Vine, The.
Vision, The.
Jarrell. Sears Roebuck.
Jonson. Fragmentum Petron. Arbitr. The Same Translated.
On Groin.
Koch. Of course you must stop her. Say anything: "Hello!" "Good-bye!"
Kunitz. She Wept, She Railed.
Lawrence. Passing Visit to Helen.
Lewis. Encounter, The.
Gates of my palace are opened wide, The.
Pharaoh has seen me in the hovels of Israel.
Soubrettes, The.
Swan's Way, The.
Tiger of Camden Town, The.
Liddy. Dream of a Strange One.
History.
Narcissus and the Young Men.
"MacDiarmid." I mind when my first wife died.
MacLeish. Humid air precipitates, The.
Passing her in the day he had but dared.
Markson. Question of Anatomy.

This Vision Comes.
To a Lady, a Part of Her.
Marlowe. 1.5: Corinnae concubitus.
2.4: Quod amet mulieres, cuiuscunque formae
sint.
3.2: Ad amicam cursum equorum spectantem.
Matthews. Lust Acts.
Melville. After the Pleasure Party.
Morrison. Soul Kitchen.
Nemerov. Don Juan to the Statue.
Landscape with Figures.
New Weapons in the Old War.
O'Hara. Poem: "I don't know as I get what
D.H. Lawrence is driving at."
Olson. As the shield goddess, Mycenae.
Hymn to the Word.
Long Distance.
Troilus.
Woman's Nipples Is the Rose of the World,
A.
Pack. Modest Boast at Meridian, A.
Piercy. For two years I broke from these
cycles, simply.
Plath. Gigolo.
Rich. Sex, as they harshly call it.
Rolfe. Manuela.
Shakespeare. Sonnet 129: "Expense of spirit in
a waste of shame, The [or Th']."
Shapiro. Kiss, The.
Sidney. Fourth Song.
Stevenson. To Minnie (With a Hand-Glass).
Thomas. Into Her Lying Down Head.
Updike. Nuda Natens.
Rockettes, The.
Van Duyn. Billings and Cooings from "The
Berkeley Barb."
Walker. She Said.
Whitman. I Am He That Aches with Love.
Native Moments.
Spontaneous Me.
Wilbur. Loves of the Puppets.
Williams, William Carlos. Canthara.
From "The Birth of Venus," Song.
Wyatt. For want of [or I] will in woe I plain.
If thou wilt mighty be, flee from the rage.
It burneth yet, alas, my heart's desire.
So unwarely was never no man caught.
Such hap as I am happed in.
Young. Flirt.
See also **Erotic Love; Sex.**

Lutes
Dunbar. Thou Art My Lute.
Herrick. Upon Linnit.
Upon Sapho, Sweetly Playing, and Sweetly
Singing.
Sidney. My lute, within thyself thy tunes
enclose.
Snodgrass. Regraduating the Lute.
Suckling. Song to a Lute, A.
Wyatt. At mo[o]st mischief.
Blame not my lute, for he must sound [or
sssnd or Sownde].
My lute, awake! Perform [the] last.

Luther, Martin
Auden. Luther.

Lying. see **Lies and Lying.**

Lynching
Carruth. Song: The Famous Vision of
America.
Dunbar. Haunted Oak, The.
"Dylan." Death of Emmett Till, The.
Ford. Plaint.
Hayden. Night, Death, Mississippi.
Hughes, Langston. Blue Bayou.
Silhouette.
Song for a Dark Girl.
Southern Mammy Sings.
Lorde. Afterimages.
McGrath. Deep South.
Patchen. Nice Day for a Lynching.
1935.
Rolfe. Georgia Nightmare.
Poem: "Girl lashed to the stake, The."
Rukeyser. Lynchings of Jesus, The.
Tate. Swimmers, The.

Lynx
Haines. Dream of the Lynx.

Hoffman. Last Lynx.
Sarton. Godhead as Lynx, The.

Lyonnesse, Cornwall
De la Mare. Sunk Lyonesse.
Hardy. When I Set Out for Lyonnesse.
Plath. Lyonnesse.

Lysergic Acid (LSD)
Beatles. Lucy in the Sky with Diamonds.
Ginsberg. Lysergic Acid.
Wales Visitation.
Gunn. At the Centre.
Fair in the Woods, The.

M

Macbeth
De la Mare. Macbeth.

Machines
Atwood. Three Desk Objects.
Auden. Engine House, The.
Pumping Engine, Cashwell, The.
Carroll, Jim. Cinco de Mayo.
Ciardi. Machine.
On the Orthodoxy and Creed of My Power
Mower.
Clark. Radio.
Crane. Supplication to the Muses on a Trying
Day.
Frost. Egg and the Machine, The.
Trial Run, A.
Ginsberg. Manhattan Thirties Flash.
Squeal.
Hesketh. Master Cotton Spinner.
Jonson. On the New Motion.
Kipling. McAndrew's Hymn.
Progress of the Spark, The.
Secret of the Machines, The.
Song of the Dynamo.
Lawrence. Departure.
Evil World-Soul, The.
Gulf, The.
Hold Back!
If You Are a Man.
Man and Machine.
Masses and Classes.
Men Like Gods.
Oh Wonderful Machine!
On and On and On.
Side-Step, O Sons of Men!
Triumph of the Machine, The.
Merton. Elegy for Five Old Ladies, An.
Exploits of a Machine Age.
Now the official nerve is analyzed.
Tune for Festive Dances in the Nineteen
Sixties, A.
Moore. To a Steam Roller.
Nash. Up from the Wheelbarrow.
We Would Refer You to Our Service
Department, If We Had One.
Nemerov. Beautiful Lawn Sprinkler, The.
Oppen. Likely as not a ruined head gasket.
Rukeyser. Power.
Wedding Presents.
Shelton. Machines, The.
Snyder. Removing the Plate of the Pump on
the Hydraulic System of the Backhoe.
Stuart. Writing Machine, The.
Tomlinson. Crane, The.
Van Duyn. Sentimental Delusion, A.
Wordsworth. Steamboats, Viaducts, and
Railways.

McKay, Eleanora Fagan. see **"Holiday, Billie"**
(Eleanora Fagan McKay).

MacLeish, Archibald
Rukeyser. Citation for Horace Gregory.
Sandburg. On a Flimmering Floom You Shall
Ride.

MacNeice, Louis
Auden. Cave of Making, The.
MacNeice. Autobiography.
Mahon. In Carrowdore Churchyard.
Muldoon. Carson.
Louis.
Wystan.
Spender. Louis MacNeice.

Macy's (department store)
Ferlinghetti. Director of Alienation.
Paley. 34th Street Song.

Mad Song (genre)
"Carroll, Lewis." Mad Gardener's Song, The.

Madness
Arnold. Summer Night, A.
Atwood. Progressive Insanities of a Pioneer.
Visit to Toronto, with Companions.
Auden. Felo de se.
Beckett. Asylum under my tread all this day.
Berg. In Washington Square.
Berrigan. DEAR CHRIS / It is 3:17 a.m. in
New York city, yes, it is.
Berry. Contrariness of the Mad Farmer, The.
Mad Farmer Revolution, The.
Meditation in the Spring Rain.
To be sane in a mad time.
Berryman. Darling I wait O in my upstairs
box.
I've found out why, that day, that suicide.
Man who made her let me climb the derrick,
The.
Mysteries, The.
Song of the Demented Priest, The.
Song of the Man Forsaken and Obsessed.
Bishop. Visits to St. Elizabeths.
Blake. Mad Song.
Madman I have been calld Fool they call thee.
To F[laxman] ("I mock thee not").
To F[laxman] ("You call me mad").
Browning, Robert. Madness.
Bukowski. Madness.
Campion. Could my poore hart whole worlds
of toungs employ.
"Carroll, Lewis." Acrostic: Around my lonely
hearth, to-night.
Mad Gardener's Song, The.
Stolen Waters.
Carruth. And he stood at his window and
shook his fist at a cloud.
Asylum, The.
Diagnosis is / Anxiety psychoneurosis, The.
Electroshock. Bang—.
Hall Five.
I Tell You For Several Years of My Madness
I Heard the Voice of Lilith Singing in the
Trees of Chicago.
John Dryden.
Lady.
Lines Written in an Asylum.
Ontological Episode of the Asylum.
Re-Acquaintance.
Reading myself, old poems, their inside truth
that was.
Simple.
To dig at Luxor, to peer.
Unnatural Unselection.
Catullus. Carmen 41: "Formianus's whore, /
long-nosed."
Clark. Silence of the Lambs, The.
Cohen. Lists, The.
Teachers.
Cowper. To Leonora Singing at Rome.
Cummings. Tell me not how electricity or.
De la Mare. Banquo.
Iago.
Motley.
Ophelia.
Dickey, William. Alligators and Paris and
North America.
Dickinson. First Day's Night had come, The.
I think I was enchanted.
Much madness is divinest sense.
Dobyns. Tenderly.
Doolittle. Gift, The.
Dove. Great Uncle Beefheart.
Duncan. In Blood's Domaine.
Dunn. Essay on Sanity.
"Dylan." Bob Dylan's 115th Dream.
Eberhart. Birth of the Spirit, The.
Killer, The.
To the Mad Poets.
Emerson. Skeptic, The.
Ferlinghetti. Love Nut, The.
Ford. Simple is madness, like a kick in the
pants.

Fox. Mother Is.
Ginsberg. Howl.
  Tonite all is well. . .What a.
  Vision 1948.
Glück. Archipelago.
Graves. Halls of Bedlam, The.
Hardy. Evening in Galilee, An.
  Forbidden Banns, The.
  Henley Regatta.
  Interloper, The.
  Mad Judy.
  Thoughts at Midnight.
Herrick. Mad Maid's Song, The.
Hill. Mad are predators. Too often lately they
  harbour, The.
Hughes, Ted. Egg-Head.
Hugo. Ghost in a Field of Mint.
  Letter to Kathy from Wisdom.
  Reconsidering the Madman.
  Right Madness on Skye, The.
  Semi-Lunatics of Kilmuir, The.
Jarrell. Germans Are Lunatics, The.
  Nursery Rhyme, A.
  Seele im Raum.
Jeffers. Cassandra.
  To the Story-Tellers.
Kipling. Kitchener's School.
Lawrence. At Last.
  Fear of Society Is the Root of All Evil.
  Money-Madness.
  Nemesis.
  Rallying-Point.
  Sane and Insane.
  Today.
  What's to Be Done.
Levine. Lights I Have Seen Before.
  On the Edge.
Lewis. He sees the dawn expanding from a
  seashell.
  His mind is an inarticulated question.
  Sensual mind in the wreaths of wine, The.
  Shattered crystal of his mind, The.
Liddy. Cantico Per Lo Tuo Amore V.
Lovelace. Cupid Far Gone.
Lowry. He plays the piano with a razor.
  Morning rain is rained, The.
  Thirty Five Mescals in Cuautla.
McAuley. Soliloquy.
Mahon. As It Should Be.
  Hearing the thunder of the intransitive weirs
Meredith. But see what living glory floods the
  west.
  Events in a Rustic Mirror.
  John, John of Ottenhaw!
Merton. Confucius and the Madman.
  Septentrion.
Millay. Siege.
Milton. To the Same ["Another Leonora
  captured the poet Torquato"].
Morgan. Catullus: Carmen xli.
Morrison. Celebration of the Lizard.
Nash. Good Night, Sweet Mind.
  Literary Scene, The.
  Machinery Doesn't Answer, Either, but You
  Aren't Married to It.
  Miriam's Lucky Day.
Nemerov. Poem of Margery Kempe, A.
Oliver. Anne.
  Aunt Elsie's Night Music.
  Clam Man.
  Robert Schumann.
Oppen. Speech at Soli, The.
  There was no other guarantee.
  Tho the world.
Owen. Mental Cases.
Paley. Poets! / Madness is a gift.
Patchen. He Thought of Mad Ellen's Ravings
  and of the Wretched Skeleton on the Rock.
  Let Us Have Madness Openly.
Plath. Life, A.
  Miss Drake Proceeds to Supper.
Poe. Conqueror Worm, The.
Raine. Medea.
"Reed." Letters to the Vatican.
Roethke. Heard in a Violent Ward.
  Lines upon Leaving a Sanitarium.
Rukeyser. Minotaur, The.

St. John. Dolls.
Sandburg. White Hands.
Schuyler. Roxy.
  Walter Scott.
Sexton. Angel of Flight and Sleigh Bells.
  Anna Who Was Mad.
  Exorcists, The.
  Flee on Your Donkey.
  For the Year of the Insane.
  Iron Hans.
  Lullaby: "It is a summer evening."
  Noon Walk on the Asylum Lawn.
  Passion of the Mad Rabbit, The.
  Ringing the Bells.
Shakespeare. Sonnet 147: "My love is as a
  fever [or feaver], longing still."
Shapiro. California Petrarchan.
Silverstein. If the World Was Crazy.
Smith, Charlotte. On Being Cautioned against
  Walking on an Headland Overlooking the
  Sea, because It Was Frequented by a Lunatic.
  Supposed To Be Written by Werter.
Smith, Stevie. Deserter, The.
  From the County Lunatic Asylum.
  Le Majeur Ydow.
Sorrentino. Cynical.
Stevenson. Storm.
Tate. Madness.
Tomlinson. Terminal Tramps.
Williams, Charles Kenneth. Cave, The.
  Flat.
Williams, Miller. Little Poem, A.
Wordsworth. On the Death of His Majesty
  (George the Third).
Wright, James. She Hid in the Trees from the
  Nurses.
Yeats. Crazed Girl, A.
  Tom the Lunatic.
Young. Madness.
  Reading Nijinsky's Diary.
Zukofsky. Ameana pulling, a foot touted high.
See also **Mental Illness.**
Madonnas
Dickinson. Only a Shrine, but Mine.
Doolittle. We have seen her/ the world over.
Muldoon. Bearded Woman, by Ribera, The.
Madrid, Spain
Creeley. Same.
McGrath. Once We Meant It.
O'Hara. Now That I Am in Madrid and Can
  Think.
Rolfe. Elegia.
  Survival Is of the Essence.
Van Duyn. Madrid, May, 1977.
  Madrid, 1974.
Young. I Arrive in Madrid.
  Madrid 1963: Some Changes.
Magazines
Hardy. Hundred Years Since, A.
Whittier. Farewell, A: "What shall I say, dear
  friends, to whom I owe."
  To Lucy Larcom.
Wilbur. Playboy.
See also **Journalism and Journalists;**
  Newspapers.
Magdalene, Mary. *see* **Mary Magdalene.**
Maggots
Haines. Insects, The.
Kipling. Bees and the Flies, The.
Magi
Eliot. Journey of the Magi.
Glück. Magi, The.
Herrick. Gold and Frankincense.
Meinke. Gift of the Magi, The.
Ralegh. On the Card[e]s, and Dice.
Rossetti. Epiphany.
  Epiphanytide.
Williams, William Carlos. Gift, The.
Yeats. Magi, The.
Magic
Bogan. Sorcerer's Daughter, The.
Browning, Robert. Natural Magic.
"Carroll, Lewis." Acrostic: Love-lighted eyes,
  that will not start.
Cohen. Etiquette.
  Magic Is Alive.
  You Do Not Have to Love Me.

Cummings. "but why should" / the / greatest.
  Emperor / sleeps in a palace of porphyry, The.
  Now air is air and thing is thing:no bliss.
  Now all the fingers of this tree(darling)have.
  Now what were motionless move(exists no).
  Perished have safe small.
  That melancholy / fellow'll play / his
  handorgan.
  To stand(alone)in some.
De la Mare. Sea-Magic.
Dickinson. Ah, Necromancy Sweet!
  Best Witchcraft is Geometry.
  I think I was enchanted.
  It is of Realms unratified.
  Magic, as it electrifies.
  To see is perhaps never quite the sorcery.
Eliot. To Walter de la Mare.
  Usk.
Ford. O.
  Yes, wave your magic.
Fox. Story of Toile, The.
Ginsberg. Magic Psalm.
Graves. At Best, Poets.
  Casse-Noisette.
  Charm for Sound Sleeping, A.
  Gorgon Mask.
  St Antony of Padua.
  Unnamed Spell, The.
Hardy. Paphian Ball, The.
Hugo. Blue Stone.
Jong. Bitter Herb.
  Deadly Nightshade.
  Henbane.
  Love Magick.
  Mandrake.
  Monkshood.
  Thorn Apple.
Keats. La Belle Dame Sans Merci.
Kunitz. Testing-Tree, The.
Lorde. Fantasy and Conversation.
  Neighbors.
  Summer Oracle.
Lowry. Magic World, The.
Meredith. Song of Courtesy, The.
  You must love the light so well.
Merton. Eye Is a Dog Howling in the
  Distance, The.
  Macarius and the Pony.
  Seven Archaic Images.
Millay. Ballad of the Harp-Weaver, The.
Olson. Bagatto.
Oppen. Occurrences, The.
Piercy. Magician, The.
Rukeyser. Second Elegy. Age of Magicians.
St. John. Merlin.
Sandburg. Impasse.
Scott. Enchanted Goblet, The.
Silverstein. Lester.
  Magical Eraser.
Stevenson. Fairy Bread.
Swift. Simile, A.
  Virtues of Sid Hamet the Magician's Rod,
  The.
Wakoski. In the Secret Room, East of the
  Sun, West of the Moon.
Wordsworth. Egyptian Maid; or, The Romance
  of the Water Lily, The.
  Wishing-Gate, The.
Magnolias
Hughes, Langston. Magnolia Flowers.
Joseph. Meteorology, A.
Sexton. Wedding Night, The.
Stevens. News and the Weather, The.
Magpies
Fletcher. Well in the Desert, The.
Kooser. Fort Robinson.
Magritte, René
Ferlinghetti. Matisse at the Modern, Magritte
  at the Met.
Tomlinson. Ceci n'est pas une Pipe.
Mail and Mailmen
Auden. Mail-train, Crewe, The.
  Night Mail, The.
Berry. Throwing away the Mail.
Bukowski. Famous Writer, The.
  Transformation and Disfiguration.
Galvin. Rural Mailboxes.

Graves. No Letter.
Hewitt. Domimie's Log, A.
S.S.K.
Hugo. Maratea Porto: The Dear Postmistress There.
Jarrell. Hope.
Mail Call.
Kipling. Overland Mail, The.
Kunitz. Reflection by a Mailbox.
Lowry. Quarrel, A.
Scribner's Sons.
McNeill. Jed Kane.
Miller. *Luftpost* (For Levy).
Nash. Ho, Varlet! My Two Cents' Worth of Penny Postcard!
Please Keep on Forwarding.
What's in a Name? Some Letter I Always Forget.
Why the Postman Has to Ring Twice, or, Yellow Envelope, Where Have You Gone?
Rossetti. Eight o'clock; / The postman's knock!
Simic. Rural Delivery.
Van Duyn. Garland for Christopher Smart, A.
Whitman. Orange Buds by Mail from Florida.
Whittier. Summons, A.
Williams, William Carlos. To Greet a Letter-Carrier.
See also **Letters.**

Maine (state)
Dobyns. Kentucky Derby Day, Belfast, Maine.
Place in Maine, A.
Eberhart. Coast of Maine.
Equivalence of Gnats and Mice.
Going to Maine.
Maine Roustabout, A.
Spite Fence.
Hartley. Fantasy and phantom—.
"Lewiston Is a Pleasant Place."
There Is an Island.
These Six or Several Houses.
Lowell. Fourth of July in Maine.
Skunk Hour.
Soft Wood.
Water.
Mahon. Lighthouse in Maine, A.
Millay. Exiled.
Oppen. Penobscot.
Schuyler. Day, The.
Penobscot.
Van Duyn. Hermit of Hudson Pond, The.
Whittier. Norembega.

Malachy, Saint
Merton. St. Malachy.

Malcolm X (Malcolm Little)
Hayden. El-Hajj Malik El-Shabazz.
Knight. For Malcolm, a Year After.
It Was a Funky Deal.
Sun Came, The.
Rukeyser. Martin Luther King, Malcolm X.
Walker. Abduction of Saints, The.
Malcolm.
Young. Malcolm's Messasge.

Mallards
Hesketh. Mallard, The.

Malls. *see* **Shopping Malls.**

Malta
Byron. Farewell to Malta.

Man, Isle of, England
"Carroll, Lewis." Limerick, A.

Man, Primitive
Atwood. Fishing for Eel Totems.
De la Mare. Owl, The ("What If To Edge Of Dream").
Heaney. Tollund Man, The.
Kipling. River's Tale, The.
Merton. Birth of the Sun, The.
Early Legend, The.
See also **Cavemen.**

Man in the Moon
Berry. Winter Night Poem for Mary.
Sorrentino. Man in the Moon, The.

Manatees
Nash. Manatee, The.

Mandalay, Burma
Kipling. Mandalay.

Mandela, Nelson
Lorde. Evening News, The.

Mandelstam, Osip
Dunn. Because We Are Not Taken Seriously.
Levertov. Deaths.
Walcott. Preparing for Exile.

Mangoes
Crane. Mango Tree, The.

Manhattan. *see* **New York City.**

Manitoba, Canada
Sandburg. Manitoba Childe Roland.

Mankind
Atwood. Charivari.
My daughter crackles paper, blows.
Beckett. D'abord / à plat sur du dur.
Berry. And I declare myself free.
Anger against Beasts.
Beginning, A.
Bloodroot is white, The.
By the excellence of his work the workman is a neighbor. By.
Discipline, A.
Farmer, Speaking of Monuments, The.
From the Distance.
In the early morning dark.
In the thought of you I imagine myself free of the weapons and the official hates that I have borne on my back like a hump.
In This World.
It is not too soon to provide by every.
It is presumptuous and irresponsible to pray for other people. A.
July, 1773.
Morning's News, The.
Slip, The.
Sometimes he thinks the earth.
To be sane in a mad time.
Walking on the River Ice.
Who has invented our enmity? Who has prescribed us.
Wish to Be Generous, The.
Berryman. Gislebertus' Eve.
Spinning Heart, The.
Traveller, The.
Bishop. In the Waiting Room.
Blake. Divine Image, The ("To Mercy, Pity, Peace, and Love").
To see a World in a Grain of Sand.
Brooks. Riders to the Blood-Red Wrath.
Browning, Elizabeth Barrett. Human Life's Mystery.
Burns. Epistle to a Young Friend.
On Scaring Some Waterfowl in Loch Turit, a Wild Scene among the Hills of Oughtertyre.
Sketch. Inscribed to the Rt. Hon. Ch. J. Fox Esq.
Song—For A' That and A' That.
To Robt. Graham of Fintry Esqr, with a Request for an Excise Division.
Twa Dogs, The.
Byron. Answer to a Beautiful Poem, Entitled "The Common Lot."
World Is a Bundle of Hay, The.
Crane. I Have That Sure Enclitic.
Cummings. Because you take life in your stride(instead.
Humanity i love you.
,Mean- / hum / a)now / (nit.
No man,if men are gods;but if gods must.
Now does our world descend.
oDE: "O / the sweet & aged people."
Of all the blessings which to man.
Pity This Busy Monster, Manunkind.
POEM(or "the divine right of majorities, that illegitimate offspring of the divine right of kings" Homer Lea).
Possibly thrice we glimpsed.
This is the vase, Here.
When serpents bargain for the right to squirm.
Davie. Christening, A.
Compline.
Gripping Serial.
Humanly Speaking.
In the Stopping Train.
Levity.
Morning.
De la Mare. All That's Past.

Hour-Glass, The.
Humanity.
Donne. To Sir Edward Herbert[,] at Juliers [or Julyers].
To the Countess of Salisbury.
Dunbar. Slow through the Dark.
Duncan. First Invention on the Theme of the Adam.
"Dylan." Slow Train.
Emerson. Life is great / Men are small.
Turtle in swamp.
Fletcher. And at these words there rose against the ark.
And God, looking out upon earth, said, "Lo, it is time / To create mankind."
As Adam, clutching earth, lay stunned within the darkness.
Fourfold is made the divine nature of man.
From Portofino Point.
Lid, The.
Now it was the ninth morning and the unseen God.
Prayer of the Antichrist, The.
Prelude: "Before the beginning of things."
Procession, The.
Thunderstorm in the Ozarks.
Fox. Clown, The.
Frost. I Will Sing You One-O.
To an Ancient.
Vantage Point, The.
Graves. Mankind and Ocean.
Gray. Ode on a Distant Prospect of Eton College.
Gunn. First Man, The.
Geyser, The.
Last Man, The.
Memoirs of the World.
Seabed, The.
Hardy. By the Earth's Corpse.
Caged Thrush Freed and Home Again, The.
Heredity.
His Country.
I Said to Love.
Thoughts at Midnight.
Hartnett. I have been stone, dust of space, sea and sphere.
Herbert. Justice (1).
Man.
Man's Medley.
Pulley, The.
Herrick. Angells.
Upon Man.
Hewitt. Corncrake.
Delos.
Garron Top.
Happy Man, The.
I Turn to Trees.
Landscape.
Mykonos.
Practical Mysticism.
Ram's Horn, The.
Torcello.
Townland of Peace.
Hopkins. Epithalamion: "Hark, hearer, hear what I do; lend a thought now, make believe."
How all is one way wrought!
Lantern Out of Doors, The.
Ribblesdale.
Sea and the Skylark, The.
To His Watch.
Housman. 'Tis five years since, "An end," said I.
Jarrell. Place of Death, The.
Tower, The.
Jeffers. All night long the rush and trampling of water.
Birth and Death.
Broken Balance, The.
Contrast.
Dawn.
End of the World.
Extinct Vertebrate, An.
Inquisitors, The.
Passenger Pigeons.
Prelude: "I drew solitude over me, on the lone shore."

Science.
To the Story-Tellers.
Torch-Bearers' Race, The.
Unformed volcanic earth, a female thing, The.
Jonson. To William, Earl[e] of Pembroke.
Joseph. Butterfly is dainty flippant fragile, The.
Genus: Homo.
Keats. Human Seasons, The.
Kipling. Divided Destinies.
Four Angels, The.
General Summary, A.
Go, stalk the red dear o'er the heather.
If.
Legends of Evil, The.
Man goes to Man! Cry the challenge though the Jungle!
Mary's Son.
Night we felt the earth would move, The.
Pilgrim's Way, A.
Prayer, The: "My brother kneels, so saith Kabir."
Lawrence. Abysmal Immortality.
But I Say unto You: Love One Another.
Cowards.
Deeper Than Love.
Deeper Than Love.
Democracy.
Difference, The.
Elemental.
Elements, The.
Factory Cities, The.
False Democracy and Real.
Flowers and Men.
For the Heroes Are Dipped in Scarlet.
Free Will.
Gentleman, The.
Gladness of Death.
Glimpses.
Gods! The Gods!, The.
Humanity Needs Pruning.
If You Are a Man.
Immoral Man.
Immorality.
Keep It Up.
Know-All.
Man, A.
Man and Machine.
Man Is More Than *Homo Sapiens*.
Men Are Not Bad.
Men Like Gods.
Michael Angelo.
Minorities in Danger.
Morality.
Morality.
Multitudes.
My Way Is Not Thy Way.
Nemesis.
Obscenity.
Only Man.
Only the Best Matters.
People.
People.
People, The.
Poison.
Retort to Whitman.
Risen Lord, The.
Sea, The.
Service.
Shades.
Side-Step, O Sons of Men!
Souls to Save.
Sun-Men.
There Are Too Many People.
There Is No Way Out.
Transformations.
Triumph of the Machine, The.
Two Ways of Living and Dying.
Universe Flows, The.
What Are the Wild Waves Saying?
What Have They Done to You?
Whatever Man Makes.
When Wilt Thou Teach the People?
Wild Things in Captivity.
Levine. Animals Are Passing from Our Lives.
Conductor of Nothing, The.

How Much Earth.
Poem of Flight, The.
"MacDiarmid." Glass of Pure Water, The.
One loves the temporal, some unique manifestation.
With the Herring Fishers.
MacLeish. Men.
Meinke. Progress.
Third Child: June Eleven, Nineteen Sixty Two.
Meredith. Alternation.
Believe me, I have studied men.
Brotherhood.
Foresight and Patience.
Men and Man.
Test of Manhood, The.
What are we first? First, animals; and next.
Merton. Bus has gone by, The.
Flower of the Fruit, The.
I Move that We Adjourn the Meeting.
Last evening a city man.
Moment of Truth, The.
Ox Mountain Parable, The.
Millay. Apostrophe to Man.
Epitaph for the Race of Man.
Milton. For man to tell how human life began.
Neruda. Bomb (II).
Gift, The.
Island (XVII), The.
Men (II), The.
Men (IV), The.
This Is Simple.
Oliver. Wild Geese.
Olson. Adamo Me.
Advantage, The.
Anubis will stare.
Applause.
Babe, The.
Bigmans II.
Blow is Creation, / & the Twist the Nasturtium, The.
Chain of memory is resurrection I am a vain man, The.
Discrete Gloss, A.
Double, double, root and branch.
Every Man His Own Matador; or for That Matter Any Member of the Family.
Fable for Slumber.
He / in the dark stall, no day now for him, to paw.
Hotel Steinplatz, Berlin, December 25 (1966).
Hour of evening—supper hour, for my neighbors—quietness, The.
In Cold Hell, in Thicket.
K, The.
Kin.
Laughing Ones, The.
Lion upon the Floor, A.
Name-Day Night.
Not to permit himself to be.
Obit.
Ode on Nativity, An.
Only the Red Fox, Only the Crow.
Post Virginal, The.
Put him this way.
Said Adam.
Seven Songs, The.
Siena.
Swimming through the air, in schools upon the highways.
Thing Was Moving, The.
2 Propositions and 3 Proof.
Whole World, The.
Writ, The.
Oppen. Parousia.
Patchen. As in the green sky.
Blind'd be the last of men.
Elegy for the Silent Voices and the Joiners of Everything.
"Gentle and Giving" and Other Sayings.
I despise these poets with their puerile little chalk-talks of the soul.
I Got the Fat Poet into a Corner.
If a Poem Can Be Headed into Its Proper Current.
In shadings of an obscure punishment.
Into another mission / Circling my exposed continent.

It Is Big Inside a Man.
It Was a Bomby Evening.
Lament for the Makers of Songs.
Man Is to Man a Beast.
Man Lives Here, A.
O fiery river / Flow out over the land.
Roses of Life, The.
Second People, The.
Shapes.
So Near—And Yet.
To Whom It May Concern.
Way men live is a lie, The.
Where Every Prospect.
Wide, wide in the rose's side.
You Must Have Some Idea Where They've Gone.
Pope. Bliss of man, The (could pride that blessing find).
Placed on this isthmus of a middle state.
What would this Man? Now upward will he soar.
Pound. Meditatio.
Ralegh. More holy than the rest, and understanding more.
Rich. For the Record.
Robinson. Octaves.
Rossetti. Day and night the Accuser makes no pause.
He Shall Go No More Out.
How great is little man! / Sun, moon, and stars respond to him.
Let Patience Have Her Perfect Work.
Lord, by what inconceivable dim road / Thou leadest man on footsore pilgrimage!
Man's life is but a working day / Whose tasks are set aright.
One Certainty, The.
Rogationtide.
That Which Hath Been Is Named Already, and It Is Known That It Is Man.
Tuesday in Holy Week.
Vanity of Vanities.
Vigil of the Annunciation.
Wednesday in Holy Week.
What is this above thy head, / O Man?
Rukeyser. Myth.
Sandburg. Chicago seems all fox and swine.
Enemy Number One.
God Is No Gentleman.
Government.
I have been woven among meshes of long ropes.
Jack.
Kindest and gentlest here are the, The.
Man, the Man-Hunter.
Masses.
Pool.
Psalm of the Bloodbank.
Sayings of Henry Stephens.
Since death is there in the light of the sun, in the song of the.
Skyscrapers Stand Proud.
Solo for Saturday Night Guitar.
Walking Man of Rodin, The.
Wilderness.
Sexton. After Auschwitz.
Earth Falls Down, The.
Two Hands.
Shelton. Why I Never Went into Politics.
Silverstein. No Difference.
Simic. Chorus for One Voice.
Smith, Stevie. All Things Pass.
Alone in the Woods.
Away, Melancholy.
Distractions and the Human Crowd.
Do Not!
From the Coptic.
From the French (2).
God and Man.
God Speaks.
Man Is a Spirit.
New Age, The.
So to Fatness Come.
Touch and Go.
Under Wrong Trees.. or Freeing the Colonial Peoples.
Will Man Ever Face Fact and Not Feel Flat?

Sorrentino. Je Connai Gens de Toutes Sortes.
Transcript, The.
Vision of the City from a Window.
What intense colloquy with the self.
Southwell. Look[e] Home.
Suckling. Ei Men Een Mathein.
Swift. On the Day of Judgement.
Turco. Dedication, A: "If it is true that."
Whitman. As I Ponder'd [or Pondered] in
Silence.
Going Somewhere.
I think I could turn and live awhile with
animals.
On the Same Picture.
One's-Self I Sing.
Our Future Lot.
Thou Reader.
Wilbur. Ceremony.
Williams, Charles Kenneth. Hounding Mercy.
Innings.
Nut, The.
Race of the Flood, The.
Ribbons.
Spirit the Triumph, The.
Then the Brother of the Wind.
Three Seasons and a Gorilla.
Williams, Miller. Living on the Surface.
Williams, William Carlos. Clouds, The.
Wordsworth. Character, A.
1811 ("Here pause: the poet claims at least
this praise").
Lines Written in Early Spring.
O'er the wide earth, on mountain and on
plain.
Poet's Epitaph, A.
There is a bondage worse, far worse, to bear.
Those words were uttered as in pensive mood.
Weak is the will of Man, his judgement blind.
Wright, James. Eternal Dice, The.
Goodbye to the Poetry of Calcium.
In Shame and Humiliation.
Secret Gratitude, The.
Winter Day in Ohio, A.
Yeats. Four Ages of Man, The.
Meditation in Time of War, A.
Sorrow of Love, The ("Brawling of a sparrow
in the eaves, The").

Mannequins
Bukowski. Trapped.
Dobyns. Passing the Word.
Jarrell. Dummies.
Nemerov. To the Mannequins.
Sandburg. Caligari.

Manners. see **Etiquette.**

Man-of-War Birds
Whitman. To the Man-of-War Bird.

Mansfield, Katherine
De la Mare. To K. M.

Manson, Charles
Cohen. Future, The.
Gunn. I spin like a solitary star, I swoon.

Mantis. see **Praying Mantis.**

Maple Sugar and Maple Syrup
Carruth. In late winter cold nights.
Hall. Maple Syrup.

Maple Trees
Ammons. Bride.
Carruth. Essay on Love.
Leaf from Mr. Dyer's Woods, A.
Sonnet: "Like the magnificent stationary
animal it is."
Sonnet: "This is our perfect silver maple's
day."
Koch. Down at the Docks.
MacLeish. Two Trees, The.
Paley. Leaves Apples.
Turco. Maple Works, The.
Updike. Maples in a Spruce Forest.
Warren. In Moonlight, Somewhere, They Are
Singing.
Wilbur. October Maples, Portland.
Williams, William Carlos. Non-Entity, The.
Wright, James. To a Troubled Friend.
Trumpets.

Maps
Atwood. Reincarnation of Captain Cook, The.

Auden. Half Way.
Have a Good Time.
Bishop. Map, The.
"Carroll, Lewis." Bellman himself they all
praised to the skies—, The.
Galvin. Old Map of Barnstable County.
Gunn. Map of the City, A.
Hewitt. School Upstairs, The.
Hugo. In Your War Dream.
Map of the Peninsula, A.
Old Map of Uhlerstown.
Ovando.
Joseph. No Map Available.
Nemerov. Mapmaker on His Art, The.
Projection.
Pack. Fathering the Map.
Paley. At the Battery.
Tate. Trout Map, The.

Marathon (race)
Dickey, James. For the Running of the New
York City Marathon.
Wilbur. Running.

Marathon, Battle of (490 B.C.)
Browning, Robert. Echetlos.
Graves. Persian Version, The.

Marble
Crane. Island Quarry.
Dickey, James. In the Marble Quarry.
Eberhart. Cousin Florence.
Hall. Columns of the Parthenon, The.
Sidney. My words, in hope to blaze my
steadfast mind.
Tomlinson. Above Carrara.

Marbles
Berryman. At Chinese Checkers.
Fenton. Obsolete Oxfordshire game of "A-
All," The.
Fox. And the lovers meet again.

March
Bishop. End of March, The.
Bogan. March Twilight.
Crane. March.
Dickinson. Dear March, Come in.
In snow thou comest.
March is the Month of Expectation.
We like March.
We like March—his shoes are Purple.
Who could be ill in March.
Dunbar. My Little March Girl.
Eberhart. Ides of March, The.
Hall. Elegy for Wesley Wells.
Housman. March.
Levine. White Iris, The.
MacLeish. March.
Matthews. March Heat.
Prince. Mortimer.
Raine. My Father's Birthday.
Schuyler. March Here.
Poem: "How about an oak leaf."
Stevens. Not Ideas about the Thing but the
Thing Itself.
Vacancy in the Park.
Tomlinson. In March.
Unstill Universe.
Updike. March: A Birthday Poem.
Wilbur. March.
Williams, William Carlos. Celebration, A.
March.
March Is a Light.
Wordsworth. Written in March [While Resting
on the Bridge at the Foot of Brother's
Water].
Wright, James. March.
Zukofsky. March First.

Marching and Marches
Beckett. Thither.
Berryman. Old Boys' blazers like a Mardi-
Gras, The.
Hewitt. Eleventh Night, The.
For One Who Did Not March.
Kipling. "Birds of Prey" March.
Columns.
Route Marchin'.
Larkin. March Past, The.
Lawrence. On the March.
MacLeish. Bearing the long lance, their

banners before them.
Twelfth Book, The.
Melville. Night-March, The.
Simic. Marching.
Stevenson. Marching Song.
Prelude: "By sunny market-place and street."
Whole day thro', in contempt and pity, The.
Warren. Small Soldiers with Drum in Large
Landscape.
See also **Parades.**

Marigolds
Herrick. How Marigolds Came Yellow.
To Marygolds.
Paley. No love / no love cried the last fling.
Williams, William Carlos. Negro Woman, A.
Zukofsky. Marigold.

Marijuana
Beatles. Get Back.
Carruth. Odds & ends: / Enosburg Falls &
Geof's cabin.
"Dylan." Queen Jane Approximately.
Rainy Day Women # 12 & 35.
Ginsberg. Consulting I Ching Smoking Pot
Listening to the Fugs Sing Blake.
Milarepa Taste.
Gunn. Bath House, The.
Smoking Pot on the Bus.
Hughes, Langston. Gauge.
Wakoski. George Washington Writes Home
About Harvesting His Hemp.
Williams, William Carlos. Wrong Door, The.

Marin County, California
Jeffers. Clouds of Evening.

Mariners. see **Sailing and Sailors.**

Markets
Beatles. Ob-La-Di Ob-La-Da.
De la Mare. Market-Place, The.
Emerson. Since the devil hopping on.
Glück. Baskets.
Hacker. Le Travail Rajeunit.
Hall. Ox Cart Man.
Hardy. No Buyers [or No Buyers: A Street
Scene].
Hayden. Market.
Hewitt. Old Corinth.
Hugo. Morning in Padova.
Pike Place Market.
Jarrell. Indian Market in Mexico, An.
Jong. Saturday Market, The.
Kunitz. Economist's Song, The.
Lorde. Keyfoods.
Signs.
Nemerov. Market-Place, The.
Sandburg. Unintentional Paint.
Wright, James. Prayer to Escape from the
Market Place, A.

Markiewicz, Constance Georgine, Countess
Yeats. In Memory of Eva Gore-Booth and
Con Markievicz.

Marlborough, John Churchill, 1st Duke of
Swift. Satirical Elegy on the Death of a Late
Famous General, A.

Marlowe, Christopher
Ford. To Christopher Marlowe.
Lowell. Marlowe.

Marriage
Ammons. Milepost.
Ashbery. Decoy.
Atwood. Habitation.
Auden. Ballad: "He offered her his paucity."
Carry her over the water.
Berg. Cherries.
Good.
Berry. Grandmother, The.
He stood on the ground.
How many times have I come to you out of
my head.
I give you what is unbounded, passing from
dark to dark.
In Rain.
Let my marriage be brought to the ground.
Marriage.
Marriage, an Elegy, A.
Our bond is no little economy based on the
exchange.
Seventeen Years.

Sometimes our life reminds me.
What I am learning to give you is my death.
Berryman. Canto Amor.
Song of the Bridegroom, The.
Sunderings and luxations, *luxe*, and grief.
Two plantations Greatgrandmother brought, The.
Betjeman. Beaumaris, December 21, 1963.
14 November, 1973.
On Leaving Wantage 1972.
Bishop. Washing hangs upon the line, A.
Bogan. Betrothed.
For a Marriage.
Boyle. Comeallye for Robert Carlton Brown, A.
Bradstreet. To My Dear and Loving Husband.
Brontë. Day Dream, A.
From a Dungeon Wall in the Southern College.
Brooks. Bronzeville Mother Loiters in Mississippi. Meanwhile, a Mississippi Mother Burns Bacon, A.
To Be in Love.
Browning, Elizabeth Barrett. Marriage of Psyche and Cupid.
Poet's Vow, The.
Romance of the Ganges, A.
Sounds.
Year's Spinning, A.
Browning, Robert. Any Wife to Any Husband.
Doctor———.
Flight of the Duchess, The.
Life in a Love.
Love in a Life.
Muckle-Mouth Meg.
My Last Duchess [Ferrara].
With Daniel Bartoli.
Bukowski. About Pain.
Not To Worry.
103 Degrees.
Burns. Another [Epigram on Said Occasion].
English Song.
Epigram on Said Occasion.
Epitaph on a Henpecked Country Squire.
Henpeck'd Husband, The.
John Anderson, My Jo.
Kellyburnbraes.
O Ay My Wife She Dang Me.
O Lay Thy Loof in Mine Lass.
O That I Had Ne'er Been Married.
On Marriage.
Tam Glen.
To Alexander Cunningham.
Whistle o'er the Lave o't.
Byron. Blues, The.
Sonnet on the Nuptials of the Marquis Antonio Cavalli with the Countess Clelia Rasponi of Ravenna.
Campion. Breath you now, while Io Hymen.
Dance, dance, and visit now the shadowes of our joy.
Full Song, A.
Pulchro pulchra datur, sociali foedere amanti.
Stars Dance, The.
Vanish, vanish hence, confusion.
Verae ut supersint nuptiae.
While dancing rests, fit place to musicke graunting.
Carew. Hymeneal[l] Dialogue, An.
Married Woman, A.
On the Marriage of T. K. and C. C.: The Morning Stormy.
"Carroll, Lewis." Game of Fives, A.
What Tottles Meant.
Carruth. August First.
Essay on Marriage.
Catullus. Carmen 61: "Hill (breeder) of Helicon."
Carmen 62: "Gather young men as the twilight gathers."
Carmen 67: "Sweet entrance to a husband's pleasure."
Hymeneal.
Chaucer. Clerk's Tale, The.
Franklin's Tale, The.
Lenvoy de Chaucer a Bukton.
Merchant's Prologue, The.

Merchant's Tale, The.
Wife of Bath's Prologue, The.
Ciardi. Men Marry What They Need.
Morning: I Know Perfectly How in a Minute You Will Stretch and Smile.
Most Like an Arch This Marriage.
To Judith Asleep.
Clough. Clergyman's Second Tale, The.
Cohen. Commentary—My Wife and I.
Commentary—This Marriage.
Commentary II—This Marriage.
Don't Go Home with Your Hard-on.
Good Fight, The.
I Like the Way You Opposed Me.
Marvellous Woman, A.
My Wife and I.
O Wife Unmasked.
She Has Given Me the Bullet.
Slowly I Married Her.
This Marriage.
Unclean Start, The.
Waiting for the Miracle.
You Have No Form.
Coleridge. Exchange, The.
Written after a Walk before Supper.
Cooper. Eve.
In the Last Few Moments Came the Old German Cleaning Woman.
Twins.
Cowper. Anti-Thelyphthora.
Catharina, the Second Part.
Impromptu ["If John marries Mary, and Mary alone"].
Love Abused.
Mutual Forbearance.
Ode on the Marriage of a Friend.
Pairing Time Anticipated.
Crashaw. Epitaph upon a Young Married Couple, An.
Epithalamium: "Come virgin tapers of pure waxe."
On Marriage.
Creeley. Ballad of the Despairing Husband.
Bed, The.
Crisis, The.
Marriage, A.
Naughty Boy.
Rocks, The.
They Say.
Wait for Me.
Wife, The.
Cummings. If there are any heavens my mother will(all by herself)have.
Davie. Autumn Imagined.
Christmas Syllabics for a Wife.
Vying.
Widower.
Dickey, William. Stella Dallas.
Dickinson. Her sweet Weight on my Heart a Night.
I am ashamed—I hide.
I'm "wife"—I've finished that.
Ourselves were wed one summer—dear.
Rearrange a "Wife's" affection!
She rose to His Requirement—dropt.
Title divine—is mine!
Wife—at Daybreak I shall be, A.
World—stands—solemner—to me, The.
Dobyns. Party, The.
Waking.
Walls To Put Up, Walls To Take Down.
Donne. Antiquary.
Epithalamion, An, or Marriage Song on the Lady Elizabeth and Count Palatine Being Married on St. Valentine's Day.
Epithalamion Made at Lincoln's Inn [or Lincolnes Inne].
Doolittle. Hymen.
Dove. Beauty and the Beast.
Kadava Kumbis Devise a Way to Marry for Love, The.
Promises.
Refrain.
Dunbar. Bridal Measure, A.
Encouragement.
Dunn. All That We Have.

Amidst the Faltering.
Sister.
"Dylan." High treachery sails / unveils.
Eliot. Dedication to My Wife, A.
Emerson. From Ibn Jemin.
She never comes to me.
Everson. God Germed in Raw Granite.
Ferlinghetti. In Golden Gate Park that day.
Report on a Happening in Washington Square San Francisco, A.
Fletcher. Marriage.
Frost. Love and a Question.
Place for a Third.
Gardner. Feminine Ending or, Abandoned, She Died.
Glück. Aphrodite.
Bridal Piece.
Edge, The.
Epithalamium: "There were others; their bodies."
From the Suburbs.
Horse.
Morning.
Graves. Advice from a Mother.
Bower-Bird.
Call It a Good Marriage.
Court of Love, A.
For Ever.
Golden Anchor.
Joan and Darby.
Lion-Gentle.
Ours is No Wedlock.
Semi-Detached.
Slice of Wedding Cake, A.
That Other World.
Through a Dark Wood.
When Love Is Not.
Griffiths. Mines in Sepia Tint, The.
News of a Marriage.
Wedding Photograph.
Gunn. Adultery.
His Rooms in College.
Hacker. Country & Western II.
Some table talk at lunch, of memory.
You rang me up this morning from Marseilles.
Hall. Dancers.
For an Exchange of Rings.
Hardy. Bride-Night Fire, The.
Catching Ballet of the Wedding Clothes, The.
Conformers, The.
Curate's Kindness, The.
Forbidden Banns, The.
Homecoming, The.
In the Night She Came.
News for Her Mother.
One Who Married above Him.
Pair He Saw Pass, The.
Poor Man and a Lady, A.
To a Bridegroom.
Hartnett. Prisoners.
Heaney. Poem: "Love, I shall perfect for you the child."
Underground, The.
Hemingway. Three traveling clocks.
Herrick. Caution, A.
Connubii Flores, or the Well-Wishes at Weddings.
Entertainment, or Porch-Verse, at the Marriage of Mr. Henry Northleigh [or Hen. Northly] and the Most Witty Mrs. Lettice Yard, The.
Epitaph on a Man who Had a Scold to His Wife.
Epitaph upon a Sober Matron, An.
Epithalamy to Sir Thomas Southwell and His Lady, An.
His Answer to a Question.
His Comfort.
Hymne to Juno, An.
No Spouse but a Sister.
Nuptiall Song, or Epithalamie, on Sir Clipseby Crew and His Lady, A.
Nuptiall Verse to Mistresse Elizabeth Lee, Now Lady Tracie.
Poet Loves a Mistress, but Not to Marry, The.
Rosemarie Branch, The.
Single Life Most Secure.
To Rosemary and Baies.

To Silvia to Wed.
Upon Loach.
Hesketh. Dilemma.
Hewitt. Breach, The.
Et Tu In Arcadia Vixisti.
Scottish Interlude.
Hill. Dead Bride, The.
Hoffman. Marriage, A.
Hopkins. Queen's Crowning, The.
Housman. Epithalamium: "He is here, Urania's
    son."
Hughes, Ted. Her Husband.
Hugo. Letter to Wright from Gooseprairie.
Park at Villammare, The.
Jarrell. Man Meets a Woman in the Street, A.
Jeffers. It was everything to me to think well
    of one man.
Of all things which are living and can form a
    judgment.
Jong. For My Husband.
Perfect Poet, The.
Truce between the Sexes, The.
Whole Point, The.
Jonson. Epithalamion: "Glad time is at his
    point arrived."
Epithalamion: or, a Song.
On Giles and Joan.
These, these are they.
Joseph. Bride to Groom.
Married People Going to Work.
Keats. Gripus.
Kipling. Betrothed, The.
Bridegroom, The.
Fall of Jock Gillespie, The.
Mare's Nest, The.
Sergeant's Weddin', The.
Koertge. Gretel.
Panty Hose.
Primary Considerations.
Quiz, The.
Two Men.
Whippersnappers.
Kooser. Old Photograph, An.
Widow Lester, The.
Kunitz. Route Six.
Larkin. Long Roots Moor Summer to Our
    Side of Earth.
Maiden Name.
Marriages.
Self's the Man.
To My Wife.
Wedding-Wind.
Whitsun Weddings, The.
Lawrence. Emotional Lies.
Gipsy.
Good Husbands Make Unhappy Wives.
Hands of the Betrothed, The.
She Looks Back.
Wedlock.
Young Wife, A.
Levertov. About Marriage.
Ache of Marriage, The.
Lewis. On Leave: Marriage.
Separation, A.
Liddy. Epithalamion I–IV: "Along a leafy
    lonely river God-shy-eyed fisher boys."
Lindsay. Ahasuerus in his prime.
Cold Sunbeams.
Epilogue to the Adventures While Preaching
    the Gospel of Beauty.
Ghosts in Love.
Perfect Marriage, The.
To Eve, Man's Dream of Wifehood as
    Described by Milton.
Lovelace. Anniversary on the Hymeneals of
    My Noble Kinsman, Thomas Stanley,
    Esquire, An.
Lowell. Flaw, The.
Man and Wife.
Our Twentieth Wedding Anniversary
    (Elizabeth).
To Speak of Woe That Is in Marriage.
Lowry. I've Said Goodbye to Shanghai.
McGrath. Anniversaries.
Dream Range, The.
MacLeish. First I will tell you something of
    these two.

Late Abed.
Old Gray Couple (1), The.
Old Gray Couple (2), The.
Poem in Prose.
Shallow Grass, The.
Unfinished History.
MacNeice. Eclogue between the Motherless.
Les Sylphides.
When clerks and navvies fondle.
McNeill. Nora O'Kane.
Wife.
Markson. Anne-on-Avon.
Marlowe. 2.19: Ad rivalem, cui uxor curae
    non erat.
Matthews. Good Company.
Meredith. Archduchess Anne.
At dinner, she is hostess, I am host.
At last we parley: we so strangely dumb.
Blue Is the Sky.
By this he knew she wept with waking eyes.
Earth and a Wedded Woman.
Friar uxorious!
He found her by the ocean's moaning verge.
Hymn to Colour.
In our old shipwrecked days there was an
    hour.
Inspiration of the Great West Wind, The.
It is no vulgar nature I have wived.
Last Wandering of Poor Willie, The.
No knightly sword to serve, nor harp of bard.
Now dawns all waxen to your seal of life.
She marries the knight she loves.
Song: Autumn.
Song: "Quick bird sings and pierces me, The."
Think not, should your husband swear.
Thus piteously Love closed what he begat.
'Tis Christmas weather, and a country house.
Yet it was plain she struggled, and that salt.
Merton. Imperfect Lover, The.
Millay. Betrothal, The.
Return from Town, The.
Milton. Their Wedded Love.
To the Nuptial Bowre.
Moore. Marriage.
Morgan. Canadaigua.
Trader, The.
Morrison. Hitchhiker, The.
Star Fish Gluttony.
Nash. Advice outside a Church.
Anniversary, The.
Aside to Husbands.
Confession to Be Traced on a Birthday Cake.
Cuckoo, The.
Don't Wait, Hit Me Now!
Down the Mousehole, and What Science
    Missed There.
I Do, I Will, I Have.
Lines To Be Mumbled At Ovington's.
Nymph and the Shepherd, or She Went That-
    a-Way, The.
Outcome of Mr. Buck's Superstition, The.
Rapunzel, Rapunzel, Let's Let Down Our
    Hair.
Solitude of Mr. Powers, The.
Song to Be Sung by the Father of Infant
    Female Children.
Strange Case of Mr. Donnybrooks's Boredom,
    The.
Strange Case of the Blackmailing Dove, The.
There'll Always Be a War between the Sexes,
    or, A Woman Can Be Sometimes Pleased,
    but Never Satisfied.
They Won't Believe, on New Year's Eve, that
    New Year's Day Will Come What May.
Tin Wedding Whistle.
Tune for an Ill-Tempered Clavichord.
Unselfish Husband, The.
What Almost Every Woman Knows Sooner or
    Later.
Nathan. Table Talk.
Washing Socks.
Nemerov. Common Wisdom, The.
Notley. But He Says I Misunderstood.
Dear Dark Continent.
O'Hara. Poem Read at Joan Mitchell's.
Olson. Bride, The.
Pack. Clayfeld Renews His Vow to Evelyn.

Clayfeld's Anniversary Song.
Clayfeld's Daughter Reveals Her Plans.
Cord of Wood, A.
Early and Late.
Leviathan.
Prayer for Prayer.
Twin, The.
Paley. Quarrel.
Patchen. And then it was that the Bridegroom
    beheld the Bride wraith- / like.
Piercy. Breaking Camp.
Laocoön is the Name of the Figure.
Married Walk in a Hot Place, A.
Plath. Epitaph for Fire and Flower.
Wreath for a Bridal.
Zoo Keeper's Wife.
Prince. Diamond, The.
Inn, The.
To a Friend on His Marriage.
Raine. Ring, The.
Ransom. Emily Hardcastle, Spinster.
Fait Accompli.
Romance of a Youngest Daughter.
"Reed." Bed, The.
Think It Over.
Rich. Any Husband to Any Wife.
Autumn Equinox.
Blue Ghazals, The.
Marriage in the 'Sixties, A.
Marriage Portion, The.
Moving in Winter.
Novella.
Perennial Answer, The.
Robinson. Eros Turannos.
London Bridge.
Rahel to Varnhagen.
Woman and the Wife, The.
Rossetti. Bride Song.
Cousin Kate.
Hour and the Ghost, The.
Lowest Room, The.
Maude Clare.
Ring Posy, A.
True Story, A.
Wife to Husband.
Rukeyser. Wedding Presents.
Sandburg. Blue Maroons.
Brim.
Couple, A.
Crimson Rambler.
Mag.
Maybe.
Put Off the Wedding Five Times and Nobody
    Comes to It.
Soiled Dove.
Two Strangers Breakfast.
Sarton. Death and the Lovers.
Sexton. Doors, Doors, Doors.
Eighth Psalm.
February 17th.
For John, Who Begs Me Not to Enquire
    Further.
Interrogation of the Man of Many Hearts, The.
Maiden without Hands, The.
Man and Wife.
Twelve-Thousand-Day Honeymoon, The.
Wedlock, The.
White Snake, The.
Shakespeare. Sonnet 13: "Oh [or O] that you
    were yourself! but, love, you are."
Sonnet 67: "Ah! wherefore with infection
    should he live."
Shapiro. New Ring, The.
Shelton. Bird in the Hand: Two Solos, A.
Building.
Everything is quiet in the garden.
Fourteenth Anniversary, The.
Grandfathering.
Housecleaning.
Promises.
Sidney. Let mother Earth now deck herself in
    flowers.
Silverstein. My Rules.
Simic. Especially forlorn human specimen,
    An.
Rough Outline.
She saw the Archangel Michael, too.

Smith, Charlotte. Epilogue [A] to *What Is She?*
To the Countess of A——. Written on the Anniversary of Her Marriage.
Truant Dove from Pilpay, The.
Smith, Stevie. Autumn.
Castle, The.
Hat, The.
I Remember.
Lady "Rogue" Singleton.
Smile, The.
Starling, The.
Wedding Photograph, The.
Spender. Polar Exploration.
Stein. Brim Beauvais.
She is that kind of a wife. She can see.
With a Wife.
Stevenson. Death.
I love to be warm by the red fireside.
It is the season now to go.
Men are Heaven's piers; they evermore.
Mine eyes were swift to know thee, and my heart.
My love was warm; for that I crossed.
My Wife.
My wife and I, in one romantic cot.
Since thou hast given me this good hope, O God.
Since years ago for evermore.
So live, so love, so use that fragile hour.
To My Wife.
Suckling. Lutea Allison.
Upon My Lord Brohall's Wedding.
Swift. Phyllis [or Phillis or Progress of Love, The].
Progress of Marriage, The.
Quiet Life and a Good Name, A.
Three Epigrams.
Tate. Nuptials.
Tennyson. Move Eastward, Happy Earth, and Leave.
Northern Farmer: New Style.
Thomas. On the Marriage of a Virgin.
Tomlinson. Farmer's Wife: at Fostons Ash, The.
Turco. Hank Fedder.
My Country Wife.
Pocoangelini 12 ("She is caught in her frail house").
Updike. Marriage Counsel.
Newlyweds, The.
Van Duyn. Fear of Flying, The.
In the Cold Kingdom.
Placet Experiri.
Time of Bees, A.
Toward a Definition of Marriage.
Winter's Tale, by a Wife, A.
Waldman. Sonnet: O Husband!
Wilbur. Six Years Later.
Williams, Charles Kenneth. Cautionary, The.
Experience.
Trash.
Williams, Miller. Husband.
Picker.
Williams, William Carlos. Ballad: "To a man and his wife."
Invocation and Conclusion.
Marriage.
Marriage of Souls, The.
Marriage Ritual, A.
Wordsworth. Composed on the Eve of the Marriage of a Friend in the Vale of Grasmere, 1812.
Yeats. Collarbone [or Collar-Bone] of a Hare, The.
Young. Two A.M.
Zukofsky. Marriage Song for Florence and Harry, A.
O dear cool you couldn't be virile—you couldn't a parent he.
Vesper out there, you vain knees can sure get up: Vesper, Olympus.
Who lives o on Helicon hill.

See also **Bigamy and Bigamists; Monogamy and Monogamists; Wedding Songs; Weddings.**

Marriage, Arranged
Burns. Altered from an Old English Song.

What can a young lassie, what shall a young lassie.
Scott. Song of Albert Graeme.
Mars (god)
Chaucer. Complaint of Mars, The.
Crashaw. Upon Venus Putting on Mars His Armes.
Herrick. Vow to Mars, A.
Meredith. Cageing of Ares, The.
Sidney. Sonnet 17: "His mother dear Cupid offended late."
Wyatt. Venus, in sport, to please therewith her dear.
Mars (planet)
Chaucer. Complaint of Mars, The.
Silverstein. Planet of Mars, The.
Marshes
Atwood. Marsh, Hawk.
Ciardi. Sea Marshes in Winter.
Dickey, James. Salt Marsh, The.
Dove. Delft.
Kinnell. Winter Sky, A.
Piercy. Cod Summer.
Snodgrass. Marsh, The.
Marsyas
Dobyns. Marsyas, Midas and the Barber.
Martens
Clare. Marten.
Eberhart. Fisher Cat, The.
Martha's Vineyard, Massachusetts
Nash. Martha's Vineyard.
Martin, Saint
Gunn. St. Martin and the Beggar.
Martins
Davie. House-martin.
Martyrs
Byron. Spell Is Broke, the Charm is Flown, The.
Thy Days Are Done.
Chaucer. Second Nun's Tale, The.
Cowper. Joy in Martyrdom.
Crashaw. Live here, great heart; and love and dy and kill.
To the Infant Martyrs.
Davie. Oxfordshire.
Dickinson. Martyr Poets—did not tell, The.
Through the strait pass of suffering.
Donne. Martyrs, The.
Glück. Jeanne d'Arc.
Herrick. Christian Militant.
Dirge of Jephthah's Daughter, The.
Sufferance.
To Groves.
Hewitt. Song for May Day.
Hill. Martyrdom of Saint Sebastian.
Martyrium.
Hopkins. Margaret Clitheroe.
Hughes, Ted. Martyrdom of Bishop Farrar, The.
Joseph. CENTERPIECE: *St. Sebastian* (Italian).
Puppet Show, The.
Lewis. Crucifixion, The.
Lowell. Colloquy in Black Rock.
Lowry. There is a sort of conspiracy about the great.
MacNeice. Springboard, The.
Meredith. Song of Theodolinda, The.
Merton. From the Legend of St. Clement.
Invocation to St. Lucy, An.
St. Agnes: A Responsory.
Milton. Sonnet 18: "Avenge O Lord thy slaughter'd Saints, whose bones."
Oliver. Sunrise.
Olson. Leader, The.
Rich. Reliquary.
Rolfe. All Ghouls' Night.
Rossetti. All Saints: Martyrs.
Martyr, A.
Martyr, A.
Martyr, The.
Martyrs' Song.
Rukeyser. Akiba.
Lynchings of Jesus, The.
Smart. King Charles the Martyr.
St. Simon and St. Jude.
Smith, Charlotte. To a Young Man Entering the World.

Southwell. Life is But Losse.
Walker. They Who Feel Death.
Whitman. Wallabout Martyrs, The.
Whittier. Barclay of Ury.
Cross, The.
Female Martyr, The.
How the Women Went from Dover.
Wilbur. Ballade to End With, A.
Wordsworth. Destined to war from very infancy.
Eagle and the Dove, The.
Wroth. Song 4: "Lovers learne to speake butt truthe."
Marvell, Andrew
MacLeish. You, Andrew Marvell.
Marx, Karl
Hewitt. Chant for the Five-Year Plan.
Lorde. Workers Rose on May Day or Postcript to Karl Marx, The.
Mary, the Virgin
Angelou. Avec Merci, Mother.
Beatles. Let It Be.
Berryman. Prayer After All, A.
Bishop. Hymn to the Virgin.
Brooks. Penitent Considers Another Coming of Mary, A.
Browning, Elizabeth Barrett. Virgin Mary to the Child Jesus, The.
Carruth. Chicory.
Chaucer. ABC, An.
Prioress's Tale, The.
Two Invocations of the Virgin, II.
Coleridge. Translation of a Passage in Ottfried's Metrical Paraphrase of the Gospel.
Virgin's Cradle-Hymn, The.
Crane. Interludium.
To Liberty.
Crashaw. Luke 2; Quærit Jesum Suum Maria.
Matthew 28; Come See the Place where the Lord Lay.
O Gloriosa Domina.
On the Blessed Virgins Bashfulnesse.
Sancta Maria Dolorum.
Tear[e], The.
Davie. Our Lady.
Donne. Annunciation.
Deliver us for thy descent.
Upon the Annunciation and Passion Falling upon One Day. 1608.
Virgin Mary, The.
Doolittle. We have seen her/ the world over.
Everson. Canticle for the Feast of the Most Precious Blood, 1954, A.
Glück. Pietà.
Winter Morning.
Graves. Birth of a Goddess.
Joseph and Mary.
Gunn. Jesus and His Mother.
Hardy. Evening in Galilee, An.
Herbert. Ana(Mary-Army)gram.
To All Angels and Saints.
Herrick. Another ("As Sun-beames pierce the glasse, and streaming in").
Observation ("Virgin-Mother stood at distance [there], The").
Upon Woman and Mary.
Virgin Mary, The ("To work a wonder, God would have her shown").
Virgin Mary, The ("Virgin Marie was [as I have read], The").
Hewitt. Ecce Homo.
Egyptian Night.
Mary's Lullaby.
May Alter.
Rhyme for Christmas Morning, A.
Hopkins. Blessed Virgin Compared to the Air We Breathe, The.
May Magnificat, The.
Rosa Mystica.
Jonson. Garland [or Ghyrlond] of the Blessèd Virgin Mary [or Marie], The.
Reverse on the Back Side, The.
Kipling. Our Lady of the Sackcloth.
Lawrence. Ballad of a Wilful Woman.
Jesus' Farewell.
Pietá.
Song to the Tune of *La Cucaracha.*

Lowell. Beyond the Alps.
"MacDiarmid." Harry Semen.
Markson. Death of the Virgin, The.
Merton. A Solis Ortus Cardine.
Blessed Virgin Mary Compared to a Window, The.
Canticle for the Blessed Virgin.
Evening of the Visitation, The.
La Salette.
Sunset. The Hour of Compline. Salve Regina.
To the Immaculate Virgin, on a Winter Night.
Morgan. Mary.
Patchen. I have lighted the candles, Mary.
Poe. Hymn: "At morn—at noon—at twilight dim."
Robinson. Gift of God, The.
Rossetti. Feast of the Annunciation.
Herself a Rose Who Bore the Rose.
Purification of St. Mary the Virgin, The.
Sexton. Angel Food Dogs, The.
For the Year of the Insane.
Jesus Suckles.
Jesus, the Actor, Plays the Holy ghost.
Mary's Song.
Simic. Psalm: "Old ones to the side."
Smart. Annunciation of the Blessed Virgin.
Smith, Stevie. Dream of Comparison, A.
Southwell. Assumption of Our Lady, The.
Conception of our Ladie, The.
Death of our Ladie, The.
Our Ladie's Nativitye.
Our Ladye's Spousalls.
Our Lady's [or Ladie's] Salutation.
Virgin Mary to Christ on the Crosse, The.
Visitation, The.
Williams, William Carlos. For Eleanor and Bill Monahan.
Wordsworth. Our Lady of the Snow.
Yeats. Mother of God, The.

Mary Magdalene
Crashaw. Weeper, The.
Donne. To Mrs. Magdalen Herbert: of St. Mary Magdalen.
Duncan. Adoration of the Virgin, The.
Herbert. Mary [or Marie] Magdalene.
Kipling. Burden, The.
Rossetti. Mary Magdalene and the Other Mary.
Southwell. Mary Magdalen's Blushe.

Mary Queen of Scots
Burns. Campbells Are Comin, The.
Lament of Mary Queen of Scots on the Approach of Spring.
Lowell. Mary Stuart.
Southwell. Decease, Release.
Wordsworth. Captivity.—Mary Queen of Scots.
Lament of Mary Queen of Scots on the Eve of a New Year.
Mary Queen of Scots.

Masefield, John
Muldoon. Profumo.
Wystan.

Masks
Atwood. Paper Bag, A.
Carroll, Jim. Borges Death Mask.
"Carroll, Lewis." Prologue: "Ladies and Gentlemen seems stiff and cold."
Carruth. Your dream: / His name was Harlequin. He wore the mask.
Creeley. Song, The: "It still makes sense."
De la Mare. Veil, The.
Dunbar. We Wear the Mask.
Dunn. Mon Semblable.
Fisher. Corner.
Ford. Masks without faces.
Graves. Women and Masks.
Hayden. Two Egyptian Portrait Masks.
Hesketh. Clown.
Hewitt. Mask, The.
Sonnet: "Among the many selves that throng my flesh."
Kunitz. Fitting of the Mask, The.
Merton. O it is not lazy to be a messenger or to live out of the shadow of some town.
Olson. Yellow of the Mask, The.
Rukeyser. Poem as Mask, The.

Sandburg. Aztec Mask.
Mask.
Snodgrass. Reichsmarschall Hermann Göring ("Dear friends, the moment's come to ask").
Thomas. O Make Me a Mask.
Updike. Modigliani's Death Mask.
Whitman. Visor'd.
Yeats. Mask, The.

Masochism
Graves. Encounter, The.
Hoffman. Marked Man, A.
Koch. To win the love of women one should first discover.
Merton. Psalm 132: A Modern Monastic Revision.
Nash. Little Miss Muffet Sat on a Prophet— and Quite Right, Too!
"Reed." Venus in Furs.

Massachusetts (state)
Bishop. In the Waiting Room.
Creeley. Picnic, The.
Eberhart. On a Squirrel Crossing the Road in Autumn, in New England.
Eliot. Cape Ann.
Emerson. God The Lord save Massachusetts.
Hymn[:] Sung at the Completion of the Concord Monument, April 19, 1836.
Kunitz. Route Six.
Lowell. For the Union Dead.
Jonathan Edwards in Western Massachusetts.
Nemerov. To the Governor & Legislature of Massachusetts.
Plath. Point Shirley.
Whittier. Album Verses.
Arisen at Last.
Bay of Seven Islands, The.
Cassandra Southwick.
Garrison of Cape Ann, The.
Haverhill.
John Underhill.
June on the Merrimac.
Kenoza Lake.
Letter to Lucy Larcom.
Massachusetts.
Massachusetts to Virginia.
Merrimac, The.
Norumbega Hall.
One of the Signers.
Our River.
Our State.
Pine-Tree, The.
Snow-Bound [or Snow-Bound; a Winter Idyl].
To Massachusetts.
Vale of the Merrimac, The.
Welcome to Lowell, A.
Witch of Wenham, The.
Wilbur. Running.

Massacre of the Innocents
Lowell. Holy Innocents, The.

Massacres
Boyle. Branded for Slaughter.
De la Mare. Massacre, The.
Glück. Slave Ship, The.
Hewitt. Bloody Brae, The.
Jeffers. Antrim.
Lowell. At the Indian Killer's Grave.
Rossetti. In the Round Tower at Jhansi, June 8, 1857.
Scott. On the Massacre of Glencoe, 1692.
Walcott. Air.
Whittier. Le Marais du Cygne.
Pentucket.

Masts
Eberhart. Broken Wing Theory.
Waiting To Lean to the Master's Command.
Olson. Mast, The.

Maternity
Beatles. Lady Madonna.
Jeffers. Haunted Country.
Robinson. Aunt Imogen.

Mathematics and Mathematicians
Auden. Last of the Old Year, The.
"Carroll, Lewis." To My Pupil.
Clark. Pharoahs Sacrifice Themselves before Her, The.
Coleridge. Mathematical Problem, A.

Davie. Bolyai, the Geometer.
Dickey, James. Math.
Fox. Johannes Kepler (1571–1630).
Gardner. Mathematics of Encounter.
Hewitt. Mathematics.
Liddy. Death of Mathmaticians, The.
Lovelace. To My Truely Valiant, Learned Friend, Who in His Booke Resolv'd the Art Gladiatory into the Mathematick's.
Olson. Lie of 10, or the Concept of Zero, The.
Rossetti. 1 and 1 are 2— / That's for me and you.
Sandburg. Arithmetic.
See also **Arithmetic.**

Matisse, Henri
Ferlinghetti. Matisse at the Modern, Magritte at the Met.
Snodgrass. Matisse: "The Red Studio."

Matterhorn
Hardy. Zermatt: To the Matterhorn.
Lowry. And who is it through the forest after the.

Maturity
Auden. Photograph of a Boy in Costume, The.
Beatles. Hey Jude.
Bunting. All the teeth ever I had are worn down and fallen out.
Like a fawn you dodge me, Molly.
Cummings. Boy and the Man, The.
Pretty a day, A.
Dickey, James. Little More, The.
Dickinson. Maturity only enhances mystery.
Dove. Obedience.
Ferlinghetti. *Firenze*, a Lifetime Later.
Fisher. Lesson in Composition, The.
Gallagher. Breasts.
Gardner. At a Summer Hotel.
Nor Good Red Herring.
That Common Moth.
Word From the Piazza del Limbo, A.
Graves. To Come of Age.
Hartley. You Who Have Done.
Hewitt. Already autumn silently / has come to sky and field and tree.
Hill. Guardians, The.
Holy Thursday.
Jonson. Ode. To Sir William Sydney, on His Birthday.
Kipling. If.
Larkin. Maturity.
Lawrence. I Heard Her Say.
Levine. How many lives were torn apart.
Last Step, The.
Lewis. Lines on a Young Girl.
Lovelace. Love Inthron'd.
Lowry. Poem Influenced By John Davenport and Cervantes.
MacLeish. Shallow Grass, The.
Markson. Johanna.
Meredith. Atlas.
Morrison. You Must Confront.
Nash. Lines to Be Scribbled on Somebody Else's Thirtieth Milestone.
Piercy. Sign.
Ransom. Eclogue: "JANE SNEED BEGAN IT: My poor John, alas."
First Travels of Max.
Semi-Centennial.
Roethke. Sententious Man, The.
Rossetti. Once.
Within the Veil.
Rukeyser. Boys of These Men Full Speed.
Sandburg. Father sees a son nearing manhood, A.
Shakespeare. Sonnet 102: "My love is strengthen'd, though more weak in seeming."
Shelton. Negative Virtues, The.
Promises.
Smith, Stevie. To Carry the Child.
Snodgrass. Seeing You Have.
Stevenson. On His Pitiable Transformation.
Wordsworth. My heart leaps up when I behold.

Mausoleums
"MacDiarmid." Skeleton of the Future, The.
Tomlinson. Mausoleum, The.

Wordsworth. Filial Piety.
See also **Cemeteries; Graves; Monuments; Tombs.**

May
Auden. May.
Berry. May Song.
Browning, Robert. Home-Thoughts, from Abroad.
  May and Death.
Burns. Song, Altered from an Old English One.
"Carroll, Lewis." What is most like a bee in May?
Cowper. Judgment of the Poets, The.
Davie. Wearing of the Green, The.
De la Mare. There Blooms No Bud in May.
Dickinson. When they come back—if Blossoms do.
Dunbar. Golden Day, A.
  In May.
Eberhart. May Evening.
  Velvet Rocks.
Emerson. May-Day.
Glück. Brooding Likeness.
Graves. Song: Olive Tree.
Herrick. Corinna's Going a-Maying.
Hewitt. Poem in May.
Hopkins. Ad Mariam.
  May Magnificat, The.
Housman. First of May, The.
MacLeish. Spring in These Hills.
Meredith. May Song.
Milton. Song: on [*or* of] May Morning.
Nash. Here We Go Quietly Nuts in May.
Nemerov. May Day Dancing, The.
Rossetti. May.
  There is but one May in the year.
Sandburg. Crossing the Ohio When Poppies Bloom in Ashtabula.
Dan.
Follies.
  Uplands in May.
Shelley. Fragment: May the Limner.
Spender. Remembering Cincinnatti, 1953.
Thomson. On May.
Whitman. Out of May's Shows Selected.
Williams, William Carlos. Bird Song.
  Locust Tree in Flower, The.
Wordsworth. Ode Composed on May Morning.
  To May.
Wyatt. You that in love find[e] luck[e] and [h]abunda[u]nce.

May Day
Emerson. May.
  May-Day.
Herrick. May-Pole, The.
Rukeyser. Cats and a Cock.

Maya
Merton. Chilam Balam.
Nemerov. Maia.
Oppen. Mayan Ground, The.

Mayflower (ship)
Plath. Mayflower.

Mayflowers. *see* **Arbutus.**

Mayo. *see* **County Mayo, Ireland.**

Mazepa, Ivan
Byron. Mazeppa.

Mead
Millay. Oh, think not I am faithful to a vow!

Meadowlarks
Dunbar. Meadow Lark, The.
Eberhart. Now Is The Air Made of Chiming Balls.

Meadows
Carruth. Lover of balsam lover of white pine.
Davie. Skelpick.
De la Mare. Crazed.
  Voices.
Duncan. Often I Am Permitted to Return to a Meadow.
Emerson. Patch of meadow & upland, A.
  Would you know what joy is hid.
Frost. Last Mowing, The.
  Rose Pogonias.
Gunn. Flooded Meadows.

Hall. Our Walk in Yorkshire.
Herrick. To Meadows [*or* Meddowes].
Hopkins. They came / Next to meadows abundant, pierced with flowers.
Joseph. Meeting Up.
Kipling. Alnaschar and the Oxen.
Lawrence. Chief Mystery, The.
Levine. Across the world / in the high mountains of the West.
Rossetti. In the meadow—what in the meadow?
  Mr. and Mrs. Scott, and I.
Sandburg. Meadow in Summer.
Simic. Pastoral: "I came to a meadow."
Wakoski. First Universe.
Wilbur. Two Voices in a Meadow.
Wright, James. Eclogue at Nash's Grove.
See also **Fields and Pastures.**

Meat
Angelou. Health-Food Diner, The.
Cohen. Person Who Eats Meat, A.
Emerson. Stout Sparta shrined the god of Laughter.
Gunn. Meat.
Hardy. Bags of Meat.
Herrick. Great Boast, Small Rost.
  Upon Lungs.
  Upon Showbread [*or* Shewbread]: Epigram.
Joseph. Just a snack for lunch.
Levine. Salami.
Lovelace. Being treated to Ellinda.
Nash. Squab, The.
Paley. Families.
Snodgrass. Boy Made of Meat, The; A Poem for Children.
Wilbur. Rillons, Rillettes.

Meath. *see* **County Meath, Ireland.**

Mechanics
Levine. Detroit Grease Shop Poem.
Wakoski. Mechanic, The.
Williams, Miller. Mecanic on Duty at All Times.
Zukofsky. Pretty.

Medals
Merton. Message to Be Inscribed on Mark Van Doren's Hamilton Medal.
Oppen. Serpent, Ouroboros / Whose tail is in his mouth: he is the root.
Sandburg. Medallion.

Medea
Byron. Translation from the Medea of Euripides.
Carruth. Sonnet: "Women in anger, it seems, become theatrical."
Lewis. Jason and Medea.
Raine. Medea.

Medici, Lorenzo de'
Davie. Tuscan Brutus, The.

Medicine
Browning, Robert. Epistle Containing the Strange Medical Experience of Karshish, the Arab Physician, An.
Burns. Death and Doctor Hornbook [A True Story].
Cohen. I Wanted to Be a Doctor.
Cowper. To Dr. Austin.
Crashaw. On Taking Physicke.
Fox. Aloe.
Graves. Apollo of the Physiologists.
Herrick. Great Maladies, Long Medicines.
  Head-Ake, The.
  Lenitie.
  Upon Leech.
Hoffman. Brainwaves.
Hopkins. Cockle's Antibilious Pills.
Jonson. You that would last long, list to my song.
Kipling. Our Fathers of Old.
Kooser. After the Funeral: Cleaning Out the Medicine Cabinet.
Lindsay. One Brief Hour of Grown-up Glory on the Gulf of Mexico.
Lowry. Homoeopathic Blues in J.
  With Sweetest Love from All the Little Animals to Their Beloved Harteebeeste.
McNeill. Granny Saunders.

Markson. On the Death, after Lying Wounded in the Thigh for Twenty-Six Days, of the Author of "Astrophel and Stella."
Meredith. Faith on Trial, A.
  Melampus.
Moore. Staff of Aesculapius, The.
Muldoon. Cure for Warts, The.
  Glanders.
Nash. Strange Case of the Lucrative Compromise, The.
Rich. 5:30 A.M.
Rossetti. Baby cry— / Oh fie!
Rukeyser. Praise of the Committee.
Schuyler. Afterward.
  What.
Sidney. Hateful cure with hate to heal, A.
Smith, Stevie. Bottle of Aspirins, The.
Stevenson. To W.E. Henley.
Turco. Pharmacy, The.
Van Duyn. Death By Aesthetics.
  Remedies, Maladies, Reasons.
See also **Hospitals; Illness; Nurses; Physicians.**

Meditation
Beatles. Inner Light, The.
Berry. Meditation in the Spring Rain.
Bly. Six Winter Privacy Poems.
Bukowski. T.M.
Carruth. Buddhist Painter Prepares to Paint, The.
Cohen. Commentary—Death to This Book.
  Death to This Book.
  Escape, The.
  Fragment from a Journal.
  I Have Not Lingered in European Monasteries.
  Peace.
  Roshi Again.
Cowper. *see also* Watching unto God in the Night-Season.
  Scenes Favourable to Meditation.
  Watching unto God in the Night-Season.
  Winter Walk at Noon, The.
Emerson. Apology, The.
Ford. I am Mantra.
Ginsberg. Cabin in the Rockies.
  Thoughts on a Breath.
  Thoughts Sitting Breathing.
  Too much industry.
Graves. Ambience.
Herbert. Content.
Levertov. Three Meditations.
Meredith. Fireside Reverie.
  I seize in a central knot.
  Meditation under Stars.
Merton. Then from tomorrow.
  When Knowledge Went North.
Oppen. Knowledge not of sorrow, you were, The.
Roethke. Meditation in Hydrotherapy.
Schwartz. This hushed surface where the doves parade.
Williams, Charles Kenneth. Listen carefully. / I'm meditating.
Wordsworth. Most Sweet It Is with Unuplifted Eyes.
Wright, Charles. Driving to Passalacqua, 1960.
Wyatt. Prologue: "Love, to give law unto his subject hearts."

Mediterranean Sea
Cummings. Sunlight was over.
Eberhart. Mediterranean Song.
Hardy. Genoa and the Mediterranean.
Lawrence. Mediterranean in January.
  Middle of the World.
Tate. Mediterranean, The.
Tomlinson. Mediterranean, The.

Medusa
Bogan. Medusa.
Bunting. I thought I saw my late wife (a very respectable woman).
Crane. Medusa.
Cullen. Medusa.
Gunn. Door opens, The.
  Dream sponsors: / Charles Manson, tongue.
Hayden. Perseus.
Nash. Medusa and the Mot Juste.
Sarton. Muse as Medusa, The.

Shelley. On the Medusa of Leonardo da Vinci in the Florentine Gallery.
Yau. Medusa.

Melampus
Meredith. Melampus.
Stevenson. As one who having wandered all night long.

Melancholy
Ammons. Correction.
Arnold. Iseult of Brittany.
Berg. Gooseberries.
Times.
Brontë. Wind, I hear it sighing, The.
Brooks. Crazy Woman, The.
Bukowski. Melancholia.
"Carroll, Lewis." Melancholetta.
Carruth. Chase in Spring, The.
Catullus. Carmen 37: "Nine posts, five doors, up the Clivus."
Ciardi. Memory of the Sad Chair, A.
Coleridge. Dejection; an Ode.
Letter to Sara Hutchinson.
Nightingale, The.
This Lime-Tree Bower My Prison.
Creeley. Medallion.
De la Mare. Old Angler, The.
Son of Melancholy, The.
Dobyns. Spleen.
Dunbar. Melancholia.
Dunn. Clarities, The.
Loneliness.
"Dylan." Meet Me in the Morning.
Emerson. Teach me I am forgotten by the dead.
Written in Naples, March, 1833.
Ferlinghetti. Thoughts to a Concerto of Telemann.
Fisher. Burnt year. Trick riders blunder about the concrete, A.
Ginsberg. Moments Return, The.
My Sad Self.
Hewitt. Northern Spring.
Keats. Ode on Melancholy.
Knott. Brighton Rock by Graham Greene.
Shorts / Excerpts ("Our farewells lack the plausibility of our departures").
Kunitz. Artist, The.
How Long Is the Night?
Liddy. Richard, Oremus.
Lowry. Hartebeeste Both Grave and Gay, The.
McGrath. Woodcut.
Nash. So Penseroso.
Olson. Your Eyes.
Plath. Poppies in July.
Robinson. Charles Carville's Eyes.
Rossetti. At Home.
If Only.
Schuyler. February 13, 1975.
Heather and Calendulas.
Shelley. Stanzas Written in Dejection, near Naples [or —December 1818, near Naples].
Sidney. Sonnet 23: "Curious wits, seeing dull pensiveness, The."
Sonnet 99: "When far-spent night persuades each mortal eye."
Smart. Melancholy.
Smith, Charlotte. To Melancholy. Written on the Banks of the Arun, October 1785.
To the Invisible Moon.
To the South Downs.
Verses Supposed to Have Been Written in the New Forest, in Early Spring.
Written in October.
Written on the Sea Shore.—October, 1784.
Smith, Stevie. Away, Melancholy.
Old Sweet Dove of Wiveton, The.
Swinburne. Itylus.
Turco. Desert of Melancholy, The.
Farewell to Melancholy.
Menu of Melancholy, The.
Moon of Melancholy, The.
That Particular Air.
Winter in Muscovy.
Wakoski. Blue Monday.
Wordsworth. World is too much with us; late and soon, The.

Wyatt. What rage is this? What furo[u]r of what kind [or kynd]?
Zukofsky. Dying away as of trees, A.
Not it was no dream of coming death.
Salt hacks, tavern boys, what skews, can't you burn alleys.
See also **Blues (mood); Dejection; Depression (psychological).**

Meleager
MacNeice. [Bad Dream] Flattest place, it seems, in Hellas.

Melons
Plath. Fiesta Melons.

Melville, Herman
Auden. Herman Melville.
Crane. At Melville's Tomb.
Dunn. Update.
Koch. You Were Wearing.
Lowry. But never fall from fealty to light.
Those who die young will look forever young.
Warning from False Cape Horn.
Olson. Letter for Melville 1951.
Rukeyser. After Melville.

Memento Mori
Graves. Half-Finished Letter, The.

Memnon
Smart. Inscriptions on an Aeolian Harp.

Memorial Day
Dunbar. Memorial Day.
Ode for Memorial Day.
Olson. Memorial Day.
Williams, William Carlos. Middle.

Memory
Angelou. I Almost Remember.
Memory, The.
Now Long Ago.
Remembering.
When You Come to Me.
Ashbery. Hop o' My Thumb.
Houseboat Days.
Some Old Tires.
Atwood. Dufferin, Simcoe, Grey.
Foundling, A.
It is not the things themselves.
Night Poem.
Nightshade on the Way to School.
Auden. Before.
Compline.
Consequences.
Elegy: "Why was it that you gave us no warning."
He Revisits the Spot.
Last Time, The.
Often the man, alone shut, shall consider.
On This Island.
Question, The ("To ask the hard question is simple").
Shock, A.
Since.
Song: "I have a little book."
Song: "Merriest cuckoo / Which haunted us in May, The."
Sunken Lane, The.
Talking to Myself.
Taller To-day.
Taller to-day, we remember similar evenings.
Whenever I see for the first time.
Beatles. In My Life.
Penny Lane.
Things We Said Today.
Yesterday.
Beckett. Ainsi a-t-on beau.
Pas davantage.
Son ombre une nuit.
Berg. And the Scream.
Fragment, 1959.
Homage to the Afterlife.
Lightbulb.
1909.
1945.
Self-Portrait at Six.
Sister Ann.
Summer Twilight.
This Cold.
Times.
To the Same Place.

Voice, The.
Why Are We Here?
Berrigan. Certain Slant of Sunlight, A.
Cranston Near the City Line.
Last Poem.
Pandora's Box, An Ode.
Berry. And then, one by one, he moved me.
At a Country Funeral.
Finally, he brought me to a hill.
Gathering, The.
His mind gone from the window.
In Memory: Stuart Egnal.
Light, The.
Meditation in the Spring Rain.
Praise, A.
We came then to his time of pain.
We stood on a height.
Wild, The.
Berryman. Cambridge friend put in,—one whom I used, A.
Clots of age, grovel and palsy, crave, The.
Crisis.
Down & Back.
Fall and rise of her midriff bells. I watch.
Heroes, The.
How far upon these songs with my strict wrist.
I didn't see anyone else, I just saw Lies.
Images of Elspeth.
In & Out.
London.
Meditation.
Meeting.
Message.
My Special Fate.
Nowhere.
Of all that weeks-long day, though call it back.
"Old Smoky" when you sing with Robin, Chris.
Recovery.
They come too thick, hail-hard, and all beside.
Two Organs.
You come blonde visiting through the black air.
Bishop. In the Middle of the Road.
Blake. Song: "Memory, hither come."
Bogan. Memory.
Boyle. Poem of Gratitude, A.
Brontë. A.G.A. to A.S.
All hushed and still within the house.
Come hither, child—who gifted thee.
From a Dungeon Wall in the Southern College.
Harp of wild and dream-like strain.
I gazed upon the cloudless moon.
I.M. to I.G.
Lines by Claudia.
Lines: "Soft unclouded blue of air, The."
M.G. For The U.S.
Mild the mist upon the hill.
O Dream, where art thou now?
O mother, I am not regretting.
R. Alcona to J. Brenzaida.
Remembrance.
Starry night shall tidings bring, The.
Still beside that dreary water.
That wind, I used to hear it swelling.
There let thy bleeding branch atone.
Warning and Reply.
What winter floods, what showers of spring.
When days of Beauty deck the earth.
Wind, I hear it sighing, The.
Brooks. Anniad, The.
Bean Eaters, The.
Browning, Elizabeth Barrett. But Fortune governed all their works[,] till when.
Dance, The.
Dead Rose, A.
Little Friend, The.
Memory and Hope.
Night and the Merry Man.
Sonnet: "Yes, call me by my pet-name! let me hear."
Browning, Robert. Appearances.
By the Fire-Side.

Dubiety.
Memorabilia.
Bukowski. Eulogy to a Hell of a Dame—.
Reunion.
Spain Sits Like a Hidden Flower in My
  Coffeepot.
Bunting. All the teeth ever I had are worn
  down and fallen out.
Let them remember Samangan, the bridge and
  tower.
Two Photographs.
Burns. Love's records, written on a heart like
  mine.
O May Thy Morn.
Byron. And Thou Art Dead, as Young and
  Fair.
Condolatory Address.
Egotism. A Letter to J.T. Becher.
If Sometimes in the Haunts of Men.
La Revanche.
Lines Written beneath a Picture.
Lines Written beneath an Elm in the
  Churchyard of Harrow.
Lines Written in an Album, at Malta.
On a Distant View of the Village and School
  of Harrow on the Hill.
Pignus Amoris.
Remember Thee! Remember Thee!
Remind Me Not, Remind Me Not.
Stanzas: "Chill and mirk is the nightly blast."
Stanzas for Music.
Stanzas for Music ("There's not a joy the
  world can give like that it takes away").
Stanzas: "Through cloudless skies, in silvery
  sheen."
Stanzas to a Lady on Leaving England.
To a Lady.
To the Hon. Mrs. George Lamb.
Carew. To T. H., a Lady Resembling My
  Mistress.
Carroll, Jim. Back Home.
Back to the streets always, ravaged and wet.
California Poem.
Moss under your fingernails it feeds, The.
Other Garden, The.
"Carroll, Lewis." Dedication: "Child of the
  pure unclouded brow."
Double Acrostic: I sing a place wherein agree.
Those Horrid Hurdy-Gurdies!
Carruth. Bearer, The.
Being as Memory, The.
Event Itself, The.
Forward! You must. Keep.
Therefore to us, time's / final lesson: be
  content.
Wind is a stealth of memory. Footsteps fall.
Ciardi. Bedlam Revisited.
Cal Coolidge and the Co.
Epilogue: The Burial of the Last Elder.
Feasts.
Five-Year Step, A.
Highest Place in Town, The.
It Took Four Flowerboats to Convoy My
  Father's Black.
Keeping.
On a Photo of Sgt. Ciardi a Year Later.
River, The.
Romancing with Our Beasts.
Shaft, The.
Survival in Missouri.
Talking Myself to Sleep at One More Hilton.
Three Views of a Mother.
Tree Trimming.
Two Saints.
What *Was* Her Name.
Clark. Ancestors.
Blue Dress.
Clemente (1934-1972).
Momentum.
1968.
What the picture tells me is itself.
Cohen. Another Family.
Big World, The.
Days of Kindness.
Disguises.
Flowers That I Left in the Ground, The.
For E. J. P.

Front Lawn.
Heirloom.
Hitler.
I Can't Forget.
I See You on a Greek Mattress.
I'd Like to Read.
Lists, The.
On Hearing a Name Long Unspoken.
So Long, Marianne.
Streetcars.
Style.
There are Some Men.
Coleridge. Lewti.
Cooper. Back.
For My Mother in Her First Illness, from a
  Window Overlooking Notre Dame.
In Silence Where We Breathe.
Inheritances.
Souvenirs.
Crane. Emblems of Conduct.
Great Western Plains, The.
Havana Rose.
Legende.
Passage.
Postscript, A.
Repose of Rivers.
Creeley. Away.
Backwards.
Ball Game, The.
Drums, The.
Every Day.
Fire, The.
First Time, The.
For Leslie.
For My Mother: Genevieve Jules Creeley.
For the Graduation.
Guido, i' vorrei che tu e Lapo ed io.
Hole, The.
I.
In London.
Just Friends.
Method of Actuality, The.
Oh, Love.
People, The.
Place, A.
Plan Is the Body, The.
Something.
Souvenir, The.
Tally, A.
Teachings, The.
Two.
Variations.
Cullen. At the Wailing Wall in Jerusalem.
To One Not There.
Youth Sings a Song of Rosebuds.
Cummings. After five / times the poem.
Along the brittle treacherous bright streets.
An(fragrance)Of / (Begins) / millions.
Buncha hardboil guys frum duh A.C. fulla.
"But / he" i / staring / into winter twi.
Clown's smirk in the skull of a baboon, A.
Dedicated to Dear Nana Clarke.
Dick Mid's large bluish face without
  eyebrows.
GrEEn's d / an / cing on hollow was.
Grin without a / face(a look), A.
How this uncouth enchanted.
I remark that this beach has been used
  too.   much Too.   originally.
In spite of everything.
In time of daffodils(who know.
It is so long since my heart has been with
  yours.
Item:is / Clumsily with of.
Ivory performing rose, The.
Jack's white horse(up).
Joys faces friends / feet terrors fate.
Memory believes / fragrance of a
  town(whose).
Now two old ladies sit peacefully knitting.
Other guineahen, The.
Out of more find than seeks.
Silently little blue elephant shyly(he was terri),
  The.
We)under)over,the thing of floating Of.
What is strictly fiercely and wholly dies.

Y is a WELL KNOWN ATHELETE'S
  BRIDE.
Davie. Abbeyforde.
Barnsley and District.
Derbyshire.
Devil on Ice.
Dudwood.
Eight Years After.
Hampshire.
Herefordshire.
Hermes and Mr Shaw.
Housekeeping.
Huntingdonshire.
Hyphens.
Northamptonshire.
Recollections of George Oppen in a Letter to
  an English Friend.
Shropshire.
Staffordshire.
Time Passing, Beloved.
De la Mare. Cage, The.
Faithless.
Fare Well.
Juliet's Nurse.
Lucy.
Memory ("Ah Memory").
Memory ("When Summer").
Miss Loo.
Mountains, The.
Music.
Old Ben.
Old Men, The.
Phantom, The.
Rachel.
Remembrance.
Rooks In October.
Sea-Magic.
Son of Melancholy, The.
To My Mother.
Treachery.
Unregarding.
Widow, The.
Winter.
Dickey, James. To Be Done in Winter.
Dickey, William. Anniversary, The.
At Your Old House.
His Death from Cancer.
Memoranda.
Things Kept.
Dickinson. Blossoms will run away.
Flower keeps it's appointment.
Heart! We [or Heart, we] will forget him!
I remember your coming as serious sweetness.
If recollecting were forgetting.
In Ebon Box, when years have flown.
Like Some Old fashioned Miracle.
Memory is a strange Bell.
Memory is the Sherry Flower.
No Passenger was known to flee.
Pile of Years is not so high, The.
Remembrance has a Rear and Front.
Show me Eternity, and I will show you
  Memory.
Some Days retired from the rest.
That sacred Closet when you sweep.
This was in the White of the Year.
Through those old Grounds of memory.
To flee from memory.
Tropic, indeed, a memory.
When Memory is full.
You cannot make Remembrance grow.
You might not know I remembered you.
Dobyns. Geese.
How To Like It.
Red Geraniums.
Slipping Away.
Song of Four Dancers.
Tenderly.
Wind Chimes.
Doolittle. At Eleusis.
Lethe.
So you have swept me back.
Dove. Anniversary.
Charm, The.
Company.
Grape Sherbet.
Nothing Down.

Pomade.
Stroke, The.
Wingfoot Lake.
Dunbar. At Sunset Time.
If I Could But Forget.
Little Lucy Landman.
Love-Song: "If Death should claim me for her own to-day."
Memory of Martha, The.
Old Homestead, The.
Old Story, The.
Parted.
Poor Withered Rose.
Retrospection.
Song, The: "My soul, lost in the music's mist."
To E. H. K.
To Pfrimmer.
When the Old Man Smokes.
Duncan. After Reading H.D.'s *Hermetic Definitions.*
There are memories everywhere then.
Rememberd, we go out, as in.
Tribal Memories.
Dunn. Briefcases.
Local Time.
Photograph Album, The.
Vanishings, The.
Whiteness.
"Dylan." Boots of Spanish Leather.
Dark Eyes.
Girl of the North Country.
I'll Remember You.
Mama, You Been on My Mind.
Something There Is About You.
Tangled Up in Blue.
This Wheel's on Fire.
Tomorrow Is a Long Time.
Eberhart. Deep Fishing.
Formative Mastership.
In the Garden.
Loss.
Memory.
Whenever I See Beauty I See Death.
Eliot. Burnt Norton.
Dans le Restauramt.
La Figlia Che Piange.
Rhapsody on a Windy Night.
Emerson. Amulet, The.
Dear are the pleasant memories.
For Nature true & like in every place.
From Frodmer's Drama "The Friends."
Memory.
Past, The.
Shall the Muse sing for thousands & not sing.
Thanks to those who go & come.
Thine Eyes Still Shined.
Where art thou / Thou beautiful dream.
Fenton. But come. Grief must have its term?
Guilt too, then.
Would come down, would ever come down.
Ferlinghetti. And she "like a young year."
Firenze, a Lifetime Later.
In woods where many rivers run.
Photo of Emily, The.
Reading Yeats I do not think.
Fletcher. Calendar in the Attic, The.
Journey Day.
Old Nursery.
Scythe, The.
Unfamiliar House, The.
Well, The.
Ford. Afternoon with André Breton, An.
It Seems You Never Were.
Weather is mild, The.
Fox. April Fool.
Dead Women.
Frost. Auspex.
Directive.
Gallagher. As If It Happened.
Backdrop With Lovers, 1931.
Bonfire.
Corona.
Devotion: That It Flow; That There Be Concentration.
Open Fire Near a Shed.
Woodcutting on Lost Mountain.

Galvin. Green Evening, A.
Mockingbird, The.
Old Woman Telling Another Version.
Gardner. Children Are Game.
Eros in May at MacDowell.
Feeling of Time.
Grocery Bouquet, The.
Summer Remembered.
Summers Ago.
Garrigue. Homage to Ghosts.
Suite.
Gildner. Edward.
Memory, A.
Poem with Levels of Meaning.
Ginsberg. Complaint of the Skeleton to Time.
Hymmnn.
Journal Night Thoughts.
Memory Gardens.
To Aunt Rose.
Glück. Lady in the Single, The.
Northwood Path.
Pond, The.
Scraps.
Song of the River.
Tango.
Graves. Plea to Boys and Girls, A.
Through Nightmare.
Griffiths. Cemaes Songs.
Christmas Night.
Elegy for John Tripp.
Few Bars Over Again, A.
Hymns and Backward Glances.
Returning I live with a huge space.
Tŷ Newydd.
Gunn. Autobiography.
Death's Door.
Memory Unsettled.
That was fifteen years ago.
Hacker. Geographer.
Hang-Glider's Daughter, The.
Letter from Goose Creek: April.
Some table talk at lunch, of memory.
Haines. Mothball Fleet: Benicia, California.
These images and their hidden voices.
Hall. Abroad Thoughts from Home.
Airstrip in Essex, 1960, An.
Beau of the Dead.
By the Exeter River.
Cider 5[dc] A Glass.
Exile.
Farm, The.
Foundations of American Industry, The.
Kicking the Leaves.
Letter to an English Poet.
Love Is Like Sounds.
Milkers Broken Up.
My Friend Felix.
1934.
"O Flodden Field."
Old Home Week.
Old Pilot, The.
Photographs of China.
September Ode.
Sleeping.
Three Movements, The.
Hardy. After a Journey.
Afterwards.
Ah, Are You Digging on My Grave?
Ancient to Ancients, An.
Beyond the Last Lamp.
Burning the Holly.
Days to Recollect.
Gentleman's Second-Hand Suit, A.
Green Slates.
I Looked Back.
In the Mind's Eye.
Joys of Memory.
Last Journey, A.
Last Time, The.
Let Me Believe.
Little Old Table, The.
Louie.
Memory and I.
Molly Gone.
Mound, The.
Not Only I.
Old Gown, The.

One We Knew.
Outside the Casement.
Procession of Dead Days, A.
Rambler, The.
Reminiscences of a Dancing Man.
Revisitation, The.
She Revisits Alone the Church of Her Marriage.
Shut Out That Moon.
Silences.
That Kiss in the Dark.
To Lizbie Browne.
Two Soldiers, The.
Unknowing.
Voice, The.
Where the Picnic Was.
Where Three Roads Joined.
Wife Comes Back, A.
Hartley. Two grey herons flying.
Hartnett. He'll to the Moors.
Mountains, Fall on Us.
Hayden. Ballad of Sue Ellen Westerfield, The.
Burly Fading One, The.
Whipping, The.
Heaney. Anahorish.
Cloistered.
Relic of Memory.
Terminus.
Underground, The.
Herrick. Upon His Sister-in-Law, Mistress Elizabeth Herrick.
Upon Parrat.
Hesketh. Autumn at Whitewell.
Call of the North.
I Am Not Resigned.
Invitation.
Love's Advocate.
Preparing to Leave.
Recapitulation.
Traitor.
Walking Back.
Hewitt. Ballad, The.
Balloons and Wooden Guns.
Bombed Public House, The.
Booleys, The.
Camaradas Y Compañeros.
Carnations.
Christmas Rhymers, Ballynure, 1941, The.
Drift of Petals, The.
Et Tu In Arcadia Vixisti.
Faded Leaf: A Chapter of Family History, The.
First Ride.
House on the Hill, The.
In Praise of Elizabeth.
Legend in His Own Lifetime.
Little Lough, The.
Mary Hagan, Islandmagee, 1919.
My Father's Ghost.
My Father's Mother.
My Teachers.
Neglected Lane, The.
Portstewart, July 1914.
Pour Hélène.
Sonnet: "I think of Glasgow, where reluctantly."
Swan.
To the Memory of James Connolly.
Two Spectres Haunt Me.
Hill. Domaine Public.
Postures.
Song from Armenia, A.
Stone Man, The.
Hoffman. Banished.
Old Reprobate.
Stop the Deathwish! Stop It! Stop!
Holmes. Dire Coasts.
Northfork October Return.
Unwanted 1943 Chappaqua Flashback.
Writing the Atheneum talk, I wonder.
Hopkins. Confirmed beauty will not bear a stress.
Hughes, Ted. Dream Time, The.
Hugo. Again, Kapowsin.
At the Cabin.
Flying, Reflying, Farming.
Freaks at Spurgin Road Field, The.

House on 15th S.W., The.
How Meadows Trick You.
Remember Graham.
Saying Goodbye to Mrs. Noraine.
Snapshot of 15th S.W., A.
Time to Remember Sangster.
Where Mission Creek Runs Hard for Joy.
Jarrell. Burning the Letters.
Dead Wingman, The.
Elementary Scene, The.
Face, The.
In Those Days.
Perfectly Free Association, A.
Player Piano, The.
Venetian Blind, The.
When I Was Home Last Christmas.
Jeffers. Ossian's Grave.
Johnson. In Rivum a Mola Stoana Lichfeldiæ
   Diffluentem.
Jong. Without Parachutes.
Jonson. Mind of the Frontispiece to a Book,
   The.
Joseph. Man in a Bar.
Summer Amnesty.
Kinnell. Apple Tree, The.
For Robert Frost.
Last River, The.
River That Is East, The.
To William Carlos Williams.
Two Seasons.
Kipling. Bells and Queen Victoria, The.
Files, The.
Fires, The.
Shock.
Knight. No Moon Floods the Memory of that
   Night.
Poem of Attrition, A.
Knott. Shorts / Excerpts ("Searching it goes").
Koch. Circus, The.
Fate.
To Marina.
With Janice.
Kunitz. Night-Piece.
Parting.
Unquiet Ones, The.
Your first dog was a Pekinese.
Larkin. Daily Things We Do, The.
Heaviest of Flowers, the Head.
I Remember, I Remember.
Morning at Last: There in the Snow.
So through that unripe day you bore your
   head.
Story.
Winter Palace, The.
Lawrence. After All Saints' Day.
After School.
Argonauts, The.
At the Cearne.
Dreams Old and Nascent.
Dreams Old and Nascent: Nascent.
Dreams Old and Nascent: Old.
Elegy: "Sun immense and rosy, The."
Forecast.
Hymn to Priapus.
Love Song, A: "Reject me not if I should say
   to you."
Piano.
Red-Herring.
Reminder.
Scent of Irises.
Southern Night.
Levertov. Note to Olga (1966), A.
Travels.
Levine. Genius.
Gift for a Believer.
Hold Me.
No One Remembers.
Winter Words.
Lewis. Bequest.
Black dog barking at the moon.
Journey, The.
Post-Script: for Gweno.
Swimmer, The.
They have clipped the wings of my doves, my
   messengers.
Ways.
Liddy. After Life.

Cantico Per Lo Tuo Amore III.
City of Dreadful Knight, The.
Coolgreany.
Cottage by the Bridge.
Deaths and Electrocutions.
Debt, The.
Dorcas.
Eugene Connolly.
Miles II.
Quarter, The.
Sound of a Moment at Scariff, The.
To the Memory of Bernard Berenson.
Lindsay. Eagle That Is Forgotten, The.
Like the woods of old Kentucky.
Longfellow. Fire of Drift-Wood, The.
My Lost Youth.
Lorde. As I Grew Up Again.
Change of Season.
Hard Love Rock.
Martha.
Movement Song.
Spring People.
Lowry. Beside Oneself.
Closed Pub, The.
For Nordahl Grieg Ship's Fireman.
Glaucous Winged Gull, The.
McAuley. Blessing.
In this trance before sleep.
Mother, sisters, brother.
Scherzo.
"MacDiarmid." Crystals like Blood.
Eemis-Stane, The.
McGrath. In Praise of Necessity.
Memorial.
Remembering Loves and Deaths.
Residencies.
MacLeish. Baccalaureate.
Crossing.
De Votre Bonheur Il ne Reste Que Vos
   Photos.
Edwin Muir.
Ever Since.
Great Contemporary Discoveries.
Memory Green.
Return.
Sentiments for a Dedication.
She was herself, not his, not anything.
Waking.
William Adams Delano.
MacNeice. Canto XII: "Now to dissolve in
   port. I take the train."
Carrick Revisited.
Casualty, The.
Jingles of the Morning, The.
Lilacs and the Roses, The.
News-Reel, The.
Pride in your history is pride.
Ravenna.
Soap Suds.
Mahon. Thinking of Inis Oírr in Cambridge,
   Mass.
Markson. Women's House of Detention.
Marvell. Gallery, The.
Matthews. Happy Childhood, A.
Housework.
School Days.
Meinke. ABC of Aerobics, The.
Everything We Do.
Melville. Age of the Antonines, The.
Stonewall Jackson.
Meredith. Change in Recurrence.
Epitaph on the Tombstone of James
   Christopher Wilson.
He where the great sun looks his last.
Youth in Memory.
Merrill. Amsterdam.
Another August.
Blue Grotto, The.
Broken Home, The.
Chimes for Yahya.
David's Night in Veliès.
Days of 1935.
Days of 1941 and '44.
Days of 1964.
Last Words.
Manos Karastefanís.
Midnight Snack, The.

Mornings in a New House.
Scenes of Childhood.
Strato in Plaster.
Tenancy, A.
Up and Down.
Urban Convalescence, An.
Vision of the Garden, A.
Merton. Early Legend, The.
Rather the flying bird, leaving no trace.
Millay. Cameo, The.
Mindful of you the sodden earth in spring.
Not only love plus awful grief.
Only until this cigarette is ended.
Sometimes, oh, often, indeed, in the midst of
   ugly adversity, beautiful.
What lips my lips have kissed, and where, and
   why.
Miller. For Mrs. Jones.
Morgan. As It Was.
Body, The.
Canadaigua.
Memories.
Past, The.
Turtle, The.
Morrison. Scour the Mind.
Muldoon. Soap-Pig, The.
Nash. All, All Are Gone, the Old Familiar
   Quotations.
Ask Daddy, He Won't Know.
Mr. Betts's Mind a Kingdom Is.
Nathan. Explanation.
Morning Song.
Nemerov. Amnesty.
Anniversary.
April.
Blue Suburban.
For the Squadron.
For W———, Who Commanded Well.
Home for the Holidays.
Lucilius.
Old Warplane, An.
Quarry, The.
Returning to Europe.
Snow Globe, The.
Sunderland.
To Clio, Muse of History.
Neruda. Oliverio Girondo.
Today How Many Hours.
Where is the child that I was.
Notley. Poem: "St. Marks Place caught at
   night in hot summer."
True Account of Talking to Judy Holiday,
   October 13, A.
O'Hara. Animals.
First Dances.
In Favor of One's Time.
In Memory of My Feelings.
Kitville.
Now That I Am in Madrid and Can Think.
Ode to Michael Goldberg ('s Birth and Other
   Births).
Poem: "That's not a cross look it's a sign of
   life."
Poem V (F) W.
Oliver. Picking Blueberries, Austerlitz, New
   York, 1957.
Olson. At Yorktown.
Chain of memory is resurrection I am a vain
   man, The.
February 10, One Year Too Late.
I have been an ability—a machine—up to.
Incunabula, 1958.
She, Thus.
Spring Song for Cagli, A.
There Is No River Which Is Called Lethe.
Thing Was Moving, The.
Twist, The.
Oppen. Cars run in a void of utensils, The.
Forms of Love, The.
It is a place.
Myth of the Blaze.
O Western Wind.
Part of the Forest.
That come before the swallow dares.
What ends / Is that.
Owen. My Shy Hand.
Roads Also, The.

To My Friend.
Unreturning, The.
Pack. Forgetting to Forget.
  Letter to My Widow.
Paley. Love.
  One day at work he cried.
  People in My Family.
Patchen. Nervousness of Memory, The.
Piercy. Valley Where I Don't Belong, A.
  What the Owl Sees.
Plath. Green Rock, Winthrop Bay.
  Thin People, The.
Poe. Sonnet to Zante.
  To F——.
Pound. Doria.
  Exile's Letter.
Prince. Babiaantje, The.
  I think of waking / In the country inn.
  In a Province.
Raine. After Fifty-five Years.
  Ah, many, many are the dead.
  Beside the river Eden.
  Campanula.
  Eider afloat in the bay.
  Flower, memory—.
  Images.
  Island Cross, The.
  It is time, heart, to recall.
  Live on in me, remembered ones.
  Petal of white rose.
  Still skies, still seas.
Ralegh. But Fortune governed all their
  works[,] till when.
  Vertue the Best Monument.
Ransom. Antique Harvesters.
  Equilibrists, The.
Rexroth. Signature of All Things, The.
Rich. Dreamwood.
  For L.G.: Unseen for Twenty Years.
  For Memory.
  From the Prison House.
  Grandmothers.
  Life and Letters.
  Living Memory.
  Mathilde in Normandy.
  Newsreel.
  Pierrot Le Fou.
  Stelae, The.
Robinson. Alma Mater.
  Souvenir.
Roethke. Dream, The.
  Memory.
  Our Lady's Winter Words.
  Praise to the End!
  Premonition, The.
  Reminder, The.
  Sententious Man, The.
Rolfe. Arctic Remembered, The.
  Barn in Wisconsin.
  Bon Voyage.
  Elegia.
  Eyes of a Boy.
  First Love.
  In the Time of Hesitation.
  Pattern of Our Lives, The.
  Poem To Delight My Friends Who Laugh at
    Science-Fiction, A.
  Primer Amor.
  Sunday Evening Revery.
  Vincent.
Rossetti. From Sunset to Star Rise.
  Have You Forgotten?
  I said within myself: I am a fool.
  I wish I could remember the [or that] first
    day.
  I wish I were a little bird.
  Last Look, The.
  Listen, and I will tell you of a face.
  Looking back along life's trodden way.
  Love Lies Bleeding.
  Memory.
  One Sea-Side Grave.
  Remember [Me].
  Shall I Forget?
  Song: "She sat and sang alway."
  They Desire a Better Country.
  Three Seasons.

Undine.
Zara.
Rukeyser. Clouds, Airs, Carried me Away.
  For Memory.
  Key, The.
  Love and its Doors and Windows.
  Sea has opened, the limit of his dream, The.
  Seventh Elegy. Dream-Singing Elegy.
  Sundays, They Sleep Late.
  What Do I Give You?
  Woman as Market.
St. John. Desire.
Sandburg. Acquaintance with Death, Sir.
  Aztec.
  Bird Footprint.
  Chords.
  Consolation Sonata.
  Drumnotes.
  Dust.
  Haunts.
  Haze.
  High Moments.
  Home Thoughts.
  Hungry and Laughing Men.
  In a Back Alley.
  Instructions.
  Keepsake Boxes.
  Kisses, Can You Come Back Like Ghosts?
  Medallion.
  Medley.
  Memoir of a Proud Boy.
  Memoranda.
  Metamorphosis.
  New Hampshire Again.
  Pearl Horizons.
  Personalia.
  Plaster.
  River Moon.
  Rose Bawn.
  Scroll.
  Shenandoah Journey.
  Stars, Songs, Faces.
  Swirl.
  Tawny.
  Throwbacks.
  Timber Wings.
  Troths.
  Two.
  Valley Song ("Sunset swept").
  Valley Song ("Your eyes").
  White Shoulders.
Sarton. Charleston Plantations.
  Der Abschied.
  Garden of Childhood, The.
  Letter to James Stephens, A.
Schuyler. Autumn Leaves.
  Hymn to Life.
Schwartz. "Lo, we descend like light. Light.
  Light."
  Poet, The.
Sexton. Angel of Beach Houses and Picnics.
  Angel of Blizzards and Blackouts.
  Baby Picture.
  Bells, The.
  Boat, The.
  Cripples and Other Stories.
  Death Baby, The.
  Divorce.
  Eighteen Days without You.
  Exorcists, The.
  February 4th.
  For Johnny Pole on the Forgotten Beach.
  Friends.
  Fury of Overshoes, The.
  Hex, The.
  Hoarder, The.
  House, The.
  I Remember.
  Inventory of Goodbyes, The.
  January 1st.
  Kind Sir: These Woods.
  Kite, The.
  Lost Lie, The.
  Love Song: "I was / the girl of the chain
    letter."
  Loving the Killer.
  Mother and Jack and the Rain.

Old.
  Speaking Bitterness.
  Those Times.
  Waking Alone.
  Walking in Paris.
  What's That.
Shakespeare. Sonnet 30: "When to the
  sessions of sweet silent thought."
  Sonnet 63: "Against my love shall be, as I am
    now."
  Sonnet 77: "Thy glass will show thee how thy
    beauties wear."
  Sonnet 122: "Thy gift, thy tables, are within
    my brain."
Shapiro. Nigger.
Shelley. Fragment: The Sepulchre of Memory.
  Letter to Maria Gisborne.
  Lines: "Far, far away, O ye."
  Ode Written October, 1819, An.
  Past, The.
  Remembrance.
  To ———: "Music, when soft voices die."
Shelton. White Hotel, The.
Simic. Lesson, The.
  Wall, A.
Smith, Charlotte. Origin of Flattery, The.
Smith, Patti. Munich.
Smith, Stevie. Northumberland House.
  Portrait (I).
  Ride, The.
  Watchful.
  Widowhood or The Home-Coming of Lady
    Ross.
Snodgrass. Disposal.
  Elm Tree, An.
  Home Town.
  Last Time, The.
  Mementos, 1.
  Reconstructions.
  Seashell, A.
  Seasoning Barn.
  Ten Days Leave.
  To a Child.
Snyder. At White River Roadhouse in the
  Yukon.
  Autumn Morning in Shokoku-ji, An.
  For Lew Welch in a Snowfall.
  For the Boy Who Was Dodger Point Lookout
    Fifteen Years Ago.
  Four Poems for Robin.
  Look Back.
  Seaman's Ditty.
  Working on the '58 Willys Pickup.
Sorrentino. Ambassador, The.
  Ars Longa.
  Bare Tree, The.
  Broadway! Broadway!
  Closet, The.
  George C. Tilyou Smiles.
  Gimlet.
  Good Night!
  He walks on the street, in.
  Memory, The.
  Miss and Hit.
  Poem: "Clear objects / one grows to love. The
    clarity, The."
  Poem for My Wife, A.
  Poem: "Living friends live / in the past so
    they bore us."
  Rose Room.
  Senorita's Bouquet, A.
  September in Kittery.
  Strambotto.
Spender. From My Diary.
  Ice.
  Photograph, The.
  Sign *Faehre nach Wilm*, The.
Stafford. Fall Journey.
  In the White Sky.
  Remembering.
  Troubleshooting.
Stevens. Debris of Life and Mind.
Stevenson. Air of Diabelli's.
  De M. Antonio.
  I have a hoard of treasure in my breast.
  To H.F. Brown.

To Minnie.
To My Mother.
Stuart. Lines.
Long Goodbye, The.
Tending.
Ties.
Widow, The.
Sutter. Mrs.
Pine Creek Parish Hall.
Swinburne. Sundew, The.
Tate. Bizarre.
Eye, The.
Mary McDonald.
Tennyson. In the Valley of Cauteretz.
Tears, Idle Tears.
Tomlinson. In Memoriam Thomas Hardy.
Movements.
Old Man at Valdez.
Poem for My Father.
Way of a World, The.
Updike. Home Movies.
July.
Leaving Church Early.
Shillington.
Solitary Pond, The.
To a Dead Flame.
Van Duyn. Photographs.
Recovery.
Speak, Memory!
Stream, The.
Woman Waiting.
Walcott. Brise Marine.
Glory Trumpeter, The.
Letter from Brooklyn, A.
Parang.
Return to D'Ennery; Rain.
Village Life, A.
Warren. Blow, West Wind.
Debate: Question, Quarry, Dream.
I Am Dreaming of a White Christmas: The
Natural History of a Vision.
Loss, of Perhaps Love, in Our World of
Contingency.
Mad Druggest, The.
Place and Time.
Small White House.
Wart, The.
Whitman. By That Long Scan of Waves.
Dying Veteran, The.
Glimpse, A.
Memories.
My Picture-Gallery.
Old Man's Thought of School, An.
Old War-Dreams.
Once I Pass'd through a Populous City.
earlier vers. of My Picture-Gallery.
Whittier. Abram Morrison.
Album Verses.
Autograph, An.
Burning Drift-Wood.
Countess, The.
Golden Wedding of Longwood, The.
Hampton Beach.
Hill-Top, The.
Homestead, The.
Kenoza Lake.
Last Walk in Autumn, The.
Lydia H. Sigourney.
Memories.
Remembrance.
Snow-Bound [*or* Snow-Bound; a Winter Idyl].
Sweet Fern.
Telling the Bees.
To My Old Schoolmaster.
Within the Gate.
Wilbur. Finished Man, A.
He Was.
Mill, The.
Mind-Reader, The.
Sirens, The.
Williams, Charles Kenneth. Ashes Ashes We
All Fall Down.
Blades.
Clay out of Silence.
Combat.
I'd forgotten and / how could I ever.
Nostalgia.

Of What Is Past.
Repression.
Still Life.
This Is a Sin.
Time: 1976.
Williams, Miller. August Evening Outside of
Nashville, An.
Documenting It.
For Victor Jara.
Rock.
Vanishing Point, The.
WW I.
Williams, William Carlos. Apparition, The.
Paterson, Book V: The River of Heaven.
Song: "You are forever April."
To a Dog Injured in the Street.
Wordsworth. Author's Voyage down the
Rhine (Thirty Years Ago).
"Beloved Vale!" I said, "when I shall con."
Bothwell Castle.
Complaint, A.
Evening Walk Addressed to a Young Lady,
An.
Her Only Pilot the Soft Breeze, the Boat.
Memory.
Remembrance of Collins, Composed upon the
Thames near Richmond.
Sonnet (To an Octogenarian).
To Joanna.
Upon Perusing the "Epistle [To Sir George
Howland Beaumont"] Thirty Years after Its
Composition.
Wright, Charles. Driving through Tennessee.
Gate City Breakdown.
Homage to Paul Cézanne.
Journal of the Year of the Ox, A.
Other Side of the River, The.
Self-Portrait ("Marostica, Val di Ser. Bassano
del Grappa").
Southern Cross, The.
Virginia Reel.
Yard Journal.
Wright, James. Christmas Greeting, A.
In Memory of Leopardi.
Summer Memory in the Crowded City, A.
Sun Tan at Dusk.
Wroth. Sonnet 7: "No time, noe roome, noe
thought, or writing can."
Sonnet: "Can the lov'd Image of thy deerest
face."
Wyatt. My sweet, alas, forget me not.
So feeble is the thread that doth the burden
stay.
When that I call unto my mind.
Yau. Flying Inland.
Radiant Silhouette III.
Reading of an Ever-Changing Tale, The.
You Must Remember.
Yeats. Broken Dreams.
Circus Animals' Desertion, The.
He Thinks of His Past Greatness When a Part
of the Constellations of Heaven.
Image from a Past Life, An.
Old Memory.
People, The.
To a Young Girl.
Tower, The.
When You Are Old.
Young. City Home Detroit.
Dancing Together.
East Boston.
Fort Collins, Colorado.
Hawk Revsited, The.
Hoboken Broken Down: A Hasty Recollection.
Houston in October.
Lesson.
Not Her, She Aint No Gypsy.
Ocean Springs Missippy.
Old Light.
Poem for Willard Motley, A.
Zimmer. Cecil Sliding Away from the
Memory of Wanda.
Curse of the Frogs, The.
Zimmer Remembering Wanda.
Zukofsky. Strange / To reach that age.
Record, The.

Memphis, Tennessee
Knight. Memo #43.
Men
Angelou. Men.
To a Man.
Atwood. Aging Female Poet Sits on the
Balcony.
Eventual Proteus.
Men with the heads of eagles.
This story was told to me by another traveller.
Werewolf Movies.
Berry. To Think of the Life of a Man.
Berryman. Huddle of Need, A.
Blake. Woman scaly & a Man all Hairy, A.
Bly. Fifty Males Sitting Together.
Bogan. Men Loved Wholly beyond Wisdom.
Boyle. Cloak for a Man Who Has No Heed
for Winter, A.
In Defense of Homosexuality.
Bradstreet. Mercury showed Apollo Bartas'
book.
Browning, Elizabeth Barrett. Island, An.
Man and Nature.
Bukowski. Cows in Art Class.
Gypsies Near Del Mar, The.
Burns. Epitaph on a Henpecked Country
Squire.
Fragment, A: "Green grow the rashes, O; /
Green grow the rashes, O; / The lasses they
hae wimble bores."
On a Dog of Lord Eglinton's.
Song: "Let not Woman e'er complain."
To Daunton Me.
Carew. Conquest by Flight.
"Carroll, Lewis." Ode To Damon.
Carruth. He said: / All right then, I *was*, o.k.?
Screwing.
Women like new brooms.
Clark. Spiritual.
Creeley. Circle, The.
Joke, The.
Sentence, The.
Cummings. This young question mark man.
De la Mare. Hare, A.
Speech.
Donne. Manliness.
Doolittle. Contest, The.
Dancer, The.
Master, The.
Dunn. Halves.
Man Who Closed Shop, The.
Not the Occult.
Eberhart. Bells of a Chinese Temple, The.
Death in the Mines.
Gnat on My Paper.
John Finley.
Man and Nature.
Man Who Was Blown Down by the Wind, A.
Marrakech.
Old Tree by the Penobscot.
Poet, The.
R. G. E.
Redemption.
Spring Mountain Climb.
To Kenya Tribesmen, the Turkana.
Vastness and Indifference of the World, The.
Waiting To Lean to the Master's Command.
Wild Life and Tamed Life.
Ford. Nubian in / Tangerine, carrying a, A.
Gallagher. Black Silk.
Woman-Enough.
Glück. Labor Day.
Palais des Arts.
Graves. Dans un Seul Lit.
Frightened Men.
Gateway, The.
Iron Palace.
Sail and Oar.
With the Gift of a Lion's Claw.
Gunn. Innocence.
Hacker. She Bitches About Boys.
Hartley. Man the Father, The.
Herrick. Gods Mirth, Mans Mourning.
To the Ladyes.
Jeffers. Of all things which are living and can
form a judgment.
Joseph. Jack and the Beanstalk.

Kipling. Female of the Species, The.
Knight. On Seeing the Black Male as #1 Sex Object in America.
Larkin. Breadfruit.
Lawrence. Fellow-Men.
Female Coercion.
How Beastly the Bourgeois Is.
I Dare Do All.
Let Us Be Men.
Men and Women.
Mournful Young Man.
She Said as Well to Me.
Sight of God, The.
Levertov. Abel's Bride.
Mutes, The.
Levine. Having Been Asked "What is a Man?" I Answer.
Lorde. Hard Love Rock II.
Seventh Sign, The.
Lowry. Epitaph on Our Gardener, Dead Near Liverpool.
Eye-Opener.
Goldeneye and Goldfish.
Hospitality.
Marathon of gulls / a chiming of chickadees, A.
Queer Poem.
"MacDiarmid." One of the Principal Causes of War.
Matthews. Men in Dark Suits.
Meinke. Arms and the Man.
Melville. On the Photograph of Corps Commander.
Meredith. Ballad of Fair Ladies in Revolt, A.
Merton. First Lesson about Man.
It would be wrong to let one man.
Man the Master.
Nash. Hearts and Flowers or What I Know about Bolivar Black.
Just Wrap It Up, and I'll Throw It Away Later.
Oh, Shucks, Ma'am, I Mean Excuse Me.
Who Understands Who Anyhow?
Nathan. Body Count.
Olson. Bigmans.
Cause, the Cause, The.
Company of Men, The.
Gloss, A.
Help Me, Venus, You Who Led Me On.
Moebius Strip, The.
This Man's Weakness Is Straw.
Troilus.
Pack. Empathy.
Plath. Gulliver.
I Want, I Want.
Pope. To a Lady with the Temple of Fame.
"Reed." Average Guy.
Men of Good Fortune.
Rich. For L.G.: Unseen for Twenty Years.
From a Survivor.
Likeness.
Mother-Right.
Natural Resources.
Phenomenology of Anger, The.
Re-forming the Crystal.
Trying to Talk with a Man.
Waking in the Dark.
Rolfe. Lanes of Death and Birth.
These Men Are Revolution.
Rossetti. Exultate Deo.
Heaven overarches earth and sea.
Surely there is an aching void within.
Two Rossettis (Brothers They), The.
Rukeyser. Light falling on that filled will drives.
Sandburg. Glimmer.
Plaster.
Three Shrines.
Schuyler. Royals.
Sexton. Assassin, The.
Smith, Stevie. Beware the Man.
Eng.
Major Macroo.
Man I Am, A.
Stevens. Paisant Chronicle.
Stevenson. Looking Forward.
Stuart. Sharp Words in the Men's Room.

Swift. Dean Swift's Answer to the Reverend Dr. Sheridan.
Thomas. I, in My Intricate Image.
I See the Boys of Summer.
Seed-at-Zero, The.
Tomlinson. Word in Edgeways, A.
Van Duyn. Cities of the Plain, The.
Wakoski. Overnight Projects with Woods.
Overweight Poem.
Those Mythical Silver Pears.
Waldman. He catches my eye, my fancy.
Mature love you say but my wounds come out through inner temple.
Williams, Charles Kenneth. Dominion: Depression.
It Is This Way with Men.
Williams, William Carlos. Atlantic City Convention, The.
Gossips, The.
Hemmed-in Males.
Men, The.
Old Men, The.
Yeats. Man Young and Old, A.
Men Improve with the Years.
Zukofsky. For you I have emptied the meaning.
Green plant grows, The.

Menageries. *see* **Zoos.**

Menopause
Carruth. "For fifteen years he never knew I never."
Lawrence. Change of Life.

Menstruation
Fox. Sunflowers.
Hacker. Peterborough.
MacLeish. Let there be shelters built in the wild fern.
Millay. Menses.
Rukeyser. Rite.
Sexton. Menstruation at Forty.
Waldman. Crack in the World.

Mental Illness
Berryman. Death Ballad.
Hell Poem, The.
I Know.
Opus Dei.
Purgatory.
Bishop. Faustina, or Rock Roses.
Bogan. Evening in the Sanitarium.
Carruth. Rise up and proclaim themselves, and his skin.
Cooper. Breslau, Spring 1918.
Dickey, James. Moon Flock.
Dickinson. Mass. Mental Health.
Dobyns. Black Dog, Red Dog.
Frenchie.
Funny.
Spiritual Chickens.
Frost. Servant to Servants, A.
Galvin. Fear of the Waldorf Cafeteria.
Gildner. Jabón.
Ginsberg. Kaddish.
Gunn. Old Meg.
Hacker. Callers, The.
Kipling. Mother's Son, The.
Larkin. Neurotics.
Lowell. Thanksgiving's Over.
Waking in the Blue.
MacLeish. Protect us help us forgive us help give.
Millay. Visit to the Asylum, A.
Morrison. Do You Have.
Owen. Chances, The.
Mental Cases.
Piercy. Years ago I had a friend.
Plath. Poem for a Birthday.
Tulips.
"Reed." Kill Your Sons.
Schuyler. Pastime.
Trip.
Sexton. Flee on Your Donkey.
Music Swims Back to Me.
Ringing the Bells.
You, Doctor Martin.
Smith, Stevie. Deserter, The.
Snodgrass. W. D. Attempts to Save Cock Robin.

Tate. Madness.
Thomas. Love in the Asylum.
Van Duyn. Serious Case, A.
Williams, Charles Kenneth. Cave, The.
Williams, Miller. On a Trailways Bus a Man Who Holds His Head Strangely Speaks to the Seat Behind Him.
Williams, William Carlos. Mental Hospital Garden, The.
Wordsworth. Oh What a Wreck! How Changed in Mien and Speech!
See also **Depression (psychological); Madness; Psychiatry and Psychiatrists.**

Mental Retardation
Gildner. When the Retarded Swim.
Gunn. As Expected.
Sweet Things.
Hugo. Letter to Wagoner from Port Townsend.
Kooser. Living Near the Rehabilitation Home.

Mephistopheles. *see* **Satan.**

Mercenaries
Clark. Sleepwalker.
Housman. Epitaph on an Army of Mercenaries.
Jonson. To Captain Hungry.
"MacDiarmid." Another Epitaph on an Army of Mercenaries.
Williams, William Carlos. Knight, The.

Merchants
Browning, Robert. Melon-Seller, The.
Dickinson. I asked no other thing.
Herrick. Upon Rook: Epigram.
Hughes, Langston. Likewise.
Mexican Market Woman.
Jonson. To My Bookseller.
Meredith. Linnet-Hawker, The.
Merton. Calicut.
Olson. Move Over.
Sidney. *speech of Dorus.*
Merchant man, whom many seas have taught, The.
See also **Business and Businessmen; Clerks.**

Mercury (god)
Browning, Elizabeth Barrett. Mercury Carries Psyche to Olympus.
Carruth. Little Old Funky Homeric Blues for Herm, A.
Your dream: / His name was Hermes, and he was all to all.
Cowper. On a Thief.
Lawrence. London Mercury.
Williams, Miller. Getting the Message.

Mercy
Ammons. Precious Weak Fields.
Angelou. On a Bright Day, Next Week.
Atwood. Not the Moon.
Beckett. Sanies II.
Berry. Poem of Thanks, A.
Browning, Elizabeth Barrett. Cry of the Human, The.
Campion. Lift up to heav'n, sad wretch, thy heavy spright.
"Carroll, Lewis." Path of Roses, The.
Chaucer. ABC, An.
Clough. In Stratis Viarum III.
Cohen. Beetle, The.
Blessed Are You.
Commentary—The Beetle.
It Is All Around Me.
Not Knowing Where to Go.
When I Have Not Rage.
You Have Sweetened Your Word.
You Who Pour Mercy into Hell.
Donne. If poisonous [or poysonous] mineral[l]s, and if that tree.
Emerson. Forbore the ant hill, shunned to tread.
Everson. Rose of Solitude, The.
Frost. Masque of Mercy, A.
Gunn. Clock, The.
Hardy. Burghers, The.
Often When Warring.
Herbert. Discipline.
Herrick. Calling, and Correcting.
Clemency.
Gods Mercy.

Mercy.
Mercy and Love.
More Mighty, the More Merciful, The.
Pittie, and Punishment.
Song: "Burne or drowne me."
To Heaven.
Hewitt. Glendun.
Habit of Mercy, The.
I saw my father die. For two long years.
William J. McClughin.
Year of Grace and My Great-Grandfather.
Hill. Redemptrice of all vows and fealties, Dame.
Hughes, Langston. Feet o' Jesus.
Litany: "Gather up / In the arms of your pity."
Hughes, Ted. Horrible Religious Error, A.
Joseph. Goddess of Nature's Diatribe to her People, The.
Kipling. Favour, The.
Shiv and the Grasshopper.
Levine. Angel Butcher.
Lindsay. Kind of Scorn, A.
Or will you let him live.
Lowry. Note, A.
Poem of God's Mercy, A.
McAuley. Go on, stir up your tiresome wavelets.
Now you lean over suicide's precipice.
Owen at Play.
Melville. Rebel Color-Bearers at Shiloh.
Meredith. At the Close.
Main Regret, The.
Merton. Litany: "Sing miserere / For the men who must die."
Milton. Answer me when I call / God of my righteousness.
Lord in thine anger do not reprehend me.
Thy gracious ear, O Lord, encline.
Thy Land to favour graciously.
To God our strength sing loud, and clear.
Patchen. Lasting Seasons, The.
Quantity of Mercy, The.
Psalms. Psalm 4: "Hear me when I call, O God of my righteousness."
Psalm 6: "O Lord, rebuke me not in thine anger."
Psalm 22: "My God, my God, why hast thou forsaken me?"
Psalm 36: "Transgression of the wicked."
Psalm 56: "Be merciful unto me. . . ."
Psalm 57: "Be merciful unto me, O God. . . ."
Psalm 72: "Give the king thy judgments, O God."
Psalm 81: "Sing aloud unto God our strength."
Psalm 85: "Lord, thou hast been favourable unto thy land."
Psalm 86: "Bow down thine ear, O Lord, hear me."
Psalm 89: "I will sing of the mercies of the Lord for ever."
Psalm 102: "Hear my prayer, O Lord, and let my cry." ["Domine exaudi orationem meam"].
Psalm 103: "Bless the Lord, O my soul."
Psalm 108: "O God, my heart is fixed."
Psalm 109: "Hold not thy peace, O God of my praise."
Psalm 118: "O give thanks unto the Lord; for he is good: because."
Psalm 123: "Unto thee lift I up mine eyes."
Psalm 136: "O give thanks unto the Lord."
Psalm 138: "I will praise thee with my whole heart."
Psalm 143: "Hear my prayer, O Lord, give ear."
Ralegh. Conjectural First Draft of the Petition to Queen Anne.
Passionate Man[']s Pilgrimage, The.
Rich. Dien Bien Phu.
Rossetti. Alas my Lord, / How should I wrestle all the livelong night.
Are Ye Not Much Better, Than They?
Before the Beginning.
Hymn: "O the bitter shame and sorrow."
O Lord, I am ashamed to seek Thy Face / As tho' I loved Thee as Thy Saints love Thee.

One of the Soldiers with a Spear Pierced His Side.
Out of the Deep.
Seven vials hold Thy wrath: but what can hold.
Sooner or later: yet at last / The Jordan must be past.
Tuesday in Holy Week.
Word for the Dumb, A.
Sandburg. Rain Winds Blow Doors Open.
Sexton. Children, The.
Shakespeare. Sonnet 145: "Those lips that Love's own hand did make."
Sidney. Psalm 22: "My God, my God, why hast thou forsaken me?"
Sonnet 40: "As good to write as for to lie and groan."
Smart. Mercy.
O Lord, thy land has favour found.
Southwell. Saint Peter's Remorse.
Spender. Girl Who Has Drowned Herself Speaks, A.
Stevenson. I am a hunchback, yellow faced.
Warren. Night is Personal.
Whittier. Brother of Mercy, The.
Captain's Well, The.
Divine Compassion.
Gift of Tritemius, The.
Giving and Taking.
How the Women Went from Dover.
"I Was a Stranger and Ye Took Me in."
King Solomon and the Ants.
Rabbi Ishmael.
Requital.
Robin, The.
Two Angels, The.
Two Rabbins, The.
Williams, Charles Kenneth. Cracks.
Wordsworth. Gravestone upon the Floor in the Cloisters of Worcester Cathedral, A.
Wright, James. Two Poems about President Harding.
Wyatt. Hear my prayer, O Lord, hear my request.
Lord hear [or here] my prayer [or prayre] and let my cry[e] pass[e].
O Lord, since in my mouth thy mighty name.

Merlin
Arnold. Iseult of Brittany.
Emerson. Merlin.
Merlin's Song.
Gunn. Merlin in the Cave: He Speculates without a Book.
Hewitt. Pendragon.
Hill. Merlin.
Merton. Merlin and the Deer.
Robinson. Merlin.
St. John. Merlin.
Wilbur. Merlin Enthralled.
Wordsworth. Egyptian Maid; or, The Romance of the Water Lilly, The.

Mermaid Tavern, London
Keats. Lines on the Mermaid Tavern.

Mermaids and Mermen
De la Mare. Old Angler, The.
Hopkins. Rowing, I reach'd a rock—the sea was low.
Vision of the Mermaids, A.
Hughes, Langston. Catch.
Joseph. Wet Sunday.
Lindsay. Dive, mermaids, with sharp swords.
Queen Mab in the Village.
Would-Be Merman, The.
Lowell. I have learned what I wanted from the mermaid.
Mermaid Emerging.
One wondered who would see and date you next.
Lowry. Alcoholic.
MacLeish. Return.
MacNeice. Merman under the Plough, The.
Morgan. Mermaid, The.
Nash. Mermaid, The.
Spenser. Mermaids, The.

Merrimac (ship). see **Monitor (ship).**

Merriment
Burns. Epistle to J. R******, Enclosing Some

Poems.
Fête Champetre, The.
Hey Ca' thro'.
Hey Tuti Tatey.
Night was still, and o'er the hill, The.
Theniel Menzies' Bony Mary.
To Clarinda.
"Carroll, Lewis." There was an ancient City, stricken down.
Clare. Merry Maid.
Herrick. Ceremonies for Christmas[se].
To Be Merry.
Lindsay. Come let us pray to the Lord of the sky.
Rossetti. Dancing on the hill-tops, / Singing in the valleys.
Summer.
Then I Commended Mirth.

Merry-Go-Rounds
Hughes, Langston. Merry-Go-Round.

Messengers
Browning, Robert. How They Brought the Good News from Ghent to Aix.
Carroll, Jim. Silver Mirrors.
Doolittle. Hermes of the Ways.
"Dylan." Wicked Messenger, The.
Frost. Bearer of Evil Tidings, The.
Glück. Messengers.
Gunn. Messenger, The.
Herrick. Present: or, The Bag of the Bee, The.
Lawrence. Love Message.
Maximus.
Lowry. Still speeding to your heart.
Merton. Cloud, The.
Hare's Message.
Messenger from the Horizon, A.
Warren. Patriotic Tour and Postulate of Joy.
Williams, Miller. Getting the Message.

Messiah
Brooks. In Emanuel's Nightmare: Another Coming of Christ.
Truth.
Cohen. You're Not Supposed to Be Here.
Lindsay. Amaranth, The.
Merton. Messias.
Pope. Messiah [a Sacred Eclogue, in Imitation of Virgil's Pollio].

Metaphor
Burns. Calf, The.
Cohen. Rose, The.
Creeley. Trees.
Davie. Poem as Abstract.
With the Grain.
Hewitt. For Stonecutters.
Hopkins. —Yes for a time they held as well.
Joseph. PROEM: Against metaphor—but how then?
Liddy. Warm Mountain Poem for Matt Liban.
"MacDiarmid." And all this here, everything I write, of course.
MacLeish. Hypocrite Auteur.
Markson. Of Writings Unfinished.
Nemerov. Sestina I: "Thickness of paint or flesh cannot deface."
Olson. Concerning Exaggeration, or How, Properly, to Heap Up.
Paley. No metaphor reinvents the job of the nurture of children.
Plath. Metaphors.
Sorcerer Bids Farewell to Seem, A.
Sidney. Sonnet 9: "Queen Virtue's court, which some call Stella's face."
Stevens. Bouquet of Roses in Sunlight.
Motive for Metaphor, The.
Pastoral Nun, A.
Poem Written at Morning.
Thomas. If I Were Tickled by the Rub of Love.
Williams, William Carlos. Sort of a Song, A.
See also **Symbols.**

Metaphysics
"Carroll, Lewis." Second Voice, The.
Graves. Synthetic Such.
Lowry. Alas, there is no still path in my soul.
You gave yourself to death but never to me.
"MacDiarmid." To My Friend the Late Beatrice Hastings.

MacNeice. London Rain.
Merton. I am doubted, therefore I am.
Nemerov. Frozen City, The.
Two Sides to an Outside: Meditation from Empson.
Rich. Incipience.
We were bound on the wheel of an endless conversation.
Robinson. Burning Book [or the Contented Metaphysician], The.
Simic. Madonnas Touched Up with a Goatee.
Stevens. Glass of Water, The.
Tomlinson. In Defence of Metaphysics.
Wakoski. Ordinary Poem.
Wright, Charles. California Dreaming.
Zukofsky. Finally a Valentine.

Meteors and Meteorites
Cooper. Meteors.
De la Mare. Spark, The.
Emerson. Wisp & meteor nightly falling.
Fletcher. Night of Stars.
Frost. Loose Mountain, A.
Gunn. Sleep by the Hot Stream.
Jarrell. Meteorite, The.
Stafford. Star in the Hills, The.
Whitman. Year of Meteors(1859–60).

Methodism
Hewitt. Eager Journey.
Whittier. Letter from a Missionary of the Methodist Episcopal Church South, in Kansas, to a Distiguished Politician.

Mexican War
Whittier. Angels of Buena Vista, The.

Mexico
Ashbery. Instruction Manual, The.
Carruth. Shirt, britches, paper.
Ceravolo. Pain Songs.
Crane. Purgatorio.
Dove. Night Watch.
"Dylan." Goin' to Acapulco.
Eberhart. Santa Claus in Oaxaca.
Ferlinghetti. Baja Beatitudes.
Baja Revisited.
Ginsberg. Siesta in Xbalba.
Graves. La Mejicana.
Hartley. And, if the Popocatapetl.
Hayden. Inference of Mexico, An.
Jarrell. Indian Market in Mexico, An.
Lawrence. Beyond the Rockies.
Coming of Quetzalcoatl, The.
First Song of Huitzilopochtli.
Jesus' Farewell.
Living Quetzalcoatl, The.
Quetzalcoatl Looks Down on Mexico.
Second Song of Huitzilopochtli.
Song of Don Ramon, The.
Third Song of Huitzilopochtli.
Welcome to Quetzalcoatl.
What Quetzalcoatl Saw in Mexico.
Levertov. Five Poems from Mexico.
Lowry. Cantinas, The.
For Under the Volcano.
Letter from Oaxaca to North Africa 1936.
Names of Mexican rivers I forgot, The.
Of the Francia.
McGrath. Tourists at Ensenada.
Merton. Ce Xochitl: The Sign of FLowers.
Ladies of Tlatilco, The.
Morgan. In Mexico.
Morrison. Hitchhiker, The.
Nathan. Outside the Wall.
Rukeyser. Gold Leaf.
Shelton. Mexico.
Sorrentino. Canta Naranja.
Jaime Valerosa y Borracho Consults His Journal.
Tomlinson. Bootblack, The.
Constitution Day.
Los Pobrecitos.
Oaxaca Bus, The.
On a Mexican Straw Christ.
On the Tlacolula Bus.
Teotihuacán.
Valle de Oaxaca.
Well, The.
Van Duyn. Into Mexico.

Warren. World Comes Galloping: A True Story, The.
Williams, William Carlos. Desert Music, The.
Hymn Among the Ruins.
Wright, James. Heights of Macchu Picchu, III, The.
Minneapolis Poem, The.
Young. Absent from the United States.
Going Back Home.
Moon Watching by Lake Chapala.

Mexico City
Carroll, Jim. Evening News.
Young. Malagueña Salerosa.
Mexico City Lover.
Ponce de León: A Morning Walk.

Mice
Auden. Owl, The.
Talking to Mice.
To a Field-mouse.
Betjeman. Diary of a Church Mouse.
Bishop. Hanging of the Mouse, The.
Bunting. Pious Cat, The.
Burns. To a Mouse [On Turning Her Up in Her Nest, with the Plough, November, 1785].
"Carroll, Lewis." Mouse's Tale, The.
Mouse's Tale, The: "We lived beneath the mat."
Carruth. Mouse, The.
Cowper. Another ["Miser, traversing his house, A"].
Cummings. Here's a little mouse)and.
Me Up at Does.
Mouse)Won / derfully is.
Dickinson. Papa above!
Eberhart. Emblem.
Equivalence of Gnats and Mice.
To the Field Mice.
Gardner. Last Trump, The.
Garrigue. Mouse, The.
Gildner. Field Mouse at My Fishing Hole, A.
Graves. One Hard Look.
Hartley. Salutations to a Mouse.
Hughes, Ted. Cat and Mouse.
Johnson. Chearful sage, when solemn dictatees fail.
Joseph. Think of the minute amount a mouse eats.
Kooser. Spring Plowing.
Kunitz. Waltzer in the House, The.
Lindsay. Mouse That Gnawed the Oak-Tree Down, The.
What Grandpa Mouse Said.
Lowry. Here him play / That sinister melody.
Old Woman who Buried Cats, The.
Three Little Dog-Gone Mice.
Moore. Camellia Sabina.
Nash. Down the Mousehole, and What Science Missed There.
Patchen. Magical Mouse, The.
Roethke. Meadow Mouse, The.
Rossetti. City Mouse and the Garden Mouse, The.
City mouse lives in a house, The.
My Mouse.
Smart. 2.6: "This was the summit of my views."
Miser and the Mouse, The.
Smith, Stevie. Cat Asks Mouse Out.
Stevens. Blue Buildings in the Summer Air, The.
Dance of the Macabre Mice.
Updike. Mouse Sex.

Michael, Saint
Garrigue. Improvisation upon the Theme of the Lady and the Unicorn, An.
Ransom. First Travels of Max.
Rossetti. St. Michael and all Angels.
Smart. St. Michael and All Angels.

Michelangelo Buonarroti
Blake. Florentine Ingratitude.
Pitiful Case, A.
Sir Joshua Praises Michael Angelo.
Browning, Robert. "Moses" of Michael Angelo, The.
"Dylan." Michelangelo would've wept.
Hugo. Maratea Porto: The Dear Postmistress There.

Lawrence. Michael Angelo.
MacLeish. Ship in the Tomb.
Prince. Old Age of Michelangelo, The.
Sun floats in sublime, The.
Smith, Patti. Florence.

Michigan (state)
Hall. Kicking the Leaves.
Letter to an English Poet.
Levine. Making It New.
Poem Circling Hamtramck, Michigan, All Night in Search of You, The.
Rain Downriver.
O'Hara. Ann Arbor Variations.
Sandburg. Dialogue.
Lake Michigan Morning.

Microbes
Auden. New Year Greeting, A.
Williams, Miller. Euglena.

Microscopes
Hesketh. Analyst.
Pack. Clayfeld's Microscope.

Midas
Campion. To his sweet Lute Apollo sung the motions of the Spheares.
Dobyns. Marsyas, Midas and the Barber.
Swift. Fable of Midas, The.
Tomlinson. Legend.

Middle Age
Auden. Walk After Dark, A.
Cohen. Good Fight, The.
Cooper. Middle Age.
Donne. Autumnal[l], The.
Love's Usury.
Glück. To Autumn.
Hall. To a Waterfowl.
Hardy. Middle-Age Enthusiasms.
Hewitt. Minor Poet's Dilemma, 1940.
Jarrell. Next Day.
Jong. Middle Aged Lovers, II.
Kunitz. End of Summer.
Lawrence. Change of Life.
So There!
Longfellow. Mezzo Cammin.
Lowell. Middle Age.
MacLeish. "Dover Beach"—a Note to That Poem.
Matthews. Good Company.
Tardy.
Nash. Crossing the Border.
Let's Not Climb the Washington Monument Tonight.
Middle, The.
Rich. Middle-aged, The.
Rukeyser. Rondel: "Now that I am fifty-six."
Schuyler. Few Days, A.
Growing Dark.
Morning of the Poem, The.
Sexton. Menstruation at Forty.
Smith, Charlotte. Thirty-Eight (Addressed to Mrs. H----Y).
Swift. On Stella's Birthday, 1718/1719.
Walcott. Nearing Forty.
Young. Mid-Life Crises: A Critical Review.

Middle Ages
Auden. Ode to the Medieval Poets.
Bly. Fire of Despair Has Been Our Savior, The.
Browning, Robert. Grammarian's Funeral, A.
Ciardi. Five-Year Step, A.
Haines. Middle Ages, The.
Hill. Requiem for the Plantagenet Kings.
Jarrell. Clock in the Tower of the Church, The.
Kipling. Dawn Wind, The.
Merton. East with Ibn Battuta.

Middlesex, England
Betjeman. Middlesex.
Slough.
Davie. Middlesex.

Midgets
Levine. Midget, The.
Lieberman. Banana Dwarf, The.
Meinke. Hero Worship at Key West on the 4th of July.
Stuart. Midget, The.

Midnight
  Creeley. La Noche.
  Two Ways of Looking in a Mirror.
  Hartley. Midnight—the City.
  Lawrence. At Midnight.
  Lewis. Midnight in India.
  Olson. At midnight, after hours of love, I ate.
  Patchen. Midnight Special.
  Stevenson. I sit up here at midnight.
  Whitman. Clear Midnight, A.

Midsummer
  "Carroll, Lewis." Little Man That Had a Little Gun, The.
  Hardy. On a Midsummer Eve.
  Mahon. Midsummer.

Mignonettes
  Lawrence. Red Geranium and Godly Mignonette.

Migraine
  Tomlinson. History of a Malady.

Migrant Workers
  Miller. Harvesters.
  Rukeyser. They pray. Security against oldness.
See also **Farmworkers.**

Migration
  Atwood. Migration: C.P.R.
  Bukowski. Fall Out.
  Carruth. It's French, of course—our name.
    And I must think.
  Hartley. Flight, The.
    Sestets.
  Hughes, Langston. Good Morning.
    New Yorkers.
  Hugo. Cripples, The.
  Longfellow. Evangeline, a Tale of Acadie.
  McNeill. Autumn Drives (Early 1800s), The.
    Backward Flight.
  Meredith. We saw the swallows gathering in the sky.
  Sandburg. Mockers Go to Kansas in Spring.
  Stevens. Wild Ducks, People and Distances.
  Tomlinson. Weatherman.
  Wilbur. Event, An.

Milan, Italy
  Cohen. Next One, The.
  Levine. And the Trains Go On.

Militarism
  Cummings. Neither awake / (there's your general).
    Why must itself up every of a park.
  "Dylan." Masters of War.
  Eliot. Coriolan.
  Emerson. One hand washes the other.
  Ginsberg. Chicago to Salt Lake by Air.
    Pentagon Exorcism.
    War Profit Litany.
  Hardy. Channel Firing.
  Hemingway. Riparto d'Assalto.
  Merton. Original Child Bomb.
  Sandburg. Mohammed Bek Hadjetlache.
  Tomlinson. Tarquinia.
  Wright, James. Undermining of the Defense Economy, The.
  Zukofsky. Motet.

Military Justice
  Kipling. Cells.
  Danny Deever.

Military Life. *see* **Army Life.**

Milk and Milking
  Eberhart. Barn, The.
  Hall. Great Day in the Cows' House.
  Herrick. Fresh Cheese and Cream.
    Upon Sibilla.
  Kinnell. Milk Bottle, The.
  Rossetti. Brownie, Brownie, let down your milk.
  Schuyler. Milk.
  Yeats. Spilt Milk.

Milkmaids
  Hardy. Milkmaid, The.
  Rossetti. Farm Walk, A.
    Rosy maiden Winifred, / With a milkpail on her head.
  Sandburg. She Opens the Barn Door Every Morning.
  Sutter. Husbandry.

Milkmen
  Gardner. Milkman, The.

Milkweed
  Frost. Pod of the Milkweed.
  Levine. Milkweed.
  Paley. In deepest summer / the milkweed flower.
  Wilbur. Two Voices in a Meadow.
  Wright, James. Milkweed.

Milky Way, The
  Fox. Names and Travelers of the Milky Way.
  Frost. Milky Way Is a Cowpath, The.

Millennium
  Clark. Millennial Icon.
  Eberhart. Young and the Old, the.
  Frost. It Is Almost the Year Two Thousand.
  Ginsberg. Rising Over Night-Blackened Detroit Streets.
  Jarrell. Clock in the Tower of the Church, The.
  Nash. Any Milleniums Today, Lady?
  Whittier. Astræa.
  Yeats. Second Coming, The.

Miller, Henry
  Williams, William Carlos. To the Dean.

Mills and Millers
  Auden. Daily Bread.
  Burns. Dusty Miller.
  Cowper. Flatting Mill, The.
  Davie. Cheshire.
  Hardy. Second Visit, The.
  Hemingway. Mitrailliatrice.
  Hesketh. Bolton-Le-Moors, 1960.
    Master Cotton Spinner.
  Hugo. Mill at Romesdal.
  Jarrell. Miller, The.
  Lawrence. Dark Satanic Mills.
    Give Us the Thebaïd.
  Lowell. Mills of the Kavanaughs, The.
  Lowry. Indian Arm.
  McNeill. Runaway Team (Written a Few Days After John Glenn's Space Flight), The.
  Robinson. Mill, The.
  Sandburg. Hemlock and Cedar.
  Tate. On the Founder of the Industrial System in the United States.
  Tomlinson. John Maydew or The Allotment.
  Turco. Mill, The.
  Whittier. Birchbrook Mill.
  Wilbur. Mill, The.

Milton, John
  Blake. And Did Those Feet in Ancient Time. Milton.
  Cowper. Complimentary Pieces to Milton.
    Stanzas on Milton's Remains.
  Duncan. Years As Catches, The.
  Hopkins. Milton.
  Johnson. New Prologue Spoken at the Representation of *Comus*, A.
  Keats. On Seeing a Lock of Milton's Hair.
  Lindsay. To Eve, Man's Dream of Wifehood as Described by Milton.
  Lowry. Schoolboy's Complaint, The.
  Marvell. On Mr Milton's "Paradise Lost."
  Meredith. Poetry of Milton, The.
  Pope. Milton's strong pinion now not heaven can bound.
  Sandburg. Our Hells.
    To the Ghost of John Milton.
  Shelley. Fragment: Milton's Spirit.
  Tate. John Milton.
  Tomlinson. Giovanni Diodati.
  Whittier. Milton.
  Wordsworth. At Vallombrosa.
    Fragment of an Intended Poem on Milton, Written in the Copy of *Paradise Lost* Which Belonged to Wordsworth at Cambridge.
    London, 1802.
    Sonnet on Milton.

Milwaukee, Wisconsin
  Young. Beauty of Milwaukee Cold with Rain, The.

Mind. *see* **Intellect and Intellectuals.**

Minerals
  "MacDiarmid." Crystals like Blood.

  Rukeyser. Disease: After-Effects, The.
See also **Mining and Miners.**

Minerva
  Byron. Curse of Minerva, The.
  Davie. Owl Minerva, The.
  Herrick. Vow to Minerva, A.
  Hill. Do words make up the majesty.
See also **Athena.**

Mining and Miners
  Auden. Lead's the Best.
    Like other men, when I go past.
    Old Colliery, The.
    Old Lead-mine, The.
    Old Mine, The.
    Rookhope (Weardale, Summer 1922).
  Davie. County Durham.
  Dunbar. Gourd, The.
  "Dylan." North Country Blues.
  Edmunds. Appalachia.
  Galvin. Photo of Miners, A.
  Heaney. Singer's House, The.
  Hugo. Helena, Where Homes Go Mad.
  Larkin. Explosion, The.
  Levine. Nitrate.
  Lindsay. What the Miner in the Desert Said.
  Owen. Miners.
  Ralegh. Calybes plough not their barren soile, The.
  Rolfe. Any Slave.
    Vincent.
  Rukeyser. Tunnel, The.
  Sandburg. Pennsylvania.
    Sayings of Henry Stephens.
  Sexton. Fury of Jewels and Coal, The.
  Snyder. Fire in the Hole.
  Tomlinson. Gladstone Street.
    Shaft, The.
  Wright, James. Miners.
See also **Coal Mining and Coal Miners; Gold Mining and Gold Miners.**

Ministers. *see* **Clergy.**

Mink
  Carruth. Brook has holes in its cover, The.
  Lowry. Welcome Home—Oh Most Beloved Harteebeeste.
  Muldoon. Mink.

Minnesota (state)
  Berryman. Minnesota Thanksgiving.
  Bly. Driving toward the Lac Qui Parle River.
  Eberhart. United 555.
  Kooser. Late Lights in Minnesota.
  McGrath. Afternoon of a McGrath.
  Wright, James. Blessing, A.
    By a Lake in Minnesota.
    Centenary Note: Inscribed to Little Crow, Leader of the Sioux Rebellion in Minnesota, 1862, A.
    Larry.
    Lying in a Hammock at William Duffy's Farm in Pine Island, Minnesota.
    Minneapolis Poem, The.
    River Down Home, The.

Minotaur
  Dobyns. Theseus Within the Labyrinth.
  Gardner. Minotaur, The.
  Lewis. Victory.
  Merton. From the Second Chapter of a Verse History of the World.
  Nemerov. On Getting Out Of Vietnam.
  Rukeyser. Minotaur, The.
  Tomlinson. Ariadne and the Minotaur.
  Turco. Minotaur.

Minstrels
  De la Mare. Unheard Melodies.
  Emerson. A.H.
  Fletcher. Joy.

Miracles
  Bishop. Miracle for Breakfast, A.
  Bly. Ants.
  Bukowski. Miracle is the Shortest Time, The.
  Carruth. It was the custom of my tribe to be silent.
  Chaucer. Prioress's Tale, The.
  Cohen. Great Feast in Quebec, A.
    Waiting for the Miracle.

Crashaw. Mark 10; The Blind Cured by the Word of Our Saviour.
Mark 7; The Dumbe Healed, and the People Enjoyned Silence.
On the Miracle of Loaves.
On the Miracle of Multiplied [*or* Multiplyed] Loaves.
To Our Lord, upon the Water Made Wine.
Creeley. Kore.
Cummings. From spiralling ecstatically this.
Dickey, James. Lazarus to the Assembled.
Dickinson. No Life can pompless pass away.
Fletcher. Fragments of Eternity.
Ginsberg. Galilee Shore.
Gunn. Lazarus Not Raised.
Hardy. Lost Pyx, The.
Hartley. Water from the Rock.
Herbert. Whitsunday.
Herrick. Widow's Tears [*or* Widdowes Teares]: or, Dirge of Dorcas, The.
Hewitt. Dedication: "I have a certain skill in phrase."
I've Known Her Turn from Bitter Phrase.
Jong. Ordinary Miracles.
Kipling. Our Lady of the Sackcloth.
Levine. Miracle, The.
Melville. Margrave's Birthnight, The.
Meredith. Glastonbury Thorn, The.
Miracle, The.
Merton. Cana.
Pack. Clayfeld Prunes His Apple Trees.
Plath. Black Rook in Rainy Weather.
Schwartz. Sonnet Suggested by Homer, Chaucer, Shakespeare, Edgar Allan Poe, Paul Valéry, James Joyce, et al.
Smart. Crucifixion of Our Blessed Lord.
Sorrentino. Shapes of Winter.
Stuart. Hermaphrodite, The.
Whitman. Miracles.
Williams, Miller. One of the Crowd on the Shore Tells How It Was.

Mirages
De la Mare. Mirage.
Hayden. Mirages, The.
Raine. Path, The.
Shapiro. Impact.
Stuart. Nomads.
Whitman. Mirages.
Whittier. Norembega.

Mirrors
Ammons. Reflective.
Atwood. Looking in a Mirror.
Tricks With Mirrors.
Berrigan. It's Important.
Bishop. Gentleman of Shalott, The.
To Be Written on the Mirror in Whitewash.
Bogan. Cupola, The.
Burns. Keekin' Glass, The.
Carew. Looking-Glass, A.
"Carroll, Lewis." Two Thieves.
Welcome Queen Alice.
Creeley. Shot.
Cummings. Clown's smirk in the skull of a baboon, A.
Ohld song / you Know.
Pieces(in darker / than small is dirtiest).
Dunbar. Looking-Glass, The.
Emerson. Such another peerless queen.
Ford. Not locking onto.
World's a mirror. Break it and you die!, The.
Fox. Susanna.
Gardner. On Looking in the Looking Glass.
Garrigue. Cracked Looking Glass.
Primer of Plato.
Graves. Foreboding, The.
Pier-Glass, The.
Spite of Mirrors.
Gunn. Behind the Mirror.
Looking Glass.
Haines. From the bed where I lay.
Hardy. At the Dinner-Table.
Cheval-Glass, The.
Honeymoon Time at an Inn.
Lament of the Looking-Glass, The.
Moments of Vision.
Herrick. Upon Sibb.
Hewitt. Mirror.

Joseph. Mirror, Mirror.
STUDY: *A Lady in her Bedroom* (Bonnard).
Kipling. Looking Glass, The.
Levertov. Looking-glass.
Liddy. Death of Lovers, The.
Lorde. Good Mirrors are Not Cheap.
Lovelace. Lucasta's Fan[ne], with a Looking-Glass[e] in It.
Lowell. Fat Man in the Mirror, The.
Lowry. Sestina in a Cantina.
MacNeice. Reflections.
Merrill. In the Hall of Mirrors.
Merton. Mirror's Mission, The.
Nemerov. Glass Dialectic.
Mirror, The.
Plath. Mirror.
"Reed." I'll Be Your Mirror.
Rossetti. Passing and Glassing.
Sandburg. Chicago Poet.
Smith, Patti. Sohl.
Stevenson. Looking-Glass River.
Tomlinson. Mirror in the Roadway, The.
Turco. Pocoangelini 38 ("You have many wrinkles").
Updike. Shaving Mirror.
Waldman. Mirror Meditation.
Warren. Nature of a Mirror, The.
Whitman. Eidolons.
This Day, O Soul.
Yau. Variations on Corpse and Mirror.
When the movie ends, the lights come on. The audience is puzzled.
When you break a mirror, you must count up the pieces to see if.
Zukofsky. With a Valentine (the 12 February).
With a Valentine (the 14 February).

Mirth
Garrigue. Note to La Fontaine, A.
Herrick. Best To Be Merry.
Gods Mirth, Mans Mourning.
His Lachrimae or Mirth, Turn'd to Mourning.
Hock-Cart, or Harvest Home, The.
Hymne, to the Lares, A.
Lyric to Mirth, A.
Meat without Mirth.
Meddow Verse; or, Aniversary to Mistris Bridget Lowman, The.
Mirth.
To All Young Men That Love.
To Live Merrily, and To Trust to Good Verses.
Upon Bran.
Kipling. To the Companions.
Lowry. I wrote: In the dark cavern of our birth.
Meinke. Gift of the Magi, The.
Meredith. To the Comic Spirit.
Milton. Mirth and Poetry.
Sonnet 21: "Cyriack, whose Grandsire on the Royal Bench."
Rolfe. Pattern of Our Lives, The.
Smart. Mirth.
Williams, William Carlos. Hic Jacet.

See also **Laughter; Merriment.**

Misanthropy
Bukowski. Being alone has always been very necessary to me. At one time I.
Ginsberg?
I had been up until 3 a.m. the night before.
I have my figures ready for the.
I pay my way in, find a seat far from everybody, sit down.
I'm Getting Back to Where I Was.
Traffic Signals.
Jeffers. Bird with the Dark Plumes, The.
Meredith. They that love not—are they not as blind camels that behold no.

Miscarriages
"MacDiarmid." Glen of Silence, The.
Plath. Barren Woman.

Mischief
Byron. Devil's Drive, The.
Clare. Young Rabbits.
Cowper. On a Mischievous Bull.
Graves. Nobody.
Herrick. Upon Pagget.

Kunitz. At breakfast mother sipped her buttermilk.
Lawrence. Flapper.
Lowry. Faking was three times married to Faking.
Three Little Dog-Gone Mice.
Ralegh. One fire than other burnes more forcibly.

Misfortune
Beckett. Ooftish.
Browning, Robert. Saint Martin's Summer.
Bukowski. Something.
Burns. Jeremiah 15th Ch. 10 V.
Lament. Occasioned by the Unfortunate Issue of a Friend's Amour, The.
Man Was Made to Mourn, a Dirge.
O raging Fortune's withering blast.
Song.—In the Character of a Ruined Farmer.
Though fickle fortune has deceiv'd me.
To a Mouse [On Turning Her Up in Her Nest, with the Plough, November, 1785].
Chaucer. Monk's Tale, The.
Coleridge. Addressed to a Young Man of Fortune.
Outcast, The.
Cowper. Shrubbery, The.
Crashaw. Upon the Faire Ethiopian Sent to a Gentlewoman.
Davie. Sext.
Dickinson. One need not be a Chamber—to be Haunted.
Donne. Fall of a Wall.
"Dylan." Ballad of Hollis Brown.
Emerson. Lo! where from Heaven's high roof.
Graves. All Except Hannibal.
Beggar Maid and King Cophetua, The.
Pandora.
Gray. Hymn to Adversity.
Hewitt. William J. McClughin.
Hughes, Langston. Juliet.
Keats. Isabella; or, The Pot of Basil.
Otho the Great.
Kooser. Tom Ball's Barn.
Kunitz. Grammar Lesson.
McAuley. Noon Apocrypha.
Meredith. Song: "Thou tremblest O my love! thy hand in mine."
Teaching of the Blows of Fortune, The.
Three Gipsies, The.
Merton. Good Fortune.
Roethke. Surly One, The.
Shelley. Tale of Society As It Is, A: From Facts, 1811.
Sidney. Fortune, Nature, Love, long have contended about me.
Smith, Charlotte. Apostrophe to an Old Tree.
Swift. Addenda Quaedam.
Thomson. Pastoral Entertainment, A.
Updike. Sleepless in Scarsdale.
Warren. Event, The.
Wroth. Sonnet 5: "How many nights have I with paine indur'd."
Sonnet 38: "What pleasure can a bannish'd creature have."
Wyatt. Being as none is, I do complain.
Double, diverse, sullen, and strange.
Ever mine [*or* myn] hap[pe] is slack and slo[w] in coming [*or* commyng].
Hap happeth oft unlooked for.
She that should most, perceiveth least.
Since love is such that, as ye wot.
To my mishap, alas, I find.
Where shall I have at mine own will.
Yeats. Ballad of Moll Magee, The.

Mishima, Yukio
Ford. Mishima.

Misogyny
Clare. "Poets are born"—and so are whores— the trade is.
Song: "I peeled bits of straw and I got switches too."
Donne. Julia.
Lorde. Need: A Chorale for Black Woman Voices.
Rich. From an Old House in America.
Swift. Journal of a Modern Lady, The.
Williams, Charles Kenneth. Madder.

Missionaries
Davie. Jesuits in North America, The.
Hewitt. Open Eye, The.
Hugo. Indian Graves at Jocko.
Mission in Carmel.
Merton. Cargo Songs.
Clever Strategem: Or, How to Handle Mystics,
A.
Poet, to His Book, The.
Oppen. Inlet.
Smart. St. Andrew.
St. James.
St. Simon and St. Jude.
Walcott. Koenig of the River.
Whittier. Missionary, The.
Vaudois Teacher, The.

Mississippi (state)
"Dylan." Oxford Town.
Eberhart. La Crosse at Ninety Miles an Hour.
Hayden. Night, Death, Mississippi.
Knight. Once on a Night in the Delta: A
Report From Hell.
Poem for Myself (or Blues for a Mississippi
Black Boy), A.
Young. Birthday Poem.

Mississippi River
Crane. River, The.
Davie. Lasalle.
Dove. Someone's Blood.
Fletcher. Down the Mississippi.
McGrath. Topography of History, The.
Ransom. Antique Harvesters.
Whitman. Mississippi at Midnight, The.

Missouri (state)
Gallagher. 3 A.M. Kitchen: My Father
Talking.
Knight. Poem to Galway Kinnell, A.

Missouri River
Whitman. Others May Praise What They Like.

Mist
Bishop. Cape Breton.
Brontë. Mild the mist upon the hill.
Burns. Lazy Mist, The.
Carruth. Pale dawnlight spooks the mist.
Ciardi. Aspect of the Air, An.
Cummings. Mi(dreamlike)st / makes / big
each dim.
Mist.
De la Mare. Mist.
Dunbar. Misty Day, A.
Fletcher. From the Japanese, VI.
Voices on the Wind.
Hewitt. Mist.
Levertov. Ground-Mist, The.
Meredith. Pasture Alp is webbed with shade,
The.
Paley. What is this whiteness on the fields?
Sandburg. Changing Light Winds.
Last Answers.
Mist Forms.
Mist Marches Across the Valley.
Mist, The.
Tomlinson. Gossamers, The.
Last of Night, The.
Mistlines.
Updike. To Evaporation.
Wilbur. Chronic Condition, A.
Williams, Charles Kenneth. Dawn.
See also **Fog.**

Mistresses
Angelou. They Went Home.
Byron. To the Sighing Strephon.
Donne. On His Mistress [*or* Mistris].
Self[e] Accuser, A.
Eberhart. Mais L'Amour Infini Me Montera
Dans L'Ame.
Herrick. Present: or, The Bag of the Bee, The.
To His Girles.
To His Mistresses.
Upon the Loss[e] of His Mistresses.
What Kind of Mistress[e] He Would Have.
Lawrence. Two Wives.
Lorde. Barren.
Meredith. Shemselnihar.
Shakespeare. Sonnet 130: "My mistress' eyes
are nothing like the sun."

Smith, Stevie. Infelice.
Stevenson. Cruel Mistress, The.
Wright, James. Gesture by a Lady with an
Assumed Name, A.

Misunderstanding
Beatles. Hello Goodbye.
She Came in Through the Bathroom Window.
She Said She Said.
We Can Work It Out.
Beckett. De pied ferme.
Carroll, Jim. To the Secret Poets of Kansas.
"Carroll, Lewis." Canto VI: Dyscomfyture.
Ciardi. Sorrow of Obedience, The.
Clark. Things About You.
Cowper. This ev'ning, Delia, you and I.
Creeley. Bird, The.
Gift, The.
Irishman's Lament on the Approaching Winter,
An.
Song: "I wouldn't / embarrass you."
Dickey, William. One Incident of Many.
Donne. Expostulation, The.
Pyramus and Thisbe.
"Dylan." Don't Fall Apart on Me Tonight.
One of Us Must Know (Sooner or Later).
Sign Language.
We Better Talk This Over.
Emerson. Out of the East, and out of the
West, no man understands me.
Star seer Copernicus / Only could earn a
curse.
Ferlinghetti. Overpopulation.
Gardner. Who Spilled the Salt?
Haines. Blood Lake, The.
Hardy. Her Confession.
Misconception.
Whaler's Wife, The.
Hewitt. Agenda.
Case of Mistaken Identity, A.
Fables for Stormont.
My Grandmother's Garter.
Salute.
Turf-Carrier [*or* Turf Carrier] on Aranmore.
Koch. Departure from Hydra, The.
Taking a Walk with You.
Lorde. Hard Love Rock II.
Sister, Morning Is a Time for Miracles.
McAuley. Photographer's Model, The.
Markson. Once in, Our Quarreling.
Rich. I was looking for a way out of a
lifetime's consolations.
Like This Together.
Pieces.
They come to you with their descriptions of
your soul.
Trying to Talk with a Man.
When We Dead Awaken.
Silverstein. Bagpipe Who Didn't Say No, The.
Stevens. Poem with Rhythms.
Virgin Carrying a Lantern, The.
Stuart. Commencement.
Updike. Zulus Live in Land without a Square.
Williams, Charles Kenneth. Cave, The.
Dirty Talker: D Line, Boston, 1973.
What Did the Man Do with the Clouds?

Mitchell, Arthur
Moore. Arthur Mitchell.

Mites
Frost. Considerable Speck, A.
Updike. Mites.

Mithridates the Great
Emerson. Mithridates.
Whittier. Mithridates at Chios.

Mittens
Carruth. Heavy gloves / or better.
Lowry. Two frozen claws / In two frozen
minutes.
See also **Gloves.**

Mobility
Hughes, Ted. Now You Have to Push.
Kunitz. Summing-up, The.
MacNeice. What ghosts of cuckoo-spit and
dew.
Nash. What the Well-Read Patient Is Talking
About, or, Look, Ma, What I Got!

Mockingbirds
Gunn. Patch Work.

Hartley. Saturday.
Jarrell. Mockingbird, The.
Moore. Bird-witted.
Nash. Listen to the Linotype.
Sandburg. Kansas Lessons.
Mockers Go to Kansas in Spring.

Models
Browning, Robert. Lady and the Painter, The.
Cohen. Paris Models.
Snow Is Falling.
Ferlinghetti. London / crossfigured / creeping
with trams.
Hardy. Figure in the Scene, The.
Statue of Liberty, The.
Merton. This is how to / This is with
imperatives.
Rossetti. In an Artist's Studio.
Yau. Picture Book.

Moderation
Cullen. Song in Spite of Myself.
Emerson. I know the appointed hour.
Herrick. Hony-Combe, The.
Love Is a Sirrup.
Meane, The ("Imparitie doth ever discord
bring").
Moderation.
Out of Time, Out of Tune.
Surfeits.
Hewitt. Coasters, The.
Memorandum for the Moderates.
MacNeice. Ode: "To-night is so coarse with
chocolate."
Oliver. Dream of Trees, A.
Smart. 3.16: To Maecenas.
Prudence.
Stevenson. In Maximum.

Modern Man
Atwood. You want to go back.
Auden. Unknown Citizen, The.
Berry. Horses.
Purification, A.
Berryman. Have a Genuine American Horror-
&-Mist on the Rocks.
Holy, as I suppose I dare to call you.
Point of Age, A.
Rock-Study with Wanderer.
Trial, The.
Bishop. Varick Street.
Carruth. All things lay in nature, even the
plastic flowers.
Bitcheries of Madison Avenue, The.
Sonnet: The Recollected Actual Voices of
Romanticism.
Sonnet: "Why complain, brothers, to you, my
writing."
Ciardi. Back through the Looking Glass to
This Side.
Magus, A.
Week That Was, The.
Cohen. I Wonder How Many People in This
City.
Coleridge. Tombless Epitaph, A.
Crane. Supplication to the Muses on a Trying
Day.
Cummings. Blue woman with sticking out
breasts hanging, A.
Boys i mean are not refined, The.
FULL SPEED ASTERN).
He does not have to feel because he thinks.
Jehovah buried,Satan dead.
Of Ever-Ever Land i speak.
Plato told / him:he couldn't.
Proud of his scientific attitude.
Red Front, The.
Season 'tis,my lovely lambs, The.
Tell me not how electricity or.
These people socalled were not given hearts.
Will i ever forget that precarious moment?
Worshipping same / they squirm and they
spawn.
Davie. Among Artisans' Houses.
Benedictus.
Mandelstam's Hope for the Best.
Mens Sana in Corpore Sano.
Through Bifocals.
To Thom Gunn in Los Altos, California.
De la Mare. Owl, The ("What If To Edge Of

Dream").
Reserved.
"Dylan." All Along the Watchtower.
Dead Man, Dead Man.
Dirge: "I hate myself for lovin' you and the weakness that it showed."
Every Grain of Sand.
Gates of Eden.
Hard Rain's A-Gonna Fall, A.
I Shall Be Free.
It's Alright, Ma (I'm Only Bleeding).
License to Kill.
Mixed Up Confusion.
No Time to Think.
Quinn the Eskimo.
Run go get out of here.
Slow Train.
Train A-Travelin'.
Eliot. Love Song of J. Alfred Prufrock, The.
Waste Land, The.
Ferlinghetti. History of the World: a TV Docu-Drama.
Home Home Home.
In Goya's greatest scenes we seem to see.
Living Theatre, The.
Lost Parents.
Sea and Ourselves at Cape Ann, The.
Triumph of the Postmodern.
Fletcher. Burning Mountain, The.
Crucifixion of the Skyscraper.
Elegy on an Empty Skyscraper.
Elegy on London.
Elegy on Tintern Abbey.
Hard Sayings.
Last Judgment, The.
1921.
Song of the Moderns.
Ford. Convalescence, The.
Special Effects.
Gardner. Loud Song, Mother, A.
Nursery Rhyme No. 2.
Sloth, The.
Garrigue. Civilization Constantly Worrying about Itself as It Goes on Doing What It Is Worrying About That It Is Doing, A.
Lead in the Water.
My Frantic Heart.
Ginsberg. Ballade of Poisons.
Birdbrain.
Grim Skeleton.
Old Pond.
Ruhr-Gebiet.
Smoke Rolling Down Street.
To the Body.
Too much industry.
Two Dreams.
Griffiths. Ciudadela, 1991.
Fruits of Virtue.
Murder.
Post Imperial.
Shamanism, Dalston.
Suffering Does for the Character.
Hall. Tomorrow.
Hardy. I Said to Love.
In St. Paul's a While Ago.
Jingle on the Times, A.
Misconception.
Wet Night, A.
Hartnett. Bereft of Its Great Poets.
No Avail.
Holmes. Berryman's Dead.
Death Drag (The Elegist).
Doctor Trustus: Man of Good Will.
Instructions for the World Librarian.
Obituary for Jan Masaryk.
Premonitory July.
Survivors, The.
Hughes, Langston. In Explanation of Our Times.
Hugo. Starting Back.
Jarrell. Old and the New Masters, The.
Jeffers. For fifty thousand years man has been dreaming of powers.
Second-Best.
Staggering Back Toward Life.
Time of Disturbance.
Joseph. Subscription.

Kipling. New Knighthood, The.
Lawrence. Classes.
Cross, The.
Cry of the Masses.
Death of Our Era, The.
Dies Irae.
Evil Is Homeless.
Fear of Society Is the Root of All Evil.
Give Us the Thebaïd.
Hold Back!
Impulse.
Latent Desire, The.
Latter-Day Sinners.
Life and the Human Consciousness.
Modern Prayer.
Real Democracy.
Religion.
Robot-Democracy.
Robot Feelings.
Tale Told by an Idiot, A.
Today.
Wellsian Futures.
What Is a Man to Do?
What Then Is Evil?
What's Wrong.
Lewis. Belief.
Now only beggars still go singing.
Southend at Dusk.
Liddy. On a Protestant Mystic.
McGrath. Citizen Dreaming, The.
MacLeish. Observations of P. Ovidus Naso on the Incidence of Sex in the Contemporary Novel.
Mahon. Gipsies.
Glengormley.
Stone Age Figure Far Below, A.
Markson. Julia Now.
Meredith. Age of petty tit-for-tat, An.
Ah for that time when open daylight pours.
London by Lamplight.
Reason.
Merrill. Clearing the Title.
Urban Convalescence, An.
Merton. Cables to the Ace.
Captives—a Psalm, The.
Day Six O'Hare Telephane.
Exploits of a Machine Age.
Letter to Pablo Antonio Cuadra Concerning Giants, A.
Tune for Festive Dances in the Nineteen Sixties, A.
Nathan. At the Well.
Nemerov. Life Cycle of Common Man.
Make Love Not War.
Neruda. Century Dying, A.
Pedro Is When.
Wars, The.
O'Hara. Naphtha.
Olson. Connection, The.
Conqueror.
Dramatis Personae.
I, Mencius, Pupil of the Master.
In Cold Hell, in Thicket.
It's Got to This.
Morning News, The.
Scream to the Editor, A.
Stone and Flower Series.
War on the Mind in a Time of Love.
Oppen. And Their Winter and Night in Disguise.
Anniversary Poem.
Book of Job and a Draft of a Poem to Praise the Paths of the Living, The.
Crowded Countries of the Bomb, The.
Enclave / Filled with their own, An.
Half free / And half mad.
Historic Pun.
I cannot even now / Altogether disengage myself.
Impossible Poem, The.
It is a place.
It is *that* light.
Now in the helicopters the casual will.
Or define / Man beyond rescue.
Philai Te Kou Philai.
They carry nativeness / To a conclusion.
To the Poets: To Make Much of Life.

Unable to begin / At the beginning, the fortunate.
Rich. Atlas of the Difficult World, An.
What kind of beast would turn its life into words?
Robinson. Modernities.
Shapiro. Crucifix in the Filing Cabinet, The.
Hospital.
Humanities Building, The.
Office Love.
Pigeons, The.
Snyder. Amitabha's Vow.
Spel Against Demons.
This Tokyo.
Spender. Man-Made World, A.
Updike. Dea ex Machina.
On the Inclusion of Miniature Dinosaurs in Breakfast Cereal Boxes.
Seven New Ways of Looking at the Moon.
Superman.
Whitman. I Was Looking a Long While.
Williams, Charles Kenneth. Cellophane.
For Children When They Grow Up.
In the Heart of the Beast.
Inches.
Long Naked Walk of the Dead, The.
Madder.
Poor Hope.
Race of the Flood, The.
Spit.
Williams, Miller. He Glimpses a Nobler Vision.
Williams, William Carlos. Exercise, An.
Wordsworth. Men of the Western World! In Fate's Dark Book.
Wright, Charles. Monastery at Vršac, The.
Yeats. Second Coming, The.
Young. Myth Science of Our Time, The.
Zimmer. History of Bears, The.

Modesty
Berry. Want of Peace, The.
Burns. Jessie—A New Scots Song.
Byron. To a Vain Lady.
Campion. Just beguiler, / Kindest love, yet only chastest.
Cowper. Of Himself.
Davie. Under a Skylight.
Herrick. Laxare Fibulam.
More Modest, More Manly.
Upon Sneape.
Kipling. English Way, The.
Lawrence. Behaviour.
Editorial Office.
She Said as Well to Me.
Meredith. Violets.
Rossetti. Listening.
Smart. Munificence and Modesty.
Mutual Subjection.
Smith, Charlotte. To an Amiable Girl.
Stevenson. Ne Sit Ancillae Tibi Amor Pudori.
Wordsworth. Ode to Apollo.
Zukofsky. Imitation.

Moles
Griffiths. Rivers Are Running Beneath Us.
Haines. Mole, The.
Hartley. Mole.
Joseph. Back to Base.
Kooser. Moles.
Merton. Bureaucrats: Diggers.
Plath. Blue Moles.
Rossetti. Handy Mole who plied no shovel, A.
Sexton. Star-Nosed Mole.

Moloch
Ginsberg. Howl.

Mona Lisa
Nash. Political Reflection.

Monarchy
Bradstreet. Four[e] Monarchies, The.
Brontë. Woe for the day; Regina's pride.
"Carroll, Lewis." Ye Fattale Cheyse.
Cowper. Heroism.
Hardy. Coronation, The.

Monasteries
Arnold. Stanzas from the Grande Chartreuse.
Byron. Elegy on Newstead Abbey.
Hoffman. Fontaine-les-Dijon Revisited.
Hopkins. Escorial, The.

Merton. Chee$e.
  Clairvaux.
  Clairvaux Prison.
  Elegy for Ernest Hemingway, An.
  In the Rain and the Sun.
  Letter to My Friends, A.
  Reader, The.
  Three Postcards from the Monastery.
  Trappist Abbey: Matins, The.
  Trappist Cemetery—Gethsemani, The.
  Winter Afternoon.
Nash. Away from It All.
Scott. Melrose by Moonlight.
Snyder. December.
Williams, William Carlos. Semblables, The.
Wordsworth. At the Convent of Camaldoli.
  At the Convent of Camaldoli, Continued.
  At the Eremite or Upper Convent of
    Camaldoli.
  Cuckoo at Laverna May 25, 1837 The.
  Nunnery.
Wright, Charles. Monastery at Vršac, The.
See also **Monks.**

Monday
Edmunds. Lunes.
Hartley. Tomorrow being Monday—.
Hughes, Langston. Blue Monday.
Nash. Every Day Is Monday.
Plath. Everlasting Monday, The.
Rossetti. Monday in Holy Week.
Wakoski. Blue Monday.

Monet, Claude
Berg. Both.
Cummings. Water-Lilies.
Hayden. Monet's "Waterlilies."
Snodgrass. Monet: "Les Nymphéas."

Money
Beatles. Can't Buy Me Love.
  You Never Give Me Your Money.
Berg. In Blue Light.
  Sad Invective.
Berry. It is *ignorant* money I declare.
Bishop. Washing hangs upon the line, A.
Boyle. Poem of Love, A.
Browning, Robert. Very Original Poem,
  Written with Even a Greater Endeavour than
  Ordinary after Intelligibility, and Hitherto
  Only Published on the First Leaf of the
  Author's Son's Account-Book.
Bukowski. $$$$$$.
Bunting. Arles, an arles for my hiring, An.
Burns. Hey for a Lass wi' a Tocher.
  Ken Ye What Meg o' the Mill Has Gotten.
  Lines Written on a Bank-Note.
  Poem: "Friend o' the Poet, tired and leal."
  Sandy and Jockie.
  What can a young lassie, what shall a young
    lassie.
Byron. For Orford and for Waldegrave.
Campion. Epigramme: "What though Harry
  braggs, let him be noble."
"Carroll, Lewis." Fame's Penny-Trumpet.
  Game of Fives, A.
  Upon the Lonely Moor.
  What Tottles Meant.
  White Knight's Ballad, The.
Carruth. As the broken front differential pops
  and jumps.
  Maybe because they're so damn frigging rich.
Ciardi. Song for an Allegorical Play.
Creeley. Something for Easter.
Cummings. Impossibly / motivated by
  midnight.
  Why / don't / be / sil / ly.
Dobyns. In a Row.
Dunbar. Real Question, The.
Dunn. Fairy Tale.
"Dylan." Money Blues.
Eberhart. Four Exposures.
Emerson. From Ibn Jemin.
Gallagher. Black Money.
Ginsberg. American Change.
Graves. S. D.
Herrick. Expenses Exhaust.
  Lyric[k] for Legacies.
  Money Gets the Mastery [*or* Masterie].
  Money Makes the Mirth.

No Man Without Money.
  Once Poore, Still Penurious.
  Upon Bunce: Epigram.
  Upon Flimsey: Epigram.
  Upon Huncks: Epigram.
  Upon Prig ("Prig now drinks Water, who
    before drank Beere").
  Upon Roots.
Hesketh. Master Cotton Spinner.
Hewitt. Collector's Choice.
  Mad Applegrower, The.
  Paid Quarterly.
Housman. When first my way to fair I took.
Hughes, Langston. Dancer.
  50–50.
  Green Memory.
  Little Lyric (of Great Importance).
  What?
Jarrell. Money.
  Nollekens.
Jonson. Elegy [*or* Elegie], An: "'Tis true, I'm
  broke! Vows, oaths, and all I had."
  Epistle to Mr Arthur Squib.
  On Bank the Usurer.
  On Lieutenant Shift.
  To Master John Burges.
  To Mr Jonson upon these Verses.
  To the Right Honourable, the Lord Treasurer
    of England. An Epigram.
Larkin. Money.
Lawrence. Altercation.
  Always This Paying.
  Kill Money.
  Money.
  Money-Madness.
  Wages.
  What Is Man Without an Income.
  Why—?
Levine. Walk with Tom Jefferson, A.
Lewis. Humanist, The.
Lowry. Cold Roast Hamlet Blues,
  Blubberhouses Blues, Ugley Blues.
  Give me the money, / Give me the money.
Markson. Accepted.
Merton. Give me a cunning dollar that tells
  me no lie.
Morrison. Money.
Nash. Bankers Are Just Like Anybody Else,
  Except Richer.
  I Burn Money.
  Ms. Found under a Serviette in a Lovely
    Home.
  Second Chime.
  Second Month It's Not Itemized, The.
  There'll Always Be a War between the Sexes,
    or, A Woman Can Be Sometimes Pleased,
    but Never Satisfied.
Nemerov. Dialogue.
  Money.
  Route Two.
Piercy. Nine of Cups, The.
Pope. Epistle IV, to Richard Boyle, Earl of
  Burlington.
  Epistle III, to Allen Lord Bathurst.
Roethke. Reckoning, The.
  Song for the Squeeze-Box.
Rossetti. Wee wee husband, / Give me some
  money.
  What will you give me for my pound?
Sandburg. Girl in a Cage.
  Great Sphinx and the Pyramids say, The.
  I am zero, naught, one ciper.
  I pledge my allegiance.
  In the light of the cold glimmer of what
    everybody knows, why should the.
  In the Shadow of the Palace.
  Let the nickels and dimes explain.
  Marshall Field the First was spick and span
    while alive.
  Mazuma, the jack, the shekels, the kale, The.
  Money, Politics, Love, and Glory.
  Nickels click off fares in the slot machines of
    the subway, the elevated, The.
  Soiled Dove.
  Theorem.
  To a Contemporary Bunkshooter.
  Two Items.

Sexton. March 4th.
Silverstein. Smart.
Stevenson. Who would think, herein to look.
Tennyson. Northern Farmer: New Style.
Van Duyn. Economics.
Wakoski. Second Universe.
Wilbur. Finished Man, A.
Williams, Charles Kenneth. Matter, The.
Williams, William Carlos. How Bad It Is to
  Say.
  Words, the Words, the Words, The.
Wright, James. To a Friendly Dun.
Young. Romance Without Finance.
Zukofsky. Song—3/4 time.
  This Fall, 1933.

Mongolia
Carruth. December now. Winter deepens and
  darkens. Stars.

Mongooses
Hartley. Ichneumon.
Kipling. At the hole where he went in.
  Darzee's Chaunt.
Moore. Snakes, Mongooses, Snake-Charmers,
  and the Like.

Monitor (ship)
Melville. In the Turret.
  Utilitarian View of the Monitor's Fight, A.

Monkeys
Emerson. On the chamber, on the stairs.
Frost. At Woodward's Gardens.
Hemingway. Kipling.
Kipling. Divided Destinies.
  Legends of Evil, The.
  Road Song of the *Bandar-Log*.
Lorde. Monkeyman.
Moore. Monkey Puzzle, The.
  Monkeys, The.
Pack. Display.
  Human Pile, The.
Sandburg. Tylor believed it important; he put
  it down; he asks us to read it, to look.
Yau. Avenue of Americans.

Monks
Blake. Monk, The.
Browning, Robert. Grammarian's Funeral, A.
  Soliloquy of the Spanish Cloister.
Byron. Fragment from the "Monk of Athos."
Cohen. Escape, The.
Coleridge. Mad Monk, The.
Dunbar. Monk's Walk, The.
Everson. Challenge, The.
  Man of God. Tall man, man of oath. Mad
    man of ignorant causes.
  Narrows of Birth, The.
Hall. Stones.
Hemingway. Earnest Liberal's Lament, The.
Hugo. With Anna at Camaldoli.
Lawrence. Apostrophe to a Buddhist Monk.
Lindsay. Strength of the Lonely, The.
Meredith. Hernani.
Merton. After the Night Office—Gethsemani
  Abbey.
  Elegy for a Trappist.
  Elegy for the Monastery Barn.
  Evening: Zero Weather.
  I do not know who is out in the snow.
  Image of True Lovers' Death, The.
  Litany: "All holy souls / pray for us fellows."
  Macarius the Younger.
  Old monk is turned loose / And can travel!,
    The.
  Practical Program for Monks, A.
  Psalm 132: A Modern Monastic Revision.
  Quickening of St. John the Baptist, The.
  St. Maedoc.
  Solitary Life.
  Special continuations: the Gethsemani
    racetrack.
  There is a little ceremony to be performed.
  Three Postcards from the Monastery.
  Trappists, Working.
  When the first signs go on.
Nash. Away from It All.
Scott. Melrose by Moonlight.
Smith, Stevie. Weak Monk, The.
Whittier. Brother of Mercy, The.

Williams, William Carlos. Venus Over the Desert.
Wordsworth. At the Convent of Camaldoli, Continued.
  At the Eremite or Upper Convent of Camaldoli.
  Cuckoo at Laverna May 25, 1837, The.
  Voice from the Side of Etna, The; or, the Mad Monk.
See also Clergy; Monasteries.

Monmouth, James Scott, Duke of
Dryden. Absalom and Achitophel, Pt. I.
  In pious times ere [*or* e'r] priest-craft did begin.
Meredith. Monmouth.

Monogamy and Monogamists
Cowper. Impromptu ["If John marries Mary, and Mary alone"].
Donne. Confined Love.
Lawrence. Love.
Shelley. Longest Journey, The.

Monotony
Hacker. Companion, The.
  Villanelle: Late Summer.
Hesketh. Yew Tree Guest House.
Levine. Lights I Have Seen Before.
MacNeice. Nature Morte.
Sandburg. Harmonica Humdrums.
  Humdrum.
Smith, Patti. Piss Factory.
Smith, Stevie. Childe Rolandine.
Williams, Charles Kenneth. Winter, / damn, / again.

Monsters
Atwood. Our leader / is a man of water.
Auden. Chimaeras, The.
"Carroll, Lewis." Horrors.
  Jabberwocky.
Creeley. Saturday Afternoon.
Cullen. To the Three for Whom the Book.
De la Mare. Gloria Mundi.
Dickey, James. Sheep Child, The.
Dunbar. Boogah Man, The.
Fox. Beasts Have Entered, The.
Graves. Dream Recalled on Waking.
Gunn. From the Highest Camp.
Hugo. Sneosdal.
Nash. Abominable Snowman, The.
  And How Keen Was the Vision of Sir Launfal?
  Dragons Are Too Seldom.
  Under the Floor.
  Wendigo, The.
Nemerov. Beyond the Pleasure Principle.
  Mythological Beast.
Rossetti. Ballad of Boding, A.
Silverstein. Worst, The.
Spenser. I saw a river swift, whose fomy billowes.
Tennyson. Kraken, The.
Turco. Grendel.
  Juggernaut.
  Nasnas.
  Sasquatch.
  Zombie.
Whittier. Double-Headed Snake of Newbury, The.
Wyatt. Vulcan begat me. Minerva me taught.
See also Demons.

Mont Blanc
Coleridge. Hymn before Sunrise, in the Vale of Chamouni.
Shelley. Mont Blanc.

Montana (state)
Carruth. Eternity Blues.
Haines. Missoula in a Dusty Light.
Hugo. Camas Prairie School.
  Degrees of Gray in Philipsburg.
  Dixon.
  Driving Montana.
  Ghosts at Garnet.
  Helena, Where Homes Go Mad.
  Lady in Kicking Horse Reservoir, The.
  Letter to Bell from Missoula.
  Letter to Goldbarth from Big Fork.
  Letter to Haislip from Hot Springs.
  Letter to Levertov from Butte.
  Letter to Oberg from Pony.
  Letter to Scanlon from Whitehall.
  Map of Montana in Italy, A.
  Night at the Napi in Browning, A.
  Only Bar in Dixon, The.
  Phoning from Sweathouse Creek.
  Reclamation at Coloma.
  Snapshot of Uig in Montana, A.
  Turtle Lake.
  2433, First Home, Last House in Missoula.
  With Kathy in Wisdom.
Matthews. Left Hand Canyon.
Wright, Charles. Mount Caribou at Night.

Months
Emerson. S.H.
Herrick. Succession of the Foure Sweet Months, The.
Kipling. Verses on Games.
Rossetti. January cold desolate; / February all dripping wet.
  Year's Windfalls, A.
Sexton. Sermon of the Twelve Acknowledgements, The.
Spenser. Mask of Mutability, The.
Stuart. Love Poems.
Yau. Return of the Hunters, The.

Montreal, Quebec
Carruth. Sonnet: "From our very high window at the Sheraton."
Cohen. Montreal.
  Streetcars.

Monuments
Bishop. Monument, The.
Carruth. French Hill.
  Therefore to us, time's / final lesson: be content.
Cohen. There are Some Men.
Emerson. Hymn[:] Sung at the Completion of the Concord Monument, April 19, 1836.
Hardy. Her Temple.
  Inscription, The.
  Monument-Maker, The.
  Old Workman, The.
  Sacred to the Memory.
Hugo. Culloden.
Jeffers. Monument.
Kipling. Grave of the Hundred Dead, The.
  Ode: "So long as memory, valour, and faith endure."
  Rhodes Memorial, Table Mountain.
Kunitz. Let the old geezers jig on Penn.
Liddy. Requiem for a Non-Croppy.
Lovelace. Black Patch on Lucasta's Face, A.
Lowell. For the Union Dead.
MacLeish. Verses for a Centennial.
Melville. Inscription: "To them who crossed the flood."
Merton. Man from Ecuador beneath the Eiffel Tower, A.
Oppen. Eros.
  Monument.
Rukeyser. City of Monuments.
Sandburg. Bronzes.
Momus.
  Ready to Kill.
  Washington Monument by Night.
Smith, Charlotte. Inscription on a Stone, in the Church-Yard at Boreham.
Spenser. I saw raysde up on yvorie pillours tall.
  Then did a sharped spyre of diamond bright.
  Virgils Gnat.
Stevens. Dance of the Macabre Mice.
Whitman. Red Jacket (from Aloft).
Whittier. Leggett's Monument.
Wordsworth. Cenotaph.
  Countess' Pillar.
  Filial Piety.
  Hart-Leap Well.
  Memorial near the Outlet of the Lake of Thun.
  Pillar of Trajan, The.
  Written with a Slate Pencil upon a Stone, the Largest of a Heap Lying near a Deserted Quarry, upon One of the Islands at Rydal.
Yeats. Three Monuments, The.

Moods
Ashbery. Crazy Weather.
Creeley. For Somebody's Marriage.
Donne. Letter to the Lady Carey, and Mistress Essex Rich, from Amiens, A.
  Oh, to vex me, contraries [*or* conraryes] meet in one.
Dunbar. Response.
Emerson. What is it to sail.
Frost. Mood Apart, A.
Graves. Song: Sullen Moods.
  Superstition.
Hartley. To H.C.
Hewitt. I've Known Her Turn from Bitter Phrase.
  My Teachers.
  Splendid Dawn, The.
Lovelace. Her Reserved Looks.
Lowry. Hartebeeste Both Grave and Gay, The.
  Morning sneat is snewing, The.
  Morning tanker gleameth, The.
  Playing alone / Drunk and bored.
  Villanelle, an Interview on Morale.
Nash. Don't Be Cross, Amanda.
Pack. Clayfeld's Metamorphosis.
Rossetti. Fluttered Wings.
  Key-Note, The.
  Rose has thorns as well as honey, A.
Schuyler. Evening.
Walker. Moody.
Yeats. Lover Asks Forgiveness because of His Many Moods.
  Moods, The.

Moon
Ammons. Catch.
Atwood. Not the Moon.
Auden. California.
  Make this night loveable.
  Moon Landing.
  Moon profaned by, A.
  This Lunar Beauty.
Berg. Both.
  Eating Outside.
  First Cold.
  Following It.
  For the Ghost of Li Po.
  New Year's.
  On This Side of the River.
  Two Fragments.
Berry. Winter Night Poem for Mary.
Bishop. Insomnia.
  Man-Moth, The.
Bly. Late Moon.
Bogan. July Dawn.
Brontë. There shines the moon, at noon of night.
Browning, Elizabeth Barrett. Night and the Merry Man.
  Romaunt of Margret, The.
Browning, Robert. Pan and Luna.
  Phases of the Moon.
Burns. Lament. Occasioned by the Unfortunate Issue of a Friend's Amour, The.
Byron. Sun of the Sleepless!
"Carroll, Lewis." Said the Moon to the Sun.
Carruth. Astigmatism breaks.
  Caught in the briary stars.
  Emptiness—you know.
  Full of the moon. In pine woods a snowlight, The.
  Insomniac Sleeps Well for Once and, The.
  Joy and Agony of Improvisation, The.
  Moon, The.
  She lay like a book.
Cohen. Days of Kindness.
Coleridge. Absence.
  Behind the thin / Grey cloud that cover'd but not hid the sky.
  Lunar Entrancement.
  Moon and the Waves, The.
  Soliloquy on the Full Moon, She Being in a Mad Passion, A.
  To the Autumnal Moon.
  To the Nightingale.
Cooper. Hunger Moon.
Crane. O Moon, Thou Cool..
  Supplication to the Muses on a Trying Day.

Creeley. Eye, The.
  Form of Women, A.
  Gesture, The.
  La Noche.
  Littleton, N.H.
  Moon, The.
  New Year's.
  Two Ways of Looking in a Mirror.
Cummings. &-moon-He-be-hind-a-mills.
  Come(all your mischief- / hatchers hatch).
  F / eeble a blu / r of cr.
  I go to this window.
  Moon falls through the autumn   Behind
    prisons she grins, The.
  Moon looked into my window, The.
  Moon over gai.
  MOOn Over tOwns mOOn.
  ! / o(rounD)moon,how.
  T,h;r:u;s,h;e:s / are / silent / now.
  Tonight the moon is round golden entire. It.
  Who / threw the silver dollar up into the tree?
  Who is this / dai / nty mademoiselle.
  Who knows if the moon's.
  Young m / oon:be kind to olde.
Davie. Some Future Moon.
De la Mare. April Moon.
  Moonlight.
  Night.
  Night.
  Unforeseen.
Dickey, James. Moon Flock.
Dickey, William. Afternoon Evening and
  Night in the Courtyard of the Museum of
  Modern Art.
Dickinson. I make His Crescent fill or lack.
  I watched the Moon around the House.
  Moon is distant from the Sea, The.
  Moon upon her fluent Route, The.
  Moon was but a Chin of Gold, The.
Doolittle. Moonrise.
Dunbar. Lover and the Moon, The.
Eberhart. Off Spectacle Island.
Edmunds. Moon.
  My Love Has Been.
Eliot. Conversation Galante.
  Rhapsody on a Windy Night.
Emerson. And since round lines are drawn.
  Atom from atom yawns as far.
  Coin the daydawn into lines.
  Earth, The.
  Excelsior.
Fisher. Last Door, The.
Ford. First owl of the evening.
Fox. Lemons, Limes.
  Megrez.
  Servants of the Emperor, The.
Frost. Freedom of the Moon, The.
  Moon Compasses.
  Two Leading Lights.
Garrigue. Enemy of Those Who Are Enemies
  of Sleep.
  Moondial.
Ginsberg. In a Moonlit Hermit's Cabin.
Graves. Between Moon and Moon.
  Colours of Night, The.
  Full Moon.
  Moon's Last Quarter, The.
  Problems of Gender.
  Song: The Far Side of Your Moon.
  Turn of the Moon.
  What Will Be, Is.
Gunn. For Signs.
  Silver Age, The.
  Wrestling.
Hall. Moon Clock.
  Moon, The.
Hardy. At Rushy-Pond.
  Seeing the Moon Rise.
  Shut Out That Moon.
  To the Moon.
Hartley. Light of Night.
Hayden. Full Moon.
Hewitt. August 1939.
  Moon, The.
  Skypiece.
Hopkins. Fragment of Anything You Like, A.
  Moonrise June 19 1876.

Hughes, Langston. March Moon.
  Winter Moon.
Hughes, Ted. Full Moon and Little Frieda.
  Harvest Moon, The.
Hugo. At Our Best.
Jarrell. Romance of Science, The.
Jeffers. At the near approach of a star...huge
  tides.
  I walk on my cliff above the Pacific Ocean
    and feel the tides.
  Moon and Five Planets.
  Our eyes by day are good enough: only the
    birds.
Jong. Dearest Man-in-the-Moon.
Jonson. Now, my cunning lady moon.
  Queen and huntress, chaste and fair.
Joseph. Moon in the morning.
Kinnell. Little Sleep's-Head Sprouting Hair in
  the Moonlight.
Kipling. Moon of Other Days, The.
  Wolf-cub at even lay hid in the corn, The.
Knott. Shorts / Excerpts ("Our farewells lack
  the plausibility of our departures").
Kunitz. Flight of Apollo, The.
Larkin. Moon Is Full Tonight, The.
Lawrence. Aware.
  Dream-Confused.
  Hostile Sun, The.
  Invocation to the Moon.
  Moon Memory.
  Moon New-Risen.
  Moonrise.
  New Moon.
  Old Song.
  Pang of Reminiscence, A.
  Prayer: "Give me the moon at my feet."
  Rebuked.
  Red Moon-Rise.
  Sea, the Sea, The.
  Southern Night.
  To Lettice, My Sister.
  Troth with the Dead.
  White Blossom, A.
Levertov. Song for Ishtar.
Levine. Late Moon.
Lindsay. Beggar Speaks, The.
  Caught in a Net.
  Censer-Moon, The.
  Drying Their Wings.
  Encyclopædia, The.
  Euclid.
  Moon Is a Painter, The.
  Moon's the North Wind's Cooky, The.
  On the Garden Wall.
  Rose of Midnight, The.
  Sense of Humor, A.
  Strength of the Lonely, The.
  What Semiramis Said.
  What the Clown Said.
  What the Coal-Heaver Said.
  What the Forester Said.
  What the Ghost of the Gambler Said.
  What the Gray-Winged Fairy Said.
  What the Hyena Said.
  What the Miner in the Desert Said.
  What the Rattlesnake Said.
  What the Snow Man Said.
  Written for a Musician.
Lorde. Gemini.
  Maiden, The.
Lowry. Fear ringed by doubt is my eternal
  moon.
  Happiness.
  Lament—June 1944.
  My two hands broke in two: and they broke
    me!
  Sonnet: "This ruin now, where moonlight
    walks alone."
  Very dark and clear with an onshore wind.
"MacDiarmid." Au Clair de la Lune.
MacLeish. Nocturne: "Earth, still heavy and
  warm with afternoon, The."
  Selene Afterwards.
  Voyage to the Moon.
Matthews. Moonlight in Vermont.
Meredith. Song: "Moon is alone in the sky,

The."
  Song of Ruark to Bhanavar the Beautiful.
  Song: "Two wedded lovers watched the rising
    moon."
Millay. Enormous moon, that rise behind these
  hills.
Morrison. Moonlight Drive.
Nemerov. Backward Look, The.
Olson. Common Place.
  Disposition, The.
  May 31, 1961.
  Moon Is the Number 18, The.
  Moonset, Gloucester, December 1, 1957, 1:58
    A.M.
  Thoughts of the Time.
Oppen. Troubled that you are not, as they say.
Patchen. Moon "Continued."
Piercy. Crescent Moon Like a Canoe.
Plath. Everlasting Monday, The.
  Maudlin.
  Metamorphoses of the Moon.
  Moon and the Yew Tree, The.
  Moonsong at Morning.
  Thalidomide.
Raine. I went out in the naked light.
  Moon golden towards the full.
  Oval the golden moon.
Rossetti. Death-Watches.
  Half Moon Shows a Face of Plaintive
    Sweetness, The.
  If the moon came from heaven, / Talking all
    the way.
  Is the Moon Tired?
  Mirrors of Life and Death.
  O Lady Moon.
Rukeyser. In Her Burning.
  Nevertheless the Moon.
Sandburg. Auctioneer.
  Baby Face.
  Back Yard.
  Balloon Faces.
  Blizzard Notes.
  Child Moon.
  Cornucopia.
  Dogheads.
  Early Moon.
  Feather Lights.
  Flux.
  Great Proud Wagon Wheels Go On, The.
  Half Moon In a High Wind.
  Horse Fiddle.
  I Sang.
  Interior.
  Light and Moonbells.
  Milk-White Moon, Put the Cows to Sleep.
  Moist Moon People.
  Moon Hammock.
  Moon Path.
  Moon Rondeau.
  Moonlight and Maggots.
  Moonset.
  Night Stuff.
  Nocturn Cabbage.
  Nocturne in a Deserted Brickyard.
  Pearl Horizons.
  River Moon.
  River Moons.
  This—For the Moon—Yes?
  Three Hills Look Different in the Moonshine.
  Timber Moon.
  Two Moon Fantasies.
  Was Ever a Dream a Drum?
  What other oaths are wanted now?
  Whitelight.
Schuyler. En Route to Southampton.
  Moon.
Sexton. Moon Song, Woman Song.
Shelley. Fragment: To the Moon.
  To the Moonbeam.
  Waning Moon, The.
Shelton. Full Daytime Moon, The.
  Full Harvest Moon, The.
  Gibbous Moon, The.
  Half-Moon, The.
  Kingdom of the Moon, The.
  Voice of the Moon, The.
  Waning Crescent Moon, The.

Sidney. Sonnet 31: "With how sad steps, O Moon, thou climb'st the skies."
Sonnet 97: "Dian, that fain would cheer her friend the Night."
When two suns do appear.
Smith, Charlotte. Lydia.
To the Invisible Moon.
To the Moon.
Written September 1791, During a Remarkable Thunder Storm, in which the Moon Was Perfectly Clear, While the Tempest Gathered in Various Directions Near the Earth.
Smith, Patti. December.
Snodgrass. Partial Eclipse.
Snyder. Once Only.
Sorrentino. Jaime Valerosa y Borracho Consults His Journal.
Stevens. God is Good. It Is a Beautiful Night.
How to Live. What to Do.
Lunar Paraphrase.
Motive for Metaphor, The.
Note on Moonlight.
Two Figures in Dense Violet Night.
Stevenson. Mile an' a Bittock, A.
Moon, The.
Tomlinson. Death of Elizabeth Grieve, The.
Foxes' Moon.
Journey, The.
Recompense, The.
Under the Moon's Reign.
Turco. Moon of Melancholy, The.
Pocoangelini 1 ("Pocoangelini sat").
Updike. Condo Moon.
Moons of Jupiter, The.
Seven New Ways of Looking at the Moon.
Wakoski. Moon Explodes in Autumn as a Milkweed Pod, The.
Searching for the Canto Fermo.
Three of Swords.
Western Music.
When You Throw Amber into the Well of the Moon.
Walcott. Morning Moon, The.
Warren. In Moonlight, Somewhere, They Are Singing.
Man in Moonlight.
Whitman. Look Down Fair Moon.
Wilbur. Five Women Bathing in Moonlight.
Williams, William Carlos. A La Lune.
Full Moon.
Moon, The.
Rigamarole.
Summer Song.
Suzanne.
To a Solitary Disciple.
View.
Wordsworth. Beauty and Moonlight.
How Beautiful the Queen of Night, on High.
Night Thought, A.
Once I Could Hail (Howe'er Serene the Sky).
Shepherd, looking eastward softly said, The.
Sweet was the walk along the narrow lane.
To the Moon (Composed by the Seaside,—on the Coast of Cumberland).
To the Moon (Rydal).
Who but Is Pleased to Watch the Moon on High.
With how sad steps, O Moon, thou climb'st the sky.
Written in a Grotto.
Wright, James. Beginning.
Divine Falling of Leaves, A.
Fear Is What Quickens Me.
Having Lost My Sons, I Confront the Wreckage of the Moon: Christmas, 1960.
Message Hidden in an Empty Wine Bottle that I Threw into a Gully of Maple Trees One Night at an Indecent Hour, A.
Moon.
Morality of Poetry, The.
Rose of the Sea.
Secret Gratitude, A.
Today I Was So Happy, So I Made this Poem.
Yeats. Cat and the Moon, The.
Crazed Moon, The.
He and She.
Phases of the Moon, The.

Young. Big Ocean-Waving, Woman-Pulling Moon.
Carolina Moon.
Coastal Moon.
Dancing Pierrot.
Here in Violet Light.
Moon, How Do I Measure Up?
Moon of No Return.
Moon Over Matter.
Moon, the Whole Moon, and Nothing but the Moon, The.
Moon Up Close in Winter by the Telescope, The.
Moon Watching by Lake Chapala.
Moonlessness.
Orchard at Night in Rain Light, The.
Pidgin Moon.
Sarajevo Moon.
Sarajevo Moonlight.
See, See, Moon.
Sing a Song of Singapore.
So is there life on you, moon?
Tutti Colori Quality of Light, The.
Waking Up in Santa Cruz at Sea.
Zukofsky. Like the oceans, or the leaves of fine Southern.

Moonflowers
Prince. Moonflower, The.

Moonshiners
McNeill. Moonshiner.
Nemerov. Moonshine.
Williams, Miller. Rituals.

Moore, Henry
Hall. "Internal and External Forms."
"King and Queen."
Notes For Nobody.
"Reclining Figure."

Moore, Marianne
Auden. Mosaic for Marianne Moore, A.
Bishop. Invitation to Miss Marianne Moore.
Boyle. For Marianne Moore's Birthday.
Cummings. Marianne Moore.
Gardner. Are Poets Ball Players?
Hartley. Marianne Moore.
Tomlinson. Over Brooklyn Bridge.
Williams, William Carlos. Marianne Moore.

Moore, Thomas
Betjeman. Ireland's Own; or the Burial of Thomas Moore.
Byron. As the Liberty Lads o'er the Sea.
My Boat Is on the Shore.

Moors (people)
Byron. Very Mournful Ballad, A.

Moors (geography)
Brontë. Blue bell is the sweetest flower, The.
"Carroll, Lewis." Upon the Lonely Moor.
Eliot. Rannoch, by Glencoe.
Emerson. She paints with white & red the moors.
Hardy. Wet Night, A.
Hesketh. Bolton-Le-Moors, 1960.
Heat-Wave.
Northern Stone.
Hughes, Ted. Wadsworth Moor.
Plath. Two Views of Withens.

Moose
Bishop. Moose, The.
Duncan. Poetry, a Natural Thing.
Haines. Horns.
Moose Calling, A.
Moosehead, The.
Hayden. Moose Wallow, The.
Pack. Ode to a Lovesick Moose.
Sexton. Moose.
Van Duyn. Moose in the Morning, Northern Maine.

Morality Plays
"Carroll, Lewis." Prologue: "Ladies and Gentlemen seems stiff and cold."
Thomson. Epilogue to Tancred and Sigismunda.

More, Sir Thomas (Saint Thomas More)
Lowell. Sir Thomas More.

Morison, Sir Henry
Jonson. To the Immortal[l] Memory [or Memorie] and Friendship of That Noble

Pair[e], Sir Lucius Cary and Sir H. [or Henry] Morison.

Mormons
Davie. Red Rock of Utah.

Morning
Ammons. Rainy Morning.
Atwood. Morning, A.
Auden. Dew steams off the thatches, The.
Early Morning.
Early Morning.
Early Morning Bathing.
Lauds.
Now from far eastern wolds, the bay.
Sunday Morning.
Berrigan. Old-Fashioned Air.
Berry. April Woods: Morning.
Architecture, An.
At night make me one with the darkness.
Plan, The.
Bishop. Sunday, 4 A.M.
Blake. Morning.
To Morning.
Bly. July Morning.
Poem in Three Parts.
Waking from Sleep.
Bogan. Italian Morning.
Morning.
Boyle. Poem on Getting up Early in the Morning (or Even Late in the Morning), When One is Old.
Browning, Robert. Year's at the spring, The.
Bukowski. 4:30 A.M.
6 A.M.
Burns. Cauld Frosty Morning.
Lover's Morning Salute to His Mistress, The.
Rosebud, The.
Up in the Morning Early.
Carroll, Jim. For Sue's Birthday.
Carruth. Sometimes When Lovers Lie Quietly Together, Unexpectedly One of Them Will Feel the Other's Pulse.
Sonnet: "Fear of falling is why the old men walk."
Ceravolo. It Is Morning.
Ciardi. At First Flower of the Easy Day.
Come Morning.
Morning: I Know Perfectly How in a Minute You Will Stretch and Smile.
Clark. Aubade: "Truck gears grinding up Marin."
Mist Sleeve Flight.
Then again by day fog drapes the boats.
Cohen. End of My Life in Art.
Cooper. In the Last Few Moments Came the Old German Cleaning Woman.
Cowper. Winter Morning Walk, The.
Crane. Annunciations.
Cummings. At just 5 a / m i hear eng.
Dawn / and now.begins / feeling.
Inthe,exquisite; / morning sure lyHer eye s exactly sit,ata little roundtable.
Lady of Silence.
O / nly this / darkness(in).
O It's Nice To Get Up In,the slipshod mucous kiss.
O the sun comes up-up-up in the opening.
Raise the shade.
When you went away it was morning.
Davie. Cold Spring in Essex.
Morning.
Nashville Mornings.
De la Mare. Assignation, The.
Imp Within, The.
Keys of Morning, The.
Martins: September.
Dickey, James. Morning, A.
Dickinson. And this of all my Hopes.
"Morning"—means "Milking"—to the Farmer.
Morning that comes but once.
Morning without you is a dwindled Dawn.
Sleep is supposed to be.
Sun—just touched the Morning, The.
To Whom the Mornings stand for Nights.
Will there really be a "Morning"?
Donne. Break[e] of Day.
Sun[ne] Rising, The.
Dunbar. Barrier, The.

In the Morning.
Morning.
Morning Song of Love.
Dunn. Halves.
   Urgencies.
"Dylan." New Morning.
Eberhart. By the Stream.
Eliot. Morning at the Window.
   Morning comes to consciousness, The.
Emerson. Written in Naples, March, 1833.
Everson. Rain on That Morning, The.
Ferlinghetti. Roman Morn.
Fisher. Billiard Table, The.
Fox. And night comes.
Frost. Valley's Singing Day, The.
Gardner. Autumn: Early Morning.
   It Rained Last Night.
Ginsberg. We Rise on Sun Beams and Fall in
   the Night.
Graves. On Rising Early.
Hacker. Aube Provençale.
   Morning: the phone jangles me from words:
   you.
Haines. It is morning again in the west.
Hall. Valley of Morning.
Hardy. On a Fine Morning.
Hartley. Come, / tired old thing.
   Go Lightly.
   Very Languor, The.
Hartnett. Last Vision of Eoghan Rua Ó
   Súilleabháin, The.
   Whom I ask for no gift.
Herbert. Matins.
Herrick. Matins [or Mattens], or Morning
   Prayer.
   To His Sweet Saviour.
Hesketh. Sun Up.
Hewitt. City Morning.
   Vida, Mykonos.
Hopkins. Dewy fields in the morning under
   the sun.
   Now more precisely touched in light and
   gloom.
   Or ever the early stirrings of skylark.
Housman. In the morning, in the morning.
   Reveille.
   Yonder see the morning blink.
Hughes, Langston. Blues at Dawn.
Hughes, Ted. Horses, The.
   Stealing Trout on a May Morning.
Jarrell. Nestus Gurley.
Joseph. Getting Up in Winter.
   Moon in the morning.
   Waking.
Knight. Boston 5:00 A.M.—10/74.
Koch. In the Morning.
Kooser. Birthday.
Larkin. Horns of the Morning, The.
   Morning at Last: There in the Snow.
   Morning Has Spread Again.
Lawrence. Dawn Verse, The.
   First Morning.
   Married in June.
   Mid-Day Verse, The.
   Morning Work.
   Next Morning.
   Wedding Morn.
Levertov. Matins.
Levine. Ordinary Morning, An.
   To My God in His Sickness.
   Wednesday.
Lindsay. In Which a Racing Auto Comes
   from the East.
   Mid-Morning.
Lowell. Waking Early Sunday Morning.
Lowry. As from All the Little Animals.
   Billetin.
   Eye-Opener.
   For Our Sweetharteebeeste on Hartebeeste
   Day.
   Fragments from the Duck Anthology to Greet
   Our Beloved Harteebeeste in the Morning
   Watch.
   Good Morning to Our Sweetest Harteebeeste!
   Happiest of Harteebeeste Days and Devoted
   Love Eterne.
   Lapis dawn is gleaming, A.

Lyrical Morning Poem.
Morning Address of Love to the Beloved
   Harteebeeste.
Morning bird is bathing, The.
Morning bird is singing, The.
Morning rain is rained, The.
Morning rain is raining / A morning pain is
   paining, The.
Morning rain is raining / The morning leg is
   paining, The.
Morning rain is weeping, The.
Morning sleet is sleeting, The.
Morning sneat is snewing, The.
Morning Song for the Harteebeeste.
Morning song of El Leon.
Morning stove is wheezing, The.
Morning tanker gleameth, The.
Reveille.
Ship will sail again, the watches sing, The.
Singing. / The morning bird. / (Humphum!).
Spark Poetry.
With Dearest Morning Love and Kisses.
With Sweetest Morning Love to Their Beloved
   Harteebeeste.
McAuley. Daybreak.
   Early Morning Walk to Work.
MacNeice. First the distant cocks. A hairfine.
   Morning Sun.
   Slow Movement.
   Sunday Morning.
Mahon. Everything Is Going to Be All Right.
   Morning.
Matthews. Blue Notes.
   Schoolboys with Dog, Winter.
Meredith. Pastoral 4: "Lo, as a tree, whose
   wintry twigs."
Merton. Aubade: Lake Erie.
Miller. Gray light awakening.
   How this morning.
Morgan. Morning. A river view.
Nash. Song Before Breakfast.
Nathan. It's a brand new morning.
Nemerov. Morning Sun.
O'Hara. Getting Up Ahead of Someone (Sun).
   Jane Awake.
   Joe's Jacket.
Oliver. Morning in a New Land.
   Morning Poem.
Olson. Clouds, The.
   Variations Done for Gerald Van de Wiele.
Plath. Sheep in Fog.
Roethke. Carnations.
Rossetti. Margaret has a milking-pail, / And
   she rises early.
Rukeyser. Song: "Voice flew out of the river
   as morning flew, A."
Sandburg. Bitter Summer Thoughts—No. 3.
   Early Hours.
   Far Rockaway Night Till Morning.
   Halsted Street Car.
   I was born in the morning of the world.
   Lake Michigan Morning.
   Margaret.
   Moon Riders.
   Pass, Friend.
Schuyler. Birds.
   Good Morning.
   In Earliest Morning.
   Morning, The.
Sexton. Fury of Sunrises, The.
   Welcome Morning.
Shakespeare. Sonnet 33: "Full many a glorious
   morning have I seen[e]."
Shapiro. Shame.
Simic. Summer Morning.
Smart. At Dressing in the Morning.
Smith, Stevie. Hendecasyllables.
Spender. Awaking.
Stevenson. About the sheltered garden ground.
   Song at Dawn.
   Winter Time [or Winter-Time].
Swift. Description of the Morning, A.
Thomas. When I woke.
Thomson. Morning in the Country, The.
Tomlinson. Drive.
   Greeting, The.
Turco. Awaken, Bells Falling.

Wakoski. Helms Bakery Man, The.
Warren. Morning.
Whittier. Waiting, The.
Wilbur. For Ellen.
   Late Aubade, A.
   Love Calls Us to the Things of This World.
   Summer Morning, A.
Williams, Charles Kenneth. Mornings:
   Catherine.
Williams, William Carlos. Morning.
   Summer Song.
Wright, Charles. California Spring.
Wright, James. Love Song to a Morning.
   Our Daily Bread.
Yau. Broken Off by the Music.
Young. Waking Up in Santa Cruz at Sea.

Morning Glories
Ciardi. Bees and Morning Glories.
Meinke. Blue Morning Glories.
Sandburg. Morning Glory Blue.

Morocco
Cohen. Morocco.
Eberhart. Marrakech.

Morris, William
Sandburg. Salvage.

Mortality
Ashbery. Absence of a Noble Presence, The.
Atwood. Aging Female Poet on Laundry Day.
   Book of Ancestors.
   Girl and Horse, 1928.
   No Name.
   We walk in the cedar groves.
Auden. After the Burial.
   Crocus stars the border, The.
   Episode, An.
   Finis.
   I chose this lean country.
   Light strives with darkness, right with wrong.
   Lullaby: "Lay your sleeping head, my love."
   Ploughing.
   Sonnet II: "It matters not that we shall cease
   to be."
   Yes and No.
Berg. At a Friend's Birthday Party in the
   Garden at Night.
   Soul, The.
   Two Little Songs.
Berrigan. Last Poem.
Berry. He has known a tunnel.
Blake. Caverns of the Grave Ive seen, The.
Bly. Ant Mansion, The.
   August Rain.
   Conversation, A.
   Defeated.
   Digging Worms.
   Empty Place, An.
   Hawk, The.
   Hollow Tree, A.
   Home in Dark Grass, A.
   July Morning.
   Kneeling Down to Look [or Peer] into a
   Culvert.
   Night.
   November Day at McClure's Beach.
   On a Ferry across Chesapeake Bay.
   Sitting on Some Rocks in Shaw Cove.
   When the Dumb Speak.
Brontë. Self-Interrogation.
Browning, Elizabeth Barrett. Stanzas: "I may
   sing; but minstrel's singing."
Burns. Song: "Sensibility how charming."
   To a Mountain Daisy [On Turning One Down,
   with the Plough, in April—1786].
Byron. Fragment, A: "When, to their airy hall,
   my fathers' voice."
   To Caroline ("Oh when shall the grave hide
   for ever my sorrow?").
   To Caroline ("When I hear you express an
   affection so warm").
Campion. Come, Cheerful Day!
   Lamentation, A.
   To the Most Illustrious and Mighty Fredericke
   the Fift, Count Palantine of the Rhein.
   What If a Day [or a Month or a Year].
   When Thou Must Home.
   Where are all thy beauties now, all hearts
   enchaining? [or harts enchayning?].

Carruth. New Hartford.
Sex.
Sonnet: "At the hospital where I had the echocardiagram."
Sonnet: "Fear of falling is why the old men walk."
Sonnet: "If I die today, which statistically speaking."
Sonnet: "It's said by the thoughtful masters that to know death."
Sonnet: "O Jesus, thou who sittest up there on the right."
Sonnet: "The loving mind in this death-haunted body."
Tanck's Song About Youth and Age.
Coleridge. Superstition.
Cowper. Happy Solitude—Unhappy Men.
Mortals around your destin'd heads.
On a Similar Occasion for the Year 1788.
On a Similar Occasion for the Year 1789.
On a Similar Occasion for the Year 1790.
On a Similar Occasion for the Year 1792.
On a Similar Occasion for the Year 1793.
Stanzas Printed on Bills of Mortality 1787–1790, 1792, 1793.
Crashaw. Out of Martiall.
Cullen. Epitaph: "She leans across a golden table."
Nothing Endures.
Sonnet: "These are no wind-blown rumors, soft say-sos."
Davie. Winter Landscapes.
De la Mare. Corner Stone, The.
Queen Wasp, A.
Self to self.
Dickinson. Because I could not stop for Death.
Exultation is the going.
"Heavenly Father"—take to thee.
I fear we think too lightly of.
Parting is one of the exactions.
Somehow myself survived the Night.
'Tis not that Dying hurts us so.
To venerate the simple days.
Visitor in Marl, A.
We knew not that we were to live.
Wounded Deer—leaps highest, A.
Donne. Farewell to Love.
First Anniversary [or Anniversarie], The.
Funeral Elegy, A.
To the Praise of the Dead, and the Anatomy.
Dunbar. Mortality.
Duncan. Erecting beyond the boundaries of all government.
Dunn. Sweetness.
Eberhart. To Evan.
Emerson. Good-bye.
Hamatreya.
Seemed to me—never maid.
To J. W.
Ferlinghetti. Paris Transformations.
Fletcher. Last Frontier, The.
Mexican Quarter.
They buried Abel at sunset in the red wet earth.
Fox. In Search of a Love Poem.
Nail of the Index Finger, The.
Galvin. Glass.
Gardner. Of Flesh and Bone.
Spendthrift.
Garrigue. Brook, The.
Last Letter to the Scholar.
Poem: "I saw the mountains in a rose-fire light."
Glück. Fortress, The.
Garden, The.
Triumph of Achilles, The.
Graves. In Her Praise.
Gray. Elegy Written in a Country Churchyard.
Griffiths. Shamanism, Dalston.
Hall. Black Faced Sheep, The.
For an Exchange of Rings.
Tubes.
Hardy. Dead and the Living One, The.
Doom and She.
Last Week in October.
Later Autumn, The.

Sine Prole.
Tenant-for-Life, The.
Herbert. Church Monuments.
Employment (2).
Frailty.
Man's Medley.
Mortification.
Virtue [or Vertue].
Herrick. Anacreontike.
Changes to Corinna, The.
Death Ends All Woe.
End Decreed, An.
Great Spirits Supervive.
His Charge to Julia at His Death.
His Own Epitaph.
Last Stroke Strike Sure, The.
Man's Dying-Place Uncertain.
Never Too Late to Dye.
None Free from Fault.
Paranæticall, or Advisive Verse, to His Friend, M. John Wicks.
Plunder, The.
Things Mortal Still Mutable.
To Enjoy the Time.
To His Kinswoman, Mistresse Susanna Herrick.
To His Sweet Saviour.
To the Reverend Shade of His Religious Father.
Upon a Young Mother of Many Children.
Upon His Departure Hence.
Upon the Troublesome Times.
Watch, The.
Hewitt. First Funeral.
Ghosts.
Hedgehog.
Hesitant Memorial.
I've seen no more than three loved persons die.
Lonely Heart, The.
Lyric: "Let but a thrush begin."
Mortal Place, The.
Pour Hélène.
Retreaded Rhymes.
Return, The.
Spectacle of Truth, The.
This is the season I think most of death.
Hill. Order of Service, An.
Holmes. Fear in the Afternoon.
Housman. Be still, my soul, be still; the arms you bear are brittle.
Chestnut casts his flambeaux, and the flowers, The.
Clunton and Clunbury.
I hoed and trenched and weeded.
I promise nothing: friends will part.
It is no gift I tender.
Oh turn not in from marching.
Rain, it streams on stone and hillock, The.
Sage to the Young Man, The.
With rue my heart is laden.
You smile upon your friend to-day.
Hugo. Remote Farm on the Dubrovnik-Sarajevo Run.
Jarrell. Author to the Reader, The.
I loved you, too. There was no use. I had no time.
Kirilov on a Skyscraper.
Jeffers. Age in Prospect.
To Death.
Wise Men in Their Bad Hours.
Johnson. On a Lady's Presenting a Sprig of Myrtle to a Gentleman.
Soon fades the rose; once past the fragrant hour.
Jong. Anti-Matter.
Color of Snow, The.
Self-Portrait in Shoulder Stand.
To X. (With Ephemeral Kisses).
Joseph. Another Old Tale.
Goddess of Nature's Diatribe to her People, The.
Man as Real (CITY; HUMAN).
To achieve knowledge, salting away Faust's stock—.
Keats. Gif Ye Wol Stonden Hardie Wight.
Ode on a Grecian Urn.

Ode to a Nightingale.
Stanzas on Some Skulls in Beauly Abbey, Near Inverness.
When I Have Fears That I May Cease to Be.
Why Did I Laugh Tonight?
Written in Disgust of Vulgar Superstition.
Kunitz. Etcher of the secret wrinkles.
O sister of the shadow.
Words of the Preacher, The.
Levertov. Earth Psalm.
Lewis. Finale.
Horace at Twenty.
Lines on a Tudor Mansion.
Sentry, The.
To a Comrade in Arms.
White frost; intricate bare branches.
Lindsay. Being the Dedication of a Morning.
Longfellow. Mezzo Cammin.
Morituri Salutamus.
Nature.
McGrath. In Early Autumn.
MacLeish. Actfive.
1892—19—.
From these night fields and waters do men raise.
Signature for Tempo.
MacNeice. Death has a look of finality.
Plant and Phantom.
Sunlight on the Garden, The.
Marvell. Picture of Little T. C. in a Prospect of Flowers, The.
Melville. Epilogue: "If Luther's day expand to Darwin's year."
Tom Deadlight.
Meredith. Dirge in Woods.
"Dream is the thought in the ghost, The."
Faith on Trial, A.
Hymn to Colour.
Last Contention, The.
Question Whither, The.
Thrush in February, The.
Merton. Meditation before an Ancient Poem.
Millay. At least, my dear.
Be sure my coming was a sharp offense.
How healthily their feet upon the floor.
Lament: "Listen, children: / Your father is dead."
Leaf and the Tree, The.
Mariposa.
Mortal Flesh, Is Not Your Place in the Ground?
Poet and His Book, The.
Pretty Love, I Must Outlive You.
Small Hands, Relinquish All.
What's this of death, from you who never will die?
When you, that at this moment are to me.
Neruda. Egoist.
Oliver. Beyond the Snow Belt.
Dream of Trees, A.
In Blackwater Woods.
Lonely, White Fields.
October.
When Death Comes.
Olson. This.
Oppen. Endlessly, endlessly, / The definition of mortality.
Population.
Owen. Anthem for Doomed Youth.
Exposure.
Send-Off, The.
Terre, A.
Paley. Drowning (II).
Fear.
Prince. Question, The.
Psalms. Psalm 39: "I said, I will take heed to my ways."
Psalm 49: "Hear this, all ye people.."
Psalm 90: "Lord, thou hast been our dwelling place in all generations."
Raine. Last night I seemed in your embrace.
Ransom. Piazza Piece.
Robinson. Pity of the Leaves, The.
Rossetti. I See That All Things Come to an End.
Rukeyser. Blue Flower, The.
Thousands of Days.

Schwartz. All Night, All Night.
Christmas Poem for Nancy.
Shapiro. Cut Flower, A.
Shelley. Dialogue, A.
Smith, Patti. Wing.
Smith, Stevie. Company.
Spender. One More New Botched Beginning.
Sleepless.
Tom's a-Cold.
Sutter. Cold, The.
Tate. Anabasis, The.
Tomlinson. After a Death.
Updike. Bath after Sailing.
Granite.
Melancholy of Storm Windows, The.
Omega.
Sea Knell.
Van Duyn. Challenger, The.
Warren. Mad Young Aristocrat on Beach.
Whitman. As at Thy Portals Also Death.
City Dead-House, The.
Quicksand Years.
This Compost.
Thought: ("As I sit with others at a great feast, suddenly while the music is playing").
Whittier. Autograph, An.
Wilbur. Ballade in Old French.
Flumen Tenebrarum.
La Rose des Vents.
Lament: "Nashe's old queens who bartered young and fair."
Lilacs, The.
To His Skeleton.
Wordsworth. Calm Is the Fragrant Air, and Loth to Lose.
Extempore Effusion upon the Death of James Hogg.
Most Alluring Clouds That Mount the Sky, The.
November, 1836.
'Tis He Whose Yester-Evening's High Disdain.
Trosachs, The.
Upon a Portrait.
Young. Mountains of California: Part 2, The.

Morticians. *see* **Undertakers.**

Moscow, Russia
Hewitt. Moscow Moment.
Mahon. After Pasternak.
Updike. Moscow.
Wilbur. Phone Booth.
Wordsworth. By Moscow Self-Devoted to a Blaze.

Moses
Cohen. Friend, When You Speak.
Dickinson. It always felt to me—a wrong.
Glück. Day Without Night.
Hopkins. Soliloquy of One of the Spies Left in the Wilderness, A.
Nemerov. Moses.

Mosquitoes
Lawrence. Mosquito Knows, The.
Mosquito, The.
Sorrentino. Mosquitoes in New Jersey.
Spender. Mosquito in Florence.
Updike. Mosquito.

Moss
Roethke. Moss-Gathering.

Motels
Nathan. Highway, The.
On the sink of the Golden Motel washroom.
Snodgrass. Leaving the Motel.

See also **Hotels.**

Mothers
Angelou. Mothering Blackness, The.
Atwood. Christmas Carols.
Letter from Persephone.
Mothers.
Red Shirt, A.
Auden. Motherhood.
Berg. Homage to the Afterlife.
Lament: "My mother wants to be burned, she told me."
Lightbulb.
Prayer: "Nobody understands so let the Rabbi."

Shoeshine.
Tashkent Blossoms, 1944.
Visit, The.
Berrigan. Certain Slant of Sunlight, A.
Berry. Poem for J.
Bishop. Infancy.
Boyle. Mothers.
Bradstreet. Epitaph on my Dear and Ever Honored Mother Mrs. Dorothy Dudley.
In Reference to Her Children, 23 June, 1659 [or 1656].
Upon My Son Samuel His Going For England.
Brooks. Big Bessie Throws Her Son into the Street.
Jessie Mitchell's Mother.
Mrs. Small.
Browning, Elizabeth Barrett. Isobel's Child.
Mother and Poet.
Mourning Mother, The.
Bukowski. Imagination and Reality.
Mother and Son.
Burns. Waukrife Minnie, A.
Campion. Fain Would I Wed.
"Carroll, Lewis." Nursery Darling, A.
Sailor's Wife, The.
Song of Love, A.
Those Horrid Hurdy-Gurdies!
Carruth. Fragment: "Who can know more deeply than I your loneliness there?"
Mother.
"My mother did it. She had to, she said. She took."
Song: So Often, So Long I Have Thought.
Ciardi. Addio.
Epithalamium at St. Michael's Cemetary.
Five-Year Step, A.
Shaft, The.
Three Views of a Mother.
Cohen. Don't Go Home with Your Hard-on.
Front Lawn.
Night Comes On, The.
Coleridge. Ode to Georgiana, Duchess of Devonshire.
Three Graves, The.
Cooper. For My Mother in Her First Illness, from a Window Overlooking Notre Dame.
My Young Mother.
Cowper. On the Receipt of My Mother's Picture out of Norfolk [the Gift of My Cousin Ann Bodham].
Crabbe. Mother, The.
Creeley. For My Mother: Genevieve Jules Creeley.
Gesture, The.
Kid.
Method of Actuality, The.
She Went to Stay.
Two.
Wind, The.
Cullen. Tribute.
Davie. Mother.
De la Mare. On the Esplanade.
Owl, The.
To My Mother.
Winter Dusk.
Dickey, James. Buckdancer's Choice.
Deborah as Scion.
Voyage of the Needle, The.
Dickey, William. Elegy Before the Time.
Stella Dallas.
Dickinson. Grief of wonder at her fate.
If Nature smiles—the Mother must.
Mama never forgets her birds.
"Mother," to me, is so sacred a Name.
Mother's dying almost stunned my spirit.
Upon the gallows hung a wretch.
Who could be motherless.
Dobyns. Tomatoes.
Doolittle. Grown Up.
No.
Dove. Bird Frau, The.
Motherhood.
Dunbar. Appreciation.
Scamp.
Turning of the Babies in the Bed, The.
Duncan. My Mother Would Be a Falconress.
Dunn. Letter Home.

Routine Things Around the House, The.
That Saturday Without a Car.
"Dylan." John Brown.
Eberhart. At Night.
Examination of Psyche: Thoughts of Home.
Orchard.
Soul Longs to Return Whence It Came, The.
Emerson. Philosophers are lined with eyes within.
Fletcher. Back Stairs, The.
Fox. Blue Dress, The.
Letters from the Island.
Mother Was a Good.
Peregrine Falcon.
Poem for My Mother.
Shipbuilder, The.
Gallagher. Coming Home.
Croce e Delizia al Cor.
Each Bird Walking.
Gildner. My Mother Writes..
Poems.
Ginsberg. Hymmnn.
Kaddish.
Glück. For My Mother.
Love Poem.
Morning.
My Cousin in April.
Nurse's Song.
Graves. Advice from a Mother.
Frosty Night, A.
Sweet-Shop Round The Corner, The.
Hacker. As yoked to her by absence as by prescence.
Autumn 1980.
Callers, The.
Fifteen to Eighteen.
Fourteen.
Iva's Birthday Poem.
Iva's Pantoum.
Mother.
Mother II.
1976.
No better lost than any other woman.
Robber Woman, The.
She twists scraps of her hair in unshelled snails.
Towards Autumn.
"What's in a park they warn girls out of?"
"Queers."
Hall. Sister by the Pond, A.
Hardy. In Childbed.
Lacking Sense, The.
Hartley. Her Daughter.
Hayden. Whipping, The.
Herrick. Upon a Lady That Dyed in Child-Bed, and Left a Daughter behind Her.
Upon a Young Mother of Many Children.
Upon the Lady Crew.
Hesketh. Mallard, The.
Hewitt. Doctor's Bag, The.
E.H.
Eye for Color, An.
First Letters.
"Forty-Four Hours" Strike, 1919, The.
Green Shoot, The.
Mother and Son.
My Grandmother's Restlessness.
My Mother.
My Widowed Mother.
No Second Troy.
Sanctuary.
Scattering, The.
Hopkins. Mothers are doubtless happier for their babes.
Hughes, Langston. Baby.
Letter.
Mama and Daughter.
Mother to Son.
Negro Mother, The.
Jarrell. Lost Children, The.
Jeffers. Solstice.
Jong. Dear Marys, Dear Mother, Dear Daughter.
Mother.
Still Life with Tulips.
Jonson. Eptiaph on Katherine, Lady Ogle.
Joseph. Jack and the Beanstalk.

Kinnell. Goodbye.
Kipling. Mother o' Mine.
Only Son, An.
Unknown Female Corpse.
Knight. Report to the Mother.
Stretching of the Belly, The.
Knott. Closet, The.
My Mother's List of Names.
Koch. On Beauty.
Lawrence. Everlasting Flowers.
Grief.
Lady Wife.
Monologue of a Mother.
She Looks Back.
Virgin Mother, The.
Levertov. Olga Poems.
Levine. Late Moon.
Look.
On the Birth of Good & Evil During the Long Winter of '28.
Lewis. Monologue.
Liddy. Dorcas.
Mothermas.
Lorde. Black Mother Woman.
Dear Toni Instead of a Letter of Congratulation..
Now That I Am Forever with Child.
Story Books on a Kitchen Table.
To the Girl Who Lives In a Tree.
Lowell. During Fever.
Mother, 1972.
Sailing Home from Rapallo.
Soft Wood.
Lowry. Marina—.
Number 8 Fireman.
Oh the Pyrrus boys are we.
"MacDiarmid." Two Parents, The.
MacLeish. Burial, The.
For the Anniversary of my Mother's Death.
Matthews. Mother.
Meredith. Little Foot-Page, The.
M. M.
Mother to Babe.
Nor had saffron and sapphire and red.
Queen Zuleima.
Recognition, The.
Merrill. After the Fire.
Millay. Ballad of the Harp-Weaver, The.
Courage that my mother had, The.
Morgan. Breasts of the loving mothers flow with milk, The.
Who will laugh / in coldest glee.
You came as sleep, warily.
You cast me from your filthy womb.
Muldoon. Ma.
Nash. Epilogue to Mother's Day, Which Is To Be Published on Any Day But Mother's Day.
Notley. Mother Mask.
O'Hara. Poem: "There I could never be a boy."
Olson. It isn't my word but my mother's.
Just Inside the Vigil of Christmas.
La Chute III.
Pack. Closer.
Drowning.
Secrets.
Trillium.
Paley. In San Salvador (I).
In San Salvador (II).
My Mother: 33 Years Later.
On the Bank Street Pier.
Some days I am lonesome I want to talk to my mother.
Patchen. Career for a Child of Five.
For the Mother of My Mother's Mother.
Niobe.
Piercy. Crescent Moon Like a Canoe.
Plath. Disquieting Muses, The.
Heavy Women.
Morning Song.
Parliament Hill Fields.
Poe. To My Mother.
Raine. Binah.
Columbines.
Dear ones in the house of the dead.
Dream.

Heirloom.
My Mother's Birthday.
"Reed." Kids, The.
Mama's Got a Lover.
Rexroth. Delia Rexroth.
Delia Rexroth.
Rich. Mother-Right.
Night-Pieces: For a Child.
Rossetti. Ballad: "Soft white lamb in the daisy meadow."
Brandons Both.
Chilly Night, A.
Crimson curtains round my mother's bed.
Crying, my little one, footsore and weary?
Death.
1885. St. Valentine's Day.
1884.
1886, St. Valentine's Day.
1878.
1879.
For Rosaline's Album.
Holy Innocents.
Johnny.
Life Out of Death.
Light Love.
Love me,—I love you / Love me, my baby.
Mother and Child.
Motherless baby and babyless mother.
On the grassy banks / Lambkins at their pranks.
Our little baby fell asleep.
Our Mothers, lovely women pitiful; / Our sisters, gracious in their life and death.
Sonnets are full of love, and this my tome.
There Is a Budding Morrow in Midnight.
To My Mother on Her Birthday.
Valentine, 1882, A.
Versi.
Wishes: Sonnet.
Rukeyser. Birth, A.
More Clues.
Night Feeding.
On the Death of Her Mother.
Question, The.
Speech of the Mother, from "The Middle of the Air."
Trinity Churchyard.
Schuyler. Name Day, A.
On the Dresser.
Sexton. Child Bearers, The.
Christmas Eve.
Division of Parts, The.
Dreaming the Breasts.
Eighth Psalm.
For the Year of the Insane.
Mothers.
Red Shoes, The.
Silverstein. Afraid of the Dark.
Loser, The.
Ma and God.
Ridiculous Rose.
Simic. Spoons with Realistic Dead Flies on Them.
Smith, Charlotte. Forest Boy, The.
Smith, Patti. Ballad of a Bad Boy.
Smith, Stevie. Human Affection.
I'll Have Your Heart.
Mother.
Mother, among the Dustbins.
Mother's Hearse, A.
N'est-ce pas assez de ne me point haïr?
Queen and the Young Princess, The.
Sad Mother, The.
She Said..
Virtuoso, The.
Snodgrass. Mother, The.
Snyder. Face in the crook of her neck.
Gen.
Sorrentino. Blackburn's Dream.
Everybody would soon change.
Spender. Furies, The.
Stafford. Clash.
My Mother Was a Soldier.
Our Kind.
Some Shadows.
Vacation Trip.
Stevenson. As in their flight the birds of song.

God gave to me a child in part.
It is not yours, O mother, to complain.
Mater Triumphans.
Mother and Daughter.
Sick Child, The.
To My Mother.
Stuart. Hidden Meanings.
Spell.
Tate. Mother and Son.
Thomas. My World Is Pyramid.
Thomson. On the Death of his Mother.
Updike. Fall.
Young Matrons Dancing.
Van Duyn. Remedies, Maladies, Reasons.
Stream, The.
Wakoski. Why My Mother Likes Liberace.
Waldman. Complaynt.
Matriarchly.
Mother & Child.
Mother's Curse.
Number Song.
Stick, The.
Warren. Revelation.
What Were You Thinking Dear Mother?
Whitman. Mother and Babe.
Sleepers, The.
Williams, Charles Kenneth. Good Mother: Out.
My Mother's Lips.
Williams, William Carlos. Crude Lament.
Dedication for a Plot of Ground.
Eternity, An.
Horse Show, The.
Painting, The.
Resemblance, The.
Two Pendants: For the Ears.
Young Woman at a Window.
Young Woman at a Window.
Wordsworth. Affliction of Margaret—, The.
By a Blest Husband Guided, Mary Came.
Complaint of a Forsaken Indian Woman, The.
Emigrant Mother, The.
Her Eyes Are Wild.
Maternal Grief.
No spade for leagues had won a rood of earth.
Sailor's Mother, The.
Three Graves, The.
To — Upon the Birth of Her First-Born Child, March, 1833.
Yeats. Song from "The Player Queen,"A.
Song of the Old Mother, The.
Young. Moving, Merging, Fading, Standing Still.
Zimmer. Once as a Child I Had Bad Dreams.
Zukofsky. Poem Beginning "The."

Mother's Day
Nash. Epilogue to Mother's Day, Which Is To Be Published on Any Day But Mother's Day.
Please Leave Father Alone.
Stafford. Mother's Day.

Mothers-in-Law
"Carroll, Lewis." What Tottles Meant.
Ciardi. Censorship.
Gunn. First Meeting with a Possible Mother-in-Law.
Koertge. He ("Bought a three-bedroom house in 1948").
Rich. Mother-in-Law.
Wakoski. Fanny's Cold Blue Eyes.

Moths
Carroll, Jim. For Sue's Birthday.
Carruth. August First.
Ceravolo. Dusk.
Crane. Moth That Made God Blind, The.
De la Mare. Moth, The.
Dickinson. Moth the hue of this, A.
Fenton. In September greasebands are put on standard apple.
Ford. Death's-head moth, A.
Frost. To a Moth Seen in Winter.
Gardner. Moth Happened, The.
That Common Moth.
Hartley. Go Lightly.
Hopkins. All as that moth call'd Underwing, alighted.
Kooser. In the Corners of Fields.
Sandburg. Goldwing Moth.

Sarton. Moth in the Schoolroom.
Schuyler. Day, The.
Smith, Charlotte. Moth, The.
Snodgrass. Lying Awake.
Stevens. Hibiscus on the Sleeping Shores.
Stuart. Audition.
Williams, William Carlos. Prelude to Winter.

Motion
Beckett. Dread Nay.
 Serena III.
Carroll, Jim. I see it passing.
 Song: "It goes, it / Goes."
Clark. Motion, 1953.
Cummings. Now what were motionless
 move(exists no).
Emerson. I sat upon the ground.
Gunn. On the Move.
Haines. Rolling Back.
Hewitt. Glendun on a Wet July Day.
Hughes, Ted. Thought-Fox, The.
Koch. On the Great Atlantic Rainway.
Kunitz. Me and the Rock.
MacNeice. Hold-up.
McNeill. Poet.
Marlowe. 3.5: Ad amnem, dum iter faceret ad
 amicam.
Pack. Invisible Hand, The.
Plath. Years.
Rukeyser. Eccentric Motion.
Snyder. Spring water in the green creek is
 clear.
Stevens. Curtains in the House of the
 Metaphysician, The.
 Place of the Solitaires, The.
 Pleasures of Merely Circulating, The.

Motion Pictures
Ashbery. Lonedale Operator, The.
Beatles. Drive My Car.
 Honey Pie.
Berryman. Dispossessed, The.
Cummings. Mind's(/ I never you never), The.
 O pr / gress verily thou art m.
Davie. Lincolnshire.
Dobyns. What You Have Come To Expect.
Duncan. Stage Directions.
Fisher. To see the film you buy a ticket.
Garrigue. Movie Actors Scribbling Letters
 Very Fast in Crucial Scenes.
Ginsberg. Methedrine Vision in Hollywood, A.
Griffiths. Chips.
Hayden. Double Feature.
Hugo. Letter to Annick from Boulder.
Jarrell. Children's Arms.
Koertge. Sidekicks.
Lawrence. Film Passion.
 When I Went to the Film.
Levertov. Film, The.
Lowry. My Beloved Harteebeeste.
"MacDiarmid." And a poetry in which as in a
 film.
McGrath. Ars Poetica: Or: Who Lives in the
 Ivory Tower?
Muldoon. Weepies, The.
Nash. Screen with the Face with the Voice,
 The.
 What's in a Name? Here's What's in a Name,
 or, I Wonder What Became of John and
 Mary.
O'Hara. Ave Maria.
 Image of Leda, An.
 To the Film Industry in Crisis.
Rich. Newsreel.
 Pierrot Le Fou.
Roethke. Double Feature.
Rukeyser. Song: Remembering Movies.
Schuyler. Simone Signoret.
Schwartz. Greatest Thing in North America,
 The.
 Metro-Goldwyn-Mayer.
Smith, Patti. Italy.
 K.O.D.A.K.
Smith, Stevie. Film Star, The.
Updike. Déjà, Indeed.
 Home Movies.
 In Memoriam.
 Movie House.

Williams, William Carlos. Light Becomes
 Darkness.
Yau. No One Ever Tried To Kiss Anna May
 Wong.
 When the movie ends and the lights come on,
 the audience is puzzled.
 When the movie ends, the lights come on. The
 audience is puzzled.
See also **Show Business.**

Motorcycles and Motorcycling
Carruth. Her Dream.
Ferlinghetti. Ladakh Buddhess Biker.
Ford. Max Ernst.
Gunn. On the Move.
 Unsettled Motorcyclist's Vision of His Death,
 The.
Hughes, Ted. Motorbike, A.
Olson. Tenemeny twilightish landscape.
"Reed." Bottoming Out.
Stafford. Fifteen.
Van Duyn. What the Motorcycle Said.

Mottoes
Byron. Ich Dien.
Kipling. Boy Scouts' Patrol Song, A.
 Ubique.
Prince. Family Mottoes.
Stein. Brim Beauvais.
 Yet Dish.
Swift. Whitshed's Motto on His Coach.

Mount Tamalpais
Clark. Life Notes.
Everson. Canticle to the Christ in the Holy
 Eucharist, A.
Oppen. Impossible Poem, The.

Mountain Climbing
Atwood. Highest Altitude.
Carruth. Mountain Fastness, The.
Dobyns. Mountain, The.
Eberhart. Spring Mountain Climb.
Frost. Time Out.
Griffiths. Climber.
Haines. On the Mountain.
 We climbed all afternoon.
Hardy. Zermatt: To the Matterhorn.
Hartley. Pilgrimage, and the Game Warden,
 The.
Kinnell. Fergus Falling.
 Flower Herding on Mount Monadnock.
Kooser. Visiting Mountains.
Rich. Phantasia for Elvira Shatayev.
Rossetti. Resurgam.
Snyder. Across Lamarck Col.
 John Muir on Mt. Ritter.
 On Climbing the Sierra Matterhorn Again after
 Thirty-One Years.
Stafford. Research Team in the Mountains,
 The.
Van Duyn. Colorado.
Wordsworth. To—, on Her First Ascent to the
 Summit of Helvellyn.

Mountain Lions
Dunn. Letting the Puma Go.
Lawrence. Mountain Lion.

Mountain Men
Carruth. John Dryden.
Hartley. Pilgrimage, and the Game Warden,
 The.
Kinnell. Fergus Falling.
Levine. 7 Years from Somewhere.
Sandburg. Proud of Their Rags.

Mountains
Atwood. Morning, A.
Auden. Everest.
 Mountains.
Tarn. The.
Brontë. Farewell To Alexandria, A.
Burns. My Heart's in the Highlands.
 Yon wild, mossy mountains sae lofty and
 wide.
Carruth. Beginning with the palest and softest
 lavender.
 In spring this mountain was a fish.
 Mountain Cabin, The.
 Mountain Fastness, The.
 Pale dawnlight spooks the mist.
Clark. In the Dark Mountains, Brilliant.

Creeley. Mountains in the Desert, The.
 Thinking.
Cummings. Fire stop thief help murder save
 the world.
Davie. Metals.
Dickey, William. Avalanche.
Dickinson. Bloom upon the Mountain—stated.
 Sweet Mountains—Ye tell Me no lie.
Dobyns. Mountain, The.
Doolittle. All Mountains.
"Dylan." Time Passes Slowly.
Eberhart. Burden.
 Skier and the Mountain, The.
Emerson. Earth, The.
 Score of airy miles will smooth, A.
Fletcher. Burning Mountain, The.
 Lines Written at Taormina, Sicily.
Ford. Mount Stavros sits on.
Frost. Fountain, a Bottle, a Donkey's Ears and
 Some Books, A.
Ginsberg. Teton Village.
Gunn. From the Highest Camp.
Haines. On a bend in the road near St. Mary.
 On the Mountain.
 Tarpaper and wind / a street rolling stones.
 Toward Many Glaciers.
 West of Logan Pass, where.
Hall. Mount Kearsarge.
 Scenic View.
 Stone Walls.
Hayden. Mountains.
Hesketh. Retreat.
 Snow Leopard.
Hewitt. Anti-Promethean Ode.
 Mourne Mountains.
Hill. God's Little Mountain.
Hoffman. Climbing Katahdin.
Hughes, Ted. Mountains.
Jeffers. Red Mountain.
 Treasure, The.
Kipling. Idiot Boy, The.
Kooser. Visiting Mountains.
Lawrence. Meeting among the Mountains.
 Men in New Mexico.
Lewis. On the Welsh Mountains.
Liddy. Blue Mountain.
 Warm Mountain Poem for Matt Liban.
Lindsay. Over the Appalachian Barricade.
Lowry. Chilliwack.
 Happiness.
 Yvonne stood there silently / the roar of the
 plane still in her ears.
McNeill. Over the Mountain.
 West Virginia.
Marvell. Epigramma in Duos Montes
 Amosclivium et Bilboreum: Farfacio
 [Epigram on Two Mountains, Almscliff and
 Bilbrough: To Fairfax].
Meredith. Swathed round in mist and crown'd
 with cloud.
Morgan. Katahdin.
Olson. From *The Song of Ullikummi.*
 Obit.
Pack. Looking at a Mountain Range While
 Listening to a Mozart Piano Concerto.
Plath. Above the Oxbow.
Raine. Man.
Robinson. Monadnock through the Trees.
 Vickery's Mountain.
Rukeyser. King's Mountain.
 Summer, the Sacramento.
Sandburg. Blue Ridge.
 Lackawanna Twilight.
 March of the Hungry Mountains.
 Smoke Blue.
Smith, Stevie. Sliding Mountain, The.
 Touch and Go.
Snyder. I have lived at Cold Mountain.
 I settled at Cold Mountain long ago.
 In the mountains it's cold.
 Meeting the Mountains.
 Poem Left in Sourdough Mountain Lookout.
 Spring water in the green creek is clear.
Stevens. In the Clear Season of Grapes.
Stevenson. To Mrs. MacMarland.
Stuart. Goshen Pass: Winter.

No Yellow Jackets on the Mountain.
This Is No Dream, This Is My Life.
Tomlinson.   At a Glance.
Gorge, The.
On the Mountain.
Updike.   Mountain Impasse.
Warren.   Vision under the October Mountain:
   A Love Poem.
Whitman.   Spirit That Form'd This Scene.
Whittier.   Mount Agiochook.
Mountain Pictures.
Williams, Charles Kenneth.   That night, /
   winter, / rain.
Williams, William Carlos.   Alighting from my
   horse to drink with you.
Wordsworth.   At Albano.
Even as a dragon's eye that feels the stress.
Fairest, brightest, hues of ether fade, The.
Farewell, A: "Farewell, thou little Nook of
   mountain-ground."
Forth from a Jutting Ridge, Around Whose
   Base.
Fragment: "Yet once again."
Fragments from the Alfoxden Note-Book (III).
Musings near Aquapendente April, 1837.
November 1.
On Hearing the "Ranz des Vaches" on the
   Top of the Pass of St Gothard.
Our Lady of the Snow.
Pelion and Ossa flourish side by side.
Stanzas Composed in the Simplon Pass.
To—, on Her First Ascent to the Summit of
   Helvellyn.
View from the Top of Black Comb.
Written with a Slate Pencil on a Stone, on the
   Side of the Mountain of Black Comb.
Young.   Mountains of California: Part 1, The.
Zukofsky.   "Further than."

See also **Hills and Mountains.**

Mourning and Mourners
Angelou.   Mourning Grace.
Atwood.   Precognition.
Auden.   Stop all the clocks, cut off the
   telephone.
Beckett.   I would like my love to die.
Je voudrais que mon amour meure.
Mort de A.D.
Bradstreet.   David's Lamentation for Saul and
   Jonathan.
Epitaph on my Dear and Ever Honored
   Mother Mrs. Dorothy Dudley.
Funeral Elegy Upon that Pattern and Patron of
   Virtue, A.
In Memory of My Dear Grandchild Anne
   Bradstreet.
In Memory of My Dear Grandchild Elizabeth
   Bradstreet Who Deceased August, 1665,
   Being a Year and a Half Old.
On My Dear Grandchild Simon Bradstreet,
   [Who Died on 16TH November, 1669, Being
   But A Month And One Day Old].
To the Memory of My Dear and Ever
   Honored Father Thomas Dudley Esq. Who
   Deceased July 31, 1653, and of His Age 77.
To the Memory of My Dear Daughter in Law,
   Mrs. Mercy Bradstreet.
Brontë.   To a Wreath of Snow.
To A.S., 1830.
Browning, Elizabeth Barrett.   Child's Grave at
   Florence, A.
Court Lady, A.
Died.
Felicia Hemans.
Grief.
Lament for Adonis.
Mourning Mother, The.
My Kate.
Bukowski.   Conversation in a Cheap Room.
Japanese Wife, The.
Burns.   Elegy on Captain Matthew Henderson
   [or Capt. M——— H———] [A *Gentleman*
   Who Held the Patent for His Honours
   Immediately from Almighty God!].
Epitaph. Here Lies Robert Fergusson, Poet.
Man Was Made to Mourn, a Dirge.
Song, A: "Thou lingering Star with lessening
   ray."

Byron.   And Thou Art Dead, as Young and
   Fair.
Bright Be the Place of Thy Soul!
Elegiac Stanzas on the Death of Sir Peter
   Parker, Bart.
Epitaph on a Friend.
Monody on the Death of the Right Hon. R. B.
   Sheridan.
Oh factious viper! whose envenom'd tooth.
On the Death of a Young Lady.
One Struggle More, and I Am Free.
Campion.   Illustrissimo, Potentissimoque
   Principi, *Frederico* Quinto, Rheni Comiti
   Palatino, Duci Bavariae, &c.
To the Most Disconsolate Great Brittaine.
To the Most Illustrious and Mighty Fredericke
   the Fift, Count Palantine of the Rhein.
To the Most Sacred Queen Anne.
What Then Is Love But Mourning?
Carew.   Another [Epitaph on the Lady Mary
   Villiers] ("Purest soul that e'er was sent,
   The").
To the Countess of Anglesey.
Chaucer.   Book of the Duchesse, The.
Ciardi.   Alec.
Cohen.   Purest of Occasions.
There are Some Men.
Coleridge.   Israel's Lament.
Sonnet [to Charles Lloyd].
Cooper.   Faithful, The.
Cowper.   Another ["Painter, this likeness is too
   strong"].
By Callimachus.
Elegy 2: On the Death of the Beadle of
   Cambridge University.
Elegy 3: On the Death of the Bishop of
   Winchester.
Epitaph on Mr. Chester.
Grief of an Heir, The.
Crashaw.   Elegy upon the Death of Mr.
   Stanninow Fellow of Queenes Colledge.
Epitaph. Upon Doctor Brooke, An.
To Pontius Washing His Blood-Stained Hands.
Upon the Death of a Gentleman.
Upon the Death of Mister Herrys.
De la Mare.   Mourn'st Thou Now?
Dickinson.   Bustle in a House, The.
That bleeding beginning that every mourner
   knows.
Donne.   Valediction, A: Forbidding Mourning.
Dunbar.   Easter Ode, An.
Weltschmertz.
"Dylan."   Ballad for a Friend.
Eberhart.   Irish Catholic.
Emerson.   My days roll by me like a train of
   dreams.
Frost.   You could sit there with the stains on
   your shoes.
Gardner.   Fly in Amber.
In Memory of Lemuel Ayers, Scene Designer,
   Dead of Cancer in His Fortieth Year.
Knowing.
Zei Gesund.
Garrigue.   Mourning, A.
Ginsberg.   Kaddish.
Glück.   Dream of Mourning, The.
Graves.   Strangling in Merrion Square, The.
Gray.   Sonnet [on the Death of Mr. Richard
   West].
Hardy.   After the Burial.
Caged Goldfinch, The.
Carrier, The.
Clock-Winder, The.
Colour, The.
Death-Day Recalled, A.
Dissemblers, The.
If You Had Known.
Mother Mourns, The.
Regret Not Me.
Roman Gravemounds, The.
Hartley.   And, should it be left like this.
Fabian Bell—His Last Visit to Cuernavaca.
O Bitter Madrigal.
Two Drowned at the Gateway.
Hartnett.   Lament for Tadhg Cronin's Children.
Hayden.   Approximations.
Herrick.   Comfort to a Lady Upon the Death

of Her Husband.
Dirge upon the Death of the Right Valiant
   Lord, Bernard Stuart, A.
False Mourning.
His Charge to Julia at His Death.
His Lachrimae or Mirth, Turn'd to Mourning.
Mad Maid's Song, The.
To Anthea: ("If, deare Anthea, my hard fate it
   be").
To His Dying Brother, Master William
   Herrick.
To His Lovely Mistresses.
To Perenna, A Mistresse ("Deare Perenna,
   prethee come").
To the Lady Crew, Upon the Death of her
   Child.
Upon a Maid[e].
Upon a Maid ("Gone she is a long, long
   way").
Upon an Old Man a Residenciarie.
Upon his Kinswoman Mrs. M. S.
Upon His Sister-in-Law, Mistress Elizabeth
   Herrick.
Upon the Much Lamented, Mr. J. Warr.
Hewitt.   Carnations.
Local Poet, A.
Memorial Service.
Hill.   Endless London / mourns for that
   knowledge.
Hughes, Langston.   Wake.
Hugo.   Elegy: "I expected him to look dead in
   the casket."
Jeffers.   Battle.
Hungerfield.
Johnson.   Stella in Mourning.
Jonson.   On My First Son [or Sonne].
To the Same [Sir John Roe].
Keats.   Ah! Ken Ye What I Met the Day.
Faery Song.
Kipling.   Gift of the Sea, The.
Last Suttee, The.
London Stone.
Kunitz.   Sacred to the Memory.
When the magician died, I wept.
Lawrence.   Mourning.
Sorrow.
Lewis.   Lady in Black.
Lovelace.   Elegie. On the Death of Mrs.
   Cassandra Cotton, An.
Lucasta Paying Her Obsequies.
Lowry.   Morning coat is walking, A.
Rain Fell Heavily, The.
McAuley.   Mourners.
"MacDiarmid."   At the Cenotaph.
I mind when my first wife died.
MacLeish.   Protect us help us forgive us help
   give.
MacNeice.   Canto XVIII: "Lament for the
   Makers. Monday comes; at noon."
Canto XX: "To Wales once more, though not
   on holiday now."
Tam Cari Capitis.
Markson.   Dante Gabriel.
Meredith.   C B M.
Merton.   Imperfect Lover, The.
Lament of a Maiden for the Warrior's Death.
Lao Tzu's Wake.
Three Friends.
Millay.   Interim.
Milton.   Elegy 2: On the Death of the Beadle
   of Cambridge University.
Elegy 3: On the Death of the Bishop of
   Winchester.
Olson.   Death of Europe, The.
Town, The.
Prince.   Eight times the autumn weather.
I can be more solitary.
In a Province.
Sky brims with the ghost of a great rage, The.
Ralegh.   11th: and Last Booke of the Ocean to
   Scinthia, The.
Songe Made by Sir Walter Rawley, A.
Ransom.   Agitato Ma Non Troppo ("I have a
   grief").
Agitato Ma Non Troppo ("This is what the
   man said").
Of Margaret ("Frost, and a leaf has quit the

tulip tree").
Of Margaret ("With the fall of the first leaf that winds rend").
"Reed." Home of the Brave.
Rich. Mourning Picture.
Valediction Forbidding Mourning, A.
Robinson. Book of Annandale, The.
Dust of Timas, The.
Reuben Bright.
Where does a dead man go?—The dead man dies.
Rolfe. Essay on Dreiser (1871-1945).
May 22nd 1939.
Rossetti. Death's Chill Between.
Song: "When I am dead, my dearest."
Rukeyser. Long Past Moncada.
One Month.
Scott. Allan-Bane's Lament.
Death of Argentine, The.
Hymn for the Dead.
Jock of Hazeldean.
Sexton. Curse against Elegies, A.
Smith, Charlotte. By the Same. Just before His Death.
Smith, Stevie. Arabella.
Spenser. Mourning Muse of Thestylis, The.
Teares of the Muses, The.
Stuart. Funeral, The.
Widow, The.
Sutter. Friends find the family.
This woman is nobody's woman.
Warming up in their truck.
Swift. Here shift the scene, to represent.
Tennyson. Dark house, by which once more I stand.
Thomas. In the White Giant's Thigh.
Thomson. Epitaph on Miss Stanley.
On the Death of his Mother.
On the Death of Mr. Aikman.
Pastoral Between Thirsis and Corydon, upon the Death of Damon, A.
Poem to the Memory of Mr. Congreve, A.
Poem to the Memory of the Righ Honourable the Lord Talbot, A.
Tomlinson. Ars Poetica.
Van Duyn. Creation, The.
Stream, The.
Walker. Natural Star.
Whitman. Hush'd be the Camps To-day.
Sobbing of the Bells, The.
When Lilacs Last in the Dooryard Bloom'd.
Whittier. Lament, A: "Circle is broken, one seat is forsaken, The."
Lines on the Death of S. Oliver Torrey.
Wilbur. Funeral of Bobò, The.
To an American Poet Just Dead.
Williams, Charles Kenneth. Le Petit Salvié.
Vehicle: Absence.
Villanelle of the Suicide's Mother.
Wordsworth. Dirge Sung by a Minstrel.
Elegiac Stanzas (Addressed to Sir G.H.B. upon the Death of His Sister-in-Law).
Elegy Written in the Same Place upon the Same Occasion.
Epitaph in the Chapel Yard of Langdale, Westmoreland.
Not without heavy grief of heart did He.
On the Death of an Unfortunate Lady.
Sonnet Written by Mr — Immediately after the Death of His Wife.
Surprised by Joy [Impatient as the Wind].
Weep not, belovèd Friends! nor let the air.
Wright, James. Angel, The.
At the Slackening of the Tide.
Centenary Note: Inscribed to Little Crow, Leader of the Sioux Rebellion in Minnesota, 1862, A.
Gesture by a Lady with an Assumed Name, A.
Girl Walking into a Shadow, A.
Listening to the Mourners.
Paul.
Poem about George Doty in the Death House, A.
Refusal, The.
Winter Day in Ohio, A.
Wyatt. Mourning my heart doth sore oppress.

Yeats. Crazy Jane Reproved.
John Kinsella's Lament for Mrs. Mary Moore.
See also **Funerals; Grief.**

Mouths
Catullus. Carmen 98: "Same can be said of you, Victius, The."
Creeley. Language, The.
Mouths Nuzz.
Cummings. Liz.
Ferlinghetti. Mouth of truth, The.
Hartley. Same Fragment—Second Look.
Stuart. Spring Song.
Waldman. Poeme en Forme de la Bouche.
Zukofsky. Do not leave me.
In the, same in (when qualm?) thick wee poetry, putrid Victi.

Movies. see **Motion Pictures.**

Moving and Movers
Berryman. Narcissus Moving.
Dickey, William. New Place, The.
Dobyns. Rootless.
Fenton. At the foot of every steep cliff or precipice in high Alpine regions.
Gunn. Last Days at Teddington.
Thoughts on Unpacking.
Haines. Flight, The.
It Must All Be Done Over.
Years ago my father read to me.
Hughes, Langston. Movies.
Hugo. Houses.
Jarrell. Moving.
Jong. Autumn Perspective.
House-Hunting in the Bicentennial Year.
Koertge. Moving Day.
Levine. I reenter a day in a late summer.
Lorde. Moving Out Or the End of Cooperative Living.
Lowry. Welcome Home, Oh Our Sweetest Harteebeeste Beloved.
Matthews. Change of Address.
Housecooling.
Moving.
Merrill. Mornings in a New House.
Nemerov. Going Away.
Rich. Moving in Winter.
Passing On.
Schuyler. Sorting, Wrapping, Packing, Stuffing.
Simic. Rosalia and her mother moved away.
Sorrentino. Ave atque Vale.
There is no instance that was not love.
Sutter. Little Litany for Moving Day, A.
Turco. Daughter Moves Out, A.
Updike. Note to the Previous Tenants.
Yau. After Moving.

Mowing and Mowers
Dickey, James. Poem: "For having left the birds that left me."
Frost. Last Mowing, The.
Mowing.
Tuft of Flowers, The.
Hewitt. Swathe Uncut, The.
Lawrence. Mowers, The.
Youth Mowing, A.
Marvell. Damon the Mower.
Mower against Gardens, The.
Mower's Song, The.
Muldoon. Coney, The.

Mozambique
"Dylan." Mozambique.

Mozart, Wolfgang Amadeus
Auden. Metalogue to The Magic Flute.
Hartley. Concert.
MacLeish. Men of My Century Loved Mozart.
Markson. Nachtmusik.
Meredith. I humm'd an air of sweet Mozart.
Pack. Clayfeld's Infancy.
Looking at a Mountain Range While Listening to a Mozart Piano Concerto.
Stevens. Mozart, 1935.
Zukofsky. Record, The.

Mud
Creeley. House, The.
Heaney. Mud Vision, The.
Hewitt. Neglected Lane, The.
Stevens. Mud Master.

Stuart. Spring Song.
Williams, William Carlos. K. McB.

Muffs
Lovelace. Her Muffe.
See also **Gloves; Mittens.**

Muhammad
Coleridge. Mahomet.
Lowell. Like Henry VIII, Mohammed got religion.
Whittier. Requital.

Mulberry Trees
Plath. Moonrise.
Smith, Charlotte. To the Mulberry-Tree.

Mules
Hughes, Langston. Me and the Mule.
Lawrence. Ass, The.
Muldoon. Mules.
Nash. Mules, The.
Patchen. Mule of water, The.
Sandburg. New Farm Tractor.

Mummies
Eberhart. On Seeing an Egyptian Mummy in Berlin, 1932.
Gardner. In the Museum.
Heaney. Punishment.
Tollund Man, The.
Kunitz. Three thousand years ago.
Merton. Mummies.
Sandburg. Mummy.
Yau. Postcards are fragments of an encyclopedia; and typical of one an- / nouncing.

Munch, Edvard
Hall. "Between the Clock and the Bed."
"Kiss, The."
"Marat's Death."
"Scream, The."
Mahon. Girls on the Bridge.

Murder and Murderers
Atwood. Robber Bridegroom, The.
Auden. Hans-in-Kelder, Hans-in-Kelder.
Victor.
Beatles. Maxwell's Silver Hammer.
Berry. Morning's News, The.
Bishop. Brazilian Tragedy.
Whom are you carrying.
Blake. Fair Elenor.
Brontë. Death Of A.G.A., The.
Browning, Robert. Forgiveness, A.
Laboratory, The [Ancien Régime].
Porphyria's Lover.
Byron. Marino Faliero, Doge of Venice.
Carew. Another [On the Duke of Buckingham].
On the Duke of Buckingham.
Song: Murdering Beauty.
Carroll, Jim. Here, every lost act.
Chaucer. Prioress's Tale, The.
Coleridge. Alice Du Clos.
Mad Monk, The.
Crashaw. To Pontius Washing His Blood-Stained Hands.
Cummings. So you're hunting for ann well i'm looking for will.
De la Mare. Banquo.
Heresy.
Macbeth.
Dickey, William. Part Song, With Concert of Recorders.
Dobyns. Night Swimmer.
Under the Green Ceiling.
Dunbar. Murdered Lover, The.
Dunn. Having Lost All Capacity.
"Dylan." Ballad of Hollis Brown.
Joey.
Lily, Rosemary, and the Jack of Hearts.
Lonesome Death of Hattie Carroll, The.
Eberhart. Am I My Neighbor's Keeper.
Snowy Owl.
Villanelle: "Christ is walking in your blood today."
Glück. Murderess, The.
Graves. Coronation Murder, The.
Dangerous Gift, The.
Nobody.
Strangling in Merrion Square, The.

Griffiths. Murder.
Gunn. Victim, The.
Hardy. Fight on Durnover Moor, The.
Flirt's Tragedy, The.
Forbidden Banns, The.
Her Second Husband Hears Her Story.
Mock Wife, The.
Single Witness, The.
Sound in the Night, A.
Hemingway. To Will Davies.
Herrick. Upon Faunus.
Upon Leech.
Hewitt. At the Newsagent's.
Case of Mistaken Identity, A.
Housman. Farewell to barn and stack and tree.
True Lover, The.
Hugo. Cattails.
With Ripley at the Grave of Albert Parenteau.
Jarrell. Eighth Air Force.
La Belle au Bois Dormant.
Jeffers. Give Your Heart to the Hawks.
Inhumanist, The.
Margrave.
Solstice.
Such Counsels You Gave to Me.
Joseph. Untitled.
Kipling. Ballad of Fisher's Boardinghouse, The.
Cain and Abel.
Cleared.
What Happened.
Knott. Brighton Rock by Graham Greene.
Two Vietnam Poems: (1966).
Koertge. Gretel.
Kunitz. Extermination Camp, The.
Lawrence. Late War, The.
Murder.
Murderous Weapons.
Lorde. Need: A Chorale for Black Woman Voices.
Lowell. Mary Stuart.
Lowry. I have known a city of dreadful night.
Illegal Heart, The.
R. Usher.
Meredith. Josepha.
Merton. Chant to Be Used in Processions around a Site with Furnaces.
Morgan. I cornered the thief in the garage at dusk.
Murder, The.
Morrison. Hitchhiker, The.
Mystery of the Dream.
Stand There Listening.
Nash. Strange Case of the Dead Divorcee, The.
Warning to Wives, A.
Nathan. I write you out of fear.
Nemerov. August, 1945.
Murder of William Remington, The.
Place of Value, The.
Neruda. Danger, The.
Wars, The.
Olson. Poemless Rhymes for the Times.
Pack. Ghost Story.
Patchen. From my high love I look at that poor world there.
If We Are to Know Where We Live.
Murder of Two Men by a Young Kid Wearing Lemon-colored Gloves, The.
Polly—An Almost-True Story.
Poe. Scenes from Politian.
Rolfe. Mystery.
St. John. Hotel of Ash.
Ostia.
Sexton. Assassin, The.
Killing the Love.
Shelton. He is ill.
Widow has burned her book, The.
Wife sits all afternoon, The.
Sidney. Sonnet 20: "Fly, fly, my friends, I have my death-wound, fly."
Smith, Patti. K.O.D.A.K.
Smith, Stevie. Bag-Snatching in Dublin.
But Murderous.
From My Notes for a Series of Lectures on Murder.
Murderer, The.

One of Many.
Who Killed Lawless Lean?
Snodgrass. Magda Goebbels ("This is the needle that we give").
Stafford. Once a man killed another, to rob him.
Swinburne. Phaedra.
Thomas. Ballad of the Long-legged Bait.
Walker. Family Of.
Killers.
1971.
Revolutionary Petunias.
Warren. Ballad of Billie Potts, The.
Crime.
Whittier. Burial of Barber.
Williams, Miller. Everything Is Fine Here How Are You.
Wordsworth. Voice from the Side of Etna, The; or, the Mad Monk.
Wright, James. At the Executed Murderer's Grave.
Life, The.
Poem about George Doty in the Death House, A.
Secret Gratitude, A.

Murfreesboro, Battle of (1862–1863)
Tate. Battle of Murfreesboro.

Muses
Beckett. Lady Love.
Berryman. I am interested alone in making ready.
Images of Elspeth.
Blake. To the Muses.
Bradstreet. Upon the Author. By a Known Friend.
Burns. Duan Second.
To Robt. Graham of Fintry Esqr, with a Request for an Excise Division.
Byron. Farewell to the Muse.
Catullus. Carmen 105: "O'Toole / attempting an entry of the *mons Parnassus.*"
Ciardi. Apology for Not Invoking the Muse, An.
Clough. If help there is not, but the Muse.
Cohen. I Bury My Girlfriend.
Cowper. Elegy 6: To Charles Deodati.
In a Letter to C.P.
Crashaw. To the Morning. Satisfaction for Sleepe.
Creeley. Door, The.
Cullen. After a Visit.
De la Mare. Child Asleep, A.
Donne. To Mr. R. W. ("Zealously my Muse doth salute all thee").
Doolittle. Thetis.
Duncan. Festivals, The.
For a Muse Meant.
Emerson. 'ΑΔΑΚΡΥΝ ΝΕΜΟΝΤΑΙ ΑΙΩΝΑ.
Best of life is presence of a muse, The.
For deathless powers to verse belong.
From Nature's beginning.
Honor bright o muse.
House, The.
I spread my gorgeous sail.
James Russell Lowell.
Loss and Gain.
Muse / Can at pleasure use, The.
Saadi held the Muse in awe.
Shall the Muse sing for thousands & not sing.
Solution.
Test, The.
Glück. Poem: "In the early evening, as now, a man is bending."
Graves. At the Gate.
Beware, Madam!
Darien.
Her Beauty.
Gray. Ode on the Pleasure Arising from Vicissitude.
Progress of Poesy, The.
Hardy. Rome: The Vatican: Sala delle Muse.
Hartnett. Falling Out, A.
Herrick. Departure of the Good Daemon, The.
His Winding-Sheet.
Hymne to the Muses, A ("O! You the Virgins nine!").
Mount of the Muses, The.

On Himselfe ("Work is done: young men, and maidens set, The").
Pride Allowable in Poets.
To His Muse.
To His Muse, Another to the Same.
To His Muse: ("Were I to give thee *Baptime,* I wo'd chuse").
To the High and Noble Prince, George, Duke, Marquesse, and Earle of Buckingham.
Hoffman. Essay on Style.
Holmes. Muse Wooing: A Song.
Johnson. Aurora Est Musis Amica.
Jong. Muse Who Came to Stay, The.
Summoning the Muse to a New House.
Jonson. And Must I Sing? What Subject Shall I Choose?
Elegy [*or* Elegie], An: "Let me be what I am, as Virgil cold."
Epistle. To My Lady Covell.
To Benjamin Rudyerd.
To My Muse.
Keats. Ode to Apollo.
Sonnet: "Where didst thou find, young Bard, thy sounding lyre?"
To George Felton Mathew.
Levertov. Illustration [—a Footnote], The.
To the Muse.
Well, The.
Liddy. Swinburne on the Playing Fields.
Lovelace. Clitophon and Lucippe.
Dedication To the Right Honorable John Lovelace. The.
On Sanazar's Being Honoured.
MacNeice. Canto VIII: "Fair; not to say radiant. The Twentyfifth of September."
Gull hundreds of miles below him, The.
Marlowe. 1.1: Quemadmodum a Cupidine pro bellis amoris scribere coactus sit.
3.1: Deliberatio poetae, utrum elegos pergat scribere an potius tragedias.
Meredith. Two Masks, The.
Milton. Elegy 6: To Charles Deodati.
Nemerov. Mythological Beast.
O'Hara. Muse Considered As a Demon Lover, The.
Olson. Atalanta.
La Chute II.
Muse / is the "fate" of the poem, The.
Prince. Tears of a Muse in America, The.
St. John. Mercenary Muse.
Shakespeare. Sonnet 38: "How can my muse want subject to invent."
Sonnet 78: "So oft I invoked thee for my Muse."
Sonnet 79: "Whilst I alone did call upon thy aid."
Sonnet 100: "Where art thou, Muse, that thou forget'st so long."
Sonnet 101: "O truant Muse, what shall be thy amends."
Sidney. I: "Loving in truth, and fain[e] in verse my love to show."
My Muse what ails this ardour.
Sonnet 3: "Let dainty wits cry on the sisters nine."
Sonnet 6: "Some lovers speak, when they their Muses entertain."
Sonnet 55: "Muses, I oft invoked your holy aid."
Sonnet 70: "My Muse may well grudge at my heav'nly joy."
Smith, Charlotte. Partial Muse, has from my earliest hours, The.
To Mr. Hayley, on Receiving Some Elegant Lines from Him.
Smith, Patti. Notice 2.
Smith, Stevie. Dear Muse.
My Muse.
Who Is This Who Howls and Mutters?
Spenser. Teares of the Muses, The.
Within this wood, out of a rocke did rise.
Stevenson. Not roses to the rose, I trow.
Pleasant river gushes, The.
Still I love to rhyme, and still more, rhyming, to wander.
Tales of Arabia.
Their Laureate to an Academy Class Dinner

Club.
To the Muse.
Swift. To Mr. Congreve.
Tennyson. Parnassus.
Thomson. Lines on Marlefield.
Ode on Æolus's Harp, An.
Poetical Epistle to Sir William Bennet, Bart. of Grubbat.
Tomlinson. Poem: It falls onto my page like rain.
Walcott. Camps hold [or held] their distance— [of] brown chestnuts and grey smoke, The.
Upstate.
Whitman. Muse in the New World, The.
Wilbur. Advice from the Muse.
Williams, Miller. Muse, The.
Wordsworth. Her Only Pilot the Soft Breeze, the Boat.
Not Love, not War, nor the Tumultuous Swell.
On Seeing a Needlecase in the Form of a Harp; the Work of E.M.S.
To Melpomene.
Wright, James. To the Muse.
Wroth. Sonnet 9: "My muse now hapy, lay thy self to rest."
Yeats. Those Images.
Zukofsky. *Barely* and *widely*.
Meantool reconnoiters Pipléa scanning Their mountain.

Museums
Atwood. Children like the block, The.
Auden. Our Bias.
Dickey, William. Afternoon Evening and Night in the Courtyard of the Museum of Modern Art.
Fenton. Pitt-Rivers Museum, Oxford, The.
Fox. Miss Pimberton Of.
Galvin. With Anne at the Peabody.
Gardner. In the Museum.
Gunn. Expression.
Hardy. Haunting Fingers.
In a Museum.
Hewitt. Diptera.
From a Museum Man's Album.
Hugo. Galileo's Chair.
Museum of Cruel Days.
Pishkun.
Jarrell. In Galleries.
Jong. At the Museum of Natural History.
Kunitz. Cold-eyed, in Naples once.
In the Great Hall of the Library.
MacNeice. Canto XXIV: "December the Twenty-third: I visit the Ancient East."
Museums.
National Gallery, The.
Time for a Smoke.
Meinke. Talk of the Paintings.
Prince. Painter's face—if, The.
Rich. Love in the Museum.
Sandburg. Dinosaur Bones, The.
Schuyler. Back.
Updike. Roman Portrait Busts.
Room 28.
Wilbur. Museum Piece.
Yau. Bare Sheets III.
I do not imagine anyone I know, including myself, would like to.
Yeats. Municipal Gallery Revisited, The.
See also **Listings for specific Museums.**

Mushrooms
Atwood. Mushrooms.
Auden. To a Toadstool.
Dickey, William. Virginia Woolf Gathers Mushrooms.
Dickinson. Mushroom is the Elf of Plants, The.
Eberhart. Mistaken Identity.
Muldoon. Gathering Mushrooms.
Oliver. Mushrooms.
Plath. Mushrooms.
Rossetti. Toadstool comes up in a night, A.
Sutter. Stalking the Wild Mushroom.
Tomlinson. Mushrooms.

Music and Musicians
Ashbery. Syringa.
Auden. Composer, The.

J.S. Bach.
Metalogue to The Magic Flute.
Music Is International.
Beatles. Sgt. Pepper's Lonely Hearts Club Band.
Sgt. Pepper's Lonely Hearts Club Band (Reprise).
Beckett. Dortmunder.
Berrigan. His piercing pince-nez. Some dim frieze.
Musick strides through these poems.
Berry. Mad Farmer in the City, The.
Music, A.
Stones, The.
Berryman. How shall I sing, western & dry & thin.
Once when they found me, some refrain "*Quoi faire?*."
Sigh as it ends . I keep an eye on your.
What can to you this music wakes my years.
Bishop. Sonnet: "I am in need of music that would flow."
View of the Capitol from the Library of Congress.
Blake. Piping Down the Valleys Wild.
Bly. Listening to the Köln Concert.
Bogan. Musician.
Song for a Slight Voice.
Sub Contra.
Brontë. Come hither, child—who gifted thee.
Brooks. Piano after War.
Browning, Elizabeth Barrett. Heaven and Earth.
Island, An.
Musical Instrument, A.
Browning, Robert. Abt Vogler.
Flute-Music, with an Accompaniment.
Master Hugues of Saxe-Gotha.
Toccata of Galuppi's, A.
Transcendentalism: A Poem in Twelve Books.
What a pretty tale you told me.
Bukowski. Bee's 5th.
Sweet Music.
Trench Warfare.
Bunting. Coryphée gravefooted precise, dance to the gracious music.
What a pity that Bela Bartok.
Burns. Amang the trees, where humming bees.
Byron. My Soul Is Dark.
Campion. Ad Io. Dolundum.
As by the streames of *Babilon.*
Dialogue Sung the First Night, A.
Follow Your Saint [Follow with Accents Sweet].
Night as well as brightest day hath her delight.
Of this Ensuing Discourse.
Peacefull westerne winde the wintrye stormes hath calmde, The.
Rose-cheeked Laura[, Come].
Song, The: "Wooe her, and win her, he that can."
Time, that leads the fatall round.
To. Campiani Epigramma de Instituto Authoris.
To his sweet Lute *Apollo* sung the motions of the Spheares.
To Music Bent Is My Retired Mind.
To the Right Noble and Vertuous Theophilus Howard, Lorde of Walden, Sonne and Heire to the Right Honorable the Earle of Suffolke.
To the Worthy Author.
Carew. Celia Singig ("You that think Love can convey").
Carroll, Jim. Fragment: Little N.Y. Ode.
It Doesn't Matter.
Music Television.
When he was young in Harlem my father.
Carruth. Æolian.
Backyard in California, A.
Cowshed Blues, The.
Expatiation on the Combining of Weathers at Thirty-Seventh and Indiana Where the Southern More or Less Crosses the Dog, An.
Freedom and Discipline.
Gray dawn seeping through stone.
He: Life is an old / casino in the park. I.
High above themselves. Above everything,

flux, ooze.
Homage to John Lyly and Frankie Newton.
How To.
Letter to Maxine Sullivan.
Listen.
Living Alone.
Paragraphs.
Sonnet: "But still, still... / In stillness mystery calls."
Tanck's Song About Earl Hines.
What a Wonder Among the Instruments Is the Walloping Tramboone!
Who Cares, Long as It's B-Flat.
Ciardi. Prayer to the Mountain, A.
Clark. On Marine Silence Street.
Cohen. Change, The.
Commentary—The Change.
Different Drum, A.
I Heard My Soul Singing.
Singer Must Die, A.
Coleridge. Ode on the Ottery and Tiverton Church Music.
To the Rev. W. J. Hort.
Tribute to Wordsworth.
Cowper. By Moschus.
Strada's Nightingale.
Crane. Black Tambourine.
Carmen de Boheme.
Crashaw. Music[k]'s Duel[l].
Upon the Death of a Freind.
Creeley. Canzone: "As would any sound make."
Greendoon's Song.
Los Guitaristas.
They.
Water Music.
Cullen. Singing in the Rain.
Cummings. Music.
Nocturne: "When the lithe moonlight silently."
Of evident invisibles / exquisite the hovering.
Oil tel duh woil doi sez.
Davie. Garland for Ivor Gurney, A.
Heart Beats.
De la Mare. Bells, The.
Clavichord.
Faint Music.
Music ("O restless").
Music ("When music").
Music Unheard.
Rose.
Sallie's Musical Box.
Dickey, James. From Time.
Dickey, William. Die Älte Frau, Die Älte Marschallin.
Dickinson. Better—than Music! For I—who heard it.
Dying at my music!
Fascinating chill that music leaves, The.
I've heard an Organ talk, sometimes.
Put up my lute!
Your relentless Music.
Doolittle. Flute Song.
So if you love me.
Dove. Definition in the Face of Unnamed Fury.
Event, The.
Jiving.
Left-Handed Cellist, The.
Robert Schumann, Or: Musical Genius Begins with Affliction.
Shakespeare Say.
Variation on Pain.
Dryden. Alexander's Feast; or, The Power of Music [or Musique].
Song for St Cecilia's Day [1687], A.
Dunbar. Concert, The.
Corn-Stalk Fiddle, THe.
Master-Player, The.
Musical, A.
Ol' Tunes, The.
Question, A.
Thou Art My Lute.
To a Lady Playing the Harp.
Valse, The.
Virginia Reel, A.
Voice of the Banjo, The.
When Malindy Sings.

Duncan. Architecture, The.
Bending the Bow.
Concert, The.
Reaper, The.
What of the structure of Rime? I said.
"Dylan." Al's wife claimed I can't be happy.
Eternal Circle.
John Wesley Harding (Liner Notes).
Lay Down Your Weary Tune.
So at last at least.
Song to Woody.
Talking New York.
Eberhart. Four Exposures.
Ives.
Kinaesthesia.
Rifkin Movement.
River Water Music.
Emerson. By art, by music, overthrilled.
From a far mountain creeping down.
I spread my gorgeous sail.
O what are heroes prophets men.
Saadi.
Thy trivial harp will never please.
Ferlinghetti. Moscow in the Wilderness,
Segovia in the Snow.
San Jose Symphony Reception.
Thoughts to a Concerto of Telemann.
Fisher. Chirico.
Home Pianist's Companion, The.
Thing About Joe Sullivan, The.
Fletcher. Joy.
Ford. And music is still a mystery!
Gildner. Page Turner, The.
Ginsberg. Portland Coliseum.
Graves. Double Bass.
Grace Notes.
Gray. Ode for Music.
Stanzas to Mr Richard Bentley.
Gunn. Before the Carnival.
Elvis Presley.
Listening to Jefferson Airplane.
Monterey.
Outdoor Concert, The.
Victim, The.
Hardy. Chapel-Organist, The.
Fiddler, The.
Haunting Fingers.
Music in a Snowy Street.
Musical Incident, A.
Selfsame Song, The.
Hartley. Concert.
Heifetz—On the Air, Bell Telephone Program.
Horowitz.
Musicologist—Preference, Prokofieff.
Herbert. Church-Music[k].
Herrick. Beucolick, or Discourse of Neatherds,
A.
Canticle to Apollo, A.
Soft Musick.
To Apollo ("Thou mighty lord and master of
the Lyre").
To his Worthy Friend M. John Hall, Student
of Grayes-Inne.
To M. Henry Lawes, the Excellent
Composer[,] of his Lyrics.
To Music.
To Music: A Song.
To Music, to Becalm a Sweet-sick Youth.
To Music, to Becalm His Fever.
Upon M. William Lawes, the Rare Musitian.
Upon Sapho, Sweetly Playing, and Sweetly
Singing.
Voice and Violl, The.
Hesketh. Changing Colour.
Hewitt. Bandstand.
Et Tu In Arcadia Vixisti.
Grandfather Robinson Dies in 1898.
Magician, The.
Music Lessons.
Hill. Music survives, composing her own
sphere.
Hoffman. Sounds, The.
Hopkins. When eyes that cast about the
heights of heaven.
Hughes, Langston. Boogie: 1 A.M.
Daybreak in Alabama.
Easy Boogie.

Juke Box Love Song.
Trumpet Player.
Hughes, Ted. Cadenza.
Hugo. From the Rain Forest Down.
Jeffers. Natural Music.
Translations from the *Medea* of Euripedes
("Err shall they not, who resolute explore").
Translations from the *Medea* of Euripedes
("The rites deriv'd from ancient days").
Johnson. Epitaph on Claudy Phillips, a
Musician, An.
To Miss —: On Her Playing upon the
Harpsichord.
To Miss Hickman Playing on the Spinet.
Translations from the *Medea* of Euripedes
("Err shall they not, who resolute explore").
Translations from the *Medea* of Euripedes
("The rites deriv'd from ancient days").
Jonson. Hum drum, sauce for a cony.
Keats. Of Late Two Dainties Were before Me
Placed.
Kipling. In the Neolithic Age.
Song of the Banjo, The.
Koch. Hearing.
Larkin. Two Guitar Pieces.
Lawrence. Listen to the Band!
Piano.
Red.
Levertov. Music, A.
Lewis. Night bibles India in her wilderness.
Liddy. Correspondences.
Unlike the moon.
Lieberman. Tartine, Strumming Her Opera.
Lindsay. Master of the Dance, The.
Longfellow. Occultation of Orion, The.
Lovelace. To a Lady That Desired Me I
Would Bear My Part with Her in a Song.
To Lucasta ("I laugh and sing, but cannot
tell").
Lowry. Born ailing on a hemisphere apart.
Here him play / That sinister melody.
Playing alone / Drunk and bored.
Port Moody.
Stoker Tom's Ukulele.
That's What I Mean.
McAuley. Allegro Moderato.
Allegro Vivace.
Scherzo.
Under the humming *continuo.*
Violas are moaning, a harpsichord chiming.
"MacDiarmid." Back to the great music,
Scottish Gaels. Too long.
Bagpipe Music.
Come, follow me into the realms of music.
Here is the gate.
McGrath. Guiffre's Nightmusic.
MacLeish. And he had used love's dream of
love before.
Beside her in the dark the chime.
Here, O wanderer, here is the hill and the
harbor.
Music and Drum.
Pablo Casals.
MacNeice. Bagpipe Music.
Mahon. Rock Music.
Markson. Strange Night.
Marvell. Music's Empire.
Matthews. Accompanist, The.
Bud Powell, Paris, 1959.
Meinke. Café Vue des Alpes.
Minuet in G.
Meredith. Flower of the Ruins, The.
I humm'd an air of sweet Mozart.
Let us sing of our beloved, let us sing of that
which is sweetest.
Phoebus with Admetus.
Song: "Might I lie where leans her lute."
To an Old Gipsy.
Merrill. Victor Dog, The.
Merton. AWFULMUSICAW.
Breath of Nature, The.
Solemn Music.
Millay. Concert, The.
On Hearing a Symphony of Beethoven.
Miller. Mixed Signals.
Milton. At a Solemn Music[k].
Moore. Melchior Vulpius.

Morgan. Music.
Morrison. Augment of Re-Birth.
I Want to Tell You.
Now Listen to This.
Paris Journal.
Translations of the Divine.
Muldoon. Ben.
Nash. Good Night, Sweet Mind.
Nathan. Wisdom of the Talmud.
Nemerov. Chromium-Plated Hat. Inlaid with
Scenes from Siegfried, A.
Four Ages, The.
Lines & Circularities.
Playing the Inventions.
Sarabande.
Notley. Desert for All of Music to Take Place.
O'Hara. Fantasy.
Radio.
Romanze, or the Music Students.
Oliver. Robert Schumann.
Olson. Her Dream, Half Remembered.
Igor Stravinsky.
2nd Musical Form, for Dave Young, A.
Oppen. Moving over the hills, crossing the
irrigation.
Pack. Beating Time.
Quasars.
Patchen. Geography of Music.
Poe. Israfel.
Pope. Ode for Music on St. Cecilia's Day.
Of a Lady Singing to Her Lute.
Pastorals.
Prince. Thyme, tufa, sage, anemone.
Raine. House of Music, A.
"Reed." Rock 'N' Roll.
Rich. At a Bach Concert.
Ninth Symphony of Beethoven Understood at
Last as a Sexual Message, The.
Recorders in Italy.
Solfeggietto.
Transcendental Etude.
Robinson. L'Envoi.
Rolfe. Nuthin but Brass.
To My Contemporaries.
Rukeyser. Asleep and Awake.
Bunk Johnson Blowing.
Certain Music, A.
Iris-Eaters, The.
Ives.
Night-Music.
Orpheus.
Spirals and Fugues.
Sandburg. Bath.
Clefs.
Clinton South of Polk.
Consolation Sonata.
Jan Kubelik.
Jazz Fantasia.
Old Music for Quiet Hearts.
To Know Silence Perfectly.
Sarton. Clavichord, The.
Evening Music.
Girl with 'Cello.
Song: "Now let us honor with violin and
flute."
Schuyler. Beautiful Funerals.
Fauré's Second Piano Quartet.
Grand Duo.
Greetings from the Chateau.
Let's All Hear It for Mildred Bailey!
Man in Blue, A.
Mood Indigo.
Rachmaninoff's Third.
Schwartz. Words for a Trumpet Chorale
Celebrating the Autumn.
Sexton. Music Swims Back to Me.
To Lose the Earth.
Wonderful Musician, The.
Shakespeare. If music and sweet poetry agree.
Sonnet 8: "Music[k] to hear[e], why hear'st
thou music[k]."
Sonnet 128: "How oft, when thou, my music,
music play'st."
Shelley. Another Fragment to Music.
Fragment: Music and Sweet Poetry.
Fragment: To Music, A.

Hymn of Pan.
Music.
Sidney. Sixth Song.
Silverstein. Dancing Pants.
Ourchestra.
Smart. For the spiritual musick is as follows.
Smith, Patti. Babelfield.
Death by Water.
Dog Dream.
High on Rebellion.
Land.
Smith, Stevie. Virtuoso, The.
Snodgrass. Regraduating the Lute.
Spender. Beethoven's Death Mask.
Late Stravinsky Listening to Late Beethoven.
Stevens. Anglais Mort à Florence.
Arrival at the Waldorf.
Peter Quince at the Clavier.
Sad Strains of a Gay Waltz.
Thunder by the Musician.
To the One of Fictive Music.
Stevenson. Land of Nod, The.
Music at the Villa Marina.
Piper, The.
Tall as a guardsman, pale as the east at dawn.
To W.E. Henley.
Stuart. Fence.
Harpist's Dream, The.
Turntables.
Thomas. Was There a Time.
Tomlinson. Chaconne for Unaccompanied
  Violin.
Consolations for Double Bass.
Da Capo.
Flute Music.
Little Night Music, A.
Melody.
Music's Trinity.
Ode to Arnold Schoenberg.
Programme Note.
Spring Symphony, The.
Words for the Madrigalist.
Turco. Dedication, A: "If it is true that."
Updike. Recital.
Vow.
Wakoski. On the Subject of Roses.
Story of Richard Maxfield, The.
Thanking My Mother for Piano Lessons.
Western Music.
Walcott. Piano Practice.
Walker. Hymn: "I well remember / A time
  when."
Whitman. Italian Music in Dakota.
Mystic Trumpeter, The.
Proud Music of the Storm.
Wilbur. C Minor.
L'Etoile.
Williams, Charles Kenneth. First Desires.
Junior High School Concert: Salle Rossini.
Prodigy, The.
Williams, Miller. Schumann Adds Trombones
  to His Second Symphony After Mendelssohn
  Conducts the First Performance.
Williams, William Carlos. Ballad: "To a man
  and his wife."
Note to Music: Brahms 1st Piano Concerto.
Ol' Bunk's Band.
Orchestra, The.
Shoot It Jimmy!
Tapiola.
Two Deliberate Exercises.
Wordsworth. I Heard (Alas! 'Twas Only in a
  Dream).
Lyre! Though Such Power Do in Thy Magic
  Live.
On the Power of Sound.
Power of Music.
Why, Minstrel, These Untuneful Murmurings.
Wright, James. Poem for Kathleen Ferrier.
Yau. All This Changing Trouble Luck and
  Suddenness.
Yeats. Crazed Girl, A.
Fiddler of Dooney, The.
Madness of King Goll, The.
Spirit Medium, The.
Young. Billie.
By Heart.

Dexter Gordon at Keystone Korner.
From Bowling Green.
Jackie McLean: Alto Saxophone.
Jazz as Was.
Lester Leaps In.
Little More Traveling Music, A.
Moss.
No Trespassing.
Poem for Dylan Thomas, A.
Selectric II.
Thelonious: An Intro.
Tune.
Zimmer. Duke Ellington Dream, The.
Zimmer's Last Gig.
Zukofsky. Atque in Perpetuum A.W.
Non Ti Fidar.
Old Poet Moves to a New Aprtment 14
  Times, The.
One lutenist played *look*; your through was
  drink.
Record, The.
Specifically, a writer of music.
Spook's Sabbath, Five Bowings.
This is after all vacation. All that.
Two Dedications: Tibor Serly.
Wish, A.
You who were made for this music.
See also **Blues (music)**; **Gospel Music.**

Music Festivals
Auden. Metalogue to The Magic Flute.
Beatles. While My Guitar Gently Weeps.
Hoffman. High Society.
Stevenson. Flower god, god of the spring,
  beautiful, bountiful.

Music Halls
Levine. At the Fillmore.
McAuley. Arched corridors. Bare white walls.
Raine. Who listens, when in the concert-hall.
Rukeyser. Paper Anniversary.

Music Lessons
Dobyns. Guitar Lesson, The.
Stevenson. Early in the morning I hear on
  your piano.

Musk Oxen
Hall. Long River, The.
Moore. Arctic Ox (or Goat), The.

Muslims
Campion. To the World.
Coleridge. Mahomet.
Merton. East with Ibn Battuta.
Moslems' Angel of Death, The.
Night of Destiny, The.
Readings from Ibn Abbad.
Whittier. Palm-Tree, The.

Mussels
Oliver. Mussels.
Plath. Mussel Hunter at Rock Harbor.

Mutability
Wyatt. Each man me telleth I change most my
  device [*or* devise].

Mutiny
Hewitt. Torcello.

Mystery
Auden. Hidden Lane, The.
Stone Walls.
Berrigan. Harum-scarum haze on the Pollock
  streets / Where Snow White sleeps among
  the silent dwarfs.
Berry. To the Unseeable Animal.
Brooks. God Works in a Mysterious Way.
Carruth. Out of the garden.
She lay like a book.
To Artemis.
Cohen. Veil, A.
Cullen. Yet Do I Marvel.
Cummings. Kind) / YM&WC / (of sort of).
Now that,more nearest even than your fate.
Should far this from mankind's unmysteries.
Silently if,out of not knowable.
Davie. I come in out of Space, and with a
  rake.
De la Mare. Interlude, An.
Snowdrop, The.
Dickey, William. Rainbow Grocery, The.
Dickinson. Mysteries of human nature, The.

Promise is firmer than a Hope, A.
Some things that fly there be.
Doolittle. Mysteries, The.
Duncan. Maiden, The.
Dunn. In the 20th Century.
Not the Occult.
Eberhart. Going.
Height of Man, The.
Humanist, The.
Mystery of the Abstract.
Only in the Dream.
Sanders Theater.
Wisdom of Insecurity, The.
Emerson. Ah strange strange strange.
But never yet the man was found.
Flute, The.
Know he who tills this lonely field.
Ferlinghetti. Hidden Door.
Graves. Women and Masks.
Hardy. No Bell-Ringing.
Third Kissing-Gate, The.
Hewitt. Hallowe'e: A Glensman Speaks.
Mass.
Our Avenue.
Providence 2.
Souterrain, The.
Hoffman. Last Arrival, The.
Hughes, Langston. Consider Me.
Hugo. Name the Mystery Fin and Win a Doll.
Joseph. Shadows Coming.
Koch. To You.
Lawrence. Terra Incognita.
Levertov. Window, A.
Liddy. Correspondences.
Lady/Lord in Doorway.
Lowry. Eels.
"MacDiarmid." Light and Shadow.
MacLeish. Autobiography.
Melville. Field Asters.
Prelusive.
Meredith. Forest History.
Here the snake across your path.
'Twas in a glimmering starlight.
Wind on the Lyre.
Merton. "Mystery of things"—where is it
  found?, The.
Truth, The.
Moore. By Disposition of Angels.
Morrison. Mystery of the Dream.
Still Wet From.
Muldoon. Why Brownlee Left.
Nash. Calling Spring VII-MMMC.
Nathan. Fourth Dimension, The.
Nemerov. There.
Neruda. At whom is the rice grinning.
Do you hear yellow detonations.
I Went.
If all rivers are sweet.
If I'm dead and don't know it.
Is it true that amber contains.
Is there anything crazier in this life.
Island (VII), The.
Island (VIII), The.
Tell me, is the rose really naked.
That solemn Senator / who claimed I had
  castles.
To whom does the raggedy condor.
What are you hiding under your hump?
When does the butterfly read.
Olson. Cole's Island.
Raine. Dreams.
Rich. Diving into the Wreck.
In my imagination I was the pivot of a fresh
  beginning.
Mare's skeleton in the clearing: another sign
  of life, The.
Of simple choice they are the villagers; their
  clothes come.
Rolfe. Cheliuskin.
Mystery.
Mystery II.
Sarton. Approach—Calcutta, The.
Light Left On, A.
Metaphysical Garden, The.
Schuyler. Eyes at the Window.
Silverstein. Bloath, The.
What's In the Sack?

Stevenson. Spaewife, The.
Updike. Agatha Christie and Beatrix Potter.
Williams, Charles Kenneth. Room.
Wright, Charles. Chinese Journal.
 Night Journal II.
Young. Still Lives.
Zukofsky. Imitation.

Mysticism
Beatles. Across the Universe.
 Because.
 Inner Light, The.
 It's All Too Much.
 Tomorrow Never Knows.
Ceravolo. Fire of Myself.
Cohen. Altar, The.
 Beetle, The.
 Commentary—The Altar.
 Commentary—The Beetle.
 Dove, The.
 Embrace, The.
 Every Pebble.
 Friend, When You Speak.
 I Have Not Lingered in European Monasteries.
 I Stopped to Listen.
 One.
 Sit Down, Master.
Cowper. Joy in Martyrdom.
Doolittle. Dead Priestess Speaks, A.
Emerson. S. R.
Fenton. Pitt-Rivers Museum, Oxford, The.
Galvin. Great Blue.
Hartley. Mystic, kneeling / in the forests of
 Malines, The.
 Mystical Forest, The.
 Richard Rolle.
Hoffman. Instructions to a Medium, to be
 Transmitted to the Shade of W.B. Yeats, the
 Latter Having Responded in a Séance Held
 on 13 June 1965, Its Hundredth Birthday.
Holmes. Samoan Head.
Hugo. Northwest Retrospective: Mark Tobey.
Lawrence. Mystic.
Lindsay. See how the generations pass.
McNeill. Light.
Merton. Cairo 1326.
 If people insist on my having.
Nemerov. Frozen City, The.
Neruda. I want the jailed / light to awaken: I
 want.
Whitman. Persian Lesson, A.
 When I Heard the Learn'd Astronomer.
Whittier. Mystic's Christmas, The.
 Vision of Echard, The.
Williams, Charles Kenneth. Cave, The.
 Halves.
 Last, The.
Wright, Charles. Holy Thursday.
 Local Journal.
Young. New Mystic, The.

Mythology
Auden. Atlantis.
Berry. Mad Farmer Revolution, The.
Bishop. Thunder.
Blake. Imitation of Spen[s]er, An.
Browning, Elizabeth Barrett. Aurora and
 Tithonus.
 Bacchus and Ariadne.
 Daughters of Pandarus, The.
 Ode to the Swallow.
 So the storms bore the daughters of Pandarus
 out into thrall.
Browning, Robert. Artemis Prologizes.
Bunting. Baudelaire in Cythera.
 Chorus of Furies.
 Empty vast days built in the waste memory
 seem a jail for.
 I thought I saw my late wife (a very
 respectable woman).
 Once, so they say, pinetrees seeded on
 Pelion's peak swam.
 What mournful stave, what bellow shakes the
 grove?
Carew. Coelum Britannicum.
 Divine Love, A.
 Fourth Song, The.
 Second Rapture, The.
Carruth. Mythology of Dark and Light, The.

Purana, Meaning Once Upon a Time.
 Spirit / whatever you are wherever.
Catullus. Carmen 63: "Plunging towards
 Phrygia over violent water."
 Carmen 64: "In old days / driving through soft
 waters."
Clark. Garland of Red, A.
Coleridge. Mighty Fountain, A.
Cooper. Atom bellies like a cauliflower, The.
 Where is the simple myth we used to have?
Crane. Atlantis.
Cullen. To the Three for Whom the Book.
Cummings. Epithalamion: "Thou aged
 unreluctant earth who dost."
 One nonsufficiently inunderstood.
Davie. Fountain of Arethusa, The.
 Fountain of Cyanë, The.
 Garland for Ronsard, A.
 On Sutton Strand.
Doolittle. Charioteer.
 Holy Satyr.
 Lais.
Dunbar. Black Samson of Brandywine.
Duncan. Fire, The.
 Stage Directions.
Eberhart. Kaire.
 Wild Swans of Inverane, The.
Eliot. Sweeney among the Nightingales.
Emerson. Hermione.
 Who gave thy cheek the mixed tint.
Everson. So the sea stands up to the shore,
 banging his chains.
Gardner. Fly in Amber.
 Folkways.
Glück. Hyacinth.
Graves. Conjunction.
 Darien.
 Good Night to the Old Gods.
 Gorgon Mask.
 Ibycus of Samos.
 In Procession.
 Instructions to the Orphic Adept.
 Judgement of Paris.
 Lyceia.
 New Legends.
 Penthesileia.
 Sirocco at Deyá.
 Song: A Phoenix Flame.
Haines. Changes.
 For Daphne at Lone Lake.
 I know three women that are you.
 You rise from your sleep.
Hardy. By the Runic Stone.
 Christmas in the Elgin Room.
 Meditation on a Holiday.
Hesketh. Snow Leopard.
Hewitt. Delos.
Hill. Orpheus and Eurydice.
Housman. Atys.
Keats. In After-Time, a Sage of Mickle Lore.
 On Visiting Staffa.
Kunitz. Spark of Laurel, A.
Lawrence. Argonauts, The.
Lovelace. Princesse Löysa drawing.
Lowry. Harpies.
 Just a Merry Little Ditty of Welcome for the
 Most Beloved Harteebeeste on Easter Sunday.
 Never in a comedian's life have I laughed till
 then!
 Outside was the roar of the sea and the
 darkness.
Merrill. Banks of a Stream Where Creatures
 Bathe.
Merton. Atlas and the Fatman.
 Gloss on the Sin of Ixion.
 Jaguar Myth, The.
 Martin's Predicament or Atlas Watches Every
 Evening.
 New Song, The.
 Zeus Is Dead.
Milton. Sabrina.
Morgan. Aegir.
 Balder.
 Freya.
 Heimdall.
 Jormungand.
 Odin's Song.

Morrison. American Prayer, An.
Nemerov. Beyond the Pleasure Principle.
 Mythological Beast.
Olson. Chronicles.
 Hour of evening—supper hour, for my
 neighbors—quietness, The.
 Stevens Song.
Piercy. Icon.
Prince. Thyme, tufa, sage, anemone.
Raine. How address you, greatest of givers.
Ralegh. Amazons with Crescent-formed shield,
 The.
 Brasen tower [or Tower] with doors [or dores]
 close barred [or bar'd], The.
 East winde with Aurora hath abiding, The.
 Joyfull Spring did ever last, The.
Robinson. As a World Would Have It.
 Lais to Aphrodite.
Rossetti. Lotus-Eaters: Ulysses to Penelope,
 The.
 Zara.
Rukeyser. Clouds, Airs, Carried me Away.
 In the Underworld.
 Mortal Girl.
Sandburg. Atlas, How Have You Been?
 From Illinois and Indiana came a later myth.
 Who made Paul Bunyan, who gave him birth
 as a myth, who joked him.
Sarton. At Delphi.
 At Lindos.
 Binding the Dragon.
 Birthday on the Acropolis.
 Furies, The.
 Narcissus.
 Proteus.
Simic. Childhood of Parmenides, The.
Snodgrass. Orpheus.
Spender. In Attica.
Swinburne. Phaedra.
Tennyson. Tithonus.
Walcott. Europa.
 From This Far.
Whittier. Dole of Jarl Thorkell, The.
 How the Robin Came.
 Robin, The.
 Vanishers, The.
Wilbur. Antéros.
 Lying.
Williams, Charles Kenneth. Hercules, Deianira,
 Nessus.
Wordsworth. Artegal and Elidure.
 Laodamia.
Wyatt. Iopas's Song.
Zukofsky. Pelion could one time prong its top
 worthy keel in pines.
 Spurred altering wake toss Attis his craft
 racing till marled in the.

N

Nabakov, Vladimir
Ferlinghetti. Deep Chess.
Matthews. Nabokov's Blues.
 Nabokov's Death.

Nakedness
Auden. Cave of Nakedness, The.
Browning, Robert. Rhyme for a Child
 Viewing a Naked Venus in a Painting of
 "The Judgement of Paris."
Bukowski. 6 A.M.
Creeley. Pool, The.
Dickey, William. You White Cunning Devils.
Donne. To His Mistress Going to Bed.
Emerson. Painting and Sculpture.
Everson. Stone Face Falls.
Fisher. Crumpled clothes come slowly off.
Fox. Help Me with the Buttons.
Gunn. Three.
Herrick. Laxare Fibulam.
 Lilly in a Cristal, The.
 Upon Electra.
Hughes, Langston. March Moon.
MacLeish. My Naked Aunt.
Millay. How Naked, How Without a Wall.
Morrison. Tales of the American Night.
Oppen. Morality Play: Preface, A.

Rukeyser. Knowledge my nakedness.
Shapiro. Shame.
Stevens. Lot of People Bathing in a Stream, A.
Nudity at the Capital.
Warren. Birth of Love.
Wright, James. Prayer to the Lord Ramakrishna, A.

Names
Angelou. Calling of Names, The.
Atwood. Squaw Lilies: Some Notes.
Beatles. I Call Your Name.
You Know My Name (Look up the Number).
Berg. Not That.
Bishop. My name is Severino.
Browning, Elizabeth Barrett. Pet-Name, The.
Browning, Robert. Names, The.
Byron. Lines Written in an Album, at Malta.
Carruth. Marge.
Names.
Septic Tanck.
Cohen. On Hearing a Name Long Unspoken.
Coleridge. Exile, An.
Names.
Crane. Name for All, A.
Creeley. It Is at Times.
Dobyns. Grief.
Donne. To Mrs. Magdalen Herbert: of St. Mary Magdalen.
Dunn. Bad Angels, The.
"Dylan." Man Gave Names to All the Animals.
Eberhart. Request.
Emerson. And though he dearly prized the bards of fame.
To every creature / Adam gave its name.
Frost. Maple.
Gallagher. Meeting, The.
Graves. My Name and I.
Name.
Gunn. Vox Humana.
Hayden. Names.
Heaney. Incertus.
Hewitt. April.
Covenanter's Grave, The.
Mortal Place, The.
My Naming.
Names We Used, The.
On the Use of Dialect Words.
Pro Tanto Quid Retribuamas.
Return (1885), The.
Ulster Names.
Hill. Pet-name, a common name. Best-selling brand, curt, A.
Hughes, Langston. In Explanation of Our Times.
Madam and the Census Man.
Hugo. Montgomery Hollow.
Jeffers. Patronymic.
Jonson. To My Lord Ignorant.
Joseph. Language Teaching: Naming.
Knott. My Mother's List of Names.
Poem (How I Lost My Pen-Name).
Shorts / Excerpts ("Suddenly I understood").
Summoning, The.
Koertge. He ("Was never called Wild Bill").
Pronouncing My Name.
Larkin. Maiden Name.
Lawrence. Name the Gods!
Levine. Making Light of It.
Renaming the Kings.
Wednesday.
Lovelace. Dedication To the Right Honorable John Lovelace. The.
Lowry. Mackerel shouldn't take, A.
"MacDiarmid." Major Road Ahead.
McGrath. Need for Dictionaries II, The.
Meinke. Indigo Buntings.
Merton. Fall, The.
Tao.
Nash. Anybody Else Hate Nicknames?
Everything's Haggis in Hoboken, or, Scots Wha Hae Hae.
Guppy, The.
Happy Ending of Mr. Train, The.
I Happen To Know.
Name Is Too Familiar, The.

Not Even for Brunch.
Sic Semper Mr. Sherman's Temper, or Kindly Place Your Order in English.
Snark Was a Boojum Was a Prawn, The.
What's in a Name? Here's What's in a Name, or, I Wonder What Became of John and Mary.
What's in a Name? Some Letter I Always Forget.
Olson. Tomorrow.
Pack. Waking to My Name.
Pope. Epigram on the Toasts of the Kit-Cat Club, Anno 1716.
Verses Occasioned by an & c. at the End of Mr. D'Urfy's Name in the Title to One of His Plays.
Robinson. Theophilus.
Rossetti. King of Kings and Lord of Lords.
Sandburg. Aster, a farewell-summer flower, stays long in the last fall weeks, An.
Blacklisted.
Corn and Beans.
Man the Moon Shooter.
Sexton. Telephone.
Sidney. Sonnet 55: "Muses, I oft invoked your holy aid."
Silverstein. Fred?
If I Had A Brontosaurus.
Smart. Fragment D.
Spenser. One day I wrote her name upon the strand.
Stafford. Story That Could Be True, A.
Stevenson. Ticonderoga: A Legend of the West Highlands.
To My Name-Child.
Updike. Clan, The.
Fritillary, The.
I Missed His Book, but I Read His Name.
Kenneths.
Van Duyn. Garland for Christopher Smart, A.
To My Godson, on His Christening.
Wakoski. Donna.
Walcott. Names.
Whitman. What Am I After All.
Whittier. Kallundborg Church.
My Namesake.
Name, A.
Wilbur. Melongène.
On Having Mis-identified a Wild Flower.
Rillons, Rillettes.
Williams, William Carlos. And Thus with All Praise.
Wright, James. Minneapolis Poem, The.
Zukofsky. Claims.

See also **Place Names.**

Nantucket, Massachusetts
Glück. Phenomenal Survivals of Death in Nantucket.
Lowell. Quaker Graveyard in Nantucket, The.
Whittier. Exiles, The.
Williams, William Carlos. Nantucket.
Yau. Nantucket.

Naples, Italy
Carruth. Two Romantic Pieces.
Ciardi. Naples.
Garrigue. Beheld in Naples.
Hugo. Brueghel in the Doria.
Napoli Again.
Sailing from Naples.
Schuyler. Dorabella's Naples Watercolor.
Shelley. Ode to Naples.
Whittier. Naples.
Prisoners of Naples, The.

Napoleon I
Blake. When France got free Europe 'twixt Fools & Knaves.
Browning, Elizabeth Barrett. Crowned and Buried.
Browning, Robert. Incident of the French Camp.
Byron. From the French.
Napoleon's Farewell.
Napoleon's Snuff-Box.
Ode from the French.
Ode to Napoleon Buonaparte.
Once Fairly Set Out on His Party of Pleasure.
Coleridge. Mighty Fountain, A.

De la Mare. Napoleon.
Emerson. Poem, Spoken Before the ΦΒΚ Society, August, 1834.
Kipling. St. Helena Lullaby, A.
Lowell. Napoleon.
Meredith. Behind the Northern curtain-folds he passed.
Bright from the shell of that much limited man.
But whom those errant moans accused.
Cannon his name.
Desire and terror then had each of each.
Flood that swept her to be slave, The.
He, did he love her? France was his weapon, shrewd.
Hugest of engines, a much limited man.
On him the long enchained, released.
Persistent through the brazen chorus round.
Poured streams of Europe's veins the flood.
To weld the nation in a name of dread.
Plath. Swarm, The.
Robinson. Island, An.
Sandburg. Statistics.
Shelley. Feelings of a Republican on the Fall of Bonaparte.
Lines Written on Hearing the News of the Death of Napoleon.
Wordsworth. Eagle and the Dove, The.
1801.
Look now on that Adventurer who hath paid.
October, 1803 ("When, looking on the present face of things").
Ode: "Who rises on the banks of Seine."
To B.R. Haydon, On Seeing His Picture of Napoleon Buonaparte on the Island of St Helena.

Napoleon III
Browning, Elizabeth Barrett. Napoleon III in Italy.
Meredith. Ode to H.I.M. Napoleon 3d.
'Tis I have seen the coming man.

Napoleonic Wars
Browning, Robert. Incident of the French Camp.
Byron. There was a sound of revelry by night.
Gildner. Johann Gaertner (1793–1887).
Hardy. Alarm, The.
Bridge of Lodi, The.
Epilogue: "We have now set forth, in our imperfect way."
Leipzig.
Peasant's Confession, The.
Prologue: "In these stern times of ours, when crimson strife."
Meredith. But whom those errant moans accused.
Poured streams of Europe's veins the flood.
Soon felt she in her shivered frame.
Wordsworth. And is it among rude untutored Dales.
Brave Schill! by death delivered, take thy flight.
By Moscow Self-Devoted to a Blaze.
1810 ("Ah! where is Pala fox?").
1810 ("O'erweening Statesman...").
Feelings of a Noble Biscayan at One of Those Funerals 1810.
Feelings of the Tyrolese.
French and the Spanish Guerrillas, The.
French Army in Russia 1812–1813, The.
Hail, Zaragoza! If with unwet eye.
Hofer.
Indignation of a High-Minded Spaniard 1810.
Invocation to the Earth; February, 1816.
Martial courage of a day is vain, The.
Memorial near the Outlet of the Lake of Thun. November, 1806.
Ode: 1815.
Ode: 1814.
Ode: The Morning of the Day Appointed for a General Thanksgiving. January 18, 1816.
On the Final Submission of the Tyrolese.
On the Same Occasion.
Spanish Guerillas 1811.
To the Men of Kent (October, 1803).

Narcissism and Narcissists
Clark. Narcissism.

Dickey, William. Narcissus Unbound.
Eberhart. If I Could Only Live at the Pitch That Is near Madness.
Ginsberg. I made love to myself.
Housman. Look not in my eyes, for fear.
Lawrence. I Know a Noble Englishman.
Nash. Swan, The.

Narcissus (botany)
Plath. Among the Narcissi.
Zukofsky. Narcissus.

Narcissus (mythology)
Auden. Narcissus.
Davie. At the Café Parnasse.
Dickey, James. Daybreak.
Dunn. Wanting to Get Closer.
Gunn. Behind the Mirror.
Lawrence. Narcissus.
Nemerov. Glass Dialectic.
Sarton. Narcissus.
Schwartz. Overture.
Prologue: "Narcissus, speaking in the first person."
Stuart. Narcissus Dreaming.
Williams, William Carlos. Narcissus in the Desert.

Narcotics. see Drug Addiction.

Nasturtiums
Gunn. Nasturtium.

Nationalism
Atwood. Two-Headed Poems.
Berry. I sit in the shade of the trees of the land I was born in.
There is no government so worthy as your son who fishes with you in silence beside the forest pool.
Brontë. Song by Julius Angora.
Dickinson. Is it Intellect that the Patriot means.
My Country, 'tis of thee.
Fisher. Nation, The.
Herrick. Lawes ("Who violates the Customes, hurts the Health").
Hewitt. Overture for an Ulster Literature.
Ulster Winter (1942).
Lindsay. Johnny Appleseed's Old Age.
Lorde. Seventh Sign, The.
Merton. Why Some Look up to Planets and Heroes.
Nash. Goody for Our Side and Your Side Too.
Patchen. We Mutually Pledge to Each Other.
Raine. Letter to Pierre Emmanuel.
Rolfe. And If You Don't See What You What, Ask for It.
Credo.
May Day Song.
Sandburg. Blood of all men of all nations being red, The.
Hope is a tattered flag and a dream out of time.
Is There Any Easy Road to Freedom?
Old Timers.
Threes.
Shapiro. Washington Cathedral.
Stevens. Imago.

Native Americans
Berry. July, 1773.
Berryman. Navajo Setting the Record Straight.
Bly. Pilgrim Fish Heads.
Schoolcraft's Diary Written on the Missouri: 1830.
Boyle. Poem for the Teesto Diné of Arizona, A.
Carruth. Rimrock, Where It Is.
Sorrow Song, The.
Crane. Sad Indian, The.
They Were There..
Cummings. Moon-in-the-Trees, / The old canoe awaits you.
Davie. Amazonian.
Frontenac.
Jesuits in North America, The.
Pontiac.
Emerson. For fifteen winter days.
Fletcher. Burning Mountain, The.
Cliff-dwelling.

On Mesa Verde.
Song of Natchez Under the Hill, The.
Frost. Vanishing Red, The.
Galvin. Saying Her Name.
Ginsberg. Rolling Thunder Stones.
Haines. Eye in the Rock, The.
Watching the Fire.
Hartley. Festival of the Corn, The.
Hemingway. Oklahoma.
Hesketh. From Walden.
Hoffman. Comanches.
Hugo. At the Cabin.
Bear Paw.
Church on Comiaken Hill, The.
Duwamish.
Indian Girl.
Letter to Hill from St. Ignatius.
Letter to Welch from Browning.
Map of Montana in Italy, A.
Night at the Napi in Browning, A.
Other Beaverbank, The.
Pishkun.
Pishkun Reservoir.
St. Ignatius Where the Salish Wail.
Tahola.
With Ripley at the Grave of Albert Parenteau.
Jeffers. Inquisitors, The.
New Mexican Mountain.
Koch. Thanksgiving.
Kunitz. Musician of the lost tribes.
Lawrence. Beyond the Rockies.
Men in New Mexico.
Lindsay. Being My Notion, as a Ferocious Small-Boy, of My Ancestral Protector.
Ghost of the Buffaloes, The.
Indian Girl Who Made Them, The.
Indians Worship Him, but He Hurries On, The.
One Brief Hour of Grown-up Glory on the Gulf of Mexico.
Lowell. At the Indian Killer's Grave.
McGrath. Buffalo Coat, The.
You Can Start the Poetry Now, Or: News from Crazy Horse.
MacLeish. Third Book, The.
Wildwest.
MacNeice. Indian Village.
McNeill. River, The.
Meinke. Exodus with Children.
Merton. Ghost Dance.
Ghost Dance: Prologue.
Morgan. Abenaki Poem.
Morrison. Wild Whore Laughs, The.
Oliver. Learning About the Indians.
Two Kinds of Deliverance.
Olson. As of Bozeman.
Buffalo Ode.
Dance, of the Grizzly Bear, The.
Men are only known in memory.
Morning News, The.
Oppen. Some of the young men.
Paley. Having Arrived by Bike at Battery Park.
Job of hunting of shooting in hunting season of, The.
"Reed." Last Great American Whale.
Rich. Apparition.
Burden Baskets.
Hohokam.
Mary Jane Colter, 1904.
Particularity.
Self-hatred.
Roethke. Longing, The.
Sandburg. Alice Corbin Is Gone.
Cahokia.
Coin, A.
Early Copper.
What did Hiamovi, the red man, Chief of.
Yes, the Dead Speak to Us.
Shelton. Navajo Song.
Reservations.
Smith, Charlotte. Supposed To Have Been Written in America.
Snyder. Anasazi.
Manzanita.
Stafford. Concealment: Ishi, the Last Wild Indian, The.

In the Oregon Country.
Returned to Say.
Tomlinson. Albuquerque.
Chief Standing Water.
Cochiti.
Jemez.
Old Man at Valdez.
Quarai.
Ute Mountain.
Waldman. White Eyes.
Whitman. Osceola.
Red Jacket (from Aloft).
Yonnondio.
Whittier. Bridal of Pennacook, The.
Fountain, The.
Funeral Tree of the Sokokis.
How the Robin Came.
Inscription: "Eagle, stooping from yon snow-blown peaks, The."
Metacom.
Mogg Megone.
Mount Agiochook.
Nauhaught, the Deacon.
On the Big Horn.
Pentucket.
Truce of Piscataqua, The.
Vanishers, The.
Williams, Charles Kenneth. Guatemala: 1964.
Williams, William Carlos. Graph.
Wordsworth. Complaint of a Forsaken Indian Woman, The.

Nativity, The
Coleridge. Translation of a Passage in Ottfried's Metrical Paraphrase of the Gospel.
Cowper. Nativity, The.
Crashaw. Come we shepheards whose blest sight.
Hymne of the Nativity, Sung by the Shepherds, A.
Glück. Nativity Poem.
Hill. Picture of a Nativity.
Lawrence. Ballad of a Wilful Woman.
Milton. On the Morning of Christs Nativity.
Smart. Nativity of Our Lord and Saviour Jesus Christ, The.
Southwell. Epiphanye, The.
Our Ladie's Nativity.
Swinburne. Christmas Carol, A.
See also **Christmas.**

Naturalists
Heaney. Death of a Naturalist.
Nash. Mr. Burgess, Meet Mr. Barmecide.
Rich. Observer, The.

Nature
Ammons. Enough.
Scarecrow.
Weight.
Arnold. Meeting.
Quiet Work.
Atwood. Boat, A.
Landcrab II.
Auden. After the Storm.
Appletreewick.
Autumn.
Bucolics.
By the Gasworks, Solihull.
Crocus stars the border, The.
Crowing of the cock, The.
Early Morning.
Earth's Praises.
Elegy: "Wagtail splutters in the stream, A."
Fall of Rome, The.
First Meeting.
Hidden Lane, The.
March.
March Song.
March Winds.
Memento Creatoris Tui.
Mill (Hempstead), The.
My Lady of the Wood.
Natural Linguistics.
Nightfall.
North, The.
Ode to Gaea.
Old Lead-mine, The.
Old Mine, The.
Rainy Afternoon, A.

Road's Your Place, The.
Sawmill, The.
Skyreholme Mill.
Song: "Crocus stars the border, The."
There is so much that I can share with you.
To a Child in Tears.
To Goethe: a Complaint.
Walk, The.
Woods in Rain.
Beatles. Julia.
Mother Nature's Son.
Berg. Alone.
Driving Out Again at Night.
Dust.
Gratitude.
1922.
Rocks, The.
Two Little Songs.
Berry. And I am here in Kentucky in the place I have made myself.
And when we speak together.
Arrival, The.
Beginning and end.
Broken Ground, The.
Design of a House, The.
Enriching the Earth.
Familiar, The.
February. A cloudy day.
Foliage has dropped, The.
For a night and a day.
Gift of Gravity, The.
Green and White.
He goes free of the earth.
Hidden Singer, The.
His love returns / and walks among the trees.
History.
I have thought of you stepping out of your doorway at dawn, your son in your tracks.
In the early morning dark.
In This World.
Independence Day.
July, 1773.
Longest night is past, The.
Look in / and see him looking out.
Man Born to Farming, The.
Man Walking and Singing, A.
Observance.
Peace. May he waken.
Peace of Wild Things, The.
Song in a Year of Catastrophe.
Song Sparrow Singing in the Fall, A.
Sowing.
Standing Ground, A.
Still sleeping, he heard.
To What Listens.
Valley holds its shadow, The.
Vision reaches the ground.
Where.
Window has forty, The.
Window. Window. / The wind's eye.
Wish to Be Generous, The.
Berryman. Mallarmé siren upside down,—rootedly!
Bishop. Brazil, January 1, 1502.
Cold Spring, A.
North Haven.
Song for the Rainy Season.
Sonnet of Intimacy.
Bly. After Drinking All Night with a Friend, We Go Out in a Boat at Dawn to See Who Can Write the Best Poem.
Fifty Males Sitting Together.
Hawk, The.
Out Picking up Corn.
Spring has come; I look up and see.
Bogan. Night.
Boyle. Spring.
To America.
Brontë. How long will you remain? The midnight hour.
I've been wandering in the greenwoods.
Only some spires of bright green grass.
Tell me, tell me, smiling child.
Was it with the fields of green.
Why do I hate that lone green dell?
Browning, Elizabeth Barrett. Hugh Stuart Boyd [His Death, 1848].

Love.
Man and Nature.
Patience Taught by Nature.
Romaunt of Margret, The.
Sea-Mew, The.
Sonnet: "Yet, love, mere love, is beautiful indeed."
Browning, Robert. Forest Thought, A.
Magical Nature.
"Oh, our manhood's prime vigour! no spirit feels waste,."
Year's at the spring, The.
Bukowski. Ants, The.
Sun Wields Mercy, The.
Bunting. Darling of Gods and Men, beneath the gliding stars.
Burns. Allan Water.
Castle Gordon—*Intended to Be Sung to Morag.*
Dainty Davie.
Humble Petition of Bruar Water to the Noble Duke of Athole, The.
Lament of Mary Queen of Scots on the Approach of Spring.
Lassie wi' the Lintwhite Locks.
Lover's Morning Salute to His Mistress, The.
My Heart's in the Highlands.
Nature's Law.
Ode to Spring.
On Scaring Some Waterfowl in Loch Turit, a Wild Scene among the Hills of Oughtertyre.
Phillis the Fair.
Rosebud, The.
Scotch Song.
Scotish Song.
Song: t'O Philly, happy be that day."
Song: "On Cessnock banks a lassie dwells."
Song. On Miss W. A.
To a Mouse [On Turning Her Up in Her Nest, with the Plough, November, 1785].
Written with a Pencil over the Chimney-Piece, in the Parlour of the Inn at Kenmore, Taymouth.
Yon wild, mossy mountains sae lofty and wide.
Byron. There be who say, in these enlightened days.
Wild Gazelle, The.
Campion. Sing a song of joy.
Carew. Divine Love, A.
Love's Force.
Protestation [A Sonnet], The.
Spring, The.
To my Friend G.N. from Wrest.
To My Worthy Friend Master George Sands [*or* Sandys], on His Translation of the Psalms.
Carroll, Jim. Birth and Death of the Sun, The.
In the Valley.
Mercury Clouds.
Night Outing, A.
Styro.
Vacation.
Withdrawal Letter.
Carruth. All Things.
Existing Pool, The.
Homecoming.
I Know, I Remember, But How Can I Help You.
My Meadow.
President's Speech, The.
Ravine, The.
Silence.
Thaw.
Underground the Darkness Is the Light.
Ceravolo. Book of Wild Flowers, The.
Chains of Mountains.
Green Lake Is Awake, The.
Note from St. Francis.
O gong of wept / O unviolet.
Pain Songs.
Water: How Weather Feels the Cotton Hotels.
Chaucer. House of Fame, The.
Ciardi. At First Flower of the Easy Day.
Bees and Morning Glories.
Credibility.
11:02 A.M. The Bird Disappeared.

Fragment: "To the laboratory then I went. What little."
No White Bird Sings.
On Wet Iota.
Thoughts on Looking into a Thicket.
Tommy's Pond.
Clare. Evening.
Evening.
February: A Thaw.
Sonnet: "I love to see the summer beaming forth."
Clark. Diary of Desert War.
Egypt, Everything.
Fireflies.
"First cold winter twilights.."
In the Dark Mountains, Brilliant.
"In This River."
Lake, The.
October.
One.
Sedge.
Sounding Chinese at Inspiration Point.
Theory of the Universe, A.
Woodtime.
Clough. Resignation—to Faustus.
That there are better things within the womb.
Cohen. Every Pebble.
I Draw Aside the Curtain.
Politics of This Book, The.
Coleridge. Barberry-Tree, The.
Inscription for a Fountain on a Heath.
Lines Composed While Climbing the Left Ascent of Brockley Coomb, in the County of Somerset, May, 1795.
Nightingale, The.
Picture, The.
To Nature.
To the Nightingale.
Unity with Nature.
Work without Hope.
Cooper. All These Dreams.
Flute Song.
Ragged and thrashing.
Rest. / A violin bow, a breeze.
Sunlight lies along my table.
Treetops are shuddering.
Wronke, Spring 1917.
Cowper. Nature Unimpaired by Time.
Retirement.
Song: "When all within is peace."
Task, The.
To the Rev. Mr. Newton.
Crane. Annunciations.
Creeley. As We Sit.
Here.
In the Fall.
Innocence, The.
Intervals.
Kid, The.
Messengers, The.
Persons.
Picnic, The.
Picture, A.
Sign.
Song: "Those rivers run from that land."
Temper, The.
Wish, A.
Cullen. Singing in the Rain.
Cummings. Beyond the stolid iron pond.
Epithalamion: "Thou aged unreluctant earth who dost."
Here's s / omething round(& so).
I thank You God for most this amazing.
If(you are i why certainly).
Let's,from some loud unworld's most rightful wrong.
Moon-in-the-Trees, / The old canoe awaits you.
Night.
Nocturne: "When the lithe moonlight silently."
O sweet spontaneous.
Sonnet: "For that I have forgot the world these days."
They have hung the sky with arrows.
When serpents bargain for the right to squirm.
Wherelings whenlings / (daughters of if but

offspring of hopefear).
Wind is a Lady with, The.
Davie. Derbyshire Turf.
I come in out of Space, and with a rake.
Orford.
Sixth Epistle.
Sylvae.
Utterings.
De la Mare. All That's Past.
April.
Awake!
Dreamer, The.
Phantom, The.
Reawakening, The.
Reserved.
Spark, The.
They Told Me.
Vacant Day, The.
Vain Questioning.
Dickey, James. For a Time and Place.
Springhouse, Menses, Held Apple, House and
  Beyond.
Dickinson. Bring me the sunset in a cup.
Changelessness / is Nature's change.
Earth has many keys, The.
Further in Summer than the Birds.
Her sovereign People.
How strange that Nature does not knock.
However you stem Nature.
I taste a liquor never brewed.
I write in the midst of Sweet-Peas.
If Nature smiles—the Mother must.
It bloomed and dropt, a Single Noon.
Moth the hue of this, A.
Narrow Fellow in the Grass, A.
Nature affects to be sedate.
Nature and God—I neither knew.
Nature can do no more.
Nature is a Haunted House.
Nature is our eldest mother.
"Nature" is what we see.
Nature must be too young to feel.
Nature, seems it to myself.
Nature—sometimes sears a Sapling.
Nature—the Gentlest Mother is.
Of Nature I shall have enough.
Sky is low—the Clouds are mean, The.
So valiant is the intimacy.
Their Barricade against the Sky.
These are the Signs to Nature's Inns.
To my quick ear the Leaves—conferred.
Touch lightly Nature's sweet Guitar.
Travel why to Nature.
Twice had Summer her fair Verdure.
Veins of other Flowers, The.
We introduce ourselves.
Were nature mortal lady.
Worthlessness of Earthly things, The.
Doolittle. Are these ashes in my hand.
Dancer, The.
If you take the moon in your hands.
Scribe.
Wash of cold river.
White World.
Dove. Fish in the Stone, The.
Dunbar. From the Porch at Runnymede.
Lapse, The.
Nature and Art.
Secret, The.
Duncan. Best of ways. That there be a law the
  Earth gives and the Mountain.
Dunn. Landscape at the End of the Century.
Snowmass Cycle, The.
"Dylan." If Dogs Run Free.
Lay Down Your Weary Tune.
Eberhart. Angels, The.
Big Rock.
Book of Nature, The.
Burden.
Centennial For Whitman.
Child, The.
Coast of Maine.
Concord Cats.
Day-Bed, The.
Death in the Mines.
Gnats.
Go to the Shine That's on a Tree.

Groundhog Revisiting, The.
Grove, The.
Hard Structure of the World, The.
Hop-Toad, The.
Illusion of Eternity, The.
Indian Pipe.
Jungle, The.
Labour them, these drenched heights.
Largess, The.
Learning from Nature.
Man Who Was Blown Down by the Wind, A.
Mind and Nature.
News.
Oak, The.
Old Tom.
On a Squirrel Crossing the Road in Autumn,
  in New England.
On Returning to a Lake in Spring.
Opulence.
Parker River, The.
Pasture, The.
Prometheus.
Recollection of Childhood.
River Water Music.
Sea-Hawk.
Skier and the Mountain, The.
Snowfall, A.
Spider, The.
Spring Mountain Climb.
Standards, The.
Summery Windermere, sweet lake!
Van Black, an Old Farmer in His Dell.
Where Are Those High and Haunting Skies.
Wild Life and Tamed Life.
Emerson. Adirondacs, The.
Ah strange strange strange.
Awed I behold once more.
Berrying.
Blackbird's song the blackbird's song, The.
Blight.
But Nature whistled with all her winds.
But never yet the man was found.
But O to see his solar eyes.
Color, taste, and smell, smaragdus, sugar, and
  musk.
Dear brother, would you know the life.
Dirge: "Knows he who tills this lonely field."
Each and All.
Experience.
Fine presentiments controlled him.
For Nature true & like in every place.
From Nature's beginning.
From the stores of eldest Matter.
Go out into Nature and plant trees.
Good is what goes on the road of Nature.
He lives not who can refuse me.
He must have / Droll fancies sometimes cross
  his quiet thoughts.
How drearily in College hall.
I leave the book, I leave the wine.
I left my dreamy page & sallied forth.
If wishes would carry me over the land.
In my garden three ways meet.
Is the pace of nature slow?
Know he who tills this lonely field.
Land was all electric, The.
Miracle, The.
Motto to "Circles."
Motto to "Nature" ("Rounded world is fair to
  see, The").
Motto to "Nature" ("Subtle chain of countless
  rings, A").
Musketaquid.
My Garden.
Nature 1 ("Winters know / Easily to shed the
  snow").
Nature 2 ("She is gamesome and good").
Nature.
Nature ("Day by day for her darlings to her
  much she added more").
Nature in Leasts.
Nature saith / I am not infinite.
Nature says, / These craggy hills that front the
  dawn.
Nature will not lose.
Natures web star broidered.
Nun's Aspiration.

October woods, wherein.
Parks & ponds are good by day.
Problem, The.
Queen rejoices in her peers, A.
See how Romance adheres.
She had wealth of mornings in her year.
She paints with white & red the moors.
Shout to the Sheperds, A.
Softens the air so cold & rude.
Song of Nature.
Tell me maiden dost thou use.
These trees like tho'ts that to visions congeal.
Though her eye seek other forms.
To every creature / Adam gave its name.
Waldeinsamkeit.
What all the books of ages paint, I have.
What never was no, & still will be.
Where the fungus broad & red.
Who saw the hid beginnings.
Why fear to die.
Woodnotes I ("For this present, hard").
Woodnotes II ("As sunbeams stream through
  liberal space").
Would you know what joy is hid.
Xenophanes.
Everson. South Coast, The.
Spikehorn.
Steelhead.
Stone Face Falls.
We in the Fields.
Fenton. For the context of the basidiocarp
  Singer states.
Frog hunts on land by vision. He escapes, A.
Genus Stephanoma, The.
In September greasebands are put on standard
  apple.
Killer Snails, The.
Kingfisher's Boxing Gloves, The.
Lollipops of the Pomeranian Baroque.
South Parks Road.
Sweden. Lapp. Pouch made from a
  blackthroated diver.
Terminal Moraine, A.
Voice disguiser with membrane of a spider's
  egg-case, A.
Ferlinghetti. Overpopulation.
Upon Reflection.
Fisher. Outlines / start to appear.
Fletcher. America.
Blue Symphony.
Elegy in a Civil War Cemetery.
From Portofino Point.
Grandfather's Grave.
Green Symphony.
On the Verandah.
Out of the waves they clomb, plant, insect,
  fish, and bird.
Sea-Sounding Bells.
They buried Abel at sunset in the red wet
  earth.
Whitman.
Ford. Will of the weed to startle, The.
Fox. Cup of Cold Water.
On the Other Side of Uji Bridge.
Pomegranates.
Frost. Design.
Fountain, a Bottle, a Donkey's Ears and Some
  Books, A.
From Iron.
On Going Unnoticed.
Our Hold on the Planet.
Something for Hope.
Time Out.
Vantage Point, The.
Gallagher. Croce e Delizia al Cor.
Refusing Silence.
Galvin. Fog Township.
Listening by a Woodpile, Night of Moon after
  Snow.
Running.
Winter Runner, The.
Gardner. It Rained Last Night.
To Thoreau on Rereading Walden.
Garrigue. Address to the Migrations.
Flux of Autumn, The.
For an Orchard Tree.
Invitation to a Hay.

Land We Did Not Know, The.
Moondial.
Thy Love Is One Thou'st Not Yet Known.
With Glaze of Tears.
Gildner.　Farm, The.
That Summer.
Ginsberg.　Bixby Canyon.
Bixby Canyon Ocean Path Word Breeze.
Carmel Valley.
Past Silver Durango Over Mexic Sierra-
　Wrinkles.
Sonora Desert-Edge.
Graves.　Ambience.
Ample Garden, The.
Around the Mountain.
Beds of Grainne and Diarmuid, The.
Climate of Thought, The.
Consortium of Stones.
Deliverance.
Endless Pavement.
Finding of Love, The.
Fragment: "Are you shaken, are you stirred."
Horizon.
Interruption.
Love in Barrenness.
Love Story, A.
Mankind and Ocean.
Meeting, The.
Nature's Lineaments.
P'eng That Was a K'un, The.
Return of the Goddess [Artemis].
She Tells Her Love while Half Asleep.
Song of Blodeuwedd, The.
Song: The Far Side of Your Moon.
To Walk on Hills.
Turn of the Moon.
Wedding, The.
Gunn.　Aqueduct.
Cool Stream, The.
Faustus Triumphant.
Last Man, The.
Rooftop, The.
Thomas Bewick.
To a Friend in Time of Trouble.
Hacker.　Crépuscule Provençale.
Languedocienne.
Haines.　In Nature.
Leaves and Ashes.
That mid-fall morning, driving north.
What did I come for? To see.
Hall.　Cold Water.
Granite and Grass.
New Hampshire.
Stories.
Hardy.　At a Bridal.
At Moonrise and Onwards.
Discouragement.
Ditty: "Beneath a knap where flown."
Five Students, The.
Genitrix Laesa.
Growth in May.
In a Wood.
Nature's Questioning.
Pat of Butter, The.
Unkindly May, An.
We Field-Women.
Hartley.　Chitter of chipmunk.
Nature.
October Afternoon.
There Are No Rocks and Trees.
Hartnett.　For My Grandmother, Bridget
　Halpin.
Naked Surgeon, The.
Heaney.　Anahorish.
Song: "Rowan like a lip-sticked girl, A."
Sweeney Astray.
Sweeney in Connacht.
Hemingway.　Grass smooth on the prairies.
Inexpressible, The.
Schwarzwald.
Herrick.　Art above Nature, to Julia.
Country Life: To His Brother, M. Tho:
　Herrick.
God, and Lord.
Painting Sometimes Permitted.
Putrefaction.
Sin ("Sin no Existence; Nature none it hath").

To Find[e] God.
Upon Man.
Upon Time.
Hesketh.　Academic.
Analyst.
Bleasdale: The Wooden Circle.
Bolton-Le-Moors, 1960.
Call of the North.
Cats.
Clown Flowers.
Dead Blackbird.
Death of a Gardener.
Edward Thomas.
Evergreen.
First Day, The.
Fisherman Poet.
From Walden.
Giraffes.
House In the Tree.
How to Do It.
I Am.
I Cannot Look into the Sun.
Joke, The.
Journey.
Limbo.
Lyric Evening.
Mary.
Northern Stone.
On Iona.
Paint Box.
Panther and the Antelope, The.
Partridge.
Prayer for Sun.
Preparing to Leave.
Recapitulation.
Reclaimed.
Reflections.
Reply to a Philistine.
Rise.
Roots.
St. Luke's Summer.
Second Childhood.
Starlings.
Survival.
Tom Rich.
Truant.
Tunnel, The.
Vine, The.
Walled In.
Ward F4.
What Is a Person?
What Is God?
Wordsworth's Old Age.
Hewitt.　Anti-Promethean Ode.
Antrim April.
Aquarium.
Autumnal.
Because I Paced My Thought.
Below the Mournes in May.
Corncrake.
Country Walk in March, A.
Country Walk in May, A.
Drift of Petals, The.
Equality.
Feathers on Turf.
First Snow in the Glens.
Flight.
Fontanel.
Garron Top.
I Turn to Trees.
Landscape.
Lettered Snow, The.
Little Glen, The.
Living Landscape, The.
Lyric: "Let but a thrush begin."
Moon, The.
Morning Hymn.
Morning Moment.
Northern Spring.
November Wood.
Now in the Spring.
October's Child.
Path Ahead, The.
Pioneer.
Poem in May.
Priest Goes through the Motions of the Play,
　The.

Ram's Horn, The.
Seeding Time.
Shortened Day, The.
Sonnets in October.
Spring of the Year.
Stoat, The.
Substance and Shadow.
Swathe Uncut, The.
Those Swans Remember; A Poem.
Three Horatian Odes.
Watchers, The.
Hill.　Elegiac Stanzas: On a Visit to Dove
　Cottage.
Two Chorale-Preludes: On Melodies by Paul
　Celan.
Hoffman.　Mother.
Holmes.　Fayetteville Dawn (1).
Hopkins.　Earth and heaven, so little known,
　The.
Epithalamion: "Hark, hearer, hear what I do;
　lend a thought now, make believe."
God's Grandeur.
I must hunt down the prize.
Inversnaid.
O what a silence is this wilderness!
O where is it, the wilderness.
Or else their cooings came from bays of trees.
Pied Beauty.
That Nature Is a Heraclitean Fire and of the
　Comfort of the Resurrection.
What being in rank-old nature should earlier
　have that breath been.
When eyes that cast about the heights of
　heaven.
Windy Day in Summer, A.
Hughes, Ted.　Earth-Numb.
Fern.
Gnat-Psalm.
Gog.
Heptonstall Old Church.
Mayday on Holderness.
Pibroch.
Rock Has Not Learned.
Song: "O lady, when the tipped cup of the
　moon blessed you."
Stealing Trout on a May Morning.
Thrushes.
West Laithe.
Widdop.
Woman in the Valley, The.
Hugo.　Culloden.
Gooseprairie.
Keen to Leaky Flowers.
Jarrell.　Field and Forest.
Rabbit hurries to the brim of its wood, The.
Jeffers.　All the Little Hoof-Prints.
Boats in a Fog.
Broken Balance, The.
Contrast.
Cycle, The.
Excesses of God, The.
For fifty thousand years man has been
　dreaming of powers.
Metamorphosis.
Natural Music.
Noon.
Not Our Good Luck.
Oh, Lovely Rock.
Place for No Story, The.
Point Joe.
Red Mountain.
Jonson.　How young and fresh I am tonight.
Joseph.　ALLEGORY: *Old Man's Fancy*
　(Poussin).
Goddess of Nature's Diatribe to her People,
　The.
Lost Hold.
Lost Sea, The.
Meeting Up.
Keats.　Hence Burgundy, Claret, and Port.
I Stood Tip-Toe upon a Little Hill.
Imitation of Spenser.
O! How I Love, on a Fair Summer's Eve.
On "The Story of Rimini."
Song of Four Faeries.
To Some Ladies.
To the Ladies Who Saw Me Crowned.

Kinnell. Feast, The.
How Many Nights.
Lastness.
Middle of the Way.
Supper after the Last, The.
Westport.
Kipling. Charm, A.
Run of the Downs, The.
Three-Part Song, A.
Kunitz. Green Ways.
Invocation: "Soul of my soul, in the ancestral wood."
Poem: "O Heart: this is a dream I had, or not a dream."
So Intricately Is This World Resolved.
Larkin. I Put My Mouth.
Long Roots Moor Summer to Our Side of Earth.
Lawrence. Corot.
Elemental.
Elements, The.
Escape.
Glory.
Gods.
Last Hours.
Letter from Town: On a Grey Morning in March.
Many Mansions.
Morality.
Paltry-Looking People.
Poverty.
Proper Pride.
Reading a Letter.
Renaissance.
Sane Universe, The.
Self-Protection.
Sinners.
Wild Common, The.
Wild Things in Captivity.
Levertov. Breathing, The.
Night on Hatchet Cove.
Lewis. *Country Gentleman, The.*
He sees the dawn expanding from a seashell.
Oh in a slim spaced forest.
Quest, The.
Wood Song.
Liddy. Correspondences.
On a Protestant Mystic.
Lindsay. Being the Dedication of a Morning.
Genesis.
I Want to Go Wandering.
Over the Appalachian Barricade.
Path in the Sky, The.
Short Walk along the Coast, A.
Longfellow. Aftermath.
Snow-Flakes.
Lorde. Echo.
Oaxaca.
October.
Return.
Lowell. Das ewig Weibliche.
Lowry. Bright as the Pleiades Upon the Soul.
Contemplation of Dead Reckoning.
Ex-Poet, The.
Happiness.
Kingfishers in British Columbia.
Kraken, Eagles, in British Columbia.
Lapis dawn is gleaming, A.
Mysterious Hint, A.
Pines write a Chinese poem upon the white-gold sun.
Two streams came from a different source, The.
Walk in Canada.
McAuley. Short Journeys Before Daybreak.
"MacDiarmid." Archin' here and arrachin there.
Back to the great music, Scottish Gaels. Too long.
Cheville.
Happy on Heimaey.
I was better with the sounds of the sea.
Poetry in which all connections will constantly render such services, A.
Wheesht, wheesht, Joyce, and let me hear.
McGrath. Autumn Song.

Return, The.
Up the Dark Valley.
MacLeish. Sunset Piece, The.
MacNeice. Evening in Connecticut.
House on a Cliff.
Jungle Clearance Ceylon.
Old Masters Abroad.
Western Landscape.
McNeill. Hill Song.
Stories at Evening (A Suburban Mother Tells Stories to Her Son).
Tillie Sage (2).
Time Is Our House.
Warning.
Mahon. Woods, The.
Marlowe. Another of the Same Nature, Made Since.
Marvell. Mower against Gardens, The.
Matthews. Human Hymn.
Wehlener Sonnenuhr Auslese 1959.
Meinke. Slow Child, The.
Vision.
Melville. Haglets, The.
Little Good Fellows, The.
Malvern Hill.
Pontoosuce.
Meredith. Change in Recurrence.
Could we know how kin we are.
Dirge in Woods.
Earth and Man.
Earth's Preference.
Earth's Secret.
Force and His Master.
Forest History.
Gentleness of Death, The.
Hans Euler.
Hard Weather.
Inspiration of the Great West Wind, The.
Invitation to the Country.
Love in the Valley.
Melampus.
Nature and Life.
Ode to the Spirit of Earth in Autumn.
Orson of the Muse, An.
Pastoral 2: "Yon upland slope which hides the sun."
Pastoral 3: "Now standing on this hedgeside path."
Pastoral 7: "Summer glows warm on the meadows, and speedwell, and gold-cups, and daisies."
Poetry of Wordsworth, The.
She drank what makes man demon at the draught.
South-West Wind in the Woodland.
Spirit of Shakespeare, The.
Succourful daughters of men are the rosed and starred.
This love of nature, that allures to take.
Three Singers to Young Blood, The.
To the High-Flyers.
We need some rallying point round which.
Whimper of Sympathy.
Woodland Peace.
Merrill. Channel 13.
In Nine Sleep Valley.
Syrinx.
Merton. Breath of Nature, The.
Bus has gone by, The.
Five Enemies, The.
Great and Small.
If I sometimes say that flowers smile.
In My End Is My Beginning.
Inner Law, The.
It would be wrong to let one man.
Man Is Born in Tao.
Metamorphosis.
Natur / aabho / rrret / vacuu / uuuum.
Natural History.
Nature loves to hide.
On a Day in August.
Ox Mountain Parable, The.
Rather the flying bird, leaving no trace.
Song: Contemplation.
Symphony for a Sea Bird.
Millay. Assault.
Doubt No More that Oberon.

God's World.
Journey.
Look how the bittersweet with lazy muscle moves aside.
Pastoral: "If it were only still!"
Milton. Morning Hymn of Adam.
Nature Does Not Suffer Decay.
Morgan. In Silence.
Loki's Song.
Njord.
White clouds, red leaves flying.
Morrison. Celebration of the Lizard.
Electric Storm.
Flowering, The.
Stand There Listening.
This Is My Forest.
Wake, A.
Nash. A Bas Ben Adhem.
Little Miss Muffet Sat on a Prophet—and Quite Right, Too!
Mr. Burgess, Meet Mr. Barmecide.
Nine Miles to the Railroad.
Nothing but Nature.
Nemerov. Companions, The.
Dependencies, The.
Elegy for a Nature Poet.
Figures of Thought.
Holding the Mirror Up to Nature.
Midsummer's Day.
Nature Morte.
Salt Garden, The.
Neruda. Are the salt and the sugar at work.
Cold.
Coming Back.
Do you hear yellow detonations.
Earth.
First Winter.
From the breach to the iron explosion.
How long would a rhinoceros last.
I entered the cave of the amethysts.
I Went.
If all rivers are sweet.
If I'm dead and don't know it.
Island (XII), The.
Men (IX), The.
Men (XVIII), The.
Quartz opens its eyes in the snow.
Star.
Stone, toppled by water and mountain, The.
Tell me, is the rose really naked.
This Is Simple.
To Puente Curvo on the Maldonado Spit in Uruguay.
To whom does the raggedy condor.
When all turned to altitude.
When does the butterfly read.
Winter.
Notley. Backyard.
O'Hara. Captain Bada.
Easter.
Oliver. Family, The.
Ghosts.
In Blackwater Woods.
Landscape.
Lilies Break Open Over the Dark Water, The.
Moths, The.
Nature.
On Winter's Margin.
Skunk Cabbage.
Snowshoe Hare, The.
Some Questions You Might Ask.
Turtle, The.
Wild Geese.
Olson. "At the boundary of the mighty world" H. (T) 620 foll.
Conqueror.
Cross-Legged, the Spider and the Web.
Day Song.
Dragon-Fly, The.
Drum World, The.
Epigon.
Every Man His Own Matador; or for That Matter Any Member of the Family.
Going from Battle to Battle.
Hour of evening—supper hour, for my neighbors—quietness, The.
Imbued / with the light.

Lower Field—Enniscorthy.
Maximus, from Dogtown-1.
May 20, 1959.
On the Shore.
Other Than.
Post Virginal, The.
Praises, The.
Said Adam.
She Who Hits at Will.
Story of an Olson, and Bad Thing, The.
Turn now and rise.
West 4 and 5.
What's Wrong with Pindar.
Will: termite mothers.
Writ, The.
Oppen. Behind their house, behind the back
 porch.
Owen. Elegy in April and September.
 From My Diary, July 1914.
Pack. It Comes to This.
 It Would Have Been Enough.
 Mountain Ash Without Cedar Waxwings.
 Orchid.
 Pantoum Approaching the Speed of Light.
 Snowy Owl, The.
 Waterfall.
Paley. Fear.
Patchen. Country Excursion.
 Deer and the Snake, The.
 Like a Mourningless Child.
 Manifold Fusions, The.
 On My Side.
 Pastoral: "Dove walks with sticky feet, The."
 Unnatural History of Peru, The.
 We Must Be Slow.
Piercy. Cod Summer.
 Development, The.
 Intruding.
 Postcard from the Garden.
 Skimpy Day at the Solstice.
Plath. Dark Wood, Dark Water.
 Wuthering Heights.
Poe. Stanzas: "How often we forget all time,
 when lone."
 Valley of Unrest, The.
Pope. Epistle I, to Sir Richard Temple, Lord
 Cobham.
 Epitaph on Sir Godfrey Kneller, in
 Westminster-Abbey, 1723.
 On His Grotto at Twickenham.
 What if the foot, ordain'd the dust to tread.
Pound. Coitus.
 Poem by the Bridge at Ten-shin.
 River Song, The.
 Spring, The.
Psalms. Psalm 65: "Praise waiteth for thee, O
 God, in Sion."
Raine. Acacia Tree.
 Amo Ergo Sum.
 Angelus.
 Canna's Basalt Crags.
 Childhood.
 Exile.
 Fateless Ones, The.
 Harvest of learning I have reaped.
 Heirloom.
 Hyacinth, The.
 I could have told much by the way.
 If, into this evening as the grass receives the
 dew.
 Into what pattern, into what music have the
 spheres whirled us.
 Marriage of Psyche, The.
 Message from Home.
 Moment, The.
 Natura Naturans.
 Night in Martindale.
 On an Ancient Isle.
 On Leaving Ullswater.
 Poet Answers the Accuser, The.
 Return, The.
 Self.
 Seventh Day.
 Soliloquy Upon Love.
 Spell of Sleep.
 Today: / This leafy apple-tree, gray.
 Traveller, The.

Triad.
Under these hills too high and bare.
What have I to regret.
Wilderness, The.
Winter Paradise.
Winter Solstice.
Word Made Flesh.
Your gift of life was idleness.
Ransom. Prometheus in Straits.
Rexroth. Autumn in California.
 Floating.
 Inversely, As the Square of Their Distances
 Apart.
 Mary and the Seasons.
 On What Planet.
 Spark in the Tinder of Knowing, The.
 Toward An Organic Philosophy.
 Young rice plants are just being.
Rich. In the Woods.
 River-fog will do for privacy, The.
 Upcountry.
Robinson. Monadnock through the Trees.
 Torrent, The.
Roethke. Bring the Day!
 Far Field, The.
 Field of Light, A.
 Genesis.
 Give a Way, Ye Gates.
 Her Time.
 I Cry, Love! Love!
 I Waited.
 Light Poem.
 Long Waters, The.
 Longing, The.
 Manifestation, The.
 Minimal, The.
 O Lull Me, Lull Me.
 O, Thou Opening, O.
 Otto.
 Praise to the End!
 Rose, The.
 Sequel, The.
 Shape of the Fire, The.
 Small, The.
 Thing, The.
 Unfold! Unfold!
 Visitant, The.
 Walk in Late Summer, A.
 Words for the Wind.
Rolfe. Dawn Song.
 More than Flesh to Fathom.
 Pastoral: "Now, on this bluest of mornings, we
 wake."
Rossetti. Are Ye Not Much Better Than
 They?
 Books In the Running Brooks.
 Cobwebs.
 Dead City, The.
 Easter Morning.
 Exultate Deo.
 Fluttered Wings.
 For Advent.
 Frisky Lamb, A.
 From early dawn until the flush of noon.
 Heartsease in my garden bed, / With
 sweetwilliam white and red.
 Hills are tipped with sunshine, while I walk /
 In shadows dim and cold.
 I Have a Message unto Thee.
 I sit among the green shady valleys oft.
 Immalee.
 In the Lane.
 Judge Not According to the Appearance.
 May.
 Minnie and Mattie.
 Patience of Hope.
 Rosy maiden Winifred, / With a milkpail on
 her head.
 Rushes in a watery place, / And reeds in a
 hollow.
 Seasons ("Crocuses and snowdrops wither").
 Seasons ("In springtime when the leaves...").
 Seasons ("Oh the cheerful budding-time").
 Sir Winter.
 Song: "Two doves upon the selfsame branch."
 Spring Fancies.

Summer ("Come, cuckoo, come").
Summer ("Hark to the song...").
Summer ("Winter is cold-hearted").
To What Purpose Is This Waste?
What Good Shall My Life Do Me?
Wintry Sonnet, A.
World's Harmonies, The.
Wouldst thou give me a heavy jewelled
 crown.
Rukeyser. Mountain: One from Bryant.
Sandburg. Just Before April Came.
 So to Speak.
 Sumach and Birds.
 Wind Horses.
Sarton. Apple Tree in May.
 Composition.
 Easter Morning.
 Fig, The.
 Guest, A.
 Invocation: "Come out of the dark earth."
 Journey toward Poetry.
 March-Mad.
 Mud Season.
 Of the Seasons.
 These Images Remain.
Schuyler. Beaded Balustrade.
 Closed Gentian Distances.
 Gulls.
 Poem: "Your enchantment / enchants me,
 stretched."
 Sonnet: "August, tasting of ripe grapes and
 afternoon sleep."
 Today.
 Under the Hanger.
 With Frank and George at Lexington.
Schwartz. If nature is life, nature is death.
 Praise Is Traditional and Appropriate.
Sexton. Buttered Greens.
Shakespeare. Sonnet 15: "When I consider
 everything that grows."
 Sonnet 68: "Thus is his cheek the map of days
 outworn."
 Sonnet 98: "From you have I been absent in
 the spring."
Shapiro. Giantess.
 Travelogue for Exiles.
Shelley. Fragment: Rome and Nature.
 Fragment: "When soft winds and sunny skies."
 Love's Philosophy.
 Mont Blanc.
 To a Skylark.
Shelton. Boojum Tree, The.
 Desert Water.
 Now while the moon pulls darkness.
 Out Here.
 Seven Preludes to Silence.
 Survival.
 Teeth of These Mountains, The.
 Wonders of the World.
Simic. Ax.
 Peaceful Kingdom.
 Strictly Bucolic.
 Summer Morning.
Smart. St. Philip and St. James.
Smith, Charlotte. Evening.
 Far on the sands, the low, retiring tide.
 Saint Monica.
 Song from the French.
 Supposed to Have Been Written in the
 Hebrides.
 Swallow, The.
 Walk by the Water, A.
 Wild Flowers.
 Written at Bignor Park in Sussex, in August,
 1799.
Smith, Patti. Suite.
Smith, Stevie. Alone in the Woods.
 Every Lovely Limb's a Desolation.
 Lady "Rogue" Singleton.
 Nature and Free Animals.
 Pretty.
 Touch and Go.
 Will Man Ever Face Fact and Not Feel Flat?
Snodgrass. Call for Clues.
 Lullaby: The Comforting of Cock Robin.
 September.
Snyder. Berry Feast, A.

Burning Island.
By Frazier Creek Falls.
Clambering up the Cold Mountain path.
Flung from demonic wombs.
For All.
Old Rotting Tree Trunk Down.
Old Woman Nature.
Piute Creek.
Ripples on the Surface.
Six Years.
Sours of the Hills.
Target Practice.
Wave.
We Make Our Vows Together with All
   Beings.
Southwell. Vale of Tear[e]s, A.
Spenser. At length, even at the time when
   Morpheus.
Stafford. How to Regain Your Soul.
Oregon Message, An.
Well Rising, The.
Stein. Study Nature.
What Does She See When She Shuts Her
   Eyes.
Stevens. Academic Discourse at Havana.
Banal Sojourn.
Botanist on Alp (No. 1).
Doctor of Geneva, The.
Dove in the Belly, The.
Dry Loaf.
Nomad Exquisite.
Sense of the Sleight-of-Hand Man, The.
Word with José Rodríguez-Feo.
Stevenson. Air of Diabelli's.
And thorns, but did the sculptor spare.
Camp, A.
House Beautiful, The.
I do not fear to own me kin.
In Lupum.
Mill-House, The.
Not undelightful, friend, our rustic ease.
On the gorgeous hills of morning.
Pleasant river gushes, The.
Song: "Light foot and tight foot."
Storm.
To Dr. Hake.
Stuart. Percussion.
Sutter. Daybreak.
Tate. Correspondences.
Tennyson. Edwin Morris.
Wish, that of the living whole, The.
Thomas. All All and All the Dry Worlds
   Lever.
Find Meat on Bones.
Foster the Light.
Process in the Weather of the Heart, A.
This Bread I Break.
Why East Wind Chills.
Thomson. Morning in the Country, The.
To Mr. Thomson, on his Blooming Winter.
Tomlinson. Discrepancies.
Four Kantian Lyrics.
Frondes Agrestes.
In Winter Woods.
Nature Poem.
Reflections.
Turco. Colony, The.
Hunting Moon.
Ice House, The.
Maple Works, The.
Meetinghouse, The.
Mill, The.
Millpond.
Tollhouse, The.
Trading Post, The.
Updike. Lamplight.
Nature.
Ode to Growth.
Penumbrae.
Solitary Pond, The.
Telephone Poles.
To a Box Turtle.
Van Duyn. Along the Road.
Ballad of Blossom, The.
Dwarf in the Woods.
End of May.
From Yellow Lake: An Interval.

Gentle Snorer, The.
Good Man, The.
Postcards from Cape Split.
Quebec Suite.
View, A.
West Branch Ponds, Kokadjo, Maine.
Wakoski. Removed from Natural Habitat.
Warren. Gold Glade.
Paul Valéry Stood on the Cliff and Confronted
   the Furious Energies of Nature.
Sound of That Wind, The.
Sunset Walk in Thaw-Time in Vermont.
Whitman. Give Me the Splendid Silent Sun.
Italian Music in Dakota.
Me Imperturbe.
Proud Music of the Storm.
Spontaneous Me.
To a President.
We Two, How Long We Were Fool'd.
Whittier. Birchbrook Mill.
Hive at Gettysburg, The.
Outdoor Reception, An.
Over-Heart, The.
Prelude: "Along the roadside, like the flowers
   of gold."
Revisited.
River Path, The.
Summer Pilgrimage, A.
Tent on the Beach, The.
Worship of Nature, The.
Wilbur. Ceremony.
Flumen Tenebrarum.
Hamlen Brook.
Mined Country.
Part of a Letter.
Problem from Milton, A.
Sunlight Is Imagination.
Williams, Charles Kenneth. Clay out of
   Silence.
Downwards.
Hounding Mercy.
Just Right.
Sky, Water.
Williams, Miller. August Evening Outside of
   Nashville, An.
Williams, William Carlos. Ballet.
Love Song: "Daisies are broken."
Martin and Katherine.
Pastoral 2: "If I talk to things."
Pastoral; "If I say I have heard voices."
Promenade.
Raleigh Was Right.
Three Sonnets.
Wanderer, The.
Wordsworth. Airey-Force Valley.
Among the Ruins of a Convent in the
   Apennines.
Barberry-Tree, The.
Between Namur and Liege.
By the Side of Rydal Mere.
Come ye that are disturbed, this steady voice.
Companion to the Foregoing [Love Lies
   Bleeding].
Composed by the Side of Grasmere Lake.
Composed on the Banks of a Rocky Stream.
Composed upon an Evening of Extraordinary
   Splendour and Beauty.
Composed While the Author Was Engaged in
   Writing a Tract, Occasioned by the
   Convention of Cintra.
Contrast; the Parrot and the Wren, The.
Dedication (Sent with These Poems, in Ms.,
   To —).
Descriptive Sketches Taken During a
   Pedestrian Tour among the Alps.
Evening Walk Addressed to a Young Lady,
   An.
Expostulation and Reply.
Fall of the Aar—Handec, The.
Filial Piety.
Fragment: "In vain did Time and Nature.."
Fragment: Redundance.
Fragments from the Alfoxden Notebook (I).
Fragments from the "Christabel" Note-book.
Highland Hut.
I love upon a stormy night.
In These Fair Vales Hath Many a Tree.

Incipient Madness.
Inscription in the Grounds of Coleorton, the
   Seat of Sir George Beaumont, BART.,
   Leicestershire.
It was an April morning: fresh and clear.
Lines Composed a Few Miles above Tintern
   Abbey on Revisiting the Banks of the Wye
   during a Tour, July 13, 1798.
Lines Written in Early Spring.
LITTLE Onward Lend Thy Guiding Hand, A.
Mark the concentrated hazels that enclose.
More May not Be by Human Art Exprest.
Motto Intended for Poems on the Naming of
   Places.
Not in the Lucid Intervals of Life.
Ode: Intimations of Immortality [from
   Recollections of Early Childhood].
Ode to Lycoris; May, 1817.
On the Projected Kendal and Windermere
   Railway.
Oxford, May 30, 1820 ("Shame on this
   faithless heart! that could allow").
Oxford, May 30, 1820 ("Ye sacred Nurseries
   of blooming Youth!").
Peter Bell; a Tale.
Proud Were Ye, Mountains, When, in Times
   of Old.
Retirement.
Rural Illusions.
So Fair, So Sweet, Withal So Sensitive.
Sonnet Composed at—Castle.
Stars Are Mansions Built by Nature's Hand,
   The.
Stray Pleasures.
Suggested at Tyndrum in a Storm.
Suggested by a Picture of the Bird of
   Paradise.
Tables Turned, The.
There is a bondage worse, far worse, to bear.
There is an Eminence,—of these our hills.
Though the Bold Wings of Poesy Affect.
Three years she grew in sun and shower.
To a Young Lady Who Had Been Reproached
   for Taking Long Walks in the Country.
To M. H.
Trosachs, The.
Vale of Esthwaite, The.
View from the Top of Black Comb.
Western clouds a deepening gloom display,
   The.
When, to the attractions of the busy world.
Written in London, September, 1802.
Written in Very Early Youth.
Wright, Charles. Bicoastal Journal.
California Spring.
Chinese Journal.
Dead Color.
December Journal.
George Trakl Journal.
Holy Thursday.
Journal of English Days, A.
Journal of One Significant Landscape, A.
Journal of Southern Rivers, A.
Laguna Dantesca.
Language Journal.
Last Journal.
Local Journal.
Lonesome Pine Special.
May Journal.
Mount Caribou at Night.
Night Journal.
Night Journal II.
Primitive Journal II.
Saturday Morning Journal.
Self-Portrait ("Someday they'll find me out,
   and my lavish hands").
Silent Journal.
Spring Abstract.
Vesper Journal.
Yard Journal.
Wright, James. Depressed by a Book of Bad
   Poetry, I Walk toward an Unused Pasture and
   Invite the Insects to Join Me.
Fit against the Country, A.
Goodbye to the Poetry of Calcium.
Horse, The.
Love Song to a Morning.

Nature Alive.
Prayer to Escape from the Market Place, A.
She Hid in the Trees from the Nurses.
Witches Waken the Natural World in Spring.
Yeats. Her Anxiety.
Indian to His Love, The.
Lake Isle of Innisfree, The.
Sorrow of Love, The ("Brawling of a sparrow in the eaves, The").
Young. Big Ocean-Waving, Woman-Pulling Moon.
Big Sur.
For Poets.
Mountains of California: Part 2, The.
No More Doors Tonight.
October Window.
Zimmer. Zimmer Directs Himself Home from the Diggings.
Zukofsky. Alba (1952).
Bird that cries like a baby, The.
Guests, The.
Mountain Laurel.
O sleep, the sky goes down behind the poplars.
Passing tall.
Prop. LXI.
So sounds grass, and if it is sun or no sun.
Song Theme.
Xenophanes.

Navaho, The
Carruth. None.
Tomlinson. Before the Dance.
Williams, William Carlos. Navajo.

Naval Battles
Donne. Burnt Ship, A.
Dryden. Cheerful soldiers, with new stores supplied, The.
Galvin. Sea Huns.
Ginsberg. Battleship Newsreel.
Hartley. Red targets blowing.
Keats. See, the Ship in the Bay Is Riding.
Kipling. Ballad of the *Clampherdown*, The.
Destroyers, The.
Verdicts, The.
Marvell. Dutch in the Medway, The.
Loyal Scot, The.
On the Victory Obtained by Blake over the Spaniards, in the Bay of Santa [*or* Sancta] Cruz, in the Island of Tenerife, 1657.
Melville. At the Cannon's Mouth.
Commemorative of a Naval Victory.
In the Turret.
Temeraire, The.
Utilitarian View of the Monitor's Fight, A.
Smith, Charlotte. Sea View, The.

Navy, France
Browning, Robert. Hervé Riel.

Navy, Great Britain
Kipling. Changelings, The.
Cruisers.
Destroyers, The.
Farewell and adieu to you, Harwich Ladies.
Lowestoft Boat, The.
Mine Sweepers.
North Sea Patrol, The.
Soldier an' Sailor Too.
Song in Storm, A.
Tin Fish.
Trade, The.
Verdicts, The.
When the Great Ark.
White Horses.
Smart. Ode to Admiral Sir George Pocock.

Navy, Spain
Marvell. Now does *Spains* Fleet her spatious wings unfold.

Navy, United States
Cohen. Commentary—It's Probably Spring.
It's Probably Spring.
Haines. Mothball Fleet: Benicia, California.
McNeill. Ballad of Joe Bittner.

Navy Life
Burns. My Bonnie [*or* Bony] Mary.
Kipling. Changelings, The.

Nazis
Dobyns. Confession.

Hill. Canaan.
Christmas Trees.
Jong. Nazi Amphitheatre, The.
Kunitz. Next to Last Things.
Mahon. Knut Hamsun in Old Age.
Merton. Chant to Be Used in Processions around a Site with Furnaces.
Epitaph for a Public Servant.
Oliver. 1945—1985: Poem for the Anniversary.
Rolfe. Witness at Leipzig.
Sandburg. Man with the Broken Fingers, The.
Snodgrass. Dr. Joseph Goebbels ("Say goodbye to the help, the ranks").
Dr. Joseph Goebbels ("Stand back, make way, you mindless scum").
HEINRICH•HIMMLER, FORMER•REICHSFUEHRER•SS—1•MAY•1945•.
HEINRICH•HIMMLER•FORMER•REICHSFUEHRER•SS—29•APRIL•1945•.
HEINRICH•HIMMLER•REICHSFUEHRER•SS—8•APRIL•1945•.
Hermann Göring, Former Reichsmarschall.
Spender. Perhaps.
Wilbur. On the Eyes of an SS Officer.
Williams, Charles Kenneth. Combat.
Spit.
Wright, James. Small Blue Heron, The.

Nebraska (state)
Kooser. Fort Robinson.
So This Is Nebraska.
Sandburg. Band Concert.
Omaha.
Sunset from Omaha Hotel Window.
Shapiro. Nebraska.
Tornado Warning.
Yau. Postcards from Nebraska.

Nebuchadnezzar
Donne. Liar, The.
Keats. Nebuchadnezzar's Dream.
Nemerov. Nebuchadnezzar, Solus.

Necrophilia
O'Hara. Ode on Necrophilia.

See also **Corpses.**

Need
Atwood. I see you fugitive, stumbling across the prarie.
You are the sun / in reverse, all energy.
Beatles. Help!
I Need You.
If I Needed Someone.
With a Little Help from My Friends.
Berg. Talking.
Berry. Wild Geese, The.
Bukowski. Everything.
Quiet Clean Girls in Gingham Dresses..
Bunting. Thrush in the syringa sings, A.
Burns. Burns Grace at Kirkudbright.
Ceravolo. Spring in This World of Poor Mutts.
Clark. Narcissism.
Cooper. Rent.
Suicide Note.
Creeley. Dream, The.
For W.C.W. ("Rhyme is after, The").
Hello.
Soup.
Dickinson. Had I not This, or This, I said.
I meant to have but modest needs.
Undue Significance a starving man attaches.
Dunn. Fable of the Water Merchants.
Sister.
Turning Fifty.
"Dylan." Don't Fall Apart on Me Tonight.
If Not for You.
Shot of Love.
Emerson. Do that which you can do.
O Hafiz! speak not of thy need.
Everson. Challenge, The.
I Am Long Weaned.
Gunn. Down in the cellars, nothing is visible.
Haines. Way We Live, The.
Herrick. No Want Where There's Little.
Want.
Hewitt. Blessing.

Iron Circle, The.
Little Bourgeois is Upset, The.
Hughes, Ted. And faces at the glutted shop-windows.
Koertge. Ubiquity of the Need for Love, The.
Kooser. Dry Winter Letter to Friends, A.
Lewis. Shattered crystal of his mind, The.
Lowry. No Time to Stop and Think.
Personal.
With Dearest Love Enfolded and Enclosed from *All* the Litle Animals.
Nemerov. Song: "Provide your friend with almanacs."
Olson. Telesphere, The.
"Reed." Strawman.
Rich. Statue.
Your dog, tranquil and innocent, dozes through.
Your silence today is a pond where drowned things live.
Rossetti. Diamond or a coal? / A diamond, if you please, A.
Motherless baby and babyless mother.
Rukeyser. Ballad Theme, A.
Shakespeare. Sonnet 75: "So are you to my thoughts as food to life."
Sorrentino. What intense colloquy with the self.
Stuart. Writing Machine, The.
Walker. Threatened.
Warren. Interjection #6: What You Sometimes Feel on Your Face at Night.
Whitman. Not Heaving from My Ribb'd Breast Only.
Young. Backtracking.
Dance of the Infidels.

See also **Poverty.**

Needles
Dickey, James. Voyage of the Needle, The.
Eberhart. Evaluation Under a Pine Tree, Lying On Pine Needles, An.

Nefertiti
Hartley. Queen Nefertiti—Small Fragment of Nose and Mouth Only.
Same Fragment—Second Look.

Neglect
Ammons. Negligence These Days.
Berry. Sowing.
Bly. Getting Up Late.
Bunting. You leave / nobody else.
Carew. My Mistress Commanding Me to Return Her Letters.
To a Lady, Not Yet Enjoyed by Her Husband.
Herrick. Neglect.
Hewitt. Failed Image.
If I had given you that love and care.
My Uncle Johnny.
Ruins Answer, The.
Survival.
Lorde. And Don't Think I Won't Be Waiting.
Need: A Chorale for Black Woman Voices.
St. Louis Out of Time.
Mahon. Disused Shed in Co. Wexford, A.
Raine. I used to watch you, sleeping.
Sarton. Hard Death, A.
Snodgrass. Coroner's Inquest.
Sorrentino. Closet, The.
Stuart. Elegies for Walker Dabney Stuart, Jr.
Wilbur. Shame.
Williams, Charles Kenneth. Souls.

Negro Spirituals. *see* Spirituals.

Negroes. *see* African Americans.

Neighbors
Atwood. First Neighbours.
We think of you as one.
Berry. By the excellence of his work the workman is a neighbor. By.
Bukowski. Experience.
Fleg.
High-Rise of the New World, The.
New Place, The.
Puzzle, The.
3:30 A.M. Conversation.
Carruth. Line, The.
Marshall Washer.
You know what?

Cummings. There are 6 doors.
De la Mare. Peeping Tom.
Dove. House on Bishop Street, The.
Dunbar. Differences.
Frost. Mending Wall.
Gardner. This Neighborhood.
Gunn. All Do Not All Things Well.
Girls Next Door, The.
Hacker. Two Cities.
Hardy. Old Neighbour and the New, The.
Heaney. Other Side, The.
Herrick. Upon Bran.
Hewitt. Company.
Folk Custom.
Halloweve: A Glensman Speaks.
Lint Pulling, The.
Hugo. What Thou Lovest Well Remains
American.
Lawrence. As Thyself!
Love Thy Neighbour.
Lorde. Cables To Rage Or I've Been Talking
On This Street Corner.
Moving Out Or the End of Cooperative
Living.
Lowry. Hypocrite! Oxford Grouper! Yahoo!
Millay. Portrait by a Neighbour.
Nash. People upstairs, The.
Piercy. Neighbor, The.
Robinson. Neighbors.
Sandburg. Neighbors.
Snodgrass. Flash Flood.
Stevenson. Ad Nepotem.
Wakoski. Night Rides of My Neighbor, Lorca,
That Prevent Sleep, The.
Wilbur. He Was.
Williams, Miller. Missing Persons.
Williams, William Carlos. Exercise No. 2.
Young. Dancing Day to Day.
Studio up over in Your Ear.

Nelson, Horatio Nelson, Viscount
Davie. Suffolk.
Graves. 1805.
Melville. *Temeraire*, The.
Meredith. October 21, 1905.
Trafalgar Day.

Nepal
Kipling. Sacrifice of Er-Heb, The.

Neptune (god)
Campion. Hymne in Praise of Neptune, A.
Hall. On a Horse Carved in Wood.
Herrick. Another to Neptune.
Kipling. Poseidon's Law.
Lawrence. Neptune's Little Affair with
Freedom.

Nero
Gray. Agrippina.
Herrick. Cruelties.

Neruda, Pablo
Dobyns. Pablo Neruda.
Ferlinghetti. General Song of Humanity, The.
Hidden Door.
Jong. To Pablo Neruda.
McGrath. Lament for Pablo Neruda.
Warrant for Pablo Neruda, A.
Rukeyser. Neruda, the Wine.
Williams, William Carlos. Tribute to Neruda
the Poet Collector of Seashells.

Ness, Loch, Scotland
Burns. Written with a Pencil, Standing by the
Fall of Fyers, near Loch-Ness.

Nests. *see* **Birds' Nests.**

Netherlands
Coleridge. Netherlands, The.
Cowper. To Lady Austen.
Hill. Lowlands of Holland, The.
Marvell. Character of Holland, The.
In Legationem Domini Oliveri St John ad
Provincias Foederatas [On the Embassy of
Lord Oliver St John to the United Provinces].

Nettles
Housman. With seed the sowers scatter.

Nevada (state)
Carruth. Too Tenuous.
Dickey, William. Gambling at Reno.
Rexroth. Toward An Organic Philosophy.
Sandburg. March of the Hungry Mountains.

Stafford. From the Move to California.
Wright, James. Gambling in Stateline, Nevada.

New England
Betjeman. Longfellow's Visit to Venice.
Bradstreet. New England.
Carruth. Begin right here. The Campground
Road. Some calls it the.
Crow's Mark.
Essay on Love.
First Version, The.
Fourth.
Ithiel Falls, below the Nazarene campground.
A name.
Keep going. *There's nothing else to do.* Past.
Marshall Washer.
Not night now. Dawn. Six o'clock, a
November morning.
Slums par excellence that were your farms!
And all.
Ugly, evil, dying. The old soft lines.
Creeley. For Anybody.
Dickinson. Field of Stubble, lying sere, A.
Robin's my Criterion for Tune, The.
Dobyns. Dancing in Vacationland.
Eberhart. Explorer on Main Street, The.
Going to Maine.
Ides of March, The.
River Water Music.
Eliot. Cousin Nancy.
Emerson. Monadnoc.
Frost. Hundred Collars, A.
Ginsberg. Autumn Gold: New England Fall.
Hall. Scenic View.
Hartley. Cobwebs and Ratholes.
World-Passport Visa.
Jong. New England Winter.
Lowell. Fourth of July in Maine.
Merrill. Summer People, The.
Nemerov. For Robert Frost, in the Autumn, in
Vermont.
Olson. Move Over.
New England March.
Oppen. Product.
Rich. Spirit of Place, The.
Rukeyser. Ives.
Schuyler. Now and Then.
Seeking.
Sexton. Expatriates, The.
Stuart. Charles River, The.
Walcott. Old New England.
Whittier. Extract from "A New England
Legend."
Mogg Megone.
Mountain Pictures.
To G. G.
Williams, William Carlos. New England.

New Guinea
Merton. Cargo Catechism.
Cargo Songs.

New Hampshire (state)
Eberhart. River Water Music.
Snowy Owl.
Three Kids.
Eliot. New Hampshire.
Emerson. Monadnoc.
Frost. Generations of Men, The.
New Hampshire.
Hall. Black Faced Sheep, The.
Elegy for Wesley Wells.
Granite and Grass.
New Hampshire.
Speeches.
Twelve Seasons.
Kinnell. Flower Herding on Mount
Monadnock.
Freedom, New Hampshire.
Matthews. On the Porch at the Frost Place,
Franconia, NH.
Robinson. Monadnock through the Trees.
Sandburg. New Hampshire Again.
Whittier. Mount Agiochook.
New Hampshire.

New Jersey (state)
Ciardi. Bicentennial.
Dunn. Smiles.
Toward the Verrazano.
Ginsberg. Bayonne Entering NYC.

Garden State.
Ode to the Setting Sun.
Paterson.
Levertov. For Floss.
Lieberman. Courtship of the Jersey Lineman.
Oppen. Undertaking in New Jersey, The.
Schuyler. Over the Hills.
Tomlinson. Ice Cream at Blauenberg.
Whitman. Patrolling Barnegat.
Williams, William Carlos. Passaic, N.J.
Semblables, The.
Young. Hoboken Broken Down: A Hasty
Recollection.

New Mexico (state)
Carruth. Coming Down to the Desert at
Lordsburg, N.M.
Shake, Well Before Using.
Hartley. Festival of the Corn, The.
Jeffers. New Mexican Mountain.
Lawrence. Autumn at Taos.
Eagle in New Mexico.
Men in New Mexico.
Sandburg. Joliet.
Santa Fe Sketches.
Tomlinson. Albuquerque.
Matachines, The.

New Orleans, Louisiana
Carruth. New Orleans.
"Dylan." Bob Dylan's New Orleans Rag.
Kinnell. Last River, The.
Larkin. For Sidney Bechet.
Morrison. Mystery of the Dream.
Sidewalkers Moved, The.
Young. New Orleans Intermissiom.

New Year
Berryman. New Year's Eve.
Bishop. January First.
Burns. Elegy on the Year 1788.
Sketch. New Year's Day. To Mrs. Dunlop.
To Miss L———.
Byron. Here's a Happy New Year! But with
Reason.
Carew. New Year's Gift. To the King, A.
New Year's Sacrifice: To Lucinda, A.
To the New Year [For the Countess of
Carlisle].
Cohen. Music Crept by Us, The.
Crashaw. Hymn for New Year's Day.
Cummings. Passing of the Year, The.
Davie. New Year Wishes for the English.
Donne. To the Countess of Bedford at New
Year's Tide.
Ginsberg. December 31, 1978.
Graves. Ancestors.
Griffiths. Doors of the Year, Well Done, The.
Hardy. At the Entering of the New Year.
New Year's Eve.
New Year's Eve in War Time, A.
Herrick. New-Year's [or New-Yeares] Gift
Sent to Sir Simeon Steward, A.
Jonson. New years [or yeares], expect new
gifts: sister, your harp[e].
New Year's Gift Sung to King Charles. 1635,
A.
Kooser. New Year's Day.
Larkin. New Year.
Lowry. And who is it through the forest after
the.
Prayer from the Wicket Gate for Forty One
Doors for Forty Two.
Though we are all a little bit disappointed this
year there won't be any fireworks.
Meredith. New Year's Eve.
Time.
Wassail for the New Year, A.
Nash. Good-By, Old Year, You Oaf or Why
Don't They Pay the Bonus.
Good Riddance, but Now What?
Put Back Those Whiskers, I Know You.
Nathan. Audit.
O'Hara. For the Chinese New Year & for Bill
Berkson.
Patchen. At the New Year.
Rich. At the Jewish New Year.
New Year Morning.
Rossetti. Hail, noble face of noble friend!
Sarton. Greeting.

Schuyler.　Empathy and New Year.
Shelton.　New Year's Eve.
Smart.　New Year.
Suckling.　On New-Year's Day 1640, to the
　King.
Swift.　New Year's Gift for Bec, A.
　To Janus.
Warren.　Late Subterfuge.
Whitman.　New Year's Day, 1848.
Wilbur.　Year's End.
Wordsworth.　Lament of Mary Queen of Scots
　on the Eve of a New Year.
Zukofsky.　Celia's Birthday Poem.
New York (state)
Ferlinghetti.　New York—Albany.
Hall.　Southwest of Buffalo.
Lindsay.　Niagara.
Morgan.　Canadaigua.
Olson.　Buffalo Ode.
Rich.　Breakfast in a Bowling Alley in Utica,
　New York.
Sandburg.　Slants at Buffalo, New York.
Schuyler.　Few Days, A.
　Morning of the Poem, The.
Walcott.　Upstate.
Wilbur.　Sleepless at Crown Point.
Williams, William Carlos.　Rapid Transit.
New York City
Angelou.　Awaking in New York.
　Times-Square-Shoeshine-Composition.
Berrigan.　American Express.
　Bean Spasms.
　February Air.
　For You.
　I Heard Brew Moore Say, One Day.
　In the 51st State.
　Red Shift.
　Seurat and Juan Gris combine this season.
　Things To Do in New York (City).
　Whitman in Black.
Bishop.　Invitation to Miss Marianne Moore.
　Letter to N. Y.
　Trouvée.
Carroll, Jim.　Ad Man's Daughter, The.
　At eighteen years of age.
　Back to the streets always, ravaged and wet.
　California Poem.
　Cough Syrup.
　Fragment: Little N.Y. Ode.
　Green Bus, The.
　Here I walked with a memory of workers in
　midtown.
　I drank cough syrup in alcoves.
　I have walked these streets so often I could.
　I stored daylight in secret attics.
　I watched a street gang heading.
　In midtown again the way you stop.
　Invisible Sleep.
　It's still gray and wet almost pink.
　Jet Fizzle.
　Love Poem: "I see myself, sad now, as in a
　mirror."
　Micky.
　Painting by Flashlight.
　Poem: "We are very much a part of the
　boredom."
　There is a stadium beside my window.
　3 hours into the afternoon of March 9th.
　To the Secret Poets of Kansas.
　What matter for thick armchairs and fine
　shelves for books?
　When he was young in Harlem my father.
Carruth.　Day　very solid　February 12th,
　1944, A.
　December now. Winter deepens and darkens.
　Stars.
Cohen.　Chelsea Hotel.
　Famous Blue Raincoat.
　Far from the Soil.
　First We Take Manhattan.
　I Am Dying.
Crane.　Tunnel, The.
Creeley.　Days and Days.
　NYC—.
Cummings.　At the ferocious phenomenon of 5
　o'clock i find myself gently decompos.
　By god i want above fourteenth.

Fragrant sag of fruit distinctly grouped, A.
Hanged / if n / y in a real hot spell.
I was sitting in mcsoreley's.　outside it was
　New York and beauti- / fully snowing.
　Noise.
　Woman / of bronze / unhappy, A.
Davie.　New York in August.
Dickey, James.　Coming Back to America.
"Dylan."　Hard Times in New York Town.
　Run go get out of here.
　Talking New York.
Eberhart.　Fragment of New York, 1929.
　Sailing to Buck's Harbor.
　Snowy Owl.
Edmunds.　December 27, 1988.
　Nocturne.
Emerson.　He walked the streets of great New
　York.
Everson.　Vision of Felicity, The.
Ferlinghetti.　Reading Yeats I do not think.
　Retired Ballerinas, Central Park West.
Ginsberg.　Back on Times Square, Dreaming of
　Times Square.
　Bayonne Entering NYC.
　Hospital Window.
　Manhattan May Day Midnight.
　Mugging.
　My Sad Self.
　345 W. 15th St.
　Two Sonnets.
　Waking in New York.
Gunn.　Iron Landscapes (and the Statue of
　Liberty).
Hartley.　Bulldog on the Roof—Avenue C.
　City Vignettes.
　Window Washer—Avenue C.
Hewitt.　My Aunt Sarah and Uncle Joe.
Hughes, Langston.　New Yorkers.
Jong.　I Live in New York.
　January in New York.
Kinnell.　Avenue Bearing the Initial of Christ
　into the New World, The.
Koch.　Thanksgiving.
Levertov.　From the Roof.
Levine.　Winter Words.
Liddy.　Poem for My Sister Nora, at the
　Reading.
Lorde.　Birthday Memorial to Seventh Street,
　A.
　New York City.
Lowell.　Inauguration Day: January 1953.
　Opposite House, The.
McGrath.　Drowned Man: Death Between Two
　Rivers, The.
MacLeish.　& Forty-Second Street.
Matthews.　107th & Amsterdam.
Merrill.　Urban Convalescence, An.
Merton.　Holy Communion: the City.
　Hymn of Not Much Praise for New York
　City.
　In the Ruins of New York.
　Queens Tunnel.
Moore.　New York.
Morgan.　Lucky black man in my dream.
　Rose dawn, in smoke, over the East River, A.
Nash.　Brief Guide to New York, A.
　I Always Say There's No Place Like New
　York in the Summer, or, That Cottage Small
　by a Waterfall Was Snapped Up Last
　February.
　I Saw Euterpe Kissing Santa Claus.
　Strange Case of Mr. Niobob's
　Transmogrification.
Nemerov.　Frozen City, The.
　Metropolitan Sunday.
　Two Poems.
O'Hara.　Adieu to Norman, Bon Jour to Joan
　and Jean-Paul.
　Commercial Variations.
　Essay on Style.
　F. (Missive & Walk) I. #53.
　For the Chinese New Year & for Bill
　Berkson.
　Poem: "Khrushchev is coming on the right
　day!"
　Rhapsody.
　Saint.

Second Avenue.
Step Away from Them, A.
Steps.
"Unfinished," The.
You Are Gorgeous and I'm Coming.
Oppen.　Antique.
　Emotions are engaged, The.
　For the people of that flow.
　It is *that* light.
　Language of New York, A.
　Whitman: "April 19, 1864."
Paley.　At the Battery.
　Bob Visits Friends.
　Having Arrived by Bike at Battery Park.
　Housing.
　Mulberry Street ends in good works.
　Nature of This City, The.
　On Mother's Day.
　On the Subway Station.
　Psalm: "Their shoes are stuccoed with sawdust
　and blood."
　34th Street Song.
　20th Street　Spring.
Piercy.　I Awoke with the Room Cold.
　Skyscrapers of the Financial District Dance
　with Gasman, The.
"Reed."　Chelsea Girls.
　Dirty Blvd.
　Hold On.
　N.Y. Telephone Conversation.
　Romeo Had Juliette.
　Tell It to Your Heart.
　Walk on the Wild Side.
Rich.　Upper Broadway.
　Wherever in this city, screens flicker.
Rukeyser.　Leaving New York, I looked back
　fourteen times.
　Night Flight : New York.
　Seventh Avenue.
Sandburg.　Eleventh Avenue Racket.
　Neighbors.
　Night Movement—New York.
　This Street Never Sleeps.
　Three Slants at New York.
Schuyler.　Alice Faye at Ruby Foo's.
　April and Its Forsythia.
　Back.
　December.
　Dining Out with Doug and Frank.
　East Window on Elizabeth Street, An.
　Few Days, A.
　Flashes.
　Greenwich Avenue.
　Hudson Ferry.
　Moon.
　Morning of the Poem, The.
　Sleep-Gummed Eyes.
　Sun Cab, A.
　This Dark Apartment.
　Thursday.
　Wonderful World.
Shapiro.　Cathedral Bells, The.
Tate.　Aeneas at New York.
Tomlinson.　Above Manhattan.
　Arrival, The.
　At the Trade Center.
　Byzantium.
　Landing, The.
　On Eleventh Street.
　On Madison.
Updike.　Summer: West Side.
Walcott.　Bleecker Street, Summer.
　Piano Practice.
　Village Life, A.
Waldman.　Giant Night.
　Snow.
Warren.　I Am Dreaming of a White
　Christmas: The Natural History of a Vision.
Whitman.　City of Orgies.
　City of Ships.
　First O Songs for a Prelude.
　Give Me the Splendid Silent Sun.
　Mannahatta: ("I was asking for something
　specific and perfect for my city").
　Mannahatta: ("My city's fit and noble name
　resumed").

Whittier. To a Poetical Trio in the City of Gotham.
Williams, William Carlos. Place (Any Place) to Transcend All Places, A.
Wright, James. To the Poets in New York.
Yau. Manhattan Miniature.
Young. Fun City Samba.
Little Poem About Jazz, A.
Zukofsky. Last cigarette / a companion, A. This Fall, 1933.
See also **Broadway, New York City; Bronx, The, New York City; Brooklyn, New York City; Harlem, New York City; Queens, New York City; Rockefeller Center, New York City.**

New Zealand
Meredith. Song of the New Zealander among the Ruins of Old London.

Newfoundland, Canada
Crane. North Labrador.
Dunn. Carpenter's Song, The.

Newgate Prison, London
Byron. Would You Go to the House by the True Gate.

Newman, John Henry, Cardinal
Rossetti. Cardinal Newman.

News
Berry. Morning's News, The.
Bishop. 12 O'Clock News.
Burns. To a Gentleman Who Had Sent Him a News-Paper, and Offered to Continue It Free of Expense.
Creeley. News, The.
Dickinson. Death obtains the Rose.
How News must feel when travelling.
I sued the News—yet feared—the News.
Myself can read the Telegrams.
Eberhart. News.
Gardner. This Room Is Full of Clocks.
Hewitt. Disaster on the Box.
S.S.K.
Jarrell. News.
Lowry. Nagging at myself something awful.
MacNeice. Canto X: "Daily news. And today? There is not so much to note."
Merton. Newscast.
Picture of Lee Ying, A.
Muldoon. Profumo.
Nash. Everybody Tells Me Everything.
Nemerov. Truth of the Matter, The.
Olson. Morning News, The.
Owen. Six o'clock in Princes Street.
"Reed." Original Wrapper, The.
Sick of You.
Sandburg. "Drama of politics doesn't interest me," said a news rewrite man, The.
Sorrentino. Morning Roundup, The.
New York Times: A Poem for the Ross Feld, The.
Stafford. Time Capsule.
Stuart. My Children Going.
Turco. Burning the News.
Van Duyn. Winter has stiffened the ground, the birds are gone.
Whitman. Nay, Tell Me Not To-day the Publish'd Shame.

Newspapers
Atwood. It Is Dangerous to Read Newspapers.
Berryman. World-Telegram.
Burns. To a Gentleman Who Had Sent Him a News-Paper, and Offered to Continue It Free of Expense.
Cowper. Reading the Newspaper.
Cummings. Insu nli gh t / o / verand.
Donne. Mercurius Gallo-Belgicus.
Eliot. *Boston Evening Transcript*, The.
Hopkins. Legetai Ti Khainon.
Hugo. Reclamation at Coloma.
Jarrell. Nestus Gurley.
Kipling. Delilah.
Flles, The.
Man Who Could Write, The.
Press, The.
Lawrence. Great Newspaper Editor to His Subordinate, The.
Lowry. Those Coke to Newcastle Blues.

Nash. I Am Full of Previous Experience.
Listen to the Linotype.
Political Reflection.
Nemerov. Daily Globe, The.
Keeping Informed in D.C.
Picture, A.
Truth of the Matter, The.
Owen. Smile, Smile, Smile.
Patchen. Pick Up the Evening Paper.
Sandburg. Press is Peculiar, The.
Schuyler. Ajaccio Violets.
Picnic Cantata, A.
Smith, Stevie. Magnificent Words.
Sorrentino. New York Times: A Poem for the Ross Feld, The.
Turco. Burning the News.
Van Duyn. To Record One Must Be Unwary.
Whitman. Nay, Tell Me Not To-day the Publish'd Shame.
Wilbur. After the Last Bulletins.
Williams, Charles Kenneth. Reading: Early Sorrow.
Williams, Miller. Newspaper Picture of Spectators at a Hotel Fire, A.
Reading the Newsapaper on Microfilm.
Zukofsky. Head Lines.
See also **Journalism and Journalists; Magazines.**

Newton, Sir Isaac
Eberhart. Quanta.
Jarrell. Emancipators, The.
Joseph. On the Nature of Scientific Law.
Pope. Epitaph Intended for Sir Isaac Newton, in Westminster Abbey.
Thomson. To the Memory of Sir Isaac Newton.
Wilbur. Worlds.

Newts
Williams, William Carlos. Ordeal, The.

Niagara Falls
Cohen. Nothing I Can Lose.
Lindsay. Niagara.
Sandburg. Tumblers of the rapids go white, go green, The.
Waldman. White Eyes.

Nicaragua
Merton. Spring has come with its smell of Nicaragua.
Miller. Nicaraguan Journal.
Paley. Dance in Jinoteca, The.
Walker. Songless.

Night
Atwood. Night Poem.
Auden. Finis.
Make this night loveable.
Nightfall.
Nocturne: "Do squamous and squiggling fish."
Skyreholme Mill.
Summer Night, A.
Walk After Dark, A.
Beckett. Dortmunder.
La nuit venue où l'âme allait.
Lueurs lisières.
Nuit qui fais tant.
Rentrer / À la nuit.
Berg. Leaves.
Berrigan. February Air.
Mountains of twine and.
Berry. At night make me one with the darkness.
Before Dark.
On the Hill Late at Night.
Thief, The.
Winter Night Poem for Mary.
Winter Nightfall.
Berryman. Conversation.
Curse, The.
Marble nor monuments where of then we spoke.
Night and the City.
Possessed, The.
Spinning Heart, The.
Bishop. Late Air.
Man-Moth, The.
Blake. Night.
Bly. Night.

Solitude Late at Night in the Woods.
Upward Moon and the Downward Moon, The.
Bogan. Night.
Boyle. Battlefield, The.
Brontë. Coldly, bleakly, drearily.
Written in Aspin Castle.
Browning, Elizabeth Barrett. Night and the Merry Man.
Romance of the Ganges, A.
Romaunt of Margret, The.
Browning, Robert. Meeting at Night.
Bukowski. 12:18 A.M.
Bunting. Night swallowed the sun as.
Burns. Night was still, and o'er the hill, The.
Song: "As I stood by yon roofless tower."
Winter Night, A.
Byron. Song: "Breeze of the night in gentler sighs."
Campion. Night as well as brightest day hath her delight.
Now Winter Nights Enlarge.
Tell me, gentle howre of night.
Carroll, Jim. Ad Man's Daughter, The.
Early Morning Crucifixion, An.
Marked by a more distant sky, I hold.
Midnight.
Sleeplessness.
"Carroll, Lewis." Echoes.
Faces in the Fire.
Carruth. Joy and Agony of Improvisation, The.
Loneliness[: An Outburst of Hexasyllables].
Moonset.
Night is a cauldron.
She lay like a book.
Snow comes / bits / of light.
Ciardi. Conversation with Leonardo, A.
Clark. "In This River.."
Sleepwalker's Way.
Clough. But that from slow dissolving pomps of dawn.
O kind protecting Darkness! as a child.
Cohen. Lady Midnight.
Night Comes On, The.
Cooper. Hunger Moon.
Cowper. Watching unto God in the Night-Season.
Crane. Fear.
In Shadow.
Persuasion, A.
Creeley. Chasing the Bird.
End of the Day, The.
Hero, The.
Old Song.
Roads.
Somewhere.
Son: "What I took in my hand."
Cullen. Night Rain.
Cummings. After all white horses are in bed.
&-moon-He-be-hind-a-mills.
Chilly,murky night, A.
Come(all your mischief- / hatchers hatch).
Do you remember when the fluttering dusk.
Helves surling out of eakspeasies per(reel)hapsingly.
Here is the ocean,this is moonlight:say.
Hokku.
Hours rise up putting off stars and it is, The.
If learned darkness from our searched world.
If night's mostness(and whom did merely day / close).
If within tonight's erect.
Is / it / because there struts a distinct silver lady.
Kind) / YM&WC / (of sort of).
Light Out), A.
Moon is hiding in, The.
Night.
Night shall eat these girls and boys.
Nite) / thatthis / crou / ched.
Nocturne: "When the lithe moonlight silently."
One day a nigger.
Out of night's almosT Floats a colour(in).
Over us if(as what dusk becomes).
Put off your faces,Death:for day is over.
Silently if,out of not knowable.
Summer Silence.

There is a / moon sole.
T,h;r:u;s,h;e:s / are / silent / now.
Tonight the moon is round golden entire. It.
Vision.
What time is it i wonder never mind.
When citied day with the sonorous homes.
When parsing warmths of dusk construe.
Windows go orange in the slowly.
Young m / oon:be kind to olde.
Davie. Evening on the Boyne.
House-martin.
Mushroom Gatherers, The.
De la Mare. Banquo.
Beware!
Birthnight: To F., The.
Fear.
Fleeting, The.
Forests.
Little Salamander, The.
Night ("All from the light...").
Night ("That shining moon...").
Noon and Night Flower.
Peace.
Snowing.
Vigil.
Dickey, James. Jewel, The.
Dickinson. Good Morning—Midnight.
Night is my favorite Day.
Night—there lay the Days between, A.
Night was wide, and furnished scant, The.
Our share of night to bear.
Some say goodnight—at night.
To Whom the Mornings stand for Nights.
When Night is almost done.
Dobyns. Giver of Gifts, The.
Leaving the Bar and Low Life at Closing, I
  Unsuccessfully Pursue Sainthood.
Doolittle. Evening.
Night.
Dove. Nigger Song: An Odyssey.
Night Watch.
To Bed.
Dunbar. At Candle-Lightin' Time.
Barrier, The.
Evening.
'Long To'ds Night.
Night.
Night, Dim Night.
Night of Love.
Summer Night, A.
Twell de Night Is Pas'.
With the Lark.
Dunn. Beyond Hammonton.
Halves.
Here and There.
Petty Thing, A.
"Dylan." On a Night Like This.
Eberhart. By the Stream.
Commitment, A.
Concord Cats.
Cover Me Over.
Hoot Owls.
Looking at the Stars.
Mystical Beast in the Shadows, The.
Off Spectacle Island.
Scouring, The.
Edmunds. Nocturne.
Passion Week Monday after Palm Sunday.
Eliot. Conversation Galante.
Rhapsody on a Windy Night.
Emerson. Always day & night.
I left my dreamy page & sallied forth.
In bounding youth the night & train.
Original—"Apropos."
Parks & ponds are good by day.
Everson. Dusk, The.
Ferlinghetti. Olbers' Paradox.
Plough of Time, The.
Fisher. Hills lie thick, The.
Of the Empirical Self and for Me.
Fletcher. At the Meeting of the Days.
City Lights.
From the Japanese, I.
Hour of Peace, The.
Houses of the city no longer hum and play,
  The.
Sorrow.

Stars, The.
White Symphony.
Ford. And no night visitors.
Garden flooded with.
Fox. And night comes.
Nightshade.
Shunga.
Frost. Acquainted with the Night.
Evening in a Sugar Orchard.
Night Light, The.
Now Close the Windows.
Two Tramps in Mud Time.
Were I in Trouble.
Garrigue. Strike of the Night, The.
Ginsberg. Spring Fashions.
Glück. Fortress, The.
Night Song.
Pond, The.
Graves. Arrears of Moonlight.
Between Moon and Moon.
Colours of Night, The.
Frosty Night, A.
Horizon.
Outlaws.
Troughs of Sea.
Visitation, The.
Gunn. All Night, Legs Pointed East.
Night Piece, The.
Haines. By the Ocean.
End of the Street, The.
Fairbanks Under the Solstice.
Foreboding.
If the Owl Calls Again.
Sometimes in our sleep.
Hall. Passage to Worship.
Hardy. Midnight on Beechen, 187–.
Night in the Old Home.
On a Heath.
On the Esplanade.
Shut Out That Moon.
Winter Night in Woodland.
Hartley. Beyond the Broken House.
Cicada.
Light of Night.
Hartnett. Naked Surgeon, The.
Hayden. O Daedalus, Fly Away Home.
Herrick. Night-Piece, to Julia, The.
No Difference in the Dark [or i'th'dark].
Old Wives Prayer, The.
To Daisies, Not to Shut So Soon[e].
To His Sweet Saviour.
Hesketh. At Four A.M.
It Was Not I.
Hewitt. Bandstand.
Roseblade's Visitants and Mine.
Sonnet: "There in the lonely quarry where at
  dawn."
Hoffman. Crack!
This Silence.
Hopkins. By One of the Old School Who Was
  Bid to Follow Mr. Browning's Flights.
How looks the night? There does not miss a
  star.
On a Poetess.
Tom's Garland: Upon the Unemployed.
Housman. Bells in tower at evening toll.
Hughes, Langston. Chord.
Gone Boy.
Harlem Night Song.
Midnight Raffle.
Night: Four Songs.
Hughes, Ted. Thought-Fox, The.
Jarrell. Breath of Night, The.
City, City!
Eine Kleine Nachtmusik.
Miller, The.
November Ghosts, The.
Over the florid capitals.
Jeffers. Hooded Night.
Night.
Night Without Sleep.
October Week-End.
Watch the Lights Fade.
Jonson. Solemn rites are well begun, The.
Joseph. Dead of Night.
Kinnell. How Many Nights.

Middle of the Way.
Ruins under the Stars.
Kipling. Morning Song in the Jungle.
Now Chil the Kite brings home the night.
Kooser. August.
Highway 30.
Hot Night in Wheat Country, A.
Late Lights in Minnesota.
Presidential Poem, A.
Sitting All Evening Alone in the Kitchen.
Summer Night, A.
Kunitz. Night-Piece.
O beautiful prey, / night-voice.
Science of the Night, The.
What wakes me now.
Larkin. Bottle Is Drunk Out by One, The.
Coming at Last to Night's Most Thankful
  Springs.
Midsummer Night, 1940.
Night-Music.
Sad Steps.
Street Lamps.
When the Night Puts Twenty Veils.
Lawrence. At the Window.
Attack, The.
Dolour of Autumn.
Elegy: "Sun immense and rosy, The."
Forecast.
Grief.
Late at Night.
Liaison.
Little Town at Evening, The.
Moon New-Risen.
Night.
Night Songs.
Nonentity.
Old Song.
Our Day Is Over.
Piccadilly Circus at Night.
Rebuked.
Red Moon-Rise.
Ruination.
Shadow of Death, The.
Southern Night.
Street Lamps.
Third Song of Huitzilopochtli.
Train at Night, A.
Weeknight Service.
Yew-Tree on the Downs, The.
Levertov. Night on Hatchet Cove.
Stems.
Lewis. Night bibles India in her wilderness.
Sentry, The.
Stars seem gilded nipples.
Welsh Night, A.
Liddy. Night / We went running to the
  garden.
Lindsay. Written for a Musician.
Longfellow. Day Is Done, The.
Lorde. Gemini.
Lovelace. Night.
Lowell. Night Sweat.
Lowry. Bosun's Song.
Don't, Have One for the Road.
Fiesta.
Heat Wave.
Morning song of El Leon.
Outward Bound.
Song for a Marimba.
Sweet night / And sleep thin, A.
McAuley. Air of an old song's in my head,
  The.
Mother, sisters, brother.
Not a sound. The house could be.
"MacDiarmid." Dying Earth, The.
Eemis-Stane, The.
McGrath. Dreams of Wild Horses, The.
Guiffre's Nightmusic.
Night Work.
Nocturne Militaire.
Such Simple Love.
MacLeish. Ancestral.
Bahamas.
Nocturne: "Earth, still heavy and warm with
  afternoon, The."
MacNeice. Canto XIV: "Battle? That is one
  way of looking at the matter, A."

Evening Indoors.
Intimations of Mortality.
Nocturne: "Dark blood of night-time, The."
Rest House, The.
Mahon. Globe in North Carolina, The.
Matthews. Driving Alongside the Housatonic
  River Alone on a Rainy April Night.
107th & Amsterdam.
Meredith. Carol of Jack Frost, A.
Child's Prayer, A.
I Chafe at Darkness.
In the Woods.
London by Lamplight.
Moonlight Night.
Night of Frost in May.
Night-Walk, The.
Night walks the earth with silver feet.
O 'tis my delight / In the dead of the night.
Postillion, The.
Sleeping City, The.
Song: "Moon is alone in the sky, The."
'Tis midnight in the skies, my dear.
'Twas in a glimmering starlight.
Merrill. House, The.
Sundown and Starlight.
Merton. Fall of Night, The.
Nights belong to / What hurts.
Nocturne: "Night has a sea which quenches
  the machine."
Song: "Come where the grieving rivers of the
  night."
When night falls / beat one drum / in honor of
  night.
Winter's Night, The.
Millay. Night is my sister, and how deep in
  love.
Winter Night.
Milton. Il Penseroso.
L'Allegro.
Morgan. Voice spoke in the night, A.
Morrison. Welcome to the American Night.
Nash. Complaint to Four Angels.
Nemerov. According to His Seasons.
Frozen City, The.
Stare of the Man from the Provinces, The.
Two Poems.
Neruda. Some Creature.
Notley. At Night the States.
Olson. Boat, The.
Dragon-Fly, The.
House, The.
Night, The.
Ode on Nativity, An.
Rosy, It Was.
Seven Songs, The.
Oppen. Animula.
Patchen. Fall of the Evening Star.
I Got the Fat Poet into a Corner.
Moon came out full, you could see the white
  breathing of the.
Night Has Been as Beautiful as Virginia.
Piercy. Longest Night, The.
Plath. By Candlelight.
Moonrise.
Poe. Evening Star.
Prince. Then came a time of great guilt, that I
  inhabited.
Raine. Banked winter cloud.
Nocturn: "Night comes, an angel stands."
Rexroth. Thin Edge of Your Pride, The.
Rich. Night.
Sleepwalking.
Roethke. Idyll: "Now as from maple to elm
  the flittermice skitter and twirl."
Rolfe. Night World.
Rossetti. Awake, Thou That Sleepest.
From Sunset to Star Rise.
Have You Forgotten?
If the moon came from heaven, / Talking all
  the way.
Is the Moon Tired?
Lord, grant us grace to rest upon Thy word.
O Lucifer, Son of the Morning!
O ye who love today, / Turn away / From
  Patience with her silver ray.
Oh knell of a passing time, / Will it never
  cease to chime?

Praying Always.
Serenade.
Smile and a Sigh, A.
Summer nights are short, / Where northern
  days are long, The.
Rukeyser. Evening Plaza, San Miguel.
Eyes of Night-Time.
Formosa.
In a Dark House.
In the Night the Sound Woke Us.
Night-Music.
Overthrow of One o'Clock at Night, The.
Study in a Late Subway.
Time Exposures.
St. John. Avenues, The.
Lucifer in Starlight.
Sandburg. Clark Street Bridge.
Far Rockaway Night Till Morning.
Good Night.
High Moments.
Interior.
Moonset.
Night Bells.
Night Movement—New York.
Night Stuff.
Night's Nothings Again.
Nightsong.
Nocturne in a Deserted Brickyard.
Pass, Friend.
Pearl Horizons.
Picnic Boat.
Shag-Bark Hickory.
Skyscraper.
Skyscraper Loves Night, The.
Special Starlight.
Tall Timber.
Window.
Schwartz. All Night, All Night.
Poem for Jacques Maritain and Leon Trotzky.
Sexton. In the Beach House.
Starry Night, The.
Shelley. Lines: "Cold earth slept below, The."
Stanzas—April, 1814.
Summer Evening Churchyard, A.
To Night.
Sidney. O night, the ease of care, the pledge
  of pleasure.
Sonnet 96: "Thought, with good cause thou
  lik'st so well the night."
Sonnet 97: "Dian, that fain would cheer her
  friend the Night."
Sonnet 99: "When far-spent night persuades
  each mortal eye."
Simic. Evening.
Trees at Night.
Smith, Charlotte. Moth, The.
Sonnet to the Forest Ytene.
To Night.
To the Moon.
Smith, Stevie. Aubade: "My dove, my doe."
Goodnight.
Light of Life, The.
Up and Down.
Snodgrass. At the Park Dance.
Snyder. Everybody Lying on Their Stomachs,
  Head toward the Candle, Reading, Sleeping,
  Drawing.
Kyoto: March.
Night.
Pine Tree Tops.
Sorrentino. Classic Case, A.
Now the night is here. Blood.
Stafford. Listening.
Stevens. Anecdote of the Prince of Peacocks.
Candle a Saint, The.
Dezembrum.
Girl in a Nightgown.
God is Good. It Is a Beautiful Night.
Men That Are Falling, The.
Rabbit as King of the Ghosts, A.
Re-statement of Romance.
Reader, The.
Sonatina to Hans Christian.
Stars at Tallapoosa.
Stevenson. Bed in Summer.
Escape at Bedtime.
Late in the nicht in bed I lay.

Late, O miller.
Moon, The.
Night and Day.
North-West Passage.
Sick Child, The.
Stormy Nights.
Summer Night.
Windy Nights.
Young Night Thought.
Stuart. Sleepwalker.
Sutter. Night Out.
Tate. Ditty: "Moon will run all consciences to
  cover, The."
Tennyson. Move Eastward, Happy Earth, and
  Leave.
Thomas. In Country Sleep.
Tomlinson. Night Transfigured.
Turco. Blood Deeper than Night.
Updike. 3 A.M.
Yes, self-obsession fills our daily clothes.
Wakoski. Helms Bakery Man, The.
Night Rides of My Neighbor, Lorca, That
  Prevent Sleep, The.
Walcott. God Rest Ye Merry, Gentlemen.
Nights in the Gardens of Port of Spain.
Warren. Birth of Love.
Eidolon.
Hands Are Paid.
Midnight Outcry.
Old Nigger on One-Mule Cart Encountered
  Late at Night When Driving Home from
  Party in the Back Country.
Walk by Moonlight in Small Town.
Whitman. After an Interval.
After the Dazzle of Day.
On the Beach at Night.
Whittier. In Peace.
Wilbur. For Ellen.
Peace of Cities, The.
Sonnet.
Terrace, The.
Williams, William Carlos. At Night.
Eternity.
From the Outside.
Good Night.
Goodnight, A.
Night.
Night Rider, The.
Peace on Earth.
Rigamarole.
Spotting the moonlight at my bedside.
Wordsworth. How Beautiful the Queen of
  Night, on High.
I Watch, and Long Have Watched [with Calm
  Regret].
Night-Piece, A.
Night Thought, A.
Western clouds a deepening gloom display,
  The.
Winter's Evening, A.
Wright, James. Morning Hymn to a Dark Girl.
Rats, The.
Winter Night, A.
Wroth. Sonnet 1: "In night yett may wee see
  some kind of light."
Sonnet 1: "When night's [or nights] black
  mantle could most darknes prove."
Sonnet 15: "Truly poore Night thou wellcome
  art to mee."
Sonnet 19: "Come darkest night, be[e]coming
  sorrow best."
Sonnet 37: "Night, welcome art thou to my
  mind destrest."
Yau. Scotch tape scars on the wall. Scared,
  The.
Sleepness Night of Eugene Delacroix, The.
Yeats. To Dorothy Wellesley.
Young. New Mode of Production, The.
New Moon Over Grove Street.
Zimmer. Zimmer with Lester Under the Moon.
Zukofsky. Aubade, 1925.
Ferry.
Snows' night's winds on the window rattling.

See also **Evening.**

Nightclubs
Berryman. Enemies of the Angels, The.
Bukowski. Very.

Cummings. Between nose-red gross.
Helves surling out of eakspeasies
per(reel)hapsingly.
In Healey's Palace I was sitting.
Infinite jukethrob smoke & swallow to dis.
Gunn. Crystal.
Hughes, Langston. Neon Signs.
MacNeice. Night Club.
"Reed." Afterhours.
Sorrentino. Sappho in Paris.

Nighthawks
Berry. September 2, 1969.

Nightingales
Auden. After Reading Keats' Ode.
Browning, Elizabeth Barrett. Bianca among
the Nightingales.
Poet and the Bird, The.
Coleridge. Nightingale, The.
To the Nightingale.
Cowper. Nightingale and Glow-Worm, The.
Strada's Nightingale.
To the Nightingale.
De la Mare. Sotto Voce.
Eberhart. Ultimate Song.
Emerson. While roses bloomed along the
plain.
Herrick. To the Nightingale, and Robin-Red-
Brest.
Hopkins. Nightingale, The.
Lawrence. Paltry-Looking People.
Lindsay. Chinese Nightingale, The.
Meredith. Poetry of Keats, The.
Three Maidens, The.
To a Nightingale.
To a Nightingale.
Milton. Sonnet 1: "O Nightingale, that on yon
bloomy spray."
Ransom. Philomela.
Rossetti. Bird Raptures.
Schuyler. Three Gardens.
Shakespeare. As it fell upon a day.
Shelley. There the voluptuous nightingales.
Smith, Charlotte. On the Departure of the
Nightingale.
Return of the Nightingale. Written in May
1791, The.
To a Nightingale.
Thomson. To the Nightingale.
Wordsworth. Cuckoo and the Nightingale,
The.
O Nightingale! thou surely art.

Nightmares
Atwood. No Name.
Brontë. Sudden chasm of ghastly light, A.
Bukowski. Rat Rises, A.
"Carroll, Lewis." Horrors.
Carruth. One called Next steps up, The.
Clark. Door Gunner to the Moment, (A Shau
Valley 1968), The.
Coleridge. Night-Mare Death in Life, The.
De la Mare. Drugged.
Dickinson. Night's capacity varies.
Fenton. Lullaby for a Summer Recess.
Vuccerìa.
Fletcher. Sharaku Dreams.
Gardner. Nightmare.
Glück. Night Piece.
Graves. Castle, The.
Dawn Bombardment.
Gratitude for a Nightmare.
Lost Jewel, The.
Nightmare of Senility.
Theme of Death, The.
Tolling Bell.
Hesketh. July 2nd, 1916.
Hugo. In Your Bad Dream.
Jarrell. Prince, The.
Quilt-Pattern, A.
Jeffers. Apology for Bad Dreams.
Nightpiece.
Lawrence. In the Dark.
Lewis. She Comes To Him in the Night.
Lorde. Conclusion.
Lowry. On Reading Redburn.
MacNeice. Bad Dream.
Merton. Saint Jason.
Nathan. Penance, The.

Nemerov. Nightmare.
Oppen. Primitive.
Raine. Bad Dream, A.
Rolfe. Georgia Nightmare.
Rossetti. Coast-Nightmare, A.
So I grew half delirious and quite sick.
Sarton. Tortured, The.
Warren. Original Sin; a Short Story.
Williams, Charles Kenneth. Dream, The.
Wright, James. Sleep.
Zimmer. Once as a Child I Had Bad Dreams.

See also **Dreams and Dreaming.**

Nihilism
Ammons. Likely Story.
Beckett. Flux cause.
Berg. To the Being We Are.
Carruth. Sonnet: "What if the psychologians,
those grand old frauds."
Creeley. Rhythm, The.
Dunn. Welcome.
Griffiths. Post Imperial.
Knott. Shorts / Excerpts ("I write these lines
to cripple the dead").
Lawrence. December Night.
Robot Feelings.
Liddy. Kerouac's Ronsard Dance.
Lowell. Nihilist as Hero, The.
Rolfe. Where Buildings Congregate.
Zukofsky. Guillaume de Machault (1300-1377)
Ballade: Plourès, dames.

Nijinsky, Vaslav
Wilbur. Grace.

Nile (river)
"Carroll, Lewis." How doth the little
crocodile.
Edmunds. Landing in Cairo.
Keats. To the Nile.
Shelley. To the Nile.

Nile, Battle of the (1798)
Moore. New York.

1930s
Auden. Bride in the 30's, A.
Morgan. Greenwich 1930's, I.
Greenwich 1930's, II.
Tomlinson. Gladstone Street.

1960s
Angelou. Riot: 60's.
Auden. Economics.
Beatles. Dig It.
Carroll, Jim. Highway Report.
Carruth. Spring 1967.
Cohen. Aquarian Age.
"Dylan." Ballad of a Thin Man.
Bringing It All Back Home.
Hurricane.
I could make you crawl.
It's Alright, Ma (I'm Only Bleeding).
Lenny Bruce.
Like a Rolling Stone.
Off the Top of My Head.
Subterranean Homesick Blues.
Tangled Up in Blue.
Times They Are A-Changin', The.
Garrigue. Resistance Meeting: Boston
Common.
Ginsberg. Beginning of a Poem of These
States.
Crossing Nation.
Hiway Poesy: L.A.–Albuquerque–Texas–
Witchita.
Iron Horse.
Kansas City to Saint Louis.
Northwest Passage.
Returning North of Vortex.
These States: Into L.A.
Violence.
Wichita Vortex Sutra.
Hacker. Nights of 1964-1966: The Old
Reliable.
Lorde. Equinox.
McGrath. Note on the Late Elections, A.
Merton. Fall '66.
Tune for Festive Dances in the Nineteen
Sixties, A.
Neruda. Century Dying, A.
Piercy. Learning Experience.

"Reed." Day John Kennedy Died, The.
Schuyler. Empathy and New Year.
Van Duyn. Christmas Card, After the
Assassinations, A.
Eros to Howard Nemerov.
What the Motorcycle Said.
Williams, Charles Kenneth. Flight.

Niobe
Carruth. Niobe, your tears.
Cowper. On Hermocratia.
On Niobe.
Donne. Niobe.
Patchen. Niobe.
Rukeyser. Niobe Now.

Nixon, Richard Milhous
Carruth. Regarding Chainsaws.
McGrath. Note on the Late Elections, A.
Paley. My Father at 85.

Noah
Cohen. Transmission, The.
Davie. Dancing Measures.
Dickinson. I am sure I feel as Noah did.
Fletcher. And at these words there rose
against the ark.
Night lay upon the ocean like a sword.
Now it was noonday, fortieth of the flood.
Graves. After the Flood.
Ark, The.
Herrick. Fast, or Lent, The.
Hewitt. Name and Number.
Kipling. Legends of Evil, The.
Rossetti. As the dove which found no rest /
For the sole of her foot, flew back.
Silverstein. Unicorn, The.
Wilbur. Still, Citizen Sparrow.

Nobility
Brontë. None of my kindred now can tell.
Burns. Elegy on Captain Matthew Henderson
[or Capt. M———— H————] [A *Gentleman*
Who Held the Patent for His Honours
Immediately from Almighty God!].
O Kenmure's on and awa, Willie.
Campion. Canto Secundo.
To the Most Illustrious and Mighty Fredericke
the Fift, Count Palantine of the Rhein.
Carew. To My Much Honoured Friend, Henry,
Lord Carey of Leppington, Upon His
Translation of Malvezzi.
Coleridge. Lines Written at the King's Arms,
Ross, Formerly the House of the "Man of
Ross."
Cowper. On Pedigree.
Cummings. For any ruffian of the sky.
Davie. Tuscan Brutus, The.
Dickinson. There is a Shame of Nobleness.
Why is it Nobleness makes us ashamed.
Gray. Impromptu.
Hall. Revolution, The.
Hardy. Man, A.
Jeffers. New Year's Eve.
Salvage.
Jonson. To the Most Noble, and above His
Titles, Robert, Earl of Somerset.
Lawrence. Death of the Baron, The.
Noble.
Nash. Ms. Found under a Serviette in a
Lovely Home.
Rossetti. Maggie a Lady.
Whittier. Countess, The.
Isabella of Austria.
Wordsworth. Song at the Feast of Brougham
Castle upon the Restoration of Lord Clifford,
the Shepherd, to the Estates and Honours of
His Ancestors.
To the Lady Fleming on Seeing the
Foundation Preparing for the Erection of
Rydal Chapel, Westmoreland.

Noblesse Oblige
Emerson. King. If farmers make my land
secure.
Lovelace. Against the Love of Great Ones.
Nash. Ms. Found under a Serviette in a
Lovely Home.

Noises
Bukowski. Trench Warfare.
"Carroll, Lewis." Oh pudgy podgy pup! / Why
did they wake you up?

Ciardi. Prayer to the Mountain, A.
Clark. Day Detail—Low Light of Afternoon.
Moodsville.
Somnambulism.
Whistle Buoy.
Coleridge. Thought, A.
Creeley. Tiny Place, A.
Cummings. After screamgroa / ning.ish:ly.
Noise.
O the sun comes up-up-up in the opening.
De la Mare. Market-Place, The.
Emerson. From a far mountain creeping down.
Fisher. Hit the bottom and spread out.
Graves. Death by Drums.
Gunn. Grasses.
Hewitt. King's Horses, The.
Listener, The.
Prisoners on the Roof, The.
Hoffman. Crack!
Kinnell. After Making Love We Hear
Footsteps.
Koch. Hearing.
Lovelace. To a Lady That Desired Me I
Would Bear My Part with Her in a Song.
Lowry. There is no poetry when you live
there.
With Sweetest Devotion from *All* the Little
Animals to Their Most Beloved Harteebeeste.
Markson. Youthful Poet's Unspoke Response
to a Woman Talking Too Loudly in His
Favorite Bookstore, The.
Morrison. Moving, A.
We Awoke, Talking.
Nash. I Didn't Say a Word, or, Who Called
That Piccolo Player a Father?
Party Next Door, The.
People upstairs, The.
Under the Floor.
Plath. Night Shift.
Rolfe. Soledad.
Rossetti. What does the donkey bray about?
Sandburg. Clinton South of Polk.
Smith, Stevie. Up and Down.
Stuart. My Children Going.
Percussion.
Tomlinson. Shout, The.
Wordsworth. Morning Exercise, A.
On the Power of Sound.
Yau. All This Changing Trouble Luck and
Suddenness.
Zukofsky. When the crickets.

Noon
Cowper. Winter Walk at Noon, The.
Davie. Lily at Noon, A.
De la Mare. Noon and Night Flower.
Sotto Voce.
Dickinson. It's like the Light.
Dunbar. Noon.
Eberhart. By the Stream.
Fisher. Hill behind the Town, The.
Jeffers. Noon.
Levine. Noon.
Lindsay. Noon.
Morgan. Noon is the hour of choice.
Nemerov. Advice from the Holy Tomb.
Stevens. What We See Is What We Think.
Wordsworth. Labourer's Noon-Day Hymn,
The.

Norfolk, England
Betjeman. Norfolk.
Davie. Norfolk.

Normandy, Invasion of (1944)
St. John. Six/Nine/Forty-Four.
Williams, Miller. Normandy Beach.

North, The, United States
Carruth. North Winter.
Melville. Fortitude of the North, The.
Whittier. Album Verses.
What State Street Said to South Carolina, and
What South Carolina Said to State Street.
Young. Leaving Home for Home.

North Carolina (state)
Glück. Cottonmouth Country.
Lorde. Poem for a Poet.
Mahon. Globe in North Carolina, The.
Muldoon. Promises, Promises.
Rukeyser. Outer Banks, The.

North Dakota (state)
Haines. Woman on the Road.
McGrath. Beyond the Red River.
Something Is Dying Here.
Wright, James. Outside Fargo, North Dakota.
Poem Written under an Archway in a
Discontinued Railroad Station, Fargo, North
Dakota, A.
To Flood Stage Again.

North Pole
Carruth. Afterword: What the Poet Had
Written.
Jarrell. 90 North.

North Wind
Graves. Love in Barrenness.
Lindsay. Moon's the North Wind's Cooky,
The.

Northamptonshire, England
Davie. Northamptonshire.

Northern Ireland
Galvin. In Ireland I Remebered the Foxes of
Truro, Massachusetts.
Heaney. Casualty.
Strand at Lough Beg, The.
Whatever You Say Say Nothing.
Kipling. Ulster.
MacNeice. Carrickfergus.
Muldoon. Mink.
More a Man Has the More a Man Wants, The.
See also **Listings for specific Counties.**

Northumberland, England
Davie. Northumberland.
Lowry. Those Coke to Newcastle Blues.
Scott. Lords Strand of Northumberland, The.
Smith, Stevie. Watchful.

Noses
Auden. Metaphor.
Coleridge. Nose, The.
Dobyns. Noses.
Hall. Nose.
Herrick. Upon Center a Spectacle-Maker with
a Flat Nose.
Upon Coone.
Upon His Julia.
Upon Lulls.
Upon Megg.
Silverstein. Longest Nose.
Warning.
Williams, William Carlos. Smell.

Nostalgia
Angelou. Just for a Time.
Auden. After the Storm.
Appletreewick.
Last Time, The.
Whenever I see for the first time.
Berg. Following It.
Good.
Berrigan. Red Shift.
Byron. Childish Recollections.
I Would I Were a Careless Child.
There Was a Time, I Need Not Name.
Campion. Wise men patience never want.
Carroll, Jim. Back Home.
Carruth. Letter to Maxine Sullivan.
November: Indian Summer.
Sonnet: "I think continually of the
differences."
Village, The.
Cohen. Queen Victoria and Me.
Coleridge. Gentle Look, The.
Lines Written in the Album at Elbingerode, in
the Har[t]z Forest.
Creeley. Old Song.
Picnic, The.
So Big.
Cummings. Boy and the Man, The.
Even if all desires things moments be.
That famous fatheads find that each.
Davie. Dudwood.
Remembering the 'Thirties.
Stratford on Avon.
Dickey, James. Two Poems of Going Home.
Dobyns. Pastel Dresses.
Doolittle. Blue-geese, white-geese, you may
say.
Dunbar. Land o' Used to Be, The.

Old High School and the New, The.
Old Memory, An.
"Dylan." Bob Dylan's Dream.
Tangled Up in Blue.
Eliot. Marina.
Everson. Blood of the Poet, The.
Ferlinghetti. Plan du Centre de Paris à Vol
D'Oiseau.
Returning to Paris with Pissarro.
Tunisian Nostalgia.
Frost. Range-finding.
Galvin. Double-Ended Dory, A.
Summer School.
Gardner. Children Are Game.
Eros in May at MacDowell.
One Sunday in 1966.
Summer Remembered.
Summers Ago.
Garrigue. Suite.
Ginsberg. After Yeats.
Europe! Europe!
Flying Elegy.
I Have Increased Power.
Mad Gleam, A.
Siesta in Xbalba.
Hall. Toy Bone, The.
Hardy. After a Journey.
Bygone Occasion, A.
Christmas in the Elgin Room.
Jog-Trot Pair, A.
Last Signal, The.
Lines to a Movement in Mozart's E-Flat
Symphony.
Lost Love.
Old Excursions.
Old Furniture.
Old Likeness, An.
On a Discovered Curl of Hair.
Paths of Former Time.
Photograph, The.
Place on the Map, The.
Places.
She Would Welcome Old Tribulations.
Two-Years' Idyll, A.
Hugo. Places and Ways to Live.
Jarrell. In Those Days.
Lot is vacant still, The.
Player Piano, The.
Times Worsen, The.
Jong. On Sending You a Lock of My Hair.
Joseph. Old Man Going.
Patient old cripple, A.
Kipling. Consolations of Memory, The.
King, The.
Lark will make her hymn to God, The.
Lovers' Litany, The.
Moon of Other Days, The.
There were three friends that buried the fourth.
Three-Decker, The.
To the Companions.
Virginity, The.
Larkin. Midsummer Night, 1940.
Lawrence. Nostalgia.
Piano.
Twenty Years Ago.
Lewis. All Day It Has Rained.
Before he sails a man may go on leave.
Bequest.
Consider this silent disciplined assembly.
From a Play.
Mountain over Aberdare, The.
On the Welsh Mountains.
Lindsay. By the Spring at Sunset.
On Suddenly Receiving a Curl Long Refused.
McAuley. Episodes for a Panel.
You'd hardly notice at first how everything.
McGrath. In Praise of Necessity.
Remembering Loves and Deaths.
Repeated Journey, The.
MacLeish. Baccalaureate.
MacNeice. Nostalgia.
Mahon. Achill.
Autobiographies.
Brighton Beach.
Going Home.
Nostalgias.
Old Snaps, The.

Melville. Æolian Harp, The.
  Age of the Antonines, The.
  Archipelago, The.
  Hearts-Of-Gold.
  Temeraire, The.
Meredith. Ah, what a dawn of splendour,
  when her sowers.
  Hungarian Air.
  It is the season of the sweet wild rose.
  O she that made the brave appeal.
  To a Skylark.
  Youth in Memory.
Merton. Memories of the Ancient World.
Muldoon. Bran.
  Ned Skinner.
Nash. Middle, The.
Nathan. Sorry.
Neruda. Ambassador, The.
  Final.
O'Hara. Commercial Variations.
Olson. Maximus, to Gloucester.
Oppen. And war.
Pack. Clayfeld's Glove.
  Clayfeld's Infancy.
Plath. Eye-Mote, The.
Rich. Living Memory.
  Location.
Robinson. Miniver Cheevy.
Roethke. Otto.
Rossetti. Farm Walk, A.
Schuyler. Alice Faye at Ruby Foo's.
  At Darragh's I.
  Morning of the Poem, The.
Sexton. 45 Mercy Street.
  Love Song for K. Owyne.
Simic. Euclid Avenue.
Smith, Charlotte. Origin of Flattery, The.
  To the Snow-Drop.
  Written in Farm Wood, South Downs, in May
  1784.
Smith, Stevie. Archie and Tina.
Snodgrass. Mementos, 1.
Snyder. Soy Sauce.
Sorrentino. Pentagram.
Stevenson. Bright is the ring of words.
  Cock's clear voice into the clearer air, The.
  Home no more home to me, whither must I
  wander?
  I dreamed of forest alleys fair.
  I know not how, but as I count.
  I saw red evening through the rain.
  Poem for a Class Re-Union.
  To Charles Baxter.
  To My Old Familiars.
  We Have Loved of Yore.
Sutter. Homing.
  Just learning to talk, I watched.
  Make no mistake. The cedar.
  Visitor, The.
Tennyson. Break, Break, Break.
  Tears, Idle Tears.
Tomlinson. Etruria Vale.
Whitman. Dying Veteran, The.
  Old Man's Thought of School, An.
Williams, Charles Kenneth. Nostalgia.
  Sanctity, The.
  Sleeping Over.
  Soon.
  Still Life.
Williams, Miller. Everything Is Fine Here
  How Are You.
  In Your Own Words Without Lying Tell
  Something of Your Background With
  Particular Attention to Anything Relating to
  the Position For Which You Are Applying.
  Press Down.
  Wiedersehen.
Williams, William Carlos. Raleigh Was Right.
Wright, Charles. Arkansas Traveller.
  Driving through Tennessee.
  Homage to Claude Lorrain.
  Italian Days.
  Journal of the Year of the Ox, A.
  Journal of True Confessions, A.
  Lonesome Pine Special.
  Lost Bodies.
  Lost Souls.

Mantova.
  Other Side of the River, The.
  Roma I.
  Roma II.
Yeats. He Remembers Forgotten Beauty.
  Meditation of the Old Fisherman, The.
Young. Afternoon After, The.
  Dance for Aging Hipsters, A.
  Dancing Together.
  Foggy Morning.
  For Janet Kafka, Dead at 30.
  Malagueña Salerosa.
  My Spanish Heart.
  Old Fashioned Cincinnati Blues, The.
  Romance.

Nothingness
Ammons. Bottommost.
Beckett. Fin fond du néant.
  Flux cause.
  Ne manquez pas à Stuttgart.
  Pas à pas.
  Rentrer / À la nuit.
  Rien nul / n'aura été.
  Something There.
Bukowski. Alone with Everybody.
  Green.
  Naked at 92 Degrees.
Carruth. Afterword: What the Poet Had
  Written.
  It was our city too. Chrome and glass.
  Little Death, The.
  Nothing I, The.
  Nothing II, The.
  Out of nothing.
  Words in a Certain Appropriate Mode.
Coleridge. On an Insignificant.
Creeley. Fancy.
  I Am Held by My Fear of Death.
  Message, The.
  Moment.
  Rhyme, The.
  Some Afternoon.
Cummings. Come nothing to my comparable
  soul.
  Don't get me wrong oblivion.
  If within tonight's erect.
  Now does our world descend.
  Only as what(out of a flophouse)floats.
  What Got him was Noth.
De la Mare. Never-To-Be.
Dickinson. By homely gift and hindered
  Words.
Dunn. Emptiness.
Eberhart. As If You Had Never Been.
  Mystery of the Abstract.
Everson. Sixty Five.
Graves. Gorge, The.
  Nothing.
Gunn. Annihilation of Nothing, The.
Herrick. Gods Presence ("God's present ev'ry
  where; but most of all").
Hesketh. Imprint.
Hughes, Langston. End.
Hughes, Ted. Swallow—rebuilding, The.
Lawrence. After All the Tragedies Are Over.
  Blank.
  Dies Irae.
  Non-Existence.
  Nullus.
  Resurrection of the Flesh.
  Worm Turns, The.
Melville. Buddha.
Merton. Abandon your body and soul into the
  abundance of light sent from above.
Gellasenheit: / Desert and void. The Uncreated
  is waste and emptiness.
  Lost Pearl, The.
  Man of Tao, The.
  Starlight and Non-Being.
  Tao.
  To a Novice ("Be a son of this instant").
  To Belong to Allah.
  Two Kings and No-Form.
  When Knowledge Went North.
  Where Is Tao?
Neruda. Search.

Olson. Lie of 10, or the Concept of Zero,
  The.
Pack. Ode to October Mist.
  Out of Nothing.
Piercy. Death of the Small Commune, The.
  Hallow Eve with Spaces for Ghosts.
  Morning Half-Life Blues, The.
  Never-Never.
  Right Thinking Man.
  S. Dead.
  Thrifty Lover, The.
Prince. Then came a time of great guilt, that I
  inhabited.
Raine. World, The.
Robinson. Man against the Sky, The.
Roethke. Abyss, The.
  Duet.
Simic. Invention of Nothing.
Smith, Stevie. Dream of Comparison, A.
Snodgrass. Eva B Hitler, geb. Braun.
Tomlinson. Event.
  Nothing: a Divagation.
Warren. Place Where Nothing Is, A.
Williams, William Carlos. To Have Done
  Nothing.
Wright, Charles. Composition in Grey and
  Pink.
  Journal of Southern Rivers, A.
  October.
Wright, James. Goodbye to the Poetry of
  Calcium.
  Stormclouds / give their morose faces to the
  sea.
See also **Nihilism.**

Notoriety
Beatles. Ballad of John and Yoko, The.
Bukowski. Best Way to Get Famous Is to Run
  Away, The.
Catullus. Carmen 79: "They nickname
  Lesbia's brother 'pulcher'."
Hewitt. Legend in His Own Lifetime.
  Nineteen Sixteen, or the Terrible Beauty.
St. John. My Tea with Madame Descartes.
Zukofsky. Lesbius has pooled her: kidney?
  whom Lesbia my—lit.

Notre Dame Cathedral
Cummings. It is winter a moon in the
  afternoon.

Nottingham, England
Davie. Nottinghamshire.
Lawrence. In Nottingham.
  Nottingham's New University.

Nova Scotia, Canada
Bishop. First Death in Nova Scotia.
  Poem: "About the size of an old-style dollar
  bill."
Dunn. Building in Nova Scotia.
Hartley. Blair Purves: Bluenose Portrait Effect
  #2.
  Cyriaque d'Etremont: Bluenose Portrait Effect
  #1.

Novels
Beatles. Paperback Writer.
Bukowski. Dear Friend.
  2nd Novel, The.
Coleridge. With Fielding's *Amelia*.
Hoffman. Great American Novel, The.
Lindsay. Raft, The.
MacLeish. Observations of P. Ovidus Naso on
  the Incidence of Sex in the Contemporary
  Novel.
Nemerov. Exasperations of a Novelist.
  Novelists.
  Reflexion of a Novelist.
  Style.
  To the Bleeding Hearts Association of
  American Novelists.
Stevens. Novel, The.

Novelty
Browning, Elizabeth Barrett. Poet, The.
Ceravolo. O Heart Uncovered.
Cowper. Sonnet 3: "As on a rugged mountain
  at the darkening of evening."
Herrick. Nothing New.
Larkin. When First We Faced, and Touching
  Showed.

MacNeice. Idle Talk.
Milton. Sonnet 3: "As on a rugged mountain at the darkening of evening."
Olson. Celestial Evening, October 1967.
"Reed." New Sensations.

November
Atwood. November.
Auden. November at Weybourne.
Brontë. Redbreast, Early in the morning.
Carruth. Once and Again.
  Tanck's Song About November.
Crane. This Way Where November..
Dickinson. Day grew small, surrounded tight, The.
  November always seemed to me.
Dunbar. Nutting Song.
Fletcher. November Days.
Frost. My November Guest.
Hardy. At Day-Close in November.
Hughes, Ted. November.
Jeffers. November Surf.
Lawrence. November by the Sea.
Levertov. Air of November.
McGrath. News and the Weather, The.
MacLeish. April in November.
  November.
Nemerov. Elegy of Last Resort.
Patchen. November in Ohio.
Sandburg. Prairie Woodland.
  Suburban Sicilian Sketches.
  Without Notice Beforehand.
Schuyler. November.
  Vermont Diary, A.
Tennyson. November in the Isle of Wight.
Tomlinson. Saving the Appearances.
Whittier. Day, A.
  St. Martin's Summer.
Williams, William Carlos. Woodpecker, The.
Wright, James. Late November in a Field.

Nuclear Accidents
Meinke. Atomic Pantoum.
Paley. In Aix.
See also **Radiation and Radiation Sickness.**

Nuclear Energy
Carruth. Phone.
Ginsberg. Nagasaki Days.
  Plutonian Ode.
Williams, Charles Kenneth. Tar.

Nuclear War
Creeley. Some Afternoon.
"Dylan." Let Me Die in My Footsteps.
  Talkin' World War III Blues.
Fox. Albert Einstein (1879–1955).
Frost. Planners, The.
Hoffman. Seals in Penobscot Bay, The.
Jeffers. Beautiful Captive, The.
  Explosion.
  Monument.
Lowell. Fall 1961.
McGrath. Nuclear Winter.
  War Resisters' Song.
Merton. Chant to Be Used in Processions around a Site with Furnaces.
  Letter to Pablo Antonio Cuadra Concerning Giants, A.
  Original Child Bomb.
Morrison. We Awoke, Talking.
Oppen. Crowded Countries of the Bomb, The.
Rich. Ultimate Act, The.
Rukeyser. Surrounded, The.
Sandburg. Call the Next Witness.
  Unknown War, The.
Walker. We Have a Map of the World.
See also **Atomic Bomb; Radiation and Radiation Sickness.**

Nudity and Nudists
Bunting. Herr Lignitz knows Old Berlin. It is near the Post Office.
Creeley. Apology, The.
Cummings. Perhaps it was Myself sits down in this chair. There were two chairs,in fact.
Dobyns. Topless.
Donne. To His Mistress Going to Bed.
Graves. Naked and the Nude, The.
Herrick. Upon Julia's Fall.
Lawrence. Elixir.
  Give Me a Sponge.

Gross, Coarse, Hideous.
  Innocent England.
  13,000 People.
Olson. Here i am, naked.
Stafford. Adults Only.
Stevens. Nudity in the Colonies.
Walker. Streaking (A Phenomenon Following the Sixties).
Wilbur. Playboy.

Numbers
Ammons. Imaginary Number.
Creeley. Numbers.
  Piece, A.
Dobyns. Toting It Up.
Donne. Primrose[, Being at Montgomery Castle, upon the Hill, on Which It Is Situate], The.
Hesketh. Joke, The.
Hughes, Langston. Madam and the Number Writer.
Koch. Magic of Numbers, The.
Lowry. Abacus, The.
Nash. Calling Spring VII-MMMC.
Neruda. Is 4 always 4 for everybody?
  2 8 3 2 5 6 7 4 5 4 9.
Olson. Lie of 10, or the Concept of Zero, The.
  2nd Musical Form, for Dave Young, A.
Pack. Number.
Rossetti. 1 and 1 are 2— / That's for me and you.
Sandburg. Child Margaret.
  City Number.
  Crossed Numbers.
  Number Man.
Simic. Figuring.
Zukofsky. To My Valentines.

Nuns
Betjeman. Felixstowe, or, The Last of Her Order.
Cohen. Sisters of Mercy.
Dobyns. Careers.
Donne. Virgins, The.
Glück. Cell, The.
Graves. Gooseflesh Abbey.
  Liadan and Curithir.
Hewitt. Age and Youth.
Hopkins. Heaven-Haven.
  Wreck of the Deutschland, The.
Hugo. Holy Family.
Lowell. Mother Marie Therese.
McAuley. Nun of St. Michan's, The.
Merton. To a Severe Nun.
Milton. Sonnet 9: "Ladie, that in the prime of earliest youth."
Pope. Vestal, The.
Rukeyser. Nuns in the Wind.
Stevenson. To Mother Maryanne.
Williams, William Carlos. Nun's Song.
Wordsworth. Nunnery.

Nursery Rhymes
Auden. Pride.
"Carroll, Lewis." Canto IV: Hys Nouryture.
  Little Man That Had a Little Gun, The.
Creeley. Names, The.
Frost. Lines Written in Dejection on the Eve of Great Success.
Gardner. Nursery Rhyme No. 1.
  Nursery Rhyme No. 2.
Robinson. Old King Cole.
Simic. Bedtime Story.
  Nursery Rhyme.

Nurses
Auden. Friends of the born nurse, The.
  In the Nursery.
Blake. Nurse's Song ("When the voices of children are heard on the green / And laughing is heard on the hill").
Browning, Elizabeth Barrett. Isobel's Child.
"Carroll, Lewis." Path of Roses, The.
De la Mare. Juliet's Nurse.
Dobyns. Dead Baby.
Gardner. Bronchitis at the Chelsea—or Salud Raul.
Glück. Nurse's Song.
Graves. Wild Cyclamen.

Hewitt. Betrayal.
  Sanctuary.
Jarrell. Well-to-Do Invalid, A.
Kipling. Dirge of Dead Sisters.
  Nurses, The.
  Nursing Sister, The.
  V.A.D. (Mediterranean).
Lawrence. Grey Nurse, The.
Lewis. Compassion.
Liddy. Josie.
Nathan. Nurse.
Poe. To M. L. S——.
Rich. Dien Bien Phu.
Stevenson. To Alison Cunningham.
Whitman. Wound-Dresser, The.
Yau. Late Night Movies I.

Nursing Homes
Kooser. Birthday.
McNeill. Ballad of the Rest Home.
Piercy. Proposal for Recycling Wastes, A.

Nymphs
Carew. Good Counsel to a Young Maid ("When you the sun-burnt pilgrim see").
  Pastoral[1] Dialogue, A.
Carruth. Afternoon of a Faun.
Doolittle. Oread.
Herrick. To the Water Nymphs, Drinking at the Fountain.
Lovelace. Amyntor's Grove.
MacLeish. How the River Ninfa Runs through the Ruined Town Beneath the Lime Quarry.
Meredith. Rape of Aurora, The.
Milton. Oracles are dumm, The.
  Sabrina.
Nash. Chloe and the Roué.
Rossetti. Water Spirit's Song, The.
Sidney. Sonnet 82: "Nymph of the garden where all beauties be."
Smith, Charlotte. To the Naiad of the Arun.
Snodgrass. Monet: "Les Nymphéas."
Spenser. I saw a spring out of a rocke forth rayle.
  Sea Nymphs, The.
Swift. Lines from Cadenus to Vanessa.
Tomlinson. Veneris Venefica Agrestis.
Wilbur. Ceremony.
  Under a Tree.
Wordsworth. Dog—An Idyllium, The.
  Fish-Women.—On Landing at Calais.
Wroth. Song 2: "Sweet Silvia in a shadie wood."
  Sonnet 3: "Juno still jealouse of her husband Jove."
  Sonnet 8: "Poore Love in chaines, and fetters like a thiefe."

O

Oafs
Nemerov. What Kind of a Guy Was He?

Oak Trees
Ammons. Grove's Way.
  Waking.
Byron. To an Oak at Newstead.
Ceravolo. Drunken Winter.
Cowper. Yardley Oak.
Creeley. Love ("Not enough. The question: what is").
Eberhart. Oak, The.
Emerson. By kinds I keep my kinds in check.
Hall. Acorns.
Heaney. Bog Oak.
Herrick. All Things Decay and Die.
Hesketh. Imprint.
Hughes, Ted. I see the oak's bride in the oak's grasp.
  Your tree—your oak.
Kipling. Tree Song, A.
Lawrence. Under the Oak.
MacLeish. Survivor.
Millay. Here in a Rocky Cup.
  Oak-Leaves, The.
Ransom. Parting, without a Sequel.
Rossetti. Toadstool comes up in a night, A.
Sandburg. Oak Arms.
  October Paint.

Meredith. Lied von Castelli.
Milton. Canzone: "Scoffing, amorous maidens
  and young men."
Morrison. Bibulous Compound Of.
Nash. Name Is Too Familiar, The.
Rich. Focus.
Rossetti. Contemptuous of his home beyond.
  Sir Eustace Grey.
Sandburg. Mist Marches Across the Valley.
  Pearl Fog.
Varren. Fog.
Wilbur. All That Is.
  Five Women Bathing in Moonlight.
Wright, James. On Minding One's Own
  Business.

Observatories. *see* Astronomy and Astronomers.

Obsessions
Berryman. Canto Amor.
  Darling I wait O in my upstairs box.
  Here too you came and sat a time once,
    drinking.
  I didn't see anyone else, I just saw Lies.
  Itself a lightning-flash ripping the dark.
  Outlaws claw mostly to a riddled end.
Brontë. A.A.A.
Bukowski. Mother and Son.
Burns. Hue and Cry of John Lewars, The.
Byron. Last Words on Greece.
Carroll, Jim. Like a rabid goat, this obsession.
Coleridge. Presence of Love, The.
  Recollections of Love.
Dickey, William. Gambling at Reno.
Dunbar. Disturber, The.
"Dylan." Love You Too Much.
  Visions of Johanna.
Eberhart. Two Loves.
Emerson. To Eva.
Graves. Double Bass.
Hemingway. If my Valentine you won't be.
Hughes, Ted. Lovesong: "He loved her and
  she loved him."
Lawrence. Release.
  What's Sane and What Isn't.
Matthews. Cloud, The.
Nash. Curl Up and Diet.
  Strange Case of the Entomologist's Heart, The.
Neruda. I entered the cave of the amethysts.
Sidney. Unto the caitiff wretch whom long
  affliction holdeth.
Silverstein. Peanut-Butter Sandwich.
  Search, The.
Snodgrass. Adolf Hitler ("More than fifty
  millions. More").
Stuart. Narcissus Dreaming.
Williams, Charles Kenneth. Resentment.
Williams, William Carlos. Love Song: First
  Version, 1915, A.
Wroth. Sonnet 23: "When every one to
  pleasing pastime hies."
Wyatt. Driven by desire to set affection.
  I am ready and ever will be.
  I might by no means surmise.
  Longer to trow ye.
  Process of time worketh such wonder.
  Shall she never out of my mind.
  Spite of their spite which they in vain.
  To whom should I sue to ease my pain?
  What would ye more of me, your slave,
    require.

Obsolescence
Hewitt. Christmas Rhymers, Ballynure, 1941,
  The.

Occult, The
Browning, Robert. Mr Sludge, "The Medium."
Ford. O.
Lieberman. Prayer against the Curse Bomb.

Occupations
Auden. Sext.
Lowry. Rich man, poor man, beggarman,
  thief.
Merton. Active Life.
Wordsworth. Poet's Epitaph, A.

Ocean. *see* Sea.

October
Angelou. Late October.
Berry. October 10.

Hall. Day I Was Older, The.
Lowell. Alfred Corning Clark.
Oblivion
Bukowski. Dow Jones: Down.
Bunting. Many well-known people have been
  packed away in cemeteries.
Campion. My Sweetest Lesbia [Let Us Live
  and Love].
Carruth. He decided to live. Alone. One room.
  Quaking.
Catullus. Carmen 5: "Lesbia / live with me."
Cowper. On the Biographia Britannica.
Creeley. Places.
Eberhart. On a Squirrel Crossing the Road in
  Autumn, in New England.
Hartley. Oblique Frontier.
Holmes. Night Music.
Hughes, Langston. Blues at Dawn.
  Shame on You.
Lawrence. Change.
  Forget.
  Know-All.
  Phoenix.
  Shadows.
  Tabernacle.
  Temples.
"MacDiarmid." Eemis-Stane, The.
Morgan. Catullus: *Carmen v.*
Neruda. Search.
Oliver. Last Days.
  Little Owl Who Lives in the Orchard.
  Moccasin Flowers.
Smith, Charlotte. To Oblivion.
Smith, Stevie. Oblivion.
Wilbur. Everness.
  Ewigkeit.
Williams, Charles Kenneth. Clay out of
  Silence.
  They Warned Him Then They Threw Him
    Away.
  What Must I Do To Be Lost?
Wordsworth. Lesbia.
Zukofsky. Drive, fast kisses.
  May we live, my Lesbia, love while we may.
Obscenity
Bukowski. Buffalo Bill.
Herrick. Lasciviousnesse.
Jonson. To Playwright.
Lawrence. Broadcasting to the G.B.P.
  Censors.
  Give Me a Sponge.
  Innocent England.
Markson. Tricentennial: 1980.
Nash. King Leer.
See also **Pornography.**
Obscurity
Cowper. Canzone: "Scoffing, amorous maidens
  and young men."
Donne. Obscure Writer, An.
Graves. Mist.
Herrick. To Cedars.
Lowry. There is a sort of conspiracy about the
  great.

Betjeman. Tregardock.
Boyle. October 1954.
Carruth. All Things.
Dunbar. October.
Eberhart. Prometheus.
  Vision through Timothy.
Emerson. October woods, wherein.
Frost. October.
Hartley. Brown Gulls.
Hayden. October.
Hewitt. Birthday Rhyme for Roberta, A.
  Lagan in October, The.
  October-Born.
  October's Child.
  Sonnets in October.
Jeffers. October Evening.
Levertov. October.
Mahon. October in Hyde Park.
Millay. October—An Etching.
Nemerov. Autumnal.
  Late Butterflies.
  Observation of October.
Oliver. October.
Paley. Arboreal Mystery, An.
Rich. Break, The.
Rossetti. Golden Holly.
Sandburg. Crabapples.
  Redhaw Rain.
  Ripe Corn.
  Wind in the corn leaves among the naked
    stalks, The.
Schuyler. Going.
  October.
  October 5, 1981.
Thomas. Especially When the October Wind.
  Poem in October.
Tomlinson. In October.
  October.
Young. Houston in October.
  October Variations, The.

Octopuses
Beatles. Octopus's Garden.
Merrill. Octopus, The.
Moore. Octopus, An.
Nash. Octopus, The.
Rolfe. Portrait of a Death.
Stafford. If I Could Be Like Wallace Stevens.

Odysseus. *see* **Ulysses.**

Oedipus
Eberhart. Oedipus.
Gallagher. Sugar.
Jarrell. Sphinx's Riddle to Oedipus, The.
Jeffers. Meditation on Saviors.
Knott. Shorts / Excerpts ("Hope...goosestep").
Lowry. Oh the Pyrrus boys are we.
Rukeyser. Myth.
Shelley. Oedipus Tyrannus; or, Swellfoot the
  Tyrant.
Spender. Oedipus Rex.
  Stranger, this is shining Colonos.
Yeats. From the "Antigone."

Offa, King of Mercia
Hill. Coins handsome as Nero's; of good
  substance and.
  King of the perennial holly-groves, the riven
    sandstone.
  Mad are predators. Too often lately they
    harbour, The.
  Not strangeness, but strange likeness.
    Obstinate.
  'Now when King Offa was alive and dead',
    they were.
  Pet-name, a common name. Best-selling brand,
    curt, A.
  Princes of Mercia were badger and raven, The.
  So much for the elves' wergild, the true
    governance.

Office Workers
Gunn. Waitress.
Jong. Paper Cuts.
Kooser. Death at the Office, A.
  They Had Torn Off My Face at the Office.
Miller. End of the Negotiable Beggar Bond
  Banquet, The.
Nash. Dance Unmacabre.
Roethke. Dolor.

Williams, William Carlos. Return to Work, The.

See also **Clerks; Secretaries.**

Officers, Military
Ciardi. Citation on Retirement.
Hughes, Ted. Retired Colonel, The.

Ogres
Auden. August 1968.
Graves. Ogres and Pygmies.
Stevenson. On Some Ghostly Companions at a Spa.

See also **Monsters; Trolls.**

O'Hara, Frank
Berrigan. Frank O'Hara.
Red Shift.
Koch. Circus, The.
Fate.
Schuyler. Beautiful Funerals.
Fauré Ballade, The.
Four Poems.
To Frank O'Hara.
Waldman. Phonecall from Frank O'Hara, A.

Ohio (state)
Crane. Porphyro in Akron.
Ferlinghetti. Ascending over Ohio.
Koch. Artist, The.
Levine. One for the Rose.
Meinke. Exodus with Children.
Oliver. River Styx, Ohio, The.
Patchen. November in Ohio.
Rolfe. Not Men Alone.
Sandburg. Crossing the Ohio When Poppies Bloom in Ashtabula.
Updike. Ohio.
Wright, James. At the Executed Murderer's Grave.
Autumn Begins in Martins Ferry, Ohio.
From a Bus Window in Central Ohio, Just before a Thunder Shower.
In Ohio.
In Response to a Rumor that the Oldest Whorehouse in Wheeling, West Virginia, Has Been Condemned.
Katy Did.
Many of Our Waters: Variaitons on a Poem by a Black Child.
Many of Our Waters: Variations on a Poem by a Black Child.
Miners.

Ohio River
Merton. City after Noon, The.
Ohio River—Louisville, The.
Ransom. Antique Harvesters.
Sandburg. Whiffs of the Ohio River at Cinncinnati.
Wright, James. Three Sentences for a Dead Swan.
To the Ohio.

Oil
Emerson. There is no evil but can speak.
Lowry. Port Moody.
Nemerov. Breaking of Rainbows, The.

Oil Industry
Griffiths. Oil Terminal.
Hoffman. Slick.
Lowry. Picture, A.
Port Moody.
Zukofsky. Arizona.

Oisin
Hewitt. Homestead.
Yeats. Wanderings of Oisin, The.

O'Keeffe, Georgia
Hartley. Perhaps Macabre.
Smith, Patti. Georgia O'Keeffe.

Oklahoma (state)
Berryman. October's both, back in the Sooner State.
Gallagher. Boat Ride.
Hartley. Are You There, Rose Trumbull?
Hemingway. Oklahoma.
Sandburg. Who was that early sodbuster in Kansas? He leaned at the gatepost and.
Stevens. Life Is Motion.
Updike. Tulsa.
Zukofsky. Belly Locks Shnooks Oakie.

Old Age
Angelou. Last Decision, The.
On Aging.
Arnold. Growing Old.
Atwood. Daguerreotype Taken in Old Age.
Some kind of ritual / for your dwindling.
Wish: Metamorphosis to Heraldic Emblem.
Auden. Song: "Merriest cuckoo / Which haunted us in May, The."
Beckett. Song: "Age is when to a man."
Berry. Boone.
Companions, The.
Freedom of Loving, The.
I stand at the cistern in front of the old barn.
Light, The.
Wilderness Starts towards Him, A.
Young Man, Thinking of the Old, The.
Berryman. Germanicus leapt upon the wild lion in Smyrna.
Betjeman. Late-flowering Lust.
Senex.
Youth and Age on Beaulieu River, Hants.
Blake. In a Myrtle [*or* Mirtle] Shade.
Bogan. Crows, The.
Boyle. Advice to the Old.
Poem on Getting up Early in the Morning (or Even Late in the Morning), When One is Old.
To a Proud Old Woman Watching the Tearing Down of the Hurricane Shed.
Brontë. From a Dungeon Wall in the Southern College.
Love and Friendship.
Brooks. Bean Eaters, The.
Old People Working (Garden, Car).
Sick Man Looks at Flowers.
Browning, Elizabeth Barrett. Bacchus and Ariadne.
Browning, Robert. Aeschylus' Soliloquy.
Grow old along with me!
Rabbi Ben Ezra.
Bukowski. Eating My Senior Citizen's Dinner at the Sizzler.
Here I Am.
I don't know where they come from.
Millionaire, The.
Patriot of Life, A.
Traffic Signals.
2 Outside, As Bones Break in My Kitchen.
Bunting. All the teeth ever I had are worn down and fallen out.
When the sword of sixty comes nigh his head.
Burns. Auld Man's Winter Thought, The.
There'll Never Be Peace Till Jamie Comes Hame.
What can a young lassie, what shall a young lassie.
Byron. Lament of Tasso, The.
Campion. Ad nobiliss. virum Gul. Percium.
Ad Rob. Caraeum Equitem Auratum Nobilissimum.
In obitum Iacobi Huissii.
Though You Are Young [*or* Yoong].
"Carroll, Lewis." Father William.
Upon the Lonely Moor.
White Knight's Ballad, The.
Carruth. Event, The.
Ciardi. Alec.
Clare. Old Man, The.
Coleridge. Love's Apparition and Evanishment.
Old Man of the Alps, The.
Pity.
Sonnet [to Charles Lloyd].
Youth and Age.
Cooper. Bermuda.
Crabbe. Ancient Mansion, The.
Crane. Fernery, The.
Creeley. Epic Expands, The.
Cullen. To France.
Cummings. Fearlessandbosomy / this / grand:gal.
Noone" autumnal this great lady's gaze.
oDE: "O / the sweet & aged people."
Old age sticks / up Keep.
Says ol man no body.
Why / do the / fingers.

Davie. Alzheimer's Disease.
Poet Redeemed & Dead.
Saw I Never the Righteous Forsaken.
De la Mare. All That's Past.
Alone.
Beneath a motionless yew.
Dust to Dust.
Fat Woman, The.
In a Library.
Karma.
Last Arrow, The.
Last Chapter, The.
Nod.
Old Angler, The.
Old Ben.
Old Men, The.
Old Susan.
Waiting.
Dickey, William. At Your Old House.
Die Älte Frau, Die Älte Marschallin.
Dunbar. Goin' Back.
Growin' Gray.
Old.
Old Story, The.
Parted.
When the Old Man Smokes.
Eberhart. White Pines, Felled 1984.
Edmunds. Doña Sebastiana.
Eliot. Gerontion.
Lines for an Old Man.
Emerson. Old Age.
Terminus ("It is time to be old").
Ferlinghetti. Just as I used to say.
Old Italians Dying, The.
Old Sailors, The.
Fox. Blue Dress, The.
Ovid.
Shipbuilder, The.
Frost. Old Man's Winter Night, An.
Provide, Provide.
Gallagher. Each Bird Walking.
Gildner. In the Social Security Office.
Uncle George at the Home.
Glück. Grandmother in the Garden.
To Florida.
Graves. Advent of Summer.
Age Gap.
Broken Girth, The.
Gentleman, The.
Great-Grandmother, The.
Grotesques.
Imminent Seventies, The.
Nightmare of Senility.
Oldest Soldier, The.
Septuagenarian, The.
Serpent's Tail.
Song:Seven Fresh Years.
Title of Poet, The.
Two Crucial Generations.
Griffiths. Education.
Geriatrics.
Gunn. At an Intersection.
Conversation of Old Men, The.
Kent.
Lines for My 55th Birthday.
Old Woman, The.
Sand Man, The.
Well Dennis O'Grady.
Haines. Deserted Cabin.
Hall. By the Exeter River.
Dump, The.
Old Home Week.
On Reaching the Age of Two Hundred.
Rocker, The.
Hardy. Aged Newspaper Soliloquizes, The.
Ancient to Ancients, An.
Faded Face, The.
He Never Expected Much.
I Look into My Glass.
Near Lanivet, 1872.
Old Workman, The.
Seventy-four and Twenty.
Singing Woman, The.
Superseded, The.
Tresses, The.
Two Rosalinds, The.
Hartley. Hiccoughs of old ladies.

Coming of Wisdom with Time, The.
Girl's Song.
Imitated from the Japanese.
In Tara's Halls.
Lamentation of the Old Pensioner, The.
Meeting.
Old Man Stirs the Fire to a Blaze, An.
Old Men Admiring Themselves in the Water,
 The.
Prayer for Old Age, A.
Quarrel in Old Age.
Sailing to Byzantium.
Spur, The.
Those Dancing Days Are Gone.
Tower, The.
Two Years Later.
When You Are Old.
Wild Old Wicked Man, The.
Zimmer. Zimmer Warns Himself with Vivid
 Images Against Old Age.
Zukofsky. Homage.
See also **Retirement and Retirees.**

"Old Ironsides." *see* Constitution (ship).

Oldham, John
Dryden. To the Memory of Mr Oldham.

Olive Trees and Olives
Graves. Oleaster, The.
Hartley. Dusty olive trees.
Herrick. Olive Branch, The.
Hewitt. Mycenae and Epidaurus.
Housman. Olive, The.
McGrath. Mediterranean.
Merrill. Olive Grove.
Smith, Charlotte. Ode to the Olive Tree.
Wilbur. Agrigentum Road, The.
 Grasse: The Olive Trees.
Williams, Miller. How the Elephant Got His
 Hump.

Olympics
Dickey, James. Olympian, The.
Eberhart. Noble Man, The.
Graves. Antorcha Y Corona, 1968.
 Torch and Crown, 1968.
Rukeyser. Voices.

Omar Khayyám
Young. Poem for Omar Khayyam (1050?-
 1123? A.D.).

Omens
Atwood. Four Auguries.
Burns. Tam Glen.
Cohen. Anthem: "Birds they sang, The."
Cowper. To a Young Friend.
Creeley. For the New Year.
De la Mare. Foreboding.
 Shadow.
Dobyns. Where We Are.

Dickinson. How can we thank each other.
Eberhart. Two Loves.
 Undercliff Evening.
Emerson. From "Bird Conversations."
 This shining hour is an edifice.
MacNeice. Creditor, The.
Milton. O Jehovah our Lord, how wondrous
 great.
Psalms. Psalm 8: "O Lord our Lord, how
 excellent.."
 Psalm 90: "Lord, thou hast been our dwelling
 place in all generations."
 Psalm 104: "Bless the Lord, O my soul.."
 Psalm 107: "O give thanks unto the Lord, for
 he is good: for.."
 Psalm 114: "When Israel went out of Egypt."
 Psalm 135: "Praise ye the Lord. Praise ye the
 name of the Lord; praise him, O ye servants
 of the Lord."
 Psalm 139: "O Lord, thou hast searched me,
 and known me."
 Psalm 147: "Praise ye the Lord: for it is
 good.."
Ralegh. First of all is God, and the same last
 is he, The.
Smart. O Praise the Lord, and bless his name.
 On the Power of the Supreme Being.
Williams, Miller. Why God Permits Evil: For
 Answers to This Question of Interest to
 Many Write Bible Answers Dept. E-7.

O'Neill, Shane
Jeffers. Shane O'Neill's Cairn.

Onions
Hesketh. Truth Game.
Matthews. Onions.
Ralegh. Egyptians [*or Aegyptians*] think[e] it
 sin[ne] to root[e] up, or to bite.
Swift. Onions.
 Onyons.
Wilbur. Shallot, A.
Williams, Charles Kenneth. Poem for the
 Governments, A.
Williams, William Carlos. To Be Hungry Is to
 Be Great.

Ontario, Canada
Davie. Frontenac.
Muldoon. Ontario.

Opera
Ashbery. Faust.
Jarrell. Love for One Orange, The.
 Seductive Piece of Business, A.
Lawrence. After the Opera.
Merrill. Matinees.
Muldoon. Chester.
Tomlinson. Night at the Opera, A.
 Programme Note.

... letter

... hidden options

... hidden

... The

... The

... r. Possum.

... opportunity

Browning, Robert. Youth and Art
Cooper. Blue Anchor, The.
Cummings. Will suddenly trees leap up from
 winter and will.
Emerson. Heartily heartily sing.
 Yet all comes out of this, that one door.
Hardy. Midnight on the Great Western.
 Musical Box, The.
 She Opened the Door.
 You on the Tower.
Kipling. Penalty, The.
Lawrence. All That We Have Is Life.
Lindsay. Empty Boats, The.
Nash. Brief Guide to New York, A.
 Doctor Fell? I Thought So.
Rolfe. Somebody and Somebody Else and
 You.
Rukeyser. What do you know of America? I
 asked a little Russian schoolgirl.
Shakespeare. Opportunity.
Shelley. Allegory, An.
Sorrentino. Cautious Circumspection Does Not
 Win the West.
 Mother, this is a ball of color.
Stuart. This Is No Dream, This Is My Life.
Whitman. And thou, America, / For the
 scheme's culmination.

Opposites
Browning, Elizabeth Barrett. Sonnet: "Unlike
 are we, unlike, O princely heart!"
Carroll, Jim. Thick veins on the back of my
 forearm.
Carruth. Mythology of Dark and Light, The.
Ford. Matin Pour Matta.
Graves. Despite and Still.
 In Broken Images.
 Laugh, The.
 Pact, The.
 Song of Contrariety.
 Song: Wherever We May Be.
Herrick. Light Lightly Pleased.
 Upon His Gray Haires.
Hesketh. Rivals, The.
Hewitt. Happy Man, The.
 W.R. Rodgers.
Kipling. Bonfires, The.
Koch. Simplicity of the Unknown Past, The.
Lovelace. Her Reserved Looks.
Melville. Art.
Merton. Homer was wrong in saying: "Would
 that conflict might perish from among gods
 and men."
Neruda. And why is the sun such a poor
 friend.
 Don't you also feel danger.
Ransom. Pink and Pale.
Rich. I was looking for a way out of a
 lifetime's consolations.
 7/26/68: II.
Robinson. Vain Gratuities.
Rukeyser. If you look at your succession of
 desires.

Silverstein. Us.
Tomlinson. Oppositions.

Oppression
Angelou. To a Freedom Fighter.
  We Saw Beyond Our Seeming.
Berryman. Sensible, coarse, and moral; in
  decent brown.
Bly. Romans Angry about the Inner World.
Bunting. They Say Etna.
Byron. On Jordan's Banks.
Carroll, Jim. Sea Battle.
"Carroll, Lewis." Elections to the Hebdomadal
  Council, The.
Carruth. I Tell You For Several Years of My
  Madness I Heard the Voice of Lilith Singing
  in the Trees of Chicago.
Cohen. I Try to Keep in Touch.
Crane. Black Tambourine.
Cummings. O to be in finland.
  Thanksgiving (1956).
Davie. Put Not Your Trust in Princes.
Dove. Parsley.
"Dylan." Baby black's / been had.
  Ballad of Donald White.
  Dear Landlord.
  George Jackson.
  I could make you crawl.
  Long Ago, Far Away.
  Money Blues.
  Neighborhood Bully.
  Rainy Day Women # 12 & 35.
  Walls of Red Wing.
Everson. If you were to try to say.
  October Tragedy.
Fisher. Wanting to get away.
Fletcher. England Again.
  Hard Sayings.
Hacker. Coda.
Hartnett. Prisoners.
Hewitt. To a Modern Irish Poet.
Hugo. Announcement.
  On Hearing a New Escalation.
Joseph. Letter to comfort a friend.
Lawrence. Being Alive.
  City-Life.
  Cry of the Masses.
  Give Us the Thebaïd.
  Gulf, The.
  Hold Back!
  Kill Money.
  Listen to the Band!
  Love as an Escape.
  Mills of God, The.
  Money-Madness.
  North Country, The.
  Poor Young Things.
  Sex Won't Work.
  Wages.
  We Die Together.
  What Have They Done to You?
McGrath. Incident in the Life of a Prophet,
  An.
  Poet of the Prison Isle: Ritsos Against the
  Colonels, The.
McNeill. Epitaph in the Imperative Mode.
Merrill. Domino.
Morrison. In This Dim Cave.
Olson. Barley or rye / blue and white green.
  Cause, the Cause, The.
  Gonfalon Raised Tonight, The.
  Kingfishers, The.
  She-Bear, The.
  She-Bear (II), The.
  To the She-Bear: *The 1st Song.*
Paley. In San Salvador (I).
  In San Salvador (II).
  Muncipal center / the morning of anger, The.
Piercy. High Frequency.
  Judgment, The.
  Tower Struck by Lightning Reversed; the
  Overturning of the Tower, The.
  Unlearning to Not Speak.
Raine. Eudaimon.
Rich. Burning of Paper instead of Children,
  The.
  Culture and Anarchy.
  For Ethel Rosenberg.

From an Old House in America.
  Heroines.
  Hunger.
  Memory says: Want to do right? Don't count
  on me.
  Mountain laurel in bloom, The.
  No one's fated or doomed to love anyone.
  North American Time.
  Over the hills in Shutesbury, Leverett.
Rolfe. Any Slave.
Rossetti. Pastime.
Rukeyser. Ann Burlak.
Shapiro. University.
  Waitress.
Shelley. Fragment: To the People of England.
  Ode Written October, 1819, An.
Smith, Charlotte. Long wintry months are
  past; the Moon that now.
  Slow in the Wintry Morn, the struggling light.
Stafford. Objector.
Waldman. Eyes in All Heads to Be Looked
  out Of.
Walker. Ndebele.
Whittier. Cassandra Southwick.
  St. John.
Williams, Charles Kenneth. Keep It.
  Poem for the Governments, A.
Yeats. Fascination of What's Difficult, The.
Young. Dude in Denver.
  Old O.O. Blues, The.
  Poem for Players, A.
  Some Recent Fiction.
  What You Seize Is What You Git.

See also **Dehumanization; Sexism; Slavery;**
  Tyranny.

Optimism
Browning, Robert. Year's at the spring, The.
Burns. Occasional Address, Spoken by Miss
  Fontenell, on Her Bnefit-Night, Decr. 4th.
  1793.—Written by Mr Burns.
Campion. If I hope, I pine; if I feare, I faint
  and die.
Carroll, Jim. Love Poem (Later).
Ceravolo. Cool Breeze.
Clough. Say not the struggle nought [*or*
  naught] availeth.
Creeley. For a Screaming Lady.
  Hi There!
  Invitation, The.
  Traveller, The.
  Wish, A.
Dunbar. Keep A-Pluggin' Away.
"Dylan." You Ain't Goin' Nowhere.
Emerson. A.H.
  Papas Blondine / Grew tall & wise.
Galvin. Great Blue.
Graves. Pact, The.
  Song: Olive Tree.
Hardy. When the clouds' swoln bosoms echo
  back the shouts of the many and strong.
Herrick. Hope Well and Have Well: or, Faire
  after Foule Weather.
Hugo. Indian Girl.
Knott. Lesson.
Lawrence. Optimist, The.
Liddy. Little Song for Ivy Day, 1991.
McGrath. Against the False Magicians.
Meredith. From labours through the night,
  outworn.
  He passed her through the sermon's dull
  defile.
  In the Sap.
  New Year's Eve.
  Open horizons round.
  Song: "Daisy now is out upon the green,
  The."
  Song: "Should thy love die; / O bury it not
  under ice-blue eyes!"
  Song: "Thou tremblest O my love! thy hand in
  mine."
  Sonnet: "Hateful are those false themes of
  speculation."
  This love of nature, that allures to take.
  Three Gipsies, The.
  Wilding little stubble flower, A.
  Will Whistle.
  World is young, the world is well, The.

Nash. Look for the Silver Lining.
  Lucy Lake.
Neruda. Cherries.
Robinson. Caput Mortuum.
Rolfe. Bequest.
  First Love.
  Primer Amor.
Silverstein. Where the Sidewalk Ends.
Smith, Stevie. Away, Melancholy.
Stevenson. Aye mon, it's true; I'm no' that
  weel.
Wyatt. Venomous thorns that are so sharp and
  keen.
Zukofsky. In Arizona / (how many years in
  the mountains).

Oracles
Hewitt. Old Corinth.
Housman. Oracles, The.
MacNeice. Oracle, The.
Meredith. Wind on the Lyre.
Merton. Oracle, The.
Milton. Oracles are dumm, The.
Raine. Oracles.
Updike. On the Way to Delphi.
Yeats. Delphic Oracle upon Plotinus, The.

Orange (color)
Sorrentino. Crown, The.

Orange Trees and Oranges
Sorrentino. Remember the story of Columbus
  and the orange?
  Variations 2.
  Zukofsky.
Swift. Oranges.
Wakoski. Slicing Oranges for Jeremiah.
  Smudging.
Walcott. In a Green Night.
Williams, William Carlos. Berket and the
  Stars.
Young. Poem with Orange.

Oratory
Burns. Collected, Harry stood awee.
  He clench'd his pamphlets in his fist.
Byron. Parenthetical Address.
Catullus. Carmen 49: "Silver-tongued among
  the sons of Rome."
Cowper. Sonnet to Henry Cowper.
Emerson. Orator.
Larkin. Nothing Significant Was Really Said.
Lovelace. To Marcus T. Cicero.
Sidney. Sonnet 58: "Doubt there hath been,
  when with his golden chain."
Smart. Disertissime Romuli Nepotum.
Stevens. United Dames of America.
Updike. Miss Moore at Assembly.
Zukofsky. Master of eloquence and Rome's
  potent line.

Orchards
Bishop. Grove, The.
Crane. There Are the Local..
Doolittle. Orchard.
Eberhart. Orchard, The.
  Recollection of Childhood.
Eliot. New Hampshire.
Frost. Evening in a Sugar Orchard.
  Good-by and Keep Cold.
  Peril of Hope.
Graves. Language of the Seasons.
Lawrence. Old Orchard, The.
McNeill. Threnody for Old Orchards.
Nemerov. To Lu Chi.
Rukeyser. Children's Orchard, The.
Sandburg. Wind Song.
Snodgrass. Old Apple Trees.
Warren. Composition in Gold and Red-Gold.
Wilbur. He Was.
  Orchard Trees, January.
Williams, William Carlos. Wild Orchard.
Wright, James. Offering for Mr. Bluehart, An.
  Two Horses Playing in the Orchard.

Orchids
Pack. Orchid.
Roethke. Orchids.
Williams, Charles Kenneth. Orchid, The.

Order
Ashbery. Ivory Tower, The.
Creeley. Peace.
  Window, The.

Davie. Ezra Pound in Pisa.
Method. For Ronald Gaskell.
Duncan. Best of ways. That there be a law the
  Earth gives and the Mountain.
Eberhart. Great Praises.
  Hard Structure of the World, The.
  Light From Above.
Emerson. But O to see his solar eyes.
  Who saw the hid beginnings.
Ford. Forms and flowers.
Fox. Lyre, The.
Hall. Lone Ranger, The.
Herbert. Family [or Familie], The.
Hewitt. I Go to School.
  Nourish Your Heart.
Hughes, Ted. I walk / Unwind with activity of
  legs.
Joseph. Instant on the Viaduct, An.
Meinke. Hermann Ludwig Ferdinand Von
  Helmholtz.
Melville. Milan Cathedral.
Merton. Each ant has his appointed task.
  Two Kings and No-Form.
Raine. Vegetation.
Sandburg. Big fish eat the little fish, The.
  Many Handles.
Silverstein. Ma and God.
Smith, Patti. Doctor Love.
Stevens. Connoisseur of Chaos.
  Idea of Order at Key West, The.
  Sad Strains of a Gay Waltz.
  Winter Bells.
Wakoski. Precision.
Wilbur. In a Bird Sanctuary.

Oregon (state)
Haines. Men Against the Sky.

Orestes (mythology)
Doolittle. Orestes Theme.
Jarrell. Orestes at Tauris.
Jeffers. Tower beyond Tragedy, The.

Organs and Organists
Dickinson. I've heard an Organ talk,
  sometimes.
Lieberman. Organist's Black Carnation, The.
Merton. Organ.

Orient
Fletcher. Over the roof-tops race the shadows
  of clouds.
Hewitt. Hollyhocks against the Wall, The.
  Sunset.
Nash. So I resigned from the Chu Chin
  Chowder and Marching Club.
Waldman. Face the Orient.

Origami
Merton. Paper Cranes.

Original Sin
Chaucer. Nun's Priest's Tale, The.
Donne. If poisonous [or poysonous]
  mineral[l]s, and if that tree.
"Dylan." Pressing On.
Glück. Murderess, The.
Herrick. Rose, The.
Liddy. Cormorants / By the pollock holes
  diving.
MacLeish. Adam in the Evening.
  Eve Answers the Burdock.
  Eve Explains Everything to the Thrush Who
  Repeats Everything.
  Eve in the Dawn.
  Eve Old.
  Eve's Riddle.
  Fall!, The.
  Serpent's Cradle Song, The.
  What the Vine Said to Eve.
Nash. Ha! Original Sin!
Thomas. Incarnate Devil.
Walcott. Orient and Immortal Wheat.
Warren. Original Sin; a Short Story.

Orioles
Dickinson. One of the ones that Midas
  touched.
  To hear an Oriole sing.
Lowell. Fall 1961.

Orion (constellation)
Dickinson. Follow wise Orion.
Everson. Orion.

Kooser. Constellation Orion, The.
Rich. Orion.
  Orion plunges like a drunken hunter.
Zukofsky. And looking to where shone Orion.

Orion (mythology)
Doolittle. Orion Dead.

Orphans
Crabbe. Richard's Youth.
Davie. Dublin Georgian (2).
Hardy. To a Motherless Child.
  Unrealized.
Herrick. To His Verses.
Levine. On My Own.
Meredith. Little Foot-Page, The.
Rossetti. Iniquity of the Fathers upon the
  Children, The.
  My baby has a father and a mother.
Rukeyser. That is what they say, who were
  broken off from love.
Smith, Stevie. Orphan Reformed, The.
  Thank You.
Williams, Charles Kenneth. Before This.

Orpheus
Atwood. Eurydice.
  Orpheus (1).
  Orpheus (2).
Auden. Orpheus.
Browning, Robert. Eurydice to Orpheus.
Campion. To. Campiani Epigramma de
  Instituto Authoris.
  Umbra.
Cowper. Ode on the Marriage of a Friend.
Davie. Orpheus.
Dobyns. Orpheus.
Fox. Lyre, The.
Herrick. Orpheus.
  Orpheus and Pluto.
Hesketh. Orpheus in the Underground.
Hill. Orpheus and Eurydice.
Joseph. Eurydice to Orpheus.
Liddy. Saint Orpheus.
  Wave of the Nineties, The.
Lovelace. Orpheus to Beasts.
  Orpheus to Woods.
Lowry. You cannot, must not, Orpheus, look
  back, my soul.
Merrill. Orfeo.
Merton. Eurydice.
Nemerov. Orphic Scenario.
Oppen. He who will not work shall not eat.
Rich. I Dream I'm the Death of Orpheus.
  Postcard.
Rukeyser. In Hades, Orpheus.
  Orpheus.
  Poem as Mask, The.
Shelley. Orpheus.
Snodgrass. Orpheus.

Ospreys
Eberhart. Ospreys in Cry.
Lieberman. Osprey Suicides, The.

Ostriches
Hesketh. Naked Ostrich.
Lovelace. Lucasta's Fan[ne], with a Looking-
  Glass[e] in It.
Moore. He "Digesteth Harde Yron."
Nash. Ostrich, The.

Ottawa, Ontario
Davie. Pontiac.

Otterburn, Battle of (1388)
Kipling. English Way, The.

Otters
Gunn. Life of the Otter, The.
Hartnett. Wounded Otter, The.
Heaney. Otter, The.
Hughes, Ted. Otter, An.

Ouija Boards
Merrill. Voices from the Other World.
"Reed." My House.

Outlaws. *see* **Crime and Criminals.**

Ovenbirds
Frost. Oven Bird, The.

Ovibos. *see* **Musk Oxen.**

Ovid (Publius Ovidius Naso)
Carruth. Ovid, Old Buddy, I Would Discourse
  with You a While.

Cowper. 5.12: "You bid me write t' amuse the
  tedious hours."
Hill. Ovid in the Third Reich.
Mahon. Ovid in Tomis.
Merton. OVID DIVO.
Pope. Sandys's Ghost, or a Proper New Ballad
  on the New Ovid's Metamorphosis as it Was
  Intended to Be.
Ransom. Philomela.
Walcott. Hotel Normandie Pool, The.

Owain Gwynedd, Prince of North Wales
Gray. Triumphs of Owen, The.

Owen, Wilfred
Hughes, Ted. Wilfred Owen's Photographs.

Owls
Atwood. Owl Song.
Auden. Below me Ticknall lay but in the
  light.
  Owl, The.
Bishop. Song for the Rainy Season.
Carroll, Jim. What matter for thick armchairs
  and fine shelves for books?
"Carroll, Lewis." Alice's Recitation.
Carruth. Arctic owl moved across the
  snowsmooth, The.
  Back of Budbill's where it dreens offn the
  ledges. Snugger.
Davie. Screech-Owl.
De la Mare. Evening.
  Owl, The ("What If To Edge Of Dream").
Dickey, James. Owl King, The.
Dickinson. Judge is like the Owl, The.
Duncan. Sentinels, The.
Eberhart. Emblem.
  Hoot Owls.
Fisher. Just beside my track through the dark.
Ford. And the first owl of.
  Black dog in a, A.
  On a high branch two.
  Owlet pulls / Pieces of meat from between
  the, The.
Frost. Questioning Faces.
Galvin. Backtalk.
  Great Horned Owls.
  Young Owls.
Graves. Like Owls.
Haines. If the Owl Calls Again.
  Prayer to the Snowy Owl.
Herrick. Vow to Minerva, A.
Hesketh. Owl.
Hewitt. Owl, The.
Hoffman. Great Owl.
Hughes, Ted. And Owl.
Kafka.
  Owl's Song.
Hugo. Snow Poem.
Jarrell. Bird of Night, The.
  Owl's Bedtime Story, The.
Lindsay. What Grandpa Mouse Said.
Merton. Christina.
Oliver. Little Owl Who Lives in the Orchard.
  Lonely, White Fields.
  Nature.
  This Morning Again It Was in the Dusty
  Pines.
  White Owl Flies Into and Out of the Field.
Pack. Snowy Owl, The.
Piercy. What the Owl Sees.
Plath. Owl.
Schuyler. Korean Mums.
Shelley. Aziola, The.
Simic. Great Horned Owl, The.
Snodgrass. Owls.
Stevens. On the Adequacy of Landscape.
Van Duyn. Ballad of Blossom, The.
Wordsworth. Leaves That Rustled on THis
  Oak-Crowned Hill, The.

Oxen
Hardy. Oxen, The.
Kipling. Beasts Are Very Wise, The.
  Between the waving tufts of jungle-grass.
Merton. Thonga Lament.
Thomson. Drooping, the labourer-ox.
Tomlinson. Oxen: Ploughing at Fiesole.
Whitman. Ox-Tamer, The.

Oxford, England
Arnold. How changed is here each spot man

makes or fills!
  Scholar-Gipsy, The.
Auden. Oxford.
Betjeman. May-Day Song for North Oxford.
  Oxford: Sudden Illness at the Bus-stop.
"Carroll, Lewis." Bachanalian Ode, A.
  Elections to the Hebdomadal Council, The.
  Maggie's Visit to Oxford.
  Majesty of Justice, The.
  New Belfry of Christ Church, Oxford, The.
  Wandering Burgess, The.
Cowper. Epigram on the Refusal of the
  University of Oxford to Subscribe to His
  Translation of Homer.
Davie. Oxfordshire.
Eberhart. To Auden on His Fiftieth.
Fenton. Pitt-Rivers Museum, Oxford, The.
Griffiths. Glyndŵr Subdued.
Hall. Christ Church Meadows, [Oxford].
Hopkins. Cheery Beggar.
  Duns Scotus's Oxford.
  Like Shuttles Fleet the Clouds.
  To Oxford.
Keats. Lines Rhymed in a Letter Received (by
  J. H. R[eynolds]) from Oxford.
Kipling. Clerks and the Bells, The.
Larkin. Poem about Oxford.
Lawrence. Oxford Voice, The.
MacNeice. Canto XII: "Now to dissolve in
  port. I take the train."
  I ought to be glad.
  Relics.
Ransom. Philomela.
Updike. Oxford, Thirty Years After.
Wordsworth. Oxford, May 30, 1820 ("Ye
  sacred Nurseries of blooming Youth!").

Oysters
"Carroll, Lewis." Walrus and the Carpenter,
  The.
Cowper. Poet, the Oyster, and Sensitive Plant,
  The.
  To Mrs. Newton.
Galvin. Winter Oysters.
Hall. Oysters and Hermits.
Heaney. Oysters.
Nash. Oyster, The.
  What, No Oysters?
Sexton. Oysters.
Swift. Oysters.
See also **Clams and Clamming; Shells.**

Ozark Mountains
Van Duyn. In the Missouri Ozarks.

P

Pacific Ocean
Davie. Out of East Anglia.
Dickey, James. Exchanges.
Frost. Once by the Pacific.
Gunn. Discovery of the Pacific, The.
Jeffers. Coast-Road, The.
  Eye, The.
  Gray Weather.
  I walk on my cliff above the Pacific Ocean
  and feel the tides.
Lowry. Pacific is a feeble symbol of death.
Oppen. California.
Whitman. Facing West from California's
  Shores.

Pacifism and Pacifists
Berryman. Pacifist's Song, The.
Bunting. Keep Troth.
Cummings. I sing of Olaf glad and big.
  I'm / asking / you dear to.
  When your honest redskin toma.
"Dylan." Hero Blues.
Housman. Oh stay at home, my lad, and
  plough.
Jeffers. Time of Disturbance.
Lowell. Memories of West Street and Lepke.
Shapiro. Conscientious Objector, The.
Walker. QPP, The.
Whittier. Brown of Ossawatomie.
  Disarmament.
See also **Conscientious Objectors.**

Paganism and Pagans
Cullen. Pagan Prayer.

Eberhart. Soul Longs to Return Whence It
  Came, The.
Emerson. To transmute crime to wisdom, & to
  stem.
Herrick. Upon Faunus.
Hewitt. May Alter.
Melville. Age of the Antonines, The.
Wordsworth. World is too much with us; late
  and soon, The.

Pain
Ammons. Glass Globe.
Angelou. Kind of Love, Some Say, A.
Atwood. Rest, The.
Auden. Sonnet: "April is here but when will
  Easter come?"
Beatles. Carry That Weight.
  Not a Second Time.
  She Said She Said.
  What You're Doing.
Berg. Bandage.
Berry. To My Children, Fearing for Them.
  Way of Pain, The.
Berryman. And does the old wound shudder
  open? Shall.
  "Broken heart.." but *can* a heart break, now?,
  A.
  Cambridge friend put in,—one whom I used,
  A.
  Venice, 182–.
Bogan. Chanson un Peu Naïve.
Browning, Elizabeth Barrett. Night and the
  Merry Man.
Bukowski. About Pain.
  Condition, The.
Burns. Address to the Tooth-Ache.
Carew. Mistake, The.
  To Master W. Montague.
  To My Inconstant Mistress [*or* Mistris].
Carroll, Jim. Cosmopolitan Sense, The.
Carruth. Poet, The.
  Tanck's Song About His Birthday.
Catullus. Carmen 85: "I hate and I love. And
  if you ask me how."
Ceravolo. Autumn-Time, Wind and the Planet
  Pluto.
Clark. Calling Infinity.
  Lyric, The: "Suffering / lament, sorrow and
  wild."
Coleridge. Two Founts, The.
Crane. Hive, The.
Creeley. Chicago.
  Flower, The.
  For Fear.
  Goodbye.
  Letter, The.
  Phone.
  Pieces.
  Snow, The.
Cullen. Saturday's Child.
  Song in Spite of Myself.
  Sonnet: "I know now how a man whose blood
  is hot."
  Sonnet: "What I am saying now was said
  before."
Dickinson. After great pain, a formal feeling
  comes.
  Anguish sometimes gives a cause.
  Crisis is sweet and yet the Heart.
  Each Scar I'll keep for Him.
  Friend Anguish reveals is, The.
  Hallowing of Pain, The.
  I heard a fly buzz—when I died.
  I never knew a broken Heart.
  I shall not murmur if at last.
  I watched her face to see which way.
  If pain for peace prepares.
  If the anguish of others helped one with one's
  own.
  It is Anguish I long conceal from you.
  It is easier to look behind at a pain.
  It is easy to work when the soul is at play.
  Months have ends—the Years—a knot, The.
  Morning after Woe, The.
  Much madness is divinest sense.
  Nearness to Tremendousness, A.
  One Anguish—in a Crowd.
  Pain—expands the Time.

Pain—has an Element of Blank.
Pain has but one Acquaintance.
  Rehearsal to Ourselves.
  There is a Languor of the Life.
  There is a pain—so utter.
  'Tis not that Dying hurts us so.
  To all except anguish.
  'Twas like a Maelstrom, with a notch.
  'Twas the old—road—through pain.
  Vastest earthly Day, The.
  Weight with Needles on the pounds, A.
  Wounded Deer—leaps highest, A.
Doolittle. Halcyon.
  Lift my head, help me up.
Dove. Variation on Pain.
Dunbar. Itching Heels.
Dunn. Vanishings, The.
Eberhart. Critic With His Pained Eye, The.
  Full of Joy Do Not Know; They Need Not,
  The.
  On Seeing an Egyptian Mummy in Berlin,
  1932.
  Truth, The.
Edmunds. Like A Green Branch.
Emerson. Intellect / Gravely broods apart on
  joy.
  Pain of love's a better fate, The.
Everson. And then that humming.
  If you were to try to say.
Ford. Ballad for Baudelaire.
  Message for Rimbaud.
Gallagher. Harmless Streets.
Galvin. Needsong.
Gardner. Accomplices, The.
  Salt.
Garrigue. For Such a Bird He Had No
  Convenient Cage.
Ginsberg. Under the World There's a Lot of
  Ass, a Lot of Cunt.
Glück. Epithalamium: "There were others;
  their bodies."
  Love Poem.
  World Breaking Apart.
Graves. Cure, The.
  Fire Walker.
  Growing Pains.
  Stolen Jewel.
Griffiths. Unmetalled Road.
Gunn. Her Pet.
  Innocence.
  Painkillers.
Hacker. Angry, I speak, and pass the hurt to
  you.
  Between us on our wide bed we cuddle an
  incubus.
  Country & Western.
Haines. I sank past bitten leaves.
Hall. Hole, The.
  To the Loud Wind.
Hardy. End of the Episode, The.
  I Thought, My Heart.
  Wish for Unconsciousness, A.
  Wound, The.
Hartley. Just one more / at the breast, she
  said—.
  Lost, Alone, The.
Hartnett. I Have Exhausted the Delighted
  Range.
Hayden. Road in Kentucky, A.
Hemingway. Poem: "Only man I ever loved,
  The."
  Portrait of a Lady.
Herrick. Persecutions Profitable.
Hesketh. Defeathered.
Hewitt. Mourne Mountains.
Hill. Ten years without you. For so it
  happens.
Hoffman. Marked Man, A.
  Woe, A.
Hughes, Ted. At the bottom of the Arctic sea,
  they say.
Jarrell. Essay on the Human Will, An.
  Field Hospital, A.
  90 North.
Jeffers. Day is a Poem, The.
  Praise Life.
  World's Wonders, The.

Joseph. Version of the Phoenix Story, A.
Kipling. Comforters, The.
Hymn to Physical Pain.
Power of the Dog, The.
Knott. Prophet in a Landscape of Immemorial Time.
Lawrence. Assuming the Burden.
Kissing and Horrid Strife.
Levertov. As It Happens.
Levine. How Much Can It Hurt?
I Could Believe.
I reenter a day in a late summer.
No One Remembers.
Lewis. Defeat.
Separation, A.
Victory.
Ways.
Liddy. After Hal'amová.
Cantico Per Lo Tuo Amore II.
Letter to Sainte-Beuve.
Lindsay. Love and Law.
Lorde. Hard Love Rock.
Lovelace. Another ("I Did believe I was in Heav'n").
Answer, The.
Guiltlesse Lady Imprisoned; after Penanced, A.
I hate and love, wouldst thou the reason know?
To Lucasta ("Like to the sentinel [or Sent'nel] stars, I watch all night").
Lowry. Autopsy on this childhood then reveals, An.
Darkness has its compensations, both.
Half of the harm that is done in this world.
Morning rain is raining / A morning pain is paining, The.
Morning rain is raining / The morning leg is paining, The.
Not all of us were heroes said my brother wit.
Poets are Godlike in that they.
Stone must be rolled away from self's pain, The.
MacLeish. Ay, sure, this is most brave.
Markson. Monody.
Merton. Not to be without words in a season of effort.
Pain Is an Eagle Clinging to Your Name.
Millay. And must I then, indeed, Pain, live with you.
Not only love plus awful grief.
Who hurt you so.
Morrison. Always a Playground Instructor.
Nathan. Great.
Nemerov. Creation of Anguish.
From the Last Dream of a Dying Woman Aged Eighty.
To the Memory of John Wheelwright.
Virgin and Martyr.
Neruda. Some Creature.
O'Hara. Savoy.
Oliver. Anne.
Olson. Cry pain, & the dogs of yrself devour.
Owen. Greater Love.
Hospital Barge at Cérisy.
Winter Song.
Pack. Hole in the Sky, A.
Paley. For George (II).
Piercy. Root Canal, The.
Raine. Descent Into Hades.
I could have told much by the way.
If I choose remorse.
Ralegh. No Pleasure, Without Some Payne.
Ransom. Moments of Minnie.
Rich. Dear Adrienne, / I feel signified by pain.
Dien Bien Phu.
I can see myself years back at Sunion.
Letters: March 1969.
Pieces.
Problem, unstated until now, is how, The.
Splittings.
That conversation we were always on the edge.
You who think I find words for everything.
Rolfe. Catalogue.
More than Flesh to Fathom.

Poem: "*Consciousness*, said Don Miguel, *is a disease.*"
Rossetti. Acme.
Ah welladay and wherefore am I here?
Balm in Gilead.
Chiefest among Ten Thousand, The.
Chilly Night, A.
Chruchyard Song of Patient Hope, A.
Dream, The.
Eva.
February 14. 1883.
Henry Hardiman.
Hope in Grief.
I said "All's over"—& I made my.
I Will Lift Up Mine Eyes unto the Hills.
Introspective.
Joy is but sorrow, / While we know.
Looking Forward.
Lord, grant me grace to love Thee in my pain.
Martyr, A.
Martyr, The.
Methinks the ills of life I fain would shun.
Monday in Holy Week.
None With Him.
O thou who tell'st me that all hope is over.
One Foot on Sea, and One on Shore.
Piteous my rhyme is / What while I muse of love and pain.
St. Bartholomew.
Sick Child's Meditation, A.
Sonnet: "Some say that love and joy are one: and so."
Spring is come again not as at first.
Vanity of Vanities.
What Sappho Would Have Said Had Her Leap Cured Instead of Killing Her.
Whom the Lord Loveth He Chasteneth.
Zara ("I dreamed that loving me he would love on").
Zara ("Now the pain beginneth and the word is spoken").
Rukeyser. Judith.
Man sits in the rocking bedroom, claws, The.
Slow Dialogue between Pain and Roosevelt.
To keep the weakness secret. To deny it and break through.
Wheels and galleries of the control of tears.
Sandburg. At a Window.
Broken Hearted Soprano.
Kisses Forgotten.
Sarton. Burial.
Humpty Dumpty.
I shall not see the end of this unweaving.
Tortured, The.
Sexton. Big Boots of Pain, The.
Grandfather, Your Wound.
Pain for a Daughter.
Shapiro. Hospital.
Shelley. Invocation to Misery.
Lament, A: "O world! O life! O time!"
To William Shelley ("My lost William, thou in whom").
Shelton. And the Greatest of These.
Sidney. Scourge of life, and death's extreme disgrace, The.
Sonnet 16: "In nature apt to like when I did see."
Thou Pain, the only guest of loathed constraint.
When Love, puffed up with rage of high disdain.
Silverstein. Crocodile's Toothache, The.
Smith, Patti. Corps de Plane.
Fleet of Deer, A.
Smith, Stevie. Doctor, The.
Lads of the Village, The.
Seymour and Chantelle or Un Peu de Vice.
Snodgrass. Flat One, A.
Sorrentino. Dominoes.
Iceman, Again, The.
Long Goodbye, The.
Open Your Mouth and Say.
You Are My Heart's Bouquet.
Spender. Nocturne: "Their six-weeks-old daughter."
Stevens. Saint John and the Back-Ache.
Stevenson. I saw red evening through the rain.

Love's Vicissitudes.
O now, although the year be done.
To F.J.S.
Suckling. If when Don Cupid's dart.
Thomas. Lie Still, Sleep Becalmed.
Updike. Pain.
Van Duyn. Ringling Brothers, Barnum and Bailey.
Wakoski. From A Go to B, If You Can Find It.
Life Is Like a Game of Cards, Or Another One of Those Metaphysical Statements from a Distant Reader.
My Knees Go Before the Firing Squad at Dawn.
Walcott. Fist, The.
Walker. Excuse.
Whitman. I Sit and Look Out.
Wilbur. Another Voice.
Arrow in the Wall, An.
Williams, Charles Kenneth. Alzheimer's: The Wife.
I Am the Bitter Name.
Image, The.
Three Seasons and a Gorilla.
Williams, Miller. Thinking about Bill, Dead of AIDS.
Williams, William Carlos. Birth of Venus, The.
Comfort.
Wordsworth. Complaint, A.
Wright, James. Blue Teal's Mother.
Prayer to the Lord Ramakrishna, A.
Refusal, The.
Wroth. Sonnet 6: "My pain[e], still smothered [or smother'd] in my grievèd bre[a]st."
Sonnet 45: "Good now bee still, and doe nott mee torment."
Wyatt. Alas, the grief and deadly wo[e]ful smart[!].
All heavy minds.
Being as none is, I do complain.
Complaining, alas, without redress.
Duress of pains and grievous smart.
Flaming sighs that boil within my breast, The.
I love, loved, and so doth she.
If I might have at mine own will.
If with complaint the pain might be expressed.
Might I as well within my song belay.
Sighs are my food, drink are my tears.
Thou sleepest fast and I with woeful heart.
Though I cannot your cruelty constrain.
Venomous thorns that are so sharp and keen.
What word is that that changeth not.
Within my breast I never thought it gain.
Yeats. Lady's First Song, The.
Young. Detroit 1958.
Zukofsky. O th'hate I move love. Quarry it fact I am, for that's so re queries.

Paine, Thomas
Cowper. Sonnet Addressed to Mr. Phillips, A.
"Dylan." As I Went Out One Morning.

Painting and Painters
Ashbery. Painter, The.
Atwood. Quattrocento.
Auden. Musée des Beaux Arts.
On Seeing Some Dutch Pictures.
Berg. Rocks, The.
Berryman. Musculatures and skulls. Later some throng.
Betjeman. On a Painting by Julius Olsson R.A.
On an Old-Fashioned Water-Colour of Oxford.
Bishop. Large Bad Picture.
Pleasure Seas.
Poem: "About the size of an old-style dollar bill."
Blake. When Sir [or Sr] Joshua Reynolds died.
Boyle. Painter Speaks—the Woman Answers, The.
Poem for a Painter Bent on Suicide.
Poem for a Painter Who Drinks Wine.
Browning, Robert. Andrea del Sarto.
Beatrice Signorini.
Face, A.
Fra Lippo Lippi.

Guardian-Angel, The.
Lady and the Painter, The.
Of Pacchiarotto, and How He Worked in
  Distemper.
Old Pictures in Florence.
Pictor Ignotus.
Bukowski. Artist.
Cows in Art Class.
Greek, The.
Promise, The.
Carew. To the Painter.
Cowper. Another ["Painter, this likeness is too
  strong"].
To Sir Joshua Reynolds.
Crane. Sunday Morning Apples.
Cummings. Of my / soul a street is.
Water-Lilies.
Davie. Death of a Painter.
De la Mare. Breughel's Winter.
Dickinson. Those fair—fictitious People.
Dobyns. Contingencies.
Dove. Agosta the Winged Man and Rasha the
  Black Dove.
Emerson. Body and Soul.
For Nature true & like in every place.
Painting and Sculpture.
Ferlinghetti. Don't let that horse.
Expressionist History of German
  Expressionism.
Matisse at the Modern, Magritte at the Met.
Painter's Dream, The.
Sarolla's women in their picture hats.
Garrigue. Figure for J.V. Meer, A.
Gunn. In Santa Maria del Popolo.
Hacker. Le Travail Rajeunit.
Haines. Blood Lake, The.
Paul Klee.
Ryder.
Hardy. Collector Cleans His Picture, The.
Hartley. Modigliani's Death Mask.
Rembrandt—Rouault—Piero.
Herrick. Painting Sometimes Permitted.
To His Nephew, to Be Prosperous in His Art
  of Painting.
To the Painter, To Draw Him a Picture.
Upon Umber: Epigram.
Hesketh. Letter to Vincent.
Poem is a Painting, A.
Hewitt. Minor Victorian Painter, A.
Sarcophagus.
Hugo. District in the City, A.
George Stubbs at Yale.
Landscapes.
Milltown Union Bar, The.
Northwest Retrospective: Mark Tobey.
Prado: Bosch: S. Antonio, The.
Prado: Number 2671, Anonimo Español, The.
S. Miniato: One by Aretino.
Wheel of Fortune.
Jong. Horse from Hell, The.
Impressionists, The.
Jonson. Picture of the Body, The.
Poem Sent Me by Sir William Burlase, A.
Joseph. Cutting Off One's Ears for Someone
  Else Is Wrong.
Kunitz. Artist, The.
Lawrence. Auto-Da-Fé.
Give Me a Sponge.
Innocent England.
Painter's Wife, The.
13 Pictures.
13,000 People.
Lewis. He Gives Her Botticelli's Birth of
  Venus as a Wedding Gift.
Humanist, The.
Lieberman. Mural of Wakeful Sleep, The.
Lovelace. Painture [or Peinture].
To My Worthy Friend Mr. Peter Lely [or
  Lilly].
Vain Painter why dost strive my face to draw.
Lowell. Rembrandt.
"MacDiarmid." Well Hung.
MacLeish. Oil Painting of the Artist as the
  Artist.
MacNeice. Canto VIII: "Fair; not to say
  radiant. The Twentyfifth of September."
Neck of an hour-glass on its side—.

Mahon. Forger, The.
Portrait of the Artist, A.
Markson. Death of the Virgin, The.
Dialogue in Milan.
History and Theory of Art.
Marvell. After two sittings, now our Lady
  State.
Meinke. Plovers.
Talk of the Paintings.
Melville. Bench of Boors, The.
Merton. Chagall.
Morgan. Master, The.
Muldoon. Bearded Woman, by Ribera, The.
Nemerov. Conversing with Paradise.
Most Expensive Picture in the World, The.
Nature Morte.
Old Picture, An.
Painting a Mountain Stream.
Sestina I: "Thickness of paint or flesh cannot
  deface."
Vermeer.
O'Hara. Having a Coke with You.
Naphtha.
On Looking at La Grande Jatte, the Czar
  Wept Anew.
Why I Am Not a Painter.
Oppen. Party on Shipboard.
Philai Te Kou Philai.
Paley. On the Ramblas / A Tree   A Girl.
Plath. Midsummer Mobile.
Pope. Epistle to Mr. Jervas, with Dryden's
  Translation of Fresnoy's Art of Painting.
To Sir Godfrey Kneller, on His Painting for
  Me the Statues of Apollo, Venus and
  Hercules.
Raine. Old Paintings on Italian Walls.
Painting by Winifred Nicholson, A.
Robinson. Her Eyes.
Rembrandt to Rembrandt.
Rossetti. In an Artist's Studio.
Rukeyser. Birth of Venus, The.
For a Mexican Painter.
Painters.
Sandburg. Four Steichen Prints.
Old Hokusai Print.
People Who Must.
Unintentional Paint.
Sarton. Dutch Interior.
Shakespeare. Sonnet 132: "I grant thou wert
  not married to my Muse."
Sonnet 133: "I never saw that you did painting
  need."
Shapiro. Dome of Sunday, The [or A].
Smith, Charlotte. Sent to the Honorable
  Mistress O'Neill, with Painted Flowers.
Smith, Patti. Georgia O'Keeffe.
Smith, Stevie. Spanish School.
Sorrentino. Particular density: in the center,
  rises, A.
Stupid painter paints. He, The.
Stevens. Prelude to Objects.
Tomlinson. Cézanne at Aix.
Composition.
Farewell to Van Gogh.
Garland for Thomas Eakins, A.
Marat Dead.
Meditation on John Constable, A.
On a Landscape by Li Ch'eng.
Paring the Apple.
Self-Portrait: David, A.
Updike. Gradations of Black.
Painted Wives.
Walcott. In the other 'eighties, a hundred
  midsummers gone.
Waldman. I Digress..
Whitman. Death's Valley.
Whittier. Raphael.
Wilbur. Dutch Courtyard, A.
Giaour and the Pacha, The.
L'Etoile.
Museum Piece.
My Father Paints the Summer.
Objects.
Williams, William Carlos. Dance, The.
Pictures from Brueghel.
Raindrops on a Briar.
Tribute to the Painters.

Wordsworth. Anacreon.
Before the Picture of the Baptist, by Raphael,
  in the Gallery at Florence.
Elegiac Stanzas Suggested by a Picture of
  Peele Castle, in a Storm [Painted by Sir
  George Beaumont].
Foregoing Subject Resumed, The.
Gleaner (Suggested By a Picture), The.
Last Supper, by Leonardo da Vinci, in the
  Refectory of the Convent of Maria della
  Grazia—Milan, The.
Picture of Daniel in the Lions' Den, at
  Hamilton Palace.
Sonnet to a Picture by Lucca Giordano in the
  Mureo Borbonico at Naples.
To a Painter ("All praise the Likeness by thy
  skill portrayed").
To a Painter ("Though I beheld at first with
  blank surprise").
To B.R. Haydon.
Upon a Portrait.
Upon seeing a Coloured Drawing of the Bird
  of Paradise in an Album.
see also Inscription in the Grounds of
  Coleorton, the Seat of Sir George Beaumont,
  BART., Leicestershire and Inscription in a
  Garden of the Same.
Wright, Charles. Looking at Pictures.
Zukofsky. 4 Other Countries.

Paleontology and Paleontologists
Wordsworth. At the Convent of Camaldoli.
See also **Dinosaurs; Evolution; Extinction;
  Fossils.**

Palestine
Hardy. Jezreel.
Lindsay. John Brown.
Whittier. Holy Land, The.
Palestine.
See also **Israel.**

Palm Sunday
Rossetti. Palm Sunday.

Palm Trees
Crane. Royal Palm.
Graves. Song: The Palm Tree.
Merton. Recipe.
Whittier. Palm-Tree, The.

Pan (god)
Browning, Elizabeth Barrett. Dead Pan, The.
Musical Instrument, A.
Psyche and Pan.
Browning, Robert. Pan and Luna.
Byron. Aristomenes.
Campion. To his sweet Lute Apollo sung the
  motions of the Spheares.
Cummings. Of evident invisibles / exquisite
  the hovering.
De la Mare. Sorcery.
They Told Me.
Eliot. Mr. Apollinax.
Emerson. Patient Pan / Drunken with nectar,
  The.
Frost. Pan with Us.
Gunn. Rites of Passage.
Hesketh. Reclaimed.
Hewitt. Summer Arcady.
Keats. Hymn to Pan.
Kipling. Pan in Vermont.
Lovelace. Princesse Löysa drawing.
Marvell. Clorinda and Damon.
Shelley. Hymn of Pan.
Sidney. Now thanked be the great god Pan.
Silvanus long in love, and long in vain.

Pancakes
Rossetti. Mix a Pancake.
Silverstein. Pancake?

Pansies
Dickinson. That a pansy is transitive.
Herrick. How Pansies or Hearts-Ease Came
  First.
To Pansies.

Pantheism and Pantheists
Coleridge. There is one Mind, one
  omnipresent Mind.
Emerson. You shall not love me for what
  daily spends.

Wordsworth. It is a beauteous Evening, calm and free.

Panthers
"Carroll, Lewis." Alice's Recitation.
Hesketh. Panther and the Antelope, The.
Nash. Panther, The.
Patchen. Black Panther and the Little Boy, The.

Papacy
Ciardi. Apartment with a View, A.
"Reed." Good Evening Mr. Waldheim.
Letters to the Vatican.
Scott. Gray Brother, The.
Whittier. To Pius IX.
See also **Catholicism and Catholics; Listings for Individual Popes.**

Paperweights
Merrill. Prism.

Parachuting and Parachutists. *see* **Sky Diving and Sky Divers.**

Parades
Hewitt. Twelfth of July, The.
Hughes, Langston. Parade.
Lindsay. Village Improvement Parade, The.
Nash. It's a Grand Parade It Will Be, Modern Design.
Olson. Memorial Day.
This Year.
"Reed." Halloween Parade, The.
Schuyler. Scarlet Tanager.
Stevenson. Whole day thro', in contempt and pity, The.
Young Night Thought.
Updike. How to Be Uncle Sam.
Whitman. Boston Ballad, A [*or* A Boston Ballad 1854].
Broadway Pageant, A.
See also **Marching and Marches.**

Paradise
Atwood. Galiano Coast: Four Entrances.
Berry. Aristocracy, The.
Fall.
Browning, Robert. Variation on Lines of Landor, A.
Byron. Impromptu.
Coleridge. Mignon's Song.
De la Mare. Dwelling-Place, The.
Three Strangers, The.
Dickinson. I lift the lid to my box of Phantoms.
I never felt at Home—Below.
Of Paradise' existence.
Paradise is of the option.
Paradise is that old mansion.
Road to Paradise is plain, The.
Writing is brief and fleeting.
You are most illustrious.
"Dylan." Ballad of Frankie Lee and Judas Priest, The.
Mozambique.
Eberhart. Adam Cast Forth.
Dream, The.
Emerson. Dear Ellen, many a golden year.
Thy songs O Hafiz.
'Tis write on Paradise's gate.
Graves. Conjunction.
East Wind, An.
Gold Cloud.
Green Castle, The.
Hidden Garden, The.
Nothing Now Astonishes.
True Joy.
Herrick. New Charon, The.
Paradise.
Kipling. When Earth's Last Picture Is Painted.
Levertov. City Psalm.
Kingdoms of Heaven.
Lovelace. Amarantha a Pastorall.
Lowry. Conversations With Goethe.
MacLeish. Tenth Book, The.
Meinke. When Eve was cloned from Adam's rib, and stood.
Merton. Paradise of Squares.
Psalm, A: "When psalms surprise me with their music."
What is beyond reproof / Is done in this building.

Pound. Blandula, Tenella, Vagula.
Rexroth. Thin Edge of Your Pride, The.
Rossetti. Afterthought, An.
As Cold Water to a Thirsty Soul, So Is Good News from a Far Country.
Beautiful For Situation.
Chiefest among Ten Thousand, The.
Earth has clear call of daily bells, / A chancel-vault of gloom and star.
Easter Tuesday.
Eye Hath Not Seen.
Flowers Appear on the Earth, The.
I Will Lift Up Mine Eyes unto the Hills.
Only Believe.
Paradise: in a Symbol.
Rivals.
So Great a Cloud of Witnesses.
That Eden of earth's sunrise cannot vie.
When wickedness is broken as a tree / Paradise comes to light, ah holy land!
Where never tempest heaveth, / Nor sorrow grieveth.
Sarton. Mediterranean.
Shapiro. California Petrarchan.
Southwell. Seek[e] Flowers of Heaven.
Tomlinson. John Maydew or The Allotment.
Whittier. Lay of Old Time, A.
Wright, Charles. May Journal.
Wright, James. Father.
Quest, The.
Yau. Paradise.
Yeats. Running to Paradise.
See also **Heaven; Eden.**

Paradise Lost
Lowry. Schoolboy's Complaint, The.
Marvell. On Mr Milton's "Paradise Lost."
Sandburg. To the Ghost of John Milton.
See also **Milton, John.**

Paradoxes
Bukowski. Genius of the Crowd, The.
Carruth. Blizzard in the mountains. Dusk. The cabin's light.
Half-turned, as if reluctant, the lady of water.
Catullus. Carmen 85: "I hate and I love. And if you ask me how."
Creeley. A.
But.
Gemini.
Here.
Look.
No.
Paradox, The.
Sanine to Leda.
Shame, The.
Time.
Xmas Poem: Bolinas.
Cullen. More Than a Fool's Song.
Dunn. Happiness.
Loves.
Snow Leopard, The.
"Dylan." Stuck Inside of Mobile with the Memphis Blues Again.
Eberhart. Hardy Perennial.
Poet, The.
Santa Claus in Oaxaca.
Ford. Matin Pour Matta.
Serenade to Leonor.
This is the story of fire without flames.
Gallagher. Not There.
Graves. Logic.
Hardy. Paradox.
Holmes. Memoirs of an Imaginary Man, The.
Knott. Lesson.
Kunitz. Bottom of the Glass, The.
King of the River.
Liddy. In the Bowling Alley.
Lovelace. I hate and love, wouldst thou the reason know?
Paradox, A.
Sidney. Sonnet 6: "Some lovers speak, when they their Muses entertain."
Warren. Paradox.
Zukofsky. And Without.
Home for Aged Bomb Throwers—U.S.S.R.
H.T.
O th'hate I move love. Quarry it fact I am, for

that's so re queries.
Train-Signal.

Parakeets
MacNeice. Budgie.
Stevens. Bird with the Coppery, Keen Claws, The.

Paralysis
Carruth. Odds & ends: / Enosburg Falls & Geof's cabin.
One called Next steps up, The.
Clark. Terminator Too.
Cohen. Poem: "I heard of a man."
Creeley. Tiger, The.
Dickinson. I've dropped my Brain—My Soul is numb.
Eliot. Love Song of J. Alfred Prufrock, The.
Garrigue. Maimed Grasshopper Speaks Up, The.
Only the Irresistible Abides.
Why the Heart Has Dreams Is Why the Mind Goes Mad.
Hughes, Ted. Green Wolf, The.
Knott. Rigor Vitus.
McGrath. Something Is Dying Here.
McNeill. Dream, The.
Sexton. Angel of Flight and Sleigh Bells.
Shapiro. Figurehead, The.

Paranoia
Creeley. Dishonest Mailmen, The.
"Dylan." Russian has three an' a half red eyes, A.
Talkin' John Birch Paranoid Blues.
Talkin' World War III Blues.
Galvin. In Ireland I Remebered the Foxes of Truro, Massachusetts.
Lewis. His mind is an inarticulated question.
Nash. Ms. Found in a Quagmire.
Neruda. Don't you also feel danger.
Sexton. Noon Walk on the Asylum Lawn.
Shakespeare. Sonnet 118: "Like as, to make our appetites more keen."
Snodgrass. W. D. Tries to Warn Cock Robin.
Warren. Loss, of Perhaps Love, in Our World of Contingency.
Something Is Going to Happen.
Williams, Charles Kenneth. Soliliquies.

Pardons and Pardoners
Browning, Robert. Martin Relph.
Chaucer. Pardoner's Prologue, The.
Creeley. Song: "God give you pardon from gratitue."
Herrick. Gods Pardon.
Pardon.
Pardons.
Rossetti. Dying Man to His Betrothed, The.
Wright, James. Our Daily Bread.

Parenthood
Berry. To My Children, Fearing for Them.
Way of Pain, The.
Ciardi. Boy.
Craft.
Encounter.
Poem for Benn's Graduation from High School, A.
Two Hours.
Coleridge. Sonnet to a Friend Who Asked[,] How I Felt When the Nurse First Presented My Infant to Me.
Cowper. To His Father.
Creeley. Name, The.
Eberhart. To Evan.
Fenton. Come and eat your Pablum.
Gardner. Daughter.
West of Childhood.
Griffiths. Children in a Walled Garden.
Still Too Quick to Hold.
Hoffman. In the Beginning.
Special Train, A.
Jonson. On My First Daughter.
Koertge. Orientation Week.
Kooser. At the End of the Weekend.
Constellation Orion, The.
Kunitz. At breakfast mother sipped her buttermilk.
I was happy you were born.
You cried. You cried.
Lorde. What My Child Learns of the Sea.

McAuley. Penance.
MacNeice. Fantasy holds the child in the man,
  the lover in the monk, the monk in the lover.
McNeill. Second Sight (My Son's First
  Springtime).
  Stories at Evening (A Suburban Mother Tells
  Stories to Her Son).
Matthews. Hope.
  Living among the Dead.
Meredith. I have a hope that's like a star.
  To a Nightingale.
Milton. To My Father.
Nash. Posies from a Second Childhood, or,
  Hark How Gaffer Do Chaffer.
  Preface to the Past.
Notley. Untitled.
Paley. No metaphor reinvents the job of the
  nurture of children.
Psalms. Psalm 127: "Except the Lord build
  the house."
Rich. Afterwake, The.
  Night-Pieces: For a Child.
Rossetti. Love me,—I love you / Love me,
  my baby.
  Three little children / On the wide wide earth.
Shakespeare. Sonnet 2: "When forty winters
  shall besiege thy brow."
Shelley. To William Shelley ("Billows on the
  beach are leaping around it, The").
Smart. If the work be not direct.
Stafford. Any Time.
  At Our House.
  For a Lost Child.
  Memorial: Son Bret, A.
  With Kit, Age Seven, at the Beach.
Turco. Minotaur.
Walcott. I once gave my daughters, separately,
  two conch shells.
Warren. Lullaby: Smile in Sleep.
  Midnight Outcry.
  Picture of Little Rory in a Municipal Park,
  The.
Williams, Miller. Trying.
Yeats. Prayer for My Daughter, A.

Parents
Auden. His peasant parents killed themselves
  with toil.
  Through the Looking-Glass.
Beatles. She's Leaving Home.
Berg. Bandage.
  God, A.
  Gratitude.
Bly. For My Son Noah, Ten Years Old.
Boyle. What Parents Do Not Yet Know.
Bukowski. Dear Pa and Ma.
Burns. Altered from an Old English Song.
"Carroll, Lewis." Three Badgers, The.
Ciardi. Bridal Photo, 1906.
  Censorship.
Cullen. Fruit of the Flower.
Cummings. If there are any heavens my
  mother will(all by herself)have.
Davie. Liverpool Epistle, A.
  No Epitaph.
Dunbar. Dilettante, The: A Modern Type.
Dunn. Local Time.
  Return, The.
Ferlinghetti. Lost Parents.
Fletcher. Calendar in the Attic, The.
Fox. Child Called *Morte*, A.
Gardner. Summers Ago.
Glück. Adult Grief.
Hall. My Son, My Executioner.
Hartley. Two Ways of Love.
Herrick. God to Be First Served.
  Primitiæ to Parents, The.
Hesketh. Journey.
Hewitt. My Parents' Courtship.
  Names We Used, The.
Housman. Culprit, The.
Jarrell. Player Piano, The.
  Quilt-Pattern, A.
Jeffers. Birthday (Autobiography).
Kooser. Book Club.
Kunitz. Quinnapoxet.
  Tutored Child, The.
  Unquiet Ones, The.

Larkin. This Be the Verse.
Liddy. Lest the hoar frost grip the iridescent
  tent of your marriage.
Lowell. Hard Way, The.
  Mother and Father 1.
  Mother and Father 2.
  Returning.
  To Daddy.
"MacDiarmid." Two Parents, The.
Meredith. First-Born, The.
Merrill. Broken Home, The.
  Childlessness.
Muldoon. Mixed Marriage, The.
Nash. Child's Guide to Parents, A.
  Father, Dear Father, Go Jump in the Lake, or,
  You're Costlier than You Think.
  Fragonard.
  Good Riddance, but Now What?
  Judgment Day.
  "My Child Is Phlegmatic.."—Anxious Parent.
  Parent, The.
  Some of My Best Friends Are Children.
Olson. One Night Ma / Lay with Pa.
Oppen. Sara in Her Father's Arms.
"Reed." Beginning of a Great Adventure.
  Endless Cycle.
Rossetti. My baby has a father and a mother.
  Why did baby die, / Making Father sigh.
  Your brother has a falcon.
Rukeyser. More Clues.
  Oh, he *is* sweet. I do love him sometimes.
Sandburg. Curse of a Rich Polish Peasant on
  His Sister Who Ran Away with a Wild Man.
Sexton. Cripples and Other Stories.
  Doors, Doors, Doors.
  Money Swing, The.
Shelley. To William Shelley ("Billows on the
  beach are leaping around it, The").
Smith, Stevie. Maximilian Esterhazy.
Snodgrass. Boy Made of Meat, The; A Poem
  for Children.
Sorrentino. Midnight Special.
  Zukofsky.
Spender. Nocturne: "Their six-weeks-old
  daughter."
Stafford. 108 East 19th.
  Vocation.
Stevenson. Before this little gift was come.
  God gave to me a child in part.
Van Duyn. Photographs.
  Relationships.
Waldman. Number Song.
Yau. Their Shadows.
Young. Son.
Zukofsky. Air.

Paris, France
Beckett. Arènes de Lutèce.
  Rue de Vaugirard.
  Sanies II.
  Zone.
Bishop. Paris, 7 A.M.
Boyle. Complaint for Mary and Marcel, A.
Cohen. Commentary—Death to This Book.
  Death to This Book.
  Paris Models.
Cummings. Along the brittle treacherous
  bright streets.
  Inthe,exquisite; / morning sure lyHer eye s
  exactly sit,ata little roundtable.
  It is winter a moon in the afternoon.
  Moon-lit snow is falling like strange candy
  into the big eyes of the, The.
  Paris;this April sunset completely utters.
  Paris,thou art not.
  Perhaps it was Myself sits down in this
  chair. There were two chairs,in fact.
  Rain Is a Handsome Animal, The.
  Red Front, The.
  16 heures / l'Etoile.
  Sometime,perhaps in Paris we will.
  Through the tasteless minute efficient room.
  Workingman with hand so hairy-sturdy.
"Dylan." For francoise hardy / at the seine's
  edge.
Ferlinghetti. In Paris in a loud dark winter.
  Paris Transformations.

Plan du Centre de Paris à Vol D'Oiseau.
  Returning to Paris with Pissarro.
Hacker. Two Cities.
Hartley. From a Paris Window—High.
  These miracles of Paris.
Hewitt. Art and Technology.
  In the Luxembourg Gardens.
Liddy. Inscribed on the Flyleaf of Richard
  Shay's Copy of Rimbaud's *Illuminations.*
  Quarter, The.
McGrath. Migration of Cities, The.
  Once We Meant It.
MacLeish. Years of the Dog.
Merrill. Days of 1971.
Merton. Man from Ecuador beneath the Eiffel
  Tower, A.
Millay. To S. V. B.—June 15, 1940.
Morrison. Paris Journal.
Nash. Absence Makes the Heart Grow Heart
  Trouble.
O'Hara. Petit Poème en Prose.
Oppen. Eros.
  Historic Pun.
Pound. In a Station of the Metro.
Ransom. Crocodile.
Rexroth. Now the Starlit Moonless Spring.
St. John. Woman and Leopard.
Sexton. Walking in Paris.
Sorrentino. Annie from Miami.
  Sappho in Paris.
Stevens. Novel, The.
Waldman. Paris Day.
Whitman. Bravo, Paris Exposition!
Wilbur. Place Pigalle.
Williams, Charles Kenneth. Le Petit Salvié.
Young. Paris.

Parker, Charlie
Creeley. Bird, the Bird, the Bird, The.

Parks
Berg. To the Same Place.
"Carroll, Lewis." Deserted Parks, The.
Ceravolo. Struggling.
Cummings. Dim / i / nu / tiv / e this park is
  e.
Eliot. Lines to a Duck in a Park.
Garrigue. Attempting to Persuade You to Go
  for a Walk in the Public Gardens.
Gunn. Back to Life.
Hacker. "That was in another country," but
  the wench.
  "What's in a park they warn girls out of?"
  "Queers."
Hewitt. Summer Park.
  Winter Park.
Hughes, Langston. Kid in the Park.
Hugo. Park at Villammare, The.
Joseph. On the Embankment.
Knight. Riverside Park.
Kunitz. Let the old geezers jig on Penn.
  Mounds rise up on every side, The.
Lawrence. Hyde Park at Night, before the
  War.
Lowell. Public Garden, The.
MacNeice. Park, The.
Millay. Armenonville.
Rukeyser. Chapultepec Park / I.
Smith, Stevie. Cousin, The.
  November.
Stevens. Vacancy in the Park.
Tomlinson. In a Brooklyn Park.
  In Verdi Square.
  Square, The.
Updike. Sunday in Boston.
Williams, Charles Kenneth. Park, The.
Williams, William Carlos. Franklin Square.

Parliament, Great Britain
Byron. New Song to the Tune of "Whare Hae
  Ye Been a' Day, My Boy Tammy O?
  Courting O' a Young Thing, Just Come Frae
  Her Mammie O?"
  Would You Go to the House by the True
  Gate.
Coleridge. Parliamentary Oscillators.
Fenton. Lullaby for a Summer Recess.
Herrick. Parliament of Roses to Julia, The.
  Upon Case.
Hughes, Ted. Wilfred Owen's Photographs.

Jonson. Panegyre, on the Happy Entrance of James, Our Sovreign, to His First High Session of Parliament in This Kingdom, the 19 of March, 1603, A.
To the Parliament.
To William, Lord Mounteagle.
Kipling. Declaration of London, The.
Lawrence. Daddy-Do-Nothing.
Milton. On the Forcers of Conscience.
Yeats. Ghost of Roger Casement, The.

Parmigianino
Ashbery. Self-Portrait in a Convex Mirror.

Parnell, Charles Stewart
Kipling. Cleared.
Liddy. Bicentennial Words for the Liberal Magistrates of 1798.
Notes towards an Ivy Leaf Video.
Poem for My Sister Nora, at the Reading.
Yeats. Come Gather Round Me Parnellites.
Parnell.
Parnell's Funeral.

Parnell, Thomas
Pope. Epistle to Robert Earl of Oxford and Earl Mortimer.

Parodies
Campion. In Barnum.
"Carroll, Lewis." Hiawatha's Photographing.
How doth the little crocodile.
Upon the Lonely Moor.
White Knight's Ballad, The.
Chaucer. Sir Thopas.
Cummings. Out of the pants which cover me.
Gardner. Nursery Rhyme No. 1.
Nursery Rhyme No. 2.
Koch. Variations on a Theme by William Carlos Williams.
Lowry. I think that I shall never see.
Meredith. It's many a penny you'll pay to go.
Manfred.
Parody of Alfred Austin.
Yes, we'll pic-nic in the woods.
Schwartz. Kilroy's Carnival; A Poetic Prologue for TV.
Zimmer. Death of the Hired Zimmer.
Leaves of Zimmer.
Zumer Is Icumen In.

Parrots
Cowper. Parrot, The.
Dove. Parsley.
Lowry. Christ I am tired of fruit im poetry.
Rossetti. I have a Poll parrot, / And Poll is my doll.
Sarton. Parrot, A.
Smith, Stevie. Parrot.
Who Killed Lawless Lean?
Wordsworth. Contrast; the Parrot and the Wren, The.
Wright, James. For the Marsh's Birthday.

Parsifal. see Arthurian Legend.

Parthenon
Hall. Columns of the Parthenon, The.
Keats. On Seeing the Elgin Marbles.
Melville. Apparition, The.
Parthenon, The.
Patchen. Saturday Night in the Parthenon.

Parties
Auden. At the Party.
Love Feast, The.
Beatles. Birthday.
I Don't Want to Spoil the Party.
Berrigan. Dinner at George & Katie Schneeman's.
Berryman. Drunks.
If not white shorts—then in a princess gown.
Meeting.
Betjeman. False Security.
Bukowski. Good Time Girl.
Social.
Burns. Extempore Reply to an Invitation.
Fête Champetre, The.
To Captain G———, on Being Asked Why I Was Not to Be of the Party with Him and His Brother K-nm-re at Syme's.
Cohen. Guests, The.
De la Mare. Feckless Dinner Party, The.
Dickey, William. Stella Dallas.

Dunbar. Party, The.
Ginsberg. In Society.
Glück. Portrait of the Queen in Tears.
Gunn. Another All-Night Party.
Falstaff.
Punch Rubicundus.
Hardy. At a Fashionable Dinner.
Harvest-Supper, The.
In the Marquee.
Lament: "How she would have loved."
Queen Caroline to Her Guests.
Hemingway. Big Dance on the Hill, The.
Hesketh. After Ecclesiastes.
Party, The.
Hoffman. Translators' Party, The.
Kooser. Book Club.
Larkin. Dance, The.
Party Politics.
Liddy. Dinner Menu a Burnt Offering, A.
Waters by this music.
Meredith. Friar uxorious!
Tuck, my treasure! Tuck, my pleasure!
Nash. Banquet, The.
Children's Party.
Drusilla.
I Know You'll Like Them.
Life of the Party, The.
Mr. Peachey's Predicament or No Mot Parades.
Next!
One Night in Oz.
Party Next Door, The.
Party, The.
There's Always an Ubblebub.
What's in a Name? Here's What's in a Name, or, I Wonder What Became of John and Mary.
O'Hara. For Grace, after a Party.
Joe's Jacket.
Plath. Yaddo: The Grand Manor.
"Reed." All Tomorrow's Parties.
Rolfe. Bal Masqué.
Sixth Winter, The.
Rukeyser. Charm for Cantinflas, A.
Three Sides of a Coin.
Sandburg. Picnic Boat.
Silverstein. Spaghetti.
Stuart. Don't Look Back.
Updike. Party Knee.
Thoughts While Driving Home.
Wilbur. Leaving.
Williams, Charles Kenneth. Flight.
On the Other Hand.
Williams, William Carlos. After the Party.
Delicacies, The.
Wright, James. To a Hostess Saying Goodnight.
Yeats. Mountain Tomb, The.

Parting
Angelou. Gamut, The.
Lie, The.
Prelude to a Parting.
Atwood. Departure from the Bush.
Newsreel: Man and Firing Squad.
Auden. At Parting.
Aubade: "At break of dawn."
Envoi: "From the red chimneys smoke climbs slow and straight."
Envoi No. 2.
Envoi: "Take up your load and go, lad."
Envoi: "You go / Now you are glad."
No trenchant parting this.
So I must go my way.
Two friends who met here and embraced are gone.
Witnesses, The.
Beatles. All My Loving.
Another Girl.
I'll Follow the Sun.
Sgt. Pepper's Lonely Hearts Club Band (Reprise).
She Loves You.
She's Leaving Home.
Think For Yourself.
Ticket to Ride.
Beckett. Da Tagte Es.
Berryman. Old Man Goes South Again Alone.

Parting as Descent.
Thrice, or I moved to sack, I saw you: how.
Bogan. Fifteenth Farewell.
Brontë. F. de Samara to A. G. A.
Browning, Elizabeth Barrett. Night and the Merry Man.
Parting Lovers.
Valediction, A: "God be with thee, my beloved,—God be with thee!"
Browning, Robert. Parting at Morning.
Rosny.
Burns. Can You Leave Me Thus, My Katy.
Clarinda.
Farewell, The: "Farewell, old Scotia's bleak domains."
Gloomy December.
Highland Lassie O.
It Was A' for Our Rightfu' King.
My Bonnie [or Bony] Mary.
Northern Lass, The.
On a Scotch Bard Gone to the West Indies.
Song: "Ae fond kiss, and then we sever."
Song: "Behold the hour, the boat arrive."
Song: "From thee, ELIZA, I must go."
Song: "Gloomy night is gath'ring fast, The."
Song: "Will ye go to the Indies, my Mary."
Wrote on the Blank Leaf of a Copy of My First Edition, Which I Sent to an Old Sweetheart, Then Married.
Byron. Childe Harold's Farewell to England.
Fare Thee Well.
Lines to Mr Hodgson.
Love's Last Adieu.
Maid of Athens, Ere We Part.
On Parting.
On the Quotation "And My True Faith Can Alter Never, Though Thou Art Gone Perhaps Forever."
Stanzas for Music.
Stanzas to a Lady on Leaving England.
Stanzas to Augusta.
To Caroline ("Think'st thou I saw thy beauteous eyes").
To Emma.
To Florence.
Well! Thou Art Happy.
When We Two Parted.
Campion. Can you, the Author of our joy, / So soone depart?
Canto Tertio.
Farewell Song, The.
Sweete, come againe.
Tarry sweete love.
Carew. On His Mistress[e] Going to Sea.
Parting, Celia Weeps.
Pastoral[l] Dialogue, A.
To His Mistress.
To My Mistress[e] in My Absence.
"Carroll, Lewis." Empress of Art, for thee I twine.
Lady Muriel's Song.
Ode To Damon.
Carruth. "Good-bye," they always whisper, "oh God," clinging.
Hah! not what's wrote down, I reckon. I'm leaving.
Poem moves north, The.
Clough. That out of sight is out of mind.
Cohen. Ain't No Cure for Love.
Hey, That's No Way to Say Goodbye.
Traitor, The.
Woman's Decision, A.
Coleridge. Ode to the Rain, An.
On My Joyful Departure from the Same City.
Cowper. On Her Endeavoring to Conceal Her Grief at Parting.
Creeley. Just Friends.
Cullen. At a Parting.
If You Should Go.
Two Who Crossed a Line (She Crosses).
Two Who Crossed a Line.
Cummings. Because / you go away i give roses who.
Goodby Betty,don't remember me.
T.A.M.
This fear is no longer dear. You are not going to America and.

Davie. Break, The.
  Fare Thee Well.
  Seeing Her Leave.
De la Mare. Adieu.
  Good-bye.
Dickinson. Auctioneer of Parting, The.
  I thought to shun the Loneliness.
  Meeting is well worth parting.
  My life closed twice before its close.
  Parting is one of the exactions.
  Parting with Thee reluctantly.
  Some say goodnight—at night.
  'Tis customary as we part.
Dobyns. Leaving the Bar and Low Life at
  Closing, I Unsuccessfully Pursue Sainthood.
Donne. His Parting from Her.
  Song: "Sweetest Love, I Do Not Go."
Doolittle. Chance.
  Orestes Theme.
Dove. Then Came Flowers.
  Thomas at the Wheel.
Dunbar. Farewell Song.
  My Love Irene.
  Parted.
  Premonition.
"Dylan." Boots of Spanish Leather.
  Don't Think Twice, It's All Right.
  Farewell Angelina.
  Farewell: "Oh it's fare thee well my darlin'
  true."
  Going, Going, Gone.
  Just Like a Woman.
  Most Likely You Go Your Way (and I'll Go
  Mine).
  You're Gonna Make Me Lonesome When You
  Go.
Emerson. Discontented Poet: A Masque, The.
Ferlinghetti. At the *Gare Bruxelles-Midi*.
  New York—Albany.
Fletcher. Memory: The Walk on the Beach.
Gallagher. All Day the Light Is Clear.
  Calm, The.
  Words Written Near a Candle.
Garrigue. Doggerel of a Diehard Who Sleeps
  in a Nest of Newspapers.
  Grief Was to Go Out, Away.
Ginsberg. Lover's Garden, A.
Glück. Aubade: "Today above the gull's call."
  Departure.
  First Goodbye.
  Here Are My Black Clothes.
  Letters, The.
Graves. As a Less than Robber.
  Hills of May, The.
  I Will Write.
  In the Vestry.
  Restless Ghost, A.
  That Was the Night.
Hacker. For K.J., Leaving and Coming Back.
  Last Time, The.
  Late August.
  Living in the Moment.
  Somewhere in a Turrent.
Hardy. After Schiller.
  At the Wicket-Gate.
  Cross-Currents.
  Days to Recollect.
  Expostulation, An.
  In the Vaulted Way.
  Leaving, A.
  Opportunity, The.
  Parting-Scene, A.
  Saying Good-bye.
  We Say We Shall Not Meet.
Hayden. Ballad of Sue Ellen Westerfield, The.
  Road in Kentucky, A.
Herrick. Dialogue Betwixt Himselfe and
  Mistresse Eliza: Wheeler, Under the Name of
  Amarillis, A.
  Farewell, The: "Sweetest Loue since wee must
  part."
  His Parting from Mistress Dorothy Keneday.
  Hymne to Sir Clipseby Crew, A.
  Lovers How They Come and Part.
  Parting Verse, Or Charge to His Supposed
  Wife When He Travelled, The.
  Parting Verse, the Feast There Ended, The.

Song upon Silvia, A.
To His Dying Brother, Master William
  Herrick.
To Larr [*or* Lar].
  Upon Parting.
Hoffman. Way He Went, The.
Hugo. Bone Hunting.
  Eileen.
  Last Day There.
  Listen, Ripley.
  Maratea Porto: Saying Good-bye to the
  Vitolos.
  Towns We Know and Leave Behind, the
  Rivers We Carry with Us, The.
Jarrell. Good-bye, Wendover; Good-bye,
  Mountain Home.
  Moving.
Jong. Driving Me Away.
Jonson. Elegy, An: "Since you must go, and I
  must bid farewell."
  Elegy, An: "That love's a bitter sweet, I ne'er
  conceive."
  To William Roe ("Roe (and my joy to name)
  th'art now, to go").
Joseph. Married People Going to Work.
Keats. On Leaving Some Friends at an Early
  Hour.
  See, the Ship in the Bay Is Riding.
  Think Not of It, Sweet One, So.
Kinnell. Fly, The.
Kipling. Appeal, The.
  Lovers' Litany, The.
  Man goes to Man! Cry the challenge though
  the Jungle!
  Parting of the Columns, The.
  Roman Centurion's Song, The.
Larkin. Love, We Must Part Now.
Lawrence. Drama, A.
  End, The.
  Going Back.
  Last Minute, The.
  Last Words to Muriel.
  Mutilation.
  Seven Seals.
  Winter's Tale, A.
Levertov. September 1961.
Lewis. And now we seek once more the
  burning breeze.
  And so we wait the tide, and when the dark.
  Christmas Holiday.
  Departure, The.
  Goodbye.
  In all the ways of going who can tell.
  Island, The.
  On Embarkation.
  Post-Script: for Gweno.
  Valediction.
Lorde. Movement Song.
  To the Girl Who Lives In a Tree.
Lovelace. Dialogue. Lucasta, Alexis.
  To Lucasta, [on] Going to the War[re]s.
McGrath. Fresco: Departure for an Imperialist
  War.
  Get Out of Town.
  When We Say Goodbye.
MacLeish. Ever Since.
  Fifth Book, The.
Marvell. Daphnis and Chloe.
Meredith. Invective of Achilles, The.
  Jack & Harry.
  Kiss, and a clasp, and an eye to eye, A.
  Schubert's "Farewell."
  To-morrow I am going.
  We sat beneath the humming pines.
Millay. To a Friend Estranged from Me.
  To S. M.
Muldoon. Holy Thursday.
Nash. Lament on the Eve of Parting.
  Song for Pier Something or Other.
Nathan. Day the Perfect Speakers Left, The.
  Hello Again.
Nemerov. Going Away.
O'Hara. Now That I Am in Madrid and Can
  Think.
Oliver. Journey, The.
Oppen. Anniversary Poem.
  Night Scene.

Owen. One Remains, The.
Plath. Departure.
Pound. Taking Leave of a Friend.
Raine. Iona.
  It is time, heart, to recall.
Rich. Continuum.
  Parting: I, The.
  Parting: II, The.
  Platform, The.
  Stepping Backward.
  Valediction Forbidding Mourning, A.
Robinson. Afterthoughts.
  Clinging Vine, The.
  John Gorham.
  Unforgiven, The.
Rolfe. Recruit.
Rossetti. I said "All's over"—& I made my.
  Light Love.
  Love Lies Bleeding.
  One Foot on Sea, and One on Shore.
  Twilight Night.
  Wife to Husband.
Rukeyser. Lat. 10 Degrees North, Long. 45
  Degrees West.
  Leaving New York, I looked back fourteen
  times.
St. John. Hotel Sierra.
Schuyler. Frank! Frank!
Scott. Farewell.
  Fitz-Eustace's Song.
Shakespeare. Good night, good rest. Ah,
  neither be my share.
  Sonnet 87: "Farewell! Thou art too dear[e] for
  my possessing."
Shelley. Buona Notte.
  Good-Night.
  Lines: "We meet not as we parted."
  On Fanny Godwin.
Sidney. Eleventh Song.
  Oft have I mused, but now at length I find.
Smith, Charlotte. Farewel, ye lawns!—by fond
  remembrance blest.
  Hymn to Love and Life.
  On Leaving a Part of Sussex.
Smith, Stevie. In My Dreams.
Snyder. Saying Farewell at the Monastery
  After Hearing the Old Master Lecture on
  "Return to the Source."
Sorrentino. Ave atque Vale.
  Marjorie.
Stuart. Long Goodbye, The.
Suckling. To My Lady E.C. at Her Going Out
  of England.
Swinburne. Before Parting.
  In the Orchard.
  Leave-taking, A.
  Triumph of Time, The.
Tate. Edges.
Thomson. Elegy on Parting, An.
  Lisy's Parting with Her Cat.
Tomlinson. Departure.
Updike. Farewell to the Shopping District of
  Antibes.
  Goodbye, Göteborg.
Van Duyn. Advice to a God.
  Fear of Flying, The.
  Peony Stalks.
Wakoski. Standing at the Door.
Waldman. Blue That Reminds Me of the Boat
  When She Left, The.
  Distance Traveled.
Walker. Even as I Hold You.
  He Said:.
  Instant of Our Parting, The.
  Mornings / of an impossible love.
Warren. To a Friend Parting.
Whitman. After the Supper and Talk.
  Good-Bye, My Fancy! ("Good-bye, my Fancy!
  / Farewell dear mate, dear love!").
  Good-Bye My Fancy ("Good-bye my fancy—
  (I had a word to say,)").
  Now Finalè to the Shore.
  Now Lift Me Close.
  Sail Out for Good, Eidólon Yacht!
  So Long!
  To the Reader at Parting.
  What Think You I Take My Pen in Hand?

Whittier. Godspeed.
Gone.
Lament, A: "Circle is broken, one seat is forsaken, The."
Lines on Leaving Appledore.
Wilbur. Leaving.
Williams, William Carlos. In the Wineshop of Chinling.
Translations from the Spanish.
Wordsworth. Cantata, from Metastasio.
Composed When a Probability Existed of Our Being Obliged to Quit Rydal Mount as a Residence.
Departure from the Vale of Grasmere. August, 1803.
Extract from the Conclusion of a Poem, Composed in Anticipation of Leaving School.
Farewell Lines.
Wright, Charles. Three Poems of Departure.
Wroth. Song 4: "Sweetest love returne againe."
Sonnet 8: "How gloewoorme like the sunn doth now apeere."
Wyatt. And wilt [or wylt] thou le[a]ve me thus?
My heart I gave thee not to do it pain.
So feeble is the thread that doth the burden stay.
Yeats. Falling of the Leaves, The.
Parting.

Partridges
Hesketh. Partridge.

Pasadena, California
Koertge. Caboose Factory, The.

Pasolini, Pier Paolo
St. John. To Pasolini.
Smith, Patti. Italy.

Passion
Arnold. Growing Old.
Ashbery. As We Know.
Atwood. Torture.
Auden. Song: "Relation seemed ordained for us."
That night when joy began.
Berg. Leaves.
Berry. And then, one by one, he moved me.
Berryman. And does the old wound shudder open? Shall.
Are we? You murmur "not." What of the night.
Astronomies and slangs to find you, dear.
Boy twenty-one, in Donne, shied like a blow.
Cadenza on Garnette.
How shall I sing, western & dry & thin.
Moths white as ghosts among these hundreds cling.
Murmuration of the shallow, Crane, A.
Old Boys' blazers like a Mardi-Gras, The.
Rackman and victim twist: sounds all these weeks.
They may, because I would not cloy your ear.
Venice, 182.
What was Ahsore, then?. Cargoed with Forget.
You in your stone home where the sycamore.
You sailed in sky-high, with your speech askew.
Bly. In the Month of May.
Bogan. Knowledge.
Second Song.
Brontë. D.G.C. to J.A.
I'm standing in the forest now.
Last Words.
Song By Julius Brenzaida To G.S.
To A.G.A.
Brooks. Love Note II: Flags.
To Be in Love.
Browning, Elizabeth Barrett. Aurora and Tithonus.
Queen Annelida and False Arcite.
Sonnet: "How do I love thee? Let me count the ways."
Vanities.
Bukowski. 6 Foot Goddess, The.
Burns. Cares o' love are sweeter far, The.
O were I on Parnassus hill.
Song: "Mark yonder pomp of costly fashion."
To Alexander Cunningham.

Byron. Last Words on Greece.
Oh! might I kiss those eyes of fire.
On Finding a Fan.
Parisina.
Remember Him Whom Passion's Power.
Stanzas to Jessy.
To ———: "But once I dared to lift my eyes."
To a Lady.
To the Sighing Strephon.
Translation from Catullus ("Equal to Jove that youth must be").
When I Roved a Young Highlander.
Campion. Beauty, Since You So Much Desire.
Fire, fire, fire, fire!
I Care Not for These Ladies.
Mistris [or Mistress] Since You So Much Desire.
Reprove not love, though fondly thou hast lost.
When the God of Merrie Love.
When Thou Must Home.
Carew. Mediocrity in Love Rejected.
Prayer to the Wind, A.
Rapture, A.
Carruth. Afternoon of a Faun.
Cross My Heart and Hope to Die, It Was the Very Same Song Exactly.
For your love given.
No love without hurt? No lovesong without distortion?
Think not of chaste snow always.
Catullus. Carmen 2: "Lesbia's sparrow! / Lesbia's plaything!"
Carmen 32: "Call me to you / at siesta."
Carmen 48: "Iuventius, / were I allowed."
Carmen 51: "Godlike the man who."
Carmen 72: "There was a time, Lesbia, when."
Carmen 75: "Reason blinded by sin, Lesbia."
Carmen 76: "If evocations of past kindness shed."
Carmen 85: "I hate and I love. And if you ask me how."
Carmen 87: "No woman loved, in truth, Lesbia."
Carmen 91: "In this hopeless & wasting love of mine."
Carmen 92: "Lesbia loads me night & day with her curses."
Carmen 104: "Do you really believe I could blacken my life."
Carmen 107: "If ever anyone anywhere, Lesbia, is looking."
Ceravolo. Passion for the Sky.
Ciardi. On Passion As a Literary Tradition.
Clough. When panting sighs the bosom fill.
Cohen. Love Is a Fire.
Coleridge. Alla Sua Amica.
Improvisatore, The.
Night-Scene, The.
Cowper. Love Pure and Fervent.
See Where the Thames, the Purest Stream.
Crane. Possessions.
Creeley. Circle.
Marriage, A.
Poem for Beginners.
Two Ways of Looking in a Mirror.
Way, The.
Cullen. Cats.
Love's Way.
Nothing Endures.
One Day We Played a Game.
Pity the Deep in Love.
Song in Spite of Myself.
Sonnet: "I have not loved you in the noblest way."
Sonnet: "Some for a little while do love, and some for long."
Cummings. Now air is air and thing is thing:no bliss.
This mind made war.
Davie. Bride of Reason, The.
Dickinson. Heart is the only workman, The.
Mob within the heart, The.
Said Death to Passion.
Voraciousness of that only gaze, The.
Doolittle. Fragment 113: "Not honey, / not the

plunder of the bee."
So if you love me.
Time breaks the barrier.
Dunbar. Passion and Love.
Duncan. Among my friends love is a great sorrow.
Beginning of Writing, The.
Circulations of the Song.
Dreamers, The.
I Am a Most Fleshly Man.
"Dylan." Baby, I'm in the Mood for You.
Don't Fall Apart on Me Tonight.
Is Your Love in Vain?
Never Gonna Be the Same Again.
Eberhart. Emily Dickinson.
Hamlet Father, The.
Sanders Theater.
Somewhere Else.
Villanelle: "Christ is walking in your blood today."
What Gives.
Emerson. Blame me not thou hoarse preacher.
I have found a nobler love.
Philosophers are lined with eyes within.
Shun passion, fold the hands of thrift.
They say, through patience, chalk.
Everson. Rose of Solitude, The.
Ferlinghetti. Café Notre Dame.
Ford. Let us make of day a delirium.
Fox. Modern woman in search of a soul.
Garrigue. Movie Actors Scribbling Letters Very Fast in Crucial Scenes.
Glück. Abishag.
Graves. All I Tell You From My Heart.
Blackening Sky.
Deliverance.
Elsewhere.
Friday Night.
In Perspective.
Lion Lover.
Lure of Murder.
Measure of Casualness, A.
Metaphor, The.
Never Such Love.
None the Wiser.
Seldom Yet Now.
Song of Contrariety.
Succubus, A.
Theme of Death, The.
Three Times In Love.
True Evil.
When and Why.
Window Pane, The.
Gunn. JVC.
Hemingway. At night I lay with you.
Killed Piave—July 8—1918.
Herrick. Caution, A.
Passion.
To Electra.
Hewitt. For R.
Host.
Lyric Sonorously Rhymed, The.
My Future Wife.
Passion.
Sonnet: "I thought tonight of all the lovers gone."
Sonnet: "There in the lonely quarry where at dawn."
Summer Arcady.
Tryst.
Hill. And you, who with your soft but searching voice.
Hopkins. Beginning of the End, The.
Jong. Living Happily Ever After.
My Love Is Too Much.
Jonson. Fair friend, 'tis true, your beauties move.
Nymph's Passion, A.
Joseph. Zenith.
Keats. Lines: "Unfelt, unheard, unseen."
Kunitz. Lovers Relentlessly.
Lawrence. Birth Night.
Both Sides of the Medal.
Deeper Than Love.
History.
Honeymoon.
Kisses in the Train.

Know Deeply, Know Thyself More Deeply.
Last Words to Miriam.
Lightning.
Love-Passage, A.
Love Storm.
Mystery.
No! Mr Lawrence!
Passing Visit to Helen.
Primal Passions, The.
Release.
Twofold.
Worm Turns, The.
Levine. At the Fillmore.
For Fran.
Lewis. On Leave: Marriage.
They Part at Daybreak, Returning Their Inevitable Ways.
Liddy. Cantico Per Lo Tuo Amore V.
Tell us, streaming lady.
Lindsay. Caught in a Net.
Firemen's Ball, The.
Queen Mab in the Village.
Lovelace. By thy fault is my mind brought to that pass.
I hate and love, wouldst thou the reason know?
Lucasta's World.
No one can boast herself so much belov'd.
That me alone you lov'd, you once did say.
To Juvencius.
Lowry. Names of Mexican rivers I forgot, The.
Save that the optimistic ones are worse.
Song for My Wife.
Sun, Aeroplane, Lovers.
"MacDiarmid." As Lovers Do.
McGrath. World; The Lovers; Falling Stars, The.
MacLeish. He had used love or lust or what's between.
Love is the way that lovers never know.
Selene Afterwards.
This was not love but love's true negative.
Wild Old Wicked Man, The.
Marlowe. 1.1: Quemadmodum a Cupidine pro bellis amoris scribere coactus sit.
1.2: Quod primo amore correptus, in triumphium duci se a Cupidine patiatur.
1.3: Ad amicam.
1.4: Amicam, qua arte, quibusve nutibus in caena, presente viro uti debeat, admonet.
1.5: Corinnae concubitus.
1.9: Ad Atticum, amantem non oportere desidiosum esse, sicuti nec militem.
1.11: Napen alloquitur, ut paratas tabellas ad Corinnam perferat.
2.1: Quod pro gigantomachia amores scribere sit coactus.
2.17: Quod Corinnae soli sit serviturus.
2.18: Ad Macrum, quod de amoribus scribat.
3.9: Ad Cererem, conquerens quod eius sacris cum amica concumbere non permittatur.
3.10: Ad amicam, a cuius amore discedere non potest.
Passionate Shepherd to His Love, The.
Meredith. Mentor and Pupils.
Remember what a night of storm.
Song: "Love within the lover's breast."
Merrill. Days of 1964.
Merton. True Man, The.
Miller. For Mrs. Jones.
Sun Now or Never (For Barbara), The.
Morgan. Voice spoke in the night, A.
Winter Poem.
Morrison. Moonlight Drive.
Nash. My Dream.
Nemerov. Earth orbits on the sun and has no sign.
Sunderland.
O'Hara. Blocks.
Hôtel Transylvanie.
My Heat.
Savoy.
Second Avenue.
Poe. Eulalie—A Song.
Romance.
Tamerlane.

Pope. Epistle I, to Sir Richard Temple, Lord Cobham.
Prince. In the Wood.
Last Attachment, A.
Ransom. Good Ships.
Spiel of [the] Three Mountebanks.
To the Scholars of Harvard.
Rich. If I lay on that beach with you.
Paula Becker to Clara Westhoff.
Since we're not young, weeks have to do time.
Sleeping, turning in turn like planets.
Roethke. Her Words.
Rossetti. Bed of Forget-Me-Nots, A.
Subject To Like Passions as We Are.
Rukeyser. Flashing Cliff, A.
Sandburg. Accordingly, they commenced by an insidious.
Aztec Mask.
Evening Sunsets Witness and Pass On, The.
Face.
Fog Numbers.
Head.
High Moments.
Honey and Salt.
Hunger and Cold.
Love Beyond Keeping.
Night's Nothings Again.
On the Breakwater.
Population Drifts.
Sarah's Letter to Peter.
Sea Chest.
They Met Young.
Three Shrines.
Under the Harvest Moon.
White Shoulders.
Sarton. Evening Music.
Scott. Spindle Song, The.
Sexton. Fierceness of Female, The.
Frenzy.
Shakespeare. Sonnet 116: "Let me not to the marriage of true minds."
Shelley. Lines: "When the lamp is shattered."
Love's Philosophy.
To ———: "When passion's trance is overpast."
To Constantia.
To the Queen of My Heart.
Sidney. My Muse what ails this ardour.
Smith, Charlotte. Supposed To Be Written by Werter.
Smith, Stevie. Francesca in Winter.
I HATE THIS GIRL.
Sorrentino. At last comes love of such a quality that it would shame me.
16 Lines.
Southwell. Christ's Bloody Sweate.
Love's Servile Lot[t].
Spender. Ice.
Stevens. Chaos in Motion and Not in Motion.
Stevenson. As in the hostel by the bridge, I sate.
I have a friend; I have a story.
My heart, when first the blackbird sings.
Ne Sit Ancillae Tibi Amor Pudori.
Suckling. Sir Toby Matthews.
Song: "Unjust decrees, that do at once exact."
Swift. Lesbia.
Swinburne. Anactoria.
Laus Veneris.
Tate. In Wintertime.
Thomson. To Seraphina.
Walcott. Return to D'Ennery; Rain.
Waldman. Cure, The.
Whitman. Native Moments.
Once I Pass'd through a Populous City.
Wilbur. Gifts, The.
Williams, Charles Kenneth. After That.
Wright, James. Idea of the Good, The.
Love Song to a Morning.
Morning Hymn to a Dark Girl.
Not in Marble Palaces.
Paul.
Pretty Redhead, The.
Quail, The.
Quest, The.
This morning / My beloved rose, before I did.

To Harvey, Who Traced the Circulation.
To the bridge of love.
To the Muse.
Wroth. Sonnet 1: "When night's [or nights] black mantle could most darknes prove."
Sonnet 3: "Yett is ther hope: Then Love butt play thy part."
Sonnet 07: "No time, noe roome, noe thought, or writing can."
Sonnet 13: "Deare fammish nott what you your self gave food."
Sonnet 21: "When last I saw thee, I did not[t] thee see."
Sonnet 48: "How like a fire doth love increase in me[e]."
Wyatt. Avising the bright beams of these fair eyes.
From thought to thought, from hill to hill love doth me lead.
Lo, what it is to love!
Perdy [or Perdie or Perdye], I said[e] it [or yt] not.
Since love is such that, as ye wot.
Take heed betime, lest ye be spied.
Your looks so often cast.
Yeats. Indian to His Love, The.
Young. Dreamjot: 1962.
Jolt.
Mexico City Lover.
Romance Without Finance.
Zukofsky. Credit me poor to say of my life *maledictory weed die.*
Decay bars one time, 'solely to know, see Catullus.'
He'll hie me, par *is* he? the God divide her.
How cast down is the mind that took to my Lesbia, culprit.
I'm a bow, my dual kiss, Ipsithilla.
Lesbia may dicker simper maul or nag talk at whom, come.
Mellowed *those,* I call *those* eyes, Juventius.
No idea, Gelli, spurred me to mirror you faithful.
No love by test, my love, 'll air then, time, say the care of all my time.
O th'hate I move love. Quarry it fact I am, for that's so re queries.
Sand: For the cigarette finished, The.
See could we quit coveting hope taunting where hope hid and.
Seek or record then the benefactor—pree or voluptuous.
Sparrow, my girl's pleasure, delight of my girl.

Passivity
Berry. Thief, The.
Carruth. You are the dreamer who dreams the world, and yet.
Creeley. As We Sit.
Cullen. Requiescam.
Glück. Game, The.
Koertge. Man like a Curtain, A.
Meredith. Woodland Peace.
Nash. I Never Even Suggested It.
"Reed." Candy Says.
Warren. Spider, The.
Wilbur. Shame.
Young. Are You the Lover or Loved?
Robbie's Dance, The.

Past
Angelou. Reverses.
Still I Rise.
Auden. April.
Before.
Below me Ticknall lay but in the light.
Maria Hat Geholfen.
Old Colliery, The.
On Seeing Some Dutch Pictures.
Progress.
Rookhope (Weardale, Summer 1922).
Beatles. Golden Slumbers.
Night Before, The.
Your Mother Should Know.
Beckett. D'où / la voix qui dit.
Dread Nay.
Pas davantage.
Rien nul / n'aura été.

Sonnet 115: "Those lines that I before have writ do lie."
Shelley. Lines: "That time is dead for ever, child!"
Past, The.
Smith, Stevie. Days of Yore, The.
In Protocreation.
Past, The.
Sorrentino. Long Gone Blues.
Open Boat, The.
pentagram.
Poem for My Wife, A.
Poem: "Living friends live / in the past so they bore us."
Poem to Read in August, A.
Simplicity.
Strambotto.
What is past is here, as we.
Spender. Barn, The.
Little Coat, The.
One More New Botched Beginning.
Tom's a-Cold.
Stafford. Some Shadows.
Stevens. Arcades of Philadelphia the Past.
Cuisine Bourgeoise.
Fish-Scale Sunrise, A.
Stuart. Opposite Field, The.
Presence.
Thomas. Because the Pleasure-Bird Whistles.
Do You Not Father Me.
Twenty-four Years.
Wakoski. Driving Gloves.
Walcott. In the other 'eighties, a hundred midsummers gone.
Waldman. After "Les Fleurs."
Warren. In the Turpitude of Time: N.D.
Letter from a Coward to a Hero.
Vision: Circa 1880, A.
Whitman. Death of General Grant.
New Year's Day, 1848.
Now Precedent Songs, Farewell.
Old Chants.
Proud Music of the Storm.
To-day and Thee.
To Get the Final Lilt of Songs.
Unnamed Lands.
With Antecedents.
Whittier. Memories.
Norsemen, The.
Wilbur. Ballade of the Ladies of Time Past.
Pardon, The.
Williams, Charles Kenneth. Blades.
Cellophane.
Combat.
Floor.
Hood.
Nostalgia.
Of What Is Past.
Past, The.
Sorrow, The.
Williams, Miller. After a Brubeck Concert.
Ghosts.
House in the Vacant Lot, The.
Wordsworth. Brugès ("Spirit of Antiquity—enshrined, The").
June, 1820.
Wright, Charles. Ars Poetica.
Bar Giamaica, 1959-60.
Looking at Pictures.
Self-Portait ("In Murray, Kentucky, I lay once").
Self-Portrait ("Marostica, Val di Ser. Bassano del Grappa").
Southern Cross, The.
Two Stories.
Wyatt. When that I call unto my mind.
Yau. Dream Life of a Coffin Factory in Lynn, Massachussetts, The.
We Are All Vultures.
Yeats. Bronze Head, A.
Circus Animals' Desertion, The.
Ego Dominus Tuus.
Image from a Past Life, An.
Seven Sages, The.
Three Marching Songs.
Young. Fort Collins, Colorado.
Geography of the Near Past.

Zukofsky. Alba (1952).
As to How Much.
I Sent Thee Late.
My nephew / And my new.
Pasternak, Boris
Davie. Death of a Voice.
Kunitz. Boris Pasternak.
Levertov. In Memory of Boris Pasternak.
Walcott. Love in the Valley.
Pastoral Verse
Auden. Chloe to Daphnis in Hyde Park.
Eberhart. Recollection of Childhood.
Summer Landscape.
Marlowe. Nimphs [or Nymph's] Reply to the Sheepheard [or Shepherd], The.
Passionate Shepherd to His Love, The.
Ralegh. Nimphs [or Nymph's] Reply to the Sheepheard [or Shepherd], The.
Sidney. Come, Dorus, come, let the songs thy sorrows signify.
Come shepherd's weeds, become your master's mind.
Feed on my sheep; my charge, my comfort, feed.
My sheep are thoughts, which I both guide and serve.
Ye [or you] goat-herd gods, [that love the grassy mountains].
Walcott. Camps hold [or held] their distance— [of] brown chestnuts and grey smoke, The.
Pastures. see **Fields and Pastures.**
Paterson, New Jersey
Williams, William Carlos. Episode 17.
Paterson.
Paths
Atwood. Paths and Thingscape.
Auden. Hidden Lane, The.
Berrigan. On the green a white boy goes / We may read about all those radio waves.
Berry. In Rain.
"Carroll, Lewis." As It Fell upon a Day.
Clark. Trout Kill on the Sacremento.
Coleridge. Long deep Lane / So overshadow'd, it might seem one bower, A.
Cummings. Seeker of truth / follow no path.
Haines. What is Life?
Hewitt. Path Ahead, The.
Way to School, The.
Kinnell. Under the Maud Moon.
Lowry. Alas, there is no still path in my soul.
Dark Path.
Rolfe. Faces No Longer White.
Rossetti. Amor Mundi.
Snyder. Elk Trails.
Off the Trail.
Path to Han-shan's place is laughable, The.
Riprap.
Stuart. Love Song.
Student, The.
Whittier. River Path, The.
Wordsworth. Simplon Pass, The.
Patience
Bishop. Patience of an Angel.
Boyle. Ode to a Maintenance Man and His Family.
Browning, Elizabeth Barrett. Patience Taught by Nature.
Perplexed Music.
Sonnet: "Oh, yes! they love through all this world of ours."
Bukowski. Object Lesson.
Chaucer. Clerk's Tale, The.
Prologue of the Monk's Tale, The.
Coleridge. Ballad of the Dark Ladié, The.
Love, Hope, and Patience in Education.
Cowper. Cantab, The.
Love Increased by Suffering.
Needless Alarm, The.
Rose, The.
Creeley. For No Clear Reason.
Indians.
Out of Sight.
Tiny Place, A.
Young Woman.
Cullen. Two Thoughts of Death.
Davie. They, to Me.

Dickinson. Patience—has a quiet Outer.
Dunbar. Plantation Melody, A.
Emerson. Fine presentiments controlled him.
Forbearance.
Go if thou wilt ambrosial Flower.
Shun passion, fold the hands of thrift.
They say, through patience, chalk.
Graves. Carol of Patience.
Patience.
Time of Waiting, A.
Hardy. Waiting Both.
Herbert. Size, The.
Herrick. Dream, The.
His Weaknesse in Woes.
Patience in Princes.
Patience, or Comforts in Crosses.
Persecutions Profitable.
Speake in Season.
To Fortune.
To God ("God is all-sufferance here").
Upon Flood, Or a Thankfull Man.
Upon God ("God when He takes my goods and chattels hence").
Hewitt. Expectancy.
How have I served you? I have let you waste.
October-Born.
To Any Dweller in Lewis Street.
Hopkins. My Own Heart.
Patience, Hard Thing!
Jarrell. Tree, The.
Kinnell. Wait.
Lawrence. Be Still!
What's to Be Done.
Lewis. Vigil: He Lies Awake in the Barracks Room, Fearful She Will Not Come, The.
Liddy. Josie.
Lowry. Pacific is a feeble symbol of death.
Nash. I'm Sure She Said Six-Thirty.
Slow Down, Mr. Ganderdonk, You're Late.
Nathan. Certain Prospects and Spectacular Diversions.
Paley. Learning From Barbara Deming.
Pope. For Sir W. Trumbull.
Psalms. Psalm 13: "How long wilt thou forget me, O Lord?"
Psalm 40: "I waited patiently for the Lord."
Rossetti. Are They Not All Ministering Spirits?
As Thy Days, So Shall Thy Strength Be.
By Way of Remembrance.
Have Patience.
Let Patience Have Her Perfect Work.
Lord, It Is Good for Us to Be Here.
O ye who love today, / Turn away / From Patience with her silver ray.
Patience must dwell with Love, for Love and Sorrow.
Sorrow hath a double voice, / Sharp today but sweet tomorrow.
Study.(A Soul), A.
Sweetness of rest when Thou sheddest rest.
Thou Knewest..Thou Oughtest Therefore.
Trees' Counselling, The.
Will of the Lord Be Done, The.
Shakespeare. Sonnet 58: "That god forbid that made me first your slave."
Sidney. Sonnet 56: "Fie, school of Patience, fie; your lesson is."
Silverstein. Melinda Mae.
Traffic Light.
Smart. Patience.
Stevenson. As starts the absent dreamer, when a train.
Stuart. Hunter, Prey.
Sutter. Visitor, The.
Whittier. Angel of Patience, The.
Williams, Charles Kenneth. In the middle / of a bite of.
Patience Is When You Stop Waiting.
Wordsworth. Force of Prayer, The; or, The Founding of Bolton Priory; A Tradition.
Wyatt. Patience, for I have wrong.
Patience for my device.
Patience of all my smart.
Patience though I have not.

Zukofsky. Do not leave me.
Sequence 1944-6.

Patients
Dobyns. In the Hospital.
Merton. Rites for the Extrusion of a Leper.
"Reed." Lady Godiva's Operation.
Schuyler. Arches.

See also **Catholicism and Catholics; Hospitals; Illness; Mental Illness.**

Patriarchy
Olson. Barley or rye / blue and white green.
Bigmans.
Bigmans II.
Fathers, The.
She-Bear (II), The.
So the Norse / were neurotic.
To the She-Bear: *The 1st Song.*
Piercy. Barbie Doll.
Plath. I Want, I Want.
Jailer, The.
Lady Lazarus.
Rich. Cartographies of Silence.
From a Survivor.
Heroines.
Hunger.
I come home from you through the early light
of spring.
Meditations for a Savage Child.
Mountain laurel in bloom, The.
Natural Resources.
No one's fated or doomed to love anyone.
Paula Becker to Clara Westhoff.
Your small hands, precisely equal to my own.
Stein. Patriarchal Poetry.
Waldman. Ancient Song Rising.

Patrick, Saint
Davie. Comforter, The.
Whittier. Proclamation, The.

Patriotic Songs, England
Thomson. Rule, Britannia!

Patriotic Songs, Scotland
Burns. Highland Laddie.
Sutors o' Selkirk.

Patriotism and Patriots
Atwood. Thoughts from Underground.
Betjeman. In Westminster Abbey.
Browning, Robert. Patriot, The [An Old
Story].
Sordello.
Burns. Dumfires Volunteers, The.
On the Death of Sir J. Hunter Blair.
Byron. Epigrams: "Oh, Castlereagh! thou art a
patriot now."
Cohen. Killers, The.
Coleridge. British Stripling's War-Song, The.
Cowper. Address to the Mob, An.
Modern Patriot, The.
Crashaw. Out of Horace.
Cummings. Come,gaze with me upon this
dome.
I sing of Olaf glad and big.
Next to of course god america i.
Dickinson. Is it Intellect that the Patriot
means.
Emerson. In an Age of Fops and Toys.
Song: "Shout for those whose course is done."
Hall. Body Politic, The.
Hemingway. To Good Guys Dead.
Hewitt. Ireland.
"Lass of Richmond Hill", or The Royal
Garden Party, The.
Neither an Elegy Nor a Manifesto.
Remembering a Conversation: Itzik Manger at
the PEN Conference, Edinburgh, 1950.
Scar, The.
Ulsterman, An.
Hopkins. What Shall I Do for the Land that
Bred Me.
Housman. New Mistress, The.
Jeffers. So Many Blood-Lakes.
Jonson. To True Soldiers.
Keats. Happy Is England! I Could Be Content.
Kipling. Recessional.
Larkin. MCMXIV.
Lawrence. As for Me, I'm a Patriot.
Canvassing for the Election.

Lindsay. Hail to the Sons of Roosevelt.
Over the Appalachian Barricade.
Yankee Doodle.
"MacDiarmid." Conception.
MacNeice. Western Landscape.
Matthews. And So.
Meredith. Loyal Soldier, The.
Patriot Engineer, The.
Song: "Who says, she is in danger."
Merton. Uncle Sam with a knife at his throat.
Owen. Dulce Et Decorum Est.
Patchen. Letter to Those Who Are About to
Die.
Pope. Epitaph on Sir William Trumbal.
Rolfe. And If You Don't See What You
Want, Ask for It.
Rukeyser. Road, The.
Scott. Caledonia.
Edinburgh From Blackford Hill.
On the Massacre of Glencoe, 1692.
Pibroch of Donuil Dhu.
Snodgrass. Fourth of July.
Thomson. Britain.
Britannia.
"From Those Eternal Regions."
Prospect, The.
To Alfred.
Updike. Minority Report.
Whitman. Beat! Beat! Drums!
I Hear America Singing.
Whittier. Barbara Frietchie.
Wordsworth. Composed by the Sea-Side, near
Calais, August, 1802.

Patrons
Burns. Brigs of Ayr, a Poem. Inscribed to J.
B*********, Esq; Ayr, The.
Dedication to G**** H******* Esq., A.
Lament for James, Earl of Glencairn.
Lines Sent to Sir John Whiteford, of
Whiteford, Bart. with the Foregoing Poem.
Sketch. Inscribed to the Rt. Hon. Ch. J. Fox
Esq.
Campion. To the Right Honourable, Both in
Birth and Vertue, Francis, Earle of
Cumberland.
Herrick. To the Honoured, Master Endimion
Porter.
To the Most Learned, Wise, and Arch-
Antiquary, M. John Selden.
To the Patron of Poets, M. End: Porter.
To the Right Honourable, Philip, Earle of
Pembroke, and Montgomerie.
Jonson. Epigram. To the Household. 1630,
An.
Humble Petition of Poor Ben to the Best of
Monarchs, Masters, Men, King Charles, The.
To Lucy, Countess of Bedford.
To Lucy, Countess[e] of Bedford, with Mr.
Donnes Satire's [or Satyres].
To Master John Burges.
To the Right Honourable, the Lord High
Treasurer of England. An Epistle Mendicant.
1631.
Prince. Epistle to a Patron, An.
Smart. On Gratitude.
Smith, Charlotte. To the Earl of Egremont.

Paul, Saint
Cohen. Future, The.
Hardy. In St. Paul's a While Ago.
Herrick. Beginnings and Endings.
Upon Paul.
Kipling. At His Execution.
Gallio's Song.
Merton. St. Paul.
Ransom. Our Two Worthies.
Robinson. Three Taverns, The.
Rossetti. Conversion of St. Paul.
In weariness and painfulness St. Paul.
St. Barnabas.
Smart. Conversion of St. Paul.

Pawnbrokers and Pawnshops
Sandburg. Kreisler.
Three Balls.

Pawnshops and Pawnbrokers
Sandburg. Street Window.

Peace
Angelou. Georgia Song, A.

Auden. Canal, Froghall, The.
Mill, The.
Punchard.
Rain.
Beatles. Within You Without You.
Beckett. Nuit qui fais tant.
Berry. In the early morning dark.
Let him escape hospital and doctor.
Mad Farmer's Love Song, The.
Marriage, an Elegy, A.
Peace. May he waken.
Peace of Wild Things, The.
Praise, A.
To Think of the Life of a Man.
Berryman. Rock-Study with Wanderer.
Bly. After Long Busyness.
After Working.
Asian Peace Offers Rejected without
Publication.
Browning, Elizabeth Barrett. First News from
Villafranca.
Burns. Song: "I murder hate by field or
flood."
When wild War's deadly blast was blawn.
Ye Jacobites By Name.
Campion. Elegeia I (1595).
Most sweet and pleasing are thy wayes, O
God.
Shewes and nightly revels, signes of joy and
peace.
To the Most Puisant and Gratious James King
of Great Britaine.
Triumph now with Joy and mirth.
Truth, sprung from heaven, shall shine.
"Carroll, Lewis." Christmas Greetings.
Path of Roses, The.
Song of Love, A.
Chaucer. Tale of Melibee, The.
Clough. In controversial foul impureness.
Cohen. Hydra 1960.
Peace.
Coleridge. Domestic Peace.
Cowper. Entire Surrender, The.
Heroism.
Nightingale and Glow-Worm, The.
Ode to Peace.
Song on Peace.
Song: "When all within is peace."
Crane. Enrich My Resignation.
In a Court.
Interior.
Meditation.
Creeley. For No Clear Reason.
Song: "How simply / for another."
Cullen. Apostrophe to the Land.
Wise, The.
Cummings. All nearness pauses,while a star
can grow.
Denied night's face / have shadowless they?
Enter no(silence is the blood whose flesh).
De la Mare. England.
Ghost, The.
Homesick.
Interlude, An.
Peace.
Vain Questioning.
Dickinson. Chilly Peace infests the Grass, A.
Peace is a fiction of our Faith.
Port of Peace has many Coves, The.
Doolittle. Trance.
Triplex.
Dunbar. At Loafing-Holt.
From the Porch at Runnymede.
"Dylan." Changing of the Guards.
Let Me Die in My Footsteps.
Eberhart. Airman Considers His Power, An.
On Seeing an Egyptian Mummy in Berlin,
1932.
Solace.
United 555.
Eliot. Song for Simeon, A.
Emerson. One hand washes the other.
Fisher. Convalescent / to get along the shop
fronts.
If I declare *Peace.*
Tranquility a manner.
Ford. When you close your eyes.

Garrigue. Thy Love Is One Thou'st Not Yet Known.
Ginsberg. Kiss Ass.
Neruda's "Que dispierte el leñador."
Graves. Love Charms.
Solomon's Seal.
Gunn. Captain in Time of Peace.
Philemon and Baucis.
Haines. Pitcher of Milk, The.
Hardy. According to the Mighty Working.
And There Was a Great Calm.
Christmas Ghost-Story, A.
Peace Peal, The.
Sick Battle-God, The.
Hartley. Where should we go.
Herbert. L'Envoy.
Peace.
Herrick. Farewell Frost; or, Welcome the Spring.
Hand and Tongue, The.
Pardons.
Peace not Permanent.
Power and Peace.
Rainbow, The.
Things of Choice, Long a Comming.
Hesketh. After Ecclesiastes.
Hewitt. Ceilidhe, The.
Comment on Verse.
Curfew Tower, The.
I Talked and Raged and Planned.
Little Glen, The.
Triad ("Three sounds of peace and rich increase").
Well-Intentioned Consul, The.
You mid the corn not yet asleep.
Hill. Mobile, immaculate and austere.
Hoffman. Stillness, A.
Hopkins. Il Mystico.
Peace.
Housman. Soldier from the wars returning.
Hughes, Langston. Projection.
Jong. Gazing Out, Gazing In.
Joseph. Chrysanth.
Rose.
Rose in the Afternoon.
Keats. O! How I Love, on a Fair Summer's Eve.
On Peace.
Kipling. American Rebellion, The.
Benfactors, The.
Peace of Dives, The.
Settler, The.
Knight. Apology for Apostasy?
Poem on the Middle East "Peace Process", A.
Koch. Pleasures of Peace, The.
Larkin. Coming.
Lawrence. Attila.
Bei Hennef.
Choice.
Compari.
Dead People.
Pax.
Peace.
Peace and War.
Secret Waters, The.
Today.
Wealth.
What Would You Fight For?
Levine. Ask the Roses.
Conductor of Nothing, The.
Miracle, The.
Lewis. East, The.
White brain crossing, The.
Lindsay. Jingo and the Minstrel, The.
Sew the Flags Together.
Tale of the Tiger Tree, The.
To Jane Addams at the Hague.
With a Rose, to Brunhilde.
Longfellow. Arsenal at Springfield, The.
Occultation of Orion, The.
Lovelace. To My Truely Valiant, Learned Friend, Who in His Booke Resolv'd the Art Gladiatory into the Mathematick's.
Lowry. And now I brood on what I think I know.
Lapis dawn is gleaming, A.

No wonder it feared peace, the knees of years.
Warning from False Cape Horn.
"MacDiarmid." Everlasting layers / Of ideas, images, feelings.
Skald's Death.
MacNeice. Apple Blossom.
Meredith. Britain.
Cageing of Ares, The.
Congress of Nations, The.
Progress.
Word from the Cannon's Mouth, A.
Merton. Advising the Prince.
Earthquake.
Guns of Fort Knox, The.
Lightly, lightly, so lightly.
Paper Cranes.
Soldiers of Peace.
Thonga Lament.
Moore. In Distrust of Merits.
Morrison. Sudden Attack.
Muldoon. Truce.
Nemerov. Peace in Our Time.
Song of Degrees, A.
Olson. May 20, 1959.
Oppen. Parousia.
Patchen. Here might have been the thinking of mountains.
How Old the World Is!
Peace in this green field.
Prince. Chapel-at-Ease.
People Rest after Conquests, The.
Psalms. Psalm 122: "I was glad when they said unto me.."
Psalm 133: "Behold, how good and how pleasant it is."
Raine. My sight with the clouds'.
Ransom. Rain.
Spiel of [the] Three Mountebanks.
Robinson. Peace on Earth.
Roethke. No Bird.
Rolfe. Lanes of Death and Birth.
Rossetti. Behold the Man!
Better So.
Counsel, A.
Discovery, A.
From the Antique.
I sit among the green shady valleys oft.
In a Certain Place.
In Patience.
Life Hidden.
Looking Forward.
Resurrection Eve.
Sir Eustace Grey.
Sleep, Sleep Happy Child; All Creation Slept and Smiled.
Song of the Star, The.
Song: "Stream moaneth as it floweth, The."
There Remaineth Therefore a Rest.
Who sits with the King in His Throne? Not a slave but a Bride.
Rukeyser. Breaking the nets of the world, in glimpses going.
Even during war, moments of delicate peace.
Flying to Hanoi.
He is breaking the nets in his wildness for the real.
Hero Speech.
It Is There.
Much later, I lie in a white seaport night.
Palos Verdes Cliffs.
Peace the great meaning has not been defined.
Song, the Brain-Coral.
Statement by Willkie after Returning from England.
Time Hinder Not Me; His Arms Reach Here and There.
Sandburg. A. E. F.
For You.
Open Letter to the Poet Archibald MacLeish Who Has Forsaken His Massachusetts Farm to Make Propaganda for Freedom.
Peace Between Wars.
Sarton. Nativity.
Work of Happiness, The.
Schuyler. May, 1972.
Schwartz. Poem to Johann Sebastian Bach.

Sonnet: "I follow thought and what the world announces."
Silverstein. Generals, The.
Simic. Summer Morning.
Smart. Peace.
Smith, Charlotte. Sonnet to the Forest Ytene.
Smith, Stevie. Dear Child of God.
In Canaan's Happy Land.
Southwell. Content and Ri[t]ch[e].
From Fortune's Reach.
Man to the Wound in Christ's Side.
Stafford. At the Un-National Monument along the Canadian Border.
Stevenson. Country of the Camisards, The.
I love to be warm by the red fireside.
Voluntary.
Sutter. Why Birch Trees Are White.
Tennyson. For I Dipped [or Dipt] into the Future.
Thomson. Nuptial song, A.
To Peace.
Walcott. Season of Phantasmal Peace, The.
Whitman. Base of All Metaphysics, The.
Halcyon Days.
O Sun of Real Peace.
Of Many a Smutch'd Deed Reminiscent.
Reconciliation.
Whittier. After Election.
Battle Autumn of 1862, The.
Disarmament.
Garrison.
Hive at Gettysburg, The.
In Peace.
Lost Occasion, The.
On the Big Horn.
Peace Autumn, The.
Peace Convention at Brussels, The.
Peace of Europe, The.
To the Thirty-Ninth Congress.
William Francis Bartlett.
Wilbur. Grasshopper, A.
Peace of Cities, The.
Williams, Charles Kenneth. Peace.
Yours.
Williams, William Carlos. And Who Do You Think "They" Are?
Peace.
Solstice.
Wordsworth. Address to Silence.
And sweet it is to see in summer time.
Danish Boy; A Fragment, The.
Emperors and Kings, How Oft Have Temples Rung.
Fairest, brightest, hues of ether fade, The.
Forsaken, The.
Fragments from Dove Cottage Manuscript 44 (II).
Invocation to the Earth; February, 1816.
Not Love, not War, nor the Tumultuous Swell.
Ode: 1815.
Ode: The Morning of the Day Appointed for a General Thanksgiving. January 18, 1816.
Rest and Be Thankful!
Scene on the Lake of Brientz.
Written in Very Early Youth.
Wright, Charles. T'ang Notebook.
Wright, James. Offering for Mr. Bluehart, An.
She Hid in the Trees from the Nurses.
Wroth. Sonnet 2: "Is to leave all, and take the thread of love."
Yeats. Against Unworthy Praise.
He Bids His Beloved Be at Peace.
Peace.
Rose of Peace, The.
Young. Available Light.
Dancing.
Dreams of Paradise.
I violinize peace.
In the Tender Woodland.

Peach Trees and Peaches
Atwood. Late August.
Blake. I asked a thief to steal me a peach.
Carruth. Springtime so impetuous. Already pink blossoms, The.
Fox. Peaches.
Lawrence. Peach.
Rossetti. Peach tree on the southern wall, The.

Sandburg. Peach Blossoms.
Spanish.
Spring Carries Surprises.
Stevens. Dish of Peaches in Russia, A.
Warren. Riddle in the Garden.

Peacocks
Dickey, William. Things Kept.
Hall. Apples.
Hopkins. Peacock's Eye, The.
Lawrence. Peacock.
Lieberman. Loves of the Peacocks.
Merrill. Peacock, The.
Moore. To the Peacock of France.
Rossetti. Look on This Picture and on This.
Smith, Charlotte. Jay in Masquerade, The.
Stevens. Domination of Black ("At night, by the fire").

Pear Trees and Pears
Doolittle. Orchard.
Pear Tree.
Hugo. Morning in Padova.
Lawrence. Pear-Blossom.
Millay. Pear Tree, The.
Stevens. Study of Two Pears.
Tomlinson. Fruit, for sculpture.
Updike. Pear like a Potato, A.
Query.
Wilbur. June Light.
Wright, James. Autumnal.

Pearl Diving
Emerson. Fit for the Pleiads' azure chord.
Wilbur. Conjuration.

Pearl Harbor
Jeffers. Pearl Harbor.
Smith, Stevie. Little Daughters of America, The.

Pearls
Browning, Robert. Pearl, a Girl, A.
Dunbar. Roses and Pearls.
Emerson. For pearls, plunge in the sea.
Graves. Pearl, The.
Herrick. Rock of Rubies: and The Quarrie of Pearls, The.
Lindsay. Pearl of Biloxi, The.
Lorde. Bridge Through My Window.
Olson. What's Wrong with Pindar.
Without the Season of Structure, Modes Lie Like Gods Thrown Down, Helpless Before the Newness Upsets Genesis When the Young Men Pour In.

Peas
Sandburg. Pods.

Peasants
Campion. Ad Rusticum.
Crabbe. Contented Peasant, The.
Dickinson. So from the mould/ Scarlet and Gold.
Hewitt. Long Bridge, The.
Lewis. Peasant Song.
Peasants, The.
Lowry. Magic World, The.
Prince. King watches at Night, The.
Sexton. Little Peasant, The.

Pedantry and Pedants
Byron. On a Change of Masters at a Great Public School.
Emerson. Borrow Urania's subtile wings.
Pedants all / They would be original.
Nash. Purist, The.
See also **Scholarship and Scholars.**

Peddling and Peddlers
Burns. Trogger, The.
Emerson. King. If farmers make my land secure.
Morgan. As It Was.
Suckling. Pedlar of Small-Wares, A.

Pedestrians
Levertov. Rainwalkers, The.

Peeping Toms. *see* **Voyeurism and Voyeurs.**

Pelicans
Eberhart. Key West.
Jeffers. Pelicans.
MacNeice. Jungle Clearance Ceylon.
Moore. Frigate Pelican, The.
Wilbur. Pelican, The.

Penelope (mythology)
Atwood. When you look at nothing.
Cowper. On Flaxman's Penelope.
Millay. Ancient Gesture, An.
Oliver. Return, The.
Stevens. World as Meditation, The.

Peninsular War (1808–14)
Wordsworth. Epigram on an Event in Col.
Evans's Redoubted Performances in Spain.
Squib on Colonel Evans, A.

Pennsylvania (state)
Sandburg. Pennsylvania.
Stevenson. Susquehanna and the Delaware, The.
Updike. Returning Native.
Whitman. Voice from Death, A.
Whittier. Chalkley Hall.
Golden Wedding of Longwood, The.
New Year, The.
Pennsylvania Pilgrim, The.
Ritner.
To Pennsylvania.
Wordsworth. To the Pennsylvanians.

Pensions and Pensioners. *see* **Old Age;**
    Retirement and Retirees.

Pentecost
Hill. Bidden Guest, The.
Olson. Pente cŏst under the body of the gull flying directly over.
Rossetti. Whitsun Day.
Whitsun Eve.
Whitsun Monday.
Whitsun Tuesday.

Peonies
Fletcher. White Symphony.
Levine. Having Been Asked "What is a Man?" I Answer.
Oliver. Peonies.

Peppers
Ciardi. Aunt Mary.

Perception
Auden. Between those happenings that prefigure it.
Beckett. Ce qu'ont les yeux.
Fin fond du néant.
Hors crâne seul dedans.
Something There.
Berg. In It.
Bogan. Late.
Brontë. I gazed upon the cloudless moon.
Campion. And would you faine the reason know.
Carruth. Diagnosis is / Anxiety psychoneurosis, The.
First Version, The.
To Know in Reverie the Only Phenomenology of the Absolute.
Catullus. Carmen 22: "I must, Varus, tell you."
Ceravolo. Chains of Mountains.
Drunken Winter.
Green Lake Is Awake, The.
Heart Feels the Water.
Water: How Weather Feels the Cotton Hotels.
White Fish in Reeds.
Ciardi. Differences.
On a Photo of Sgt. Ciardi a Year Later.
Selectivity.
Three Views of a Mother.
Coleridge. Apologia pro Vita Sua.
Lunar Entrancement.
Reason for Love's Blindness.
Creeley. "Do You Think.."
Echo.
End, The.
Enough.
Family, The.
For Love.
Here.
Man, The.
Cullen. For Helen Keller.
Cummings. &(all during the / dropsin).
But if i should say.
For prodigal read generous.
Hate blows a bubble of despair into.
I shall imagine life.

If up's the word;and a world grows greener.
Love's absence is illusion,alias time.
Mr youse needn't be so spry.
One's not half two. It's two are halves of one.
So shy shy shy(and with a).
Somewhere I have never travelled,gladly beyond.
This little bride & groom are.
This mind made war.
What freedom's not some under's mere above.
Dickinson. Perception of an object costs.
Tint I cannot take—is best, The.
Doolittle. If you take the moon in your hands.
Duncan. First Invention on the Theme of the Adam.
"Dylan." John Wesley Harding (Liner Notes).
Tangled Up in Blue.
Emerson. Astræa.
Heartily heartily / Nothing be false.
High heart, O Hafiz! though not thine.
I live among ideal men.
Memory.
Motto to "Illusions."
No song so tuneful, quoth the fox.
Seyd planted where the deluge ploughed.
Fenton. Terminal Moraine, A.
This Octopus Exploits Women.
Wild Ones[, The].
Ferlinghetti. Poet as Fisherman.
Fisher. Eye ascending / is gone up, The.
Idea of defence, The.
Red and the Black, The.
Sliding the tongue-leaved.
World / arranged in zones, A.
Ford. Break up conventional.
Impossibility of Dying in Your Arms Does Not Sadden Me, The.
Fox. Almagest, Last Letter to Zakarias.
Angel of Death, The.
Fata Morgana.
Gallagher. Accomplishment.
Gardner. Conversation at Midnight with Oscar Williams.
Who Spilled the Salt?
Garrigue. Maimed Grasshopper Speaks Up, The.
Ginsberg. Guru.
I learned a world from each.
Land O'Lakes, Wisconsin: Vajrayana Seminary.
Marijuana Notation.
Terms in Which I Think of Reality, The.
Who.
Graves. In Perspective.
Like Owls.
Utter Rim, The.
Griffiths. Belonging.
Hardy. Alike and Unlike.
House of Silence, The.
In Her Precincts.
Prophetess, The.
Protean Maiden, The.
Seven Times, The.
So Various.
Week, A.
Winsome Woman, A.
Hewitt. Glen of Light, The.
Touch of Things, The.
Hoffman. In Provence.
Hugo. Distances.
Jarrell. Jamestown.
Orient Express, The.
Picture in the Paper, A.
Seele im Raum.
When you and I were all.
Joseph. Descartes—You There?
Lady.
Kipling. Conundrum of the Workshops, The.
Looking Glass, The.
Story of Ung, The.
Two-Sided Man, The.
We and They.
Knott. Feeding the Sun.
Koch. On Beauty.
Kunitz. Organic Bloom.

Levertov. Letter to William Kinter of
  Muhlenberg, A.
Lewis. *Country Gentleman, The.*
He sees the dawn expanding from a seashell.
Poet, The.
Sensual mind in the wreaths of wine, The.
Shadows.
Liddy. Blue Mountain.
"MacDiarmid." Everlasting layers / Of ideas,
  images, feelings.
McGrath. Proverbs of the Middle World.
MacLeish. Seeing.
Markson. Women's House of Detention.
Nemerov. Companions, The.
This is about the stillness in moving things.
Olson. Cross-Legged, the Spider and the Web.
Oppen. Not to reduce the thing to nothing.
Paley. Life.
Patchen. Always Another Viewpoint.
Piercy. In the Men's Room(s).
Raine. Angelus.
  Elementals, The.
  Message.
  Mirage, The.
  Shadow.
Ransom. Painted Head.
Rich. Can it be growing colder when I begin.
Rolfe. Casualty.
Rukeyser. Phaneron.
  Seeming, The.
  Shooting Gallery.
Schuyler. Freely Espousing.
  View, A.
Silverstein. Hector the Collector.
Smith, Patti. Easter.
  Translators.
Smith, Stevie. Not Waving but Drowning.
Snyder. Men ask the way to Cold Mountain.
  Nooksack Valley.
  Through the Smoke Hole.
  When men see Han-Shan.
Sorrentino. Meeting, The.
Stevens. Bouquet of Roses in Sunlight.
  Idea of Order at Key West, The.
  Lack of Repose, The.
  Snow Man, The.
  Thinking of a Relation between the Images of
    Metaphors.
  Thirteen Ways of Looking at a Blackbird.
  What We See Is What We Think.
  Woman Looking at a Vase of Flowers.
Stevenson. Foreign Children.
Tomlinson. Appearance.
  Gap, The.
  Greeting, The.
  Reflections.
  Variant on a Scrap of Conversation.
Turco. Pocoangelini 7 ("Sir. Your Head. It is
  stuck into the sand").
Updike. Revelation.
Van Duyn. Spell of Conjunctivitis, A.
Walcott. Map of Europe, A.
Waldman. I Digress..
Whitman. Of the Terrible Doubt of
  Appearances.
  Song of the Rolling Earth, A.
Whittier. Hill-Top, The.
  Star of Bethlehem, The.
Williams, Charles Kenneth. It's over now. I
  watch.
Williams, Miller. Little Poem, A.
Williams, William Carlos. Flattery.
  Men, The.
  New Clouds, The.
  Shadows.
  Short Poem.
Wordsworth. Fish-Women.—On Landing at
  Calais.
  Glad Sight Wherever New with Old.
  Hint from the Mountains for Certain Political
    Pretenders.
  Morning Exercise, A.
  Ode to Lycoris.
  To ———: "Let other bards of angels sing."
  To a Painter ("All praise the Likeness by thy
    skill portrayed").
  To a Painter ("Though I beheld at first with

blank surprise").
  Yarrow Visited [September, 1814].
Wright, Charles. Cryopexy.
  Dead Color.
  Yard Journal.
Yeats. Nativity, A.
Young. Drawing.
  How the Rainbow Works.
  Process.
  Still Lives.
Zukofsky. Home for Aged Bomb Throwers—
  U.S.S.R.
  Suffenus is, stay Varus,—whom you've
    proven—is the.

Percy, Sir Henry
Kipling. English Way, The.

Perfection
Betjeman. Planster's Vision, The.
Carruth. Excellence requires / leaf-rakers to
  sweep one spot.
  Woman, The.
Cowper. R.S.S.
Creeley. Sign.
Cummings. I / never / guessed any /
  thing(even a).
Dickey, William. Androids.
Donne. Negative Love.
Eberhart. In a Hard Intellectual Light.
  Meditation, A.
  Memory.
  Noble Man, The.
  Orchard, The.
Fox. To the Man Who Watches Spiders.
Graves. Judges, The.
  Those Who Came Short.
Herrick. God ("In God there's nothing, but 'tis
  known to be").
  Gods Grace.
  His Request to Julia.
Hughes, Ted. Bride and Groom Lie Hidden
  for Three Days.
Kunitz. Single Vision.
Lawrence. Only the Best Matters.
Lowry. Sun was almost shining, The.
Meinke. Hôtel Lion d'Or.
Merton. Apologies.
  Empty Boat, The.
  Perfect act is empty. Who can see it?, The.
  Perfect Joy.
Millay. Inert Perfection.
Oliver. Buck Moon—From the Field Guide to
  Insects.
  Ponds, The.
Olson. As the Dead Prey upon Us.
Paley. She did good. She stood up like a.
Raine. Statues.
Rossetti. Love and Hope.
  Thou Art Fairer Than the Children of Men.
Silverstein. My Rules.
Stevens. Asides on the Oboe.
  Poems of Our Climate, The.
Stevenson. Had I the power that have the will.
Tomlinson. Images of Perfection.
  Parsnips.
  Perfection, The.
  Rhymes.
Walker. Perfection.
Yeats. Before the World Was Made.
  Old Tom Again.

Perfumes
Cowper. Lines after the Manner of Homer.
Donne. Perfume, The.
Ford. Trees with white perfumed.
Herrick. Another on Her.
  Love Perfumes All Parts.
  On a Perfum'd Lady.
  Pomander Bracelet, The.
  To His Mistresses.
  Upon Julia's Unlacing Her Self.

Perplexity
Creeley. Echo.
  For No Clear Reason.
  Form of Adaptation, A.
  Lady in Black.
  Rain (2) ("Thoughtful of you, I was /
    anticipating change in").
  Still.

  Trees.
  Wanting You.
Gunn. Birthday Poem.
Liddy. Donn na Duimche.
  Poem for My Sister Nora, at the Reading.

Persecution
"Carroll, Lewis." Mouse's Tale, The.
Cohen. Lovers.
Cooper. And here is that part of my dream I
  would like to forget.
Donne. Confessors, The.
"Dylan." Groom's Still Waiting at the Altar,
  The.
  Neighborhood Bully.
  Talkin' John Birch Paranoid Blues.
Fox. Johannes Kepler (1571–1630).
Hayden. From the Corpse Woodpiles, from the
  Ashes.
Hewitt. In This Year of Grace.
Kunitz. Next to Last Things.
  To a Slave Named Job.
Longfellow. Jewish Cemetery at Newport,
  The.
  Proclamation, The.
MacNeice. Turf-Stacks.
  Visit to Rouen.
Snodgrass. Adolf Hitler ("More than fifty
  millions. More").
  HEINRICH•HIMMLER•REICHSFUEHRER•SS
  —8•APRIL•1945•.
Warren. Elijah on Mount Carmel.
Whittier. Banished from Massachusetts.
  Barclay of Ury.
  Exiles, The.
  How the Women Went from Dover.
  King's Missive, The.
  Witch of Wenham, The.

Persephone
Atwood. Letter from Persephone.
Browning, Elizabeth Barrett. Psyche and
  Proserpine.
Campion. Umbra.
Creeley. Kore.
Glück. Pomegranate.
Graves. Food of the Dead.
Joseph. Persephone Returns.
Lawrence. Purple Anemones.
Meredith. Now the meadows with crocus
  besprent.
Smith, Stevie. Persephone.
Spenser. Garden of Proserpina, The.
Williams, William Carlos. Misericordia.

Perseus
Hayden. Perseus.
Hill. Slime; the residues of refined tears.
MacNeice. Perseus.
Plath. Perseus.

Perseverance
Atwood. Beyond truth, / tenacity: of those.
  Orpheus (2).
Beatles. I'll Get You.
Bukowski. History of a Tough Motherfucker,
  The.
Burns. I dream'd I lay where flowers were
  springing.
  O, for Ane-and-Twenty Tam.
  Though fickle fortune has deceiv'd me.
Campion. Turn all thy thoughts to eyes.
Carew. Eternity of Love Protested.
"Carroll, Lewis." Canto VI: Dyscomfyture.
Carruth. Because in the heart / of darkness I
  could not see.
  Well, beat on, beat on.
Ciardi. Lung Fish, The.
Clark. As the Human Village Prepares for Its
  Fate.
  Dark Continent.
  "Like Musical Instruments.."
Clough. Say not the struggle nought [*or
  naught*] availeth.
Cooper. He came all this way.
Creeley. Circle.
  Gesture, The.
  Marriage, A.
  Oh No.
  You.
Cullen. Thorn Forever in the Breast, A.

Dunbar. Joggin' Erlong.
Dunn. All That We Have.
Competition.
"Dylan." Baby, I'm in the Mood for You.
Pressing On.
Eliot. East Coker.
Little Gidding.
Emerson. Artist.
Cloud upon cloud / Clouds after rain.
Love.
Skeptic, The.
Suum Cuique ("Rain has spoiled the farmer's day, The").
Garrigue. Bad Times Song.
For Anybody's Martyr's Song.
Hardy. Why Do I?
Herbert. Employment (2).
Pilgrimage, The.
Herrick. End, The.
Perseverance.
Purposes.
Hesketh. Betterwear Man, The.
Hewitt. Ars Poetica.
Brothers, The.
Colony, The.
Last Call, The.
My Great-Grandfather's Refusal.
Vers Libre.
Hopkins. Il Mystico.
Jarrell. Knight, Death, and the Devil, The.
Joseph. Beyond Descartes.
But they could do something about that.
Inverts.
Letter to comfort a friend.
Man as Real (CITY; HUMAN).
Stay close, little tortoise, dig in.
This day our daily..
Kipling. Last Lap, The.
Old Men, The.
Larkin. Continuing to Live.
Lawrence. To Let Go Or to Hold on—?
Liddy. Death of Artists, The.
Lindsay. Babylon, Babylon, Babylon the Great.
Longfellow. Psalm of Life, A.
Lovelace. Apostasy of One and But One Lady, The.
McGrath. Woodcut.
Matthews. Why We Are Truly a Nation.
Meredith. Ah for that time when open daylight pours.
Eastward of Paris morn is high.
From labours through the night, outworn.
Hilda's Morning and Evening Dose of Rhyme.
Lady C. M., The.
Last Wandering of Poor Willie, The.
On her lost arm love bade her look.
She shall rise worthier of her prototype.
She snatched at heaven's flame of old.
Song: "Should thy love die; / O bury it not under ice-blue eyes!"
Teaching of the Blows of Fortune, The.
Wilding little stubble flower, A.
Moore. Nevertheless.
Olson. Adamo Me.
Gloss, A.
Return, The.
Story of an Olson, and Bad Thing, The.
Oppen. Also he has set the world.
From Disaster.
Paley. On certain days I am not in love.
Piercy. Phyllis Wounded.
To Be of Use.
Rich. Can it be growing colder when I begin.
For a Sister.
Rolfe. Communists.
Guerrillas, The.
Sandburg. Beat, Old Heart.
Upstream.
Schwartz. Maxims of Sisyphus, The.
"O New York boy, this is Life, Life in which."
Poem: How Marvelous Man's Kind Is.
Sexton. Live.
Smith, Charlotte. Apostrophe to an Old Tree.
Heath, The.
Hymn to Love and Life.

Sorrentino. Evening News, The.
Stafford. My Mother Was a Soldier.
Stevenson. As Daniel, bird-alone, in that far land.
Tennyson. Ulysses.
Whitman. Noiseless Patient Spider.
To You ("Whoever you are, I fear you are walking the walks of dreams").
Williams, Charles Kenneth. Resentment.
War.
Williams, William Carlos. Agony Among the Crowd, The.
Pink Locust, The.
Problem, The.
Wordsworth. When Haughty Expectations Prostrate Lie.

Persia. see **Iran and Iranians.**

Persian Wars (500 B.C.–449 B.C.)
Graves. Persian Version, The.

Persians
Dickey, William. Love among the Manichees.
Emerson. Shah Sandschar, whose lowest slave.
Who gave thy cheek the mixed tint.
Graves. Persian Version, The.
Lindsay. Rhyme for All Zionists, A.
Patchen. Empire of Persia, The.
Williams, Charles Kenneth. Allies: According to Herodotus.

Persimmon Trees
Snyder. Persimmons, The.

Peru
Patchen. Unnatural History of Peru, The.

Pessimism
Auden. "O where are you going?" said reader to rider.
Berg. Crutches.
Soul, The.
Carruth. On Being Asked to Write a Poem Against the War in Vietnam.
Sonnet: "At the hospital where I had the echocardiagram."
Ceravolo. Cross Fire.
Creeley. Business, The.
Changes, The.
I Am Held by My Fear of Death.
Turn, The.
Wall, A.
Cullen. For a Pessimist.
Dickinson. His little Hearse like Figure.
Dunbar. What's the Use.
Dunn. Bad Angels, The.
Emerson. See & hear the fraud, the malice of the change of fortune.
Gallagher. Boat Ride.
Hardy. Epitaph on a Pessimist.
Lorde. Conclusion.
Lowell. Waking Early Sunday Morning.
MacNeice. Aubade: "Having bitten on life like a sharp apple."
Canto XXIII: "December continues mild. The rose garden."
Meredith. I Chafe at Darkness.
Not solely that the Future she destroys.
Nash. No Woe Is Gossamer to Mr. Bessemer.
When You Say That, Smile! or All Right Then, Don't Smile.
Rexroth. August 22, 1939.
Rich. Ghost of a Chance.
Smith, Stevie. Lot's Wife.
Snodgrass. Diplomacy: The Father.
Warren. Letter about Money, Love, or Other Comfort, If Any.
Zukofsky. And Without.

Peter, Saint
Browning, Elizabeth Barrett. Look, The.
Meaning of the Look, The.
Two Sayings, The.
View Across the Roman Campagna.
Crashaw. Act 5; Sicke Implore St. Peter's Shadow, The.
On St. Peter Casting Away His Nets at Our Saviours Call.
On Saint Peter Cutting of Malchus His Eare.
"Dylan." I'd Hate to Be You on That Dreadful Day.
Hardy. In the Servants' Quarters.

Herrick. Peter-penny, The.
Merton. House of Caiphas, The.
Rossetti. I followed Thee, my God, I followed Thee / To see the end.
St. Peter.
St. Peter once: "Lord, dost Thou wash my feet?"
Vigil of St. Peter.
Smart. St. Peter.
Southwell. Author to the Reader, The ("Deare eye, that daynest to let fall a looke").
Wilbur. Peter.

Peterloo Massacre (1819)
Shelley. Song to the Men of England.

Petra, Jordan
Whittier. "Rock" in El Ghor, The.

Petrarch (Francesco Petrarca)
Berryman. Swarthy when young; who took the tonsure; sign.
Chaucer. Clerk's Prologue, The.
Lowry. Thing to know is how to write a verse, The.

Petrels
Whitman. To the Man-of-War Bird.

Pets
Cowper. Epitaph on a Hare.
Epitaphium Alterum.
On Mrs. Throckmorton's Bulfinch.
Retired Cat, The.
Creeley. If You.
Dickey, William. Chickens in San Francisco.
Gunn. Her Pet.
Hardy. Last Words to a Dumb Friend.
Herrick. Upon His Spaniel[l] Tracie [or Tracy].
Upon Mudge.
Upon the Death of His Sparrow; an Elegie.
Hewitt. Pet Shop, The.
Larkin. Take One Home for the Kiddies.
MacNeice. Pet Shop.
Roethke. Meadow Mouse, The.
Rossetti. Dog lies in his kennel, The.
Word for the Dumb, A.
Sidney. Sonnet 83: "Good brother Philip, I have borne you long."
Silverstein. If I Had A Brontosaurus.
Smith, Stevie. Croft.
Heber.
Mrs. Blow and her Animals.
Shooting Incident, The.
Snyder. Nansen.
Spender. Boy, Cat, Canary.
Updike. Another Dog's Death.
Wilbur. Marché aux Oiseaux.
Williams, Charles Kenneth. My Fly.
Williams, Miller. Animals.
Yeats. Two Songs of a Fool.

Peyote
Carruth. Sorrow Song, The.

Phaeton
Meredith. Phaéthôn.

Phantoms
De la Mare. Captive, The.
Reverie.
Which?
Graves. Sea Horse, The.
Jong. Man under the Bed, The.
Meredith. Phantasy.

Pheasants
Ammons. Down Low.
Cowper. Thanks for a Gift of Pheasants.
Creeley. Happy love, this.
Eberhart. I Walked Out to the Graveyard to See the Dead.
Plath. Pheasant.
Pope. See! from the brake the whirring Pheasant springs.

Philadelphia, Pennsylvania
Kipling. Philadelphia.
Tomlinson. Garland for Thomas Eakins, A.
Whittier. Pennsylvania Hall.
Relic, The.

Philanthropy and Philanthropists
Meredith. Angela Burdett-Coutts.
Whitman. Outlines for a Tomb.

See also **Charity.**

Philippines
Kipling.   White Man's Burden, The.

Philistines
Hesketh.   Reply to a Philistine.
Pound.   Les Millwin.

Philodendrons
Ammons.   Night Post.

Philomela
Herrick.   Charon and Phylomel, a Dialogue Sung.
Ransom.   Philomela.
Wordsworth.   Translation of Virgil's Georgic IV. 511–15.

Philosophy and Philosophers
Auden.   Voltaire at Ferney.
Blake.   Mock On, Mock On, Voltaire, Rousseau.
Bly.   Meditation on Philosophy, A.
Burns.   Letter to J———s T———t, Gl—nc———r.
Carruth.   Sonnet: "In the mind of the kiss occurs a thought so rich."
Survival as Tao, Beginning at 5:00 A.M.
Chaucer.   Consolation of Philosophy, The ("De Consolacione Philosophie").
Clough.   Away, haunt not thou me.
Look you, my simple friend, 'tis one of those.
Coleridge.   Drinking versus Thinking.
Philosophical Trinity, A.
Cowper.   Philosopher and the King, The.
Cummings.   Will out of the kindness of their hearts a few philosophers tell me.
Dobyns.   General and the Tango Singer, The.
Eberhart.   Great Principles Are Thrown Down by Time.
Emerson.   It takes a philosopher or fool.
Philosophers are lined with eyes within.
Graves.   Nothing.
Hardy.   Drinking Song.
Our Old Friend Dualism.
Hesketh.   Child's Guide to Philosophy, A.
Credo.
Hoffman.   Natural Philosopher, A.
Holmes.   Doctor Trustus: Man of Good Will.
Jarrell.   Charles Dodgson's Song.
Zeno.
Jeffers.   Great Men.
What's the best life for a man?
Lowry.   In Cape Code with Conrad Aiken.
"MacDiarmid."   To My Friend the Late Beatrice Hastings.
MacNeice.   Canto XIX: "All out!" the voices cry in the Park, "All out!"
Melville.   Fragments of a Lost Gnostic Poem of the Twelfth [or 12th] Century.
Meredith.   Garden of Epicurus, The.
Merton.   Legacy of Herakleitos, The.
Logos Our Teacher, The.
Origen.
Philosophers, The.
Song for the Death of Averroës.
Milton.   Philosopher on His Way to His Death Suddenly Sent This Message to a Certain King Who Had Unawares Condemned Him, Unrecognized and Innocent, When He Was Seized by Chance Among Criminals, A.
Nemerov.   Epitaph on a Philosopher the Reports of Whose Death Have Been Grossly Minimized.
Philosophy.
Two Views of a Philosopher.
Patchen.   Shapes and Intensities of This Man, This Confucius, The.
Robinson.   Captain Craig.
Rolfe.   Credo.
Sandburg.   Lovable Babblers.
Two Neighbors.
Schuyler.   Bleeding Gums.
Unlike Joubert.
Scott.   Thorsgill.
Simic.   Madonnas Touched Up with a Goatee.
Smith, Stevie.   Distractions and the Human Crowd.
On the Death of a German Philosopher.
Stevens.   To an Old Philosopher in Rome.
Tomlinson.   In Defence of Metaphysics.

Lacunae.
Machiavelli in Exile.
Whitman.   Base of All Metaphysics, The.
Roaming in Thought.
Whittier.   Follen.
To ———: "Maiden! with the fair brown tresses."
Wordsworth.   To the Utilitarians.
Zukofsky.   Song—3/4 time.

Phoebus Apollo. see **Apollo.**

Phoenix
Atwood.   Eating Fire.
Carruth.   Fact of the Matter, The.
Cullen.   That Bright Chimeric Beast.
Dickinson.   I knew a Bird that would sing as firm.
Emerson.   Phoenix, The.
Hughes, Ted.   And the Phoenix Has Come.
Jonson.   Phoenix Analysed, The.
Lawrence.   Phoenix.
Merrill.   About the Phoenix.
Merton.   Owl and Phoenix.
Nash.   Phœnix, The.
Nemerov.   Phoenix, The.
Raine.   Traveller, The.
Sarton.   Phoenix, The.
Spenser.   I saw a phoenix in the wood alone.
I saw the bird that can the sun endure.

Photography and Photographers
Atwood.   Daguerreotype Taken in Old Age.
This Is a Photograph of Me.
Auden.   I Am Not a Camera.
Beckett.   Rue de Vaugirard.
Berg.   Bread.
Lightbulb.
Talking.
Visit, The.
Bukowski.   Photographs.
"Carroll, Lewis."   Double Acrostic: I sing a place wherein agree.
Hiawatha's Photographing.
Ciardi.   Bridal Photo, 1906.
On a Photo of Sgt. Ciardi a Year Later.
Thanks to a Botanist, A.
Cohen.   Photograph, The.
Creeley.   Chance, The.
Dickinson.   Picture of the pretty Home, The.
Dobyns.   Living Room, The.
Dunbar.   Photograph, The.
Dunn.   Photograph Album, The.
Photograph in the Hallway, The.
Split: 1962.
Ferlinghetti.   Photo of Emily, The.
Gallagher.   Time Lapse with Tulips.
Galvin.   Photo of Miners, A.
Glück.   Pictures of the People in the War.
Still Life.
Griffiths.   Spanish Providence, A.
Gunn.   Song of a Camera.
Hall.   Photographs of China.
Hewitt.   Collector's Choice.
Hughes, Ted.   Six Young Men.
Hugo.   Iowa Déjà Vu.
Old Scene.
Snapshot of 15th S.W., A.
Snapshot of the Auxiliary, A.
Larkin.   Lines on a Young Lady's Photograph Album.
Lowry.   Betty and Gerald Noxon.
McAuley.   Photographer's Model, The.
Mahon.   Old Snaps, The.
Matthews.   Nabokov's Blues.
Photo of the Author with a Favorite Pig.
Portrait, The.
Melville.   On the Photograph of Corps Commander.
Merrill.   David's Night in Veliès.
Nemerov.   Old Photograph, An.
Photograph of a Girl, The.
Picture, A.
Olson.   There they were.
Oppen.   From a Photograph.
Paley.   In San Salvador (I).
Rich.   Photograph of the Unmade Bed, The.
St. John.   Hotel Sierra.
My Tea with Madame Descartes.
Schuyler.   Shaker.

Schwartz.   Poem: "You, my photographer, you, most aware."
Simic.   Baby Pictures of Famous Dictators.
Smith, Stevie.   Photograph, The.
Sorrentino.   Hit Album, A.
Spender.   Photograph, The.
Stafford.   Archival Print, An.
Stuart.   Opposite Field, The.
Rescue.
Water's Fine, I'm Fine, The.
Sutter.   Hoarfrost and Fog.
Lost in Antarctica.
Turco.   Photograph, The.
Updike.   Camera.
Exposure.
Little Poems.
Snapshots.
Van Duyn.   Photographs.
Wakoski.   Photos, The.
Wilbur.   Looking into History.
Williams, Charles Kenneth.   Floor.
Williams, Miller.   Newspaper Picture of Spectators at a Hotel Fire, A.
Story, The.
Williams, William Carlos.   View by Color Photography on a Commercial Calendar.
Wright, Charles.   Looking at Pictures.
Yau.   Picture Book.
Postcards are fragments of an encyclopedia; and typical of one an- / nouncing.
Return of the Hunters, The.
Sheets dangling from the line, The.

See also **Cameras.**

Physicians
Auden.   Art of Healing, The.
Give me a doctor, partridge-plump.
Boyle.   December 1989.
Browning, Robert.   Artemis Prologizes.
Classicality Applied to Tea-Dealing: A Fancy Inspired by Westbourne Grove.
Doctor———.
Epistle Containing the Strange Medical Experience of Karshish, the Arab Physician, An.
You are sick, that's sure—they say.
Bukowski.   Stethoscope Case, A.
Burns.   Death and Doctor Hornbook [A True Story].
To Dr Maxwell, on Miss Jessy Staig's Recovery.
Cooper.   After Fever.
Crane.   Havana Rose.
Crashaw.   On Taking Physicke.
De la Mare.   Of a Son.
Dunbar.   To Dan.
Herrick.   Physitians.
Upon a Physitian.
Hewitt.   Doctor's Bag, The.
Hughes, Langston.   Interne at Provident.
Johnson.   On the Death of Dr [or Mr] Robert Levet [a Practiser in Physic].
Jonson.   Had old Hippocrates, or Galen.
To Doctor Empiric[k].
Kipling.   Doctors.
Lawrence.   Scientific Doctor, The.
Lowry.   Thou was not born for death, immortal Duck.
Nash.   Cousin Euphemia Knows Best, or, Physician, Heal Somebody Else.
Paley.   Every day he went out, forsaking.
Plath.   Surgeon at 2 A.M., The.
Rukeyser.   Arthur Peyton.
Sexton.   Doctor of the Heart, The.
Doctors.
Surgeon, The.
Smith, Stevie.   Doctor, The.
Stevenson.   To W.E. Henley.
Swift.   To Dr. Helsham.
To Dr. Sheridan.
Whittier.   Healer, The.
Williams, William Carlos.   Cold Front, A.
Complaint.
Le Médecin Malgré Lui.
Poor, The.
To Close.
Young Love.

See also **Hospitals; Medicine; Nurses.**

Physics and Physicists
Auden. After Reading a Child's Guide to Modern Physics.
Eberhart. Quanta.
Lawrence. Relativity.
Pack. Clayfeld Among the Quarks.
Reversing.
Tomlinson. On the Principle of Blowclocks.
Updike. Cosmic Gall.
Mobile of Birds.
News from the Underworld.

Pianos
Bukowski. Chopin Bukowski.
Dickey, James. From Time.
Frost. Investment, The.
Gardner. Music Room, The.
Hardy. Duettist to her Pianoforte, A.
Hartley. Concert.
Hewitt. Music Lessons.
Lawrence. Piano.
Piano, The.
Meinke. Minuet in G.
Nash. Piano Tuner, Untune Me That Tune.
Oppen. O withering seas.
Rukeyser. Gradus ad Parnassum.
Sandburg. Chords.
Stevens. Mozart, 1935.
Two Tales of Liadoff.
Stevenson. Early in the morning I hear on your piano.
Updike. Player Piano.
Wakoski. Joyce Carol Oates Plays the Saturn Piano.

Picasso, Pablo
Cooper. In a Room with Picassos.
Cummings. Picasso / you give us Things.
Smith, Patti. Picasso Laughing.
Williams, William Carlos. Genius, The.

Picnics and Barbecues
Betjeman. Archaeological Picnic, The.
Creeley. Souvenir, The.
"Dylan." Talking Bear Mountain Picnic Massacre Blues.
Fox. At the Edge of the Suburbs.
Hardy. Where the Picnic Was.
Hewitt. Portstewart, July 1914.
Matthews. Visionary Picnic, The.
Muldoon. Truce.
Plath. Whitsun.
Roethke. Thing, The.
Rossetti. Mr. and Mrs. Scott, and I.
Schuyler. Picnic Cantata, A.
Tennyson. Audley Court.
Wilbur. Terrace, The.
Williams, Charles Kenneth. Holiday: / every / yard or, A.

Piero della Francesca
Hartley. Rembrandt—Rouault—Piero.
Sarton. Nativity.

Pies
Dunbar. Reluctance.
"Dylan." Country Pie.

Piety
Byron. Queries to Casuists.
Chaucer. Chaucer's Retraction.
Friar's Tale, The.
Man of Law's Tale, The.
Parson's Prologue, The.
Parson's Tale, The.
Prioress's Tale, The.
Second Nun's Prologue, The.
Second Nun's Tale, The.
Coleridge. Lines Suggested by the Last Words of Berengarius.
Crashaw. Acts 21; I Am Ready Not Onely To Be Bound but To Dye.
Epitaph upon Mr. Ashton, a Conformable Citizen, An.
In Amorem Divinum.
It Is Better To Go into Heaven with One Eye.
Luke 7; She Began To Wash His Feet with Teares and Wipe Them with the Haires of Her Head.
On St. *Peter* Casting Away His Nets at Our Saviours Call.
Recommendation, The.

Donne. From needing danger, to be[e] good.
Hymn [*or* Hymne] to Christ, at the Author's Last Going into Germany, A.
If faithful soul[e]s be alike glorified [*or* glorifi'd].
Oh, to vex me, contraries [*or* conraryes] meet in one.
Glück. Jeanne d'Arc.
Herrick. Another, to His Saviour.
Chewing [of] the Cud, The.
Gods Commands.
His Offering, with the Rest, at the Sepulcher.
To God, His Gift.
To Keep a True Lent.
Hewitt. Nettles of Offence.
Novice, The.
Lowry. Those Coke to Newcastle Blues.
Meredith. Certain People, A.
Milton. Blest is the man who hath not walk'd astray.
Psalms. Psalm 1: "Blessed is the man that walketh.."
Psalm 119: "Blessed are the undefiled in the way."
Rossetti. St. Elizabeth of Hungary.
Smith, Stevie. Unpopular, Lonely and Loving.

Pigeons
Ammons. Filling in the Dots.
Bishop. Paris, 7 A.M.
Cohen. Event, The.
Eberhart. Incidence of Flight.
Fox. Night and Day.
Hartley. Ladies and the Pigeons, The.
Jeffers. Passenger Pigeons.
Kooser. Five P.M.
Larkin. Pigeons.
Nash. Squab, The.
Rossetti. 4th May Morning.
Sandburg. Pigeon.
Timber Wings.
Understandings in Blue.
Zukofsky. Madrigal for 3 Voices, A.

Pigs
Atwood. Pig Song.
Berry. For the Hog Killing.
"Carroll, Lewis." Pig-Tale, The.
Cowper. Love of the World Reproved, The.
Dobyns. White Pig.
Gunn. Moly.
Hall. Eating the Pig.
Herrick. Upon Spokes.
Hughes, Ted. View of a Pig.
Kinnell. Saint Francis and the Sow.
Kipling. Dark children of the mere and marsh.
Lawrence. Food of the North.
Levine. Animals Are Passing from Our Lives.
L'Homme et La Bête.
Lowry. Pigs—For T.H.
Matthews. Photo of the Author with a Favorite Pig.
Nash. Pig, The.
Plath. Sow.
Rolfe. Ballad: "What are we having for dinner tonight?"
Rossetti. If a pig wore a wig, / What could we say?
Sexton. Hog.
Hutch.
Silverstein. Wild Boar.
Snyder. Mother of the Buddhas, Queen of Heaven, Mother of the Sun; Marici, Goddess of the Dawn.
Warren. Go it, Granny—Go it, Hog!
Williams, Miller. One of the Crowd on the Shore Tells How It Was.
Williams, William Carlos. To a Mexican Pig-Bank.

Pike (fish)
Hughes, Ted. Pike.

Pike's Peak
Schuyler. Money Musk.

Pilgrim Fathers
Emerson. Boston Hymn.
Longfellow. Courtship of Miles Standish, The.
Muldoon. Promises, Promises.
Whittier. Banished from Massachusetts.

John Underhill.
Mayflowers, The.

Pilgrimages and Pilgrims
Arnold. Resignation.
Berry. Springs, The.
Chaucer. Canterbury Tales, The.
General Prologue, The.
Cummings. Chaucer.
De la Mare. Decoy, The.
Fisher. Pilgrim disposition—, The.
Hall. Woolworth's.
Herrick. To His Brother Nicolas Herrick.
Lowry. Pilgrim passes through the town by night, A.
Melville. Sketch, A.
Merton. Mecca.
Pilgrims' Song.
Prince. His Dog and Pilgrim.
Rossetti. After This the Judgement.
Uphill [*or* Up-Hill].
Scott. Lords Strand of Northumberland, The.
Spender. Marston.
Whittier. Summer Pilgrimage, A.
Yeats. Pilgrim, The.

Pilots
Beckett. Zone.
Dickey, James. Patience: In the Mill.
Doolittle. R.A.F.
Hall. Man in the Dead Machine, The.
Jarrell. Pilot from the Carrier, A.
Kipling. Hymn of the Triumphant Airman.
R.A.F. (Aged Eighteen).
Matthews. Black Box.
Merton. Comedy Card for a Serious Case.
Pack. Black Hole, The.
Robinson. Pilot, The.
Sandburg. To Beachey, 1912.
Smith, Patti. Amelia Earhart.

See also **Air Warfare.**

Pindar
Duncan. Poem Beginning with a Line by Pindar, A.
MacNeice. Pindar is Dead.
Smart. To Antonius Julus, the Son of Mark Antony, of the Triumvirate.

Pine Island, Minnesota
Wright, James. Lying in a Hammock at William Duffy's Farm in Pine Island, Minnesota.

Pine Trees
Ammons. Recording.
Carruth. Snow's downstrokes climb softly up the conifer.
Cooper. Feathers.
Eberhart. Evaluation Under a Pine Tree, Lying On Pine Needles, An.
Old Tree by the Penobscot.
White Pines, Felled 1984.
Emerson. I sat upon the ground.
Nature in Leasts.
Galvin. Pitch Pines.
Muldoon. Yggdrasil.
Plath. Black Pine Tree in an Orange Light.
Sidney. Do not disdain, O straight upraised pine.
You goodly pines, which still with brave ascent.
Smith, Stevie. Now Pine-Needles.
Snyder. Foxtail Pine.
January.
KuLOWSCARONiwoqqóbī.
Lodgepole / cone/seed waits for fire.
Lodgepole Pine: the wonderful reproductive.
Pines, under pines.
Warren. Return: An Elegy, The.
Wordsworth. Pine of Monte Mario at Rome, The.

Ping-pong
Meinke. Ping-Pong.

Pioneers
Atwood. Progressive Insanities of a Pioneer.
Eberhart. Statue of Liberty.
Emerson. Forerunners.
Fletcher. Burning Mountain, The.
Haines. There Are No Such Trees in Alpine, California.

Hesketh.   He Saved Others..
Hugo.   Three Stops to Ten Sleep.
Kipling.   Lost Legion, The.
  Voortrekker, The.
McGrath.   Seekers, The.
  Underground, The.
MacLeish.   Fourth Book, The.
McNeill.   Gabriel MacElmain, Pioneer.
Olson.   April Today Main Street.
  Bigmans II.
  Some Good News.
Rich.   Face to Face.
  From an Old House in America.
Van Duyn.   That was in 1875, and we come
  through.
  That was in 1875, then we moved here.
Whitman.   Pioneers! O Pioneers!
Whittier.   Pass of the Sierra, The.
Williams, William Carlos.   Poem: "Daniel
  Boone, the father of Kentucky."

Pipers
Blake.   Piping Down the Valleys Wild.
Browning, Robert.   Pied Piper of Hamelin,
  The.
Silverstein.   One Who Stayed, The.
Stevenson.   Piper, The.

Piracy and Pirates
Frost.   Discovery of the Madeiras, The.
Kipling.   Rhyme of the Three Captains, The.
Morgan.   Pirate Poem.
Plath.   Bluebeard.
Silverstein.   Pirate Captain Jim.
Stevenson.   Pirate Story.

Pisa, Italy
Melville.   Pisa's Leaning Tower.
Shelley.   Evening: Ponte al Mare, Pisa.

Pitt, William
Burns.   On Mr. Pitt's [or Pit's] Hair-Powder
  Tax.
Coleridge.   Pitt.

Pittsburgh, Pennsylvania
"Reed."   Small Town.

Pity
Blake.   Terror in the house does roar.
Campion.   Good men, shew, if you can tell.
Carruth.   To her, to be her, that her hurt and
  wrong be mine.
Chaucer.   Complaint unto Pity, The.
  Introduction to the Pardoner's Tale.
Clark.   I'm on an Island.
Cohen.   You Tore Your Shirt.
Coleridge.   Addressed to a Young Man of
  Fortune.
  Dungeon, The.
  Love.
  To a Young Ass.
Cowper.   On Envy.
  Pity for Poor Africans.
Creeley.   In an Act of Pity.
  Variation, A.
De la Mare.   Blind Boy, The.
  Catechism, The.
Dickinson.   I cried at Pity—not at Pain.
  'Tis easier to pity those when dead.
Eberhart.   When Doris Danced.
Fisher.   Absolute / Pity / Advancing.
Fox.   Transvestite, The.
Garrigue.   False Country of the Zoo.
Graves.   Man of Evil.
  Pity.
Hall.   September Ode.
Hardy.   Her Dilemma.
Hartley.   Lost, Alone, The.
Herrick.   His Ejaculation to God.
  Pitie to the Prostrate.
Hewitt.   Blessing.
  How have I served you? I have let you waste.
  Lyric: "Let this last lyric of a passing day."
  Mister Faintheart Middleclass.
  Providence 3.
Hughes, Langston.   Lover's Return.
Keats.   I Cry Your Mercy, Pity, Love—Ay,
  Love!
Kinnell.   To a Child in Calcutta.
Kunitz.   Tutored Child, The.
Lovelace.   A La Bourbon.
  Ode To My Lady H.

Lowry.   But I shall live when you are dead
  and damned.
  Jokes Amidships.
  Jokes in the Galley.
  Jokes on the Poop.
  On board the Matsue Maru.
  Song: "Pity the blind and the halt but yet
  pity."
MacLeish.   Pity's Sake.
Markson.   Sister's Son.
Meredith.   They say, that Pity in Love's
  service dwells.
Millay.   Pity me not because the light of day.
Raine.   I used to watch you, sleeping.
Rolfe.   Are You Now or Have You Ever Been.
Rossetti.   Good Lord, today / I scarce find
  breath to say.
  Plague, The.
  Vanity of Vanities.
Schuyler.   Self-Pity Is a Kind of Lying, Too.
Shakespeare.   Sonnet 111: "O, for my sake do
  you with Fortune chide."
Shelley.   To Harriet ("Thy look of love has
  power to calm").
Sidney.   Sonnet 44: "My words I know do
  well set forth my mind."
  Sonnet 45: "Stella oft sees the very face of
  woe."
Smith, Stevie.   In the Park.
Sorrentino.   Nightpiece.
Spender.   Coward, The.
Stevenson.   To Mother Maryanne.
Wilbur.   Pity.
Williams, Charles Kenneth.   Beginning of
  April, The.
  Scar.
  Ten Below.
Wright, James.   American Twilights, 1957.
  At the Executed Murderer's Grave.
  Inscription for the Tank.
  Pretty Redhead, The.
  What the Earth Asked Me.
Wroth.   Song: "Beeing past the paines of
  love."
Yeats.   Pity of Love, The.

Pius IX, Pope
Whittier.   Dream of Pio Nono, The.
  From Perugia.
  To Pius IX.

Pius XII, Pope
Whittier.   Prisoners of Naples, The.

Pixies. see Fairies.

Pizza
Nash.   Pizza, The.

Place Names
Carruth.   I don't say you can't find him in
  New Hampshire.
  Well, I've said that Robert Frost had curiosity.
  West Bolton is due north of Bolton, East.
Hartley.   Fantasy and phantom—.
Hopkins.   Bellisle! that is a fabling name, but
  we.
Merton.   Place Names.
Sandburg.   Localities.

Plague
Dove.   Fiammetta Breaks Her Peace.
Melville.   In the Desert.
Moore.   Animals Sick of the Plague, The.
Rossetti.   Plague, The.

Plains. see Prairies.

Planets
Bogan.   At a Party.
Carruth.   Introspectional.
Frost.   A-Wishing Well.
Jeffers.   Moon and Five Planets.
"MacDiarmid."   Bonnie Broukit Bairn, The.
Rexroth.   On What Planet.
Sandburg.   Bright Conversation with Saint-Ex.
Sorrentino.   Lost in the Stars.
Updike.   Exposé.
Whitman.   After an Interval.

Plants
Berg.   Wife Talks to Herself, A.
Berry.   April Woods: Morning.
  Broken Ground, The.
Burns.   On Chloris Requesting Me to Give Her
  a Spray of a Sloe-Thorn in Full Blossom.

Carruth.   Lichen is a hardy plant.
Cowper.   On a Plant of Virgin's Bower.
  Poet, the Oyster, and Sensitive Plant, The.
  Sonnet 3: "As on a rugged mountain at the
  darkening of evening."
De la Mare.   Miracle, The.
Dickinson.   Plants went into camp last night,
  The.
Eberhart.   Forms of the Human.
Emerson.   Spices in the plants that run.
Fox.   Aloe.
  She Used to Water the Plants.
Glück.   Tree House, The.
Gunn.   Mandrakes.
  Rooftop, The.
  Yellow Pitcher Plant.
Hardy.   At the Royal Academy.
Hesketh.   Tom Rich.
  Truant.
  Vine, The.
Hill.   Sorrel.
Hopkins.   From any hedgerow, any copse.
Johnson.   On a Lady's Presenting a Sprig of
  Myrtle to a Gentleman.
Jonson.   Garland [or Ghyrlond] of the Blessèd
  Virgin Mary [or Marie], The.
Joseph.   Summer Amnesty.
Kipling.   Veil them, cover them, wall them
  round.
Levertov.   For Floss.
Levine.   Later Still.
"MacDiarmid."   Bracken Hills in Autumn.
  Happy on Heimaey.
McNeill.   Garden Moment.
  Potherbs (Of the Edible Wild Plants My
  Granny Taught Me).
Meredith.   Song in the Songless.
Millay.   Hawkweed, The.
Milton.   Sonnet 3: "As on a rugged mountain
  at the darkening of evening."
Moore.   Nevertheless.
Muldoon.   Thrush.
Pack.   Bounty.
Piercy.   High Frequency.
Raine.   Vegetation.
Rich.   Corpse-Plant, The.
Roethke.   Cuttings ("Sticks-in-a-drowse droop
  over sugary loam").
  Cuttings ("This urge, wrestle, resurrection of
  dry sticks").
  Moss-Gathering.
  Root Cellar.
Rossetti.   Rushes in a watery place, / And
  reeds in a hollow.
Sandburg.   Aster, a farewell-summer flower,
  stays long in the last fall weeks, An.
Schuyler.   Blossoming Oakwood.
  Three Gardens.
  What Ails My Fern?
Sexton.   Love Plant, The.
Smart.   Country Squire and the Mandrake, The.
Smith, Charlotte.   Flora.
  To the Goddess of Botany.
Smith, Stevie.   Stroke, The.
Stevens.   Anecdote of Canna.
  Botanist on Alp (No. 1).
Stevenson.   To A Gardener.
Swinburne.   Sundew, The.
Wilbur.   Children of Darkness.
  Fern-Beds in Hampshire County.
  Seed Leaves.
Williams, William Carlos.   It Is a Small Plant.
Young.   Look Good, Smell Good, Feel.
See also Listings for specific Plants.

Plath, Sylvia
Ciardi.   Trying to Feel Something.
Jong.   In Sylvia Plath Country.
Knott.   Fear of Domesticity.
Sexton.   Sylvia's Death.
Updike.   Upon Looking into Sylvia Plath's
  Letters Home.
Wilbur.   Cottage Street, 1953.

Plato
Auden.   No, Plato, No.
Berg.   It Is.
Clough.   Uranus.

Cowper. On the Platonic Idea as Aristotle Understood It.
Dunn. Essay on the Personal.
Eberhart. Commitment, A.
Great Principles Are Thrown Down by Time.
Lawrence. For the Heroes Are Dipped in Scarlet.
Liddy. Lesbos.
Mahon. Death and the Sun.
Milton. On the Platonic Idea as Aristotle Understood It.
Prince. Plato says that in Heaven there is.
Raine. Afternoon sunlight plays.
Sidney. Sonnet 21: "Your words my friend (right healthful caustics) blame."
Yeats. His Bargain.
Statistics.
What Then?

Platonic Love
Ceravolo. Cool Breeze.
Lighthouse.
Eberhart. Hand, The.
Koertge. Ubiquity of the Need for Love, The.
Lowry. Dream of the Departing Soldier.
St. John. My Friend.
Sandburg. Little Word, Little White Bird.
Schuyler. Dear Joe.
Looking Forward to See Jane Real Soon.
Night, The.
Poem: "Your enchantment / enchants me, stretched."
Sky Eats Up the Trees, The.
Tomorrow.

Platypuses
Gunn. Mammal is with her young. She is unique, The.
Nash. Platypus, The.

Play
Angelou. Harlem Hopscotch.
Blake. Nurse's Song ("When the voices of children are heard on the green / And laughing is heard on the hill").
Carew. To the Reader of Master William Davenant's Play [*The Wits*].
Cowper. Impromptu ["So I have seen the maids in vain"].
Dickinson. It is easy to work when the soul is at play.
Eberhart. Wild Life and Tamed Life.
Everson. Spotfire.
Ginsberg. Bop Lyrics.
Gunn. Aquarium, The.
Cool Stream, The.
Hide and Seek.
Jack Straw sits.
Menace, The.
Seesaw.
Hartley. Diabolo.
Lawrence. Disagreeable Advice.
Man at Play on the River, A.
McAuley. Owen at Play.
Markson. Recitation before Bed.
Meinke. Minuet in G.
Meredith. Alternation.
And tho' my friar's mandate is severe.
I say, that but for black Foakes'-day.
Nemerov. Warning: Children at Play.
Ransom. Old Man Playing with Children.
Rossetti. Clever little Willie wee, / Bright eyed, blue eyed little fellow.
Frisky Lamb, A.
I caught a little ladybird / That flies far away.
Playing at bob cherry / Tom and Nell and Hugh.
Sandburg. Props.
Silverstein. Acrobats, The.
Simic. Game, The.
Smith, Stevie. I Like to Play with Him.
Snyder. Hop, Skip, and Jump.
Sorrentino. She whom no one ever found.
Stevenson. At the Seaside [*or* Sea-Side].
Behold, as goblins dark of mien.
Block City.
Dumb Soldier, The.
Hayloft, The.
Historical Associations.
Land of Counterpane, The.

Land of Story-Books, The.
Little Land, The.
My Treasures.
Pirate Story.
Wordsworth. Intent on Gathering Wool from Hedge and Brake.
Young. Squirrels.

Playhouses. *see* **Theater and Theaters.**
Playmates
Gunn. Seesaw.
Kipling. Playmate, The.
Mahon. Lost Girls, The.
Morrison. You Think I Don't Know.
Rossetti. Clever little Willie wee, / Bright eyed, blue eyed little fellow.
On the grassy banks / Lambkins at their pranks.
Playing at bob cherry / Tom and Nell and Hugh.
Silverstein. Tree House.
Stevenson. De Erotio Puella.
Gardener, The.
Home from the daisied meadows, where you linger yet.
Marching Song.
My Kingdom.
My Shadow.
Night and Day.
Poem for a Class Re-Union.
To Any Reader.
To Willie and Henrietta.
Unseen Playmate, The.
Stuart. Girl at Play.
Williams, Charles Kenneth. Gift, The.

Pleasure
Beatles. Please Please Me.
Berrigan. Many Happy Returns.
Peace.
Burns. Down the Burn Davie.
Greybeard, old wisdom, may boast of his treasures, The.
Here's, a bottle and an honest friend.
My bottle is a holy pool.
My Love She's But a Lassie Yet.
Sandy and Jockie.
Song: "I murder hate by field or flood."
Wisdom and Science—honor'd Powers!
Byron. Translation from Anacreon.
Campion. Stars Dance, The.
Tell me, gentle howre of night.
What is a day, what is a yeere.
"Carroll, Lewis." Stolen Waters.
Carruth. "Ecstasy is the / disaster of pleasure": this.
Catullus. Carmen 31: "Apple of islands, Sirmio, & bright peninsulas, set."
Cowper. Progress of Error, The.
Crashaw. Out of Petronius.
Creeley. For Arthur Okamura.
For Martin.
Was.
Woman, The.
Cummings. I'm very fond of.
Out of a supermetamathical subpreincestures.
Dickinson. Expectation—is Contentment.
Stagnant pleasure like a Pool, A.
There is an arid Pleasure.
Dunn. Between Angels.
From the Manifesto of the Selfish.
Eberhart. Labour then, these drenched heights.
Thrush Song at Dawn.
Emerson. Mask thy wisdom with delight.
See how Romance adheres.
Gray. Ode on the Pleasure Arising from Vicissitude.
Gunn. Modes of Pleasure.
Modes of Pleasure.
Sweet Things.
Hacker. Canzone: "Consider the three functions of the tongue."
Hall. Digging.
Set of Seasons, A.
Hardy. Before and after Summer.
Catullus: XXXI.
Child and the Sage, The.
Great Things.
You on the Tower.

Hartley. Royal Love Child, The.
Herrick. On Himself ("Wearied Pilgrim, I have wandered here, A").
On Himselfe: ("Born[e] I was to meet with Age").
On Himselfe ("I fear no Earthly Powers").
On Himselfe ("Let me not live, if I not love").
To the Maids to Walke Abroad.
Hewitt. Clink of Rhyme, The.
My Father.
Spring Restored, The.
Tricycle, The.
Jeffers. Pleasures.
Johnson. Short Song of Congratulation [*or* To a Young Heir], A.
Jonson. Come on, come on! And where you go.
Joseph. Living Off Other People—Welfare.
Lewis. *Civil Servant, The.*
Mine Host.
Liddy. Poison, The.
Vir II.
Waters by this music.
Lorde. Sacrifice.
MacLeish. Starved Lovers.
Markson. Hygiene.
Melville. Montaigne and His Kitten.
Merton. Song: Sensation Time at the Home, A.
Millay. Portrait.
Olson. Whole World, The.
Pack. Bear on the Unicycle, The.
Ecstasy of the Rat, The.
Patchen. Pleasures of This Gentle Day.
Ralegh. No Pleasure, Without Some Payne.
Rossetti. Candlemas Dialogue, A.
Do This, and He Doeth It.
Goblin Market.
Lay Up for Yourselves Treasures in Heaven.
Mariana.
Memento Mori.
Passing away the bliss, / The anguish passing away.
River Thames (?).
Sorrow hath a double voice, / Sharp today but sweet tomorrow.
What?
Where love is, there comes sorrow / Today or else tomorrow.
Yea, I Have a Goodly Heritage.
Shelley. Birth of Pleasure, The.
Love, Hope, Desire and Fear.
Sidney. Get hence foul[e] grief[e], the canker of the mind[e].
Smith, Patti. Babelogue.
Smith, Stevie. Dear Little Sirmio.
Snyder. Under the Skin of It.
Sorrentino. Sonnet with X's.
Southwell. Man's Civil[l] War[re].
Stevenson. Youth and Love II ("To the heart of youth the world is a highwayside").
Warren. Interjection #8: Or, Sometimes, Night.
Wilbur. L'Invitation au Voyage.
Ode to Pleasure.
Simile for Her Smile, A.
Statues.
Wroth. Sonnet 11: "Unprofitably pleasing, and unsound."
Yeats. Chambermaid's First Song, The.
Zukofsky. Cocktails / and signs of.
Peninsular arm, Sirmio, insular arm, well.

Pleiades
Emerson. Fit for the Pleiads' azure chord.
Schuyler. Just before Fall.
Whitman. On the Beach at Night.

Plowing and Plowmen
Auden. Ploughing.
Burns. Ploughman, The.
Everson. Winter Ploughing.
Frost. Plowmen.
Haines. Old ladders shorten, pulled down.
Heaney. Follower.
Hewitt. On a January Train Journey.
Hopkins. Harry Ploughman.
Housman. When smoke stood up from Ludlow.
Sandburg. Plowboy.

Stevens. Ploughing on Sunday.
Tomlinson. Lines.
Whitman. As I Watch'd the Ploughman
  Ploughing.

Plum Trees and Plums
Atwood. Late August.
Carroll, Jim. Eugene, Orgeon.
Carruth. Bears at Raspberry Time.
Glück. Flowering Plum.
Millay. Plum Gatherer, The.
Snyder. Aged Tamba Temple Plum Tree Song.
Williams, William Carlos. This Is Just to Say.
  To a Poor Old Woman.

Plumbing and Plumbers
Nash. Pipe Dreams.
Schwartz. Albert Einstein to Archibald
  MacLeish.

Plunder and Plundering
Fenton. Nest of Vampires.
Herrick. Rapine Brings Ruine.
Hewitt. Colony, The.

Plymouth, England
Davie. Among Artisans' Houses.
  For an Age of Plastics. [Plymouth].
Hardy. Marble-Streeted Town, The.
Spender. Air Raid across the Bay at Plymouth.

Poaching and Poachers
Ciardi. Feasts.
Crabbe. Smugglers and Poachers.
Kipling. Ballad of Minepit Shaw, The.
  Rhyme of the Three Sealers, The.
Wright, James. Lifting Illegal Nets by
  Flashlight.

Pocahontas
Lindsay. Our Mother Pocahontas.
Nash. Captain John Smith.

Poe, Edgar Allan
Boyle. Statement for El Greco and William
  Carlos Williams, A.
Carruth. Mild Winter.
Ford. Bad Habit, The.
Ginsberg. Haunting Poe's Baltimore.
  To Poe: Over the Planet, Air Albany–
  Baltimore.
Gunn. Readings in French.
Koch. You Were Wearing.
Levine. On the Edge.
Lindsay. Wizard in the Street, The.
Smith, Stevie. After-Thought, The.
Tomlinson. Bells: a Period Piece, The.

Poetic Meter
"Carroll, Lewis." Tèma con Variazioni.
Eberhart. Why.
Koch. Art of Poetry, The.
Markson. Preference of Metre.
Stevenson. From Wishing-Land.
Tennyson. Hendecasyllabics.

Poetics
Ammons. Double Exposure.
  Substantial Planes.
  Theory Center.
Ashbery. Paradoxes and Oxymorons.
  What Is Poetry.
Auden. Dichtung und Wahrheit.
Bishop. My Last Poem.
Browning, Elizabeth Barrett. Earth and Her
  Praisers.
Browning, Robert. How It Strikes a
  Contemporary.
  One Word More.
  Prologue: "Poet's age is sad: for why?, The."
Bukowski. Beauti-ful.
Byron. E Nihilo Nihil.
  To Lord Thurlow.
Campion. Ad Librum.
  Goe, numbers, boldly passe, stay not for ayde.
  Neither buskin now, nor bayes.
"Carroll, Lewis." Poeta Fit, Non Nascitur.
  Rhyme? and Reason?
  Ye Capete Knyghte.
Carruth. Birth of Venus, The.
  Chronological.
  Godhulivela.
  Impossible Indispensability of the Ars Poetica,
  The.
  Lamoille River Valley otherwise known, The.

Master, Grieved with Age, The.
  Meadow House.
  Sonnet: "To see a woman long oppressed by
  fear."
  Tabula Rasa.
  Why speak of the use / of poetry? Poetry.
Catullus. Carmen 16: "Pedicabo et irrumabo."
  Carmen 50: "Other day we spent, The."
Clark. Terminator Too.
Clough. About what sort of thing.
  Veni.
Cohen. Another Room.
  Commentary—Another Room.
  Commentary—How to Speak Poetry.
  Commentary—The News You Really Hate.
  Far from the Soil.
  For E. J. P.
  How to Speak Poetry.
  My Greed.
  News You Really Hate, The.
  Next One, The.
  On Seeing Kabir's Poems on Her Dressing
  Table.
  Only Poem, The.
  Poems Don't Love Us Any More, The.
  Reason I Write, The.
  This Is War.
Coleridge. Homeric Hexameter, The.
  Metrical Feet.
  Ovidian Elegiac Metre, The.
Cowper. Ode: Secundum Artem, An.
  Poetic Pains.
  Table Talk.
Creeley. Dishonest Mailmen, The.
  Epic Expands, The.
  Method, A.
Cullen. After a Visit.
  Poet, The.
  Sonnet: "What I am saying now was said
  before."
  That Bright Chimeric Beast.
  To an Unknown Poet.
Cummings. Here's a little mouse)and.
  If i have made,my lady,intricate.
  Little joe gould has lost his teeth and doesn't
  know where.
  My Prayer.
  No man,if men are gods;but if gods must.
  Out of the pants which cover me.
  Phonograph may(if it likes)be prophe, The.
  Since feeling is first.
  Sonnet entitled how to run the world).
  To start,to hesitate;to stop.
Davie. Oak Openings.
  Or, Solitude.
  Poem as Abstract.
De la Mare. Happy Encounter, The.
Dickinson. All the letters I can write.
  To learn the Transport by the Pain.
  To see the Summer Sky.
Doolittle. Heliodora.
Dunbar. To E. H. K.
Duncan. Poetry, a Natural Thing.
Eberhart. At the End of the War.
  Deep Fishing.
  Emerson's Concord.
  Killer, The.
  Life and Death.
  Long Term Suffering.
  Meaningless Poem.
  Moment of Vision, The.
  News.
  Place, The.
  Poem as Trajectory, The.
  Poetry and Games.
  Refrains.
  Sacrifice, The.
  To William Carlos Williams.
  21st Century Man.
  Undercliff Evening.
  Winter Kill.
  Worldly Failure.
Edmunds. Back Home.
Eliot. Note on War Poetry, A.
Emerson. I grieve that better souls than mine.
  Merlin.
  Motto to "The Poet."

Poet ("To clothe the fiery thought").
  Seyd planted where the deluge ploughed.
  Test, The.
  William does thy frigid soul.
Fenton. Letter to John Fuller.
Fisher. In Touch.
  It Is Writing.
  Necessaries.
  Poem: "Small / poem / the unit of feeling,
  The."
Fletcher. From the Japanese, III.
  Truth of the Matter, The.
  Vowels, The.
Ford. Prison Life.
  So you'd eat the ear of Van Gogh!
  War.
Fox. In the Land of Shinar.
Frost. In a Poem.
Gallagher. Redwing.
  Refusing Silence.
Gardner. Are Poets Ball Players?
  Fright among the Runes.
  Homo Gratia Artis.
  Roundelay: "Blood-red bird with one green
  eye, A."
  To Thoreau on Rereading Walden.
  When a Warlock Dies.
  Writing Poetry.
Ginsberg. City Midnight Junk Strains.
  Contest of Bards.
  Grim Skeleton.
  G.S. Reading Poesy at Princeton.
  I attempted to concentrate.
  Reading French Poetry.
  Returning to the Country for a Brief Visit.
  To an Old Poet in Peru.
Graves. De Arte Poetica.
  Poem: A Reminder.
Gray. Behold, where Dryden's less
  presumptuous car.
Hacker. Feeling and Form.
  I still balk at my preference for rhyme.
  Rhetoric.
  Riposte.
  Untoward Occurance at Embassy Poetry
  Reading.
Hartley. Courage for Lost Poems.
Hartnett. Poet as Mastercraftsman, The.
Herbert. Jordan (1).
  Jordan (2).
  Quidditie [or Quiddity], The.
  Sonnet: "My God, where is that ancient heat
  towards Thee."
  Sonnet: "Sure Lord, there is enough in thee to
  dry."
Herrick. His Prayer for Absolution.
  Verses.
Hesketh. Poem is a Painting, A.
Hewitt. After Reading Sonnets by Rev.
  Charles Turner (1864) and The New Day,
  Sonnets by Dr T. Gordon Hake (1890).
  Emily Dickinson.
  I Cannot Make a Song Tonight.
  I Turned My Touch to Campion.
  Lyric Sonorously Rhymed, The.
  North-West Passage: An Old Man Dying.
  Poetry, Then..
  Retreaded Rhymes.
  Sonnet: "I thought tonight of all the lovers
  gone."
  To a Modern Irish Poet.
Hill. Anguish bloated by the replete scream.
  Four Poems Regarding the Endurance of
  Poets.
  History as Poetry.
Hoffman. Comanches.
  Essay on Style.
  Poem, The: "Arriving at last."
  Words.
Hugo. Lecture.
  Snow Poem.
Jong. Perfect Poet, The.
  Zen & the Art of Poetry.
Jonson. Elegy [or Elegie], An: "Let me be
  what I am, as Virgil cold."
  Fit of Rhyme [or Rime] against Rhyme [or

Rime], A.
Proludium.
Joseph. PROEM: *Against metaphor—but how then?*
Knight. And Tell Me Poet, Can Love Exist in Slavery?
Genesis.
Haiku: "Eastern guard tower."
Knott. Keeper, The.
Koch. Art of Poetry, The.
Invention of Poetry, The.
Pleasures of Peace, The.
Secret, The.
Stones of Time, The.
Levertov. Grey Sparrow Addresses the Mind's Ear.
Kingdoms of Heaven.
Prayer, The.
Levine. Genius.
Lewis. Destruction.
Poet, The.
Liddy. As in poetry.
Hounds can't / Come in, The.
Lady/Lord in Doorway.
Letter to Eamonn Wall, A.
Letter to Sainte-Beuve.
Thursdays Are Sacred.
Wave of the Nineties, The.
White Thought in a White Shade, A.
Lovelace. Commendatory Poems.
Dedication to Anne Lovelace, The.
On Sanazar's Being Honoured.
To My Noble Kinsman T.S. Esq.
Lowell. Randall Jarrell 1. October 1965.
Lowry. Bright as the Pleiades Upon the Soul.
Christ I am tired of fruit im poetry.
Epitaph: "Dear Scipio Sprague / sans plague sans blague."
Ex-Poet, The.
Foul, or Twenty-Five.
Give me a poem / To wring the hearts of men.
Note.
Note For a Poem.
Plagiarist, The.
Poem about a poem that can't be written, A.
Poets are Godlike in that they.
Save that the optimistic ones are worse.
Thing to know is how to write a verse, The.
What the Gardener Said to Mrs. Trail.
"MacDiarmid." Poetry that goes all the way, A.
McGrath. Against the False Magicians.
Flint and Steel.
You Can Start the Poetry Now, Or: News from Crazy Horse.
MacLeish. Ars Poetica.
Theory of Poetry.
Marlowe. 1.1: Quemadmodum a Cupidine pro bellis amoris scribere coactus sit.
2.1: Quod pro gigantomachia amores scribere sit coactus.
3.14: Ad Venerem, quod elegis finem imponat.
Meredith. Confession.
Empty Purse: A Sermon to our Later Prodigal Son, The.
He who has looked upon Earth.
To R.H.H. with Daphne.
Tuck, Demitroïa, / Ariadne, and Froyja.
Millay. I will put Chaos into fourteen lines.
Miller. How this morning.
On Getting My Poems Back from the Typist.
Nash. Brief Guide to Rhyming, or, How Be the Little Busy Doth?, A.
Notley. World's Bliss.
O'Hara. To Gottfried Benn.
Olson. Later Note on Letter #15, A.
Muse / is the "fate" of the poem, The.
You know, verse.
Oppen. And Their Winter and Night in Disguise.
Cars on the highway filled with speech.
Five Poems about Poetry.
It is difficult now to speak of poetry.
Latitude, Longitude.
Lighthouses, The.
Little Pin: Fragment, The.

Not the symbol but the scene this pavement leads.
O withering seas.
Or, in that light, New arts!
Semite.
Song, the Winds of Downhill.
Tell the beads of the chromosomes like a rosary.
Thirties. And / A spectre, The.
To the Poets: To Make Much of Life.
Translucent Mechanics, The.
Two Romance Poems.
Who Shall Doubt.
Patchen. I despise these poets with their puerile little chalk-talks of the soul.
Often Was It.
Poem Written after Reading Certain Poets Sired by the English School and Bitched by the C.P.
Poems which are written by the soul.
Poe. Enigma, An.
Pound. Coda.
Ité.
Salvationists.
Prince. Being *incontentabile* / Like Foscolo, in making verse.
Byron-Shelley Conversation, A.
Not a *Paris Review* Interview.
Renouncing an Epigram.
Rich. Poetry: I.
Rossetti. Charades.
New Enigmas.
Roundel seems to fit a round of days, A.
Rukeyser. Sixth Night: Waking, The.
Sandburg. Cups of Coffee.
Impossible Iambics.
Letters to Dead Imagists.
Now They Bury Her Again.
Sketch of a Poet.
Tentative (First Model) Definitions of Poetry.
Schuyler. What.
Schwartz. Apollo Musagete, Poetry, and the Leader of the Muses.
Journey of a Poem Compared to All the Sad Variety of Travel, The.
Philology Recapitulates Ontology, Poetry Is Ontology.
Poet, The.
Sonnet on Famous and Familiar Sonnets and Experiences.
Shakespeare. Sonnet 54: "O [*or* Oh], how much more doth beauty beauteous seem."
Sonnet 79: "Whilst I alone did call upon thy aid."
Sidney. Sonnet 15: "You that do search for every purling spring."
Sonnet 74: "I never drank of Aganippe well."
Smart. Epistle to John Sherratt, Esq., An.
For the spiritual musick is as follows.
Snyder. As for Poets.
Axe Handles.
How Poetry Comes to Me.
What You Should Know to Be a Poet.
Sorrentino. Address to the National Council on the Arts.
Billy McCoy.
Canzone: "On the tropical coast of Java."
Cautious Circumspection Does Not Win the West.
Mysteries Sacred and Profane.
Remember the story of Columbus and the orange?
Stuart. Charles River, The.
Exutive Discovers Poetry, The.
Suckling. That box, fair mistress, which thou gavest to me.
To My Friend Will. Davenant, upon His Poem of "Madagascar."
Sutter. Declaration of Dependence.
Work, The.
Thomas. In My Craft or Sullen Art.
Turco. Poem: "It is time to write a poem."
Wakoski. Ordinary Poem.
Poet at Carpenter's Bench.
What Happened.
With Words.

Whitman. I am the poet of the Body and I am the poet of the Soul.
Williams, Charles Kenneth. Yours.
Williams, Miller. Form and Theory of Poetry.
Let Me Tell You.
On Hearing About the Death of Mitzi Mayfair.
Paying Some Attention to His Birthday the Associate Professor Goes About His Business Considering What He Sees and a Kind of Praise.
Style.
Today is Wednesday.
Williams, William Carlos. Come On!
Coronal, A.
Defense.
Dish of Fruit, The.
Entity, The.
Phoenix and the Tortoise, The.
Poet and His Poems, The.
Riposte.
Uses of Poetry, The.
Wordsworth. Scorn Not the Sonnet [Critic,You Have Frowned].
To the Poet, John Dyer.
Valedictory Sonnet.
Wright, James. Many of Our Waters: Variaitons on a Poem by a Black Child.
Yau. Dragon's Blood II.
Seance Music.
Yeats. He Gives His Beloved Certain Rhymes.
Spirit Medium, The.
Zimmer. Sonnet: Zimmer Imagines Himself Being Poet-in-Residence.
Zukofsky. Her face the Book of—Love Delights in—Praises.
It's a Gay Li-ife.
Lines of this new song are nothing, The.
"Mantis," An Interpretation.
Old Poet Moves to a New Aprtment 14 Times, The.
Peri Poietikes.
Piping, beaus, I'll go *whoosh* and I'll rumble you.
Song—3/4 time.
William Carlos Williams Alive!
Yesterday, Licinius, what a day it was.

Pogroms. *see* Massacres.

Poison
Bishop. Giant Toad.
Burns. Lord Ronald My Son.
Donne. To Sir Edward Herbert[,] at Juliers [*or* Julyers].
Emerson. At last the poet spoke.
There resides in the grieving.
Graves. Poisoned Day.
Herrick. Upon Love ("Christall Violl Cupid brought, A").
Hoffman. Crop-Dusting.
Lovelace. Toad and Spyder, The.
Lowry. Homoeopathic Blues in J.
Nemerov. ..And Is Silent.
Sandburg. Anecdote of Hemlock for Two Athenians.
Spenser. Hideous dragon, dreadfull to behold, A.
Williams, Miller. How the Elephant Got His Hump.

Poker
Dunn. Woman with Five Hearts, The.
Nemerov. Day on the Big Branch, A.
Myth & Ritual.
Sexton. Rowing Endeth, The.

Poland
Berryman. 1 September 1939.
Davie. In Chopin's Garden.
Edmunds. Treblinka.
Stevens. Colloquy with a Polish Aunt.

Police Stations and Police
Beatles. Piggies.
Brooks. Negro Hero.
Cummings. 16 heures / l'Etoile.
Fenton. GIRL ATTACKED.
Haines. About the hour the December moon.
Hewitt. At the Newsagent's.
Case of Mistaken Identity, A.
Troubles, 1922, The.
Two Spectres Haunt Me.

Hughes, Langston. Third Degree.
Who But the Lord?
Kipling. Tour, The.
Lawrence. Gross, Coarse, Hideous.
Man in the Street, The.
Lowell. Opposite House, The.
MacNeice. Mahavveray.
Matthews. Lust.
Morrison. Sidewalkers Moved, The.
Patchen. Letter to a Policemen in Kansas City, A.
Rich. Frame.
Sandburg. Stripes.
Van Duyn. That was my grandfather, nearly went to prison.
Warren. Jet Must Be Hunting for Something, The.
Williams, Charles Kenneth. Crime.

Politics and Politicians

Atwood. Beyond the white hill which maroons us.
Investigator is here, The.
Is this what we wanted.
Torture.
Auden. O where would those choleric boys.
Partition.
When Statesmen gravely say, "We must be realistic."
Who will cure the nation's ill?
Why are the public buildings so high? How come you don't know?
Berg. Mother Political.
Blake. Blind-Man's Buff.
Boyle. Poem for February First 1975, A.
Browning, Elizabeth Barrett. August Voice, An.
Italy and the World.
Summing Up in Italy.
Tale of Villafranca, A.
Bunting. Duke Valentine had been in Lombardy with the King.
Burns. Act Sederunt of the Session—A Scots Ballad.
Author's Earnest Cry and Prayer, to the Right Honorable and Honorable, the Scotch Representatives in the House of Commons, The.
Awa Whigs Awa.
Ballad, A: "While Prose-work and rhymes."
Collected, Harry stood awee.
Epigram on James Baillie Swan.
Epistle to Robt. Graham Esq: of Fintry on the Election for the Dumfries String of Boroughs, Anno 1790.
Extempore [on the *Loyal Natives'* Verses].
Fête Champetre, The.
Five Carlins—A Ballad—Tune, Chevy Chase, The.
He clench'd his pamphlets in his fist.
In politics if thou would'st mix.
Ode to the Departed Regency-Bill—1789.
On Mr. Burke by an Opponent and a Friend to Mr. Hastings.
On the Death of the Late Lord President Dundas.
Solemn League and Covenant, The.
Song: "O, Logan, sweetly didst thou glide."
Carroll, Jim. Inauguration Day.
"Carroll, Lewis." Elections to the Hebdomadal Council, The.
Carruth. Republicans? We've got a few. In fact.
Your dream: / His name was Herod. No? How close.
Catullus. Carmen 10: "Alfenus Varus / buttonholes me."
Carmen 29: "What man could stomach the sight."
Cohen. Any System.
Killers, The.
Wrong Man, The.
Coleridge. Character, A.
Verses Addressed to J. Horne Tooke and the Company Who Met on 28 June 1796 to Celebrate His Poll at the Westminster Election.
Cowper. On Thurlow.

Crabbe. Election, The.
Creeley. Menu, The.
Cummings. Ballad of an Intellectual.
F is for foetus(a).
Next to of course god america i.
Nobody could / in superhuman flights.
Opening of the chambers close.
Politician, A.
Red-rag and pink-flag.
Salesman is an it that stinks excuse, A.
This evangelist / buttons with his big gollywog voice.
Way to hump a cow is not, The.
When muckers pimps and tratesmen.
Davie. Barnsley and District.
Elect, The.
Right Wing Sympathies.
Dryden. To My Honoured [*or* Honour'd] Kinsman, John Driden [of Chesterton in the County of Huntingdon, Esquire].
Dunbar. Speakin' at de Cou't-House.
Dunn. Introduction to the 20th Century.
Response to a Letter from France.
To a Terrorist.
"Dylan." I Shall Be Free No. 10.
You tell me about politics.
Eberhart. Rape of the Cataract, The.
Eliot. Coriolan.
Emerson. Van Buren.
Fenton. Lullaby for a Summer Recess.
Ferlinghetti. Sandinista Avioncitos.
Frost. Build Soil.
No Holy Wars for Them.
To a Thinker.
Ginsberg. America.
These States: to Miami Presidential Convention.
Thoughts on a Breath.
Glück. Exile.
Hacker. Untoward Occurance at Embassy Poetry Reading.
Herrick. To His Kinsman, Sir Tho. Soame.
To Sir John Berkeley, Governour of Exeter.
True Safety.
Hewitt. Agenda.
Any Rich Suburban Church.
As You Like It.
Bangor, Spring 1916.
Carson at Six Road Ends.
Fables for Stormont.
King Concerned, The.
Labour Victory, A.
Prime Minister.
Reference, The.
Those Morning Walks.
To Be Used in an Address Delivered at the Unveiling of a Plaque Commemorating "George A. Birmingham."
Well-Intentioned Consul, The.
Hughes, Langston. Corner Meeting.
Hugo. Letter to Gildner from Wallace.
Jarrell. English Garden in Austria, An.
State, The.
Jeffers. Greater Grandeur.
Ink-Sack.
Sinverguenza.
Stars Go Over the Lonely Ocean, The.
Johnson. Translation of the Latin Epitaph on Sir Thomas Hanmer, Written by Doctor Freind, A.
Jonson. New Cry, The.
To Robert, Earl of Salisbury ("Who can consider thy right courses run").
To the Parliament.
To the Same [Robert, Earl of Salisbury] [Upon the Accension of the Treasurership to Him].
To Thomas, Lord Chancellor.
Keats. Otho the Great.
Kipling. Dead Statesman, A.
Declaration of London, The.
Things and the Man.
Knight. On Watching Politicians Perform at Martin Luther King's Funeral.
Kunitz. Daughters of the Horseleech, The.
Lawrence. Hard-Boiled Conservatives.
Hibiscus and Salvia Flowers.
Liddy. Maud Gonne Rode Out on a White

Horse to Coolgreany.
New O'Dwyer's dim lights. "You hate, The."
Roses of Parnell & Mellowes, The.
Sister Beach, Sister Garden.
Talking to Clare as.
Lindsay. Bryan, Bryan, Bryan, Bryan.
What the Moon Saw.
Why I Voted the Socialist Ticket.
Lowell. Words.
Lowry. Where Did That One Go to, 'Erbert.
McAuley. Irish Bull, An.
"MacDiarmid." Left-wing poetry represents a rise in the price of bread.
McGrath. Note on the Late Elections, A.
Merrill. Popular Demand.
Roger Clay's Proposal.
Merton. Man with One Foot and the Marsh Pheasant, The.
Note in Honor of Machiavelli, A.
Original Child Bomb.
Public Affairs.
Spring has come with its smell of Nicaragua.
Suddenly in the night the sirens.
Morrison. L'America.
Nash. Election Day Is a Holiday.
Nemerov. To the Rulers.
Olson. Issue, Mood.
Memory, Mind, and Will.
Rufus Woodpecker visited the President.
Oppen. Now we do most of the killing.
Patchen. I Don't Want to Startle You but They Are Going to Kill Most of Us.
Piercy. Curse of the Earth Magician on a Metal Land.
Pope. Epitaph on James Craggs, Esq., in Westminster Abbey.
Epitaph on Sir William Trumbal.
Ransom. Primer for Statesmen.
"Reed." Good Evening Mr. Waldheim.
Original Wrapper, The.
Rich. Atlas of the Difficult World, An.
Robinson. On the Way.
Rukeyser. Until I stand on the January platform.
Sandburg. "Drama of politics doesn't interest me," said a news rewrite man, The.
Money, Politics, Love, and Glory.
Under the Capitol Dome.
Shelley. Similes for Two Political Characters of 1819.
Sidney. Sonnet 30: "Whether the Turkish new moon minded be."
Smith, Stevie. Hast Du Dich Verirrt?
Snodgrass. Reichsmarschall Hermann Göring ("And why, Herr Reichsmarschall, is Italy").
Spender. Helmut.
Stevenson. Old Chimæras, old receipts, The.
Sutter. November Seven, Nineteen Eighty-Four.
Swift. Dog and the Thief, The.
Simile, A.
Thomson. Britain.
Rome.
Tomlinson. Machiavelli in Exile.
Updike. Sin City, D.C.
Washington: Tourist View.
Waldman. It Sounds It.
Warren. Terror.
Whitman. Song for Certain Congressmen.
Thought ("Of obedience, faith, adhesiveness").
Thoughts: ("Of public opinion").
To a President.
Whittier. King Solomon and the Ants.
Lost Statesman, The.
One of the Signers.
Samuel J. Tilden.
Thiers.
To a Poetical Trio in the City of Gotham.
To a Southern Statesman.
To William H. Seward.
Wilson.
Wilbur. Miltonic Sonnet for Mr. Johnson on His Refusal of Peter Hurd's Official Portrait, A.
Williams, Charles Kenneth. Interrogation II.
Politics.

Williams, Miller. Senator Explains a Vote,
  The.
Wordsworth. Blest Statesman He, Whose
  Mind's Unselfish Will.
Composed after Reading a Newspaper of the
  Day.
Help for the Memory of the Grand
  Independent; A New Song, A.
Hint from the Mountains for Certain Political
  Pretenders.
Placard for a Poll Bearing an Old Shirt.
Prelude, Prefixed to the Volume Entitled
  "Poems Chiefly of Early and Late Years."
Protest against the Ballot.
Sonnets upon the Punishment of Death.
Squib on Colonel Evans, A.
To the Utilitarians.
Wright, James. Eisenhower's Visit to Franco,
  1959.
Yeats. Politics.
Young. Politics As History.
Zukofsky. "Immediate Aim, The."
  Varus old crony had me visit his love.
  Whose hoax to put up with, outstare, protest
    patience.
Pollock, Jackson
Dunn. He/She.
Pollution
Auden. Curse, A.
Gardner. Part of the Darkness.
Ginsberg. Ballade of Poisons.
  Homework.
  Swirls of Black Dust on Avenue D.
Graves. Poisoned Day.
Hoffman. April, An.
Hugo. Cataldo Mission.
Lawrence. Obscenity.
Lewis. Rhondda, The.
Matthews. Waste Carpet, The.
Neruda. Bomb (II).
Olson. Every Man His Own Matador; or for
  That Matter Any Member of the Family.
Raine. Polluted tide, / Desecrated earth
    destroyed.
  What message from imagined Paradise.
Sandburg. Record is a scroll of many
  indecipherable scrawls, The.
Sexton. As It Was Written.
Smith, Stevie. Friends of the River Trent.
Snyder. Bomb Test.
See also **Ecology and Ecologists.**
Polyandry. *see* **Bigamy and Bigamists;**
  Marriage; Monogamy and Monogamists.
Pomegranates
Fox. Pomegranates.
Lawrence. Andraitx—Pomegranate Flowers.
  Pomegranate.
Pomp
Meredith. Cool you proceed at speed.
Pompeii, Italy
Dickey, James. In the Lupanar at Pompeii.
Galvin. For a Little Girl of Pompeii.
Muldoon. Chinook.
Shelley. At Pompeii.
  Ode to Naples.
Updike. Pompeii.
Walcott. Early Pompeian.
Ponds. *see* **Lakes and Ponds.**
Ponies
Betjeman. Hunter Trials.
Ciardi. Tommy's Pond.
"Dylan." New Pony.
Moore. Blue Bug.
Sandburg. Half Way.
Wright, James. Blessing, A.
Pony Express
Emerson. Too late the anxious fire came.
Pool (game)
Carruth. Capper Kaplinski at the North Side
  Cue Club.
Matthews. Eternally Undismayed Are the
  Poolshooters.
Poorhouses
Hardy. Curate's Kindness, The.
Pope, Alexander
Cowper. Then Pope, as harmony itself exact.

Johnson. To Eliza Plucking Laurel in Mr
  Pope's Gardens.
Pope. Dialogue, A.
Swift. Dr. Swift to Mr. Pope.
Tate. Mr. Pope.
Poplar Trees
Carruth. Four greens / the poplar trunk.
Cowper. Poplar Field, The.
Doolittle. Mid-day.
Fisher. Poplars, The.
Hopkins. Binsey Poplars (Felled 1879).
Sandburg. Follies.
  Moonset.
  Poplar and Elm.
Smart. To My Worthy Friend, Mr. T.B. One
  of the People Called Quakers.
Snodgrass. Silver Poplars.
Wilbur. Poplar, Sycamore.
See also **Aspen Trees.**
Poppies
Doolittle. Choros Sequence.
  Sea Poppies.
Fletcher. Poppies of the Red Year.
Levine. Holding On.
Oliver. Poppies.
Olson. When do poppies bloom   I ask myself,
  stopping again.
Plath. Poppies in July.
  Poppies in October.
St. John. Black Poppy (At the Temple).
Sandburg. Crossing the Ohio When Poppies
  Bloom in Ashtabula.
  Poppies.
Porcupines
Atwood. Porcupine Meditation.
  Porcupine Tree.
Kinnell. Porcupine, The.
Nash. Porcupine, The.
Sexton. Porcupine.
Pornography
Carruth. Sonnet: "Yes. After all my arguments
  with myself."
Ciardi. Blue Movie.
Hacker. Pornographic Poem.
Shapiro. Adult Bookstore.
Updike. In Memoriam Felis Felis.
Williams, Charles Kenneth. Floor.
Williams, William Carlos. Drugstore Library.
  Picture of a Nude in a Machine Shop.
See also **Obscenity.**
Portland, Maine
Glück. Portland, 1968.
Longfellow. My Lost Youth.
Portraits
Ashbery. Self-Portrait in a Convex Mirror.
Auden. Portrait.
Bishop. Family Portrait.
Browning, Elizabeth Barrett. On a Portrait of
  Wordsworth by B. R. Haydon.
  Portrait, A.
  Two Sketches.
Browning, Robert. Likeness, A.
  My Last Duchess [Ferrara].
Burns. C——d faithful likeness, friend
  Painter, would'st seize?
Byron. To Mary on Receiving Her Picture.
Coleridge. Lines on a Portrait of a Lady.
  Melancholy.
  To the Young Artist.
Cowper. Denner's Old Woman.
  On Hayley's Portrait.
  On His Portrait.
  On Receiving Hayley's Picture.
  On the Engraver of His Pourtrait.
  On the Receipt of My Mother's Picture out of
    Norfolk [the Gift of My Cousin Ann
    Bodham].
  Tears of a Painter, The.
De la Mare. Portrait, A.
  Son of Melancholy, The.
Dickinson. Brow is that of Deity, The.
  Portraits are to daily faces.
Donne. His Picture.
  Phryne.
Eliot. Lines for Cuscuscaraway and Mirza
  Murad Ali Beg.

Ferlinghetti. It was a face which darkness
  could kill.
  Jack of Hearts, The.
  Ladakh Buddhess Biker.
  Love Nut, The.
  Mouth of truth, The.
  That fellow on the boattrain who insisted.
Fisher. Self-Portraits and Their Mirrors.
Graves. Face in the Mirror, The.
Griffiths. Consequences.
  Courting Prosperity.
Hardy. Enemy's Portrait, The.
  Family Portraits.
  On the Portrait of a Woman About to Be
    Hanged.
Herrick. On Julia's Picture.
  Upon a Painted Gentlewoman.
Hewitt. Portrait, The.
  Portraits on the Walls.
Hopkins. On the Portrait of Two Beautiful
  Young People.
Jong. In Defense of the English Portrait
  School.
Jonson. Picture of the Body, The.
  Poem Sent Me by Sir William Burlase, A.
  To the Reader ("This figure, that thou here
    seest put").
Lawrence. Portraits.
Lindsay. Moon Is a Painter, The.
Lovelace. Upon the Curtain[e] of Lucasta's
  Picture [It Was Thus Wrought].
Lowell. Charles V by Titian.
MacLeish. Contemporary Portrait.
Melville. Formerly a Slave.
Meredith. Fireside Reverie.
Pope. On Lady Mary Wortley Montagu's
  Portrait.
Raine. Oval Portrait: Jessie Wilkie, The.
Rossetti. In an Artist's Studio.
Sandburg. Cartoon.
  Even Numbers.
  Fog Portrait.
  His Own Face Hidden.
  Paula.
  Portrait.
  Sins of Kalamazoo, The.
  Slants at Buffalo, New York.
  Under a Telephone Pole.
  Winter Milk.
Sarton. Portrait by Holbein.
Sexton. Portrait of an Old Woman on the
  College Tavern Wall.
Swift. Portrait from the Life, A.
Tomlinson. Against Portraits.
Wilbur. Miltonic Sonnet for Mr. Johnson on
  His Refusal of Peter Hurd's Official Portrait,
  A.
Wordsworth. Effusion in the Pleasure-Ground
  on the Banks of the Bran, Near Dunkeld.
  Lines Suggested By a Portrait from the Pencil
    of F. Stone.
  On a Portrait of the Duke of Wellington upon
    the Field of Waterloo, by Haydon.
  Recollection of the Portrait of King Henry
    Eighth, Trinity Lodge, Cambridge.
  Sonnet to a Picture by Lucca Giordano in the
    Mureo Borbonico at Naples.
  To a Painter ("All praise the Likeness by thy
    skill portrayed").
  To B.R. Haydon, On Seeing His Picture of
    Napoleon Buonaparte on the Island of St
    Helena.
  To the Author's Portrait.
  Upon a Portrait.
  Upon the Sight of the Portrait of a Female
    Friend.
See also **Painting and Painters; Photography
  and Photographers.**
Ports. *see* **Harbors and Ports.**
Portugal
Young. Saudades: The Portuguese Blues.
Possums. *see* **Opossums.**
Posterity
Burns. Nature's Law.
  Perish their names, however great or brave.
Catullus. Carmen 77: "Whom I have trusted to
  no end (Rufus)."

Carmen 95: "Nine harvests & nine winters since its inception."
Carmen 116: "Conscientiously bringing my mind to bear on this problem."
Eberhart. R. G. E.
Emerson. Cup of life is not so shallow, The.
Future, The.
Nature says, / These craggy hills that front the dawn.
Nature will not lose.
Thank the gods thy governors.
Who knows this or that?
Hardy. John and Jane.
Life Laughs Onward.
Sine Prole.
Herrick. On Himselfe ("Live by thy Muse thou shalt; when others die").
To His Verses.
To His Worthy Friend, M. Arthur Bartly.
To the Earle of Westmerland.
Upon His Verses.
Jonson. Epigram on the Prince's Birth. 1630, An.
Epistle to Elizabeth, Countess of Rutland.
Kipling. Disciple, The.
England's Answer.
Heritage, The.
MacLeish. Epistle to Be Left in the Earth.
Sentiments for a Dedication.
Neruda. What will the Poles think of my hat.
Psalms. Psalm 49: "Hear this, all ye people.."
Sandburg. Call the Next Witness.
Enemy Number One.
Shapiro. Manhole Covers.
Snyder. For the Children.
Surrounded by Wild Turkeys.
Tomlinson. Against Extremity.
Whitman. From My Last Years.
Full of Life Now.
L. of G.'s Purport.
My Legacy.
No Labor-Saving Machine.
Poem of Remembrances for a Girl or a Boy of These States.
Whittier. Autograph, An.
Name, A.
Wordsworth. Poet to His Grandchild; Sequel to "A Plea for Authors."
Zukofsky. Rufey my how frustrate unquickened and craved the tie I'm equal.
Sigh paid to be studious when I moved went on to (queer) once.
Zmyrna, my own Cinna, nine harvests passed making his hymn.

Postmen. see **Mail and Mailmen.**

Potatoes
Heaney. Digging.
Lindsay. Potatoes' Dance, The.
Matthews. This Spud's for You.
Wakoski. Duchess Potatoes, The.
Wilbur. Potato.

Potomac River
Sandburg. Potomac River Mist.
Potomac Town in February.
Smoke Rose Gold.
Whitman. By Broad Potomac's Shore.

Pottery and Potters
Cowper. Epigram of Homer, An.
Hewitt. With a Little Book of Pottery.
Merton. Ladies of Tlatilco, The.
Sandburg. Jug.
Schuyler. Andrew Lord Poems.
Snyder. Firing, The.
Williams, William Carlos. Stone Crock, The.

Pound, Ezra
Berryman. Heroes, The.
Bunting. On the Fly-Leaf of Pound's Cantos.
Carruth. Gnarled wind blurs the light, my hurt and another's.
West Bolton is due north of Bolton, East.
Davie. Ezra Pound in Pisa.
On a Proposed Celebration of Ezra Pound.
Ferlinghetti. Pound at Spoleto.
Hall. Sestina: "Hang it all, Ezra Pound, there is only the one sestina."
Koch. Art of Poetry, The.
Levertov. September 1961.

Lowry. Another Immorality.
Thing to know is how to write a verse, The.
MacLeish. Ezry.
Olson. Lustrum for You, E.P., A.
Williams, William Carlos. To My Friend Ezra Pound.
Wright, Charles. Landscape with Seated Figure and Olive Trees.

Poverty
Angelou. Bump d'Bump.
Ashbery. Street Musicians.
Beckett. Confections.
Sanies II.
Bishop. Miracle for Breakfast, A.
Pink Dog.
Blake. Holy Thursday (" 'Twas on a Holy Thursday, their innocent faces clean").
Holy Thursday ("Is this a holy thing to see").
I wander tho each dirty street.
London ("I wander through each chartered street").
Bly. Man Writes to a Part of Himself, A.
Boyle. Poem for a Painter Bent on Suicide.
World Tour.
Brooks. Bean Eaters, The.
Lovers of the Poor, The.
Browning, Elizabeth Barrett. Song for the Ragged Schools of London, A.
Bukowski. I was out there again today. There are some creatures out there.
Meek Have Inherited, The.
Trench Warfare.
Bunting. Gin the Goodwife Stint.
Burns. Address of Beelzebub.
Auld Rob Morris.
Country Lassie.
Jeremiah 15th Ch. 10 V.
Lines Written on a Bank-Note.
New Psalm for the Chapel of Kilmarnock, on the Thanksgiving-Day for His Majesty's Recovery, A.
O Mally's Meek, Mally's Sweet.
O That I Had Ne'er Been Married.
Penitential Thought, in the Hour of Remorse—Intended for a Tragedy, A.
Poem on Life.
Ronalds of the Bennals, The.
Song—For A' That and A' That.
Song: "Mark yonder pomp of costly fashion."
Song: "O poortith cauld, and restless love."
Sonnet—On Hearing a Thrush Sing on a Morning Walk in January.
Why Should Na Poor Folk Mowe.
Campion. Epigramme: "Why droopst thou, Trefeild? Will Hurst the Banker."
In Crispinum.
In Nervam.
Carroll, Jim. In midtown again the way you stop.
"Carroll, Lewis." First Voice, The.
Peter and Paul.
Carruth. If It Were Not for You.
John Dryden.
Song of the Two Crows.
Chaucer. Clerk's Tale, The.
Complaint of Chaucer to His Purse, The.
Introduction to the Man of Law's Tale.
Clare. Impromptu on Winter.
Tramp, The.
Crabbe. Alms-House and Trustees, The.
Poor and Their Dwellings, The.
Richard's Youth.
Cullen. Death to the Poor.
Saturday's Child.
Cummings. Unnoticed woman from whose kind large flesh.
Davie. Back of Affluence.
Right Lads, The.
De la Mare. Slum Child, The.
Dickinson. I play at Riches—to appease.
None can experience stint.
Dobyns. Dancing in Vacationland.
Donne. Deliver us for thy descent.
Dunbar. Companion's Progress, A.
Precedent.
"Dylan." Ballad of Hollis Brown.
I Am a Lonesome Hobo.

Like a Rolling Stone.
Money Blues.
North Country Blues.
Too Much of Nothing.
Emerson. Chartist's Complaint, The.
Have ye seen the caterpillar.
It is certain that who his mind.
New England Capitalist.
Fletcher. Fuel Vendor, The.
Joy.
Ford. Poverty is always / Imaginary. The.
Sharp eyes, hoodlum skin.
Frost. Equalizer, An.
Galvin. 1847.
Stone Arabia Farm.
Glück. Bridal Piece.
Letter from Provence.
Griffiths. Horse's Mouth, The.
Patchworks.
Gunn. Tenderloin.
Haines. Hunger.
On the Road.
Hall. Wreckage, The.
Hardy. Reminder, The.
Hartnett. Listen, / if I came to you, out of the wind.
Herrick. Plunder, The.
Poore Mans Part, The.
Poores Portion, The.
Poverty and Riches.
Poverty the Greatest Pack.
To God, His Good Will.
To His Deere God.
Upon Adam Peapes.
Upon Boreman. Epig.
Upon Flood, Or a Thankfull Man.
Upon Grubs.
Upon Her Almes.
Upon Tubbs.
Hewitt. Agitator.
Art and Technology.
Doctor Muses, The.
Fairy Thresher, The.
Irishman in Coventry, An.
Island Folk Tale, An.
Rank-and-Filer, The.
Scissors For a One-Armed Tailor.
Simple-Minded Christian, The.
Turf-Carrier [or Turf Carrier] on Aranmore.
Housman. When first my way to fair I took.
Hughes, Langston. Ballad of the Man Who's Gone.
Consider Me.
Dime.
Down and Out.
Ennui.
Madam and the Charity Child.
Madam and the Rent Man.
Necessity.
Hugo. Back of Gino's Place.
Between the Bridges.
Maratea Porto.
South Italy, Remote and Stone.
Squatter on Company Land, The.
Tinker Camp, The.
What the Brand New Freeway Won't Go By.
Jeffers. Blind Horses.
Jonson. Elegy [or Elegie], An: "'Tis true, I'm broke! Vows, oaths, and all I had."
To Alchemists.
To the Right Honourable, the Lord High Treasurer of England. An Epistle Mendicant. 1631.
Kinnell. To a Child in Calcutta.
Kipling. Last of the Light Brigade, The.
Masque of Plenty, The.
Lawrence. Altercation.
Poverty.
Young Fathers.
Lewis. Indian Day.
Karanje Village.
Lindsay. Beggar's Valentine, The.
Honor Among Scamps.
Prologue to "Rhymes to be Traded for Bread."
Lovelace. On the Best, Last, and Only Remaining Comedy of Mr. Fletcher.

Lowry. Hospitality.
I sing the joy of poverty, not such.
McAuley. Child of ten, no more, A.
"MacDiarmid." Glass of Pure Water, The.
Hokum.
In the Slums of Glasgow.
Left-wing poetry represents a rise in the price of bread.
McGrath. Long Way Outside Yellowstone, A.
Tourists at Ensenada.
Trouble with the Times, The.
MacNeice. My Mary.
Slum Song.
Merton. Anger.
Letter to America, A.
Millay. Ballad of the Harp-Weaver, The.
Miller. Free Clinic.
No and I don't know where.
Spade a Spade (Grocery for the Poor), A.
When you live in your car.
Morrison. In This Dim Cave.
Nash. Lines Indited with All the Depravity of Poverty.
Nathan. Ellora.
Likeness, The.
Nemerov. Poverty Programs, The.
Oppen. Street.
Streets, in a poor district.
Patchen. Down in Ol' Dontcaradama.
I Can't Understand! I Can't Understand!
It's a Smallworld.
Piercy. Half Past Home.
Pound. Garret, The.
Prince. Drypoints of the Hasidim.
Ralegh. Have speciall care, that valiant povertie.
"Reed." Dirty Blvd.
Rexroth. Bad Old Days, The.
Robinson. Poor Relation, The.
Rolfe. Homage to Karl Marx.
Rossetti. Who Have a Form of Godliness.
Rukeyser. Chapultepec Park / II.
Silence of Volcanoes.
Scott. Palmer, The.
Shakespeare. Sonnet 125: "Were't aught to me I bore the canopy."
Shelton. Death Row.
Heaven of the Poor, The.
Negative Virtues, The.
Smith, Charlotte. Dead Beggar, an Elegy Addressed to a Lady, The.
Female Exile. Written at Brighthelmstone in November 1792, The.
Written for the Benefit of a Distressed Player, Detained at Brighthelmstone for Debt, November 1792.
Smith, Stevie. Alfred the Great.
Spender. Elementary School Classroom in a Slum, An.
Hamburg, 1929.
In Railway Halls.
Stafford. Dedication, A: "We stood by the library. It was an August night."
Stevens. Dry Loaf.
Good Man Has No Shape, The.
Stevenson. System.
Sutter. Icehouse.
Taconite Harbor.
Swift. Phyllis [or Phillis or Progress of Love, The].
Updike. Eurydice.
Van Duyn. Ja, we had it hard.
Wakoski. Civilization.
Walcott. Laventille.
Walker. Facing the Way.
Talking to My Grandmother Who Died Poor.
Warren. Vital Statistics.
Whittier. Poor Voter on Election Day, The.
Williams, William Carlos. Pastoral; "When I was younger."
Poor, The.
Poor, The.
Proletarian Portrait.
To a Poor Old Woman.
Wordsworth. Alice Fell; or, Poverty.
Fragment: The Baker's Cart.
I Know an Aged Man Constrained to Dwell.

No spade for leagues had won a rood of earth.
Placard for a Poll Bearing an Old Shirt.
Prelude, Prefixed to the Volume Entitled "Poems Chiefly of Early and Late Years."
Wright, James. Before a Cashier's Window in a Department Store.
In Terror of Hospital Bills.
Poor Washed Up by Chicago Winter, The.
Yeats. Ballad of Moll Magee, The.
Young. January.

See also **Need.**

Power
Ammons. Kingpin.
Atwood. Fist, withered and strung, The.
Holding my arms down.
I am sitting on the / edge of the impartial.
I see you fugitive, stumbling across the prarie.
Procedures for Underground.
There are so many things I want.
Through this forest / burned and sparse, the tines.
Torture.
We hear nothing these days.
Women's Issue, A.
You did it / it was you who started the countdown.
You stand at the door / bright as an icon.
Auden. Epitaph on a Tyrant.
Managers, The.
March Winds.
Speech.
Berry. Dark with power.
To Think of the Life of a Man.
Boyle. Weather.
Browning, Robert. Reverie.
Bunting. Darling of Gods and Men, beneath the gliding stars.
Carroll, Jim. Fragment, A: "When I see a rabbit."
Clark. Commanders, The.
Milky Turqoise Cloud.
Dickey, James. Power and Light.
Dickinson. One crown that no one seeks.
Power is a familiar growth.
Doolittle. Pygmalion.
Dunn. Beautiful Women.
Eberhart. And the first, the father, with indomitable will.
Birth of the Spirit, The.
Death in the Mines.
Man's Greed and Envy Are So Great.
Request for Offering.
Sea-Hawk.
Sea-Ruck.
Snowfall, A.
Transfer, The.
Waiting To Lean to the Master's Command.
Words.
Emerson. From high to higher forces.
Motto to "Power."
Power.
Vain against him were hostile blows.
Ford. Little boys, faces smeared.
Gardner. Nursery Rhyme No. 1.
Graves. Powers Unconfessed.
Griffiths. Murder.
Gunn. Legal Reform.
Loot.
Hacker. Rune of the Finland Woman.
Hayden. Wheel, The.
Hemingway. Roosevelt.
Herrick. Bad Princes Pill Their People.
Credit of the Conqueror, The.
Cruelty Base in Commanders.
Factions.
Gods Power.
His Power.
More Mighty, the More Merciful, The.
Power and Peace.
Strength to Support Soveraigty.
Hesketh. Master Cotton Spinner.
Retreat.
Hewitt. Bangor, Spring 1916.
Colonial Consequence.
Curfew Tower, The.
Great Headmaster, A.
He Suggests a Solution.

His Majesty's Inspectors.
Monarch, The.
Moon, The.
Moscow Moment.
Outside the Creeds.
Hughes, Ted. Ghost Crabs.
Jeffers. Be Angry at the Sun.
Blind Horses.
For fifty thousand years man has been dreaming of powers.
Machine, The.
Reference to a Passage in Plutarch's Life of Sulla.
To the Children.
What Odd Expedients.
Lawrence. Escape.
Revolutionary, The.
Liddy. Bicentennial Words for the Liberal Magistrates of 1798.
Lindsay. Queen of Bubbles, The.
Lowry. Ye pow'rs who make mankind your care.
McAuley. She opened the lower button of her blouse.
"MacDiarmid." Poetry like a lance at rest, A.
Meredith. Cannon his name.
Capitalist, The.
Merton. Active Life.
Advising the Prince.
Cracking the Safe.
Inner Law, The.
Kingly Man, The.
Owl and Phoenix.
Time is a child playing draughts.
Morgan. Loki's Song.
Morrison. Leave the Informed Sense.
Nemerov. Political Reflexion [or Reflection].
To Clio, Muse of History.
Neruda. Who can persuade the sea.
Olson. Lion upon the Floor, A.
Oppen. Now we do most of the killing.
Power ruptures at a thousand holes.
Power, which hides what it can.
Pack. Wolf Pack, The.
Patchen. Poem in the Form of a Letter: to Lauro de Bosis.
Piercy. Nine of Cups, The.
Prince. Strafford.
Ransom. Judith of Bethulia.
L'etat C'est Moi.
Robinson. Old King's New Jester, The.
Sunken Crown, The.
Rolfe. Homage to Karl Marx.
Kill the Umpire!
These Men Are Revolution.
Rossetti. O glorious sea that in each climbing wave.
What Hath God Wrought!
Yea, if Thou wilt, Thou canst put up Thy sword.
Rukeyser. Not leaves, not lightning, not the greatness of rivers.
Structure is rising. It takes on shape, it takes on meaning, A.
To follow the hard sunlight on the northern harbor.
Tree of rivers flowing through our lives, A.
Sandburg. Fireborn Are at Home in Fire, The.
From what graveyards and sepulchers have they come.
I am zero, naught, one ciper.
Let the nickels and dimes explain.
Mazuma, the jack, the shekels, the kale, The.
When was it long ago the murmurings began.
Sarton. Binding the Dragon.
Sexton. Admonitions to a Special Person.
Shapiro. Essay on Chess.
Office Love.
Shelley. Cancelled Stanza.
Daemon of the World, The; A Fragment.
Fragment: "I would not be a king—enough."
Smart. On the Power of the Supreme Being.
Snodgrass. Dr. Joseph Goebbels ("Stand back, make way, you mindless scum").
Examination, The.
Hermann Göring, Former Reichsmarschall.
Southwell. Scorne Not the Leaste.

Spender.   War God, The.
Thomas.   Hand That Signed the Paper, The.
Warren.   All is nothing, nothing all.
Wilbur.   She.
Williams, Charles Kenneth.   Beginning of
   April, The.
Wordsworth.   Calais, August, 1802.
   What if our numbers barely could defy.
Wroth.   Song 6: "You happy blessed eyes."
   Sonnet 7: "Love leave to urge, thou know'st
      thou hast the hand."
   Sonnet 13: "Deare fammish nott what you
      your self gave food."
Wyatt.   Of Carthage he, that worthy warrior.
Yeats.   Poet Pleads with the Elemental Powers,
   The.
Zukofsky.   Ferry.
   Two Dedications: D.R.
   You who were made for this music.

Prairies
Carruth.   But once winds lightened, freshening
   fair from the West.
   Song: The Famous Vision of America.
Dickinson.   To make a prairie it takes a clover
   and one bee.
Hugo.   High Grass Prairie.
Kipling.   Prairie, The.
Lindsay.   Prairie Battlements, The.
Roethke.   In Praise of Prairie.
Sandburg.   Haze.
   Interior.
   Prairie.
   Prairie Waters by Night.
   Prairie Woodland.
   Rusty Crimson.
   Two Nocturns.
   Who was that early sodbuster in Kansas? He
      leaned at the gatepost and.
Stafford.   Prairie Town.
Whitman.   Prairie States, The.

Praxiteles
Ferlinghetti.   In hintertime Praxiteles.

Prayer
Ammons.   Figuring Belief.
Angelou.   Thank You, Lord.
Atwood.   Three Praises.
Auden.   Prayer.
Beckett.   Sanies II.
Berry.   Don't pray for the rain to stop.
   It is presumptuous and irresponsible to pray
      for other people. A.
   Prayer after Eating.
   Purification, A.
Berryman.   Night and the City.
Betjeman.   In Westminster Abbey.
Bradstreet.   Deliverance from a Fit of Fainting.
   For the Restoration of My Dear Husband from
      a Burning Ague.
   From Another Sore Fit.
   Here Follow[es] Some Verses upon the
      Burning of Our House [July 10th, 1966.
      Copied Out of a Loose Paper].
   In My Solitary Hours in My Dear Husband
      His Absence.
   In Thankful Acknowledgement for the Letters
      I Received from My Husband Out Of
      England.
   In Thankful[l] Remembrance for My Dear
      Husband[']s Safe Arrival[l].
   My thankful heart with glorying tongue.
   Upon My Daughter Hannah Wiggin her
      Recovery from a Dangerous Fever.
   Upon My Dear and Loving Husband His
      Going into England.
   Upon My Son Samuel His Going For England.
   What God is like to him I serve?
Browning, Elizabeth Barrett.   Earth and Her
   Praisers.
   Isobel's Child.
Browning, Robert.   Guardian-Angel, The.
Burns.   Holy Willie's Prayer.
   Lying at a Reverend Friend's House One
      Night, the Author Left the Following *Verses*
      in the Room Where He Slept.
Campion.   Out of My Soul's Depth.
Carruth.   Chronological.
Chaucer.   Prologue of the Prioress's Tale.

Clough.   O Qui Me—!
   Qui Laborat, Orat.
Cohen.   All My Life.
   Blessed Are You.
   Commentary—Beside My Son.
   Commentary II—This Marriage.
   Holy Is Your Name.
   I Lost My Way.
   If It Be Your Will.
   In the Eyes of Men.
   It Is All Around Me.
   It Is to You I Turn.
   Not Knowing Where to Go.
   Sit Down, Master.
   You Have Sweetened Your Word.
   You Who Pour Mercy into Hell.
   You Who Question Souls.
Coleridge.   He Prayeth Best.
   He Prayeth Well.
Cowper.   Fragment: "He came to him in the
   extasy of pray'r."
Crashaw.   Authors Motto, The.
   C[h]aritas Nimia; or, The Dear[e] Bargain.
   Christs Victory.
   Compline.
   Dies Irae.
   Evensong.
   For the Hour of Prime.
   Howres for the Hours of Matines, The.
   Lauda Sion Salvatorem.
   O Gloriosa Domina.
   Ode on a Prayer-Book.
   On Mr. G. Herberts Booke, The Temple.
   Out of Euphormio.
   Out of *Grotius* his Tragedy of *Christes*
      Sufferinges.
   Prayer, A.
   To the Name above Every Name, the Name of
      Jesus, a Hymn.
   Two Went Up into the Temple To Pray.
   Vexilla Regis.
Cullen.   Pagan Prayer.
Cummings.   Ballade of Soul.
   Noster was a ship of swank, The.
Davie.   Benedictus.
   Bowing the Head.
   Nones.
   Prime.
   Thirty-Ninth Psalm, Adapted, The.
De la Mare.   Motley.
   Prayer, A.
Dickey, James.   Approaching Prayer.
Dickinson.   At least—to pray—is left—is left.
   "Heavenly Father"—take to thee.
   My period had come for Prayer.
   Of Course—I prayed.
   Prayer is the little implement.
   We pray—to Heaven.
Donne.   And whilst [or whil'st] this universal
   choir [or universall Quire].
   Hear[e] us, O hear[e] us Lord; to thee.
   Hymn to God the Father, A.
   Litany, A.
   That we[e] may change to evenness[e].
Doolittle.   If You Will Let Me Sing.
   Prayer: "White, O white face."
   Triplex.
Dunbar.   Crisis, The.
"Dylan."   Father of Night.
Eberhart.   Father, stabilise me. My legs.
Eliot.   Song for Simeon, A.
Emerson.   Dervish whined to *Said*, The.
   I am alone. Sad is my solitude.
   I know this perilous love-lane.
   Many our needs, yet we spare prayers.
   Think not the gods receive thy prayer.
   When success exalts thy lot.
Fletcher.   Prayer of the Antichrist, The.
Gardner.   Ballade: "You who outlive us, you,
   our mortal brothers."
Ginsberg.   Father Guru.
Glück.   Cell, The.
Graves.   Awakening, The.
   Grace Notes.
Gunn.   Well Dennis O'Grady.
Hall.   Grace, A.
Hartley.   O where have I wandered—out.

Hartnett.   Poem for Lara, 10.
   Prisoners.
Hayden.   Incense of the Lucky Virgin.
Heaney.   Stone from Delphi.
Herbert.   Antiphon: "Let all the world in ev'ry
   corner sing / *My God and King.*"
   Antiphon (2): "Praised be the God of love."
   Bag, The.
   Denial[l].
   Evensong.
   Gratefulness.
   Home.
   Jordan (1).
   Matins.
   Obedience.
   Offering, An.
   Praise (3).
   Praise (2).
   Prayer (1): "Prayer the Church's banquet,
      Angels' age."
   Prayer (2).
   Temper (1), The.
   Wreath, A.
Herrick.   Another Grace for a Child.
   Another ("Shame of mans face is no more,
      The").
   Confusion of Face.
   Devotion Makes the Deity.
   Evensong.
   Gods Gifts Not Soon[e] Granted.
   Gods Prt.
   Heart, The.
   His Prayer for Absolution.
   His Wish.
   Hymne to the Muses, An.
   Matins [or Mattens], or Morning Prayer.
   Old Wives Prayer, The.
   Pray and Prosper.
   Prayer.
   Prayers Must Have Poise.
   Psalme or Hymne to the Graces, A.
   Thanksgiving to God for His House, A.
   To Anthea ("Anthea I am going hence").
   To Apollo ("Thou mighty lord and master of
      the Lyre").
   To God: an Anthem, Sung in the Chapel at
      White-Hall, Before the King.
   To God ("Come to me God; but do not
      come").
   To God ("God! to my little meale and oyle").
   To God, in Time of Plundering.
   To God ("Pardon me God").
   To God ("Work is done, The").
   To His Sweet Saviour.
   To Julia ("Help me, Julia, for to pray").
   To Julia ("I am zeellesse, prethee pray").
   To Julia in the Temple.
   To Silvia ("No more my Silvia, do I mean to
      pray").
   Upon Spenke.
   Vow to Minerva, A.
Hewitt.   For a Moment of Darkness over the
   Nations.
   Glendun.
   Hill-Farm, The.
   Isaac McKeown.
   Novice, The.
   Whit Monday.
Hill.   Cycle.
   Hymns to Our Lady of Chartres.
   This is the ash-pit of the lily-fire.
Hopkins.   My prayers must meet a brazen
   heaven.
Hughes, Langston.   Prayer Meeting.
   Sinner.
Johnson.   On Losing the Power of Speech.
   Prayer: "Summe Deus, cui caeca patent
      penetralia cordis."
Jonson.   To Heaven.
Keats.   God of the Meridian.
   Ode to May. Fragment.
Kinnell.   How Many Nights.
Kipling.   Obedient, The.
   Prayer, The: "My brother kneels, so saith
      Kabir."
   Rabbi's Song, The.
   Recessional.

Kunitz. Extermination Camp, The.
Larkin. Come Then to Prayers.
Compline.
Lawrence. Ah, Muriel!
Grey Nurse, The.
Hands of God, The.
Litany of Grey Nurses.
Lord's Prayer.
Maiden's Prayer.
Message to Perfidious Soldier.
No Joy in Life.
Pietá.
Prophet in the Rose Garden, The.
Levertov. Prayer, The.
Levine. Jewish Graveyards, Italy.
To Cipriano, in the Wind.
Lewis. And so we wait the tide, and when the dark.
Liddy. Litany of Satan, The.
Lindsay. Invocation for "The Map of the Universe."
Look You, I'll Go Pray.
Lorde. October.
Release Time.
Lowry. Christ, slashed with an axe, in the humped church.
I set this down as humble prayer.
No prayer for the people.
Prayer from the Wicket Gate for Forty One Doors for Forty Two.
Prayer: "I pray that I may form a prayer, oh Lord."
Prayer: "Oh thou who art not above."
McGrath. Restless Night, The.
MacNeice. Jam Lucis Orto Sidere.
Prayer before Birth.
Prayer in Mid-Passage.
Meredith. Child's Prayer, A.
Merrill. Santo.
Merton. Christina.
Evening Prayer.
Fugitive.
Great Prayer.
Ibn Abbad Described by a Friend (Ibn Qunfud).
Litany: "All holy souls / pray for us fellows."
Prayer to Saint Anatole.
Reader, The.
Theory of Prayer.
To the Immaculate Virgin, on a Winter Night.
Two States of Prayer.
Whitsun Canticle, A.
Write a prayer to a computer?
Millay. Poem and Prayer for an Invading Army.
Miller. For Those Who Pray for the Souls of Broken Dolls.
Milton. Jehovah to my words give ear.
Lord in thine anger do not reprehend me.
Morrison. American Prayer, An.
Soft Parade, The.
Thank You, O Lord.
Olson. Hear my prayer my father.
Pack. Prayer for Prayer.
Poe. Hymn: "At morn—at noon—at twilight dim."
Psalms. Psalm 5: "Give ear to my words, O Lord, consider my meditation."
Psalm 6: "O Lord, rebuke me not in thine anger."
Psalm 61: "Hear my cry, O God.."
Psalm 77: "I cried unto God with my voice.."
Psalm 116: "I love the Lord.."
Raine. Spell of Sleep.
Ralegh. Authours Epitaph, Made by Himself, The.
Rossetti. Alas my Lord, / How should I wrestle all the livelong night.
Ash Wednesday.
Changing Chimes.
Christmas Carol, A: "Thank God, thank God, we do believe."
Eleventh Hour, The.
End Is Not Yet, The.
Exceeding Bitter Cry, An.
Exultate Deo.
For H.P.

I Do Set My Bow in the Cloud.
Imitated From the Arpa Evangelica: Page 121.
Last Answer, The.
O Lord, I cannot plead my love of Thee.
Palm Sunday.
Praying Always.
St. Andrew's Church.
Sinner's own fault? So it was, The.
Take No Thought for The Morrow.
That Which Hath Been Is Named Already, and It Is Known That It Is Man.
Then Shall Ye Shout.
There Remaineth Therefore a Rest to the People of God.
They Toil Not, Neither Do They Spin.
Thou, God, Seest Me.
Thro' burden and heat of the day.
Way of the World, The.
What Is That to Thee? Follow Thou Me.
When My Heart Is Vexed I Will Complain ("Fields are white to harvest, look and see, The").
World's Harmonies, The.
Rukeyser. Place-Rituals.
St. John. Interlude: Hephaestion's Prayer.
Sandburg. Fire Dreams.
On Lang Syne Plantation they had a prayer.
Our Prayer of Thanks.
Prayer after World War.
Sarton. Prayer before Work.
Schuyler. Our Father.
Sexton. Cigarettes and Whiskey and Wild, Wild Women.
Ninth Psalm.
Praying on a 707.
Praying to Big Jack.
Second Psalm.
Smart. Hope.
Jubilate Agno.
Prayer.
Smith, Stevie. In the Park.
Why Are the Clergy..?
Spender. Rejoice in the Abyss.
Stevenson. All influences were in vain.
As one who having wandered all night long.
Good Boy, A.
House Beautiful, The.
Last night we had a thunderstorm in style.
Prayer: "I ask good things that I detest."
System.
This gloomy northern day.
Thought, A.
Thomas. Complaint on the Miseries of Life, A.
Conversation of Prayer, The.
Vision and Prayer.
Thomson. Paraphrase on the Latter Part of the Sixth Chapter of St. Matthew's, A.
Psalm CIV Paraphrased.
Tomlinson. Weeper in Jalisco.
Warren. Answer to Prayer.
Whittier. Andrew Rykman's Prayer.
Dedication: "I would the gift I offer here."
Garrison of Cape Ann, The.
Prayer of Agassiz, The.
Prayer-Seeker, The.
Swan Song of Parson Avery, The.
Truce of Piscataqua, The.
Wish of To-day, The.
Williams, Miller. Vision and Prayer.
Wordsworth. Devotional Incitements.
Force of Prayer, The; or, The Founding of Bolton Priory; A Tradition.
On a High Part of the Coast in Cumberland.
Upon the Late General Fast. March, 1832.
Wright, James. Confession to J. Edgar Hoover.
Elegy for the Poet Morgan Blum, An.
Prayer in My Sickness, A.
Prayer to the Lord Ramakrishna, A.
Trying to Pray.
Wyatt. O Lord, since in my mouth thy mighty name.
Prologue: "Love, to give law unto his subject hearts."
Yeats. Blessed, The.
Mohini Chatterjee.

Prayer for My Daughter, A.
Prayer for My Son, A.
Praying Mantis
Carroll, Jim. Praying Mantis.
Ford. There's that praying.
Nash. Praying Mantis, The.
Zukofsky. "Mantis."
"Mantis," An Interpretation.
Preaching and Preachers
Cummings. Skinny voice / of the leatherfaced, The.
This evangelist / buttons with his big gollywog voice.
Davie. Gathered Church, A.
Emerson. ʼΑΔΑΚΡΥΝ ΝΕΜΟΝΤΑΙ ΑΙΩΝΑ.
Herrick. Upon Parson Beanes.
Hewitt. Demagogue.
Jenny Geddes.
Last Crusade, The.
Hugo. No Bells to Believe.
Kipling. At His Execution.
Mulholland's Contract.
Lindsay. As I built cob-houses with small cousins on the floor.
MacNeice. All is well, said the voice from the tiny pulpit.
Preacher, The.
Merton. Prayer and Sermon of Ibn Abbad.
Roethke. Judge Not.
Smith, Stevie. Where Are You Going?
Stevenson. Lowden Sabbath Morn, A.
Wind is without there and howls in the trees, The.
Sutter. As a boy my father preached to trees.
Tomlinson. For Miriam.
Whitman. Child's Amaze, A.
Whittier. Daniel Wheeler.
Preacher, The.
To J. P.
See also **Clergy.**
Precocity
Koertge. He ("Told me that I shouldn't have books like that").
Predators
Clark. Silence of the Lambs, The.
Donne. Whale, The.
Eberhart. Ospreys in Cry.
Swallows Return, The.
Fenton. Killer Snails, The.
Haines. Dream of the Lynx.
Goshawk, The.
Hesketh. Gone Away.
Mallard, The.
Panther and the Antelope, The.
Hughes, Ted. Eagle.
That Moment.
Lewis. Tiger of Camden Town, The.
Lindsay. Spider and the Ghost of the Fly, The.
What Grandpa Mouse Said.
Lovelace. Lady with a Falcon on Her Fist, A.
Lowry. Dodder, The.
Merrill. Violent Pastoral.
Morrison. Promises.
Owen. Arms and the Boy.
Rossetti. Handy Mole who plied no shovel, A.
Shelley. Bigotry's Victim.
Snodgrass. Lullaby: The Comforting of Cock Robin.
Tomlinson. How Still the Hawk.
Predestination
Eberhart. Sacrifice, The.
Hardy. Subalterns, The.
Herrick. Another ("Art thou not destin'd? then, with hast, go on").
Predestination.
Hesketh. Imagination.
Hewitt. My First Reported Words.
Psychometrist's Remarkable Forecast, The.
Hughes, Ted. Whether you say it, think it, know it.
Lindsay. North Star Whispers to the Blacksmith's Son, The.
Nemerov. Western Approaches, The.
Rossetti. If I Could Trust Mine Own Self.
Pregnancy
Berry. Poem for J.

Berryman. Damned.
Boyle. Waterfront for Allan Ross MacDougall, A.
Burns. To the Weaver's Gin Ye Go.
Wha'll M-w Me Now.
Ceravolo. Pregnant, I Come.
Crane. Stark Major.
Creeley. "For Some Weeks.."
Dickey, James. At the Home for Unwed Mothers.
Dickinson. Boston Lying-In.
Dove. Weathering Out.
Dunn. Building in Nova Scotia.
Fox. Letters from the Island.
River and Light.
Graves. Name.
Gunn. Baby Song.
Hacker. 1973.
Hartley. Blessed Event.
Heaney. Act of Union.
Hughes, Langston. What? So Soon!
Jeffers. Loving Shepherdess, The.
Jong. Another Language.
Anti-Conception.
Buddha in the Womb, The.
Gardener.
Lawrence. Youth Mowing, A.
Liddy. In the Bowling Alley.
Lorde. Now That I Am Forever with Child.
McNeill. Aubade to Fear (Heavy with Child).
Life-Force.
Lullaby:"Herda, herda, herda, sing my sisters."
Mahon. Ford Manor.
Unborn Child, An.
Markson. Anne-on-Avon.
Footnotes to "Anne-on-Avon."
Meinke. Monk can do his work on bended knees, A.
Pack. Clayfeld's Infancy.
Clayfeld's Microscope.
Look, there it is—I'm sure that is the oak.
Piercy. Provocation of the Dream, The.
Plath. Heavy Women.
Metaphors.
Rich. There Are Such Springlike Nights.
Rukeyser. All the Little Animals.
Tunnel, The.
Unborn Song.
Sandburg. Poppies.
Snyder. Berry Feast, A.
Spender. Dream, The.
One.
Updike. March: A Birthday Poem.
Origin of Laughter, The.
Waldman. 8/9.
Song: Time Drawes Neere.
Wright, James. Trouble.
Young. For Arl in Her Sixth Month.
Night before Michael Was Born, The.

Prehistoric Man. *see* **Cavemen; Man, Primitive.**

Prejudice
Berry. In the thought of you I imagine myself free of the weapons and the official hates that I have borne on my back like a hump.
Brooks. Men of careful turns, haters of forks in the road.
Ciardi. My Tribe.
Dunbar. To Miss Mary Britton.
Hacker. For Jean Migrenne.
Hewitt. Demagogue.
From the Tibetan.
Happy Boy, A.
Lines for a Dead Alderman.
Minister.
Strangers and Neighbors.
Kipling. Jobson's Amen.
Stranger, The.
Tommy.
Moore. Labors of Hercules, The.
Ralegh. If a Phoenician born I am, what then?
Rolfe. June 19, 1953.
Rukeyser. What Do We See?
Sandburg. Blood of all men of all nations being red, The.
Man, the Man-Hunter.

Shelley. Bigotry's Victim.
Smart. Moderation.
Snodgrass. W. D. Tries to Warn Cock Robin.

See also **Racial Prejudice; Racism and Racists; Sexism.**

Presbyterianism and Presbyterians
Milton. On the Forcers of Conscience.

Presence
Coleridge. Angel Visitant, An.
Creeley. As real as thinking.
Fire, The.
Here.
Like They Say.
Photo.
Smell of gum wrappers as of Saturday afternoon at movies.
Two Times ("Image / docteur").
Woman, The.
Eliot. Mélange Adultère de Tout.
Emerson. Dearest, where thy shadow falls.
Fisher. Dawn birds at noon.
Gallagher. Hands of the Blindman, The.
Herrick. Gods Presence ("God's evident, and may be said to be").
Presence and Absence.
Knott. Goodbye.
Kunitz. Very Tree.
Levertov. Presence, The.
Thread, The.
Wings, The.
Liddy. From This Distance: The Last Poem of the Clare Bards in Praise of the MacDonnells of Kilkee.
Lowry. Welcome Home oh Harteebeeste beloved who doth with thy.
Olson. Cole's Island.
Rich. City.
Williams, Miller. House in the Vacant Lot, The.
Wright, Charles. Each year the dead grow less dead, and nudge.
Young. Available Light.
Blues Don't Change, The.
Kicking.
Orchard at Night in Rain Light, The.
Total Incandescence.
Yes, the Secret Mind Whispers.
Zukofsky. Air.
Whatever makes this happening.
You three:—my wife.

Presents. *see* **Gifts and Giving.**

Presidency, The, United States
Berryman. Presidential flags! and the General is here.
Carroll, Jim. Inauguration Day.
Hall. Presidentiad, The.
Hemingway. Roosevelt.
Hoffman. Shaking the President's Hand.
Jeffers. Woodrow Wilson.
Lindsay. Bryan, Bryan, Bryan, Bryan.
Roosevelt.
MacLeish. State Funeral: March 31, 1969.
Olson. Hustings, The ("Future sucks, The").
Hustings, The ("Under the eyes").
Rufus Woodpecker visited the President.
Wakoski. Uncle Sam in the White House.
Whitman. Sobbing of the Bells, The.
To the States, To Identify the 16th, 17th, or 18th Presidentiad.
Whittier. Song, A: "Beneath thy skies, November!"

Presley, Elvis
Gunn. Elvis Presley.
Painkillers.
Sandburg. Graceland.

Presumption
Catullus. Carmen 105: "O'Toole / attempting an entry of the *mons Parnassus.*"
Cummings. But granted that it's nothing paradoxically enough beyond mere personal.
Space being(don't forget to remember)Curved.
Dickinson. Presumption has it's Affliction.
"Dylan." License to Kill.
With God on Our Side.
Graves. Cliff Edge, The.
Kipling. Lollius.

Neruda. This Is Simple.
Rich. Apparition.
Williams, Charles Kenneth. Next to the Last Poem about God, The.
Shame.
Wright, Charles. March Journal.
Zukofsky. Meantool reconnoiters Pipléa scanning Their mountain.

Pretension
Ammons. Camels.
Burns. Epitaph Extempore, on a Person Nicknamed the Marquis, Who Desired Burns to Write One on Him.
Monody on Maria.
Toadeater, The.
Campion. Heart's Music.
Chaucer. Epilogue to the Man of Laws' Tale, The.
Clare. Braggart.
Clough. Go foolish thoughts, and join the throng.
Davie. Owl Minerva, The.
Donne. Satire 4: "Well, I may now receive, and die: my sin."
Upon Mr. Thomas Coryat's Crudities.
Eberhart. Laocoön.
Eliot. Portrait of a Lady.
Emerson. Early after the night long revel.
Park, The.
Romany Girl, The.
Hewitt. Island Folk Tale, An.
Memorial Service.
Old Men Sitting.
On Reading Terence de Vere White on Landor.
Victorian Steps Out, A.
Hughes, Langston. Warning: Augmented.
Hughes, Ted. Once I said lightly.
Jonson. On English Monsieur.
To Sir Annual Tilter.
Lawrence. Gentleman, The.
Natural Complexion.
To Be Superior.
Tolerance.
Markson. Dante Gabriel.
See Susan Read.
Nash. Reflections on the Vernacular.
There Were Giants in Those Days or Maybe There Weren't.
What's in a Name? Here's What's in a Name, or, I Wonder What Became of John and Mary.
Olson. Issues from the Hand of God.
Pope. To Eustace Budgell, Esq., on His Translation of the Characters of Theophrastus.
Shapiro. University.
Spender. Art Student.

Pride
Angelou. Phenomenal Woman.
Auden. Pride.
Pride.
Beatles. I've Just Seen a Face.
Bukowski. Poem for Liz.
Burns. Ronalds of the Bennals, The.
Song: "As I cam down by yon castle wa' ."
Song: "Mark yonder pomp of costly fashion."
Toadeater, The.
Campion. Do Not, Oh, Do Not Prize.
Carruth. Tanck's Brag.
Tanck's Song About Pride.
Ceravolo. Wild Provoke of the Endurance Sky.
Cohen. When I Have Not Rage.
Cowper. Truth.
Crashaw. On Nanus Mounted on an Ant.
Creeley. "For Some Weeks.."
Gangster.
Cullen. Advice to a Beauty.
To an Unknown Poet.
Dickey, William. For Every Last Batch When the Next One Comes Along.
Dickinson. Poor little Heart!
Dobyns. Body's Curse, The.
Emerson. Bended to fops who bent to him.
Bluebeard. Let the gentle wife prepare.
Good-bye.

Fletcher. End of Job, The.
Then the archangels all together abandoned the black menacing sky.
Frost. Haec Fabula Docet.
Galvin. Last Man in the Quabbin, The.
Gardner. Abraham and Isaac.
Graves. Child with Veteran.
My Ghost.
Pride of Love.
Progress, The.
Questions in a Wood.
Unicorn and the White Doe.
Hacker. Iva's Birthday Poem.
Hardy. Dear, The.
Whaler's Wife, The.
Hartley. Old Lady in the Park.
She had a way of doing.
Herbert. Church Monuments.
Flower, The.
Vanity [or Vanitie] (1).
Herrick. Pride Allowable in Poets.
Sobriety in Search.
To Dianeme ("Sweet, be not proud of those two eyes").
To His Honour'd Friend, Sir Thomas Heale.
Upon Tubbs.
Hewitt. Ars Poetica.
Ballad, The.
Country Talk.
Grandfather Robinson Dies in 1898.
Minotaur.
Montelepre.
My Uncle Willy.
On Reading Terence de Vere White on Landor.
Spring Restored, The.
Stone.
Ulster Names.
What Little Happened There.
Hopkins. Of virtues I most warmly bless.
Hughes, Langston. Ballad of the Girl Whose Name Is Mud.
Madam and the Census Man.
Hughes, Ted. Haunting, A.
Jeffers. Rock and Hawk.
Kipling. English Flag, The.
Islanders, The.
Legend of Mirth, The.
Knott. Two Vietnam Poems: (1966).
Lawrence. Conceit.
Finding Your Level.
Fireflies in the Corn.
Humiliation.
Proper Pride.
Levine. Animals Are Passing from Our Lives.
Lewis. Song: "I lay in sheets of softest linen."
Lindsay. Kind of Scorn, A.
Lowry. More Impatience.
No Kraken Shall Be Found Till Sought By Name.
Song for My Wife.
Meinke. Father.
Meredith. Believe me, I have studied men.
Bellerophon.
Creed.
Reason.
Were men of such importance as they deem.
Morrison. Fear is a Porch.
Nash. Platitudinous Reflection.
Neruda. This Is Simple.
O'Hara. Savoy.
Oppen. Ozymandias.
Prince. Young question of *What it is for* stays always, The.
Ralegh. Have speciall care, that valiant povertie.
Ransom. Overtures.
Rossetti. Dead City, The.
Helen Grey.
Standing Afar Off for the Fear of Her Torment.
Surely there is an aching void within.
Young Men Aye Were Fickle Found Since Summer Trees Were Leafy.
Rukeyser. Bubble of Air.
Sandburg. Acquaintance with Death, Sir.
Blood of all men of all nations being red, The.

Primer Lesson.
Proud and Beautiful.
Proud of Their Rags.
Proud Torsos.
Skyscrapers Stand Proud.
Swell People.
Sarton. Exchange of Gifts, An.
Franz, a Goose.
Hard Death, A.
Memory of Swans.
Scott. Boat Song.
Invocation: "Harp of the North! that mouldering long hast hung."
Sexton. Civil War, The.
Shakespeare. Sonnet 91: "Some glory in their birth, some in their skill."
Shelley. Ozymandias [of Egypt].
Sidney. Now thanked be the great god *Pan.*
Sonnet 27: "Because I oft, in dark abstracted guise."
Sonnet 53: "In martial sports I had my cunning tried."
Silverstein. Battle, The.
Invention.
Snodgrass. Flash Flood.
Sorrentino. Fixture, A.
Stafford. Our Kind.
Stevenson. Foreign Children.
Thomson. To the God of Fond Desire.
Updike. Commencement, Pingree School.
Warren. I had once poured oil on his head.
Whitman. Inca's Daughter, The.
Punishment of Pride, The.
Whittier. Cities of the Plain, The.
Judith at the Tent of Holofernes.
Maids of Attitash, The.
Yankee Girl, The.
Williams, Charles Kenneth. Spirit the Triumph, The.
Wordsworth. Lines: "Nay, Traveller! rest. This lonely Yew-tree stands."
Pilgrim's Dream; or, The Star and the Glow-Worm, The.
Wright, James. In Shame and Humiliation.
Winter Night, A.
Yeats. Peacock, The.

Priests. *see* **Clergy.**

Primitive Man. *see* **Man, Primitive.**

Primroses
Burns. Primrose, The.
Donne. Primrose[, Being at Montgomery Castle, upon the Hill, on Which It Is Situate], The.
Hardy. Unplanted Primrose, The.
Herrick. Primrose, The.
Hesketh. Imagination.
Reply to a Philistine.
Wordsworth. Primrose of the Rock, The.
Tuft of Primroses, The.

Princes and Princesses
Byron. Fragment of an Epistle to Thomas Moore.
Sonnet to the Prince Regent.
Campion. To the Most High and Mighty Prince Charles.
Coleridge. On a Late Connubial Rupture in High Life.
Crashaw. Upon the birth of the Princesse Elizabeth.
Davie. Put Not Your Trust in Princes.
De la Mare. Heresy.
Mourn'st Thou Now?
Emerson. Prince the ball of heaven should.
Shah Sandschar, whose lowest slave.
Graves. Frog and the Golden Ball, The.
Herrick. Bad Princes Pill Their People.
Gentlenesse.
Pollicie in Princes.
Prevision, or Provision.
To the Right Gratious Prince, Lodwick, Duke of Richmond and Lenox.
Hesketh. Unicorn.
Hewitt. Iron and Stone.
MacLeish. Acknowledgement.
Meredith. Beauty Rohtraut.
When the South sang like a nightingale.
Patchen. Legend for a Little Child.

Plath. Princess and the Goblins, The.
Rossetti. Royal Princess, A.
Sexton. Twelve Dancing Princesses, The.
Sidney. Since wailing is a bud of causeful sorrow.
Smith, Stevie. Days of Yore, The.
Forlorn Sea, The.
Voices about the Princess Anemone.
Sorrentino. Ultima Despedida del Principe Poniatowski de Su Familia.
Stevenson. To an Island Princess.
To Mesdames Zassetsky and Garschine.
Stuart. Sunburst.
Wilbur. Up, Jack.
Yau. Some fish we peel back, leaving only the bones. Others devour us.

Princeton University
Eberhart. Half-bent Man.

Printing and Printers
Boyle. Print from a Lucite Block.
Hughes, Langston. Madam's Calling Cards.
Kipling. Press, The.
Pope. Translator, The.
Verses Occasioned by an &c. at the End of Mr. D'Urfy's Name in the Title to One of His Plays.
Verses to be Prefix'd before Bernard Lintot's New Miscellany.
Sutter. Night Shift: the Composing Room.
Updike. Tune, in American Type.
Whitman. Font of Type, A.

Prisoners of War
Brontë. Gleneden's Dream.
Organ swells, the trumpets sound, The.
Dickey, James. Performance, The.
Fenton. Prison Island.
Vuccerìa.
Hewitt. Man from the Mountains, The.
Jarrell. Stalag Luft.
Lawrence. Prisoner at Work in a Turkish Garden.
Prisoners at Work in the Rain.
Patchen. What Happened in the Camps.
Prince. Coeur de Lion.
Rukeyser. Breaking Open.
Scott. Lay of the Imprisoned Huntsman.
Smith, Charlotte. Written at the Same Place, on Seeing a Seaman Return Who Had Been Imprisoned at Rochfort.
Williams, Miller. Wiedersehen.

Prisons and Prisoners
Angelou. Prisoner.
Brontë. Ierne's eyes were glazed and dim.
M.A. Written on the Dungeon Wall.
Still, let my tyrants know, I am not doomed to wear.
Written in the Gaaldine Prison Caves to A.G.A.
Written on Returning to the P. of I. on the 10th of January, 1827.
Browning, Elizabeth Barrett. Prisoner, The.
Bunting. Let his days be few and let.
Burns. Fragment—Epistle from Esopus to Maria.
Lament of Mary Queen of Scots on the Approach of Spring.
Byron. Oh You, Who in All Names Can Tickle the Town.
Sonnet on Chillon.
Campion. To My Honourable Friend, Sr. Thomas Mounson, *Knight and Baronet.*
Carruth. Lana.
Clare. Ballad: "Summer morning is risen."
Coleridge. Dungeon, The.
Cooper. Breslau, Spring 1918.
Crabbe. Condemned Felon, The.
Cullen. Thoughts in a Zoo.
Cummings. But if a living dance upon dead minds.
Mind is its own beautiful prisoner, The.
Moon falls through the autumn   Behind prisons she grins, The.
De la Mare. In the Dock.
Monologue, The.
One in the Public Gallery.
Dickey, James. When.
Dickinson. How soft this Prison is.

Of Paul and Silas it is said.
Prison gets to be a friend, A.
Dobyns. Walls To Put Up, Walls To Take Down.
Donne. Oh my black[e] soul[e]! now thou art summoned.
Doolittle. Prisoners.
Dunbar. Garret, The.
Sympathy.
"Dylan." Ballad of Donald White.
George Jackson.
Walls of Red Wing.
Eberhart. In Prisons of Established Craze.
Fenton. Prison Island.
Ford. Prison Life.
Frost. Line-Gang, The.
Ginsberg. Meaningless Institution, A.
Sometime Jailhouse Blues.
Graves. Certain Mercies.
Philosopher, The.
Reduced Sentence, A.
Gunn. In the Tank.
La Prisonnière.
Hayden. Prisoners, The.
Hemingway. Captives.
Hewitt. At the Newsagent's.
Housman. Oh who is that young sinner with the handcuffs on his wrists?
Hugo. Bridge of Sighs, The.
In Your Dream after Falling in Love.
Letter to Birch from Deer Lodge.
Jarrell. O My Name It Is Sam Hall.
Officers' Prison Camp Seen from a Troop-Train, An.
Prisoners.
Wild Birds, The.
Jong. Prisoner, The.
Joseph. Catch.
Dog Body and Cat Mind.
Keats. Written on the Day That Mr. Leigh Hunt Left Prison.
Kipling. Captive, The.
Cells.
Half-Ballad of Waterval.
We now, held in captivity.
Knight. Cell Song.
Fable: "Once upon a today and yesterday and nevermore there were 7 men."
For Freckle-Faced Gerald.
Haiku: "Eastern guard tower."
He Sees Through Stone.
Idea of Ancestry, The.
Penal Farm, The.
Rehabilitation & Treatment in the Prisons of America.
Warden Said to Me the Other Day, The.
WASP Woman Visits a Black Junkie in Prison, A.
Knott. Shorts / Excerpts ("Suddenly I understood").
Lawrence. Sisters, I am sorry for this foreign man.
Levine. Heaven.
Lewis. They have clipped the wings of my doves, my messengers.
Lindsay. Gamblers, The.
Lovelace. To Althea, from Prison.
To Lucasta, from Prison.
Vintage to the Dungeon, The.
Lowell. In the Cage.
Memories of West Street and Lepke.
Lowry. Nocturne: "This evening Venus signs alone."
Sestina in a Cantina.
There was an old Consul called Firmin.
Merton. Aegeus in Prison.
But did you ever know the whole world was once held prisoner in a bank?
Tropics.
Miller. For Han Shan on His Cold Mountain.
For Phil.
Room in a Penitentiary.
Paley. Women's Prison: El Salvador / The Ballad of Visiting Day, The.
Patchen. He Is Guarded by Crowds and Shackled with Formalities.
How Jimsey O'Roon and Peter Stack, Coal

Miners, Came to Be Put in the Ferbettville (Pa.) Jail Early One Saturday Night.
Theory of Nato-geography as Advanced by the Tiaphidian Man, With a Comment on the Character of His Penal System, A.
Plath. Jailer, The.
Pope. Epistle to Robert Earl of Oxford and Earl Mortimer.
Prince. Campanella.
Ralegh. My Body in the Walls Captived.
Rich. From the Prison House.
Prisoners, The.
Rossetti. Epitaph: "Slave yet wearing on my head a crown, A."
Tasso and Leonora.
Sandburg. Bars.
Teamster's Farewell, A.
Shelley. Fragment: To a Friend Released from Prison.
Shelton. Harry Orchard.
Simic. Drawn to Perspective.
Prisoner, The.
Rough Outline.
Smith, Charlotte. Written for the Benefit of a Distressed Player, Detained at Brighthelmstone for Debt, November 1792.
Smith, Stevie. Commuted Sentence, The.
Sorrentino. Vapid Transit.
Spender. Prisoners, The.
Walcott. Forest of Europe.
Warren. Penological Study: Southern Exposure.
Whitman. Singer in the Prison, The.
Whittier. Prisoner for Debt, The.
Williams, Charles Kenneth. Saturday.
Wordsworth. Captivity.—Mary Queen of Scots.
Convict, The.
I Know an Aged Man Constrained to Dwell.
When Philoctetes in the Lemnian Isle.
Wright, James. American Twilights, 1957.
Young. Visiting Day.

Privacy
Auden. Private faces in public places.
Carroll, Jim. To the National Endowment for the Arts.
Carruth. Sonnet: "Last night, I don't know if from habit or intent."
Cohen. Cross Didn't Fall on Me, A.
Threat.
Davie. Against Confidences.
Dickinson. I'm Nobody! Who are you?
To my quick ear the Leaves—conferred.
Dunn. Corners.
Fairy Tale.
How to Be Happy: Another Memo to Myself.
Secret Life, A.
Gardner. Milkman, The.
Graves. Secrecy.
Herrick. His Wish to Privacie.
Hesketh. Defeathered.
Hewitt. Dissertation II.
Hedgehog: For R., The.
On the Preservation of Work Sheets.
Kinnell. There Are Things I Tell to No One.
Lewis. *Civil Servant, The.*
Moore. Injudicious Gardening.
Nash. I Spy, or, The Depravity of Privacy.
Mrs. Purvis Dreads Room Service.
My Daddy.
Piercy. Somehow.
Plath. Eavesdropper.
Sidney. Sonnet 54: "Because I breathe not love to every one."
Sorrentino. Prince Rupert's Drop.
Warren. And Don't Forget Your Corset Cover, Either.
See also **Solitude.**

Privateers
Kipling. When the Great Ark.

Prizefighting and Prizefighters
Hartley. Three Friends: Outline for a Picture.

Procrastination
"Carroll, Lewis." Punctuality.
Ceravolo. Wind Is Blowing West, The.
Dunbar. Lapse, The.
Hewitt. No Cresta Run.

One I Loved, The.
Pour Hélène.
Nash. I'll Get One Tomorrow.
Procrastination Is All of the Time.

Prodigal Son
Bishop. Prodigal, The.
Crashaw. Luke 15; On the Prodigall.
Kipling. Prodigal Son, The.
Rossetti. Prodigal Son, A.

Prodigality
Lowry. Exile's Return.
Marlowe. 1.8: Execratur lenam, quae puellam suam meretricia arte instituebat.
Southwell. Prodigall Chyld's Soule Wracke, The.

Progress
Ammons. Progress Report.
Atwood. Alternate Thoughts from Underground.
Is / Not.
Auden. Moon Landing.
Recitative by Death.
We've covered enough ground since that awkward day.
Berry. Against the War in Vietnam.
Horses.
Manifesto: the Mad Farmer Liberation Front.
Streets, guns, machines.
Want of Peace, The.
Betjeman. Inexpensive Progress.
Browning, Elizabeth Barrett. Rhapsody of Life's Progress, A.
Clough. To think that men of former days.
Cummings. Jehovah buried,Satan dead.
O pr / gress verily thou art m.
Of all the blessings which to man.
Pity This Busy Monster, Manunkind.
Davie. Mustered into the Avant-Garde.
"Dylan." Ain't Gonna Grieve.
License to Kill.
Paths of Victory.
Eberhart. On Shooting Particles beyond the World.
Parker River, The.
United 555.
Emerson. Once the priest / Lived in an age.
Fenton. Kingfisher's Boxing Gloves, The.
South Parks Road.
Terminal Moraine, A.
Frost. Some Science Fiction.
Galvin. Last Man in the Quabbin, The.
Graves. Personal Packaging, Inc.
Gunn. Considering the Snail.
Hall. Elegy for Wesley Wells.
Red Branch, The.
Hardy. Christmas: 1924.
Discouragement.
Hundred Years Since, A.
Inscriptions for a Peal of Eight Bells.
Hewitt. Admonition to Science.
Ceilidhe, The.
Drift of Petals, The.
Lint Pulling, The.
Hughes, Ted. Do Not Pick Up the Telephone.
Rock Has Not Learned.
Hugo. Announcement.
Letter to Oberg from Pony.
Making Certain It Goes On.
Plans for Altering the River.
Starting Back.
Jeffers. Broken Balance, The.
Cycle, The.
Decaying Lambskins.
Dog in the Sky, The.
Torch-Bearers' Race, The.
What is Worthless?
Kipling. Benfactors, The.
Secret of the Machines, The.
Levine. 7 Years from Somewhere.
Liddy. In a Blue Smoke.
Lindsay. Rhyme About an Electrical Advertising Sign, A.
McAuley. Spokane Perspective.
McGrath. Legendary Progress.
Portents.
McNeill. Hard Road, The.
Mahon. Consolations of Philosophy.

Meinke. Hermann Ludwig Ferdinand Von Helmholtz.
Progress.
Meredith. Congress of Nations, The.
Labourer, The.
Progress.
Progression.
World's Advance, The.
Merton. Natur / aabho / rrret / vacuu / uuuum.
Old monk is turned loose / And can travel!, The.
Millay. We have gone too far; we do not know how to stop: impetus.
Nash. Caesar Knifed Again, or, Culture Biz Gets Hep, Boffs Profs.
First Chime.
Look What You Did, Christopher!
No Wonder Our Fathers Died.
Up from the Wheelbarrow.
What, No Sheep?
Nathan. Progress Report.
Nemerov. Great Society, Mark X, The.
Wheel King, The.
Oppen. Building of the Skyscraper, The.
Technologies.
Three wide / Funnels raked aft, and the masts slanted, The.
Paley. Bob Visits Friends.
Ralegh. Strong Ilion thou shalt see with walls and towers high.
Rich. Amnesia.
Robinson. Modernities.
Town Down the River, The.
Rukeyser. Book of the Dead, The.
Breaking the nets of the world, in glimpses going.
Trophies.
Sandburg. Bitter Summer Thoughts.
Four Preludes on Playthings of the Wind.
Great Sphinx and the Pyramids say, The.
Hunger and only hunger changes worlds?
People, yes, The.
People, yes, the people, The.
Prairie.
Response of wild birds, The.
Sea moves always, the wind moves always, The.
Smoke Blue.
There have been thousands of Andy Adams.
Unemployed / Without a stake in the country, The.
Who shall speak for the people?
Who were those editors picking the most.
Schwartz. Kilroy's Carnival; A Poetic Prologue for TV.
When a hundred years had passed nature seemed to man / a clock.
Shelton. Machines, The.
New Road, The.
Snyder. L M F B R.
Sutter. Witch Tree.
Tomlinson. Gladstone Street.
Quarry, The.
Return to Hinton.
Way In, The.
Whitman. Going Somewhere.
Williams, Charles Kenneth. Spirit the Triumph, The.
Williams, Miller. Love and How It Becomes Important in Our Day to Day Lives.
Main Street.
Wordsworth. Nunnery.
Steamboats, Viaducts and Railways.

Prometheus
Browning, Elizabeth Barrett. Prometheus Bound.
Wail of Prometheus Bound, The.
Byron. Prometheus.
Campion. Full Song, A.
Song, A: "Come away; bring thy golden theft."
Cowper. On the Inventor of Guns.
Dunbar. Prometheus.
Graves. Prometheus.
Milton. On the Inventor of Gunpowder.
Rich. Always the Same.
Swift. Prometheus.

Tomlinson. Prometheus.

Promises
Beatles. All My Loving.
If I Fell.
Tell Me What You See.
Wait.
Browning, Elizabeth Barrett. Sonnet: "But only three in all God's universe."
Sonnet "First time that the sun rose on thine oath, The."
Burns. Thou hast left me ever, Jamie.
Byron. Endorsement to the Deed of Separation, in the April of 1816.
Catullus. Carmen 82: "My eyes in your pledge, Quintius."
Carmen 110: "Men always praise an honest whore."
Cohen. I'm Your Man.
Cowper. Epigram of Homer, An.
Dickinson. Promise is firmer than a Hope, A.
Emerson. But God will keep his promise yet.
She never comes to me.
Gardner. Collage of Echoes.
Graves. As All Must End.
Court of Love, A.
Earlier Lovers.
Elsewhere.
Falcon Woman, The.
Impossible, The.
Lion-Gentle.
Oath, The.
Purification.
Rose, The.
Scared Child, The.
Song: Basket of Blossom.
Song: The Promise.
To Tell and Be Told.
Until We Both.
Vow, The.
Herrick. Gods Time Must End Our Trouble.
Rainbow; or Curious Covenant, The.
To God ("Thou hast promis'd, Lord, to be").
To His Conscience.
To His Mistress[e].
Housman. Westward on the high-hilled plains.
Knott. My Mother's List of Names.
Larkin. Is It Now Or For Always.
Lovelace. To Quintius.
Lowry. Promises made drunk should be kept drunk.
MacLeish. America Was Promises.
Broken Promise.
Meredith. Hernani.
Song: "Thou steppest from thy splendour."
Milton. Why do the Gentiles tumult, and the Nations.
Psalms. Psalm 2: "Why do the heathen rage."
Robinson. Vickery's Mountain.
Rossetti. Moonshine.
Promises like Pie-Crust.
Rukeyser. Loan, The.
Risen Image Shines, The.
St. John. Blue Waves.
Until the Sea Is Dead.
Shakespeare. Did not the heavenly rhetoric of thine eye.
Sidney. O words, which fall like summer dew on me!
Smart. To the Rev. Mr. Powell.
Stuart. Breakwater.
Finding One of the Ghosts.
Swift. Twelve Articles.
Swinburne. Old Saying, An.
Warren. What Was the Promise That Smiled from the Maples at Evening?
Whittier. Curse of the Charter-Breakers, The.
Wright, James. Assignation, The.
Devotions.
Wroth. Song 4: "Lovers learne to speake butt truthe."
Wyatt. Thy promise was to love me best.
What should I say.
Yeats. Deep-sworn Vow, A.
Under Saturn.
Zukofsky. Aufilena—bonnie, simple, laud and they're amicable.

Quinti, see if't be wish of cool eyes day bear your Catullus.
Pronunciation
Knott. Summoning, The.
Lowry. French Pronunciation Simplified for Julian Trevelyan.
Nash. Brief Guide to Rhyming, or, How Be the Little Busy Doth?, A.
Strange Case of the Renegade Lyric Writer, The.
Tomlinson. Class.
Zukofsky. Claims.
Propaganda
Hewitt. Agenda.
Meredith. On the Danger of War.
Sandburg. Always the storm of propaganda blows.
Propertius, Sextus
Hill. Old Poet with Distant Admirers.
Lowell. Ghost, The.
Property
Berryman. Two plantations Greatgrandmother brought, The.
Burns. Extempore—On Being Shown a Beautiful County Seat Belonging to the Same [Maxwell of Cardoness].
Inventory, The.
Frost. Trespass.
Hugo. 2433, First Home, Last House in Missoula.
Lawrence. Lord Tennyson and Lord Melchett.
Property and No-Property.
Property Question, The.
Solomon's Baby.
St George and the Dragon.
Way Out, The.
MacNeice. Property! Property! Let us extend.
Merton. Cracking the Safe.
Sandburg. "Drama of politics doesn't interest me," said a news rewrite man, The.
Have you seen men handed refusals.
Who shall speak for the people?
Smart. 2.15: Upon the Luxury of the Age He Lived in.
Sutter. Little Litany for Moving Day, A.
Waldman. Sonnet: O Husband!
Whitman. Thoughts ("Of ownership—as if one fit to own things could not at pleasure enter upon all, and incorporate them into himself or herself").
Wilbur. Dutch Courtyard, A.
Young. What Have You Got of Your Own.
Prophecy and Prophets
Atwood. Here are the holy birds.
Blake. Memorable Fancy, A ("Prophets Isaiah and Ezekiel dined with me, and, The").
Bukowski. Day the Epileptic Spoke, The.
Ciardi. Annals.
Crashaw. Matthew 23; Yee Build the Sepulchres of the Prophets.
Davie. Pentecost.
Woe unto Thee!
Dickey, William. Ezekiel's Rabbit.
Donne. Prophets, The.
Emerson. Gods walk in the breath of the woods, The.
History & prophecy are alike.
Ginsberg. Prophecy, A.
Graves. Christmas Robin, The.
Young Sibyl, The.
Herrick. Prognostick, A.
Hewitt. New Jerusalem 1.
Hill. Day clacks and birds, The.
They slew by night.
Hopkins. Not kind! to freeze me with forecast.
Jeffers. Blood-Guilt, The.
Meditation on Saviors.
Kipling. Disciple, The.
Last Ode, The.
Prophets at Home.
Lawrence. Anaxagoras.
Prophet.
Prophet in the Rose Garden, The.
Lindsay. Scissors-Grinder, The.
Lorde. Equinox.
McGrath. End of the World, The.
Incident in the Life of a Prophet, An.

MacLeish. Eve's First Prophecy.
Seeing.
Meredith. Creation and the Prophet.
Song of the New Zealander among the Ruins of Old London.
Merton. Advice to a Young Prophet.
Black Stone on Top of a White Stone.
Dzules.
Elias—Variations on a Theme.
Ghost Dance.
Good Fortune.
La Salette.
Landscape, Prophet and Wild-dog.
Prophet.
Rolfe. Prophecy in Stone.
Rukeyser. Second Elegy. Age of Magicians.
Shakespeare. Sonnet 14: "Not from the stars do I my judgement pluck."
Sonnet 106: "When in the chronicle of wasted time."
Sidney. Thy elder care shall from thy careful face.
Smart. Fragment C.
Holy Innocents, The.
Spender. Pylons, The.
Swift. Windsor Prophecy, The.
Tennyson. Dead Prophet, The.
Tomlinson. Lesson, The.
Portrait of the Artist I.
Providence.
Whittier. Cobbler Keezar's Vision.
Prophecy of Samuel Sewall, The.
What of the Day?
Wilbur. Advice to a Prophet.
Williams, William Carlos. Portent.
Wordsworth. Composed at the Same Time and on the Same Occasion.
Cuckoo at Laverna May 25, 1837, The.
Picture of Daniel in the Lions' Den, at Hamilton Palace.
Zukofsky. Nor did the prophet.

See also **Oracles.**

Prose
Bishop. Rainy Season; Sub-Tropics.

Proserpina [*or* Proserpine]. *see* **Persephone.**

Prostitution and Prostitutes
Auden. Economics.
Beckett. Scene.
Bishop. Brazilian Tragedy.
Bukowski. Artist.
Fear.
Pacific Telephone.
Prayer in Bad Weather.
Price, The.
Quiet Clean Girls in Gingham Dresses..
Catullus. Carmen 6: "Your most recent acquisition, Flavius."
Carmen 41: "Formianus's whore, / long-nosed."
Carmen 42: "From the quarters of the compass."
Carmen 43: "O elegant whore!"
Carmen 110: "Men always praise an honest whore."
Chaucer. Cook's Tale, The.
Shipman's Tale, The.
Clare. Scandal.
Cullen. Black Magdalens.
For Daughters of Magdalen.
Cummings. Between the breasts / of bestial.
Curtains part) / the peacockappareled.
Dick Mid's large bluish face without eyebrows.
First she like a piece of ill-oiled.
Five Americans.
In making Marjorie god hurried.
"Kitty." sixteen,5'1[mM],white,prostitute.
Little ladies more / than dead exactly dance.
Twentyseven bums give a prostitute the once.
Waddling / madam star, The.
Wanta / spendsix / dollars Kid.
When you rang at Dick Mid's Place.
Dickey, James. Mercy.
Dickey, William. Confidence.
Dobyns. To Pull into Oneself as into a Locked Room.
Walls To Put Up, Walls To Take Down.

Donne. Klockius.
Self[e] Accuser, A.
"Dylan." Bob Dylan's New Orleans Rag.
Eliot. Sweeney Erect.
Griffiths. Fruits of Virtue.
Hardy. Chapel-Organist, The.
Julie-Jane.
Reluctant Confession.
Ruined Maid, The.
Hemingway. FOR THE HARLOT HAS A HARDLOT.
Sequal.
Herrick. Upon Doll.
Upon Jack.
Upon Slouch.
Upon Snare, an Usurer.
Holmes. Suzy Q, The.
Hughes, Langston. Evening Song.
Natcha.
Ruby Brown.
Sliver of Sermon.
Hugo. End of Krim's Pad, The.
Galleria Umberto I.
Jonson. Epigram on the Court Pucell, An.
On Bawds and Usurers.
On Cashiered Capt[ain] Surly.
On Gypsy.
On the New Hot-House.
To Hornet.
Knight. As You Leave Me.
Harlem.
Violent Space, The.
Lewis. Indolence.
Soubrettes, The.
Liddy. Quarter, The.
Lindsay. Trap, The.
Lovelace. La Bella Bona Roba.
Miller. Hookah.
Morgan. Catullus: *Carmen xli.*
Olson. Bigmans.
Plath. Strumpet Song.
"Reed." Street Hassle: Street Hassle.
Street Hassle: Waltzing Matilda.
Walk on the Wild Side.
St. John. Una Vita Violenta (1955).
Sandburg. Harrison Street Court.
It Is Much.
Trafficker.
Woman with a Past.
Sexton. Buying the Whore.
Jesus Raises Up the Harlot.
Snodgrass. Home Town.
Sorrentino. That you allow yourself this vast neglect of me.
Sutter. Halloween on Hennepin.
Swift. Beautiful Young Nymph Going to Bed, A.
Turco. Bordello.
Whitman. City Dead-House, The.
To a Common Prostitute.
Wilbur. Place Pigalle.
Williams, Charles Kenneth. Gas Station, The.
Medusa.
Williams, William Carlos. King!, The.
Wright, James. In Response to a Rumor that the Oldest Whorehouse in Wheeling, West Virginia, Has Been Condemned.
Morning Hymn to a Dark Girl.
Young. Ho.
Zukofsky. Ameana pulling, a foot touted high.
At hest, hendecasyllabics, what is this.
Aufilena—*bonnie, simple,* laud and they're amicable.
Flavius—that delicate lass—to Catullus.
Salvé, next, minimal, poor little nosey.

Protest, Social
Angelou. Take Time Out.
Atwood. Notes towards a Poem That Can Never Be Written.
Beatles. Blackbird.
Continuing Story of Bungalow Bill, The.
Revolution.
Bly. At a March against the Vietnam War.
Brooks. First fight. Then fiddle. Ply the slipping string.
Lovers of the Poor, The.
People protest in sprawling lightless ways.

Browning, Elizabeth Barrett. Song for the Ragged Schools of London, A.
Clough. Latest Decalogue, The.
Cullen. Scottsboro, Too, Is Worth Its Song.
Cummings. Season 'tis,my lovely lambs, The.
16 heures / l'Etoile.
Davie. Barnsley and District.
Thanks to Industrial Essex.
Dickinson. Much madness is divinest sense.
"Dylan." Ain't Gonna Grieve.
Blowin' in the Wind.
Chimes of Freedom.
Death of Emmett Till, The.
Hard Rain's A-Gonna Fall, A.
Jim Jim / where is our party?
Let Me Die in My Footsteps.
Lonesome Death of Hattie Carroll, The.
Long Ago, Far Away.
Maggie's Farm.
Playboys and Playgirls.
Subterranean Homesick Blues.
Times They Are A-Changin', The.
Emerson. Ode, Inscribed to W. H. Channing.
Garrigue. Resistance Meeting: Boston Common.
Ginsberg. America.
Anti-Vietnam War Peace Mobilization.
Death to Van Gogh's Ear!
Going to Chicago.
Grant Park: August 28, 1968.
Nagasaki Days.
Verses Written for Student Antidraft Registration Rally 1980.
Haines. About the hour the December moon.
People fell back, a field of wheat, The.
Hewitt. At the Newsagent's.
Paper Banners.
Prisoners on the Roof, The.
Reference, The.
Jong. Student Revolution.
Kunitz. Demonstrations in the streets.
This Day This World.
Lawrence. How Beastly the Bourgeois Is.
Stand Up!
Lorde. Revolution Is One Form of Social Change.
Workers Rose on May Day or Postcript to Karl Marx, The.
Lowell. Memories of West Street and Lepke.
McAuley. Aor Against the Termagant from California Who Confused Instruction With Indignation.
McGrath. Blues for the Old Revolutionary Woman.
Meredith. Old Chartist, The.
Millay. Apostrophe to Man.
Morrison. Sidewalkers Moved, The.
Paley. Definition.
If you have acquired a taste for happiness.
Responsibility.
Street Corner Dialogue.
Rexroth. Bad Old Days, The.
Rich. Burning of Paper instead of Children, The.
Education of a Novelist.
For a Russian Poet.
For a Sister.
From the Prison House.
Leaflets.
Tear Gas.
To Frantz Fanon.
Rolfe. Communists.
Rukeyser. Boys in the Branches.
For Kayle Boyle.
How We Did It.
Wherever.
Shelley. Song to the Men of England.
Stafford. Peace Walk.
Walker. Chic Freedom's Reflection.
Whittier. Astræa.
Calef in Boston.
Human Sacrifice, The.
Men of Old, The.
Panorama, The.
Problem, The.
Quaker of the Olden Time, The.
Reformer, The.

To the Reformers of England.
Voices, The.
Wilbur. For the Student Strikers.
Williams, Charles Kenneth. In the Heart of the Beast.
Keep It.
Wordsworth. On the Projected Kendal and Windermere Railway.
Placard for a Poll Bearing an Old Shirt.
Protest against the Ballot.
Zukofsky. "Immediate Aim, The."

Protestantism and Protestants
Campion. Debetur alto iure Principium Iovi.
Crashaw. Upon the Ensuing Treatises [of Mr. Shelford].
Davie. Short Run to Camborne.
Donne. Show me dear[e] Christ, thy spouse, so bright and clear.
Eberhart. New England Protestant.
Herbert. British Church, The.
see also To the Lady Elizabeth Queen of Bohemia.
To the Lady Elizabeth Queen of Bohemia.
Hill. Christmas Trees.
Lawrence. Protestant Churches, The.
Liddy. Island / Of the hungry bishop, The.
To the Liberal Magistrates.
Vir VI.
Smart. Fifth of November, The.
King's Restoration, The.
Swift. On the Words "Brother Protestants and Fellow Christians."

Proust, Marcel
Ferlinghetti. Late Impressionist Dream.
Gunn. Readings in French.
Jarrell. Man Meets a Woman in the Street, A.
Merrill. For Proust.
Nash. Leda's Fortunate Gaffe.
Schuyler. Stun.

Provence, France
Browning, Robert. Count Gismond.
Glück. Letter from Provence.
Hartley. Corniche—Marseille.
Dusty olive trees.
Les Baux.
Hoffman. In Provence.
Koch. Ma Provence.
MacLeish. Voyage en Provence.
Millay. Cap D'Antibes.
Memory of Cassis.
Tomlinson. Hill Walk.
Wilbur. Grasse: The Olive Trees.
Williams, William Carlos. To Ford Madox Ford in Heaven.

Providence
Ammons. Providence.
Cowper. Epistle to Lady Austen.
Expostulation.
Fable, A: "Raven, while with glossy breast, A."
Emerson. Motto to "New England Reformers."
Herrick. Gods Providence.
Gods Time Must End Our Trouble.
Hewitt. Whit Monday.
Tomlinson. Providence.

Providence, Rhode Island
Berrigan. Things to Do in Providence.
Young. Providence, Rhode Island.

Prudes
Beatles. Hello Goodbye.
Cummings. "Gay" is the captivating cognomen of a Young Woman of cambridge,mass.
Lawrence. Young and Their Moral Guardians, The.
Nash. First Limick.
Pope. Answer to the Following Question of Mrs. Howe.

Psyche (mythology)
Browning, Elizabeth Barrett. Marriage of Psyche and Cupid.
Mercury Carries Psyche to Olympus.
Psyche and Cerberus.
Psyche and Pan.
Psyche and Proserpine.
Psyche and the Eagle.
Psyche and Venus.

Psyche Gazing on Cupid.
Psyche Propitiating Ceres.
Psyche Wafted by Zephyrus.
Duncan. Poem Beginning with a Line by Pindar, A.
Keats. Ode to Psyche.
MacLeish. Psyche with the Candle.
Merrill. From the Cupola.
Olson. West 4 and 5.
Swift. On Psyche.

Psychiatry and Psychiatrists
Carruth. Ekstase, Alptraum, Schlaf in einem Nest von Flammen.
Electroshock. Bang—.
Jong. Walking through the Upper East Side.
Olson. True Numbers.
"Reed." Kill Your Sons.
Sarton. Christmas Letter to a Psychiatrist.
Walker. After the Shrink.
See also **Mental Illness**.

Psychoanalysis and Psychoanalysts
Berg. Visiting the Stone.
Carruth. Sonnet: "Freedom in love? It has been questioned. Think."
Cummings. Listen my children and you.
Doolittle. Dedication: "When everything was over."
Master, The.
Fletcher. 1921.
Jong. Walking through the Upper East Side.
Markson. Memo to His Lady's Therapist.
O'Hara. To a Poet.
Sexton. Cripples and Other Stories.
Hoarder, The.
Letters to Dr. Y.
Said the Poet to the Analyst.
Van Duyn. Birthday Card for a Psychiatrist.
Williams, Charles Kenneth. Child Psychology.

Psychological Testing
Merton. Studies of man's friendly competitor the rat have shown.

Puberty
Gardner. Nor Good Red Herring.
Lewis. Lines on a Young Girl.
Lorde. Generation II.
Rukeyser. Rite.
Sutter. Husbandry.

Publishing and Publishers
Byron. For Orford and for Waldegrave.
Strahan, Tonson, Lintot of the Times.
You Ask for a "Volume of Nonsense."
"Carroll, Lewis." Poeta Fit, Non Nascitur.
Herrick. To the Right Honourable Mildmay, Earl of Westmorland.
Hewitt. Pavane for a Dead Professor.
Koch. Supposing that one walks out into the air.
Thank You.
Lawrence. To Pino.
Roethke. Reply to a Lady Editor.
Smith, Stevie. To an American Publisher.
Updike. Rack of Paperbacks, A.
Whittier. Lines on the Portrait of a Celebrated Publisher.

Pudding
Nash. Yorkshire Pudding.

Puddles
Ammons. Equilibrations.
Fletcher. Sands, The.
Sandburg. Lumber Yard Pools at Sunset.
Schuyler. Sparks.

Puerto Ricans
Kinnell. Avenue Bearing the Initial of Christ into the New World, The.

Puerto Rico
Carruth. In filthy Puerto Rico lives a bird with no.
Paley. Bridges.
Williams, William Carlos. Prelude in Boricua.

Pumpkins
Carruth. Metaphysical.
Sandburg. Theme in Yellow.
Wakoski. Pumpkin Pie, Or Reassurances Are Always Fake Though We Love Them, Only Physics Counts.
Whittier. Pumpkin, The.

Punctuality
"Carroll, Lewis." Punctuality.
Frost. Lone Striker, A.
Nash. There's Always an Ubblebub.
Updike. Time's Fool.

Punctuation
Hartley. Watching.
Tomlinson. Hyphens.
Wilbur. &.
Games One.

Punishment
Arnold. Sick King in Bokhara, The.
Beckett. Noire soeur.
Burns. Ode, Sacred to the Memory of Mrs. —— of ——.
Ciardi. Boy.
Poem for Benn's Graduation from High School, A.
Cummings. Poets yeggs and thirsties.
"Dylan." Hard Rain's A-Gonna Fall, A.
I'd Hate to Be You on That Dreadful Day.
Percy's Song.
Seven Curses.
Emerson. Merlin's Song.
Nemesis.
Traitors tho' plumed & steel equipped.
Glück. Game, The.
Graves. Wreath, The.
Hardy. In Weatherbury Stocks.
Hayden. Whipping, The.
Heaney. Punishment.
Herrick. Gods Providence.
Hell Fire ("One onely fire has Hell; but yet it shall").
No Escaping the Scourging.
Patience in Princes.
Persecutions Purifie.
Pittie, and Punishment.
Rewards and Punishments.
Sin Severely Punisht.
Sinners.
Smart.
Sufferings.
To God ("Make, make me Thine").
Whips.
Will the Cause of Woe, The.
Hewitt. Curfew Tower, The.
I Still Had a Friend.
Jonson. On Reformed Gamester.
Kipling. Ballad of the King's Jest, The.
Ballad of the King's Mercy, The.
Lament of the Border Cattle Thief, The.
Kunitz. System, The.
Lawrence. Punisher, The.
Lindsay. City That Will Not Repent, The.
Lowry. Soul, The.
Soul's Pentonville, The.
Marlowe. 2.2: Ad Bagoum, ut custodiam puellae sibi commissae laxiorem habeat.
Milton. On the Gunpowder Plot.
Which way I fly is Hell; my self am Hell.
Morrison. Always a Playground Instructor.
Neruda. What forced labor / for Hitler in Hell?
Patchen. Lions of fire, The.
Ralegh. Nine furlongs strecht lies Tityus, who for his wicked deedes.
Ransom. Man without Sense of Direction.
"Reed." Blue Mask, The.
Rolfe. Pastoral—1954.
Political Prisoner 123456789.
Rossetti. Brother Bruin.
By the Waters of Babylon. B.C. 570.
Rukeyser. Chapman.
Spenser. Kingly bird, that beares Joves thunder-clap, The.
Warren. Friends of the Family, or Bowling a Sticky Cricket.
Wet Hair: If Now His Mother Should Come.
Whittier. Branded Hand, The.
Wife of Manoah to Her Husband, The.
Williams, Charles Kenneth. Man Who Owns Sleep, The.
Wordsworth. When Philoctetes in the Lemnian Isle.
Wright, James. Song for the Middle of the Night, A.

Young. Lesson.

Punks
Ginsberg. Punk Rock Your My Big Crybaby.

Puns
Campion. Verba volant; verum: quid enim velocius illis?
Crashaw. Upon Ford's Two Tragedies, "Loves Sacrifice" and "The Broken Heart."
Jonson. On the New Hot-House.
Ralegh. From the Diary of John Manningham of the Middle Temple.
Tomlinson. Misprint.
Zukofsky. All of December Toward New Year's.
Checkers, checkmate and checkerboard.
Hyacinth.
I's (Pronounced *Eyes*).
No One Inn.
"One oak fool box";—the pun.

Puppets and Puppeteers
Cummings. A(ncient)a / weigh / tless.
Joseph. Puppet Show, The.
Puppeteer.

Puppies
Dickey, William. Anniversary, The.
Kipling. His Apologies.
Williams, William Carlos. Stormy.

Purcell, Henry
Hopkins. Henry Purcell.

Purgatory
Fletcher. Reunion.
Milton. On the Same ["James derided the Purgatorial fire of the soul"].

Puritanism and Puritans
Bly. Pilgrim Fish Heads.
Campion. Epigramme: "Drue feasts no Puritans; the churles, he saith."
Epigramme: "Drue gives thee money, yet thou thankst not him."
Donne. Cross, The.
Eberhart. Opposition.
Jonson. On Lip the Teacher.
Lowell. After the Surprising Conversions.
Meredith. Certain People, A.
Wilbur. Puritans, The.

Purity
Brontë. Not a vapour had stained the breezeless blue.
Browning, Elizabeth Barrett. Prospect, The.
Sonnet: "Pardon, oh, pardon, that my soul should make."
Burns. Scottish Song.
Carew. To the Painter.
Carroll, Jim. Little Ode on St. Anne's Day.
Carruth. Ignis.
Ciardi. Evil Eye, The.
Two Egrets.
Clough. From the contamination / Of laudation.
Cowper. Love Pure and Fervent.
Swallow, The.
Creeley. Love ("Thing comes / of itself, The").
Dickinson. Candor—my tepid friend.
Doolittle. Daemon initiate, spirit.
"Dylan." Watered-Down Love.
Eberhart. Supreme Authority of the Imagination, The.
Emerson. Papas Blondine / Grew tall & wise.
Everson. And then that humming.
Song the Body Dreamed in the Spirit's Mad Behest, The.
Fletcher. There was a pool that rippled in the silence of the north.
Ford. Happy? The very eye of the world.
Garrigue. Improvisation upon the Theme of the Lady and the Unicorn, An.
Graves. Purification.
Herbert. Superliminare.
Herrick. Another New-Yeeres Gift, or Song for the Circumcision.
Julia's Churching, or Purification.
North and South.
Parasceve, or Preparation, The.
Persecutions Purifie.
To God ("Pardon me God").

To Julia ("Offer thy gift").
To Perenna ("When I thy parts runne o're, I can't espie").
To Silvia ("I am holy, while I stand").
Upon Jone and Jane.
Hoffman. Breathing Purely.
Kunitz. Deciduous Branch.
Hermetic Poem.
Vita Nuova.
Levine. Genius.
Lindsay. General William Booth Enters into Heaven.
Lovelace. Her Muffe.
Lucasta at the Bath.
Lowry. Prayer: "I pray that I may form a prayer, oh Lord."
MacNeice. Individualist Speaks, The.
McNeill. Verb, The.
Meredith. Margaret's Bridal-Eve.
Merton. Night-Flowering Cactus.
Nash. Reflection On a Wicked World.
Nemerov. Earthquake in the West, The.
Neruda. Stone, toppled by water and mountain, The.
Patchen. Ecstasy of the Pure.
Rolfe. Poisoned Air Befouled the Whole Decade, The.
Rossetti. Isidora.
Lord, make me pure: / Only the pure shall see Thee as Thou art.
Purification of St. Mary the Virgin, The.
They Shall Be as White as Snow.
Thou Art Fairer Than the Children of Men.
Thy lilies drink the dew, / Thy lambs the rill, and I will drink them too.
Whitsun Monday.
Sandburg. White Ash.
White Hands.
Shapiro. Back, The.
Snyder. To Fire.
Thomson. To Seraphina.
Warren. Rebuke of the Rocks.
Williams, Charles Kenneth. Acids.
Kingdom of Stinking Wishes, The.
Wright, James. All the Beautiful are Blameless.
Eclogue at Nash's Grove.
Wroth. Sonnet 3: "His flames ar joyes, his bands true lovers might."
Young. Art of Benny Carter, The.

Pursuit
Clough. To spend unsolaced years of pain.
Cowper. Song on Peace.
Doolittle. Pursuit.
"Dylan." Billy.
Gypsy Lou.
Eberhart. 1934.
Frost. Escapist—Never.
Griffiths. Continuity.
Hall. Cops and Robbers.
Hoffman. Koch.
Koch. Which cannot be begun, however, until you meet somebody.
Kooser. Looking for You, Barbara.
Pocket Poem.
Lowry. Some years ago he started to escape.
MacNeice. Canto XVI: "Young man cannot answer. Is this life?, The."
Explorations.
Meredith. Song: "When on my faithful charger."
With the Huntress.
Youthful Quest, The.
Merton. Tower of the Spirit, The.
Nash. Chloe and the Roué.
Emancipation of Mr. Poplin, or, Skoal to the Skimmerless.
Plath. Pursuit.
Robinson. Dear Friends.
Young. Backtracking.
Zukofsky. Sequence 1944-6.

Pushers
Angelou. Pusher, The.
Gunn. Street Song.
"Reed." I'm Waiting for the Man.

See also **Drug Addiction.**

Pushkin, Aleksandr Sergeyevich
Davie. Pushkin. A Didactic Poem.

Pygmalion
Wordsworth. Lady Whom You here Behold, The.
Prithee, Gentle Lady, List.

Pygmies
Graves. Ogres and Pygmies.

Pyramids
Hugo. Politely like Snakes in the Oats.

Pyramus and Thisbe
Donne. Pyramus and Thisbe.

Q

Quail
Shelton. Territorial Rights.
Wright, James. Quail, The.

Quakers. *see* **Friends, Society of.**

Quarrels
Burns. Holy Tulzie, The.
Byron. Brave Champions! Go On with the Farce.
"Carroll, Lewis." Two Brothers, The.
Cowper. Lily and the Rose, The.
On Madan's Answer to Newton.
Written in a Quarrel.
Creeley. One Way.
Dobyns. Separations.
Doolittle. Halcyon.
Dryden. Malcontents, The.
Dunbar. After the Quarrel.
Dunn. Dinner, The.
He/She.
"Dylan." Something's Burning, Baby.
Frost. From Plane to Plane.
Herrick. Epitaph on a Man who Had a Scold to His Wife.
Upon Jolly and Jilly.
Hughes, Langston. Early Evening Quarrel.
Koch. At the Poem Society a black-haired man stands up to say.
Kunitz. Quarrel, The.
Lawrence. Henriette.
Lowry. Quarrel, A.
With Great Love Oh Beloved Harteebeeste from El Leon.
McGrath. News and the Weather, The.
Markson. Once, in Our Quarreling.
Muldoon. Sushi.
Nash. Birdies, Don't Make Me Laugh.
Don't Wait, Hit Me Now!
Frailty, Thy Name Is a Misnomer.
I Do, I Will, I Have.
I Never Even Suggested It.
Nothing but Nature.
They Won't Believe, on New Year's Eve, that New Year's Day Will Come What May.
Olson. Common Place.
Paley. Quarrel.
We quarreled / Alone I.
Plath. Snowman on the Moor, The.
Pope. Epigram: "My Lord complains, that Pope, stark mad with gardens."
Prince. Token, The.
Rich. Novella.
Rukeyser. After Their Quarrel.
St. John. Art of Argument, the Argument of Art, The.
Schuyler. Was It.
Shakespeare. Sonnet 40: "Take all my loves, my Love, yea, take them all."
Sonnet 117: "Accuse me thus; that I have scanted all."
Sonnet 120: "That you were once unkind befriends me now."
Sonnet 139: "O, call me not to justify the wrong."
Sorrentino. Crisis, The.
Williams, Charles Kenneth. Color of Time, The.
Peace.
Toil.

See also **Anger.**

Quarries
Hardy. Green Slates.
Jeffers. Bixby's Landing.
Rukeyser. Sand-Quarry with Moving Figures.
Tomlinson. Above Carrara.
Quarry, The.
Wordsworth. Written with a Slate Pencil upon a Stone, the Largest of a Heap Lying near a Deserted Quarry, upon One of the Islands at Rydal.

Quebec (province), Canada
Atwood. 1837 War in Retrospect.
Van Duyn. Quebec Suite.

Quebec (city), Canada
Atwood. Disembarking at Quebec.
Eberhart. Sainte Anne De Beaupré.
Lowry. So he would rather have written those lines.

Queen Anne's Lace
Williams, William Carlos. Queen-Anne's-Lace.

Queens
Browning, Elizabeth Barrett. Crowned and Wedded.
Nature's Remorses.
Campion. Dance now and sing the joy and love we owe.
To the Most Sacred Queen Anne.
Welcome to this flowrie place.
"Carroll, Lewis." Red Queen's Lullaby, The.
Welcome Queen Alice.
Crashaw. To the Queen, an Apologie for the Length of the Following Panegyricke.
De la Mare. Gold.
Queen Djenira.
Emerson. Queen rejoices in her peers, A.
Such another peerless queen.
Hall. Pictures of Philippa.
Herrick. To the Queene.
Twelfe Night, or King and Queene.
Hewitt. With E.M.F. on 28th December 1965.
Housman. 1887.
Jonson. Epigram to the Queen, Then Lying In. 1630, An.
Ode, or Song, by All the Muses, An.
Kipling. And you may lead a thousand men.
Bells and Queen Victoria, The.
There was never a queen like Balkis.
Marvell. In Eandem Reginae Sueciae Transmissam [To Christina, Queen of Sweden].
Letter to Doctor Ingelo, A.
Meredith. Queen Zuleima.
Plath. Queen's Complaint, The.
Prince. Vivat.
Ralegh. Conjectural First Draft of the Petition to Queen Anne.
Over the Medes and light Sabaeans reigns[*or* raignes].
Sir Walter Ralegh to the Queen.
Sir Walter Ralegh's [*or* S.W. Raghlies] Petition to the Queene 1618.
Rossetti. I sit a queen, and am no widow, and shall see no sorrow.
She Came from The Uttermost Part of the Earth.
Succession of Kings, The.
Sidney. To one whose state is raised over all.
Wilbur. Lament: "Nashe's old queens who bartered young and fair."
Yeats. Old Age of Queen Maeve, The.
See also **Listings for specific Queens.**

Queens, New York City
Ferlinghetti. Queens Cemetery, Setting Sun.
Hoffman. Flushing Meadows, 1939.
Merton. Queens Tunnel.

Questions
Auden. Question, The ("To ask the hard question is simple").
Beckett. Que ferais-je sans ce monde sans visage sans questions.
What would I do without this world faceless incurious.
Berg. Bandage.
Ollie, Answer Me.
Bishop. Mountain, The.

Browning, Elizabeth Barrett. Question and Answer.
Sonnet: "My poet, thou canst touch on all the notes."
Carew. First of Jealousy. Dialogue, The.
Incommunicability of Love.
Methodus Amandi.
"Carroll, Lewis." Ode To Damon.
Upon the Lonely Moor.
Creeley. Ballad, A: "We have a song for the death in her body."
Down Home.
Fire.
Lover, The.
Pedigree, The.
Riddle, The.
Cummings. Will out of the kindness of their hearts a few philosophers tell me.
Will you teach a.
De la Mare. Last Chapter, The.
Vain Questioning.
Which Way?
Dunbar. Mystery, The.
Duncan. Among my friends love is a great sorrow.
"Dylan." Blowin' in the Wind.
Eberhart. Configuration.
Old Question.
Question Mark.
Emerson. Sphinx, The.
Gildner. Mark Only One Circle.
Graves. Possibly.
What is Love?
When and Why.
Herrick. Upon Love, by Way of Question and Answer.
Hesketh. Child's Guide to Philosophy, A.
From the Day Room.
I Am.
Naked Ostrich.
Hewitt. Ars Poetica.
Dissertation I.
I Remember.
Mathematics.
Who Was C.B. Fry?
Kipling. I keep six honest serving-men.
Levine. How Much Can It Hurt?
Late Answer, A.
Lowry. No words assess, no pencil knows.
Years standing round in a ring, The.
Matthews. Civilization and Its Discontents.
Oppen. Gesture, The.
Owen. Asleep.
Maundy Thursday.
Patchen. Investigation of Certain Interesting Questions.
Naked Land, The.
Prince. Question, The.
Robinson. Still through the dusk of dead, blank-legended.
Two Men.
Rolfe. Ballad of the Noble Intentions.
Ballad: "What are we having for dinner tonight?"
Rossetti. Grown Cold.
Maiden May.
Of Him That Was Ready to Perish.
Until the Day Break.
Rukeyser. Private Life of the Sphinx.
Sandburg. Brass Keys.
Haze.
Honey and Salt.
How Much?
Little Word, Little White Bird.
Man in the street is fed, The.
Money, Politics, Love, and Glory.
Oomba.
Out of White Lips.
Questionnaire.
Sphinx, A.
Who shall speak for the people?
Sexton. Fury of Sunsets, The.
Sidney. Sonnet 31: "With how sad steps, O Moon, thou climb'st the skies."
Silverstein. What's In the Sack?
Snodgrass. W. D. Sits in Kafka's Chair and Is

Interrogated Concerning the Assumed Death of Cock Robin.
Sorrentino. Barely Aware of the Insistent Loud Roars.
Crool Time.
Oranges Returned, The.
Zukofsky.
Stevens. Questions Are Remarks.
Stuart. Begging on North Main.
Tomlinson. Question, The.
Whitman. To the States.
Williams, Charles Kenneth. Question, The.
Wright, James. What the Earth Asked Me.
Yau. If you asked.
Reading of an Ever-Changing Tale, The.
Yeats. At Algeciras—a Meditation upon Death.

Quests
Ashbery. And I'd Love You to Be in It.
Browning, Robert. Childe Roland to the Dark Tower Came.
Carruth. Journey to a Known Place.
Second Version, The.
Clark. Dark Continent.
Cooper. She is like that man.
Cowper. Four Ages, The.
De la Mare. Mistress Fell.
Dickinson. Each Life Converges to some Centre.
Dunn. Homage to the Divers.
"Dylan." Isis.
Eliot. Waste Land, The.
Emerson. Beauty.
Fisher. Near Garmsley Camp.
Graves. White Goddess, The.
Hartnett. He'll to the Moors.
Herrick. Sobriety in Search.
Hoffman. Another Border.
Another Country.
Exploration.
Over the Rim.
Sacred Fount, The.
Vows.
Wanderer, The.
Wherever.
Hopkins. I must hunt down the prize.
Hughes, Ted. October Salmon, An.
Kipling. Because I sought it far from men.
Kunitz. Pivot, The.
Levine. To get west you go east.
Lindsay. Dive, mermaids, with sharp swords.
I Went Down into the Desert.
Indian Girl Tells the Hero Where to Go to Get the Laughing Bell, The.
Mouse That Gnawed the Oak-Tree Down, The.
Lowry. Ballad: "Twas in the springtime of the year."
Crane over seas and forests seeks her home, The.
Poem Influenced By John Davenport and Cervantes.
That's What I Mean.
MacLeish. Whether before have been.
MacNeice. Good Dream.
Oracle, The.
This Way Out.
O'Hara. Ode to Tanaquil Leclercq.
Poe. Eldorado.
Robinson. Sage, The.
Siege Perilous.
Still through the dusk of dead, blank-legended.
Roethke. Journey to the Interior.
Rossetti. Confluents.
Darkness and light are both alike to Thee.
Discovery, A.
How One Chose.
Lady Montrevor.
My Old Friends.
Of Him That Was Ready to Perish.
Resurgam.
What is the beginning? Love. What the course? Love still.
Yet A Little While.
Rukeyser. Brilliant, the full-bodied, the real of the world in their powers, The.
Searching / Not Searching.
Sandburg. Circle of Doors.

Sexton. God-Monger, The.
 Gods.
Stevens. Pediment of Appearance, The.
Warren. Pursuit.
Whittier. In Quest.
Wordsworth. Alas! what boots the long
 laborious quest.
Wright, James. Quest, The.

Quilts and Quilting
Cowper. To Mrs. King.
Dunbar. Quilting, The.
Griffiths. Patchworks.
Piercy. Looking at Quilts.
Sutter. Old Mrs. Court and Her Quilt.

Quinces
Tomlinson. Green Quinces.

Quotidian
Hall. Coffee Cup, The.
 Widows, The.
Herrick. Upon Mudge.
Lewis. Mountain over Aberdare, The.
Nash. I Must Tell You about My Novel.
Schuyler. Few Days, A.
 Red Brick and Brown Stone.
Williams, Miller. Glass Darkly, A.
 Love Poem.
 Rock.

R

Rabbis
Hayden. Rabbi, The.
Nemerov. Debate with the Rabbi.
Schwartz. Rabbi to Preach.
Whittier. Rabbi Ishmael.

Rabbits
Bukowski. Look:, The.
Carroll, Jim. Fragment, A: "When I see a
 rabbit."
Carruth. Tracks of the snowshoe rabbit across
 the.
Clare. Young Rabbits.
De la Mare. Dry August Burned.
Dunbar. Winter's Approach.
Garrigue. Iowa City Zoo.
Haines. Goshawk, The.
Hesketh. Very Small Casualty, A.
Joseph. Animal Story, An.
Larkin. Myxomatosis.
Lawrence. Rabbit Snared in the Night.
Millay. Rabbit, The.
Muldoon. Coney, The.
Nash. Rabbits, The.
Piercy. Sojourners.
Plath. Rabbit Catcher, The.
Rossetti. When the cows come home the milk
 is coming.
Sexton. Passion of the Mad Rabbit, The.
Stevens. Rabbit as King of the Ghosts, A.
Zimmer. Wanda and Zimmer.

See also **Hares; Jackrabbits.**

Raccoons
Rexroth. Raccoon.
Sexton. Raccoon.
Snyder. True Night.

Rachel (Bible)
Burns. Patriarch, The.
Smart. Holy Innocents, The.

Rachmaninov, Sergei
Carruth. Freedom and Discipline.
O'Hara. On Rachmaninoff's Birthday.
 On Rachmaninoff's Birthday ("Blue windows,
 blue rooftops").
Schuyler. Rachmaninoff's Third.

Racial Prejudice
Angelou. Bump d'Bump.
 No No No No.
Blake. Little Black Boy, The.
Bly. Hatred of Men with Black Hair.
Boyle. Communication to Nancy Cunard, A.
 Poem about Black Power, A.
 Testament for My Students, 1968–1969.
Brooks. Ballad of Rudolph Reed, The.
 Bronzeville Woman in a Red Hat.

Browning, Elizabeth Barrett. Runaway Slave
 at Pilgrim's Point, The.
Cullen. Colors.
 For a Lady I Know.
 Incident.
 Tableau.
 Uncle Jim.
Eberhart. Request for Offering.
Hacker. 1973.
Hughes, Langston. Cross.
 Merry-Go-Round.
Lorde. Poem for Women in Rage, A.
 Revolution Is One Form of Social Change.
"MacDiarmid." With the Herring Fishers.
Merton. Plessy vs Ferguson: Theme and
 Variations.
"Reed." I Wanna Be Black.
Walcott. Blues.
 Gulf, The.
Walker. First, They Said.
 It is true--/ I've always loved.
 January 10, 1973.
 Once.
 Right to Life, The: What Can the White Man
 Say to the Black Woman?
 South: The Name of Home.
Warren. Event, The.
Whittier. On a Prayer-Book.
Williams, Charles Kenneth. Racists.
Young. Dance for Militant Dilettantes, A.
 Your Basic Black Poet.

See also **Racism and Racists.**

Racing and Racers. *see* **Crew and Crew
 Racing; Horse Racing; Track Athletics.**

Racism and Racists
Angelou. Miss Scarlet, Mr. Rhett and other
 Latter-Day Saints.
 No No No No.
Brooks. Chicago Defender Sends a Man to
 Little Rock, The.
 Negro Hero.
 White Troops Had Their Orders but the
 Negroes Looked Like Men.
Carruth. Named she was a Smith, born Smith,
 but how related.
Cohen. Opium and Hitler.
Cullen. Ballad of the Brown Girl, The.
 Black Christ, The.
 Incident.
Cummings. YgUDuh / ydoan / yunnuhstan.
"Dylan." Death of Emmett Till, The.
 Hurricane.
 Only a Pawn in Their Game.
 Oxford Town.
Fletcher. Elegy on a Nordic White Protestant.
Ford. Plaint.
Gardner. Little Rock Arkansas 1957.
Hayden. Frederick Douglass.
 From the Corpse Woodpiles, from the Ashes.
Hewitt. Test, The.
Hughes, Langston. Argument.
 As I Grew Older.
 Ballad of the Landlord.
 Blue Bayou.
 Children's Rhymes.
 Comment on Curb.
 Dream Boogie: Variation.
 Good Morning.
 Harlem.
 I, Too.
 In Explanation of Our Times.
 Island.
 Lunch in a Jim Crow Car.
 Movies.
 Mulatto.
 Not a Movie.
 Parade.
 Puzzled.
 Same in Blues.
 Southern Mammy Sings.
 Tell Me.
 West Texas.
Knight. Fable: "Once upon a today and
 yesterday and nevermore there were 7 men."
 Once on a Night in the Delta: A Report From
 Hell.

Rehabilitation & Treatment in the Prisons of
 America.
Lorde. Afterimages.
 Suffer the Children.
 Who Said It Was Simple.
McGrath. Deep South.
Merton. Picture of a Black Child with a White
 Doll.
 Plessy vs Ferguson: Theme and Variations.
Rich. Frame.
Rolfe. June 19, 1953.
Sandburg. Sayings of Henry Stephens.
Stafford. Serving with Gideon.
Walcott. Blues.
Williams, William Carlos. Impromptu: The
 Suckers.
Young. Midnight Special Revisited, The.

See also **Racial Prejudice.**

Radiation and Radiation Sickness
Piercy. Long Death, The.

See also **Nuclear Accidents; Nuclear War.**

Radio
Clark. Radio.
Creeley. Mary's Fancy.
Dunn. Coming Home, Garden State Parkway.
Hesketh. Retreat.
Mahon. Morning Radio.
O'Hara. Radio.
Rolfe. Radio Madrid—1937.
Sorrentino. Morning Roundup, The.

Rahab
Merton. Rahab's House.

Railroad Wrecks
Whittier. Conductor Bradley.

Railroads
Betjeman. Great Central Railway, Sheffield
 Victoria to Banbury.
 Metropolitan Railway, The.
Crane. River, The.
Davie. Northern Metres.
Hall. Sister on the Tracks, A.
Heaney. Railway Children, The.
Kipling. Public Waste.
Koch. Railway Stationery, The.
Levine. Conductor of Nothing, The.
Nash. Riding on a Railroad Train.
Roethke. Night Journey.
Rukeyser. There is a knotless line westward,
 past terraces.
 Up past the burnt hills. Distance and the
 crowd.
 Young Men, The.
Sandburg. Caboose Thoughts.
 Child of the Romans.
 Five Towns on the B. and O.
 Jack.
 Old Flagman, The.
 Pods.
 Slow Program.
 Still Life.
 Work Gangs.
Turco. Depot, The.
 Trestle, The.
Wakoski. There's Plenty of Anguish at the
 Railroad.
Whitman. To a Locomotive in Winter.
Wilbur. Stop.
Williams, William Carlos. Period Piece: 1834.
Wordsworth. At Furness Abbey ("Well may
 yon Railway Labourers to THIS ground").
 On the Projected Kendal and Windermere
 Railway.
 Proud Were Ye, Mountains, When, in Times
 of Old.
 Steamboats, Viaducts and Railways.
Wright, James. Outside Fargo, North Dakota.

See also **Trains; Locomotives.**

Railway Stations
Eberhart. Analogue of Unity in Multeity.
Graves. Between Trains.
Griffiths. In the Railway Hotel at Cordoba.
Jarrell. La Belle au Bois Dormant.
 Traveler, The.
Wilbur. For the New Railway Station in
 Rome.
 Stop.

Wright, James. Poem Written under an Archway in a Discontinued Railroad Station, Fargo, North Dakota, A.

Railway Travel
Beatles. One after 909.
Berryman. On the London Train.
Davie. In the Stopping Train.
De la Mare. Railway Junction, The.
Ginsberg. Patna-Benares Express.
  Sunset.
Hardy. Faintheart in a Railway Train.
Jarrell. Orient Express, The.
Lawrence. Honeymoon.
  Train at Night, A.
Merton. Kandy Express.
  Night Train, The.
Nash. Riding on a Railroad Train.
Rukeyser. Street corner to corner he will talk all day.
Sandburg. Slabs of the Sunburnt West.
Schuyler. En Route to Southampton.
Stevenson. From a Railway Carriage.
Updike. English Train Compartment.
Wilbur. In the Smoking-Car.

Rain
Ammons. After Yesterday.
  Mediation.
  Rainy Morning.
  Release.
  Soaker.
Auden. Farglow.
  Friendship.
  Job.
  Rain.
  Rainy Afternoon, A.
  Woods in Rain.
Beatles. Rain.
Berg. It Is.
Berry. Don't pray for the rain to stop.
  Falling Asleep.
  In Rain.
  Let me wake in the night.
  Rain.
  Warm day in December, A.
  Winter Rain, The.
Berryman. Our love conducted as in tropic rain.
  Where the lane from the highway swerves the first drops fell.
Bishop. Imber Nocturnus.
  Rain Towards Morning.
  Sestina: "September rain falls on the house."
Bly. August Rain.
  Reading in Fall Rain.
Boyle. Thunderstorm in South Dakota.
Brontë. 'Tis evening now, the sun descends.
Bukowski. Star, The.
Carroll, Jim. Eugene, Orgeon.
  Little Ode on St. Anne's Day.
  3 hours into the afternoon of March 9th.
Carruth. Far-removed Mountain Men, The.
  Missing the Bo in the Henhouse.
Ceravolo. Down.
Clare. Clown, The.
Coleridge. Ode to the Rain, An.
Cooper. Letters.
  Morning on the St. John's.
Cowper. To Lady Austen.
Creeley. Falling.
  Funny.
  Midnight.
  Out.
  Place, A.
  Rain, The.
  Rain ("Things one sees through").
  Rain (2) ("Thoughtful of you, I was / anticipating change in").
  Rose, The.
Cullen. Night Rain.
  Singing in the Rain.
Cummings. But the other / day i was passing a certain.
  Dim / i / nu / tiv / e this park is e.
  Early Summer Sketch.
  I have found what you are like.
  N(o)w / the / how / dis(appeared cleverly)world.

Now comes the good rain farmers pray for(and).
O / nly this / darkness(in).
  Sky a silver, The.
  Sonnet: "Rain-drop on the eyelids of the earth, A."
  Take for example this.
  When rain whom fear.
  You asked me to come:it was raining a little.
Davie. Rain on South-East England.
  Though Dry, Not Dry.
Dickey, James. Six, The.
Dickinson. Drop fell on the Apple Tree, A.
  Like Rain it sounded till it curved.
Dobyns. Rain Song.
  Six Poems on Moving.
Dunbar. Drizzle.
  Rain-Songs.
  Time to Tinker 'Roun'!
Dunn. Afterlife.
  Urgencies.
"Dylan." Hard Rain's A-Gonna Fall, A.
Eberhart. Point-pushed by the wind, rain.
Edmunds. El Niño.
  Like A Green Branch.
Emerson. All day the rain.
  He lives not who can refuse me.
  In bounding youth the night & train.
  More sweet than my refrain.
Everson. Rain on That Morning, The.
  We in the Fields.
Fisher. Downpour that subdued everybody and, The.
  Sloping and tapering away.
Fletcher. Dahlias, The.
  Flickering of incessant rain.
  Old South, The.
  Rain in the Desert.
  Spattering of the rain upon pale terraces, The.
Ford. Garden flooded with.
  I thought I heard Indra's.
Frost. In Time of Cloudburst.
Gallagher. Ever After.
  Hands of the Blindman, The.
  Message for the Sinecurist.
  Open Fire Near a Shed.
  Second Language.
  Sudden Journey.
  Women's Tug of War at Lough Arrow.
Gardner. It Rained Last Night.
Garrigue. Rain Song.
Graves. Around the Mountain.
  Turn of the Moon.
Haines. Rain Glass, The.
Hall. Sun, The.
Hardy. Autumn Rain-Scene, An.
  Expectation and Experience.
  On the Doorstep.
  Rain on a Grave.
  Sundial on a Wet Day, The.
  Thunderstorm in Town, A.
  We Sat at the Window.
  Weathers [or Weather].
  Wet August, A.
Hartnett. Listen, / if I came to you, out of the wind.
Heaney. Gifts of Rain.
Hesketh. Autumn at Whitewell.
Hewitt. For a Moment of Darkness over the Nations.
  Gathering Praties.
  Haymaking in the Low Meadow.
  Sap in the Sticks Again.
  Season's End.
Hopkins. Now the rain.
Hughes, Langston. In Time of Silver Rain.
Hughes, Ted. Heptonstall.
Hugo. No Bells to Believe.
Jeffers. Distant Rainfall.
Jong. Rain is My Home, The.
Joseph. Wet Sunday.
Kinnell. Under the Maud Moon.
  Westport.
Koch. On the Great Atlantic Rainway.
Larkin. Card-Players, The.
Lawrence. Autumn Rain.

Malade.
  There Is Rain in Me.
Levine. Jewish Graveyards, Italy.
  Making It New.
  Rain Downriver.
  White Iris, The.
Lewis. All Day It Has Rained.
  On the Welsh Mountains.
  Poet, The.
Liddy. Cracks in the Pavement.
  Vir IV.
Lindsay. Song of the Sturdy Snails, The.
Lorde. My Fifth Trip to Washington Ended in Northeast Delaware.
Lowry. Afternoon Nocturne.
  Billetin.
  Duckturne.
  Fragments from the Duck Anthology to Greet Our Beloved Harteebeeste in the Morning Watch.
  Happiest of Harteebeeste Days and Devoted Love Eterne.
  Heat Wave.
  Morning bird is singing, the.
  Morning rain is rained, The.
  Morning rain is raining / A morning pain is paining, The.
  Morning rain is raining / The morning leg is paining, The.
  Morning rain is sleeting, The.
  Morning rain is weeping, The.
  Poem: "Wet streets in Liverpool."
  Poor Butterfly that stamped.
  Rain Fell Heavily, The.
  Report on Conditions.
  3 Happy Little Ducks.
"MacDiarmid." Dying Earth, The.
MacLeish. De Votre Bonheur Il ne Reste Que Vos Photos.
MacNeice. Glass Falling.
  June Thunder.
  London Rain.
  Wild grass in spate in a rainy wind.
  Wiper, The.
Mahon. Kinsale.
Matthews. Record Flood.
  Taken at the Flood.
Meredith. Desired as Summer rain.
  Earth and a Wedded Woman.
  Song: "I would I were the drop of rain."
Merrill. Childlessness.
Merton. Song: "When rain, (sings light) rain has devoured my house."
  Spring Storm.
Millay. If it should rain—(the sneezy moon).
Morgan. When it rained and rained.
Muldoon. Boundary Commission, The.
Nash. Tomorrow, Partly Cloudy.
Nathan. Solemn Music.
Nemerov. Ending, An.
Neruda. I Went.
O'Hara. Poem: "Now the violets are all gone, the rhinoceroses, the cymbals."
Oliver. Marengo.
  Rain in Ohio.
Oppen. Two Romance Poems.
Paley. I don't think / the rain will end.
Patchen. Biography of Southern Rain.
Piercy. Rainy 4th.
Raine. Summit, The.
  These watery diamond spheres.
Ransom. Rain.
Rexroth. Mary and the Seasons.
Rich. Rain of Blood, The.
Roethke. Cycle, The.
  Interlude.
Rolfe. More than Flesh to Fathom.
Rossetti. And is this August weather? nay not so.
  If all were rain and never sun.
  O wind, why do you never rest.
  Winter Rain.
Sandburg. Lumber Yard Pools at Sunset.
  Monotone.
  New Weather.
  People know what the land knows, The.
  Rain Winds Blow Doors Open.

Redhaw Rain.
Santa Fe Sketches.
Summer Grass.
Three Balls.
Without Notice Beforehand.
Sarton. Japanese Prints.
Schuyler. Fauré's Second Piano Quartet.
Poem: "I got my hair cut."
Rain.
Running Footsteps.
Standing and Watching.
Suddenly.
Schwartz. First Night of Fall and Falling Rain, The.
Poem: "In the morning, when it was raining."
Sexton. Fury of Rain Storms, The.
Mother and Jack and the Rain.
Shapiro. And Now, the Weather.
Shelley. Cloud, The.
Fragment: Rain ("Fitful alternations of the rain, The").
Fragment: Rain ("Gentleness of rain was in the wind, The").
Shelton. San Juan's Day.
Silverstein. Lazy Jane.
Rain.
Smith, Stevie. Suburb.
Stevens. Human Arrangement.
Stevenson. I am like one that has sat alone.
I love to be warm by the red fireside.
Rain.
Tropic Rain.
Swift. Description of a City Shower, A.
Tomlinson. During Rain.
What It Was Like.
Updike. Code, The.
Raining in Magens Bay.
Sunday Rain.
Wash.
Walcott. Dark August.
Mud. Clods. The sucking heel of the rain-flinger.
Return to D'Ennery; Rain.
Warren. Holly and Hickory.
Whitman. Lingering Last Drops.
Voice of the Rain, The.
Wilbur. My Father Paints the Summer.
Williams, Charles Kenneth. It Is Teeming.
Souls.
That night, / winter, / rain.
Williams, William Carlos. Advent of Today.
Contemporania.
Dark Day, The.
From the Inside.
Hermaphroditic Telephones, The.
Idyl: "Wine of the grey sky."
Rain.
Self-Portrait 2.
Wordsworth. Rains at length have ceased, the winds are stilled, The.
Wright, James. Down to the Dregs.
Gemela.
Living by the Red River.
Rain.
Young. Beauty of Milwaukee Cold with Rain, The.
Zukofsky. Prop. LXI.
Rains, the rains, The.

Rain-in-the-Face
Whittier. On the Big Horn.

Rainbows
Dunbar. Place Where the Rainbow Ends, The.
Dunn. American Film, An.
Emerson. Sun athwart the cloud thought it no sin, The.
What are all the flowers.
Fisher. Land, The.
Frost. Iris by Night.
Graves. Nothing Now Astonishes.
Herrick. Rainbow; or Curious Covenant, The.
Rainbow, The.
Hopkins. Rainbow, The.
Kipling. So we settled it all when the storm was done.
Lawrence. Rainbow.
Rainbow, The.
"MacDiarmid." Watergaw, The.

MacLeish. Rainbow at Evening.
Melville. Canticle, A.
Nemerov. Breaking of Rainbows, The.
Raine. Rainbow, beautiful and clear light, A.
Rossetti. Boats sail on the rivers, / And ships sail on the seas.
If all were rain and never sun.
Sandburg. Bubbles.
Fins.
Gold Mud.
Out of the Rainbow End.
Tomlinson. Double Rainbow, The.
Wordsworth. My heart leaps up when I behold.

Rainey, Gertrude ("Ma")
Young. Dance for Ma Rainey, A.

Ralegh, Sir Walter
Beatles. I'm So Tired.
Spenser. Colin Clouts Come Home Againe.

Rameses II, King of Egypt
Kunitz. Three thousand years ago.
Shelley. Ozymandias [of Egypt].

Rams. see **Sheep.**

Ranches
Everson. Residual Years, The.
Hugo. Montana Ranch Abandoned.

Rape
Atwood. Women's Issue, A.
Bukowski. 99 to One.
Campion. Umbra.
Catullus. Carmen 77: "Whom I have trusted to no end (Rufus)."
Davie. Fountain of Cyané, The.
Eberhart. Snowy Owl.
Edmunds. December 27, 1988.
Gunn. Helen's Rape.
Hacker. Why We Are Going Back to Paradise Island.
Kipling. Raped and Revenged.
Larkin. Deceptions.
Lindsay. Trap, The.
Lovelace. Amarantha a Pastorall.
Mock Charon, A.
MacLeish. Rape of the Swan, The.
Meredith. Falling of Sally, The.
Rape of Aurora, The.
Olson. Hymn to Proserpine.
O'Ryan.
Piercy. Rape Poem.
Rich. Rape.
Rolfe. Mystery.
Shakespeare. Rape of Lucrece, The.
Smith, Patti. Rape.
Robert Bresson.
Swift. Excellent New Ballad, An.
Walker. Thing Itself, The.
Williams, William Carlos. Raper from Passenack, The.
Zimmer. Wanda and the Fish.
Zukofsky. Rufey my how frustrate unquickened and craved the tie I'm equal.

Raphael Santi
Blake. Pretty Epigram for [Those] the Entertainment of Those Who [Pay] Have Paid Great Sums in the Venetian & Flemish Ooze, A.
Rafael Sublime Majestic Graceful Wise.
Hardy. Cardinal Bembo's Epitaph on Raphael.
Lovelace. Amyntor's Grove.
Whittier. Raphael.
Wordsworth. Before the Picture of the Baptist, by Raphael, in the Gallery at Florence.

Rationalism and Rationalists
Blake. Mock On, Mock On, Voltaire, Rousseau.
Eberhart. Blessed Are the Angels in Heaven.
Recapitulation, The.
Oppen. Constant singing / Of the radios, and the art, The.
Rationality.

See also **Intellect and Intellectuals; Reason.**

Rats
Atwood. Rat Song.
Browning, Robert. Pied Piper of Hamelin, The.

Dickinson. Rat is the conciest Tenant, The.
Rat surrendered here, A.
Emerson. Van Buren.
Hall. Poem With One Fact.
Hoffman. Rats.
Hughes, Ted. Rat's Dance, The.
Lowry. There was an old Consul called Firmin.
Matthews. Change of Address.
Olson. Will: the rat.
Pack. Ecstasy of the Rat, The.
Sandburg. Rat Riddles.
Silverstein. Drats.
Simic. Note.
Smith, Stevie. To a Dead Vole.
Sorrentino. L the simple shape.
Nightpiece.
Updike. Rats.
Williams, William Carlos. Rat, The.
Wright, James. Eclogue at Nash's Grove.
Rats, The.

Rattlesnakes
Atwood. Eating Snake.
Dickey, James. Blowgun and Rattlesnake.
Everson. Rattlesnake August.
Lindsay. What the Rattlesnake Said.
Tomlinson. Abiquiu.
Warren. Rattlesnake Country.

Ravenna, Italy
MacNeice. Ravenna.

Ravens
Bukowski. All I Know.
Carruth. Mild Winter.
Coleridge. Raven, The.
Cowper. Fable, A: "Raven, while with glossy breast, A."
De la Mare. Omen, The.
Hughes, Ted. Ravens.
Poe. Raven, The.
Rich. Raven, The.
Robinson. Raven, The.
Rossetti. Bird's-Eye View, A.

Reading and Readers
Ashbery. Sonnet: "Each servant stamps the reader with a look."
Berg. Music.
1911.
Prayer: "Nobody understands so let the Rabbi."
Talking.
Unfinished Double Sonnet.
Why Are We Here?
With Akhmatova at the Black Gates.
Berryman. Olympus.
Bly. Reading in Fall Rain.
Bukowski. As I Lay Dying.
Hustle, The.
Little Girls, The.
Professors, The.
Byron. Answer to Some Elegant Verses.
I Read the "Christabel."
To Harriet ("Harriet! To see such Circumspection").
To Hook the Reader, You, John Murray.
To the Author of a Sonnet Beginning " 'Sad Is My Verse,' You Say, 'And Yet No Tear' ."
Campion. Ad ampliss. totius Angliae Cancellarium, Fr. Ba.
Ad Ed. Mychelburnum.
Ad Guil. Camdenum.
Ad Io. Davisium.
Epigramma: "Quid tu te numeris immisces? anne medentem."
In Honour of the Author by Tho: Campion Doctor in Physicke. To the Reader.
To the Reader.
"Carroll, Lewis." Madrigal: "He shouts amain, he shouts again."
Poeta Fit, Non Nascitur.
Three Little Maids.
Carruth. Dedication in These Days.
He reads there, only a boy, fifteen, in the dingy.
In Memoriam.
Ray.
Tanck's Song About Women.
Cohen. I Decided.

Coleridge. To the Author of "The Robbers."
Creeley. Irish.
The.
Cummings. For prodigal read generous.
Davie. His Themes.
Two Widows in Tashkent.
De la Mare. Old Susan.
Omen, The.
Vigil.
Winter Dusk.
Dickinson. It is still as distinct as Paradise.
There is no Frigate like a Book.
Dobyns. Katia Reading.
Song of the Wrong Response.
Dove. Reading Hölderlin on the Patio with the
Aid of a Dictionary.
Dunbar. End of the Chapter, The.
Duncan. Human Communion. Traces, The.
Emerson. He must have / Droll fancies
sometimes cross his quiet thoughts.
I grieve that better souls than mine.
What all the books of ages paint, I have.
Fisher. Correspondence.
Gallagher. His Shining Helmet; Its Horsehair
Crest.
Reading Aloud.
Graves. Colophon.
Gunn. His Rooms in College.
Hartley. Any Page of Thomas Mann's.
Perusing Mallarmé in Maine.
Herrick. Another [To His Booke].
Another [To His Booke].
Glorie.
His Wish to God.
Ode to Sir Clipsebie Crew, An.
To His Booke ("Be bold my Booke, nor be
abasht, or feare").
To His Booke ("Come thou not neere those
men, who are like Bread").
To Momus.
To My Ill Reader.
To the Sour[e] Reader.
To Vulcan.
Hewitt. Big Room, The.
Encounter With R.J. Welch, The Antiquary.
Eye for Color, An.
Reading.
Hugo. Keen to Leaky Flowers.
Jarrell. Reader, The.
Jonson. To Groom Idiot.
To the Reader ("Pray thee, take care, that
tak'st my book[e] in hand").
Joseph. Knock Knock.
Keats. On Receiving a Curious Shell, and a
Copy of Verses, from the Same Ladies.
Written on a Blank Space at the End of
Chaucer's Tale of "The Floure and the Lefe."
Koertge. Reading at the Local High School.
Sometimes.
Kooser. Selecting a Reader.
Larkin. Fiction and the Reading Public.
Study of Reading Habits, A.
Lawrence. Reading a Letter.
Reading in the Evening.
Levertov. To the Reader.
Liddy. Miles.
Longfellow. Day Is Done, The.
Lovelace. To My Truely Valiant, Learned
Friend, Who in His Booke Resolv'd the Art
Gladiatory into the Mathematick's.
Lowry. Thoughts to Be Erased from My
Destiny.
McGrath. Ars Poetica: Or: Who Lives in the
Ivory Tower?
Praises IV.
Use of Books, The.
You Can Start the Poetry Now, Or: News
from Crazy Horse.
Mahon. Death and the Sun.
Meinke. Dear Reader.
Robert Frost in Warsaw.
Meredith. Hail, Common Sense! most rare of
all!
He who has looked upon Earth.
Rosalind.
Thou pirate nested over Alde!
You like not that French novel? Tell me why.

Merton. Reading Translated Poets, Feb. 1.
Olson. I'm With You.
Sexton. Sweeney.
Simic. Chorus for One Voice.
Smith, Charlotte. Should the lone Wanderer,
fainting on his way.
Smith, Stevie. To an American Publisher.
Sorrentino. Woman Irritable because of Her
Menses.
Southwell. Author to the Reader, The ("Deare
eye, that daynest to let fall a looke").
Author to the Reader, The ("Deare eye that
doost peruse my Muses stile").
Stevens. House Was Quiet and the World Was
Calm, The.
Lack of Repose, The.
Large Red Man Reading.
Novel, The.
Phosphor Reading by His Own Light.
Reader, The.
Stevenson. After Reading "Antony and
Cleopatra."
Envoy: "Go, little book, and wish to all."
Go, little book—the ancient phrase.
I, now, O friend, whom noiselessly the snows.
Picture-Books in Winter.
So shall this book wax like unto a well.
To Any Reader.
To Master Andrew Lang.
Who would think, herein to look.
Tomlinson. Double Rainbow, The.
Dream, A.
Hyphens.
Walcott. Volcano.
Whitman. For Us Two, Reader Dear.
Thou Reader.
To the Reader at Parting.
Who Is Now Reading This?
Whoever You Are Holding Me Now in Hand.
Whittier. Lines on a Fly-Leaf.
Wordsworth. Illustrated Books and
Newspapers.
Lines Written on a Blank Leaf in a Copy of
the Author's Poem "The Excursion", upon
Hearing of the Death of the Late Vicar of
Kendal.
Yeats. Ribh at the Tomb of Baile and Aillinn.
Zukofsky. After reading.
Reading and Talking.

Reagan, Ronald W.
"Reed." Original Wrapper, The.
Williams, Charles Kenneth. Bishop Tutu's
Visit to the White House: 1984.

Real Estate
Sandburg. Real Avenue News.
Sutter. Real Estate.

Reality
Ammons. Turning.
Atwood. Comic Books vs. History.
Double Voice, The.
How To Tell One Country from Another.
There are two islands / at least, they do not
exclude each other.
Browning, Robert. Statue and the Bust, The.
Bukowski. Nice Try.
Nothing Subtle.
Trick to Dull Our Bleeding, A.
Burns. Fragment: "Why, why tell thy lover."
Carroll, Jim. To the Secret Poets of Kansas.
Carruth. Une Présence Absolue.
Ciardi. Credibility.
Differences.
For Instance.
Fragment of a Bas Relief.
Knothole in Spent Time, A.
On a Photo of Sgt. Ciardi a Year Later.
On the Patio.
One Jay at a Time.
To a Lovely Lady Gone to Theory.
Clark. Color of Stepped on Gum, The.
Realism.
Coleridge. Phantom or Fact?
Cooper. Approaching my life I am terrified.
Creeley. As real as thinking.
City, The.
"Do You Think."
Echo.

Numbers.
Place, A.
Province, The.
Surgeons.
"There."
Token, A.
Cummings. &(all during the / dropsin).
As freedom is a breakfastfood.
But observe;although / once is never the
beginning of.
Dive for dreams / or a slogan may topple you.
Dominic has / a doll wired.
Great advantage of being alive, The.
Hate blows a bubble of despair into.
I shall imagine life.
If.
In a middle of a room.
Love is a place.
Lucky means finding / Holes where.
My darling since / you and.
My sweet old etcetera.
Now air is air and thing is thing:no bliss.
Of Ever-Ever Land i speak.
Out of the lie of no.
There is a here and.
This little bride & groom are.
This mind made war.
When serpents bargain for the right to squirm.
De la Mare. I Sit Alone.
Looking Glass, The.
Dove. Anti-Father.
Duncan. Imagining in Writing.
What of the structure of Rime? I said.
Writing as Writing.
Dunn. Here and There.
"Dylan." Gates of Eden.
Idiot Wind.
Eberhart. Ceremonial.
Commas in Wintertime.
Kaire.
Looking Head On.
Mystery of the Abstract.
On the Subtle Man.
Poem as Trajectory, The.
Propositions.
Reality.
Stopping a Kaleidoscope.
Vision through Timothy.
Way Out, A.
Emerson. But as this fugitive sunlight.
Proteus.
Fenton. Skip, The.
Ferlinghetti. Sarolla's women in their picture
hats.
Sueño Real.
Sweet and various the woodlark.
Fisher. For Realism.
Ford. Large bead on the.
Real dreams. More real than.
Fox. Phekda.
Visitor, The.
Gallagher. Candle, Lamp & Firefly.
Gardner. Cowardice.
Ginsberg. Imaginary Universes.
Metaphysics.
Trembling of the Veil, The.
Griffiths. Few Bars Over Again, A.
Hardy. At Waking.
Beauty, The.
History of an Hour, The.
Just the Same.
There Seemed a Strangeness.
To Sincerity.
Tragedian to Tragedienne.
Hesketh. Moving Staircase.
Tunnel, The.
Hewitt. Blossomed Thorn, The.
Glen of Light, The.
Orientations.
Parallels Never Meet.
Hoffman. Reflections.
Jarrell. Jamestown.
Märchen, The.
Picture in the Paper, A.
Jeffers. Boats in a Fog.
Real and Half Real.

Jonson. Epigram. To William, Earl of
Newcastle, An.
Keats. And What Is Love? It Is a Doll
Dressed Up.
Lawrence. Demiurge.
Red Geranium and Godly Mignonette.
Ultimate Reality.
Levertov. Ground-Mist, The.
Liddy. Pools where it offers to our curiosity,
The.
Lovelace. Cinna seems poor in show.
Lowry. Correcting Manuscript.
Song for My Wife.
MacLeish. Einstein.
MacNeice. News-Reel, The.
Plain Speaking.
Under the Mountain.
McNeill. Stoic (Circa 1907).
Markson. Agree.
At the Lion's Head.
Merton. If I sometimes say that flowers smile.
"Mystery of things"—where is it found?, The.
Truth, The.
Where Is Tao?
Morrison. Cock-pit.
Form Is an Angel, The.
Hope Is Just.
Nathan. Creed.
Scroll, The.
Nemerov. Maia.
Neruda. Child of the Moon.
Don't you also feel danger.
O'Hara. Poem: "Now the violets are all gone,
the rhinoceroses, the cymbals."
Olson. A B Cs (3—for Rimbaud).
Applause.
Concerning Exaggeration, or How, Properly, to
Heap Up.
Discrete Gloss, A.
He treads on edges of being where the drop.
Moon Is the Number 18, The.
Put him this way.
Signs.
There Are Sounds.
Piercy. Erasure.
Raine. Bad Dream, A.
World: / Image on water, waves.
Ransom. Somewhere Is Such a Kingdom.
"Reed." Legendary Hearts.
Robinson. Prophet of dead words defeats
himself, The.
Rolfe. Any Slave.
Conscript's Song.
Guerrillas, The.
Paris—Christmas 1938.
Portrait of a Death.
Postscript to a War.
Rossetti. Hopeless Case, A.
Rukeyser. When the true things meet us at the
place we reach, they are all.
Sandburg. Moonlight and Maggots.
Schuyler. Letter to a Friend: Who Is Nancy
Daum?
Sexton. Self in 1958.
Snodgrass. Mouse, The.
Snyder. Milton by Firelight.
Nanao Knows.
Truth Like the Belly of a Woman Turning,
The.
Sorrentino. Door that opens on, A.
Evils of the City.
Let's Call This.
Particular density: in the center, rises, A.
Perceive.
Something plus something else is not one
thing.
Toward the End of Winter.
What is past is here, as we.
Where are the rose-colored cities.
Stevens. Add This to Rhetoric.
Angel Surrounded by Paysans.
Bed of Old John Zeller, The.
Bouquet of Roses in Sunlight.
Holiday in Reality.
Jasmine's Beautiful Thoughts Underneath the
Willow.
Man Carrying Thing.

Not Ideas about the Thing but the Thing Itself.
Novel, The.
Paisant Chronicle.
Repetitions of a Young Captain.
Saint John and the Back-Ache.
So-and-So Reclining on Her Couch.
Tomlinson. Observation of Facts.
Updike. Reel.
Van Duyn. Causes.
Waldman. Baby Breakdown.
Out There.
Warren. Court-Martial.
Whitman. Ambition.
That Shadow My Likeness.
Wilbur. Antiworlds.
Hole in the Floor, A.
Thyme Flowering among Rocks.
Williams, Charles Kenneth. Beginning of
April, The.
Harm.
Williams, William Carlos. Paterson.
Wordsworth. Hint from the Mountains for
Certain Political Pretenders.
Oxford, May Thirtieth, Eighteen Twenty
("Shame on this faithless heart! that could
allow").
To the Utilitarians.
Yarrow Visited [September, 1814].
Wright, Charles. Last Journal.
Local Journal.
Wright, James. How close to becoming spirit
something is.
Life.
Yeats. Meru.
Realists, The.
Young. Singular Yen, A.

Reaping and Reapers
Berry. Mad Farmer Revolution, The.
Hartley. Five Women.
Hewitt. Load.
Rolfe. Somebody and Somebody Else and
You.
Wordsworth. Solitary Reaper, The.

Reason
Auden. Those who will not reason.
Blake. Mock On, Mock On, Voltaire,
Rousseau.
Reason and Imagination.
Bogan. Sonnet: "Since you would claim the
sources of my thought."
Campion. And would you faine the reason
know.
Carew. Lover, upon an Accident Necessitating
His Departure, Consults with Reason, A.
Love's Force.
Carroll, Jim. I Am Not Kurt Schwitters.
Tenth Try, The.
"Carroll, Lewis." Misunderstandings.
Warden's Charm, The.
Carruth. Persimmon wind, lost names raining.
Thwart.
Chaucer. Lak of Stedfastnesse.
O thou, whose all-creating hands sustain.
Clough. When panting sighs the bosom fill.
Coleridge. Mythology in an Age of Reason.
Reason.
Cowper. By Philemon.
Report of an Adjudged Case.
Creeley. Poem for Beginners.
Davie. Bride of Reason, The.
Donne. If poisonous [or poysonous]
mineral[l]s, and if that tree.
Dove. Geometry.
Eberhart. Fables of the Moon.
Recapitulation, The.
Somewhere Else.
Emerson. And Ellen, when the greybeard
years.
Brave Empedocles defying fools, The.
Hard is it to persuade the public mind of its
plain duty & true interest.
Everson. You, God.
Frost. Masque of Reason, A.
Graves. Ageless Reason.
Synthetic Such.
Within Reason.
Hardy. Philosophical Fantasy, A.

Hesketh. Integration.
Hewitt. Disaster on the Box.
Hugo. Dwelling.
Jeffers. Contemplation of the Sword.
McGrath. Little Odyssey of Jason Quint, of
Science, Doctor, The.
Matthews. Another Beer.
Psychopathology of Everyday Life, The.
Melville. Reasonable Constitution, A.
Meredith. As mighty thews burst manacles,
she went mad.
To the Comic Spirit.
Nash. Passionate Pagan and the Dispassionate
Public, The.
Nathan. Diver, The.
Plath. Death of Myth-making, The.
Pope. Epistle I, to Sir Richard Temple, Lord
Cobham.
O thou, whose all-creating hands sustain.
On a Certain Lady at Court.
Rolfe. Conscript's Song.
Postscript to a War.
Rossetti. In the Willow Shade.
Sandburg. Transient tar-paper shack, The.
Sidney. Reason, tell me thy mind, if here be
reason.
Sonnet 5: "It is most true that eyes are formed
to serve."
Sonnet 10: "Reason, in faith thou art well
served, that still."
Sonnet 18: "With what sharp checks I in
myself am shent."
Sonnet 71: "Who will in fairest book of
Nature know."
Smart. Reason and Imagination.
Smith, Charlotte. Hope. A Rondeau.
Written near a Port on a Dark Evening.
Stevens. Pieces.
Suckling. Love, Reason, Hate, did once
bespeak.
Williams, Charles Kenneth. Love: Wrath.
Vehicle: Violence.
Wordsworth. Alas! what boots the long
laborious quest.
Wroth. Sonnet 10: "Bee from court of Love,
and reason torne."
Zukofsky. Can a mote of sunlight defeat its
purpose.
Junction, A.
Snows' night's winds on the window rattling.
Tall and singularly dark you pass among the
breakers—.
To My Valentines.

See also **Intellect and Intellectuals; Rationalism
and Rationalists.**

Rebellions and Rebels
Atwood. 1837 War in Retrospect.
Beatles. Come Together.
Cry Baby Cry.
Berry. Manifesto: the Mad Farmer Liberation
Front.
Browning, Robert. Italian in England, The.
Through the Metidja to Abd-el-Kadr.
Bukowski. This.
Burns. Birth-Day Ode. December 31st 1787,
A.
Johnie Cope.
Strathallan's Lament.
Campion. Bravely deckt, come forth, bright
day.
Carroll, Jim. I stored daylight in secret attics.
Carruth. Smallish Son, The.
Sonnet: "To rebel is suitable philosophical
tactics."
Sonnet: "To rebel. So I have saved my life,
not once."
Ciardi. Encounter.
Cohen. First We Take Manhattan.
Rebellion, The.
Coleridge. Foster-Mother's Tale, The.
Cowper. Modern Patriot, The.
Crashaw. Upon the Powder Day.
Cummings. Boys i mean are not refined, The.
Crazy jay blue) / demon laughshriek.
If i / or anybody don't.
Timeless / ly this / (merely and whose).
Dunbar. Conquerors, The.

"Dylan." My Back Pages.
  Outlaw Blues.
  Times They Are A-Changin', The.
  When the Ship Comes In.
Eberhart. Throwing the Apple.
Emerson. Uriel.
Fenton. Wild Ones[, The].
Frost. Not Quite Social.
Ginsberg. Elegy Che Guevara.
Haines. In the middle of America.
  Thereafter on that cold.
Hardy. At Shag's Heath.
Heaney. Requiem for the Croppies.
Hesketh. Retreat.
Hewitt. Mobile Mollusc, A.
  Rebel, The.
Hoffman. Twentieth Century, The.
Hughes, Langston. In Explanation of Our
  Times.
Hugo. Braes, The.
Jong. Lullabye for a Dybbuk.
  Rain is My Home, The.
Joseph. Dog Body and Cat Mind.
Kipling. Ballad of Boh Da Thone, The.
  Ballad of the Red Earl, The.
  Pict Song, A.
  Rebel, The.
  Ulster.
Koertge. I Wanted My Name on the Side of a
  Building I Wanted to Be as Feared as the
  Word Biopsy.
Kunitz. Demonstrations in the streets.
  This Day This World.
Lawrence. Don'ts.
Lindsay. Factory Windows Are Always
  Broken.
Lorde. Relevant Is Different Points on the
  Circle.
McGrath. Restless Night, The.
MacNeice. Canto XV: "Been here before?
  Whether he has or no."
  Les Neiges d'Antan.
  Million simmering kettles: in the Destroyer's
  shrine, A.
Meinke. Uncle Jim.
Meredith. Monmouth.
Merton. NORMS / Grraa aa aa lll.
Morrison. Crossroads, The.
Nash. Child Is Father to the Man, But with
  More Authority, The.
O'Hara. On Seeing Larry Rivers' *Washington
  Crossing the Delaware* at the Museum of
  Modern Art.
Olson. Put him this way.
  Stevens Song.
Paley. Women's Prison: El Salvador / The
  Ballad of Visiting Day, The.
Piercy. Eight of Swords, The.
Plath. Bull of Bendylaw, The.
Pope. Shut, shut the door, good *John*!
  fatigu'd, I said.
Rich. North American Time.
  Phenomenology of Anger, The.
  Tear Gas.
  You: air-driven reft from the tuber-bitten
  soil.
Rolfe. Ballad of the Noble Intentions.
  Entry.
  Idiot Joe Prays in Pershing Square and Gets
  Hauled in for Vagrancy.
  Letter.
  May Day Song.
Rukeyser. For Kayle Boyle.
Silverstein. I Won't Hatch.
Smith, Patti. Fleet of Deer, A.
  High on Rebellion.
Thomas. Find Meat on Bones.
Walker. Rage.
Whitman. We Two Boys Together Clinging.
Whittier. Bolivar.
  Dream of Pio Nono, The.
  From Perugia.
  Garibaldi.
  Italy.
  Kossuth.
  Slaves of Martinique, The.

Song of the Vermonters, 1779, The.
  Toussaint L'Ouverture.
Williams, William Carlos. In San Marco,
  Venezia.
  Poem for Norman Macleod, A.
Wordsworth. At Bologna, in Remembrance of
  the Late Insurrections, 1837.
  At Bologna, in Remembrance of the Late
  Insurrections, 1837, Continued: "As leaves
  are to the tree wheron they grow."
  At Bologna, in Remembrance of the Late
  Insurrections, 1837, Continued: "Hard task!
  exclaim the undisciplined, to lean."
  Eagle and the Dove, The.
  Just Vengeance Claims Thy Soul for Rights
  Invaded?
Wright, James. Centenary Note: Inscribed to
  Little Crow, Leader of the Sioux Rebellion in
  Minnesota, 1862, A.
Yeats. Upon a House Shaken by the Land
  Agitation.

See also **Revolution and Revolutionaries.**

Rebirth
Berry. Autumn Burning, An.
  Envoy: "Love, all day there has been at the
  edge of my mind."
  Farm travels in snow, The.
  Song in a Year of Catastrophe.
Bly. Home in Dark Grass, A.
Carruth. One day music / begins.
  Primavera, The.
  Stone, The.
  Where the snow bank leans.
Cohen. This Is for You.
Cullen. For My Grandmother.
Cummings. I thank You God for most this
  amazing.
  Now does our world descend.
  When god lets my body be.
  Who before dying demands not rebirth.
Dickey, James. For a Time and Place.
Dobyns. Song for Making the Birds Come.
Doolittle. But it won't be that way.
  In the Rain.
  It is no madness to say.
Eberhart. Return of Odysseus, The.
Everson. In All These Acts.
  Song the Body Dreamed in the Spirit's Mad
  Behest, The.
Ferlinghetti. I am waiting for my case to
  come up.
  Wild Dreams of a New Beginning.
Frost. Onset, The.
Gardner. West of Childhood.
Garrigue. Spring Song II.
Glück. Cottonmouth Country.
Graves. Ages of Oath, The.
  Song: The Palm Tree.
  Survivor, The.
Hardy. For Life I Had Never Cared Greatly.
Hartley. Vast rose of July.
Hewitt. Morning Hymn.
Hoffman. New Birth, A.
  Shell.
Holmes. Chinese Poets.
Hughes, Langston. In Time of Silver Rain.
Hughes, Ted. Wino.
Joseph. Geranium.
Kinnell. Saint Francis and the Sow.
  Wait.
Kunitz. Poem: "O Heart: this is a dream I
  had, or not a dream."
  Reckoning, The.
  Vita Nuova.
  When the Dead Arise.
  When the magician died, I wept.
Levine. Belief.
  Let Me Begin Again.
  Told.
  Waking an Angel.
McGrath. Drowned Man: Death Between Two
  Rivers, The.
  Passages.
MacNeice. April Manifesto, An.
Merton. On the Anniversary of My Baptism.
Millay. Renascence.
Nathan. It's a brand new morning.

Oliver. Alligator Poem.
  Meeting, A.
Piercy. Butt of Winter, The.
  Inside Chance, The.
Raine. Journey, The.
Rolfe. Not Men Alone.
Rossetti. All the world is out in leaf.
  Shut Out.
Sandburg. Falltime.
  October Paint.
  Uplands in May.
Shelley. But Greece and her foundations are.
Smith, Patti. Neo Boy.
Snodgrass. Seasoning Barn.
Stevenson. Cock's clear voice into the clearer
  air, The.
  Flower god, god of the spring, beautiful,
  bountiful.
Stuart. Major Work.
Thomas. I Dreamed My Genesis.
  I Have Longed to Move Away.
  Saint About to Fall, A.
Warren. World Is a Parable, The.
Whittier. April.
  First Flowers, The.
Wilbur. Alatus.
  April 5, 1974.
  Black Birch in Winter, A.
  Children of Darkness.
  Flumen Tenebrarum.
  Lilacs, The.
  Orchard Trees, January.
  Rondeau: "Year has cast its cloak away, The."
  Shad-Time.
  Then.
  To Ishtar.
Wordsworth. Peter Bell; a Tale.
Wright, James. Come Forth.
  Mary Bly.
  Moon.
  On the Skeleton of a Hound.

See also **Renewal; Regeneration.**

Rebuilding
Griffiths. Guesthouse, The.
Holmes. Weekend Away.
Pack. Letter to My Widow.

Recipes
Silverstein. Recipe For A Hippopotamus
  Sandwich.

Recognition
Berg. No Word.
Berry. Recognition, The.
Browning, Robert. Popularity.
Bukowski. On Being Recognized.
  Some of My Readers.
Carroll, Jim. Micky.
Cooper. Conversation by the Body's Light.
Creeley. Smell of gum wrappers as of
  Saturday afternoon at movies.
Dickinson. You'll know Her—by Her Foot.
Ferlinghetti. One of These Days.
Hardy. He Did Not Know Me.
  Poet's Thoughts, A.
Herrick. To his Faithfull Friend, Master John
  Crofts, Cup-bearer to the King.
Hewitt. Owl, The.
Kunitz. Open the Gates.
Lindsay. Prayer to All the Dead Among Mine
  Own People, A.
Lowry. More Impatience.
MacLeish. Speech to the Detractors.
MacNeice. Elegy for Minor Poets.
Patchen. I always return to this place.
Piercy. If They Come in the Night.
Ransom. Jack's Letter.
Sorrentino. People in Hell are clothed.
  Something plus something else is not one
  thing.
Tomlinson. Insistence of Things, The.
Whitman. Death and Burial of McDonald
  Clarke, a Parody, The.
  Last Droplets.
  Long, Long Hence.
Wilbur. Foggy Street.
Williams, Charles Kenneth. Philadelphia:
  1978.
Williams, Miller. Divorce.

Young. Sleepy Day at Half Moon Bay.

Reconciliation
Beatles. It Won't Be Long.
Berg. In Death I Know Well Enough All Things End in Emptiness.
Bly. Conversation with a Holy Woman Not Seen for Many Years.
Carruth. Fathers die, but sons.
Gods.
Chaucer. Pardoner's Tale, The.
Cohen. Coming Back to You.
Cowper. Alexander Selkirk.
Creeley. Operation, The.
De la Mare. Reconciliation.
Donne. Expostulation, The.
Frost. Dream Pang, A.
Graves. *Song*: Reconciliation.
Hardy. At the Word "Farewell."
Herrick. To the Rose; a Song.
Hoffman. When my wiser brother.
Jong. If You Come Back.
Lovelace. To Ellinda, That Lately I Have Not Written.
Lowry. Harteebeeste with flying hoof, The.
Melville. America.
Meredith. War.
Nash. Nothing but Nature.
Oliver. Visitor, A.
Piercy. Night Letter.
Ransom. Armageddon.
Parting at Dawn.
Robinson. Partnership.
Story of the Ashes and the Flame, The.
Schuyler. Was It.
Shakespeare. Sonnet 119: "What potions have I drunk of Siren tears."
Shelley. Cancelled Stanza.
Whitman. While Not the Past Forgetting.
Wyatt. Alas, dear heart! what hap [*or* hope] had I.
How oft have I, my dear [*or* dere] and cruel[l] foe.
Yeats. Reconciliation.

Reconstruction, United States
Dunbar. To the South.
Piercy. Community.
Whittier. Howard at Atlanta.
To the Thirty-Ninth Congress.

Record Players
Creeley. Love ("Tracking through this").
Cummings. Phonograph may(if it likes)be prophe, The.
Stuart. Turntables.

Red (color)
Atwood. Red Shirt, A.
Beatles. Yes It Is.
Donne. Oh my black[e] soul[e]! now thou art summoned.
Eberhart. Vermont Idyll.
Hughes, Langston. When Sue Wears Red.
Hugo. Red Stone.
Notley. Red Zinnias.
Raine. Quenching the Red.
Rukeyser. Salamander.

Red Jacket (Seneca Chief)
Whitman. Red Jacket (from Aloft).

Redemption
Auden. Ballad of Barnaby, The.
Beatles. Getting Better.
Brontë. Lines: "Soft unclouded blue of air, The."
Brooks. Truth.
Campion. Author of light, revive my dying spright.
Come Let Us Sound With Melodie.
Seek the Lord.
View Mee, Lord.
Carruth. Bitcheries of Madison Avenue, The.
Cohen. Isaiah.
Cowper. Longing To Be with Christ.
Song of Mercy and Judgment, A.
De la Mare. I Sit Alone.
Dickinson. Danger is not at first.
Summer day on which you came, The.
To congratulate the Redeemed is perhaps superfluous.
Work is a bleak redeemer.

"Dylan." Honey, Just Allow Me One More Chance.
Eberhart. Art, the holy care of life.
Redemption.
Graves. Gold and Malachite.
Point of No Return.
Herbert. Faith.
Holy Baptism (1).
Jews, The.
Love (2).
Nature.
Parody [*or* Parodie], A.
Pulley, The.
Redemption.
Repentance.
Sion.
Vanity (2).
World, The.
Herrick. Christs Incarnation.
To Julia, the Flaminica Dialis, or Queen-Priest.
Hewitt. Turban, The.
Hill. Brazed city / reorders its own, The.
Hopkins. God's Grandeur.
To him who ever thought with love of me.
Jeffers. Redeemer, A.
Lindsay. Look You, I'll Go Pray.
Rhymer's Reply: Incense and Splendor, The.
McAuley. Penance.
Secret.
MacLeish. Infinite Reason, The.
MacNeice. Jam Lucis Orto Sidere.
Return, The.
Merton. Biography, The.
Cana.
Holy Communion: the City.
I Have Called You.
Rahab's House.
Ut Queant.
Milton. Atonement, The.
Nemerov. Carol: "Now is the world withdrawn all."
Oppen. That Land.
Ralegh. Passionate Man[']s Pilgrimage, The.
Robinson. Dark House, The.
Rossetti. God Is Our Hope and Strength.
Rejoice with Me.
Whatsoever Is Right, That Shall Ye Receive.
Smart. Epiphany.
Hymn to the Supreme Being.
Plenteous Redemption.
Southwell. Presentation, The.
Synne's Heavy Loade.
Spenser. Most glorious lord of life that on this day.
Stevenson. Tempest tossed and sore afflicted, sin defiled and care oppressed.
Thomas. There Was a Saviour.
Warren. Sunset Walk in Thaw-Time in Vermont.
Wilbur. Proof, The.
Wordsworth. After-Thought ("Oh Life! without thy chequered scene").

Redwings
Ammons. Bay Bank.

Redwood Trees. *see* **Sequoia Trees.**

Reeds
Browning, Elizabeth Barrett. Reed, A.
Cowper. On the Reed.
Herrick. Poet Hath Lost His Pipe, The.
Tomlinson. Reeds.

Refinement
Lovelace. Song: "Strive not, vain Lover, to be fine."
Sarton. Lady with a Falcon.
Stuart. Interlude at the Grand Hotel, An.

Reflections
Atwood. Being with you / here, in this room.
My face, my other faces.
Tricks With Mirrors.
Auden. California.
Narcissus.
Berg. Rocks, The.
Berry. Porch over the River, The.
Bishop. Gentleman of Shalott, The.
To Be Written on the Mirror in Whitewash.
Bukowski. Anthony.
Face While Shaving.

Layover.
One Night Stand.
Sleep.
10 Lions and the End of the World.
Burns. I Love My Jean.
Carew. To T. H., a Lady Resembling My Mistress.
Carruth. Full of the moon. In pine woods a snowlight, The.
Once on a night in spring.
Point, The.
Rhopaloceral.
Sonnet: "How is it, tell me, that this new self can be—."
There where pines darken the water above the brookbed.
Cohen. Window, The.
Creeley. Awakening, The.
Eye, The.
For Joel.
It Is at Times.
Kind of Act Of, The.
De la Mare. Looking Glass, The.
Reflections.
Dickey, William. His Death from Cancer.
Emerson. Sea reflects the rosy sky, The.
Ferlinghetti. At midnight on the next balcony.
Heaven / was only half as far that night.
Fletcher. Sands, The.
Frost. For Once, Then, Something.
Gallagher. My Mother Remembers That She Was Beautiful.
Graves. Foreboding, The.
Spite of Mirrors.
Griffiths. Anglo-Welshman and his friends, The.
Decision.
Getting It Wrong, Again.
Spanish Providence, A.
Hemingway. Along with Youth.
Hesketh. Recapitulation.
Hewitt. On the Grand Dublin Canal: Musing on the "Two Nations" Theory.
Jarrell. Game at Salzburg, A.
Joseph. Bound upon a Wheel.
Cloud.
Descartes—You There?
Man as Matter (ISLAND; PHYSICS).
Mirror, Mirror.
STUDY: *A Lady in her Bedroom* (Bonnard).
Kinnell. Still Time, The.
Knight. Belly Song.
Knott. Shorts / Excerpts ("I keep a TV monitor on my chest").
Lewis. Consider this silent disciplined assembly.
Lorde. Birthday Memorial to Seventh Street, A.
Lovelace. Song: "Strive not, vain Lover, to be fine."
McGrath. Proverbs of the Middle World.
World of the Perfect Tear, The.
MacNeice. Corner Seat.
Perdita.
To Hedli.
McNeill. Involved (The Spider).
Markson. At Malcolm Lowry's Grave.
Merrill. In the Hall of Mirrors.
Merton. Faces of Girls Looking at Themselves in the River.
Lake, The.
Miller. Invincible Summer.
Late September.
Panhandle (For Annette).
Putting Up Snow Fence.
Start Up the Music Again.
Stumble into the great red sunset.
Morgan. Choice, The.
Reflection, The.
Morrison. If Only I.
In That Year.
Start Again.
Sudden Attack.
To Be Alone.
Nemerov. Mirror, The.
Raine. Golden Leaf, The.
Loch, The.

Message.
Peace of Mind.
"Reed." I'll Be Your Mirror.
Rexroth. Between Two Wars.
Delia Rexroth.
Fish Peddler and Cobbler.
On What Planet.
Pausing in my sixth d-ecade.
Signature of All Things, The.
Rolfe. Biography.
Kentucky.
Rukeyser. Asylum Song.
Sandburg. Chicago Poet.
Hungry and Laughing Men.
Old Music for Quiet Hearts.
Pool of Bethesda.
Sarton. Charleston Plantations.
Myself to Me.
Nostalgia for India.
Schuyler. Sparks.
Shelton. Letter From an Inland Province.
Out Here.
Sorrentino. Billy McCoy.
Stevens. Golden Woman in a Silver Mirror, A.
Poem with Rhythms.
Stevenson. Mother and Daughter.
Stuart. Narcissus Dreaming.
Tomlinson. Below Tintern.
Canal.
Given Grace, A.
Reflections.
Windshield, The.
Turco. Fetch.
Moon of Melancholy, The.
Reflections at Forty-Nine.
Warren. Late Subterfuge.
Wilbur. Aspen and the Stream, The.
Wroth. Sonnet 46: "Love, thou hast all, for now thou hast mee made."
Young. Fun City Samba.
Move Continuing, The.
Some Spice for Jack Spicer.

Refugees
Boyle. New Emigration, The.
Browning, Robert. Italian in England, The.
Carruth. This nation was asylum when we came.
Cummings. Belgium.
Duncan. Bring It Up from the Dark.
Ginsberg. September on Jessore Road.
Griffiths. Refugees.
Hacker. Days of 1944: Three Friends.
Hardy. Appeal to America on Behalf of the Belgian Destitute, An.
Cry of the Homeless.
On the Belgian Expatriation.
Jarrell. Refugees, The.
To the New World.
Lewis. Polish girls singing, in the wind's soughing.
Longfellow. Evangeline, a Tale of Acadie.
MacNeice. Refugees.
Merton. Picture of Lee Ying, A.
Miller. Dislocado.
Rolfe. Are You Now or Have You Ever Been.
Rukeyser. Another Day (Day Lilies, Yellow Daisies).
Another Day (You can't come).
Fourth Elegy. The Refugees.
Story, A.
Smith, Charlotte. Disillusion with the French Revolution.
Long wintry months are past; the Moon that now.
Stuart. Leavetaking.

Regeneration
Berry. Country where he lives, The.
Slip, The.
Sycamore, The.
Bukowski. Numb Your Ass and Your Brain and Your Heart—.
Cohen. Believe Me, Edith.
Song for Abraham Klein.
You Tore Your Shirt.
Hall. Day I Was Older, The.
Herrick. Sonnet of Perilla, A.

To Anthea: ("Sick is Anthea, sickly is the spring").
Upon Trigg.
Holmes. Premonitory July.
Melville. Of Wickedness the Word.
Oliver. Rabbit, The.
Three Poems for James Wright.
Paley. In deepest summer / the milkweed flower.
Shapiro. Leg, The.
Wright, Charles. Mount Caribou at Night.

See also **Rebirth; Renewal.**

Regret
Angelou. Refusal.
Beatles. I'll Follow the Sun.
Berg. Kiss, The.
Last Elegy.
Berrigan. Paul Blackburn.
Berryman. All I did wrong, all the Grand Guignol years.
Darling I wait O in my upstairs box.
Our lives before hopelessly our mistake!—.
Spot of poontang on a five-foot piece, A.
Swarthy when young; who took the tonsure; sign.
You, Chris, *contrite* I never thought to see.
You sailed in sky-high, with your speech askew.
Brontë. Why ask to know what date, what clime?
Brooks. Mother, The.
Bukowski. Oh, Yes.
Bunting. Slinking by the jug-and-bottle.
Burns. Remorse.
Byron. Herod's Lament for Mariamne.
Lament of Tasso, The.
To the Sighing Strephon.
"Carroll, Lewis." Faces in the Fire.
Carruth. In Tobey Woods.
Clough. Oh, I have done those things that my Soul fears.
Cohen. Ain't No Cure for Love.
Coleridge. Elegy Imitated from One of Akenside's Blank-Verse Inscriptions.
Mad Monk, The.
Cowper. Another ["At three-score winters' end I died"].
Crane. Meditation.
Pastorale.
Creeley. Eye, The.
Oh Mabel.
Prejudice, The.
Teachings, The.
"You've Tried the World, Try Jesus."
Cullen. Song of Sour Grapes, A.
Cummings. As Joe Gould says in.
It really must / be Nice,never to.
Dickinson. No matter—now—Sweet.
Within my reach!
Doolittle. So you have swept me back.
Dunbar. Debt, The.
Life's Tragedy.
Old Memory, An.
"Dylan." Ballad in Plain D.
Honey, Just Allow Me One More Chance.
I Threw It All Away.
One More Night.
You're a Big Girl Now.
Fenton. Skip, The.
Fox. If He Had Not Had Two Hands Tattooed on His Chest.
Gallagher. Love Poem to Be Read to an Illiterate Friend.
Same Kiss After Many Years, The.
Tableau Vivant.
Ginsberg. Green Valentine Blues.
Sickness Blues.
Glück. Song of the River.
Griffiths. Choice of Flowers, The.
Gunn. Incident on a Journey.
Hacker. 1976.
Hall. Tubes.
Hardy. Beauty's Soliloquy during Her Honeymoon, A.
Dead Bastard, The.
Fetching Her.
Lady of Forebodings, The.

Month's Calendar, The.
Question of Marriage, A.
Song to Aurore.
Watcher's Regret, A.
Hayden. Ballad of Sue Ellen Westerfield, The.
Heaney. Sweeney's Lament on Alisa Craig.
Hewitt. And, by that act of giving, my slow hand.
Betrayal.
Instead of an Elegy.
My Own and Not My Own.
Of course, the gruffest prompting comes from age.
One I Loved, The.
Search, The.
Holmes. Too-Late Words to My Father.
Hopkins. But what indeed is ask'd of me?
Housman. How clear, how lovely bright.
Westward on the high-hilled plains.
When the bells justle in the tower.
Hughes, Langston. Reverie on the Harlem River.
Kipling. Follow Me 'Ome.
Penalty, The.
Tarrant Moss.
Koch. To Marina.
Kunitz. Illumination, The.
Quarrel, The.
Lawrence. Ah, Muriel!
End, The.
Everlasting Flowers.
Last Words to Muriel.
Married in June.
Mutilation.
Pear-Blossom.
Sick.
Sigh No More.
Levine. Uncle.
Lewis. Odyssey, The.
Swan's Way, The.
Liddy. Lesbos.
Lowry. Quarrel, A.
MacLeish. Eve to the Storm of Thunder.
MacNeice. Slow Starter, The.
Mahon. After the Titanic.
Meredith. Main Regret, The.
Not solely that the Future she destroys.
Merrill. Renewal, A.
Merton. Regret, The.
Nash. Raven, Don't Stay Away from My Door—A Chant for April First.
Nathan. Waving Good-Bye.
Olson. All things stand out against the sky.
February 10, One Year Too Late.
Owen. Strange Meeting.
Terre, A.
Piercy. Never-Never.
Visiting a Dead Man on a Summer Day.
Poe. Bridal Ballad.
Pound. Villanelle: The Psychological Hour.
Raine. Columbines.
Ransom. Hilda.
Parting, without a Sequel.
"Reed." Hello It's Me.
Rossetti. Soeur Louise De La Miséricorde.
Sandburg. Choices.
Wistful.
Schuyler. Salute.
Sexton. Anna Who Was Mad.
Lament: "Someone is dead."
Shakespeare. Lover's Complaint, A.
Sonnet 133: "I never saw that you did painting need."
Shelley. Time Long Past.
Sidney. Fifth Song.
Sonnet 33: "I might, unhappy word, O me, I might."
Smith, Charlotte. Farewel, ye lawns!—by fond remembrance blest.
Smith, Stevie. La Gretchen de Nos Jours (I).
Piggy to Joey.
Warden, The.
Snodgrass. Eva B Hitler, geb. Braun.
Valediction, A.
Sorrentino. Light, my light, let me never be again.
Swift. Apology to the Lady Carteret, An.

Tate. Sulpicia to Cerinthus.
Updike. Academy.
Report of Health.
Wakoski. Apology, An.
Walcott. Parang.
Warren. Keepsakes.
Reading Late at Night, Thermometer Falling.
Sound of That Wind, The.
Whittier. Maud Muller.
Wilbur. Sirens, The.
Williams, Charles Kenneth. Time: 1976.
Wordsworth. Repentance; A Pastoral Ballad.
Voice from the Side of Etna, The; or, the Mad Monk.
Wroth. O pardon, Cupid I confess my fault.
Sonnet 24: "Once did I heere an aged father say."
Wyatt. Had I wist that now I wot.
Yeats. Down by the Salley Gardens.
Imitated from the Japanese.
Men Improve with the Years.
People, The.

Reincarnation
Atwood. Metempsychosis.
Clark. Eternity.
Dobyns. Red Geraniums.
Donne. Progress[e] of the Soul[e], The.
Galvin. Inventing Ballygalvin.
Glück. Easter Season.
Graves. Serpent's Tail.
Hardy. Transformations.
Holmes. Samoan Head.
Jeffers. Resurrection.
Jong. Aura.
Levine. Fox, The.
Let Me Be.
Lewis. Village Funeral: Maharashtra.
Mahon. Deaths.
Lives.
Neruda. Today Isn't Everything.
Snyder. For/From Lew.
Stevens. Good Man Has No Shape, The.

Reindeer
Moore. Rigorists.
Silverstein. Santa and the Reindeer.

Rejection
Angelou. Refusal.
Beatles. Don't Bother Me.
No Reply.
One after 909.
Ticket to Ride.
Yes It Is.
Yesterday.
You Won't See Me.
You've Got to Hide Your Love Away.
Beckett. Cascando.
Betjeman. Caprice.
Browning, Elizabeth Barrett. Amy's Cruelty.
Denial, The.
False Step, A.
Sonnet: "I lift my heavy heart up solemnly."
Sonnet: "I see thine image through my tears tonight."
Bukowski. Beds, Toilets, You and Me—.
Change of Habit, A.
Chicago.
Defeat.
Eat Your Heart Out.
For Al—.
I Made a Mistake.
I park, get out, lock the car, it's a perfect day, warm and.
Love Is a Dog from Hell.
My women of the past keep trying to locate me.
Numb Your Ass and Your Brain and Your Heart—.
One to the Breastplate.
Retreat, The.
Turnabout.
Waving and Waving Goodbye.
Bunting. Trinacria.
You leave / nobody else.
You, with my enemy, strolling down my street.
Burns. Auld Rob Morris.
Craigieburn-Wood—A Song.

Eppie McNab.
Fair Eliza.
Gloomy December.
Here's to Thy Health My Bonie Lass.
Jeremiah 15th Ch. 10 V.
Let Me in This Ae Night.
Lord Gregory.
Open the Door to Me, Oh!
Talk not to me of savages.
To Captain G———, on Being Asked Why I Was Not to Be of the Party with Him and His Brother K-nm-re at Syme's.
Campion. Art Thou That She.
Aye me, that love should natures workes accuse!
Dolus.
Faire If You Expect Admiring.
Fire that must flame is with apt fuell fed.
Good men, shew, if you can tell.
If any hath the heart to kill.
If I urge my kinde desires.
If she forsake me, I must die.
Leave prolonging thy distresse.
Now let her change and spare not.
Shall I Come, Sweet Love.
Shall I then hope when faith is fled?
So Quicke, So Hot, So Mad is Thy Fond Sute.
Where shall I refuge seeke, if you refuse mee?
Carew. My Mistress Commanding Me to Return Her Letters.
To My Inconstant Mistress [or Mistris].
Catullus. Carmen 60: "Hard. Hard. As she-cat whelped in desert mountains."
Carmen 99: "Purloining while you played in honeyed youth."
Chaucer. Complaint unto His Lady, A.
Complaynt d'Amours.
To Rosamounde.
Coleridge. Ad Vilmum Axiologum.
Alla Sua Amica.
Elegy Imitated from One of Akenside's Blank-Verse Inscriptions.
Kiss, The.
Love and Friendship Opposite.
Lover's Complaint to His Mistress, A.
Cowper. Symptoms of Love, The.
Creeley. In an Act of Pity.
Invoice, The.
Cummings. I spoke to thee.
Nobody loved this.
Dickey, William. Here There Are Three of Us Driving South in This Expensive Car.
Læstrygonians, The.
Stella Dallas.
Dickinson. Could I—then—shut the door.
Poor little Heart!
Donne. Damp[e], The.
Love's Deity [or Deitie].
Dove. Aircraft.
Dryden. Disdain Punished.
Song: "Farewell ungrateful[l] traitor [or traytor]."
Dunbar. Jilted.
"Dylan." All Over You.
Oh, Sister.
Quit Your Low Down Ways.
Gardner. Letter from Slough Pond.
Ginsberg. Lack Love.
Glück. Fire, The.
Game, The.
Hesitate to Call.
My Life Before Dawn.
12. 6. 71.
Graves. As All Must End.
Confess, Marpessa.
Discarded Love Poem, The.
Love as Lovelessness.
Song: How Can I Care?
Song: Though Once True Lovers.
Wall, The.
Gray. Amatory Lines.
Gunn. Carnal Knowledge.
Monster, The.
Hardy. Daughter Returns, A.
Love-Letters, The.
One Who Married above Him.
She Did Not Turn.

They Would Not Come.
Torn Letter, The.
Two Serenades.
Hemingway. Big Dance on the Hill, The.
Herrick. Cruell Maid, The.
His Covenant or Protestation to Julia.
To Myrrha Hard-Hearted.
To Pansies.
Hesketh. Meths Men, The.
Hewitt. Montelepre.
Outside the Creeds.
Wedding Present, The.
Hughes, Langston. Ballad of the Gypsy.
Black Pierrot, A.
Late Last Night.
Hughes, Ted. Song, The: "Did not want the air."
Jonson. Song. To Celia ("Drink to me only with thine eyes").
Keats. Stanzas: "You say you love; but with a voice."
Knott. Consolations of Sociobiology, The.
Kunitz. How Long Is the Night?
Larkin. Since the Majority of Me.
Lawrence. Lilies in the Fire.
Reminder.
Repulsed.
Turned Down.
Lewis. *Vigil: She Tarries, Far-Off, in a Strange Anguish, The.*
Longfellow. Meanwhile the stalwart Miles Standish was marching steadily northward.
Lorde. Dozens, The.
Lovelace. Love Conquer'd.
To Lucasta ("Like to the sentinel [or Sent'nel] stars, I watch all night").
"MacDiarmid." First Love.
MacNeice. 'Drunk again! Where do you think you are?'
Markson. Occupation.
On Being Denied for Being Already Took.
Vow, The.
Marlowe. Nimphs [or Nymph's] Reply to the Sheepheard [or Shepherd], The.
Meinke. Love Poem 1990.
Melville. Sketch, A.
Meredith. Lord Dusiote sprang from priest and squire.
Madam would speak with me. So, now it comes.
My Lady has Diana's brows.
No state is enviable. To the luck alone.
Roar through the Tall Twin Elm-Trees, A.
Schubert's "Farewell."
Millay. Love me no more, now let the god depart.
Morrison. Curses & Invocations.
Don't Start That.
O'Hara. Mayakovsky.
Meditations in an Emergency.
Pack. Hole in the Sky, A.
Robot Romance.
Paley. I Gave Away That Kid.
Piercy. I am sitting on a kitchen chair.
Plath. Jilted.
To a Jilted Lover.
Prince. Wind in the Tree, The.
Ralegh. 11th: and Last Booke of the Ocean to Scinthia, The.
Fayne Would I But I Dare Not.
Nimphs [or Nymph's] Reply to the Sheepheard [or Shepherd], The.
Poem Put into My Lady Laiton's Pocket by Sr W. Rawleigh, A.
Shall I, Like an Hermit, Dwell.
Ransom. Romance of a Youngest Daughter.
Robinson. Job the Rejected.
Rossetti. Amore E Dispetto.
Corydon's Lament and Resolution.
Despised and Rejected.
Jessie Cameron.
No, Thank You, John.
Schuyler. Sleep.
Shelley. To ———: "One word is too often profaned."
Sidney. Eighth Song.
Ninth Song.

Smith, Stevie. Lady "Rogue" Singleton.
Pad, Pad.
Sorrowful Girl, The.
Sorrentino. At twenty love disintegrates.
Fixture, A.
Old Tale.
Stuart. Girl of My Dreams Is Dying.
Once More for My Lady.
Suckling. Proffered Love Rejected.
Swinburne. Leave-taking, A.
Tennyson. Locksley Hall.
Thomas. Not from This Anger.
Thomson. To the Nightingale.
Verses Addressed to Amanda.
Warren. Be Something Else.
Whitman. Sometimes with One I Love.
Whittier. Isabel.
Williams, William Carlos. Birds and Flowers.
Wordsworth. Ellen Irwin; or, The Braes of
Kirtle.
Wroth. Sonnet 14: "Except my hart which you
beestow'd before."
Wyatt. All in thy sight my life doth whole
depend.
Disdain me not without desert.
Like as the swan towards her death.
Lively sparks that issue from those eyes, The.
My heart I gave thee not to do it pain.
Pass forth, my wonted cries.
That time that mirth did steer my ship.
When first mine eyes did view and mark.
Zukofsky. None but a lioness moaned this,
Libya's mountains.
Surreptitious you at bay doom loot is, my
little Juventi.

Relatives
Berryman. Poem for Bhain, A.
Bukowski. What to Do with Contributor's
Copies?
Eberhart. To Harriet Monroe.
Herrick. To His Kinsman, Master Thomas
Herrick, Who Desired to Be in His Book.
To His Sister in Law, M. Susanna Herrick.
Lorde. And What About the Children.
Nash. I Must Tell You about My Novel.
Robinson. Poor Relation, The.
Sandburg. Destroyers.
Stevenson. Fixed is the doom; and to the last
of years.
Young. 2 takes from *Love in Los Angeles*.

Relativity
Auden. Law like Love.
Carew. To the Reader of Master William
Davenant's Play [*The Wits*].
Carruth. Final Version, The.
Cullen. Sonnet: "Some for a little while do
love, and some for long."
Cummings. Space being(don't forget to
remember)Curved.
Dunbar. Comparison.
Hardy. King's Experiment, The.
Hewitt. Glendun.
On the Canal.
Kunitz. Change.
Lawrence. Relativity.
MacNeice. Perspectives.
What is truth? says Pilate.
Matthews. Minuscule Things.
Merton. Sound of passing cars, (if a car
comes), The.
Olson. Discrete Gloss, A.
Rolfe. Many an Outcast.
Snodgrass. These Trees Stand.
Warren. Brotherhood in Pain.
Interjection #2: Caveat.
Williams, Miller. Journalist Buys a Pig Farm,
The.

Relief
Beatles. Hard Day's Night, A.
Ceravolo. Ocean.
Cohen. Paper-Thin Hotel.
Cowper. R.S.S. Written in a Fit of Illness.
Creeley. For Anybody.
Jack's Blues.
Dickinson. Summer day on which you came,
The.

Dobyns. Santiago: Five Men in the Street:
Number One.
"Dylan." Queen Jane Approximately.
Emerson. Sunshine was he.
Gardner. Minotaur, The.
Hartley. Look down ever-intimate one.
Herrick. Griefes.
Sauce for Sorrowes.
Lewis. Lying in the hospital he often thought.
Mending, with books and papers and a fan.
Lindsay. Johnny Appleseed Speaks of the
Appleblossom Amaranth That Will Come to
This City.
What the Miner in the Desert Said.
With a Bouquet of Twelve Roses.
Nash. Middle of the Month, The.
Rich. Break, The.
Rolfe. Song: "There is indeed now reason for
rejoicing."
Rossetti. Lord, comest Thou to me?
Smith, Stevie. Bottle of Aspirins, The.
Stevenson. Ad Martialem.
Wordsworth. On the Death of His Majesty
(George the Third).
Zimmer. Entering the Storm, Unable to Swim,
Zimmer, Rollo, and Cecil Are Saved.

Religion
Beckett. Home Olga.
Whoroscope.
Berg. Nothingness.
Prayer: "Nobody understands so let the
Rabbi."
Sunday Afternoon.
Berry. Desolation.
Meditation in the Spring Rain.
Song (1).
Berryman. Handshake, the Entrance, The.
Betjeman. Matlock Bath.
Bishop. Hymn to the Virgin.
Patience of an Angel.
Blake. All Religions Are One.
Garden of Love, The.
Lacedemonian Instruction.
Mock On, Mock On, Voltaire, Rousseau.
Opposition Is True Friendship.
There Is No Natural Religion.
Browning, Elizabeth Barrett. Sabbath Morning
at Sea, A.
Browning, Robert. Confessional, The.
Easter-Day.
Holy-Cross Day.
Burns. Ballad, A: "While Prose-work and
rhymes."
Epistle to a Young Friend.
Epistle to John Goldie in Kilmarnock, Author
of, the Gospel Recovered.
Holy Fair, The.
Holy Tulzie, The.
Kirk of Scotland's Garland—a New Song,
The.
Letter to J——s T——t, Gl—nc——r.
Ordination, The.
Postscript [To W. S*****n, Ochiltree].
To the Rev. John McMath, Inclosing a Copy
of *Holy Willie's Prayer*, Which He Had
Requested.
Byron. Spirit Pass'd Before Me, A.
Were My Bosom As False As Thou Deem'st
It to Be.
Campion. To the Right, Noble, and Vertuous,
Henry Lord Clifford, Sonne and Heyre to the
Right Honourable, Francis, Earle of
Cumberland.
Carroll, Jim. Sea Battle.
Carruth. Sonnet: "Was Yahweh chosen by the
chosen people?"
Chaucer. Canterbury Tales, The.
Consolation of Philosophy, The ("De
Consolacione Philosophie").
Clark. Parish: A Satire, The.
Cohen. Be with Me.
Hurry to Your Dinner.
Magic Is Alive.
Rebellion, The.
Rose, The.
Transmission, The.
Coleridge. Catullian Hendecasyllables.

Cowper. Table Talk.
Crashaw. On the Frontispiece of Isaacsons
Chronologie Explained.
Upon the Ensuing Treatises [of Mr. Shelford].
Creeley. After Lorca.
Cummings. Candles and / Here Comes a glass
box.
Like most godhouses this particular house.
This evangelist / buttons with his big gollywog
voice.
Dickey, James. Circuit.
Eagle's Mile, The.
Tapestry and Sail.
Dickey, William. Fred and the Holy Grail.
Love among the Machinees.
You White Cunning Devils.
Dickinson. I'm ceded—I've stopped being
Theirs.
Some keep the Sabbath going to Church.
Donne. Satire 3: "Kind pity [*or* Kinde pitty]
chokes my spleen[e]; brave scorn forbids."
To the Countess of Bedford ("Honour is so
sublime perfection").
To the Countess of Bedford ("Madam, /
Reason is Our Soul's Left Hand, Faith Her
Right").
Doolittle. Priest.
Dove. Receiving the Stigmata.
Dryden. Dim, as the borrow'd beams of moon
and stars.
Thus man by his own strength to Heaven
would soar.
Tradition.
Dunbar. Faith.
How Lucy Backslid.
Possession.
Spiritual, A.
Temptation.
Edmunds. Hill Village, A.
Eliot. Choruses from "The Rock."
Hippopotamus, The.
Mr. Eliot's Sunday Morning Service.
Song for Simeon, A.
Emerson. Dervish whined to *Said*, The.
Problem, The.
Song of Seyd [*or* Seid] Nimetollah of
Kuhistan.
Fletcher. Epilogue: "By the glare of the
guttering torch."
Frost. Innate Helium.
Gallagher. If Blood Were Not as Powerful as
It Is.
Linoleum.
Glück. Winter Morning.
Graves. Awakening, The.
Good Night to the Old Gods.
Griffiths. Under Mynydd-y-Tŵr.
Gunn. Vigil of Corpus Christi, The.
Hall. Religious Articles.
Hardy. Christmas: 1924.
Dream Question, A.
Graveyard of Dead Creeds, The.
Quid Hic Agis?
Respectable Burgher, The.
Whispered at the Church-Opening.
Hemingway. Neothomist Poem.
Herrick. Slavery.
Hewitt. After the Fire.
Consequences.
Dilemma, The.
Ellendene.
Going to Church.
Grim Dean, who sleeps within his pulpit's
shade.
Habit of Mercy, The.
Hill-Farm, The.
Immortality.
Lonely Heart, The.
Methodists.
My Great-Grandfather's Refusal.
Open Eye, The.
Portstewart, July 1914.
Priest Goes through the Motions of the Play,
The.
Rite, Lubitavish, Glenaan.
Rome Sunday[,] June 1960.
St Rosalie: Monte Pellegrino.

Tryst.
When the Bell Rings in the Steeple.
Hopkins. But what indeed is ask'd of me?
On the Portrait of Two Beautiful Young
People.
Wreck of the Deutschland, The.
Housman. New Year's Eve.
Hughes, Langston. Mystery.
Hughes, Ted. Martyrdom of Bishop Farrar,
The.
Jeffers. Great Men.
Theory of Truth.
Kinnell. Avenue Bearing the Initial of Christ
into the New World, The.
Kipling. Buddha at Kamakura.
Disciple, The.
MacDonough's Song.
Knott. Funny Poem.
Larkin. Church Going.
Water.
Lawrence. Bells.
Future Religion.
Quetzalcoatl Looks Down on Mexico.
Religion.
Resurrection of the Flesh.
Spiral Flame.
Liddy. After Kraske.
Art Is Not for Grown-ups.
Every Evening in Axel's.
Kerouac's Ronsard Dance.
Spring tide swept 'em to the hills.
Vir X.
Lindsay. I walk the forest by the Daniel
Boone trail.
I Went Down into the Desert.
Incense.
On the Building of Springfield.
Soul of the City Receives the Gift of the Holy
Spirit, The.
Sun Says His Prayers, The.
Lorde. Release Time.
When the Saints Come Marching In.
Winds of Orisha, The.
Lovelace. Apostasy of One and But One
Lady, The.
Lowell. Like Henry VIII, Mohammed got
religion.
Tenth Muse.
McAuley. Late Afternoon, Running: Close
Reasoning, Listening Closely.
Prelude in Darkness.
"MacDiarmid." Covenanters, The.
Credo.
To My Friend the Late Beatrice Hastings.
Two Memories.
MacLeish. Two Priests, The.
MacNeice. After anemones, after almond.
Carol: "To end all carols, darling."
Oh but my doubt is a sea harsher than this
that I see.
Preacher, The.
Spermologies fallen on stony ground. Stone of
relentlessness, stone of crime.
Tall story over a dark sanctum, A.
Melville. Fragments of a Lost Gnostic Poem
of the Twelfth [or 12th] Century.
Ungar and Rolfe.
Meredith. Martin's Puzzle.
Merton. Baroque Gravure, A.
There Is a Way.
Morgan. May 1, 1974.
Muldoon. Our Lady of Ardboe.
Nash. Birth Comes to the Archbishop.
Seven Spiritual Ages of Mrs. Marmaduke
Moore, The.
Nemerov. Boom!
Olson. Applause.
Concerning Exaggeration, or How, Properly, to
Heap Up.
Pack. Prayer for Prayer.
Patchen. Mohammed.
Ralegh. Ah wretched they that worship
vanities.
I sacrifice to God the Beefe, which you adore.
Rich. Air without Incense.
Rolfe. 1949 (After Reading a News Item).
Rossetti. Dream, A.

Lord, dost Thou look on me, and will not I.
Ruined Cross, The.
Sonnet: "Some say that love and joy are one:
and so."
Three Nuns.
Rukeyser. Gates, The.
St. John. Wavelength.
Sandburg. Broken Tabernacles.
To a Contemporary Bunkshooter.
Schuyler. I Sit Down to Type.
Scott. Gray Brother, The.
Sexton. With Mercy for the Greedy.
Sidney. Leave me, O Love which reachest but
to dust.
Smith, Patti. Thread.
Smith, Stevie. From the County Lunatic
Asylum.
Religious Man, A.
Spender. Landscape near an Aerodrome, The.
Stevens. Blue Buildings in the Summer Air,
The.
Sunday Morning.
Stevenson. All influences were in vain.
Angler rose, he took his rod, The.
Embro Hie Kirk.
If I could arise and travel away.
Stout marches lead to certain ends.
Well-Head, The.
Wind is without there and howls in the trees,
The.
Updike. Comp. Religion.
Earthworm.
Whittier. Cassandra Southwick.
Hymn for the Opening of Plymouth Church.
In the "Old South."
Mary Garvin.
Miriam.
Pennsylvania Pilgrim, The.
Preacher, The.
Worship.
Wilbur. Matthew VIII, 28 ff.
Pelican, The.
Williams, William Carlos. Choral: The Pink
Church.
Host, The.
Semblables, The.
Wordsworth. Composed in One of the
Catholic Cantons.
Ecclesiastical Sonnets.
Lines Written as a School Exercise at
Hawkshead, Anno Aetatis 14.
Processions Suggested on a Sabbath Morning
in the Vale of Chamouny.
Wright, Charles. Looking at Pictures.
Yeats. Church and State.
Wisdom.
Zukofsky. Poem Beginning "The."

See also **Faith.**

Religious Life
Arnold. Dover Beach.
Beatles. Inner Light, The.
Berg. On the Steps.
Berryman. Terce.
Betjeman. Anglo-Catholic Congresses.
Holy Trinity, Sloane Street.
Huxley Hall.
Lenten Thoughts of a High Anglican.
Lincolnshire Church, A.
Undenominational.
Wantage Bells.
Brooks. Firstly Inclined to Take What It Is
Told.
Byron. Fragment from the "Monk of Athos."
Cowper. Olney Hymns.
Crane. Emblems of Conduct.
Crashaw. Description of a Religious House
and Condition of Life.
On Mr. G. Herberts Booke, The Temple.
To [Mrs. M. R.] Councel Concerning Her
Choise.
Davie. Advent.
Baptist Childhood, A.
Church Militant.
God Saves the King.
Inditing a Good Matter.
Nones.
Prime.

Priory of St Saviour, Glendalough, The.
Selina, Countess of Huntingdon.
Their Rectitude Their Beauty.
Dickinson. I prayed, at first, a little Girl.
I've heard an Organ talk, sometimes.
Ourselves we do inter with sweet derision.
This is a Blossom of the Brain.
Who were "the Father and the Son."
You love the Lord—you cannot see.
Donne. To the Countess of Bedford at New
Year's Tide.
Fenton. Kingfisher's Boxing Gloves, The.
Herbert. Affliction (1).
Content.
Dulness[e].
H[oly] Communion, The.
Invitation, The.
Perirrhanterium.
Herrick. Thanksgiving to God for His House,
A.
Hewitt. Methodists.
Hoffman. Another Border.
Visitation, A.
Hopkins. Barnfloor and Winepress.
Glimmer'd along the square-cut steep.
Half-way House, The.
I wake and feel the fell of dark, not day.
Il Mystico.
In Honour of St. Alphonsus Rodriguez.
Let me be to Thee as the circling bird.
Lines for a Picture of St. Dorothea.
Margaret Clitheroe.
Morning, Midday, and Evening Sacrifice.
On St. Winefred.
St. Dorothea.
Summa.
Times are nightfall, look, their light grows
less, The.
To Seem the Stranger.
Voice from the World, A.
Jonson. To Heaven.
Kipling. Song of Kabir, A.
Lawrence. Vicar's Son.
Liddy. Cliffs with sea breaking at their.
Requiem for a Non-Croppy.
Lindsay. Where Is the Real Non-Resistant?
Marlowe. 3.12: De Iunonis festo.
Meredith. Angelic Love.
Creed.
Jump-to-Glory Jane.
St. Thérèse.
Story of Sir Arnulph, The.
To Cardinal Manning.
Twilight Music.
Merton. Clever Strategem: Or, How to Handle
Mystics, A.
Elegy for a Trappist.
La Comparsa en Oriente.
Letter to a Sufi Who Has Abandoned Sufism
to Study Law.
Moment of Truth, The.
Practical Program for Monks, A.
Quickening of St. John the Baptist, The.
Ranter and Their Pleads, The.
Solitary Life.
Three Postcards from the Monastery.
When in the Soul of the Serene Disciple.
Nemerov. Boom!
Common Saw, A.
Ransom. Prometheus in Straits.
Rich. Eben Haëzer.
Roethke. Abyss, The.
Right Thing, The.
Rossetti. Portrait, A.
Quinquagesima.
Snyder. December.
Tōji.
Southwell. Content and Ri[t]ch[e].
Tate. True Believer.
Whittier. Adjustment.
Brother of Mercy, The.
Chapel of the Hermits, The.
Ezekiel.
Hermit of the Thebaid, The.
Hymn of the Dunkers.
Hymns of the Brahmo Somaj.
Knight of St. John, The.

My Soul and I.
Reward, The.
Shadow and the Light, The.
Two Elizabeths, The.
Wordsworth. At the Convent of Camaldoli,
Continued.
Decay of Piety.
For the Spot Where the Hermitage Stood on
St Herbert's Island, Derwent-Water.
See also **Clergy; Convents; Monasteries;
Monks; Nuns; Rabbis.**

Religious Wars
Coleridge. Sancti Dominici Pallium.
Crashaw. On the Gunpowder-Treason.
Upon the Gunpowder Treason ("Reach me a
quill").
Hewitt. Conversations in Hungary, August
1969.
In This Year of Grace.
Jonson. Epistle to a Friend, to Persuade Him
to the Wars, An.
Lindsay. Foreign Missions in Battle Array.
King Arthur's Men Have Come Again.
See how the generations pass.

Rembrandt, Harmenszoon van Rijn
Blake. Florentine Ingratitude.
Hartley. Rembrandt—Rouault—Piero.
Lowell. Rembrandt.
Robinson. Rembrandt to Rembrandt.

Remorse
Beatles. Getting Better.
Girl.
You've Got to Hide Your Love Away.
Bly. Getting Up Late.
Brontë. A.G.A. to A.S.
Come, walk with me.
If grief for grief can touch thee.
Lady, in your Palace Hall.
O Dream, where art thou now?
Starry night shall tidings bring, The.
Still beside that dreary water.
There let thy bleeding branch atone.
When days of Beauty deck the earth.
Where were ye all? and where wert thou?
Browning, Elizabeth Barrett. Nature's
Remorses.
Burns. Penitential Thought, in the Hour of
Remorse—Intended for a Tragedy, A.
Prayer, in the Prospect of Death, A.
Remorse.
Coleridge. Invocation, An: "Hear, sweet spirit,
hear the spell."
De la Mare. Thus Her Tale.
Dickinson. Remorse—is Memory—awake.
Donne. Hymn to God the Father, A.
Emerson. Amulet, The.
Gallagher. Same Kiss After Many Years, The.
Tableau Vivant.
Hardy. His Heart.
Hartley. Beyond the Broken House.
Herrick. Mora Sponsi, the Stay of the
Bridegroome.
Penitencie.
Hewitt. Bloody Brae, The.
Housman. Rain, it streams on stone and
hillock, The.
Lewis. Journey, The.
Lorde. Separation.
Lowry. Hangover—Reading Rilke, Schnitzler
or Someone, A.
Sunrise.
Walls of remorse are steep, there is no belay,
The.
Mahon. After the Titanic.
Nash. Clean Conscience Never Relaxes, A.
Hearts of Gold.
Nemerov. Remorse for Time, The.
Raine. If I choose remorse.
Rolfe. Hunter Went Killing: A Fable, A.
Letter for One in Russia.
Not Hatred.
Words Found on a Cave's Wall.
St. John. Boathouse, The.
Sandburg. Remorse.
Sidney. Sonnet 93: "O fate, O fault, O curse,
child of my bliss."
Stevenson. Stormy Nights.

Warren. Death I have entered is a death, The.
Williams, Charles Kenneth. Beginning of
April, The.
Conscience.
With Ignorance.

Renaissance
Browning, Robert. Fra Lippo Lippi.
Hill. Humanist, The.
Pre-Raphaelite Notebook, A.
Kipling. Dawn Wind, The.

Renewal
Angelou. Recovery.
Request.
Atwood. Departure from the Bush.
Head against White.
In this house (in a dying orchard.
Last Day.
Beatles. Getting Better.
Here Comes the Sun.
I've Got a Feeling.
Berry. Anniversary, An.
Rain.
Setting Out.
Berryman. Caravan.
Under new management, Your Majesty.
Brontë. Here, with my knee upon thy stone.
Burns. John Barleycorn [a Ballad].
Campion. Peacefull westerne winde the
wintrye stormes hath calmde, The.
Carroll, Jim. In the Valley.
Little Ode on St. Anne's Day.
Carruth. Coming Down to the Desert at
Lordsburg, N.M.
One day music / begins.
Return to Love.
Cohen. You Have the Lovers.
Crane. Interludium.
Creeley. Rose, The.
Cummings. Love is the every only god.
Mist.
N(o)w / the / how / dis(appeared
cleverly)world.
Now that fierce few.
Paris;this April sunset completely utters.
Semi-Spring.
Sonnet: "Rain-drop on the eyelids of the earth,
A."
Spring is like a perhaps hand.
When faces called flowers float out of the
ground.
Davie. Orford.
De la Mare. Fleeting, The.
Oh, Why?
Dickinson. Then will I not repine.
Dobyns. Santiago: Five Men in the Street:
Number One.
Donne. Cales and Guiana.
Father, The.
To Mr. R. W. ("Kindly I envy thy song's [or
songs] perfection").
Eberhart. Parker River, The.
Everson. Of such touch given.
Galvin. Apple Trees, The.
Ginsberg. Eastern Ballad, An.
Hardy. Something that Saved Him, The.
Hartley. Being new inside—so that outside,
the outside.
Hesketh. From the Day Room.
It Was Not I.
Hewitt. Bombed Public House, The.
Take the intention then and let me live.
Hill. Veni Coronaberis.
Hoffman. Incubus.
Jeffers. Point Pinos and Point Lobos.
Practical People.
Shiva.
Joseph. For a New Year.
Kipling. Pan in Vermont.
Rector's Memory, A.
Song of Seven Cities, The.
Lawrence. Climbing Down.
First Morning.
Flowers.
Love Comes Late.
New Heaven and Earth.
New Word, The.
Phoenix.

Real Democracy.
Sleep and Waking.
Sun in Me.
Welcome to Quetzalcoatl.
Levertov. Seedtime.
Levine. Let Me Begin Again.
Told.
Lewis. After Dunkirk.
Mid-Winter.
Mahon. One of These Nights.
Melville. American Aloe on Exhibition, The.
Meredith. Now was her face white waves in
the tempest's sharp flame-blink.
Merrill. Variations: The Air Is Sweetest That
a Thistle Guards.
Merton. Earthquake.
Litany: "It yawns at me the cavernous gulf."
Responsory, A.
Oliver. Marengo.
Morning in a New Land.
Roses.
Olson. Chain of memory is resurrection   I am
a vain man, The.
Going from Battle to Battle.
La Torre.
Paley. In the Bus.
Piercy. Ache's End.
"Reed." Rock 'N' Roll.
Roethke. Renewal, The.
Vernal Sentiment.
Rossetti. Easter Carol, An.
First Spring Day, The.
Go In Peace.
Greatest of These Is Charity, The.
Seasons.
Vigil of all Saints.
Wintry Sonnet, A.
Sandburg. Bath.
Shakespeare. Sonnet 56: "Sweet love, renew
thy force; be it not said."
Sonnet 108: "What's in the brain that ink may
character."
Shelley. Zucca, The.
Smith, Stevie. New Age, The.
Sorrentino. What is past is here, as we.
Southwell. Times [or Tymes] Go[e] By
Turn[e]s.
Stevens. Adult Epigram.
Walcott. City's Death by Fire, A.
Walker. These Mornings of Rain.
Whitman. Soon Shall the Winter's Foil Be
Here.
Whittier. Chicago.
Cypress-Tree of Ceylon, The.
Dream of Summer, A.
Easter Flower Gift, An.
My Psalm.
Wilbur. Rondeau: "Year has cast its cloak
away, The."
Then.
Williams, Charles Kenneth. Bread.
Williams, William Carlos. Paterson: The Falls.
Rewaking, The.
Wordsworth. From the Dark Chambers of
Dejection Freed.
I Watch, and Long Have Watched [with Calm
Regret].
Ode Composed on May Morning.
To May.
Young. April Blue.
James Cotton Band at Keytstone, The.
Zukofsky. Chrysanthemum.
I walk in the old street.
See also **Rebirth; Regeneration.**

Repentance
Burns. To Mr. S. McKenzie.
Campion. Awake, Awake! [Thou Heavy
Sprite].
Lift up to heav'n, sad wretch, thy heavy
spright.
Loe, when backe mine eye.
Chaucer. Parson's Tale, The.
Cohen. Bird on the Wire.
Not Knowing Where to Go.
We Cry Out.
Cowper. Tale, Founded on a Fact, A.
Dickinson. Renunciation—is a piercing Virtue.

Donne. At the round earth's imagined corners, blow.
Heaney. Sweeney's Last Poem.
Herbert. Business.
Cross[e], The.
Discipline.
Mary [or Marie] Magdalene.
Parody [or Parodie], A.
Reprisal[l], The.
Rose, The.
Sighs and Groans [or Grones].
Sinner, The.
Sin's Round.
Storm, The.
Trinity Sunday.
Herrick. Bad May Be Better.
Calling, and Correcting.
Cunctation in Correction.
Penitence ("Doctors").
Penitence ("Who after").
Penitencie ("Man's transgression").
Position in the Hebrew Divinity, A.
Sin ("There is no evill that we do commit").
Sinners.
To God ("God, who me gives a will").
Hewitt. Evangelist.
Year of Grace and My Great-Grandfather.
Jeffers. At the Birth of an Age.
Jonson. Hymn[e] to God the Father, A.
Kipling. Supplication of the Black Aberdeen.
Lindsay. When Peter Jackson Preached in the Old Church.
Lowell. Death of Alexander.
Melville. Mortmain Reappears.
Meredith. He where the great sun looks his last.
Merton. Epitaph for a Public Servant.
Millay. Penitent, The.
Milton. Eve Penitent.
Nash. Reminiscent Reflection.
Pope. Epigram in a Maid of Honour's Prayer-Book.
Prince. Campanella.
Rossetti. Ash Wednesday.
Convent Threshold, The.
Cried Out with Tears.
Divine and Human Pleading.
O Lord, I am ashamed to seek Thy Face / As tho' I loved Thee as Thy saints love Thee.
Smart. Ash Wednesday. First Day of Lent.
Smith, Patti. Burning Roses.
Smith, Stevie. Repentance of Lady T, The.
Stevenson. Apologetic Postscript of a Year Later.
Look of Death is both severe and mild, The.
Williams, Charles Kenneth. Penance.
Wordsworth. Upon the Late General Fast. March, 1832.

Repression
Bishop. Sonnet: "Caught—the bubble."
Bly. Executive's Death, The.
Browning, Elizabeth Barrett. Sonnet: "And therefore if to love can be desert."
"Carroll, Lewis." Elections to the Hebdomadal Council, The.
Carruth. "My mother did it. She had to, she said. She took."
Coleridge. Two Founts, The.
Cummings. Red-rag and pink-flag.
Dunn. Beneath the Sidewalk.
Hemingway. Little Mr. Wilson / Wrote a little book.
Lawrence. Hands of the Betrothed, The.
Virgin Youth.
Lowry. Noble City Full of Pigeons or Everyone a Hypocrite Including Me.
McGrath. Warrant for Pablo Neruda, A.
Shapiro. Buick.
Williams, Charles Kenneth. Repression.
Williams, Miller. Well-Ordered Life, The.
Williams, William Carlos. Slow Movement.

Reproach
Atwood. You did it / it was you who started the countdown.
Beatles. Another Girl.
If I Needed Someone.
Bly. Executive's Death, The.

"Carroll, Lewis." Duchess's Lullaby, The.
Chaucer. Chaucer's Wordes unto Adam, his Owne Scriveyn.
Creeley. Mirror, The.
Cullen. For an Atheist.
Everson. Man of God. Tall man, man of oath.
Mad man of ignorant causes.
Graves. Dialogue on the Headland.
Reproach.
Hardy. Her Reproach.
Jonson. Epigram on the Court Pucell, An.
Epistle to a Friend, An ("Censure not sharply then, but me advise").
MacLeish. You Also, Gaius Valerius Catullus.
Merton. What is beyond reproof / Is done in this building.
Pound. Jewel Stairs' Grievance, The.
Psalms. Psalm 74: "O God, why hast thou cast us off for ever?"
"Reed." Temporary Thing.
Snodgrass. W. D. Tries to Warn Cock Robin.
Stevenson. My Conscience!

Reptiles
Wilbur. Nights rolled upon the river's face.

Reputation
Byron. Lines Written in the Travellers' Book at Orchomenus.
Campion. Ad Leam.
Respect my faith, regard my service past.
Donne. Epitaph on Himself.
From tempting Satan to tempt us.
Graves. Deed of Gift.
Herrick. Care a Good Keeper.
Honours Are Hindrances.
Poetry Perpetuates the Poet.
To His Honoured Kinsman Sir William Soame.
Upon Pievish.
Jeffers. Old Wolf My Father, The.
Jonson. To Sir Edward Herbert.
MacLeish. Poetical Remains.
Nash. Lines to Be Embroidered on a Bib, or, The Child Is Father of the Man, but Not for Quite a While.
Pope. To a Lady with the Temple of Fame.
Robinson. Flammonde.
Shakespeare. Sonnet 111: "O, for my sake do you with Fortune chide."
Yeats. Father and Child.

Rescues
Atwood. My beautiful wooden leader.
Carew. Lady, Rescued from Death by a Knight, Who in the Instant Leaves Her, Complains Thus, A.
Fox. Shipbuilder, The.
Joseph. Washing is jerked from shade into the sun, The.
Kunitz. Customs Collector's Report, The.
Lieberman. Kofukuji Arsonists, The.
MacNeice. Burnt Bridge, The.
Matthews. Search Party, The.
Pack. Dwarf and Doctor Freud, The.
Ransom. Lady Lost.
Rolfe. Death by Water.
Silverstein. Peanut-Butter Sandwich.

Reservations, Native American
Edmunds. Taos.
Shelton. Reservations.

Resistance
Atwood. Last year I abstained / this year I devour.
Not you I fear but that other.
Returning to the room: / I notice how.
Roominghouse, Winter.
Berry. Beware of the machinery of longevity. When a man's life is over.
If a man finds it necessary to eat garbage, he should resist.
Campion. Bar Not the Door.
Carew. Boldness[e] in Love.
Protestation [A Sonnet], The.
Carruth. All my life that's been / the watchword: Resist! Resist!
"My mother did it. She had to, she said. She took."
Cohen. Prayer for Messiah.

This Is War.
Welcome to These Lines.
Creeley. Sea, The.
Cullen. In Spite of Death.
Dunn. Essay on Sanity.
Emerson. O what is Heaven but the fellowship.
Ferlinghetti. Short Story on a Painting of Gustav Klimt.
Frost. One Step Taken Backward.
Herrick. To Virgins.
Will To Be Working, A.
Hesketh. Cross.
Hewitt. Providence 1.
Tribunes, The.
Hill. De Jure Belli ac Pacis.
Knott. Prophet in a Landscape of Immemorial Time.
Kunitz. To a Slave Named Job.
Lawrence. Metal for Resistance.
Merton. For the Spanish Poet Miguel Hernandez.
Miller. To be against to resist everything.
Oliver. Rain.
Plath. Resolve.
Rukeyser. Don Baty, the Draft Resister.
Women and poets see the truth arrive.
Silverstein. One Who Stayed, The.
Williams, Charles Kenneth. Drought.
Peace.
Wyatt. What no, Perdy [or Perdie or perdie][!] ye may be sure[!].
Young. Geography of the Near Past.

Resorts
Catullus. Carmen 37: "Nine posts, five doors, up the Clivus."
Cohen. Another Room.
Commentary—Another Room.
Hughes, Langston. Seashore through Dark Glasses (Atlantic City).
Mahon. Last Resort, The.
Zukofsky. Salt hacks, tavern boys, what skews, can't you burn alleys.

Respectability
Bukowski. Soul.
Campion. Epigramme: "Lockly spits apace, the rhewme he cals it."
Uni eqo mallem placuisse docto.
Davie. Grudging Respect.
"Dylan." Jack o' diamonds / jack o' diamonds.
Eberhart. Hop-Toad, The.
New England Bachelor, A.
Emerson. O Boston city lecture-hearing.
Frost. Considerable Speck, A.
Hewitt. After Reading Sonnets by Rev. Charles Turner (1864) and The New Day, Sonnets by Dr T. Gordon Hake (1890).
Bangor, Spring 1916.
College Fence, The.
In a Suburban Avenue.
In Memorium: D.H. Lawrence.
In Recollection of Drumcliffe, September 1948.
Little Death, The.
Lonely Heart, The.
My Father's Ghost.
96 Clifton Park Avenue and the Robinsons.
Strangers and Neighbors.
To Robert Telford Hewitt.
Watercolour, The.
Lindsay. Hearth Eternal, The.
McNeill. Warning.
"Reed." Kids, The.
Temporary Thing.
Sandburg. 'Boes.
Memoir.
Silver Nails.
Sorrentino. Transcript, The.
Stafford. Thanksgiving for My Father, A.
Well Rising, The.
Stevenson. To Auntie.
Stuart. Return, The.
Warren. Before the knowledge in me, he, beautiful, down in the dirt, kneels.
What Were You Thinking Dear Mother?

Responsibility
Angelou. On Working White Liberals.
Atwood. It was not my fault, these animals.
Berry. In the predicament of other lives.
Burns. Libel Summons.
Creeley. Easter.
Dobyns. Short Rides.
Dunn. For Fathers of Girls.
"Dylan." Masters of War.
Up to Me.
Who Killed Davey Moore?
Hewitt. Carol Singers from the Church, The.
Fame.
Function.
Scattering, The.
Hughes, Ted. When Men Got to the Summit.
Joseph. Living Off Other People—Welfare.
Warning.
Kipling. Natural Theology.
Question, The.
Refined Man, The.
Reformers, The.
Levertov. Part, The.
MacNeice. They call me crafty, I robbed my
brother.
Yours Next.
Meredith. Atlas.
I am not of those miserable males.
Merton. What is beyond reproof / Is done in
this building.
Written Next to a Blue Flower.
"Reed." It Wasn't Me.
Rich. For the Record.
Rukeyser. Despisals.
Simic. Man, The.
Sorrentino. Perceive.
Stevenson. What glory for a boy of ten.
Williams, Charles Kenneth. Alzheimer's: The
Husband.
Another Dollar.
Williams, Miller. After You Die You Don't
Give a Piddling Damn.
Wright, Charles. Self-Portrait ("Someday
they'll find me out, and my lavish hands").

Rest
Berry. As the vision of labor grows.
February. A cloudy day.
My life's wave is at its crest.
Requiem: "We will see no more."
Song (2).
Winter Nightfall.
Bukowski. Pace is the Essence.
Cowper. Inscription for a Moss-House.
Inscription for an Hermitage.
Repose in God.
Testimony of Divine Adoption, The.
Cummings. Rain or hail / sam done.
When the proficient poison of pure sleep.
Davie. Felicity's Fourth Order.
De la Mare. Last Coachload, The.
Dunbar. Noddin' by de Fire.
Eberhart. Bells of a Chinese Temple, The.
Cover Me Over.
Fletcher. Hour of Peace, The.
Gardner. Collage of Echoes.
Gunn. Crosswords.
Hardy. A.H., 1855–1912.
Drizzling Easter Morning, A.
Epeisodia.
Herbert. Pulley, The.
Herrick. End of His Work, The.
Rest.
Rest Refreshes.
Keats. To One Who Has Been Long in City
Pent.
Kipling. Alnaschar and the Oxen.
Lawrence. Last Hours.
Levine. Holding On.
Sleepless Night, A.
Lovelace. Ant, The.
"MacDiarmid." Everlasting layers / Of ideas,
images, feelings.
MacLeish. Ninth Book, The.
Tenth Book, The.
MacNeice. Gorged on red, green, purple,
tomatoes, peppers, aubergine.
Sunday in the Park.

Marvell. Second Chorus from Seneca's
Tragedy "Thyestes", The.
Merton. Hat Salesman and a Capable Ruler,
A.
Oliver. Creeks.
Prince. People Rest after Conquests, The.
Rossetti. Better So.
Burial Anthem.
Cardinal Newman.
Counsel, A.
Death Is Swallowed Up in Victory.
I toiled on, but thou.
Let Them Rejoice in Their Beds.
Lotus-Eaters: Ulysses to Penelope, The.
Love loveth Thee, and wisdom loveth Thee.
Martyr, A.
My Old Friends.
Sir Eustace Grey.
Sleeping at last, the trouble and tumult over.
Sonnet from the Psalms.
Sweetness of rest when Thou sheddest rest.
Then I Commended Mirth.
There Remaineth Therefore a Rest to the
People of God.
Three Nuns.
Thro' burden and heat of the day.
Today's Burden.
What will it be, O my soul, what will it be.
Simic. History.
Smith, Charlotte. Sleeping Woodman. Written
in April 1790, The.
Smith, Stevie. Road Up.
Snodgrass. Lullaby: The Comforting of Cock
Robin.
Spender. Dusk.
Stevens. Two Versions of the Same Poem.
Yellow Afternoon.
Stevenson. All influences were in vain.
I whom Apollo sometime visited.
Lo, now, my guest, if aught amiss were said.
Warren. Hands Are Paid.
Switzerland.
Whitman. Ended Day, An.
Evening Lull, An.
We All Shall Rest at Last.
Whittier. Autumn Thoughts.
Wilbur. Sonnet.
Wordsworth. Inscription for a Seat by a
Roadside, Half Way up a Steep Hill, Facing
the South.
Inscription for a Seat by the Pathway Side
Ascending to Windy Brow.
Labourer's Noon-Day Hymn, The.
Rest and Be Thankful!
Written with a Slate Pencil on a Stone, on the
Side of the Mountain of Black Comb.
Yeats. He Bids His Beloved Be at Peace.
Lover's Song, The.
Young. No Trespassing.

Restaurants
Brooks. I Love Those Little Booths at
Benvenuti's.
Bukowski. Eating My Senior Citizen's Dinner
at the Sizzler.
Krutz.
Plate Glass Window, A.
Cummings. Item.
One April dusk the.
Hugo. Pizzeria S. Biagio.
Keats. Lines on the Mermaid Tavern.
Mahon. Chinese Restaurant in Portrush, The.
Muldoon. Holy Thursday.
Nash. Try It Suns. and Hols.; It's Closed
Then.
Schuyler. Dining Out with Doug and Frank.
Tomlinson. Hero Sandwiches.
Updike. To an Usherette.
Williams, William Carlos. Brilliant Sad Sun.

Restlessness
Ciardi. Three A.M. and Then Five.
Creeley. Midnight.
On Vacation.
Surf: An Elegy, The.
De la Mare. Out Of Bounds.
Dobyns. Syracuse Nights.
Uprising.
"Dylan." One Too Many Mornings.

Gunn. All Night, Legs Pointed East.
Hewitt. New Jerusalem 2.
Longfellow. Seaweed.
Lowell. At the Altar.
Lowry. Joseph Conrad.
Oliver. Whelks.
Oppen. Little Hole, The.
Prince. Babiaantje, The.
Stevens. Well Dressed Man with a Beard,
The.
Stevenson. All night through, raves or broods.
Updike. Poisoned in Nassau.
Young. I Arrive in Madrid.

Restraint
Browning, Elizabeth Barrett. Sonnet: "And
therefore if to love can be desert."
Bukowski. Hey, Ezra, Listen to This.
Bunting. Now that sea's over that island.
Campion. Kind in every kinde.
Carruth. They Accuse Me of Not Talking.
Cooper. Wronke, Spring 1917.
De la Mare. Imagination's Pride, The.
Doolittle. She Contrasts with Herself
Hippolyta.
Dunn. Hard Work 1956.
Emerson. Art thou wise, four things resign.
Glück. Palais des Arts.
Graves. Fetter, The.
Hill. Masque of Blackness, The.
Lawrence. Passing Visit to Helen.
Lowry. Conversations With Goethe.
Morrison. In This Dim Cave.
Piercy. Work of Artifice, A.
Psalms. Psalm 39: "I said, I will take heed to
my ways."
Rich. Unsaid Word, An.
Wyatt. Though I myself be bridled of my
mind.

Resurrection, The
"Carroll, Lewis." After Three Days.
Davie. Attar of Roses.
Dickey, James. Gila Bend.
Dickinson. And with what body do they
come?
Business enough indeed.
I lift the lid to my box of Phantoms.
No Crowd that has occurred.
Donne. Resurrection.
Resurrection, Imperfect.
Upon the Annunciation and Passion Falling
upon One Day. 1608.
"Dylan." In the Garden.
Graves. To Bring the Dead to Life.
Herbert. Dawning, The.
Easter.
Herrick. God Has a Twofold Part.
Resurrection, Possible, and Probable, The.
Resurrection, The.
Hopkins. That Nature Is a Heraclitean Fire
and of the Comfort of the Resurrection.
Lawrence. Resurrection.
Lindsay. Hope of the Resurrection, The.
Merton. Trappist Cemetery—Gethsemani, The.
Rossetti. Easter Even.
In resurrection is it awfuller.
Resurrection Eve.
Smart. Easter Day.
Spenser. Most glorious lord of life that on this
day.
Updike. Seven Stanzas at Easter.
Wordsworth. Composed in One of the Valleys
of Westmoreland, on Easter Sunday.

Retirement and Retirees
Cowper. Retirement.
Dove. Satisfaction Coal Company, The.
Hartley. Daily Library Visitor.
Herrick. Mr. Robert Hericke His Farwell unto
Poetrie.
Koertge. He ("Used to do most everything
himself").
Lowell. Charles Vby Titian.
Terminal Days at Beverly Farms.
Marvell. Garden, The.
Upon the Hill and Grove at Bilbrough.
Smith, Stevie. Bandol (Var).
Williams, Charles Kenneth. Alzheimer's: The

Husband.
Rungs.
See also **Old Age.**

Retribution
Bukowski. Trying to Get Even.
  Turnabout.
Carroll, Jim. Growing Up.
Cowper. Expostulation.
  Time-piece, The.
"Dylan." All Over You.
  When the Ship Comes In.
Gardner. Of Mercy.
Herrick. To Myrrha Hard-Hearted.
Jeffers. Home.
Kipling. Justice.
Lindsay. Voice of the Earthquake, The.
Lowry. Plingen plangen auf gefangen.
Pack. South Bronx, 1939.
Ralegh. 3.2: "Seldome the villaine, though
  much hast he make."
Scott. Gray Brother, The.
Warren. Red Mullet, The.

Reunions
Arnold. Meeting.
Beatles. It Won't Be Long.
  Long and Winding Road, The.
  Long Long Long.
  Wait.
Beckett. Alba.
  Arènes de Lutèce.
Berry. Kentucky River Junction.
  Meeting, A.
Berryman. Dew is drying fast, a last drop
  glistens, The.
  Hello.
  Infallible symbolist!—Tanker driven ashore.
  Today is it? Is it today? I shudder.
Bradstreet. On My Son's Return Out of
  England.
Browning, Elizabeth Barrett. Exile's Return,
  The.
  Sonnet: "Thou comest! all is said without a
  word."
Burns. Banks of Cree.
  Lassie Lie near Me.
Campion. Lords Welcome, sung before the
  Kings Good-night, The.
Carew. Upon Master W. Montague, His
  Return from Travel.
Carruth. Family Reunion.
Clark. "My heart in pieces."
Cohen. Coming Back to You.
Cowper. On the Queens's Visit to London.
Cullen. Two Who Crossed a Line.
Eberhart. Inchiquin Lake, Penobscot Bay.
  Return, The.
Glück. My Life Before Dawn.
Graves. Brief Reunion.
Hacker. For K.J., Leaving and Coming Back.
  Somewhere in a Turrent.
  When you told me that he was in jail.
Hardy. Minute before Meeting, The.
  Revisitation, The.
  Song of the Soldiers' Wives and Sweethearts.
  Two Soldiers, The.
  Woman Who Went East, The.
Hartley. Return of the Native.
Hesketh. Party, The.
Hughes, Langston. Lover's Return.
Hugo. Way a Ghost Behaves, The.
Joseph. Married People Going to Work.
Kipling. Friends, The.
  Widower, The.
Koch. Fate.
Kunitz. Father and Son.
Lawrence. Chief Mystery, The.
  Reach Over.
  Return.
McGrath. Celebration.
  Once We Meant It.
  Poem: "How could I have come so far?"
MacLeish. Hotel Breakfast.
MacNeice. Bluebells.
  Happy Families.
Meredith. At last we parley: we so strangely
  dumb.
  He found her by the ocean's moaning verge.

Lord Dusiote sprang from priest and squire.
  Nor had saffron and sapphire and red.
Owen. Unreturning, The.
Pack. Cord of Wood, A.
Plath. Family Reunion.
Rich. Face to Face.
Rossetti. Last Words of St. Telemachus, The.
  Lord Thomas and Fair Margaret.
Rukeyser. More of a Corpse than a Woman.
Schuyler. Reunion, A.
Stevenson. Stormy evening closes now in
  vain, The.
Stuart. Return, The.
Turco. Street Meeting.
Updike. Oxford, Thirty Years After.
Whittier. Reunion, The.
  To a Friend.
Williams, William Carlos. Visit.

Revelation (Bible)
Blake. Mental Traveller, The.
Carruth. Lamoille River Valley otherwise
  known, The.
Herrick. To God ("Do with me, God! as Thou
  didst deal with John").
Sarton. Storm of Angels, A.

Revelry
Brontë. Through the hours of yesternight.
Carruth. In the snowy woods of morning.
Cohen. Closing Time.
Ford. O.
Herrick. Tinkers Song, The.
  Twelfe Night, or King and Queene.
Keats. Song: "Spirit here that reignest!"

Revenge
Beatles. I'll Cry Instead.
  Rocky Raccoon.
Browning, Robert. Forgiveness, A.
Bukowski. 20 minutes later.
Bunting. Faridun watched the road.
Burns. Bonie Laddie, Highland Laddie.
  Where Helen Lies.
Byron. And Dost Thou Ask the Reason of My
  Sadness?
Carew. In the Person of a Lady To Her
  Inconstant Servant.
  To My Inconstant Mistress [*or* Mistris].
Carruth. "They tossed my baby like a cat in
  the air."
Chaucer. Reeve's Tale, The.
Creeley. Lady Bird.
Davie. Revenge for Love.
Dickinson. Mine Enemy is growing old.
Donne. Apparition, The.
Emerson. When devils bite.
Gardner. Of Mercy.
Graves. Return.
  Wreath, The.
Hardy. Brother, The.
  Sacrilege, The.
Herbert. Reprisal[l], The.
Herrick. Bubble; a Song, The.
  Revenge.
Hewitt. My Teachers.
Hughes, Ted. Kreutzer Sonata.
Jeffers. At the Birth of an Age.
  At the Fall of an Age.
  Love and the Hate, The.
  Medea.
Kipling. Heriot's Ford.
Pagett, M. P.
  Raped and Revenged.
Lawrence. Vengeance Is Mine.
  Welcome Death.
Lovelace. Cupid Far Gone.
MacLeish. MacLeish goes up the.
Melville. Martyr, The.
Meredith. King Harald's Trance.
Merton. Dialog with Mister Clapcott.
Milton. Heroic Vengeance.
  Immortal Hate.
  Oh [*or* O] how comely it is and how reviving.
Plath. Lady Lazarus.
  Shrike, The.
Sandburg. Mascots.
Shakespeare. Rape of Lucrece, The.
Sidney. Fifth Song.
Silverstein. Crocodile's Toothache, The.

Smith, Stevie. King Hamlet's Ghost.
Williams, Miller. Rubaiyat for Sue Ella
  Tucker.

Revere, Paul
Longfellow. Landlord's Tale: Paul Revere's
  Ride, The.

Revivalism and Revivalists
Dunbar. Whistling Sam.
Lindsay. I walk the forest by the Daniel
  Boone trail.
Rich. Revivalist in Boston, A.
See also **Evangelism and Evangelists; Religion.**

Revolution and Revolutionaries
Beatles. Revolution.
Browning, Elizabeth Barrett. Italy and the
  World.
Burns. Robert Bruce's March to Bannockburn.
Carroll, Jim. Highway Report.
Carruth. Now tell me if we don't need a
  revolution! Black.
  Sonnet: "All revolutions in modern times have
  led."
  Tsar, who knew you? Who.
  You—Spanish-speaking.
Catullus. Carmen 54: "If not by all that his
  friends boast."
Cohen. Any System.
  Cherry Orchards.
  Commentary—A Working Man.
  One of These Days.
  This Is My Voice.
  Working Man, A.
Cooper. Poetry As Continuity.
Cummings. Red Front, The.
Dickinson. Revolution is the Pod.
"Dylan." Times They Are A-Changin', The.
Emerson. Boston.
Ferlinghetti. Sandinista Avioncitos.
Frost. Semi-Revolution, A.
Gallagher. That Kind of Thing.
Ginsberg. Neruda's "Que dispierte el leñador."
Glück. Exile.
Gunn. Court Revolt, The.
Haines. Sweater of Vladimir Ussachevsky,
  The.
Hall. Revolution, The.
Hardy. Sergeant's Song, The.
Herrick. Warre.
Hewitt. "Lass of Richmond Hill", or The
  Royal Garden Party, The.
  Poem: "My name is Revolution—let me
  speak."
  Tribunes, The.
  Twisted Heart, The.
Hughes, Langston. Roland Hayes Beaten
  (Georgia: 1942).
Knight. On the Yard.
Lawrence. Fight! O My Young Men.
  It's Either You Fight or You Die.
  Minorities in Danger.
  O! Start a Revolution.
  Revolutions as Such!
  Sane Revolution, A.
  Softly, Then, Softly.
Lorde. NOW.
McGrath. Blues for the Old Revolutionary
  Woman.
  Incident in the Life of a Prophet, An.
  Lament for Pablo Neruda.
  Praises IV.
  Underground, The.
  Vision of Three Angels Viewing the Progress
  of Socialism.
  Warrant for Pablo Neruda, A.
MacLeish. Background with Revolutionaries.
  Revolution of the Children.
Meredith. Amid the plash of scarlet mud.
  As mighty thews burst manacles, she went
  mad.
  Banners from East, from South.
  Banners from South, from East.
  Lo, where hurricane flocks of the North-wind
  rattle their thunder.
  Not yet had History's Ætna smoked the skies.
  Now her glut of vengeance left her grey.
  Now was her face white waves in the
  tempest's sharp flame-blink.

Merton. Letters to Che: Canto Bilingue.
Never Call a Babysitter in a Thunderstorm.
Miller. Hasta la Victoria Siempre.
Nicaraguan Journal.
Muldoon. Lunch with Pancho Villa.
Nathan. Coup.
Law and Order.
Patchen. Ladder, The.
O What a Revolution!
Small but Brilliant Fire Blazed in the Grate, A.
To Whom It May Concern.
Pope. Shut, shut the door, good *John*!
fatigu'd, I said.
Rich. To Frantz Fanon.
Uncle Speaks in the Drawing Room, The.
Rolfe. Brigadas Internacionales.
Communists.
Homage to Karl Marx.
Room with Revolutionists.
These Men Are Revolution.
Three Who Died.
Unit Meeting.
Rossetti. Royal Princess, A.
Rukeyser. Child and Mother.
Sandburg. Dynamiter.
Who was that antique Chinese crook who put
over his revolution and.
Sarton. Ballad of the Sixties.
We'll to the Woods No More, the Laurels Are
Cut Down.
Schwartz. Poem for Jacques Maritain and
Leon Trotzky.
Snyder. Revolution in the Revolution in the
Revolution.
Walcott. Elegy: "Our hammock swung
between Americas."
Waldman. How the Sestina (Yawn) Works.
Revolution.
Walker. Facing the Way.
Lost My Voice? Of Course.
Well.
Whitman. To a Foil'd European
Revolutionaire.
Transpositions.
Williams, Miller. Allende at the End.
Yeats. From the "Antigone."
Great Day, The.
Young. Myth Science of Our Time, The.
Zukofsky. Otho's scooped nut its
pusillanimity.
See also **Rebellions and Rebels.**

Revolutionary War, American. *see* **American
Revolution.**

Rewards
Coleridge. Good Great Man, The.
Herrick. Gods Gifts Not Soon[e] Granted.
Nothing Free-Cost.
Recompence.
Rewards.
Rewards and Punishments.
Hewitt. Epitaph for a Gardener.
Habit of Mercy, The.
Jonson. To Mr Ben Jonson in His Journey, by
Mr Craven.
Lindsay. Dancing for a Prize.
Merton. Keng Sang Chu.
Milton. Jehovah to my words give ear.
Psalms. Psalm 5: "Give ear to my words, O
Lord, consider my meditation."
Psalm 15: "Lord, who shall abide in thy
tabernacle?"
Psalm 17: "Hear the right, O Lord."
Psalm 18: "I will love thee, O Lord, my
strength."
Psalm 112: "Praise ye the Lord. Blessed."
Smart. Thee will I love, O Lord, my tow'r.
Stevenson. Tempest tossed and sore afflicted,
sin defiled and care oppressed.
To all that love the far and blue.

Reynolds, Sir Joshua
Blake. Cripple every step Drudges & labours,
The.
Florentine Ingratitude.
Pitiful Case, A.
Sir Jo[s]hua praised Rubens with a Smile.
To the Royal Academy.
When Sir [*or* Sr] Joshua Reynolds died.

Cowper. To Sir Joshua Reynolds.
Wordsworth. Anacreon.

Rhine (river), Germany
Coleridge. Cologne.
Lowry. April 1937 In the Oaxaca Train.
In the Oaxaca Train.
Wordsworth. Author's Voyage down the
Rhine (Thirty Years Ago).
Germans on the Heights of Hochheim, The.
In a Carriage, upon the Banks of the Rhine.

Rhinoceroses
Ciardi. Bird in Whatever Name, The.
Nash. Rhinoceros, The.

Rhode Island (state)
Whittier. Spiritual Manifestation, A.

Rhythm
Carruth. Sometimes When Lovers Lie Quietly
Together, Unexpectedly One of Them Will
Feel the Other's Pulse.
Creeley. Rhythm, The.
Duncan. Book of Resemblances, A.
Eberhart. Long Swing, The.
Fox. On Some Such Morning.
Jeffers. Rearmament.
Knight. Ilu, the Talking Drum.
Rukeyser. To Enter That Rhythm Where the
Self Is Lost.

Ribbons
Carew. Upon a Ribbon [*or* Ribband].
Herrick. Bracelet; to Julia, The.
Upon a Black Twist, Rounding the Arm of the
Countess of Carlisle.
Upon Julia's Ribband.

Rice
Bly. Dawn in Threshing Time.
Oliver. Rice.

**Richard I (Richard Coeur de Lion), King of
England**
Chaucer. Lak of Stedfastnesse.
Meredith. Richard Lionheart.
Prince. Coeur de Lion.

Richard II, King of England
Lowell. Coleridge and Richard II.

Richard III, King of England
Lowell. Bosworth Field.

Richardson, Samuel
Cowper. Ode on *Sir Charles Grandison.*

Riches. *see* **Wealth.**

Riddles
Beckett. Tailpiece.
Carroll, Jim. My blond niece speaks in
riddles.
"Carroll, Lewis." Four Riddles.
Puzzles from Wonderland.
Riddle, A.
White Queen's Riddle, The.
Cohen. You Know Who I Am.
Cowper. Ænigma, An.
Manual, A.
Riddle: "I am just two and two, I am warm, I
am cold."
De la Mare. Riddle, A.
Riddlers, The.
Dickinson. Riddle we can guess, The.
Jarrell. What's the Riddle.
Lindsay. Two Old Crows.
Lowry. Abacus, The.
MacLeish. What Riddle Asked the Sphinx.
MacNeice. Riddle.
Meredith. Riddle for Men, The.
Nash. Unanswered by Request.
Poe. Valentine, A.
Rossetti. Charades.
New Enigmas.
Peacock has a score of eyes, The.
Pin has a head, but has no hair, A.
There is one that has a head without an eye.
Sandburg. Gang in its working clothes, The.
Riddles and Whims.
Sidney. Sonnet 37: "My mouth doth water,
and my breast doth swell."
Silverstein. Toucan, The.
Simic. Solving the Riddle.
Snodgrass. Riddle: "So small it is, there must
be at least two."

Swift. Answer to Delany's Riddle, The.
Probatur Aliter.
Riddling Letter, A ("Sir, / Pray discruciate
what follows: / The dullest beast, and
gentleman's liquor").
Wilbur. Eight Riddles from Symphosius.
Riddle, A.
Some Riddles from Symphosius.
Two Riddles from Aldhelm.

Rifles
Haines. Denali Road.
Hall. Merle Bascom's .22.
Kipling. Brown Bess.
Meinke. Cabaret Voltaire.
Sandburg. A. E. F.

Righteousness
Cummings. World is very big, and we, The.
Davie. Woe unto Thee!
"Dylan." Ain't No Man Righteous, No Not
One.
Do Right to Me Baby (Do Unto Others).
Property of Jesus.
Trouble in Mind.
When You Gonna Wake Up?
Haines. Circles and Squares.
Let the inhuman, drab machines.
Lindsay. Galahad, Knight Who Perished.
Rhymer's Reply: Incense and Splendor, The.
Statue of Old Andrew Jackson, The.
Lowry. From This Acceptance, Sir, We Might
Proceed.
Oh gentle Jesus of the hymnal once.
MacNeice. Canto I: "August. Render to
Caesar. Speak parrot: a gimmick for Poll."
'Drunk again! Where do you think you are?'
Take this old man with the soldierly straight
back.
Under the surface of flux and of fear there is
an underground movement.
Meredith. Blest is the sword that leaps from
sheath.
Milton. Blest is the man who hath not walk'd
astray.
Pack. Clayfeld's Campaign.
Pope. Version of the First Psalm, for the Use
of a Young Lady, A.
Psalms. Psalm 1: "Blessed is the man that
walketh."
Psalm 11: "In the name of the Lord."
Psalm 15: "Lord, who shall abide in thy
tabernacle?"
Psalm 19: "Heavens declare the glory of God,
The."
Psalm 26: "Judge me, O Lord; for I have
walked in mine integrity."
Psalm 32: "Blessed is he whose transgression
is forgiven, whose sin is covered."
Psalm 34: "I will bless the Lord at all times."
Psalm 35: "Plead my cause, O Lord, with
them that strive with me."
Psalm 37: "Fret not thyself because of
evildoers."
Psalm 50: "Mighty God, even the Lord, hath
spoken, The."
Psalm 58: "Do ye indeed speak righteousness,
O congregation?"
Psalm 101: "I will sing of mercy and
judgment."
Psalm 112: "Praise ye the Lord. Blessed."
Psalm 141: "Lord, I cry unto thee."
Ralegh. Lie, The.
Rossetti. Escape to the Mountain.
I have done with hope.
Sidney. Speak Thou for me against wrong-
speaking foes.
Warren. Harvard '61: Battle Fatigue.
Wyatt. Although thou see th'outrageous climb
aloft.
O happy are they that have forgiveness got.

Riley, James Whitcomb
Dunbar. James Whitcomb Riley.
Kipling. To James Whitcomb Riley.

Rilke, Rainer Maria
Dunn. Smiles.
Eberhart. Portrait of Rilke.
Lewis. To Rilke.
"MacDiarmid." Seamless Garment, The.

MacLeish. Infinite Reason, The.
Merton. Rilke's Epitaph.
Nemerov. On Reading "The Love and Death of Cornet Christopher Rilke."
O'Hara. Poem: "To be idiomatic in a vacumm."
Rich. After a Sentence in "Malte Laurids Brigge."
Paula Becker to Clara Westhoff.

Rimbaud, Arthur
Auden. Rimbaud.
Berg. Music.
Berrigan. Sweeter than sour apples flesh to boys.
Carruth. Sonnet: "Cindy, I've used my writing all my life."
Cohen. Not Going Back.
Ferlinghetti. Sweet and various the woodlark.
Ford. Message for Rimbaud.
Lowry. On Reading Edmund Wilson's Remarks about Rimbaud.
"MacDiarmid." Greatest poets undergo a kind of crisis in their art, The.
MacLeish. Aeterna Poetae Memoria.
Against Illuminations.
Olson. Put him this way.
Schuyler. Fauré Ballade, The.
Smith, Patti. Dream of Rimbaud.
Rimbaud Dead.
Sorrentino. Canzone: "On the tropical coast of Java."

Rings
Crabbe. On Receiving from a Lady a Present of a Ring.
Cummings. Girl's Ring, A.
Donne. Jet Ring Sent, A.
Eberhart. Oak, The.
Graves. Golden Anchor.
St Antony of Padua.
Song: Three Rings for Her.
With a Gift of Rings.
Herrick. Jimmall Ring, or True-Love-Knot, The.
Ring Presented to Julia, A.
Hewitt. Booleys, The.
Lovelace. Sonnet: "Depose your finger of that Ring."
Marlowe. 2.15: Ad annulum, quem dono amicae dedit.
Pack. Clayfeld Renews His Vow to Evelyn.
Rossetti. Ring upon her finger, / Walks the bride, A.
Sexton. Wedding Ring Dance, The.
Shapiro. New Ring, The.
Stevenson. These rings, O my beloved pair.
Wakoski. Ring, The.
Ringless.

Rin-Tin-Tin
Hoffman. In the Days of Rin-Tin-Tin.

Riots and Rioters
Angelou. Riot: 60's.
Cowper. Address to the Mob, An.
On the Burning of Lord Mansfield's Library.
On the Same.
Griffiths. Horse's Mouth, The.
Melville. House-Top, The.
Piercy. Curse of the Earth Magician on a Metal Land.
Williams, Miller. Aesthetic Distance.

Risorgimento
Whittier. Dream of Pio Nono, The.
From Perugia.
Italy.
Prisoners of Naples, The.
To Pius IX.

Rituals
Atwood. Some Objects of Wood and Stone.
Carew. New Year's Sacrifice: To Lucinda, A.
To the King, at His Entrance into Saxham: By Master John Crofts.
Dickey, William. Pruned Roses, The.
Eberhart. Lorca.
Hall. Eating the Pig.
Herrick. Another New-Yeeres Gift, or Song for the Circumcision.
Frankincense, The.
New-Yeeres Gift, or Circumcisions Song, Sung

to the King in the Presence at White Hall, The.
Perfume, The.
Steam in Sacrifice.
Sweetnesse in Sacrifice.
To Julia ("Help me, Julia, for to pray").
To Julia ("Offer thy gift").
To Julia, the Flaminica Dialis, or Queen-Priest.
To the Reverend Shade of His Religious Father.
Hewitt. Dedication: "I have a certain skill in phrase."
Holy Place, A.
St Rosalie: Monte Pellegrino.
Swathe Uncut, The.
Lawrence. Bells.
Lewis. Holi.
McGrath. Reading the Names of the Vietnam War Dead.
Merton. Seven Archaic Images.
There is a little ceremony to be performed.
Olson. Morning News, The.
Ransom. First Travels of Max.
Rukeyser. Three Black Women.
Snyder. Uluru Wild Fig Song.
Tomlinson. Cochiti.
Harvest Festival: at Ozleworth.
On a Mexican Straw Christ.
Whittier. Dead Feast of the Kol-Folk, The.
Funeral Tree of the Sokokis.
Williams, Miller. Glass Darkly, A.
Rituals.
Yeats. Collarbone [or Collar-Bone] of a Hare, The.

Rivalry
Bukowski. Who in the Hell is Tom Jones?
Burns. Auld Rob Morris.
Dean of Faculty—a New Ballad, The.
Epistle to Robt. Graham Esq: of Fintry on the Election for the Dumfries String of Boroughs, Anno 1790.
Campion. Epigramme: "Phoebe all the rights Elisa claymeth."
Carew. Fly That Flew into My Mistress'[s] Eye, A.
To My Rival.
Truce in Love Intreated.
"Carroll, Lewis." Size and Tears.
Creeley. Carnival, The.
Emerson. By the unacknowledged tie.
Hesketh. Rivals, The.
Kipling. Cain and Abel.
Lowry. Plingen plangen auf gefangen.
Markson. Recitation before Bed.
Melville. Battle of Stone River, Tennessee.
Meredith. Archduchess Anne.
Internal Harmony.
Nemerov. Deposition, The.
Suckling. My dearest rival, lest [or least] our love.
To His Rival.
Upon Two Sisters.
Williams, Charles Kenneth. Hood.
Zimmer. Ancient Wars, The.
Games in the Field, The.
Zimmer Finds Imbellis in the Ancient Graves.

See also **Competition.**

Rivers
Auden. River Profile.
Beckett. Fleuves et océans.
Berry. Heron, The.
March Snow.
March 22, 1968.
Observance.
Porch over the River, The.
Rising, the river.
River Bridged and Forgot, The.
River is rising, The.
Slip, The.
Bishop. Santarém.
Bly. Schoolcraft's Diary Written on the Missouri: 1830.
Browning, Elizabeth Barrett. Romance of the Ganges, A.
Sounds.
Bukowski. I Was Born to Hustle Roses Down the Avenues of the Dead.

Burns. Afton Water.
Banks of Nith, The.
Banks of the Devon, The.
Fragment, A: "One night as I did wander."
Jessie—A New Scots Song.
Written with a Pencil, Standing by the Fall of Fyers, near Loch-Ness.
Byron. Stanzas to the Po.
Campion. Fire, fire, fire, fire!
Carew. To My Mistress Sitting by a River's Side; an Eddy.
Carruth. In Russia.
Clough. From thy far sources 'mid mountains airily climbing.
Cohen. Suzanne [Takes You Down].
Coleridge. Sonnet to the River Otter.
Cooper. Leaving Water Hyacinths.
Morning on the St. John's.
Cowper. Comparison, A.
Crane. River, The.
Creeley. Memory, The.
Davie. Evening on the Boyne.
Green River.
Late Anniversary, A.
Ox-Bow.
Skelpick.
De la Mare. Voices.
Dickinson. I like to see it lap the Miles.
Doolittle. He marked the pattern of the sky.
Pursuit.
Wash of cold river.
Dove. Event, The.
In the Bulrush.
Dryden. Song of the River Thames, A.
Dunbar. On the River.
Duncan. Source.
"Dylan." Watching the River Flow.
Eberhart. Hatred of the Old River.
La Crosse at Ninety Miles an Hour.
Lost Children, The.
Parker River, The.
Pasture, The.
Eliot. Dry Salvages, The.
Virginia.
Emerson. Far seen the river glides below.
Musketaquid.
Two Rivers.
Everson. River-Root: as even under high drifts, those fierce wind-grappled cuts of the Rockies.
Ferlinghetti. Hilarious God.
Reading Apollinaire by the Rogue River.
River Still To Be Found, A.
Fisher. Butterton Ford.
Fletcher. Elegy on a Nordic White Protestant.
Flood Symphony, The.
Old South, The.
On the Banks of the Sumida.
Fox. River and Light.
Frost. Too Anxious for Rivers.
Gallagher. Reading Aloud.
Galvin. Trying to Flatter Twelve Mile River.
Garrigue. There Is a Dark River.
Hacker. Going Back to the River.
Hall. Long River, The.
Photographs of China.
Hardy. On Sturminster Foot-Bridge.
Hartley. Androscoggin.
Bend of the Androscoggin, The.
Heaney. Broagh.
New Song, A.
Herrick. Proof to No Purpose.
To Dean-bourn, a Rude River in Devon, by Which Sometimes He Lived.
Hesketh. Call of the North.
Hill. Rivers bring down. the sea.
Hughes, Langston. Life Is Fine.
Negro Speaks of Rivers, The.
Reverie on the Harlem River.
Hughes, Ted. Salmon Eggs.
Hugo. At the Cabin.
At the Stilli's Mouth.
Bad Vision at the Skagit.
Ballad of the Upper Bumping.
Beaverbank.
Birthday.
Colors of a Bird, The.

Duwamish.
Duwamish Head.
Duwamish No. 2.
For Jennifer, 6, on the Teton.
Fort Benton.
From the Rain Forest Down.
Gooseprairie.
Hideout.
Index.
Introduction to the Hoh.
Keokuk.
Making Certain It Goes On.
Map of the Peninsula, A.
Other Beaverbank, The.
Ovando.
Plans for Altering the River.
Plunking the Skagit.
River Now, The.
Skykomish River Running.
Small Oil Left in the House We Rented in
  Boulder, The.
Snoqualmie.
Spinning the Sava.
Tahola.
To Die in Milltown.
Towns We Know and Leave Behind, the
  Rivers We Carry with Us, The.
Underwater Autumn.
West Marginal Way.
Where Jennie Used to Swim.
Where Mission Creek Runs Hard for Joy.
Jeffers. Heavy and yellow with the clay wrack
  from the flooded valley.
Johnson. In Rivum a Mola Stoana Lichfeldiæ
  Diffluentem.
Translation of the Beginning of *Rio Verde.*
Joseph. Non-communicant.
River Rising in India.
Kinnell. Last River, The.
River That Is East, The.
Kipling. Ford o' Kabul River.
Song of the Fifth River.
Larkin. Thaw.
Lawrence. Kiss, A.
Man at Play on the River, A.
River Roses.
Levertov. Music, A.
Levine. Noon.
Renaming the Kings.
Lewis. Rhondda, The.
River Temple: Wai, The.
Liddy. I am telling you, kid.
Lovelace. Lucasta, Taking the Waters at
  Tunbridge.
Lowry. Names of Mexican rivers I forgot,
  The.
Yvonne stood there silently / the roar of the
  plane still in her ears.
"MacDiarmid." Ah, sweetheart, what a pool!
  Broad, deep, strong, silent, and sedate!
McGrath. Beyond the Red River.
Edge of the River, The.
History.
Return to Marsh Street.
MacLeish. What Any Lover Learns.
McNeill. American Boating Song.
Ballad of New River.
Marlowe. 3.5: Ad amnem, dum iter faceret ad
  amicam.
Melville. Muster, The.
Meredith. By the Passeyr.
Pictures of the Rhine.
Rhine-Land.
Song: "I would I were the drop of rain."
Song: "Over the ferry, and over the ferry."
There is for me no sweeter holiday.
Merrill. Current, The.
River Poem.
Miller. Near Old Fort Pike on the Des Moines
  River.
River of long standing, bridge abut-ment.
Morgan. Decisions of afternoon: as.
Noon is the hour of choice.
River in the dream, The.
Sun tells stories, The.
Two bodies in the river.
What voice is it that speaks.

Nemerov. Dead River.
Neruda. Stone, toppled by water and
  mountain, The.
Oliver. Snowshoe Hare, The.
Olson. There Is No River Which Is Called
  Lethe.
Oppen. Coastal Strip.
I saw from the bus.
River of our substance.
Travelogue.
Paley. On the Bank Street Pier.
Patchen. Anna Karenina and the Love-sick
  River.
Piercy. Let Us Gather at the River.
Plath. Lorelei.
Poe. To the River———.
Pope. River, The.
Raine. Beside the river Eden.
"I am the stream," I said.
It crossed my mind.
Never twice that river.
Seen from the train.
Ransom. Rain.
Rich. Concord River.
Roethke. Long Alley, The.
Meditation at Oyster River.
River Incident.
Rossetti. River Thames (?).
Rose, The.
Whitsun Monday.
Rukeyser. Dam, The.
Gullies as deep as halls held these surveyors.
Rock Flow, River Mix.
Sandburg. Chromo.
Cornfield Ridge and Stream.
Letter S.
On a Railroad Right of Way.
Prairie Woodland.
River Moons.
River Roads.
They Ask Each Other Where They Came
  From.
Schwartz. Overture.
Prologue: "Narcissus, speaking in the first
  person."
Smith, Charlotte. To the River Arun.
Walk by the Water, A.
Smith, Stevie. Friends of the River Trent.
River Deben, The.
River God, The.
River Humber, The.
Snyder. River in the Valley.
Spenser. Rivers Come to the Hall of Proteus
  for the Marriage of the Thames and the
  Medway, The.
Rivers of Ireland, The.
Stafford. Ask Me.
By a River in the Osage Country.
Ceremony.
In the Deep Channel.
Looking across the River.
Stevens. Completely New Set of Objects, A.
Countryman, The.
Frogs Eat Butterflies. Snakes Eat Frogs. Hogs
  Eat Snakes. Men Eat Hogs.
Indian River.
Metaphor as Degeneration.
River of Rivers in Connecticut, The.
This Solitude of Cataracts.
Stevenson. Air of Diabelli's.
Epistle to Albert Dew-Smith.
Keepsake Mill.
Know you the river near to Grez.
Looking-Glass River.
Susquehanna and the Delaware, The.
Where Go the Boats?
Stuart. Leavetaking.
Tomlinson. Below Tintern.
Race, The.
Severnside.
Turco. Ferry, The.
Whitman. As Consequent, Etc.
Whittier. June on the Merrimac.
Merrimac, The.
Mystery, A.
Our River.
R. S. S., at Deer Island on the Merrimac.

Red River Voyageur, The.
River Path, The.
To G. G.
Vale of the Merrimac, The.
Wilbur. Aspen and the Stream, The.
Glance from the Bridge, A.
Problem from Milton, A.
Puritans, The.
Shad-Time.
Williams, Charles Kenneth. Sky, Water.
Williams, William Carlos. Flowing River, A.
Mind Hesitant, The.
Mists over the River.
River Rhyme.
River Rhyme II.
Sluggishly.
Wordsworth. Avon, The.
Between Namur and Liege.
Composed upon Westminster Bridge,
  September 3, 1802.
Fall of the Aar—Handec, The.
Hymn for the Boatmen, as They Approach the
  Rapids under the Castle of Heidelberg.
Stanzas Composed in the Simplon Pass.
Wright, James. Living by the Red River.
Morning Hymn to a Dark Girl.
RIP.
To the Poets in New York.
Yau. Rumors.
Zukofsky. Not much more than being.
World autumn, The.

See also **Brooks and Streams; Listings for
  specific Rivers.**

Roaches. *see* **Cockroaches.**

Roads
Auden. Lovers' Lane.
Beatles. Why Don't We Do It in the Road.
Bishop. In the Middle of the Road.
Bly. Three Kinds of Pleasures.
Burns. Epigram on Rough Roads.
"Carroll, Lewis." Lays of Sorrow, No. 2.
Carruth. Am I wrong? The roads.
Creeley. Poem for Bob Leed.
  Traveller, The.
Dickey, James. Craters.
Dickinson. Little Road—not made of Man, A.
Dove. Corduroy Road.
Early Morning on the Tel Aviv-Haifa
  Freeway.
Dunbar. On the Road.
  Riding to Town.
Roadway, A.
To the Road.
"Dylan." Down the Highway.
  Highway 61 Revisited.
Fenton. South Parks Road.
Fisher. Lazily into the curve.
Frost. Middleness of the Road, The.
Road Not Taken, The.
Galvin. Old Woodsroads.
Tar.
Hardy. By Henstridge Cross at the Year's
  End.
Roman Road, The.
Weary Walker, The.
Heaney. On the Road.
Hughes, Langston. Bound No'th Blues.
Hugo. Blond Road, The.
End of Krim's Pad, The.
Goodbye, Iowa.
In Your Small Dream.
Late Summer, Drummond.
Letter to Gale from Ovando.
Medicine Bow.
Reconsidering the Madman.
Kipling. Arterial.
Fox-Hunting.
Song of French Roads, A.
Way through the Woods, The.
Knight. Outside St. Louis.
Larkin. No Road.
Lawrence. On the Road.
Levine. To get west you go east.
Lowry. Walk in Canada.
McGrath. Winter Roads.
MacLeish. Companions.
McNeill. Roads, The.

Nash. I'll Take the High Road Commission.
Song of the Open Road.
Nathan. To Somewhere.
Patchen. Appian Way, The.
Shelton. New Road, The.
Sidney. Sonet 84: "Highway, since you my
chief Parnassus be."
Tomlinson. Arizona Highway.
Bridges.
Question, The.
Whitman. Afoot and light-hearted I take to the
open road.
Williams, Charles Kenneth. I know / nothing
anymore.
Williams, William Carlos. Autumn.
Wordsworth. Massy Ways Carried across
These Heights, The.
Road extended o'er a heath, The.
Wright, Charles. Lonesome Pine Special.
See also Streets.
**"Rob Roy" (Robert MacGregor, Scottish
freebooter)**
Wordsworth. Rob Roy's Grave.
Robbers. *see* **Crime and Criminals.**
Robeson, Paul
Hayden. Homage to Paul Robeson.
Robespierre, Maximilien Marie Isidore
Carruth. As Rousseau was another, singing.
Lowell. Robespierre and Mozart as Stage.
Robin Hood
Keats. Robin Hood.
Robins
Auden. Robin, The.
Cowper. Epitaph on a Free but Tame
Redbreast.
Invitation to the Redbreast.
Cummings. Christ but they're few.
Sentinel robins two / guard me and you.
De la Mare. Robin, A.
Dickinson. Come show thy Durham Breast.
I knew a Bird that would sing as firm.
I raise only robins on my farm.
Quite empty, quite at rest.
Robin for the Crumb, The.
Robin is a Gabriel, The.
Robin is the One, The.
"Robins?" They are writing now, The.
Hardy. Robin, The.
Herrick. To Robin Redbreast.
To the Nightingale, and Robin-Red-Brest.
Upon Mistress Elizabeth Wheeler under the
Name of Amarillis.
Keats. Song: "Stay, ruby-breasted warbler,
stay."
Kunitz. Robin Redbreast.
Melville. Little Good Fellows, The.
Meredith. To Robin Redbreast.
Nash. Who Called That Robin a Piccolo
Player?
Rossetti. Bread and Milk for Breakfast.
I am a King, / Or an Emperor rather.
Key-Note, The.
Wrens and robins in the hedge.
Thomson. Fowls of heaven, The.
Whittier. How the Robin Came.
Robin, The.
Wordsworth. Driven in by autumn's
sharpening air.
I Know an Aged Man Constrained to Dwell.
Redbreast Chasing the Butterfly, The.
Redbreast, The [Suggested in a Westmoreland
Cottage].
Robinson Crusoe
Bishop. Crusoe in England.
Infancy.
Jarrell. Island, The.
Lowry. Mr. Lowry's Good Friday under a
Real Cactus.
Old Freighter in an Old Port.
Oppen. We are pressed, pressed on each other.
Robinson, Jackie
Knight. Belly Song.
Robots
Dickey, William. Androids.
Jonson. On the New Motion.

Pack. Robot.
Robot Romance.
Rochester, John Wilmot, 2d Earl of
Markson. Tricentennial: 1980.
Pope. Verses Left by Mr. Pope, on His Lying
in the Same Bed which Wilmot, the
Celebrated Earl of Rochester, Slept in, at
Adderbury, then Belonging to the Duke of
Argyle, Bridges. July 9th, 1739.
Rockefeller Center, New York City
Schuyler. December.
Rockets. *see* **Space and Space Travel.**
Rocking Chairs
Bishop. Sunday at Key West.
Hall. Rocker, The.
Rocks. *see* **Stones and Rocks.**
Rocky Mountains
Haines. Nine thousand feet in the Rockies.
Lawrence. Beyond the Rockies.
Waldman. For J.A. As Dusk Deepens Canyon.
Rodin, Auguste
Hall. Notes For Nobody.
Roethke, Theodore
Ciardi. Was a Man.
Davie. July, 1964.
Roland
Lowell. Death of Count Roland.
MacLeish. Silent Slain, The.
Roller Skating and Roller Skaters. *see* **Skiing
and Skiers.**
Roman Catholicism. *see* **Catholicism and
Catholics.**
Romanticism and Romantics
Auden. To Goethe: a Complaint.
Bogan. Romantic, The.
Browning, Elizabeth Barrett. Romaunt of
Margret, The.
Bukowski. Spain Sits Like a Hidden Flower in
My Coffeepot.
Carruth. Sonnet: The Recollected Actual
Voices of Romanticism.
Two Romantic Pieces.
Cummings. Let's live suddenly without
thinking.
Davie. Derbyshire.
De la Mare. Mercutio.
Dunn. American Film, An.
Jarrell. English Garden in Austria, An.
Jong. Death of a Romantic.
"MacDiarmid." Poetry in which all
connections will constantly render such
services, A.
MacNeice. All Over Again.
Meinke. Easter in Neuchâtel.
Shell, The.
Rexroth. I Dream of Leslie.
Inversely, As the Square of Their Distances
Apart.
Now the Starlit Moonless Spring.
Robinson. Miniver Cheevy.
Stevens. Re-statement of Romance.
Stevenson. Her name is as a word of old
romance.
I will make you brooches and toys for your
delight.
Tate. To a Romantic.
To a Romantic Novelist.
To the Romantic Traditionists.
Rome, Italy
Auden. Roman Wall Blues.
Browning, Elizabeth Barrett. View Across the
Roman Campagna.
Browning, Robert. Protus.
Two in the Campagna.
Bukowski. Anthony.
Byron. Rome by Metella's Tomb.
Carruth. Eternal City.
Catullus. Carmen 10: "Alfenus Varus /
buttonholes me."
Ciardi. Apartment with a View, A.
S.P.Q.R. A Letter from Rome.
Clough. Amours de Voyage.
Rome ("Rome disappoints me much").
Cooper. Roman Dream.
Cowper. Boadicea: An Ode.

Cummings. 4.6: "O, blessed of the gods."
I met a man under the moon.
"Dylan." When I Paint My Masterpiece.
Edmunds. Bella Roma.
Emerson. Alone in Rome! Why Rome is
lonely too.
Ancient lady who dwelt in Rome, An.
Poem on Eloquence by R. W. Emerson.
Ferlinghetti. Roman Morn.
Graves. Cuirassiers of the Frontier, The.
Gunn. Silver Age, The.
Hardy. Rome: At the Pyramid of Cestius near
the Graves of Shelley and Keats.
Rome: Building a New Street in the Ancient
Quarter.
Rome: On the Palatine.
Hewitt. Of course, the gruffest prompting
comes from age.
Hoffman. At the Roman Wall, 1956.
Hugo. Castel Sant'Angelo.
Gull Hardly Explained, The.
Jarrell. Lament of the Children of Israel in
Rome.
Jonson. To My Chosen Friend the Learnèd
Translator of Lucan, Thomas May, Esquire.
To Sir Henry [*or* Henrie] Savile [upon His
Translation of Tacitus].
To the Same; on the Same.
Kipling. British-Roman Song, A.
Pict Song, A.
Rimini.
Roman Centurion's Song, The.
Romulus and Remus.
Song to Mithras, A.
Kunitz. Thief, The.
Lovelace. Hand by which no King but
Serjeant dies, The.
Lowell. Cicero, the Sacrificial Killing.
Marcus Cato 234–149 B.C.
Marcus Cato 95–42 B.C.
Meredith. Square along the couch, and stark.
Milton. Rome ("Brought our saviour to the
western side").
Rome ("The City which thou seest no other
deem").
Patchen. Appian Way, The.
Piercy. Track of the Master Builder, The.
Pope. On the Statue of *Cleopatra*, Made into
a Fountain by *Leo* the Tenth.
Prince. Walks in Rome.
Rolfe. 1949 (After Reading a News Item).
Rossetti. True Story, A.
Rukeyser. Lost Romans, The.
St. John. Last Night with Rafaella.
Lucifer in Starlight.
To Pasolini.
Shapiro. Room in Rome, A.
Shelley. Fragment: A Roman's Chamber.
Fragment: Rome and Nature.
Smart. Secular Ode, A.
Spenser. Antique Babel, empresse of the East,
The.
Ruines of Time, The.
Ruines of Rome.
Then was the faire Dodonian tree far seene.
Thou stranger, which for Rome in Rome here
seekest.
What time the Romaine Empire bore the raine.
Stevenson. Ad Quintilianum.
In Maximum.
Thomson. Rome.
Walcott. Companion in Rome, whom Rome
makes as old as Rome.
Warren. What Day Is.
Wilbur. Baroque Wall-Fountain in the Villa
Sciarra, A.
For the New Railway Station in Rome.
Piazza di Spagna, Early Morning.
Williams, Miller. Aesthetic Distance.
Evening: A Studio in Rome.
Lost in Ladispoli.
Wordsworth. At Rome ("Is this, ye Gods, the
Capitolian Hill?").
At Rome.—Regrets.—In Allusion to Niebuhr
and Other Modern Historians.
At Rome.—Regrets.—In Allusion to Niebuhr
and Other Modern Historians, Continued.

At Rome ("They—who have seen the noble Roman's scorn").
Eagle and the Dove, The.
From the Alban Hills, Looking towards Rome.
Pine of Monte Mario at Rome, The.
Roman Antiquities.
Roman Antiquities Discovered at Bishopstone, Herefordshire.
Sonnet: "Why should we weep or mourn, Angelic boy."
Wright, Charles. Roma I.
Roma II.
Zukofsky. Varus old crony had me visit his love.

Romeo and Juliet
Davie. Bride of Reason, The.
Hughes, Langston. Juliet.
"Reed." Legendary Hearts.
Romeo Had Juliette.

Ronsard, Pierre de
Davie. Garland for Ronsard, A.

Roofing and Roofers
Berry. New Roof, The.
Bukowski. 2 Outside, As Bones Break in My Kitchen.
Gildner. Shy Roofer, The.
Heaney. Thatcher.
Levine. Roofs.
Rich. Roofwalker, The.
Williams, Charles Kenneth. Tar.
Williams, William Carlos. Fine Work with Pitch and Copper.

Rooks
Auden. Rookery, The.
Hewitt. September Lull.
Plath. Black Rook in Rainy Weather.
Prospect.

Rooming Houses. *see* **Boarding Houses.**

Roosevelt, Franklin Delano
Jeffers. Wilson in Hell.
Rukeyser. Slow Dialogue between Pain and Roosevelt.
Sandburg. When Death Came April Twelve 1945.
Williams, William Carlos. Death by Radio.

Roosevelt, Theodore
Dunbar. For Theodore Roosevelt.
Hall. President and Poet.
Kipling. Great-Heart.
Lindsay. In Which Roosevelt Is Compared to Saul.
Roosevelt.
Robinson. Revealer, The.

Roosters
Auden. Early Morning.
Bishop. Roosters.
Burns. To Alexander Findlater.
Chaucer. His comb was redder than the fine coral.
Nun's Priest's Tale, The.
Ciardi. Come Morning.
Dickey, James. Gamecock.
Gardner. Cock-a-Hoop.
Graves. Cock in Pullet's Feathers.
Hall. Henyard Round, The.
Herrick. Cock-Crow.
Hewitt. Hen and the Cock: A Glens Folk Rhyme, The.
Meredith. Full loud & fresh crows Chaunticlere!
Prestige.
Nash. Rooster, The.
Piercy. Valley Where I Don't Belong, A.
Rossetti. "Kookoorookoo! kookoorookoo!" / Crows the cock before the morn.
Smart. Story of a Cock and a Bull, A.
Smith, Stevie. Cock-a-Doo.
Stevens. Bantams in Pine-Woods.

See also **Chickens.**

Rope
Dobyns. Ten Feet of Rope.
Longfellow. Ropewalk, The.
Nemerov. Rope's End, The.
Silverstein. Jumping Rope.
Turco. Ropewalk, The.

Rosary
Browning, Elizabeth Barrett. Lay of the Brown Rosary, The.
Heaney. Trial Runs.
Smith, Stevie. Violent Hand, The.

Roses
Ashbery. White Roses.
Berg. Uncle Will, the Gardener.
Bishop. Faustina, or Rock Roses.
Blake. My Pretty Rose Tree.
Sick Rose, The.
Bly. Bouquet of Ten Roses, A.
Brontë. Love and Friendship.
Browning, Elizabeth Barrett. Dead Rose, A.
Lay of the Early Rose, A.
Song of the Rose.
Browning, Robert. Women and Roses.
Bukowski. Destroying Beauty.
Burns. Banks O' Doon, The.
Banks o' Doon, The: "Ye flowery banks o' bonie Doon."
Rosebud, The.
Byron. Translation from Anacreon.
Campion. Song: "Now hath Flora rob'd [*or* robbed] her bowers."
Welcome to this flowrie place.
Carew. On a Damask[e] Rose, Sticking upon a Lady's Breast.
Red and White Roses.
Carroll, Jim. In the Deep Green Vase.
"Carroll, Lewis." Lesson in Latin, A.
Love among the Roses.
Ciardi. On the Patio.
Cohen. Not Going Back.
Rose, The.
Coleridge. Rose, The.
Cowper. Lily and the Rose, The.
Rose, The.
To Gravina.
Creeley. Question, The.
Rose, The.
Sanine to Leda.
Cummings. &(all during the / dropsin).
Dedication: "White rose my soul, The."
Every one of the red roses opened.
Rose / is dying the, The.
These from my mother's greatgrandmother's rosebush white.
Un(bee)mo / vi / n(in)g.
De la Mare. Epitaph, An: "Last, Stone, a little yet."
Rose in Candlelight, A.
Rose in Water, A.
Dickey, James. Deborah as Scion.
Dickinson. Bird must sing to earn the Crumb, The.
Essential oils—are wrung.
Full fed Rose on meals of Tint, A.
Go not too near a House of Rose.
If I should cease to bring a Rose.
Many can boast a hollyhock.
Nobody knows this little Rose.
Where Roses would not dare to go.
Doolittle. Garden.
Sea Rose.
White Rose.
Dunbar. Fulfilment.
Poor Withered Rose.
Promise.
Roses.
Roses and Pearls.
She Gave Me a Rose.
Eliot. Little Gidding.
Emerson. By breath of beds of roses drawn.
By kinds I keep my kinds in check.
God only knew how Saadi dined.
Thy poems Hafiz shame the rose leaves.
Everson. Rose of Solitude, The.
Ford. And the first owl of.
Bedraggled rose, The.
Krishna climbs up there.
They need no other.
Fox. Five Stanzas for My Two Brothers.
Frost. Rose Family, The.
Garrigue. One for the Roses.
Glück. Brennende Liebe.
Graves. Florist Rose, The.

Rose, The.
Song: Sword and Rose.
Song: To a Rose.
Hall. Old Roses.
Hardy. Fading Rose, The.
Spell of the Rose, The.
Hartley. Nature.
Herbert. Rose, The.
Herrick. Funeral[l] Rites of the Rose, The.
How Roses Came Red ("Roses at first").
How Roses Came Red ("'Tis Said").
Meditation for His Mistress[e], A.
Parliament of Roses to Julia, The.
Rosarie, The.
Showre of Roses, The.
To Roses in Julia's Bosome.
Upon a Virgin Kissing a Rose.
Upon Her Blush.
Upon One Lillie, Who Marryed with a Maid Call'd Rose.
Upon Roses.
Upon the Roses in Julias Bosome.
Vow to Venus, A.
Hesketh. Sally.
What Is a Person?
Hewitt. Providence 1.
Hopkins. All as that moth call'd Underwing, alighted.
Joseph. Rose.
Rose in the Afternoon.
Keats. To a Friend Who Sent Me Some Roses.
Kipling. Answer, The.
Blue Roses.
Lawrence. All of Roses.
Cabbage-Roses.
Grapes.
Grey Nurse, The.
Guelder Roses.
I Am like a Rose.
Love Storm.
Married in June.
Prophet in the Rose Garden, The.
River Roses.
Rose Is Not a Cabbage, A.
Rose of All the World.
Rose of England, The.
Roses.
Roses on the Breakfast Table.
Song-Day in Autumn.
Levine. One for the Rose.
Liddy. Price, The.
Lindsay. Rose of Midnight, The.
Wedding of the Rose and the Lotus, The.
With a Bouquet of Twelve Roses.
With a Rose, to Brunhilde.
Lowry. Rain Fell Heavily, The.
"MacDiarmid." Little White Rose, The.
Meinke. Sonnet on the Death of the Man Who Invented Plastic Roses.
Melville. Rosary Beads.
Meredith. It is the season of the sweet wild rose.
Wild Rose, The.
Young Usurper, The.
Merton. Rilke's Epitaph.
Neruda. Herbalist's Rose, The.
Oliver. Roses.
Paley. Bee! / drowning in, A.
Patchen. As Frothing Wounds of Roses.
Roses of Life, The.
Who Walks There?
Piercy. You lay in bed depressed, passive as butter.
Raine. Dream of Roses, A.
Petal of white rose.
Rose.
Rossetti. Brandons Both.
Floral Teaching.
Hope is like a harebell trembling from its birth.
I have but one rose in the world.
Lily has a smooth stalk, / Will never hurt your hand, The.
Lily has an air, / And the snowdrop a grace, The.
Maiden May.

October Garden, An.
Queen Rose.
Rose Plant in Jericho, A.
Rose that blushes rosy red, The.
Rose, The ("Gentle, gentle").
Rose, The ("O Rose").
Rose with such a bonny blush, The.
Solitary Rose, The.
Summer Is Ended.
Summer Wish, A.
Where shall I find a white rose blowing?
Rukeyser. Among Grass.
Fighting for Roses.
Sandburg. Dust.
Great Hunt, The.
Little Word, Little White Bird.
Poems Done on a Late Night Car.
Public Letter to Emily Dickinson.
Red and White.
Rose Bawn.
Throw Roses.
Whirls.
Sarton. Lion and the Rose, The.
Schuyler. Horse-Chestnut Trees and Roses.
Princess Di.
Rose of Marion, The.
Shelton. Harry Orchard.
Smith, Charlotte. To a Green-Chafer, on a
White Rose.
Smith, Stevie. Broken Heart, The.
Saint Anthony and the Rose of Life.
Stevens. Bouquet of Roses in Sunlight.
Sutter. Driftrose.
First Hard Frost, The.
Tennyson. Roses on the Terrace, The.
Tomlinson. Fireflies.
Rose-hips.
Wakoski. Light.
On the Subject of Roses.
Poetry, the Unpredictable.
Roses Were Talking, The.
Warren. Two Poems about Suddenly and a
Rose.
Whittier. Winter Roses.
Wilbur. Beautiful Changes, The.
Williams, William Carlos. Act, The.
Crimson Cyclamen, The.
Poem: "Rose fades, The."
Rose, The ("Rose is obsolete, The").
Rose, The ("Stillness of the Rose, The").
Rosebush in an Unlikely Garden, A.
To Flossie.
Wordsworth. Waterfall and the Eglantine, The.
Wright, James. Rosebushes.
Yeats. Lover Tells of the Rose in His Heart,
The.
Secret Rose, The.
To the Rose upon the Rood of Time.
Zukofsky. Roses.
Starglow.

Rousseau, Henri
Plath. Yadwigha, on a Red Couch, among
Lilies.

Rousseau, Jean Jacques
Blake. Mock On, Mock On, Voltaire,
Rousseau.
Carruth. As Rousseau was another, singing.
I am a fanatic lover of liberty, considering it.
Davie. Rousseau in His Day.
Whittier. Chapel of the Hermits, The.

Rowing and Rowers
Bly. After Drinking All Night with a Friend,
We Go Out in a Boat at Dawn to See Who
Can Write the Best Poem.
Coleridge. Water Ballad.
Eberhart. Loon Call, A.
Kipling. Akbar's Bridge.
Galley-Slave, the.
Lowell. Mills of the Kavanaughs, The.
Sexton. Rowing.
Rowing Endeth, The.
Smith, Stevie. River Deben, The.
Tomlinson. Rower.
Wright, James. On Minding One's Own
Business.

See also **Crew and Crew Racing.**
Royalty
Angelou. Let's Majeste.
Auden. Bank Holiday.
Beatles. Cry Baby Cry.
Her Majesty.
Berryman. Once when they found me, some
refrain "*Quoi faire?*."
Browning, Elizabeth Barrett. August Voice,
An.
Browning, Robert. Cristina.
Burns. Birth-Day Ode. December 31st 1787,
A.
Lines on Stirling.
O'er the Water to Charlie.
Scots Ballad.
Carew. Coelum Britannicum.
For a Picture Where a Queen Laments over
the Tomb of a Slain Knight.
Fourth Song, The.
Third Song, The.
De la Mare. Maerchen.
Dickey, William. Stella Dallas.
Dickinson. One dignity delays for all.
Dryden. All human[e] things are subject to
decay.
Frost. How Hard It Is to Keep from Being
King When It's in You and in the Situation.
Graves. Coronation Murder, The.
Gunn. Julian the Apostate.
Herrick. Dialogue Betwixt Himselfe and
Mistresse Eliza: Wheeler, Under the Name of
Amarillis, A.
Princes and Favourites.
Ultimus Heroum: or, To the Most Learned,
and to the Right Honourable, Henry,
Marquesse of Dorchester.
Hewitt. Colmcille.
"Lass of Richmond Hill", or The Royal
Garden Party, The.
Hopkins. Queen's Crowning, The.
Keats. Cap and Bells; or, The Jealousies, The.
Otho the Great.
Liddy. Kerouac's Ronsard Dance.
River Video, The.
Meredith. 'Tis I have seen the coming man.
Prince. Moult sont Prud'hommes les
Templiers.
Rossetti. I am a King, / Or an Emperor rather.
If I Were a Queen.
Royal Princess, A.
Succession of Kings, The.
Scott. Song of Albert Graeme.
Silverstein. Farmer and the Queen, The.
Smith, Stevie. Lord Barrenstock.
Spenser. Prosopopoia: or Mother Hubberds
Tale.
Stevenson. To Kalakaua.
Thomson. To His Royal Highness the Prince
of Wales.
Updike. Visions of Mackenzie King, The.
Wordsworth. Calais, August, 1802.
Wroth. Pamphilia to Amphilanthus.
Yeats. Fallen Majesty.

See also **Kings; Princes and Princesses; Queens.**
Rubens, Peter Paul
Blake. I Rubens am a Statesman & a Saint.
Pretty Epigram for [Those] the Entertainment
of Those Who [Pay] Have Paid Great Sums
in the Venetian & Flemish Ooze, A.
Rafael Sublime Majestic Graceful Wise.
Swelld limbs with no outline that you can
descry.
To English Connoisseurs.

Rugs and Carpets
Merrill. Carpet Not Bought, A.
Silverstein. Helping.

Ruins
Berry. Supplanting, The.
Boyle. Stones of a Seventeenth Century
Village, The.
Brontë. Old Hall of Elbë, ruined, lonely now.
Browning, Robert. Love among the Ruins.
Burns. Lines on Stirling.
Byron. Newstead Abbey.
Carruth. Rimrock, Where It Is.
Ciardi. Naples.

Coleridge. On a Ruined House in a Romantic
Country.
Cummings. Earth like a tipsy.
Ponder,darling,these busted statues.
De la Mare. Corner Stone, The.
Not Only.
Dove. Ants of Argos, The.
Nestor's Bathtub.
Sightseeing.
Eberhart. Dry Rot, The.
Emerson. For fifteen winter days.
I will be drunk and down with wine.
Fletcher. Cliff-dwelling.
Hall. Traffic.
Hugo. Carloway Broch.
Chysauster.
Clachard.
Death of the Kapowsin Tavern.
Fort Casey, without Guns.
Paestum.
Standing Stones of Callanish, The.
Kinnell. Ruins under the Stars.
Kipling. City of Brass, The.
Lowry. Sonnet: "This ruin now, where
moonlight walks alone."
McGrath. Need for Stoicism in the Stoa of
Attalus, The.
MacLeish. Sheep in the Ruins, The.
Melville. Off Cape Colona.
Ravaged Villa, The.
Merton. Dry Places.
In the Ruins of New York.
Nemerov. Guide to the Ruins.
Quarry, The.
Oppen. Mayan Ground, The.
There are things / We live among "and to see
them."
Pope. Epistle V, to Mr. Addison.
Rich. Villa Adriana.
Robinson. House on the Hill, The.
Rossetti. Ruin.
St. John. Black Poppy (At the Temple).
Shelley. Fragment: The Vine-Shroud.
Lines Written During the Castlereagh
Administration.
Ozymandias [of Egypt].
Smith, Charlotte. Descriptive Ode, Supposed
to Have Been Written under the Ruins of
Rufus's Castle, A.
On Passing Over a Dreary Tract of Country,
and Near the Ruins of a Deserted Chapel,
During a Tempest.
Saint Monica.
Written at Penshurst, in Autumn 1788.
Tomlinson. Idrigill.
Ruin, The.
Walcott. Ruins of a Great House.
Whittier. Homestead, The.
Wilbur. For the New Railway Station in
Rome.
Williams, William Carlos. Hymn Among the
Ruins.
Wordsworth. At Furness Abbey ("Here, where,
of havoc tired and rash undoing").
At Furness Abbey ("Well have yon Railway
Labourers to THIS ground").
Brownie, The.
Brownie's Cell, The.
Church of San Salvador Seen from the Lake
of Lugano.
Composed among the Ruins of a Castle in
North Wales.
Earl of Breadalbane's Ruined Mansion, and
Family Burial-Place, near Killin, The.
Fort Fuentes.
Massy Ways Carried across These Heights,
The.
Pillar of Trajan, The.
Yarrow Visited [September, 1814].
Zukofsky. 4 Other Countries.

Rumor
Burns. Verses: "I am a keeper of the law."
Byron. What News, What News? Queen
Orraca.
Chaucer. Maniple's Tale, The.
Clark. Love (after La Rochefoucauld).
Creeley. Photo.

Emerson. South Wind.
Herrick. Lips Tongueless[e].
Suspition upon His Over-much Familiarity with a Gentlewoman, The.
Jeffers. Old Wolf My Father, The.
Kipling. Ballad of the King's Jest, The.
Runners, The.
Kooser. Skeleton in the Closet, The.
Tomlinson. Rumour.
Wright, Charles. Virginia Reel.
See also **Fame; Gossip and Gossips; Reputation.**

Running and Runners
Davie. Pacer in the Fresco. John the Baptist, The.
Dickey, James. Sprinter at Forty, The.
Eberhart. Track.
Galvin. Running.
Gildner. Runner, The.
Herrick. Upon Patrick a Footman.
Hoffman. Finish, The.
Jogger.
Runner.
Housman. To an Athlete Dying Young.
Knott. Shorts / Excerpts ("Searching it goes").
Lowry. Welcome Home Oh Sweetest Harteebeeste with Quadruple Devotion from All the Little Animals.
McAuley. Running in Snow.
Ten-Mile Run.
Miller. Down the Lanes and Paths (For Stack).
Nash. Birthday on the Beach.
Piercy. Morning Athletes.
Robinson. Mighty Runner, A.
Stafford. Run before Dawn.
Wakoski. Red Runner.
Warren. Paradox.
Whitman. Runner, The.
Wilbur. Running.
Williams, Charles Kenneth. Or.
Williams, Miller. Running into Things.

Russell, Lucy, Countess of Bedford
Jonson. Author ad Librum.
On Lucy Countess[e] of Bedford.
To Lucy, Countess[e] of Bedford, with Mr. Donnes Satire's [or Satyres].

Russia
Beatles. Back in the USSR.
Bly. Aban Kavost and Ivar Oakeson.
Carruth. In Russia.
Cooper. Poetry As Continuity.
Creeley. She Went to Stay.
Edmunds. White Nights, 1938.
Ferlinghetti. Moscow in the Wilderness, Segovia in the Snow.
Hewitt. Chant for the Five-Year Plan.
Jarrell. Love for One Orange, The.
Jeffers. Teheran.
Larkin. When the Russian Tanks Roll Westward.
Lawrence. Now It's Happened.
Meredith. Crisis, The.
Three Eagles and the Sleepy Lion, The.
Moore. Combat Cultural.
O'Hara. On Looking at La Grande Jatte, the Czar Wept Anew.
Paley. Song Stanzas of Private Luck.
Rolfe. Poem for May First.
Three Who Died.
Rukeyser. Willkie: Words from Russia.
Stevens. Dish of Peaches in Russia, A.
Updike. Poem for a Far Land.
Postcards from Soviet Cities.
Williams, William Carlos. Russia.
Wordsworth. French Army in Russia 1812–1813, The.
On the Same Occasion.
Russian Fugitive, The.

Russian Revolution
Cummings. Red Front, The.
Hewitt. Chant for the Five-Year Plan.
Kipling. Russia to the Pacifists.
Tomlinson. At Trotsky's House.
Dream, A.

Russians, The
Berryman. Communist.
Byron. Fragment of an Epistle to Thomas Moore.

Davie. Hearing Russian Spoken.
Rolfe. Cheliuskin.
Rukeyser. What do you know of America? I asked a little Russian schoolgirl.
Williams, William Carlos. Foreign.
When Fresh, It Was Sweet.

Ruth (Bible)
Carruth. Tanck's Song About Fear of Falling.

Ruth, George Herman ("Babe")
Bukowski. End, The.

Rydal Water, England
Wordsworth. By the Side of Rydal Mere.

Ryder, Albert Pinkham
Haines. Ryder.
Hartley. Albert Ryder—Moonlightist.
Rukeyser. Ryder.

S

Sabbath
Auden. Sabbath, The.
Browning, Elizabeth Barrett. Sabbath Morning at Sea, A.
Coleridge. Reproof and Reply, The.
Dickinson. Some keep the Sabbath going to Church.
Herbert. Sunday.
Herrick. Sabbaths.
MacNeice. Sunday in the Park.
Sunday Morning.
Smith, Patti. Grant.
Stevenson. Lowden Sabbath Morn, A.
Walcott. Sabbaths, W.I.
See also **Sunday.**

Sacco-Vanzetti Case
Cullen. Not Sacco and Vanzetti.
Lewis. Sacco Writes to His Son.
Millay. As men have loved their lovers in times past.
Justice Denied in Massachusetts.
Where can the heart be hidden in the ground.

Sacraments. see Baptism; Eucharist; Extreme Unction; Marriage.

Sacrifices
Browning, Elizabeth Barrett. Sonnet: "If I leave all for thee, wilt thou exchange."
Bukowski. Minor Impulse to Complain, A.
Byron. Jephtha's Daughter.
Carew. Cruel Mistress, A.
Carroll, Jim. My body has been perforated.
Carruth. No Supervening Thought of Grace.
Ciardi. Lamb, The.
Clark. Angel's Choice.
Cohen. Came So Far for Beauty.
Prayer for Messiah.
Coleridge. To Nature.
Cowper. Gratitude and Love to God.
Perfect Sacrifice, The.
Self-Diffidence.
Truth and Divine Love Rejected by the World.
Crane. Possessions.
Dunn. Fable of the Water Merchants.
"Dylan." What Can I Do for You?
Emerson. And when I am entombed in my place.
Beauty.
Love / Asks nought his brother cannot give.
They strew in the path of kings and czars.
To Rhea.
Everson. Passion Week.
Fletcher. Crucifixion, The.
Ginsberg. Voice of Rock, The.
Glück. Late Snow.
Winter Morning.
Hardy. Aristodemus the Messenian.
Heaney. Tollund Man, The.
Hemingway. Kipling.
Herbert. Obedience.
Herrick. Ass[e], The.
Cheerfulnesse in Charitie: or, The Sweet Sacrifice.
Good Friday: Rex Tragicus or, Christ Going to His Cross[e].
Hymne to Love, An.
Lip Labour.

Perfume, The.
Sacrifice, by Way of Discourse betwixt Himselfe and Julia, The.
Scar[e]-Fire, The.
Smell of the Sacrifice, The.
Steam in Sacrifice.
Sweetnesse in Sacrifice.
To God, His Good Will.
Vow to Mars, A.
Vow to Minerva, A.
Hewitt. Burnt Post, The.
Housman. If it chance your eye offend you.
Hughes, Ted. Contender, The.
God, A.
Knight, The.
Jeffers. I have been warned. It is more than thirty years since I wrote.
Joseph. Muse.
Kipling. Convoy Escort.
Heritage, The.
Sacrifice of Er-Heb, The.
They killed a Child to please the Gods.
Knott. Feeding the Sun.
Lawrence. Old Idea of Sacrifice, The.
Self-Sacrifice ("Self-sacrifice, after all").
Self-Sacrifice ("Self-sacrifice is").
Shedding of Blood.
Lewis. Parable.
Lindsay. Doll's "Arabian Nights," A.
Johnny Appleseed's Hymn to the Sun.
Where Is the Real Non-Resistant?
Lowry. Iphigenia in Aulis. Agamemnon Speaks:.
McAuley. Ritual.
McGrath. Offering.
MacLeish. Tenth Book, The.
Markson. We Love, But Cannot Live.
Melville. At the Cannon's Mouth.
Meredith. Angelic Love.
Antigone.
Henceforth of her the Gods are known.
Mother who gave birth to Jeanne, The.
Shipwreck of Idomeneus, The.
Merton. Ce Xochitl: The Sign of FLowers.
Seven Archaic Images.
Olson. Dura.
Owen. To Eros.
Piercy. Market Economy, The.
Psalms. Psalm 51: "Have mercy upon me, O God.."
Rich. Leaflets.
Rolfe. All Ghouls' Night.
Ballad of the Noble Intentions.
Poem: "Girl lashed to the stake, The."
Rossetti. Johnny.
Lord God of Hosts, most Holy and most High.
My God, wilt Thou accept, and will not we / Give aught to Thee?
Slain from the Foundation of the World.
Take Care Of Him.
Shelton. Farmer's Testimony, The.
Silverstein. Me-Stew.
Simic. Help Wanted.
Smart. Faith.
Sorrentino. Totem, The.
Stevens. Cy Est Pourtraicte, Madame Ste Ursule, et Les Unze Mille Vierges.
Stevenson. My love was warm; for that I crossed.
Tennyson. Charge of the Light Brigade, The.
Warren. Love and Knowledge.
Ransom.
You Never Knew Her Either, Though You Thought You Did.
Whittier. Two Loves, The.
Wyatt. Rue on me, Lord, for thy goodness and grace.

Sacrilege
Lindsay. City That Will Not Repent, The.
MacNeice. Although we say we disbelieve.
Psalms. Psalm 106: "Praise ye the Lord. O give thanks.."
Whittier. Official Piety.
Sabbath Scene, A.

Sade, Donatien Alphonse François, Marquis de
Carruth. Sonnet: "To have been Diogenes.
Why not? Or de Sade."

Graves. Encounter, The.
Holmes. Sade on Calvary.
Nash. Literary Scene, The.

Sadism and Sadists
Beatles. If I Fell.
Bukowski. Beast, The.
On the Failure of a Poet.
Regard Me.
Koch. To win the love of women one should
first discover.
Merton. Psalm 132: A Modern Monastic
Revision.

Sadness
Arnold. Isolation: To Marguerite.
Auden. Eyes look into the well.
Lady[,] Weeping at the Crossroads.
To a Child in Tears.
Berg. Roses.
Berryman. It was the sky all day I grew to
and saw.
Bogan. Didactic Piece.
Solitary Observation Brought Back from a
Sojourn in Hell.
Brontë. Had there been falsehood in my
breast.
Inspiring music's thrilling sound, The.
Old church tower and garden wall, The.
Bukowski. All the Casualties.
Melancholia.
Bunting. Faridun watched the road.
This I write, mix ink with tears.
Burns. Address to the Woodlark.
My Nannie's Awa'.
Scotch Song.
Campion. Can you, the Author of our joy, /
So soone depart?
"Carroll, Lewis." Canto VII: Sad
Souvenaunce.
Melancholetta.
Carruth. Cows at Night, The.
Cross My Heart and Hope to Die, It Was the
Very Same Song Exactly.
Catullus. Carmen 30: "Alfenus from Cremona
/ forsakes the friendship of friends."
Carmen 38: "Angst, / ennui & angst."
Creeley. Air: "The Love of a Woman."
Disappointment, The.
Illness, An.
Love ("Tracking through this").
Oh Mabel.
Passage, The.
Total Parts of a World, The.
Dickey, William. New Place, The.
Dickinson. How happy I was if I could forget.
I should not dare to be so sad.
Dobyns. Black Dog, Red Dog.
What You Have Come To Expect.
Dunn. Letter About Myself to You.
Loveliness.
Woman on Edgehill Road, The.
"Dylan." Sad-Eyed Lady of the Lowlands.
To Ramona.
Where Are You Tonight? (Journey through
Dark Heat).
You're a Big Girl Now.
Eberhart. Despair.
I turned where the sun came up and he held
my hand.
Emerson. I am alone. Sad is my solitude.
Everson. Rattlesnake August.
Frost. Hannibal.
Gallagher. Dim House, Bright Face.
Hardy. Christmastide.
Place on the Map, The.
Woman in the Rye, The.
Herbert. Storm, The.
Herrick. Christs Sadnesse.
Wounded Heart, The.
Hesketh. And Fall.
Clown.
Hewitt. Mist.
Season's Return.
Housman. In my own shire, if I was sad.
Hughes, Langston. Late Last Night.
Miss Blues'es Child.
Hugo. Art of Poetry, The.
Doing the House.

Jarrell. Three Bills.
Kipling. Roman Centurion's Song, The.
Knott. Brighton Rock by Graham Greene.
Two Vietnam Poems: (1966).
Larkin. Femmes Damnees.
Levine. Buying and Selling.
Midget, The.
Lewis. Chanson Triste.
Swallows are nesting in the hovels of Israel,
The.
Liddy. Dear Anima, Show These Words.
For Jimin in Manchuria II.
Holden, a Thought From Abroad.
To the Memory of Sylvia Plath: A Personal
Note.
Lowry. I've Said Goodbye to Shanghai.
Love of a Seagull.
Names of Mexican rivers I forgot, The.
Outward Bound.
When I am in the purgatory of the unread.
"MacDiarmid." Love-sick Lass, The.
MacNeice. And love hung still as crystal over
the bed.
Mahon. Dejection.
Matthews. Loyal.
Meredith. Ask, is Love divine.
Dark on the ridge of the cold salt wave.
Fair Bedfellow, The.
Millay. Anguish, The.
Ashes of Life.
Macdougal Street.
Spring and the Fall, The.
To a Young Girl.
To the Wife of a Sick Friend.
Nash. So Penseroso.
Nemerov. View from an Attic Window, The.
Owen. Happiness.
Pack. Leviathan.
Patchen. Great Sadnesses, The.
Two Ghosts Together.
Pope. Winter, the Fourth Pastoral, or Daphne.
Prince. Mortimer.
Sea View.
White sunlight and the dripping oars!
Rich. Mirror in Which Two Are Seen as One,
The.
Roethke. Dolor.
Elegy: "Should every creature be as I have
been."
Rossetti. At Home.
Corydon's Lament and Resolution.
Faithless Shepherdess, The.
Golden Silences.
Hear what the mournful linnets say.
I have but one rose in the world.
In resurrection is it awfuller.
Trees' Counselling, The.
Unforgotten.
Why did baby die, / Making Father sigh.
Zara.
Sandburg. And This Will Be All?
Swell People.
Schuyler. So Good.
Shapiro. Confession, The.
Shelley. Cancelled Passage.
Invocation to Misery.
On a Faded Violet.
Stanzas—April, 1814.
To Mary Shelley ("World is dreary, The / And
I'm weary").
To Mary, Who Died in This Opinion.
To William Shelley ("My lost William, thou
in whom").
Simic. Terms, The.
Smith, Charlotte. By the Same. To Solitude.
To a Nightingale.
To Hope.
Sorrentino. Toward the End of Winter.
Spenser. Being one day at my window all
alone.
Suckling. Invocation, The: "Ye juster Powers
of Love and Fate."
Wakoski. Cobra Lilies in the Supermarket.
Walker. S M.
Williams, Miller. Living on the Surface.
Williams, William Carlos. Sadness of the Sea,

The.
Twelve Line Poem.
Wordsworth. Sonnet on Seeing Miss Helen
Maria Williams Weep at a Tale of Distress.
Wright, James. American Wedding.
Breath of Air, A.
Dawn brings with it, The.
De Profundis.
Yau. Cascade.
Yeats. He Reproves the Curlew.
Young. Detroit 1958.
There Is a Sadness.
Zimmer. Lester Tells of the End of the
Summer.
Zukofsky. Alfenus, remember *kind intimacies*?
false? They elated us.
As to How Much.
H.T.
My last—Cornificius—your Catullus'.
Tam Cari Capitis.

Sailing and Sailors
Angelou. Martial Choreograph.
Auden. Fleet Visit.
Berryman. Conversation.
What was Ashore, then?... Cargoed with
Forget.
Bishop. Imaginary Iceberg, The.
Santarém.
Unbeliever, The.
Bogan. Putting to Sea.
Browning, Robert. Hervé Riel.
Burns. On the Seas and Far Away.
Byron. Farewell Petition to J.C.H., Esq.
Island, The.
Julian [A Fragment].
Lines to Mr Hodgson.
Oh How I Wish That an Embargo.
Stanzas: "Through cloudless skies, in silvery
sheen."
Campion. Come a shore, come, merrie mates.
"Carroll, Lewis." Acrostic: Maidens! if you
love the tale.
Double Acrostic: I sing a place wherein agree.
Hunting of the Snark, The.
Lady Muriel's Song.
Sailor's Wife, The.
Carruth. Terra.
Catullus. Carmen 4: "My bean-pod boat you
see here."
Carmen 63: "Plunging towards Phrygia over
violent water."
Clough. Come home, come home! and where
an home hath he.
Mari Magno II.
Qua Cursum Ventus.
Ye flags of Piccadilly, / Where I posted up
and down.
Cohen. Another Room.
Commentary—Another Room.
Unclean Start, The.
Coleridge. Catullian Hendecasyllables.
Rime of the Ancient Mariner, The.
Cooper. Meteors.
Crane. So Dream Thy Sails.
Traveller Born, A.
Cummings. So standing.our eyes filled with
the wind,and the.
Davie. Admiral to His Lady, The.
After the Calamitous Convoy (July 1942).
Commodore Barry.
Lady Cochrane.
Norfolk.
Trevenen.
De la Mare. Never More, Sailor.
Dickey, James. Expanses.
Tapestry and Sail.
Dickinson. Adrift! A little boat adrift!
Exultation is the going.
It tossed—and tossed.
On this wondrous sea.
Once more, my now bewildered Dove.
Sailor cannot see the North, The.
'Twas such a little little boat.
Where Ships of Purple—gently toss.
Whether my bark went down at sea.
Donne. Calm[e], The.
Hymn [or Hymne] to Christ, at the Author's

Last Going into Germany, A.
Storm[e], The.
Doolittle. In Our Town.
Look-out, The.
Sea Heroes.
Shrine, The.
Dunbar. Sailor's Song, A.
Eberhart. American Hakluyt.
Going Backward Going Forward.
Sailing to Buck's Harbor.
Sea Burial from the Cruiser *Reve*.
Voyage, The.
Waiting To Lean to the Master's Command.
Emerson. For fifteen winter days.
I love thy music, mellow bell.
I spread my gorgeous sail.
Northman.
What is it to sail.
Fletcher. Clipper-Ships.
Night of Stars.
Sailboats.
Snow at Sea.
Frost. Flower Boat, The.
Ginsberg. Dakar Doldrums.
Glück. Archipelago.
Graves. Furious Voyage, The.
Hardy. Sea Fight, The.
Hartley. Like ice his blood.
Heaney. North.
Hemingway. Rail ends do not meet, The.
Herrick. Ship-Wrack.
Hewitt. Braes O' Layde, The.
For Any Women Who Pass This House.
Hired Lad's Farewell, The.
Little Ships.
Minotaur.
To Piraeus.
Vida, Mykonos.
Volunteer, The.
Witch, The.
Hill. Guardians, The.
Housman. Land of Biscay, The.
Oh were he and I together.
R. L. S.
Hughes, Langston. Long Trip.
Port Town.
Seascape.
Young Sailor.
Hugo. Bay of Resolve.
Picnic in the Saracen Ruin, The.
Sailing Dalmatia.
Sailing from Naples.
Jarrell. O weary mariners, here shaded, fed.
Joseph. Exorcism.
Kipling. Anchor Song.
Ballad of Fisher's Boardinghouse, The.
Ballad of the "Bolivar", The.
Coastwise Lights, The.
Coiner, The.
Departure, A.
Exiles' Line, The.
First Chantey, The.
Frankie's Trade.
French Wars, The.
In the Matter of One Compass.
Last Chantey, The.
McAndrew's Hymn.
Merchantmen, The.
Mulholland's Contract.
Nurses, The.
Poseidon's Law.
Rhyme of the Three Sealers, The.
Sea-Wife, The.
Second Voyage, The.
Song of Diego Valdez, The.
Song of the Dead, The.
Song of the Red War-Boat.
Thorkild's Song.
Truthful Song, The.
Wet Litany, The.
When the cabin port-holes are dark and green.
When the Great Ark.
With Drake in the Tropics.
Koch. Poem: "Thing / To do / Is organize / The Sea, The."
Levertov. Leaving Forever.
Levine. Let Me Begin Again.

Lewis. And now we seek once more the burning breeze.
Exultantly he drives his screaming pinnace.
Run-In, The.
Song (On Seeing Dead Bodies Floating Off the Cape).
Southend at Dusk.
Troopship in the Tropics, A.
Lindsay. Song in July, A.
Lowry. And yet I am of England too; odi et amo.
Bosun's Song.
Cap and gown instead of a sweatrag, A.
Danish Sailor's Song.
Days Like Smitten Cymbals of Brass, The.
Epitaph: "Dear Scipio Sprague / sans plague sans blague."
Freighter 1940.
Fyrbøterer.
Glory of the Sea, The.
In Memoriam; Ingvald Bjorndal and His Comrade.
Jokes Amidships.
Joseph Cconrad.
Look Out! The Bloody Bosun.
Old Freighter in an Old Port.
On board the Matsue Maru.
Roar of the Sea and the Darkness, The.
Sailors, The.
Ship.
Ship stands drawn like a jewelled dagger, A.
Ship will sail again, the watches sing, The.
Stars have simple paradigms, The.
Stowaway, The.
Visiting the Wreck: An Able Seaman Explains.
Voyage of Kevin O'Riordine, The.
When I am in the purgatory of the unread.
"MacDiarmid." Wreck of the *Swan*, The.
McGrath. Excursion: Or: O Columbus!, The.
MacLeish. Bernál Díaz' Preface to his Book.
But men have known.
Lines for a Prologue.
Seafarer.
Second Book, The.
Ship's Log.
Yacht for Sale.
MacNeice. Passage Steamer.
Mahon. Hearing the thunder of the intransitive weirs
Marlowe. 2.11: Ad amicam navigantem.
Marvell. Bermudas.
Meinke. Dead Tree, The.
Night Watch on the Chesapeake.
Melville. Billy in the Darbies.
Commemorative of a Naval Victory.
Haglets, The.
In the Turret.
Jack Roy.
Since as in night's deck-watch ye show.
Tom Deadlight.
Meredith. Camelus Saltat: Continued.
Last Contention, The.
Olive Branch, The.
Periander.
Shipwreck of Idomeneus, The.
Merton. Drake in the Southern Sea.
Morgan. History.
Morrison. Ah, The Rule.
O'Hara. To the Harbormaster.
Oliver. Magellan.
Olson. Mast, The.
Morning News, The.
Rosy, It Was.
Shut in kept off.
Six Inch Chapter—in Verse, A.
Patchen. Plate of Steaming Fish, A.
Plath. Channel Crossing.
Pound. Canto 1: "And then went down to the ship."
Canto 2: "Hang it all, Robert Browning."
Seafarer, The.
Ralegh. Moist[e]ned Osyer [*or* osier] of the hoarie Willow, The.
Robinson. Lost Anchors.
Pasa Thalassa Thalassa.
Pilot, The.

Return of Morgan and Fingal, The.
Wise Brothers, The.
Rolfe. Dedication, A.
Rossetti. Ballad of Boding, A.
I have a little husband / And he is gone to sea.
O Sailor, Come Ashore.
Rukeyser. Suite for Lord Timothy Dexter.
Sandburg. All Day Long.
Baltic Fog Notes.
Deep Sea Wandering.
From the Shore.
Lief the Lucky.
Old Deep Sing-Song.
Sea Slant.
Waiting.
Way of the World, The.
Young Sea.
Schwartz. Late Autumn in Venice.
To Helen.
Scott. Voyage to Arran, The.
Sexton. Love Song for K. Owyne.
Silverstein. Homemade Boat.
Smith, Charlotte. Beachy Head.
To the Morning Star. Written Near the Sea.
Smith, Stevie. Die Lorelei.
Look!
Snyder. Engine Room, S.S. Sappa Creek, The.
Longitude 170° West, Latitude 35° North.
7.IV.64.
Twelve Hours Out of New York After Twenty-Five Days at Sea.
Stevenson. Christmas at Sea.
Far-Farers, The.
Farewell: "Farewell, and when forth."
Good Play, A.
I am like one that for long days had sate.
Lo! in thine honest eyes I read.
Man sails the deep a while.
My Bed Is a Boat.
My Ship and I.
Nor judge me light, tho' light at times I seem.
Since years ago for evermore.
Sing me a song of a lad that is gone.
Skerryvore.
Stormy evening closes now in vain, The.
To all that love the far and blue.
To My Father.
To N.V. de G.S.
Wind blew shrill and smart, The.
Yes, I remember, and still remember wailing.
Turco. Schooner, The.
Updike. Bath after Sailing.
Sails on All Saints' Day.
Walcott. Sea-Chantey, A.
Warren. Masts at Dawn.
Whitman. In Cabin'd Ships at Sea.
Old Age's Ship & Crafty Death's.
Old Salt Kossabone.
Sail Out for Good, Eidólon Yacht!
Ship Ahoy!
Ship Starting, The.
Song for All Seas, All Ships.
Twenty Years.
Whittier. Bay of Seven Islands, The.
Branded Hand, The.
Slave-Ships, The.
Wilbur. Regatta, The.
Superiorities.
Williams, William Carlos. Jean Sans Terre at the Final Port.
Seafarer.
Yachts, The.
Wordsworth. As when, upon the smooth pacific deep.
By a Retired Mariner (A Friend of the Author).
Composed by the Sea-Shore.
Sailor's Mother, The.
There never breathed a man who, when his life.
Wyatt. My galley [*or* galy] charged with forgetfulness.
Yeats. Colonel Martin.
Shadowy Waters, The.
Zukofsky. Facile as can be the boat you see, my guests, says.

Spurred altering wake toss Attis his craft racing till marled in the.

St. Agnes' Eve
Keats. Eve of St. Agnes, The.
Merton. Prelude: For the Feast of St. Agnes, A.

St. Cecilia's Day
Swift. Dean to Himself on St. Cecilia's Day, The.

Saint Lawrence (river), Canada
Carruth. Plains of snow. The buntings whirl like rung.
Cohen. Light as the Breeze.

St. Louis, Missouri
Lorde. St. Louis Out of Time.

St. Mark's Eve
Keats. Eve of St. Mark, The.

St. Patrick's Day
Nash. It's a Grand Parade It Will Be, Modern Design.

St. Paul's Cathedral
Hardy. In St. Paul's a While Ago.
MacNeice. Homage to Wren.
Wordsworth. St Paul's.

Saint Peter's Church, Rome
Clough. From far and near / He drew the scattered ciphers.
Wordsworth. Near Rome, in Sight of St Peter's.

Saint Petersburg [*formerly* Leningrad], Russia
Mahon. Night Drive.
Updike. Leningrad.

St. Stephen's Day
Hewitt. St Stephen's Day.

St. Valentine's Day. *see* **Valentine's Day.**

Saints
Auden. You're a long way off becoming a saint.
Berry. Springs, The.
Betjeman. Saint Cadoc.
Brontë. Heaven's glory shone where he was laid.
Chaucer. Second Nun's Prologue, The.
Second Nun's Tale, The.
Cohen. What Is a Saint.
Cummings. Candles and / Here Comes a glass box.
Davie. Terce.
Dickinson. No matter where the Saints abide.
Dove. Catherine of Alexandria.
Ford. Through him (The Diamond).
Graves. St Antony of Padua.
Gunn. Here Come the Saints.
Hartley. Miracle Cary, and His Twelve Loaves—Twelve Fishes.
Herbert. To All Angels and Saints.
Herrick. Teares: ("Teares of Saints more sweet by farre, The").
Temptations ("Those Saints, which God loves best").
To Groves.
To Julia ("Saints-bell calls; and *Julia*, I must read, The").
Upon a Maide ("Hence a blessed soule is fled").
Hewitt. Two Irish Saints.
Hill. In Piam Memoriam.
Hopkins. For a Picture of Saint Dorothea.
In Honour of St. Alphonsus Rodriguez.
Lines for a Picture of St. Dorothea.
On St. Winefred.
St. Dorothea.
St. Thecla.
Jeffers. Delusion of Saints.
Lawrence. St John.
St Luke.
St Mark.
St Matthew.
Liddy. To the Memory of Sylvia Plath: A Personal Note.
MacLeish. What Riddle Asked the Sphinx.
MacNeice. Stylite.
Merton. Burial Place of Ibn Abbad, The.
Clairvaux.
Invocation to St. Lucy, An.
Listen, Saints.

Macarius and the Pony.
Prayer to Saint Anatole.
Rievaulx: St. Ailred.
St. Agnes: A Responsory.
St. Alberic.
Two Desert Fathers.
Nemerov. Situation Does Not Change, The.
Rich. Reliquary.
Rolfe. Munich.
Rossetti. Alas, alas! for the self-destroyed / Vanish as images from a glass.
All Flesh Is Grass.
All Saints ("As grains of sand").
All Saints ("They are flocking from the East").
All Saints ("They have brought gold").
All Saints: Martyrs.
As dying, and behold we live!
Before the Throne, and Before the Lamb.
Cast down but not destroyed, chastened not slain.
Dear Angels and dear disembodied Saints.
Embertide.
Every One That Is Perfect Shall Be as His Master.
Eye Hath Not Seen.
General Assembly and Church of the Firstborn, The.
Hark! the Alleluias of the great salvation.
I Gave a Sweet Smell.
Jerusalem of fire / And gold and pearl and gem.
Joy of Saints, like incense turned to fire, The.
Let Them Rejoice in Their Beds.
Lift up thine eyes to seek the invisible.
Our life is long. Not so, wise Angels say.
St. Barnabas.
St. Bartholomew.
St. Elizabeth of Hungary.
St. Mark.
So Great a Cloud of Witnesses.
Thy Servant Will Go and Fight with This Philistine.
To Every Seed His Own Body.
Vigil of all Saints.
Vigil of St. Bartholomew.
Vigil of the Annunciation.
What are these lovely ones, yea, what are these?
What is this above thy head, / O Man?
Who would wish back the Saints upon our rough.
St. John. Francesco and Clare.
Scott. Saint of Holy Island, The.
Sexton. Saints Come Marching In, The.
Smart. All Saints.
Elegance.
St. Barnabas.
St. Bartholomew.
St. James.
St. John the Evangelist.
St. Luke.
St. Mark.
St. Matthew.
St. Matthias.
Tennyson. St. Simeon Stylites.
Thomas. Saint About to Fall, A.
Tomlinson. Santa Maria delle Nevi.
Weeper in Jalisco.
Walker. Abduction of Saints, The.
Whittier. Legend of St. Mark, The.
Two Elizabeths, The.
Wordsworth. St Catherine of Ledbury.

Salads
Cowper. Salad, The.

Salem, Massachusetts
Eberhart. Salem.
Longfellow. Prologue: "Delusions of the days that once have been."

Sales Clerks. *see* **Clerks.**

Salesmen
Berry. By the excellence of his work the workman is a neighbor. By.
Cummings. Salesman is an it that stinks excuse, A.
Hesketh. Betterwear Man, The.
Kooser. Salesman, The.
Levine. Buying and Selling.

Sandburg. Fish Crier.
Smith, Stevie. In Canaan's Happy Land.

Salisbury, England
Hardy. In a Cathedral City.

Salmon
"Carroll, Lewis." Mock Turtle's Song, The: "Beneath the waters of the sea."
Hughes, Ted. October Salmon, An.
Salmon Eggs.
That Morning.
Liddy. Enchanter of Yellow Gold to the Old Friend, The.
Lowry. Salmon Drowns Eagle.
Muldoon. Chinook.

Salt
Fisher. Only Image, The.
Gardner. Salt.
Lawrence. Boundary Stone, The.
Salt.
Spilling the Salt.
Levine. Nitrate.

Salt Lake City, Utah
Ginsberg. Chicago to Salt Lake by Air.

Salvation
Bradstreet. As spring the winter doth succeed.
As weary pilgrim, now at rest.
From Another Sore Fit.
My soul, rejoice thou in thy God.
Occasional Meditations: "By night, when others soundly slept."
What God is like to him I serve?
Brooks. Truth.
Browning, Elizabeth Barrett. Sonnet: "My own Beloved, who hast lifted me."
Chaucer. Parson's Tale, The.
Cooper. Now it's our turn. Three a.m.
Crane. Recitative.
Crashaw. Matthew 8; I Am Not Worthy that Thou Should'st Come Under my Roofe.
Matthew 16:25; Whosoever Shall Loose His Life.
Matthew 22; Neither Durst Any Man from that Day Aske Him Any More Questions.
Cullen. Shroud of Color, The.
Davie. Except the Lord Build the House.
Dickinson. Province of the Saved, The.
Summer day on which you came, The.
Donne. At the round earth's imagined corners, blow.
Batter my heart, three-personed [*or* three person'd] God; for you.
Deliver us for thy descent.
Father, part of his double interest.
Son[ne] of God hear[e] us, and since thou.
This is my play's [*or* playes] last scene, here heavens appoint.
Wilt thou love God, as he thee? [*or* thee!] then digest.
"Dylan." Covenant Woman.
Every Grain of Sand.
I Shall Be Released.
Saved.
Saving Grace.
What Can I Do for You?
When He Returns.
Eberhart. Lord, stabilise me. My legs.
Suite in Prison.
Eliot. Hippopotamus, The.
Emerson. God The Lord save Massachusetts.
Everson. Vision of Felicity, The.
Graves. Song: Lift-Boy.
Heaney. On the Road.
Herbert. Bunch of Grapes, The.
Business.
Call, The.
Clasping of Hands.
Conscience.
Dialogue, A.
Divinity.
Ephesians 4:30. Grieve not the Holy Spirit, etc.
Giddiness.
Holdfast, The.
Holy Baptism (1).
Love Unknown.
Man's Medley.
Peace.

Perseverance.
Water-Course, The.
Herrick. All Things Run Well for the
  Righteous.
Charroll Presented to Dr. Williams Bp. of
  Lincolne as a Newyears Guift, A.
Cloaths for Continuance.
Purgatory.
To Christ.
To His Saviour.
Hewitt. Cobweb.
Epitaph for a Conscript, 1940.
Heart of Joy, The.
Hopkins. Myself unholy, from myself unholy.
Jarrell. Song: Not There.
Jonson. Hymn[e] on the Nativity [or Nativitie]
  of My Saviour, A.
Joseph. Washing is jerked from shade into the
  sun, The.
Kipling. Mulholland's Contract.
Lawrence. Huitzilopochtli Gives the Black
  Blade of Death.
Nothing to Save.
Salvation.
Levine. Hear Me.
Lewis. Crucifixion, The.
Liddy. To the Memory of Sylvia Plath: A
  Personal Note.
Lindsay. Daniel.
Galahad, Knight Who Perished.
General William Booth Enters into Heaven.
Look You, I'll Go Pray.
Merciful Hand, The.
Rhymer's Reply: Incense and Splendor, The.
Speak Now for Peace.
Lowry. Ladder, The.
Merton. Biography, The.
Peril, The.
Prose in Advent Time.
Soldiers of Peace.
Milton. Thou Shepherd that dost Israel keep.
Morrison. Now Listen to This.
Nemerov. Morality, A.
Oliver. In Blackwater Woods.
Piercy. Let Us Gather at the River.
Psalms. Psalm 20: "Lord hear thee in the day
  of trouble, The."
Psalm 21: "King shall rejoice in thy strength,
  O Lord, The."
Psalm 37: "Fret not thyself because of
  evildoers."
Psalm 80: "Give ear, O Shepherd of Israel."
Ralegh. Authours Epitaph, Made by Himself,
  The.
Ransom. Rose, The.
Rossetti. Chill blank world. Yet over the
  utmost sea, A.
Christian and Jew. A Dialogue.
I lift mine eyes to see: earth vanisheth.
I, Lord, Thy foolish sinner low and small.
Isidora.
Lord, hast Thou so loved us, and will not we.
Lord, I am here.—But, child, I look for thee.
Lord Jesu, Thou art sweetness to my soul.
Lord, Save Us, We Perish.
None Other Lamb None Other Name.
O foolish Soul! to make thy count / For
  languid falls and much forgiven.
O mine enemy / Rejoice not over me!
Peace I Leave with You.
Thy Friend and Thy Father's Friend Forget
  Not.
Smith, Stevie. Ah, Will the Saviour?
Breughel.
Conviction (i).
Man I Am, A.
Tate. Cross, The.
Whittier. Crucifixion, The.
Cry of a Lost Soul, The.
Over-Heart, The.
Williams, Charles Kenneth. Yours.
Wordsworth. Composed During a Storm.
Wyatt. Although thou see th'outrageous climb
  aloft.

Samarkand
Emerson. Take my heart in thy hand, O
  beautiful boy of Schiraz!

Samson
Cohen. Transmission, The.
Cooper. Gaza.
Crashaw. Samson to His De[or a]lilah.
Emerson. Samson stark at Dagon's knee.
Graves. Angry Samson.
Lindsay. How Samson Bore Away the Gates
  of Gaza.
Longfellow. Warning, The.
Lowry. And Samson said if yo' shave ma
  hair.
Meredith. Dalila.
Milton. Blindness of Samson, The.
But what is strength without a double share.
Come, come, no time for lamentation now.
Oh [or O] how comely it is and how reviving.
Ways of God to Men, The.
Morgan. Samson.
Tomlinson. Bone.

San Francisco, California
Ferlinghetti. Report on a Happening in
  Washington Square San Francisco, A.
They were putting up the statue.
Ginsberg. Continuation of a Long Poem of
  These States.
Gunn. Hitching into Frisco.
Invitation, An.
San Francisco Streets.
Sand Man, The.
Hugo. At Cronkhite.
Lindsay. City That Will Not Repent, The.
St. Francis of San Francisco.
Olson. Who slays the Spanish sun.
Oppen. Niece.
Some San Francisco Poems.
Rukeyser. Bunk Johnson Blowing.
Sandburg. Portrait of a Child Settling Down
  for an Afternoon Nap.
Schuyler. Blossoming Oakwood.
Shadowy Room.
Snyder. Night Herons.
North Beach Alba.
Updike. Scenic.
Young. Berkeley Pome.
Zukofsky. Head Lines.

Sanctuaries
Dobyns. Place in Maine, A.
Eberhart. Bower, The.
Grove, The.
Jong. This Element.
Lowry. My hate is as a wind that buffets me.
Sandburg. Palladiums.
Wordsworth. By the Side of Rydal Mere.

"Sand, George" (Amandine Aurore Lucie
  Dupin, Baronne Dudevant)
Browning, Elizabeth Barrett. To George Sand:
  A Desire.
To George Sand: A Recognition.
Waldman. George Sand.

Sand
Creeley. All That Is Lovely in Men.
De la Mare. Mermaids, The.
Eberhart. Ceremony By the Sea, A.
Emerson. Asmodaean feat be mine, The.
Chladni strewed on glass the sand.
Gunn. Sand Man, The.
Kinnell. Feast, The.
Rossetti. I dug and dug amongst the snow.
Sandburg. Flux.
Schwartz. Song: "Under the yellow sea."
Spenser. One day I wrote her name upon the
  strand.
Stevenson. At the Seaside [or Sea-Side].
Thomas. We Lying by Seasand.
Tomlinson. Writing on Sand.

Sandpipers
Bishop. Sandpiper.
Carruth. Summer's Early End at Hudson's
  Bay.
Nemerov. Sandpipers.
Sandburg. Sand Scribblings.
Sandpipers.
Stuart. Birds, The.

Sanitary Engineering and Sanitary Engineers.
  see Sewers; Garbage and Garbage Men.

Santa Barbara, California
Rexroth. Song at the Winepresses, A.

Santa Claus
Eberhart. Santa Claus in Oaxaca.
Moore. Saint Nicholas.
Nemerov. Santa Claus.
Sexton. Santa.
Silverstein. Santa and the Reindeer.

Santa Fe Trail
Sandburg. Slabs of the Sunburnt West.

Santayana, George
Lowell. For George Santayana.
Stevens. To an Old Philosopher in Rome.

Sappho
Herrick. Apron of Flowers, The.
To Sapho ("Sapho, I will chuse to go").
Upon Sapho.
Millay. Of what importance, O my lovely
  girls, my dancers, O my lovely boys.
Sappho Crosses the Dark River into Hades.
Olson. For Sappho, Back.
Pope. Sappho to Phaon.
Robinson. Doricha.
Sexton. Red Dance, The.
Swinburne. Sapphics.
Williams, William Carlos. Sappho, Be
  Comforted.
To a Lovely Old Bitch.
Wordsworth. Alcaeus to Sappho.
Wright, James. Erinna to Sappho.
Sappho.

Sarah (Bible)
Nemerov. Nicodemus.
Van Duyn. Cities of the Plain, The.

Sarajevo, Yugoslavia
Dobyns. Somewhere It Still Moves.
Hugo. Yards of Sarajevo, The.
Nemerov. Sarajevo.
Young. Moon Over Matter.
Sarajevo Moon.
Sarajevo Moonlight.

Sarto, Andrea del
Browning, Robert. Andrea del Sarto.

Satan
Auden. Et in Arcadia Ego.
Berryman. Whether There Is Sorrow in the
  Demons.
Bishop. Rainbow.
Blake. I rose up at the dawn of day.
Memorable Fancy, A ("As I was walking
  among the fires of hell").
Memorable Fancy, A ("Once I saw a Devil in
  a flame of fire").
Voice of the Devil, The.
Browning, Robert. Doctor———.
Ponte dell' Angelo, Venice.
Burns. Address to the Deil.
Epigram on Capt. Francis Grose, the
  Celebrated Antiquary.
On J-hn M-r-ne, Laird of L-gg-n.
Poem on Life.
To a Painter.
Byron. Devil's Drive, The.
On Sam Rogers.
Coleridge. Devil's Thoughts, The.
Crashaw. Luke 11; Upon the Dumbe Devill
  Cast Out, and the Slanderous Jewes Put to
  Silence.
Cullen. Dictum.
For a Mouthy Woman.
Cummings. Devil crept in eden wood.
Davie. Ironist, The.
Dickinson. Devil, had we fidelity, The.
We read in a tremendous Book.
Donne. As due by many titles I resign[e].
"Dylan." Man Gave Names to All the
  Animals.
Man of Peace.
Trouble in Mind.
Eberhart. Assassin, The.
Emerson. For Lucifer, that old athlete.
Fletcher. As Adam, clutching earth, lay
  stunned within the darkness.
End of Job, The.
In the still evening of the sixth long day.
New Beatitudes, The.
Now it was the ninth morning and the unseen
  God.

Prayer of the Antichrist, The.
Prelude: "Before the beginning of things."
Herrick. Another ("In the morning when ye rise").
Satan.
To Julia ("Help me, Julia, for to pray").
Upon Pink an Ill-Fac'd Painter.
Hill. Bibliographers, The.
Hopkins. Dark-out Lucifer detesting this, The.
Kipling. Conundrum of the Workshops, The.
Lawrence. Lucifer.
Old Archangels.
Root of Our Evil, The.
When Satan Fell.
Liddy. Litany of Satan, The.
Lindsay. Simon Legree—A Negro Sermon.
Lovelace. Triumphs of Philamore and Amoret, The.
Lowell. At the Altar.
Lowry. Devil is a gentleman, The.
This business of evil / Like brokers the weevil.
Who made this suicide pact of love?
Matthews. It Don't Mean a Thing if it Ain't Got That Swing.
Meredith. Lucifer in Starlight.
Milton. As when of old some orator renowed.
Immortal Hate.
Meanwhile [or Mean while] the Adversary of God and Man.
Satan and His Host.
Satan Beholds Adam and Eve in Eden.
Satan ("He ceased; and Satan stayed not to reply").
Satan's Journey.
Satan's Soliloquy.
Nemerov. Lucifer.
Poem of Margery Kempe, A.
Olson. He is the Devil. He whores Nature.
Love is a word in his Mouth. He has no Mouth.
Plath. Sonnet to Satan.
Rich. Lucifer in the Train.
Rossetti. O Lucifer, Son of the Morning!
Three Enemies, The.
Shapiro. Tree of Guilt, The.
Shelley. Devil's Walk, The.
Fragment: Satan Broken Loose.
Smith, Stevie. Fallen, Fallen.
God and the Devil.
I Was So Full.
Thomas. Incarnate Devil.
Whitman. Punishment of Pride, The.

Satie, Erik
Merrill. Angel.

Satire and Satirists
Campion. Verba volant; verum: quid enim velocius illis?
De la Mare. Satire, The.
Graves. Research and Development: Classified.
Hacker. Pornographic Poem.
Herrick. On Poet Prat.
Hewitt. To Be Used in an Address Delivered at the Unveiling of a Plaque Commemorating "George A. Birmingham."
Liddy. Cracks in the Pavement.
MacNeice. Satirist, The.
Prince. Renouncing an Epigram.
Shelley. Fragment of a Satire on Satire.
Spenser. Prosopopoia: or Mother Hubberds Tale.

Satiric Verse
Carroll, Jim. Sure.
"Carroll, Lewis." Duchess's Lullaby, The.
Father William.
Mad Hatter's Song, The.
Melodies.
Meredith. Empedocles.
Jump-to-Glory Jane.
Pope. Alas, young man! your days can ne'er be long.
Swift. On Reading Dr. Young's Satires.
See also **Satire and Satirists.**

Saturday
Beckett. Samedi répit.
Ceravolo. I Like to Collapse.
Smart. For Saturday.

Zukofsky. Dying away as of trees, A.
See also **Sabbath.**

Saul (Bible)
Auden. Pride.
Bradstreet. David's Lamentation for Saul and Jonathan.
Browning, Robert. "Oh, our manhood's prime vigour! no spirit feels waste."
Saul.
Byron. Saul.
Song of Saul before His Last Battle.
Lindsay. Hail to the Sons of Roosevelt.
In Which Roosevelt Is Compared to Saul.
Merton. St. Paul.
Smith, Stevie. Man Saul, The.
Warren. Saul at Gilboa.
Wilbur. Water Walker.

Saunas. see **Baths and Bathing.**

Sawmills and Sawyers
Auden. Sawmill, The.
Carruth. Regarding Chainsaws.

Scanderbeg (George Castriot)
Spenser. Wherefore doth vaine Antiquitie so vaunt.

Scandinavia and Scandinavians
Lowry. For Nordahl Grieg Ship's Fireman.
Peter Gaunt and the Canals.
Miller. From Oslo.
Kattegat.

Scarecrows
De la Mare. Scarecrow, The.
Lindsay. What the Scarecrow Said.
Nemerov. Sonnet at Easter.
Stuart. Ballad of the Scarecrow, The.
Wilbur. Sonnet.
Wright, James. Dog in a Cornfield.

Schiller, Johanne Christoph Friedrich von
Coleridge. To the Author of "The Robbers."

Schoenberg, Arnold
Tomlinson. Ode to Arnold Schoenberg.

Scholarship and Scholars
Arnold. Scholar-Gipsy, The.
Auden. I'm afraid there's many a spectacled sod.
Browning, Robert. Development.
Grammarian's Funeral, A.
"Carroll, Lewis." Fame's Penny-Trumpet.
Cowper. Retaliation.
Cullen. Cats.
Cummings. Ballad of the Scholar's Lament.
Voices to voices, lip to lip.
Donne. To Mr S. B.
Eberhart. Lucubration.
Emerson. Scholar is a ball thats spent.
Frost. Lesson for Today, The.
Graves. Complaint and Reply.
Hewitt. Going to Church.
Pavane for a Dead Professor.
Hughes, Ted. Tutorial.
Johnson. Be gone ye blockheads, *Heraclitus* cries.
Kinnell. Schoolhouse, The.
Lovelace. Prologue to the Scholars, A.
Merton. Origen.
Nemerov. To a Scholar in the Stacks.
Stevens. On the Manner of Addressing Clouds.
Turco. Old Professor and the Sphinx, The.
Yeats. Gratitude to the Unknown Instructors.
Scholars, The.
See also **Pedantry and Pedants; Students; Teaching and Teachers; Libraries and Librarians.**

School and Schools
Atwood. Comic Books vs. History.
Auden. Schoolchildren.
Browning, Elizabeth Barrett. Song for the Ragged Schools of London, A.
Browning, Robert. Epigram on School Days.
Bunting. Song of the Ackworth Clock, The.
Burns. Tale, A.
Ciardi. Knothole in Spent Time, A.
Poem for Benn's Graduation from High School, A.
Clough. Effusions of a School-Patriarch, The.

Coleridge. Sonnet on Quitting Christ's Hospital.
Davie. Sorting the Personae.
Dickey, James. Mangham.
Dunbar. Old High School and the New, The.
Wadin' in de Crick.
Eberhart. Long Term Suffering.
Emerson. How drearily in College hall.
It takes a philosopher or fool.
Frost. Not of School Age.
To the Right Person.
Gildner. First Practice.
Glück. School Children, The.
Gunn. Drive to Los Alamos, A.
Hardy. He Revisits His First School.
High-School Lawn, The.
Hesketh. Paint Box.
Hewitt. Bangor, Spring 1916.
Big Room, The.
First Letters.
For Deirdre.
I Go to School.
Miss Murdoch.
School Upstairs, The.
Hill. Cowan Bridge; At the Site of 'Lowood School.'
Hughes, Langston. Graduation.
Kinnell. Schoolhouse, The.
Kipling. Kitchener's School.
School Song, A.
Waster, The.
Larkin. Administration.
By Day, a Lifted Study-Storehouse.
School in August, The.
Lawrence. Best of School, The.
Children Singing in School.
Last Lesson of the Afternoon.
School on the Outskirts.
Schoolmaster [A], The.
Snowy Day at School, A.
Snowy Day in School, A.
Levine. On My Own.
Lorde. Bees, The.
Release Time.
Lowry. Der Tag.
MacNeice. I ought to be glad.
Matthews. School Days.
Schoolboys with Dog, Winter.
Merton. News from the School at Chartres.
Moore. Student, The.
Morgan. Past, The.
Muldoon. Anseo.
Oliver. Spring in the Classroom.
Paley. For Danny.
Piercy. Learning Experience.
Rukeyser. Backside of the Academy, The.
Sexton. Elegy in the Classroom.
Silverstein. Chester.
Sick.
Simic. School for Dark Thoughts.
Smith, Stevie. At School.
Parents.
Si Peu Séduisante.
To School!
Snyder. June.
Sorrentino. Girl at Sixteen with Lightning.
Spender. Elementary School Classroom in a Slum, An.
Stevenson. Come, here is adieu to the city.
Wakoski. Overnight Projects with Woods.
Warren. School Lesson Based on Word of Tragic Death of Entire Gillum Family.
Whitman. Old Man's Thought of School, An.
Whittier. At School-Close.
In School-Days.
To My Old Schoolmaster.
Vanishers, The.
Williams, Charles Kenneth. Hood.
Soon.
Wright, James. Little Girl on Her Way to School, A.
Zimmer. Father Animus and Zimmer.
Zimmer in Grade School.
Zimmer's Head Thudding against the Blackboard.

Schoolmasters.
See also **Colleges and Universities.**
Schoolmasters. *see* **Teaching and Teachers.**
Schopenhauer, Arthur
Carruth. World as Will and Representation,
The.
Lawrence. Schoolmaster [B], The.
Schubert, Franz
Schuyler. Grand Duo.
Schwartz, Delmore
Koch. Pleasures of Peace, The.
Lowell. To Delmore Schwartz.
Muldoon. Louis.
"Reed." My House.
Science and Scientists
Ammons. Exotic.
Auden. Ode to Terminus.
Ciardi. Credibility.
Fragment: "To the laboratory then I went.
What little."
Cummings. Beware beware beware / because
because because.
But granted that it's nothing paradoxically
enough beyond mere personal.
Kind) / YM&WC / (of sort of).
Of Ever-Ever Land i speak.
Pity This Busy Monster, Manunkind.
Proud of his scientific attitude.
Space being(don't forget to remember)Curved.
Who before dying demands not rebirth.
De la Mare. Happy Encounter, The.
Dickinson. Science will not trust us.
Fenton. For the context of the basidiocarp
Singer states.
Genus Stephanoma, The.
Kingfisher's Boxing Gloves, The.
Psychopharmacological drugs.
South Parks Road.
Fox. Albert Einstein (1879–1955).
Almagest, Last Letter to Zakarias.
Frost. Any Size We Please.
Reflex, A.
Why Wait for Science.
Graves. Research and Development: Classified.
Herrick. Knowledge.
Hesketh. Analyst.
He Saved Others.
Hewitt. Admonition to Science.
Jarrell. Charles Dodgson's Song.
Emancipators, The.
Romance of Science, The.
Jeffers. Curb Science?
Mathematicians and physics men, The.
Science.
Staggering Back Toward Life.
Joseph. On the Nature of Scientific Law.
Koch. Poem: "Thing / To do / Is organize /
The Sea, The."
Larkin. Ape Experiment Room.
Lawrence. Anaxagoras.
Scientific Doctor, The.
"MacDiarmid." Poetry and Science.
McGrath. Little Odyssey of Jason Quint, of
Science, Doctor, The.
MacLeish. Dr. Sigmund Freud Discovers the
Sea Shell.
MacNeice. Little dapper man but with shiny
elbows, A.
Meinke. Hermann Ludwig Ferdinand Von
Helmholtz.
Monk can do his work on bended knees, A.
Merton. Learning of many things does not
teach understanding, or else it would have
taught Hesiod and Pythagoras, The.
Nash. Purist, The.
Patchen. It Depends on Whose Science.
Poe. Sonnet—To Science.
Pope. Epitaph Intended for Sir Isaac Newton,
in Westminster Abbey.
Rich. Meditations for a Savage Child.
Rukeyser. Gyroscope, The.
Updike. Bitter Life, A.
In Praise of $(C_{10}H_9O_5)$x.
V. B. Nimble, V. B. Quick.
Williams, Miller. Associate Professor Delivers
an Exhortation to His Failing Students, The.
He Speaks to His Arguing Friends and to
Himself.

Wordsworth. Lines Written as a School
Exercise at Hawkshead, Anno Aetatis 14.
Science Fiction
Stuart. Next Step, The.
Scopes Trial. *see* **Evolution.**
Scorn
Carew. Looking-Glass, A.
To My Mistress Sitting by a River's Side; an
Eddy.
Catullus. Carmen 53: "I laughed. Calvus. I
laughed today."
De la Mare. Iago.
Emerson. Quoth Saadi, when I stood before.
Glück. Horse.
Hemingway. Defense of Luxembourg.
Hewitt. Triad ("Three things that men may
scorn").
Lorde. Poem for Women in Rage, A.
Lowry. They will be ashamed after they are
dead.
Ransom. Moments of Minnie.
Two Gentlemen Scholars.
Stevenson. O now, although the year be done.
Wyatt. I see my plaint with open ears.
Zukofsky. Risible nice go when from mud a
crony.
Scorpions
Boyle. Landscape for Wyn Henderson, A.
Scotland
Berryman. Scots Poem.
Burns. Act Sederunt of the Session—A Scots
Ballad.
Address of Beelzebub.
Address to Edinburgh.
Amang the trees, where humming bees.
Author's Earnest Cry and Prayer, to the Right
Honorable and Honorable, the Scotch
Representatives in the House of Commons,
The.
Awa Whigs Awa.
Banks of Nith, The.
Banks of the Devon, The.
Battle of Sherra-Moor, The.
Birks of Aberfeldy, The [Composed on the
Spot].
Birth-Day Ode. December 31st 1787, A.
Bonie Laddie, Highland Laddie.
Ca' the Ewes [*or* Yowes] [to the Knowes].
Caledonia.
Campbells Are Comin, The.
Castle Gordon—*Intended to Be Sung to
Morag.*
Cotter's Saturday Night [Inscribed to Robert
Aiken [*or* R. A****], Esq.], The.
Dainty Davie.
Duan First.
Duan Second.
Dumfires Volunteers, The.
Epistle to Mr Tytler of Woodhouselee, Author
of a Defence of Mary Queen of Scots.
Epistle to Robt. Graham Esq: of Fintry on the
Election for the Dumfries String of Boroughs,
Anno 1790.
Epitaph. Here Lies Robert Fergusson, Poet.
Extempore [on the *Loyal Natives'* Verses].
Five Carlins—A Ballad—Tune, Chevy Chase,
The.
Frae the friends and Land I love.
Geordie [An Old Ballad].
Halloween.
Here's a Health to Them That's Awa'.
Highland Balou, The.
Highland Laddie.
It Was A' for Our Rightfu' King.
Jessie—A New Scots Song.
John Barleycorn [a Ballad].
Kirk of Scotland's Garland—a New Song,
The.
Lines on Stirling.
Lines Written on a Bank-Note.
My Heart's in the Highlands.
Nithsdale's Welcome Hame.
O Kenmure's on and awa, Willie.
Ode [for General Washington's Birthday].
On the Death of Sir J. Hunter Blair.
On the Death of the Late Lord President
Dundas.

On the Late Captain Grose's Peregrinations
thro' Scotland, Collecting the Antiquities of
That King.
Prologue: "When by a generous Public's kind
acclaim."
Robert Bruce's March to Bannockburn.
Scotch Drink.
Scots Ballad.
Scots Prologue, *For Mrs. Sutherland's Benefit
Night,* Spoken at the Theatre Dumfries.
Song: "As I stood by yon roofless tower."
Song. On Miss W. A.
Song: "Their groves o' sweet myrtle let
Foreign Lands reckon."
Such a Parcel of Rogues in a Nation.
Sutors o' Selkirk.
Tam Lin.
Tam o' Shanter [A Tale].
There'll Never Be Peace Till Jamie Comes
Hame.
To a Haggis.
To W. S*****n, Ochiltree.
Toast, A.
Up and Warn A' Willie.
While new-ca'd kye rowte at the stake.
White Cockade, The.
Written with a Pencil over the Chimney-Piece,
in the Parlour of the Inn at Kenmore,
Taymouth.
Yon wild, mossy mountains sae lofty and
wide.
Campion. Ad Invictissimum Serenissimumque
Iacobvm *Magnae Britanniae Regem.*
Epigram, An: "Merlin, the great King Arthur
being slaine."
Epigramma: "Haeredem (ut spes est) pariet
nova nupta Scot Anglum."
To the Most Puisant and Gratious James King
of Great Britaine.
Davie. Strathnaver.
Hugo. Ayr.
Braes, The.
Cairn in Loch An Duin, The.
Carloway Broch.
Clearances, The.
Clouds of Uig, The.
Drums in Scotland.
Duntulm Castle.
Glen Uig.
Graves in Uig.
Greystone Cottage.
Langaig.
Mill at Romesdal.
Piping to You on Skye from Lewis.
St. John's Chapel.
Sneosdal.
Standing Stones of Callanish, The.
Trumpan.
Jonson. On the Union.
Keats. Lines Written in the Highlands after a
Visit to Burns's Country.
There was a naughty boy.
Lowry. Ye pow'rs who make mankind your
care.
"MacDiarmid." Back to the great music,
Scottish Gaels. Too long.
Conception.
Dìreadh III.
Gairmscoile.
Here in the hauf licht waitin' till the clock.
I'm weary o' the shapes mere chance can
thraw.
John Maclean (1879-1923).
Little White Rose, The.
Scotland.
Scotland Small?
Vision of Scotland, A.
Raine. For the Visitors' Book.
Scott. Ambuscade, The.
Autumn on Tweedside.
Boat Song.
Branksome Hall.
Brooch of Lorn, The.
Caledonia.
Dawn and Sunrise.
Douglas and Marmion.
Edinburgh From Blackford Hill.

English Advance at Flodden, The.
Farewell.
Fiery Cross, The.
Hellvellyn.
Invocation: "Harp of the North! that mouldering long hast hung."
Loch Coruisk.
Lochinvar.
Lords Strand of Northumberland, The.
Melrose by Moonlight.
Norham Castle.
On the Massacre of Glencoe, 1692.
Pibroch of Donuil Dhu.
Ride to Stirling, The.
Trossachs, The.
Voyage to Arran, The.
Stevenson. Embro Hie Kirk.
Heather Ale: A Galloway Legend.
On the gorgeous hills of morning.
Scotsman's Return from Abroad, The.
Tomlinson. Mr. Brodsky.
Of Lady Grange.
Whittier. Burns.
Memory, A.
Wordsworth. Bothwell Castle.
Brownie's Cell, The.
Composed at Cora Linn in Sight of Wallace's Tower.
Composed in the Glen of Loch Etive.
Effusion in the Pleasure-Ground on the Banks of the Bran, Near Dunkeld.
Help for the Memory of the Grand Independent; A New Song, A.
Highland Broach, The.
Highland Hut.
On the Sight of a Manse in the South of Scotland.
Suggested by a View from an Eminence in Inglewood Forest.

Scots, The
Burns. Address to Edinburgh.
Author's Earnest Cry and Prayer, to the Right Honorable and Honorable, the Scotch Representatives in the House of Commons, The.
Battle of Sherra-Moor, The.
Birth-Day Ode. December 31st 1787, A.
Cock up Your Beaver.
Cotter's Saturday Night [Inscribed to Robert Aiken [or R. A****], Esq.], The.
Five Carlins—A Ballad—Tune, Chevy Chase, The.
Gude Wallace.
Here's a Health to Them That's Awa'.
Highland Laddie.
Johnie Cope.
O Kenmure's on and awa, Willie.
Ode [for General Washington's Birthday].
On Miss J. Scott, of Ayr.
Pray who are these Natives the Rabble so ven'rate.
Robert Bruce's March to Bannockburn.
Scotch Drink.
Such a Parcel of Rogues in a Nation.
To a Haggis.
Toast, A.
Verses Intended to Be Written below a Noble Earl's Picture.
Whistle. A Ballad, The.
Byron. Address Intended to be Recited at the Caledonian Meeting.
Graves. Single Fare.
Hewitt. My Father's Voice.
Kipling. Fall of Jock Gillespie, The.
McAndrew's Hymn.
"MacDiarmid." Hokum.
Weapon, The.
Nash. Everything's Haggis in Hoboken, or, Scots Wha Hae Sae.
Genealogical Reflection.
Scott. Allan-Bane's Lament.
Death of Marmion, The.
Stevenson. Maker to Posterity, The.
Ticonderoga: A Legend of the West Highlands.

Scott, Sir Walter
Schuyler. Eyes at the Window.
Walter Scott.
Wordsworth. On the Departure of Sir Walter Scott from Abbotsford, for Naples.
Yarrow Revisited.

Scottish Highlands
Burns. Bannocks o' Bear-Meal.
Highland Widow's Lament, The.
Killiecrankie.
My Heart's in the Highlands.
Verse Composed and Repeated by Burns, to the Master of the House, on Taking Leave at a Place in the Highlands, Where He Had Been Hospitably Entertained, A.
Byron. Address Intended to be Recited at the Caledonian Meeting.
When I Roved a Young Highlander.
Stevenson. In the highlands, in the country places.
On the gorgeous hills of morning.

Scottsboro Case
Boyle. Communication to Nancy Cunard, A.
Cullen. Scottsboro, Too, Is Worth Its Song.

Screams
Carroll, Jim. My Debt.
Creeley. Turn, The.
Everson. In the Breach.
Hall. "Scream, The."
Hughes, Ted. Dawn's Rose.
Tomlinson. Scream, The.
Warren. Scream, The.

Scribes
Chaucer. Chaucer's Wordes unto Adam, his Owne Scriveyn.

See also **Secretaries.**

Sculpture and Sculptors
Berryman. Ecce Homo.
Browning, Elizabeth Barrett. Hiram Powers' "Greek Slave."
Byron. In This Beloved Marble View.
Carew. Carver. To His Mistress, The.
Davie. Ars Poetica.
At the Synod in St Patrick's.
Sculptures in Hungary.
De la Mare. Image, The.
Dobyns. Mermaid.
Doolittle. Gift.
Wooden Animal.
Eberhart. Cousin Florence.
Laocoön.
Looking Head On.
Edmunds. Gaea.
Emerson. Painting and Sculpture.
Sonnet of Michel Angelo Buonaroti.
Ferlinghetti. Goya & the Sleep of Reason.
In hintertime Praxiteles.
Hall. Notes For Nobody.
"Reclining Figure."
Hardy. Children and Sir Nameless, The.
Question of Marriage, A.
Hartley. King Amenemhat III.
Hewitt. Chinese Fluteplayer.
Modelled Head, The.
Municipal Gallery Revisited, October 1954.
Hugo. Bassetti's Lions.
Jarrell. Bronze David of Donatello, The.
Keats. On Seeing the Elgin Marbles.
Knott. Sculpture, The.
Kunitz. To a Slave Named Job.
Lawrence. London Mercury.
Meinke. Helen.
Meredith. In Paris, at the Louvre, there have I seen.
Merrill. Dream (Escape from the Sculpture Museum) and Waking.
Merton. Celebrating Giacometti.
Moore. No Swan So Fine.
Piercy. For Jeriann's Hands.
Plath. Sculptor.
Sandburg. Face.
Head.
Mask.
Shapiro. Calder, A.
Stevenson. And thorns, but did the sculptor spare.

Tomlinson. Maillol.
Portrait in Stone.
Updike. Roman Portrait Busts.
Wilbur. Giacometti.
Williams, William Carlos. Gothic Candor.
Yeats. Bronze Head, A.
Statues, The.
Zukofsky. 1892-1941.

Sea
Ammons. Immediacy.
Reading.
Undersea.
Arnold. Dover Beach.
Auden. Bank Holiday.
On This Island.
Beatles. Octopus's Garden.
Beckett. Dieppe.
Dieppe.
Fleuves et océans.
La Mouche.
Berry. Farmer and the Sea, The.
Berryman. Ceremony and Vision.
Betjeman. Bay in Anglesey, A.
East Anglian Bathe.
Hearts Together.
Winter Seascape.
Bishop. At the Fishhouses.
Cootchie.
Key of Water, The.
Large Bad Picture.
Map, The.
Pleasure Seas.
Quai d'Orléans.
Rainbow.
Riverman, The.
Seascape.
Song: "Summer is over upon the sea."
Twelfth Morning; or What You Will.
Wave, The.
Bly. Calm Day at Drake's Bay.
On a Ferry across Chesapeake Bay.
Sitting on Some Rocks in Shaw Cove.
Two Sounds When We Sit by the Ocean.
Boyle. Dedicated to Robert McAlmon.
Poem of Gratitude, A.
Seascape for an Engraver.
Waterfront for Allan Ross MacDougall, A.
Browning, Elizabeth Barrett. Earth and Her Praisers.
Man and Nature.
Sea-Mew, The.
Sea-side walk, A.
Sounds.
Browning, Robert. Amphibian.
Bukowski. Beach Trip.
Gypsies Near Del Mar, The.
Monday Beach, Cold Day.
Shit Time.
Bunting. I am agog for foam. Tumultuous come.
Now we've no hope of going back.
Under the olive trees.
Vessels thrown awry by strong gusts.
Burns. Song: "As I stood by yon roofless tower."
Byron. And I have loved thee, Ocean! and my joy.
Carew. On His Mistress[e] Going to Sea.
Carroll, Jim. California Poem.
Early Morning Crucifixion, An.
Found it once more in the ocean's rush.
Poem: "My footsteps in the shallow."
Your Daughter.
"Carroll, Lewis." Coronach.
Double Acrostic: I sing a place wherein agree.
Lady of the Ladle, The.
Mock Turtle's Song, The: "Beneath the waters of the sea."
Sailor's Wife, The.
Three Voices, The.
Carruth. Aqua.
Eons gone by the sea.
Far-removed Mountain Men, The.
In deep winter the sea roams.
Sigh, you seven seas.
Ceravolo. Ocean.
Ciardi. Sea Burial.

Clark. Culebra Cascabel.
Eos.
"Walked into State."
Coleridge. Complaint of Ninathóma, The.
Cooper. Atom bellies like a cauliflower, The.
Cowper. To Mr. Newton [on His Return from Ramsgate].
Crabbe. Sea: A Summer and Winter View, The.
Crane. And Bees of Paradise.
At Melville's Tomb.
Ave Maria.
Mermen, The.
Sea Raised Up, The.
Voyages.
Creeley. As You Come.
Place.
Sea.
Cullen. For Joseph Conrad.
Cummings. As is the sea marvelous.
Because i love you)last night.
Beyond the brittle towns asleep.
God gloats upon Her stunning flesh. Upon.
Here is the ocean,this is moonlight:say.
How many moments must(amazing each).
I remark that this beach has been used
too. much Too. originally.
Maggie and milly and molly and may.
What is / a / voyage / ?
Davie. North Sea, in a Snowstorm, The.
North Sea, The.
Our Lady.
Where Depths Are Surfaces.
De la Mare. Flotsam.
Good Company.
Mermaids, The.
Never-To-Be.
Sea-Magic.
Thule.
Dickey, James. Daybreak.
Expanses.
Immortals.
Lakes of Värmland.
Dickinson. Drop, that wrestles in the Sea, The.
Escaping backward to perceive.
How slow the Wind.
I started Early—Took my Dog.
My River runs to thee.
We send the Wave to find the Wave.
Doolittle. Blue-geese, white-geese, you may say.
Hermes of the Ways.
Hermonax.
Oread.
Other Sea-Cities.
Sea-Choros.
Sea Gods.
Sea Heroes.
Sea Lily.
Thetis.
Time breaks the barrier.
Dunbar. Fisher Child's Lullaby, The.
Mystic Sea, The.
On the Sea Wall.
Sea speaks to me of you, The.
Wind and the Sea, The.
Duncan. Achilles' Song.
Dunn. Atlantic City.
Eberhart. Deep Fishing.
Froth.
Going Backward Going Forward.
Man and Nature.
Moment of Equilibrium among the Islands.
Off Spectacle Island.
Old Tree by the Penobscot.
Ospreys in Cry.
Recognition.
Sea-Ruck.
Sea Storm.
Ship Burning and a Comet All in One Day, A.
Tree Swallows.
Verbalist of Summer, The.
Voyage, The.
Eliot. River is within us, the sea is all about us, The.
Emerson. All day the waves assailed the rock.
At Sea, September 1833.

For fifteen winter days.
From Alcuin.
Heavy blue chain, The.
Plunge in yon angry waves.
Sea reflects the rosy sky, The.
Sea-Shore.
Trimountain.
What is it to sail.
Fenton. This Octopus Exploits Women.
Ferlinghetti. Grottamare.
Old Sailors, The.
Sea and Ourselves at Cape Ann, The.
Fisher. Ocean-lights go flashing.
Fletcher. Black Rock, The.
Calm, The.
Empty Days, The.
Gale, The.
Groundswell, The.
Gulf Stream.
Midsummer Dawn at Sea.
Night Wind, The.
On the Beach.
Sea-Sounding Bells.
Sea-Violins.
Snow at Sea.
Tide of Storms.
Tide, The.
Ford. This same sea, there.
Fox. On This Shore.
Servants of the Emperor, The.
Frost. Does No One at All Ever Feel This Way in the Least?
Neither Out Far nor In Deep.
Once by the Pacific.
Glück. Inlet, The.
Meridian.
Phenomenal Survivals of Death in Nantucket.
Portland, 1968.
Swans.
Graves. Beach, The.
Door, The.
Mankind and Ocean.
Griffiths. Anglo-Welshman and his friends, The.
For the Irish Sea.
Misrule, Towyn, 1990.
Oil Terminal.
Optimism.
Returning I live with a huge space.
Gunn. Lerici.
Hacker. Across the mud flats and the wide roads, over rivers and borders.
Haines. By the Ocean.
Hall. Blue Wing, The.
On a Horse Carved in Wood.
Sea, The.
Hardy. Once at Swanage.
Hartley. Indian Point.
Listening to the Music.
Hemingway. Oily Weather.
Rail ends do not meet, The.
Herrick. Faire Shewes Deceive.
Gods Mercy.
Proof to No Purpose.
Hesketh. Credo.
On Iona.
Waiting.
Hewitt. Hired Lad's Farewell, The.
Lost *Argo*, Islandmagee, Summer 1919.
Minotaur.
Songs I Sing, The.
Sonnet: "By the sea's edge, on gravel and on sand."
Vida, Mykonos.
Hill. Lowlands of Holland, The.
Ode on the Loss of the Titanic.
Rivers bring down. The sea.
Wreaths.
Hopkins. Sea Took Pity, The.
Hughes, Langston. Sea Calm.
Hughes, Ted. Mayday on Holderness.
Relic.
Still-Life.
Hugo. Alki Beach.
Bay of Recovery.
Cape Alava.
Changes in Policy at Taholah.

Cornwall, Touring.
Duntulm Castle.
Maratea Antica.
Maratea Porto: The Bitter Man.
Mendocino, Like You Said.
Near Kalalock.
Note from Capri to Richard Ryan on the Adriatic Floor.
Ocean on Monday.
One Son North to Naples.
Pike Place Market.
Point No Point.
Port Townsend, 1974.
Road Ends at Tahola.
Salt Water Story.
Shark Island.
Tiberio's Cliff.
Jarrell. Birth of Venus, The.
Iceberg, The.
Jeffers. All night long the rush and trampling of water.
Beach, The.
Evening Ebb.
Eye, The.
July Fourth by the Ocean.
Morro Bay.
November Surf.
Ocean.
Ocean.
Ocean's Tribute, The.
Place for No Story, The.
Their Beauty Has More Meaning.
Watch the Lights Fade.
Winged Rock.
Jong. People Who Live.
Surgery of the Sea, The.
Unrequited.
Joseph. February Floods, 1953.
Lost Continent, The.
Recovered from the Sea.
Tides.
Keats. On the Sea.
Kipling. Anchor Song.
Beat off in our last fight were we?
Bell Buoy, The.
Deep-Sea Cables, The.
Dykes, The.
First Chantey, The.
Gift of the Sea, The.
In the Matter of One Compass.
Last Chantey, The.
Lukannon.
Merchantmen, The.
North Sea Patrol, The.
Oh! hush thee, my baby, the night is behind us.
Poseidon's Law.
Sea and the Hills, The.
Sea-Wife, The.
Song of the Dead, The.
Song of the Red War-Boat.
V.A.D. (Mediterranean).
Wet Litany, The.
Koch. Poem: "Thing / To do / Is organize / The Sea, The."
Kunitz. Indian Summer at Land's End.
Mulch, The.
Larkin. Absences.
To the Sea.
Lawrence. Desire Goes Down into the Sea.
Forte Dei Marmi.
Mana of the Sea.
November by the Sea.
Sea, The.
Sea, the Sea, The.
Spray.
They Say the Sea Is Loveless.
Levine. We sat by the shore.
Lewis. Across seven thousand miles of sea and time.
And now we seek once more the burning breeze.
Liddy. Sea / Is not distinguished by.
Wave of the Nineties, The.
Lindsay. Chanting of the Whales, The.
Queen Mab in the Village.

Song in July, A.
Would-Be Merman, The.
Longfellow. Seaweed.
Lorde. Maiden, The.
Lovelace. Lucasta, Taking the Waters at
  Tunbridge.
Sanazar's Hexaflick.
Lowell. Near the Ocean.
Water.
Lowry. Alcoholic.
Asperin tree outside told me to say, The.
Byzantium: Or Where the Great Life Begins.
Cook in the Galley, The.
Eels.
Injured Choriant or Paeonic.
Iphigenia in Aulis. Agamemnon Speaks:.
Jokes Amidships.
Jokes in the Galley.
Jokes on the Poop.
Ladder, The.
Lines Written on Reading Dostoievski.
Look Out! The Bloody Bosun.
Marina—.
Morning Address of Love to the Beloved
  Harteebeeste.
Morning Song for the Harteebeeste.
Number 8 Fireman.
On board the Matsue Maru.
Outside was the roar of the sea and the
  darkness.
Outward Bound.
Pacific is a feeble symbol of death.
Pilgrim passes through the town by night, A.
Reflection to Windward.
Sestina in a Cantina.
Stars have simple paradigms, The.
Western Ocean, The.
Wild Cherry, The.
"MacDiarmid." I was better with the sounds
  of the sea.
On the Ocean Floor.
Water of Life.
McGrath. Encounter.
Poem: "Through the fog / The gulls."
MacLeish. Boatmen of Santorin, The.
For the Anniversary of my Mother's Death.
Hurricane.
Land's End.
Lost Speakers, The.
Men of My Century Loved Mozart.
Out of Sleep Awakened.
Return.
MacNeice. Atlantic Tunnel, The.
Broken bollard, rusted hawser.
Canto V: "Hence these arrears, this filing
  cabinet crammed."
Leaving Barra.
Left-Behind, The.
North Sea, The.
Round the Corner.
Sailing Orders.
Sea, The.
Thalassa.
Upon This Beach.
Which being so, which beauties being
  evanescent but also recurrent.
White rolling battlements on rumbling lead.
Mahon. Hearing the thunder of the intransitive
  weirs
Sea in Winter, The.
Markson. I Ate My Love Alive.
Meinke. Night Watch on the Chesapeake.
Melville. Far Off-Shore.
March to the Sea, The.
Pebbles.
Meredith. Dark on the ridge of the cold salt
  wave.
Him loved she. Lo, now was he veiled.
Olive Branch, The.
Wind & sea are as playmates.
Merrill. Island in the Works.
Merton. Autumn Floods.
Song: "Bottom of the sea has come, The."
Millay. Exiled.
Inland.
Mist in the Valley.
Milton. But now my oat proceeds.

Earth was form'd, but in the womb as yet,
  The.
Moore. Grave, A.
Morgan. I remember the sea when I was six.
Komë Berenikes floating.
Morrison. Horse Latitudes.
Moonlight Drive.
Nash. Beginner's Guide to the Ocean, A.
Nemerov. Salt Garden, The.
Neruda. Another One.
Bomb (II).
Different Ship, A.
Search.
Who can persuade the sea.
Oliver. Sea, The.
Olson. Adamo Me.
Disposition, The.
Easter.
Flower grows, The.
Maximus, at the Harbor.
Sea is an archeology: eight fathom down, on
  Dogger bank, the bones, The.
Shut in kept off.
Thy Gleeman Who Flattered Thee.
Oppen. Animula.
Bahamas.
Book of Job and a Draft of a Poem to Praise
  the Paths of the Living, The.
Coastal Strip.
Confession.
Inlet.
River of our substance.
Silver as / The needle's eye.
Squall.
Theological Definition, A.
Translucent Mechanics, The.
Patchen. Fog Over the Sea and the Sun Going
  Down.
Sea Has Caves and Urns, The.
Piercy. Road Behind the Last Dune, The.
Plath. Aquatic Nocturne.
Full Fathom Five.
Man in Black.
Point Shirley.
Winter Ship, A.
Poe. City in the Sea, The.
Prince. And yet the Sibyl parches, caught and
  clutched within a fist of dust!
Sky brims with the ghost of a great rage, The.
Raine. All that is: / The unbroken surface of
  the sea.
I went out in the naked light.
Lindisfarne.
Moment, The.
My feet in the ever-moving sea.
Petal of white rose.
There Shall Be No More Sea.
Turner's Seas.
"Reed." Since Half the World is H$_2$O.
Rich. Homecoming.
Roethke. On the Quay.
Rose, The.
Rolfe. Brickyards at Beacon.
Rossetti. By the Sea.
Heaven overarches earth and sea.
His Banner over Me Was Love.
Horses of the Sea, The.
O glorious sea that in each climbing wave.
Roses on a brier, / Pearls from out the bitter
  sea.
Song: "Oh what comes over the sea."
Was Thy Wrath against the Sea?
Water Spirit's Song, The.
Wind has such a rainy sound, The.
Rukeyser. After Melville.
Believing in Those Inexorable Laws.
Child and Mother.
Green Limits.
In the Night the Sound Woke Us.
Landscape with Wave Approaching.
Network that emerges. At the ocean, A.
Outer Banks, The.
Running of the Grunion, The.
Sea Mercy.
Suite for Lord Timothy Dexter.
Summer, the Sacramento.
Sandburg. Adelaide Crapsey.

Alone and Not Alone.
Baltic Fog Notes.
Be Ready.
Bones.
Bottom of the sea accomodates mountain
  ranges, The.
Breathing of the earth, The.
Changing Light Winds.
Chasers.
Deep Sea Wandering.
Docks.
Evening Sea Wind.
Fins.
Fog Portrait.
Have Me.
How Yesterday Looked.
In the heave of the hankering sea.
Kin.
No matter how thick or how thin you slice it
  it's still baloney.
Nocturn IV: "Claims of the sea, of the tide,
  move out, The."
North Atlantic.
On the Breakwater.
Pink nipples of the earth in springtime, The.
Sand Scribblings.
Sea Chest.
Sea Hold, The.
Sea moves always, the wind moves always,
  The.
Sea Slant.
Sea-Wash.
Sea Wisdom.
Sketch.
Spray.
Thimble Islands.
Throw Roses.
Two Nocturns.
Two Women.
Under.
Way of the World, The.
Sarton. Sun Boat.
Schuyler. Amy Lowell Thoughts.
Crystal Lithium, The.
Schwartz. Famous Resort in Late Autumn,
  The.
Song: "Under the yellow sea."
To Helen.
Sexton. Consecrating Mother, The.
In Excelsis.
There You Were.
Shelley. From the Greek of Moschus.
Smith, Charlotte. Elegy: "Dark gathering
  clouds involve the threatening skies."
Sea View, The.
Studies by the Sea.
Written in the Church-yard at Middleton in
  Sussex.
Written on the Sea Shore.—October, 1784.
Smith, Stevie. Death's Ostracism.
Engine Drain, The.
Forlorn Sea, The.
Will Ever?
Snyder. Rainbow Body.
Real Work, The.
Sorrentino. Sinking, Swimming.
Spender. Seascape.
Stevens. Idea of Order at Key West, The.
Infanta Marina.
Page from a Tale.
Sea Surface Full of Clouds.
Somnambulisma.
Two Versions of the Same Poem.
Stevenson. At the Seaside [or Sea-Side].
Bour-Tree Den, The.
Fair Isle at Sea—thy lovely name.
To My Father.
To N.V. de G.S.
Yes, I remember, and still remember wailing.
Stuart. Breakwater.
Flatfish.
Tennyson. Break, Break, Break.
Calm is the morn without a sound.
Crossing the Bar.
Kraken, The.
Tomlinson. Aesthetic.
Last of Night, The.

Marine.
Mediterranean, The.
Sea Change.
Sea is Open to the Light, The.
Sea Poem.
Turco. Pilot, The.
Roc.
Updike. Bitter Life, A.
Sand Dollar.
Sea Knell.
Shipbored.
Winter Ocean.
Walcott. I can sense it coming from far, too,
Maman, the tide.
Missing the Sea.
Sea is History, The.
Something primal in our spine makes the child
swing.
Warren. End of Season.
Foreign Shore, Old Woman, Slaughter of
Octopus.
Mediterranean Beach, Day after Storm.
True Nature of Time, The.
Whitman. After the Sea-Ship.
As I Ebb'd with the Ocean of Life.
By That Long Scan of Waves.
From Montauk Point.
Had I the Choice.
In Cabin'd Ships at Sea.
Out of the Cradle Endlessly Rocking.
Out of the Rolling Ocean the Crowd.
Patrolling Barnegat.
Ship Starting, The.
Song for All Seas, All Ships.
To the Man-of-War Bird.
With Husky-Haughty Lips, O Sea!
World below the Brine, The.
You sea! I resign myself to you also—I guess
what you mean.
Whittier. Cable Hymn, The.
Hampton Beach.
Ocean.
Palatine, The.
Wilbur. Beacon, The.
Conjuration.
From the Lookout Rock.
Games One.
Waters, The.
Wellfleet: The House.
Williams, William Carlos. Cod Head, The.
Flowers by the Sea.
In Harbor.
Sadness of the Sea, The.
Sea, The.
Yachts, The.
Wordsworth. Address to the Ocean.
At Dover.
At the Isle of Wight. 1793.
Beauty and Moonlight.
By the Sea-Side.
Composed by the Sea-Shore.
Fact, and an Imagination or, Canute and
Alfred, on the Sea-Shore, A.
Fish-Women.—On Landing at Calais.
Lines Written While Sailing in a Boat at
Evening.
On Being Stranded near the Harbour of
Boulogne.
To Melpomene.
Wright, James. American Wedding.
Cold Divinities, The.
Fishermen, The.
I am Freed.
Morality of Poetry, The.
Old Age Compensation.
On the City Ramparts of Cádiz.
Rose of the Sea.
Rosebushes.
Snowstorms in the Midwest.
Stormclouds / give their morose faces to the
sea.
Way to Make a Living, A.
Wyatt. My galley [or galy] charged with
forgetfulness.
Young. Sometimes With the Waves.
Zukofsky. It's hard to see but think of a sea.
Like the oceans, or the leaves of fine

Southern.
World autumn, The.
See also **Sailing and Sailors.**
Sea Battles. *see* **Naval Battles.**
Sea Chanteys
Fletcher. Clipper-Ships.
Lindsay. Sea Serpent Chantey, The.
Sea Creatures
Carruth. Aqua.
De la Mare. Sunk Lyonesse.
Emerson. Lobster-car, boat, or fishbasket.
Fenton. This Octopus Exploits Women.
Graves. Sea Horse, The.
Hemingway. Translations from the Esquimaux:
There Are Seasons.
Lindsay. There's a snake on the western wave.
Moore. Fish, The.
Sea Unicorns and Land Unicorns.
Nash. Snark Was a Boojum Was a Prawn,
The.
Olson. His house / in the branches of.
West Gloucester.
Stuart. Snorkeling in the Caribbean.
Williams, William Carlos. Sea-Elephant, The.
Sea Gulls. *see* **Gulls.**
Sea Hawks
Eberhart. Ospreys in Cry.
Sea-Hawk.
Sea Monsters and Sea Serpents
Carruth. Aqua.
Lindsay. Sea Serpent Chantey, The.
Tennyson. Kraken, The.
Sea Shells. *see* **Shells.**
Sea Voyages. *see* **Voyages.**
Seacoasts
Atwood. Galiano Coast: Four Entrances.
Berryman. Ceremony and Vision.
Browning, Elizabeth Barrett. Soul's Travelling,
The.
Carruth. Ducks, waking at sea.
Études de Plusiers Paysages de l'Âme.
Crane. To Liberty.
Davie. Emigrant, to the Receding Shore.
Porec.
Portland.
De la Mare. Flotsam.
Doolittle. Shrine, The.
When I Am a Cup.
Emerson. Lobster-car, boat, or fishbasket.
Seashore.
Fisher. Real things move.
Straight into the sea fog.
Fox. On This Shore.
Graves. Sea Side.
Griffiths. Chiming at Trwyn Du, The.
Guesthouse, The.
Wedding Photograph.
Hartley. In Robin Hood Cove.
Lapping of waters / thick, upon razorblade.
Serving the Curve.
Hopkins. Sea and the Skylark, The.
Jeffers. Point Pinos and Point Lobos.
Keats. To Ailsa Rock.
Larkin. I Dreamed of an Out-Thrust Arm of
Land.
Liddy. Shore.
MacLeish. Under an elm tree where the river
reaches.
Mahon. Chinese Restaurant in Portrush, The.
Day Trip to Donegal.
Merrill. Summer People, The.
Nemerov. Still Life I.
Oliver. Winter.
Olson. By Cure of—Sulfa.
Compleynt Blossoms April to July.
On the Shore.
Purgatory Blind.
Plath. Finisterre.
Two Lovers and a Beachcomber by the Real
Sea.
Whitsun.
Roethke. Her Time.
Shy Man, The.
St. John. Reef, The.
Schuyler. Crystal Lithium, The.
Sexton. In the Beach House.

Smith, Charlotte. Evening Walk by the Sea-
Side, An.
Smith, Stevie. Engine Drain, The.
Numbers.
Stevenson. Light-Keeper, The.
Skerryvore.
Skerryvore: the Parallel.
Thomas. Author's Prologue.
Tomlinson. Cronkhite Beach.
Fiascherino.
Icos.
Two Poems on titles proposed by Octavio and
Marie José Paz.
Turco. Ropewalk, The.
Williams, William Carlos. Cod Head, The.
Metric Figure.
Wordsworth. At the Isle of Wight. 1793.
Narrow girdle of rough stones and crags, A.
See also **Shores; Beaches.**
Seafaring and Seafarers. *see* **Sailing and
Sailors.**
Seals
Bly. Dead Seal [near McClure's Beach], The.
Eberhart. Off Spectacle Island.
Seals, Terns, Time.
Hoffman. Seals in Penobscot Bay, The.
Kipling. Angutivaun Taina.
Lukannon.
Oh! hush thee, my baby, the night is behind
us.
Rhyme of the Three Sealers, The.
You mustn't swim till you're six weeks old.
Lowell. Soft Wood.
Lowry. Billets Doux for the Harteebeeste.
Just a Merry Little Ditty of Welcome for the
Most Beloved Harteebeeste on Easter Sunday.
Welcome Home—Oh Most Beloved
Harteebeeste.
Sexton. Seal.
Smith, Stevie. Hymn to the Seal.
Updike. Seal in Nature.
Seamstresses
Bishop. House Guest.
Seashores. *see* **Shores; Beaches.**
Seasickness
Meredith. *Irene* ducks and runs amuck, The.
Rich. It was your vision of the pilot.
Seasons
Auden. From the very first coming down.
In Due Season.
In Due Season.
Berry. Familiar, The.
Farm travels in snow, The.
Finches, The.
Let the great song come.
Song (4).
Bishop. Song for the Rainy Season.
Bly. Spring has come; I look up and see.
Bogan. Zone.
Boyle. Glad Day for Laurence Vail, A.
Bradstreet. Four Seasons of the Year, The.
Brontë. Fall, leaves, fall; die, flowers, away.
M.G. For The U.S.
Browning, Robert. Lovers' Quarrel, A.
Burns. Address, to the Shade of Thomson, on
Crowning His Bust, at *Ednam, Roxburgh-
shire*, with Bays.
Bonie Bell.
Carroll, Jim. For Elizabeth.
In Four Seasons.
Carruth. In spring this mountain was a fish.
Clare. February: A Thaw.
Clough. In Stratis Viarum IV.
July's Farewell.
Cooper. High deck. Blue skies overhead.
White distance, A.
Cowper. See'st thou yon mountains laden with
deep snow.
Winter Nosegay, The.
Cummings. 4.7: "Farewell,runaway
snows! For the meadow is green,and the
tree stands."
All ignorance toboggans into know.
Autumn is:that between here and there.
Coming of May, The.
Goo-dmore-ning(en / ter)nize-aday(most).

In time of daffodils(who know.
Metamorphosis.
Open green those / (dear).
Skating.
Song: "But we've the may / (for you are in love)."
Summer is over / —it's no use demanding.
Yes is a pleasant country.
You are like the snow only.
Davie. Meteorologist, September.
De la Mare. Children of Stare, The.
Episodes.
Futility.
In Vain.
Memory.
Willow, The.
Dickinson. I remember the leaves were falling.
Now the Grass is Glass.
Summer begins to have the look.
'Twas later when the summer went.
Twice had Summer her fair Verdure.
Donne. Love's Growth.
Dunbar. Foolin' wid de Seasons.
Love's Seasons.
Roses.
Eberhart. Hornets by the Sill.
Seasons, The.
Spider, The.
Emerson. In my garden three ways meet.
Softens the air so cold & rude.
Thermometer.
To Ellen, at the South.
Galvin. First Night of Fall, The.
Graves. Language of the Seasons.
Mid-Winter Waking.
Haines. Poem: "Immense sadness / of approaching winter, The."
Hall. September Ode.
Set of Seasons, A.
Sister by the Pond, A.
Twelve Seasons.
Hardy. Before and after Summer.
June Leaves and Autumn.
Master and the Leaves, The.
Seasons of Her Year, The.
We Field-Women.
Hartley. "Lewiston Is a Pleasant Place."
Hartnett. Oatwoman, The.
Herrick. After Autumne, Winter.
Hesketh. Autumn at Whitewell.
Days.
Death of a Gardener.
I Cannot Look into the Sun.
Journey.
St. Luke's Summer.
Winter Daffodils.
Hewitt. Autumn Gale.
Autumnal.
Birthday Rhyme for Roberta, A.
For a Mild Season.
For R.S. Thomas.
Glens of Atrim, The.
Lagan in October, The.
Load.
Season's End.
Seeding Time.
Sonnet in Autumn.
Threshing, The.
Values.
Vigil.
Hughes, Ted. October Dawn.
Woman in the Valley, The.
Hugo. Making Certain It Goes On.
Keats. Human Seasons, The.
To Autumn.
Kinnell. Winter Sky, A.
Kipling. Two Months.
Kooser. Late February.
Kunitz. Deciduous Branch.
Larkin. All Catches Alight.
We See the Spring Breaking across Rough Stone.
Levine. Later Still.
New Season.
Voice, The.
Walk with Tom Jefferson, A.
Winter Words.

Lewis. Patrol, The.
Lindsay. Lame Boy and the Fairy, The.
Sweethearts of the Year.
Lorde. Change of Season.
Father, the Year Has Fallen.
Return.
What My Child Learns of the Sea.
Lovelace. Grasse-Hopper, The.
Lowry. Minstrel in Labrador, A.
MacNeice. April Manifesto, An.
August.
Canto VI: "Everydayness is good; particular-dayness."
Canto XI: "Golden guineas filter through the mist, The."
Solvitur Acris Hiems.
Spring Voices.
Mahon. October in Hyde Park.
Melville. Little Good Fellows, The.
Pontoosuce.
Meredith. Appeasement of Demeter, The.
Wild Rose and the Snowdrop, The.
Merrill. Under Libra: Weights and Measures.
Merton. Vine, The.
Nash. It's Never Fair Weather.
One Third of a Calendar.
Nemerov. Anniversary.
Fall Song.
First Snow.
Late Summer.
Madrigal: "She is the darkness where I wander."
Old Days, The.
O'Hara. Ann Arbor Variations.
July Is Over and There's Very Little Trace.
Poem: "So many echoes in my head."
Owen. Winter Song.
Pack. Trying to Separate.
Patchen. Nocturne for the Heirs of Light.
Piercy. Snow, Snow.
Wind is the Wall of the Year.
Plath. Couriers, The.
Ransom. Vaunting Oak.
Rexroth. Another Spring.
Toward An Organic Philosophy.
Rolfe. Pastoral: "Now, on this bluest of mornings, we wake."
Rossetti. Autumn.
Autumn Violets.
Cor Mio.
Daughter of Eve, A.
Diamond or a coal? / A diamond, if you please, A.
Gone for Ever.
Grown and Flown.
If Only.
January cold desolate; / February all dripping wet.
Key-Note, The.
Mirrors of Life and Death.
Mr. and Mrs. Scott, and I.
Months: A Pageant, The.
O wind, where have you been.
Once for All. (Margaret).
Seasons.
Seasons.
Seasons.
Tempus Fugit.
Under Willows.
Year's Windfalls, A.
Rukeyser. After Their Quarrel.
Sandburg. Autumn Movement.
Brown Gold.
Bug Spots.
Cheap Blue.
Corn Hut Talk.
Cornfield Ridge and Stream.
First Sonata for Karlen Paula.
Lesson.
Never Two Songs the Same.
Outstraw green turns gold turns ashen and, The.
Pink nipples of the earth in springtime, The.
Prairie.
Year, The.
Sarton. Apple Tree in May.
First Autumn, The.

March-Mad.
Mud Season.
Of the Seasons.
Schuyler. Almanac, An.
Bluet, The.
Hymn to Life.
Looking Forward to See Jane Real Soon.
Poem: "Wind tears up the sun, The."
Thursday.
Shakespeare. Sonnet 97: "How like a winter hath my absence been[e]."
Sonnet 98: "From you have I been absent in the spring."
Shelley. Stanza: "If I walk in Autumn's even."
Smith, Charlotte. Close of Summer, The.
Composed During a Walk on the Downs, in November 1787.
Snowdrops.
Song from the French.
Smith, Stevie. Saffron.
Snodgrass. September in the Park.
Setting Out.
Sorrentino. There is no instance that was not love.
Spenser. Mask of Mutability, The.
Stevens. Meditation Celestial & Terrestrial.
Metamorphosis.
Motive for Metaphor, The.
Two Illustrations That the World Is What You Make of It.
Stevenson. Autumn Fires.
Come, here is adieu to the city.
House Beautiful, The.
In autumn when the woods are red.
It blows a snowing gale in the winter of the year.
Over the land is April.
Spring Song.
Summer sun shone round me, The.
Stuart. Funeral, The.
Tate. Seasons of the Soul.
These Deathy Leaves.
Thomas. Here in This Spring.
Thomson. Hymn on the Seasons, A.
Tomlinson. Northern Spring.
Prelude, A.
Weathercocks, The.
Updike. Calendar.
Melancholy of Storm Windows, The.
Snowdrops 1987.
Van Duyn. Fall.
Wilbur. April 5, 1974.
Courtyard Thaw, A.
Fall in Corrales.
In the Elegy Season.
Storm in April, A.
Then.
Two Quatrains for First Frost.
Two Songs in a Stanza of Beddoes'.
Winter Spring.
Williams, William Carlos. Another Year.
Wordsworth. Ode to Lycoris; May, 1817.
September, 1819 ("Sylvan slopes with corn-clad fields, The").
Thoughts on the Seasons.
Wright, Charles. Journal of English Days, A.
Journal of One Significant Landscape, A.
Wright, James. Fit against the Country, A.
Mary Bly.
Seasonless, The.
Three Steps to the Graveyard.
To a Troubled Friend.
To the August Fallen.
Wroth. Song: "Springing time of my first loving, The."
Song 1: "Sweet lett mee injoye thy sight."
Song 3: "Come merry spring delight us."
Yeats. Wheel, The.

Seattle, Washington
Ginsberg. Afternoon Seattle.
Hugo. Letter to Peterson from the Pike Place Market.
Updike. Seattle Uplift.

Seaweed
Lawrence. Sea-Weed.
Longfellow. Seaweed.
Melville. Tuft of Kelp, The.

Seclusion
Auden. Thank You, Fog.
Browning, Robert. Dubiety.
 Prologue: "O the old wall here! How I could
  pass."
Donne. Satire 1: "Away thou fondling motley
  humourist."
Hayden. Soledad.
Hewitt. Distances, The.
Levertov. Closed World, The.
 Night on Hatchet Cove.
Mahon. Craigvara House.
 Woods, The.
Melville. Garden of Metrodorus, The.
Nathan. Powerful Little Stove, A.
Ralegh. Like to a Hermit[e] Poor[e].
Rich. Holding Out.
 Letter from the Land of Sinners.
Shapiro. Intellectual, The.
Shelley. Fragment: "Follow to the deep
  wood's weeds."
Sorrentino. Diaghilev Did Not Say "Étonnez-
  Moi."
Stafford. Oregon Message, An.
Stuart. Charles River, The.
Walcott. As John to Patmos.
Warren. Dark Woods.

Second Coming
Browning, Robert. Earth Breaks Up.
"Dylan." Are You Ready?
 Slow Train.
 When He Returns.
Hartley. Elias Gove—or, The Second Coming.
Jarrell. Clock in the Tower of the Church,
 The.
Merton. Peril, The.
Oppen. Parousia.

See also **Millennium.**

Second World War. *see* **World War II.**

Secrecy and Secrets
Angelou. In a Time.
Atwood. This is the secret: these hearts.
Auden. Household, A.
 Lost Secret, The.
 Nor was that final, for about that time.
 Secrets.
Beatles. Do You Want to Know a Secret?
Berg. With Akhmatova at the Black Gates.
Berrigan. Bulbs burn phosphorescent, white,
 The.
 Scorpio.
Berryman. Cadenza on Garnette.
Blake. Never seek [or pain] to tell thy love.
Browning, Elizabeth Barrett. Deserted Garden,
 The.
Bunting. Envoi to the Reader.
Burns. I Love My Love in Secret.
 Song: "O whistle, and I'll come to ye, my
  lad."
Carew. Secrecy [or Secresie] Protested.
"Carroll, Lewis." Atalanta in Camden-Town.
 She's All My Fancy Painted Him.
 Song of Love, A.
Carruth. There where pines darken the water
 above the brookbed.
Catullus. Carmen 6: "Your most recent
  acquisition, Flavius."
 Carmen 102: "If, Cornelius, we entrust our
  secrets."
Cohen. Master Song.
 Warning.
Cowper. Apology, An.
 On Her Endeavoring to Conceal Her Grief at
  Parting.
Creeley. Ear, The.
 Innocence, The.
Davie. Dule of a Dewsbury Matron.
De la Mare. Empty House, The.
 Image, The.
 Portrait, A.
 Voice, The.
Dickey, William. History of the Moon, The.
Dickinson. Life is the finest secret.
 Murmur in the Trees—to note, A.
 Secret told, A.
 "Secrets" is a daily word.

Donne. Perfume, The.
 Undertaking, The.
Dunn. Secret Life, A.
Emerson. By breath of beds of roses drawn.
 Dull uncertain brain, A.
 On a raisin stone.
 Secret that should not be blown, The.
 Sphinx, The.
Fisher. Arrival, The.
Ford. If someone asked you to be happy.
Frost. Secret Sits, The.
Graves. Love and Night.
 Secrecy.
 Secret Theatre.
 Song: Just Friends.
 Strayed Message, The.
 Three Years Waiting.
 Ugly Secret, The.
 Unposted Letter.
Griffiths. Ciudadela, 1991.
Gunn. Outdoor Concert, The.
Hacker. After the Revolution.
 More circumspect good friend, if by "deceive."
 Sestina: "For a week now our bodies have
  whispered."
Hall. Mr. Wakeville on Interstate 90.
Hardy. Her Secret.
Hesketh. Clown.
Hewitt. Ecce Homo.
 Free Mason.
 Gentle Bush, The.
 House at Ballyholme, The.
 Roseblade's Visitants and Mine.
 W.R.R.
Hill. Turtle Dove, The.
Hughes, Langston. Personal.
Jonson. Nymph's Passion, A.
 To One that Desired Me Not to Name Him.
 To Person Guilty ("Guilty, be wise; and
  though thou know'st the crimes").
 To Person Guilty ("Guilty, because I bad you
  late be wise").
Kinnell. There Are Things I Tell to No One.
Kipling. Delilah.
Lawrence. Liaison.
 Tease.
Levertov. Secret, The.
Lovelace. To the Same Ayre in English, Thus.
Lowry. Never seek to tell thy stove.
 Spiderweb.
McGrath. Poem: "You out there, so secret."
MacLeish. Le Secret Humain.
 Night Dream, The.
Meredith. She had a secret—bonny Bess!
Merton. Take, O take the key of Rome.
Muldoon. Hedgehog.
Nash. Mr. Barcalow's Breakdown.
Nathan. Fourth Dimension, The.
Nemerov. To watch water, to watch running
 water.
Neruda. How long would a rhinoceros last.
Pack. Secrets.
Patchen. Strange, Moving Lights of People
 Handle Holinesses Unknown, The.
Plath. Secret, A.
Rich. They come to you with their
  descriptions of your soul.
 Whatever it was: the grains of the glacier
  caked in the boot-cleats.
 When We Dead Awaken.
Rolfe. Entry.
Rossetti. Brandons Both.
 Seeking Rest.
 Winter: My Secret.
Rukeyser. Private Life of the Sphinx, The.
Sandburg. Has-Been, The.
Shelley. Fragment: A Roman's Chamber.
Silverstein. Me and My Giant.
 Tree House.
Simic. Suitcase Strapped with a Rope, A.
Smith, Stevie. Portrait (I).
Stuart. Coming To.
 Urban Hunting Scenes.
Warren. Ballad of Mister Dutcher and the Last
 Lynching in Gupton.
Whitman. Riddle Song, A.

To You ("Let us twain walk aside from the
  rest").
Williams, Charles Kenneth. Secrets.
 Trash.
Williams, Miller. Love in the Cathedral.
Wordsworth. Protest against the Ballot.
 Said Secrecy to Cowardice and Fraud.
Zukofsky. Flavius—that delicate lass—to
 Catullus.
 Secret I take it a commitment hushed to feed
  amic—.

Secretaries
Piercy. Secretary Chant, The.

See also **Scribes.**

Sectarianism
Ferlinghetti. Buddha in the Woodpile, A.
Herbert. Church-Rents and Schisms.
Meredith. Jump-to-Glory Jane.

Security
Berg. Sad Invective.
Berry. This comes after silence. Was it
 something I said.
Browning, Elizabeth Barrett. Sonnet: "Thou
 comest! all is said without a word."
Bukowski. Pace is the Essence.
 Promenade.
 Sad Poem, A.
Creeley. Places.
Cullen. For a Poet.
Cummings. Of Ever-Ever Land i speak.
Dickey, William. New Place, The.
Dobyns. Shaving.
Dunbar. Farm Child's Lullaby, The.
Eberhart. Wisdom of Insecurity, The.
Fisher. This is where the game gets dirty.
Gunn. Hug, The.
 La Prisonnière.
 Reassurance, The.
Hacker. Robber Woman, The.
Herrick. Bellman, The.
 No Shipwrack of Vertue. To a Friend.
 Old Wives Prayer, The.
 Suspicion Makes Secure.
 True Safety.
Hugo. Crinan Canal.
Joseph. Love and Justice.
Koch. Locks.
Kooser. Empty Place, An.
Lawrence. Song of a Man Who Is Loved.
Liddy. Woodenbridge Golf Club.
McGrath. Poem: "When I carry my little son
 in the cold."
MacNeice. Riding in Cars.
Matthews. Burglary.
Meredith. Song: "My darling's love shall close
 me up."
Merton. Wholeness.
Piercy. Behold: A Relationship.
 Many people have a thing they want to
  protect.
Roethke. Reckoning, The.
Rossetti. Safe where I cannot lie yet, / Safe
 where I hope to lie too.
Rukeyser. Another Day. In a Field of Peace
 the Child, Playing. The Child Preparing for
 Daytime Sleep.
Sarton. Because What I Want Most Is
 Permanence.
Wilbur. Dead Still.

Seduction
Beckett. Serena II.
Bukowski. Escape, The.
 3:30 A.M. Conversation.
Burns. As I Went Out Ae May Morning.
 Had I the Wyte She Bade Me.
 Jumpin John.
 Taylor, The.
 Wha Is That at My Bower-Door?
Campion. Bar Not the Door.
 Be Wise, and Fly Not.
 Faire If You Expect Admiring.
 Follow Your Saint [Follow with Accents
  Sweet].
 If thou longst so much to learne (sweet boy)
  what 'tis to love.
 It Fell on a Summer's [or Sommers] Day [or
  Daie].

My Love Hath Vowd.
O Love, where are thy Shafts, thy Quiver, and thy Bow?
Think'st thou to seduce me then with words that have no meaning?
Thrice Toss[e] These Oaken Ashes in the Air [or Ayre].
Turne Backe You Wanton Flier.
Unlesse there were consent twixt hell and heaven.
Where She Her Sacred Bower Adorns.
Your Fair[e] Look[e]s Inflame [My Desire].
Carruth. Green Mountain Idyl.
Sonnet: "Honey, darling, baby...but no endearments."
Catullus. Carmen 35: "Fetch, papyrus / our soft-measured poet."
Cohen. Death of a Lady's Man.
Lady Midnight.
Coleridge. Wills of the Wisp, The.
De la Mare. Decoy, The.
Emerson. Thou who with thy long hair.
Fletcher. Scene from a Drama.
Graves. Scared Child, The.
Song: The Sigil.
Gunn. Odysseus on Hermes.
To a Dead Graduate Student.
Hall. Conduct and Work.
Hardy. Dark-Eyed Gentleman, The.
Herrick. Delight in Disorder.
Hughes, Ted. Speech Out of Shadow.
Hugo. Letter to Snyder from Montana.
Jong. Man under the Bed, The.
Ritratto.
Kipling. To a Lady, Persuading Her to a Car.
Lorde. On a Night of the Full Moon.
Marvell. Fair Singer, The.
Meredith. Daphne.
Penetration and Trust.
Teaching of the Nude, The.
Morrison. Promises.
Wedding-Dress, The.
Woman's Voice.
Ransom. April Treason.
Judith of Bethulia.
Rexroth. Floating.
Rukeyser. Mrs. Walpurga.
Schuyler. Tom's Attempt to Seduce Big Brother Steve.
Stevens. Hand as a Being, The.
Plot against the Giant, The.
Waldman. Romance.
Williams, Charles Kenneth. Medusa.
Zukofsky. Poet I'm too near your and my sod daily.

Seeds
Berry. Outside the window.
Seeds, The.
Bishop. What's that shining in the leaves.
Carruth. Tanck's Song About November.
Dunbar. Seedling, The.
Haines. Sun on Your Shoulder, The.
Hewitt. Seeding Time.
Housman. I hoed and trenched and weeded.
Joseph. This nut withering on the shelf.
Lindsay. Indians Worship Him, but He Hurries On, The.
Meredith. Seed-Time.
Nash. Caraway Seed, The.
Nemerov. Cabinet of Seeds Displayed, A.
Pack. Bounty.
Piercy. Seedlings in the Mail.
Thomas. Seed-at-Zero, The.
Whittier. Utterance.
Wilbur. Seed Leaves.

Seine (river), France
Wilbur. Mirabeau Bridge.
Wordsworth. Ode: "Who rises on the banks of Seine."

Self
Ammons. Chasm.
Increment.
Progress Report.
Self.
Angelou. Reverses.
Atwood. Looking in a Mirror.
More and More.

Solipsism While Dying.
You refuse to own / yourself, you permit.
Auden. Alone.
Contrast, A.
Dawn.
Lullaby: "Din of work is subdued, The."
Prime.
Prologue at Sixty.
Quique Amavit.
Speech.
Talking to Myself.
Beatles. Let Me Mine.
Berg. Between Us.
Crutches.
Eating Outside.
Gratitude.
Leaves.
Lowell: Self-Portrait.
Music.
Self-Portrait at Six.
Summer Twilight.
Three Voices.
To My Friends.
Berrigan. Last Poem.
Berryman. Defensio in Extremis.
Matins.
Prayer for the Self, A.
Sext.
Views of Myself.
Blake. Fly, The.
Little Fly.
Bly. Chinese Tomb Guardians.
Man Locked Inside the Oak, The.
Bogan. Man Alone.
Brooks. My Dreams, My Works, Must Wait Till after Hell.
Sundays of Satin-Legs Smith, The.
Browning, Elizabeth Barrett. Isobel's Child.
Browning, Robert. At the "Mermaid."
House.
Reverie.
Carruth. Blizzard in the mountains. Dusk. The cabin's light.
Okay, Fulke Greville: "None can well behold."
Sonnet: "Freedom in love? It has been questioned. Think."
Then ultimately asylum is the soul.
What does this wind say, plunging upon the land.
Catullus. Carmen 22: "I must, Varus, tell you."
Carmen 23: "Friend Furius, / who has no slaves & no money.""
Carmen 46: "Now spring bursts."
Ceravolo. Grow.
Ciardi. Dialogue with Outer Space.
Coleridge. Phantom.
What Is Life?
Cooper. Knowledge That Comes through Experience, The.
Cowper. Divine Love Endures No Rival.
Necessity of Self-Abasement.
Self-Diffidence.
Self-Love and Truth Incompatible.
Creeley. Answer, The.
Billfold.
But You.
"Do You Think."
For a Friend.
Form of Women, A.
Intervals.
Mirror, The.
Mountains in the Desert, The.
Not Again.
Pattern, The.
Person.
Poem for D. H. Lawrence.
Pool, The.
Puritan Ethos, The.
Skeleton, The.
Some Place.
Song: "You look out and you see people."
Than I.
Walls.
Wife, The.
Cullen. For Myself.
Cummings. Dive for dreams / or a slogan may

topple you.
Doveglion.
Ecco a letter starting "dearest we."
God,Thine the hand that doth extend.
How generous is that himself the sun.
How this uncouth enchanted.
I am a beggar always.
I am a little church(no great cathedral).
I go to this window.
It's / so damn sweet when Anybody.
Maggie and milly and molly and may.
Nobody wears a yellow.
Noone and a star stand,am to am.
One day a nigger.
These from my mother's greatgrandmother's rosebush white.
Total stranger one black day, A.
When / (day's amazing murder with).
Davie. Expecting Silence.
They, to Me.
Vespers.
De la Mare. How Blind!
Moment, The.
Queen Wasp, A.
Dickinson. I am alive—I guess.
I could not weigh myself, Myself.
I heard, as if I had no Ear.
I often wish I was a grass.
Me from Myself—to banish.
One need not be a Chamber to be Haunted.
Perhaps you smile at me.
Soto! Explore thyself!
Those that die seem near me.
We meet no Stranger.
We must be less than Death.
Donne. Self Love.
Doolittle. Are we unfathomable night.
At least I have the flowers of myself.
Pygmalion.
Dunbar. Advice.
Vagrants.
Duncan. Roots and Branches.
Dunn. Biography in the First Person.
Snowmass Cycle, The.
Welcome.
"Dylan." I and I.
I end up then.
Eberhart. Birth and Death.
Gnat on My Paper.
I Walked Out to the Graveyard to See the Dead.
In the Garden.
Laocoön.
Mistaken Identity.
1934.
Soul.
Throwing Yourself Away.
Vision through Timothy.
Eliot. Little Gidding.
Ferlinghetti. Mock Confessional.
Plan du Centre de Paris à Vol D'Oiseau.
True Confessional.
Fisher. Of the Empirical Self and for Me.
Red and the Black, The.
Releases.
To come out ready capitalized, with outlines.
Winking drop on the lens.
Frost. Any Size We Please.
Iota Subscript.
Gallagher. Black Silk.
Sudden Journey.
Gardner. Your Fearful Symmetries.
Gildner. 8/22/38–8/22/68.
Ginsberg. End, The.
Graves. From the Embassy.
Our Self.
Second-Fated, The.
Griffiths. Getting It Wrong, Again.
Gunn. Interruption.
Legal Reform.
Plan of Self-Subjection, A.
Hartley. Inner Distance.
Like a lustrous bird threading the maze.
Hayden. Names.
Herrick. On Himselfe ("Lost to the world").
Hesketh. Return.
Hewitt. Comment on Verse.

I Talked and Raged and Planned.
I Told My Heart to Rest.
Interim.
Response, The.
Sonnet: "Among the many selves that throng my flesh."
Hoffman. Companion, The.
Himself.
Testament.
Wanderer, The.
When my wiser brother.
Holmes. Fayetteville Dawn (2).
Memoirs of an Imaginary Man, The.
Hopkins. Candle Indoors, The.
—I am like a slip of comet.
I wake and feel the fell of dark, not day.
Times are nightfall, look, their light grows less, The.
Jarrell. Children Selecting Books in a Library.
Face, The.
Let's love each other for what we are.
Story, A.
Venetian Blind, The.
Woman at the Washington Zoo, The.
Jeffers. Fog.
Jong. Alphabet Poem: To the Letter I.
At the Edge of the Body.
Lullabye for a Dybbuk.
Poet Writes in I, The.
Keats. Ode on Indolence.
Kipling. Mother's Son, The.
Knight. Cop-Out Session.
Report to the Mother.
Welcome Back, Mr. Knight: Love of My Life.
Knott. Beddybye.
Death.
(Face) (Autumn) (En Face).
Shorts / Excerpts ("Night, in whose death did your ennui take refuge?").
Sonnet: "Way the world is not, The."
Koch. Alive for an Instant.
Kunitz. Organic Bloom.
Single Vision.
Larkin. Conscript.
Counting.
Self's the Man.
Lawrence. Dissolute.
Eloi, Eloi, Lama Sabachthani?
Escape.
I Am in a Novel.
Nonentity.
Rose of All the World.
Self-Sacrifice.
Self-Sacrifice.
There Is Rain in Me.
Underneath.
Unhappy Souls.
Wild Common, The.
Levertov. In Mind.
Looking-glass.
Levine. Baby Villon.
Liddy. Bright Crown of Freedom, The.
Lorde. Good Mirrors are Not Cheap.
Lovelace. Song: "In mine one [or own] monument I lie [or lye]."
Lowell. Fat Man in the Mirror, The.
Lowry. Conversations With Goethe.
God help those and others who.
Imprisoned in a Liverpool of self.
Lake, a sea itself, whose gentle crash, A.
Stone must be rolled away from self's pain, The.
"MacDiarmid." Wind-bags, The.
MacLeish. Eve's Now-I-Lay-Me.
MacNeice. Carrick Revisited.
How, yes how! To achieve in a world of flux and bonfires.
Man woman and child.
Once-in-Passing, The.
Merrill. Dreams About Clothes.
Remora.
Syrinx.
Merton. Inner Law, The.
Lao Tzu's Wake.
Man of Tao, The.
Morgan. Being, I.
Nathan. Conversation Piece.

Hello Again.
Hole.
Just Looking, Thank You.
Third Wish, The.
Nemerov. Angel and Stone.
Companions, The.
Earthquake in the West, The.
Flame of a Candle, The.
Glass Dialectic.
Knowledge.
Mirror, The.
Returning to Europe.
Salt Garden, The.
Sanctuary, The.
Neruda. Dying.
Egoist.
One Comes Back.
Successions.
O'Hara. Mayakovsky.
To the Harbormaster.
Oliver. Journey, The.
Olson. As the Dead Prey upon Us.
"At the boundary of the mighty world" H. (T) 620 foll.
Dogwood Comes Out Yellow, The.
Key West.
Love.
Motion, The.
My belly / sounds like an owl.
My poor dumb body.
Of the United States.
Pavement, The.
Twist, The.
Piercy. Unlearning to Not Speak.
Plath. I Am Vertical.
In Plaster.
Nick and the Candlestick.
Ravaged Face, The.
Raine. All things new / But I: no shadow.
Amo Ergo Sum.
Blue butterflies' eyed wings.
Harvest of learning I have reaped.
"I am the stream," I said.
It crossed my mind.
Live on in me, remembered ones.
Night Sky.
Night Thought.
Poet Answers the Accuser, The.
Self.
This little house / No smaller than the world.
Today as I / Looked up at the sky's great face.
Two Invocations of Death.
What have I to regret.
Rich. Delta.
Double Monologue.
Integrity.
Moth Hour.
Our Whole Life.
Rain on the West Side Highway.
They come to you with their descriptions of your soul.
Trying to Talk with a Man.
Upper Broadway.
What kind of beast would turn its life into words?
When We Dead Awaken.
Roethke. Journey to the Interior.
Prayer before Study.
Renewal, The.
Sensibility! O La!
Rossetti. Hymn: "O the bitter shame and sorrow."
Our heaven must be within ourselves / Our home and heaven the work of faith.
Thread of Life, The.
Rukeyser. Easter Eve 1945.
Light falling on that filled will drives.
Not to Be Printed, Not to Be Said, Not to Be Thought.
Red bridge fastening this city to the forest, A.
Song from Puck Fair.
Then I Saw What the Calling Was.
To Enter That Rhythm Where the Self Is Lost.
Sandburg. Chicago Poet.
Sexton. Ballad of the Lonely Masturbator, The.

Bat.
Civil War, The.
For John, Who Begs Me Not to Enquire Further.
Going Gone.
House, The.
Old Dwarf Heart.
Other, The.
Second Psalm.
Self in 1958.
Shakespeare. Sonnet 10: "For shame! deny that thou bear'st love to any."
Sonnet 80: "O, how I faint when I of you do write."
Sonnet 88: "When thou shalt be dispos'd to set me light."
Sonnet 89: "Say that thou didst forsake me for some fault."
Shelley. Fragment: "Methought I was a billow in the crowd."
Fragment: Wedded Souls.
Simic. Charles Simic.
My Shoes.
Quiet Talk with Oneself, A.
Smith, Stevie. Portrait (II).
Sorrentino. Billy McCoy.
Spender. Solipsist.
Stevens. Idiom of the Hero.
Man on the Dump, The.
On the Adequacy of Landscape.
Stevenson. Youth and Love I ("Once only by the garden gate").
Tate. Meaning of Life, The.
Thomas. How Shall My Animal.
I, in My Intricate Image.
Out of the Sighs.
Tomlinson. Something: a Direction.
Updike. Amoeba.
Yes, self-obsession fills our daily clothes.
Van Duyn. Pot-au-feu.
Wakoski. My Trouble.
Walcott. At the Queen's Park Hotel, with its white, high-ceilinged rooms.
Hotel Normandie Pool, The.
Love after Love.
My double, tired of morning, closes the door.
Prelude: "I, with legs crossed along the daylight, watch."
Waldman. Dialogue Between the Self & the Soul.
Eyes in All Heads to Be Looked out Of.
Whitman. Ah Poverties, Wincings, and Sulky Retreats.
Are You the New Person Drawn toward Me?
I celebrate myself, and sing myself.
Small the Theme of My Chant.
That Shadow My Likeness.
Trippers and askers surround me.
Walt Whitman.
Wilbur. Leaving.
Williams, Charles Kenneth. Bad Mouth.
One of the Muses.
Or.
Resentment.
Shade, The.
Thinking Thought.
Twice More.
Williams, William Carlos. Danse Russe.
Self-Portrait 1.
Self, The.
Wright, Charles. Self-Portrait ("Charles on the Trevisan, night bridge").
Wroth. Sonnet 46: "Love, thou hast all, for now thou hast mee made."
Wyatt. Once [or Ons], as methought, Fortune me kissed [or kist or kyst].
Yau. Choral Amphisbaena.
Yeats. Dialogue of Self and Soul, A.
Young. Self-Portrait: Holding On.
Seventh April.
Tiny Self-Portrait.
What Have You Got of Your Own.
Zukofsky. Furius, with no key to service, no key.
Memory of V. I. Ulianov.
Not it was no dream of coming death.
Suffenus is, stay Varus,—whom you've

proven—is the.
Warm gale, a dose of spring—revert to the pores.

Self-Deceit

Beatles. And Your Bird Can Sing.
I'll Be Back.
Nowhere Man.
Berrigan. New Personal Poem.
Berryman. Tongue there is wags, down in the dark wood O, A.
Creeley. One Way.
Davie. Brilliance.
Everson. Annul in Me My Manhood.
But now having seen.
Gallagher. Ever After.
Gardner. Not At All What One Is Used To.
Ginsberg. In Society.
Ode: My 24th Year.
Hardy. Collector Cleans His Picture, The.
Dissemblers, The.
Jeffers. Self-Criticism in February.
Lawrence. Men Like Gods.
Liddy. Dream of a Strange One.
Lovelace. Sonnet: "When I by Thy Faire Shape Did Sweare."
MacNeice. Alcohol.
Canto XIV: "Battle? That is one way of looking at the matter, A."
Merton. To a Severe Nun.
Nash. Happy Ending of Mr. Train, The.
Plath. Fearful, The.
Other Two, The.
Ransom. Parting at Dawn.
Rich. Power.
Sandburg. If you can imagine love letters written back and forth between Mary.
Smith, Stevie. Infelice.
No Respect.
Snodgrass. Locked House, A.
Stuart. Elect, The.
Swinburne. Ballad of Life, A.
Whittier. Changeling, The.
Haschish, The.
Williams, William Carlos. Love Charm, The.
Wright, Charles. May Journal.

Self-Doubt

Berryman. Anomalous I linger, and ignore.
Huddle of Need, A.
Somber Prayer.
Bukowski. 35 Seconds.
Byron. Soliloquy of a Bard in the Country.
Ceravolo. Grass.
In My Crib.
Soul in Migration.
Creeley. Chicago.
Song, The: "It still makes sense."
Cullen. Self Criticism.
Doolittle. Centaur Song.
Gallagher. Rhododendrons.
Ginsberg. Fragment 1956.
Graves. My Ghost.
Hewitt. Belfastman Abroad Argues with Himself.
Modelled Head, The.
Pangur Ban.
Hill. Lachrimae Amantis.
Jeffers. Love the Wild Swan.
Koch. Days and Nights.
Koertge. Man like a Curtain, A.
Lowry. Conversations With Goethe.
Half of the harm that is done in this world.
Minstrel in Labrador, A.
Villaknell.
MacLeish. Tyrant of Syracuse.
MacNeice. Oh but my doubt is a sea harsher than this that I see.
Neruda. One Comes Back.
Whom can I ask / what I meant to achieve in this world?
Olson. Day Song, the Day After.
Maximus, to Himself.
Purgatory Blind.
Rich. Dialogue.
Letters: March 1969.
Roofwalker, The.
Sexton. Lessons in Hunger.
Shakespeare. Sonnet 46: "Mine eye and heart

are at a mortal war."
Sonnet 76: "Why is my verse so barren of new pride."
Sonnet 131: "Thou art as tyrannous, so as thou art."
Snodgrass. Dostoievsky Warns W. D. about Wearing Raskolnikov's Hat.
Swift. On Burning a Dull Poem.
Updike. Thoughts While Driving Home.
Walcott. Codicil.
Walk, The.
Williams, Charles Kenneth. Body, The.
Cautionary, The.
Solid, The.
Wright, Charles. Laguna Blues.
Yeats. Stream and Sun at Glendalough.
Zukofsky. Tam Cari Capitis.
You three:—my wife.

Self-Knowledge

Ammons. Chasm.
Angelou. When I Think about Myself.
Arnold. Self-Dependence.
Ashbery. And Others, Vaguer Presences.
Atwood. You refuse to own / yourself, you permit.
Beatles. Across the Universe.
Dig a Pony.
Get Back.
Hey Bulldog.
I've Got a Feeling.
Berg. Don't Forget.
In the Evening.
Berrigan. Around the Fire.
It's Important.
Browning, Robert. Reverie.
Carruth. Aer.
Sonnet: "How is it, tell me, that this new self can be—."
True, I happen. So.
Ceravolo. Floating Gardens.
O Heart Uncovered.
Ciardi. Birthday.
Dialogue with Outer Space.
Knowing Bitches.
Creeley. Awakening, The.
Loop, A.
Reason, A.
Return.
Cummings. Total stranger one black day, A.
De la Mare. Memory.
Self to self.
Dickinson. Though we are each unknown to ourself.
Duncan. After a Long Illness.
Dunn. In the House.
Introduction to the 20th Century.
"Dylan." Bob Dylan's Blues.
Dirge: "I hate myself for lovin' you and the weakness that it showed."
Guess I'm Doin' Fine.
I and I.
It Ain't Me, Babe.
Joan Baez in Concert, Part 2.
Lay Down Your Weary Tune.
Love Is Just a Four-Letter Word.
Man in Me, The.
Run go get out of here.
Gallagher. Into the Known.
Story of a Citizen, The.
Gardner. Conversation at Midnight with Oscar Williams.
Jean Sans Terre The Chest of Drawers.
Not At All What One Is Used To.
Garrigue. Circle, The.
Ginsberg. Sather Gate Illumination.
Shrouded Stranger, The.
Glück. Gemini.
Graves. Spite of Mirrors.
Griffiths. Expectations.
Hacker. Rhetoric.
Hall. Abroad Thoughts from Home.
Hardy. Beauty, The.
Surview [or Surview: Cogitavi Vias Meas].
Hartley. Holding in reserve.
Hewitt. Mirror.
Style.
Hugo. Duwamish Head.

Jeffers. Self-Criticism in February.
Joseph. Meeting Up.
Mirror, Mirror.
STUDY: *A Lady in her Bedroom* (Bonnard).
Kipling. Glories, The.
Knott. At the Crossroads.
Larkin. If My Darling.
Reasons for Attendance.
Lawrence. After All the Tragedies Are Over.
Know Deeply, Know Thyself More Deeply.
Know Thyself.
Know Thyself, and That Thou Art Mortal.
Levertov. Three Meditations.
Lewis. Quest, The.
Lorde. For Each of You.
McGrath. Seekers, The.
You Taught Me.
MacLeish. What Adam Said.
MacNeice. Aubade for Infants.
Merton. Keng's Disciple.
Morrison. You Think I Don't Know.
Nash. Sage of Darien, The.
Nemerov. Glass Dialectic.
Neruda. Cold.
Conditions.
Heavy Surf, A.
Pardon Me.
Star.
Olson. Cross-Legged, the Spider and the Web.
In Cold Hell, in Thicket.
Lamp, The.
Moonset, Gloucester, December 1, 1957, 1:58 A.M.
Newly Discovered "Homeric" Hymn, A.
Sit by the Window and Refuse.
Stevens Song.
Swimming through the air, in schools upon the highways.
Wholly absorbed / into my own conduits to.
Oppen. Confession.
From a Phrase of Simone Weil's and Some Words of Hegel's.
Hills, The.
Knowledge not of sorrow, you were, The.
Myself I Sing.
Product.
Semite.
There are things / We live among "and to see them."
Which is ours, which is ourselves.
World, World—.
Owen. Show, The.
Pack. Human Pile, The.
Raine. Bad Dream, A.
Ransom. Crocodile.
"Reed." I'll Be Your Mirror.
There Is No Time.
Rich. Afterward.
August.
Can it be growing colder when I begin.
Essential Resources.
Every peak is a crater. This is the law of volcanoes.
I can see myself years back at Sunion.
Letter from the Land of Sinners.
Stranger, The.
Roethke. Lines upon Leaving a Sanitarium.
O, Thou Opening, O.
Open House.
Rolfe. Ballad of the Noble Intentions.
Catalogue of I.
Melancholy Comus, The.
Sunday Evening Revery.
Sandburg. If you can imagine love letters written back and forth between Mary.
In the heave of the hankering sea.
Questionnaire.
Who knows the people, the migratory harvest hands and berry pickers.
Sarton. Myself to Me.
Schwartz. "All is forgiven when guilt is accepted."
Apollo Musagete, Poetry, and the Leader of the Muses.
Maxims of Sisyphus, The.
Overture.
Sexton. Kind Sir: These Woods.

Shakespeare. Sonnet 121: "'Tis better to be vile than vile esteem'd."
Silverstein. Magic.
Simic. Quiet Talk with Oneself, A.
Smith, Charlotte. Partial Muse, has from my earliest hours, The.
Smith, Stevie. Do Not!
Stafford. Story That Could Be True, A.
Stevens. Of Modern Poetry.
Prelude to Objects.
Tate. Homily.
Meaning of Life, The.
Tomlinson. How It Happened.
Van Duyn. Essay on Criticism, An.
Three Valentines to the Wide World.
Walcott. Harbour, The.
Whitman. Out from Behind This Mask.
Perfections.
Wilbur. Driftwood.
Williams, Charles Kenneth. Bad Mouth.
Becoming Somebody Else.
Beyond.
Did I write this.
Failure.
Jetsam.
What we are / given.
Williams, Miller. Rebecca at Play.
Williams, William Carlos. Sale, The.
Slow Movement.
Wordsworth. Ode to Lycoris.
Wright, Charles. California Dreaming.
Chinese Journal.
Gate City Breakdown.
Self-Portrait ("Someday they'll find me out, and my lavish hands").
Wright, James. Three Stanzas From Goethe.
Yeats. Two Trees, The.
Young. Dancing.
Dancing All Alone.
Zukofsky. Cars once steel and green, now old.
How many / Times round.
Sand: For the cigarette finished, The.

Self-Pity
Beatles. I'm a Loser.
Misery.
Tell Me Why.
Think For Yourself.
Berryman. Languid the songs I wish I willed . I try.
Bukowski. About My Very Tortured Friend, Peter.
Empire of Coins, An.
Reprieve and Admixture.
Coleridge. Addressed to a Young Man of Fortune.
Creeley. Love ("Tracking through this").
Dunn. Petty Thing, A.
When the Revolution Came.
Hewitt. Emily Dickinson.
Kipling. Natural Theology.
Lawrence. Self-Pity.
Tragedy.
Liddy. Icarus.
Markson. Occupation.
Neruda. Conditions.
Rolfe. Catalogue.
Schuyler. Self-Pity Is a Kind of Lying, Too.
Sexton. Killing the Spring.
Sidney. Loved I am, and yet complain[e] of Love.
Smith, Stevie. Analysand.
Sad Heart, The.
Warren. Interjection #5: Solipsism and Theology.
Williams, Charles Kenneth. Fat.
Thinking Thought.
Wroth. Sonnet 42: "If ever love had force in huma[i]ne brest?"
Yeats. Sad Shepherd, The.
Zukofsky. Guillaume de Machault (1300-1377) Ballade: Plourès, dames.
In the midst of things.

Self-Reliance
Arnold. Self-Dependence.
Brontë. Strong I stand, though I have borne.
Weaned from life and torn away.
Browning, Robert. At the "Mermaid."

Ceravolo. Data.
Clark. Withdrawal.
Creeley. Xmas Poem: Bolinas.
"Dylan." Bob Dylan's Blues.
Restless Farewell.
Trust Yourself.
Emerson. Poet is at home, A.
Power.
Simple people each with basket or tool, The.
Frost. Figure in the Doorway, The.
Hewitt. Ars Poetica.
Leaf.
My Father.
Jong. Becoming a Nun.
Knight. Evolutionary Poem No. 1.
Evolutionary Poem No. 2.
Lawrence. Deeper Than Love.
McNeill. Ballad of Miss Sally.
Melville. In a Garret.
Nash. Compliments of a Friend.
Neruda. Bird.
Olson. Maximus to Himself June 1964.
Rich. Dark lintels, the blue and foreign stones, The.
Song: "You're wondering if I'm lonely."
Rolfe. Brigadas Internacionales.
May Day Song.
Rossetti. I seek among the living & I seek.
Smith, Charlotte. Lark's Nest, The.
Smith, Stevie. Company.
Sorrentino. Edges, The.
Spenser. By Her That Is Most Assured to Her Self.
Zukofsky. Catullus viii.
Peri Poietikes.

Self-Restraint
Brontë. All day I've toiled, but not with pain.
Campion. Harden now thy tyred hart, with more than flinty rage.
Catullus. Carmen 8: "Break off / fallen Catullus."
"Dylan." Heart of Mine.
Eberhart. Throwing Yourself Away.
Everson. Annul in Me My Manhood.
Glück. Reproach, The.
Hewitt. Passion.
Jeffers. Nightpiece.
Knott. Closet, The.
Depressionism.
McNeill. When the Scientists Told Me of the Expanding Universe.
Markson. Vow, The.
Stafford. Clash.
Stevenson. My Conscience!
Williams, Charles Kenneth. Thinking Thought.
Williams, William Carlos. Defiance to Cupid.
Zukofsky. Catullus vii.
Miss her, Catullus? don't be so inept to rail.

Self-Righteousness
Burns. Holy Willie's Prayer.
Crane. Ah! the divine infatuation.
Dunn. Moralists.
Gallagher. That Kind of Thing.
Hewitt. Breastplate.
Colmcille.
I've seen no more than three loved persons die.
Mobile Mollusc, A.
Jong. Perfect Poet, The.
Lawrence. Censors.
Lindsay. Drunkards in the Street, The.
Kind of Scorn, A.
McAuley. After Yeats, After Ronsard, PaceHopkins.
MacNeice. Over the roofs and cranes, blistered cupola and hungry smokestack.
O'Hara. Spleen.
Williams, Miller. Promotion, The.

Selfishness
Ammons. Coming Right Up.
Auden. Candles Gutter Low, The.
Berry. It is presumptuous and irresponsible to pray for other people. A.
Blake. Proverbs of Hell.
Burns. Friend Commissar, since we're met and are happy.

There's a youth in this city, it were a great pity.
Carruth. Tanck's Song About the Younger Generation.
Cowper. Against Interested Love.
Retired Cat, The.
Davie. At the Cradle of Genius.
Bowing the Head.
Doolittle. You'll go on, talking away.
Dunbar. Career, A.
Dunn. From the Manifesto of the Selfish.
Ford. Some flowers wickedly.
Gardner. Spendthrift.
Larkin. Love.
None of the Books Have Time.
Lawrence. All I Ask.
Chimaera.
Conceit.
Furniture.
Immorality.
Intimates.
Painter's Wife, The.
Sphinx.
To a Certain Friend.
True Love at Last.
Ultimate Reality.
Vengeance Is Mine.
Woe.
Lindsay. Curse for Kings, A.
Lowry. Half of the harm that is done in this world.
Meredith. Quake, quake, let us turn Quaker all!
Society.
Nash. Doctor Fell? I Thought So.
Medusa and the Mot Juste.
Olson. Cinos.
Piercy. Always you were dancing before the altar of guilt.
You speak of the collective.
Rich. Boundary.
Roethke. Poetaster.
Shakespeare. Sonnet 62: "Sin [or Sinne] of self-love [or selfe-love] possesseth all mine eye [or eie]."
Shapiro. Intellectual, The.
Silverstein. Just Me, Just Me.
Smith, Stevie. Analysand.
Egocentric.
Major Macroo.
Snyder. Spel Against Demons.
Swift. To Stella.
Tennyson. Character, A.
Williams, Charles Kenneth. Like Little Birds.
Williams, Miller. Promotion, The.

Semele
Graves. Ambrosia of Dionysus and Semele, The.
Lovelace. Against the Love of Great Ones.

Seneca
Merton. Seneca.

Senility
Atwood. Some kind of ritual / for your dwindling.
Berry. Wilderness Starts towards Him, A.
Dobyns. Dead Baby.
Graves. Nightmare of Senility.
Hall. By the Exeter River.
Hesketh. From the Day Room.
Hewitt. My Widowed Mother.
When my wife's sister's husband came to die.
Koertge. My Grandmother.
Levertov. Old Adam, The.
Lieberman. Stubby Carrot.
Paley. My Father at 89.
Tomlinson. Last Days of the Miser.
Williams, Charles Kenneth. Tails.
Williams, William Carlos. Another Old Woman.
Two Pendants: For the Ears.

Sennacherib, King of Assyria
Byron. Destruction of Sennacherib, The.

Senses
Angelou. Senses of Insecurity.
Atwood. Fortification, A.
Nothing.
Beatles. It's All Too Much.

Bishop. Thy senses are too different to please me.
Blake. Memorable Fancy, A ("As I was walking among the fires of hell").
Bogan. Spirit's Song.
Browning, Robert. Transcendentalism: A Poem in Twelve Books.
Catullus. Carmen 13: "I shall expect / you in to dine."
Ceravolo. Chains of Mountains.
Drunken Winter.
Grow.
May.
Water: How Weather Feels the Cotton Hotels.
Creeley. For Helen.
Penitent, The.
Pryaer, A.
Two.
Variations.
Way.
Davie. And of the sixth sense, the infinitesimal suffix.
Seur, near Blois.
Dickinson. Light exists in Spring, A.
Dunn. Afterlife.
Emerson. Color, taste, and smell, smaragdus, sugar, and musk.
Go into the garden.
I call her beautiful;—she says.
Griffiths. Nearness.
Herrick. Eyes before the Eares, The.
Hewitt. Bifocal in Gaza.
Bleeze.
Glen of Light, The.
Last Summer, For Roberta (1975), The.
Living Landscape, The.
Nourish Your Heart.
October-Born.
On the Canal.
Variations on a Theme.
Will.
Lawrence. Cabbage-Roses.
Deepest Sensuality, The.
Renaissance.
Satisfaction.
Sense of Truth.
Liddy. Cantico Per Lo Tuo Amore II.
Lovelace. Fabullus I will treat you handsomely.
Mahon. Thinking of Inis Oírr in Cambridge, Mass.
Merrill. Amsterdam.
Merton. Holy Sacrament of the Altar, The.
My gaze is clear as a sunflower.
Olson. Red Mallows.
Raine. Hieros Gamos.
Instrument, The.
Roethke. Prayer: "If I must of my Senses lose."
St. John. Day of the Sentry, The.
Sandburg. Slabs of the Sunburnt West.
Schuyler. Freely Espousing.
Shakespeare. Sonnet 151: "In faith, I do[e] not love thee with mine eyes."
Sidney. Seventh Song.
Sorrentino. In a fantastic light.
Spender. Never Being.
Stevens. Arcades of Philadelphia the Past.
Dish of Peaches in Russia, A.
Poem Written at Morning.
Thomas. When All My Five and Country Senses See.
Wilbur. Lamarck Elaborated.
Zukofsky. All Wise.
Canapés, my Fabullus, at home any.
We are crossing the bridge now.
When the crickets.

Sensitivity
Beatles. It's Only Love.
Burns. Rusticity's ungainly form.
Creeley. Pryaer, A.
Gunn. Saturnalia.
Herrick. Vertue Is Sensible of Suffering.
Hesketh. Mary.
Levertov. O Taste and See.
Lindsay. Song for Elizabeth, A.
Lowry. Only thing that Jack had, The.

Meredith. Triad of British Evils, A.
Merton. Written Next to a Blue Flower.
Nash. That's Funny, Wasn't It? No, It Won't Be.
Nemerov. View from an Attic Window, The.
Owen. Insensibility.
Rossetti. "Immurata" Sister, An.
Smith, Stevie. Rencontres Funestes.
Van Duyn. Death By Aesthetics.

Sensuality
Atwood. Nothing.
Beatles. And I Love Her.
Savoy Truffle.
Catullus. Carmen 45: "Phyllis Corydon clutched to him."
Ceravolo. Fly.
Creeley. Flesh.
Flower, The.
Cullen. Cat, The.
Cummings. After your poppied hair inaugurates.
Emperor / sleeps in a palace of porphyry, The.
Moon is hiding in, The.
My lady is an ivory garden.
My love / thy hair is one kingdom.
Nearer:breath of my breath:take not thy tingling.
Of evident invisibles / exquisite the hovering.
Since feeling is first.
Sometimes i am alive because with.
(Swooning)a pillar of youngly.
Through the tasteless minute efficient room.
What is thy mouth to me?
You said Is / there anything which.
Yours is the music for no instrument.
Eberhart. Giantess, The.
Everson. Dark God of Eros, Christ of the buried brood.
Ferlinghetti. Away above a harborful.
Fox. Shunga.
Visitor, The.
Gallagher. Backdrop With Lovers, 1931.
Hacker. Canzone: "Consider the three functions of the tongue."
Knott. (Sideshow).
Levertov. Eros at Temple Stream.
Liddy. Cantico Per Lo Tuo Amore II.
Correspondences.
Lesbos.
Spring tide swept 'em to the hills.
Thursdays Are Sacred.
Vir IV.
You Came By on Bamboo Stilts, Playing Horse..
O'Hara. Poem: "Twin spheres full of fur and noise."
Owen. Purple.
Pound. Alba ("As cool as the pale wet leaves").
Encounter, The.
House of Splendour, The.
Ransom. Rose, The.
Rich. Floating Poem, Unnumbered, The.
Rukeyser. Child in the Great Wood.
Song: Lying in Daylight.
Snyder. Running Water Music II.
Stein. Lifting Belly.
Sonatina Followed by Another, A.
Van Duyn. Annual and Perennial Problem, An.
Death By Aesthetics.
With Warm Regards to Miss Moore and Mr. Ransom.
Wakoski. Belly Dancer.
Whitman. From Pent-up Aching Rivers.
To the Garden the World.
Williams, William Carlos. Crystal Maze, A.
Sappho.
Translation.
Wordsworth. Septimius and Acme.
Yeats. Chosen.
Zukofsky. Acme, Septimius, sighs so amorous.
Happier, happier, now.
Madison, Wis., Remembering the Bloom of Monticello (1931).

Separation
Angelou. My Life Has Turned to Blue.

Arnold. Farewell, A: "My horse's feet beside the lake."
Forsaken Merman, The.
Isolation: To Marguerite.
Ashbery. Recent Past, The.
Atwood. If I were a foreigner, as you say.
Postcard.
Auden. Amor Vincit Omnia.
At Parting.
Envoi: "From the red chimneys smoke climbs slow and straight."
Envoi: "You go / Now you are glad."
Felo de se.
Happy Tree, The.
In a Train.
On Receiving a Christmas Card.
On the frontier at dawn getting down.
Tea-time in November.
Visit, A.
Beatles. I'm So Tired.
P.S. I Love You.
Beckett. Cascando.
Berg. Last Meeting.
Milk.
1911.
Thread.
Berry. Except.
In place with you, as I come and go.
Kentucky River Junction.
To search for what belongs where it is.
Berryman. Bell to sore knees vestigial crowds, let crush.
Crouched on a ridge sloping to where you pour.
He Resigns.
How shall I do, to pass the weary time.
Loves are the summer's. Summer like a bee.
One note, a daisy, and a photograph.
Sullen brook hardly would satisfy, A.
They come too thick, hail-hard, and all beside.
Tyranny of your car—so far resembles.
Wasp skims nearby up the bright warm air, A.
When I recall I could believe you'd go.
You should be gone in winter, that Nature mourn.
Betjeman. Pershore Station, or a Liverish Journey First Class.
Bishop. Argument.
Time has come to call a halt, The.
Blake. Memorable Fancy, A ("I was in a printing house in Hell & I saw the method in").
Bly. Man Writes to a Part of Himself, A.
Boyle. And Winter.
Night Letter, A.
Thunderstorm in South Dakota.
Brontë. A.G.A. to A.E.
Alcona, in its changing mood.
Companions, all day long we've stood.
I gazed within thine earnest eyes.
I see around me tombstones grey.
It is too late to call thee now.
Last Words.
O mother, I am not regretting.
Song: "O between distress and pleasure."
There shines the moon, at noon of night.
Thousand sounds of happiness, A.
'Tis moonlight, summer moonlight.
Where were ye all? and where wert thou?
Wind was rough which tore, The.
Written on Returning to the P. of I. on the 10th of January, 1827.
Yes, holy be thy resting place.
Browning, Elizabeth Barrett. Catarina to Camoens.
Sonnet: "Go from me. Yet I feel that I shall stand."
Browning, Robert. In a Gondola.
In Three Days.
Last Ride Together, The.
Lovers' Quarrel, A.
Too Late.
Waring.
Bukowski. All the Casualties..
Communion.
Day I Kicked Away a Bankroll, The.
Bunting. Hi, tent-boy, get that tent down.

Burns. Bonie Lad That's Far Awa, The.
English Song.
For the Sake o' Somebody.
Frae the friends and Land I love.
Here Awa' There Awa ["Here awa', there
    awa' wandering, Willie"].
Highland Balou, The.
Highland Mary.
How lang and dreary is the night.
I Look to the North.
Jockey's Ta'en the Parting Kiss.
Musing on the roaring ocean.
My Bonnie [or Bony] Mary.
My Harry was a gallant gay.
My Nannie's Awa'.
Northern Lass, The.
On the Seas and Far Away.
Sae Far Awa.
Shepherd's Wife, The.
Song: "Behold the hour, the boat arrive."
Song: "From thee, ELIZA, I must go."
Song: "O, Logan, sweetly didst thou glide."
Song: "Will ye go to the Indies, my Mary."
There Was a Bonie Lass.
To William Creech.
Winter It Is Past, The.
Young Highland Rover, The.
Byron. Epistle to Augusta.
Fare Thee Well.
On Parting.
When We Two Parted.
Campion. Harden now thy tyred hart, with
    more than flinty rage.
Carew. Elegy on the La: Pen: Sent to My
    Mistress Out of France, An.
On His Mistress[e] Going to Sea.
To Her in Absence; a Ship.
To Mistress Katherine Neville, on Her Green
    Sickness.
Carroll, Jim. Moss under your fingernails it
    feeds, The.
Poem: "It's sad this vision required."
Torn Canvas.
Catullus. Carmen 8: "Break off / fallen
    Catullus."
Carmen 30: "Alfenus from Cremona / forsakes
    the friendship of friends."
Carmen 37: "Nine posts, five doors, up the
    Clivus."
Carmen 46: "Now spring bursts."
Clark. Momentum.
Clough. Were I with you or you with me.
Coleridge. On a Late Connubial Rupture in
    High Life.
Separation from Asra.
Something Childish, but Very Natural.
Wedded Love.
Cooper. In the Last Few Moments Came the
    Old German Cleaning Woman.
Letters.
Yesterday a letter / spoke of our parting.
Cowper. Bid adieu, my sad heart, bid adieu to
    thy peace.
Hope, like the short-liv'd ray that gleams
    awhile.
Written after Leaving Her at New Burns.
Crashaw. Alexias.
Creeley. Ballad of the Despairing Husband.
Enough.
Envoi: "Particulars they want."
For Rainer Gerhardt.
Irishman's Lament on the Approaching Winter,
    An.
Kid.
Knokke.
Sight, A.
Cullen. Dictum.
Therefore, Adieu.
To One Not There.
Cummings. Ballad of Love.
Clown's smirk in the skull of a baboon, A.
It is so long since my heart has been with
    yours.
Or who and who.
S.F.D.
T.A.M.
Up into the silence the green.

We miss you,jack—tactfully you(with one
    cocked).
When my sensational moments are no more.
When thou art dead,dead,and far from the
    splendid sin.
You being in love.
Dickinson. Air is soft as Italy, The.
Busy missing you.
Crumbling elms and evergreens, The.
Morning without you is a dwindled Dawn.
Today or this noon.
Dobyns. Separate Time, A.
This Life.
Waking.
Doolittle. Toward the Piraeus.
Dove. Someone's Blood.
Dunbar. Comrade.
Lyric, A: "My lady love lives far away."
Duncan. Passage over Water.
"Dylan." Down the Highway.
Girl of the North Country.
If You See Her, Say Hello.
Simple Twist of Fate.
Something's Burning, Baby.
You're a Big Girl Now.
Edmunds. Farewell: "Farewell, my love,
    goodbye."
Lancaster Street.
Eliot. Portrait of a Lady.
Emerson. Ah strange strange strange.
Atom from atom yawns as far.
Last Farewell, The.
To Eva.
Unity.
Who ever suffered as I from separation?
Ferlinghetti. In Golden Gate Park that day.
Third World Calling.
Two Amsterdams.
Two Scavengers in a Truck, Two Beautiful
    People in a Mercedes.
Wild Life Cameo, Early Morn.
Ford. Activity without / Attachment. One link
    with the.
Seeking out corpses.
Two people can be.
Fox. Alioth.
Peregrine Falcon.
Frost. Flower-Gathering.
Gallagher. Bird-Window-Flying.
Kidnap[p]er.
With Stars.
Gardner. Accomplices, The.
Garrigue. Requiem: "In the sudden white
    silence, where are you?"
With Glaze of Tears.
Ginsberg. Message.
Glück. From the Japanese.
Hesitate to Call.
Horse.
Night Song.
Return, The.
Rosy.
World Breaking Apart.
Graves. Fortunate Child.
Full Moon.
Her Brief Withdrawal.
I Will Write.
In the Vestry.
Sentence, The.
Snapped Thread, The.
Song: Of Course.
Song: The Clocks of Time.
Tower of Love, The.
True Magic.
Griffiths. Contact.
Everyone Watches the Sunset.
Gunn. During an Absence.
June.
Separation, The.
Hacker. Across the mud flats and the wide
    roads, over rivers and borders.
Companion, The.
Crépusule Provençale.
Going Back to the River.
Home, and I've.
If we talk, we're too tired to make love; if
    we.

Letter from Goose Creek: April.
Living in the Moment.
Satisfied loves eat big breakfasts. I.
Separate Lives.
Somewhere in a Turrent.
Villanelle: "Every day our bodies seperate."
You rang me up this morning from Marseilles.
Hardy. After the Visit.
Amabel.
At Castle Boterel.
Difference, The.
Going of the Battery, The.
Her Song.
I Say, "I'll Seek Her."
In a Cathedral City.
In Death Divided.
In Vision I Roamed.
My Cicely.
Old Gown, The.
On the Departure Platform.
Tarrying Bridegroom, The.
They Would Not Come.
To Louisa in the Lane.
Walk, The.
When Wearily We Shrink Away.
Herrick. His Sailing from Julia.
Pastorall Sung to the King: Montano, Silvio,
    and Mirtillo, Shepards, A.
Presence and Absence.
Hesketh. I Cannot Look into the Sun.
Love without Frontiers.
Orpheus in the Underground.
Single Footprints.
Hewitt. Mother and Son.
Scattering, The.
Housman. As through the wild green hills of
    Wyre.
He would not stay for me; and who can
    wonder?
Now hollow fires burn out to black.
Oh were he and I together.
White in the moon the long road lies.
Winds out of the west land blow, The.
Hughes, Langston. Afro-American Fragment.
Dream.
So Long.
Hughes, Ted. Calves harshly parted from their
    mamas.
Sheep.
Jarrell. Story, A.
Street Has Changed, The.
Keats. Endymion: Poetic Romance.
Kipling. Love Song of Har Dyal, The.
Rimini.
Song in the Desert, A.
Widower, The.
Knight. For a Brookline Lady I Love.
Memo #5.
Upon Your Leaving.
Knott. Shorts / Excerpts ("Other strangers than
    our own may remember").
Shorts / Excerpts ("Our farewells lack the
    plausibility of our departures").
Summoning, The.
Kunitz. After the Last Dynasty.
Father and Son.
Parting.
Tristia.
Unquiet Ones, The.
Larkin. As a War in Years of Peace.
Within the Dream You Said.
Lawrence. Mother's Son in Salonika.
Mutilation.
Reach Over.
Separated.
Walk Warily.
Lewis. Chanson Triste.
Separation, A.
Way Back, The.
Liddy. Sister Beach, Sister Garden.
Lorde. Memorial III—from a Phone Booth on
    Broadway.
Lovelace. Amyntor from beyond the Sea to
    Alexis.
Another ("I Did believe I was in Heav'n").
Sonnet: "When I by Thy Faire Shape Did
    Sweare."

To Lucasta, [on] Going beyond the Seas.
To Lucasta, [on] Going to the War[re]s.
Lowry. I bet you don't know who I am.
Slough of Despond: Or the House of Hope, The.
To account for this, but it cannot be.
McAuley. To His Host, Who Has Asked Him To Stay Longer.
MacLeish. Eve's Now-I-Lay-Me.
They say they are one flesh.
MacNeice. And love hung still as crystal over the bed.
And the Lord was not in the whirlwind.
Bluebells.
Letter from India.
This Way Out.
When clerks and navvies fondle.
Markson. *Sans.*
Marvell. Definition of Love, The.
Morrison. Don't Start That.
I Want to Tell You.
Nash. Tin Wedding Whistle.
Nemerov. De Anima.
Neruda. Men (XVIII), The.
Olson. Boats' lights in the dawn going so swiftly the, The.
Newly Discovered "Homeric" Hymn, A.
Pack. Departing Words to a Son.
Remains.
Trying to Separate.
Plath. Monologue at 3 A.M.
Parliament Hill Fields.
Rival, The.
Pope. Epistle to Miss [*or* Miss Teresa] Blount, on Her Leaving the Town after the Coronation.
Prince. Eight times the autumn weather.
For Fugitives.
Sea View.
Strambotti.
Raine. Crossing the sound I summoned you in thought.
I went out in the naked light.
Poet is of those, The.
Ransom. Injured Sire.
Jack's Letter.
Overtures.
Spectral Lovers.
Two Gentlemen Scholars.
Two in August.
Rich. Across a city from you, I'm with you.
Boundary.
Natural Resources.
Pieces.
Prisoners, The.
Rain on the West Side Highway.
Splittings.
Rossetti. Come back to me, who wait and watch for you.
Cor Mio.
Dream, A.
Dream, The.
Echo from Willowwood, An.
Goodbye in fear, goodbye in sorrow.
Had Fortune parted us / Fortune is blind.
Husband and Wife.
I have a little husband / And he is gone to sea.
I said "All's over"—& I made my.
If.
In July / No goodbye.
Isidora.
Last Words of St. Telemachus, The.
Many in aftertimes will say of you.
May.
Meeting.
Next of Kin.
One Foot on Sea, and One on Shore.
Parting after parting, / Sore loss and gnawing pain.
Rosalind.
Two Parted.
Rukeyser. Meeting, The.
Story, A.
Young Girl of the Mississippi Valley, The.
Sexton. Eighteen Days without You.
Keeping the City.

Shakespeare. Sonnet 36: "et me confess that we two must be twain."
Sonnet 39: "O, how thy worth with manners may I sing."
Sonnet 44: "If the dull substance of my flesh were thought."
Sonnet 45: "Other two, slight air and purging fire, The."
Sonnet 47: "Betwixt mine eye and heart a league is took."
Sonnet 57: "Being your slave, what should I do[e] but tend."
Sonnet 97: "How like a winter hath my absence been[e]."
Sonnet 98: "From you have I been absent in the spring."
Sonnet 99: "Forward violet thus did I chide, The."
Shapiro. Glass Poem.
Haircut.
Homewreck.
V-Letter.
Shelton. Disintegration.
Sidney. Sonnet 87: "When I was forced from Stella ever dear."
Sonnet 89: "Now that of absence the most irksome night."
Snodgrass. First Leaf, The.
Locked House, A.
Snyder. Fear Not.
Sorrentino. Evening News, The.
Long Goodbye, The.
Spender. Absence.
Double Shame, The.
Not to You.
Room above the Square, The.
Song: "Stranger, you who hide my love."
Stevenson. As in their flight the birds of song.
Dedication: "My first gift and my last, to you."
Farewell to the Farm.
Fixed is the doom; and to the last of years.
I love to be warm by the red fireside.
If I had wings, my lady, like a dove.
Swallows travel to and fro.
To My Wife.
Stuart. Commencement.
Song for Champagne Saturday.
Tennyson. Fatima.
Updike. Report of Health.
Walker. Walker.
Warren. To a Friend Parting.
Whitman. Complaint, A.
Whitman. Complaint, A. ("Good-bye, my Fancy! / Farewell dear mate, dear love!").
Hours Continuing Long.
Out of the Rolling Ocean the Crowd.
Whittier. Amy Wentworth.
Memories.
Williams, Miller. Memphis, 2 P.M.
Sale.
Williams, William Carlos. I Will Sing a Joyous Song.
Letter, A.
Long Banister Lane.
Wordsworth. Complaint, A.
To ———: "O dearer far than light and life are dear."
Tradition of Oker Hill in Darley Dale, Derbyshire, A.
Wright, Charles. Dead Color.
March Journal.
Wright, James. Morning Hymn to a Dark Girl.
On the City Ramparts of Cádiz.
Wyatt. If it be so that I forsake thee.
Young. Only Race There Is, The.
What Is the Blues?
Zukofsky. Alfenus, remember *kind intimacies*? false? They elated us.
Catullus viii.
Finally a Valentine.
Miss her, Catullus? don't be so inept to rail.
Salt hacks, tavern boys, what skews, can't you burn alleys.
Warm gale, a dose of spring—revert to the pores.

Sepoy Rebellion
Kipling. Veterans, The.

Rossetti. In the Round Tower at Jhansi, June 8, 1857.
September
Auden. September.
Carruth. Essay on Love.
This Song.
Dickinson. September's Baccalaureate.
Eberhart. In the Garden.
Graves. September Landscape.
Hall. September Ode.
Hartley. And Now—September.
Housman. Tell Me Not Here [It Needs Not Saying].
Kinnell. Blackberry Eating.
Kipling. Two Months.
Merton. Morning. Good for foliage to resist the faithful wind.
Miller. Late September.
Nemerov. Crossing, The.
Sandburg. Dragoons, I tell you the white hydrangeas turn rust and go soon.
Home Fires.
Proud Torsos.
Snodgrass. September.
Wordsworth. September, 1815.
Sequoia Trees
Gunn. Lights among Redwood.
Jeffers. Summit Redwood, The.
Serenity
Berg. Iowa.
To Charlie.
Brontë. Awaking morning laughs from heaven.
Clough. Sweet streamlet bason! at thy side.
Coleridge. Hope and Tranquillity.
Ode to Tranquillity.
Creeley. Picture, A.
Davie. West Virginia's Auburn.
Eberhart. Parker River, The.
Fletcher. Buddha and Christ.
Glück. Porcelain Bowl.
Haines. Divided, the Man is Dreaming.
Hayden. Monet's "Waterlilies."
Hewitt. First Snow in the Glens.
Little Lough, The.
Monastary, Tourliani, Mykonos.
Ocean, 1940.
Watchers, The.
Hopkins. She Schools the Flighty Pupils of Her Eyes.
Knott. Obsolescent and His Deity (Polyptych), An.
Lewis. River Temple: Wai, The.
Liddy. Attention: First Lady of the Festival.
Sound of a Moment at Scariff, The.
MacLeish. White of her Colonial, The.
Melville. Off Cape Colona.
Merton. True Man, The.
Prince. Moonflower, The.
Sandburg. Flanders.
Peace, Night, Sleep.
Three Pieces on the Smoke of Autumn.
Snodgrass. At the Park Dance.
Snyder. Once at Cold Mountain, troubles cease.
Stevens. Rabbit as King of the Ghosts, A.
Wilbur. From the Lookout Rock.
Horses, The.
Zukofsky. And to paradise which is a port.
Not much more than being.
Sand: For the cigarette finished, The.
So sounds grass, and if it is sun or no sun.
Serfs. *see* **Slavery.**
Sermons
Browning, Robert. Impromptu on Hearing a Sermon by the Rev. T. R—Pronounced "Heavy."
Dickey, James. May Day Sermon to the Women of Gilmer County, Georgia, by a Woman Preacher Leaving the Baptist Church.
Hopkins. On One Who Borrowed His Sermons.
Hughes, Langston. Sunday Morning Prophecy.
Merton. Prayer and Sermon of Ibn Abbad.
Stevenson. You looked so tempting in the pew.
Servants
Angelou. When I Think about Myself.

Bishop. Cootchie.
Eliot. Aunt Helen.
Emerson. Be of good cheer, brave spirit; steadfastly.
Frost. Blueberries.
Glück. Abishag.
Hall. Revolution, The.
Herrick. To His Maid Prew.
Upon Prue [or Prew], His Maid.
Hewitt. Domestic Help.
Hughes, Langston. Madam and Her Madam.
Madam's Past History.
Porter.
Ruby Brown.
Jonson. On Mill, My Lady's Woman.
Kipling. Servant When He Reigneth, A.
Lawrence. Young Soldier with Bloody Spurs, The.
Liddy. Cantico Per Lo Tuo Amore IV.
Lindsay. Aladdin and the Jinn.
MacNeice. My Mary.
Morgan. Scotch Mary.
Muldoon. Big House, The.
Rossetti. Prodigal Son, A.
Smith, Charlotte. Inscription on a Stone, in the Church-Yard at Boreham.
Stevenson. Ne Sit Ancillae Tibi Amor Pudori.
Old Chimæras, old receipts, The.
Stuart. Sunburst.
Wilbur. Complaint.
Good Servant, The.
Summer Morning, A.
Wyatt. Heart and service to you proffered, The.

Service (botany)
Davie. Life of Service, The.

Service Stations. *see* **Gasoline Stations.**

Sestina (form)
Bishop. Miracle for Breakfast, A.
Sestina: "September rain falls on the house."
Cooper. Morning on the St. John's.
Hall. Sestina: "Hang it all, Ezra Pound, there is only the one sestina."
Pound. Sestina: Altaforte.

See also **Sestina in Title and First Line Index.**

Seurat, Georges
Bishop. Pleasure Seas.
O'Hara. On Looking at *La Grande Jatte*, the Czar Wept Anew.

Seven Deadly Sins
De la Mare. Quiet.

Severn River, England
Tennyson. Danube to the Severn gave, The.
Wordsworth. When Severn's Sweeping Flood Had Overthrown.

Seville, Spain
Garrigue. Giralda, The.
Levine. Memory of rain falling slowly, The.

Sewall, Samuel
Whittier. Samuel E. Sewall.

Sewers
Kipling. Municipal.

Sewing
Berg. Thread.
Bishop. House Guest.
Dickinson. Don't put up my Thread and Needle.
Dunbar. Quilting, The.
Hall. Sew.
Kunitz. Girl with Sampler.
Matthews. Needle's Eye, the Lens, The.
Sutter. Old Mrs. Court and Her Quilt.
Wordsworth. On Seeing a Needlecase in the Form of a Harp; the Work of E.M.S.

See also **Seamstresses; Tailoring and Tailors.**

Sex
Ammons. Their Sex Life.
Angelou. Remembrance.
Zorro Man, A.
Atwood. Pre-Amphibian.
Beatles. Come Together.
Happiness Is a Warm Gun.
Hard Day's Night, A.
Helter Skelter.
Love You To.

Savoy Truffle.
Why Don't We Do It in the Road.
Beckett. À elle l'acte calme.
Dread Nay.
Être là sans mâchoires sans dents.
Serena III.
Berrigan. Dinner at George & Katie Schneeman's.
Poem upon the page is as massive as, The.
Berryman. Damned.
Faith like the warrior ant swarming, enslaving.
Freshman Blues.
Huddle of Need, A.
Keep your eyes open when you kiss: do: when.
Spot of poontang on a five-foot piece, A.
Bishop. Exchanging Hats.
Key of Water, The.
Blake. Long John Brown & Little Mary Bell.
Bukowski. Alone with Everybody.
Another Bed.
Ashes.
Ass But No Class.
Cold Plums.
Conversation on Morality, Eternity and Copulation, A.
Dead Now.
End of a Short Affair, The.
Fuck.
Good Life, The.
How Come You're Not Unlisted?
I Fall into It Without Trying.
Layover.
Like a Flower in the Rain.
Love Poem, A.
Making It.
Mercy, Wherever You Are, Come Running in to Me and Grab Me in Your Good Arms—.
Moaning and Groaning.
Night I Fucked My Alarm Clock, The.
99 to One.
One of the Hottest.
Place Didn't Look Bad, The.
Prayer in Bad Weather.
Problems About the Other Woman.
Red Up and Down.
Scarlet.
6 Foot Goddess, The.
Sweaty Day in August, A.
This Then—.
T.M.
Trying to Get Even.
225 Pounds.
Waving and Waving Goodbye.
Bunting. Dear be still! Time's start of us lengthens slowly.
May my libation of flat beer stood overnight.
Burns. Adam A———'s Prayer.
As I Went Out Ae May Morning.
Ballad, A: "While Prose-work and rhymes."
Bob o' Dumblane, The.
Bonie Mary.
Can Ye Labor Lea.
Captain's Lady, The.
Come rede me, dame, come tell me, dame.
Deuks Dang o'er My Daddie, The.
Duncan Gray ["Weary fa' you, Duncan Gray"].
Fornicator. A New Song, The.
Gie the Lass her Fairin'.
Godly Girzie.
Here's His Health in Water.
I'm Owre [or O'er] Young to Marry Yet.
Jolly Gauger, The.
Lea-Rig, The.
Libel Summons.
Muirland Meg.
O Saw Ye My Maggie.
Ode to Spring.
On a Bank of Flowers.
Patriarch, The.
Ploughman, The.
Robert Burns' Answer [to Epistle from a Taylor].
Scroggam.
Shepherd's Wife, The.
Song: "I'll tell you a tale of a wife."

Song: "My girl she's airy, she's buxom and gay."
Taylor fell thro' the bed, thimble an' a', The.
There's News Lasses News.
Trogger, The.
Waukrife Minnie, A.
Wha Is That at My Bower-Door?
Wha'll M-w Me Now.
Why Should Na Poor Folk Mowe.
Campion. In se.
Let us now sing of Loves delight.
Carroll, Jim. Epiphany.
Green Bus, The.
On Susan's Birthday.
Poem: "We are very much a part of the boredom."
Poem: "Yesterday you past / into your lips.. your hips."
Savage Bubbles.
To the National Endowment for the Arts.
Vacation.
"Carroll, Lewis." She's All My Fancy Painted Him.
Carruth. Alive.
August.
Capper Kaplinski at the North Side Cue Club.
"For fifteen years he never knew I never."
He thinks how, often when his semen spews.
Making love in the cabin, not to himself.
Pray You Young Woman.
Sex.
Sonnet: "From our very high window at the Sheraton."
Sonnet: "Thy sting sufficeth, Death. If Heidegger first."
Sonnet: "Yes. After all my arguments with myself."
Tanck's Song About Youth and Age.
Then rapture is self in itself entranced. And love?
Three Songs.
Valentine.
Woman's Genitals, The.
Your dream: / His name is Heraclitus, and he is huge.
Catullus. Carmen 6: "Your most recent acquisition, Flavius."
Carmen 10: "Alfenus Varus / buttonholes me."
Carmen 13: "I shall expect / you in to dine."
Carmen 21: "Impresario of neediness."
Carmen 28: "In Piso's suite / are empty pockets."
Carmen 32: "Call me to you / at siesta."
Carmen 55: "Where / if it's not too much to ask."
Carmen 56: "Matter for mirth, Cato, & a smile, A."
Carmen 57: "*Caesar Mamurraque!* / A peerless pair of brazen buggers."
Carmen 61: "Hill (breeder) of Helicon."
Carmen 62: "Gather young men as the twilight gathers."
Carmen 67: "Sweet entrance to a husband's pleasure."
Carmen 71: "If every anyone / was deservedly plagued by a goat under his armpits."
Carmen 88: "What, Gellius, of the man."
Carmen 89: "Gellius is thin. / So?"
Carmen 94: "Stuffing, O'Toole naturally stuffs with his tool."
Carmen 112: "Naso! an elevated personage."
Ceravolo. Pregnant, I Come.
Sea Level.
Chaucer. Shipman's Tale, The.
Ciardi. Blue Movie.
Censorship.
Cohen. All Right, Edith.
Chelsea Hotel.
Commentary—My Wife and I.
Death of a Lady's Man.
Dream, The.
End of My Life in Art.
Far from the Soil.
Hurry to Your Dinner.
Is This What You Wanted.
Letter.
Light as the Breeze.

Memories.
My Wife and I.
Rebellion, The.
This Wretch.
You Have the Lovers.
Cooper. Circle, a Square, a Triangle and a Ripple of Water, A.
Obligations.
Creeley. Alba.
Curse.
Let something else be / the question—.
Woman, The.
Cummings. Amiable putrescence carpenters, An.
&-moon-He-be-hind-a-mills.
Bed is not very big, The.
Between the breasts / of bestial.
Devil crept in eden wood.
Dirty colours of her kiss have just, The.
Don't cries to please my.
First she like a piece of ill-oiled.
Five Americans.
Her / flesh / Came / at.
Her careful distinct sex whose sharp lips comb.
I like my body when it is with your.
I will be / M o ving in the Street of her.
In making Marjorie god hurried.
Innerly / UningstrolL / (stamens & pistil).
Irreproachable ladies firmly lewd.
Light cursed falling in a singular block.
Light Out), A.
Luminous tendril of celestial wish.
May i feel said he.
Moan / (is) / ing / the she of the.
My deathly body's deadly lady.
My strength becoming wistful in a glib.
Noise.
O by the by / has anybody seen.
O It's Nice To Get Up In,the slipshod mucous kiss.
Poor But TerFLY / went(flesh is grass).
Raise the shade.
She being Brand.
She had that softness which is falsity.
She,straddling my lap.
So you're hunting for ann well i'm looking for will.
Sunlight was over.
When the spent day begins to frail.
When you went away it was morning.
Whereas by dark really released,the modern.
Who's most afraid of death?thou.
Davie. Under a Skylight.
Dickey, James. Form.
Dickey, William. Androids.
Making Love.
Dobyns. Desire.
Dunbar. Confirmation.
Duncan. I Am a Most Fleshly Man.
Mirror, The.
Dunn. Cleanliness.
Decorum.
Having Lost All Capacity.
Man Who Closed Shop, The.
Some Things I Wanted to Say to You.
Vanishings, The.
"Dylan." Bob Dylan's New Orleans Rag.
Get Your Rocks Off!
Hazel.
If You Gotta Go, Go Now.
Wanted Man.
Eberhart. Request for Offering.
Edmunds. Like A Green Branch.
Thirteen Years.
Everson. And it creams: from under her elbow a suffix of light, a sheen of kept being.
And the storm swings in from the sea with a smashing of floats.
But masked of the self.
But now having seen.
Challenge, The.
Man of God. Tall man, man of oath. Mad man of ignorant causes.
Sea: / And in its flaw the sprung silence.
So him in dream.

Song the Body Dreamed in the Spirit's Mad Behest, The.
Ferlinghetti. Imaginary Happening, London, An.
Love Nut, The.
See / it was like this when.
What could she say to the fantastic foolybear.
Fisher. Passive Partner, The.
Fox. Like a Woman in the Kitchen.
Your Nipples.
Gardner. Compleat Anglers, The.
Gimboling.
Lines to a Seagreen Lover.
Ginsberg. After Thoughts.
Archetype Poem, The.
Change: *Kyoto-Tokyo Express*, The.
C'mon Jack.
Fie My Fum.
Kaddish.
Maybe Love.
Pull My Daisy.
Pussy Blues.
Glück. Edge, The.
First Goodbye.
Labor Day.
Marathon.
Memo from the Cave.
Mock Orange.
Murderess, The.
My Life Before Dawn.
Night Song.
Portrait of the Queen in Tears.
Return, The.
Song of Obstacles.
Wound, The.
Graves. Dans un Seul Lit.
Death Grapple, The.
Deed of Gift.
Ecstasy of Chaos.
Encounter, The.
Fact of the Act.
In Time of Absence.
Measure of Casualness, A.
Metaphor, The.
Starred Coverlet, The.
Visitation, The.
What Did You Say?
Woman of Greece.
Gunn. Adultery.
Amorous Debate, An.
At the Barriers.
Barren Leaves.
Carnal Knowledge.
Hot in his mind, Tom watches Dobbin fuck.
Loot.
Menace, The.
Miracle, The.
Modes of Pleasure.
New York.
Pig Pig she cries.
Saturnalia.
Tenderloin.
Hacker. Gino hummed an epithalamium.
Hall. Material.
Hemingway. Little Mr. Wilson / Wrote a little book.
Herrick. Delaying Bride, The.
Epithalamy to Sir Thomas Southwell and His Lady, An.
Good-Night, or Blessing, The.
On Himselfe ("Young I was, but [or who] now am old").
Poet Loves a Mistress, but Not to Marry, The.
To a Maid.
To Anthea ("Ah my Anthea! must my heart still break?").
To Anthea ("Come Anthea, know thou this").
To Electra ("I'll [or Ile] come to thee in all those shapes").
Upon a Lady Faire, but Fruitlesse.
Upon Doll.
Upon Groynes.
Upon Jolly and Jilly.
Vision to Electra, The.
Hewitt. Dry Summer, Islandmagee, 1921.
Jeffers. Tamar.
Jong. Land of Fuck, The.

Jonson. Fragmentum Petron. Arbitr. The Same Translated.
To Pertinax Cob.
Keats. O Blush Not So! O Blush Not So!
Kinnell. After Making Love We Hear Footsteps.
Knott. Poem (the Starfish One).
Rigor Vitus.
Koertge. Sex Object.
Lawrence. After Many Days.
At the Cearne.
Cross, The.
I Know a Noble Englishman.
Jeune Fille, The.
Jewess and the V.C., The.
Leave Sex Alone.
London Mercury.
Love as an Escape.
Love on the Farm.
Men and Women.
Puss-Puss!
Red Moon-Rise.
Rose of All the World.
Scent of Irises.
Sex and Trust.
Sex Isn't Sin.
Sex Won't Work.
Spiritual Woman, A.
What's Sane and What Isn't.
Wild Things in Captivity.
Young Want to Be Just, The.
Lewis. Desperate, The.
Exultantly he drives his screaming pinnace.
Gates of my palace are opened wide, The.
Holi.
Indolence.
Lines on a Young Girl.
Marriage Bed, The.
Mid-Winter.
Miniature on a Book of Hours.
On a Bereaved Girl.
Peace.
Swan's Way, The.
Under each starry leafless tree.
Liddy. Correspondences.
Donn na Duimche.
Dream of a Strange One.
Evening at Axel's.
Hounds can't / Come in, The.
Notes towards an Ivy Leaf Video.
Orpheus in Connaught.
Poison, The.
Quarter, The.
Richard, Oremus.
Voyage to Cytherea, A.
Wine of Lovers.
Lovelace. Fabullus I will treat you handsomely.
Lowell. Like Henry VIII, Mohammed got religion.
McAuley. Artist, Reclining, The.
Glory.
Mnemosyne: The Empty Room.
McGrath. Love in a Bus.
Rediscovery.
MacLeish. Eve in the Dawn.
Eve's Rebuke to Her Child.
German Girls! The German Girls!, The.
Hearts' and Flowers'.
Observations of P. Ovidus Naso on the Incidence of Sex in the Contemporary Novel.
Wild Old Wicked Man, The.
You Also, Gaius Valerius Catullus.
MacNeice. And love hung still as crystal over the bed.
Canto II: "'On the other hand,' said Gavin—or could have said."
Canto XI: "Golden guineas filter through the mist, The."
Markson. Memo to His Lady's Therapist.
Nachtmusik.
On Being Denied for Being Already Took.
Marlowe. 1.5: Corinnae concubitus.
2.4: Quod amet mulieres, cuiuscunque formae sint.
Matthews. Accompanist, The.

It Don't Mean a Thing if it Ain't Got That Swing.
Meinke. Helen.
Miller. Distance Between Us.
Milton. To the Nuptial Bowre.
Morgan. From a Forgotten Book.
We took a room at the Westbury.
Morrison. Enter the Slip.
Lament for the Death of My Cock.
Soul Kitchen.
Woman's Voice.
Nash. Nevertheless.
Nathan. Diver, The.
Neruda. Physics.
O'Hara. Captain Bada.
Ode to Michael Goldberg ('s Birth and Other Births).
Poem: "Twin spheres full of fur and noise."
Poem: "When I am feeling depressed and anxious sullen."
Olson. As the shield goddess, Mycenae.
From *The Song of Ullikummi*.
Hymn to the Word.
Long Distance.
Maximus of Gloucester.
One Night Ma / Lay with Pa.
Picture, The.
Under every green tree, sex.
Oppen. Half free / And half mad.
Pack. Clayfeld's Operatic Debut.
Early and Late.
Modest Boast at Meridian, A.
Patchen. Figure Motioned with Its Mangled Hand Toward the Wall Behind It, The.
Heaven and Earth.
I compel you to question me about my motives.
New Being, The.
On the South-West Coast of Erehwemos Stands a Romantic Little Village.
Queer Client and the Forest-Inn, The.
Waking into Sleep.
Piercy. Beds that are mirrors.
Cats Like Angels.
Crabs.
For two years I broke from these cycles, simply.
Greater Grand Rapids Lover, The.
In the pit of the night our bodies merge.
Lansing Bad Penny Come Again Blues, The.
Meditation in My Favorite Position.
Seeking from women nurturance, feedback, idea.
Some Collisions Bring Luck.
Trying to enter each other.
When we mesh badly, with scraping and squeaking.
You are an opening in me.
You Ask Why Sometimes I Say Stop.
You lay in bed depressed, passive as butter.
Plath. Gigolo.
Ralegh. Brasen tower [*or* Tower] with doors [*or* dores] close barred [*or* bar'd], The.
"Reed." Some Kinda Love.
Rich. Demon Lover, The.
For L.G.: Unseen for Twenty Years.
Sex, as they harshly call it.
That "old last act"! / And yet sometimes.
Waking in the Dark.
Roethke. Four for Sir John Davies.
Moment, The.
Sensualists, The.
Rukeyser. Anemone.
Double Ode.
Drunken Girl.
Flattered by grief, the changeable spirit.
Loan, The.
Mortal Girl.
Orgy.
Speed of Darkness, The.
Transgress, The.
Tunnel, The.
Watchers, The.
Wedding Presents.
Welcome from War.
What I See.
Sexton. Angel of Fire and Genitals.

Ballad of the Lonely Masturbator, The.
Barefoot.
Farmer's Wife, The.
Jesus Awake.
Old Dwarf Heart.
Song for a Lady.
Us.
When Man Enters Woman.
Shapiro. First Time, The.
Smith, Patti. Judith Revisited.
Smith, Stevie. Conviction (iv).
Snyder. Song of the Slip.
Song of the Tangle.
Stein. Lifting Belly.
Stuart. I Can't Live Without You.
Suckling. Health to the nut-brown lass, A.
Sutter. Love Poem.
Talking To Grandpa Eastman.
Third Use of the Penis, The.
Warmth.
Thomas. Into Her Lying Down Head.
My World Is Pyramid.
Turco. Hank Fedder.
Jasper Olson.
Lovers.
Updike. Cunts.
Elderly Sex.
Fellatio.
In Memoriam Felis Felis.
Mouse Sex.
No More Access to Her Underpants.
Squirrels Mating.
Van Duyn. Billings and Cooings from "The Berkeley Barb."
Wakoski. Emerald Ice.
Some Constantly Besieged Castle.
Waldman. He catches my eye, my fancy.
3 Epiphanies.
Walker. She Said:.
Whitman. Ages and Ages Returning at Intervals.
Wilbur. Late Aubade, A.
Under a Tree.
Williams, Charles Kenneth. Cautionary, The.
Combat.
Crawl.
Madder.
Nut, The.
Portions of Manslayer.
Saint Sex.
Soliloquies.
Williams, Miller. Original Sin.
Rubaiyat for Sue Ella Tucker.
Williams, William Carlos. April is the Saddest Month.
Wright, James. Moral Poem Freely Accepted from Sappho, A.
Yau. Bare Sheets I.
Zukofsky. Aurelius, father, assure that the o numb.
Canapés, my Fabullus, at home any.
Flavius—that delicate lass—to Catullus.
Gellius is thin why yes: kiddin'? quite a bonny mater.
I'm a bow, my dual kiss, Ipsithilla.
Meantool amuck with her. Muck with her mean tool ah? Geared I.
Mool 'tis homos,' Naso 'n' queer take 'im mool 'tis ho most *he.*
O dear cool you couldn't be virile—you couldn't a parent he.
O ram ridicule home, Cato, the jokes some.
Piso's own comates, his, corps an inane as.
"Pull! crew" 's convenient to reprobate kin hides.
Quid, fact it is Gelli? quick'ning mother, at (queer) sis, all three.
Rum asks—see, fortune won't molest you.
Securer a bo? no sacred armpits lair hops as that he-goat's.
Varus old crony had me visit his love.
Vesper out there, you vain knees can sure get up: Vesper, Olympus.
Who lives o on Helicon hill.

See also **Erotic Love; Homosexuality and Homosexuals.**

Sexism
Dickinson. Over the fence.
Fox. Caroline Herschel (1750–1848).
Gallagher. Conversation with a Fireman from Brooklyn.
Jong. Truce between the Sexes, The.
Koch. Sleeping with Women.
Koertge. Two Men.
Lorde. Revolution Is One Form of Social Change.
Who Said It Was Simple.
Markson. Sexist Stanza.
Piercy. Barbie Doll.
We will be equal, we say, new man and new woman.
Rich. Snapshots of a Daughter-in-Law.
Stevenson. Mater Triumphans.
Yeats. Nativity, A.

Sexton, Anne
Ciardi. Trying to Feel Something.
Jong. Dear Anne Sexton, I.
Dear Anne Sexton, II.
Knott. Fear of Domesticity.
Sexton. Ambition Bird, The.
Angel Food Dogs, The.
Baby Picture.
Cigarettes and Whiskey and Wild, Wild Women.
Double Image, The.
Fourth Psalm.
Gods.
Hurry Up Please It's Time.
Is It True?
January 1st.
Letters to Dr. Y.
Said the Poet to the Analyst.
Speaking Bitterness.
Sweeney.
Talking to Sheep.
Tenth Psalm.
Williams, Charles Kenneth. Suicide: Anne.

Sexual Abuse
Dobyns. Gun, The.
"Reed." Betrayed.
Smith, Patti. Rape.
Williams, Miller. Everything Is Fine Here How Are You.
Late Show.

Sexual Exploitation
Betjeman. Shattered Image.
Bukowski. Frozen Food Section.
Girl on the Bus Stop Bench, The.
Girls Coming Home.
Girls in Pantyhose.
Catullus. Carmen 15: "*My love & I* are yours to command."
Cohen. Disguises.
Kunitz. She Wept, She Railed.
Zukofsky. Commend to you my cares for the love I love.

Sexuality
Auden. Because sap fell away.
Crowing of the cock, The.
Berg. Homage to the Afterlife.
Lament: "My mother wants to be burned, she told me."
Not That.
Rubber Rats.
Sticks.
Bukowski. Girls at the Green Hotel, The.
Making It.
Sex.
Sexpot.
You.
Burns. Fragment, A: "Green grow the rashes, O; / Green grow the rashes, O; / The lasses they hae wimble bores."
Catullus. Carmen 45: "Phyllis Corydon clutched to him."
Clark. Parish: A Satire, The.
Creeley. Dear Dorothy.
Hands, The.
Hole, The.
Cummings. "Gay" is the captivating cognomen of a Young Woman of cambridge,mass.

Dickey, William. Performances.
  You White Cunning Devils.
Donne. To His Mistress Going to Bed.
Dunn. Desire.
Everson. Annul in Me My Manhood.
  Cutting the Firebreak.
Ferlinghetti. Dark Portrait, A.
Ford. After the drama.
  Astride the chiffonier of post-oral conductions.
  Flag of Ecstasy.
  Illness, The.
  Modesty, chastity.
  This year's jackfruit hang.
Fox. At the Edge of the Suburbs.
  Grandmother.
  Help Me with the Buttons.
  Juggler, The.
  Mother Is.
  Nightshade.
  Ornithology.
  Your Nipples.
Ginsberg. Typical Affair, A.
Graves. Cry Faugh!
Gunn. Courage, a Tale.
Hacker. Adult Entertainment.
  Days of 1959.
  If we talk, we're too tired to make love; if
    we.
Jong. Becoming a Nun.
  Egyptology.
  Gardener.
Larkin. Annus Mirabilis.
  Two Portraits of Sex.
Levertov. Mutes, The.
Liddy. Art Is Not for Grown-ups.
  Dear Anima, Show These Words.
  Delphine and Hippolyta.
  Epithalamion I–IV: "Along a leafy lonely river
    God-shy-eyed fisher boys."
  Love Songs of Corca Bascinn.
Lowry. Canny Castor, Punching Pollux.
McAuley. She opened the lower button of her
    blouse.
Melville. After the Pleasure Party.
Morrison. Flesh of Her.
Notley. September's Book.
Olson. Assuming the Soul Is a Bitch.
  Cause, the Cause, The.
  Help Me, Venus, You Who Led Me On.
  Mazdaism / has overcome.
  White Horse.
  Woman's Nipples Is the Rose of the World,
    A.
Piercy. Cats Like Angels.
  You Ask Why Sometimes I Say Stop.
Rich. Dialogue.
Rukeyser. Along History.
Schuyler. Tom.
Schwartz. Love and Marilyn Monroe.
Sexton. When the Glass of My Body Broke.
Smith, Patti. After/Words.
  Anna of the Harbor.
  Dream of Rimbaud.
  Health Lantern.
  Jeanne D'Arc.
  Seventh Heaven.
  Suite.
  Witt.
Sorrentino. Où Sont Ils, Où, Vierge Souvráin?
Stuart. Sexual Disappointments.
Van Duyn. Billings and Cooings from "The
    Berkeley Barb."
Whitman. As Adam Early in the Morning.
  Behold This Swarthy Face.
  From Pent-up Aching Rivers.
  Spontaneous Me.
  To the Garden the World.
Wilbur. Catch, The.
Williams, Charles Kenneth. Love:
    Beginnnings.
  Saint Sex.
Williams, William Carlos. Transitional.
Wordsworth. Septimius and Acme.
Yeats. From the "Antigone."
  Her Triumph.
  Whence Had They Come?

Zukofsky. Acme, Septimius, sighs so amorous.
  Immature Pebbles.

Shadbush. *see* **Service (botany)**.

Shadows
Ammons. Recovery.
Atwood. Night Poem.
Auden. By the Fire.
Beckett. Son ombre une nuit.
Bishop. Imber Nocturnus.
Bogan. Division.
  Mark, The.
Browning, Elizabeth Barrett. Romaunt of
    Margret, The.
Campion. Follow Thy Fair Sun[ne] [Unhappy
    Shadow].
  Shadowes before the shining sunne do vanish.
Carruth. Coming of Snow, The.
  Shadow sprang out, The.
Clark. Last Poem (after Robert Desnos), The.
Cooper. Hunger Moon.
Cummings. Mrs / and mr across the way are
    kind of.
De la Mare. Death-Dream, The.
  Fear.
  Music Unheard.
  Phantom, The.
  Shade, The.
  Shadow.
  Tired Cupid, The.
  Where?
  Where Is Thy Victory?
Dickey, William. History of the Moon, The.
  Silver Creek Falls.
Dickinson. Like Men and Women Shadows
    walk.
Donne. Lecture upon the Shadow, A.
Eberhart. Hand and the Shadow, The.
Fisher. From an English Sensibility.
Gallagher. Into the Known.
Glück. Hawk's Shadow.
Hardy. In the Garden.
Hewitt. Difficult Man, A.
  Substance and Shadow.
Hill. Of Coming-into-Being and Passing-
    Away.
Jonson. Song, A: "Come, let us here enjoy the
    shade."
Lawrence. Shades.
  Sympathy.
Lindsay. Caught in a Net.
Lowry. Indian Arm.
  Sonnet: "This ruin now, where moonlight
    walks alone."
  Sun, Aeroplane, Lovers.
McGrath. When We Say Goodbye.
MacNeice. Our shadows now grow long in the
    sun.
Mahon. Katie at the Pool.
Matthews. Driving Alongside the Housatonic
    River Alone on a Rainy April Night.
Merton. Mirror's Mission, The.
Patchen. And forth from that shadow of a
    shadow.
Raine. Afternoon sunlight plays.
Rossetti. In the Willow Shade.
St. John. Shadow.
Sandburg. Evening Questions.
  Losses.
  Out of the Rainbow End.
  Shadows Fall Blue on the Mountains.
  Sketch.
  Smoke Shapes.
  Wall Shadows.
Schuyler. Light Within, The.
Silverstein. Shadow Wash.
Simic. Position without a Magnitude.
Smith, Stevie. Conviction (iii).
Stevens. Poem with Rhythms.
Stevenson. Armies in the Fire.
  My Shadow.
Tomlinson. All Afternoon.
  White Van, The.
Turco. Stone and Shadow.
Updike. Long Shadow.
Waldman. Light & Shadow.
Wilbur. Gnomons.
  Sunlight Is Imagination.

Williams, Charles Kenneth. It's over now. I
    watch.
Williams, Miller. Friend, The.
Williams, William Carlos. Halfworld, The.
Wright, James. Girl Walking into a Shadow,
    A.
  RIP.
  Shadow and the Real, The.
Yau. Radiant Silhouette I.
Yeats. New Faces, The.
Zukofsky. All of December Toward New
    Year's.
  Can a mote of sunlight defeat its purpose.

**Shaftesbury, Anthony Ashley Cooper, 1st Earl
of**
Dryden. Absalom and Achitophel, Pt. I.
  In pious times ere [*or* e'r] priest-craft did
    begin.
  Of these the false Achitophel was first.

Shakers (First Church of The Millennium)
Hall. Religious Articles.
Schuyler. Shaker.

Shakespeare, William
Arnold. Shakespeare.
Auden. Sea and the Mirror, The.
Bogan. To an Artist, to Take Heart.
Browning, Robert. Names, The.
Bukowski. Kings Are Gone, The.
"Carroll, Lewis." Prologue to "La Guida Di
    Bragia."
Carruth. Sonnet: "Well, Jim says that the
    couplet at the end."
Crane. To Shakespeare.
Cullen. Cor Cordium.
De la Mare. Ariel.
Dickinson. He has had his Future.
Eberhart. Broken Pen, The.
  Hamlet Father, The.
Emerson. 'ΑΔΑΚΡΥΝ ΝΕΜΟΝΤΑΙ ΑΙΩΝΑ.
  Shakspeare.
  Turtle in swamp.
Gray. William Shakespeare to Mrs Anne,
    Regular Servant to the Rev. Mr Precentor of
    York.
Hardy. To Shakespeare.
Hewitt. Magician, The.
Hopkins. Shakspere.
Jeffers. Shakespeare's Grave.
Jonson. To the Memory of My Beloved, the
    Author Mr [*or* Master] William Shakespeare[:
    And What He Hath Left Us].
  To the Reader ("This figure, that thou here
    seest put").
Joseph. Not a Rootless Lily.
Keats. On Sitting Down to Read "King Lear"
    Once Again.
Kipling. Coiner, The.
  Craftsman, The.
Lawrence. When I Read Shakespeare.
Lowry. Search, The.
  Shakespeare should have come to Acapulco.
  Shakespeare's house is safe and sound.
MacLeish. Verses for a Centennial.
Markson. Anne-on-Avon.
Melville. Coming Storm, The.
Meredith. Poetry of Shakespeare, The.
  Rosalind.
  Spirit of Shakespeare: Continued, The.
  Spirit of Shakespeare, The.
Milton. On Shakespear[e].
Robinson. Ben Jonson Entertains a Man from
    Stratford.
Stevenson. After Reading "Antony and
    Cleopatra."
Suckling. Supplement of an Imperfect Copy of
    Verses of Mr. William Shakespeare's, By the
    Author, A.
Van Duyn. Birthday Card for a Psychiatrist.
Whitman. Shakspeare-Bacon's Cipher.
Wilbur. Up, Jack.
Zukofsky. Stratford-on-Avon.

Shamans
Lieberman. Sunday: My Throat Afire.
Muldoon. Glanders.
Rich. Particularity.

Shame
Angelou. Memory, The.

Auden. September.
Beatles. You've Got to Hide Your Love Away.
Berry. Do Not Be Ashamed.
Brontë. A.A.A.
Browning, Elizabeth Barrett. Sonnet: "Can it be right to give what I can give."
Bunting. Verse and Version.
Burns. Rantin Laddie, The.
Wha'll M-w Me Now.
Carruth. Am I wrong? The roads.
I hurt. Hungrier flowers try my rank ground.
Catullus. Carmen 79: "They nickname Lesbia's brother 'pulcher' ."
Chaucer. Physician's Tale, The.
Crashaw. Out of Horace.
Creeley. Shame, The.
Song: "I wouldn't / embarrass you."
Davie. Berkshire.
Machineries of Shame.
Dickinson. Embarrassment of one another.
His Cheek is his Biographer.
Seraphic shame generosity causes, The.
Shame is the shawl of Pink.
There is a Shame of Nobleness.
Donne. Triple Fool, The.
Dunn. Something.
With No Experience in Such Matters.
Emerson. If curses be the wage of love.
Everson. Encounter, The.
Man of God. Tall man, man of oath. Mad man of ignorant causes.
Gardner. Fall in Massachusetts.
Hardy. Spectres That Grieve.
Herrick. Another ("Shame of mans face is no more, The").
Shame, No Statist.
Sins Loathed, and Yet Loved.
Upon Peason.
Hewitt. Our Sunday School Teacher.
Joseph. There are more accidents in the home than on the roads.
Lawrence. Rallying-Point.
Lewis. Swan's Way, The.
Lowry. Oh gentle Jesus of the hymnal once. They will be ashamed after they are dead.
MacLeish. Conversation in a Belfry.
Meredith. Falling of Sally, The.
'Tis Christmas weather, and a country house.
Morrison. I Bring These.
Oliver. Strawberry Moon.
Olson. Translation, A.
Psalms. Psalm 25: "Unto thee, O Lord, do I lift up my soul."
"Reed." It Wasn't Me.
Rolfe. Political Prisoner 123456789.
Rossetti. Behold the Man!
Sarton. Who Wakes.
Shakespeare. Sonnet 72: "O! Lest the world should task you to recite."
Shapiro. Shame.
Smart. Lord and Master, to thine altar.
Wilbur. Shame.
Williams, Charles Kenneth. Shame.
Wright, James. In Shame and Humiliation.
In Terror of Hospital Bills.
Zukofsky. In that this happening.
Lesbius has pooled her: kidney? whom Lesbia my—lit.

Shaped Poetry
"Carroll, Lewis." Mock Turtle's Song, The.
Mouse's Tale, The.
Mouse's Tale, The: "We lived beneath the mat."
Herbert. Colossians 3:3.
Herrick. Pillar of Fame, The.

Sharecroppers
Hughes, Langston. Share-Croppers.

Sharks
"Carroll, Lewis." Alice's Recitation.
Dickey, James. Shark's Parlor, The.
Gunn. Cannibal.
Haines. Inside the shell of our skulls.
Lowry. Boatmen swing their lanterns on the Caribbean, The.
Melville. Maldive Shark, The.
Nash. Shark, The.

Shaving
Fisher. Small Room, The.
Hewitt. Holy Place, A.
Jarrell. Transient Barracks.
Lowry. That she could cook.
Nash. And Three Hundred and Sixty-Six in Leap Year.
Simic. Shaving at Night.
Updike. Upon Shaving Off One's Beard.
Walcott. My double, tired of morning, closes the door.

Shaw, George Bernard
Eberhart. Explorer on Main Street, The.
Williams, William Carlos. For G.B.S., Old.

Shaw, Robert Gould
Dunbar. Robert Gould Shaw.
Lowell. For the Union Dead.

Sheep
Atwood. November.
Berry. Birth (Near Port William), The.
Browning, Elizabeth Barrett. Sounds.
Burns. Death and Dying Words of Poor Mailie, the Author's Only Pet Yowe, an Unco Mournfu' Tale, The.
Poor Mailie's Elegy.
Cowper. Needless Alarm, The.
Cummings. After-Glow.
Davie. Skelpick.
Hall. Black Faced Sheep, The.
Kill, The.
Our Walk in Yorkshire.
Hardy. Sheep Fair, A.
Hewitt. Easter Flock.
Glenaan.
Iron Pot, The.
Sheep Fair.
Hopkins. Io.
Hughes, Ted. Sheep.
Jarrell. Country Was, The.
Larkin. To a Very Slow Air.
Lowry. Courage is not standing on the crosstrees.
MacLeish. Mark's Sheep.
MacNeice. Come, my sheep, my goats, graze where the shoots are tender.
Paley. Families.
Rossetti. Lambs of Grasmere, 1860, The.
Sandburg. Sheep.
Suburban Sicilian Sketches.
Sexton. Sheep.
Talking to Sheep.
Sidney. Feed on my sheep; my charge, my comfort, feed.
Leave off my sheep: it is no time to feed.
My sheep are thoughts, which I both guide and serve.
Simic. Strictly Bucolic.
Wakoski. First Universe.
Wilbur. Grace.
See also **Lambs.**

Sheffield, England
Betjeman. Edwardian Sunday, Broomhill, Sheffield, An.

Shelley, Percy Bysshe
Browning, Robert. Memorabilia.
Sun-treader, life and light be thine for ever!
Cullen. Cor Cordium.
Gunn. Lerici.
Hardy. Rome: At the Pyramid of Cestius near the Graves of Shelley and Keats.
Shelley's Skylark.
Lowry. Port has a sweeter name than Saigon, The.
Meredith. Poetry of Shelley, The.
Millay. To a Poet that Died Young.
Nash. You and Me and P.B. Shelley.
Oppen. Boy's Room.
Prince. Byron-Shelley Conversation, A.
Rukeyser. From a Play: Publisher's Song.

Shells
"Carroll, Lewis." Lays of Sorrow, No. 1.
Graves. Judges, The.
Hartley. These shells are paradox.
Wingaersheek Beach.
Hesketh. On Iona.
Hugo. Beachthieves.

Lovelace. Snail [*or* Snayl], The.
MacLeish. Dr. Sigmund Freud Discovers the Sea Shell.
Triumph of the Shell, The.
Meinke. Shell, The.
Moore. Paper Nautilus, The.
Nemerov. Shells.
Spiral Shell, A.
Oliver. Whelks.
Pack. Secrets.
Raine. On a Shell-strewn Beach.
Shells.
Snodgrass. Seashell, A.
Tomlinson. Shell, The.
Walcott. I once gave my daughters, separately, two conch shells.
Williams, William Carlos. Tribute to Neruda the Poet Collector of Seashells.
Wordsworth. Curious child, who dwelt upon a tract, A.
See also **Snails; Clams and Clamming; Oysters.**

Shellshock
Hughes, Ted. Dream Time, The.
Owen. Chances, The.
Conscious.
Dead-Beat, The.
Dulce Et Decorum Est.
Mental Cases.

Shenandoah River and Shenandoah Valley
Melville. Portent, The.
Sandburg. Shenandoah.
Shenandoah Journey.

Shepherds and Shepherdesses
Blake. Shepherd, The.
Carew. Pastoral[l] Dialogue, A.
Coleridge. Hunting Song.
Cummings. After-Glow.
De la Mare. Nod.
Doolittle. Shepherd, The.
Emerson. Shout to the Sheperds, A.
Hall. Black Faced Sheep, The.
Hardy. Sheep-Boy, An.
Unkindly May, An.
Hartley. Shepherd of the morning.
Herbert. Twenty-third Psalm, The.
Herrick. Pastorall Sung to the King: Montano, Silvio, and Mirtillo, Shepards, A.
Hewitt. In the Lenin Library, Dushanbe.
Hopkins. Pure gold lily, but by the pure gold lily, A.
Richard.
Shepherd's Brow, The.
Whose braggart 'scutcheon, whose complaisant crest.
Jeffers. Loving Shepherdess, The.
Silent Shepherds, The.
Lawrence. St Mark.
MacNeice. Eclogue by a Five-Barred Gate.
Nuts in May.
Marlowe. Another of the Same Nature, Made Since.
Nimphs [*or* Nymph's] Reply to the Sheepheard [*or* Shepherd], The.
Passionate Shepherd to His Love, The.
Marvell. Clorinda and Damon.
Merrill. Violent Pastoral.
Merton. Fall of Night, The.
Pope. Pastorals.
Ralegh. Nimphs [*or* Nymph's] Reply to the Sheepheard [*or* Shepherd], The.
Rossetti. Faithless Shepherdess, The.
Good Shepherd, The.
Hymn for Christmas Day, A.
Lambs of Grasmere, 1860, The.
Shakespeare. My flocks feed not.
Sidney. Come, *Espilus*, come now declare thy skill.
Come shepherd's weeds, become your master's mind.
My sheep are thoughts, which I both guide and serve.
Ye [*or* you] goat-herd gods, [that love the grassy mountains].
Smith, Charlotte. Blest is yon shepherd, on the turf reclined.
Spenser. Colin Clouts Come Home Againe.
Wakoski. First Universe.

Williams, William Carlos. Maid, The.
Wordsworth. Idle Shepherd-Boys, The; or,
  Dungeon-Ghyll Force. A Pastoral.
  Last of the Flock, The.
  Michael [A Pastoral Poem].
  Norman Boy, The.
  Shepherd, looking eastward softly said, The.
  Song at the Feast of Brougham Castle upon
    the Restoration of Lord Clifford, the
    Shepherd, to the Estates and Honours of His
    Ancestors.
Yeats. Shepherd and Goatherd.
  Song of the Happy Shepherd, The.

Sheridan, Philip Henry
Melville. Sheridan at Cedar Creek.
Whitman. Interpolation Sounds.

Sheridan, Richard Brinsley
Coleridge. To Richard Brinsley Sheridan, Esq.

Sherman, William Tecumseh, Union general
Ferlinghetti. Sherman's March Reglitterized.
Melville. March to the Sea, The.
Whitman. Ethiopia Saluting the Colors.
Whittier. Howard at Atlanta.

Shields
Sarton. Baroque Image.
Sidney. Sonnet 13: "Phoebus was judge
  between Jove, Mars, and Love."

Shiloh, Battle of (1862)
Hill. Shiloh Church, 1862: Twenty–Three
  Thousand.
Melville. Rebel Color-Bearers at Shiloh.
  Shiloh [A Requiem].

Ships and Shipbuilding
Auden. Ship, The.
Bishop. Casabianca.
  Large Bad Picture.
  Song: "Summer is over upon the sea."
Byron. Oh How I Wish That an Embargo.
Carew. To Her in Absence; a Ship.
Carruth. Well, beat on, beat on.
Ciardi. Benefits of an Education, The.
Clough. Qua Cursum Ventus.
Davie. Reminded of Bougainville.
De la Mare. Sea-Magic.
Dunbar. Ships That Pass in the Night.
Edmunds. Landing in Cairo.
Emerson. Letters.
Fletcher. Calm, The.
  Midsummer Dawn at Sea.
Fox. Shipbuilder, The.
Gallagher. Still Moment at Dun Laoghaire.
Glück. Slave Ship, The.
Graves. Former Attachment, A.
  Shot, The.
Griffiths. Oil Terminal.
Haines. Mothball Fleet: Benicia, California.
Hartley. New Rains.
Hemingway. Worker, The.
Herrick. No Shipwrack of Vertue. To a
  Friend.
Hugo. Bay of Sad Loss.
  Ness.
Joseph. CENTERPIECE: St. Sebastian (Italian).
Kipling. Ballad of the "Bolivar", The.
  Big Steamers.
  Cruisers.
  Derelict, The.
  Destroyers, The.
  Junk and the Dhow, The.
  King Henry VII. And the Shipwrights.
  Liner She's a Lady, The.
  Mary Gloster, The.
  Such As in Ships.
  Truthful Song, The.
Kooser. Afterlife, The.
Larkin. North Ship, The.
Lawrence. Argonauts, The.
  Greeks Are Coming!, The.
  Ships in Bottles.
Lindsay. Johnny Appleseed's Ship Comes In.
Lowry. After Labour Day.
  Alcoholic.
  And yet I am of England too; odi et amo.
  Boatmen swing their lanterns on the
    Caribbean, The.
  Burnt pier: the last passenger: the farewells,
    The.

Cook in the Galley, The.
  For Nordahl Grieg Ship's Fireman.
  Freighter 1940.
  From Helsinki to Liverpool with Lumber.
  Iron Thoughts Sail Out at Evening.
  Like the black iron steps.
  Look Out! The Bloody Bosun.
  No Kraken Shall Be Found Till Sought By
    Name.
  Old Freighter in an Old Port.
  Outside was the roar of the sea and the
    darkness.
  Picture, A.
  Ship.
  Ship is Turning Homeward, The.
  Ship of war sails in the grey morning, The.
  Ship stands drawn like a jewelled dagger, A.
  Ship will sail again, the watches sing, The.
  S.O.S Sinking fast by both bow and stern.
  Stars have simple paradigms, The.
  Stowaway, The.
  Villanelle, an Interviewo on Morale.
  Voyage of Kevin O'Riordine, The.
  When I am in the purgatory of the unread.
MacLeish. Ship of Fools.
  Under an elm tree where the river reaches.
MacNeice. Atlantic Tunnel, The.
  Death of an Old Lady.
  North Sea, The.
  Passage Steamer.
Mahon. Old Roscoff.
Markson. Of Writings Unfinished.
Melville. *Temeraire*, The.
Meredith. *Irene* ducks and runs amuck, The.
  Olive Branch, The.
Neruda. Different Ship, A.
Oppen. Carpenter's Boat.
  City of Keansburg, The.
  On that water / Grey with morning.
  Taste, The.
  Three wide / Funnels raked aft, and the masts
    slanted, The.
Plath. On Deck.
  Winter Ship, A.
Prince. White sunlight and the dripping oars!
Ransom. Good Ships.
Rolfe. Cheliuskin.
  Death by Water.
  Ship, The.
Rossetti. Boats sail on the rivers, / And ships
    sail on the seas.
Rukeyser. Cruise, The.
Sandburg. Sketch.
Snyder. Goofing Again.
  Oil.
  Sappa Creek, The.
Spenser. Looking far foorth into the ocean
    wide.
Stevenson. Fixed is the doom; and to the last
    of years.
  My Ship and I.
  Where Go the Boats?
Stuart. Last Words.
Tomlinson. Barque Nornen.
  Faring, The.
  Ship's Waiters.
Turco. Leviathan.
  Schooner, The.
Updike. Azores.
  Shipbored.
Whitman. Aboard at a Ship's Helm.
  After the Sea-Ship.
  Beauty of the Ship, The.
  Dismantled Ship, The.
  Patrolling Barnegat.
  Ship Starting, The.
  Song for All Seas, All Ships.
  Would You Hear of an Old-Time [or Old-
    Fashioned] Sea fight?
Whittier. Ship-Builders, The.
  To a Cape Ann Schooner.
Williams, William Carlos. In Harbor.
Wordsworth. Where lies the Land to which
  yon Ship must go?
  With Ships the sea was sprinkled far and nigh.
Zukofsky. Hill.

See also **Boats and Boating; Freighters;**
  Steamers; Yachts.

Shipwrecks
Bunting. Vessels thrown awry by strong gusts.
Byron. Julian [A Fragment].
  Ship, called the most holy *Trinidada*, The.
Carruth. No, I was wrecked here.
Clark. Time.
Coleridge. To a Lady.
Cowper. Castaway, The.
  On the Loss of the *Royal George.*
De la Mare. Wreck, The.
Dickinson. Glee—The great storm is over.
"Dylan." Talking Bear Mountain Picnic
  Massacre Blues.
Fletcher. Wreck, The.
Graves. Furious Voyage, The.
Hardy. Convergence of the Twain, The.
Herrick. Safety on the Shore.
  Ship-Wrack.
Hopkins. Loss of the Eurydice, The.
  Nightingale, The.
  On Saturday sailed from Bremen.
  Sea Took Pity, The.
  Wreck of the Deutschland, The.
Hughes, Ted. I can understand the haggard
  eyes.
Longfellow. Wreck of the *Hesperus*, The.
Lowry. Tashtego Believed Red.
  Voyage of Kevin O'Riordine, The.
McAuley. Vigil.
"MacDiarmid." Wreck of the *Swan*, The.
McGrath. Offering.
Mahon. Old Roscoff.
Markson. Of Writings Unfinished.
Marvell. Unfortunate Lover, The.
Melville. Æolian Harp, The.
  Berg, The.
  Far Off-Shore.
  Haglets, The.
  Off Cape Colona.
Oppen. Obsessed, bewildered / By the
  shipwreck.
  Squall.
Raine. Turner's Seas.
Rich. Diving into the Wreck.
Rolfe. Ship, The.
Rossetti. Bird's-Eye View, A.
Schwartz. Poem: "You, my photographer, you,
  most aware."
Smith, Charlotte. Descriptive Ode, Supposed
  to Have Been Written under the Ruins of
  Rufus's Castle, A.
Spenser. After, at sea a tall ship did appeare.
  Much richer then that vessell seem'd to bee.
Stuart. Last Words.
Tomlinson. Barque Nornen.
Walcott. Castaway, The.
Whittier. Dead Ship of Harpswell, The.
  Palatine, The.
  Skipper Ireson's Ride.
  Swan Song of Parson Avery, The.
  Three Bells, The.
  Wreck of Rivermouth, The.
Wordsworth. I find it written of SIMONIDES.

Shirts
Housman. From the wash the laundress sends.
Sandburg. Shirt: ("I remember once I ran...")
  Shirt: ("My shirt is a token and a symbol...")
  Summer Shirt Sale.
Simic. Shirt.

Shiva
Jeffers. Shiva.
Kipling. Shiv and the Grasshopper.

Shoes and Shoemakers
Berg. Shoeshine.
  Through Glass.
Cowper. Let Banister now lend his aid.
  Verses Written at Bath on Finding the Heel of
    a Shoe.
Dobyns. Receivers of the World's Attention.
Hardy. Satin Shoes, The.
Herrick. Gain and Gettings.
  Sho[o]e Tying, The.
  Upon Cob.
  Upon Pimpe.
  Upon Prigg ("Prigg, when he comes to houses,

oft doth use").
Upon Rush.
Upon Smeaton.
Hughes, Langston. Bad Morning.
Jong. Ode to My shoes.
Liddy. Miles II.
MacNeice. Empty Shoes.
Miller. Meditations on an Old Shoe.
Patchen. Daft Little Shoe Clerk Decided It Would Be Fun to Go Up and See What Things Are Like above the Sky, The.
Old Pair of Shoes, An.
Sexton. Fury of Overshoes, The.
Red Shoes, The.
Simic. My Shoes.
Sutter. Shoe Shop.
Warren. Shoes In Rain Jungle.
Whittier. Shoemakers, The.
Williams, Charles Kenneth. Time: 1978.
Williams, William Carlos. Nightingales, The.
Thinker, The.

Shopping and Shops
Browning, Robert. Shop.
Bukowski. Lovely Couple, A.
Ginsberg. Supermarket in California, A.
Gunn. Wind in the Street.
Hacker. Fourteen.
Hall. Green Shelf, The.
Hewitt. Rotterdam.
Larkin. Scratch on the Scratch Pad.
Lowry. Welcome Home Oh Harteebeeste.
McGrath. Trouble with the Times, The.
MacNeice. Christmas Shopping.
Miller. In the typewriter shop.
Nash. Friendly Touch, The.
I Remember Yule.
Just Wrap It Up, and I'll Throw It Away Later.
Nemerov. Night before Christmas, The.
Olson. In an Automotive Store.
Simic. Grocery.

Shopping Malls
Hugo. Letter to Matthews from Barton Street Flats.

Shores
Browning, Robert. Meeting at Night.
Bunting. Now we've no hope of going back.
Carroll, Jim. Early Morning Crucifixion, An.
Narrows, The.
"Carroll, Lewis." Mock Turtle's Song, The.
Ciardi. Sea Marshes in Winter.
Cohen. She Has Given Me the Bullet.
Coleridge. On Revisiting the Sea-Shore, after Long Absence.
Eliot. Cape Ann.
Frost. Once by the Pacific.
Hardy. On the Esplanade.
Hesketh. Waiting.
Hughes, Langston. Moonlight Night: Carmel.
Hugo. Alki Beach.
At Cronkhite.
Cape Nothing.
First South and Cambridge.
Mendocino, Like You Said.
Meridian.
Resulting from Magnetic Interference.
With Melissa on the Shore.
Kipling. Lukannon.
Larkin. To the Sea.
Liddy. Shore.
Lorde. Bridge Through My Window.
MacNeice. Littoral.
Lugubrious, Salubrious Seaside, The.
Meredith. Mark where the pressing wind shoots javelin-like.
Orchard and the Heath, The.
Millay. I shall go back again to the bleak shore.
Oppen. Book of Job and a Draft of a Poem to Praise the Paths of the Living, The.
California.
Coastal Strip.
Guest Room.
Little Pin: Fragment, The.
O withering seas.
Penobscot.
Primitive.

Speech at Soli, The.
Taste, The.
Two Romance Poems.
Patchen. Turner.
Roethke. Rose, The.
Young Girl, The.
St. John. Shore, The.
Until the Sea Is Dead.
Smith, Charlotte. On Being Cautioned against Walking on an Headland Overlooking the Sea, because It Was Frequented by a Lunatic.
Written in a Tempestuous Night, on the Coast of Sussex.
Written near a Port on a Dark Evening.
Written on the Sea Shore.—October, 1784.
Snyder. Wild Edge, The.
Stevenson. At the Seaside [or Sea-Side].
Thomas. We Lying by Seasand.
Wakoski. On Barbara's Shore.
Whitman. As I Ebb'd with the Ocean of Life.
From Montauk Point.
Patrolling Barnegat.
Paumanok.
Whittier. Burning Drift-Wood.
Young. Big Sur.
Zukofsky. Ferry.
See also **Beaches; Seacoasts.**

Show Business
Rolfe. Nuthin but Brass.
Stuart. Barker, The.
That'll Be the Day.
Young. Ian.
See also **Acting and Actors; Motion Pictures; Theater and Theaters.**

Shrews
Burns. Kellyburnbraes.
Pinned to Mrs R———'s Carriage.
Gardner. Masked Shrew, The.
Hardy. She Charged Me.
Hoffman. Shrew.
Nash. Introduction, The.

Shrines
Berry. Springs, The.
Sandburg. Three Shrines.
See also **Mausoleums; Monuments.**

See also **Shropshire, England**
Davie. Shropshire.
Housman. On Wenlock Edge the wood's in trouble.

Shrouds
De la Mare. Snow.
Hartley. John Donne in His Shroud.

Sibyl
Eberhart. Difficulty of Ideas, The.
Frost. Our Doom to Bloom.
Graves. Young Sibyl, The.
Hopkins. Spelt from Sibyl's Leaves.
Prince. And yet the Sibyl parches, caught and clutched within a fist of dust!

Sicily
Eberhart. Mediterranean Song.
Fletcher. Lines Written at Taormina, Sicily.
Hewitt. Agrigento, Sicily.
Hugo. Docking at Palermo.
Maratea Porto.
Lawrence. Almond Blossom.
Bare Almond-Trees.
Hibiscus and Salvia Flowers.
Sandburg. Suburban Sicilian Sketches.

Sickness. *see* **Illness.**

Siddons, Mrs. Sarah
Coleridge. Mrs. Siddons.

Sideshows
Gardner. Three Rings or Five rings.
Williams, Miller. Firebreathers at the Café Deux Magots, The.

Sidmouth, Henry Addington, Viscount
Shelley. Similes for Two Political Characters of 1819.

Sidney, Sir Philip
Bradstreet. Elegy Upon that Honorable and Reknowned Knight Sir Philip Sydney, An.
Campion. De obitu Phil. Sydnaei equitis aurati generosissimi.

Donne. Upon the Translation of the Psalms by Sir Philip Sidney, and the Countess of Pembroke His Sister.
Jonson. To Elizabeth, Countess of Rutland.
To Mary, Lady Wroth ("How well, fair crown of your fair sex, might he").
To Mrs Phillip Sidney.
Markson. On the Death, after Lying Wounded in the Thigh for Twenty-Six Days, of the Author of "Astrophel and Stella."
Ralegh. Epitaph upon the Right Hono[u]rable Sir Philip Sidney Knight, Lord Governor of Flushing, An.
Spenser. Another of the Same.
Astrophel.
Elegie, or Friends Passion, for His Astrophill, An.
Epitaph upon the Right Honourable Sir Phillip Sidney, Knight: Lord Governor of Flushing, An.
Mourning Muse of Thestylis, The.
Pastorall Aeglogue upon the Death of Sir Phillip Sidney, Knight, etc, A.
Such skill, matcht with such courage as he had.

Siegfried
Fletcher. August, 1940.

Sierra Nevada Mountains
Jeffers. Ascent to the Sierras.
Levine. Wednesday.
Whittier. Pass of the Sierra, The.

Siestas
Catullus. Carmen 32: "Call me to you / at siesta."
Zukofsky. I'm a bow, my dual kiss, Ipsithilla.

Sight
Auden. Heard and Seen.
Crane. Visible the Untrue, The.
Creeley. For Allen.
Ice Cream.
Night Sky, A.
Statue, The.
Window, The.
De la Mare. Window, The.
Frost. Wish to Comply, A.
Gallagher. Reading Aloud.
Graves. Gift of Sight.
Herrick. Upon His Eye-Sight Failing Him.
Upon One-Ey'd Broomsted.
Hesketh. Reply to a Philistine.
Hewitt. Spectacle of Truth, The.
To Any Dweller in Lewis Street.
Koch. On Beauty.
Liddy. Blue Mountain.
Lowell. Eye and Tooth.
Myopia: a Night.
McAuley. Exile on His Failing Vision, The.
Merton. What we see of things is the things themselves.
Olson. Well.
Pack. Einstein's Pegasus.
Sandburg. What other oaths are wanted now?
Sidney. Beauty hath force to catch the human sight.
If mine eyes can speak to do hearty errand.
Sonnet 105: "Unhappy sight, and hath she vanished by."
Stevens. Note on Moonlight.
Poem Written at Morning.
Red Fern, The.
Tattoo.
Woman Looking at a Vase of Flowers.
Tomlinson. Sight and Flight.
Williams, William Carlos. Eyeglasses, The.
Zukofsky. In Arizona / (how many years in the mountains).

Silence
Atwood. Investigator is here, The.
Auden. At last, down in the lane.
Canal, Froghall, The.
Dark Fiddler, The.
Homage to Clio.
Punchard.
Beckett. Bon bon il est un pays.
Musique de l'indifférence.
Silence tel que ce qui fut.
Berg. Answer, The.

Behind Us.
Iowa.
Milk.
Sketch.
Berry. Elegy: "All day our eyes could find no resting place."
Except.
He Has Lived through Another Night.
Silence, The.
Sorrel Filly, The.
To Gary Snyder.
Where.
Bogan. Poem in Prose.
Brontë. How still, how happy! These [or Those] are words.
Browning, Elizabeth Barrett. Hugh Stuart Boyd [Legacies].
Substitution.
"Carroll, Lewis." Solitude.
Carruth. But if the wind should fall and silence spread.
Line, The.
Silence.
Sonnet: "But still, still... / In stillness mystery calls."
Sonnet: "The hubbub of the Hall of Languages, our Babel."
Tanck's Song About Silence.
This hour is best, darkening.
To Artemis.
Cohen. Gift.
I Stopped to Listen.
Poem: "I heard of a man."
Summer Haiku.
You're Not Supposed to Be Here.
Coleridge. Eros aei lalethros hetairos.
Silent City, A.
Cooper. In Silence Where We Breathe.
Sunlight lies along my table.
Creeley. After Mallarmé.
Apple Uppfle.
Eye, The.
Going to Bed.
Kitchen.
Return.
Song, A: "I had wanted a quiet testament."
Sound.
Waiting.
Words.
Cummings. & sun & / sil / e / nce.
Because / an obstreperous grin minutely floats.
Do you remember when the fluttering dusk.
Enter no(silence is the blood whose flesh).
Hush) / noones / are coming.
Silence / .is / a / looking.
Summer Silence.
These children singing in stone a.
De la Mare. Autumn.
Bells, The.
Dark Château, The.
Echo.
Faint Music.
Fear.
Listeners, The.
Market-Place, The.
Myself.
Quiet.
Silence.
Snowflake, The.
Stranger, The.
Swallows Flown.
Taciturn, The.
Time Passes.
Where?
Dickinson. Cherishing that is speechless, The.
Death's Waylaying not the sharpest.
I fear a Man of frugal Speech.
Night is my favorite Day.
Silence is all we dread.
Silence' oblation to the Ear.
There is no Silence in the Earth—so silent.
To those who can estimate silence.
Words the happy say, The.
Dobyns. Silence.
Dunbar. Silence.
Duncan. Sentinels, The.
Dunn. After the Argument.

Legacy.
Secret Life, A.
Those of Us Who Think We Know.
Woman on Edgehill Road, The.
Eberhart. Bower, The.
Emblem.
Grave Piece.
Hatred of the Old River.
Parker River, The.
Snow Cascades.
Velvet Rocks.
Why.
Emerson. And had Hafiz.
As I walked in the woods.
Dangerous gift & grace is mine, A.
Future, The.
Merops.
Pedants all / They would be original.
Silence.
While roses bloomed along the plain.
Ferlinghetti. He with the Beating Wings.
Garrigue. Thy Love Is One Thou'st Not Yet Known.
Ginsberg. Funny Death.
Glück. Exile.
Horse.
Graves. Black Goddess, The.
Nobody.
Touch My Shut Lips.
Yet Unsayable, The.
Hacker. Against Silence.
Haines. People fell back, a field of wheat, The.
Hall. Je Suis une Table.
Hardy. Duettist to her Pianoforte, A.
He Resolves to Say No More.
I Look in Her Face.
Silences.
Herrick. Silence.
Hesketh. Vision.
Hewitt. Drypoint.
Memorandum for the Moderates.
Hoffman. This Silence.
Hugo. Greystone Cottage.
Or Another Place.
Jeffers. Northern Heather.
Knott. Sonnet: "Way the world is not, The."
Kunitz. Silence.
Lawrence. Listening.
Poor Bit of a Wench!
Sickness.
Silence: (Come, holy silence...).
Silence: (Since I lost you...).
Winter-Lull.
Levine. Face, The.
Last Step, The.
Silent in America.
Winter Words.
Lieberman. Psychodrama: Tokyo Mime Film.
Lorde. Suspension.
Lovelace. To Ellinda, That Lately I Have Not Written.
Lowry. Iphigenia in Aulis. Agamemnon Speaks:.
Poets are Godlike in that they.
McAuley. Fire's gone down: burnt pine, The.
Not a sound. The house could be.
"MacDiarmid." Glen of Silence, The.
MacLeish. Epitaph for John McCutcheon.
Lost Speakers, The.
Wood Dove at Sandy Spring, The.
Markson. Traveler's Tale.
Meinke. Arms and the Man.
Myth.
Meredith. Meeting.
Nature and Life.
Night-Walk, The.
Pastoral 5: "Now from the meadow floods the wild duck clamours."
We stood in the garden alone.
Merrill. Dandelion Sermon, The.
Merton. Action and Non-Action.
In Silence.
Love Winter When the Plant Says Nothing.
O Sweet Irrational Worship.
St. Alberic.
Song: If You Seek.

Millay. Ode to Silence.
Moore. Silence.
Nash. That Reminds Me.
Oppen. Clarity / In the sense of *transparence*.
Patchen. Limpidity of Silences.
Piercy. At the Core.
Plath. Courage of Shutting-Up, The.
Munich Mannequins, The.
Poe. Sonnet—Silence.
Pope. On Silence.
Raine. Once I heard your voice.
Rich. Cartographies of Silence.
Ghazal V.
Hohokam.
Particularity.
That conversation we were always on the edge.
This apartment full of books could crack open.
Your silence today is a pond where drowned things live.
Rolfe. Soledad.
To My Contemporaries.
Rossetti. Golden Silences.
I See That All Things Come to an End.
I seek among the living & I seek.
I sit among the green shady valleys oft.
Introspective.
Sonnet from the Psalms.
Then Shall Ye Shout.
Way of the World, The.
Rukeyser. Breathing Landscape.
Sandburg. Alone and Not Alone.
Answer, The.
Aprons of Silence.
At the Gates of Tombs.
First Sonata for Karlen Paula.
Gong of Time, The.
Gypsy.
Honey and Salt.
Is There Any Easy Road to Freedom?
Sandhill People.
Speech.
To Know Silence Perfectly.
What did Hiamovi, the red man, Chief of.
Year, The.
Schuyler. "From the next .."
Sometimes.
Schwartz. Choir and Music of Solitude and Silence, The.
"Lo, we descend like light. Light. Light."
"O Death, great captain, lift anchor!"
Poem to Johann Sebastian Bach.
Sexton. Silence, The.
Shelley. Fragment: Apostrophe to Silence.
Summer Evening Churchyard, A.
Simic. Dismantling the Silence.
Smart. Silence.
Smith, Stevie. King Hamlet's Ghost.
Nor We of Her to Him.
Snyder. Without.
Stevens. Creations of Sound, The.
Less and Less Human, O Savage Spirit.
Stevenson. About the sheltered garden ground.
Late, O miller.
Suckling. Why so pale and wan, fond lover?
Sutter. He would never say any of this.
What the Country Man Knows By Heart.
When loons laugh he does not.
Why he lives there he can't say.
Tomlinson. Awakening, The.
Hand at Callow Hill Farm, The.
Wakoski. Steely Silence.
Walcott. Oddjob, a Bull Terrier.
Whitman. After the Dazzle of Day.
Wilbur. Games Two.
Williams, Charles Kenneth. One of the Muses.
Patience Is When You Stop Waiting.
Williams, William Carlos. Silence.
Stillness.
Wordsworth. Address to Silence.
Wright, Charles. George Trakl Journal.
Night Journal II.
Silent Journal.
Wright, James. Arriving in the Country Again.
Echo for the Promise of Georg Trakl's Life.
In the Face of Hatred.

Snowstorms in the Midwest.
Sparrows in a Hillside Drift.
Wroth. Sonnet 37: "Night, welcome art thou to my mind destrest."
Yeats. After Long Silence.
Maid Quiet.
Young. Curative Powers of Silence, The.
Koto Music/Singing.
Zukofsky. Or a Valentine.

Silk
Herrick. Upon Franck.
Upon Julia's Clothes.
Schuyler. Steaming Ties.
Smith, Charlotte. To the Mulberry-Tree.

Silkworms
Cowper. Silk Worm, The.

Silver
Davie. On Generous Lines.
Dunbar. Real Question, The.
Emerson. At Plymouth in the friendly crowd.
High heart, O Hafiz! though not thine.
Hewitt. Silver Was the Barbèd Hook.
Sorrentino. Variations 2.
Swift. Simile, A.
Wakoski. Silver.

Similes. *see* **Metaphor.**

Simon of Cyrene
Cullen. Simon the Cyrenian Speaks.

Simplicity
Berry. In the early morning dark.
Throwing away the Mail.
Browning, Elizabeth Barrett. Mountaineer and Poet.
Burns. Song: "Adown winding Nith I did wander."
Song: "Behind yon hills where Lugar flows."
Song: "Mark yonder pomp of costly fashion."
Song: "O poortith cauld, and restless love."
Campion. *Jacke* and *Jone*, they thinke no ill.
Clark. Slow Life.
Coleridge. To Simplicity.
Cowper. 1.38: Simplicity.
Another Translation of the Same Ode.
Ease is the weary merchant's pray'r.
On a Fowler.
Retirement.
Creeley. "Bolinas and Me."
Pryaer, A.
Song: "How simply / for another."
Wall, A.
Davie. Love-Poems: for Mairi MacInnes.
Dickinson. My life has been too simple and stern.
Doolittle. There is no sign-post to say.
"Dylan." Bob Dylan's Dream.
Sign on the Window.
Emerson. For what need I of book or priest.
I live among ideal men.
Poet ("To clothe the fiery thought").
Fisher. Sky, the Sea, The.
Galvin. Defending the Provinces.
Gunn. Corridor, The.
Haines. Way We Live, The.
Hall. Clown, The.
Hartley. Logic.
Herbert. Wreath, A.
Herrick. Covetous Still Captives, The.
Expenses Exhaust.
No Want Where There's Little.
Hewitt. Lyric: "Chestnut and beech / sycamore and willow."
My Mother.
Resource.
W.R.R.
Hoffman. Breathing Purely.
Hopkins. Horace: Persicos Odi, Puer, Apparatus.
Shepherd's Brow, The.
Hugo. Christmas with Shepherds in Brefaro.
Getty.
Jeffers. Wind-Struck Music, The.
Jonson. Still to be neat, still to be dressed [*or* Drest].
Knott. Shorts / Excerpts ("Night, in whose death did your ennui take refuge?").
Larkin. Modesties.
Lewis. To Rilke.

Liddy. As in poetry.
Lowry. I set this down as humble prayer.
"MacDiarmid." Covenanters, The.
Meinke. Blue Morning Glories.
Merton. Five Enemies, The.
Importance of Being Toothless, The.
Turtle, The.
When the Shoe Fits.
Nash. I Will Arise and Go Now.
"My Child Is Phlegmatic..."—Anxious Parent.
Reflection on Ingenuity.
Olson. It's Got to This.
Oppen. Penobscot.
Ransom. Captain Carpenter.
Rolfe. In Praise Of.
Rossetti. Farm Walk, A.
Sandburg. Fellow Citizens.
Oomba.
Shelton. Kind of Glory, A.
Sidney. Sonnet 28: "You that with allegory's curious frame."
Smart. 2.16: To Grosphus.
To His Servant.
Sorrentino. As with a Simple Gesture of the Fingers.
Detail, A.
In a fantastic light.
Stevenson. Camp, A.
Whittier. To James T. Fields.
Wilbur. Baroque Wall-Fountain in the Villa Sciarra, A.
Happy the Man.
Wordsworth. Farmer of Tilsbury Vale, The.
Young. Real Time.
Zukofsky. Madison, Wis., Remembering the Bloom of Monticello (1931).
You three:—my wife.

Sin
Beckett. Dortmunder.
Berry. Purification, A.
Berryman. Curse, The.
Gislebertus' Eve.
Blake. Was Jesus Chaste? or did he.
Washer Womans Song, The.
Bradstreet. Flesh and the Spirit, The.
Brontë. A.A.A.
There let they bleeding branch atone.
Browning, Elizabeth Barrett. Lay of the Brown Rosary, The.
Weeping Saviour, The.
Browning, Robert. Adam, Lilith, and Eve.
Burns. Song: "I'll tell you a tale of a wife."
Byron. Prayer of Nature, The.
Campion. View Mee, Lord.
Chaucer. Pardoner's Tale, The.
Parson's Tale, The.
Physician's Tale, The.
Reeve's Prologue, The.
Summoner's Tale, The.
Clough. Here am I yet, another twelvemonth spent.
Cowper. Epistle to a Protestant Lady in France, An.
Testimony of Divine Adoption, The.
Crane. This Way Where November..
Crashaw. But Men loved Darkness[e] Rather Than [*or* Then] Light.
John 3; But Men Loved Darknesse Rather than Light.
On Saint Peter Cutting of Malchus His Eare.
Creeley. Kind of Act Of, The.
Cullen. For Daughters of Magdalen.
Cummings. Now dis "daughter" uv eve(who aint precisely slim)sim.
Davie. Dancing Measures.
Levity.
Vengeance Is Mine, Saith the Lord.
Vespers.
Witness.
Donne. Licentious Person, A.
Son[ne] of God hear[e] us, and since thou.
Spit in my face ye [*or* you] Jew[e]s, and pierce my side.
Dunbar. Distinction.
How Lucy Backslid.
"Dylan." Trouble in Mind.
Eberhart. Adam Cast Forth.

Emerson. Puff of air or dry or damp, A.
Sun athwart the cloud thought it no sin, The.
Gardner. Triolet: "Bad die old, The."
Glück. Murderess, The.
Hall. Conduct and Work.
Hemingway. I'm off'n wild wimmen.
Little drops of grain alcohol.
Herbert. Agony [*or* Agonie], The.
Church-Lock and Key.
Confession.
Foil, The.
Good Friday.
Judgement.
Love.
Sin: "O that I could a sin once see!"
Sin (1).
Sinner, The.
Sin's Round.
Storm, The.
Herrick. Another ("Sin is an act so free, that if we shall").
Another ("Sin is the cause of death").
Bad May Be Better.
Baptisme.
Bell-Man, The.
Christs Incarnation.
Cock-Crow.
Eucharist, The.
Evill.
Eye, The.
God Has a Twofold Part.
Gods Pardon.
Good, and Bad.
Loading and Unloading.
Long Life.
Mirth.
More Potent, Lesse Peccant.
None Free from Fault.
Our Owne Sinnes Unseen.
Pain[e] Ends in Pleasure.
Pardon.
Penitencie.
Position in the Hebrew Divinity, A.
Prescience.
Sin.
Sin and Strife.
Sin Seen.
Sin Severely Punisht.
Sin ("Sin leads the way, but as it goes, it feels").
Sin ("Sin never slew a soule, unless there went").
Sin ("Sin no Existence; Nature none it hath").
Sin ("Sin once reacht up to Gods eternall Sphere").
Sin ("There is no evill that we do commit").
Sins Loathed, and Yet Loved.
Soule, The.
Three Fatal[l] Sisters.
To God: an Anthem, Sung in the Chapel at White-Hall, Before the King.
To His Conscience.
Upon Groynes.
Will To Be Working, A.
Hopkins. Glimmer'd along the square-cut steep.
Myself unholy, from myself unholy.
Housman. Epitaph, An: "Stay, if you list, O passer by the way."
Stars, I have seen them fall.
Hughes, Langston. Madam and the Minister.
Sinner.
Jeffers. Give Your Heart to the Hawks.
Original Sin.
Jonson. Epode: "Not to know vice at all, and keep[e] true state."
Of Life and Death.
Sinner's Sacrifice, The.
Larkin. High Windows.
Lawrence. Demon Justice.
En Masse.
Eve.
God and the Holy Ghost.
Humility.
In a Spanish Tram-Car.
Irreverent Thoughts.
Latter-Day Sinners.

Little Wowser, The.
Sex Isn't Sin.
Sinners.
Spanish Privilege.
Lewis. Miniature on a Book of Hours.
On a Bereaved Girl.
Liddy. Homage to Conor Cruise O'Brien.
Lindsay. Unpardonable Sin, The.
Lovelace. Amarantha a Pastorall.
Mock Charon, A.
Lowell. Worst Sinner, Jonathan Edwards'
God, The.
McAuley. Secret.
MacLeish. Serpent's Riddle, The.
MacNeice. Blasphemies, The.
Meum Est Propositum.
Merton. Biography, The.
On the Anniversary of My Baptism.
Sponge Full of Vinegar, The.
Milton. No more of talk where God or Angel
Guest.
Pensive here I sat.
Nash. Ha! Original Sin!
Inter-Office Memorandum.
Nevertheless.
Portrait of the Artist as a Prematurely Old
Man.
Nemerov. Let sin be preordained.
Poem of Margery Kempe, A.
Olson. Sin is inferiority. The mother's
cooperation in the birth of her daughter.
Patchen. I compel you to question me about
my motives.
Wide, wide in the rose's side.
Psalms. Psalm 51: "Have mercy upon me, O
God."
Raine. It is in us they burn.
Ralegh. Diseases, famine, enemies, in us no
change have wrought.
Rossetti. Afterward He Repented, and Went.
Ash Wednesday.
Behold, I stand at the door and knock.
Cannot Sweeten.
For Thine Own Sake, O My God.
He Shall Go No More Out.
If thou be dead, forgive and thou shalt live.
Lord, what have I to offer? sickening fear.
O Christ my God Who seest the unseen.
O Lord, when Thou didst call me, didst Thou
know.
Sinner's own fault? So it was, The.
Standing Afar Off for the Fear of Her
Torment.
Surely there is an aching void within.
Weigh all my faults and follies righteously.
Who shall my wandering thoughts steady &
fix.
Rukeyser. Sun on the faces. On the knotted
rocks.
Sandburg. Quotations.
Scott. Gray Brother, The.
Shakespeare. Sonnet 35: "No more be grieved
at that which thou hast done."
Sonnet 94: "They that have power to hurt[e],
and will do[e] none."
Sonnet 119: "What potions have I drunk of
Siren tears."
Sidney. Sonnet 14: "Alas, have I not pain
enough, my friend."
Smith, Patti. Oath.
Smith, Stevie. Man I Am, A.
Oh What Is the Thing He Done?
Recognition Not Enough.
Southwell. Man's Civil[l] War[re].
Prodigall Chyld's Soule Wracke, The.
Saint Peter's Remorse.
Synne's Heavy Loade.
Stevenson. Look of Death is both severe and
mild, The.
You looked so tempting in the pew.
Swinburne. Phaedra.
Tate. Ah, Christ, I love you rings to the wild
sky.
Tennyson. St. Simeon Stylites.
Vision of Sin, The.
Thomas. It Is the Sinner's Dust-Tongued Bell.

Walker. Compulsory Chapel.
Mississippi Winter II.
Warren. Original Sin; a Short Story.
Whittier. Two Rabbins, The.
Wilbur. Pelican, The.
Williams, Miller. Picker.
Williams, William Carlos. From "The Birth of
Venus," Song.
Wordsworth. Rid of a vexing and a heavy
load.
Wyatt. Rue on me, Lord, for thy goodness
and grace.

See also **Original Sin; Seven Deadly Sins; Vice.**

Singing and Singers
Angelou. Shaker, Why Don't You Sing?
Singer Will Not Sing, The.
Auden. At last, down in the lane.
Beatles. All Together Now.
Ob-La-Di Ob-La-Da.
Only a Northern Song.
Berry. Architecture, An.
Law That Marries All Things, The.
Man Walking and Singing, A.
Song Sparrow Singing in the Fall, A.
To Go By Singing.
Bogan. M., Singing.
Boyle. Complaint for Mary and Marcel, A.
Browning, Elizabeth Barrett. King's Gift, The.
Seraph and Poet, The.
Browning, Robert. On Singers.
Carew. Celia Singing ("You that think Love
can convey").
Celia Singing ("Hark, how my Celia, with the
choice").
Ciardi. No White Bird Sings.
Clark. Every Day.
Cohen. Tower of Song, The.
Coleridge. On a Volunteer Singer.
Cowper. Catharina.
To Leonora Singing at Rome.
To the Same ["Why, credulous Naples, do you
vaunt your clear-voiced Siren"].
Creeley. Air: "The Love of a Woman."
Poem for Bob Leed.
Xmas.
Cullen. Colored Blues Singer.
Cummings. All which isn't singing is mere
talking.
Now(more near ourselves than we).
These children singing in stone a.
Until and i heard.
Voices to voices, lip to lip.
You shall sing my songs, O earth.
De la Mare. In Vain.
Rachel.
Dickey, James. Buckdancer's Choice.
Folk Singer of the Thirties, A.
Dickinson. I shall keep singing!
Dunbar. Banjo Song, A.
Deacon Jones' Grievance.
Lesson, The.
Question, A.
When Malindy Sings.
When Sam'l Sings.
With the Lark.
"Dylan." Eternal Circle.
Joan Baez in Concert, Part 2.
Minstrel Boy.
Song to Woody.
Yes, I am a thief of thoughts.
Emerson. Saadi.
Everson. Bard.
Ferlinghetti. Carrara, Looking Seaward.
Fisher. Why They Stopped Singing.
Fletcher. Joy.
Ford. Chanson Pour Billie.
He's out on the loggia.
Fox. Cetus, a Letter from Jonah.
Frost. Aim Was Song, The.
Our Singing Strength.
Valley's Singing Day, The.
Gardner. Incantate the Cockatrice.
Graves. Bards, The.
Hacker. Elegy: "Crying from exile, I."
Hall. Blue Wing, The.
Hardy. He Inadvertently Cures His Love-
Pains.

To a Lady Playing and Singing in the
Morning.
Heaney. Singer's House, The.
Herrick. Againe.
Another ("Wassaile the Trees, that they may
beare").
His Lachrimae or Mirth, Turn'd to Mourning.
Poet Hath Lost His Pipe, The.
Upon a Gentlewoman with a Sweet Voice.
Upon a Hoarse Singer.
Upon Comely a Good Speaker but an Ill
Singer.
Upon Her Voice.
Upon Julia's Voice.
Upon Linnit.
Upon Sapho, Sweetly Playing, and Sweetly
Singing.
Voice and Violl, The.
Hewitt. Black and White.
Moscow Moment.
Hoffman. Awoke into a Dream of Singing.
Singing.
Hughes, Langston. Harlem Night Song.
Hughes, Ted. Owl's Song.
Hugo. Langaig.
Jonson. And Must I Sing? What Subject Shall
I Choose?
Musical Strife; in a Pastoral Dialogue, The.
Kinnell. Last Songs.
Kipling. Army Headquarters.
In the Neolithic Age.
Last Rhyme of True Thomas, The.
Recantation, A.
Lawrence. Piano.
Liddy. I Hear the Wife of the Governor of
Wisconsin Singing.
Little Song for Ivy Day, 1991.
Lindsay. How a Little Girl Sang.
Lorde. Day They Eulogized Mahalia, The.
For My Singing Sister.
Lovelace. Dialogue. Lute and Voice, A.
To Lucasta ("I laugh and sing, but cannot
tell").
Lowry. Another Immorality.
Duck Train—Vocal Arctic Fox-Trot.
Mackerel shouldn't take, A.
Marching down the road to China.
Singing. / The morning bird. / (Humphum!).
With Sweetest Devotion from *All* the Little
Animals to Their Most Beloved Harteebeeste.
McAuley. Caruso.
Interlude, with Alter Ego.
"MacDiarmid." Archin' here and arrachin
there.
Empty Vessel.
Wheesht, wheesht, Joyce, and let me hear.
MacNeice. Death of an Actress.
Marvell. Fair Singer, The.
Meinke. Aunt Mary.
Indigo Buntings.
Melville. Jack Roy.
Milton. To Leonora Singing in Rome.
To the Same ["Another Leonora captured the
poet Torquato"].
To the Same ["Why, credulous Naples, do you
vaunt your clear-voiced Siren"].
Nash. It's Snug to Be Smug.
Screen with the Face with the Voice, The.
Strange Case of the Renegade Lyric Writer,
The.
O'Hara. Day Lady Died, The.
Olson. Green Man, The.
Patchen. Irate Songster, The.
Pope. Pastorals.
Pound. Cino.
Raine. Ancient Speech, The.
Robinson. Eutychides.
Rolfe. Nuthin but Brass.
Rossetti. All Saints.
Before the Throne, and Before the Lamb.
Easter Day.
Eleanor.
Joy of Saints, like incense turned to fire, The.
Love me,—I love you / Love me, my baby.
Sing me a song— / What shall I sing?
Songs in a Cornfield.
Then Shall Ye Shout.

Rukeyser. Seventh Elegy. Dream-Singing Elegy.
Sandburg. I Sang.
Splinter.
Schuyler. Beautiful Funerals.
Janis Joplin's Dead: Long Live Pearl.
Let's All Hear It for Mildred Bailey!
Sexton. Fury of Guitars and Sopranos, The.
Shelley. Fragment: To One Singing.
Smith, Stevie. Singing Cat, The.
Songster, The.
Sorrentino. In the blue, singa.
Stevens. Idea of Order at Key West, The.
Stevenson. Bright is the ring of words.
Come, my little children, here are songs for you.
Singing.
To Dr. Hake.
Stuart. Gospel Singer.
Lines.
Tomlinson. At Wells: Polyphony.
Wakoski. Lady Who Sang, The.
Whitman. Chanting the Square Deific.
Dead Tenor, The.
I Hear America Singing.
Singer in the Prison, The.
To a Certain Cantatrice.
Whittier. Singer, The.
Williams, Charles Kenneth. Mornings: Catherine.
Williams, William Carlos. Late Singer, The.
Wordsworth. On Approaching the Staub-Bach, Lauterbrunnen.
On Hearing the "Ranz des Vaches" on the Top of the Pass of St Gothard.
Solitary Reaper, The.
Wyatt. Marvel [or Marvaill] no more although [or all tho].
My lute, awake! Perform [the] last.
Young. Jungle Strut.
Poem for Lena Horne, A.
See also **Tenors.**

Sinkholes
Ford. Pleasure boat, pleasure boat where has it gone?

Sioux, The
Everson. Black Hills, The.
Oliver. Ghosts.
Wright, James. Centenary Note: Inscribed to Little Crow, Leader of the Sioux Rebellion in Minnesota, 1862, A.

Sirens (mythology)
Atwood. Siren Song.
Cowper. To the Same ["Why, credulous Naples, do you vaunt your clear-voiced Siren"].
De la Mare. Alexander.
Not that way.
Hoffman. There.
Milton. At a Solemn Music[k].
To the Same ["Why, credulous Naples, do you vaunt your clear-voiced Siren"].
Wilbur. Merlin Enthralled.
Sirens, The.

Sirens (warning devices)
Merton. Suddenly in the night the sirens.
Wilbur. Fire-Truck, A.

Sisters
Bogan. Sleeping Fury, The.
Browning, Elizabeth Barrett. Bertha in the Lane.
Byron. Epistle to Augusta.
Campion. To the Most Princely and Vertuous the Lady Elizabeth.
"Carroll, Lewis." Three sisters at breakfast were feeding the cat.
Coleridge. On Receiving an Account That His Only Sister's Death Was Inevitable.
On Seeing a Youth Affectionately Welcomed by a Sister.
To a Friend [Charles Lamb] Together with an Unfinished Poem.
To Two Sisters.
De la Mare. Brother and Sister.
Reflections.
Rose.

Dickey, James. Veer-Voices: Two Sisters under Crows.
Dickinson. One Sister have I in our house.
Dunn. Sister.
Emerson. Elizabeth Hoar.
Hearst thou, sweet spirit, thou hast heard before.
Kind & holy were the words.
Fletcher. Old Nursery.
Gallagher. Still Moment at Dun Laoghaire.
Glück. Descending Figure.
Silverpoint.
Tango.
Gunn. Girls Next Door, The.
Hardy. Logs on the Hearth.
Herrick. To My Dearest Sister M. Mercie Herrick.
Hewitt. Her situation seemed a piteous thing.
My Sister.
On Choosing Some Verses for My Sister's Cremation.
On Colinward: The Scattering.
Keats. Acrostic.
Kunitz. My Sisters.
Lorde. Family Resemblance, A.
Lowry. Oh the Pyrrus boys are we.
Plath. Babysitters, The.
Prince. To My Sister.
"Reed." Little Sister.
Rich. Sisters.
Transit.
Women.
Roethke. To My Sister.
Rossetti. For there is no friend like a sister.
Goblin Market.
Lowest Room, The.
Maiden-Song.
Noble Sisters.
Our Mothers, lovely women pitiful; / Our sisters, gracious in their life and death.
Sister Maude.
Summer Is Ended, The.
Rukeyser. Two Years.
Sexton. One-Eye, Two-Eyes, Three-Eyes.
Silverstein. For Sale.
Smith, Stevie. Barlow.
Suckling. Upon Two Sisters.
Waldman. Sisters.
Walker. For My Sister Molly Who in the Fifties.
Telling.
Whittier. Singer, The.
Sisters, The.
To My Friend on the Death of His Sister.
To My Sister.
Williams, Charles Kenneth. Kin.
Wordsworth. Forth from a Jutting Ridge, Around Whose Base.
Fragment: "Witness Thou."
Seven Sisters, or, the Solitude of Binnorie, The.

Sisyphus
Glück. Mountain, The.
Mahon. Death and the Sun.
Schwartz. Maxims of Sisyphus, The.

Skateboarding and Skateboarders
Gunn. Skateboard.

Skating and Skaters
Atwood. Woman Skating.
Bukowski. Skaters, The.
Cummings. Skating.
Fox. Figure Eights.
Johnson. Translations of Roy's Verses on Skaters.
Kipling. DECEMBER (*Skating*).
Matthews. School Figures.
Morgan. Night Skater, The.
Rukeyser. Boys of These Men Full Speed.
Stevenson. Duddingstone.
Wordsworth. Skating.
See also **Skateboarding and Skateboarders.**

Skeletons
Carruth. Imagine bird bones.
There! Whitman's skull—.
Hartley. Perhaps Macabre.
Hesketh. Skeleton Bride.
Lovelace. La Bella Bona Roba.

Morrison. Maids Are Bickering.
Wilbur. To His Skeleton.
Wright, James. On the Skeleton of a Hound.
Yau. Nantucket.
See also **Bones.**

Skepticism. *see* **Doubt.**

Skiing and Skiers
Cummings. Skies may be blue;yes.
Eberhart. Skier and the Mountain, The.
Jarrell. January 1938.
Merrill. Up and Down.
Rich. Transit.
Updike. Tsokadze O Altitudo.
Wakoski. Skier, The.
Warren. Skiers.

Skin
Angelou. Passing Time.
Creeley. Skeleton, The.
Fox. Angel of Death, The.
Herrick. Lawne, The.
To Electra.
Upon Blinks.
Hesketh. Truth Game.
Knott. Shorts / Excerpts ("Our farewells lack the plausibility of our departures").
Larkin. Skin.
Olson. Her skin / covered me, illuminated.
Silverstein. Colors.
Smith, Patti. Schinden.
Williams, Charles Kenneth. Scar.
Williams, Miller. Book, The.

Skulls
Beckett. Hors crâne seul dedans.
Eberhart. Meditation, A.
Gardner. Only Relic, The.
Hewitt. Sheep Skull, The.
Hoffman. Northern Lights.
Keats. Stanzas on Some Skulls in Beauly Abbey, Near Inverness.
"MacDiarmid." Perfect.
Markson. Skull.
Morgan. Skulls, The.
Nemerov. Decorated Skull in a University Museum.
Tomlinson. Skullshapes.
Tiger Skull.

Skunks
Eberhart. Dead Skunk.
Heaney. Skunk, The.
Jeffers. Skunks.
Lowell. Skunk Hour.
Oliver. Certain Sharpness in the Morning Air, A.

Sky
Ashbery. Variant.
Auden. Dawn.
Summer Night, A.
Berg. Endings.
Carroll, Jim. Love Rockets.
Song: "In minute gestures / that jet wetly slight."
Carruth. I Know, I Remember, But How Can I Help You.
Like a frozen lake the sky in the bitterest.
Sky like fishblood.
Sky yellow sky.
Ceravolo. Passion for the Sky.
Clark. Sky.
"sun shoots high..", The.
Warm ripe days. The sun floods the ridge with color.
Coleridge. Indifference of the Heavens, The.
'Twas not a mist, nor was it quite a cloud.
Crane. To the Cloud Juggler.
Creeley. From Pico & the Women: A Life.
Traveller, The.
Water.
Cummings. If up's the word;and a world grows greener.
Like a little bear twilight.
Luminous tendril of celestial wish.
The / sky / was / can dy lu.
These(whom;pretends / blue nothing).
They have hung the sky with arrows.
Vision.
Davie. If I Take the Wings of the Morning.

De la Mare. Bright Life.
Mermaids, The.
Dickinson. Competitions of the sky, The.
It troubled me as once I was.
Lightly stepped a yellow star.
Not what the stars have done.
Of Yellow was the outer Sky.
Slash of Blue, A.
Sun retired to a cloud, The.
Wild Blue sky abreast of Winds, A.
Dunn. Danse Manhattanique.
Meditation on Two Themes.
Eberhart. Child, The.
Grove, The.
Light From Above.
Looking At The Stars.
Looking at the Stars.
Standards, The.
Summery Windermere, sweet lake!
Emerson. But O to see his solar eyes.
Low December vault in June be up-lifted high.
Sea reflects the rosy sky, The.
That wandering fire to me appears.
Ferlinghetti. Poet as Fisherman.
Fisher. Leaving July.
Fletcher. Isle Iranim.
Lid, The.
Frost. A-Wishing Well.
Astrometaphysical.
Garrigue. Invocation to Old Windylocks.
Hewitt. Skypiece.
Hoffman. Evening.
Hugo. Mission to Linz.
Jeffers. Their Beauty Has More Meaning.
Kinnell. Daybreak.
Levertov. Clouds.
Levine. We sat by the shore.
Lowry. Morning Address of Love to the
Beloved Harteebeeste.
Meredith. Blue Is the Sky.
South-Wester, The.
Winter Heavens.
Nemerov. Above.
Olson. Rosy, It Was.
Signs.
Thoughts of the Time.
Oppen. Behind their house, behind the back
porch.
Raine. Night Sky.
Today as I / Looked up at the sky's great
face.
Rossetti. Fluttered Wings.
Mirrors of Life and Death.
Rukeyser. Haying Before Storm.
Preamble.
Sandburg. Be Ready.
Broken Sky.
In the heave of the hankering sea.
Love in Labrador.
People will live on, The.
Schuyler. Blue.
Schwartz. When I Remember the Advent.
Smith, Stevie. Coeur Simple.
Snyder. Blue Sky, The.
Stevens. Candle a Saint, The.
Dezembrum.
Stevenson. Summer Night.
To the Commissioners of Northern Lights.
Tomlinson. Images of Perfection.
Sky Writing.
Warren. Nature of a Mirror, The.
Whitman. After an Interval.
On the Beach at Night.
On the Beach at Night Alone.
Year of Meteors (1859–60).
Williams, William Carlos. At Night.
Conquest.
Desolate Field, The.
Naked.
Peace on Earth.
Tree and Sky.
Wordsworth. Volant Tribe of Bards on Earth
Are Found, A.
Wright, James. Divine Falling of Leaves, A.
Yau. Beneath sky's broken tiles, ancient barns
are embedded in plaster.
Engines of Gloom and Affection.

Young. Grizzly Peak.
Zukofsky. Close your eyes.
See also **Constellations; Stars.**
Sky Diving and Sky Divers
Morrison. Planes Are Groaning Mothers.
Skye, Isle of, Scotland
Hugo. Map of Skye, A.
Johnson. Ode, De Skia Insula.
Skia, An Ode on the Isle of Skye.
Skylarks. see Larks; Meadowlarks.
Skyscrapers
Fletcher. Crucifixion of the Skyscraper.
Elegy on an Empty Skyscraper.
Oppen. City of the corporations, A.
So spoke of the existence of things.
Piercy. Gasman Invites the Skyscrapers to
Dance.
Skyscrapers of the Financial District Dance
with Gasman, The.
Sandburg. Good Morning, America.
Hold down the skylines now with your
themes.
Prayers of Steel.
Skyscraper.
Skyscraper Loves Night, The.
Skyscrapers Stand Proud.
Tomlinson. All Afternoon.
Slander
Byron. Epitaph for Joseph Blacket.
Clare. Scandal.
Coleridge. Lines on a Friend.
Cowper. To Warren Hastings.
Trail of Admiral Keppel, The.
Donne. Expostulation, The.
Herrick. Accusation.
No Despight to the Dead.
Hewitt. Passion.
MacLeish. Black Day, The.
Pope. To the Earl of Burlington Asking Who
Writ the Libels against Him.
Shakespeare. Sonnet 70: "That thou art
blamed shall not be thy defect."
Sonnet 140: "Be wise as thou art cruel; do not
press."
Yeats. Against Unworthy Praise.
He Thinks of Those Who Have Spoken Evil
of His Beloved.
**Slaughter of the Innocents. see Massacre of the
Innocents.**
Slaughterhouses
Nash. Calf, The.
Oliver. Farm Country.
Simic. Travelling Slaughterhouse.
Slavery
Angelou. My Guilt.
One More Round.
Slave Coffle.
Song for the Old Ones.
Southeast Arkanasia.
Berry. My Great-Grandfather's Slaves.
Browning, Elizabeth Barrett. Hiram Powers'
"Greek Slave."
Runaway Slave at Pilgrim's Point, The.
Burns. Slave's Lament, The.
Catullus. Carmen 106: "When an auctioneer's
seen with a good-looking boy."
Cohen. I Am Punished.
Cowper. Charity.
Epigram: "To purify their wine some people
bleed."
Morning Dream, The.
Negro's Complaint, The.
Oh for a lodge in some vast wilderness.
Pity for Poor Africans.
Sonnet to Wilberforce.
Sweet Meat Has Sour Sauce.
Cullen. Negro Mother's Lullaby, A.
De la Mare. Gloria Mundi.
Dickey, James. Slave Quarters.
Dove. Abduction, The.
Adolescence—I.
Belinda's Petition.
House Slave, The.
Kentucky, 1833.
Pamela.
Slave's Critique of Practical Reason, The.

Transport or Slaves From Maryland to
Mississippi, The.
Dunbar. Ante-Bellum Sermon, An.
Corn-Song, A.
Deserted Plantation, The.
News, The.
Old Cabin, The.
Parted.
Sympathy.
To the South.
Emerson. Boston Hymn.
God The Lord save Massachusetts.
I am not black in my mind.
Pilgrims, The.
Glück. Slave Ship, The.
Hacker. Inheritances.
Part of a True Story.
Sword.
Hayden. Ballad of Nat Turner, The.
Frederick Douglass.
Middle Passage.
Runagate Runagate.
Hughes, Langston. Aunt Sue's Stories.
Kipling. Galley-Slave, The.
Song of the Galley-Slaves.
Knight. And Tell Me Poet, Can Love Exist in
Slavery?
Lawrence. Liberty's Old Old Story.
Moth and Rust.
Lindsay. Simon Legree—A Negro Sermon.
Longfellow. Slave Singing at Midnight, The.
Warning, The.
Melville. Formerly a Slave.
Misgivings.
Robinson. Sonnet: "Master and the slave go
hand in hand, The."
Rolfe. Kentucky.
Rossetti. Epitaph: "Slave yet wearing on my
head a crown, A."
Rukeyser. Secrets of American Civilization.
Sandburg. Mammy Hums.
Nigger.
Osawatomie.
Smith, Stevie. Was It Not Curious?
Stevenson. Ad Olum.
Ad Quintilianum.
Daughter of Herodias, The.
Plain as the glistering planets shine.
Tate. Times have changed. Why do you make
a fuss, The.
Thomson. Greece.
Walker. Early Losses: a Requiem.
Right to Life, The: What Can the White Man
Say to the Black Woman?
Whitman. Blood-Money.
Runaway Slave, The.
Song for Certain Congressmen.
Wounded Person, The.
Whittier. Astræa at the Capitol.
At Washington.
Branded Hand, The.
Christian Slave, The.
Clerical Oppressors.
Crisis, The.
Expostulation.
Farewell, The: "Gone, gone,—sold and gone."
For Righteousness' Sake.
Haschish, The.
Hunters of Men, The.
Hymn: "O Thou, whose presence went
before."
Ichabod[!].
Kathleen.
Legend of St. Mark, The.
Letter, A.
Letter from a Missionary of the Methodist
Episcopal Church South, in Kansas, to a
Distiguished Politician.
Lines on the Portrait of a Celebrated
Publisher.
Massachusetts to Virginia.
Mithridates at Chios.
Moral Warfare, The.
New Exodus, The.
Official Piety.
Panorama, The.
Pastoral Letter, The.

Ritner.
Sabbath Scene, A.
Sentence of John L. Brown, The.
Slave-Ships, The.
Slaves of Martinique, The.
Song for the Time, A.
Song of Slaves in the Desert.
Sumner.
Texas.
To a Southern Statesman.
To Delaware.
To George B. Cheever.
To Massachusetts.
To the Memory of Thomas Shipley.
To William Lloyd Garrison.
Yankee Girl, The.
Yorktown.
Wordsworth.   To Thomas Clarkson, on the
    Final Passing of the Bill for the Abolition of
    the Slave Trade. March, 1807.
Zukofsky.   Cute boy arm in elbow prize con
    man, kid, what do we see.

Sleds
Stafford.   Sayings from the Northern Ice.

See also **Sleighs.**

Sleep
Atwood.   Pre-Amphibian.
    Variation on the Word *Sleep*.
Auden.   Lullaby: "Din of work is subdued,
    The."
Beatles.   Golden Slumbers.
    Goodnight.
    I'm Only Sleeping.
Beckett.   Sleep till death.
Berry.   Birth (Near Port William), The.
    Deepest sleep holds us, The.
    Design of a House, The.
    His love returns / and walks among the trees.
    Let me wake in the night.
    Poem of Thanks, A.
    Sleep.
    What we leave behind to sleep.
    Winter Nightfall.
Berryman.   Henry by Night.
Bishop.   Insomnia.
    Sleeping on the Ceiling.
    Sleeping Standing Up.
    Unbeliever, The.
Bly.   Falling Asleep.
Bogan.   Tears in Sleep.
Brontë.   Sleep brings no joy to me.
Browning, Elizabeth Barrett.   Child Asleep, A.
    Isobel's Child.
    Sleep, The.
    Sleeping and Watching.
Burns.   Afton Water.
    Ay Waukin O.
    On a Bank of Flowers.
Byron.   Song: "Breeze of the night in gentler
    sighs."
Campion.   As on a day Sabina fell asleepe.
    Awake, thou spring of speaking grace, mute
    rest becomes not thee.
    Come, Cheerful Day!
    In eosdem.
    In Lycium et Clytham.
    It Fell on a Summer's [or Sommers] Day [or
    Daie].
Carroll, Jim.   Fear and Trembling.
"Carroll, Lewis."   Canto V: Byckerment.
    Canto VII: Sad Souvenaunce.
    Nursery Darling, A.
    Red Queen's Lullaby, The.
Carruth.   Hard journey—yes, A.
    Insomniac Sleeps Well for Once and, The.
    'Tis a fine deceit.
Ciardi.   After Sunday Dinner We Uncles
    Snooze.
Clark.   Autorotation without Gravity.
    Bathed.
    "Before Dawn..."
    Every Day.
    Mist Sleeve Flight.
    Night Patrol.
    Nodding.
    Pillow.

Cohen.   Song to Make Me Still.
    You Have Sweetened Your Word.
Coleridge.   Ode to Sleep.
    Pains of Sleep, The.
    Something Childish, but Very Natural.
    Virgin's Cradle-Hymn, The.
    Wish for Dreamful Sleep, A.
Cooper.   My Young Mother.
Cowper.   On the Picture of a Sleeping Child.
Crabbe.   World of Dreams, The.
Crashaw.   To the Morning. Satisfaction for
    Sleepe.
Creeley.   Don't Sign Anything.
    Je Vois dans le Hasard Tous les Biens Que
    J'espere.
    Plan, The.
    Sing Song.
    Sleep.
    Thinking.
Cullen.   Night Rain.
Cummings.   As any(men's hells having
    wrestled with).
    Fl / a / tt / ene / d d.
    If you and i awakening.
    If you can't eat you got to.
    Light Out), A.
    Love was—entire excellently steep.
    Now winging selves sing sweetly, while
    ghosts(there).
    Un(bee)mo / vi / n(in)g.
    Us if therefore must forget ourselves.
    When you are silent,shining host by guest.
    White guardians of the universe of sleep.
    Why why / How many winds make wonderful.
    You are tired, / (I think).
De la Mare.   Awake!
    Forests.
    Galliass, The.
    Homesick.
    Nocturne: "'Tis not my voice now speaks; but
    as a bird."
    Nod.
    Queen Djenira.
    Sleep.
    Sleeper, The ("As Ann came in...").
    Sleeper, The ("The Lovely, sleeping...").
    Tailor, The.
    Thule.
    Visionary, The.
    Where Is Thy Victory?
Dickey, James.   Heads.
Dickinson.   I had no Cause to be awake.
    On that specific Pillow.
    Sleep is supposed to be.
Doolittle.   No.
Dove.   Lines Muttered in Sleep.
Dunbar.   At Night.
    Ere Sleep Comes Down to Soothe the Weary
    Eyes.
    Farm Child's Lullaby, The.
    Fisher Child's Lullaby, The.
    Good-Night.
    Johnny Speaks.
    Lullaby: "Bedtime's come fu' little boys."
    Lullaby: "Kiver up yo' haid, my little lady."
    Sand-Man, The.
Duncan.   Banners, The.
    Four Songs the Night Nurse Sang.
    In Waking.
Dunn.   Insomnia.
    Night Truths.
Eberhart.   Caravan of Silence.
    Secret Heart, The.
    Ur Burial.
Emerson.   Eternal Watcher, who doth wake,
    The.
Fisher.   Gone down / from the upper air.
    I have slept shallow a long while.
    Report on August.
    Roused from a double.
    She sleeps, in the day, in the silence.
Fletcher.   Hour of Peace, The.
Ford.   Sandman, I'd tear you limb from limb.
    Someone made up my eyes.
Fox.   Dog Days.
    Hands.

Gallagher.   Under Stars.
    Willingly.
Gardner.   That Princeling.
Garrigue.   Rain Song.
Graves.   Charm for Sound Sleeping, A.
    Coronet of Moonlight.
    Death Grapple, The.
    Friday Night.
    Rose, The.
    She Tells Her Love while Half Asleep.
    Song: Once More.
    Through Nightmare.
    Twin of Sleep, The.
Gunn.   Conversation, The.
    Differences, The.
    Down panic, down. The castle is still here.
    For Signs.
    Hug, The.
    Incident on a Journey.
    Night Piece, The.
    Phaedra in the Farm House.
    Sacred Heart.
    Sleep by the Hot Stream.
    Touch.
Hacker.   You made algebra: his tastes in food.
Haines.   Sleep.
Hall.   Moon Clock.
    Passage to Worship.
    Six Naps in One Day.
    Sleeping.
Herrick.   Bellman, The.
    Epitaph upon a Virgin, An.
    To Daisies, Not to Shut So Soon[e].
    Upon a Child.
    Upon His Kinswoman Mistris Elizabeth
    Herrick.
    Upon Mistress Elizabeth Wheeler under the
    Name of Amarillis.
Hewitt.   Response, The.
Housman.   I lay me down and slumber.
Hughes, Langston.   Fired.
    Morning After.
Jarrell.   Afterwards.
    Dreams.
    Prayer at Morning, A.
    Variation on "To Say to Go to Sleep," A.
Keats.   To Sleep.
Kinnell.   After Making Love We Hear
    Footsteps.
    Little Sleep's-Head Sprouting Hair in the
    Moonlight.
Kipling.   City of Sleep, The.
    Oh! hush thee, my baby, the night is behind
    us.
    Sleepy Sentinel, The.
Knott.   Death.
Koch.   Sleeping with Women.
Koertge.   Sleep.
Kooser.   After My Grandmother's Funeral.
Larkin.   How to Sleep.
    Midwinter Waking.
Lawrence.   Ah life, God, Law, whatever name
    you have.
    Baby Asleep after Pain, A.
    In the Dark.
    Is not the wondrous sense of being flung.
    Martyr à la Mode.
    Sleep.
    Song of the Grey Dog, The.
    To Toss the Troubled Night Long.
Levertov.   Tide, The.
Levine.   Making Light of It.
Lewis.   Monologue.
    Peace.
    She Comes To Him in the Night.
    Songs of Sleep.
Lieberman.   Siesta.
Lorde.   Dreams Bite.
Lowell.   Sleepless.
Lowry.   Just some love and kisses.
    Oh and / Who is it unforlorn.
    Sweet night / And sleep thin, A.
McGrath.   In Sickness Like Sleep.
    Such Simple Love.
MacLeish.   Ancestral.
    Waking.

Way-Station.
Words in Time.
MacNeice. Cradle Song for Eleanor.
Cradle Song for Miriam.
Rest House, The.
McNeill. Donna MacElmain.
Pioneer Lullaby.
Matthews. And So.
Sleep.
Meinke. Third Child: June Eleven, Nineteen
Sixty Two.
Melville. Bench of Boors, The.
Meredith. Full loud & fresh crows
Chaunticlere!
Song: "Flower unfolds its dawning cup, The."
Merrill. About the Phoenix.
Dream (Escape from the Sculpture Museum)
and Waking.
Merton. From empty windows / Voice of dead
eyes.
Hidden harmony is better than the open, The.
Miller. Moment of Sleep (For Schnu), A.
Milton. Elegiac Verses.
Slothful Sleep.
Nash. Cat Naps Are Too Good for Cats.
Complaint to Four Angels.
Pappy Wants a Poppy.
Plea for a League of Sleep, A.
What, No Sheep?
Nemerov. To the Memory of John
Wheelwright.
O'Hara. Jane Awake.
Sleeping on the Wing.
Oliver. Sleeping in the Forest.
White Flowers.
White Night.
Owen. Asleep.
Sleeping Beauty, The.
Plath. Ghost's Leavetaking, The.
Sleepers, The.
Prince. Book, The.
Raine. Behind the lids of sleep.
From vague regions of sleep I come again.
Spell of Sleep.
Ransom. Janet Waking.
Rich. Night.
Sleepwalking.
Rolfe. Night World.
Night World.
Sentry.
Rossetti. Angels at the foot,/ And Angels at
the head.
Chill, A.
Crying, my little one, footsore and weary?
Daughter of Eve, A.
Holy Innocents.
Hopeless Case, A.
Lie a-bed, / Sleepy head, / Shut up eyes, bo-
peep.
Lullaby, oh lullaby! / Flowers are closed and
lambs are sleeping.
O Death Where Is Thy Sting?
Our little baby fell asleep.
So I grew half delirious and quite sick.
Song of Flight, A.
Sound Sleep.
There Remaineth Therefore a Rest for the
People of God.
Rukeyser. Another Day. In a Field of Peace
the Child, Playing. The Child Preparing for
Daytime Sleep.
Child Asleep, A.
He starts awake in the city. Orion believing.
Watchers, The.
Water Night.
Sandburg. Atlas, How Have You Been?
Bringers.
Drowsy.
Peace, Night, Sleep.
Portrait of a Child Settling Down for an
Afternoon Nap.
Sheep.
Sleep is a suspension midway.
Sleep Song.
Sleepyheads.
Smoke Shapes.

Wind Song.
Work Gangs.
Schuyler. Watching You.
Schwartz. Sonnet: "I follow thought and what
the world announces."
Scott. Ellen's Song.
Sexton. Three Green Windows.
Shelley. Fragment: The Deserts of Dim Sleep.
To ———: "When passion's trance is
overpast."
Sidney. Lock up, fair lids, the treasure of my
heart.
Second Song.
Sonnet 32: "Morpheus, the lively son of
deadly sleep."
Sonnet 38: "This night, while sleep begins
with heavy wings."
Sonnet 39: "Come sleep, O sleep, the certain
knot of peace."
Simic. Pillow, The.
Smith, Charlotte. To Sleep.
To Tranquillity.
When welcome slumber sets my spirit free.
Smith, Stevie. Goodnight.
Siesta.
Sorrentino. Calling Dr. Dunninger.
Spender. One.
Stevens. Anecdote of the Prince of Peacocks.
Hymn from a Watermelon Pavilion.
Old Man Asleep, An.
To the Roaring Wind.
Stevenson. Bed in Summer.
Come, my little children, here are songs for
you.
Escape at Bedtime.
Good Boy, A.
Home from the daisied meadows, where you
linger yet.
My Bed Is a Boat.
Stout marches lead to certain ends.
Sun's Travels, The.
Young Night Thought.
Stuart. Dressing.
Fireworks.
My Children Going.
Sleepwalker.
Thomas. I Fellowed Sleep.
In Country Sleep.
Lie Still, Sleep Becalmed.
Tomlinson. Arizona Highway.
Updike. Pillow.
Stunt Flier, The.
To a Waterbed.
Waldman. Napping in the Shadow of Day.
Warren. Lullaby: A Motion Like Sleep.
Lullaby: Moonlight Lingers.
Wilbur. Dead Still.
In Limbo.
Walking to Sleep.
Williams, Charles Kenneth. Man Who Owns
Sleep, The.
Waking Jed.
Williams, Miller. Man Who Stays Up Late,
The.
Williams, William Carlos. Death the Barber.
Goodnight, A.
Phoenix Dying, sel.
Wordsworth. Come, gentle sleep, death's
image though thou art.
Grateful is Sleep, my life in stone bound fast.
Slumber did my spirit seal, A.
To Sleep ("Flock of sheep that leisurely pass
by, A").
To Sleep ("Fond words have oft been spoken
to thee, sleep!").
To Sleep ("O gentle Sleep! do they belong to
thee").
Wright, Charles. Homage to Cesare Pavese.
Wright, James. American Wedding.
Gemela.
I Want to Sleep.
In the Cold House.
March.
Sleep.
Winter Night, A.
Wroth. Sonnet 16: "Sleepe fy possess mee
nott, nor doe nott fright."

Yeats. Lullaby: "Beloved, may your sleep be
sound."
Young. Falling Asleep in a Darkening Room.
It Is God that Moves in Your Heart.
Zukofsky. Alba (1952).
Atque in Perpetuum A.W.
Like the oceans, or the leaves of fine
Southern.
O sleep, the sky goes down behind the
poplars.
Tall and singularly dark you pass among the
breakers—.
When the crickets.

Sleeping Beauty
Angelou. Let's Majeste.
Carruth. Dornröschen, princess.
Sleeping Beauty, The.
Knight. Portrait of Mary.
Nemerov. Sleeping Beauty.
Sexton. Briar Rose (Sleeping Beauty).

Sleepwalking and Sleepwalkers. see
Somnambulism and Somnambulists.

Sleet
Lowry. Morning sleet is sleeting, The.

Sleighs
Cummings. So many selves(so many fiends
and gods).
Lowry. I am speeding through the northern
lights.

Sligo. see **County Sligo, Ireland.**

Sloth
Campion. Lighten, heavy hart, thy spright.
Dobyns. Sloth.
Lewis. Indolence.
Lowry. Magic World, The.
Nash. Procrastination Is All of the Time.
Where There's a Will, There's Velleity.
Sandburg. Galoots.
Smart. 3.12: To Neobule.
Smith, Stevie. Lament of a Slug-a-Bed's Wife.

Sloths
Gardner. Sloth, The.
Roethke. Sloth, The.

Slough, England
Betjeman. Slough.

Slugs
Lewis. Slug, The.
Roethke. Slug.
See also **Snails.**

Slums
Brooks. Lovers of the Poor, The.
De la Mare. Slum Child, The.
Dove. Teach Us to Number Our Days.
Glück. Letter from Provence.
Hayden. Summertime and the Living.
Hewitt. Aristocratic Area.
Suburb.
MacNeice. Slum Song.
Merton. Aubade—Harlem.
Oppen. Bicycles and the Apex, The.
Patchen. Slums, The.
Spender. Elementary School Classroom in a
Slum, An.
Walcott. Laventille.

Smallpox
Jonson. Epigram. To the Small-Pox, An.
Muldoon. Meeting the British.

Smart, Christopher
Browning, Robert. With Christopher Smart.
Van Duyn. Garland for Christopher Smart, A.

Smells
Auden. Smelt and Tasted.
Catullus. Carmen 98: "Same can be said of
you, Victius, The."
Clare. Bean Field, The.
Coleridge. Cologne.
On My Joyful Departure from the Same City.
Cummings. Whereas by dark really
released,the modern.
Davie. Kingship.
De la Mare. Pot Of Musk, A.
Donne. Perfume, The.
Emerson. We wish like the glass.
Gunn. At the Back of the North Wind.
Fennel.
Grasses.

Hall. Repeated Shapes, The.
Herbert. Odour, The. (2 Corinthians 2).
Herrick. Another on Her.
  Frankincense, The.
  On a Perfum'd Lady.
  On Julia's Breath.
  Perfume, The.
  To Cherry-Blossomes.
  To the Most Fair and Lovely Mistress Anne Soame, Now Lady Abdie.
  Upon a Sowre-Breath Lady.
  Upon Burr.
  Upon Coone.
  Upon Gorgonius.
  Upon His Kinswoman Mistresse Bridget Herrick.
  Upon Julia's Sweat.
  Upon Julia's Unlacing Her Self.
  Upon Skoles.
Hewitt. Big Room, The.
  Carnations.
  Hay.
  Leaving for Holiday.
Jonson. On Sir Cod the Perfumed.
  To Sir Cod.
  To the Same Sir Cod.
Kipling. Lichtenberg.
Lawrence. Swing Song of a Girl and a Soldier.
"MacDiarmid." Happy on Heimaey.
McGrath. Praises IV.
Meredith. Tuck, thou graceless sinner!—.
Olson. Of Mathilde.
  Perfume / of Flowers!, The.
  Perfume!, The.
Sandburg. Blossom Themes.
Sorrentino. In Memoriam P.B.
  Memory, A.
Stuart. Hunter, Prey.
Swift. Lady's Dressing Room, The.
Tomlinson. Hay.
Whittier. Sweet Fern.
Williams, Charles Kenneth. Hog Heaven.
Williams, William Carlos. Smell.
  Sonnet in Search of an Author.
Zukofsky. In the, same in (when qualm?) thick wee poetry, putrid Victi.

Smiles
Angelou. I Almost Remember.
Auden. In Schrafft's.
Berg. One.
Blake. Smile, The.
Burns. Song: "Full well thou knowest I love thee dear."
Byron. I Saw Thee Weep.
"Carroll, Lewis." Two Acrostics: Round the wondrous globe / Maidens, if a maid you meet.
Catullus. Carmen 39: "Because he has bright white teech, Eg- / natius whips out a."
Creeley. Happy Man, The.
  Oh No.
Cummings. Chas sing does(who).
  "Kitty." sixteen,5'1[mM],white,prostitute.
  You which could grin three smiles into a dead.
Dickinson. Her smile was shaped like other smiles.
  They might not need me—yet they might.
Dunbar. Made to Order Smile, The.
  Philosophy.
  Response.
Dunn. In the 20th Century.
  Smiles.
  Turning Fifty.
  Welcome.
Graves. One Hard Look.
Hartley. Fabian Bell—His Last Visit to Cuernavaca.
Lovelace. Lucasta Weeping.
Lowry. To Herr Toller, Who Hanged Himself.
Patchen. But the Beast of the Wood came as a smiling man.
Shelley. What Mary is when she is a little smiles.
Smith, Stevie. Smile, The.
Sorrentino. Beautiful Soup.

Wilbur. Simile for Her Smile, A.
Wordsworth. What Heavenly Smiles! O Lady Mine.
Zukofsky. Egnatius, candid as his horse-bit white dentures.

Smith, Bessie
Carruth. Named she was a Smith, born Smith, but how related.
Hayden. Homage to the Empress of the Blues.

Smith, John (1580–1631)
Nash. Captain John Smith.
Olson. Some Good News.

Smoke
Brontë. What is that smoke that ever still.
Carruth. Woodsmoke at 70.
Creeley. Smoke.
Galvin. Woodsmoke.
Hartley. Brown Gulls.
Hesketh. Invitation.
Lowry. Picture, A.
  Port Moody.
Nathan. Winter Morning of the Village.
Oppen. And war.
Rukeyser. This is going to be about smoke.
Sandburg. Smoke.
  Smoke Shapes.
Tomlinson. Night-Piece: The Near and the Far.
Williams, William Carlos. Classic Scene.

Smoking and Smokers
Angelou. Health-Food Diner, The.
Berg. What I Wanted to Say.
Bishop. Giant Toad.
Creeley. In a Boat Shed.
  Sound.
Dunbar. Companion's Progress, A.
  My Corn-Cob Pipe.
  When the Old Man Smokes.
Fisher. Klonk! The smoker's trick.
Lowry. Men With Coats Thrashing.
Sandburg. Crimson.
Snyder. Makings.
Stevenson. Epistle to Albert Dew-Smith.
Tomlinson. Milieux.
Williams, William Carlos. M.B.
Young. Life at the Back of the Plane.

Smuggling and Smugglers
Kipling. Poor Honest Men.
  Smuggler's Song, A.

Snails
Bishop. Giant Snail.
"Carroll, Lewis." Mock Turtle's Song, The.
Cowper. Snail, The.
Fenton. Killer Snails, The.
Fisher. Out in the early morning, by empty roads.
Gardner. Widow's Yard, The.
Gunn. Considering the Snail.
Hoffman. Auricle's Oracle.
Hughes, Langston. Snail.
Lindsay. Haughty Snail-King, The.
  Song of the Sturdy Snails, The.
  Visit to Mab, The.
Lovelace. Another ("The centaur, siren I forgo").
  Snail [or Snayl], The.
MacLeish. Out of Sleep Awakened.
Moore. To a Snail.
Piercy. Spring Offensive of the Snail, The.
Sarton. Eine Kleine Snailmusik.
Sexton. Snail.
Silverstein. Warning.
See also **Slugs.**

Snakebites
Dickey, James. Snakebite.
  Venom.

Snakes
Atwood. After Heraclitus.
  Bad Mouth.
  Psalm to Snake.
  Quattrocento.
  She.
  Snake Woman.
Berry. Snake, The.
Burns. On Mr. Burke by an Opponent and a Friend to Mr. Hastings.

Carruth. Mix the Ingredients.
Cowper. Colubriad, The.
De la Mare. Dream, A.
Dickey, James. Blowgun and Rattlesnake.
  Goodbye to Serpents.
  Poisoned Man, The.
  Venom.
Dickinson. In Winter in my Room.
  Narrow Fellow in the Grass, A.
  Sweet is the swamp with its secrets.
Doolittle. Helios and Athene.
Duncan. Albigenses, The.
"Dylan." Man Gave Names to All the Animals.
Eberhart. Ode to the Chinese Paper Snake.
Fox. Beasts Have Entered, The.
  Letter from the Snake Woman.
Hartley. Little Green Snake.
Herrick. Silken Snake, The.
Hoffman. Summerhouse, The.
Hopkins. Cold whip-adder unespied, The.
Hughes, Ted. Cleopatra to the Asp.
  Horrible Religious Error, A.
Hugo. Taneum Creek.
Kipling. At the hole where he went in.
  Darzee's Chaunt.
  Poison of Asps.
Kooser. Frozen Stream, A.
Kunitz. Separation, The.
Lawrence. He drank enough.
  Snake.
Lowell. Serpent, The.
  Snake.
McNeill. Passage of Time, The.
Matthews. Snake, The.
Millay. To a Snake.
Moore. Snakes, Mongooses, Snake-Charmers, and the Like.
Nash. Asp, The.
  Cobra, The.
Nathan. Snake Charming.
O'Hara. In Memory of My Feelings.
Oliver. Water Snake.
Oppen. Serpent, Ouroboros / Whose tail is in his mouth: he is the root.
Pack. Invisible Hand, The.
Patchen. Deer and the Snake, The.
  Who Walks There?
Plath. Medallion.
  Snakecharmer.
Roethke. Serpent, The.
  Snake.
Sexton. Snake.
Shelley. Fragment: "Wake the serpent not— lest he."
Silverstein. Boa Constrictor.
Warren. Snake, The.
Whittier. Double-Headed Snake of Newbury, The.
Wilbur. Fable, A.
Williams, Charles Kenneth. Tails.
See also **Listings for specific Snakes.**

Snapdragons
Lawrence. Snap-Dragon.
Zukofsky. Butter-and-Eggs.

Sneezing
"Carroll, Lewis." Duchess's Lullaby, The.
Ford. When the coolie blew.

Snobbery and Snobs
Beatles. And Your Bird Can Sing.
  Girl.
Bukowski. Being alone has always been very necessary to me. At one time I.
  O, We Are the Outcasts.
  Parts of an Opera, Parts of a Guitar, Part of Nowhere.
Burns. Epigram: "Whoe'er he be that sojourns here."
  Song: "Tibby I hae seen the day."
"Carroll, Lewis." Canto III: Scarmoges.
  Canto IV: Hys Nouryture.
Dickey, William. Being Asked To Define Bourgeois Individuality.
Dunbar. Jealous.
Glück. My Neighbor in the Mirror.
Griffiths. Crossing Lady-Stanley, Here, 1868.
Hemingway. Big Dance on the Hill, The.

Hughes, Langston. High to Low.
Low to High.
Meredith. Fusion.
Miss Millicent Maxse was fond of her Ma.
Moore. Labors of Hercules, The.
Nash. Ms. Found under a Serviette in a
Lovely Home.
Now Tell Me About Yourself.
Sandburg. Balloon Faces.
Smith, Stevie. Parents.
Sorrentino. White Lemons.
See also **Social Class.**
Snoring
Hughes, Langston. Morning After.
Nash. Arthur.
Snorkeling and Snorkelers
Lieberman. Coral Reef, The.
Flying below Sea Level.
Skin-Flying into the Storm Center.
Stuart. Snorkeling in the Caribbean.
Snow
Ammons. Capture.
Crinkling Trails.
Grisly Grit.
Preexistence.
Scour, The.
Settlement.
Snow Roost.
Twangs & Little Twists.
Auden. To-night when a full storm surrounds
the house.
Berg. Between Us.
Day, A.
Iowa.
This Cold.
To My Friends.
Berrigan. For You.
Berry. He has known a tunnel.
March Snow.
March 22, 1968.
Blake. Soft Snow.
Bly. Dream on the Night of First Snow, A.
Night of First Snow.
Six Winter Privacy Poems.
Snowfall in the Afternoon.
Brontë. Farewell To Alexandria, A.
It was night, and on the mountains.
Carew. To My Mistress [*or* Mistris], I
Burning in Love.
Carroll, Jim. On the Rush.
Carruth. After the thaw after.
Again on dark looms.
Brook has holes in its cover, The.
Cold hunger tripped her but her years.
Coming of Snow, The.
Continuo.
Eons gone by the sea.
Essay on Marriage.
In cold / the snow.
In freshfallen snow.
In late winter cold nights.
Layer upon layer / late winter snow.
Let my snow-tracks lead.
Lichen and liverwort.
Night is a cauldron.
Out of nothing.
Sky like fishblood.
Snow / ice / bitter wind.
Snow comes / bits / of light.
Snow's downstrokes climb softly up the
conifer.
Sound of Snow, The.
Tamarack with needles lost, The.
Three sixteen seventy.
Tracks of the snowshoe rabbit across the.
Where two boots labored yesterday across the.
Winter's tale is told in, A.
Cohen. Snow Is Falling.
Coleridge. Reed-roof'd Village, still bepatch'd
with snow, The.
Two Round Spaces on the Tombstone, The.
Creeley. As Now It Would Be Snow.
Snow, The.
To And.
Xmas Poem: Bolinas.
Cummings. Ballade: "White night roared with
a huge north-wind, The."

Beautiful / is the / unmea.
Blossoming are people / nimbler than Really.
Comedian stands on a corner,the sky is, The.
I was sitting in mcsoreley's.   outside it was
New York and beauti- / fully snowing.
Infinite jukethrob smoke & swallow to dis.
One / t / hi / s / snowflake.
SNO / a white idea(Listen).
Snow means that / life is a black cannonadin.
Snow)says!Says / over un / graves.
This man's heart / is true to his.
De la Mare. Snow.
Snowdrop, The.
Snowflake, The.
Snowing.
There Blooms No Bud in May.
Winter ("Green Mistletoe!").
Winter ("Clouded wth snow").
Dickey, James. Snow on a Southern State.
Snow Thickets.
To Be Done in Winter.
Dickey, William. Avalanche.
Dickinson. I remember the leaves were falling.
It sifts from Leaden Sieves.
Snow beneath whose chilly softness.
Snow that never drifts, The.
Verily it snows.
Dunbar. Grievance, A.
Snowin'.
Dunn. Loneliness.
Eberhart. Homage to the North.
Skier and the Mountain, The.
Snow Cascades.
Snowfall, A.
Edmunds. My Love Has Been.
Emerson. All the great & good.
Snow-Storm, The.
Fletcher. From the Japanese, V.
Grey Symphony.
Snow at Sea.
Symphony of Snow.
White Symphony.
Fox. Cup of Cold Water.
Frost. Afterflakes.
Desert Places.
Dust of Snow.
Onset, The.
Patch of Old Snow, A.
Snow.
Stopping by Woods on a Snowy Evening.
Storm Fear.
Gallagher. My Mother Remembers That She
Was Beautiful.
Snowheart.
Gildner. Poem: "My daughter and I lie in the
snow."
Glück. Late Snow.
Graves. Like Snow.
She Tells Her Love while Half Asleep.
Hall. Love Is Like Sounds.
Snow, The.
Hardy. Light Snow-Fall after Frost, A.
Snow in the Suburbs.
Hayden. Snow.
Hesketh. After Verlaine.
Snow Leopard.
Hewitt. First Snow in the Glens.
Hoffman. Snow.
Housman. Eight O'Clock.
Hughes, Langston. Angels Wings.
Jarrell. Winter's Tale, The.
Kooser. Dry Winter Letter to Friends, A.
First Snow.
Walking to Work.
Lawrence. Snowy Day at School, A.
Levine. Snow.
Lindsay. What the Snow Man Said.
Longfellow. Cross of Snow, The.
Snow-Flakes.
Lorde. Woman Thing, The.
Lowry. Contemplation of Dead Reckoning.
Morning rain is sleeting, The.
Walk in Canada.
McAuley. Behind a brightening cloud.
"MacDiarmid." Lourd on My Hert.
McGrath. Afternoon of a McGrath.
Everything in Order.

MacLeish. Snow Fall, The.
MacNeice. Snow.
McNeill. Snow Angels.
Matthews. Spring Snow.
Visionary Picnic, The.
Meinke. Running with the Hyenas.
Merton. I do not know who is out in the
snow.
Millay. Snow Storm, The.
Nash. Jangle Bells.
Nemerov. First Snow.
From a Record of Disappointment.
White water now in the snowflake's prison.
Winter Lightning, The.
Neruda. Quartz opens its eyes in the snow.
O'Hara. Second Avenue.
Oliver. First Snow.
Olson. Hotel Steinplatz, Berlin, December 25
(1966).
Li Po.
She Who Hits at Will.
Snow, The.
Patchen. Snow is deep on the ground, The.
Piercy. Snow in May.
Snow, Snow.
Raine. What does this day bestow?
Rich. Snow.
Rossetti. I dug and dug amongst the snow.
O wind, why do you never rest.
Seasons.
There's Snow on the Fields.
Rukeyser. Another Day. For a Moment
Slipping Back, Again the Unreal King.
Sandburg. Red and White.
Sarton. First Snow.
Girl with 'Cello.
Snow Light, The.
Schuyler. Afterward.
April and Its Forsythia.
Blizzard.
Empathy and New Year.
February 13, 1975.
Snow, The.
White City, A.
Sexton. Letter Written During a January
Northeaster.
Oh.
Snow.
Smith, Stevie. Angel Face.
Spender. Driving through Snow.
Face of the Dam: Vivian Jones.
Stafford. Near.
Stevens. Snow Man, The.
Sutter. Snowman, The.
Tomlinson. Santa Maria delle Nevi.
Snow Sequence.
Snow Signs.
Tree, The.
Turco. Covered Bridge, The.
Updike. Dream and Reality.
Flurry.
Snowdrops 1987.
Van Duyn. Who says the world is mud? For
the fifth day.
Waldman. Snow.
Warren. Time as Hypnosis.
Wilbur. First Snow in Alsace.
Storm in April, A.
Williams, Charles Kenneth. Snow: I.
Snow: II.
Williams, Miller. Waiting for the Paper to be
Delivered.
Williams, William Carlos. Naked.
Polar Bear, The.
Snow Begins, The.
Wright, James. Blue Teal's Mother.
In Fear of Harvests.
Seasonless, The.
Snowstorms in the Midwest.
Sparrows in a Hillside Drift.
To the August Fallen.
Winter Night, A.
Yau. Cenotaph of Snow.
Zimmer. Lester Tells of Wanda and the Big
Snow.
Zukofsky. After reading.
As to How Much.

Cactus rose-mauve and gray, twin overturned. (Ryokan's scroll).

See also **Snowflakes; Snowmen.**

Snow White
Jarrell.   Ways and the Peoples, The.
Sexton.   Snow White and the Seven Dwarfs.

Snowdrops
Hughes, Ted.   Snowdrop.
Meredith.   When stormy day is cold & gray.
Rossetti.   Baby lies so fast asleep / That we cannot wake her.
Schuyler.   Snowdrop, The.
Smith, Charlotte.   To the Snow-Drop.
Wordsworth.   To a Snow-Drop.

Snowflakes
Bly.   Watering the Horse.
Ceravolo.   Migratory Noon.
Clark.   Song of the Drowned Ghost in the Pool's, The.
Cummings.   S(/ these out of in).
Dickinson.   Snow flakes / I counted till they danced so.
Nemerov.   Snowflakes.

See also **Snow.**

Snowmen
Lindsay.   What the Snow Man Said.
MacNeice.   Snow Man, The.
Nash.   Abominable Snowman, The.
Nemerov.   Journey of the Snowmen.
Plath.   Snowman on the Moor, The.
Schwartz.   Poem: "Old man in the crystal morning after snow."
Wilbur.   Boy at the Window.

Soap
Cohen.   I Have Two Bars of Soap.
MacNeice.   Soap Suds.
Muldoon.   Soap-Pig, The.
Silverstein.   Dirtiest Man in the World, The.
Instructions.

Sobriety
Cowper.   Truth.
Eberhart.   Old Dichotomy: Choosing Sides.
Herrick.   Abstinence.
Excesse.
Sobriety in Search.
Keats.   Character of Charles Brown.
Lowry.   Fear ringed by doubt is my eternal moon.
Poem: "When drunk he crawled home on his knees."
Promises made drunk should be kept drunk.
When I was young I broke all drinking records.
Markson.   To a Mexican Poet Who Has Forsaken Drink.
Whittier.   Brewing of Soma, The.
Drunkard to His Bottle, The.
Yeats.   Drunken Man's Praise of Sobriety, A.

Soccer
Beckett.   Ascension.

Social Class
Angelou.   Bump d'Bump.
Sepia Fashion Show.
Beatles.   Honey Pie.
Lady Madonna.
Mean Mr. Mustard.
Betjeman.   False Security.
Wembley Lad, A.
Brooks.   Beverly Hills, Chicago.
Bukowski.   Darlings.
I was out there again today. There are some creatures out there.
Private First Class.
Sparks.
Bunting.   As appleblossom to crocus.
Burns.   Toadeater, The.
When She Cam Ben She Bobbed.
Byron.   To E———.
Catullus.   Carmen 24: "Best sprig of the clan."
Clark.   Parish: A Satire, The.
Cullen.   For a Lady I Know.
Cummings.   Come,gaze with me upon this dome.
Little joe gould has lost his teeth and doesn't know where.
Dunn.   Truck Stop: Minnesota.

Eberhart.   Blessed Are the Angels in Heaven.
Gnats.
Hop-Toad, The.
Lament of a New England Mother, The.
Maine Roustabout, A.
Nostalgia for Edith Sitwell.
Emerson.   And man of wit & mark.
Fenton.   This Octopus Exploits Women.
Griffiths.   Courting Prosperity.
Hacker.   Grizzled doorman lets the doctors' wives, The.
Hardy.   Lady Vi.
Question of Marriage, A.
Hewitt.   Conacre.
He Suggests a Solution.
Hughes, Langston.   Graduation.
Low to High.
Keats.   Pensive They Sit, and Roll Their Languid Eyes.
Kipling.   Banquet Night.
Knight.   WASP Woman Visits a Black Junkie in Prison, A.
Knott.   Funny Poem.
Lawrence.   Amo Sacrum Vulgus.
Are You Pining?
Be a Demon!
Classes.
Climbing Up.
Have Done With It.
Masses and Classes.
Middle-Class Children.
Middle Classes, The.
O! Start a Revolution.
Rise in the World, A.
Saddest Day, The.
Softly, Then, Softly.
True Democracy.
Up He Goes!
What Is He?
Working Man, The.
Liddy.   Lady Fitzwilliam.
May Day Song.
River Video, The.
Lindsay.   Drunkards in the Street, The.
MacNeice.   My Mary.
Under the surface of flux and of fear there is an underground movement.
Matthews.   Left Hand Canyon.
Moore.   People's Surroundings.
Piercy.   Market Economy, The.
Pound.   Garden, The.
Rukeyser.   Gradus ad Parnassum.
Smith, Stevie.   Parents.
Stein.   Little Novel, A.
Stevens.   Theory.
Stevenson.   Eh, man Henley, you're a Don!
Link your arm in mine, my lad.
Old Chimæras, old receipts, The.
Van Duyn.   That was my grandfather, nearly went to prison.
Whitman.   Song for Occupations, A.
Whittier.   Maud Muller.
Our Country.
Problem, The.
Wordsworth.   Composed after Reading a Newspaper of the Day.
Zukofsky.   O quick floss silk of the Juventii, form.

See also **Snobbery and Snobs.**

Social Protest. *see* **Protest, Social.**

Social Work and Social Workers
Cohen.   Lists, The.

Socialism
Carruth.   My Father's Face.
Cohen.   Disguises.
Dunn.   Response to a Letter from France.
Frost.   Build Soil.
Jarrell.   Night before the Night before Christmas, The.
Lawrence.   Hibiscus and Salvia Flowers.
Lindsay.   Net to Snare the Moonlight, A.
Why I Voted the Socialist Ticket.
McGrath.   Vision of Three Angels Viewing the Progress of Socialism.
Merton.   Radicals.
Rolfe.   Homage to Karl Marx.
Sandburg.   Dynamiter.

Tomlinson.   Rich, The.
Young.   Moon Over Matter.

Socrates
Carruth.   Anent Socrates, or Somebody.

Sodom
Duncan.   This Place Rumord to Have Been Sodom.
Nemerov.   Lot Later.
Van Duyn.   Cities of the Plain, The.
Whittier.   Cities of the Plain, The.
Wilbur.   Lot's Wife.

Softball
Hugo.   Missoula Softball Tournament.
Knott.   Mitts and Gloves.

Solace
Auden.   Everest.
Plane Tree, The.
Beatles.   Let It Be.
Browning, Elizabeth Barrett.   Isobel's Child.
Catullus.   Carmen 2: "Lesbia's sparrow! / Lesbia's plaything!"
Cohen.   Our Lady of Solitude.
De la Mare.   Sunday, A.
Dunn.   Atlantic City.
Guardian Angel, The.
"Dylan."   Shelter from the Storm.
Ford.   No beings but.
Hardy.   On a Fine Morning.
Herrick.   Comfort to a Lady Upon the Death of Her Husband.
Mirth.
Miseries.
Ode to Master Endymion Porter, upon His Brother's Death, An.
To the Lady Crew, Upon the Death of her Child.
To the Willow-Tree.
Nash.   I Can Hardly Wait for the Sandman.
Neruda.   I Come Back from a Journey.
Ransom.   Winter Remembered.
Sandburg.   Old Music for Quiet Hearts.
Sarton.   Return.
Stevenson.   So shall this book wax like unto a well.
Wilbur.   Avowal, The.
Zukofsky.   Sparrow, my girl's pleasure, delight of my girl.

Soldiers
Atwood.   Beyond the white hill which maroons us.
Machine. Gun. Nest.
Projected Slide of an Unknown Soldier.
Auden.   O What Is That Sound [Which So Thrills the Ear].
Ode: "Though aware of our rank and alert to obey orders."
Roman Wall Blues.
Berryman.   Captain's Song, The.
White Feather.
Bly.   As the Asian War Begins.
Teeth Mother Naked at Last, The.
Boyle.   Letter to Francis Picabia, A.
Brooks.   Gay Chaps at the Bar.
Looking.
Browning, Elizabeth Barrett.   Forced Recruit, The.
Parting Lovers.
Bukowski.   Troops, The.
Burns.   Bonie Dundee.
Charlie He's My Darling.
Extempore.
Highland Laddie.
I'll Mak You Be Fain to Follow Me.
It Was A' for Our Rightfu' King.
There Was a Bonie Lass.
When wild War's deadly blast was blawn.
Byron.   As the Liberty Lads o'er the Sea.
There was a sound of revelry by night.
Campion.   In Barnum.
Clark.   Forty Days.
Cowper.   Epitaph, An: "Here lies one, who never drew."
On Miltiades.
Dickey, James.   Drinking from a Helmet.
Enclosure, The.
Dickinson.   Bless God, he went as soldiers.
Dobyns.   Favorite Iraqi Soldier.

Dunbar. Colored Soldiers, The.
Dirge for a Soldier.
Our Martyred Soldiers.
Veteran, The.
When Dey 'Listed Colored Soldiers.
Emerson. In an Age of Fops and Toys.
Voluntaries.
Fenton. At the foot of every steep cliff or
  precipice in high Alpine regions.
Ferlinghetti. Along the Appian Way / children
  are playing.
Fisher. To the Memory of Wyndham Lewis.
Ford. Do birds need to fly so much.
Soldiers walk around.
Frost. Not to Keep.
Soldier, A.
Gardner. Cock-a-Hoop.
Graves. Oldest Soldier, The.
Griffiths. Island with Army, Pines and Wind.
Gunn. As Expected.
Captain in Time of Peace.
Corporal, The.
Incident on a Journey.
Innocence.
Market at Turk.
Haines. Dusk of the Revolutionaries.
Flight, The.
Invaders, The.
Hardy. Budmouth Dears.
Casterbridge Captains, The.
Colonel's Soliloquy, The.
Dance at the Phoenix, The.
Departure.
Dolls, The.
Drummer Hodge.
Man He Killed, The.
Men Who March Away.
Military Appointment, A.
My Love's Gone a-Fighting.
Often When Warring.
Panthera.
Parting-Scene, A.
Sitting on the Bridge.
Subalterns, The.
Hartley. Soldier on His Knees in the Snow.
This Piece of Eucharist.
Hayden. Dream, The.
Heaney. Toome Road, The.
Trial Runs.
Visitant.
Hemingway. All armies are the same.
Champs d'Honneur.
Poem to Mary (Second Poem).
Shock Troops.
There was Ike and Tony and Jaque and me.
Herrick. To the Right Gratious Prince,
  Lodwick, Duke of Richmond and Lenox.
Hewitt. Bogside, Derry, 1971.
Golden Boy, The.
Paraphrase of Verses by Mayakovsky.
Roman Fort, The.
Ulster Winter (1942).
YCVS and the Ulster Division, The.
Hopkins. Soldier, The.
Housman. Day of Battle, The.
Deserter, The.
Epitaph on an Army of Mercenaries.
Farewell to a name and a number.
Grenadier.
Here dead lie we because we did not choose.
I did not lose my heart in summer's even.
In valleys green and still.
Lancer.
New Mistress, The.
Oh stay at home, my lad, and plough.
Recruit, The.
Soldier from the wars returning.
Street sounds to the soldiers' tread, The.
Hughes, Ted. Grass-blade is not without, The.
Haunting, A.
Six Young Men.
Two Minute's Silence.
Warriors of the North, The.
Hugo. Bannerman's Island.
Where We Crashed.
Jarrell. Absent with Official Leave.
Description of Some Confederate Soldiers, A.

Eighth Air Force.
Good-bye, Wendover; Good-bye, Mountain
  Home.
Gunner.
Learners, The.
Lines, The.
Lullaby, A: "For wars his life and half a
  world away."
Mail Call.
New Georgia.
O My Name It Is Sam Hall.
Port of Embarkation.
Prisoners.
Sick Nought, The.
Soldier Walks under the Trees of the
  University, The.
Soldier [T. P.].
Jonson. On Sir John Roe ("What two brave
  perils of the private sword").
To Sir Horace Vere.
To Sir John Radcliffe.
To the Same; on the Same.
To True Soldiers.
Kinnell. Vapor Trail Reflected in the Frog
  Pond.
Kipling. Absent-Minded Beggar, The.
Arithmetic on the Frontier.
Back to the Army Again.
Ballad of East and West, The.
Belts.
"Birds of Prey" March.
Bobs.
Boots.
Bridge-Guard in the Karroo.
British-Roman Song, A.
Brown Bess.
Cells.
Chant-Pagan.
Cholera Camp.
Columns.
Danny Deever.
Dedication from "Barrack-Room Ballads."
'Eathen, The.
Expert, The.
Follow Me 'Ome.
For All We Have and Are [1914].
Fuzzy-Wuzzy.
Gentlemen-Rankers.
Gunga Din.
Instructor, The.
Irish Guards, The.
Jacket, The.
Lichtenberg.
Loot.
M. I.
Married Man, The.
Men That Fought at Minden, The.
Oonts.
Parting of the Columns, The.
Pharaoh and the Sergeant.
Piet.
Private Ortheris's Song.
Pro-Consuls, The.
Recessional.
Return, The.
Rimini.
Roman Centurion's Song, The.
Route Marchin'.
Sappers.
Screw-Guns.
Service Man, The.
Shillin' a Day.
Shut-Eye Sentry, The.
Snarleyow.
Soldier an' Sailor Too.
Soldier, Soldier.
Song of the Old Guard, The.
Song to Mithras, A.
Stellenbosch.
That Day.
To Thomas Atkins.
Tommy.
Troopin'.
Ubique.
Vineyard, The.
Widow at Windsor, The.
Widow's Party, The.

Wilful-Missing.
Young British Soldier, The.
Kunitz. Careless Love.
Customs Collector's Report, The.
Larkin. Homage to a Government.
MCMXIV.
Lawrence. Child and the Soldier, The.
Girl in Cairo, The.
Guards.
Jewess and the V.C., The.
Maiden's Prayer.
Mesopotamia.
Message to Perfidious Soldier.
Mother's Son in Salonika.
Munitions.
Obsequial Ode.
Swing Song of a Girl and a Soldier.
Tommies in the Train.
Levine. Planting.
To P.L., 1916–1937.
Lewis. After Dunkirk.
All Day It Has Rained.
Assault Convoy, The.
Boy who climbed the creaking stairs, The.
Dawn on the East Coast.
From a Play.
Greetings.
I within me holding.
Infantry.
Lady in Black.
Lines on a Tudor Mansion.
Odi et Amo.
Patrol, The.
Peasants, The.
Public Gardens, The.
Raid, The.
Run-In, The.
Sentry, The.
She Wakes Early, While He Still Sleeps.
To a Comrade in Arms.
Unknown Soldier, The.
Way Back, The.
White brain crossing, The.
White frost; intricate bare branches.
Lindsay. Yankee Doodle.
Lovelace. To a Lady with Child that Asked
  [or Ask'd] an Old Shirt.
To Lucasta, [on] Going to the War[re]s.
To My Truely Valiant, Learned Friend, Who
  in His Booke Resolv'd the Art Gladiatory
  into the Mathematick's.
Lowry. And partly they deserve dishonest
  death.
"MacDiarmid." Another Epitaph on an Army
  of Mercenaries.
McGrath. All the Dead Soldiers.
Blues for Warren.
In the Sleep of Reason.
Nocturne Militaire.
Ode for the American Dead in Asia.
MacLeish. Fourteenth Book, The.
Lines for an Interment.
Memorial Rain.
MacNeice. Bottleneck.
Legend of the Dead Soldier, The.
Meinke. Soldiers with Green Leggings.
Melville. Ball's Bluff.
On the Grave.
Meredith. Atkins.
Flat as to an eagle's eye.
Grandfather Bridgeman.
Merrill. Peter.
Milton. Parthians, The.
Sonnet 8: "Captain or Colonel, or Knight in
  Arms."
Morgan. Hideyoshi.
Morrison. Times Change, Damaged.
Muldoon. Truce.
Nemerov. Fable of the War, A.
For the Squadron.
Grand Central, with Soldiers, in Early
  Morning.
Old Soldiers' Home, The.
Soldier Who Lived Through the War, The.
Olson. King's Mountain.
This Year.

Oppen. I cannot even now / Altogether disengage myself.
Owen. Anthem for Doomed Youth.
Apologia Pro Poemate Meo.
Arms and the Boy.
Disabled.
Dulce Et Decorum Est.
Exposure.
Fragment: "Not one corner of a foreign field."
Futility.
Insensibility.
Mental Cases.
Send-Off, The.
Show, The.
Soldier's Dream.
Spring Offensive.
Strange Meeting.
Terre, A.
To a Comrade in Flanders.
Training.
Paley. I Gave Away That Kid.
Patchen. Being so hideous that the air weeps blood.
Class of 1934.
Constant Bridegrooms, The.
Known Soldier, The.
Letter to the Young Men, A.
This Man Was Your Brother.
Pope. Epitaph on General Henry Withers, in Westminster-Abbey, 1729.
Prince. He Compares Old Customs with Those of His Kingdom.
Soldiers Bathing.
Watching Song.
Robinson. Field of Glory, The.
Rolfe. Entry.
What Does the Novice Soldier Think.
Rossetti. Come cheer up, my lads, 'tis to glory we steer!
Rukeyser. One Soldier.
Sandburg. Among the Red Guns.
And They Obey.
Buttons.
Dunes.
Fight.
House.
John Ericsson Day Memorial, 1918.
Killers.
Medallion.
Old Timers.
Places.
Remembered Women.
Tumblers of the rapids go white, go green, The.
Scott. Ellen's Song.
Norham Castle.
Shelton. Soldiers Returning, The.
Smith, Charlotte. Forest Boy, The.
Smith, Stevie. Private Means Is Dead.
Soldier Dear to Us, A.
Snodgrass. Ten Days Leave.
Spender. Stopwatch and an Ordnance Map, A.
Two Armies.
Stevens. Gigantomachia.
Repetitions of a Young Captain.
Woman Sings a Song for a Soldier Come Home, A.
Stevenson. Ticonderoga: A Legend of the West Highlands.
Voluntary.
Suckling. Soldier, A.
Tennyson. Charge of the Light Brigade, The.
Warren. Small Soldiers with Drum in Large Landscape.
Whitman. Adieu to a Soldier.
Army Corps on the March, An.
Artilleryman's Vision, The.
As Toilsome I Wander'd Virginia's Woods.
Ashes of Soldiers.
Ashes of Soldiers: Epigraph.
Bravest Soldiers, The.
By the Bivouac's Fitful Flame.
Camps of Green.
Cavalry Crossing a Ford.
Centenarian's Story, The.
How Solemn as One by One.
Hush'd be the Camps To-day.

I Saw Old General at Bay.
March in the Ranks Hard-Prest, and the Road Unknown, A.
O Tan-Faced Prairie-Boy.
Race of Veterans.
Sight in Camp [or] Sight in Camp in the Daybreak Gray and Dim, A.
Spirit Whose Work Is Done.
Wound-Dresser, The.
Whittier. Lost Occasion, The.
Wilbur. Place Pigalle.
Williams, Charles Kenneth. Creams.
Williams, Miller. Voice of America.
Wordsworth. Character of the Happy Warrior.
Epigram on an Event in Col. Evans's Redoubted Performances in Spain.
Pelayo.
Squib on Colonel Evans, A.
Wright, James. Confession to J. Edgar Hoover.
Speak.
Yeats. Irish Airman Foresees His Death, An.
Young. Some Recent Fiction.
Suicide.

See also **War.**

Solipsism
Atwood. Solipsism While Dying.
Brontë. It's over now; I've known it all.
Creeley. La Noche.
Not Again.
Dobyns. Mountain, The.
Housman. Good creatures, do you love your lives.
Plath. Soliloquy of the Solipsist.
Stevens. Chocorua to Its Neighbor.
Landscape with Boat.

Solitude
Atwood. Georgia Beach.
Auden. Alone ("Each lover has a theory...").
Alone ("Soundless is the Winter Darkness").
Farglow.
Grow thin by walking and go inland.
Lauds.
Mill (Hempstead), The.
Song: "Past all your knowing."
Two Climbs.
Visit, A.
Walk, The.
Beatles. Dear Prudence.
Fixing a Hole.
Nowhere Man.
Beckett. Bois seul.
Bon bon il est un pays.
Lueurs lisières.
Universe-Solitude.
Berg. Alone.
One.
Writing Class.
Berry. Cold, The.
Except.
I have come to the end.
Stay Home.
Berryman. Meditation.
Song of the Man Forsaken and Obsessed.
Bly. After Long Busyness.
Falling Asleep.
"Out of the Rolling Ocean, the Crowd . . ."
Six Winter Privacy Poems.
Solitude Late at Night in the Woods.
Brontë. And like myself lone, wholly lone.
Away, away, resign me now.
Blue bell is the sweetest flower, The.
I am the only being whose doom.
Little while, a little while, A.
Redbreast, Early in the morning.
That wind, I used to hear it swelling.
There are two trees in a lonely field.
To Imagination.
Written in Aspin Castle.
Browning, Elizabeth Barrett. Sonnet: "I lived with visions for my company."
Sonnet: "Thou hast thy calling to some palace floor."
Browning, Robert. Aeschylus' Soliloquy.
Amphibian.
Prologue: "O the old wall here! How I could pass."
Bukowski. Being alone has always been very

necessary to me. At one time I.
Chopin Bukowski.
Defeat.
Hangover and Sick Leave.
Patriot of Life, A.
2nd Novel, The.
Somebody Always Breaking My Dainty Solitude..
Burns. Song: "Had I a cave on some wild, distant shore."
Strathallan's Lament.
Byron. Lines: "Dear Becher, you tell me to mix with mankind."
"Carroll, Lewis." Solitude.
Carruth. Alive.
Aqua.
It was the custom of my tribe to be silent.
Living Alone.
No, I was wrecked here.
Simple.
Clare. I Am.
Love and Solitude.
Song: "I peeled bits of straw and I got switches too."
Clark. Calling Infinity.
Cohen. Came So Far for Beauty.
Deep Happiness, A.
Diamonds in the Mine.
Seems So Long Ago, Nancy.
Sit Down, Master.
Sky.
Travel.
Welcome to These Lines.
Window, The.
Cooper. Builder of Houses, The.
Coda.
Earthquake, The.
Inheritances.
Middle Age.
Cowper. Alexander Selkirk.
Child of God Longing To See Him Beloved, A.
God Neither Known Nor Loved by the World.
Happy Solitude—Unhappy Men.
Inscription for a Moss-House.
Love Faithful in the Absence of the Beloved.
Love Increased by Suffering.
Scenes Favourable to Meditation.
Secrets of Divine Love Are To Be Kept, The.
Self-Love and Truth Incompatible.
To the Nightingale.
Watching unto God in the Night-Season.
Creeley. Flower, The.
Cummings. Among / these / red pieces of.
BrIght / bRight s??? big / (soft).
Dim / i / nu / tiv / e this park is e.
I will cultivate within.
Nothing is more exactly terrible than.
Davie. Compline.
Expecting Silence.
Or, Solitude.
Pietà.
De la Mare. April Moon.
Captive, The.
Epitaph, An: "Last, Stone, a little yet."
Estranged.
Haunted.
I Sit Alone.
Solitude.
Dickey, James. Gila Bend.
Heads.
One, The.
Three, The.
Dickinson. Society for me my misery.
There is a solitude of space.
Dobyns. Santiago: Forestal Park.
Way It Goes or the Proper Use of Leisure Time, The.
Dove. Daystar.
Weathering Out.
Dunbar. Career, A.
Lost Dream, A.
Dunn. Corners.
Room and the World, The.
Snowmass Cycle, The.

Eberhart. Contend with steepness, the dark air.
Ode to Silence.
Emerson. As I walked in the woods.
Civil world will much forgive, The.
Comrade of the snow & wind.
I am alone. Sad is my solitude.
I have no brothers & no peers.
Lover's Petition.
Manners.
O What have I to do.
Pale Genius roves alone.
Fenton. Chosun.
Pitt-Rivers Museum, Oxford, The.
Vacant Possession, A.
Fisher. Gone down / from the upper air.
Ford. And no night visitors.
Place in which to, A.
Frost. Acquainted with the Night.
Desert Places.
Good Hours.
Most of It, The.
Gallagher. Amplitude.
On Your Own.
Glück. Beginning, The.
Summer.
12. 6. 71.
Graves. Singleness in Love.
Song: Crown of Stars.
Unicorn and the White Doe.
Griffiths. Chiming at Trwyn Du, The.
Hairdresser, Age 55, Dalston.
Taking Shelter.
Gunn. L'Epreuve.
Memoirs of the World.
Hacker. Dear Jool, I Miss You in Saint-
Saturnin.
Going Back to the River.
Home, and I've.
Haines. Hermitage, The.
Poem of the Forgotten.
Hardy. Midnight on Beechen, 187–.
Hartley. Eagle wants no friends, The.
In Those Exquisite Areas.
Solitude is kind.
Hartnett. Green Room.
Poet Dreams and Resolves, The.
Hayden. Road in Kentucky, A.
Hemingway. Stevenson.
Herrick. His Wish to Privacie.
Meat without Mirth.
Not To Love.
To Julia ("Permit me, Julia, now to goe
away").
Upon the Loss[e] of His Mistresses.
Hesketh. Bull Alone.
Emily Dickinson.
Hewitt. Birthday Rhyme for Roberta, A.
Company.
Conacre.
Distances, The.
Eager Journey.
Epithalamion: "O who will share with me."
Father's Death, A.
Halloweve: A Glensman Speaks.
Little Glen, The.
Little House, The.
My Grandmother's Restlessness.
R.K.
To Any Dweller in Lewis Street.
Hill. Men Are a Mockery of Angels.
Hoffman. Hermit of Cape Rosier, The.
Solitary, A.
Hughes, Langston. Crossing.
Hughes, Ted. For Billy Holt.
Hugo. Camas Prairie School.
Cornwall, Touring.
Dixon.
Duwamish No. 2.
High Grass Prairie.
Invasion North.
Letter to Bell from Missoula.
Living Alone.
Repairing the House, the Church, Restoring
the Music.
Salt Water Story.
Sandbanks, The.
Shark Island.

Jarrell. Ghost, a Real Ghost, A.
Le Poète Contumace.
90 North.
Jeffers. Fog.
Pleasures.
Jong. Beast, Book, Body.
I Sit at My Desk Alone.
Joseph. Back to Base.
Reported Missing.
Wet Sunday.
Keats. O Solitude! If I Must With Thee
Dwell.
Kinnell. There Are Things I Tell to No One.
Kipling. For to Admire.
Kunitz. Death In Moonlight.
Hermetic Poem.
No Word.
River Road.
Larkin. Best Society.
Kick Up the Fire, and Let the Flames Break
Loose.
Reasons for Attendance.
Ugly Sister.
Wants.
Lawrence. Deeper Than Love.
Delight of Being Alone.
Desire.
Effort of Love, The.
Image-Making Love.
Lonely, Lonesome, Loney—O!
Man Reaches a Point.
People.
Song of a Man Who Is Not Loved.
Tarantella.
Uprooted, The.
Levertov. Losing Track.
Shalom.
Liddy. Tray-Carrier of Laurels, Liam Miller.
Lovelace. Calling Lucasta from Her
Retirement.
Song: "In mine one [*or* own] monument I lie
[*or* lye]."
Lowry. Jokes on the Poop.
McAuley. Fire's gone down: burnt pine, The.
"MacDiarmid." I was better with the sounds
of the sea.
McGrath. Emblems of Exile.
From a Long Way Out of Pah-Gatzin-Kay.
Letter for Marian, A.
Near Pah-Gotzin-Kay.
Night Work.
Ordonnance.
Perpetual Motion.
Poem: "You out there, so secret."
Progress of the Soul, The.
Return, The.
Topography of History, The.
MacLeish. Definition of the Frontiers.
MacNeice. Lake in the Park, The.
Merman under the Plough, The.
Postcript to Iceland.
Solitary Travel.
Markson. Monody.
Traveler's Tale.
Marvell. Garden, The.
Meinke. Arms and the Man.
You stand in isolation like the first bloom.
Meredith. If thou art sorrowful, hide thy face!
Sleeping City, The.
Merrill. Hourglass.
Merton. Song for Nobody.
Song: If You Seek.
Song: "When rain, (sings light) rain has
devoured my house."
Things and people goodbye / It is not that I
prefer.
Tower of the Spirit, The.
Morgan. At sunset the hills turn purple.
Nathan. Jubilee.
Powerful Little Stove, A.
Nemerov. Loon's Cry, The.
Observation of October.
Paraphrase from Notebooks.
Small Moon.
These Words Also.
Winter Exercise.
Neruda. Another.

Egoist.
Island (XVII), The.
Some Creature.
O'Hara. Autobiographia Literaria.
Essay on Style.
1951.
Poem: "Eager note on my door said "Call
me", The."
Rant, A.
Olson. Blow is Creation, / & the Twist the
Nasturtium, the.
Oppen. Leviathan.
Myself I Sing.
Night Scene.
Piercy. All Clear.
Death of the Small Commune, The.
Going In.
Plath. Wuthering Heights.
Pope. Ode on Solitude.
Prince. False Bay.
For the Deserted.
I can be more solitary.
Sky brims with the ghost of a great rage, The.
Raine. I am old, I am alone.
Ralegh. Like to a Hermit[e] Poor[e].
Rexroth. Spark in the Tinder of Knowing,
The.
Rich. Night in the Kitchen.
Roadway, The.
Sleepwalking.
Robinson. Aaron Stark.
Roethke. Pure Fury, The.
Rolfe. Soledad.
Rossetti. Hopeless Case, A.
Novice, The.
Scarce tolerable life, which all life long.
Solitary Rose, The.
Rukeyser. Key, The.
Pouring Milk Away.
Speech for the Assistant, from Houdini.
Sandburg. Have Me.
Sarton. Gestalt at Sixty.
Glass of Water, A.
House in Winter, The.
Sexton. For John, Who Begs Me Not to
Enquire Further.
Fury of Abandonment, The.
Shakespeare. Sonnet 4: "Unthrifty loveliness,
why dost thou spend."
Shelley. Fragment: Thoughts Come and Go in
Solitude.
Invocation: "Earth, ocean, air, belovèd
brotherhood!"
Solitary, The.
Stanzas—April, 1814.
There was a poet whose untimely tomb.
Shelton. Alone.
Stranger.
Sidney. O sweet woods, the delight of
solitariness!
Simic. Solitude.
Smith, Charlotte. Blest is yon shepherd, on the
turf reclined.
By the Same. To Solitude.
On Passing Over a Dreary Tract of Country,
and Near the Ruins of a Deserted Chapel,
During a Tempest.
Supposed to Have Been Written in the
Hebrides.
Written at Weymouth in Winter.
Smith, Stevie. Failed Spirit, The.
Forgive Me, Forgive Me.
Forgot!
Lot's Wife.
Recluse, The.
Snodgrass. Song: "Sweet beast, I have gone
prowling."
Snyder. Clambering up the Cold Mountain
path.
In a tangle of cliffs I chose a place.
I've lived at Cold Mountain—how many
autumns.
Mid-August at Sourdough Mountain Lookout.
Sorrentino. Woman Irritable because of Her
Menses.
Stafford. Run before Dawn.
Stevens. Anglais Mort à Florence.

Stevenson. De Hortis Julii Martialis.
I love to be warm by the red fireside.
I saw red evening through the rain.
In the green and gallant Spring.
On Some Ghostly Companions at a Spa.
Soon our friends perish.
Stuart. Real World, The.
Tate. Light.
These generations that have sealed your heart.
Tennyson. Palace of Art, The.
Thomas. Ears in the Turrets Hear.
Thomson. Hymn on Solitude.
Tomlinson. Chaconne for Unaccompanied Violin.
Farmer's Wife: at Fostons Ash, The.
Updike. Oddly Lovely Day Alone, An.
Pillow.
Solitary Pond, The.
Walcott. Letter from Brooklyn, A.
Winding Up.
Walker. These Mornings of Rain.
Wilbur. Clearness.
Mirabeau Bridge.
Williams, Charles Kenneth. On the Roof.
Solid, The.
Trappers.
Williams, Miller. La Ultima Carta: A Young Wife Writes to Her Husband in the Mountains.
Williams, William Carlos. Danse Russe.
Wordsworth. Cento Made By Wordsworth, A.
For the Spot Where the Hermitage Stood on St Herbert's Island, Derwent-Water.
Fragments from Dove Cottage Manuscript 44 (II).
Solitary Reaper, The.
There is an Eminence,—of these our hills.
Written in Very Early Youth.
Wright, James. Echo for the Promise of Georg Trakl's Life.
Prayer to Escape from the Market Place, A.
Rose of the Sea.
Two Postures beside a Fire.
Yau. Casual solitude that is beyond casualness, A.
Yeats. Apparitions, The.
Lake Isle of Innisfree, The.
Young. Mid-Life Crises: A Critical Review.
Saudades: The Portuguese Blues.
Still Lives.
Zukofsky. Even if love convey.
Judge and the Bird, The.
Whatever makes this happening.

Solomon (Bible)
Auden. Extract.
Browning, Robert. Solomon and Balkis.
Cohen. Transmission, The.
Graves. Solomon's Seal.
Herbert. Sion.
Hewitt. Free Mason.
Hill. Solomon's Mines.
Lewis. Encounter, The.
Lindsay. King Solomon and the Queen of Shiba.
Merton. King Solomon: my master and the imbeciles.
Nemerov. False Solomon's Seal.
Rossetti. Consider the Lilies of the Field.
Whittier. King Solomon and the Ants.
Yeats. On Woman.
Solomon and the Witch.
Solomon to Sheba.

Somerset, England
Coleridge. This Lime-Tree Bower My Prison.
Davie. Somerset.

Somnambulism and Somnambulists
Clark. Autorotation without Gravity.
Culebra Cascabel.
Door Gunner to the Moment, (A Shau Valley 1968), The.
Forty Days.
Night Patrol.
Sleepwalker.
Sleepwalker's Way.
Somnambulism.

Son
Carroll, Jim. Poem on My Son's Birthday.

Carruth. Son, The.
Catullus. Carmen 33: "Vibennius & son, renowned."
Cullen. Fruit of the Flower.
Griffiths. Continuity.
Hemingway. Across the Board.
Hesketh. I Give Death to a Son.
Levine. My Son and I.
1933.
Sandburg. Boy and Father.
Waldman. Stick, The.
Williams, Charles Kenneth. Sorrow, The.
Zukofsky. Offer 'em up to me—bullneck crook of the baths.
To My Baby Paul.

Songs
Auden. To Goethe: a Complaint.
Berry. Bird Killer, The.
Silence, The.
Song Sparrow Singing in the Fall, A.
Song (3).
Berryman. "Old Smoky" when you sing with Robin, Chris.
Bishop. Songs for a Colored Singer.
Sonnet: "I am in need of music that would flow."
Browning, Elizabeth Barrett. Deserted Garden, The.
Last Translation, The.
Byron. Here's to Her Who Long.
In the Valley of Waters.
To the Hon. Mrs. George Lamb.
Campion. Peacefull westerne winde the wintrye stormes hath calmde, The.
"Carroll, Lewis." Miss Jones.
Carruth. It was the custom of my tribe to be silent.
Clark. Song of the Drowned Ghost in the Pool's, The.
Coleridge. Tribute to Wordsworth.
Crane. Song for Happy Feast Days, A.
Creeley. Fragments: "Decorous, and forbearing further correction."
Here.
Mary's Fancy.
Song, A: "I had wanted a quiet testament."
Davie. If I Take the Wings of the Morning.
Woodpigeons at Raheny.
De la Mare. Fool's Song, The.
Interlude, An.
Linnet, The.
Nocturne: "'Tis not my voice now speaks; but as a bird."
Rooks In October.
Sotto Voce.
Dickey, James. Buckdancer's Choice.
Donne. Triple Fool, The.
Doolittle. If You Will Let Me Sing.
Dunbar. Compensation.
Corn-Song, A.
Joggin' Erlong.
Just Whistle a Bit.
Keep a Song Up on de Way.
Ol' Tunes, The.
Poet and His Song, The.
Prometheus.
Remembered.
Songs.
Duncan. Reaper, The.
Eberhart. Evening Bird Song.
Later or Sooner.
Sacrifice, The.
Thrush Song at Dawn.
To William Carlos Williams.
Ultimate Song.
Emerson. Ah, could I hide me in my song.
Blackbird's song the blackbird's song, The.
Dull uncertain brain, A.
Fit for the Pleiads' azure chord.
High heart, O Hafiz! though not thine.
If bright the sun, he tarries.
Merlin's Song.
To Ellen, at the South.
Everson. Bard.
October Tragedy.
Fenton. Killer Snails, The.

Nothing.
Song That Sounds like This, The.
Ferlinghetti. Dove sta amore / Where lies love.
Gallagher. If Poetry Were Not a Morality.
Gardner. Incantate the Cockatrice.
Garrigue. Song in Sligo.
Strike of the Night, The.
Graves. Grace Notes.
Haunted House, The.
Hall. Whip-Poor-Will.
Hardy. Any Little Old Song.
Bridge of Lodi, The.
Donaghadee.
On the Tune Called the Old-Hundred-and-Fourth.
Sitting on the Bridge.
Hesketh. At Four A.M.
Fisherman Poet.
Jolly Good Fellow, A.
Mary.
Partridge.
Starlings.
Hewitt. For Roberta in the Garden.
July.
Lilibulero.
Man from Malabar, The.
My Great-Grandfather's Refusal.
Survival.
Hughes, Langston. Gypsy Melodies.
Sliver.
Hughes, Ted. I suppose you just gape and let your gaspings.
Song, The: "Did not want the air."
Keats. Song: "Stay, ruby-breasted warbler, stay."
Larkin. Love Songs in Age.
Lawrence. Children Singing in School.
Song of Death.
Zeppelin Nights.
Liddy. Holden, a Thought From Abroad.
I Hear the Wife of the Governor of Wisconsin Singing.
Song about Sinn Fein for Serena.
Lindsay. In Praise of Songs That Die.
Last Song of Lucifer, The.
Lowry. Bird in the Tree, The.
Duck Train—Vocal Arctic Fox-Trot.
Fragments from the Duck Anthology to Greet Our Beloved Harteebeeste in the Morning Watch.
How overjoyed I am to get your letter.
I sing the joy of poverty, not such.
Joseph Cconrad.
My two hands broke in two: and they broke me!
McAuley. Caruso.
McGrath. Little Song about Charity, A.
MacLeish. Linden Branch, The.
Lost Speakers, The.
MacNeice. Off the Peg.
Meinke. Stille Nacht, Heilege Nacht.
Meredith. Lark Ascending, The.
Noise of the hollow ground, A.
Rhine-Land.
Nemerov. Banqauet, The.
Olson. Name-Day Night.
Song, The: "More than the sennet of the solstice pipe."
Paley. When she was young she wanted.
Roethke. Light Listened.
Reply, The.
Song, The: "I met a ragged man."
Voice, The.
Rossetti. Blind from my birth, / Where flowers are springing.
In the Day of His Espousals.
Key-Note, The.
Lord, give me love that I may love Thee much.
Lord, grant us grace to rest upon Thy word.
Paradise: in a Symbol.
Summer nights are short, / Where northern days are long, The.
Way of the World, The.
When a mounting skylark sings / In the sunlit

summer morn.
World's Harmonies, The.
Rukeyser. Another Day (I will now sing).
Another Day (Miss Lorence).
Segre Song.
This Place in the Ways.
Sandburg. Bee Song.
Evening Waterfall.
Far Rockaway Night Till Morning.
Frog Songs.
Horse Fiddle.
Kansas Lessons.
Mammy Hums.
Man and Dog on an Early Winter Morning.
Potato Blossom Songs and Jigs.
Singing Nigger.
Three Violins.
Work Gangs.
Sarton. Song: "Now let us honor with violin and flute."
Scott. Hunting Song.
Sexton. Little Uncomplicated Hymn, A.
Shelley. To a Skylark.
Sidney. Doubt you to whom my Muse these notes intendeth [or entendeth].
Third Song.
Snodgrass. Song: "Sweet beast, I have gone prowling."
Sorrentino. In the blue, singa.
L the simple shape.
Lecture on Time and Space, The.
You Are My Heart's Bouquet.
Spenser. Within this wood, out of a rocke did rise.
Stevens. Country Words.
Stevenson. Song of the Road, A.
Spring Carol.
Still I love to rhyme, and still more, rhyming, to wander.
To H.F. Brown.
Stuart. Audition.
Suckling. Ballad[e] [upon a Wedding], A.
Whitman. Chanting the Square Deific.
My Canary Bird.
Unexpress'd, The.
Wilbur. Cicadas.
Plain Song for Comadre, A.
Song, A: "As at the bottom of a seething well."
Williams, William Carlos. Botticellian Trees, The.
I Will Sing a Joyous Song.
Rendezvous.
Sicilian Emigrant's Song.
Wordsworth. Reverie of Poor Susan, The.
Wright, James. Cold Divinities, The.
Humming a Tune for an Old Lady in West Virginia.
Morality of Poetry, The.
Poem for Kathleen Ferrier.
Written in a Copy of Swift's Poems, for Wayne Burns.
Yau. Ten Songs.
Yeats. Coat, A.
Lover Speaks to the Hearers of His Songs in Coming Days, The.
Three Marching Songs.
Young. Dock Song Crazy.
Malagueña Salerosa.
Song skips around, The.
Zukofsky. Letter of Poor Birds, The.
To my wash-stand.
Two Dedications: Tibor Serly.
What are these songs.

Sonnets
Bogan. Single Sonnet.
Burns. Sonnet upon Sonnets, A.
Carruth. Sonnet: "Well, Jim says that the couplet at the end."
Creeley. Apology, The.
Dunbar. Poet and the Baby, The.
Emerson. O follow the sonnet's flight.
Hoffman. Sonnet, The: "Sonnet, she told the crowd of bearded, The."
Keats. If by Dull Rhymes Our English Must Be Chained.

Lowry. Asperin tree outside told me to say, The.
Poe. Enigma, An.
Rossetti. Sonnets are full of love, and this my tome.
Wordsworth. Nuns fret not at their convent's narrow room.
Scorn Not the Sonnet [Critic, You Have Frowned].

Sonora Desert
Shelton. Requiem for Sonora.

Sons
Berry. Gathering, The.
I have thought of you stepping out of your doorway at dawn, your son in your tracks.
Poem for J.
Berryman. Holy, & holy. The damned are said to say.
Sympathy, a Welcome, A.
Bishop. Travelling in the Family.
Bly. More of the fathers are dying each day.
Prodigal Son, The.
Bradstreet. On My Son's Return Out of England.
Upon My Son Samuel His Going For England.
Brooks. Big Bessie Throws Her Son into the Street.
Byron. To My Son.
Campion. To the Most Sacred Queen Anne.
"Carroll, Lewis." Tèma con Variazioni.
Carruth. Fathers die, but sons.
Little Fire in the Woods, The.
Missing the Bo in the Henhouse.
Of Brook and Stone.
Reading myself, old poems, their inside truth that was.
Smallish Son, The.
Song: The Young Man with the Guitar, Testing.
Sonnet: "The Bo was three when we slugged through Arizona."
Ciardi. One Morning.
Poem for Benn's Graduation from High School, A.
Prayer to the Mountain, A.
Cohen. Beside My Son.
Commentary—Beside My Son.
You Who Question Souls.
Coleridge. Sonnet on Receiving a Letter Informing Me of the Birth of a Son.
To the Rev. George Coleridge.
Cowper. To His Father.
Creeley. Variation, A.
Davie. Barnsley Cricket Club.
De la Mare. Virtue.
Dickey, James. Bee, The.
Fathers and Sons.
Duncan. My Mother Would Be a Falconress.
Eberhart. Examination of Psyche: Thoughts of Home.
Emerson. What from this barren being do we reap.
Fletcher. On My Father's Hundredth Birthday.
Gallagher. Each Bird Walking.
Glück. Seconds.
Hall. Fathers and Sons.
Hardy. Geographical Knowledge.
Whitewashed Wall, The.
Herrick. Correction.
Hewitt. Cushkib Fair.
Father Explains, A.
My Grandmother's Garter.
Hughes, Langston. Letter.
Jonson. Nor do you think that their legs is all.
On My First Son [or Sonne].
To My L[ord] the King, on the Christening His Second Son James.
Kipling. My Boy Jack.
Recantation, A.
Son, A.
Koertge. Royce Newport Money.
Kooser. At the End of the Weekend.
Constellation Orion, The.
Lawrence. Mother's Son in Salonika.
Vicar's Son.
Levertov. Son, The.
Levine. Across the world / in the high

mountains of the West.
Face, The.
Look.
Starlight.
Lewis. Lady in Black.
McGrath. Enemy, The.
Poem: "My little son comes running with open arms!"
Poem: "My little son, laughing, singing."
Poem: "When I carry my little son in the cold."
McNeill. Hill Daughter.
Meinke. Advice to My Son.
Father.
This is a poem to my son Peter.
Meredith. Ah! little Angel, child of bliss!
And tho' my friar's mandate is severe.
Dear Heaven! for this sweet pledge of life.
Dear, my friend & honour'd madam! of hard facts I'm not a hoarder.
Of Robin Redbreast's babes I told.
Periander.
Shipwreck of Idomeneus, The.
When my little son leaps in my sight.
Yet what is this? the spring returns.
Merton. To Sons: Not to Be Numb.
Milton. To My Father.
Morgan. Sometimes I hear my father's voice, sometimes my son's, in mine.
Olson. In an Automotive Store.
On the equator east of my son I Orion bequeath to him my riches.
Oppen. Daedalus: The Dirge.
Pack. Clayfeld's Son Selects His Specialty.
Plath. For a Fatherless Son.
Robinson. Old King Cole.
Rossetti. Johnny.
Sexton. Hangman, The.
Two Sons.
Shakespeare. Sonnet 7: "Lo! in the orient when the gracious light."
Shelton. Letter to a Dead Father.
Letting Go.
Smith, Charlotte. Forest Boy, The.
Smith, Stevie. Correspondence between Mr. Harrison in Newcastle and Mr. Sholto Peach Harrison in Hull.
Upon a Grave.
Stafford. Memorial: Son Bret, A.
Stevenson. As in their flight the birds of song.
Last Sight, The.
Stuart. Taking the Wheel.
Tate. Mother and Son.
Turco. Corral.
Whitman. Dirge for Two Veterans.
Vigil Strange I Kept on the Field One Night.
Williams, Charles Kenneth. Easter.
Instinct.
Williams, William Carlos. Genesis.
Wordsworth. Affliction of Margaret—, The.
Wright, James. Father.
Having Lost My Sons, I Confront the Wreckage of the Moon: Christmas, 1960.
Revelation, The.
Two Postures beside a Fire.
Youth.
Yeats. Prayer for My Son, A.
Young. Foggy Morning.
Son.
Zukofsky. Record, The.
So That Even a Lover.

Sophocles
Arnold. To a Friend.

Sorcery and Sorcerers
Graves. At Best, Poets.
Lindsay. Sorceress!, The.

Sorrow
Ashbery. Variant.
Auden. Dark Fiddler, The.
Envoi No. 2.
Nightfall.
Portrait.
Sower, The.
Suppose they met, the inevitable procedure.
Beatles. Carry That Weight.
Long and Winding Road, The.

Misery.
While My Guitar Gently Weeps.
Beckett.   Enueg II.
I would like my love to die.
Je voudrais que mon amour meure.
Samedi répit.
Scarcely Disfigured.
Berg.   Uncle Will, the Gardener.
Berryman.   Fare Well.
Mallarmé siren upside down,—rootedly!
Sometimes the night echoes to prideless
  wailing.
What can to you this music wakes my years.
Blake.   On Another's Sorrow.
Bogan.   If We Take All Gold.
Boyle.   Branded for Slaughter.
Evening Grass, The.
Letter to Archibald Craig, A.
Mothers.
On the Death of My Student, the Poet Serafin.
Bradstreet.   For the Restoration of My Dear
  Husband from a Burning Ague.
Brontë.   From our evening fireside now.
Geraldine.
Harp of wild and dream-like strain.
I am the only being whose doom.
Inspiring music's thrilling sound, The.
Lady to Her Guitar, The.
May flowers are opening.
Night is darkening round me, The.
O God of heaven! the dream of horror.
Redbreast, Early in the morning.
She dried her tears, and they did smile.
Browning, Elizabeth Barrett.   Court Lady, A.
Cry of the Children, The.
Dead Rose, A.
Last Translation, The.
Mask, The.
My Heart and I.
My Kate.
Psyche Wafted by Zephyrus.
Sonnet: "Accuse me not, beseech thee, that I
  wear."
Sonnet: "Heavy heart, Beloved, have I borne,
  A."
Sonnet: "I see thine image through my tears
  tonight."
Sonnet: "My letters! All dead paper, mute and
  white."
Sonnet: "When we first met and loved, I did
  not build."
Year's Spinning, A.
Bukowski.   All I Know.
Bunting.   Verse and Version.
Burns.   Banks O' Doon, The (Ye banks and
  braes).
Banks o' Doon, The: "Ye flowery banks o'
  bonie Doon."
Cares o' love are sweeter far, The.
Craigieburn-Wood—A Song.
Despondency, an Ode.
Fair Eliza.
Fair Jenny.
Gloomy December.
Man Was Made to Mourn, a Dirge.
Musing on the roaring ocean.
Saw Ye My Phely (Quasi Dicat, Phillis).
Song: "Ae fond kiss, and then we sever."
Song: "Farewell, thou stream that winding
  flows."
Sonnet on the Death of Robert Riddel, Esq. of
  Glen Riddel, April 1794.
Wae Is My Heart.
Where Helen Lies.
Byron.   And Dost Thou Ask the Reason of My
  Sadness?
By the Rivers of Babylon We Sat Down and
  Wept.
Impromptu, in Reply to a Friend.
My Soul Is Dark.
Oh! Weep for Those.
Campion.   Let him that will be free and keep
  his hart from care.
No grave for woe, yet earth my watrie teares
  devoures.
Carew.   Conquest by Flight.
Epitaph on the Lady Mary Villiers.

Lover, upon an Accident Necessitating His
  Departure, Consults with Reason, A.
Parting, Celia Weeps.
To Celia, upon Love's Ubiquity.
Upon the Sickness of E.S.
"Carroll, Lewis."   Coronach.
Carruth.   Essay.
For Papa.
Marshall Washer.
Reflexive.
Chaucer.   Anelida and Arcite.
Balade of Complaint, A.
Book of the Duchesse, The.
Complaint unto His Lady, A.
Complaynt d'Amours.
Merchant's Prologue, The.
Clark.   Momentum.
"My heart in pieces."
What the picture tells me is itself.
Coleridge.   Anthem for the Children of Christ's
  Hospital.
On a Discovery Made Too Late.
Cowper.   Bid adieu, my sad heart, bid adieu to
  thy peace.
Joy of the Cross, The.
No Sorrow Peculiar to the Sufferer.
Shrubbery, The.
Testimony of Divine Adoption, The.
Crabbe.   Ruth.
Crashaw.   Alexias.
To Pontius Washing His Blood-Stained Hands.
Creeley.   Late Comer, The.
Cullen.   Any Human to Another.
Lament: "Now let all lovely things embark."
Love Tree, The.
Pagan Prayer.
Saturday's Child.
Two Who Croseed a Line (She Crosses).
Variations on a Theme.
Cummings.   Always before your voice my
  soul.
But being not amazing:without love.
My little heart is so wonderfully sorry.
Though your sorrows not.
Davie.   Seeing Her Leave.
De la Mare.   At Ease.
Dove, The.
Forgiveness.
Ghost, The.
Hamlet.
Old Summerhouse, The.
Stratagem, The.
Dickinson.   Faithful "I am sorry", A.
I wish I might say one liquid word.
Love's stricken "why."
One need not be a Chamber—to be Haunted.
Sorrow almost resents love.
Sorrow, benighted with Fathoms.
That Sorrow dare to touch the Loved.
There are Sweets of Pathos.
To divulge itself is Sorrow's Right.
We read the words but know them not.
Donne.   Lamentations of Jeremy, for the Most
  Part According to Tremeullius.
Doolittle.   For Bryher and Perdita.
Dunbar.   Song, The: "My soul, lost in the
  music's mist."
Duncan.   Among my friends love is a great
  sorrow.
Kingdom of Jerusalem, The.
"Dylan."   Black Crow Blues.
Corrina, Corrina.
Shot of Love.
Tomorrow Is a Long Time.
Emerson.   Bended to fops who bent to him.
I am an exile from my home; heavily.
Out of the East, and out of the West, no man
  understands me.
Red rose blooms, The.
Where art thou / Thou beautiful dream.
Yet sometimes to the sorrow stricken.
Ferlinghetti.   Elegy to Dispel Gloom, An.
Fletcher.   Sorrow.
Fox.   If He Had Not Had Two Hands Tattooed
  on His Chest.
Frost.   Love and a Question.
My November Guest.

Gallagher.   Four Dancers at an Irish Wedding.
Stepping Outside.
Gardner.   Feminine Ending or, Abandoned, She
  Died.
Glück.   Elms.
Portland, 1968.
Return, The.
Seated Figure.
Graves.   Dream of Hell, A.
Hooded Flame.
Lost Love.
Love as Lovelessness.
Primrose Bed, The.
Song: Though Once True Lovers.
Song: Victims of Calumny.
Wand, The.
Griffiths.   Choice of Flowers, The.
Hacker.   Separate Lives.
Hardy.   I Rose and Went to Rou'tor Town.
Penance.
Sunday Morning Tragedy, A.
Hartley.   Royal Love Child, The.
Hemingway.   Killed Piave—July 8—1918.
Herrick.   Bad Season Makes the Poet Sad,
  The.
Griefe ("Consider sorroowes, how they are
  aright").
Griefe ("Sorrowes divided amongst many,
  lesse").
Miseries.
Roaring.
Sauce for Sorrowes.
Sin and Strife.
Sorrowes.
Sorrows Succeed.
To Dianeme ("I co'd but see thee").
To His Angrie God.
To the Willow-Tree.
Upon Her Weeping.
Hewitt.   Grandfather Robinson Dies in 1898.
Host.
Hill.   Sorrel.
Workable fancy. Old petulant, A.
Hoffman.   Ode to Joy.
That Morning.
Housman.   They say my verse is sad: no
  wonder.
When first my way to fair I took.
Hughes, Langston.   Island.
Troubled Woman.
Jeffers.   Distant Rainfall.
Steelhead, Wild Pig, the Fungus.
Keats.   O Thou Whose Face Hath Felt the
  Winter's Wind.
Think Not of It, Sweet One, So.
Welcome Joy, and Welcome Sorrow.
Kinnell.   Burn, The.
Kipling.   Man goes to Man! Cry the challenge
  though the Jungle!
Power of the Dog, The.
Song in the Desert, A.
Larkin.   Many Famous Feet Have Trod.
Lawrence.   Goodnight.
Grey Evening.
Human Face, The.
Loss.
Sympathy.
Levertov.   To Speak.
Levine.   Red Dust.
Lewis.   Motifs.
Lovelace.   Amyntor from beyond the Sea to
  Alexis.
Calling Lucasta from Her Retirement.
Dialogue. Lucasta, Alexis.
Lowry.   Child may find no words for its
  sorrow, A.
I met the spirit of tragedy in the wood.
Jokes Aloft.
Resurgent sorrow is a sea in the cave.
Searching in a ravaged heart for anguish.
What the Gardener Said to Mrs. Trail.
MacLeish.   Before March.
It is time we should accept.
MacNeice.   Canto XVIII: "Lament for the
  Makers. Monday comes; at noon."
Markson.   Lament: "My love is gone."
Meredith.   By this he knew she wept with

waking eyes.
Joy is Fleet.
Sorrows and Joys.
We sat beneath the humming pines.
Merrill. Black Swan, The.
Millay. Kin to Sorrow.
Sorrow.
Milton. Lycidas.
Which way I fly is Hell; my self am Hell.
Morrison. Lament for the Death of My Cock.
Nathan. Learning Experience.
Neruda. Oliverio Girondo.
O'Hara. Aus Einem April.
Owen. Roads Also, The.
Winter Song.
Patchen. O sorrow it is.
Poe. Bridal Ballad.
Haunted Palace, The.
To ———: "I heed not that my earthly lot."
Valley of Unrest, The.
Pound. Song of the Bowmen of Shu.
Prince. Sky brims with the ghost of a great rage, The.
Raine. Spell Against Sorrow.
Two Invocations of Death.
Who stands at my door in the storm and rain.
Ralegh. 11th: and Last Booke of the Ocean to Scinthia, The.
End of the Boo[c]k[e]s, of the Ocean's Love to Cynthia [or Scinthia], and the Beginning[e] of the 12 [or 22] Boo[c]k, Entreating of Sorrow, The.
Like to a Hermit[e] Poor[e].
Rexroth. Delia Rexroth.
Robinson. To you that sit with Sorrow like chained slaves.
Rolfe. Catalogue.
Recruit.
Rossetti. Acme.
Ah welladay and wherefore am I here?
Chruchyard Song of Patient Hope, A.
Daughter of Eve, A.
Dost Thou Not Care?
Good Friday.
Goodbye in fear, goodbye in sorrow.
I Gave a Sweet Smell.
I sit a queen, and am no widow, and shall see no sorrow.
Lord, give me love that I may love Thee much.
Luscious and Sorrowful.
Memento Mori.
Of each sad word which is more sorrowful.
One woe is past. Come what come will.
Our Mothers, lovely women pitiful; / Our sisters, gracious in their life and death.
Patience must dwell with Love, for Love and Sorrow.
Present and Future.
Shut Out.
Sorrow hath a double voice, / Sharp today but sweet tomorrow.
Under the ivy bush / One sits sighing.
Where love is, there comes sorrow / Today or else tomorrow.
Where shall I find a white rose blowing?
Whom the Lord Loveth He Chasteneth.
Rukeyser. Foghorn in Horror.
Sandburg. Fellow Citizens.
Poems Done on a Late Night Car.
Sarton. Gestalt at Sixty.
Winter Carol.
Scott. Allan-Bane's Lament.
Spindle Song, The.
Shelley. To Mary Shelley ("My dearest Mary, wherefore hast thou gone").
Sidney. I joy in grief, and do detest all joys.
My lute, within thyself thy tunes enclose.
Sonnet 104: "Envious wits, what hath been mine offence."
Sonnet 108: "When sorrow (using mine own fire's might)."
Sonnet 95: "Yet sighs, dear sighs, indeed true friends you are."
Sonnet 97: "Dian, that fain would cheer her friend the Night."
Silverstein. Poor Angus.

Simic. Especially forlorn human specimen, An.
Smith, Charlotte. Evening.
On the Departure of the Nightingale.
Verses Intended to Have Been Prefixed to the Novel of Emmeline, but Then Suppressed.
Smith, Patti. Sheep Lady from Algiers, The.
Smith, Stevie. I Do Not Speak.
Satin-Clad.
Sorrowful Girl, The.
Sorrentino. Solitary Man Discovered in a Field of Daisies.
You Are My Heart's Bouquet.
Southwell. Mary Magdalen's Blushe.
Mary Magdalen's Complaint at Christ's Death.
Vale of Tear[e]s, A.
Stevenson. Infinite shining heavens, The.
Stuart. Elegies for Walker Dabney Stuart, Jr.
Swinburne. Anactoria.
Complaint of the Fair Armoress [or Armouress], The.
In the Orchard.
Tennyson. Mariana in the South.
Thomson. Lisy's Parting with Her Cat.
Walcott. Oddjob, a Bull Terrier.
Return to D'Ennery; Rain.
Whitman. I Sit and Look Out.
Wilbur. Song, A: "As at the bottom of a seething well."
Williams, Charles Kenneth. After That.
When.
Williams, William Carlos. Bella Donna Iu.
Waiting.
Wordsworth. Elegiac Verses in Memory of My Brother, John Wordsworth.
Wright, James. Trumpets.
Wroth. Song 2: "All night I weep[e], all day I cry, Ay me[e]."
Sonnet 4: "Forbeare darke night, my joyes now budd againe."
Sonnet 9: "Be[e] you all pleased [or pleas'd]? your pleasures grieve not[t] me[e]."
Sonnet 11: "You endless torments that my rest opress."
Sonnet 12: "Cloy'd with the torments of a tedious night."
Sonnet 20: "Sunn which glads, the earth att his bright sight, The."
Wyatt. All ye that know of care and heaviness.
I know not where my heavy sighs to hide.
Joy so short alas, the pain so near, The.
Yeats. Cloak, the Boat, and the Shoes, The.
Sad Shepherd, The.
Young. Alba.
Zimmer. Father Animus and Zimmer.
Zukofsky. In that this happening.

See also **Funerals; Grief; Mourning and Mourners.**

Soul

Angelou. Willie.
Atwood. Soul, Geologically, A.
Beatles. Within You Without You.
Beckett. La nuit venue où l'âme allait.
Berg. Unfinished Double Sonnet.
Berryman. Defensio in Extremis.
Faith like the warrior ant swarming, enslaving.
Blake. Voice of the Devil, The.
Browning, Elizabeth Barrett. Felicia Hemans.
Finite and Infinite.
Hugh Stuart Boyd [His Death, 1848].
Insufficiency.
Prospect, The.
Sonnet: "I thank all who have loved me in their hearts."
Soul's Expression, The.
Browning, Robert. You are sick, that's sure—they say.
Burns. [On] Maxwell of Cardoness.
Campion. Are you what your faire lookes expresse?
Carruth. Then ultimately asylum is the soul.
Ceravolo. Fire of Myself.
Clough. But if as (not by that the soul desired.
Nay draw not yet the cork, my friend.

That there are better things within the womb.
These vulgar ways that round me be.
Cohen. I Heard My Soul Singing.
Coleridge. Body Imaging Soul.
Psyche.
To a Lady.
Cowper. Aspirations of the Soul after God.
Crane. Bridge of Estador, The.
Cullen. For an Evolutionist and His Opponent.
Sonnet Dialogue.
Cummings. Cambridge ladies who live in furnished souls, The.
Dedication: "White rose my soul, The."
If being mortised with a dream.
Into a truly / curving form.
Of my / soul a street is.
On souls robbed of their birth-right's better part.
Out of the mountain of his soul comes.
These people socalled were not given hearts.
This is a rubbish of human rind.
Three wealthy sisters swore they'd never part.
De la Mare. Reconciliation.
Where?
Dickey, William. Self Prepares for an Unwilling Journey, The.
Dickinson. Dare you see a Soul at the White Heat?
Difference between Despair, The.
Go slow, my soul, to feed thyself.
How lonesome to be an Article!
I cannot see my soul but know 'tis there.
Its Hour with itself.
No Rack can torture me.
Of all the Souls that stand create.
Of nearness to her sundered Things.
Single Screw of Flesh, A.
Soul has Bandaged moments, The.
Soul selects her own Society, The.
Soul should always stand ajar, The.
Soul that hath a Guest, The.
Soul unto itself, The.
Soul's distinct connection, The.
Spirit is the Conscious Ear, The.
Spirit lasts, but in what mode, The.
To try to speak, and miss the way.
Too little way the House must lie.
You cannot take itself.
Donne. Ecstasy, The.
Harbinger to the Progress, The.
Our Companie in the Next World.
Poor soul, in this thy flesh what dost thou know?
Progress[e] of the Soul[e], The.
Resurrection, Imperfect.
To Sir Henry Goodyer ("Who makes the past, a pattern for next year").
To the Countess of Bedford ("Honour is so sublime perfection").
To the Countess of Bedford ("To have written then, when you writ, seemed to me").
To the Countess of Salisbury.
What if this present were the world's last night?
Doolittle. At least I have the flowers of myself.
Dunbar. Light was on the golden sands, The.
Vagrants.
Eberhart. Anima.
Configuration.
Emily Dickinson.
Jungle, The.
Lucubration.
Mistaken Identity.
My Bones Flew Apart.
Nothing But Change.
Refrains.
Rifkin Movement.
Soul.
Truncated Bird, The.
Truth, The.
Wisdom of Insecurity, The.
Worldly Failure.
Eliot. Animula.
Emerson. And the best gift of God.
Atom displaces all atoms beside, The.
Crowning hour when bodies vie with souls,

The.
Dost thou not hear me Ellen.
Few are free / All might be.
Γνωθι Σεαυτον.
I call her beautiful;—she says.
Pale Genius roves alone.
S. R.
Soul, The.
Stand up, that we may sacrifice the soul.
Though her eye seek other forms.
When thy soul / Is filled with a just image fear not thou.
Where o where is the message which today.
World is a bride superbly dressed, The.
Ford. Dampness in the air.
Glück. Day Without Night.
Gemini.
Graves. Sun-Face and Moon-Face.
Virgin Mirror.
Hall. Sister by the Pond, A.
Hartley. Giant and Saint.
Heaney. Spoonbait, The.
Herbert. Colossians 3:3.
Virtue [or Vertue].
Herrick. Another ("Thou bidst me come; I cannot come; for why").
Great Spirits Supervive.
How His Soule Came Ensnared.
Love Palpable.
Need.
On Himselfe ("Some parts may perish; dye thou canst not all").
Paradise.
Soul Is the Salt, The.
Tapers.
Hesketh. After Verlaine.
Defeathered.
Integration.
Wordsworth's Old Age.
Hill. Let mind be more precious than soul; it will not.
Hoffman. Felled Tree, A.
Hopkins. Caged Skylark, The.
Housman. Be still, my soul, be still; the arms you bear are brittle.
Hughes, Langston. To Artina.
Jeffers. Animula.
Cruel Falcon, The.
Kipling. Tomlinson.
Larkin. Spirit Wooed, The.
Lawrence. At Midnight.
Behaviour.
Dissolute.
End, The Beginning, The.
Fatigue.
Glory of Darkness.
Healing.
Mid-Day Verse, The.
Moon Memory.
Shadows.
Souls to Save.
Tarantella.
There Is Rain in Me.
Underneath.
Unhappy Souls.
Lewis. On a Bereaved Girl.
Tiger of Camden Town, The.
Lindsay. Prayer to All the Dead Among Mine Own People, A.
Lowry. Alas, there is no still path in my soul.
Born ailing on a hemisphere apart.
Dried Up River is like the Soul, A.
Exile's Return.
From This Acceptance, Sir, We Might Proceed.
Give me a poem / To wring the hearts of men.
Hunger.
I sing the joy of poverty, not such.
Joseph Cconrad.
No words assess, no pencil knows.
Perhaps for Eridanus.
Prelude To Mammon.
Soul, The.
You were in hell fire? had been all your life?
"MacDiarmid." O Ease My Spirit.
McGrath. Revisionist Poem—Octavio Paz.

MacLeish. Adam's Jealousy: Eve's Answer.
Eve's Child.
Midsummer Dawn.
What the Lion Said to the Child.
What the Serpent Said to Adam.
Mahon. Soles.
Marvell. Dialogue between the Resolved Soul and Created Pleasure, A.
Dialogue between the Soul and [the] Body, A.
On a Drop of Dew.
Ros.
Meredith. Soul, The.
Merton. Dirty Souls.
Hidden harmony is better than the open, The.
It is hard to fight / against one's heart's desire.
Some Bloody Mutiny.
Moore. What Are Years?
Morrison. Form Is an Angel, The.
Nathan. Fourth Dimension, The.
Hieroglyph.
Spirit.
Nemerov. Banqauet, The.
Flame of a Candle, The.
Speculation.
Spy, The.
Tale.
There.
Neruda. Heavy Surf, A.
Oliver. Maybe.
Some Questions You Might Ask.
Olson. As though there were no flowing.
Assuming the Soul Is a Bitch.
Chain of memory is resurrection I am a vain man, The.
Dogwood Comes Out Yellow, The.
Love.
Maximus, from Dogtown-1.
Of the United States.
Proper Soul / in the Proper Body, The.
Quail.
To a Poet Who Read in Gloucester Before the Cape Ann Historical Literary and Scientific Society.
Owen. Fragment: "As bronze may be much beautified."
O World of Many Worlds.
Show, The.
This is the Track.
Patchen. To Be Holy, Be Wholly Your Own.
Poe. Ulalume [or Ulalume—a Ballad].
Pope. Most souls, 'tis true, but peep out once an age.
Raine. Dead, The.
High Summer.
Instrument, The.
Night Thought.
Nocturn: "Night comes, an angel stands."
Ralegh. Lie, The.
"Reed." Dime Store Mystery.
Roethke. Her Reticence.
Journey to the Interior.
Light Breather, A.
Motion, The.
Renewal, The.
Restored, The.
Song: "This fair parcel of summer's."
Tranced, The.
Rolfe. Melancholy Comus, The.
Rossetti. As the dove which found no rest / For the sole of her foot, flew back.
Baby's cradle with no baby in it, A.
Castle-Builder's World, A.
Confluents.
From early dawn until the flush of noon.
I Will Lift Up Mine Eyes unto the Hills.
Introspective.
O foolish Soul! to make thy count / For languid falls and much forgiven.
Of My Life.
Pause, A.
Soul rudderless, unbraced.
To the End.
What is it Jesus saith unto the soul?
Ye Have Forgotten the Exhortation.
Sandburg. Under a Hat Rim.
Sarton. All Souls.

Sexton. Civil War, The.
God-Monger, The.
Shakespeare. Sonnet 26: "Lord of my love, to whom in vassalage."
Sonnet 74: "But be contented: when that fell arrest."
Sonnet 146: "Poor[e] soul[e], the centre of my sinful[l] earth."
Shelley. Fragment: Wedded Souls.
Simic. Evening with the Master, An.
Smith, Stevie. Animula, Vagula, Blandula.
Childe Rolandine.
Man Is a Spirit.
My Soul.
Scorpion.
Spender. Conscript, The.
Man-Made World, A.
Spiritual Explorations.
Stevens. Anecdote of Men by the Thousand.
Invective against Swans.
Lions in Sweden.
Swinburne. Ballad of Life, A.
Tennyson. How Pure at Heart and Sound in Head.
Wakoski. Eat your Rose Hips, C'est La Vie.
Walcott. Saddhu of Couva, The.
Waldman. Dialogue Between the Self & the Soul.
Warren. Interjection #7: Remarks of Soul to Body.
Whitman. Come, said my soul.
Noiseless Patient Spider.
Whittier. My Soul and I.
Wilbur. Love Calls Us to the Things of This World.
Williams, Charles Kenneth. Interrogation II.
Williams, William Carlos. Man to a Woman, A.
Virtuous Agent, The.
Wordsworth. It is no spirit who from heaven hath flown.
No mortal object did these eyes behold.
Wright, James. Heights of Macchu Picchu, III, The.
I Want to Sleep.
Not in Marble Palaces.
Wroth. Song: "Deerest if I by my deserving."
Yeats. Dialogue of Self and Soul, A.
Lady's Second Song, The.
Lady's Third Song, The.
Young. Leaving Rochester.

Sound
Angelou. Sounds Like Pearls.
Auden. Heard and Seen.
Beckett. Roundelay: "On all that strand."
Berrigan. Crystal.
Browning, Elizabeth Barrett. Sounds.
"Carroll, Lewis." Ye Fattale Cheyse.
Ciardi. Selectivity.
Size of Song, The.
Cooper. All is closed in.
Creeley. As You Come.
Hart Crane 2.
Herd.
Place.
Sound.
Sounds.
Dickey, James. Sleepers.
Dickinson. Of all the Sounds despatched abroad.
Spirit is the Conscious Ear, The.
Eberhart. Sea-Ruck.
Emerson. Chladni strewed on glass the sand.
From a far mountain creeping down.
Fisher. Discovering the Form.
Ford. Consider the sound.
Haines. We climbed all afternoon.
Hartley. B. is for Bach—.
Hewitt. Glendun on a Wet July Day.
Triad ("Three sounds of peace and rich increase").
Hoffman. Crack!
Hugo. Sound Track Conditional.
Koch. Hearing.
Kooser. Man with the Hearing Aid, The.
Kunitz. One summer, like a stone.
Levertov. Overheard.

Lovelace. To a Lady That Desired Me I Would Bear My Part with Her in a Song.
"MacDiarmid." Come, follow me into the realms of music. Here is the gate.
MacNeice. Ear, The.
McNeill. Memoria.
Mahon. Ford Manor.
Miller. Mixed Signals.
Nathan. Soundings, The.
Olson. There Are Sounds.
Owen. All Sounds Have Been As Music.
Pack. Beating Time.
Patchen. Listen / Listen / O what is that sound.
Raine. House of Music, A.
Who listens, when in the concert-hall.
Rich. We were bound on the wheel of an endless conversation.
Rossetti. Wind has such a rainy sound, The.
Sandburg. So to Speak.
Young Bullfrogs.
Schuyler. "From the next."
Stafford. Listening.
Stevens. Certain Phenomena of Sound.
Continual Conversation with a Silent Man.
How to Live. What to Do.
Jumbo.
No Possum, No Sop, No Taters.
Page from a Tale.
Two Figures in Dense Violet Night.
Tomlinson. In the Studio.
Sea Poem.
Whip, The.
Whitman. Proud Music of the Storm.
That Music Always Round Me.
Williams, Miller. Logos.
Staying.
Wordsworth. Cuckoo at Laverna May 25, 1837 The.
Morning Exercise, A.
On Approaching the Staub-Bach, Lauterbrunnen.
On the Power of Sound.
To the Cuckoo.
Unremitting Voice of Nightly Streams, The.
Wright, James. Depressed by a Book of Bad Poetry, I Walk toward an Unused Pasture and Invite the Insects to Join Me.
Poem for Kathleen Ferrier.
Young. John Coltrane Dance, The.
Koto Music/Singing.
Zukofsky. Two Dedications: Tibor Serly.

Soup
Angelou. This Winter Day.
"Carroll, Lewis." Turtle Soup.
Galvin. Kale Soup.
Hesketh. Animals' Last Words.
Piercy. Digger Indians were too primitive, The.
Sandburg. Soup.
Silverstein. Me-Stew.
Sky Seasoning.
Simic. Soup, The.
Van Duyn. Goya's "Two Old People Eating Soup."

South, The, United States
Angelou. Georgia Song, A.
Miss Scarlet, Mr. Rhett and other Latter-Day Saints.
Southeast Arkanasia.
Carruth. Wind is a stealth of memory.
Footsteps fall.
Davie. University of the South, The.
Dickey, James. Spring-Shock.
Dove. Nothing Down.
Dunbar. Chrismus on the Plantation.
Plantation Child's Lullaby, The.
"Dylan." Oxford Town.
Fletcher. Elegy on a Nordic White Protestant.
Gulf Stream.
Old South, The.
Passing of the South, The.
Towards the North Star.
Hayden. Tour 5.
Hughes, Langston. Not a Movie.
One-Way Ticket.

Silhouette.
South, The.
Lorde. Afterimages.
McGrath. Deep South.
Nash. First Families Move Over!
Rolfe. Homecoming (August 7, 1934).
Rukeyser. Lynchings of Jesus, The.
Schuyler. Procession.
Sorrentino. Drifting South.
Walker. Hymn: "I well remember / A time when."
It is true--/ I've always loved.
Once.
South: The Name of Home.
Whitman. O Magnet-South.
Whittier. To a Southern Statesman.
What State Street Said to South Carolina, and What South Carolina Said to State Street.
Young. Sunday Sonnet for My Mother's Mother, A.

South Africa
Kipling. Chant-Pagan.
English Flag, The.
Parting of the Columns, The.
Settler, The.
South Africa.
Two Kopjes.
Knight. Poem for the Liberation of Southern Africa.
Television Speaks.
Lorde. Evening News, The.
Williams, Charles Kenneth. Bishop Tutu's Visit to the White House: 1984.

South African War. see Boer War.

South America. see Listings for specific South American Countries.

South Carolina (state)
Whittier. At Port Royal.
Hymn Sung at Christmas by the Scholars of St. Helena's Island, S.C.

South Dakota (state)
Boyle. Thunderstorm in South Dakota.
Wright, James. Having Lost My Sons, I Confront the Wreckage of the Moon: Christmas, 1960.
Sitting in a Small Screenhouse on a Summer Morning.

South Sea Islands
Merton. East with Malinowski.

South Wind
Emerson. South Wind.
Lindsay. Moon's the North Wind's Cooky, The.
Sandburg. South Wind Says So, The.

Southey, Robert
Byron. Dedication: "Bob Southey! You're a poet--poet-laureate."
"Carroll, Lewis." Father William.
Coleridge. To Robert Southey.

Soviet Union. see Russia.

Soy Sauce
Snyder. Soy Sauce.

Space and Space Travel
Ammons. Spaceship.
Auden. Moon Landing.
Clark. Millennial Icon.
Moira.
Moira's Messages.
Dickey, James. Apollo.
Eberhart. Dam Neck, Virginia.
On Shooting Particles beyond the World.
Emerson. Coil of space the cones of light, The.
Frost. But outer Space.
Ginsberg. In a Moonlit Hermit's Cabin.
Jeffers. Dog in the Sky, The.
Kunitz. Flight of Apollo, The.
Larkin. Time and Space Were Only Their Disguises.
Lawrence. Space.
MacLeish. What Eve Sang.
Merton. Why Some Look up to Planets and Heroes.
Rolfe. Three Who Died.
Sexton. Venus and the Ark.

Updike. Exposé.
Moons of Jupiter, The.
Open Letter to Voyager II, An.
Skyey Developments.
Williams, William Carlos. Gossips, The.
Heel & Toe to the End.
World Contracted to a Recognizable Image, The.

Spain
Browning, Robert. Cristina.
Byron. Girl of Cadiz, The.
Carroll, Jim. El Hombre del Ombre.
Crane. Imperator Victus.
Emerson. For fifteen winter days.
Ferlinghetti. Goya & the Sleep of Reason.
Hemingway. Poem Is By Maera, The.
To a Tragic Poetess.
Hewitt. Camaradas Y Compañeros.
Hughes, Ted. You Hated Spain.
Jeffers. Sinverguenza.
Kipling. When the Great Ark.
Lawrence. At the Bank in Spain.
Spanish Privilege.
Spanish Wife, The.
Levine. Face, The.
Holding On.
Let Me Begin Again.
Midget, The.
On the Murder of Lieutenant José Del Castillo by the Falangist Bravo Martinez, July 12, 1936.
Salami.
MacLeish. Spanish Lie, The.
MacNeice. And I remember Spain.
Marvell. On the Victory Obtained by Blake over the Spaniards, in the Bay of Santa [or Sancta] Cruz, in the Island of Tenerife, 1657.
Millay. Say that We Saw Spain Die.
Plath. Alicante Lullaby.
Rexroth. Autumn in California.
Requiem for the Spanish Dead.
Rolfe. City of Anguish.
Elegia.
Elegy for Our Dead.
In the Time of Hesitation.
Song: "Through all the cowering world, crouching, shrinking."
Rukeyser. Word of Mouth.
Shelley. Ode Written October, 1819, An.
Smith, Stevie. Spanish School.
Spender. Port Bou.
Updike. All crises pass, though not the condition of crisis.
Land is dry enough to make the rivers, The.
Neumático punturado—we stopped.
These islands of history amid traffic snarls.
Van Duyn. Madrid, May, 1977.
Madrid, 1974.
Whitman. Spain, 1873–74.
Spanish Lady, The.
Wordsworth. And is it among rude untutored Dales.
Avaunt all specious pliancy of mind.
Composed While the Author Was Engaged in Writing a Tract, Occasioned by the Convention of Cintra.
1810.
Hail, Zaragoza! If with unwet eye.
Pelayo.
Spanish Guerillas 1811.
Wright, James. Eisenhower's Visit to Franco, 1959.
In Memory of a Spanish Poet.
On the City Ramparts of Cádiz.
Young. My Spanish Heart.
Topsy: Part 2.

Spanish-American War
Kipling. White Man's Burden, The.

Spanish Armada
Campion. Ad Thamesin.
Kipling. Together.

Spanish Civil War. see Civil War, Spain.

Spankings
Dunbar. When a Feller's Itchin' to be Spanked.
Hayden. Whipping, The.
Herrick. Upon Pagget.

Sparrows
Ammons. Anxiety.
Berry. Sparrow.
Bukowski. Farewell Thing While Breathing, A.
Byron. Translation from Catullus ("Ye Cupids, droop each little head").
Carruth. Snow, The.
Sparrows.
Catullus. Carmen 2: "Lesbia's sparrow! / Lesbia's plaything!"
Carmen 3: "Who loves beauty / vel her statues."
Ciardi. Minus One.
Cowper. Sparrows Self-Domesticated.
Cummings. N / ot eth / eold almos.
Dickinson. Sparrow took a Slice of Twig, A.
Dunbar. Sparrow, The.
Dunn. With No Experience in Such Matters.
Emerson. Sparrow is rich in her nest, THe.
Gunn. Sparrow.
Herrick. Upon the Death of His Sparrow; an Elegie.
Jarrell. Augsburg Adoration, The.
Levine. Goodbye.
Millay. English Sparrows.
Milton. How lovely are thy dwellings fair!
Nathan. To Transcend the Cat.
Oppen. Stranger's Child.
Psalms. Psalm 84: "How amiable are thy tabernacles.."
Psalm 84: "How amiable are thy tabernacles, O Lord of hosts!"
Rossetti. Yea, the Sparrow Hath Found Her an House.
Sidney. Sonnet 83: "Good brother Philip, I have borne you long."
Smith, Stevie. When the Sparrow Flies.
Williams, William Carlos. Breakfast.
Pastoral 1; "Old man who goes about, The."
Pastoral: "Little sparrows, The."
Sleeping Brute, The.
Sparrow, The.
Sparrows among Dry Leaves.
To a Sparrow.
Wordsworth. Death of a Starling, The.
Sparrow's Nest, The.
Wright, James. Elegy in a Firelit Room.
Sparrows in a Hillside Drift.
Zukofsky. Lament, o graces of Venus, and Cupids.
Sparrow, my girl's pleasure, delight of my girl.

Sparta, Greece
Browning, Robert. Pheidippides.
Cowper. By Palladas.
From Julianus.
McNeill. To the Boys in Freshman History (Thermopylae, 480 B.C.).

Spas
Merton. Song: Sensation Time at the Home, A.
Warren. End of Season.

Speech
Auden. Short Ode to a Philologist, A.
Speech.
Berry. Silence, The.
Bogan. Henceforth, from the Mind.
Boyle. After New York—May Seventeenth.
April Thirtieth 1960.
"Carroll, Lewis." Bellman himself they all praised to the skies—, The.
Carruth. I'm from Connecticut. But please, not Stamford.
Sonnet: "Key-reist, I am fed and sick unto death with this."
Sonnet: "Well, she told me I had an aura. 'What?' I said."
Steeple bush, hardhack.
Catullus. Carmen 84: "'*H*advantageous' breathes Arrius heavily."
Clough. Light words they were, and lightly, falsely said.
Creeley. Charm, The.
Pattern, The.
Shame, The.
Words.

Davie. Advise me, draftsman of the drifting sands.
I love the way the weave, when two or three or.
I love the way the weave, when two or three or.
De la Mare. Speech.
Dickinson. How precious Thought and Speech are!
Emerson. Merops.
Poem on Eloquence by R. W. Emerson.
There is no evil but can speak.
Gallagher. Gray Eyes.
Gardner. And Thou No Breath at All?
Graves. Cool Web, The.
Herrick. Teares are Tongues.
Upon Julia's Fall.
Hewitt. Dedication of "The Rhyming Weavers."
Names We Used, The.
On the Use of Dialect Words.
Hoffman. In the Beginning.
Levertov. Sequence, A.
MacLeish. Speech to a Crowd.
Morgan. Saying.
Oppen. Which is ours, which is ourselves.
Psalms. Psalm 64: "Hear my voice, O God, in my prayer."
Rich. Apology.
Rukeyser. Effort at Speech between Two People.
In Our Time.
Sandburg. Basket.
Speech.
Sidney. Sonnet 55: "Muses, I oft invoked your holy aid."
Sonnet 58: "Doubt there hath been, when with his golden chain."
Smart. Silence.
Sorrentino. Meeting, The.
Stevens. Chocorua to Its Neighbor.
Creations of Sound, The.
Page from a Tale.
Search for Sound Free from Motion.
Sketch of the Ultimate Politician.
To the Roaring Wind.
Whittier. Summons, A.
Williams, Charles Kenneth. Don't.
My Mother's Lips.
Williams, Miller. Logos.
Wright, Charles. May Journal.
Primitive Journal II.
Zukofsky. '*c-hommodating* he'd bait, seeking *accomodating* willed.
1959 Valentine.

See also **Screams; Talk.**

Speed
Browning, Elizabeth Barrett. Soul's Travelling, The.
Cohen. Hurry to Your Dinner.
Emerson. Is the pace of nature slow?
Frost. Master Speed, The.
Gardner. Triolet: "Bad die old, The."
Herrick. Haste Hurtfull.
Kipling. Braggart, The.
Carmen Circulare.
Justice's Tale, The.
Sepulchral.
To Motorists.
Tour, The.
Lindsay. Journey Starts Swiftly, The.
Nash. Ho, Varlet! My Two Cents' Worth of Penny Postcard!
It Would Have Been Quicker to Walk, or, Don't Tell Me We're There Already.
Mrs. Purvis Dreads Room Service.
Slow Down, Mr. Ganderdonk, You're Late.
We Don't Need to Leave Yet, Do We? Or, Yes We Do.
Pack. Red Shift, The.
Rossetti. Swift and sure the swallow.
Rukeyser. Lover as Fox.
Speed, We Say.
Study in a Late Subway.
Target Practice.

Spelling
Nash. What's in a Name? Some Letter I Always Forget.

Spelling Bees
Dunbar. Spellin'-Bee, The.

Spender, Stephen
Eberhart. Face, Ocean.

Spenser, Edmund ("Colin Clout")
Campion. Ad Ed. Spencerum.
Keats. Specimen of an Induction to a Poem. Spenser! A Jealous Honourer of Thine.
Koch. Art of Poetry, The.
Meredith. Poetry of Spenser, The.
Ralegh. Vision upon This Concei[p]t of the Faerie [or Faery] Queen[e], A.
Wordsworth. Gentle Spenser.
White Doe of Rylstone, The; or, The Fate of the Nortons.

Sphinx
Auden. Sphinx, The.
Duncan. Huon of Bordeaux.
Eberhart. Sphinx.
Emerson. Sphinx, The.
Hayden. Sphinx.
MacLeish. What Riddle Asked the Sphinx.
Nash. Thirteenth Labor of Hercules, The.
Rukeyser. Myth.
Private Life of the Sphinx.
Sandburg. Sphinx, A.

Spider Webs
Bukowski. Escape, The.
Eberhart. Spider, The.
Hayden. Web, The.
Lowry. Sonnet: "This ruin now, where moonlight walks alone."
Spiderweb.
Meredith. Garden Idyl, A.
Nemerov. End of Summer School, The.
Rich. Knot, The.
Sandburg. Sun Dancer.
Webs.
Smith, Charlotte. Gossamer, The.
To the Insect of the Gossamer.
Williams, Charles Kenneth. Spider Psyche.

Spiders
Ammons. Planet Actions.
Trigger.
Beckett. Morte parmi.
Bukowski. Death Wants More Death.
Escape, The.
Spider, The.
Ciardi. Thoughts on Looking into a Thicket.
Dickinson. Alone and in a Circumstance.
Spider as an Artist, The.
Spider holds a Silver Ball, A.
Spider sewed at Night, A.
Eberhart. Spider, The.
Fox. To the Man Who Watches Spiders.
Frost. Design.
Graves. Philosopher, The.
Hall. Some Oddities.
Lawrence. Malade.
Lindsay. Spider and the Ghost of the Fly, The.
Lowell. Mr. Edwards and the Spider.
Lowry. Spiderweb.
McNeill. Involved (The Spider).
Meredith. Garden Idyl, A.
Outer and Inner.
Plath. Spider.
Rich. Knot, The.
Sandburg. Drowsy.
Sun Dancer.
Schwartz. Spiders.
Smith, Stevie. On Walking Slowly after an Accident.
Wakoski. Coins and Coffins under My Bed.
Elizabeth and the Golden Oranges.
Whitman. Noiseless Patient Spider.
Williams, Charles Kenneth. Spider Psyche.

Spies. *see* **Spying and Spies.**

Spinning and Spinners
Burns. Bess[y] and Her Spinning-Wheel.
Weary Pund o' Tow, The.
Hewitt. Iron Pot, The.
Hugo. Bad Eyes Spinning the Rock.

Wordsworth. Grief, thou hast lost an ever ready friend.
Song for the Spinning Wheel (Founded upon a Belief Prevalent among the Pastoral Vales of Westmoreland).
Through Cumbrian wilds, in many a mountain cove.

Spinoza, Baruch
Muldoon. Ontario.

Spinsters
Auden. Miss Gee.
Beatles. Eleanor Rigby.
Byron. Epigram on an Old Lady Who Had Some Curious Notions Respecting the Soul.
Campion. Epigramme: "Kate can fancy only berdles husbands."
In Laurentiam.
Hardy. Retty's Phases.
Hartley. Spinsters.
This Lady Rides a Languid Dromedary toward Her Dear-God.
Herrick. To the Little Spinners.
Upon Himself ("Mop-eyed I am, as some have said").
Plath. Ella Mason and Her Eleven Cats.
Spinster.
Smith, Stevie. Gnädiges Fräulein.
Mrs Simpkins.

Spiritualism and Spiritualists
Brontë. I'm happiest when most away.
O wander not so far away!
Strong I stand, though I have borne.
Browning, Elizabeth Barrett. Sleep, The.
Duncan. Circulations of the Song.
Eberhart. Recapitulation, The.
Emerson. Be of good cheer, brave spirit; steadfastly.
Leave me, Fear! thy throbs are base.
Hartley. To the Nameless One.
Kipling. En-dor.
Levine. Holding On.
Voice, The.
Lorde. October.
Oya.
Signs.
Winds of Orisha, The.
MacNeice. When the indefinable / Moment apprises.
Markson. Loss.
Merton. Ranter and Their Pleads, The.
Morrison. It Has Been Said.
Star Fish Gluttony.
This Is My Forest.
O'Hara. Ode to Tanaquil Leclercq.
Patchen. Cloth of the Tempest, The.
In the footsteps of the walking air.
Temple, A.
Rexroth. Suchness.
Sarton. Action of Therapy, The.
Annunciation.
Behind What Little Mirror..
Olive Grove, The.
Storm of Angels, A.
These Pure Arches.
Smith, Stevie. From the County Lunatic Asylum.
Mrs Simpkins.
Stuart. Gospel Singer.
Wright, Charles. To Giacomo Leopardi in the Sky.
Wright, James. How close to becoming spirit something is.
On the Skeleton of a Hound.

Spirituals
Hughes, Langston. Note on Commercial Theatre.
Spirituals.
Tambourines.
Sarton. At Muzot.
Prayer before Work.

Spittoons
Cummings. As that named Fred.

Sports
Beckett. Ascension.
"Dylan." Catfish.
Gildner. First Practice.
Hesketh. Gone Away.

Hewitt. Away Match: June 1924.
On Dunmore's Waste.
Housman. Twice a week the winter thorough.
Jonson. Epigram to My Jovial Good Friend Mr Robert Dover, on His Great Instauration of His Hunting and Dancing at Cotswold, An.
To Sir Henry Goodyere.
Kipling. FEBRUARY (*Coursing*).
Verses on Games.
Lowry. Though I Have More.
Pack. Camp Wakonda, 1940.
Sandburg. One of the Cherokees on Oklahoma, having a million or so from oil.
Sidney. Sonnet 53: "In martial sports I had my cunning tried."
Updike. Sometime Sportsman Greets the Spring, The.
Wright, James. Mad Fight Song for William S. Carpenter, 1966, A.

See also **Athletics and Athletes; Games; Listings for specific Sports.**

Spring
Ammons. Resurrections.
Atwood. Spring again, can I stand it.
Auden. Alston Moor.
April in a Town.
Elegy: "Wagtail splutters in the stream, A."
March.
March Song.
March Winds.
Spring will come, The.
Weeks of blizzard over, The.
Beatles. Here Comes the Sun.
Berry. Another Descent.
Farm travels in snow, The.
March 22, 1968.
Purification, A.
Returning.
Berryman. Caravan.
I wished, all the mild days of middle March.
Bishop. Cold Spring, A.
Blake. Echoing [*or* Ecchoing] Green, The.
Spring.
Thou hearest the nightingale begin the song of spring.
To Spring.
When the Green Woods Laugh.
Bly. Early Spring Between Madison and Bellingham.
Spring has come; I look up and see.
Boyle. O This Is Not Spring.
Spring.
Bradstreet. As spring the winter doth succeed.
Brontë. May flowers are opening.
Browning, Robert. Home-Thoughts, from Abroad.
Year's at the spring, The.
Bunting. Weeping oaks grieve, chestnuts raise.
Burns. Auld Man's Winter Thought, The.
Gardener wi' His Paddle—or, The Gardener's March, The.
Lament of Mary Queen of Scots on the Approach of Spring.
O Were My Love Yon Lilac[k] Fair.
Ode to Spring.
Scotch Song.
Song, Altered from an Old English One.
Byron. Stanzas: "Could Love for ever."
Campion. Elegia I (1619).
Peaceful Western Wind, The.
Carew. Spring, The.
Carruth. Chase in Spring, The.
Incident of May.
One day music / begins.
Primavera, The.
Spring Notes from Robin Hill.
Springtime so impetuous. Already pink blossoms.
Tanck's Song About His Unicameral Mind.
Where the snow bank leans.
Wise child is born, The.
Catullus. Carmen 46: "Now spring bursts."
Ceravolo. Spring.
Spring in This World of Poor Mutts.
Warmth.
Chaucer. Knight's Tale, The.

Ciardi. Saturday, March 6.
Clare. Dying Child, The.
February: A Thaw.
Cohen. Commentary—It's Probably Spring.
Coleridge. Answer to a Child's Question.
Lines to a Beautiful Spring in a Village.
Cowper. Elegy 5: On the Coming of Spring.
To the Rev. Mr. Newton.
Crane. Lachrymae Christi.
Crashaw. Out of Virgil, in the Praise of the Spring.
Creeley. Spring.
Cullen. Spring Reminiscence.
To John Keats, Poet, at Springtime.
Cummings. And this day it was Spring..us.
Ardensteil-henarub-izabeth) / this noN.
Because it's / Spring / thingS.
But the other / day i was passing a certain.
"but why should" / the / greatest.
Darling!because my blood can sing.
Greedy the people, The.
Here's to opening and upward,to leaf and to sap.
If(among / silent skies).
In / Spring comes(no- / one).
In Just- / spring   when the world is mud-.
Let us lie here in the disturbing grass.
(Listen) / this a dog barks and.
Metamorphosis.
Never could anyone / who simply lives to die.
Nouns to nouns / wan / wan.
Now i lay(with everywhere around).
O sweet spontaneous.
Rain Is a Handsome Animal, The.
Semi-Spring.
Skies may be blue;yes.
Sometimes / in)Spring a someone will lie(glued).
Sonnet: "Long since, the flicker brushed with shameless wing."
Spring is like a perhaps hand.
Spring omnipotent goddess thou dost.
Spring!may— / everywhere's here.
Spring(side / walks are)is.
Sweet spring is your.
There are so many tictoc.
Tonight the moon is round golden entire. It.
Trees / were in(give).
Weazened Irrefutable unastonished.
When / from a sidewalk.
When faces called flowers float out of the ground.
Yes is a pleasant country.
You asked me to come:it was raining a little.
Davie. Orford.
Oriental Visitor, An.
Spring Song, A.
Wearing of the Green, The.
De la Mare. Reawakening, The.
Riddle, A.
Spectre, The.
Dickinson. Bee! I'm expecting you!
Before you thought of Spring.
Dear March, Come in.
I cannot meet the Spring unmoved.
I dreaded that first Robin, so.
I have a Bird in spring.
Inundation of the Spring, The.
Light exists in Spring, A.
Little Madness in the Spring, A.
Notice that is called the Spring, The.
Ones that disappeared are back, The.
Spring comes on the World.
Spring is a happiness so beautiful.
Spring is the Period.
Spring's first conviction is a wealth.
That sweet Physician, an approaching spring.
Trusting the happy flower.
Violets are by my side, The.
When they come back—if Blossoms do.
Donne. Love's Growth.
Doolittle. Late Spring.
Dunbar. Come and Kiss Me Sweet and Twenty.
Little Lucy Landman.
Song: "De bee hit sip some honey f'om de matermony vine."

Spring Fever.
Spring Song.
Spring Wooing, A.
When Winter Darkening All Around.
Dunn. Beneath the Sidewalk.
Eberhart. Apple Buds.
Day-Bed, The.
On Returning to a Lake in Spring.
Pasture, The.
Scarf of June, The.
Spring was never his fort. Suspect at first.
This Fevers Me.
Three Kids.
Where Are Those High and Haunting Skies.
Edmunds. Letter to Jeffrey Gustavson.
Emerson. April.
For Genius made his cabin wide.
Gentle Spring has charmed the earth.
Good Charles the springs adorer.
May.
May-Day.
Musketaquid.
Fletcher. November Days.
Spattering of the rain upon pale terraces, The.
Symphony of Snow.
Frost. Cloud Shadow, A.
Prayer in Spring, A.
Spring Pools.
Galvin. Fog Township.
Gardner. Disenchanted, The.
Eros in May at MacDowell.
Grocery Bouquet, The.
Tango for Zither.
West of Childhood.
Garrigue. Spring Song II.
Gildner. It's Spring, Lover.
Ginsberg. Easter Sunday.
Glück. Easter Season.
Flowering Plum.
For Jane Myers.
Letter from our Man in Blossomtime.
My Cousin in April.
Shad-Blow Tree, The.
Graves. Primrose Bed, The.
Song: Fig Tree in Leaf.
Spring 1974.
Gray. Ode on the Spring.
Haines. And When the Green Man Comes.
Hall. Love Is Like Sounds.
Hardy. Backward Spring, A.
Growth in May.
If It's Ever Spring Again.
Joys of Memory.
Spring Call, The.
Year's Awakening, The.
Herrick. Apron of Flowers, The.
Farewell Frost; or, Welcome the Spring.
Meddow Verse; or, Aniversary to Mistris
Bridget Lowman, The.
Succession of the Foure Sweet Months, The.
Hesketh. Edward Thomas.
From the Day Room.
Reflections.
Winter Daffodils.
Hewitt. Antrim April.
Evening in Spring.
For a Mild Season.
Late Spring.
March Day.
Mid-April.
Northern Spring.
Now in the Spring.
Season's Return.
Spring of the Year.
Suburban Spring in Warwickshire.
We too have gone down little roads in spring.
Hill. Cycle.
Hoffman. Thaw.
Hopkins. Ad Mariam.
Furl of fresh-leaved dogrose down, The.
May Magnificat, The.
See how Spring opens with disabling cold.
Spring.
Spring and Death.
Spring and Fall.
Housman. Loveliest of trees, the cherry now.

Oh see how thick the goldcup flowers.
Spring Morning.
Hughes, Ted. Swifts.
Jarrell. Trees in Spring, The.
Jonson. Come forth, come forth, the gentle
Spring.
Joseph. Anthropomorphism Reversed.
Chorale.
First Spring Dawn.
Geranium.
Puppeteer.
Keats. After Dark Vapours Have Oppressed
Our Plains.
Extracts from an Opera.
I Stood Tip-Toe upon a Little Hill.
Kinnell. Apple Tree, The.
Kipling. Cuckoo Song.
In Springtime.
Pan in Vermont.
Koch. Desire for Spring.
Kooser. Late February.
Larkin. Coming.
First Sight.
Fragment from May.
May Weather.
Spring.
Spring Warning.
Lawrence. Campions.
Come Spring, Come Sorrow.
Craving for Spring.
Disagreeable Advice.
Drained Cup, The.
Enkindled Spring, The.
Spring Morning.
Levertov. Another Spring.
Levine. Nitrate.
Sleepless Night, A.
To Cipriano, in the Wind.
Waking an Angel.
Lewis. Holi.
Mid-Winter.
Lindsay. Sweetheart Spring.
Lovelace. Female Glory.
Lowry. Born ailing on a hemisphere apart.
Kraken, Eagles, in British Columbia.
Years standing round in a ring, The.
McGrath. Black Train, The.
What We Think We Know.
Winter Roads.
MacLeish. March.
Sowing of the Dead Corn, The.
MacNeice. Another Cold May.
April Manifesto, An.
March gave clear days.
Pale Panther, The.
Solvitur Acris Hiems.
Spring Cleaning.
Spring Voices.
That is the end of the news. The humanist.
McNeill. Second Sight (My Son's First
Springtime).
Meredith. Death of Winter, The.
Fresh Spring has come with flower and leaf to
warn.
Fullness of love sleeps in us like a sea.
I saw young Spring leap over the hills.
Invitation to the Country.
May Song.
Postillion, The.
Song: "Daisy now is out upon the green,
The."
Song: Spring.
Song: The Wren.
Sweet o' the Year, The.
Tardy Spring.
When stormy day is cold & gray.
Merton. April.
City's Spring, The.
Sowing of Meanings, The.
Spring: Monastery Farm.
What Troubles I Have Seen in Birdlegged
Spring.
Millay. New England Spring, 1942.
Spring.
Spring and the Fall, The.
Spring in the Garden.
Spring Song.

Milton. Elegy 5: On the Coming of Spring.
Nash. Eternal Vernal, or, In All My Dreams
My Fair Face Beams, The.
Individualist, The.
Passionate Pagan and the Dispassionate Public,
The.
Spring Song.
Nemerov. Zalmoxis.
Neruda. Same Story.
O'Hara. Captain Bada.
Easter.
Oliver. Spring.
Two Kinds of Deliverance.
Olson. Day Song.
Day Song, the Day After.
It's SPRing AgAIN!
Variations Done for Gerald Van de Wiele.
Owen. Spring Offensive.
Pack. Modest Boast at Meridian, A.
Paley. Love.
Patchen. Shadows and Spring Flowers.
Piercy. Inside Chance, The.
Snow, Snow.
Plath. April Aubade.
Prologue to Spring.
Pope. Spring, the First Pastoral, or Damon.
Prince. Keeper's Wood.
Raine. April's new apple buds on an old
lichened tree.
Flower, memory—.
I felt, under my old breasts, this April day.
Winter Solstice.
Ralegh. Joyfull Spring did ever last, The.
Plants and trees made poore and old, The.
Ransom. Birthday of an Aging Seer.
Semi-Centennial.
Rexroth. Mary and the Seasons.
Rich. There Are Such Springlike Nights.
Roethke. Bring the Day!
Light Comes Brighter, The.
Vernal Sentiment.
Rossetti. Amen.
Another Spring.
Bride Song, A.
Child's Talk in April.
Cor Mio.
Days are clear, / Day after day, The.
Death-Watches.
Easter Carol, An.
First Spring Day, The.
L. E. L.
May.
One Swallow Does Not Make a Summer.
St. Valentine's Day 1881.
Spring.
Spring Fancies.
Spring is come again not as at first.
There Is a Budding Morrow in Midnight.
To Mary Rossetti.
What Sappho Would Have Said Had Her Leap
Cured Instead of Killing Her.
What's in a Name?
Who Hath Despised the Day of Small Things?
Wintry Sonnet, A.
Rukeyser. Fighting for Roses.
Gift-Poem.
Wooden Spring.
Sandburg. Blossom Themes.
Child Face.
Crisscross.
Elm Buds.
Frog Songs.
Lines Written for Gene Kelly to Dance To.
New Song for Indiana Ophelias.
Population Drifts.
Spring Carries Surprises.
Spring Cries.
Spring Grass.
Spring Wind.
Three Spring Notations on Bipeds.
Understandings in Blue.
Wind Sings Welcome in Early Spring, The.
Sarton. Metamorphosis.
Schuyler. Industrial Archaeology.
May 24th or So.

Spring.
Thinness.
3/23/66.
Schwartz. News of the Gold World of May.
Sexton. It is a Spring Afternooon.
Killing the Spring.
Shelley. Cloud, The.
Fragment: May the Limner.
Question, The.
Smart. 1.4: To Sextius, a Person of Consular
Dignity.
Smith, Charlotte. April.
Early Butterfly, The.
Ode to the Missel Thrush.
To Spring.
To the Muse.
Violets.
Written in Farm Wood, South Downs, in May
1784.
Smith, Stevie. Written at the Close of Spring.
Snyder. Migration of Birds.
Morning star is not a star, The.
Sixth-Month Song in the Foothills.
What Have I Learned.
Stevens. Celle Qui Fût Héaulmiette.
Depression before Spring.
Indian River.
Meditation Celestial & Terrestrial.
Stevenson. Come, here is adieu to the city.
Flower god, god of the spring, beautiful,
bountiful.
Spring Carol.
Spring Song.
Summer sun shone round me, The.
When aince Aprile has fairly come.
Stuart. Spring Song.
Swinburne. Hounds of Spring, The.
Interlude, An.
Tennyson. In the Spring.
To Mary Boyle.
Thomas. From Love's First Fever to Her
Plague.
Here in This Spring.
Holy Spring.
Thomson. Song: "When blooming spring."
To Amanda ("Come, dear Amanda, quit the
town").
To Amanda ("Unless with my Amanda blest").
Tomlinson. Hesitation, The.
Northern Spring.
Order of Saying, The.
Updike. Melting.
Query.
Sometime Sportsman Greets the Spring, The.
Spring Song.
Styles of Bloom.
Touch of Spring.
Van Duyn. Notes from a Suburban Heart.
Waldman. Lindsay Speaks.
Warren. Deciduous Spring.
Whitman. First Dandelion, The.
Out of May's Shows Selected.
Soon Shall the Winter's Foil Be Here.
Whittier. April.
First Flowers, The.
Mayflowers, The.
My Psalm.
Pageant, The.
Wind of March, The.
Wilbur. April 5, 1974.
Avowal, The.
Cicadas.
Next Door.
Rondeau: "Year has cast its cloak away, The."
Seed Leaves.
To Ishtar.
Winter Spring.
Williams, Charles Kenneth. Spring: another /
joke. / This run-down.
Williams, William Carlos. April.
Bird Song.
Bitter World of Spring, The.
Della Primavera Transportata al Morale.
Hermaphroditic Telephones, The.
In spring you sleep and never know when the
morn comes.
Late Singer, The.

March.
May 1st Tomorrow.
Memory of April.
Shadow, The.
She Who Turns Her Head.
Spring and All.
Spring is Here Again, Sir.
Spring Song.
Spring Strains.
Two Aspects of April.
Wordsworth. 3.13: Translation of Horace's
Ode III, xiii.
In Part from Moschus's Lament for Bion.
Lines Written in Early Spring.
Ode Composed on May Morning.
Ode to Lycoris; May, 1817.
Poor Robin.
Stray Pleasures.
Thoughts on the Seasons.
To a Snow-Drop.
To Lady Beaumont.
To May.
To My Sister.
To S.H.
To the Cuckoo.
Vernal Ode.
Written in March [While Resting on the
Bridge at the Foot of Brother's Water].
Wright, James. March.
Spring Images.
Two Spring Charms.
Witches Waken the Natural World in Spring.
Zukofsky. Ah spring, when with a thaw of
blue.
And Without.
Chrysanthemum.
Ears beringed with fuzz.
—"Her Soil's Birth."
Home for Aged Bomb Throwers—U.S.S.R.
I walk in the old street.
Immature Pebbles.
Last cigarette / a companion, A.
Stubbing the cloud-fields—the searchlight,
high.
Warm gale, a dose of spring—revert to the
pores.

Springfield, Illinois
Lindsay. On the Building of Springfield.
Soul of the City Receives the Gift of the Holy
Spirit, The.

Springs
Berry. Springs, The.
Gunn. Geyser, The.
Herrick. How Springs Came First.
Hugo. Hot Springs.
Snyder. Spring, The.
Wordsworth. Suggested by Mr W. Westall's
Views of the Caves, etc., in Yorkshire.
Wroth. Sonnet 44: "How fast thou hast'st (O
spring) with sweetest speed."

Spruce Trees
Ammons. Crow Ride.
Carruth. Think not of chaste snow always.
Rukeyser. Blue Spruce.
Schuyler. Buried at Springs.
Light from Canada.

Spying and Spies
Auden. Control of the passes was, he saw, the
key.
Secret Agent, The.
Bukowski. Breakout.
Cohen. Field Commander Cohen.
You Went to Work.
De la Mare. Peeping Tom.
Dunn. What They Wanted.
Jonson. On Spies.
Kipling. Spies' March, The.
Lawrence. Police Spies.
Morgan. His Last Case.
Silverstein. For Sale.
Wilbur. Agent, The.

Squash (botany)
Galvin. Fall Squashes.
Wilbur. Melongène.

Squid
Nash. Squid, The.

Squires
Chaucer. Introduction to the Squire's Tale.

Squirrels
Ammons. Bulletin.
Twangs & Little Twists.
Winter Sanctuaries.
Creeley. Love ("Thing comes / of itself,
The").
Dickinson. Saucer holds a Cup, A.
Eberhart. On a Squirrel Crossing the Road in
Autumn, in New England.
Emerson. Fable: "Mountain and the squirrel,
The."
Fletcher. Midwinter Sunset.
McAuley. For the Humanism Class at
Fairchild Airforce Base, in Place of a Session
on the Book of Job.
McGrath. What We Think We Know.
Nash. Squirrel, The.
O'Hara. Pastoral Dialogue, A.
Schuyler. Deep Winter.
Updike. Squirrels Mating.
Wright, James. Today I Was So Happy, So I
Made this Poem.
Yeats. Appointment, An.
To a Squirrel at Kyle-na-no.
Young. Squirrels.

Sri Lanka
Merton. Kandy Express.

Stables
Gunn. Phaedra in the Farm House.
Turco. Stable, The.

Stained Glass
Hardy. Young Glass-Stainer, The.
Kipling. Chartres Windows.
Lewis. Belief.
Scott. Melrose by Moonlight.

Stairs
Hughes, Langston. Mother to Son.
Lindsay. Sweet Briars of the Stairways.

Stalin, Joseph
Cohen. Future, The.
Dunn. Introduction to the 20th Century.
Lowell. Stalin.

Standish, Miles
Longfellow. Courtship of Miles Standish, The.

Starfish
Bly. Starfish, The.
Ford. In the tentacles.
Kinnell. Daybreak.
Knott. Poem (the Starfish One).
Liddy. As in poetry.
Oliver. Starfish.
Pack. Secrets.

Starlings
Hardy. Starlings on the Roof.
Hayden. Plague of Starlings, A.
Hesketh. Starlings.
Schuyler. So Good.
Smith, Stevie. British Song, A.
Wilbur. Writer, The.
Williams, William Carlos. Aginst the Sky.
Maneuver [or Manoeuvre], The.

Stars
Auden. More Loving One, The.
Berry. Star, The.
Blake. Song: "How sweet I roamed [or
roam'd] from field to field."
To the Evening Star.
Brontë. Stars.
Browning, Elizabeth Barrett. Heaven and
Earth.
Romance of the Ganges, A.
Romaunt of Margret, The.
Browning, Robert. My Star.
Byron. On the Star of "The Legion of
Honour."
Campion. Song, A: "Come away; bring thy
golden theft."
Carroll, Jim. Birth and Death of the Sun, The.
For John Donne.
Prologue: "Starting with little in mind."
Tenth Try, The.
Carruth. They gave me in trust.
Ceravolo. Star Song.
Clough. Uranus.

Cohen. Cross Didn't Fall on Me, A.
Coleridge. 'Twas not a mist, nor was it quite a cloud.
Creeley. Colors.
Cullen. To Endymion.
Cummings. All stars are(and not one star only)love.
I was considering how.
Over us if(as what dusk becomes).
De la Mare. Birthnight: To F., The.
Flight, The.
Night.
O Childish Mind!
Dickinson. Moon upon her fluent Route, The.
My best Acquaintances are those.
Not what the stars have done.
Outer—from the Inner, The.
Doolittle. Sirius: / what mystery is this?
Two Poems for Christmas, 1937.
Dunbar. Love Is a Star.
Starry Night, A.
Eberhart. Looking At The Stars.
Looking at the Stars.
Emerson. Atom from atom yawns as far.
Earth, The.
I have supped with the gods tonight.
If he go apart.
On that night the poet went.
Teach me your mood, O patient stars!
To the Shah, from Enweri ("From thy worth and weight the stars gravitate").
To the Shah, from Enweri ("Not in their houses stand the stars").
Wisp & meteor nightly falling.
Everson. Orion.
Ferlinghetti. Plough of Time, The.
Rebels, The.
Fletcher. Night of Stars.
Stars, The.
Towards the North Star.
Fox. Cetus, a Letter from Jonah.
Finding the Andromeda Nebula.
Lyre, The.
Names and Travelers of the Milky Way.
Poem for My Mother.
Frost. Bravado.
Canis Major.
Literate Farmer and the Planet Venus, The.
On Making Certain Anything Has Happened.
Skeptic.
Star in a Stoneboat, A.
Stars.
Take Something Like a Star.
Gallagher. Rijl.
Glück. Under Taurus.
Gunn. Blackie, the Electric Rembrandt.
My Sad Captains.
Hardy. Waiting Both.
Hayden. Stars.
Herbert. Star[re], The.
Hesketh. No Reply at Christmas.
Hewitt. Atlas.
Nebula.
Omens and Auguries.
Hoffman. Far-Off Light.
Hopkins. His gilded rowels.
How looks the night? There does not miss a star.
Lover's Stars, The.
Night's lantern / Pointed with piercèd lights, and breaks of rays.
Sky minted into golden sequins, The.
Star most spiritual, principal, preeminent, A.
Starlight Night, The.
Stars waving their indivisible rays.
Stars were packed so close that night, The.
Housman. Stars, I have seen them fall.
Hughes, Ted. Fire-Eater.
Hugo. Lecture.
Jarrell. Evening Star, The.
Lament: "All is far."
Jeffers. At the near approach of a star..huge tides.
Epic Stars, The.
My Dear Love.
Nova.
October Week-End.

Polar ice-caps are melting, the mountain glaciers, The.
Keats. Bright Star! Would I Were Steadfast as Thou Art.
Kinnell. Daybreak.
Kipling. Astrologer's Song, An.
Penalty, The.
Larkin. Far Out.
Lawrence. In a Boat.
Like the Green Candles of Malintzi.
Lord of the Morning Star.
Son of the Morning Star.
Lewis. Stars seem gilded nipples.
Under each starry leafless tree.
Liddy. Sergeant Valentine Function, at Hollyfort.
Lindsay. He Nears the Goal.
Indian Girl Tells the Hero Where to Go to Get the Laughing Bell, The.
Star of My Heart.
Longfellow. Occultation of Orion, The.
Lorde. Separation.
Lovelace. Paradox, A.
Lowry. And, when you go—much as a meteor.
Byzantium: Or Where the Great Life Begins.
Doggerel.
Happiness.
Stars have simple paradigms, The.
Very dark and clear with an onshore wind.
MacLeish. Epistle to Be Left in the Earth.
Pole Star.
Signal, The.
MacNeice. Star-Gazer.
Meinke. Fixed Stars.
Fourth of July.
Meredith. Lucifer in Starlight.
Meditation under Stars.
Star Sirius, The.
Union in Disseverance.
When I saw the jewelled girdle tied at her waist I thought of.
Winter Heavens.
Merton. Fighters.
Glass Orchard.
Secret of the Burning Stars, The.
Tonight There Is a Showing of Champion Lights.
Muldoon. Ontario.
Nemerov. Speculation.
Pack. Stellar Thanksgiving.
Patchen. Stars go to sleep so peacefully, The.
Plath. Stars over the Dordogne.
Poe. Evening Star.
Prince. Then came a time of great guilt, that I inhabited.
Raine. Banked winter cloud.
Star of Bethlehem.
Rich. Planetarium.
Rossetti. If stars dropped out of heaven, / And if flowers took their place.
Song of the Star, The.
What do the stars do / Up in the sky.
Rukeyser. Cats and a Cock.
Darkness Music.
Song: The Star in the Nets of Heaven.
Sandburg. Baby Toes.
Bright Conversation with Saint-Ex.
Broken Hearted Soprano.
Cadenza.
In the long flat panhandle of Texas.
Monkey of Stars.
Offering and Rebuff.
Silver Point.
Special Starlight.
Star Silver.
Stars.
Summer Stars.
There Are Different Gardens.
We Have Gone Through Great Rooms Together.
Yellow Evening Star.
Schwartz. When I Remember the Advent.
Shelley. To a Star.
Sidney. Sonnet 26: "Though dusty wits dare scorn astrology."

Sonnet 48: "Soul's joy, bend not those morning stars from me."
Silverstein. Flag.
Smith, Charlotte. By the Same. To the North Star.
Sorrentino. Lost in the Stars.
Stevens. Chocorua to Its Neighbor.
Dezembrum.
Stevenson. Escape at Bedtime.
Infinite shining heavens, The.
Song: "Light foot and tight foot."
Suckling. Bright star o' th' lower orb, twinkling inviter.
Updike. Skyey Developments.
White Dwarf.
Walcott. Star.
Warren. Stargazing.
Whitman. On the Beach at Night.
On the Beach at Night Alone.
When I Heard the Learn'd Astronomer.
Wilbur. Games One.
In the Field.
Star in the sky. How many words and tears, A.
Under Cygnus.
Williams, William Carlos. At Night.
El Hombre.
Flight to the City.
Wordsworth. Composed by the Side of Grasmere Lake.
I Watch, and Long Have Watched [with Calm Regret].
It is no spirit who from heaven hath flown.
Pilgrim's Dream; or, The Star and the Glow-Worm, The.
Stars Are Mansions Built by Nature's Hand, The.
To the Evening Star over Grasmere Water.
Wright, James. To the Evening Star: Central Minnesota.
Wroth. Song: "Birds doe sing, day doth apeere, The."
Sonnet 41: "You blessed starrs which doe heavns glory show."
Young. How Stars Start.
Zimmer. I Go Out in the Long Nights.
Zukofsky. And looking to where shone Orion. Memory of V. I. Ulianov.
See also **Astronomy and Astronomers.**

Statistics
Gildner. Statistics.
Hoffman. Open Letter, Returning a Questionnaire Unanswered.

Statue of Liberty. *see* **Liberty, Statue of.**

Statues
Atwood. My beautiful wooden leader.
Berryman. Boston Common.
Statue, The.
Bogan. Statue and Birds.
Browning, Robert. Protus.
Statue and the Bust, The.
Bukowski. Experience.
Clark. Statue.
Crane. To the Empress Josephine's Statue.
Creeley. Figures, The.
Statue, The.
Cummings. Great Dante stands in Florence, looking down.
Eberhart. Angels, The.
Anxiety I Felt in Guanajuato, The.
Statue of Liberty.
Fisher. From the 'Town Guide.'
Haines. Old, root-crowded cemetery, An.
Hardy. Statue of Liberty, The.
Hartley. Queen Nefertiti—Small Fragment of Nose and Mouth Only.
Same Fragment—Second Look.
Herrick. To His Honoured Kinsman, Sir Richard Stone.
Hewitt. Iron and Stone.
Moscow Moment.
Hoffman. In the Graeco-Roman Room.
Old Bug up There.
Kunitz. At the Porch of the Caryatids.
Lieberman. God's Measurements.
Lindsay. Statue of Old Andrew Jackson, The.
Lorde. Sacrifice.

MacNeice. Stylite.
Merrill. Bronze.
Santo.
Merton. Idol of Sarapis, The.
Nemerov. Don Juan to the Statue.
Statues in the Public Gardens, The.
Neruda. Island (VII), The.
Island (VIII), The.
Island (XII), The.
Men (XIX), The.
Oppen. Giovanni's *Rape of the Sabine Women*
at Wildenstein's.
Whitman: "April 19, 1864."
Plath. Colossus, The.
Touch-and-Go.
Pope. On the Statue of *Cleopatra*, Made into
a Fountain by *Leo* the Tenth.
Raine. Statues.
Sandburg. Cheap Rent.
Has-Been, The.
Shapiro. Statue of Liberty.
Shelley. Ozymandias [of Egypt].
Spender. Cyril Connolly.
Stevens. Dance of the Macabre Mice.
Tomlinson. In Verdi Square.
Thunder in Tuscany.
Wilbur. Statues.
Wordsworth. Lady Whom You here Behold,
The.
Prithee, Gentle Lady, List.
Yeats. Statues, The.

Steak
Creeley. Naughty Boy.

Steam Baths. see Baths and Bathing.

Steam Rollers and Steam Rolling
Moore. To a Steam Roller.

Steamers
Fletcher. Steamers.
Kipling. McAndrew's Hymn.
Lowry. After Labour Day.
MacLeish. Steamboat Whistle, The.
Nash. Song for Pier Something or Other.
See also **Ships and Shipbuilding.**

Steel
Carruth. Listen, in night's last tender hour.
Hartley. Laughter of Steel 1.
Laughter of Steel 2.
Sandburg. Bar of steel--it is only, A.
Laughing Blue Steel.
Prayers of Steel.
Smoke and Steel.
Tomlinson. Etruria Vale.
Steel.
Williams, Charles Kenneth. Hooks.
See also **Iron.**

Steeples
Frost. Steeple on the House, A.
Moore. Steeple-Jack, The.
Williams, William Carlos. To a Solitary
Disciple.

Steers. see Oxen.

Stein, Gertrude
Lowry. Those Coke to Newcastle Blues.
Muldoon. More a Man Has the More a Man
Wants, The.

Stenographers. see Scribes; Secretaries.

Stepfathers and Stepmothers
Smith, Stevie. Papa Love Baby.
Whittier. Kathleen.

Stephen, Saint
Smart. St. Stephen.

Stepmothers. see Stepfathers and Stepmothers.

Sterne, Laurence
Muldoon. Yggdrasill.

Stevedores. see Longshoremen.

Stevens, Wallace
Dobyns. Party, The.
Duncan. Erecting beyond the boundaries of all
government.
Eberhart. At The Canoe Club.
Roethke. Rouse for Stevens, A.
Schuyler. Fauré Ballade, The.

Stevenson, Robert Louis
Kipling. Child's Garden, A.
Lowry. On Reading R.L.S.

Still Lifes
Atwood. Against Still Life.
Sandburg. Still Life.
Smith, Patti. Georgia O'Keeffe.
Sorrentino. Everything Is a Still-Life.
Stevens. Dish of Peaches in Russia, A.
Tomlinson. Fruit, for sculpture.
Given Grace, A.
Montage.
Paring the Apple.
View, The.
Turco. Meetinghouse, The.
Wilbur. Objects.
Zukofsky. Che Di Lor Suona Su Nella Tua
Vita.

Stockholm, Sweden
Sandburg. Mohammed Bek Hadjetlache.
Savoir Faire.
Two Items.
Young. Dear Old Stockholm.

Stoicism
Brontë. Old Stoic, The.
Dickinson. It might be lonelier.
Edmunds. Letter to Jeffrey Gustavson.
Lovelace. Sir Thomas Wortley's Sonnet
Answered.
McNeill. Stoic (Circa 1907).
Rossetti. Study. (A Soul), A.
Schwartz. "O New York boy, this is Life, Life
in which."

Stonecutting and Stonecutters
Davie. "Sculpture" of Rhyme, The.
To a Brother in the Mystery.
Fisher. Emblem.
Hewitt. For Stonecutters.
Jeffers. Old Stone-Mason, The.
To the Stone-Cutters.
Levertov. Stonecarver's Poem, The.
Wright, James. In a Viennese Cemetery.

Stonehenge, England
Lowry. Shakespeare's house is safe and sound.
Rich. Dark lintels, the blue and foreign stones,
The.
Wordsworth. Salisbury Plain and Stonehenge.

Stones and Rocks
Ammons. Digging Wonder.
Pebble's Story.
Stoning Down.
Atwood. Some Objects of Wood and Stone.
Auden. Stone Walls.
Stone Walls.
Berry. Dance, A.
Stones, The.
Bishop. In the Middle of the Road.
Carruth. Almanach du Printemps Vivarois.
Essay on Stone.
La colline du mystère. Solitary here. The
stone.
Naming for Love.
On Canann Mountain Meadow.
Song of the Two Crows.
Stone, The.
Cooper. Rock Climbing.
Creeley. After Mallarmé.
Divisions.
"I Keep to Myself Such Measures."
Poem, A: "If the water forms."
Davie. Twilight on the Waste Lands.
De la Mare. Epitaph, An: "Last, Stone, a little
yet."
Taciturn, The.
Dickey, James. Six, The.
Dickinson. How happy is the little Stone.
Too cold is this.
"Dylan." Get Your Rocks Off!
Eberhart. Big Rock.
La Crosse at Ninety Miles an Hour.
Sphinx.
Edmunds. Stone.
Emerson. Rubies.
Upon a rock yet uncreate.
Fox. Sentence, A.
Frost. Of the Stones of the Place.
Graves. Consortium of Stones.
Haines. Eye in the Rock, The.
Nine thousand feet in the Rockies.
On a bend in the road near St. Mary.

Hall. Granite and Grass.
Waters.
Hartley. Stones to Wind.
Topaz of the Sixties, The.
Heaney. Granite Chip.
Sandstone Keepsake.
Hewitt. Stone.
Hughes, Ted. Still-Life.
Stone, The.
Hugo. Blue Stone.
Brown Stone.
Clachard.
Gold Stone.
Gray Stone.
Green Stone.
Red Stone.
Jeffers. To the Stone-Cutters.
Kipling. By the Hoof of the Wild Goat.
Levine. Breath.
Renaming the Kings.
Liddy. Island / Of the hungry bishop, The.
Lowry. Child may find no words for its
sorrow, A.
McAuley. Creed.
"MacDiarmid." Crystals like Blood.
On a Raised Beach.
McGrath. Passages.
McNeill. Grave Creek Inscribed Stone, The.
Matthews. Flood Plain.
Olson. Other Than.
Stone and Flower Series.
Plath. Child's Park Stones.
Raine. Rock.
Stone on High Crag.
Summit, The.
Roethke. Harsh Country, The.
Rolfe. Cell, The.
Sandburg. Chasers.
Slabs of the Sunburnt West.
Shelton. All day I lifted stones.
How to Amuse a Stone.
Stones, The.
Silverstein. Joey.
Stone Telling.
Simic. Stone.
Stuart. Spring Song.
Sticks and Stones.
Tomlinson. In Defence of Metaphysics.
Stone Speech.
Updike. Phenomena.
Warren. At the Hour of the Breaking of the
Rocks.
Interjection #2: Caveat.
Rebuke of the Rocks.
Wilbur. From the Lookout Rock.
Giacometti.
On the Marginal Way.
Thyme Flowering among Rocks.
Two Voices in a Meadow.
Williams, William Carlos. Rock-Old Dogma,
The.
Wordsworth. Inscription on a Rock at Rydal
Mount.
Mark the concentrated hazels that enclose.
To Joanna.
Who fancied what a pretty sight.
Zukofsky. For Zadkine.

Storms
Auden. Before.
February Dawn, A.
First Things First.
Job.
Berryman. Of all that weeks-long day, though
call it back.
Your shining—where?—rays my wide room
with gold.
Bishop. Electrical Storm.
Little Exercise.
Norther—Key West, A.
Brontë. How loud the storm sounds round the
Hall!
Browning, Robert. Adam, Lilith, and Eve.
Burns. Strathallan's Lament.
Tam o' Shanter [A Tale].
Winter Night, A.
Byron. Julian [A Fragment].
Stanzas: "Chill and mirk is the nightly blast."

Carroll, Jim. Cold Faces.
"Carroll, Lewis." Sailor's Wife, The.
Carruth. Listen.
  Mountain Cabin, The.
  Three sixteen seventy.
Cowper. Thunder Storm, A.
Crane. Echoes.
  Eternity.
Cummings. N(o)w / the / how / dis(appeared
  cleverly)world.
Davie. Admiral to His Lady, The.
  North Sea, in a Snowstorm, The.
  Remembering the 'Thirties.
  Sing unto the Lord a New Song.
De la Mare. Macbeth.
Dickinson. Awful Tempest mashed the air,
  An.
  Cap of Lead across the sky, A.
  Clouds their Backs together laid, The.
  Glee—The great storm is over.
  It sounded as if the Streets were running.
  It struck me—every Day.
  Symptom of the Gale, The.
  There is a tall—pale snow storm.
  Wind begun to knead the Grass, The.
  Wind drew off, The.
  Wind took up the Northern Things, The.
Donne. Storm[e], The.
Doolittle. Storm.
Dunbar. Changing Time.
  Right's Security.
  Rising of the Storm, The.
Dunn. Ordinary Days.
Eberhart. Contend with steepness, the dark air.
  Labour them, these drenched heights.
  Scouring.
  Sea Storm.
Edmunds. Like A Green Branch.
Emerson. Seemed, tho' the soft sheen all
  enchants.
  Snow-Storm, The.
Everson. Storm-Surge.
  We in the Fields.
Fletcher. Thunderstorm in the Ozarks.
  Tide of Storms.
Ford. Poem for Paul Eluard.
Frost. Line-Storm Song, A.
  Lodged.
  Our Singing Strength.
  Snow.
  Storm Fear.
Graves. Apple Island.
  Rhea.
  Sirocco at Deyá.
  Window Pane, The.
Hardy. Night-Time in Mid-Fall.
  She Hears the Storm.
  Thunderstorm in Town, A.
Hartley. Three Loving Men.
Hayden. Electrical Storm.
Herbert. Storm, The.
Herrick. His Hope or Sheet-Anchor.
Hewitt. Storm, The.
  Turban, The.
Holmes. Storm in the Ozarks.
Hopkins. Strike, churl; hurl, cheerless wind,
  then; heltering hail.
  Why if it be so, for the dismal morn.
Hughes, Ted. Wind.
Hugo. Bay of Sad Loss.
  How to Use a Storm.
  Night with Cindy at Heitman's, A.
  Point No Point.
  Storm in Acquafredda.
  Triangle for Green Men.
  Trumpan.
Jarrell. Night before the Night before
  Christmas, The.
  November Ghosts, The.
Jeffers. Gale in April.
  Storm blowing up, rain and dark weather and
  the roaring wind, The.
Kinnell. Westport.
Kipling. Before a Midnight Breaks in Storm.
  Egg-Shell, The.
  Song of the Red War-Boat.

Storm Cone, The.
  When the cabin port-holes are dark and green.
Lawrence. Lightning.
  Love Storm.
  Passing-Bell, A.
  Storm in the Black Forest.
Lieberman. Santana.
  Skin-Flying into the Storm Center.
Lindsay. Storm-Flower, The.
Lorde. Oaxaca.
  Suspension.
Lowry. Contemplation of Dead Reckoning.
  Danish Sailor's Song.
  Lighthouse invites the storm and lights it, The.
  Lying awake beside a sleeping girl.
  Oh Storms / Oh The Seal!
  Outside was the roar of the sea and the
  darkness.
  Reflection to Windward.
"MacDiarmid." Dying Earth, The.
  Wind-bags, The.
McGrath. History.
MacLeish. April in November.
  But men have known.
  November.
Melville. Misgivings.
Meredith. Hard Weather.
  Him loved she. Lo, now was he veiled.
  Inspiration of the Great West Wind, The.
  Roar through the Tall Twin Elm-Trees, A.
  Shipwreck of Idomeneus, The.
  There fell a sudden rain.
  When stormy day is cold & gray.
Merton. Spring Storm.
  Storm at Night, The.
Morrison. Hurricane and Eclipse.
Nash. Watched Example Never Boils, A.
Nemerov. Brainstorm.
  Lightning Storm on Fuji.
  Storm Windows.
  Sunday at the End of Summer.
Oliver. Lightning.
Plath. Insolent Storm Strikes at the Skull.
Ransom. Miriam Tazewell.
Rich. Attention.
  Eastport to Block Island.
  Storm Warnings.
Roethke. Storm, The.
Rossetti. His Banner over Me Was Love.
  Love and Death.
Rukeyser. Jetty. Dover, The.
  Ringling.
Sandburg. Blizzard Notes.
  Storms Begin Far Back.
  Way of the World, The.
Sarton. Snow Light, The.
Schuyler. Crocus Night.
  Running Footsteps.
Schwartz. Famous Resort in Late Autumn,
  The.
Sexton. Letter Written During a January
  Northeaster.
Shelley. Vision of the Sea, A.
Smith, Charlotte. Elegy: "Dark gathering
  clouds involve the threatening skies."
  Pilgrim, The.
  Written in a Tempestuous Night, on the Coast
  of Sussex.
  Written September 1791, During a Remarkable
  Thunder Storm, in which the Moon Was
  Perfectly Clear, While the Tempest Gathered
  in Various Directions Near the Earth.
Snyder. It.
Spenser. After, at sea a tall ship did appeare.
  Much richer then that vessell seem'd to bee.
  Then did a sharped spyre of diamond bright.
  Then heavenly branches did I see arise.
Stafford. Found in a Storm.
Stevenson. Epistle to Charles Baxter.
  It blows a snowing gale in the winter of the
  year.
  Last night we had a thunderstorm in style.
  Moon is sinking—the tempestuous weather,
  The.
  Storm.
  Stormy Nights.
  To the Stormy Petrel.

Wind is without there and howls in the trees,
  The.
Swift. Description of a City Shower, A.
  Storm, The.
Thomas. Shall Gods Be Said to Thump The
  Clouds.
Tomlinson. After the Storm.
  Awakening, The.
  Insufficiency of Earth, An.
  Thunder in Tuscany.
Walcott. Before that thundercloud breaks from
  its hawsers.
  Dark August.
  Wind-scraped headland, a sludgy, dishwater
  sea, A.
Warren. Summer Storm (Circa 1916), and
  God's Grace.
Whitman. Patrolling Barnegat.
  Proud Music of the Storm.
Whittier. Palatine, The.
  Sisters, The.
  Storm on Lake Asquam.
Wilbur. March.
  Storm in April, A.
Williams, Charles Kenneth. Baby, I don't
  want.
  Snow: I.
  Storm, The.
Williams, William Carlos. Dark Day, The.
  Lady speaks, The.
  Spring Storm.
  Storm, The.
Wordsworth. Composed During a Storm.
  Fragment of a "Gothic" Tale.
  I love upon a stormy night.
  Whirl-blast from behind the hill, A.
Wright, James. At Thomas Hardy's Birthplace,
  1953.
  From a Bus Window in Central Ohio, Just
  before a Thunder Shower.
  Snowstorms in the Midwest.
  Stormclouds / give their morose faces to the
  sea.
Yeats. Mad as the Mist and Snow.
  Pity of Love, The.
Zimmer. Entering the Storm, Unable to Swim,
  Zimmer, Rollo, and Cecil Are Saved.

See also **Blizzards; Tornadoes; Hurricanes.**

Storytelling and Storytellers
Angelou. When I Think about Myself.
Atwood. It's the story that counts.
  True Stories.
Auden. In the Nursery.
Berryman. How far upon these songs with my
  strict wrist.
"Carroll, Lewis." Dedication: "All in the
  golden afternoon."
  Dedication: "Child of the pure unclouded
  brow."
Carruth. Winter's tale is told in, A.
  Your dream: / His name was Hilarity but he
  never laughed.
Chaucer. Canon's Yeoman's Prologue, The.
  Clerk's Prologue, The.
  Cook's Prologue, The.
  Epilogue to the Nun's Priest's Tale.
  Franklin's Prologue, The.
  Introduction to the Man of Law's Tale.
  Introduction to the Pardoner's Tale.
  Introduction to the Squire's Tale.
  Manciple's Prologue, The.
  Parson's Prologue, The.
  Prologue of the Nun's Priest's Tale, The.
  Prologue to Sir Thopas.
Clark. Tire, The.
Coleridge. Love.
Creeley. Hero.
  Story, The.
  Than I.
  They Say.
  Think.
De la Mare. Martha.
Dickinson. Ended, ere it begun.
Dove. Roast Possum.
Dunbar. Cabin Tale, A.
Dunn. Parable of the Fictionist.

Ford. Andromache, I think of you! / When the war goes on forever.
Gallagher. Boat Ride.
Galvin. Old Woman Telling Another Version.
Graves. Devil's Advice to Story-Tellers, The.
To Juan at the Winter Solstice.
Hall. Stories.
Hewitt. Ballad, The.
Curfew Tower, The.
Fairy-Man at Layde, The.
Fairy Thresher, The.
Fame.
Gentle Bush, The.
Golden Boy, The.
Jenny Geddes.
MacDonnell's Question.
Ossian's Grave, Lubitavish, County Antrim.
This Narrative.
Word, The.
Hoffman. Tale-Teller, The.
Hughes, Langston. Aunt Sue's Stories.
Jong. Artist as an Old Man, The.
Kipling. Captive, The.
Coiner, The.
To James Whitcomb Riley.
Knott. Keeper, The.
Lieberman. Saltcod Red.
Lindsay. Yet Gentle Will the Griffin Be.
Lowry. Wolf, wolf, cried the boy in the fable.
Markson. Hartnett in Worcester.
Merrill. Kostas Tympakianákis.
Muldoon. Frog, The.
Nash. Fee Fi Ho Hum, No Wonder Baby Sucks Her Thumb.
There Were Giants in Those Days or Maybe There Weren't.
Olson. As I went in and out I heard pieces.
Pack. Coincidence.
Paley. Poem About Storytelling, A.
"Reed." Ferryboat Bill.
That's the Story of My Life.
Robinson. Captain Craig.
Lost Anchors.
Stafford's Cabin.
Rolfe. Bequest.
Rossetti. If the sun could tell us half / That he hears and sees.
Sing me a song— / What shall I sing?
St. John. Gin.
Sandburg. Deep in the dusty chattels of the tombs.
Fire Pages.
Iglits and His Wife.
Legends.
One of the Cherokees in Oklahoma, having a million or so from oil.
They have yarns / Of a skyscraper so tall they had to put hinges.
Who made Paul Bunyan, who gave him birth as a myth, who joked him.
Sexton. Gold Key, The.
Rowing.
Story for Rose on the Midnight Flight to Boston, A.
Wallflower.
Sidney. Sonnet 45: "Stella oft sees the very face of woe."
Simic. Bedtime Story.
Point, The.
Sorrentino. Beautiful Soup.
Fiction, The.
Open Boat, The.
Stevenson. Et Tu In Arcadia Vixisti.
Land of Story-Books, The.
Of Schooners, Islands, and Maroons.
Picture-Books in Winter.
Tales of Arabia.
Woodman, The.
Tomlinson. Dialectic.
Wakoski. How Do You Tell a Story?
Walcott. Man Who Loved Islands, The.
Warren. Dragon Country: To Jacob Boehme.
Tell Me a Story.
Whittier. Tent on the Beach, The.
Wilbur. Fable, A.
Folk Tune.

Williams, Charles Kenneth. Herakles.
Near the Haunted Castle.
Wordsworth. Motto Intended for Poems on the Naming of Places.
Yau. Genghis Chan: Private Eye III.
Yeats. Grey Rock, The.
Under the Moon.

Stowe, Harriet Beecher
Dunbar. Harriet Beecher Stowe.
Schuyler. Reunion, A.
Whittier. Greeting, A.

Strafford, Thomas Wentworth, 1st Earl of
Prince. Strafford.

Strangers
Auden. At the Maison Lyons.
Before.
Berg. Behind Us.
Brontë. And now the house-dog stretched once more.
Bunting. Orotava Road, The.
Cohen. Stranger Song, The.
Crane. Tunnel, The.
Cummings. Once like a spark.
De la Mare. Exile.
Galliass, The.
Mistress Fell.
Peeping Tom.
Stranger, The.
Stranger, The.
Three Strangers, The.
Who?
Donne. Tale of a Citizen and His Wife, A.
Dunn. Woman on Edgehill Road, The.
Ferlinghetti. Ladakh Buddhess Biker.
Frost. Love and a Question.
Gallagher. Hug, The.
Gardner. Loud Song, Mother, A.
This Neighborhood.
Garrigue. Stranger, The.
Graves. Fortunate Child.
Gunn. First Meeting with a Possible Mother-in-Law.
Hacker. His Wife at Bellevue.
Heaney. Making Strange.
Herrick. Once Seen, and No More.
Hesketh. Limbo.
Hewitt. Diptera.
Fair Game.
From the Chinese of Wang Li Shi.
In a Lurgan Pub.
Man from Malabar, The.
Man from the Mountains, The.
Salute.
Search, The.
Tinker's Answer, The.
To Piraeus.
Kinnell. Flying Home.
Kipling. Stranger, The.
Larkin. Strangers.
MacNeice. Restaurant Car.
When the stranger came out of the night.
Markson. Traveler's Tale.
Merton. When night falls / beat one drum / in honor of night.
With great speed I set the young man free.
Morrison. L.A. Woman.
Pack. Coincidence.
Paley. Stranger calling a dog whistled, A.
Patchen. Stranger, The.
Piercy. Learning to manage the process.
Robinson. Flammonde.
Fleming Helphenstine.
Sandburg. Two Strangers Breakfast.
Sarton. Strangers.
Shelton. Encounter.
Strangers.
Sorrentino. They Die Over and Over. In the Movies.
Stuart. My Hostess at the Renovated Inn.
Timeshare.
Turco. Blood Deeper than Night.
Whitman. This Moment Yearning and Thoughtful.
To a Stranger.
To You ("Stranger, if you passing meet me and desire to speak to me, why should you not speak to me?").

Wilbur. Transit.
Williams, Charles Kenneth. On the Other Hand.
Young. Manhattan March, The 1970s.
Sing a Song of Singapore.

Strawberries
Millay. Strawberry Shrub, The.
Paley. False strawberry is.
When the wild strawberry leaves turn.
Plath. Bitter Strawberries.
Wordsworth. Foresight.

Streams. see **Brooks and Streams.**

Street People. see **Homeless, The.**

Street Performers
Ashbery. Street Musicians.
Cummings. At the head of this street a gasping organ is waving moth-eaten.
It is winter a moon in the afternoon.

Streetcars
Cohen. Streetcars.
Hewitt. Double-Ended Tram, The.
Levine. On the Birth of Good & Evil During the Long Winter of '28.
Lowry. Fisherman's Return.
Sandburg. Halsted Street Car.

Streets
Angelou. Letter to an Aspiring Junkie.
Bishop. Along Galeana Street.
Crane. Euclid Avenue.
Creeley. Colors.
Place, A.
Return.
Cummings. As usual i did not find him in cafes,the more dissolute atmosphere.
At the head of this street a gasping organ is waving moth-eaten.
Dobyns. Street, The.
Dunn. Beneath the Sidewalk.
Desire.
Eberhart. Fragment of New York, 1929.
Fisher. Butterton Ford.
Galvin. Assembling a Street.
Gunn. Release, The.
San Francisco Streets.
Hewitt. Mile-Long Street, The.
River Streets, The.
Hughes, Langston. Dive.
Larkin. Street Lamps.
Lawrence. Street Lamps.
Levertov. Whisper, The.
Levine. On the Corner.
These Streets.
McAuley. Spokane Perspective.
MacNeice. Street Scene.
Nemerov. Frozen City, The.
O'Hara. Step Away from Them, A.
Olson. Stone and Flower Series.
Owen. Six o'clock in Princes Street.
St. John. Avenues, The.
Sandburg. Streets Too Old.
Schuyler. Back.
Shapiro. Manhole Covers.
Tomlinson. Mirror in the Roadway, The.
Williams, William Carlos. Attic Which Is Desire, The.
Term, The.
Yau. Avenue of Americans.

See also **Roads.**

Strength
Arnold. Growing Old.
Auden. Pick a quarrel, go to war.
Though thy rafters are grown rotten.
Bly. Indigo Bunting, The.
Bogan. Single Sonnet.
Browning, Elizabeth Barrett. Weakest Thing, The.
Bukowski. John Dillinger Marches On.
Bunting. Hymn to Alias Thor.
Burns. Prayer, under the Pressure of Violent Anguish, A.
Carruth. Sonnet: The Recollected Actual Voices of Romanticism.
Cohen. True Love Leaves No Traces.
Coleridge. Eagle and the Tortoise, The.
O Spirit blest! / Whether th' eternal Throne around.

Creeley. Song, The: "It still makes sense."
Cullen. Minutely Hurt.
  To the Swimmer.
Dickinson. I hope you may sometime be.
  Not to discover weakness is.
Dunbar. Warrior's Prayer, The.
Dunn. Sudden Light and the Trees, The.
  That Saturday Without a Car.
Eberhart. Birth of the Spirit, The.
Edmunds. Black Bull, The.
Emerson. Compensation ("Wings of Time are black and white, The").
  I leave the book, I leave the wine.
  Samson stark at Dagon's knee.
  Vain against him were hostile blows.
  With the key of the secret he marches faster.
Fletcher. Black Rock, The.
Ford. Butterfly and the Bull, The.
  Rise to capture the.
Garrigue. For J.
Graves. Lion Lover.
  Superstition.
Gunn. Diagrams.
  Exercise, The.
Herbert. Constancy.
Herrick. By Use Comes Easinesse.
  Christian Militant.
  Upon Julias Recovery.
Hewitt. Mary Hagan, Islandmagee, 1919.
  Providence 1.
Hughes, Ted. Lark begins to go up, The.
Jeffers. Contemplation of the Sword.
  Give Your Heart to the Hawks.
  Rock and Hawk.
Joseph. Birthday Poem.
Kipling. Departure, A.
  Preface, A: "To all to whom this little book may come."
Lawrence. Hills, The.
Lovelace. Valiant Love.
Lowry. May well befall the common weal.
  What Sigbj[do]orn Said.
  What the Irish Soldier Said.
McNeill. Sol Brady.
Meredith. Angel, be ye ne'er in doubt, An.
  Burden of Strength, The.
  Lady C. M., The.
Notley. 30th Birthday.
Olson. Double, double, root and branch.
Oppen. Kind of Garden: A Poem for my Sister, A.
Patchen. Sturdy Legs, That.
Piercy. For Strong Women.
  Icon.
  Woman in the Ordinary, The.
Plath. Mushrooms.
Psalms. Psalm 62: "Truly my soul waiteth upon God."
  Psalm 68: "Let God arise, let his enemies be scattered."
Ransom. Agitato Ma Non Troppo ("I have a grief").
  Agitato Ma Non Troppo ("This is what the man said").
  Spiel of [the] Three Mountebanks.
Rich. Phantasia for Elvira Shatayev.
  Power.
Rossetti. And Now Why Tarriest Thou?
  Helpmeet For Him, A.
  If I Had Words.
  Martyr, A.
  O glorious sea that in each climbing wave.
  Our Widowed Queen.
  Resurgam.
  Study. (A Soul), A.
Rukeyser. When the young man reaches his full height.
Sandburg. Love Beyond Keeping.
  Telegram.
  Upstream.
Smart. Arouse—and let thy foes disperse.
  Strong is the horse upon his speed.
Smith, Charlotte. To Fortitude.
Smith, Stevie. I Do Not Speak.
Snodgrass. W. D. Lifts Ten Times the Weight of His Own Body.
Tennyson. Will.

Whittier. Help.
  Our State.
Wordsworth. Translation of a Celebrated Greek Song.
Wroth. Sonnet 47: "O stay mine eyes, shed nott thes fruitles tears."
Yeats. Wild Old Wicked Man, The.

Strikes and Strikers
Berryman. Thanksgiving: Detroit.
Frost. Lone Striker, A.
Hewitt. "Forty-Four Hours" Strike, 1919, The.
McGrath. Triumphal March.
Miller. When you live in your car.
Rukeyser. Time of finks and nobles, A.

String. see Rope.

Striptease
Beckett. Serena III.
Cummings. Sh estiffl / ystrut sal.
Dobyns. Topless.
Muldoon. Gypsy.
Olson. As the shield goddess, Mycenae.
Rukeyser. Burlesque.
St. John. Doors, The.
  Swan at Sheffield Park, The.
Sandburg. Three Slants at New York.
Zimmer. Worrying About You All the Time.

Strokes
Dove. Recovery.
  Stroke, The.
Hall. Green Shelf, The.
Pack. Last Drowning, The.
Plath. Paralytic.
Rukeyser. Resurrection of the Right Side.

Stuart, Charles Edward (The Young Pretender)
Burns. O'er the Water to Charlie.

Stuart, James Francis Edward (The Old Pretender)
Burns. There'll Never Be Peace Till Jamie Comes Hame.
  Up and Warn A' Willie.

Students
Angelou. Communication II.
Ashbery. And You Know.
Berg. Day, A.
  Iowa.
Betjeman. Cricket Master.
  'Varsity Students' Rag, The.
Blake. School Boy, The.
Boyle. Testament for My Students, 1968–1969.
Browning, Elizabeth Barrett. Student, The.
"Carroll, Lewis." To My Pupil.
Cowper. Elegy 1: To Charles Deodati.
Dunn. Temporarily.
Griffiths. Glyndŵr Subdued.
Gunn. To a Dead Graduate Student.
Hemingway. How Ballad Writing Affects Our Seniors.
Hoffman. At the Roman Wall, 1956.
  Battle of Hastings, The.
Hughes, Langston. Theme for English B.
Jarrell. Randall Jarrell, Office Hours 10-11.
Kinnell. Correspondence School Instructor Says Goodbye to His Poetry Students, The.
  Schoolhouse, The.
Koertge. If Other Students.
  Loving Ugly.
  Reading at the Local High School.
  "These Students Couldn't Write Their Way out of a Paper Bag"—Anonymous.
Lawrence. Study.
Liddy. In a Blue Smoke.
Lorde. Workers Rose on May Day or Postcript to Karl Marx, The.
Lowry. Schoolboy's Complaint, The.
McAuley. Lecture.
MacNeice. I ought to be glad.
Milton. Elegy 1: To Charles Deodati.
Moore. Student, The.
Nemerov. September, the First Day of School.
O'Hara. Romanze, or the Music Students.
Owen. Bold Horatius.
Snodgrass. Campus on the Hill, The.
Stevenson. Poem for a Class Re-Union.
  Their Laureate to an Academy Class Dinner Club.

Stuart. Student, The.
Whitman. To a Western Boy.
Wilbur. For the Student Strikers.
Williams, Miller. Paying Some Attention to His Birthday the Associate Professor Goes About His Business Considering What He Sees and a Kind of Praise.
Young. Teaching.

Stupidity
Cummings. Ballad of an Intellectual.
  "Economic secu / rity" is a cu.
  That famous fatheads find that each.
  Yonder deadfromtheneckup graduate of a.
De la Mare. Pollie.
Emerson. To be wise the dull brain so earnestly throbs.
Hartley. For the Shut Eye.
Hewitt. Aquarium.
  Folk Custom.
Lawrence. Life and the Human Consciousness.
"MacDiarmid." Lourd on My Hert.
Nash. It Would Have Been Quicker to Walk, or, Don't Tell Me We're There Already.
Rapunzel, Rapunzel, Let's Let Down Our Hair.
Williams, William Carlos. Education a Failure.
  For a Low Voice.
  Hey Red!
  These Purists.
Wright, James. Presentation of Two Birds to My Son, A.

Submarines
Beatles. Yellow Submarine.
Hewitt. Brown's Bay, Islandmagee, Spring 1917.
Kipling. Farewell and adieu to you, Harwich Ladies.
  Tin Fish.

Submission
Angelou. Song for the Old Ones.
Atwood. There are so many things I want.
  You stand at the door / bright as an icon.
Berryman. Christian to Try: "I am so coxed in it."
Browning, Elizabeth Barrett. Sonnet: "And yet, because thou overcomest so."
Bunting. Like a fawn you dodge me, Molly.
  Shall I sulk because my love has a double heart?
Carruth. "Shock? Is that what you're asking? My dear, I was a."
Cohen. Master Song.
Cooper. Treetops are shuddering.
Cowper. Attempt at the Manner of Waller, An.
  Divine Justice Amiable.
  Dog and the Water-Lily, The.
Dickey, James. Leap, The.
Donne. Why are we[e] by all creatures waited on?
"Dylan." Gotta Serve Somebody.
Frost. Reluctance.
Gunn. In Santa Maria del Popolo.
Herbert. Submission.
Herrick. Obedience in Subjects.
  To Anthea, Who May Command Him Anything.
Hewitt. My Father's Death in Hospital.
Kunitz. Master and Mistress.
Meredith. But whom those errant moans accused.
  Ireland.
  To A.M.
Nash. Tweedledee and Tweedledoom.
Neruda. Star.
Piercy. Nine of Cups, The.
  Unclench Yourself.
Prince. Epistle to a Patron, An.
Rossetti. Lord, what have I that I may offer Thee?
Rukeyser. Long Enough. Long Enough.
Sidney. Since, shunning pain, I ease can never find.
Stevenson. On His Pitiable Transformation.
  To Will H. Low.
Tomlinson. Oxen: Ploughing at Fiesole.

Warren. Jet Must Be Hunting for Something, The.
Whittier. Common Question, The.

Suburbs and Suburban Life
Angelou. Through the Inner City to the Suburbs.
Atwood. City Planners, The.
Letter from Persephone.
Beatles. Good Morning Good Morning.
Penny Lane.
Berg. Oblivion.
Betjeman. Hertfordshire.
Middlesex.
Slough.
Bishop. Flood, The.
Ciardi. On the Orthodoxy and Creed of My Power Mower.
Suburban.
Cowper. London Suburbs.
Cummings. E / cco the uglies / t.
Davie. Hertfordshire.
Hall. Poem With One Fact.
Hardy. Snow in the Suburbs.
Hewitt. Ellendene.
Suburb.
Jeffers. Carmel Point.
Lawrence. Flat Suburbs, S.W., in the Morning.
Suburbs on a Hazy Day.
McGrath. Excursion: Or: O Columbus!, The.
Markson. Youthful Poet's Unspoke Response to a Woman Talking Too Loudly in His Favorite Bookstore, The.
Nemerov. Suburban Prophecy.
Oppen. Bicycles and the Apex, The.
Piercy. Development, The.
"Reed." Families.
Roethke. Idyll: "Now as from maple to elm the flittermice skitter and twirl."
Sandburg. Suburban Sicilian Sketches.
Schuyler. Man in Blue, A.
Sky Eats Up the Trees, The.
Smith, Stevie. Suburb.
Suburban Classes, The.
Updike. Short Days, The.
Sleepless in Scarsdale.
Suburban Madrigal.
Van Duyn. Evening Stroll in the Suburbs.
Walking the Dog: A Diatribe.
Wilbur. To an American Poet Just Dead.
Williams, Miller. Love Poem.

Subways
Betjeman. Metropolitan Railway, The.
Carroll, Jim. But everything has worked out fine.
Crane. Tunnel, The.
Edmunds. December 27, 1988.
Glück. Cripple in the Subway, The.
Hesketh. Orpheus in the Underground.
Hughes, Langston. Midnight Raffle.
Subway Rush Hour.
Merrill. After the ball.
Oppen. Roots of words, The.
Vulcan.
Paley. On the Subway Station.
Pound. In a Station of the Metro.
Virginal, A.
Rukeyser. Study in a Late Subway.
Sandburg. Subway.
Tate. Subway, The.
Walcott. Village Life, A.

Success
Ammons. Success Story.
Upshot, The.
Auden. Managers, The.
Carruth. My brother and I, without hope.
Dickinson. Success is counted sweetest.
Success is dust, but an aim.
We grow accustomed to the Dark.
"Dylan." Catfish.
I Pity the Poor Immigrant.
Emerson. Cloud upon cloud / Clouds after rain.
Fate ("That you are fair or wise or vain").
When success exalts thy lot.
Graves. Fragment of a Lost Poem.
Hemingway. Poetry.
Herrick. Merits Make the Man.

Poets Good Wishes for the Most Hopefull and Handsome Prince, the Duke of Yorke, The.
Pray and Prosper.
Regression Spoiles Resolution.
To His Nephew, to Be Prosperous in His Art of Painting.
To Worthy Friend, M. Tho. Falconbirge.
Wassaile, The.
Hewitt. Coasters, The.
My Brooklyn Uncle.
Uncle Sam and Aunt Edie.
Jonson. Elegy, An: "Can beauty that did prompt me first to write."
Kipling. If.
Winners, The.
Larkin. Success Story.
Lawrence. Are You Pining?
Played-Out Game, A.
Lowry. Poem Inspired By Auden and Clare's Snail.
Success is like some horrible disaster.
Meinke. Wishing He Had a Theory in Key West.
Meredith. Aimée.
Morrison. Very Brave.
Nash. Kindly Unhitch That Star, Buddy.
Pack. Clayfeld's Campaign.
Robinson. Old Trails.
Rukeyser. Everything here is real and of our joy.
Smith, Charlotte. To a Querulous Acquaintance.
Spender. Public Son of a Public Man, The.
Stevenson. Ad Se Ipsum.
Men marvel at the works of man.
Sutter. Celebration of Rust, A.
Good Night, A.
Whittier. Seeking of the Waterfall, The.
Williams, Charles Kenneth. Spirit the Triumph, The.
Yeats. To a Friend Whose Work Has Come to Nothing.
Young. Poem for Dorothy Dandridge, A.

Sudan
Kipling. Fuzzy-Wuzzy.
Kitchener's School.

Suez Canal
Hoffman. 1956.
Nemerov. Reflexions on the Seizure of the Suez, and on a Proposal to Line the Banks of That Canal with Billboard Advertisements.

Suffering
Atwood. You did it / it was you who started the countdown.
Auden. Musée des Beaux Arts.
Berg. Talking.
Berry. Let him escape hospital and doctor.
Berryman. On the London Train.
Bradstreet. Upon Some Distemper of Body.
Brontë. Far, far away is mirth withdrawn.
Stars.
That dreary lake, that midnight sky.
Brooks. My Dreams, My Works, Must Wait Till after Hell.
Browning, Elizabeth Barrett. Convinced by Sorrow.
Bukowski. Crunch, The.
462-0614.
Burns. Prayer, under the Pressure of Violent Anguish, A.
Byron. Epistle to a Friend.
What Matter the Pangs of a Husband and Father.
Carroll, Jim. Like a rabid goat, this obsession.
Misery may be folded.
Carruth. Saving Way, The.
Catullus. Carmen 76: "If evocations of past kindness shed."
Ceravolo. Indian Suffering.
Cohen. Avalanche.
Creeley. Revelation, The.
Cullen. Harsh World That Lashest Me.
Magnets.
Shroud of Color, The.
Thorn Forever in the Breast, A.
Davie. Grazia Deledda, Young.
Dickinson. For each ecstatic instant.

For the comprehension of Suffering.
I wish one could be sure the suffering.
It is a Suffering, to have a sea.
Through the strait pass of suffering.
Time does go on.
Unto a broken heart.
Dobyns. Noise the Hairless Make, The.
Dunbar. Prayer, A: "O lord, the hard-won miles."
We Wear the Mask.
Eberhart. Edgar Lee Masters.
Emerson. Borrowing from the French.
From the Persian of Hafiz.
Heroism.
Untruth is become the mode.
Everson. Canticle to the Christ in the Holy Eucharist, A.
I Am Long Weaned.
If you were to try to say.
In All These Acts.
Fletcher. Buddha and Christ.
Crucifixion, The.
Sea-Violins.
Fox. Raccoon, A.
Glück. Autumnal.
Elms.
Pictures of the People in the War.
Poem: "In the early evening, as now, a man is bending."
Seated Figure.
Graves. Records.
Stolen Jewel.
Griffiths. Suffering Does for the Character.
Haines. House of the Injured, The.
Hunger.
Hayden. Soledad.
Herbert. Love Unknown.
Repentance.
Herrick. Christs Suffering.
Comforts in Contentions.
Great Grief, Great Glory.
His Saviour['s] Words, Going to the Cross[e].
Patience, or Comforts in Crosses.
Satisfaction for Sufferings.
Suffer Thou that Canst not Shift.
Sufferance.
Sufferings.
To God ("Thou hast promis'd, Lord, to be").
Hesketh. Bull Alone.
Meths Men, The.
Reflections.
Hewitt. Emily Dickinson.
Her situation seemed a piteous thing.
My Father's Death in Hospital.
Hughes, Ted. Emily Brontë.
God, A.
Jeffers. Calm and Full the Ocean.
King of Beasts, The.
We Are Those People.
Joseph. River Rising in India.
Kunitz. Welcome the Wrath.
Lawrence. Bei Hennef.
End, The.
Man Hauling a Wagon.
Lewis. Assault Convoy, The.
Belief.
Boy who climbed the creaking stairs, The.
East, The.
Indian Day.
Odyssey, The.
Song: "O have you seen the thorn that grows."
Liddy. At a Czech Tomb in Tuam.
Price, The.
Lindsay. Who Knows?
Lowry. And yet his suffering got involved with all this.
Poem to be Placed at the Conclusion of a Long Obscure Passionate and Eloquent Book of Poems.
McAuley. Child of ten, no more, A.
Markson. A.D. 2029.
Matthews. Why We Are Truly a Nation.
Meinke. Flatbush.
Melville. Armies of the Wilderness, The.
Pebbles.
Meredith. Martin's Puzzle.
Riddle for Men, The.

War.
What are we first? First, animals; and next.
Year's Sheddings, The.
Millay. Ancient Gesture, An.
Fatal Interview.
Felicity of Grief!—even Death being kind.
Here is a wound that never will heal, I know.
Pity me not because the light of day.
That Love at length should find me out and bring.
Nash. What the Well-Read Patient Is Talking About, or, Look, Ma, What I Got!
Nemerov. From the Last Dream of a Dying Woman Aged Eighty.
Virgin and Martyr.
Olson. All You Can Do.
Ode on Nativity, An.
Patchen. I Can't Understand! I Can't Understand!
Piercy. Burying Blues for Janis.
Ransom. Necrological.
Rich. It was your vision of the pilot.
Robinson. As a World Would Have It.
Rossetti. Endure Hardness.
Love Attacked.
Sick Child's Meditation, A.
There's Snow on the Fields.
What is it Jesus saith unto the soul?
Yes, I too could face death and never shrink.
Sidney. How Is My Sun.
Lady, reserved by the heav'ns to do pastors' company honour.
Sonnet 2: "Not at [the] first sight, nor with a dribbed shot."
Sonnet 47: "What, have I thus betrayed my liberty?"
Sonnet 57: "Woe, having made with many fights his own."
Sonnet 86: "Alas, whence came this change of looks? If I."
Simic. Great Infirmities.
Smith, Charlotte. Sighing I see yon little troop at play.
Southwell. Christ's Bloody Sweate.
Dyer's Phancy Turned to a Sinner's Complainte.
Love's Gardyne Greife.
Saint Peter's Afflicted Mynde.
Saint Peter's Remorse.
Spender. Epilogue to a Human Drama.
Stevenson. Counterblast—1886, The.
Counterblast Ironical, The.
To F.J.S.
Walker. At First.
Diamonds on Liz's Bosom, The.
Warren. History.
Keep That Morphine Moving, Cap.
Moral Assessment.
Ransom.
Riddle in the Garden.
There once, on that goat island, I.
Whittier. Christian Slave, The.
Watchers, The.
Williams, Charles Kenneth. Dog, The.
On the Roof.
This Is a Sin.
Williams, William Carlos. Complaint.
Wright, James. In Memory of Leopardi.
Three Stanzas From Goethe.
Wroth. Song: "O[h] me[e] the time is [or has] come to part."
Sonnet 5: "How many nights have I with paine indur'd."
Sonnet 6: "Ô strive nott still to heape disdaine on mee."
Sonnet 28: "Griefe, killing griefe: have nott my torments binn."
Sonnet 39: "Iff I were giv'n to mirthe 't'wowld be more cross."
Sonnet 44: "How fast thou hast'st (O spring) with sweetest speed."
Wyatt. All ye that know of care and heaviness.
Alone musing, / Remembering.
At last withdraw your cruelty.
Complaining, alas, without redress.
Farewell, all my welfare.

Fortune, what aileth thee.
I love, loved, and so doth she.
I see my plaint with open ears.
Might I as well within my song belay.
My love is like unto th'eternal fire.
Now must I learn to feign.
O miserable sorrow withouten cure!
Suffering in sorrow, in hope to attain.
To make an end of all this strife.
To whom should I sue to ease my pain?
When that I call unto my mind.
With serving still.
Ye know my heart, my lady dear.
Yeats. Fascination of What's Difficult, The.
Zukofsky. Seek or record then the benefactor—pree or voluptuous.
See also **Pain.**

Suffolk, England
Davie. Suffolk.
Tomlinson. Hedgerows.
Poem for My Father.

Suffrage. see Voting and Voters.

Sugar
Gallagher. Sugar.
Merrill. Domino.

Sugar Cane
Emerson. Wilt thou life's best elixir drain?

Suicide
Angelou. Chicken-Licken.
Ashbery. Illustration.
Auden. Suicide.
Beatles. Day in the Life, A.
Yer Blues.
Berryman. Death Ballad.
I've found out why, that day, that suicide.
Of Suicide.
Betjeman. Suicide on Junction Road Station after Abstention from Evening Communion in North London.
Bishop. Don't Kill Yourself.
Boyle. Evening Grass, The.
Poem for a Painter Bent on Suicide.
Brontë. F. de Samara to A. G. A.
O hinder me by no delay.
Bukowski. Almost Made Up Poem, An.
Green.
Suicide.
Carroll, Jim. At eighteen years of age.
Love Story.
"Carroll, Lewis." Lady of the Ladle, The.
Lays of Sorrow, No. 1.
Carruth. Re-Acquaintance.
Tanck's Song About Dying Young.
Ciardi. Trying to Feel Something.
Cohen. Photograph, The.
Purest of Occasions.
Seems So Long Ago, Nancy.
Threat.
Coleridge. Suicide's Argument, The.
Cooper. I did not protest. I spoke nothing but the truth.
Nightmare of the Suburbs, A.
Ragged and thrashing.
Suicide Note.
Creeley. Hart Crane.
Two Times ("It takes so long to look down").
What's for Dinner.
Cullen. Ballad of the Brown Girl, The.
Mood.
Cummings. In a middle of a room.
Will i ever forget that precarious moment?
De la Mare. Suicide, The.
Dickey, James. Leap, The.
Dickinson. He scanned it—staggered.
Dobyns. Japanese Girl with Red Table.
Seeing Off a Friend.
Dunbar. Right to Die, The.
"Dylan." Ballad of Hollis Brown.
Clean-Cut Kid.
Run go get out of here.
Eberhart. Flow of Thought.
Hardy Perennial.
How It Is.
On Returning to a Lake in Spring.
Parker River, The.
Suicide Note.
Edmunds. Back Home.

Fenton. Letter to John Fuller.
Ferlinghetti. And she "like a young year."
Fletcher. End of Job, The.
Gallagher. Their Heads Bent Toward Each Other Like Flowers.
Graves. Call It a Good Marriage.
Song: Lift-Boy.
Suicide in The Copse, The.
Gunn. Elegy: "I can almost see it."
Hall. Carlotta's Confession.
Hardy. Newcomer's Wife, The.
Plena Timoris.
Second Night, The.
War-Wife of Catknoll, The.
Hartley. And, should it be left like this.
Spirits Are Organized Men.
Hemingway. If my Valentine you won't be.
Montparnasse.
To a Tragic Poetess.
Hesketh. It Was Not I.
Hewitt. Ophelia.
What Little Happened There.
Hoffman. Center of Attention, The.
Holmes. Berryman's Dead.
Dying Lawrence.
Obituary for Jan Masaryk.
Housman. Good creatures, do you love your lives.
It nods and curtseys and recovers.
Shot? so quick, so clean an ending?
Sinner's Rue.
Hughes, Langston. Lament over Love.
Suicide's Note.
Hugo. Cape Nothing.
Death in the Aquarium.
District in the City, A.
Letter to Sister Madeline from Iowa City.
Jeffers. Give Your Heart to the Hawks.
Mara.
Joseph. Recovered from the Sea.
Knight. Black Poet Leaps to His Death, A.
For Black Poets Who Think of Suicide.
Knott. Ant Dodger.
Fear of Domesticity.
Goodbye.
Shorts / Excerpts ("I keep a TV monitor on my chest").
Kooser. Failed Suicide, The.
Kunitz. Portrait, The.
Lewis. Suicide, The.
Liddy. He'd be alive today if he wasn't pretty.
Night / We went running to the garden.
Lovelace. Dialogue. Lucasta, Alexis.
What doubt'st thou hand? sad Cato 'tis to kill.
Lowell. After the Surprising Conversions.
Marcus Cato 95–46 B.C.
Lowry. Thoughts to Be Erased from My Destiny.
To Herr Toller, Who Hanged Himself.
Who made this suicide pact of love?
MacNeice. Springboard, The.
Suicide, The.
McNeill. Martha MacElmain.
Mahon. Antarctica.
Markson. Relevance.
Matthews. You Dance Up There.
Meinke. Because.
Heart's Location, The.
Merrill. Roger Clay's Proposal.
Merton. Songs.
Millay. Pond, The.
Suicide, The.
Milton. Then both ourselves and seed at once to free.
Nash. Asp, The.
Nemerov. To D——, Dead by Her Own Hand.
Olson. Diaries of Death.
Here i am, naked.
You, Hart Crane.
Oppen. In Alsace, during the war.
They carry nativeness / To a conclusion.
Owen. S.I.W.
Plath. Edge.
Lady Lazarus.
Lesbos.
Suicide off Egg Rock.

Poe. Scenes from Politian.
"Reed." Bed, The.
It Wasn't Me.
Rich. From a Survivor.
I can see myself years back at Sunion.
Whatever it was: the grains of the glacier caked in the boot-cleats.
Robinson. Bokardo.
Growth of "Lorraine," The.
Mill, The.
Richard Cory.
Roethke. Kitty-Cat Bird, The.
Rossetti. In the Round Tower at Jhansi, June 8, 1857.
Jessie Cameron.
Rukeyser. Double Dialogue: *Homage to Robert Frost.*
Exile of Music.
F.O.M.
Gates, The.
Power of Suicide, The.
Suicide Blues.
Victims, a Play for the Home, The.
Sandburg. Neither wife nor child had Mr. Eastman and the manner of his death.
Schuyler. Night, The.
Trip.
Virginia Woolf.
Schwartz. Sequel, the Conclusion, the Endlessness, The.
Sexton. Double Image, The.
Red Dance, The.
Risk, The.
Suicide Note.
Wanting to Die.
Shakespeare. Sonnet 66: "Tired [*or* Tyr'd, *or* Tir'd] with all these, for restful death I cry."
Shelton. She has three pills left in the bottle.
Smith, Stevie. Death Came to Me.
Death in the Rose Garden.
Dido's Farewell to Aeneas.
Doctor, The.
Does No Love Last?
Exeat.
Father for a Fool, A.
I Am.
Starling, The.
Suicide's Epitaph.
Snodgrass. Adolf Hitler ("More than fifty millions. More").
Magda Goebbels ("This is the needle that we give").
Spender. Girl Who Has Drowned Herself Speaks, A.
Spenser. Who travels [*or* trauels] by the wearie wandring way.
Stevenson. Celestial Surgeon, The.
Tate. Suicide.
Tennyson. Two Voices, The.
Van Duyn. Hermit of Hudson Pond, The.
Wakoski. Justice Is Reason Enough.
Some Brilliant Sky.
Warren. Confederate Veteran Tries to Explain the Event, A.
Event, The.
Place Where the Boy Pointed, The.
Whitman. Inca's Daughter, The.
Williams, Charles Kenneth. Suicide: Anne.
Williams, Miller. Rituals.
Williams, William Carlos. Death of See, The.
Wordsworth. Argument for Suicide.
Near the Same Lake [Thrasymene].
'Tis said that some have died for love.
Wright, James. Minneapolis Poem, The.
Wyatt. Horrible of hue, hideous to behold.
Zukofsky. Send regards to Ida the bitch.

Sumac
Sandburg. Sumach and Birds.
Schuyler. 8/12/70.

Summer
Ammons. Circling Splinters.
Ashbery. Summer.
Auden. Summer quickens grass, The.
Berryman. And Plough-month peters out . its thermal power.
Loves are the summer's. Summer like a bee.
October's both, back in the Sooner State.

Bishop. Late Air.
Song: "Summer is over upon the sea."
Summer's Dream, A.
Blake. School Boy, The.
To Summer.
Bogan. Dark Summer.
Song for a Lyre.
Summer Wish.
Brontë. 'Twas one of those dark, cloudy days.
Burns. Ay Waukin O.
Birks of Aberfeldy, The [Composed on the Spot].
On a Bank of Flowers.
Winter It Is Past, The.
Carruth. Ravine, The.
Song: "Summer burns on the edges of day."
Speaking for Them.
Summer, The.
Ceravolo. Risk.
Ciardi. Catalpa, The.
On the Orthodoxy and Creed of My Power Mower.
Clare. Sonnet: "I love to see the summer beaming forth."
Cummings. Do you remember when the fluttering dusk.
Early Summer Sketch.
O It's Nice To Get Up In,the slipshod mucous kiss.
O purple finch / please tell me why.
Out of midsummer's blazing most not night.
Summer Silence.
Summer Song.
Sunset.
Davie. Barnsley Cricket Club.
Hardness of Light, The.
Viper-Man.
De la Mare. Vacant Day, The.
Dickey, William. Kindness, A.
Dickinson. Acts of Light which beautified, The.
As imperceptibly as Grief.
As Summer into Autumn slips.
Bee is not afraid of me, The.
Consulting summer's clock.
How near this suffering Summer.
I know a place where Summer strives.
I trust you may have the dearest summer.
It will be Summer—eventually.
Last of Summer is Delight, The.
Midsummer, was it, when They died.
Revolution is the Pod.
Slips of the last rose of summer, The.
So much Summer.
Soft Sea washed around the House, A.
Some one prepared this mighty show.
Something in a summer's Day, A.
Summer for thee, grant I may be.
Summer has been wide and deep, The.
Summer has two Beginnings.
Summer laid her simple Hat.
Summer that we did not prize, The.
Summer—we all have seen.
There came a Day at Summer's full.
There is a June when Corn is cut.
These are the days when Birds come back—.
To see the Summer Sky.
'Twas here my summer paused.
We wear our sober Dresses when we die.
What shall I do when the Summer troubles.
When Roses cease to bloom, Sir.
Your coming is a symptom of Summer.
Doolittle. Blue-geese, white-geese, you may say.
Dunbar. Boy's Summer Song, A.
In Summer.
In Summer Time.
Song, A: "On a summer's day as I sat by a stream."
Song of Summer.
Summer in the South.
Summer Night, A.
Summer Pastoral, A.
Summer's Night, A.
Two Songs.
Dunn. Nova Scotia.
"Dylan." In the Summertime.

Eberhart. Great Praises.
Project, The.
Spring Man.
Summer Landscape.
To the Field Mice.
Van Black, an Old Farmer in His Dell.
Verbalist of Summer, The.
Eliot. New Hampshire.
Emerson. In this sour world, o summerwind.
Everson. In the Ripeness of the Weed.
Fletcher. Memory: The Walk on the Beach.
Ford. Wall ritual. These.
Galvin. Long Pond Summer.
Gardner. At a Summer Hotel.
Grocery Bouquet, The.
Summer Remembered.
Summers Ago.
Garrigue. Moondial.
Thy Love Is One Thou'st Not Yet Known.
Gildner. Always in Late Summer Now, in the City.
That Summer.
Glück. Letter from Provence.
Solstice.
Summer.
Graves. Advent of Summer.
Haines. Green smoke and white ash.
It was late summer.
Hall. Whip-Poor-Will.
Hardy. Before and after Summer.
Best She Could, The.
It Never Looks Like Summer.
On the Esplanade.
Summer Schemes.
This Summer and Last.
We Sat at the Window.
When Oats Were Reaped.
Hartley. And Now—September.
Summer Evening.
Summer is done—.
Yesterday, in the night.
Hayden. Summertime and the Living.
Heaney. Summer Home.
Herrick. Succession of the Foure Sweet Months, The.
Hesketh. Buttercup Children, The.
Rise.
Hewitt. Away Match: June 1924.
Black and White.
Eleventh Night, The.
Portstewart, 1914.
Since June was hot on head and hand.
Summer Arcady.
Summer Park.
Hoffman. Summer Solstice.
Hopkins. Summer Malison, The.
Windy Day in Summer, A.
Hugo. Taneum Creek.
Jarrell. All or None.
Jonson. Epithalamion: or, a Song.
Joseph. Certain Weathers.
Meteorology, A.
Summer Amnesty.
Zenith.
Kinnell. Two Seasons.
Kipling. Two Months.
Koch. Summery Weather.
Kooser. Sunday Morning.
Kunitz. End of Summer.
Summer Solstice.
Larkin. Mother, Summer, I.
Summer Nocturne.
Levine. I reenter a day in a late summer.
Making Light of It.
Lindsay. Sweetheart Summer.
Lowell. Long Summer.
WIldrose.
Lowry. Very dark and clear with an onshore wind.
McGrath. Black Train, The.
Poem: "Long wound of the summer—, The."
MacLeish. Danger in the Air, The.
Humid air precipitates, The.
Long Hot Summer.
MacNeice. Solstice.
Matthews. Moonlight in Vermont.
On the Porch at the Frost Place, Franconia,

NH.
Writer-in-Residence.
Meredith. It is the season of the sweet wild rose.
July.
Longest Day, The.
Out in the yellow meadows, where the bee.
Pastoral 1: "How sweet on sunny afternoons."
Pastoral 7: "Summer glows warm on the meadows, and speedwell, and gold-cups, and daisies."
Song: The Wren.
Song: "Two wedded lovers watched the rising moon."
To a Nightingale.
Merrill. Another August.
Summer People, The.
Millay. Three Songs from "The Lamp and the Bell."
Morgan. Canadaigua.
Morrison. Dancing & Thrashing.
I Walked Thru.
Paris Journal.
Nash. Fahrenheit *Gesundheit.*
I Always Say There's No Place Like New York in the Summer, or, That Cottage Small by a Waterfall Was Snapped Up Last February.
Man Bites Dog-Days.
September Is Summer, Too.
Summer Serenade.
Summergreen for President.
Nemerov. End of Summer School, The.
Late Summer.
Summer's Elegy.
Notley. Poem: "St. Marks Place caught at night in hot summer."
O'Hara. Summer Breezes.
Owen. From My Diary, July 1914.
Paley. Connections: Vermont Vietnam (I).
St. Johnswort!
Patchen. This Summer Day.
This summer earth.
Piercy. Cod Summer.
Plath. Frog Autumn.
Pope. Summer, The Second Pastoral, or Alexis.
Rexroth. When We with Sappho.
Rich. Holiday.
6/21.
This high summer we love will pour its light.
Roethke. Song: "This fair parcel of summer's."
Rolfe. Winter's Ghost Plagues Them.
Rossetti. Bitter for Sweet.
Cor Mio.
Fly Away, Fly Away.
Have You Forgotten?
In the Lane.
October Garden, An.
Seasons.
Summer.
Summer.
Summer.
Summer Is Ended.
Summer Wish, A.
When a mounting skylark sings / In the sunlit summer morn.
Rukeyser. Children's Orchard, The.
Letter, Unposted.
Summer, the Sacramento.
Sandburg. Bird Talk.
Bitter Summer Thoughts.
Bitter Summer Thoughts—No. 3.
Cricket Match.
Crisscross.
Foxgloves.
Mask.
Meadow in Summer.
Potato Blossom Songs and Jigs.
Silver Wind.
Small Homes.
Summer Grass.
Summer Shirt Sale.
Summer Stars.
Timber Wings.

Under the Harvest Moon.
Village in Late Summer.
Sarton. Flower-Arranging Summer, A.
We Sat Smoking at a Table..
Schuyler. Buried at Springs.
Haze.
Jelly Jelly.
Overcast, Hot.
Shimmer.
Schwartz. Words for a Trumpet Chorale Celebrating the Autumn.
Sexton. I Remember.
In the Beach House.
Loving the Killer.
Shakespeare. Sonnet 18: "Shall I compare thee to a summer's day?"
Shelley. Summer and Winter.
Summer Evening Churchyard, A.
Shelton. August.
Simic. Summer Morning.
Smith, Charlotte. Close of Summer, The.
To the Mulberry-Tree.
Where the green leaves exclude the summer beam.
Written at Exmouth, Midsummer, 1795.
Sorrentino. Captain Marvell.
Lecture on Time and Space, The.
Pastorale: "Rushing darkness of the summer evening, The."
Spender. Lost Days.
Stevens. Banal Sojourn.
Beginning, The.
Credences of Summer.
Meditation Celestial & Terrestrial.
Stevenson. Summer Night.
Summer sun shone round me, The.
Stuart. River, The.
Swift. Part of a Summer, The.
Tate. Idyl: "In a valley late bees with whining gold."
Thomson. Home from his morning task the swain retreats.
Tomlinson. Conspiracy, The.
Lesson, The.
Witnesses, The.
Updike. Island Sun.
July.
Summer: West Side.
Van Duyn. End of May.
Walcott. Before that thundercloud breaks from its hawsers.
Bleecker Street, Summer.
Lesson for This Sunday, A.
Midsummer stretches beside me with its cat's yawn.
Midsummer, Tobago.
Sun has fired my face to terra-cotta, The.
Whittier. At School-Close.
Dream of Summer, A.
June on the Merrimac.
Summer by the Lakeside.
Summer Pilgrimage, A.
Wilbur. Exeunt.
June Light.
My Father Paints the Summer.
Praise in Summer.
Song, A: "As at the bottom of a seething well."
Two Songs in a Stanza of Beddoes'.
Williams, Charles Kenneth. Shade, The.
Williams, William Carlos. At the Faucet of June.
Botticellian Trees, The.
Ivy Crown, The.
Primrose.
Summer Song.
Wordsworth. Longest Day; Addressed to My Daughter, The.
Wright, James. Eleutheria.
Yau. Rubbing her sable with long thoughtful.
Young. Summer.
Zukofsky. Anew, sun, to fire summer.

Sumner, Charles
Dickinson. When Continents expire.
Whittier. Sumner.
To Charles Sumner.

Sun
Ammons. Late November.
Photosynthesis.
Transducer.
Worky Shallows.
Atwood. Despite us / there is only one universe, the sun.
Auden. Flowers and Stationmaster.
Sunshine.
Beatles. Good Day Sunshine.
Here Comes the Sun.
I'll Follow the Sun.
Sun King.
Berry. April Woods: Morning.
Boyle. Glad Day for Laurence Vail, A.
Brontë. How golden bright from earth and heaven.
It will not shine again.
Will the day be bright or cloudy?
Browning, Elizabeth Barrett. Man and Nature.
Byron. On the Eyes of Miss A——— H——— —.
Ossian's Address to the Sun in "Carthon."
Version of Ossian's Address to the Sun, A.
Campion. Follow Thy Fair Sun[ne] [Unhappy Shadow].
Shadowes before the shining sunne do vanish.
Carroll, Jim. Child Growing Up with the Sun, A.
Judging the Pageant.
Song: "In minute gestures / that jet wetly slight."
"Carroll, Lewis." Facts.
Said the Moon to the Sun.
Carruth. Introspectional.
Saving Way, The.
Sun, The.
Catullus. Sunne may set and rise, The.
Ceravolo. Red Sun.
Risk.
Clark. Culebra Cascabel.
Sky.
Coleridge. Sun-shine lies on the cottage-wall, The.
Crashaw. On a Foule Morning, Being Then to Take a Journey.
Creeley. Anger.
Flowers.
Gesture, The.
To the One in the Gray Coat.
Cummings. How generous is that himself the sun.
Davie. Sunburst.
De la Mare. Mist.
Twice Lovely.
Dickey, James. Sun.
Dickinson. After the Sun comes out.
Blazing in Gold and quenching in Purple.
Daisy follows soft the Sun, The.
Had I not seen the Sun.
How good his Lava Bed.
My God—He sees thee.
Pattern of the sun, The.
Sun and Fog contested, The.
Sun is gay or stark, The.
Sun is one—and on the Tare, The.
Sun—just touched the Morning, The.
Sun kept stooping—stooping—low!, The.
Sun retired to a cloud, The.
Thank her dear power for having come.
To interrupt His Yellow Plan.
We can but follow to the Sun.
We would'nt mind the sun, dear.
When I have seen the Sun emerge.
Who is the East?
Donne. Resurrection, Imperfect.
Sun[ne] Rising, The.
Doolittle. Helios.
Eberhart. Autumnal.
I Will Not Dare to Ask One Question.
Key West.
Let the Tight Lizard on the Wall.
Opulence.
Perception as a Guided Missile.
Spring Man.
Emerson. But as this fugitive sunlight.

He lives not who can refuse me.
Sun is the sole inconsumable fire, The.
Everson. August.
Ferlinghetti. Man Who Rode Away, The.
Fisher. Treasure House, The.
Fletcher. America.
Ford. Clouds covered it, The.
Soleil d'automne. Do.
Trees with white perfumed.
Frost. Two Leading Lights.
Gallagher. Corona.
Zero.
Glück. Silverpoint.
Graves. Blessed Sun.
Chink, The.
Lament for Pasiphaë.
Near Eclipse, The.
Problems of Gender.
Song: The Far Side of Your Moon.
What Will Be, Is.
Gunn. Sunlight.
Value of Gold, The.
Wrestling.
Hall. Sun, The.
Hardy. Coming Up Oxford Street: Evening.
Sun's Last Look on the Country Girl, The.
Herbert. Son[ne], The.
Hesketh. Bleasdale: The Wooden Circle.
I Cannot Look into the Sun.
Prayer for Sun.
Sundowner.
What Is a Person?
Winter Daffodils.
Hewitt. April Awake.
Aristocratic Area.
Matin sur le Port.
Minor Victorian Painter, A.
St Stephen's Day.
School Upstairs, The.
Winter Day.
Hill. Of Coming-into-Being and Passing-
Away.
Prayer to the Sun, A.
Hoffman. I Am the Sun.
Hopkins. —I am like a slip of comet.
Sun just risen, The.
Housman. Revolution.
Hughes, Langston. Sun Song.
Hughes, Ted. Crow's Last Stand.
Hugo. Storm in Acquafredda.
Jarrell. Archangel's' Song, The.
Jeffers. Nova.
Jong. Sunjuice.
Jonson. So breaks the sun earth's rugged
chains.
Joseph. Against the Personality Cult.
Certain Weathers.
Kipling. Hymn of the Triumphant Airman.
Knott. Feeding the Sun.
Larkin. Solar.
Lawrence. Aristocracy of the Sun.
Democracy.
Drill in the Heat.
Elements, The.
Forte Dei Marmi.
Hostile Sun, The.
Immorality.
Mid-Day Verse, The.
Space.
Sun in Me.
Sun-Men.
Sun-Women.
Tropic.
Lieberman. Banana Dwarf, The.
Lindsay. Indian Summer Day on the Prairie,
An.
Sun Says His Prayers, The.
Sunshine.
What the Rattlesnake Said.
Lovelace. Lucasta Weeping.
Lucasta's Fan[ne], with a Looking-Glass[e] in
It.
Paradox, A.
Lowry. And, when you go—much as a
meteor.
Happiness.
Indian Arm.

Not all of us were heroes said my brother wit.
Sun, Aeroplane, Lovers.
Windows from a Machine Shop.
"MacDiarmid." My Love Is to the Light of
Lights.
MacLeish. Autumn.
Ha, but the sun among us.
Men of My Century Loved Mozart.
No Lamp Has Ever Shown Us Where to
Look.
Old Man to the Lizard, The.
Salute.
MacNeice. Morning Sun.
Spring Sunshine.
Sunlight on the Garden, The.
Meredith. Pastoral 6: "How barren would this
valley be."
Phaéthôn.
Sunrise.
Then said she, quick as the cries.
Merrill. Dandelion Sermon, The.
Little Fanfare for Felix Magowan.
Merton. Birth of the Sun, The.
Poem: "Watching, among the rifled branches,
for the sun, our hero."
Moore. Sun.
Morgan. Sun tells stories, The.
Nemerov. Sunglasses, The.
Neruda. First Winter.
O'Hara. True Account of Talking to the Sun
at Fire Island, A.
Oliver. Sun, The.
Olson. Advantage, The.
Maya Against Itzas.
Right in My Eye.
Owen. Futility.
Pack. Autumn Warmth.
Stepping Out.
Paley. Oh the dreamer said.
One Day.
Woman invented fire and called it, A.
Patchen. Blood of the Sun.
Colony of the Sun, The.
World Whose Sun Retreats Before the Brave,
A.
Piercy. Noon of the Sunbather.
Sun, The.
Raine. Childhood Memory.
Holy Isles, The.
Sun.
To the Sun.
What can I tell you, future ones.
What message from imagined Paradise.
Ralegh. Sunne may set and rise, The.
"Reed." Fly into the Sun.
Rossetti. Death-Watches.
If all were rain and never sun.
If the sun could tell us half / That he hears
and sees.
Let Everything That Hath Breath Praise the
Lord.
Mirrors of Life and Death.
O ye who love today, / Turn away / From
Patience with her silver ray.
Rose with such a bonny blush, The.
Song of Flight, A.
Sunshine.
Rukeyser. In Her Burning.
Panacea.
Sun-Artist, The.
Sandburg. Cahokia.
Haze Gold.
Monotone.
What other oaths are wanted now?
Women Washing Their Hair.
Schuyler. We Walk.
Schwartz. "Interpretation! that's the act of
mind."
Poem: "In the morning, when it was raining."
Sexton. Sun, The.
Yellow.
Shakespeare. Sonnet 7: "Lo! in the orient
when the gracious light."
Sonnet 34: "Why didst thou promise such a
beauteous day."
Shelley. Fragment: "Unrisen splendour of the

brightest sun."
Prologue in Heaven.
Sidney. Sonnet 22: "In highest way of heav'n
the sun did ride."
Sonnet 76: "She comes, and straight therewith
her shining twins do move."
Silverstein. Invention.
Joey.
Smith, Charlotte. To the Sun.
Sorrentino. How I loved that melody.
Stevens. Brave Man, The.
Fading of the Sun, A.
Latest Freed Man, The.
News and the Weather, The.
Of Hartford in a Purple Light.
Page from a Tale.
Sense of the Sleight-of-Hand Man, The.
Sun This March, The.
Woman in Sunshine, The.
Stevenson. Night and Day.
Summer Sun.
Sun's Travels, The.
Thomas. How Soon the Servant Sun.
Tomlinson. De Sole.
Head Hewn with an Axe.
On a Theme of Pasternak.
Wakoski. Sun.
Sun with Hands for Rays.
Whitman. Give Me the Splendid Silent Sun.
Thou Orb Aloft Full-Dazzling.
Wilbur. Black November Turkey, A.
Courtyard Thaw, A.
For Ellen.
Grasse: The Olive Trees.
I.
Poplar, Sycamore.
Sun and Air.
Sunlight Is Imagination.
Wellfleet: The House.
Williams, William Carlos. Conquest.
Daisy.
Hula-Hula.
Light Hearted William.
Metric Figure.
Sun Bathers, The.
Sun, The.
Wordsworth. Eclipse of the Sun, 1820, The.
What is it that tells my soul the Sun is
setting?
Wright, James. Shadow and the Real, The.
Wroth. Sonnet 20: "Sunn which glads, the
earth att his bright sight, The."
Zukofsky. Ask of the sun.
Can a mote of sunlight defeat its purpose.
Close your eyes.
—"Her Soil's Birth."
Tall and singularly dark you pass among the
breakers—.

Sunburn
Sidney. Sonnet 22: "In highest way of heav'n
the sun did ride."

Sunday
Berg. Rubber Rats.
Berrigan. Sandy's Sunday Best.
Bishop. Sunday at Key West.
Sunday, 4 A.M.
Brooks. Sundays of Satin-Legs Smith, The.
Clough. O Qui Me—!
Cooper. In the Last Few Moments Came the
Old German Cleaning Woman.
Cowper. Tale, Founded on a Fact, A.
Creeley. Midnight.
De la Mare. Sunday, A.
Dickinson. Organ is moaning, The.
Dove. Kentucky, 1833.
Gardner. One Sunday in 1966.
Hardy. Farmer Dunman's Funeral.
Hayden. Those Winter Sundays.
Hewitt. Word, The.
Hugo. Carnival Inside, The.
Koertge. Sunday.
Kooser. Sunday Morning.
MacNeice. Another Sunday Morning.
Mahon. Another Sunday Morning.
Nemerov. Metropolitan Sunday.
Sunday.
Sunday at the End of Summer.

Olson. Proensa.
Schuyler. June 30, 1974.
Picnic Cantata, A.
Sunday.
Sexton. Fury of Sundays, The.
Smart. For Sunday.
Stevens. Sunday Morning.
Updike. Leaving Church Early.
Sunday.
Walcott. Lesson for This Sunday, A.
Sabbaths, W.I.
Williams, William Carlos. Sunday.
See also **Sabbath.**

Sundews
Swinburne. Sundew, The.

Sundials
Cooper. Sundial, The.
Graves. *Song*: The Sundial's Lament.
Hardy. Sundial on a Wet Day, The.
Wilbur. Gnomons.

Sunflowers
Blake. Ah, Sun-Flower [*or* Ah! Sun-Flower].
Fox. Sunflowers.
Ginsberg. Sunflower Sutra.
Hesketh. Clown Flowers.
Comparison with a Sunflower.
Letter to Vincent.
Levertov. For Floss.
McAuley. I lounge on the warm step,
watching the child.
Oliver. Sunflowers, The.
Sandburg. Cripple.
Updike. Sunflower.
Williams, William Carlos. Sunflowers.

Sunrise
Angelou. Plagued Journey, A.
Berryman. Prime.
Bogan. July Dawn.
Ceravolo. Passion for the Sky.
Clark. Warm ripe days. The sun floods the
ridge with color.
Cowper. Sunset and Sunrise.
De la Mare. Sunrise.
Dickey, James. Morning, A.
Dickinson. I had no Cause to be awake.
I'd rather recollect a setting.
I'll tell you how the Sun rose.
Sun went down—no Man looked on, The.
Sunrise runs for Both, The.
Donne. Sun[ne] Rising, The.
Hardy. Life and Death at Sunrise.
Herrick. Maiden-Blush, The.
Hewitt. Morning Moment.
Housman. Reveille.
Lowry. Sestina in a Cantina.
Merrill. Radiometer.
Morrison. Wild Whore Laughs, The.
Oliver. Buddha's Last Instruction, The.
Sun, The.
Sunrise.
Oppen. Light / Of the closed pages, tightly
closed, packed against each other, The.
Plath. Southern Sunrise.
Roethke. Unextinguished, The.
Rolfe. Dawn Song.
Sexton. Fury of Sunrises, The.
Stevens. Fish-Scale Sunrise, A.
Whittier. Waiting, The.

Sunset
Atwood. Sunset II.
Auden. Moment, A.
Bly. Evening When the Full Moon Rose as
the Sun Set, An.
Bogan. March Twilight.
Brontë. Evening sun was sinking down, The.
Fair sinks the summer evening now.
'Tis evening now, the sun descends.
Byron. Sunset over the Aegean.
Clare. *Song*: "Dying gales of sweet even."
Clark. "Sun shoots high," The.
Coleridge. Sunset, A.
Cowper. Sunset and Sunrise.
Cummings. Beyond the brittle towns asleep.
E / cco the uglies / t.
Finis.
Of this sunset(which is so).
Paris;this April sunset completely utters.

Sunset.
This(let's remember)day died again and.
Who are you,little i.
Writhe and / gape of tortured.
Dickinson. Crickets sang, The.
Fairer through Fading—as the Day.
How the old Mountains drip with Sunset.
I send Two Sunsets.
I'd rather recollect a setting.
Ignorance a Sunset, An.
I'll tell you how the Sun rose.
Sun in reining to the West, The.
Sun went down—no Man looked on, The.
Sunset at Night—is natural.
Sunset stopped on Cottages, The.
Sunset that screens, reveals.
Dunbar. Sunset.
Eberhart. Sea-Ruck.
Fisher. At sunset over the water.
Dusk.
Fletcher. Midwinter Sunset.
Frost. Acceptance.
Graves. Allie.
Land of Whipperginny, The.
Hartley. Summer Evening.
Hesketh. All Hallows.
Hewitt. Autumn Valley.
Leaf.
Jeffers. Ocean's Tribute, The.
Joseph. Instant on the Viaduct, An.
Kinnell. Daybreak.
Lawrence. Fall of Day, The.
Foreign Sunset.
In Trouble and Shame.
Love on the Farm.
Our Day Is Over.
Ruination.
Sunset.
Sunset Verse, The.
Levertov. Coming Fall, The.
Lindsay. Sunset.
Lowry. October Sunset.
Sestina in a Cantina.
MacLeish. Cummings.
Matthews. Every Tub.
Meredith. Union in Disseverance.
Merton. Sundown.
Sundown.
Oliver. Sun, The.
Rich. Colophon.
Robinson. Dark Hills, The.
Sandburg. Aloof.
Evening Sunsets Witness and Pass On, The.
Flash Crimson.
Flat Waters of the West in Kansas.
Flux.
Harvest Sunset.
Hits and Runs.
Hoof Dusk.
Letter S.
Little Sketch.
Lumber Yard Pools at Sunset.
Maroon with Silver Frost.
Mist Forms.
Plowboy.
Runaway Colors.
Rusty Crimson.
Slabs of the Sunburnt West.
Slow Program.
Smoke Rose Gold.
Sunset from Omaha Hotel Window.
Sunsets.
Thimble Islands.
Three Slants at New York.
Valley Song.
Yellow Evening Star.
Schuyler. Poem: "This beauty that I see."
Sunset.
Schwartz. Purple black cloud at sunset: it is
late August.
Scott. Trossachs, The.
Sexton. Fury of Sunsets, The.
Sidney. Why dost thou haste away.
Smart. Sweets of Evening, The.
Smith, Charlotte. Pilgrim, The.
Sorrentino. Red sun is going down
somewhere, A.

Stevenson. I saw red evening through the rain.
Song: "Light foot and tight foot."
Tate. Dusk.
Tennyson. Crossing the Bar.
Move Eastward, Happy Earth, and Leave.
Tomlinson. In the Intensity of Final Light.
Landing, The.
Nocturnal.
Perfection, The.
Praeludium.
Suggestions for the Improvement of a Sunset.
Whitman. Prairie Sunset, A.
Song at Sunset.
Whittier. Sunset on the Bearcamp.
What the Traveller Said at Sunset.
Williams, William Carlos. Winter Sunset.
Wright, Charles. Dog Day Vespers.
Young. Where the Danube and Sava Rivers
Meet.

Superiority
Emerson. Such another peerless queen.
Who compares a poem.
Lawrence. Amo Sacrum Vulgus.
Are You Pining?
Conceit.
Finding Your Level.
Have Done With It.
Prestige.
Saddest Day, The.
To Be Superior.
Owen. Bold Horatius.
Rich. Artificial Intelligence.
Rolfe. Many an Outcast.
Wilbur. Superiorities.
Williams, Charles Kenneth. Ribbons.

Supermarkets
Bukowski. Frozen Food Section.
Gildner. High-Class Bananas, The.
Ginsberg. Supermarket in California, A.
Meinke. Supermarket.
Miller. Spade a Spade (Grocery for the Poor),
A.
Nemerov. Grace to Be Said at the
Supermarket.

Supernatural
Burns. Tam Lin.
Tam o' Shanter [A Tale].
Coleridge. Rime of the Ancient Mariner, The.
Eberhart. Undercliff Evening.
Graves. Watch, The.
Hardy. She Saw Him, She Said.
Herrick. Upon God ("God is not only said to
be").
Keats. La Belle Dame Sans Merci.
Longfellow. Skeleton in Armor [*or* Armour],
The.
Poe. Raven, The.
Ulalume [*or* Ulalume—a Ballad].
Silverstein. Magic.
Warren. Eidolon.
Williams, Miller. Gift of Prophecy Lost, The.

Superstition
Auden. Like other men, when I go past.
Burns. Epistle to John Goldie in Kilmarnock,
Author of, the Gospel Recovered.
Halloween.
Holy Fair, The.
Ciardi. Daemons.
Evil Eye, The.
Coleridge. Priestley.
Superstition.
Dove. Cholera.
Graves. Superstition.
Hardy. Honeymoon Time at an Inn.
In the Garden.
Signs and Tokens.
Herrick. Charme, or an Allay for Love, A.
Observation.
Hewitt. Fairy Thresher, The.
For a Moment of Darkness over the Nations.
Orientations.
Tumbling Spore, The.
Keats. Gif Ye Wol Stonden Hardie Wight.
Kipling. Bees and the Flies, The.
Our Fathers of Old.
Melville. American Aloe on Exhibition, The.

Nash. Outcome of Mr. Buck's Superstition, The.
Oppen. Occurrences, The.
Rich. For the Conjunction of Two Planets.
Sandburg. Come on, superstition, and get my goat.
Smith, Stevie. From the Italian.
Williams, Miller. Believing in Symbols.

Supper
Nash. Out Is Out.
Roethke. Supper with Lindsay.

Supplication
Atwood. People come from all over to consult me, bringing their limbs.
Browning, Elizabeth Barrett. Supplication for Love, A.
Herrick. Another, to God ("Lord, do not beat me").
To His Ever-Loving God.
Lowry. Perhaps for Eridanus.
Psalms. Psalm 130: "Out of the depths have I cried unto thee, O Lord."
Psalm 140: "Deliver me, O Lord, from the evil man."
Psalm 141: "Lord, I cry unto thee."
Psalm 142: "I cried unto the Lord with my voice."
Psalm 143: "Hear my prayer, O Lord, give ear."
Rich. Statue.
Wyatt. F[f]rom depth of[f] sin[n] and from a deep despair [or diepe dispaire].
Hear my prayer, O Lord, hear my request.

Surfing and Surfers
Gunn. From the Wave.
Tomlinson. Moment, The.
See also **Swimming and Swimmers.**

Surgery
"Carroll, Lewis." Photography Extraordinary.
Cohen. I Wanted to Be a Doctor.
Gardner. Mea Culpa.
Graves. Surgical Ward: Men.
Hesketh. Brain Child.
Kunitz. My Surgeons.
Lewis. "Your leg must go. Okay?" the surgeon said.
MacNeice. Fresh from the knife and coming to.
Meinke. Uncle Jim.
Plath. Surgeon at 2 A.M., The.
Sexton. Operation, The.
Shelton. Surgery.
Stuart. Prayer, A.
See also **Hospitals; Medicine; Physicians.**

Surprise
Auden. Buzzards.
Berry. Aristocracy, The.
Carruth. Ideas hit life like / planks hitting water. Some skim.
Out of the garden.
Catullus. Carmen 107: "If ever anyone anywhere, Lesbia, is looking."
Ciardi. Saturday, March 6.
Creeley. Hello.
Lady in Black.
People, The.
Something.
Swinging Down Central.
Warning, The.
Water (2).
Window, The.
Dickinson. As if some little Arctic flower.
Facts by our side are never sudden.
Incredible never surprises us, The.
Surprise is like a thrilling—pungent.
Graves. At First Sight.
Grotesques.
Hardy. Collector Cleans His Picture, The.
Discovery, The.
Experience, An.
Hewitt. Filled Stocking, The.
Great Headmaster, A.
Joseph. Shadows Coming.
Knott. Sonnet: "Way the world is not, The."
Lawrence. Love Comes Late.
MacLeish. Revenant, The.

Meinke. Poet, Trying to Surprise God, The.
Melville. Lone Founts.
Olson. Fish is the Flower of Water, A.
Pound. Pagani's, November 8.
Rolfe. Death by Water.
Rossetti. Her Seed; It Shall Bruise Thy Head.
Sandburg. People, yes, the people, The.
Simic. Stone.
Stuart. Elegies for Walker Dabney Stuart, Jr.
Warren. Into Broad Daylight.
Whittier. Hazel Blossoms.
Williams, Charles Kenneth. Easter.
Zukofsky. Strange / To reach that age.
See could we quit coveting hope taunting where hope hid and.

Surrealism and Surrealists
Beatles. Glass Onion.
I Am the Walrus.
Lucy in the Sky with Diamonds.
Beckett. Lady Love.
Brooks. Surrealist and Omega, A.
Carroll, Jim. Cosmopolitan Sense, The.
Clark. Trout Kill on the Sacramento.
Creeley. "You've Tried the World, Try Jesus."
Ferlinghetti. Matisse at the Modern, Magritte at the Met.
Fisher. Duchamp and Man Ray.
Shines coldly away.
Ford. Afternoon with André Breton, An.
Hartley. Cellaphon–a Favorite Word with Picabia.
Eilshemius.
Muldoon. Salvador.
Olson. Maximus Letter # Whatever.
Simic. Landscape with Crutches, A.
Van Duyn. Dwarf in the Woods.
Waldman. Paul Eluard.

Survival
Angelou. Alone.
Song for the Old Ones.
Ashbery. Untilted.
Atwood. Place: Fragments, A.
Roominghouse, Winter.
They Are Hostile Nations.
Berry. Poem: "Willing to die, / you give up."
Sitting among the bluebells.
Vision, A.
Berryman. Surviving Love.
Byron. Julian [A Fragment].
Carroll, Jim. For Your Birthday.
Carruth. Smallish Son, The.
Sonnet: "To rebel. So I have saved my life, not once."
Tanck's Song About Survival.
Ciardi. Gift, The.
Clare. Marten.
Clark. As the Human Village Prepares for Its Fate.
Cohen. As the Mist Leaves No Scar.
True Love Leaves No Traces.
Cooper. Blue Anchor, The.
Creeley. Door, The.
Swinging Down Central.
You.
Cullen. Harsh World That Lashest Me.
Only the Polished Skeleton.
Donne. Prohibition, The.
Dove. Zeppelin Factory, The.
Dunn. Loves.
Privilege.
Workers.
Eberhart. Caught there, then, on the Rock. At Corregidor.
Fisher Cat, The.
Let the Tight Lizard on the Wall.
Man's Type.
My mind was heavy and my luck was dark.
To the Field Mice.
Emerson. With the key of the secret he marches faster.
Fenton. Children in Exile.
Ford. Brought in tame from the.
What hard work it takes.
Garrigue. Bad Times Song.
For J.
Glück. Inlet, The.
Phenomenal Survivals of Death in Nantucket.

Graves. Survivor, The.
Uncalendared Love.
Gunn. Rastignac at 45.
Hardy. Heredity.
Hemingway. Poem, 1928.
Hesketh. Fox, The.
Moving Staircase.
Survival.
Survivors.
Hewitt. Epitaph to a Man Not Dead.
Survival.
Triad ("Three things that men may scorn").
Hughes, Ted. How Water Began to Play.
Notes for a Little Play.
Hugo. Cripples, The.
Hideout.
Lone Lake, Whidbey.
Snapshot of Uig in Montana, A.
Joseph. Beyond Descartes.
Birthday Poem.
LANDSCAPE: *Jungle Days* (Dutch).
Man as Cannibal (PLAIN; BIOLOGY).
Stay close, little tortoise, dig in.
Kinnell. Bear, The.
Under the Maud Moon.
Kipling. England's Answer.
Lorde. Brown Menace or Poem to the Survival of Roaches, The.
McGrath. Nuclear Winter.
Revisionist Poem: Machado.
Three Functions of Irony.
World of the Perfect Tear, The.
MacLeish. Geography of this Time.
MacNeice. Canto IV: "To work. To my own office, my own job."
Meredith. Swift fall the blows, and men upbraid.
Whimper of Sympathy.
Merton. Faction du Muet.
Miller. In Celebration of Surviving.
Riding the bus in the evening again.
River of long standing, bridge abut-ment.
Nemerov. Soldier Who Lived Through the War, The.
To My Least Favorite Reviewer.
Who Did Not Die in Vain.
Neruda. Island (VIII), The.
Oliver. Rabbit, The.
Swimming Lesson, The.
Piercy. Best Defense is Offensive, The.
Rolfe. Guerrillas, The.
Marching Song of the Children of Darkness.
Survival Is of the Essence.
War Guilt.
Where Buildings Congregate.
Rukeyser. His father is lost and away.
Sandburg. Hunger and only hunger changes worlds?
Stafford. My Mother Was a Soldier.
Thinking for Berky.
Stevens. Sense of the Sleight-of-Hand Man, The.
Whitman. True Conquerors.
Williams, Charles Kenneth. Faint Praise.
Williams, Miller. Survivor, The.
Wyatt. Alas! my dear, the word thou spakest.

Susanna (Bible)
Stevens. Peter Quince at the Clavier.

Sussex, England
Davie. Sussex.
Kipling. Alnaschar and the Oxen.
Puck's Song.
Run of the Downs, The.
Sussex.
Three-Part Song, A.
Very Many People.

Suttee
Kipling. Last Suttee, The.

Swallows
Browning, Elizabeth Barrett. Ode to the Swallow.
Coleridge. Swallows interweaving there mid the paired, The.
Terrible and loud / As the strong Voice that from the Thunder-cloud.
Cooper. Little Vesper, A.

Cowper. Swallow, The.
To the Swallow.
De la Mare. Swallows Flown.
Eberhart. Summer Landscape.
Swallows Return, The.
Tree Swallows.
Garrigue. This Swallows' Empire.
Hartley. Buttons for Swallows.
Swallows.
Hopkins. Earth and heaven, so little known,
The.
Meredith. Swallow came from over the sea,
The.
Nemerov. Blue Swallows, The.
Rossetti. Fly Away, Fly Away.
Smith, Charlotte. Swallow, The.
Snyder. Sixth-Month Song in the Foothills.
Swinburne. Itylus.
Tennyson. O Swallow, Swallow, flying, flying
South.
Williams, Miller. Evening: A Studio in Rome.

Swamps
Ceravolo. Caught in the Swamp.
Heaney. Bogland.
Moore. I May, I Might, I Must.
Oliver. Crossing the Swamp.
Rain.
Silverstein. Yipiyuk, The.
Walcott. Swamp, The.
Whittier. Le Marais du Cygne.

Swans
Bogan. Winter Swan.
Carruth. Burning Dawn.
Wild Swans at Norfolk, The.
Coleridge. On a Volunteer Singer.
Doolittle. Leda.
Duncan. Four Songs the Night Nurse Sang.
Eberhart. Wild Swans of Inverane, The.
Fisher. In a dull hour thinking of the swan.
Glück. Palais des Arts.
Swans.
Herrick. To Apollo ("Phoebus! when that I a
Verse").
Hewitt. Flight.
Swan.
Swan's Nest.
Jarrell. Black Swan, The.
Jeffers. Flight of Swans.
It was good of my father, whom I hated at
times.
Love the Wild Swan.
Lawrence. Give Us Gods.
Swan.
Won't It Be Strange—?
McAuley. Dying Swan, The.
"MacDiarmid." Two Memories.
MacLeish. Rape of the Swan, The.
Merrill. Black Swan, The.
Millay. Wild Swans.
Moore. No Swan So Fine.
Nash. Swan, The.
Oliver. Swan, The.
Swans on the River Ayr.
Patchen. Cruelkind Swans, The.
Lives of the Swan.
Roethke. Swan, The.
St. John. Swan at Sheffield Park, The.
Sarton. Memory of Swans.
Swans, The.
Smith, Stevie. Bereaved Swan, The.
Stevens. Academic Discourse at Havana.
Invective against Swans.
Tennyson. Dying Swan, The.
Tomlinson. Canal.
Van Duyn. Leda.
Leda Reconsidered.
Wright, James. Three Sentences for a Dead
Swan.
Yeats. Leda and the Swan.
Wild Swans at Coole, The.

Sweden
Cowper. To Christina.
Dickey, James. Lakes of Värmland.
Hemingway. Battle of Copenhagen, The.
Marvell. Letter to Doctor Ingelo, A.
Moore. Carriage from Sweden, A.
Stevens. Lions in Sweden.

Sutter. Swedish Lesson.
Wordsworth. Call not the royal Swede
unfortunate.

Swift, Jonathan
Berryman. Cloud and Flame.
Bogan. Hypocrite Swift.
Jarrell. Boyg, Peer Gynt, the One Only One,
The.
Liddy. Proverbs of Corca Bascinn.
Mahon. Dawn at Saint Patrick's.
Pope. Happy Life of a Country Parson, The.
Lines on a Drawing of a Monument to Swift's
Grandfather.
Stuart. Prayer, A.
Swift. Author upon Himself, The.
Author's Manner of Living, The.
Here shift the scene, to represent.
Life and Genuine Character of Dr Swift, The.
Verses on the Death of Dr. Swift, D.S.P.D.
Wright, James. Written in a Copy of Swift's
Poems, for Wayne Burns.
Yeats. Swift's Epitaph.

Swimming and Swimmers
Atwood. Younger Sister, Going Swimming.
Auden. Early Morning Bathing.
Browning, Robert. Amphibian.
Byron. Written after Swimming from Sestos to
Abydos.
Cullen. To the Swimmer.
Dickey, James. Awaiting the Swimmer.
Lifeguard, The.
Night Pool, The.
Olympian, The.
Dickinson. Water is deeper than the land, The.
Dunn. Primer for Swimming at Black Point,
A.
Glück. Swimmer, The.
Gunn. He grins, he plunges into orgy. It
moves about.
Hugo. Swimmer at Lake Edward, The.
Where Jennie Used to Swim.
Levine. Belle Isle, 1949.
Lewis. Swimmer, The.
Liddy. Afterword.
Lieberman. Diving Ballet, The.
Swimming Pool Pastoral.
Tarpon.
Lowry. !Bulletin!
Mackerel shouldn't take, A.
3 Happy Little Ducks.
McAuley. Pool at the Y.
Mahon. Katie at the Pool.
Matthews. Puberty.
Merrill. Swimming by Night.
Millay. Above These Cares.
Miller. Swimming in the last of September.
Oliver. Swimming Lesson, The.
Olson. All Havens Astern.
"Reed." Since Half the World is H$_2$O.
Sexton. Nude Swim, The.
Smith, Stevie. Come On, Come Back.
Stuart. Rescue.
River, The.
Water's Fine, I'm Fine, The.
Tomlinson. Swimming Chenango Lake.
Updike. You Who Swim.
Waldman. True Story of Being at the Pool.
Young. Sleepy Day at Half Moon Bay.
See also **Surfing and Surfers.**

Swinburne, Algernon Charles
Hardy. Refusal, A.
Singer Asleep, A.
Meredith. There was a young poet of Chelsea.

Swings
Eberhart. Long Swing, The.
Stevenson. Swing, The.

Switzerland
Dickinson. Our lives are Swiss.
Hardy. Lausanne: In Gibbon's Old Garden:
11–12 p.m.
Jeffers. After Lake Leman.
It was good of my father, whom I hated at
times.
Meinke. Cabaret Voltaire.
Café du Pont.
Hôtel de la Truite.
Hôtel Lion d'Or.

Shelley. Mont Blanc.
Updike. Switzerland.
Williams, William Carlos. View by Color
Photography on a Commercial Calendar.
Wordsworth. Descriptive Sketches Taken
During a Pedestrian Tour among the Alps.
Effusion in the Presence of the Painted Tower
of Tell, at Altorf.
Elegiac Stanzas.
Feelings of the Tyrolese.
Hofer.
Memorial near the Outlet of the Lake of Thun.
On Hearing the "Ranz des Vaches" on the
Top of the Pass of St Gothard.
Our Lady of the Snow.
Thought[s] of a Briton on the Subjugation of
Switzerland.
Town of Schwytz, The.

Swordfish
Dickey, James. Undersea Fragment in Colons.
Spenser. Toward the sea turning my troubled
eye.

Swords
Coleridge. Song: "Though veiled in spires of
myrtle wreath."
De la Mare. Massacre, The.
Dobyns. Six Poems on Moving.
Emerson. And as the light divided the dark.
Everson. Attila.
Herrick. Upon Pagget.
Hill. Clash of salutation. As keels thrust into
shingle.
Kipling. Runes on Weland's Sword, The.
Lovelace. One stabbe could not fierce Cato's
Life unty.
When brave chast Arria to her Pætus gave.
"Reed." My Friend George.
Smith, Stevie. Frozen Lake, The.
Sorrentino. Charles and Arthur.
Wakoski. Three of Swords.

Symbiosis
Carruth. I Could Take.
Meredith. Woodman and Echo.
Oliver. Fish, The.
Hunter's Moon—Eating the Bear.

Symbols
Berry. Below.
Burns. Posie, The.
Primrose, The.
Byron. Ich Dien.
Carroll, Jim. Caves, The.
Carruth. Sonnet: " 'Whut do you spose thet
thing is,' Oi said. 'Whut?' ."
De la Mare. Assignation, The.
Rose in Candlelight, A.
Doolittle. Sheltered Garden.
Dove. Five Elephants.
Eberhart. Flag, The.
Everson. Blood of the Poet, The.
Garrigue. Figure for J.V. Meer, A.
With Glaze of Tears.
Hardy. Sign-Seeker, A.
Herbert. Church-Floor[e], The.
Herrick. Primrose, The.
Hewitt. Crossing, The.
Man Fish and Bird.
Those Swans Remember; A Poem.
Hugo. Clachard.
Joseph. Little dots.
Kipling. English Flag, The.
Levertov. Whisper, The.
Liddy. Correspondences.
MacNeice. In Lieu.
Merrill. To a Butterfly.
Olson. A B Cs (3—for Rimbaud).
A B Cs (2).
Lie of 10, or the Concept of Zero, The.
2nd Musical Form, for Dave Young, A.
Troilus.
Pack. Landscape Goat.
Raine. How address you, greatest of givers.
Rich. Design in Living Colors.
Rossetti. Rose, The.
Roses blushing red and white, / For delight.
Sandburg. Shirt.
Sorrentino. Give Them Blood.
Wilbur. 1.

Williams, Miller. Believing in Symbols.
Williams, William Carlos. Formal Design, A.
  Rose, The.
  Still Lifes.
See also **Metaphor.**

Sympathy
Angelou. Poor Girl.
  To a Freedom Fighter.
Atwood. Rest, The.
Brontë. Sympathy.
Cowper. Mutual Forbearance.
  Poet, the Oyster, and Sensitive Plant, The.
  To Miss Macartney.
Creeley. Friend, The.
  Phone.
Cullen. Magnets.
Cummings. Our touching hearts slenderly
  comprehend.
Dobyns. Frenchie.
Dove. Variation on Gaining a Son.
Dunbar. Passion and Love.
  Sympathy.
Dunn. Beautiful Women.
"Dylan." Baby black's / been had.
  Baby, Stop Crying.
  Sad-Eyed Lady of the Lowlands.
  Tell Me, Momma.
  Train A-Travelin'.
Galvin. Tar.
Gardner. That "Craning of the Neck."
Garrigue. For Such a Bird He Had No
  Convenient Cage.
Herrick. Sadness of Things for Sappho's
  Sickness, The.
Hewitt. Memorial Service.
Holmes. Sweet Charity.
Kipling. Recantation, A.
Lawrence. Retort to Whitman.
Lewis. This stunted pine whose knotted roots.
Liddy. Richard, Oremus.
Mahon. Gipsies.
Melville. Arch, The.
Neruda. Men (IV), The.
Rich. For a Sister.
  For the Dead.
  River-fog will do for privacy, The.
  Roots.
  White Night.
Sandburg. Choose.
Sidney. Sonnet 44: "My words I know do
  well set forth my mind."
Silverstein. Benjamin Bunnn.
  Point of View.
Thomson. Sent to George Lyttleton, Esq.,
  Soon After the Death of His Wife.
Wilbur. Another Voice.
  Next Door.
Williams, Charles Kenneth. Bringing It Home.
  Color of Time, The.
  Saturday.
Wordsworth. Feel for the Wrongs of Universal
  Ken.
  Fragments from the Alfoxden Notebook (I).
Yeats. Words.

Synagogues
Schuyler. Sometimes.
Stevens. Winter Bells.
Tomlinson. On Eleventh Street.

Synge, John Millington
Yeats. In Memory of Major Robert Gregory.
  Municipal Gallery Revisited, The.

Synthesis
Carruth. Making love in the cabin, not to
  himself.
Rolfe. Melancholy Comus, The.

Syphilis
Campion. Epigramme: "Lockly spits apace, the
  rhewme he cals it."
Hemingway. FOR THE HARLOT HAS A
  HARLOT.
Wilbur. Pangloss's Song: A Comic-Opera
  Lyric.
See also **Venereal Disease.**

Syria
Merton. Syria.
Walcott. There was one Syrian, with his
  bicycle, in our town.

Syrinx. *see* **Pan (god).**

T

Tagus River, Spain and Portugal
Merton. Tagus is finer than the creek, The.
Wyatt. Tagus farewell, that westward with thy
  streams.

Tahiti
Eberhart. Sailing to Buck's Harbor.
Stevenson. Song of Rahéro: A Legend of
  Tahiti, The.
  To an Island Princess.

Tailoring and Tailors
Burns. Taylor, The.
De la Mare. Tailor, The.
Nash. Consider the Lapel, Sir.
Paley. In Hanoi 1969.

Talk
Angelou. Thirteens (Black), The.
  Thirteens (White), The.
Beckett. Écoute-les / s'ajouter.
  Silence tel que ce qui fut.
Betjeman. Reproof Deserved; or After the
  Lecture.
"Carroll, Lewis." Second Voice, The.
Chaucer. Manciple's Tale, The.
Coleridge. Eros aei lalethros hetairos.
Cummings. All which isn't singing is mere
  talking.
De la Mare. On the Esplanade.
Emerson. Burn your literary verses.
Fisher. Mouth-Talk.
Fox. Like a Woman in the Kitchen.
  Modern woman in search of a soul.
Graves. She to Him.
  Yet Unsayable, The.
Hall. "Internal and External Forms."
Hewitt. Country Walk in May, A.
Hopkins. You ask why can't Clarissa hold her
  tongue.
Kinnell. For Robert Frost.
Kipling. Puzzler, The.
Lawrence. Effort of Love, The.
  Let Us Talk, Let Us Laugh.
Markson. Sexist Stanza.
Nash. Let's Not Play Lotto, Let's Just Talk.
Roethke. Boy and the Bush, The.
Silverstein. With His Mouth Full of Food.
See also **Speech.**

Talmud, The
Nathan. Wisdom of the Talmud.

Tamerlane
Poe. Tamerlane.

Tanagers
Eberhart. Truncated Bird, The.
Schuyler. Scarlet Tanager.

Tangier, Morocco
Beckett. Ne manquez pas à Tanger.

Tannhäuser
Swinburne. Laus Veneris.

Taos, New Mexico
Edmunds. High Road to Taos, The.
Hughes, Langston. House in Taos, A.
Jeffers. New Mexican Mountain.

Tapestries
Jong. Tapestry, with Unicorn.
Nemerov. Tapestry, The.
Rich. Aunt Jennifer's Tigers.

Tarantulas
Dunn. To a Friend in Love with the Wrong
  Man Again.

Taste
Auden. Smelt and Tasted.
Browning, Robert. De Gustibus.
Hacker. Between us on our wide bed we
  cuddle an incubus.
Canzone: "Consider the three functions of the
  tongue."
Hewitt. My Naming.
Lawrence. My Naughty Book.
"MacDiarmid." It is possible that a change
  may come.
Sorrentino. Lemonade Panel, The.

Stevens. Floral Decorations for Bananas.

Tattoos (skin markings)
Fenton. Adult: That's a tattooed man.
  GIRL ATTACKED.
Gunn. Blackie, the Electric Rembrandt.
Hartley. He Too Wore a Butterfly.
Hayden. Tattooed Man, The.
Kooser. Tattooed Lady, The.
St. John. Last Night with Rafaella.

Taverns
Arnold. At Some Lone Alehouse.
Burns. At Whigham's Inn, Sanquar.
  Versicles on Sign-Posts.
De la Mare. Falstaff.
  Good Company.
Dunbar. At the Tavern.
Jonson. Over the Door at the Entrance into
  the Apollo.
Keats. Lines on the Mermaid Tavern.
Lowry. Jokes Aloft.
  Old Blake was warm, he got down to the hub.
  Poem Influenced By John Davenport and
  Cervantes.
  We Sit Unhackled Drunk and Mad to Edit.
  Xochitepec.
"MacDiarmid." Old Wife in High Spirits.
Robinson. Tavern, The.
Sexton. Portrait of an Old Woman on the
  College Tavern Wall.
Turco. Tavern, The.
Wordsworth. Cumberland Water Authority.

Taxes
Beatles. Taxman.
Burns. De'il's [*or* Deil's] Awa wi' th' [*or* the]
  Exciseman, The.
  Inventory, The.
  Jolly Gauger, The.
  Lines *Written on a Window, at the King's
  Arms Tavern, Dumfries.*
  On Mr. Pitt's [*or* Pit's] Hair-Powder Tax.
  To Alexander Findlater.
Cowper. Yearly Distress, The.
Stevenson. Song of the Road, A.

Taxidermy
Fox. In the taxidermist's shop.

Taxis
Carruth. Tanck's Song About the
  Transportation Business.
Creeley. NYC—.
Davie. Mother.
Dickey, James. Spring-Shock.
Gallagher. Open Fire Near a Shed.
Gunn. Night Taxi.
Knight. Memo #2.
MacNeice. Taxis, The.
Matthews. 107th & Amsterdam.
Morgan. Lucky black man in my dream.
Nash. It Would Have Been Quicker to Walk,
  or, Don't Tell Me We're There Already.
  Strange Case of the Pleasing Taxi-Driver, The.
Sandburg. Madison and 42nd.
Schuyler. Sun Cab, A.
Williams, Charles Kenneth. Travelers.

Taylor, Bayard
Whittier. Bayard Taylor.

Tea
Auden. Tea-time in November.
Betjeman. How to Get On in Society.
Browning, Robert. Classicality Applied to Tea-
  Dealing: A Fancy Inspired by Westbourne
  Grove.
"Carroll, Lewis." Welcome Queen Alice.
Dickinson. Little package of Ceylon, The.
Johnson. Parodies of Bishop Percy's *Hermit of
  Warkworth.*
MacNeice. Poussin.
Meredith. Bumble Bee—the Bumble Bee, The.
Silverstein. Bloath, The.

Teaching and Teachers
Angelou. Communication II.
Atwood. My daughter crackles paper, blows.
Berg. Coat, The.
  In It.
Lowell. Self-Portrait.
  Writing Class.
Berry. My mind was overborne with

questions.
To be at home on its native ground.
Berryman. College of cocktails, a few gentlemen.
Professor's Song, A.
Some sketch sweat' out, unwilling swift & crude.
Boyle. Poem in One Sentence, A.
Testament for My Students, 1968–1969.
Burns. On a Schoolmaster in Cleish Parish, Fifeshire.
"Carroll, Lewis." Misunderstandings.
To My Pupil.
Carruth. How To.
Cohen. Teachers.
This Is My Voice.
Cowper. By Moschus.
Cummings. To William F. Bradbury.
Davie. To a Teacher of French.
Dunn. Teacher Answering Young Radicals.
Eberhart. I Went to See Irving Babbitt.
Mysticism Has Not the Patience To Wait for God's Revelation.
Emerson. S. R.
Teach your child to earn his meal.
Gildner. Eeny, Meeny, Miney, Mo, Miss Beech.
Letter to a Substitute Teacher.
Glück. Mountain, The.
Griffiths. Education.
Gunn. Autumn Chapter in a Novel.
His Rooms in College.
Hall. Brief Lives.
Herrick. Eare-rings.
Upon Fone a School-master. Epigram.
Hewitt. Consequences.
Going up to Dublin.
Middle Infant.
Minor Victorian Painter, A.
Miss Murdoch.
Music Lessons.
My Teachers.
96 Clifton Park Avenue and the Robinsons.
Our Sunday School Teacher.
Paid Quarterly.
School Upstairs, The.
Teacher's Residence, The.
Hugo. Letter to Haislip from Hot Springs.
Letter to Kizer from Seattle.
Letter to Mayo from Missoula.
Jonson. To William Camden.
Kinnell. Correspondence School Instructor Says Goodbye to His Poetry Students, The.
Kipling. Centaurs, The.
Koertge. If Other Students.
Larkin. Schoolmaster.
Lawrence. Best of School, The.
Discipline.
Schoolmaster [A], The.
Schoolmaster [B], The.
Snowy Day in School, A.
Lieberman. Homage to Austin Warren.
Love, the Barber.
Lindsay. Master of the Dance, The.
Lowry. Pilgrim passes through the town by night, A.
Prayer: "Oh thou who art not above."
McAuley. Lecture.
McGrath. You Taught Me.
Meinke. Minuet in G.
Myrtle the Turtle.
Teaching Poetry at a Country School in Florida.
Merrill. Three Chores.
Merton. Learning of many things does not teach understanding, or else it would have taught Hesiod and Pythagoras, The.
Millay. Cairn, The.
Nash. Caesar Knifed Again, or, Culture Biz Gets Hep, Boffs Profs.
Purist, The.
Oliver. Spring in the Classroom.
Pack. Clayfeld's Operatic Debut.
Paley. Learning From Barbara Deming.
One day at work he cried.
Prince. Mine old dear enemy.
"Reed." Teach the Gifted Children.

Rossetti. Hollow-Sounding and Mysterious.
O Christ our All in each, our All in all!
Quinquagesima.
Rukeyser. Another Day (You sit there).
Sandburg. Mr. Attila.
Scripture.
Silverstein. Chester.
Snodgrass. April Inventory.
Campus on the Hill, The.
Stevenson. Here he comes, big with statistics.
Long time I lay in little ease.
Tomlinson. High Summer.
Instead of an Essay.
Updike. Humanities Course.
Whittier. At School-Close.
Memorial, A.
To My Old Schoolmaster.
Williams, Miller. Associate Professor Delivers an Exhortation to His Failing Students, The.
Paying Some Attention to His Birthday the Associate Professor Goes About His Business Considering What He Sees and a Kind of Praise.
Williams, William Carlos. Ballad: "To a man and his wife."
Wordsworth. Address to the Scholars of the Village School of—1798.
See also **Scholarship and Scholars.**
Teahouses. *see* **Tea.**
Team Spirit
Kipling. Song in Storm, A.
Teamsters. *see* **Trucks and Truckers.**
Tears
Angelou. Tears.
Beatles. I'll Cry Instead.
Beckett. Samedi répit.
Bishop. Reprimand, The.
What's that shining in the leaves.
Bogan. Solitary Observation Brought Back from a Sojourn in Hell.
Tears in Sleep.
Brontë. She dried her tears, and they did smile.
Browning, Elizabeth Barrett. Sonnet: "I see thine image through my tears tonight."
Tears.
Byron. I Saw Thee Weep.
Lines to a Lady Weeping.
Tear, The.
Carew. Conquest by Flight.
Elegy on the La: Pen: Sent to My Mistress Out of France, An.
Carroll, Jim. Winter's Age.
"Carroll, Lewis." Canto VII: Sad Souvenaunce.
Lays of Sorrow, No. 1.
Only a Woman's Hair.
Sailor's Wife, The.
Third Voice, The.
Willow-Tree, The.
Carruth. Eye of / the hut, The.
Crashaw. John 16; Verily I Say unto You, Yee Shall Weep and Lament.
Tear[e], The.
Creeley. Sea, The.
De la Mare. Forgiveness.
Irrevocable, The.
To E. T.: 1917.
Dickinson. Each Scar I'll keep for Him.
Honest Tear, An.
It's such a little thing to weep.
Donne. Twicknam [or Twickenham] Garden.
Valediction, A: Of Weeping.
Dunbar. Fount of Tears, The.
"Dylan." Baby, Stop Crying.
Emerson. Should I shed my tears.
Gardner. Fly in Amber.
Ginsberg. Tears.
Graves. Love as Lovelessness.
Scared Child, The.
Three Words Only.
Hardy. Had You Wept.
Hartley. Tear Is an Intellectual Thing, A.
Herbert. Grief.
Herrick. Another upon Her Weeping.
Deluge, The.
His Parting from Mistress Dorothy Keneday.

Seest thou those diamonds which she wears.
Teare Sent to Her from Stanes, The.
Teares, and Laughter.
Teares are Tongues.
Teares: ("God from our eyes all teares..").
Teares ("Teares most prevaile; with teares too thou mayst move").
Teares: ("Teares of Saints more sweet by farre, The").
To Primroses Filled with Morning Dew.
Upon Electra's Teares.
Upon Her Weeping.
Upon Shopter.
Upon Teares.
Hill. Slime; the residues of refined tears.
Jonson. Slow, slow, fresh fount, keep time with my salt tears.
Kinnell. There Are Things I Tell to No One.
Kipling. To James Whitcomb Riley.
Kunitz. Night when Coleridge, The.
Lawrence. Punisher, The.
Levine. Told.
Lovelace. Lucasta Paying Her Obsequies.
Lucasta Weeping.
To His Deare Brother Colonel F.L.
Lowry. Poem: "Wet streets in Liverpool."
McGrath. World of the Perfect Tear, The.
Marvell. Eyes and Tears.
Meinke. Myth.
You stand in isolation like the first bloom.
Meredith. By this he knew she wept with waking eyes.
Pope. Weeping.
Rich. Peeling Onions.
Rolfe. Hunter Went Killing: A Fable, A.
Rossetti. Heart Knoweth Its Own Bitterness, The.
Sonnet from the Psalms.
Three Moments.
Sandburg. Bundles.
Smith, Stevie. Satin-Clad.
Sorrentino. George C. Tilyou Smiles.
Southwell. Vale of Tear[e]s, A.
Stevenson. Small is the trust when love is green.
Suckling. Upon L.M. Weeping.
Tennyson. Tears, Idle Tears.
Wakoski. Cobra Lilies in the Supermarket.
Walker. S M.
Whitman. Tears.
Williams, Charles Kenneth. Dirty Talker: D Line, Boston, The.
Good Mother: Out.
Rampage, The.
Villanelle of the Suicide's Mother.
Wordsworth. Away, away, it is the air.
Sonnet on Seeing Miss Helen Maria Williams Weep at a Tale of Distress.
Yeats. He Reproves the Curlew.
Technology and Technologists
Auden. Progress.
Recitative by Death.
Carruth. "I've Never Seen Such a Real Hard Time Before": Three-Part Invention.
Cummings. In heavenly realms of hellas dwelt.
Emerson. Adirondacs, The.
Ferlinghetti. Overpopulation.
Fletcher. America.
Elegy on Tintern Abbey.
Last Judgment, The.
1921.
Song of the Moderns.
Hesketh. Bolton-Le-Moors, 1960.
He Saved Others..
Master Cotton Spinner.
Hughes, Ted. Do Not Pick Up the Telephone.
Jarrell. Machine-Gun, The.
Winter's Tale, The.
Kipling. *after* Horace, *Book* 5, *Ode* 3.
Lawrence. Dies Irae.
Lindsay. Illinois Village, The.
"MacDiarmid." And thus a poetry which fully understands.
MacNeice. Here too, as in my childhood, twilight.
Matthews. Waste Carpet, The.

Nash. Second Chime.
Updike. Telephone Poles.
Waldman. White Eyes.
Williams, Charles Kenneth. Work.

Tecumseh (Shawnee Chief)
Oliver. Tecumseh.

Teddy Bears
Williams, Charles Kenneth. Souls.

Teenagers
Ciardi. Craft.
Poem for Benn's Graduation from High
School, A.
Prayer to the Mountain, A.
Gildner. Around the Horn.
Blue Like the Heavens.
Burn-Out.
Griffiths. Out of a Descended Generation.
Hall. Material.
Updike. Due Respect.
Williams, William Carlos. No Good Too.

Teeth
Catullus. Carmen 39: "Because he has bright
white teech, Eg- / natius whips out a."
Cummings. Mame.
Davie. Machineries of Shame.
Edmunds. Monday.
Hardy. Gap in the White, The.
Herrick. Candor of Julias Teeth, The.
Rock of Rubies: and The Quarrie of Pearls,
The.
To Women, to Hide Their Teeth, if They Be
Rotten or Rusty.
Upon Bridget.
Upon Franck: ("Franck wo'd go scoure her
teeth; and setting to't").
Upon Horne.
Upon Lucie.
Upon One Who Said She Was Always
Young.
Upon Ursley.
Lowry. Good Morning to Our Sweetest
Harteebeeste!
Piercy. Root Canal, The.
Rukeyser. Back Tooth.
Silverstein. Wild Boar.
Updike. Orthodontia.
Zukofsky. Egnatius, candid as his horse-bit
white dentures.
See also **Dentistry and Dentists; Toothaches.**

Telegrams
Davie. Nineteen-Seventeen.
Kipling. Mare's Nest, The.
Sandburg. Telegram.

Telegraph
Joseph. Lost Continent, The.
Kipling. Deep-Sea Cables, The.
Nash. Why the Postman Has to Ring Twice,
or, Yellow Envelope, Where Have You
Gone?
Woman Pulls the Wires.
Whittier. Cable Hymn, The.

Telephones and Telephoning
Angelou. Telephone, The.
Beatles. You Know My Name (Look up the
Number).
Bukowski. 462-0614.
Good One, A.
How Come You're Not Unlisted?
Macho Man.
9 Rings.
Pacific Telephone.
Wrong Number.
Carruth. Phone.
Cummings. Your little voice / Over the wires
came leaping.
"Dylan." Long-Distance Operator.
Gardner. Telephone, The.
Ginsberg. I Am a Victim of Telephone.
Hughes, Langston. Madam and the Phone Bill.
Hughes, Ted. Do Not Pick Up the Telephone.
Koertge. In the Underground Station.
Waiting.
Kunitz. No Word.
Lorde. Memorial III—from a Phone Booth on
Broadway.
Merrill. Doodler, The.

Nathan. Breathing Exercises.
Nemerov. Dial Tone, The.
Piercy. Hand Games.
Plath. Words Heard, by Accident, over the
Phone.
Sandburg. Manual System.
Pick-Offs.
Under a Telephone Pole.
Stafford. Farm on the Great Plains, The.
Updike. Why the Telephone Wires Dip and
the Poles Are Cracked and Crooked.
Wilbur. Phone Booth.
Williams, Charles Kenneth. Call, The.
Williams, William Carlos. Thing, The.

Television
Bukowski. Numb Your Ass and Your Brain
and Your Heart—.
Carroll, Jim. Epiphany.
Inauguration Day.
Music Television.
Carruth. Rule of the majority is / strictly
enforced in all matters, The.
Clark. Daring to Be the Same.
Eberhart. How It Is.
Ferlinghetti. History of the World: a TV
Docu-Drama.
Ginsberg. Television Was a Baby Crawling
toward That Deathchamber.
Gunn. Death's Door.
Hugo. Note to R. H. from Strongsville.
Knight. Television Speaks.
Merrill. Channel 13.
Morrison. American Prayer, An.
Nemerov. Late Late Show.
Mousemeal.
TV.
Way of Life, A.
O'Hara. Poem: "O sole mio, hot diggety, nix
'I wather think I can' ."
"Reed." Video Violence.
Schwartz. Kilroy's Carnival; A Poetic
Prologue for TV.
Silverstein. Jimmy Jet and His TV Set.
Stuart. Common Ground.
Next Step, The.
Waldman. How the Sestina (Yawn) Works.
Williams, Miller. Late Show.

Tell, William
Coleridge. Ode to Georgiana, Duchess of
Devonshire.
Tell's Birth-Place.
Wordsworth. Effusion in the Presence of the
Painted Tower of Tell, at Altorf.

Temperance
Emerson. Way of love is unlimited, The.
Lindsay. On Reading Omar Khayyam.
Smart. Temperance.
Whittier. Brewing of Soma, The.
Disenthralled, The.
Drunkard to His Bottle, The.
Khan's Devil, The.

Temptation
Brooks. Song in the Front Yard, A.
Burns. Poem on Life.
Byron. To a Lady Who Presented to the
Author a Lock of Hair Braided with His
Own, and Appointed a Night in December to
Meet Him in the Garden.
Carew. Separation of Lovers.
To a Lady, Not Yet Enjoyed by Her Husband.
To His Jealous Mistress.
Willing Prisoner to His Mistress, The.
Ciardi. Temptation.
Clark. "Because They Are Desiring.."
Cowper. Temptation.
Cullen. Street Called Crooked, The.
De la Mare. Outskirts, The.
Stratagem, The.
Dickey, William. You White Cunning Devils.
Dickinson. I often wonder how.
Dobyns. Short Rides.
Donne. Thou hast made me, and shall thy
work[e] decay?
Doolittle. Why Have You Sought?
Dunbar. After Many Days.
Reluctance.
Temptation.

"Dylan." Pressing On.
Trouble in Mind.
Emerson. Go into the garden.
Garrigue. Demon Came to Me, A.
Gunn. In Time of Plague.
Hall. Small Fig Tree, A.
Herbert. Quip, The.
Self-Condemnation.
Sin (1).
Herrick. Parting Verse, Or Charge to His
Supposed Wife When He Travelled, The.
Sin ("Sin never slew a soule, unlesse there
went").
Temptations ("No man is tempted so, but may
o'recome").
Temptations ("Temptations hurt not, though
they have accesse").
Temptations ("Those Saints, which God loves
best").
Jarrell. Conversation with the Devil, A.
Lorde. Generation.
Monkeyman.
To a Girl Who Knew What Side Her Bread
Was Buttered On.
Lowry. Just some love and kisses.
MacLeish. What the Serpent Said to Adam.
MacNeice. Canto III: "To work—To
Beaconsfield. A suburban train."
Marlowe. 1.8: Execratur lenam, quae puellam
suam meretricia arte instituebat.
Marvell. Dialogue between the Resolved Soul
and Created Pleasure, A.
Meredith. I am not of those miserable males.
In Paris, at the Louvre, there have I seen.
She had a secret—bonny Bess!
Will o' the Wisp.
Milton. As when of old some orator renowed.
Temptation of Eve, The.
Tempter Disarmed, The.
Morrison. Can We Resolve the Past.
Crossroads, The.
Nash. Never Mind the Overcoat, Button Up
That Lip.
Pope. *Adam* had fallen twice, if for an apple.
Ransom. Tall Girl, The.
Rossetti. Goblin Market.
O Lord, when Thou didst call me, didst Thou
know.
Prince's Progress, The.
World, The.
Shakespeare. Sonnet 144: "Two loves I have
of comfort and despair."
Silverstein. One Who Stayed, The.
Southwell. Fortune's Falsehoode.
Lewd Love Is Loss[e].
Stuart. Confirmation.
Swinburne. Ballad of Death, A.
Tennyson. Œnone.
Williams, Charles Kenneth. Medusa.
Yeats. All Things Can Tempt Me.

Ten Commandments
Clough. Latest Decalogue, The.
Coleridge. Reproof and Reply, The.
Lawrence. Know Thyself.
Stevenson. If I could arise and travel away.

Tennessee (state)
Cohen. I Try to Keep in Touch.
Lindsay. Preface to "Bob Taylor's Birthday."
Melville. Shiloh [A Requiem].
Nash. Fourth Limick.

Tennis
Betjeman. Olympic Girl, The.
Brooks. Old Tennis Player.
Jarrell. Northern Snows, The.

Tennyson, Alfred Tennyson, 1st Baron
"Carroll, Lewis." Melancholetta.
Lawrence. Lord Tennyson and Lord Melchett.

Tenors
Whitman. Dead Tenor, The.

Tents
Frost. Silken Tent, The.

Termites
Nash. Termite, The.

Terns
Eberhart. Seals, Terns, Time.
Piercy. Gracious Goodness.

Snyder. Straits of Malacca 24 Oct 1957.

Terror
Blake. Terror in the house does roar.
Bukowski. There Once Was a Woman Who Put Her Head into an Oven.
Carruth. Your dream: / His name was Hitler and he lived over.
Clark. Door Gunner to the Moment, (A Shau Valley 1968), The.
De la Mare. Gloria Mundi.
Dickey, William. Performances.
Eberhart. And the first, the father, with indomitable will.
Transfer, The.
World War.
Ford. ABC's.
Gunn. Old Woman, The.
Hewitt. Sparrowhawk.
Kinnell. How Many Nights.
Lowry. Alternative.
Fear ringed by doubt is my eternal moon.
Injured Choriant or Paeonic.
Oppen. Primitive.
Rolfe. About Eyes.
Song: "Through all the cowering world, crouching, shrinking."
Schwartz. "O Death, great captain, lift anchor!"
Warren. Terror.

Terrorism and Terrorists
Carruth. Essay on Death.
Dunn. To a Terrorist.
Galvin. In Ireland I Remebered the Foxes of Truro, Massachusetts.
Hoffman. Princess Casamassima, The.
Merrill. Casual Wear.

Texas (state)
Ferlinghetti. Buddha in the Woodpile, A.
Gallagher. Crêpes Flambeau.
Ginsberg. Guru Om.
Hughes, Langston. West Texas.
Miller. Panhandle (For Annette).
Rukeyser. I used to press tools in the Texas oil fields.
Sandburg. In the long flat panhandle of Texas.
Sorrentino. Big Brown Eyes.
Coast of Texas.
Deux Morceaux en Forme de Banane.
Whittier. Texas.
Williams, William Carlos. Desert Music, The.
Yau. Texas Sprawl.
Young. Midnight Special Revisited, The.

Thames (river), England
Betjeman. Henley-on-Thames.
Campion. Ad Thamesin.
"Carroll, Lewis." Double Acrostic: Two little girls near London dwell.
Cowper. See Where the Thames, the Purest Stream.
De la Mare. Old Summerhouse, The.
Dryden. Song of the River Thames, A.
Gunn. Conversation of Old Men, The.
Herrick. His Tears to Thamesis [or Thamasis].
Hesketh. Orpheus in the Underground.
Kipling. River's Tale, The.
Sidney. Sonnet 103: "O happy Thames, that didst my Stella bear."
Spenser. Rivers Come to the Hall of Proteus for the Marriage of the Thames and the Medway, The.
Wordsworth. Remembrance of Collins, Composed upon the Thames near Richmond.

Thankfulness
Beatles. She Loves You.
Thank You Girl.
Berry. Poem of Thanks, A.
Sorrel Filly, The.
Bradstreet. My thankful heart with glorying tongue.
On My Son's Return Out of England.
Upon My Daughter Hannah Wiggin her Recovery from a Dangerous Fever.
Burns. Burns Grace at Kirkudbright.
Ciardi. Memo: Preliminary Draft of a Prayer to God the Father.
Dickinson. I know not how to thank you.

"Thank you" ebbs between us.
Thank you in my heart obstructs, The.
Gunn. Lines for a Book.
Herbert. Antiphon: "Let all the world in ev'ry corner sing / My God and King."
Herrick. Gods Bounty ("Gods Bounty, that ebbs lesse and lesse").
Nash. Oh, Stop Being Thankful All over the Place.
Pack. Number.
Sandburg. Our Prayer of Thanks.
Stevenson. Since thou hast given me this good hope, O God.
System.
Thought, A.
See also **Gratitude.**

Thanksgiving
Angelou. Thank You, Lord.
Berryman. Thanksgiving: Detroit.
Bradstreet. In Thankful[l] Remembrance for My Dear Husband[']s Safe Arrival[l].
Burns. Grace before Dinner, Extempore, A.
Cummings. I thank You God for most this amazing.
Dunbar. Thanksgiving Poem, A.
Emerson. Grace.
Glück. Thanksgiving.
Hartley. Robin Hood Cove—Georgetown, Maine.
Herrick. Another Grace for a Child.
Thanksgiving.
Thanksgiving to God for His House, A.
To God, in Time of Plundering.
Koch. Thanksgiving.
Liddy. Jours-Fixes.
Merton. Prayer of Thanksgiving Written for Victor Hammer, A ("O Thou Father of splendor, Giver of light").
Millay. Thanksgiving Dinner.
Psalms. Psalm 30: "I will extol thee, O Lord; for thou hast lifted me up."
Psalm 75: "Unto thee, O God, do we give thanks."
Psalm 92: "It is a good thing to give thanks unto the Lord."
Psalm 95: "O come, let us sing unto the Lord."
Psalm 116: "I love the Lord.."
Psalm 118: "O give thanks unto the Lord; for he is good: because.."
Psalm 136: "O give thanks unto the Lord.."
Sandburg. Fire Dreams.
Snyder. Prayer for the Great Family.
Whittier. Pumpkin, The.

Thanksgiving Day
Berryman. Minnesota Thanksgiving.
Carruth. Family Reunion.
Cummings. Thanksgiving (1956).
Dickinson. One Day is there of the Series.
Dobyns. Cemetery Nights IV.
Dunbar. Signs of the Times.
Whittier. Harvest Hymn.

Theater and Theaters
Burns. Prologue: "When by a generous Public's kind acclaim."
Scots Prologue, *For Mrs. Sutherland's Benefit Night*, Spoken at the Theatre Dumfries.
Byron. Address.
Elegy: "Behold the blessings of a lucky lot!"
Good Plays Are Scarce.
Occasional Prologue Delivered Previous to the Performance of "The Wheel of Fortune" at a Private Theatre, An.
"Carroll, Lewis." Prologue: "Ladies and Gentlemen seems stiff and cold."
Prologue to "La Guida Di Bragia."
Prologue: "Wiffie! I'm *sure* that something *is* the matter."
Clark. Silence of the Lambs, The. Theatre.
Crabbe. Arrival of the Players, The.
Dunbar. Curtain.
Duncan. Stage Directions.
Ferlinghetti. Living Theatre, The.
Fletcher. Scene from a Drama.
Frost. It Bids Pretty Fair.
Garrigue. Studies for an Actress.

Graves. Secret Theatre.
Hewitt. Lines on the Opening of the Belgrade Theatre.
Hughes, Langston. Note on Commercial Theatre.
Johnson. Prologue Spoken by Mr[.] Garrick at the Opening of the Theatre in Drury Lane, 1747.
Jonson. Ode to Himself.
Ode. To Himself, An.
To My Dear Son, and Right-Learnèd Friend, Master Joseph Rutter.
Kunitz. Downtown at the Front St. Bi-jo (spelt Bijou).
Five..four..three..two..one.
Lovelace. Epilogue, The: "Stubborne Author of the trifle, Crime, The."
MacLeish. Brooks Atkinson.
Meredith. Motley.
There was a fair footman of Torrington Square.
Two Masks, The.
Nash. Boop-Boop-Adieup, Little Group!
Do, Do, Do What You Done, Done, Done Before, Before, Before.
How to Harry a Husband, or, Is That Accessory Really Necessary?
Theatrical Reflection.
Wednesday Matinee.
O'Hara. Mexican Guitar, A.
Pope. On a Lady Who P-ssed [or P———st] at the Tragedy of Cato.
Prologue Design'd for Mr. Durfy's Last Play.
Prologue to a Play for Mr. Dennis's Benefit, in 1733, when He Was Old, Blind, and in Great Distress, a Little before His Death, A.
"Reed." Doin' the Things That We Want To.
Rukeyser. Girl at the Play.
Sandburg. In a Breath.
Props.
Simic. Note.
Position without a Magnitude.
Smith, Charlotte. Epilogue [A] to *What Is She?*
Epiologue [B] to *What Is She?*
Epilogue [C] to *What Is She?*
Prologue to *What is She?* A Comedy, in Five Acts.
Prologue to William Godwin, *Antonio: or, The Soldier's Return.*
Snyder. Feathered Robe, The.
Stevenson. Behold, as goblins dark of mien.
Suckling. Epilogue: "And how, and how, in faith—a pretty plot."
Epilogue: "Plays are like feasts; and every act should be."
Prologue: "'Fore love, a mighty session; and (I fear)."
Prologue: "I've thought upon't; and cannot tell which way."
Prologue to the Court ("Those common passions, hopes, and fears, that still").
Prologue to the Court ("'Tis strange, perchance you'll think, that she, that died").
Prologue: "Wit in a prologue poets justly may."
Thomson. Epilogue to Agamemnon.
Prologue to Mallet's Mustapha.
Prologue to Tancred and Sigismunda.
Updike. Mime.
Movie House.
Williams, William Carlos. Writer's Prologue to a Play in Verse.
Young. Identities.
See also **Show Business.**

Theft. *see* **Crime and Criminals; Thieves.**

Theology
Cowper. Man on the dubious waves of error toss'd.
Dickinson. He preached upon "Breadth" till it argued him narrow.
Donne. Doctors, The.
Eliot. Mr. Eliot's Sunday Morning Service.
Hardy. Respectable Burgher, The.
Merton. Cargo Catechism.
Duns Scotus.
Hagia Sophia.

Hymn for the Feast of Duns Scotus.
Origen.
Stevens. Les Plus Belles Pages.

Theresa, Saint, of Avila
Crashaw. Flaming Heart, The.
Hymn to the Name and Hono[u]r of the
Admirable Saint[e] T[h]eresa, A.
Meredith. St. Thérèse.
Merton. It rained dark and cold on the Day of
St. Theresa of the Heart.
Wilbur. Teresa.

Theseus
Catullus. Carmen 64: "In old days / driving
through soft waters."
Dobyns. Theseus Within the Labyrinth.
Graves. Theseus and Ariadne.
Lewis. Victory.
Lowry. Canny Castor, Punching Pollux.
Nemerov. On Getting Out Of Vietnam.
Zukofsky. Pelion could one time prong its top
worthy keel in pines.
See also **Minotaur.**

Thieves
Berry. Thief, The.
Bukowski. Promise, The.
Stolen.
Walls, The.
Burns. Hughie Graham.
"Carroll, Lewis." Miss Jones.
Two Thieves.
Catullus. Carmen 12: "While everyone else is
laughing & drinking."
Carmen 42: "From the quarters of the
compass."
Chaucer. Reeve's Tale, The.
Cohen. I Have Two Bars of Soap.
Coleridge. Reproof and Reply, The.
Cowper. Ode to Rouse.
On a Thief.
To a Young Lady Who Stole a Pen.
Dickey, James. Spring-Shock.
Dickinson. He that is robbed and smiles.
Sweets of Pillage, can be known, The.
Dobyns. Crossroads.
Santiago: Market Day in Winter.
Graves. Thief.
Thieves, The.
Gunn. Idea of Trust, The.
Hacker. Little Robber Girl Gets On in the
Wide World, The.
Robber Woman, The.
Hartley. She Sauntered Most Elegantly Down.
Herrick. Christmasse-Eve, Another Ceremonie.
Upon Letcher: Epigram.
Upon Prigg ("Prigg, when he comes to houses,
oft doth use").
Upon Shark.
Kipling. Ballad of Fisher's Boardinghouse,
The.
General Summary, A.
Lament of the Border Cattle Thief, The.
Loot.
Kunitz. Thief, The.
Lawrence. Thief in the Night.
Lovelace. Mock Charon, A.
Lowry. Oh the Pyrrus boys are we.
Markson. Youthful Poet's Unspoke Response
to a Woman Talking Too Loudly in His
Favorite Bookstore, The.
Meredith. Au voleur, au voleur, au voleur!—.
Merton. Cracking the Safe.
Milton. To John Rouse.
Nash. Strange Case of the Irksome Prude,
The.
Pack. Stolen Clothes.
Plath. Fable of the Rhododendron Stealers.
Sandburg. Rakeoff and the Getaway, The.
Silverstein. Razor-Tailed Wren, The.
Smith, Stevie. Bag-Snatching in Dublin.
Stafford. Once a man killed another, to rob
him.
Swift. Mrs. Harris's Petition.
Wakoski. Hermit, The.
Williams, William Carlos. Berket and the
Stars.
Childe Harold to the Round Tower Came.
Wright, James. Gesture by a Lady with an

Assumed Name, A.
Offering for Mr. Bluehart, An.
Young. Dude in Denver.
Zukofsky. At hest, hendecasyllabics, what is
this.
Marrucinus Asinius, that sinister.
See also **Crime and Criminals.**

Thinness
"Carroll, Lewis." Size and Tears.
Catullus. Carmen 89: "Gellius is thin. / So?"
Lorde. Song for a Thin Sister.
Nash. Curl Up and Diet.
Zukofsky. Gellius is thin why yes: kiddin'?
quite a bonny mater.

Thirst
Dickey, James. Diabetes.
Dickinson. I could not drink it, Sweet.
Lowry. Prelude To Mammon.
Ralegh. Here Tantalus in water seek[e]s for
water, and doth miss[e].
Wilbur. Ballade for the Duke of Orléans.
See also **Hunger.**

Thistles
Hughes, Ted. Thistles.
Merrill. Variations: The Air Is Sweetest That
a Thistle Guards.
Williams, Charles Kenneth. Drought.
Williams, William Carlos. Thistle.

Thomas, Saint
Crashaw. Adoro Te. The Hymn of Saint
Thomas in Adoration of the Blessed
Sacrament.
Hill. Canticle for Good Friday.
Smart. St. Thomas.

Thomas, Dylan
Berryman. In Memoriam (1914–1953).
Carruth. Aw, Dylan, have you left us? Have
you gone?
Ciardi. Thousandth Poem for Dylan Thomas,
The.
Ferlinghetti. Belated Palinode for Dylan
Thomas.
Gardner. When a Warlock Dies.
Garrigue. Mourning, A.
Markson. Dylan.
I Saw Old Dylan.
Olson. Dylan Thomas, and Now Matthew
Mead—as He Himself, "To Edward Thomas."
Rexroth. Thou Shalt Not Kill.
Young. Poem for Dylan Thomas, A.

Thomas, Edward ("Edward Eastaway")
Hewitt. Minor Poet's Dilemma, 1940.
Lewis. All Day It Has Rained.
To Edward Thomas.
Walcott. Homage to Edward Thomas.

Thomas Aquinas, Saint
Herrick. Sin ("Sin no Existence; Nature none
it hath").
Hopkins. S. Thomae Aquinatis Rhythmus ad
SS. Sacramentum.
Merton. St. Thomas Aquinas.
Stevens. Les Plus Belles Pages.

Thomas More, Saint. *see* **More, Sir Thomas
(Saint Thomas More).**

Thomson, James (1700–1748)
Thomson. Address to the Shade of Thomson.
Ode on the Death of [Mr.] Thomson.

Thor
Bunting. Hymn to Alias Thor.
Morgan. Thor.

Thoreau, Henry David
Carruth. Concerning Necessity.
Not night now. Dawn. Six o'clock, a
November morning.
Gardner. To Thoreau on Rereading Walden.
Hesketh. From Walden.
Oliver. Going to Walden.
Olson. Fish is the Flower of Water, A.
Rich. Walden 1950.

Thought
Beatles. Fixing a Hole.
Fool on the Hill, The.
There's a Place.
Think For Yourself.
Beckett. Ask of all-healing, all consoling
thought.

Berry. Awake at Night.
Breaking.
Clear Days, The.
His mind gone from the window.
Light, The.
This is the wind's eye.
Thought of Something Else, The.
When I think of death I see.
Where.
Berryman. Possessed, The.
Bishop. Wit, The.
Bogan. Henceforth, from the Mind.
Sonnet: "Since you would claim the sources of
my thought."
Brontë. Enough of Thought, Philosopher.
Browning, Elizabeth Barrett. Pain in Pleasure.
Browning, Robert. Transcendentalism: A Poem
in Twelve Books.
Byron. If Sometimes in the Haunts of Men.
Carroll, Jim. How Relaxed.
"Carroll, Lewis." First Voice, The.
Misunderstandings.
Photography Extraordinary.
Ceravolo. O gong of wept / O unviolet.
Ciardi. Birds, Like Thoughts.
Clough. O happy they whose hearts receive.
Coleridge. Constancy to an Ideal Object.
Her Thoughts.
Life.
Love's Sanctuary.
Cooper. In Silence Where We Breathe.
Creeley. After Mallarmé.
Change.
Circle, The.
Dimensions.
Echo.
Edge, The.
Enough.
Fancy.
For a Bus on Its Side and the Man Inside It.
"I Keep to Myself Such Measures.."
Juggler's Thought.
Lion and the Dog, The.
Measure, The.
NYC—.
On Acid.
Plan Is the Body, The.
Rocks, The.
Some Place.
Time.
"To Work Is to Contradict Contradications, to
Do Violence to Natural Violence.."
Young Woman.
Davie. Gardens No Emblems.
When you have shoved aside the scribbled
worksheet.
De la Mare. Idleness.
Mist.
Young Girl, A.
Dickinson. How precious Thought and Speech
are!
I felt a Cleaving in my Mind.
If wrecked upon the Shoal of Thought.
It is solemn to remember.
One need not be a Chamber to be Haunted.
One need not be a Chamber—to be Haunted.
There seems a spectral power.
We cannot believe for each other.
Dunbar. Unexpressed.
Duncan. Illustrative Lines.
Dunn. Not the Occult.
Eberhart. Broken Pen, The.
Emerson. But as this fugitive sunlight.
Coil of space the cones of light, The.
Comrade or the book is good, The.
Ever the Rock of Ages melts.
I wear no badge; no tinsel star.
Idealism.
Love and Thought.
Motto to "Intellect."
My Thoughts.
O Hafiz, give me thought.
Oil & Wine, / Sparkling gems, & rich attire.
Pale Genius roves alone.
Terminus ("For thought & not praise").
What avails it me.
When thou sittest moping.

Fisher. Today / let us think.
Ford. Eagle carries / Off a single sheep.
  Carry, An.
Mishima.
Frost. All Revelation.
  Bond and Free.
  Etherealizing.
  Never Naught Song, A.
Graves. Climate of Thought, The.
  Thieves, The.
  To Sleep.
  Utter Rim, The.
Gray. Ode on the Pleasure Arising from
  Vicissitude.
Gunn. At the Centre.
  Confessions of the Life Artist.
  Dream sponsors: / Charles Manson, tongue.
  L'Epreuve.
  Lines for a Book.
  Merlin in the Cave: He Speculates without a
  Book.
Hall. Poem, The: "It discovers by night."
Hardy. Aerolite, The.
  Freed the Fret of Thinking.
Hartley. Brown Gulls.
  If It Were the Eye.
  Inner Distance.
  Soliloquy in Dogtown, Cape Ann.
Hewitt. Ars Poetica.
  Because I Paced My Thought.
  Blossomed Thorn, The.
  Breastplate.
  Doctor's Bag, The.
  I Turned My Touch to Campion.
  I Write For.
  Mauberly's Son: A Summary.
  Those Morning Walks.
  Values.
Hoffman. Reflections.
Joseph. To achieve knowledge, salting away
  Faust's stock—.
Keats. O! How I Love, on a Fair Summer's
  Eve.
Kipling. Seven Watchmen.
  Two-Sided Man, The.
Knott. Poem (How I Lost My Pen-Name).
  Prophet in a Landscape of Immemorial Time.
Kunitz. Motion of Wish.
  Unquiet Ones, The.
Lawrence. Cerebral Emotions.
  Climb Down, O Lordly Mind.
  Demiurge.
  Prophet.
  Red Geranium and Godly Mignonette.
  Sex Isn't Sin.
  Thought.
Lewis. Run-In, The.
Lovelace. Song: "Strive not, vain Lover, to be
  fine."
Lowry. Bosun's Song.
  Iron Thoughts Sail Out at Evening.
"MacDiarmid." At My Father's Grave.
  Light and Shadow.
  To Hell wi' Happiness!
MacNeice. Turf-Stacks.
Matthews. Theme of the Three Caskets, The.
Meredith. When Will was at home in his
  palace of zinc.
Merrill. Dedication: "Hans, there are moments
  when the whole mind."
  From the Cupola.
  River Poem.
Merton. If people insist on my having.
  My gaze is clear as a sunflower.
  What we see of things is the things
  themselves.
Moore. Mind Is an Enchanting Thing, The.
Nathan. Conversation Piece.
Nemerov. Figures of Thought.
  Idea.
  Knowledge.
  One Way.
  This is about the stillness in moving things.
  Thought.
  Two Sides to an Outside: Meditation from
  Empson.
O'Hara. Colloque Sentimental.

Day and Night in 1952.
Heroic Sculpture.
Poem: "And tomorrow morning at 8 o'clock in
  Springfield, Massachusetts."
Olson. At midnight, after hours of love, I ate.
Moon Is the Number 18, The.
My belly / sounds like an owl.
My poor dumb body.
Night, The.
Shenandoah.
Under every green tree, sex.
Writ, The.
Owen. Spells and Incantation (a Fragment).
Plath. Apprehensions.
  Natural History.
Pope. Epistle I, to Sir Richard Temple, Lord
  Cobham.
Raine. Man.
Rich. Ghost of a Chance.
Robinson. Garden, The.
  Never until our souls are strong enough.
Roethke. Genesis.
  Give Way, Ye Gates.
  Prayer before Study.
Rolfe. Bon Voyage.
  What Does the Novice Soldier Think.
Rukeyser. Notes for a Poem.
  Rang and rang, rang in a small boy's head.
Sandburg. Aprons of Silence.
  Back Yard.
  Bundles.
  Caboose Thoughts.
  Chillicothe.
  Crimson.
  Dialogue.
  Home Thoughts.
  Many Hats.
  Murmurings in a Field Hospital.
  Offering and Rebuff.
  Pool of Bethesda.
  Potato Blossom Songs and Jigs.
  Sandhill People.
  Santa Fe Sketches.
  Sea only knows the bottom of the ship, The.
  Sixteen Months.
Schuyler. Evening Wind.
  Unlike Joubert.
Sexton. February 3rd.
  January 24th.
Shakespeare. Sonnet 47: "Betwixt mine eye
  and heart a league is took."
  Sonnet 85: "My tongue-tied Muse in manners
  holds her still."
Shelley. Fragment: Thoughts Come and Go in
  Solitude.
Sidney. My sheep are thoughts, which I both
  guide and serve.
  Sonnet 96: "Thought, with good cause thou
  lik'st so well the night."
Simic. Stream, The.
Smith, Stevie. After-Thought, The.
  Blood Flows Back, The.
  Lord Say-and-Seal.
  Night Thoughts.
  Thought Is Superior.
  White Thought, The.
Sorrentino. Dominoes.
Stevens. Bed of Old John Zeller, The.
  Crude Foyer.
  Looking across the Fields and Watching the
  Birds Fly.
  Man Carrying Thing.
  Quiet Normal Life, A.
  Saint John and the Back-Ache.
  What We See Is What We Think.
Stuart. Sharp Words in the Men's Room.
  Umpire.
  We Never Close.
Tomlinson. Flame.
  Movements.
Turco. Tick.
Van Duyn. Insight.
  Two Poems, with Birds.
Waldman. I Digress.
Whitman. Aboard at a Ship's Helm.
Wilbur. Event, An.

Fire-Truck, A.
  Praise in Summer.
Williams, Charles Kenneth. That night, /
  winter, / rain.
Williams, William Carlos. Fruit, The.
  Gentle Man, The.
  Ogre, The.
  To the Shade of Po Chü-I.
Wordsworth. Character, A.
  On the Banks of a Rocky Stream.
  Those words were uttered as in pensive mood.
  Travelling.
Wright, James. Breath of Air, A.
Yau. Serenade: "Windows reflect the fuscous
  clouds."
Yeats. Meru.
  Results of Thought, The.
Young. After Visiting Arl at the Hospital.
Zukofsky. Claims.
  It's hard to see but think of a sea.
  Judge and the Bird, The.
  Sequence 1944-6.
See also **Intellect and Intellectuals; Reason.**
Three Kings. *see* **Magi.**
Three Mile Island, Pennsylvania
  Williams, Charles Kenneth. Tar.
Three Wisemen. *see* **Magi.**
Thrushes
  Browning, Elizabeth Barrett. Deserted Garden,
  The.
  Bunting. Thrush in the syringa sings, A.
  Burns. Sonnet—On Hearing a Thrush Sing on
  a Morning Walk in January.
  Cummings. Might these be thrushes climbing
  through almost(do they).
  Music.
  Eberhart. Ultimate Song.
  Frost. Come In.
  Ginsberg. Voznesensky's "Silent Tingling."
  Hardy. Caged Thrush Freed and Home Again,
  The.
  Darkling Thrush, The.
  Proud Songsters.
  Reminder, The.
  Hoffman. Voice of the Woodthrush, Played at
  Half Speed, The.
  Hughes, Ted. Thrushes.
  Lieberman. Song of the Thrush.
  MacLeish. Thrush in the Gaelic Islands, The.
  Meredith. Thrush in February, The.
  Millay. This / Is mine, and I can hold it.
  Rossetti. Dead in the cold, a song-singing
  thrush.
  Smith, Charlotte. Ode to the Missel Thrush.
  Wilbur. On Having Mis-identified a Wild
  Flower.
  Williams, William Carlos. Woodthrush, The.
  Wordsworth. Hark! 'Tis the Thrush,
  Undaunted, Undeprest.
Thumbs
  Sandburg. Personality.
  Silverstein. Thumbs.
Thunder
  Bishop. Thunder.
  Cowper. Thunder Storm, A.
  Dickinson. Farthest Thunder that I heard, The.
  Emerson. When wrath & terror changed
  Jove's regal port.
  Kinnell. Another Night in the Ruins.
  Lorde. Oaxaca.
  Lowry. Black thunderclouds mass up against
  the wind.
  Volcano is dark and suddenly thunder, The.
  MacNeice. June Thunder.
  Meredith. Clash in Arms of the Achaians and
  Trojans.
  Nash. Watched Example Never Boils, A.
  Sandburg. Blizzard Notes.
  Stevenson. Last night we had a thunderstorm
  in style.
  Tomlinson. Whip, The.
Thyme
  Wilbur. Thyme Flowering among Rocks.
  Zukofsky. Thyme.
Tides
  Beckett. Fleuves et océans.

Bly. Calm Day at Drake's Bay.
Coleridge. Moon and the Waves, The.
Hall. Stones.
Hartley. Signatures of Multiple Things.
Hewitt. Moon, The.
Hill. Wreaths.
Jeffers. At the near approach of a star..huge tides.
Joseph. Tides.
Levertov. Tide, The.
Nash. Beginner's Guide to the Ocean, A.
Paley. Women let the tide go out, The.
Piercy. Smalley Bar.
Sandburg. From the Shore.
 Sketch.
 Under.
Sutter. Driftrose.
Tomlinson. In the Estuary.
 Promise, The.
Wilbur. Conjuration.
Zukofsky. Strange / To reach that age.

Tigers
Blake. Tiger [or Tyger][!], The.
Bunting. Muzzle and jowl and beastly brow.
Creeley. Tiger, The.
Dickinson. Dying Tiger—moaned for Drink, A.
Ford. Tonguless crocodile / Meets eyeless tiger darted.
Griffiths. Continuity.
Hughes, Ted. Tiger-Psalm.
Lewis. Tiger of Camden Town, The.
Lindsay. Tale of the Tiger Tree, The.
Lowry. Byzantium: Or Where the Great Life Begins.
Moore. Tippoo's Tiger.
O'Hara. Chez Jane.
Olson. Afternoon.
Oppen. Myth of the Blaze.
Smith, Stevie. Little Boy Sick.
Tomlinson. Tiger Skull.
Walker. There are no tigers.

Tightropes and Tightrope Walkers
Dunn. Man Who Never Loses His Balance, The.
Hesketh. Credo.
Smith, Patti. Ballad of Hagan Waker, The.
Williams, Charles Kenneth. Vehicle: Conscience.
See also **Acrobatics and Acrobats.**

Till, Emmett
Brooks. Last Quatrain of the Ballad of Emmett Till, The.
"Dylan." Death of Emmett Till, The.
Lorde. Afterimages.

Time
Ammons. Glacials.
 Over and Done With.
 Soul's Seas.
 This.
 Time Spans.
 Timing.
Angelou. In a Time.
Ashbery. As You Came from the Holy Land.
 Ivory Tower, The.
 Saying It to Keep It from Happening.
 Wind thrashes the maple seed-pods, The.
Atwood. Beauharnois.
 Dufferin, Simcoe, Grey.
 There are two islands / at least, they do not exclude each other.
 There Is Only One of Everything.
Auden. As I Walked Out One Evening.
 Clocks cannot tell our time of day.
 Homage to Clio.
 If I Could Tell You.
 Sunday Morning.
 Waste.
Beckett. Home Olga.
 Je suis ce cours de sable qui glisse.
 My way is in the sand flowing.
 Somme toute / tout compte fait.
Berry. Anger against Beasts.
 Anniversary, An.
 Dance, The.
 Design of a House, The.
 Discipline, A.

For a night and a day.
For the Rebuilding of a House.
From the Distance.
He Takes His Time.
Meadow, The.
Seventeen Years.
Vision reaches the ground.
Wheel, The.
Berryman. Presidential flags! and the General is here.
 Statue, The.
Bishop. Anaphora.
 January First.
 Paris, 7 A.M.
 While Someone Telephones.
Blake. From Cratetos.
Bogan. Come, Break with Time.
 Mark, The.
Boyle. Advice to the Old.
Bradstreet. Contemplations.
Brontë. O evening, why is thy light so sad?
 Self-Interrogation.
 Tell me, tell me, smiling child.
 There shines the moon, at noon of night.
Browning, Elizabeth Barrett. Hugh Stuart Boyd [Legacies].
 Sonnet: "I thought once how Theocritus had sung."
Browning, Robert. Prologue: "Poet's age is sad: for why?, The."
 Speculative.
Bunting. At Briggflatts Meetinghouse.
Burns. Bonie Bell.
 Lazy Mist, The.
 Prologue: "No song nor dance I bring from yon great city."
 Sketch. New Year's Day. To Mrs. Dunlop.
Byron. Answer to a Beautiful Poem, Entitled "The Common Lot."
 Stanzas: "Could Love for ever."
 Stanzas for Music ("There's not a joy the world can give like that it takes away").
 To a Youthful Friend.
 To an Oak at Newstead.
 To Time.
Campion. De horologio portabili.
 Time, that leads the fatall round.
 To the Right, Noble, and Vertuous, Henry Lord Clifford, Sonne and Heyre to the Right Honourable, Francis, Earle of Cumberland.
Carew. Persuasions to Enjoy.
Carroll, Jim. Caves, The.
 For John Donne.
 In Time, AIDS.
 New Year 1970.
 Winter's Age.
"Carroll, Lewis." Acrostic: Is all our Life, then, but a dream.
 Faces in the Fire.
 Facts.
 Punctuality.
 Three Sunsets.
Carruth. Chronological.
 Horologikos.
 I came to this place one November day.
Ciardi. Bridal Photo, 1906.
 Epilogue: The Burial of the Last Elder.
 January 1.
 S.P.Q.R. A Letter from Rome.
 Thanks to a Botanist, A.
Clark. Color of Stepped on Gum, The.
 On Marine Silence Street.
 Personal Angel Glimpsed.
 Pharoahs Sacrifice Themselves before Her, The.
 Retro.
Clough. He sate, no stiller stands a rock.
 Roused by importunate knocks.
Coleridge. Bitter Reflection, A.
 Hope and Time.
Cooper. Sundial, The.
Cowper. Comparison, A.
Crane. My Grandmother's Love Letters.
 Sonnet: "Ere elfish Night shall sift another day."
 Tenderness and Resolution.
 Time Cannot Be Worn..

Crashaw. On the Frontispiece of Isaacsons Chronologie Explained.
Creeley. Again.
 "Do You Think.."
 Echo.
 For the Graduation.
 For the Graduation: Bolinas, 1972.
 Kitchen.
 Love ("Not enough. The question: what is").
 Master of All.
 Measure, The.
 Moment.
 New Year's.
 Of Years.
 Re C—.
 Rescue, The.
 Sea.
 Sitting Here.
 Still.
 They.
 Time.
 Time, The.
 Tunnel, The.
 Up in the Air.
Cummings. 2.14: "Ah, Postumus, fleet-footed are the years!"
 All ignorance toboggans into know.
 Anyone lived in a pretty how town.
 As is the sea marvelous.
 Being to timelessness as it's to time.
 Chérie / the very,picturesque,last Day.
 Faithfully tinying at twilight voice.
 Fire stop thief help murder save the world.
 Hours rise up putting off stars and it is, The.
 How many moments must(amazing each).
 I say no world.
 If everything happens that can't be done.
 If(touched by love's own secret)we,like homing.
 In time's a noble mercy of proportion.
 Love is a guess / that deepens.
 Love's absence is illusion,alias time.
 Much i cannot) / tear up the world:& toss.
 Night shall eat these girls and boys.
 Not time's how(anchored in what mountaining roots).
 Now is a ship / which captain am.
 Once White & Gold / daisy in the dust.
 Out of more find than seeks.
 Out of the mountain of his soul comes.
 Ponder,darling,these busted statues.
 Skies may be blue;yes.
 Stand with your lover on the ending earth.
 Summer is over / —it's no use demanding.
 There are so many tictoc.
 This is the garden:clours come and go.
 Time,be kind;herself and i.
 True lovers in each happening of their hearts.
 What time is it?it is by every star.
 Whatever's merely wilful, / and not miraculous.
 When hair falls off and eyes blur And.
 When the proficient poison of pure sleep.
 When unto nights of autumn do complain.
 Wherelings whenlings / (daughters of if but offspring of hopefear).
 Where's Madge then / Madge and her men?
 Which is the very.
 Workingman with hand so hairy-sturdy.
Davie. And Our Eternal Home.
 First Epistle.
 I love the way the weave, when two or three or.
 Love and the Times.
 Mens Sana in Corpore Sano.
 Preoccupation's Gift.
 Time Passing, Beloved.
 Winter Landscape Near Ely, A.
De la Mare. Beneath a motionless yew.
 Clear Eyes.
 Decoy, The.
 Flight, The.
 Foreboding.
 Memory.
 Moment, The.
 Music.
 Not Only.

Of a Son.
Polonius.
Quiet Enemy, The.
Thule.
Time Passes.
Dickey, James. Daughter.
From Time.
Dickinson. Clock strikes one that just struck two, The.
Forever—is composed of Nows.
Great Streets of silence led away.
Hour is a Sea, An.
Is it a joyous expanse of Year.
Look back on Time, with kindly eyes.
Sic transit gloria mundi.
Some time is longer than the rest.
There comes a warning like a spy.
They say that "Time assuages."
Things that never can come back, are several, The.
Time does go on.
Time feels so vast that were it not.
Time is short and full.
Time's wily Chargers will not wait.
Too happy Time dissolves itself.
We talked with each other about each other.
Donne. Computation, The.
Dove. Hill Has Something to Say, The.
Dunbar. King is Dead, The.
Love Despoiled.
Time to Tinker 'Roun'!
Dunn. Each from Different Heights.
"Dylan." Ballad for a Friend.
Coming from the Heart (The Road Is Long).
I'll Keep It with Mine.
Restless Farewell.
Time Passes Slowly.
Tomorrow Is a Long Time.
Eberhart. Address to you.
Cemetery, The.
Formative Mastership.
Garden God, The.
Human Being is a Lonely Creature, The.
Illusion of Eternity, The.
Light From Above.
Light, Time, Dark.
Man and Nature.
My Bones Flew Apart.
Nothing But Change.
Poem as Trajectory, The.
Return, The.
Sanders Theater.
Soldier Rejects His Times Addressing His Contemporaries, A.
Standards, The.
Time Passes.
Usurper.
What Gives.
You Think They Are Permanent But They Pass.
Eliot. Burbank with a Baedeker: Beistein with a Cigar.
Burnt Norton.
East Coker.
Little Gidding.
Emerson. Alas, Alas, that I am betrayed.
All day the waves assailed the rock.
Brother, no decrepitude.
Compensation ("Wings of Time are black and white, The").
Crowning hour when bodies vie with souls, The.
Dangerous gift & grace is mine, A.
Days.
Ever the Rock of Ages melts.
From Omar Chiam.
How drearily in College hall.
I know the appointed hour.
Nun's Aspiration.
On bravely through the sunshine & the showers.
Past, The.
Patient Pan / Drunken with nectar, The.
Poet of poets / Is Time, the distiller.
Pour the wine! pour the wine!
Seashore.
Test, The.

This shining hour is an edifice.
To every creature / Adam gave its name.
To the Clock.
Valedictory Poem.
Wo is me woe's me when I think.
Woods.
Ferlinghetti. Hilarious God.
Fisher. Linear.
Magritte Imitated Himself.
Ford. And take your time.
Day has twenty-four hours, The.
Face of the Earth, The.
Not everyone has plenty of time to die in.
Fox. Susanna.
Frost. I Could Give All to Time.
Nothing Gold Can Stay.
Galvin. First Night of Fall, The.
Gardner. Feeling of Time.
Ginsberg. In Death, Cannot Reach What Is Most Near.
Glück. For My Mother.
Inlet, The.
Magi, The.
Saturnalia.
Shad-Blow Tree, The.
Graves. Broken Neck.
Counting the Beats.
Flowering Aloe, The.
Gold Cloud.
In Time.
Joan and Darby.
Lost World, A.
Love Story, A.
Song: From Otherwhere or Nowhere.
Song: The Clocks of Time.
Song: The Queen of Time.
Song: The Sundial's Lament.
Spring 1974.
Time.
Uncalendared Love.
Gunn. Inherited Estate, The.
Hacker. I'll tell you what I don't want: an affair.
Haines. Alive in the World.
Hall. At Delphi.
"Between the Clock and the Bed."
Columns of the Parthenon, The.
Day I Was Older, The.
Exile.
Sea, The.
Shudder [, The].
Hardy. Absolute Explains, The.
Anniversary, An.
Best Times.
Clasped Skeleton, The.
Clock of the Years, The.
Clock-Winder, The.
Commonplace Day, A.
Copying Architecture in an Old Minster.
During Wind and Rain.
Her Initials.
Hundred Years Since, A.
In a Eweleaze near Weatherbury.
In a Former Resort after Many Years.
Inquiry, An.
Long Plighted.
Man Who Forgot, The.
New Dawn's Business, The.
Old Furniture.
Perhaps, long hence, when I have passed away.
Places.
Second Attempt, A.
Second Visit, The.
Self-Unconscious.
She, to Him.
Sheep Fair, A.
So, Time.
Sunshade, The.
Ten Years Since.
Tenant-for-Life, The.
They Are Great Trees.
This Summer and Last.
Week, A.
When Wearily We Shrink Away.
Where They Lived.
Woman Who Went East, The.

Hartley. Flight, The.
Invitation.
Herbert. Life.
Time.
Herrick. Death Ends All Woe.
His Poetry His Pillar.
No Time in Eternity.
Present Time But Pleaseth, The.
Sabbaths.
To a Friend("Looke in my Book, and herein see").
Upon Time.
Watch, The.
Hesketh. All Hallows.
Bleasdale: The Wooden Circle.
Brief Encounter.
Buttercup Children, The.
Call of the North.
Comparison with a Sunflower.
Days.
Fox, The.
Love's Advocate.
Mill Clock, The.
So Little It Can Take.
Traitor.
Violet at Ninety.
Walking Back.
Widowhood.
Winter Daffodils.
Hewitt. Anti-Promethean Ode.
Awareness of Time.
Balloons and Wooden Guns.
Comment on Verse.
End of the World, The.
Expectancy.
First Honey.
For a September Afternoon of Unexpected Brightness.
Here at the Tide's Turn.
Iron and Stone.
Morning Moment.
Northern Spring.
Omens and Auguries.
Poem: "Consider Wordsworth in his withered age."
Poet's Trade, The.
Pour Hélène.
R.P.M.
Sonnet in Autumn.
Ulsterman.
Whit Monday.
Young Womanhood.
Holmes. Fear in the Afternoon.
Hopkins. To His Watch.
Housman. On Wenlock Edge the wood's in trouble.
Jarrell. Bad Music, The.
Kirilov on a Skyscraper.
Lament: "All is far."
Man with the axe stands profound and termless, The.
Old orchard in the middle of the forest, The.
Picture in the Paper, A.
When you and I were all.
Jeffers. All night long the rush and trampling of water.
Diagram.
Gray Weather.
It flows out of mystery into mystery: there is no beginning—.
Little Scraping, A.
Old Stone-Mason, The.
Polar ice-caps are melting, the mountain glaciers, The.
Soliloquy.
Stone Axe, The.
Johnson. In Rivum a Mola Stoana Lichfeldiæ Diffluentem.
Jong. Near the Black Forest.
Jonson. Hour-Glass [or Houre-Glasse], The.
Joseph. For a New Year.
No Map Available.
On the Embankment.
Persephone Returns.
Timetable for a Town.
Visiting.

Tempus Fugit.
Time flies, hope flags, life plies a wearied wing.
Time lengthening, in the lengthening seemeth long.
Time passeth away with its pleasure and pain.
Time seems not short: / If so I call to mind.
Touching "Never."
Unforgotten.
You who looked on passed ages as a glass.
Rukeyser.   Clouds, Airs, Carried me Away.
Eel.
Night Flight : New York.
Overthrow of One o'Clock at Night, The.
Poem: "Green going through the jungle of those years."
Speech of the Mother, from "The Middle of the Air."
Sundays, They Sleep Late.
Thousands of Days.
Three Sides of a Coin.
Time Exposures.
Time Hinder Not Me; His Arms Reach Here and There.
Sandburg.   Altgeld.
Among the shapes and shadow-shapes.
Bitter Summer Thoughts.
Blue Ridge.
Bronzes.
Counting.
Cumulatives.
Deep in the dusty chattels of the tombs.
Deep roots moving in lush soil to send a silver-gray beech tree.
Eleventh Avenue Racket.
Flowers Tell Months.
Four Preludes on Playthings of the Wind.
Gong of Time, The.
Harmonica Humdrums.
Has-Been, The.
Junk Man, The.
Keepsake Boxes.
Kin.
Languages.
Let Love Go On.
Limited.
Losses.
Man the Moon Shooter.
Mist, The.
Moon Hammock.
North Atlantic.
People will live on, The.
Poobahs rise and hold their poobah sway, The.
Record is a scroll of many indecipherable scrawls, The.
Sacred legion of the justborn, The.
Santa Fe Sketches.
Solo for Saturday Night Guitar.
Stars, Songs, Faces.
Streets Too Old.
Striped Cats, Old Men and Proud Stockings.
Sunset from Omaha Hotel Window.
Transient tar-paper shack, The.
Turn of the Wheel.
Under.
Variations on a Theme.
We'll see what we'll see.
Who were those editors picking the most.
Wind on the Way, The.
Without the daily chores of the people.
Sarton.   Now I Become Myself.
On Being Given Time.
These Images Remain.
Schuyler.   Hymn to Life.
Schwartz.   "At last! the present darkness! all is known!"
When a hundred years had passed nature seemed to man / a clock.
Sexton.   For Mr. Death Who Stands with His Door Open.
Road Back, The.
Shakespeare.   Sonnet 12: "When I do count the clock that tells the time."
Sonnet 16: "But wherefore do not you a mightier way."
Sonnet 19: "Devouring Time, blunt thou the lion's paws."

Sonnet 60: "Like as the waves make towards the pebbled shore."
Sonnet 64: "When I have seen by Time's fell hand defac'd."
Sonnet 65: "Since brass, nor stone, nor earth, nor boundless sea."
Sonnet 77: "Thy glass will show thee how thy beauties wear."
Sonnet 123: "No, Time, thou shalt not boast that I do change."
Sonnet 124: "If my dear love were but the child of state."
Sonnet 126: "O thou, my lovely boy, who in thy power."
Shapiro.   Drug Store.
Shelley.   Fragment: Love the Universe To-day.
Ozymandias [of Egypt].
Time.
Sidney.   O stealing time, the subject of delay.
Smart.   To Posthumus.
Smith, Charlotte.   Horologe of the Fields, The.
Smith, Patti.   True Music.
Smith, Stevie.   All Things Pass.
Grange, The.
How Slowly Time Lengthens.
Intimation of Immortality.
Out of Time.
What Is the Time?; or, St. Hugh of Lincoln.
Snyder.   Four Poems for Robin.
I settled at Cold Mountain long ago.
One Year.
Years, The.
Spender.   In 1929.
In Railway Halls.
Spenser.   One day, whiles that my daylie cares did sleepe.
Ruines of Time, The.
Whilom, as antique stories tellen us.
Stevens.   Analysis of a Theme.
Martial Cadenza.
This Solitude of Cataracts.
Stevenson.   For Richmond's Garden Wall.
Light as my heart was long ago.
Mirror Speaks, The.
Nay, but I fancy somehow, year by year.
Strong man's hand, the snow-cool head of age, The.
Sun's Travels, The.
There where the land of love.
Though deep indifference should drowse.
Stuart.   Casting.
Suckling.   Lover's Clock, The.
Swift.   Power of Time, The.
To Janus.
Swinburne.   Triumph of Time, The.
Thomas.   Force That through the Green Fuse Drives the Flower, The.
Hold Hard, These Ancient Minutes in the Cuckoo's Month.
Then Was My Neophyte.
When, Like a Running Grave.
Tomlinson.   During Rain.
End, The.
In the Fullness of Time.
Maintenant.
One World.
Sound of Time, The.
Wind.
Turco.   Attic Poem.
Cat, The.
Forest Beyond the Glass, The.
Girl You Thought You Loved, The.
Habitation, The.
Ice House, The.
Mill, The.
Reflections at Forty-Nine.
Ropewalk, The.
Schooner, The.
Street Meeting.
Tollhouse, The.
Vigilance.
Van Duyn.   Homework.
Wakoski.   Sour Milk.
Walcott.   Prelude: "I, with legs crossed along the daylight, watch."
Warren.   Arrogant Law.
Bearded Oaks.

Forever O'Clock.
I am the past time, am old, but.
Interjection #1: The Need For Re-evaluation.
Late Subterfuge.
Mortmain.
Natural History.
Nature of a Mirror, The.
Sunset Walk in Thaw-Time in Vermont.
There's a Grandfather's Clock in the Hall.
Whitman.   As Consequent, Etc.
For Him I Sing.
From My Last Years.
Hours Continuing Long.
Life and Death.
Or, from That Sea of Time.
Quicksand Years.
To Think of Time.
Who Learns My Lesson Complete.
Whittier.   Autograph, An.
Greeting.
Hampton Beach.
Homestead, The.
Past and Coming Year, The.
Reunion, The.
Winter Roses.
Wilbur.   Agrigentum Road, The.
Ballade in Old French.
Death, from a Distance.
Gnomons.
Mill, The.
Mirabeau Bridge.
On the Marginal Way.
Shad-Time.
To Madame du Châtelet.
Wellfleet: The House.
Year's End.
Williams, Charles Kenneth.   When / you were small, I.
Williams, Miller.   Ghost of His Wife Comes to Tell Him How It Is.
House in the Vacant Lot, The.
Reading the Newsapaper on Microfilm.
Sir.
Sitting Alone at Sunrise: Problems in the Space-Time Continuum.
Summer Afternoon an Old Man Gives Some Thought to the Central Questions, A.
Williams, William Carlos.   A, B & C of It, The.
Clock of the Years, The.
Counter, The.
Prelude, A; "I know only the bare rocks of today."
Tailpiece.
Time the Hangman.
To a Woman Seen Once.
Wordsworth.   Among the Ruins of a Convent in the Apennines.
At Furness Abbey ("Here, where, of havoc tired and rash undoing").
"Beloved Vale!" I said, "when I shall con."
Calm Is the Fragrant Air, and Loth to Lose.
Composed among the Ruins of a Castle in North Wales.
Cuckoo-Clock, The.
Fragment: "In vain did Time and Nature.."
Go Back to Antique Ages, If Thine Eyes.
Longest Day; Addressed to My Daughter, The.
Massy Ways Carried across These Heights, The.
Pillar of Trajan, The.
September, 1819 ("Departing summer hath assumed").
Sequel to *Beggars* Composed Many Years After.
Sonnet: "If grief dismiss me not to them that rest."
'Tis He Whose Yester-Evening's High Disdain.
To ———: "Look at the fate of summer flowers."
To a Painter ("All praise the Likeness by thy skill portrayed").
Wright, Charles.   Journal of English Days, A.
Light Journal.
Lost Souls.
March Journal.

Monastery at VrLOWSCARONac, The.
Portrait of the Artist with Hart Crane.
Southern Cross, The.
Yard Journal.
Wright, James. Devotions.
Fishermen, The.
RIP.
Sitting in a Small Screenhouse on a Summer Morning.
Three Steps to the Graveyard.
To the August Fallen.
Today I Was So Happy, So I Made this Poem.
Wroth. Song 5: "Time only cause of my unrest."
Sonnet 5: "Like to huge clowds of smoke which well may hide."
Sonnet 32: "How fast thou fliest, O Time, on loves swift wings."
Yeats. Gyres, The.
His Bargain.
Lamentation of the Old Pensioner, The.
Moods, The.
Peace.
Tom at Cruachan.
Young. Continuing.
Eternity.
Fort Collins, Colorado.
Hot House.
Imitation Dance, The.
Poem for Omar Khayyam (1050?-1123? A.D.).
Why a Hush Should Not Be Rushed.
Zukofsky. For Selma Gubin's Umbrellas.
Has the sum.
I Sent Thee Late.

Tinkers
Herrick. Tinkers Song, The.
Plath. Tinker Jack and the Tidy Wives.
Wordsworth. Tinker, The.

Tintern Abbey
Stevenson. Thou strainest through the mountain fern.

Tiresias
Gunn. Book of the Dead, The.

Titanic (ship)
Hardy. Convergence of the Twain, The.
Hewitt. Late Spring, 1912.
Hill. Ode on the Loss of the Titanic.
Knight. Dark Prophecy: I Sing of Shine.
Lowry. Lusty Advice of a Fortune-Teller.
S.O.S Sinking fast by both bow and stern.

Tithonus
Browning, Elizabeth Barrett. Aurora and Tithonus.
Tennyson. Tithonus.

Titian (Tiziano Vecellio)
Lovelace. Amyntor's Grove.
Lowell. Charles V by Titian.

Titmice
De la Mare. Titmouse.
See also **Chickadees.**

Titus (Roman Emperor)
Wordsworth. Perhaps some needful service of the State.

Toads
Bishop. Giant Toad.
Eberhart. Hop-Toad, The.
Gildner. Toads in the Greenhouse.
Rossetti. Hopping frog, hop here and be seen.
Sexton. March 7th.
Wilbur. Death of a Toad, The.

Toadstools. *see* **Mushrooms.**

Tobacco
Byron. Napoleon's Snuff-Box.
Cowper. To Mr. Newton.
To the Rev. William Bull.
Eberhart. Tobacconist of Eighth Street, The.
Kipling. Poor Honest Men.
Melville. Herba Santa.
Turco. Tobacco Shed, The.

Tobago. *see* **Trinidad and Tobago.**

Toes
Knott. Beddybye.
Silverstein. My Beard.
Yipiyuk, The.
Updike. In Extremis.

See also **Feet.**

Toledo, Spain
Boyle. Statement for El Greco and William Carlos Williams, A.
Williams, William Carlos. High Bridge above the Tagus River at Toledo, The.

Tolerance
Browning, Elizabeth Barrett. Adequacy.
Dunbar. Accountability.
Fenton. Chosun.
Hewitt. You mid the corn not yet asleep.
Hughes, Langston. Live and Let Live.
Lawrence. Tolerance.
Nash. Nevertheless.
Yes and No.
Plath. Companionable Ills, The.

Toller, Ernst
Auden. In Memory of Ernst Toller.
Rolfe. May 22nd 1939.

Tollund Man
Heaney. Tollund Man, The.

Tombs
Berry. Farmer among the Tombs, The.
Brontë. Darkness was overtraced on every face.
Start not! upon the minister wall.
Wide cathedral aisles are lone, The.
Carew. Another [Epitaph on Lady Mary Villiers] ("This little vault, this narrow room").
Coleridge. Love's Burial-Place.
Two Round Spaces on the Tombstone, The.
Cowper. Another.
Another ["Take to thy bosom, gentle earth, a swain"].
Epitaph, An: "My name—my country—what are they to thee."
Stanzas on Milton's Remains.
Davie. Under St Paul's.
De la Mare. Stranger, The.
Dickey, James. Tomb Stone.
Dickinson. Admirations—and Contempts—of time, The.
Dimple in the Tomb, A.
It was a Grave, yet bore no Stone.
Sweet hours have perished here.
Donne. Fall of a Wall.
Niobe.
Eberhart. I Will Not Dare to Ask One Question.
Emerson. And when I am entombed in my place.
Fletcher. From the Japanese, VI.
In the Garden of Dreams.
Hall. Southwest of Buffalo.
Hardy. Obliterate Tomb, The.
Herbert. Church Monuments.
Herrick. His Winding-Sheet.
To Robin Redbreast.
Upon a Flie.
Upon the Lady Crew.
Jeffers. Broadstone, The.
Low Sky, The.
Kipling. Burden, The.
Larkin. Arundel Tomb, An.
Lindsay. Trial of the Dead Cleopatra in Her Beautiful and Wonderful Tomb, The.
Lovelace. On the Death of Mrs. Elizabeth Filmer.
Merton. Tomb Cover of Imam Riza.
Morrison. It Has Been Said.
Nash. Funebrial Reflection.
Lather as You Go.
Patchen. Old lean over the tombstones, the, The.
Pope. Epitaph Intended for Mr. Rowe, in Westminster Abbey.
Epitaph on the Monument of the Honourable Robert Digby, and of his Sister Mary, erected by their Father the Lord Digby, in the Church of Sherborne in Dorsetshire, 1727.
Pound. Tomb of Akr Caar, The.
Rossetti. Dead in the cold, a song-singing thrush.
Stevens. Worms at Heaven's Gate, The.
Stevenson. Here you rest among the valleys,

maiden known to but a few.
To Priapus.
See also **Cemeteries; Graves; Monuments; Mausoleums.**

Tongues
Creeley. Charm, The.
Hacker. Canzone: "Consider the three functions of the tongue."
Herrick. Hand and Tongue, The.
Meinke. Poet to His Tongue, The.
Zukofsky. Michtam.

Tools
Ammons. Utensil.
Berry. Adze, The.
Ciardi. Measurements.
Eberhart. Broken Pen, The.
Hewitt. Ars Poetica.
Lowry. Note.
Sandburg. Laughing Blue Steel.
Sutter. Tools.
Wordsworth. To the Spade of a Friend (An Agriculturist).
Yau. Electric Drills.

Toothaches
Burns. Address to the Tooth-Ache.
Carew. Tooth-Ache Cured by a Kiss, The.
Herrick. Upon Gorgonius.
Lowry. With Sweetest Love from All the Little Animals to Their Beloved Harteebeeste.
Piercy. Root Canal, The.
See also **Teeth.**

Torah, The
Cohen. My Teacher.

Tornadoes
Ammons. Spring Tornado.
Eberhart. Contend with steepness, the dark air.
MacNeice. Crouched upon sea-chiselled gravel, staring out and up at the sea.
Shapiro. Tornado Warning.

Toronto, Ontario
Atwood. Visit to Toronto, with Companions.

Tortoises
Atwood. Elegy for the Giant Tortoises.
Carruth. Cross My Heart and Hope to Die, It Was the Very Same Song Exactly.
Coleridge. Eagle and the Tortoise, The.
Joseph. Stay close, little tortoise, dig in.
Kunitz. Jonathan, the last of the giant tortoises.
Lawrence. Baby Tortoise.
Lui et Elle.
Tortoise Family Connections.
Tortoise Gallantry.
Tortoise-Shell.
Tortoise Shout.
Nash. Tortoise, The.

Torture
Atwood. Torture.
Beckett. Noire soeur.
Berryman. Song of the Tortured Girl, The.
Bly. Romans Angry about the Inner World.
Carew. Song: Murdering Beauty.
Carruth. He remembers: / There was this big house they called the Hatch.
Clark. Calling Infinity.
Cohen. Failure of a Secular Life, The.
Heirloom.
What I'm Doing Here.
Dickey, William. Post-Therapy Room.
Fenton. Vuccerìa.
Fisher. Instruments of Torture, The.
Gunn. I am the man on the rack.
Hemingway. In a magazine.
Hesketh. Cross.
Different.
Jeffers. Memoir.
Lieberman. Dungeon Amorist, The.
Lindsay. Dangerous Little Boy Fairies, The.
Lorde. Barren.
Lowry. What the Irish Soldier Said.
Paley. In San Salvador (II).
Plath. Hanging Man, The.
Prince. Campanella.
"Reed." Blue Mask, The.
Rolfe. Witness at Leipzig.
Sandburg. Man with the Broken Fingers, The.

Simic. Rough Outline.
Walker. Torture.
Williams, Charles Kenneth. Another Dollar.
Interrogation II.

Touch
Atwood. Axiom.
Beatles. I Want to Hold Your Hand.
Graves. Touch My Shut Lips.
Gunn. Touch.
Hall. Fête.
Jong. Touch.
Kinnell. Poem of Night.
Lawrence. Initiation Degrees.
Night.
Touch.
Touch Comes.
Rossetti. De Profundis.
Sexton. Touch, The.
Sutter. Warmth.
Williams, Charles Kenneth. Medusa.

Tourism and Tourists
Atwood. At the Tourist Centre in Boston.
Auden. Day-dreams of a Tourist.
Bishop. Arrival at Santos.
Carruth. Baler, The.
Clough. Resignation—to Faustus.
Cummings. Memorabilia.
Dobyns. Dancing in Vacationland.
Eliot. Burbank with a Baedeker: Beistein with
a Cigar.
Ferlinghetti. Baja Revisited.
Frost. Importer, An.
Hall. Christ Church Meadows, [Oxford].
Hemingway. I Like Americans.
I Like Candians.
Hewitt. Double-Ended Tram, The.
Lake Bled, Slovenia.
Montelepre.
Kunitz. Thief, The.
Lawrence. Tourists.
Lieberman. Dungeon Amorist, The.
Lindsay. Within the town of Buffalo.
Lowry. Betty and Gerald Noxon.
MacNeice. Gorged on red, green, purple,
tomatoes, peppers, aubergine.
Merrill. Casual Wear.
Morrison. Dancing & Thrashing.
Rich. Tourist and the Town, The.
Shelton. Reservations.
Tomlinson. Ice Cream at Blauenberg.
Teotihuacán.
Updike. Moscow.
Waldman. Going In.
Paris Day.
Whittier. Christian Tourists, The.
Wordsworth. On Seeing Some Tourists of the
Lakes Pass by Reading; a Practice Very
Common.
Zukofsky. 4 Other Countries.
Stratford-on-Avon.

Toussaint L'Ouverture, François Dominique
Whittier. Toussaint L'Ouverture.
Wordsworth. To Toussaint L'Ouverture.

Towns
Auden. April in a Town.
Humpty Dumpty.
No Change of Place.
Berry. He Looks out the Window at the
Town.
Betjeman. From the Great Western.
Small Towns of Ireland, The.
Browning, Robert. Up at a Villa—Down in
the City.
Davie. Oriental Visitor, An.
Townend, 1976.
Dove. Small Town.
Dunbar. Possum Trot.
Eberhart. Retrospective Forelook.
Fisher. Sloping and tapering away.
Frost. Serious Step Taken Lightly, A.
Ginsberg. Reflections in Sleepy Eye.
Hall. Town of Hill, The.
Hewitt. Mile-Long Street, The.
Mortal Place, The.
Hugo. After a Train Trip, One Town Remains.
Belt.
Larkin. Here.

Lawrence. End of Another Home Holiday.
Inheritance, The.
Little Town at Evening, The.
Transformations.
Whether or Not.
Lindsay. Springfield of the Far Future, The.
Lowry. Old Freighter in an Old Port.
Port has a sweeter name than Saigon, The.
Welcome Home Oh Harteebeeste.
Merrill. Summer People, The.
Miller. No and I don't know where.
Moore. Steeple-Jack, The.
Olson. Chronicles.
Gonfalon Raised Tonight, The.
Town, The.
Oppen. Undertaking in New Jersey, The.
Patchen. It's My Town!
Just outside Tombstone.
Knowledge of Old Towns, The.
"Reed." Small Town.
Rukeyser. Gauley Bridge.
Sandburg. Between Two Hills.
Chromo.
Five Towns on the B. and O.
Gone.
Joliet.
Potomac Town in February.
Schuyler. Elizabethans Called It Dying, The.
Smith, Stevie. Avondale.
Snyder. Arts Council Meets in Eureka, The.
Suckling. Sir, / Whether these lines do find
you out.
Tomlinson. Sconset.
Two Views of Two Ghost Towns.
Updike. Upon Learning That a Town Exists in
Virginia Called Upperville.
Van Duyn. In the Missouri Ozarks.
Whittier. Haverhill.
Williams, Miller. Main Street.
Williams, William Carlos. Invitation.
Wordsworth. Brugès ("Bruges I saw attired
with golden light").
Brugès ("Spirit of Antiquity—enshrined, The").
Incident at Brugès.
Yau. Dear . . .
Yeats. Happy Townland, The.
Young. Leaving Syracuse.
See also **Cities; Villages.**

Toys
Bishop. Cirque d'Hiver.
Bukowski. Look:, The.
Ginsberg. Ghost May Come, A.
Hewitt. Lead Soldiers and Regimental
Uniforms.
Lost *Argo*, Islandmagee, Summer 1919.
Larkin. Tops.
Nemerov. Instructions for Use of This Toy.
Snow Globe, The.
Patchen. Orange Bears, The.
Sandburg. Upstairs.
Simic. Toy Factory.
Stevenson. Block City.
Dumb Soldier, The.
Land of Counterpane, The.
My Treasures.
Williams, William Carlos. Chinese Toy, A.

Track Athletics
Auden. Runner.
Whitman. Runner, The.

Tractors
Auden. Traction Engine, The.
Hewitt. Thresher, The.
Hughes, Ted. Tractor.
Sandburg. New Farm Tractor.
Tomlinson. Lines.

Tradition
Berrigan. Penn Station.
Davie. Livingshayes.
Ford. Before his father.
Fox. Guillermo's Wedding.
Gardner. Folkways.
Graves. Traditionalist, The.
Hall. Family, The.
Herrick. Fast, or Lent, The.
Hewitt. Eleventh Night, The.
From the Tibetan.
Little People, A.

Long Bridge, The.
Man from Malabar, The.
Minotaur.
My Parents' Courtship.
Strangers and Neighbors.
Tinker's Answer, The.
True Smith of Tieveragh, The.
Wake, The.
Kipling. Irish Guards, The.
Land, The.
Lorde. Generation.
Lovelace. To a Lady with Child that Asked
[or Ask'd] an Old Shirt.
"MacDiarmid." Here in the hauf licht waitin'
till the clock.
Mahon. Last of the Fire Kings, The.
Nash. Epstein, Spare That Yule Log!
Neruda. XIX, The.
Patchen. Letter to the Inventors of a Tradition,
A.
Prince. He Compares Old Customs with Those
of His Kingdom.
Rich. At the Jewish New Year.
8/1/68.
Cartographies of Silence.
Ghazal V.
7/14/68: i.
7/16/68: ii.
Rules break like a thermometer, The.
Study of History.
Tear Gas.
This apartment full of books could crack open.
Shapiro. Humanities Building, The.
Necropolis.
Shelton. Local Knowledge.
Wordsworth. Fancy and Tradition.
Highland Broach, The.
Young England—What Is Then Become of
Old.

Trafalgar, Battle of (1805)
Hardy. Night of Trafalgar, The.
Meredith. October 21, 1905.
Trafalgar Day.

Traffic
Beckett. Lueurs lisières.
Dobyns. Santiago: la Avenida Pedro de
Valdivia.
Hall. Traffic.
Kipling. Advertisement, The.
Meinke. Myth.
Nash. It Would Have Been Quicker to Walk,
or, Don't Tell Me We're There Already.
Poor Mr. Strawbridge.
Strange Case of Mr. Niobob's
Transmogrification, The.
O'Hara. Walking to Work.
Sandburg. Blue Island Intersection.
Silverstein. Traffic Light.
Wilbur. Simile for Her Smile, A.
Young. Beauty of Milwaukee Cold with Rain,
The.

Traffic Accidents. *see* **Automobile Accidents.**
Traherne, Thomas
Wilbur. "World without Objects Is a Sensible
Emptiness, A."

Trains
Auden. Flowers and Stationmaster.
Mail-train, Crewe, The.
Betjeman. Parliament Hill Fields.
Bogan. Train Tune.
Clark. "Enforced lapse..., The."
Cummings. Will i ever forget that precarious
moment?
Davie. Buckinghamshire.
Dickinson. I like to see it lap the Miles.
Train went through a burial gate, A.
Dunbar. Ballade: "By Mystic's banks I held
my dream."
"Dylan." It Takes a Lot to Laugh, It Takes a
Train to Cry.
Train A-Travelin'.
Eberhart. Analogue of Unity in Multeity.
Gallagher. Devotion: That It Flow; That There
Be Concentration.
Not There.
Garrigue. On Going by Train to White River
Junction, Vt.

Glück. Chicago Train, The.
Hacker. Friend (this is an imaginary letter).
Hall. Sister on the Tracks, A.
Transcontinent.
Hardy. Faintheart in a Railway Train.
Midnight on the Great Western.
Hesketh. Leave Train, The.
Limbo.
Hewitt. Frontier, The.
On a January Train Journey.
Prelude to Consternation.
Hoffman. City of Satisfactions, The.
Special Train, A.
Hughes, Langston. Lunch in a Jim Crow Car.
Hugo. After a Train Trip, One Town Remains.
Argo.
Elegy: "I expected him to look dead in the casket."
Late Summer, Drummond.
Yards of Sarajevo, The.
Jarrell. Orient Express, The.
Joseph. Instant on the Viaduct, An.
Kunitz. Me and the Rock.
Larkin. Like the Train's Beat.
Lawrence. À La Maniere De D. H. Lawrence.
Honeymoon.
Red Moon-Rise.
Tommies in the Train.
Train, The.
Levine. And the Trains Go On.
Lowry. April 1937 In the Oaxaca Train.
Duck Train—Vocal Arctic Fox-Trot.
In the Oaxaca Train.
Picture, A.
With Sweetest Morning Love to Their Beloved Harteebeeste.
McGrath. End of the Line, The.
Repeated Journey, The.
Something Is Dying Here.
MacLeish. Arrival and Departure.
Way-Station.
MacNeice. Canto III: "To work—To Beaconsfield. A suburban train."
Canto XX: "To Wales once more, though not on holiday now."
Contact, A.
Figure of Eight.
Hold-up.
Restaurant Car.
Slow Movement.
Train to Dublin.
Trains in the Distance.
McNeill. First Train (1895).
Merton. Every evening the L & N.
Long freight train / Wakes me in my cell, The.
Millay. Travel.
Miller. On some night a train is going past the library.
Nash. Dr. Fell and Points West.
Now You See It, Now I Don't.
September Morn.
Unwinged Ones, The.
Nathan. Soundings, The.
Nemerov. Clock With No Hands, A.
Home for the Holidays.
Junction, on a Warm Afternoon, The.
Notley. It Would.
Olson. Landscape, Without Color.
Morning News, The.
Patchen. Little Black Train, The.
Plath. Getting There.
Rich. Sunday Evening.
Roethke. Night Journey.
Rukeyser. Grand Central Station.
Sandburg. Limited.
Window.
Schwartz. All Night, All Night.
Sorrentino. Simplicity.
Spender. Express, The.
Sign *Faehre nach Wilm*, The.
Stevenson. From a Railway Carriage.
Tomlinson. Night-Train, The.
Warren. Ballad: Between the Boxcars.
Whitman. To a Locomotive in Winter.
Williams, William Carlos. Overture to a

Dance of Locomotives.
To freight cars in the air.
Yau. Dragon's Blood IV.
Zukofsky. And to paradise which is a port.
See also **Railroads; Locomotives.**
Traitors. *see* **Treason and Traitors.**
Trakl, Georg
Berryman. Drugs Alcohol Little Sister.
Silverstein. Sarah Cynthia Sylvia Stout Would Not Take the Garbage Out.
Williams, Charles Kenneth. Neglect.
Tramps. *see* **Vagabonds.**
Transcience. *see* **Change.**
Transformation
Atwood. Carrying Food Home in Winter.
Fist, withered and strung, The.
It was not my fault, these animals.
Songs of the Transformed.
Auden. After.
Dawn.
Evolution of the Dragon, The.
To a Small Buddha.
We, knowing the family history.
Berg. Eating Outside.
God, A.
Music.
Boyle. Poem for Arthur, A.
Brontë. H.A. and A.S.
Browning, Robert. Rephan.
Carruth. Wheel of Being I, The.
Clark. Sky.
Cohen. Cuckold's Song, The.
Creeley. Song: "Grit / of things, The."
Statue, The.
Cullen. Protest.
That Bright Chimeric Beast.
Dickinson. He touched me, so I live to know.
Duncan. Banners, The.
Dunn. Parable of the Fictionist.
Emerson. Character.
He could condense cerulean ether.
Life is great / Men are small.
Everson. Encounter, The.
Ferlinghetti. Paris Transformations.
Fisher. Upper corner—probably, The.
Ford. Curse for the War Machine, A.
Fox. Beasts Have Entered, The.
Offering.
Gallagher. Present.
Willingly.
Galvin. Transmigration.
Glück. Undertaking, The.
Hacker. Sea Coming Indoors, The.
Haines. I left the graveyard by a chosen path.
Instructions to a Sentry.
Hall. Digging.
Je Suis une Table.
"King and Queen."
Hardy. Transformations.
Hoffman. Possession.
Hugo. Reading at the Old Federal Courts Building, St. Paul.
Kipling. 'Eathen, The.
Wonder, The.
Kunitz. Illusionist, The.
Transformations.
Levertov. Unknown, The.
Liddy. Kerouac's Ronsard Dance.
Prayers of a Pagan.
Vir XII.
Lieberman. Skin Song.
McGrath. Revisionist Poem—Octavio Paz.
Marlowe. 3.11: Dolet amicam suam ita suis carminibnus innotuisse ut rivales multos sibi pararit.
Merrill. Transfigured Bird.
Merton. Keng's Disciple.
Macarius and the Pony.
Transformation: For the Sacred Heart, The.
Morrison. Time Works Like Acid.
Nemerov. Singular Metamorphosis, A.
Oliver. Spring Azures.
Pack. Orchid.
Piercy. At the big round table in the university.
Raine. At the day's end I found.
Childhood.

I felt, under my old breasts, this April day.
If, into this evening as the grass receives the dew.
"Reed." Andy's Chest.
Rukeyser. Child of the root, among your apples and forests.
Sarton. In Time Like Air.
Shapiro. Haircut.
I Am an Atheist Who Says His Prayers.
Sidney. Transformed in show, but more transformed in mind.
Smith, Patti. Amazing Tale of Skunkdog, The.
Neo Boy.
Sohl.
Smith, Stevie. Friskers, or, Gods and Men.
Frog Prince, The.
Sorrentino. Abstraction, The.
Calling Dr. Dunninger.
Stevenson. Behold, as goblins dark of mien.
Tomlinson. Door, The.
Faring, The.
Metamorphosis, The.
Palm of the Hand.
Prometheus.
Under the Moon's Reign.
Van Duyn. Leda Reconsidered.
Wilbur. Beautiful Changes, The.
Wright, Charles. October.
Zukofsky. After reading.
Checkers, checkmate and checkerboard.
Daruma.
Marriage Song for Florence and Harry, A.
Rains, the rains, The.
Song Theme.
Transience
Auden. As I Walked Out One Evening.
Berg. You.
Berrigan. Ann Arbor Song.
Browning, Elizabeth Barrett. Change Upon Change.
Sonnet: "I thank all who have loved me in their hearts."
Browning, Robert. Prologue: "Poet's age is sad: for why?, The."
Rephan.
Speculative.
Bunting. At Briggflatts Meetinghouse.
Burns. Epitaph: "Lo worms enjoy the seat of bliss."
Hey for a Lass wi' a Tocher.
Song: "Sensibility how charming."
Campion. Loe, when backe mine eye.
To Music Bent Is My Retired Mind.
What If a Day [or a Month or a Year].
Where are all thy beauties now, all hearts enchaining? [*or* harts enchayning?].
Carruth. Point, The.
Song: The Old, Old Man.
Two Romantic Pieces.
Woodsmoke at 70.
Catullus. Carmen 70: "Lesbia says she'ld rather marry me."
Sunne may set and rise, The.
Crane. Passage.
Creeley. Step, A.
Time, The.
Cummings. Christ but they're few.
Cruelly,love / walk the autumn long.
Touching you i say(it being Spring).
Without the mercy of / your eyes your.
Dove. Connections.
"Dylan." Eternal Circle.
Gypsy Lou.
It's All Over Now, Baby Blue.
Eberhart. Groundhog, The.
Eliot. Burnt Norton.
Dry Salvages, The.
East Coker.
Mélange Adultère de Tout.
Emerson. Yet sometimes to the sorrow stricken.
Frost. Nothing Gold Can Stay.
Gardner. Spendthrift.
Waltz for Accordion.
Garrigue. Address to the Migrations.
From Venice Was That Afternoon.
This Swallows' Empire.

Hardy. Obliterate Tomb, The.
Plaint to Man, A.
Roman Gravemounds, The.
St. Launce's Revisited.
Self-Unconscious.
Sunshade, The.
Thought in Two Moods, A.
Hayden. Theme and Variation.
Herbert. Virtue [or Vertue].
Herrick. Best To Be Merry.
Corinna's Going a-Maying.
Putrefaction.
To a Bed of Tulips.
To Blossoms.
To Daffodils [or Daffadills].
To Dianeme ("Sweet, be not proud of those two eyes").
To Enjoy the Time.
To Live Freely.
Upon Craw.
Hesketh. Moving Staircase.
Words.
Hewitt. Glenarriffe and Parkmore.
Last Summer, For Roberta (1975), The.
Lonsdale Street.
Mykonos.
Old Mill-Race, The.
Sonnet: "I thought tonight of all the lovers gone."
Sonnet: "Since brooding men put beauty in a rime."
Hill. Even now one is amazed.
Holmes. Old Saybrook House, The.
Storm in the Ozarks.
Housman. Along the field as we came by.
Jeffers. To the Stone-Cutters.
Johnson. Translation of Horace Odes IV vii ("Diffugere nives").
Joseph. Even Over the Flat Land.
Kooser. In a Country Cemetery in Iowa.
Levine. Sweet Will.
Lewis. Encirclement.
Horace at Twenty.
Midnight in India.
Song: "Oh journeyman, Oh journeyman."
White frost; intricate bare branches.
Lindsay. Firemen's Ball, The.
Wizard Wind, The.
Longfellow. Morituri Salutamus.
Lovelace. Female Inconstancy.
McAuley. Coming & Going.
McGrath. Return, The.
MacNeice. Sunlight on the Garden, The.
Marlowe. 1.10: Ad puellam, ne pro amore praemia poscat.
Nimphs [orNymph's] Reply to the Sheepheard[orShepherd], The.
Melville. Malvern Hill.
Meredith. Creed.
Foresight and Patience.
From lamplight and an aged leaf.
I play for Seasons; not Eternities!
In the Dry.
Song: "O the wind, the wind, the wind doth blow."
Song: "Pass we to another land."
Stave of Roving Tim, A.
Time.
Unknown Fair Faces.
Nemerov. Autumnal.
Dandelions.
Equations of a Villanelle.
Paraphrase from Notebooks.
Situation Does Not Change, The.
Neruda. Men (IV), The.
Olson. La Chute.
Pope. Stanzas: "At length, my soul! thy fruitless hopes give o'er."
Ralegh. As You Came from the Holy Land [of Walsingham].
Nimphs [orNymph's] Reply to the Sheepheard[orShepherd], The.
Plants and trees made poore and old, The.
Poem of Sir Walter Rawleighs, A.
Sunne may set and rise, The.
Ransom. Blue Girls.

Eclogue: "JANE SNEED BEGAN IT: My poor John, alas."
Rich. 7/14/68: i.
Robinson. Man against the Sky, The.
Rossetti. Bed of Forget-Me-Nots, A.
Days are clear, / Day after day, The.
Dead Bride, The.
Death Is Swallowed Up in Victory.
Earth and Heaven.
End of Time, The.
Have Patience.
I Have a Message unto Thee.
I said within myself: I am a fool.
Joy is but sorrow, / While we know.
Love Attacked.
Love Ephemeral.
Love hath a name of Death.
May.
Memento Mori.
Patience of Hope.
Present and Future.
Seasons.
Tempus Fugit.
Time of Waiting, The.
St. John. Day of the Sentry, The.
Sandburg. At the Gates of Tombs.
Autumn Movement.
Caboose Thoughts.
Flash Crimson.
Jabberers.
Mist, The.
One memorial stone reads.
Out of the Rainbow End.
Runaway Colors.
Shakespeare. Sonnet 18: "Shall I compare thee to a summer's day?"
Shapiro. Premises.
Shelley. Fragment: "When a lover clasps his fairest."
Ozymandias [of Egypt].
To ———: "When passion's trance is overpast."
Smart. To L. Manlius Torquatus.
Smith, Charlotte. Horologe of the Fields, The.
To a Butterfly in a Window.
To the Insect of the Gossamer.
Walk in the Shrubbery, A.
Written at Penshurst, in Autumn 1788.
Southwell. Upon the Image of Death.
Stuart. Audition.
Tennyson. Break, Break, Break.
Tears, Idle Tears.
Turco. Schooner, The.
Wilbur. Ballade in Old French.
Ballade of the Ladies of Time Past.
La Rose des Vents.
Looking into History.
To Madame du Châtelet.
To the Etruscan Poets.
Transit.
Two Voices in a Meadow.
Wellfleet: The House.
Williams, Miller. After the Revolution for Jesus a Secular Man Prepares His Final Remarks.
Wordsworth. Most Alluring Clouds That Mount the Sky, The.
Wright, Charles. Last Journal.
March Journal.
Portrait of the Artist with Hart Crane.
Wright, James. Eleutheria.
To a Troubled Friend.
Wyatt. Each man me telleth I change most my device [or devise].
I see the change from that that was.
Is it possible.
Zukofsky. Cars once steel and green, now old.
Junction, A.
Newly say dickered my love air my own would marry me all.
Passing tall.

Translation and Translators
Burns. To Mr. E——— on His Translation of and Commentaries on Martial.
Carew. To My Much Honoured Friend, Henry, Lord Carey of Leppington, Upon His Translation of Malvezzi.

Davie. Mandelstam, on Dante.
Mandelstam's Hope for the Best.
Donne. Upon the Translation of the Psalms by Sir Philip Sidney, and the Countess of Pembroke His Sister.
Fenton. Lines for Translation into Any Language.
Fisher. Style.
Gallagher. Poem in Translation, A.
Hacker. For Jean Migrenne.
Herbert. To the Right Hon. the Lord Chancellor (Bacon).
Hewitt. August 1939.
Gloss, on the Difficulties of Translation.
Jonson. On the Author, Work, and Translator.
To Clement Edmonds, on His Caesar's Commentaries Observed, and Translated.
To Mr Joshua Sylvester.
To My Chosen Friend the Learnèd Translator of Lucan, Thomas May, Esquire.
To My Worthy and Honoured Friend, Mr George Chapman, on His Translation of Hesiod's Works and Days.
To Sir Henry [or Henrie] Savile [upon His Translation of Tacitus].
To the Same; on the Same.
Keats. On First Looking into Chapman's Homer.
Marvell. To His Worthy Friend Doctor Witty upon His Translation of the "Popular Errors."
Merrill. Lost in Translation.
Merton. Reading Translated Poets, Feb. 1.
When class was in the garden at Greylands.
Nash. What Is Bibbidi-Bobbidi-Boo in Sanskrit?
Nemerov. Translation.
Patchen. And in Another Place Uses the Same Phrase.
Pope. Sandys's Ghost, or a Proper New Ballad on the New Ovid's Metamorphosis as it Was Intended to Be.
To Eustace Budgell, Esq., on His Translation of the Characters of Theophrastus.
Translator, The.
Ralegh. To the Translator of Lucan [or Lucan's Pharsalia, 1614].
Rich. Translations.
Sorrentino. Impromptu Solo on a Balcony.
Suckling. To His Much Honoured the Lord Lepington upon His Translation of Malvezzi, His "Romulus" and "Tarquin."

Transmutation
Emerson. Builder of heaven, The.

Trapezes and Trapeze Artists
Hartley. Trapezist's Despair.
Joseph. Overbold, The.
Koch. Circus, The.
MacNeice. Trapezists.
Plath. Aerialist.
Stuart. His Granddaughter Arrives.

Trapping and Trappers
Simic. Day Marked with a Small White Stone, A.
Snyder. "One Should Not Talk to a Skilled Hunter about What Is Forbidden by the Buddha."

Trash. see Garbage and Garbage Men.

Traveling and Travelers
Angelou. Traveler, The.
Arnold. Scholar-Gipsy, The.
Ashbery. Old heavens, you used to tweak above us.
Wind thrashes the maple seed-pods, The.
Atwood. Bus to Alliston, Ontario, The.
Journey to the Interior.
You think you are safe at last.
Auden. Inn Song.
On the Circuit.
Song: "Past all your knowing."
Beatles. Magical Mystery Tour.
Beckett. Zone.
Berry. Air and Fire.
Dear relatives and friends, when my last breath.
Traveling at Home.
Berryman. Away.
Friendless.

London.
Point of Age, A.
Recovery.
Traveller, The.
Travelling South.
Betjeman.　Back from Australia.
Mind's Journey to Diss, A.
Bishop.　Arrival at Santos.
Moose, The.
Over 2000 Illustrations and a Complete
　Concordance.
Questions of Travel.
Santarém.
Travelling in the Family.
Bly.　Driving toward the Lac Qui Parle River.
Bradstreet.　Upon My Son Samuel His Going
　For England.
Browning, Robert.　Home-Thoughts, from the
　Sea.
Bukowski.　On the Continent.
Winter Comes to a Lot of Places in August.
Bunting.　Birthday Greeting.
Burns.　Bonie Lass Made the Bed to Me, The.
Epigram on Rough Roads.
Highland Balou, The.
Ken ye ought o' Captain Grose?
Byron.　He who, grown aged in this world of
　woe.
Lines to Mr Hodgson.
Once Fairly Set Out on His Party of Pleasure.
To a Lady.
Carew.　Upon Master W. Montague, His
　Return from Travel.
Carroll, Jim.　On Tour.
"Carroll, Lewis."　Coronach.
Carruth.　Hard journey—yes, A.
In Russia.
Journey to a Known Place.
Catullus.　Carmen 46: "Now spring bursts."
Carmen 63: "Plunging towards Phrygia over
　violent water."
Chaucer.　Canterbury Tales, The.
In May, that moder is of monthes glade.
Troilus and Criseyde [or Criseide].
Clark.　One.
Rojo.
Clough.　O Theos Meta Sou.
Once more the wonted road I tread.
Cohen.　Next One, The.
Road to Larissa, The.
Suzanne [Takes You Down].
Travel.
Unclean Start, The.
Winter Lady.
You Went to Work.
Coleridge.　Delinquent Travellers, The.
Perspiration: A Travelling Eclogue.
Cowper.　1.5: "'Twas a long journey lay before
　us."
Distressed Travellers, The.
Elegy 4: To Thomas Young.
Crane.　River, The.
Traveller Born, A.
Creeley.　Berlin: First Night & Early Morning.
Poem for Beginners.
Davie.　Christian Hero, A.
Epistle. To Enrique Caracciolo Trejo.
Mr Sharp in Florence.
Nashville Mornings.
Siloam.
Spring Song, A.
Sunday Morning.
Wide France.
De la Mare.　Last Coachload, The.
Listeners, The.
Railway Junction, The.
Three Strangers, The.
Dickey, James.　Baggage King, The.
Dickey, William.　Fred and the Holy Grail.
Dickinson.　Go traveling with us!
Road was lit with Moon and star, The.
Dobyns.　Somewhere It Still Moves.
Donne.　Upon Mr. Thomas Coryat's Crudities.
Doolittle.　O for wings.
Dove.　Sahara Bus Trip, The.
Dunbar.　Keep a Song Up on de Way.
Dunn.　Listener, The.

"Dylan."　Black Crow Blues.
California.
Don't Think Twice, It's All Right.
Down the Highway.
Dusty Old Fairgrounds.
Farewell: "Oh it's fare thee well my darlin'
　true."
Goin' to Acapulco.
If I Don't Be There by Morning.
Last Thoughts on Woody Guthrie.
Lo and Behold!
Motorpsycho Nightmare.
My Life in a Stolen Moment.
Rambling, Gambling Willie.
Romance in Durango.
Song to Woody.
Tangled Up in Blue.
Wanted Man.
Yea! Heavy and a Bottle of Bread.
Eliot.　Lune de Miel.
Emerson.　At Sea, September 1833.
I care not whither I may go.
I never went out of my country.
If wishes would carry me over the land.
Last Farewell, The.
Saadi loved the new & old.
Una.
Everson.　Wise, The.
Fisher.　At the end of the familiar.
Castle, The.
From here to there—.
He is going to the woman.
Riding out of the built-up.
Fox.　April Fool.
Frost.　Rogers Group, A.
Gallagher.　Devotion: That It Flow; That There
　Be Concentration.
Garrigue.　Pays Perdu.
Ginsberg.　Auto Poesy: On the Lam from
　Bloomington.
Beginning of a Long Poem of These States.
Continuation of a Long Poem of These States.
Hiway Poesy: L.A.–Albuquerque–Texas–
　Witchita.
Kansas City to Saint Louis.
Message II.
Glück.　To Florida.
Graves.　Advocates.
Around the Mountain.
Cloak, The.
Furious Voyage, The.
Legs, The.
Next Time, The.
Gunn.　Discovery of the Pacific, The.
Hacker.　Across the mud flats and the wide
　roads, over rivers and borders.
Country & Western.
Haines.　It Must All Be Done Over.
Poem for a Cold Journey.
Sunlight struck before us.
There Are No Such Trees in Alpine,
　California.
Hall.　Abroad Thoughts from Home.
Hardy.　How She Went to Ireland.
Meditation on a Holiday.
Hayden.　Tour 5.
Heaney.　Stations of the West, The.
Hemingway.　Travel Poem.
Herrick.　Salutation.
To His Brother Nicolas Herrick.
Hesketh.　Limbo.
Unicorn.
Hewitt.　Aesthete's Renunciation.
Dusty Roads.
Frontier, The.
Little Ships.
Riders, The.
Roll Call.
Teetotal Master.
Hoffman.　Stone, A.
Trip, A.
Hugo.　Argo.
Belt.
Docking at Palermo.
Driving Montana.
Goodbye, Iowa.
Last Words from Maratea.

Maratea Porto.
Montesano Unvisited.
North.
Picnic in the Saracen Ruin, The.
Walking Praed Street.
Jarrell.　See-er of Cities, The.
Jonson.　On the Famous Voyage.
To the London Reader, on the Odcombian
　Writer, Polytopian Thomas the Traveller.
To the Right Noble Tom, Tell-Troth of His
　Travels, the Coriat of Odcombe, and His
　Book Now Going to Travel.
Keats.　Keen, Fitful Gusts Are Whispering
　Here and There.
Sweet, Sweet Is the Greeting of Eyes.
There was a naughty boy.
Kipling.　As the Bell Clinks.
Bother, The.
Fastness.
Friends, The.
Gipsy Trail, The.
I've never sailed the Amazon.
Sestina of the Tramp-Royal.
Song of Kabir, A.
Song of Seventy Horses.
Song of Travel, A.
When the cabin port-holes are dark and green.
Koch.　Departure from Hydra, The.
Lunch.
Larkin.　Arrivals, Departures.
Autobiography at an Air-Station.
Local Snivels through the Field, The.
Nursery Tale.
Lawrence.　On the Road.
Travel Is Over.
Levertov.　Travels.
Levine.　To get west you go east.
Lewis.　Troopship in the Tropics, A.
Liddy.　Attention: First Lady of the Festival.
Vir XI.
Lorde.　My Fifth Trip to Washington Ended in
　Northeast Delaware.
Lowry.　Ballad: "Twas in the springtime of the
　year."
Betty and Gerald Noxon.
Canadian Turned Back at the Border, The.
Love and wisdom have no home.
Ten fifty eight may arrive.
With Sweet Sweet Love from All Your
　Amused Little Animals.
Young Man From Oaxaca, The.
McAuley.　Draft Balance Sheet.
McGrath.　Driving toward Boston I Run across
　One of Robert Bly's Old Poems.
Edge of the River, The.
Epitaph: "Again, traveller, you have come a
　long way led by that star."
Long Way Outside Yellowstone, A.
Love in a Bus.
Poem: "How could I have come so far?"
Poem—Unfinished Poem.
Repeated Journey, The.
Tourists at Ensenada.
MacLeish.　Arrival and Departure.
Cinema of a Man.
Ever Since.
Old Man's Journey.
Tourist Death.
Voyage.
Why the Face of a Clock is not Truly a
　Circle.
MacNeice.　Ravenna.
Solitary Travel.
Splinters under the nails, weals on the
　buttocks.
Markson.　Quietude.
Traveler's Tale.
Matthews.　Human Hymn.
Meinke.　Aunt Gertrud.
Meredith.　Familiar Things.
Last Wandering of Poor Willie, The.
Meeting, The.
Pictures of the Rhine.
Will o' the Wisp.
Merrill.　Bronze.
Clearing the Title.
Days of 1971.

Flèche d'Or.
Friend of the Fourth Decade, The.
Last Mornings in California.
Santorini: Stopping the Leak.
Summer People, The.
Thousand and Second Night, The.
Merton. Ash Wednesday.
East with Ibn Battuta.
Landfall, The.
Like the flights of ducks.
Old monk is turned loose / And can travel!, The.
Prophet.
Song of the Traveller, The.
Welcome.
Millay. Travel.
Unexplorer, The.
Miller. From Oslo.
No and I don't know where.
Milton. Elegy 4: To Thomas Young.
Morrison. Ah, The Rule.
Untrampled Footsteps.
Muldoon. Identities.
Making the Move.
Nash. Buses Headed for Scranton, The.
Change Here for Wichita Falls, or, Has Anybody Seen My Wanderlust?
Everybody Eats Too Much Anyhow.
Have a Seat behind the Potted Palm, Sir.
Hi-Ho the Ambulance-O.
My Trip Daorba.
Traveler's Rest.
Unwinged Ones, The.
You Bet Travel Is Broadening.
Nathan. Highway, The.
Nemerov. Home for the Holidays.
Sestina II: "No waste is trackless: all terrain the lost."
Sightseers.
Song of Degrees, A.
Neruda. I Come Back from a Journey.
O'Hara. Biotherm [for Bill Berkson].
Mary Desti's Ass.
Terrestrial Cuckoo, A.
You Are Gorgeous and I'm Coming.
Oliver. Dreams.
Olson. De Los Cantares.
Encounter, The.
Landscape, Without Color.
Oppen. Party on Shipboard.
Travelogue.
Patchen. Evidence? What Evidence.?
Pope. Mary Gulliver to Capt. Lemuel Gulliver.
Ralegh. To his Singular Friend, William Lithgow.
Rich. Itinerary.
Road to the great canyon always feels, The.
Turning the Wheel.
White Night.
Roethke. Harsh Country, The.
Night Journey.
Rossetti. Lord, by what inconceivable dim road / Thou leadest man on footsore pilgrimage!
Uphill [or Up-Hill].
Rukeyser. Adventures, Midnight.
Ajanta.
During the journey there come moments of waking.
Grand Central Station.
Man in a plane looks at the surface of land, A.
Otherworld.
Road, The.
Willkie in the Gulliver.
Sandburg. Red Son, The.
Road and the End, The.
Schuyler. New Yorker, A.
Rose of Marion, The.
Voyage Autour de Mes Cartes Postales.
Schwartz. Journey of a Poem Compared to All the Sad Variety of Travel, The.
Scott. Voyage to Arran, The.
Shelley. World's Wanderers, The.
Shelton. Crossing, The.
Sidney. Sonet 84: "Highway, since you my chief Parnassus be."

Simic. Midpoint.
Pillow, The.
Travelling.
Smith, Patti. Notice.
Smith, Stevie. Louise.
Where Are You Going?
Snyder. In my first thirty years of life.
One Year.
Sorrentino. Fragments of an Old Song 1.
My hated birthday looms. In the rude and wretched country.
See America First.
Simplicity.
Stafford. In Fur.
Stein. Marry Nettie.
Painted Lace.
Sonatina Followed by Another, A.
Stevenson. As starts the absent dreamer, when a train.
Bour-Tree Den, The.
Cock's clear voice into the clearer air, The.
End of Travel, An.
Far-Farers, The.
From a Railway Carriage.
It's forth across the roaring foam, and on towards the west.
Land of Nod, The.
My Bed Is a Boat.
North-West Passage.
Scotsman's Return from Abroad, The.
Since years ago for evermore.
Song of the Road, A.
Susquehanna and the Delaware, The.
To all that love the far and blue.
To Kalakaua.
To N.V. de G.S.
To W.E. Henley.
Travel.
Tropics vanish, and meseems that I, The.
Vagabond, The.
Yes, I remember, and still remember wailing.
Sutter. Trying to Dream Up an Answer.
Tomlinson. Or Traveller's Joy.
Updike. Accumulation.
Airport.
Back from Vacation.
Capacity.
Goodbye, Göteborg.
Land is dry enough to make the rivers, The.
Postcards from Soviet Cities.
Somewhere.
Van Duyn. Into Mexico.
Small Excursion, A.
Walcott. Fortunate Traveller, The.
Our houses are one step from the gutter.
Plastic curtains.
Warren. Dream He Never Knew the End of, The.
Switzerland.
Whitman. On Journeys through the States.
Promise to California, A.
Whittier. To a Cape Ann Schooner.
To a Friend.
Wilbur. Happy the Man.
L'Invitation au Voyage.
Williams, Charles Kenneth. Travelers.
Wordsworth. Descriptive Sketches Taken During a Pedestrian Tour among the Alps.
Italian Itinerant, and the Swiss Goatherd, The.
Memorials of a Tour in Italy, 1837.
Memorials of a Tour of the Continent; 1820.
Most Sweet It Is with Unuplifted Eyes.
No spade for leagues had won a rood of earth.
Poems Composed or Suggested During a Tour, in the Summer of 1833.
Road extended o'er a heath, The.
Stepping Westward.
Travelling.
Waggoner, The.
Wright, Charles. Self-Portait ("Pictures in the air have few visitors, The").
Wright, James. Sitting in a Small Screenhouse on a Summer Morning.
Stages on a Journey Westward.
Wroth. Sonnet 10: "Weary traveller who tired sought, The."
Young. Leaving Home for Home.

Leaving Rochester.
Leaving Syracuse.
Zukofsky. Jaunt.
Spurred altering wake toss Attis his craft racing till marled in the.
Warm gale, a dose of spring—revert to the pores.

Treason and Traitors
Brontë. M. Douglas to E.R. Gleneden.
Burns. Such a Parcel of Rogues in a Nation.
Crashaw. On the Gunpowder-Treason.
Upon the Gunpowder Treason ("Grow plumpe, leane Death").
Upon the Gunpowder Treason ("Reach me a quill").
Cullen. La Belle, La Douce, La Grande.
De la Mare. Ballad of Christmas, A.
Dickinson. Treason of an Accent, The.
Treason of an accent, The.
When the Astronomer stops seeking.
Hall. Body Politic, The.
Herrick. Treason.
Jeffers. War-Guilt Trials.
Kipling. Ballad of the Red Earl, The.
MacLeish. Treason Crime, The.
Rich. For Ethel Rosenberg.
Scott. On the Massacre of Glencoe, 1692.

Treasures
Dickinson. Where the Treasure is.
Dunn. Homage to the Divers.
Emerson. I will be drunk and down with wine.
Hemingway. Black-Ass Poem After Talking to Pamela Churchill.
Lindsay. He waits by the door of his cave.
Morgan. Pirate Poem.
Rossetti. Lay Up for Yourselves Treasures in Heaven.
Silverstein. Hector the Collector.
Search, The.

Treaties
Hewitt. Peace Pact.
Hill. Apostles: Versailles, 1919, The.
Meinke. Soldiers with Green Leggings.
Thomas. Hand That Signed the Paper, The.
Whittier. Crisis, The.

Tree of Life
Fletcher. As Adam, clutching earth, lay stunned within the darkness.
Rukeyser. Speaking Tree, The.
Shapiro. Tree of Guilt, The.

Tree Surgeons
Hall. Stump.
Williams, Charles Kenneth. Elms.

Tree Toads. *see* **Toads.**

Trees
Ammons. Leaning Up.
Mediation.
North Street.
Scarecrow.
Shading Flight In.
Whitelash of Air Rapids.
Winter Scene.
Ashbery. Some Trees.
Atwood. Porcupine Tree.
Auden. Happy Tree, The.
November at Weybourne.
Plane Tree, The.
Reflections in a Forest.
Berg. New Year's.
No Word.
Berrigan. Each tree stands alone in stillness.
Berry. Foliage has dropped, The.
For the Future.
I sit in the shade of the trees of the land I was born in.
Planting Trees.
Porch over the River, The.
Sycamore gathers / out of the sky, white, The.
Sycamore, The.
Through elm, buckeye, thorn.
We pile the brush high.
Woods.
Bishop. To a Tree.
Blake. In a Myrtle [or Mirtle] Shade.
Boyle. April Thirtieth 1960.

Brontë. There are two trees in a lonely field.
  Woods, you need not frown on me.
Browning, Elizabeth Barrett. Where's Agnes?
Bunting. Not to thank dogwood nor.
Burns. Amang the trees, where humming bees.
  Tree of Liberty, The.
Campion. Bring away this Sacred Tree.
Carruth. Anxious View of a Tree.
  August.
  Block.
  "I've Never Seen Such a Real Hard Time
    Before": Three-Part Invention.
  My Meadow.
  Shake, Well Before Using.
  Trees, The.
  Trees, the naked trees.
  Way of the Conventicle of the Trees, The.
Ceravolo. Happiness in the Trees.
Ciardi. Tree Trimming.
Clark. Lake, The.
Coleridge. Barberry-Tree, The.
  Broad-breasted Pollards with broad-branching
    head.
  Tree of Mystery, The.
Crane. Mango Tree, The.
Creeley. Air: "Cat Bird Singing."
  For Helen.
  Hunger.
  In the Fall.
  Kid, The.
  To Bobbie.
  Trees.
  Turn, The.
Cullen. Love Tree, The.
Cummings. I am going to utter a tree,Noboby.
  Into the smiting / sky tense.
  Now all the fingers of this tree(darling)have.
  Rosetree,rosetree / —you're a song to
    see:whose.
  Timeless / ly this / (merely and whose).
  Trees / were in(give).
Davie. Democrats.
  Intervals in a Busy Life.
  Mushroom Gatherers, The.
De la Mare. Foreboding.
  Three Cherry Trees, The.
Dickey, James. Autumn.
  One, The.
  Seeking the Chosen.
  Trees and Cattle.
Dickinson. Antiquated Tree, An.
  Still as the Profile of a Tree.
Duncan. Four Songs the Night Nurse Sang.
Dunn. Under the Black Oaks.
Eberhart. Burden.
  Christmas Tree.
  Go to the Shine That's on a Tree.
  There Is an Evil in the Air.
Emerson. Go out into Nature and plant trees.
  See yonder leafless trees against the sky.
  Where is Skrymir? Giant Skrymir?
  Where the fungus broad & red.
Everson. High Embrace, A.
  Passion Week.
Fisher. Starting to Make a Tree.
Fletcher. Dogwood.
  Trees, like great jade elephants, The.
Frost. Axe-Helve, The.
  Birches.
  Encounter, An.
  On a Tree Fallen across the Road.
  Sound of Trees, The.
  Sycamore.
  Tree at My Window.
  Wild Grapes.
Gallagher. Clearing.
  Some with Wings, Some with Manes.
  Woodcutting on Lost Mountain.
Garrigue. Country Villa.
Ginsberg. Trembling of the Veil, The.
Glück. Flowering Plum.
  Shad-Blow Tree, The.
  Tree House, The.
Graves. Advocates.
  Woman and Tree.
Gunn. Exercise, The.
  Hampstead; the Horse Chestnut Trees.

Kind of Ethics, A.
Philemon and Baucis.
Waking in a Newly Built House.
Haines. And When the Green Man Comes.
  Brand.
  Here is the place I came to.
  Instructions to a Sentry.
  Poem About Birch Trees.
  Red Trees in the Wind.
  Tree that Became a House, The.
  Tree, The.
Hall. Tree and the Cloud, The.
Hardy. At Day-Close in November.
  Everything Comes.
  They Are Great Trees.
  Throwing a Tree.
  To a Tree in London.
  Tree and the Lady, The.
  Tree, The.
  Without Ceremony.
Heaney. Sweeney Praises the Trees.
Herrick. All Things Decay and Die.
  Another ("Wassaile the Trees, that they may
    beare").
  To Blossoms.
  To Groves.
  To Sycamores.
  Upon the Losse of His Finger.
Hesketh. All Hallows.
  Evergreen.
  Prayer for Sun.
  Reflections.
  Roots.
Hewitt. I Turn to Trees.
  In That Fair and Pleasant Land.
  Lagan in October, The.
  Late Spring.
  Lyric ("Chestnut and beech / sycamore and
    willow."
  November Wood.
  Suburban Spring in Warwickshire.
  Timber.
Hoffman. Felled Tree, A.
  Testament.
  Tree.
Hopkins. Binsey Poplars (Felled 1879).
  Distance / Dappled with diminish'd trees.
Hughes, Langston. Little Green Tree.
Hughes, Ted. Dead Farms, Dead Leaves.
Kipling. Tree Song, A.
Kooser. Walking Beside a Creek.
Kunitz. Deciduous Branch.
  War against the Trees, The.
Larkin. Trees, The.
Lawrence. Erotic.
  Reality of Peace, 1916.
  Trees in the Garden.
  Winter in the Boulevard.
Levertov. Message.
  Novices, The.
  Stems.
Levine. Sleepless Night, A.
Liddy. Bicentennial Words for the Liberal
    Magistrates of 1798.
  Notes towards a Video of Avondale House.
Lindsay. He Climbs the Hill Where the Tree
    Grows.
  Spice-Tree, The.
Lorde. Ballad from Childhood.
  Song: "Wild trees have bought me."
Lovelace. Orpheus to Woods.
Lowry. Bird in the Tree, The.
  Fragment: "Dead tree that, frozen, utters at the
    top, The."
  Happiness.
  Hypocrite! Oxford Grouper! Yahoo!
  I think that I shall never see.
  Walk in Canada.
McGrath. Long Goodbye.
MacLeish. Farm, The.
  Man's Work, A.
  March.
  Words to be Spoken.
MacNeice. Tree of Guilt, The.
  Tree Party.
McNeill. Clearing, The.
  Corner Tree.

Mahon. Going Home.
Meredith. Pastoral 4: "Lo, as a tree, whose
    wintry twigs."
Merrill. Trees Listening to Bach.
Merton. Cocoa Tree.
  Silver bird is E backward in cool pond water,
    The.
  Useless Tree, The.
Millay. City Trees.
  Counting-out Rhyme.
  Grow not too high, grow not too far from
    home.
  Leaf and the Tree, The.
Moore. Sycamore, The.
Morgan. Sun tells stories, The.
  Tree, The.
Muldoon. Wind and Tree.
Nash. Song of the Open Road.
Nemerov. Learning by Doing.
  Learning the Trees.
  Thought of Trees, The.
  Trees.
Oliver. Black Walnut Tree, The.
Olson. 2 Propositions and 3 Proof.
Oppen. Building of the Skyscraper, The.
  Return.
Pack. Cracked Apple Tree, The.
  Unburying the Birch.
Paley. Arboreal Mystery, An.
Patchen. Under a Tree.
Plath. I Am Vertical.
  On the Plethora of Dryads.
  Polly's Tree.
  Winter Trees.
Raine. Acacia Tree.
  Forest is multitude.
  Tree of night is spangled with a thousand
    stars, The.
Rich. For the Felling of an Elm in the
    Harvard Yard.
  Tree, The.
  Trees, The.
Robinson. Archibald's Example.
Rossetti. Dumb Friend, A.
  Mirrors of Life and Death.
  Trees' Counselling, The.
Rukeyser. Boys in the Branches.
Sandburg. Branches.
  Deep roots moving in lush soil to send a
    silver-gray beech tree.
  Hemlock and Cedar.
  Lesson.
  Little Sketch.
  Never Two Songs the Same.
  Prairie Woodland.
  Proud Torsos.
  Shag-Bark Hickory.
  Tall Timber.
  Without Notice Beforehand.
Schuyler. Amy Lowell Thoughts.
  Autumn Leaves.
  Noon Office.
Shapiro. Calder, A.
Simic. December Trees.
  Peaceful Trees.
  Trees at Night.
Smith, Charlotte. Apostrophe to an Old Tree.
  On thy grey bark, in witness of my flame.
Snodgrass. These Trees Stand.
Snyder. Groves are down, The.
Sorrentino. Transcript, The.
Spenser. Then heavenly branches did I see
    arise.
Stevenson. Foreign Lands.
Stuart. Charles River, The.
  Leaf Eater, The.
  Sticks and Stones.
Sutter. Can you believe it?
  Cedarhome.
  I didn't used to care much.
  Just learning to talk, I watched.
  Make no mistake. The cedar.
  Witch Tree.
Tomlinson. Poem: "Upended, it crouches on
    broken limbs."
  Scar, The.
  Tree.

Tree, The.
Witnesses, The.
Updike. Planting Trees.
Van Duyn. To Record One Must Be Unwary.
Warren. Return, The.
Whittier. Sycamores, The.
Wood Giant, The.
Wilbur. Alatus.
Black Birch in Winter, A.
Chronic Condition, A.
Courtyard Thaw, A.
Fern-Beds in Hampshire County.
Orchard Trees, January.
Poplar, Sycamore.
Under a Tree.
Wood, A.
Williams, William Carlos. Approach of Winter.
Flowers Alone, The.
Hunter, The.
Hurricane, The.
Locust Tree in Flower, The.
Tree.
Tree and Sky.
Trees.
Trees, The.
Winter Trees.
Yellow Tree Peony, The.
Young Sycamore.
Wordsworth. Barberry-Tree, The.
Desponding Father! Mark This Altered Bough.
Hart's-Horn Tree, near Penrith.
see also Written at the Request of Sir George Beaumont, BART., and in His Name, for an Urn, Placed by Him at the Termination of a Newly-Planted Avenue, in the Same Grounds *and* Inscription in a Garden of the Same.
Laodamia.
Nutting.
Tradition of Oker Hill in Darley Dale, Derbyshire, A.
see also Inscription in the Grounds of Coleorton, the Seat of Sir George Beaumont, BART., Leicestershire *and* Inscription in a Garden of the Same.
Yew-Trees.
Wright, James. Seasonless, The.
Zimmer. Final Affection, A.
Zukofsky. As to How Much.
Gamut.
George Washington.
In Arizona / (how many years in the mountains).
Like the oceans, or the leaves of fine Southern.
Pretty.
See also **Listings for specific Trees.**

Trench Warfare
Owen. Anthem for Doomed Youth.
Exposure.

Trinidad and Tobago
Berryman. Old Man Goes South Again Alone.
Walcott. Egypt, Tobago.
Midsummer, Tobago.
Spoiler's Return, The.

Trinity, The
Herbert. Trinity Sunday.
Ungratefulness.
Herrick. Number of Two, The.
To God ("God's undivided, One in Persons Three").
Jonson. Reverse on the Back Side, The.
Sinner's Sacrifice, The.
Merton. Freedom as Experience.
Hymn for the Feast of Duns Scotus.
Rossetti. All Saints: Martyrs.
Trinity Sunday.
Smart. Trinity Sunday.
Whittier. Trust.
Yeats. Ribh Denounces Patrick.

Triolet (form)
Hardy. How Great My Grief.
See also **Triolet in Title and First Line Index.**

Tristram and Isolde
Carruth. Your dream: / His name was Hegel, a dear sweet man.

Triviality
Hugo. Park at Villammare, The.
Nash. What to Do until the Doctor Goes or It's Tomorrow Than You Think.
Neruda. What will the Poles think of my hat.
Sandburg. Aprons of Silence.
Wilbur. Ballade of Forgiveness.
Lightness.
What's Good for the Soul is Good for Sales.
Williams, Charles Kenneth. Regulars, The.

Troilus and Cressida
Wordsworth. Troilus and Cresida.

Trojan War
Chaucer. Troilus and Criseyde [*or* Criseide].
Doolittle. After Troy.
Burnished-head / By burnished-head.
Chorus of the Women of Chalkis.
Crowd of the Greek force, The.
It is not for me, the day.
Now sing, O slight girls.
Marlowe. 2.12: Exultat, quod amica potitus sit.
Meredith. Achilles over the Trench.
Helen on the Skaian Gates.
Marshalling of the Achaians.
Night Watch of the Trojans before Troy.
Nourishment before Battle.
Odysseus Encircled.
Shield of Achilles, The.
Merton. Greek Women, The.
Pound. Canto 1: "And then went down to the ship."
Wilbur. Helen.
Yeats. Leda and the Swan.

Trolleys. *see* **Streetcars.**

Trolls
Smith, Stevie. Her-zie.
Whittier. Brown Dwarf of Rügen, The.
Kallundborg Church.

Trossachs, The, Scotland
Wordsworth. Trosachs, The.

Troubadours
Browning, Robert. Rudel to the Lady of Tripoli.
Sordello.
Carruth. In France, through archways, the archaic stonework.
Then here was where it began, dear sleeping princess.
Hardy. Dead Man Walking, The.

Trout
Dickey, James. Winter Trout.
Hughes, Ted. Night Arrival of Sea-Trout.
Hugo. Skykomish River Running.
Trout.
Liddy. River Video, The.
Wilbur. Hamlen Brook.

Troy
Carruth. What does this wind say, plunging upon the land.
Doolittle. It is not for me, the day.
Now sing, O slight girls.
Gunn. Wound, The.
Hewitt. Motives.
Lovelace. Asse Eating the Ænieds, The.
MacLeish. Excavation of Troy.
Meredith. Night Watch of the Trojans before Troy.
Merton. Like Ilium.
Nash. First Limick.
Nemerov. Home for the Holidays.
Pound. Canto 4: "Palace in smoky light."
Shakespeare. Troy Depicted.
Walcott. Map of the New World.
See also **Trojan War.**

Truancy
Fisher. Truants.
Graves. Death Room, The.
Hewitt. I Still Had a Friend.

Trucks and Truckers
Bukowski. Jack-Knife.
Carruth. Poem moves north, The.
Gunn. Trucker, A.
Lieberman. Siesta.
Miller. Behind a large truck.
Silverstein. Traffic Light.

Snyder. Why Log Truck Drivers Rise Earlier than Students of Zen.
Tomlinson. At Barstow.

Trujillo Molina, Rafael Leonidas
Dove. Parsley.

Trumpets
Tomlinson. Valle de Oaxaca.
Whitman. Mystic Trumpeter, The.
Wordsworth. Horn of Egremont Castle, The.
Wright, James. Trumpets.

Trust
Angelou. Sounds Like Pearls.
Beatles. Don't Let Me Down.
Berg. Oblivion.
Berry. How many times have I come to you out of my head.
Bogan. Heard by a Girl.
Brontë. Now trust a heart that trusts in you.
Carroll, Jim. Poem: "Some trust the wolf."
Catullus. Carmen 82: "My eyes are in your pledge, Quintius."
Carmen 91: "In this hopeless & wasting love of mine."
Carmen 102: "If, Cornelius, we entrust our secrets."
Cowper. Simple Trust.
Crashaw. Happy me! o happy sheepe!
Creeley. For Friendship.
Form of Adaptation, A.
Cummings. Nothing false and possible is love.
Donne. Anagram, The.
Doolittle. Now let the cycle sweep us here and there.
Dunn. This Late in the Century.
"Dylan." Let's Keep It Between Us.
Tell Me That It Isn't True.
Fox. Acrobat, The.
Graves. Beware, Madam!
Broken Compact.
Loving True, Flying Blind.
Oath, The.
Through a Dark Wood.
What is Love?
Gunn. Idea of Trust, The.
Hacker. Morning: the phone jangles me from words: you.
Hardy. Woman's Trust, A.
Herrick. Eyes before the Eares, The.
Multitude.
Hewitt. Ram's Horn, The.
Larkin. Out in the Lane I Pause.
Lawrence. Being Alive.
Emotional Friend, The.
Sex and Trust.
Trust.
Lovelace. To Quintus.
Lowry. I met a man who had got drunk with Christ.
MacLeish. Treason Crime, The.
Merton. Come Dance in Baronies.
Morrison. End of the Rainbow, The.
Piercy. Behold: A Relationship.
In the pit of the night our bodies merge.
It Breaks.
My old friend, how we sustain.
Psalms. Psalm 23: "Lord is my shepherd, I shall not want, The."
Psalm 27: "Lord is my light and my salvation, The."
Psalm 31: "In thee, O Lord, do I put my trust. . . ."
Psalm 57: "Be merciful unto me, O God. . . ."
Psalm 71: "In thee, O Lord, do I put my trust."
Psalm 125: "They that trust in the Lord shall be as mount Zion."
Rossetti. In Patience.
Judge Nothing before the Time.
Leaf from leaf Christ knows; / Himself the Lily and the Rose.
Palm Sunday.
Sidney. Lord, the Lord my shepherd is, The.
Stevenson. Mine eyes were swift to know thee, and my heart.
Thomas. Ears in the Turrets Hear.
Williams, Miller. Husband.

Wroth. Sonnet 10: "Bee from court of Love, and reason torne."
Zukofsky. No idea, Gelli, spurred me to mirror you faithful.
Peri Poietikes.
Quinti, see if't be wish of cool eyes day bear your Catullus.
Secret I take it a commitment hushed to feed amic—.

Truth, Sojourner
Hayden. Sojourner Truth.

Truth
Ammons. Turning.
Angelou. Accident.
Atwood. True Stories.
Auden. Dichtung und Wahrheit.
He watched the stars and noted birds in flight.
History of Truth, The.
Beatles. All You Need Is Love.
Berry. Forsaking all others, we.
Song (1).
Bradstreet. Of the Four Humors in Man's Constitution.
Brontë. There was a time when my cheek burned.
Browning, Elizabeth Barrett. Best Thing in the World, The.
Browning, Robert. Pippa Passes.
Reverie.
Summum Bonum.
Bukowski. Funny.
It's Not Who Lived Here.
Byron. To Romance.
Campion. Truth, sprung from heaven, shall shine.
Vain Men, Whose Follies.
Carew. Disdain Returned.
"Carroll, Lewis." Misunderstandings.
Catullus. Carmen 109: "Joy of my life! you tell me this."
Chaucer. Lak of Stedfastnesse.
Truth.
Clough. It fortifies my soul to know.
Look you, my simple friend, 'tis one of those.
Old things need not be therefore true.
Truth is a golden thread seen here and there.
Cohen. Singer Must Die, A.
Cowper. Garden, The.
Moralizer Corrected, The.
Truth.
Crane. Visible the Untrue, The.
Creeley. Bed, The.
Echo.
Fancy.
Mind's Heart.
My Love.
Wisdom.
Cullen. To Certain Critics.
Cummings. As freedom is a breakfastfood.
If a cheerfulest Elephantangelchild should sit.
Life is more true than reason will deceive.
My darling since / you and.
Out of the lie of no.
Seeker of truth / follow no path.
What freedom's not some under's mere above.
When / (day's amazing murder with).
Davie. Standings.
De la Mare. Catechism, The.
Dickinson. Counterfeit—a Plated Person, A.
I died for Beauty—but was scarce.
Opinion is a flitting thing.
Quicker deceit dies, The.
Tell all the Truth but tell it slant.
That it is true, Master.
Things of which we want the proof, The.
Truth—is as old as God.
Truth—is stirless, The.
Dunn. What They Wanted.
"Dylan." All Along the Watchtower.
Just Like Tom Thumb's Blues.
Nothing Was Delivered.
Eberhart. Airman Considers His Power, An.
Anima.
Austere Poem.
Ceremonial.
Flow of Thought.
Four Exposures.

Froth.
Full of Joy Do Not Know; They Need Not, The.
Humanist, The.
I Walked Out to the Graveyard to See the Dead.
Incomparable Light, The.
Kaire.
Mystery of the Abstract.
R. G. E.
Soul.
Time Passes.
Truth, The.
Way Out, A.
Eliot. Hippopotamus, The.
Emerson. Dull uncertain brain, A.
Easy to match what others do.
Hard is it to persuade the public mind of its plain duty & true interest.
Harp, The.
Heartily heartily / Nothing be false.
I live among ideal men.
Now tells the flower.
Panoply of Paradise is mine.
Papas Blondine / Grew tall & wise.
Sacrifice.
Shun passion, fold the hands of thrift.
There is in all the sons of men.
Uriel.
Everson. Narrows of Birth, The.
Wise, The.
Ferlinghetti. Elegy on the Death of Kenneth Patchen, An.
Mouth of truth, The.
Fisher. Red and the Black, The.
Wish.
Fletcher. August, 1940.
Glück. Day Without Night.
Graves. Arrow Shots.
Broken Compact.
Chink, The.
Compact.
Dilemma, The.
End of Play.
Expect Nothing.
Love Charms.
Pier-Glass, The.
Poet's Curse, The.
Prepared Statement, The.
Seven Years.
Terraced Valley, The.
To Put It Simply.
Truth Is Poor Physic.
Whole Love.
Hardy. To a Lady.
Hemingway. Ultimately.
Herrick. Truth and Error.
Truth and Falsehood.
Truth ("Truth is best found out by the time, and eyes").
Hesketh. Truth Game.
Hewitt. Bloody Brae, The.
Colney Hatch.
Dichotomy.
Eye for Color, An.
Feathers on Turf.
Frost.
Ossian's Grave, Lubitavish, County Antrim.
Poem: "Consider Wordsworth in his withered age."
Since June was hot on head and hand.
Spectacle of Truth, The.
To Be Used in an Address Delivered at the Unveiling of a Plaque Commemorating "George A. Birmingham."
Hill. Crack of a starting pistol. Jean Jaurès.
Hoffman. Companion, The.
Far-Off Light.
Instructions to a Medium, to be Transmitted to the Shade of W.B. Yeats, the Latter Having Responded in a Séance Held on 13 June 1965, Its Hundredth Birthday.
It cannot come because desired.
Problems of Knowledge.
Reflections.
Hopkins. Summa.
Jeffers. Advice to Pilgrims.

Cassandra.
Curb Science?
Faith.
Mathematicians and physics men, The.
Silent Shepherds, The.
Theory of Truth.
To the Story-Tellers.
What's the best life for a man?
Jonson. From The Touchstone of Truth.
Joseph. Lost Hold.
On the Nature of Scientific Law.
Kipling. Fabulists, The.
Legend of Truth, A.
Poseidon's Law.
Kooser. Skeleton in the Closet, The.
Larkin. Send No Money.
Lawrence. Elemental.
Satisfaction.
Search for Truth.
Sense of Truth.
Levertov. Ground-Mist, The.
Illustration [—a Footnote], The.
Levine. I Was Born in Lucerne.
Jewish Graveyards, Italy.
Poem of Flight, The.
Roofs.
Suit, The.
Liddy. After Kraske.
At castle shadowed mouth of the / Doonbeg.
Lindsay. Beyond the Moon.
Lowry. After all, the vision was like but subtly sea-changed.
Elsinore was the battlements of Oaxaca.
Slough of Despond: Or the House of Hope, The.
MacLeish. Love is the way that lovers never know.
Throwing a careless pebble in the lake.
MacNeice. Canto I: "August. Render to Caesar. Speak parrot: a gimmick for Poll."
What is truth? says Pilate.
Matthews. Bad.
Meinke. Supermarket.
Meredith. Song: "Thou steppest from thy splendour."
To Cardinal Manning.
Merton. Philosophers, The.
Truth, The.
Millay. Anguish, The.
Moore. Enough.
Morgan. Skulls, The.
Nathan. Conversation Piece.
Creed.
Feeding the Ducks.
Loophole, The.
Thirty Rings.
Nemerov. Earthquake in the West, The.
Old Photograph, An.
Questions.
Seeing Things.
Sestina I: "Thickness of paint or flesh cannot deface."
To Clio, Muse of History.
Two Pair.
Neruda. Don't you also feel danger.
Is 4 always 4 for everybody?
Little Devils.
Pedro Is When.
Olson. Kingfishers, The.
Oppen. And truth? O, / Truth!
Leviathan.
To insist that what is true is good, no matter, no matter.
Patchen. Shapes and Intensities of This Man, This Confucius, The.
Sure There Is Food.
Raine. Halt, The.
Ralegh. Conjectural First Draft of the Petition to Queen Anne.
Lie, The.
Rich. Burden Baskets.
Double Monologue.
5:30 A.M.
Frame.
7/16/68: i.
Robinson. Sainte-Nitouche.

Though the sick beast infect us, we are fraught.
Roethke. Adamant, The.
Open House.
Rolfe. Bequest.
Poisoned Air Befouled the Whole Decade, The.
Rossetti. All night I dream you love me well.
Hark! the Alleluias of the great salvation.
So I began my walk of life; no stop.
That Which Hath Been Is Named Already, and It Is Known That It Is Man.
Rukeyser. Ballad of Orange and Grape.
Believing in Those Inexorable Laws.
Poem as Mask, The.
Say it depends on the interpretation.
Sandburg. Accomplished Facts.
Do You Want Affidavits?
Good Morning, America.
On the Way.
Troths.
Who Am I?
Schwartz. Poem: "Window winter."
Shakespeare. Phoenix and the Turtle, The.
Sonnet 14: "Not from the stars do I my judgement pluck."
Sonnet 101: "O truant Muse, what shall be thy amends."
Shelley. Sonnet: To a Balloon Laden with Knowledge.
Smart. Truth.
Smith, Stevie. Magna Est Veritas.
Stafford. Turn Over Your Hand.
Stevens. Gigantomachia.
Man on the Dump, The.
On the Road Home.
Suckling. Welcome, welcome, mortal wight.
Updike. Fever.
Walker. Confession.
Whitman. All Is Truth.
Whittier. Brown of Ossawatomie.
Calef in Boston.
Friend's Burial, The.
Miriam.
Preacher, The.
Quaker Alumni, The.
Ritner.
To ———: "Maiden! with the fair brown tresses."
To George B. Cheever.
Utterance.
Wilbur. Clearness.
Epistemology.
Lying.
Williams, Charles Kenneth. Near the Haunted Castle.
Refuge, Serpent-Riders.
Williams, Miller. Journalist Buys a Pig Farm, The.
Williams, William Carlos. Fool's Song, The.
Hard Listener, The.
Wordsworth. In Allusion to Various Recent Histories and Notices of the French Revolution, Continued.
Lines Written as a School Exercise at Hawkshead, Anno Aetatis 14.
To ———: "Let other bards of angels sing."
Where Lies the Truth? Has Man in Wisdom's Creed.
Wright, Charles. Language Journal.
Wright, James. Accusation, The.
How close to becoming spirit something is.
Wroth. Song: "Fairest, and still truest eyes."
Sonnet 5: "Like to huge clowds of smoke which well may hide."
Sonnet 8: "Hee that shunns love doth love him self the less."
Sonnet 40: "Itt is nott love which you poore fooles do deeme."
Wyatt. Mistrustful minds be moved.
Take heed therfore, lest ye be spied.
To cause accord or to ag[g]re[e].
What should I say.
Within my breast I never thought it gain.
Yeats. Leaders of the Crowd, The.
Song of the Happy Shepherd, The.

Young. Dancing Naked.
Reading Nijinsky's Diary.
Zukofsky. You could then, my heart, wit, eye, mean in proposing love our aim.
Tubman, Harriet
Hacker. Part of a True Story.
Hayden. Runagate Runagate.
Tulips
Emerson. O'er the garden water goes the wind alone.
Gallagher. Time Lapse with Tulips.
Herrick. Meditation for His Mistress[e], A.
To a Bed of Tulips.
Jong. Still Life with Tulips.
Levertov. Tulips, The.
MacNeice. Another Cold May.
Plath. Tulips.
Sandburg. Garden Wireless.
Schuyler. February.
Schwartz. News of the Gold World of May.
Smith, Charlotte. To an Amiable Girl.
Williams, William Carlos. Tulip Bed, The.
When I saw.
Zukofsky. Tulip.
Tumbleweeds
Carruth. Shake, Well Before Using.
Turkey
Byron. Stanzas: "Chill and mirk is the nightly blast."
Carroll, Jim. Sure.
Griffiths. Doors of the Year, Well Done, The.
Hemingway. They All Made Peace—What Is Peace?
Lawrence. Prisoner at Work in a Turkish Garden.
Sisters, I am sorry for this foreign man.
Meredith. Wassail for the New Year, A.
Merrill. Thousand and Second Night, The.
Yánnina.
Turkeys
Dunbar. Soliloquy of a Turkey.
Lawrence. Turkey-Cock.
Nash. Turkey, The.
Pack. Wild Turkeys in Paradise.
Wilbur. Black November Turkey, A.
Turner, Joseph Mallord William
Carruth. Excursus of Reassurance in Begonia Time, An.
Raine. Turner's Seas.
Turner, Nat
Hayden. Ballad of Nat Turner, The.
Turtle Doves
Cowper. Doves, The.
See also **Doves.**
Turtles
"Carroll, Lewis." Mock Turtle's Song, The.
Turtle Soup.
Lindsay. Little Turtle, The.
Lowell. Bringing a Turtle Home.
Neo-Classical Urn, The.
Returning Turtle.
Meinke. Myrtle the Turtle.
Morgan. Turtle, The.
Nash. Turtle, The.
Nemerov. Mud Turtle, The.
Oliver. Turtle, The.
Roethke. Myrtle.
Silverstein. Bagpipe Who Didn't Say No, The.
Updike. To a Box Turtle.
Williams, Charles Kenneth. In the middle / of a bite of.
Shells.
Williams, William Carlos. Turtle, The.
See also **Tortoises.**
Tuscany
Fletcher. From Portofino Point.
Tomlinson. Thunder in Tuscany.
Tuskegee Institute
Dunbar. Tuskegee Song.
"Twain, Mark" (Samuel Langhorne Clemens)
Hoffman. Mark Twain, 1909.
Lindsay. Three Poems About Mark Twain.
Stein. Mark Twain Centenary.
Twelfth Night
Hardy. Burning the Holly.
Herrick. Twelfe Night, or King and Queene.

Twickenham, England
Donne. Twicknam [*or* Twickenham] Garden.
Twilight
Auden. Nightfall.
Beckett. Roundelay: "On all that strand."
Berry. Before Dark.
Bogan. Short Summary.
Boyle. Two Twilights for William Carlos Williams.
Carruth. Anima.
Eternal City.
Like a frozen lake the sky in the bitterest.
October. Twilight / flutters like cloth of silver.
Twilight Comes.
Under the hill a winter twilight.
Ceravolo. Dusk.
Clark. Warm ripe days. The sun floods the ridge with color.
Crane. Interior.
Creeley. End of the Day, The.
Cummings. A- / float on some.
If in beginning twilight of winter will stand.
Like a little bear twilight.
Nine birds(rising / through a gold moment)climb.
Somebody knew Lincoln somebody Xerxes.
Sonnet: "No sunset, but a grey, great, struggling sky."
Sunset)edges become swiftly.
This out of within itself moo.
This(let's remember)day died again and.
Twi- / is -Light bird.
Utterly and amusingly I am pash.
When parsing warmths of dusk construe.
De la Mare. Evening.
Market-Place, The.
Reverie.
Voices.
Dickey, James. Dusk of Horses, The.
Dunbar. Twilight.
Eberhart. Four Lakes' Days.
Solace.
Everson. Dusk, The.
Fisher. Thin smoke, A.
Gunn. Back to Life.
Herrick. To Anthea Lying in Bed.
Twilight ("Twilight is no other thing [we say], The").
Twilight ("Twilight, no other thing is, Poets say").
Hesketh. Lyric Evening.
Sundowner.
Hewitt. Apparition.
November Park.
Winter Day.
Kunitz. Twilight.
Lawrence. Bei Hennef.
Dawn Verse, The.
Sunset.
Sunset Verse, The.
Twilight.
Lewis. Patrol, The.
Longfellow. Children's Hour, The.
McGrath. Up the Dark Valley.
Meredith. Along the garden terrace, under which.
Ballad of Past Meridian, A.
Evening, after a Picture.
Longest Day, The.
Pastoral 3: "Now standing on this hedgeside path."
There fell a sudden rain.
Twilight Music.
Prince. Handfast Point.
Robinson. Twilight Song.
Rossetti. Twilight Calm.
Sandburg. Bringers.
Dreams in the Dusk.
Hoof Dusk.
Lackawanna Twilight.
Smoke Shapes.
Sarton. Evening Walk in France.
Schuyler. Song: "Light lies layered in the leaves, The."
Shelley. Summer Evening Churchyard, A.
Smart. Sweets of Evening, The.

Smith, Charlotte. Written near a Port on a Dark Evening.
Spender. Dusk.
Tomlinson. Tramontana at Lerici.
Under the Moon's Reign.
Whitman. Twilight.
Williams, Miller. Staying.
Wordsworth. Hail, Twilight, sovereign of one peaceful hour!
When slow from pensive twilight's latest gleams.
Wright, James. By a Lake in Minnesota.
Cold Divinities, The.
Sun Tan at Dusk.
Twilights.
Yau. Cascade.
See also **Evening; Sunset.**

Twins
Graves. Twins.
Kooser. Soul of Twins, The.
Matthews. Twins.
Rukeyser. Destruction of Grief.
Shapiro. Twins, The.
Van Duyn. Twins, The.
Wilbur. Gemini.

Typing and Typists
Cummings. Pound pound pound / on thy cold grey corona oh P.
Koertge. Panty Hose.

Tyranny
Auden. Epitaph on a Tyrant.
Blake. Grey Monk, The.
Browning, Robert. Instans Tyrannus.
Burns. Altered from an Old English Song.
Fragment—on Glenriddel's Fox Breaking His Chain, A.
Ode [for General Washington's Birthday].
Perish their names, however great or brave.
Byron. On a Royal Visit to the Vaults.
On Jordan's Banks.
Windsor Poetics.
Clark. Commanders, The.
Cohen. Your Eyes.
Cummings. F is for foetus(a).
Davie. Creon's Muse.
Fenton. Chosun.
Gray. Tophet.
Herrick. Duty to Tyrants.
Empires.
Kings and Tyrants.
Lawes ("When Lawes full power have to sway, we see").
Love.
Jarrell. English Garden in Austria, An.
State, The.
Jeffers. Ave Caesar.
Kipling. Benfactors, The.
Greek National Anthem, The.
Old Issue, The.
Lowell. Bosworth Field.
MacLeish. Tyrant of Syracuse.
Melville. Timoleon.
Meredith. Banners from East, from South.
Despots of Manchester, Oligarchs!
Hugest of engines, a much limited man.
Now had her glut of vengeance left her grey.
Solon.
Poe. Tamerlane.
Rukeyser. Third Elegy. The Fear of Form.
Shelley. Song to the Men of England.
Smith, Stevie. Christmas.
Leader, The.
Spenser. Hard by a rivers side a virgin faire.
Warren. Apology for Domitian.
Wordsworth. 1811 ("Here pause: the poet claims at least this praise").
Imitation of Juvenal — Satire VIII.
Is there a power that can sustain and cheer.
Ode: "Who rises on the banks of Seine."

U

UFOs. *see* **Flying Saucers.**

Uganda
Walker. In Uganda an Early King.

Ugliness
Brontë. And now the house-dog stretched once more.
Browning, Robert. And were I not, as a man may say, cautious.
Burns. I do confess thou art sae fair.
Keekin' Glass, The.
Sic a Wife as Willie Had.
Byron. If for Silver, or for Gold.
On Sam Rogers.
Catullus. Carmen 97: "As God is my witness where is the difference between."
Cowper. On a Similar Character.
On an Ugly Fellow.
To Demosthenis.
Creeley. For Martin.
Cummings. Dress was a suspicious madder,importing the cruelty of roses, The.
N / Umb a / stree / t's wintr.
Of an it ignoblest he, The.
Donne. Anagram, The.
Comparison, The.
Herrick. Upon Blanch: ("Blanch swears her Husband's lovely; when a scald").
Upon Deb.
Upon Jollies Wife.
Upon Madam Ursly.
Upon Ursley.
Jeffers. Carmel Point.
Lowry. Warning from False Cape Horn.
Merton. When a Hideous Man.
Millay. Still will I harvest beauty where it grows.
Who hurt you so.
Rich. Wherever in this city, screens flicker.
Robinson. Rat, The.
Rossetti. What is this above thy head, / O Man?
Sidney. What length of verse can serve brave *Mopsa*'s good to show?
Suckling. Deformed Mistress, The.
Turco. Lafe Grat.
Williams, Charles Kenneth. Becoming Somebody Else.
Portions of Manslayer.
Williams, William Carlos. In Sisterly Fashion.
Wyatt. Ye old mule, that thin[c]k your self so fair [*or* fayre].
Zukofsky. No it would not mean a damn (quick whim referred to pure.

Ukrainians
Hartley. Kuzan—First Avenue.

Ulysses
Cowper. On Flaxman's Penelope.
Doolittle. Calypso.
Graves. Ulysses.
Gunn. Book of the Dead, The.
Odysseus on Hermes.
Lewis. Odyssey, The.
Lovelace. To a Lady That Desired Me I Would Bear My Part with Her in a Song.
Lowry. Reflection to Windward.
MacLeish. Eplenor.
Old Man's Journey.
Muldoon. Making the Move.
Nathan. Family Circle.
Nemerov. About Ulysses, the learned have reached two.
Pope. Argus.
Pound. Canto 1: "And then went down to the ship."
Rossetti. Lotus-Eaters: Ulysses to Penelope, The.
Schwartz. Sonnet Suggested by Homer, Chaucer, Shakespeare, Edgar Allan Poe, Paul Valéry, James Joyce, et al.
Spenser. Virgils Gnat.
Stevens. World as Meditation, The.
Tennyson. "Courage!" he said, and pointed toward the land.
To Ulysses.
Ulysses.
Yau. Return of Ulysses I.
Return of Ulysses II.

Umbrellas
Dickinson. Parasol is the umbrella's daughter, The.

Hall. Umbrella, The.
Zukofsky. For Selma Gubin's Umbrellas.

Uncertainty
Ashbery. Gazing Grain, The.
Auden. Belief.
Finis.
Joy.
Mill, The.
Tale, A.
To a Toadstool.
We've covered enough ground since that awkward day.
Beatles. Something.
Strawberry Fields Forever.
Beckett. Enueg II.
Browning, Robert. Dubiety.
Bukowski. Guru.
Saying Goodbye to Love.
Clark. Coral.
Coleridge. Superstition.
Uncertainty in Love.
Creeley. Two.
Dickey, William. One Incident of Many.
Dickinson. If you were coming in the Fall.
Dobyns. Refusing the Necessary.
Doolittle. Are we unfathomable night.
Fragment 36: "I know not what to do."
"Dylan." Señor (Tales of Yankee Power).
Gallagher. Message for the Sinecurist.
Graves. In No Direction.
When and Why.
Why of the Weather, The.
Griffiths. Fluidity, Charmouth.
Hacker. Lines Declining a Transatlantic Dinner Invitation.
Hardy. Come Not; Yet Come!
Hartley. What Is Sacrament.
Hayden. Traveling through Fog.
Herrick. Things Mortal Still Mutable.
Hewitt. Hand over Hand.
Jong. Middle Aged Lovers, I.
MacNeice. Entirely.
Les Sylphides.
Meum Est Propositum.
What ghosts of cuckoo-spit and dew.
McNeill. Aubade to Fear (Heavy with Child).
Markson. As in the Aftermath.
Melville. Pisa's Leaning Tower.
Meredith. Chambers of my heart are many, dear, The.
Merrill. About the Phoenix.
Merton. Like the flights of ducks.
Soda Fountains.
Neruda. Let's Wait.
O'Hara. Cornkind.
Meditations in an Emergency.
Olson. Fish is the Flower of Water, A.
Oppen. Department of Plants and Structures— obsolete, the old name.
Pack. Look, there it is—I'm sure that is the oak.
Piercy. What Feeling Is This?
Raine. Sphere, The.
"Reed." Make Up Mind.
Rich. You are beside me like a wall; I touch you with my fingers and.
Rolfe. To Thine Own Self.
Undersea Poem.
Schwartz. At This Moment of Time.
Shelton. To You.
Smith, Stevie. Reason, The.
Thomas. Should Lanterns Shine.
Tomlinson. Barometer, The.
Warren. Mango on the Mango Tree, The.
Whittier. Song of Slaves in the Desert.
Williams, Miller. La Ultima Carta: A Young Wife Writes to Her Husband in the Mountains.

Uncles
Ciardi. Alec.
Cowper. On the Astrologers.
Cullen. Uncle Jim.
Cummings. My uncle / Daniel fought in the civil.
Nobody loses all the time.
Dove. Great Uncle Beefheart.
Ferlinghetti. Old Sailors, The.

Hayden. Burly Fading One, The.
Hewitt. Magician, The.
My Brooklyn Uncle.
My Uncle.
My Uncle Johnny.
My Uncle Willy.
Teacher's Residence, The.
Uncle Dick and Aunt Bertha.
Volunteer, The.
Knight. My Uncle is My Honor and a Guest in My House.
Levine. Uncle.
Meinke. Uncle Jim.
Uncle Joe.
Patchen. Wouldn't You Be after a Jaunt of 964,000,000,000,000 Million Miles?
Piercy. Landed Fish.
Plath. Stopped Dead.
Wright, James. Willy Lyons.

Underground Railroad
Hayden. Runagate Runagate.

Underhill, John
Whittier. John Underhill.

Undertakers
Herrick. Upon Luske.
Hugo. Digging Is an Art.
Kipling. Undertaker's Horse, The.
Nash. Tweedledee and Tweedledoom.
Sandburg. To Certain Journeymen.

Underwear
Ferlinghetti. Underwear.
Hemingway. I Like Americans.
Herrick. Upon Skoles.

Unemployment
Angelou. Contemporary Announcement.
Bukowski. Fall Out.
Hello, Willie Shoemaker.
Hall. Waiting on the Corners.
Hewitt. Ex-Serviceman, The.
New Jerusalem.
Ruins Answer, The.
Hopkins. Tom's Garland: Upon the Unemployed.
Lawrence. British Workman and the Government, The.
Miller. Wondered why the building was so small.
Sandburg. Muckers.
Spender. Unemployed.
Sutter. My dad's old man was a carpenter.
Taconite Harbor.
Williams, Charles Kenneth. Fast Food.

Unicorns
Cullen. That Bright Chimeric Beast.
Duncan. Banners, The.
Festivals, The.
Ferlinghetti. With bells for hooves in sounding streets.
Garrigue. Improvisation upon the Theme of the Lady and the Unicorn, An.
Graves. Unicorn and the White Doe.
Hall. Some Oddities.
Hesketh. Unicorn.
Jarrell. Unicorn, The.
Moore. Sea Unicorns and Land Unicorns.
Sarton. Lady and the Unicorn, The.

Unidentified Flying Objects. *see* **Flying Saucers.**
Union of Soviet Socialist Republics. *see* **Russia.**
Unions. *see* **Labor Unions.**
United Nations. *see* **World Federation.**
United States
Angelou. Request.
Berryman. American Lights, Seen from Off Abroad.
Presidential flags! and the General is here.
Burns. Slave's Lament, The.
Carruth. Bitcheries of Madison Avenue, The.
Ciardi. Box Comes Home, A.
Cohen. Democracy.
Creeley. America.
Cummings. Next to of course god america i.
Opening of the chambers close.
Poem, or Beauty Hurts Mr. Vinal.
Season 'tis,my lovely lambs, The.
Davie. From the New World.
Dickey, James. Coming Back to America.

Dickinson. My country need not change her gown.
Sweet Land of Liberty.
Duncan. Before the Judgment.
"Dylan." Lonesome Death of Hattie Carroll, The.
Russian has three an' a half red eyes, A.
With God on Our Side.
Eberhart. Yonder.
Emerson. Ode Sung in the Town Hall.
Frost. Gift Outright, The.
Record Stride, A.
Serious Step Taken Lightly, A.
Ginsberg. America.
Vow, A.
Hardy. On an Invitation to the United States.
Hughes, Langston. I, Too.
Jeffers. Eagle Valor, Chicken Mind.
Historical Choice.
Invasion.
Shine, Perishing Republic.
Kipling. American, An.
Choice, The.
Deep-Sea Cables, The.
Question, The.
Vineyard, The.
White Man's Burden, The.
Lawrence. American Eagle, The.
O! Americans.
MacLeish. American Letter.
Colloquy for the States.
Empire Builders.
Men.
Muldoon. Immram.
Notley. At Night the States.
Olson. Hustings, The ("Future sucks, The").
Of the United States.
Rufus Woodpecker visited the President.
Patchen. Letter to Those Who Are About to Die.
Roethke. Night Journey.
Stevenson. In the States.
Tate. Historical Epitaphs.
Updike. Air Show.
Minority Report.
Whitman. America.
For You O Democracy.
From Paumanok Starting I Fly Like a Bird.
I Hear America Singing.
Passage to India.
Poem of Remembrances for a Girl or a Boy of These States.
Starting from Paumanok.
States!
Thou Mother with Thy Equal Brood.
To the Leaven'd Soil They Trod.
To the States, To Identify the 16th, 17th, or 18th Presidential.
Virginia—the West.
Wandering at Morn.
Whittier. On Receiving an Eagle's Quill from Lake Superior.
Vow of Washington, The.

Unity
Ammons. Roundel.
Beatles. All Together Now.
Come Together.
Word, The.
Beckett. Universe-Solitude.
Berry. All the lives this place.
And I am here in Kentucky in the place I have made myself.
At night make me one with the darkness.
Falling Asleep.
Going into the city, coming.
Hidden Singer, The.
Law That Marries All Things, The.
Little farm, motherland, made.
Man Born to Farming, The.
Man who does not ask too much, A.
My mind was overborne with questions.
On the Hill Late at Night.
Silence, The.
Sowing the seed, / my hand is one with the earth.
Wheel, The.
Bishop. Sonnet of Intimacy.

Bradstreet. Letter to Her Husband, Absent upon Public[k] Employment, A.
To My Dear and Loving Husband.
Carroll, Jim. I am trying to abide by the clues.
Mercury Clouds.
Tenth Try, The.
Carruth. Border is what creates illegal aliens, The.
Contra Mortem.
He thinks in wonder how love was all that was.
Okay, Fulke Greville: "None can well behold."
Rhopaloceral.
Voided by too many hopes betrayed, too many.
Ceravolo. Autumn Break.
White Fish in Reeds.
Clark. Warm ripe days. The sun floods the ridge with color.
Cooper. Racetrack, The.
Cowper. Song, A: "Sparkling eye, the mantling cheek."
Donne. Prophets, The.
Eberhart. Parker River, The.
Emerson. All that thy virgin soul can ask be thine.
Dear Ellen, many a golden year.
Flute, The.
I cannot find a place so lonely.
Love and Thought.
Motto to "Nature" ("Rounded world is fair to see, The").
None spares another yet it pleases me.
Poet of poets / Is Time, the distiller.
Principle of all things; entrails made.
Rex.
Though her eye seek other forms.
Unity.
Xenophanes.
Everson. August.
God Germed in Raw Granite.
Ford. Even when the heart of the world is found.
Seis Hermanos.
Fox. On Some Such Morning.
On This Shore.
Gardner. Loud Song, Mother, A.
Mathematics of Encounter.
Ginsberg. Change: *Kyoto-Tokyo Express*, The.
Glück. Hawk's Shadow.
Pond, The.
Song of Invisible Boundaries.
Graves. Cliff and Wave.
Fast Bound Together.
Song: Twinned Heart.
Three Locked Hoops.
To Tell and Be Told.
Toast to Death, A.
Gunn. Ruthlessly gentle, gently ruthless we move.
Saturnalia.
Hartley. Day is dark—the night, The.
Herbert. Clasping of Hands.
Herrick. God is One.
JEHOVAH.
Power and Peace.
Hewitt. I Turn to Trees.
Response, The.
Hoffman. Resolution.
Holmes. Chinese Poets.
Jonson. On the Union.
Kunitz. Geometry of Moods.
Poem: "O Heart: this is a dream I had, or not a dream."
Prophecy on Lethe.
Levertov. Part, The.
Lewis. And now we seek once more the burning breeze.
Beloved Beware.
On Leave: Marriage.
Lindsay. In Memory of My Friend, Joyce Kilmer, Poet and Soldier.
Incense.
Sew the Flags Together.
Traveller-Heart, The.
What the Forester Said.

V

Eberhart. Four Lakes' Days.
Hoffman. Summerhouse, The.
Hopkins. Penmaen Pool.
Knight. For a Brookline Lady I Love.
Kooser. Sunday Morning.
Merrill. Santorini: Stopping the Leak.
  Up and Down.
Merton. Miami You Are About to Be
  Surprised.
Morrison. Dancing & Thrashing.
Nash. I Always Say There's No Place Like
  New York in the Summer, or, That Cottage
  Small by a Waterfall Was Snapped Up Last
  February.
  Tomorrow, Partly Cloudy.
Nemerov. Sightseers.
O'Hara. Summer Breezes.
Schuyler. New Yorker, A.
  You're.
Stafford. Any Time.
Stevens. Gray Stones and Gray Pigeons.
Stevenson. O Lady fair and sweet.
Updike. Antigua.
  Back from Vacation.
  Island Sun.
  Poisoned in Nassau.
Van Duyn. Postcards from Cape Split.
Williams, William Carlos. On a Proposed Trip
  South.

Vacuum Cleaners and Vacuum Cleaning
Nemerov. Vacuum, The.
Stuart. Leaf Eater, The.

Vagabonds
Bukowski. Insane Always Loved Me, The.
  Swans Walk My Brain in April It Rains, The.
Clare. Lout, The: "No sort of learning ever
  hurts his head."
Clark. Silence of the Lambs, The.
Crane. River, The.
Dobyns. Freight Cars.
"Dylan." California.
  Down the Highway.
  Drifter's Escape.
  Gypsy Lou.
  Long Time Gone.
  Rambling, Gambling Willie.
Frost. Old Barn at the Bottom of the Fogs,
  The.
  Two Tramps in Mud Time.
  Unstamped Letter in Our Rural Letter Box,
  An.
Hardy. Trampwoman's Tragedy, A.
  Vagrant's Song.
Hayden. Rag Man, The.
Hughes, Ted. November.
Kinnell. Memory of Wilmington.
Kipling. Sestina of the Tramp-Royal.
Koertge. Caboose Factory, The.
Lawrence. Embankment at Night, before the
  War: Outcasts.
McGrath. Long Way Outside Yellowstone, A.
Mahon. Knut Hamsun in Old Age.
Miller. If you can't make a joke.
Sandburg. 'Boes.
Stevenson. Vagabond, The.
Tate. Traveller, The.
Tomlinson. Terminal Tramps.
  Thief's Journal, The.
Williams, Charles Kenneth. Harm.
Williams, William Carlos. R R Bums, The.

Valentine's Day
Boyle. Valentine for Harry Crosby, A.
"Carroll, Lewis." Valentine, A.
Carruth. Valentine.
Chaucer. Parlement of Foules, The.
Dickinson. Awake ye muses nine, sing me a
  strain divine.
Donne. Epithalamion, An, or Marriage Song
  on the Lady Elizabeth and Count Palatine
  Being Married on St. Valentine's Day.
Hemingway. Valentine.
Herrick. To his deare Valentine, Mistresse
  Margaret Falconbrige.
  To His Valentine, on S. Valentines Day.
Moore. For February 14th.
  Saint Valentine.

Nash. Strange Case of Mr. Ballantine's
  Valentine, The.
Poe. Valentine, A.
Rossetti. 1880.
  1885. St. Valentine's Day.
  1884.
  1886, St. Valentine's Day.
  1878.
  1879.
  February 14. 1883.
  St. Valentine's Day 1881.
  Valentine, 1882, A.
  Valentines From C.G.R.
Schuyler. February 13, 1975.
  Sleep.
Schwartz. Salute Valentine.
Silverstein. Won't You?
Stevenson. Wind is without there and howls in
  the trees, The.
Thomson. On Mrs. Mendez' Birthday.
Williams, William Carlos. On St. Valentine's
  Day.
Zukofsky. Happiest February.
  1959 Valentine.
  On Valentine's Day to Friends.
  This year / that Valentine is / late.

Valentino, Rudolph
Lawrence. Film Passion.

Valéry, Paul
Nemerov. Master at a Mediterranean Port,
  The.

Valkyries
Gray. Fatal Sisters, The.

Valleys
Browning, Elizabeth Barrett. Man and Nature.
Byron. Lachin y Gair.
Carroll, Jim. In the Valley.
Coleridge. Lines Composed While Climbing
  the Left Ascent of Brockley Coomb, in the
  County of Somerset, May, 1795.
Davie. Low Lands.
Dickey, James. Mexican Valley.
Eberhart. Summery Windermere, sweet lake!
Hewitt. Glendun.
Lawrence. Misery.
McGrath. Up the Dark Valley.
Meredith. Pastoral 6: "How barren would this
  valley be."
  Pasture Alp is webbed with shade, The.
Olson. Afica.
Patchen. Down in the Lone Valley.
Plath. Above the Oxbow.
Sandburg. Lackawanna Twilight.
  Mist Forms.
  Mist Marches Across the Valley.
  Moist Moon People.
  Santa Fe Sketches.
  They Ask Each Other Where They Came
  From.
  Valley Song.
  Valley Song.
Wordsworth. Airey-Force Valley.
Yeats. He Tells a Valley Full of Lovers.

Value
Ammons. Immoderation.
  Likely Story.
  Success Story.
Beatles. In My Life.
Berry. There is no government so worthy as
  your son who fishes with you in silence
  beside the forest pool.
Burns. On Being Asked Why God Had Made
  Miss D——— So Little and Mrs A———
  So Big.
  Sweetest May.
Carruth. He goes out with his chainsaw into
  the cold bright.
Cowper. To Sir John Fenn.
Dickinson. How precious Thought and Speech
  are!
  I took one Draught of Life.
  Nothing inclusive of a human Heart.
Fisher. Least, The.
  Red and the Black, The.
Gallagher. Refusing Silence.
Hacker. Riposte.
Herrick. Merits Make the Man.

Hewitt. Administration.
  Feathers on Turf.
  For Stonecutters.
  Hour with E.M.F. at Ninety, An.
  Values.
  Variations on a Theme.
Larkin. To Put One Brick upon Another.
  "MacDiarmid." Poetry in which all
  connections will constantly render such
  services, A.
Merton. Useless Tree, The.
Moore. Values in Use.
Nathan. Bladder Song.
  So?
Nemerov. Place of Value, The.
Oliver. Buddha's Last Instruction, The.
  Sun, The.
Raine. I've read all the books but one.
Rich. At Hertford House.
Sandburg. Again?
  Buyers and Sellers.
  How Much?
  Very Very Important.
Shakespeare. Sonnet 52: "So am I as the rich,
  whose blessed key."
Shelley. Fragment: "What men gain fairly—·
  that they should possess."
Smith, Stevie. Valuable.
Snodgrass. Old Jewelry.
Walker. We Alone.

Vampires
Byron. But thou, false infidel! shall writhe.
Kipling. Vampire, The.
Merrill. Narrow Escape, A.
Sandburg. Baby Vamps.
  Testimony Regarding a Ghost.
Smith, Patti. Doctor Love.
Smith, Stevie. Great Unaffected Vampires and
  the Moon.
Wilbur. Undead, The.
Zimmer. Zimmer Fearing Anemia.

Van Doren, Mark
Hayden. Ballad of Remembrance, A.
MacLeish. Danger in the Air, The.
  Mark Van Doren and the Brook.
Merton. Message to Be Inscribed on Mark
  Van Doren's Hamilton Medal.

Van Gogh, Vincent
Berg. Unfinished Double Sonnet.
Ford. So you'd eat the ear of Van Gogh!
Fox. Sunflowers.
Hesketh. Letter to Vincent.
  Poem is a Painting, A.
Joseph. Cutting Off One's Ears for Someone
  Else Is Wrong.
Snodgrass. Van Gogh: "The Starry Night."
Tomlinson. Farewell to Van Gogh.
  Van Gogh.
Walker. If There Was Any Justice.

Vanbrugh, Sir John
Swift. Vanbrug's House.

Vancouver, British Columbia
Lowry. Beneath the Malebolge lies Hastings
  street.
  Burnt pier: the last passenger: the farewells,
  The.
  Noble City Full of Pigeons or Everyone a
  Hypocrite Including Me.
  Welcome Home Our Own.
Olson. West 6.

Vane, Sir Henry (1613-62)
Milton. Sonnet 17: "Vane, young in yeares,
  but in sage counsell old."

Vanity
Berry. Praise.
  Though He Can't Know Death, He Must
  Study Dying.
Berryman. Vespers.
Bradstreet. Flesh and the Spirit, The.
  Vanity of All Worldly Things, The.
Browning, Elizabeth Barrett. Vanities.
Bukowski. Beach Trip.
Bunting. Renowned author of, The.
Burns. Song: "As I cam down by yon castle
  wa'."
  There's a youth in this city, it were a great
  pity.

Byron. All Is Vanity, Saith the Preacher.
To ———: "Oh! well I know your subtle Sex."
To a Vain Lady.
Campion. Ad Chloen.
Epigramme: "All in sattin Oteny will be suited."
Epigramme: "Cease, fond wretch, to love, so oft deluded."
Ev'ry Dame affects good fame, what ere her doings be.
Carew. Ingrateful[l] Beauty Threatened.
"Carroll, Lewis." Miss Jones.
Clough. Go foolish thoughts, and join the throng.
Cohen. Window, The.
Cowper. Glory to God Alone.
Necessity of Self-Abasement.
On a Similar Character.
Self-Love and Truth Incompatible.
Truth and Divine Love Rejected by the World.
Creeley. Apple Uppfle.
Cummings. Cambridge ladies who live in furnished souls, The.
De la Mare. Reflections.
Dickinson. Ribbons of the Year.
Dobyns. Vanity.
Donne. When senses, which thy so[u]ldiers are.
Dunn. Wanting to Get Closer.
"Dylan." When He Returns.
Gardner. Spendthrift.
Ginsberg. Very Dove, A.
Graves. Vain and Careless.
Vanity.
Gunn. Lines for a Book.
Hardy. Lady Vi.
Herbert. Vanity (2).
Vanity [or Vanitie] (1).
Herrick. Upon Rook: Epigram.
Hewitt. Ireland.
My Naming.
Pangur Ban.
Peter Peri (1899-1967).
Hopkins. Hope holds to Christ.
Keats. When They Were Come unto the Faery's Court.
Lawrence. Intimates.
Narcissus.
Natural Complexion.
Tragedy.
True Love at Last.
Ultimate Reality.
Melville. Camoëns.
Fortitude of the North, The.
Meredith. Song: "Fair and false! No dawn will greet."
Merrill. Peacock, The.
Nash. Evening Out, The.
Manatee, The.
Theatrical Reflection.
Oppen. To C. T.
Piercy. Barbie Doll.
Rossetti. Beauty Is Vain.
If love is not worth loving, then life is not worth living.
One Certainty, The.
St. Andrew's Church.
Soeur Louise De La Miséricorde.
Testimony, A.
Then Whose Shall Those Things Be?
Vain Shadow, A.
Vanity of Vanities.
Rukeyser. Letter, Unposted.
Sarton. Narcissus.
Sexton. Snow White and the Seven Dwarfs.
Shakespeare. Sonnet 1: "From fairest creatures we desire increase."
Sonnet 134: "Who is it that says most? which can say more."
Shelley. Ozymandias [of Egypt].
Smith, Charlotte. Dictatorial Owl, The.
Jay in Masquerade, The.
Moth, The.
To My Lyre.
Wheat-Ear, The.
Smith, Stevie. Adelaide Abner.

Devil-My-Wife, The.
Face, The.
Hat, The.
Spenser. Hideous dragon, dreadfull to behold, A.
It was the time, when rest, soft sliding downe.
On high hills top I saw a stately frame.
Soone after this I saw an elephant.
Then did a sharped spyre of diamond bright.
Swift. Lady's Dressing Room, The.
Tennyson. Character, A.
Whitman. Fame's Vanity.
Whittier. Common Question, The.
Williams, Charles Kenneth. Mirror, The.
Williams, Miller. Love and How It Becomes Important in Our Day to Day Lives.
Wordsworth. Column Intended by Buonaparte for a Triumphal Edifice in Milan, Now Lying by the Way-Side in the Simplon Pass, The.
Emperors and Kings, How Oft Have Temples Rung.
Soft As a Cloud Is Yon Blue Ridge.
Wild Duck's Nest, The.
Yeats. Two Trees, The.
See also **Pride.**
Variety
Bukowski. Ten minutes before post time.
Emerson. Three Dimensions, The.
MacNeice. Plurality.
Merton. Great and Small.
Zukofsky. With a Valentine (the 14 February).
Vaudeville
Muldoon. Gypsy.
Vaughan, Henry
Davie. Monmouthshire.
Vegetables
Cohen. Person Who Eats Meat, A.
Dickey, William. More Under Saturn.
Haines. Cauliflower, The.
Harvest.
Jarrell. My aunt kept turnips in a flock.
Jong. Eggplant Epithalamion, The.
Fruits & Vegetables.
McGrath. Praises.
Rossetti. Lily has a smooth stalk, / Will never hurt your hand, The.
Schuyler. Under the Hanger.
Sorrentino. Disappearance of Oilcloth, The.
Swift. Asparagus.
Wilbur. Melongène.
Williams, Charles Kenneth. Modern, The.
Williams, William Carlos. Child and Vegetables.
See also **Listings for specific Vegetables.**
Vegetarians
Dove. Why I Turned Vegetarian.
Eberhart. Explorer on Main Street, The.
Silverstein. Point of View.
Venereal Disease
Catullus. Carmen 57: "Caesar Mamurraque! / A peerless pair of brazen buggers."
Crane. National Fugue.
Zukofsky. "Pull! crew" 's convenient to reprobate kin hides.
Vengeance
Brontë. Gleneden's Dream.
Browning, Robert. First-Born of Egypt, The.
Clough. Alcaics.
Cowper. Cock-Fighters Garland.
De la Mare. Thus Her Tale.
Dunbar. Vengeance is Sweet.
Eberhart. Request for Offering.
Graves. Return.
Herrick. Abels Bloud.
To the Fever, Not To Trouble Julia.
Hughes, Langston. Hard Daddy.
Lowry. Plingen plangen auf gefangen.
"MacDiarmid." Focherty.
Meredith. Hans Euler.
Milton. Be not thou silent now at length.
Paley. I cannot keep my mind on Jerusalem.
Psalms. Psalm 55: "Give ear to my prayer, O God."
Psalm 58: "Do ye indeed speak righteousness, O congregation?"
Psalm 69: "Save me, O God.."

Psalm 79: "O God, the heathen are come.."
Psalm 83: "Keep not thou silence, O God."
Psalm 94: "O Lord God, to whom vengeance belongeth."
Psalm 109: "Hold not thy peace, O God of my praise."
Psalm 110: "Lord said unto my Lord, The."
Psalm 129: "Many a time have they afflicted me from my youth."
Psalm 149: "Praise ye the Lord. Sing unto the Lord a new song."
Ralegh. 3.2: "Seldome the villaine, though much hast he make."
Ransom. On the Road to Wockensutter.
"Reed." My Friend George.
Rossetti. Will These Hands Ne'er Be Clean? Zara.
Smart. Hosanna! God be prais'd.
Whittier. Cities of the Plain, The.
Sicilian Vespers, The.
Wright, James. Devotions.
Wroth. Sonnet: "Lett griefe as farr bee from your deerest brest."
Venice, Italy
Betjeman. Longfellow's Visit to Venice.
Browning, Robert. Goldoni.
In a Gondola.
Toccata of Galuppi's, A.
Byron. I stood in Venice on the Bridge of Sighs.
Ode on Venice.
Venice.
Eliot. Burbank with a Baedeker: Beistein with a Cigar.
Garrigue. From Venice Was That Afternoon.
Housman. Far known to sea and shore.
Hugo. Bridge of Sighs, The.
Jong. Venice, November, 1966.
Lowell. Old snapshot from Venice 1952.
Melville. In a Bye-Canal.
Venice.
Schwartz. Late Autumn in Venice.
Tomlinson. Death in Venice.
Venice.
Wordsworth. On the Extinction of the Venetian Republic.
Venus (goddess)
Auden. Venus Will Now Say a Few Words.
Browning, Elizabeth Barrett. Psyche and Venus.
Campion. Come a shore, come, merrie mates.
Carew. Carver. To His Mistress, The.
On Sight of a Gentlewoman's Face in the Water.
Carruth. Birth of Venus, The.
Chaucer. Complaint of Mars, The.
Knight's Tale, The.
Parlement of Foules, The.
Romance [or Romaunt] of the Rose, The.
Crashaw. Out of Euphormio.
Upon the Same.
Upon Venus Putting on Mars His Armes.
De la Mare. Blind Boy, The.
Encounter, The.
Mercutio.
Eberhart. Giantess, The.
Glück. Letter from our Man in Blossomtime.
Hardy. Well-Beloved, The.
Herrick. Bag of the Bee, The.
Cloud, The.
How Lillies Came White.
How Violets Came Blue.
Hymne to Venus, and Cupid, A.
Short Hymne to Venus, A.
Vow to Venus, A.
Wounded Cupid, The.
Jarrell. Birth of Venus, The.
Lawrence. What Does She Want?
Lewis. Defeat.
He Gives Her Botticelli's Birth of Venus as a Wedding Gift.
Lovelace. Against the Love of Great Ones.
Paris's Second Judgement.
Princesse Löysa drawing.
Lowry. Nocturne: "This evening Venus signs alone."
Reflection to Windward.

Olson. Ring of, The.
Prince. Gregory Nazianzen.
Rossetti. Venus's Looking-Glass.
Rukeyser. Birth of Venus, The.
Shakespeare. Venus and Adonis.
Sidney. Now was our heav'nly vault deprived of the light.
Sonnet 17: "His mother dear Cupid offended late."
Smith, Stevie. Votaries of Both Sexes Cry First to Venus.
Swinburne. Laus Veneris.
Thomson. Nuptial song, A.
Wroth. Song: "Say Venus how long have I lov'd, and serv'd you heere?"
Sonnet 9: "But wher they may returne with honors grace."
Sonnet 9: "My muse now hapy, lay thy self to rest."
Sonnet 12: "Bee given to him who triumphs in his right."
Venus unto the Gods a sure did move.
Wyatt. Venus, in sport, to please therewith her dear.
See also **Aphrodite.**

Venus (planet)
Bogan. Evening-Star.
Brontë. Cold, clear, and blue, the morning heaven.
Chaucer. Complaint of Mars, The.
Frost. Literate Farmer and the Planet Venus, The.
Lowry. Consolation.
Millay. Truce for a Moment.
Olson. Objects, The.
Sexton. Venus and the Ark.
Updike. Milady Reflects.
Wordsworth. To the Planet Venus.
To the Planet Venus, an Evening Star.

Veracruz, Mexico
Hayden. Veracruz.

Verdi, Giuseppe
Tomlinson. In Verdi Square.

Verdun, Battle of (1916)
Lowell. Verdun.

Vergil. see **Virgil** [or Vergil].

Verlaine, Paul
Robinson. Verlaine.
Sorrentino. Le Bateau d'Amour Descried on the Briny.

Vermont (state)
Carruth. All things lay in nature, even the plastic flowers.
Maybe because they're so damn frigging rich.
My Meadow.
Slums par excellence that were your farms! And all.
This Song.
Vermont.
Wise child is born, The.
Eberhart. Play, The.
River Water Music.
Kipling. Pan in Vermont.
Matthews. Moonlight in Vermont.
Nash. Kipling's Vermont.
Paley. Connections: Vermont Vietnam (I).
Connections: Vermont Vietnam (II).
Rich. Living Memory.
Schuyler. Afterward.
Evenings in Vermont.
Now and Then.
Vermont Diary, A.
Updike. Vermont.
Warren. Fall Comes in Back-Country Vermont.
Whittier. Song of the Vermonters, 1779, The.

Verona, Italy
St. John. Doors, The.
Wright, Charles. Homage to Claude Lorrain.

Versailles, France
Moore. No Swan So Fine.
Patchen. Grand Palace of Versailles, The.
Rich. Versailles.

Veterans
Dobyns. Funny.
Dunbar. Veteran, The.

Fenton. Better for the widow, that she should not live in fear of surprise, The.
But come. Grief must have its term? Guilt too, then.
Children in Exile.
Doctor Gliedschirm, skin specialist, surgeries 14–16 hours or by appointment.
His wife nods, and a secret smile.
How comforting it is, once or twice a year. Vuccerìa.
Would come down, would ever come down.
Graves. Child with Veteran.
Hall. Man in the Dead Machine, The.
Hardy. San Sebastian.
Hewitt. Father Explains, A.
Kipling. All the world over, nursing their scars.
Chant-Pagan.
Clerks and the Bells, The.
Expert, The.
Last of the Light Brigade, The.
Scholars, The.
Troopin'.
Veterans, The.
Vineyard, The.
Knight. At a VA Hospital in the Middle of the United States of America: An Act in a Play.
Oppen. I cannot even now / Altogether disengage myself.
Seated Man.
"Reed." Xmas in February.
Sandburg. And So Today.
Graves.
Schuyler. Scarlet Tanager.
Whitman. Dying Veteran, The.
Williams, Charles Kenneth. From My Window.
Williams, Miller. WW I.
See also **Soldiers.**

Veterans Day. see **Armistice.**

Vice
Beckett. Ce qu'a de pis.
Out of Sight in the Direction of My Body.
Chaucer. Second Nun's Prologue, The.
Emerson. Γνωθι Σεαυτον.
This world is tedious.
To transmute crime to wisdom, & to stem.
Herrick. Nothing New.
Of Love ("Instruct me now, what love will do").
Two Things Odious.
Hewitt. One I Loved, The.
W.R.R.
Jeffers. Vices.
Kinnell. Last Songs.
Lawrence. What's Sane and What Isn't.
Marlowe. 3.4: Ad virum servantem coniugem.
Morrison. Feast Green Beast.
Nash. So That's Who I Remind Me Of.
O'Hara. Poem V (F) W.
Turco. Simon Judson.
See also **Sin.**

Vicksburg Campaign (1862–63)
Gildner. Dear and most Loved wife it is with pleasure.
Dear and Mutch Loved One with pleasure I take.
Dear Cecelia we hav hat some warm times.
Dear Cecelia well its shel and shel and.
Dear loved one did I mention General Grants.
Dear loved one well the last 2 days I spent.
Dear wife and bosom friend I hat seen hart.
Dear wife and friend I dozed but now will try.
Dear wife and friend I hav not mutch to write.
Dear wife I feal prety rested now.
Dear woman I again take pen in hand.
Dear woman I am sor a littel bit.
Dear woman I am well and hope you ar.
Dear woman I was glat to hear from you.
I went with General Logans men and we.
Letters from Vicksburg.
Mrs. Blood. Dear Madam. Yours of Sept. 13.
Some boys ar playing cards but I dont feal.
We left the River seven days ago.

Victoria, Queen of England
Browning, Elizabeth Barrett. Crowned and

Wedded.
Victoria's Tears.
Young Queen, The.
Cohen. Queen Victoria and Me.
Hardy. V.R. 1819–1901.
Housman. 1887.
Kipling. Ave Imperatrix!
Bells and Queen Victoria, The.
What the People Said.
Widow at Windsor, The.
Widow's Party, The.
Lawrence. Deadly Victorians, The.
Meredith. At the Funeral.
Nash. Don't Look Now.
Tennyson. To the Queen.
Whitman. For Queen Victoria's Birthday.
Wordsworth. Lines Inscribed in a Copy of His Poems Sent to the Queen for the Royal Library at Windsor.
Ode on the Installation of His Royal Highness Prince Albert as Chancellor of the University of Cambridge, July, 1847.

Victory
Ciardi. Memory of the Sad Chair, A.
V-J Day.
Coleridge. Verses Addressed to J. Horne Tooke and the Company Who Met on 28 June 1796 to Celebrate His Poll at the Westminster Election.
Dickinson. Neither fearing Extinction.
Triumph—may be of several kinds.
Victory comes late.
Donne. Death[,] be not proud, though some have called thee.
Emerson. Archangel Hope / Looks to the azure cope, The.
Hardy. Young Churchwarden, The.
Hartley. V—Is for Victory as You Can Plainly See.
Herrick. Care a Good Keeper.
Credit of the Conquerer, The.
End, The.
Last Stroke Strike Sure, The.
To the King, upon His Taking of Leicester.
To the Lord Hopton, on His Fight in Cornwall.
Hewitt. Valediction Lines to My WEA Students.
Hoffman. Victor, The.
Jarrell. Terms.
Jeffers. Moments of Glory.
Kipling. Darzee's Chaunt.
Hymn of the Triumphant Airman.
Lawrence. Triumph.
Lovelace. Of Cato.
Sonnet. To Generall Goring.
Mahon. Home Front, The.
Marlowe. 2.12: Exultat, quod amica potitus sit.
Melville. Canticle, A.
Dupont's Round Fight.
Meredith. Banners from South, from East.
Soon felt she in her shivered frame.
Prince. People Rest after Conquests, The.
Ralegh. If Croesus over Halys goe.
Ransom. Judith of Bethulia.
Roethke. Favorite, The.
Rolfe. At the Moment of Victory.
Marching Song of the Children of Darkness.
Swift. Ode to the King.
Whitman. Old Salt Kossabone.
Over the Carnage Rose Prophetic a Voice.
True Conquerors.
Turn O Libertad.
Whittier. Emancipation Group, The.
Wordsworth. Anticipation. October, 1803.
By Moscow Self-Devoted to a Blaze.
Germans on the Heights of Hochheim, The.
Occasioned by the Battle of Waterloo February, 1816.
Occasioned by the Battle of Waterloo (the Last Six Lines Intended for an Inscription) February, 1816.
Ode: 1815.
Ode: 1814.
On the Same Occasion.
Siege of Vienna Raised by John Sobieski February, 1816.

Wroth. Sonnet 47: "O stay mine eyes, shed nott thes fruitles tears."

Vienna, Austria
Cohen. Take This Waltz (After Lorca).
Merrill. Dream of Old Vienna, A.
Williams, William Carlos. Lustspiel.

Vienna, Siege of (1683)
Wordsworth. Siege of Vienna Raised by John Sobieski February, 1816.

Vietnam
Berg. Mother Political.
Berry. Against the War in Vietnam.
Dark with power.
Bly. Asian Peace Offers Rejected without Publication.
At a March against the Vietnam War.
Driving through Minnesota during the Hanoi Bombings.
Teeth Mother Naked at Last, The.
Bukowski. Simplicity of Everything in Viet Nam, The.
Carruth. And I was past caring so many, too many men.
Birds of Vietnam, The.
Clark. Door Gunner to the Moment, (A Shau Valley 1968), The.
Duncan. Up Rising.
Dunn. Turning Fifty.
Edmunds. Highlands 1966, The.
Garrigue. Resistance Meeting: Boston Common.
Ginsberg. Wichita Vortex Sutra.
Kinnell. Vapor Trail Reflected in the Frog Pond.
Knott. Two Vietnam Poems: (1966).
Levertov. Altars in the Street, The.
What Were They Like?
McGrath. Reading the Names of the Vietnam War Dead.
MacLeish. National Security.
Merton. Twenty Three Point Prospectus for Small College in the Badlands.
Morrison. I Fucked the Dregs.
Nathan. Penance, The.
Nemerov. On Getting Out Of Vietnam.
Notley. White Phosphorus.
Paley. Bridges.
Connections: Vermont Vietnam (I).
Connections: Vermont Vietnam (II).
In Hanoi 1969.
My Father at 85.
That Country.
Two Villages.
"Reed." Xmas in February.
Rich. Dien Bien Phu.
Newsreel.
Rukeyser. Flying to Hanoi.
Schuyler. May, 1972.
Shapiro. Vietnam Memorial.
Stuart. Speakers from the Vietnam War.
Tomlinson. Tarquinia.
Williams, Charles Kenneth. From My Window.
In the Heart of the Beast.

Vikings
Heaney. Viking Dublin: Trial Pieces.
Kipling. Dane-Geld.
Song of the Red War-Boat.
Longfellow. Skeleton in Armor [or Armour], The.
Lowry. What Sigbj[do]orn Said.
MacNeice. North Sea, The.
Whittier. Dole of Jarl Thorkell, The.
Norsemen, The.

Village Idiots
Graves. Villagers and Death, The.

Villages
Betjeman. Dear Old Village, The.
Village Inn, The.
Carruth. Village, The.
Coleridge. Reed-roof'd Village, still bepatch'd with snow, The.
Haines. Thousands of years passed.
Hall. Village in East Anglia, A.
Levine. Pili's Wall.
Longfellow. Part the First.
Ropewalk, The.

Tale of Acadie, A.
Village Blacksmith, The.
"MacDiarmid." Island Funeral.
McGrath. Ah.. to the Villages!
Merton. Tagus is finer than the creek, The.
Nathan. Winter Morning of the Village.
Oppen. Founder, The.
Patchen. Authority of Krajova, The.
Kibali-Ituri.
On the South-West Coast of Erehwemos Stands a Romantic Little Village.
Village Tudda, The.
Robinson. Dead Village, The.
Sandburg. Pods.
Weeds.
Smith, Charlotte. Written on Passing by Moon-Light through a Village, While the Ground Was Covered with Snow.
Smith, Stevie. Brickenden, Hertfordshire.
Williams, William Carlos. Wind of the Village.
Yau. Radiant Silhouette V.
Young. Leaving Rochester.

See also **Cities; Towns.**

Villanelle (form)
Bishop. One Art.
Hugo. Freaks at Spurgin Road Field, The.

See also **Villanelle in Title and First Line Index.**

Villon, François, the Virgin
Sandburg. François Villon Forgotten.

Vinci, Leonardo da. *see* **Leonardo da Vinci.**

Vines
Dickey, James. Kudzu.
Eberhart. Stealth and Subtleties of Growth.
Everson. August.
Lawrence. Erotic.
MacLeish. Population Explosion.
Merton. Vine, The.
Patchen. Vines with Their.
Rossetti. Passion Flower hath sprung up tall, The.
Tomlinson. Old Man's Beard.
Zukofsky. Vines.

Violence
Atwood. You fit into me.
Beckett. Dread Nay.
Berryman. Letter to His Brother.
Boyle. Poem for February First 1975, A.
Bukowski. I Don't Need a Bedsheet with Slits for Eyes to Kill You In.
Carruth. Mountain, The.
Cohen. Hydra 1960.
Creeley. Answer, The.
Names.
Reason, A.
Cummings. Come from his gal's.
Davie. Battered Wife, The.
Dobyns. How Could You Ever Be Fine.
Under the Green Ceiling.
Dunn. White Collar.
Eberhart. Dream, A.
My Golden and My Fierce Assays.
Galvin. In Ireland I Remembered the Foxes of Truro, Massachusetts.
Gardner. Of Conscience.
Ginsberg. Violence.
Glück. Edge, The.
Egg, The.
Seconds.
Griffiths. Mines in Sepia Tint, The.
Gunn. Mirror for Poets, A.
Hacker. Why We Are Going Back to Paradise Island.
Haines. I saw in that glittering distance.
Hardy. On the Doorstep.
Hayden. For King, for Robert Kennedy.
Locus.
Hemingway. Blood is thicker than water.
In a magazine.
Hewitt. At the Newsagent's.
Encounter Nineteen Twenty.
Legend in His Own Lifetime.
Mortal Place, The.
Neither an Elegy Nor a Manifesto.
Postscript, 1984.

Sonnet: "When I have read your hard and lively words."
Tribunes, The.
Troubles, 1922, The.
Two Spectres Haunt Me.
Ulster Landowner's Song, An.
William Conor RHA, 1881–1968.
Hoffman. Power.
Hughes, Langston. Third Degree.
Jeffers. Bloody Sire, The.
Explosion.
Knott. (Sideshow).
Lawrence. Love-Passage, A.
Shedding of Blood.
Levine. Letters for the Dead.
Lewis. River Temple: Wai, The.
Liddy. He'd be alive today if he wasn't pretty.
Requiem for a Non-Croppy.
MacLeish. Black Humor.
Marlowe. 1.7: Ad pacandam amicam, quam verberaverat.
2.14: In amicam, quod abortivum ipsa fecerit.
Meinke. Growing Deaf.
Ping-Pong.
Meredith. Candid Friend who strikes because he loves, The.
Merton. Hopeless and Felons.
Morgan. From a Forgotten Book.
Hideyoshi.
Morrison. Sidewalkers Moved, The.
Nash. It Figures.
Nathan. Body Count.
Law and Order.
Nemerov. Trial and Death, a Double Feature.
Oliver. Murderer's House, The.
Olson. Anecdotes of the Late War.
Laughing Ones, The.
Trinacria.
Pack. Twin, The.
"Reed." Hold On.
Kicks.
Video Violence.
Rich. 5:30 A.M.
Perennial Answer, The.
Violence.
Your small hands, precisely equal to my own.
Rukeyser. Second Elegy. Age of Magicians.
This is going to be about smoke.
Waking this Morning.
Sandburg. In the folded and quiet yesterdays.
Sexton. Wifebeater, The.
Shapiro. California Petrarchan.
Fly, The.
Girls Fighting, Broadway.
Shelley. Cancelled Stanza.
Shelton. Reaching For the Gun.
Smith, Stevie. Violent Hand, The.
Stevenson. Daughter of Herodias, The.
Walcott. Blues.
Wilbur. Tywater.
Williams, Charles Kenneth. Crime, The.
Hounding Mercy.
How Humble We Were before This.
In the Heart of the Beast.
Innings.
Nut, The.
Poor Hope.
Rabbit Fights for His Life the Leopard Eats Lunch, The.
Williams, William Carlos. Birth of Venus, The.
Drunk and the Sailor, The.
Mezzo Forte.
To All Gentleness.
Wordsworth. In the Sound of Mull.
Wyatt. Vulcan begat me. Minerva me taught.

Violets
Cohen. Song: "I almost went to bed."
Doolittle. For Bryher and Perdita.
Sea Violet.
Dunbar. To a Violet Found on All Saints' Day.
Fletcher. Alpine Violets.
Herrick. How Violets Came Blue.
Meditation for His Mistress[e], A.
To Violets.
Lawrence. Violets for the Dead.

Lowry. Dodder, The.
Meredith. Dearest Dimpling, we believe.
  Violets.
  We violets white and blue.
Rossetti. Autumn Violets.
  O wind, where have you been.
  Who Hath Despised the Day of Small Things?
Shelley. On a Faded Violet.
Smith, Charlotte. Violets.
Wakoski. Precisely, Not Violets.
Zukofsky. Violet.

Violins
Creeley. Canzone: "As would any sound
  make."
Ford. Glass violin is broken, The.
Gallagher. Bonfire.
Hardy. To My Father's Violin.
Sandburg. Clefs.
  Kreisler.
  Three Violins.

Virgil [or Vergil]
Auden. Secondary Epic.
Cowper. On Receiving Heyne's Virgil.
  On the Author of Letters on Literature.
Creeley. Heroes.
Kipling. Last Ode, The.
Tennyson. To Virgil [or Vergil].

Virgin Islands
Williams, William Carlos. Calypsos.

Virgin Mary. see Mary, the Virgin.

Virginia (state)
Burns. Slave's Lament, The.
Eliot. Virginia.
Jarrell. Jamestown.
Moore. Virginia Britannia.
Nash. First Families Move Over!
Sarton. Monticello.
Tate. On the Great Conciliator: Now Honored
  in the Old Dominion.
Whitman. As Toilsome I Wander'd Virginia's
  Woods.
  Virginia—the West.
Whittier. Farewell, The: "Gone, gone,—sold
  and gone."
  Randolph of Roanoke.
Wright, Charles. Virginia Reel.

Virginity and Virgins
Auden. They noticed that virginity was
  needed.
Blake. On the Virginity of the Virgin Mary &
  Johanna Southcott.
Burns. Bonie Lass Made the Bed to Me, The.
Campion. Her rosie cheekes, her ever smiling
  eyes.
Carew. Maria Wentworth.
  Obsequies to the Lady Anne Hay.
Carruth. "Shock? Is that what you're asking?
  My dear, I was a."
Catullus. Carmen 61: "Hill (breeder) of
  Helicon."
  Carmen 62: "Gather young men as the twilight
  gathers."
Cummings. She being Brand.
Donne. Virgins, The.
Ferlinghetti. Deflowering.
  They were putting up the statue.
  With bells for hooves in sounding streets.
Graves. Purification.
  Virgin Mirror.
Hardy. Bad Example, The.
Herrick. Charmes.
  Dirge of Jephthah's Daughter, The.
  How Primroses Came Green.
  To Anthea ("Lets call for Hymen if agreed
  thou art").
  To [the] Virgins, to Make Much of Time.
  To Violets.
  To Virgins.
  Upon a Crooked Maid.
  Upon a Virgin.
  Upon Doll.
  Upon his Kinswoman Mrs. M. S.
  Why Flowers Change Color.
Hopkins. St. Thecla.
Jonson. Epigram on the Court Pucell, An.
Lawrence. Virgin Youth.
Lewis. Peace.

Lovelace. To Lucasta. Ode Lyrick.
Lowry. Ballad: "Twas in the springtime of the
  year."
MacNeice. Corona Virginum.
Merton. Five Virgins, The.
Milton. Chastity ("I Mean That Too, But Yet
  a Hidden Strength").
  Temperance and Virginity.
Morrison. Always a Playground Instructor.
Plath. Virgin in a Tree.
Ransom. Her Eyes.
Rukeyser. Unborn Song.
Shapiro. First Time, The.
Sidney. Ye living powers enclosed in stately
  shrine.
Smith, Patti. After/Words.
  Jeanne D'Arc.
Thomas. On the Marriage of a Virgin.
Williams, Miller. Original Sin.
Williams, William Carlos. From a Book.
Zukofsky. Vesper out there, you vain knees
  can sure get up: Vesper, Olympus.
  Who lives o on Helicon hill.

Virtue
Browning, Elizabeth Barrett. Sonnet: "Because
  thou hast the power and own'st the grace."
Burns. Dedication to G**** H******* Esq.,
  A.
  Extempore Verses on Dining with Lord Daer.
  For G. H. Esq.
  For the Author's Father.
  Lines Addressed to Mr. John Ranken.
  O Kenmure's on and awa, Willie.
  On Mr. James Gracie.
  To Miss Ainslie, in Church.
  To Miss Graham of Fintray.
Byron. Lines to a Lady Weeping.
  Sketch, A.
  Stanzas to Augusta.
Campion. Epigramme: "If fancy can not erre
  which vertue guides."
  Man of Life Upright, The.
  O griefe, O spight, to see poore Vertue
  scorn'd.
  Some can flatter, some can faine.
  Thou Joy'st, Fond Boy.
  To My Worthy Friend, Mr. John Mounson,
  Sonne and Heyre to Sir Thomas Mounson,
  Knight and Baronet.
  What is a day, what is a yeere.
  Why presumes thy pride on that, that must so
  private be.
Carew. Complement, The.
  Divine Mistress, A.
  Epitaph on the Lady S.: Wife of Sir W.S.
  Feminine Honour.
  In Praise of His Mistress.
  Ingrateful[l] Beauty Threatened.
  Married Woman, A.
  Obsequies to the Lady Anne Hay.
  Pastoral[l] Dialogue, A.
  To A.D., Unreasonable, Distrustful of Her
  Own Beauty.
  To My Rival.
  To the Painter.
Chaucer. Complaint unto Pity, The.
  Lak of Stedfastnesse.
Cowper. Another Version.
  Charity.
  In Memory of John Thorton.
  Ode on *Sir Charles Grandison*.
  On a Good Man.
  Progress of Error, The.
  R.S.S.
  To Miss Macartney.
  Translation of Verses to Lloyd.
Crashaw. Upon the Death of Mister Herrys.
Cullen. Tribute.
Davie. Mamertinus on Rhetoric, A.D. 291.
  Selina, Countess of Huntingdon.
  Three Moral Discoveries.
De la Mare. Virtue.
Donne. Elegy on the Lady Markham.
  Elegy upon the Death of Mistress Boulstred,
  An.
  Letter to the Lady Carey, and Mistress Essex
  Rich, from Amiens, A.

Obsequies to the Lord Harrington, Brother to
  the Lady Lucy, Countess of Bedford.
  To the Countess of Bedford ("Madam, / You
  have refined me, and to worthiest things").
  To the Countess of Bedford ("To have written
  then, when you writ, seemed to me").
Emerson. Alone in Rome! Why Rome is
  lonely too.
  Cloud upon cloud / Clouds after rain.
  Γν&ohgr;θι Σεαυτον.
  In the deep heart of man a poet dwells.
  Leave me, Fear! thy throbs are base.
  Loss and Gain.
  This effervescing gentleman who despises a
  secret.
  Untruth is become the mode.
Graves. Golden Anchor.
  In the Name of Virtue.
  Young Cordwainer, The.
Hartley. Family Album in Red Plush.
Herbert. Charms and Knots.
  Constancy.
  Foil, The.
  Virtue [or Vertue].
Herrick. Abstinence.
  Choose for the Best.
  Excesse.
  Feare.
  Gold, before Goodnesse.
  Just Man, A.
  Leprosie in Cloathes.
  No Shipwrack of Vertue. To a Friend.
  On Himself ("Wearied Pilgrim, I have
  wandered here, A").
  Parcell-gil't-Poetry.
  Pleasures Pernicious.
  Purposes.
  To His Honoured Kinsman Sir William
  Soame.
  To His Peculiar Friend Sir Edward Fish,
  Knight Baronet.
  To the Most Accomplisht Gentleman Master
  Michael Oulsworth.
  Vertue.
  Vertue Best United.
  Vertue Is Sensible of Suffering.
Hewitt. When my wife's sister's husband
  came to die.
Hopkins. Of virtues I most warmly bless.
Jonson. Come on, come on! And where you
  go.
  Epigram on Sir Edward Coke, when He Was
  Lord Chief Justice of England, An.
  Epigram. To the Honoured————, Countess
  of————, An.
  Epode: "Not to know vice at all, and keep[e]
  true state."
  Eye of looking back were well, An.
  Ode. To Sir William Sydney, on His Birthday.
  To Sir William Uvedale.
  Who, Virtue, can thy power forget.
Kipling. Portent, The.
Lovelace. On the Death of Mrs. Elizabeth
  Filmer.
MacLeish. Good Man in a Bad Time, A.
  Speech to the Detractors.
Merton. Confucius and the Madman.
  Keng Sang Chu.
  Man of Tao, The.
Moore. Blessed Is the Man.
Nash. Hand Me Down My Old School Sliding
  Pads, or, There's a Hint of Strawberry
  Leaves in the Air.
  Stitch Too Late Is My Fate, A.
Patchen. Virtue.
Pope. Epitaph on John Knight, Who Died Oct.
  2, 1733.
  Epitaph on Mrs. Corbet, Who Died of a
  Cancer in Her Breast.
  Version of the First Psalm, for the Use of a
  Young Lady, A.
Prince. Gregory Nazianzen.
Ralegh. More holy than the rest, and
  understanding more.
  Vertue the Best Monument.
"Reed." That's the Story of My Life.
Rolfe. Blues.

Sidney. Sonnet 4: "Virtue, alas, now let me take some rest."
Sonnet 25: "Wisest scholar of the wight most wise, The."
Sonnet 52: "Strife is grown between Virtue and Love, A."
Sonnet 62: "Late tired with woe, e'en ready for to pine."
Sonnet 68: "Stella, the only planet of my light."
Sonnet 71: "Who will in fairest book of Nature know."
Smart. To Mrs. Dacosta.
Smith, Stevie. Exeat.
Last Turn of the Screw, The.
Southwell. To the Christian Reader of "Short Rules of Good Life."
Wordsworth. Inscription for a Seat by the Pathway Side Ascending to Windy Brow.
October, 1803 ("These times strike monied worldlings with dismay").
Wright, James. Moral Poem Freely Accepted from Sappho, A.

Viruses
Graves. Virus, The.

Vishnu
Ford. Bala Krishna's voice.
Illness, The.
Juggernaut chanting.
Krishna climbs up there.
Shaven heads, rubber.
Lewis. Karanje Village.

Vision
Beckett. Son ombre une nuit.
Berry. As the vision of labor grows.
Evening comes / when we finish work and go, An.
Through elm, buckeye, thorn.
Vision, A.
Vision must have severity.
Vision reaches the ground.
Berryman. Apparition, The.
Browning, Elizabeth Barrett. Isobel's Child.
Poet, The.
Prospect, The.
Browning, Robert. Cardinal and the Dog, The.
Carew. On Sight of a Gentlewoman's Face in the Water.
Carruth. Being as Prevision, The.
Nothing I, The.
Clark. Blue Dress.
Clough. Upon the water in the boat.
Cohen. Every Pebble.
Future Night, A.
Crane. Hieroglyphic.
I Rob My Breast.
Wine Menagerie, The.
Creeley. People.
Cummings. All worlds have halfsight,seeing either with.
Davie. Hill Field, The.
Hypochondriac Logic.
De la Mare. Visionary, The.
What?
Dickinson. My family of Apparitions.
Eberhart. Birth of the Spirit, The.
Dream, The.
Goal of Intellectual Man, The.
Going.
Great Principles Are Thrown Down by Time.
In a Hard Intellectual Light.
In after Time.
Life as Visionary Spirit.
Lucubration.
May Evening.
Memory.
Moment of Vision, The.
Mystical Beast in the Shadows, The.
Quarrel with a Cloud.
Stopping a Kaleidoscope.
Testimony.
Virgin, The.
Vision.
Vision through Timothy.
Emerson. I live among ideal men.
In dreamy woods, what forms abound.
Why should I live.

Fenton. Frog hunts on land by vision. He escapes,
Fisher. Eye ascending / is gone up, The.
From the wrecked byre.
How does he come to be wearing that suit.
Intruder, The.
Poem not a Picture, A.
Sign, The.
Simple Location.
Travesties of the world.
Fox. Fata Morgana.
Finding the Andromeda Nebula.
Phekda.
Gallagher. Devotion: That It Flow; That There Be Concentration.
Garrigue. Poem: "I saw the mountains in a rose-fire light."
Graves. Like Owls.
Gunn. Unsettled Motorcyclist's Vision of His Death, The.
Hall. Apples.
Hardy. At a Seaside Town in 1869.
In Vision I Roamed.
She Who Saw Not.
Hartley. Eagle of the Inner Eye.
What Have We All—a Soliloquy of Essences.
Hesketh. Vision.
Hewitt. Fool's Cap, The.
Hoffman. Possession.
Jarrell. Orient Express, The.
Kipling. Chartres Windows.
Levertov. Depths, The.
Kingdoms of Heaven.
Puñal.
Sequence, A.
Lindsay. Town of American Visions, The.
Lowry. Western Ocean, The.
McGrath. Incident in the Life of a Prophet, An.
Markson. This Vision Comes.
Meinke. Vision.
Meredith. He tells it, who knew the law.
Him loved she. Lo, now was he veiled.
Merrill. Blue Eye, The.
Octopus, The.
Remora.
Merton. Macarius and the Pony.
Nash. And How Keen Was the Vision of Sir Launfal?
Nathan. Scroll, The.
Season's Greetings.
Nemerov. Frozen City, The.
I Only Am Escaped Alone to Tell Thee.
Maia.
Seeing Things.
Two Girls.
O'Hara. Day and Night in 1952.
Pound. Apparuit.
Raine. Poet is of those, The.
Rossetti. Blind from my birth, / Where flowers are springing.
Shapiro. Dome of Sunday, The [or A].
Glass Poem.
Shelton. Point of View.
Sorrentino. Handbook of Versification.
Stevens. Delightful Evening.
Stuart. Mystic.
Student, The.
Swift. Occasioned by Sir William Temple's Late Illness and Recovery.
Tomlinson. Appearance.
At a Glance.
At the Edge.
Face and Image.
Mistlines.
Poem: "Muscles which move the eyeballs."
Ponte Veneziano.
Skullshapes.
Through Binoculars.
Through Closed Eyes.
Tout Entouré de Mon Regard.
Walcott. Hotel Normandie Pool, The.
Wilbur. Beacon, The.
Eye, The.
Poplar, Sycamore.
Sketch, A.
Young. Sea Level.

Visiting and Visitors
Beatles. Blue Jay Way.
Bishop. Faustina, or Rock Roses.
Byron. Oh You, Who in All Names Can Tickle the Town.
"Carroll, Lewis." Maggie's Visit to Oxford.
Cowper. Letter in Verse.
On His Approaching Visit to Hayley.
To My Dearest Cousin, on Her Removal of us from Silver End, to Weston.
To the Rev. Mr. Newton.
Dickinson. Little poem we will write unto our Cousin John, A.
Dunbar. Opportunity.
Visitor, The.
Fenton. Doctor Gliedschirm, skin specialist, surgeries 14–16 hours or by appointment.
Graves. Silent Visit.
Hartley. Corillyn is Dark.
Herrick. Night-Piece, to Julia, The.
Ode to Sir Clipsebie Crew, An.
Panegyric to Sir Lewis Pemberton, A.
Hewitt. Glenaan.
Portrait, The.
Revenant.
Joseph. Visiting.
Levertov. Presence, The.
Lewis. Corfe Castle.
Encounter, The.
Lindsay. Visit to Mab, The.
Lowry. Tribute to the Renowned Harteebeeste, A.
MacLeish. Danger in the Air, The.
MacNeice. Return to Lahore.
Nash. Grin and Bear Left.
On Waking to the Third Rainy Morning of a Long Week End.
Visit From Dr. Fell, A.
Visit, The.
O'Hara. Poem: "Eager note on my door said 'Call me'," The.
Paley. Bob Visits Friends.
Rolfe. Unit Assignment.
Rossetti. Enrica, 1865.
Schuyler. After Joe Was at the Island.
Snodgrass. Vuillard: "The Mother and Sister of the Artist."
Sorrentino. Poet Tires of Those Who Disparage His City, The.
See America First.
Stein. Little Novel, A.
Turco. Visitor.
Van Duyn. Gentle Snorer, The.
Williams, Charles Kenneth. Bishop Tutu's Visit to the White House: 1984.
End of Drought.
Sleeping Over.
Young. Dance for Li Po, A.
New Orleans Intermission.
One West Coast.
Visiting Day.

Vitality
Cullen. Counter Mood.
Epilogue: "Lily, being white not red, The."
I Have a Rendezvous with Life.
Life's Rendezvous.
Emerson. Nature 2 ("She is gamesome and good").
Fox. Exposing Fox and Artifice.
Hughes, Langston. Demand.
Koch. Departure from Hydra, The.
Lawrence. Vitality.
What's Wrong.
Stevens. Dove in the Belly, The.
Stevenson. Old lady (so they say) but I, The.
Young. Foggy Morning.

Vivaldi, Antonio
Carruth. Begin right here. The Campground Road. Some calls it the.

Vocations. see **Occupations.**

Vogler, Georg Joseph
Browning, Robert. Abt Vogler.

Voices
Beckett. D'où / la voix qui dit.
Berg. Endings.
Berry. Song in a Year of Catastrophe.

Berryman. "Old Smoky" when you sing with Robin, Chris.
Blake. I wander thro each dirty street.
London ("I wander through each chartered street").
Carew. Eyes of a Blind Man.
Carroll, Jim. Their voice, as one, was heavy.
Clark. Sounding Chinese at Inspiration Point.
Tones of voice are petty, The.
Up in Here.
Creeley. Air: "Cat Bird Singing."
Messengers, The.
There.
Cummings. Gert.
Voices to voices, lip to lip.
De la Mare. Voice, The.
Dickey, James. Sleepers.
Dunbar. Musical, A.
Eberhart. Transformation.
Emerson. In dreamy woods, what forms abound.
Hall. Friend Revisited, A.
White Apples.
Herrick. Againe.
Poet Hath Lost His Pipe, The.
Upon a Gentlewoman with a Sweet Voice.
Upon Her Voice.
Upon Julia's Voice.
Upon Sapho, Sweetly Playing, and Sweetly Singing.
Voice and Violl, The.
Hesketh. Imprint.
Hewitt. My Father's Voice.
Sonnet: "When I have read your hard and lively words."
Kinnell. Lastness.
Knott. Shorts / Excerpts ("Suddenly I understood").
Summoning, The.
Levine. Voice, The.
Liddy. I Hear the Wife of the Governor of Wisconsin Singing.
Lovelace. To a Lady That Desired Me I Would Bear My Part with Her in a Song.
MacNeice. Schizophrene.
Meinke. Uncle Jim.
Nash. I Didn't Say a Word, or, Who Called That Piccolo Player a Father?
Raine. Once I heard your voice.
Triad.
Winds.
Rich. Strangers are an endangered species.
Rolfe. Eyes of a Blind Man.
Rossetti. If I Had Words.
What does the donkey bray about?
Rukeyser. Song: "Voice flew out of the river as morning flew, A."
Sorrentino. Silences.
Stafford. Long Distance.
Stuart. Barker, The.
Spell.
Tomlinson. At Wells: Polyphony.
Shout, The.
Their Voices Rang.
Williams, William Carlos. Pastoral; "If I say I have heard voices."
Wordsworth. Fragment: "Yet once again."
Wright, James. For the Marsh's Birthday.
Speak.
To the Poets in New York.
Yau. When you break a mirror, you must count up the pieces to see if.
Yeats. Everlasting Voices, The.
Zukofsky. Mirror oval sabres playing, The.

See also Screams; Speech; Talk.

Volcanoes
Bishop. Crusoe in England.
Clark. Desert Wars.
Cowper. Heroism.
Dickey, William. Heroine, The.
Dickinson. I have never seen "Volcanoes."
On my volcano grows the Grass.
Volcanoes be in Sicily.
When Etna basks and purrs.
Everson. Lava Bed.
Hartley. And, if the Popocatapetl.
Hewitt. Disaster on the Box.

Keats. Upon My Life, Sir Nevis, I Am Piqued.
Lawrence. Peace.
Lowry. Volcano is dark and suddenly thunder, The.
Yvonne stood there silently / the roar of the plane still in her ears.
Melville. Apparition, The.
Rich. Every peak is a crater. This is the law of volcanoes.
Snyder. Burning Island.
Walcott. Volcano.
Williams, William Carlos. Catastrophic Birth.
Voltaire, François Marie Arouet de
Auden. Voltaire at Ferney.
Blake. Mock On, Mock On, Voltaire, Rousseau.
Gallagher. Survival of a Heart.
Voodoo
Cohen. Tower of Song, The.
Voting and Voters
"Carroll, Lewis." Elections to the Hebdomadal Council, The.
Hewitt. I saw my father die. For two long years.
Jenny Geddes.
Labour Victory, A.
Hughes, Langston. Not a Movie.
Lawrence. Flapper Vote.
Lindsay. Bryan, Bryan, Bryan, Bryan.
Why I Voted the Socialist Ticket.
Nash. Election Day Is a Holiday.
Nathan. Election, The.
Olson. Hustings, The ("Under the eyes").
Pack. Clayfeld's Campaign.
Swift. Dog and the Thief, The.
Whittier. After Election.
Eve of Election, The.
Poor Voter on Election Day, The.
Quakers Are Out, The.
Wordsworth. Help for the Memory of the Grand Independent; A New Song, A.
Protest against the Ballot.
Said Secrecy to Cowardice and Fraud.
See also Campaigns, Political; Woman Suffrage.
Vowels
Burns. Tale, A.
"Carroll, Lewis." Puzzle.
Knott. Summoning, The.
Voyages
Berryman. First Night at Sea.
Carruth. Blizzard in the mountains. Dusk. The cabin's light.
Death, The.
Ship, The.
Cowper. Figurative Description of the Procedure of Divine Love, A.
Crane. Voyages.
Cummings. What is / a / voyage / ?
De la Mare. Galliass, The.
Dickey, William. Læstrygonians, The.
Eberhart. Moment of Equilibrium among the Islands.
Perception as a Guided Missile.
Voyage, The.
Emerson. Thine Eyes Still Shined.
Herrick. His Sailing from Julia.
Plaudite, or End of Life, The.
Hewitt. Open Eye, The.
Sonnet: "I think of Glasgow, where reluctantly."
Larkin. North Ship, The.
Lowry. Happiest of Hartebeeste Days and Devoted Love Eterne.
Marina—.
No Kraken Shall Be Found Till Sought By Name.
Ship.
Ship will sail again, the watches sing, The.
Sweet Good Night Poem to Our Beloved Hartebeeste from All the Little Animals.
Morgan. Now that at last I must forego.
Nash. I Want a Drink of Water, but Not from the Thermos.
Rossetti. Today's Burden.
Sexton. Crossing the Atlantic.
Simic. Navigator.

Spender. Cornet Cornelius Rilke.
Marston.
Stevenson. Christmas at Sea.
Turco. Moon of Melancholy, The.
Walcott. As John to Patmos.
Harbour, The.
Voyageurs
De la Mare. Mirage.
Oliver. No Voyage.
Voyeurism and Voyeurs
Bukowski. Girl on the Bus Stop Bench, The.
Girls Coming Home.
Girls in Pantyhose.
New Place, The.
Coleridge. Picture, The.
Dickey, James. Fiend, The.
Gunn. Corridor, The.
Release, The.
Taylor Street.
Venetian Blind.
Hardy. Seen by the Waits.
Meredith. Teaching of the Nude, The.
Shapiro. Dome of Sunday, The [*or* A].
Sorrentino. Man in the Moon, The.
Spenser. Nymphs and Graces Dancing, The.
Stuart. Timeshare.
Van Duyn. Voyeur, The.
Warren. Her Hat.
Wilbur. Eye, The.
Williams, Miller. Late Show.
Wright, James. Girl in a Window, A.
Vuillard, Edouard
Rich. Pictures by Vuillard.
Snodgrass. Vuillard: "The Mother and Sister of the Artist."
Vulcan
Auden. Shield of Achilles, The.
Herrick. To Vulcan.
Jonson. Execration upon Vulcan, An.
Vulnerability
Beckett. Thither.
Bly. Fifty Males Sitting Together.
Bukowski. Iron Mike.
Carroll, Jim. It seems I have misplaced the directions for childhood.
Creeley. Not Now.
Pieces.
Something.
Dickey, James. Attempted Departure.
Dunn. Landscape, The.
Man Who Never Loses His Balance, The.
Ferlinghetti. It was a face which darkness could kill.
Gardner. Sonnet for My Acquaintances.
Graves. Injuries.
Gunn. Odysseus on Hermes.
Jeffers. To a Young Artist.
MacNeice. Les Neiges d'Antan.
Morrison. Fear is a Porch.
Piercy. Rape Poem.
You Ask Why Sometimes I Say Stop.
Ransom. Winter Remembered.
Rich. Antinoüs: The Diaries.
8/8/68: ii.
July seventeenth nineteen sixty eight.
Storm Warnings.
Shapiro. First Time, The.
Snodgrass. Through the Nursery Window.
Warren. Where Purples Now the Fig.
Wright, Charles. Dead are a cadmium blue, The.
Young. Mid-Life Crises: A Critical Review.
Vulpius, Melchior
Moore. Melchior Vulpius.
Vultures
Atwood. Vultures.
Beckett. Vulture, The.
Hill. Rivers bring down. The sea.
Jeffers. Vulture.
Oliver. Field near Linden, Alabama.
Vultures.
Piercy. Best Defense is Offensive, The.
Rexroth. Vulture.
Wilbur. Still, Citizen Sparrow.

See also **Buzzards.**

W

Wagner, Richard
Browning, Robert. Impromptu on Richard Wagner.
Hugo. December 24 and George McBride Is Dead.

Wagon Trains
Sandburg. Great Proud Wagon Wheels Go On, The.
Turco. That Particular Air.

Wagtails
Roethke. Wagtail, The.

Wailing Wall, The
Cullen. At the Wailing Wall in Jerusalem.

Waiters and Waitresses
Bukowski. Krutz.
Cullen. Atlantic City Waiter.
Dunn. Truck Stop: Minnesota.
Fox. To Do More Than Hair.
Gallagher. Crêpes Flambeau.
Gunn. Waitress.
Kooser. Hairnet with Stars, A.
Muldoon. Holy Thursday.
Nash. Banquet, The.
  Coffee with the Meal.
  Suppose He Threw It in Your Face.
  Try It Suns. and Hols.; It's Closed Then.
Piercy. What You Waited For.
Sorrentino. Insane Waiters, The.
Stevens. Attempt to Discover Life.
Tomlinson. Ship's Waiters.
Williams, William Carlos. Atlantic City Convention, The.

Waiting Rooms
Bishop. In the Waiting Room.
Creeley. Illness, An.
Hardy. In a Waiting-Room.
Mahon. Image from Beckett, An.
Nash. Thoughts Thought While Waiting for a Pronouncement from a Doctor, an Editor, a Big Executive, the Department of Internal Revenue or Any Other Momentous Pronouncer.
Nemerov. Waiting Rooms.

Wakes
Herrick. Wake, The.
Hewitt. Wake, The.
Merton. Lao Tzu's Wake.

Waking
Angelou. Awaking in New York.
Atwood. Fortification, A.
  Pre-Amphibian.
Auden. Early Morning.
Berry. Deepest sleep holds us, The.
  Let me wake in the night.
Berryman. Who for those ages ever without some blood.
Bishop. Love Lies Sleeping.
Bly. Awakening.
  Poem in Three Parts.
  Waking from Sleep.
Burns. Lover's Morning Salute to His Mistress, The.
Carruth. In wavering shadow and silted with soot, her face.
Ciardi. Morning: I Know Perfectly How in a Minute You Will Stretch and Smile.
Clark. Afternoons.
  Eos.
Coleridge. Something Childish, but Very Natural.
Crane. Paraphrase.
Cummings. Raise the shade.
De la Mare. Awake!
  Break of Morning.
  Imp Within, The.
  Queen Djenira.
  Sleeper, The.
Dobyns. Music One Looks Back On, The.
Donne. Good Morrow, The.
Duncan. In Waking.
  Song of the Borderguard, The.

"Dylan." When You Gonna Wake Up?
Emerson. Eternal Watcher, who doth wake, The.
Fox. And night comes.
Garrigue. Waking, I Always Waked You Awake.
Ginsberg. Morning.
Gunn. My coldness wakes me.
  Waking in a Newly Built House.
Hall. Exile.
Hardy. Four in the Morning.
Hewitt. Et Tu In Arcadia Vixisti.
Hoffman. Waking, A.
Hopkins. By One of the Old School Who Was Bid to Follow Mr. Browning's Flights.
Jarrell. Venetian Blind, The.
Joseph. Waking.
Lawrence. Chief Mystery, The.
  Coming Awake.
  Quite Forsaken.
Lewis. *She Comes To Him in the Night.*
Lowell. Waking Early Sunday Morning.
Lowry. From *The Gleanings of a Gadwall.*
  On Reading Redburn.
  Reveille.
  Spark Poetry.
MacLeish. Eve Quiets Her Children.
  Waking.
Miller. Poets, The.
  Rising Up.
Milton. Elegiac Verses.
Nash. Nature Knows Best.
  Pappy Wants a Poppy.
Nathan. Soundings, The.
Nemerov. Zalmoxis.
O'Hara. Getting Up Ahead of Someone (Sun).
  Jane Awake.
  Sonnet for Jane Freilicher, A.
Raine. Campanula.
  From vague regions of sleep I come again.
Roethke. Waking, The.
Rossetti. Our little baby fell asleep.
  Song of Flight, A.
Rukeyser. Child wakes in the morning to enter a country, The.
Schuyler. Sleep-Gummed Eyes.
Simic. Poem: "Every morning I forget how it is."
Smith, Stevie. Hendecasyllables.
Stevenson. Time to Rise.
Stuart. Dressing.
  Percussion.
Thomas. When I woke.
Turco. Awaken, Bells Falling.
Wilbur. Love Calls Us to the Things of This World.
Williams, Charles Kenneth. Waking Jed.
Wright, James. I Try to Waken and Greet the World Once Again.
  Sun Tan at Dusk.

Walden Pond, Massachusetts
Emerson. In my garden three ways meet.
  In Walden wood the chickadee.
Hesketh. From Walden.
Oliver. Going to Walden.

Waldenses
Zimmer. Day Zimmer Lost Religion, The.

Wales
Carruth. Aw, Dylan, have you left us? Have you gone?
Clough. When soft September brings again.
Davie. Barnsley, 1966.
Ferlinghetti. Spirit of the Crusades.
Ginsberg. Wales Visitation.
Graves. Welsh Incident.
Lewis. Before he sails a man may go on leave.
  Olwen and Taliesin.
  Welsh Night, A.
Shelley. On Leaving London for Wales.
Thomas. Author's Prologue.
Walcott. Wales.

See also **Welsh, The.**

Walking and Walkers
Auden. Grow thin by walking and go inland.
  Walks.

Beckett. Arènes de Lutèce.
  Enueg I.
Berry. History.
  I dream of you walking at night along the streams.
  Man Walking and Singing, A.
Bishop. Night City.
Bly. Out Picking up Corn.
Browning, Elizabeth Barrett. Sea-side walk, A.
Bukowski. Promenade.
Burns. Dainty Davie.
Carroll, Jim. But everything has worked out fine.
"Carroll, Lewis." Second Voice, The.
Clark. "Walked into State.."
Cowper. Away goes Sussex William with his pack.
  Winter Morning Walk, The.
  Winter Walk at Noon, The.
Crane. In Shadow.
Creeley. "Bolinas and Me."
  But.
  For Betsy and Tom.
  Oh Mabel.
  Out.
  Place.
  Somebody Died.
  Song: "Grit / of things, The."
  Walking.
De la Mare. On the Esplanade.
Dunbar. Spring Wooing, A.
Dunn. This Late in the Century.
Eberhart. Track.
Fisher. Walking at dusk often.
Frost. Bravado.
  Encounter, An.
  Good Hours.
  Late Walk, A.
  Meeting and Passing.
Graves. Legs, The.
  To Walk on Hills.
Hacker. April Interval.
Haines. We were away for a long time.
Hall. Our Walk in Yorkshire.
  Second Stanza, A.
Hardy. Weary Walker, The.
Hartnett. Visit to Croom, 1745, A.
Hewitt. Country Walk in May, A.
  My Future Wife.
  Those Morning Walks.
Hughes, Langston. Harlem Night Song.
Kipling. I am the Most Wise Baviaan, saying in most wise tones.
Knight. Green Grass and Yellow Balloons.
Koch. Spring.
Liddy. Patrick Kavanagh's Dublin.
Lowry. No Time to Stop and Think.
McAuley. Late Morning Talk.
Mahon. Four Walks in the Country Near Saint-Brieuc.
Meredith. Night-Walk, The.
O'Hara. F. (Missive & Walk) I. #53.
  Petit Poème en Prose.
  Poem: "Let's take a walk, you."
  Walking to Work.
Olson. Pavement, The.
Patchen. And they walked in the ancient wonder of the morning light.
Plath. Hardcastle Crags.
  Letter in November.
  Song for a Summer's Day.
Roethke. I Waited.
Rossetti. Once for All. (Margaret).
Schuyler. Walk, The.
Sexton. Noon Walk on the Asylum Lawn.
Smith, Stevie. Bag-Snatching in Dublin.
  November.
  On Walking Slowly after an Accident.
Sorrentino. He walks on the street, in.
Stevenson. In autumn when the woods are red.
Tomlinson. Comedy.
Warren. Walk by Moonlight in Small Town.
Williams, William Carlos. Love Song: "Daisies are broken."
Wordsworth. Evening Walk Addressed to a Young Lady, An.
  Stepping Westward.

Wall Street

To a Young Lady Who Had Been Reproached for Taking Long Walks in the Country.
Young. New Autumn, New York.
New Moon Over Grove Street.
Ponce de León: A Morning Walk.
Zukofsky. I walk in the old street.

Wall Street, New York City

Lowry. Morning coat is walking, A.
Piercy. Skyscrapers of the Financial District
Dance with Gasman, The.
Rukeyser. Paper Anniversary.

Wallace, Sir William

Burns. Gude Wallace.
Ode [for General Washington's Birthday].
Robert Bruce's March to Bannockburn.
Gunn. Adolescence.
Wordsworth. Composed at Cora Linn in Sight of Wallace's Tower.

Wallflowers

"Dylan." Wallflower.

Walls

Auden. Bawbee.
Stone Walls.
Stone Walls.
Bukowski. Walls, The.
Carruth. I came to this place one November day.
Creeley. Walls.
De la Mare. Daisy, The.
Dickey, James. Wall and Cloud.
Donne. Fall of a Wall.
Eberhart. In Prisons of Established Craze.
Frost. Atmosphere.
Mending Wall.
Triple Bronze.
Hall. Stone Walls.
Hughes, Langston. Mellow.
Kipling. Romulus and Remus.
Lieberman. Bulwark.
O'Hara. Variations on Pasternak's "Mein Liebchen, Was Willst Du Noch Mehr?"
Plath. Apprehensions.
Sandburg. Wall Shadows.
Schuyler. Blue.
Sexton. Wall, The.
Simic. Wall, A.
Tomlinson. Churchyard Wall, The.
Rubh An' Dunain.
Stone Walls: at Chew Magna.
Wilbur. Caserta Garden.
Williams, William Carlos. On Gay Wallpaper.

See also **Fences.**

Walnut Trees and Walnuts

Oliver. Black Walnut Tree, The.
Pack. Walnut.
Wright, James. Nature Alive.

Walpole, Robert, 1st Earl of Orford

Swift. Character of Sir Robert Walpole, The.

Walruses

"Carroll, Lewis." Walrus and the Carpenter, The.
Wilbur. Castles and Distances.

Waltzes and Waltzing

Cohen. Take This Waltz (After Lorca).
Gardner. Waltz for Accordion.
Hemingway. Lines to a Young Lady on Her Having Very Nearly Won a Vögel.
Roethke. My Papa's Waltz.
Stevens. Sad Strains of a Gay Waltz.

Wanderlust

Auden. Wanderer, The.
Byron. To a Lady.
Catullus. Carmen 46: "Now spring bursts."
Davie. English Revenant, An.
De la Mare. Journey, The.
Dobyns. Rootless.
"Dylan." Long Time Gone.
Tangled Up in Blue.
Eberhart. Address to you.
I turned where the sun came up and he held my hand.
Frost. Encounter, An.
Into My Own.
Ginsberg. Ready to Roll.
Hall. Abroad Thoughts from Home.

Hardy. Vagrant's Song.
Wanderer, The.
Hewitt. Dusty Roads.
Tiphead.
Kipling. Anchor Song.
Explorer, The.
Feet of the Young Men, The.
Sestina of the Tramp-Royal.
Song of Travel, The.
Larkin. House on the Edge of the Serious Wood, The.
One Man Walking a Deserted Platform.
Poetry of Departures.
So You Have Been, Despite Parental Ban.
Lawrence. Restlessness.
Nash. Nymph and the Shepherd, or She Went That-a-Way, The.
Shelley. Fragment: A Wanderer.
Shelton. And the Scars Will Be Covered.
White Hotel, The.
Smith, Charlotte. Truant Dove from Pilpay, The.
Smith, Stevie. Lightly Bound.
Wanderer, The.
Tennyson. Ulysses.
Whitman. Afoot and light-hearted I take to the open road.
Williams, William Carlos. Wanderer, The: A Rococo Study.
Wordsworth. Song for the Wandering Jew.
Yeats. Madness of King Goll, The.
Young. City Home Detroit.
Zukofsky. Warm gale, a dose of spring— revert to the pores.

Wang Wei

Berryman. Note to Wang Wei.
Williams, William Carlos. To Wang Wei.

War

Arnold. Dover Beach.
Atwood. As for the women, who did not.
1837 War in Retrospect.
Auden. Danse Macabre.
Missing.
Spring unsettles sleeping partnerships, The.
Beatles. Continuing Story of Bungalow Bill, The.
Berg. Tashkent Blossoms, 1944.
Berry. Against the War in Vietnam.
Window grows fragile, The.
Berryman. Luftmenschen dream, the men who live on air.
River Rouge, 1932.
Betjeman. Invasion Exercise on the Poultry Farm.
Bishop. Wading at Wellfleet.
Blake. Gwin, King of Norway.
Prologue to King John.
War Song [to Englishmen], A.
Bly. As the Asian War Begins.
Counting Small-boned Bodies.
Driving through Minnesota during the Hanoi Bombings.
Teeth Mother Naked at Last, The.
War and Silence.
Boyle. American Citizen.
Only Bird That Sang, The.
People's Cry, The.
Brontë. Douglas's Ride.
Far, far away is mirth withdrawn.
Loud without the wind roaring.
On the Fall of Zalona.
Rodric Lesley. 1830.
Song by Julius Angora.
Sudden chasm of ghastly light, A.
Brooks. Looking.
Progress, The.
White Troops Had Their Orders but the Negroes Looked Like Men.
Browning, Elizabeth Barrett. Dance, The.
First News from Villafranca.
Garibaldi.
Italy and the World.
Parting Lovers.
Browning, Robert. Arcades Ambo.
Pheidippides.
Rosny.
Sordello.

Bukowski. Conversation on Morality, Eternity and Copulation, A.
Night They Took Whitey, The.
Soirée.
22,000 Dollars in 3 Months.
Bunting. Duke Valentine had been in Lombardy with the King.
Jengiz to Chang Chun: China.
Stuck in the mud they are saying: "We were sad."
Burns. Battle of Sherra-Moor, The.
Killiecrankie.
My Bonnie [or Bony] Mary.
Robert Bruce's March to Bannockburn.
Song: "O, Logan, sweetly didst thou glide."
There Was a Bonie Lass.
Up and Warn A' Willie.
When wild War's deadly blast was blawn.
Byron. By the Rivers of Babylon We Sat Down and Wept.
Siege of Corinth, The.
Song of Saul before His Last Battle.
Song to the Suliotes.
Translation of the Famous Greek War Song Deute Paides Tov Ellenon.
Very Mournful Ballad, A.
Campion. Raving warre, begot / In the thirstye sands.
Carew. On Mistress N.
Carroll, Jim. Love Story.
Traffic.
"Carroll, Lewis." Path of Roses, The.
Carruth. Algeria.
And I was past caring so many, too many men.
Birds of Vietnam, The.
Cappadocian Song.
Of course make love not.
On Being Asked to Write a Poem Against the War in Vietnam.
President's Speech, The.
Sanskrit root word, The.
Sonnet: "To the aged, trembling, illiterate woman yesterday."
When Howitzers Began.
Winds; words of the wind; rumor of great walls pierced.
Chaucer. Tale of Melibee, The.
Ciardi. Baboon and the State, The.
Bashing the Babies.
Graph, The.
To Lucasta, About That War.
Clark. Commanders, The.
Desert Wars.
Diary of Desert War.
Eternity.
Forty Days.
Sleepwalker's Fate.
Clough. Alteram Partem.
Cohen. Captain, The.
Welcome to These Lines.
Coleridge. British Stripling's War-Song, The.
Fire, Famine, and Slaughter.
Cooper. Breslau, November-December 1917.
For a Boy Born in Wartime.
Meteors.
Crashaw. Beginning of Heliodorus, The.
Cummings. Along the justexisting road to Roupy.
Hello is what a mirror says.
I sing of Olaf glad and big.
I'm / asking / you dear to.
My sweet old etcetera.
Next to of course god america i.
Where's Jack Was / General Was.
Davie. English Revenant, An.
Montcalm.
De la Mare. Marionettes, The.
Motley.
Truce.
Dickey, James. Between Two Prisoners.
Drinking from a Helmet.
Lakes of Värmland.
Dickey, William. Virginia Woolf Gathers Mushrooms.
Dickinson. Their Barricade against the Sky.
There's the Battle of Burgoyne.

Dobyns. Somewhere It Still Moves.
Donne. Love's War.
Doolittle. Telesila.
Dryden. All, All of a Piece Throughout.
Duncan. Fire, The.
  Up Rising.
Dunn. Wind in a Jar.
"Dylan." John Brown.
  Masters of War.
  Talkin' World War III Blues.
  With God on Our Side.
Eberhart. Airman Considers His Power, An.
  At the End of the War.
  Caught there, then, on the Rock. At
  Corregidor.
  Fury of Aerial Bombardment, The.
  Protagonists.
  World War.
Eliot. Note on War Poetry, A.
Emerson. Land was all electric, The.
Everson. Eastward the armies.
Fenton. But come. Grief must have its term?
  Guilt too, then.
  But when so many had died, so many and at
  such speed.
  Cambodia.
  Children in Exile.
  Chosun.
  Dead Soldiers.
  His wife nods, and a secret smile.
  In a Notebook.
  It is not what they built. It is what they
  knocked down.
  Nest of Vampires.
  Prison Island.
  Staffordshire Murderer, A.
  Wind.
  Would come down, would ever come down.
Fisher. Entertainment of War, The.
Ford. Curse for the War Machine, A.
  War.
Gallagher. Harmless Streets.
Gardner. Nursery Rhyme No. 1.
  Nursery Rhyme No. 2.
Garrigue. Resistance Meeting: Boston
  Common.
Glück. Pictures of the People in the War.
Graves. All Except Hannibal.
  Apples and Water.
  Armistice Day, 1918.
  Field-Postcard, The.
  Spoils.
Gray. Death of Hoel, The.
  Ruin seize thee, ruthless King!
  Triumphs of Owen, The.
Gunn. Adolescence.
  Last Man, The.
Hacker. Before the War.
  February of the merely real, A.
Haines. Dusk of the Revolutionaries.
  Invaders, The.
  Pitcher of Milk, The.
  Subversive leaves, you fall.
  Sun keeps its promises, The.
Hall. Body Politic, The.
Hardy. Channel Firing.
  Chorus of the Pities.
  Epilogue: "We have now set forth, in our
  imperfect way."
  In Time of "The Breaking of Nations."
  Last Chorus.
  Man He Killed, The.
  Night of Trafalgar, The.
  Often When Warring.
  Sick Battle-God, The.
Hemingway. Arsiero, Asiago, / Half a hundred
  more.
  Battle of Copenhagen, The.
  Defense of Luxembourg.
  Poem, 1928.
  Poetry.
  They All Made Peace—What Is Peace?
  To Good Guys Dead.
Herrick. Blame.
  Clemency.
  Eyes, The.
  Hand and Tongue, The.

Hope Heartens.
  Multitude.
  Pardons.
  Possesions.
  Rainbow, The.
  Things of Choice, Long a Comming.
  To the Lord Hopton, on His Fight in
  Cornwall.
  Vow to Mars, A.
  Warre.
Hesketh. July 2nd, 1916.
  More than Grass.
Hewitt. Already autumn silently / has come to
  sky and field and tree.
  Antrim April.
  Bloody Brae, The.
  Bogside, Derry, 1971.
  Brown's Bay, Islandmagee, Spring 1917.
  Colmcille.
  Compton Wynates, Warwickshire.
  Feathers on Turf.
  Motives.
  Peace Pact.
  Portstewart, July 1914.
  Return, The.
  Roman Fort, The.
  Second Front: Double Summertime, July 1943.
  To the People of Dresden.
  Uncle Sam and Aunt Edie.
  Volunteer, The.
  YCVS and the Ulster Division, The.
  You mid the corn not yet asleep.
Hill. Salute us all, Christus with your iron.
Hoffman. Victor, The.
Housman. Day of Battle, The.
  Deserter, The.
  Oh is it the jar of nations.
  Recruit, The.
Hughes, Langston. Green Memory.
  Relief.
Hughes, Ted. Bayonet Charge.
  Dead man in his cave beginning to sweat,
  The.
  Dream Time, The.
  Grass-blade is not without, The.
  Haunting, A.
  Mascot, The.
  Retired Colonel, The.
  So the leaves trembled.
  Thistles.
  Two Minute's Silence.
  Warriors of the North, The.
  Wit's End.
  Woman Unconscious, A.
Hugo. Culloden.
  Guns at Fort Flagler.
  In Your War Dream.
  Where We Crashed.
Jarrell. Automaton, The.
  Come to the Stone.
  Dream of Waking, The.
  Eighth Air Force.
  Fat, aging, the child clinging to her hand.
  Germans Are Lunatics, The.
  Lullaby, A: "For wars his life and half a
  world away."
  Machine-Gun, The.
  Nursery Rhyme, A.
  Pilot from the Carrier, A.
  Rising Sun, The.
  Sick Nought, The.
  Soldier, The.
  War, A.
  When Achilles fought and fell.
  Wide Prospect, The.
Jeffers. Air-Raid Rehearsals.
  Antrim.
  At the Birth of an Age.
  Bloody Sire, The.
  Bowl of Blood, The.
  Calm and Full the Ocean.
  Carmel.
  Dead to Clemenceau: November 1929, The.
  Eagle Valor, Chicken Mind.
  Eye, The.
  Fantasy.
  Fire.

Historical Choice.
I saw a regiment of soldiers shuffling and
  stumbling.
King of Beasts, The.
Moments of Glory.
Moon and Five Planets.
Neutrals, The.
Orca.
Real and Half Real.
Rearmament.
Skunks.
So Many Blood-Lakes.
Staggering Back Toward Life.
That Noble Flower.
To Kill in War Is Not Murder.
Urchin, The.
We Are Those People.
What Odd Expedients.
What of It?
Wilson in Hell.
Jonson. Epigram. To William, Earl of
  Newcastle, An.
  Speech According to Horace, A.
Joseph. Trying to Understand Violence.
Keats. If shame can on a soldier's vein-
  swoll'n front.
  See, the Ship in the Bay Is Riding.
Kinnell. Dead Shall Be Raised Incorruptible,
  The.
  Vapor Trail Reflected in the Frog Pond.
Kipling. Anvil, The.
  Benfactors, The.
  Boots.
  Changelings, The.
  Cold Iron.
  Dane-Geld.
  Departure, A.
  Dutch in the Medway, The.
  Edgehill Fight.
  For All We Have and Are [1914].
  Ford o' Kabul River.
  French Wars, The.
  Fuzzy-Wuzzy.
  Grave of the Hundred Dead, The.
  Gunga Din.
  Hymn before Action.
  Storm Cone, The.
  That Day.
  Together.
  Widow's Party, The.
  With Scindia to Delhi.
Knott. Two Vietnam Poems: (1966).
Kunitz. Foreign Affairs.
  Harsh Judgment, The.
  Hemorrhage, The.
  Last Picnic, The.
  Signal from the House, The.
Larkin. Homage to a Government.
  MCMXIV.
Lawrence. At the Front.
  Attack, The.
  Attila.
  Bombardment.
  Combative Spirit, The.
  Future War.
  Going Back.
  Late War, The.
  Maiden's Prayer.
  Noise of Battle.
  On the March.
  Peace and War.
  Rondeau of a Conscientious Objector.
  Song of a Man Who Has Come Through.
  War-Baby.
  Winter-Lull.
Levertov. Life at War.
Levine. And the Trains Go On.
  Baby Villon.
  Heaven.
  How many lives were torn apart.
  How Much Can It Hurt?
  Planting.
  To Cipriano, in the Wind.
Lewis. All Day It Has Rained.
  Assault Convoy, The.
  Autumn, 1939.
  Bivouac.

Christmas Holiday.
Defeated: for Wales, The.
Destruction.
East, The.
Easter at Christmas.
From a Play.
Goodbye.
I within me holding.
Lines on a Tudor Mansion.
Midnight in India.
Now as a lover would.
Now only beggars still go singing.
Odi et Amo.
Odyssey, The.
On Embarkation.
Peasants, The.
Raiders' Dawn.
Run-In, The.
She Comes To Him in the Night.
She Remains.
She Wakes Early, While He Still Sleeps.
They Part at Daybreak, Returning Their
Inevitable Ways.
This stunted pine whose knotted roots.
White brain crossing, The.
Liddy. Maud Gonne Rode Out on a White
Horse to Coolgreany.
Lindsay. Curse for Kings, A.
King Arthur's Men Have Come Again.
Scissors-Grinder, The.
Unpardonable Sin, The.
Voice of St. Francis of Assisi, The.
Yankee Doodle.
Longfellow. Arsenal at Springfield, The.
Part the First.
Lovelace. To Lucasta, [on] Going to the
War[re]s.
To My Truely Valiant, Learned Friend, Who
in His Booke Resolv'd the Art Gladiatory
into the Mathematick's.
Lowry. Courage is not standing on the
crosstrees.
I don't want to criticize war.
I met a man who had got drunk with Christ.
Marching down the road to China.
Not all of us were heroes said my brother wit.
Ship of war sails in the grey morning, The.
Slough of Despond: Or the House of Hope,
The.
McAuley. Aor Against the Philistine Who
Destroyed Lovely Dublin Vistas With His
Ugly Erections, Then Absconded to London.
Aor Against the Warmonger.
"MacDiarmid." Left-wing poetry represents a
rise in the price of bread.
McGrath. Encounter.
Fresco: Departure for an Imperialist War.
Nocturne Militaire.
Ordonnance.
Theory, A.
MacLeish. German Girls! The German Girls!,
The.
Invocation to the Social Muse.
National Security.
Silent Slain, The.
Spanish Lie, The.
Thirteenth Book, The.
True History of Bernál Díaz.
Two Poems from the War.
What the Old Women Say.
MacNeice. Aftermath.
Bad Lord Byron went to the firing, helmet and
dogs and all.
Canto X: "Daily news. And today? There is
not so much to note."
Carrickfergus.
Close the vein! It is Easter Eve.
Death of an Actress.
Galway.
Mixer, The.
On the Four Masters.
On the Grettir Saga.
Richard Coeur-de-Lion.
Rites of War.
Swing-Song.
To the Lords of Convention'—The horses
went by.

Unoccupied Zone, The.
War Heroes.
Mahon. Afterlives.
Marlowe. 1.9: Ad Atticum, amantem non
oportere desidiosum esse, sicuti nec militem.
2.14: In amicam, quod abortivum ipsa fecerit.
2.18: Ad Macrum, quod de amoribus scribat.
Meinke. Monkey's Paw, The.
Ode to Good Men Fallen Before Hero Come.
Soldiers with Green Leggings.
Melville. Apathy and Enthusiasm.
Conflict of Convictions, The.
Utilitarian View of the Monitor's Fight, A.
Meredith. Alternation.
At the Close.
Behold, the Gods are with her, and are known.
Call, The.
Clash in Arms of the Achaians and Trojans.
England before the Storm.
Field-Marshal Radetzky.
Friend, when the thundercloud is low.
Grandfather Bridgeman.
Hatton's "God of War."
He, did he love her? France was his weapon,
shrewd.
Look not for spreading boughs.
Lord of old has dealt in blood, The.
New Era the Army of the Future the Egg of
an Army, The.
On the Danger of War.
Paris and Diomedes.
She drank what makes man demon at the
draught.
Song: "Twelve arrows, and a bow, and spear."
Square along the couch, and stark.
Three Eagles and the Sleepy Lion, The.
To Colonel Charles.
To the Merry Men of France.
Under the thin hoop of gold.
Vengeance of Apollo, The.
War.
Ye noble Lords who bravely fight.
Merrill. Nike.
Merton. Advising the Prince.
Fable for a War.
Great Men of Former Times, The.
Lent in a Year of War.
Long Enough.
Night Train, The.
Poem: 1939.
Millay. Apostrophe to Man.
Come home, victorious wounded!—let the
dead.
Invocation to the Muses.
Memory of England.
Poem and Prayer for an Invading Army.
Read history: so learn your place in Time.
To the Maid of Orleans.
Milton. Sonnet 18: "Avenge O Lord thy
slaughter'd Saints, whose bones."
What Though the Field Be Lost?
Moore. In Distrust of Merits.
To Military Progress.
Morgan. Door, The.
From a Forgotten Book.
Morrison. Ah, The Rule.
Planes Are Groaning Mothers.
Muldoon. Meeting the British.
Nathan. Reading of History, A.
Nemerov. Armistice.
Bacterial War, The.
Fable of the War, A.
For the Squadron.
For W——, Who Commanded Well.
Memory of the War, A.
Old Soldiers' Home, The.
Old Warplane, An.
On Getting Out Of Vietnam.
Peace in Our Time.
Redeployment.
Returning to Europe.
September Shooting.
Soldier Who Lived Through the War, The.
To Clio, Muse of History.
Trial and Death, a Double Feature.
Olson. Encounter, The.
Trinacria.

Oppen. And war.
In Alsace, during the war.
Myth of the Blaze.
Survival: Infantry.
Wars that are just? A simpler question: In the
event.
Which act is / Violence.
Owen. Apologia Pro Poemate Meo.
Arms and the Boy.
At a Calvary near the Ancre.
Calls, The.
Chances, The.
Conscious.
Disabled.
Dulce Et Decorum Est.
Exposure.
Fragment: "Cramped in that funnelled hole,
they watched the dawn."
Futility.
Insensibility.
Inspection.
Last Laugh, The.
Le Christianisme.
Letter, The.
Mental Cases.
Next War, The.
Parable of the Old Man and the Young, The.
Send-Off, The.
Sentry, The.
Show, The.
S.I.W.
Six o'clock in Princes Street.
Smile, Smile, Smile.
Soldier's Dream.
Sonnet: "Be slowly lifted up, thou long black
arm."
Spring Offensive.
Strange Meeting.
Terre, A.
Paley. Connections: Vermont Vietnam (II).
People in My Family.
Two Villages.
Patchen. Among Ourselves and with All
Nations.
And He Had Wilder Moments.
And When Freedom Is Achieved.
Attila.
Avarice and Ambition Only Were the First
Builders of Towns and Founders of Empire.
Battle of Unameit, The.
Behold, One of Several Little Christs.
Being so hideous that the air weeps blood.
Billion Freedoms, The.
Boxers Hit Harder When Women Are Around.
But the Images of His Former Dreams Still
Haunted Him.
Can the Harp Shoot Through Its Propellers?
Class of 1934.
Climate of War, The.
Encounter at Nightfall.
Eve of St. Agony, or the Middle Class Was
Sitting on Its Fat.
Executions in Moscow, The.
Fields of Earth.
Firing, The.
First Crusades, The!
Gatherers of wild seed and froststained fruit.
Heine, Too, Lived in Germany.
How at the midnight of his age the Poet hurls
himself on the.
Hymn to a Trench Gun.
I despise these poets with their puerile little
chalk-talks of the soul.
I saw three hundred fat cattle putting their
forlornly comic faces.
Known Soldier, The.
Last Full Measure of Devotion, The.
Leaflet (One).
Leaflet (Two).
Letter to the Young Men, A.
Letter to Those Who Are About to Die.
Little hill climbs up to the village and puts its
green hands, The.
Loyalty Is the Life You Are.
O Howling Cells.
Old Lean Over the Tombstones, The.
Peter's Diary in Goodentown.

Poem: "Feeling chilled in that cold country."
Poem in the Form of a Letter: to Lauro de Bosis.
Soldier and the Star, The.
Stars go to sleep so peacefully, The.
Strange thing I said to Sam is the way they die, The.
There are no losses.
These Have Gone with Silent Hands, Seeking.
These Unreturning Destinies.
This Early Day.
This Man Was Your Brother.
Though I Had Much More To Say.
Thus Far So Nobly Advanced.
We Mutually Pledge to Each Other.
What Happened in the Camps.
What I'd like to know is.
When in the Course of Human Events.
You May All Go Home Now.
Piercy. Knight of Swords, The.
Peaceable Kingdom, The.
Plath. Thin People, The.
Pound. Lament of the Frontier Guard.
Sestina: Altaforte.
Prince. Cefalù.
Inn, The.
Painter's face—if, The.
Soldiers Bathing.
Ralegh. Giants did advance their wicked hand, The.
Robinson. Field of Glory, The.
Rolfe. After Tu Fu (A.D. 713-770).
At the Moment of Victory.
In the Time of Hesitation.
Postscript to a War.
Radio Madrid—1937.
These Men Are Revolution.
Rossetti. For One Sake.
Massacre of Perugia, The.
Rukeyser. All Souls.
Another Day. Paul in the Mountains of Fantasy. Paul Tells His Adventure.
Chapultepec Park / II.
Child Asleep, The.
Correspondences.
Cruise, The.
Deep in the Century of Opposites.
Don Baty, the Draft Resister.
Eighth Elegy. Children's Elegy.
Facing Sentencing.
Father dreams that he was hid in a tree, The.
His Head is Full of Faces.
How We Did It.
It Is There.
Käthe Kollwitz.
Lat. 10 Degrees North, Long. 45 Degrees West.
Letter to the Front.
Long Past Moncada.
Looking.
M-Day's Child is Fair of Face.
Mendings.
My toes feel like nothing they are so cold.
Noguchi.
Not Yet.
Now he plays with the other children.
One Soldier.
Otherworld.
Poem: "I lived in the first century of world wars."
Poem Out of Childhood.
Power of war leads to a plan of lives, The.
Sixth Elegy. River Elegy.
Sundays, They Sleep Late.
Tenth Elegy. Elegy in Joy.
This is going to be about smoke.
Welcome from War.
What Have You Brought Home from the Wars?
When he began to witness, it was not to a journey.
Who in One Lifetime.
Sandburg. Among the Red Guns.
And They Obey.
Bas-Relief.
Black Horizons.
Buttons.

Choices.
Crimson Changes People.
Dunes.
Fight.
Forgotten Wars.
From the people the countries get their names.
Graves.
House.
Iron.
Jan, the Son of Thomas.
John Ericsson Day Memorial, 1918.
Killers.
Long Guns.
Memoir.
Memoir of a Proud Boy.
Mr. Longfellow and His Boy.
Murmurings in a Field Hospital.
New Feet.
Old Osawatomie.
Out of White Lips.
Peace Between Wars.
People is Everyman, everybody, The.
Places.
Prayer after World War.
Ready to Kill.
Remembered Women.
Salvage.
Smoke.
Statistics.
Three Pieces on the Smoke of Autumn.
Threes.
Unknown War, The.
Wars.
You can drum on immense drums.
Sarton. We'll to the Woods No More, the Laurels Are Cut Down.
Schuyler. May, 1972.
Scott. Ambuscade, The.
Bale-Fire, The.
Branksome Hall.
Defenceless Border, The.
Douglas and Marmion.
English Advance at Flodden, The.
Fiery Cross, The.
Melrose by Moonlight.
Norham Castle.
On the Massacre of Glencoe, 1692.
Sexton. Papa and Mama Dance, The.
Shapiro. Conscientious Objector, The.
Scyros.
Shelley. Ode Written October, 1819, An.
War Is the Statesman's Game.
Shelton. War.
Silverstein. Generals, The.
Simic. Place, The.
Smith, Charlotte. Long wintry months are past; the Moon that now.
Smith, Patti. Babelfield.
Corps de Plane.
Smith, Stevie. Bye Baby Bother.
Come On, Come Back.
Poets Are Silent, The.
Who Shot Eugenie?
Snodgrass. After Experience Taught Me..
Dr. Joseph Goebbels, Minister for Propaganda.
Sorrentino. Veterans of Foreign Wars.
Spender. Conscript, The.
Cornet Cornelius Rilke.
Epilogue to a Human Drama.
Hamburg, 1929.
In 1929.
Shadow of War.
Two Armies.
Stafford. Dedication, A: "We stood by the library. It was an August night."
1940.
Time Capsule.
Stevens. Dry Loaf.
Examination of the Hero in a Time of War.
Gigantomachia.
Stevenson. Country of the Camisards, The.
Lost Occasion, The.
Loud and low in the chimney.
Our Lady of the Snows.
Prelude: "By sunny market-place and street."
Strange are the ways of men.
To the Stormy Petrel.

Vanquished Knight, The.
Voluntary.
Stuart. Last Words.
Speakers from the Vietnam War.
Suckling. This moiety war.
Swinburne. May Janet.
Tate. Ode to Our Young Pro-consuls of the Air.
Tennyson. Battle of Brunanburh.
Chaos! Cosmos! Cosmos, Chaos! who can tell how all will end?
Thomas. Hand That Signed the Paper, The.
Turco. Fort, The.
Walcott. Beachhead.
Those grooves in that forehead of sand-coloured flesh.
Walker. Enemy, The.
Warren. Court-Martial.
Interjection #4: Bad Year, Bad War: A New Year's Card, 1969.
Natural History I.
Shoes In Rain Jungle.
Sirocco.
Whitman. As I Ponder'd [or Pondered] in Silence.
Beat! Beat! Drums!
Columbian's Song, The.
Mystic Trumpeter, The.
Old War-Dreams.
Respondez!
To Thee Old Cause.
Whittier. Judith at the Tent of Holofernes.
Wilbur. Agent, The.
Another Voice.
First Snow in Alsace.
Fourth of July, The.
Looking into History.
Mined Country.
On Freedom's Ground.
Peace of Cities, The.
Place Pigalle.
Williams, Charles Kenneth. Creams.
Dream, The.
How Humble We Were before This.
I Am the Bitter Name.
Little Shirt, The.
War.
Williams, Miller. La Ultima Carta: A Young Wife Writes to Her Husband in the Mountains.
Normandy Beach.
Williams, William Carlos. Illegitimate Things.
These.
Threnody: "Christian coin, The."
Wanderings of the Tribe, The.
War, the Destroyer.
Wordsworth. Anticipation. October, 1803.
1811 ("Power of Armies is a visible thing, The").
Germans on the Heights of Hochheim, The.
Is there a power that can sustain and cheer.
Lines on the Expected Invasion 1803.
Ode: 1814.
Say, what is Honour?—"Tis the finest sense."
Sonnet in the Pass of Killicranky.
Wright, James. Mad Fight Song for William S. Carpenter, 1966, A.
Yeats. Irish Airman Foresees His Death, An.
Meditations in Time of Civil War.
On Being Asked for a War Poem.
Rose of Battle, The.
Valley of the Black Pig, The.
What Was Lost.
Young. Suicide.
Zukofsky. "One oak fool box";—the pun.

See also **Soldiers; War Casualties; War Dead; Listings for specific Wars and Battles.**

War Casualties

Bly. Driving through Minnesota during the Hanoi Bombings.
Boyle. Dedicated to *Terre des Hommes*.
Bukowski. On Seeing an Old Civil War Painting with My Love.
Simplicity of Everything in Viet Nam, The.
"Carroll, Lewis." Path of Roses, The.
Carruth. Song: So Often, So Long I Have

Thought.
There was this girl 18, 19 and slight.
Clark. Sleepwalker's Fate.
Cummings. It's jolly / odd what pops into.
Doolittle. R.A.F.
Dove. Bird Frau, The.
"Dylan." John Brown.
Eberhart. Protagonists.
World War.
Emerson. Inscription on a Well in Memory of the Martyrs of the War.
Fenton. Better for the widow, that she should not live in fear of surprise, The.
Bus is waiting at the southern gate, The.
But when so many had died, so many and at such speed.
Children in Exile.
Dead Soldiers.
How comforting it is, once or twice a year.
Prison Island.
Staffordshire Murderer, A.
Vacant Possession, A.
Ferlinghetti. Third World Calling.
Ford. War.
Hacker. Before the War.
Hardy. At the War Office, London.
Hemingway. All armies are the same.
Poem to Mary (Second Poem).
Hewitt. YCVS and the Ulster Division, The.
Hughes, Langston. Casualty.
Jarrell. Field Hospital, A.
Sick Nought, The.
Terms.
Ward in the States, A.
Kinnell. Dead Shall Be Raised Incorruptible, The.
Knight. At a VA Hospital in the Middle of the United States of America: An Act in a Play.
Lawrence. Casualty.
Lewis. Assault Convoy, The.
Greetings.
Lady in Black.
Mending, with books and papers and a fan.
Three endless weeks of sniping all the way.
White brain crossing, The.
Muldoon. Field Hospital, The.
Owen. Chances, The.
Conscious.
Dead-Beat, The.
Disabled.
Futility.
Letter, The.
Mental Cases.
Sentry, The.
Terre, A.
Patchen. This Man Was Your Brother.
Rolfe. Epitaph: "Deep in this earth."
War Guilt.
Rukeyser. Bringing.
Leg in a Plaster Cast, A.
Stevens. Woman Sings a Song for a Soldier Come Home, A.
Whitman. March in the Ranks Hard-Prest, and the Road Unknown, A.
Wound-Dresser, The.
Williams, Charles Kenneth. From My Window.
War.
Williams, William Carlos. Item.
Zukofsky. "One oak fool box";—the pun.

See also **Soldiers; War Dead.**

War Dead
Betjeman. In Memory of Basil, Marquess of Dufferin and Ava.
Bly. War and Silence.
Bogan. To My Brother: Killed: Hammont Wood: October, 1918.
Bradstreet. Elegy Upon that Honorable and Reknowned Knight Sir Philip Sydney, An.
Brontë. Rodric Lesley. 1830.
Brooks. Appendix to the Anniad.
Browning, Elizabeth Barrett. Forced Recruit, The.
Mother and Poet.
Browning, Robert. Incident of the French Camp.

Burns. It Was A' for Our Rightfu' King.
Lovely Lass o' Inverness, The.
Byron. On the Star of "The Legion of Honour."
Ciardi. Box Comes Home, A.
Elegy Just in Case.
Survival in Missouri.
V-J Day.
Cummings. Belgium.
Earth like a tipsy.
First Jock he / was kilt a handsome.
I'm / asking / you dear to.
Look at this) / a 75 done.
Dickey, James. Hunting Civil War Relics at Nimblewill Creek.
Island, The.
Performance, The.
Dickinson. It feels a shame to be Alive.
My Triumph lasted till the Drums.
Dunbar. Memorial Day.
Our Martyred Soldiers.
Unsung Heroes, The.
Eberhart. Anxiety I Felt in Guanajuato, The.
Ceremony By the Sea, A.
Eliot. To the Indians Who Died in Africa.
Emerson. Hymn[:] Sung at the Completion of the Concord Monument, April 19, 1836.
Fenton. Doctor Gliedschirm, skin specialist, surgeries 14–16 hours or by appointment.
Graves. Devil's Advice to Story-Tellers, The.
Gray. Death of Hoel, The.
Haines. Certain Dead.
Hardy. At the War Office, London.
Casterbridge Captains, The.
Drummer Hodge.
I Looked Up from My Writing.
Man He Killed, The.
Sea Fight, The.
Son's Portrait, The.
Souls of the Slain, The.
Wife in London, A.
Hartley. K. von F.—1914—Arras-Bouquoi.
Heaney. In Memoriam Francis Ledwidge.
Hesketh. More than Grass.
Hewitt. Volunteer, The.
Hill. Dear lords of life, stump-toothed, with ragged breath.
Funeral Music.
Housman. Astronomy.
Day of Battle, The.
Defeated, The.
Epitaph on an Army of Mercenaries.
Farewell to a name and a number.
Here dead lie we because we did not choose.
On the idle hill of summer.
Recruit, The.
Hughes, Ted. Six Young Men.
Hugo. G. I. Graves in Tuscany.
Note from Capri to Richard Ryan on the Adriatic Floor.
Jarrell. Burning the Letters.
Come to the Stone.
Dead in Melanesia, The.
Dead Wingman, The.
Death of the Ball Turret Gunner, The.
For the Madrid Road.
Gunner.
Losses.
New Georgia.
1945: The Death of the Gods.
Protocols.
Second Air Force.
Subway from New Britain to the Bronx, The.
Jeffers. Drunken Charlie.
Love and the Hate, The.
Resurrection.
Kipling. American Rebellion, The.
Children, The.
Death-Bed, A.
Dirge of Dead Sisters.
Epitaphs of the War [1914–1918].
General Joubert.
Gethsemane.
Hyænas [or Hyenas], The.
King's Pilgrimage, The.
London Stone.
Lord Roberts.

Memories.
Mesopotamia.
My Boy Jack.
Ode: "So long as memory, valour, and faith endure."
Recantation, A.
Rimmon.
Soldier, Soldier.
Knight. Poem for Black Relocation Centers, A.
Larkin. MCMXIV.
Levertov. Two Variations.
Lewis. Finale.
Raid, The.
Raiders' Dawn.
Unknown Soldier, The.
White frost; intricate bare branches.
Lowell. For the Union Dead.
Holy Innocents, The.
"MacDiarmid." Another Epitaph on an Army of Mercenaries.
At the Cenotaph.
McGrath. All the Dead Soldiers.
Ode for the American Dead in Asia.
Reading the Names of the Vietnam War Dead.
MacLeish. Family Group.
Lines for an Interment.
Memorial Rain.
Young Dead Soldiers, The.
MacNeice. This then is our answer under.
Melville. Inscription: "To them who crossed the flood."
Meredith. Blest is the sword that leaps from sheath.
Ever invoking fire from heaven, the fire.
Good Comrade, The.
Merton. Bombarded City, The.
For My Brother: Reported Missing In Action, 1943.
Long Enough.
Two British Airmen.
Nathan. Meadow Foam.
Nemerov. For W——, Who Commanded Well.
Neruda. Wars, The.
Owen. Anthem for Doomed Youth.
Asleep.
Dulce Et Decorum Est.
Fragment: "As bronze may be much beautified."
Fragment: "I saw his round mouth's crimson deepen as it fell."
Futility.
Greater Love.
Has Your Soul Sipped?
Inspection.
Last Laugh, The.
Miners.
Next War, The.
Send-Off, The.
Strange Meeting.
Paley. I Gave Away That Kid.
Ransom. Necrological.
St. John. Six/Nine/Forty-Four.
Sandburg. Grass.
Scott. Coronach.
Death of Marmion, The.
Hymn for the Dead.
Shakespeare. Sonnet 25: "Let those who are in favour with their stars."
Snodgrass. Flat One, A.
Inquest.
Stevens. Death of a Soldier, The.
Dutch Graves in Bucks County.
Tate. Ode to the Confederate Dead.
Tennyson. Charge of the Light Brigade, The.
Warren. History among the Rocks.
Whitman. As Toilsome I Wander'd Virginia's Woods.
Ashes of Soldiers.
Ashes of Soldiers: Epigraph.
Bravest Soldiers, The.
Camps of Green.
Come Up from the Fields Father.
Dirge for Two Veterans.
Look Down Fair Moon.
Pensive on Her Dead Gazing.

Reconciliation.
Sight in Camp [or] Sight in Camp in the
Daybreak Gray and Dim, A.
Vigil Strange I Kept on the Field One Night.
Yeats. Irish Airman Foresees His Death, An.
See also **Soldiers.**

War of the Grand Alliance
Browning, Robert. Hervé Riel.

Warblers
Galvin. Glass.
Lying to Fall Warblers.
Stevens. Meditation Celestial & Terrestrial.

Warning
Berry. Warning to My Readers, A.
Boyle. After the Earth Quaked.
Bukowski. I Don't Need a Bedsheet with Slits
for Eyes to Kill You In.
Carew. Deposition from Love, A.
Chaucer. Lenvoy de Chaucer a Bukton.
De la Mare. Beware!
Not that way.
Outskirts, The.
Dove. Primer for the Nuclear Age.
Eberhart. Going Backward Going Forward.
Everson. Scout, The.
Graves. Gorgon Mask.
Hemingway. Advice to a Son.
Modern Version of Polonius' Advice, A.
Herrick. Bellman, The.
Upon Luggs.
Hewitt. Encounter With R.J. Welch, The
Antiquary.
Housman. I wake from dreams and turning.
Kipling. Bell Buoy, The.
Kunitz. Rover.
Lorde. For Each of You.
MacLeish. For if the sun breed maggots in a
dead.
MacNeice. To a Communist.
Pack. Twin, The.
Piercy. Girl in White.
Plath. Admonitions.
Ralegh. Sir Walter Ra[u]le[i]gh to His
Son[ne].
Rolfe. Little Ballad for Americans—1954.
Sexton. Admonitions to a Special Person.
Smith, Stevie. Advice to Young Children.
Beware the Man.
Songe d'Athalie.
Wakoski. Warning to the Man in Receiving at
Sears, A.
Warren. Pondy Woods.
Yeats. Never Give All the Heart.

Warren, Robert Penn
Tate. To a Romantic.

Warsaw, Poland
Davie. Meeting of Cultures, A.
Meinke. Robert Frost in Warsaw.

Warts
Muldoon. Cure for Warts, The.

Warwickshire, England
Davie. Warwickshire.

Washing
Bishop. Under the Window: Ouro Prêto.
Gallagher. Ritual of Memories, The.
Herrick. Another ("In the morning when ye
rise").
Sincerity.
Psalms. Psalm 51: "Have mercy upon me, O
God.."
Sandburg. Brainwashing.
Silverstein. Shadow Wash.
Snyder. February.
Williams, Charles Kenneth. They wash you /
when.
Wyatt. Rue on me, Lord, for thy goodness
and grace.
See also **Baths and Bathing.**

Washing Machines. *see* **Laundry and
Laundering.**

Washington, Booker Taliaferro
Dunbar. Booker T. Washington.
To Booker T. Washington.

Washington, George
Berryman. Washington in Love.

Boyle. Statement for El Greco and William
Carlos Williams, A.
Burns. Ode [for General Washington's
Birthday].
Emerson. Hard is it to persuade the public
mind of its plain duty & true interest.
Nash. Watchman, What of the First First
Lady?
O'Hara. On Seeing Larry Rivers' *Washington
Crossing the Delaware* at the Museum of
Modern Art.
Oppen. I am the father of no country.
Tate. On the Martyr of Harpers Ferry.
Tomlinson. Ice Cream at Blauenberg.
Updike. February 22.
Wakoski. George Washington Slept Here.
George Washington: The Whole Man.
George Washington Writes Home About
Harvesting His Hemp.
George Washington's Camp Cups.
Patriotic Poem.
Second Universe.
Whitman. Washington's Monument, February,
1885.
Whittier. Vow of Washington, The.
Zukofsky. George Washington.

Washington (state)
Hugo. Anacortes-Sydney Run, The.
Bad Vision at the Skagit.
Fort Casey, without Guns.
Orcas in the Eyes.
Plunking the Skagit.
Port Townsend.
Tahola.
White Center.
McGrath. Beyond Seattle.
Snyder. Mid-August at Sourdough Mountain
Lookout.
Text, The.

Washington, D.C
Bishop. View of the Capitol from the Library
of Congress.
Dove. Banneker.
D. C.
Eberhart. Gods of Washington, D.C., The.
Emerson. One night he dreamed of a palace
fair.
Fox. Nail of the Index Finger, The.
Lowell. July in Washington.
Piercy. Gift of Light, A.
Rich. Capital, The.
Rukeyser. City of Monuments.
Sandburg. And So Today.
Smoke Rose Gold.
Tangibles.
Schuyler. Hymn to Life.
Shapiro. Washington Cathedral.
Snyder. It Pleases.
Travelling to the Capital.
Tate. Aeneas at Washington.
Updike. Sin City, D.C.
Washington.
Washington: Tourist View.
Whitman. How Solemn as One by One.
Whittier. Astræa at the Capitol.
At Washington.

Washington Monument
Sandburg. Washington Monument by Night.
Whitman. Washington's Monument, February,
1885.

Wasps
De la Mare. Queen Wasp, A.
Dickey, James. Springhouse, Menses, Held
Apple, House and Beyond.
Dunn. To a Friend in Love with the Wrong
Man Again.
Eberhart. New Hampshire, February.
Frost. Waspish.
Nash. Wasp, The.
Nemerov. Invocation: "Wasp, climbing the
window pane."
Spenser. Mighty lyon, lord of all the wood, A.

Watches
Auden. Parable.
Bukowski. Gold Pocket Watch, A.
Gallagher. Kidnap[p]er.
Herrick. Watch, The.

Hughes, Langston. Could Be.
Nash. I Had No Idea It Was So Late.
Simic. Watch Repair.
Updike. Omega.
See also **Clocks.**

Water
Ammons. For Doyle Fosso.
Arnold. But the majestic river floated on.
Auden. Damming Stream.
Beckett. Fleuves et océans.
Berry. Wet Time, A.
Winter Rain, The.
Bishop. Elegy for Maria Alves.
Under the Window: Ouro Prêto.
Bly. Awakening.
Bogan. To Be Sung on the Water.
Bunting. Flat land lies under water, The.
Stones trip Coquet burn.
Carew. To My Mistress Sitting by a River's
Side; an Eddy.
Carroll, Jim. August.
Blue Poles.
Distances, The.
Epiphany.
Mercury Clouds.
Narrows, The.
Their voice, as one, was heavy.
Window in Cherry Valley, A.
Your Daughter.
Carruth. And the water/ the rising water.
Aqua.
Existing Pool, The.
Far-removed Mountain Men, The.
Ceravolo. Heart Feels the Water.
Coleridge. Netherlands, The.
Crashaw. To Our Lord, upon the Water Made
Wine.
Creeley. Act of Love, The.
Birds, The.
Birthday, A.
Divisions.
Down Home.
Falling.
Flowers.
For an Anniversary.
For Lewis, to Say It.
For Marisol.
For You.
Funny.
Just Friends.
1971.
Poem, A: "If the water forms."
Pool, The.
Rocks, The.
Sea.
Shot.
Sign.
Spring.
Stomping with Catullus.
The.
Total Parts of a World, The.
Water.
Water (2).
Wish, A.
Davie. Waterfall at Powerscourt, The.
Dickey, James. Circuit.
Eagle's Mile, The.
Rain Guitar, The.
Remnant Water.
Dickinson. I think that the Root of the Wind
is Water.
Doolittle. Pool, The.
Dunbar. Gourd, The.
Pool, The.
Duncan. There are memories everywhere then.
Remembe[r]d, we go out, as in.
Dunn. Fable of the Water Merchants.
Eberhart. Froth.
Garden God, The.
Ichetucknee.
Loon Call, A.
Sea-Ruck.
Standards, The.
Emerson. As the drop feeds its fated flower.
Water.
You shall not love me for what daily spends.
Everson. River-Root: as even under high

drifts, those fierce wind-grappled cuts of the Rockies.
Wader, / Watcher by water.
Fisher. Civic water / with lilies and flies.
In long shapes over the channel's.
Passing Newbridge-on-Wye.
Rudiments.
So, the water gate.
Ford. Wind is the breath of it.
Fox. Cup of Cold Water.
River and Light.
Gallagher. Corona.
If Blood Were Not as Powerful as It Is.
Reading Aloud.
Ritual of Memories, The.
Women's Tug of War at Lough Arrow.
Garrigue. Clovers, The.
For the Fountains and Fountaineers of Villa d'Este.
Pays Perdu.
Gunn. Cool Stream, The.
Geysers, The.
He grins, he plunges into orgy. It moves about.
Sleep by the Hot Stream.
Hacker. Pantoum.
Haines. That mid-fall morning, driving north.
To My Father.
Hall. Child, The.
Waters.
Hartnett. Sad Singing in Darkness.
Heaney. Drink of Water, A.
Herrick. Another ("In the morning when ye rise").
Proof to No Purpose.
To the Water Nymphs, Drinking at the Fountain.
Hesketh. Boy Drowning.
Integration.
Mallard, The.
Protean Lover.
Hewitt. Footing Turf.
Glendun on a Wet July Day.
Old Mill-Race, The.
Spring Restored, The.
Those Swans Remember; A Poem.
Hopkins. I hear a noise of waters drawn away.
Hughes, Ted. How Water Began to Play.
Man Seeking Experience Enquires His Way of a Drop of Water, The.
Jarrell. Well Water.
Jonson. Daughters of the subtle flood.
Now Dian, with her burning face.
Joseph. Lost Sea, The.
Kinnell. Feast, The.
Kipling. Native Water-Carrier (M.E.F.).
Ripple Song, A.
Koch. Boiling Water, The.
Kunitz. King of the River.
Larkin. Water.
Lawrence. Four, The.
Hark in the Dusk!
Secret Waters, The.
Third Thing, The.
Wild Common, The.
Levertov. Fountain, The.
Ripple, The.
Well, The.
Levine. Belief.
Gift for a Believer.
Lovelace. Lucasta at the Bath.
Lucasta, Taking the Waters at Tunbridge.
Lowell. Water.
Lowry. Indian Arm.
Mackerel shouldn't take, A.
Poem: "Wet streets in Liverpool."
Port Moody.
Two streams came from a different source, The.
McAuley. Confession, The.
"MacDiarmid." Glass of Pure Water, The.
Water of Life.
MacLeish. What Any Lover Learns.
MacNeice. Genesis.
Our shadows now grow long in the sun.
Our Sister Water.
Rest House, The.

Markson. Hygiene.
Matthews. Flood Plain.
Puberty.
Waters, The.
Miller. Saw 'er at a temple on the outskirts of Hangzhou.
Milton. Forthwith the sounds and seas, each creek and bay.
Morgan. Jormungand.
Oliver. At Blackwater Pond.
Olson. Carrying water to the Youth in Honor of Sappho Jane Harrison & Miss Duncan if She Had.
His house / in the branches of.
I Weep, Fountain of Jazer.
Other Than.
Small Birds, to Agree with the Leaves, Come in the Fall.
Snow, The.
Stone and Flower Series.
Story, A.
Pack. Last Drowning, The.
Red Shift, The.
Reversing.
Patchen. All Is Safe.
Piercy. Unclench Yourself.
Raine. Bright cloud, / Bringer of rain to far fields.
Golden Flowers.
Loch, The.
Monessie Gorge.
Night in Martindale.
Peace of Mind.
There Shall Be No More Sea.
Water.
Ransom. Persistent Explorer.
"Reed." Since Half the World is H$_2$O.
Roethke. Cycle, The.
Long Alley, The.
Rossetti. Lord, we are rivers running to Thy sea.
Mirrors of Life and Death.
Water Spirit's Song, The.
Rukeyser. Asylum Song.
Boys in the Branches.
Delta Poems.
Divining Water.
Mrs. Walpurga.
Song, from "Mr. Amazeen on the River."
Wind arrow, wind rose, the wind currents in air.
Sandburg. Landscape.
Metamorphosis.
Pool of Bethesda.
Prairie Waters by Night.
Sarton. Glass of Water, A.
In Time Like Air.
Italian Garden.
Schuyler. Edge in the Morning, The.
Sexton. Water.
Silverstein. Dirtiest Man in the World, The.
Smith, Patti. Death by Water.
Smith, Stevie. Abominable Lake, The.
Sorrentino. Detail, A.
Stuart. Narcissus Dreaming.
Sticks and Stones.
Water's Fine, I'm Fine, The.
Suckling. Upon Sir John Lawrence's Bringing Water over the Hills [to My L. Middlesex His House at Witten].
Tomlinson. Logic.
On Water.
Updike. To Evaporation.
Van Duyn. Elementary Attitudes.
Wakoski. Water.
Whittier. Captain's Well, The.
Wilbur. Water Walker.
Wordsworth. Suggested by Mr W. Westall's Views of the Caves, etc., in Yorkshire.
Unremitting Voice of Nightly Streams, The.
Wright, James. All the Beautiful are Blameless.
Humming a Tune for an Old Lady in West Virginia.
To Flood Stage Again.
To the bridge of love.
Young. H$_2$O.

Zimmer. Cecil Sliding Away from the Memory of Wanda.
Zukofsky. And to paradise which is a port. Only water—.
To my wash-stand.
Ways, The.
When the crickets.
Xenophanes.

Water Lilies
Cummings. Water-Lilies.
Wordsworth. Egyptian Maid; or, The Romance of the Water Lilly, The.

Waterbeds
Updike. Insomnia the Gem of the Ocean.
To a Waterbed.

Watercolors
Plath. Watercolor of Grantchester Meadows.

Waterfalls
Burns. Humble Petition of Bruar Water to the Noble Duke of Athole, The.
Written with a Pencil, Standing by the Fall of Fyers, near Loch-Ness.
Carruth. Ithiel Falls, below the Nazarene campground. A name.
Coleridge. Thought, A.
Davie. Waterfall at Powerscourt, The.
Dickey, James. Twin Falls, The.
Dickey, William. Silver Creek Falls.
Everson. Stone Face Falls.
Hardy. Under the Waterfall.
Hartley. West Pitch at the Falls.
Hopkins. It was a hard thing to undo this knot.
Noise of falls I am possessèd by, A.
Kinnell. Falls, The.
"MacDiarmid." Of My First Love.
Meredith. By the Passeyr.
Merrill. McKane's Falls.
Oliver. Waterfall, The.
Pack. Coincidence.
Rondo of the Familiar.
Waterfall.
Snyder. By Frazier Creek Falls.
Stevens. Doctor of Geneva, The.
Tomlinson. Death of Elizabeth Grieve, The.
Race, The.
Whittier. Seeking of the Waterfall, The.
Williams, William Carlos. Paterson: The Falls.
Wordsworth. Fall of the Aar—Handec, The.
Louisa; After Accompanying Her on a Mountain Excursion.
On Approaching the Staub-Bach, Lauterbrunnen.
To the Torrent at the Devil's Bridge, North Wales, 1824.
Waterfall and the Eglantine, The.

Waterfowl
Burns. On Scaring Some Waterfowl in Loch Turit, a Wild Scene among the Hills of Oughtertyre.
Wordsworth. Water Fowl.
See also **Listings for specific Waterfowl.**

Watergate. *see* **Nixon, Richard Milhous.**

Waterloo, Battle of (1815)
Byron. There was a sound of revelry by night.
Hardy. Peasant's Confession, The.
Lowell. Waterloo.
Meredith. Behind the Northern curtain-folds he passed.
Desire and terror then had each of each.
Wordsworth. After Visiting the Field of Waterloo.
Occasioned by the Battle of Waterloo February, 1816.
Occasioned by the Battle of Waterloo (the Last Six Lines Intended for an Inscription) February, 1816.
Ode: 1815.
Ode: The Morning of the Day Appointed for a General Thanksgiving. January 18, 1816.

Watermelons
Simic. Watermelons.

Watertowers
Auden. Watertowers, The.
Who stands, the crux left of the watershed.

Waterwheels
Auden. Skyreholme Mill.

Watteau, Jean-Antoine
Walcott. Watteau.

Watts, Isaac
"Carroll, Lewis." How doth the little crocodile.

Waugh, Evelyn
Liddy. Homage to Conor Cruise O'Brien.

Waves
Arnold. But the majestic river floated on.
Bishop. Wave, The.
Browning, Elizabeth Barrett. Sea-Mew, The.
"Carroll, Lewis." Lady of the Ladle, The.
Cooper. Racetrack, The.
De la Mare. Miracle, The.
Dickey, James. Daybreak.
Emerson. All day the waves assailed the rock.
Fletcher. Sea-Violins.
Tide, The.
Gunn. From the Wave.
Hall. Sea, The.
Hartley. How like the sea / to be.
Life ahead, life behind—.
Herrick. Just Man, A.
Hugo. Port Townsend, 1974.
Larkin. And the Wave Sings Because It Is Moving.
Lawrence. What Are the Wild Waves Saying?
MacLeish. "Dover Beach"—a Note to That Poem.
Oliver. Winter.
Rich. Wave, The.
Sandburg. All Day Long.
Fins.
From the Shore.
Stuart. Birds, The.
Turco. Roc.
Whitman. By That Long Scan of Waves.
Wilbur. Beacon, The.
Waters, The.
Williams, Miller. Staying.
Williams, William Carlos. Sound of Waves, The.
Yeats. Nineteenth Century and After, The.
Young. Sometimes With the Waves.
Zukofsky. I Sent Thee Late.

Wealth
Brooks. Beverly Hills, Chicago.
Burns. Auld Rob Morris.
Epistle to Captn Willm Logan at Park.
My Lady's Gown There's Gairs upon't.
Ode, Sacred to the Memory of Mrs. ——— of ———.
Ronalds of the Bennals, The.
Song: "Mark yonder pomp of costly fashion."
Song: "Tibby I hae seen the day."
Twa Dogs, The.
"Carroll, Lewis." Canto III: Scarmoges.
First Voice, The.
Carruth. Our own hearts too like, seems's-zo, whenever.
Catullus. Carmen 114: "O'Tool is generally accounted."
Carmen 115: "O'Toole is the proud master of."
Chaucer. Miller's [or Milleres] Tale, The.
Coleridge. Lines Written at the King's Arms, Ross, Formerly the House of the "Man of Ross."
Cowper. On a True Friend.
On Late-acquired Wealth or Riches.
R.S.S.
Crane. All This..
Cummings. Ci-gît l Foetus(unborn to not die).
IKEY(GOLDBERG)'S WORTH I'M.
It's just like a coffin's.
Lord John Unalive(having a fortune of fifteengrand).
Davie. Garden Party, The.
Dickinson. Because 'twas Riches I could own.
I made slow Riches but my Gain.
Your Riches—taught me—Poverty.
Donne. Deliver us for thy descent.
Satire 2: "Sir: though (I thank God for it) I do hate."

Dunbar. Place Where the Rainbow Ends, The.
Precedent.
"Dylan." Lonesome Death of Hattie Carroll, The.
Emerson. Chartist's Complaint, The.
Compensation ("Wings of Time are black and white, The").
Have ye seen the caterpillar.
I have no hoarded treasure.
Oil & Wine, / Sparkling gems, & rich attire.
Who gave thy cheek the mixed tint.
Ferlinghetti. Two Scavengers in a Truck, Two Beautiful People in a Mercedes.
Fox. Sentence, A.
Frost. Equalizer, An.
Lovely Shall Be Choosers, The.
Hemingway. Road to Avallon, The.
Herrick. Adversity ("Love is maintain'd by wealth; when all is spent").
Amber Bead, The.
Any Way for Wealth.
Gold, before Goodnesse.
His Grange, or Private Wealth.
Poverty and Riches.
Reverence to Riches.
To His Deere God.
Upon Croot.
Hewitt. Ellendene.
Ex-Serviceman, The.
Hill. To the (Supposed) Patron.
Hugo. Approaching the Castle.
Jarrell. Three Bills.
Johnson. Short Song of Congratulation [or To a Young Heir], A.
Vanity of Wealth, The.
Joseph. Living Off Other People—Welfare.
Kipling. Lollius.
Knott. Funny Poem.
Koertge. Royce Newport Money.
Lawrence. Bathing Resort.
Choice.
Poverty.
Riches.
Liddy. City Life.
Lovelace. On the Best, Last, and Only Remaining Comedy of Mr. Fletcher.
Lowry. Hospitality.
Morning coat is walking, A.
MacNeice. Godfather.
Melville. In a Garret.
Merton. Come to your windows, rich women.
Songs of Experience; India, One.
Morgan. Greenwich 1930's, II.
Nash. Eheu! Fugaces, or, What a Difference a Lot of Days Make.
I Yield to My Learned Brother or Is There a Candlestick Maker in the House?
Lines Indited with All the Depravity of Poverty.
Pride Goeth Before a Raise or Ah, There, Mrs. Cadwallader-Smith.
Reflection of the Fallibility of Nemesis.
Terrible People, The.
O'Hara. Commercial Variations.
Olson. Allegory of Wealth, The.
Friend, The.
Pope. Epistle IV, to Richard Boyle, Earl of Burlington.
Epistle III, to Allen Lord Bathurst.
On His Grotto at Twickenham.
Ralegh. Queene anone commands the waightie bowle, The.
"Reed." Men of Good Fortune.
Rich. Uncle Speaks in the Drawing Room, The.
Robinson. Bewick Finzer.
Old Story, The.
Richard Cory.
Rossetti. Light of Light.
She Came from The Uttermost Part of the Earth.
There's Snow on the Fields.
Rukeyser. Gradus ad Parnassum.
Sandburg. Child of the Romans.
Graceland.
Neither wife nor child had Mr. Eastman and the manner of his death.

Schuyler. New Yorker, A.
Schwartz. Dream of Whitman Paraphrased, Recognized and Made More Vivid by Renoir, A.
Sexton. "Daddy" Warbucks.
Money Swing, The.
Sidney. Sonnet 24: "Rich fools there be, whose base and filthy heart."
Sonnet 37: "My mouth doth water, and my breast doth swell."
Smith, Charlotte. To a Querulous Acquaintance.
Smith, Stevie. Satin-Clad.
Villains.
Sorrentino. People in Hell are clothed.
White Lemons.
Stevens. Good Man Has No Shape, The.
Stevenson. System.
To A Gardener.
Tomlinson. Rich, The.
Updike. Handkerchiefs of Khaibar Khan, The.
Whitman. Thought: ("Of persons arrived at high positions, ceremonies, wealth, scholarships, and the like").
Whittier. Maids of Attitash, The.
Problem, The.
Wilbur. Summer Morning, A.
Williams, Charles Kenneth. Allies: According to Herodotus.
Williams, William Carlos. Look, there goes the young lady across the street.
Wordsworth. Vale of Esthwaite, The.
Yeats. Witch, The.
Zukofsky. Firmum is all too known fails so Meantool a Dives.
Meantool inhabits in style three times ten hewed acres, forty.

Weapons
Atwood. Children like the block, The.
Cummings. It's jolly / odd what pops into. Look at this) / a 75 done.
Dickey, James. Lakes of Värmland.
Emerson. Vain against him were hostile blows.
Haines. In Oberlin the university park.
Hayden. Zeus over Redeye.
Hemingway. In a magazine.
Kipling. Benfactors, The.
Song of the Men's Side.
Morrison. We Awoke, Talking.
Owen. Arms and the Boy.
Soldier's Dream.
Stuart. Urban Hunting Scenes.
Tomlinson. Bone.
Wilbur. Giaour and the Pacha, The.

Weariness
Auden. Last Bus, Saturday Night.
Beckett. Enueg II.
Enueg I.
Berry. As the vision of labor grows.
Beginning, A.
Sleep.
Berryman. I break my pace now for a sonic boom.
Why can't, Chris, why shouldn't they fall in love?
Brontë. Lines: "Far away is the land of rest."
Browning, Elizabeth Barrett. My Heart and I.
Burns. Lord Ronald My Son.
Carruth. August First.
Creeley. Eros.
Cullen. Mood.
Dunbar. Goin' Home.
Glück. Islander, The.
Hemingway. Captives.
Herrick. To Sycamores.
Joseph. To Keep Each Other Warm.
Lawrence. Fatigue.
Foreign Sunset.
Nonentity.
Prisoners at Work in the Rain.
Well in Africa, The.
Lowry. Reflection to Windward.
Waking wassails of wistful welcome.
MacLeish. He had used love or lust or what's between.
Markson. As in the Aftermath.

Nash. Every Day Is Monday.
Olson. Knowing All Ways, Including the Transposition of Continents.
Rich. White Night.
Rossetti. Along the highroad the way is too long.
Annie.
Dost Thou Not Care?
Ellen Middleton.
For Thine Own Sake, O My God.
From the Antique.
Have Patience.
Hills are tipped with sunshine, while I walk / In shadows dim and cold.
How One Chose.
I love you and you know it—this at least.
I sit among the green shady valleys oft.
I toiled on, but thou.
I Will Arise.
In Progress.
Is the Moon Tired?
Looking Forward.
Lord, by what inconceivable dim road / Thou leadest man on footsore pilgrimage!
Mid-Lent.
Of My Life.
Out of the Deep.
Sleeping at last, the trouble and tumult over.
There Remaineth Therefore a Rest for the People of God.
Three Nuns.
Thro' burden and heat of the day.
Vigil of the Presentation.
Weary in Well-Doing.
What to Do?
Who Have a Form of Godliness.
Whole Head Is Sick, and the Whole Heart Faint, The.
Yawn, A.
Yes, I too could face death and never shrink.
Zion Said.
Shakespeare. Sonnet 27: "Weary with toil, I haste me to my bed."
Sonnet 50: "How heavy do I journey on the way."
Shelley. Fragment: Death in Life.
Spender. Driving through Snow.
Wright, Charles. Primitive Journal.

Weasels
Hughes, Ted. Strawberry Hill.
Moore. Wood Weasel, The.
Wright, James. Blue Teal's Mother.

Weather
Ammons. Down Low.
Weathering.
Ashbery. Crazy Weather.
Beatles. Rain.
Berg. First Cold.
Berry. Dance, A.
Elegy: "All day our eyes could find no resting place."
Warm day in December, A.
Window. Window. / The wind's eye.
Bogan. Fiend's Weather.
Boyle. Weather.
Brontë. Will the day be bright or cloudy?
Carroll, Jim. But everything has worked out fine.
Clark. Greeks, The.
Magic Arrival No. 7.
Cooper. Bermuda.
If the weather breaks.
Crashaw. On a Foule Morning, Being Then to Take a Journey.
Creeley. Business, The.
To Bobbie.
Cummings. Painted wind has sprung, A.
De la Mare. April.
Scarecrow, The.
Dickinson. Sun and Fog contested, The.
Dunn. Worker's Creed, A.
Eberhart. Flux.
Emerson. Thermometer.
Fisher. Downpour that subdued everybody and, The.
Grey weather beating across the upland.
Sloping and tapering away.

Frost. Voice Ways.
Graves. Language of the Seasons.
Love Story, A.
Weather of Olympus, The.
Why of the Weather, The.
Hardy. Division, The.
Weathers [or Weather].
Herrick. Fair[e] Days; or, Dawn[e]s Deceitful[l].
Hope Well and Have Well: or, Faire after Foule Weather.
Hesketh. Ward F4.
Hewitt. Footing Turf.
St Stephen's Day.
Winter Park.
Hughes, Langston. Strange Hurt.
Hugo. Walking Praed Street.
Kooser. How to Foretell a Change in the Weather.
Lowry. Report on Conditions.
MacLeish. New England Weather.
Mahon. Kinsale.
Nash. It's Never Fair Weather.
Nemerov. April.
Observation of October.
To Lu Chi.
Walking Down Westgate in the Fall.
Weather of the World, The.
Olson. Some partial cloudiness will flow locally, mostly.
Ralegh. 3.24: "Nor Southerne heat nor Northerne snow."
Roethke. Dinky.
Sandburg. Broken Sonnet.
New Weather.
Schuyler. Advent.
April and Its Forsythia.
Flashes.
October 5, 1981.
Overcast, Hot.
So Good.
3/23/66.
Sorrentino. Morning Roundup, The.
Stevenson. Blast—1875, The.
Moon is sinking—the tempestuous weather, The.
Spring Song.
Summer sun shone round me, The.
Sutter. Hoarfrost and Fog.
Tomlinson. Barometer, The.
Discrepancies.
In the Balance.
Windshield, The.
Updike. Code, The.
Walcott. Oddjob, a Bull Terrier.
Whitman. New Year's Day, 1848.
Wilbur. Chronic Condition, A.
Foggy Street.
Williams, Charles Kenneth. Storm, The.
Wordsworth. At Albano.
Zukofsky. Passing tall.
Rains, the rains, The.

Weathervanes
Graves. Arrow on the Vane.
Merton. Weathercock on the Cathedral of Quito, The.
Tomlinson. Weathercocks, The.

Weaving and Weavers
Burns. Cardin o't, The.
Gallant Weaver, The.
To the Weaver's Gin Ye Go.
Carruth. Being as Memory, The.
Doolittle. Archer.
Emerson. Natures web star broidered.
Haines. Weaver, The.
Herrick. To the Little Spinners.
"MacDiarmid." Seamless Garment, The.
Yeats. Fragments; "Locke sank into a swoon."

Webster, Daniel
Emerson. On thee has God conferred.
Poem, Spoken Before the ΦBK Society, August, 1834.
Webster.
Whittier. Ichabod[!].

Webster, John
Eliot. Whispers of Immortality.

Wedding Songs
Herrick. Nuptiall Song, or Epithalamie, on Sir Clipseby Crew and His Lady, A.
Upon a Maid That Died [or Dyed] the Day She Was Married [or Marryed].
Housman. Epithalamium: "He is here, Urania's son."
Shelley. Another Version of the Same.
Bridal Song, A: "Golden gates of Sleep unbar, The."
Epithalamium: "Night, with all thine eyes look down!"
Sidney. Let mother Earth now deck herself in flowers.

Weddings
Bly. My Father's Wedding.
Burns. Mauchline Wedding, The.
Song: "Mark yonder pomp of costly fashion."
Campion. Illustrissimo, Potentissimoque Principi, *Frederico* Quinto, Rheni Comiti Palatino, Duci Bavariae, &c.
Song: "Now hath Flora rob'd [or robbed] her bowers."
Carew. Hymneal Song, on the Nuptials of the Lady Ann Wentworth and the Lord Lovelace.
"Carroll, Lewis." Willow-Tree, The.
Cummings. Logeorge / lo / wellifitisn't eddy how's the boy.
This little bride & groom are.
De la Mare. Episodes.
Donne. Eclogue 1613. December 26.
Dove. In the Old Neighborhood.
Variation on Gaining a Son.
Dunbar. To Dan.
Eberhart. Groundhog Revisiting, The.
Wedding on Cape Rosier, A.
Fisher. Don't Ask.
Fox. Guillermo's Wedding.
Gallagher. Four Dancers at an Irish Wedding.
Glück. Morning.
Graves. Wedding, The.
Hall. Wedding Party.
Hardy. At a Hasty Wedding.
Church and the Wedding, The.
Country Wedding, The.
Wedding Morning, The.
Heaney. Wedding Day.
Herrick. Bride-Cake, The.
Connubii Flores, or the Well-Wishes at Weddings.
Delaying Bride, The.
Hewitt. St Rosalie: Monte Pellegrino.
Hopkins. At the Wedding March.
Jong. Here Comes.
Jonson. Epithalamion: "Glad time is at his point arrived."
Epithalamion: or, a Song.
Epithalamion: "Up, youths and virgins, up, and praise."
Now, now begin to set.
Think yet how night doth waste.
Larkin. Whitsun Weddings, The.
Lawrence. Wedding Morn.
Merton. Five Virgins, The.
Nash. Here Usually Comes the Bride.
Patchen. Letter on the Use of Machine Guns at Weddings, A.
Poe. To ———: "I saw thee on thy bridal day."
Robinson. On the Night of a Friend's Wedding.
Rossetti. Boy Johnny.
"Ding a ding," / The sweet bells sing.
Love from The North.
Ring upon her finger, / Walks the bride, A.
St. John. Wedding Preparations in the Country.
Sandburg. Thin Strips.
Wedding Postponed.
Sarton. Lady and the Unicorn, The.
Scott. Lochinvar.
Sexton. How We Danced.
Wedding Ring Dance, The.
Sorrentino. Hit Album, A.
Senorita's Bouquet, A.
Stevenson. It is the season now to go.
Suckling. Ballad[e] [upon a Wedding], A.

Whittier. Bridal of Pennacook, The.
Wilbur. Wedding Toast, A.
Wright, James. American Wedding.
Zukofsky. My nephew / And my new.
See also **Marriage.**

Weeds
Ammons. Reflective.
Auden. By the Gasworks, Solihull.
Berg. Red Weed.
Berry. May Song.
Bishop. Weed, The.
De la Mare. Bindweed, The.
  Twice Lovely.
Dickey, James. Weeds.
Eberhart. Stealth and Subtleties of Growth.
Everson. In the Ripeness of the Weed.
Hughes, Ted. Thistles.
Lindsay. Dandelion, The.
Millay. Weeds.
Patchen. There Are Two.
Roethke. Long Live the Weeds.
  Weed Puller.
Sandburg. Bright Conversation with Saint-Ex.
  Weeds.
Updike. Bindweed.
Zukofsky. Weeds.

Weekends
Angelou. Weekend Glory.
"Dylan." One More Weekend.
  Silent Weekend.
Gunn. Hotblood on Friday.
Hesketh. Single Footprints.
Lowry. Der Tag.
Sorrentino. Morning Roundup, The.

Weeping. see Tears.

Welcome
Angelou. Arrival.
Berry. I sit in the shade of the trees of the
  land I was born in.
  Long Hunter, The.
Campion. Dance now and sing the joy and
  love we owe.
"Carroll, Lewis." Bruno's Song.
Eberhart. Statue of Liberty.
Herrick. Free Welcome.
  To His Kinsman, Master Thomas Herrick,
  Who Desired to Be in His Book.
  To the King, upon His Welcome to Hampton-
  Court.
Keats. Sweet, Sweet Is the Greeting of Eyes.
Lowry. Waking wassails of wistful welcome.
Silverstein. Farmer and the Queen, The.
  Invitation.
Stevenson. Hail, guest, and enter freely! All
  you see.
  Lo, now, my guest, if aught amiss were said.
Suckling. Welcome, welcome, mortal wight.
Whittier. Welcome to Lowell, A.

Welfare
Angelou. Momma Welfare Roll.
Miller. End of the Negotiable Beggar Bond
  Banquet, The.

Wellington, Arthur Wellesley, 1st Duke of
Byron. Oh, Wellington! (or "Villainton") for
  fame.
  You are "the best of cut-throats:"—do not
  start.
Tennyson. Bury the Great Duke.
Wordsworth. On a Portrait of the Duke of
  Wellington upon the Field of Waterloo, by
  Haydon.

Wells
Dickey, James. Underground Stream, The.
Dickinson. I know where Wells grow—
  Droughtless Wells.
  Well upon the Brook, The.
  What mystery pervades a well!
Fletcher. Well, The.
Hall. Wells.
Heaney. Personal Helicon.
Hewitt. Gentle Bush, The.
Jarrell. Well Water.
Kunitz. One summer, like a stone.
Lawrence. Well in Africa, The.
Rich. Well, The.
Sexton. What the Bird with the Human Head
  Knew.

Tomlinson. Well, The.
Wakoski. When You Throw Amber into the
  Well of the Moon.
Wordsworth. Hart-Leap Well.

Welsh, The
Davie. Monmouthshire.
Housman. Welsh Marches, The.
Lewis. Defeated: for Wales, The.
See also **Wales.**

Werewolves
Atwood. Wereman, The.
  Werewolf Movies.
Wilbur. Beasts.

Wessex, England
Hardy. Milestone by the Rabbit-Burrow, The.
  Spring Call, The.
  Wessex Heights.
MacNeice. Wessex Guidebook.

West, The, United States
Atwood. Backdrop Addresses Cowboy.
Berry. July, 1773.
Carruth. But once winds lightened, freshening
  fair from the West.
Crane. Great Western Plains, The.
Davie. Sunday Morning.
Dunbar. Welcome Address.
"Dylan." Lily, Rosemary, and the Jack of
  Hearts.
Eberhart. Rape of the Cataract, The.
Everson. Scout, The.
Fletcher. Burning Mountain, The.
  Requiem for a Twentieth-Century Outlaw.
Garrigue. Grand Canyon, The.
Hacker. Country & Western.
Hall. Lone Ranger, The.
Hugo. After a Train Trip, One Town Remains.
  Keokuk.
  Topographical Map.
Knight. Clay County.
McGrath. Buffalo Coat, The.
  Something Is Dying Here.
MacLeish. Landscape as a Nude.
  Wildwest.
MacNeice. Western Landscape.
Merrill. McKane's Falls.
Nathan. If you start in loneliness.
Oliver. Dreams.
Olson. Men are only known in memory.
Pedens, who re-walked the trails, hobbyists,
  The.
Ransom. On the Road to Wockensutter.
Rukeyser. Sun on the faces. On the knotted
  rocks.
  There is a knotless line westward, past
  terraces.
Schuyler. Money Musk.
Whitman. Promise to California, A.
Wright, James. Stages on a Journey Westward.

West, Richard
Gray. Sonnet [on the Death of Mr. Richard
  West].

West Indies
Crane. O Carib Isle!
Creeley. Problem, The.
Lorde. Za Ki Tan Ke Parlay Lot.
MacLeish. St. Philip's Church in Antigua.
Walcott. Tales of the Islands.

West Virginia (state)
Davie. West Virginia's Auburn.
McNeill. West Virginia.
Rukeyser. West Virginia.
Wright, James. Mad Fight Song for William
  S. Carpenter, 1966, A.

West Wind
Herrick. To the Western Wind.
Koch. West Wind.
Shelley. Ode to the West Wind.

Westminster Abbey
Betjeman. In Westminster Abbey.
Hardy. Refusal, A.
Lewis. Westminster Abbey.

Whales and Whaling
Donne. Whale, The.
Fisher. Whale Knot, The.
Fox. Cetus, a Letter from Jonah.

Haines. Whale in the Blue Washing Machine,
  The.
Hoffman. Armada of Thirty Whales, An.
Hugo. Letter to Bly from La Push.
Jeffers. Ocean.
  Ocean's Tribute, The.
Jong. Elegy for a Whale.
Joseph. In Memory of God.
Kunitz. Ambergris.
Lindsay. Chanting of the Whales, The.
Lowry. Fiesta.
  Warning from False Cape Horn.
Meinke. Death of the Pilot Whales, The.
Milton. And God created the great whales,
  and each.
Leviathan.
Morgan. Whale Poem.
Oliver. Humpbacks.
Pack. Champ.
  Leviathan.
  Remains.
Piercy. Why the Soup Tastes Like the *Daily
  News.*
Raine. Whales.
"Reed." Last Great American Whale.
Roethke. Whale, The.
Sarton. Jonah.
Sexton. Whale.
Silverstein. Melinda Mae.
Spenser. Toward the sea turning my troubled
  eye.
Tomlinson. Littleton Whale, The.
Turco. Leviathan.

Wharves
Bishop. Bight, The.
  Summer's Dream, A.
Ciardi. Benefits of an Education, The.

Wheat
De la Mare. Gold.
Heaney. Harvest Bow, The.
Herrick. Larr's Portion, and the Poets Part.
Hewitt. Swathe Uncut, The.
Merton. Landscape: Wheatfields.
Sandburg. Buckwheat.

Wheatley, Phillis
Hayden. Letter from Phillis Wheatley, A.

Wheelbarrows
Williams, William Carlos. Red Wheelbarrow,
  The.

Wheelchairs
Owen. Disabled.

Wheeling, West Virginia
Wright, James. In Response to a Rumor that
  the Oldest Whorehouse in Wheeling, West
  Virginia, Has Been Condemned.

Wheels
Bishop. Wading at Wellfleet.
Carruth. Ignis.
  Wheel of Being II, The.
Dobyns. Six Poems on Moving.
"Dylan." This Wheel's on Fire.
Emerson. There is no evil but can speak.
Gunn. Wheel of Fortune, The.
Hewitt. Wheel, The.
Lowry. Oh, poor Mary Ann / When she got to
  the top.
Nemerov. Extract from Memoirs.
Piercy. Twelve-Spoked Wheel Flashing, The.
Simic. Ballad of the Wheel, The.
Wilbur. 1.

Whippoorwills
Cummings. Whippoorwill this / moonday into.
Dickinson. Feather from the Whippoorwill, A.
Dunbar. Whip-Poor-Will and Katy-Did.
Frost. Nature Note, A.
Hall. Whip-Poor-Will.

Whiskey
Burns. Author's Earnest Cry and Prayer, to
  the Right Honorable and Honorable, the
  Scotch Representatives in the House of
  Commons, The.
  John Barleycorn [a Ballad].
  Scotch Drink.
  Third Epistle to J. Lapraik.
  Willie Brew'd [*or* Brewed] a Peck o' Maut.
Hughes, Langston. Bar.

Lowry. Alternative.
Beside Oneself.
When you were starving, you waited—how long?
Meinke. Poet to His Tongue, The.
Merton. WHISKE / WHI SK.
Nemerov. Moonshine.
Williams, William Carlos. Centenarian, The.

Whistler, James Abbott McNeill
Williams, William Carlos. Period Piece: 1834.

Whistling and Whistlers
Berry. First, The.
Bishop. Behind Stowe.
Clark. Whistle Buoy.
Dunbar. Breaking the Charm.
Just Whistle a Bit.
Whistling Sam.

White (color)
Berry. Green and White.
Carew. Red and White Roses.
Creeley. Blue.
Gift, The.
Dickey, James. Expanses.
Donne. Oh my black[e] soul[e]! now thou art summoned.
Dunn. Whiteness.
Eberhart. Emblem.
Fisher. White Cloud, White Blossom.
Fox. Alkaid.
Blanc de Blanc.
White and the River.
Hartley. Wingaersheek Beach.
Herrick. To Electra.
Hesketh. Emily Dickinson.
Hewitt. April Awake.
Grey and White.
Hughes, Langston. Angels Wings.
Levertov. Wings, The.
Liddy. White Thought in a White Shade, A.
Lowry. About Ice.
And now the seagulls feed on the front porch.
Courage is not standing on the crosstrees.
I am speeding through the northern lights.
Matthews. Spring Snow.
Meinke. Liquid Paper.
Rossetti. Ballad: "Soft white lamb in the daisy meadow."
They Shall Be as White as Snow.
Whitsun Eve.
Sandburg. Clean Curtains.
March of the Hungry Mountains.
Schuyler. White.
Simic. What the White Had to Say.
White.
Smith, Patti. Judith Revisited.
Sorrentino. 16 Lines.
Walcott. Goats and Monkeys.
Williams, Charles Kenneth. Fast Food.

Whitefield, George
Davie. Homage to George Whitefield.
Whittier. Preacher, The.

Whitman, Walt
Berrigan. Whitman in Black.
Bukowski. When the Berry Bush Dies I'll Swim Down the Green River with My Hair on Fire.
Carruth. There! Whitman's skull—.
Crane. Cape Hatteras.
Eberhart. Emerson's Concord.
Ferlinghetti. Poem for Old Walt.
Fletcher. Whitman.
Ford. He Cut His Finger on Eternity.
Gallagher. Simple Sonatina.
Ginsberg. Supermarket in California, A.
Hoffman. Crossing Walt Whitman Bridge.
Hughes, Langston. Old Walt.
Liddy. Cantico.
Lowry. Port has a sweeter name than Saigon, The.
Thing to know is how to write a verse, The.
MacLeish. In and Come In.
Meredith. Orson of the Muse, An.
Pound. Pact, A.
Smith, Stevie. Dear Karl.
Tomlinson. Crossing Brooklyn Ferry.
Whitman. Now Precedent Songs, Farewell.

Williams, William Carlos. End of the Rope, The.

Whitsunday. *see* **Pentecost.**

Whittier, John Greenleaf
Dunbar. Whittier.
Koch. You Were Wearing.
Whitman. As the Greek's Signal Flame.

Widows and Widowers
Atwood. At first I was given centuries.
Auden. Miner's Wife, The.
Betjeman. Variation on a Theme by Newbolt.
Burns. Highland Widow's Lament, The.
Carew. To the Countess of Anglesey.
Crashaw. Old Widow[e]'s Mites, The.
Davie. Two Widows in Tashkent.
Widowers.
De la Mare. Juliet's Nurse.
Widow, The.
Dobyns. Footstep.
Glück. Racer's Widow, The.
Hall. Widows, The.
Hardy. At the Draper's.
In a London Flat.
Memorial Brass, The: 186–.
Rash Bride, The.
Widow Betrothed, The.
Heaney. Afterwards, An.
Hemingway. Poem to Miss Mary.
Herrick. Upon an Old Woman.
Upon Hanch a Schoolmaster.
Widow's Tears [or Widdowes Teares]: or, Dirge of Dorcas, The.
Hesketh. Dilemma.
Widowhood.
Hewitt. My Grandmother's Restlessness.
My Widowed Mother.
Hughes, Langston. Widow Woman.
Hugo. Letter to Annick from Boulder.
Jarrell. Burning the Letters.
Widow's Song, The.
Jonson. Epigram. To the Honoured——, Countess of——, An.
Kipling. Akbar's Bridge.
Widower, The.
Kooser. Widow, A.
Lowell. For Sale.
Merton. Widow of Naim, The.
Milton. Sonnet 23: "Mee thought I saw my late espoused saint."
Nathan. Widowhood.
Plath. Widow.
Robinson. Book of Annandale, The.
Roethke. Ballad of the Clairvoyant Widow.
Rossetti. Our Widowed Queen.
Shakespeare. Sonnet 9: "Is it for fear to wet a widow's eye."
Simic. Whispers in the Next Room.
Smith, Stevie. Autumn.
Silence and Tears.
Widowhood or The Home-Coming of Lady Ross.
Stuart. Widow, The.
Swift. Fable of the Widow and Her Cat, A.
Thomson. Sent to George Lyttleton, Esq., Soon After the Death of His Wife.
Williams, Miller. And Then.
Widow, The.
Williams, William Carlos. Widow's Lament in Springtime, The.
Wordsworth. To a Sexton.
Widow on Windmere Side, The.

Wight, Isle of, England
Tennyson. At Farringford.
November in the Isle of Wight.

Wigs
"Carroll, Lewis." Majesty of Justice, The.
Cowper. On an Old Woman.

Wilberforce, William
Cowper. Sonnet to Wilberforce.

Wilde, Oscar
Betjeman. Arrest of Oscar Wilde at the Cadogan Hotel, The.
Liddy. Your Pleasure in my Cemetery.
Lowry. Soul, The.

Wildebeests. *see* **Gnus.**

Wilderness
Atwood. Further Arrivals.
Journey to the Interior.
Berry. His love returns / and walks among the trees.
Homecoming, A.
Look in / and see him looking out.
Peace of Wild Things, The.
Setting Out.
Boyle. For an American.
Clark. Door to the Forest, The.
Fireflies.
Eberhart. Fisher Cat, The.
Old Dichotomy: Choosing Sides.
Wild Life and Tamed Life.
Emerson. Comrade of the snow & wind.
I to my garden went.
Everson. High Embrace, The.
Fox. Ovid.
Gardner. Part of the Darkness.
Graves. In the Wilderness.
Rocky Acres.
Hopkins. Wildness.
Jeffers. Last Conservative, The.
Morro Bay.
Kinnell. Lastness.
Under the Maud Moon.
Kipling. Pelicans in the Wilderness (A Grave near Halfa).
Lorde. Song: "Wild trees have bought me."
Lowry. Welcome Home Oh Most Loved and Famed Harteebeeste.
Milton. So spake our morning star then in his rise.
Nemerov. Two Poems.
Pack. Waterfall.
Patchen. Sovereign of the wilderness!
Rexroth. Living Pearl, A.
Robinson. Wilderness, The.
Sandburg. Wilderness.
Yes, the Dead Speak to Us.
Shelton. Requiem for Sonora.
Snyder. Above Pate Valley.
Arktos.
At Tower Peak.
Elk Trails.
Message from Outside.
Straight-Creek—Great Burn.
Stafford. In Fur.
Warren. Sound of That Wind, The.
Whitman. Italian Music in Dakota.
Spirit That Form'd This Scene.
Wilbur. Castles and Distances.
Williams, William Carlos. Song: "I'd rather read an account."
Wright, James. Nature Alive.

Wildflowers
Blake. Wild Flower's Song, The.
Levine. Across the world / in the high mountains of the West.
Lowry. Isle of Man Wildflowers.
Melville. Field Asters.
Paley. Then the flowers became very wild.
Sandburg. Windflower Leaf.
Smith, Charlotte. Close of Summer, The.
Heath, The.
Wild Flowers.
Tomlinson. Under the Bridge.
Williams, William Carlos. Queen-Anne's-Lace.
Wildflower, The.

William III, King of England (William of Orange)
Byron. Conquest, The.

William of Orange. *see* **William III, King of England (William of Orange).**

Williams, William Carlos
Berg. William Carlos Williams Reading His Poems.
Berrigan. In Joe Brainard's collage its white arrow.
Boyle. For Marianne Moore's Birthday.
Statement for El Greco and William Carlos Williams, A.
Two Twilights for William Carlos Williams.
United States, The.
Carruth. Fourth.

Creeley. For W.C.W. ("Pleasure of the wit sustains, The").
For W.C.W. ("Rhyme is after, The").
Eberhart. Mystery of the Abstract.
To William Carlos Williams.
Ginsberg. Death News.
Hoffman. Words for Dr. Williams.
Kinnell. To William Carlos Williams.
Koch. Variations on a Theme by William Carlos Williams.
Levertov. September 1961.
Lowell. William Carlos Williams.
Rexroth. Letter to William Carlos Williams, A.
Stevens. Nuances of a Theme by Williams.
Zukofsky. William Carlos Williams Alive!

Willow Herbs
Herrick. Willow Garland, The.

Willow Trees
Bly. Hunting Pheasants in a Cornfield.
"Carroll, Lewis." Willow-Tree, The.
Crane. Repose of Rivers.
De la Mare. Willow, The.
Herrick. To the Willow-Tree.
Levertov. Willows of Massachusetts, The.
"MacDiarmid." Sauchs in the Reuch Heuch Hauch, The.
Merrill. Willow.
Pack. Thrasher in the Willow by the Lake, The.
Rossetti. In the Willow Shade.
Under the ivy bush / One sits sighing.
Sandburg. Prairie Waters by Night.
Williams, William Carlos. Epitaph; "Old willow with hollow branches, An."
Willow Poem.
Wright, James. Elegy in a Firelit Room.

Wills
Boyle. Funeral in Hungary.
Clough. Like one that in a dream would fain arise.
Coleridge. Epitaphium Testamentarium.
Dickinson. To fulfill the will of a powerless friend.
Donne. Disinherited.
Will, The.
Eberhart. And the first, the father, with indomitable will.
Hewitt. Braes O' Layde, The.
Kinnell. In the Twentieth Century of my trespass on earth.
Kipling. *Mary Gloster*, The.
Larkin. Last Will and Testament.
Lewis. Bequest.
Merrill. Will, The.
Rossetti. Bruised Reed Shall He Not Break, A.
Schuyler. Earth's Holocaust.
Williams, Miller. For Lucinda, Robert, and Karyn.

Wilmot, John, 2d Earl of Rochester. *see* **Rochester, John Wilmot, 2d Earl of.**

Wilson, Woodrow
Jeffers. Wilson in Hell.
Woodrow Wilson.

Wiltshire, England
Davie. Wiltshire.

Winchester, England
Betjeman. Hike on the Downs, A.
Cowper. Elegy 3: On the Death of the Bishop of Winchester.
Milton. Elegy 3: On the Death of the Bishop of Winchester.

Wind
Ammons. Meeting the Opposition.
Reorganization.
Scour, The.
Small Song.
Still Frame.
Auden. Lost Secret, The.
March Winds.
Winds.
Beckett. Enueg I.
Berrigan. Each tree stands alone in stillness.
Berry. Birth (Near Port William), The.
We pile the brush high.

Bogan. Zone.
Brontë. Night Wind, The.
Sun Has Set, The.
Wind, I hear it sighing, The.
Browning, Robert. Englishman in Italy, The.
Campion. Peaceful Western Wind, The.
Carew. Prayer to the Wind, A.
Carruth. Aer.
Again on dark looms.
Continuo.
Snow / ice / bitter wind.
Then from beyond, from nowhere, from the wilderness.
This wind this / screaming parrot.
What does this wind say, plunging upon the land.
Clark. Day Detail—Low Light of Afternoon.
Coleridge. Death Wish, A.
Homeric Hexameter, The.
Cooper. Jittoku, Buddhist Mystic—15th Century.
Crane. Persuasion, A.
Creeley. Hart Crane 2.
Hélas.
Still Life Or.
Wind, The.
Cummings. Painted wind has sprung, A.
What if a much of a which of a wind.
Wind has blown the rain away and blown, A.
Wind is a Lady with, The.
Davie. Aubade: "I wish for you that when you wake."
Conditioned Air, A.
Wind at Penistone, The.
De la Mare. Echo.
Dickinson. Duties of the Wind are few, The.
How lonesome the Wind must feel Nights.
How slow the Wind.
I saw the wind within her.
I think that the Root of the Wind is Water.
South Wind—has a pathos, A.
Spry Arms of the Wind, The.
There came a Wind like a Bugle.
Wind begun to knead the Grass, The.
Wind—tapped like a tired Man, The.
Wind that rose, A.
Wind took up the Northern Things, The.
Doolittle. Sea-Choros.
Wind Sleepers, The.
Dunbar. Chase, The.
Plantation Child's Lullaby, The.
Till the Wind Gets Right.
Wind and the Sea, The.
Dunn. Wind in a Jar.
"Dylan." Blowin' in the Wind.
Eberhart. Listing.
Eliot. Wind Sprang Up at Four o'Clock, The.
Emerson. Bird was gone the ghastly trees, The.
God only knew how Saadi dined.
Heartily heartily / Nothing be false.
I sat upon the ground.
In this sour world, o summerwind.
O'er the garden water goes the wind alone.
Roguish wind and I, The.
Snow-Storm, The.
Treacherous wind pipes a lewd song, The.
Winds are cold, the days are dark, The.
Fisher. Wind at Night, The.
Fletcher. Flickering of incessant rain.
From the Chinese.
From the Japanese, IV.
Gale, The.
Lines Written at Taormina, Sicily.
Midwinter Sunset.
Night Wind, The.
Voices on the Wind.
Frost. Aim Was Song, The.
Brown's Descent; or, The Willy-Nilly.
To the Thawing Wind.
Wind and Window Flower.
Graves. Arrow on the Vane.
East Wind, An.
Falcon Woman, The.
Sirocco at Deyá.
Weather of Olympus, The.

Griffiths. Decision.
Island with Army, Pines and Wind.
Gunn. At the Back of the North Wind.
Cat and the Wind, The.
Conversation of Old Men, The.
Elegy on the Dust.
Exercise, The.
Sketch of the Great Dejection, A.
Hacker. Languedocienne.
Haines. On the Road.
Hall. To the Loud Wind.
Hardy. Wind's Prophecy, The.
Hartley. Les Baux.
Hesketh. After Verlaine.
Imprint.
Naked Ostrich.
Roots.
Hewitt. Autumn Gale.
Bandstand.
Bell, The.
Matin sur le Port.
Providence 1.
Rotterdam.
Sonnet: "There in the lonely quarry where at dawn."
Hopkins. Wind, that passes by so fleet, The.
Housman. Winds out of the west land blow, The.
Hughes, Ted. Wind.
Wind Flashes the Grass, A.
Hugo. Birthday.
Dog Lake with Paula.
Spinazzola: Quella Cantina Là.
Jeffers. Gale in April.
Joseph. Certain Weathers.
Kipling. Dawn Wind, The.
Fires, The.
Thorkild's Song.
Koch. West Wind.
Kooser. In an Old Apple Orchard.
There Is Always a Little Wind.
Larkin. Climbing the Hill within the Deafening Wind.
Portrait.
Who Whistled for the Wind, That It Should Break.
Lawrence. At the Window.
Birdcage Walk.
Suspense.
Wind, the Rascal, The.
Levine. Voice, The.
Lindsay. Wizard Wind, The.
Lorde. Blackstudies.
Bloodbirth.
Lowell. These Winds.
Lowry. Ballad: "Twas in the springtime of the year."
Black thunderclouds mass up against the wind.
Bright as the Pleiades Upon the Soul.
Iphigenia in Aulis. Agamemnon Speaks:.
Morning bird is bathing, The.
Very dark and clear with an onshore wind.
With Sweetest Morning Love to Their Beloved Harteebeeste.
"MacDiarmid." Moment in Eternity, A.
MacLeish. Linden Trees, The.
Mistral Over the Graves.
MacNeice. Nocturne: "Dark blood of night-time, The."
Sleeping Winds.
Mahon. North Wind: Portrush.
Meredith. Inspiration of the Great West Wind, The.
Song: "O the wind, the wind, the wind doth blow."
South-West Wind in the Woodland.
Stave of Roving Tim, A.
Wind & sea are as playmates.
Merrill. House, The.
Millay. I woke in the night and heard the wind, and it blowing half a gale.
Miller. Wind, The.
Morrison. Maids Are Bickering.
Muldoon. Wind and Tree.
Nash. Word on Wind, A.
Neruda. Heavy Surf, A.
O'Hara. To Hell with It.

Oppen. That come before the swallow dares.
West.
Pack. Still Passing.
Raine. Lifelong ago such days.
Summit, The.
Wind.
Winds.
Ralegh. Joyfull Spring did ever last, The.
Roethke. Big Wind.
Mid-Country Blow.
Song: "From whence cometh song?"
Words for the Wind.
Rossetti. Hollow-Sounding and Mysterious.
Mirrors of Life and Death.
O wind, where have you been.
O wind, why do you never rest.
Playing at bob cherry / Tom and Nell and
Hugh.
Song of Flight, A.
Who Has Seen the Wind?
Wind has such a rainy sound, The.
Sandburg. Baby Song of the Four Winds.
Bitter Summer Thoughts—No. 3.
Blossom Themes.
Changing Light Winds.
Corn Prattlings.
Dan.
Evening Sea Wind.
Field People.
Four Preludes on Playthings of the Wind.
Head.
How Yesterday Looked.
Landscape.
Man and Dog on an Early Winter Morning.
Meadow in Summer.
Never Two Songs the Same.
North Atlantic.
Rain Winds Blow Doors Open.
Ripe Corn.
Sand Scribblings.
Sleep Impression.
Spring Wind.
Whirls.
Wind carves sand into shapes, The.
Wind on the Way, The.
Wind Song.
Windflower Leaf.
Windy City, The.
Schuyler. Day, The.
Evening Wind.
Shelley. Dirge, A: "Rough wind, that moanest
loud."
Shelton. Sonora.
Simic. Two Riddles.
Smith, Charlotte. To the Winds.
Smith, Stevie. When the Wind.
Stafford. Wind World.
Stevens. Chaos in Motion and Not in Motion.
How to Live. What to Do.
Page from a Tale.
To the Roaring Wind.
Valley Candle.
Wind Shifts, The.
Stevenson. English Breeze, An.
It blows a snowing gale in the winter of the
year.
Storm.
Wind, The.
Windy Nights.
Tomlinson. At the Hill Fort.
Embassy.
Insufficiency of Earth, An.
Wind.
Updike. Wind.
Wakoski. Wind Secrets.
Warren. Blow, West Wind.
Wind.
Whitman. To the Sun-set Breeze.
Wilbur. Agrigentum Road, The.
From the Lookout Rock.
Poplar, Sycamore.
Regatta, The.
Sleepless at Crown Point.
Williams, Charles Kenneth. Listen carefully. /
I'm meditating.
Williams, William Carlos. Black Winds, The.
January.

Porous.
Wind Increases, The.
Winds, The.
Wordsworth. Flower Garden at Coleorton Hall,
Leicestershire, A.
September, 1815.
There was a spot.
Wright, James. Autumnal.
Listening to the Mourners.
Spring Images.
Two Spring Charms.
Zukofsky. Cars once steel and green, now old.
Close your eyes.
Wire.

See also **North Wind; Tornadoes; West Wind.**
Windflowers. *see* **Anemones.**
Windhovers. *see* **Falcons.**

Windmills
Fletcher. Windmills, The.
Hall. Swan.

Window Washing and Window Washers
Hartley. Window Cleaner to Nude Manikin.
Window Washer—Avenue C.
Hayden. Performers, The.
Simic. Window Washer.

Windows
Beckett. Rentrer / À la nuit.
Berry. Cold Pane, The.
Foliage has dropped, The.
His mind gone from the window.
How fine / to have a long-legged house.
Longest night is past, The.
Look in / and see him looking out.
Now that April with sweet rain.
Outside the window.
Rising, the river.
River is rising, The.
Still sleeping, he heard.
Sycamore gathers / out of the sky, white, The.
There is a sort of vertical.
This is the wind's eye.
Warm day in December, A.
Window grows fragile, The.
Window has forty, The.
Window. Window. / The wind's eye.
Bukowski. Liberty.
Carruth. Window / the icicle / the gleaming
moon, The.
Cowper. Lines Written upon a Window-
Shutter at Weston.
Creeley. Box, The.
Goodbye.
Poem for D. H. Lawrence.
Cummings. You / in win / ter who sit.
Donne. Valediction, A: Of My Name in the
Window.
Fisher. Mounted on all four walls, the neat.
Haines. Door turned its white face, A.
Hardy. Love Watches a Window.
Knott. (Poem): "Like a room."
Koch. Simplicity of the Unknown Past, The.
Levertov. Crack, The.
Lindsay. Factory Windows Are Always
Broken.
Longfellow. Ropewalk, The.
Lowry. Windows from a Machine Shop.
Patchen. Opening the Window.
Sandburg. Clean Curtains.
Foolish About Windows.
Panels.
Schuyler. In Wiry Winter.
Silverstein. My Hobby.
Simic. Window Washer.
Tomlinson. Poem: "Space / window / that
looks into itself."
View, The.
Warren. Problem in Spatial Composition, A.
Williams, Miller. Evening: A Studio in Rome.
Williams, William Carlos. Young Woman at a
Window.
Young. October Window.

Windsor Forest, England
Pope. Windsor-Forest [*or* Windsor Forest].
Wine
Bogan. To Wine.
Browning, Elizabeth Barrett. Wine of Cyprus.

Bunting. Light of my eyes, there *is* something
to be said.
Byron. Fill high the bowl with Samian wine!
Cowper. Elegy 6: To Charles Deodati.
Crashaw. To Our Lord, upon the Water Made
Wine.
Doolittle. Wine Bowl.
Dove. Champagne.
Emerson. Bacchus.
Borrow Urania's subtile wings.
Boy bring the bowl full of wine.
Bring wine release me.
Builder of heaven, The.
By art, by music, overthrilled.
Come!—the palace of heaven rests on aëry
pillars.
Drink wine, and the heaven.
For his constant dwelling place has Hafiz.
Friends to me are frozen wine.
From the Persian of Hafiz.
I will be drunk and down with wine.
Lo! where from Heaven's high roof.
On a raisin stone.
Pour the wine! pour the wine!
Reach me wine No counsel weakens the
conclusion of the lot.
She had wealth of mornings in her year.
So long as there's a trace.
To be wise the dull brain so earnestly throbs.
Wine resembles the Lord Jesus.
Herrick. Anacrontik Verse.
Bachanalian Verse, A.
His Farewell [*or* Fare-well] to Sack.
How He Would Drinke His Wine.
Ode to Sir Clipsebie Crew, An.
To Live Merrily, and To Trust to Good
Verses.
To Youth.
Upon Vinegar.
Welcome to Sack, The.
Hopkins. Barnfloor and Winepress.
Hugo. Cantina Iannini.
Jonson. Dedication of the King's New Cellar.
To Bacchus, The.
Epigram. To the Household. 1630, An.
Swell me a bowl with lusty wine.
Kooser. How to Make Rhubarb Wine.
Liddy. Vir II.
Lindsay. On Reading Omar Khayyam.
What Semiramis Said.
Lovelace. Being treated to Ellinda.
Fly about a Glass[e] of Burnt Claret, A.
Loose Saraband, A: ("Nay, prethee [*or* prithee]
dear, draw nigher").
Of a Drunkard.
Vintage to the Dungeon, The.
Melville. Vine and Clarel.
Millay. Wine from These Grapes.
Milton. Bacchus.
Elegy 6: To Charles Deodati.
Moore. Camellia Sabina.
Piercy. Gift of Light, A.
Ralegh. I have no wine of Gaza, nor Falerna
wine.
Rukeyser. Neruda, the Wine.
Schuyler. This Soft October.
Shelley. Fragment: Wine of the Fairies.
Suckling. Hall, a hall, A.
Tate. Progress of Œnia, The.
Updike. Pale Bliss.
Wilbur. Wedding Toast, A.
Yeats. Drinking Song, A.
Zukofsky. To My Baby Paul.

Wings
"Carroll, Lewis." Canto III: Scarmoges.
Dickey, James. Moon Flock.
Dickinson. Hours have Wings.
Herbert. Easter Wings.
Hopkins. Ecquis Binas.
Lindsay. How the Wings Were Made.
Indian Girl Who Made Them, The.
Lowry. Simple Seabird's Tribute to Her
Harteebeeste, A.
Waldman. Leonardo.
Wright, James. To the August Fallen.

Winter
Ammons. Around Here.

Angelou. This Winter Day.
Atwood. Midwinter, Presolstice.
Auden. Alone.
  Dark Fiddler, The.
  Frost.
  Winter Afternoon.
Beckett. Vive morte ma seule saison.
Berg. Sketch.
Berry. Boone.
  Cold, The.
  Companions, The.
  Dance, A.
  Elegy: "All day our eyes could find no resting
    place."
  February 2, 1968.
  Finches, The.
  Foliage has dropped, The.
  He has known a tunnel.
  Longest night is past, The.
  Winter Nightfall.
Berryman. Bell to sore knees vestigial crowds,
  let crush.
  Winter-Piece to a Friend Away, A.
Bishop. Colder the Air, The.
  Paris, 7 A.M.
Blake. Song 3rd By an Old Shepherd.
  To Winter.
Bly. Six Winter Privacy Poems.
  Three Kinds of Pleasures.
Boyle. And Winter.
  Christmas Carol for Emanuel Carnevali, A.
  Cloak for a Man Who Has No Heed for
    Winter, A.
  O This Is Not Spring.
  Valentine for Harry Crosby, A.
  Winter Fable, A.
Brontë. Castle Wood.
  I.M. to I.G.
  Upon her soothing breast.
Burns. Auld Man's Winter Thought, The.
  Cauld Is the E'enin Blast.
  Gloomy December.
  Impomptu, on Mrs. W. Riddell's Birthday, 4th
    Novr. 1793.
  Song: "On Cessnock banks a lassie dwells."
  Up in the Morning Early.
  Winter, a Dirge.
  Winter Night, A.
Campion. Ad nobiliss. virum Gul. Percium.
  Now Winter Nights Enlarge.
Carroll, Jim. Invisible Sleep.
  Loft, The.
  Winter's Age.
  You hear the call.
"Carroll, Lewis." Three Children.
Carruth. Book, The.
  December now. Winter deepens and darkens.
  Stars.
  I know there is a country where we go.
  Mild Winter.
  North Winter.
  Snow, The.
  Tanck's Epilogue.
  To Artemis.
  Twilight Comes.
Ceravolo. Contrast.
Clare. Impromptu on Winter.
  January: A Winters Day.
  Winter Evening.
Clark. "First cold winter twilights."
Cohen. Dark at Four O'Clock.
  Marvellous Woman, A.
Cooper. Feathers.
  No More Elegies.
Cowper. Winter Evening, The.
Crane. This Way Where November.
Creeley. Interview, The.
  Irishman's Lament on the Approaching Winter,
    An.
  Something for Easter.
Cummings. 1.4: "Fetters of winter are
    shattered,shatter, The."
  Ballade: "White night roared with a huge
    north-wind, The."
  "But / he" i / staring / into winter twi.
  Enter no(silence is the blood whose flesh).
  Glory is fallen out of, The.

I was sitting in mcsoreley's.   outside it was
  New York and beauti- / fully snowing.
Infinite jukethrob smoke & swallow to dis.
Moon-lit snow is falling like strange candy
  into the big eyes of the, The.
N / Umb a / stree / t's wintr.
Nor woman / (just as it be).
Numb(and / that was).
Skating.
Will suddenly trees leap up from winter and
  will.
You / in win / ter who sit.
Davie. January.
  Westmorland.
  Winter Talent, A.
  Winter's Talents.
De la Mare. Alone.
  Fairy in Winter, The.
  Tryst, The.
  Winter.
  Winter.
Dickey, James. To Be Done in Winter.
Dickey, William. More Under Saturn.
Dickinson. Conjecturing a Climate.
  How luscious is the dripping.
  I remember the leaves were falling.
  Jay his Castanet has struck, The.
  No event of Wind or Bird.
  Not at Home to Callers.
  These are the days that Reindeer love.
  This is a stern Winter.
  'Twas here my summer paused.
  Winter is good—his Hoar Delights.
  Winter under cultivation.
  Winters are so short, The.
Dobyns. Song for Making the Birds Come.
Donne. Nocturnal[l] upon Saint Lucy's [or S.
  Lucies] Day, Being the Shortest Day, A.
Doolittle. Blue-geese, white-geese, you may
  say.
Dove. November for Beginners.
  Snow King, The.
Dunbar. Jack Frost at Bedtime.
  Plantation Child's Lullaby, The.
  Warm Day in Winter, A.
  When Winter Darkening All Around.
  Winter-Song.
  Winter's Approach.
  Winter's Day, A.
Dunn. Kindness.
  "Dylan." Winterlude.
Eberhart. Christmas Tree.
  Commas in Wintertime.
  Emblem.
  Homage to the North.
  Man of Autumn, The.
  Snow Cascades.
  Spider, The.
Eliot. Little Gidding.
Emerson. Seemed, tho' the soft sheen all
  enchants.
  Titmouse, The.
Fletcher. From the Japanese, II.
  From the Japanese, V.
  Grey Symphony.
  November Days.
  Symphony of Snow.
  White Symphony.
Ford. Theatre of winter, The.
Fox. Ice Fishing.
  White and the River.
Frost. Birches.
  Good Hours.
  Hillside Thaw, A.
  My Butterfly.
  Old Man's Winter Night, An.
  Onset, The.
  Reluctance.
  Stopping by Woods on a Snowy Evening.
  To a Moth Seen in Winter.
  Winter Eden, A.
Glück. Early December in Croton-on-Hudson.
  Illuminations.
  Saturnalia.
Graves. Frosty Night, A.
  Mid-Winter Waking.
Gunn. At the Back of the North Wind.

Hacker. Christmas Crown, A.
Haines. End of the Street, The.
  Snowy Night.
  Winter News.
Hall. Stump.
Hardy. At Middle-Field Gate in February.
  Birds at Winter Nightfall.
  Faithful Swallow, The.
  Farm-Woman's Winter, The.
  Frozen Greenhouse, The.
  I Need Not Go.
  Ice on the Highway.
  Music in a Snowy Street.
  Neutral Tones.
  Prospect, The.
  Robin, The.
  Spellbound Palace, A.
  Unrealized.
  Winter in Durnover Field.
  Winter Night in Woodland.
Hartley. Watching.
Hartnett. Mo Ghrá Thú.
Hayden. Those Winter Sundays.
Heaney. Sweeney's Lament on Alisa Craig.
Hesketh. Invitation.
  Letter to Vincent.
  Meths Men, The.
  No Reply at Christmas.
  Owl.
  Winter Daffodils.
Hewitt. For a Mild Season.
  Winter Day ("From the first").
  Winter Day ("When sun was").
Hoffman. February.
  Thaw.
Holmes. Cold Window.
Hopkins. Winter with the Gulf Stream.
Housman. In midnights of November.
Hughes, Langston. Midwinter Blues.
Hughes, Ted. Couples Under Cover.
  Roe-Deer.
  Snowdrop.
Hugo. Letter to Hill from St. Ignatius.
  Letter to Scanlon from Whitehall.
  Orcas in the Eyes.
  Reconsidering the Madman.
Jarrell. Northern Snows, The.
  Windows.
  Winter's Tale, The.
Johnson. Winter's Walk, The.
Jong. January in New York.
  New England Winter.
Jonson. Elegy, An: "Since you must go, and I
    must bid farewell."
Joseph. Anthropomorphism Reversed.
  Getting Up in Winter.
  Puppeteer.
  Road from Glastonbury, The.
  To Keep Each Other Warm.
  Unlooked-For Season, The.
Keats. In Drear-nighted December.
Kinnell. Bear, The.
  Two Seasons.
  Winter Sky, A.
Knight. Indianapolis Winter, 1973.
Knott. Widower's Winter.
Kooser. Dry Winter Letter to Friends, A.
  First Snow.
  Walking Beside a Creek.
Larkin. And Now the Leaves Sudddenly Lose
    Strength.
  Gathering Wood.
  Slight Relax of Air Where Cold Was, A.
  Winter.
  Winter Nocturne.
Lawrence. Drained Cup, The.
  Parliament Hill in the Evening.
  To Clarinda.
  Winter in the Boulevard.
  Winter-Lull.
Levertov. Crack, The.
Levine. On the Birth of Good & Evil During
  the Long Winter of '28.
  Walk with Tom Jefferson, A.
Lewis. Mid-Winter.
Lindsay. Sweetheart Winter.
Longfellow. Snow-Flakes.

Lorde. Cables To Rage Or I've Been Talking On This Street Corner.
Father, the Year Has Fallen.
Woman Thing, The.
Lowell. Inauguration Day: January 1953.
Lowry. Fragment: "Dead tree that, frozen, utters at the top, The."
Platinum sun rising. / Platinum frost on porch.
Walk in Canada.
"MacDiarmid." Lourd on My Hert.
McGrath. Black Train, The.
Don't Think You Know My Name!
Face of the Precipice is Black with Lovers, The.
Melville. Apathy and Enthusiasm.
Meredith. Death of Winter, The.
Or the single path— / Which the cool moon sheds.
Parody of Alfred Austin.
Time.
Merton. Early Blizzard.
Evening: Zero Weather.
Love Winter When the Plant Says Nothing.
Messenger, The.
Regret, The.
Winter Afternoon.
Winter's Night, The.
Millay. Winter Night.
Miller. For Barbara.
Winter Dawn.
Morgan. Beginning is a cold wind, The.
Winter Poem.
Nash. Summergreen for President.
Word about Winter, A.
Nathan. Audit.
Haakon Jarl.
Master of the Winter Landscape, The.
Winter Morning of the Village.
Nemerov. Central Park.
First Snow.
From a Record of Disappointment.
Rent in the Screen, The.
Spell before Winter, A.
Winter Exercise.
Neruda. Winter.
O'Hara. Music.
Poem: "I watched an armory combing its bronze bricks."
Poem In January.
Oliver. Winter in the Country.
Wolf Moon.
Olson. Personality and dourness of winter, The.
Song, The: "More than the sennet of the solstice pipe."
Winter After, The.
Winter Solstice.
Oppen. From a Photograph.
Owen. Exposure.
Paley. Winter Afternoon.
Patchen. Winter at the Inn.
Winter Poem.
Wolf of winter, The.
Piercy. Breaking Camp.
Butt of Winter, The.
Longest Night, The.
Skimpy Day at the Solstice.
Plath. By Candlelight.
Magnolia Shoals.
Private Ground.
Wintering.
Pope. Winter, the Fourth Pastoral, or Daphne.
Pound. Villonaud for This Yule.
Raine. Winter Paradise.
Winter Solstice.
Rich. Purely Local.
Roethke. Coming of the Cold, The.
Rolfe. Sixth Winter, The.
Where Buildings Congregate.
Rossetti. Amen.
Autumn.
Bread and Milk for Breakfast.
Crying, my little one, footsore and weary!
1885. St. Valentine's Day.
1886, St. Valentine's Day.
Endure Hardness.
Grown and Flown.

I dug and dug amongst the snow.
One Swallow Does Not Make a Summer.
St. Valentine's Day 1881.
Sir Winter.
Song: "Stream moaneth as it floweth, The."
Tempus Fugit.
There Is a Budding Morrow in Midnight.
There's Snow on the Fields.
Where shall I find a white rose blowing?
Winter: My Secret.
Wintry Sonnet, A.
Rukeyser. Certain Music, A.
Flashing Cliff, A.
Sandburg. Aloof.
Blossom Themes.
Haze Gold.
Hemlock and Cedar.
Man and Dog on an Early Winter Morning.
Winter Gold.
Winter Weather.
Sarton. First Snow.
House in Winter, The.
On a Winter Night.
Snow Light, The.
Winter Carol.
Schuyler. Deep Winter.
Empathy and New Year.
In January.
Schwartz. Poem: "Window winter."
Sexton. Landscape Winter.
Shelley. Dirge for the Year.
Summer and Winter.
Shelton. Winter.
Silverstein. Snowman.
Simic. February.
Winter Night.
Smith, Charlotte. Laplander, The.
To a Geranium Which Flowered during the Winter.
Written at Weymouth in Winter.
Snyder. Thin Ice.
Sorrentino. Shapes of Winter.
Spender. Ice.
Stafford. Sayings from the Northern Ice.
Stevens. Meditation Celestial & Terrestrial.
No Possum, No Sop, No Taters.
Poesie Abrutie.
Snow Man, The.
Stevenson. Epistle to Charles Baxter.
Ille Terrarum.
In the green and gallant Spring.
Picture-Books in Winter.
Summer sun shone round me, The.
Winter.
Winter Time [or Winter-Time].
Sutter. Hoarfrost and Fog.
Tate. In Wintertime.
Tennyson. Song: "Spirit haunts the last year's hours, A."
Thomas. Hold Hard, These Ancient Minutes in the Cuckoo's Month.
Winter's Tale, A.
Thomson. Now, when the cheerless empire of the sky.
To Mr. Thomson, on his Blooming Winter.
Tomlinson. Fox, The.
In Winter Woods.
Maine Winter.
Nine Variations in a Chinese Winter Setting.
Snow Fences, The.
Winter.
Winter Encounters.
Winter-Piece.
Updike. Late January.
Winter Ocean.
Working Outdoors in Winter.
Van Duyn. Two Poems for Sub-Zero Times.
Wakoski. Winter Ode.
Winter Poem for Tony Weinburger Written on the Occassion of Feeling Very Happy, A.
Walcott. Love in the Valley.
Warren. Answer to Prayer.
Time as Hypnosis.
Whitman. Sounds of the Winter.
Whittier. Flowers in Winter.
Frost Spirit, The.
Letter to Lucy Larcom.

Pressed Gentian, The.
Red Riding-Hood.
Snow-Bound [or Snow-Bound; a Winter Idyl].
To E. C. S.
Winter Roses.
Wilbur. April 5, 1974.
Courtyard Thaw, A.
Orchard Trees, January.
Sonnet.
Storm in April, A.
Two Songs in a Stanza of Beddoes'.
Winter Spring.
Year's End.
Williams, Charles Kenneth. Reading: Winter.
That night, / winter, / rain.
Winter, / damn, / again.
Williams, Miller. Waiting for the Paper to be Delivered.
Williams, William Carlos. Approach of Winter.
Arrival.
Bare Tree, The.
Birds and Flowers.
Cold Night, The.
December.
Descent of Winter, The.
Jersey Lyric.
Midwinter.
Soughing Wind, The.
These.
This Is Pioneer Weather.
To a Woodpecker.
Winter.
Winter Quiet.
Winter Trees.
Woodthrush, The.
Wordsworth. Composed Near Calais on the Road Leading to Ardres, August 7, 1802.
French Army in Russia 1812–1813, The.
On the Same Occasion.
Wright, James. Elegy in a Firelit Room.
Frontier, The.
I slouch in bed.
Late November in a Field.
Our Daily Bread.
Poor Washed Up by Chicago Winter, The.
Seasonless, The.
Sparrows in a Hillside Drift.
Winter Night, A.
Yeats. Withering of the Boughs, The.
Young. Ars Poetica.
Zukofsky. Home for Aged Bomb Throwers— U.S.S.R.
Run on, you still dead to the sound of a name.
Winters, Yvor
Gunn. To Yvor Winters, 1955.
Wisconsin (state)
Bly. Three Kinds of Pleasures.
Dickey, James. For the Death of Vince Lombardi.
Eberhart. La Crosse at Ninety Miles an Hour.
Wisdom
Arnold. Shakespeare.
Atwood. Procedures for Underground.
Beckett. Better on your arse than on your feet.
Berry. Heaviness of His Wisdom, The.
Blake. Voice of the Ancient Bard, The.
Browning, Elizabeth Barrett. Wisdom Unapplied.
Bukowski. Counsel.
Kings Are Gone, The.
Burns. Occasional Address, Spoken by Miss Fontenell, on Her Benefit-Night, Decr. 4th. 1793.—Written by Mr Burns.
Byron. R. C. Dallas.
Campion. Canto Quarto.
"Carroll, Lewis." Misunderstandings.
My First is singular at best.
When the King found that his money was nearly all.
Cowper. Prudent Simplicity.
When little more than boy in age.
Wisdom.
Crane. Praise for an Urn.
Creeley. Wisdom.
Cullen. Threnody for a Brown Girl.

Wisdom Cometh with the Years.
Wise, The.
Cummings. If up's the word;and a world grows greener.
May my heart always be open to little.
Sitting in a tree-.
There is a here and.
Who were so dark of heart they might not speak.
You shall above all things be glad and young.
Davie. Hot Hands.
Measured Tread, A.
Obiter Dicta.
De la Mare. Catechism, The.
In a Library.
Moonlight.
Dickinson. I worked for chaff and earning Wheat.
If the foolish, call them "flowers."
We learned the Whole of Love.
Donne. Temple.
Dunbar. At Cheshire Cheese.
"Dylan." In the Garden.
Eberhart. And the first, the father, with indomitable will.
My Golden and My Fierce Assays.
Mysticism Has Not the Patience To Wait for God's Revelation.
Sagacity.
Emerson. Art thou wise, four things resign.
He walked the streets of great New York.
Mask thy wisdom with delight.
O What have I to do.
Prudence.
To be wise the dull brain so earnestly throbs.
To transmute crime to wisdom, & to stem.
Whilst I disdain the populace.
Who knows this or that?
Whoso alas is young.
Everson. Wise, The.
Fox. Letter from the Snake Woman.
Frost. Boeotian.
Gardner. Collage of Echoes.
Graves. Myrrhina.
Within Reason.
Hacker. Rune of the Finland Woman.
Hardy. Child and the Sage, The.
Heaney. Master, The.
Hesketh. Truant.
Hewitt. Bleeze.
Once Alien Here.
Raindrop.
Response, The.
Sonnet: "Our love is full of memorable things."
Touch of Things, The.
When my wife's sister's husband came to die.
Jarrell. Head of Wisdom, The.
Jeffers. Come Little Birds.
Prescription of Painful Ends.
Wise Men in Their Bad Hours.
Jonson. Lord Bacon's Birthday.
Ode, An: "High-spirited friend, / I send not balms, nor corsives to your wound."
Kipling. King's Job, The.
Playmate, The.
Kooser. Sure Signs.
Lawrence. Fresh Water.
Race and Battle.
Salt of the Earth.
Lewis. *Merchants Wife, The.*
Mine Host.
Quest, The.
Lowry. Love and wisdom have no home.
Morning coat is walking, A.
MacLeish. No doubt he'd once had eyes to see.
With Age Wisdom.
Melville. Lone Founts.
Meredith. All other joys of life he strove to warm.
Discipline of Wisdom, The.
Earth and Man.
Earth's Secret.
I seize in a central knot.
In the Sap.
My Theme: Continued.

Reason.
Three Singers to Young Blood, The.
We need some rallying point round which.
Wisdom of Eld, The.
Merrill. World and the Child, The.
Yánnina.
Merton. Action and Non-Action.
Hagia Sophia.
Importance of Being Toothless, The.
Of all those discourses I have heard.
St. Alberic.
Way of man has no wisdom, but the way of God has, The.
Wholeness.
Wisdom.
Wisdom is one thing: it is to know the thought by which all things are steered through all things.
Nash. If Fun Is Fun, Isn't That Enough?
Sage of Darien, The.
Nemerov. Interview, An.
Olson. Christmas.
Dance, of the Grizzly Bear, The.
He, Who, in His Abandnoned Infancy, Spoke of Jesus, Caesar, Those Who Beg, and Hell.
In the Hills South of Capernaum, Port.
Oppen. Quotations.
Patchen. Lao Tsze.
Pope. Epistle I, to Sir Richard Temple, Lord Cobham.
Ralegh. From wisedome Fortune differs farre.
Ransom. Semi-Centennial.
Tall Girl, The.
To the Scholars of Harvard.
Robinson. Sage, The.
When one that you and I had all but sworn.
Rolfe. Brigadas Internacionales.
Rossetti. Answer, An.
Counterblast on Penny Trumpet.
Let Everything That Hath Breath Praise the Lord.
Love loveth Thee, and wisdom loveth Thee.
Passing and Glassing.
She Came from The Uttermost Part of the Earth.
To Lalla, Reading My Verses Topsy-Turvy.
Was Thy Wrath against the Sea?
Yea, the Sparrow Hath Found Her an House.
Sandburg. Brass Keys.
Crossing the Paces.
Gypsy.
Has-Been, The.
Is Wisdom a Lot of Language?
Jabberers.
Let Them Ask Your Pardon.
Three Fragments for Fishers of Destiny.
Smith, Charlotte. Dictatorial Owl, The.
Swallow, The.
Thirty-Eight (Addressed to Mrs. H----Y).
Smith, Stevie. Everything Is Swimming.
Homage to John Cowper Powys.
Is It Wise?
Portrait (II).
To Dean Inge Lecturing on Origen.
Snyder. There's a naked bug at Cold Mountain.
Spender. Auden at Milwaukee.
Swift. On Wisdom's Defeat in a Learned Debate.
Swinburne. At Eleusis.
Old Saying, An.
Thomas. Should Lanterns Shine.
Updike. Mountain Impasse.
Whitman. Song of Prudence.
When I Heard the Learn'd Astronomer.
Williams, Miller. Ruby Tells All.
Woman on the Porch, The.
Williams, William Carlos. Invitation.
Wordsworth. Lines: "Nay, Traveller! rest. This lonely Yew-tree stands."
Resolution and Independence.
Though narrow be that old Man's cares, and near.
Yeats. Another Song of a Fool.
Coming of Wisdom with Time, The.
Seven Sages, The.

See also **Reason; Libraries and Librarians.**

Wisemen. *see* **Magi.**

Wishes
Auden. Song of the Beggars.
Berry. Wish to Be Generous, The.
Carew. New Year's Gift. To the King, A.
Catullus. Carmen 31: "Apple of islands, Sirmio, & bright peninsulas, set."
Clare. "Poets are born"—and so are whores—the trade is.
Cowper. Poet's New-Year's Gift, The.
Creeley. Apple Uppfle.
For Rainer Gerhardt.
Fragments: "Decorous, and forbearing further correction."
Friend, The.
Going.
In London.
Picnic, The.
Song: "Were I myself more blithe."
Wish, A.
Cummings. Come a little further—why be afraid.
Luminous tendril of celestial wish.
O by the by / has anybody seen.
One day a nigger.
So many selves(so many fiends and gods).
Davie. Aubade: "I wish for you that when you wake."
New Year Wishes for the English.
Dunn. Something.
"Dylan." Forever Young.
Eberhart. Despair.
To Auden on His Fiftieth.
Verbalist of Summer, The.
Emerson. If wishes would carry me over the land.
Galvin. Willow, Wishbone, Warblers.
Ginsberg. What I'd Like to Do.
Graves. Richard Roe and John Doe.
Griffiths. Doors of the Year, Well Done, The.
Hardy. Catullus: XXXI.
Could I but Will.
Herrick. His Wish ("Fat be my Hinde").
Poets Good Wishes for the Most Hopefull and Handsome Prince, the Duke of Yorke, The.
Upon Batt.
Upon Gubbs.
Jarrell. Man in Majesty.
Man Meets a Woman in the Street, A.
Kunitz. Motion of Wish.
Larkin. Born Yesterday.
I Am Washed upon a Rock.
Lawrence. Labour Battalion.
Liddy. Prayers of a Pagan.
Translate into Latin for my Epitaph.
Lindsay. Aladdin and the Jinn.
Lowry. I do not wish to live.
Patchen. I Never Had Any Other Desire So Strong.
Rolfe. Cell, The.
Song for a Birth Day in Exile.
Rossetti. I planted a hand / And there came up a palm.
I wish I were a little bird.
Wishes: Sonnet.
Rukeyser. Course.
Sandburg. Ambassadors of Grief.
Do You Want Affidavits?
Good Night.
Mag.
Old Hokusai Print.
Poems Done on a Late Night Car.
Wanting the Impossible.
Wistful.
Shakespeare. On a day, alack the day!
Silverstein. Silver Fish, The.
Smith, Stevie. Dear Little Sirmio.
Stevens. Bed of Old John Zeller, The.
Poem with Rhythms.
Stevenson. Envoy: "Go, little book, and wish to all."
Whittier. Wishing Bridge, The.
Wordsworth. Wishing-Gate, The.
Wright, James. Moon.
Yau. Cascade.
Zukofsky. Letter of Poor Birds, The.

Peninsular arm, Sirmio, insular arm, well.
Wish, A.

Wit
Beckett. Long after Chamfort.
Bishop. Wit, The.
Campion. De Epigrammate.
"Carroll, Lewis." Father William.
Emerson. And man of wit & mark.
From Nature's beginning.
Herrick. His Losse.
To His Honoured Friend, Sir John Mynts.
To Perenna ("Thou say'st I'm dull; if edge-lesse so I be").
Hewitt. On a Country Bus Forty Years Ago.
On Reading Wallace Stevens' *Collected Poems* after Many Years.
To Be Used in an Address Delivered at the Unveiling of a Plaque Commemorating "George A. Birmingham."
Hopkins. Denis, / Whose motionable, alert, most vaulting wit.
Lowry. Jokes Amidships.
Meredith. Glee.
Pope. Impromptu to Lady Winchelsea.
In the *lines* that you sent, are the *Muses* and *Graces*.
They may talk of the *goddesses* in *Ida* veils.
They say *Argyll*'s a wit, for what?
You *Bellenden, Griffin*, and little *Lepell*.
Ralegh. In the Grace of Wit, of Tongue and Face.
Suckling. Prologue of the Author's to a Masque at Witten, A.

Witchcraft and Witches
Bishop. Riverman, The.
Burns. Tam o' Shanter [A Tale].
Catullus. Carmen 90: "Let there stem (Gellius)."
Cummings. Hist whist / little ghostthings.
De la Mare. Journey, The.
Dickey, William. Dolls Play at Hansel and Gretel.
Dickinson. Best Witchcraft is Geometry.
Witchcraft has not a Pedigree.
Witchcraft was hung, in History.
Eberhart. Salem.
Frost. Two Witches.
Gardner. Fall in Massachusetts.
When a Warlock Dies.
Graves. Against Witchcraft.
Hag-Ridden.
Two Witches, The.
Gray. Fatal Sisters, The.
Herrick. Hag, The ("Hag is astride, The").
Hag[g], The ("Staff[e] is now greased [or greas'd], The").
Upon an Old Woman.
Hesketh. Lyric Evening.
Hewitt. Witch, The.
Housman. Her strong enchantments failing.
Hughes, Ted. Witches.
Jong. Baby-Witch.
Bitter Herb.
Figure of the Witch.
For all those who died.
Her Broom, or the Ride of the Witch.
How to Name Your Familiar.
Kipling. Egg-Shell, The.
Lindsay. Sorceress!, The.
Longfellow. Prologue: "Delusions of the days that once have been."
Lorde. Neighbors.
Meredith. Hecate.
Merton. Notes for a New Liturgy.
Plath. Vanity Fair.
Prince. Stolen Heart, The.
Rich. November 1968.
Rolfe. Poem: "Girl lashed to the stake, The."
Sarton. Intruder, An.
Sexton. Witch's Life, The.
Silverstein. Magic.
Smith, Stevie. Little Boy Lost.
Small Lady, The.
Van Duyn. Such things there are, we don't know.
Whittier. Changeling, The.

Mabel Martin.
Witch of Wenham, The.
Williams, Miller. For Lucy, on Her Birthday.
Wright, James. Witches Waken the Natural World in Spring.
Yeats. Song of Wandering Aengus, The.
Zukofsky. Now seed their Magus (of Gelli's mother wrestling confounded).

Wives
Berry. How many times have I come to you out of my head.
Marriage.
Berryman. For you am I collared to quit my dear.
Burns. Broom Besoms ["I maun hae a wife, whatsoe'er she be"].
English Song.
Henpeck'd Husband, The.
Kellyburnbraes.
My Wife's a Wanton Wee Thing.
My Wife's a Winsome Wee Thing.
Sic a Wife as Willie Had.
Weary Pund o' Tow, The.
Campion. What is it that all men possesse, among themselves conversing?
Carroll, Jim. Torn Canvas.
"Carroll, Lewis." Sailor's Wife, The.
Chaucer. Merchant's Prologue, The.
Prologue of the Monk's Tale, The.
Coleridge. Happy Husband, The.
Life in Death.
Cowper. To Mary.
Creeley. Obscene Poem, An.
Sing Song.
Cummings. S.T.
Davie. Battered Wife, The.
Christmas Syllabics for a Wife.
Dickinson. Many an angel, with its needle.
Donne. Anagram, The.
Since she whom I loved [or lov'd] hath paid [or payd] her last debt.
Tale of a Citizen and His Wife, A.
Dunbar. To a Poet and a Lady.
To Alice Dunbar.
Eliot. Dedication to My Wife, A.
Emerson. All the great & good.
Dust unto dust! and shall no more be said.
Hearst thou, sweet spirit, thou hast heard before.
I am alone. Sad is my solitude.
She never comes to me.
Where art thou / Thou beautiful dream.
Written in Naples, March, 1833.
Frost. Paul's Wife.
Gildner. My Coed Wife.
Hall. Mr. and Mrs. Billings.
Hardy. Every Artemisia.
I Sometimes Think.
Two Wives, The.
Wife Comes Back, A.
Wives in the Sere.
Woman's Fancy, A.
Hartnett. Retreat of Ita Cagney, The.
Hewitt. My dear spouse died—a tumour on the brain.
My Future Wife.
This is the season I think most of death.
Hill. Fortified in their front parlours, at Yuletide men.
Hoffman. As I Was Going to Saint-Ives.
Jarrell. Next Day.
Well-to-Do Invalid, A.
Jonson. Epistle. To Katharine, Lady Aubigny.
Joseph. Just a snack for lunch.
Knight. Portrait of Mary.
Koertge. Panty Hose.
Primary Considerations.
Lawrence. Good Husbands Make Unhappy Wives.
Lady Wife.
Painter's Wife, The.
She Was a Good Little Wife.
Spanish Wife, The.
Two Wives.
Levine. For Fran.
Lindsay. To Eve, Man's Dream of Wifehood as Described by Milton.

Lorde. Evening News, The.
Lowell. Old Flame, The.
Lowry. Correcting Manuscript.
Only thing that Jack had, The.
Song for My Wife.
MacLeish. Late Abed.
Poem in Prose.
Markson. Dante Gabriel.
Quietude.
Recitation before Bed.
Matthews. Narcissus Blues.
Meinke. Surfaces.
Meredith. M. M.
Milton. Sonnet 23: "Mee thought I saw my late espoused saint."
Morgan. Abenaki Poem.
Nash. Always Marry an April Girl.
How to Harry a Husband, or, Is That Accessory Really Necessary?
Machinery Doesn't Answer, Either, but You Aren't Married to It.
Very Funny, Very Funny.
Warning to Wives, A.
Watchman, What of the First First Lady?
Nemerov. Lot's Wife.
Pope. Version of the First Psalm, for the Use of a Young Lady, A.
Robinson. Evangelist's Wife, An.
Roethke. Wish for a Young Wife.
Rolfe. Letter.
Rossetti. Helpmeet For Him, A.
Husband and Wife.
I caught a little ladybird / That flies far away.
I have a little husband / And he is gone to sea.
Rosalind.
Wee wee husband, / Give me some money.
Sexton. For My Lover, Returning to His Wife.
Interrogation of the Man of Many Hearts, The.
Simic. Thus.
Smart. Apollo and Daphne.
Smith, Stevie. Be Off!
Devil-My-Wife, The.
Major Macroo.
Stevenson. So live, so love, so use that fragile hour.
To My Wife.
To the Stormy Petrel.
Tennyson. June Bracken and Heather.
Tomlinson. Farmer's Wife: at Fostons Ash, The.
Portrait of Mrs. Spaxton.
Turco. Hank Fedder.
My Country Wife.
Updike. Living with a Wife.
Painted Wives.
Waldman. Sonnet: O Husband!
Walker. In Uganda an Early King.
Whittier. New Wife and the Old, The.
Williams, Charles Kenneth. Alzheimer's: The Wife.
Signs.
Williams, William Carlos. Mezzo Forte.
Young Housewife, The.
Wordsworth. Fragment: A Somersetshire Tragedy.
Wright, James. Complaint.
Paul.
Zukofsky. Record, The.
See also **Marriage.**

Wolfe, James
Davie. Montcalm.

Wollstonecraft, Mary
Browning, Robert. Mary Wollstonecraft and Fuseli.

Wolverines
Dickey, James. For the Last Wolverine.

Wolves
Gildner. Life of the Wolf, The.
Graves. Lyceia.
Gunn. Allegory of the Wolf Boy, The.
Haines. Wolves.
Hall. Wolf Knife.
Hoffman. Blood.
Hughes, Ted. Howling of Wolves, The.
Hugo. Letter to Stafford from Polson.
Kipling. Hunting Song of the Seeonee Pack.

Law of the Jungle, The.
Only Son, The.
Wolf-cub at even lay hid in the corn, The.
Lawrence. Red Wolf, The.
Lowry. Pacific is a feeble symbol of death.
Queer Poem.
Wolf, wolf, cried the boy in the fable.
MacNeice. Wolves.
Nathan. Around the Fire.
Nemerov. Wolves in the Zoo.
Pack. Wolf Pack, The.
Rexroth. Wolf.
Spenser. I saw a wolfe under a rockie cave.
Tate. Wolves, The.
Williams, William Carlos. Wolf, A.

Woman Suffrage
Hardy. Woman I Met, The.
See also **Voting and Voters.**

Wombats
Nash. Wombat, The.

Women
Angelou. Family Affairs.
Lady Luncheon Club.
Phenomenal Woman.
Woman Me.
Woman Work.
Atwood. Aging Female Poet Sits on the Balcony.
As for the women, who did not.
At first I was given centuries.
Christmas Carols.
Marrying the Hangman.
This story was told to me by another traveller.
Torture.
Women's Issue, A.
Auden. Bach and the Lady.
Helen.
Beckett. À elle l'acte calme.
Elles viennent.
Scene.
Serena II.
They come.
Universe-Solitude.
Berg. Rubber Rats.
Berry. Earth and Fire.
Mad Farmer in the City, The.
Marriage.
Berryman. To a Woman.
Young Woman's Song.
Betjeman. Business Girls.
Station Syren.
Blake. Pair of Stays to mend the Shape, A.
Woman scaly & a Man all Hairy, A.
Bogan. Changed Woman, The.
Evening in the Sanitarium.
Portrait.
Women.
Boyle. Carnival 1927.
Bradstreet. Mercury showed Apollo Bartas' book.
Prologue: "To sing of wars, of captain[e]s, and of kings."
Brooks. Sadie and Maud.
Weaponed Woman.
Browning, Elizabeth Barrett. Isobel's Child.
Lord Walter's Wife.
Browning, Robert. Lady and the Painter, The.
Pearl, a Girl, A.
Bukowski. Beginning, A.
Cows in Art Class.
Girls From Nowhere.
Love Poem, A.
Me.
My women of the past keep trying to locate me.
Sandra.
Tonight.
Burns. Answer, The [To the Guidwife of Wauchope-House].
Beware o' Bonie Ann.
Bonnie Peg.
Epitaph on a Henpecked Country Squire.
Fragment, A: "Green grow the rashes, O; / Green grow the rashes, O; / The lasses they hae wimble bores."
Fragment: "Altho' my bed were in yon muir."
Grim Grizzle.

Hue and Cry of John Lewars, The.
Ken Ye What Meg o' the Mill Has Gotten.
Lassie wi' the Lintwhite Locks.
Muirland Meg.
My Peggy's Face.
O leave novels, ye Mauchline belles.
O Mally's Meek, Mally's Sweet.
O saw ye bonny Lesley.
On Being Asked Why God Had Made Miss D——— So Little and Mrs A——— So Big.
On Miss J. Scott, of Ayr.
Rights of Woman—Spoken by Miss Fontenelle on Her Benefit Night, The.
She's fair and fause that causes my smart.
Should he escape the slaughter of thine Eyes.
Song, Altered from an Old English One.
Song: "I'll tell you a tale of a wife."
Song: "In Mauchline there dwells six proper young Belles."
Song: "Let not Woman e'er complain."
Song: "My girl she's airy, she's buxom and gay."
Song. On Miss P——— K———, A.
Song. On Miss W. A.
Song: "Tho' women's minds, like winter winds."
Tarbolton Lasses, The.
Theniel Menzies' Bony Mary.
There was twa wives, and twa witty wives.
There's News Lasses News.
Tibbie Fowler.
To Chloris.
To Maria.
To the Beautiful Miss Eliza J———n, on Her Principles of Liberty and Equality.
Yon wild, mossy mountains sae lofty and wide.
Byron. Egotism. A Letter to J.T. Becher.
Girl of Cadiz, The.
In her first passion woman loves her lover.
To ———: "Oh! well I know your subtle Sex."
To Eliza.
To Harriet ("Harriet! To see such Circumspection").
Campion. Ev'ry Dame affects good fame, what ere her doings be.
I Care Not for These Ladies.
If Love loves truth, then women doe not love.
In Sannium.
In se.
See Where She Flies.
So many loves have I neglected.
Vain Men, Whose Follies.
What is it that all men possesse, among themselves conversing?
Why presumes thy pride on that, that must so private be.
Young and Simple though I Am.
Carew. Conquest by Flight.
Feminine Honour.
To My Mistress Sitting by a River's Side; an Eddy.
"Carroll, Lewis." Only a Woman's Hair.
Path of Roses, The.
Carruth. Anima.
Assignment.
Cross My Heart and Hope to Die, It Was the Very Same Song Exactly.
Down there like. Maybe not the same, of course.
He thinks of classical women.
I Tell You For Several Years of My Madness I Heard the Voice of Lilith Singing in the Trees of Chicago.
Reversions, always.
Sonnet: "Most brainy woman, the sexuality of your thought."
Sonnet: "To see a woman long oppressed by fear."
Sonnet: "Women in anger, it seems, become theatrical."
Tanck's Song About Women.
Woman, The.
Woman's Genitals, The.
Women like new brooms.

Catullus. Carmen 110: "Men always praise an honest whore."
Chaucer. Against Women Unconstant [or A Ballade against Woman Inconstant].
Epilogue to the Merchant's Tale.
Legend of Good Women, The.
Tale of Melibee, The.
Wife of Bath's Prologue, The.
Wife of Bath's Tale, The.
Ciardi. To Judith Asleep.
Cohen. Commentary—My Wife and I.
I Knelt Beside a Stream.
My Wife and I.
Paris Models.
There Are No Traitors.
Coleridge. Hunting Song.
Love's Burial-Place.
To a Lady.
Crane. Ah! without the moon, what white nights.
Creeley. Air: "The Love of a Woman."
All That Is Lovely in Men.
Circle, The.
Dream, The.
Finger, The.
For Irving.
Form of Adaptation, A.
Hands, The.
Irish.
Letter, The.
Memory, The.
Name, The.
Paradox, The.
Person.
Photo.
Prejudice, The.
Sentence, The.
Son: "What I took in my hand."
Story, The.
Three Ladies, The.
Whip, The.
Woman, The.
Young Woman.
Cullen. Cat, The.
Cummings. Any man is wonderful.
As Joe Gould says in.
Ballade: "White night roared with a huge north-wind, The."
Between the breasts / of bestial.
By little accurate saints thickly which tread.
Cleopatra built / like a smooth arrow or.
Dress was a suspicious madder,importing the cruelty of roses, The.
Ev erythingex Cept: / that / 's what she's.
Fabulous against ,a,fathoming jelly.
Fearlessandbosomy / this / grand:gal.
Five Americans.
"Gay" is the captivating cognomen of a Young Woman of cambridge,mass.
Hips lOOsest OOping shoulders blonde& pastoral hair,strong.
I have seen her a stealthily frail.
Impossibly / motivated by midnight.
In making Marjorie god hurried.
Inthe,exquisite; / morning sure lyHer eye s exactly sit,ata little roundtable.
Irreproachable ladies firmly lewd.
Is there a flower(whom).
Like a, A / grey / rock wanderin.
Little ladies more / than dead exactly dance.
My girl's tall with hard long eyes.
My lady is an ivory garden.
My smallheaded pearshaped.
Perhaps it is to feel strike.
Pretty a day, A.
Puella Mea.
She sits dropping on a caret of clenched arms.
2 shes / both not quite / young perfectly.
Which is the very.
Who(at / her nons- / elf).
You are like the snow only.
De la Mare. Here Sleeps.
Dickey, James. Enclosure, The.
Two Women.
Weeds.
Dickinson. Title divine—is mine!
What Soft—Cherubic Creatures.

Donne. Community.
Love's Progress.
Manliness.
Primrose[, Being at Montgomery Castle, upon the Hill, on Which It Is Situate], The.
Song: "Go, and catch a falling star."
To the Countess of Huntingdon ("Madam, / Man to God's image, Eve, to man's was made").
Twicknam [or Twickenham] Garden.
Doolittle. Dancer, The.
Huntress.
Master, The.
Dove. For Kazuko.
Spy.
Dunbar. Made to Order Smile, The.
On the Dedication of Dorothy Hall.
Turning of the Babies in the Bed, The.
Duncan. Bending the Bow.
Maiden, The.
Tribal Memories.
Dunn. Eggs.
Halves.
Listener, The.
Not the Occult.
Routine Things Around the House, The.
"Dylan." Eternal Circle.
Just Like a Woman.
Sara.
She Belongs to Me.
Spanish Harlem Incident.
Eberhart. Apple Buds.
Bells of a Chinese Temple, The.
Lament of a New England Mother, The.
Legend of Viable Women, A.
Marrakech.
Redemption.
Ruby Daggett.
Spring Mountain Climb.
To Harriet Monroe.
To Kenya Tribesmen, the Turkana.
Vastness and Indifference of the World, The.
Eliot. Cousin Nancy.
Emerson. All that thy virgin soul can ask be thine.
Romany Girl, The.
Seemed to me—never maid.
Everson. But masked of the self.
But now having seen.
Sea: / And in its flaw the sprung silence.
So him in dream.
Wader, / Watcher by water.
Fenton. Voice disguiser with membrane of a spider's egg-case, A.
Fletcher. Father's Thought of His Daughter, The.
Marriage.
Fox. At Nightfall.
Caroline Herschel (1750–1848).
Dead Women.
Nightshade.
Onna-E, Pictures of Women.
Sunflowers.
To the Man Who Watches Spiders.
Gallagher. Breasts.
Conversation with a Fireman from Brooklyn.
From Dread in the Eyes of Horses.
On Your Own.
Story of a Citizen, The.
Woman Who Raised Goats, The.
Glück. Aphrodite.
Autumnal.
Palais des Arts.
Porcelain Bowl.
Graves. Above the Edge of Doom.
Antorcha Y Corona, 1968.
At Best, Poets.
Batxóca.
Dans un Seul Lit.
Gateway, The.
Hung Wu Vase, The.
In Her Praise.
Iron Palace.
La Mejicana.
Lyceia.
Portrait, The.
Robbers' Den.

Ruby and Amethyst.
Sail and Oar.
Secret Land, The.
She Is No Liar.
Snap-Comb Wilderness, The.
Song: Crown of Stars.
Song: Dew-Drop and Diamond.
Three-Faced, The.
To Beguile and Betray.
Torch and Crown, 1968.
Traditionalist, The.
Undead, The.
What Can We Not Ask?
White Goddess, The.
With the Gift of a Lion's Claw.
Women and Masks.
Hacker. Another poet, woman and alive.
Ballad of Ladies Lost and Found.
Coda.
Country & Western.
Elegy: "Crying from exile, I."
I will never be only a Lesbian.
Mother II.
Pantoum.
Peterborough.
Prayer for my Daughter.
Shirland Road.
Sisterhood.
Towards Autumn.
Haines. For Anne, at a Little Distance.
Woman on the Road.
Hall. Blue Wing, The.
Hardy. Ballet, The.
Chosen, The.
Conjecture.
Coquette, and After, The.
Countenance, A.
Donaghadee.
Dream or No, A.
Elopement, The.
Her Definition.
I Knew a Lady.
Ice on the Highway.
On Stinsford Hill at Midnight.
One Ralph Blossom Soliloquizes.
Protean Maiden, The.
Rejected Member's Wife, The.
Rival, The.
So Various.
We Field-Women.
Winsome Woman, A.
Without, Not within Her.
Hartley. Five Women.
Fork of Annie, The.
Passionate Rebuke.
Sister, The.
Woman Distorts, with Hunger, The.
Hartnett. I saw magic on a green country road.
Heaney. Wife's Tale, The.
Hemingway. I'm off'n wild wimmen.
Lady Poets With Foot Notes, The.
Herrick. Defence for Women, A.
Deniall in Women No Disheartning to Men.
Descripcion; of a Woman, The.
I Call and I Call.
In Praise of Women.
Little and Loud.
No Fault in Women.
On Himselfe ("Let me not live, if I not love").
Request to the Graces, An.
Saint Distaffs Day, or the Morrow after Twelth Day.
Short and Long Both Likes.
To His Girles.
To the Ladyes.
Upon Jone and Jane.
Upon Some Women.
Women Uselesse.
Hewitt. Lyric Sonorously Rhymed, The.
Paper Banners.
Sonnets for Roberta (1954).
Variations on a Theme.
Holmes. Women in A.M.
Hughes, Langston. Preference.
Troubled Woman.
Hugo. At Our Best.

Letter to Blessing from Missoula.
Snapshot of the Auxiliary, A.
To Women.
Jarrell. Next Day.
Jeffers. Of all things which are living and can form a judgment.
Jong. Blood & Honey.
Commandments, The.
Deaths of the Goddesses, The.
Woman Enough.
Jonson. Another. In Defense of Their Inconstancy [or Inconstancie]. A Song.
Had those that dwell in error foul.
In the Person of Womankind [A Song Apologetic].
Phoenix Analysed, The.
Satirical Shrub, A.
Song. That Women Are But Men's Shadows.
Joseph. Recovered from the Sea.
Sunripe.
Women at Streatham Hill.
Keats. Woman! When I Behold Thee Flippant, Vain.
Kipling. Female of the Species, The.
"I have a thousand men," said he.
Ladies, The.
Lady Geraldine's Hardship.
Mary, Pity Women!
Song of the Lathes, The.
Vampire, The.
Knight. Genesis 11.
Knott. Fear of Domesticity.
Koch. Sleeping with Women.
Koertge. Coign of Vantage.
Two Men.
Kunitz. Blessing of Women, A.
Larkin. Deep Analysis.
Femmes Damnees.
In Times When Nothing Stood.
Large Cool Store, The.
Letter to a Friend about Girls.
Mythological Introduction.
Lawrence. Dominant Woman.
Don't Look at Me.
Ego-Bound Women.
Energetic Women.
Female Coercion.
Flapper.
Frost Flowers.
I Wish I Knew a Woman.
In a Spanish Tram-Car.
It's No Good!
Men and Women.
Mournful Young Man.
One Woman to All Women.
Other Women Have Reared in Me.
Peacock.
Spirits Summoned West.
To Women, as Far as I'm Concerned.
Valentine's Night.
Volcanic Venus.
What Ails She?
Women Want Fighters for Their Lovers.
Wonderful Spiritual Women.
Levertov. Abel's Bride.
Hypocrite Women.
In Mind.
Mutes, The.
Stepping Westward.
Liddy. Bicentennial Words for the Liberal Magistrates of 1798.
Clare De Lughnasa.
Katherine Young.
Lady/Lord in Doorway.
Lorde. For My Singing Sister.
Hard Love Rock II.
Keyfoods.
Need: A Chorale for Black Woman Voices.
NOW.
Poem for Women in Rage, A.
Seventh Sign, The.
Lovelace. Clitophon and Lucippe.
Female Glory.
Lowry. Curse, A.
Harpies.
Letter from Oaxaca to North Africa 1936.
"MacDiarmid." His attitude towards woman is

the basic point.
One of the Principal Causes of War.
Two Parents, The.
Vision of Scotland, A.
McGrath. Behold the Woman.
Excursion: Or: O Columbus!, The.
MacLeish. Contemporary Portrait.
Eve's Child.
Shallow Grass, The.
Steamboat Whistle, The.
Markson. Sexist Stanza.
Marlowe. 2.4: Quod amet mulieres,
cuiuscunque formae sint.
2.14: In amicam, quod abortivum ipsa fecerit.
3.2: Ad amicam cursum equorum spectantem.
Meinke. Arms and the Man.
50 on 50.
Melville. Marchioness of Brinvilliers, The.
Meredith. Across his path the spouseless Lady
cast.
Ballad of Fair Ladies in Revolt, A.
Full faith I have she holds that rarest gift.
Marian: "She can be as wise as we."
My lady unto Madam makes her bow.
No knightly sword to serve, nor harp of bard.
One fairest of the ripe unwedded left.
Squireless Kate.
Sweetheart of the Csikos, The.
This golden head has wit in it. I live.
Merrill. Sundown and Starlight.
Merton. Greek Women, The.
Mecca.
There Has to Be a Jail for Ladies.
Millay. I, being born a woman and distressed.
Miller. Saw 'er at a temple on the outskirts of
Hangzhou.
Milton. Woman.
Moore. Sojourn in the Whale.
Morgan. Bianca.
Morrison. America As Bullring Arena.
Flesh of Her.
Nash. Allow Me, Madam, But It Won't Help.
Cousin Euphemia Knows Best, or, Physician,
Heal Somebody Else.
Frailty, Thy Name Is a Misnomer.
I Never Even Suggested It.
It's about Time.
Just Wrap It Up, and I'll Throw It Away
Later.
Lines to a Three-Name Lady.
Oh, Please Don't Get Up!
Oh, Shucks, Ma'am, I Mean Excuse Me.
That Reminds Me.
Thoughts Thought after a Bridge Party.
Wednesday Matinee.
What's the Use.
Who Understands Who Anyhow?
Woman Pulls the Wires.
Nathan. Body Count.
Nemerov. Lore.
Young Woman.
Oliver. Strawberry Moon.
Olson. Anubis will stare.
As the shield goddess, Mycenae.
Barley or rye / blue and white green.
Cause, the Cause, The.
Conversation Galante.
Easter.
Ferrini—I.
For a Lady of Whom I Speak.
For Sappho, Back.
Help Me, Venus, You Who Led Me On.
I Believe in You.
Mazdaism / has overcome.
Moebius Strip, The.
Of Lady, of Beauty, of Stream.
O'Ryan.
Proensa.
She.
She-Bear, The.
She-Bear (II), The.
She, Thus.
So the Norse / were neurotic.
Soul, The.
To the She-Bear: The 1st Song.
Translation, A.
Troilus.

Woman's Nipples Is the Rose of the World,
A.
Oppen. Boy's Room.
Hills, The.
Kind of Garden: A Poem for my Sister, A.
Like the wind in the trees and the bells.
Morality Play: Preface, A.
O Western Wind.
Of This All Things..
Only that it should be beautiful.
People, the People, The.
Source, The.
Pack. Empathy.
Paley. On the Fourth Floor.
On the Ramblas / A Tree   A Girl.
Song Stanzas of Private Luck.
That Country.
Woman invented fire and called it, A.
Women let the tide go out, The.
Patchen. Letter on the Use of Machine Guns
at Weddings, A.
Piercy. Burying Blues for Janis.
For Strong Women.
Juan's Twilight Dance.
Looking at Quilts.
Phyllis Wounded.
Right to Life.
Sabbath of Mutual Respect, The.
Unlearning to Not Speak.
We will be equal, we say, new man and new
woman.
Window of the Woman Burning, The.
Woman in the Ordinary, The.
Plath. Ariel.
Childless Woman.
Female Author.
Old Ladies' Home.
Two Sisters of Persephone.
Vanity Fair.
Poe. To Helen ("I saw thee once—once
only—years ago").
Pope. Epistle [II,] to a Lady[: Of the
Characters of Women].
Impromptu to Lady Winchelsea.
On a Certain Lady at Court.
On the Countess of Burlington Cutting Paper.
To a Lady with the Temple of Fame.
Version of the First Psalm, for the Use of a
Young Lady, A.
Pound. Portrait d'une Femme.
Tame Cat.
Prince. Creation Myth.
Rich. After Twenty Years.
Blood-Sister.
Cartographies of Silence.
Culture and Anarchy.
Dark lintels, the blue and foreign stones, The.
Education of a Novelist.
Essential Resources.
Every peak is a crater. This is the law of
volcanoes.
Floating Poem, Unnumbered, The.
For Julia in Nebraska.
For L.G.: Unseen for Twenty Years.
From a Survivor.
From an Old House in America.
Heroines.
Hunger.
I come home from you through the early light
of spring.
Meditations for a Savage Child.
Mirror in Which Two Are Seen as One, The.
Mountain laurel in bloom, The.
Natural Resources.
No one's fated or doomed to love anyone.
Orion plunges like a drunken hunter.
Over the hills in Shutesbury, Leverett.
Paula Becker to Clara Westhoff.
Phantasia for Elvira Shatayev.
Phenomenology of Anger, The.
Planetarium.
Poem of Women.
Re-forming the Crystal.
Roots.
Rules break like a thermometer, The.
Self-hatred.
Sleeping, turning in turn like planets.

Snapshots of a Daughter-in-Law.
Strangers are an endangered species.
That conversation we were always on the
edge.
This apartment full of books could crack open.
To Judith, Taking Leave.
Transit.
Translations.
Upcountry.
Waking in the Dark.
When/Then.
White Night.
Woman Dead in Her Forties, A.
Women.
Your small hands, precisely equal to my own.
Roethke. I Knew a Woman.
She.
Rolfe. Blues.
Lanes of Death and Birth.
Rossetti. From the Antique.
Helpmeet For Him, A.
"Immurata" Sister, An.
Lady Isabella.
Listen, and I will tell you of a face.
Passing and Glassing.
Rukeyser. Burning Bush.
Cries from Chiapas.
Judith.
Käthe Kollwitz.
Letter to the Front.
More of a Corpse than a Woman.
Mrs. Walpurga.
Myth.
Painters.
Rite.
Searching / Not Searching.
Song from Puck Fair.
Waterlily Fire.
Wreath of Women.
Sandburg. Adelaide Crapsey.
Bitter Summer Thoughts—No. XXII.
Cadenza.
Cartoon.
Glimmer.
Lief the Lucky.
Night Stuff.
Pigeon.
Remembered Women.
Shag-Bark Hickory.
Three Shrines.
Two Women.
Two Women and Their Fathers.
Working Girls.
Sarton. My Sisters, O My Sisters.
Schuyler. Sestina: "I have reached, alas, the
long shadow."
Velvet Roses.
Schwartz. Dream of Whitman Paraphrased,
Recognized and Made More Vivid by Renoir,
A.
Sonnet on Famous and Familiar Sonnets and
Experiences.
Sexton. Breast, The.
Consorting with Angels.
Eighth Psalm.
Fierceness of Female, The.
Her Kind.
Hurry Up Please It's Time.
In Celebration of My Uterus.
Rapunzel.
To Like, to Love.
Shapiro. Back, The.
Buick.
Dome of Sunday, The [or A].
Giantess.
Girls Fighting, Broadway.
Recognition of Eve, The.
Waitress.
Shelton. Her.
Sidney. What tongue can her perfections tell.
Smith, Patti. Amelia Earhart.
Sheep Lady from Algiers, The.
Suite.
Smith, Stevie. Dear Female Heart.
Feminine Charm.
Fool, The.
Girls!

House of Mercy, A.
Lady of the Well-Spring, The.
Wretched Woman.
Snodgrass. Seeing You Have..
Vuillard: "The Mother and Sister of the
 Artist."
Snyder. Alabaster.
Could She See the Whole Real World with
 Her Ghost Breast Eyes Shut under a Blouse
 Lid?
Love.
Sorrentino. Verlaine's Innocents.
Stevens. Apostrophe to Vincentine, The.
Ordinary Women, The.
Woman in Sunshine, The.
Stevenson. About my fields, in the broad sun.
Her name is as a word of old romance.
Now bare to the beholder's eye.
To Madame Garschine.
Suckling. Health to the nut-brown lass, A.
Prologue: "'Fore love, a mighty session; and (I
 fear)."
She's pretty to walk with.
There never yet was woman made.
Verses: "I confirm'd a woman can."
Swift. Answer, An.
Cassinus and Peter.
Dean Swift's Answer to the Reverend Dr.
 Sheridan.
Death and Daphne.
Furniture of a Woman's Mind, The.
Hardship Put upon Ladies, The.
Journal of a Modern Lady, The.
Lady's Dressing Room, The.
Tennyson. Dream of Fair Women, A.
Thomas. In the White Giant's Thigh.
Tomlinson. Black Nude.
Rhenish Winter.
Turco. Pocoangelini 5 ("Pocoangelini said").
Updike. Cunts.
Klimt and Schiele Confront the Cunt.
Van Duyn. Cities of the Plain, The.
Wakoski. Belly Dancer.
Overnight Projects with Woods.
Reaching Out with the Hands of the Sun.
Those Mythical Silver Pears.
To the Thin and Elegant Woman Who Resides
 Inside of Alix Nelson.
Waldman. Fast Speaking Woman.
Philosophia Perennis.
Walker. Pagan.
Well.
Woman Is Not a Potted Plant, A.
Whitman. Unfolded Out of the Folds.
Woman Waits for Me, A.
Whittier. To a Friend.
Wilbur. Catch, The.
She.
Williams, Charles Kenneth. Dominion:
 Depression.
Williams, William Carlos. And Thus with All
 Praise.
Atlantic City Convention, The.
Classic Picture.
Cold Night, The.
Conventional Ballad.
Crystal Maze, A.
Fertile.
Girl, The.
In the 'Sconset Bus.
Mama.
Mounted as an Amazon.
Portrait of a Lady.
Portrait of a Woman in Bed.
Profile of a Lady.
Queen-Anne's-Lace.
Three Sonnets.
To a Chinese Woman.
To a Friend Concerning Several Ladies.
To an Old Jaundiced Woman.
To Daphne and Virginia.
Woman Walking.
Wordsworth. Epitaph in Grasmere Church.
Fish-Women.—On Landing at Calais.
Lines Written in the Album of the Countess of
 Lonsdale.
Lo! Where She Stands Fixed in a Saint-like

Trance.
She was a phantom of delight.
Three Cottage Girls, The.
To —, in Her Seventieth Year.
To the Lady E.B. and the Hon. Miss P.
Wright, James. Down to the Dregs.
So She Said.
Witches Waken the Natural World in Spring.
Yau. January 18, 1979.
Radiant Silhouette II.
Yeats. Crazy Jane Talks with the Bishop.
First Confession, A.
He Tells a Valley Full of Lovers.
Heart of the Woman, The.
Lady's First Song, The.
Lady's Second Song, The.
Michael Robartes and the Dancer.
No Second Troy.
On Woman.
Prayer for My Daughter, A.
Presences.
Thought from Propertius, A.
To an Isle in the Water.
Woman Homer Sung, A.
Young. Dear Old Stockholm.
Head of a Woman.
Zukofsky. After Charles Sedley.
Aufilena—*bonnie, simple,* laud and they're
 amicable.
One lutenist played *look;* your through was
 drink.

Wood
Bly. Old Boards.
Carruth. Block.
Cohen. Joan of Arc.
Dunbar. To Pfrimmer.
Eberhart. Dry Rot, The.
Frost. Wood-Pile, The.
Garrigue. Circle, The.
Haines. Legend of Paper Plates, The.
Hardy. Workbox, The.
Kipling. Tree Song, A.
Koch. Down at the Docks.
Koertge. Coign of Vantage.
Kunitz. Knot, The.
Trompe L'oeil.
Larkin. Gathering Wood.
Lawrence. Bowls.
Lowell. Soft Wood.
Lowry. Note.
Song for a Marimba.
There's something burning, you said, when we
 were hammering.
Welcome Home Oh Most Loved and Famed
 Harteebeeste.
McAuley. Ritual.
MacLeish. Cat in the Wood, The.

Woodpeckers
Creeley. Like They Say.
Dunn. Honesty.
Hoffman. On the Extinction of a Species.
Williams, William Carlos. To a Woodpecker.
Woodpecker, The.

Woods
Ammons. Spruce Woods.
Auden. Lovers' Lane.
Woods.
Berry. Bird Killer, The.
Grace.
History.
Independence Day.
Now that April with sweet rain.
Satisfactions of the Mad Farmer, The.
Stay Home.
Winter Night Poem for Mary.
Woods.
Carruth. Bearer, The.
Blizzard trampling past has left.
Existence Before Essence.
Far-removed Mountain Men, The.
Line, The.
Little Fire in the Woods, The.
No Supervening Thought of Grace.
Once More.
Poet, The.
Primavera, The.
Trees, The.

Clare. Gipsies: "Gipsies seek wide sheltering
 woods again, The."
Clark. Woodtime.
Cooper. Graveyard, The.
De la Mare. Last Coachload, The.
Tom's Angel.
Tryst, The.
Emerson. As I walked in the woods.
I to my garden went.
In dreamy woods, what forms abound.
Miracle, The.
October woods, wherein.
These trees like tho'ts that to visions congeal.
Titmouse, The.
Woods.
Garrigue. Invocation to Old Windylocks.
Glück. Early December in Croton-on-Hudson.
Graves. Green Woods of Unrest, The.
Gunn. Fair in the Woods, The.
Here Come the Saints.
Hewitt. First Snow in the Glens.
Hopkins. Time was late and the wet yellow
 woods, The.
Woods in Spring.
Housman. We'll to the woods no more.
Kinnell. Fergus Falling.
Winter Sky, A.
Knight. Talking in the Woods with Karl
 Amorelli.
Levertov. Breathing, The.
Liddy. Lady Fitzwilliam.
Lowry. Bright as the Pleiades Upon the Soul.
Markson. Birches.
Meredith. Daphne.
Enter these enchanted woods.
In the Woods.
Love of the Woods.
On Combe Bottom: Surrey.
Open hither, open hence.
Will o' the Wisp.
You must love the light so well.
Youthful Quest, The.
Nemerov. Deep Woods.
Oppen. But So As by Fire.
Paley. Then Vera stopped at the flower called
 fireweed.
Patchen. Beyond the Dark Cedars.
Prince. Keeper's Wood.
Roethke. Light Poem.
Praise to the End!
Rukeyser. Then I Saw What the Calling Was.
Schuyler. Just before Fall.
Schwartz. Poem: "Window winter."
Praise Is Traditional and Appropriate.
Smith, Charlotte. Lines Composed in Passing
 through a Forest in Germany.
Smith, Stevie. Brickenden, Hertfordshire.
I Rode with My Darling.
Little Boy Lost.
Stafford. At a little pond in the woods.
Stevenson. Woodman, The.
Tomlinson. At the Edge.
Turco. Colony, The.
Warren. Dark Night of the Soul.
Dark Woods.
Wilbur. Children of Darkness.
Fern-Beds in Hampshire County.
Williams, William Carlos. Source, The.
To a Wood Thrush.
Wordsworth. Fragments from the "Christabel"
 Note-book.
How sweet it is, when mother Fancy rocks.
Nutting.
Yeats. Ragged Wood, The.
Young. In the Tender Woodland.
Zukofsky. Guests, The.

See also **Forests.**

Wool
Hewitt. Country Walk in March, A.
Nash. Shinking Song.

Woolf, Virginia
Schuyler. Virginia Woolf.

Woolworth Building, New York City
Sandburg. Again?

Worcestershire, England
Davie. Worcestershire.

Words
Ammons. *De* / on one, The.
Atwood. You can't live here without
  breathing.
Auden. Base words are uttered only by the
  base.
  Words.
Beckett. Mots survivants.
  Tailpiece.
Berg. Sketch.
Berry. And when we speak together.
  Autumn Burning, An.
  Meditation in the Spring Rain.
Browning, Elizabeth Barrett. Sonnet: "And
  wilt thou have me fashion into speech."
Bukowski. Hey, Ezra, Listen to This.
  Itch, Come and Gone.
Carruth. Wheel of Being I, The.
Clough. Go foolish thoughts, and join the
  throng.
Creeley. Diction.
  Epic Expands, The.
  Gemini.
  Language, The.
  Numbers.
  Oh, Love.
  Phone.
  Thinking.
  Token, A.
  Trees.
  Waiting.
  Water Music.
  Words.
Cullen. Karenge Ya Marenge.
Cummings. Here is little Effie's Head.
  Little joe gould has lost his teeth and doesn't
  know where.
Dickey, James. Basics.
Dickinson. Amazing human [*or* Human] heart
  [*or* Heart].
  Could mortal lip divine.
  How vast is the chastisement of Beauty.
  I hesitate which word to take.
  Man may make a Remark, A.
  To tell the Beauty would decrease.
  Word is dead, A.
Dobyns. Name-Burning.
  Ways of Keys, The.
Dove. Ö.
Duncan. For a Muse Meant.
  I ask the unyielding Sentence that shows Itself
  forth in the language.
  Poem in Stretching, A.
  Upon Taking Hold.
Dunn. He/She.
  Those of Us Who Think We Know.
  What.
Eberhart. Ideal and the Real, The.
  Words.
Emerson. And as the light divided the dark.
  I will not hesitate to speak the word.
  On thee has God conferred.
  S. R.
Fisher. Irreversible.
Ford. That first and last word.
Fox. There was, perhaps, a time.
Frost. Beyond Words.
  Ends.
Gallagher. Love Poem to Be Read to an
  Illiterate Friend.
  When You Speak to Me.
Gardner. Homo Gratia Artis.
Graves. Dance of Words.
  Forbidden Words.
  Tilth.
  Word, The.
Gunn. For a Birthday.
  Words.
Hacker. Forage Sestina.
Hartley. Word and Its Meaning, A.
  Yielding the Initiative.
Heaney. In Illo Tempore.
Hesketh. Brain Child.
  Poem is a Painting, A.
  Protean Lover.
  Shaping Spirit, The.
  Words.

Hewitt. My First Reported Words.
  North-West Passage: An Old Man Dying.
  On the Use of Dialect Words.
Hill. Do words make up the majesty.
Hoffman. Words.
Hughes, Langston. Refugee in America.
Koch. Permanently.
Larkin. Talking in Bed.
Lawrence. Conundrums.
Levine. Words.
Lewis. Prologue: The Grinder.
Liddy. White Thought in a White Shade, A.
Lorde. Coal.
Lowry. Au clair de la lune.
  Blepharipappus Glandulosus or White Tidy-
  Tips.
  Bright as the Pleiades Upon the Soul.
  Ex-Poet, The.
  Give me a poem / To wring the hearts of
  men.
  I sing the joy of poverty, not such.
  I wrote: In the dark cavern of our birth.
  Outward Bound.
  Poem to be Placed at the Conclusion of a
  Long Obscure Passionate and Eloquent Book
  of Poems.
  They will be ashamed after they are dead.
  Though we are but *sea* birds.
  What the Gardener Said to Mrs. Trail.
MacLeish. Reproach to Dead Poets.
  They Come No More, Those Words, Those
  Finches.
MacNeice. Idle Talk.
  Plain Speaking.
Markson. Preference of Metre.
Matthews. Straight Life.
Merrill. Dedication: "Hans, there are moments
  when the whole mind."
  Nightgown.
Merton. Duke Hwan and the Wheelwright.
  Sartre said Francis Ponge had a moss-complex.
  Tower of Babel.
Millay. It is the fashion now to wave aside.
Moore. Avec Ardeur.
Muldoon. Quoof.
Nash. Do You Plan to Speak Bantu? or
  Abbreviation is the Thief of Sanity.
  Literary Scene, The.
  Reflections on the Vernacular.
Nemerov. One Way.
Neruda. Pedro Is When.
Notley. Jack Would Speak through the
  Imperfect Medium of Alice.
Olson. A B Cs.
  A B Cs (3—for Rimbaud).
  Abstract #1, Yucatan.
  New Poem.
Pack. After Returning from Camden Harbor.
  Neanderthal Poem, "Ah," Number One.
  Villanelle for Pamela.
Patchen. To Be Charmed.
Piercy. At the Core.
  Athena in the Front Lines.
  Little Scandal, A.
  Meetings Like Hungry Beaks.
Plath. Conversation among the Ruins.
  Munich Mannequins, The.
  Poems, Potatoes.
  Sorcerer Bids Farewell to Seem, A.
  Words.
Pope. Verses Occasioned by an &c. at the
  End of Mr. D'Urfy's Name in the Title to
  One of His Plays.
Raine. Night in Martindale.
  Word Made Flesh.
"Reed." Murder Mystery, The.
Rossetti. City plum is not a plum, A.
  If I Had Words.
Rukeyser. Ballad of Orange and Grape.
  Forerunners.
  Rune.
Sandburg. Basket.
  Crossing the Paces.
  Different Kinds of Good-by.
  Is Wisdom a Lot of Language?
  Little Girl, Be Careful What You Say.
  Monosyllabic.

People is Everyman, everybody, The.
  Precious Moments.
  Seventeen Months.
  Speech.
  Threes.
Schuyler. Freely Espousing.
Sexton. Words.
Smith, Stevie. La Speakerine de Putney.
  Lord Say-and-Seal.
Sorrentino. Fiction, The.
  Language Barrier, The.
Spender. Word.
Stafford. How These Words Happened.
  In the Night Desert.
Stein. More Grammar for a Sentence.
  New.
  Practice of Oratory.
Stevens. Certain Phenomena of Sound.
  Search for Sound Free from Motion.
Stevenson. To Sydney.
Stuart. Coming To.
Thomas. Especially When the October Wind.
  Once It Was the Colour of Saying.
Tomlinson. Double Rainbow, The.
  Ritornello.
Walcott. Those grooves in that forehead of
  sand-coloured flesh.
Whitman. Font of Type, A.
  Song of the Answerer.
Wilbur. Compass.
  Games Two.
Williams, Miller. Little Poem, A.
  Logos.
  Words.
Williams, William Carlos. Fragment: "As for
  him who."
  Offering.
Wright, James. In Shame and Humiliation.
  Morality of Poetry, The.
Yau. Bare Sheets II.
Yeats. Old Memory.
  Song of the Happy Shepherd, The.
  Words.
Zukofsky. Non Ti Fidar.
  Peri Poietikes.
  (Ryokan's scroll).
  Translation, The.
  You three:—my wife.

See also **Language.**

Wordsworth, William
Arnold. And Wordsworth! Ah, pale ghosts,
  rejoice!
  Memorial Verses.
  Wordsworth's Grave.
  Youth of Nature, The.
Browning, Elizabeth Barrett. On a Portrait of
  Wordsworth by B. R. Haydon.
Browning, Robert. Lost Leader, The.
Byron. Braziers, It Seems, Are Preparing to
  Pass, The.
  Dedication: "Bob Southey! You're a poet--
  poet-laureate."
  Epilogue: "There's something in a stupid ass."
"Carroll, Lewis." Upon the Lonely Moor.
  White Knight's Ballad, The.
Carruth. All things lay in nature, even the
  plastic flowers.
Coleridge. Hexameters.
  To a Gentleman.
  To W. Wordsworth.
  Tribute to Wordsworth.
Davie. Hawkshead and Dachau in a Christmas
  Glass.
Ferlinghetti. I am waiting for my case to
  come up.
Fletcher. Elegy on Tintern Abbey.
Griffiths. From Waterloo Bridge, Ensuing
  Dark.
Hesketh. Wordsworth's Old Age.
Hopkins. Child is Father to the Man, The.
Lowry. Another than Wordsworth dropped his
  live work.
  Schoolboy's Complaint, The.
"MacDiarmid." Greatest poets undergo a kind
  of crisis in their art, The.
Meredith. Poetry of Wordsworth, The.

Shelley. All things that Peter saw and felt. To Wordsworth.
Stevenson. Thou strainest through the mountain fern.
Whittier. Wordsworth.
Wordsworth. 1811 ("Here pause: the poet claims at least this praise").

Work and Workers
Angelou. One More Round.
Woman Work.
Beatles. Hard Day's Night, A.
Berry. Adze, The.
From the Distance.
My life's wave is at its crest.
Satisfactions of the Mad Farmer, The.
Vision reaches the ground.
Berryman. Animal Trainer, The.
Browning, Elizabeth Barrett. Work.
Work and Contemplation.
Bukowski. Fragile!
Green.
How I Got Started.
Sparks.
Transformation and Disfiguration.
Burns. Extemporaneous Effusion on Being Appointed to the Excise, An.
Merry Hae I Been Teethin a Heckle.
Carroll, Jim. Here I walked with a memory of workers in midtown.
Ciardi. Cal Coolidge and the Co.
Elegy: "My father was born with a spade in his hand and traded it."
Cohen. Commentary—A Working Man.
Working Man, A.
Creeley. On Vacation.
"To Work Is to Contradict Contradictions, to Do Violence to Natural Violence."
Cummings. At the ferocious phenomenon of 5 o'clock i find myself gently decompos.
Davie. Felicity's Fourth Order.
With the Grain.
Dickinson. It is easy to work when the soul is at play.
Some—Work for Immortality.
Work is a bleak redeemer.
Donne. From needing danger, to be[e] good.
Dove. Satisfaction Coal Company, The.
Zeppelin Factory, The.
Dunbar. Not They Who Soar!
Too Busy.
Dunn. Carpenter's Song, The.
Checklist.
Hard Work 1956.
Local Time.
Eberhart. Clam Diggers and Diggers of Sea Worms, The.
My mind was heavy and my luck was dark.
Emerson. Comrade or the book is good, The.
On bravely through the sunshine & the showers.
When thou sittest moping.
Everson. Muscat Pruning.
Fletcher. Flood Symphony, The.
Ford. What hard work it takes.
Gallagher. Black Money.
Ginsberg. Bricklayer's Lunch Hour, The.
Graves. Work-Room.
Griffiths. Expectations.
Gunn. To a Friend in Time of Trouble.
Haines. Harvest.
Pickers.
Hall. Foundations of American Industry, The. 1934.
Stump.
Valley of Morning.
Hardy. At the Aquatic Sports.
Four in the Morning.
Unkindly May, An.
You on the Tower.
Herrick. Beginning, Difficult.
First Work, and Then Wages.
Heaven.
No Paines, No Gaines.
Nothing Free-Cost.
To His Nephew, to Be Prosperous in His Art of Painting.

Upon Cuffe. Epig.
Upon Strut.
Hewitt. Ex-Serviceman, The.
Executives Third Tier.
Return (1885), The.
Song of the Shipyard Men, The.
Housman. When smoke stood up from Ludlow.
Hughes, Langston. Blue Bayou.
Buddy.
Elevator Boy.
Fired.
Gone Boy.
Necessity.
Johnson. Gnothi Seauton (Post Lexicon Anglicanum Auctum et Emendatum).
Kipling. Imperial Rescript, An.
Jubal and Tubal Cain.
King's Job, The.
Mary's Son.
Sons of Martha, The.
Koch. Thank You.
Larkin. Dedicated, The.
Lawrence. But I Say unto You: Love One Another.
City-Life.
Foreign Sunset.
Labour Battalion.
Man Hauling a Wagon.
Moon Memory.
People, The.
Prisoners at Work in the Rain.
Sex Won't Work.
Wages.
What Is He?
What Is Man Without an Income.
Why—?
Work.
Levine. Look.
Sweet Will.
You Can Have It.
Lindsay. Sweet Briars of the Stairways.
Longfellow. Village Blacksmith, The.
Lowry. !Bulletin!
Cook in the Galley, The.
Der Tag.
Epitaph on Our Gardener, Dead Near Liverpool.
Glory of the Sea, The.
Heat Wave.
Morning rain is raining / The morning leg is paining, The.
"Portly & middleaged" can never.
Stowaway, The.
Welcome Home—Oh Most Beloved Harteebeeste.
With Sweetest Love from All the Little Animals As from 2 Old Friends.
McGrath. Little Song about Charity, A.
Proletarian in Abstract Light.
Mahon. Studio, The.
Matthews. Writer-in-Residence.
Meredith. I say, that but for black Foakes'-day.
Merrill. Three Chores.
Merton. Letter to a Sufi Who Has Abandoned Sufism to Study Law.
Trappists, Working.
Nash. Introspective Reflection.
Will Consider Situation.
Nemerov. Sunday at the End of Summer.
Neruda. Child of the Moon.
Negative Hands.
Olson. Praises, The.
Oppen. Debt.
Paley. Every day he went out, forsaking.
Patchen. In Order to.
No one ever works alone.
Roethke. Gentle, The.
Rossetti. Can I know it?—Nay.— / Shall I know it?—Yea.
Candlemas Dialogue, A.
Crying, my little one, footsore and weary?
4th May Morning.
I fancy the good fairies dressed in white.
I toiled on, but thou.
I Will Arise.

In Patience.
In weariness and painfulness St. Paul.
Margaret has a milking-pail, / And she rises early.
Our life is long. Not so, wise Angels say.
Pastime.
Pocket handkerchief to hem, A.
Septuagesima.
There Remaineth Therefore a Rest to the People of God.
Today's Burden.
Until the Day Break.
Weary in Well-Doing.
Where Neither Rust Nor Moth Doth Corrupt.
Would that I were a turnip white.
Yet A Little While.
Rukeyser. Statement: Philippa Allen.
Sandburg. Big oil tanks squat next the railroad.
Blue Island Intersection.
Have you seen men handed refusals.
Hazardous Occupations.
In a winter sunset near Springfield, Illinois.
Moon Riders.
Noon Hour.
Smoke and Steel.
Stripes.
Two Women and Their Fathers.
Who can make a poem of the depths of weariness.
Silverstein. Bang-Klang.
Simic. Man, The.
Thus.
Smith, Patti. Work Song.
Smith, Stevie. Childe Rolandine.
Snyder. Painting the North San Juan School.
Yase: September.
Spender. Face of the Dam: Vivian Jones.
Unemployed.
Stein. Tillie.
Stevenson. About my fields, in the broad sun.
I meanwhile in the populous house apart.
Link your arm in mine, my lad.
Strong man's hand, the snow-cool head of age, The.
To A Gardener.
Who would think, herein to look.
Warren. Morning.
Work.
Whitman. Song for Occupations, A.
Whittier. Dedication: "I would the gift I offer here."
Mrs. Choate's House-Warming.
Seed-Time and Harvest.
Wilbur. Plain Song for Comadre, A.
Summer Morning, A.
Williams, Charles Kenneth. Fast Food.
Sanctity, The.
Work.
Williams, William Carlos. Rogation Sunday.
Well Disciplined Bargeman, The.
Wordsworth. At Furness Abbey ("Well have yon Railway Labourers to THIS ground").
Labourer's Noon-Day Hymn, The.
Wright, James. Youth.
Yeats. Spirit Medium, The.
Zimmer. Work.
See also **Labor and Laborers.**

World. *see* **Earth.**

World Federation
Tennyson. For I Dipped [*or* Dipt] into the Future.

World War I
Bunting. Keep Troth.
Carroll, Jim. Traffic.
Cummings. Belgium.
Bigness of cannon, The.
Come,gaze with me upon this dome.
Earth like a tipsy.
It's jolly / odd what pops into.
Lis / -ten / you know what i mean when.
Look at this) / a 75 done.
My sweet old etcetera.
Opening of the chambers close.
Fletcher. America.
Graves. Armistice Day, 1918.
Field-Postcard, The.

Hall. Six Naps in One Day.
Hardy. And There Was a Great Calm.
Appeal to America on Behalf of the Belgian Destitute, An.
Before Marching and After.
Call to National Service, A.
Channel Firing.
Cry of the Homeless.
England to Germany in 1914.
I Met a Man.
In Time of "The Breaking of Nations."
In Time of Wars and Tumults.
Jezreel.
Men Who March Away.
New Year's Eve in War Time, A.
Often When Warring.
On the Belgian Expatriation.
Peace Peal, The.
Pity of It, The.
Sea Fight, The.
Then and Now.
War-Wife of Catknoll, The.
Hartley. Ironies out of St. George's.
K. von F.—1914—Arras-Bouquoi.
Heaney. In Memoriam Francis Ledwidge.
Hesketh. July 2nd, 1916.
Hewitt. Portstewart, 1914.
Hill. Apostles: Versailles, 1919, The.
Mystery of the Charity of Charles Péguy, The.
To the Nieuport Scout.
Hugo. Yards of Sarajevo, The.
Jarrell. 1914.
Kipling. Beginnings, The.
Changelings, The.
Children, The.
Choice, The.
Clerks and the Bells, The.
Covenant, The.
Death-Bed, A.
Epitaphs of the War [1914–1918].
Farewell and adieu to you, Harwich Ladies.
For All We Have and Are [1914].
Gethsemane.
Justice.
King's Pilgrimage, The.
Legend of Truth, A.
London Stone.
Lord Roberts.
Lowestoft Boat, The.
Memories.
Mesopotamia.
Mine Sweepers.
My Boy Jack.
Nativity, A.
North Sea Patrol, The.
Ode: "So long as memory, valour, and faith endure."
Outlaws, The.
Question, The.
Recantation, A.
Scholars, The.
Song at Cock-Crow, A.
Song in Storm, A.
Song of French Roads, A.
Song of the Lathes, The.
Tin Fish.
Trade, The.
Verdicts, The.
Vineyard, The.
Larkin. MCMXIV.
Lawrence. Reality of Peace, 1916.
Song of a Man Who Has Come Through.
Tommies in the Train.
Town in 1917.
Nemerov. Sarajevo.
Oppen. Niece.
Owen. Anthem for Doomed Youth.
Apologia Pro Poemate Meo.
Calls, The.
Chances, The.
Conscious.
Disabled.
Dulce Et Decorum Est.
Futility.
Greater Love.
Inspection.
Last Laugh, The.
Letter, The.

Next War, The.
1914.
Parable of the Old Man and the Young, The.
Send-Off, The.
Sentry, The.
Show, The.
S.I.W.
Smile, Smile, Smile.
Spring Offensive.
Terre, A.
To a Comrade in Flanders.
Pound. Coming of War, The; Actaeon.
There died a myriad.
These fought in any case.
Sandburg. Four Brothers, The.
Jaws.
Liars, The.
Million Young Workmen, 1915, A.
Spender. In 1929.
Tomlinson. Poem for My Father.
Williams, Miller. WW I.
Yeats. On Being Asked for a War Poem.
Young. Sarajevo Moon.

World War II
Auden. Here war is harmless like a monument.
Berryman. Dangerous Year, The.
Moon and the Night and the Men, The.
Nineteen Thirty-Eight.
1 September 1939.
Rock-Study with Wanderer.
White Feather.
Betjeman. Before Invasion, 1940.
In Westminster Abbey.
South London Sketch, 1944.
Bukowski. Troops, The.
Carruth. Any fire will do - you who are sleeping.
Mountain, The.
People burned, came apart, suffocated, melted.
Ciardi. Elegy Just in Case.
Graph, The.
Memory of the Sad Chair, A.
Naples.
V-J Day.
Cohen. Hitler.
It Uses Us!
Music Crept by Us, The.
Cullen. La Belle, La Douce, La Grande.
Cummings. Why must itself up every of a park.
YgUDuh / ydoan / yunnuhstan.
Davie. Eight Years After.
Elect, The.
Huntingdonshire.
In Chopin's Garden.
1945.
Reminded of Bougainville.
Well-Found Poem.
Dickey, James. Firebombing, The.
Two Poems of the Military.
Doolittle. Ancient Wisdom Speaks.
Body and Soul.
Christmas 1944.
Ecce Sponsus.
May 1943.
Dove. Aircraft.
Aurora Borealis.
Edmunds. Treblinka.
Eliot. Defense of the Islands.
To the Indians Who Died in Africa.
Fenton. But come. Grief must have its term?
Guilt too, then.
His wife nods, and a secret smile.
It is not what they built. It is what they knocked down.
Ferlinghetti. L'Occupation Obsédée.
Fletcher. August, 1940.
Griffiths. From Waterloo Bridge, Ensuing Dark.
Gunn. Berlin in Ruins.
Hacker. Days of 1944: Three Friends.
Hesketh. More than Grass.
Hill. Canaan.
De Jure Belli ac Pacis.
Hughes, Langston. World War II.
Hugo. April in Cerignola.
Docking at Palermo.

Eighteen Days in a Tuscan World.
Galleria Umberto I.
Letter to Matthews from Barton Street Flats.
Letter to Simic from Boulder.
Napoli Again.
Paestum.
Pizzeria S. Biagio.
Sailing from Naples.
Spinazzola: Quella Cantina Là.
Tretitoli, Where the Bomb Group Was.
View from Cortona, A.
Viva La Resistènza.
Jarrell. Absent with Official Leave.
Angels at Hamburg, The.
Burning the Letters.
Camp in the Prussian Forest, A.
Dead in Melanesia, The.
Dead Wingman, The.
Death of the Ball Turret Gunner, The.
Eighth Air Force.
Field Hospital, A.
Front, A.
Germans Are Lunatics, The.
Good-bye, Wendover; Good-bye, Mountain Home.
Leave.
Losses.
Lullaby, A: "For wars his life and half a world away."
Machine-Gun, The.
Metamorphoses, The.
New Georgia.
1945: The Death of the Gods.
Pilot from the Carrier, A.
Pilots, Man Your Planes.
Port of Embarkation.
Range in the Desert, The.
Rising Sun, The.
Second Air Force.
Sick Nought, The.
Siegfried.
Soldier, The.
Stalag Luft.
Subway from New Britain to the Bronx, The.
To the New World.
Transient Barracks.
Truth, The.
Ward in the States, A.
Jeffers. Battle.
Fourth Act.
Greater Grandeur.
Invasion.
Miching Mallecho.
Nerves.
Ordinary Newscaster, An.
Pearl Harbor.
Shine, Empire.
War-Guilt Trials.
Lewis. After Dunkirk.
Burma Casualty.
Peasants, The.
Raiders' Dawn.
Sweet Mother Chruch, beleaguered on the hill.
Liddy. Eugene Connolly.
His Refugees.
Lowell. Exile's Return, The.
Holy Innocents, The.
Mad Negro Soldier Confined at Munich, A.
McGrath. Blues for Warren.
MacNeice. Lilacs and the Roses, The.
Neutrality.
Streets of Laredo, The.
Mahon. Home Front, The.
One of These Nights.
Meinke. Stille Nacht, Heilege Nacht.
Merton. Fable for a War.
For My Brother: Reported Missing In Action, 1943.
Poem: "Light plays like a radio in the iron tree."
Moore. In Distrust of Merits.
Keeping Their World Large.
Nathan. Letter to the Patrol Twenty Years After.
Meadow Foam.
Nemerov. August, 1945.
Memory of the War, A.

Oliver. 1945—1985: Poem for the Anniversary.
Olson. Town, The.
Oppen. In Alsace, during the war.
  Of Hours.
Pack. Fathering the Map.
Patchen. I Don't Want to Startle You but They Are Going to Kill Most of Us.
Rolfe. Munich.
Rukeyser. Breaking Open.
  Do you know Hitler? Does he like you?
  His gay words, words of delight.
  Willkie: Words from Russia.
St. John. Six/Nine/Forty-Four.
Sandburg. Man with the Broken Fingers, The.
Shapiro. Progress of Faust, The.
Smith, Stevie. I Remember.
  Voices against England in the Night.
Spender. War God, The.
Tate. Ode to Our Young Pro-consuls of the Air.
Tomlinson. On the Tlacolula Bus.
Updike. Munich.
Wilbur. On the Eyes of an SS Officer.
Williams, Miller. We.
Williams, William Carlos. Sleeping Brute, The.

Worldliness
Clough. From the contamination / Of laudation.
  These vulgar ways that round me be.
Donne. Satire 1: "Away thou fondling motley humourist."
  Since she whom I loved [or lov'd] hath paid [or payd] her last debt.
Eberhart. To Harriet Monroe.
Herrick. Temporall Goods.
Hill. Of Rumor, of Clamor.
Zukofsky. Song for the Year's End, A.
See also **Libraries and Librarians.**

World's Fair (1939)
Hall. Tomorrow.
Hoffman. Flushing Meadows, 1939.
Sorrentino. 1939 World's Fair.

Worms
Atwood. Song of the Worms.
Blake. Sick Rose, The.
Dickinson. Our little Kinsmen—after Rain.
Eberhart. Grave's a seed will get some monstrous bloom, The.
Hartley. There Is Spit upon the Daisy Stem.
Lawrence. Worm Either Way.
Levertov. Earth Worm, The.
Lindsay. Song of the Garden-Toad, The.
"MacDiarmid." Ex Vermibus.
MacLeish. Triumph of the Shell, The.
Rossetti. Handy Mole who plied no shovel, A.
Sandburg. Worms and the Wind.
Sexton. Earthworm.
  Fury of Flowers and Worms, The.
Silverstein. Early Bird.
Simic. Interlude.
Smith, Stevie. Reversionary.
Stevens. Worms at Heaven's Gate, The.
Updike. Earthworm.

Worry
Beatles. Don't Pass Me By.
Berry. To My Children, Fearing for Them.
Davie. On Not Deserving.
"Dylan." I'll Be Your Baby Tonight.
  Sign on the Cross.
  Tell Me, Momma.
Emerson. Borrowing from the French.
Galvin. Needsong.
Hacker. As yoked to her by absence as by prescence.
Hall. Jealous Lovers, The.
Herrick. His Change.
Hesketh. Mill Clock, The.
Hewitt. Storm, The.
Kooser. Leaky Faucet, The.
  Looking for You, Barbara.
  Pocket Poem.
Levertov. Who Is at My Window.
Lowry. Goldeneye and Goldfish.
Nash. Tin Wedding Whistle.
Patchen. Catfish River Lullaby.

Sandburg. Curse of a Rich Polish Peasant on His Sister Who Ran Away with a Wild Man.
Schuyler. Letter to a Friend: Who Is Nancy Daum?
  Shadowy Room.
Sidney. Sonnet 86: "Alas, whence came this change of looks? If I."
Williams, Charles Kenneth. Experience.
Wordsworth. Affliction of Margaret—, The.
Zimmer. Worrying About You All the Time.
  Zimmer with Lester Under the Moon.

Worship and Worshipers
Browning, Robert. Boy and the Angel, The.
  Numpholeptos.
Bunting. O, it is godlike to sit selfpossessed.
Byron. On the Day of the Destruction of Jerusalem by Titus.
Carew. New Years Gift. To the Queen, A.
  New Year's Sacrifice: To Lucinda, A.
Clark. Daring to Be the Same.
  You (V) (after Holderlin).
Cohen. Hallelujah.
  If It Be Your Will.
Coleridge. Eolian Harp, The.
  Love's Sanctuary.
Cummings. Lady / i pray to what is unimaginable.
  Lean candles hunger in.
  Unto thee i / burn incense.
Dickinson. Because the Bee may blameless hum.
  Some keep the Sabbath going to Church.
  We shun because we prize her Face.
Doolittle. Hippolytus Temporizes.
  Magician [Master].
Eliot. Blessed sister, holy mother, spirit of the fountain.
Emerson. Sursum Corda.
Hall. Passage to Worship.
Hardy. Afternoon Service at Mellstock.
Hemingway. I think that I have never trod.
Herbert. Antiphon (2): "Praised be the God of love."
  Christmas.
  Gratefulness.
  Holy Scriptures (1), The.
  Love (2).
  Misery [or Miserie].
  Praise (2).
  Prayer (1): "Prayer the Church's banquet, Angels' age."
  Sunday.
  Temper (1), The.
  Temper (2), The.
Hesketh. Bleasdale: The Wooden Circle.
  What Is God?
Hewitt. Novice, The.
  Sonnet: "I have no time to worship. I must live."
Hill. Eia, with handbells, jews' harps, risible.
Hopkins. Pied Beauty.
Housman. New Year's Eve.
Hughes, Langston. Testimonial.
Keats. Ode to May. Fragment.
Kipling. L'Envoi; Departmental Ditties.
  Will they gape for the husks that ye proffer.
Lawrence. Absolute Reverence.
  Worship.
Lieberman. Banana Madonna, The.
  Wreckage of the Pagoda Moons.
Lindsay. At Mass.
  Beyond the Moon.
  Johnny Appleseed's Hymn to the Sun.
Lowry. Old Blake was warm, he got down to the hub.
Markson. Sister's Son.
Marlowe. 3.12: De Iunonis festo.
Merton. After the Night Office—Gethsemani Abbey.
  Evening: Zero Weather.
  In the Rain and the Sun.
  O Sweet Irrational Worship.
  Song for Our Lady of Cobre.
  Trappists, Working.
  Word—a Responsory, The.
Olson. Winter Solstice.
Pack. Dead King, The.
Psalms. Psalm 29: "Give unto the Lord, O ye

mighty."
  Psalm 33: "Rejoice in the Lord, O ye righteous."
  Psalm 34: "I will bless the Lord at all times."
  Psalm 66: "Make a joyful unto God, all ye lands."
  Psalm 96: "O sing unto the Lord a new song."
  Psalm 97: "Lord reigneth, The; let the earth rejoice."
  Psalm 98: "O sing unto the Lord a new song."
  Psalm 100: "Make a joyful noise unto the Lord, all ye lands."
  Psalm 111: "Praise ye the Lord. I will praise."
  Psalm 117: "O praise ye the Lord, all ye nations."
  Psalm 134: "Behold, bless ye the Lord, all ye servants of the Lord."
  Psalm 138: "I will praise thee with my whole heart."
  Psalm 145: "I will extol thee, my God, O king."
  Psalm 146: "Praise ye the Lord. Praise the Lord."
  Psalm 147: "Praise ye the Lord: for it is good."
  Psalm 148: "Praise ye the Lord. Praise ye the Lord from the heavens."
  Psalm 149: "Praise ye the Lord. Sing unto the Lord a new song."
  Psalm 150: "Praise ye the Lord. Praise God in his sanctuary."
Rossetti. All Saints: Martyrs.
  Antipas.
  Ash Wednesday.
  Charity Never Faileth.
  Christmas Day.
  Christmastide.
  Epiphany.
  Epiphanytide.
  Eva.
  I love you and you know it—this at least.
  Imitated From the Arpa Evangelica: Page 121.
  Jesus alone:—if thus it were to me.
  Lift up thine eyes to seek the invisible.
  Not Yours But You.
  O Lord, on Whom we gaze and dare not gaze, / Increase our faith that gazing we may see.
  Sursum Corda.
  Valentines From C.G.R.
  Vigil of the Presentation.
  Worship God.
Sandburg. Cahokia.
Smart. Attend to the music divine.
  Hallelujah! kneel and sing / Praises to the heav'nly king.
  Hosanna! God be prais'd.
  Hosanna! praise the Lord, and bless.
  O Frame the strains anew.
  Rejoice in God, ye saints above.
Sorrentino. Totem, The.
Southwell. Child[e] My Choice [or Choyse], A.
Stevenson. Relic taken, what avails the shrine?, The.
Whittier. First-Day Thoughts.
  Hymns from the French of Lamartine.
  Meeting, The.
  Worship.
Wordsworth. Fragment: Redundance.
See also **Churches; Prayer; Religion.**

Wreaths
"MacDiarmid." Last Song, A.
  One of the Principal Causes of War.
Whitman. Pallid Wreath, The.
Whittier. Birthday Wreath, The.

Wrecks
Hall. Blue Wing, The.
  Stump.
  Wreckage, The.

Wren, Sir Christopher
MacNeice. Homage to Wren.

Wrens
De la Mare. Jenny Wren.
Meredith. Song: The Wren.
Rossetti. Wrens and robins in the hedge.
Sandburg. People of the Eaves, I Wish You Good Morning.

Silverstein. Razor-Tailed Wren, The.
Upstairs.
Wordsworth. Contrast; the Parrot and the
Wren, The.
Wren's Nest, A.

Wrestling and Wrestlers
Gunn. Wrestling.
Hewitt. Jacob and the Angel.
Owen. Antaeus: A Fragment.
Tomlinson. Wrestlers on the Vase, The.
Van Duyn. Outlandish Agon.

Wright, James
Hugo. Last Words to James Wright.
Oliver. Three Poems for James Wright.

Wright, Richard
Muldoon. Carson.

Writing and Writers
Angelou. Artful Pose.
Conceit, A.
Impeccable Conception.
Ashbery. And "Ut Pictura Poesis" Is Her
Name.
Or in My Throat.
Sonnet: "Each servant stamps the reader with
a look."
Atwood. Aging Female Poet Reads Little
Magazines.
Words Continue Their Journey, The.
Auden. Dichtung und Wahrheit.
Nones.
Novelist, The.
Richard Jefferies.
To E.T.
Beatles. Paperback Writer.
Berg. God, A.
Iowa.
You.
Berrigan. Academy of the future is opening its
doors, The.
Ann Arbor Song.
Dear Ron: hello. Your name is now a
household name.
Final Sonnet, A.
Grace to be born and live as variously as
possible.
How strange to be gone in a minute / Bearden
is dead Gallup is dead Margie is dead.
I like to beat people up.
In Anselm Hollo's Poems.
It is a human universe: & I.
It is night. You are asleep. And beautiful
tears.
Musick strides through these poems.
On the 15th day of November in the year of
the motorcar.
Personal Poem #9.
Poem: "Of morning, Iowa City, blue."
Seurat and Juan Gris combine this season.
Tambourine Life.
Words for Love.
Berry. Warning to My Readers, A.
Berryman. All we were going strong last night
this time.
Antitheses.
Cold rewards trail in, when the man is blind,
The.
Damn You, Jim D., You Woke Me Up.
Friendless.
He made, a thousand years ago, a-many songs.
Her & It.
Heroes, The.
Home Ballad, The.
How far upon these songs with my strict
wrist.
Message.
Monkhood.
Of Suicide.
Poet hunched, so, whom the worlds admire,
The.
Relations.
They come too thick, hail-hard, and all beside.
They may, because I would not cloy your ear.
Two Organs.
Bishop. Rainbow.
Blake. Blakes apology for His Catalogue.
When Klopstock England defied.
Bly. After Drinking All Night with a Friend,
We Go Out in a Boat at Dawn to See Who

Can Write the Best Poem.
Words Rising.
Bogan. Poem in Prose.
Boyle. On the Death of My Student, the Poet
Serafin.
Poem for Vida Hadjebi Tabrizi, A.
Poets.
Bradstreet. Another to Mrs. Anne Bradstreet,
Author of this Poem.
Elegy Upon that Honorable and Reknowned
Knight Sir Philip Sydney, An.
I cannot wonder at Apollo now.
In Honor of Du Bartas, 1641.
In Praise of the Author, Mistress Anne
Bradstreet, Virtue's True and Lively Pattern.
Prologue: "To sing of wars, of captain[e]s, and
of kings."
To Her Most Honored Father Thomas Dudley,
Esquire, These Humbly Presented.
To My Dear Sister, the Author of these
Poems.
Upon the Author.
Upon the Author. By a Known Friend.
Brontë. Alone I sat; the summer day.
Aye, there it is! It wakes to-night.
How long will you remain? The midnight
hour.
Night Wind, The.
Plead for Me.
Browning, Elizabeth Barrett. Insufficiency.
North and the South, The.
Poet and the Bird, The.
Sonnet: "My poet, thou canst touch on all the
notes."
Sonnet: "Thou hast thy calling to some palace
floor."
Vision of Poets, A.
Browning, Robert. At the "Mermaid."
Thus I wrote in London, musing on my
betters.
Bukowski. About My Very Tortured Friend,
Peter.
After the Reading.
Ah.
As Crazy As I Ever Was.
Beauti-ful.
Clean Old Man.
Dear Friend.
Famous Writer, The.
Farewell, Foolish Objects.
462-0614.
Gloomy Lady.
Horse on Fire.
How Come You're Not Unlisted?
How to Be a Great Writer.
Hustle, The.
I Am Visited by an Editor and a Poet.
I Have Lived in England.
Interviewed by a Guggenheim Recipient.
Lady Poet, The.
Last Generation, The.
Letter from the North.
Literary Life, The.
Little Girls, The.
My Comrades.
Note to the Boys in the Back Room, A.
O, We Are the Outcasts.
Old Buddy, An.
Old Gang, The.
Old Man, Dead in a Room.
On and Off the Road.
On Being Recognized.
Result.
Sad-Eyed Mules of Men.
Sad Poem, A.
2nd Novel, The.
Sickness, The.
Suggestion for an Arrangement.
Suicide.
This Poet.
Tonight.
Unkind Poem, An.
Very.
Word on the Quick and Modern Poem-Makers,
A.
Writing Is a State of Trance.
Bunting. Against the Tricks of Time.
Envoi to the Reader.

Narciss, my numerous cancellations prefer.
Reading X's Collected Works.
Renowned author of, The.
That volatile poet called Jonathan.
What the Chairman Told Tom.
Burns. Address, to the Shade of Thomson, on
Crowning His Bust, at *Ednam, Roxburgh-*
shire, with Bays.
Answer, The [To the Guidwife of Wauchope-
House].
Bard's Epitaph, A.
Dear Cimon Gray, / The other day.
Elegy on the Death of Robert Ruisseaux.
Epistle to Davie, a Brother Poet.
Epistle to J. L*****k, an Old Scotch Bard.
Epitaph. Here Lies Robert Fergusson, Poet.
Extempore—on Some Commemorations of
Thomson.
Extempore—To Mr. Gavin Hamilton.
Fragment—Epistle from Esopus to Maria.
Ill-fated Genius! Heaven-taught Fergusson.
O were I on Parnassus hill.
On a Scotch Bard Gone to the West Indies.
On Fergusson.
Robert Burns' Answer [to Epistle from a
Taylor].
Second Epistle to Davie.
Sketch.
To Captain Riddell.
To Mr. E——— on His Translation of and
Commentaries on Martial.
To Peter Stuart.
To R***** G***** of F*****, Esq.
While new-ca'd kye rowte at the stake.
Byron. Another Simple Ballat.
Answer to Some Elegant Verses.
Ballad: "Of all the twice ten thousand bards."
Canto the Eleventh.
Dear Doctor, I Have Read Your Play.
E Nihilo Nihil.
Epitaph for Joseph Blacket.
From the French.
Good Plays Are Scarce.
My Dear Mr. Murray.
Next comes the dull disciple of thy school.
No Infant Sotheby, Whose Dauntless Head.
To a Knot of Ungenerous Critics.
To Harriet ("Harriet! To see such
Circumspection").
To Hook the Reader, You, John Murray.
To the Countess of Blessington.
When Thurlow This Damn'd Nonsense Sent.
Campion. Ad Carolum Fitz Geofridum.
Ad Ed. Mychelburnum.
Ad Io. Davisium.
Ad Librum.
Ad Nashum.
De Catullo et Martiale.
De obitu Phil. Sydnaei equitis aurati
generosissimi.
Eiusdem ad Authorem.
Epigramma: "Quid tu te numeris immisces?
anne medentem."
Incipit Thomas Campianus Medicinae Doctor.
In Peragrantissimi, Itinerosissimi,
Montiscandentissimique Peditis, Thomae
Coryati, viginti-hebdomadarium *Diarium, sex*
pedibus gradiens, partim vero claudicans,
Encomiasticon.
Long have mine eies gaz'd with delight.
Writer to his Booke, The.
Carew. Fancy, A.
To Ben Jonson.
To My Honoured Friend, Master Thomas May,
Upon His Comedy *The Heir.*
To My Worthy Friend, Master Davenant Upon
His Excellent Play, *The Just Italian.*
Carroll, Jim. It Doesn't Matter.
Not surprisingly / I lost track of the seasons.
"Carroll, Lewis." Three Children.
Carruth. Apology for Using the Word "Heart"
in Too Many Poems, An.
Assignment.
Cowshed Blues, The.
Dedication in These Days.
Essay on Marriage.
Expectantly and fearfully I sing.
Fourth.

Freedom and Discipline.
Hey, Basho, you there!
Lamoille River Valley otherwise known, The.
Master, Grieved with Age, The.
Morning ice on the window.
Notes from Robin Hill Cottage.
On Being Asked to Write a Poem Against the War in Vietnam.
Poet, The.
Post-Impressionist Susurration for the First of November, 1983, A.
RAVAGE, v.t. To lay waste; to subject.
Reading myself, old poems, their inside truth that was.
Shirt, britches, paper.
Sonnet: "Cindy, I've used my writing all my life."
Sonnet: "It's said by the thoughtful masters that to know death."
Sonnet: "Most brainy woman, the sexuality of your thought."
Sonnet: Sin.
Sonnet: "Well, Jim says that the couplet at the end."
Sonnet: "While you stood talking at the counter, cutting."
Sonnet: "Yes. After all my arguments with myself."
Sonnet: "You rose from our embrace and the small light spread."
Stepping Backward.
Tanck's Epilogue.
Tanck's Prolegomenon.
'Thee knows. Must thee not knowe?' I so saying.
Today my poems seem / only the spells I muttered.
True, I happen. So.
When I Wrote a Little.
Catullus. Carmen 14: "If, my irrepressible Calvus, I didn't".
Carmen 16: "Pedicabo et irrumabo."
Carmen 22: "I must, Varus, tell you."
Carmen 35: "Fetch, papyrus / our soft-measured poet."
Carmen 49: "Silver-tongued among the sons of Rome."
Carmen 50: "Other day we spent, The."
Carmen 54: "If not by all that his friends boast."
Carmen 65: "Although entangled in prolonged grief."
Carmen 68: "Borne down by bitter misfortune."
Carmen 95: "Nine harvests & nine winters since its inception."
Carmen 116: "Conscientiously bringing my mind to bear on this problem."
Ciardi. Annals.
Apology for Not Invoking the Muse, An.
Bicentennial.
Gift, The.
Highest Place in Town, The.
Thousandth Poem for Dylan Thomas, The.
Trying to Feel Something.
Clark. "Enforced lapse ..., The."
Things About You.
Clough. If to write, rewrite, and write again.
Cohen. I Bury My Girlfriend.
Price of This Book, The.
Coleridge. Character, A.
Lines to a Comic Author, on an Abusive Review.
Silver Thimble, The.
To a Friend [Charles Lamb] Who Had Declared His Intention of Writing No More Poetry.
To the Author of Poems.
Cooper. Coda.
Inheritances.
Long View from the Suburbs.
Cowper. 5.12: "You bid me write t' amuse the tedious hours."
Ah brother Poet! send me of your shade.
Epistle to Robert Lloyd, Esq., An.
In Memory of John Thorton.
My pens are all spilt, and my ink-glass is dry.
Ode to Apollo.

On the Author of Letters on Literature.
Sonnet to Mrs. Unwin.
To Dr. Darwin.
To Gravina.
To William Hayley, Esq.: In Reply to His Solicitation to Write with Him in a Literary Work.
Crane. Passage.
Porphyro in Akron.
Crashaw. On Mr. G. Herberts Booke, The Temple.
Upon Ford's Two Tragedies, "Loves Sacrifice" and "The Broken Heart."
Creeley. Apology, The.
Citizen.
Re C—.
Sound.
Trees.
Waiting.
Cullen. To Certain Critics.
Cummings. Chaucer.
Fame Speaks.
It was a goodly co.
Pound pound pound / on thy cold grey corona oh P.
To start,to hesitate;to stop.
We miss you,jack—tactfully you(with one cocked).
Davie. Agave in the West.
Bent, The.
Cambridgeshire.
Catullus on Friendship.
Depravity: Two Sermons.
Epistle. To Enrique Caracciolo Trejo.
First Epistle.
Fourth Epistle.
God of Details, The.
H. D.
His Themes.
Hypochondriac Logic.
July, 1964.
Leicestershire.
Love-Poems: for Mairi MacInnes.
Method. For Ronald Gaskell.
Mustered into the Avant-Garde.
North & South.
Oak Openings.
Obiter Dicta.
Pastor Errante.
Poet Redeemed & Dead.
Preoccupation's Gift.
Pushkin. A Didactic Poem.
Recollections of George Oppen in a Letter to an English Friend.
Rejoinder to a Critic.
Resolutions.
Revulsion.
Savannah.
"Sculpture" of Rhyme, The.
Second Epistle.
Sixth Epistle.
Somerset.
Summer Lightning.
Surrey.
To a Bad Poet.
To Certain English Poets.
To Thom Gunn in Los Altos, California.
When you have shoved aside the scribbled worksheet.
Wild Boar Clough.
Winter's Talents.
Wombwell on Strike.
Woodpigeons at Raheny.
Zip!
De la Mare. Scribe, The.
Dickey, James. False Youth: Autumn: Clothes of the Age.
For Robert Bhain Campbell.
To Landrum Guy, Beginning to Write at Sixty.
Dickey, William. Virginia Woolf Gathers Mushrooms.
Dickinson. All the letters I can write.
Going—to—Her!
Going to Him! Happy letter!
If it had no pencil.
Missing All—prevented Me, The.
Word dropped careless on a Page, A.

Writing is brief and fleeting.
Your thoughts don't have words every day.
Dobyns. Passing the Word.
Place in Maine, A.
Donne. Sappho to Philaenis.
Satire 2: "Sir: though (I thank God for it) I do hate."
To E. of D. with Six Holy Sonnets.
To Mr. R. W. ("Kindly I envy thy song's [or songs] perfection").
To Mr. R. W. ("Muse not that by thy mind thy body is led").
To Mr S. B.
To Mr. T. W. ("All hail, sweet poet, more full of more strong fire").
To Mr. T. W. ("At once, from hence, my lines and I depart").
To Mr. T. W. ("Haste thee harsh verse as fast as thy lame measure").
Valediction, A: Of the Book.
Doolittle. Fragment 36: "I know not what to do."
Heliodora.
Poet, The.
Dove. At the German Writers Conference in Munich.
Nexus.
Dryden. Prologue to the University of Oxford, 1674.
Dunbar. Choice, A.
Confirmation.
Crumb, a Crumb, and a Little Seed, A.
Inspiration.
Lapse, The.
Misapprehension.
Poet and His Song, The.
Poet and the Baby, The.
Poet, The.
Prometheus.
Then and Now.
To a Poet and a Lady.
Duncan. After Reading H.D.'s *Hermetic Definitions*.
Ballad of the Enamord Image, The.
Banners, The.
Beginning of Writing, The.
Bending the Bow.
Book of Resemblances, A.
Circulations of the Song.
Descriptions of Imaginary Poetries.
Festivals, The.
Helmet of Goliath, The.
Illustrative Lines.
Imagining in Writing.
In Blood's Domaine.
Kingdom of Jerusalem, The.
Poem in Stretching, A.
Poetry, a Natural Thing.
Poetry Disarranged.
Source.
Dunn. Almost Everyone.
Because We Are Not Taken Seriously.
Decorum.
Essay on the Personal.
Temporarily.
Eberhart. Broken Pen, The.
Face, Ocean.
Flow of Thought.
Ideal and the Real, The.
Long Term Suffering.
Man and Nature.
1934.
Question Mark.
Request.
Testament, A.
Yonder.
Edmunds. Fire, The.
Moon.
White Nights, 1938.
Eliot. Whispers of Immortality.
Emerson. And he like me is not too proud.
By the unacknowledged tie.
God only knew how Saadi dined.
Gods walk in the breath of the woods, The.
His instant thought the Poet spoke.
Husband has the nearest acres, The.
I shall go from my sickbed to heaven.

In the kingdom of Poesy Hafiz waves like a banner.
Lament not, o Hafiz, the distribution.
Letters ("My tongue is prone to lose the way").
O Hafiz! speak not of thy need.
Poet ("Ever the poet *from* the land").
Poet is at home, A.
Poets are colorpots.
Saadi held the Muse in awe.
Saadi loved the new & old.
Thy poems Hafiz shame the rose leaves.
Thy songs O Hafiz.
Who compares a poem.
William does thy frigid soul.
Everson. Answer, The.
Ferlinghetti. Adieu À Charlot.
Constantly risking absurdity.
Elegy on the Death of Kenneth Patchen, An.
Heaven / was only half as far that night.
In Paris in a loud dark winter.
Jack of Hearts, The.
L'Occupation Obsédée.
Mock Confessional.
Poem for Old Walt.
Poet as Fisherman.
Populist Manifesto.
Sea and Ourselves at Cape Ann, The.
Triste Corbiére.
Uses of Poetry.
Fisher. I saw what there was to write and I wrote it.
Making of the Book, The.
News for the Ear.
Occasional Poem 7.1.72.
Sets.
Fletcher. Clown's Song.
Golden Demon, The.
Sorrow.
Ford. Mishima.
Not everyone has plenty of time to die in.
St.-John Perse.
Fox. Megrez.
Frost. It takes all sorts of in- and outdoor schooling.
Lost Follower, The.
On Being Chosen Poet of Vermont.
Gardner. Are Poets Ball Players?
Fright among the Runes.
This Room Is Full of Clocks.
Writing Poetry.
Garrigue. Cortège for Colette.
In Memory.
Last Letter to the Scholar.
Mourning, A.
There Is a Dark River.
Ginsberg. After All, What Else Is There to Say?
Howl.
Names, The.
On Burroughs, Work.
Poem Rocket.
Glück. Exile.
Mountain, The.
Poem: "In the early evening, as now, a man is bending."
Graves. At the Gate.
Crucibles of Love.
Field-Postcard, The.
Last Poem, A.
Laureate, The.
Plea to Boys and Girls, A.
Poem: A Reminder.
Reader over My Shoulder, The.
Singleness in Love.
Something to Say.
Three Years Waiting.
Title of Poet, The.
To Be Poets.
Unpenned Poem, The.
Wall, The.
Work Drafts.
Work-Room.
Gray. Long Story, A.
Progress of Poesy, The.
Stanzas to Mr Richard Bentley.
Griffiths. Christmas Night.
Elegy for John Tripp.

Hymns and Backward Glances.
Tŷ Newydd.
Unwritten Chapters.
Gunn. Drive to Los Alamos, A.
Expression.
Interruption.
J Car, The.
JVC.
Mirror for Poets, A.
Plan of Self-Subjection, A.
Hacker. Art of a Novel, The.
Feeling and Form.
Late August Letter.
Riposte.
Rooms in Bloomsbury.
Untoward Occurance at Embassy Poetry Reading.
Why We Are Going Back to Paradise Island.
Hall. To a Waterfowl.
Hardy. Epitaph for George Moore.
George Meredith (1828-1909).
I Looked Up from My Writing.
Hartnett. Bereft of Its Great Poets.
Falling Out, A.
I Have Exhausted the Delighted Range.
I say farewell to English verse.
Man Who Wrote Yeats, the Man Who Wrote Mozart, The.
Mountains, Fall on Us.
Notes on My Contemporaries.
Old Catechism, The.
Sibelius in Silence.
This road is not new.
Heaney. Afterwards, An.
Digging.
From the Frontier of Writing.
Scribes, The.
Wolfe Tone.
Hemingway. And everything the author knows.
First Poem to Mary in London.
How Ballad Writing Affects Our Seniors.
Lady Poets With Foot Notes, The.
Lines to Be Read at the Casting of Scott FitzGerald's Balls into the Sea from Eden Roc (Antibes, Alpes Maritimes).
Portrait of a Lady.
Robert Graves.
Sequal.
To a Tragic Poetess.
Herbert. Jordan (2).
Posy [*or* Posie], The.
Sonnet: "My God, where is that ancient heat towards Thee."
Sonnet: "Sure Lord, there is enough in thee to dry."
Herrick. Departure of the Good Daemon, The.
Glorie.
His Desire.
His Poetry His Pillar.
His Prayer to Ben[.] Jo[h]nson.
His Request to Julia.
Mr. Robert Hericke His Farwell unto Poetrie.
Most Words, Lesse Workes.
Not Every Day Fit for Verse.
On Himselfe ("Ile sing no more, nor will I longer write").
On Himselfe ("Live by thy Muse thou shalt; when others die").
Poets.
Pride Allowable in Poets.
To Cedars.
To God ("Do with me, God! as Thou didst deal with John").
To His Book ("Before the Press scarce one co'd see").
To His Booke ("While thou didst keep thy candor undefil'd").
To His Honour'd Friend, Sir Thomas Heale.
To His Muse: ("Were I to give thee *Baptime*, I wo'd chuse").
To His Muse ("Whither, mad maiden, wilt thou roame?").
To His Verses.
To M. Denham, on His Prospective Poem.
To the Generous Reader.
To the Reverend Shade of His Religious Father.

Upon His Verses.
Upon Master Fletchers Incomparable Playes.
Upon Nis.
When He Would Have His Verses Read.
Writing.
Hewitt. Clink of Rhyme, The.
Country Walk in May, A.
Dedication: "I have a certain skill in phrase."
Domimie's Log, A.
First Honey.
Fontanel.
Function.
I Cannot Make a Song Tonight.
I Write For.
In Memorium: D.H. Lawrence.
Interim.
Limitations.
Local Poet, A.
Mauberly's Son: A Summary.
On Reading Wallace Stevens' *Collected Poems* after Many Years.
On the Preservation of Work Sheets.
Poem: "Consider Wordsworth in his withered age."
Poetry, Then..
Reading.
Real Estate.
Seedsman, The.
Sonnet: "Since brooding men put beauty in a rime."
Style.
Vers Libre.
Holmes. Bad Turn, A.
Vocation, The.
Hopkins. Modern Poets.
On a Poetess.
We live to see.
Housman. They say my verse is sad: no wonder.
Hughes, Langston. Theme for English B.
Hughes, Ted. Famous Poet.
Hugo. Ashville.
Letter to Ammons from Maratea.
Letter to Birch from Deer Lodge.
Letter to Gildner from Wallace.
Letter to Goldbarth from Big Fork.
Letter to Haislip from Hot Springs.
Letter to Kathy from Wisdom.
Letter to Kizer from Seattle.
Letter to Logan from Milltown.
Letter to Mayo from Missoula.
Letter to Peterson from the Pike Place Market.
Letter to Reed from Lolo.
Letter to Snyder from Montana.
Note to R. H. from Strongsville.
Poem for Zen Hofman.
Reading at the Old Federal Courts Building, St. Paul.
Second Chances.
Snow Poem.
Tony.
Jarrell. Author to the Reader, The.
Le Poète Contumace.
Jeffers. Eagle and hawk with their great claws and hooked heads.
George Sterling.
Goethe, they say, was a great poet, Pindar, perhaps, was a great poet.
Hand.
Let Them Alone.
Love the Wild Swan.
Mathematicians and physics men, The.
On an Anthology of Chinese Poems.
On Building with Stone.
Second-Best.
Johnson. Prologue Spoken by Mr[.] Garrick at the Opening of the Theatre in Drury Lane, 1747.
Prologue to Garrick's *Lethe*.
Prologue to Goldsmith's *The Good Natur'd Man*.
Jong. Alphabet Poem: To the Letter I.
Commandments, The.
Good Carpenters.
Insomnia & Poetry.
Lives of the Poets: Three Profiles, The.
My death.
Ode to My shoes.

On Reading a Vast Anthology.
Poet Writes in *I*, The.
Poetry Suit, The.
Reading, A.
What You Need to Be a Writer.
Jonson.　Here Follow Certain Other Verses, as
　Charms to Unlock the Mystery of the
　Crudities.
In Authorem.
Ode Allegoric.
Ode to Himself.
On Playwright ("Playwright, by chance,
　hearing some toys I had writ").
On Playwright ("Playwright convict of public
　wrongs to men").
On Poet-Ape.
On the Honoured Poems of His Honoured
　Friend, Sir John Beaumont, Baronet.
Sonnet to the Noble Lady, the Lady Mary
　Wroth, A.
To Alphonso Ferrabosco, on His Book.
To Francis Beaumont.
To His Friend the Author upon His *Richard.*
To Mrs Alice Sutcliffe, on Her Divine
　Meditations.
To My Dear Son, and Right-Learnèd Friend,
　Master Joseph Rutter.
To My Old Faithful Servant: And (by His
　Continued Virtue) My Loving Friend: The
　Author of this Work, Mr Rich[ard] Brome.
To My Truly-Beloved Friend, Mr Browne: on
　His Pastorals.
To My Worthy Friend, Master Edward Filmer,
　on His Work Published.
To the Author.
To the London Reader, on the Odcombian
　Writer, Polytopian Thomas the Traveller.
To the Right Noble Tom, Tell-Troth of His
　Travels, the Coriat of Odcombe, and His
　Book Now Going to Travel.
To the Same [Benjamin Rudyerd] ("Writing
　thyself, or judging others' writ").
To Thomas Palmer [on His Book "The Sprite
　of Trees and Herbs"].
Vision of Ben Jonson, on the Muses of His
　Friend M. Drayton, The.
Joseph.　Abstract Study—Circles.
Bound upon a Wheel.
Knock Knock.
PROEM: *Against metaphor—but how then?*
Translation.
Keats.　House of Mourning Written by Mr
　Scott, The.
Ode: "Bards of passion and of mirth."
Ode to Apollo.
On Leaving Some Friends at an Early Hour.
On Receiving a Laurel Crown from Leigh
　Hunt.
On Seeing a Lock of Milton's Hair.
Poet, The.
Sleep and Poetry.
To J. H. Reynolds, Esq.
To My Brother George.
Where's the Poet? Show Him! Show Him.
Kipling.　Coiner, The.
Craftsman, The.
Dedication, A: "And they were stronger hands
　than mine."
Jane's Marriage.
Prelude to "Departmental Ditties."
Samuel Pepys.
When 'Omer Smote 'Is Bloomin' Lyre.
Knight.　Apology for Apostasy?
Black Poet Leaps to His Death, A.
For Black Poets Who Think of Suicide.
Green Grass and Yellow Balloons.
Memo #9.
On the Projects Playground.
Poem to Galway Kinnell, A.
Knott.　Poem (How I Lost My Pen-Name).
Shorts / Excerpts ("I write these lines to
　cripple the dead").
Koch.　Art of Poetry, The.
Circus, The.
Days and Nights.
Fresh Air.
Pleasures of Peace, The.
Koertge.　Reading at the Local High School.

"These Students Couldn't Write Their Way out
　of a Paper Bag"—Anonymous.
Kunitz.　Mens Creatrix.
Spark of Laurel, A.
Larkin.　Good for You, Gavin.
Literary World, The.
Waiting for Breakfast, While She Brushed Her
　Hair.
Writer, A.
Lawrence.　Correspondence in After Years.
Fate and the Younger Generation.
I Am in a Novel.
My Naughty Book.
Levertov.　Common Ground, A.
Novel, The.
Prayer, The.
Secret, The.
Walk through the Notebooks, A.
Levine.　My Poets.
On the Edge.
Theory of Prosody, A.
Lewis.　Prologue: The Grinder.
To Edward Thomas.
Liddy.　Miles III.
On a Protestant Mystic.
Scott Rautmann, Saturday Night.
Swinburne on the Playing Fields.
Lieberman.　Homage to Austin Warren.
Lindsay.　Apology for the Bottle Volcanic, An.
Dream of All the Springfield Writers, The.
On Receiving One of Gloriana's Letters.
Raft, The.
Lovelace.　Dedication To the Right Honorable
　John Lovelace. The.
On Sanazar's Being Honoured.
One stabbe could not fierce Cato's Life unty.
To Marcus T. Cicero.
Lowell.　Ford Madox Ford ("Lobbed ball
　plops, then dribbles to the cup, The").
Marlowe.
Reading Myself.
Lowry.　Arctic fox / With snow white hocks,
　The.
As to report, / Within his court.
He wrote for the dead, but the ubiquitous
　dead.
I set this down as humble prayer.
I wrote: In the dark cavern of our birth.
Need it be so niggardly of meaning too?
Pijijiapan.
Poets are Godlike in that they.
"Portly & middleaged" can never.
Save that the optimistic ones are worse.
Song: "Pity the blind and the halt but yet
　pity."
Thing to know is how to write a verse, The.
Thoughts to Be Erased from My Destiny.
McAuley.　Examination, The.
"MacDiarmid."　And all this here, everything I
　write, of course.
Caledonian Antisyzygy, The.
Dìreadh III.
Gairmscoile.
Here in the hauf licht waitin' till the clock.
Hokum.
Poetry and Science.
To a Friend and Fellow Poet.
McGrath.　Ars Poetica: Or: Who Lives in the
　Ivory Tower?
For a Critic Who Tries to Write Poems.
Ordonnance.
Poet of the Prison Isle: Ritsos Against the
　Colonels, The.
Uses of the Lost Poets.
MacLeish.　Cummings.
Edwin Muir.
Epistle to Léon-Paul Fargue.
Great Contemporary Discoveries.
Poet.
Reasons for Music.
Reproach to Dead Poets.
Where a Poet's From.
MacNeice.　Autolycus.
Canto II: "'On the other hand,' said Gavin—or
　could have said."
Canto IV: "To work. To my own office, my
　own job."
Elegy for Minor Poets.

Epitaph for Liberal Poets.
To Hedli ("Acting younger").
To Hedli ("Because the velvet").
To Posterity.
To the Public.
Mahon.　Attic, The.
Beyond the Pale.
Craigvara House.
De Quincey in Later Life.
Knut Hamsun in Old Age.
Sea in Winter, The.
Table Talk.
Markson.　Borrowed Line.
Cummings.
Dante Gabriel.
Hartnett in Worcester.
Lowry.
Occupation.
Of Writings Unfinished.
On the Death, after Lying Wounded in the
　Thigh for Twenty-Six Days, of the Author of
　"Astrophel and Stella."
Prosody.
See Susan Read.
Sister's Son.
Skull.
Tardy Poet: 1978.
To a Mexican Poet Who Has Forsaken Drink.
Tricentennial: 1980.
Youthful Poet's Unspoke Response to a
　Woman Talking Too Loudly in His Favorite
　Bookstore, The.
Marvell.　Illustrissimo Viro Domino Lanceloto
　Josepho de Maniban Grammatomanti [To
　That Renowned Man Lord Lancelot Joseph
　de Maniban Graphologist].
Matthews.　Cat, The.
Little Blue Nude.
Meinke.　Hermann Ludwig Ferdinand Von
　Helmholtz.
In Gentler Times.
Liquid Paper.
Playing Shuffleboard, Drunk, in Key West,
　Fla.
Poet to His Tongue, The.
Poet, Trying to Surprise God, The.
Teaching Poetry at a Country School in
　Florida.
Wishing He Had a Theory in Key West.
Writing the Great American Poem in Key
　West.
Meredith.　As often in a bun.
Au voleur, au voleur, au voleur!—.
But see what living glory floods the west.
Camelus Saltat.
Confession.
Empty Purse: A Sermon to our Later Prodigal
　Son, The.
Hail, Common Sense! most rare of all!
Later Alexandrian, A.
Milton.
My Theme.
Poetry of Chaucer, The.
Poetry of Coleridge, The.
Poetry of Keats, The.
Poetry of Milton, The.
Poetry of Shakespeare, The.
Poetry of Shelley, The.
Poetry of Southey, The.
Poetry of Spenser, The.
Poetry of Wordsworth, The.
Spirit of Shakespeare: Continued, The.
There stood in her street a poor exile of
　Queen Je'n.
There was a young poet of Chelsea.
To Alex. Smith, the "Glasgow Poet," on His
　Sonnet to "Fame."
To Carlyle.
To R.H.H. with Daphne.
Tuck, Demitroïa, / Ariadne, and Froyja.
While Janet eyes the Lanthorn's Magic.
Merrill.　Angel.
Clearing the Title.
From a Notebook.
From the Cupola.
Marsyas.
Prism.
Merton.　Ceremony for Edward Dahlberg.

I do not bother with rhymes.
I think poetry must / I think it must.
In the Rain and the Sun.
Message to Be Inscribed on Mark Van
　Doren's Hamilton Medal.
Nombril Walketh on the Loam.
Poet, to His Book, The.
Poetry Ends with Me.
Prologo.
Strife between the Poet and Ambition, The.
Three Sisters, The.
Miller.　For Juan Rulfo.
Moore.　Novices.
Morrison.　Paris Journal.
Muldoon.　Armageddon, Armageddon.
　Lunch with Pancho Villa.
　7, Middagh Street.
Nemerov.　Epitaph: "Of the Great World he
　knew not much."
　Exasperations of a Novelist.
　In the Glass of Fashion.
　Make Big Money at Home! Write Poems in
　　Spare Time!
　Novelists.
　On the Platform.
　Praising the Poets of That Country.
　Reflexion of a Novelist.
　Style.
　To Lu Chi.
　To the Bleeding Hearts Association of
　　American Novelists.
　Winter Lightning, The.
Neruda.　Cherries.
　Child of the Moon.
　Conditions.
　Herbalist's Rose, The.
　Little Devils.
　Negative Hands.
　XIX, The.
　Pardon Me.
　Sitting Down.
Notley.　Homer's Art.
　Jack Would Speak through the Imperfect
　　Medium of Alice.
O'Hara.　Adieu to Norman, Bon Jour to Joan
　and Jean-Paul.
　Answer to Voznesensky and Evtushenko.
　Ashes on a Saturday Afternoon.
　Avenue A.
　Critic, The.
　Getting Up Ahead of Someone (Sun).
　Les Luths.
　Memorial Day 1950.
　My Heart.
　Ode on Causality.
　Ode: Salute to the French Negro Poets.
　Personal Poem.
　Pleasant Thought from Whitehead, A.
　Poem: "I ran through the snow like a young
　　Czarevitch!"
　Poem: "I watched an armory combing its
　　bronze bricks."
　Poem: "To be idiomatic in a vacumm."
　Poetry.
　Post the Lake Poets Ballad.
　Spirit Ink, The.
　To a Poet.
　To Gottfried Benn.
　To Hell with It.
　Today.
　"Unfinished," The.
　Why I Am Not a Painter.
　Young Poet, A.
Oliver.　Morning.
　Some Herons.
　Stanley Kunitz.
Olson.　Black Mt. College Has a Few Words
　for a Visitor.
　Collected Poems of, The.
　Dylan Thomas, and Now Matthew Mead—as
　　He Himself, "To Edward Thomas."
　Got Me Home, the Light Snow Gives the Air,
　　Falling.
　Maximus of Gloucester.
　New Poem.
　Peograms.
　To a Poet Who Read in Gloucester Before the
　　Cape Ann Historical Literary and Scientific

Society.
West 6.
Oppen.　Boy's Room.
　Of Hours.
　Silver as / The needle's eye.
　Whether, as the intensity of seeing increases,
　　one's distance.
Owen.　On My Songs.
Pack.　Landscape Goat.
　Villanelle for Pamela.
Paley.　In France.
　On the Ramblas / A Tree　A Girl.
　Poets! / Madness is a gift.
　Responsibility.
　Traveler.
Patchen.　And in Another Place Uses the Same
　Phrase.
　I Got the Fat Poet into a Corner.
Plath.　Female Author.
　Notes to a Neophyte.
　On the Difficulty of Conjuring Up a Dryad.
　Stillborn.
Pope.　Epigram from the French: "Sir, I admit
　your general [or gen'ral] Rule."
　Epitaph for One Who Would Not Be Buried
　　in Westminster Abbey ("Heroes, and Kings!
　　your distance keep").
　Epitaph on Charles Earl of Dorset.
　Epitaph on Mr. Elijah Fenton, at Easthamstead
　　in Berks, 1730.
　Impromptu to Lady Winchelsea.
　In the lines that you sent, are the Muses and
　　Graces.
　On Lady Mary Wortley Montagu's Portrait.
　On Mr. Gay, in Westminster Abbey, 1732.
　Presentation Verses to Nathaniel Pigott.
　Prologue Design'd for Mr. Durfy's Last Play.
　Prologue to a Play for Mr. Dennis's Benefit,
　　in 1733, when He Was Old, Blind, and in
　　Great Distress, a Little before His Death, A.
　Prologue to the Three Hours after Marriage.
　Sandys's Ghost, or a Proper New Ballad on
　　the New Ovid's Metamorphosis as it Was
　　Intended to Be.
　They say Argyll's a wit, for what?
　Three Gentle Shepherds, The.
　To Belinda on the Rape of the Lock.
　To Eustace Budgell, Esq., on His Translation
　　of the Characters of Theophrastus.
　To Mr. Thomas Southern, on His Birth-Day,
　　1742.
　Translator, The.
　Umbra.
　Verses to Be Placed under the Picture of
　　England's Arch-Poet: Containing a Compleat
　　Catalogue of His Works.
　Where'er you find the cooling western breeze.
Pound.　Epitaphs: "Fu I loved the high cloud
　and the hill."
Prince.　Finis Coronat Opus.
Raine.　My day's plan to write.
　Poet Answers the Accuser, The.
　Poet is of those, The.
　Testimony.
Ralegh.　Epitaph upon the Right Hono[u]rable
　Sir Philip Sidney Knight, Lord Governor of
　Flushing, An.
　If Synthia Be a Queene, a Princes, and
　　Supreame.
　Phoenicians first (if Fame may credit have).
　To the Translator of Lucan [or Lucan's
　　Pharsalia, 1614].
　Walter Rawley [or Ralegh or Rawely] of the
　　Middle Temple, in Commendation of the
　　Steel[e] Glass[e].
Ransom.　Conrad Sits in Twilight.
　Master's in the Garden Again.
　Survey of Literature.
Rexroth.　Thou Shalt Not Kill.
Rich.　Focus.
　Juvenilia.
　North American Time.
　This apartment full of books could crack open.
　Upper Broadway.
　What kind of beast would turn its life into
　　words?
　Woman waking behind grimed blinds slatted
　　across a courtyard, A.

Robinson.　Dark House, The.
　Momus.
　Shadrach O'Leary.
　Sonnet: "Master and the slave go hand in
　　hand, The."
　Sonnet: "Oh for a poet—for a beacon bright."
Roethke.　Reply to a Lady Editor.
　Supper with Lindsay.
Rolfe.　Catalogue of I.
　Essay on Dreiser (1871-1945).
　Poem: "Consciousness, said Don Miguel, is a
　　disease."
　Room with Revolutionists.
　To My Contemporaries.
Rossetti.　How many authors are my first!
　Roundel seems to fit a round of days, A.
　Would that I were a turnip white.
　You who looked on passed ages as a glass.
Rukeyser.　Artifact.
　Louis Sonnet, A.
　Poem White Page White Page Poem.
　Song: Love in Whose Rich Honor.
　Work, for the Day Is Coming.
　Writer, The.
Sandburg.　Enemy Number One.
　Jack London and O. Henry.
　Many Handles.
　One Modern Poet.
　Pencils.
　Sketch of a Poet.
　Tentative (First Model) Definitions of Poetry.
Sarton.　My Sisters, O My Sisters.
Schuyler.　Dec. 28, 1974.
　Dining Out with Doug and Frank.
　Fauré Ballade, The.
　Money Musk.
　Morning of the Poem, The.
　O Sleepless Night.
　Perhaps.
　To Frank O'Hara.
　Virginia Woolf.
　Wystan Auden.
Schwartz.　America, America!
　Apollo Musagete, Poetry, and the Leader of
　　the Muses.
　Come, let us rejoice in James Joyce, in the
　　greatness of this poet.
　Poet, The.
Sexton.　Ambition Bird, The.
　Black Art, The.
　Errand, The.
　Fallen Angels, The.
　February 20th.
　Frenzy.
　Portrait of an Old Woman on the College
　　Tavern Wall.
Shakespeare.　If music and sweet poetry agree.
　Sonnet 17: "Who will believe my verse in
　　time to come."
　Sonnet 21: "So is it not with me as with that
　　Muse."
　Sonnet 23: "As an unperfect actor on the
　　stage."
　Sonnet 32: "If thou survive my well-contented
　　day."
　Sonnet 76: "Why is my verse so barren of
　　new pride."
　Sonnet 78: "So oft I invoked thee for my
　　Muse."
　Sonnet 79: "Whilst I alone did call upon thy
　　aid."
　Sonnet 80: "O, how I faint when I of you do
　　write."
　Sonnet 86: "Was it the proud full sail of his
　　great verse."
　Sonnet 100: "Where art thou, Muse, that thou
　　forget'st so long."
　Sonnet 103: "Alack, what poverty my Muse
　　brings forth."
　Sonnet 108: "What's in the brain that ink may
　　character."
　Sonnet 110: "Alas, 'tis true I have gone here
　　and there."
　Sonnet 115: "Those lines that I before have
　　writ do lie."
　Sonnet 131: "Thou art as tyrannous, so as
　　thou art."
Sidney.　I: "Loving in truth, and fain[e] in

verse my love to show."
My words, in hope to blaze my steadfast mind.
Sonnet 3: "Let dainty wits cry on the sisters nine."
Sonnet 15: "You that do search for every purling spring."
Sonnet 34: "Come, let me write. 'And to what end?' To ease."
Sonnet 50: "Stella, the fullness of my thoughts of thee."
Sonnet 55: "Muses, I oft invoked your holy aid."
Sonnet 58: "Doubt there hath been, when with his golden chain."
Sonnet 70: "My Muse may well grudge at my heav'nly joy."
Sonnet 90: "Stella, think not that I by verse seek fame."
Silverstein. It's Dark In Here.
Simic. Description.
  Evening with the Master, An.
  Poem: "My father writes all day, all night."
Smart. Disertissime Romuli Nepotum.
  To Ethelinda.
Smith, Charlotte. Partial Muse, has from my earliest hours, The.
  Prologue to *What is She?* A Comedy, in Five Acts.
  Sent to the Honorable Mistress O'Neill, with Painted Flowers.
  To a Friend.
  To Miss C—on Being Desired To Attempt Writing a Comedy.
  To Mr. Hayley, on Receiving Some Elegant Lines from Him.
  To My Lyre.
  To the Naiad of the Arun.
  To the River Arun.
  Written at Bristol in the Summer of 1794.
  Written at Penshurst, in Autumn 1788.
Smith, Patti. Notice.
  Ps/alm 23 Revisited.
Smith, Stevie. Full Well I Know.
  How Far Can You Press a Poet?
  Lads of the Village, The.
  Mrs. Arbuthnot.
  My Muse.
  Old Ghosts.
  Pearl.
  Poet!
  Poet Hin, The.
  Poets Are Silent, The.
  Souvenir de Monsieur Poop.
  To an American Publisher.
  To School!
  Voice from the Tomb (1).
  What Is She Writing? Perhaps It Will Be Good.
Snyder. As for Poets.
Sorrentino. Address to the National Council on the Arts.
  At last comes love of such a quality that it would shame me.
  Interesting Glass, The.
  Poet Tires of Those Who Disparage His City, The.
  September in Kittery.
  Stupid painter paints. He, The.
Stein. Comedy like That, A.
  Subject-Cases: The Background of a Detective Story.
Stevens. Creations of Sound, The.
  Planet on the Table, The.
  Prelude to Objects.
  Ultimate Poem Is Abstract, The.
Stevenson. Dedication: "My first gift and my last, to you."
  From Wishing-Land.
  Go, little book—the ancient phrase.
  Had I the power that have the will.
  Henry James.
  I meanwhile in the populous house apart.
  I, now, O friend, whom noiselessly the snows.
  Indefensible impulse of my blood, The.
  Long time I lay in little ease.
  Not roses to the rose, I trow.
  O Henley, in my hours of ease.

Of Schooners, Islands, and Maroons.
Over the land is April.
Pleasant river gushes, The.
Since years ago for evermore.
Still I love to rhyme, and still more, rhyming, to wander.
Their Laureate to an Academy Class Dinner Club.
Thou strainest through the mountain fern.
To Andrew Lang.
To Charles Baxter.
To Doctor John Brown.
To friends at home, the lone, the admired, the lost.
To H.F. Brown.
To Master Andrew Lang.
To Sydney.
To the Muse.
Who would think, herein to look.
Yes, I remember, and still remember wailing.
Stuart. Sticks and Stones.
  Writing Machine, The.
Suckling. Epilogue: "And how, and how, in faith—a pretty plot."
  Epilogue: "Plays are like feasts; and every act should be."
  Prologue to the Court ("Those common passions, hopes, and fears, that still").
  Prologue: "Wit in a prologue poets justly may."
  Session[s] of the Poets, A.
  To My Friend Will. Davenant, on His Other Poems.
  To My Friend Will. Davenant, upon His Poem of "Madagascar."
  Upon T.C. Having the Pox.
Sutter. Declaration of Dependence.
  Motto above my table says, The.
  Work, The.
Tate. To a Romantic Novelist.
Tennyson. Prefatory Poem to My Brother's Sonnets.
  What Hope Is Here for Modern Rhyme.
Thomas. Author's Prologue.
  Especially When the October Wind.
  In My Craft or Sullen Art.
  My Hero Bares His Nerves.
  On No Work of Words.
Thomson. Address to the Shade of Thomson.
  Lines on Marlefield.
  To Mr. Thomson.
  To Mr. Thomson, on his Blooming Winter.
Tomlinson. Antecedents.
  Art of Poetry, The.
  Biography of the Author: A Cento, A.
  Macduff.
  Nature Poem.
  Oppositions.
  Parsnips.
  Poem: It falls onto my page like rain.
  Portrait of the Artist I.
  Portrait of the Artist II.
Turco. Conceit.
  Desert of Melancholy, The.
  Poem: "It is time to write a poem."
Updike. Angels, The.
  At the End of the Rainbow.
  Kenneths.
  Literary Dublin.
  Marching through a Novel.
  Miss Moore at Assembly.
  Ode, An: "I'm going to write a novel, hey."
Van Duyn. Day in Late October, A.
  Eros to Howard Nemerov.
  Essay on Criticism, An.
  Lives of the Poets.
  Moose in the Morning, Northern Maine.
  Quiet Afternoon at Home, A.
  To Poets' Worksheets in the Air-Conditioned Vault of a Library.
  Vision Test, The.
Wakoski. Poet at Carpenter's Bench.
  What Happened.
  With Words.
  Write.
Walcott. At the Queen's Park Hotel, with its white, high-ceilinged rooms.
  Camps hold [*or* held] their distance— [of]

brown chestnuts and grey smoke, The.
  Codicil.
  Hotel Normandie Pool, The.
  Islands.
  Man Who Loved Islands, The.
  Volcano.
Waldman. How the Sestina (Yawn) Works.
  Paul Eluard.
Warren. Flaubert in Egypt.
  Psychological Profile.
Whitman. Ages and Ages Returning at Intervals.
  As I Lay with My Head in Your Lap Camerado.
  As I Sit Writing Here.
  Death and Burial of McDonald Clarke, a Parody, The.
  Excelsior.
  Font of Type, A.
  For Us Two, Reader Dear.
  Here the Frailest Leaves of Me.
  Last Droplets.
  Not Youth Pertains to Me.
  Now Precedent Songs, Farewell.
  Old Chants.
  Shakspeare-Bacon's Cipher.
  So Far, and So Far, and On toward the End.
  Thou Reader.
  Thoughts—6: "Of What I Write."
  To a Certain Civilian.
  To Get the Final Lilt of Songs.
  To Soar in Freedom and in Fullness of Power.
  Unexpress'd, The.
  You Lingering Sparse Leaves of Me.
Whittier. Fitz-Greene Halleck.
  Greeting, A.
  Mulford.
  Proem: "I love the old melodious lays."
  To a Poetical Trio in the City of Gotham.
  To Lydia Maria Child.
Wilbur. Advice from the Muse.
  Beasts.
  Cottage Street, 1953.
  To an American Poet Just Dead.
  To the Etruscan Poets.
Williams, Charles Kenneth. Critic, The.
  Did I write this.
  One of the Muses.
  Yours.
Williams, Miller. Journalist Buys a Pig Farm, The.
  Let Me Tell You.
  Muse, The.
  Today is Wednesday.
Williams, William Carlos. Apology.
  Cure, The.
  Flower, The.
  La Flor.
  Lines on Receiving *The Dial's* Award: 1927.
  Our (American) Ragcademicians.
  Rhymed Address: The Lobster.
  To an Elder Poet.
  Tolstoy.
  Transitional.
  Uses of Poetry, The.
  Wind Increases, The.
Wordsworth. Distressful gift! this Book receives.
  Her Only Pilot the Soft Breeze, the Boat.
  In the First Page of an Album by One Whose Handwriting Is Wretchedly Bad.
  Let More Ambitious Poets Take the Heart.
  Ode to Apollo.
  Orchard Pathway, The.
  Poet and the Caged Turtledove, The.
  Poet!—He Hath Put His Heart to School, A.
  Poet's Epitaph, A.
  Scorn Not the Sonnet [Critic,You Have Frowned].
  Stanzas Written in My Pocket-Copy of Thomson's "Castle of Indolence."
  There Is a Pleasure in Poetic Pains.
  Though Pulpits and the Desk May Fail.
  Though the Bold Wings of Poesy Affect.
  To ———: "Happy feeling from the bosom thrown."
  To ———: "If these brief Records, by the

Muses' art."
Torquato Tasso rests within this tomb.
Wright, Charles. Ars Poetica.
  California Dreaming.
  Childhood's Body.
  Dog Day Vespers.
  Journal of English Days, A.
  Journal of the Year of the Ox, A.
  Light Journal.
  Portrait of the Artist with Hart Crane.
  Roma II.
  Spring Abstract.
Wright, James. Learning from MacDiarmid.
  This morning / My beloved rose, before I did.
  To a Dead Drunk.
  To the Poets in New York.
Wyatt. My pen, take pain a little space.
Yau. Spin, Spell, Spill.
  You Must Remember.
Yeats. Ego Dominus Tuus.
  Model for the Laureate, A.
  On Being Asked for a War Poem.
  Pardon, old fathers, if you still remain.
  To a Poet, Who Would Have Me Praise
    Certain Bad Poets, Imitators of His and
    Mine.
  Under Saturn.
Young. Boogie With O.O. Gabugah.
  Election Night Pome.
  Loneliness.
  People of Letters.
  Poetry.
  Prestidigitator 1, The.
  Realism.
  Reggie's Version.
  Some Spice for Jack Spicer.
  Yes, the Secret Mind Whispers.
  Your Basic Black Poet.
Zimmer. Zimmer Loathing the Gentry.
Zukofsky. *Barely* and *widely.*
  Checkers, checkmate and checkerboard.
  Cold how mean, fortune consuming you
    oppresses your care, your.
  "Mantis," An Interpretation.
  Master of eloquence and Rome's potent line.
  N.Y.
  Not that I look to my eyes more than your
    love.
  Otho's scooped nut its pusillanimity.
  Piping, beaus, I'll go *whoosh* and I'll rumble
    you.
  Poet I'm too near your and my sod daily.
  Sigh paid to be studious when I moved went
    on to (queer) once.
  Song—3/4 time.
  Suffenus is, stay Varus,—whom you've
    proven—is the.
  Yesterday, Licinius, what a day it was.
  Yet see (may as I do) a confect of my cure—
    a dolor.
  Zmyrna, my own Cinna, nine harvests passed
    making his hymn.
See also **Handwriting.**

Wyatt, Sir Thomas
Clark. "Himself let him unknown contain."

Wyeth, Andrew
Muldoon. My Grandfather's Wake.
Wilbur. Wyeth's Mild Cans.

X

Xenophanes
Emerson. Xenophanes.
Hardy. Xenophanes, the Monist of Colophon.

X-Rays
Graves. Broken Neck.
Hoffman. Northern Lights.

Y

Yachts
Eberhart. Sailing to Buck's Harbor.
Williams, William Carlos. Yachts, The.
See also **Boats and Boating; Sailing and Sailors.**

Yaks
Roethke. Yak, The.

Yale University
Hugo. Overlooking Yale.
Nash. Eight O'Clock Peril, The.

Yankees (New York baseball team)
Moore. Baseball and Writing.
Updike. Tao in the Yankee Stadium Bleachers.

Yarrow [*or* Yarrow Water], Scotland
Wordsworth. Yarrow Revisited.
  Yarrow Unvisited [1803].
  Yarrow Visited [September, 1814].

Years
Burns. Elegy on the Year 1788.
Carroll, Jim. New Year 1970.
"Carroll, Lewis." Facts.
Dunbar. King is Dead, The.
Eberhart. Parker River, The.
  Placation of Reality.
  White Pines, Felled 1984.
  Young and the Old, the.
Haines. Calendar, The.
Hardy. End of the Year 1912.
Hartley. New Morning—and the Years Are
  Ours.
Hewitt. Winter Day.
Lowry. Abacus, The.
  Years standing round in a ring, The.
Moore. What Are Years?
Olson. Year Is a Great Circle or the Year Is a
  Great Mistake, The.

Yeats, John Butler
Liddy. Cantico.

Yeats, William Butler
Auden. Earth, receive an honoured guest.
  In Memory of W. B. Yeats.
Berryman. Away.
Davie. Church of Ireland.
Eberhart. Young and the Old, the.
Ferlinghetti. Reading Yeats I do not think.
Hartnett. Man Who Wrote Yeats, the Man
  Who Wrote Mozart, The.
Hoffman. Instructions to a Medium, to be
  Transmitted to the Shade of W.B. Yeats, the
  Latter Having Responded in a Séance Held
  on 13 June 1965, Its Hundredth Birthday.
Liddy. Maud Gonne Rode Out on a White
  Horse to Coolgreany.
Muldoon. Wystan.
Roethke. Dying Man, The.
Schwartz. Yeats Died Saturday in France.
Tate. Winter Mask.
Yeats. Circus Animals' Desertion, The.
  Under Ben Bulben.

Yellow (color)
Creeley. Edge, The.
  Yellow.
Dickinson. Nature rarer uses Yellow.
Eberhart. Vermont Idyll.
Fisher. Oh yellow head.
Herrick. How Marigolds Came Yellow.
Olson. Yellow of the Mask, The.
Sandburg. Crucible.
Williams, William Carlos. Primrose.
Zukofsky. Judge and the Bird, The.

Yew Trees
Ammons. Night Chill.
Herrick. To the Yew and Cypress to Grace
  His Funeral.
Lawrence. Yew-Tree on the Downs, The.
Plath. Little Fugue.
  Moon and the Yew Tree, The.
Tennyson. Old yew, which graspest at the
  stones.
Wordsworth. Yew-Trees.

Yiddish
Sandburg. Home Fires.

York, England
Tomlinson. Near York.

Yorkshire, England
Davie. Northern Metres.
  Yorkshire.
Merton. Rievaulx: St. Ailred.
Wordsworth. Composed after a Journey across
  the Hamilton Hills, Yorkshire.

Yoruba
Lorde. Oya.
  Winds of Orisha, The.

Young, Lester
Young. Lester Leaps In.

Youth
Ashbery. Our Youth.
Auden. Consequences.
  Ebes Anthos Apollumenon.
  Gipsy Girl, The.
  Thomas Prologizes.
Beckett. Ascension.
  Gnome.
Berg. Two Fragments.
Berry. Young Man, Thinking of the Old, The.
Berryman. Down & Back.
  Drunks.
  Heroes, The.
  If not white shorts—then in a princess gown.
  In & Out.
  My Special Fate.
  Nowhere.
  Olympus.
  Song of the Young Hawaiian, The.
  Two Organs.
Betjeman. Youth and Age on Beaulieu River,
  Hants.
Blake. School Boy, The.
  Voice of the Ancient Bard, The.
Bogan. Tale, A.
Boyle. Career.
Brontë. There was a time when my cheek
  burned.
Brooks. We Real Cool.
Browning, Robert. Evelyn Hope.
  Rabbi Ben Ezra.
  She was fifteen—had great eyes.
  Spoils of Youth, The.
  Youth and Art.
Bukowski. Too Late.
Burns. I'm Owre [*or* O'er] Young to Marry
  Yet.
  Lovely Polly Stewart.
  My Bonie Laddie's Young but He's Growin
  Yet.
  Prologue: "No song nor dance I bring from
  yon great city."
Byron. All Is Vanity, Saith the Preacher.
  Childish Recollections.
  Stanzas to a Lady on Leaving England.
  Stanzas Written on the Road between Florence
  and Pisa.
  To a Youthful Friend.
  To Edward Noel Long, Esq.
  To George, Earl Delawarr.
  When I Roved a Young Highlander.
Campion. Canto Secundo.
  First Love.
  My Dearest Mistress.
  There Is a Garden in Her Face.
  Though You Are Young [*or* Yoong].
Carew. To My Cousin (C.R.) Marrying My
  Lady (A.).
Carroll, Jim. At eighteen years of age.
  Back to the streets always, ravaged and wet.
  I watched a street gang heading.
  Nightclubbing.
"Carroll, Lewis." Acrostic: Around my lonely
  hearth, to-night.
  Air is bright with hues of light, The.
  Father William.
  Lady of the Ladle, The.
Carruth. Bleakness in the town.
  Last year of youth, The.
  Sonnet: "To rebel is suitable philosophical
  tactics."
  Tanck's Song About the Younger Generation.
  That I Had Had Courage When Young.
Clark. Her voice is heard, and then the
  child's.
Clough. Dance on, dance on, we see, we see.
  How often sit I, poring o'er.
  Thesis and Antithesis.
Coleridge. Character of Wallenstein, The.
  Foster-Mother's Tale, The.
  On a Cataract.
  Sonnet to William Linley.
  Sonnet [to Charles Lloyd].
  Youth and Age.
Cooper. Pencil Sketch of Self & Other.
Cowper. Inscription for the Tomb of

Hamilton.
Such were the trophies, that, in earlier days.
Upon a Venerable Rival.
Crabbe. Phoebe Dawson.
Crane. Legend.
Creeley. Ball Game, The.
For the Graduation.
Prejudice, The.
Cullen. Wisdom Cometh with the Years.
Youth Sings a Song of Rosebuds.
Cummings. Boy and the Man, The.
I have seen her a stealthily frail.
Noone" autumnal this great lady's gaze.
Old age sticks / up Keep.
You shall above all things be glad and young.
Young / man sitting, The.
Davie. Garden Party, The.
Hampshire.
Herefordshire.
1945.
Zion.
De la Mare. Age.
Dreams.
Foreboding.
Karma.
Keep Innocency.
Dickey, James. Leap, The.
Dickinson. Youth, like Indian Summer.
Donne. Love's Usury.
Obsequies to the Lord Harrington, Brother to
the Lady Lucy, Countess of Bedford.
Dunbar. At Cheshire Cheese.
Ione.
Old Homestead, The.
Old Story, The.
Retrospection.
Dunn. Tenderness.
Vanishings, The.
"Dylan." Bob Dylan's Dream.
Forever Young.
My Back Pages.
Times They Are A-Changin', The.
Eberhart. Haystack, The.
Lovely were the fruit trees in the evening.
Portrait of Rilke.
Emerson. Dear are the pleasant memories.
Fame.
He must have / Droll fancies sometimes cross
his quiet thoughts.
I rake no coffined clay, nor publish wide.
In an Age of Fops and Toys.
Merlin's Song.
On prince or bride no diamond stone.
Stout Sparta shrined the god of Laughter.
Valedictory Poem.
Whoso alas is young.
Why honor the new men.
Written in Sickness.
Everson. Answer, The.
Ferlinghetti. In hintertime Praxiteles.
John Lennon in the Porto Santo Stefano.
Morlaix: Into the Future with Neil Young.
Pennycandystore beyond the El, The.
Ford. Baby's in Jail; the Animal Day Plays
Alone.
In the playpen of.
Frost. Birches.
In a Vale.
Precaution.
What Fifty Said.
Gallagher. Backdrop With Lovers, 1931.
Galvin. Summer School.
Gardner. Milkman, The.
Glück. Morning.
Graves. Song:Seven Fresh Years.
Tousled Pillow.
Gray. Ode on a Distant Prospect of Eton
College.
Griffiths. Under Mynydd-y-Tŵr.
Hacker. Days of 1959.
Haines. For Anne, at a Little Distance.
Poem of the Forgotten.
Hall. Friend Revisited, A.
Hardy. Memory and I.
Passer-By, The.
Rival, The.
Seventy-four and Twenty.
Young Man's Exhortation, A.

Hartley. Light-Heavy at Prayer.
Surprise Package.
There Are No Names.
These exquisite mementos.
Hartnett. He'll to the Moors.
Sibelius in Silence.
Heaney. Guttural Muse, The.
Incertus.
Herbert. Answer, The.
Herrick. Advice to a Maid.
Meane, The ("Tis much among the filthy to be
clean").
Song, A: "Loose no time nor youth but be."
To Be Merry.
To [the] Virgins, to Make Much of Time.
To Youth.
Upon a Lady Faire, but Fruitlesse.
Youth, and Age.
Hesketh. Call of the North.
House In the Tree.
Walled In.
Hewitt. Age and Youth.
Agitator.
Bogside, Derry, 1971.
Boy Seen in a Bus Journey.
First Honey.
Happy Boy, A.
I Learn About Art.
Incident, An.
Mainland, The.
Middle Infant.
Young Womanhood.
Holmes. Unwanted 1943 Chappaqua
Flashback.
Writing the Atheneum talk, I wonder.
Hopkins. On the Portrait of Two Beautiful
Young People.
Housman. Lads in their hundreds to Ludlow
come in for the fair, The.
Loitering with a vacant eye.
On forelands high in heaven.
Sage to the Young Man, The.
Think no more, lad; laugh, be jolly.
West, The.
Westward on the high-hilled plains.
When I was one-and-twenty.
Hughes, Ted. Couples Under Cover.
Jarrell. Face, The.
Jeffers. After Lake Leman.
Age in Prospect.
Miching Mallecho.
Oysters.
Johnson. Short Song of Congratulation [or To
a Young Heir], A.
Joseph. Birthday Poem.
Kinnell. Meditation Among the Tombs.
Kipling. My Rival.
R.A.F. (Aged Eighteen).
Knight. For Freckle-Faced Gerald.
Kunitz. Demonstrations in the streets.
Downtown at the Front St. Bi-jo (spelt Bijou).
For Proserpine.
Larkin. Having Grown Up in Shade of Church
and State.
How Distant.
Pour Away That Youth.
Sad Steps.
Wild Oats.
Lawrence. Beware, O My Dear Young Men.
Dreams Old and Nascent.
Fight! O My Young Men.
Grudge of the Old, The.
It's Either You Fight or You Die.
Latter-Day Sinners.
Maybe.
Mournful Young Man.
Old People.
Poor Young Things.
Signs of the Times.
So There!
Stop It.
Tarts.
Vitality.
White Horse, The.
Young and Their Moral Guardians, The.
Young Are Not Mean in Material Things, The.
Young Want to Be Just, The.
Youth Mowing, A.

Levine. Last Step, The.
You Can Have It.
Lewis. Horace at Twenty.
Lines on a Tudor Mansion.
Liddy. Tips of the fronds become swollen,
The.
Waters by this music.
Lindsay. Leaden-eyed, The.
My Lady Is Compared to a Young Tree.
Longfellow. My Lost Youth.
Lorde. Generation.
Mentor.
Spring People.
Lowry. Beside Oneself.
"Portly & middleaged" can never.
Those who die young will look forever young.
When I was young I broke all drinking
records.
"MacDiarmid." Of My First Love.
MacLeish. He had used love or lust or what's
between.
No doubt he'd once had eyes to see.
Yacht for Sale.
Years of the Dog.
MacNeice. Canto XXII: "So this is
Glastonbury. A green hill far away."
Cyclist, The.
Sailing Orders.
Taken for Granted.
When We Were Children.
McNeill. Hounds, The.
Mahon. Autobiographies.
Markson. Imitative Fragment.
Melville. Lone Founts.
On the Slain Collegians.
Meredith. Amid the plash of scarlet mud.
Earth's Preference.
One fairest of the ripe unwedded left.
Time and Sentiment.
When the South sang like a nightingale.
Years Had Worn Their Season's Belt, The.
Youth in Memory.
Merrill. Tenancy, A.
Merton. My birthday was in March, when the
weather was furious.
When class was in the garden at Greylands.
Millay. Being Young and Green.
Miller. Some days / the sunlight has a clarity.
Milton. I with foolish mind and heedless zeal
formerly.
Sonnet 7: "How soon hath Time the suttle
theef of youth."
Morgan. Turtle, The.
Nash. There's Nothing Like Instinct,
Fortunately.
You Can Be a Republican, I'm a Genocrat.
Nathan. Tendril.
Nemerov. Blue Suburban.
Boy with Book of Knowledge.
Interview, An.
Young Woman.
Neruda. Ambassador, The.
Notley. When I Was Alive.
O'Hara. Animals.
Blocks.
Ode to Michael Goldberg ('s Birth and Other
Births).
Young Poet, A.
Olson. All things stand out against the sky.
Gloss, A.
Toss, for John Cage, A.
Owen. Anthem for Doomed Youth.
Parable of the Old Man and the Young, The.
Sonnet, to a Child.
Paley. Question.
Patchen. Street Corner College.
Plath. Tinker Jack and the Tidy Wives.
Words for a Nursery.
Poe. Happiest Day, the Happiest Hour, The.
Lake: To———, The.
Prince. Afterword on Rupert Brooke.
Fretted discoloured towers and domes.
Sea View.
Sun shines on the gliding river, The.
Youth and Age.
Raine. Long ago I thought you young, bright
daimon.
Oval Portrait: Jessie Wilkie, The.

Ralegh. Plants and trees made poore and old, The.
Poem of Sir Walter Rawleighs, A.
Ransom. Piazza Piece.
Vision by Sweetwater.
Rexroth. Thou Shalt Not Kill.
Rich. At Majority.
Middle-aged, The.
Recorders in Italy.
Robinson. Bon Voyage.
Roethke. Feud.
Her Words.
Sententious Man, The.
Rossetti. Dream-Love.
I Have a Message unto Thee.
Maiden May.
My old admiration before I was twenty.
Till Tomorrow.
Versi.
Whole Head Is Sick, and the Whole Heart Faint, The.
Young Death.
Rukeyser. Bringing.
Delta Poems.
Down from Chicago Bryan came.
Drowning Young Man, The.
Eel.
Poem Out of Childhood.
Sexton. Angel of Beach Houses and Picnics.
Fury of Sundays, The.
Mother and Daughter.
Young.
Shakespeare. Crabbed age and youth cannot live together.
Sonnet 3: "Look in thy glass, and tell the face thou viewest."
Sonnet 126: "O thou, my lovely boy, who in thy power."
Sidney. Sonnet 21: "Your words my friend (right healthful caustics) blame."
Smith, Charlotte. To a Young Man Entering the World.
Smith, Stevie. Eng.
From the French (1).
Lord Mope.
Snodgrass. Home Town.
To a Child.
Snyder. Go Round.
Sorrentino. Oú Sont Ils, Oú, Vierge Souvrain?
Razzmatazz.
Spender. Art Student.
Generous Days, The.
Uncreating Chaos (Double Portrait in a Mirror), The.
Us.
Stevens. Pediment of Appearance, The.
Stevenson. Flower god, god of the spring, beautiful, bountiful.
Here you rest among the valleys, maiden known to but a few.
I look across the ocean.
In Memoriam F. A. S.
In the States.
It is the season now to go.
Light as my heart was long ago.
Link your arm in mine, my lad.
On His Pitiable Transformation.
Sing me a song of a lad that is gone.
To a Youth.
To what shall I compare her.
To Will H. Low.
To Willie and Henrietta.
Unforgotten II, The ("She rested by the Broken Brook").
When the sun comes after rain.
Youth and Love II ("To the heart of youth the world is a highwayside").
Suckling. Against Fruition ("Stay here, fond youth, and ask no more, be wise").
Swift. Receipt to Restore Stella's Youth, A.
Swinburne. Les Noyades.

Thomas. I See the Boys of Summer.
Once below a Time.
Process in the Weather of the Heart, A.
Updike. Youth's Progress.
Van Duyn. What the Motorcycle Said.
Walcott. Glory Trumpeter, The.
Orient and Immortal Wheat.
Parang.
Prelude: "I, with legs crossed along the daylight, watch."
Warren. Folly on Royal Street before the Raw Face of God.
Whitman. We Two Boys Together Clinging.
Youth, Day, Old Age and Night.
Whittier. Fountain, The.
June on the Merrimac.
Wilbur. Star System, The.
To Madame du Châtelet.
Williams, Charles Kenneth. Love: Beginnnings.
Prodigy, The.
World's Greatest Tricycle-Rider, The.
Williams, William Carlos. Deceptrices, The.
Invocation and Conclusion.
Sea, The.
To Wish Myself Courage.
Young Woman at a Window.
Wordsworth. Author's Voyage down the Rhine (Thirty Years Ago).
Edward VI.
Elegiac Stanzas.
Evening Walk Addressed to a Young Lady, An.
Inscription for a Seat by a Roadside, Half Way up a Steep Hill, Facing the South.
Wright, James. Trouble.
Wroth. Sonnet 24: "Once did I heere an aged father say."
Wyatt. Lament my loss[e], my labo[u]r, and my pain [or payne].
Since love is such that, as ye wot.
There was never file half so well filed.
Yeats. Brown Penny.
Crazy Jane Grown Old Looks at the Dancers.
Down by the Salley Gardens.
His Phoenix.
Image from a Past Life, An.
Man Young and Old, A.
Meditation of the Old Fisherman, The.
Old Memory.
Owen Aherne and His Dancers.
To a Young Girl.
Two Years Later.
Whence Had They Come?
Who Goes with Fergus?
Young Man's Song.
Youth and Age.
Young. Sweet Sixteen Lines.
Zukofsky. Strange / To reach that age.
Homage.

Yucatán, Mexico
Merton. Chilam Balam.
Dzules.

Yugoslavia
Davie. Porec.
Vindication of Jovan Babic, The.
Hugo. Letter to Simic from Boulder.
Museum of Cruel Days.
Remote Farm on the Dubrovnik-Sarajevo Run.
Sailing Dalmatia.
Spinning the Sava.
Young. Belgrade Moon.
In a Twinkling, the green.

Yukio Mishima. *see* **Mishima, Yukio.**

Yukon Territory
Robinson. Klondike, The.

Z

Zen Buddhism
Beatles. Across the Universe.

Dunn. Something Like Happiness.
Merton. Abandon your body and soul into the abundance of light sent from above.
Snyder. December.
On Vulture Peak.
Wakoski. Fourth Universe.
See also **Buddha and Buddhism.**

Zeppelins. *see* **Dirigibles.**

Zeus
Clark. Change.
Doolittle. Muse, / tell me of this man of wit.
Zeus-Provider.
Merton. Wisdom is one thing: it is to know the thought by which all things are steered through all things.
Zeus Is Dead.
Nash. Leda's Fortunate Gaffe.
Olson. Borne down by the inability to lift the heaviness.
Ralegh. Brasen tower [or Tower] with doors [or dores] close barred [or bar'd], The.
Yeats. Leda and the Swan.

Zinnias
Hayden. Zinnias.
Notley. Red Zinnias.
Zukofsky. Zinnia.

Zion
Byron. In the Valley of Waters.
Davie. Except the Lord Build the House.
Zion.
Hughes, Ted. Mount Zion.
Merton. Sundown.
Milton. Among the holy Mountains high.
Psalms. Psalm 48: "Great is the Lord.."
Psalm 87: "His foundation is in the holy mountains."

Zionism
"Dylan." Neighborhood Bully.

Zipcodes
Updike. ZIP Code Ode.

Zodiac
Davie. Zodiac, The.
Dickey, William. Sagittarius, Scorpio Rising.
Ford. Your Horoscope.
Lawrence. Astronomical Changes.
Merrill. Under Libra: Weights and Measures.
O'Hara. Poem: "Now it is the 27th."
Olson. Year Is a Great Circle or the Year Is a Great Mistake, The.
Sorrentino. Come from the whirling zodiac.
Yeats. Chosen.

Zola, Émile
Dobyns. Cézanne and Zola.
Robinson. Zola.

Zoos
Bukowski. Rain or Shine.
Cullen. Thoughts in a Zoo.
Dickey, James. Encounter in the Cage Country.
Gardner. At the Zoo.
Garrigue. False Country of the Zoo.
Iowa City Zoo.
Hughes, Ted. Jaguar, The.
Jarrell. Woman at the Washington Zoo, The.
MacLeish. Boy in the Roman Zoo.
Meinke. Running with the Hyenas.
Sandburg. Elephants Are Different to Different People.
Sarton. Ballad of Johnny, The.
Updike. Menagerie at Versailles in 1775, The.
Zoo Bats.
Van Duyn. Marriage, with Beasts.

Zulus
Davie. Ordinary God.
Lawrence. Immoral Man.
Merton. Notes for a New Liturgy.
Updike. Zulus Live in Land without a Square.